PETERSON'S®
GRADUATE & PROFESSIONAL PROGRAMS

AN OVERVIEW

2020

© 2020 Peterson's®

Previous editions © 1966, 1967, 1968, 1969, 1970, 1971, 1972, 1973, 1974, 1975, 1976, 1977, 1978, 1979, 1980, 1981, 1982, 1983, 1984, 1985, 1986, 1987, 1988, 1989, 1990, 1991, 1992, 1993, 1994, 1995, 1996, 1997, 1998, 1999, 2000, 2001, 2002, 2003, 2004, 2005, 2006, 2007, 2008, 2009, 2010, 2011, 2012, 2013, 2014, 2015, 2016, 2017, 2018, 2019

ISSN 1093-8443
ISBN: 978-0-7689-4318-4

Printed in the United States of America

10 9 8 7 6 5 4 3 2 1   21 20 19

Fifty-fourth Edition

CONTENTS

A Note from the Peterson's Editors

The six volumes of Peterson's *Graduate and Professional Programs*, the only annually updated reference work of its kind, provide wide-ranging information on the graduate and professional programs offered by accredited colleges and universities in the United States, U.S. territories, and Canada and by those institutions outside the United States that are accredited by U.S. accrediting bodies. More than 44,000 individual academic and professional programs at nearly 2,300 institutions are listed. Peterson's *Graduate and Professional Programs* have been used for more than fifty years by prospective graduate and professional students, placement counselors, faculty advisers, and all others interested in postbaccalaureate education.

Graduate & Professional Programs: An Overview contains information on institutions as a whole, while the other books in the series are devoted to specific academic and professional fields:

- *Graduate Programs in the Biological/Biomedical Sciences & Health-Related Medical Professions*

- *Graduate Programs in Business, Education, Information Studies, Law & Social Work*

- *Graduate Programs in Engineering & Applied Sciences*

- *Graduate Programs in the Humanities, Arts & Social Sciences*

- *Graduate Programs in the Physical Sciences, Mathematics, Agricultural Sciences, the Environment & Natural Resources*

The books may be used individually or as a set. For example, if you have chosen a field of study but do not know what institution you want to attend or if you have a college or university in mind but have not chosen an academic field of study, it is best to begin with the Overview guide.

Graduate & Professional Programs: An Overview presents several directories to help you identify programs of study that might interest you; you can then research those programs further in the other books in the series by using the Directory of Graduate and Professional Programs by Field, which lists 500 fields and gives the names of those institutions that offer graduate degree programs in each.

For geographical or financial reasons, you may be interested in attending a particular institution and will want to know what it has to offer. You should turn to the Directory of Institutions and Their Offerings, which lists the degree programs available at each institution. As in the Directory of Graduate and Professional Programs by Field, the level of degrees offered is also indicated.

All books in the series include advice on graduate education, including topics such as admissions tests, financial aid, and accreditation. **The Graduate Adviser** includes two essays and information about accreditation. The first essay, "The Admissions Process," discusses general admission requirements, admission tests, factors to consider when selecting a graduate school or program, when and how to apply, and how admission decisions are made. Special information for international students and tips for minority students are also included. The second essay, "Financial Support," is an overview of the broad range of support available at the graduate level. Fellowships, scholarships, and grants; assistantships and internships; federal and private loan programs, as well as Federal Work-Study; and the GI bill are detailed. This essay concludes with advice on applying for need-based financial aid. "Accreditation and Accrediting Agencies" gives information on accreditation and its purpose and lists institutional accrediting agencies first and then specialized accrediting agencies relevant to each volume's specific fields of study.

With information on more than 40,000 graduate programs in more than 500 disciplines, Peterson's *Graduate and Professional Programs* give you all the information you need about the programs that are of interest to you in three formats: **Profiles** (capsule summaries of basic information), **Displays** (information that an institution or program wants to emphasize), and **Close-Ups** (written by administrators, with more expansive information than the **Profiles**, emphasizing different aspects of the programs). By using these various formats of program information, coupled with **Appendixes** and **Indexes** covering directories and subject areas for all six books, you will find that these guides provide the most comprehensive, accurate, and up-to-date graduate study information available.

Peterson's publishes a full line of resources with information you need to guide you through the graduate admissions process. Peterson's publications can be found at college libraries and career centers and your local bookstore or library—or visit us on the Web at www.petersons.com.

Colleges and universities will be pleased to know that Peterson's helped you in your selection. Admissions staff members are more than happy to answer questions, address specific problems, and help in any way they can. The editors at Peterson's wish you great success in your graduate program search!

THE GRADUATE ADVISER

The Admissions Process

Generalizations about graduate admissions practices are not always helpful because each institution has its own set of guidelines and procedures. Nevertheless, some broad statements can be made about the admissions process that may help you plan your strategy.

Factors Involved in Selecting a Graduate School or Program

Selecting a graduate school and a specific program of study is a complex matter. Quality of the faculty; program and course offerings; the nature, size, and location of the institution; admission requirements; cost; and the availability of financial assistance are among the many factors that affect one's choice of institution. Other considerations are job placement and achievements of the program's graduates and the institution's resources, such as libraries, laboratories, and computer facilities. If you are to make the best possible choice, you need to learn as much as you can about the schools and programs you are considering before you apply.

The following steps may help you narrow your choices.

- Talk to alumni of the programs or institutions you are considering to get their impressions of how well they were prepared for work in their fields of study.
- Remember that graduate school requirements change, so be sure to get the most up-to-date information possible.
- Talk to department faculty members and the graduate adviser at your undergraduate institution. They often have information about programs of study at other institutions.
- Visit the websites of the graduate schools in which you are interested to request a graduate catalog. Contact the department chair in your chosen field of study for additional information about the department and the field.
- Visit as many campuses as possible. Call ahead for an appointment with the graduate adviser in your field of interest and be sure to check out the facilities and talk to students.

General Requirements

Graduate schools and departments have requirements that applicants for admission must meet. Typically, these requirements include undergraduate transcripts (which provide information about undergraduate grade point average and course work applied toward a major), admission test scores, and letters of recommendation. Most graduate programs also ask for an essay or personal statement that describes your personal reasons for seeking graduate study. In some fields, such as art and music, portfolios or auditions may be required in addition to other evidence of talent. Some institutions require that the applicant have an undergraduate degree in the same subject as the intended graduate major.

Most institutions evaluate each applicant on the basis of the applicant's total record, and the weight accorded any given factor varies widely from institution to institution and from program to program.

The Application Process

You should begin the application process at least one year before you expect to begin your graduate study. Find out the application deadline for each institution (many are provided in the **Profile** section of this guide). Go to the institution's website and find out if you can apply online. If not, request a paper application form. Fill out this form thoroughly and neatly. Assume that the school needs all the information it is requesting and that the admissions officer will be sensitive to the neatness and overall quality of what you submit. Do not supply more information than the school requires.

The institution may ask at least one question that will require a three- or four-paragraph answer. Compose your response on the assumption that the admissions officer is interested in both what you think and how you express yourself. Keep your statement brief and to the point, but, at the same time, include all pertinent information about your past experiences and your educational goals. Individual statements vary greatly in style and content, which helps admissions officers differentiate among applicants. Many graduate departments give considerable weight to the statement in making their admissions decisions, so be sure to take the time to prepare a thoughtful and concise statement.

If recommendations are a part of the admissions requirements, carefully choose the individuals you ask to write them. It is generally best to ask current or former professors to write the recommendations, provided they are able to attest to your intellectual ability and motivation for doing the work required of a graduate student. It is advisable to provide stamped, preaddressed envelopes to people being asked to submit recommendations on your behalf.

Completed applications, including references, transcripts, and admission test scores, should be received at the institution by the specified date.

Be advised that institutions do not usually make admissions decisions until all materials have been received. Enclose a self-addressed postcard with your application, requesting confirmation of receipt. Allow at least ten days for the return of the postcard before making further inquiries.

If you plan to apply for financial support, it is imperative that you file your application early.

ADMISSION TESTS

The major testing program used in graduate admissions is the Graduate Record Examinations (GRE®) testing program, sponsored by the GRE Board and administered by Educational Testing Service, Princeton, New Jersey.

The Graduate Record Examinations testing program consists of a General Test and six Subject Tests. The General Test measures critical thinking, verbal reasoning, quantitative reasoning, and analytical writing skills. It is offered as an Internet-based test (iBT) in the United States, Canada, and many other countries.

The GRE® revised General Test's questions were designed to reflect the kind of thinking that students need to do in graduate or business school and demonstrate that students are indeed ready for graduate-level work.

- **Verbal Reasoning**—Measures ability to analyze and evaluate written material and synthesize information obtained from it, analyze relationships among component parts of sentences, and recognize relationships among words and concepts.
- **Quantitative Reasoning**—Measures problem-solving ability, focusing on basic concepts of arithmetic, algebra, geometry, and data analysis.
- **Analytical Writing**—Measures critical thinking and analytical writing skills, specifically the ability to articulate and support complex ideas clearly and effectively.

The computer-delivered GRE® revised General Test is offered year-round at Prometric™ test centers and on specific dates at testing locations outside of the Prometric test center network. Appointments are scheduled on a first-come, first-served basis. The GRE® revised General Test is also offered as a paper-based test three times a year in areas where computer-based testing is not available.

You can take the computer-delivered GRE® revised General Test once every twenty-one days, up to five times within any continuous rolling twelve-month period (365 days)—even if you canceled your scores on a previously taken test. You may take the paper-based GRE® revised General Test as often as it is offered.

Three scores are reported on the revised General Test:

1. A **Verbal Reasoning score** is reported on a 130–170 score scale, in 1-point increments.

2. A **Quantitative Reasoning score** is reported on a 130–170 score scale, in 1-point increments.

3. An **Analytical Writing score** is reported on a 0–6 score level, in half-point increments.

The GRE® Subject Tests measure achievement and assume undergraduate majors or extensive background in the following six disciplines:

- Biology
- Chemistry
- Literature in English
- Mathematics
- Physics
- Psychology

The Subject Tests are available three times per year as paper-based administrations around the world. Testing time is approximately 2 hours and 50 minutes. You can obtain more information about the GRE® by visiting the ETS website at **www.ets.org** or consulting the *GRE® Information Bulletin*. The *Bulletin* can be obtained at many undergraduate colleges. You can also download it from the ETS website or obtain it by contacting Graduate Record Examinations, Educational Testing Service, P.O. Box 6000, Princeton, NJ 08541-6000; phone: 609-771-7670 or 866-473-4373.

If you expect to apply for admission to a program that requires any of the GRE® tests, you should select a test date well in advance of the application deadline. Scores on the computer-based General Test are reported within ten to fifteen days; scores on the paper-based Subject Tests are reported within six weeks.

Another testing program, the Miller Analogies Test® (MAT®), is administered at more than 500 Controlled Testing Centers in the United States, Canada, and other countries. The MAT® computer-based test is now available. Testing time is 60 minutes. The test consists of 120 partial analogies. You can obtain the *Candidate Information Booklet,* which contains a list of test centers and instructions for taking the test, from **www.milleranalogies.com** or by calling 800-328-5999 (toll-free).

Check the specific requirements of the programs to which you are applying.

How Admission Decisions Are Made

The program you apply to is directly involved in the admissions process. Although the final decision is usually made by the graduate dean (or an associate) or the faculty admissions committee, recommendations from faculty members in your intended field are important. At some institutions, an interview is incorporated into the decision process.

A Special Note for International Students

In addition to the steps already described, there are some special considerations for international students who intend to apply for graduate study in the United States. All graduate schools require an indication of competence in English. The purpose of the Test of English as a Foreign Language (TOEFL®) is to evaluate the English proficiency of people who are nonnative speakers of English and want to study at colleges and universities where English is the language of instruction. The TOEFL® is administered by Educational Testing Service (ETS) under the general direction of a policy board established by the College Board and the Graduate Record Examinations Board.

The TOEFL iBT® assesses four basic language skills: listening, reading, writing, and speaking. The Internet-based test is administered at secure, official test centers. The testing time is approximately 4 hours.

The TOEFL® is also offered in a paper-based format in areas of the world where internet-based testing is not available. In 2017, ETS launched a revised TOEFL® paper-based Test, that more closely aligned to the TOEFL iBT® test. This revised paper-based test consists of three sections—listening, reading, and writing. The testing time is approximately 3 hours.

You can obtain more information for both versions of the TOEFL® by visiting the ETS website at **www.ets.org/toefl**. Information can also be obtained by contacting TOEFL® Services, Educational Testing Service, P.O. Box 6151, Princeton, NJ 08541-6151. Phone: 609-771-7100 or 877-863-3546 (toll free).

International students should apply especially early because of the number of steps required to complete the admissions process. Furthermore, many United States graduate schools have a limited number of spaces for international students, and many more students apply than the schools can accommodate.

International students may find financial assistance from institutions very limited. The U.S. government requires international applicants to submit a certification of support, which is a statement attesting to the applicant's financial resources. In addition, international students *must* have health insurance coverage.

Tips for Minority Students

Indicators of a university's values in terms of diversity are found both in its recruitment programs and its resources directed to student success. Important questions: Does the institution vigorously recruit minorities for its graduate programs? Is there funding available to help with the costs associated with visiting the school? Are minorities represented in the institution's brochures or website or on their faculty rolls? What campus-based resources or services (including assistance in locating housing or career counseling and placement) are available? Is funding available to members of underrepresented groups?

At the program level, it is particularly important for minority students to investigate the "climate" of a program under consideration. How many minority students are enrolled and how many have graduated? What opportunities are there to work with diverse faculty and mentors whose research interests match yours? How are conflicts resolved or concerns addressed? How interested are faculty in building strong and supportive relations with students? "Climate" concerns should be addressed by posing questions to various individuals, including faculty members, current students, and alumni.

Information is also available through various organizations, such as the Hispanic Association of Colleges & Universities (HACU), and publications such as *Diverse Issues in Higher Education* and *Hispanic Outlook* magazine. There are also books devoted to this topic, such as *The Multicultural Student's Guide to Colleges* by Robert Mitchell.

Financial Support

The range of financial support at the graduate level is very broad. The following descriptions will give you a general idea of what you might expect and what will be expected of you as a financial support recipient.

Fellowships, Scholarships, and Grants

These are usually outright awards of a few hundred to many thousands of dollars with no service to the institution required in return. Fellowships and scholarships are usually awarded on the basis of merit and are highly competitive. Grants are made on the basis of financial need or special talent in a field of study. Many fellowships, scholarships, and grants not only cover tuition, fees, and supplies but also include stipends for living expenses with allowances for dependents. However, the terms of each should be examined because some do not permit recipients to supplement their income with outside work. Fellowships, scholarships, and grants may vary in the number of years for which they are awarded.

In addition to the availability of these funds at the university or program level, many excellent fellowship programs are available at the national level and may be applied for before and during enrollment in a graduate program. A listing of many of these programs can be found at the Council of Graduate Schools' website, **https://cgsnet.org/**. There is a wealth of information in the "Programs" and "Awards" sections.

Assistantships and Internships

Many graduate students receive financial support through assistantships, particularly involving teaching or research duties. It is important to recognize that such appointments should not be viewed simply as employment relationships but rather should constitute an integral and important part of a student's graduate education. As such, the appointments should be accompanied by strong faculty mentoring and increasingly responsible apprenticeship experiences. The specific nature of these appointments in a given program should be considered in selecting that graduate program.

TEACHING ASSISTANTSHIPS

These usually provide a salary and full or partial tuition remission and may also provide health benefits. Unlike fellowships, scholarships, and grants, which require no service to the institution, teaching assistantships require recipients to provide the institution with a specific amount of undergraduate teaching, ideally related to the student's field of study. Some teaching assistants are limited to grading papers, compiling bibliographies, taking notes, or monitoring laboratories. At some graduate schools, teaching assistants must carry lighter course loads than regular full-time students.

RESEARCH ASSISTANTSHIPS

These are very similar to teaching assistantships in the manner in which financial assistance is provided. The difference is that recipients are given basic research assignments in their disciplines rather than teaching responsibilities. The work required is normally related to the student's field of study; in most instances, the assistantship supports the student's thesis or dissertation research.

ADMINISTRATIVE INTERNSHIPS

These are similar to assistantships in application of financial assistance funds, but the student is given an assignment on a part-time basis, usually as a special assistant with one of the university's administrative offices. The assignment may not necessarily be directly related to the recipient's discipline.

RESIDENCE HALL AND COUNSELING ASSISTANTSHIPS

These assistantships are frequently assigned to graduate students in psychology, counseling, and social work, but they may be offered to students in other disciplines, especially if the student has worked in this capacity during his or her undergraduate years. Duties can vary from being available in a dean's office for a specific number of hours for consultation with undergraduates to living in campus residences and being responsible for both counseling and administrative tasks or advising student activity groups. Residence hall assistantships often include a room and board allowance and, in some cases, tuition assistance and stipends. Contact the Housing and Student Life Office for more information.

Health Insurance

The availability and affordability of health insurance is an important issue and one that should be considered in an applicant's choice of institution and program. While often included with assistantships and fellowships, this is not always the case and, even if provided, the benefits may be limited. It is important to note that the U.S. government requires international students to have health insurance.

The GI Bill

This provides financial assistance for students who are veterans of the United States armed forces. If you are a veteran, contact your local Veterans Administration office to determine your eligibility and to get full details about benefits. There are a number of programs that offer educational benefits to current military enlistees. Some states have tuition assistance programs for members of the National Guard. Contact the VA office at the college for more information.

Federal Work-Study Program (FWS)

Employment is another way some students finance their graduate studies. The federally funded Federal Work-Study Program provides eligible students with employment opportunities, usually in public and private nonprofit organizations. Federal funds pay up to 75 percent of the wages, with the remainder paid by the employing agency. FWS is available to graduate students who demonstrate financial need. Not all schools have these funds, and some only award them to undergraduates. Each school sets its application deadline and workstudy earnings limits. Wages vary and are related to the type of work done. You must file the Free Application for Federal Student Aid (FAFSA) to be eligible for this program.

Loans

Many graduate students borrow to finance their graduate programs when other sources of assistance (which do not have to be repaid) prove insufficient. You should always read and understand the terms of any loan program before submitting your application.

FEDERAL DIRECT LOANS

Federal Direct Loans. The Federal Direct Loan Program offers a variable-fixed interest rate loan to graduate students with the Department of Education acting as the lender. Students receive a new rate with each new loan, but that rate is fixed for the life of the loan. Beginning with loans made on or after July 1, 2013, the interest rate for loans made each July 1st to June 30th period are determined based on the last 10-year Treasury note auction prior to June 1st of that year, plus an added percentage. The interest rate can be no higher than 9.5%.

Beginning July 1, 2012, the Federal Direct Loan for graduate students is an unsubsidized loan. Under the *unsubsidized* program, the grad borrower pays the interest on the loan from the day proceeds are issued and is responsible for paying interest during all periods. If the borrower chooses not to pay the interest while in school, or during the grace periods, deferment, or forbearance, the interest accrues and will be capitalized.

Graduate students may borrow up to $20,500 per year through the Direct Loan Program, up to a cumulative maximum of $138,500, including undergraduate borrowing. No more than $65,500 of the $138,500 can be from subsidized loans, including loans the grad borrower may have received for periods of enrollment that began before July 1, 2012, or for prior undergraduate borrowing. You may borrow up to the cost of attendance at the school in which you are enrolled or will attend, minus estimated financial assistance from other federal, state, and private sources, up to a maximum of $20,500. Grad borrowers who reach the aggregate loan limit over the course of their education cannot receive additional loans; however, if they repay some of their loans to bring the outstanding balance below the aggregate limit, they could be eligible to borrow again, up to that limit.

Under the *subsidized* Federal Direct Loan Program, repayment begins six months after your last date of enrollment on at least a half-time basis. Under the *unsubsidized* program, repayment of interest begins within thirty days from disbursement of the loan proceeds, and repayment of the principal begins six months after your last enrollment on at least a half-time basis. Some borrowers may choose to defer interest payments while they are in school. The accrued interest is added to the loan balance when the borrower begins repayment. There are several repayment options.

Federal Perkins Loans. The Federal Perkins Loan is available to students demonstrating financial need and is administered directly by the school. Not all schools have these funds, and some may award them to undergraduates only. Eligibility is determined from the information you provide on the FAFSA. The school will notify you of your eligibility.

Eligible graduate students may borrow up to $8,000 per year, up to a maximum of $60,000, including undergraduate borrowing (even if your previous Perkins Loans have been repaid). The interest rate for Federal Perkins Loans is 5 percent, and no interest accrues while you remain in school at least half-time. Students who are attending less than half-time need to check with their school to determine the length of their grace period. There are no guarantee, loan, or disbursement fees. Repayment begins nine months after your last date of enrollment on at least a half-time basis and may extend over a maximum of ten years with no prepayment penalty.

Federal Direct Graduate PLUS Loans. Effective July 1, 2006, graduate and professional students are eligible for Graduate PLUS loans. This program allows students to borrow up to the cost of attendance, less any other aid received. These loans have a fixed interest rate (7.08% for loans first disbursed on or after July 1, 2019, and before July 1, 2020) and interest begins to accrue at the time of disbursement. Beginning with loans made on or after July 1, 2013, the interest rate for loans made each July 1st to June 30th period are determined based on the last 10-year Treasury note auction prior to June 1st of that year. The interest rate can be no higher than 10.5%. The PLUS loans do involve a credit check; a PLUS borrower may obtain a loan with a cosigner if his or her credit is not good enough. Grad PLUS loans may be deferred while a student is in school and for the six months following a drop below half-time enrollment. For more information, you should contact a representative in your college's financial aid office.

Deferring Your Federal Loan Repayments. If you borrowed under the Federal Direct Loan Program, Federal Direct PLUS Loan Program, or the Federal Perkins Loan Program for previous undergraduate or graduate study, your payments may be deferred when you return to graduate school, depending on when you borrowed and under which program.

There are other deferment options available if you are temporarily unable to repay your loan. Information about these deferments is provided at your entrance and exit interviews. If you believe you are eligible for a deferment of your loan payments, you must contact your lender or loan servicer to request a deferment. The deferment must be filed prior to the time your payment is due, and it must be re-filed when it expires if you remain eligible for deferment at that time.

SUPPLEMENTAL (PRIVATE) LOANS

Many lending institutions offer supplemental loan programs and other financing plans, such as the ones described here, to students seeking additional assistance in meeting their education expenses. Some loan programs target all types of graduate students; others are designed specifically for business, law, or medical students. In addition, you can use private loans not specifically designed for education to help finance your graduate degree.

If you are considering borrowing through a supplemental or private loan program, you should carefully consider the terms and be sure to read the fine print. Check with the program sponsor for the most current terms that will be applicable to the amounts you intend to borrow for graduate study. Most supplemental loan programs for graduate study offer unsubsidized, credit-based loans. In general, a credit-ready borrower is one who has a satisfactory credit history or no credit history at all. A creditworthy borrower generally must pass a credit test to be eligible to borrow or act as a cosigner for the loan funds.

Many supplemental loan programs have minimum and maximum annual loan limits. Some offer amounts equal to the cost of attendance minus any other aid you will receive for graduate study. If you are planning to borrow for several years of graduate study, consider whether there is a cumulative or aggregate limit on the amount you may borrow. Often this cumulative or aggregate limit will include any amounts you borrowed and have not repaid for undergraduate or previous graduate study.

The combination of the annual interest rate, loan fees, and the repayment terms you choose will determine how much you will repay over time. Compare these features in combination before you decide which loan program to use. Some loans offer interest rates that are adjusted monthly, quarterly, or annually. Some offer interest rates that are lower during the in-school, grace, and deferment periods and then increase when you begin repayment. Some programs include a loan origination fee, which is usually deducted from the principal amount you receive when the loan is disbursed and must be repaid along with the interest and other principal when you graduate, withdraw from school, or drop below half-time study. Sometimes the loan fees are reduced if you borrow with a qualified cosigner. Some programs allow you to defer interest and/or principal payments while you are enrolled in graduate school. Many programs allow you to capitalize your interest payments; the interest due on your loan is added to the outstanding balance of your loan, so you don't have to repay immediately, but this increases the amount you owe. Other programs allow you to pay the interest as you go, which reduces the amount you later have to repay. The private loan market is very competitive, and your financial aid office can help you evaluate these programs.

Applying for Need-Based Financial Aid

Schools that award federal and institutional financial assistance based on need will require you to complete the FAFSA and, in some cases, an institutional financial aid application.

If you are applying for federal student assistance, you **must** complete the FAFSA. A service of the U.S. Department of Education, the FAFSA is free to all applicants. Most applicants apply online at **www.fafsa.ed.gov**. Paper applications are available at the financial aid office of your local college.

After your FAFSA information has been processed, you will receive a Student Aid Report (SAR). If you provided an e-mail address on the FAFSA, this will be sent to you electronically; otherwise, it will be mailed to your home address.

Follow the instructions on the SAR if you need to correct information reported on your original application. If your situation changes after you file your FAFSA, contact your financial aid officer to discuss amending your information. You can also appeal your financial aid award if you have extenuating circumstances.

If you would like more information on federal student financial aid, visit the FAFSA website or download the most recent version of *Do You Need Money for College* at www.studentaid.ed.gov/sa/sites/default/files/2018-19-do-you-need-money.pdf. This guide is also available in Spanish.

The U.S. Department of Education also has a toll-free number for questions concerning federal student aid programs. The number is 1-800-4-FED AID (1-800-433-3243). If you are hearing impaired, call toll-free, 1-800-730-8913.

Summary

Remember that these are generalized statements about financial assistance at the graduate level. Because each institution allots its aid differently, you should communicate directly with the school and the specific department of interest to you. It is not unusual, for example, to find that an endowment vested within a specific department supports one or more fellowships. You may fit its requirements and specifications precisely.

Accreditation and Accrediting Agencies

Colleges and universities in the United States, and their individual academic and professional programs, are accredited by nongovernmental agencies concerned with monitoring the quality of education in this country. Agencies with both regional and national jurisdictions grant accreditation to institutions as a whole, while specialized bodies acting on a nationwide basis—often national professional associations—grant accreditation to departments and programs in specific fields.

Institutional and specialized accrediting agencies share the same basic concerns: the purpose an academic unit—whether university or program—has set for itself and how well it fulfills that purpose, the adequacy of its financial and other resources, the quality of its academic offerings, and the level of services it provides. Agencies that grant institutional accreditation take a broader view, of course, and examine university-wide or college-wide services with which a specialized agency may not concern itself.

Both types of agencies follow the same general procedures when considering an application for accreditation. The academic unit prepares a self-evaluation, focusing on the concerns mentioned above and usually including an assessment of both its strengths and weaknesses; a team of representatives of the accrediting body reviews this evaluation, visits the campus, and makes its own report; and finally, the accrediting body makes a decision on the application. Often, even when accreditation is granted, the agency makes a recommendation regarding how the institution or program can improve. All institutions and programs are also reviewed every few years to determine whether they continue to meet established standards; if they do not, they may lose their accreditation.

Accrediting agencies themselves are reviewed and evaluated periodically by the U.S. Department of Education and the Council for Higher Education Accreditation (CHEA). Recognized agencies adhere to certain standards and practices, and their authority in matters of accreditation is widely accepted in the educational community.

This does not mean, however, that accreditation is a simple matter, either for schools wishing to become accredited or for students deciding where to apply. Indeed, in certain fields the very meaning and methods of accreditation are the subject of a good deal of debate. For their part, those applying to graduate school should be aware of the safeguards provided by regional accreditation, especially in terms of degree acceptance and institutional longevity. Beyond this, applicants should understand the role that specialized accreditation plays in their field, as this varies considerably from one discipline to another. In certain professional fields, it is necessary to have graduated from a program that is accredited in order to be eligible for a license to practice, and in some fields the federal government also makes this a hiring requirement. In other disciplines, however, accreditation is not as essential, and there can be excellent programs that are not accredited. In fact, some programs choose not to seek accreditation, although most do.

Institutions and programs that present themselves for accreditation are sometimes granted the status of candidate for accreditation, or what is known as "preaccreditation." This may happen, for example, when an academic unit is too new to have met all the requirements for accreditation. Such status signifies initial recognition and indicates that the school or program in question is working to fulfill all requirements; it does not, however, guarantee that accreditation will be granted.

Institutional Accrediting Agencies—Regional

MIDDLE STATES COMMISSION ON HIGHER EDUCATION

Accredits institutions in Delaware, District of Columbia, Maryland, New Jersey, New York, Pennsylvania, Puerto Rico, and the Virgin Islands.

Dr. Elizabeth Sibolski, President
Middle States Commission on Higher Education
3624 Market Street, Second Floor West
Philadelphia, Pennsylvania 19104
Phone: 267-284-5000
Fax: 215-662-5501
E-mail: info@msche.org
Website: www.msche.org

NEW ENGLAND ASSOCIATION OF SCHOOLS AND COLLEGES

Accredits institutions in Connecticut, Maine, Massachusetts, New Hampshire, Rhode Island, and Vermont.

Dr. Barbara E. Brittingham, President/Director
Commission on Institutions of Higher Education
3 Burlington Woods Drive, Suite 100
Burlington, Massachusetts 01803-4531
Phone: 855-886-3272 or 781-425-7714
Fax: 781-425-1001
E-mail: cihe@neasc.org
Website: https://cihe.neasc.org

THE HIGHER LEARNING COMMISSION

Accredits institutions in Arizona, Arkansas, Colorado, Illinois, Indiana, Iowa, Kansas, Michigan, Minnesota, Missouri, Nebraska, New Mexico, North Dakota, Ohio, Oklahoma, South Dakota, West Virginia, Wisconsin, and Wyoming.

Dr. Barbara Gellman-Danley, President
The Higher Learning Commission
230 South LaSalle Street, Suite 7-500
Chicago, Illinois 60604-1413
Phone: 800-621-7440 or 312-263-0456
Fax: 312-263-7462
E-mail: info@hlcommission.org
Website: www.hlcommission.org

NORTHWEST COMMISSION ON COLLEGES AND UNIVERSITIES

Accredits institutions in Alaska, Idaho, Montana, Nevada, Oregon, Utah, and Washington.

Dr. Sandra E. Elman, President
8060 165th Avenue, NE, Suite 100
Redmond, Washington 98052
Phone: 425-558-4224
Fax: 425-376-0596
E-mail: selman@nwccu.org
Website: www.nwccu.org

SOUTHERN ASSOCIATION OF COLLEGES AND SCHOOLS

Accredits institutions in Alabama, Florida, Georgia, Kentucky, Louisiana, Mississippi, North Carolina, South Carolina, Tennessee, Texas, and Virginia.

Dr. Belle S. Wheelan, President
Commission on Colleges
1866 Southern Lane
Decatur, Georgia 30033-4097
Phone: 404-679-4500 Ext. 4504
Fax: 404-679-4558
E-mail: questions@sacscoc.org
Website: www.sacscoc.org

WESTERN ASSOCIATION OF SCHOOLS AND COLLEGES

Accredits institutions in California, Guam, and Hawaii.

Jamienne S. Studley, President
WASC Senior College and University Commission
985 Atlantic Avenue, Suite 100
Alameda, California 94501
Phone: 510-748-9001
Fax: 510-748-9797
E-mail: wasc@wscuc.org
Website: https://www.wscuc.org/

Institutional Accrediting Agencies—Other

ACCREDITING COUNCIL FOR INDEPENDENT COLLEGES AND SCHOOLS
Michelle Edwards, President
750 First Street NE, Suite 980
Washington, DC 20002-4223
Phone: 202-336-6780
Fax: 202-842-2593
E-mail: info@acics.org
Website: www.acics.org

DISTANCE EDUCATION ACCREDITING COMMISSION (DEAC)
Leah Matthews, Executive Director
1101 17th Street NW, Suite 808
Washington, DC 20036-4704
Phone: 202-234-5100
Fax: 202-332-1386
E-mail: info@deac.org
Website: www.deac.org

Specialized Accrediting Agencies

ACUPUNCTURE AND ORIENTAL MEDICINE
Mark S. McKenzie, LAc MsOM DiplOM, Executive Director
Accreditation Commission for Acupuncture and Oriental Medicine
8941 Aztec Drive, Suite 2
Eden Prairie, Minnesota 55347
Phone: 952-212-2434
Fax: 301-313-0912
E-mail: info@acaom.org
Website: www.acaom.org

ALLIED HEALTH
Kathleen Megivern, Executive Director
Commission on Accreditation of Allied Health Education Programs (CAAHEP)
25400 US Hwy 19 North, Suite 158
Clearwater, Florida 33763
Phone: 727-210-2350
Fax: 727-210-2354
E-mail: mail@caahep.org
Website: www.caahep.org

ART AND DESIGN
Karen P. Moynahan, Executive Director
National Association of Schools of Art and Design (NASAD)
Commission on Accreditation
11250 Roger Bacon Drive, Suite 21
Reston, Virginia 20190-5248
Phone: 703-437-0700
Fax: 703-437-6312
E-mail: info@arts-accredit.org
Website: http://nasad.arts-accredit.org

ATHLETIC TRAINING EDUCATION
Pamela Hansen, CAATE Director of Accreditation
Commission on Accreditation of Athletic Training Education (CAATE)
6850 Austin Center Blvd., Suite 100
Austin, Texas 78731-3184
Phone: 512-733-9700
E-mail: pamela@caate.net
Website: www.caate.net

AUDIOLOGY EDUCATION
Meggan Olek, Director
Accreditation Commission for Audiology Education (ACAE)
11480 Commerce Park Drive, Suite 220
Reston, Virginia 20191
Phone: 202-986-9500
Fax: 202-986-9550
E-mail: info@acaeaccred.org
Website: https://acaeaccred.org/

AVIATION
Dr. Gary J. Northam, President
Aviation Accreditation Board International (AABI)
3410 Skyway Drive
Auburn, Alabama 36830
Phone: 334-844-2431
Fax: 334-844-2432
E-mail: gary.northam@auburn.edu
Website: www.aabi.aero

BUSINESS
Stephanie Bryant, Executive Vice President and Chief Accreditation Officer
AACSB International—The Association to Advance Collegiate Schools of Business
777 South Harbour Island Boulevard, Suite 750
Tampa, Florida 33602
Phone: 813-769-6500
Fax: 813-769-6559
E-mail: stephanie.bryant@aacsb.edu
Website: www.aacsb.edu

BUSINESS EDUCATION
Dr. Phyllis Okrepkie, President
International Assembly for Collegiate Business Education (IACBE)
11374 Strang Line Road
Lenexa, Kansas 66215
Phone: 913-631-3009
Fax: 913-631-9154
E-mail: iacbe@iacbe.org
Website: www.iacbe.org

CHIROPRACTIC
Dr. Craig S. Little, President
Council on Chiropractic Education (CCE)
Commission on Accreditation
8049 North 85th Way
Scottsdale, Arizona 85258-4321
Phone: 480-443-8877 or 888-443-3506
Fax: 480-483-7333
E-mail: cce@cce-usa.org
Website: www.cce-usa.org

CLINICAL LABORATORY SCIENCES
Dianne M. Cearlock, Ph.D., Chief Executive Officer
National Accrediting Agency for Clinical Laboratory Sciences
5600 North River Road, Suite 720
Rosemont, Illinois 60018-5119
Phone: 773-714-8880 or 847-939-3597
Fax: 773-714-8886
E-mail: info@naacls.org
Website: www.naacls.org

CLINICAL PASTORAL EDUCATION
Trace Haythorn, Ph.D., Executive Director/CEO
Association for Clinical Pastoral Education, Inc.
One West Court Square, Suite 325
Decatur, Georgia 30030-2576
Phone: 678-363-6226
Fax: 404-320-0849
E-mail: acpe@acpe.edu
Website: www.acpe.edu

DANCE
Karen P. Moynahan, Executive Director
National Association of Schools of Dance (NASD)
Commission on Accreditation
11250 Roger Bacon Drive, Suite 21
Reston, Virginia 20190-5248
Phone: 703-437-0700
Fax: 703-437-6312
E-mail: info@arts-accredit.org
Website: http://nasd.arts-accredit.org

DENTISTRY
Dr. Kathleen T. O'Loughlin, Executive Director
Commission on Dental Accreditation
American Dental Association
211 East Chicago Avenue
Chicago, Illinois 60611
Phone: 312-440-2500
E-mail: accreditation@ada.org
Website: www.ada.org

DIETETICS AND NUTRITION
Mary B. Gregoire, Ph.D., Executive Director; RD, FADA, FAND
Academy of Nutrition and Dietetics
Accreditation Council for Education in Nutrition and Dietetics (ACEND)
120 South Riverside Plaza
Chicago, Illinois 60606-6995
Phone: 800-877-1600 or 312-899-0040
E-mail: acend@eatright.org
Website: www.eatright.org/cade

EDUCATION PREPARATION
Christopher Koch, President
Council for the Accreditation of Educator Preparation (CAEP)
1140 19th Street NW, Suite 400
Washington, DC 20036
Phone: 202-223-0077
Fax: 202-296-6620
E-mail: caep@caepnet.org
Website: www.caepnet.org

ENGINEERING
Michael Milligan, Ph.D., PE, Executive Director
Accreditation Board for Engineering and Technology, Inc. (ABET)
415 North Charles Street
Baltimore, Maryland 21201
Phone: 410-347-7700
E-mail: accreditation@abet.org
Website: www.abet.org

FORENSIC SCIENCES
Nancy J. Jackson, Director of Development and Accreditation
American Academy of Forensic Sciences (AAFS)
Forensic Science Education Program Accreditation Commission (FEPAC)
410 North 21st Street
Colorado Springs, Colorado 80904
Phone: 719-636-1100
Fax: 719-636-1993
E-mail: njackson@aafs.org
Website: www.fepac-edu.org

FORESTRY
Carol L. Redelsheimer
Director of Science and Education
Society of American Foresters
10100 Laureate Way
Bethesda, Maryland 20814-2198
Phone: 301-897-8720 or 866-897-8720
Fax: 301-897-3690
E-mail: membership@safnet.org
Website: www.eforester.com

HEALTHCARE MANAGEMENT
Commission on Accreditation of Healthcare Management Education (CAHME)
Anthony Stanowski, President and CEO
6110 Executive Boulevard, Suite 614
Rockville, Maryland 20852
Phone: 301-298-1820
E-mail: info@cahme.org
Website: www.cahme.org

HEALTH INFORMATICS AND HEALTH MANAGEMENT
Angela Kennedy, EdD, MBA, RHIA, Chief Executive Officer
Commission on Accreditation for Health Informatics and Information Management Education (CAHIIM)
233 North Michigan Avenue, 21st Floor
Chicago, Illinois 60601-5800
Phone: 312-233-1134
Fax: 312-233-1948
E-mail: info@cahiim.org
Website: www.cahiim.org

HUMAN SERVICE EDUCATION
Dr. Elaine Green, President
Council for Standards in Human Service Education (CSHSE)
3337 Duke Street
Alexandria, Virginia 22314
Phone: 571-257-3959
E-mail: info@cshse.org
Website: www.cshse.org

INTERIOR DESIGN
Holly Mattson, Executive Director
Council for Interior Design Accreditation
206 Grandview Avenue, Suite 350
Grand Rapids, Michigan 49503-4014
Phone: 616-458-0400
Fax: 616-458-0460
E-mail: info@accredit-id.org
Website: www.accredit-id.org

JOURNALISM AND MASS COMMUNICATIONS
Patricia Thompson, Executive Director
Accrediting Council on Education in Journalism and Mass Communications (ACEJMC)
201 Bishop Hall
P.O. Box 1848
University, MS 38677-1848
Phone: 662-915-5504
E-mail: pthomps1@olemiss.edu
Website: www.acejmc.org

LANDSCAPE ARCHITECTURE
Nancy Somerville, Executive Vice President, CEO
American Society of Landscape Architects (ASLA)
636 Eye Street, NW
Washington, DC 20001-3736
Phone: 202-898-2444
Fax: 202-898-1185
E-mail: info@asla.org
Website: www.asla.org

LAW
Barry Currier, Managing Director of Accreditation & Legal Education
American Bar Association
321 North Clark Street, 21st Floor
Chicago, Illinois 60654
Phone: 312-988-6738
Fax: 312-988-5681
E-mail: legaled@americanbar.org
Website: https://www.americanbar.org/groups/legal_education/accreditation.html

LIBRARY
Karen O'Brien, Director
Office for Accreditation
American Library Association
50 East Huron Street
Chicago, Illinois 60611-2795
Phone: 800-545-2433, ext. 2432 or 312-280-2432
Fax: 312-280-2433
E-mail: accred@ala.org
Website: http://www.ala.org/aboutala/offices/accreditation/

MARRIAGE AND FAMILY THERAPY
Tanya A. Tamarkin, Director of Educational Affairs
Commission on Accreditation for Marriage and Family Therapy
    Education (COAMFTE)
American Association for Marriage and Family Therapy
112 South Alfred Street
Alexandria, Virginia 22314-3061
Phone: 703-838-9808
Fax: 703-838-9805
E-mail: coa@aamft.org
Website: www.aamft.org

MEDICAL ILLUSTRATION
Kathleen Megivern, Executive Director
Commission on Accreditation of Allied Health Education Programs
    (CAAHEP)
25400 US Highway 19 North, Suite 158
Clearwater, Florida 33756
Phone: 727-210-2350
Fax: 727-210-2354
E-mail: mail@caahep.org
Website: www.caahep.org

MEDICINE
Liaison Committee on Medical Education (LCME)
Robert B. Hash, M.D., LCME Secretary
American Medical Association
Council on Medical Education
330 North Wabash Avenue, Suite 39300
Chicago, Illinois 60611-5885
Phone: 312-464-4933
E-mail: lcme@aamc.org
Website: www.ama-assn.org

Liaison Committee on Medical Education (LCME)
Heather Lent, M.A., Director
Accreditation Services
Association of American Medical Colleges
655 K Street, NW
Washington, DC 20001-2399
Phone: 202-828-0596
E-mail: lcme@aamc.org
Website: www.lcme.org

MUSIC
Karen P. Moynahan, Executive Director
National Association of Schools of Music (NASM)
Commission on Accreditation
11250 Roger Bacon Drive, Suite 21
Reston, Virginia 20190-5248
Phone: 703-437-0700
Fax: 703-437-6312
E-mail: info@arts-accredit.org
Website: http://nasm.arts-accredit.org/

NATUROPATHIC MEDICINE
Daniel Seitz, J.D., Ed.D., Executive Director
Council on Naturopathic Medical Education
P.O. Box 178
Great Barrington, Massachusetts 01230
Phone: 413-528-8877
E-mail: https://cnme.org/contact-us/
Website: www.cnme.org

NURSE ANESTHESIA
Francis R.Gerbasi, Ph.D., CRNA, COA Executive Director
Council on Accreditation of Nurse Anesthesia Educational Programs
    (CoA-NAEP)
American Association of Nurse Anesthetists
222 South Prospect Avenue
Park Ridge, Illinois 60068-4001
Phone: 847-655-1160
Fax: 847-692-7137
E-mail: accreditation@coa.us.com
Website: http://www.coacrna.org

NURSE EDUCATION
Jennifer L. Butlin, Executive Director
Commission on Collegiate Nursing Education (CCNE)
One Dupont Circle, NW, Suite 530
Washington, DC 20036-1120
Phone: 202-887-6791
Fax: 202-887-8476
E-mail: jbutlin@aacn.nche.edu
Website: www.aacn.nche.edu/accreditation

Marsal P. Stoll, Chief Executive Officer
Accreditation Commission for Education in Nursing (ACEN)
3343 Peachtree Road, NE, Suite 850
Atlanta, Georgia 30326
Phone: 404-975-5000
Fax: 404-975-5020
E-mail: mstoll@acenursing.org
Website: www.acenursing.org

NURSE MIDWIFERY
Heather L. Maurer, M.A., Executive Director
Accreditation Commission for Midwifery Education (ACME)
American College of Nurse-Midwives
8403 Colesville Road, Suite 1550
Silver Spring, Maryland 20910
Phone: 240-485-1800
Fax: 240-485-1818
E-mail: info@acnm.org
Website: www.midwife.org/Program-Accreditation

NURSE PRACTITIONER
Gay Johnson, CEO
National Association of Nurse Practitioners in Women's Health
Council on Accreditation
505 C Street, NE
Washington, DC 20002
Phone: 202-543-9693 Ext. 1
Fax: 202-543-9858
E-mail: info@npwh.org
Website: www.npwh.org

NURSING
Marsal P. Stoll, Chief Executive Director
Accreditation Commission for Education in Nursing (ACEN)
3343 Peachtree Road, NE, Suite 850
Atlanta, Georgia 30326
Phone: 404-975-5000
Fax: 404-975-5020
E-mail: info@acenursing.org
Website: www.acenursing.org

OCCUPATIONAL THERAPY
Heather Stagliano, DHSc, OTR/L, Executive Director
The American Occupational Therapy Association, Inc.
4720 Montgomery Lane, Suite 200
Bethesda, Maryland 20814-3449
Phone: 301-652-6611 Ext. 2682
TDD: 800-377-8555
Fax: 240-762-5150
E-mail: accred@aota.org
Website: www.aoteonline.org

OPTOMETRY
Joyce L. Urbeck, Administrative Director
Accreditation Council on Optometric Education (ACOE)
American Optometric Association
243 North Lindbergh Boulevard
St. Louis, Missouri 63141-7881
Phone: 314-991-4100, Ext. 4246
Fax: 314-991-4101
E-mail: accredit@aoa.org
Website: www.theacoe.org

OSTEOPATHIC MEDICINE
Director, Department of Accreditation
Commission on Osteopathic College Accreditation (COCA)
American Osteopathic Association
142 East Ontario Street
Chicago, Illinois 60611
Phone: 312-202-8048
Fax: 312-202-8202
E-mail: predoc@osteopathic.org
Website: www.aoacoca.org

PHARMACY
Peter H. Vlasses, PharmD, Executive Director
Accreditation Council for Pharmacy Education
135 South LaSalle Street, Suite 4100
Chicago, Illinois 60603-4810
Phone: 312-664-3575
Fax: 312-664-4652
E-mail: csinfo@acpe-accredit.org
Website: www.acpe-accredit.org

PHYSICAL THERAPY
Sandra Wise, Senior Director
Commission on Accreditation in Physical Therapy Education (CAPTE)
American Physical Therapy Association (APTA)
1111 North Fairfax Street
Alexandria, Virginia 22314-1488
Phone: 703-706-3245
Fax: 703-706-3387
E-mail: accreditation@apta.org
Website: www.capteonline.org

PHYSICIAN ASSISTANT STUDIES
Sharon L. Luke, Executive Director
Accredittion Review Commission on Education for the Physician Assistant, Inc. (ARC-PA)
12000 Findley Road, Suite 275
Johns Creek, Georgia 30097
Phone: 770-476-1224
Fax: 770-476-1738
E-mail: arc-pa@arc-pa.org
Website: www.arc-pa.org

PLANNING
Jesmarie Soto Johnson, Executive Director
American Institute of Certified Planners/Association of Collegiate Schools of Planning/American Planning Association
Planning Accreditation Board (PAB)
2334 West Lawrence Avenue, Suite 209
Chicago, Illinois 60625
Phone: 773-334-7200
E-mail: smerits@planningaccreditationboard.org
Website: www.planningaccreditationboard.org

PODIATRIC MEDICINE
Heather Stagliano, OTR/L, DHSc, Executive Director
Council on Podiatric Medical Education (CPME)
American Podiatric Medical Association (APMA)
9312 Old Georgetown Road
Bethesda, Maryland 20814-1621
Phone: 301-581-9200
Fax: 301-571-4903
Website: www.cpme.org

PSYCHOLOGY AND COUNSELING
Jacqueline Remondet, Associate Executive Director, CEO of the Accrediting Unit,
Office of Program Consultation and Accreditation
American Psychological Association
750 First Street, NE
Washington, DC 20002-4202
Phone: 202-336-5979 or 800-374-2721
TDD/TTY: 202-336-6123
Fax: 202-336-5978
E-mail: apaaccred@apa.org
Website: www.apa.org/ed/accreditation

Kelly Coker, Executive Director
Council for Accreditation of Counseling and Related Educational Programs (CACREP)
1001 North Fairfax Street, Suite 510
Alexandria, Virginia 22314
Phone: 703-535-5990
Fax: 703-739-6209
E-mail: cacrep@cacrep.org
Website: www.cacrep.org

Richard M. McFall, Executive Director
Psychological Clinical Science Accreditation System (PCSAS)
1101 East Tenth Street
IU Psychology Building
Bloomington, Indiana 47405-7007
Phone: 812-856-2570
Fax: 812-322-5545
E-mail: rmmcfall@pcsas.org
Website: www.pcsas.org

PUBLIC HEALTH
Laura Rasar King, M.P.H., MCHES, Executive Director
Council on Education for Public Health
1010 Wayne Avenue, Suite 220
Silver Spring, Maryland 20910
Phone: 202-789-1050
Fax: 202-789-1895
E-mail: Lking@ceph.org
Website: www.ceph.org

PUBLIC POLICY, AFFAIRS AND ADMINISTRATION
Crystal Calarusse, Chief Accreditation Officer
Commission on Peer Review and Accreditation
Network of Schools of Public Policy, Affairs, and Administration (NASPAA-COPRA)
1029 Vermont Avenue, NW, Suite 1100
Washington, DC 20005
Phone: 202-628-8965
Fax: 202-626-4978
E-mail: copra@naspaa.org
Website: accreditation.naspaa.org

RADIOLOGIC TECHNOLOGY
Leslie Winter, Chief Executive Officer Joint Review Committee on Education in Radiologic Technology (JRCERT)
20 North Wacker Drive, Suite 2850
Chicago, Illinois 60606-3182
Phone: 312-704-5300
Fax: 312-704-5304
E-mail: mail@jrcert.org
Website: www.jrcert.org

REHABILITATION EDUCATION
Frank Lane, Ph.D., Executive Director
Council for Accreditation of Counseling and Related Educational Programs (CACREP)
1001 North Fairfax Street, Suite 510
Alexandria, Virginia 22314
Phone: 703-535-5990
Fax: 703-739-6209
E-mail: cacrep@cacrep.org
Website: www.cacrep.org

RESPIRATORY CARE
Thomas Smalling, Executive Director
Commission on Accreditation for Respiratory Care (CoARC)
1248 Harwood Road
Bedford, Texas 76021-4244
Phone: 817-283-2835
Fax: 817-354-8519
E-mail: tom@coarc.com
Website: www.coarc.com

SOCIAL WORK
Dr. Stacey Borasky, Director of Accreditation
Office of Social Work Accreditation
Council on Social Work Education
1701 Duke Street, Suite 200
Alexandria, Virginia 22314
Phone: 703-683-8080
Fax: 703-519-2078
E-mail: info@cswe.org
Website: www.cswe.org

SPEECH-LANGUAGE PATHOLOGY AND AUDIOLOGY
Kimberlee Moore, Accreditation Executive Director
American Speech-Language-Hearing Association
Council on Academic Accreditation in Audiology and Speech-Language
    Pathology
2200 Research Boulevard #310
Rockville, Maryland 20850-3289
Phone: 301-296-5700
Fax: 301-296-8750
E-mail: accreditation@asha.org
Website: http://caa.asha.org

TEACHER EDUCATION
Christopher A. Koch, President
National Council for Accreditation of Teacher Education (NCATE)
Teacher Education Accreditation Council (TEAC)
1140 19th Street, Suite 400
Washington, DC 20036
Phone: 202-223-0077
Fax: 202-296-6620
E-mail: caep@caepnet.org
Website: www.ncate.org

TECHNOLOGY
Michale S. McComis, Ed.D., Executive Director
Accrediting Commission of Career Schools and Colleges
2101 Wilson Boulevard, Suite 302
Arlington, Virginia 22201
Phone: 703-247-4212
Fax: 703-247-4533
E-mail: mccomis@accsc.org
Website: www.accsc.org

TECHNOLOGY, MANAGEMENT, AND APPLIED ENGINEERING
Kelly Schild, Director of Accreditation
The Association of Technology, Management, and Applied Engineering
(ATMAE)
275 N. York Street, Suite 401
Elmhurst, Illinois 60126
Phone: 630-433-4514
Fax: 630-563-9181
E-mail: Kelly@atmae.org
Website: www.atmae.org

THEATER
Karen P. Moynahan, Executive Director
National Association of Schools of Theatre Commission on
    Accreditation
11250 Roger Bacon Drive, Suite 21
Reston, Virginia 20190
Phone: 703-437-0700
Fax: 703-437-6312
E-mail: info@arts-accredit.org
Website: http://nast.arts-accredit.org/

THEOLOGY
Dr. Bernard Fryshman, Executive VP
Emeritus and Interim Executive Director
Association of Advanced Rabbinical and Talmudic Schools (AARTS)
Accreditation Commission
11 Broadway, Suite 405
New York, New York 10004
Phone: 212-363-1991
Fax: 212-533-5335
E-mail: k.sharfman.aarts@gmail.com

Frank Yamada, Executive Director
Association of Theological Schools in the United States and Canada
    (ATS)
Commission on Accrediting
10 Summit Park Drive
Pittsburgh, Pennsylvania 15275
Phone: 412-788-6505
Fax: 412-788-6510
E-mail: ats@ats.edu
Website: www.ats.edu

Dr. Timothy Eaton, President
Transnational Association of Christian Colleges and Schools (TRACS)
Accreditation Commission
15935 Forest Road
Forest, Virginia 24551
Phone: 434-525-9539
Fax: 434-525-9538
E-mail: info@tracs.org
Website: www.tracs.org

VETERINARY MEDICINE
Dr. Karen Brandt, Director of Education and Research
American Veterinary Medical Association (AVMA)
Council on Education
1931 North Meacham Road, Suite 100
Schaumburg, Illinois 60173-4360
Phone: 847-925-8070 Ext. 6674
Fax: 847-285-5732
E-mail: info@avma.org
Website: www.avma.org

How to Use These Guides

As you identify the particular programs and institutions that interest you, you can use both the *Graduate & Professional Programs: An Overview* volume and the specialized volumes in the series to obtain detailed information.

- *Graduate Programs in the Biological/Biomedical Sciences & Health-Related Professions*
- *Graduate Programs in Business, Education, Information Studies, Law & Social Work*
- *Graduate Programs in Engineering & Applied Sciences*
- *Graduate Programs the Humanities, Arts & Social Sciences*
- *Graduate Programs in the Physical Sciences, Mathematics, Agricultural Sciences, the Environment & Natural Resources*

Each of the specialized volumes in the series is divided into sections that contain one or more directories devoted to programs in a particular field. If you do not find a directory devoted to your field of interest in a specific volume, consult "Directories and Subject Areas" (located at the end of each volume). After you have identified the correct volume, consult the "Directories and Subject Areas in This Book" index, which shows (as does the more general directory) what directories cover subjects not specifically named in a directory or section title.

Each of the specialized volumes in the series has a number of general directories. These directories have entries for the largest unit at an institution granting graduate degrees in that field. For example, the general Engineering and Applied Sciences directory in the *Graduate Programs in Engineering & Applied Sciences* volume consists of **Profiles** for colleges, schools, and departments of engineering and applied sciences.

General directories are followed by other directories, or sections, that give more detailed information about programs in particular areas of the general field that has been covered. The general Engineering and Applied Sciences directory, in the previous example, is followed by nineteen sections with directories in specific areas of engineering, such as Chemical Engineering, Industrial/Management Engineering, and Mechanical Engineering.

Because of the broad nature of many fields, any system of organization is bound to involve a certain amount of overlap. Environmental studies, for example, is a field whose various aspects are studied in several types of departments and schools. Readers interested in such studies will find information on relevant programs in the *Graduate Programs in the Biological/Biomedical Sciences & Health-Related Professions* volume under Ecology and Environmental Biology and Environmental and Occupational Health; in the *Graduate Programs in the Physical Sciences, Mathematics, Agricultural Sciences, the Environment & Natural Resources* volume under Environmental Management and Policy and Natural Resources; and in the *Graduate Programs in Engineering & Applied Sciences* volume under Energy Management and Policy and Environmental Engineering. To help you find all of the programs of interest to you, the introduction to each section within the specialized volumes includes, if applicable, a paragraph suggesting other sections and directories with information on related areas of study.

Directory of Institutions and Their Offerings

This directory lists institutions in alphabetical order and includes beneath each name the academic fields in which each institution offers graduate programs. The degree level in each field is also indicated, provided that the institution has supplied that information in response to Peterson's Annual Survey of Graduate and Professional Institutions.

An M indicates that a master's degree program is offered; a D indicates that a doctoral degree program is offered; an O signifies that other advanced degrees (e.g., certificates or specialist degrees) are offered; and an * (asterisk) indicates that a **Close-Up** and/or **Display** is

located in this volume. See the index, "Close-Ups and Displays," for the specific page number.

Profiles of Academic and Professional Programs in the Specialized Volumes

Each section of **Profiles** has a table of contents that lists the Program Directories, **Displays**, and **Close-Ups**. Program Directories consist of the **Profiles** of programs in the relevant fields, with **Displays** following if programs have chosen to include them. **Close-Ups,** which are more individualized statements, are also listed for those graduate schools or programs that have chosen to submit them.

The **Profiles** found in the 500 directories in the specialized volumes provide basic data about the graduate units in capsule form for quick reference. To make these directories as useful as possible, **Profiles** are generally listed for an institution's smallest academic unit within a subject area. In other words, if an institution has a College of Liberal Arts that administers many related programs, the **Profile** for the individual program (e.g., Program in History), not the entire College, appears in the directory.

There are some programs that do not fit into any current directory and are not given individual **Profiles**. The directory structure is reviewed annually in order to keep this number to a minimum and to accommodate major trends in graduate education.

The following outline describes the **Profile** information found in the guides and explains how best to use that information. Any item that does not apply to or was not provided by a graduate unit is omitted from its listing. The format of the **Profiles** is constant, making it easy to compare one institution with another and one program with another.

A ★ graphic next to the school's name indicates the institution has additional detailed information in a "Premium Profile" on Petersons.com. After reading their information here, you can learn more about the school by visiting www.petersons.com and searching for that particular college or university's graduate program.

Identifying Information. The institution's name, in boldface type, is followed by a complete listing of the administrative structure for that field of study. (For example, University of Akron, Buchtel College of Arts and Sciences, Department of Theoretical and Applied Mathematics, Program in Mathematics.) The last unit listed is the one to which all information in the **Profile** pertains. The institution's city, state, and ZIP code follow.

Offerings. Each field of study offered by the unit is listed with all postbaccalaureate degrees awarded. Degrees that are not preceded by a specific concentration are awarded in the general field listed in the unit name. Frequently, fields of study are broken down into subspecializations, and those appear following the degrees awarded; for example, "Offerings in secondary education (M.Ed.), including English education, mathematics education, science education." Students enrolled in the M.Ed. program would be able to specialize in any of the three fields mentioned.

Professional Accreditation. Some **Profiles** indicate whether a program is professionally accredited. Because it is possible for a program to receive or lose professional accreditation at any time, students entering fields in which accreditation is important to a career should verify the status of programs by contacting either the chairperson or the appropriate accrediting association.

Jointly Offered Degrees. Explanatory statements concerning programs that are offered in cooperation with other institutions are included in the list of degrees offered. This occurs most commonly on a regional basis (for example, two state universities offering a cooperative Ph.D. in special education) or where the specialized nature of the institutions encourages joint efforts (a J.D./M.B.A. offered by a law school at an institution with no formal business programs and an institution with a business school but lacking a law school). Only programs that are truly cooperative are listed; those involving only limited course work at another institution are not. Interested students should contact the heads of such units for further information.

Program Availability. This may include the following: part-time, evening/weekend, online only, 100% online, blended/hybrid learning, and/or minimal on-campus study. When information regarding the availability of part-time or evening/weekend study appears in the **Profile**, it means that students are able to earn a degree exclusively through such study. Blended/hybrid learning describes those courses in which some traditional in-class time has been replaced by online learning activities. Hybrid courses take advantage of the best features of both face-to-face and online learning.

Faculty. Figures on the number of faculty members actively involved with graduate students through teaching or research are separated into full- and part-time as well as men and women whenever the information has been supplied.

Students. Figures for the number of students enrolled in graduate and professional programs pertain to the semester of highest enrollment from the 2017–18 academic year. These figures are broken down into full- and part-time and men and women whenever the data have been supplied. Information on the number of matriculated students enrolled in the unit who are members of a minority group or are international students appears here. The average age of the matriculated students is followed by the number of applicants, the percentage accepted, and the number enrolled for fall 2017.

Degrees Awarded. The number of degrees awarded in the calendar year is listed. Many doctoral programs offer a terminal master's degree if students leave the program after completing only part of the requirements for a doctoral degree; that is indicated here. All degrees are classified into one of four types: master's, doctoral, first professional, and other advanced degrees. A unit may award one or several degrees at a given level; however, the data are only collected by type and may therefore represent several different degree programs.

Degree Requirements. The information in this section is also broken down by type of degree, and all information for a degree level pertains to all degrees of that type unless otherwise specified. Degree requirements are collected in a simplified form to provide some very basic information on the nature of the program and on foreign language, thesis or dissertation, comprehensive exam, and registration requirements. Many units also provide a short list of additional requirements, such as fieldwork or an internship. For complete information on graduation requirements, contact the graduate school or program directly.

Entrance Requirements. Entrance requirements are broken down into the four degree levels of master's, doctoral, first professional, and other advanced degrees. Within each level, information may be provided in two basic categories: entrance exams and other requirements. The entrance exams are identified by the standard acronyms used by the testing agencies, unless they are not well known. Other entrance requirements are quite varied, but they often contain an undergraduate or graduate grade point average (GPA). Unless otherwise stated, the GPA is calculated on a 4.0 scale and is listed as a minimum required for admission. Additional exam requirements/recommendations for international students may be listed here. Application deadlines for domestic and international students, the application fee, and whether electronic applications are accepted may be listed here. Note that the deadline should be used for reference only; these dates are subject to change, and students interested in applying should always contact the graduate unit directly about application procedures and deadlines.

Expenses. The typical cost of study for the 2018–2019 academic year (2017–18 if 2018–19 figures were not available) is given in two basic categories: tuition and fees. Cost of study may be quite complex at a graduate institution. There are often sliding scales for part-time study, a different cost for first-year students, and other variables that make it impossible to completely cover the cost of study for each graduate program. To provide the most usable information, figures are given for full-time study for a full year where available and for part-time study in terms of a per-unit rate (per credit, per semester hour, etc.). Occasionally, variances may be noted in tuition and fees for reasons such as the type of program, whether courses are taken during the day or evening, whether courses are at the master's or doctoral level, or other institution-specific reasons. Respondents were also given the opportunity to provide more specific and detailed tuition and fees information at the unit level. When provided, this information will appear in

place of any typical costs entered elsewhere on the university-level survey. Expenses are usually subject to change; for exact costs at any given time, contact your chosen schools and programs directly. Keep in mind that the tuition of Canadian institutions is usually given in Canadian dollars.

Financial Support. This section contains data on the number of awards administered by the institution and given to graduate students during the 2017–18 academic year. The first figure given represents the total number of students receiving financial support enrolled in that unit. If the unit has provided information on graduate appointments, these are broken down into three major categories: fellowships give money to graduate students to cover the cost of study and living expenses and are not based on a work obligation or research commitment, research assistantships provide stipends to graduate students for assistance in a formal research project with a faculty member, and teaching assistantships provide stipends to graduate students for teaching or for assisting faculty members in teaching undergraduate classes. Within each category, figures are given for the total number of awards, the average yearly amount per award, and whether full or partial tuition reimbursements are awarded. In addition to graduate appointments, the availability of several other financial aid sources is covered in this section. Tuition waivers are routinely part of a graduate appointment, but units sometimes waive part or all of a student's tuition even if a graduate appointment is not available. Federal Work Study is made available to students who demonstrate need and meet the federal guidelines; this form of aid normally includes 10 or more hours of work per week in an office of the institution. Institutionally sponsored loans are low-interest loans available to graduate students to cover both educational and living expenses. Career-related internships or fieldwork offer money to students who are participating in a formal off-campus research project or practicum. Grants, scholarships, traineeships, unspecified assistantships, and other awards may also be noted. The availability of financial support to part-time students is also indicated here.

Some programs list the financial aid application deadline and the forms that need to be completed for students to be eligible for financial awards. There are two forms: FAFSA, the Free Application for Federal Student Aid, which is required for federal aid, and the CSS PROFILE®.

Faculty Research. Each unit has the opportunity to list several keyword phrases describing the current research involving faculty members and graduate students. Space limitations prevent the unit from listing complete information on all research programs. The total expenditure for funded research from the previous academic year may also be included.

Unit Head and Application Contact. The head of the graduate program for each unit may be listed with academic title, phone and fax numbers, and e-mail address. In addition to the unit head's contact information, many graduate programs also list a separate contact for application and admission information, followed by the graduate school, program, or department's website. If no unit head or application contact is given, you should contact the overall institution for information on graduate admissions.

Displays and Close-Ups

The **Displays** and **Close-Ups** are supplementary insertions submitted by deans, chairs, and other administrators who wish to offer an additional, more individualized statement to readers. A number of graduate school and program administrators have attached a **Display** ad near the **Profile** listing. Here you will find information that an institution or program wants to emphasize. The **Close-Ups** are by their very nature more expansive and flexible than the **Profiles**, and the administrators who have written them may emphasize different aspects of their programs. All of the **Close-Ups** are organized in the same way (with the exception of a few that describe research and training opportunities instead of degree programs), and in each one you will find information on the same basic topics, such as programs of study, research facilities, tuition and fees, financial aid, and application procedures. If an institution or program has submitted a **Close-Up**, a boldface cross-reference appears below its **Profile**. As with the **Displays**, all of the **Close-Ups** in the guides have been submitted by choice; the absence of a **Display** or **Close-Up** does not reflect any type of editorial judgment on the part of Peterson's, and their presence in the guides should not be taken as an indication of status, quality, or approval. Statements regarding a university's objectives and accomplishments are a reflection of its own beliefs and are not the opinions of the Peterson's editors.

Appendixes

This section contains two appendixes. The first, "Institutional Changes Since the 2018 Edition," lists institutions that have closed, merged, or changed their name or status since the last edition of the guides. The second, "Abbreviations Used in the Guides," gives abbreviations of degree names, along with what those abbreviations stand for. These appendixes are identical in all six volumes of *Peterson's Graduate and Professional Programs*.

Indexes

There are three indexes presented here. The first index, "Close-Ups and Displays," gives page references for all programs that have chosen to place **Close-Ups** and **Displays** in this volume. It is arranged alphabetically by institution; within institutions, the arrangement is alphabetical by subject area. It is not an index to all programs in the book's directories of **Profiles**; readers must refer to the directories themselves for **Profile** information on programs that have not submitted the additional, more individualized statements. The second index, "Directories and Subject Areas in Other Books in This Series", gives book references for the directories in the specialized volumes and also includes cross-references for subject area names not used in the directory structure, for example, "Computing Technology (see Computer Science)." The third index, "Directories and Subject Areas in This Book," gives page references for the directories in this volume and cross-references for subject area names not used in this volume's directory structure.

Data Collection Procedures

The information published in the directories and Profiles of all the books is collected through Peterson's Annual Survey of Graduate and Professional Institutions. The survey is sent each spring to nearly 2,300 institutions offering postbaccalaureate degree programs, including accredited institutions in the United States, U.S. territories, and Canada and those institutions outside the United States that are accredited by U.S. accrediting bodies. Deans and other administrators complete these surveys, providing information on programs in the 500 academic and professional fields covered in the guides as well as overall institutional information. While every effort has been made to ensure the accuracy and completeness of the data, information is sometimes unavailable or changes occur after publication deadlines. All usable information received in time for publication has been included. The omission of any particular item from a directory or Profile signifies either that the item is not applicable to the institution or program or that information was not available. Profiles of programs scheduled to begin during the 2018–19 academic year cannot, obviously, include statistics on enrollment or, in many cases, the number of faculty members. If no usable data were submitted by an institution, its name, address, and program name appear in order to indicate the availability of graduate work.

Criteria for Inclusion in This Guide

To be included in this guide, an institution must have full accreditation or be a candidate for accreditation (preaccreditation) status by an institutional or specialized accrediting body recognized by the U.S. Department of Education or the Council for Higher Education Accreditation (CHEA). Institutional accrediting bodies, which review each institution as a whole, include the six regional associations of schools and colleges (Middle States, New England, North Central, Northwest, Southern, and Western), each of which is responsible for a specified portion of the United States and its territories. Other institutional accrediting bodies are national in scope and accredit specific kinds of institutions (e.g., Bible colleges, independent colleges, and rabbinical and Talmudic schools). Program registration by the New York State Board of Regents is considered to be the equivalent of institutional accreditation, since the board requires that all programs offered by an institution meet its standards before recognition is granted. A Canadian institution must be chartered and authorized to grant degrees by the provincial government, affiliated with a chartered institution, or accredited by a recognized U.S. accrediting body. This guide also includes institutions outside the United States that are accredited by these U.S. accrediting bodies. There are recognized specialized or professional accrediting bodies in more than fifty different fields, each of which is authorized to accredit institutions or specific programs in its particular field. For specialized institutions that offer programs in one field only, we designate this to be the equivalent of institutional accreditation. A full explanation of the accrediting process and complete information on recognized institutional (regional and national) and specialized accrediting bodies can be found online at **www.chea.org** or at **www.ed.gov/admins/finaid/accred/index.html**.

DIRECTORY OF GRADUATE AND PROFESSIONAL PROGRAMS BY FIELD

ACCOUNTING

Institution	Degree
Abilene Christian University	M
Adelphi University	M
Adrian College	M
Alabama State University	M
Albany State University	M
Albertus Magnus College	M
Alfred University	M
American Business & Technology University	M
American InterContinental University Online	
American International College	M,D,O
American Public University System	M,D
American University	M,O
American University of Sharjah	M,D
Anderson University (IN)	M,D
Andrews University	M
Angelo State University	M
Appalachian State University	M
Argosy University, Atlanta	M,D
Argosy University, Chicago	M,D
Argosy University, Hawai'i	M,D,O
Argosy University, Los Angeles	M,D
Argosy University, Northern Virginia	M,D,O
Argosy University, Orange County	M,D,O
Argosy University, Phoenix	M,D
Argosy University, Seattle	M,D
Argosy University, Tampa	M,D
Argosy University, Twin Cities	M,D
Arizona State University at the Tempe campus	M,D
Arkansas State University	M
Ashland University	M
Assumption College	M,O
Auburn University	M
Auburn University at Montgomery	M
Augustana University	M
Aurora University	M
Averett University	M
Azusa Pacific University	M
Babson College	M,O
Baker College Center for Graduate Studies–Online	M,D
Baldwin Wallace University	M
Ball State University	M
Barry University	M
Baruch College of the City University of New York	M,D*
Bayamón Central University	M
Baylor University	M
Bay Path University	M
Belmont University	M
Benedictine University	M
Bentley University	M,D
Binghamton University, State University of New York	M
Bloomfield College	M
Bloomsburg University of Pennsylvania	M
Bluffton University	M
Bob Jones University	M,D,O
Boise State University	M
Boston College	M
Bowling Green State University	M
Bradley University	M
Brandman University	M
Brenau University	M
Bridgewater State University	M
Brock University	M
Brooklyn College of the City University of New York	M
Bryant University	M
Cabrini University	M,D
Cairn University	M,O
California Baptist University	M
California Polytechnic State University, San Luis Obispo	M
California State Polytechnic University, Pomona	M
California State University, East Bay	M
California State University, Fullerton	M
California State University, Los Angeles	M
California State University, Sacramento	M
California State University, San Bernardino	M
California Western School of Law	M,D
Calvin College	M
Canisius College	M
Capella University	M,D
Carnegie Mellon University	D
Case Western Reserve University	M,D
The Catholic University of America	M
Centenary University	M
Central Connecticut State University	M
Central Michigan University	M,O
Chaminade University of Honolulu	M*
Chapman University	M*
Charleston Southern University	M
Chatham University	M
Christian Brothers University	M,O
City University of Seattle	M,O
Clarion University of Pennsylvania	M
Clark Atlanta University	M
Clark University	M
Clayton State University	M
Clemson University	M
Cleveland State University	M
Coastal Carolina University	M,O
The College at Brockport, State University of New York	M
College of Charleston	M
The College of Saint Rose	M
College of Staten Island of the City University of New York	M
The College of William and Mary	M
Colorado State University	M
Colorado State University–Global Campus	M
Colorado Technical University Aurora	
Colorado Technical University Colorado Springs	M,D
Columbia College (MO)	M
Columbia University	M,D
Cornell University	M,D
Creighton University	M,D
Culver-Stockton College	M
Daemen College	M
Dallas Baptist University	M
Davenport University	M
Delaware Valley University	M
Delta State University	M
DePaul University	M,D
DeSales University	M
DeVry University–Folsom Campus	
Dominican College	M
Dominican University	M
Drake University	M
Drexel University	M,D,O*
Duke University	D
Duquesne University	M
East Carolina University	M
East Central University	M
Eastern Connecticut State University	M
Eastern Illinois University	M
Eastern Michigan University	M
Eastern Washington University	M
East Tennessee State University	M
Edgewood College	M
Elms College	M,O
Emory University	M,D
Emporia State University	M
Everglades University	M
Fairfield University	M,O
Fairleigh Dickinson University, Florham Campus	M
Fairleigh Dickinson University, Metropolitan Campus	M,O
Fitchburg State University	M
Florida Agricultural and Mechanical University	M
Florida Atlantic University	M
Florida Gulf Coast University	M
Florida International University	M
Florida National University	M
Florida Southern College	M
Florida State University	M,D
Fontbonne University	M
Fordham University	M,D
Franklin University	M
Freed-Hardeman University	M
Friends University	M
George Fox University	M,D
George Mason University	M
The George Washington University	M
Georgia College & State University	M
Georgia Southern University	M
Georgia State University	M
Golden Gate University	M,D,O
Gonzaga University	M
Governors State University	M
The Graduate Center, City University of New York	D
Grand Canyon University	M
Grand Valley State University	M
Harvard University	D*
HEC Montreal	M,D,O
Hendrix College	M
Herzing University Online	M
Hodges University	M
Hofstra University	M,O
Holy Family University	M
Hood College	M,O
Howard University	M
Hunter College of the City University of New York	M
IGlobal University	M
Illinois State University	M
Indiana Tech	M
Indiana University Kokomo	M,O
Indiana University Northwest	M,O
Indiana University–Purdue University Indianapolis	M
Indiana University South Bend	M,O
Indiana Wesleyan University	M,O
Instituto Tecnologico de Santo Domingo	M,O
Inter American University of Puerto Rico, Aguadilla Campus	M
Inter American University of Puerto Rico, Arecibo Campus	M
Inter American University of Puerto Rico, Barranquitas Campus	M
Inter American University of Puerto Rico, Metropolitan Campus	M
Inter American University of Puerto Rico, Ponce Campus	M
Inter American University of Puerto Rico, San Germán Campus	M,D
Iona College	M,O
Iowa State University of Science and Technology	M
Ithaca College	M
Jackson State University	M
Jacksonville University	M
James Madison University	M
John Carroll University	M
Johnson & Wales University	M
Juniata College	M
Kansas State University	M
Kean University	M
Keiser University	M
Kennesaw State University	M
Kent State University	M,D
King University	M
Lakeland University	M
Lamar University	M
La Roche University	M
La Salle University	M,O
La Sierra University	M,O
Lehigh University	
Lehman College of the City University of New York	M
Lenoir-Rhyne University	M
Lewis University	M
Liberty University	M,D
Lipscomb University	M,O
Long Island University–LIU Brooklyn	M,O
Long Island University–LIU Post	M
Louisiana State University and Agricultural & Mechanical College	M,D
Louisiana Tech University	M,D
Loyola Marymount University	M
Loyola University Chicago	M
Maharishi University of Management	M,D
Manhattanville College	M,O
Marist College	M
Marquette University	M
Marshall University	M
Maryville University of Saint Louis	M,O
McGill University	M,D,O
Mercer University	M
Mercy College	M
Mercyhurst University	M,O
Merrimack College	M
Metropolitan State University of Denver	M
Miami University	M
Michigan State University	M,D
Middle Tennessee State University	M
Millennia Atlantic University	M
Millsaps College	M
Minnesota State University Mankato	M
Misericordia University	M
Mississippi College	M
Mississippi State University	M
Missouri State University	M
Missouri Western State University	M
Molloy College	M,O
Monmouth University	M,O
Monroe College	M
Montana State University	M
Montclair State University	M,O
Moravian College	M
Morgan State University	M,D
Mount Aloysius College	M
Murray State University	M
National American University (TX)	M
National University	M,O
Neumann University	M
New England College	M
New Jersey City University	M,O
New York University	M,D*
Niagara University	M
North Carolina Agricultural and Technical State University	M
North Carolina State University	M
North Dakota State University	M
Northeastern Illinois University	M
Northeastern State University	M
Northeastern University	M
Northern Illinois University	M
Northern Kentucky University	M,O
Northwest Christian University	M
Northwestern University	M,D
Nova Southeastern University	M
Oakland University	M
Ohio Christian University	M
Ohio Dominican University	M
Ohio Northern University	M
The Ohio State University	M
Oklahoma Christian University	M
Oklahoma State University	M,D
Old Dominion University	M
Oral Roberts University	M
Oregon State University	M,D
Our Lady of the Lake University	M
Pace University	M,O
Pacific Lutheran University	M
Pacific States University	M,O
Penn State Erie, The Behrend College	M
Penn State Harrisburg	M,O
Penn State University Park	M,D*
Pepperdine University	M
Pittsburg State University	M
Plymouth State University	M
Polytechnic University of Puerto Rico, Miami Campus	M
Polytechnic University of Puerto Rico, Orlando Campus	M
Pontifical Catholic University of Puerto Rico	M,O
Post University	M
Prairie View A&M University	M
Providence College	M
Purdue University Northwest	M
Queens College of the City University of New York	M
Quinnipiac University	M
Ramapo College of New Jersey	M
Regent University	M,D,O
Regis University	M,O
Rhode Island College	M,O
Rhodes College	M
Rider University	M,O
Robert Morris University Illinois	M
Rochester Institute of Technology	M
Rockhurst University	M,O
Rocky Mountain College	M
Roosevelt University	M
Rutgers University–Newark	M,D
Sacred Heart University	M,O
St. Ambrose University	M
St. Bonaventure University	M
St. Edward's University	M
St. Francis College	M
St. John's University (NY)	M
St. Joseph's College, Long Island Campus	M
St. Joseph's College, New York	M
Saint Joseph's College of Maine	M
Saint Joseph's University	M,O
Saint Leo University	M,D
Saint Louis University	M*
Saint Mary's College of California	
Saint Mary's University of Minnesota	M
Saint Peter's University	M
St. Thomas University	M,O
Samford University	M
Sam Houston State University	M
San Diego State University	M
San Francisco State University	M
Seattle University	M
Seton Hall University	M,O
Seton Hill University	M
Shorter University	M
Siena College	M
Slippery Rock University of Pennsylvania	M
Southeast Missouri State University	M
Southern Adventist University	M
Southern Illinois University Carbondale	M,D
Southern Illinois University Edwardsville	M
Southern Methodist University	M
Southern New Hampshire University	M,D,O
Southern Oregon University	M,O
Southern Utah University	M
Southwestern Adventist University	M
State University of New York at New Paltz	M
State University of New York College at Geneseo	M
State University of New York College at Old Westbury	M
State University of New York Polytechnic Institute	M
Stephen F. Austin State University	M
Stetson University	M
Stony Brook University, State University of New York	M,O
Stratford University (VA)	M,D
Strayer University	M
Suffolk University	M,O
Syracuse University	M
Tabor College	M
Tarleton State University	M
Temple University	M,D*
Tennessee Technological University	M
Tennessee Wesleyan University	M
Texas A&M International University	M
Texas A&M University	M
Texas A&M University–Central Texas	M,O
Texas A&M University–Commerce	M
Texas A&M University–Corpus Christi	M
Texas A&M University–San Antonio	M
Texas A&M University–Texarkana	M
Texas Christian University	M
Texas Lutheran University	M
Texas State University	M
Texas Tech University	M,D
Texas Woman's University	M
Thomas Edison State University	M
Towson University	M
Trinity University	M
Troy University	M
Truman State University	M
Tulane University	M,D
Union University	M
Universidad del Este	M
Universidad del Turabo	M
Universidad Metropolitana	M
Université de Sherbrooke	M
Université du Québec à Montréal	M,O
Université du Québec à Trois-Rivières	M
Université du Québec en Outaouais	M,O
Université Laval	M,O
University at Buffalo, the State University of New York	M,D
The University of Akron	M
The University of Alabama	M,D
The University of Alabama at Birmingham	M
The University of Alabama in Huntsville	M,O
University of Alberta	D
The University of Arizona	M
University of Arkansas	M
University of Baltimore	M
University of Bridgeport	M
The University of British Columbia	D
University of California, Berkeley	D,O
University of California, Davis	M
University of California, Irvine	M
University of California, Los Angeles	M,D
University of California, Riverside	M,D
University of Central Arkansas	M
University of Central Florida	M
University of Central Missouri	M,D,O
University of Charleston	M
University of Chicago	M,O
University of Cincinnati	M,D
University of Colorado Denver	M
University of Connecticut	M
University of Dallas	M,D

University of Dayton	M
University of Delaware	M
University of Denver	M
University of Detroit Mercy	M,O
The University of Findlay	M,D
University of Florida	M,D
University of Georgia	M
University of Hartford	M,O
University of Hawaii at Manoa	M,D
University of Houston	M,D
University of Houston–Clear Lake	M
University of Houston–Downtown	M
University of Houston–Victoria	M
University of Idaho	M
University of Illinois at Chicago	M
University of Illinois at Springfield	M
University of Illinois at Urbana–Champaign	M,D
The University of Iowa	M,D
The University of Kansas	M
University of Kentucky	M
University of La Verne	M
University of Lethbridge	M,D
University of Louisiana at Lafayette	M
University of Louisville	M
The University of Manchester	M
University of Mary Hardin-Baylor	M
University of Maryland University College	M,O
University of Massachusetts Amherst	M,D
University of Massachusetts Boston	M
University of Massachusetts Dartmouth	M,O
University of Memphis	M,D
University of Miami	M,D
University of Michigan	M,D
University of Michigan–Dearborn	M
University of Michigan–Flint	M,O
University of Minnesota, Twin Cities Campus	M,D
University of Mississippi	M,D
University of Missouri	M,D,O
University of Missouri–Kansas City	M
University of Missouri–St. Louis	M,D,O
University of Montana	M
University of Nebraska at Kearney	M
University of Nebraska at Omaha	M
University of Nebraska–Lincoln	M,D
University of Nevada, Las Vegas	M,O
University of Nevada, Reno	M
University of New Hampshire	M
University of New Haven	M,O
University of New Orleans	M
University of North Alabama	M
The University of North Carolina at Chapel Hill	M,D
The University of North Carolina at Charlotte	M
The University of North Carolina at Greensboro	M,O
The University of North Carolina Wilmington	M
University of Northern Colorado	M
University of Northern Iowa	M
University of North Florida	M
University of North Texas	M,D,O
University of North Texas at Dallas	M
University of Notre Dame	M*
University of Oklahoma	M*
University of Oregon	M
University of Pennsylvania	M,D*
University of Phoenix–Bay Area Campus	M,D
University of Phoenix–Central Valley Campus	M
University of Phoenix–Dallas Campus	M
University of Phoenix–Hawaii Campus	M
University of Phoenix–Houston Campus	M
University of Phoenix–Las Vegas Campus	M
University of Phoenix–Online Campus	M,O
University of Phoenix–Phoenix Campus	M,O
University of Phoenix–Sacramento Valley Campus	M
University of Phoenix–San Antonio Campus	M
University of Phoenix–San Diego Campus	M
University of Pittsburgh	M,D*
University of Puerto Rico–Río Piedras	M,D
University of Rhode Island	M
University of Rochester	M,D*
University of St. Francis (IL)	M,O
University of St. Thomas (TX)	M
University of St. Thomas (MN)	M
University of Saskatchewan	M
The University of Scranton	M
University of South Africa	M,D
University of South Alabama	M
University of South Carolina	M
University of South Dakota	M
University of Southern California	M
University of Southern Indiana	M
University of Southern Maine	M

University of Southern Mississippi	M
University of South Florida	M,D
The University of Tampa	M,O
The University of Tennessee	M,D
The University of Tennessee at Chattanooga	M
The University of Texas at Arlington	M,D
The University of Texas at Austin	M,D
The University of Texas at Dallas	M
The University of Texas at El Paso	M
The University of Texas at San Antonio	M,D
The University of Texas at Tyler	M
The University of Texas of the Permian Basin	M
The University of Texas Rio Grande Valley	M
University of the Cumberlands	M
University of the Incarnate Word	M
University of the Sacred Heart	M,O
The University of Toledo	M
The University of Tulsa	M
University of Utah	M,D
University of Vermont	M
University of Virginia	M
University of Washington	M,D
University of Washington, Tacoma	M
University of Waterloo	M
University of West Florida	M
University of West Georgia	M
University of Wisconsin–Madison	M,D
University of Wisconsin–Whitewater	M
University of Wyoming	M
Upper Iowa University	M
Ursuline College	M
Utah State University	M
Utah Valley University	M
Utica College	M
Valdosta State University	M
Vanderbilt University	M*
Villanova University	M
Virginia Commonwealth University	M,O
Virginia International University	M,O
Virginia Polytechnic Institute and State University	M,D
Wagner College	M
Wake Forest University	M
Walden University	M,D,O
Warner University	M
Washburn University	M
Washington & Jefferson College	M,O
Washington State University	M
Washington University in St. Louis	M
Wayland Baptist University	M,D
Wayne State University	M,D,O
Webber International University	M
Weber State University	M
Webster University	M
Western Carolina University	M
Western Connecticut State University	M
Western Governors University	M
Western Illinois University	M
Western Michigan University	M
Western New England University	M
Westfield State University	M
West Liberty University	M
Westminster College (UT)	M,O
West Texas A&M University	M
West Virginia University	M,D,O
Wheeling Jesuit University	M
Wichita State University	M
Wilfrid Laurier University	M,D
Wilkes University	M
William Paterson University of New Jersey	M,O
Wilmington University	M,D
Wilson College	M
Wingate University	M
Worcester State University	M
Wright State University	M
Xavier University	M*
Yale University	D
Yeshiva University	M
York College of Pennsylvania	M
York University	M,D
Youngstown State University	M

ACOUSTICS

Naval Postgraduate School	M,D
Penn State University Park	M,D*
Rensselaer Polytechnic Institute	D
The University of Kansas	M,D,O

ACTUARIAL SCIENCE

Ball State University	M
Boston University	M
California State University, East Bay	M
Central Connecticut State University	M,O
Columbia University	M
Florida State University	M,D
Georgia State University	M
Governors State University	M
Lock Haven University of Pennsylvania	M
Maryville University of Saint Louis	M
Middle Tennessee State University	M
The Ohio State University	M,D
Oregon State University	M,D
Roosevelt University	M
St. John's University (NY)	M
Simon Fraser University	M,D
Temple University	M*
Université du Québec à Montréal	O

University of Illinois at Urbana–Champaign	M,D
The University of Iowa	M,D
The University of Manchester	M,D
University of Nebraska–Lincoln	M
The University of Texas at Austin	M,D
The University of Texas at Dallas	M,D
University of Waterloo	M,D
University of Wisconsin–Madison	D
University of Wisconsin–Milwaukee	M,D*
Youngstown State University	M

ACUPUNCTURE AND ORIENTAL MEDICINE

Academy for Five Element Acupuncture	M
Academy of Chinese Culture and Health Sciences	M
Acupuncture & Integrative Medicine College, Berkeley	M
Acupuncture and Massage College	M
American Academy of Acupuncture and Oriental Medicine	M,D
American College of Acupuncture and Oriental Medicine	M
American Institute of Alternative Medicine	M
AOMA Graduate School of Integrative Medicine	M,D
Arizona School of Acupuncture and Oriental Medicine	M
Atlantic Institute of Oriental Medicine	M,D
Bastyr University	M,D
California Institute of Integral Studies	M,D
Canadian Memorial Chiropractic College	O
Colorado School of Traditional Chinese Medicine	M
Daoist Traditions College of Chinese Medical Arts	M,D
Dongguk University Los Angeles	M
Dragon Rises College of Oriental Medicine	M
Eastern School of Acupuncture and Traditional Medicine	M
East West College of Natural Medicine	M
Emperor's College of Traditional Oriental Medicine	M,D
Five Branches University	M,D
Florida College of Integrative Medicine	M
Institute of Clinical Acupuncture and Oriental Medicine	M
Institute of Taoist Education and Acupuncture	M
Maryland University of Integrative Health	M,D,O
MCPHS University	M
Midwest College of Oriental Medicine	M,O
National University of Health Sciences	M,D
National University of Natural Medicine	M
New York Chiropractic College	M
New York College of Health Professions	M
New York College of Traditional Chinese Medicine	M
Northwestern Health Sciences University	M
Oregon College of Oriental Medicine	M,D
Pacific College of Oriental Medicine	M,D
Pacific College of Oriental Medicine–Chicago	M
Pacific College of Oriental Medicine-New York	M
Phoenix Institute of Herbal Medicine & Acupuncture	M
Seattle Institute of East Asian Medicine	M
South Baylo University	M
Southern California University of Health Sciences	M,D
Southwest Acupuncture College	M
Swedish Institute, College of Health Sciences	M
Texas Health and Science University	M,D
University of Bridgeport	M
University of East-West Medicine	M,D
Virginia University of Integrative Medicine	M,D,O
Wongu University of Oriental Medicine	M
Won Institute of Graduate Studies	M,O
Yo San University of Traditional Chinese Medicine	M

ACUTE CARE/CRITICAL CARE NURSING

Augusta University	D
Barry University	M,O
Case Western Reserve University	M,O
The College of New Rochelle	M,O
Columbia University	M
Drexel University	M*
Duke University	M,D,O
Elms College	M,D
Georgetown University	M,D
Goldfarb School of Nursing at Barnes-Jewish College	M
Grand Canyon University	M,D,O

Indiana University–Purdue University Indianapolis	M
Inter American University of Puerto Rico, Arecibo Campus	M
Inter American University of Puerto Rico, Barranquitas Campus	M
Marquette University	M,D,O
Maryville University of Saint Louis	M,D
Moravian College	M
Mount Carmel College of Nursing	M,D
New York University	M,D,O*
Northeastern University	M,D,O
Point Loma Nazarene University	M
Purdue University Northwest	M
San Francisco State University	M,O
Southern Adventist University	M,D
Tennessee Technological University	D
Texas Tech University Health Sciences Center	M,D,O
Texas Woman's University	M,D
Universidad de Iberoamerica	M,D
The University of Alabama in Huntsville	M,D,O
University of Cincinnati	M,D
University of Guelph	M,D,O
University of Illinois at Chicago	M,O
University of Miami	M,D
The University of North Carolina at Charlotte	M,D,O
University of Northern Colorado	M,D
University of Pennsylvania	M*
University of Puerto Rico–Medical Sciences Campus	M
University of Rhode Island	M,D,O
University of Rochester	M,D*
University of South Africa	M,D
University of South Carolina	M,O
University of South Florida	M,D,O
The University of Texas Health Science Center at San Antonio	M,D,O
University of Virginia	M,D
Wayne State University	M,D
Winona State University	M,D
Wright State University	M

ADDICTIONS/SUBSTANCE ABUSE COUNSELING

Adler Graduate School	M
Adler University	O
Alliant International University–Los Angeles	M
Antioch University New England	M
Argosy University, Hawai'i	O
Arkansas State University	M,O
Assumption College	O
Bay Path University	M
Cambridge College	M,O
Capella University	M,D
The College of New Jersey	M,O
College of St. Joseph	M
Coppin State University	M
East Carolina University	M,D,O
Fairfield University	M,O
The George Washington University	M
Governors State University	M
Hazelden Betty Ford Graduate School of Addiction Studies	M,O
Houston Baptist University	M
Indiana University Northwest	M,O
Indiana University South Bend	M,O
Indiana Wesleyan University	M
Johnson & Wales University	M
Kean University	M
Lenoir-Rhyne University	M
Lewis & Clark College	M
Liberty University	M,D,O
Loma Linda University	M,D,O
Long Island University–Hudson	M,O
Maryville University of Saint Louis	M
Metropolitan State University	M
Monmouth University	M,O
Montclair State University	O
Northern Vermont University–Johnson	M
Northwest Nazarene University	M
Nova Southeastern University	M,D,O
Oral Roberts University	M
Pace University	M
Palm Beach Atlantic University	M
Plymouth State University	M
Post University	M
Regent University	M,D,O
Salve Regina University	M,O
Stephens College	M,O
Stony Brook University, State University of New York	M,O
Syracuse University	M,O
Texas Tech University Health Sciences Center	M
United States International University–Africa	M
Universidad Central del Caribe	M
University of California, Berkeley	O
University of Central Oklahoma	M
University of Cincinnati	M,D,O
University of Detroit Mercy	M,D,O
University of Illinois at Springfield	M,O
University of Indianapolis	M,D
University of Lethbridge	M,D
University of Louisville	M,D,O
University of Nevada, Las Vegas	M,D,O
University of New Hampshire	M,O
The University of North Carolina at Charlotte	M,D,O
University of South Dakota	M
University of Southern Maine	M,O
University of South Florida	M,D

---

*M—masters degree; D—doctorate; O—other advanced degree; *—Close-Up and/or Display*

The University of Tennessee at Martin — M
Viterbo University — M
Walden University — M,D
Washburn University — M
Waynesburg University — M,D
Winona State University — M,O

ADULT EDUCATION

Alverno College — M
Antioch University Seattle — M
Argosy University, Chicago — M,D,O
Argosy University, Hawai'i — M,D
Argosy University, Phoenix — M,D,O
Argosy University, Seattle — M,D
Athabasca University — M,O
Auburn University — M,D,O
Aurora University — M,D
Ball State University — M,D
Buffalo State College, State University of New York — M,O
California Baptist University — M
Capella University — M,D
Carroll University — M
Chicago State University — M
Cleveland State University — M,D,O
Colorado State University — M,D
Concordia University (Canada) — M,O
Coppin State University — M
Cornell University — M,D
Dallas Theological Seminary — M,D,O
Delaware State University — M
DePaul University — M
East Carolina University — M,O
Eastern Washington University — M
Florida Agricultural and Mechanical University — M,D
Florida Atlantic University — M,D,O
Florida International University — M,D,O
The George Washington University — O
Grand Valley State University — M
Indiana University of Pennsylvania — M
Instituto Tecnologico de Santo Domingo — M,O
Kansas State University — M,D,O
Lesley University — M,D,O
Marshall University — M
Memorial University of Newfoundland — M,D,O
Michigan State University — M,D,O
Montana State University — M,D,O
Morehead State University — M,O
Mount Saint Vincent University — M
National Louis University — M,D,O
North Carolina Agricultural and Technical State University — M,D
North Carolina State University — M,D
Northern Illinois University — M,D
Northwestern Oklahoma State University — M
Northwestern State University of Louisiana — M
Oregon State University — M,D
Penn State Harrisburg — M,D,O
Penn State University Park — M,D,O*
Plymouth State University — D
Point Park University — M,D
Regent University — M,D,O
St. Francis Xavier University — M
Saint Joseph's College of Maine — M
San Francisco State University — M
Seattle University — M,O
Southern Arkansas University–Magnolia — M
State University of New York Empire State College — M
Teachers College, Columbia University — M,D
Texas A&M University–Kingsville — M
Texas A&M University–Texarkana — M
Texas State University — M,D
Trident University International — M
Troy University — M
Universidad del Este — M
Universidad Metropolitana — M,D,O
University of Alberta — M,D,O
University of Arkansas — M,D
University of Arkansas at Little Rock — M,D
The University of British Columbia — M,D
University of Calgary — M,D
University of Central Arkansas — M,O
University of Central Oklahoma — M
University of Colorado Denver — M
University of Connecticut — M,O
University of Georgia — D,O
University of Houston–Victoria — M,O
University of Manitoba — M
University of Memphis — M,D,O
University of Minnesota, Twin Cities Campus — M,D,O
University of Missouri — M,D,O
University of Missouri–St. Louis — M,O
University of Nebraska–Lincoln — M,D,O
The University of North Carolina at Greensboro — M
University of North Florida — M
University of Oklahoma — M,D*
University of Phoenix–Bay Area Campus — M,D,O
University of Phoenix–Online Campus — M,O
University of Phoenix–Phoenix Campus — M
University of Phoenix–Sacramento Valley Campus — M,O
University of Regina — M
University of South Africa — M,D

University of South Dakota — M,D,O
University of Southern Maine — M,O
University of South Florida — M,D,O
The University of Tennessee — M,D
University of the District of Columbia — O
The University of West Alabama — M
University of Wisconsin–Milwaukee — M,D,O*
University of Wisconsin–Platteville — M
Virginia Commonwealth University — M
Walden University — M,D,O
Western Kentucky University — M,D,O
Western Washington University — M
Widener University — M,D

ADULT NURSING

Adelphi University — M
Allen College — M,D
Azusa Pacific University — M
Bloomsburg University of Pennsylvania — M,D
Boston College — M,D
California Baptist University — M
Clarkson College — M,O
College of Staten Island of the City University of New York — M,O
Columbia University — M,O
Creighton University — M,D,O
Daemen College — M,D,O
Duke University — M,D,O
Eastern Michigan University — M,O
Emory University — M
Felician University — M,O
Florida International University — M,D
Florida Southern College — M
George Mason University — M,D,O
The George Washington University — M,D,O
Georgia State University — M,D,O
Gwynedd Mercy University — M,D
Hunter College of the City University of New York — M
Jacksonville University — M,D,O
Kent State University — M,D
La Salle University — M,D,O
Lehman College of the City University of New York — M
Lewis University — M,D
Loma Linda University — M
Long Island University–LIU Brooklyn — M,O
Loyola University Chicago — M
Madonna University — M
Marian University (WI) — M
Marquette University — M,D,O
Maryville University of Saint Louis — M,D
Medical University of South Carolina — M,D
Monmouth University — M,D,O
Mount Carmel College of Nursing — M,D
Mount Saint Mary College — M,O
Neumann University — M,O
New York University — M,D,O*
North Park University — M
Nova Southeastern University — M,D
Old Dominion University — M,D
Purdue University Fort Wayne — M,O
Purdue University Northwest — D
Quinnipiac University — D
Research College of Nursing — M
Rush University — D,O
Rutgers University–Newark — M,D,O
St. Catherine University — M,D
St. Joseph's College, Long Island Campus — M
St. Joseph's College, New York — M
Saint Mary's College — D
Saint Peter's University — M,D,O
Seattle Pacific University — M,O
Seton Hall University — M,D
Shenandoah University — M,D,O
Southern Adventist University — M
South University — M
Spalding University — M,D,O
Stony Brook University, State University of New York — M,D,O
Temple University — D*
Texas Christian University — M,O
Texas Woman's University — M,D
Troy University — M,D
Universidad del Turabo — M,O
University at Buffalo, the State University of New York — M,D,O
The University of Alabama at Birmingham — M,D
University of Central Arkansas — M,D
University of Cincinnati — M,D
University of Colorado Colorado Springs — M,D
University of Colorado Denver — M,D
University of Delaware — M,O
University of Hawaii at Manoa — M,D,O
University of Illinois at Chicago — M,O
The University of Kansas — M,D,O
University of Massachusetts Amherst — M,D
University of Massachusetts Medical School — M,D,O
University of Miami — M,D
University of Missouri — M,D,O
University of Missouri–Kansas City — M,D
University of Missouri–St. Louis — D,O
The University of North Carolina at Chapel Hill — M,D,O
The University of North Carolina at Greensboro — M,D,O
University of Pennsylvania — M*
University of Puerto Rico–Medical Sciences Campus — M

University of Rhode Island — M,D,O
University of Rochester — M,D*
University of San Diego — M
University of South Carolina — M
University of Southern Maine — M,D,O
University of South Florida — M,D,O
The University of Tampa — M
The University of Texas at Austin — M,D
University of Wisconsin–Eau Claire — M,D
University of Wisconsin–Madison — D
University of Wisconsin–Oshkosh — M
Ursuline College — M,D
Villanova University — M,D,O
Virginia Commonwealth University — M,D,O
Walden University — M,D,O
Walsh University — M,D
Wayne State University — M,D
Western Connecticut State University — M,D
William Paterson University of New Jersey — M,D,O
Wilmington University — M,D
Winona State University — M,D,O
Wright State University — M

ADVERTISING AND PUBLIC RELATIONS

Academy of Art University — M
Ball State University — M
Boston University — M
California Baptist University — M
Central Connecticut State University — M,O
Colorado State University — M
DePaul University — M
Georgetown University — M
Hofstra University — M
Iona College — M
Kansas State University — M
Kent State University — M
La Salle University — M,O
Lasell College — M,O
La Sierra University — M
Liberty University — M,D
Lindenwood University — M
Marquette University — M,O
Marshall University — M,O
Michigan State University — M
Mississippi College — M
Monmouth University — M,O
Montana State University Billings — M
Montclair State University — M
Mount Saint Vincent University — M
Murray State University — M
New York University — M*
Northern Kentucky University — M,O
Quinnipiac University — M
Rowan University — M
San Diego State University — M
Savannah College of Art and Design — M
Seton Hall University — M
Southeastern Louisiana University — M
Southern Illinois University Edwardsville — M
Southern Methodist University — M
Southern New Hampshire University — M,D,O
Suffolk University — M
Syracuse University — M
Universidad Autonoma de Guadalajara — M,D
Université Laval — O
The University of Alabama — M
University of Colorado Boulder — M,D
University of Florida — M
University of Houston — M
University of Illinois at Urbana–Champaign — M
University of Maryland, College Park — M,D
University of Miami — M,D
University of Nebraska–Lincoln — M
University of North Texas — M,D,O
University of Saint Mary — M
University of Southern California — M
University of Southern Mississippi — M,D
The University of Tennessee — M,D
The University of Texas at Austin — M,D
University of the Sacred Heart — M
University of Wisconsin–Stevens Point — M
Virginia Commonwealth University — M
Virginia International University — M
Wayne State University — M,D,O
Webster University — M
Western New England University — M
William Woods University — M,D,O

AEROSPACE/AERONAUTICAL ENGINEERING

Air Force Institute of Technology — M,D
Arizona State University at the Tempe campus — M,D
Auburn University — M,D
California Institute of Technology — M,D,O
California Polytechnic State University, San Luis Obispo — M
California State Polytechnic University, Pomona — M
Carleton University — M,D
Case Western Reserve University — M,D
The Citadel, The Military College of South Carolina — M,O
Concordia University (Canada) — M
Cornell University — M,D
École Polytechnique de Montréal — M,D,O
Embry-Riddle Aeronautical University–Daytona — M,D
Embry-Riddle Aeronautical University–Worldwide — M
Florida Institute of Technology — M
The George Washington University — M,D,O

Georgia Institute of Technology — M,D
Illinois Institute of Technology — M,D
Inter American University of Puerto Rico, Bayamón Campus — M
Iowa State University of Science and Technology — M,D
Johns Hopkins University — M*
Kent State University — M
Massachusetts Institute of Technology — M,D,O
McGill University — M,D
Middle Tennessee State University — M
Mississippi State University — M,D
Missouri University of Science and Technology — M,D
Naval Postgraduate School — M,D,O
North Carolina State University — M,D
The Ohio State University — M,D
Old Dominion University — M,D
Penn State University Park — M,D*
Princeton University — M,D
Purdue University — M,D
Rensselaer Polytechnic Institute — M,D
Rutgers University–New Brunswick — M,D
San Diego State University — M,D
San Jose State University — M
Stevens Institute of Technology — M,O
Syracuse University — M,D
Texas A&M University — M,D
Université Laval — M
University at Buffalo, the State University of New York — M,D
The University of Alabama — M,D
The University of Alabama in Huntsville — M,D
The University of Arizona — M,D
University of California, Davis — M,D,O
University of California, Irvine — M,D
University of California, Los Angeles — M,D
University of California, San Diego — M,D
University of Central Florida — M
University of Central Missouri — M,D,O
University of Cincinnati — M,D
University of Colorado Boulder — M,D
University of Colorado Colorado Springs — M,D
University of Dayton — M,D
University of Florida — M,D
University of Illinois at Urbana–Champaign — M,D
The University of Kansas — M,D
The University of Manchester — M,D
University of Maryland, College Park — M,D
University of Miami — M,D
University of Michigan — M,D
University of Minnesota, Twin Cities Campus — M,D
University of Missouri — M,D
University of Nevada, Las Vegas — M,D,O
University of Notre Dame — M,D
University of Oklahoma — M,D*
University of Ottawa — M,D
University of Puerto Rico–Mayagüez — M
University of Southern California — M,D,O
The University of Tennessee — M,D
The University of Texas at Arlington — M,D
The University of Texas at Austin — M,D
University of Toronto — M,D
University of Virginia — M,D
University of Washington — M,D
Utah State University — M,D
Virginia Polytechnic Institute and State University — M,D,O
Washington University in St. Louis — M,D
Webster University — M,D,O
Western Michigan University — M,D
West Virginia University — M,D
Wichita State University — M,D
Worcester Polytechnic Institute — M,D
Wright State University — M

AFRICAN-AMERICAN STUDIES

Boston University — M
Capital University — M
Carnegie Mellon University — D
Clark Atlanta University — M,D
Columbia University — M,D
Cornell University — M,D
Eastern Michigan University — O
Georgia State University — M
Harvard University — D*
Indiana University Bloomington — M,D
Michigan State University — M,D
Morgan State University — M,D
North Carolina Agricultural and Technical State University — M
Northwestern University — D
Oblate School of Theology — M,D,O
The Ohio State University — M,D
Rutgers University–New Brunswick — D
Syracuse University — M
Temple University — M,D*
University at Albany, State University of New York — M
University of California, Berkeley — D
University of California, Los Angeles — M
University of California, Santa Barbara — D
The University of Kansas — M,O
University of Louisville — M
University of Massachusetts Amherst — M,D
University of Memphis — M,D,O
University of Wisconsin–Madison — M,D
Wayne State University — M,D,O

Yale University — D

AFRICAN STUDIES

Arizona State University at the Tempe campus — M,D,O
California State University, Long Beach — M
Carnegie Mellon University — D
Claremont Graduate University — M,D,O
College of Staten Island of the City University of New York — M
Columbia University — M,D
Cornell University — M,D
Florida International University — M*
Harvard University — D*
Howard University — M
Indiana University Bloomington — M
Lehigh University — M,O
Michigan State University — M,D
New York University — M,D,O*
Northwestern University — O
The Ohio State University — M,D
Ohio University — M
Rice University — D
Rutgers University–New Brunswick — D
Stony Brook University, State University of New York — M,O
Syracuse University — M
University at Albany, State University of New York — M
The University of Arizona — M,D,O
University of California, Los Angeles — M
University of Illinois at Urbana–Champaign — M
The University of Kansas — M,O
University of Louisville — M
University of Michigan — M
The University of North Carolina at Charlotte — O
University of Pennsylvania — M,D*
University of Pittsburgh — O*
University of South Florida — M,D,O
The University of Texas at Austin — M,D
University of Wisconsin–Madison — M,D
University of Wisconsin–Milwaukee — D*
Yale University — M

AGRICULTURAL ECONOMICS AND AGRIBUSINESS

Alcorn State University — M
American University of Beirut — M
Arizona State University at the Tempe campus — D
Auburn University — M,D
Colorado State University — M,D
Cornell University — M,D
Delaware Valley University — M
Illinois State University — M
Instituto Centroamericano de Administración de Empresas — M
Iowa State University of Science and Technology — M,D
Kansas State University — M,D
Louisiana State University and Agricultural & Mechanical College — M,D
McGill University — M
Michigan State University — M,D
Mississippi State University — M
New Mexico State University — M,D
North Carolina Agricultural and Technical State University — M
North Carolina State University — M,D
North Dakota State University — M
Northwest Missouri State University — M
The Ohio State University — M,D
Oklahoma State University — M,D
Penn State University Park — M,D,O*
Purdue University — M,D
Rutgers University–New Brunswick — M
South Carolina State University — M
Southern Illinois University Carbondale — M
Texas A&M University — M,D
Texas A&M University–Kingsville — M,D
Texas Tech University — M,D
Tropical Agriculture Research and Higher Education Center — M,D
Tuskegee University — M
Universidad del Este — M
Université Laval — M
University of Alberta — M,D
The University of Arizona — M
University of Arkansas — M
The University of British Columbia — M
University of California, Berkeley — D
University of California, Davis — M,D
University of California, Santa Barbara — M,D
University of Connecticut — M
University of Delaware — M
University of Florida — M,D
University of Georgia — M,D
University of Guelph — M,D
University of Idaho — M
University of Illinois at Urbana–Champaign — M,D
University of Kentucky — M,D
University of Maine — M
University of Manitoba — M,D
University of Maryland, College Park — M,D
University of Massachusetts Amherst — M,D
University of Missouri — M,D

University of Nebraska–Lincoln — M,D
University of Puerto Rico–Mayagüez — M
University of Saskatchewan — M,D,O
The University of Tennessee at Martin — M
University of Vermont — M
University of Wisconsin–Madison — M,D
University of Wyoming — M,D
Utah State University — M,D
Virginia Polytechnic Institute and State University — M
Washington State University — M
West Texas A&M University — M

AGRICULTURAL EDUCATION

Alcorn State University — M,O
Arkansas State University — M,O
California Polytechnic State University, San Luis Obispo — M
California State University, Chico — M
Clemson University — M
Colorado State University — M
Cornell University — M
Eastern Kentucky University — M
Iowa State University of Science and Technology — M
Ithaca College — M
Kansas State University — M
Louisiana State University and Agricultural & Mechanical College — M,D
Mississippi State University — M,D
Montana State University — M
Murray State University — M,O
North Carolina Agricultural and Technical State University — M
North Dakota State University — M
Northwest Missouri State University — M
The Ohio State University — M
Oklahoma State University — M,D
Oregon State University — M,D
Penn State University Park — M,D,O*
Purdue University — M,D,O
Saint Leo University — M,D
South Dakota State University — M
State University of New York at Oswego — M
Tennessee State University — M
Texas A&M University — M,D
Texas State University — M
Texas Tech University — M,D
The University of Arizona — M,O
University of Arkansas — M
University of Connecticut — M
University of Delaware — M
University of Florida — M
University of Illinois at Urbana–Champaign — M
University of Missouri — M,D,O
University of Nebraska–Lincoln — M
University of Puerto Rico–Mayagüez — M
The University of Tennessee — M
University of Wisconsin–River Falls — M
Utah State University — M
West Virginia University — M,D

AGRICULTURAL ENGINEERING

Cornell University — M,D
Illinois Institute of Technology — M
Instituto Tecnológico y de Estudios Superiores de Monterrey, Campus Monterrey — M,D
Iowa State University of Science and Technology — M,D
Kansas State University — M,D
Louisiana State University and Agricultural & Mechanical College — M,D
McGill University — M,D
North Carolina State University — M,D,O
North Dakota State University — M,D
The Ohio State University — M,D
Oklahoma State University — M,D
Oregon State University — M,D
Penn State University Park — M,D*
Purdue University — M,D
South Dakota State University — M,D
Texas A&M University — M,D
Université Laval — M
The University of Arizona — M,D
University of Arkansas — M,D
University of Florida — M,D,O
University of Illinois at Urbana–Champaign — M,D
University of Kentucky — M,D
University of Nebraska–Lincoln — M,D
The University of Tennessee — M
University of Wisconsin–Madison — M,D
Virginia Polytechnic Institute and State University — M,D
Washington State University — M,D

AGRICULTURAL SCIENCES—GENERAL

Alabama Agricultural and Mechanical University — M,D
Alcorn State University — M
Angelo State University — M
Arkansas State University — M,O
Auburn University — M,D
Brigham Young University — M,D
California Polytechnic State University, San Luis Obispo — M
California State Polytechnic University, Pomona — M
California State University, Chico — M

Clemson University — M,D
Colorado State University — M,D
Dalhousie University — M
Illinois State University — M
Instituto Tecnológico y de Estudios Superiores de Monterrey, Campus Monterrey — M,D
Iowa State University of Science and Technology — M,D
Kansas State University — M,D,O
Louisiana State University and Agricultural & Mechanical College — M,D
Louisiana Tech University — M,D,O
McGill University — M,D
McNeese State University — M
Michigan State University — M,D
Mississippi State University — M,D
Missouri State University — M
Montana State University — M
Morehead State University — M
Murray State University — M,O
New Mexico State University — M,D
North Carolina Agricultural and Technical State University — M
North Carolina State University — M,D,O
North Dakota State University — M,D
Northwest Missouri State University — M
The Ohio State University — M,D
Oklahoma State University — M,D
Penn State University Park — M,D,O*
Prairie View A&M University — M
Purdue University — M,D
Sam Houston State University — M
South Dakota State University — M,D
Southern Arkansas University–Magnolia — M
Southern Illinois University Carbondale — M
Southern University and Agricultural and Mechanical College — M
Stephen F. Austin State University — M
Tarleton State University — M
Tennessee State University — M,D
Tennessee Technological University — D
Texas A&M University — M,D
Texas A&M University–Commerce — M
Texas A&M University–Kingsville — M,D
Texas Tech University — M,D
Tropical Agriculture Research and Higher Education Center — M,D
Universidad Nacional Pedro Henriquez Urena — M
Université Laval — M,D,O
University of Alberta — M,D,O
The University of Arizona — M,D,O
University of Arkansas — M
The University of British Columbia — M,D
University of California, Davis — M
University of Connecticut — M,D
University of Delaware — M,D
University of Florida — M,D,O
University of Georgia — M,D
University of Guelph — M,D,O
University of Hawaii at Manoa — M,D
University of Illinois at Urbana–Champaign — M
The University of Iowa — M,D,O
University of Kentucky — M,D
University of Lethbridge — M,D
University of Maine — M,D,O
University of Manitoba — M,D
University of Maryland, College Park — M,D
University of Maryland Eastern Shore — M
University of Minnesota, Twin Cities Campus — M,D
University of Missouri — M,D
University of Nebraska–Lincoln — M,D
University of Nevada, Reno — M,D
University of New Hampshire — M,D
University of Puerto Rico–Mayagüez — M
University of Saskatchewan — M,D,O
University of South Africa — M,D
The University of Tennessee — M,D
The University of Tennessee at Martin — M
The University of Texas Rio Grande Valley — M
University of Vermont — M,D,O
University of Wisconsin–Madison — M,D
University of Wisconsin–River Falls — M
University of Wyoming — M,D
Utah State University — M,D
Virginia Polytechnic Institute and State University — M,D,O
Western Kentucky University — M
West Texas A&M University — M,D
West Virginia University — M,D

AGRONOMY AND SOIL SCIENCES

Alabama Agricultural and Mechanical University — M,D
Alcorn State University — M
Auburn University — M,D
Colorado State University — M,D
Cornell University — M,D
Dalhousie University — M
Iowa State University of Science and Technology — M,D
Kansas State University — M,D,O
Louisiana State University and Agricultural & Mechanical College — M,D

McGill University — M,D
Michigan State University — M,D
Mississippi State University — M,D
North Carolina Agricultural and Technical State University — M
North Carolina State University — M,D
North Dakota State University — M,D
The Ohio State University — M,D
Oklahoma State University — M,D
Oregon State University — M,D
Penn State University Park — M,D*
Purdue University — M,D
Southern Illinois University Carbondale — M
Tennessee State University — M,D
Texas A&M University — M,D
Texas A&M University–Kingsville — M
Texas Tech University — M
Tuskegee University — M
Université Laval — M,D
University of Alberta — M,D
The University of Arizona — M,D,O
University of Arkansas — M,D
The University of British Columbia — M,D
University of California, Davis — M,D
University of California, Riverside — M,D
University of Connecticut — M,D
University of Delaware — M,D
University of Florida — M,D
University of Georgia — M,D
University of Guelph — M,D
University of Idaho — M,D
University of Illinois at Urbana–Champaign — M,D
University of Kentucky — M,D
University of Manitoba — M,D
University of Minnesota, Twin Cities Campus — M,D
University of Missouri — M,D,O
University of Nebraska–Lincoln — M,D
University of Puerto Rico–Mayagüez — M
University of Saskatchewan — M
University of Vermont — M,D,O
University of Wisconsin–Madison — M,D
University of Wyoming — M,D
Utah State University — M,D
Virginia Polytechnic Institute and State University — M,D,O
Washington State University — M,D
West Virginia University — M,D

ALLIED HEALTH—GENERAL

Alabama State University — M,D
American College of Healthcare Sciences — M,O
Andrews University — M
Athabasca University — M,O
A.T. Still University — M,D,O
Augusta University — D
Belmont University — M,D
Bennington College — O
Boston University — M,D
Brock University — M,D
Canisius College — M,O
Cleveland State University — M
Concordia University, St. Paul — M,D
Creighton University — M,D
Dominican College — M,D
Drexel University — M,D,O*
Duquesne University — M,D,O
East Carolina University — M,D,O
Eastern Kentucky University — M
East Tennessee State University — M,D
Emory University — M,D
Ferris State University — M
Florida Agricultural and Mechanical University — M,D
Florida Gulf Coast University — M,D
Georgia Southern University — M,D,O
Georgia State University — M
Grand Valley State University — M,D
Hampton University — M
Harding University — M,D
Howard University — M,D
Idaho State University — M,D,O
Ithaca College — M,D
Jacksonville University — M,D
Loma Linda University — M,D
Long Island University–LIU Post — M,O
Marymount University — M,D,O
Maryville University of Saint Louis — M,D,O
Medical University of South Carolina — M,D
Mercy College — M,D
Midwestern University, Glendale Campus — M,D
Minnesota State University Mankato — M,D,O
Misericordia University — M,D
New Jersey City University — M
Northeastern University — M,D,O
Northern Arizona University — M,D,O
Northern Kentucky University — M
Nova Southeastern University — M,D
Oakland University — M,D,O
The Ohio State University — M
Old Dominion University — M
Oregon State University — M
Purdue University — M,D
Quinnipiac University — M
Regis University — M,D,O
Rosalind Franklin University of Medicine and Science — M,D,O
Rutgers University–Newark — M,D,O
Saint Louis University — M,D,O*

Sam Houston State University	M
Seton Hall University	D
Shenandoah University	M,D,O
South Carolina State University	M
Temple University	M,D*
Tennessee State University	M,D,O
Texas Christian University	M,D,O
Texas State University	M,D
Texas Woman's University	M,D
Towson University	M
University at Buffalo, the State University of New York	M,D,O
The University of Alabama at Birmingham	M,D,O
University of Detroit Mercy	M,D,O
University of Florida	M,D,O
University of Illinois at Chicago	M,D,O
The University of Kansas	M,D,O
University of Kentucky	M,D
University of Maryland, Baltimore	M
University of Massachusetts Lowell	M
University of Memphis	M,O
University of Mississippi Medical Center	M
University of Nebraska Medical Center	M,D,O
University of Nevada, Las Vegas	M,D,O
University of New Mexico	M,D,O
The University of North Carolina at Chapel Hill	M,D
University of Northern Iowa	M,D
University of North Florida	M,D,O
University of Oklahoma Health Sciences Center	M,D,O
University of Phoenix–Las Vegas Campus	M
University of Puerto Rico–Medical Sciences Campus	M,D,O
University of South Alabama	M,D
University of South Dakota	M,D,O
The University of Tennessee Health Science Center	M,D
The University of Texas at El Paso	D
The University of Texas Medical Branch	M,D
University of Vermont	M,D,O
University of Wisconsin–Milwaukee	M,D,O*
Virginia Commonwealth University	D
Western University of Health Sciences	M,D
Wichita State University	M,D

ALLOPATHIC MEDICINE

Albany Medical College	D
Albert Einstein College of Medicine	D
American University of Beirut	M,D
Augusta University	D
Baylor College of Medicine	D
Boston University	D
Brown University	D
California Northstate University	D
Case Western Reserve University	D
Central Michigan University	D
Charles R. Drew University of Medicine and Science	D
Columbia University	M,D
Creighton University	D
Dalhousie University	M,D
Dartmouth College	D
Drexel University	D*
Duke University	D
East Carolina University	D
Eastern Virginia Medical School	D
East Tennessee State University	D
Emory University	D
Florida Atlantic University	M,D
Florida International University	M,D
Florida State University	D
Geisinger Commonwealth School of Medicine	D
Georgetown University	D
The George Washington University	D
Harvard University	D*
Hofstra University	D
Howard University	D
Icahn School of Medicine at Mount Sinai	D
Indiana University–Purdue University Indianapolis	M,D
Instituto Tecnologico de Santo Domingo	M,D
Johns Hopkins University	D*
Loma Linda University	M,D
Louisiana State University Health Sciences Center	M,D
Louisiana State University Health Sciences Center at Shreveport	D
Marshall University	D
Mayo Clinic Alix School of Medicine	D
McGill University	M,D
Medical College of Wisconsin	D
Medical University of South Carolina	D
Meharry Medical College	D
Mercer University	M,D
Michigan State University	D
Morehouse School of Medicine	D
New York Medical College	D
New York University	M,D*
Northeast Ohio Medical University	D
Northwestern University	D
Nova Southeastern University	D
The Ohio State University	D
Oregon Health & Science University	D
Penn State Hershey Medical Center	M,D
Pontificia Universidad Catolica Madre y Maestra	D
Queen's University at Kingston	D
Quinnipiac University	D

Rosalind Franklin University of Medicine and Science	D
Rowan University	D
Rush University	D
Rutgers University–Newark	D
Rutgers University–New Brunswick	D
Saint Louis University	D*
San Juan Bautista School of Medicine	M,D
Seton Hall University	D
Stanford University	D
State University of New York Downstate Medical Center	M,D
State University of New York Upstate Medical University	D
Stony Brook University, State University of New York	D
Temple University	D*
Texas A&M University	M,D
Texas Tech University Health Sciences Center	D
Texas Tech University Health Sciences Center El Paso	D
Thomas Jefferson University	D
Tufts University	D
Tulane University	D
Uniformed Services University of the Health Sciences	M,D*
Universidad Autonoma de Guadalajara	D
Universidad Central del Caribe	M,D
Universidad Central del Este	D
Universidad de Ciencias Medicas	M,D,O
Universidad de Iberoamerica	M,D
Universidad Iberoamericana	D
Universidad Nacional Pedro Henriquez Urena	D
Université de Montréal	D
Université de Sherbrooke	D
Université Laval	D,O
University at Buffalo, the State University of New York	D
The University of Alabama at Birmingham	D
University of Alberta	D
The University of Arizona	M,D
University of Arkansas for Medical Sciences	D
The University of British Columbia	M,D
University of Calgary	D
University of California, Berkeley	D
University of California, Davis	D
University of California, Irvine	D
University of California, Los Angeles	D
University of California, Riverside	D
University of California, San Diego	D
University of California, San Francisco	D
University of Central Florida	M,D
University of Chicago	D
University of Cincinnati	D
University of Colorado Denver	D
University of Connecticut Health Center	D
University of Florida	D
University of Hawaii at Manoa	D
University of Illinois at Chicago	D
The University of Iowa	D
The University of Kansas	D
University of Kentucky	D
University of Louisville	D
University of Lynchburg	D
University of Manitoba	M
University of Maryland, Baltimore	D
University of Massachusetts Medical School	D
University of Miami	D
University of Michigan	D
University of Minnesota, Duluth	D
University of Minnesota, Twin Cities Campus	M,D
University of Mississippi Medical Center	D
University of Missouri	D
University of Missouri–Kansas City	M,D
University of Nebraska Medical Center	D,O
University of Nevada, Reno	D
University of New Mexico	D
The University of North Carolina at Chapel Hill	D
University of Oklahoma Health Sciences Center	D
University of Ottawa	M,D
University of Pennsylvania	D*
University of Pittsburgh	D*
University of Puerto Rico–Medical Sciences Campus	D
University of Rochester	D*
University of Saskatchewan	D
University of South Alabama	D
University of South Carolina	D
University of South Dakota	D,O
University of Southern California	D
University of South Florida	M,D
The University of Tennessee Health Science Center	D
The University of Texas at Austin	D
The University of Texas Health Science Center at Houston	D
The University of Texas Health Science Center at San Antonio	M,D
The University of Texas Medical Branch	D
The University of Texas Rio Grande Valley	D
The University of Texas Southwestern Medical Center	D
The University of Toledo	M,D,O

University of Toronto	M,D
University of Utah	D
University of Vermont	M,D,O
University of Virginia	M,D
University of Washington	D
The University of Western Ontario	M,D
University of Wisconsin–Madison	D
Vanderbilt University	M,D*
Virginia Commonwealth University	D
Virginia Polytechnic Institute and State University	D
Wake Forest University	D
Washington State University	M,D
Washington University in St. Louis	D
Western Michigan University Homer Stryker MD School of Medicine	D
West Virginia University	M,D
Wright State University	D
Yale University	D

AMERICAN INDIAN/NATIVE AMERICAN STUDIES

Central Michigan University	M
Montana State University	M
Navajo Technical University	M
Northeastern State University	M
Northern Arizona University	O
Trent University	M,D
The University of Arizona	M,D
University of California, Davis	M,D
University of California, Los Angeles	M
The University of Kansas	M,O
University of Lethbridge	M,D
University of Manitoba	M
University of New Mexico	M,D
University of Oklahoma	M*
University of South Dakota	M,D,O
The University of Tulsa	M,D,O

AMERICAN STUDIES

American Public University System	M,D
American University	M
Appalachian State University	M
Baylor University	D
Boston University	D
Bowling Green State University	M,D
Brown University	M,D
California State University, Fullerton	M
The Catholic University of America	M,D
Central Michigan University	M,O
Claremont Graduate University	M,D,O
Clark University	M
The College at Brockport, State University of New York	M
College of Staten Island of the City University of New York	M
The Colorado College	M
Columbia University	M,D
Cornell University	M,D
Drew University	M,D,O
East Carolina University	M
Emory & Henry College	M
Fairfield University	M
Florida State University	M,D
Georgetown University	M,D
The George Washington University	M,D
Harvard University	D*
Indiana University–Purdue University Indianapolis	M,D
Inter American University of Puerto Rico, Metropolitan Campus	M,D
James Madison University	M
Kennesaw State University	M
Lake Forest College	M
La Salle University	M,O
Lehigh University	M,D,O
Michigan State University	M
Monmouth University	M
New Mexico Highlands University	M
New York University	M,D*
Northwestern Oklahoma State University	M
Northwestern University	D
Penn State Harrisburg	M,D,O
Pepperdine University	M
Portland State University	M
Providence College	M
Purdue University	M,D
Regent University	M
Rice University	D
Rutgers University–Newark	M,D
Saint Louis University	M,D*
Salisbury University	M
Stockton University	M,O
Texas Christian University	M,O
Trinity College (United States)	M
Universidad de las Américas Puebla	M
University at Buffalo, the State University of New York	M
The University of Alabama	M
University of Colorado Denver	M
University of Delaware	M,D
University of Hawaii at Manoa	M,D,O
The University of Iowa	M,D
The University of Kansas	M,D
University of Louisiana at Lafayette	M
University of Maryland, College Park	M
University of Massachusetts Amherst	M,D
University of Massachusetts Boston	M
University of Michigan	D
University of Michigan–Flint	M,D
University of Minnesota, Twin Cities Campus	D
University of Missouri–St. Louis	M,D
University of New Mexico	M,D
University of Southern California	D
University of Southern Maine	M,O

University of South Florida	M,D
The University of Texas at Austin	M,D
University of Utah	M,D
University of West Florida	M
University of Wisconsin–Madison	M,D
University of Wyoming	M
Utah State University	M
Washington State University	M,D
Wilfrid Laurier University	M,D
Yale University	D
Youngstown State University	M

ANALYTICAL CHEMISTRY

Auburn University	M,D
Binghamton University, State University of New York	M,D
Brigham Young University	M,D
California State University, Los Angeles	M
Cornell University	D
Eastern New Mexico University	M
Florida State University	D
Georgetown University	D
The George Washington University	M,D
Georgia State University	M,D
Governors State University	M
Howard University	M,D
Illinois Institute of Technology	M,D
Indiana University Bloomington	M,D
Iowa State University of Science and Technology	M,D
Laurentian University	M
Marquette University	M,D
McMaster University	M,D
Old Dominion University	M,D
Oregon State University	M,D
Purdue University	M,D
Rutgers University–Newark	M,D
Seton Hall University	M,D
Southern University and Agricultural and Mechanical College	M
University of Calgary	M,D
University of Cincinnati	M,D
University of Georgia	M,D
University of Louisville	M,D
The University of Manchester	M,D
University of Maryland, College Park	M,D
University of Massachusetts Lowell	M,D
University of Memphis	M,D
University of Michigan	M,D
University of Missouri	D
University of Missouri–Kansas City	M,D
University of Montana	M,D
University of Nebraska–Lincoln	M,D
University of Oklahoma	M,D*
University of Regina	M,D
The University of Tennessee	M,D
The University of Texas at Austin	D
The University of Toledo	M,D
Virginia Commonwealth University	M,D
Wake Forest University	M,D
Wayne State University	M,D
Youngstown State University	M

ANATOMY

Albert Einstein College of Medicine	D
Augusta University	M
Barry University	M
Boston University	M
Case Western Reserve University	M
Columbia University	M
Creighton University	M
Dalhousie University	M,D
Des Moines University	M
Duke University	D
D'Youville College	M
East Carolina University	M,D
East Tennessee State University	M
Howard University	M,D
Indiana University–Purdue University Indianapolis	M,D
Johns Hopkins University	D*
Liberty University	M
Loma Linda University	D
Louisiana State University Health Sciences Center	D
Louisiana State University Health Sciences Center at Shreveport	M,D
McGill University	M
New York Academy of Art	M
New York Chiropractic College	M
The Ohio State University	M,D
Palmer College of Chiropractic	M
Penn State Hershey Medical Center	M,D
Purdue University	M,D
Rosalind Franklin University of Medicine and Science	D
Rush University	M,D
Saint Louis University	M,D*
State University of New York Upstate Medical University	M,D
Stony Brook University, State University of New York	M
Universidad Central del Caribe	M,D
Universidad de Ciencias Medicas	M,D,O
Université Laval	O
University at Buffalo, the State University of New York	M,D
University of California, Irvine	M,D
University of California, Los Angeles	M,D
University of Chicago	D
University of Colorado Denver	M,D
University of Connecticut Health Center	D
University of Guelph	D
University of Illinois at Chicago	M
The University of Iowa	D
The University of Kansas	M,D

University of Kentucky — D
University of Louisville — M,D
University of Manitoba — M,D
University of Mississippi Medical Center — M,D
University of Missouri — M,D
University of North Texas Health Science Center at Fort Worth — M,D
University of Prince Edward Island — M,D
University of Puerto Rico–Medical Sciences Campus — M,D
University of Rochester — D*
University of Saskatchewan — M,D
University of South Florida — M,D
The University of Tennessee — M,D
University of Utah — D
The University of Western Ontario — M,D
Virginia Commonwealth University — M
Wake Forest University — D
Wayne State University — M,D,O
Wright State University — M
Youngstown State University — M

ANESTHESIOLOGIST ASSISTANT STUDIES
Case Western Reserve University — M
Emory University — M
Medical College of Wisconsin — M
Nova Southeastern University — M
Quinnipiac University — M
South University (GA) — M
Université Laval — O
University of Colorado Denver — M
University of Guelph — M,D,O

ANIMAL BEHAVIOR
Arizona State University at the Tempe campus — M,D
Bucknell University — M
Cornell University — D
Emory University — D
Hunter College of the City University of New York — M,O
Illinois State University — M,D
University of California, Davis — D
University of Massachusetts Amherst — M,D
University of Minnesota, Twin Cities Campus — M,D
University of Montana — M,D,O
The University of Tennessee — M,D
The University of Texas at Austin — D
University of Washington — M,D

ANIMAL SCIENCES
Alcorn State University — M
American University of Beirut — M
Auburn University — M
Bergin University of Canine Studies — M
Boise State University — M,D
Brigham Young University — M,D
California State University, Fresno — M
Clemson University — M,D
Colorado State University — M,D
Cornell University — M
Dalhousie University — M
Fort Valley State University — M
Iowa State University of Science and Technology — M,D
Kansas State University — M,D
Louisiana State University and Agricultural & Mechanical College — M,D
McGill University — M,D
Michigan State University — M,D
Mississippi State University — M,D
Missouri Western State University — M
Montana State University — M,D
North Carolina Agricultural and Technical State University — M
North Carolina State University — M,D
North Dakota State University — M,D
The Ohio State University — M,D
Oklahoma State University — M,D
Oregon State University — M
Penn State University Park — M,D*
Purdue University — M,D
Rutgers University–New Brunswick — M
South Dakota State University — M,D
Southern Illinois University Carbondale — M
Sul Ross State University — M
Texas A&M University — M,D
Texas A&M University–Kingsville — M
Texas Tech University — M
Tufts University — M
Tuskegee University — M
Universidad Nacional Pedro Henriquez Urena — M
Université Laval — M,D
The University of Arizona — M,D
University of Arkansas — M,D
The University of British Columbia — M,D
University of California, Davis — M,D
University of Connecticut — M,D
University of Delaware — M,D
University of Florida — M,D
University of Georgia — M,D
University of Guelph — M,D
University of Hawaii at Manoa — M
University of Idaho — M,D
University of Illinois at Urbana–Champaign — M,D
University of Kentucky — M,D
University of Manitoba — M,D
University of Maryland, College Park — M,D
University of Massachusetts Amherst — M,D

University of Minnesota, Twin Cities Campus — M,D
University of Missouri — M,D
University of Nebraska–Lincoln — M,D
University of Nevada, Reno — M,D
University of New Hampshire — M,D
University of Puerto Rico–Mayagüez — M
University of Rhode Island — M,D
University of Saskatchewan — M,D
The University of Tennessee — M,D
University of Vermont — M,D
University of Wisconsin–Madison — M,D
University of Wyoming — M,D
Utah State University — M,D
Virginia Polytechnic Institute and State University — M,D
Washington State University — M,D
West Texas A&M University — M
West Virginia University — M,D

ANTHROPOLOGY
American University — M,D,O
American University of Beirut — M,D
Arizona State University at the Tempe campus — M,D,O
Ball State University — M,O
Binghamton University, State University of New York — M,D
Biola University — M,D,O
Boise State University — M
Boston University — M,D
Brandeis University — M
Brigham Young University — M
Brown University — M,D
California State University, Chico — M
California State University, East Bay — M
California State University, Fullerton — M
California State University, Long Beach — M
California State University, Los Angeles — M
California State University, Northridge — M
California State University, Sacramento — M
Carleton University — M
Case Western Reserve University — M,D
The Catholic University of America — M
Central European University — M,D
Central Washington University — M
Clemson University — M
Colorado State University — M
Columbia University — M,D
Concordia University (Canada) — M,D
Cornell University — D
Dalhousie University — M
East Carolina University — M
Eastern New Mexico University — M
Edinboro University of Pennsylvania — M
Emory University — D
Florida Atlantic University — M
George Mason University — M,D
The George Washington University — M,D
Georgia State University — M
The Graduate Center, City University of New York — D
Harvard University — M,D*
Humboldt State University — M
Hunter College of the City University of New York — M
Idaho State University — M
Indiana University Bloomington — M,D
Iowa State University of Science and Technology — M
Johns Hopkins University — D*
Kent State University — M
Louisiana State University and Agricultural & Mechanical College — M,D
McGill University — M,D
McMaster University — M,D
Memorial University of Newfoundland — M,D
Mercyhurst University — M
Michigan State University — M,D
Minnesota State University Mankato — M
Mississippi State University — M
Monmouth University — M
New Mexico Highlands University — M
The New School — M,D
New York University — M,D*
North Carolina State University — M
North Dakota State University — M
Northern Arizona University — M
Northern Illinois University — M
Northwestern University — D
The Ohio State University — M,D
Oregon State University — M
Penn State University Park — M,D*
Portland State University — M,D,O
Princeton University — D
Purdue University — M,D
Rice University — M,D
Rutgers University–New Brunswick — M
San Diego State University — M
San Francisco State University — M
San Jose State University — M
Simon Fraser University — M
Sonoma State University — M
Southern Illinois University Carbondale — M,D
Southern Methodist University — M,D
Stanford University — M,D
Stony Brook University, State University of New York — M,D

Syracuse University — M,D
Teachers College, Columbia University — M,D
Temple University — D*
Texas A&M University — M
Texas State University — M
Texas Tech University — M
Trent University — M
Tulane University — D
Universidad de las Américas Puebla — M
Université de Montréal — M,D
Université Laval — M,D
University at Albany, State University of New York — M,D
University at Buffalo, the State University of New York — M,D
The University of Alabama — M,D
The University of Alabama at Birmingham — M
University of Alaska Anchorage — M
University of Alaska Fairbanks — M,D
University of Alberta — M,D
The University of Arizona — M,D,O
University of Arkansas — M
The University of British Columbia — M,D
University of California, Berkeley — D
University of California, Davis — M,D
University of California, Irvine — M,D
University of California, Los Angeles — M,D
University of California, Riverside — M,D
University of California, San Diego — D
University of California, San Francisco — D
University of California, Santa Barbara — M,D
University of California, Santa Cruz — D
University of Central Florida — M
University of Chicago — D
University of Cincinnati — M
University of Colorado Boulder — M,D
University of Colorado Denver — M
University of Connecticut — M,D
University of Denver — M
University of Florida — M,D
University of Georgia — M,D
University of Guelph — M,D
University of Hawaii at Manoa — M,D
University of Houston — M
University of Idaho — M
University of Illinois at Chicago — M,D
University of Illinois at Urbana–Champaign — M,D
University of Indianapolis — M
The University of Iowa — M,D
The University of Kansas — M,D
University of Kentucky — M,D
University of Lethbridge — M,D
University of Louisville — M
University of Maine — D
The University of Manchester — M,D
University of Manitoba — M,D
University of Maryland, College Park — M
University of Massachusetts Amherst — M,D
University of Memphis — M
University of Michigan — D
University of Minnesota, Duluth — M
University of Minnesota, Twin Cities Campus — M,D
University of Mississippi — M,D
University of Missouri — M,D
University of Montana — M,D
University of Nebraska–Lincoln — M
University of Nevada, Las Vegas — M,D
University of Nevada, Reno — M,D
University of New Brunswick Fredericton — M
University of New Mexico — M,D
The University of North Carolina at Chapel Hill — M,D
The University of North Carolina at Charlotte — M
University of North Georgia — M
University of North Texas — M,D,O
University of Oklahoma — M,D*
University of Oregon — M
University of Ottawa — M
University of Pennsylvania — M,D*
University of Pittsburgh — M,D*
University of Regina — M
University of Rhode Island — M
University of Saskatchewan — M
University of South Africa — M,D
University of South Carolina — M,D
University of Southern Mississippi — M
University of South Florida — M,D,O
The University of Tennessee — M,D
The University of Texas at Arlington — M
The University of Texas at Austin — M,D
The University of Texas at El Paso — M,O
The University of Texas at San Antonio — M,D
University of Toronto — M,D
The University of Tulsa — M,D
University of Utah — M,D
University of Victoria — M,D
University of Virginia — M,D
University of Washington — M,D
University of Waterloo — M
The University of Western Ontario — M,D
University of West Florida — M
University of Wisconsin–Madison — D

University of Wisconsin–Milwaukee — M,D,O*
University of Wyoming — M,D
Utah State University — M,D
Vanderbilt University — M,D*
Washington State University — M,D
Washington University in St. Louis — D
Wayne State University — M,D
Western Kentucky University — M
Western Michigan University — M
Western Washington University — M
Wichita State University — M
Yale University — M,D
York University — M,D

APPLIED ARTS AND DESIGN—GENERAL
Academy of Art University — M
Alfred University — M
Arizona State University at the Tempe campus — M,D
The Art Institute of Dallas, a branch of Miami International University of Art & Design — M
Bowling Green State University — M
California College of the Arts — M
California Institute of the Arts — M,O
California State University, Fresno — M
California State University, Fullerton — M
California State University, Los Angeles — M
Carnegie Mellon University — M,D
College for Creative Studies — M
Concordia University (Canada) — M,O
Drexel University — M,D*
Emily Carr University of Art + Design — M
Fashion Institute of Technology — M
Ferris State University — M
Florida Atlantic University — M
Howard University — M
Illinois Institute of Technology — M,D
Indiana University Bloomington — M
Iowa State University of Science and Technology — M,D
Louisiana State University and Agricultural & Mechanical College — M
Maryland Institute College of Art — M
Massachusetts College of Art and Design — M,O
Miami International University of Art & Design — M
Minneapolis College of Art and Design — M
The New School — M
New York Institute of Technology — M
New York University — M*
North Carolina State University — M
Northeastern University — M
NSCAD University — M
Oklahoma State University — M,D
Pacific Northwest College of Art — M
Pratt Institute — M,O
Purdue University — M,D
Rhode Island School of Design — M
Rutgers University–New Brunswick — M
San Diego State University — M
San Francisco State University — M
Savannah College of Art and Design — M
School of Visual Arts (NY) — M
Southern Illinois University Carbondale — M
Stanford University — M,D,O
Stephen F. Austin State University — M
Suffolk University — M
Syracuse University — M
Texas State University — M
University of Alberta — M
University of Baltimore — M
University of Bridgeport — M
University of California, Berkeley — O
University of California, Los Angeles — M
University of Central Oklahoma — M
University of Cincinnati — M
University of Connecticut — M
University of Delaware — M
University of Illinois at Chicago — M
University of Illinois at Urbana–Champaign — M,D
The University of Kansas — M
University of Kentucky — M
University of Louisville — M,D
University of Michigan — M,D
University of Minnesota, Twin Cities Campus — M,D,O
University of North Texas — M,D,O
University of Notre Dame — M
University of Oklahoma — M,D*
University of Oregon — M
The University of Texas at Austin — M
University of Washington — M
University of Wisconsin–Madison — M,D
University of Wisconsin–Milwaukee — M*
Western Carolina University — M
Western Michigan University — M
Yale University — M
York University — M

APPLIED BEHAVIOR ANALYSIS
Antioch University New England — M,O
Arcadia University — M
Arizona State University at the Tempe campus — M,D
Assumption College — M,O
Aurora University — M,D

---

*M—masters degree; D—doctorate; O—other advanced degree; *—Close-Up and/or Display*

Ball State University — M
Bay Path University — M
Cairn University — M,O
Caldwell University — M,D,O
California State University, Fresno — M,O
California State University, Sacramento — M
California State University, Stanislaus — M
Capella University — M
The Chicago School of Professional Psychology — M,D
The Chicago School of Professional Psychology at Downtown Los Angeles — M,D
The Chicago School of Professional Psychology at San Diego — M,D
College of Saint Elizabeth — M,O
Drake University — M,D,O
Drexel University — M,D*
Elms College — M,O
Endicott College — M,D,O
Fairfield University — M,O
Florida International University — M,D
Florida State University — M
Georgian Court University — M,O
Hofstra University — M,D,O
James Madison University — M
Lindenwood University — M,D,O
Lipscomb University — M,D,O
Long Island University–LIU Brooklyn — M,O
Long Island University–LIU Post — M,O
Long Island University–Riverhead — M,O
Mary Baldwin University — M
McNeese State University — M,O
Mercyhurst University — M
Missouri State University — M,O
Monmouth University — M
Montana State University Billings — M
National University — M,O
Niagara University — M,D,O
Northeastern University — M,D,O
Northern Michigan University — M
Northern Vermont University–Johnson — M
Oakland University — M,O
Oklahoma City University — M
Oklahoma State University — M,D,O
Penn State Harrisburg — M,D,O
Philadelphia College of Osteopathic Medicine — M,D,O*
Queens College of the City University of New York — M
Regis College (MA) — M,D,O
Rollins College — M
Rowan University — M,O
Sage Graduate School — M
St. Cloud State University — M
Saint Louis University — M,D*
Saint Peter's University — M,O
Salve Regina University — M,O
Shenandoah University — M
Simmons University — M,D,O
Teachers College, Columbia University — M,D,O
Temple University — M,D,O*
Tennessee Technological University — D
University of California, Riverside — M,D,O
The University of Kansas — M,D,O
University of Louisville — M,D,O
University of Massachusetts Dartmouth — M,O
University of Memphis — M,D,O
University of Michigan–Dearborn — M
University of Nebraska at Omaha — M,D
University of Nebraska Medical Center — M,D
University of Nevada, Reno — M,D
The University of North Carolina Wilmington — M,D
University of North Florida — M
University of North Texas — M,D,O
University of Oklahoma — M,D
University of Pittsburgh — M,D*
University of Southern Maine — M,O
University of South Florida — M,D
The University of Texas at San Antonio — M,O
University of Utah — M,D,O
University of West Florida — M
Wayne State University — M,D,O
Western New England University — M
Westfield State University — M
Wright State University — M

APPLIED ECONOMICS
Auburn University — M,D
Auburn University at Montgomery — M
Brandeis University — M
Buffalo State College, State University of New York — M
Clemson University — M,D
Cornell University — M,D
DePaul University — M
East Carolina University — M
Florida State University — M,D
Georgia Southern University — M,O
HEC Montreal — M,D
Johns Hopkins University — M*
Mills College — M
New York University — M,D,O*
Ohio University — M
Oregon State University — M,D
St. Cloud State University — M
San Jose State University — M
Southern Methodist University — M,D
Southern New Hampshire University — M,D,O
Texas Tech University — M,D

Thomas Jefferson University — M,D,O
The University of Arizona — M
University of California, Los Angeles — M
University of California, Santa Cruz — M
University of Cincinnati — M
University of Georgia — M,D
University of Houston — M,D
University of Illinois at Urbana–Champaign — M,D
University of Massachusetts Boston — M,D
University of Michigan — M
University of Minnesota, Twin Cities Campus — M,D
University of Nevada, Las Vegas — M,O
University of New Brunswick Fredericton — M
The University of North Carolina at Charlotte — M,O
The University of North Carolina at Greensboro — M
University of North Dakota — M
University of Oklahoma — M,D*
University of Pennsylvania — D*
University of Vermont — M
University of Wisconsin–Madison — M,D
University of Wyoming — M
Utah State University — M,D
Virginia Polytechnic Institute and State University — M,D
Washington & Jefferson College — M,O
Western Kentucky University — M
Western Michigan University — M,D
Wright State University — M

APPLIED MATHEMATICS
Air Force Institute of Technology — M,D
Arizona State University at the Tempe campus — M,D,O
Auburn University — M,D
Bowie State University — M
Brown University — M,D
California Baptist University — M
California Institute of Technology — D
California State Polytechnic University, Pomona — M
California State University, Fullerton — M
California State University, Long Beach — M,D
California State University, Los Angeles — M
California State University, Northridge — M
Case Western Reserve University — M,D
Central European University — M,D
Claremont Graduate University — M,D
Colorado School of Mines — M,D
Columbia University — M,D
Cornell University — M,D
Dalhousie University — M,D
Delaware State University — M,D
DePaul University — M,D
École Polytechnique de Montréal — M,D,O
Elizabeth City State University — M
Florida Atlantic University — M,D
Florida Institute of Technology — M,D
Florida State University — M,D
The George Washington University — M,D,O
Hampton University — M
Harvard University — M,D*
Howard University — M,D
Hunter College of the City University of New York — M
Illinois Institute of Technology — M,D
Indiana University Bloomington — M,D
Indiana University of Pennsylvania — M
Indiana University–Purdue University Indianapolis — M,D
Indiana University South Bend — M,O
Inter American University of Puerto Rico, San Germán Campus — M
Iowa State University of Science and Technology — M,D
Jackson State University — M
Johns Hopkins University — M,D,O*
Kent State University — M,D
Lehigh University — M,D
Long Island University–LIU Post — M,O
Manhattan College — M
McGill University — M,D
Michigan State University — M,D
Missouri University of Science and Technology — M,D
Montclair State University — M
Naval Postgraduate School — M,D
New Jersey Institute of Technology — M,D,O
New Mexico Institute of Mining and Technology — M,D
North Carolina Agricultural and Technical State University — M
North Dakota State University — M
Northeastern Illinois University — M
Northeastern University — M,D
Northwestern University — M,D
Oakland University — M,D
Oklahoma State University — M,D
Old Dominion University — M,D
Oregon State University — M,D
Princeton University — D
Purdue University Fort Wayne — M,O
Queens College of the City University of New York — M
Rensselaer Polytechnic Institute — M,D
Rice University — M,D
Rochester Institute of Technology — M,D
Rutgers University–Camden — M
Rutgers University–New Brunswick — M,D
St. John's University (NY) — M

San Diego State University — M
Santa Clara University — M,D,O
Simon Fraser University — M,D
Southern Illinois University Edwardsville — M
Southern Methodist University — M,D
Stevens Institute of Technology — M
Stony Brook University, State University of New York — M,D,O
Temple University — M,D*
Texas Christian University — M,D
Towson University — M
The University of Akron — M
The University of Alabama — M,D
The University of Alabama at Birmingham — D
The University of Alabama in Huntsville — M,D
University of Alberta — M,D,O
The University of Arizona — M,D
University of Arkansas at Little Rock — M,O
University of California, Berkeley — M,D
University of California, Davis — M,D
University of California, Irvine — M,D
University of California, Merced — M,D
University of California, San Diego — M,D
University of California, Santa Barbara — M,D
University of California, Santa Cruz — M,D
University of Central Arkansas — M
University of Central Missouri — M,D,O
University of Central Oklahoma — M
University of Chicago — D
University of Cincinnati — M,D
University of Colorado Boulder — M,D
University of Colorado Colorado Springs — M
University of Colorado Denver — M,D
University of Connecticut — M
University of Dayton — M
University of Delaware — M,D
University of Georgia — M,D
University of Guelph — M,D
University of Houston — M,D
University of Illinois at Urbana–Champaign — M,D
The University of Iowa — D
The University of Kansas — M,D,O
University of Kentucky — M,D
University of Louisville — M,D
The University of Manchester — M,D
University of Maryland, Baltimore County — M,D
University of Maryland, College Park — M,D
University of Massachusetts Amherst — M,D
University of Memphis — M,D
University of Michigan–Dearborn — M
University of Minnesota, Duluth — M
University of Missouri — M,D
University of New Hampshire — M,D,O
The University of North Carolina at Charlotte — M,D
University of Northern Iowa — M
University of Notre Dame — M,D
University of Pennsylvania — D*
University of Pittsburgh — M,D*
University of Puerto Rico–Mayagüez — M
University of Rhode Island — M,D
University of Southern California — M,D
University of South Florida — M,D
The University of Tennessee — M,D
The University of Tennessee at Chattanooga — M
The University of Texas at Arlington — M,D
The University of Texas at Austin — M,D
The University of Texas at Dallas — M,D
The University of Texas at San Antonio — M
The University of Toledo — M,D
University of Washington — M,D
University of Waterloo — M,D
The University of Western Ontario — M,D
University of Wisconsin–Milwaukee — M,D*
University of Wisconsin–Stout — M
Utah State University — M,D
Virginia Commonwealth University — M
Washington State University — M,D
Wayne State University — M
West Chester University of Pennsylvania — M,O
Western Michigan University — M,D
Wichita State University — M
Worcester Polytechnic Institute — M,D,O
Wright State University — M
Yale University — M,D
York University — M,D
Youngstown State University — M

APPLIED PHYSICS
Air Force Institute of Technology — M,D
Binghamton University, State University of New York — M,D
California Institute of Technology — M,D
Carnegie Mellon University — M,D
Christopher Newport University — M
Colorado School of Mines — M,D
Columbia University — M,D
Cornell University — M,D
East Carolina University — M
Georgia Southern University — M
Harvard University — M,D*
Idaho State University — M,D
Illinois Institute of Technology — M,D

Iowa State University of Science and Technology — M,D
Johns Hopkins University — M,O*
Laurentian University — M
Louisiana Tech University — M,D,O
Michigan Technological University — M,D
Naval Postgraduate School — M,D,O
New Jersey Institute of Technology — M,D,O
Northern Arizona University — M,D
Northwestern University — D
Rice University — M,D
Rutgers University–Newark — M,D
Southern Illinois University Carbondale — M,D
Stanford University — M,D
Texas A&M University — M,D
Towson University — M
University of Arkansas — M,D
University of California, San Diego — M,D
University of Massachusetts Boston — M
University of Michigan — D
University of Missouri–St. Louis — M,D
The University of North Carolina at Charlotte — M,D
University of South Florida — M,D
The University of Texas at Austin — M,D
University of Washington — M,D
Virginia Commonwealth University — M
Yale University — M,D

APPLIED PSYCHOLOGY
Adler University — M
Antioch University New England — M,D,O
Arizona State University at the Tempe campus — M
Athabasca University — M,O
California State University, Chico — M
The Catholic University of America — M,D
Central Michigan University — M,D
The Chicago School of Professional Psychology at San Diego — M,D
The Chicago School of Professional Psychology: Online — M,O
Clayton State University — M
Clemson University — M,D
DEREE - The American College of Greece — M
Eastern Washington University — M
Fairfield University — M,O
Fordham University — M,D
Francis Marion University — M,O
The George Washington University — D
Laurentian University — M
Liberty University — M,D,O
London Metropolitan University — M,D
Loras College — M
Lynn University — M
Mississippi State University — M,D
New York University — M,D,O*
North Carolina State University — D
Oklahoma State University — M,D,O
Old Dominion University — D
Penn State Erie, The Behrend College — M
Penn State Harrisburg — M,D,O
Rutgers University–New Brunswick — M,D
Sacred Heart University — M
Saint Mary's University (Canada) — M,D
Tarleton State University — M
Teachers College, Columbia University — M,D
University of Arkansas at Little Rock — M
University of Baltimore — M
University of Calgary — M,D
University of Guelph — M,D
University of Maryland, Baltimore County — D
University of Pennsylvania — M*
University of Pittsburgh — M,D*
University of Regina — M,D
University of South Carolina Aiken — M,D
The University of Tennessee — M,O
The University of Texas at El Paso — M,O
University of West Florida — M
University of Windsor — M,D
University of Wisconsin–Stout — M
Walden University — M,D,O
William James College — M,D,O

APPLIED SCIENCE AND TECHNOLOGY
Colorado State University–Pueblo — M
Harvard University — M,O*
Kansas State University — M
Louisiana State University and Agricultural & Mechanical College — M
Missouri State University — M,O
Naval Postgraduate School — M,D
Saint Mary's University (Canada) — M
Southeastern Louisiana University — M
Thomas Edison State University — M,O
University of Arkansas at Little Rock — M,D
University of California, Berkeley — D
University of California, Davis — M,D
University of Colorado Denver — M
University of Mississippi — M,D

APPLIED SOCIAL RESEARCH
American University — M,O
California State University, Dominguez Hills — M
Concordia University Irvine — M
Florida State University — M,D
Hunter College of the City University of New York — M
Laurentian University — M
Loma Linda University — M,D

The New School — M,D
New York University — M*
Portland State University — M
Queens College of the City
  University of New York — M

APPLIED STATISTICS

American University — M,O
Bay Path University — M
Bowling Green State University — M
Brigham Young University — M
California State University, East
  Bay — M
California State University, Long
  Beach — M
Clemson University — M,D
Cleveland State University — M
Colorado School of Mines — M,D
Cornell University — M,D
DePaul University — M,D
Florida State University — M,D
Fordham University — M,D
Indiana University Bloomington — M,D
Indiana University–Purdue
  University Indianapolis — M
Instituto Tecnológico y de
  Estudios Superiores de Monterrey,
  Campus Monterrey — M,D
Kennesaw State University — M
Louisiana State University and
  Agricultural & Mechanical College — M
Loyola University Chicago — M
McMaster University — M
Michigan State University — M,D
Minnesota State University Mankato — M
New Jersey Institute of Technology — M,D,O
New Mexico State University — M,D,O
New York University — M*
Northern Arizona University — M
Oakland University — M
Penn State University Park — M,D*
Portland State University — M,D,O
Purdue University Fort Wayne — M,O
Rochester Institute of Technology — M,O
Rutgers University–New
  Brunswick — M,D
Southern Methodist University — M,D
Syracuse University — M
Teachers College, Columbia
  University — M,D
The University of Alabama — M,D
University of Arkansas at Little
  Rock — M,O
University of California, Santa
  Barbara — M,D
University of Chicago — M
University of Colorado Denver — M,D
University of Guelph — M,D
University of Illinois at
  Urbana–Champaign — M,D
The University of Kansas — M,D,O
University of Memphis — M,D
University of Michigan — M,D
The University of North Carolina
  Wilmington — M,O
University of Northern Colorado — M,D
University of Notre Dame — M,D
University of Pittsburgh — M,D*
University of South Carolina — M,D,O
The University of Tennessee at
  Chattanooga — M
The University of Texas at San
  Antonio — M,D
University of the Incarnate Word — M,D
University of Wyoming — M,D
Villanova University — M
Virginia Polytechnic Institute and
  State University — M,D
West Chester University of
  Pennsylvania — M,O
Western Illinois University — M
Worcester Polytechnic Institute — M,D,O
Wright State University — M

AQUACULTURE

American University of Beirut — M
Auburn University — M,D
Dalhousie University — M
Memorial University of
  Newfoundland — M
Oregon State University — M,D
Purdue University — M,D
Texas A&M University–Corpus
  Christi — M
University of Arkansas at Pine
  Bluff — M,D
University of Florida — M,D
University of Guelph — M
University of Rhode Island — M,D

ARCHAEOLOGY

American University of Beirut — M,D
Arizona State University at the
  Tempe campus — M,D,O
Boston University — M,D
Brown University — D
Bryn Mawr College — M,D
California State University,
  Northridge — M
California State University, San
  Bernardino — M
Columbia University — M,D
Cornell University — M,D
Florida State University — M,D
Gordon-Conwell Theological
  Seminary — M,D
The Graduate Center, City
  University of New York — D
Harvard University — M,D*
Illinois State University — M
Indiana University Bloomington — M,D
Indiana University of Pennsylvania — M

Johns Hopkins University — D*
Massachusetts Institute of
  Technology — M,D,O
Memorial University of
  Newfoundland — M,D
Mercyhurst University — M
New York University — M,D*
Princeton University — D
Rice University — M,D
St. Cloud State University — M,O
San Francisco State University — M
Simon Fraser University — M,D
Southern Methodist University — M,D
Stanford University — M,D
Trinity International University — M,D,O
Universidad de las Américas
  Puebla — M
Université Laval — M,D
University of Alberta — M
The University of British Columbia — M
University of California, Berkeley — M,D
University of California, Los
  Angeles — M,D
University of Chicago — D
University of Colorado Denver — M
University of Denver — M
University of Lethbridge — M
The University of Manchester — D
University of Massachusetts Boston — M
University of Memphis — M,D,O
University of Michigan — M,D
University of Minnesota, Twin
  Cities Campus — M,D
University of Missouri — M,D
University of Nebraska–
  Lincoln — M,D
University of New Mexico — M,D
The University of North Carolina
  at Chapel Hill — M,D
University of Oklahoma — M,D*
University of Pennsylvania — M,D*
University of Rhode Island — M
University of Saskatchewan — M
University of South Africa — M,D
University of South Florida — M,D,O
The University of Tennessee — M,D
The University of Texas at Austin — M,D
University of West Florida — M
University of Wisconsin–
  Madison — D
Washington State University — M,D
Washington University in St. Louis — M,D
Wheaton College — M
Yale University — M

ARCHITECTURAL ENGINEERING

California Polytechnic State
  University, San Luis Obispo — M
California State University,
  Fullerton — M
Carnegie Mellon University — M,D
Drexel University — M,D*
Illinois Institute of Technology — M,D
Kansas State University — M
Lawrence Technological University — M,D
Milwaukee School of Engineering — M
Penn State University Park — M,D*
University of California, San
  Diego — M
University of Colorado Boulder — M,D
University of Detroit Mercy — M
The University of Kansas — M
University of Louisiana at
  Lafayette — M
University of Massachusetts
  Amherst — M,D
University of Miami — M,D
University of Nebraska–
  Lincoln — M,D
The University of Texas at Austin — M,D
University of Wyoming — M,D

ARCHITECTURAL HISTORY

Arizona State University at the
  Tempe campus — D
Cornell University — M,D
The Graduate Center, City
  University of New York — D
Harvard University — D*
Massachusetts Institute of
  Technology — M,D
New York University — M*
Roger Williams University — M
Savannah College of Art and Design — M
University of California, Berkeley — M,D
University of Colorado Denver — D
University of Pittsburgh — M,D*
The University of Texas at Austin — M,D
University of Virginia — M,D

ARCHITECTURE

Academy of Art University — M
Andrews University — M
Arizona State University at the
  Tempe campus — M,D
Athabasca University — M,O
Auburn University — M
Ball State University — M
Boston Architectural College — M
California Baptist University — M
California College of the Arts — M
California Polytechnic State
  University, San Luis Obispo — M
California State Polytechnic
  University, Pomona — M
Carleton University — M
Carnegie Mellon University — M
The Catholic University of America — M,O
City College of the City
  University of New York — M
Clemson University — M,D
Columbia University — M,D

Cooper Union for the Advancement
  of Science and Art — M
Cornell University — M,D
Cranbrook Academy of Art — M
Dalhousie University — M
Florida Agricultural and
  Mechanical University — M
Florida International University — M
Florida State University — M
Georgia Institute of Technology — M,D
Harvard University — M,D*
Illinois Institute of Technology — M,D
Indiana University Bloomington — M
Instituto Tecnológico y de
  Estudios Superiores de Monterrey,
  Campus Estado de México — M,D
Instituto Tecnológico y de
  Estudios Superiores de Monterrey, Campus
  Irapuato — M,D
Iowa State University of Science
  and Technology — M
Judson University — M
Kansas State University — M
Kent State University — M
Lawrence Technological University — M,O
London Metropolitan University — M,D
Louisiana State University and
  Agricultural & Mechanical College — M
Louisiana Tech University — M,D,O
Marywood University — M
Massachusetts College of Art and
  Design — M
Massachusetts Institute of
  Technology — M,D
McGill University — M,D,O
Miami University — M
Montana State University — M
Morgan State University — M
New Jersey Institute of Technology — M,D
The New School — M
NewSchool of Architecture and
  Design — M
New York Institute of Technology — M
North Carolina State University — M
North Dakota State University — M
Northeastern University — M
The Ohio State University — M,D
Penn State University Park — M,D*
Pontificia Universidad Catolica
  Madre y Maestra — M
Portland State University — M
Prairie View A&M University — M
Pratt Institute — M
Princeton University — M,D
Rensselaer Polytechnic Institute — M
Rhode Island School of Design — M
Rice University — M,D
Rochester Institute of Technology — M
Roger Williams University — M,O
Savannah College of Art and Design — M
School of Architecture at Taliesin — M
Southern California Institute of
  Architecture — M
Southern Illinois University
  Carbondale — M
Syracuse University — M
Temple University — M*
Texas A&M University — M
Texas Tech University — M,D
Thomas Jefferson University — M
Tulane University — M
Universidad Autonoma de
  Guadalajara — M,D
Universidad Nacional Pedro
  Henriquez Urena — M
Université Laval — M
The University of Arizona — M
The University of British Columbia — M
University of Calgary — M,D
University of California, Berkeley — M,D
University of California, Los
  Angeles — M,D
University of Cincinnati — M
University of Colorado Denver — M
University of Florida — M,D
University of Hartford — M
University of Hawaii at Manoa — D
University of Houston — M
University of Idaho — M
University of Illinois at Chicago — M
University of Illinois at
  Urbana–Champaign — M,D
The University of Kansas — M,D,O
University of Kentucky — M
The University of Manchester — M,D
University of Manitoba — M
University of Maryland, College
  Park — M
University of Massachusetts
  Amherst — M
University of Memphis — M
University of Miami — M
University of Michigan — M
University of Minnesota, Twin
  Cities Campus — M
University of Missouri — M,D
University of Nebraska–
  Lincoln — M,D
University of Nevada, Las Vegas — M,O
University of New Mexico — M,D
The University of North Carolina
  at Charlotte — M
The University of North Carolina
  at Greensboro — M,O
University of Notre Dame — M
University of Oregon — M
University of Pennsylvania — M,D,O*
University of Puerto Rico–
  Río Piedras — M
University of Southern California — M
University of South Florida — M

The University of Tennessee — M
The University of Texas at
  Arlington — M
The University of Texas at Austin — M
The University of Texas at San
  Antonio — M
University of the District of
  Columbia — M
University of Toronto — M
University of Virginia — M
University of Washington — M,D,O
University of Waterloo — M
University of Wisconsin–
  Milwaukee — M,D,O*
Washington State University — M
Washington University in St. Louis — M
Wentworth Institute of Technology — M
Woodbury University — M
Yale University — M,D

ARCHIVES/ARCHIVAL ADMINISTRATION

Claremont Graduate University — M,D,O
Clayton State University — M
Columbia University — M*
Drexel University — M*
East Tennessee State University — M,O
Middle Tennessee State University — M,D,O
Montclair State University — M
New York University — M,D,O*
Queens College of the City
  University of New York — M,O
The University of British Columbia — M
University of California, Los
  Angeles — M,D,O
University of California,
  Riverside — M,D
University of Manitoba — M,D
University of Massachusetts Boston — M
University of Oklahoma — M,D,O*
University of Rochester — M*
University of South Carolina — M
Wayne State University — M,O

ART/FINE ARTS

Academy of Art University — M
Adelphi University — M
Alfred University — M,D
Anna Maria College — M,O
Arizona State University at the
  Tempe campus — M,D
ArtCenter College of Design — M
Azusa Pacific University — M
Ball State University — M
Bard College — M
Barry University — M
Bob Jones University — M,D,O
Boise State University — M
Boston University — M
Bowling Green State University — M
Bradley University — M
Brandeis University — O
Brooklyn College of the City
  University of New York — M
Butler University — M
California College of the Arts — M
California Institute of the Arts — M,O
California State University, Chico — M
California State University,
  Fresno — M
California State University,
  Fullerton — M
California State University, Long
  Beach — M
California State University, Los
  Angeles — M
California State University,
  Northridge — M
California State University,
  Sacramento — M
California State University, San
  Bernardino — M
Carlow University — M
Carnegie Mellon University — M
Central Washington University — M
Christie's Education — O
City College of the City
  University of New York — M
Claremont Graduate University — M
Clemson University — M
The College at Brockport, State
  University of New York — M
College for Creative Studies — M
Colorado State University — M
Columbia College Chicago — M
Columbia University — M,D
Columbus College of Art & Design — M
Concordia University (Canada) — M
Cornell University — M
Cranbrook Academy of Art — M
Drew University — M,D,O
Duke University — M,D
East Carolina University — M
Eastern Illinois University — M
Eastern Michigan University — M
East Tennessee State University — M
Edinboro University of
  Pennsylvania — M
Emily Carr University of Art +
  Design — M
Fairleigh Dickinson University,
  Metropolitan Campus — M
Ferris State University — M
Florida Atlantic University — M
Florida International University — M,O
Florida State University — M
Fontbonne University — M
Fort Hays State University — M
Full Sail University — M
George Mason University — M
The George Washington University — M,O
Georgia Southern University — M

Georgia State University — M
Governors State University — M
Hollins University — M
Hood College — M,O
Houston Baptist University — M
Howard University — M
Hunter College of the City University of New York — M
Idaho State University — M
Illinois State University — M
Indiana State University — M
Indiana University Bloomington — M
Indiana University of Pennsylvania — M
Indiana University–Purdue University Indianapolis — M
Institute for Doctoral Studies in the Visual Arts — D
Inter American University of Puerto Rico, San Germán Campus — M
Iowa State University of Science and Technology — M
Ithaca College — M
Jacksonville University — M
James Madison University — M
Kansas State University — M
Kent State University — M
Laguna College of Art & Design — M
Lake Forest College — M
Lee University — M,O
Lehman College of the City University of New York — M
Lesley University — M,D,O
Liberty University — M
Long Island University–LIU Post — M
Louisiana State University and Agricultural & Mechanical College — M
Louisiana Tech University — M,D,O
Maine College of Art — M
Maryland Institute College of Art — M,O
Marywood University — M
Massachusetts College of Art and Design — M,O
Miami University — M
Michigan State University — M
Mills College — M
Minneapolis College of Art and Design — M,O
Minnesota State University Mankato — M
Mississippi College — M
Missouri State University — M
Montana State University — M
Montclair State University — M
Moore College of Art & Design — M
Morehead State University — M
New Hampshire Institute of Art — M
New Jersey City University — M
The New School — M
New York Academy of Art — M
New York Institute of Technology — M
New York Studio School of Drawing, Painting and Sculpture — M,O*
New York University — M,D,O*
Norfolk State University — M
Northern Illinois University — M
Northern Vermont University–Johnson — M
Northwestern State University of Louisiana — M
Northwestern University — M
Nova Southeastern University — M,D,O
NSCAD University — M
The Ohio State University — M
Ohio University — M
Otis College of Art and Design — M
Pacific Northwest College of Art — M
Paris College of Art — M
Penn State University Park — M,D,O*
Pennsylvania Academy of the Fine Arts — M,O
Pensacola Christian College — M,D,O
Pontifical Catholic University of Puerto Rico — M
Portland State University — M
Pratt Institute — M
Prescott College — M
Purchase College, State University of New York — M
Purdue University — M,D
Queens College of the City University of New York — M
Radford University — M
Rensselaer Polytechnic Institute — D
Rhode Island College — M
Rhode Island School of Design — M
Rochester Institute of Technology — M
Rutgers University–New Brunswick — M
San Diego State University — M
San Francisco Art Institute — M,O
San Francisco State University — M
Savannah College of Art and Design — M
School of Visual Arts (NY) — M
Sotheby's Institute of Art–London — M
Sotheby's Institute of Art–New York — M
Southern Illinois University Carbondale — M
Southern Illinois University Edwardsville — M
Southern Methodist University — M
Southwest University of Visual Arts — M,O
Spring Hill College — M,O
Stanford University — M,D
State University of New York at New Paltz — M
State University of New York at Oswego — M
Stephen F. Austin State University — M
Stony Brook University, State University of New York — M
Sul Ross State University — M

Syracuse University — M
Temple University — M*
Texas A&M University — M
Texas A&M University–Commerce — M,D,O
Texas A&M University–Corpus Christi — M
Texas Christian University — M
Texas Southern University — M
Texas Tech University — M,D
Texas Woman's University — M
Thomas Jefferson University — M
Tiffin University — M
Towson University — M
Tufts University — M,O
Tulane University — M
United Theological Seminary of the Twin Cities — M,D,O
Universidad del Turabo — M
Université du Québec à Chicoutimi — M
Université du Québec à Montréal — M
Université Laval — M
University at Albany, State University of New York — M
University at Buffalo, the State University of New York — M
The University of Alabama — M
University of Alaska Fairbanks — M
University of Alberta — M
The University of Arizona — M
University of Arkansas — M
University of Arkansas at Little Rock — M
The University of British Columbia — M,D
University of California, Berkeley — M,O
University of California, Davis — M
University of California, Irvine — M,D
University of California, Los Angeles — M
University of California, Riverside — M
University of California, San Diego — M,D
University of California, Santa Barbara — M
University of California, Santa Cruz — M,D
University of Central Florida — M
University of Chicago — M
University of Cincinnati — M
University of Colorado Boulder — M
University of Colorado Denver — M,O
University of Dayton — M
University of Delaware — M
University of Denver — M
University of Florida — M,D
University of Georgia — M,D
University of Guam — M
University of Guelph — M
University of Hartford — M
University of Hawaii at Manoa — M
University of Houston — M
University of Idaho — M
University of Illinois at Chicago — M,D
University of Illinois at Urbana–Champaign — M
University of Indianapolis — M
The University of Iowa — M
The University of Kansas — M,D
University of Kentucky — M
University of Lethbridge — M,D
University of Maine — M
The University of Manchester — M,D
University of Maryland, College Park — M
University of Massachusetts Amherst — M
University of Massachusetts Dartmouth — M,O
University of Memphis — M,O
University of Miami — M
University of Michigan — M
University of Michigan–Flint — M
University of Minnesota, Duluth — M
University of Minnesota, Twin Cities Campus — M
University of Mississippi — M,D
University of Missouri — M
University of Missouri–Kansas City — M,D
University of Montana — M
University of Nebraska at Omaha — M
University of Nebraska–Lincoln — M
University of Nevada, Las Vegas — M
University of Nevada, Reno — M
University of New Mexico — M
University of New Orleans — M
The University of North Carolina at Chapel Hill — M
The University of North Carolina at Greensboro — M
University of North Dakota — M
University of Northern Colorado — M
University of Northern Iowa — M
University of North Texas — M,D,O
University of Notre Dame — M
University of Oklahoma — M,D*
University of Oregon — M
University of Pennsylvania — M,O*
University of Regina — M
University of Rochester — D*
University of Saint Francis (IN) — M
University of Saskatchewan — M
The University of Scranton — M
University of South Alabama — M
University of South Carolina — M
University of South Dakota — M
University of Southern California — M,D,O
University of South Florida — M
The University of Tennessee — M

The University of Texas at Arlington — M
The University of Texas at Austin — M
The University of Texas at El Paso — M
The University of Texas at San Antonio — M
The University of Texas at Tyler — M
The University of Texas Rio Grande Valley — M
The University of the Arts — M
University of Utah — M
University of Victoria — M
University of Washington — M
University of Waterloo — M
University of Windsor — M
University of Wisconsin–Madison — M
University of Wisconsin–Milwaukee — M,O*
University of Wisconsin–River Falls — M
University of Wisconsin–Stout — M
University of Wisconsin–Superior — M
Utah State University — M
Vermont College of Fine Arts — M
Virginia Commonwealth University — M,D
Warren Wilson College — M
Washington State University — M
Washington University in St. Louis — M
Wayne State University — M
Webster University — M
Western Carolina University — M
Western Connecticut State University — M
West Texas A&M University — M
West Virginia University — M,D
Wichita State University — M
Wilson College — M
Winthrop University — M
Yale University — M
York University — M,D

ART EDUCATION

Academy of Art University — M
Adelphi University — M
Alabama Agricultural and Mechanical University — M
American University of Puerto Rico — M
Arcadia University — M,D,O
Arizona State University at the Tempe campus — M,D
Art Academy of Cincinnati — M
Boston University — M
Bowling Green State University — M
Bridgewater State University — M
Brigham Young University — M
Brooklyn College of the City University of New York — M
Buffalo State College, State University of New York — M
California State University, Long Beach — M
California State University, Los Angeles — M
California State University, Northridge — M
Carthage College — M,O
Case Western Reserve University — M
Central Connecticut State University — M,O
Chatham University — M
Cleveland State University — M
The College of New Rochelle — M
The Colorado College — M
Colorado State University–Pueblo — M
Columbus State University — M
Concordia University (United States) — M,D
Concordia University (Canada) — M,D
Concordia University Wisconsin — M
Converse College — M
Delaware State University — M
East Carolina University — M
Eastern Illinois University — M
Eastern Kentucky University — M
Eastern Michigan University — M
Edinboro University of Pennsylvania — M
Fitchburg State University — M,O
Florida International University — M,D,O
Florida State University — M,D
Fontbonne University — M
Framingham State University — M
George Mason University — M
The George Washington University — M
Georgia State University — M
Harding University — M,O
Harvard University — M*
Hofstra University — M,D,O
Indiana University Bloomington — M,D,O
James Madison University — M
Kean University — M
Kennesaw State University — M
Kent State University — M
Kutztown University of Pennsylvania — M
Lake Forest College — M
Lehman College of the City University of New York — M
Lesley University — M,D,O
Long Island University–LIU Post — M,D,O
Manhattanville College — M,O
Mansfield University of Pennsylvania — M
Maryland Institute College of Art — M
Marywood University — M
Massachusetts College of Art and Design — M,O
McNeese State University — O
Miami University — M

Minnesota State University Mankato — M
Mississippi College — M,D,O
Montclair State University — M
Moore College of Art & Design — M
Morehead State University — M
Nazareth College of Rochester — M
New Hampshire Institute of Art — M
New Jersey City University — M
New York University — M,O*
The Ohio State University — M,D
Penn State University Park — M,D,O*
Piedmont College — M,D,O
Plymouth State University — M
Pratt Institute — M,O
Purdue University — M,D,O
Queens College of the City University of New York — M,O
Rhode Island College — M
Rhode Island School of Design — M
Rochester Institute of Technology — M
Rocky Mountain College of Art + Design — M
Saint Michael's College — M,O
Salem College — M
Salem State University — M
School of Visual Arts (NY) — M
Simon Fraser University — M,D
Southern Connecticut State University — M
Southwestern Oklahoma State University — M
Spalding University — M
State University of New York at Oswego — M
Stephen F. Austin State University — M
Sul Ross State University — M
Syracuse University — M
Teachers College, Columbia University — M,D,O
Temple University — M*
Texas Tech University — M
Texas Woman's University — M
Towson University — M,O
Tufts University — M,D,O
The University of Akron — M
The University of Alabama at Birmingham — M
The University of Arizona — M,D
University of Arkansas at Little Rock — M
The University of British Columbia — M,D
University of Central Florida — M,O
University of Cincinnati — M
University of Denver — M,O
University of Florida — M,D
University of Illinois at Urbana–Champaign — M,D
University of Indianapolis — M
The University of Iowa — M,D
The University of Kansas — M
University of Kentucky — M
University of Louisville — M,D,O
University of Maryland, Baltimore County — M
University of Massachusetts Amherst —
University of Massachusetts Dartmouth — M
University of Minnesota, Twin Cities Campus — M
University of Missouri — M,D,O
University of Montana — M
University of Nebraska at Kearney — M
University of New Mexico — M
The University of North Carolina at Charlotte — M,D,O
The University of North Carolina at Pembroke — M
University of Northern Colorado — M
University of Northern Iowa — M
University of North Texas — M,D,O
University of Rio Grande — M
University of St. Francis (IL) — M,D,O
University of South Alabama — M,D
University of South Carolina — M,D
University of South Dakota — M
The University of Tennessee — M,D,O
The University of Texas at Austin — M
The University of Texas at El Paso — M
The University of the Arts — M
The University of Toledo — M,D,O
University of Utah — M
University of Victoria — M,D
University of Wisconsin–Milwaukee — M,D,O*
University of Wisconsin–Superior — M
Vermont College of Fine Arts — M
Virginia Commonwealth University — M,D
Wayne State University — M,D,O
Western Kentucky University — M
Western Michigan University — M
West Virginia University — M,D
William Carey University — M,O
Winthrop University — M

ART HISTORY

Academy of Art University — M
American University — M
American University of Beirut — M,D
Arizona State University at the Tempe campus — M,D
Bard Graduate Center — M,D
Binghamton University, State University of New York — M,D
Boston University — M,D,O
Bowling Green State University — M
Brooklyn College of the City University of New York — M
Brown University — D
Bryn Mawr College — M,D
California State University, Chico — M
California State University, Fullerton — M

California State University, Los Angeles — M
California State University, Northridge — M
Caribbean University — M,D
Carleton University — M
Case Western Reserve University — M,D
Christie's Education — M
City College of the City University of New York — M
Cleveland State University — M
Colorado State University — M
Columbia College Chicago — M
Columbia University — M,D
Concordia University (Canada) — M
Cornell University — D
Dominican University of California — M
Duke University — M,D
Emory University — D
Fashion Institute of Technology — M
Florida State University — M,D
George Mason University — M
The George Washington University — M
Georgia State University — M
The Graduate Center, City University of New York — D
Graduate Theological Union — M,D,O
Harvard University — D*
Howard University — M
Hunter College of the City University of New York — M
Illinois State University — M
Indiana University Bloomington — M,D
James Madison University — M
John Cabot University — M
Johns Hopkins University — M,D*
Kent State University — M
Lancaster Theological Seminary — M,D,O
Lindenwood University — M
Louisiana State University and Agricultural & Mechanical College — M
Massachusetts Institute of Technology — M,D
McGill University — M,D
Montana State University — M
New Mexico State University — M
New York University — M,D*
Northwestern University — D
The Ohio State University — M,D
Ohio University — M
Oklahoma State University — M
Penn State University Park — M,D*
Purchase College, State University of New York — M
Queens College of the City University of New York — M
Rice University — D
Richmond, The American International University in London — M
Roger Williams University — M,O
Rutgers University–New Brunswick — M,D,O
San Francisco Art Institute — M
Savannah College of Art and Design — M
School of Visual Arts (NY) — M
Southern Methodist University — M,D
Stony Brook University, State University of New York — M,D
Sul Ross State University — M
Syracuse University — M
Temple University — M,D*
Texas Christian University — M
Texas Tech University — M
Texas Woman's University — M
Towson University — M
Tufts University — M
Tulane University — M,D
Université de Montréal — M
Université du Québec à Montréal — M,D
Université Laval — M,D
University at Buffalo, the State University of New York — M,D
The University of Alabama — M
The University of Alabama at Birmingham — M
University of Alberta — M
The University of Arizona — M,D
University of Arkansas at Little Rock — M
The University of British Columbia — M,D
University of California, Berkeley — D
University of California, Davis — M
University of California, Los Angeles — M,D
University of California, Riverside — M,D
University of California, San Diego — M,D
University of California, Santa Barbara — D
University of Chicago — M,D
University of Cincinnati — M
University of Colorado Boulder — M
University of Delaware — M,D
University of Denver — M
University of Florida — M,D
University of Georgia — M,D
University of Hawaii at Manoa — M
University of Houston — M
University of Illinois at Chicago — M,D
University of Illinois at Urbana–Champaign — M,D
The University of Iowa — M,D
The University of Kansas — M,D
University of Kentucky — M
University of Louisville — M,D
The University of Manchester — D
University of Maryland, College Park — M,D

University of Massachusetts Amherst — M
University of Massachusetts Dartmouth — M
University of Memphis — M,O
University of Miami — M
University of Michigan — M,D
University of Minnesota, Twin Cities Campus — M,D
University of Missouri — M,D
University of Montana — M
University of Nebraska–Lincoln — M
University of New Mexico — M,D
The University of North Carolina at Chapel Hill — M,D
University of Northern Colorado — M
University of North Texas — M,D,O
University of Notre Dame — M
University of Oklahoma — M,D*
University of Oregon — M
University of Pennsylvania — M,D*
University of Pittsburgh — M,D*
University of Rochester — D*
University of St. Thomas (MN) — M,O
University of South Africa — M,D
University of South Carolina — M
University of Southern California — M,D,O
University of South Florida — M
The University of Texas at Austin — M,D
The University of Texas at Dallas — M,D
The University of Texas at San Antonio — M
The University of Texas at Tyler — M,D
University of Toronto — M,D
University of Utah — M
University of Victoria — M,D
University of Virginia — M,D
University of Washington — M,D
University of Wisconsin–Madison — M,D
University of Wisconsin–Milwaukee — M*
University of Wisconsin–Superior — M
Virginia Commonwealth University — M,D
Washington University in St. Louis — M,D
Wayne State University — M
Webster University — M
West Virginia University — M,D
Williams College — M
Yale University — D
York University — M,D

ARTIFICIAL INTELLIGENCE/ROBOTICS

The American University in Cairo — M,D,O
Brandeis University — M
California State University, Northridge — M
Carnegie Mellon University — M,D
College of Staten Island of the City University of New York — M
Cornell University — M,D
Georgia Institute of Technology — D
Illinois Institute of Technology — M,D
Indiana University Bloomington — D
Instituto Tecnológico y de Estudios Superiores de Monterrey, Campus Monterrey — M,D
Johns Hopkins University — M*
Lawrence Technological University — M,O
New York University — M,D*
Northwestern University — M
Oregon State University — M,D
Portland State University — M,D,O
Queen's University at Kingston — M
South Dakota School of Mines and Technology — M
Stevens Institute of Technology — M,D,O
Temple University — M,D*
Tufts University — M,D
University of California, Riverside — M,D
University of California, San Diego — M,D
University of Georgia — M
University of Michigan — M
University of Nebraska at Omaha — M,D
University of Pennsylvania — M*
University of Pittsburgh — M,D*
University of Rochester — M,D*
University of Southern California — M,D
Villanova University — M
Worcester Polytechnic Institute — M,D

ARTS ADMINISTRATION

American University — M,O
The American University of Rome — M
Arizona State University at the Tempe campus — M,D
Baruch College of the City University of New York — M*
Boston University — M,O
Brooklyn College of the City University of New York — M
Carnegie Mellon University — M
Christie's Education — M
Claremont Graduate University — M
The College at Brockport, State University of New York — M,O
College of Charleston — O
Colorado State University — M
Drexel University — M*
Eastern Michigan University — M
Fashion Institute of Technology — M
Florida State University — M,D
George Mason University — M
Goucher College — M
HEC Montreal — O
Indiana University Bloomington — M

Kutztown University of Pennsylvania — M
Le Moyne College — M
London Metropolitan University — M,D
Montclair State University — M
Moore College of Art & Design — M*
New York University — M*
Northeastern University — M
Northwestern University — M
The Ohio State University — M
Pratt Institute — M
Purchase College, State University of New York — M
Rhode Island College — M
Rider University — M
Rocky Mountain College of Art + Design — M
Roosevelt University — M,O
Rowan University — M
Ryerson University — M
St. Thomas University — M
Savannah College of Art and Design — M
Seattle University — M
Sotheby's Institute of Art–London — M
Sotheby's Institute of Art–New York — M
Southern Methodist University — M
Southern Utah University — M
Teachers College, Columbia University — M,D,O
Temple University — M,D*
Universidad del Turabo — M
University at Buffalo, the State University of New York — M
The University of Akron — M
University of Cincinnati — M,D
University of Kentucky — M
The University of Manchester — D
University of Michigan–Flint — M
University of New Orleans — M
The University of North Carolina at Charlotte — M,O
University of Southern California — M
University of Wisconsin–Madison — M
Valparaiso University — M
Winthrop University — M

ARTS JOURNALISM

Academy of Art University — M
Syracuse University — M

ART THERAPY

Adler Graduate School — M
Adler University — M,D
Albertus Magnus College — M
Athabasca University — M,O
California State University, Los Angeles — M
Cedar Crest College — M
The College of New Rochelle — M
Concordia University (Canada) — M
Drexel University — M,O*
Eastern Virginia Medical School — M
Edinboro University of Pennsylvania — M,O
Emporia State University — M
Florida State University — M,D
The George Washington University — M,O
Georgia College & State University — M
Goddard College — M
Hofstra University — M,O
Indiana University–Purdue University Indianapolis — M
Lesley University — M,D,O
Long Island University–LIU Post — M
Marywood University — M,O
Mount Mary University — M,O
Naropa University — M
Nazareth College of Rochester — M
New York University — M*
Notre Dame de Namur University — M,D
Ottawa University — M
Phillips Graduate University — M
Pratt Institute — M
Prescott College — M
Saint Mary-of-the-Woods College — M,O
School of Visual Arts (NY) — M
Seton Hill University — M
Southern Illinois University Edwardsville — M
Southwestern College (NM) — M
Springfield College — M,O
University of Louisville — M,D
University of Maryland, College Park — M,D,O
University of Wisconsin–Superior — M
Ursuline College — M

ASIAN-AMERICAN STUDIES

Binghamton University, State University of New York — M,O
California State University, Long Beach — M
San Francisco State University — M
Stony Brook University, State University of New York — M
University of California, Los Angeles — M

ASIAN LANGUAGES

Cornell University — M,D
Harvard University — M,D*
Indiana University Bloomington — M,D
The Ohio State University — M,D
St. John's College (NM) — M
Stanford University — M,D
University of California, Berkeley — M,D
University of California, Irvine — M,D

University of California, Los Angeles — M,D
University of California, Santa Barbara — M,D
University of Chicago — D
University of Hawaii at Manoa — M,D
University of Illinois at Urbana–Champaign — M,D
The University of Iowa — M
The University of Kansas — M,O
University of Michigan — D
University of Minnesota, Twin Cities Campus — D
University of Oregon — M,D
University of Southern California — M,D
The University of Texas at Austin — M,D
University of Washington — M,D
University of Wisconsin–Madison — M,D
Washington University in St. Louis — M,D
Yale University — D

ASIAN STUDIES

American University — O
Binghamton University, State University of New York — M,O
Brown University — D
California State University, Long Beach — M
College of Staten Island of the City University of New York — M
Columbia University — M,D,O
Cornell University — M,D
Dallas Baptist University — M
Duke University — M,O
Florida International University — M
Florida State University — M
Georgetown University — M
The George Washington University — M
Harvard University — M,D*
Indiana University Bloomington — M,D
Johns Hopkins University — M,D,O*
Maharishi University of Management — M
McGill University — M
New York University — M,D*
The Ohio State University — M
Ohio University — M
Princeton University — D
Rutgers University–New Brunswick — M,D
St. John's College (NM) — M
St. John's University (NY) — M
San Diego State University — M
Seton Hall University — M
Stanford University — M
Stony Brook University, State University of New York — M
United Theological Seminary of the Twin Cities — M,D,O
University of Alberta — M
The University of Arizona — M,D
University of Bridgeport — M
The University of British Columbia — M,D
University of California, Berkeley — M
University of California, Los Angeles — M,D
University of California, Riverside — M
University of California, Santa Barbara — M,D
University of Chicago — M,D
University of Colorado Boulder — M,D
University of Hawaii at Manoa — O
University of Illinois at Urbana–Champaign — M,D
The University of Iowa — M
The University of Kansas — M,O
The University of Manchester — D
University of Michigan — M,D,O
University of Minnesota, Twin Cities Campus — D
University of Oregon — M
University of Pennsylvania — M,D*
University of Pittsburgh — M,O*
University of San Francisco — M
University of Southern California — M,D
The University of Texas at Austin — M,D
University of Toronto — M,D
University of Utah — M
University of Victoria — M
University of Virginia — M
University of Washington — M,D
University of Wisconsin–Madison — M,D
Washington University in St. Louis — M,D
Yale University — M

ASTRONOMY

Boston University — M,D
Brigham Young University — M,D
California Institute of Technology — D
Case Western Reserve University — M,D
Columbia University — M,D
Cornell University — D
Dartmouth College — D
George Mason University — M,D
Georgia State University — D
Harvard University — D*
Hunter College of the City University of New York — M
Indiana University Bloomington — M,D
Johns Hopkins University — D*
Louisiana State University and Agricultural & Mechanical College — M,D
Michigan State University — M,D
Minnesota State University Mankato — M
Northwestern University — D
The Ohio State University — M,D
Ohio University — M,D
Penn State University Park — M,D*
Princeton University — D

Queen's University at Kingston	M,D
Rensselaer Polytechnic Institute	M
Rice University	M,D
Rutgers University–New Brunswick	M,D
Saint Mary's University (Canada)	M,D
San Diego State University	M
San Francisco State University	M
Stony Brook University, State University of New York	D
Texas A&M University	M,D
Texas Tech University	M,D
Université de Moncton	M
The University of Alabama	M,D
The University of Alabama in Huntsville	M,D
The University of Arizona	D
The University of British Columbia	M,D
University of Calgary	M,D
University of California, Los Angeles	M,D
University of California, Santa Cruz	D
University of Chicago	D
University of Delaware	M,D
University of Florida	M,D
University of Hawaii at Manoa	M,D
University of Illinois at Urbana–Champaign	M,D
The University of Iowa	M
The University of Kansas	M,D
University of Kentucky	M,D
The University of Manchester	M,D
University of Maryland, College Park	M,D
University of Massachusetts Amherst	M,D
University of Michigan	D
University of Missouri	M,D
University of Nebraska–Lincoln	M,D
University of Nevada, Las Vegas	M,D
The University of North Carolina at Chapel Hill	M,D
University of Rochester	D*
University of South Carolina	M,D
The University of Texas at Austin	M,D
University of Toronto	M,D
University of Victoria	M,D
University of Virginia	M,D
University of Washington	M,D
The University of Western Ontario	M,D
University of Wisconsin–Madison	D
Wesleyan University	M
West Chester University of Pennsylvania	M,O
Yale University	M,D
York University	M,D

ASTROPHYSICS

Air Force Institute of Technology	M,D
Arizona State University at the Tempe campus	M,D
Cornell University	D
Harvard University	D*
Indiana University Bloomington	M,D
Iowa State University of Science and Technology	M,D
Louisiana State University and Agricultural & Mechanical College	M,D
McMaster University	D
Michigan State University	M,D
New Mexico Institute of Mining and Technology	M,D
New Mexico State University	M,D
Penn State University Park	M,D*
Princeton University	D
Rochester Institute of Technology	M,D
Texas Christian University	M,D
Tufts University	M,D
University of Alaska Fairbanks	M,D
University of Alberta	M,D
University of California, Berkeley	D
University of California, Los Angeles	M,D
University of California, Santa Cruz	D
University of Chicago	D
University of Colorado Boulder	M,D
The University of Manchester	M,D
University of Michigan	D
University of Minnesota, Twin Cities Campus	M,D
University of Missouri–St. Louis	M,D
The University of North Carolina at Chapel Hill	M,D
University of North Dakota	M,D
The University of Toledo	M,D
University of Toronto	M,D
University of Victoria	M,D
Yale University	M,D

ATHLETIC TRAINING AND SPORTS MEDICINE

Adrian College	M
A.T. Still University	M,D,O
Azusa Pacific University	M
Barry University	M
Baylor University	M,D
Bellarmine University	M,D
Bloomsburg University of Pennsylvania	M
Boston University	M,D
Bridgewater College	M
Brigham Young University	M
California Baptist University	M
California State University, Long Beach	M
California University of Pennsylvania	M
Campbell University	M

The College of St. Scholastica	M
Drake University	M,D
Eastern Michigan University	M,O
East Stroudsburg University of Pennsylvania	M
Florida International University	M
Franklin College	M
Gannon University	M
George Mason University	M,O
Georgia Southern University	M,O
Georgia State University	M,O
Grand View University	M,O
High Point University	M,D
Idaho State University	M
Indiana State University	M,D
Indiana University Bloomington	M,D
Indiana Wesleyan University	M,D
Inter American University of Puerto Rico, Metropolitan Campus	M
Kent State University	M,D
Lebanon Valley College	M
Lenoir-Rhyne University	M
Life University	M
Lock Haven University of Pennsylvania	M
London Metropolitan University	M,D
Long Island University–LIU Brooklyn	M,D,O
Manchester University	M
Marshall University	M
Mercer University	M,D
Merrimack College	M
Missouri State University	M
Montana State University Billings	M
Moravian College	M,D
North Dakota State University	M,D
Northern Arizona University	M
Ohio University	M
Old Dominion University	M
Oregon State University	M
Pacific University	M,D
Plymouth State University	M
Saint Louis University	M,D*
Salisbury University	M
Samford University	M,D
Seton Hall University	M
Shenandoah University	M,D,O
South Dakota State University	M,D
Spalding University	M
Springfield College	M
Stephen F. Austin State University	M
Tarleton State University	M
Temple University	M,D*
Texas A&M University	M
Texas State University	M
Texas Tech University Health Sciences Center	M
Thomas Jefferson University	M
Trinity International University	M
Universidad del Turabo	M
University of Arkansas	M
University of Central Florida	M
University of Central Oklahoma	M
University of Evansville	M
The University of Findlay	M,D
University of Florida	M,D
University of Idaho	M,D
The University of Iowa	M,D
University of Kentucky	M
University of Lynchburg	M
University of Miami	M,D
University of Nebraska at Omaha	M,D
The University of North Carolina at Chapel Hill	M
The University of North Carolina at Greensboro	M,D
University of Northern Iowa	M
University of North Georgia	M
University of Pittsburgh	M*
University of St. Augustine for Health Sciences	M
University of South Florida	M,D
The University of Tennessee	M,D
The University of Tennessee at Chattanooga	M
The University of Texas at Arlington	M,D
The University of Toledo	M,D
University of Wisconsin–La Crosse	M
University of Wisconsin–Milwaukee	M,D*
University of Wisconsin–Stevens Point	M
Wayne State University	M,D
Weber State University	M
West Chester University of Pennsylvania	M,O
Western Michigan University	M
West Virginia University	M,D
West Virginia Wesleyan College	M
Xavier University	M*
Youngstown State University	M

ATMOSPHERIC SCIENCES

Bard College	M,O
Carnegie Mellon University	D
City College of the City University of New York	M,D
Colorado State University	M,D
Columbia University	M,D
Cornell University	M,D
Florida State University	M,D
George Mason University	D
Georgia Institute of Technology	M,D
Hampton University	M,D
Howard University	M,D
Indiana University Bloomington	M,D
Jackson State University	M,D
Massachusetts Institute of Technology	M,D
McGill University	M,D
Mississippi State University	M,D

New Mexico Institute of Mining and Technology	M,D
North Carolina State University	M,D
Northern Arizona University	M,D,O
The Ohio State University	M,D
Oregon State University	M,D
Princeton University	D
Purdue University	M,D
Rutgers University–New Brunswick	M,D
South Dakota School of Mines and Technology	M,D
Stony Brook University, State University of New York	M,D
Texas Tech University	M,D
Université du Québec à Montréal	M,D,O
University at Albany, State University of New York	M,D
The University of Alabama in Huntsville	M,D
University of Alaska Fairbanks	M,D
The University of Arizona	M,D
The University of British Columbia	M,D
University of California, Davis	M,D
University of California, Los Angeles	M,D
University of Chicago	D
University of Colorado Boulder	M,D
University of Guelph	M,D
University of Houston	M,D
University of Illinois at Urbana–Champaign	M,D
The University of Kansas	M,D,O
The University of Manchester	M,D
University of Maryland, Baltimore County	M,D
University of Michigan	M,D
University of Nevada, Reno	M,D
University of North Dakota	M,D
University of Utah	M,D
University of Washington	M,D
University of Wisconsin–Madison	M,D
University of Wisconsin–Milwaukee	M,D*
University of Wyoming	M,D
Yale University	D

AUTOMOTIVE ENGINEERING

Clemson University	M,D,O
College for Creative Studies	M
Lawrence Technological University	M
Minnesota State University Mankato	M
University of Michigan	M,D
University of Michigan–Dearborn	M
The University of Tennessee at Chattanooga	M
University of Wisconsin–Madison	M,D
Wayne State University	M,O

AVIATION

Embry-Riddle Aeronautical University–Daytona	M
Embry-Riddle Aeronautical University–Prescott	M
Everglades University	M
Florida Institute of Technology	M,D
Lewis University	M
National Test Pilot School	M
Oklahoma State University	M,D,O
Southeastern Oklahoma State University	M
University of North Dakota	M
The University of Tennessee	M

AVIATION MANAGEMENT

Arizona State University at the Tempe campus	M
Delta State University	M
Embry-Riddle Aeronautical University–Worldwide	M
Middle Tennessee State University	M
Midwest University	M,D
National American University (TX)	M,D
Purdue University	M
Southeastern Oklahoma State University	M
Vaughn College of Aeronautics and Technology	M

BACTERIOLOGY

Illinois State University	M,D
The University of Iowa	M,D
University of Prince Edward Island	M,D
University of Wisconsin–Madison	M

BIOCHEMICAL ENGINEERING

Brown University	M,D
Cornell University	M,D
Drexel University	M*
Lehigh University	M,D
Rutgers University–New Brunswick	M,D
University of California, Irvine	M,D
University of Connecticut	M,D
University of Georgia	M
The University of Iowa	M,D
The University of Manchester	M,D
University of Maryland, Baltimore County	M,D,O
The University of Western Ontario	M,D
Villanova University	M,O

BIOCHEMISTRY

Albert Einstein College of Medicine	D
American University of Beirut	M,D
Arizona State University at the Tempe campus	M,D
Auburn University	M,D
Augusta University	M,D
Baylor College of Medicine	D

Baylor University	M,D
Boston College	M,D
Boston University	M,D
Bradley University	M
Brandeis University	M,D
Brigham Young University	M,D
Brown University	M,D
California Institute of Technology	M,D
California Polytechnic State University, San Luis Obispo	M
California State University, East Bay	M
California State University, Long Beach	M
California State University, Los Angeles	M
California State University, Northridge	M
California State University, Sacramento	M
Carnegie Mellon University	M,D
Case Western Reserve University	M,D
City College of the City University of New York	M,D
Clark University	D
Colorado State University	M,D
Colorado State University–Pueblo	M
Columbia University	M,D
Cornell University	M,D
Dalhousie University	M,D
Dartmouth College	M,D
Drexel University	M,D*
Duke University	D
East Carolina University	M,D
Eastern New Mexico University	M
East Tennessee State University	D
Emory University	D
Florida Institute of Technology	M
Florida State University	M,D
George Mason University	M,D
Georgetown University	M,D
The George Washington University	D
Georgia State University	M,D
The Graduate Center, City University of New York	D
Harvard University	D*
Howard University	M,D
Hunter College of the City University of New York	M,D
Illinois Institute of Technology	M,D
Illinois State University	M,D
Indiana University Bloomington	M,D
Indiana University–Purdue University Indianapolis	M,D
Irell & Manella Graduate School of Biological Sciences	D
Johns Hopkins University	M,D*
Kansas State University	M,D
Kennesaw State University	M
Laurentian University	M
Lehigh University	M,D
Loma Linda University	M,D
Louisiana State University and Agricultural & Mechanical College	M,D
Louisiana State University Health Sciences Center at Shreveport	M,D
Loyola University Chicago	M,D
Massachusetts Institute of Technology	D
Mayo Clinic Graduate School of Biomedical Sciences	D
McGill University	M,D
McMaster University	M,D
Medical College of Wisconsin	D
Medical University of South Carolina	M,D
Meharry Medical College	D
Memorial University of Newfoundland	M,D
Miami University	M,D
Michigan State University	M,D
Michigan Technological University	M,D,O
Mississippi College	M
Mississippi State University	M,D
Montana State University	M,D
Montclair State University	M
Mount Allison University	M
New York Medical College	M
North Carolina State University	D
North Dakota State University	M,D
Northern Illinois University	M,D
Northwestern University	D
The Ohio State University	M,D
Ohio University	M,D
Oklahoma State University	M,D
Old Dominion University	M,D
Oregon Health & Science University	M,D
Oregon State University	M,D
Pace University	M
Penn State Hershey Medical Center	M,D
Penn State University Park	M,D*
Purdue University	M,D
Rensselaer Polytechnic Institute	M,D
Rice University	M,D
Rosalind Franklin University of Medicine and Science	D
Rush University	M,D
Rutgers University–Newark	M,D
Rutgers University–New Brunswick	M,D
Saint Louis University	D*
San Diego State University	M,D
San Francisco State University	M
Seton Hall University	M,D
Simon Fraser University	M,D,O
Sonoma State University	M
South Dakota State University	M,D
Southern Illinois University Carbondale	M,D
Southern University and Agricultural and Mechanical College	M
Stanford University	D

State University of New York College of Environmental Science and Forestry — M,D
State University of New York Upstate Medical University — M,D
Stevens Institute of Technology — M,D,O
Stony Brook University, State University of New York — D
Texas A&M University — M,D
Texas Christian University — M,D
Texas State University — M
Thomas Jefferson University — D
Tufts University — D
Tulane University — M
Universidad Central del Caribe — M,D
Université de Moncton — M
Université de Montréal — M,D,O
Université de Sherbrooke — M,D
Université Laval — M,D,O
University at Buffalo, the State University of New York — M,D
The University of Alabama at Birmingham — D
University of Alaska Fairbanks — M,D
University of Alberta — M,D
The University of Arizona — M,D
University of Arkansas for Medical Sciences — M,D,O
The University of British Columbia — M,D
University of Calgary — M,D
University of California, Berkeley — D
University of California, Davis — M,D
University of California, Irvine — M,D
University of California, Los Angeles
University of California, Merced — M,D
University of California, Riverside — M,D
University of California, San Diego — M,D
University of California, San Francisco — D
University of California, Santa Barbara — D
University of California, Santa Cruz — M,D
University of Cincinnati — M,D
University of Colorado Boulder — M,D
University of Colorado Denver — D
University of Connecticut Health Center — D
University of Dayton — M
University of Delaware — M,D
University of Florida — D
University of Georgia — M,D
University of Guelph — M,D
University of Houston — M,D
University of Idaho — M,D
University of Illinois at Chicago — M,D
University of Illinois at Urbana–Champaign — M,D
The University of Iowa — M,D
The University of Kansas — D
University of Kentucky — M,D
University of Lethbridge — M,D
University of Louisville — M,D
The University of Manchester — M,D
University of Manitoba — M,D
University of Maryland, Baltimore — M,D
University of Maryland, College Park — M,D
University of Massachusetts Amherst — M,D
University of Massachusetts Dartmouth — M,D
University of Massachusetts Lowell — M,D
University of Massachusetts Medical School — M,D
University of Miami — D
University of Michigan — M,D
University of Minnesota, Duluth — M,D
University of Minnesota, Twin Cities Campus — D
University of Mississippi Medical Center — D
University of Missouri — M,D
University of Missouri–Kansas City — D
University of Missouri–St. Louis — M,D
University of Montana — D
University of Nebraska–Lincoln — M,D
University of Nebraska Medical Center — M
University of Nevada, Las Vegas — M,D
University of Nevada, Reno — M,D
University of New Hampshire — M,D
University of New Mexico — M,D
The University of North Carolina at Chapel Hill — M,D
The University of North Carolina at Greensboro — M
University of North Texas — M,D,O
University of North Texas Health Science Center at Fort Worth — M,D
University of Notre Dame — M,D
University of Oklahoma — M,D*
University of Oklahoma Health Sciences Center — M,D
University of Oregon — M,D
University of Ottawa — M,D
University of Pennsylvania — D*
University of Puerto Rico–Medical Sciences Campus — M,D
University of Regina — M,D
University of Rhode Island — M,D
University of Rochester — D*
University of Saint Joseph — M,D
University of Saskatchewan — M,D
The University of Scranton — M

University of South Carolina — M,D
University of Southern California — M
University of Southern Mississippi — M,D
The University of Tennessee — M,D
The University of Texas at Austin — D
The University of Texas at Dallas — M,D
The University of Texas at El Paso — M,D
The University of Texas Health Science Center at Houston — M,D
The University of Texas Health Science Center at San Antonio — M,D
The University of Texas Medical Branch — D
The University of Texas Southwestern Medical Center — D
University of the Sciences — M,D
The University of Toledo — M,D
University of Toronto — M,D
University of Utah — M,D
University of Vermont — M,D
University of Victoria — M,D
University of Virginia — D
University of Washington — D
University of Waterloo — M,D
The University of Western Ontario — M,D
University of Windsor — M,D
University of Wisconsin–Madison — M,D
University of Wisconsin–Milwaukee — M,D*
Utah State University — M,D*
Vanderbilt University — M,D*
Virginia Commonwealth University — M,D
Virginia Polytechnic Institute and State University — M,D
Wake Forest University — D
Washington State University — M,D
Washington University in St. Louis — D
Wayne State University — M,D,O
Weill Cornell Medicine — M,D
Wesleyan University — D
West Virginia University — M,D
Worcester Polytechnic Institute — M,D
Wright State University — M
Yale University — D
Youngstown State University — M

BIOENGINEERING

Alfred University — M,D
Baylor College of Medicine — D
California Institute of Technology — M,D
Carnegie Mellon University — M,D
Clemson University — M,D,O
Colorado School of Mines — M,D
Colorado State University — M,D
Cornell University — M,D
Dalhousie University — M,D
Florida Atlantic University — M,D
George Mason University — D
Georgia Institute of Technology — M,D
Harvard University — M,D*
Illinois Institute of Technology — M,D
Johns Hopkins University — M,D*
Kansas State University — M,D
Lehigh University — M,D
Louisiana State University and Agricultural & Mechanical College — M,D
Massachusetts Institute of Technology — M,D
McGill University — M,D
Mississippi State University — M,D
New York Institute of Technology — M
North Carolina Agricultural and Technical State University — M
North Carolina State University — M,D,O
Northeastern University — M,D,O
Northern Arizona University — M,D
Northwestern University — D
The Ohio State University — M,D
Oklahoma State University — M,D
Oregon State University — M,D
Penn State University Park — M,D*
Princeton University — M,D
Rice University — M,D
Santa Clara University — M,D,O
South Dakota School of Mines and Technology — D
Stanford University — M,D
Syracuse University — M,D
Temple University — M,D*
Texas A&M University — M,D
Tufts University — M,D,O
University at Buffalo, the State University of New York — M,D,O
University of Arkansas — M,D
The University of British Columbia — M,D
University of California, Berkeley — M,D
University of California, Davis — M,D
University of California, Los Angeles — M,D
University of California, Merced — M,D
University of California, Riverside — M,D
University of California, San Diego — M,D
University of California, San Francisco — D
University of California, Santa Barbara — M,D
University of Chicago — D
University of Colorado Denver — M,D
University of Dayton — M
University of Denver — M,D
University of Florida — M,D,O
University of Guelph — M,D
University of Hawaii at Manoa — M,D
University of Idaho — M,D
University of Illinois at Chicago — M,D
University of Illinois at Urbana–Champaign — M,D
The University of Kansas — M,D

University of Louisville — M,D
University of Maryland, College Park — M,D
University of Michigan–Dearborn — M
University of Missouri — M,D
University of Nebraska–Lincoln — M,D
University of Notre Dame — M,D
University of Ottawa — M,D
University of Pennsylvania — M,D*
University of Pittsburgh — M,D*
University of Puerto Rico–Mayagüez — M,D
University of Saskatchewan — M,D
The University of Texas at Arlington — M,D
The University of Toledo — M,D
University of Utah — M,D
University of Vermont — D
University of Washington — M,D
Utah State University — M,D
Virginia Polytechnic Institute and State University — M,D
Washington State University — M,D
Wilkes University — M

BIOETHICS

Albany Medical College — M,D,O
Case Western Reserve University — M
Clarkson University — M,O
Cleveland State University — M,O
Columbia University — M
Creighton University — M
Duke University — M
Duquesne University — M,D,O
Emory University — M
Hofstra University — M,D,O
Icahn School of Medicine at Mount Sinai — M
Indiana University–Purdue University Indianapolis — M,D,O
Instituto Tecnologico de Santo Domingo — M,O
Johns Hopkins University — M,D*
Kansas City University of Medicine and Biosciences — M
Loma Linda University — M,O
Loyola Marymount University — M
Loyola University Chicago — M,D,O
McGill University — M,D,O
Medical College of Wisconsin — M,O
Northeast Ohio Medical University — M,D,O
Saint Louis University — D,O*
Stony Brook University, State University of New York — M,D
Trinity International University — M,D
Université de Montréal — M,D,O
University of Louisville — M,D
University of Mary — M
University of Pennsylvania — M*
University of Pittsburgh — M*
University of South Dakota — D,O
University of South Florida — O
The University of Tennessee — M,D
University of Toronto — M,D
University of Washington — M
Washington State University — M,D,O
Washington University in St. Louis — M

BIOINFORMATICS

Arizona State University at the Tempe campus — M,D
Boston University — M,D
Brandeis University — M
California State University Channel Islands — M
California State University, Dominguez Hills — M
Clemson University — M,D,O
Dalhousie University — M,D
Duke University — D,O
Emory University — M,D
Endicott College — M
George Mason University — M,D,O
Georgetown University — M,O
Georgia Institute of Technology — M,D
Georgia State University — M,D
Grand Valley State University — M
Hood College — M,O
Hunter College of the City University of New York — M
Indiana University Bloomington — M,D,O
Indiana University–Purdue University Indianapolis — M,D
Iowa State University of Science and Technology — M,D
Johns Hopkins University — M*,O
Lawrence Technological University — M
Lewis University — M
Loyola University Chicago — M
Marquette University — M,D
Massachusetts Institute of Technology — M,D
McGill University — M,D
Morgan State University — M
New Mexico State University — M,D
New York University — M,D,O*
North Dakota State University — M,D
Northeastern University — M,D
Nova Southeastern University — M,D
Oregon Health & Science University — M,D,O
Oregon State University — M,D
Penn State Hershey Medical Center — M,D
Rice University — M,D
Rochester Institute of Technology — M
Rowan University — M
Rutgers University–Newark — M,D
Saint Louis University — M*
Simon Fraser University — M,D,O

State University of New York at Oswego — M
Stony Brook University, State University of New York — M,D,O
Tufts University — M,D
Université de Montréal — M,D
University at Buffalo, the State University of New York — M,D
The University of Alabama at Birmingham — D
University of Arkansas at Little Rock — M,D
University of Arkansas for Medical Sciences — M,D
The University of British Columbia — M,D
University of California, Los Angeles — M,D
University of California, Riverside — D
University of California, San Diego — D
University of California, San Francisco — D
University of California, Santa Cruz — M,D
University of Chicago — M
University of Cincinnati — D,O
University of Colorado Denver — D
University of Georgia — M,D
University of Idaho — M,D
University of Illinois at Chicago — M,D
University of Illinois at Urbana–Champaign — M,D,O
The University of Iowa — M,D,O
University of Louisville — M,D
University of Maine — M,D
The University of Manchester — M,D
University of Maryland, College Park — D
University of Massachusetts Medical School — M,D
University of Memphis — M,D
University of Michigan — M,D
University of Minnesota Rochester — M,D
University of Missouri — M
University of Missouri–Kansas City — M,D,O
University of Nebraska at Omaha — M,D
University of Nebraska–Lincoln — M,D
University of Nebraska Medical Center — M,D
The University of North Carolina at Chapel Hill — D
The University of North Carolina at Charlotte — M,D,O
University of Pittsburgh — M,D,O*
University of Rochester — M,D*
University of Southern California — D
University of South Florida — M,D,O
The University of Tennessee at Chattanooga — M,O
The University of Texas at El Paso — M,D
The University of Texas Health Science Center at Houston — M,D,O
The University of Texas Medical Branch — D
University of the Sciences — M
The University of Toledo — M,O
University of Utah — M,D,O
University of Washington — M,D
University of Wisconsin–Madison — M,D
Vanderbilt University — M,D*
Virginia Polytechnic Institute and State University — M,D
Wayne State University — M,D
Wesleyan University — D
Worcester Polytechnic Institute — M,D
Yale University — D

BIOLOGICAL AND BIOMEDICAL SCIENCES—GENERAL

Acadia University — M
Adelphi University — M
Alabama Agricultural and Mechanical University — M,D
Alabama State University — M,D
Albert Einstein College of Medicine — D
Alcorn State University — M
American Museum of Natural History–Richard Gilder Graduate School — D
American University — M
American University of Beirut — M,D
Andrews University — M
Angelo State University — M
Appalachian State University — M
Arizona State University at the Tempe campus — M,D
Arkansas Colleges of Health Education — M
Arkansas State University — M,O
A.T. Still University — M,D
Auburn University — M,D
Austin Peay State University — M
Ball State University — M
Barry University — M
Baylor College of Medicine — M,D
Baylor University — M,D
Bemidji State University — M
Binghamton University, State University of New York — M,D
Bloomsburg University of Pennsylvania — M
Boise State University — M,D
Boston College — D
Boston University — M,D
Bowling Green State University — M,D
Bradley University — M

---

*M—masters degree; D—doctorate; O—other advanced degree; *—Close-Up and/or Display*

Institution	Degrees
Brandeis University	M,D,O
Brigham Young University	M,D
Brock University	M,D
Brooklyn College of the City University of New York	M
Brown University	M,D
Bucknell University	M
Buffalo State College, State University of New York	M
Cabrini University	M
California Institute of Technology	D
California Polytechnic State University, San Luis Obispo	M
California State Polytechnic University, Pomona	M
California State University, Bakersfield	M
California State University, Chico	M
California State University, Dominguez Hills	M
California State University, East Bay	M
California State University, Fresno	M
California State University, Fullerton	M
California State University, Long Beach	M
California State University, Los Angeles	M
California State University, Northridge	M
California State University, Sacramento	M
California State University, San Bernardino	M
California State University, San Marcos	M
Carleton University	M,D
Carnegie Mellon University	M,D
Case Western Reserve University	M,D
The Catholic University of America	M,D
Cedars-Sinai Medical Center	M,D
Central Connecticut State University	M,D
Central Michigan University	M
Central Washington University	M
Chatham University	M
Chicago State University	M
The Citadel, The Military College of South Carolina	M,O
City College of the City University of New York	M,D
Clark Atlanta University	M,D
Clarkson University	M
Clark University	M,D
Clayton State University	M
Clemson University	M,D
Cleveland State University	M
Cold Spring Harbor Laboratory	D
The College at Brockport, State University of New York	M,O
College of Staten Island of the City University of New York	M
Colorado State University	M,D
Colorado State University–Pueblo	M
Columbia University	M,D,O
Columbus State University	M
Concordia University (Canada)	M,D,O
Cornell University	D
Creighton University	M,D
Dalhousie University	M,D
Dartmouth College	D
Delaware State University	M
Delta State University	M
DePaul University	M,D
Des Moines University	M
Dominican University of California	M
Drew University	M,D,O
Drexel University	M,D,O*
Duke University	M,D
Duquesne University	D
East Carolina University	M
Eastern Illinois University	M
Eastern Kentucky University	M
Eastern Mennonite University	M
Eastern Michigan University	M
Eastern New Mexico University	M
Eastern Virginia Medical School	M,D
Eastern Washington University	M
East Stroudsburg University of Pennsylvania	M
East Tennessee State University	M,D
Elizabeth City State University	M
Elms College	M
Emory University	D
Emporia State University	M
Fairleigh Dickinson University, Florham Campus	M
Fairleigh Dickinson University, Metropolitan Campus	M
Fisk University	M
Fitchburg State University	M
Florida Atlantic University	M,D
Florida Institute of Technology	M,D
Florida International University	M,D
Florida State University	M,D
Fordham University	M,D,O
Fort Hays State University	M
Frostburg State University	M
Geisinger Commonwealth School of Medicine	M
George Mason University	M,D,O
Georgetown University	D
The George Washington University	M
Georgia College & State University	M
Georgia Institute of Technology	M,D
Georgia Southern University	M
Georgia State University	M,D
Gerstner Sloan Kettering Graduate School of Biomedical Sciences	D*
Goucher College	O
The Graduate Center, City University of New York	D
Grand Valley State University	M
Hampton University	M
Harvard University	M,D,O*
Hofstra University	M
Hood College	M
Howard University	M,D
Humboldt State University	M
Hunter College of the City University of New York	M,D
Icahn School of Medicine at Mount Sinai	M,D
Idaho State University	M,D
Illinois Institute of Technology	M,D
Illinois State University	M,D
Indiana State University	M,D
Indiana University Bloomington	M,D
Indiana University of Pennsylvania	M
Indiana University–Purdue University Indianapolis	M,D
Inter American University of Puerto Rico, Barranquitas Campus	M
Iowa State University of Science and Technology	M,D
Irell & Manella Graduate School of Biological Sciences	D
Jackson State University	M
Jacksonville State University	M
James Madison University	M
John Carroll University	M
Johns Hopkins University	M,D*
Kansas City University of Medicine and Biosciences	M
Kansas State University	M,D
Keck Graduate Institute	M,D,O
Kennesaw State University	M
Kent State University	M,D
Kutztown University of Pennsylvania	M,D
Lake Erie College of Osteopathic Medicine	M,D,O
Lakehead University	M
Lamar University	M
Laurentian University	M,D
Lee University	M,O
Lehigh University	M,D
Lehman College of the City University of New York	M
Liberty University	M,D
London Metropolitan University	M,D
Long Island University–LIU Brooklyn	M,D,O
Long Island University–LIU Post	M,O
Louisiana State University and Agricultural & Mechanical College	M,D
Louisiana State University Health Sciences Center	D
Louisiana State University Health Sciences Center at Shreveport	M
Louisiana State University in Shreveport	M
Louisiana Tech University	M,D,O
Loyola University Chicago	M,D
Loyola University Chicago	M,D
Manhattanville College	M,O
Marquette University	M,D
Marshall University	M,D
Massachusetts Institute of Technology	M,D
McGill University	M,D
McMaster University	M,D
Medical College of Wisconsin	M,D,O
Medical University of South Carolina	M,D
Meharry Medical College	D
Memorial University of Newfoundland	M,D,O
Miami University	M,D
Michigan State University	M,D
Michigan Technological University	M,D
Middle Tennessee State University	M
Midwestern State University	M
Midwestern University, Downers Grove Campus	M
Midwestern University, Glendale Campus	M
Mills College	O
Minnesota State University Mankato	M
Mississippi College	M
Mississippi State University	M,D
Missouri State University	M
Missouri University of Science and Technology	M
Missouri Western State University	M
Montana State University	M,D
Montclair State University	M
Morehead State University	M
Morehouse School of Medicine	M,D
Morgan State University	M,D
Mount Allison University	M
Murray State University	M
National University	M,O
New Jersey Institute of Technology	M,D,O
New Mexico Institute of Mining and Technology	M,D
New York Medical College	M,D
New York University	M,D*
North Carolina Agricultural and Technical State University	M
North Carolina Central University	M
North Carolina State University	M,D,O
North Dakota State University	M,D
Northeastern Illinois University	M
Northeastern University	M,D
Northern Arizona University	M,D
Northern Illinois University	M,D
Northern Michigan University	M
Northwestern University	D
Northwest Missouri State University	M
Nova Southeastern University	M,D
Oakland University	M,D,O
Occidental College	M
The Ohio State University	M,D
Ohio University	M,D
Oklahoma State University	M,D
Oklahoma State University Center for Health Sciences	M,D
Old Dominion University	M,D
Oregon Health & Science University	M,D,O
Oregon State University	M,D
Pace University	M,O
Penn State Hershey Medical Center	M,D
Penn State University Park	M,D*
Philadelphia College of Osteopathic Medicine	M*
Pittsburg State University	M
Point Loma Nazarene University	M
Ponce Health Sciences University	D
Pontifical Catholic University of Puerto Rico	M
Portland State University	M,D
Purdue University	M,D
Purdue University Fort Wayne	M
Purdue University Northwest	M
Queens College of the City University of New York	M,O
Queen's University at Kingston	M,D
Quinnipiac University	M
Regis University	M
Rensselaer Polytechnic Institute	M,D
Rhode Island College	M,O
Rochester Institute of Technology	M
The Rockefeller University	M,D*
Rocky Vista University	M
Rosalind Franklin University of Medicine and Science	M,D
Rowan University	M
Rutgers University–Camden	M
Rutgers University–Newark	M,D,O
Rutgers University–New Brunswick	M,D
St. Cloud State University	M
Saint Francis University	M
St. Francis Xavier University	M
St. John Fisher College	M
St. John's University (NY)	M,D
Saint Joseph's University	M
Saint Louis University	M,D*
Salisbury University	M
Sam Houston State University	M
San Diego State University	M,D
Sanford Burnham Prebys Medical Discovery Institute	D
San Francisco State University	M
San Jose State University	M
The Scripps Research Institute	D
Seton Hall University	M,D
Shippensburg University of Pennsylvania	M
Simon Fraser University	M,D,O
Smith College	M
Sonoma State University	M
South Carolina State University	M
South Dakota State University	M,D
Southeastern Louisiana University	M
Southeast Missouri State University	M
Southern Connecticut State University	M
Southern Illinois University Carbondale	M,D
Southern Illinois University Edwardsville	M
Southern Methodist University	M,D
Southern University and Agricultural and Mechanical College	M
Stanford University	M,D
State University of New York at Fredonia	M,O
State University of New York College at Oneonta	M
State University of New York Downstate Medical Center	M,D
State University of New York Upstate Medical University	M,D
Stephen F. Austin State University	M
Stevenson University	M
Stony Brook University, State University of New York	M,D,O
Sul Ross State University	M
Syracuse University	M,D
Tarleton State University	M
Teachers College, Columbia University	M,D
Temple University	M,D*
Tennessee State University	D
Tennessee Technological University	M
Texas A&M International University	M
Texas A&M University	M,D
Texas A&M University–Commerce	M,O
Texas A&M University–Corpus Christi	M,D
Texas A&M University–Kingsville	M
Texas Christian University	M,D
Texas Southern University	M
Texas State University	M
Texas Tech University	M,D
Texas Tech University Health Sciences Center	M,D
Texas Tech University Health Sciences Center El Paso	M
Texas Woman's University	M,D
Thomas Jefferson University	M,D,O
Towson University	M,D
Trent University	M,D
Troy University	M,O
Truett McConnell University	M
Tufts University	M,D,O
Tulane University	M,D
Tuskegee University	M,D
Uniformed Services University of the Health Sciences	M,D*
Universidad Central del Caribe	M,D
Universidad de Ciencias Medicas	M,D,O
Université de Moncton	M
Université de Montréal	M,D
Université de Sherbrooke	M,D,O
Université du Québec à Montréal	M,D
Université du Québec en Abitibi-Témiscamingue	M,D
Université du Québec, Institut National de la Recherche Scientifique	M,D,O
Université Laval	M,D,O
University at Albany, State University of New York	M,D
University at Buffalo, the State University of New York	M,D
The University of Akron	M,D
The University of Alabama	M,D
The University of Alabama at Birmingham	M,D
The University of Alabama in Huntsville	M,D
University of Alaska Anchorage	M
University of Alaska Fairbanks	M,D,O
University of Alberta	M,D
The University of Arizona	M,D
University of Arkansas	M,D
University of Arkansas at Little Rock	M
University of Arkansas for Medical Sciences	M,D,O
University of Calgary	M,D
University of California, Berkeley	D
University of California, Irvine	M,D
University of California, Los Angeles	M,D
University of California, Merced	M,D
University of California, Riverside	M,D
University of California, San Diego	M,D
University of California, San Francisco	D
University of Central Arkansas	M
University of Central Florida	M,D,O
University of Central Missouri	M,D,O
University of Central Oklahoma	M
University of Chicago	D
University of Cincinnati	M,D,O
University of Colorado Denver	M,D
University of Connecticut Health Center	D
University of Dayton	M,D
University of Delaware	M,D
University of Denver	M,D
University of Florida	M,D
University of Georgia	D
University of Guam	M
University of Guelph	M,D
University of Hawaii at Manoa	M,D
University of Holy Cross	M,D
University of Houston	M,D
University of Houston–Clear Lake	M
University of Houston–Victoria	M
University of Idaho	M,D
University of Illinois at Chicago	M,D
University of Illinois at Springfield	M
University of Illinois at Urbana–Champaign	M,D
University of Indianapolis	M
The University of Iowa	M,D
The University of Kansas	D
University of Kentucky	M,D
University of Lethbridge	M,D
University of Louisiana at Lafayette	M,D
University of Louisiana at Monroe	M
University of Louisville	M,D
University of Maine	M,D
The University of Manchester	M,D
University of Manitoba	M,D,O
University of Maryland, Baltimore	M,D,O
University of Maryland, Baltimore County	M,D
University of Maryland, College Park	M,D
University of Massachusetts Amherst	M,D
University of Massachusetts Boston	M,D
University of Massachusetts Dartmouth	M
University of Massachusetts Lowell	M
University of Massachusetts Medical School	M,D
University of Memphis	M,D
University of Miami	M,D
University of Michigan	M,D
University of Michigan–Flint	M
University of Minnesota, Duluth	M,D
University of Minnesota, Twin Cities Campus	M
University of Mississippi	M,D
University of Mississippi Medical Center	M,D
University of Missouri	M,D,O
University of Missouri–Kansas City	M,D
University of Missouri–St. Louis	M,D,O
University of Montana	M,D
University of Nebraska at Kearney	M
University of Nebraska at Omaha	M,O
University of Nebraska–Lincoln	M,D
University of Nebraska Medical Center	M,D
University of Nevada, Las Vegas	M,D
University of Nevada, Reno	M

University of New Brunswick Fredericton — M,D
University of New Brunswick Saint John
University of New England — M
University of New Hampshire — M,D
University of New Mexico — M,D
University of New Orleans — M
The University of North Carolina at Chapel Hill — M,D
The University of North Carolina at Charlotte — M,D
The University of North Carolina at Greensboro — M
The University of North Carolina Wilmington — M,D
University of North Dakota — M,D
University of Northern Colorado — M
University of Northern Iowa — M
University of North Florida — M
University of North Texas — M,D,O
University of North Texas Health Science Center at Fort Worth — M,D
University of Notre Dame — M,D
University of Oklahoma Health Sciences Center — M,D
University of Oregon — M,D
University of Ottawa — M,D
University of Pennsylvania — M,D*
University of Pittsburgh — M,D*
University of Prince Edward Island — M,D
University of Puerto Rico–Mayagüez — M
University of Puerto Rico–Medical Sciences Campus
University of Puerto Rico–Río Piedras — M,D
University of Regina — M,D
University of Rhode Island — M,D
University of Rochester — M,D*
University of Saint Joseph — M
University of San Francisco — M
University of Saskatchewan — M,D
University of South Alabama — M,D
University of South Carolina — M,D,O
University of South Dakota — M,D
University of Southern California — M,D,O
University of Southern Maine — M
University of Southern Mississippi — M,D
University of South Florida — M,D
The University of Tennessee — M,D
The University of Tennessee Health Science Center — M,D
The University of Tennessee–Oak Ridge National Laboratory — M,D
The University of Texas at Arlington — M,D
The University of Texas at Austin — M,D
The University of Texas at Dallas — M,D
The University of Texas at El Paso — M,D
The University of Texas at San Antonio — M,D
The University of Texas at Tyler — M
The University of Texas Health Science Center at Houston — M,D
The University of Texas Health Science Center at San Antonio — D
The University of Texas Medical Branch — M,D
The University of Texas of the Permian Basin — M
The University of Texas Rio Grande Valley — M
The University of Texas Southwestern Medical Center — M,D
University of the Incarnate Word — M
University of the Pacific — M
The University of Toledo — M,D,O
The University of Tulsa — M,D
University of Utah — M,D,O
University of Vermont — M,D
University of Victoria — M,D
University of Virginia — M,D
University of Washington — M,D
University of Waterloo — M,D
The University of Western Ontario — M,D
University of West Florida — M
University of West Georgia — M,O
University of Windsor — M,D
University of Wisconsin–La Crosse — M
University of Wisconsin–Madison
University of Wisconsin–Milwaukee — M,D*
University of Wisconsin–Oshkosh
Utah State University — M,D
Vanderbilt University — M,D*
Villanova University — M
Virginia Commonwealth University — M,D,O
Virginia Polytechnic Institute and State University — M,D
Virginia State University
Wake Forest University — M
Walla Walla University — M
Washington State University — M,D
Washington University in St. Louis — D
Wayne State University — M,D
Weill Cornell Medicine — M
Wesleyan University — D
West Chester University of Pennsylvania — M,O
Western Carolina University — M
Western Illinois University — M,O
Western Kentucky University — M
Western Michigan University — M,D,O
Western University of Health Sciences — M
Western Washington University — M
West Liberty University — M

West Texas A&M University — M
West Virginia University — M
Wichita State University — M
Wilfrid Laurier University — M
William Paterson University of New Jersey — M,D,O
Winthrop University — M
Worcester Polytechnic Institute — M,D
Wright State University — M,D
Yale University — D
York University — M,D
Youngstown State University — M

BIOLOGICAL ANTHROPOLOGY

Cornell University — D
Duke University — D
Harvard University — M,D*
Kent State University — M
Mercyhurst University — M
San Francisco State University — M
University of Colorado Denver — M
University of Michigan — D
The University of Tennessee — M,D
University of Wisconsin–Madison — D

BIOMATHEMATICS

Florida State University — M,D
University of California, Los Angeles — M,D

BIOMEDICAL ENGINEERING

American University of Beirut — M,D
American University of Sharjah — M,D
Arizona State University at the Tempe campus — M,D
Baylor College of Medicine — D
Baylor University — M,D
Binghamton University, State University of New York — M,D
Boston University — M,D
Brown University — M,D
California Polytechnic State University, San Luis Obispo — M
Carleton University — M
Carnegie Mellon University — M,D
Case Western Reserve University — M,D
The Catholic University of America
City College of the City University of New York — M,D
Clemson University — M,D,O
Cleveland State University — D
Colorado State University — M,D
Columbia University — M,D
Cornell University — M,D
Dalhousie University — M,D
Dartmouth College — M,D
Drexel University — M,D*
Duke University — M,D
East Carolina University — M,D
Ecole Polytechnique de Montréal — M,D,O
Florida Agricultural and Mechanical University — M,D
Florida Institute of Technology — M,D
Florida International University — M,D
Florida State University — M,D
The George Washington University — M,D
Georgia Institute of Technology — D
Harvard University — D*
Illinois Institute of Technology — M,D
Indiana University–Purdue University Indianapolis — M,D
Johns Hopkins University — M,D,O*
Lawrence Technological University — M,D
Louisiana Tech University — M,D,O
Marquette University — M,D
Massachusetts Institute of Technology — M,D
Mayo Clinic Graduate School of Biomedical Sciences — M,D
McGill University — M,D
Mercer University — M
Michigan Technological University — M,D
Mississippi State University — M,D
New Jersey Institute of Technology — M,D
Northwestern University — M,D
The Ohio State University — M,D
Ohio University — M
Old Dominion University — M,D
Oregon Health & Science University — M,D
Purdue University — M,D
Rensselaer Polytechnic Institute — M,D
Rice University — M,D
Rose-Hulman Institute of Technology — M
Rutgers University–Newark — O
Rutgers University–New Brunswick — M,D
St. Cloud State University — M
Saint Louis University — M,D*
South Dakota School of Mines and Technology — M,D
Southern Illinois University Carbondale — M
Stanford University — M,D,O
State University of New York Downstate Medical Center — M,D
Stevens Institute of Technology — M,D,O
Stony Brook University, State University of New York — M,D,O
Tennessee State University — M,D
Texas A&M University — M,D
Tufts University — M,D
Tulane University — M,D,O
Université de Montréal — M,D,O
University at Buffalo, the State University of New York — M,D
The University of Akron — M,D
The University of Alabama at Birmingham — M,D
University of Alberta — M,D

The University of Arizona — M,D
University of Arkansas — M
The University of British Columbia — M,D
University of Calgary — M,D
University of California, Davis — M,D
University of California, Irvine — M,D
University of California, Los Angeles — M,D
University of Central Oklahoma — M,D
University of Cincinnati — M,D
University of Connecticut — M,D
University of Florida — M,D,O
University of Houston — D
The University of Iowa — M,D
University of Kentucky — M,D
University of Maine — M,D
University of Massachusetts Boston — D
University of Massachusetts Dartmouth — D
University of Memphis — M,D
University of Miami — M,D
University of Michigan — M,D
University of Minnesota, Twin Cities Campus — M,D
University of Nebraska–Lincoln — M,D
University of Nevada, Las Vegas — M,D,O
University of Nevada, Reno — M,D
University of New Haven — M
University of New Mexico — M,D
The University of North Carolina at Chapel Hill — M,D
University of North Texas — M,D,O
University of Ottawa — M
University of Portland — M
University of Rhode Island — M,D
University of Rochester — M,D*
University of Saskatchewan — M,D
University of Southern California — M,D
University of South Florida — M,D,O
The University of Tennessee — M,D
The University of Tennessee Health Science Center — M,D
The University of Texas at Austin — M,D
The University of Texas at Dallas — M,D
The University of Texas at San Antonio — M,D
The University of Texas Health Science Center at San Antonio — M,D
The University of Texas Southwestern Medical Center — M,D
The University of Toledo — D
University of Toronto — M,D
University of Vermont — M
University of Virginia — M,D
University of Wisconsin–Madison — M,D
University of Wisconsin–Milwaukee — M,D*
Vanderbilt University — M,D*
Virginia Commonwealth University — M,D
Virginia Polytechnic Institute and State University — M,D
Wake Forest University — M,D
Washington University in St. Louis — M,D
Wayne State University — M,D,O
Wichita State University — M
Widener University — M
Worcester Polytechnic Institute — M,D,O
Wright State University — M
Yale University — M,D

BIOMETRY

Cornell University — M,D
San Diego State University — M
University of Wisconsin–Madison — M

BIOPHYSICS

Albert Einstein College of Medicine — D
Baylor College of Medicine — D
Boston University — M,D
Brandeis University — M,D
California Institute of Technology — D
Carnegie Mellon University — M,D
Case Western Reserve University — M,D
Columbia University — M,D
Cornell University — D
Dalhousie University — M,D
East Carolina University — M,D
Harvard University — D*
Howard University — M,D
Illinois State University — M
Iowa State University of Science and Technology — M,D
Johns Hopkins University — D*
Northwestern University — D
The Ohio State University — M,D
Oregon State University — M,D
Purdue University — D
Rensselaer Polytechnic Institute — M,D
Rosalind Franklin University of Medicine and Science — M,D
Stanford University — D
Stony Brook University, State University of New York — D
Texas Christian University — M,D
Université de Sherbrooke
Université du Québec à Trois-Rivières — M,D
University at Buffalo, the State University of New York — M,D
University of California, Berkeley — D
University of California, Davis — M,D
University of California, Irvine — D
University of California, San Diego — M,D
University of California, San Francisco — D

University of California, Santa Barbara — D
University of Chicago — D
University of Cincinnati — D
University of Colorado Denver — M
University of Connecticut — M,D
University of Guelph — M,D
University of Illinois at Chicago — M,D
University of Illinois at Urbana–Champaign — M,D
The University of Iowa — M,D
The University of Kansas — M,D
The University of Manchester — M,D
University of Maryland, College Park — D
University of Miami — D
University of Michigan — D
University of Minnesota, Duluth — M,D
University of Minnesota, Twin Cities Campus — M,D
University of Mississippi Medical Center — D
University of Missouri–Kansas City — D
The University of North Carolina at Chapel Hill — M,D
University of Regina — M,D
University of Rochester — D*
University of Southern California — D
The University of Texas Medical Branch — D
University of Toronto — M,D
University of Virginia — M,D
University of Washington — M,D
The University of Western Ontario — M,D
University of Wisconsin–Madison — D
Vanderbilt University — M,D*
Washington State University — M,D
Weill Cornell Medicine — M,D
Yale University — D

BIOPSYCHOLOGY

American University — M,D,O
Argosy University, Atlanta — M,D,O
Argosy University, Twin Cities — M,D,O
Binghamton University, State University of New York — D
Boston University — M
Carnegie Mellon University — D
Cornell University — D
Drexel University — M,D*
Duke University — D
Florida State University — M,D
The Graduate Center, City University of New York — D
Harvard University — D*
Howard University — M,D
Liberty University — M,D
Louisiana State University and Agricultural & Mechanical College — M,D
Memorial University of Newfoundland — D
Northwestern University — D
Oregon Health & Science University — D
Palo Alto University — D
Penn State University Park — M,D*
Philadelphia College of Osteopathic Medicine — M,D,O*
Rutgers University–Newark — D
Rutgers University–New Brunswick — D
The University of British Columbia — M,D
University of Connecticut — M,D
University of Michigan — D
University of Minnesota, Twin Cities Campus — D
University of Nebraska–Lincoln — M,D
The University of North Carolina at Chapel Hill — D
University of Oklahoma Health Sciences Center — M,D
University of Oregon — D
The University of Texas at Austin — D
University of Windsor — M,D
University of Wisconsin–Madison — D
Wayne State University — M,D,O

BIOSTATISTICS

American University — M,O
American University of Beirut — M,D
Boston University — M,D
Brown University — M,D
California State University, East Bay — M
Case Western Reserve University — M,D
Columbia University — M,D
Dartmouth College — M,D
Drexel University — M,D,O*
Duke University — M
East Tennessee State University — M,D,O
Emory University — M,D
Florida International University — M,D
Florida State University — M,D
George Mason University — M,D
Georgetown University — M,O
The George Washington University — M,D
Georgia Southern University — M,D
Georgia State University — M
Grand Valley State University — M
Harvard University — M,D*
Indiana University Bloomington — M,D
Indiana University–Purdue University Indianapolis — M,D,O
Iowa State University of Science and Technology — M,D
Johns Hopkins University — M,D*
Kent State University — M,D
Loma Linda University — M,D

Institution	Degree
Louisiana State University Health Sciences Center	M,D
McGill University	M,D
Medical College of Wisconsin	D
Medical University of South Carolina	M,D
Middle Tennessee State University	M
Monroe College	M
New Jersey Institute of Technology	M,D,O
New York Medical College	M,D,O
Northwestern University	D
The Ohio State University	M,D
Old Dominion University	M,D
Oregon State University	M,D
Penn State Hershey Medical Center	D
Rice University	M,D
Rutgers University–New Brunswick	M,D,O
San Diego State University	M,D
Southern Methodist University	M,D
Stanford University	M,D
Texas A&M University	M,D
Tufts University	M,D,O
Tulane University	M,D
University at Albany, State University of New York	M,D
University at Buffalo, the State University of New York	M,D
The University of Alabama at Birmingham	M,D
University of Alberta	M,D,O
The University of Arizona	M,D
University of Arkansas for Medical Sciences	M,D,O
University of California, Berkeley	M,D
University of California, Davis	M,D
University of California, Los Angeles	M,D
University of California, San Diego	D
University of Cincinnati	M,D
University of Colorado Denver	M,D
University of Florida	M,D,O
University of Illinois at Chicago	M,D
The University of Iowa	M,D,O
The University of Kansas	M,D,O
University of Kentucky	D
University of Maryland, Baltimore	M,D
University of Maryland, Baltimore County	M,D
University of Maryland, College Park	M,D
University of Massachusetts Amherst	M,D
University of Memphis	M,D
University of Miami	M,D
University of Michigan	M,D
University of Minnesota, Twin Cities Campus	M,D
University of Nebraska Medical Center	D
The University of North Carolina at Chapel Hill	M,D
University of North Texas Health Science Center at Fort Worth	M,D,O
University of Oklahoma Health Sciences Center	
University of Pennsylvania	M,D*
University of Pittsburgh	M,D*
University of Puerto Rico–Medical Sciences Campus	M
University of Rochester	M*
University of South Carolina	M,D
University of Southern California	M,D
University of Southern Mississippi	M
University of South Florida	O
The University of Texas Health Science Center at Houston	M,D,O
The University of Toledo	M,O
University of Toronto	M,D
University of Utah	M,D
University of Vermont	M
University of Washington	M,D
University of Waterloo	M,D
The University of Western Ontario	M,D
University of Wisconsin–Milwaukee	M,D,O*
Virginia Commonwealth University	M,D
Washington University in St. Louis	M,D,O
Weill Cornell Medicine	M
West Virginia University	M
Yale University	M,D

BIOSYSTEMS ENGINEERING

Institution	Degree
Auburn University	M,D
Clemson University	M,D
Michigan State University	M,D
North Dakota State University	M,D
South Dakota State University	M,D
The University of Arizona	M,D
University of Manitoba	M,D
University of Minnesota, Twin Cities Campus	M,D
The University of Tennessee	M,D

BIOTECHNOLOGY

Institution	Degree
Adelphi University	M
American University	M
The American University in Cairo	M,D,O
Arizona State University at the Tempe campus	M,D
Arkansas State University	M,O
Azusa Pacific University	M
Brandeis University	M
Brigham Young University	M,D
Brock University	M,D
Brown University	M
California State University Channel Islands	M
California State University, Fullerton	M
California State University, San Marcos	M
Carnegie Mellon University	M
The Catholic University of America	M,D
Claflin University	M,D
Clarkson University	M,D
College of Staten Island of the City University of New York	M
Columbia University	M,D
Concordia University (Canada)	M,D,O
Cornell University	M,D
Duquesne University	M
East Carolina University	M
Eastern Virginia Medical School	M
Florida Institute of Technology	M,D
The George Washington University	M,D,O
Harvard University	M,O*
Howard University	M,D
Husson University	M
Illinois State University	M
Indiana University Bloomington	M,D
Instituto Tecnológico y de Estudios Superiores de Monterrey, Campus Monterrey	M,D
Inter American University of Puerto Rico, Barranquitas Campus	M
Inter American University of Puerto Rico, Bayamón Campus	M
Johns Hopkins University	M*
Kean University	M
Marywood University	M
McGill University	M,D,O
Middle Tennessee State University	M,D
Mount St. Mary's University (MD)	M
New Mexico State University	M,D
Northeastern University	M,D
Northwestern University	M,D
Oregon State University	M,D
Penn State University Park	M,D*
Pontifical John Paul II Institute for Studies on Marriage and Family	M,D,O
Purdue University	D
Purdue University Northwest	M
Roosevelt University	M
St. John's University (NY)	M
San Francisco State University	M
Simon Fraser University	M,D,O
Southeastern Oklahoma State University	M
Stephen F. Austin State University	M
Temple University	M,D*
Tennessee State University	M,D
Texas Tech University	M,D
Texas Tech University Health Sciences Center	M
Thomas Jefferson University	M
Tufts University	M,D,O
Universidad de las Américas Puebla	M
University at Buffalo, the State University of New York	M
The University of Alabama at Birmingham	M
The University of Alabama in Huntsville	M,D
University of Alberta	M,D
University of Calgary	M
University of California, Irvine	M
University of Delaware	M,D
University of Guelph	M,D
University of Houston–Clear Lake	M
The University of Kansas	M
The University of Manchester	M,D
University of Maryland, Baltimore County	M,O
University of Maryland University College	M,O
University of Massachusetts Amherst	M,D
University of Massachusetts Boston	M,D
University of Massachusetts Dartmouth	D
University of Minnesota, Twin Cities Campus	M
University of Missouri–St. Louis	M,D
University of Nevada, Reno	M
University of North Texas Health Science Center at Fort Worth	M,D
University of Pennsylvania	M*
University of Rhode Island	M,D
University of San Francisco	M
University of Southern California	M
University of South Florida	M,D,O
The University of Texas at Dallas	M,D
The University of Texas at San Antonio	M,D
The University of Texas Health Science Center at Tyler	M
University of the Sciences	M
University of Toronto	M
University of Utah	D
University of Washington	D
University of Wyoming	D
Virginia Polytechnic Institute and State University	M,D
West Virginia State University	M
William Paterson University of New Jersey	M,D,O
Worcester Polytechnic Institute	M,D
Worcester State University	M
Yeshiva University	M

BOTANY

Institution	Degree
Auburn University	M,D
Central Washington University	M
Claremont Graduate University	M,D
Colorado State University	M,D
Dalhousie University	M,D
Emporia State University	M
Illinois State University	M,D
Kent State University	M,D
North Dakota State University	M,D
Oklahoma State University	M,D
Oregon State University	M,D
Purdue University	M,D
The University of British Columbia	M,D
University of California, Riverside	M,D
University of Connecticut	M,D
University of Florida	M,D
University of Guelph	M,D
University of Hawaii at Manoa	M,D
University of Maine	M,D
University of Manitoba	M,D
The University of North Carolina at Chapel Hill	M,D
University of Wisconsin–Madison	M,D
University of Wisconsin–Oshkosh	M
University of Wyoming	M,D

BROADCAST JOURNALISM

Institution	Degree
American University	M
The American University in Cairo	M,O
Kent State University	M
Northwestern University	M
Quinnipiac University	M
Syracuse University	M
University of Maryland, College Park	M,D
University of Miami	M,D
University of the Sacred Heart	M,O

BUILDING SCIENCE

Institution	Degree
Arizona State University at the Tempe campus	M,D
Carnegie Mellon University	M,D
Georgia Institute of Technology	M,D
Pontificia Universidad Catolica Madre y Maestra	M
University of California, Berkeley	M,D

BUSINESS ADMINISTRATION AND MANAGEMENT—GENERAL

Institution	Degree
Abilene Christian University	M
Adams State University	M
Adelphi University	M
Alabama Agricultural and Mechanical University	M
Alabama State University	M
Alaska Pacific University	M
Albany State University	M
Albertus Magnus College	M
Albizu University, Miami Campus	M,D
Alcorn State University	M
Alfred University	M
Alliant International University–Los Angeles	D
Alliant International University–San Diego	M
Alvernia University	M
Alverno College	M
Amberton University	M
American Business & Technology University	M
American College Dublin	M
The American College of Financial Services	M
American College of Thessaloniki	M,O
American Graduate University	M,O
American InterContinental University Houston	M
American InterContinental University Online	M
American International College	M,D,O
American Jewish University	M
American National University	M
American Public University System	M,D
American Sentinel University	M
American University	M,O
American University in Bulgaria	M
The American University in Cairo	M,O
The American University in Dubai	M
American University of Armenia	M
American University of Beirut	M
The American University of Paris	M
American University of Sharjah	M,D
Anaheim University	M,D,O
Anderson University (IN)	M,D
Anderson University (SC)	M
Angelo State University	M
Anna Maria College	M,O
Antioch University Los Angeles	M
Antioch University New England	M
Antioch University Santa Barbara	M
Apollos University	M,D
Appalachian State University	M
Aquinas College (MI)	M
Arcadia University	M
Argosy University, Atlanta	M,D
Argosy University, Chicago	M,D
Argosy University, Hawai'i	M,D,O
Argosy University, Los Angeles	M,D
Argosy University, Northern Virginia	M,D,O
Argosy University, Orange County	M,D,O
Argosy University, Phoenix	M,D
Argosy University, Seattle	M,D
Argosy University, Tampa	M,D
Argosy University, Twin Cities	M,D
Arizona State University at the Tempe campus	M,D
Arkansas State University	M
Arkansas Tech University	M
Ashland University	M
Ashworth College	M
Aspen University	M,O
Assumption College	M,O
Athabasca University	M,D,O
Atlantis University	M,D
Auburn University	M,D
Auburn University at Montgomery	M
Augsburg University	M
Augusta University	M
Aurora University	M
Austin Peay State University	M
Averett University	M
Avila University	M
Azusa Pacific University	M
Babson College	M,O
Baker College Center for Graduate Studies–Online	M,D
Baker University	M
Bakke Graduate University	M,D
Baldwin Wallace University	M
Ball State University	M,O
Barry University	M,O
Baruch College of the City University of New York	M,D,O*
Bayamón Central University	M
Baylor University	M
Belhaven University (MS)	M
Bellarmine University	M
Bellevue University	M,D
Belmont University	M
Benedictine College	M
Benedictine University	M,D
Bentley University	M,D,O
Berkeley College–Woodland Park Campus	M
Berry College	M
Bethel University (IN)	M
Bethel University (MN)	M,D,O
Bethel University (TN)	M
Binghamton University, State University of New York	M,D
Biola University	M
Black Hills State University	M
Bloomsburg University of Pennsylvania	M,O
Bluffton University	M
Bob Jones University	M,D,O
Boise State University	M
Boston College	M
Boston University	M,D
Bowie State University	M
Bowling Green State University	M
Bradley University	M
Brandeis University	M
Brandman University	M
Brenau University	M
Brescia University	M
Bridgewater State University	M
Briercrest Seminary	M
Brigham Young University	M
Broadview University–West Jordan	M
Brock University	M
Brooklyn College of the City University of New York	M
Bryan College	M
Bryant University	M
Bryan University	M
Butler University	M
Cairn University	M,O
Caldwell University	M
California Baptist University	M
California Coast University	M
California Institute of Advanced Management	M
California Intercontinental University	M,D
California International Business University	M,D
California Lutheran University	M,O
California Miramar University	M
California Polytechnic State University, San Luis Obispo	M
California State Polytechnic University, Pomona	M
California State University, Bakersfield	M
California State University Channel Islands	M
California State University, Chico	M
California State University, Dominguez Hills	M
California State University, East Bay	M
California State University, Fresno	M
California State University, Fullerton	M
California State University, Long Beach	M
California State University, Los Angeles	M,O
California State University, Monterey Bay	M
California State University, Northridge	M
California State University, Sacramento	M
California State University, San Bernardino	M
California State University, Stanislaus	M
California University of Management and Sciences	M,D
California University of Pennsylvania	M
Cambridge College	M
Cameron University	M
Campbellsville University	M,D
Campbell University	M
Canisius College	M
Cape Breton University	M
Capella University	M
Capital University	M
Capitol Technology University	M,D
Cardinal Stritch University	M
Carleton University	M,D
Carlow University	M
Carnegie Mellon University	M
Carroll University	M
Carson-Newman University	M
Case Western Reserve University	M,D
The Catholic University of America	M,D
Cedar Crest College	M
Cedarville University	M,D
Centenary College of Louisiana	M
Centenary University	M

Institution	Degree
Central Connecticut State University	M
Central European University	M,D
Central Michigan University	M,O
Chadron State College	M
Chaminade University of Honolulu	M
Champlain College	M*
Chapman University	M*
Charleston Southern University	M
Charter College	M
Chatham University	M
Christian Brothers University	M,O
The Citadel, The Military College of South Carolina	M
City College of the City University of New York	M
City University of Seattle	M,O
Claflin University	M
Claremont Graduate University	M,D,O
Clarion University of Pennsylvania	M
Clark Atlanta University	M
Clarke University	M
Clarkson University	M,O
Clark University	M
Clayton State University	M
Cleary University	M,O
Clemson University	M,D
Cleveland State University	M,D
Coastal Carolina University	M,O
Coker College	M
College of Charleston	M
College of Saint Elizabeth	M
College of St. Joseph	M
The College of Saint Rose	M
The College of St. Scholastica	M,O
College of Staten Island of the City University of New York	M
The College of William and Mary	M
Colorado Christian University	M
Colorado Mesa University	M
Colorado State University	M
Colorado State University–Global Campus	M
Colorado State University–Pueblo	M
Colorado Technical University Aurora	M
Colorado Technical University Colorado Springs	M,D
Columbia College (MO)	M
Columbia College Chicago	M
Columbia Southern University	M,D
Columbia University	M,D
Columbus State University	M,O
Concordia University (United States)	M
Concordia University (Canada)	M,D,O
Concordia University Chicago	M,D
Concordia University Irvine	M
Concordia University, St. Paul	M
Concordia University Wisconsin	M
Copenhagen Business School	M,D
Corban University	M
Cornell University	M,D
Cornerstone University	M,O
Creighton University	M
Culver-Stockton College	M
Cumberland University	M
Curry College	M,O
Daemen College	M,D,O
Dakota State University	M
Dalhousie University	M,O
Dallas Baptist University	M,D
Dartmouth College	M
Davenport University	M
Defiance College	M
Delaware State University	M
Delaware Valley University	M
Delta State University	M
DePaul University	M,D
DeSales University	M
DeVry College of New York–Midtown Manhattan Campus	M
DeVry University–Alpharetta Campus	M
DeVry University–Arlington Campus	M
DeVry University–Charlotte Campus	M
DeVry University–Chesapeake Campus	M
DeVry University–Chicago Campus	M
DeVry University–Chicago Loop Campus	M
DeVry University–Cincinnati Campus	M
DeVry University–Columbus Campus	M
DeVry University–Decatur Campus	M
DeVry University–Folsom Campus	M
DeVry University–Fremont Campus	M
DeVry University–Ft. Washington Campus	M
DeVry University–Henderson Campus	M
DeVry University–Irving Campus	M
DeVry University–Jacksonville Campus	M
DeVry University–Long Beach Campus	M
DeVry University–Miramar Campus	M
DeVry University–Morrisville Campus	M
DeVry University–Nashville Campus	M
DeVry University–North Brunswick Campus	M
DeVry University Online	M
DeVry University–Orlando Campus	M
DeVry University–Phoenix Campus	M
DeVry University–Pomona Campus	M
DeVry University–San Diego Campus	M,O
DeVry University–Seven Hills Campus	M,O
DeVry University–Tinley Park Campus	M
Doane University	M
Dominican College	M
Dominican University	M
Dominican University of California	M
Drake University	M
Drexel University	M,D,O*
Drury University	M
Duke University	M,D,O
Duquesne University	M
D'Youville College	M
East Carolina University	M,D,O
Eastern Illinois University	M
Eastern Kentucky University	M
Eastern Mennonite University	M
Eastern Michigan University	M,O
Eastern Nazarene College	M
Eastern New Mexico University	M
Eastern Oregon University	M
Eastern University	M,D,O
Eastern Washington University	M
East Tennessee State University	M
East Texas Baptist University	M
ECPI University	M
Edgewood College	M
Elmhurst College	M
Elms College	M,O
Elon University	M
Embry-Riddle Aeronautical University–Daytona	M
Embry-Riddle Aeronautical University–Worldwide	M
Emmanuel College (United States)	M,O
Emory University	M,D
Emporia State University	M
Endicott College	M
ESSEC Business School	M,D
Everglades University	M
Fairfield University	M,O
Fairleigh Dickinson University, Florham Campus	M,O
Fairleigh Dickinson University, Metropolitan Campus	M
Fairmont State University	M
Fashion Institute of Technology	M
Faulkner University	M
Fayetteville State University	M
Felician University	M,D
Ferris State University	M
Fisher College	M
Fitchburg State University	M
Florida Agricultural and Mechanical University	M
Florida Atlantic University	M
Florida Gulf Coast University	M
Florida Institute of Technology	M
Florida Memorial University	M
Florida National University	M
Florida Southern College	M
Florida State University	M,D
Fontbonne University	M
Fordham University	M,D
Fort Hays State University	M
Framingham State University	M
Franciscan University of Steubenville	M
Francis Marion University	M
Franklin Pierce University	M,D,O
Franklin University	M
Freed-Hardeman University	M
Fresno Pacific University	M
Frostburg State University	M
Full Sail University	M
Gannon University	M
Gardner-Webb University	M
Geneva College	M
George Fox University	M,D
George Mason University	M
Georgetown University	M
The George Washington University	M,D,O
Georgia College & State University	M
Georgia Institute of Technology	M,D
Georgian Court University	M,O
Georgia Southern University	M,O
Georgia Southwestern State University	M
Georgia State University	M,D
Goddard College	M
Golden Gate University	M,D,O
Goldey-Beacom College	M
Gonzaga University	M
Governors State University	M
The Graduate Center, City University of New York	D
Grand Canyon University	M,D
Grand Valley State University	M
Granite State College	M
Grantham University	M,O
Gwynedd Mercy University	M
Hallmark University	M
Hamline University	M,D
Hampton University	M,D
Harding University	M
Hardin-Simmons University	M
Harvard University	M,D,O*
Hawai'i Pacific University	M
HEC Montreal	M,D,O
Heidelberg University	M
Henderson State University	M
Herzing University Online	M
High Point University	M,D
Hodges University	M
Hofstra University	M,O
Holy Family University	M
Holy Names University	M
Hood College	M,O
Houston Baptist University	M,D
Howard Payne University	M
Howard University	M
Hult International Business School (United States)	M
Humboldt State University	M
Huntington University	M,D
Husson University	M
Idaho State University	M,O
IGlobal University	M
Illinois Institute of Technology	M,D
Illinois State University	M
Independence University	M
Indiana State University	M
Indiana Tech	M
Indiana University Bloomington	M,D
Indiana University Kokomo	M,O
Indiana University Northwest	M
Indiana University of Pennsylvania	M
Indiana University–Purdue University Indianapolis	M
Indiana University South Bend	M,O
Indiana University Southeast	M
Indiana Wesleyan University	M,O
Instituto Centroamericano de Administración de Empresas	M
Instituto Tecnologico de Santo Domingo	M,O
Instituto Tecnológico y de Estudios Superiores de Monterrey, Campus Central de Veracruz	M
Instituto Tecnológico y de Estudios Superiores de Monterrey, Campus Ciudad de México	M,D
Instituto Tecnológico y de Estudios Superiores de Monterrey, Campus Ciudad Juárez	M
Instituto Tecnológico y de Estudios Superiores de Monterrey, Campus Ciudad Obregón	M
Instituto Tecnológico y de Estudios Superiores de Monterrey, Campus Cuernavaca	M
Instituto Tecnológico y de Estudios Superiores de Monterrey, Campus Estado de México	M,D
Instituto Tecnológico y de Estudios Superiores de Monterrey, Campus Guadalajara	M
Instituto Tecnológico y de Estudios Superiores de Monterrey, Campus Irapuato	M,D
Instituto Tecnológico y de Estudios Superiores de Monterrey, Campus Laguna	M
Instituto Tecnológico y de Estudios Superiores de Monterrey, Campus León	M
Instituto Tecnológico y de Estudios Superiores de Monterrey, Campus Monterrey	M,D
Instituto Tecnológico y de Estudios Superiores de Monterrey, Campus Querétaro	M
Instituto Tecnológico y de Estudios Superiores de Monterrey, Campus Sonora Norte	M
Instituto Tecnológico y de Estudios Superiores de Monterrey, Campus Toluca	M
Inter American University of Puerto Rico, Aguadilla Campus	M
Inter American University of Puerto Rico, Arecibo Campus	M
Inter American University of Puerto Rico, Barranquitas Campus	M
Inter American University of Puerto Rico, Fajardo Campus	M
Inter American University of Puerto Rico, Guayama Campus	M
Inter American University of Puerto Rico, Metropolitan Campus	M
Inter American University of Puerto Rico, San Germán Campus	M,D
International Technological University	M,D
International University in Geneva	M,D
The International University of Monaco	M
Iona College	M,O
Iowa State University of Science and Technology	M,D
Ithaca College	M
Jackson State University	M
Jacksonville State University	M
Jacksonville University	M,D
James Madison University	M
John Brown University	M
John Carroll University	M
John F. Kennedy University	M
Johns Hopkins University	M,O*
Johnson & Wales University	M
Judson University	M
Juniata College	M
Kansas State University	M,O
Kansas Wesleyan University	M
Kean University	M
Keiser University	M,D
Kennesaw State University	M,D
Kent State University	M
Kent State University at Stark	M
Kettering University	M
Keuka College	M
Keystone College	M
King University	M
Kutztown University of Pennsylvania	M
Lake Erie College	M
Lake Forest Graduate School of Management	M
Lakeland University	M
Lamar University	M
La Salle University	M,O
Lasell College	M,O
La Sierra University	M,O
Laurentian University	M
Lawrence Technological University	M,D,O
Lebanese American University	M
Lebanon Valley College	M
Lee University	M
Lehigh University	M
Lehman College of the City University of New York	M
Le Moyne College	M
Lenoir-Rhyne University	M
LeTourneau University	M
Lewis University	M
Liberty University	M,D
LIM College	M
Limestone College	M
Lincoln Memorial University	M
Lincoln University (CA)	M,D
Lindenwood University	M,O
Lindenwood University–Belleville	M
Lipscomb University	M,O
Long Island University–LIU Brooklyn	M,O
Long Island University–LIU Post	M
Longwood University	M
Louisiana State University and Agricultural & Mechanical College	M,D
Louisiana State University in Shreveport	M
Louisiana Tech University	M,D,O
Lourdes University	M
Loyola Marymount University	M
Loyola University Chicago	M,O
Loyola University Maryland	M
Loyola University New Orleans	M
Lynn University	M
Maastricht School of Management	M,D
Madonna University	M
Maharishi University of Management	M,D
Malone University	M
Manhattan College	M
Marconi International University	M,D
Marian University (WI)	M
Marist College	M,O
Marlboro College	M
Marquette University	M,O
Marshall University	M,O
Maryland Institute College of Art	M
Marymount California University	M
Marymount University	M,O
Maryville University of Saint Louis	M,O
Marywood University	M
Massachusetts College of Liberal Arts	M,O
Massachusetts Institute of Technology	M,D
McGill University	M,D,O
McKendree University	M
McMaster University	M,D
McNeese State University	M
Medaille College	M
Melbourne Business School	M,D,O
Memorial University of Newfoundland	M
Mercer University	M
Mercer University	M
Mercy College	M
Meredith College	M
Merrimack College	M
Messiah College	M,O
Methodist University	M
Metropolitan College of New York	M
Metropolitan State University	M,D,O
Miami University	M
Michigan State University	M,D
Michigan Technological University	M
Mid-America Christian University	M
MidAmerica Nazarene University	M
Middle Tennessee State University	M
Midway University	M
Midwestern State University	M
Millennia Atlantic University	M
Milligan College	M,O
Millikin University	M
Millsaps College	M
Mills College	M
Milwaukee School of Engineering	M
Minnesota State University Mankato	M
Minnesota State University Moorhead	M
Minot State University	M
Misericordia University	M
Mississippi College	M,O
Mississippi State University	M,D
Missouri Baptist University	M,O
Missouri Southern State University	M
Missouri State University	M
Missouri University of Science and Technology	M
Missouri Western State University	M
Molloy College	M,O
Monmouth University	M,O
Monroe College	M
Montclair State University	M,O
Moravian College	M
Morehead State University	M

M—masters degree; D—doctorate; O—other advanced degree; *—Close-Up and/or Display

Institution	Degree
Morgan State University	M,D
Mount Aloysius College	M
Mount Marty College	M
Mount Mary University	M
Mount Mercy University	M
Mount St. Joseph University	M
Mount Saint Mary College	M
Mount Saint Mary's University (CA)	M,D,O
Mount St. Mary's University (MD)	M
Mount Vernon Nazarene University	M
Murray State University	M
National American University (TX)	M,D
National Louis University	M
National University	M,O
National University College	M
Naval Postgraduate School	M
Nazareth College of Rochester	M
Nebraska Christian College of Hope International University	M
Neumann University	M
New Charter University	M
New England College	M
New Jersey City University	M,O
New Jersey Institute of Technology	M,D,O
Newman University	M
New Mexico Highlands University	M
New Mexico State University	D
New York Institute of Technology	M,D,O
New York Medical College	M,D,O
New York University	M,D,O*
Niagara University	M
Nicholls State University	M
Nichols College	M
North Carolina Agricultural and Technical State University	M
North Carolina Central University	M
North Carolina State University	M
North Central College	M
Northcentral University	M,D,O
North Dakota State University	M
Northeastern Illinois University	M
Northeastern State University	M
Northeastern University	M
Northern Arizona University	M,O
Northern Illinois University	M
Northern Kentucky University	M,O
Northern Michigan University	M
North Park University	M
Northwest Christian University	M
Northwestern Polytechnic University	M,D
Northwestern University	M,D
Northwest Missouri State University	M
Northwest Nazarene University	M
Northwest University	M
Northwood University, Michigan Campus	M
Norwich University	M
Notre Dame de Namur University	M
Notre Dame of Maryland University	M
Nova Southeastern University	M
Nyack College	M
Oakland City University	M
Oakland University	M,O
Oglala Lakota College	M
Ohio Christian University	M
Ohio Dominican University	M
The Ohio State University	M,D
Ohio University	M
Oklahoma Baptist University	M
Oklahoma Christian University	M
Oklahoma City University	M
Oklahoma State University	M,D
Old Dominion University	M,D
Olivet Nazarene University	M
Open University	M
Oral Roberts University	M
Oregon State University	M,D
Ottawa University	M
Otterbein University	M
Our Lady of the Lake University	M
Pace University	M,D,O
Pacific Lutheran University	M
Pacific States University	M,O
Pacific University	M
Palm Beach Atlantic University	M
Park University	M,O
Penn State Erie, The Behrend College	M
Penn State Great Valley	M,O
Penn State Harrisburg	M,O
Penn State University Park	M,D*
Pensacola Christian College	M,D,O
Pfeiffer University	M
Phillips Theological Seminary	M,D
Piedmont College	M
Pittsburg State University	M
Plymouth State University	M
Point Loma Nazarene University	M
Point Park University	M
Point University	M
Polytechnic University of Puerto Rico	M
Polytechnic University of Puerto Rico, Miami Campus	M
Polytechnic University of Puerto Rico, Orlando Campus	M
Pontifical Catholic University of Puerto Rico	M,D,O
Pontificia Universidad Catolica Madre y Maestra	M
Portland State University	M,D,O
Post University	M
Prairie View A&M University	M
Presidio Graduate School (CA)	M,O
Providence College	M
Purdue University	M,D
Purdue University Fort Wayne	M
Purdue University Global	M
Purdue University Northwest	M

Institution	Degree
Queen's University at Kingston	M,D
Queens University of Charlotte	M
Quincy University	M
Quinnipiac University	M
Radford University	M
Ramapo College of New Jersey	M
Reformed University	M
Regent's University London	M
Regent University	M,D,O
Reinhardt University	M
Rensselaer at Hartford	M
Rensselaer Polytechnic Institute	M,D
Rice University	M
Rider University	M
Rivier University	M
Robert Morris University	M
Robert Morris University Illinois	M
Roberts Wesleyan College	M
Rochester Institute of Technology	M
Rockford University	M
Rockhurst University	M,O
Rogers State University	M
Roger Williams University	M
Rollins College	M
Roosevelt University	M
Roseman University of Health Sciences	M,O
Rosemont College	M
Rowan University	M,O
Royal Military College of Canada	M
Rutgers University–Camden	M
Rutgers University–Newark	M,D
Ryerson University	M
Sacred Heart University	M,O
Sage Graduate School	M
Saginaw Valley State University	M
St. Ambrose University	M,D
St. Bonaventure University	M
St. Catherine University	M
St. Cloud State University	M
Saint Francis University	M
St. John Fisher College	M
St. John's University (NY)	M
St. Joseph's College, Long Island Campus	M
St. Joseph's College, New York	M
Saint Joseph's College of Maine	M
Saint Joseph's University	M,O
Saint Leo University	M,D
Saint Louis University	M*
Saint Martin's University	M
Saint Mary's College of California	M
Saint Mary's University (Canada)	M,D
St. Mary's University (United States)	M
Saint Mary's University of Minnesota	M,D
St. Norbert College	M
Saint Peter's University	M
St. Thomas Aquinas College	M
St. Thomas University	M,O
Saint Vincent College	M
Saint Xavier University	M,O
Salem International University	M
Salem State University	M
Salisbury University	M
Salve Regina University	M,O
Samford University	M
Sam Houston State University	M
San Diego State University	M
San Francisco State University	M
San Ignacio University	M
Santa Clara University	M
Savannah State University	M
Schiller International University (United States)	M
Schiller International University (Germany)	M
Schiller International University (Spain)	M
Schreiner University	M
Seattle Pacific University	M
Seattle University	M,O
Seton Hall University	M,O
Seton Hill University	M
Shenandoah University	M,O
Shippensburg University of Pennsylvania	M,D,O
Shorter University	M
Siena College	M
Silver Lake College of the Holy Family	M
Simmons University	M
Simon Fraser University	M,D,O
SIT Graduate Institute	M
Slippery Rock University of Pennsylvania	M
Sonoma State University	M
South Carolina State University	M
Southeastern Louisiana University	M
Southeastern Oklahoma State University	M
Southeastern University (FL)	M,D
Southeast Missouri State University	M
Southern Adventist University	M
Southern Arkansas University–Magnolia	M
Southern Connecticut State University	M
Southern Illinois University Carbondale	M,D
Southern Illinois University Edwardsville	M
Southern Methodist University	M
Southern Nazarene University	M
Southern New Hampshire University	M,D,O
Southern Oregon University	M,O

Institution	Degree
Southern States University	M
Southern University and Agricultural and Mechanical College	M
Southern Utah University	M
Southern Wesleyan University	M
South University	M
South University	M
South University (TX)	M
South University (SC)	M
South University (GA)	M
South University (AL)	M
South University	M
Southwest Baptist University	M
Southwestern Adventist University	M
Southwestern College (KS)	M
Southwestern College (KS)	M
Southwestern Oklahoma State University	M
Southwest Minnesota State University	M
Southwest University	M
Spring Arbor University	M
Springfield College	M
Spring Hill College	M
Stanford University	M,D
State University of New York at New Paltz	M
State University of New York at Oswego	M
State University of New York College at Geneseo	M
State University of New York College at Old Westbury	M
State University of New York Empire State College	M
State University of New York Polytechnic Institute	M
Stephen F. Austin State University	M
Stetson University	M
Stevens Institute of Technology	M,O
Stockton University	M
Stony Brook University, State University of New York	M,O
Stratford University (VA)	M,D
Strayer University	M
Suffolk University	M
Sullivan University	M,D
Sul Ross State University	M
Syracuse University	M,D
Tabor College	M
Tarleton State University	M
Temple University	M,D*
Tennessee State University	M
Tennessee Technological University	M
Tennessee Wesleyan University	M
Texas A&M International University	M,D
Texas A&M University	M
Texas A&M University–Central Texas	M,O
Texas A&M University–Commerce	M
Texas A&M University–Corpus Christi	M
Texas A&M University–Kingsville	M
Texas A&M University–San Antonio	M
Texas A&M University–Texarkana	M
Texas Christian University	M
Texas Health and Science University	M,D
Texas Southern University	M
Texas State University	M
Texas Tech University	M,D
Texas Wesleyan University	M
Texas Woman's University	M
Thomas College	M
Thomas Edison State University	M
Thomas Jefferson University	M
Thomas More University	M
Thomas University	M
Thompson Rivers University	M
Tiffin University	M
Trevecca Nazarene University	M
Trident University International	M,D
Trine University	M
Trinity International University	M,D,O
Trinity University	M
Trinity Washington University	M
Trinity Western University	M
Troy University	M
Truett McConnell University	M
Tulane University	M,D
Tusculum University	M
Union University	M
United States International University–Africa	M
Universidad Autonoma de Guadalajara	M,D
Universidad de las Americas, A.C.	M
Universidad de las Américas Puebla	M
Universidad del Este	M,D
Universidad del Turabo	M,D
Universidad Iberoamericana	M,D
Universidad Metropolitana	M
Université de Moncton	M
Université de Sherbrooke	M,D,O
Université du Québec à Chicoutimi	M
Université du Québec à Montréal	M,D,O
Université du Québec à Rimouski	M,O
Université du Québec à Trois-Rivières	M
Université du Québec en Abitibi-Témiscamingue	M
Université Laval	M,D,O
University at Albany, State University of New York	M

Institution	Degree
University at Buffalo, the State University of New York	M,D
The University of Akron	M
The University of Alabama	M,D
The University of Alabama at Birmingham	M
The University of Alabama in Huntsville	M,O
University of Alaska Anchorage	M
University of Alaska Fairbanks	M
University of Alberta	M,D
University of Antelope Valley	M
The University of Arizona	M,D,O
University of Arkansas	M,D
University of Arkansas at Little Rock	M,O
University of Baltimore	M,O
University of Bridgeport	M
The University of British Columbia	M,D
University of Calgary	M,D
University of California, Berkeley	M,D,O
University of California, Davis	M
University of California, Irvine	M,D
University of California, Los Angeles	M,D
University of California, Riverside	M,D
University of California, San Diego	M,D
University of Central Arkansas	M
University of Central Florida	M,D,O
University of Central Missouri	M,D,O
University of Charleston	M
University of Chicago	M,D,O
University of Cincinnati	M,D
University of Colorado Boulder	M,D
University of Colorado Colorado Springs	M
University of Colorado Denver	M
University of Connecticut	M,D
University of Dallas	M,D
University of Dayton	M
University of Delaware	M
University of Denver	M
University of Detroit Mercy	M,O
University of Dubuque	M
University of Fairfax	M
The University of Findlay	M,D
University of Florida	M,D
University of Georgia	M,D
University of Guam	M
University of Guelph	M,D
University of Hartford	M
University of Hawaii at Manoa	M
University of Holy Cross	M,D
University of Houston	M,D
University of Houston–Clear Lake	M
University of Houston–Downtown	M
University of Houston–Victoria	M
University of Idaho	M
University of Illinois at Chicago	M,D
University of Illinois at Springfield	M
University of Illinois at Urbana–Champaign	M,D
University of Indianapolis	M,O
The University of Iowa	M,D
The University of Kansas	M,D
University of Kentucky	M,D
University of La Verne	M,D,O
University of Lethbridge	M,D
University of Louisiana at Lafayette	M
University of Louisiana at Monroe	M,O
University of Louisville	M,D
University of Lynchburg	M
University of Maine	M
University of Management and Technology	M,D,O
The University of Manchester	M
University of Manitoba	M,D
University of Mary	M
University of Mary Hardin-Baylor	M
University of Maryland, College Park	M,D
University of Maryland University College	M,D,O
University of Mary Washington	M
University of Massachusetts Amherst	M,D
University of Massachusetts Boston	M
University of Massachusetts Dartmouth	M,O
University of Massachusetts Lowell	M,D
University of Memphis	M,D
University of Miami	M,D
University of Michigan	M,D
University of Michigan–Dearborn	M
University of Michigan–Flint	M,O
University of Minnesota, Duluth	M
University of Minnesota Rochester	M,D
University of Minnesota, Twin Cities Campus	M,D
University of Mississippi	M,D
University of Missouri	M,D
University of Missouri–Kansas City	M,D
University of Missouri–St. Louis	M,D,O
University of Mobile	M
University of Montana	M
University of Montevallo	M
University of Mount Olive	M
University of Nebraska at Kearney	M
University of Nebraska at Omaha	M,O
University of Nebraska–Lincoln	M,D
University of Nevada, Las Vegas	M,O
University of Nevada, Reno	M

University of New Brunswick Fredericton — M
University of New Brunswick Saint John
University of New Hampshire — M,O
University of New Haven — M
University of New Mexico — M
University of New Orleans — M
University of North Alabama — M
The University of North Carolina at Chapel Hill — M,D
The University of North Carolina at Charlotte — M,D,O
The University of North Carolina at Greensboro — M,O
The University of North Carolina at Pembroke — M
The University of North Carolina Wilmington — M
University of North Dakota — M
University of Northern Colorado — M
University of Northern Iowa — M
University of North Florida — M
University of North Georgia — M
University of North Texas — M,D,O
University of North Texas at Dallas — M
University of Northwestern Ohio — M
University of Northwestern– St. Paul — M
University of Notre Dame — M
University of Oklahoma — M,D,O*
University of Oregon — M,D
University of Ottawa — M
University of Pennsylvania — M,D*
University of Phoenix–Bay Area Campus — M,D
University of Phoenix– Central Valley Campus — M
University of Phoenix–Dallas Campus — M
University of Phoenix–Hawaii Campus — M
University of Phoenix– Houston Campus — M
University of Phoenix–Las Vegas Campus — M
University of Phoenix–Online Campus — M,D,O
University of Phoenix– Phoenix Campus — M,O
University of Phoenix– Sacramento Valley Campus — M
University of Phoenix–San Antonio Campus — M
University of Phoenix–San Diego Campus — M
University of Pikeville — M
University of Pittsburgh — M,D*
University of Portland — M
University of Puerto Rico– Mayagüez — M
University of Puerto Rico– Río Piedras — M,D
University of Redlands — M
University of Regina — M,O
University of Rhode Island — M,D
University of Richmond — M
University of Rochester — M,D*
University of St. Francis (IL) — M,O
University of Saint Francis (IN) — M
University of Saint Joseph — M
University of Saint Mary — M
University of St. Thomas (TX) — M
University of St. Thomas (MN) — M
University of San Diego — M
University of San Francisco — M
University of Saskatchewan — M,D
The University of Scranton — M
University of Sioux Falls — M
University of South Africa — M,D
University of South Alabama — M,D
University of South Carolina — M,D
University of South Carolina Aiken — M
University of South Dakota — M
University of Southern California — M,D
University of Southern Indiana — M
University of Southern Maine — M,O
University of Southern Mississippi — M
University of South Florida — M
University of South Florida, St. Petersburg — M
University of South Florida Sarasota-Manatee — M
The University of Tampa — M,O
The University of Tennessee — M,D
The University of Tennessee at Chattanooga — M
The University of Tennessee at Martin — M
The University of Texas at Austin — M,D
The University of Texas at Dallas — M,D
The University of Texas at El Paso — M,D,O
The University of Texas at San Antonio — M,D,O
The University of Texas at Tyler — M
The University of Texas of the Permian Basin — M
The University of Texas Rio Grande Valley — M,D
University of the Cumberlands — M
University of the District of Columbia — M
University of the Incarnate Word — M
University of the Pacific — M
University of the People — M
University of the Potomac — M
University of the Sacred Heart — M
University of the Southwest — M
University of the Virgin Islands — M
University of the West — M

The University of Toledo — M
University of Toronto — M,D
The University of Tulsa — M
University of Utah — M,D,O
University of Vermont — M
University of Victoria — M
University of Virginia — M,D,O
University of Washington — M,D
University of Washington, Bothell — M
University of Washington, Tacoma — M
University of Waterloo — M
The University of West Alabama — M
The University of Western Ontario — M,D
University of West Florida — M
University of West Georgia — M
University of West Los Angeles — M
University of Windsor — M
University of Wisconsin–Eau Claire — M
University of Wisconsin– Green Bay — M
University of Wisconsin– Madison — M
University of Wisconsin– Milwaukee — M,D,O*
University of Wisconsin– Oshkosh — M
University of Wisconsin– Parkside — M
University of Wisconsin– River Falls — M
University of Wisconsin– Whitewater — M
University of Wyoming — M
Upper Iowa University — M
Urbana University–A Branch Campus of Franklin University — M
Ursuline College — M
Utah State University — M
Utah Valley University — M
Valdosta State University — M
Valparaiso University — M,O
Vancouver Island University — M
Vanderbilt University — M*
Villanova University — M
Virginia Commonwealth University — M,D
Virginia International University — M,O
Virginia Polytechnic Institute and State University — M,D
Virginia Wesleyan University — M
Viterbo University — M
Wagner College — M
Wake Forest University — M,D,O
Walden University — M
Walsh College of Accountancy and Business Administration — M
Walsh University — M
Warner University — M
Washburn University — M
Washington Adventist University — M
Washington State University — M,D
Washington University in St. Louis — M,D
Wayland Baptist University — M,D
Waynesburg University — M,D
Wayne State College — M
Wayne State University — M,D,O
Webber International University — M
Weber State University — M,O
Webster University — M,D,O
Wesleyan College — M
Wesley College — M
West Chester University of Pennsylvania — M,O
Westcliff University — M,D
Western Carolina University — M
Western Connecticut State University — M
Western Governors University — M
Western Illinois University — M,O
Western Kentucky University — M
Western Michigan University — M
Western New England University — M
Western New Mexico University — M
Western Washington University — M
West Liberty University — M
Westminster College (UT) — M,O
West Texas A&M University — M
West Virginia University — M,D,O
West Virginia Wesleyan College — M
Wheeling Jesuit University — M
Whitworth University — M
WHU - Otto Beisheim School of Management — M
Wichita State University — M
Widener University — M
Wilfrid Laurier University — M,D
Wilkes University — M
Willamette University — M
William Carey University — M
William Paterson University of New Jersey — M,O
William Woods University — M,O
Wilmington University — M,D
Wilson College — M
Wingate University — M
Winston-Salem State University — M
Winthrop University — M
Woodbury University — M
Worcester Polytechnic Institute — M,D,O
Worcester State University — M
Wright State University — M
Xavier University — M*
Yale University — M,D
Yeshiva University — M
York College of Pennsylvania — M
York University — M,D
Youngstown State University — M

BUSINESS ANALYTICS
Abilene Christian University — M
American Public University System — M,D

Ashland University — M
Babson College — M,O
Baldwin Wallace University — M,O
Bentley University — M,D
Boston University — M,D
California Polytechnic State University, San Luis Obispo — M
California State University, East Bay — M
California State University, Fullerton — M
California University of Pennsylvania — M
Case Western Reserve University — M
Central European University — M,D
Clark University — M
Cleary University — M,O
Clemson University — M
The College of Saint Rose — M
The College of William and Mary — M
Columbia University — M
Creighton University — M,D
Dakota State University — M,D,O
DePaul University — M,D
Duke University — M
Fairfield University — M,O
The George Washington University — M,O
Golden Gate University — M,D,O
Grand Canyon University — M
HEC Montreal — M
Hult International Business School (United States) — M
Iowa State University of Science and Technology — M
Johns Hopkins University — M*
Kent State University — M
La Salle University — M,O
Lenoir-Rhyne University — M
Lewis University — M
Loyola University Chicago — M,O
Marist College — M,O
Merrimack College — M
Metropolitan State University — M,D,O
Michigan State University — M
Montclair State University — M
National University — M,O
Northwestern University — M,D
Northwest Missouri State University — M
Nova Southeastern University — M
Point Park University — M
Queen's University at Kingston — M,D
Regent University — M,D,O
Rensselaer Polytechnic Institute — M
Robert Morris University Illinois — M
Rockhurst University — M,O
St. John's University (NY) — M
Saint Joseph's University — M
Saint Mary's College of California — M
Santa Clara University — M
Seattle University — M,O
Shippensburg University of Pennsylvania — M,D,O
Southern Illinois University Edwardsville — M
Southern Methodist University — M
Southern New Hampshire University — M,D,O
Stevens Institute of Technology — M,O
Suffolk University — M
Syracuse University — M
Texas A&M University– Commerce — M
Texas Woman's University — M
Thomas Jefferson University — M
Tulane University — M,D
University at Albany, State University of New York — M
University at Buffalo, the State University of New York — M,D
The University of Alabama in Huntsville — M,O
The University of British Columbia — M
University of California, Davis — M
University of California, Irvine — M
University of California, Los Angeles — M,D
University of California, San Diego — M,D
University of Central Oklahoma — M
University of Cincinnati — M,D
University of Connecticut — M,D
University of Dallas — M,D
University of Denver — M
University of Georgia — M
The University of Iowa — M
The University of Manchester — M
University of Massachusetts Boston — M
University of Miami — M,D
University of Michigan– Dearborn — M
The University of North Carolina at Charlotte — M,D,O
University of Notre Dame — M
University of Oklahoma — M,O*
University of Pittsburgh — D*
University of St. Francis (IL) — M,O
University of St. Thomas (MN) — M
University of South Dakota — M,O
The University of Tampa — M,O
The University of Tulsa — M
University of Wisconsin– Milwaukee — M,O*
Villanova University — M
Virginia Polytechnic Institute and State University — M,D
Wake Forest University — M
Walsh College of Accountancy and Business Administration — M

West Chester University of Pennsylvania — M,O
West Virginia University — M,D,O
William Paterson University of New Jersey — M,O
York University — M,D

BUSINESS EDUCATION
Alabama Agricultural and Mechanical University — M,O
Arkansas State University — O
Ball State University — M,O
Bloomsburg University of Pennsylvania — M
Bowling Green State University — M
Buffalo State College, State University of New York — M
Canisius College — M,O
Capella University — D
Chadron State College — M,O
Clemson University — M,D
Colorado Christian University — M
East Carolina University — M,O
Eastern Kentucky University — M,O
Florida Agricultural and Mechanical University — M
Hofstra University — M,D,O
Indiana University of Pennsylvania — M
Inter American University of Puerto Rico, Metropolitan Campus — M
Inter American University of Puerto Rico, San Germán Campus — M
Johnson & Wales University — M
Lock Haven University of Pennsylvania — M
Louisiana State University and Agricultural & Mechanical College — M,D
Manhattanville College — M,O
Maryville University of Saint Louis — M,O
Middle Tennessee State University — M
Milwaukee School of Engineering — M,O
Mississippi College — M,D,O
Morehead State University — M,O
New York University — M,O*
North Carolina Agricultural and Technical State University — M
North Carolina State University — M
Nova Southeastern University — M
Old Dominion University — M,D
Pontifical Catholic University of Puerto Rico — M,D
Regis University — M,O
Salve Regina University — M,O
South Carolina State University — M
Spalding University — M
State University of New York at Oswego — M*
Temple University — M
Thomas College — M
University of Delaware — M,D
University of Georgia — M,D,O
University of Missouri — M,D,O
The University of North Carolina at Charlotte — D
University of South Carolina — M,D
University of the Cumberlands — M,D,O
The University of Toledo — M,D,O
University of West Georgia — M,D,O
University of Wisconsin– Whitewater — M
Utah State University — D
Washington State University — M,D
Wayne State College — M
West Chester University of Pennsylvania — M,O

CANADIAN STUDIES
Carleton University — M,D
Queen's University at Kingston — M,D
Saint Mary's University (Canada) — M,O
Trent University — M,D
Université de Saint-Boniface — M
Université de Sherbrooke — M,D
Université du Québec à Chicoutimi — M
University at Buffalo, the State University of New York — M,D
University of Lethbridge — M,D
University of Manitoba — D
University of Ottawa — D
University of Saskatchewan — M,D
Wilfrid Laurier University — M,D

CANCER BIOLOGY/ONCOLOGY
Augusta University — D
Baylor College of Medicine — D
Case Western Reserve University — D
Duke University — D
Emory University — D
Gerstner Sloan Kettering Graduate School of Biomedical Sciences — D*
Grand Valley State University — M
Irell & Manella Graduate School of Biological Sciences — D
McMaster University — M,D
Medical University of South Carolina — D
Meharry Medical College — D
Memorial University of Newfoundland — M,D
New York University — M,D*
Oregon Health & Science University — D
Purdue University — D
Rutgers University–New Brunswick — M,D
Saint Francis University — M
Thomas Jefferson University — D
Tufts University — D
Université Laval — O

M—masters degree; D—doctorate; O—other advanced degree; *—Close-Up and/or Display

University at Buffalo, the State University of New York — M
The University of Alabama at Birmingham — D
University of Alberta — M,D
The University of Arizona — D
University of Calgary — M,D
University of Chicago — D
University of Cincinnati — D
University of Colorado Denver — D
University of Delaware — M,D
The University of Kansas — M,D
The University of Manchester — M,D
University of Manitoba — D
University of Maryland, Baltimore — D
University of Massachusetts Medical School — M,D
University of Miami — D
University of Michigan — M,D
University of Minnesota, Twin Cities Campus — D
University of Nebraska Medical Center — D
University of North Texas Health Science Center at Fort Worth — M,D
University of Pennsylvania — D*
University of Regina — D
University of Southern California — D
University of South Florida — M,D
The University of Texas Health Science Center at Houston — D
The University of Texas Southwestern Medical Center — D
University of the District of Columbia — M
The University of Toledo — M,D
University of Utah — M,D
University of Wisconsin–La Crosse — M
University of Wisconsin–Madison — D
Wake Forest University — D
Wayne State University — M,D,O
West Virginia University — D

CARDIOVASCULAR SCIENCES
Albany Medical College — M,D
Augusta University — D
Baylor College of Medicine — D
Johns Hopkins University — M,D*
Marquette University — M
McMaster University — M,D
Medical University of South Carolina — D
Memorial University of Newfoundland — M,D
Midwestern University, Glendale Campus —
Milwaukee School of Engineering — M
Quinnipiac University — M
Université Laval — O
University of Calgary — M,D,O
University of Guelph — M,D,O
University of Mary — M
University of South Dakota — M,D
University of South Florida — O
The University of Toledo — M,D

CELL BIOLOGY
Albany College of Pharmacy and Health Sciences — M
Albany Medical College — M,D
Albert Einstein College of Medicine — D
American University of Beirut — M,D
Appalachian State University — M
Arizona State University at the Tempe campus — M,D
Auburn University — M,D
Augusta University — D
Baylor College of Medicine — D
Boston University — M,D
Brandeis University — M,D
Brown University — M,D
California Institute of Technology — D
California State University, Sacramento — M
Carnegie Mellon University — M,D
Case Western Reserve University — D
The Catholic University of America — M,D
Columbia University — M,D
Cornell University — D
Dartmouth College — D
Drexel University — M,D*
Duke University — D,O
East Carolina University — M,D
Emory University — D
Emporia State University — M
Florida Institute of Technology — M
Florida State University — M,D
Georgia State University — M,D
Grand Valley State University — M
Harvard University — D*
Illinois Institute of Technology — M,D
Illinois State University — M,D
Indiana State University — M,D
Indiana University Bloomington — M,D
Indiana University–Purdue University Indianapolis — M,D
Iowa State University of Science and Technology — M,D
Irell & Manella Graduate School of Biological Sciences — D
Johns Hopkins University — D*
Kent State University — M,D
Lehigh University — M,D
Liberty University — M,D
Louisiana State University Health Sciences Center — D
Louisiana State University Health Sciences Center at Shreveport — M,D
Loyola University Chicago — M,D
Marquette University — M,D
Massachusetts Institute of Technology — D

McGill University — M,D
McMaster University — M,D
Medical University of South Carolina — D
Michigan State University — M,D
Missouri State University — M
New York Medical College — M,D
North Carolina State University — M,D
North Dakota State University — D
Northeastern Illinois University — M
Northwestern University — D
The Ohio State University — M,D
Ohio University — M,D
Oregon Health & Science University — D
Oregon State University — D
Penn State Hershey Medical Center —
Penn State University Park — M,D*
Purdue University — M,D
Quinnipiac University — M
Rice University — M,D
Rosalind Franklin University of Medicine and Science — D
Rush University — M,D
Rutgers University–Newark — D
Rutgers University–New Brunswick — M,D
San Diego State University — M,D
San Francisco State University — M
Southern Methodist University — M,D
State University of New York Downstate Medical Center — D
State University of New York Upstate Medical University — M,D
Stony Brook University, State University of New York — M,D
Texas Tech University Health Sciences Center — M,D
Thomas Jefferson University — D
Tufts University — D
Tulane University — M,D
Uniformed Services University of the Health Sciences — M,D*
Universidad Central del Caribe — M,D
Université de Montréal — M,D
Université de Sherbrooke — M,D
Université Laval — M,D
University at Buffalo, the State University of New York — M,D
The University of Alabama at Birmingham — D
University of Alberta — M,D
The University of Arizona — M,D
University of Arkansas — M,D
The University of British Columbia — M,D
University of California, Berkeley — D
University of California, Davis — M,D
University of California, Irvine — M,D
University of California, Los Angeles — M,D
University of California, Riverside — M,D
University of California, San Francisco — D
University of California, Santa Barbara — M,D
University of California, Santa Cruz — M,D
University of Chicago — D
University of Cincinnati — D
University of Colorado Boulder — M,D
University of Colorado Denver — M,D
University of Connecticut — D
University of Connecticut Health Center — D
University of Delaware — M,D
University of Denver — M,D
University of Florida — M,D
University of Georgia — M,D
University of Guelph — M,D
University of Illinois at Chicago — M,D
University of Illinois at Urbana–Champaign — M,D
The University of Iowa — M,D
The University of Kansas — M,D
The University of Manchester — M,D
University of Maryland, Baltimore — M,D
University of Maryland, Baltimore County — D
University of Maryland, College Park — M,D
University of Massachusetts Amherst — M,D
University of Miami — D
University of Michigan — M,D
University of Minnesota, Twin Cities Campus — M,D
University of Missouri–Kansas City — D
University of Montana — D
University of Nevada, Reno — M,D
University of New Haven — M
University of New Mexico — M,D
The University of North Carolina at Chapel Hill — M,D
University of Notre Dame — M,D
University of Oklahoma Health Sciences Center — M,D
University of Ottawa — M,D
University of Pennsylvania — D*
University of Pittsburgh — D*
University of Puerto Rico–Río Piedras — M,D
University of Rhode Island — M,D
University of Saskatchewan — M,D
University of South Carolina — M,D
University of South Dakota — M,D
University of Southern California — M,D
University of South Florida — M,D
The University of Texas at Austin — D
The University of Texas at Dallas — M,D
The University of Texas at San Antonio — M,D
The University of Texas Health Science Center at Houston — M,D

The University of Texas Health Science Center at San Antonio — M,D
The University of Texas Medical Branch — D
The University of Texas Southwestern Medical Center — D
University of the Sciences — M
University of Toronto — M,D
University of Vermont — D
University of Virginia — D
University of Washington — D
The University of Western Ontario — M,D
University of Wisconsin–La Crosse — M
University of Wisconsin–Madison — D
University of Wisconsin–Milwaukee — M,D*
University of Wyoming — D
Vanderbilt University — M,D*
Washington University in St. Louis — D
Wayne State University — M,D,O
Weill Cornell Medicine — M,D
Wesleyan University — D
Yale University — D

CELTIC LANGUAGES
Harvard University — D*

CERAMIC SCIENCES AND ENGINEERING
Alfred University — M,D
Missouri University of Science and Technology — M,D

CHEMICAL ENGINEERING
American University of Sharjah — M,D
Arizona State University at the Tempe campus — M,D
Auburn University — M,D
Brigham Young University — M,D
Brown University — M,D
Bucknell University — M
California Institute of Technology — D
Carnegie Mellon University — M,D
Case Western Reserve University — M,D
City College of the City University of New York — M,D
Clarkson University — M,D
Clemson University — M,D
Cleveland State University — M,D
Colorado School of Mines — M,D
Colorado State University — M,D
Columbia University — M,D
Cooper Union for the Advancement of Science and Art — M
Cornell University — M,D
Dalhousie University — M,D
Dartmouth College — M,D
Drexel University — M,D*
École Polytechnique de Montréal — M,D,O
Fairleigh Dickinson University, Florham Campus — M,O
Florida Agricultural and Mechanical University — M,D
Florida Institute of Technology — M,D
Florida State University — M,D
Georgia Institute of Technology — M,D
Howard University — M,D
Illinois Institute of Technology — M,D
Instituto Tecnológico y de Estudios Superiores de Monterrey, Campus Monterrey — M,D
Iowa State University of Science and Technology — M,D
Johns Hopkins University — M,D*
Kansas State University — M,D,O
Lamar University — M,D
Lehigh University — M,D
Louisiana State University and Agricultural & Mechanical College — M,D
Manhattan College — M
Massachusetts Institute of Technology — M,D
McGill University — M,D
McMaster University — M,D
McNeese State University — M
Miami University — M
Michigan State University — M,D
Michigan Technological University — M,D
Mississippi State University — M,D
Missouri University of Science and Technology — M,D
Montana State University — M,D
New Jersey Institute of Technology — M,D
North Carolina Agricultural and Technical State University — M
North Carolina State University — M,D
Northeastern University — M,D,O
Northwestern University — M,D
The Ohio State University — M,D
Ohio University — M,D
Oklahoma State University — M,D
Oregon State University — M,D
Penn State University Park — M,D*
Princeton University — M,D
Purdue University — M,D
Queen's University at Kingston — M,D
Rensselaer Polytechnic Institute — M,D
Rice University — M,D
Rose-Hulman Institute of Technology — M
Rowan University — M,D
Royal Military College of Canada — M,D
Rutgers University–New Brunswick — M,D
San Jose State University — M
South Dakota School of Mines and Technology — M,D
Stanford University — M,D
Stevens Institute of Technology — M,D,O
Syracuse University — M,D
Tennessee Technological University — M

Texas A&M University — M,D
Texas A&M University–Kingsville — M
Tufts University — M,D
Tulane University — M,D
Universidad de las Américas Puebla — M
Université de Sherbrooke — M,D
Université Laval — M,D
University at Buffalo, the State University of New York — M,D,O
The University of Akron — M,D
The University of Alabama — M,D
The University of Alabama in Huntsville — M,D
University of Alberta — M,D
The University of Arizona — M,D
University of Arkansas — M,D
The University of British Columbia — M,D
University of Calgary — M,D
University of California, Berkeley — M,D
University of California, Davis — M,D
University of California, Irvine — M,D
University of California, Los Angeles — M,D
University of California, Riverside — M,D
University of California, San Diego — M,D
University of California, Santa Barbara — M,D
University of Cincinnati — M,D
University of Colorado Boulder — M,D
University of Connecticut — M,D
University of Dayton — M
University of Delaware — M,D
University of Florida — M,D,O
University of Houston — M,D
University of Idaho — M,D
University of Illinois at Chicago — M,D
University of Illinois at Urbana–Champaign — M,D
The University of Iowa — M,D
The University of Kansas — M,D,O
University of Kentucky — M,D
University of Louisiana at Lafayette — M
University of Louisville — M,D
University of Maine — M,D
The University of Manchester — M,D
University of Maryland, Baltimore County — M,D
University of Maryland, College Park — M,D
University of Massachusetts Amherst — M,D
University of Massachusetts Lowell — M,D
University of Michigan — M,D,O
University of Minnesota, Twin Cities Campus — M,D
University of Mississippi — M,D
University of Missouri — M,D
University of Nebraska–Lincoln — M,D
University of Nevada, Reno — M,D
University of New Brunswick Fredericton — M,D
University of New Hampshire — M,D
University of New Mexico — M,D
University of North Dakota — M,D
University of Notre Dame — M,D
University of Ottawa — M,D
University of Pennsylvania — M,D*
University of Pittsburgh — M,D*
University of Puerto Rico–Mayagüez — M,D
University of Rhode Island — M,D,O
University of Rochester — M,D*
University of Saskatchewan — M,D
University of South Africa — M
University of South Alabama — M
University of South Carolina — M,D
University of Southern California — M,D,O
University of South Florida — M,D,O
The University of Tennessee — M,D
The University of Tennessee at Chattanooga — M
The University of Texas at Austin — M,D
The University of Toledo — M,D
University of Toronto — M,D
The University of Tulsa — M,D
University of Utah — M,D
University of Virginia — M,D
University of Washington — M,D
University of Waterloo — M,D
The University of Western Ontario — M,D
University of Wisconsin–Madison — D
University of Wyoming — M,D
Vanderbilt University — M,D*
Villanova University — M,O
Virginia Polytechnic Institute and State University — M,D
Washington State University — M,D
Washington University in St. Louis — M,D
Wayne State University — M,D,O
Western Michigan University — M,D
West Virginia University — M,D
Widener University — M
Worcester Polytechnic Institute — M,D
Yale University — M,D

CHEMICAL PHYSICS
Columbia University — M,D
Cornell University — D
Harvard University — D*
Kent State University — M,D
Lewis University — M
Marquette University — M,D
McMaster University — M,D
Michigan State University — M,D
The Ohio State University — M,D
Tufts University — M,D

University of Illinois at
Urbana–Champaign — M,D
University of Louisville — M,D
University of Maryland, College
Park — M,D
University of Minnesota, Twin
Cities Campus — M,D
University of Nevada, Reno — D
The University of Tennessee — M,D
University of Utah — M,D
Virginia Commonwealth University — M,D
Wesleyan University — D

CHEMISTRY
Acadia University — M
American University — M
The American University in Cairo — M,D,O
American University of Beirut — M
Arizona State University at the
Tempe campus — M,D
Arkansas State University — M,O
Auburn University — M,D
Ball State University — M
Baylor University — M,D
Binghamton University, State
University of New York — M,D
Boise State University — M
Boston College — M,D
Boston University — M,D
Bowling Green State University — M,D
Bradley University — M
Brandeis University — M,D
Brigham Young University — M,D
Brock University — M,D
Brooklyn College of the City
University of New York — M,D
Brown University — D
Bryn Mawr College — M,D
Bucknell University — M
Cabrini University — M,D
California Institute of Technology — M,D
California Polytechnic State
University, San Luis Obispo — M
California State Polytechnic
University, Pomona — M
California State University, East
Bay — M
California State University,
Fresno — M
California State University,
Fullerton — M
California State University, Long
Beach — M
California State University, Los
Angeles — M
California State University,
Northridge — M
California State University,
Sacramento — M
Carleton University — M,D
Carnegie Mellon University — D
Case Western Reserve University — M,D
Central Michigan University — M
Central Washington University — M
City College of the City
University of New York — M,D
Clark Atlanta University — M,D
Clarkson University — M,D
Clark University — D
Clemson University — M,D
Cleveland State University — M,D
The College at Brockport, State
University of New York — M,O
Colorado School of Mines — M,D
Colorado State University — M,D
Colorado State University–
Pueblo — M
Columbia University — M,D
Columbus State University — M,O
Concordia University (Canada) — M,D
Cornell University — D
Dalhousie University — M,D
Dartmouth College — M,D
Delaware State University — M,D
DePaul University — M,D
Drew University — M,D,O
Drexel University — M,D*
Duke University — D
Duquesne University — M
East Carolina University — M
Eastern Illinois University — M
Eastern Kentucky University — M
Eastern Michigan University — M
Eastern New Mexico University — M
East Tennessee State University — M
Emory University — D
Fairleigh Dickinson University,
Florham Campus — M
Fairleigh Dickinson University,
Metropolitan Campus — M
Fisk University — M
Florida Agricultural and
Mechanical University — M
Florida Atlantic University — M,D
Florida Institute of Technology — M,D
Florida International University — M,D
Furman University — M
George Mason University — M,D
Georgetown University — D
The George Washington University — M,D
Georgia Institute of Technology — M,D
Georgia State University — M,D
The Graduate Center, City
University of New York — M,D
Hampton University — M*
Harvard University — D*
Howard University — M,D
Hunter College of the City
University of New York — D
Idaho State University — M,D
Illinois Institute of Technology — M,D

Indiana University Bloomington — M,D
Indiana University of Pennsylvania — M
Indiana University–Purdue
University Indianapolis — M,D
Instituto Tecnológico y de
Estudios Superiores de Monterrey,
Campus Monterrey — M,D
Iowa State University of Science
and Technology — M,D
Jackson State University — M,D
Johns Hopkins University — M,D*
Kansas State University — M,D
Kennesaw State University — M
Kent State University — M,D
Lakehead University — M
Lamar University — M
Laurentian University — M
Lehigh University — M,D
Lewis University — M
Long Island University–LIU
Brooklyn — M,D,O
Louisiana State University and
Agricultural & Mechanical College — M,D
Louisiana Tech University — M,D,O
Loyola University Chicago — M,D
Manhattanville College — M,O
Marquette University — M,D
Marshall University — M
Massachusetts Institute of
Technology — D
McGill University — M,D
McMaster University — M,D
McNeese State University — M
MCPHS University — M,D
Memorial University of
Newfoundland — M,D
Miami University — M,D
Michigan State University — M,D
Michigan Technological University — M,D
Middle Tennessee State University — M
Mississippi College — M
Mississippi State University — M,D
Missouri State University — M
Missouri University of Science and
Technology — M,D
Missouri Western State University — M
Montana State University — M,D
Montclair State University — M
Morgan State University — M
Mount Allison University — M
Murray State University — M
New Jersey Institute of Technology — M,D,O
New Mexico Highlands University — M
New Mexico Institute of Mining and
Technology — M,D
New York University — M,D*
North Carolina Agricultural and
Technical State University — M
North Carolina Central University — M
North Carolina State University — M,D
North Dakota State University — M,D
Northeastern Illinois University — M
Northeastern University — M,D
Northern Arizona University — M
Northern Illinois University — M,D
Northwestern University — D
Oakland University — M,D
The Ohio State University — M,D
Oklahoma State University — M,D
Old Dominion University — M,D
Oregon State University — M,D
Pace University — M,O
Penn State University Park — M,D*
Pittsburg State University — M
Pontifical Catholic University of
Puerto Rico — M
Portland State University — M,D
Prairie View A&M University — M
Princeton University — D
Purdue University — M,D
Queens College of the City
University of New York — M,D
Queen's University at
Kingston — M,D
Rensselaer Polytechnic Institute — M,D
Rice University — M,D
Rochester Institute of Technology — M,D
Roosevelt University — M
Royal Military College of Canada — M,D
Rutgers University–Camden — M
Rutgers University–Newark — M,D
Rutgers University–New
Brunswick — M,D
Sacred Heart University — M
St. Francis Xavier University — M
St. John Fisher College — M
St. John's University (NY) — M
Saint Louis University — M,D*
Sam Houston State University — M
San Diego State University — M
San Francisco State University — M
San Jose State University — M
The Scripps Research Institute — D
Seton Hall University — M,D
Simon Fraser University — M,D
Smith College — M
South Dakota State University — M,D
Southeast Missouri State
University — M
Southern Connecticut State
University — M
Southern Illinois University
Carbondale — M,D
Southern Illinois University
Edwardsville — M
Southern Methodist University — M,D
Southern University and
Agricultural and Mechanical
College — M
Stanford University — D

State University of New York at
New Paltz — M,O
State University of New York at
Oswego — M
State University of New York
College of Environmental Science
and Forestry — M,D
Stephen F. Austin State University — M
Stevens Institute of Technology — M,D,O
Stevenson University — M
Stony Brook University, State
University of New York — M,D
Syracuse University — M,D
Teachers College, Columbia
University — M,D
Temple University — M,D*
Tennessee State University — M
Tennessee Technological University — M,D
Texas A&M University — M,D
Texas A&M University–
Commerce — M,O
Texas A&M University–Corpus
Christi — M,D
Texas A&M University–
Kingsville — M
Texas Christian University — M,D
Texas Southern University — M
Texas State University — M
Texas Tech University — M,D
Texas Woman's University — M,D
Trent University — M
Tufts University — M,D
Tulane University — M,D
Tuskegee University — M
Universidad del Turabo — M,D
Université de Moncton — M
Université de Montréal — M,D
Université de Sherbrooke — M,D,O
Université du Québec
à Montréal — M,D
Université du Québec
à Trois-Rivières — M
Université Laval — M,D
University at Albany, State
University of New York — M,D
University at Buffalo, the State
University of New York — M,D
The University of Akron — M,D
The University of Alabama — M,D
The University of Alabama at
Birmingham — M,D
The University of Alabama in
Huntsville — M,D
University of Alaska Fairbanks — M,D
University of Alberta — M,D
The University of Arizona — M,D
University of Arkansas — M,D
University of Arkansas at Little
Rock — M
The University of British Columbia — M,D
University of Calgary — M,D
University of California, Berkeley — D
University of California, Davis — M,D
University of California, Irvine — M,D
University of California, Los
Angeles — M,D
University of California, Merced — M,D
University of California,
Riverside — M,D
University of California, San
Diego — M,D
University of California, San
Francisco — D
University of California, Santa
Barbara — M,D
University of California, Santa
Cruz — M,D
University of Central Florida — M,D,O
University of Chicago — D
University of Cincinnati — M,D
University of Colorado Boulder — M,D
University of Colorado Denver — M
University of Connecticut — M,D
University of Dayton — M
University of Delaware — M,D
University of Denver — M,D
University of Detroit Mercy — M,D
University of Florida — M,D
University of Georgia — M,D
University of Guelph — M,D
University of Hawaii at Manoa — M,D
University of Houston — M,D
University of Houston–Clear
Lake — M
University of Idaho — M,D
University of Illinois at Chicago — M,D
University of Illinois at
Urbana–Champaign — M,D
The University of Iowa — D
The University of Kansas — M,D
University of Kentucky — M,D
University of Lethbridge — M,D
University of Louisville — M,D
University of Maine — M,D
The University of Manchester — M,D
University of Manitoba — M,D
University of Maryland, Baltimore
County — M,D,O
University of Maryland, College
Park — M,D
University of Maryland Eastern
Shore — M,D
University of Massachusetts
Amherst — M,D
University of Massachusetts Boston — M,D
University of Massachusetts
Dartmouth — M,D
University of Massachusetts Lowell — M,D
University of Memphis — M,D
University of Miami — M,D
University of Michigan — M,D

University of Minnesota, Duluth — M
University of Minnesota, Twin
Cities Campus — M,D
University of Mississippi — M,D
University of Missouri — D
University of Missouri–
Kansas City — M,D
University of Missouri–St.
Louis — M,D
University of Montana — M,D
University of Nebraska–
Lincoln — M,D
University of Nevada, Las Vegas — M,D
University of Nevada, Reno — M,D
University of New Brunswick
Fredericton — M,D
University of New Hampshire — M,D
University of New Mexico — M,D
University of New Orleans — M,D
The University of North Carolina
at Chapel Hill — M,D
The University of North Carolina
at Charlotte — M,D
The University of North Carolina
at Greensboro — M
The University of North Carolina
Wilmington — M
University of North Dakota — M,D
University of Northern Colorado — M,D
University of North Texas — M,D,O
University of Notre Dame — M,D
University of Oklahoma — M,D*
University of Oregon — M,D
University of Ottawa — M,D
University of Pennsylvania — M,D*
University of Pittsburgh — M,D*
University of Prince Edward Island — M,D
University of Puerto Rico–
Mayagüez — M,D
University of Puerto Rico–
Río Piedras — M,D
University of Regina — M,D
University of Rhode Island — M,D
University of Rochester — D*
University of Saint Joseph — M
University of San Francisco — M
University of Saskatchewan — M,D
The University of Scranton — M
University of South Alabama — M
University of South Carolina — M,D
University of South Dakota — M,D
University of Southern California — D
University of Southern Mississippi — M,D
University of South Florida — M,D
The University of Tennessee — M,D
The University of Texas at
Arlington — M,D
The University of Texas at Austin — D
The University of Texas at Dallas — M,D
The University of Texas at El Paso — M,D
The University of Texas at San
Antonio — M,D
The University of Texas Rio Grande
Valley — M
University of the Sciences — M,D
The University of Toledo — M,D
University of Toronto — M,D
University of Utah — M,D
University of Vermont — M,D
University of Victoria — M,D
University of Virginia — M,D
University of Washington — M,D
University of Waterloo — M,D
The University of Western Ontario — M,D
University of Windsor — M,D
University of Wisconsin–
Madison — M,D
University of Wisconsin–
Milwaukee — M,D*
University of Wyoming — M,D
Utah State University — M,D
Vanderbilt University — M,D*
Villanova University — M
Virginia Commonwealth University — M,D
Virginia Polytechnic Institute and
State University — M,D
Wake Forest University — M,D
Washington State University — M,D
Washington University in St. Louis — D
Wayne State University — M,D
Wesleyan University — D
West Chester University of
Pennsylvania — O
Western Carolina University — M
Western Illinois University — M
Western Kentucky University — M
Western Michigan University — M,D,O
Western Washington University — M
West Texas A&M University — M
West Virginia University — M,D
Wichita State University — M,D
Wilfrid Laurier University — M
Worcester Polytechnic Institute — M,D
Wright State University — M
Yale University — D
York University — M,D
Youngstown State University — M

CHILD AND FAMILY STUDIES
Alabama Agricultural and
Mechanical University — M
Amberton University — M
Arizona State University at the
Tempe campus — M,D
Asbury University — M
Assumption College — M,O
Auburn University — M,D
Bank Street College of Education — M
Brandeis University — M,D
Brigham Young University — M,D
Brock University — M

M—masters degree; D—doctorate; O—other advanced degree; *—Close-Up and/or Display

California State University, East Bay	M
California State University, Los Angeles	M
Capella University	M
Central Michigan University	M,O
Central Washington University	M
Colorado State University	M,D
Concordia University (Canada)	M
Concordia University, St. Paul	M
Concordia University Wisconsin	M
Cornell University	M,D
Dallas Theological Seminary	M,D,O
East Carolina University	M,D
Eastern University	D
Fairfield University	M,O
Florida State University	M,D
Iowa State University of Science and Technology	M,D,O
Kansas State University	M,D,O
Kent State University	M
Liberty University	M,D,O
Loma Linda University	M,D,O
London Metropolitan University	M,D
Miami University	M
Michigan State University	M,D
Mississippi State University	M,D
Missouri State University	M
Montclair State University	M,D,O
Mount Saint Vincent University	M
North Carolina Agricultural and Technical State University	M
North Dakota State University	M,D,O
Northern Illinois University	M
The Ohio State University	M,D
Ohio University	M
Oklahoma State University	M
Omega Graduate School	M,D
Oregon State University	M,D
Penn State University Park	M,D*
Purdue University	M,D
Purdue University Northwest	M
Queens College of the City University of New York	M,O
Roberts Wesleyan College	M
St. Cloud State University	M
San Diego State University	M
San Jose State University	M
South Carolina State University	M
Spring Arbor University	M
State University of New York at Oswego	M
Syracuse University	M,D
Texas State University	M
Texas Tech University	M,D
Texas Woman's University	M,D
Towson University	M,O
Tufts University	M,D
The University of Akron	M
The University of Alabama	M
The University of Arizona	M,D,O
University of Central Oklahoma	M
University of Colorado Denver	M,D
University of Connecticut	M,D
University of Delaware	M,D
University of Denver	M,D,O
University of Georgia	M
University of Guelph	M,D
University of Illinois at Springfield	M,O
University of Kentucky	M,D
University of La Verne	M
University of Maryland, College Park	M,D
University of Massachusetts Amherst	M,D,O
University of Minnesota, Twin Cities Campus	M,D
University of Missouri	M,D
University of Montana	M,D,O
University of Nebraska–Lincoln	M,D
University of Nevada, Reno	M
University of New Hampshire	M,O
University of New Mexico	M,D
University of North Alabama	M
The University of North Carolina at Charlotte	M,D,O
The University of North Carolina at Greensboro	M,D
University of North Texas	M,D,O
University of Rhode Island	M
University of Southern California	M,D
University of Southern Mississippi	M
University of South Florida	M,D,O
The University of Tennessee	M,D
The University of Tennessee at Martin	M
The University of Texas at Austin	M,D
The University of Texas at Dallas	M,D
University of Utah	M
University of Victoria	M,D
University of Wisconsin–Madison	M,D
Utah State University	M,D
Walden University	M,D
Washington University in St. Louis	M,D

CHILD DEVELOPMENT

Adler University	M
California State University, Los Angeles	M
California State University, Sacramento	M,D,O
California State University, San Bernardino	M
Chaminade University of Honolulu	M
East Carolina University	M
Erikson Institute	M
Fielding Graduate University	M,D,O
Kansas State University	M,D,O
Lee University	M
Michigan State University	M,D
Montclair State University	M,O

Mount Saint Mary College	M,O
North Carolina Agricultural and Technical State University	M
North Dakota State University	M
Ohio University	M
Purdue University	M,D
Purdue University Northwest	M,D
Rutgers University–Camden	M,D
San Diego State University	M
Sarah Lawrence College	M
Texas Woman's University	M,D
Tufts University	M,D
The University of Akron	M
University of California, Davis	M
University of Florida	M
University of La Verne	M
University of Minnesota, Twin Cities Campus	M,D
University of Nebraska–Lincoln	M,D
The University of North Carolina at Charlotte	M,D,O
The University of Tennessee at Martin	M
The University of Texas at Austin	M,D
The University of West Alabama	M,O
University of Wyoming	M
Whittier College	M

CHINESE

Arizona State University at the Tempe campus	M,D
Brandeis University	M
DePaul University	M
Harvard University	D*
Hunter College of the City University of New York	M
Indiana University Bloomington	M,D
Middlebury College	M
New York University	M,D,O*
The Ohio State University	M,D
Saginaw Valley State University	M
San Francisco State University	M
Stanford University	M,D
University of Alberta	M
University of California, Berkeley	D
University of California, Irvine	M,D
University of Colorado Boulder	M,D
University of Delaware	M
University of Hawaii at Manoa	M,D,O
The University of Iowa	M
The University of Manchester	D
University of Massachusetts Amherst	M
University of Oregon	M,D
University of Pittsburgh	M*
University of Washington	M,D
University of Wisconsin–Madison	M,D
Washington University in St. Louis	M,D

CHIROPRACTIC

Canadian Memorial Chiropractic College	D,O
Cleveland University–Kansas City	D
D'Youville College	D
Institut Franco-Européen de Chiropraxie	D
Life Chiropractic College West	D
Life University	D
Logan University	D
National University of Health Sciences	M,D
New York Chiropractic College	D
Northwestern Health Sciences University	D
Palmer College of Chiropractic	D
Parker University	D
Sherman College of Chiropractic	D
Southern California University of Health Sciences	D
Texas Chiropractic College	D
Université du Québec à Trois-Rivières	D
University of Bridgeport	D
University of Western States	D

CIVIL ENGINEERING

American University of Beirut	M,D
American University of Sharjah	M,D
Arizona State University at the Tempe campus	M,D
Auburn University	M,D
Boise State University	M
Bradley University	M
Brigham Young University	M,D
Bucknell University	M
California Baptist University	M
California Institute of Technology	M,D,O
California Polytechnic State University, San Luis Obispo	M
California State Polytechnic University, Pomona	M
California State University, Fresno	M
California State University, Fullerton	M
California State University, Long Beach	M
California State University, Los Angeles	M
California State University, Northridge	M
California State University, Sacramento	M
Carleton University	M,D
Carnegie Mellon University	M,D
Case Western Reserve University	M,D
The Catholic University of America	M,D,O
The Citadel, The Military College of South Carolina	M,O
City College of the City University of New York	M,D
Clarkson University	M,D

Clemson University	M,D
Cleveland State University	M,D
Colorado School of Mines	M,D
Colorado State University	M,D
Columbia University	M,D
Concordia University (Canada)	M,D,O
Cooper Union for the Advancement of Science and Art	M
Cornell University	M,D
Dalhousie University	M,D
Drexel University	M,D*
Duke University	M,D
École Polytechnique de Montréal	M,D,O
Embry-Riddle Aeronautical University–Daytona	M
Florida Agricultural and Mechanical University	M,D
Florida Atlantic University	M
Florida Institute of Technology	M,D
Florida International University	M,D
Florida State University	M,D
George Mason University	M,D
The George Washington University	M,D,O
Georgia Institute of Technology	M,D
Georgia Southern University	M
Howard University	M
Idaho State University	M
Illinois Institute of Technology	M,D
Instituto Tecnológico y de Estudios Superiores de Monterrey, Campus Monterrey	M,D
Iowa State University of Science and Technology	M,D
Jackson State University	M,D
Johns Hopkins University	M,D,O*
Kansas State University	M,D
Kennesaw State University	M
Lawrence Technological University	M,D
Lehigh University	M,D
Louisiana State University and Agricultural & Mechanical College	M,D
Loyola Marymount University	M
Manhattan College	M
Marquette University	M,D,O
Massachusetts Institute of Technology	M,D,O
McGill University	M,D
McMaster University	M,D
McNeese State University	M
Memorial University of Newfoundland	M,D
Merrimack College	M
Michigan State University	M,D
Michigan Technological University	M,D
Milwaukee School of Engineering	M
Mississippi State University	M,D
Missouri University of Science and Technology	M,D
Montana State University	M
Morgan State University	M,D,O
New York University	M,D*
North Carolina Agricultural and Technical State University	M
North Carolina State University	M,D
North Dakota State University	M,D
Northeastern University	M,D,O
Northern Arizona University	M
Northwestern University	M,D
Norwich University	M
The Ohio State University	M,D
Ohio University	M,D
Oklahoma State University	M,D
Old Dominion University	M,D
Oregon State University	M,D
Penn State Harrisburg	M,O
Penn State University Park	M,D*
Polytechnic University of Puerto Rico	M
Portland State University	M,D,O
Princeton University	M,D
Purdue University	M,D
Purdue University Fort Wayne	M
Queen's University at Kingston	M,D
Rensselaer Polytechnic Institute	M,D
Rice University	M,D
Rose-Hulman Institute of Technology	M
Rowan University	M
Royal Military College of Canada	M,D
Rutgers University–New Brunswick	M,D
Saint Martin's University	M
San Diego State University	M
San Jose State University	M
Santa Clara University	M,D,O
South Carolina State University	M
South Dakota School of Mines and Technology	M
South Dakota State University	M
Southern Illinois University Carbondale	M,D
Southern Illinois University Edwardsville	M
Southern Methodist University	M,D
Stevens Institute of Technology	M,D,O
Stony Brook University, State University of New York	M,D,O
Syracuse University	M,D
Temple University	M,D,O*
Tennessee State University	M
Tennessee Technological University	M
Texas A&M University	M,D
Texas A&M University–Kingsville	M
Texas State University	M
Tufts University	M,D
United States Merchant Marine Academy	M
Université de Moncton	M
Université de Sherbrooke	M,D
Université Laval	M,D,O

University at Buffalo, the State University of New York	M,D
The University of Akron	M,D
The University of Alabama	M,D
The University of Alabama at Birmingham	M,D
The University of Alabama in Huntsville	M,D
University of Alaska Fairbanks	M,D,O
University of Alberta	M,D
University of Arkansas	M,D
The University of British Columbia	M,D
University of Calgary	M,D
University of California, Berkeley	M,D
University of California, Davis	M,D,O
University of California, Irvine	M,D
University of California, Los Angeles	M,D
University of Central Florida	M,D,O
University of Cincinnati	M,D
University of Colorado Boulder	M,D
University of Colorado Denver	M,D
University of Connecticut	M,D
University of Dayton	M
University of Delaware	M,D
University of Detroit Mercy	M,D
University of Florida	M,D
University of Hawaii at Manoa	M,D
University of Houston	M,D
University of Idaho	M,D
University of Illinois at Chicago	M,D
University of Illinois at Urbana–Champaign	M,D
The University of Iowa	M,D
The University of Kansas	M,D
University of Kentucky	M,D
University of Louisiana at Lafayette	M
University of Louisville	M,D
University of Maine	M,D
The University of Manchester	M,D
University of Manitoba	M,D
University of Maryland, College Park	M,D
University of Massachusetts Amherst	M,D
University of Massachusetts Dartmouth	M
University of Massachusetts Lowell	M,D
University of Memphis	M,D,O
University of Miami	M,D
University of Michigan	M,D,O
University of Minnesota, Twin Cities Campus	M,D,O
University of Mississippi	M,D
University of Missouri	M,D
University of Missouri–Kansas City	M,D,O
University of Nebraska–Lincoln	M,D
University of Nevada, Reno	M,D
University of New Brunswick Fredericton	M,D
University of New Hampshire	M,D
University of New Haven	M
University of New Mexico	M,D
University of New Orleans	M
The University of North Carolina at Charlotte	M,D
University of North Dakota	M,D
University of North Florida	M
University of Notre Dame	M,D
University of Oklahoma	M,D*
University of Ottawa	M,D
University of Pittsburgh	M,D*
University of Portland	M
University of Puerto Rico–Mayagüez	M,D
University of Rhode Island	M,D
University of Saskatchewan	M,D
University of South Alabama	M
University of South Carolina	M,D
University of Southern California	M,D,O
University of South Florida	M,D,O
The University of Tennessee	M,D
The University of Tennessee at Chattanooga	M
The University of Texas at Arlington	M,D
The University of Texas at Austin	M,D
The University of Texas at El Paso	M,D,O
The University of Texas at San Antonio	M,D
The University of Texas at Tyler	M
The University of Toledo	M,D
University of Toronto	M,D
University of Utah	M,D
University of Vermont	M,D
University of Virginia	M,D
University of Washington	M,D
University of Waterloo	M,D
The University of Western Ontario	M,D
University of Windsor	M,D
University of Wisconsin–Madison	M
University of Wisconsin–Milwaukee	M,D*
University of Wyoming	M,D
Utah State University	M,D,O
Vanderbilt University	M,D*
Villanova University	M
Virginia Polytechnic Institute and State University	M,D,O
Washington State University	M,D
Wayne State University	M,D
Wentworth Institute of Technology	M
Western Michigan University	M
Western New England University	M
West Virginia University	M
Widener University	M
Worcester Polytechnic Institute	M,D,O
Youngstown State University	M

CLASSICS

Asbury University	M
Bethel Seminary	M,D,O
Boston College	M
Boston University	M,D
Brandeis University	M
Brock University	M,D
Brown University	M,D
Bryn Mawr College	M,D
The Catholic University of America	M,D,O
Columbia University	M,D
Cornell University	D
Dalhousie University	M,D
Duke University	D
Duquesne University	M
Fordham University	M,D
The Graduate Center, City University of New York	M,D
Harvard University	D*
Heritage Christian University	M
Hunter College of the City University of New York	M
Indiana University Bloomington	M,D
Johns Hopkins University	D*
Knox Theological Seminary	M
McMaster University	M,D
Memorial University of Newfoundland	M
New York University	M,D,O*
The Ohio State University	M,D
Princeton University	D
Queen's University at Kingston	M
Rutgers University–New Brunswick	M,D
San Francisco State University	M,D
Stanford University	M,D
Tufts University	M
Tulane University	M
Université de Montréal	M
University at Buffalo, the State University of New York	M,D,O
University of Alberta	M
The University of Arizona	M
The University of British Columbia	M,D
University of Calgary	M,D
University of California, Berkeley	M,D
University of California, Irvine	M,D
University of California, Los Angeles	M,D
University of California, Riverside	D
University of California, Santa Barbara	M,D
University of Chicago	M,D
University of Cincinnati	M,D
University of Colorado Boulder	M,D
University of Florida	M,D
University of Georgia	M
University of Illinois at Urbana–Champaign	M,D
The University of Iowa	M,D
The University of Kansas	M
University of Kentucky	M
The University of Manchester	D
University of Manitoba	M
University of Maryland, College Park	M
University of Massachusetts Amherst	M
University of Massachusetts Boston	M
University of Michigan	M,D,O
University of Minnesota, Twin Cities Campus	M,D
University of Missouri	M,D
University of Nebraska–Lincoln	M
University of New Brunswick Fredericton	M
The University of North Carolina at Chapel Hill	M,D
The University of North Carolina at Greensboro	M
University of Oregon	M
University of Ottawa	M,D
University of Pennsylvania	M,D*
University of South Africa	M,D
University of Southern California	M,D
The University of Texas at Austin	M,D
University of Toronto	M,D
University of Vermont	M,O
University of Victoria	M,D
University of Virginia	M,D
University of Washington	M,D
The University of Western Ontario	M
University of Wisconsin–Madison	M,D
University of Wisconsin–Milwaukee	M,O*
Villanova University	M
Washington University in St. Louis	M,D
Yale University	M,D

CLINICAL LABORATORY SCIENCES/MEDICAL TECHNOLOGY

Albany College of Pharmacy and Health Sciences	M
Austin Peay State University	M
Baylor College of Medicine	M,D
The Catholic University of America	M,D
Dominican University of California	M
Duke University	M
Fairleigh Dickinson University, Metropolitan Campus	M
Inter American University of Puerto Rico, Metropolitan Campus	M
Lipscomb University	M
Mayo Clinic Graduate School of Biomedical Sciences	M,D
Medical College of Wisconsin	M
Michigan State University	M

Milwaukee School of Engineering	M
Northern Michigan University	M
Northwestern University	M
Pontifical Catholic University of Puerto Rico	O
Rush University	M
Rutgers University–Newark	M
Rutgers University–New Brunswick	M
State University of New York Upstate Medical University	M
Tarleton State University	M
Thomas Jefferson University	M,D,O
Tufts University	
Universidad de las Américas Puebla	M
Université de Sherbrooke	M,D
University at Buffalo, the State University of New York	M
The University of Alabama at Birmingham	M,D
University of Alberta	M,D
University of California, San Diego	M,D
University of Colorado Denver	M,D
University of Florida	M,D
University of Maryland, Baltimore	M,D
University of Massachusetts Lowell	M
University of Minnesota, Twin Cities Campus	M
University of Nebraska Medical Center	M,O
University of New Mexico	M,O
University of North Dakota	M,D
University of Pennsylvania	M*
University of Pittsburgh	D*
University of Puerto Rico–Medical Sciences Campus	M,O
University of Rhode Island	M
University of Southern Mississippi	M
The University of Tennessee Health Science Center	M,D
The University of Texas at Austin	M,D
The University of Texas Health Science Center at San Antonio	D
The University of Texas Medical Branch	M,D
The University of Texas Rio Grande Valley	M
University of Utah	M
University of Vermont	M,D,O
University of Washington	M
Virginia Commonwealth University	M
Wake Forest University	M

CLINICAL PSYCHOLOGY

Abilene Christian University	M
Acadia University	M
Adams State University	M,D
Adelphi University	D
Adler Graduate School	M
Adler University	M,D
Alabama Agricultural and Mechanical University	M,O
Albizu University	M,D
Albizu University, Miami Campus	M,D
Alliant International University–Fresno	D
Alliant International University–Los Angeles	D
Alliant International University–Sacramento	D
Alliant International University–San Diego	M,D
Alliant International University–San Francisco	M,D,O
American International College	M,D,O
American University	M,D
American University of Beirut	M,D
Andrews University	M
Antioch University Los Angeles	M
Antioch University New England	M,D
Antioch University Santa Barbara	M,D
Antioch University Seattle	M,D
Appalachian State University	M
Argosy University, Atlanta	M,D,O
Argosy University, Chicago	M,D
Argosy University, Hawai i	M,D,O
Argosy University, Los Angeles	M,D
Argosy University, Northern Virginia	M,D
Argosy University, Orange County	M,D
Argosy University, Phoenix	M,D
Argosy University, Seattle	M,D,O
Argosy University, Tampa	M,D
Argosy University, Twin Cities	M,D,O
Arizona State University at the Tempe campus	M,D
Arkansas State University	M,O
Ashland Theological Seminary	M,O
Auburn University at Montgomery	M,O
Augusta University	M,O
Austin Peay State University	M
Azusa Pacific University	D
Ball State University	M,D
Barry University	M
Baylor University	D
Bay Path University	M
Benedictine University	M
Bethel Seminary	M,D,O
Binghamton University, State University of New York	D
Biola University	D
Bowling Green State University	M,D
Bradley University	M
Brigham Young University	M,D
California Lutheran University	M,D
California State University, Dominguez Hills	M
California State University, Fullerton	M

California State University, Northridge	M
California State University, San Bernardino	M
California University of Pennsylvania	M
Capella University	M,D
Cardinal Stritch University	M
Case Western Reserve University	D
The Catholic University of America	M,D
Central Michigan University	D
Chestnut Hill College	M,D,O
The Chicago School of Professional Psychology	M,D
The Chicago School of Professional Psychology at Downtown Los Angeles	M,D
The Chicago School of Professional Psychology at Irvine	D
The Chicago School of Professional Psychology at San Diego	M,D
The Chicago School of Professional Psychology at Xavier University of Louisiana	D
The Chicago School of Professional Psychology: Online	M
Chicago State University	M
City College of the City University of New York	M,D
Clark University	D
Clayton State University	M
Clemson University	M,D,O
College of St. Joseph	M
College of Staten Island of the City University of New York	M
Columbus State University	M,D,O
Concordia University (Canada)	D,O
Dalhousie University	M,D
DePaul University	M,D
Divine Mercy University	M,D
Drexel University	D*
Duke University	D
Duquesne University	M,D,O
East Carolina University	M,D,O
East Central University	M
Eastern Illinois University	M,O
Eastern Kentucky University	M,O
Eastern Michigan University	M,D
Eastern Virginia Medical School	D
Eastern Washington University	M
East Tennessee State University	M,D
Edinboro University of Pennsylvania	M,O
Emory University	D
Emporia State University	M
Evangel University	M
Fairfield University	M,O
Fairleigh Dickinson University, Florham Campus	M
Fairleigh Dickinson University, Metropolitan Campus	M,D
Fielding Graduate University	D,O
Fisk University	M
Florida Gulf Coast University	M
Florida International University	M,D,O
Florida State University	D
Fordham University	D
Franciscan University of Steubenville	M
Francis Marion University	M,O
Fuller Theological Seminary	M,D,O
Gallaudet University	M,D
Gannon University	M
Geneva College	M
George Fox University	M,D,O
George Mason University	M,D,O
The George Washington University	M,D
Georgian Court University	M,O
Georgia Southern University	M,D
Georgia State University	D
Goddard College	M
Grace College	M
The Graduate Center, City University of New York	D
Hawai i Pacific University	M
Hodges University	M
Hofstra University	M,D
Hood College	M
Howard University	M,D
Husson University	M
Idaho State University	D
Illinois Institute of Technology	M,D
Illinois State University	M,D,O
Immaculata University	M,D
Indiana State University	M,D
Indiana University of Pennsylvania	M,D
Indiana University–Purdue University Indianapolis	M,D
Indiana University South Bend	M,O
Jackson State University	M,D
James Madison University	D
John Brown University	M,O
Johns Hopkins University	M,D*
Johnson & Wales University	M
Johnson University	M,D,O
Judson University	M
Kean University	M,D
Kent State University	M,D
LaGrange College	M
Lakehead University	M,D
Lamar University	M
La Salle University	M
Lenoir-Rhyne University	M
Lesley University	M,D,O
Lewis University	M
Liberty University	M,D,O
Lipscomb University	M,O
Lock Haven University of Pennsylvania	M
Loma Linda University	D
London Metropolitan University	M,D

Long Island University–Brentwood Campus	M,O
Long Island University–LIU Brooklyn	M,D,O
Long Island University–LIU Post	M,D,O
Louisiana State University and Agricultural & Mechanical College	M,D
Louisiana Tech University	M,D,O
Loyola University Chicago	M,D,O
Loyola University Maryland	M,D,O
Loyola University New Orleans	M
Madonna University	M
Marquette University	M,D
Marshall University	M,D,O
Marymount University	M
Marywood University	M,D
McGill University	M,D
McKendree University	M
Medaille College	M,D
Memorial University of Newfoundland	M,D
Mercer University	M,D
Merrimack College	M,O
Messiah College	M,O
Michigan School of Psychology	M,D
MidAmerica Nazarene University	M
Middle Tennessee State University	M,O
Midwestern State University	M
Midwestern University, Downers Grove Campus	D
Midwestern University, Glendale Campus	D
Millersville University of Pennsylvania	M
Milligan College	M,O
Minnesota State University Mankato	M,D
Mississippi State University	M,D,O
Missouri State University	M,O
Molloy College	M
Montclair State University	M
Morehead State University	M
Mount Mary University	M,O
Murray State University	M,O
National University	M,O
Neumann University	M,D,O
New Mexico Highlands University	M
The New School	M,D
Nicholls State University	M,O
Norfolk State University	M
North Carolina Agricultural and Technical State University	M,D
North Carolina Central University	M
North Dakota State University	M,D
Northeastern Illinois University	M
Northern Kentucky University	M
Northern State University	M
Northwestern State University of Louisiana	M
Northwestern University	D
Northwest Nazarene University	M
Notre Dame de Namur University	M
Nova Southeastern University	M,D,O
The Ohio State University	D
Ohio University	D
Oklahoma State University	M,D
Old Dominion University	D
Oregon State University	M,D
Pace University	M,D
Pacifica Graduate Institute	M,D
Pacific University	M,D
Palo Alto University	M,D
Penn State Erie, The Behrend College	M
Penn State Harrisburg	M,D,O
Philadelphia College of Osteopathic Medicine	M,D,O*
Pillar College	M
Pittsburg State University	M
Plymouth State University	O
Point Loma Nazarene University	M
Point Park University	M,D
Ponce Health Sciences University	D
Pontifical Catholic University of Puerto Rico	D
Pontificia Universidad Catolica Madre y Maestra	M
Post University	M
Prairie View A&M University	M,D
Purdue University	D
Queen's University at Kingston	M,D
Quincy University	M
Radford University	M
Regent University	M,D,O
Richmont Graduate University	M,O
Rider University	M,O
Rivier University	M
Roberts Wesleyan College	M,D
Roger Williams University	M
Roosevelt University	M
Rosalind Franklin University of Medicine and Science	M,D
Rowan University	M,O
Rutgers University–New Brunswick	M,D
St. John's University (NY)	M,D,O
Saint Louis University	M,D*
Saint Michael's College	M
Sam Houston State University	M,D,O
San Diego State University	M,D
San Francisco State University	M,O
San Jose State University	M
Saybrook University	D
Seattle Pacific University	M,D
Shippensburg University of Pennsylvania	M,D
Siena Heights University	M,O
Slippery Rock University of Pennsylvania	M
Sofia University	M,D

---

*M—masters degree; D—doctorate; O—other advanced degree; *—Close-Up and/or Display*

Sonoma State University	M
Southeastern Oklahoma State University	M
Southern Illinois University Carbondale	M,D
Southern Illinois University Edwardsville	M
Southern Methodist University	D
Southern New Hampshire University	M
Spalding University	M,D,O
Springfield College	M,D,O
State University of New York at New Paltz	M,O
State University of New York at Plattsburgh	M,O
Stephens College	M,O
Suffolk University	M,D,O
Syracuse University	M,D
Teachers College, Columbia University	M,D
Texas A&M University–Central Texas	M,O
Texas A&M University–Corpus Christi	M
Texas A&M University–San Antonio	M
Texas State University	M
Texas Tech University	M,D
Texas Tech University Health Sciences Center	M
Trinity Washington University	M
Uniformed Services University of the Health Sciences	D*
Union College (KY)	M
Union Institute & University	M
Universidad de Iberoamerica	M,D
Université Laval	D
University at Albany, State University of New York	M,D
The University of Akron	M
The University of Alabama	D
The University of Alabama at Birmingham	M,D
University of Alaska Anchorage	M
University of Bridgeport	M
The University of British Columbia	M,D
University of Calgary	M,D
University of California, San Diego	D
University of California, Santa Barbara	M,D,O
University of Central Florida	M,D
University of Cincinnati	D
University of Colorado Denver	M,D
University of Connecticut	M,D
University of Dayton	M,O
University of Delaware	D
University of Denver	M,D,O
University of Detroit Mercy	M,D,O
University of Florida	M,D
University of Guelph	M,D
University of Hartford	M,D
University of Hawaii at Manoa	M,D,O
University of Houston	M,D
University of Houston–Clear Lake	M
University of Indianapolis	M,D
The University of Kansas	M,D
University of La Verne	D
University of Louisiana at Monroe	M
University of Louisville	D
University of Lynchburg	M
The University of Manchester	M,D
University of Manitoba	M
University of Mary Hardin-Baylor	M
University of Maryland, Baltimore County	M,D
University of Maryland, College Park	M,D
University of Massachusetts Amherst	M,D
University of Massachusetts Boston	D
University of Massachusetts Dartmouth	M,O
University of Memphis	M,D,O
University of Miami	M,D
University of Michigan	D
University of Michigan–Dearborn	M
University of Minnesota, Twin Cities Campus	D
University of Missouri–St. Louis	M,D,O
University of Montana	M,D,O
University of Nebraska–Lincoln	M,D
University of Nevada, Las Vegas	M,D,O
University of Nevada, Reno	D
University of New Brunswick Saint John	M,D
University of New Mexico	D
University of North Alabama	M
The University of North Carolina at Chapel Hill	D
The University of North Carolina at Greensboro	M,D
The University of North Carolina Wilmington	M,D
University of North Dakota	M,D
University of Northern Colorado	M
University of North Texas	M,D,O
University of North Texas at Dallas	M
University of Oklahoma	M,O*
University of Oregon	D
University of Phoenix–Phoenix Campus	M
University of Pittsburgh	M,D*
University of Puerto Rico–Río Piedras	M,D
University of Regina	M,D
University of Rhode Island	M,D
University of Rochester	D*
University of Saint Francis (IN)	M,O
University of Saint Joseph	M
University of San Francisco	D
The University of Scranton	M
University of South Africa	M,D
University of South Alabama	M,D,O
University of South Carolina	M,D
University of South Carolina Aiken	M
University of South Dakota	M,D
University of Southern California	M,D
University of South Florida	D
The University of Tennessee	M,D
The University of Texas at Austin	M,D
The University of Texas at El Paso	M,D
The University of Texas at Tyler	M
The University of Texas of the Permian Basin	M
The University of Texas Rio Grande Valley	M
The University of Texas Southwestern Medical Center	D
University of the Cumberlands	D
The University of Toledo	M,D
The University of Tulsa	M,D
University of Utah	M,D,O
University of Vermont	M,D
University of Victoria	M,D
University of Virginia	D
University of Washington	M,D
The University of West Alabama	M
University of Windsor	M,D
University of Wisconsin–Madison	D
University of Wisconsin–Parkside	M
University of Wisconsin–Stout	M
Utah State University	M,D
Valparaiso University	M
Vanguard University of Southern California	M
Virginia Commonwealth University	D
Virginia State University	M,D
Walden University	M,D,O
Washburn University	M
Washington State University	M,D
Waynesburg University	M
Wayne State University	M,D
West Chester University of Pennsylvania	M,D,O
Western Connecticut State University	M
Western Illinois University	M,O
Western Kentucky University	M,O
Western Michigan University	M,D
Westminster College (PA)	M
West Virginia University	M,D
Wheaton College	M,D
Wichita State University	D
Widener University	D
William James College	M,D,O
William Paterson University of New Jersey	M,D,O
Wilmington University	M
Winona State University	M,O
Wisconsin School of Professional Psychology	M,D
The Wright Institute	D
Wright State University	D
Xavier University	M,D*
Yale University	D
Yeshiva University	D

CLINICAL RESEARCH

Albert Einstein College of Medicine	D
American University of Beirut	M,D
American University of Health Sciences	M
Augusta University	M
Boston University	M
Case Western Reserve University	M,D
Clemson University	M,D,O
Duke University	M
Eastern Michigan University	M,O
Emory University	M
Fordham University	M
Icahn School of Medicine at Mount Sinai	M,D
Johns Hopkins University	M,D*
Loyola University Chicago	M
Medical College of Wisconsin	M
Medical University of South Carolina	M
Memorial University of Newfoundland	M
Morehouse School of Medicine	M
National University of Natural Medicine	M
New York University	M*
Northwestern University	M,O
Oregon Health & Science University	M
Palmer College of Chiropractic	M
Stanford University	M
Thomas Jefferson University	M,O
Trident University International	M,D,O
University of California, Berkeley	O
University of California, Davis	M
University of California, Los Angeles	M
University of California, San Diego	M
University of Colorado Denver	M,D
University of Connecticut Health Center	M
University of Florida	M,D,O
The University of Iowa	M,D
The University of Kansas	M
University of Kentucky	M
University of Maryland, Baltimore	M,D
University of Massachusetts Medical School	M,D
University of Michigan	M
University of Minnesota, Twin Cities Campus	M
The University of North Carolina at Chapel Hill	M,D
The University of North Carolina Wilmington	M,D,O
University of Pittsburgh	M,O*
University of Puerto Rico–Medical Sciences Campus	M,O
University of Rochester	M*
University of Southern California	M,D,O
University of South Florida	M,D,O
The University of Texas Health Science Center at San Antonio	M
University of Virginia	M
University of Washington	M,D
University of Wisconsin–Madison	M,D
Walden University	M,D,O
Washington University in St. Louis	M

CLOTHING AND TEXTILES

Alabama Agricultural and Mechanical University	M
Auburn University	M,D
Central Michigan University	M,O
Cornell University	M,D
Drexel University	M*
Eastern Michigan University	M
Fashion Institute of Technology	M
Georgia State University	M
Iowa State University of Science and Technology	M,D
Kansas State University	M,D
LIM College	M
Mississippi State University	M,D
New Mexico State University	M
The New School	M
North Carolina State University	M,D
Oklahoma State University	M,D
Rutgers University–Newark	M
Savannah College of Art and Design	M
Thomas Jefferson University	M
The University of Akron	M
The University of Alabama	M
University of Alberta	M,D
University of California, Davis	M
University of Delaware	M
University of Georgia	M,D
The University of Manchester	M
University of Minnesota, Twin Cities Campus	M,D,O
University of Missouri	M,D
University of Nebraska–Lincoln	M,D
University of Rhode Island	M,O
The University of Tennessee	M,D
University of the Incarnate Word	M
Washington State University	M
Wayne State University	M

COGNITIVE SCIENCES

American University	M,D,O
Arizona State University at the Tempe campus	M,D
Ball State University	M
Binghamton University, State University of New York	D
Brandeis University	M,D
Brigham Young University	D
Brown University	M,D
Carleton University	D
Carnegie Mellon University	D
Case Western Reserve University	M
Central European University	D
Claremont Graduate University	M,D,O
Cornell University	D
Dartmouth College	D
Duke University	D
Emory University	D
Florida International University	M,D
Florida State University	D
George Mason University	M,D,O
The George Washington University	D
Georgia State University	D
The Graduate Center, City University of New York	D
Grand Canyon University	D
Harvard University	M,D*
Illinois State University	M,D,O
Indiana University Bloomington	D
Iowa State University of Science and Technology	M,D
Johns Hopkins University	M,D*
Louisiana State University and Agricultural & Mechanical College	M,D
Massachusetts Institute of Technology	D
Michigan Technological University	M,D,O
Mississippi State University	M,D
The New School	M,D
New York University	M,D,O*
North Carolina State University	M,D
North Dakota State University	M,D
Northwestern University	D
The Ohio State University	D
Oregon State University	M,D
Purdue University	D
Queen's University at Kingston	M,D
Rensselaer Polytechnic Institute	D
Rice University	M,D
Rochester Institute of Technology	O
Rutgers University–Newark	D
Rutgers University–New Brunswick	D
Syracuse University	D
Texas Christian University	M,D
Tufts University	M,D
University at Albany, State University of New York	M,D
The University of British Columbia	M,D
University of California, Merced	M,D
University of California, San Diego	D
University of California, Santa Barbara	M,D
University of Connecticut	M,D
University of Delaware	M,D
University of Guelph	M,D
The University of Kansas	M,D
University of Louisville	D
University of Maryland, Baltimore County	D
University of Maryland, College Park	D
University of Massachusetts Amherst	M,D
University of Massachusetts Boston	M
University of Michigan	D
University of Minnesota, Twin Cities Campus	D
University of Nebraska–Lincoln	M,D,O
University of Nevada, Reno	M,D
University of New Mexico	D
The University of North Carolina at Chapel Hill	D
The University of North Carolina at Charlotte	M,D,O
The University of North Carolina at Greensboro	M,D
University of Notre Dame	D
University of Oregon	M,D
University of Rochester	D*
University of Southern California	M,D
University of South Florida	D
The University of Texas at Dallas	M,D
University of Washington	M,D
University of Wisconsin–Madison	D
Wayne State University	M,D
Wilfrid Laurier University	M,D
Yale University	D

COMMUNICATION—GENERAL

Abilene Christian University	M
American University	M,D
The American University in Cairo	M,D,O
The American University of Paris	M
Andrews University	M
Angelo State University	M
Arizona State University at the Tempe campus	M,D
Arkansas State University	M,O
Ashland University	M
Auburn University	M,O
Austin Peay State University	M
Ball State University	M,O
Baylor University	M
Bay Path University	M
Bellarmine University	M
Boise State University	M
Boston University	M,D
Bowling Green State University	M,D
Bryant University	M,O
Cabrini University	M,D
California Baptist University	M
California State University, Chico	M
California State University, East Bay	M
California State University, Fresno	M
California State University, Fullerton	M
California State University, Long Beach	M
California State University, Los Angeles	M
California State University, Northridge	M
California State University, Sacramento	M
California State University, San Bernardino	M,D
Carleton University	M,D
Carnegie Mellon University	M,D
Central Connecticut State University	M,O
Central Michigan University	M
Chapman University	M*
Chatham University	M
Clarion University of Pennsylvania	M
Clarks Summit University	M,D
Clark University	M
Clemson University	M
Cleveland State University	M,D,O
The College at Brockport, State University of New York	M
The College of New Rochelle	M,O
Columbia College Chicago	M
Columbia University	M,D
Concordia University (Canada)	M,D,O
Cornell University	M,D
Dallas Baptist University	M
DePaul University	M
DEREE - The American College of Greece	M
Drake University	M
Drexel University	M*
Drury University	M
Duquesne University	M,D
Eastern Illinois University	M
Eastern Michigan University	M
Eastern New Mexico University	M
Eastern University	M,O
Eastern Washington University	M
East Stroudsburg University of Pennsylvania	M
East Tennessee State University	M,O
Edinboro University of Pennsylvania	M
Fairfield University	M
Fairleigh Dickinson University, Metropolitan Campus	M
Fitchburg State University	M,O
Florida Atlantic University	M,O
Florida International University	M,D
Fordham University	M,D
Fordham University	M,D
Fort Hays State University	M

Institution	Degrees
George Mason University	M,D,O
Georgetown University	M
The George Washington University	M
Georgia State University	M,D
Governors State University	M
Grand Valley State University	M
Harvard University	M,O*
Hawai'i Pacific University	M
Howard University	M,D
Idaho State University	M
Illinois Institute of Technology	M,D
Illinois State University	M
Indiana State University	M
Indiana University of Pennsylvania	D
Indiana University–Purdue University Indianapolis	M,D
Indiana University South Bend	M,D
Instituto Tecnologico de Santo Domingo	M,O
Instituto Tecnológico y de Estudios Superiores de Monterrey, Campus Ciudad Obregón	M
Instituto Tecnológico y de Estudios Superiores de Monterrey, Campus Monterrey	M,D
International University in Geneva	M,D
James Madison University	M
Johns Hopkins University	M,O*
Kansas State University	M,D,O
Kean University	M
Kennesaw State University	M
Kent State University	M
La Salle University	M,O
Lasell College	M,O
La Sierra University	M
Lawrence Technological University	M
Liberty University	M
Lindenwood University	M,O
Lindenwood University–Belleville	M
Louisiana State University and Agricultural & Mechanical College	M,D
Loyola University Chicago	M,O
Lynn University	M,O
Marist College	M
Marquette University	M,O
Marshall University	M
Marywood University	M
McGill University	M,D
Michigan State University	M,O
Minnesota State University Mankato	M,O
Mississippi College	M
Mississippi State University	M,D
Missouri State University	M,O
Monmouth University	M,O
Montana State University Billings	M
Moore College of Art & Design	M
Morehead State University	M
Mount Saint Vincent University	M
New York Institute of Technology	M
New York University	M,D*
Norfolk State University	M
North Carolina State University	M
North Dakota State University	M
Northeastern State University	M
Northern Arizona University	M,O
Northern Illinois University	M
Northern Kentucky University	M,O
Northwestern University	M,D
Notre Dame of Maryland University	M
The Ohio State University	M,D
Ohio University	M,D
Old Dominion University	M,O
Pace University	M
Penn State Harrisburg	M,D,O
Penn State University Park	M,D*
Pepperdine University	M
Pittsburg State University	M
Point Park University	M
Purdue University	M,D
Purdue University Fort Wayne	M
Purdue University Northwest	M
Queen's University of Kingston	M,D
Queens University of Charlotte	M
Quinnipiac University	M
Regent University	M,D
Rochester Institute of Technology	M
Roosevelt University	M
Rutgers University–New Brunswick	D
Sacred Heart University	M
Saginaw Valley State University	M
Saint Louis University	M*
St. Mary's University (United States)	M
St. Thomas University	M,D,O
Sam Houston State University	M
San Diego State University	M
San Jose State University	M
Seton Hall University	M
Shippensburg University of Pennsylvania	M
Simon Fraser University	M
South Dakota State University	M
Southeastern Louisiana University	M
Southern Illinois University Carbondale	M,D
Southern Utah University	M
Spring Arbor University	M
Stanford University	M,D
State University of New York at Oswego	M
Stephen F. Austin State University	M
Stevens Institute of Technology	M,D,O
Stevenson University	M
Syracuse University	M,D
Tarleton State University	M
Teachers College, Columbia University	M,D
Temple University	M,D*
Texas A&M University	M,D
Texas A&M University–Corpus Christi	M
Texas Christian University	M
Texas Southern University	M
Texas State University	M
Texas Tech University	M
Tiffin University	M
Towson University	M
Trinity Washington University	M
Troy University	M
Université de Montréal	M
Université du Québec à Montréal	M,D
Université du Québec à Trois-Rivières	M,O
University at Albany, State University of New York	M,D
University at Buffalo, the State University of New York	M,D
The University of Akron	M
The University of Alabama	M,D
The University of Alabama at Birmingham	M
University of Alaska Fairbanks	M
University of Alberta	M
The University of Arizona	M,D
University of Arkansas	M
University of Bridgeport	M
University of California, Davis	M
University of California, San Diego	D
University of California, Santa Barbara	D
University of California, Santa Cruz	O
University of Central Missouri	M,D,O
University of Cincinnati	M
University of Colorado Boulder	M,D
University of Colorado Colorado Springs	M
University of Colorado Denver	M,D
University of Connecticut	M,D
University of Dayton	M
University of Delaware	M
University of Denver	M,O
University of Dubuque	M
University of Florida	M,D
University of Georgia	M,D
University of Hartford	M
University of Hawaii at Manoa	M,O
University of Houston	M
University of Illinois at Chicago	M,D
University of Illinois at Springfield	M
University of Illinois at Urbana–Champaign	M,D
The University of Iowa	M,D
The University of Kansas	M,D,O
University of Louisiana at Lafayette	M
University of Louisiana at Monroe	M
University of Louisville	M
University of Maine	M,D
University of Maryland, Baltimore County	M
University of Maryland, College Park	M,D
University of Massachusetts Amherst	M,D
University of Memphis	M,D
University of Miami	M,D
University of Michigan	D
University of Michigan–Flint	M
University of Minnesota, Twin Cities Campus	M,D,O
University of Missouri	M,D
University of Missouri–St. Louis	M
University of Montana	M
University of Nebraska at Omaha	M,O
University of Nebraska–Lincoln	M,D
University of Nevada, Las Vegas	M
University of New Mexico	M,D
The University of North Carolina at Chapel Hill	M,D,O
The University of North Carolina at Charlotte	M
The University of North Carolina at Greensboro	M
University of North Dakota	D
University of Northern Colorado	M
University of Northern Iowa	M
University of North Texas	M,D,O
University of Oklahoma	M,D*
University of Oregon	M,D
University of Ottawa	M
University of Pennsylvania	D*
University of Pittsburgh	M,D*
University of Portland	M
University of Puerto Rico–Río Piedras	M
University of Rhode Island	M
University of San Francisco	M
University of South Africa	M,D
University of South Alabama	M,D
University of South Dakota	M
University of Southern California	M
University of Southern Indiana	M
University of Southern Mississippi	M
University of South Florida	M,D
The University of Tennessee	M,D
The University of Tennessee at Martin	M
The University of Texas at Arlington	M
The University of Texas at Austin	M,D
The University of Texas at Dallas	M,D
The University of Texas at El Paso	M
The University of Texas at San Antonio	M
The University of Texas at Tyler	M
The University of Texas Rio Grande Valley	M,D
University of the Incarnate Word	M
University of the Pacific	M
University of the Sacred Heart	M,O
The University of Toledo	O
University of Utah	M,D
University of Washington	M,D
University of West Florida	M
University of Windsor	M
University of Wisconsin–Madison	M,D
University of Wisconsin–Milwaukee	M,D,O*
University of Wisconsin–Stevens Point	M
University of Wisconsin–Superior	M
University of Wisconsin–Whitewater	M
University of Wyoming	M
Utah State University	M
Valparaiso University	M,O
Villanova University	M
Virginia Commonwealth University	D
Virginia Polytechnic Institute and State University	M,D,O
Wake Forest University	M
Walden University	M,D,O
Walla Walla University	M
Washington State University	M,D
Wayne State College	M
Wayne State University	M,D,O
Weber State University	M
Webster University	M,O
West Chester University of Pennsylvania	M
Western Illinois University	M
Western Kentucky University	M,O
Western Michigan University	M
Western New England University	M
Westminster College (UT)	M
West Texas A&M University	M
West Virginia University	M,D
Wichita State University	M,D
Wilfrid Laurier University	M
York University	M,D

COMMUNICATION DISORDERS

Institution	Degrees
Abilene Christian University	M
Adelphi University	M,D
Alabama Agricultural and Mechanical University	M
Albizu University	M,D
Albizu University, Miami Campus	M,D
Andrews University	M
Appalachian State University	M
Arizona State University at the Tempe campus	M,D
Arkansas State University	M,O
A.T. Still University	M,D,O
Auburn University	M
Baldwin Wallace University	M
Ball State University	M,D
Barry University	M
Baylor University	M
Biola University	M,O
Bloomsburg University of Pennsylvania	M,D
Boston University	M,D
Bowling Green State University	M,D
Bridgewater State University	M
Brooklyn College of the City University of New York	M,D
Buffalo State College, State University of New York	M
California Baptist University	M
California State University, Chico	M
California State University, East Bay	M
California State University, Fresno	M
California State University, Fullerton	M
California State University, Long Beach	M
California State University, Los Angeles	M
California State University, Northridge	M
California State University, Sacramento	M
California State University, San Marcos	M
California University of Pennsylvania	M
Calvin College	M
Canisius College	M,O
Case Western Reserve University	M,D
Central Michigan University	M
Chapman University	M*
Clarion University of Pennsylvania	M
Cleveland State University	M
The College of Saint Rose	M
Dalhousie University	M,D
Duquesne University	M,D
East Carolina University	M
Eastern Kentucky University	M
Eastern Michigan University	M
Eastern New Mexico University	M
Eastern Washington University	M
East Stroudsburg University of Pennsylvania	M
East Tennessee State University	M,D
Edinboro University of Pennsylvania	M
Elmhurst College	M
Florida Atlantic University	M
Florida International University	M
Fontbonne University	M
Fort Hays State University	M
Francis Marion University	M
Gallaudet University	M,D,O
The George Washington University	M
Georgia Southern University	M
Georgia State University	M,D
Governors State University	M
The Graduate Center, City University of New York	D
Grand Valley State University	M
Hampton University	M
Harding University	M
Hofstra University	M,D,O
Howard University	M,D
Hunter College of the City University of New York	M
Idaho State University	M,D
Illinois State University	M
Indiana State University	M,D,O
Indiana University Bloomington	M,D
Indiana University of Pennsylvania	M
Iona College	M
Ithaca College	M
Jackson State University	M
Jacksonville University	M
James Madison University	M,D
Kansas State University	M,D,O
Kean University	M,D
Kent State University	M,D,O
Lamar University	M,D
La Salle University	M
Lebanon Valley College	M
Lehman College of the City University of New York	M
Lewis & Clark College	M
Lindenwood University	M,D,O
Loma Linda University	M,D
Long Island University–LIU Brooklyn	M,D,O
Long Island University–LIU Post	M,D,O
Longwood University	M
Louisiana State University and Agricultural & Mechanical College	M,D
Louisiana State University Health Sciences Center	M,D
Louisiana Tech University	M,D,O
Loyola University Maryland	M
Marquette University	M,O
Marshall University	M
Maryville University of Saint Louis	M
Marywood University	M
Massachusetts Institute of Technology	M,D
McGill University	M,D
Mercy College	M
MGH Institute of Health Professions	M,O
Miami University	M
Michigan State University	M,D
Midwestern University, Downers Grove Campus	M
Midwestern University, Glendale Campus	M
Minnesota State University Mankato	M
Minot State University	M
Misericordia University	M
Mississippi University for Women	M,D,O
Missouri State University	M,D
Molloy College	M
Monmouth University	M,D,O
Montclair State University	M,D
Moravian College	M,D
Murray State University	M,O
Nazareth College of Rochester	M
New York Medical College	M,D,O
New York University	M,D*
North Carolina Central University	M
Northeastern State University	M
Northeastern University	M,D,O
Northern Arizona University	M
Northern Illinois University	M,D
Northwestern University	M,D
Nova Southeastern University	M,D
The Ohio State University	M,D
Ohio University	M,D
Oklahoma State University	M
Old Dominion University	M
Our Lady of the Lake University	M
Pace University	M
Pacific University	M
Penn State University Park	M,D,O*
Portland State University	M
Purdue University	M,D
Queens College of the City University of New York	M,O
Radford University	M
Rockhurst University	M
Rocky Mountain University of Health Professions	D
Rush University	M,D
Sacred Heart University	M
St. Ambrose University	M
St. Cloud State University	M
St. John's University (NY)	M,D
Saint Joseph's University	M,D,O
Saint Louis University	M*
Saint Mary's College	M
Saint Xavier University	M
Salus University	M,D,O
Samford University	M,D
San Diego State University	M,D
San Francisco State University	M
San Jose State University	M
Seton Hall University	M
South Carolina State University	M
Southeastern Louisiana University	M

*M—masters degree; D—doctorate; O—other advanced degree; *—Close-Up and/or Display*

Southeast Missouri State University — M
Southern Connecticut State University — M
Southern Illinois University Carbondale — M
Southern Illinois University Edwardsville — M
Southern University and Agricultural and Mechanical College — M
State University of New York at Fredonia — M,O
State University of New York at Plattsburgh — M
State University of New York College at Cortland — M
Stephen F. Austin State University — M
Stockton University — M
Syracuse University — M,D
Teachers College, Columbia University — M,D,O
Temple University — M,D*
Tennessee State University — M
Texas A&M University–Kingsville — M
Texas Christian University — M
Texas State University — M
Texas Tech University Health Sciences Center — M,D
Texas Woman's University — M
Touro College — M,D
Towson University — M,D
Truman State University — M
Universidad del Turabo — M
Université de Montréal — M
Université Laval — M
University at Buffalo, the State University of New York — M,D
The University of Akron — M
The University of Alabama — M
University of Alberta — M
The University of Arizona — M,D,O
University of Arkansas — M
University of Arkansas for Medical Sciences — M,D
The University of British Columbia — M,D
University of California, San Diego — D
University of Central Arkansas — M,D
University of Central Florida — M,O
University of Central Missouri — M,D,O
University of Central Oklahoma — M
University of Cincinnati — M,D
University of Colorado Boulder — M,D
University of Connecticut — M
University of Delaware — M
University of Florida — M,D
University of Georgia — M,D,O
University of Hawaii at Manoa — M
University of Houston — M
University of Illinois at Urbana–Champaign — M,D
The University of Iowa — M,D
The University of Kansas — M,D
University of Kentucky — M
University of Louisiana at Lafayette — M,D
University of Louisiana at Monroe — M
University of Louisville — M,D
University of Maine — M
The University of Manchester — M,D
University of Mary — M
University of Maryland, College Park — M,D
University of Massachusetts Amherst — M,D
University of Memphis — M,D
University of Minnesota, Duluth — M
University of Minnesota, Twin Cities Campus — M,D
University of Mississippi — M,D
University of Missouri — M,D
University of Montana — M,O
University of Montevallo — M
University of Nebraska at Kearney — M
University of Nebraska at Omaha — M
University of Nebraska–Lincoln — M,D
University of Nevada, Reno — M,D
University of New Hampshire — M
University of New Mexico — M
The University of North Carolina at Chapel Hill — M,D
The University of North Carolina at Greensboro — M,D
University of North Dakota — M
University of Northern Colorado — M
University of Northern Iowa — M
University of North Florida — M
University of North Texas — M,D,O
University of Oklahoma Health Sciences Center — M,D,O
University of Oregon — M,D
University of Ottawa — M
University of Pittsburgh — M,D*
University of Puerto Rico–Medical Sciences Campus — M,D
University of Redlands — M
University of Rhode Island — M
University of South Alabama — M,D
University of South Carolina — M,D
University of South Dakota — M
University of Southern Mississippi — M,D
University of South Florida — M,D,O
The University of Tennessee — M,D,O
The University of Tennessee Health Science Center — M,D
The University of Texas at Austin — M,D
The University of Texas at Dallas — M,D
The University of Texas at El Paso — M
The University of Texas Health Science Center at San Antonio — M,D

The University of Texas Rio Grande Valley — M
University of the District of Columbia — M
University of the Pacific — M,D
The University of Toledo — M,D,O
University of Toronto — M,D
The University of Tulsa — M
University of Utah — M,D
University of Vermont — M
University of Virginia — M,D
University of Washington — M,D
The University of Western Ontario — M
University of West Georgia — M,D,O
University of Wisconsin–Eau Claire — M
University of Wisconsin–Madison — M,D
University of Wisconsin–Milwaukee — M*
University of Wisconsin–River Falls — M
University of Wisconsin–Stevens Point — M,D
University of Wisconsin–Whitewater — M
University of Wyoming — M
Utah State University — M,D,O
Valdosta State University — M,D,O
Vanderbilt University — M,D*
Washington State University — M
Washington University in St. Louis — M,D
Wayne State University — M,D
Webster University — M
West Chester University of Pennsylvania — M
Western Carolina University — M
Western Illinois University — M
Western Kentucky University — M
Western Michigan University — M
Western Washington University — M
West Texas A&M University — M
West Virginia University — M,D
Wichita State University — M,D
William Paterson University of New Jersey — M,D,O
Worcester State University — M
Yeshiva University — M

COMMUNITY COLLEGE EDUCATION

Argosy University, Chicago — M,D,O
Argosy University, Los Angeles — M,D
Argosy University, Northern Virginia — M,D,O
Argosy University, Orange County — M,D
Argosy University, Phoenix — M,D,O
Argosy University, Seattle — M,D
Argosy University, Tampa — M,D,O
Arkansas State University — M,D,O
California State University, San Bernardino — M
California State University, Stanislaus — D
Central Michigan University — M,D,O
Drew University — M,D,O
East Carolina University — M,D,O
Eastern Michigan University — M,D,O
Elizabeth City State University — M
Ferris State University — D
Lenoir-Rhyne University — M
Marymount University — M,O
Mississippi State University — M,D,O
Morgan State University — M
National American University (TX) — M,D
North Carolina State University — M,D
Northern Arizona University — M,D,O
Old Dominion University — M,D
University of Arkansas at Little Rock — M,D
University of Central Florida — M,O
University of Memphis — M,D,O
University of Northern Iowa — M
University of South Florida — M,D,O
Wingate University — M,D,O

COMMUNITY HEALTH

Adelphi University — M,O
Adler University — M
American University of Beirut — M,D
Arizona State University at the Tempe campus — M,D,O
Baylor University — M
Bloomsburg University of Pennsylvania — M,D
Boston University — M,D
Brooklyn College of the City University of New York — M
Brown University — M,D
Canisius College — M,O
Clark University — M
The College at Brockport, State University of New York — M
Columbia University — M,D
Daemen College — M
Dalhousie University — M
Eastern Kentucky University — M
East Tennessee State University — M,D,O
George Mason University — M,O
The George Washington University — M,D
Georgia Southern University — M,D
Icahn School of Medicine at Mount Sinai — M,D
Idaho State University — O
Independence University — M
Indiana University Bloomington — M,D
Indiana University–Purdue University Indianapolis — M,D,O
Johns Hopkins University — M,D*
Long Island University–LIU Brooklyn — M
Louisiana State University Health Sciences Center — M,D
Medical College of Wisconsin — D

Memorial University of Newfoundland — M,D,O
Midwestern State University — M,O
Minnesota State University Mankato — M,O
Monroe College — M
New Jersey City University — M
New York University — M,D*
North Dakota State University — M
Old Dominion University — *
Quinnipiac University — D
Saint Louis University — M*
San Francisco State University — M
Southern Illinois University Carbondale — M
State University of New York College at Cortland — M
State University of New York College at Potsdam — M
State University of New York Downstate Medical Center — M
Stony Brook University, State University of New York — M,D,O
Suffolk University — M
Teachers College, Columbia University — M,D,O
Tulane University — M,D
Universidad de Ciencias Medicas — M,D,O
Université de Montréal — M,D,O
Université Laval — M,D,O
University at Buffalo, the State University of New York — M,D,O
The University of Alabama — M
The University of Alabama at Birmingham — M
University of Alberta — M,D
University of Arkansas — M,D
University of Calgary — M,D
University of California, Los Angeles — M,D
University of Colorado Denver — M,D,O
University of Illinois at Chicago — M,D
University of Illinois at Springfield — M,O
University of Illinois at Urbana–Champaign — M,D
The University of Iowa — M,D
The University of Kansas — M,D,O
University of Louisville — M
University of Manitoba — M,D,O
University of Massachusetts Amherst — M,D
University of Miami — M,D
University of Minnesota, Twin Cities Campus — M
University of Montana — M
University of Nevada, Las Vegas — M,D,O
University of New Mexico — M
The University of North Carolina at Charlotte — M,D,O
The University of North Carolina at Greensboro — M,D
University of Northern British Columbia — M,D,O
University of Northern Colorado — M
University of Northern Iowa — M
University of North Florida — M,O
University of Ottawa — D,O
University of Phoenix–Central Valley Campus — M
University of Phoenix–Hawaii Campus — M
University of Pittsburgh — M,D,O*
University of Saskatchewan — M,D
University of South Florida — O
The University of Tennessee — M,D
The University of Texas Health Science Center at Houston — M,D,O
University of Toronto — M,D
University of Vermont — M
University of Virginia — M,D
University of Washington — M,D
University of Wisconsin–La Crosse — M
University of Wisconsin–Milwaukee — D*
University of Wyoming — M,D
Virginia Commonwealth University — M,D
Virginia State University — M,D
Walden University — M,D,O
Washington State University — M,D,O
William James College — M,D,O

COMMUNITY HEALTH NURSING

Allen College — M,D
American University of Beirut — M
Binghamton University, State University of New York — M,D,O
Hampton University — M,D
Hunter College of the City University of New York — M
Husson University — M,O
Independence University — *
Johns Hopkins University — *
Kean University — M
La Salle University — M,D,O
Louisiana State University Health Sciences Center — M,D,O
Oregon Health & Science University — M,O
Rush University — D
San Francisco State University — M,O
University of Hartford — M
University of Hawaii at Manoa — M,D,O
University of Illinois at Chicago — M,O
The University of Kansas — M,D,O
University of Maryland, Baltimore — M,D,O
University of Massachusetts Amherst — M
University of Massachusetts Dartmouth — M,D
University of North Dakota — M,D,O
University of Puerto Rico–Medical Sciences Campus — M
University of South Carolina — M
The University of Texas at Austin — M,D

The University of Texas Health Science Center at San Antonio — M,D,O
The University of Toledo — M,O
University of Washington, Tacoma — M
Wayne State University — M,D
Worcester State University — M*

COMPARATIVE AND INTERDISCIPLINARY ARTS

Brigham Young University — M
Florida Atlantic University — D
Goddard College — M
Ohio University — D
Simon Fraser University — M

COMPARATIVE LITERATURE

American University — M
The American University in Cairo — M,O
Arizona State University at the Tempe campus — M,D,O
Binghamton University, State University of New York — M,D
Brock University — M
Brown University — D
California State University, Northridge — M
Carleton University — D
Carnegie Mellon University — M,D
Case Western Reserve University — M
Claremont Graduate University — M,D
Columbia University — M,D
Cornell University — D
Dartmouth College — M
Duke University — D
East Carolina University — M,D,O
Emory University — D,O
Fairleigh Dickinson University, Metropolitan Campus — M
Florida Atlantic University — M
Georgetown University — M,D
The Graduate Center, City University of New York — M,D
Harrison Middleton University — M,D
Harvard University — D*
Hunter College of the City University of New York — M
Indiana University Bloomington — M,D
Johns Hopkins University — D*
Louisiana State University and Agricultural & Mechanical College — M,D
New York University — M,D*
Northwestern University — M,D
Penn State University Park — M,D*
Princeton University — D
Purdue University — M,D
Rutgers University–New Brunswick — M,D
San Francisco State University — M
Stanford University — D
Stony Brook University, State University of New York — M,D,O
Université de Montréal — M,D
Université de Sherbrooke — M,D
Université du Québec à Chicoutimi — M
Université du Québec à Montréal — M,D
Université du Québec à Rimouski — M,D
Université du Québec à Trois-Rivières — M
Université Laval — M,D
University at Buffalo, the State University of New York — M,D
University of Arkansas — M,D
University of California, Berkeley — D
University of California, Davis — D
University of California, Irvine — M,D
University of California, Los Angeles — M,D
University of California, Riverside — M,D
University of California, Santa Barbara — D
University of California, Santa Cruz — M,D
University of Chicago — M,D
University of Georgia — M,D
University of Guelph — D
University of Houston — M
University of Illinois at Urbana–Champaign — M,D
University of Maryland, College Park — M,D
University of Massachusetts Amherst — M,D
University of Memphis — M,D,O
University of Michigan — D
University of Minnesota, Twin Cities Campus — D
University of Nebraska–Lincoln — M,D
University of New Mexico — M,D
University of Notre Dame — M
University of Oregon — M,D
University of Pennsylvania — M,D*
University of Puerto Rico–Río Piedras — M
University of South Carolina — M,D
University of Southern California — D
University of South Florida — O
The University of Texas at Austin — M,D
The University of Texas at Dallas — M,D
University of Toronto — M,D
University of Utah — M,D
University of Washington — M,D
The University of Western Ontario — M,D
University of Wisconsin–Madison — M,D
University of Wisconsin–Milwaukee — M,O*
Washington University in St. Louis — M,D
Western Kentucky University — M
Yale University — D

COMPUTATIONAL BIOLOGY

Albert Einstein College of Medicine	D
Baylor College of Medicine	D
Carnegie Mellon University	M,D
Claremont Graduate University	M,D
Cornell University	D
Duke University	D,O
George Mason University	M,D,O
Harvard University	M*
Iowa State University of Science and Technology	M,D
Lewis University	M
Massachusetts Institute of Technology	D
New York University	D*
Oregon Health & Science University	M,D,O
Oregon State University	M,D
Princeton University	D
Rutgers University–Camden	M,D
Rutgers University–Newark	M
Rutgers University–New Brunswick	D
Saint Louis University	M*
University of California, Irvine	D
University of Colorado Denver	M,D
University of Idaho	M,D
University of Illinois at Urbana–Champaign	M,D
The University of Iowa	M,D,O
The University of Kansas	D
University of Maryland, College Park	D
University of Massachusetts Medical School	M,D
University of Minnesota Rochester	M,D
The University of North Carolina at Chapel Hill	D
University of Pennsylvania	D*
University of Pittsburgh	D*
University of Rochester	M,D*
University of Southern California	D
University of South Florida	M,D
The University of Texas Medical Branch	D
University of Wyoming	D
Washington University in St. Louis	D
Wayne State University	M,D
Weill Cornell Medicine	D
Worcester Polytechnic Institute	M,D
Yale University	D

COMPUTATIONAL SCIENCES

American University of Beirut	M,D
California Institute of Technology	M,D
Chapman University	M,D*
Claremont Graduate University	M,D
Cornell University	M,D
Duke University	M,D
Florida State University	M,D
George Mason University	M,D,O
Georgia Institute of Technology	M,D
Hampton University	M
Harvard University	M,D*
Marquette University	M,D
Massachusetts Institute of Technology	M
McGill University	M,D
Memorial University of Newfoundland	M
Michigan Technological University	M,D,O
Middle Tennessee State University	D
Morgan State University	M,D
North Carolina Agricultural and Technical State University	M
The Ohio State University	M,D
Oregon State University	M,D
Princeton University	D
Purdue University	D
Rice University	M
St. John's University (NY)	M
Sam Houston State University	M,D
San Diego State University	M,D
Simon Fraser University	M,D
South Dakota State University	M,D
Southern Illinois University Edwardsville	M
Southern Methodist University	M,D
Stanford University	M,D
Texas A&M University–Commerce	M,O
University at Buffalo, the State University of New York	D,O
The University of Alabama at Birmingham	D
University of Alaska Fairbanks	M,D
University of California, San Diego	M,D
University of California, Santa Barbara	M,D
University of Central Oklahoma	M
University of Chicago	M
University of Colorado Denver	M,D
The University of Iowa	D
University of Lethbridge	M
University of Manitoba	M
University of Massachusetts Boston	D
University of Memphis	M
University of Michigan–Dearborn	M
University of Minnesota, Duluth	M
University of Minnesota, Twin Cities Campus	M,D
University of Notre Dame	M,D
University of Pennsylvania	M,D*
University of Pittsburgh	M,D,O*
University of Puerto Rico–Mayagüez	M,D
University of Southern Mississippi	M,D
The University of Tennessee at Chattanooga	D
The University of Texas at Austin	M,D
University of Utah	M
University of Washington	M,D
Valparaiso University	M
Western Michigan University	M,D

COMPUTER AND INFORMATION SYSTEMS SECURITY

American InterContinental University Online	M
American Public University System	M,D
Augusta University	M
Austin Peay State University	M
Bay Path University	M
Benedictine University	M
Boston University	M,D,O
Brandeis University	M
California State University, San Bernardino	M
California State University, San Marcos	M
California University of Pennsylvania	M
Capella University	M,D
Capitol Technology University	M
Cardinal Stritch University	M
Carnegie Mellon University	M
Central Michigan University	O
Champlain College	M
City University of Seattle	M,O
Claremont Graduate University	M,D,O
College of Saint Elizabeth	M,O
College of Staten Island of the City University of New York	M
Colorado Christian University	M
Colorado Technical University Aurora	M
Colorado Technical University Colorado Springs	M,D
Columbus State University	M,O
Concordia University (Canada)	M,D,O
Concordia University, Nebraska	M
Concordia University of Edmonton	M
Concordia University, St. Paul	M
Davenport University	M
DePaul University	M,D
DeSales University	M,O
Drury University	O
East Carolina University	M,D,O
Eastern Illinois University	M
Eastern Michigan University	O
EC-Council University	M
ECPI University	M
Embry-Riddle Aeronautical University–Daytona	M
Embry-Riddle Aeronautical University–Worldwide	M
Endicott College	M,O
Fairfield University	M,O
Florida Institute of Technology	M
Florida International University	M,D
Florida State University	M,D
George Mason University	M
The George Washington University	M,D,O
Georgia Institute of Technology	M
Georgia Southern University	M,O
Hampton University	M
Harrisburg University of Science and Technology	M
Hofstra University	M
Hood College	M,O
Illinois Institute of Technology	M,D
Indiana University Bloomington	M,D
Indiana University–Purdue University Indianapolis	M,D,O
The Institute of World Politics	M,D,O
Inter American University of Puerto Rico, Guayama Campus	M
Iona College	M,O
James Madison University	M
Johns Hopkins University	M,O*
Johnson & Wales University	M
Keiser University	M
Kennesaw State University	M,O
Kent State University	M
Lawrence Technological University	M,D,O
Lewis University	M
Liberty University	M,D
Lindenwood University	M,O
Lipscomb University	M,O
London Metropolitan University	M,D
Long Island University–Riverhead	M,O
Louisiana Tech University	M,D
Marymount University	M,D,O
Maryville University of Saint Louis	M,O
Marywood University	M
Mercy College	M
Mercyhurst University	M
Metropolitan State University	M,D,O
Middle Georgia State University	M
Mississippi College	M
Missouri Western State University	M
National University	M
Naval Postgraduate School	M,D
New Jersey City University	M,D,O
New Jersey Institute of Technology	M,D,O
New York Institute of Technology	M
New York University	M*
Niagara University	M
Northcentral University	M,D,O
Northeastern University	M,D,O
Northern Kentucky University	M,O
Northwestern University	M
Norwich University	M
Nova Southeastern University	M,D
Our Lady of the Lake University	M
Pace University	M,D,O
Penn State Great Valley	M,O
Portland State University	M,D,O

Purdue University	M
Purdue University Global	M
Quinnipiac University	M
Regent University	M
Regis University	M,O
Robert Morris University	M,D
Robert Morris University Illinois	M
Rochester Institute of Technology	M,O
Roger Williams University	M
Rowan University	O
Sacred Heart University	M
Saginaw Valley State University	M
St. Cloud State University	M
Saint Leo University	M,D
St. Mary's University (United States)	M,O
Saint Mary's University of Minnesota	M
Salem International University	M
Salve Regina University	M,O
Sam Houston State University	M,D
The SANS Technology Institute	M
Seattle Pacific University	M
Southern Arkansas University–Magnolia	M
Southern New Hampshire University	M
Southern Utah University	M
State University of New York Polytechnic Institute	M
Stephen F. Austin State University	M
Stevens Institute of Technology	M,O
Stevenson University	M
Stratford University (VA)	M,D
Strayer University	M
Syracuse University	M,O
Temple University	M,D*
Thomas Edison State University	M
Trident University International	M,D
Tuskegee University	M
Universidad del Este	M
Université de Sherbrooke	M
University at Albany, State University of New York	M
University of Advancing Technology	M
The University of Alabama at Birmingham	M
The University of Alabama in Huntsville	M,D,O
University of Colorado Colorado Springs	M,D
University of Dallas	M,D
University of Dayton	M
University of Denver	M,D
University of Detroit Mercy	M,D,O
University of Fairfax	M,D
University of Houston	M
University of Louisville	M,D,O
University of Maryland, Baltimore County	M,O
University of Maryland University College	M,O
University of Michigan–Dearborn	D
University of Minnesota, Twin Cities Campus	M
University of Missouri–St. Louis	M,D,O
University of Nebraska at Omaha	M,D,O
University of Nevada, Las Vegas	M,D,O
University of New Hampshire	M,O
University of New Haven	M
University of New Mexico	M
The University of North Carolina at Charlotte	M,D,O
University of Rhode Island	M,D,O
University of San Diego	M
University of Southern California	M,D
University of South Florida	M,D
The University of Tampa	M,O
The University of Texas at Austin	M,D
The University of Texas at El Paso	M,D,O
The University of Texas at San Antonio	M,D,O
The University of Texas at Tyler	M
The University of Tulsa	M,D
University of Utah	M,O
University of Washington	M,D
University of West Florida	M
University of Wisconsin–Madison	M
Utah Valley University	O
Utica College	M
Valparaiso University	M*
Vanderbilt University	M
Virginia International University	M,O
Virginia Polytechnic Institute and State University	M,O
Walden University	M,D,O
Walsh College of Accountancy and Business Administration	M
Webster University	M
West Chester University of Pennsylvania	M,O
Western Governors University	M
West Virginia University	M,D,O
Wilmington University	M

COMPUTER ART AND DESIGN

Academy of Art University	M
Alfred University	M
ArtCenter College of Design	M
Bowling Green State University	M
California College of the Arts	M
Carnegie Mellon University	M
Chatham University	M
City College of the City University of New York	M
Claremont Graduate University	M
Concordia University (Canada)	M,O
Cornell University	M,D
DePaul University	M,D

DigiPen Institute of Technology	M
Drexel University	M,D*
East Tennessee State University	M
Emily Carr University of Art + Design	M
Full Sail University	M
Georgia Institute of Technology	M,D
Georgian Court University	M,O
Goucher College	M
Indiana University–Purdue University Indianapolis	M
International Technological University	M
Lindenwood University–Belleville	M
Lynn University	M,O
Minneapolis College of Art and Design	O
New Mexico Highlands University	M
The New School	M
New York Institute of Technology	M
North Carolina State University	M,D
Northern Vermont University–Johnson	M
The Ohio State University	M
Old Dominion University	M
Purchase College, State University of New York	M
Purdue University	M,D
Rensselaer Polytechnic Institute	D
Rhode Island School of Design	M
Rochester Institute of Technology	M
Savannah College of Art and Design	M
School of Visual Arts (NY)	M
Syracuse University	M
Texas State University	M
Universidad Autonoma de Guadalajara	M
Universidad de las Américas Puebla	M
University of Alaska Fairbanks	M
University of California, Santa Cruz	M,D
University of Central Arkansas	M
University of Central Florida	M
University of Denver	M
University of Florida	M,D
University of Maryland, Baltimore County	M
University of Montana	M
University of Pennsylvania	M,D*
University of Rhode Island	M
University of Southern California	M
University of South Florida, St. Petersburg	M
University of Victoria	M
University of Wisconsin–Milwaukee	M,O*
Virginia International University	M,O

COMPUTER EDUCATION

Arcadia University	M,D,O
Ball State University	M,D,O
Eastern Washington University	M
Illinois Institute of Technology	M,D
Kent State University	M,D,O
Lesley University	M,D,O
Mississippi College	M,D,O
Ohio University	M,D
Teachers College, Columbia University	M,D
Thomas College	M
University of Bridgeport	M,D,O
University of Illinois at Chicago	D
University of Phoenix–Central Valley Campus	M
University of Phoenix–Online Campus	M,O
University of Phoenix–San Diego Campus	M

COMPUTER ENGINEERING

Air Force Institute of Technology	M,D
American University of Beirut	M,D
American University of Sharjah	M,D
Arizona State University at the Tempe campus	M,D
Atlantis University	M
Auburn University	M,D
Baylor University	M,D
Boise State University	M,D
Boston University	M,D,O
Brigham Young University	M,D
Brown University	M,D
Bucknell University	M
California State University, Chico	M
California State University, Fresno	M
California State University, Fullerton	M
California State University, Long Beach	M
Carnegie Mellon University	M,D
Case Western Reserve University	M,D
The Citadel, The Military College of South Carolina	M,O
Clemson University	M,D
Colorado Technical University Aurora	M
Colorado Technical University Colorado Springs	M
Columbia University	M,D
Concordia University (Canada)	M,D
Cornell University	M,D
Dalhousie University	M,D
Dartmouth College	M,D
Drexel University	M*
Duke University	M,D
East Carolina University	M,D,O
École Polytechnique de Montréal	M,D,O

Institution	Degree
Fairfield University	M,O
Fairleigh Dickinson University, Metropolitan Campus	M
Florida Atlantic University	M,D
Florida Institute of Technology	M,D
Florida International University	M,D
George Mason University	M,D,O
The George Washington University	M,D,O
Georgia Institute of Technology	M,D
Grand Valley State University	M
Illinois Institute of Technology	M,D
Indiana State University	M
Indiana University–Purdue University Indianapolis	M,D
Instituto Tecnológico y de Estudios Superiores de Monterrey, Campus Chihuahua	M,O
International Technological University	M
Iowa State University of Science and Technology	M,D
Johns Hopkins University	M,D,O*
Kansas State University	M
Lakehead University	M
Lawrence Technological University	M,D
Lehigh University	M,D
Louisiana State University and Agricultural & Mechanical College	M,D
Manhattan College	M
Marquette University	M,D,O
Marshall University	M
Massachusetts Institute of Technology	M,D,O
McGill University	M,D
Memorial University of Newfoundland	M,D
Mercer University	M
Miami University	M
Michigan Technological University	M,D,O
Mississippi State University	M,D
Missouri University of Science and Technology	M,D
Montana State University	M,D
Naval Postgraduate School	M,D,O
New Jersey Institute of Technology	M,D
New York Institute of Technology	M,D*
New York University	M
Norfolk State University	M
North Carolina Agricultural and Technical State University	M,D
North Carolina State University	M,D
North Dakota State University	M,D
Northeastern University	M,D,O
Northern Arizona University	M,D
Northwestern Polytechnic University	M,D
Northwestern University	M,D
Oakland University	M,D
The Ohio State University	M,D
Oklahoma Christian University	M
Oklahoma State University	M,D
Old Dominion University	M,D
Oregon Health & Science University	M,D
Oregon State University	M,D
Penn State University Park	M,D*
Polytechnic University of Puerto Rico	M
Portland State University	M,D
Purdue University	M,D
Purdue University Fort Wayne	M
Purdue University Northwest	M
Queen's University at Kingston	M,D
Rensselaer at Hartford	M
Rensselaer Polytechnic Institute	M,D
Rice University	M,D
Rochester Institute of Technology	M,D
Rose-Hulman Institute of Technology	M
Royal Military College of Canada	M,D
Rutgers University–New Brunswick	M,D
St. Mary's University (United States)	M
San Jose State University	M
Santa Clara University	M,D,O
Southern Illinois University Carbondale	M,D
Southern Methodist University	M,D
Stevens Institute of Technology	M,D,O
Stony Brook University, State University of New York	M,D
Syracuse University	M,D
Tennessee State University	M,D
Texas A&M University	M,D
Universidad del Turabo	M
The University of Akron	M,D
The University of Alabama	M,D
The University of Alabama at Birmingham	M,D
The University of Alabama in Huntsville	M,D
University of Alberta	M,D
The University of Arizona	M,D
University of Arkansas	M,D
University of Bridgeport	M,D
The University of British Columbia	M,D
University of Calgary	M,D
University of California, Davis	M,D
University of California, Los Angeles	M,D
University of California, Riverside	M
University of California, San Diego	M,D
University of California, Santa Barbara	M,D
University of California, Santa Cruz	M,D
University of Central Florida	M,D
University of Cincinnati	M,D
University of Colorado Boulder	M,D
University of Connecticut	M,D
University of Dayton	M,D
University of Delaware	M,D
University of Denver	M,D
University of Detroit Mercy	M
University of Florida	M,D
University of Houston–Clear Lake	M
University of Illinois at Chicago	M,D
University of Illinois at Urbana–Champaign	M,D
The University of Iowa	M,D
The University of Kansas	M
University of Louisville	M,D,O
University of Maine	M,D
University of Manitoba	M,D
University of Maryland, Baltimore County	M,D
University of Maryland, College Park	M,D
University of Massachusetts Amherst	M,D
University of Massachusetts Dartmouth	M,D,O
University of Massachusetts Lowell	M,D
University of Memphis	M,D,O
University of Miami	M,D
University of Michigan	M,D
University of Michigan–Dearborn	M,D
University of Minnesota, Duluth	M
University of Minnesota, Twin Cities Campus	M,D
University of Missouri	M,D
University of Missouri–Kansas City	M,D,O
University of Nebraska–Lincoln	M,D
University of Nevada, Reno	M,D
University of New Brunswick Fredericton	M,D
University of New Haven	M
University of New Mexico	M,D
The University of North Carolina at Charlotte	M,D,O
University of North Texas	M,D,O
University of Notre Dame	M,D
University of Oklahoma	M,D*
University of Ottawa	M,D
University of Pittsburgh	M,D*
University of Puerto Rico–Mayagüez	M,D
University of Regina	M,D
University of Rhode Island	M,D
University of Rochester	M,D*
University of San Diego	M
University of South Alabama	M
University of South Carolina	M,D
University of Southern California	M,D,O
University of South Florida	M,D
The University of Tennessee	M,D
The University of Texas at Arlington	M,D
The University of Texas at Austin	M,D
The University of Texas at Dallas	M,D
The University of Texas at El Paso	M,D,O
The University of Texas at San Antonio	M,D
University of Toronto	M,D
University of Utah	M,D
University of Victoria	M,D
University of Virginia	M,D
University of Washington	M,D
University of Washington, Bothell	M
University of Washington, Tacoma	M
University of Waterloo	M,D
The University of Western Ontario	M,D
University of Wisconsin–Milwaukee	M,D*
Villanova University	M,O
Virginia Polytechnic Institute and State University	M,D,O
Washington State University	M,D
Washington University in St. Louis	M,D
Wayne State University	M,D
Weber State University	M
Western Michigan University	M,D
West Virginia University	M,D
Wichita State University	M,D
Worcester Polytechnic Institute	M,D,O
Wright State University	M,D
Youngstown State University	M

COMPUTER SCIENCE

Institution	Degree
Acadia University	M
Air Force Institute of Technology	M
Alabama Agricultural and Mechanical University	M
Alcorn State University	M
American Sentinel University	M
The American University in Cairo	M,D,O
American University of Armenia	M
American University of Beirut	M,D
Appalachian State University	M
Arizona State University at the Tempe campus	M,D
Arkansas State University	M
Auburn University	M,D
Ball State University	M
Baylor University	M,D
Binghamton University, State University of New York	M,D
Boise State University	M,O
Boston University	M,D,O
Bowie State University	M
Bowling Green State University	M
Bradley University	M
Brandeis University	M,D
Bridgewater State University	M
Brigham Young University	M,D
Brock University	M
Brooklyn College of the City University of New York	M
Brown University	M,D
California Institute of Technology	M,D
California Polytechnic State University, San Luis Obispo	M
California State Polytechnic University, Pomona	M
California State University, Channel Islands	M
California State University, Chico	M
California State University, Dominguez Hills	M
California State University, East Bay	M
California State University, Fresno	M
California State University, Fullerton	M
California State University, Long Beach	M
California State University, Los Angeles	M
California State University, Northridge	M
California State University, Sacramento	M
California State University, San Bernardino	M
California State University, San Marcos	M
Capitol Technology University	M
Carleton University	M,D
Carnegie Mellon University	M,D
Case Western Reserve University	M,D
The Catholic University of America	M,D
Central Connecticut State University	M,O
Central Michigan University	M
Chicago State University	M
Christopher Newport University	M
City College of the City University of New York	M,D
City University of Seattle	M,O
Clark Atlanta University	M,D
Clarkson University	M,D
Clemson University	M,D
Coastal Carolina University	M,D,O
College of Charleston	M
The College of Saint Rose	M,O
College of Staten Island of the City University of New York	M
Colorado School of Mines	M,D
Colorado State University	M,D
Colorado Technical University Aurora	M
Colorado Technical University Colorado Springs	M,D
Columbia University	M,D
Columbus State University	M
Concordia University (Canada)	M,D,O
Concordia University, Nebraska	M
Cornell University	M,D
Dakota State University	M,D,O
Dalhousie University	M,D
Dartmouth College	M,D
DePaul University	M,D
DigiPen Institute of Technology	M
Drexel University	M,D,O*
Duke University	M,D
East Carolina University	M,D,O
Eastern Illinois University	M
Eastern Michigan University	M,O
Eastern Washington University	M
East Stroudsburg University of Pennsylvania	M
East Tennessee State University	M,O
École Polytechnique de Montréal	M,D,O
Elizabeth City State University	M
Emory University	M,D
Fairleigh Dickinson University, Florham Campus	M
Fairleigh Dickinson University, Metropolitan Campus	M
Fitchburg State University	M
Florida Atlantic University	M,D
Florida Institute of Technology	M,D
Florida International University	M,D
Florida Polytechnic University	M
Fontbonne University	M
Fordham University	M
Franklin University	M
Frostburg State University	M
Gannon University	M
George Mason University	M,D,O
Georgetown University	M,D
The George Washington University	M,D,O
Georgia Institute of Technology	M,D
Georgia Southern University	M
Georgia Southwestern State University	M,O
Georgia State University	M,D
Governors State University	M
The Graduate Center, City University of New York	D
Grand Valley State University	M
Hampton University	M
Harvard University	M,D*
Hood College	M,O
Howard University	M
Illinois Institute of Technology	M,D
Indiana State University	M
Indiana University Bloomington	M,D,O
Indiana University–Purdue University Indianapolis	M,D,O
Indiana University South Bend	M,O
Instituto Tecnológico y de Estudios Superiores de Monterrey, Campus Central de Veracruz	M
Instituto Tecnológico y de Estudios Superiores de Monterrey, Campus Ciudad de México	M,D
Instituto Tecnológico y de Estudios Superiores de Monterrey, Campus Cuernavaca	M,D
Instituto Tecnológico y de Estudios Superiores de Monterrey, Campus Estado de México	M,D
Instituto Tecnológico y de Estudios Superiores de Monterrey, Campus Irapuato	M,D
Instituto Tecnológico y de Estudios Superiores de Monterrey, Campus Monterrey	M,D
Inter American University of Puerto Rico, Fajardo Campus	M
Inter American University of Puerto Rico, Guayama Campus	M
Inter American University of Puerto Rico, Metropolitan Campus	M
Iona College	M
Iowa State University of Science and Technology	M,D
Jackson State University	M
Jacksonville State University	M
James Madison University	M
Johns Hopkins University	M,D,O*
Kansas State University	M,D
Kennesaw State University	M
Kent State University	M,D
Kutztown University of Pennsylvania	M
Lakehead University	M
Lamar University	M
La Salle University	M,O
Lawrence Technological University	M,O
Lebanese American University	M
Lehigh University	M,D
Lehman College of the City University of New York	M
Lewis University	M
Long Island University–LIU Brooklyn	M,O
Louisiana State University and Agricultural & Mechanical College	M,D
Louisiana State University in Shreveport	M
Louisiana Tech University	M,D,O
Loyola University Chicago	M
Maharishi University of Management	M
Marist College	M,O
Marquette University	M,D
Marshall University	M
Massachusetts Institute of Technology	M,D,O
McGill University	M,D
McMaster University	M,D
McNeese State University	M
Memorial University of Newfoundland	M,D
Merrimack College	M
Metropolitan State University	M
Michigan State University	M,D
Middle Tennessee State University	M
Midwestern State University	M
Mills College	M,O
Minnesota State University Mankato	M,O
Mississippi College	M
Mississippi State University	M,D
Missouri State University	M
Missouri University of Science and Technology	M,D
Monmouth University	M
Monroe College	M
Montana State University	M,D
Montclair State University	M,O
Morgan State University	M
Murray State University	M
National University	M
Naval Postgraduate School	M,D,O
New Jersey Institute of Technology	M,D,O
New Mexico Highlands University	M
New Mexico Institute of Mining and Technology	M,D
New York Institute of Technology	M
New York University	M,D,O*
Norfolk State University	M
North Carolina Agricultural and Technical State University	M,D
North Carolina State University	M,D
North Central College	M
Northcentral University	M,D,O
North Dakota State University	M,D,O
Northeastern Illinois University	M
Northeastern University	M,D
Northern Arizona University	M,D
Northern Illinois University	M
Northern Kentucky University	M,O
Northwestern Polytechnic University	M,D
Northwestern University	M,D
Northwest Missouri State University	M
Notre Dame College (OH)	M,O
Nova Southeastern University	M,D
Oakland University	M,D
The Ohio State University	M,D
Ohio University	M,D
Oklahoma Christian University	M
Oklahoma City University	M
Oklahoma State University	M,D
Old Dominion University	M,D
Oregon Health & Science University	M,D
Oregon State University	M,D
Pace University	M,D,O
Pacific States University	M
Penn State Harrisburg	M,O
Penn State University Park	M,D*
Polytechnic University of Puerto Rico	M
Portland State University	M,D,O
Prairie View A&M University	M,D
Princeton University	M,D
Purdue University	M,D
Purdue University Fort Wayne	M
Purdue University Northwest	M
Queens College of the City University of New York	M

University	Degree
Queen's University at Kingston	M,D
Regis University	M,O
Rensselaer at Hartford	M
Rensselaer Polytechnic Institute	M,D
Rice University	M,D
Rivier University	M
Rochester Institute of Technology	M,D
Roosevelt University	M
Rowan University	M,D
Royal Military College of Canada	M
Rutgers University–Camden	M
Rutgers University–New Brunswick	M
Sacred Heart University	M
Saginaw Valley State University	M
St. Cloud State University	M,O
St. Francis Xavier University	M
Saint Joseph's University	M,O
Saint Louis University	M*
St. Mary's University (United States)	M
Saint Xavier University	M
Sam Houston State University	M,D
San Diego State University	M
San Francisco State University	M
Santa Clara University	M,D,O
Seattle University	M
Shippensburg University of Pennsylvania	M,O
Simon Fraser University	M,D
Sofia University	M,D
Southern Adventist University	M
Southern Arkansas University–Magnolia	M
Southern Connecticut State University	M
Southern Illinois University Carbondale	M,D
Southern Illinois University Edwardsville	M
Southern Methodist University	M,D
Southern Oregon University	M
Southern University and Agricultural and Mechanical College	M
Stanford University	M,D
State University of New York Polytechnic Institute	M
Stevens Institute of Technology	M,D,O
Stony Brook University, State University of New York	M,D,O
Stratford University (VA)	M,D
Syracuse University	M
Télé-université	M,D
Temple University	M,D*
Tennessee Technological University	M,D
Texas A&M University	M,D
Texas A&M University–Corpus Christi	M
Texas A&M University–Kingsville	M
Texas Southern University	M
Texas State University	M,D
Towson University	M
Toyota Technological Institute at Chicago	D
Trent University	M
Troy University	M
Tufts University	M,D,O
Universidad Autonoma de Guadalajara	M,D
Universidad de las Américas Puebla	M,D
Université de Moncton	M,O
Université de Montréal	M,D
Université du Québec à Trois-Rivières	M
Université du Québec en Outaouais	M,D,O
Université Laval	M,D
University at Albany, State University of New York	M,D
University at Buffalo, the State University of New York	M,D,O
University of Advancing Technology	M
The University of Akron	M,D
The University of Alabama	M,D
The University of Alabama at Birmingham	M,D
The University of Alabama in Huntsville	M,D,O
University of Alaska Fairbanks	M
University of Alberta	M,D
The University of Arizona	M,D
University of Arkansas	M,D
University of Arkansas at Little Rock	M,D
University of Bridgeport	M,D
The University of British Columbia	M,D
University of Calgary	M,D
University of California, Berkeley	M,D
University of California, Davis	M,D
University of California, Irvine	M,D
University of California, Los Angeles	M,D
University of California, Merced	M,D
University of California, Riverside	M,D
University of California, San Diego	M,D
University of California, Santa Barbara	M,D
University of California, Santa Cruz	M,D
University of Central Arkansas	M
University of Central Florida	M,D,O
University of Central Missouri	M,D,O
University of Central Oklahoma	M
University of Chicago	M,D
University of Cincinnati	M,D
University of Colorado Boulder	M,D
University of Colorado Denver	M,D
University of Connecticut	M,D
University of Dayton	M
University of Delaware	M,D
University of Denver	M,D
University of Detroit Mercy	M,D,O
University of Fairfax	M,D
University of Florida	M,D
University of Georgia	M,D
University of Guelph	M,D
University of Hawaii at Manoa	M,D,O
University of Houston	M,D
University of Houston–Clear Lake	M
University of Houston–Victoria	M
University of Idaho	M
University of Illinois at Chicago	M,D
University of Illinois at Springfield	M
University of Illinois at Urbana–Champaign	M,D
The University of Iowa	M,D
The University of Kansas	M,D
University of Kentucky	M,D
University of Lethbridge	M,D
University of Louisville	M,D,O
University of Maine	M,D,O
University of Management and Technology	M,O
The University of Manchester	M,D
University of Manitoba	M,D
University of Maryland, Baltimore County	M,D
University of Maryland, College Park	M,D
University of Maryland Eastern Shore	M
University of Massachusetts Amherst	M,D
University of Massachusetts Boston	M,D
University of Massachusetts Dartmouth	M,O
University of Massachusetts Lowell	M,D
University of Memphis	M,D
University of Miami	M,D
University of Michigan	M,D
University of Michigan–Dearborn	D
University of Michigan–Flint	M
University of Minnesota, Duluth	M
University of Minnesota, Twin Cities Campus	M,D
University of Mississippi	M,D
University of Missouri	M,D
University of Missouri–Kansas City	M,D,O
University of Missouri–St. Louis	M,D
University of Montana	M,D
University of Nebraska at Omaha	M,O
University of Nebraska–Lincoln	M,D
University of Nevada, Reno	M,D
University of New Brunswick Fredericton	M,D
University of New Hampshire	M,D
University of New Haven	M,O
University of New Mexico	M,D
University of New Orleans	M,D
The University of North Carolina at Chapel Hill	M,D
The University of North Carolina at Charlotte	M,D
The University of North Carolina at Greensboro	M
The University of North Carolina Wilmington	M
University of North Dakota	M
University of Northern British Columbia	M,D,O
University of North Florida	M
University of North Texas	M,D,O
University of Notre Dame	M,D
University of Oregon	M,D
University of Ottawa	M,D
University of Pennsylvania	M,D*
University of Pittsburgh	M,D*
University of Portland	M
University of Puerto Rico–Mayagüez	M,D
University of Regina	M,D
University of Rhode Island	M,D;O
University of Rochester	M,D*
University of San Francisco	M
University of Saskatchewan	M,D
University of South Alabama	M,D
University of South Carolina	M,D
University of South Dakota	M,D
University of Southern California	M,D
University of Southern Maine	M,O
University of Southern Mississippi	M,D
University of South Florida	M,D
The University of Tennessee	M,D
The University of Tennessee at Chattanooga	M,O
The University of Texas at Arlington	M,D
The University of Texas at Austin	M,D
The University of Texas at Dallas	M,D
The University of Texas at El Paso	M,D,O
The University of Texas at San Antonio	M,D
The University of Texas at Tyler	M
The University of Texas of the Permian Basin	M
The University of Texas Rio Grande Valley	M
University of the District of Columbia	M
The University of Toledo	M,D
University of Toronto	M,D
The University of Tulsa	M,D
University of Utah	M,D
University of Vermont	M,D
University of Victoria	M,D
University of Virginia	M,D
University of Washington	M,D
University of Waterloo	M,D
The University of Western Ontario	M,D
University of West Florida	M
University of West Georgia	M
University of Windsor	M,D
University of Wisconsin–Madison	M,D
University of Wisconsin–Milwaukee	M,D*
University of Wisconsin–Parkside	M
University of Wisconsin–Platteville	M
University of Wyoming	M,D
Utah State University	M,D
Vanderbilt University	M,D*
Villanova University	M,D
Virginia Commonwealth University	M,D
Virginia International University	M,O
Virginia Polytechnic Institute and State University	M,D,O
Wake Forest University	M
Washington State University	M,D
Washington University in St. Louis	M,D
Wayne State University	M,D
Webster University	M
Wentworth Institute of Technology	M
Wesleyan University	M,D
West Chester University of Pennsylvania	M,O
Western Illinois University	M
Western Kentucky University	M
Western Michigan University	M,D
Western Washington University	M
West Virginia University	M,D
Wichita State University	M,D
Winston-Salem State University	M
Worcester Polytechnic Institute	M,D,O
Wright State University	M,D
Yale University	M,D
York University	M,D
Youngstown State University	M

CONDENSED MATTER PHYSICS

University	Degree
Iowa State University of Science and Technology	M,D
Memorial University of Newfoundland	M,D
Rutgers University–New Brunswick	M,D
University of Alberta	M,D
The University of Manchester	M,D
University of Victoria	M,D

CONFLICT RESOLUTION AND MEDIATION/PEACE STUDIES

University	Degree
Abilene Christian University	M,O
American Public University System	M,D
American University	M,D,O
The American University of Paris	M
The American University of Rome	M
Anabaptist Mennonite Biblical Seminary	M,O
Arcadia University	M
Bethany Theological Seminary	M,O
Bethel University (TN)	M
Brandeis University	M,D
California State University, Dominguez Hills	M
California University of Pennsylvania	M
Cambridge College	M
Carleton University	M,O
Champlain College	M
Colgate Rochester Crozer Divinity School	M,D,O
Colorado Technical University Aurora	M
Colorado Technical University Colorado Springs	M,D
Columbia University	M
Cornell University	M,D
Creighton University	M,D,O
Dallas Baptist University	M
Drew University	M,D,O
Eastern Mennonite University	M,O
Fresno Pacific University	M,O
George Mason University	M,D,O
Georgetown University	M
Henley-Putnam School of Strategic Security	M
The Institute of World Politics	M,D,O
Kansas State University	M,D,O
Kennesaw State University	M,D
Kent State University	M,D
Lesley University	M,D,O
Lipscomb University	M,O
London Metropolitan University	M,D
Middlebury Institute of International Studies at Monterey	M
Montclair State University	M,O
Naval Postgraduate School	M,D
New York University	M*
Norwich University	M
Nova Southeastern University	M,D,O
Old Dominion University	M
Portland State University	M
Regent University	M
Royal Roads University	M,O
Saint Mary's College of California	M
St. Mary's University (United States)	M,O
Saint Paul University	M
Salisbury University	M
Salve Regina University	M,D
SIT Graduate Institute	M,O
Southern Methodist University	M,O
Syracuse University	O
Trident University International	M,D
United States International University–Africa	M
United Theological Seminary of the Twin Cities	M,D,O
Universidad del Turabo	M
Université de Sherbrooke	M,D,O
University of Arkansas at Little Rock	O
University of Baltimore	M
University of Bridgeport	M
University of Denver	M,D,O
University of Hawaii at Manoa	M,O
The University of Manchester	D
University of Massachusetts Amherst	M
University of Massachusetts Boston	M,O
University of Massachusetts Lowell	M
University of Missouri	M,D
University of New Brunswick Fredericton	M
University of New Haven	M,O
The University of North Carolina at Greensboro	M,O
The University of North Carolina Wilmington	M
University of Notre Dame	M,D
University of Phoenix–Online Campus	M,O
University of San Diego	M
University of the Sacred Heart	M
University of Victoria	M,D
University of Wisconsin–Milwaukee	M,D,O*
Walden University	M,D,O
Wayne State University	M,D,O
Wilfrid Laurier University	D
Willamette University	M,D
Yeshiva University	M,D

CONSERVATION BIOLOGY

University	Degree
Antioch University New England	M
Arizona State University at the Tempe campus	M,D
California State University, Sacramento	M
California State University, Stanislaus	M
Central Michigan University	M
Colorado State University	M,D
Columbia University	M,D
Cornell University	M,D
Florida Institute of Technology	M
Fordham University	M,D,O
Frostburg State University	M
Illinois State University	M,D
North Dakota State University	M,D
Oregon State University	M,D
State University of New York College of Environmental Science and Forestry	M,D
Texas State University	M
Tropical Agriculture Research and Higher Education Center	M,D
University of Alberta	M,D
University of Central Florida	M,D,O
University of Hawaii at Hilo	M
University of Illinois at Urbana–Champaign	M,D
University of Maryland, College Park	M
University of Minnesota, Twin Cities Campus	M,D
University of Missouri	M,D,O
University of Nevada, Reno	D
University of New Hampshire	M
The University of West Alabama	M
University of Wisconsin–Madison	M
University of Wisconsin–Stout	M

CONSTRUCTION ENGINEERING

University	Degree
The American University in Cairo	M,D,O
Arizona State University at the Tempe campus	M,D
Auburn University	M
Bradley University	M
Clemson University	M,D
Colorado School of Mines	M,D
Columbia University	M,D
Concordia University (Canada)	M,D,O
George Mason University	M,D
Illinois Institute of Technology	M,D
Iowa State University of Science and Technology	M,D
Lawrence Technological University	M,D
Marquette University	M,D,O
Massachusetts Institute of Technology	M,D,O
Montana State University	M,D
Ohio University	M,D
Oregon State University	M,D
Pittsburg State University	M
Stanford University	M,D,O
Stevens Institute of Technology	M,O
The University of Alabama	M,D
The University of Alabama at Birmingham	M
University of Alberta	M,D
University of Michigan	M,D,O
University of Missouri–Kansas City	M,D,O
University of New Brunswick Fredericton	M,D

*M—masters degree; D—doctorate; O—other advanced degree; *—Close-Up and/or Display*

University of Puerto Rico–Mayagüez	M,D
University of Southern Mississippi	M
University of Virginia	D
University of Washington	M,D
University of Wisconsin–Madison	M
Wentworth Institute of Technology	M

CONSTRUCTION MANAGEMENT

The American University in Dubai	M
Arizona State University at the Tempe campus	M,D
Brigham Young University	M
California Baptist University	M
California State University, Chico	M
California State University, East Bay	M
California State University, Northridge	M
Carnegie Mellon University	M,D
Central Connecticut State University	M,O
Clemson University	M,D
Colorado State University	M
Columbia University	M,D
Drexel University	M*
East Carolina University	M,O
Eastern Michigan University	M,O
Farmingdale State College	M
Florida International University	M
Georgia Southern University	M
Illinois Institute of Technology	M
Instituto Tecnologico de Santo Domingo	M,O
Kennesaw State University	M
Louisiana State University and Agricultural & Mechanical College	M,D
Manhattan College	M
Marquette University	M,D,O
Michigan State University	M
Missouri State University	M
New England Institute of Technology	M
NewSchool of Architecture and Design	M
New York University	M*
North Dakota State University	M,O
Norwich University	M
Pittsburg State University	M
Polytechnic University of Puerto Rico, Miami Campus	M
Polytechnic University of Puerto Rico, Orlando Campus	M
Purdue University	M
Purdue University Fort Wayne	M
South Dakota School of Mines and Technology	M
Stevens Institute of Technology	M,O
Texas A&M University	M
Thomas Jefferson University	M
Universidad de las Américas Puebla	M
The University of Alabama at Birmingham	M
University of Alaska Fairbanks	M,D,O
University of Arkansas at Little Rock	M
University of California, Berkeley	O
University of Denver	M
University of Florida	M
University of Houston	M
The University of Kansas	M
University of New Mexico	M,D
The University of North Carolina at Charlotte	M,O
University of North Florida	M
University of Southern California	M,D,O
The University of Tennessee at Chattanooga	M,O
The University of Texas at Arlington	M,D
The University of Texas at El Paso	M,D,O
University of Washington	M
University of Wisconsin–Stout	M
Wentworth Institute of Technology	M
Western Carolina University	M

CONSUMER ECONOMICS

Colorado State University	M
Cornell University	M,D
Kansas State University	M,D,O
North Dakota State University	M,O
Ohio University	M
Oklahoma State University	M,D
Purdue University	M,D
South Dakota State University	M
State University of New York at Oswego	M
Texas Tech University	M,D
Université Laval	O
The University of Alabama	M
University of Guelph	M
University of Idaho	M
University of Illinois at Urbana–Champaign	M,D
University of Missouri	D
University of Nebraska–Lincoln	M,D
University of South Carolina	M,D
The University of Tennessee	M,D
University of Wisconsin–Madison	M,D
University of Wyoming	M
Utah State University	M

CORPORATE AND ORGANIZATIONAL COMMUNICATION

American University	M
Ashland University	M
Austin Peay State University	M
Baruch College of the City University of New York	M*
Bellevue University	M

Boston University	M
Bowie State University	M,O
Bryant University	M,O
California State University, San Bernardino	M
Carnegie Mellon University	M
City College of the City University of New York	M
Columbia University	M
Concordia University, St. Paul	M
Concordia University Wisconsin	M
Cornell University	M,D
DePaul University	M
Drexel University	M*
East Carolina University	M,D,O
Eastern Michigan University	M,O
Fairleigh Dickinson University, Florham Campus	M
Florida State University	M,D
Franklin University	M
Georgia Southern University	M,O
HEC Montreal	O
High Point University	M,D
Howard University	M,D
Illinois Institute of Technology	M
Iowa State University of Science and Technology	M,D
La Salle University	M,O
Lasell College	M,O
Loyola University Chicago	M
Manhattanville College	M,O
Marist College	M
Minnesota State University Mankato	M,O
Mississippi College	M
Montclair State University	M
Murray State University	M
New Mexico State University	M,D
New York University	M*
Northeastern University	M
Northwestern University	M,D
Ohio University	M,D
Radford University	M
Regent University	M,D
Regis College (MA)	M
Rider University	M
Roosevelt University	M
Rowan University	O
St. Bonaventure University	M
Seton Hall University	M
Southern Illinois University Edwardsville	M
Spalding University	M
State University of New York at Oswego	M
Suffolk University	M
Temple University	M,D*
Texas Christian University	M
Towson University	M
Troy University	M
Universidad Autonoma de Guadalajara	M,D
Universidad Iberoamericana	M,D
Université de Sherbrooke	M
University of Alaska Fairbanks	M
University of Colorado Denver	M
University of Illinois at Urbana–Champaign	M
University of Nebraska–Lincoln	M,D
University of Oklahoma	M,D*
University of Portland	M
University of Southern California	M
University of South Florida	M,O
University of Wisconsin–Stevens Point	M
University of Wisconsin–Whitewater	M
Washington State University	M,D
Webster University	M
Western Kentucky University	M,O
West Virginia University	M,O

COUNSELING PSYCHOLOGY

Abilene Christian University	M
Adelphi University	M
Adler Graduate School	M
Adler University	M
Alabama Agricultural and Mechanical University	M,O
Alaska Pacific University	M
Albizu University, Miami Campus	M,D
Alfred University	M,D,O
Amberton University	M
American International College	M,D
Amridge University	M,D
Andrews University	M,D
Anna Maria College	M
Antioch University New England	M
Appalachian State University	M
Arcadia University	M
Argosy University, Chicago	D
Argosy University, Hawai'i	D
Argosy University, Los Angeles	M,D
Argosy University, Northern Virginia	M,D
Argosy University, Orange County	M,D
Argosy University, Phoenix	M
Argosy University, Seattle	M,D
Argosy University, Tampa	M,D
Arizona State University at the Tempe campus	D
Assumption College	M,O
Athabasca University	M,O
Austin Peay State University	M
Avila University	M
Ball State University	M,D
Baruch College of the City University of New York	M*
Bastyr University	M
Becker College	M
Bethel University (MN)	M,D,O
Boston College	M,D
Boston Graduate School of Psychoanalysis	M

Boston University	M
Bowie State University	M
Bradley University	M
Brandman University	M
Brooklyn College of the City University of New York	M,D,O
Caldwell University	M,O
California Baptist University	M
California State University, Bakersfield	M
California State University, Fresno	M
California State University, San Bernardino	M
California State University, Stanislaus	M
California University of Pennsylvania	M
Cambridge College	M,O
Capella University	M
Carlow University	M,D,O
Centenary University	M
Central Michigan University	M,D,O
Central Washington University	M
Chaminade University of Honolulu	M
Chatham University	M,D
Chestnut Hill College	M
City University of Seattle	M
Cleveland State University	M,D
The College at Brockport, State University of New York	M,O
The College of New Rochelle	M,O
College of Saint Elizabeth	M,D
College of St. Joseph	M
The College of Saint Rose	M,O
College of Staten Island of the City University of New York	M,O
Colorado Christian University	M
Concordia University Chicago	M
Dallas Baptist University	M
Delaware Valley University	M
DePaul University	M
Dominican University of California	M
Duquesne University	M,D,O
Eastern Nazarene College	M
Eastern University	M,O
Eastern Washington University	M
East Texas Baptist University	M
Edinboro University of Pennsylvania	M,O
Emporia State University	M
Evangel University	M
Fairfield University	M,O
Fairleigh Dickinson University, Florham Campus	M
Felician University	M,D
Fitchburg State University	M
Florida International University	M,D,O
Fordham University	M,D
Fort Valley State University	M
Framingham State University	M
Franciscan University of Steubenville	M
Francis Marion University	M,O
Frostburg State University	M
Gallaudet University	M,D,O
Gannon University	M
Gardner-Webb University	M
Geneva College	M
George Fox University	M,O
Georgian Court University	M,O
Georgia Southern University	M
Georgia State University	M,O
Governors State University	M
Hardin-Simmons University	M
Heidelberg University	M
Henderson State University	M,O
Hodges University	M
Hofstra University	M
Holy Family University	M
Holy Names University	M
Houston Baptist University	M
Howard University	D
Humboldt State University	M
Husson University	M
Idaho State University	M,D,O
Illinois State University	M,D,O
Immaculata University	M,D,O
Indiana University Northwest	M,O
Indiana University South Bend	M,O
Indiana Wesleyan University	M
Instituto Tecnologico de Santo Domingo	M,O
Inter American University of Puerto Rico, Aguadilla Campus	M
Inter American University of Puerto Rico, Metropolitan Campus	M,D
Inter American University of Puerto Rico, San Germán Campus	M,D
Iona College	M,O
Iowa State University of Science and Technology	M,D
Jacksonville University	M
James Madison University	D
John Brown University	M,O
John Carroll University	M,O
John F. Kennedy University	M
Kean University	M
Kent State University	M
Kutztown University of Pennsylvania	M
Lamar University	M
Lancaster Bible College	M,D
La Salle University	M
Lee University	M
Lehigh University	M,D,O
Lenoir-Rhyne University	M
Lesley University	M,D,O
LeTourneau University	M
Lewis & Clark College	M
Lewis University	M
Liberty University	M,D,O
Lindenwood University	M,D,O
Lindsey Wilson College	M,D

Lipscomb University	M,O
Lock Haven University of Pennsylvania	M
London Metropolitan University	M,D
Long Island University–Brentwood Campus	M,O
Long Island University–Hudson	M,O
Long Island University–LIU Brooklyn	M,O
Long Island University–LIU Post	M,D,O
Louisiana Tech University	M,D,O
Loyola Marymount University	M*
Loyola University Chicago	M
Loyola University Maryland	M,D,O
Lynn University	M
Manhattan College	M,O
Marian University (IN)	M
Marist College	M,O
Marquette University	M,D
Marymount University	M
Marywood University	M
McGill University	M,D,O
McKendree University	M
McNeese State University	M,O
Medaille College	M,D
Mercy College	M,O
Messiah College	M,O
Mid-America Christian University	M
Middle Tennessee State University	M
Midwestern State University	M
Minnesota State University Mankato	M,D
Mississippi College	M
Missouri State University	M
Monmouth University	M,O
Montana State University Billings	M
Moody Theological Seminary–Michigan	M,O
Morehead State University	M
Mount Mary University	M,O
Mount Saint Mary's University (CA)	M,D,O
Naropa University	M
National University	M,O
Nebraska Christian College of Hope International University	M
New England College	M
New Mexico Highlands University	M
New York University	M,D,O*
Niagara University	M,D,O
North Dakota State University	M,D
Northeastern University	M,D,O
Northern Arizona University	M,D,O
Northern Kentucky University	M
Northern State University	M
Northwest Christian University	M
Northwestern Oklahoma State University	M
Northwest University	M,D
Nova Southeastern University	M,D,O
Nyack College	M
Oakland University	M,D,O
Old Dominion University	M,D,O
Ottawa University	M
Our Lady of the Lake University	D
Pace University	M,D
Pacifica Graduate Institute	M
Palm Beach Atlantic University	M
Palo Alto University	M
Philadelphia College of Osteopathic Medicine	M,D,O*
Phoenix Seminary	M,D,O
Prescott College	M
Providence University College & Theological Seminary	M,D,O
Purdue University Northwest	M
Queens College of the City University of New York	M,O
Radford University	D
Regent University	M,D,O
Regis College (MA)	M,D,O
Rhode Island College	M,O
Rivier University	M,D,O
Rosemont College	M
Rutgers University–New Brunswick	M
Sage Graduate School	M
St. Bonaventure University	M,O
St. Edward's University	M
St. John Fisher College	M
St. John's University (NY)	M
Saint Martin's University	M
St. Mary's University (United States)	M
Saint Mary's University of Minnesota	M,D,O
Saint Paul University	M
St. Thomas University	M
Salem State University	M
Salve Regina University	M,O
Santa Clara University	M,O
Saybrook University	M
The Seattle School of Theology and Psychology	M
Seton Hall University	M,D
Siena Heights University	M,O
Simpson University	M
Slippery Rock University of Pennsylvania	M
Sofia University	M,D
Sonoma State University	M
Southeastern Oklahoma State University	M
Southeastern University (FL)	M
Southeast Missouri State University	M,O
Southern Adventist University	M
Southern California Seminary	M,D
Southern Illinois University Carbondale	M,D
Southern Nazarene University	M
Southern Oregon University	M
South University	M

South University | M
South University (TX) | M
South University (SC) | M
South University (GA) | M
South University (AL) | M
South University | M
Southwestern Assemblies of God University | M,O
Southwestern College (NM) | M,O
Spring Arbor University | M
Springfield College | M,D,O
State University of New York at New Paltz | M,O
State University of New York at Oswego | M
State University of New York at Plattsburgh | M,O
State University of New York College at Old Westbury | M
Suffolk University | M,D,O
Tarleton State University | M
Teachers College, Columbia University | M,D
Temple University | M,D,O*
Tennessee State University | M
Texas A&M International University | M
Texas A&M University | M,D
Texas A&M University–Texarkana | M
Texas Tech University | M,D
Texas Woman's University | M,D,O
Touro College | M,D
Towson University | M
Trinity Christian College | M
Trinity International University | M,D,O
Trinity International University Florida | M
Trinity Washington University | M
Trinity Western University | M
Truett McConnell University | M
Union College (KY) | M
United States International University–Africa | M
Universidad del Turabo | M,D,O
Universidad Metropolitana | M
University at Albany, State University of New York | M,D,O
University at Buffalo, the State University of New York | M,D,O
The University of Akron | M,D
University of Alberta | M
The University of Arizona | M
University of Baltimore | M
University of Bridgeport | M
The University of British Columbia | M,D,O
University of Calgary | M,D
University of California, Berkeley | O
University of California, Santa Barbara | M,D,O
University of Central Arkansas | M
University of Central Missouri | M
University of Central Oklahoma | M
University of Colorado Denver | M
University of Connecticut | M,O
University of Dayton | M,O
University of Denver | M,D,O
University of Florida | M,D
University of Hawaii at Hilo | M
University of Houston | M,D
University of Houston–Victoria | M
University of Indianapolis | M,D
The University of Iowa | M,D,O
The University of Kansas | M
University of Kentucky | M,D,O
University of Lethbridge | M,D
University of Louisiana at Monroe | M
University of Louisville | M,D
University of Lynchburg | M
The University of Manchester | M,D
University of Mary Hardin-Baylor | M
University of Maryland, College Park | M,D,O
University of Massachusetts Boston | M,D
University of Memphis | M,D
University of Miami | D
University of Minnesota, Twin Cities Campus | D
University of Missouri | M,D,O
University of Missouri–Kansas City | M,D,O
University of Montana | M,D,O
University of Nebraska at Kearney | M,O
University of Nebraska–Lincoln | M,D,O
University of Nevada, Las Vegas | M,D,O
The University of North Carolina at Greensboro | M,D,O
The University of North Carolina at Pembroke | M
University of North Dakota | M,D
University of Northern Colorado | D
University of Northern Iowa | M
University of North Florida | M
University of North Georgia | M
University of North Texas | M,D,O
University of Notre Dame | D
University of Oregon | M,D
University of Pennsylvania | M*
University of Phoenix–Las Vegas Campus | M
University of Phoenix–Phoenix Campus | M
University of Providence | M
University of Puget Sound | M
University of Rhode Island | M
University of Saint Francis (IN) | M,O
University of Saint Joseph | M
University of Saint Mary | M
University of St. Thomas (MN) | M,D
University of San Diego | M

University of San Francisco | M
University of Saskatchewan | M,D
The University of Scranton | M
University of South Africa | M,D
University of South Alabama | M,D,O
University of South Dakota | M,D,O
University of Southern Maine | M,O
University of South Florida | M,D,O
The University of Tennessee | M,D
The University of Texas at Austin | M,D
The University of Texas at Tyler | M
University of the Cumberlands | M
University of the District of Columbia | M
University of the Southwest | M
University of Utah | M,D,O
University of Vermont | M
University of Victoria | M,D
The University of Western Ontario | M,D
University of West Florida | M
University of Wisconsin–Madison | D
University of Wisconsin–Milwaukee | M,D,O*
University of Wisconsin–Stout | M
Utah State University | M,D
Virginia Commonwealth University | M,D
Viterbo University | M
Walden University | M,D,O
Walsh University | M
Washington Adventist University | M
Washington State University | M,D
Wayland Baptist University | M
Waynesburg University | M,D
Wayne State University | M,D
Webster University | M
Western Kentucky University | M
Western Michigan University | M,D
Western Washington University | M
Westfield State University | M
Westminster College (UT) | M
West Virginia University | M,D
Wheaton College | M,D
William Carey University | M
William James College | M,D,O
William Paterson University of New Jersey | M,D,O
Wilmington University | M
Winebrenner Theological Seminary | M,D
The Wright Institute | M
Xavier University | M*
Yeshiva University | M

COUNSELOR EDUCATION

Acadia University | M
Adams State University | M,D
Adler Graduate School | M
Adler University | D
Alabama Agricultural and Mechanical University | M,O
Alabama State University | M,D,O
Albany State University | M,O
Alcorn State University | M,O
Alfred University | M,D,O
Alliant International University–San Francisco | M
Amberton University | M
American International College | M,D,O
Amridge University | M,D
Angelo State University | M
Antioch University Seattle | M,D
Appalachian State University | M
Argosy University, Atlanta | M,D,O
Argosy University, Chicago | D
Argosy University, Northern Virginia | M,D
Argosy University, Tampa | M,D,O
Arizona State University at the Tempe campus | M
Arkansas State University | M,O
Arkansas Tech University | M,D,O
Ashland Theological Seminary | M,O
Athabasca University | M,O
Auburn University at Montgomery | M,O
Augusta University | M
Austin Peay State University | M
Azusa Pacific University | M
Ball State University | M,D
Barry University | M,O
Bayamón Central University | M,O
Becker College | M
Bellevue University | M
Bloomsburg University of Pennsylvania | M
Bob Jones University | M,D,O
Boise State University | M,O
Bowie State University | M
Bowling Green State University | M
Bradley University | M
Brandman University | M,D
Brandon University | M,O
Bridgewater State University | M,O
Brooklyn College of the City University of New York | M
Buena Vista University | M
California Baptist University | M
California Lutheran University | M,D
California State University, Bakersfield | M
California State University, Dominguez Hills | M
California State University, East Bay | M
California State University, Fresno | M
California State University, Fullerton | M
California State University, Long Beach | M,D

California State University, Los Angeles | M,D
California State University, Northridge | M
California State University, Sacramento | M,D,O
California State University, San Bernardino | M
California State University, Stanislaus | M
California University of Pennsylvania | M
Cambridge College | M,O
Campbell University | M
Canisius College | M
Capella University | M,D
Carson-Newman University | M
Carthage College | M,O
Central Connecticut State University | M,O
Central Methodist University | M
Central Michigan University | M
Chadron State College | M
Chapman University | M,D,O*
Chicago State University | M
The Citadel, The Military College of South Carolina | M
City University of Seattle | M,O
Clark Atlanta University | M
Clarks Summit University | M
Clemson University | M
Cleveland State University | M,D,O
The College at Brockport, State University of New York | M,O
The College of New Jersey | M
College of St. Joseph | M
The College of Saint Rose | M,O
The College of William and Mary | M,D
Colorado State University | M,D
Columbia International University | M
Columbus State University | M,D,O
Concordia University Chicago | M
Concordia University Irvine | M
Concordia University Wisconsin | M
Creighton University | M
Dallas Baptist University | M
Delta State University | M,D,O
DePaul University | M,D
Doane University | M
Drake University | M,D,O
Duquesne University | M,D,O
East Carolina University | M,D,O
Eastern Illinois University | M
Eastern Kentucky University | M
Eastern Mennonite University | M
Eastern Michigan University | M,O
Eastern New Mexico University | M
Eastern Washington University | M
East Tennessee State University | M
Edinboro University of Pennsylvania | M,O
Emporia State University | M
Evangel University | M
Fairfield University | M,O
Faulkner University | M
Fitchburg State University | M,O
Florida Agricultural and Mechanical University | M
Florida Atlantic University | M,D
Florida International University | M,D,O
Fordham University | M,D
Fort Hays State University | M
Fort Valley State University | M,O
Freed-Hardeman University | M
Fresno Pacific University | M
Frostburg State University | M
Gallaudet University | M,D,O
Geneva College | M
George Fox University | M,O
George Mason University | M
The George Washington University | M,D,O
Georgian Court University | M
Georgia Southern University | M
Georgia State University | M,O
Grambling State University | M,D,O
Gwynedd Mercy University | M,D
Hampton University | M,D,O
Harding University | M,O
Hardin-Simmons University | M,O
Henderson State University | M,O
Heritage University | M
Hofstra University | M,O
Houston Baptist University | M
Howard University | M
Hunter College of the City University of New York | M
Husson University | M
Idaho State University | M,D,O
Indiana State University | M,D,O
Indiana University Bloomington | M,D,O
Indiana University of Pennsylvania | M
Indiana University–Purdue University Indianapolis | M,O
Indiana University South Bend | M
Indiana University Southeast | M
Indiana Wesleyan University | M
Inter American University of Puerto Rico, Arecibo Campus | M
Inter American University of Puerto Rico, Metropolitan Campus | M,D
Inter American University of Puerto Rico, San Germán Campus | M,D
Iowa State University of Science and Technology | M,D
Jackson State University | M
Jacksonville State University | M
John Brown University | M,O
John Carroll University | M,O
Johnson University | M,D,O
Kansas State University | M,D,O
Kean University | M

Kent State University | M,D,O
Kutztown University of Pennsylvania | M
Lakeland University | M
Lamar University | M
Lancaster Bible College | M,D
La Sierra University | M,O
Lee University | M
Lehigh University | M,D,O
Lehman College of the City University of New York | M
Lenoir-Rhyne University | M
Lewis University | M
Liberty University | M,D,O
Lincoln Memorial University | M
Lincoln University (MO) | M
Lindenwood University–Belleville | M
Lindsey Wilson College | M,D
Loma Linda University | M,D,O
Long Island University–Brentwood Campus | M,O
Long Island University–Hudson | M,O
Long Island University–LIU Brooklyn | M,O
Longwood University | M
Louisiana State University and Agricultural & Mechanical College | M,D,O
Louisiana State University in Shreveport | M
Loyola Marymount University | M
Loyola University Chicago | M,O
Loyola University Maryland | M
Malone University | M
Manhattan College | M,O
Marian University (IN) | M
Marquette University | M
Marshall University | M
Marymount University | M
Marywood University | M
McDaniel College | M
McNeese State University | M
Mercer University | M
Mercy College | M,O
Messiah College | M,O
Michigan State University | M,D,O
Middle Tennessee State University | M
Midwestern State University | M
Midwest University | M,D
Milligan College | M
Minnesota State University Mankato | M,D
Minnesota State University Moorhead | M,D,O
Mississippi College | M,O
Mississippi State University | M,D,O
Missouri Baptist University | M,O
Missouri State University | M
Montana State University Billings | M
Montana State University–Northern | M
Montclair State University | M,D
Morehead State University | M
Mount Mary University | M,O
Murray State University | M,D,O
Naropa University | M
National Louis University | M,D,O
National University | M,O
New Jersey City University | M
New Mexico Highlands University | M
New York Institute of Technology | M,O
New York University | M,D,O*
Niagara University | M,O
Nicholls State University | M,O
North Carolina Agricultural and Technical State University | M,D
North Carolina Central University | M,D
North Carolina State University | M,D
North Dakota State University | M,D
Northeastern Illinois University | M
Northern Arizona University | M,D,O
Northern Illinois University | M,D
Northern Kentucky University | M
Northern State University | M
Northern Vermont University–Johnson | M
Northern Vermont University–Lyndon | M
Northwest Christian University | M
Northwestern Oklahoma State University | M
Northwestern State University of Louisiana | M,O
Northwest Nazarene University | M
Nova Southeastern University | M,D,O
Nyack College | M
Ohio University | M,D
Oklahoma City University | M
Old Dominion University | M,D,O
Oregon State University | M,D
Ottawa University | M
Our Lady of the Lake University | M
Palm Beach Atlantic University | M
Penn State University Park | M,D,O*
Phillips Graduate University | M
Pittsburg State University | M
Plymouth State University | M
Point Loma Nazarene University | M
Pontifical Catholic University of Puerto Rico | M
Prairie View A&M University | M,D
Prescott College | M,D
Providence College | M
Purdue University Fort Wayne | M,O
Purdue University Northwest | M
Queens College of the City University of New York | M,O
Quincy University | M
Radford University | M
Regent University | M,D,O
Regis University | M,D,O

---

*M—masters degree; D—doctorate; O—other advanced degree; *—Close-Up and/or Display*

Institution	Degrees
Rhode Island College	M,O
Richmont Graduate University	M
Rider University	M,O
Rivier University	M,D,O
Roberts Wesleyan College	M,D
Rollins College	M
Rosemont College	M
Rowan University	M
Rutgers University–New Brunswick	M
Sage Graduate School	M,O
St. Bonaventure University	M,O
St. Cloud State University	M
St. John's University (NY)	M,O
Saint Mary's College of California	M,O
St. Mary's University (United States)	D
Saint Peter's University	M
St. Thomas University	M,O
Saint Xavier University	M
Salem College	M
Salem State University	M
Sam Houston State University	M,D
San Diego State University	M
San Jose State University	M
Santa Clara University	M,O
Seattle Pacific University	M,D,O
Seattle University	M,O
Seton Hall University	M,D
Shippensburg University of Pennsylvania	M,D
Simon Fraser University	M
Slippery Rock University of Pennsylvania	M
South Carolina State University	M
South Dakota State University	M
Southeastern Louisiana University	M
Southeastern Oklahoma State University	M
Southeastern University (FL)	M
Southeast Missouri State University	M,O
Southern Adventist University	M
Southern Arkansas University–Magnolia	M
Southern Connecticut State University	M,O
Southern Methodist University	M,O
Southern University and Agricultural and Mechanical College	M
Southwestern Oklahoma State University	M
Spalding University	M
Springfield College	M,D,O
State University of New York at New Paltz	M,O
State University of New York at Plattsburgh	M,O
State University of New York College at Oneonta	M,O
Stephen F. Austin State University	M
Stephens College	M,O
Stetson University	M
Suffolk University	M,D,O
Sul Ross State University	M
Syracuse University	M
Texas A&M International University	M
Texas A&M University–Central Texas	M,O
Texas A&M University–Commerce	M,D,O
Texas A&M University–Corpus Christi	M,D
Texas A&M University–Kingsville	M
Texas A&M University–San Antonio	M
Texas Christian University	M,D
Texas Southern University	M,D
Texas State University	M
Texas Tech University	M,D
Texas Woman's University	M,D
Trevecca Nazarene University	M,D
Trinity Washington University	M
Troy University	M
Universidad del Turabo	M
Université de Moncton	M
Université Laval	M,D
University at Buffalo, the State University of New York	M,D,O
The University of Akron	M,D
The University of Alabama	M,D,O
The University of Alabama at Birmingham	M
University of Alaska Fairbanks	M,O
University of Alberta	M,D
The University of Arizona	M
University of Arkansas	M
University of Arkansas at Little Rock	M
University of Central Arkansas	M
University of Central Florida	M,O
University of Central Missouri	M,D,O
University of Central Oklahoma	M
University of Cincinnati	M,D,O
University of Colorado Colorado Springs	M,D
University of Colorado Denver	M,D
University of Connecticut	M,D
University of Dayton	M,O
University of Florida	M,D,O
University of Georgia	M,D,O
University of Guam	M
University of Holy Cross	M,D
University of Houston–Clear Lake	M
University of Houston–Victoria	M,O
University of Idaho	M
University of Illinois at Urbana–Champaign	M,D,O
The University of Iowa	M,D

Institution	Degrees
University of La Verne	M,D,O
University of Lethbridge	M,D
University of Louisiana at Lafayette	M
University of Louisiana at Monroe	M
University of Louisville	M,D
University of Lynchburg	M
University of Manitoba	M
University of Mary Hardin-Baylor	M
University of Maryland, College Park	M,D,O
University of Maryland Eastern Shore	M
University of Massachusetts Amherst	M,D,O
University of Massachusetts Boston	M
University of Memphis	M,D
University of Miami	M,O
University of Minnesota, Twin Cities Campus	M
University of Mississippi	M
University of Missouri–Kansas City	M,D,O
University of Missouri–St. Louis	D
University of Montana	M,D,O
University of Montevallo	M
University of Nebraska at Kearney	M,O
University of Nebraska at Omaha	M
University of Nevada, Las Vegas	M,D,O
University of Nevada, Reno	M,D,O
University of New Mexico	M,D
University of New Orleans	M,D
University of North Alabama	M
The University of North Carolina at Chapel Hill	M
The University of North Carolina at Charlotte	M
The University of North Carolina at Greensboro	M
The University of North Carolina at Pembroke	M
University of Northern Colorado	M,D
University of Northern Iowa	M
University of North Florida	M,D
University of North Texas	M,D,O
University of North Texas at Dallas	M
University of Pennsylvania	M*
University of Phoenix–Las Vegas Campus	M
University of Phoenix–Phoenix Campus	M
University of Puerto Rico–Río Piedras	M,D
University of Puget Sound	M
University of Rochester	M,D*
University of Saint Francis (IN)	M,O
University of Saint Joseph	M
University of St. Thomas (TX)	M,D
University of San Diego	M
University of San Francisco	M
The University of Scranton	M
University of South Africa	M,D
University of South Alabama	M,D,O
University of South Carolina	D,O
University of South Dakota	M,D,O
University of Southern California	M
University of Southern Maine	M,O
University of Southern Mississippi	M
University of South Florida	M,D,O
The University of Tennessee	M,D,O
The University of Tennessee at Chattanooga	M,D,O
The University of Tennessee at Martin	M
The University of Texas at Austin	M,D
The University of Texas at El Paso	M
The University of Texas at San Antonio	M,D
The University of Texas of the Permian Basin	M
The University of Texas Rio Grande Valley	M
University of the Cumberlands	M,D,O
University of the Southwest	M
The University of Toledo	M,D,O
University of Utah	M,D,O
University of Vermont	M
University of Victoria	M,D
University of Virginia	M,D,O
The University of West Alabama	M,O
University of West Georgia	M,D,O
University of Wisconsin–Madison	M
University of Wisconsin–Oshkosh	M
University of Wisconsin–River Falls	M,O
University of Wisconsin–Superior	M
University of Wyoming	M,D
Utah State University	M,D
Valdosta State University	M,O
Villanova University	M
Virginia Commonwealth University	M,D
Virginia Polytechnic Institute and State University	M,D
Virginia State University	M
Wake Forest University	M
Walden University	M,D
Walsh University	M
Waynesburg University	M,D
Wayne State College	M
Wayne State University	M,D,O
West Chester University of Pennsylvania	M,O
Western Connecticut State University	M
Western Illinois University	M
Western Kentucky University	M
Western Michigan University	M,D
Western Washington University	M
Westfield State University	M

Institution	Degrees
Westminster College (PA)	M
West Texas A&M University	M
West Virginia University	M,D
Whitworth University	M
Wichita State University	M,D,O
Widener University	M,D
William Paterson University of New Jersey	M,O
Wilmington University	M,D
Winona State University	M,O
Winthrop University	M
Wright State University	M
Xavier University	M*
Xavier University of Louisiana	M
Youngstown State University	M,D,O

CRIMINAL JUSTICE AND CRIMINOLOGY

Institution	Degrees
Adler University	M
Adrian College	M
Albany State University	M
Albertus Magnus College	M
Alliant International University–San Francisco	M
American Public University System	M,D
American University	M,D
American University of Puerto Rico	M
Anderson University (SC)	M
Angelo State University	M
Anna Maria College	M
Arizona State University at the Tempe campus	M,D,O
Arkansas State University	M,O
Ashworth College	M
Auburn University at Montgomery	M
Ball State University	M,O
Bellevue University	M
Boise State University	M
Boston University	M
Bowling Green State University	M,D
Bridgewater State University	M
Buffalo State College, State University of New York	M
Cabrini University	M,D
California Coast University	M
California State University, Fresno	M
California State University, Long Beach	M
California State University, Los Angeles	M
California State University, Sacramento	M
California State University, San Bernardino	M
California State University, Stanislaus	M
California University of Pennsylvania	M
Calumet College of Saint Joseph	M
Capella University	M,D
Cardinal Stritch University	M
Caribbean University	M,D
Carnegie Mellon University	M
The Catholic University of America	M
Central Connecticut State University	M
Chaminade University of Honolulu	M
Charleston Southern University	M
Chicago State University	M
Clark Atlanta University	M
Clayton State University	M
Clemson University	M
Coker College	M
College of Saint Elizabeth	M,O
Colorado State University–Global Campus	M
Colorado Technical University Aurora	M
Colorado Technical University Colorado Springs	M
Columbia College (MO)	M
Columbia College (SC)	M
Columbia Southern University	M
Columbus State University	M
Concordia University, St. Paul	M
Coppin State University	M
Curry College	M
Dallas Baptist University	M
Delaware Valley University	M
Delta State University	M
DeSales University	M,O
East Carolina University	M,O
East Central University	M
Eastern Kentucky University	M
Eastern Michigan University	M
East Tennessee State University	M,O
Fairleigh Dickinson University, Metropolitan Campus	M
Fairmont State University	M
Faulkner University	M
Fayetteville State University	M
Ferris State University	M
Florida Agricultural and Mechanical University	M
Florida Atlantic University	M
Florida Gulf Coast University	M
Florida International University	M,D
Florida State University	M,D
Franklin University	M
Gannon University	M
George Mason University	M,D
The George Washington University	M
Georgia College & State University	M
Georgian Court University	M,O
Georgia Southern University	M,O
Georgia State University	M,D,O
Governors State University	M
The Graduate Center, City University of New York	D
Grambling State University	M
Grand Valley State University	M
Guilford College	M
Hilbert College	M
Holy Family University	M

Institution	Degrees
Howard Payne University	M
Husson University	M
Illinois State University	M
Indiana State University	M
Indiana University Bloomington	M,D
Indiana University Northwest	M,O
Indiana University of Pennsylvania	M,D
Indiana University–Purdue University Indianapolis	M,O
Inter American University of Puerto Rico, Aguadilla Campus	M
Inter American University of Puerto Rico, Barranquitas Campus	M
Inter American University of Puerto Rico, Metropolitan Campus	M
Inter American University of Puerto Rico, Ponce Campus	M
Iona College	M,O
Jackson State University	M
Jacksonville State University	M
John Jay College of Criminal Justice of the City University of New York	M,D
Johnson & Wales University	M
Kean University	M
Keiser University	M
Kennesaw State University	M
Kent State University	M,D
Keuka College	M
Lamar University	M
Lasell College	M,O
Lewis University	M
Liberty University	M,D,O
Lincoln University (MO)	M
Lindenwood University	M,O
Lindenwood University–Belleville	M
Loma Linda University	M,D
London Metropolitan University	M,D
Long Island University–Brentwood Campus	M,O
Long Island University–LIU Post	M,O
Loyola University Chicago	M
Loyola University New Orleans	M
Lynn University	M
Madonna University	M
Marshall University	M
Marywood University	M
McNeese State University	M
Mercer University	M,D
Mercyhurst University	M,O
Methodist University	M
Metropolitan State University	M
Michigan State University	M,D
Middle Tennessee State University	M
Midwestern State University	M
Minnesota State University Mankato	M
Mississippi College	M,O
Mississippi Valley State University	M
Missouri Southern State University	M
Missouri State University	M,O
Molloy College	M
Monmouth University	M,O
Monroe College	M
Morehead State University	M
Mount Mercy University	M
National American University (TX)	M,D
National University	M
New Jersey City University	M,D,O
Niagara University	M
Norfolk State University	M
North Carolina Central University	M
North Dakota State University	M,D
Northeastern State University	M
Northeastern University	M,D
Northern Arizona University	M
Norwich University	M
Nova Southeastern University	M,D,O
Oklahoma City University	M
Old Dominion University	M,D
Penn State Harrisburg	M,D,O
Penn State University Park	M,D*
Point Park University	M
Pontifical Catholic University of Puerto Rico	M
Pontificia Universidad Catolica Madre y Maestra	M
Portland State University	M
Purdue University Global	M
Radford University	M,O
Regent University	M,D,O
Regis University	M
Robert Morris University Illinois	M
Rochester Institute of Technology	M
Roger Williams University	M
Rowan University	M
Rutgers University–Camden	M
Rutgers University–Newark	M,D
Sacred Heart University	M
St. Ambrose University	M
St. Cloud State University	M
St. John's University (NY)	M
Saint Joseph's University	M,O
Saint Leo University	M
Saint Louis University	M*
Saint Mary's University (Canada)	M
St. Mary's University (United States)	M
Saint Peter's University	M
St. Thomas University	M,O
Salem State University	M
Salve Regina University	M,O
Sam Houston State University	M,D
San Diego State University	M
San Francisco State University	M
San Jose State University	M
Seattle University	M,O
Shippensburg University of Pennsylvania	M
Simon Fraser University	M,D
Simpson College	M

Institution	Degree
Slippery Rock University of Pennsylvania	M
Southeast Missouri State University	M
Southern Illinois University Carbondale	M,D
Southern New Hampshire University	M
Southern University and Agricultural and Mechanical College	M
Southern University at New Orleans	M
South University	M
South University (SC)	M
South University (GA)	M
South University (AL)	M
South University	M
Southwestern College (KS)	M
Southwest University	M
Stockton University	M
Suffolk University	M
Sul Ross State University	M
Tarleton State University	M
Temple University	M,D*
Tennessee State University	M
Texas A&M International University	M
Texas A&M University–Central Texas	M,O
Texas A&M University–Commerce	M,D,O
Texas A&M University–Kingsville	M
Texas Christian University	M
Texas Southern University	M,D
Texas State University	M,D
Tiffin University	M
Trident University International	M
Trine University	M
Troy University	M
Universidad del Este	M
Universidad del Turabo	M
Université de Montréal	M,D
University at Albany, State University of New York	M,D
The University of Alabama	M
The University of Alabama at Birmingham	M
University of Alaska Fairbanks	M
University of Alberta	M,D
University of Antelope Valley	M
University of Arkansas at Little Rock	M,D
University of Baltimore	M
University of California, Irvine	M
University of Central Florida	M,D,O
University of Central Missouri	M,D,O
University of Central Oklahoma	M
University of Cincinnati	M,D
University of Colorado Colorado Springs	M
University of Colorado Denver	M,D
University of Delaware	M,D
University of Denver	M,O
University of Detroit Mercy	M,D,O
University of Florida	M
University of Guelph	M,D
University of Houston–Clear Lake	M
University of Houston–Downtown	M
University of Illinois at Chicago	M,D
University of Louisiana at Monroe	M
University of Louisville	M,D
University of Lynchburg	M
University of Management and Technology	M,O
The University of Manchester	M,D
University of Maryland, College Park	M,D
University of Maryland Eastern Shore	M
University of Massachusetts Lowell	M
University of Memphis	M
University of Michigan–Dearborn	M
University of Michigan–Flint	M
University of Minnesota, Duluth	M
University of Mississippi	M,D
University of Missouri–Kansas City	M
University of Missouri–St. Louis	M,D
University of Montana	M
University of Nebraska at Omaha	M,D,O
University of Nevada, Las Vegas	M,D
University of Nevada, Reno	M
University of New Haven	M,D,O
University of North Alabama	M
The University of North Carolina at Charlotte	M
The University of North Carolina at Greensboro	M
The University of North Carolina at Pembroke	M
The University of North Carolina Wilmington	M
University of North Dakota	D
University of Northern Colorado	M
University of North Florida	M
University of North Georgia	M
University of North Texas	M,D,O
University of North Texas at Dallas	M
University of Oklahoma	M,O*
University of Ottawa	M,D
University of Pennsylvania	M,D*
University of Phoenix–Bay Area Campus	M
University of Phoenix–Dallas Campus	M
University of Phoenix–Online Campus	M
University of Phoenix–Phoenix Campus	M
University of Phoenix–San Antonio Campus	M
University of Pittsburgh	M*
University of Providence	M
University of Regina	M
University of San Diego	M
University of South Africa	M,D
University of South Carolina	M,D
University of South Dakota	M
University of Southern Mississippi	M,D
University of South Florida	M,D,O
University of South Florida Sarasota-Manatee	M
The University of Tampa	M
The University of Tennessee	M,D
The University of Tennessee at Chattanooga	M
The University of Texas at Arlington	M
The University of Texas at Dallas	M,D
The University of Texas at San Antonio	M
The University of Texas at Tyler	M
The University of Texas of the Permian Basin	M
The University of Texas Rio Grande Valley	M
University of the Fraser Valley	M
The University of Toledo	M,O
University of Toronto	M,D
University of West Florida	M
University of West Georgia	M,D,O
University of Windsor	M,D
University of Wisconsin–Milwaukee	M,O*
University of Wisconsin–Platteville	M
Urbana University–A Branch Campus of Franklin University	M
Utica College	M
Virginia Commonwealth University	M
Virginia State University	M
Walden University	M,D,O
Waldorf University	M
Washburn University	M
Washington State University	M,D
Wayland Baptist University	M
Waynesburg University	M,D
Wayne State University	M
Webber International University	M
Webster University	M,D,O
West Chester University of Pennsylvania	M
Western Illinois University	M,O
Western Kentucky University	M
Western Oregon University	M
Westfield State University	M
West Texas A&M University	M
West Virginia State University	M
Wichita State University	M
Widener University	M
Wilfrid Laurier University	M
Wilmington University	M
Wright State University	M
Xavier University	M*
Youngstown State University	M

CULTURAL ANTHROPOLOGY

Institution	Degree
Brandeis University	M,D
California Institute of Integral Studies	M,D,O
Concordia University (Canada)	M,D
Cornell University	D
Duke University	D
The Graduate Center, City University of New York	D
Memorial University of Newfoundland	M,D
Rice University	M,D
San Francisco State University	M
Southern Illinois University Edwardsville	M
Southern Methodist University	M,D
University of California, Santa Barbara	M,D
University of California, Santa Cruz	D
University of Denver	M
University of Michigan	D
The University of Tennessee	M,D
University of Wisconsin–Madison	D
Washington State University	M,D

CULTURAL STUDIES

Institution	Degree
American University	M,D,O
The American University of Paris	M
Appalachian State University	M
Arizona State University at the Tempe campus	M,D
Assemblies of God Theological Seminary	M,D
Athabasca University	M,O
Biola University	M,D,O
Boston University	M
Brock University	M
Carnegie Mellon University	D
Central Michigan University	M
Chapman University	M,D,O*
Charlotte Christian College and Theological Seminary	M,D
Claremont Graduate University	M,D,O
Columbia International University	M,D,O
Concordia University Irvine	M,D
Cornell University	M,D
Drew University	M,D,O
Eastern Michigan University	O
Florida State University	M,D
Gardner-Webb University	M,D
George Fox University	M,D,O
George Mason University	D
Georgia State University	M,O
Goucher College	M
Grace Theological Seminary	M,D,O
Graduate Theological Union	M,D,O
Greensboro College	M
Johnson University	M,D,O
Lincoln Christian University	M
Maranatha Baptist University	M
McMaster University	M,D
Nazarene Theological Seminary	M,D,O
New Mexico State University	M,D,O
New York University	M,D,O*
North Central College	M
Northern Kentucky University	M,O
Northwest University	M
Old Dominion University	M,D,O
Pacific Northwest College of Art	M
Plymouth State University	M
Regent University	M,D
St. Francis Xavier University	M
San Francisco State University	M
School of Visual Arts (NY)	M
Simmons University	M,D,O
Simon Fraser University	D
Southern Illinois University Carbondale	M
Stanford University	M,D
Stony Brook University, State University of New York	M,D
Taylor College and Seminary	M,O
Texas A&M University	M
Texas A&M University–Kingsville	M
Texas Tech University	M,D
Trent University	D
Trinity College (United States)	M
Union Institute & University	M,D
Union University	M
University of Alaska Fairbanks	M
University of Arkansas	M,D
University of California, Davis	M,D
University of California, Irvine	D
University of California, Riverside	D
University of California, Santa Barbara	M,D
University of Dayton	M
University of Denver	M,O
University of Hawaii at Hilo	M,D
University of Hawaii at Manoa	O
University of Houston	M
University of Houston–Clear Lake	M
The University of Kansas	M,D
University of Louisiana at Lafayette	M,D
University of Louisville	M,D
The University of Manchester	M,D
University of Massachusetts Boston	M
University of Minnesota, Twin Cities Campus	D
University of Montana	M,D,O
University of New Mexico	M,D
University of North Carolina at Asheville	M,O
The University of North Carolina at Charlotte	M,O
University of Oklahoma	M,D*
University of Pittsburgh	O*
University of Saskatchewan	M
University of Southern California	D
University of Southern Indiana	M
University of Southern Maine	M,O
The University of Texas at Austin	M,D
The University of Texas at San Antonio	M,D
University of the Sacred Heart	M
University of Utah	M,D
University of Washington, Bothell	M
Washington State University	M,D
Wayne State University	M,D
West Chester University of Pennsylvania	M,O
Wilfrid Laurier University	M
Wilson College	M

CURRICULUM AND INSTRUCTION

Institution	Degree
Acadia University	M
Adams State University	M
American College of Education	M
American InterContinental University Online	M
Andrews University	M,D,O
Angelo State University	M
Appalachian State University	M
Arcadia University	M,D,O
Arizona State University at the Tempe campus	M
Arlington Baptist University	M
Auburn University	M,D,O
Augusta University	M,O
Aurora University	M,D
Averett University	M
Azusa Pacific University	M
Ball State University	M,D
Barry University	D,O
Baylor University	M,D
Berry College	M
Biola University	M,O
Black Hills State University	M
Bloomsburg University of Pennsylvania	M
Bluffton University	M
Bob Jones University	M,D,O
Boise State University	M,D,O
Boston College	M
Bowling Green State University	M
Bradley University	M
Brandman University	M,D
Brandon University	M,O
Brescia University	M
Buena Vista University	M
Cabrini University	M,D
California Baptist University	M
California Coast University	M,D
California State Polytechnic University, Pomona	M
California State University, Chico	M
California State University, Fresno	M
California State University, Los Angeles	M
California State University, Northridge	M
California State University, Sacramento	M,D,O
California State University, Stanislaus	M
Calvary University	M
Calvin College	M
Cambridge College	M,D,O
Capella University	M,D
Caribbean University	M,D
Carlow University	M
Carson-Newman University	M
Castleton University	M
Central Michigan University	M,D,O
Central Washington University	M
Chapman University	M,D,O*
City University of Seattle	M,O
Clarion University of Pennsylvania	M
Clark Atlanta University	M
Clarks Summit University	M
Clemson University	M,D,O
Coker College	M
The College at Brockport, State University of New York	M,O
The College of Idaho	M
The College of Saint Rose	M,O
The College of William and Mary	M
Colorado Christian University	M
Columbia International University	M,D,O
Columbus State University	M,D,O
Concordia University (United States)	M,D
Concordia University Ann Arbor	M
Concordia University Chicago	M
Concordia University Irvine	M
Concordia University, St. Paul	M,D,O
Coppin State University	M
Cornell University	M,D
Dakota Wesleyan University	M
Dallas Baptist University	M
Delaware State University	M
Delaware Valley University	M
DePaul University	M,D
DeVry University–Folsom Campus	M
Doane University	M,D,O
Drexel University	M,D*
Drury University	M
Duquesne University	M,O
East Carolina University	M,O
Eastern Illinois University	M
Eastern Kentucky University	M
Eastern Mennonite University	M
Eastern Michigan University	M,O
Eastern New Mexico University	M
Eastern Washington University	M
East Tennessee State University	M,O
Emporia State University	M
Evangel University	M,D
Fairleigh Dickinson University, Metropolitan Campus	M,O
Faulkner University	M
Ferris State University	M
Fitchburg State University	M
Florida Atlantic University	M,D,O
Florida Gulf Coast University	M
Florida International University	M,D,O
Florida State University	M,D,O
Fontbonne University	M
Fordham University	M,O
Framingham State University	M
Franciscan University of Steubenville	M
Franklin Pierce University	M,D,O
Freed-Hardeman University	M,O
Fresno Pacific University	M
Frostburg State University	M,D
Furman University	M,O
Gannon University	M,O
Gardner-Webb University	M,D,O
George Mason University	M
The George Washington University	M,D,O
Georgia College & State University	M
Georgia Southern University	M,D
Georgia State University	M,D
Graceland University (IA)	M
Grambling State University	M,D,O
Grand Canyon University	M,D,O
Grand Valley State University	M
Harvard University	M*
Henderson State University	M
Hood College	M,O
Houston Baptist University	M,D
Illinois State University	M,D
Indiana State University	M,D
Indiana University Bloomington	M,D,O
Indiana University of Pennsylvania	D
Indiana University–Purdue University Indianapolis	M,O
Inter American University of Puerto Rico, Arecibo Campus	M
Inter American University of Puerto Rico, Barranquitas Campus	M
Inter American University of Puerto Rico, Metropolitan Campus	M,D
Inter American University of Puerto Rico, San Germán Campus	D

*M—masters degree; D—doctorate; O—other advanced degree; *—Close-Up and/or Display*

Iowa State University of Science and Technology	M,D
Iowa Wesleyan University	M
John Brown University	M
Kansas State University	M,D,O
Kean University	M
Kennesaw State University	O
Kent State University	M,D,O
Kent State University at Stark	M
Kutztown University of Pennsylvania	M,D
LaGrange College	M,O
Lasell College	M,O
La Sierra University	M,D,O
Lee University	M,O
Lehigh University	M,D,O
Lesley University	M,D,O
LeTourneau University	M
Lewis & Clark College	M
Lewis University	M
Lincoln Memorial University	M,D,O
Louisiana State University in Shreveport	M,D
Louisiana Tech University	M,D,O
Lourdes University	M
Loyola University Chicago	M,D
Loyola University Maryland	M
Malone University	M
Marian University (WI)	M,D
Marquette University	M,D,O
Martin Luther College	M,O
Marygrove College	M
Marymount University	M
Massachusetts College of Liberal Arts	M,O
McDaniel College	M
McGill University	M,D,O
McKendree University	M,D,O
McNeese State University	M
Medaille College	M
Memorial University of Newfoundland	M,D,O
Mercer University	M,D,O
Mercer University	M,D,O
Messiah College	M
Metropolitan State University	M
Michigan State University	M,D,O
Middle Tennessee State University	M,O
Midwestern State University	M
Misericordia University	M
Mississippi College	M,D,O
Mississippi State University	M,D,O
Mississippi University for Women	M
Montana State University	M,D,O
Montana State University Billings	M
Montclair State University	M
Moravian College	M
Morehead State University	M,O
Mount Saint Vincent University	M
National Louis University	M,D,O
Newman University	M
New Mexico Highlands University	M
Nicholls State University	M
North Carolina State University	M,D
Northern Arizona University	M,D
Northern Illinois University	M,D
Northern Michigan University	M
Northern State University	M
Northern Vermont University– Johnson	M
Northern Vermont University– Lyndon	M
Northwestern Oklahoma State University	M
Northwestern State University of Louisiana	
Northwest Nazarene University	M,D,O
Notre Dame de Namur University	M
Oakland City University	M,D
Ohio Dominican University	M
Ohio University	M,D
Ohio Valley University	M
Oklahoma State University	M,D
Old Dominion University	M,D
Olivet Nazarene University	M,D
Oral Roberts University	M,D
Ottawa University	M
Our Lady of the Lake University	M
Pacific Lutheran University	M
Park University	M,O
Penn State Harrisburg	M,D,O
Penn State University Park	M,D,O*
Penn State York	M,O
Pensacola Christian College	M,D,O
Peru State College	M
Piedmont College	M,D,O
Piedmont International University	M,D
Plymouth State University	D
Point Park University	M,D
Pontifical Catholic University of Puerto Rico	M,D
Post University	M
Prairie View A&M University	M,D,O
Purdue University	M,D,O
Quincy University	M
Randolph College	M
Regent University	M,D,O
Regis University	M,O
Rivier University	M,D,O
St. Catherine University	M
St. Francis Xavier University	M
St. John's University (NY)	D
Saint Joseph's University	M,D,O
Saint Louis University	M,D*
Saint Vincent College	M
Saint Xavier University	M
Salem International University	M
Salisbury University	M,D
Sam Houston State University	M,D
San Diego State University	M
San Jose State University	M
Shawnee State University	M
Shaw University	M
Shepherd University (WV)	M

Shippensburg University of Pennsylvania	M
Simon Fraser University	M,D
Simpson University	M
Sitting Bull College	M
Sonoma State University	M,O
South Dakota State University	M
Southeastern Louisiana University	M
Southeastern University (FL)	M,D
Southern Arkansas University– Magnolia	M
Southern Illinois University Carbondale	M,D
Southern Illinois University Edwardsville	M
Southern New Hampshire University	M,D,O
Southwestern Adventist University	M
Southwestern Assemblies of God University	M
Southwestern College (KS)	M,D
Stanford University	M,D
State University of New York at Fredonia	M
State University of New York at Oswego	M
State University of New York at Plattsburgh	M
State University of New York College at Potsdam	M
Syracuse University	M,D,O
Tarleton State University	M
Teachers College, Columbia University	M,D
Tennessee State University	M
Tennessee Technological University	M,O
Texas A&M International University	M
Texas A&M University	M,D
Texas A&M University–Central Texas	M,O
Texas A&M University– Commerce	M,D,O
Texas A&M University–Corpus Christi	M,D
Texas A&M University– Texarkana	M
Texas Christian University	M,D
Texas Southern University	M,D
Texas Tech University	M,D
Texas Woman's University	M,D
Trevecca Nazarene University	M,O
Trinity Baptist College	M
Trinity Washington University	M
Tusculum University	M
Universidad Adventista de las Antillas	M
Universidad del Turabo	M,D
Universidad Metropolitana	M
Université de Montréal	M,D,O
Université Laval	M,D
University at Albany, State University of New York	M,D,O
University at Buffalo, the State University of New York	M,D,O
The University of Akron	M
The University of Alabama at Birmingham	O
University of Arkansas	M,D,O
University of Arkansas at Little Rock	M
The University of British Columbia	M,D
University of Calgary	M,D
University of California, Davis	M,D
University of California, San Diego	M
University of Central Arkansas	M,O
University of Central Florida	M,O
University of Cincinnati	M,D
University of Colorado Boulder	M,D
University of Colorado Colorado Springs	M,D
University of Connecticut	M,D
University of Delaware	M,D,O
University of Denver	M,D,O
University of Detroit Mercy	M,D,O
University of Florida	M,D,O
University of Hawaii at Manoa	M,D
University of Houston–Clear Lake	M
University of Houston– Downtown	M
University of Houston– Victoria	M,O
University of Idaho	M,O
University of Illinois at Chicago	M,D
University of Illinois at Urbana–Champaign	M,D,O
University of Indianapolis	M
University of Jamestown	M
The University of Kansas	M,D
University of Kentucky	M,D
University of Louisiana at Lafayette	M
University of Louisiana at Monroe	M,D
University of Louisville	M,D,O
University of Lynchburg	M
University of Manitoba	M
University of Mary	M,D
University of Mary Hardin-Baylor	M
University of Maryland, College Park	M,D,O
University of Massachusetts Lowell	M,D
University of Memphis	M,D,O
University of Michigan– Dearborn	D,O
University of Michigan–Flint	M,D,O
University of Minnesota, Twin Cities Campus	M,D
University of Missouri	M,D,O
University of Missouri– Kansas City	M,D,O
University of Missouri–St. Louis	M
University of Montana	M
University of Nebraska at Kearney	M

University of Nebraska– Lincoln	M,D,O
University of Nevada, Las Vegas	M,D,O
University of Nevada, Reno	D
University of New England	M,D,O
University of New Hampshire	D,O
University of New Orleans	M
The University of North Carolina at Chapel Hill	M,D
The University of North Carolina at Charlotte	M,D,O
The University of North Carolina at Greensboro	M,D,O
The University of North Carolina Wilmington	M,D
University of Northern Colorado	M,D
University of Northern Iowa	D
University of North Georgia	M
University of North Texas	M,D
University of North Texas at Dallas	M
University of Oklahoma	M,D*
University of Oregon	M,D
University of Phoenix– Central Valley Campus	M
University of Phoenix–Dallas Campus	M
University of Phoenix–Hawaii Campus	M
University of Phoenix– Houston Campus	M
University of Phoenix–Las Vegas Campus	M
University of Phoenix–Online Campus	M,D,O
University of Phoenix– Phoenix Campus	M
University of Phoenix– Sacramento Valley Campus	M,O
University of Phoenix–San Antonio Campus	M
University of Phoenix–San Diego Campus	M
University of Puerto Rico– Río Piedras	M,D
University of Regina	M
University of Rochester	M,D*
University of St. Francis (IL)	M,D,O
University of Saint Joseph	M
University of St. Thomas (TX)	M,D
University of San Diego	M
University of San Francisco	M,D
University of Saskatchewan	M,D,O
The University of Scranton	M
University of South Africa	M,D
University of South Carolina	D
University of South Dakota	M
University of Southern Mississippi	M,D
University of South Florida Sarasota-Manatee	M
The University of Tampa	M
The University of Tennessee	M,D,O
The University of Tennessee at Martin	M
The University of Texas at Arlington	M
The University of Texas at Austin	M,D
The University of Texas at El Paso	M,D
The University of Texas at San Antonio	M,D
The University of Texas Rio Grande Valley	M,D
University of the Pacific	M,D,O
University of the Southwest	M
The University of Toledo	M,D,O
University of Vermont	M
University of Victoria	M,D
University of Virginia	M,D,O
University of Washington	M,D
The University of Western Ontario	M,D
University of West Florida	M,O
University of Wisconsin– Madison	M,D
University of Wisconsin– Milwaukee	M,D,O*
University of Wisconsin– Oshkosh	M
University of Wisconsin– Superior	M
University of Wyoming	M,D
Utah State University	D
Vanguard University of Southern California	M
Virginia Commonwealth University	D
Virginia Polytechnic Institute and State University	M,D,O
Virginia Union University	M
Walden University	M
Walla Walla University	M
Warner University	M
Washburn University	M
Washington State University	M,D
Waynesburg University	M,D
Wayne State College	M
Wayne State University	M,D,O
Weber State University	M
Western Connecticut State University	M
Western Illinois University	M
Western New England University	M
West Texas A&M University	M
West Virginia University	M,D
Wichita State University	M
William Woods University	M,D,O
Wisconsin Lutheran College	M
Worcester State University	M,O
Wright State University	O
Xavier University of Louisiana	M
Youngstown State University	M

DANCE

Arizona State University at the Tempe campus	M,D
Bennington College	M

California Institute of the Arts	M,O
California State University, Long Beach	M
Case Western Reserve University	M
The College at Brockport, State University of New York	M
Eastern Michigan University	M
Florida State University	M
The George Washington University	M,O
Hollins University	M
Jacksonville University	M
Mills College	M
New York University	M,D,O*
Northern Illinois University	M
The Ohio State University	M,D
Saint Mary's College of California	M
Sam Houston State University	M
Sarah Lawrence College	M
Smith College	M
Temple University	M,D*
Texas Woman's University	M,D
Tulane University	M
Université du Québec à Montréal	M
University at Buffalo, the State University of New York	M,D
The University of Arizona	M
University of California, Irvine	M
University of California, Los Angeles	M,D
University of California, Riverside	M
University of California, San Diego	M,D
University of Colorado Boulder	M,D
University of Hawaii at Manoa	M,D
University of Illinois at Urbana–Champaign	M
The University of Iowa	M
University of Maryland, Baltimore County	M
University of Maryland, College Park	M
University of Michigan	M
University of New Mexico	M
The University of North Carolina at Greensboro	M
University of Oklahoma	M*
University of Oregon	M
The University of Texas at Austin	M,D
The University of the Arts	M
University of Washington	M
University of Wisconsin– Milwaukee	M,O*
Washington University in St. Louis	M
Wayne State University	M,D,O
Wilson College	M
York University	M,D

DATA SCIENCE/DATA ANALYTICS

American University	M
Austin Peay State University	M
Azusa Pacific University	M,O
Boston University	M
Brandman University	M
Buffalo State College, State University of New York	M
Central European University	D
Claremont Graduate University	M,D,O
Clarion University of Pennsylvania	M
College of Saint Elizabeth	M
College of Staten Island of the City University of New York	M,O
Colorado Technical University Aurora	
Colorado Technical University Colorado Springs	M,D
Columbia University	M
DePaul University	M,D
DeSales University	M,O
Elmhurst College	M
Fairfield University	M,O
Fitchburg State University	M
Florida International University	M,D
Fordham University	M
George Mason University	M,D,O
The Graduate Center, City University of New York	
Grand Canyon University	D
HEC Montreal	D
IGlobal University	M
Illinois Institute of Technology	M,D
Indiana University Bloomington	M,O
Indiana University–Purdue University Indianapolis	M,D,O
Johnson & Wales University	M
Kansas State University	M,O
Keck Graduate Institute	M
Kennesaw State University	M,D,O
Lawrence Technological University	M,O
Lewis University	M
Lipscomb University	M,O
London Metropolitan University	M,D
Manhattan College	M
Maryville University of Saint Louis	M
Merrimack College	M
Metropolitan State University	M,D,O
Michigan Technological University	M,D,O
Montclair State University	O
National University	M
New College of Florida	M
New Jersey Institute of Technology	M
The New School	M
New York University	M*
Northcentral University	M
Northeastern University	M,D
Northwestern University	M
Ohio Dominican University	M
Oregon State University	M
Penn State Great Valley	M,O
Queens College of the City University of New York	M

Radford University	M
Regis University	M,O
Robert Morris University	M,D
Rochester Institute of Technology	O
Rockhurst University	M,O
St. John's University (NY)	M
Saint Mary's College	M
Saint Mary's University of Minnesota	M
Saint Peter's University	M
Seattle Pacific University	M
Slippery Rock University of Pennsylvania	M
Southern Arkansas University–Magnolia	M
Southern Methodist University	M,D
Southern New Hampshire University	M,D,O
Stockton University	M
Suffolk University	M
Syracuse University	M,O
Texas Tech University	M
Tufts University	M,D
University at Buffalo, the State University of New York	M,D
The University of Arizona	M
University of California, Berkeley	M
University of California, San Diego	M
University of Colorado Denver	M
University of Denver	M,D
University of Houston–Downtown	M
University of Illinois at Springfield	M
University of Louisville	M,D,O
University of Maryland, Baltimore County	M
University of Maryland University College	M,O
University of Massachusetts Dartmouth	M
University of Michigan	M,D,O
University of Michigan–Dearborn	M,D
University of Minnesota, Twin Cities Campus	M
University of Mississippi	M,D
University of Nebraska at Omaha	M,D,O
University of Nevada, Las Vegas	M,O
The University of North Carolina at Charlotte	M,O
The University of North Carolina Wilmington	M
University of Pennsylvania	M*
University of Pittsburgh	M,D,O*
University of Rochester	M*
University of St. Thomas (MN)	M
University of San Francisco	M
University of Southern Indiana	M
University of South Florida	M,D,O
The University of Tennessee	D
The University of Texas at Dallas	M,D
The University of Texas Health Science Center at Houston	M,D,O
University of Vermont	M
University of Virginia	M
University of Washington	M,D
University of West Florida	M
University of Wisconsin–La Crosse	M
University of Wisconsin–Stevens Point	M
Virginia International University	M,O
Walsh College of Accountancy and Business Administration	M
Washington University in St. Louis	M
Wayne State University	M,D,O
Weill Cornell Medicine	
Western Governors University	M
Worcester Polytechnic Institute	M,D,O
Yeshiva University	M

DECORATIVE ARTS

Bard Graduate Center	M,D
The George Washington University	M
Sotheby's Institute of Art–London	M
Sotheby's Institute of Art–New York	M

DEMOGRAPHY AND POPULATION STUDIES

Bowling Green State University	M,D
Cornell University	M,D
Florida State University	M,D
Harvard University	M,D*
Johns Hopkins University	M,D*
Miami University	M,D
New York University	M,D*
Princeton University	D,O
Université de Montréal	M,D
Université du Québec, Institut National de la Recherche Scientifique	M,D,O
University at Albany, State University of New York	M,D,O
University of Alberta	M,D
University of California, Berkeley	M,D
University of California, Irvine	M
University of Colorado Denver	D
University of Guelph	M,D
University of Hawaii at Manoa	O
University of Pennsylvania	M,D*
University of Puerto Rico–Medical Sciences Campus	M
The University of Texas at San Antonio	D
The University of Texas Medical Branch	D
University of Wisconsin–Madison	M,D

DENTAL HYGIENE

Eastern Washington University	M
Idaho State University	M
Missouri Southern State University	M
The Ohio State University	M,D
Old Dominion University	M
Texas Woman's University	M,D
Université de Montréal	O
University of Alberta	O
University of Bridgeport	M
University of Michigan	M
University of Missouri–Kansas City	M,D,O
University of New Mexico	M
The University of North Carolina at Chapel Hill	M,D
West Virginia University	M,D

DENTISTRY

A.T. Still University	M,D,O
Augusta University	D
Boston University	M,D,O
Case Western Reserve University	D
Columbia University	D
Creighton University	D
East Carolina University	D
Harvard University	M,D,O*
Howard University	D,O
Idaho State University	O
Indiana University–Purdue University Indianapolis	M,D,O
Jacksonville University	M,O
Loma Linda University	M,D,O
Louisiana State University Health Sciences Center	D
Marquette University	M,D,O
McGill University	M,D,O
Medical University of South Carolina	D
Meharry Medical College	D
Midwestern University, Downers Grove Campus	D
Midwestern University, Glendale Campus	D
New York University	D*
Nova Southeastern University	M,D
The Ohio State University	M,D
Oregon Health & Science University	D,O
Roseman University of Health Sciences	M,D,O
Rutgers University–Newark	M,D,O
Saint Louis University	M*
Southern Illinois University Edwardsville	D
Stony Brook University, State University of New York	D,O
Temple University	D*
Texas A&M University	M
Tufts University	D
Universidad Central del Este	D
Universidad Iberoamericana	D
Universidad Nacional Pedro Henriquez Urena	D
Université Laval	D
The University of Alabama at Birmingham	D
University of Alberta	D
The University of British Columbia	D
University of California, Los Angeles	D,O
University of California, San Francisco	D
University of Colorado Denver	D,O
University of Connecticut Health Center	D,O
University of Detroit Mercy	M,D,O
University of Florida	D,O
University of Illinois at Chicago	D
The University of Iowa	M,D,O
University of Kentucky	D
University of Louisville	M,D
The University of Manchester	M,D
University of Manitoba	D
University of Maryland, Baltimore	D,O
University of Michigan	D
University of Minnesota, Twin Cities Campus	D
University of Mississippi Medical Center	M,D
University of Missouri–Kansas City	M,D,O
University of Nebraska Medical Center	M,D,O
University of Nevada, Las Vegas	M,D,O
University of New England	D
The University of North Carolina at Chapel Hill	D
University of Oklahoma Health Sciences Center	D,O
University of Pennsylvania	D*
University of Pittsburgh	M,D,O*
University of Puerto Rico–Medical Sciences Campus	D
University of Saskatchewan	D
University of Southern California	D
The University of Tennessee Health Science Center	D
The University of Texas Health Science Center at Houston	M,D
The University of Texas Health Science Center at San Antonio	M,D,O
University of the Pacific	M,D,O
University of Toronto	D
University of Utah	D
University of Washington	D
The University of Western Ontario	D
Virginia Commonwealth University	M,D
Western University of Health Sciences	M,D
West Virginia University	M,D

DEVELOPMENTAL BIOLOGY

Albert Einstein College of Medicine	D
Baylor College of Medicine	D
Brigham Young University	M,D
California Institute of Technology	D
California State University, Sacramento	M
Carnegie Mellon University	M,D
Columbia University	M,D
Cornell University	M,D
Dalhousie University	M,D
Duke University	O
Emory University	D
Illinois State University	M,D
Iowa State University of Science and Technology	M,D
Irell & Manella Graduate School of Biological Sciences	D
Johns Hopkins University	D*
Louisiana State University Health Sciences Center	D
Marquette University	M,D
Massachusetts Institute of Technology	D
Medical University of South Carolina	D
New York University	M,D*
Northwestern University	D
The Ohio State University	M,D
Oregon Health & Science University	D
Penn State Hershey Medical Center	D
Purdue University	M,D
Rutgers University–New Brunswick	M,D
San Francisco State University	M
Stanford University	M,D
Stony Brook University, State University of New York	M,D
Thomas Jefferson University	M
Tufts University	D
The University of Alabama at Birmingham	D
The University of British Columbia	M,D
University of California, Davis	M,D
University of California, Irvine	M,D
University of California, Los Angeles	M,D
University of California, Riverside	M,D
University of California, San Francisco	D
University of California, Santa Barbara	M,D
University of California, Santa Cruz	M,D
University of Chicago	D
University of Cincinnati	D
University of Colorado Boulder	M,D
University of Colorado Denver	M,D
University of Connecticut	M,D
University of Connecticut Health Center	D
University of Delaware	M,D
University of Hawaii at Manoa	M,D
University of Illinois at Urbana–Champaign	D
The University of Kansas	D
The University of Manchester	M,D
University of Massachusetts Amherst	D
University of Miami	D
University of Michigan	M,D
University of Minnesota, Twin Cities Campus	M,D
University of Montana	D
The University of North Carolina at Chapel Hill	M,D
University of Pennsylvania	D*
University of Pittsburgh	D*
University of South Carolina	D
University of Southern California	D
The University of Texas Southwestern Medical Center	D
Vanderbilt University	M,D*
Washington University in St. Louis	D
Wesleyan University	D
West Virginia University	M,D
Yale University	D

DEVELOPMENTAL EDUCATION

East Tennessee State University	M,O
Ferris State University	M
Grambling State University	M,D,O
Instituto Tecnológico y de Estudios Superiores de Monterrey, Campus Ciudad Obregón	M
National Louis University	M,D,O
Penn State Harrisburg	M,D,O
Rutgers University–New Brunswick	M
Sam Houston State University	M,D
Texas State University	M,D
The University of Iowa	M,D
Walden University	M,D,O

DEVELOPMENTAL PSYCHOLOGY

Adler University	M
Andrews University	M,D
Arizona State University at the Tempe campus	M,D
Azusa Pacific University	M
Bay Path University	M
Boston College	M,D
Boston Graduate School of Psychoanalysis	O
Bowling Green State University	M,D
Brandeis University	M,D
Capella University	M
Carnegie Mellon University	D
Chatham University	M,D

DEVELOPMENTAL BIOLOGY (continued)

Claremont Graduate University	M,D,O
Clark University	D
Clayton State University	M
Cornell University	M,D
Delaware Valley University	M
Duke University	D
Emory University	M,O
Erikson Institute	M,D,O
Fielding Graduate University	M,D
Florida International University	D
Florida State University	D
Fordham University	M,D,O
George Mason University	D
Georgia State University	D
The Graduate Center, City University of New York	D*
Harvard University	M,D
Howard University	M
Humboldt State University	M,D,O
Illinois State University	D
Indiana University Bloomington	M,D
La Salle University	M,D
Liberty University	M,D
Louisiana State University and Agricultural & Mechanical College	M,D,O
Loyola University Chicago	D
McGill University	M,D*
New York University	D
North Carolina State University	D
North Dakota State University	M,D
The Ohio State University	M
Pace University	M
Pontificia Universidad Catolica Madre y Maestra	M,D
Queen's University at Kingston	M,D,O
Regis University	M,O
San Francisco State University	M,D
Teachers College, Columbia University	M,D
Texas Christian University	M,D
Université de Montréal	M,D
The University of Alabama at Birmingham	M,D
The University of British Columbia	M,D
University of Connecticut	D
University of Denver	D
University of Houston	M,D
University of Illinois at Chicago	M,D
The University of Kansas	M,D
University of Louisville	M,D
The University of Manchester	D
University of Maryland, Baltimore County	M,D
University of Maryland, College Park	M,D
University of Massachusetts Amherst	M,D
University of Miami	M,D,O*
University of Michigan	M
University of Montana	M,D
University of Nebraska–Lincoln	D
University of New Mexico	D
The University of North Carolina at Chapel Hill	M,D
The University of North Carolina at Greensboro	D
University of Notre Dame	D
University of Oregon	M,D*
University of Pittsburgh	D*
University of Rochester	D
University of Southern California	M,D
The University of Texas at Austin	D
University of Utah	D
University of Vermont	M,D
University of Victoria	M,D
University of Washington	D
University of Wisconsin–Madison	M,D,O*
University of Wisconsin–Milwaukee	M
Viterbo University	M,D
Washington University in St. Louis	D
Wilfrid Laurier University	
Yale University	

DISABILITY STUDIES

Brandeis University	D
Brock University	M,O
Chapman University	M,D,O*
Montclair State University	M,O
Syracuse University	O
University of Hawaii at Manoa	O
University of Illinois at Chicago	M,D
University of Manitoba	M
University of Northern British Columbia	M,D,O
University of Pittsburgh	O*
Utah State University	M,D
York University	M,D

DISTANCE EDUCATION DEVELOPMENT

Athabasca University	M,D,O
Barry University	O
Boise State University	M,D,O
Brandeis University	M
California Baptist University	M
Capella University	M,D
Carlow University	M,O
Clemson University	M,O
Coastal Carolina University	M,O
College of Saint Elizabeth	M,O
Colorado Christian University	M
Dallas Baptist University	M
East Carolina University	M,O
Eastern Michigan University	M,O
Emporia State University	M
Endicott College	O
The George Washington University	M,D,O
Kansas State University	M,D,O

M—masters degree; D—doctorate; O—other advanced degree; *—Close-Up and/or Display

Keiser University	M
Lenoir-Rhyne University	M
Lesley University	M,D,O
Millersville University of Pennsylvania	M,D
National University	M,O
Nova Southeastern University	M,D,O
Post University	M
Regent University	M,D,O
Télé-université	M,D
Thomas Edison State University	M,O
University at Buffalo, the State University of New York	M,D,O
University of Colorado Denver	M
University of Maryland, Baltimore County	M,O
University of Maryland University College	M
University of Nevada, Las Vegas	M,D,O
University of South Florida	O
Virginia Polytechnic Institute and State University	M,O
Walden University	M,D,O
Waynesburg University	M,D
Wayne State University	M,D,O
Western Illinois University	M,O
Wilkes University	M

EARLY CHILDHOOD EDUCATION

Alabama Agricultural and Mechanical University	M,D,O
Alabama State University	M,O
Albany State University	M,O
Albright College	M
American International College	M,D,O
Anna Maria College	M,O
Antioch University New England	M
Arcadia University	M
Arkansas State University	M,D,O
Auburn University at Montgomery	M,O
Avila University	M,O
Bank Street College of Education	M
Barry University	M,D,O
Bayamón Central University	M,O
Binghamton University, State University of New York	M
Biola University	M,O
Bloomsburg University of Pennsylvania	M
Boise State University	M
Boston College	M,D,O
Brandman University	M
Brenau University	M,O
Bridgewater State University	M
Brooklyn College of the City University of New York	M,O
Buffalo State College, State University of New York	M
Cabrini University	M,D
California State University, Dominguez Hills	M
California State University, East Bay	M
California State University, Fresno	M
California State University, Northridge	M
California State University, Sacramento	M,D,O
California University of Pennsylvania	M
Cambridge College	M,D,O
Canisius College	M
Capella University	M
Caribbean University	M,D
Carlow University	M
Carroll University	M
The Catholic University of America	M,O
Central Connecticut State University	M
Central Michigan University	M,O
Chaminade University of Honolulu	M
Champlain College	M
Chatham University	M
Chestnut Hill College	M
Chicago State University	M
The Citadel, The Military College of South Carolina	M,O
City College of the City University of New York	M
Clarion University of Pennsylvania	M
Clemson University	M,D,O
Cleveland State University	M
The College at Brockport, State University of New York	M
College of Charleston	M
The College of New Jersey	M
The College of New Rochelle	M
College of Saint Elizabeth	M
The College of Saint Rose	M,O
College of Staten Island of the City University of New York	M
Colorado Christian University	M
Columbia International University	M,D,O
Columbus State University	M,O
Concordia University (United States)	M,D
Concordia University Chicago	M
Concordia University, Nebraska	M
Concordia University, St. Paul	M,D,O
Concordia University Wisconsin	M
Daemen College	M
Dallas Baptist University	M,D
DePaul University	M
Dickinson State University	M
Dominican University	M
Duquesne University	M
East Carolina University	M
Eastern Connecticut State University	M
Eastern Illinois University	M
Eastern Michigan University	M
Eastern Nazarene College	M,O
Eastern New Mexico University	M

Eastern University	M,O
Eastern Washington University	M
East Stroudsburg University of Pennsylvania	M
East Tennessee State University	M,D,O
Edinboro University of Pennsylvania	M
Elms College	M,O
Emporia State University	M
Endicott College	M
Erikson Institute	M,D
Fairleigh Dickinson University, Florham Campus	M,O
Fairleigh Dickinson University, Metropolitan Campus	M
Fielding Graduate University	M,D,O
Fitchburg State University	M
Five Towns College	M,D
Florida Atlantic University	M,D
Florida International University	M,D,O
Fontbonne University	M
Fordham University	M,O
Framingham State University	M
Furman University	M,O
Gallaudet University	M,D,O
Gateway Seminary	M,D,O
George Mason University	M
The George Washington University	M
Georgia College & State University	M
Georgia Southwestern State University	M,D,O
Georgia State University	M,D,O
Gordon College	M,O
Governors State University	M
Grand Canyon University	M,D,O
Grand Valley State University	M
Harding University	M,O
Hebrew College	M,O
Henderson State University	M,O
Hofstra University	M,D,O
Holy Family University	M
Hunter College of the City University of New York	M,D,O
Indiana University–Purdue University Indianapolis	M,O
Inter American University of Puerto Rico, Guayama Campus	M
Iona College	M
Jackson State University	M,D,O
Jacksonville State University	M
James Madison University	M
Jose Maria Vargas University	M
Kansas State University	M,D,O
Kean University	M
Kennesaw State University	M
Kent State University	M,D,O
Keuka College	M
Keystone College	M
Lander University	M
La Salle University	M,O
Lee University	M,O
Lehigh University	M,D,O
Lehman College of the City University of New York	M
Le Moyne College	M,O
Lesley University	M,D,O
Lewis University	M
Lincoln University (PA)	M
London Metropolitan University	M,D
Long Island University– Brentwood Campus	M,O
Long Island University– Hudson	M,O
Long Island University–LIU Brooklyn	M,O
Long Island University–LIU Post	M,D,O
Long Island University– Riverhead	M,O
Louisiana Tech University	M,D,O
Loyola University Maryland	M,O
Lynn University	M,D
Manhattan College	M,O
Manhattanville College	M,O
Martin Luther College	M
Marygrove College	M,O
Maryville University of Saint Louis	M,D
Marywood University	M
McNeese State University	O
Mercer University	M,D,O
Mercer University	M,D,O
Mercy College	M
Middle Tennessee State University	M,O
Millersville University of Pennsylvania	M
Milligan College	M,D,O
Mills College	M
Mississippi State University	M,D,O
Missouri Southern State University	M
Missouri State University	M
Missouri Western State University	M
Molloy College	M,O
Monmouth University	M,O
Mount St. Joseph University	M,O
Murray State University	M
National Louis University	M,D,O
Nazareth College of Rochester	M
New Jersey City University	M
New Mexico State University	M,D,O
New York Institute of Technology	M
New York University	M*
Niagara University	M,O
Norfolk State University	M
North Carolina Agricultural and Technical State University	M
Northeastern Illinois University	M
Northeastern State University	M
Northern Arizona University	M,D,O
Northern Illinois University	M
Northwestern College	M
Northwestern State University of Louisiana	M

Northwest Missouri State University	M,D,O
Oakland University	M,D,O
Oklahoma City University	M
Old Dominion University	M,D
Ottawa University	M
Pace University	M,O
Pacific Oaks College	M
Pacific University	M
Piedmont College	M,D,O
Pontificia Universidad Catolica Madre y Maestra	M
Prescott College	M,D
Queens College of the City University of New York	M,O
Radford University	M
Regent University	M
Reinhardt University	M
Rhode Island College	M
Rider University	M
Rivier University	M,D,O
Roberts Wesleyan College	M
Rockford University	M
Roosevelt University	M
Rutgers University–New Brunswick	M,D
Saginaw Valley State University	M
St. Ambrose University	M
St. Bonaventure University	M
St. Catherine University	M
St. John's University (NY)	M,D,O
Saint Joseph's University	M
Saint Mary's College of California	M
Saint Xavier University	M
Salem State University	M
San Francisco State University	M,D,O
San Ignacio University	M
Shenandoah University	M,D,O
Shippensburg University of Pennsylvania	M
Siena Heights University	M
Sonoma State University	M,O
South Carolina State University	M
Southern New Hampshire University	M,D,O
Southern Oregon University	M
Southwestern College (KS)	M,D
Southwestern Oklahoma State University	M
Southwest Minnesota State University	M
Springfield College	M,O
Spring Hill College	M
State University of New York at Fredonia	M
State University of New York at New Paltz	M
State University of New York at Oswego	M
State University of New York at Plattsburgh	O
State University of New York College at Cortland	M
State University of New York College at Potsdam	M
Stephen F. Austin State University	M
Syracuse University	M
Teachers College, Columbia University	M,D
Teachers College of San Joaquin	M,D
Tennessee Technological University	M,O
Texas A&M University– Commerce	M,D,O
Texas A&M University–Corpus Christi	M,D
Texas A&M University– Kingsville	M
Texas A&M University–San Antonio	M
Texas State University	M
Texas Woman's University	M,D
Theological University of the Caribbean	M,D
Towson University	M,O
Trident University International	M
Trinity Washington University	M
Troy University	M,O
Universidad del Turabo	M
University at Buffalo, the State University of New York	M,D,O
The University of Alabama at Birmingham	M,D
University of Alaska Anchorage	M,O
University of Arkansas	M
University of Bridgeport	M,D,O
University of Central Missouri	M
University of Central Oklahoma	M
University of Colorado Denver	M,D
University of Dayton	M
University of Denver	M
University of Florida	M,D,O
University of Hartford	M
University of Hawaii at Manoa	M
University of Houston–Clear Lake	M
University of Illinois at Chicago	M,D
The University of Kansas	M,D,O
University of Kentucky	M,D
University of Louisiana at Lafayette	M
University of Louisville	M,D,O
University of Maine	M,D,O
University of Maine at Farmington	M
University of Maryland, Baltimore County	M
University of Massachusetts Amherst	M,D,O
University of Massachusetts Boston	D
University of Memphis	M,D,O
University of Miami	M,O
University of Michigan– Dearborn	M
University of Michigan–Flint	M,D,O

University of Minnesota, Twin Cities Campus	M,D,O
University of Mississippi	M,D,O
University of Missouri	M,D,O
University of Missouri–St. Louis	M
University of Montana	M,D
University of Nebraska at Kearney	M
University of Nebraska– Lincoln	M,D
University of Nevada, Las Vegas	M,D,O
University of New England	M,D,O
University of New Hampshire	M
University of New Mexico	D
The University of North Carolina at Chapel Hill	M,D
The University of North Carolina at Charlotte	M,D,O
The University of North Carolina at Greensboro	M,D,O
The University of North Carolina Wilmington	M
University of North Dakota	M
University of Northern Iowa	M
University of North Georgia	M
University of North Texas	M,D,O
University of Oklahoma	M,D*
University of Phoenix–Bay Area Campus	M,D,O
University of Phoenix–Online Campus	M,O
University of Phoenix– Phoenix Campus	M
University of Pittsburgh	M*
University of Puerto Rico– Rio Piedras	M
University of South Alabama	M,D
University of South Carolina	M,D
University of South Carolina Upstate	M
University of South Dakota	M,D,O
University of South Florida	M,D,O
The University of Tennessee	M,D,O
The University of Texas at Austin	M,D
The University of Texas at San Antonio	M,D
The University of Texas at Tyler	M
The University of Texas of the Permian Basin	M
The University of Texas Rio Grande Valley	M
University of the District of Columbia	M
University of the Sacred Heart	M,O
University of the Southwest	M
The University of Toledo	M,D,O
University of Utah	M,D
University of Vermont	M
University of Victoria	M,D
University of Virginia	M,D
The University of West Alabama	M,O
University of West Georgia	M,D,O
University of Wisconsin– Milwaukee	M*
University of Wisconsin– Oshkosh	M
Upper Iowa University	M
Virginia Commonwealth University	M
Viterbo University	M,O
Wagner College	M
Walden University	M,D,O
Wayne State College	M
Wayne State University	M,D,O
Webster University	M,O
Wesleyan College	M
West Chester University of Pennsylvania	M,O
Western Kentucky University	M,O
Western Oregon University	M
Westfield State University	M
West Virginia University	M,D
Westminster College (PA)	M
Wichita State University	M
Widener University	M,D
William Paterson University of New Jersey	M,O
Worcester State University	M,O
Xavier University	M*

EAST EUROPEAN AND RUSSIAN STUDIES

Boston College	M
Brown University	M,D
Carleton University	M,O
Columbia University	M,D
Cornell University	M,D
Florida State University	M
Georgetown University	M
The George Washington University	M
Harvard University	M*
Indiana University Bloomington	M,O
The Ohio State University	M,D
Stanford University	M
University of Alberta	M,D
The University of British Columbia	M,D
University of Colorado Boulder	M,D
University of Illinois at Chicago	M,D
University of Illinois at Urbana–Champaign	M
The University of Kansas	M,O
The University of Manchester	D
University of Michigan	M,O
The University of North Carolina at Chapel Hill	M
University of Pittsburgh	O*
The University of Texas at Austin	M
University of Toronto	M
University of Washington	M,D
Yale University	M,D

ECOLOGY

Baylor University	D
Brown University	D
California State University, Stanislaus	M

Institution	Degree
Central Washington University	M
Columbia University	M,D
Cornell University	M,D
Dalhousie University	D
Dartmouth College	D
Duke University	D,O
Eastern Kentucky University	M
Emory University	D
Florida Institute of Technology	M,D
Florida State University	M,D
Frostburg State University	M
Illinois State University	M,D
Indiana State University	M,D
Indiana University Bloomington	M,D,O
Inter American University of Puerto Rico, Bayamón Campus	M
Iowa State University of Science and Technology	M,D
Kent State University	M,D
Laurentian University	M,D,O
Lesley University	M,D
Marquette University	D
Michigan State University	M,D
Montana State University	M
Montclair State University	M
Naropa University	M
Northeastern Illinois University	M
The Ohio State University	M,D
Ohio University	M,D
Oklahoma State University	M,D
Old Dominion University	D
Oregon State University	M,D
Penn State University Park	M,D*
Princeton University	D
Purdue University	M,D
Rice University	M,D
Rutgers University–New Brunswick	M,D
San Diego State University	M,D
San Francisco State University	M
San Jose State University	M
Stanford University	M,D
State University of New York College of Environmental Science and Forestry	M,D
Stony Brook University, State University of New York	M,D
Tulane University	M,D
Universidad Nacional Pedro Henriquez Urena	M
University at Buffalo, the State University of New York	M,D,O
University of Alberta	M,D
The University of Arizona	M,D
University of California, Davis	M,D
University of California, Irvine	M,D
University of California, Los Angeles	M,D
University of California, Santa Barbara	M,D
University of California, Santa Cruz	M,D
University of Chicago	D
University of Colorado Boulder	M
University of Colorado Denver	M
University of Connecticut	M,D
University of Delaware	M,D
University of Denver	M,D
University of Florida	M,D,O
University of Georgia	M,D
University of Guelph	M,D
University of Illinois at Urbana–Champaign	M,D
The University of Kansas	M,D
The University of Manchester	M,D
University of Manitoba	M,D
University of Maryland, College Park	M,D
University of Michigan	M,D
University of Minnesota, Twin Cities Campus	M,D
University of Missouri	M,D
University of Montana	M,D
University of Nevada, Reno	D
University of New Haven	M
The University of North Carolina at Chapel Hill	M,D
University of Notre Dame	M,D
University of Oklahoma	M,D*
University of Oregon	M,D
University of Pittsburgh	D*
University of Puerto Rico–Río Piedras	M,D
University of Rhode Island	M,D
University of Rochester	M,D*
University of South Carolina	M,D
University of South Florida	M,D
The University of Tennessee	M,D
The University of Texas at Austin	D
The University of Texas at San Antonio	M
The University of Toledo	M,D
University of Toronto	M,D
University of Washington	M,D
University of Wisconsin–Madison	M
University of Wyoming	M,D
Utah State University	M,D
Washington University in St. Louis	D
Wesleyan University	D
Western Illinois University	D
Yale University	D

ECONOMIC DEVELOPMENT

Institution	Degree
Albany State University	M
The American University in Cairo	M,O
Ball State University	M,O
Boston University	M
The Catholic University of America	M
Claremont Graduate University	M,D,O
Cleveland State University	M,O
Concordia University (Canada)	O
Cornell University	M,D
East Carolina University	M,O
East Tennessee State University	M,O
Fordham University	D
Georgetown University	M,D
Georgia Institute of Technology	M,D
Georgia State University	M,D,O
Indiana University Bloomington	M,D,O
Johnson & Wales University	M
Murray State University	M
New Mexico State University	M,D,O
Northeastern University	M
Southern New Hampshire University	M,D,O
State University of New York Empire State College	M
Thomas Edison State University	M
Troy University	M
Université de Sherbrooke	D
University at Buffalo, the State University of New York	M,D,O
University of Central Arkansas	M,O
University of Colorado Denver	M
University of Houston–Victoria	M
University of Massachusetts Lowell	M
University of New Hampshire	M
University of North Alabama	M
The University of North Carolina at Greensboro	M,D,O
University of Pennsylvania	M,O*
University of Puerto Rico–Río Piedras	M
University of Southern California	M
University of Southern Mississippi	M
Vanderbilt University	M,D*
Wayne State University	M,D,O
Western Illinois University	M
Williams College	M
Yale University	M

ECONOMICS

Institution	Degree
Albany State University	M
American University	M,D,O
The American University in Cairo	M,O
American University of Armenia	M
American University of Beirut	M,D
Andrews University	M
Arizona State University at the Tempe campus	D
Assumption College	M,O
Auburn University	M
Bard College	M
Baruch College of the City University of New York	M*
Baylor University	M
Binghamton University, State University of New York	M,D
Boise State University	M
Boston College	D
Boston University	M
Bowling Green State University	M
Brandeis University	M,D
Brock University	M
Brooklyn College of the City University of New York	M
Brown University	D
Buffalo State College, State University of New York	M
California Polytechnic State University, San Luis Obispo	M
California State Polytechnic University, Pomona	M
California State University, East Bay	M
California State University, Fullerton	M
California State University, Long Beach	M
California State University, Los Angeles	M
California University of Management and Sciences	M,D
Campbellsville University	M,D
Carleton University	M,D
Carnegie Mellon University	D
Central European University	M,D
Central Michigan University	M
City College of the City University of New York	M
Claremont Graduate University	M,D,O
Clark Atlanta University	M
Clark University	D
Clemson University	M,D
Cleveland State University	M,O
Colorado State University	M,D
Columbia University	M,D
Concordia University (Canada)	M,D
Copenhagen Business School	M,D
Cornell University	M,D
Dalhousie University	M,D
DePaul University	M,D
Drexel University	M,D,O*
Duke University	M,D
Eastern Illinois University	M
Eastern Michigan University	M,O
Emory University	D
Florida Atlantic University	M,D
Florida International University	M,D
Florida State University	M,D
Fordham University	M,D,O
George Mason University	M,D
Georgetown University	D
The George Washington University	M,D
Georgia Institute of Technology	M,D
Georgia State University	M,D
The Graduate Center, City University of New York	D
Harvard University	D*
Howard University	M,D
Hunter College of the City University of New York	M
Illinois State University	M
Indiana University Bloomington	M,D
Indiana University–Purdue University Indianapolis	M
Instituto Tecnologico de Santo Domingo	M,O
Instituto Tecnológico y de Estudios Superiores de Monterrey, Campus Ciudad de México	M,O
Iowa State University of Science and Technology	M,D
Johns Hopkins University	D*
Kansas State University	M,D
Kent State University	M
Lakehead University	M
Lee University	M,O
Lehigh University	M,D
Louisiana State University and Agricultural & Mechanical College	M
Loyola University Chicago	M
Marquette University	M,O
Massachusetts Institute of Technology	M,D
McGill University	M,D
McMaster University	M,D
Memorial University of Newfoundland	M
Miami University	M
Michigan State University	M,D
Middle Tennessee State University	M,D
Mississippi State University	M,D
Morgan State University	M
Murray State University	M
The New School	M,D
New York University	M,D,O*
North Carolina State University	M,D
Northeastern University	M,D
Northern Illinois University	M,D
Northwestern University	D
Oakland University	M,O
The Ohio State University	M,D
Ohio University	M
Oklahoma State University	M,D
Old Dominion University	M
Pace University	O
Penn State University Park	M,D*
Pepperdine University	M
Peru State College	M
Portland State University	M,D,O
Princeton University	D,O
Purdue University	D
Queen's University at Kingston	M,D
Regent University	M,D,O
Regis University	M,O
Rice University	M,D
Roosevelt University	M
Rutgers University–Newark	M,D
Rutgers University–New Brunswick	M,D
St. Cloud State University	M
San Diego State University	M
San Francisco State University	M
San Jose State University	M
Simon Fraser University	M,D
South Dakota State University	M
Southern Illinois University Carbondale	M,D
Southern Illinois University Edwardsville	M
Southern Methodist University	M,D
Southern New Hampshire University	M,D,O
Stanford University	D
State University of New York College of Environmental Science and Forestry	M,D
Stony Brook University, State University of New York	M,D
Syracuse University	M,D
Teachers College, Columbia University	M,D
Temple University	M,D*
Texas A&M University	M,D
Texas Tech University	M,D
Troy University	M
Tufts University	M,D
Tulane University	M,D
Universidad de las Américas Puebla	M
Université de Moncton	M
Université de Montréal	M,D,O
Université de Sherbrooke	M
Université du Québec à Montréal	M,D
Université Laval	M,D
University at Albany, State University of New York	M,D,O
University at Buffalo, the State University of New York	M,D,O
The University of Akron	M
The University of Alabama	M,D
University of Alberta	M,D
The University of Arizona	M,D
University of Arkansas	M,D
The University of British Columbia	M,D
University of California, Berkeley	D
University of California, Davis	M,D
University of California, Irvine	M,D
University of California, Los Angeles	D
University of California, Riverside	M,D
University of California, San Diego	D
University of California, Santa Barbara	M,D
University of California, Santa Cruz	D
University of Chicago	M,D,O
University of Cincinnati	D
University of Colorado Boulder	M,D
University of Colorado Denver	M
University of Connecticut	M,D
University of Delaware	M,D
University of Denver	M
University of Detroit Mercy	M,D,O
University of Florida	M,D
University of Georgia	M,D
University of Guelph	M,D
University of Hawaii at Manoa	M,D
University of Houston	M,D
University of Illinois at Chicago	M,D
University of Illinois at Urbana–Champaign	M,D
The University of Iowa	D
The University of Kansas	M,D
University of Kentucky	M,D
University of Lethbridge	M,D
University of Maine	M
University of Manitoba	M,D
University of Maryland, Baltimore County	M,D
University of Maryland, College Park	M,D
University of Massachusetts Amherst	M,D
University of Massachusetts Lowell	M,O
University of Memphis	M,D
University of Miami	M,D
University of Michigan	M,D
University of Minnesota, Twin Cities Campus	M,D
University of Mississippi	M,D
University of Missouri	M,D
University of Missouri–Kansas City	M,D
University of Missouri–St. Louis	M
University of Montana	M
University of Nebraska at Omaha	M
University of Nebraska–Lincoln	M,D
University of Nevada, Las Vegas	M
University of Nevada, Reno	M
University of New Brunswick Fredericton	M
University of New Hampshire	M,D
University of New Mexico	M,D
University of New Orleans	D
The University of North Carolina at Chapel Hill	M,D
The University of North Carolina at Charlotte	M,O
The University of North Carolina at Greensboro	D
University of North Florida	M
University of North Texas	M,D,O
University of Notre Dame	D
University of Oklahoma	M,D*
University of Oregon	M,D
University of Ottawa	M,D
University of Pennsylvania	M,D*
University of Pittsburgh	M,D*
University of Puerto Rico–Río Piedras	M
University of Regina	M,D,O
University of Rhode Island	M,D
University of Rochester	D*
University of San Francisco	M
University of Saskatchewan	M,O
University of South Africa	M,D
University of South Carolina	M,D
University of Southern California	M,D
University of South Florida	M,D
The University of Tennessee	M,D
The University of Texas at Arlington	M
The University of Texas at Austin	M,D
The University of Texas at Dallas	M,D
The University of Texas at El Paso	M
The University of Texas at San Antonio	M
The University of Toledo	M,D,O
University of Toronto	M,D
University of Utah	M,D
University of Vermont	M,D,O
University of Victoria	M,D
University of Virginia	M,D
University of Washington	D
University of Waterloo	M,D
The University of Western Ontario	M,D
University of Windsor	M
University of Wisconsin–Madison	D
University of Wisconsin–Milwaukee	M,D*
University of Wyoming	M,D
Utah State University	M
Vanderbilt University	M,D*
Virginia Commonwealth University	M
Virginia Polytechnic Institute and State University	M,D
Virginia State University	M
Washington State University	M,D,O
Washington University in St. Louis	D
Wayne State University	M,D
Western Illinois University	M
Western Michigan University	M,D
West Texas A&M University	M
West Virginia University	M,D,O
Wichita State University	M
Wilfrid Laurier University	M,D
Wright State University	M
Yale University	M,D
Yeshiva University	M,D
York University	M,D
Youngstown State University	M

EDUCATION—GENERAL

Institution	Degree
Abilene Christian University	M,O

*M—masters degree; D—doctorate; O—other advanced degree; *—Close-Up and/or Display*

Institution	Degree
Acacia University	M
Acadia University	M,D
Adams State University	M
Adelphi University	M,D,O
Alabama Agricultural and Mechanical University	M,D,O
Alabama State University	M,D,O
Alaska Pacific University	M
Albany State University	M,O
Albertus Magnus College	M
Albright College	M
Alcorn State University	M,O
Alfred University	M
Alliant International University–Los Angeles	M,O
Alliant International University–Sacramento	M,O
Alliant International University–San Diego	M,O
Alliant International University–San Francisco	M,O
Alvernia University	M
Alverno College	M
American College of Education	M
American InterContinental University Online	M
American International College	M,D
American Jewish University	M,O
American University	M,O
The American University in Cairo	M
The American University in Dubai	M
American University of Beirut	M,D
American University of Puerto Rico	M
Anderson University (IN)	M
Anderson University (SC)	M
Andrews University	M,D,O
Anna Maria College	M,O
Antioch University Los Angeles	M
Antioch University New England	M,O
Antioch University Santa Barbara	M
Antioch University Seattle	M
Aquinas College (MI)	M
Aquinas College (TN)	M
Arcadia University	M,D,O
Argosy University, Atlanta	M,D,O
Argosy University, Chicago	M,D,O
Argosy University, Hawai'i	M,D
Argosy University, Los Angeles	M,D
Argosy University, Northern Virginia	M,D,O
Argosy University, Orange County	M,D,O
Argosy University, Phoenix	M,D,O
Argosy University, Seattle	M,D
Argosy University, Tampa	M,D,O
Argosy University, Twin Cities	M,D,O
Arizona State University at the Tempe campus	M,D,O
Arkansas State University	M,D,O
Arkansas Tech University	M,D,O
Arlington Baptist University	M
Ashland University	M,D
Athabasca University	M,D,O
Auburn University	M,D,O
Auburn University at Montgomery	M,D,O
Augsburg University	M
Augustana University	M
Augusta University	M,D,O
Aurora University	M,D
Austin College	M
Austin Peay State University	M,O
Averett University	M
Avila University	M,O
Azusa Pacific University	M,D
Baker University	M,D
Baldwin Wallace University	M
Ball State University	M,D,O
Bank Street College of Education	M
Bard College	M
Barry University	M,D,O
Bayamón Central University	M,O
Baylor University	M,D,O
Belhaven University (MS)	M,D,O
Bellarmine University	M,D,O
Bemidji State University	M
Benedictine College	M
Berry College	M,O
Bethany College	M
Bethel University (IN)	M
Bethel University (MN)	M,D,O
Binghamton University, State University of New York	M,D,O
Biola University	M,O
Bishop's University	M,O
Bloomsburg University of Pennsylvania	M,O
Bluefield College	M
Bluffton University	M
Boise State University	M,D,O
Boston College	M,D,O
Boston University	M,D,O
Bowie State University	M
Bradley University	M,D,O
Brandman University	M,D
Brandon University	M,O
Brenau University	M,O
Bridgewater State University	M,O
Brigham Young University	M,D,O
Brock University	M,D
Brooklyn College of the City University of New York	M,O
Brown University	M
Bucknell University	M
Buena Vista University	M
Buffalo State College, State University of New York	M
Butler University	M,O
Cairn University	M,O
Caldwell University	M,D,O
California Baptist University	M
California Coast University	M
California Lutheran University	M,D
California Polytechnic State University, San Luis Obispo	M
California State University, Bakersfield	M,D
California State University, Dominguez Hills	M
California State University, East Bay	M
California State University, Fresno	M,D
California State University, Long Beach	M,D
California State University, Los Angeles	M,D,O
California State University, Monterey Bay	M
California State University, Northridge	M,D
California State University, Sacramento	M,D,O
California State University, San Bernardino	M
California State University, San Marcos	M,D
California State University, Stanislaus	M,D
California University of Pennsylvania	M,D
Calvary University	M
Calvin College	M
Cambridge College	M,D,O
Cameron University	M
Campbellsville University	M
Campbell University	M
Canisius College	M,D
Capella University	M,D
Cardinal Stritch University	M,D
Caribbean University	M,D
Carlow University	M,O
Carroll University	M
Carson-Newman University	M
Carthage College	M,O
Castleton University	M,O
The Catholic University of America	M
Cedar Crest College	M
Centenary College of Louisiana	M
Centenary University	M,D
Central Connecticut State University	M,D,O
Central Methodist University	M
Central Michigan University	M,D,O
Central Washington University	M
Chadron State College	M
Chaminade University of Honolulu	M
Chapman University	M,D,O*
Charleston Southern University	M
Chatham University	M,D
Chestnut Hill College	M
Cheyney University of Pennsylvania	M,O
Chicago State University	M,D
Chowan University	M
Christian Brothers University	M
Christopher Newport University	M
The Citadel, The Military College of South Carolina	M,O
City College of the City University of New York	M,O
City University of Seattle	M,O
Claremont Graduate University	M,D,O
Clarion University of Pennsylvania	M
Clark Atlanta University	M,D,O
Clarke University	M
Clarkson University	M
Clark University	M,D
Clayton State University	M
Clemson University	M,D,O
Cleveland State University	M,D,O
Coastal Carolina University	M,O
The College at Brockport, State University of New York	M,O
College of Charleston	M,O
The College of Idaho	M
College of Mount Saint Vincent	M,O
The College of New Jersey	M,O
The College of New Rochelle	M,O
College of Saint Elizabeth	M,O
College of St. Joseph	M
College of Saint Mary	M
The College of Saint Rose	M,O
The College of St. Scholastica	M,O
College of Staten Island of the City University of New York	M,O
The College of William and Mary	M,D,O
Colorado Christian University	M
The Colorado College	M
Colorado Mesa University	M,O
Colorado State University	M,D
Colorado State University–Global Campus	M
Colorado State University–Pueblo	M
Columbia College (MO)	M
Columbia College (SC)	M
Columbia International University	M,D,O
Columbus State University	M,D,O
Concordia College	M
Concordia University (United States)	M,D
Concordia University (Canada)	M,O
Concordia University Chicago	M,D,O
Concordia University Irvine	M
Concordia University, Nebraska	M
Concordia University, St. Paul	M,D,O
Concordia University Texas	M
Concordia University Wisconsin	M
Concord University	M
Coppin State University	M
Corban University	M
Cornell University	M,D
Cornerstone University	M,O
Covenant College	M
Crandall University	M
Creighton University	M
Cumberland University	M
Curry College	M
Daemen College	M
Dakota State University	M
Dakota Wesleyan University	M
Dallas Baptist University	M
Defiance College	M
Delaware State University	M,D
Delta State University	M,D,O
DePaul University	M,D
DeSales University	M,O
Dickinson State University	M
Doane University	M,D,O
Dominican College	M
Dominican University	M
Dominican University of California	M
Dordt College	M
Drake University	M,D,O
Drew University	M,D,O
Drexel University	M,D*
Drury University	M
Duke University	M
Duquesne University	M,D,O
D'Youville College	M
Earlham College	M
East Carolina University	M,D,O
East Central University	M
Eastern Connecticut State University	M
Eastern Illinois University	M,O
Eastern Kentucky University	M
Eastern Mennonite University	M
Eastern Michigan University	M,D,O
Eastern Nazarene College	M,O
Eastern New Mexico University	M
Eastern Oregon University	M
Eastern Washington University	M
East Stroudsburg University of Pennsylvania	M,D
East Tennessee State University	M,D,O
East Texas Baptist University	M
Edgewood College	M,D,O
Elizabeth City State University	M
Elms College	M,O
Elon University	M
Embry-Riddle Aeronautical University–Worldwide	M
Emmanuel College (United States)	M,O
Emory & Henry College	M,D
Emory University	M,D
Emporia State University	M,D
Evangel University	M
The Evergreen State College	M
Fairfield University	M,O
Fairleigh Dickinson University, Florham Campus	M,O
Fairleigh Dickinson University, Metropolitan Campus	M,O
Fairmont State University	M
Faulkner University	M
Felician University	M,O
Ferris State University	M
Fielding Graduate University	M,D
Florida Agricultural and Mechanical University	M,D
Florida Atlantic University	M,D,O
Florida Gulf Coast University	M
Florida Memorial University	M
Florida Southern College	M,D
Florida State University	M,D,O
Fontbonne University	M
Fordham University	M,D,O
Fort Hays State University	M,O
Franciscan University of Steubenville	M
Francis Marion University	M
Freed-Hardeman University	M,O
Fresno Pacific University	M,O
Frostburg State University	M,D
Furman University	M,O
Gallaudet University	M,D,O
Gannon University	M,O
Gardner-Webb University	M,D,O
Geneva College	M
George Fox University	M,D,O
George Mason University	M,D,O
Georgetown College	M
The George Washington University	M,D,O
Georgia College & State University	M,O
Georgian Court University	M,O
Georgia Southern University	M,D,O
Georgia Southwestern State University	M,O
Georgia State University	M,D,O
Goddard College	M
Gonzaga University	M,D
Gordon College	M,O
Goucher College	M,O
Governors State University	M
Graceland University (IA)	M
Grambling State University	M,D,O
Grand Canyon University	M,D,O
Grand Valley State University	M
Gratz College	M,D
Greensboro College	M
Greenville University	M
Gwynedd Mercy University	M,D
Hamline University	M,D
Hampton University	M,D,O
Hannibal-LaGrange University	M
Harding University	M,D
Hardin-Simmons University	M,D
Harrison Middleton University	M,D
Harvard University	M,D*
Hastings College	M
Hebrew College	M,O
Hebrew Union College–Jewish Institute of Religion (NY)	M
Heidelberg University	M
Henderson State University	M,O
Heritage University	M
Hofstra University	M,D,O
Hollins University	M
Holy Family University	M,D
Holy Names University	M,O
Hood College	M,O
Hope International University	M
Houston Baptist University	M,D
Howard University	M,D,O
Humboldt State University	M
Hunter College of the City University of New York	M,D,O
Idaho State University	M,D,O
Illinois College	M
Indiana State University	M,D,O
Indiana University Bloomington	M,D,O
Indiana University East	M
Indiana University Northwest	M,O
Indiana University of Pennsylvania	M,D,O
Indiana University–Purdue University Indianapolis	M,O
Indiana University South Bend	M,O
Indiana University Southeast	M
Institute for Christian Studies	M,D
Instituto Tecnologico de Santo Domingo	M,O
Instituto Tecnológico y de Estudios Superiores de Monterrey, Campus Central de Veracruz	M
Instituto Tecnológico y de Estudios Superiores de Monterrey, Campus Ciudad de México	M,D
Instituto Tecnológico y de Estudios Superiores de Monterrey, Campus Ciudad Juárez	M
Instituto Tecnológico y de Estudios Superiores de Monterrey, Campus Ciudad Obregón	M
Instituto Tecnológico y de Estudios Superiores de Monterrey, Campus Estado de México	M,D
Instituto Tecnológico y de Estudios Superiores de Monterrey, Campus Irapuato	M,D
Instituto Tecnológico y de Estudios Superiores de Monterrey, Campus Sonora Norte	M
Inter American University of Puerto Rico, Arecibo Campus	M
Inter American University of Puerto Rico, Barranquitas Campus	M
Inter American University of Puerto Rico, Metropolitan Campus	M,D
International Baptist College and Seminary	M
Iona College	M
Iowa State University of Science and Technology	M,D
Jackson State University	M,D,O
Jacksonville State University	M,O
John Brown University	M
John Carroll University	M
Johns Hopkins University	M,D,O*
Johnson & Wales University	M
Johnson University	M,D,O
Kansas State University	M,D,O
Kean University	M
Keiser University	M
Kennesaw State University	M,D,O
Kent State University	M,D,O
Kent State University at Stark	M
King's College	M
Kutztown University of Pennsylvania	M,D
LaGrange College	M,O
Lake Erie College	M,O
Lake Forest College	M
Lakehead University	M,D
Lakeland University	M
Lamar University	M,D,O
Lander University	M
Langston University	M
La Salle University	M,O
Lasell College	M,O
La Sierra University	M,D,O
Lee University	M,O
Lehigh University	M,D,O
Lehman College of the City University of New York	M
Le Moyne College	M,O
Lenoir-Rhyne University	M
Lesley University	M,D,O
Lewis University	M,D
Liberty University	M,D,O
Lincoln Memorial University	M,D,O
Lindenwood University	M,D,O
Lindenwood University–Belleville	M
Lipscomb University	M,D,O
Lock Haven University of Pennsylvania	M
London Metropolitan University	M,D
Long Island University–LIU Brooklyn	M,O
Long Island University–LIU Post	M,D,O
Longwood University	M
Louisiana College	M
Louisiana State University and Agricultural & Mechanical College	M,D,O
Louisiana State University in Shreveport	M,D
Louisiana Tech University	M,D,O
Loyola Marymount University	M,D
Loyola University Chicago	M,D,O
Loyola University Maryland	M,O
Loyola University New Orleans	M
Lynn University	M,D
Madonna University	M
Malone University	M
Manhattan College	M,O
Manhattanville College	M,D,O
Mansfield University of Pennsylvania	M
Maranatha Baptist University	M
Marian University (IN)	M,D
Marian University (WI)	M,D
Marist College	M,O
Marquette University	M,D,O
Marshall University	M,D,O
Martin Luther College	M

Institution	Degree
Mary Baldwin University	M
Marymount University	M
Maryville University of Saint Louis	M,D
Marywood University	M
Massachusetts College of Liberal Arts	M,O
McGill University	M,D,O
McKendree University	M,D,O
McNeese State University	O
McPherson College	M
Medaille College	M
Memorial University of Newfoundland	M,D,O
Mercer University	M,D,O
Mercer University	M,D,O
Mercy College	M,O
Meredith College	M,O
Merrimack College	M,O
Metropolitan State University of Denver	M
Miami University	M,D,O
Michigan State University	M,D
MidAmerica Nazarene University	M
Middle Tennessee State University	M,D,O
Midway University	M
Midwestern State University	M,D
Midwest University	M,D
Millersville University of Pennsylvania	M,D,O
Milligan College	M,D,O
Mills College	M,D,O
Minnesota State University Mankato	M,D,O
Minnesota State University Moorhead	M,D,O
Misericordia University	M
Mississippi College	M,D,O
Mississippi State University	M,D,O
Mississippi University for Women	M
Mississippi Valley State University	M
Missouri Baptist University	M
Missouri Southern State University	M
Molloy College	M,O
Monmouth University	M,D,O
Montana State University	M,D,O
Montana State University Billings	M,O
Montana State University–Northern	
Montclair State University	M,D,O
Moravian College	M
Morehead State University	M,O
Morgan State University	M
Morningside College	M
Mount Mary University	M
Mount Mercy University	M
Mount St. Joseph University	M
Mount Saint Mary College	M,O
Mount Saint Mary's University (CA)	M,D,O
Mount St. Mary's University (MD)	M
Mount Saint Vincent University	M
Mount Vernon Nazarene University	M
Multnomah University	M
Murray State University	M,D,O
Muskingum University	M
National Louis University	M,D,O
National University	M,O
Nazareth College of Rochester	M
Neumann University	M
New England College	M,D
New Jersey City University	M,D
Newman University	M
New Mexico Highlands University	M
New Mexico State University	M,D,O
New York University	M,D,O*
Niagara University	M,D,O
Nicholls State University	M
Nipissing University	M,O
Norfolk State University	M
North Carolina Agricultural and Technical State University	M,D
North Carolina Central University	M
North Carolina State University	M,D,O
North Central College	M
Northcentral University	M,D,O
North Dakota State University	M,D,O
Northeastern Illinois University	M
Northeastern State University	M
Northern Arizona University	M,D,O
Northern Illinois University	M,D,O
Northern Kentucky University	M,D,O
Northern Michigan University	M
Northern State University	M
Northern Vermont University–Johnson	M
Northern Vermont University–Lyndon	M
North Greenville University	M,D
North Park University	M
Northwest Christian University	M
Northwestern College	M,O
Northwestern Oklahoma State University	M
Northwestern State University of Louisiana	M,O
Northwestern University	M,D
Northwest Missouri State University	M,D,O
Northwest Nazarene University	M,D,O
Northwest University	M
Notre Dame de Namur University	M
Notre Dame of Maryland University	M
Nova Southeastern University	M,D,O
Oakland City University	M,D
Oakland University	M,D,O
Ohio Dominican University	M
The Ohio State University	M,D,O
The Ohio State University at Mansfield	M
The Ohio State University at Marion	M
The Ohio State University at Newark	M
Ohio University	M,D
Ohio Valley University	M
Oklahoma State University	M,D,O
Old Dominion University	M,D,O
Olivet Nazarene University	M
Open University	M
Oral Roberts University	M,D
Oregon State University	M,D
Oregon State University–Cascades	M
Ottawa University	M
Otterbein University	M
Pace University	M,O
Pacific Lutheran University	M
Pacific Oaks College	M
Pacific Union College	M
Pacific University	M
Palm Beach Atlantic University	M
Park University	M,O
Penn State Harrisburg	M,D,O
Penn State University Park	M,D,O*
Penn State York	M,O
Peru State College	M
Piedmont College	M,D,O
Pittsburg State University	M,O
Plymouth State University	O
Point Loma Nazarene University	M
Point Park University	M,D
Pontifical Catholic University of Puerto Rico	M,D
Portland State University	M,D
Post University	M
Prairie View A&M University	M,D
Prescott College	M,D
Purdue University	M,D,O
Purdue University Fort Wayne	M,O
Purdue University Global	M
Purdue University Northwest	M
Queens College of the City University of New York	M,D
Queen's University at Kingston	M,D
Queens University of Charlotte	M
Quincy University	M
Quinnipiac University	M,O
Randolph College	M
Regent University	M,D,O
Regis College (MA)	M,D
Regis University	M
Reinhardt University	M
Relay Graduate School of Education	M
Rhode Island College	D
Rice University	M
Rider University	M,O
Rivier University	M,D,O
Roberts Wesleyan College	M
Rockford University	M
Rockhurst University	M
Roger Williams University	M,O
Rollins College	M
Roosevelt University	M
Rosemont College	M
Rowan University	M,D,O
Rutgers University–New Brunswick	M,D
Sacred Heart University	M,O
Sage Graduate School	M,D,O
Saginaw Valley State University	M,O
St. Ambrose University	M
St. Bonaventure University	M,O
St. Catherine University	M,O
St. Cloud State University	M,D,O
St. Edward's University	M,O
Saint Francis University	M
St. Francis Xavier University	M
St. John Fisher College	M,D,O
St. John's University (NY)	M,D,O
St. Joseph's College, New York	M
Saint Joseph's College of Maine	M
Saint Joseph's University	M,D,O
Saint Leo University	M,D,O
Saint Louis University	M,D*
Saint Martin's University	M
Saint Mary's College of California	M,D,O
St. Mary's College of Maryland	M
St. Mary's University (United States)	M
Saint Mary's University of Minnesota	M,O
Saint Michael's College	M,D,O
Saint Peter's University	M,D,O
St. Thomas Aquinas College	M,O
St. Thomas University	M,D,O
Saint Vincent College	M
Saint Xavier University	M
Salem College	M
Salem International University	M
Samford University	M,D,O
Sam Houston State University	M,D
San Diego Christian College	M
San Diego State University	M,D
San Francisco State University	M
San Ignacio University	M
Santa Clara University	M
Sarah Lawrence College	M
Schreiner University	M,O
Seattle Pacific University	D
Seattle University	M,D,O
Seton Hall University	M,D,O
Shawnee State University	M
Shenandoah University	M,D,O
Shippensburg University of Pennsylvania	M,D
Siena Heights University	M,O
Sierra Nevada College	M
Silver Lake College of the Holy Family	M
Simon Fraser University	M,D,O
Simpson College	M
Simpson University	M
Sinte Gleska University	M
Slippery Rock University of Pennsylvania	M,D
Smith College	M
Sonoma State University	M,O
South Carolina State University	M
South Dakota State University	M,D
Southeastern Louisiana University	M,D
Southeastern Oklahoma State University	M
Southeastern University (FL)	M,D
Southern Adventist University	M
Southern Arkansas University–Magnolia	M
Southern Connecticut State University	M,D,O
Southern Illinois University Carbondale	M,D
Southern Illinois University Edwardsville	M,D,O
Southern Methodist University	M,D
Southern New Hampshire University	M,D,O
Southern Oregon University	M
Southern University and Agricultural and Mechanical College	M,D
Southern Utah University	M,O
Southern Wesleyan University	M
Southwest Baptist University	M
Southwestern Adventist University	M,O
Southwestern Assemblies of God University	M
Southwestern College (KS)	M,D
Southwestern Oklahoma State University	M,O
Southwest Minnesota State University	M
Spalding University	M,D
Spring Arbor University	M
Springfield College	M
Spring Hill College	M
Stanford University	M,D
State University of New York at Fredonia	M
State University of New York at New Paltz	M,O
State University of New York at Oswego	M,O
State University of New York College at Cortland	M,O
State University of New York College at Geneseo	M
State University of New York College at Old Westbury	M
State University of New York College at Oneonta	M,O
State University of New York Empire State College	M
Stephen F. Austin State University	M
Stetson University	M
Stevenson University	M
Stockton University	M
Strayer University	M
Sul Ross State University	M,O
Sweet Briar College	M
Syracuse University	M,D,O
Taft University System	M
Tarleton State University	M,D,O
Teachers College, Columbia University	M,D
Teachers College of San Joaquin University	M,D
Temple University	M,D,O*
Tennessee State University	M,D,O
Tennessee Technological University	M
Texas A&M International University	M
Texas A&M University	M,D
Texas A&M University–Commerce	M,D,O
Texas A&M University–Corpus Christi	M,D
Texas A&M University–Kingsville	M,D,O
Texas A&M University–San Antonio	M
Texas A&M University–Texarkana	M
Texas Christian University	M,D
Texas Southern University	M,D
Texas State University	M,D,O
Texas Tech University	M,D,O
Texas Wesleyan University	M
Texas Woman's University	M,D,O
Thomas More University	M
Thomas University	M
Thompson Rivers University	M
Tiffin University	M
Touro College	M
Touro University California	M,D
Towson University	M
Trevecca Nazarene University	M,O
Trident University International	M
Trinity International University	M
Trinity University	M
Trinity Washington University	M
Troy University	M,O
Truman State University	M
Tufts University	M,D,O
Tusculum University	M
Union College (KY)	M
Union Institute & University	D
Union University	M,D,O
Universidad Autonoma de Guadalajara	M,D
Universidad de las Americas, A.C.	M
Universidad de las Américas Puebla	M
Universidad del Turabo	M,D
Universidad Metropolitana	M
Université de Moncton	M
Université de Montréal	M,D,O
Université de Saint-Boniface	M
Université de Sherbrooke	M,O
Université du Québec à Chicoutimi	M,D
Université du Québec à Montréal	M,D,O
Université du Québec à Rimouski	M,D,O
Université du Québec à Trois-Rivières	M,D
Université du Québec en Abitibi-Témiscamingue	M,D,O
Université du Québec en Outaouais	M,D,O
Université Laval	M,D,O
Université Sainte-Anne	M
University at Albany, State University of New York	M,D,O
University at Buffalo, the State University of New York	M,D,O
The University of Akron	M
The University of Alabama at Birmingham	M,D,O
University of Alaska Anchorage	M,O
University of Alaska Fairbanks	M,O
University of Alaska Southeast	M
The University of Arizona	M,D,O
University of Arkansas	M,D,O
University of Arkansas at Little Rock	M,D,O
University of Arkansas at Monticello	M
University of Arkansas at Pine Bluff	M
University of Bridgeport	M,D,O
The University of British Columbia	M,D,O
University of California, Berkeley	M,D,O
University of California, Davis	M,D
University of California, Irvine	M,D
University of California, Los Angeles	M,D
University of California, Riverside	M,D,O
University of California, San Diego	M,D
University of California, Santa Barbara	M,D,O
University of California, Santa Cruz	M,D
University of Central Arkansas	M,O
University of Central Missouri	M,D,O
University of Central Oklahoma	M
University of Cincinnati	M,D,O
University of Colorado Boulder	M,D
University of Colorado Colorado Springs	M,D
University of Colorado Denver	M,D,O
University of Connecticut	M,D
University of Delaware	M,D,O
University of Denver	M,D,O
The University of Findlay	M,D
University of Florida	M,D,O
University of Georgia	M,D,O
University of Guam	M
University of Hartford	M,D
University of Hawaii at Hilo	M
University of Hawaii at Manoa	M,D,O
University of Holy Cross	M,D
University of Houston	M,D
University of Houston–Clear Lake	M,D
University of Houston–Victoria	M,O
University of Idaho	M,D,O
University of Illinois at Chicago	M,D
University of Illinois at Springfield	M,O
University of Illinois at Urbana–Champaign	M,D,O
University of Indianapolis	M
The University of Iowa	M,D,O
University of Jamestown	M
The University of Kansas	M,D,O
University of Kentucky	M,D,O
University of La Verne	M,O
University of Lethbridge	M,D
University of Louisiana at Lafayette	M,D
University of Louisiana at Monroe	M,D
University of Louisville	M,D,O
University of Maine	M,D,O
University of Maine at Farmington	M
The University of Manchester	M,D
University of Manitoba	M,D
University of Mary	M,D
University of Mary Hardin-Baylor	M,D
University of Maryland, Baltimore County	M,O
University of Maryland, College Park	M,D,O
University of Maryland Eastern Shore	M
University of Maryland University College	M
University of Mary Washington	M
University of Massachusetts Amherst	M,D,O
University of Massachusetts Boston	M,D,O
University of Massachusetts Dartmouth	M,D,O
University of Massachusetts Lowell	M,D,O
University of Memphis	M,D,O
University of Miami	M,D,O
University of Michigan	M,D,O

*M—masters degree; D—doctorate; O—other advanced degree; *—Close-Up and/or Display*

University	Code
University of Michigan–Dearborn	M
University of Michigan–Flint	M,D,O
University of Minnesota, Duluth	M,D
University of Minnesota, Twin Cities Campus	M,D,O
University of Mississippi	M,D,O
University of Missouri	M,D,O
University of Missouri–Kansas City	M,D,O
University of Missouri–St. Louis	M,D,O
University of Mobile	M
University of Montana	M,D,O
University of Montevallo	M,O
University of Nebraska at Kearney	M,O
University of Nebraska at Omaha	M,D,O
University of Nevada, Las Vegas	M,D,O
University of Nevada, Reno	M,D,O
University of New Brunswick Fredericton	M,D
University of New England	M,D,O
University of New Hampshire	M,D,O
University of New Mexico	M,D,O
University of North Alabama	M,O
The University of North Carolina at Chapel Hill	M,D
The University of North Carolina at Charlotte	M,D,O
The University of North Carolina at Greensboro	M,D,O
The University of North Carolina at Pembroke	M
The University of North Carolina Wilmington	M,D
University of North Dakota	M,D,O
University of Northern British Columbia	M,D,O
University of Northern Colorado	M,D,O
University of Northern Iowa	M,D,O
University of North Florida	M,D
University of North Georgia	M
University of North Texas	M,D,O
University of Northwestern–St. Paul	M
University of Notre Dame	M
University of Oklahoma	M,D,O*
University of Oregon	M,D
University of Ottawa	M
University of Pennsylvania	M,D,O*
University of Phoenix–Bay Area Campus	M,D,O
University of Phoenix–Central Valley Campus	M
University of Phoenix–Dallas Campus	M
University of Phoenix–Hawaii Campus	M
University of Phoenix–Houston Campus	M
University of Phoenix–Las Vegas Campus	M
University of Phoenix–Online Campus	M,O
University of Phoenix–Phoenix Campus	M
University of Phoenix–Sacramento Valley Campus	M,O
University of Phoenix–San Diego Campus	M
University of Pikeville	M
University of Pittsburgh	M,D*
University of Portland	M,D
University of Prince Edward Island	M,D
University of Puerto Rico–Río Piedras	M,D
University of Puget Sound	M
University of Redlands	M,D,O
University of Regina	M,D,O
University of Rhode Island	M,D
University of Rio Grande	M
University of Rochester	M,D*
University of St. Francis (IL)	M,D,O
University of Saint Francis (IN)	M
University of Saint Joseph	M
University of Saint Mary	M
University of St. Thomas (MN)	M,D,O
University of St. Thomas (TX)	M,D
University of San Diego	M,D,O
University of San Francisco	M,D
University of Saskatchewan	M,D,O
The University of Scranton	M
University of Sioux Falls	M,O
University of South Africa	M,D
University of South Alabama	M,D,O
University of South Carolina	M,D,O
University of South Carolina Upstate	M
University of South Dakota	M,D,O
University of Southern California	M,D
University of Southern Indiana	M,D
University of Southern Maine	M,D,O
University of Southern Mississippi	M,D,O
University of South Florida	M,D,O
University of South Florida, St. Petersburg	M
The University of Tampa	M
The University of Tennessee	M,D,O
The University of Tennessee at Chattanooga	M,D,O
The University of Tennessee at Martin	M
The University of Texas at Arlington	M,D
The University of Texas at Austin	M,D
The University of Texas at El Paso	M,D
The University of Texas of the Permian Basin	M
The University of Texas Rio Grande Valley	M
University of the Cumberlands	M,D,O
University of the Incarnate Word	M,D
University of the Pacific	M,D,O
University of the Sacred Heart	M,O
University of the Southwest	M
University of the Virgin Islands	M,D,O
The University of Toledo	M,D,O
University of Toronto	M,D
University of Utah	M,D
University of Vermont	M,D
University of Victoria	M,D
University of Virginia	M,D,O
University of Washington	M,D
University of Washington, Bothell	M
University of Washington, Tacoma	M
The University of West Alabama	M,O
The University of Western Ontario	M,D
University of West Georgia	M,D,O
University of Windsor	M,D
University of Wisconsin–Eau Claire	M
University of Wisconsin–Green Bay	M
University of Wisconsin–La Crosse	M,O
University of Wisconsin–Madison	M,D,O
University of Wisconsin–Milwaukee	M,D,O*
University of Wisconsin–Oshkosh	M
University of Wisconsin–Platteville	M
University of Wisconsin–River Falls	M
University of Wisconsin–Stevens Point	M,D
University of Wisconsin–Stout	M,D,O
University of Wisconsin–Superior	M
University of Wisconsin–Whitewater	M,O
Upper Iowa University	M
Urbana University–A Branch Campus of Franklin University	M
Utah State University	M,D,O
Utah Valley University	M
Utica College	M,O
Valley City State University	M
Valparaiso University	M,O
Vanderbilt University	M,D*
Vanguard University of Southern California	M
Villanova University	M
Virginia Commonwealth University	M,D,O
Virginia International University	M
Virginia Polytechnic Institute and State University	M,D
Virginia State University	M,D
Virginia Union University	M
Virginia Wesleyan University	M
Viterbo University	M,O
Wagner College	M
Wake Forest University	M
Walden University	M,D,O
Walla Walla University	M
Walsh University	M
Warner Pacific University	M
Warner University	M
Washburn University	M
Washington State University	M,D
Washington University in St. Louis	M,D
Wayland Baptist University	M
Wayne State College	M,O
Wayne State University	M,D
Weber State University	M
Webster University	M,O
Wesleyan College	M
Wesley College	M
West Chester University of Pennsylvania	M,D,O
Westcliff University	M
Western Carolina University	M,D
Western Connecticut State University	M,D
Western Governors University	M,O
Western Illinois University	M,D,O
Western Michigan University	M,D,O
Western New Mexico University	M
Western Oregon University	M
Western State Colorado University	M
Western Washington University	M
Westfield State University	M
West Liberty University	M
Westminster College (UT)	M
West Texas A&M University	M
West Virginia University	M,D
Wheaton College	M
Whittier College	M
Whitworth University	M
Wichita State University	M,D,O
Widener University	M,D
Wilkes University	M,D
William Carey University	M,O
William Jessup University	M
William Jewell College	M
William Paterson University of New Jersey	M,O
Williams Baptist College	M
Wilmington College	M
Wilmington University	M,D
Wilson College	M
Wingate University	M,D,O
Winona State University	O
Winston-Salem State University	M
Winthrop University	M,D
Wittenberg University	M
Worcester State University	M,O
Wright State University	M,O
Xavier University	M,D*
York College of Pennsylvania	M
York University	M,D
Youngstown State University	M,D,O

EDUCATIONAL LEADERSHIP AND ADMINISTRATION

University	Code
Abilene Christian University	M,D,O
Acacia University	M
Acadia University	M
Adams State University	M
Alabama State University	M,D,O
Albany State University	M,O
Alliant International University–San Diego	M,D,O
Alliant International University–San Francisco	M,D,O
Alverno College	M
American College of Education	M
American InterContinental University Online	M
American International College	M
American Public University System	M,D
American University	M,O
The American University in Cairo	M
American University of Beirut	M,D
Anderson University (SC)	M
Andrews University	M,D,O
Angelo State University	M
Antioch University New England	M,O
Appalachian State University	M,O
Arcadia University	M,D,O
Argosy University, Atlanta	M,D,O
Argosy University, Chicago	M,D,O
Argosy University, Hawai'i	M,D
Argosy University, Los Angeles	M,D
Argosy University, Northern Virginia	M,D,O
Argosy University, Orange County	M,D
Argosy University, Phoenix	M,D,O
Argosy University, Seattle	M,D
Argosy University, Tampa	M,D,O
Argosy University, Twin Cities	M,D,O
Arizona State University at the Tempe campus	M,D
Arkansas State University	M,D,O
Arkansas Tech University	M,D,O
Arlington Baptist University	M
Asbury University	M
Ashland University	M,D
Auburn University	M,D,O
Auburn University at Montgomery	M,O
Augusta University	M,O
Aurora University	M,D
Averett University	M
Azusa Pacific University	M,D
Baldwin Wallace University	M
Ball State University	M,D,O
Bank Street College of Education	M
Barry University	M,D,O
Baruch College of the City University of New York	M,O*
Bayamón Central University	M,O
Baylor University	M,O
Bay Path University	M
Belhaven University (MS)	M,D,O
Bellarmine University	M,D,O
Benedictine College	M
Berry College	O
Bethel University (MN)	M,D,O
Bethel University (TN)	M
Binghamton University, State University of New York	M,D,O
Bloomsburg University of Pennsylvania	M
Bluffton University	M
Bob Jones University	M,D,O
Boise State University	M,D,O
Bowie State University	M,D
Bowling Green State University	M,D,O
Bradley University	M
Brandeis University	M
Brandman University	M,D
Brandon University	M,O
Bridgewater State University	M,O
Brooklyn College of the City University of New York	M
Buffalo State College, State University of New York	O
Butler University	M,O
Cabrini University	M,D
Cairn University	M,O
Caldwell University	M,D,O
California Baptist University	M
California Coast University	M,D
California Lutheran University	M,D
California State Polytechnic University, Pomona	D
California State University, Bakersfield	M,D
California State University, East Bay	M,D
California State University, Fresno	M,D
California State University, Fullerton	M,D
California State University, Long Beach	M,D
California State University, Northridge	M,D
California State University, Sacramento	M,D,O
California State University, San Bernardino	M,D
California State University, San Marcos	M,D
California State University, Stanislaus	M,D
California University of Pennsylvania	M,D
Calumet College of Saint Joseph	M
Calvary University	M
Cambridge College	M,D,O
Cameron University	M
Campbellsville University	M
Campbell University	M
Canisius College	M,O
Capella University	M,D
Cardinal Stritch University	M,D
Caribbean University	M,D
Carroll University	M
Carson-Newman University	M
Carthage College	M,O
Castleton University	M
The Catholic University of America	M,O
Centenary University	M,D
Central Connecticut State University	M,D,O
Central Michigan University	M,D,O
Central Washington University	M
Chadron State College	M,O
Chaminade University of Honolulu	M
Chapman University	M,D,O*
Charleston Southern University	M
Chestnut Hill College	M
Cheyney University of Pennsylvania	M,O
Chicago State University	M,D
Christian Brothers University	M
The Citadel, The Military College of South Carolina	M,O
City College of the City University of New York	M,O
City University of Seattle	M,D,O
Claremont Graduate University	M,D,O
Clark Atlanta University	M,D,O
Clarke University	M
Clarks Summit University	M
Clemson University	M,D,O
Cleveland State University	M,D,O
Coastal Carolina University	M,O
The College at Brockport, State University of New York	M,O
The College of New Jersey	M,O
The College of New Rochelle	M,O
College of Saint Elizabeth	M,D,O
College of Saint Mary	M
The College of Saint Rose	M,O
College of Staten Island of the City University of New York	O
The College of William and Mary	M,D
Colorado Mesa University	M,D
Colorado State University	M,D
Colorado State University–Global Campus	M
Columbia College (MO)	M
Columbia College (SC)	M
Columbia International University	M,D,O
Columbus State University	M,D,O
Concordia University (United States)	M,D
Concordia University Ann Arbor	M
Concordia University Chicago	M,D
Concordia University Irvine	M
Concordia University, Nebraska	M
Concordia University, St. Paul	M,D,O
Concordia University Wisconsin	M
Concord University	M
Converse College	M,O
Creighton University	M,D
Dakota Wesleyan University	M
Dallas Baptist University	M,D
Dallas Theological Seminary	M,D,O
Delaware State University	M,D
Delaware Valley University	M
Delta State University	M,D,O
DePaul University	M,D
DeVry University–Folsom Campus	M
Doane University	M,D,O
Drake University	M,D
Drexel University	M,D*
Drury University	M
Duquesne University	M,D,O
D'Youville College	M,D
East Carolina University	M,D,O
Eastern Illinois University	M,O
Eastern Kentucky University	M
Eastern Michigan University	M,D,O
Eastern Nazarene College	M,O
Eastern New Mexico University	M
Eastern University	M,D,O
Eastern Washington University	M
East Tennessee State University	M,D,O
Edinboro University of Pennsylvania	M
Elizabeth City State University	M
Elmhurst College	M
Emporia State University	M
Endicott College	M,D
Evangel University	M,D
Fairleigh Dickinson University, Florham Campus	M
Fairleigh Dickinson University, Metropolitan Campus	M
Fayetteville State University	M,D
Felician University	M,O
Ferris State University	D
Fitchburg State University	M,O
Florida Agricultural and Mechanical University	M,D
Florida Atlantic University	M,D,O
Florida Gulf Coast University	M
Florida International University	M,D,O
Florida State University	M,D,O
Fordham University	M,D,O
Fort Hays State University	M,O
Fort Lewis College	M,O
Framingham State University	M
Franciscan University of Steubenville	M
Freed-Hardeman University	M,O
Fresno Pacific University	M
Frostburg State University	M,D
Furman University	M
Gannon University	D,O
Gardner-Webb University	M,D,O
Gateway Seminary	M,D,O
Geneva College	M
George Fox University	M,D,O
George Mason University	M,D,O
The George Washington University	M,D,O
Georgia College & State University	M,O
Georgian Court University	M,O
Georgia Southern University	M,D,O
Georgia State University	M,D,O
Gonzaga University	M,D

Gordon College	M,O
Goucher University	M,O
Governors State University	M,D
Graceland University (IA)	M,D,O
Grambling State University	M,D,O
Grand Canyon University	M,D,O
Grand Valley State University	M,O
Grand View University	M,O
Granite State College	M
Gratz College	M,D
Gwynedd Mercy University	M,D
Hampton University	M,D
Harding University	M,O
Hardin-Simmons University	D
Harvard University	M,D*
Hawai'i Pacific University	M
Henderson State University	M,O
Heritage University	M
High Point University	M,D·
High Tech High Graduate School of Education	M
Hofstra University	M,D,O
Holy Family University	M,D
Hood College	M,O
Hope International University	M
Houston Baptist University	M,D
Howard Payne University	M
Howard University	M,D,O
Hunter College of the City University of New York	D,O
Husson University	M,O
Huston-Tillotson University	M
Idaho State University	M,D
Illinois State University	M,D,O
Immaculata University	M,D,O
Indiana State University	M,D,O
Indiana University Bloomington	M,D,O
Indiana University Northwest	M,O
Indiana University of Pennsylvania	D,O
Indiana University–Purdue University Indianapolis	M,O
Indiana University South Bend	M,O
Indiana Wesleyan University	M,O
Instituto Tecnologico de Santo Domingo	M,O
Instituto Tecnológico y de Estudios Superiores de Monterrey, Campus Central de Veracruz	M
Instituto Tecnológico y de Estudios Superiores de Monterrey, Campus Ciudad Juárez	M
Instituto Tecnológico y de Estudios Superiores de Monterrey, Campus Estado de México	M,D
Instituto Tecnológico y de Estudios Superiores de Monterrey, Campus Irapuato	M,D
Inter American University of Puerto Rico, Aguadilla Campus	M
Inter American University of Puerto Rico, Arecibo Campus	M
Inter American University of Puerto Rico, Barranquitas Campus	M
Inter American University of Puerto Rico, Fajardo Campus	M
Inter American University of Puerto Rico, Metropolitan Campus	M,D
Iona College	M
Iowa State University of Science and Technology	M,D
Jackson State University	M,D,O
Jacksonville State University	M,O
Jacksonville University	M
James Madison University	M
Johnson & Wales University	D
Kansas State University	M,D,O
Kean University	M,D
Keiser University	M,D,O
Kennesaw State University	M,D,O
Kent State University	M,D,O
Keystone College	M
Kutztown University of Pennsylvania	M
Lamar University	M,D
La Salle University	M,O
Lasell College	M
La Sierra University	M,D,O
Lee University	M,O
Lehigh University	M,D,O
Le Moyne College	M,O
Lenoir-Rhyne University	M
Lesley University	M,D,O
LeTourneau University	M
Lewis & Clark College	M,D,O
Lewis University	M,D
Lincoln Memorial University	M,D,O
Lincoln University (PA)	M
Lindenwood University	M,D,O
Lindenwood University–Belleville	M
Lindsey Wilson College	M
Lipscomb University	M,D,O
Lock Haven University of Pennsylvania	M
Long Island University–Brentwood Campus	M,O
Long Island University–Hudson	M,O
Long Island University–LIU Brooklyn	M,O
Long Island University–LIU Post	M,D,O
Loras College	M
Louisiana College	M
Louisiana State University and Agricultural & Mechanical College	M,D,O
Louisiana State University in Shreveport	M,D
Louisiana Tech University	M,D,O
Lourdes University	M
Loyola Marymount University	M,D
Loyola University Chicago	M,D,O
Loyola University Maryland	M,O
Lynn University	M,D
Madonna University	M
Malone University	M
Manhattan College	M
Manhattanville College	M,D,O
Marconi International University	M,D
Marian University (WI)	M,D
Marquette University	M,D,O
Marshall University	M
Martin Luther College	M
Mary Baldwin University	M
Marygrove College	M,O
Maryville University of Saint Louis	M,D
Marywood University	M,D
Massachusetts College of Liberal Arts	M,O
McDaniel College	M
McGill University	M,D,O
McKendree University	M,D,O
McNeese State University	M,O
Memorial University of Newfoundland	M,D,O
Mercer University	M,D,O
Mercer University	M,D,O
Mercy College	M,O
Mercyhurst University	M,O
Miami University	M,D
Michigan State University	M,D,O
Middle Tennessee State University	M,O
Midwestern State University	M
Millersville University of Pennsylvania	M,D
Milligan College	M,D,O
Mills College	M
Minnesota State University Mankato	M
Minnesota State University Moorhead	M,D,O
Mississippi College	M,D,O
Mississippi State University	M,D,O
Mississippi University for Women	M
Missouri Baptist University	M,O
Missouri State University	M,O
Monmouth University	M,D,O
Montana State University	M,D,O
Montclair State University	M,D
Morehead State University	M,O
Morgan State University	M,D
Mount Holyoke College	M
Mount Mercy University	M
Murray State University	M,D,O
National American University (TX)	M,D
National Louis University	M,D,O
National University	M,O
Nebraska Christian College of Hope International University	M
Neumann University	M,D
New England College	M,D
New Jersey City University	M
Newman University	M
New Mexico Highlands University	M
New York Institute of Technology	O
New York University	M,D,O*
Niagara University	M,D,O
Nicholls State University	M
Norfolk State University	M
North American University	M
North Carolina Agricultural and Technical State University	M,D
North Carolina Central University	M
North Carolina State University	M,D
North Central College	M
North Dakota State University	M,O
Northeastern Illinois University	M
Northeastern State University	M
Northeastern University	M,D
Northern Arizona University	M,D,O
Northern Illinois University	M,D,O
Northern Kentucky University	M,D,O
Northern Michigan University	M
Northern State University	M,O
Northwestern Oklahoma State University	M
Northwestern State University of Louisiana	M,O
Northwestern University	M
Northwest Missouri State University	M,D,O
Northwest Nazarene University	M,D,O
Notre Dame de Namur University	M
Notre Dame of Maryland University	M,D
Oakland City University	M,D
Oakland University	M,D,O
Oglala Lakota College	M
Ohio Dominican University	M
The Ohio State University	M,D,O
Ohio University	M,D
Oklahoma State University	M,D
Old Dominion University	M,D,O
Olivet Nazarene University	M
Oral Roberts University	M,D
Oregon State University	M,D
Ottawa University	M,O
Park University	M,O
Penn State University Park	M,D,O*
Pensacola Christian College	M,D,O
Piedmont International University	M,D
Pittsburg State University	M,O
Plymouth State University	M,D,O
Point Loma Nazarene University	M
Point Park University	M,D
Pontifical Catholic University of Puerto Rico	D
Post University	M
Prairie View A&M University	M,D
Prescott College	M
Providence College	M
Purdue University	M,D,O
Purdue University Fort Wayne	M,O
Purdue University Global	M,O
Purdue University Northwest	M
Queens College of the City University of New York	M,O
Queens University of Charlotte	M
Quincy University	M
Quinnipiac University	M
Radford University	M
Ramapo College of New Jersey	M
Regent University	M,D,O
Regis College (MA)	M,D
Regis University	M
Rhode Island College	M,O
Rivier University	M,D,O
Robert Morris University Illinois	M
Rocky Mountain College	M
Roosevelt University	M
Rowan University	M,D,O
Rutgers University–Camden	M
Rutgers University–New Brunswick	M,D
Sacred Heart University	O
Sage Graduate School	D
Saginaw Valley State University	M,O
St. Ambrose University	M
St. Bonaventure University	M
St. Cloud State University	M,D
Saint Francis University	M
St. Francis Xavier University	M
St. John Fisher College	M,D
St. John's University (NY)	M,D,O
St. Joseph's College, New York	M
Saint Joseph's College of Maine	M
Saint Joseph's University	M,D,O
Saint Leo University	M,D,O
Saint Louis University	M,D,O*
Saint Mary's College of California	M,D,O
St. Mary's University (United States)	M
Saint Mary's University of Minnesota	M,D,O
Saint Michael's College	M,O
Saint Peter's University	M,O
St. Thomas Aquinas College	M,O
St. Thomas University	M,D,O
Saint Vincent College	M
Saint Xavier University	M
Salem International University	M
Salem State University	M
Salisbury University	M
Samford University	M,D,O
Sam Houston State University	M,D
San Diego State University	M
San Francisco State University	M,D,O
San Ignacio University	M
San Jose State University	M,D
Santa Clara University	M,O
Schreiner University	M
Seattle Pacific University	M,D,O
Seattle University	M,D,O
Seton Hall University	D,O
Shasta Bible College	M
Shippensburg University of Pennsylvania	M,D
Siena Heights University	M,O
Sierra Nevada College	M
Silver Lake College of the Holy Family	M
Simon Fraser University	M,D
Simpson University	M
SIT Graduate Institute	M
Slippery Rock University of Pennsylvania	M,D
Soka University of America	M
Sonoma State University	M
South Dakota State University	M
Southeastern Louisiana University	M,D
Southeastern Oklahoma State University	M
Southeastern University (FL)	M,D
Southeast Missouri State University	M,D,O
Southern Adventist University	M
Southern Arkansas University–Magnolia	M
Southern Connecticut State University	M,D,O
Southern Illinois University Carbondale	M,D
Southern Illinois University Edwardsville	M,D,O
Southern Methodist University	M,D
Southern New Hampshire University	M,D,O
Southern Oregon University	M
Southern University and Agricultural and Mechanical College	M,D
Southwest Baptist University	M,O
Southwestern Adventist University	M
Southwestern Assemblies of God University	M
Southwestern College (KS)	M,D
Southwestern Oklahoma State University	M
Southwest Minnesota State University	M
Spalding University	M,D
Springfield College	M,D,O
Stanford University	M
State University of New York at New Paltz	M,O
State University of New York at Oswego	O
State University of New York at Plattsburgh	O
State University of New York College at Cortland	O
Stephen F. Austin State University	M,D
Stetson University	M
Stevenson University	M
Stony Brook University, State University of New York	M,O
Suffolk University	M,O
Sul Ross State University	M
Syracuse University	M,D,O
Tarleton State University	M,D,O
Teachers College, Columbia University	M,D
Teachers College of San Joaquin	M
Temple University	M,D*
Tennessee Technological University	M,O
Texas A&M International University	M
Texas A&M University	M,D
Texas A&M University–Central Texas	M,O
Texas A&M University–Commerce	M,D,O
Texas A&M University–Corpus Christi	M,D
Texas A&M University–Kingsville	M,D
Texas A&M University–San Antonio	M
Texas A&M University–Texarkana	M
Texas Christian University	M,D
Texas Southern University	M,D
Texas State University	M,D
Texas Tech University	M,D
Texas Woman's University	M,D
Thomas Edison State University	M,O
Thomas More University	M
Tiffin University	M
Touro College	M
Towson University	M,O
Trevecca Nazarene University	M,D,O
Trident University International	M,D
Trinity Baptist College	M
Trinity University	M
Trinity Washington University	M
Trinity Western University	M
Troy University	M,O
Union College (KY)	M
Union University	M,D,O
Universidad Adventista de las Antillas	M
Universidad del Turabo	M,D
Universidad Iberoamericana	M
Universidad Metropolitana	M
Université de Moncton	M
Université de Montréal	M,D,O
Université de Sherbrooke	M
Université du Québec à Trois-Rivières	O
Université Laval	M,D,O
University at Albany, State University of New York	M,D,O
University at Buffalo, the State University of New York	M,D,O
The University of Akron	M,O
The University of Alabama	M,D,O
The University of Alabama at Birmingham	M,D,O
University of Alaska Anchorage	M,O
University of Alaska Southeast	M
University of Alberta	M,D,O
The University of Arizona	M,D,O
University of Arkansas	M,D,O
University of Arkansas at Little Rock	M,D,O
University of Arkansas at Monticello	M
University of Bridgeport	M,D,O
The University of British Columbia	M,D
University of Calgary	M,D
University of California, Berkeley	M,D
University of California, Irvine	M,D
University of California, Los Angeles	D
University of California, Riverside	M,D,O
University of California, San Diego	M,D
University of Central Arkansas	M,O
University of Central Florida	M,O
University of Central Missouri	M,D,O
University of Central Oklahoma	M
University of Cincinnati	M,D,O
University of Colorado Colorado Springs	M,D
University of Colorado Denver	M,D,O
University of Connecticut	M
University of Dayton	M,D,O
University of Delaware	M,D,O
University of Denver	M,D,O
University of Detroit Mercy	M,D,O
The University of Findlay	M,D
University of Florida	M,D,O
University of Georgia	D,O
University of Guam	M
University of Hartford	D
University of Hawaii at Manoa	M,D
University of Holy Cross	M,D
University of Houston	M,D
University of Houston–Clear Lake	M,D
University of Houston–Victoria	M,O
University of Idaho	M,D
University of Illinois at Chicago	M,D
University of Illinois at Springfield	M,O
University of Illinois at Urbana–Champaign	M,D,O
University of Indianapolis	M,D
The University of Iowa	M,D,O
The University of Kansas	M,D
University of Kentucky	M,D,O

*M—masters degree; D—doctorate; O—other advanced degree; *—Close-Up and/or Display*

University of La Verne	M,D,O
University of Lethbridge	M,D
University of Louisiana at Lafayette	M,D
University of Louisville	M,D,O
University of Lynchburg	M,D
University of Maine	M,D,O
University of Maine at Farmington	M
University of Manitoba	M
University of Mary	M
University of Mary Hardin-Baylor	M,D
University of Maryland, College Park	M,D,O
University of Maryland Eastern Shore	D
University of Massachusetts Amherst	M,D,O
University of Massachusetts Boston	M,D,O
University of Massachusetts Dartmouth	D
University of Memphis	M,D,O
University of Michigan–Dearborn	M,D,O
University of Michigan–Flint	M,D,O
University of Minnesota, Twin Cities Campus	M,D
University of Mississippi	M,D,O
University of Missouri	M,D,O
University of Missouri–Kansas City	M,D,O
University of Missouri–St. Louis	D
University of Mobile	M
University of Montana	M,D,O
University of Montevallo	M,O
University of Mount Union	M
University of Nebraska at Kearney	M,O
University of Nebraska at Omaha	M,D,O
University of Nebraska–Lincoln	M,D,O
University of Nevada, Las Vegas	M,D,O
University of Nevada, Reno	M,D,O
University of New England	M,D,O
University of New Hampshire	M,O
University of New Mexico	M,D,O
University of New Orleans	M,D
University of North Alabama	M,O
The University of North Carolina at Chapel Hill	M,D
The University of North Carolina at Charlotte	M,D,O
The University of North Carolina at Greensboro	M,D,O
The University of North Carolina at Pembroke	M
The University of North Carolina Wilmington	M,D
University of North Dakota	M,D,O
University of Northern Colorado	M,D,O
University of Northern Iowa	M,D
University of North Florida	M,D
University of North Georgia	D,O
University of North Texas	M,D,O
University of North Texas at Dallas	M
University of Oklahoma	M,D*
University of Oregon	M,D
University of Pennsylvania	M,D*
University of Phoenix–Bay Area Campus	M,D,O
University of Phoenix–Hawaii Campus	M
University of Phoenix–Las Vegas Campus	M
University of Phoenix–Online Campus	M,D,O
University of Phoenix–Phoenix Campus	M
University of Pikeville	M
University of Pittsburgh	M,D*
University of Portland	M,D
University of Prince Edward Island	M,D
University of Puerto Rico–Río Piedras	M,D
University of Regina	M
University of Rio Grande	M
University of Rochester	M,D*
University of St. Francis (IL)	M,D,O
University of St. Thomas (MN)	M,D,O
University of St. Thomas (TX)	M,D
University of San Diego	M,D,O
University of San Francisco	M,D
University of Saskatchewan	M,D,O
The University of Scranton	M
University of Sioux Falls	M,O
University of South Africa	M,D
University of South Alabama	M,D
University of South Carolina	M,D,O
University of South Dakota	M,D,O
University of Southern California	D
University of Southern Indiana	M,D
University of Southern Maine	M,O
University of Southern Mississippi	M,D,O
University of South Florida	M,D,O
University of South Florida, St. Petersburg	M
University of South Florida Sarasota-Manatee	M
The University of Tampa	M
The University of Tennessee	M,D,O
The University of Tennessee at Chattanooga	M,D,O
The University of Tennessee at Martin	M
The University of Texas at Arlington	M,D
The University of Texas at Austin	M,D
The University of Texas at El Paso	M,D
The University of Texas at San Antonio	M,D
The University of Texas of the Permian Basin	M
The University of Texas Rio Grande Valley	M,D
University of the Cumberlands	M,D,O
University of the Pacific	M,D,O
University of the Southwest	M
University of the Virgin Islands	M,D,O
The University of Toledo	M,D,O
University of Vermont	M,D
University of Victoria	M,D
University of Virginia	M,D,O
University of Washington	M,D
University of Washington, Bothell	M
University of Washington, Tacoma	M
The University of West Alabama	M,O
University of West Florida	M,D
University of West Georgia	M,D,O
University of Wisconsin–Madison	M,D,O
University of Wisconsin–Milwaukee	M,D,O*
University of Wisconsin–Oshkosh	M
University of Wisconsin–Stevens Point	M,D
University of Wisconsin–Superior	M,O
University of Wisconsin–Whitewater	M
University of Wyoming	M,D,O
Upper Iowa University	M
Ursuline College	M
Utah Valley University	M
Valdosta State University	M,D,O
Valparaiso University	M,O
Vanderbilt University	D*
Vanguard University of Southern California	M
Villanova University	M
Virginia Commonwealth University	M,D
Virginia Polytechnic Institute and State University	M,D,O
Virginia State University	M
Virginia Theological Seminary	M,D
Viterbo University	M,O
Walden University	M,D,O
Waldorf University	M
Walla Walla University	M
Washburn University	M
Washington State University	M,D
Wayland Baptist University	M
Waynesburg University	M,D
Wayne State College	M,O
Wayne State University	M,D,O
West Chester University of Pennsylvania	M,D,O
Western Connecticut State University	D
Western Governors University	M,O
Western Illinois University	M,D,O
Western Kentucky University	M,D,O
Western Michigan University	M,D,O
Western New Mexico University	M
Western State Colorado University	M
Western Washington University	M
West Liberty University	M
Westminster College (PA)	M
West Texas A&M University	M
West Virginia University	M,D
Wheeling Jesuit University	M
Whittier College	M
Whitworth University	M
Wichita State University	M,D,O
Widener University	M,D
Wilkes University	M,D
William Paterson University of New Jersey	M,O
William Woods University	M,D,O
Wilmington University	M,D
Wingate University	M,D,O
Winona State University	M,O
Winthrop University	M
Wisconsin Lutheran College	M
Worcester State University	M,O
Wright State University	O
Xavier University	M,D*
Xavier University of Louisiana	M
Yeshiva University	M,D,O
York College of Pennsylvania	M
Youngstown State University	M,D,O

EDUCATIONAL MEASUREMENT AND EVALUATION

American InterContinental University Online	M
American University	M,O
Arizona State University at the Tempe campus	D
Ball State University	M,D,O
Brandeis University	O
Cambridge College	M,D,O
Claremont Graduate University	M,D,O
Clemson University	M,D,O
College of Saint Mary	M
Duquesne University	M
Eastern Michigan University	M,O
Florida State University	M,D,O
Georgetown University	M
Georgia Southern University	M,D,O
Georgia State University	M,D
Houston Baptist University	M,D
Indiana University Bloomington	M,D,O
Iowa State University of Science and Technology	M,D
James Madison University	M,D
Kent State University	M,D
Louisiana State University and Agricultural & Mechanical College	M,D,O
Loyola University Chicago	M,D,O
McNeese State University	M,O
Michigan State University	M,D
Missouri State University	O
Missouri Western State University	M,O
Montclair State University	O
Mount Saint Vincent University	M
New Mexico State University	M,D,O
North Carolina State University	D
Ohio University	M,D
Old Dominion University	D
Rutgers University–New Brunswick	M
Seton Hall University	M,D,O
Southern Connecticut State University	M,D,O
Southwestern Oklahoma State University	M
Sul Ross State University	M,O
Syracuse University	M,D,O
Teachers College, Columbia University	M,D
Teachers College of San Joaquin	M
Tennessee Technological University	D
Texas A&M University–San Antonio	M
Université Laval	M,D,O
University of Arkansas	M,D
The University of British Columbia	M,D,O
University of Calgary	M,D
University of California, Riverside	M,D,O
University of Colorado Boulder	D
University of Colorado Denver	M,D
University of Denver	M,D,O
University of Florida	M,D,O
University of Illinois at Chicago	M,D
The University of Iowa	M,D,O
The University of Kansas	M,D
University of Kentucky	M,D
University of Louisville	M,D
University of Maryland, College Park	M,D
University of Massachusetts Amherst	M,D,O
University of Memphis	M,D
University of Miami	M,D
University of Michigan–Dearborn	M
University of Minnesota, Twin Cities Campus	M,O
University of Missouri–St. Louis	M,O
University of Nebraska–Lincoln	M,D,O
The University of North Carolina at Chapel Hill	M,D
The University of North Carolina at Greensboro	D
University of Northern Colorado	M,D
University of Northern Iowa	M
University of North Texas	M,D,O
University of Pennsylvania	M,D*
University of Pittsburgh	M,D*
University of Puerto Rico–Río Piedras	M
University of St. Thomas (TX)	M,D
University of Saskatchewan	M,D
University of South Carolina	M,D
University of Southern Mississippi	O
University of South Florida	O
The University of Tennessee	M,D,O
The University of Texas at El Paso	M
The University of Texas at San Antonio	M,D
The University of Toledo	M,D,O
University of Victoria	M,D
University of Virginia	M,D,O
University of Washington	M,D
University of Wisconsin–Milwaukee	M,D,O*
Utah State University	M,D
Virginia Commonwealth University	D
Virginia Polytechnic Institute and State University	M,D,O
Walden University	M,D,O
Washington University in St. Louis	D
Wayland Baptist University	M
Wayne State University	M,D,O
Western Michigan University	M
West Texas A&M University	M
Wilkes University	M,D

EDUCATIONAL MEDIA/INSTRUCTIONAL TECHNOLOGY

Adelphi University	M
Alabama Agricultural and Mechanical University	M,O
Alabama State University	M,D,O
Alverno College	M
American College of Education	M
American InterContinental University Online	M
American University	M,O
Antioch University New England	M,O
Appalachian State University	M,O
Arcadia University	M,D,O
Argosy University, Atlanta	M,D,O
Argosy University, Orange County	M,D
Argosy University, Phoenix	M,D,O
Argosy University, Seattle	M,D
Argosy University, Twin Cities	M,D,O
Arizona State University at the Tempe campus	M,O
Arkansas Tech University	M,D,O
Auburn University	M,D,O
Auburn University at Montgomery	M
Augustana University	M
Augusta University	D
Aurora University	M,D
Avila University	M
Azusa Pacific University	M
Baldwin Wallace University	M
Ball State University	M,D,O
Barry University	M
Bay Path University	M
Bellevue University	M
Bloomsburg University of Pennsylvania	M
Boise State University	M,D,O
Bowling Green State University	M
Brandman University	M
Bridgewater State University	M
Brigham Young University	M
Buffalo State College, State University of New York	M
California Baptist University	M
California State University, East Bay	M
California State University, Fullerton	M
California State University, Northridge	M
California State University, Sacramento	M,D,O
California State University, Stanislaus	M
Cambridge College	M,D,O
Canisius College	M,O
Capella University	M,D
Caribbean University	M,D
Central Michigan University	M,D,O
Chestnut Hill College	M,O
Clarion University of Pennsylvania	
Cleveland State University	D
Coastal Carolina University	M,O
Coker College	M
College of Mount Saint Vincent	M,O
Colorado Christian University	M
Colorado State University–Pueblo	M
Concordia University (United States)	M,D
Concordia University (Canada)	M,O
Concordia University Chicago	M
Concordia University Irvine	M
Concordia University, St. Paul	M,D,O
Dakota State University	M
Dallas Baptist University	M
Delaware Valley University	M
DeSales University	M,O
DeVry University–Folsom Campus	M
Drexel University	M,D*
Drury University	M
Duquesne University	M,D,O
East Carolina University	M,O
Eastern Connecticut State University	M
Eastern Michigan University	M,O
Eastern New Mexico University	M
East Stroudsburg University of Pennsylvania	M
East Tennessee State University	M,O
Emporia State University	M,O
Fairfield University	M,O
Fairleigh Dickinson University, Florham Campus	M,O
Fairleigh Dickinson University, Metropolitan Campus	M
Fairmont State University	M
Florida Atlantic University	M
Florida International University	M,D,O
Florida State University	M,D,O
Fontbonne University	M
Fort Hays State University	M
Framingham State University	M
Franklin University	M
Fresno Pacific University	M
Frostburg State University	M,D
Full Sail University	M
George Fox University	M,O
George Mason University	M
The George Washington University	M,O
Georgia College & State University	M
Georgian Court University	M,O
Georgia Southern University	M,O
Georgia State University	M,D
Goucher College	M,O
Graceland University (IA)	M
Grambling State University	M,D,O
Grand Canyon University	M,D,O
Grand Valley State University	M
Harrisburg University of Science and Technology	M
Harvard University	M,O*
Hofstra University	M,D,O
Houston Baptist University	M,D
Idaho State University	M,D
Indiana State University	M,D
Indiana University Bloomington	M,D
Indiana University of Pennsylvania	M,D
Indiana University South Bend	M,O
Instituto Tecnológico y de Estudios Superiores de Monterrey, Campus Central de Veracruz	M
Instituto Tecnológico y de Estudios Superiores de Monterrey, Campus Ciudad de México	M,D
Instituto Tecnológico y de Estudios Superiores de Monterrey, Campus Ciudad Juárez	M,D
Instituto Tecnológico y de Estudios Superiores de Monterrey, Campus Estado de México	M,D
Instituto Tecnológico y de Estudios Superiores de Monterrey, Campus Irapuato	M,D
Inter American University of Puerto Rico, Metropolitan Campus	M
Iowa State University of Science and Technology	M,D
Jacksonville State University	M
James Madison University	M
Johnson University	M
Kansas State University	M,D,O
Keiser University	D,O
Kennesaw State University	M,D,O
Kent State University	M,D,O
Kutztown University of Pennsylvania	M
Lamar University	M,O
La Salle University	M,O
Lawrence Technological University	M,D
Lehigh University	M,D
Lenoir-Rhyne University	M
Lesley University	M,D,O

Lewis University	M
Lindenwood University	M,D,O
Lipscomb University	M
Long Island University–LIU Post	M,D,O
Longwood University	M
Louisiana State University and Agricultural & Mechanical College	M,D,O
Loyola University Maryland	M
Manhattan College	M
Marconi International University	M,D
Marian University (WI)	M,O
Marlboro College	M,O
Martin Luther College	M
Marygrove College	M,O
Massachusetts College of Liberal Arts	M,O
McDaniel College	M
McNeese State University	M,O
Memorial University of Newfoundland	M,D,O
Michigan State University	M,D,O
MidAmerica Nazarene University	M
Middle Tennessee State University	M,O
Midwestern State University	M
Misericordia University	M,D
Mississippi State University	M,D,O
Missouri Southern State University	M
Missouri State University	M,O
Molloy College	M,O
Montana State University Billings	M
Morehead State University	M,O
Murray State University	M,D,O
National Louis University	M,D,O
National University	M,O
Nazareth College of Rochester	M
New Jersey City University	M,D
New York Institute of Technology	M,O
New York University	M,D,O*
North Carolina Agricultural and Technical State University	M
North Carolina Central University	M
North Carolina State University	M,D
Northeastern State University	M
Northern Arizona University	M,O
Northern Illinois University	M,D
Northern State University	M
Northwestern State University of Louisiana	M,O
Northwestern University	M,D
Northwest Missouri State University	M
Nova Southeastern University	M,D,O
Ohio University	M,D
Old Dominion University	M,D,O
Ottawa University	M
Pace University	M
Penn State University Park	M,D,O*
Pittsburg State University	M
Post University	M
Purdue University	M,D,O
Purdue University Global	M
Purdue University Northwest	M
Quinnipiac University	M
Ramapo College of New Jersey	M
Regent University	M,D,O
Rockford University	M
Rowan University	M,O
Saginaw Valley State University	M
St. Cloud State University	M,O
St. John Fisher College	M
Saint Mary's University of Minnesota	M
St. Thomas University	M,D,O
Saint Vincent College	M
Saint Xavier University	M
Salem State University	M
Samford University	M,D,O
San Diego State University	M,D
San Francisco State University	M
Seattle Pacific University	M
Seton Hall University	M
Seton Hill University	M
Simon Fraser University	M,D
Slippery Rock University of Pennsylvania	M,D
Southern Illinois University Edwardsville	M,O
Southern New Hampshire University	M,D,O
Southern University and Agricultural and Mechanical College	M
Stanford University	M
State University of New York College at Potsdam	M
State University of New York Empire State College	M
Stockton University	M
Strayer University	M
Syracuse University	M,O
Tarleton State University	M
Teachers College, Columbia University	M,D
Tennessee Technological University	M,O
Texas A&M University	M,D
Texas A&M University–Commerce	M,D,O
Texas A&M University–Corpus Christi	M,D
Texas A&M University–Kingsville	M
Texas A&M University–Texarkana	M
Texas State University	M
Texas Tech University	M,D
Thomas Edison State University	M,O
Tiffin University	M
Touro College	M
Towson University	M
Trevecca Nazarene University	M
Trident University International	M,D
Université Laval	M,D
University at Albany, State University of New York	M,D,O
University at Buffalo, the State University of New York	M,D,O
University of Alaska Southeast	M
University of Alberta	M,D
University of Arkansas	M
University of Arkansas at Little Rock	M
University of Central Arkansas	M
University of Central Florida	M,O
University of Central Missouri	M,D,O
University of Central Oklahoma	M
University of Colorado Denver	M
University of Connecticut	M,D
University of Dayton	M,D
The University of Findlay	M,D
University of Georgia	M,O
University of Hawaii at Manoa	M,D
University of Houston–Clear Lake	M
University of Houston–Victoria	M,O
The University of Kansas	M,D
University of Kentucky	M,D
University of Louisiana at Lafayette	M
University of Maine	M,D,O
University of Maine at Farmington	M
University of Maryland, Baltimore County	M,O
University of Maryland, College Park	M,D,O
University of Maryland University College	M
University of Massachusetts Amherst	M,D,O
University of Massachusetts Boston	M,O
University of Memphis	M,D,O
University of Michigan–Dearborn	M
University of Michigan–Flint	M,D,O
University of Minnesota, Twin Cities Campus	M,D,O
University of Missouri	D
University of Nebraska at Kearney	M
University of Nevada, Las Vegas	M,D,O
University of New Hampshire	M,O
University of New Mexico	M,D,O
The University of North Carolina at Charlotte	M,D,O
The University of North Carolina at Greensboro	M,D,O
The University of North Carolina Wilmington	M
University of North Dakota	M
University of Northern Iowa	M
University of North Florida	M,D
University of Oklahoma	M,D,O*
University of Pennsylvania	M*
University of Phoenix–Online Campus	D,O
University of Saint Joseph	M
University of San Francisco	M,D
University of Sioux Falls	M,O
University of South Africa	M,D
University of South Alabama	M,D,O
University of South Carolina	M
University of South Carolina Aiken	M
University of South Dakota	M
University of Southern Mississippi	M,D
University of South Florida	O
The University of Tampa	M
The University of Tennessee	M,D,O
The University of Texas at Austin	M,D
The University of Texas at San Antonio	M,D
The University of Texas Rio Grande Valley	M,D
University of the Sacred Heart	M
The University of Toledo	M,D,O
University of Utah	M,D,O
University of Virginia	M,D
University of Washington	M,D
The University of West Alabama	M,O
University of West Florida	M,D
University of West Georgia	M,D,O
University of Wisconsin–Milwaukee	M*
University of Wyoming	M,D
Utah State University	M,D,O
Utah Valley University	M
Valley City State University	M
Virginia Commonwealth University	M
Virginia Polytechnic Institute and State University	M,O
Walden University	M,D,O
Warner University	M
Wayland Baptist University	M
Waynesburg University	M,D
Wayne State University	M,O
Webster University	M,O
West Chester University of Pennsylvania	M,O
Western Connecticut State University	M
Western Governors University	M,O
Western Illinois University	M,O
Western Kentucky University	M,O
Western Michigan University	M,D,O
Western Oregon University	M
West Texas A&M University	M
West Virginia University	M,D
Widener University	M,D
Wilkes University	M,D
William Paterson University of New Jersey	M,O
William Woods University	M,O
Wilmington University	M,O
Wilson College	M
Wisconsin Lutheran College	M
Worcester Polytechnic Institute	M,D
York College of Pennsylvania	M

EDUCATIONAL POLICY

American University	M,O
American University of Beirut	M,D
Arizona State University at the Tempe campus	D
Ball State University	D
Brigham Young University	M,D
California State University, Sacramento	M,D,O
Cleveland State University	D
Cornell University	M
Eastern Michigan University	M
Florida State University	M,D,O
The George Washington University	M,D,O
Georgia State University	M,D,O
Harvard University	M*
Howard University	M,D,O
Illinois State University	M,D
Indiana University Bloomington	M,D,O
Loyola University Chicago	M,D
Marquette University	M,D,O
Michigan State University	D
New York University	M,D*
Niagara University	M,D,O
Northwest Missouri State University	M,D,O
The Ohio State University	M,D,O
Oregon State University	M,D
Penn State University Park	M,D,O*
Rutgers University–Camden	M
Rutgers University–New Brunswick	D
Stanford University	M
Teachers College, Columbia University	M,D
University at Albany, State University of New York	M,D,O
University of Alberta	M,D,O
University of Arkansas	D
The University of British Columbia	M,D
University of California, Riverside	M,D,O
University of Colorado Boulder	M,D
University of Colorado Denver	M,D,O
University of Denver	M,D
University of Florida	M,D,O
University of Georgia	D,O
University of Hawaii at Manoa	D
University of Illinois at Chicago	M,D
University of Illinois at Urbana–Champaign	M,D,O
The University of Iowa	M,D,O
The University of Kansas	M,D
University of Kentucky	M,D
University of Maryland, Baltimore County	M,D
University of Massachusetts Amherst	M,D,O
University of Massachusetts Boston	D
University of Massachusetts Dartmouth	M,D,O
University of Minnesota, Twin Cities Campus	M,D
University of Missouri–St. Louis	D
University of Mobile	M
The University of North Carolina Wilmington	M
University of Northern Colorado	M,D,O
University of Pennsylvania	M,D*
University of Pittsburgh	D*
University of Rochester	M,D*
University of Southern California	D
The University of Texas at Arlington	M,D
University of Vermont	D
University of Virginia	D
University of Washington	M,D
The University of Western Ontario	M
University of Wisconsin–Madison	M,D,O
University of Wisconsin–Milwaukee	M,O*
Virginia Polytechnic Institute and State University	M,D,O
Wayne State University	M,D,O
West Chester University of Pennsylvania	M,D,O

EDUCATIONAL PSYCHOLOGY

Alliant International University–Irvine	M,D,O
Alliant International University–Los Angeles	M,D,O
Alliant International University–San Diego	M,D,O
Alliant International University–San Francisco	M,D,O
American International College	M,D,O
Andrews University	M,D
Ball State University	M,D
Baylor University	M,D
Boston College	M,D
California Coast University	M,D
California State University, Long Beach	M,D
California State University, Northridge	M
Capella University	M,D
Chapman University	M,D,O*
Clark Atlanta University	M
The College of Saint Rose	M,O
Eastern Michigan University	M,O
Edinboro University of Pennsylvania	M,O
Florida State University	M,D,O
Fordham University	M,D
Fordham University	M,D
George Mason University	M,O
Georgia State University	M,D
The Graduate Center, City University of New York	D
Harvard University	M*
Holy Names University	M,O
Howard University	D
Immaculata University	M,D,O
Indiana University Bloomington	M,D,O
Indiana University of Pennsylvania	M,O
Instituto Tecnologico de Santo Domingo	M,O
John Carroll University	M,O
Kent State University	M
La Sierra University	M,O
McGill University	M,D,O
Memorial University of Newfoundland	M,O
Miami University	M,O
Michigan School of Psychology	M,D
Michigan State University	M,D,O
Mississippi State University	M,D,O
Mount Saint Vincent University	M
National Louis University	M,D,O
New York University	M,D*
Northern Arizona University	M,D,O
Northern Illinois University	M,D,O
Oklahoma State University	M,D,O
Old Dominion University	D
Penn State University Park	M,D,O*
Philadelphia College of Osteopathic Medicine	M,D,O*
Pontifical Catholic University of Puerto Rico	M
Regent University	M,D,O
Rutgers University–New Brunswick	M,D
Simon Fraser University	M,D
Southern Illinois University Carbondale	M,D
State University of New York College at Oneonta	M,O
Teachers College, Columbia University	M,D,O
Temple University	M,D,O*
Tennessee Technological University	M,O
Texas A&M University	M,D
Texas A&M University–Central Texas	M,O
Texas A&M University–Commerce	M,D,O
Texas Tech University	M,D
Universidad de Iberoamerica	M,D
Université de Moncton	M
Université de Montréal	M,D,O
Université du Québec à Trois-Rivières	M,D
Université du Québec en Outaouais	M
Université Laval	M,D
University at Buffalo, the State University of New York	M,D,O
University of Alberta	M,D,O
The University of Arizona	M,D,O
University of California, Davis	M,D
University of California, Riverside	M,D,O
University of Colorado Boulder	M,D
University of Connecticut	M,D,O
University of Georgia	O
University of Hawaii at Manoa	M,D
University of Illinois at Chicago	M,D
University of Illinois at Urbana–Champaign	M,D,O
The University of Iowa	M,D,O
The University of Kansas	M,D
University of Kentucky	M,D,O
University of Louisville	M,D
The University of Manchester	M,D
University of Manitoba	M
University of Memphis	M,D
University of Minnesota, Twin Cities Campus	M,D,O
University of Missouri	M,D,O
University of Missouri–St. Louis	D
University of Nebraska–Lincoln	M,D,O
University of Nevada, Reno	M,D,O
University of New Mexico	M,D
The University of North Carolina at Chapel Hill	M,D
University of Northern Colorado	M,D
University of Northern Iowa	M
University of North Texas	M,D,O
University of Oklahoma	M,D*
University of Regina	M
University of Saskatchewan	M,D
University of South Africa	M,D
University of South Carolina	M,D
University of South Dakota	M,D,O
University of Southern California	D
University of Southern Maine	M,O
University of South Florida	M,D,O
The University of Tennessee	M,D,O
The University of Texas at Austin	M,D
The University of Texas at El Paso	M
The University of Texas at San Antonio	M,O
The University of Texas Rio Grande Valley	M
University of the Pacific	M,D,O
The University of Toledo	M,D,O
University of Victoria	M,D
University of Virginia	M,D,O
University of Washington	M,D
The University of Western Ontario	M
University of Wisconsin–Madison	M,D

*M—masters degree; D—doctorate; O—other advanced degree; *—Close-Up and/or Display*

University of Wisconsin–
  Milwaukee — M,D,O*
Virginia Commonwealth University — D
Walden University — M,D,O
Washington State University — M,D
Wayne State University — M,D,O
Webster University — M,O
West Virginia University — M,D
Wichita State University — M,D
Widener University — M,D

EDUCATION OF STUDENTS WITH SEVERE/MULTIPLE DISABILITIES

California Baptist University — M
California State University, East
  Bay — M
California State University,
  Northridge — M
Chapman University — M,D,O*
Cleveland State University — M
Georgia State University — M,D
Hofstra University — M,D,O
Hunter College of the City
  University of New York — M
Lesley University — M,D,O
Murray State University — M,O
Norfolk State University — M
Rhode Island College — M,O
Simmons University — M,D,O
Syracuse University — M
Teachers College, Columbia
  University — M,D,O
The University of Arizona — M,D,O
University of Central Oklahoma — M
University of Illinois at
  Urbana–Champaign — M,D,O
University of New Mexico — M,D,O
University of South Florida — O
University of Utah — M,D
University of Washington — M,D
Western Kentucky University — M,O
West Liberty University — M

EDUCATION OF THE GIFTED

Albizu University, Miami Campus — M,D
Arkansas State University — M,D,O
Ball State University — M,D,O
Barry University — M,D,O
Canisius College — M,O
Carthage University — M,O
The College of New Rochelle — O
Colorado Mesa University — M,O
Converse College — M
Eastern New Mexico University — M
Emporia State University — M
Florida Gulf Coast University — M
George Mason University — M
Grand Canyon University — M,D,O
Hardin-Simmons University — M
Hofstra University — M,D,O
James Madison University — M
Kent State University — M,D,O
Lindenwood University — M,D,O
Lynn University — M,D
Mary Baldwin University — M
McNeese State University — M
Meredith College — M,O
Midwest University — M,D
Millersville University of
  Pennsylvania — M
Mississippi University for Women — M
Morehead State University — M,O
Nebraska Christian College of Hope
  International University — M
Northeastern Illinois University — M
Pacific University — M
Regent University — M,D,O
St. Bonaventure University — M,O
St. John's University (NY) — D,O
St. Thomas University — M,D,O
Samford University — M,D,O
Southeastern University (FL) — M,D
Southern Arkansas University–
  Magnolia — M
Southern Methodist University — M,D
Teachers College, Columbia
  University — M,D
Tennessee Technological University — D
University at Buffalo, the State
  University of New York — M,D,O
The University of Alabama — M,D,O
University of Arkansas at Little
  Rock — M,O
University of Central Arkansas — M,O
University of Connecticut — O
University of Louisiana at
  Lafayette — M
University of Minnesota, Twin
  Cities Campus — M
University of Nebraska at Kearney — M
The University of North Carolina
  at Charlotte — M,D,O
University of Northern Colorado — M,D
University of North Texas — M,D,O
University of Southern Maine — M,O
The University of Toledo — M,D,O
University of Virginia — M,D,O
Viterbo University — M,O
Western Washington University — M
West Virginia University — ,M,D
Whitworth University — M
Wichita State University — M
William Carey University — M,O
Wilmington University — M,D

ELECTRICAL ENGINEERING

Air Force Institute of Technology — M,D
Alfred University — M,D
The American University in Cairo — M,D,O
American University of Beirut — M,D
American University of Sharjah — M,D
Arizona State University at the
  Tempe campus — M,D,O
Arkansas Tech University — M
Auburn University — M,D

Baylor University — M,D
Binghamton University, State
  University of New York — M,D
Boise State University — M,D
Boston University — M,D
Bradley University — M
Brigham Young University — M,D
Brown University — M,D
Bucknell University — M
California Institute of Technology — M,D,O
California Polytechnic State
  University, San Luis Obispo — M
California State Polytechnic
  University, Pomona — M
California State University, Chico — M
California State University,
  Fresno — M
California State University,
  Fullerton — M
California State University, Long
  Beach — M
California State University, Los
  Angeles — M
California State University,
  Northridge — M
California State University,
  Sacramento — M
Capitol Technology University — M,D
Carleton University — M,D
Carnegie Mellon University — M,D
Case Western Reserve University — M,D
The Catholic University of America — M,D
The Citadel, The Military College
  of South Carolina — M,O
City College of the City
  University of New York — M,D
Clarkson University — M,D
Clemson University — M,D
Cleveland State University — M,D
College of Staten Island of the
  City University of New York — M
Colorado School of Mines — M,D
Colorado State University — M,D
Colorado Technical University
  Aurora — M
Colorado Technical University
  Colorado Springs — M
Columbia University — M,D
Concordia University (Canada) — M,D
Cooper Union for the Advancement
  of Science and Art — M
Cornell University — M,D
Dalhousie University — M,D
Dartmouth College — M,D
Drexel University — M*
Duke University — M,D
École Polytechnique de
  Montréal — M,D,O
Embry-Riddle Aeronautical
  University–Daytona — M
Fairfield University — M,O
Fairleigh Dickinson University,
  Metropolitan Campus — M
Farmingdale State College — M
Florida Agricultural and
  Mechanical University — M,D
Florida Atlantic University — M,D
Florida Institute of Technology — M,D
Florida International University — M,D
Florida State University — M,D
Gannon University — M
George Mason University — M,D,O
The George Washington University — M,D,O
Georgia Institute of Technology — M,D
Georgia Southern University — M
Grand Valley State University — M
Harvard University — M,D*
Howard University — M,D
Illinois Institute of Technology — M,D
Indiana University–Purdue
  University Indianapolis — M,D
Instituto Tecnológico y de
  Estudios Superiores de Monterrey,
  Campus Chihuahua — M,O
Instituto Tecnológico y de
  Estudios Superiores de Monterrey,
  Campus Monterrey — M,D
Inter American University of
  Puerto Rico, Bayamón Campus — M
International Technological
  University — M,D
Iowa State University of Science
  and Technology — M,D
Johns Hopkins University — M,D,O*
Kansas State University — M,D
Kennesaw State University — M
Kettering University — M
Lakehead University — M
Lamar University — M,D
Lawrence Technological University — M,D
Lehigh University — M,D
Louisiana State University and
  Agricultural & Mechanical College — M,D
Loyola Marymount University — M
Manhattan College — M
Marquette University — M,D,O
Marshall University — M
Massachusetts Institute of
  Technology — M,D,O
McGill University — M,D
McMaster University — M,D
McNeese State University — M
Memorial University of
  Newfoundland — M,D
Mercer University — M
Miami University — M
Michigan State University — M,D
Michigan Technological University — M,D,O
Mississippi State University — M,D
Missouri University of Science and
  Technology — M,D
Montana State University — M,D
Montana Tech of The University of
  Montana — M

Morgan State University — M,D,O
National University — M
Naval Postgraduate School — M,D,O
New Jersey Institute of Technology — M,D
New Mexico Institute of Mining and
  Technology — M
New York Institute of Technology — M
New York University — M,D*
Norfolk State University — M
North Carolina Agricultural and
  Technical State University — M,D
North Carolina State University — M,D
North Dakota State University — M,D
Northeastern University — M,D,O
Northern Arizona University — M,D
Northern Illinois University — M,D
Northwestern Polytechnic
  University — M,D
Northwestern University — M,D
Oakland University — M,D
The Ohio State University — M,D
Ohio University — M,D
Oklahoma Christian University — M
Oklahoma State University — M,D
Old Dominion University — M,D
Oregon Health & Science University — M,D
Oregon State University — M,D
Penn State Harrisburg — M,O
Penn State University Park — M,D*
Pittsburg State University — M
Polytechnic University of Puerto
  Rico — M
Portland State University — M,D
Prairie View A&M University — M,D
Princeton University — M,D
Purdue University — M,D
Purdue University Fort Wayne — M,D
Purdue University Northwest — M
Queen's University at
  Kingston — M,D
Rensselaer at Hartford — M
Rensselaer Polytechnic Institute — M,D
Rice University — M,D
Rochester Institute of Technology — M,D
Rose-Hulman Institute of
  Technology — M
Rowan University — M
Royal Military College of Canada — M,D
Rutgers University–New
  Brunswick — M,D
St. Cloud State University — M
St. Mary's University
  (United States) — M
San Diego State University — M
San Francisco State University — M
San Jose State University — M
Santa Clara University — M,D,O
South Dakota School of Mines and
  Technology — M
South Dakota State University — M,D
Southern Illinois University
  Carbondale — M,D
Southern Illinois University
  Edwardsville — M
Southern Methodist University — M,D
Stanford University — M,D
Stevens Institute of Technology — M,D,O
Stony Brook University, State
  University of New York — M,D
Syracuse University — M,D
Temple University — M,D*
Tennessee State University — M,D
Tennessee Technological University — M
Texas A&M University — M,D
Texas A&M University–
  Kingsville — M
Texas State University — M
Tufts University — M,D,O
Tuskegee University — M
Universidad de las Américas
  Puebla — M,D
Universidad del Turabo — M
Université de Moncton — M
Université de Sherbrooke — M,D
Université du Québec
  à Trois-Rivières — M,D
Université Laval — M,D
University at Buffalo, the State
  University of New York — M,D
The University of Akron — M,D
The University of Alabama — M,D
The University of Alabama at
  Birmingham — M,D
The University of Alabama in
  Huntsville — M,D
University of Alaska Fairbanks — M
University of Alberta — M,D
The University of Arizona — M,D
University of Arkansas — M,D
University of Bridgeport — M
The University of British Columbia — M,D
University of Calgary — M,D
University of California, Berkeley — M,D
University of California, Davis — M,D
University of California, Irvine — M,D
University of California, Los
  Angeles — M,D
University of California, Merced — M,D
University of California,
  Riverside — M,D
University of California, San
  Diego — M,D
University of California, Santa
  Barbara — M,D
University of California, Santa
  Cruz — M,D
University of Central Florida — M,D
University of Central Oklahoma — M
University of Cincinnati — M,D
University of Colorado Boulder — M,D
University of Colorado Denver — M,D
University of Connecticut — M,D
University of Dayton — M,D
University of Delaware — M,D

University of Denver — M,D
University of Detroit Mercy — M,D
University of Florida — M,D
University of Hawaii at Manoa — M,D
University of Houston — M,D
University of Idaho — M,D
University of Illinois at Chicago — M,D
University of Illinois at
  Urbana–Champaign — M,D
The University of Iowa — M,D
The University of Kansas — M,D
University of Kentucky — M,D
University of Louisiana at
  Lafayette — M,D
University of Louisville — M,D
University of Maine — M,D
The University of Manchester — M,D
University of Manitoba — M,D
University of Maryland, Baltimore
  County — M,D
University of Maryland, College
  Park — M,D
University of Massachusetts
  Amherst — M,D
University of Massachusetts
  Dartmouth — M,D,O
University of Massachusetts Lowell — M,D
University of Memphis — M,D,O
University of Miami — M,D
University of Michigan — M,D
University of Michigan–
  Dearborn — M,D
University of Minnesota, Duluth — M
University of Minnesota, Twin
  Cities Campus — M,D
University of Mississippi — M,D
University of Missouri — M,D
University of Missouri–
  Kansas City — M,D,O
University of Nebraska–
  Lincoln — M,D
University of Nevada, Reno — M,D
University of New Brunswick
  Fredericton — M,D
University of New Hampshire — M,D,O
University of New Haven — M
University of New Mexico — M,D
University of New Orleans — M
The University of North Carolina
  at Charlotte — M,D
University of North Dakota — M,D
University of North Florida — M
University of North Texas — M,D,O
University of Notre Dame — M,D
University of Oklahoma — M,D*
University of Ottawa — M,D
University of Pennsylvania — M,D*
University of Pittsburgh — M,D*
University of Portland — M
University of Puerto Rico–
  Mayagüez — M,D
University of Rhode Island — M,D
University of Rochester — M,D*
University of St. Thomas (MN) — M,O
University of Saskatchewan — M,D,O
University of South Alabama — M
University of South Carolina — M,D
University of Southern California — M,D,O
University of South Florida — M,D
The University of Tennessee — M,D
The University of Tennessee at
  Chattanooga — M
The University of Texas at
  Arlington — M,D
The University of Texas at Austin — M,D
The University of Texas at Dallas — M,D
The University of Texas at El Paso — M,D,O
The University of Texas at San
  Antonio — M,D
The University of Texas at Tyler — M
The University of Texas Rio Grande
  Valley — M
University of the District of
  Columbia — M
The University of Toledo — M,D
University of Toronto — M,D
The University of Tulsa — M,D
University of Utah — M,D
University of Vermont — M,D
University of Victoria — M,D
University of Virginia — M,D
University of Washington — M,D
University of Waterloo — M,D
The University of Western Ontario — M,D
University of Windsor — M,D
University of Wisconsin–
  Madison — M,D
University of Wisconsin–
  Milwaukee — M,D*
University of Wyoming — M,D
Utah State University — M,D
Vanderbilt University — M,D*
Villanova University — M,O
Virginia Polytechnic Institute and
  State University — M,D
Washington State University — M,D
Wayne State University — M,D
Western Michigan University — M,D
Western New England University — M
West Virginia University — M
Wichita State University — M
Widener University — M
Wilkes University — M
Worcester Polytechnic Institute — M,D,O
Wright State University — M,D
Yale University — M,D
Youngstown State University — M

ELECTRONIC COMMERCE

California State University,
  Fullerton — M
Claremont Graduate University — M,D,O
Dalhousie University — M,D
DePaul University — M,D

Eastern Michigan University	M,O
Fairleigh Dickinson University, Metropolitan Campus	M
Fordham University	M,D
HEC Montreal	M
Instituto Tecnológico y de Estudios Superiores de Monterrey, Campus Central de Veracruz	M
Instituto Tecnológico y de Estudios Superiores de Monterrey, Campus Ciudad Juárez	M
Instituto Tecnológico y de Estudios Superiores de Monterrey, Campus Estado de México	M,D
Instituto Tecnológico y de Estudios Superiores de Monterrey, Campus Irapuato	M,D
Lewis University	M
Northwestern University	M
Pace University	O
Stevens Institute of Technology	M,O
Towson University	M,O
Universidad del Este	M
Université de Montréal	M,D
Université de Sherbrooke	M
Université Laval	M
University at Buffalo, the State University of New York	M,D,O
The University of Akron	M
University of New Brunswick Saint John	M
University of North Florida	M
University of Ottawa	M,D,O
University of Phoenix–Dallas Campus	M
University of Phoenix–Houston Campus	M
University of Phoenix–San Antonio Campus	M

ELECTRONIC MATERIALS

Colorado School of Mines	M,D
Princeton University	D
University of Arkansas	M,D
University of Memphis	M
Wayne State University	M

ELEMENTARY EDUCATION

Acacia University	M
Adelphi University	M
Alabama Agricultural and Mechanical University	M,D,O
Alaska Pacific University	M
Albright College	M
Alcorn State University	M,O
American International College	M,D,O
American University of Beirut	M,D
American University of Puerto Rico	M
Anderson University (SC)	M
Andrews University	M,D,O
Anna Maria College	M,O
Antioch University New England	M,O
Appalachian State University	M
Aquinas College (TN)	M
Arcadia University	M,D,O
Argosy University, Atlanta	M,D,O
Argosy University, Chicago	M,D,O
Argosy University, Hawai i	M,D,O
Argosy University, Los Angeles	M,D
Argosy University, Northern Virginia	M,D,O
Argosy University, Orange County	M,D
Argosy University, Phoenix	M,D,O
Argosy University, Seattle	M,D
Argosy University, Tampa	M,D,O
Argosy University, Twin Cities	M,D,O
Arizona State University at the Tempe campus	M
Arkansas State University	M,D,O
Arkansas Tech University	M,D,O
Auburn University at Montgomery	M,O
Augusta University	M,O
Avila University	M,O
Ball State University	M,D,O
Bank Street College of Education	M
Barry University	M,D,O
Barton College	M
Bayamón Central University	M,O
Bellarmine University	M,D,O
Bethel University (MN)	M,D,O
Blue Mountain College	M
Bob Jones University	M,D,O
Boston College	M,D,O
Bowie State University	M
Brandeis University	M,O
Brandman University	M
Bridgewater State University	M
Brooklyn College of the City University of New York	M,O
Brown University	M,D
Cabrini University	M,D
California Lutheran University	M,D
California State University, Fullerton	M
California State University, Long Beach	M
California State University, Los Angeles	M
California State University, Northridge	M
California State University, Sacramento	M,D,O
California State University, Stanislaus	M
California University of Pennsylvania	M
Calvary University	M
Cambridge College	M,D,O
Campbell University	M
Canisius College	M,O
Capella University	M,D

Caribbean University	M,D
Carroll University	M
Carson-Newman University	M
Catawba College	M
Centenary College of Louisiana	M
Central Connecticut State University	M,O
Central Michigan University	M,D,O
Chadron State College	M
Chaminade University of Honolulu	M
Chapman University	M,D,O*
Charleston Southern University	M
Chatham University	M
Chestnut Hill College	M
Cheyney University of Pennsylvania	M
Chicago State University	M
City University of Seattle	M,O
Clemson University	M,D,O
College of Charleston	M
The College of New Jersey	M
The College of New Rochelle	M
College of Saint Elizabeth	M,O
College of St. Joseph	M
College of Staten Island of the City University of New York	M
Colorado Christian University	M
The Colorado College	M
Columbia College (SC)	M
Columbia International University	M,D,O
Concordia University (United States)	M,D
Concordia University Chicago	M
Concordia University, Nebraska	M
Converse College	M
Creighton University	M
Curry College	M,O
Dallas Baptist University	M
Delta State University	M,D,O
DePaul University	M,D
Dominican College	M
Dominican University	M
Drew University	M,D,O
Drury University	M
Duquesne University	M
D'Youville College	M,D
East Carolina University	M,O
Eastern Connecticut State University	M
Eastern Illinois University	M
Eastern Kentucky University	M
Eastern Nazarene College	M,O
Eastern New Mexico University	M
Eastern Oregon University	M
Eastern University	M,O
Eastern Washington University	M
East Stroudsburg University of Pennsylvania	M
East Tennessee State University	M,O
Elizabeth City State University	M
Elms College	M,O
Elon University	M
Emporia State University	M
Endicott College	M
Fairfield University	M
Faulkner University	M
Fayetteville State University	M
Fitchburg State University	M
Florida Agricultural and Mechanical University	M
Florida Atlantic University	M
Florida Gulf Coast University	M
Florida International University	M,D,O
Florida Memorial University	M
Fontbonne University	M
Fordham University	M,O
Framingham State University	M,D,O
Franklin Pierce University	M,D,O
Frostburg State University	M,D
Gallaudet University	M
George Mason University	M
The George Washington University	M
Georgia Southern University	M,O
Georgia State University	M,D,O
Gonzaga University	M,D
Gordon College	M,O
Goucher College	M,O
Grand Canyon University	M,D,O
Grand Valley State University	M
Greensboro College	M
Greenville University	M
Harding University	M
Hawai i Pacific University	M
High Point University	M,D
Hofstra University	M,D,O
Holy Family University	M
Hood College	M,O
Hope International University	M
Houston Baptist University	M
Howard University	M
Huntington University	M
Idaho State University	M
Indiana University Bloomington	M,D,O
Indiana University Northwest	M,O
Indiana University South Bend	M,O
Indiana University Southeast	M
Inter American University of Puerto Rico, Aguadilla Campus	M
Inter American University of Puerto Rico, Arecibo Campus	M
Inter American University of Puerto Rico, Barranquitas Campus	M
Inter American University of Puerto Rico, Guayama Campus	M
Inter American University of Puerto Rico, Metropolitan Campus	M
Inter American University of Puerto Rico, Ponce Campus	M
Inter American University of Puerto Rico, San Germán Campus	M
Iowa State University of Science and Technology	M,D

Ithaca College	M
Jackson State University	M,D,O
Jacksonville State University	M
James Madison University	M
Johnson & Wales University	M
Kansas State University	M,D,O
Keuka College	M
Kutztown University of Pennsylvania	M
Lake Forest College	M
Lancaster Bible College	M,D
Langston University	M
Lasell College	M,O
Lee University	M,O
Lehigh University	M,D
Lehman College of the City University of New York	M
Le Moyne College	M,O
Lesley University	M,D,O
Lewis & Clark College	M
Lewis University	M
Lincoln University (MO)	M
Lock Haven University of Pennsylvania	M
Long Island University–Brentwood Campus	M,O
Long Island University–Hudson	M,O
Long Island University–Riverhead	M,O
Longwood University	M
Louisiana State University and Agricultural & Mechanical College	M,D,O
Louisiana Tech University	M,D,O
Loyola Marymount University	M
Loyola University Chicago	M
Loyola University Maryland	M,O
Manhattan College	M,O
Manhattanville College	M,O
Mansfield University of Pennsylvania	M
Marquette University	M,D,O
Mars Hill University	M
Mary Baldwin University	M
Marygrove College	M,O
Marymount University	M
Maryville University of Saint Louis	M,D
Marywood University	M
McDaniel College	M,O
McNeese State University	M,O
Medaille College	M
Mercy College	M
Meredith College	M,O
Metropolitan College of New York	M
Metropolitan State University of Denver	M,O
Middle Tennessee State University	M,O
Milligan College	M,D,O
Minot State University	M
Mississippi College	M,D,O
Mississippi State University	M,D,O
Missouri State University	M,D,O
Monmouth University	M
Montana State University Billings	M
Morehead State University	M
Morgan State University	M
Mount Saint Vincent University	M
Murray State University	M,O
National Louis University	M
Nazareth College of Rochester	M
Nebraska Christian College of Hope International University	M
Neumann University	M
New Jersey City University	M
New York Institute of Technology	M
New York University	M*
Niagara University	M,O
Nicholls State University	M
North Carolina Agricultural and Technical State University	M
North Carolina State University	M
Northeastern Illinois University	M
Northeastern University	M
Northern Arizona University	M,D
Northern Illinois University	M
Northwest Christian University	M
Northwestern Oklahoma State University	M
Northwestern State University of Louisiana	M
Northwestern University	M
Northwest Missouri State University	M,D,O
Nyack College	M
Oakland City University	M,D
Oakland University	M,O
Oklahoma City University	M
Old Dominion University	M,O
Olivet Nazarene University	M
Oregon State University	M
Ottawa University	M
Pace University	M,O
Pacific Union College	M
Pacific University	M
Pfeiffer University	M
Point Park University	M,D
Prescott College	M,D
Providence College	M
Purdue University	M,D,O
Purdue University Fort Wayne	M,O
Queens College of the City University of New York	M,O
Queens University of Charlotte	M
Quinnipiac University	M
Regent University	M,D,O
Regis College (MA)	M,D
Regis University	M,O
Rhode Island College	M
Rider University	M
Rivier University	M,D,O

Rockford University	M
Rollins College	M
Roosevelt University	M
Rosemont College	M
Rutgers University–New Brunswick	M,D
Sage Graduate School	M
St. John Fisher College	M,O
St. John's University (NY)	M
Saint Joseph's University	M,D,O
Saint Mary's University of Minnesota	M
Saint Peter's University	M,O
St. Thomas Aquinas College	M
St. Thomas University	M,D,O
Saint Xavier University	M
Salem College	M
Salem State University	M
Samford University	M,D,O
San Diego State University	M
San Francisco State University	M
San Jose State University	M,O
Seton Hill University	M
Shippensburg University of Pennsylvania	M
Siena Heights University	M,O
Sierra Nevada College	M
Simmons University	M,D,O
Sinte Gleska University	M
Slippery Rock University of Pennsylvania	M
Smith College	M
South Carolina State University	M
Southeastern Louisiana University	M
Southeastern University (FL)	M,D
Southeast Missouri State University	M,D,O
Southern Connecticut State University	M,O
Southern New Hampshire University	M
Southern Oregon University	M
Southern University and Agricultural and Mechanical College	M,D
Southwestern College (KS)	M,D
Southwestern Oklahoma State University	M
Spalding University	M
Springfield College	M,O
Spring Hill College	M
Stanford University	M
State University of New York at New Paltz	M
State University of New York at Oswego	M
State University of New York at Plattsburgh	M,O
State University of New York College at Oneonta	M
State University of New York College at Potsdam	M
Stephen F. Austin State University	M
Sul Ross State University	M
Tarleton State University	M
Teachers College, Columbia University	M,D
Tennessee State University	M,D
Tennessee Technological University	M,O
Texas A&M University–Commerce	M,D,O
Texas A&M University–Corpus Christi	M
Texas State University	M
Texas Tech University	M,D
Towson University	M
Trevecca Nazarene University	M,O
Trinity Washington University	M
Troy University	M,O
Tufts University	M,D
Union College (KY)	M
Universidad del Este	M
Universidad Metropolitana	M
Université de Sherbrooke	M,O
University at Buffalo, the State University of New York	M,D,O
The University of Akron	M
The University of Alabama	M,D,O
The University of Alabama at Birmingham	M
University of Alaska Southeast	M
University of Alberta	M,D
The University of Arizona	M,D
University of Arkansas at Pine Bluff	M
University of Bridgeport	M,D,O
University of California, Irvine	M,D
University of Central Florida	M
University of Central Missouri	M,D,O
University of Central Oklahoma	M
University of Colorado Denver	M
University of Connecticut	M,D
University of Dayton	M
University of Florida	M,D,O
University of Hartford	M
University of Illinois at Chicago	M,D
University of Indianapolis	M
The University of Iowa	M,D
University of Kentucky	M,D
University of La Verne	M,D,O
University of Louisiana at Monroe	M
University of Louisville	M,D,O
University of Mary Hardin-Baylor	M
University of Maryland, Baltimore County	M
University of Mary Washington	M
University of Massachusetts Amherst	M,D,O
University of Memphis	M,D,O
University of Minnesota, Twin Cities Campus	M
University of Mississippi	M,D,O

*M—masters degree; D—doctorate; O—other advanced degree; *—Close-Up and/or Display*

University of Missouri	M,D,O
University of Missouri–St. Louis	M
University of Montevallo	M
University of Nebraska at Kearney	M
University of Nebraska at Omaha	M
University of Nevada, Las Vegas	M,D,O
University of Nevada, Reno	M
University of New Hampshire	M,O
University of New Mexico	M
University of North Alabama	M,O
The University of North Carolina at Charlotte	M,O
The University of North Carolina at Greensboro	D
The University of North Carolina at Pembroke	D
The University of North Carolina Wilmington	M
University of North Dakota	M
University of Northern Colorado	M
University of Northern Iowa	M
University of North Florida	M
University of Oklahoma	M,D*
University of Pennsylvania	M*
University of Phoenix–Bay Area Campus	M,D,O
University of Phoenix–Central Valley Campus	M
University of Phoenix–Hawaii Campus	M
University of Phoenix–Las Vegas Campus	M
University of Phoenix–Online Campus	M,O
University of Phoenix–Phoenix Campus	M
University of Phoenix–Sacramento Valley Campus	M,O
University of Phoenix–San Diego Campus	M*
University of Pittsburgh	M*
University of Puget Sound	M
University of St. Francis (IL)	M,D,O
University of Saint Joseph	M
University of Saint Mary	M
University of St. Thomas (TX)	M,D
University of South Alabama	M,D
University of South Carolina	M,D
University of South Carolina Upstate	M
University of South Dakota	M
University of Southern Indiana	M
University of Southern Mississippi	M,D
University of South Florida	M,D,O
University of South Florida, St. Petersburg	M
University of South Florida Sarasota-Manatee	M
The University of Tennessee	M,D,O
The University of Tennessee at Chattanooga	M,D,O
The University of Tennessee at Martin	M
The University of Texas Rio Grande Valley	M,D
University of the Cumberlands	M,D,O
University of the District of Columbia	M
The University of Toledo	M,D,O
University of Utah	M,D,O
University of Vermont	M
University of Virginia	M,D,O
University of Washington, Tacoma	M
The University of West Alabama	M,O
University of West Florida	M
University of Wisconsin–Milwaukee	M*
University of Wisconsin–River Falls	M
University of Wisconsin–Stevens Point	M
Utah State University	M
Utah Valley University	M
Valdosta State University	M
Valley City State University	M
Valparaiso University	M,O
Vanderbilt University	M*
Virginia Commonwealth University	M
Wagner College	M
Walden University	M,D,O
Warner University	M
Washington State University	M,D
Washington University in St. Louis	M
Wayland Baptist University	M
Wayne State College	M
Wayne State University	M,D,O
Webster University	M,O
Western Governors University	M,O
Western Kentucky University	M,O
Western New Mexico University	M
Western Washington University	M
Westfield State University	M
West Virginia University	M
Wheaton College	M
Whittier College	M
Whitworth University	M
Widener University	M,D
William Carey University	M,O
William Paterson University of New Jersey	M,O
Wilmington University	M,D
Wilson College	M
Wingate University	M,D,O
Worcester State University	M,O
Wright State University	M*
Xavier University	M*

EMERGENCY MANAGEMENT

Adelphi University	O
Anna Maria College	M,O
Arizona State University at the Tempe campus	M,D
Arkansas State University	M,O

Arkansas Tech University	M
Ball State University	M,O
Benedictine University	M
Boston University	M
California State University, Long Beach	M
California State University Maritime Academy	M
Capella University	M
Columbia Southern University	M
Drexel University	M*
Endicott College	M,O
Florida International University	M
Fordham University	M
Georgetown University	M
The George Washington University	M,D,O
Georgia State University	M,D,O
Grand Canyon University	M
Indiana University–Purdue University Indianapolis	M,O
Jacksonville State University	M,D
Lander University	M
Lasell College	M,O
Liberty University	M,D,O
London Metropolitan University	M
Massachusetts Maritime Academy	M
Metropolitan College of New York	M
National University	M
New York Medical College	M
Norwich University	M
Nova Southeastern University	M,D,O
Oklahoma State University	M,D
Pace University	M
Park University	M,O
Post University	M
Regent University	M
Royal Roads University	M,O
Rutgers University–New Brunswick	M,D,O
Saint Leo University	M,D
Saint Louis University	M*
San Diego State University	M
Sul Ross State University	M
Syracuse University	O
Thomas Jefferson University	M
Trident University International	M,D,O
Trine University	M
Tulane University	M,D
Université de Montréal	O
University at Albany, State University of New York	M,D,O
University of Alaska Fairbanks	M
University of Central Florida	M,O
University of Chicago	M
University of Colorado Denver	M,D
University of Delaware	M,D
University of Denver	M,O
University of Florida	M
University of Hawaii at Manoa	O
University of Illinois at Springfield	M,O
University of Maryland, Baltimore County	M,D,O
University of Nebraska Medical Center	M
University of Nevada, Las Vegas	M,D,O
University of New Haven	M,O
The University of North Carolina at Charlotte	M,O
The University of North Carolina at Pembroke	M
University of North Texas	M,D,O
University of South Florida	O
The University of Texas Rio Grande Valley	M
The University of Toledo	M,O
Upper Iowa University	M
Virginia Commonwealth University	M,O
Walden University	M,D,O
Waldorf University	M
Wheaton College	M
York University	M

EMERGENCY MEDICAL SERVICES

Creighton University	M
Drexel University	M*
San Diego State University	M,D
Université Laval	O
University of Guelph	M,D,O

ENERGY AND POWER ENGINEERING

Appalachian State University	M
Arizona State University at the Tempe campus	M,D
Carnegie Mellon University	M,D
The Catholic University of America	M,D
Clarkson University	M
Cornell University	M,D
Dartmouth College	M,D
Florida State University	M,D
Georgia Southern University	M
Instituto Tecnologico de Santo Domingo	M,D,O
Inter American University of Puerto Rico, Bayamón Campus	M
Kansas State University	M,D
Lawrence Technological University	M,D
Lehigh University	M,D
New Jersey Institute of Technology	M,D
New York Institute of Technology	O
North Carolina Agricultural and Technical State University	M,D
Northeastern University	M,D,O
Saginaw Valley State University	M
San Francisco State University	M
Santa Clara University	M,D
Southern Illinois University Carbondale	D
Stanford University	M,D,O
Texas A&M University–Kingsville	D
Texas Tech University	M,D
Universidad Autonoma de Guadalajara	M,D

University at Buffalo, the State University of New York	M,D
University of Alberta	M,D
The University of British Columbia	M
University of Calgary	M,D
University of Colorado Colorado Springs	M,D
University of Illinois at Urbana–Champaign	M,D
The University of Iowa	M,D
University of Massachusetts Lowell	M,D
University of Memphis	M,D,O
University of Michigan	M,D
University of Michigan–Dearborn	M
The University of North Carolina at Charlotte	M,O
University of North Texas	M,D,O
University of Puerto Rico–Mayagüez	M,D
The University of Tennessee	D
The University of Tennessee at Chattanooga	M,O
The University of Texas at El Paso	M,D,O
Washington State University	M,D
Wayne State University	M,O
West Virginia University	M
Worcester Polytechnic Institute	M,D,O

ENERGY MANAGEMENT AND POLICY

American College Dublin	M
American University of Armenia	M
Boston University	M,D
Clarkson University	M,O
Colorado School of Mines	M,D
Colorado State University	M
Duke University	M,O
Eastern Illinois University	M
Franklin Pierce University	M,D,O
Indiana University Bloomington	M,D,O
Instituto Tecnologico de Santo Domingo	M,D,O
Johns Hopkins University	M,O*
Kansas State University	M,D
New York Institute of Technology	O
Norwich University	M
Oklahoma Baptist University	M
Oklahoma City University	M
Portland State University	M,D,O
Rice University	M,D
Samford University	M
SIT Graduate Institute	M
Stony Brook University, State University of New York	M
Tulane University	M,D
Université du Québec, Institut National de la Recherche Scientifique	M,D
University of Calgary	M,D
University of California, Berkeley	M,D
University of California, San Diego	M
University of Colorado Denver	M
University of Delaware	M,D
University of Illinois at Urbana–Champaign	M
University of Mary	M
University of Phoenix–Bay Area Campus	M,D
University of Phoenix–Online Campus	M,O
University of Phoenix–Phoenix Campus	M,O
University of Pittsburgh	M*
University of San Francisco	M
The University of Texas at Tyler	M
The University of Tulsa	M
Vermont Law School	M
Waynesburg University	M,D

ENGINEERING AND APPLIED SCIENCES—GENERAL

Air Force Institute of Technology	M,D
Alabama Agricultural and Mechanical University	M,D
Alfred University	M,D
The American University in Cairo	M,D,O
American University of Beirut	M,D
Arizona State University at the Tempe campus	M,D,O
Arkansas State University	M
Arkansas Tech University	M
Atlantis University	M
Auburn University	M,D,O
Austin Peay State University	M
Binghamton University, State University of New York	M,D
Boise State University	M,D,O
Boston University	M,D
Bradley University	M
Brigham Young University	M,D
Brown University	M,D
Bucknell University	M
California Institute of Technology	M,D,O
California State University, Chico	M
California State University, East Bay	M
California State University, Fresno	M
California State University, Fullerton	M
California State University, Los Angeles	M
California State University, Northridge	M
California State University, Sacramento	M
Carleton University	M,D
Case Western Reserve University	M,D
The Catholic University of America	M,D,O
Central Connecticut State University	M
Central Michigan University	M
Christian Brothers University	M

The Citadel, The Military College of South Carolina	M,O
City College of the City University of New York	M,D
Clarkson University	M,D,O
Clemson University	M,D,O
Cleveland State University	M,D
Colorado School of Mines	M,D,O
Colorado State University	M,D
Colorado State University–Pueblo	M
Columbia University	M,D
Concordia University (Canada)	M,D,O
Cooper Union for the Advancement of Science and Art	M
Cornell University	M,D
Dalhousie University	M,D
Dartmouth College	M,D
Drexel University	M,D,O*
Duke University	M,D
Eastern Illinois University	M,O
Eastern Michigan University	M
École Polytechnique de Montréal	M,D,O
Fairfield University	M,O
Fairleigh Dickinson University, Metropolitan Campus	M
Florida Agricultural and Mechanical University	M,D
Florida Atlantic University	M,D
Florida Institute of Technology	M,D
Florida International University	M,D
Florida Polytechnic University	M
Florida State University	M,D
George Mason University	M,D,O
The George Washington University	M,D,O
Georgia Institute of Technology	M,D
Georgia Southern University	M,O
Gonzaga University	M,O
Grand Valley State University	M
Grantham University	M
Harvard University	M,D*
Hofstra University	M
Howard University	M,D
Idaho State University	M,D,O
Illinois Institute of Technology	M,D
Indiana State University	M
Instituto Tecnologico de Santo Domingo	M,O
Instituto Tecnológico y de Estudios Superiores de Monterrey, Campus Ciudad Obregón	M
Instituto Tecnológico y de Estudios Superiores de Monterrey, Campus Monterrey	M,D
James Madison University	M
Johns Hopkins University	M,D,O*
Kansas State University	M,D,O
Kennesaw State University	M
Lakehead University	M
Lamar University	M,D
Laurentian University	M,D
Lawrence Technological University	M,D
Lehigh University	M,D,O
LeTourneau University	M
Louisiana State University and Agricultural & Mechanical College	M,D
Louisiana Tech University	M,D,O
Manhattan College	M
Marquette University	M,D,O
Marshall University	M,O
Massachusetts Institute of Technology	M,D,O
McGill University	M,D,O
McMaster University	M,D
McNeese State University	M
Memorial University of Newfoundland	M,D
Mercer University	M
Merrimack College	M
Miami University	M
Michigan State University	M,D
Michigan Technological University	M,D,O
Milwaukee School of Engineering	M
Mississippi State University	M,D
Missouri Western State University	M
Montana State University	M,D
Montana Tech of The University of Montana	M
Morgan State University	M,D,O
National University	M
New Jersey Institute of Technology	M,D
New Mexico State University	M,D,O
New York Institute of Technology	M,O
New York University	M,D,O*
North Carolina Agricultural and Technical State University	M,D
North Carolina State University	M,D,O
North Dakota State University	M,D,O
Northeastern University	M,D,O
Northern Arizona University	M,D,O
Northern Illinois University	M
Northwestern Polytechnic University	M,D
Northwestern University	M,D
Oakland University	M,D,O
The Ohio State University	M,D
Ohio University	M,D
Oklahoma Christian University	M
Oklahoma State University	M,D
Old Dominion University	M,D
Open University	M
Oregon State University	M,D
Penn State Great Valley	M,O
Penn State Harrisburg	M,O
Penn State University Park	M,D*
Pontificia Universidad Catolica Madre y Maestra	M
Portland State University	M,D
Prairie View A&M University	M,D
Princeton University	M,D
Purdue University	M,D,O
Purdue University Fort Wayne	M,O
Purdue University Northwest	M

Institution	Degrees
Queen's University at Kingston	
Rensselaer at Hartford	M
Rensselaer Polytechnic Institute	M,D
Rice University	M,D
Robert Morris University	M
Rochester Institute of Technology	M,D,O
Rose-Hulman Institute of Technology	M
Rowan University	M
Royal Military College of Canada	M,D
Saginaw Valley State University	M
St. Cloud State University	M,O
San Diego State University	M,D
San Francisco State University	M
Santa Clara University	M,D,O
Seattle University	M,D
Simon Fraser University	M,D
South Dakota School of Mines and Technology	M,D
South Dakota State University	M,D
Southern Illinois University Carbondale	M,D
Southern Illinois University Edwardsville	M
Southern Methodist University	M,D
Southern University and Agricultural and Mechanical College	M
Stanford University	M,D,O
Stevens Institute of Technology	M,D,O
Stony Brook University, State University of New York	M,D,O
Syracuse University	M,D,O
Temple University	D*
Tennessee State University	M,D
Tennessee Technological University	M,D
Texas A&M University–Kingsville	M,D
Texas State University	M
Texas Tech University	M,D
Tufts University	M,D
Tuskegee University	M,D
Universidad de las Américas Puebla	M,D
Universidad del Turabo	M
Université de Moncton	M
Université de Sherbrooke	M,D,O
Université du Québec à Chicoutimi	M,D
Université du Québec à Rimouski	M
Université du Québec, École de technologie supérieure	M,D,O
Université du Québec en Abitibi-Témiscamingue	M,O
Université Laval	M,D,O
University at Albany, State University of New York	M,D,O
University at Buffalo, the State University of New York	M,D,O
The University of Akron	M,D
The University of Alabama	M,D
The University of Alabama at Birmingham	D
The University of Alabama in Huntsville	M,D
University of Alaska Fairbanks	D
The University of Arizona	M,D,O
University of Arkansas	M,D
University of Bridgeport	M,D
The University of British Columbia	M,D
University of Calgary	M,D
University of California, Berkeley	M,D,O
University of California, Davis	M,D,O
University of California, Irvine	M,D
University of California, Los Angeles	M,D
University of California, Merced	M,D
University of California, Santa Barbara	M,D
University of California, Santa Cruz	M,D,O
University of Central Florida	M,D,O
University of Central Oklahoma	M
University of Cincinnati	M,D
University of Colorado Boulder	M,D
University of Colorado Colorado Springs	M,D
University of Colorado Denver	M,D
University of Connecticut	M,D
University of Delaware	M,D
University of Denver	M,D
University of Detroit Mercy	M,D,O
University of Florida	M,D,O
University of Guelph	M,D
University of Hartford	M
University of Hawaii at Manoa	M,D
University of Houston	M,D
University of Idaho	M,D
University of Illinois at Chicago	M,D
University of Illinois at Urbana–Champaign	M,D
The University of Iowa	M,D
The University of Kansas	M,D,O
University of Kentucky	M,D
University of Louisville	M,D,O
University of Maine	M,D
University of Manitoba	M,D
University of Maryland, Baltimore County	M,D,O
University of Maryland, College Park	M
University of Massachusetts Amherst	M,D
University of Massachusetts Dartmouth	D
University of Massachusetts Lowell	M,D
University of Memphis	M,D,O
University of Miami	M,D
University of Michigan	M,D,O
University of Michigan–Dearborn	M,D
University of Minnesota, Twin Cities Campus	M,D,O
University of Mississippi	M,D
University of Missouri	M,D,O
University of Missouri–Kansas City	M,D,O
University of Nebraska–Lincoln	M,D
University of Nevada, Las Vegas	M,D,O
University of Nevada, Reno	M,D
University of New Brunswick Fredericton	M,D,O
University of New Haven	M,D
University of New Mexico	M,D
University of New Orleans	M,D
The University of North Carolina at Charlotte	M,D,O
University of North Dakota	D
University of North Texas	M,D,O
University of Notre Dame	M,D
University of Ottawa	M,D
University of Pennsylvania	M,D*
University of Pittsburgh	M,D*
University of Portland	M
University of Puerto Rico–Mayagüez	M,D
University of Regina	M,D
University of Rhode Island	M,D,O
University of Rochester	M,D*
University of St. Thomas (MN)	M,D,O
University of Saskatchewan	M,D,O
University of South Africa	M
University of South Alabama	M,D
University of South Carolina	M,D
University of Southern California	M,D,O
University of Southern Indiana	M,D
University of South Florida	M,D,O
The University of Tennessee	M,D
The University of Texas at Arlington	M,D
The University of Texas at Austin	M,D
The University of Texas at Dallas	M,D
The University of Texas at El Paso	M,D,O
The University of Texas at San Antonio	M,D
University of the District of Columbia	M
University of the Pacific	M
The University of Toledo	M
University of Toronto	M,D
The University of Tulsa	M,D
University of Utah	M,D
University of Vermont	M,D
University of Victoria	M,D
University of Virginia	M,D
University of Washington	M,D,O
University of Waterloo	M,D
The University of Western Ontario	M,D
University of Windsor	M,D
University of Wisconsin–Madison	M,D
University of Wisconsin–Milwaukee	M,D*
University of Wisconsin–Platteville	M
University of Wyoming	M,D
Utah State University	M,D,O
Vanderbilt University	M,D*
Villanova University	M
Virginia Commonwealth University	M,D
Virginia Polytechnic Institute and State University	M,D
Washington State University	M,D,O
Washington University in St. Louis	M,D
Wayne State University	M,D,O
Western Michigan University	M,D
Western New England University	M
West Texas A&M University	M
West Virginia University	M,D
Wichita State University	M,D
Widener University	M
Wilkes University	M
Worcester Polytechnic Institute	M,D,O
Wright State University	M
Yale University	M,D
Youngstown State University	M,O

ENGINEERING DESIGN

Institution	Degrees
Harvard University	M,D*
Northwestern University	M
Ohio Dominican University	M
Penn State University Park	M*
Rochester Institute of Technology	M
San Diego State University	M,D
Stanford University	M,D,O
Stevens Institute of Technology	M
The University of Alabama at Birmingham	M
University of Michigan	M,D
Worcester Polytechnic Institute	M,D,O

ENGINEERING MANAGEMENT

Institution	Degrees
Air Force Institute of Technology	M
American University of Beirut	M,D
American University of Sharjah	M,D
Arkansas State University	M
California State Polytechnic University, Pomona	M
California State University, East Bay	M
California State University, Long Beach	M,D
California State University Maritime Academy	
California State University, Northridge	M
Case Western Reserve University	M
The Catholic University of America	M,O
Central Michigan University	M,D
The Citadel, The Military College of South Carolina	M,D
Clarkson University	M
Colorado School of Mines	M
Cornell University	M,D
Dartmouth College	M
Drexel University	M,O*
Duke University	M
Eastern Michigan University	M
Embry-Riddle Aeronautical University–Worldwide	M
Florida Institute of Technology	M
Florida International University	M
Gannon University	M
The George Washington University	M,D,O
Georgia Southern University	M,O
Indiana Tech	M
Instituto Tecnológico y de Estudios Superiores de Monterrey, Campus Chihuahua	M,O
International Technological University	M
Johns Hopkins University	M*
Kansas State University	M
Kennesaw State University	M
Kettering University	M
Lawrence Technological University	M,D,O
Lehigh University	M,D,O
LeTourneau University	M
Long Island University–LIU Post	M
Louisiana Tech University	M,D,O
Loyola Marymount University	M
Marquette University	M,D,O
Marshall University	M
Massachusetts Institute of Technology	M
McNeese State University	M
Mercer University	M
Merrimack College	M
Middle Tennessee State University	M
Milwaukee School of Engineering	M
Missouri University of Science and Technology	M,D
National University	M
Naval Postgraduate School	M,D,O
New England Institute of Technology	M
New Jersey Institute of Technology	M,D
New Mexico Institute of Mining and Technology	M
Northeastern University	M,D,O
Northwestern University	M
Oakland University	M
Oklahoma Christian University	M
Old Dominion University	M,D
Oregon State University	M,D
Penn State Great Valley	M,O
Penn State Harrisburg	M,O
Point Park University	M
Polytechnic University of Puerto Rico	M
Polytechnic University of Puerto Rico, Orlando Campus	M
Portland State University	M
Robert Morris University	M
Rochester Institute of Technology	M
Rose-Hulman Institute of Technology	M
Saint Martin's University	M
St. Mary's University (United States)	M
Santa Clara University	M,D,O
South Dakota School of Mines and Technology	M
Southern Illinois University Carbondale	M
Southern Methodist University	M,D
Southern New Hampshire University	M,D,O
Stanford University	M,D
Stevens Institute of Technology	M,D,O
Syracuse University	M
Tarleton State University	M
Temple University	M,O*
Texas A&M University	M,D
Texas Tech University	M,D
Trine University	M
Tufts University	M
Université de Sherbrooke	M,O
University at Buffalo, the State University of New York	M,D,O
The University of Alabama at Birmingham	M
University of Alberta	M,D
The University of Arizona	M,D,O
University of California, Berkeley	M,D
University of California, Irvine	M
University of Colorado Boulder	M
University of Dayton	M
University of Denver	M,D
University of Detroit Mercy	M,D
The University of Kansas	M,O
University of Louisville	M,D,O
University of Management and Technology	M
The University of Manchester	M,D
University of Maryland, Baltimore County	M,O
University of Michigan–Dearborn	M
University of Minnesota, Duluth	M
University of Missouri–Kansas City	M,D,O
University of Nebraska–Lincoln	M,D
University of New Brunswick Fredericton	M
University of New Haven	M
University of New Orleans	M
The University of North Carolina at Charlotte	M,O
University of Ottawa	M,O
University of Puerto Rico–Mayagüez	M,D
University of Regina	M,D
University of St. Thomas (MN)	M,O
University of Southern California	M,D,O
University of Southern Indiana	M
University of South Florida	M,D
The University of Tennessee	M,D
The University of Tennessee at Chattanooga	M,O
The University of Texas at Arlington	M
The University of Texas at Tyler	M
The University of Texas Rio Grande Valley	M
University of Vermont	M
University of Waterloo	M,D
Valparaiso University	M,O
Virginia Polytechnic Institute and State University	M,O
Washington State University	M,O
Wayne State University	M,D,O
Western Michigan University	M,D
Western New England University	M,D
Wichita State University	M,D
Widener University	M
Wilkes University	M

ENGINEERING PHYSICS

Institution	Degrees
Air Force Institute of Technology	M,D
Cornell University	M,D
École Polytechnique de Montréal	M,D,O
Embry-Riddle Aeronautical University–Daytona	M,D
Louisiana Tech University	M,D,O
McMaster University	M
Queen's University at Kingston	M,D
Rensselaer Polytechnic Institute	M,D
Stanford University	M,D
University of California, San Diego	M
University of Central Oklahoma	M
University of Oklahoma	M,D*
University of Saskatchewan	M,D
University of Virginia	M,D
University of Wisconsin–Madison	M,D
Yale University	M,D

ENGLISH

Institution	Degrees
Abilene Christian University	M
Acadia University	M
The American University in Cairo	M,O
American University of Beirut	M,D
Andrews University	M
Angelo State University	M
Appalachian State University	M
Arcadia University	M
Arizona State University at the Tempe campus	M,D,O
Arkansas State University	M,O
Arkansas Tech University	M
Asbury University	M
Auburn University	M,D,O
Austin Peay State University	M
Azusa Pacific University	M
Ball State University	M,D
Bard College	M
Baylor University	M,D
Bemidji State University	M
Binghamton University, State University of New York	M,D
Bob Jones University	M,D,O
Boston College	M,D
Boston University	M,D
Bowie State University	M
Bowling Green State University	M,D
Bradley University	M
Brandeis University	M
Bridgewater State University	M
Brock University	M
Brooklyn College of the City University of New York	M
Brown University	M,D
Bucknell University	M
Buffalo State College, State University of New York	M
Cabrini University	M
California Polytechnic State University, San Luis Obispo	M
California State Polytechnic University, Pomona	M
California State University, Bakersfield	M
California State University, Chico	M
California State University, Dominguez Hills	M,O
California State University, East Bay	M
California State University, Fresno	M
California State University, Fullerton	M
California State University, Long Beach	M
California State University, Los Angeles	M,O
California State University, Northridge	M
California State University, Sacramento	M
California State University, San Bernardino	M
California State University, San Marcos	M
California State University, Stanislaus	M,O

M—masters degree; D—doctorate; O—other advanced degree; *—Close-Up and/or Display

University	Degrees
Carleton University	M,D
Carnegie Mellon University	M,D
Case Western Reserve University	M,D
The Catholic University of America	M,D,O
Central Connecticut State University	M,O
Central Michigan University	M
Central Washington University	M
Chapman University	M*
Chicago State University	M
The Citadel, The Military College of South Carolina	M
City College of the City University of New York	M
Claremont Graduate University	M,D
Clark Atlanta University	M,D
Clarks Summit University	M
Clark University	M
Cleveland State University	M
The College at Brockport, State University of New York	M,O
College of Charleston	M
The College of New Jersey	M
College of Staten Island of the City University of New York	M
Colorado State University	M
Columbia College Chicago	M
Columbia University	M,D
Concordia University (Canada)	M,D
Converse College	M
Cornell University	M,D
Creighton University	M
Dalhousie University	M,D
DePaul University	M
Drew University	M,D,O
Duke University	D
Duquesne University	M,D
East Carolina University	M,D,O
Eastern Illinois University	M
Eastern Kentucky University	M
Eastern Michigan University	M
Eastern New Mexico University	M
Eastern Washington University	M
East Tennessee State University	M,O
Emory University	D,O
Emporia State University	M
Fairleigh Dickinson University, Metropolitan Campus	M
Fitchburg State University	M,O
Florida Atlantic University	M
Florida Gulf Coast University	M
Florida International University	M
Fordham University	M,D
Fort Hays State University	M
Framingham State University	M
Gannon University	M
Gardner-Webb University	M
George Mason University	M,D,O
Georgetown University	M
The George Washington University	M,D
Georgia College & State University	M
Georgia Southern University	M
Georgia State University	M,D
Governors State University	M
The Graduate Center, City University of New York	D
Grambling State University	M,D,O
Grand Valley State University	M
Harvard University	M,D,O*
Heritage University	M
Hofstra University	M
Hollins University	M,O
Houston Baptist University	M,D
Howard University	M,D
Humboldt State University	M
Idaho State University	M,D,O
Illinois State University	M,D
Indiana State University	M
Indiana University Bloomington	M,D
Indiana University of Pennsylvania	M,D
Indiana University–Purdue University Indianapolis	M,O
Indiana University South Bend	M,O
Inter American University of Puerto Rico, Metropolitan Campus	M
Iona College	M
Iowa State University of Science and Technology	M,D
Jackson State University	M
Jacksonville State University	M
James Madison University	M
John Carroll University	M
Johns Hopkins University	D*
Kansas State University	M,D
Kent State University	M,D
Kutztown University of Pennsylvania	M
Lakehead University	M
Lamar University	M,O
La Salle University	M
La Sierra University	M,O
Lee University	M,D
Lehigh University	M
Lehman College of the City University of New York	M
Liberty University	M,D,O
Lipscomb University	M,D,O
Long Island University–LIU Brooklyn	M,O
Long Island University–LIU Post	M,D
Louisiana State University and Agricultural & Mechanical College	M,D,O
Louisiana Tech University	M
Loyola Marymount University	M,O
Loyola University Chicago	M,O
Manhattan College	M,O
Manhattanville College	M,D
Marquette University	M,D
Marshall University	M
Mary Baldwin University	M,O
Marymount University	M,D
McGill University	M,D
McMaster University	

University	Degrees
McNeese State University	M
Memorial University of Newfoundland	M,D
Mercy College	M
Miami University	M,D
Michigan State University	M,D
Middlebury College	M
Middle Tennessee State University	M,D
Midwestern State University	M,D
Mills College	M
Minnesota State University Mankato	M,O
Mississippi College	M
Mississippi State University	M
Missouri State University	M,O
Monmouth University	M
Montana State University	M
Montclair State University	M
Morehead State University	M
Morgan State University	M,D
Mount Mary University	M
Mount Saint Mary's University (CA)	M,D,O
Murray State University	M,D,O
National University	M,O
New Mexico Highlands University	M
New York University	M,D*
North Carolina Agricultural and Technical State University	M
North Carolina Central University	M
North Carolina State University	M
North Dakota State University	M,D
Northeastern Illinois University	M
Northeastern State University	M
Northeastern University	M,D
Northern Arizona University	M,D,O
Northern Illinois University	M,D
Northern Kentucky University	M,O
Northern Michigan University	M,O
Northwestern State University of Louisiana	M
Northwestern University	M,D
Northwest Missouri State University	M,O
Oakland University	M
Ohio Dominican University	M
The Ohio State University	M,D
Ohio University	M,D
Oklahoma State University	M,D
Old Dominion University	M,D
Oregon State University	M
Our Lady of the Lake University	M
Pace University	M,O
Penn State University Park	M,D*
Pittsburg State University	M
Portland State University	M
Princeton University	D
Purdue University	M,D
Purdue University Fort Wayne	M,O
Purdue University Northwest	M
Queens College of the City University of New York	M
Queen's University at Kingston	M,D
Radford University	M
Rhode Island College	M,O
Rice University	M,D
Rivier University	M
Rutgers University–Camden	M
Rutgers University–Newark	M
Rutgers University–New Brunswick	D
St. Cloud State University	M
St. John's University (NY)	M,D
Saint Louis University	M,D*
Saint Louis University–Madison Campus	M
St. Mary's University (United States)	M
Salem State University	M
Salisbury University	M
Sam Houston State University	M
San Diego State University	M
San Francisco State University	M
Seton Hall University	M
Simmons University	M,D,O
Simon Fraser University	M,D
Slippery Rock University of Pennsylvania	M
Sonoma State University	M
South Carolina State University	M
South Dakota State University	M
Southeastern Louisiana University	M
Southeast Missouri State University	M
Southern Connecticut State University	M
Southern Illinois University Carbondale	M,D
Southern Illinois University Edwardsville	M,O
Southern Methodist University	M,D
Southern New Hampshire University	M
Spring Hill College	M,O
Stanford University	M,D
State University of New York at Fredonia	M,O
State University of New York at Oswego	M
State University of New York College at Cortland	M
Stephen F. Austin State University	M
Stony Brook University, State University of New York	M,D,O
Sul Ross State University	M
Syracuse University	M,D
Tarleton State University	M
Temple University	M,D*
Tennessee Technological University	M
Texas A&M International University	M
Texas A&M University	M,D
Texas A&M University–Commerce	M,D,O
Texas A&M University–Corpus Christi	M

University	Degrees
Texas A&M University–Kingsville	M
Texas A&M University–San Antonio	M
Texas A&M University–Texarkana	M
Texas Christian University	M,D
Texas Southern University	M
Texas State University	M
Texas Tech University	M,D
Texas Woman's University	M,D
Tiffin University	M
Trinity College (United States)	M
Trinity Western University	M
Truman State University	M
Tufts University	M,D
Tulane University	M
Universidad de las Américas Puebla	M
Université de Montréal	M,D
Université Laval	M,D
University at Albany, State University of New York	M,D
University at Buffalo, the State University of New York	M,D,O
The University of Akron	M,D
The University of Alabama	M,D
The University of Alabama at Birmingham	M
The University of Alabama in Huntsville	M,O
University of Alaska Anchorage	M
University of Alaska Fairbanks	M
University of Alberta	M,D
The University of Arizona	M,D
University of Arkansas	M,D
The University of British Columbia	M,D
University of California, Berkeley	D
University of California, Davis	M,D
University of California, Irvine	M,D
University of California, Los Angeles	M,D
University of California, Riverside	M,D
University of California, San Diego	M,D
University of California, Santa Barbara	D
University of California, Santa Cruz	M,D
University of Central Arkansas	M
University of Central Florida	M,D,O
University of Central Missouri	M,D,O
University of Central Oklahoma	M
University of Chicago	M,D
University of Cincinnati	M,D
University of Colorado Boulder	M,D
University of Colorado Denver	M
University of Connecticut	M,D
University of Dayton	M
University of Delaware	M,D
University of Denver	M,D
University of Florida	M,D
University of Georgia	M,D
University of Guam	M
University of Guelph	M
University of Hawaii at Manoa	M
University of Houston–Clear Lake	M
University of Houston–Downtown	M
University of Illinois at Chicago	M,D
University of Illinois at Springfield	M,O
University of Illinois at Urbana–Champaign	M,D
University of Indianapolis	M
The University of Iowa	M,D
The University of Kansas	M,D
University of Kentucky	M,D
University of La Verne	M,O
University of Lethbridge	M,D
University of Louisiana at Lafayette	M,D
University of Louisiana at Monroe	M
University of Louisville	M,D
University of Maine	M
The University of Manchester	D
University of Manitoba	M,D
University of Maryland, Baltimore County	M
University of Maryland, College Park	M,D
University of Massachusetts Amherst	M,D
University of Massachusetts Boston	M
University of Memphis	M,D,O
University of Miami	M,D
University of Michigan	M,D,O
University of Michigan–Flint	M
University of Minnesota, Duluth	M
University of Minnesota, Twin Cities Campus	M,D
University of Mississippi	M,D
University of Missouri	M,D
University of Missouri–Kansas City	M,D
University of Missouri–St. Louis	M
University of Montana	M
University of Montevallo	M
University of Nebraska at Kearney	M
University of Nebraska at Omaha	M,O
University of Nebraska–Lincoln	M,D
University of Nevada, Las Vegas	M,D
University of Nevada, Reno	M,D
University of New Brunswick Fredericton	M,D
University of New Hampshire	M,D
University of New Mexico	M,D
University of New Orleans	M
University of North Alabama	M

University	Degrees
The University of North Carolina at Chapel Hill	M,D
The University of North Carolina at Charlotte	M,O
The University of North Carolina at Greensboro	M,D
The University of North Carolina Wilmington	M
University of North Dakota	M,D
University of Northern Colorado	M
University of Northern Iowa	M
University of North Florida	M
University of North Texas	M,D,O
University of Notre Dame	M,D
University of Oklahoma	M,D*
University of Oregon	M,D
University of Ottawa	M
University of Pennsylvania	M,D*
University of Pittsburgh	M,D*
University of Puerto Rico–Mayagüez	M
University of Puerto Rico–Río Piedras	M,D
University of Regina	M,D
University of Rhode Island	M,D
University of Rochester	M,D*
University of St. Thomas (MN)	M,O
University of Saskatchewan	M,D
University of South Africa	M,D
University of South Alabama	M
University of South Carolina	M,D
University of South Dakota	M,D
University of Southern California	M,D
University of Southern Indiana	M
University of Southern Mississippi	M,D
University of South Florida	M,D,O
The University of Tennessee	M,D
The University of Tennessee at Chattanooga	M
The University of Texas at Arlington	M,D
The University of Texas at Austin	M,D
The University of Texas at El Paso	M,D,O
The University of Texas at San Antonio	M,D
The University of Texas at Tyler	M
The University of Texas of the Permian Basin	M
The University of Texas Rio Grande Valley	M
The University of the South	M
The University of Toledo	M,O
University of Toronto	M,D
The University of Tulsa	M,D
University of Utah	M,D
University of Vermont	M,D
University of Victoria	M,D
University of Virginia	M,D
University of Washington	M,D
University of Waterloo	M,D
The University of Western Ontario	M,D
University of West Florida	M
University of West Georgia	M,O
University of Windsor	M
University of Wisconsin–Eau Claire	M
University of Wisconsin–Madison	M,D
University of Wisconsin–Milwaukee	M,D*
University of Wisconsin–Oshkosh	M
University of Wyoming	M
Utah State University	M
Valdosta State University	M
Valparaiso University	M
Vanderbilt University	M,D*
Villanova University	M
Virginia Commonwealth University	M
Virginia Polytechnic Institute and State University	M,D,O
Wake Forest University	M
Washington State University	M,D
Washington University in St. Louis	M,D
Wayne State University	M,D
Weber State University	M
West Chester University of Pennsylvania	M,O
Western Carolina University	M,O
Western Connecticut State University	M
Western Illinois University	M,O
Western Kentucky University	M
Western Michigan University	M,D
Western Washington University	M
Westfield State University	M
West Texas A&M University	M
West Virginia University	M,D
Wichita State University	M,D
Wilfrid Laurier University	M,D
William Paterson University of New Jersey	M,D,O
Wilson College	M
Winona State University	M
Winthrop University	M
Wright State University	M
Xavier University	M*
Yale University	M,D
York University	M,D
Youngstown State University	M

ENGLISH AS A SECOND LANGUAGE

University	Degrees
Acacia University	M
Adelphi University	M,O
Albizu University, Miami Campus	M,D
Albright College	M
Alliant International University–San Diego	M,D,O
Alliant International University–San Francisco	M,O
American College of Education	M
American University	M,O
The American University in Cairo	M,O
American University of Armenia	M

American University of Beirut	M,D
American University of Sharjah	M,D
Anaheim University	M,D,O
Andrews University	M,D,O
Angelo State University	M
Arizona State University at the Tempe campus	M,D,O
Arkansas Tech University	M
Asbury University	M,D
Aurora University	M,O
Avila University	M
Azusa Pacific University	M
Ball State University	M
Barry University	M,D,O
Binghamton University, State University of New York	M
Biola University	M,D,O
Bishop's University	M,O
Boise State University	M
Boricua College	M
Brigham Young University	M
Brock University	M
Brown University	M,D
Buena Vista University	M
Cabrini University	M,D
California Baptist University	M
California State University, Dominguez Hills	M,O
California State University, East Bay	M
California State University, Fresno	M
California State University, Long Beach	M,O
California State University, Sacramento	M
California State University, Stanislaus	M,O
Cambridge College	M,D,O
Canisius College	M,O
Carson-Newman University	M
Central Michigan University	M
Central Washington University	M
City College of the City University of New York	M
Cleveland State University	M
Coastal Carolina University	M,O
College of Charleston	O
College of Mount Saint Vincent	M,O
The College of New Jersey	M,O
The College of New Rochelle	M,O
College of Saint Elizabeth	M,O
College of Saint Mary	M
College of Staten Island of the City University of New York	M,O
Colorado Mesa University	M,O
Columbia International University	M,D,O
Columbus State University	O
Concordia University (United States)	M,D
Concordia University (Canada)	M,O
Cornerstone University	M,O
Dallas Baptist University	M
DeSales University	M
Dominican University	M
Duquesne University	M
East Carolina University	M,D,O
Eastern Michigan University	M,O
Eastern Nazarene College	M,O
Eastern New Mexico University	M
Eastern University	M,O
Eastern Washington University	M
East Tennessee State University	M,O
Elms College	M,O
Emporia State University	M,O
Erikson Institute	M,O
Fairfield University	M
Florida Atlantic University	M,D,O
Florida Gulf Coast University	M
Florida International University	M,D,O
Florida State University	M,D,O
Fordham University	M,O
Framingham State University	M,O
Fresno Pacific University	M,O
Furman University	M,O
Gannon University	O
George Fox University	M,O
George Mason University	M
Gonzaga University	M
Gordon College	M
Grand Canyon University	M,D,O
Grand Valley State University	M
Greensboro College	M
Hamline University	M,D
Harding University	M
Hawai'i Pacific University	M,O
Henderson State University	M,O
Heritage University	M
Hofstra University	M,D,O
Holy Family University	M
Houston Baptist University	M,D
Humboldt State University	M
Hunter College of the City University of New York	M
Huntington University	M,D
Idaho State University	M,D,O
Immaculata University	M
Indiana State University	M,D,O
Indiana University Bloomington	M,D
Indiana University of Pennsylvania	M,D
Indiana University–Purdue University Indianapolis	M,O
Inter American University of Puerto Rico, Arecibo Campus	M
Inter American University of Puerto Rico, Barranquitas Campus	M
Inter American University of Puerto Rico, Metropolitan Campus	M
Inter American University of Puerto Rico, Ponce Campus	M

Inter American University of Puerto Rico, San Germán Campus	M
Iowa State University of Science and Technology	M
James Madison University	M
Kansas State University	M,D,O
Kean University	M
Kennesaw State University	M
Kent State University	M,D
Langston University	M
La Salle University	M,O
Lasell College	M
Lee University	M,O
Lehman College of the City University of New York	M
Le Moyne College	M,O
Lesley University	M,D,O
Lewis University	M
Lindenwood University	M,D,O
Long Island University–Hudson	M,O
Long Island University–LIU Brooklyn	M,O
Long Island University–LIU Post	M,D,O
Long Island University–Riverhead	M
Madonna University	M
Manhattanville College	M,O
Marlboro College	M
Mary Baldwin University	M
McDaniel College	M
Mercy College	M,O
Meredith College	M
Messiah College	M
Metropolitan State University	M
Michigan State University	M,D
MidAmerica Nazarene University	M
Middlebury Institute of International Studies at Monterey	M
Middle Tennessee State University	M,O
Midwest University	M,D
Minnesota State University Mankato	M,O
Mississippi College	M
Missouri State University	M
Missouri Western State University	M
Molloy College	M,O
Monmouth University	M,D,O
Montclair State University	M
Mount Saint Vincent University	M
Multnomah University	M
Murray State University	M,D,O
Nazareth College of Rochester	M
New Jersey City University	M
Newman University	M
New Mexico State University	M,D,O
The New School	M
New York University	M,D,O*
Niagara University	M,O
Northeastern Illinois University	M
Northern Arizona University	M,D,O
Northern Michigan University	M
Northwest Christian University	M
Northwest Missouri State University	M,D,O
Notre Dame of Maryland University	M
Nyack College	M
Oakland University	M
Ohio Dominican University	M
Oklahoma City University	M
Old Dominion University	M
Pacific University	M
Penn State Harrisburg	M,D,O
Penn State University Park	M,D*
Penn State York	M,O
Pittsburg State University	M,O
Pontifical Catholic University of Puerto Rico	M
Portland State University	M
Post University	M
Providence University College & Theological Seminary	M,D,O
Purdue University Fort Wayne	M,O
Queens College of the City University of New York	M
Quincy University	M
Regent University	M,D,O
Rhode Island College	M
Rider University	M
Rowan University	O
Rutgers University–New Brunswick	M,D
St. John's University (NY)	M,O
Saint Michael's College	M
St. Thomas University	M,D,O
Saint Xavier University	M
Salem College	M
Salem State University	M
San Diego State University	M,O
San Francisco State University	M
San Jose State University	M
Seattle Pacific University	M,O
Seattle University	M
Simon Fraser University	M
SIT Graduate Institute	M
Slippery Rock University of Pennsylvania	M
Southeastern University (FL)	M,D
Southeast Missouri State University	M
Southern Connecticut State University	M
Southern Illinois University Carbondale	M
Southern Illinois University Edwardsville	M,O
Southern Methodist University	M,O
Southern New Hampshire University	M,D,O
Southwest Minnesota State University	M

State University of New York at Fredonia	M
State University of New York at New Paltz	M,O
State University of New York College at Cortland	M
Stony Brook University, State University of New York	M
Syracuse University	M,O
Taylor College and Seminary	M,O
Teachers College, Columbia University	M,D,O
Temple University	M*
Tennessee Technological University	M
Texas A&M University–Commerce	M,D,O
Texas A&M University–Kingsville	M,D
Touro College	M
Trevecca Nazarene University	M,O
Trinity Western University	M
Troy University	M
Universidad del Este	M
Universidad del Turabo	M
University at Buffalo, the State University of New York	M,D,O
The University of Alabama	M,D
The University of Alabama at Birmingham	M,O
The University of Alabama in Huntsville	M,O
University of Alberta	M,D
The University of Arizona	M,D
University of Arkansas at Little Rock	M
The University of British Columbia	M,D
University of California, Berkeley	O
University of California, Los Angeles	M,D,O
University of California, Riverside	M,D,O
University of Central Florida	M,O
University of Central Missouri	M,D,O
University of Central Oklahoma	M
University of Cincinnati	M,D
University of Colorado Colorado Springs	M,D
University of Dayton	M
University of Delaware	M,D,O
The University of Findlay	M,D
University of Florida	M,D,O
University of Guam	M
University of Hawaii at Manoa	M,D,O
University of Illinois at Chicago	M,D
University of Illinois at Urbana–Champaign	M,D
The University of Iowa	M,D
University of Louisiana at Lafayette	M,D
University of Manitoba	M
University of Maryland, Baltimore County	M,O
University of Maryland, College Park	M,D,O
University of Massachusetts Amherst	M,D,O
University of Massachusetts Dartmouth	M,D,O
University of Memphis	M,D,O
University of Minnesota, Twin Cities Campus	M,D,O
University of Missouri–St. Louis	M
University of Nebraska at Kearney	M
University of Nebraska at Omaha	M
University of Nevada, Las Vegas	M,D,O
University of Nevada, Reno	M
University of New Mexico	M,D
The University of North Carolina at Chapel Hill	M
The University of North Carolina at Charlotte	M,D,O
The University of North Carolina at Greensboro	M,D,O
The University of North Carolina Wilmington	M
University of Northern Colorado	M,D
University of Northern Iowa	M
University of North Florida	M
University of North Texas	M,D,O
University of Pennsylvania	M*
University of Phoenix–Online Campus	M,O
University of Phoenix–San Diego Campus	M
University of Pittsburgh	D,O*
University of Portland	M,D
University of Puerto Rico–Río Piedras	M
University of St. Francis (IL)	M,D,O
University of Saint Joseph	M
University of St. Thomas (TX)	M,D
University of San Diego	M
University of Saskatchewan	M
University of South Africa	M,D
University of South Carolina	M,D,O
University of South Dakota	M
University of Southern California	M
University of Southern Indiana	M
University of Southern Maine	M,O
University of Southern Mississippi	M
University of South Florida	M,D,O
The University of Tennessee	M,D,O
The University of Texas at Arlington	M
The University of Texas at El Paso	M,O
The University of Texas at San Antonio	M,D,O
The University of Texas of the Permian Basin	M

The University of Texas Rio Grande Valley	M
University of the Southwest	M
The University of Toledo	M,D,O
University of Washington	M,D
University of Wisconsin–Madison	M,D
University of Wisconsin–Milwaukee	M,D,O*
University of Wisconsin–River Falls	M
Upper Iowa University	M
Utah Valley University	M
Valley City State University	M
Valparaiso University	M,O
Virginia International University	M
Walden University	M,D,O
Washington State University	M,D
Wayland Baptist University	M
Wayne State College	M
Wayne State University	M,D,O
Webster University	M,O
West Chester University of Pennsylvania	M,O
Westcliff University	M
Western Carolina University	M,O
Western Illinois University	M,O
Western Kentucky University	M
Western New Mexico University	M
Wilkes University	M,D
William Paterson University of New Jersey	M,D,O
Wilmington University	M,D
Winona State University	M
Worcester State University	M,O

ENGLISH EDUCATION

Alabama Agricultural and Mechanical University	M,O
Alabama State University	M
Albany State University	M
Andrews University	M,D,O
Anna Maria College	M,O
Appalachian State University	M
Arcadia University	M,D,O
Arkansas State University	M
Arkansas Tech University	M
Binghamton University, State University of New York	M
Bloomsburg University of Pennsylvania	M
Bob Jones University	M,D,O
Boise State University	M
Boston College	M,D,O
Brooklyn College of the City University of New York	M
Brown University	M
Buffalo State College, State University of New York	M
California Baptist University	M
California State University, Northridge	M
Campbellsville University	M
Caribbean University	M,D
Carthage College	M,O
Central Connecticut State University	M,O
Chadron State College	M,O
Chatham University	M
The Citadel, The Military College of South Carolina	M,O
City College of the City University of New York	M,O
Clayton State University	M
The College at Brockport, State University of New York	M,O
College of St. Joseph	M
College of Staten Island of the City University of New York	M
The Colorado College	M
Columbus State University	M,O
Converse College	M
Delta State University	M
Duquesne University	M
East Carolina University	M,D,O
Eastern Kentucky University	M
Eastern Michigan University	M
Eastern University	M,O
Elms College	M,O
Fitchburg State University	M,O
Florida Agricultural and Mechanical University	M
Florida Gulf Coast University	M
Florida International University	M,D,O
Florida State University	M,D,O
Gardner-Webb University	M
George Mason University	M
Georgia Southwestern State University	M,O
Georgia State University	M,D
Grand Valley State University	M
Hampton University	M
Harding University	M,O
Hofstra University	M,D,O
Houston Baptist University	M
Hunter College of the City University of New York	M
Indiana University of Pennsylvania	D
Iona College	M
Ithaca College	M
Jackson State University	M
Kansas State University	M,D,O
Kennesaw State University	M
Kent State University	M,D
Kutztown University of Pennsylvania	M
Lake Forest College	M
Lehman College of the City University of New York	M
Le Moyne College	M,O
Lewis University	M

Lincoln Memorial University — M,D,O
Lipscomb University — M,D
London Metropolitan University — M,D
Manhattanville College — M,O
Marymount University — M,O
Metropolitan State University — M
Millersville University of Pennsylvania — M
Mississippi College — M,D,O
Missouri State University — M,O
Molloy College — M,O
Montclair State University — M,O
Morehead State University — M,O
Murray State University — M,D,O
National Louis University — M,D,O
New Mexico State University — M,D
New York Institute of Technology — M
New York University — M,D,O*
North Carolina Agricultural and Technical State University — M
Northeastern Illinois University — M
Northwest Missouri State University — M,O
Oregon State University — M
Plymouth State University — M
Purdue University — M,D,O
Purdue University Fort Wayne — M,O
Queens College of the City University of New York — M,O
Quinnipiac University — M
Rhode Island College — M
Rowan University — O
Rutgers University–New Brunswick — M
St. John Fisher College — M
San Francisco State University — M,O
Simon Fraser University — M,D
Slippery Rock University of Pennsylvania — M
Smith College — M
South Carolina State University — M
Southeastern Louisiana University — M
Southern Illinois University Edwardsville — M,O
State University of New York at Fredonia — M,O
State University of New York at New Paltz — M,O
State University of New York at Plattsburgh — M
State University of New York College at Cortland — M
State University of New York College at Geneseo — M
State University of New York College at Old Westbury — M
State University of New York College at Potsdam — M
Syracuse University — M
Teachers College, Columbia University — M,D,O
Temple University — M*
Texas Woman's University — M
Trinity Washington University — M
University at Buffalo, the State University of New York — M,D,O
The University of Akron — M
The University of Alabama in Huntsville — M,O
The University of Arizona — M,D
University of Arkansas at Pine Bluff — M
University of Central Florida — M,O
University of Colorado Denver — M
University of Connecticut — M,D
University of Florida — M,D,O
University of Georgia — M,D
University of Indianapolis — M
The University of Iowa — M,D
University of Manitoba — M
University of Maryland, Baltimore County — M
University of Michigan — D
University of Minnesota, Twin Cities Campus — M
University of Missouri — M,D,O
University of Montana — M
University of New Mexico — M,D
The University of North Carolina at Chapel Hill — M
The University of North Carolina at Greensboro — M,D
The University of North Carolina at Pembroke — M
University of Northern Colorado — M,D
University of Northern Iowa — M
University of North Georgia — M
University of Oklahoma — M,D*
University of Pennsylvania — M,D*
University of Phoenix–Online Campus — M,O
University of Pittsburgh — M,D*
University of Puerto Rico–Mayagüez — M
University of St. Francis (IL) — M,D,O
University of South Carolina — M,D
University of Southern Mississippi — M,D
University of South Florida, St. Petersburg — M
University of South Florida Sarasota-Manatee — M
The University of Tennessee — M,D,O
The University of Texas at El Paso — M,D,O
University of the District of Columbia — M
University of the Sacred Heart — M,O
The University of Toledo — M,D
University of Victoria — M,D
University of Virginia — M,D
University of Washington — M,D
The University of West Alabama — M
University of Wisconsin–La Crosse — M,O

University of Wisconsin–Milwaukee — M,D*
University of Wisconsin–Stevens Point — M
Valdosta State University — M
Valley City State University — M
Vanderbilt University — M*
Wagner College — M
Wayland Baptist University — M
Wayne State College — M
Wayne State University — M,D,O
West Chester University of Pennsylvania — M,O
Western Governors University — M,O
Western Kentucky University — M
Western Michigan University — M
Western New England University — M
West Virginia University — M,D
Widener University — M,D
William Carey University — M,O
William Jessup University — M
Worcester State University — M

ENTERTAINMENT MANAGEMENT

Berklee College of Music — M
California Intercontinental University — M
California State University, Northridge — M,O
Carnegie Mellon University — M
Columbia College Chicago — M
Full Sail University — M,O
Hofstra University — M
Point Park University — M
Southern New Hampshire University — M,D,O
Syracuse University — M
Universidad Autonoma de Guadalajara — M,D
University of Colorado Denver — M
University of Dallas — M,D
University of Massachusetts Amherst — M
University of South Carolina — M
Valparaiso University — M
William Paterson University of New Jersey — M,O

ENTOMOLOGY

Auburn University — M,D
Clemson University — M,D
Colorado State University — M,D
Cornell University — M,D
Illinois State University — M,D
Iowa State University of Science and Technology — M,D
Kansas State University — M,D
Louisiana State University and Agricultural & Mechanical College — M,D
McGill University — M,D
Michigan State University — M,D
North Carolina State University — M,D
North Dakota State University — M,D
The Ohio State University — M,D
Oklahoma State University — M,D
Penn State University Park — M,D*
Purdue University — M,D
Rutgers University–New Brunswick — M,D
Simon Fraser University — M,D,O
State University of New York College of Environmental Science and Forestry — M,D
Texas A&M University — M,D
The University of Arizona — M,D
University of Arkansas — M,D
University of California, Davis — M,D
University of California, Riverside — M,D
University of Delaware — M,D
University of Georgia — M,D
University of Guelph — M,D
University of Hawaii at Manoa — M,D
University of Idaho — M,D
University of Illinois at Urbana–Champaign — M,D
University of Kentucky — M,D
University of Maine — M,D
University of Manitoba — M,D
University of Maryland, College Park — M,D
University of Minnesota, Twin Cities Campus — M,D
University of Missouri — M,D
University of Nebraska–Lincoln — M,D
The University of Tennessee — M,D
University of Vermont — M,D,O
University of Wisconsin–Madison — M,D
University of Wyoming — M,D
Virginia Polytechnic Institute and State University — M,D
Washington State University — M,D
West Virginia University — M,D

ENTREPRENEURSHIP

Albizu University, Miami Campus — M,O
American College of Thessaloniki — M,O
American University — M,D,O
Anaheim University — M,D,O
Arizona State University at the Tempe campus — M,D
Ashland University — M
Azusa Pacific University — M
Babson College — M,O
Bakke Graduate University — M,D
Baruch College of the City University of New York — M,D*
Baylor University — D
Bay Path University — M
Benedictine University — M
Brandeis University — M
Brandman University — M
Brigham Young University — M
Cairn University — M,O

California Institute of Advanced Management — M
California Intercontinental University — M,D
California Lutheran University — M,O
California State University, San Bernardino — M
California University of Pennsylvania — M
Cambridge College — M
Cameron University — M
Capella University — M,D
Carnegie Mellon University — D
City Vision University — M
Clarion University of Pennsylvania — M
Clemson University — M,D
Cogswell Polytechnical College — M
Columbia University — M
Dallas Baptist University — M
Dartmouth College — D
Delaware Valley University — M
DePaul University — M,D
Dickinson State University — M
Drexel University — M*
Duke University — M,O
Eastern Michigan University — M,O
East Tennessee State University — M,O
Elms College — M,O
Embry-Riddle Aeronautical University–Worldwide — M
Emory University — M
Everglades University — M
Fairleigh Dickinson University, Florham Campus — M,O
Fairleigh Dickinson University, Metropolitan Campus — M,O
Felician University — M,D
Florida Atlantic University — M
Fordham University — M,D
Georgia State University — M,D
Golden Gate University — M,D,O
Grand Canyon University — M
Harrisburg University of Science and Technology — M,O
HEC Montreal — M,O
Hult International Business School (United States) — M
IGlobal University — M
Illinois Institute of Technology — M
Indiana University–Purdue University Indianapolis — M
International University in Geneva — M,D
The International University of Monaco — M
James Madison University — M
Kansas State University — M,O
Lehigh University — M
Lenoir-Rhyne University — M
Lindenwood University — M
Loyola University Chicago — M
Manhattanville College — M
Marlboro College — M
Marquette University — M,O
McGill University — M,D,O
Mercer University — M
Mercyhurst University — M,O
Midwest University — M,D
Monroe College — M
Nebraska Christian College of Hope International University — M
North Carolina State University — M
Northeastern University — M
Northwestern University — M,D
Nova Southeastern University — M
Oakland University — M,O
Oklahoma State University — M,D
Old Dominion University — M,O
Oral Roberts University — M
Pace University — M
Penn State Great Valley — M,O
Penn State University Park — M*
Peru State College — M
Point Loma Nazarene University — M
Pontificia Universidad Catolica Madre y Maestra — M
Purchase College, State University of New York — M
Purdue University Global — M
Queen's University at Kingston — M
Regent University — M,D,O
Rensselaer Polytechnic Institute — M
Rochester Institute of Technology — M
Rockhurst University — M,O
Rollins College — M
Salve Regina University — M
Samford University — M
San Diego State University — M
San Francisco State University — M
Seton Hall University — M,O
Seton Hill University — M
SIT Graduate Institute — M
South Carolina State University — M
Southeastern University (FL) — M,D
Southeast Missouri State University — M
Southern Methodist University — M
Southern New Hampshire University — M,D,O
South University (GA) — M
Stevens Institute of Technology — M,O
Stony Brook University, State University of New York — M,O
Suffolk University — M
Syracuse University — M
Temple University — M,D*
Texas A&M University — M
Tufts University — M
Tulane University — M,D
United States International University–Africa — M
Université Laval — M,O
University at Albany, State University of New York — M

The University of Alabama in Huntsville — M,O
University of Arkansas at Little Rock — O
University of Baltimore — M
University of Bridgeport — M
University of California, Davis — M
University of California, Merced — M,D
University of Central Florida — M,O
University of Chicago — M,O
University of Colorado Denver — M
University of Delaware — M,D
University of Florida — M,D,O
University of Hawaii at Manoa — M,O
University of Houston–Victoria — M
University of Louisiana at Lafayette — M
University of Louisville — M,D
The University of Manchester — M
University of Massachusetts Amherst — M,D
University of Massachusetts Lowell — M,D
University of Minnesota, Twin Cities Campus — D
University of New Brunswick Fredericton — M
University of New Mexico — M
University of Notre Dame — M
University of Oklahoma — M,D,O*
University of Pennsylvania — M*
University of Pikeville — M
University of Portland — M
University of Rhode Island — M,D,O
University of Rochester — M*
University of San Francisco — M
University of Sioux Falls — M
University of Southern California — M
University of South Florida — M,O
The University of Tampa — M,O
The University of Texas at Austin — M
The University of Texas at Dallas — M,D
University of Washington — M,D
University of Waterloo — M
The University of Western Ontario — M,D
University of West Los Angeles — M
University of Wisconsin–Milwaukee — M,D,O*
Ursuline College — M
Virginia International University — M,O
Walden University — M,D,O
Washington University in St. Louis — M
Wayne State University — M,D,O
Western Carolina University — M
Wichita State University — M
Wilkes University — M
William Paterson University of New Jersey — M,O
Wingate University — M

ENVIRONMENTAL AND OCCUPATIONAL HEALTH

American University of Beirut — M,D
Augusta University — M
Boise State University — M,O
Boston University — M,D
California State University, Fullerton — M
California State University, Northridge — M
Capella University — M,D
Clemson University — M,D
Colorado State University — M
Columbia Southern University — M
Columbia University — M,D
Duke University — O
East Carolina University — M,D,O
Eastern Kentucky University — M
East Tennessee State University — M,D,O
Embry-Riddle Aeronautical University–Worldwide — M
Emory University — M,D
Florida International University — M,D
Fort Valley State University — M
Gannon University — M
The George Washington University — D
Georgia Southern University — M,D,O
Harvard University — M,D*
Indiana State University — M
Indiana University Bloomington — M,D
Indiana University of Pennsylvania — M,D
Indiana University–Purdue University Indianapolis — M,D,O
Johns Hopkins University — M,D*
Kent State University — M,D
Lehigh University — M,O
Lewis University — M
Loma Linda University — M
Louisiana State University Health Sciences Center — M,D
McGill University — M,D
Meharry Medical College — M
Mercer University — M,D
Mississippi Valley State University — M
Murray State University — M
New York Medical College — M,D,O
Oakland University — M
Old Dominion University — M
Oregon State University — M,D
Purdue University — M,D
Rochester Institute of Technology — M
Rutgers University–New Brunswick — M,D,O
San Diego State University — M,D
Southeastern Oklahoma State University — M
Syracuse University — M
Temple University — M,D*
Texas A&M University — D
Towson University — M
Trident University International — M,D,O
Tufts University — M,D
Tulane University — M,D

Uniformed Services University of the Health Sciences	M,D*
Universidad Autonoma de Guadalajara	M,D
Universidad de Ciencias Medicas	M,D,O
Université de Montréal	M
Université du Québec à Montréal	O
Université Laval	O
University at Albany, State University of New York	M,D
The University of Alabama at Birmingham	M,D
University of Alberta	M,D
University of Arkansas for Medical Sciences	M,D,O
University of California, Berkeley	M,D
University of California, Irvine	M,D
University of California, Los Angeles	M,D
University of Central Missouri	M,D,O
University of Cincinnati	M,D
University of Colorado Denver	O
University of Florida	M,D,O
University of Georgia	M,D
University of Illinois at Chicago	M,D
University of Illinois at Springfield	M,O
The University of Iowa	M,D,O
University of Maryland, College Park	M
University of Massachusetts Amherst	M,D
University of Memphis	M,D
University of Miami	M
University of Michigan	M,D
University of Minnesota, Twin Cities Campus	M,D,O
University of Nebraska Medical Center	D
University of Nevada, Reno	M,D
University of New Haven	M
The University of North Carolina at Chapel Hill	M,D
University of Oklahoma Health Sciences Center	M,D
University of Pennsylvania	M*
University of Pittsburgh	M,D*
University of Puerto Rico–Medical Sciences Campus	M,D
University of Saint Francis (IN)	M
University of South Alabama	M
University of South Carolina	M,D
University of Southern California	M
University of South Florida	O
The University of Texas at Tyler	M
The University of Texas Health Science Center at Houston	M,D,O
University of the Sacred Heart	M
The University of Toledo	M,D,O
University of Toronto	M,D
University of Vermont	M,O
University of Washington	M,D
University of Wisconsin–Milwaukee	M,D,O*
University of Wisconsin–Whitewater	M
West Virginia University	M,D
Yale University	M,D

ENVIRONMENTAL BIOLOGY

Chatham University	M
Dalhousie University	M
Dartmouth College	D
Emporia State University	M
Georgia State University	M,D
Governors State University	M
Hampton University	M
Hood College	M,O
Massachusetts Institute of Technology	M,D,O
Missouri University of Science and Technology	M
Morgan State University	D
Nicholls State University	M
Ohio University	M,D
Oregon State University	M,D
Regis University	M
Rutgers University–New Brunswick	M,D
State University of New York College of Environmental Science and Forestry	M,D
Universidad del Turabo	M,D
University of Alberta	M,D
University of California, Santa Cruz	M,D
University of Guelph	M,D
University of Louisiana at Lafayette	M,D
University of Louisville	M,D
The University of Manchester	M,D
University of Massachusetts Amherst	M,D
University of Southern California	M,D
University of South Florida	M,D
University of Wisconsin–Madison	D
Washington University in St. Louis	D
Youngstown State University	M

ENVIRONMENTAL DESIGN

Arizona State University at the Tempe campus	D
ArtCenter College of Design	M
Columbia University	M
Cornell University	M
Kansas State University	D
Kent State University	M
Michigan State University	M,D

North Carolina Agricultural and Technical State University	M
Texas Tech University	M,D
Université de Montréal	M,D,O
University of Calgary	M,D
University of California, Berkeley	M,D
University of California, Irvine	D
University of Georgia	M,D
The University of Manchester	M,D
Virginia Polytechnic Institute and State University	M,D
Yale University	M,D

ENVIRONMENTAL EDUCATION

Alaska Pacific University	M
Antioch University New England	M,D,O
Arcadia University	M,O
Ball State University	M,O
Brooklyn College of the City University of New York	M
Chatham University	M
Concordia University (United States)	M
Concordia University Wisconsin	M
Florida Atlantic University	M
Goshen College	M
Hamline University	M,D
Instituto Tecnologico de Santo Domingo	M,D,O
Mary Baldwin University	M
Montclair State University	M
New York University	M*
Oregon State University	M,D
Prescott College	M,D
Royal Roads University	M,O
Slippery Rock University of Pennsylvania	M
Southern Connecticut State University	M,O
Southern Oregon University	M
State University of New York College at Cortland	M
Université du Québec à Montréal	M,D,O
University of Florida	M,D,O
University of South Africa	M,D
University of Victoria	M,D
Western Washington University	M

ENVIRONMENTAL ENGINEERING

Air Force Institute of Technology	M,D
The American University in Cairo	M,D,O
Arizona State University at the Tempe campus	M,D
California Institute of Technology	M,D
California Polytechnic State University, San Luis Obispo	M
California State University, Fullerton	M
Carleton University	M,D
Carnegie Mellon University	M,D
The Catholic University of America	M,D
Clarkson University	M,D
Clemson University	M,D
Cleveland State University	M,D
Colorado School of Mines	M,D
Columbia University	M,D
Concordia University (Canada)	M,D,O
Cornell University	M,D
Dalhousie University	M,D
Drexel University	M,D*
Duke University	M,D
École Polytechnique de Montréal	M,D,O
Florida Atlantic University	M
Florida International University	M,D
Florida State University	M,D
Gannon University	M
The George Washington University	M,D,O
Georgia Institute of Technology	M,D
Harvard University	M,D*
Idaho State University	M
Illinois Institute of Technology	M,D
Instituto Tecnologico de Santo Domingo	M,O
Instituto Tecnológico y de Estudios Superiores de Monterrey, Campus Ciudad de México	M,D
Instituto Tecnológico y de Estudios Superiores de Monterrey, Campus Monterrey	M,D
Iowa State University of Science and Technology	M,D
Jackson State University	M,D
Johns Hopkins University	M,D,O*
Kansas State University	M,D
Kennesaw State University	M
Lakehead University	M
Lehigh University	M,D
Louisiana State University and Agricultural & Mechanical College	M,D
Manhattan College	M
Marquette University	M,D,O
Marshall University	M
Massachusetts Institute of Technology	M,D,O
McGill University	M,D
Memorial University of Newfoundland	M
Mercer University	M
Michigan State University	M
Michigan Technological University	M,D
Missouri University of Science and Technology	M,D
Montana State University	M,D
Montana Tech of The University of Montana	M
New Jersey Institute of Technology	M
New Mexico Institute of Mining and Technology	M
New Mexico State University	M,D

New York Institute of Technology	M
North Dakota State University	M,D
Northeastern University	M,D,O
Northwestern University	M,D
Norwich University	M
Ohio University	M,D
Oklahoma State University	M,D
Old Dominion University	M,D
Oregon Health & Science University	M,D
Oregon State University	M,D
Penn State Harrisburg	M,O
Penn State University Park	M,D*
Polytechnic University of Puerto Rico, Miami Campus	M
Polytechnic University of Puerto Rico, Orlando Campus	M
Portland State University	M,D
Princeton University	M,D
Purdue University	M,D
Rensselaer Polytechnic Institute	M,D
Rice University	M,D
Rose-Hulman Institute of Technology	M
Rutgers University–New Brunswick	M,D
Southern Illinois University Carbondale	D
Southern Illinois University Edwardsville	M
Southern Methodist University	M,D
State University of New York College of Environmental Science and Forestry	M,D,O
Stevens Institute of Technology	M,D,O
Syracuse University	M
Temple University	M,D,O*
Tennessee State University	M,D
Texas A&M University–Kingsville	M,D
Tufts University	M,D
Universidad Central del Este	M
Universidad Nacional Pedro Henriquez Urena	M
Université de Sherbrooke	M
Université Laval	M,D
University at Buffalo, the State University of New York	M,D
The University of Alabama	M,D
The University of Alabama in Huntsville	M,D
University of Alaska Fairbanks	M,D,O
University of Alberta	M,D
The University of Arizona	M,D
University of Arkansas	M,D
University of Calgary	M,D
University of California, Berkeley	M,D
University of California, Davis	M,D,O
University of California, Irvine	M,D
University of California, Los Angeles	M,D
University of California, Merced	M,D
University of California, Riverside	M,D
University of Central Florida	M,D
University of Cincinnati	M,D
University of Colorado Boulder	M,D
University of Colorado Denver	M,D
University of Connecticut	M,D
University of Dayton	M
University of Delaware	M,D
University of Detroit Mercy	M,D
University of Florida	M,D,O
University of Georgia	M
University of Guelph	M,D
University of Hawaii at Manoa	M,D
University of Illinois at Urbana–Champaign	M,D
The University of Iowa	M,D
The University of Kansas	M,D
The University of Manchester	M,D
University of Maryland, Baltimore County	M,D
University of Maryland, College Park	M,D
University of Massachusetts Amherst	M,D
University of Massachusetts Lowell	M,D
University of Memphis	M,D,O
University of Michigan	M,D,O
University of Mississippi	M,D
University of Missouri	M,D
University of Nebraska–Lincoln	M,D
University of New Brunswick Fredericton	M,D
University of New Hampshire	M,D
University of New Haven	M
The University of North Carolina at Chapel Hill	M,D
The University of North Carolina at Charlotte	M,D
University of North Dakota	M,D
University of Notre Dame	M,D
University of Oklahoma	M,D*
University of Pittsburgh	M,D*
University of Puerto Rico–Mayagüez	M,D
University of Regina	M,D
University of Rhode Island	M,D
University of South Alabama	M
University of Southern California	M,D,O
University of South Florida	M,D
The University of Tennessee	M
The University of Texas at Austin	M,D
The University of Texas at El Paso	M,D,O
The University of Texas at San Antonio	M,D
The University of Texas at Tyler	M
University of Utah	M,D
University of Vermont	M,D
University of Washington	M,D

University of Waterloo	M,D
The University of Western Ontario	M,D
University of Windsor	M,D
University of Wisconsin–Madison	M
University of Wyoming	M
Utah State University	M,D,O
Vanderbilt University	M,D*
Villanova University	M,O
Virginia Polytechnic Institute and State University	M,O
Washington State University	M,D
Washington University in St. Louis	M,D
Worcester Polytechnic Institute	M,D,O
Yale University	M,D
Youngstown State University	M

ENVIRONMENTAL LAW

Chapman University	M,D*
Florida State University	M,D
Georgetown University	M,D
Golden Gate University	M,D
Lehigh University	M,D
Lewis & Clark College	M,D
Montclair State University	O
Pace University	M,D
St. Mary's University (United States)	M
Stanford University	M,D
University at Buffalo, the State University of New York	M,O
University of Calgary	M,O
University of Colorado Denver	M,D
University of Florida	M,D
University of Houston	M,D
University of Pittsburgh	M*
The University of Tulsa	M,D,O
Vermont Law School	M
Western Michigan University Thomas M. Cooley Law School	M,D

ENVIRONMENTAL MANAGEMENT AND POLICY

Adelphi University	M
Air Force Institute of Technology	M
American Public University System	M,D
American University	M,D,O
American University of Beirut	M,D
Antioch University New England	M,D
Arizona State University at the Tempe campus	M
Ball State University	M,O
Bard College	M,D
Baylor University	M
Bemidji State University	M
Binghamton University, State University of New York	M,D
California State University, Fullerton	M
Central European University	M,D
Central Washington University	M
The Citadel, The Military College of South Carolina	M,O
Clarkson University	M
Clark University	M,D
Clemson University	M,D
Cleveland State University	M
College of the Atlantic	M
Colorado State University	M
Columbia University	M
Columbus State University	M
Concordia University (Canada)	M,D,O
Cornell University	M,D
Dalhousie University	M
Drexel University	M*
Duke University	D
Duquesne University	M,O
The Evergreen State College	M
Florida Gulf Coast University	M
Florida Institute of Technology	M
Florida International University	M,D
George Mason University	M
The George Washington University	M
Georgia Institute of Technology	M
Georgia State University	M,D,O
Harvard University	M,O*
Humboldt State University	M
Idaho State University	M
Illinois Institute of Technology	M
Indiana University Bloomington	M,D,O
Indiana University Northwest	M
Indiana University of Pennsylvania	M
Instituto Tecnologico de Santo Domingo	M,D,O
Instituto Tecnológico y de Estudios Superiores de Monterrey, Campus Estado de México	M,D
Instituto Tecnológico y de Estudios Superiores de Monterrey, Campus Irapuato	M,D
Inter American University of Puerto Rico, Metropolitan Campus	M
James Madison University	M
Johns Hopkins University	M,O*
Lake Forest College	M
Lehigh University	M,O
Long Island University–LIU Post	M,O
Louisiana State University and Agricultural & Mechanical College	M,D
McGill University	M,D
Middlebury Institute of International Studies at Monterey	M
Millersville University of Pennsylvania	M
Missouri State University	M,O
Montclair State University	M,D
Morehead State University	M
New Jersey Institute of Technology	M,D,O
The New School	O
New York Institute of Technology	M

New York University	M*
Northeastern Illinois University	M,O
Northeastern University	M,D
Northern Arizona University	M,D,O
The Ohio State University	M,D
Ohio University	M,O
Oregon State University	M,D
Pace University	M
Penn State University Park	M*
Point Park University	M
Polytechnic University of Puerto Rico	M
Polytechnic University of Puerto Rico, Miami Campus	M
Polytechnic University of Puerto Rico, Orlando Campus	M
Portland State University	M,D,O
Prescott College	M
Purdue University	M,D
Rice University	M
Royal Roads University	M,O
St. Edward's University	M
Samford University	M
San Francisco State University	M
San Jose State University	M
Shippensburg University of Pennsylvania	M
Simon Fraser University	M,D,O
SIT Graduate Institute	M
Slippery Rock University of Pennsylvania	M
Southeast Missouri State University	M
Southern Illinois University Carbondale	M,D
Southern Illinois University Edwardsville	M
Southern New Hampshire University	M,D,O
State University of New York College of Environmental Science and Forestry	M,D
Stony Brook University, State University of New York	M,O
Tennessee Technological University	M
Texas Southern University	M,D
Texas Tech University	M,D
Thomas Edison State University	M
Towson University	M
Trent University	M,D
Tropical Agriculture Research and Higher Education Center	M,D
Troy University	M
Tufts University	M,D,O
Universidad Autonoma de Guadalajara	M,D
Universidad del Turabo	M,D
Universidad Metropolitana	M
Université de Montréal	O
Université du Québec à Chicoutimi	M
Université du Québec, Institut National de la Recherche Scientifique	M,D
Université Laval	M,D,O
University of Alaska Fairbanks	M
University of Alberta	M,D
The University of Arizona	M,D
The University of British Columbia	M,D
University of Calgary	M,D,O
University of California, Berkeley	M,D,O
University of California, San Diego	M
University of California, Santa Barbara	M,D
University of California, Santa Cruz	D
University of Central Missouri	M,D,O
University of Chicago	M
University of Colorado Boulder	M,D
University of Colorado Denver	M,D,O
University of Dayton	M,D
University of Delaware	M,D
University of Denver	M,O
The University of Findlay	M,D
University of Guelph	M,D
University of Hawaii at Manoa	M,D,O
University of Houston–Clear Lake	M
University of Illinois at Springfield	M
University of Maine	D
The University of Manchester	M,D
University of Maryland, Baltimore County	M,D
University of Maryland Eastern Shore	M,D
University of Maryland University College	M
University of Massachusetts Amherst	M,D
University of Massachusetts Dartmouth	M,O
University of Michigan	M,D
University of Minnesota, Twin Cities Campus	M,D
University of Montana	M
University of Nevada, Reno	M
University of New Brunswick Fredericton	M,D
University of New Hampshire	M
University of New Haven	M
University of New Mexico	M
The University of North Carolina Wilmington	M
University of Northern British Columbia	M,D,O
University of Oregon	M,D
University of Pennsylvania	M*
University of Puerto Rico–Río Piedras	M
University of Rhode Island	M,D
University of South Africa	M,D
University of South Alabama	M,D
University of South Carolina	M

University of South Florida	M,D,O
University of South Florida, St. Petersburg	M
The University of Tennessee	M,D
The University of Texas at Austin	M
University of Washington	M,D
University of Waterloo	M,D
University of Wisconsin–Green Bay	M
Utah State University	M,D
Vanderbilt University	M,D*
Vermont Law School	M
Virginia Commonwealth University	M
Virginia Polytechnic Institute and State University	M,D,O
Webster University	M
Wesley College	M
Western State Colorado University	M
Wilfrid Laurier University	M,D
Wilmington University	M,D
Yale University	M,D
York University	M,D
Youngstown State University	M,O

ENVIRONMENTAL SCIENCES

Adelphi University	M
Alaska Pacific University	M
American University	M,O
American University of Beirut	M,D
Antioch University New England	M,D
Arizona State University at the Tempe campus	M,D,O
Arkansas State University	M
Ball State University	D
Baylor University	D
Boston University	M,D
Brigham Young University	M,D
California Institute of Technology	M,D
California State Polytechnic University, Pomona	M
California State University, Chico	M
California State University, East Bay	M
California State University, Northridge	M
California State University, San Bernardino	M
Carnegie Mellon University	D
Christopher Newport University	M
Clarkson University	M,D
Clark University	M
Clemson University	M,D
Cleveland State University	M,D
The College at Brockport, State University of New York	M
College of Charleston	M
College of Staten Island of the City University of New York	M
Colorado School of Mines	M,D
Columbia University	M,D
Columbus State University	M,O
Cornell University	M,D
Dalhousie University	M
DePaul University	M,D
Drexel University	M,D*
Duke University	M,D
Duquesne University	M,O
Florida Agricultural and Mechanical University	M,D
Florida Gulf Coast University	M
Florida Institute of Technology	M,D
Florida State University	M,D
Gannon University	M
George Mason University	M,D
The Graduate Center, City University of New York	D
Harvard University	M,D*
Howard University	M,D
Humboldt State University	M
Idaho State University	M,O
Indiana University Bloomington	M,D,O
Instituto Tecnologico de Santo Domingo	M,D,O
Instituto Tecnológico y de Estudios Superiores de Monterrey, Campus Ciudad de México	M,D
Inter American University of Puerto Rico, San Germán Campus	M
Iowa State University of Science and Technology	M,D
Jackson State University	M
Johns Hopkins University	M,O*
Kansas State University	M,D,O
Laurentian University	M
Lehigh University	M,D
Lincoln University (MO)	M
Louisiana State University and Agricultural & Mechanical College	M,D
Loyola Marymount University	M
Marshall University	M
Massachusetts Institute of Technology	M,D,O
McNeese State University	M
Memorial University of Newfoundland	M,D
Mercer University	M
Miami University	M
Michigan State University	M,D
Minnesota State University Mankato	M
Montana State University	M,D
Montclair State University	M
Murray State University	M,O
New Jersey Institute of Technology	M,D,O
North Carolina Agricultural and Technical State University	M
North Carolina Central University	M
North Dakota State University	M,D
Northeastern University	M,D
Northern Arizona University	M,D,O
Oakland University	M,D
The Ohio State University	M,D
Oklahoma State University	M,D,O
Old Dominion University	M,D
Oregon Health & Science University	M,D

Oregon State University	M,D
Pace University	M
Penn State Harrisburg	M,O
Penn State University Park	M*
Pontifical Catholic University of Puerto Rico	M
Portland State University	M,D,O
Queens College of the City University of New York	M
Rice University	M,D
Rochester Institute of Technology	M
Rutgers University–Newark	M,D
Rutgers University–New Brunswick	M,D
Sitting Bull College	M
South Dakota School of Mines and Technology	D
Southeast Missouri State University	M
Southern Connecticut State University	M,O
Southern Illinois University Carbondale	D
Southern Illinois University Edwardsville	M
Southern University and Agricultural and Mechanical College	M
Stanford University	M,D,O
State University of New York College of Environmental Science and Forestry	M,D
Stephen F. Austin State University	M
Stockton University	M
Tarleton State University	M
Tennessee Technological University	M,D
Texas A&M University–Commerce	M,O
Texas A&M University–Corpus Christi	M
Texas Christian University	M
Texas Tech University	M,D
Thompson Rivers University	M
Towson University	M,O
Tuskegee University	M,D
Universidad del Turabo	M,D
Universidad Nacional Pedro Henriquez Urena	M
Université de Sherbrooke	M,O
Université du Québec à Montréal	M,D,O
Université du Québec à Trois-Rivières	M,D
Université du Québec en Abitibi-Témiscamingue	M,D
Université Laval	M,D
University at Buffalo, the State University of New York	M,D
University of Alberta	M,D
The University of Arizona	M,D,O
University of California, Berkeley	M,D
University of California, Davis	M,D
University of California, Los Angeles	M,D
University of California, Riverside	M
University of California, Santa Barbara	M,D
University of Chicago	M
University of Cincinnati	M,D
University of Colorado Colorado Springs	M
University of Colorado Denver	M
University of Guam	M
University of Guelph	M,D
University of Hawaii at Hilo	M
University of Houston–Clear Lake	M
University of Idaho	M,D
University of Illinois at Springfield	M
University of Illinois at Urbana–Champaign	M,D
The University of Kansas	M,D
University of Lethbridge	M,D
University of Louisiana at Lafayette	M,D
The University of Manchester	M,D
University of Manitoba	M,D
University of Maryland, Baltimore	M,D
University of Maryland, Baltimore County	M,D
University of Maryland, College Park	M,D
University of Maryland Eastern Shore	M,D
University of Massachusetts Boston	M,D
University of Massachusetts Lowell	M,D
University of Michigan	M,D
University of Michigan–Dearborn	M
University of Missouri	M,D,O
University of Montana	M
University of Nevada, Las Vegas	M,D,O
University of Nevada, Reno	M
University of New Haven	M
University of New Orleans	M,D
The University of North Carolina at Chapel Hill	M,D
The University of North Carolina Wilmington	M
University of North Texas	M,D,O
University of Oklahoma	M,D*
University of Pennsylvania	M,D
University of Pittsburgh	M,D*
University of Prince Edward Island	M,D
University of Puerto Rico–Mayagüez	M
University of Puerto Rico–Río Piedras	M,D
University of Rhode Island	M,D
University of San Diego	M
University of Saskatchewan	M,D
University of South Africa	M,D

University of South Florida	M,D
University of South Florida, St. Petersburg	M
The University of Tennessee at Chattanooga	M
The University of Texas at Arlington	M,D
The University of Texas at El Paso	M,D
The University of Texas at San Antonio	M,D
The University of Texas Rio Grande Valley	M
University of the Virgin Islands	M
The University of Toledo	M,D
University of Toronto	M,D
University of Utah	M,D
University of Vermont	M
University of Virginia	M,D
University of Waterloo	M
The University of Western Ontario	M,D
University of West Florida	M
University of Windsor	M,D
University of Wisconsin–Green Bay	M
University of Wisconsin–Madison	M
University of Wisconsin–Milwaukee	M,D*
Vanderbilt University	M*
Virginia Polytechnic Institute and State University	M,O
Washington State University	M,D
Wesleyan University	M
Western Illinois University	D
Western Washington University	M
West Texas A&M University	M
Wichita State University	M
Wilfrid Laurier University	M,D
Wright State University	D
Yale University	M,D

EPIDEMIOLOGY

American University of Beirut	M,D
Boston University	M,D
Brown University	M,D
California State University, Northridge	M
Capella University	M
Case Western Reserve University	D
Colorado State University	M,D
Columbia University	M
Daemen College	M
Dalhousie University	M,D
Dartmouth College	M,D
Drexel University	M,D,O*
East Tennessee State University	M,D,O
Emory University	M,D
Florida International University	M,D
George Mason University	M,O
Georgetown University	M,O
The George Washington University	M
Georgia Southern University	M,D
Harvard University	M,D*
Indiana University Bloomington	M,D
Indiana University–Purdue University Indianapolis	M,D,O
Johns Hopkins University	M,D*
Kent State University	M,D
Liberty University	M,D
Loma Linda University	M,D
Louisiana State University Health Sciences Center	M,D
McGill University	M,D
Medical University of South Carolina	M,D
Memorial University of Newfoundland	M,D,O
Michigan State University	M
Monroe College	M
New York Medical College	M,D,O
North Carolina State University	M,D
Northwestern University	D
Oregon State University	M,D
Ponce Health Sciences University	M,D
Purdue University	M,D
Queen's University at Kingston	M,D
Rutgers University–Newark	M,O
Rutgers University–New Brunswick	M,D,O
San Diego State University	M,D
Stanford University	M,D
Temple University	M,D*
Texas A&M University	M,D
Tufts University	M,D,O
Tulane University	M,D
Université Laval	M,D
University at Albany, State University of New York	M,D
University at Buffalo, the State University of New York	M,D
The University of Alabama at Birmingham	M,D
University of Alberta	M,D
The University of Arizona	M,D
University of Arkansas for Medical Sciences	M,D,O
University of California, Berkeley	M,D
University of California, Davis	M,D
University of California, Irvine	M,D
University of California, Los Angeles	M,D
University of California, San Diego	D
University of Cincinnati	M,D
University of Colorado Denver	M,D,O
University of Florida	M,D
University of Guelph	M,D
University of Hawaii at Manoa	D
University of Illinois at Chicago	M,D
University of Illinois at Springfield	M,O
The University of Iowa	M,D
The University of Kansas	M

University of Kentucky — D
University of Maryland, Baltimore — M,D,O
University of Maryland, Baltimore County — M,D,O
University of Maryland, College Park — M,D
University of Massachusetts Amherst — M,D
University of Memphis — M,D
University of Michigan — M,D
University of Minnesota, Twin Cities Campus — M,D
University of Nebraska Medical Center — D
University of New Mexico — M
The University of North Carolina at Chapel Hill — M,D
University of North Texas Health Science Center at Fort Worth — M,D,O
University of Oklahoma Health Sciences Center — M,D
University of Ottawa — M*
University of Pennsylvania — M,D
University of Pittsburgh — M,D*
University of Prince Edward Island — M
University of Puerto Rico– Medical Sciences Campus — M
University of Rochester — D*
University of Saskatchewan — M,D
University of South Carolina — M,D
University of Southern California — M,D
University of Southern Mississippi — M,D
University of South Florida — O
The University of Tennessee Health Science Center — M,D
The University of Texas Health Science Center at Houston — M,D,O
The University of Toledo — M,O
University of Toronto — M,O
University of Vermont — M,O
University of Washington — M,D
The University of Western Ontario — M,D
University of Wisconsin– Madison — M,D
University of Wisconsin– Milwaukee — M,D,O*
Virginia Commonwealth University — M,D
Walden University — M,D,O
Washington University in St. Louis — M,D
Weill Cornell Medicine — M
West Virginia University — M,D
Yale University — M,D

ERGONOMICS AND HUMAN FACTORS

Arizona State University at the Tempe campus — M
Bentley University — M
California State University, Long Beach — M
The Catholic University of America — M,D
Clemson University — M,D
Cornell University — M
Embry-Riddle Aeronautical University–Daytona — M,D
Georgia Institute of Technology — M,D
Harvard University — M,D*
Indiana University Bloomington — M,D
Michigan Technological University — M,D,O
Mississippi State University — M,D
North Carolina State University — D
Old Dominion University — D
Purdue University — M,D
Queen's University at Kingston — M,D
Tufts University — O
Université de Montréal — O
Université du Québec à Montréal — O
The University of Alabama — M
University of Cincinnati — M,D
The University of Iowa — M,D,O
University of Miami — M
University of Wisconsin– Madison — M,D
University of Wisconsin– Milwaukee — M*
Wright State University — M,D

ETHICS

American University — M,D,O
Anabaptist Mennonite Biblical Seminary — M,O
Arizona State University at the Tempe campus — M,D
Azusa Pacific University — M
Chicago Theological Seminary — M,D
Claremont Graduate University — M,D
Claremont Lincoln University — M
Claremont School of Theology — M,D
Columbia University — M
Duke University — M,O
Emory University — M,D
Epic Bible College — M,D
Fordham University — M,O
Freed-Hardeman University — M*
George Mason University — M
Georgetown University — M,D
Graduate Theological Union — M,D,O
Greensboro College — M
John Brown University — M
Lancaster Theological Seminary — M,D,O
Lebanon Valley College — M
Lee University — M
Loyola University Chicago — M
Lutheran Theological Seminary Saskatoon — M,D
Marquette University — M,D
New England College of Business and Finance — M
Northwestern University — M
Oregon State University — M

Phillips Theological Seminary — M,D
Pontifical John Paul II Institute for Studies on Marriage and Family — M,D,O
Santa Clara University — M,D,O
Schreiner University — M
Southeastern Baptist Theological Seminary — M,D
Spring Hill College — M,O
Stevens Institute of Technology — M,O
Suffolk University — M,O
Texas State University — M
Université de Sherbrooke — M,D,O
Université du Québec à Chicoutimi — O
Université du Québec à Rimouski — M,O
Université Laval — O
University of Chicago — D
University of Detroit Mercy — M,O
University of Maryland, Baltimore — O
The University of North Carolina at Charlotte — M,O
University of North Florida — M,O
University of Pennsylvania — M,D*
University of St. Thomas (MN) — M,D
University of South Africa — M,D
The University of Tennessee at Chattanooga — M,O
Valparaiso University — M,O
Viterbo University — M,O
West Chester University of Pennsylvania — M,O
Xavier University — M*

ETHNIC STUDIES

Colorado State University — M
Cornell University — M,D
DePaul University — M
Minnesota State University Mankato — M
Northern Arizona University — O
San Francisco State University — M
United Theological Seminary of the Twin Cities — M,D,O
Université Laval — M,D
The University of British Columbia — M
University of California, Berkeley — D
University of California, Riverside — D
University of California, San Diego — D
University of Colorado Boulder — M
University of Colorado Denver — M,O
University of New Mexico — M,D

EVOLUTIONARY BIOLOGY

Arizona State University at the Tempe campus — M,D
Brown University — D
Columbia University — M,D
Cornell University — D
Dartmouth College — D
Emory University — D
Florida State University — M,D
Harvard University — D*
Illinois State University — M,D
Indiana State University — M,D
Indiana University Bloomington — M,D
Iowa State University of Science and Technology — M,D
Johns Hopkins University — D*
Michigan State University — D
Montclair State University — M
The Ohio State University — M,D
Ohio University — M,D
Oklahoma State University — D
Princeton University — D
Purdue University — M,D
Rice University — M,D
Rutgers University–New Brunswick — M,D
Stony Brook University, State University of New York — M,D
Tulane University — M,D
University at Buffalo, the State University of New York — M,D,O
University of Alberta — M,D
The University of Arizona — M,D
University of California, Davis — D
University of California, Irvine — M,D
University of California, Los Angeles — M,D
University of California, Riverside — M,D
University of California, Santa Barbara — M,D
University of California, Santa Cruz — M,D
University of Chicago — D
University of Colorado Boulder — M,D
University of Delaware — M,D
University of Denver — M,D
University of Guelph — M,D
University of Illinois at Urbana–Champaign — M,D
The University of Iowa — M,D
The University of Kansas — M,D
University of Louisiana at Lafayette — M,D
The University of Manchester — M,O
University of Maryland, College Park — M,D
University of Massachusetts Amherst — M,D
University of Miami — M,D
University of Michigan — M,D
University of Minnesota, Twin Cities Campus — M,D
University of Missouri — M,D
University of Nevada, Reno — M,D
University of New Hampshire — D

The University of North Carolina at Chapel Hill — M,D
University of Notre Dame — M,D
University of Oklahoma — M,D*
University of Oregon — M,D
University of Pittsburgh — D*
University of Puerto Rico– Río Piedras — M,D
University of Rhode Island — M,D
University of South Carolina — M,D
University of Southern California — D
University of South Florida — M,D
The University of Tennessee — M
The University of Texas at Austin — D
University of Toronto — M,D
Washington University in St. Louis — D
Wesleyan University — D
Yale University — D

EXERCISE AND SPORTS SCIENCE

Adams State University — M
American International College — M,D,O
Appalachian State University — M
Arizona State University at the Tempe campus — M,D
Arkansas State University — M,O
Ashland University — M
Auburn University — M,D,O
Auburn University at Montgomery — M
Austin Peay State University — M
Ball State University — M,D
Barry University — M
Baylor University — M,D
Benedictine University — M
Bloomsburg University of Pennsylvania — M
Brigham Young University — M,D
Brooklyn College of the City University of New York — M
California Baptist University — M
California State University, Fresno — M
California State University, Long Beach — M
California State University, Sacramento — M
California University of Pennsylvania — M
Carroll University — M
Central Connecticut State University — M,O
Central Michigan University — M,D
The Citadel, The Military College of South Carolina — M,O
The College of St. Scholastica — M
Colorado State University — M,D
Columbus State University — M
Concordia University (Canada) — M
Concordia University Chicago — M
Concordia University, St. Paul — M,D
Delaware State University — M
Delta State University — M
East Carolina University — M,D,O
Eastern Kentucky University — M
Eastern Michigan University — M
Eastern New Mexico University — M
Eastern Washington University — M
East Tennessee State University — M
Fairmont State University — M
Florida Atlantic University — M
Florida State University — M,D
Gannon University — M
Gardner-Webb University — M
George Mason University — M,O
The George Washington University — M
Georgia College & State University — M
Georgia State University — M
Hofstra University — M,O
Howard University — M
Indiana University Bloomington — M,D
Indiana University of Pennsylvania — M
Inter American University of Puerto Rico, Metropolitan Campus — M
Iowa State University of Science and Technology — M
Ithaca College — M
James Madison University — M
Kean University — M
Kennesaw State University — M
Kent State University — M,D
Lakehead University — M
Liberty University — M,D
Life University — M
Lipscomb University — M
Logan University — M
Long Island University–LIU Brooklyn — M,D,O
Manhattanville College — M,O
Marshall University — M
Marywood University — M
McNeese State University — M
Memorial University of Newfoundland — M
Merrimack College — M
Miami University — M
Middle Tennessee State University — M,D
Midwestern State University — M
Mississippi State University — M,D
Montclair State University — M,O
New Mexico Highlands University — M
North Dakota State University — M,D
Northeastern Illinois University — M
Northeastern University — M,D,O
Northern Michigan University — M
Northwest Missouri State University — M
Oakland University — M,D,O
Ohio University — M,D
Old Dominion University — M
Pittsburg State University — M
Point Loma Nazarene University — M

Purdue University — M,D
Queens College of the City University of New York — M,O
Queen's University at Kingston — M,D
Rowan University — M
Sacred Heart University — M
St. Ambrose University — M
Saint Mary's College of California — M
San Diego State University — M
Smith College — M
Sonoma State University — M
South Dakota State University — M,D
Southeast Missouri State University — M
Southern Connecticut State University — M
Southern Illinois University Edwardsville — M
Southern Utah University — M
Springfield College — M,D,O
Syracuse University — M
Tennessee State University — M
Texas A&M University– Commerce — M,D,O
Texas Tech University — M
Texas Woman's University — M,D
United States Sports Academy — M
University at Buffalo, the State University of New York — M,D,O
The University of Akron — M
The University of Alabama — M,D
University of Alberta — M,D
University of Arkansas at Little Rock — M
University of California, Davis — M,O
University of Central Florida — M
University of Central Oklahoma — M
University of Connecticut — M,D
University of Dayton — M
University of Florida — M,D
University of Houston — M,D
University of Houston–Clear Lake — M
University of Idaho — M,D
The University of Iowa — M,D
The University of Kansas — M,D
University of Kentucky — M,D
University of Lethbridge — M,D
University of Louisiana at Monroe — M
University of Louisville — M,D,O
University of Maine — M,D,O
University of Mary — M
University of Mary Hardin-Baylor — M
University of Massachusetts Boston — M,D
University of Memphis — M
University of Miami — M
University of Minnesota, Twin Cities Campus — M,D
University of Mississippi — M,D
University of Montana — M
University of Nebraska at Kearney — M
University of Nebraska at Omaha — M,D
University of Nebraska– Lincoln — M,D
University of Nevada, Las Vegas — M,D
University of New Brunswick Fredericton — M
University of New Mexico — D
University of North Alabama — M
The University of North Carolina at Chapel Hill — M
The University of North Carolina at Pembroke — M
University of Northern Colorado — M,D
University of North Florida — M,D
University of Oklahoma — M,D*
University of Pittsburgh — M,D*
University of Puerto Rico– Mayagüez — M
University of Puerto Rico– Río Piedras — M
University of Rhode Island — M
University of South Alabama — M
University of South Carolina — M
University of South Dakota — M
The University of Tampa — M
The University of Tennessee — M,D,O
The University of Texas at Arlington — M,D
The University of Texas at Austin — M,D
The University of Texas Rio Grande Valley — M
University of the Pacific — M
The University of Toledo — M,D
University of West Florida — M
University of Wisconsin–La Crosse — M
University of Wisconsin– Milwaukee — M,D*
University of Wyoming — M
Valdosta State University — M
Virginia Commonwealth University — M
Virginia Polytechnic Institute and State University — M,D
Wake Forest University — M
Washington State University — M
Wayne State College — M
Wayne State University — M
West Chester University of Pennsylvania — M,O
Western Michigan University — M
Western Washington University — M
West Texas A&M University — M
West Virginia University — M
Wichita State University — M
William Paterson University of New Jersey — M,D,O

*M—masters degree; D—doctorate; O—other advanced degree; *—Close-Up and/or Display*

EXPERIMENTAL PSYCHOLOGY

Azusa Pacific University — M
Bowling Green State University — M,D
Brooklyn College of the City University of New York — M,D
California State University, Fresno — M,O
California State University, Northridge — M
Case Western Reserve University — D
The Catholic University of America — M,D
Central Michigan University — M,D
Central Washington University — M
Cornell University — D
Duke University — D
Eastern Washington University — M
East Tennessee State University — D
Fairleigh Dickinson University, Metropolitan Campus — M,O
The Graduate Center, City University of New York — D
Harvard University — D*
Howard University — M,D
Idaho State University — D
Iona College — M,O
James Madison University — M
Kent State University — M,D
Lakehead University — M
Laurentian University — M
McGill University — M,D
McNeese State University — M,O
Memorial University of Newfoundland — M,D
Middle Tennessee State University — M,O
Missouri State University — M,O
Morehead State University — M
Murray State University — M,O
Nova Southeastern University — M,D,O
Ohio University — D
Radford University — M
Rivier University — M
Rochester Institute of Technology — M
Saint Louis University — M,D*
San Jose State University — M
Seton Hall University — M
Southern Illinois University Carbondale — M,D
Texas A&M University–Central Texas — M,O
Texas Christian University — M,D
Texas Tech University — M,D
Towson University — M
The University of Alabama — D
University of Central Oklahoma — M
University of Cincinnati — D
University of Connecticut — M,D
University of Idaho — M,D
University of Louisville — D
University of Maryland, College Park — M,D
University of Massachusetts Dartmouth — M,O
University of Memphis — M,D,O
University of Mississippi — M,D
University of Montana — M,D,O
University of New Brunswick Saint John — M,D
University of Regina — M,D
University of South Carolina — M,D
The University of Tennessee — M,D
The University of Tennessee at Chattanooga — M
The University of Texas at Arlington — M,D
The University of Texas at El Paso — M,D
The University of Texas of the Permian Basin — M
The University of Texas Rio Grande Valley — M
The University of Toledo — M,D
University of Vermont — D
University of Victoria — M,D
The University of West Alabama — M
University of West Florida — M
University of Wisconsin–Oshkosh — M
Washington State University — M,D
Western Illinois University — M,O
Western Kentucky University — M,O
Western Washington University — M

FACILITIES MANAGEMENT

Cornell University — M
Liberty University — M,D
Maastricht School of Management — M,D
Massachusetts Maritime Academy — M
Pratt Institute — M
Purdue University Fort Wayne — M
Université Laval — M,O
University of California, Berkeley — O
University of New Haven — M,O
The University of North Carolina at Charlotte — M,O
Wentworth Institute of Technology — M

FAMILY AND CONSUMER SCIENCES-GENERAL

Alabama Agricultural and Mechanical University — M
Ball State University — M
California State University, Northridge — M
Central Michigan University — M,O
Central Washington University — M
Clemson University — D,O
Florida State University — M,D
Fontbonne University — M
Hofstra University — M,D,O
Illinois State University — M
Iowa State University of Science and Technology — M
Kansas State University — M,D,O
Lamar University — M

Louisiana State University and Agricultural & Mechanical College — M,D
North Carolina Agricultural and Technical State University — M
North Dakota State University — M
The Ohio State University — M,D
Oklahoma State University — M,D
Queens College of the City University of New York — M,O
Saint Peter's University — M
Sam Houston State University — M
San Francisco State University — M
South Carolina State University — M
South Dakota State University — M
Stephen F. Austin State University — M
Tennessee State University — M,D
Texas A&M University–Kingsville — M
Texas Southern University — M
Texas State University — M
Tufts University — M,D
The University of Alabama — M,D
University of Alberta — M,D
The University of Arizona — D
University of Arkansas — M
University of Central Arkansas — M
University of Central Oklahoma — M
University of Colorado Denver — M,D
University of Florida — M
University of Georgia — M,D
University of Houston — M
University of Maryland, College Park — M,D
University of Missouri — M,D,O
University of Nebraska–Lincoln — M,D
University of Puerto Rico–Río Piedras — M
University of South Africa — M,D
The University of Tennessee — D
The University of Tennessee at Martin — M
The University of Texas at Austin — M,D
University of Wisconsin–Madison — M,D
University of Wisconsin–Stevens Point — O
Utah State University — M,D
Western Michigan University — M

FAMILY NURSE PRACTITIONER STUDIES

Albany State University — M
Allen College — M,D
Alvernia University — M,D,O
Alverno College — M,D
American International College — M,D,O
Anderson University (SC) — M,D
Angelo State University — M
Arizona State University at the Tempe campus — M,D,O
Ashland University — D
Auburn University at Montgomery — M
Augsburg University — M,D
Augusta University — D
Austin Peay State University — M
Azusa Pacific University — M,D
Ball State University — M,D,O
Barry University — M,O
Bellarmine University — M,D
Bellin College — M
Binghamton University, State University of New York — M,D,O
Bloomsburg University of Pennsylvania — M,D
Bowie State University — M
Bradley University — M,D,O
Brenau University — M
Brigham Young University — M
California Baptist University — M
California State University, Bakersfield — M
California State University, San Marcos — M
Carlow University — M,O
Carson-Newman University — M
Case Western Reserve University — M
Cedarville University — M,D
Clarion University of Pennsylvania — M
Clarke University — D
Clarkson College — M,O
Clayton State University — M
Clemson University — M,D,O
College of Mount Saint Vincent — M,O
The College of New Rochelle — M,O
Colorado Mesa University — M,D,O
Columbia University — M,O
Columbus State University — M
Concordia University Wisconsin — M,D
Coppin State University — M,O
Cox College — M
Creighton University — M,D,O
Delta State University — M,D
DePaul University — M,D
DeSales University — M,D,O
Dominican College — M
Drexel University — M*
Duke University — M,D,O
Duquesne University — M,O
D'Youville College — M,D,O
Eastern Kentucky University — M
East Tennessee State University — M,D,O
Edinboro University of Pennsylvania — M,D
Elms College — M,D
Emory University — M
Endicott College — M,O
Fairfield University — M,D
Felician University — M,O
Florida National University — M
Florida Southern College — M
Florida State University — D,O
Franciscan Missionaries of Our Lady University — M

Francis Marion University — M
Fresno Pacific University — M
Frontier Nursing University — M,D,O*
Gannon University — M,O
Gardner-Webb University — M,D
George Mason University — M,D,O
Georgetown University — M,D
The George Washington University — M,D,O
Georgia Southern University — M
Georgia Southwestern State University — M,O
Georgia State University — M,D,O
Goshen College — M
Graceland University (IA) — M,D,O
Grambling State University — M,O
Grand Canyon University — M,D,O
Gwynedd Mercy University — M,D
Hampton University — M,D
Hardin-Simmons University — M
Hofstra University — M
Holy Names University — M
Houston Baptist University — M
Howard University — M
Hunter College of the City University of New York — D
Husson University — M,O
Illinois State University — M,D,O
Indiana State University — M,D
Indiana University Kokomo — M
Indiana University–Purdue University Indianapolis — M
Indiana University South Bend — M
Jacksonville University — M
James Madison University — M,D
Johns Hopkins University — D*
Keiser University — M
Kent State University — M,D
King University — M,D,O
La Salle University — M,D,O
Le Moyne College — M,O
Lewis University — M,D
Liberty University — M,D
Lincoln Memorial University — M
Long Island University–Brentwood Campus — M
Long Island University–LIU Brooklyn — M,O
Long Island University–LIU Post — M,O
Louisiana State University Health Sciences Center — M,D,O
Loyola University Chicago — M,D,O
Loyola University New Orleans — M,D
Malone University — M
Marian University (IN) — M,D
Marquette University — M,D,O
Marymount University — M,D
Maryville University of Saint Louis — M,D
McGill University — M,D,O
McMurry University — M
McNeese State University — M
Medical University of South Carolina — M,D
Mercer University — M,D,O
Middle Tennessee State University — M,O
Midwestern State University — M
Millersville University of Pennsylvania — M,D,O
Minnesota State University Mankato — M,D
Missouri State University — M,D
Molloy College — M,D,O
Montana State University — M,D,O
Morningside College — M
Mount Carmel College of Nursing — M,D
Mount Saint Mary College — M,O
Murray State University — D
National University — M,O
New Mexico State University — M,D,O
New York University — M,D,O*
Nicholls State University — M
Northeastern University — M,D,O
Northern Arizona University — M,D,O
Nova Southeastern University — M,D
Oakland University — M,O
Ohio University — M,D
Old Dominion University — M
Olivet Nazarene University — M
Oregon Health & Science University — M
Otterbein University — M,D,O
Pace University — M,D
Pacific Lutheran University — D
Palm Beach Atlantic University — M,D
Point Loma Nazarene University — M
Purdue University — M,D,O
Purdue University Fort Wayne — M,O
Purdue University Northwest — M
Queen's University at Kingston — M,D,O
Quinnipiac University — D
Ramapo College of New Jersey — M
Regis College (MA) — M,D,O
Research College of Nursing — M
Rivier University — M,D
Rocky Mountain University of Health Professions — D
Rush University — M,D
Rutgers University–Camden — D
Rutgers University–Newark — M,D,O
Sacred Heart University — M,D,O
Sage Graduate School — M
Saginaw Valley State University — M,D
Saint Francis Medical Center College of Nursing — M,D,O
Saint Joseph's College of Maine — M,O
Saint Mary's College — D
Salisbury University — D
Samford University — M,D,O
Samuel Merritt University — M,D,O
San Francisco State University — M
Seattle Pacific University — M,O
Shenandoah University — M,D,O
Simmons University — M,D

Sonoma State University — M
Southern Adventist University — M,D
Southern Connecticut State University — M,D
Southern Illinois University Edwardsville — M,D,O
Southern University and Agricultural and Mechanical College — M,D,O
South University — M
South University — M
South University — M
Spalding University — M,D,O
State University of New York Downstate Medical Center — M,O
State University of New York Polytechnic Institute — M,O
State University of New York Upstate Medical University — M
Stephen F. Austin State University — M
Stony Brook University, State University of New York — M,D,O
Temple University — D*
Tennessee State University — M
Tennessee Technological University — M,D
Texas A&M International University — M
Texas A&M University — M
Texas A&M University–Corpus Christi — M,D
Texas Christian University — D
Texas State University — M
Texas Tech University Health Sciences Center — M,D,O
Texas Woman's University — M,D
Troy University — M,D
Tusculum University — M
Uniformed Services University of the Health Sciences — M,D*
Union University — M
United States University — M
Universidad del Turabo — M,O
University at Buffalo, the State University of New York — M,D,O
The University of Alabama at Birmingham — M,D
The University of Alabama in Huntsville — M,D,O
The University of Arizona — M,D,O
University of Central Arkansas — M,O
University of Colorado Denver — M,D
University of Connecticut — M
University of Delaware — M,O
University of Detroit Mercy — M,D,O
University of Hawaii at Manoa — M,D,O
University of Houston — M
University of Illinois at Chicago — M,O
University of Indianapolis — M,D
University of Louisiana at Lafayette — M,D
University of Louisville — M,D
University of Maine — M,O
University of Mary — M,O
University of Mary Hardin-Baylor — M,D,O
University of Maryland, Baltimore — M,D,O
University of Massachusetts Amherst — M
University of Massachusetts Lowell — M
University of Massachusetts Medical School — M,D,O
University of Memphis — M,O
University of Miami — M,O
University of Michigan–Flint — M,D,O
University of Minnesota, Twin Cities Campus — M,D
University of Missouri — M,D,O
University of Missouri–Kansas City — M,D
University of Missouri–St. Louis — D,O
University of Nevada, Las Vegas — M,D,O
University of New Hampshire — M,D,O
The University of North Carolina at Chapel Hill — M,D,O
The University of North Carolina at Charlotte — M,D,O
The University of North Carolina Wilmington — M,D,O
University of North Dakota — M,D,O
University of Northern Colorado — M,D
University of North Florida — M,D,O
University of North Georgia — M,D
University of Pennsylvania — M,O*
University of Phoenix–Hawaii Campus — M
University of Phoenix–Online Campus — M
University of Phoenix–Phoenix Campus — M,O
University of Phoenix–Sacramento Valley Campus — M
University of Portland — M,D
University of Puerto Rico–Medical Sciences Campus — M
University of Rhode Island — M
University of Rochester — M,D*
University of St. Francis (IL) — M,D,O
University of Saint Francis (IN) — M,D,O
University of Saint Joseph — M,D
University of San Diego — M,D
The University of Scranton — M
University of South Carolina — M
University of Southern Indiana — M,D,O
University of Southern Maine — M,D,O
University of South Florida — M,D,O
The University of Tampa — M
The University of Tennessee at Chattanooga — M,D,O
The University of Tennessee Health Science Center — D,O
The University of Texas at Arlington — M,D
The University of Texas at Austin — M,D
The University of Texas at El Paso — M,D,O
The University of Texas at Tyler — M,D

The University of Texas Health Science Center at San Antonio — M,D,O
The University of Toledo — M,O
The University of Tulsa — D
University of Victoria — M,D
University of Wisconsin–Eau Claire — M,D
University of Wisconsin–Milwaukee — M,D,O*
University of Wisconsin–Oshkosh — M
Ursuline College — M,D
Valdosta State University — M
Villanova University — M,D,O
Virginia Commonwealth University — M
Wagner College — M,D,O
Walden University — M,D,O
Washington State University — M,D,O
West Coast University — M
Westminster College (UT) — M
West Texas A&M University — M
West Virginia Wesleyan College — M,D,O
Wilmington University — M,D
Winona State University — M,D,O
Winston-Salem State University — M,D
Wright State University — M

FILM, TELEVISION, AND VIDEO PRODUCTION

Academy of Art University — M
American Film Institute Conservatory — M
American University — M
Arizona State University at the Tempe campus — M
ArtCenter College of Design — M
Azusa Pacific University — M
Bard College — M
Bob Jones University — M,D,O
Boston University — M
Bowling Green State University — M,D
Brooklyn College of the City University of New York — M
California College of the Arts — M
California Institute of the Arts — M,O
California State University, Fullerton — M
California State University, Northridge — M
Carleton University — M
Carnegie Mellon University — M
Central Michigan University — M
Chapman University — M*
Chatham University — M
Columbia College Chicago — M
Columbia University — M
Concordia University (Canada) — M,D
DePaul University — M,D
Drexel University — M*
Florida Atlantic University — M,O
Florida State University — M
Georgia State University — M,D
Governors State University — M
Hollins University — M
Howard University — M
Johns Hopkins University — M*
Lake Forest College — M
Lindenwood University — M
Lipscomb University — M
Loyola Marymount University — M
Maryland Institute College of Art — M
Massachusetts College of Art and Design — M,O
Miami International University of Art & Design — M
Minneapolis College of Art and Design — M
Missouri State University — M,O
Montana State University — M
Mount Saint Mary's University (CA) — M,D,O
National University — M
New York Film Academy — M
New York University — M*
Northwestern University — M,D
Ohio University — M
Quinnipiac University — M
Regent University — M,D
Rochester Institute of Technology — M
Sacred Heart University — M
St. Thomas University — M
San Diego State University — M
San Francisco State University — M
San Jose State University — M
Savannah College of Art and Design — M
School of Visual Arts (NY) — M
Stanford University — M,D
Stephen F. Austin State University — M
Stevens Institute of Technology — M
Stony Brook University, State University of New York — M
Syracuse University — M
Temple University — M*
Universidad Autonoma de Guadalajara — M,D
The University of British Columbia — M
University of California, Los Angeles — M,D
University of California, Santa Barbara — D
University of Central Arkansas — M
University of Central Florida — M
University of Colorado Boulder — M
The University of Iowa — M
University of Memphis — M,D
University of Miami — M,D
University of Mississippi — M,D
University of Montana — M
University of Nevada, Las Vegas — M,O
University of New Orleans — M

The University of North Carolina at Greensboro — M
University of North Carolina School of the Arts — M
University of North Texas — M,D,O
University of Regina — M
University of Rhode Island — M,D
University of Southern California — M
The University of Texas at Arlington — M,D
The University of Texas at Austin — M,D
University of the Sacred Heart — M,O
University of Victoria — M
University of Wisconsin–Milwaukee — M,O*
Vermont College of Fine Arts — M
Virginia Commonwealth University — M,D
Watkins College of Art, Design, & Film — M
Western State Colorado University — M
York University — M,D

FILM, TELEVISION, AND VIDEO THEORY AND CRITICISM

Brooklyn College of the City University of New York — M
California College of the Arts — M
Central Michigan University — M
Claremont Graduate University — M,D
College of Staten Island of the City University of New York — M
Columbia University — M
Concordia University (Canada) — M
DePaul University — M
Emory University — M,D,O
Hollins University — M
National University — M,O
New York University — M,D*
Ohio University — M
San Francisco State University — M
Savannah College of Art and Design — M
Texas A&M University–Commerce — M,D,O
Tiffin University — M
Université de Montréal — M,D
Université Laval — M,D
University at Buffalo, the State University of New York — M,D,O
The University of Arizona — M
The University of British Columbia — D
University of California, Berkeley — D
University of California, Santa Cruz — D
University of Chicago — D
The University of Iowa — M,D
The University of Kansas — M,D
University of Miami — M,D
University of Michigan — D,O
University of Oklahoma — M,D*
University of Pittsburgh — M,D,O*
University of Southern California — M,D
University of South Florida — M
University of Toronto — M,D
University of Wisconsin–Madison — M,D
University of Wisconsin–Milwaukee — M,D*
Walla Walla University — M,D
Wayne State University — M,D
Wilfrid Laurier University — M,D
Yale University — D

FINANCE AND BANKING

Adelphi University — M
American Business & Technology University — M
The American College of Financial Services — M
American College of Thessaloniki — M,O
American InterContinental University Online — M
American University — M,O
The American University in Cairo — M,O
The American University in Dubai — M
American University of Beirut — M,D
Andrews University — M
Argosy University, Atlanta — M,D
Argosy University, Chicago — M,D
Argosy University, Hawai`i — M,D,O
Argosy University, Los Angeles — M,D
Argosy University, Northern Virginia — M,D,O
Argosy University, Orange County — M,D,O
Argosy University, Phoenix — M,D
Argosy University, Seattle — M,D
Argosy University, Tampa — M,D
Argosy University, Twin Cities — M,D
Arizona State University at the Tempe campus — M
Ashland University — M
Aspen University — M,O
Assumption College — M,O
Auburn University — M
Azusa Pacific University — M
Babson College — M,O
Baker College Center for Graduate Studies–Online — M,D
Barry University — O
Baruch College of the City University of New York — M,D*
Bayamón Central University — M
Bellevue University — M
Benedictine University — M
Bentley University — M
Binghamton University, State University of New York — D
Bluffton University — M
Boston College — M
Brandeis University — M,D
Brandman University — M

Bridgewater State University — M
Brigham Young University — M
Brooklyn College of the City University of New York — M
California College of the Arts — M
California Intercontinental University — M,D
California Lutheran University — M,O
California State University, East Bay — M
California State University, Fullerton — M
California State University, Los Angeles — M
California State University, San Bernardino — M
Capella University — M,D
Carnegie Mellon University — D
Case Western Reserve University — M
Central European University — M,D
Central Michigan University — M
Charleston Southern University — M
City University of Seattle — M
Clarion University of Pennsylvania — M
Clark University — M
Cleary University — M,O
College for Financial Planning — M
The College of Saint Rose — O
Colorado State University — M
Colorado State University–Global Campus — M
Colorado Technical University Aurora — M
Colorado Technical University Colorado Springs — M,D
Columbia Southern University — M
Columbia University — M,D
Concordia University (Canada) — M,D,O
Concordia University Wisconsin — M
Cornell University — D
Creighton University — M
Culver-Stockton College — M
Curry College — M,O
Dalhousie University — M
Dallas Baptist University — M
Davenport University — M
Delaware Valley University — M
DePaul University — M,D
DeSales University — M
DeVry University–Folsom Campus — M
Drew University — M,D,O
Drexel University — M,D,O*
Duke University — M,D,O
Duquesne University — M
Eastern Michigan University — M,O
Elms College — M,O
Embry-Riddle Aeronautical University–Daytona — M
Embry-Riddle Aeronautical University–Worldwide — M
Emory University — M,D
Fairfield University — M,O
Fairleigh Dickinson University, Florham Campus — M,O
Fairleigh Dickinson University, Metropolitan Campus — M,O
Florida Agricultural and Mechanical University — M
Florida International University — M
Florida National University — M
Florida State University — M,D
Fordham University — M,D
Gannon University — M
Geneva College — M
George Fox University — M,D
Georgetown University — M
The George Washington University — M,D
Georgia State University — M,D,O
Golden Gate University — M,D,O
Goldey-Beacom College — M
Gordon College — M
The Graduate Center, City University of New York — D
Grand Canyon University — M
Hawai`i Pacific University — M
HEC Montreal — M,D,O
Hofstra University — M,O
Holy Family University — M
Holy Names University — M
Howard University — M
Hult International Business School (United States) — M
IGlobal University — M
Illinois Institute of Technology — M,D
Indiana University Bloomington — M,D,O
Indiana University–Purdue University Indianapolis — M
Indiana University South Bend — M,O
Indiana University Southeast — M
Instituto Centroamericano de Administración de Empresas — M
Instituto Tecnologico de Santo Domingo — M,O
Instituto Tecnológico y de Estudios Superiores de Monterrey, Campus Central de Veracruz — M
Instituto Tecnológico y de Estudios Superiores de Monterrey, Campus Ciudad de México — M,D
Instituto Tecnológico y de Estudios Superiores de Monterrey, Campus Ciudad Obregón — M
Instituto Tecnológico y de Estudios Superiores de Monterrey, Campus Cuernavaca — M
Instituto Tecnológico y de Estudios Superiores de Monterrey, Campus Estado de México — M,D

Instituto Tecnológico y de Estudios Superiores de Monterrey, Campus Guadalajara — M
Instituto Tecnológico y de Estudios Superiores de Monterrey, Campus Irapuato — M,D
Instituto Tecnológico y de Estudios Superiores de Monterrey, Campus Monterrey — M
Inter American University of Puerto Rico, Aguadilla Campus — M
Inter American University of Puerto Rico, Arecibo Campus — M
Inter American University of Puerto Rico, Metropolitan Campus — M
Inter American University of Puerto Rico, Ponce Campus — M
Inter American University of Puerto Rico, San Germán Campus — M,D
The International University of Monaco — M
Iona College — M,O
Iowa State University of Science and Technology — M
Jacksonville University — M
John F. Kennedy University — M
Johns Hopkins University — M,D,O*
Johnson & Wales University — M
Kansas State University — M,D,O
Kent State University — D
King University — M
Lake Forest Graduate School of Management — M
Lakeland University — M
La Salle University — M,O
La Sierra University — M,D,O
Lawrence Technological University — M
Lehigh University — M
Lewis University — M
Liberty University — M,D
Lincoln University (CA) — M,D
Lincoln University (PA) — M
Lipscomb University — M,O
Long Island University–LIU Post — M
Louisiana State University and Agricultural & Mechanical College — M,D
Louisiana Tech University — M,D
Loyola University Chicago — M
Loyola University Maryland — M
Manhattanville College — M,O
Marquette University — M,O
Maryville University of Saint Louis — M,O
Marywood University — M
McGill University — M,D,O
Metropolitan College of New York — M
Michigan State University — M,D
Mississippi College — M,O
Mississippi State University — M,D
Molloy College — M,O
Monmouth University — M,O
Monroe College — M
Montclair State University — M
Mount Saint Mary College — M
Murray State University — M
Naval Postgraduate School — M
New Charter University — M
New England College of Business and Finance — M
New Jersey City University — M
Newman University — M
New Mexico State University — M,D
The New School — M
New York Institute of Technology — M
New York University — M,D*
Niagara University — M
North Central College — M
Northeastern State University — M
Northeastern University — M
Northern State University — M
North Greenville University — M,D
Northwestern University — M,D
Norwich University — M
Notre Dame de Namur University — M
Nova Southeastern University — M
Oakland University — M,O
Ohio Christian University — M
Ohio Dominican University — M
The Ohio State University — M
Ohio University — M
Oklahoma Christian University — M
Oklahoma State University — M,D
Old Dominion University — D
Oral Roberts University — M
Oregon State University — M,D
Ottawa University — M
Our Lady of the Lake University — M
Pace University — M,D,O
Pacific Lutheran University — M
Pacific States University — M,O
Pacific University — M
Park University — M,O
Penn State Great Valley — M,O
Penn State Harrisburg — M,D,O
Polytechnic University of Puerto Rico, Miami Campus — M
Polytechnic University of Puerto Rico, Orlando Campus — M
Pontifical Catholic University of Puerto Rico — M
Pontificia Universidad Catolica Madre y Maestra — M
Portland State University — M
Post University — M
Princeton University — M
Providence College — M
Purdue University — M
Purdue University Global — M
Queens College of the City University of New York — M

---

*M—masters degree; D—doctorate; O—other advanced degree; *—Close-Up and/or Display*

Institution	Degree
Queen's University at Kingston	M,D
Quinnipiac University	M
Regent's University London	M
Regent University	M,D,O
Regis University	M,O
Rhode Island College	M,O
Rider University	M
Robert Morris University Illinois	M
Rochester Institute of Technology	M
Rockhurst University	M,O
Rollins College	M
Rutgers University–Newark	M,D
Sacred Heart University	M,D,O
St. John's University (NY)	M
Saint Joseph's University	M,O
Saint Louis University	M*
Saint Mary's College of California	M
Saint Peter's University	M
St. Thomas Aquinas College	M
Saint Xavier University	M
Samford University	M
Sam Houston State University	M
San Diego State University	M
San Francisco State University	M
Santa Clara University	M
Schiller International University (United States)	M
Seattle University	M,O
Seton Hall University	M,O
Shippensburg University of Pennsylvania	M,D,O
Simon Fraser University	M,D,O
Slippery Rock University of Pennsylvania	M
Southeast Missouri State University	M
Southern Adventist University	M
Southern Illinois University Edwardsville	M
Southern Methodist University	M
Southern New Hampshire University	M,D,O
Southwestern Adventist University	M
State University of New York Polytechnic Institute	M
Stevens Institute of Technology	M,O
Stony Brook University, State University of New York	M,O
Strayer University	M
Suffolk University	M
Syracuse University	M,D
Télé-université	M,D
Temple University	M,D*
Tennessee Technological University	M
Texas A&M International University	M
Texas A&M University	M
Texas A&M University–Commerce	M
Texas A&M University–Corpus Christi	M
Texas Tech University	M,D
Thomas Edison State University	M
Tiffin University	M
Trident University International	M,D
Troy University	M
Tulane University	M,D
United States International University–Africa	M
Universidad Central del Este	M
Universidad de las Americas, A.C.	M
Universidad de las Américas Puebla	M
Universidad Metropolitana	M
Université de Sherbrooke	M
Université du Québec à Montréal	O
Université du Québec à Trois-Rivières	O
Université du Québec en Outaouais	M,O
Université Laval	M,O
University at Albany, State University of New York	M,D,O
University at Buffalo, the State University of New York	M,D
The University of Akron	M
The University of Alabama	M,D
The University of Alabama at Birmingham	M
The University of Alabama in Huntsville	M,O
University of Alaska Fairbanks	M
University of Alberta	M,D
The University of Arizona	M
University of Baltimore	M
University of Bridgeport	M
The University of British Columbia	D
University of California, Berkeley	D,O
University of California, Davis	M
University of California, Los Angeles	M,D
University of California, Riverside	M,D
University of California, San Diego	M,D
University of California, Santa Barbara	M,D
University of California, Santa Cruz	M
University of Central Missouri	M,D,O
University of Chicago	M,O
University of Cincinnati	M,D
University of Colorado Denver	M
University of Connecticut	M,D,O
University of Dallas	M,D
University of Dayton	M
University of Delaware	M
University of Denver	M
University of Detroit Mercy	M,D,O
University of Florida	M,D,O
University of Hawaii at Manoa	M,D
University of Houston	M
University of Houston–Clear Lake	M
University of Houston–Downtown	M
University of Houston–Victoria	M
University of Illinois at Chicago	M
University of Illinois at Urbana–Champaign	M,D
The University of Iowa	M,D
The University of Kansas	M,D
University of La Verne	M
University of Lethbridge	M,D
University of Louisiana at Lafayette	M
University of Maine	M
The University of Manchester	M
University of Maryland University College	M
University of Massachusetts Amherst	M,D
University of Massachusetts Boston	M,D
University of Massachusetts Dartmouth	M,O
University of Memphis	M,D
University of Miami	M,D
University of Michigan–Dearborn	M
University of Michigan–Flint	M,O
University of Minnesota, Twin Cities Campus	M,D
University of Mississippi	M,D
University of Missouri	M,D
University of Missouri–Kansas City	M,D
University of Nebraska–Lincoln	M,D
University of Nevada, Reno	M
University of New Haven	M,O
University of New Orleans	M
University of North Alabama	M
The University of North Carolina at Chapel Hill	D
The University of North Carolina at Charlotte	M,O
The University of North Carolina at Greensboro	M,O
University of North Florida	M
University of North Texas	M,D,O
University of Notre Dame	M
University of Oregon	D
University of Ottawa	D,O
University of Pennsylvania	M,D*
University of Pittsburgh	M,D*
University of Portland	M
University of Puerto Rico–Mayagüez	M
University of Puerto Rico–Río Piedras	M,D
University of Rhode Island	M,D
University of Rochester	M,D*
University of St. Francis (IL)	M,O
University of Saint Mary	M
University of St. Thomas (TX)	M
University of San Francisco	M
University of Saskatchewan	M
The University of Scranton	M
University of Southern Maine	M
University of South Florida	M,D
The University of Tampa	M,O
The University of Tennessee	M,D
The University of Tennessee at Martin	M
The University of Texas at Arlington	M,D
The University of Texas at Austin	M,D
The University of Texas at Dallas	M
The University of Texas at San Antonio	M,D
The University of Texas Rio Grande Valley	M,D
University of the West	M
The University of Toledo	M
University of Toronto	M
University of Utah	M,D
University of Virginia	M
University of Washington, Tacoma	M
University of Waterloo	M
University of West Alabama	M
The University of Western Ontario	M,D
University of Wisconsin–Madison	M,D
University of Wisconsin–Whitewater	M
University of Wyoming	M
Upper Iowa University	M
Ursuline College	M
Utah State University	M
Valparaiso University	M,O
Vancouver Island University	M
Vanderbilt University	M*
Villanova University	M
Virginia Commonwealth University	M
Virginia International University	M,O
Virginia Polytechnic Institute and State University	M,D
Wagner College	M
Walden University	M,D,O
Walsh College of Accountancy and Business Administration	M
Washington University in St. Louis	M,D
Waynesburg University	M,D
Wayne State University	M,D,O
Webster University	M
Western Michigan University Thomas M. Cooley Law School	M
West Texas A&M University	M,D
West Virginia University	M
Wilfrid Laurier University	M,D
Wilkes University	M
William Paterson University of New Jersey	M,O
Wilmington University	M,D
Wingate University	M
Xavier University	M*
Yale University	D
York College of Pennsylvania	M
York University	M,D
Youngstown State University	M

FINANCIAL ENGINEERING

Institution	Degree
Baruch College of the City University of New York	M*
Claremont Graduate University	M
Columbia University	M,D
HEC Montreal	M,D
The International University of Monaco	M
North Carolina State University	M
Princeton University	M,D
Rensselaer Polytechnic Institute	M
Stevens Institute of Technology	M,D,O
Temple University	M*
University of California, Berkeley	M
University of California, Los Angeles	M,D
University of Illinois at Urbana–Champaign	M

FIRE PROTECTION ENGINEERING

Institution	Degree
Oklahoma State University	M
University of Maryland, College Park	M
University of New Haven	M,O
The University of North Carolina at Charlotte	M,O
Worcester Polytechnic Institute	M,D,O

FISH, GAME, AND WILDLIFE MANAGEMENT

Institution	Degree
Arkansas Tech University	M
Auburn University	M,D
Brigham Young University	M,D
Central Washington University	M
Clemson University	M,D
Colorado State University	M,D
Cornell University	M,D
Frostburg State University	M
Humboldt State University	M
Iowa State University of Science and Technology	M,D
Louisiana State University and Agricultural & Mechanical College	M,D
McGill University	M,D
Memorial University of Newfoundland	M,O
Michigan State University	M,D
Mississippi State University	M,D
Montana State University	M,D
The Ohio State University	M,D
Oregon State University	M,D
Penn State University Park	M,D*
Purdue University	M,D
Simon Fraser University	M,D,O
South Dakota State University	M,D
State University of New York College of Environmental Science and Forestry	M,D
Sul Ross State University	M
Tarleton State University	M
Tennessee Technological University	M
Texas A&M University	M,D
Texas A&M University–Kingsville	M,D
Texas State University	M
Texas Tech University	M,D
Université du Québec à Rimouski	M,D,O
University of Alaska Fairbanks	M,D
University of Arkansas at Pine Bluff	M,D
University of Delaware	M,D
University of Florida	M,D,O
University of Maine	M,D
University of Maryland Eastern Shore	M,D
University of Massachusetts Amherst	M,D
University of Miami	M,D
University of Missouri	M,D,O
University of Montana	M,D
University of New Hampshire	M
University of North Dakota	M,D
University of Rhode Island	M,D
The University of Tennessee	M
University of Washington	M,D
University of Wisconsin–Madison	M,D
Utah State University	M,D
Virginia Polytechnic Institute and State University	M,D
West Virginia University	M,D

FOLKLORE

Institution	Degree
The George Washington University	M,D
Indiana University Bloomington	M,D
Memorial University of Newfoundland	M,D
Penn State Harrisburg	M,D,O
University of Alberta	M,D
University of California, Berkeley	M
University of Louisiana at Lafayette	M,D
The University of North Carolina at Chapel Hill	M
University of Oregon	M
The University of Texas at Austin	M,D
University of Wisconsin–Madison	M,D
Utah State University	M

FOOD SCIENCE AND TECHNOLOGY

Institution	Degree
Alabama Agricultural and Mechanical University	M,D
American University of Beirut	M
The American University of Rome	M
Auburn University	M,D,O
Boston University	M
Brigham Young University	M
California Polytechnic State University, San Luis Obispo	M
Chapman University	M*
Clemson University	M,D
Colorado State University	M,D
Cornell University	M,D
Dalhousie University	M,D
Drexel University	M*
Florida State University	M,D
Illinois Institute of Technology	M
Iowa State University of Science and Technology	M,D
Kansas State University	M,D
London Metropolitan University	M,D
Louisiana State University and Agricultural & Mechanical College	M,D
McGill University	M,D
Memorial University of Newfoundland	M,D
Michigan State University	M,D
Mississippi State University	M,D
New Mexico State University	M
New York University	M,D*
North Carolina Agricultural and Technical State University	M
North Carolina State University	M,D
North Dakota State University	M,D
The Ohio State University	M,D
Oklahoma State University	M,D
Oregon State University	M,D
Penn State University Park	M,D*
Portland State University	M,D,O
Purdue University	M,D
Rutgers University–New Brunswick	M,D
South Dakota State University	M,D
Texas A&M University	M,D
Texas Tech University	M,D
Texas Woman's University	M,D
Tuskegee University	M
Universidad de las Américas Puebla	M
Université de Moncton	M
Université Laval	M
University at Buffalo, the State University of New York	M,D,O
University of Arkansas	M,D
The University of British Columbia	M,D
University of California, Davis	M,D
University of Delaware	M,D
University of Florida	M,D
University of Georgia	M,D
University of Guelph	M,D
University of Hawaii at Manoa	M
University of Idaho	M,D
University of Illinois at Urbana–Champaign	M,D
University of Kentucky	M,D
University of Manitoba	M,D
University of Maryland, College Park	M,D
University of Maryland Eastern Shore	M,D
University of Massachusetts Amherst	M,D
University of Minnesota, Twin Cities Campus	M,D
University of Mississippi	M,D
University of Missouri	M,D
University of Nebraska–Lincoln	M,D
University of Puerto Rico–Mayagüez	M
University of Rhode Island	M,D
University of Saskatchewan	M,D
University of Southern California	M,D,O
University of Southern Mississippi	M
The University of Tennessee	M,D
The University of Tennessee at Martin	M
University of Vermont	M,D
University of Wisconsin–Madison	M,D
University of Wisconsin–Stout	M
University of Wyoming	M,D
Utah State University	M,D
Washington State University	M,D
Wayne State University	M,D,O
West Virginia University	M,D

FOREIGN LANGUAGES EDUCATION

Institution	Degree
Andrews University	M,D,O
Appalachian State University	M
Arizona State University at the Tempe campus	M,D
Augusta University	M,O
Binghamton University, State University of New York	M
Boston College	M,D,O
Brandeis University	M
Brigham Young University	M
Brooklyn College of the City University of New York	M
California State University, Sacramento	M
Caribbean University	M,D
Central Connecticut State University	M,O
Cleveland State University	M
College of Charleston	M
The Colorado College	M
Colorado State University–Pueblo	M
Columbia University	M,D
Concordia College	M
Cornell University	M,D
Delaware State University	M
DePaul University	M
Duquesne University	M
Eastern Michigan University	M,O
Eastern University	M,O
Elms College	M,O
Florida International University	M,D,O

George Mason University	M
The George Washington University	M
Georgia Southern University	M
Georgia State University	M,O
Harding University	M,O
Hofstra University	M,D,O
Hunter College of the City University of New York	M
Indiana State University	M,D,O
Indiana University Bloomington	M,D
Indiana University–Purdue University Indianapolis	M,O
Inter American University of Puerto Rico, Arecibo Campus	M
Inter American University of Puerto Rico, Barranquitas Campus	M
Inter American University of Puerto Rico, Metropolitan Campus	M
Iona College	M
James Madison University	M
Kean University	M
Lamar University	M
Le Moyne College	M,O
Lewis University	M
London Metropolitan University	M,D
Manhattanville College	M,O
Marquette University	M
McGill University	M,D,O
Michigan State University	D
Middlebury Institute of International Studies at Monterey	M
Middle Tennessee State University	M
Minnesota State University Mankato	M
Mississippi State University	M
Molloy College	M,O
Morehead State University	M
New York University	M,D,O*
Northern Arizona University	M
Pace University	M,O
Portland State University	M
Purdue University	M,D,O
Queens College of the City University of New York	M,O
Quinnipiac University	M
Rhode Island College	M
Rider University	M
Rivier University	M
Rutgers University–New Brunswick	M,D
Saginaw Valley State University	M
St. John Fisher College	M
Saint Xavier University	M
Shippensburg University of Pennsylvania	M
Southern Connecticut State University	M
Southern Oregon University	M
Spalding University	M
State University of New York at Plattsburgh	M
State University of New York College at Old Westbury	M
Stony Brook University, State University of New York	M,O
Texas A&M International University	M
Texas A&M University–Kingsville	M
Universidad del Este	M
Université du Québec en Outaouais	O
University at Buffalo, the State University of New York	M,D,O
University of Arkansas at Little Rock	M
University of California, Irvine	M,D
University of Central Florida	M,O
University of Connecticut	M,D
University of Dayton	M
University of Delaware	M
University of Florida	M,D
University of Hawaii at Hilo	M,D
University of Hawaii at Manoa	M,D,O
University of Illinois at Chicago	M,D
University of Illinois at Urbana–Champaign	M,D
University of Indianapolis	M
The University of Iowa	M,D
University of Kentucky	M
University of Maine	M
University of Maryland, Baltimore County	M
University of Maryland, College Park	D
University of Massachusetts Amherst	M
University of Michigan	M,D
University of Minnesota, Twin Cities Campus	M
University of Mississippi	M,D
University of Missouri	M,D,O
University of Nebraska at Kearney	M
University of Nebraska at Omaha	M
The University of North Carolina at Chapel Hill	.
The University of North Carolina at Charlotte	M,D,O
The University of North Carolina at Greensboro	M,D,O
University of Northern Colorado	M,D
University of Northern Iowa	M
University of Oklahoma	M,D*
University of Pittsburgh	M,D*
University of Puerto Rico–Río Piedras	M,D
University of South Carolina	M,D
University of Southern Mississippi	O
University of South Florida	O
The University of Tennessee	M,D,O
University of the Sacred Heart	M,O
The University of Toledo	M,D,O
University of Vermont	M,O

University of Victoria	M
University of Virginia	M,D,O
University of Wisconsin–Milwaukee	M,O*
Vanderbilt University	M,D*
Wagner College	M
Washington State University	M
Wayne State University	M,D,O
West Chester University of Pennsylvania	M,O
Western Kentucky University	M
Worcester State University	M

FORENSIC NURSING

Aspen University	M
Duquesne University	M,O
Fitchburg State University	M,O
Monmouth University	M,D,O
Texas A&M University	M

FORENSIC PSYCHOLOGY

Adler University	M
Alliant International University–Fresno	D
Alliant International University–Irvine	D
Alliant International University–Los Angeles	D
Alliant International University–Sacramento	D
Alliant International University–San Diego	D
Alliant International University–San Francisco	M,D
American International College	M,D,O
Argosy University, Atlanta	M,D,O
Argosy University, Chicago	D
Argosy University, Hawai'i	M
Argosy University, Los Angeles	M,D
Argosy University, Northern Virginia	M,D
Argosy University, Orange County	M,D
Argosy University, Phoenix	M,D
Argosy University, Twin Cities	M,D,O
California Baptist University	M
Castleton University	M
The Chicago School of Professional Psychology	M,D
The Chicago School of Professional Psychology at Downtown Los Angeles	D
The Chicago School of Professional Psychology at Irvine	D
The Chicago School of Professional Psychology: Online	M,O
Drexel University	D*
Fairleigh Dickinson University, Metropolitan Campus	M
The George Washington University	M,D,O
Holy Names University	M
Immaculata University	M,D,O
John Jay College of Criminal Justice of the City University of New York	M,D
Kean University	M
Liberty University	M
London Metropolitan University	M,D
Marymount University	M
Montclair State University	O
Nova Southeastern University	M,D,O
Pontificia Universidad Catolica Madre y Maestra	M
Post University	M
Prairie View A&M University	M,D
Roger Williams University	M
Sage Graduate School	M
Tiffin University	M
Universidad de Iberoamerica	M,D
Universidad del Turabo	M,D,O
University of Central Oklahoma	M
University of Denver	M,D,O
University of Houston–Victoria	M
University of Louisiana at Monroe	M
University of New Haven	M,O
University of North Dakota	M
Walden University	M,D,O
Westfield State University	M
William James College	M,D,O

FORENSIC SCIENCES

Alabama State University	M
Alliant International University–Irvine	D
Arcadia University	M
Bay Path University	M
Boston University	M
Buffalo State College, State University of New York	M
Carlow University	M
Cedar Crest College	M
Champlain College	M
DeSales University	M,O
Duquesne University	M
Emporia State University	M
Florida Gulf Coast University	M
Florida International University	M,D
George Mason University	M
The George Washington University	M,O
Georgia State University	M,O
Golden Gate University	M,O
Indiana University–Purdue University Indianapolis	M,O
Iona College	M,O
James Madison University	M
John Jay College of Criminal Justice of the City University of New York	M,D
La Salle University	M,O
Long Island University–LIU Brooklyn	M,D
Marshall University	M,O

McGill University	M,D,O
Mercyhurst University	M
Michigan State University	M,D
Middle Georgia State University	M
Missouri Western State University	M,O
National University	M,O
Niagara University	M
Oklahoma State University Center for Health Sciences	M
Pace University	M
Penn State University Park	M*
Philadelphia College of Osteopathic Medicine	M*
St. Joseph's College, Long Island Campus	M
St. Joseph's College, New York	M
Saint Leo University	M,D
Salve Regina University	M,O
Sam Houston State University	M,D
Seattle University	M,O
Stevenson University	M
Stratford University (VA)	M,D
Syracuse University	M,O
Towson University	M
Universidad del Turabo	M
University at Albany, State University of New York	M
The University of Alabama at Birmingham	M
University of California, Davis	M
University of Central Oklahoma	M
University of Charleston	M
University of Colorado Denver	M
University of Detroit Mercy	M,O
University of Florida	M,O
University of Houston–Victoria	M
University of Illinois at Chicago	M
University of Maryland, Baltimore	M
University of New Haven	M,O
University of North Texas Health Science Center at Fort Worth	M,D
University of Rhode Island	M,D,O
University of St. Francis (IL)	M,O
University of Southern Mississippi	M,D
University of South Florida	M,D,O
Virginia Commonwealth University	M
Webster University	M
West Virginia University	M,D

FORESTRY

Auburn University	M,D
California Polytechnic State University, San Luis Obispo	M
Clemson University	M,D
Cornell University	M,D
Harvard University	M*
Humboldt State University	M
Iowa State University of Science and Technology	M,D
Lakehead University	M,D
Louisiana State University and Agricultural & Mechanical College	M,D
McGill University	M,D
Michigan State University	M,D
Michigan Technological University	M,D
Mississippi State University	M,D
North Carolina State University	M,D
Northern Arizona University	M,D
The Ohio State University	M,D
Oklahoma State University	M,D
Oregon State University	M,D
Penn State University Park	M,D*
Purdue University	M,D
Southern Illinois University Carbondale	M
Southern University and Agricultural and Mechanical College	M
State University of New York College of Environmental Science and Forestry	M,D
Stephen F. Austin State University	M,D
Texas A&M University	M,D
Tropical Agriculture Research and Higher Education Center	M,D
Université du Québec en Abitibi-Témiscamingue	M,D
Université Laval	M,D
University of Alberta	M,D
The University of Arizona	M,D
University of Arkansas at Monticello	M
The University of British Columbia	M,D
University of California, Berkeley	M,D
University of Florida	M,D
University of Georgia	M,D
University of Kentucky	M,D
University of Maine	M,D
University of Massachusetts Amherst	M,D
University of Minnesota, Twin Cities Campus	M,D
University of Missouri	M,D,O
University of Montana	M,D
University of New Brunswick Fredericton	M,D
University of New Hampshire	M
The University of Tennessee	M
University of Toronto	M,D
University of Vermont	M,D,O
University of Washington	M,D
University of Wisconsin–Madison	M,D
Utah State University	M,D
Virginia Polytechnic Institute and State University	M,D
West Virginia University	M,D
Yale University	M,D

FOUNDATIONS AND PHILOSOPHY OF EDUCATION

Antioch University New England	M,O
Arkansas State University	M,D,O
Ball State University	D
Bank Street College of Education	M
Binghamton University, State University of New York	D
Chicago State University	M
Columbia University	M,D
Curry College	M,O
DePaul University	M,D
Duquesne University	M
Eastern Michigan University	M
Eastern Washington University	M
Fairfield University	M,O
Fairleigh Dickinson University, Metropolitan Campus	M
Florida State University	M,D,O
Georgia State University	M,D
Harvard University	M,O*
Indiana University Bloomington	M,D,O
Iowa State University of Science and Technology	M,D
Kent State University	M,D
Marquette University	M,D,O
McGill University	M,D,O
Mount Saint Vincent University	M
New York University	M,D*
Northern Arizona University	M,D,O
Northern Illinois University	M,D,O
Northern Vermont University–Johnson	M
Penn State University Park	M,D,O*
Purdue University	M,D,O
Rutgers University–New Brunswick	M,D
Saint Louis University	M,D*
Simon Fraser University	M,D
Southern Illinois University Edwardsville	M
Spring Hill College	M
Syracuse University	M,D,O
Teachers College, Columbia University	M,D,O
University at Buffalo, the State University of New York	M,D,O
The University of British Columbia	M,D
University of California, Riverside	M,D,O
University of Central Oklahoma	M
University of Cincinnati	M,D
University of Hawaii at Manoa	M,D
University of Houston–Clear Lake	M
The University of Iowa	M,D,O
University of Manitoba	M
University of Maryland, College Park	M,D,O
University of Minnesota, Twin Cities Campus	M,D
University of New Mexico	M,D
University of Pennsylvania	M,D*
University of Pittsburgh	M,D*
University of Rochester	D*
University of Saskatchewan	M,D,O
University of South Africa	M,D
University of South Carolina	D
The University of Tennessee	M,D,O
The University of Texas of the Permian Basin	M
The University of Toledo	M,D,O
University of Victoria	M,D
University of Washington	M,D
University of Wisconsin–Milwaukee	M,D,O*
Wayne State University	M,D,O
West Chester University of Pennsylvania	M,O
Western Illinois University	M,O
Widener University	M,D
William Paterson University of New Jersey	M,D,O

FRENCH

American University	M,O
Arizona State University at the Tempe campus	M
Asbury University	M
Binghamton University, State University of New York	M
Boston College	M
Bowling Green State University	M
Brooklyn College of the City University of New York	M
Brown University	D
California State University, Long Beach	M
California State University, Los Angeles	M
Carleton University	M
Case Western Reserve University	M
Central Connecticut State University	M,O
Colorado State University	M
Columbia University	M,D
Concordia University (Canada)	M,O
Cornell University	D
Dalhousie University	M,D
DePaul University	M
Drew University	M,D,O
Duke University	D
Emory University	D
Florida Atlantic University	M
Florida State University	M,D
George Mason University	M
Georgia State University	M,O
The Graduate Center, City University of New York	D
Harvard University	M,D*
Howard University	M

*M—masters degree; D—doctorate; O—other advanced degree; *—Close-Up and/or Display*

Hunter College of the City University of New York	M
Illinois State University	M
Indiana University Bloomington	M,D
Johns Hopkins University	M,D*
Kansas State University	M
Kent State University	M,D
Lake Forest College	M
Louisiana State University and Agricultural & Mechanical College	M,D
McGill University	M,D
McMaster University	M
Memorial University of Newfoundland	M
Miami University	M
Michigan State University	M
Middlebury College	M,D
Middle Tennessee State University	M
Millersville University of Pennsylvania	M
Minnesota State University Mankato	M
Montclair State University	M
New York University	M,D,O*
North Carolina State University	M
Northern Illinois University	M
Northwestern University	D,O
The Ohio State University	M,D
Ohio University	M
Penn State University Park	M,D*
Portland State University	M
Princeton University	D
Purdue University	M,D
Queens College of the City University of New York	M
Queen's University at Kingston	M,D
Rutgers University–New Brunswick	M,D
St. John Fisher College	M
Saint Louis University	M*
San Francisco State University	M
Simon Fraser University	M
Southern Oregon University	M
Stanford University	M,D
State University of New York at New Paltz	M,O
State University of New York College at Geneseo	M
Stony Brook University, State University of New York	M
Syracuse University	M
Tufts University	M
Tulane University	M,D
Université de Moncton	M,D
Université de Montréal	M,D
Université de Sherbrooke	M,D
Université du Québec à Chicoutimi	O
University at Buffalo, the State University of New York	M,D,O
The University of Alabama	M,D
University of Alberta	M,D
The University of Arizona	M
University of Arkansas	M
The University of British Columbia	M,D
University of California, Berkeley	D
University of California, Davis	D
University of California, Irvine	M,D
University of California, Los Angeles	M,D
University of California, Santa Barbara	D
University of Chicago	D
University of Cincinnati	M,D
University of Colorado Boulder	M,D
University of Delaware	M
University of Florida	M,D
University of Georgia	M,D
University of Guelph	M
University of Hawaii at Manoa	M
University of Illinois at Chicago	M
University of Illinois at Urbana–Champaign	M,D
The University of Iowa	M,D
The University of Kansas	M,D
University of Lethbridge	M,D
University of Louisiana at Lafayette	M,D
University of Louisville	M,O
University of Maine	M
The University of Manchester	D
University of Manitoba	M,D
University of Maryland, College Park	M,D
University of Massachusetts Amherst	M
University of Memphis	M
University of Miami	D
University of Michigan	D
University of Minnesota, Twin Cities Campus	M,D
University of Missouri	M,D
University of Missouri–Kansas City	M
University of Montana	M
University of Nebraska–Lincoln	M,D
University of New Mexico	M,D
The University of North Carolina at Chapel Hill	M,D
The University of North Carolina at Greensboro	M
University of North Texas	M,D,O
University of Notre Dame	M
University of Oklahoma	M,D*
University of Oregon	M
University of Ottawa	M,D
University of Pennsylvania	M,D*
University of Pittsburgh	M,D*
University of Regina	M
University of Saskatchewan	M
University of South Africa	M,D
University of South Carolina	M
University of Southern Mississippi	M

University of South Florida	M,D
The University of Tennessee	M,D
The University of Texas at Arlington	M
The University of Texas at Austin	M,D
The University of Toledo	M
University of Toronto	M,D
University of Utah	M,D
University of Victoria	M
University of Virginia	M,D
University of Washington	M,D
University of Waterloo	M
The University of Western Ontario	M,D
University of Wisconsin–Madison	M,D,O
University of Wisconsin–Milwaukee	M,O*
University of Wyoming	M,D*
Vanderbilt University	M,D*
Washington University in St. Louis	D
Wayne State University	M,D
West Chester University of Pennsylvania	M,O
Western Kentucky University	M
Yale University	M,D
York University	M,D

GAME DESIGN AND DEVELOPMENT

Academy of Art University	M
Concordia University (Canada)	M,D,O
DePaul University	M,D
Full Sail University	M
Iona College	M
Long Island University–LIU Post	M
Michigan State University	M
New York University	M*
Rochester Institute of Technology	M
Sacred Heart University	M
Savannah College of Art and Design	M
University of Advancing Technology	M
University of California, Santa Cruz	M,D
The University of North Carolina at Charlotte	M,O
University of Pennsylvania	M,D*
University of Southern California	M,D
University of Utah	M
Virginia International University	M,O
Worcester Polytechnic Institute	M

GENDER STUDIES

Adler University	M
American University	M,D,O
The American University in Cairo	M,O
Arizona State University at the Tempe campus	M,D,O
Brandeis University	M,D
Carnegie Mellon University	D
Central European University	M,D
Central Michigan University	M
The College of New Jersey	O
Cornell University	M,D
Delta State University	M
DePaul University	M
Dominican University of California	M
Eastern Michigan University	M,O
George Mason University	M
The George Washington University	O
Georgia State University	M,O
Indiana University Bloomington	D
Indiana University Northwest	M,O
Instituto Tecnologico de Santo Domingo	M,O
Kansas State University	O
Loyola University Chicago	M
Memorial University of Newfoundland	M,D
Middle Tennessee State University	O
Minnesota State University Mankato	M,D,O
Murray State University	M,D,O
New York University	M*
Northern Arizona University	O
Northwestern University	O
The Ohio State University	M,D
Old Dominion University	M,O
Oregon State University	M,D
Queen's University at Kingston	M,D
Rutgers University–New Brunswick	M,D
Saint Mary's University (Canada)	M
San Diego State University	O
Simmons University	M,D,O
Simon Fraser University	M,D
Stony Brook University, State University of New York	O
Texas Woman's University	M,D
University at Albany, State University of New York	M
University at Buffalo, the State University of New York	M
The University of Arizona	M,D,O
The University of British Columbia	M,D
University of California, Los Angeles	M,D
University of Chicago	M
University of Colorado Denver	M,O
University of Florida	M,O
University of Lethbridge	M,D
University of Maryland, Baltimore County	O
University of Memphis	O
University of Michigan–Flint	M
The University of North Carolina at Charlotte	M,D,O
The University of North Carolina at Greensboro	M,O
University of Northern British Columbia	M,D,O
University of Northern Iowa	M
University of Oklahoma	O*
University of Rhode Island	M,D,O
University of South Florida	M,O

The University of Toledo	O
University of Toronto	M,D
University of Wisconsin–Milwaukee	M,O*
Wayne State University	M,D,O
Wilfrid Laurier University	M
York University	M,D

GENETIC COUNSELING

Augustana University	M
Baylor College of Medicine	M
Bay Path University	M
Boston University	M
Brandeis University	M
California State University, Stanislaus	M
Case Western Reserve University	M,D
Emory University	M
Icahn School of Medicine at Mount Sinai	M,D
Johns Hopkins University	M,D*
Long Island University–LIU Post	M,O
McGill University	M,D
Northwestern University	M
Sarah Lawrence College	M
Thomas Jefferson University	M
Université de Montréal	O
The University of Alabama at Birmingham	M
University of Arkansas for Medical Sciences	M,D
The University of British Columbia	M
University of California, Irvine	M
University of Cincinnati	M
University of Colorado Denver	M
University of Manitoba	M
University of Maryland, Baltimore	M
University of Michigan	M,D
University of Minnesota, Twin Cities Campus	M,D
The University of North Carolina at Greensboro	M
University of Oklahoma Health Sciences Center	M
University of Pittsburgh	M,D,O*
University of South Carolina	M
The University of Texas Health Science Center at Houston	M,D
University of Toronto	M,D
University of Wisconsin–Madison	M,D
Wayne State University	M,D,O

GENETICS

Albert Einstein College of Medicine	D
Baylor College of Medicine	D
Boston University	D
Brandeis University	M,D
California Institute of Technology	D
Carnegie Mellon University	M,D
Clemson University	M,D,O
Columbia University	M,D
Cornell University	D
Dartmouth College	D
Drexel University	M,D*
Duke University	D
Emory University	D
Harvard University	M,D*
Illinois State University	M,D
Indiana University Bloomington	M,D
Iowa State University of Science and Technology	M,D
Irell & Manella Graduate School of Biological Sciences	D
Johns Hopkins University	M,D*
Kansas State University	M,D
Kent State University	M,D
Marquette University	M,D
Massachusetts Institute of Technology	D
Mayo Clinic Graduate School of Biomedical Sciences	D
McMaster University	M,D
Medical University of South Carolina	D
Michigan State University	M,D
Mississippi State University	M,D
New York University	M,D*
The Ohio State University	M,D
Oregon Health & Science University	D
Oregon State University	M,D
Purdue University	M,D
Rutgers University–New Brunswick	M,D
Stanford University	D
Stony Brook University, State University of New York	M,D
Thomas Jefferson University	D
Tufts University	M,D
Université de Montréal	O
Université du Québec à Chicoutimi	M
University at Buffalo, the State University of New York	M,D
The University of Alabama at Birmingham	D
University of Alberta	M,D
The University of Arizona	M,D
The University of British Columbia	M,D
University of Calgary	M,D
University of California, Davis	M,D
University of California, Irvine	D
University of California, Riverside	D
University of California, San Francisco	D
University of Chicago	D
University of Colorado Denver	D
University of Connecticut	M,D
University of Connecticut Health Center	D
University of Delaware	M,D
University of Florida	D

University of Georgia	M,D
University of Hawaii at Manoa	M,D
University of Illinois at Chicago	D
The University of Iowa	M,D
The University of Manchester	M,D
University of Massachusetts Amherst	M,D
University of Miami	M,D
University of Minnesota, Twin Cities Campus	M,D
University of New Hampshire	M,D
University of New Mexico	M,D
The University of North Carolina at Chapel Hill	M,D
University of North Dakota	M,D
University of North Texas Health Science Center at Fort Worth	M,D
University of Notre Dame	M,D
University of Oregon	M,D
University of Pennsylvania	D*
University of Puerto Rico–Río Piedras	M
University of Rochester	M,D*
The University of Tennessee	M,D
The University of Texas Health Science Center at Houston	M,D
The University of Texas MD Anderson Cancer Center	M
The University of Texas Southwestern Medical Center	D
University of Washington	M,D,O
University of Wisconsin–Madison	M,D
University of Wyoming	D
Van Andel Institute Graduate School	D
Virginia Polytechnic Institute and State University	M,D
Washington State University	M,D
Washington University in St. Louis	M,D
Wesleyan University	D
West Virginia University	M,D
Yale University	D

GENOMIC SCIENCES

Albert Einstein College of Medicine	D
Augusta University	D
Black Hills State University	M
Boston University	D
Case Western Reserve University	M,D
Concordia University (Canada)	M,D,O
Cornell University	D
Duke University	D
Manchester University	M
Massachusetts Institute of Technology	M,D
North Carolina State University	M,D
North Dakota State University	M,D
Oregon State University	M,D
Penn State Hershey Medical Center	M,D
Purdue University	D
Thomas Jefferson University	D
University at Buffalo, the State University of New York	M,D
The University of Alabama at Birmingham	D
University of California, Riverside	D
University of California, San Francisco	D
University of Chicago	D
University of Cincinnati	M,D
University of Colorado Denver	D
University of Connecticut	M,D
University of Georgia	M,D
University of Maryland, Baltimore	M,D
University of Maryland, College Park	D
University of Pennsylvania	D*
University of Rochester	D*
University of Southern California	D
The University of Tennessee	M,D
The University of Tennessee–Oak Ridge National Laboratory	M,D
The University of Texas Health Science Center at Houston	M,D,O
The University of Toledo	M,O
University of Washington	D
Wake Forest University	M
Washington University in St. Louis	M
Wayne State University	M,D,O
Wesleyan University	M
Yale University	D

GEOCHEMISTRY

California Institute of Technology	M,D
Colorado School of Mines	M,D
Cornell University	M,D
Georgia State University	M,D
Indiana University Bloomington	M,D
Massachusetts Institute of Technology	M,D
McMaster University	M,D
Missouri University of Science and Technology	M,D
Montana Tech of The University of Montana	M
New Mexico Institute of Mining and Technology	M,D
Ohio University	M
Oregon State University	M,D
University of California, Los Angeles	M,D
University of Hawaii at Manoa	M,D
The University of Manchester	M,D
University of Nevada, Reno	M,D
Yale University	D

GEODETIC SCIENCES

The Ohio State University	M,D
Université Laval	M,D
University of New Brunswick Fredericton	M,D

GEOGRAPHIC INFORMATION SYSTEMS

Acadia University	M
Appalachian State University	M
Arizona State University at the Tempe campus	M,D,O
Auburn University at Montgomery	M
Ball State University	M,O
Boston University	M,D
Central Michigan University	M
Chicago State University	M
Claremont Graduate University	M,D,O
Clark University	M
Cleveland State University	M,O
East Carolina University	M,O
Eastern Illinois University	M
Eastern Michigan University	M,O
East Tennessee State University	M
Elizabeth City State University	M
Elmhurst College	M
Florida State University	M,D
George Mason University	M,D
Georgia Institute of Technology	M,D
Georgia State University	O
The Graduate Center, City University of New York	M
Hood College	M,O
Hunter College of the City University of New York	M,O
Idaho State University	M,O
Indiana University of Pennsylvania	M,O
Indiana University–Purdue University Indianapolis	M,O
Johns Hopkins University	M,O*
Kansas State University	M
Kent State University	M,D
Millersville University of Pennsylvania	M
Montclair State University	O
Naval Postgraduate School	M,D,O
North Carolina Central University	M
North Carolina State University	M,D
Northeastern Illinois University	M,O
Northeastern University	M
Northern Arizona University	M,O
Northern Kentucky University	M,O
Northwest Missouri State University	M,O
Oregon State University	M
Saint Mary's University of Minnesota	M,O
Salisbury University	M
Sam Houston State University	M
San Francisco State University	M
San Jose State University	M,O
State University of New York College of Environmental Science and Forestry	M,D
Stony Brook University, State University of New York	O
Temple University	M,D,O*
Texas A&M University–Corpus Christi	M,D
Texas State University	M,D
Université du Québec à Montréal	O
Université Laval	M,O
University at Albany, State University of New York	M,O
University at Buffalo, the State University of New York	M,D
The University of Alabama	M,D
University of Alaska Fairbanks	M
The University of Arizona	M,D,O
University of Central Arkansas	M,O
University of Colorado Denver	M,D
University of Denver	M,D,O
University of Florida	M,D
The University of Iowa	M,D,O
The University of Kansas	M,D,O
University of Lethbridge	M,D
University of Maryland, Baltimore County	M,O
University of Memphis	M
University of Minnesota, Twin Cities Campus	M,D
University of Missouri	M,D,O
University of Nebraska at Omaha	M,O
University of New Hampshire	O
University of New Haven	M
University of North Alabama	M
The University of North Carolina at Charlotte	M,D
The University of North Carolina at Greensboro	M,D,O
The University of North Carolina Wilmington	M,O
University of North Dakota	M
University of North Texas Health Science Center at Fort Worth	M,D,O
University of Pennsylvania	M,D,O*
University of Pittsburgh	M,D*
University of Redlands	M
University of Southern California	M,O
University of South Florida	M,D,O
The University of Texas at Dallas	M,D
The University of Toledo	M,D,O
University of Utah	M
University of West Florida	M
University of West Georgia	M,O
University of Wisconsin–Madison	M,D,O
University of Wisconsin–Milwaukee	M,D,O*
Virginia Commonwealth University	O
West Chester University of Pennsylvania	M,O
Western Illinois University	M,O
Western Michigan University	M,O

GEOGRAPHY

Appalachian State University	M

Arizona State University at the Tempe campus	M,D,O
Auburn University	M
Ball State University	M,O
Binghamton University, State University of New York	M
Brock University	M
California State University, East Bay	M
California State University, Fullerton	M
California State University, Long Beach	M
California State University, Los Angeles	M
California State University, Northridge	M
Carleton University	M,D
Central Connecticut State University	M
Central Washington University	M
Clark University	D
Concordia University (Canada)	M,D,O
East Carolina University	M,O
East Stroudsburg University of Pennsylvania	M
Florida State University	M,D
Fort Hays State University	M
George Mason University	M,D,O
The George Washington University	M,O
Georgia State University	M,D
Hunter College of the City University of New York	M,O
Indiana University Bloomington	D
Indiana University of Pennsylvania	M,O
Kansas State University	M,D,O
Kent State University	M,D
Louisiana State University and Agricultural & Mechanical College	M,D
Marshall University	M
McGill University	M,O
McMaster University	M,O
Memorial University of Newfoundland	M
Miami University	M
Michigan State University	M,D
Minnesota State University Mankato	M
Mississippi State University	M,D
Missouri State University	M,O
Northeastern Illinois University	M,O
Northern Arizona University	M,O
Northern Illinois University	M,D
The Ohio State University	M,D
Ohio University	M
Oklahoma State University	M,D
Oregon State University	M,D
Penn State University Park	M,D*
Portland State University	M,D
Queen's University at Kingston	M,D
Rutgers University–New Brunswick	M,D
St. Cloud State University	M,O
Salem State University	M
San Diego State University	M,D
San Francisco State University	M
San Jose State University	M,O
Shippensburg University of Pennsylvania	M
Simon Fraser University	M,D
South Dakota State University	M
Southern Illinois University Carbondale	M,D
Southern Illinois University Edwardsville	M
Syracuse University	M,D
Temple University	M,D,O*
Texas A&M University	M,D
Texas State University	M,D
Texas Tech University	M,D
Thomas Jefferson University	M
Towson University	M
Trent University	M,D
Université de Montréal	M,D,O
Université de Sherbrooke	M,D
Université du Québec à Montréal	M
Université Laval	M,D
University at Albany, State University of New York	M,O
University at Buffalo, the State University of New York	M,D
The University of Alabama	M,D
The University of Arizona	M,D,O
University of Arkansas	M
The University of British Columbia	M,D
University of Calgary	M,D
University of California, Berkeley	D
University of California, Davis	M,D
University of California, Los Angeles	M,D
University of California, Santa Barbara	M,D
University of Central Arkansas	M,D
University of Cincinnati	M,D
University of Colorado Boulder	M,D
University of Colorado Colorado Springs	M
University of Connecticut	M,D
University of Delaware	M,D
University of Denver	M,D
University of Florida	M,D
University of Georgia	M,D
University of Guelph	M,D
University of Hawaii at Manoa	M,D
University of Idaho	M,D
University of Illinois at Chicago	M
University of Illinois at Urbana–Champaign	M,D
The University of Iowa	M,D,O
The University of Kansas	M,D,O

University of Kentucky	M,D
University of Lethbridge	M,D
University of Louisville	M
The University of Manchester	M,D
University of Manitoba	M,D
University of Maryland, Baltimore County	M,D
University of Maryland, College Park	M,D
University of Massachusetts Amherst	M
University of Memphis	M,D,O
University of Miami	M
University of Minnesota, Twin Cities Campus	M,D
University of Missouri	M,O
University of Montana	M
University of Nebraska at Omaha	M,O
University of Nebraska–Lincoln	M,D
University of Nevada, Reno	M,D
University of New Mexico	M
The University of North Carolina at Chapel Hill	M,D
The University of North Carolina at Charlotte	M,D
The University of North Carolina at Greensboro	M,D,O
University of North Dakota	M
University of Northern Iowa	M
University of North Texas	M,D,O
University of Oklahoma	M,D*
University of Oregon	M,D
University of Ottawa	M,D
University of Prince Edward Island	M
University of Regina	M,D
University of Saskatchewan	M,D
University of South Africa	M,D
University of South Carolina	M,D
University of Southern California	M,O
University of Southern Mississippi	M,D
University of South Florida	O
The University of Tennessee	M,D
The University of Texas at Austin	M,D
The University of Texas at Dallas	M,D
The University of Toledo	M,D,O
University of Toronto	M,D
University of Utah	M,D
University of Victoria	M,D
University of Washington	M,D
University of Waterloo	M,D
The University of Western Ontario	M,D
University of Wisconsin–Madison	M,D,O
University of Wisconsin–Milwaukee	M,D*
University of Wyoming	M
Utah State University	M,D
Virginia Polytechnic Institute and State University	M,D
West Chester University of Pennsylvania	M,O
Western Illinois University	M,O
Western Michigan University	M,D,O
Western Washington University	M
West Virginia University	M,D
Wilfrid Laurier University	M,D
York University	M,D

GEOLOGICAL ENGINEERING

Arizona State University at the Tempe campus	M,D
Colorado School of Mines	M,D
Missouri University of Science and Technology	M,D
Montana Tech of The University of Montana	M
New Mexico Institute of Mining and Technology	M
South Dakota School of Mines and Technology	M,D
The University of Akron	M
University of Alaska Fairbanks	M
The University of Arizona	M,D,O
The University of British Columbia	M,D
University of Hawaii at Manoa	M,D
University of Idaho	M,D
University of Minnesota, Twin Cities Campus	M,D,O
University of Mississippi	M,D
University of Nevada, Reno	M,D
University of North Dakota	M,D
University of Oklahoma	M,D,O*
University of Saskatchewan	M,D
University of Utah	M,D
University of Wisconsin–Madison	M,D

GEOLOGY

Acadia University	M
American University of Beirut	M
Arizona State University at the Tempe campus	M,D
Auburn University	M
Ball State University	M,D
Binghamton University, State University of New York	M,D
Boston College	M
Bowling Green State University	M
Brigham Young University	M
Brooklyn College of the City University of New York	M,D
California Institute of Technology	M,D
California State Polytechnic University, Pomona	M
California State University, Bakersfield	M
California State University, Chico	M
California State University, East Bay	M

California State University, Fresno	M
California State University, Fullerton	M
California State University, Long Beach	M
California State University, Los Angeles	M
California State University, Northridge	M
Case Western Reserve University	M,D
Central Washington University	M
City College of the City University of New York	M
Colorado School of Mines	M,D
Cornell University	M,D
Duke University	M,D
East Carolina University	M,O
Eastern Kentucky University	M,D
Florida Atlantic University	M,D
Florida State University	M,D
Fort Hays State University	M
Georgia State University	M
Humboldt State University	M
Idaho State University	M,O
Indiana University–Purdue University Indianapolis	M,D
Iowa State University of Science and Technology	M,D
Kansas State University	M
Kent State University	M,D
Lakehead University	M
Laurentian University	M,D
Lehigh University	M,D
Louisiana State University and Agricultural & Mechanical College	M,D
Massachusetts Institute of Technology	M,D
McMaster University	M,D
Memorial University of Newfoundland	M,D
Miami University	M,D
Mississippi State University	M,D
Missouri State University	M,O
Missouri University of Science and Technology	M,D
Montana Tech of The University of Montana	M
New Mexico Institute of Mining and Technology	M,D
Northern Arizona University	M,D,O
Northern Illinois University	M,D
Northwestern University	D
The Ohio State University	M,D
Ohio University	M
Oklahoma State University	M,D
Oregon State University	M,D
Portland State University	M,D,O
Queens College of the City University of New York	M
Queen's University at Kingston	M,D
Rensselaer Polytechnic Institute	M,D
Rutgers University–Newark	M
Rutgers University–New Brunswick	M,D
St. Francis Xavier University	M
San Diego State University	M
San Jose State University	M
South Dakota School of Mines and Technology	M,D
Southern Illinois University Carbondale	M,D
Southern Methodist University	M,D
Stephen F. Austin State University	M
Sul Ross State University	M
Syracuse University	M,D
Temple University	M,D*
Texas A&M University	M,D
Université du Québec à Montréal	M,D,O
Université Laval	M,D
University at Buffalo, the State University of New York	M,D
The University of Akron	M
The University of Alabama	M,D
University of Arkansas	M
The University of British Columbia	M,D
University of Calgary	M,D
University of California, Berkeley	M,D
University of California, Davis	M,D
University of California, Los Angeles	M,D
University of California, Riverside	M,D
University of Cincinnati	M,D
University of Colorado Boulder	M,D
University of Connecticut	M,D
University of Delaware	M,D
University of Florida	M,D
University of Georgia	M,D
University of Hawaii at Manoa	M,D
University of Houston	M,D
University of Idaho	M,D
University of Illinois at Chicago	M,D
University of Illinois at Urbana–Champaign	M,D
The University of Kansas	M,D
University of Kentucky	M,D
University of Maine	M,D
University of Manitoba	M,D
University of Maryland, College Park	M,D
University of Memphis	M,D,O
University of Minnesota, Duluth	M,D
University of Minnesota, Twin Cities Campus	M,D
University of Mississippi	M,D
University of Missouri	M,D
University of Montana	M,D
University of Nevada, Reno	M,D

M—masters degree; D—doctorate; O—other advanced degree; *—Close-Up and/or Display

University of New Brunswick Fredericton	M,D
University of New Hampshire	M
The University of North Carolina at Chapel Hill	M,D
University of North Dakota	M,D
University of Oklahoma	M,D*
University of Oregon	M,D
University of Pittsburgh	M,D*
University of Puerto Rico– Mayagüez	M
University of Regina	M,D
University of Rochester	M,D*
University of Saskatchewan	M,D,O
University of South Carolina	M,D
University of Southern Mississippi	M,D
University of South Florida	M,D,O
The University of Tennessee	M,D
The University of Texas at Arlington	M,D
The University of Texas at Austin	M,D
The University of Texas at El Paso	M,D
The University of Texas at San Antonio	M
The University of Texas of the Permian Basin	M
The University of Toledo	M,D
University of Toronto	M,D
University of Utah	M,D
University of Vermont	M
University of Washington	M,D
The University of Western Ontario	M,D
University of Wisconsin– Madison	M,D
University of Wisconsin– Milwaukee	M,D*
University of Wyoming	M,D
Utah State University	M
Vanderbilt University	M*
Washington State University	M,D
Wayne State University	M
Western Kentucky University	M
Western Washington University	M
West Virginia University	M,D
Wichita State University	M
Wright State University	O
Yale University	D

GEOPHYSICS

Boise State University	M,D
Boston College	M
Bowling Green State University	M
California Institute of Technology	M,D
Colorado School of Mines	M,D
Cornell University	M,D
Idaho State University	M,O
Indiana University Bloomington	M,D
Louisiana State University and Agricultural & Mechanical College	M,D
Massachusetts Institute of Technology	M,D
Memorial University of Newfoundland	M,D
Michigan Technological University	M,D
Missouri University of Science and Technology	M,D
New Mexico Institute of Mining and Technology	M,D
Oregon State University	M,D
Rice University	M
Saint Louis University	M,D*
Southern Methodist University	M,D
Stanford University	M,D
Texas A&M University	M,D
University of Alaska Fairbanks	M
University of Alberta	M,D
The University of British Columbia	M,D
University of Calgary	M,D
University of California, Berkeley	M,D
University of California, Los Angeles	M,D
University of California, San Diego	M,D
University of Chicago	D
University of Colorado Boulder	M,D
University of Hawaii at Manoa	M,D
University of Houston	M,D
University of Manitoba	M,D
University of Memphis	M,D,O
University of Miami	M,D
University of Minnesota, Twin Cities Campus	M,D
University of Nevada, Reno	M,D
University of Oklahoma	M,D*
University of Rhode Island	M,D
The University of Texas at El Paso	M,D
The University of Tulsa	M,D
University of Utah	M,D
University of Washington	M,D
The University of Western Ontario	M,D
University of Wisconsin– Madison	M,D
University of Wyoming	M,D
Wright State University	M
Yale University	D

GEOSCIENCES

Arizona State University at the Tempe campus	M,D
Ball State University	M
Baylor University	M,D
Boise State University	M,D
Boston University	M,D
Brock University	M
Brooklyn College of the City University of New York	M
Brown University	D
California State University, Chico	M
California State University, San Bernardino	M
Carleton University	M,D
Case Western Reserve University	M,D
City College of the City University of New York	M
Colorado State University	M,D

Columbia University	M,D
Cornell University	M,D
Dalhousie University	M,D
Dartmouth College	M,D
Duke University	M,D
Eastern Michigan University	M
East Tennessee State University	M,O
Emporia State University	M,O
Florida Atlantic University	M,D
Florida Institute of Technology	M,D
Florida International University	M,D
Florida State University	M,D
Fort Hays State University	M
George Mason University	M,D,O
Georgia Institute of Technology	M,D
Georgia State University	M,D,O
The Graduate Center, City University of New York	D
Harvard University	M,D*
Hunter College of the City University of New York	M
Idaho State University	M,O
Indiana University Bloomington	M,D
Indiana University–Purdue University Indianapolis	M,D
Iowa State University of Science and Technology	M,D
Jackson State University	M,D
Johns Hopkins University	M,D*
Lehigh University	M,D
Long Island University–LIU Post	M,O
Manhattanville College	M,O
Massachusetts Institute of Technology	M,D
McGill University	M,D
McMaster University	M,D
Memorial University of Newfoundland	M,D
Michigan State University	M,D
Middle Tennessee State University	O
Mississippi State University	M,D
Missouri State University	M,O
Montana State University	M,D
Montana Tech of The University of Montana	M
Montclair State University	M
Murray State University	M,O
New Mexico Institute of Mining and Technology	M,D
North Carolina Central University	M
North Carolina State University	M,D
Northwestern University	D
The Ohio State University	M,D
Pace University	M,O
Penn State University Park	M,D*
Princeton University	D
Purdue University	M,D
Queens College of the City University of New York	M
Rice University	M,D
St. Francis Xavier University	M
Saint Louis University	M,D*
St. Thomas University	M,D,O
San Francisco State University	M
Simon Fraser University	M
South Dakota State University	D
Southern Illinois University Carbondale	M,D
Stanford University	M,D,O
State University of New York at New Paltz	M,O
Stony Brook University, State University of New York	M,D
Teachers College, Columbia University	M,D
Temple University	M,D*
Tennessee Technological University	D
Texas Tech University	M,D
Université du Québec à Chicoutimi	M
Université du Québec à Montréal	M,D,O
Université du Québec, Institut National de la Recherche Scientifique	M,D
Université Laval	M,D
University at Buffalo, the State University of New York	M,D
The University of Akron	M
The University of Alabama	M,D
The University of Alabama in Huntsville	M,D
University of Alberta	M,D
The University of Arizona	M,D
University of Arkansas at Little Rock	O
University of Calgary	M,D
University of California, Irvine	M,D
University of California, Los Angeles	M,D
University of California, San Diego	M,D
University of California, Santa Barbara	M,D
University of California, Santa Cruz	M,D
University of Chicago	D
University of Florida	M,D
University of Illinois at Chicago	M,D
University of Illinois at Urbana–Champaign	M,D
The University of Iowa	M,D
University of Louisiana at Lafayette	M
University of Lynchburg	M
University of Maine	M,D
The University of Manchester	M,D
University of Massachusetts Amherst	M,D
University of Michigan	M,D
University of Missouri– Kansas City	M,D
University of Montana	M,D

University of Nebraska– Lincoln	M,D
University of Nevada, Las Vegas	M,D
University of New Hampshire	M
University of New Haven	M
University of New Mexico	M,D
University of New Orleans	M,D
The University of North Carolina at Charlotte	M,D
The University of North Carolina Wilmington	M,O
University of North Dakota	M,D
University of Northern Colorado	M
University of Northern Iowa	M
University of Notre Dame	M,D
University of Ottawa	M,D
University of Pennsylvania	M,D*
University of Rhode Island	M,D,O
University of Rochester	M,D*
University of South Carolina	M,D
University of Southern California	M,D
University of South Florida	M,D
The University of Texas at Austin	M,D
The University of Texas at Dallas	M,D
The University of Texas Rio Grande Valley	M
The University of Tulsa	M,D
University of Victoria	M,D
University of Waterloo	M,D
The University of Western Ontario	M,D
University of Windsor	M,D
Virginia Polytechnic Institute and State University	M,D
Washington University in St. Louis	D
Wesleyan University	M
West Chester University of Pennsylvania	M,O
Western Connecticut State University	M
Western Kentucky University	M
Western Michigan University	M,D,O
Yale University	D
York University	M,D

GEOTECHNICAL ENGINEERING

The Citadel, The Military College of South Carolina	M,O
Clemson University	M,D
Cornell University	M,D
Drexel University	M,D*
École Polytechnique de Montréal	M,D,O
Illinois Institute of Technology	M,D
Iowa State University of Science and Technology	M,D
Kansas State University	M,D
Kennesaw State University	M
Louisiana State University and Agricultural & Mechanical College	M,D
Massachusetts Institute of Technology	M,D,O
McGill University	M,D
Missouri University of Science and Technology	M,D
Northwestern University	M,D
Norwich University	M
Ohio University	M,D
Old Dominion University	M
Oregon State University	M,D
Penn State University Park	M,D*
Southern Illinois University Edwardsville	M
Southern Methodist University	M,D
Stanford University	M,D,O
Tufts University	M,D
University of Alberta	M,D
University of Calgary	M,D
University of California, Berkeley	M,D
University of Colorado Denver	M,D
University of Dayton	M
University of Delaware	M,D
University of Massachusetts Amherst	M,D
University of Memphis	M,D,O
University of New Brunswick Fredericton	M,D
University of Puerto Rico– Mayagüez	M,D
University of Rhode Island	M,D
University of Southern California	M,D,O
University of South Florida	M,D
The University of Texas at Austin	M,D
University of Washington	M,D
University of Wisconsin– Madison	M

GERMAN

Arizona State University at the Tempe campus	M
Bowling Green State University	M
Brown University	D
California State University, Long Beach	M
Central Connecticut State University	M,O
Columbia University	M,D
Cornell University	M,D
Dalhousie University	M
DePaul University	M
Duke University	D
Florida State University	M
Georgetown University	M,D
Georgia State University	O
Harvard University	D*
Illinois State University	M
Indiana University Bloomington	M,D
Johns Hopkins University	M,D*
Kansas State University	M
Kent State University	M,D
McGill University	M
Memorial University of Newfoundland	M
Michigan State University	M,D
Middlebury College	M,D
Middle Tennessee State University	M

Millersville University of Pennsylvania	M
New York University	M,D*
Northwestern University	D
The Ohio State University	M,D
Penn State University Park	M,D*
Portland State University	D
Princeton University	D
Purdue University	M,D
Rutgers University–New Brunswick	M,D
San Francisco State University	M
Stanford University	M,D
Tufts University	M
Université de Montréal	M
University at Buffalo, the State University of New York	M,D,O
The University of Alabama	M,D
University of Alberta	M,D
The University of Arizona	M,D
University of Arkansas	M,D
The University of British Columbia	M,D
University of Calgary	M,D
University of California, Berkeley	D
University of California, Davis	M,D
University of California, Irvine	M,D
University of California, Los Angeles	M,D
University of Chicago	M,D
University of Cincinnati	M,D
University of Colorado Boulder	M
University of Delaware	M
University of Florida	M,D
University of Georgia	M
University of Illinois at Chicago	M,D
University of Illinois at Urbana–Champaign	M,D
University of Kentucky	M
University of Lethbridge	M,D
The University of Manchester	D
University of Manitoba	M
University of Maryland, College Park	M,D
University of Massachusetts Amherst	M,D
University of Michigan	M,D,O
University of Minnesota, Twin Cities Campus	M,D
University of Missouri	M
University of Montana	M
University of Nebraska– Lincoln	M,D
University of New Mexico	M,D
The University of North Carolina at Chapel Hill	D
University of Oklahoma	M,D*
University of Oregon	M,D
University of Pennsylvania	M,D*
University of South Africa	M,D
University of South Carolina	M,D
The University of Tennessee	M,D
The University of Texas at Austin	M,D
The University of Toledo	M
University of Toronto	M,D
University of Vermont	M
University of Victoria	M
University of Virginia	M
University of Washington	M,D
University of Waterloo	M,D
University of Wisconsin– Madison	M,D
University of Wisconsin– Milwaukee	M,O*
University of Wyoming	M
Vanderbilt University	M,D*
Washington University in St. Louis	D
Wayne State University	M,D
West Chester University of Pennsylvania	M,O
Western Kentucky University	M
Yale University	D

GERONTOLOGICAL NURSING

Allen College	M,D
Alvernia University	M,D,O
American University of Beirut	M
Arizona State University at the Tempe campus	M,D,O
Augusta University	D
Azusa Pacific University	M,D
Ball State University	M,D,O
Binghamton University, State University of New York	M,D,O
Boise State University	M,D,O
Boston College	M,D
California State University, Stanislaus	M
Capella University	M
Caribbean University	M,D
Case Western Reserve University	M
Clemson University	M,D,O
College of Staten Island of the City University of New York	M,O
Columbia University	M,O
Creighton University	M,D,O
Duke University	M,D,O
East Tennessee State University	M,D,O
Elms College	M,D
Fairleigh Dickinson University, Florham Campus	M
Felician University	M,O
Florida Southern College	M
George Mason University	M,D,O
Goldfarb School of Nursing at Barnes-Jewish College	M
Graceland University (IA)	M,D,O
Gwynedd Mercy University	M
Hofstra University	M
Hunter College of the City University of New York	M,D
Independence University	M
Indiana University–Purdue University Indianapolis	M,D,O
Jacksonville University	M,D,O

James Madison University	M,D
Johns Hopkins University	D*
Kent State University	M,D
Keuka College	M
La Salle University	M,D,O
Lehman College of the City University of New York	M
Loma Linda University	M
Louisiana State University Health Sciences Center	M,D,O
Marquette University	M,D,O
Maryville University of Saint Louis	M,D
Medical University of South Carolina	M,D
Mercer University	M,D,O
MGH Institute of Health Professions	M
Middle Georgia State University	M
Molloy College	M,D,O
Monmouth University	M,D,O
Morningside College	M
Mount Carmel College of Nursing	M,D
Neumann University	M,O
New York University	M,D,O*
Northeastern University	M,D,O
Nova Southeastern University	M,D
Oakland University	M,O
Old Dominion University	M,D
Oregon Health & Science University	M
Point Loma Nazarene University	M
Purdue University	M,D,O
Purdue University Fort Wayne	M
Research College of Nursing	M
Rush University	D,O
Rutgers University–Camden	D
Sage Graduate School	M,O
St. Catherine University	M,D
Saint Francis Medical Center College of Nursing	M,D,O
St. Joseph's College, Long Island Campus	
St. Joseph's College, New York	M
Saint Mary's College	D
Salem State University	M
San Jose State University	M,O
Seattle Pacific University	M,O
Seton Hall University	M,D
Shenandoah University	M,D,O
Southern Adventist University	M,D
Southern University and Agricultural and Mechanical College	M,D,O
Stony Brook University, State University of New York	M,D,O
Tennessee Technological University	D
Texas Christian University	M,O
Texas Tech University Health Sciences Center	M,D,O
Texas Woman's University	M,D
Uniformed Services University of the Health Sciences	M,D*
University at Buffalo, the State University of New York	M,D,O
The University of Alabama at Birmingham	M,D
The University of Alabama in Huntsville	M,D,O
University of Cincinnati	M,D
University of Colorado Colorado Springs	M,D
University of Connecticut	M,O
University of Delaware	M,O
University of Illinois at Chicago	M,O
The University of Kansas	M,D
University of Louisville	M,D
University of Maryland, Baltimore	M,D,O
University of Massachusetts Amherst	M,D
University of Massachusetts Lowell	M
University of Massachusetts Medical School	M,D,O
University of Minnesota, Twin Cities Campus	M,D
University of Missouri	M,D,O
University of Missouri–Kansas City	M,D
University of Missouri–St. Louis	D,O
The University of North Carolina at Chapel Hill	M,D,O
The University of North Carolina at Charlotte	M,D,O
The University of North Carolina at Greensboro	M,D,O
University of North Dakota	M
University of Pennsylvania	M*
University of Phoenix–Bay Area Campus	M,D
University of Phoenix–Phoenix Campus	M,O
University of Pittsburgh	D*
University of Puerto Rico–Medical Sciences Campus	M
University of Rhode Island	M,D,O
University of Rochester	M,D*
University of San Diego	M,D
University of Southern Maine	M,D,O
University of South Florida	M,D,O
The University of Tennessee at Chattanooga	M,D,O
The University of Tennessee Health Science Center	D,O
The University of Texas at Austin	M,D
The University of Texas Health Science Center at San Antonio	M,D,O
The University of Tulsa	D
University of Utah	M,O
University of Wisconsin–Eau Claire	M,D
University of Wisconsin–Madison	D
Ursuline College	M,D
Valdosta State University	M
Villanova University	M,D,O
Walden University	M,D,O
Wayne State University	M,D
West Chester University of Pennsylvania	M,D,O
Western Connecticut State University	M,D
William Paterson University of New Jersey	M,D,O
Wilmington University	M,D
Winona State University	M,D,O
Wright State University	M
York College of Pennsylvania	M

GERONTOLOGY

Adelphi University	M,O
Alliant International University–Los Angeles	M
Arizona State University at the Tempe campus	M,D,O
Arkansas State University	M,D,O
California State University, Fullerton	M
California State University, Long Beach	M
Capella University	M
Central Michigan University	M,O
The College at Brockport, State University of New York	M,O
Concordia University Chicago	M
DeSales University	M,D,O
Duke University	M,D,O
East Carolina University	M,O
Eastern Michigan University	O
East Tennessee State University	M,D,O
Georgia State University	M,O
Kansas State University	M,D
Kent State University	M,D
Lakehead University	M,D
La Salle University	M,D,O
Loma Linda University	M,D
Long Island University–LIU Brooklyn	M,O
Long Island University–LIU Post	M,O
Marywood University	M
McDaniel College	M,O
Mercer University	M,D
Miami University	M,D
Middle Tennessee State University	O
Minnesota State University Mankato	M
Morehead State University	M
Mount Saint Vincent University	M
North Dakota State University	D,O
Northeastern Illinois University	M
Oregon Health & Science University	M,O
Sage Graduate School	M
St. Cloud State University	M,O
San Diego State University	M
San Francisco State University	M
Simon Fraser University	M,D
Temple University	D*
Texas Christian University	D
Texas State University	M
Texas Tech University	M
Université de Sherbrooke	M
Université Laval	O
The University of Akron	D
University of Arkansas at Little Rock	O
University of Central Missouri	M,D,O
University of Central Oklahoma	M
University of Georgia	O
University of Illinois at Springfield	M,O
University of Indianapolis	M,D,O
The University of Kansas	D
University of Kentucky	D,O
University of La Verne	M,O
University of Louisiana at Monroe	M,O
University of Louisville	M,D,O
University of Maryland, Baltimore	M,D
University of Maryland, Baltimore County	M,D
University of Massachusetts Boston	M,D,O
University of Michigan–Flint	M,D,O
University of Nebraska at Omaha	M,D,O
University of Nebraska–Lincoln	M,D
The University of North Carolina at Charlotte	M,D,O
The University of North Carolina at Greensboro	M,O
The University of North Carolina Wilmington	M
University of Northern Colorado	M,D
University of North Texas	M,D,O
University of Phoenix–Central Valley Campus	M
University of Phoenix–Hawaii Campus	M
University of Puerto Rico–Medical Sciences Campus	M,O
University of Regina	M
University of South Carolina	O
University of Southern California	M,D,O
University of Southern Indiana	M,D,O
University of South Florida	M,D,O
The University of Tennessee	M
The University of Toledo	M,O
University of Utah	M,O
University of Wisconsin–Milwaukee	M,D,O*
Virginia Commonwealth University	M,D,O
Walden University	M,D,O
Washington University in St. Louis	M,D,O
Wayne State University	M,D,O

Webster University	M
West Chester University of Pennsylvania	M,O
Wichita State University	M
Youngstown State University	M

GRAPHIC DESIGN

Academy of Art University	M
ArtCenter College of Design	M
Atlantic University College	M
Bob Jones University	M,D,O
Bowling Green State University	M
Bradley University	M
California College of the Arts	M
California Institute of the Arts	M,O
California State University, Fullerton	M
California State University, Los Angeles	M
Central Connecticut State University	M
Central Washington University	M
City College of the City University of New York	M
East Carolina University	M
Florida Atlantic University	M
Full Sail University	M
George Mason University	M
Georgia Southern University	M
Georgia State University	M
Illinois State University	M
Indiana State University	M
Indiana University–Purdue University Indianapolis	M
Inter American University of Puerto Rico, San Germán Campus	M
Iowa State University of Science and Technology	M
Kent State University	M
Liberty University	M
Louisiana State University and Agricultural & Mechanical College	M
Louisiana Tech University	M,D,O
Lynn University	M,O
Maryland Institute College of Art	M
Marywood University	M
Minneapolis College of Art and Design	M,O
Morehead State University	M
New York Institute of Technology	M
North Carolina State University	M
Ohio University	M
Oklahoma State University	M
Otis College of Art and Design	M
Pensacola Christian College	M,D,O
Pittsburg State University	M,O
Pratt Institute	M
Rhode Island School of Design	M
Rochester Institute of Technology	M
San Diego State University	M
Savannah College of Art and Design	M
School of Visual Arts (NY)	M
State University of New York at Oswego	M
Suffolk University	M
Temple University	M*
Texas State University	M
Texas Woman's University	M
Université Laval	M
University of Baltimore	D
University of Cincinnati	M
University of Guam	M
University of Illinois at Chicago	M
University of Illinois at Urbana–Champaign	M
University of Memphis	M,O
University of Miami	M
University of Minnesota, Duluth	M
University of Notre Dame	M
University of Pennsylvania	M,O*
University of South Dakota	M
The University of Tennessee	M
University of Utah	M
Vermont College of Fine Arts	M
Wayne State University	M
West Virginia University	M,D
Yale University	M

HAZARDOUS MATERIALS MANAGEMENT

Humboldt State University	M
Indiana University Bloomington	M,D,O
Jackson State University	M,D
Marquette University	M,D,O
New Mexico Institute of Mining and Technology	M
Rutgers University–New Brunswick	M,D
University of Colorado Denver	M
The University of Manchester	M,D
University of New Haven	M
University of South Carolina	M,D
University of Southern California	M,D,O

HEALTH COMMUNICATION

Arkansas State University	M,O
Boston University	M
Chatham University	M
The College of New Jersey	M
Cornell University	M,D
DePaul University	M
East Carolina University	M
Fontbonne University	M
Gannon University	M
The George Washington University	M,D
Indiana University–Purdue University Indianapolis	M,D
Johns Hopkins University	M,D*
Kansas State University	M
Lasell College	M,O
Marquette University	M,O
Michigan State University	M

Ohio University	M,D
Rider University	M
Southeastern Louisiana University	M
Southern Illinois University Edwardsville	M
State University of New York at Oswego	M
Stony Brook University, State University of New York	M,O
Tufts University	M,D,O
University of Florida	M,D,O
University of Houston	M
University of Missouri	M,D
The University of North Carolina at Chapel Hill	M,D,O
University of Oklahoma	M,D*
University of St. Thomas (MN)	M
University of Southern California	M,D
Wayne State University	M,D,O

HEALTH EDUCATION

Adelphi University	M
Alabama State University	M
Albany State University	M,O
Alcorn State University	M,O
Allen College	M,D
Arcadia University	M
Arizona State University at the Tempe campus	D
Arkansas State University	M,D,O
Auburn University	M,D,O
Austin Peay State University	M
Baldwin Wallace University	M
Baylor University	M,D
Benedictine University	M
Boston University	M
Brandeis University	D
California Baptist University	M
California State University, Long Beach	M
California State University, Northridge	M,O
Cambridge College	M,D,O
Central Washington University	M
Clark University	M
Cleveland State University	M
Cleveland University–Kansas City	M
The College at Brockport, State University of New York	M
College of Saint Mary	D
Colorado State University–Pueblo	M
Columbus State University	M
Concordia University (United States)	M,D
Concordia University Wisconsin	M,D
Daemen College	M
Dalhousie University	M
Delta State University	M
Drew University	M,D,O
East Carolina University	M
Eastern Kentucky University	M
Eastern Michigan University	M,O
Eastern University	M,O
East Stroudsburg University of Pennsylvania	M
Emory University	M,D
Fairfield University	M,D
Florida State University	M,D
Fort Hays State University	M
Georgia College & State University	M
Georgia Southern University	M,D
Georgia State University	M
Harding University	M,O
Hofstra University	M,D,O
Howard University	M
Idaho State University	M
Illinois State University	M
Indiana State University	M,D
Indiana University Bloomington	M,D
Indiana University of Pennsylvania	M
Indiana University–Purdue University Indianapolis	M,D
Inter American University of Puerto Rico, Metropolitan Campus	M
Inter American University of Puerto Rico, San Germán Campus	M
Ithaca College	M
Jackson State University	M
James Madison University	M
John F. Kennedy University	M
Johns Hopkins University	M,D*
Kansas State University	M,D
Keiser University	M
Kent State University	M,D
Lake Erie College of Osteopathic Medicine	M,D,O
Lehman College of the City University of New York	M
Lock Haven University of Pennsylvania	M
Logan University	M,D
Loma Linda University	M,D
Longwood University	M
Marshall University	M
Marymount University	M
Marywood University	D
Massachusetts College of Liberal Arts	M,O
McNeese State University	O
Meredith College	M,O
Merrimack College	M
Middle Tennessee State University	M
Minnesota State University Mankato	M,O
Mississippi University for Women	M,D,O
Montana State University	M
Montclair State University	M
Morehead State University	M
New Jersey City University	M
New Mexico Highlands University	M

M—masters degree; D—doctorate; O—other advanced degree; *—Close-Up and/or Display

New York Medical College	M,D,O
Nicholls State University	M
Northeastern State University	M
Northwestern State University of Louisiana	M
Northwest Missouri State University	M
Nova Southeastern University	M,D,O
Oklahoma State University	M,D,O
Old Dominion University	M,D
Penn State Harrisburg	M,D,O
Pennsylvania College of Health Sciences	M
Pittsburg State University	M
Plymouth State University	M
Prairie View A&M University	M
Purdue University	M,D
Rhode Island College	M,O
Rosalind Franklin University of Medicine and Science	
Rutgers University–Newark	M,D
Rutgers University–New Brunswick	M,D,O
Sage Graduate School	M
Saint Francis University	M
Saint Joseph's College of Maine	M
San Francisco State University	M
Southeastern Louisiana University	M
Southern Connecticut State University	M
Southern Illinois University Carbondale	M,D
Southern Illinois University Edwardsville	M,D,O
Southwestern Oklahoma State University	M
State University of New York College at Cortland	M
Stony Brook University, State University of New York	M,O
Teachers College, Columbia University	M,D,O
Tennessee Technological University	M
Texas A&M University	M,D
Texas A&M University–Kingsville	M
Texas Southern University	M
Texas State University	M
Texas Woman's University	M,D
Thomas Jefferson University	M,D,O
Trident University International	M
Union College (KY)	M
The University of Alabama	M,D
University of Arkansas	M,D
University of Arkansas at Little Rock	M,D
University of Arkansas for Medical Sciences	M,D,O
University of Central Arkansas	M
University of Cincinnati	M,D
University of Colorado Denver	M
University of Florida	M,D,O
University of Georgia	M,D
University of Houston	M
University of Illinois at Chicago	M
University of Illinois at Springfield	M,O
The University of Kansas	M,D,O
University of Louisville	M,D,O
University of Maryland, College Park	M,D
University of Massachusetts Amherst	M,D
University of Michigan	M,D
University of Michigan–Flint	M
University of Missouri	M,D,O
University of Missouri–Kansas City	M
University of Montana	M
University of Nebraska at Omaha	M,D
University of New Mexico	M
The University of North Carolina at Pembroke	M
University of Northern Colorado	M
University of Northern Iowa	M
University of Oklahoma Health Sciences Center	D
University of Phoenix–Online Campus	M,O
University of Pittsburgh	M,D*
University of Puerto Rico–Medical Sciences Campus	M
University of Rhode Island	M
University of St. Augustine for Health Sciences	M,D
University of South Africa	M,D
University of South Alabama	M
University of South Carolina	M,D,O
University of Southern California	M
University of South Florida	M,D
The University of Tennessee	M
The University of Texas at Austin	M,D
The University of Texas at San Antonio	M
The University of Texas at Tyler	M
The University of Toledo	M,D
University of Utah	M,D
University of Waterloo	M,D
University of Wisconsin–La Crosse	M
University of Wyoming	M
Utah State University	M,D
Virginia State University	M,D
Walden University	M,D,O
Washburn University	M
Wayne State University	M,D,O
Western Illinois University	M
Western Michigan University	D,O
Western Oregon University	M
Western University of Health Sciences	M
Widener University	M,D
Worcester State University	M,O

Wright State University	M

HEALTH INFORMATICS

Adelphi University	M,D,O
American Public University System	M,D
American Sentinel University	M
Arkansas Tech University	M
Augusta University	M
Barry University	O
Bay Path University	M
Belmont University	D
Benedictine University	M
Boston University	M,O
Brandeis University	M
Brooklyn College of the City University of New York	M,O
Canisius College	M,O
Capella University	M
Chatham University	M
Claremont Graduate University	M,D,O
Clarkson University	M
The College of St. Scholastica	M,D,O
Colorado Mesa University	M,D,O
Dakota State University	M,D
Dartmouth College	M,D
DePaul University	M,D
DeSales University	M,O
Duke University	M
East Carolina University	M,O
Emory University	M,D
George Mason University	M,D,O
Georgia Southwestern State University	M,O
Georgia State University	M,D,O
Grand Canyon University	M,D,O
Hofstra University	M,O
Indiana University Bloomington	M,D
Indiana University–Purdue University Indianapolis	M,D
Jacksonville University	M
Kennesaw State University	M,O
Kent State University	M
Liberty University	M,D
Lipscomb University	M,D
Logan University	M,D
Louisiana Tech University	M,D,O
Marshall University	M
Marymount University	M,O
Mercer University	M,D
Middle Georgia State University	M,O
Midwestern State University	M,O
Millennia Atlantic University	M
Montana Tech of The University of Montana	O
National University	M,O
Northeastern University	M,D
Northern Kentucky University	M,O
Northwestern University	M,D
Nova Southeastern University	M,D,O
Oregon Health & Science University	M,D,O
Regis University	M
Roberts Wesleyan College	M
Rochester Institute of Technology	M
Rutgers University–New Brunswick	M
Sacred Heart University	M
St. Catherine University	M
St. Joseph's College, Long Island Campus	M
St. Joseph's College, New York	M
Saint Joseph's University	M
Samford University	M
Slippery Rock University of Pennsylvania	M
Southern Illinois University Edwardsville	M
Southern New Hampshire University	M,D,O
State University of New York at Oswego	M
Stephens College	M,O
Stony Brook University, State University of New York	M,D,O
Temple University	M,D*
Texas State University	M
Trident University International	M,D,O
The University of Alabama at Birmingham	M
University of Central Florida	M,O
University of Cincinnati	M
University of Colorado Denver	M
The University of Findlay	M
University of Illinois at Chicago	M,O
University of Illinois at Urbana–Champaign	M,D,O
The University of Iowa	M,D,O
The University of Kansas	M,O
University of Lynchburg	O
University of Maryland, Baltimore County	M
University of Maryland University College	M
University of Michigan	M,D
University of Michigan–Dearborn	M
University of Michigan–Flint	M
University of Minnesota, Twin Cities Campus	M,D
University of Missouri	M,O
University of New England	M,D,O
The University of North Carolina at Charlotte	M,O
University of Phoenix–Online Campus	M,O
University of Pittsburgh	M*
University of Puerto Rico–Medical Sciences Campus	M
University of St. Augustine for Health Sciences	M
University of San Diego	M,D
University of San Francisco	M
University of South Carolina Upstate	M
University of South Florida	M,D,O

The University of Tennessee Health Science Center	M,D
The University of Texas Health Science Center at Houston	M,D,O
University of Toronto	M
University of Victoria	M
University of Virginia	M
University of Washington	M,D
University of Waterloo	M,D
University of Wisconsin–Milwaukee	M,D*
Virginia International University	M,O
Walden University	M,D,O
Weill Cornell Medicine	M

HEALTH LAW

Boston University	M,D
Case Western Reserve University	M,D
DePaul University	M,D
Drexel University	M,D*
Florida State University	M,D
Georgetown University	M,D
Hofstra University	M,D,O
Indiana University–Purdue University Indianapolis	M,D,O
Loyola University Chicago	M,D,O
Nova Southeastern University	M,D
St. Mary's University (United States)	M
Seattle University	M,D
Seton Hall University	M,D
Southern Illinois University Carbondale	M
Suffolk University	M,D
Université de Sherbrooke	M,D,O
University of California, San Francisco	M
University of Houston	M,D
The University of Manchester	M,D
University of Pittsburgh	M*
The University of Tulsa	M,D,O
Widener University	M,D

HEALTH PHYSICS/RADIOLOGICAL HEALTH

East Carolina University	M,D
Georgetown University	M
Georgia Institute of Technology	M,D
Idaho State University	M,D
Illinois Institute of Technology	M,D
McMaster University	M
Midwestern State University	M
Northwestern State University of Louisiana	M
Oregon State University	M,D
Purdue University	M,D
Quinnipiac University	M
Radiological Technologies University VT	M
Rutgers University–Newark	M
San Diego State University	M
Thomas Jefferson University	M
Université Laval	O
University of Alberta	M,D
University of Arkansas for Medical Sciences	M,D
University of Cincinnati	M
University of Kentucky	M
University of Massachusetts Lowell	M
University of Michigan	M,D,O
University of Missouri	M
University of Nevada, Las Vegas	M,D,O
University of Oklahoma Health Sciences Center	M,D
University of Toronto	M,D
Virginia Commonwealth University	D
Weber State University	M

HEALTH PROMOTION

Adler University	M
American College of Healthcare Sciences	M,O
American University	M,O
American University of Beirut	M,D
Arizona State University at the Tempe campus	M,D
Ball State University	M
Boise State University	M,O
Bridgewater State University	M
Brigham Young University	M,D
California Baptist University	M
California State University, Fresno	M
California State University, Fullerton	M
Claremont Graduate University	M,D
Cleveland University–Kansas City	M
Concord University	M
Creighton University	M
East Carolina University	M
Eastern Kentucky University	M
Eastern Michigan University	M,O
Emory University	M
Fairmont State University	M
Florida Atlantic University	M
Florida International University	M,D
George Mason University	M,O
Georgetown University	M,D
Georgia College & State University	M
Goddard College	M
Harvard University	M,D*
Immaculata University	M
Independence University	M
Indiana University Bloomington	M,D
Instituto Tecnologico de Santo Domingo	M
Kent State University	M,D
Lehman College of the City University of New York	M
Liberty University	M,D,O
Lindenwood University	M
Lock Haven University of Pennsylvania	M
Manhattanville College	M,O

Maryland University of Integrative Health	M,O
Marymount University	M
McNeese State University	M
Merrimack College	M
Morehead State University	M
Mount St. Joseph University	M,O
National University	M,O
Nebraska Methodist College	M
New York University	M,D,O*
Old Dominion University	M
Oregon State University	M,D
Plymouth State University	M,O
Portland State University	M,D
Queen's University at Kingston	M,D
Rosalind Franklin University of Medicine and Science	M
Rowan University	M
San Diego State University	M,D
Simmons University	M,D,O
Sonoma State University	M
Southern Methodist University	M,D
Springfield College	M,D,O
Stony Brook University, State University of New York	M,O
Tennessee Technological University	M
Tulane University	M
Union Institute & University	M
Universidad del Turabo	M
The University of Alabama	M,D
University of Alberta	M,O
University of Arkansas	M,D
University of Arkansas for Medical Sciences	M,D,O
University of Central Oklahoma	M
University of Chicago	M,D
University of Cincinnati	M,D
University of Delaware	M,D
University of Georgia	M,D
The University of Kansas	M,D,O
University of Kentucky	M,D
University of Lynchburg	M
University of Massachusetts Lowell	D
University of Memphis	M,O
University of Michigan	M,D
University of Mississippi	M,D
University of Missouri	M,O
University of Nebraska–Lincoln	M,D
University of Nebraska Medical Center	D
University of North Alabama	M
The University of North Carolina at Chapel Hill	M
University of Northern Iowa	M
University of Oklahoma	M,D*
University of Oklahoma Health Sciences Center	M,D
University of Puerto Rico–Medical Sciences Campus	O
University of South Carolina	M,D,O
University of Southern California	M
The University of Tennessee	M
The University of Texas Health Science Center at Houston	M,D,O
The University of Toledo	M,D,O
University of Toronto	M,D
University of Utah	M,D
University of Vermont	M
University of West Florida	M
University of Wisconsin–Milwaukee	M,D,O*
University of Wisconsin–Parkside	M
University of Wisconsin–Stevens Point	M
University of Wyoming	M
Utah State University	M,D
Walden University	M,D,O
Wilfrid Laurier University	M
Wright State University	M

HEALTH PSYCHOLOGY

Adler University	M
Alliant International University–Los Angeles	D
Appalachian State University	M
Argosy University, Atlanta	M,D,O
Argosy University, Chicago	D
Argosy University, Northern Virginia	M,D
Argosy University, Twin Cities	M,D,O
Bastyr University	M,O
California State University, Dominguez Hills	M
Central Michigan University	M,D
Chatham University	M,D
Claremont Graduate University	M,D
Drexel University	D*
Duke University	D
East Carolina University	M,D,O
Georgian Court University	M,O
John F. Kennedy University	M
La Salle University	M,D
Lesley University	M,D,O
North Dakota State University	M,D
Northern Kentucky University	M,D
Oklahoma State University	M,D,O
Oregon State University	M,D,O
Penn State Harrisburg	M,D,O
Prescott College	M
Rhode Island College	M,O
Rutgers University–New Brunswick	D
San Diego State University	M,D
Saybrook University	M,D
Southwestern College (NM)	O
United States International University–Africa	M
The University of Alabama at Birmingham	
The University of British Columbia	M,D
University of Colorado Denver	D

University of Florida	M,D
University of Michigan–Dearborn	M
University of New Mexico	D
The University of North Carolina at Chapel Hill	M,D
The University of North Carolina at Charlotte	M,D,O
University of Pittsburgh	D*
The University of Texas at Arlington	M,D
University of the Sciences	M
Virginia Commonwealth University	D
Virginia State University	M,D
Viterbo University	M
Walden University	M,D,O
Yeshiva University	D

HEALTH SERVICES MANAGEMENT AND HOSPITAL ADMINISTRATION

Abilene Christian University	M
Adelphi University	M
AdventHealth University	M
Alaska Pacific University	M
Albany State University	M
Albertus Magnus College	M
American InterContinental University Online	M
American Sentinel University	M
American University	M,O
American University of Beirut	M
Anderson University (SC)	M
Antioch University Midwest	M
Aquinas Institute of Theology	M,D,O
Argosy University, Atlanta	M,D
Argosy University, Chicago	M,D
Argosy University, Hawai'i	M,D,O
Argosy University, Los Angeles	M,D
Argosy University, Northern Virginia	M,D,O
Argosy University, Orange County	M,D,O
Argosy University, Phoenix	M,D
Argosy University, Seattle	M,D
Argosy University, Tampa	M,D
Argosy University, Twin Cities	M,D
Arizona State University at the Tempe campus	M,D
Arkansas State University	M,D,O
Ashland University	M
Ashworth College	M
Assumption College	M,O
Atlantis University	M
A.T. Still University	M,D,O
Baker College Center for Graduate Studies–Online	M,D
Baldwin Wallace University	M
Barry University	M,O
Baruch College of the City University of New York	M*
Bay Path University	M
Belhaven University (MS)	M
Bellevue University	M
Belmont University	M
Benedictine University	M
Binghamton University, State University of New York	M,D
Bluffton University	M
Boston University	M,D
Bradley University	M,D,O
Brandeis University	M
Brandman University	M
Brenau University	M
Brigham Young University	M
Broadview University–West Jordan	M
Brooklyn College of the City University of New York	M
Bryan College	M
California Baptist University	M
California Coast University	M
California Intercontinental University	M,D
California State University, Bakersfield	M
California State University, Chico	M
California State University, East Bay	M
California State University, Fresno	M
California State University, Long Beach	M
California State University, Los Angeles	M,O
California State University, Northridge	M
California State University, San Bernardino	M
California University of Pennsylvania	M
Cambridge College	M
Capella University	M,D
Cardinal Stritch University	M
Carlow University	M
Carnegie Mellon University	M
Case Western Reserve University	M
The Catholic University of America	M
Cedarville University	M,D
Central Michigan University	M,D,O
Champlain College	M
The Chicago School of Professional Psychology: Online	M
Clarion University of Pennsylvania	M
Clarkson University	M
Cleary University	M,O
Cleveland State University	M
The College at Brockport, State University of New York	M
College of Saint Elizabeth	M
College of Staten Island of the City University of New York	M

Colorado State University–Global Campus	M
Columbia Southern University	M
Columbia University	M
Columbus State University	M
Concordia University Irvine	M
Concordia University, St. Paul	M
Concordia University Wisconsin	M
Copenhagen Business School	M,D
Cornell University	M,D
Creighton University	M,D
Daemen College	M
Dalhousie University	M,D
Dallas Baptist University	M
Dartmouth College	M,D
Davenport University	M
Delta State University	M,D
DeSales University	M
Des Moines University	M
Dominican College	M
Drew University	M,D,O
Duke University	M,O
Duquesne University	M,D
D'Youville College	M,D,O
East Carolina University	M,O
Eastern Kentucky University	M
Eastern Mennonite University	M
Eastern Michigan University	M,O
Eastern University	M
East Tennessee State University	M,D,O
Elmhurst College	M
Elms College	M,O
Emory University	M,D
Fairleigh Dickinson University, Florham Campus	M
Fairleigh Dickinson University, Metropolitan Campus	M
Felician University	M
Ferris State University	M
Florida Atlantic University	M
Florida Institute of Technology	M
Florida International University	M,D
Florida National University	M
Fordham University	M,D
Framingham State University	M
Franciscan Missionaries of Our Lady University	M,D
Francis Marion University	M
Franklin Pierce University	M,D,O
Friends University	M
George Mason University	M,D
The George Washington University	M,D,O
Georgia Institute of Technology	M
Georgia Southern University	M,D
Georgia State University	M,D,O
Goldey-Beacom College	M
Governors State University	M
Grambling State University	M
Grand Canyon University	M,D,O
Grand Valley State University	M
Grantham University	M
Gwynedd Mercy University	M
Harvard University	M,D*
Herzing University Online	M
Hilbert College	M
Hodges University	M
Hofstra University	M,O
Holy Family University	M
Husson University	M
IGlobal University	M
Independence University	M
Indiana Tech	M
Indiana University Bloomington	M,D
Indiana University Kokomo	M
Indiana University Northwest	M,O
Indiana University of Pennsylvania	M
Indiana University–Purdue University Indianapolis	M,D,O
Indiana University South Bend	M,O
Indiana Wesleyan University	M,O
Institute of Public Administration	M,O
Iona College	M
John F. Kennedy University	M
Johns Hopkins University	M,D*
Kean University	M
Keiser University	M
Kennesaw State University	M
Kent State University	M,D
King's College	M
King University	M
Lake Erie College	M
Lake Forest Graduate School of Management	M
Lakeland University	M
Lasell College	M
Lawrence Technological University	M,D,O
Lebanon Valley College	M
Lehigh University	M,O
Lenoir-Rhyne University	M
LeTourneau University	M
Lewis University	M
Lindenwood University	M,O
Lindenwood University-Belleville	M
Lipscomb University	M,O
Lock Haven University of Pennsylvania	M
Loma Linda University	M,D
London Metropolitan University	M,D
Long Island University–Brentwood Campus	M,O
Long Island University–Hudson	M,O
Long Island University–LIU Brooklyn	M,O
Long Island University–LIU Post	M,O
Louisiana State University Health Sciences Center	M,D

Louisiana State University in Shreveport	M
Loyola University Chicago	M
Madonna University	M
Marshall University	M
Marymount University	M
Maryville University of Saint Louis	M,O
Marywood University	M
MCPHS University	M
Medical University of South Carolina	M,D
Meharry Medical College	M
Mercy College	M
Mercy College of Ohio	M
Midwestern State University	M,O
Milligan College	M,O
Milwaukee School of Engineering	M
Minnesota State University Moorhead	M,O
Misericordia University	M
Mississippi College	M
Molloy College	M,D,O
Monroe College	M
Montana State University Billings	M
Moravian College	M
Mount Aloysius College	M
Mount St. Joseph University	D
Mount Saint Mary College	M
Mount Saint Mary's University (CA)	M,D,O
Mount St. Mary's University (MD)	M
National American University (TX)	M,D
National University	M,O
Nebraska Methodist College	M
New Charter University	M
New England College	M
New Jersey City University	M
New Jersey Institute of Technology	M,D
New York Medical College	M,D,O
New York University	M,D,O*
Niagara University	M
Northeast Ohio Medical University	M,D,O
Northern Arizona University	D
Northwestern University	M,D
Ohio Christian University	M
Ohio Dominican University	M
The Ohio State University	M,D
Ohio University	M
Oklahoma Christian University	M
Oklahoma State University Center for Health Sciences	M
Oregon Health & Science University	M,O
Oregon State University	M,D
Our Lady of the Lake University	M
Pace University	M
Pacific University	M
Park University	M,O
Penn State Great Valley	M,O
Penn State Harrisburg	M,D,O
Penn State University Park	M,D*
Pennsylvania College of Health Sciences	M
Pfeiffer University	M
Philadelphia College of Osteopathic Medicine	M,D,O*
Point Loma Nazarene University	M
Point Park University	M
Portland State University	M,D,O
Post University	M
Purdue University Global	M,O
Quinnipiac University	M
Regent University	M,D,O
Regis College (MA)	M,D,O
Regis University	M,D,O
Rhode Island College	M
Rice University	M
Robert Morris University Illinois	M
Roberts Wesleyan College	M
Rochester Institute of Technology	M,O
Rockhurst University	M,O
Roger Williams University	M
Rosalind Franklin University of Medicine and Science	M,O
Rush University	M,D
Rutgers University–Camden	M,O
Rutgers University–Newark	M,D,O
Rutgers University–New Brunswick	M,D,O
Sage Graduate School	M
Saginaw Valley State University	M
St. Ambrose University	M,D
St. Catherine University	M
St. Joseph's College, Long Island Campus	M
St. Joseph's College, New York	M
Saint Joseph's College of Maine	M
Saint Joseph's University	M,O
Saint Leo University	M,D
Saint Louis University	M,D*
Saint Mary-of-the-Woods College	M
Saint Mary's University of Minnesota	M
St. Norbert College	M
Saint Peter's University	M
St. Thomas University	M,O
Saint Xavier University	M,O
Salve Regina University	M
Samford University	M
San Diego State University	M,D
San Francisco State University	M
Seton Hall University	M,D
Seton Hill University	M
Shenandoah University	M,D,O
Shippensburg University of Pennsylvania	M,D,O
Siena Heights University	M,O
Simmons University	M

South Carolina State University	M
Southeastern University (FL)	M,D
Southern Adventist University	M
Southern Illinois University Carbondale	M
Southern Nazarene University	M
Southern New Hampshire University	M,D,O
South University	M
South University (SC)	M
South University (GA)	M
South University (AL)	M
South University	M
Southwest Baptist University	M
Stevenson University	M
Stony Brook University, State University of New York	M,D,O
Stratford University (VA)	M,D
Strayer University	M
Suffolk University	M
Syracuse University	O
Temple University	M*
Texas A&M University	M,D
Texas A&M University–Corpus Christi	M,D
Texas Health and Science University	M,D
Texas Southern University	M
Texas State University	M
Texas Tech University	M,D
Texas Tech University Health Sciences Center	M
Texas Woman's University	M
Thomas Jefferson University	M,D,O
Tiffin University	M
Towson University	M,O
Trevecca Nazarene University	M
Trident University International	M,D,O
Trinity University	M
Trinity Western University	M,O
Troy University	M
Tufts University	M,D,O
Tulane University	M,D
Uniformed Services University of the Health Sciences	M,D*
Union Institute & University	M
Universidad de Ciencias Medicas	M,D,O
Universidad de Iberoamerica	M,D
Université de Montréal	M,O
University at Albany, State University of New York	M,D,O
University at Buffalo, the State University of New York	M,D
The University of Alabama at Birmingham	M,D
The University of Alabama in Huntsville	M,D,O
University of Alberta	M,D
University of Arkansas for Medical Sciences	M,D,O
University of Arkansas–Fort Smith	M
University of Baltimore	M
The University of British Columbia	M,D
University of California, Berkeley	D
University of California, Irvine	M
University of California, Los Angeles	M,D
University of California, San Diego	M
University of Central Florida	M,O
University of Chicago	M,O
University of Colorado Denver	M
University of Connecticut	M,D
University of Dallas	M,D
University of Denver	M,O
University of Detroit Mercy	M,D,O
University of Evansville	M
The University of Findlay	M,D
University of Florida	M,D
University of Holy Cross	M,D
University of Houston–Clear Lake	M
University of Illinois at Chicago	M,D
University of Illinois at Urbana–Champaign	M,D
The University of Iowa	M,D
The University of Kansas	M,D
University of Kentucky	M
University of La Verne	M,D,O
University of Louisville	M
University of Management and Technology	M
University of Mary	M
University of Maryland, Baltimore County	M,D,O
University of Maryland, College Park	M,D
University of Maryland University College	M
University of Massachusetts Amherst	M,D
University of Massachusetts Dartmouth	M
University of Memphis	M,D
University of Miami	M,D
University of Michigan	M,D
University of Michigan–Flint	M,O
University of Minnesota, Twin Cities Campus	M,D
University of Missouri	M,O
University of Nebraska Medical Center	M,D
University of Nevada, Las Vegas	M
University of New England	M,D,O
University of New Mexico	M
University of New Orleans	M
University of North Alabama	M
The University of North Carolina at Chapel Hill	M,D
The University of North Carolina at Charlotte	M,D,O

Institution	Degree
The University of North Carolina at Pembroke	M
University of Northern Colorado	M
University of North Florida	M
University of North Texas	M,D,O
University of North Texas Health Science Center at Fort Worth	M,D,O
University of Oklahoma	M,O*
University of Oklahoma Health Sciences Center	M,D
University of Ottawa	M
University of Pennsylvania	M,D*
University of Phoenix–Bay Area Campus	M,D
University of Phoenix–Central Valley Campus	M
University of Phoenix–Hawaii Campus	M
University of Phoenix–Houston Campus	M
University of Phoenix–Online Campus	M,D,O
University of Phoenix–Phoenix Campus	M,O
University of Phoenix–Sacramento Valley Campus	M
University of Phoenix–San Antonio Campus	M
University of Pikeville	M
University of Pittsburgh	M,D,O*
University of Portland	M
University of Puerto Rico–Medical Sciences Campus	M
University of Regina	M,D,O
University of Rhode Island	M,D,O
University of Rochester	M,D*
University of St. Augustine for Health Sciences	M
University of St. Francis (IL)	M,O
University of Saint Francis (IN)	M
University of Saint Mary	M
University of St. Thomas (MN)	M
University of San Francisco	M
The University of Scranton	M
University of Sioux Falls	M
University of South Africa	M,D
University of South Carolina	M,D
University of South Dakota	M,O
University of Southern California	M,D
University of Southern Indiana	M
University of Southern Maine	M
University of Southern Mississippi	M
University of South Florida	O
The University of Tennessee	M
The University of Texas at Arlington	M
The University of Texas at Dallas	M,D
The University of Texas at El Paso	M,D,O
The University of Texas at Tyler	M,D
The University of Texas Health Science Center at Houston	M,D,O
The University of Texas Health Science Center at Tyler	M
The University of Texas Rio Grande Valley	M
University of the Incarnate Word	M,D
University of the Sciences	M,D
The University of Toledo	M,O
University of Toronto	M
University of Utah	M,D
University of Vermont	M,O
University of Virginia	M
University of Washington	M
The University of Western Ontario	M,D
University of West Florida	M
University of West Georgia	M,D,O
University of Wisconsin–Milwaukee	M,D*
University of Wisconsin–Oshkosh	M
University of Wyoming	M,D
Ursuline College	M
Utica College	M
Valdosta State University	M
Valparaiso University	M
Vanderbilt University	M*
Villanova University	M
Virginia Commonwealth University	M,D
Virginia International University	M,O
Viterbo University	M
Walden University	M,D,O
Walsh University	M
Washington Adventist University	M
Washington State University	M
Wayland Baptist University	M
Waynesburg University	M,D
Wayne State University	M,D
Weber State University	M
Webster University	M,D,O
Weill Cornell Medicine	M
West Chester University of Pennsylvania	M,O
West Coast University	M,D
Western Carolina University	M
Western Connecticut State University	M
Western Governors University	M
Western Kentucky University	M
Western Michigan University	M,D,O
Widener University	M
Wilkes University	M
William Woods University	M,D,O
Wilmington University	M,D
Wilson College	M
Wingate University	M
Winston-Salem State University	M
Worcester State University	M
Xavier University	M*
Yale University	M,D
York College of Pennsylvania	M
Youngstown State University	M

HEALTH SERVICES RESEARCH

Institution	Degree
Albany College of Pharmacy and Health Sciences	M,D
American University of Beirut	M,D
Boston University	M,D
Brown University	D
Clarkson University	M
Dartmouth College	M,D
Emory University	M,D
Florida Agricultural and Mechanical University	M,D
George Mason University	M,D,O
The George Washington University	M,D,O
Lakehead University	M,D
McMaster University	M,D
Northwestern University	D
Old Dominion University	M
Penn State Hershey Medical Center	M
Stanford University	M,D
Texas A&M University	M,D
Thomas Jefferson University	M,D,O
The University of Alabama at Birmingham	M,D
University of Alberta	M,D
University of Arkansas for Medical Sciences	M,D,O
University of Cincinnati	M
University of Colorado Denver	M,D
University of Florida	M,D
University of Illinois at Chicago	M,D
University of La Verne	M,D
University of Maryland, Baltimore	M,D
University of Massachusetts Medical School	M,D
University of Minnesota, Twin Cities Campus	M,D
University of Nebraska Medical Center	M,D
University of New Brunswick Fredericton	M
The University of North Carolina at Charlotte	D
University of North Texas Health Science Center at Fort Worth	M,D,O
University of Ottawa	D,O
University of Pennsylvania	M*
University of Pittsburgh	M*
University of Puerto Rico–Medical Sciences Campus	M
University of Rochester	D*
University of Southern California	D
The University of Tennessee Health Science Center	M,D
University of Utah	M,D
University of Virginia	M
University of Washington	M,D
Virginia Commonwealth University	D
Washington University in St. Louis	M,O
Wayne State University	M,D
Weill Cornell Medicine	M

HIGHER EDUCATION

Institution	Degree
Abilene Christian University	M
Alliant International University–San Diego	M,D,O
Alliant International University–San Francisco	M,D,O
Andrews University	M,D,O
Angelo State University	M
Appalachian State University	M,O
Argosy University, Atlanta	M,D,O
Argosy University, Chicago	M,D,O
Argosy University, Hawai'i	M,D
Argosy University, Los Angeles	M,D
Argosy University, Northern Virginia	M,D,O
Argosy University, Orange County	M,D
Argosy University, Phoenix	M,D
Argosy University, Seattle	M,D
Argosy University, Tampa	M,D
Argosy University, Twin Cities	M,D,O
Arizona State University at the Tempe campus	M
Auburn University	M,D,O
Azusa Pacific University	M,D
Ball State University	M,D
Barry University	M,D
Baruch College of the City University of New York	M*
Bay Path University	M
Bellarmine University	M,D,O
Bowling Green State University	D
California Baptist University	M
California Lutheran University	M,D
California State University, Long Beach	M,D
California State University, Sacramento	M,D,O
Capella University	M,D
Cardinal Stritch University	M,D
Central Michigan University	M,D,O
Central Washington University	M
Chicago State University	M,D
Claremont Graduate University	M,D,O
Clemson University	M,D,O
Cleveland State University	D
College of Saint Elizabeth	M,D,O
The College of Saint Rose	M,O
Colorado State University	M,D
Columbia College (SC)	M
Columbus State University	M,D,O
Concordia University (United States)	M,D
Dallas Baptist University	M,D
Delta State University	D
DePaul University	M,D
DeVry University–Folsom Campus	M,D
Drexel University	M,D*
East Carolina University	M,O
Eastern Kentucky University	M
Eastern Michigan University	M,D,O
Fitchburg State University	M,O
Florida Atlantic University	M,D,O
Florida International University	M,D,O
Florida State University	M,D,O
Geneva College	M
George Mason University	M,D,O
The George Washington University	M,D,O
Georgia Southern University	M,D
Grambling State University	M,D,O
Grand Valley State University	M
Hardin-Simmons University	D
Hofstra University	M,D,O
Houston Baptist University	M,D
Illinois State University	M,D
Indiana State University	M,D,O
Indiana University Bloomington	M,D,O
Indiana University of Pennsylvania	M,D
Indiana Wesleyan University	M
Inter American University of Puerto Rico, Metropolitan Campus	M
Iowa State University of Science and Technology	M,D
Jackson State University	M,D,O
James Madison University	M
Johnson University	M,D,O
Kent State University	M,D
Lee University	M,O
Lewis University	M
Lincoln Memorial University	M,D,O
Lincoln University (MO)	M
London Metropolitan University	M,D
Louisiana State University and Agricultural & Mechanical College	M,D,O
Louisiana Tech University	M,D,O
Loyola Marymount University	M
Loyola University Chicago	M,D
Mary Baldwin University	M
Maryville University of Saint Louis	M,D
Marywood University	M,D
McKendree University	M,D,O
Mercer University	M,D,O
Mercer University	M,D,O
Mercyhurst University	M,O
Messiah College	M
Michigan State University	M,D
Minnesota State University Mankato	M
Mississippi College	M
Mississippi State University	M,D,O
Missouri State University	M
Montana State University	M,D,O
Morehead State University	M,O
Morgan State University	M,D
National American University (TX)	M,D
National University	M,O
New England College	M,D
New Mexico State University	M,D
New York University	M,D*
North Dakota State University	O
Northeastern University	M
Northern Arizona University	M,D,O
Northern Illinois University	M,D
Northwest Missouri State University	M,D,O
Oakland University	M,D,O
Ohio University	M,D
Oklahoma State University	M,D
Old Dominion University	M,D,O
Oral Roberts University	M,D
Oregon State University	M,D
Penn State University Park	M,D,O*
Phillips Theological Seminary	M
Plymouth State University	D,O
Purdue University	M,D,O
Purdue University Global	M,D
Regent University	M,D,O
Regis College (MA)	M,D
Robert Morris University Illinois	M
Rowan University	M
St. Cloud State University	D
Saint Louis University	M,D,O*
Saint Peter's University	M,D
Salem State University	M
Sam Houston State University	M,D
San Diego State University	M
San Jose State University	M,D
Seton Hall University	D
Siena Heights University	M,O
Southeast Missouri State University	M,D,O
Southern Arkansas University–Magnolia	M
Southern Illinois University Carbondale	M
Southern Illinois University Edwardsville	M
Southern Methodist University	M,D
Southern New Hampshire University	M,D,O
Southwestern College (KS)	M,D
Springfield College	M,D,O
Stony Brook University, State University of New York	M,O
Syracuse University	M,D
Taylor University	M
Teachers College, Columbia University	M,D
Texas A&M University–Commerce	M,D,O
Texas Southern University	M,D
Texas State University	M,D
Texas Tech University	M,D
Tiffin University	M
Trident University International	M,D
Union University	M,D,O
Universidad Central del Este	M,D
Université de Sherbrooke	M,O
University at Albany, State University of New York	M,D
University at Buffalo, the State University of New York	M,D,O
The University of Alabama	M,D
The University of Arizona	M,D
University of Arkansas	M,D,O
University of Arkansas at Little Rock	M,D
The University of British Columbia	M,D
University of California, Riverside	M,D,O
University of Central Florida	M,O
University of Connecticut	M
University of Delaware	M,D,O
University of Denver	M,D,O
University of Florida	M,D
University of Georgia	M,D
University of Houston	M,D
University of Houston–Victoria	M,O
The University of Iowa	M,D
The University of Kansas	M,D
University of Kentucky	M,D
University of La Verne	M
University of Louisville	M,D,O
University of Lynchburg	M
University of Maine	M,D,O
University of Manitoba	M
University of Mary Hardin-Baylor	M,D
University of Massachusetts Amherst	M,D,O
University of Massachusetts Boston	D
University of Memphis	M,D
University of Miami	M,D,O
University of Minnesota, Twin Cities Campus	M,D
University of Mississippi	M,D,O
University of Missouri	M,D,O
University of Missouri–Kansas City	M,D
University of Missouri–St. Louis	M,O
University of Nevada, Las Vegas	M,D
University of New Hampshire	O
University of New Mexico	O
University of New Orleans	M,D
University of North Alabama	M
The University of North Carolina at Greensboro	D
The University of North Carolina Wilmington	M,D
University of Northern Colorado	M,D
University of Northern Iowa	M
University of North Georgia	D
University of North Texas	M,D,O
University of Oklahoma	M,D*
University of Pennsylvania	M,D*
University of Phoenix–Bay Area Campus	M,D,O
University of Phoenix–Online Campus	D,O
University of Pittsburgh	M,D*
University of Puerto Rico–Mayagüez	M
University of Rochester	M,D*
University of San Diego	M,D,O
University of South Carolina	M
University of South Dakota	M,D,O
University of Southern California	D
University of Southern Maine	M,O
University of Southern Mississippi	M,D,O
University of South Florida	M,D,O
The University of Texas at Arlington	M,D
The University of Texas at San Antonio	M,D
The University of Toledo	M,D,O
University of Utah	M,D
University of Vermont	M
University of Virginia	M,D,O
University of Washington	M,D
The University of West Alabama	M
University of Wisconsin–La Crosse	M,D
University of Wisconsin–Madison	M,D,O
University of Wisconsin–Milwaukee	M,O*
Upper Iowa University	M
Wagner College	M
Walden University	M,D,O
Walsh University	M
Wayland Baptist University	M
West Chester University of Pennsylvania	M,O
Western Illinois University	M
Western Kentucky University	M
Western Michigan University	M,D
Western Washington University	M
West Virginia University	M,D
William Paterson University of New Jersey	M,O
Wilmington University	M,O

HISPANIC AND LATIN AMERICAN LANGUAGES

Institution	Degree
Boston University	M,D
Brigham Young University	M
California State University, San Marcos	M
Cornell University	D
The Graduate Center, City University of New York	D
Indiana University Bloomington	M,D
Michigan State University	M,D
Queens College of the City University of New York	M
Stony Brook University, State University of New York	M,D
Université de Montréal	M,D
University of California, Berkeley	D
University of California, Los Angeles	D
University of California, Santa Barbara	M,D
University of Colorado Boulder	M,D
University of Illinois at Chicago	M,D
University of Massachusetts Amherst	M,D
University of Minnesota, Twin Cities Campus	M,D
The University of North Carolina at Greensboro	M,O

The University of Texas at Austin	M,D
University of Washington	M

HISPANIC STUDIES

Brown University	D
California State University, Los Angeles	M
California State University, Northridge	M
California State University, San Marcos	M
The Catholic University of America	M,D
The Citadel, The Military College of South Carolina	O
Columbia University	M,D
La Salle University	M,O
Louisiana State University and Agricultural & Mechanical College	M
McGill University	M,D
Michigan State University	M,D
Oregon State University	M
Pontifical Catholic University of Puerto Rico	M,D
St. Thomas University	M,O
Stephen F. Austin State University	M
Texas A&M University–Kingsville	D
University of Alberta	M,D
The University of British Columbia	M,D
University of California, Riverside	M,D
University of California, Santa Barbara	M,D
University of Houston	M,D
University of Illinois at Chicago	M,D
University of Kentucky	M,D
University of Nevada, Las Vegas	M,O
The University of North Carolina at Greensboro	M,O
The University of North Carolina Wilmington	M,O
University of Puerto Rico–Mayagüez	M
University of Puerto Rico–Río Piedras	M,D
The University of Texas at Austin	M
University of Victoria	M
Villanova University	M

HISTORIC PRESERVATION

The American University of Rome	M
Arkansas State University	M
Ball State University	M
Boston Architectural College	M
Boston University	M
Buffalo State College, State University of New York	M,O
Clemson University	M,O
Cleveland State University	M,O
College of Charleston	M
Columbia University	M,D,O
Cornell University	M,D
Delaware State University	M
Eastern Michigan University	M,O
The George Washington University	M,D
Georgia State University	M,D
Goucher College	M
Morgan State University	M,D
New York University	*
Penn State Harrisburg	M,D,O
Plymouth State University	M
Pratt Institute	M
Roger Williams University	M,O
Rutgers University–New Brunswick	M,D,O
St. Cloud State University	M
Savannah College of Art and Design	M
Southeast Missouri State University	M,O
Universidad Nacional Pedro Henríquez Ureña	M
University at Buffalo, the State University of New York	M,D,O
University of California, Los Angeles	M
University of Colorado Denver	M,D
University of Delaware	M,D
University of Florida	M,D
University of Georgia	M
University of Hawaii at Manoa	O
The University of Kansas	M,D,O
University of Kentucky	M
University of Maryland, College Park	M,O
University of Massachusetts Amherst	M
University of New Mexico	O
University of North Alabama	M
The University of North Carolina at Greensboro	M,O
University of Oregon	M
University of Pennsylvania	M,O*
University of Rochester	M*
University of South Carolina	M
University of Southern California	M
The University of Texas at Austin	M
University of Vermont	M
University of Washington	O
Ursuline College	M

HISTORY

Adams State University	M
American Public University System	M,D
American University	M,D
American University of Beirut	M,D
Appalachian State University	M
Arizona State University at the Tempe campus	M,D,O
Arkansas State University	M,O
Arkansas Tech University	M
Ashland University	M
Auburn University	M,D,O

Ball State University	M
Bard College	M
Baylor University	M,D
Binghamton University, State University of New York	M,D
Bob Jones University	M,D,O
Boise State University	M
Boston College	M,D
Boston University	M,D
Bowling Green State University	M,D
Brandeis University	M,D
Brock University	M
Brooklyn College of the City University of New York	M,D
Brown University	M,D
Buffalo State College, State University of New York	M
Cabrini University	M,D
California Polytechnic State University, San Luis Obispo	M
California State Polytechnic University, Pomona	M
California State University, Bakersfield	M
California State University, Chico	M
California State University, East Bay	M
California State University, Fresno	M
California State University, Fullerton	M
California State University, Long Beach	M
California State University, Los Angeles	M
California State University, Northridge	M
California State University, San Marcos	M
California State University, Stanislaus	M
Carleton University	M,D
Carnegie Mellon University	D
Case Western Reserve University	M,D
The Catholic University of America	M,D
Central Connecticut State University	M,O
Central European University	M,O
Central Michigan University	M,O
Central Washington University	M
Centro de Estudios Avanzados de Puerto Rico y el Caribe	M,D
Chicago State University	M
The Citadel, The Military College of South Carolina	M,O
City College of the City University of New York	M
Claremont Graduate University	M,D,O
Clark University	D
Clayton State University	M
Clemson University	M
Cleveland State University	M
The College at Brockport, State University of New York	M
College of Charleston	M
College of Staten Island of the City University of New York	M
Colorado State University	M
Columbia University	M,D
Columbus State University	M,O
Concordia University (Canada)	M,D
Converse College	M
Cornell University	M,D
Dalhousie University	M,D
DePaul University	M
Dominican University of California	M
Drew University	M,D,O
Duke University	M,D
Duquesne University	M
East Carolina University	M
Eastern Illinois University	M
Eastern Kentucky University	M
Eastern Michigan University	M
Eastern Washington University	M
East Stroudsburg University of Pennsylvania	M
East Tennessee State University	M,O
Edinboro University of Pennsylvania	M
Emory & Henry College	M,D
Emory University	D
Emporia State University	M
Fairleigh Dickinson University, Metropolitan Campus	M
Fitchburg State University	M
Florida Agricultural and Mechanical University	M
Florida Atlantic University	M
Florida Gulf Coast University	M
Florida International University	M,D
Florida State University	M,D
Fordham University	M,D
Fort Hays State University	M
George Mason University	M,D,O
Georgetown University	M,D
The George Washington University	M,D
Georgia Southern University	M,O
Georgia State University	M,D
The Graduate Center, City University of New York	D
Harvard University	D*
Howard University	M,D
Hunter College of the City University of New York	M
Idaho State University	M
Illinois State University	M
Indiana State University	M
Indiana University Bloomington	M,D
Indiana University of Pennsylvania	M
Indiana University–Purdue University Indianapolis	M

Inter American University of Puerto Rico, Barranquitas Campus	M
Inter American University of Puerto Rico, Metropolitan Campus	M,D
Iona College	M
Iowa State University of Science and Technology	M,D
Jackson State University	M
Jacksonville State University	M
James Madison University	M
Johns Hopkins University	D*
Kansas State University	M,D
Kent State University	M,D
Lake Forest College	M
Lakehead University	M
Lamar University	M
La Salle University	M,O
Laurentian University	M
Lee University	M,O
Lehigh University	M,D
Lehman College of the City University of New York	M
Liberty University	M
Lincoln University (MO)	M
Long Island University–LIU Post	M,O
Louisiana State University and Agricultural & Mechanical College	M,D
Louisiana Tech University	M,D,O
Loyola University Chicago	M,D
Marquette University	M,D
Marshall University	M,O
McGill University	M,D
McMaster University	M,D
Memorial University of Newfoundland	M
Miami University	M
Michigan State University	M,D
Middle Tennessee State University	M
Midwestern State University	M
Minnesota State University Mankato	M
Mississippi College	M,O
Mississippi State University	M,D
Missouri State University	M,D
Monmouth University	M
Montana State University	M,D
Morgan State University	M,D
Murray State University	M
New Jersey Institute of Technology	M,D,O
New Mexico Highlands University	M
The New School	M,D
New York University	M,D,O*
North Carolina Central University	M
North Carolina State University	M
North Dakota State University	M,D
Northeastern Illinois University	M
Northeastern University	M,D
Northern Arizona University	M
Northern Illinois University	M,D
Northwestern University	M,D
Norwich University	M
Oakland University	M
The Ohio State University	M,D
Ohio University	M,D
Oklahoma State University	M,D
Old Dominion University	M
Open University	M
Penn State University Park	M,D*
Pittsburg State University	M
Pontifical Catholic University of Puerto Rico	M
Portland State University	D
Providence College	M
Purdue University	M,D
Purdue University Northwest	M
Queens College of the City University of New York	M
Rhode Island College	M
Rice University	M,D
Roosevelt University	M
Rowan University	M,O
Rutgers University–Camden	M
Rutgers University–Newark	M
Rutgers University–New Brunswick	D
St. Cloud State University	M,D
St. John's University (NY)	M,D
Saint Louis University	M,D*
Saint Mary's University (Canada)	M
Salem State University	M
Salisbury University	M
Sam Houston State University	M
San Diego State University	M
San Francisco State University	M
San Jose State University	M
Sarah Lawrence College	M
Seton Hall University	M
Shippensburg University of Pennsylvania	M
Simmons University	M,D,O
Simon Fraser University	M,D
Slippery Rock University of Pennsylvania	M
Smith College	M
Sonoma State University	M
Southeastern Louisiana University	M
Southeast Missouri State University	M,O
Southern Connecticut State University	M
Southern Illinois University Carbondale	M,D
Southern Illinois University Edwardsville	M
Southern Methodist University	M,D
Southern New Hampshire University	M
Southern University and Agricultural and Mechanical College	M

Southwestern Assemblies of God University	M
Stanford University	M,D
State University of New York at Oswego	M
State University of New York College at Cortland	M
Stephen F. Austin State University	M
Stony Brook University, State University of New York	M,D
Sul Ross State University	M
Syracuse University	M,D
Tarleton State University	M
Temple University	M,D*
Texas A&M International University	M
Texas A&M University	M,D
Texas A&M University–Central Texas	M,O
Texas A&M University–Commerce	M,D,O
Texas A&M University–Corpus Christi	M
Texas Christian University	M,D
Texas Southern University	M
Texas State University	M
Texas Tech University	M,D
Texas Woman's University	M
Trinity Western University	M
Troy University	M
Tufts University	M,D
Tulane University	M,D
Union Institute & University	M
Université de Moncton	M
Université de Montréal	M
Université de Sherbrooke	M
Université du Québec à Montréal	M,D
Université Laval	M,D
University at Albany, State University of New York	M,D,O
University at Buffalo, the State University of New York	M,D,O
The University of Akron	M,D
The University of Alabama	M,D
The University of Alabama at Birmingham	M
The University of Alabama in Huntsville	M
University of Alaska Fairbanks	M
University of Alberta	M,D
The University of Arizona	M,D,O
University of Arkansas	M,D
The University of British Columbia	M,D
University of Calgary	M,D
University of California, Berkeley	M,D
University of California, Davis	M,D
University of California, Irvine	M,D
University of California, Los Angeles	M,D
University of California, Riverside	M,D
University of California, San Diego	M,D
University of California, Santa Barbara	D
University of California, Santa Cruz	M,D
University of Central Arkansas	M
University of Central Florida	M
University of Central Missouri	M,D,O
University of Central Oklahoma	M
University of Chicago	D
University of Cincinnati	M,D
University of Colorado Boulder	M,D
University of Colorado Colorado Springs	M
University of Colorado Denver	M
University of Connecticut	M,D
University of Delaware	M,D
University of Denver	M,O
University of Florida	M,D
University of Georgia	M,D
University of Guelph	M,D
University of Hawaii at Manoa	M,D
University of Houston	M,D
University of Houston–Clear Lake	M
University of Idaho	M,D
University of Illinois at Chicago	M,D
University of Illinois at Springfield	M
University of Illinois at Urbana–Champaign	M,D
University of Indianapolis	M
The University of Iowa	M,D
The University of Kansas	M,D
University of Kentucky	M,D
University of Louisiana at Lafayette	M,D
University of Louisiana at Monroe	M
University of Louisville	M,O
University of Maine	M,D
The University of Manchester	D
University of Manitoba	M,D
University of Maryland, Baltimore County	M
University of Maryland, College Park	M,D
University of Massachusetts Amherst	M,D
University of Massachusetts Boston	M
University of Memphis	M,D
University of Miami	M,D
University of Michigan	D,O
University of Minnesota, Twin Cities Campus	M,D
University of Mississippi	M,D
University of Missouri	M,D
University of Missouri–Kansas City	M,D

History (continued)

University of Missouri–St. Louis	M,O
University of Montana	M,D
University of Nebraska at Kearney	M,D
University of Nebraska at Omaha	M
University of Nebraska–Lincoln	M,D
University of Nevada, Las Vegas	M,D
University of Nevada, Reno	M,D
University of New Brunswick Fredericton	M,D
University of New Hampshire	M,D
University of New Mexico	M,D
University of New Orleans	M
University of North Alabama	M
The University of North Carolina at Chapel Hill	M,D
The University of North Carolina at Charlotte	M
The University of North Carolina at Greensboro	M,D,O
The University of North Carolina Wilmington	M
University of North Dakota	M
University of Northern British Columbia	M,D,O
University of Northern Colorado	M
University of Northern Iowa	M
University of North Florida	M
University of North Georgia	M
University of North Texas	M,D,O
University of Notre Dame	M,D
University of Oklahoma	M,D*
University of Oregon	M,D
University of Ottawa	M,D
University of Pennsylvania	M,D*
University of Pittsburgh	M,D*
University of Puerto Rico–Río Piedras	M,D
University of Regina	M
University of Rhode Island	M
University of Rochester	M,D*
University of Saskatchewan	M,D
University of South Africa	M,D
University of South Alabama	M
University of South Carolina	M,D,O
University of South Dakota	M
University of Southern California	D
University of Southern Mississippi	M,D
University of South Florida	M,D
The University of Tennessee	M,D
The University of Texas at Arlington	M,D
The University of Texas at Austin	M,D
The University of Texas at Dallas	M,D
The University of Texas at El Paso	M,D
The University of Texas at San Antonio	M
The University of Texas at Tyler	M
The University of Texas of the Permian Basin	M
The University of Texas Rio Grande Valley	M
The University of Toledo	M,D
University of Toronto	M,D
University of Utah	M,D
University of Vermont	M
University of Victoria	M,D
University of Virginia	M,D
University of Washington	M,D
University of Waterloo	M,D
The University of West Alabama	M
The University of Western Ontario	M,D
University of West Florida	M
University of West Georgia	M,O
University of Windsor	M
The University of Winnipeg	M
University of Wisconsin–Eau Claire	M
University of Wisconsin–Madison	M,D
University of Wisconsin–Milwaukee	M,D*
University of Wyoming	M
Utah State University	M
Vanderbilt University	M,D*
Villanova University	M
Virginia Commonwealth University	M
Washington State University	M
Washington University in St. Louis	D
Wayland Baptist University	M
Wayne State University	M,D,O
West Chester University of Pennsylvania	M
Western Carolina University	M
Western Connecticut State University	M
Western Illinois University	M
Western Kentucky University	M
Western Michigan University	M,D
Western Washington University	M
West Texas A&M University	M
West Virginia University	M,D
Wichita State University	M
Wilfrid Laurier University	M,D
William Paterson University of New Jersey	M,D,O
Winthrop University	M
Worcester State University	M
Wright State University	M
Yale University	M,D
York University	M,D
Youngstown State University	M

HISTORY OF MEDICINE

The College at Brockport, State University of New York	M,O
Indiana University Bloomington	M,D
McGill University	M,D
Rutgers University–New Brunswick	D
The University of Manchester	M,D
University of Minnesota, Twin Cities Campus	M,D
University of Wisconsin–Madison	M,D
Yale University	M,D

HISTORY OF SCIENCE AND TECHNOLOGY

Arizona State University at the Tempe campus	M,D
Brown University	D
Carnegie Mellon University	D
Cornell University	M,D
Drexel University	M*
Georgia Institute of Technology	M,D
Harvard University	M,D*
Indiana University Bloomington	M,D
Johns Hopkins University	M,D*
Massachusetts Institute of Technology	D
Oregon State University	M,D
Princeton University	D
Rensselaer Polytechnic Institute	M,D
Rutgers University–New Brunswick	D
University of California, Berkeley	D
University of California, San Diego	D
University of California, San Francisco	M,D
University of Delaware	M,D
The University of Manchester	M,D
University of Minnesota, Twin Cities Campus	M,D
University of Notre Dame	M,D
University of Oklahoma	M,D*
University of Pennsylvania	M,D*
University of Pittsburgh	D*
University of Toronto	M,D
University of Wisconsin–Madison	M,D
Yale University	M,D

HIV/AIDS NURSING

University of Delaware	M,O

HOLOCAUST AND GENOCIDE STUDIES

Chapman University	M*
Clark University	D
College of Saint Elizabeth	M,O
Gratz College	M,D
Kean University	M
Stockton University	M
Texas A&M University–Commerce	M,D,O
University of South Florida	O
West Chester University of Pennsylvania	M,O

HOME ECONOMICS EDUCATION

Alabama Agricultural and Mechanical University	M,O
Central Washington University	M
Eastern Kentucky University	M
Louisiana State University and Agricultural & Mechanical College	M,D
Montana State University	M
Purdue University	M,D,O
South Carolina State University	M
Texas Tech University	M,D
The University of British Columbia	M,D
University of Nebraska–Lincoln	M,D
Utah State University	M
Wayne State College	M

HOMELAND SECURITY

Angelo State University	M
Arizona State University at the Tempe campus	M,D
Aurora University	M
Ball State University	M,O
Capella University	M
The Citadel, The Military College of South Carolina	M,O
Columbus State University	M
Drexel University	M*
Endicott College	M,O
Fairleigh Dickinson University, Metropolitan Campus	M
Georgian Court University	M,O
Henley-Putnam School of Strategic Security	M
Indiana University–Purdue University Indianapolis	M,O
The Institute of World Politics	M,D,O
Johns Hopkins University	M,O*
Keiser University	M
Lasell College	M,O
Liberty University	M
London Metropolitan University	M,D
Long Island University–Riverhead	M,O
Missouri State University	M,O
Monmouth University	M,O
National Defense University	M
National University	M
Naval Postgraduate School	M,D
Nichols College	M
Northeastern University	M,D
Northwestern State University of Louisiana	M
Notre Dame College (OH)	M,O
Pace University	M
Penn State Harrisburg	M,D,O
Post University	M
Regent University	M
Rider University	M
St. John's University (NY)	M
St. Mary's University (United States)	M,O
Salve Regina University	M,O
Sam Houston State University	M
Southern Illinois University Carbondale	M
Texas A&M University–Commerce	M,D,O
Thomas Edison State University	M

Tiffin University	M
Towson University	M,O
Tulane University	M
University at Albany, State University of New York	M,D,O
University of Alaska Fairbanks	M
University of Central Florida	M,O
University of Colorado Denver	M,D
University of Denver	M,D,O
University of Illinois at Springfield	M,O
University of Management and Technology	M
University of Oklahoma Health Sciences Center	M
University of Phoenix–Online Campus	M
University of Phoenix–Phoenix Campus	M
University of Southern California	M,O
University of the District of Columbia	M
Upper Iowa University	M
Virginia Commonwealth University	M,O
Walden University	M,D,O
Wayland Baptist University	M
Western Kentucky University	M
Western Michigan University Thomas M. Cooley Law School	M,D
Wilmington University	M,D

HORTICULTURE

Auburn University	M,D
Colorado State University	M,D
Cornell University	M,D
Dalhousie University	M
Iowa State University of Science and Technology	M,D
Kansas State University	M,D
Louisiana State University and Agricultural & Mechanical College	M,D
Michigan State University	M,D
Mississippi State University	M,D
North Carolina State University	M,D,O
North Dakota State University	M,D
The Ohio State University	M,D
Oklahoma State University	M,D
Oregon State University	M,D
Penn State University Park	M,D*
Purdue University	M,D
Rutgers University–New Brunswick	M,D
Texas A&M University	M,D
Texas A&M University–Kingsville	M,D
Texas Tech University	M,D
Universidad Nacional Pedro Henriquez Urena	M
University of Arkansas	M
University of California, Davis	M
University of Delaware	M
University of Florida	M,D
University of Georgia	M,D
University of Guelph	M,D
University of Hawaii at Manoa	M,D
University of Maine	M,D,O
University of Manitoba	M,D
University of Maryland, College Park	M,D
University of Missouri	M,D
University of Nebraska–Lincoln	M,D
University of Puerto Rico–Mayagüez	M
University of South Africa	M,D
University of Vermont	M,D,O
University of Washington	M,D
University of Wisconsin–Madison	M,D
Utah State University	M,D
Virginia Polytechnic Institute and State University	M,D
Washington State University	M,D
West Virginia University	M,D

HOSPICE NURSING

Central Connecticut State University	M
Madonna University	M

HOSPITALITY MANAGEMENT

Alabama Agricultural and Mechanical University	M
American International College	M,D,O
Boston University	M
California State Polytechnic University, Pomona	M
California State University, Northridge	M,O
Cornell University	M,D
DePaul University	M,D
Drexel University	M*
East Carolina University	M
Eastern Michigan University	O
Ecole Hôtelière de Lausanne	M
ESSEC Business School	M,D
Fairleigh Dickinson University, Florham Campus	M
Fairleigh Dickinson University, Metropolitan Campus	M
Florida International University	M
Georgetown University	M,D
The George Washington University	M,O
Glion Institute of Higher Education	M
Husson University	M
IGlobal University	M
Johnson & Wales University	M
Kansas State University	M,D
Kent State University	M
Lasell College	M,O
Les Roches International School of Hotel Management	M
Michigan State University	M

Monroe College	M
Morgan State University	M
New York University	M,D*
North Carolina Agricultural and Technical State University	M
Oklahoma State University	M,D
Penn State University Park	M,D*
Pontificia Universidad Catolica Madre y Maestra	M
Purdue University	M,D
Rochester Institute of Technology	M
Roosevelt University	M
San Diego State University	M
San Francisco State University	M
San Ignacio University	M
Schiller International University (United States)	M
South University (GA)	M
Stratford University (MD)	M
Strayer University	M
Syracuse University	M,O
Temple University	M,D*
Texas Tech University	M,D
Thomas Edison State University	M
The University of Alabama	M
University of Central Florida	M,D,O
University of Delaware	M
The University of Findlay	M,D
University of Guelph	M
University of Houston	M
University of Kentucky	M
University of Louisiana at Lafayette	M
University of Massachusetts Amherst	M,D
University of Memphis	M,O
University of Mississippi	M,D
University of Missouri	M,D
University of Nevada, Las Vegas	M,D
University of New Orleans	M
University of North Texas	M,D,O
University of South Carolina	M,D
University of South Florida Sarasota-Manatee	M
The University of Tennessee	M
University of the Pacific	M
Virginia International University	M,O

HUMAN-COMPUTER INTERACTION

Brandeis University	M
Carnegie Mellon University	M,D
Cornell University	M,D
Dalhousie University	M,D
DePaul University	M,D
Georgia Institute of Technology	M
Harrisburg University of Science and Technology	M
Indiana University Bloomington	M,D
Indiana University–Purdue University Indianapolis	M,D
Iowa State University of Science and Technology	M,D
Rochester Institute of Technology	M
State University of New York at Oswego	M
Tufts University	O
University of Baltimore	M
University of Illinois at Urbana–Champaign	M,D,O
University of Rochester	M,D*
University of Washington	M,D,O

HUMAN DEVELOPMENT

Alabama Agricultural and Mechanical University	M
Argosy University, Chicago	D
Arizona State University at the Tempe campus	M,D
Auburn University	M,D
Ball State University	M,D,O
Bradley University	M
Brigham Young University	M,D
Brock University	M,D
California State University, Fresno	M,D
Central Michigan University	M,O
Claremont Graduate University	M,D,O
Colorado State University	M,D
Cornell University	M,D
Duke University	D
Erikson Institute	M,O
Fielding Graduate University	M,D,O
Florida State University	M,D
Georgetown University	M,D
The George Washington University	M
Georgia State University	M
Harvard University	M*
Iowa State University of Science and Technology	M,D,O
Kansas State University	M,D,O
Kent State University	M,D
Laurentian University	M
Lindsey Wilson College	M
Marywood University	D
Michigan State University	M,D
Mississippi State University	M,D
Montana State University	M
Murray State University	M,D,O
National Louis University	M,D,O
New York University	M,D,O*
Northern Arizona University	O
Northwestern University	D
The Ohio State University	M,D
Oregon State University	M,D
Pacific Oaks College	M
Penn State University Park	M,D*
Purdue University	M,D
Saint Mary's University of Minnesota	M
Syracuse University	M,D
Texas A&M University–Corpus Christi	M,D
Texas Tech University	M,D
Tufts University	M,D
The University of Alabama	M

The University of Arizona — M,D,O
The University of British Columbia — M,D,O
University of California, Berkeley — M,D
University of California, Davis — D
University of Central Oklahoma — M
University of Chicago — D
University of Colorado Denver — M,D
University of Connecticut — M,D
University of Dayton — M,O
University of Delaware — M,D
University of Guelph — M,D
University of Illinois at Chicago — M,D
University of Illinois at Springfield — M
University of Illinois at Urbana–Champaign — M,D
University of Maine — M,D,O
University of Maryland, College Park — M,D
University of Missouri — M,D
University of Nebraska–Lincoln — M,D,O
University of Nevada, Reno — M
University of New Mexico — M,D
The University of North Carolina at Greensboro — M,D
University of North Texas — M,D,O
University of Pennsylvania — M,D*
University of Rhode Island — M
University of Rochester — M,D*
University of St. Thomas (MN) — D
University of South Africa — M,D
University of South Dakota — M,D,O
The University of Texas at Austin — M,D
University of Utah — M
University of Victoria — M,D
University of Washington — M,D
University of Wisconsin–Madison — M,D
Utah State University — M,D
Washington State University — D
Wright Graduate University for the Realization of Human Potential — M,D,O

HUMAN GENETICS
Baylor College of Medicine — D
Case Western Reserve University — M,D
Emory University — M
Louisiana State University Health Sciences Center — D
McGill University — M,D
Memorial University of Newfoundland — M,D
Sarah Lawrence College — M
Thomas Jefferson University — M
Tulane University — M
University of California, Los Angeles — M,D
University of Chicago — D
University of Manitoba — M,D
University of Maryland, Baltimore — M,D
University of Michigan — M,D
University of Pennsylvania — M*
University of Pittsburgh — M,D,O*
University of Utah — M,D
Vanderbilt University — D*
Virginia Commonwealth University — M,D
Washington University in St. Louis — D

HUMANITIES
Adams State University — M
The American University in Cairo — M,O
Antioch University New England — M
California Institute of Integral Studies — M,D,O
California State University, Dominguez Hills — M
Central Michigan University — M
Claremont Graduate University — M,D,O
The Colorado College — M
Colorado School of Mines — O
Concordia University (Canada) — D
Dominican University of California — M
Duke University — M
Faulkner University — M,D
Georgetown University — M,D
The Graduate Center, City University of New York — M
Harrison Middleton University — M
Hollins University — M
Hood College — M
Illinois Institute of Technology — M,D
Instituto Tecnologico de Santo Domingo — M,O
Instituto Tecnológico y de Estudios Superiores de Monterrey, Campus Central de Veracruz — M
Instituto Tecnológico y de Estudios Superiores de Monterrey, Campus Ciudad de México — M,D
Instituto Tecnológico y de Estudios Superiores de Monterrey, Campus Ciudad Juárez — M
Instituto Tecnológico y de Estudios Superiores de Monterrey, Campus Estado de México — M,D
Instituto Tecnológico y de Estudios Superiores de Monterrey, Campus Irapuato — M,D
John Carroll University — M
Laurentian University — M
Loyola University Chicago — M
Marshall University — M,O
Memorial University of Newfoundland — M
Mount Saint Mary's University (CA) — M,D,O
New York University — M,O*
Northeast Ohio Medical University — M,D,O
Nova Southeastern University — M,D,O
Old Dominion University — M,O

Penn State Harrisburg — M,D,O
Pepperdine University — M
Prescott College — M
Roosevelt University — M
St. Edward's University — M
Salve Regina University — M,D
Sam Houston State University — M,D,O
San Francisco State University — M
Simon Fraser University — M
Tiffin University — M
Towson University — M
Trinity Western University — M
Union Institute & University — D
United Theological Seminary of the Twin Cities — M,D,O
University at Buffalo, the State University of New York — M
University of California, Merced — M,D
University of California, Santa Cruz — D
University of Chicago — M
University of Colorado Denver — M,O
University of Houston–Clear Lake — M
University of Louisville — M,D
University of South Florida — M
The University of Texas at Dallas — M,D
The University of Texas Medical Branch — M,D
University of Utah — M
Virginia Polytechnic Institute and State University — M,D,O
Wayland Baptist University — M
Wilson College — M
Wright State University — M
York University — M,D

HUMAN RESOURCES DEVELOPMENT
Abilene Christian University — M
Amberton University — M
Antioch University Los Angeles — M
Barry University — M,D
Bowie State University — M
California State University, Sacramento — M
Claremont Graduate University — M,D,O
Clemson University — M,D,O
The College of New Rochelle — M,O
Drexel University — M,D*
Florida International University — M,D,O
The George Washington University — M,D,O
Grantham University — M,O
HEC Montreal — O
Illinois Institute of Technology — M,D
Indiana State University — M
Indiana Tech — M
Indiana University of Pennsylvania — M
Inter American University of Puerto Rico, Metropolitan Campus — M
Inter American University of Puerto Rico, San Germán Campus — M,D
Iowa State University of Science and Technology — M,D
La Salle University — M,O
Lawrence Technological University — M,O
Lincoln Memorial University — M,D,O
Louisiana State University and Agricultural & Mechanical College — M,D
Marquette University — M
McDaniel College — M
Midwestern State University — M
Mississippi State University — M,D,O
National Louis University — M
New York University — M*
North Carolina State University — M
Northeastern Illinois University — M
Ottawa University — M
Penn State Great Valley — M,O
Penn State University Park — M*
Pittsburg State University — M
Regent University — M,D,O
Rochester Institute of Technology — M
Rockhurst University — M,O
Rollins College — M
Roosevelt University — M
South Dakota State University — M
Texas A&M University — M
Towson University — M
Tusculum University — M
Universidad Central del Este — M
Universidad Iberoamericana — M,D
University of Arkansas — M,D,O
University of Bridgeport — M
University of Houston — M
University of Louisville — M,D,O
University of Minnesota, Twin Cities Campus — M,D,O
University of Nebraska at Omaha — M,D,O
University of Regina — M
The University of Scranton — M
University of South Africa — M,D
University of South Florida — O
The University of Tennessee — M
The University of Texas at Tyler — M
University of Wisconsin–Stout — M
Villanova University — M
Virginia Commonwealth University — M
Waldorf University — M
Webster University — M,D,O
Western Seminary — M
William Woods University — M,D,O
Xavier University — M,D*

HUMAN RESOURCES MANAGEMENT
Adelphi University — M,O
Albany State University — M
Albertus Magnus College — M
Amberton University — M
American InterContinental University Online — M

American University — M,O
American University of Beirut — M
Anderson University (SC) — M
Ashland University — M
Ashworth College — M
Assumption College — M,O
Averett University — M
Avila University — M
Baker College Center for Graduate Studies–Online — M,D
Baldwin Wallace University — M
Barry University — O
Baruch College of the City University of New York — M,D*
Belhaven University (MS) — M
Bellevue University — M,D
Benedictine University — M
Brandman University — M
Brigham Young University — M
Bryan College — M
Buffalo State College, State University of New York — M,O
California Coast University — M
California Intercontinental University — M,D
California State University, East Bay — M
California State University, Sacramento — M
Capella University — M,D
Caribbean University — M,D
Carlow University — M
The Catholic University of America — M
Central Michigan University — M,O
Charleston Southern University — M
City University of Seattle — M,O
Claremont Graduate University — M
Clarkson University — M,O
Clayton State University — M
Cleveland State University — M
College of Saint Elizabeth — M
Colorado State University–Global Campus — M
Colorado Technical University Aurora — M
Colorado Technical University Colorado Springs — M,D
Columbia College (MO) — M
Columbia Southern University — M
Columbia University — M
Columbus State University — M,O
Concordia University, St. Paul — M
Concordia University Wisconsin — M
Cornell University — M
Dallas Baptist University — M
Davenport University — M
Delaware Valley University — M
DePaul University — M,D
DeSales University — M
DeVry University–Folsom Campus — M
East Central University — M
Eastern Michigan University — M,O
Embry-Riddle Aeronautical University–Daytona — M
Embry-Riddle Aeronautical University–Worldwide — M
Emmanuel College (United States) — M,O
Everglades University — M
Fairleigh Dickinson University, Florham Campus — M
Fairleigh Dickinson University, Metropolitan Campus — M,O
Fitchburg State University — M
Florida Institute of Technology — M
Florida International University — M,D
Florida State University — M,D
Framingham State University — M
Franklin Pierce University — M,D,O
Gannon University — M
George Fox University — M,D
George Mason University — M
Georgetown University — M,D
The George Washington University — M,O
Georgia State University — M,D
Golden Gate University — M,D,O
Goldey-Beacom College — M
Grambling State University — M
Grand Canyon University — M
Grantham University — M,O
Hawai'i Pacific University — M
HEC Montreal — M,D,O
Herzing University Online — M
Hofstra University — M,O
Holy Family University — M
Houston Baptist University — M
Howard University — M
Idaho State University — M,D
IGlobal University — M
Indiana Tech — M
Indiana University South Bend — M,O
Indiana Wesleyan University — M,O
Instituto Tecnologico de Santo Domingo — M,O
Instituto Tecnológico y de Estudios Superiores de Monterrey, Campus Cuernavaca — M
Inter American University of Puerto Rico, Aguadilla Campus — M
Inter American University of Puerto Rico, Arecibo Campus — M
Inter American University of Puerto Rico, Barranquitas Campus — M
Inter American University of Puerto Rico, Bayamón Campus — M
Inter American University of Puerto Rico, Fajardo Campus — M
Inter American University of Puerto Rico, Metropolitan Campus — M
Inter American University of Puerto Rico, Ponce Campus — M

Inter American University of Puerto Rico, San Germán Campus — M,D
Iona College — M,O
James Madison University — M
John F. Kennedy University — M
Johnson & Wales University — M
King University — M
La Roche University — M,O
La Salle University — M,O
Lasell College — M,O
La Sierra University — M,O
Lebanon Valley University — M
Lewis University — M
Lincoln University (CA) — M,D
Lincoln University (PA) — M
Lindenwood University — M,O
Lindenwood University–Belleville — M
London Metropolitan University — M,D
Long Island University–LIU Brooklyn — M,O
Loyola University Chicago — M
Manhattanville College — M,O
Marquette University — M,O
Marshall University — M
Marygrove College — M,O
Marymount University — O
Maryville University of Saint Louis — M,O
McKendree University — M
McMaster University — M,D
Mercy College — M
Mercyhurst University — M,O
Michigan State University — M,D
Middle Tennessee State University — M,D
Millennia Atlantic University — M
Misericordia University — M
Monroe College — M
Montclair State University — M
Moravian College — M
Mount Mercy University — M
Murray State University — M
National American University (TX) — M,D
National Louis University — M
National University — M,O
Nazareth College of Rochester — M
New Mexico Highlands University — M
New York Institute of Technology — M,O
New York University — M*
Niagara University — M
North Carolina Agricultural and Technical State University — M
North Central College — M
North Greenville University — M,D
Northwestern University — M,D
Northwest Missouri State University — M
Norwich University — M
Nova Southeastern University — M
Oakland University — M,O
Ohio Christian University — M
The Ohio State University — M,D
Oklahoma Christian University — M
Ottawa University — M
Pace University — M
Penn State Great Valley — M,O
Penn State Harrisburg — M,D,O
Penn State University Park — M*
Polytechnic University of Puerto Rico, Miami Campus — M
Polytechnic University of Puerto Rico, Orlando Campus — M
Pontifical Catholic University of Puerto Rico — M,O
Pontificia Universidad Catolica Madre y Maestra — M
Portland State University — M,D,O
Purdue University — M,D
Purdue University Global — M
Regent's University London — M
Regent University — M,D,O
Regis University — M,O
Robert Morris University — M
Robert Morris University Illinois — M
Rollins College — M
Roosevelt University — M
Rutgers University–Newark — M,D
Rutgers University–New Brunswick — M,D
Sacred Heart University — M,O
St. Ambrose University — M,D
Saint Francis University — M
St. Joseph's College, Long Island Campus — M
St. Joseph's College, New York — M
Saint Joseph's University — M
Saint Leo University — M,D
Saint Mary's University of Minnesota — M
St. Peter's University — M
St. Thomas University — M,O
Salve Regina University — M,O
San Diego State University — M
San Ignacio University — M
Savannah State University — M
Seattle Pacific University — M
Southern New Hampshire University — M,D,O
State University of New York Polytechnic Institute — M
Stevens Institute of Technology — M
Stony Brook University, State University of New York — M,O
Strayer University — M
Tarleton State University — M*
Temple University — M,D
Tennessee State University — M
Tennessee Technological University — M
Texas A&M University — M
Texas A&M University–Central Texas — M,O

Institution	Degree
Texas State University	M
Texas Woman's University	M
Thomas College	M
Thomas Edison State University	M
Tiffin University	M
Towson University	M
Trident University International	M,D
Trinity International University	M,D
Trinity Washington University	M
Troy University	M
United States International University–Africa	M
Universidad del Este	M
Universidad del Turabo	M
Universidad Metropolitana	M
University at Albany, State University of New York	M,D,O
University at Buffalo, the State University of New York	M,D,O
The University of Alabama in Huntsville	M,O
University of Bridgeport	M
University of California, Berkeley	O
University of Cincinnati	M
University of Colorado Denver	M
University of Connecticut	M,D
University of Dallas	M
University of Denver	M,O
University of Florida	M
University of Hawaii at Manoa	M
University of Houston–Clear Lake	M
University of Houston–Downtown	M
University of Illinois at Urbana–Champaign	M,D,O
The University of Kansas	M,D
University of La Verne	M,O
University of Lethbridge	M,D
University of Louisiana at Lafayette	M
University of Louisville	M,D,O
The University of Manchester	M
University of Mary	M
University of Memphis	M,O
University of Minnesota, Twin Cities Campus	M
University of Missouri–St. Louis	M,D,O
University of Nebraska at Kearney	M
University of New Haven	M,O
University of New Mexico	M
University of Northern Colorado	M
University of North Florida	M
University of North Texas	M,D,O
University of North Texas at Dallas	M
University of Oklahoma	M,D,O*
University of Phoenix–Bay Area Campus	M,D
University of Phoenix–Central Valley Campus	M
University of Phoenix–Dallas Campus	M
University of Phoenix–Hawaii Campus	M
University of Phoenix–Houston Campus	M
University of Phoenix–Las Vegas Campus	M
University of Phoenix–Online Campus	M,O
University of Phoenix–Phoenix Campus	M,O
University of Phoenix–Sacramento Valley Campus	M
University of Phoenix–San Antonio Campus	M
University of Phoenix–San Diego Campus	M
University of Pittsburgh	M,D*
University of Puerto Rico–Mayagüez	M
University of Puerto Rico–Río Piedras	M,D
University of Regina	M,O
University of Rhode Island	M,O
University of St. Francis (IL)	M,O
University of Saint Mary	M
University of South Carolina	M
University of South Dakota	M
University of Southern Indiana	M
University of South Florida	M
The University of Texas at Arlington	M
University of the Sacred Heart	M
University of Toronto	M,D
University of Wisconsin–Madison	M,D
University of Wisconsin–Milwaukee	M,O*
Upper Iowa University	M
Utah State University	M
Virginia Commonwealth University	M
Virginia International University	M,O
Walden University	M,D,O
Walsh College of Accountancy and Business Administration	M
Warner University	M
Wayland Baptist University	M,D
Waynesburg University	M,D
Wayne State University	M,D
Webster University	M,D,O
West Chester University of Pennsylvania	M,O
Wilfrid Laurier University	M,D
Wilkes University	M
William Paterson University of New Jersey	M,O
Wilmington University	M,D
York University	M,D

HUMAN SERVICES

Institution	Degree
Abilene Christian University	M,O
Albertus Magnus College	M
Albizu University, Miami Campus	M,D
Amridge University	M,D
Bellevue University	M
Boricua College	M
Brandeis University	M
California State University, Sacramento	M
Capella University	M
Chestnut Hill College	M,O
Concordia University Chicago	M
Concordia University, St. Paul	M
Coppin State University	M
Eastern Michigan University	O
East Tennessee State University	M
Ferris State University	M
Georgia State University	M,O
Governors State University	M
Judson University	M
Kansas State University	M,D,O
Kent State University	M,D,O
Lehigh University	M,D,O
Lenoir-Rhyne University	M
Liberty University	M,D,O
Lincoln University (PA)	M
Lock Haven University of Pennsylvania	M
Louisiana Tech University	M,D,O
McDaniel College	M
Mercer University	M,D
Minnesota State University Mankato	M
Murray State University	M,D,O
National Louis University	M,D,O
National University	M,O
New England College	M
Northeastern University	M
Pontifical Catholic University of Puerto Rico	M,D
Post University	M
Purdue University Northwest	M
Regent University	M,D,O
Roberts Wesleyan College	M
Rosemont College	M
St. Cloud State University	M
St. Joseph's College, Long Island Campus	M
St. Joseph's College, New York	M
Saint Leo University	M
South Carolina State University	M
Southeastern University (FL)	M
Springfield College	M
Texas Southern University	M
Thomas University	M
Universidad del Turabo	M
Université de Montréal	D
University of Baltimore	M
University of Bridgeport	M
University of Central Missouri	M,D,O
University of Colorado Colorado Springs	M,D
University of Idaho	M,O
University of Illinois at Springfield	M,O
University of Illinois at Urbana–Champaign	M,D
University of Maryland, Baltimore County	M,D
University of Massachusetts Boston	M
University of Nebraska at Kearney	M
University of Northern Iowa	M
University of North Georgia	M
University of Northwestern–St. Paul	M
University of Oklahoma	M,O*
University of Providence	M
Upper Iowa University	M
Walden University	M,D
Warner Pacific University	M
Washburn University	M
Webster University	M
Western Michigan University	D,O
West Virginia University	M,D
Wichita State University	M
Wilmington University	M
Winona State University	M,O
Youngstown State University	M

HYDRAULICS

Institution	Degree
Drexel University	M,D*
École Polytechnique de Montréal	M,D,O
McGill University	M,D
Old Dominion University	M,D
Stevens Institute of Technology	M,D,O
University of Colorado Denver	M,D
The University of Iowa	M,D

HYDROGEOLOGY

Institution	Degree
Clemson University	M,D
East Carolina University	M,O
Indiana University Bloomington	M,D
Montana Tech of The University of Montana	M
Oregon State University	M,D
University of Hawaii at Manoa	M,D
University of Nevada, Reno	M,D
University of South Florida	O

HYDROLOGY

Institution	Degree
Boise State University	M,D
California State University, Bakersfield	M
Colorado School of Mines	M,D
Cornell University	M,D
Drexel University	M,D*
Idaho State University	M,D
Massachusetts Institute of Technology	M,D,O
New Mexico Institute of Mining and Technology	M,D
New Mexico State University	M,D
Oregon State University	M,D
Portland State University	M,D,O
Stanford University	M,D,O
Stevens Institute of Technology	M,D,O
Temple University	M,O*
Université du Québec, Institut National de la Recherche Scientifique	M,D
The University of Arizona	D,O
University of Calgary	M,D
University of California, Davis	M,D
University of Colorado Denver	M,D
University of Florida	M,D
University of Minnesota, Twin Cities Campus	M,D
University of Mississippi	M,D
University of Nevada, Reno	M,D
University of New Brunswick Fredericton	M,D
University of New Hampshire	M
University of Rhode Island	M,D,O
University of Southern Mississippi	M,D
University of Washington	M,D

ILLUSTRATION

Institution	Degree
Academy of Art University	M
Bob Jones University	M,D,O
California College of the Arts	M
California State University, Fullerton	M
East Carolina University	M
Fashion Institute of Technology	M
Hollins University	M,O
Kent State University	M
Maryland Institute College of Art	M
Marywood University	M
Mills College	M,O
Minneapolis College of Art and Design	M
Savannah College of Art and Design	M
School of Visual Arts (NY)	M
Syracuse University	M
Western Connecticut State University	M

IMMUNOLOGY

Institution	Degree
Albany Medical College	M,D
Albert Einstein College of Medicine	D
American University of Beirut	M,D
Baylor College of Medicine	D
Boston University	D
California Institute of Technology	D
Colorado State University	M,D
Creighton University	M,D
Dalhousie University	M,D
Dartmouth College	M,D
Drexel University	M,D*
Duke University	D
East Carolina University	M,D
Emory University	D
Georgetown University	M,D
The George Washington University	D
Illinois State University	M,D
Indiana University–Purdue University Indianapolis	M,D
Iowa State University of Science and Technology	M,D
Irell & Manella Graduate School of Biological Sciences	D
Johns Hopkins University	M,D*
London Metropolitan University	M,D
Louisiana State University Health Sciences Center	D
Louisiana State University Health Sciences Center at Shreveport	M,D
Loyola University Chicago	M,D
Massachusetts Institute of Technology	D
Mayo Clinic Graduate School of Biomedical Sciences	D
McGill University	M,D
McMaster University	M,D
Medical University of South Carolina	M,D
Meharry Medical College	D
Memorial University of Newfoundland	M,D
Montana State University	M,D
New York Medical College	M,D
New York University	M,D*
Old Dominion University	M
Oregon Health & Science University	M
Oregon State University	M,D
Penn State Hershey Medical Center	M,D
Purdue University	M,D
Rosalind Franklin University of Medicine and Science	D
Rush University	M,D
Rutgers University–Newark	D
Rutgers University–New Brunswick	M,D
Saint Louis University	D*
Stanford University	D
State University of New York Upstate Medical University	M,D
Stony Brook University, State University of New York	M,D
Thomas Jefferson University	D
Tufts University	D
Tulane University	M
Uniformed Services University of the Health Sciences	D*
Universidad Central del Caribe	M,D
Université de Montréal	M,D
Université de Sherbrooke	M,D
Université du Québec, Institut National de la Recherche Scientifique	M,D
Université Laval	M,D
University at Buffalo, the State University of New York	M,D
The University of Alabama at Birmingham	D
University of Alberta	M,D
The University of Arizona	D
University of Arkansas for Medical Sciences	M,D,O
The University of British Columbia	M,D
University of Calgary	M,D
University of California, Berkeley	D
University of California, Davis	M,D
University of California, Los Angeles	M,D
University of Chicago	D
University of Cincinnati	M,D
University of Colorado Denver	D
University of Connecticut Health Center	D
University of Florida	D
University of Guelph	M,D,O
University of Illinois at Chicago	D
The University of Iowa	M,D
University of Kentucky	D
University of Louisville	M,D
The University of Manchester	M,D
University of Manitoba	M,D
University of Maryland, Baltimore	D
University of Massachusetts Medical School	M,D
University of Miami	D
University of Michigan	M,D
University of Minnesota, Duluth	M,D
University of Minnesota, Twin Cities Campus	D
University of Missouri	D
University of Montana	D
University of Nebraska Medical Center	M,D
The University of North Carolina at Chapel Hill	M,D
University of North Texas Health Science Center at Fort Worth	M,D
University of Oklahoma Health Sciences Center	M,D
University of Ottawa	M,D
University of Pennsylvania	D*
University of Pittsburgh	D*
University of Prince Edward Island	M,D
University of Rochester	M,D*
University of Saskatchewan	M,D
University of South Dakota	M,D
University of Southern California	M
University of Southern Maine	M
University of South Florida	M,D
The University of Texas Health Science Center at Houston	M,D
The University of Texas Health Science Center at San Antonio	M,D
The University of Texas Medical Branch	M,D
The University of Texas Southwestern Medical Center	D
The University of Toledo	M,D
University of Toronto	M,D
University of Washington	D
The University of Western Ontario	M,D
Vanderbilt University	M,D*
Virginia Commonwealth University	M,D
Wake Forest University	D
Washington State University	M,D
Washington University in St. Louis	D
Wayne State University	M,D,O
Weill Cornell Medicine	M,D
West Virginia University	M,D
Wright State University	M
Yale University	D

INDUSTRIAL/MANAGEMENT ENGINEERING

Institution	Degree
American University of Armenia	M
Arizona State University at the Tempe campus	M,D
Auburn University	M,D,O
Binghamton University, State University of New York	M,D
Bradley University	M
Buffalo State College, State University of New York	M
California Polytechnic State University, San Luis Obispo	M
California State University, Fresno	M
California State University, Northridge	M
Clemson University	M,D
Colorado State University–Pueblo	M
Columbia University	M,D
Concordia University (Canada)	M,D,O
Cornell University	M,D
Dalhousie University	M,D
Eastern Kentucky University	M
École Polytechnique de Montréal	M,D,O
Florida Agricultural and Mechanical University	M,D
Florida State University	M,D
Georgia Institute of Technology	M,D
Illinois State University	M
Instituto Tecnologico de Santo Domingo	M,O
Instituto Tecnológico y de Estudios Superiores de Monterrey, Campus Chihuahua	M,O
Instituto Tecnológico y de Estudios Superiores de Monterrey, Campus Ciudad de México	M,D
Instituto Tecnológico y de Estudios Superiores de Monterrey, Campus Laguna	M
Instituto Tecnológico y de Estudios Superiores de Monterrey, Campus Monterrey	M,D
Iowa State University of Science and Technology	M,D
Kansas State University	M,D
Lawrence Technological University	M,D
Lehigh University	M,D,O
Mississippi State University	M,D
Montana State University	M,D

Montana Tech of The University of
Montana — M
Morgan State University — M,D,O
New Jersey Institute of Technology — M,D
North Carolina Agricultural and
Technical State University — M,D
North Carolina State University — M,D
North Dakota State University — M,D
Northeastern University — M,D,O
Northern Illinois University — M
Northwestern University — M,D
The Ohio State University — M,D
Ohio University — M,D
Oklahoma State University — M,D
Oregon State University — M,D
Penn State University Park — M,D*
Purdue University — M,D
Purdue University Fort Wayne — M
Rensselaer Polytechnic Institute — M
Rochester Institute of Technology — M
Rutgers University–New
Brunswick — M,D
St. Mary's University
(United States) — M
San Jose State University — M
Southern Illinois University
Edwardsville — M,D
Stanford University — M,D
Texas A&M University — M,D
Texas A&M University–
Kingsville — M
Texas Southern University — M
Texas State University — M
Universidad de las Américas
Puebla — M
Université de Moncton — M
Université du Québec
à Trois-Rivières — M,O
Université Laval — O
University at Buffalo, the State
University of New York — M,D,O
The University of Alabama in
Huntsville — M,D
The University of Arizona — M,D,O
University of Arkansas — M,D
University of California, Berkeley — M,D
University of Central Florida — M,D,O
University of Cincinnati — M,D
University of Florida — M,D,O
University of Houston — M,D
University of Illinois at Chicago — M,D
University of Illinois at
Urbana–Champaign — M,D
The University of Iowa — M,D
University of Louisville — M,D,O
University of Manitoba — M,D
University of Massachusetts
Amherst — M,D
University of Massachusetts
Dartmouth — M,O
University of Massachusetts Lowell — D
University of Miami — M,D
University of Michigan — M,D
University of Michigan–
Dearborn — M,D
University of Minnesota, Twin
Cities Campus — M,D
University of Missouri — M,D
University of Nebraska–
Lincoln — M,D
University of New Haven — M,O
University of Pittsburgh — M,D*
University of Puerto Rico–
Mayagüez — M
University of Regina — M,D
University of Rhode Island — M,D
University of Southern California — M,D,O
University of South Florida — M,D,O
The University of Tennessee — M,D
The University of Texas at
Arlington — M,D
The University of Texas at Austin — M,D
The University of Texas at El Paso — M
The University of Toledo — M,D
University of Toronto — M,D
University of Washington — M,D
University of Windsor — M,D
University of Wisconsin–
Madison — M,D
University of Wisconsin–
Milwaukee — M,D*
University of Wisconsin–
Stout — M
Virginia Polytechnic Institute and
State University — M,O
Wayne State University — M,D,O
Western Carolina University — M
Western Michigan University — M
Western New England University — M
West Virginia University — M,D
Wichita State University — M,D
Wright State University — M
Youngstown State University — M

INDUSTRIAL AND LABOR RELATIONS

Baruch College of the City
University of New York — M*
Carnegie Mellon University — D
Cleveland State University — M
Cornell University — M,D
Georgetown University — D
Georgia State University — M
Indiana University of Pennsylvania — M
Inter American University of
Puerto Rico, Metropolitan Campus — M,D
McMaster University — M
Memorial University of
Newfoundland — M
Michigan State University — M,D
New York Institute of Technology — M,O
The Ohio State University — M

Penn State University Park — M*
Queen's University at
Kingston — M
Rutgers University–New
Brunswick — M,D
State University of New York
Empire State College — M
Temple University — M,O*
Université de Montréal — M,D,O
Université du Québec
à Trois-Rivières — O
Université du Québec
en Outaouais — M,D,O
Université Laval — M,D
University of Alberta — D
University of California, Berkeley — D
University of Cincinnati — M
University of Illinois at
Urbana–Champaign — M,D
The University of Manchester — M
University of Massachusetts
Amherst — M
University of Minnesota, Twin
Cities Campus — M
University of Rhode Island — M,O
University of Toronto — M,D
University of Wisconsin–
Milwaukee — M,O*
Wayne State University — M,D
West Virginia University — M,D,O

INDUSTRIAL AND MANUFACTURING MANAGEMENT

American InterContinental
University Online — M
Baruch College of the City
University of New York — M,D*
Bluffton University — M
California State University, East
Bay — M
Carnegie Mellon University — M,D
Case Western Reserve University — M,D
Cedarville University — M,D
Central Connecticut State
University — M,O
Central Michigan University — M
Colorado Technical University
Aurora — M
Colorado Technical University
Colorado Springs — M,D
Duke University — M,D,O
East Carolina University — M,D,O
Emory University — M
Everglades University — D
Georgetown University — D*
Harvard University — D*
HEC Montreal — M
Illinois Institute of Technology — M
Instituto Tecnologico de Santo
Domingo — M,O
Instituto Tecnológico y de
Estudios Superiores de Monterrey,
Campus Estado de México — M,D
Instituto Tecnológico y de
Estudios Superiores de Monterrey,
Campus Irapuato — M,D
Inter American University of
Puerto Rico, Metropolitan Campus — M
Inter American University of
Puerto Rico, San Germán Campus — M,D
Lawrence Technological University — M,D
Marquette University — M,O
McGill University — M,D,O
Milligan College — M,O
Milwaukee School of Engineering — M
Mississippi State University — M,D
Northern Illinois University — M
Northwestern University — M,D
Oakland University — M,O
Penn State Erie, The Behrend
College — M
Polytechnic University of Puerto
Rico — M
Polytechnic University of Puerto
Rico, Miami Campus — M
Polytechnic University of Puerto
Rico, Orlando Campus — M
Regis University — M,O
Rochester Institute of Technology — M
San Francisco State University — M
Southern New Hampshire University — M,D,O
Stevens Institute of Technology — M
Texas A&M University–
Kingsville — M
Universidad de las Américas
Puebla — M
The University of Alabama — M
University of Arkansas — M
University of Bridgeport — M
University of Central Missouri — M,D,O
University of Chicago — M,O
University of Cincinnati — D
The University of Manchester — M,D
University of Michigan–Flint — M,O
University of New Haven — M,O
The University of North Carolina
at Charlotte — M,D,O
University of North Texas — M,D,O
University of Pittsburgh — M*
University of Portland — M
University of Puerto Rico–
Mayagüez — M,D
University of Puerto Rico–
Río Piedras — M,D
University of Rochester — D*
University of Southern Indiana — M
The University of Tennessee — M,D
The University of Texas at Austin — M,D
The University of Texas at Dallas — M,D
The University of Texas at Tyler — M
University of Utah — M,D,O

Wayne State University — M,D
Wilkes University — M

INDUSTRIAL AND ORGANIZATIONAL PSYCHOLOGY

Adler University — M,D
Albizu University — M,D
Albizu University, Miami Campus — M,D
Alliant International
University–Fresno — M,D
Alliant International
University–Los Angeles — M,D
Alliant International
University–San Diego — M,D
Alliant International
University–San Francisco — M,D
American InterContinental
University Online — M
Angelo State University — M
Anna Maria College — M
Argosy University, Atlanta — M,D,O
Argosy University, Chicago — M,D
Argosy University, Phoenix — M
Argosy University, Tampa — M,D
Argosy University, Twin Cities — M,D,O
Austin Peay State University — M
Azusa Pacific University — M
Baruch College of the City
University of New York — M,D*
Bayamón Central University — M,D
Bowling Green State University — M,D
Brooklyn College of the City
University of New York — M,D
California State University, Long
Beach — M
California State University,
Sacramento — M
California State University, San
Bernardino — M
Capella University — M,D
Central Michigan University — M,D
Chatham University — M,D
The Chicago School of Professional
Psychology — M,D,O
The Chicago School of Professional
Psychology at Downtown Los
Angeles — M
The Chicago School of Professional
Psychology at San Diego — M,D
The Chicago School of Professional
Psychology: Online — M,D,O
Claremont Graduate University — M,D,O
Clemson University — M,D
East Carolina University — M,D,O
Eastern Kentucky University — M,O
Elmhurst College — M
Emporia State University — M
Fairleigh Dickinson University,
Florham Campus — M
Florida International University — M,D
George Mason University — M,D,O
The Graduate Center, City
University of New York — D
Grand Canyon University — D
Hofstra University — M,D
Illinois Institute of Technology — M,D
Illinois State University — M,D,O
Indiana University–Purdue
University Indianapolis — M,D
Inter American University of
Puerto Rico, Metropolitan Campus — M,D
Iona College — M,O
Kean University — M
Keiser University — M,D
La Salle University — M
Liberty University — M,D,O
London Metropolitan University — M,D
Louisiana Tech University — M,D,O
Meredith College — M
Middle Tennessee State University — M,O
Minnesota State University Mankato — M,D
Missouri State University — M,O
Missouri University of Science and
Technology — M
Montclair State University — M
New York University — M,D,O*
North Carolina State University — D
Northern Kentucky University — M,O
Ohio University — D
Old Dominion University — D
Philadelphia College of
Osteopathic Medicine — M,D,O*
Pontifical Catholic University of
Puerto Rico — D
Purdue University — D
Radford University — M
Rice University — M,D
Roosevelt University — M,D
Sacred Heart University — M
St. Cloud State University — M
Saint Louis University — M,D*
Saint Mary's University
(Canada) — M,D
St. Mary's University
(United States) — M
San Diego State University — M,D
San Francisco State University — M,O
San Jose State University — M
Seattle Pacific University — M,D
South Dakota State University — M
Southeastern Louisiana University — M
Southern Illinois University
Edwardsville — M
Springfield College — M,D,O
Teachers College, Columbia
University — M,D
Thomas Edison State University — M,O
Touro College — M,D
University at Albany, State
University of New York — M,D
The University of Akron — M,D

The University of Alabama in
Huntsville — M
University of Connecticut — M,D
University of Detroit Mercy — M,D,O
University of Guelph — M,D
University of Houston — M,D
The University of Manchester — M
University of Maryland, Baltimore
County — M
University of Maryland, College
Park — M,D
University of Minnesota, Twin
Cities Campus — D
University of Nebraska at Omaha — M,D,O
University of New Haven — M,O
The University of North Carolina
at Charlotte — M,D,O
University of Phoenix–Online
Campus — M,D,O
University of Puerto Rico–
Río Piedras — M,D
University of South Africa — M,D
University of South Florida — D
The University of Tennessee — D
The University of Tennessee at
Chattanooga — M
The University of Texas at
Arlington — M,D
University of the Incarnate Word — M,D
The University of Tulsa — M,D
University of West Florida — M
University of Wisconsin–
Oshkosh — M
Valdosta State University — M,O
Vanguard University of Southern
California — M
Walden University — M,D,O
Wayne State University — M,D
West Chester University of
Pennsylvania — M,D,O
Western Kentucky University — M,O
Western Michigan University — M,D
William James College — M,D,O
Wright State University — D
Xavier University — M,D*

INDUSTRIAL DESIGN

Academy of Art University — M
ArtCenter College of Design — M
Auburn University — M
California College of the Arts — M
Carleton University — M
Georgia Institute of Technology — M
Iowa State University of Science
and Technology — M
The New School — M
North Carolina State University — M
The Ohio State University — M
Pratt Institute — M
Purdue University — M,D
Rhode Island School of Design — M
Rochester Institute of Technology — M
Savannah College of Art and Design — M
Thomas Jefferson University — M
University of Cincinnati — M
University of Detroit Mercy — M,D
University of Illinois at
Urbana–Champaign — M
University of Notre Dame — M
The University of the Arts — M
University of Washington — M
Wayne State University — M

INDUSTRIAL HYGIENE

California State University,
Northridge — M
Eastern Kentucky University — M
Montana Tech of The University of
Montana — M
New York Medical College — M,D,O
Old Dominion University — M
The University of Alabama at
Birmingham — M,D
University of Central Missouri — M,D,O
University of Cincinnati — M,D
The University of Iowa — M,D,O
University of Michigan — M,D
University of Minnesota, Twin
Cities Campus — M,D
University of Puerto Rico–
Medical Sciences Campus — M
University of South Carolina — M,D
The University of Toledo — M,D,O
University of Wisconsin–
Stout — M
West Virginia University — M,D

INFECTIOUS DISEASES

Georgetown University — M,D
The George Washington University — M,D,O
Johns Hopkins University — M,D*
Loyola University Chicago — M,D,O
Montana State University — M,D
North Carolina State University — M,D
North Dakota State University — M
Thomas Jefferson University — O
Tufts University — M,D
Uniformed Services University of
the Health Sciences — D*
Université Laval — O
The University of British Columbia — M,D
University of Calgary — M,D
University of California, Berkeley — M
University of Georgia — D
University of Guelph — M,D,O
University of Manitoba — M,D
University of Minnesota, Twin
Cities Campus — M,D
University of Nebraska Medical
Center — M,D
University of Pittsburgh — M,D*
University of South Florida — M,D

---

*M—masters degree; D—doctorate; O—other advanced degree; *—Close-Up and/or Display*

The University of Texas Health Science Center at Houston — M,D
University of Washington — D
Washington State University — M,D
Yale University — D

INFORMATION SCIENCE
Alcorn State University — M
American InterContinental University Atlanta
American InterContinental University Online — M
American University of Armenia — M
Arizona State University at the Tempe campus — M
Arkansas Tech University — M
Aspen University — M,O
Ball State University — M,O
Barry University — M
Bellevue University — M
Bentley University — M
Bradley University — M
Brigham Young University — M
Brooklyn College of the City University of New York — M,O
California State University, Fullerton — M
Capitol Technology University — M,D
Carleton University — M,D
Carnegie Mellon University — M,D
Case Western Reserve University — M,D
The Citadel, The Military College of South Carolina
Claremont Graduate University — M,D,O
Clarion University of Pennsylvania — M
Clark Atlanta University — M
Clark University — M
The College of Saint Rose — M,O
Cornell University — D
Dakota State University — M,D,O
DePaul University — M,D
Drexel University — M,D,O*
East Tennessee State University — M,O
Florida Institute of Technology — M
Florida International University — M,D
Gannon University — M
George Mason University — M,D,O
Georgia State University — M,D,O
Grand Valley State University — M
Hardin-Simmons University — M
Harvard University — M,D,O*
Hood College — M,O
Indiana University Bloomington — M,D,O
Indiana University–Purdue University Indianapolis — M
Instituto Tecnologico de Santo Domingo — M,O
Instituto Tecnológico y de Estudios Superiores de Monterrey, Campus Cuernavaca — M,D
Instituto Tecnológico y de Estudios Superiores de Monterrey, Campus Estado de México — M,D
Instituto Tecnológico y de Estudios Superiores de Monterrey, Campus Irapuato — M,D
Instituto Tecnológico y de Estudios Superiores de Monterrey, Campus Monterrey — M,D
Instituto Tecnológico y de Estudios Superiores de Monterrey, Campus Sonora Norte — M
Iowa State University of Science and Technology — M
Kennesaw State University — M,O
Kent State University — M
Lawrence Technological University — M,D,O
Lehigh University — M
Loyola University Chicago — M
Marshall University — M
Maryville University of Saint Louis — M,O
Massachusetts Institute of Technology
Minnesota State University Mankato — M,O
Missouri University of Science and Technology — M
Monroe College — M
Naval Postgraduate School — M,D,O
New Jersey Institute of Technology — M,D,O
Northern Kentucky University — M,O
Northwestern University — M
Nova Southeastern University — M,D
Oklahoma State University — M,D
Old Dominion University — D
Pace University — M,D,O
Penn State Great Valley — M,O
Penn State University Park — M,D*
Purdue University Fort Wayne — M
Regis University — M,O
Rensselaer at Hartford — M
Rensselaer Polytechnic Institute — M
Robert Morris University — M,D
Rochester Institute of Technology — M,D
Rutgers University–New Brunswick — M
Sacred Heart University — M
St. John's University (NY)
St. Mary's University (United States) — M
Sam Houston State University — M,D
Shippensburg University of Pennsylvania — M,O
Southern Methodist University — M,D
Southern States University — M
State University of New York Polytechnic Institute — M
Stevens Institute of Technology — M
Strayer University — M
Syracuse University — M,D
Temple University — M,D*
Texas Woman's University
Thomas Edison State University — M,O
Towson University — M,D

Trevecca Nazarene University — M,D
Université de Sherbrooke — M,D
University at Albany, State University of New York — M,D
The University of Alabama at Birmingham — M,D
University of Arkansas at Little Rock — M,D,O
University of California, Irvine — M,D
University of California, Merced — M,D
University of Central Missouri — M,D,O
University of Cincinnati — M,O
University of Colorado Boulder — D
University of Colorado Denver — M,D
University of Delaware — M,D
University of Denver — M,O
University of Fairfax — M,D
University of Florida — M,D
University of Hawaii at Manoa — M,D
University of Houston — M,D
University of Houston–Clear Lake — M
University of Illinois at Urbana–Champaign — M,D,O
The University of Iowa — M,D,O
University of Kentucky — M,D
University of Maine — M,D,O
University of Maryland, Baltimore County — M,D
University of Maryland University College — M
University of Michigan — M,D
University of Michigan–Dearborn — M,D
University of Michigan–Flint — M
University of Nebraska at Omaha — M,D,O
University of Nebraska–Lincoln — M,D
University of North Alabama — M
The University of North Carolina at Charlotte — M,O
University of North Texas — M,D,O
University of Oregon — M,D
University of Ottawa — M,O
University of Pennsylvania — M,D*
University of Pittsburgh — M,D,O*
University of Puerto Rico–Mayagüez — M,D
University of Puerto Rico–Río Piedras — M,O
University of St. Thomas (MN) — M,O
University of South Africa — M,D
University of South Carolina Upstate — M
University of Southern Mississippi — M,O
University of South Florida — M
The University of Tennessee — M
The University of Texas at El Paso — M,D,O
The University of Texas at San Antonio — M,D,O
University of the Sacred Heart — O
University of Washington — M,D
University of Waterloo — M,D
University of Wisconsin–Parkside — M
University of Wisconsin–Stout — M
Western Governors University — M
Youngstown State University — M

INFORMATION STUDIES
The Catholic University of America — M,O
Central Connecticut State University — M
Columbia University — M
Cornell University — D
Dalhousie University — M
Dominican University — M,D,O
Lock Haven University of Pennsylvania — M
Louisiana State University and Agricultural & Mechanical College — M
Mansfield University of Pennsylvania — M
McGill University — M,D,O
Metropolitan State University — M,D,O
Monmouth University — M
North Carolina Central University — M
Pratt Institute — M,O
Queens College of the City University of New York — M,O
Queen's University at Kingston — M,D
Rutgers University–New Brunswick — M,D
St. Catherine University — M
St. John's University (NY) — M,O
Southern Connecticut State University — M,O
Syracuse University — M
Universidad del Turabo — M
Université de Montréal — M,D
University at Buffalo, the State University of New York — M,O
The University of Alabama — M,D
University of Alberta — M
The University of Arizona — M,D
The University of British Columbia — M,D
University of California, Berkeley — M,D
University of California, Los Angeles — M,D,O
University of Hawaii at Manoa — M,O
University of Illinois at Urbana–Champaign — M,D,O
The University of Iowa — M,D
University of Maryland, College Park — M,D
University of Michigan — M,D
University of Missouri — D
The University of North Carolina at Chapel Hill — M,D,O
The University of North Carolina at Greensboro — M
University of Oklahoma — M,D,O*

University of Puerto Rico–Río Piedras — M,O
University of Rhode Island — M
University of South Carolina — M,D,O
University of South Florida — M,O
The University of Texas at Austin — M,D
University of Toronto — M,D
The University of Western Ontario — M,D
University of Wisconsin–Madison — M,D
University of Wisconsin–Milwaukee — M,D,O*
Valdosta State University — M
Wayne State University — M,O

INORGANIC CHEMISTRY
Auburn University — M,D
Binghamton University, State University of New York — M,D
Boston College — M,D
Brandeis University — M,D
Cornell University — D
Florida State University — M,D
Georgetown University — D
The George Washington University — M,D
Harvard University — D*
Howard University — M,D
Illinois Institute of Technology — M,D
Indiana University Bloomington — M,D
Iowa State University of Science and Technology — M,D
Marquette University — M,D
Massachusetts Institute of Technology — D
McMaster University — M,D
Old Dominion University — M,D
Purdue University — M,D
Rice University — M,D
Rutgers University–Newark — M,D
Rutgers University–New Brunswick — M,D
Seton Hall University — M,D
Southern University and Agricultural and Mechanical College — M
University of Calgary — M,D
University of Cincinnati — M,D
University of Louisville — M,D
The University of Manchester — M,D
University of Maryland, College Park — M,D
University of Massachusetts Lowell — M,D
University of Memphis — M,D
University of Miami — M,D
University of Michigan — M,D
University of Missouri–Kansas City — M,D
University of Montana — M,D
University of Nebraska–Lincoln — M,D
University of Notre Dame — M,D
University of Oklahoma — M,D*
University of Regina — M,D
University of Rochester — D*
The University of Tennessee — M,D
The University of Texas at Austin — D
The University of Toledo — M,D
Virginia Commonwealth University — M,D
Wake Forest University — M,D
Wesleyan University — D
Yale University — D
Youngstown State University — M

INSURANCE
California State University, Fullerton — M
Florida State University — M,D
Georgia State University — M,D,O
Olivet College — M
Pontificia Universidad Catolica Madre y Maestra
St. John's University (NY) — M
Temple University — D*
University of Colorado Denver — M
University of Florida — M,D,O
University of Pennsylvania — M,D*
University of Wisconsin–Madison — M,D
Western Michigan University Thomas M. Cooley Law School — M,D

INTELLECTUAL PROPERTY LAW
Case Western Reserve University — M,D
DePaul University — M,D
Drexel University — M,D*
Fordham University — M,D
Golden Gate University — M,D
Hofstra University — M,D,O
Indiana University–Purdue University Indianapolis — M,D,O
Michigan State University College of Law — M,D
Montclair State University — M,O
Santa Clara University — M,D,O
Suffolk University — M,D
Texas A&M University — M,D
University of Baltimore — M,D
University of Houston — M,D
University of New Hampshire — M,D
University of Pittsburgh — M*
University of San Francisco — M
University of Washington — M,D
Western Michigan University Thomas M. Cooley Law School — M,D
Yeshiva University — M,D

INTERDISCIPLINARY STUDIES
Alaska Pacific University — M
Amberton University — M
Antioch University New England — M
Arizona State University at the Tempe campus — M
Athabasca University — M,O
Baylor University — D
Boise State University — M

Bowling Green State University — M,D
Buffalo State College, State University of New York — M
California State University, Bakersfield — M
California State University, East Bay — M
California State University, San Bernardino — M
California State University, Stanislaus — M
Cambridge College — M,D,O
Campbell University — M
Central Washington University — M
The Citadel, The Military College of South Carolina — M,O
Clarkson University — M,D
Colorado State University — M,D
Concordia University (Canada) — M,D
Dalhousie University — D
Dallas Baptist University — M
DePaul University — M
Eastern Washington University — M
Emory University — D
Fitchburg State University — O
Florida Gulf Coast University — M
Florida Institute of Technology — M
Fresno Pacific University — M
Frostburg State University — M,D
George Mason University — M
Georgetown University — M,D
Goddard College — M
Grand Rapids Theological Seminary of Cornerstone University — M
Harrison Middleton University — M,D
Hiram College — M
Hollins University — M
Indiana University Southeast — M,O
Iowa State University of Science and Technology — M
Kansas State University — M
Lehigh University — M,D
Lesley University — M,D,O
Long Island University–LIU Post — M
Marquette University — D
Marywood University — D
Massachusetts College of Art and Design — M,O
Michigan Technological University — M,D,O
Mills College — M
Minnesota State University Mankato — M
Montana State University Billings — M
Montana Tech of The University of Montana — M
Murray State University — M,O
New Mexico State University — M,D
New York University — M*
Niagara University — M
Northeastern University — M,D,O
Nova Southeastern University — M,D,O
The Ohio State University — M,D
Oregon State University — M
Regent University — M,D,O
Rensselaer Polytechnic Institute — M,D
Rochester Institute of Technology — M
Rosalind Franklin University of Medicine and Science — D
Rutgers University–New Brunswick — D
San Diego State University — M
Sonoma State University — M
Southern Illinois University Edwardsville — M
Southern Oregon University — M
Southern Utah University — M
State University of New York at Fredonia — M,O
Stephen F. Austin State University — M
Teachers College, Columbia University — M,D
Texas A&M University–Texarkana — M
Texas State University — M
Texas Tech University — M,D
Trinity Western University — D
Tufts University — D
Tulane University — D
Union Institute & University — D
University at Buffalo, the State University of New York — M
The University of Alabama — D
University of Alaska Fairbanks — M,D
The University of Arizona — M,D
University of Arkansas at Little Rock — M
University of California, Santa Barbara — D
University of California, Santa Cruz — M,D
University of Central Oklahoma — M
University of Cincinnati — D
University of Colorado Colorado Springs — M
University of Dayton — M,D
University of Florida — M,D
University of Houston–Victoria — M
University of Idaho — M
University of Illinois at Chicago — M
University of Illinois at Springfield — M
University of Illinois at Urbana–Champaign — D
The University of Kansas — D
University of Louisville — M,D
University of Maine — M,D
University of Manitoba — M,D
University of Massachusetts Medical School — M,D
University of Memphis — M,D,O
University of Minnesota, Twin Cities Campus — D

University of Missouri–Kansas City	D
University of Montana	M,D
University of New Brunswick Fredericton	M,D
University of North Alabama	M
The University of North Carolina at Charlotte	M,D,O
University of Northern British Columbia	M,D,O
University of North Texas	M,D,O
University of Oregon	M
University of Ottawa	D,O
University of Pittsburgh	D*
University of Regina	M
University of South Dakota	M
University of South Florida	M,D
The University of Tennessee at Martin	M
The University of Texas at Dallas	M
The University of Texas at El Paso	M
The University of Texas at San Antonio	M
The University of Texas at Tyler	M
The University of Texas Health Science Center at San Antonio	D
The University of Texas Rio Grande Valley	M
University of Vermont	M
University of Virginia	M
University of Washington, Tacoma	M
The University of Western Ontario	M
Virginia Commonwealth University	M
Virginia Polytechnic Institute and State University	M,D
Virginia State University	M
Walden University	M,D,O
Washington State University	D
Western Kentucky University	M,O
Western New Mexico University	M
West Texas A&M University	M
Worcester Polytechnic Institute	M,D,O
York University	M

INTERIOR DESIGN

Academy of Art University	M
Ball State University	M
Boston Architectural College	M
Brenau University	M
California State Polytechnic University, Pomona	M
Chatham University	M
Cornell University	M
Drexel University	M*
Eastern Michigan University	M
Endicott College	M
Florida International University	M,O
Florida State University	M
The George Washington University	M
Georgia State University	M
Interior Designers Institute	M
Iowa State University of Science and Technology	M
Kansas State University	M
Lawrence Technological University	M,O
Marymount University	M
Marywood University	M
Miami University	M
Michigan State University	M,D
Moore College of Art & Design	M
The New School	M
New York School of Interior Design	M
The Ohio State University	M
Paris College of Art	M
Pontificia Universidad Catolica Madre y Maestra	M
Pratt Institute	M
Purdue University	M,D
Queens University of Charlotte	M
Rhode Island School of Design	M
San Diego State University	M
Savannah College of Art and Design	M
Suffolk University	M
Texas Tech University	M,D
Thomas Jefferson University	M
University of California, Berkeley	O
University of Cincinnati	M
University of Florida	M,D
University of Georgia	M,D
University of Kentucky	M
University of Manitoba	M
University of Massachusetts Amherst	M
University of Minnesota, Twin Cities Campus	M,D,O
University of Nebraska–Lincoln	M,D
The University of North Carolina at Greensboro	M,O
University of North Texas	M,D,O
University of Oregon	M
The University of Tennessee at Chattanooga	M
The University of Texas at Austin	M
Virginia Commonwealth University	M,D
Washington State University	M
Wayne State University	M

INTERNATIONAL AFFAIRS

American Graduate School in Paris	M,D
American Public University System	M,D
American University	M,D,O
The American University in Cairo	M,O
American University of Armenia	M
American University of Beirut	M,D
The American University of Paris	M
Anabaptist Mennonite Biblical Seminary	M,O
Baruch College of the City University of New York	M*
Baylor University	M

Boston University	M
Brigham Young University	M
Brock University	M
Brooklyn College of the City University of New York	M
Carleton University	M,D
The Catholic University of America	M,D
Central Connecticut State University	M
Central European University	M,D
Central Michigan University	M,O
Chapman University	M*
City College of the City University of New York	M
Claremont Graduate University	M,D
Cleveland State University	M
Columbia University	M
Concordia University Irvine	M
Cornell University	D
Dallas Baptist University	M
DePaul University	M
East Carolina University	M,O
Eastern University	M
Embry-Riddle Aeronautical University–Worldwide	M
Fairleigh Dickinson University, Metropolitan Campus	M
Florida International University	M,D
Florida State University	M
Fordham University	M,O
George Mason University	M
Georgetown University	M,D
The George Washington University	M,D
Georgia Institute of Technology	M
Harvard University	D*
Indiana University Bloomington	M
Indiana University South Bend	M,O
The Institute of World Politics	M,D,O
Instituto Tecnologico de Santo Domingo	M,O
Instituto Tecnológico y de Estudios Superiores de Monterrey, Campus Ciudad Obregón	M
International University in Geneva	M,D
Johns Hopkins University	M,D,O*
Kennesaw State University	M
Lebanese American University	M
Lesley University	M,D,O
Liberty University	M,D
Lipscomb University	M,O
London Metropolitan University	M,D
Marquette University	M,D
McMaster University	M,D
Middlebury Institute of International Studies at Monterey	M
Middle Tennessee State University	M
Missouri State University	M
Morgan State University	M
New England College	M
The New School	M
New York University	M,D*
North Carolina State University	M
Northeastern University	M
Northwestern University	M,D,O
Norwich University	M
Ohio University	M
Oklahoma State University	M,D,O
Old Dominion University	M,D
Penn State University Park	M*
Pepperdine University	M
Pontificia Universidad Catolica Madre y Maestra	M
Portland State University	M
Princeton University	M,D
Queen's University at Kingston	M,D
Regent's University London	M
Regent University	M
Richmond, The American International University in London	M
Rutgers University–Camden	M
Rutgers University–Newark	M,D
Rutgers University–New Brunswick	M,D
St. Mary's University (United States)	M,O
Salve Regina University	M,D,O
San Francisco State University	M
Schiller International University	M
Seton Hall University	M,O
Simon Fraser University	M
SIT Graduate Institute	M
Syracuse University	M
Teachers College, Columbia University	M,D,O
Texas A&M University	M,O
Texas State University	M
Troy University	M
Tufts University	M,D
United States International University–Africa	M
Universidad de las Americas, A.C.	M
Universidad Nacional Pedro Henriquez Urena	M
Université de Montréal	M,O
Université Laval	M,D
University of Bridgeport	M
The University of British Columbia	M
University of California, Berkeley	M
University of California, San Diego	M,D
University of California, Santa Barbara	M,D
University of California, Santa Cruz	D
University of Chicago	M
University of Colorado Denver	M,O
University of Connecticut	M
University of Delaware	M,D
University of Denver	M,D,O
University of Florida	M

University of Georgia	M,D
University of Hawaii at Manoa	O
University of Indianapolis	M
The University of Kansas	M
University of Kentucky	M
University of Maine	M
The University of Manchester	D
University of Massachusetts Boston	M
University of Miami	M,D
University of Michigan–Flint	M
The University of North Carolina at Chapel Hill	M
University of Northern British Columbia	M,D,O
University of North Georgia	M
University of North Texas	M,D,O
University of Notre Dame	M
University of Oklahoma	M*
University of Oregon	M*
University of Pennsylvania	M*
University of Pittsburgh	M,D,O*
University of San Diego	M
University of San Francisco	M
University of South Carolina	M,D
University of Southern California	M,D
University of South Florida	O
University of the Pacific	M,D
University of Toronto	M
University of Utah	M,D
University of Virginia	M,D
University of Washington	M,D
University of Waterloo	M,D
University of Wyoming	M
Virginia International University	M
Virginia Polytechnic Institute and State University	M,D
Walden University	M,D,O
Webster University	M
Western Michigan University	M,D
Wilfrid Laurier University	M,D
Yale University	M
York University	M

INTERNATIONAL AND COMPARATIVE EDUCATION

American University	M,O
The American University in Cairo	M
Andrews University	M
Bowling Green State University	M
California Baptist University	M
California State University, Dominguez Hills	M
The College of New Jersey	M,O
Drexel University	M,D*
East Carolina University	M,O
Florida International University	M,D,O
Florida State University	M,D,O
Gallaudet University	M,D,O
The George Washington University	M,D,O
Harvard University	M*
Indiana University Bloomington	M,D,O
Louisiana State University and Agricultural & Mechanical College	M,D
Loyola University Chicago	M,D
Middlebury Institute of International Studies at Monterey	M
New York University	M,D,O*
St. John's University (NY)	D
SIT Graduate Institute	M
Stanford University	M,D
Teachers College, Columbia University	M,D
University at Albany, State University of New York	M,D,O
University of Bridgeport	M,D,O
University of Massachusetts Amherst	M,D,O
University of Minnesota, Twin Cities Campus	M,D
University of Pennsylvania	M*
University of Pittsburgh	M,D*
University of San Francisco	M,D
University of South Africa	M,D
University of Wisconsin–Madison	M,D,O
Walden University	M,D,O
Wilkes University	M,D

INTERNATIONAL BUSINESS

Abilene Christian University	M
Amberton University	M
American Business & Technology University	M
American College Dublin	M
American InterContinental University Atlanta	M
American InterContinental University Online	M
The American University in Dubai	M
The American University of Paris	M
Anaheim University	M,D,O
Argosy University, Atlanta	M,D
Argosy University, Chicago	M,D
Argosy University, Hawai'i	M,D,O
Argosy University, Los Angeles	M,D
Argosy University, Northern Virginia	M,D,O
Argosy University, Orange County	M,D,O
Argosy University, Phoenix	M,D
Argosy University, Seattle	M,D
Argosy University, Tampa	M,D
Argosy University, Twin Cities	M,D
Arizona State University at the Tempe campus	M,D
Ashland University	M
Ashworth College	M
Assumption College	M,O
Azusa Pacific University	M
Baldwin Wallace University	M
Barry University	O

Baruch College of the City University of New York	M,D*
Benedictine University	M
Boston University	M
Brandeis University	M,D
Brandman University	M
Brooklyn College of the City University of New York	M
California Intercontinental University	M,D
California Lutheran University	M,O
California State University, Fullerton	M
California State University, Los Angeles	M
California State University, San Bernardino	M
California University of Management and Sciences	M,D
Canisius College	M
Central European University	M,D
Central Michigan University	M,O
Christian Brothers University	M,O
City University of Seattle	M,O
Clarkson University	M,O
Clayton State University	M
Colorado State University–Global Campus	M
Columbia University	M
Concordia University Wisconsin	M
Copenhagen Business School	M,D
Daemen College	M
Dallas Baptist University	M
Delaware Valley University	M
DePaul University	M,D
Duke University	M,O
D'Youville College	M
Eastern Michigan University	M,O
Embry-Riddle Aeronautical University–Worldwide	M
Emory University	M
ESSEC Business School	M,D
Fairleigh Dickinson University, Florham Campus	M,O
Fairleigh Dickinson University, Metropolitan Campus	M
Florida Atlantic University	M
Florida Institute of Technology	M
Florida International University	M,D
Franklin University Switzerland	M
George Mason University	M
Georgetown University	M,O
The George Washington University	M,D
Georgia Institute of Technology	M
Georgia State University	M
Golden Gate University	M,D,O
Goldey-Beacom College	M
Hallmark University	M
Harding University	M
Hawai'i Pacific University	M
HEC Montreal	M,D
Hofstra University	M,O
Hope International University	M
Houston Baptist University	M
Howard University	M
Hult International Business School (United States)	M
IGlobal University	M
Indiana Tech	D
Instituto Tecnologico de Santo Domingo	M,O
Instituto Tecnológico y de Estudios Superiores de Monterrey, Campus Central de Veracruz	M
Instituto Tecnológico y de Estudios Superiores de Monterrey, Campus Chihuahua	M,O
Instituto Tecnológico y de Estudios Superiores de Monterrey, Campus Ciudad de México	M,D
Instituto Tecnológico y de Estudios Superiores de Monterrey, Campus Cuernavaca	M
Instituto Tecnológico y de Estudios Superiores de Monterrey, Campus Irapuato	M,D
Instituto Tecnológico y de Estudios Superiores de Monterrey, Campus Monterrey	M
Inter American University of Puerto Rico, Metropolitan Campus	M,D
Inter American University of Puerto Rico, San Germán Campus	M,D
International University in Geneva	M,D
The International University of Monaco	M
Iona College	M,O
John Brown University	M
Kean University	M
Keiser University	M,D
Lake Forest Graduate School of Management	M
La Salle University	M,O
Lenoir-Rhyne University	M
Lewis University	M
Liberty University	M,D
Lincoln University (CA)	M,D
Long Island University–LIU Post	M
Loyola University Chicago	M
Madonna University	M
Maine Maritime Academy	M
Marconi International University	M,D
Marquette University	M,O
McGill University	M,D,O
McKendree University	M
Midwest University	M
Milwaukee School of Engineering	M
National American University (TX)	M,D
National University	M,O

*M—masters degree; D—doctorate; O—other advanced degree; *—Close-Up and/or Display*

Nebraska Christian College of Hope International University	M
Newman University	M
New Mexico Highlands University	M
New York University	M,D*
Niagara University	M
Northeastern University	M
Northern Arizona University	M
Northwestern University	M,D
Northwest University	M
Norwich University	M
Nova Southeastern University	M
Oakland University	M,O
Oklahoma Christian University	M
Oklahoma State University	M,D
Old Dominion University	M
Oral Roberts University	M
Pace University	M,O
Pacific States University	M,O
Park University	M,O
Pittsburg State University	M
Point Park University	M
Polytechnic University of Puerto Rico	M
Polytechnic University of Puerto Rico, Miami Campus	M
Polytechnic University of Puerto Rico, Orlando Campus	M
Pontifical Catholic University of Puerto Rico	M
Pontificia Universidad Catolica Madre y Maestra	M
Portland State University	M
Providence College	M
Purdue University	M
Purdue University Global	M
Queen's University at Kingston	M
Regent's University London	M
Rochester Institute of Technology	M
Rockhurst University	M,O
Rollins College	M
Rutgers University–Newark	D
St. John's University (NY)	M,O
Saint Joseph's University	M,O
Saint Louis University	M,D*
Saint Peter's University	M
St. Thomas University	M,O
Salem International University	M
San Francisco State University	M
San Ignacio University	M
Schiller International University (United States)	M
Schiller International University (Germany)	M
Schiller International University	M
Schiller International University (Spain)	M
Seton Hall University	M,O
SIT Graduate Institute	M
Southeastern University (FL)	M,D
Southern New Hampshire University	M,D,O
Southern Oregon University	M,O
State University of New York Empire State College	M
Stevens Institute of Technology	M
Suffolk University	M
Temple University	M,D*
Tennessee Technological University	M
Texas A&M International University	M,D
Texas A&M University–Corpus Christi	M
Thomas Edison State University	M
Tiffin University	M
Trident University International	M,D
Trinity Western University	M
Tufts University	M,D
Tulane University	M,D
United States International University–Africa	M
Universidad Autonoma de Guadalajara	M,D
Universidad Metropolitana	M
Université de Sherbrooke	M
Université du Québec, École nationale d'administration publique	M,O
Université Laval	M,O
University at Buffalo, the State University of New York	M,D
University of Alberta	M
University of Baltimore	M
University of Bridgeport	O
University of California, San Diego	M
University of Chicago	M,O
University of Colorado Denver	M
University of Dallas	M,D
University of Florida	M,D
University of Hawaii at Manoa	M,D
University of Houston–Downtown	M
University of Houston–Victoria	M
University of Kentucky	M
University of La Verne	M
University of Lethbridge	M,D
University of Louisiana at Lafayette	M
University of Louisville	M
The University of Manchester	M
University of Mary Hardin-Baylor	M
University of Massachusetts Boston	M
University of Miami	M,D
University of Michigan–Flint	M,O
University of New Brunswick Saint John	M
University of New Haven	M
University of New Mexico	M
University of North Alabama	M
The University of North Carolina Wilmington	M
University of North Florida	M

University of Pennsylvania	M*
University of Phoenix–Bay Area Campus	M,D
University of Phoenix–Central Valley Campus	M
University of Phoenix–Dallas Campus	M
University of Phoenix–Hawaii Campus	M
University of Phoenix–Houston Campus	M
University of Phoenix–Las Vegas Campus	M
University of Phoenix–Online Campus	M,O
University of Phoenix–Phoenix Campus	M,O
University of Phoenix–Sacramento Valley Campus	M
University of Phoenix–San Antonio Campus	M
University of Phoenix–San Diego Campus	M
University of Pittsburgh	O*
University of Puerto Rico–Río Piedras	M,D
University of Regina	M,O
University of St. Thomas (TX)	M
University of San Francisco	M
The University of Scranton	M
University of South Carolina	M
The University of Tampa	M,O
The University of Texas at Dallas	M
The University of Texas at El Paso	M,D,O
University of the West	M
The University of Toledo	M
University of Virginia	M,D
University of Washington	M,D,O
The University of Western Ontario	M,D
University of Wisconsin–Oshkosh	M
Vancouver Island University	M
Villanova University	M
Virginia International University	M,O
Viterbo University	M
Walden University	M,D,O
Walsh College of Accountancy and Business Administration	M
Warner University	M
Wayland Baptist University	M,D
Webber International University	M
Webster University	M
Wilkes University	M
Xavier University	M*
York University	M,D

INTERNATIONAL DEVELOPMENT

American University	M,D,O
Andrews University	M
Athabasca University	M
Clark University	M
Dalhousie University	M
Duke University	M
Eastern University	M
Fordham University	M,O
Georgetown University	M
The George Washington University	M,D
Harvard University	M*
Hope International University	M
Indiana University Bloomington	M,D,O
Johns Hopkins University	M,D,O*
Marymount California University	M
McGill University	M,D,O
Middlebury Institute of International Studies at Monterey	M
Norwich University	M
Ohio University	M
Old Dominion University	M,D
Rutgers University–Camden	M
Saint Mary's University (Canada)	M,O
St. Mary's University (United States)	M,O
Saint Mary's University of Minnesota	M
Tufts University	M
Tulane University	M,D
University of California, San Diego	M
University of Denver	M,D,O
University of Florida	M,D,O
University of Guelph	M,D
University of Hawaii at Manoa	M,D,O
The University of Manchester	M,D
University of Massachusetts Boston	M,D
University of Minnesota, Twin Cities Campus	M
University of New Brunswick Fredericton	M
University of New Mexico	M,D
University of Ottawa	M
University of Pittsburgh	M,D*
University of San Francisco	M
University of Southern Mississippi	M,D
Walden University	M,D,O

INTERNATIONAL ECONOMICS

American University	M,D,O
Baruch College of the City University of New York	M*
Claremont Graduate University	M,D,O
Cleveland State University	M
Fordham University	M,D,O
Fordham University	M,D,O
The Institute of World Politics	M,D,O
Johns Hopkins University	M,D,O*
The New School	M,D
Pace University	O
University of California, San Diego	M
University of New Mexico	M,D
Valparaiso University	M
Wayne State University	M,D
Wichita State University	M
Wilfrid Laurier University	M

Yale University	M

INTERNATIONAL HEALTH

Arizona State University at the Tempe campus	M,D,O
A.T. Still University	M,D,O
Boston University	M,D
Brandeis University	M,D
Cedarville University	M,D
Central Michigan University	M,D,O
Clark University	M
Clemson University	M,D,O
The College of New Jersey	M
Duke University	M
East Tennessee State University	M,D,O
Emory University	M
Endicott College	M,O
George Mason University	M,O
Georgetown University	M,D
The George Washington University	M,D
Harvard University	M,D*
Indiana University–Purdue University Indianapolis	M,D,O
Johns Hopkins University	M,D*
Liberty University	M
Loma Linda University	M
Medical University of South Carolina	M
National University of Natural Medicine	M
New York Institute of Technology	O
New York Medical College	M,D,O
New York University	M,D*
Northwestern University	M
Oregon State University	M,D
Park University	M,O
St. Catherine University	M
San Diego State University	M,D
Seton Hall University	M,O
Simon Fraser University	M,D,O
Syracuse University	M
Trident University International	M,D,O
Tulane University	M,D
Uniformed Services University of the Health Sciences	M,D*
University of Alberta	M,D
University of California, Riverside	M,D
University of California, San Diego	D
University of Colorado Denver	M
University of Denver	M,D,O
University of Florida	M,D
University of Maryland, Baltimore	M,D,O
University of Michigan	M,D
University of Minnesota, Twin Cities Campus	M,D
University of Missouri	M,O
University of Northern Colorado	M
University of North Texas Health Science Center at Fort Worth	M,D,O
University of Pennsylvania	M*
University of Pittsburgh	M,D,O*
University of Southern California	M,O
University of South Florida	O
The University of Toledo	M,O
University of Vermont	M,O
University of Washington	M,D
Walden University	M,O
Washington University in St. Louis	M,D
William James College	M,D,O
Yale University	M,D

INTERNATIONAL TRADE POLICY

Baruch College of the City University of New York	M*
The George Washington University	M
Middlebury Institute of International Studies at Monterey	M
University at Buffalo, the State University of New York	M,D
Valparaiso University	M

INTERNET AND INTERACTIVE MULTIMEDIA

Academy of Art University	M
Agnes Scott College	M
Alfred University	M
Ball State University	M
Boston University	M,O
Brandeis University	M
Brooklyn College of the City University of New York	M
California State University, East Bay	M
Champlain College	M
College of Saint Elizabeth	M
Concordia University (Canada)	M,D,O
DePaul University	M,D
Elon University	M
Fairfield University	M,O
Full Sail University	M
Georgetown University	M
Georgia Institute of Technology	M,D
Ithaca College	M
Kutztown University of Pennsylvania	M
Liberty University	M
Lindenwood University	M
Lindenwood University–Belleville	M
Lindsey Wilson College	M
London Metropolitan University	M,D
Long Island University–LIU Post	M
Louisiana State University and Agricultural & Mechanical College	M
Lynn University	M,O
Minneapolis College of Art and Design	M
Montclair State University	M
Mount Mary University	M
National University	M
New Mexico Highlands University	M
The New School	M

New York University	M*
Northeastern University	M
Northwestern University	M
The Ohio State University	M
Ohio University	M
Pace University	M
Pratt Institute	M
Quinnipiac University	M
Rochester Institute of Technology	O
Rocky Mountain College of Art + Design	M
Sam Houston State University	M
San Diego State University	M
Savannah College of Art and Design	M
School of Visual Arts (NY)	M
Southern New Hampshire University	M,D,O
State University of New York at Oswego	M
Stonehill College	M
Texas Woman's University	M
Thomas Jefferson University	M
Touro College	M
Towson University	M,O
Universidad Autonoma de Guadalajara	M,D
University of Advancing Technology	M
The University of British Columbia	M
University of California, Santa Cruz	M,D
University of Chicago	M
University of Colorado Boulder	D
University of Miami	M
University of Montana	M
University of North Texas	M,D,O
University of Pennsylvania	M,O*
University of Southern California	M,D,O
University of South Florida	M,O
The University of Tennessee	M
The University of Texas at Dallas	M,D
University of the Sacred Heart	M,O
University of Utah	M,D
Virginia Polytechnic Institute and State University	M,D
Walla Walla University	M
Webster University	M
Wilmington University	M
Worcester Polytechnic Institute	M

INTERNET ENGINEERING

Dalhousie University	M,D
New Jersey Institute of Technology	M,D
Wilmington University	M

INVESTMENT MANAGEMENT

Alaska Pacific University	M,O
Creighton University	M,D
Fordham University	M,D
The George Washington University	M,D
Hofstra University	M,O
Johns Hopkins University	M,O*
Lincoln University (CA)	M,D
Loyola University Maryland	M
Manhattanville College	M,O
Marywood University	M
Midwest University	M,D
New York University	M*
Pace University	M,O
Regent University	M,D,O
Sacred Heart University	M,D,O
Saint Mary's College of California	M
Southern New Hampshire University	M,D,O
Temple University	M,O*
University of Houston–Downtown	M
University of Notre Dame	M
University of Wisconsin–Madison	D
University of Wisconsin–Milwaukee	M,O*
Walsh College of Accountancy and Business Administration	M

ITALIAN

Binghamton University, State University of New York	M
Boston College	M
Brown University	D
Central Connecticut State University	M,O
Columbia University	M,D
Cornell University	D
DePaul University	M
Drew University	M,D,O
Duke University	D
Florida State University	M
The Graduate Center, City University of New York	M,D
Harvard University	M,D*
Hunter College of the City University of New York	M
Indiana University Bloomington	M,D
Johns Hopkins University	M,D*
McGill University	M,D
Middlebury College	M,D
New York University	M,D,O*
Northwestern University	D,O
The Ohio State University	M,D
Queens College of the City University of New York	M
Rutgers University–New Brunswick	M,D
San Francisco State University	M
Stanford University	M,D
Stony Brook University, State University of New York	M
University of Alberta	M,D
University of California, Berkeley	D
University of California, Los Angeles	M,D
University of Chicago	D
University of Georgia	M,D
University of Illinois at Urbana–Champaign	M,D

Institution	Degree
University of Massachusetts Amherst	M
University of Michigan	D
The University of North Carolina at Chapel Hill	M,D
University of Notre Dame	M
University of Oregon	M
University of Pennsylvania	M,D*
University of Pittsburgh	M,D*
University of South Africa	M,D
The University of Tennessee	D
The University of Texas at Austin	M,D
University of Toronto	M,D
University of Victoria	M
University of Washington	M,D
University of Wisconsin–Madison	M,D
Wayne State University	M,D
Yale University	D

JAPANESE

Institution	Degree
Arizona State University at the Tempe campus	M
Columbia University	M,D
DePaul University	M
Harvard University	D*
Indiana University Bloomington	M,D
Kent State University	M,D
New York University	M,D,O*
The Ohio State University	M,D
Portland State University	M
Purdue University	M
San Francisco State University	M
Stanford University	M,D
University of Alberta	M
University of California, Berkeley	D
University of California, Irvine	M,D
University of Colorado Boulder	M,D
University of Hawaii at Manoa	M,D,O
The University of Manchester	D
University of Massachusetts Amherst	M
University of Oregon	M,D
University of Pittsburgh	M*
University of Washington	M
University of Wisconsin–Madison	M,D
Washington University in St. Louis	M,D

JEWISH STUDIES

Institution	Degree
Academy for Jewish Religion California	M
American Jewish University	M
Biola University	M,D,O
Brandeis University	M,D
Brooklyn College of the City University of New York	M
Central Yeshiva Tomchei Tmimim-Lubavitch	M
Columbia University	M,D
Concordia University (Canada)	M
Cornell University	M,D
Criswell College	M
Dallas Theological Seminary	M,D,O
Graduate Theological Union	M,D,O
Gratz College	M,O
Harvard University	M,D*
Hebrew College	M,O
Hebrew Union College–Jewish Institute of Religion (NY)	M
Indiana University Bloomington	M
The Jewish Theological Seminary	M,D
McGill University	M
New York University	M,D*
Reconstructionist Rabbinical College	M,D,O
Rice University	D
Rutgers University–New Brunswick	M,O
Seton Hall University	M,O
Southern Evangelical Seminary	M,D,O
Spertus Institute for Jewish Learning and Leadership	M,D
Telshe Yeshiva–Chicago	O
Touro College	M
Towson University	M,O
University of California, San Diego	M,D
University of Connecticut	M,D
University of Florida	M,D
University of Maryland, College Park	M
University of Michigan	M,D,O
University of St. Michael's College	M,D,O
University of Wisconsin–Madison	M,D
Washington University in St. Louis	M
Yeshiva University	M,D

JOURNALISM

Institution	Degree
American University	M
The American University in Cairo	M,O
Arizona State University at the Tempe campus	M,D
Arkansas State University	M
Arkansas Tech University	M
Ball State University	M
Baylor University	M
Boston University	M
California State University, Northridge	M
Carleton University	M
Clarion University of Pennsylvania	M
Columbia University	M
Concordia University (Canada)	M,O
CUNY Craig Newmark Graduate School of Journalism	M
DePaul University	M
Florida Agricultural and Mechanical University	M
Florida International University	M
Full Sail University	M
Georgetown University	M,D
Harvard University	M,O*
Hofstra University	M
Iowa State University of Science and Technology	M
Kansas State University	M
Kent State University	M
Lindenwood University	M
Marquette University	M,O
Marshall University	M,O
Michigan State University	M
Morgan State University	M
Murray State University	M
National University	M
New York University	M,D,O*
Northeastern University	M
Northwestern University	M
Ohio University	M,D
Point Park University	M
Quinnipiac University	M
Regent University	M,D
Sacred Heart University	M
South Dakota State University	M
Southeastern Louisiana University	M
Stony Brook University, State University of New York	M,O
Syracuse University	M
Temple University	M*
Université Laval	O
The University of Alabama	M
The University of Arizona	M
University of Arkansas	M
The University of British Columbia	M
University of California, Berkeley	M
University of Colorado Boulder	M,D
University of Florida	M,D
University of Georgia	M
University of Illinois at Springfield	M
University of Illinois at Urbana–Champaign	M
The University of Iowa	M,D
The University of Kansas	M,D
University of King's College	M
University of Maryland, College Park	M,D
University of Memphis	M,O
University of Miami	M,D
University of Mississippi	M
University of Missouri	M,D
University of Montana	M
University of Nebraska–Lincoln	M
University of Nevada, Las Vegas	M
University of Nevada, Reno	M
The University of North Carolina at Chapel Hill	M,D,O
University of North Texas	M,D,O
University of Oregon	M,D
University of Puerto Rico–Río Piedras	M
University of Regina	M
University of South Carolina	M,D
University of Southern California	M
University of South Florida	M,O
University of South Florida, St. Petersburg	M
The University of Tennessee	M,D
The University of Texas at Austin	M,D
The University of Western Ontario	M
University of Wisconsin–Madison	M,D
Virginia Commonwealth University	M
Wayne State University	M,D,O
West Virginia University	M,O

KINESIOLOGY AND MOVEMENT STUDIES

Institution	Degree
Alabama Agricultural and Mechanical University	M
A.T. Still University	M,D,O
Azusa Pacific University	M
Ball State University	M,D,O
Barry University	M
Baylor University	M,D
Boise State University	M
Bowling Green State University	M
Brooklyn College of the City University of New York	M
California State Polytechnic University, Pomona	M
California State University, Chico	M
California State University, Fresno	M
California State University, Long Beach	M
California State University, Los Angeles	M,O
California State University, Northridge	M
Canisius College	M
Columbia University	M,D
Dalhousie University	M
Dallas Baptist University	M
East Carolina University	M,D,O
Eastern Michigan University	M
East Tennessee State University	M
East Texas Baptist University	M
Fresno Pacific University	M
Georgia College & State University	M
Georgia Southern University	M
Georgia State University	D
Hardin-Simmons University	M
Houston Baptist University	M
Humboldt State University	M
Indiana University Bloomington	M,D
Indiana University–Purdue University Indianapolis	M,O
Inter American University of Puerto Rico, San Germán Campus	M
Iowa State University of Science and Technology	M,D
Jacksonville University	M
James Madison University	M
Kansas State University	M,D
Lakehead University	M
Lamar University	M
Louisiana State University and Agricultural & Mechanical College	M,D
Louisiana Tech University	M,D,O
McDaniel College	M
McGill University	M,D,O
McMaster University	M,D
Memorial University of Newfoundland	M
Michigan State University	M,D
Michigan Technological University	M
Mississippi College	M
Mississippi State University	M
Missouri State University	M
New York University	M,D,O*
Northeastern State University	M
Northwestern University	D
The Ohio State University	M,D
Old Dominion University	M,D
Oregon State University	M,D
Penn State University Park	M,D,O*
Point Loma Nazarene University	M
Prairie View A&M University	M
Purdue University	M,D
Saint Mary's College of California	M
Sam Houston State University	M
San Diego State University	M
San Francisco State University	M
San Jose State University	M
Sarah Lawrence College	M
Simon Fraser University	M
Sonoma State University	M
Southeastern Louisiana University	M
Southeastern University (FL)	M,D
Southern Arkansas University–Magnolia	M
Southern Illinois University Carbondale	M
Southern Illinois University Edwardsville	M
Southwestern Oklahoma State University	M
Stephen F. Austin State University	M
Syracuse University	M,D,O
Tarleton State University	M
Teachers College, Columbia University	M,D
Temple University	M,D*
Tennessee Technological University	M,D
Texas A&M University	M,D
Texas A&M University–Commerce	M,D,O
Texas A&M University–Corpus Christi	M,D
Texas A&M University–Kingsville	M
Texas A&M University–San Antonio	M
Texas Christian University	M
Texas Tech University	M
Université de Montréal	M,D,O
Université de Sherbrooke	M,O
Université du Québec à Montréal	M
Université Laval	M,D
The University of Alabama	M,D
University of Alberta	M,D
University of Arkansas	M,D
The University of British Columbia	M,D
University of Calgary	M,D
University of Central Arkansas	M
University of Central Florida	M
University of Central Missouri	M,D,O
University of Colorado Boulder	M,D
University of Delaware	M
University of Florida	M,D
University of Georgia	M,D
University of Hawaii at Manoa	M,D
University of Houston	M,D
University of Idaho	M
University of Illinois at Chicago	M,D
University of Illinois at Urbana–Champaign	M,D
University of Kentucky	M,D
University of Lethbridge	M,D
University of Maine	M,D,O
University of Mary	M
University of Maryland, College Park	M,D
University of Massachusetts Amherst	M,D
University of Michigan	M,D
University of Minnesota, Twin Cities Campus	M,D
University of Mississippi	M,D
University of Nebraska at Omaha	M,D
University of Nevada, Las Vegas	M,D
University of New Hampshire	M,O
University of North Alabama	M
The University of North Carolina at Chapel Hill	D
The University of North Carolina at Charlotte	M
The University of North Carolina at Greensboro	M,D
University of North Dakota	M
University of Northern Iowa	M
University of North Georgia	M
University of North Texas	M,D,O
University of Ottawa	M
University of Puerto Rico–Mayagüez	M
University of Regina	M,D
University of Saskatchewan	M,D
University of South Alabama	M
University of South Dakota	M
University of Southern California	M,D
The University of Tennessee	M,D
The University of Texas at Arlington	M,D
The University of Texas at Austin	M,D
The University of Texas at El Paso	M
The University of Texas at San Antonio	M
The University of Texas at Tyler	M
The University of Texas of the Permian Basin	M
The University of Texas Rio Grande Valley	M
University of the Incarnate Word	M,D
University of Toronto	M,D
The University of Tulsa	M
University of Utah	M,D
University of Victoria	M
University of Virginia	M,D
University of Waterloo	M,D
The University of Western Ontario	M
University of Windsor	M
University of Wisconsin–Madison	M,D
University of Wisconsin–Milwaukee	M,D*
University of Wyoming	M
Utah State University	M
Washington University in St. Louis	D
Wayne State University	M,D
West Chester University of Pennsylvania	M,O
Western Illinois University	M
Wilfrid Laurier University	M
York University	M,D

LANDSCAPE ARCHITECTURE

Institution	Degree
Academy of Art University	M
Arizona State University at the Tempe campus	M,D
Auburn University	M
Ball State University	M
Boston Architectural College	M
California State Polytechnic University, Pomona	M
City College of the City University of New York	M
Colorado State University	M,D
Columbia University	M
The Conway School	M
Cornell University	M
Florida Agricultural and Mechanical University	M
Florida International University	M
Harvard University	M,D*
Illinois Institute of Technology	M,D
Iowa State University of Science and Technology	M
Kansas State University	M
Kent State University	M
Louisiana State University and Agricultural & Mechanical College	M
Mississippi State University	M
Morgan State University	M
North Carolina State University	M
North Dakota State University	M
The Ohio State University	M,D
Oklahoma State University	M
Penn State University Park	M,D*
Polytechnic University of Puerto Rico	M
Pontificia Universidad Catolica Madre y Maestra	M
Rhode Island School of Design	M
Rutgers University–New Brunswick	M
State University of New York College of Environmental Science and Forestry	M
Texas A&M University	M,D
Texas Tech University	M
The University of Arizona	M
The University of British Columbia	M
University of Calgary	M,D
University of California, Berkeley	M,D,O
University of Colorado Denver	M
University of Connecticut	M,D
University of Florida	M,D
University of Georgia	M
University of Guelph	M
University of Idaho	M
University of Illinois at Urbana–Champaign	M,D
The University of Manchester	M,D
University of Manitoba	M
University of Maryland, College Park	M
University of Massachusetts Amherst	M
University of Michigan	M
University of Minnesota, Twin Cities Campus	M
University of New Mexico	M
University of Oregon	M,D
University of Pennsylvania	M,O*
University of Southern California	M
The University of Tennessee	M
The University of Texas at Arlington	M
The University of Texas at Austin	M
University of Toronto	M
University of Virginia	M
University of Washington	M
University of Wisconsin–Madison	M,D

*M—masters degree; D—doctorate; O—other advanced degree; *—Close-Up and/or Display*

Utah State University	M
Virginia Polytechnic Institute and State University	M,D
Washington State University	M
Washington University in St. Louis	M
West Virginia University	M,D

LATIN AMERICAN STUDIES

American University	M,O
Brown University	M,D
California State University, Los Angeles	M
Centro de Estudios Avanzados de Puerto Rico y el Caribe	M,D
College of Staten Island of the City University of New York	M
Columbia University	M,D
Cornell University	M,D
Duke University	M
Georgetown University	M
The George Washington University	M,O
Georgia State University	M,O
Indiana University Bloomington	M
La Salle University	M,O
Michigan State University	D
New York University	M*
Northeastern Illinois University	M
The Ohio State University	M
Ohio University	M
San Diego State University	M
Simon Fraser University	M,O
Texas Christian University	M
Tulane University	M,D
University at Albany, State University of New York	M,D,O
The University of Arizona	M
University of California, Los Angeles	M
University of California, San Diego	M
University of California, Santa Barbara	M
University of Chicago	M
University of Connecticut	M
University of Florida	M,O
University of Illinois at Chicago	M
University of Illinois at Urbana–Champaign	M
The University of Kansas	M,O
University of Louisiana at Lafayette	M
The University of Manchester	D
University of Massachusetts Dartmouth	M,D
University of Miami	M
University of New Mexico	M,D
The University of North Carolina at Chapel Hill	M,D,O
The University of North Carolina at Charlotte	M,D,O
University of Notre Dame	M
University of Pittsburgh	O*
University of Southern California	D
University of South Florida	M,D,O
The University of Texas at Austin	M
The University of Texas at Dallas	M
University of Utah	M
University of Wisconsin–Madison	M,D
University of Wisconsin–Milwaukee	M,O*
Vanderbilt University	M*
Yale University	D

LAW

Abraham Lincoln University	D
Albany Law School	M,D
Alliant International University–San Francisco	D
American University	M,O
The American University in Cairo	M,O
American University of Armenia	M
The American University of Paris	M
Appalachian School of Law	D
Arizona State University at the Tempe campus	M,D
Atlanta's John Marshall Law School	M,D
Ave Maria School of Law	D
Barry University	D
Baylor University	D
Belmont University	D
Boston College	D
Boston University	M,D
Brigham Young University	M,D
Brooklyn Law School	M,D
California Western School of Law	D
Campbell University	D
Capital University	M,D
Case Western Reserve University	M,D
The Catholic University of America	M,D
Central European University	M,D
Champlain College	M
Chapman University	M,D*
Charleston School of Law	D
City University of New York School of Law	M,D
Cleveland State University	M,D,O
The College of William and Mary	M,D
Columbia University	M,D
Concordia University (United States)	D
Concord Law School	D
Cornell University	M,D
Creighton University	M,D,O
Dalhousie University	M,D
DePaul University	M,D
Drake University	M,D
Drexel University	M,D*
Duke University	M,D
Dunlap-Stone University	M
Duquesne University	M,D
Elon University	D
Emory University	M,D,O
Empire College	M,D

Faulkner University	D
Florida Agricultural and Mechanical University	D
Florida Coastal School of Law	D
Florida International University	M,D
Florida State University	M,D
Fordham University	M,D
Friends University	M
George Mason University	M,D
Georgetown University	M,D
The George Washington University	M,D
Georgia State University	D
Golden Gate University	D
Gonzaga University	D
Harvard University	M,D*
Hofstra University	M,D,O
Howard University	M,D
Humphreys University	D
Illinois Institute of Technology	M,D
Indiana University Bloomington	M,D,O
Indiana University–Purdue University Indianapolis	M,D,O
Instituto Tecnológico y de Estudios Superiores de Monterrey, Campus Ciudad de México	O
Inter American University of Puerto Rico School of Law	D
John F. Kennedy University	D
The John Marshall Law School	M,D
The Judge Advocate General's School, U.S. Army	M
Lewis & Clark College	M,D
Liberty University	M
Lincoln Memorial University	D
London Metropolitan University	M,D
Louisiana State University and Agricultural & Mechanical College	M,D
Loyola Marymount University	M,D
Loyola University Chicago	M,D,O
Loyola University New Orleans	M,D
Marquette University	D
Massachusetts School of Law at Andover	D
McGill University	M,D,O
Mercer University	M,D
Michigan State University College of Law	M,D
Mississippi College	D,O
Mitchell Hamline School of Law	M,D
Montclair State University	M,O
New England Law–Boston	M,D
New York Law School	M,D
New York University	M,D,O*
North Carolina Central University	D
Northeastern University	M,D
Northern Illinois University	D
Northern Kentucky University	D
Northwestern University	M,D
Nova Southeastern University	M,D
Ohio Northern University	M,D
The Ohio State University	M,D
Oklahoma City University	M,D
Pace University	M,D
Penn State University–Dickinson Law	M,D
Penn State University Park	M,D*
Pontifical Catholic University of Puerto Rico	D
Pontificia Universidad Catolica Madre y Maestra	M
Purdue University Global	M
Queen's University at Kingston	M,D
Quinnipiac University	M,D
Regent University	M,D
Roger Williams University	M,D
Rutgers University–Camden	D
Rutgers University–Newark	D
St. John's University (NY)	M,D
Saint Joseph's University	M,O
Saint Louis University	M,D*
St. Mary's University (United States)	M,D
St. Thomas University	M,D
Samford University	M,D
San Joaquin College of Law	D
The Santa Barbara and Ventura Colleges of Law–Santa Barbara	M,D
The Santa Barbara and Ventura Colleges of Law–Ventura	M,D
Santa Clara University	M,D,O
Seattle University	M,D
Seton Hall University	M,D
Southern Illinois University Carbondale	M,D
Southern Methodist University	M,D
Southern University and Agricultural and Mechanical College	D
South Texas College of Law Houston	M,D
Southwestern Law School	M,D
Stanford University	M,D
Stetson University	M,D
Suffolk University	M,D
Syracuse University	M,D
Taft University System	M,D
Temple University	M,D,O*
Texas A&M University	M,D
Texas Southern University	D
Texas Tech University	D
Thomas Jefferson School of Law	M,D
Touro College	M,D
Trinity International University	M,D
Tufts University	M,D
Tulane University	M,D
Universidad Autonoma de Guadalajara	M,D
Universidad Central del Este	D
Universidad Iberoamericana	D
Université de Montréal	M,D,O
Université de Sherbrooke	M,D,O
Université du Québec à Montréal	O
Université Laval	M,D,O

University at Buffalo, the State University of New York	M,D
The University of Akron	M,D
The University of Alabama	M,D
University of Alberta	M,D
The University of Arizona	M,D
University of Arkansas	M,D
University of Arkansas at Little Rock	D
University of Baltimore	M,D
The University of British Columbia	M,D
University of Calgary	M,D,O
University of California, Berkeley	M,D
University of California, Davis	M,D
University of California, Hastings College of the Law	M,D
University of California, Irvine	D
University of California, Los Angeles	M,D
University of Chicago	M,D
University of Cincinnati	M,D
University of Colorado Boulder	D
University of Connecticut	D
University of Dayton	M
University of Denver	M,D,O
University of Detroit Mercy	D
University of Florida	M,D
University of Georgia	M,D
University of Hawaii at Manoa	M,D,O
University of Houston	M,D
University of Idaho	M,D
University of Illinois at Urbana–Champaign	M,D
The University of Iowa	M,D
The University of Kansas	M,D
University of Kentucky	D
University of La Verne	D
University of Louisville	D
University of Maine	D
The University of Manchester	M,D
University of Manitoba	M
University of Maryland, Baltimore	M,D
University of Maryland, College Park	
University of Massachusetts Dartmouth	D
University of Memphis	D
University of Miami	M,D
University of Michigan	M,D
University of Minnesota, Twin Cities Campus	M,D
University of Mississippi	M,D
University of Missouri	M,D
University of Missouri–Kansas City	M,D
University of Montana	D
University of Nebraska–Lincoln	M,D
University of Nevada, Las Vegas	M,D
University of New Hampshire	M,D,O
University of New Mexico	D
University of North Alabama	M
The University of North Carolina at Chapel Hill	M,D
University of North Dakota	D
University of North Texas at Dallas	D
University of Notre Dame	M,D
University of Oklahoma	M,D*
University of Oregon	M,D
University of Ottawa	M,D
University of Pennsylvania	M,D*
University of Pittsburgh	M*
University of Puerto Rico–Río Piedras	M,D
University of Richmond	D
University of St. Thomas (MN)	M,D
University of San Diego	M,D,O
University of San Francisco	D
University of Saskatchewan	M,D
University of South Africa	M,D
University of South Carolina	D
University of South Dakota	D
University of Southern California	M,D
The University of Tennessee	D
The University of Texas at Austin	M,D
The University of Texas at Dallas	M,D
University of the District of Columbia	M,D
University of the Pacific	M,D
The University of Toledo	M,D,O
University of Toronto	M,D
The University of Tulsa	M,D,O
University of Utah	M,D
University of Victoria	M,D
University of Virginia	M,D
University of Washington	M,D
The University of Western Ontario	M,D,O
University of West Los Angeles	D
University of Wisconsin–Madison	M,D
University of Wyoming	D
Vanderbilt University	M,D*
Vermont Law School	D
Villanova University	M,D
Wake Forest University	M,D
Walden University	M,D,O
Washburn University	M,D
Washington and Lee University	D
Washington University in St. Louis	M,D
Wayne State University	M,D
Western Michigan University Thomas M. Cooley Law School	M,D
Western New England University	M,D
Western State College of Law at Argosy University	D
West Virginia University	M,D
Widener University	M,D
Willamette University	M,D
Yale University	M,D
Yeshiva University	M,D
York University	M,D

LEGAL AND JUSTICE STUDIES

Arizona State University at the Tempe campus	M,D,O
Auburn University at Montgomery	M
Binghamton University, State University of New York	M,D
Brock University	M
California University of Pennsylvania	M
Campbellsville University	M
Capital University	M
Carleton University	M,O
Case Western Reserve University	M
The Catholic University of America	M,D,O
Central European University	M,D
Columbia University	M,D
The George Washington University	M,D,O
Georgian Court University	M,O
Golden Gate University	M,D
Governors State University	M
Harrison Middleton University	M,D
Harvard University	D*
Hodges University	M
Hofstra University	M,D,O
Illinois Institute of Technology	M,D
Indiana University South Bend	M,O
John Jay College of Criminal Justice of the City University of New York	M,D
Liberty University	M
Loyola University Chicago	M,O
Marlboro College	M
Marygrove College	M,O
Michigan State University College of Law	M,D
Mississippi College	M,O
Montclair State University	O
National Paralegal College	M
National University	M
New York University	M,D*
Northeastern University	M,D
Nova Southeastern University	M,D
Pace University	M,D
Prairie View A&M University	M,D
Prescott College	M
Purdue University Global	M,O
Queen's University at Kingston	M,D
Regent University	M,D
Rhode Island College	M
Royal Roads University	M,O
Rutgers University–New Brunswick	M,D
St. John's University (NY)	M,D
Saint Leo University	M,D
St. Mary's University (United States)	M
San Francisco State University	M
The Santa Barbara and Ventura Colleges of Law–Santa Barbara	M,D
The Santa Barbara and Ventura Colleges of Law–Ventura	M,D
Simon Fraser University	M,D
Southern Illinois University Carbondale	M
Southern New Hampshire University	M,D,O
Stanford University	M,D
Taft University System	M,D
Temple University	M,D*
Texas State University	M
Texas Tech University	M,D
Touro College	M,D
Trident University International	M,D,O
Universidad Autonoma de Guadalajara	M,D
Université Laval	O
University at Buffalo, the State University of New York	M,D
University of Baltimore	M
University of Calgary	M,O
University of California, Berkeley	D
University of Charleston	M
University of Denver	M,O
University of Illinois at Springfield	M
University of Massachusetts Lowell	M
University of Montana	M
University of Nebraska–Lincoln	M
University of Nevada, Reno	M
University of New Hampshire	M,D,O
University of Pennsylvania	M,D*
University of Pittsburgh	M*
University of San Diego	M,D,O
University of South Florida	O
University of the District of Columbia	M,D
University of the Sacred Heart	M
University of Washington	M,D
University of Windsor	M
Vermont Law School	M
Washburn University	M
Weber State University	M
Webster University	M,O
Western Michigan University Thomas M. Cooley Law School	M,D
West Virginia University	M,D
Wilfrid Laurier University	D

LEISURE STUDIES

Bowling Green State University	M
California State University, Long Beach	M
Dalhousie University	M
East Carolina University	M,O
Howard University	M
Indiana University Bloomington	M,D
Penn State University Park	M,D*
Prescott College	M
San Francisco State University	M
Southeast Missouri State University	M
Southern Connecticut State University	M

Texas State University	M
Universidad Metropolitana	M
Université du Québec à Trois-Rivières	M,O
University of Illinois at Urbana–Champaign	M,D
The University of Iowa	M
University of Nebraska at Kearney	M
The University of Tennessee	M,D
The University of Toledo	M,D
University of Utah	M,D
University of Victoria	M
University of Waterloo	M,D
University of West Florida	M

LIBERAL STUDIES

Abilene Christian University	M
Alaska Pacific University	M
Albertus Magnus College	M
Alvernia University	M
Arizona State University at the Tempe campus	M
Arkansas Tech University	M
Auburn University at Montgomery	M
Baker University	M
Barry University	M
Binghamton University, State University of New York	M
Brooklyn College of the City University of New York	M
Cardinal Stritch University	M
Clayton State University	M
Coastal Carolina University	M
The College at Brockport, State University of New York	M
College of Staten Island of the City University of New York	M
The Colorado College	M
Colorado State University	M
Converse College	M
Dallas Baptist University	M
Dartmouth College	M
Delta State University	M
DePaul University	M
Dominican University of California	M
Drew University	M,D,O
Duke University	M
Eastern Washington University	M
East Tennessee State University	M,O
Florida International University	M
Fort Hays State University	M
Georgetown University	M,D
The Graduate Center, City University of New York	M
Hampton University	M,D,O
Harvard University	M,O*
Hawai`i Pacific University	M
Henderson State University	M
Hollins University	M
Houston Baptist University	M
Indiana University Northwest	M
Indiana University–Purdue University Indianapolis	M,D,O
Indiana University South Bend	M,O
Jacksonville State University	M
Johns Hopkins University	M,O*
Kean University	M
Kent State University	M
Lake Forest College	M
Louisiana State University and Agricultural & Mechanical College	M
Louisiana State University in Shreveport	M
Madonna University	M
McDaniel College	M,O
Metropolitan State University	M
Mississippi College	M
The New School	M
North Central College	M
Northern Arizona University	M
Northern Kentucky University	M
Northwestern University	M
Notre Dame of Maryland University	M
Oakland University	M
Queens College of the City University of New York	M
Reed College	M
Rice University	M
Rollins College	M
Rutgers University–Camden	M
St. Edward's University	M
St. John's College (MD)	M
St. John's College (NM)	M
St. John's University (NY)	M
St. Norbert College	M
San Diego State University	M
San Francisco State University	M
Simon Fraser University	M
Southern Methodist University	M
Spring Hill College	M,O
State University of New York College at Old Westbury	M
State University of New York Empire State College	M
Stony Brook University, State University of New York	M,O
Texas A&M University–Central Texas	M,O
Texas Christian University	M
Thomas Edison State University	M
Towson University	M
Tulane University	M
University at Albany, State University of New York	M
University of Central Oklahoma	M
University of Chicago	M
University of Delaware	M
University of Detroit Mercy	M,D,O
University of Memphis	M
University of Miami	M
University of Michigan–Flint	M

University of Minnesota, Duluth	M
University of New Hampshire	M
University of North Carolina at Asheville	M,O
The University of North Carolina at Charlotte	M,D,O
The University of North Carolina at Greensboro	M
The University of North Carolina Wilmington	M
University of Pennsylvania	M*
University of St. Thomas (TX)	M
University of Southern Indiana	M
University of South Florida	M,D
University of South Florida, St. Petersburg	M
University of South Florida Sarasota-Manatee	M
The University of Texas at El Paso	M
University of the Virgin Islands	M
The University of Toledo	M
University of Wisconsin–Milwaukee	M*
Vanderbilt University	M*
Villanova University	M
Virginia Polytechnic Institute and State University	M,O
Wake Forest University	M
Washburn University	M
Wesleyan University	M,O
Western Illinois University	M
Wichita State University	M
Winthrop University	M

LIBRARY SCIENCE

Appalachian State University	M,O
The Catholic University of America	M,O
Chicago State University	M
Clarion University of Pennsylvania	M
Dalhousie University	M
Drexel University	M,D,O*
East Carolina University	M,O
Eastern Kentucky University	M
East Tennessee State University	M,O
Emporia State University	M,D,O
Indiana University Bloomington	M,D,O
Indiana University–Purdue University Indianapolis	M,O
Instituto Tecnológico y de Estudios Superiores de Monterrey, Campus Irapuato	M,D
Inter American University of Puerto Rico, Barranquitas Campus	M
Inter American University of Puerto Rico, San Germán Campus	M
Kent State University	M
Kutztown University of Pennsylvania	M
Long Island University–Brentwood Campus	M,O
Long Island University–LIU Post	M,D,O
Louisiana State University and Agricultural & Mechanical College	M
Mansfield University of Pennsylvania	M
McDaniel College	M
McGill University	M,D,O
McNeese State University	O
North Carolina Central University	M
Old Dominion University	M,O
Olivet Nazarene University	M
Pratt Institute	M,O
Queens College of the City University of New York	M,O
Rowan University	M,D,O
Rutgers University–New Brunswick	D
St. Catherine University	M
St. John's University (NY)	M,O
Sam Houston State University	M
Southern Arkansas University–Magnolia	M
Southern Connecticut State University	M,O
Syracuse University	M
Tennessee Technological University	M,O
Texas A&M University–Commerce	M,D,O
Texas Woman's University	M
Trevecca Nazarene University	M,O
Universidad del Turabo	M
Université de Montréal	M,D
University at Buffalo, the State University of New York	M,O
The University of Alabama	M,D
University of Alberta	M
The University of Arizona	M,D
The University of British Columbia	M,D
University of California, Los Angeles	M,D,O
University of Central Arkansas	M
University of Central Missouri	M,D,O
University of Central Oklahoma	M
University of Denver	M,D,O
University of Hawaii at Manoa	M,O
University of Houston–Clear Lake	M
University of Illinois at Urbana–Champaign	M,D,O
The University of Iowa	M,D
University of Kentucky	M
University of Maryland, College Park	M,O
University of Missouri	D
University of Nebraska at Kearney	M
The University of North Carolina at Chapel Hill	M,D
The University of North Carolina at Greensboro	M
University of Oklahoma	M,D,O*

University of Pittsburgh	M,D*
University of Puerto Rico–Río Piedras	M,O
University of Rhode Island	M
University of South Carolina	M,D,O
University of Southern Mississippi	M,O
University of South Florida	M
University of Washington	M,D
The University of Western Ontario	M,D
University of Wisconsin–Eau Claire	M
University of Wisconsin–Madison	M,D
University of Wisconsin–Milwaukee	M,D,O*
Valdosta State University	M
Valley City State University	M
Wayne State University	M,O

LIGHTING DESIGN

The New School	M
New York School of Interior Design	M
Rensselaer Polytechnic Institute	M,D
University of Washington	M,D,O

LIMNOLOGY

Cornell University	D
Oregon State University	M,D
University of Alaska Fairbanks	M,D
University of Florida	M,D

LINGUISTICS

Arizona State University at the Tempe campus	M,D,O
Ball State University	M
Biola University	M,D,O
Boston College	M
Boston University	M,D
Brandeis University	M
Brigham Young University	M
Brown University	M,D
California State University, Fresno	M
California State University, Fullerton	M
California State University, Long Beach	M,O
California State University, Northridge	M
Carleton University	M
Carnegie Mellon University	M,D
Case Western Reserve University	M
Concordia University (Canada)	M,O
Cornell University	M,D
Dallas International University	M,O
East Carolina University	M,D,O
Eastern Michigan University	M
Florida Atlantic University	M
Florida International University	M
Gallaudet University	M,D,O
George Mason University	M,D,O
Georgetown University	M,D
Georgia State University	M,D
The Graduate Center, City University of New York	M,D
Grand Valley State University	M
Harvard University	D*
Hofstra University	M
Indiana State University	M,D,O
Indiana University Bloomington	M,D
Instituto Tecnologico de Santo Domingo	M,O
Iowa State University of Science and Technology	M,D
Kent State University	M,D
Massachusetts Institute of Technology	D
McGill University	M,D
Memorial University of Newfoundland	M
Michigan State University	M,D
Montclair State University	M,O
New York University	M,D*
Northeastern Illinois University	M
Northern Arizona University	M,D,O
Northwestern University	D
Oakland University	M,O
The Ohio State University	M,D
Ohio University	M
Old Dominion University	M
Penn State University Park	M,D*
Purdue University	M,D
Queens College of the City University of New York	M,O
Rice University	M,D
Rutgers University–New Brunswick	D
San Diego State University	M,O
San Francisco State University	M
San Jose State University	M,O
Simon Fraser University	M,D
Southern Illinois University Carbondale	M
Stanford University	M,D
Stony Brook University, State University of New York	M
Syracuse University	M
Teachers College, Columbia University	M,D,O
Texas A&M University–Commerce	M,D,O
Trinity Western University	M
Universidad de las Américas Puebla	M
Université de Montréal	M,D,O
Université de Sherbrooke	M,D
Université du Québec à Chicoutimi	M
Université du Québec à Montréal	M,D
Université Laval	M,D

University at Buffalo, the State University of New York	M,D
University of Alaska Fairbanks	M,D
University of Alberta	M,D
The University of Arizona	M,D
The University of British Columbia	M,D
University of Calgary	M,D
University of California, Berkeley	D
University of California, Davis	M,D
University of California, Los Angeles	M,D
University of California, San Diego	D
University of California, Santa Barbara	M,D
University of California, Santa Cruz	M,D
University of Chicago	M,D
University of Colorado Boulder	M,D
University of Colorado Denver	M
University of Connecticut	M,D
University of Delaware	M,D
The University of Findlay	M,D
University of Florida	M,D,O
University of Georgia	M,D
University of Hawaii at Manoa	M,D
University of Houston	M,D
University of Illinois at Chicago	M
University of Illinois at Urbana–Champaign	M,D
The University of Iowa	M,D
The University of Kansas	M,D
University of Louisville	M,D
The University of Manchester	D
University of Manitoba	M,D
University of Maryland, Baltimore County	M
University of Maryland, College Park	M,D
University of Massachusetts Amherst	M,D
University of Massachusetts Boston	M,D
University of Memphis	M,D,O
University of Michigan	D
University of Minnesota, Twin Cities Campus	M,D
University of Montana	M,D
University of New Hampshire	M,D
University of New Mexico	M,D
The University of North Carolina at Chapel Hill	M
The University of North Carolina at Charlotte	M,O
University of North Dakota	M
University of North Texas	M,D,O
University of Oregon	M,D
University of Ottawa	M
University of Pennsylvania	M,D*
University of Pittsburgh	M,D*
University of Puerto Rico–Río Piedras	M,D
University of Rochester	M*
University of Saskatchewan	M
University of South Africa	M,D
University of South Carolina	M,D,O
University of Southern California	M,D
University of South Florida	M,D
The University of Tennessee	D
The University of Texas at Arlington	M,D
The University of Texas at Austin	M,D
The University of Texas at El Paso	M,O
University of Toronto	M,D
University of Utah	M,D
University of Victoria	M,D
University of Virginia	M
University of Washington	M,D
University of Wisconsin–Madison	M,D
University of Wisconsin–Milwaukee	M,D,O*
Virginia International University	M
Wayne State University	M
Wesley Biblical Seminary	M
Yale University	D
York University	M,D

LOGISTICS

Air Force Institute of Technology	M,D
Albany State University	M
American Public University System	M
Athens State University	M
Benedictine University	M
Case Western Reserve University	M,D
Central Connecticut State University	M,O
Central Michigan University	M,O
Colorado Technical University Colorado Springs	M,D
Copenhagen Business School	M,D
East Carolina University	M,D,O
Embry-Riddle Aeronautical University–Worldwide	M
Florida Institute of Technology	M
Friends University	M
George Mason University	M
Georgia College & State University	M
Georgia Institute of Technology	M
Georgia Southern University	D
HEC Montreal	M
Maryville University of Saint Louis	M,O
Massachusetts Institute of Technology	M
Michigan State University	M,D
Naval Postgraduate School	M
North Dakota State University	M
Norwich University	M
The Ohio State University	M
Polytechnic University of Puerto Rico, Miami Campus	M

---

*M—masters degree; D—doctorate; O—other advanced degree; *—Close-Up and/or Display*

Pontifical Catholic University of Puerto Rico	O
Pontificia Universidad Catolica Madre y Maestra	M
Purdue University Global	M
Rutgers University–Newark	M
Shippensburg University of Pennsylvania	M,D,O
Trident University International	M,D
Universidad del Turabo	M
University at Buffalo, the State University of New York	M,D
The University of Alabama in Huntsville	M,O
University of Alaska Anchorage	M
University of Dallas	M,D
University of Houston	M
The University of Kansas	M
University of Louisville	M,D,O
University of Missouri–St. Louis	M,D,O
The University of North Carolina at Charlotte	M,O
University of North Florida	M
University of North Texas	M,D,O
University of St. Francis (IL)	M,O
University of South Africa	M,D
University of Southern Mississippi	M
The University of Tennessee	M,D
The University of Tennessee at Chattanooga	M,O
The University of Texas at Arlington	M
University of Washington	O
Virginia International University	M,O
Wright State University	M

MANAGEMENT INFORMATION SYSTEMS

Adelphi University	M
Air Force Institute of Technology	M
American Business & Technology University	M
American InterContinental University Atlanta	M
American Sentinel University	M,D,O
American University	M
American University of Armenia	M
Argosy University, Atlanta	M,D
Argosy University, Chicago	M,D
Argosy University, Hawai'i	M,D,O
Argosy University, Los Angeles	M,D
Argosy University, Northern Virginia	M,D,O
Argosy University, Orange County	M,D,O
Argosy University, Phoenix	M,D
Argosy University, Seattle	M,D
Argosy University, Tampa	M,D
Argosy University, Twin Cities	M,D
Arizona State University at the Tempe campus	M,D
Arkansas State University	O
Ashland University	M
Aspen University	M,O
Auburn University at Montgomery	M
Baker College Center for Graduate Studies–Online	M
Ball State University	M,O
Barry University	O
Baruch College of the City University of New York	M,D*
Baylor University	M
Bay Path University	M
Bellevue University	M
Benedictine University	M
Binghamton University, State University of New York	D
Boston University	M,O
Bowie State University	M,O
Brandeis University	M
Broadview University–West Jordan	M
California Intercontinental University	M,D
California Lutheran University	M,O
California State Polytechnic University, Pomona	M
California State University, Fullerton	M
California State University, Los Angeles	M
California State University, Monterey Bay	M
California State University, San Bernardino	M
California University of Management and Sciences	M,D
Capella University	M,D
Capitol Technology University	M
Carnegie Mellon University	M,D
The Catholic University of America	M,O
Central Michigan University	M,O
Central Penn College	M
Charleston Southern University	M
City College of the City University of New York	M,D
City University of Seattle	M,O
Claremont Graduate University	M,D,O
Clark University	M
Clemson University	M,D
Cleveland State University	D
Coastal Carolina University	M,D,O
College of Charleston	M
The College of St. Scholastica	M
Colorado State University	M
Colorado State University–Global Campus	M
Concordia University Wisconsin	M
Copenhagen Business School	M,D
Daemen College	M
Dakota State University	M,D,O
Dalhousie University	M
Dallas Baptist University	M
DePaul University	M,D

DeSales University	M,O
DeVry University–Folsom Campus	M
Dominican University	M,D,O
Drexel University	M,D,O*
Duquesne University	M
East Carolina University	M,D,O
Eastern Michigan University	M,O
ECPI University	M
Elmhurst College	M
Embry-Riddle Aeronautical University–Worldwide	M
Emory University	M,D
Endicott College	M
Fairfield University	M,O
Fairleigh Dickinson University, Metropolitan Campus	M,O
Ferris State University	M
Florida Agricultural and Mechanical University	M
Florida Atlantic University	M
Florida Gulf Coast University	M
Florida Institute of Technology	M
Florida International University	M,D
Florida State University	M,D,O
Fordham University	M,D
Franklin Pierce University	M,D,O
Friends University	M
George Mason University	M
The George Washington University	M,D
Georgia College & State University	M
Georgia Institute of Technology	M
Georgia Southern University	M,O
Georgia Southwestern State University	M
Georgia State University	M,D,O
Golden Gate University	M,D,O
Goldey-Beacom College	M
Governors State University	M
The Graduate Center, City University of New York	D
Grand Valley State University	M
Grantham University	M,O
Harrisburg University of Science and Technology	M
Hawai'i Pacific University	M
HEC Montreal	M,O
Hodges University	M
Hofstra University	M,O
Holy Family University	M
Hood College	M
Howard University	M
Idaho State University	M,O
IGlobal University	M
Illinois Institute of Technology	M,D
Illinois State University	M
Indiana University Bloomington	M,D,O
Indiana University Northwest	M,O
Instituto Tecnologico y de Estudios Superiores de Monterrey, Campus Central de Veracruz	M
Instituto Tecnológico y de Estudios Superiores de Monterrey, Campus Ciudad de México	M,D
Instituto Tecnológico y de Estudios Superiores de Monterrey, Campus Ciudad Juárez	M
Instituto Tecnológico y de Estudios Superiores de Monterrey, Campus Ciudad Obregón	M
Instituto Tecnológico y de Estudios Superiores de Monterrey, Campus Estado de México	M,D
Instituto Tecnológico y de Estudios Superiores de Monterrey, Campus Irapuato	M,D
Instituto Tecnológico y de Estudios Superiores de Monterrey, Campus Laguna	M
Inter American University of Puerto Rico, Aguadilla Campus	M
Inter American University of Puerto Rico, Fajardo Campus	M
Inter American University of Puerto Rico, Metropolitan Campus	M
Inter American University of Puerto Rico, San Germán Campus	M,D
Iona College	M,O
Iowa State University of Science and Technology	M,D
James Madison University	M
Johns Hopkins University	M,O*
Johnson & Wales University	M
Kean University	M
Keiser University	M
Kent State University	D
Lake Erie College	M
Le Moyne College	M
Lenoir-Rhyne University	M
Lewis University	M
Lincoln University (CA)	M,D
Lindenwood University	M,O
Lipscomb University	M,O
London Metropolitan University	M
Long Island University–LIU Post	M
Louisiana State University and Agricultural & Mechanical College	M,D
Louisiana Tech University	M,D
Loyola University Chicago	M,O
Loyola University Maryland	M
Marist College	M,O
Marquette University	M,O
Marymount University	M,O
Marywood University	M
McGill University	M,D,O
McMaster University	D
Metropolitan State University	M,D
Michigan State University	M,D
Middle Georgia State University	M
Middle Tennessee State University	M
Minot State University	M
Mississippi State University	M,D
Montclair State University	M

Morehead State University	M
Morgan State University	D
Murray State University	M
National American University (TX)	M,D
National University	M,O
Naval Postgraduate School	M,D,O
New England Institute of Technology	M
New Jersey Institute of Technology	M,D,O
Newman University	M
New Mexico State University	M
New York University	M,D*
Northeastern University	M,D,O
Northern Illinois University	M
Northwestern University	M
Northwest Missouri State University	M
Nova Southeastern University	M,D
Oakland University	M,D,O
The Ohio State University	M,D
Oklahoma State University	M,D
Old Dominion University	M,D
Our Lady of the Lake University	M
Pace University	M,D,O
Pacific States University	M,O
Park University	M,O
Penn State Harrisburg	M,O
Penn State University Park	M,D*
Point Park University	M
Polytechnic University of Puerto Rico	M
Pontifical Catholic University of Puerto Rico	M,O
Prairie View A&M University	M,D
Purdue University	M
Purdue University Global	M
Queen's University at Kingston	M,D
Radford University	M
Regent's University London	M
Regis University	M,O
Rivier University	M
Robert Morris University	M,D
Robert Morris University Illinois	M
Rochester Institute of Technology	O
Rose-Hulman Institute of Technology	M
Rutgers University–Newark	M,D
St. John's University (NY)	M
Saint Peter's University	M
San Diego State University	M
San Francisco State University	M
Santa Clara University	M
Schiller International University (United States)	M
Schiller International University (Germany)	M
Seattle Pacific University	M
Shippensburg University of Pennsylvania	M,D,O
Southeastern Oklahoma State University	M
Southern Illinois University Edwardsville	M
Southern Methodist University	M
Southern New Hampshire University	M,D,O
Southern University at New Orleans	M
South University	M
South University	M
South University (TX)	M
South University (AL)	M
South University	M
Stevens Institute of Technology	M,D,O
Stratford University (VA)	M,D
Strayer University	M
Suffolk University	M
Syracuse University	M,D,O
Tarleton State University	M
Temple University	M,D*
Tennessee Technological University	M
Texas A&M International University	M,D
Texas A&M University	M
Texas A&M University–Central Texas	M,O
Texas Southern University	M
Texas State University	M
Texas Tech University	M,D
Touro College	M
Trident University International	M,D,O
Trine University	M
Troy University	M
Tulane University	M
Tuskegee University	M
United States International University–Africa	M
Universidad del Este	M
Universidad del Turabo	D
Universidad Metropolitana	M
Université de Sherbrooke	M,O
Université du Québec à Montréal	M
Université Laval	M,O
University at Albany, State University of New York	M,D,O
University at Buffalo, the State University of New York	M,D,O
The University of Akron	M
The University of Alabama at Birmingham	M
The University of Alabama in Huntsville	M,O
The University of Arizona	M,O
University of Arkansas	M
University of Arkansas at Little Rock	M,O
University of Baltimore	M
University of Bridgeport	M
The University of British Columbia	D
University of California, Berkeley	M,D,O
University of Central Missouri	M,D,O
University of Cincinnati	M,D
University of Colorado Denver	M,D
University of Connecticut	M,D
University of Dallas	M,D

University of Delaware	M,D
University of Detroit Mercy	M,D,O
University of Florida	M,D,O
University of Hawaii at Manoa	M,D,O
University of Houston–Clear Lake	M
University of Houston–Victoria	M
University of Illinois at Chicago	M,D
University of Illinois at Springfield	M
University of Illinois at Urbana–Champaign	M,D,O
The University of Kansas	M
University of La Verne	M
University of Lethbridge	M,D
University of Management and Technology	M,O
University of Mary Hardin-Baylor	M
University of Maryland University College	M
University of Massachusetts Boston	M
University of Memphis	M,D
University of Michigan–Dearborn	M
University of Michigan–Flint	M,O
University of Minnesota, Twin Cities Campus	M,D
University of Mississippi	M,D
University of Missouri–St. Louis	M,D,O
University of Nebraska at Kearney	M
University of Nebraska at Omaha	M,D,O
University of Nebraska–Lincoln	M
University of Nevada, Las Vegas	M,O
University of Nevada, Reno	M
University of New Hampshire	M,O
University of North Alabama	M
The University of North Carolina at Chapel Hill	D
The University of North Carolina at Charlotte	M,D,O
The University of North Carolina at Greensboro	M,D,O
The University of North Carolina Wilmington	M
University of North Florida	M
University of North Texas	M,D,O
University of Oklahoma	M,D,O*
University of Oregon	M
University of Pennsylvania	M,D*
University of Phoenix–Bay Area Campus	M,D
University of Phoenix–Central Valley Campus	M
University of Phoenix–Dallas Campus	M
University of Phoenix–Hawaii Campus	M
University of Phoenix–Houston Campus	M
University of Phoenix–Las Vegas Campus	M
University of Phoenix–Online Campus	M
University of Phoenix–Sacramento Valley Campus	M
University of Phoenix–San Antonio Campus	M
University of Phoenix–San Diego Campus	M
University of Pittsburgh	M,D*
University of Redlands	M
University of Rochester	M,D*
University of San Francisco	M
The University of Scranton	M
University of South Africa	M
University of South Alabama	M,D
University of South Florida	M,D,O
The University of Tampa	M,O
The University of Texas at Arlington	M,D
The University of Texas at Austin	M,D
The University of Texas at Dallas	M
The University of Texas Rio Grande Valley	M
University of the Sacred Heart	M
University of the West	M
University of Utah	M,D,O
University of Washington	M,D
University of Wisconsin–Madison	D
Utah State University	M
Valparaiso University	M
Virginia Commonwealth University	M
Virginia International University	M,O
Virginia Polytechnic Institute and State University	M,D,O
Walden University	M,D,O
Wayland Baptist University	M,D
Wayne State University	M,D,O
Webster University	M,D,O
West Chester University of Pennsylvania	M,O
Western Governors University	M
Wichita State University	M
Wilmington University	M,D
Winston-Salem State University	M
Worcester Polytechnic Institute	M,D,O
Wright State University	M

MANAGEMENT OF TECHNOLOGY

Air Force Institute of Technology	M,D
Arizona State University at the Tempe campus	M
Athabasca University	M,D,O
Atlantis University	M
Boston University	M
California Lutheran University	M,O
California State University, Los Angeles	M
Cambridge College	M
Campbellsville University	M,D

Capella University	M,D
Carleton University	M
The Catholic University of America	M,O
Central Connecticut State University	M,O
Central European University	M,D
Champlain College	M
City University of Seattle	M,O
Colorado School of Mines	M,D
Colorado Technical University Aurora	M
Colorado Technical University Colorado Springs	M,D
Columbia University	M
Duke University	M,O
East Carolina University	M,D,O
Eastern Michigan University	D
École Polytechnique de Montréal	M,D,O
Embry-Riddle Aeronautical University–Worldwide	M
Fairfield University	M,O
Fairleigh Dickinson University, Florham Campus	M,O
Farmingdale State College	M
George Mason University	M
Georgetown University	M,D
The George Washington University	M
Golden Gate University	M,D,O
Grand Canyon University	M
Harrisburg University of Science and Technology	M
Harvard University	D*
Herzing University Online	M
Illinois State University	M
Indiana State University	M,D
Indiana University–Purdue University Indianapolis	M
Instituto Centroamericano de Administración de Empresas	M
Instituto Tecnológico y de Estudios Superiores de Monterrey, Campus Cuernavaca	M,D
Instituto Tecnológico y de Estudios Superiores de Monterrey, Campus Irapuato	M,D
Iona College	M,O
John F. Kennedy University	M
Johns Hopkins University	M,O*
Kansas State University	M
Keiser University	M
Kennesaw State University	M
La Salle University	M,O
Lewis University	M
Lipscomb University	M,O
London Metropolitan University	M
Louisiana Tech University	M,D,O
Marquette University	M,D
Marshall University	M,O
Mercer University	M
Montclair State University	M
National University	M
New Jersey Institute of Technology	M,D,O
North Carolina State University	M,D
Northern Kentucky University	M
Pacific States University	M,O
Pittsburg State University	M,O
Polytechnic University of Puerto Rico	M
Polytechnic University of Puerto Rico, Orlando Campus	M
Portland State University	M,D
Purdue University	M
Rutgers University–Newark	D
Ryerson University	M
St. Ambrose University	M
Seton Hall University	M,O
Simon Fraser University	M,D,O
South Dakota School of Mines and Technology	M
Southeast Missouri State University	M
State University of New York Polytechnic Institute	M
Stevens Institute of Technology	M,D,O
Stevenson University	M
Stony Brook University, State University of New York	M
Stratford University (VA)	M,D
Texas A&M University–Commerce	M,O
Texas State University	M,O
Towson University	M,O
University of Advancing Technology	M
The University of Alabama in Huntsville	M,O
University of Bridgeport	M,D
University of California, Los Angeles	M,D
University of California, Santa Barbara	
University of Central Missouri	M,D,O
University of Colorado Denver	M
University of Dallas	M,D
University of Delaware	M
University of Illinois at Urbana–Champaign	M,D
University of Maryland, Baltimore County	M
University of Massachusetts Dartmouth	M
University of Miami	M,D
University of Minnesota, Twin Cities Campus	
University of New Mexico	M
University of Phoenix–Bay Area Campus	M,D
University of Phoenix–Central Valley Campus	M

University of Phoenix–Dallas Campus	M
University of Phoenix–Hawaii Campus	M
University of Phoenix–Houston Campus	M
University of Phoenix–Las Vegas Campus	M
University of Phoenix–Online Campus	M,O
University of Phoenix–Phoenix Campus	M,O
University of Phoenix–Sacramento Valley Campus	M
University of Phoenix–San Antonio Campus	M
University of Phoenix–San Diego Campus	M
University of Portland	M
University of St. Thomas (MN)	M,O
University of South Florida	O
The University of Texas at Dallas	M
The University of Texas at San Antonio	M,D,O
University of Toronto	M
University of Virginia	M
University of Washington	M
University of Waterloo	M,D
University of Wisconsin–Madison	M
University of Wisconsin–Milwaukee	M,O*
Washington State University	M,O
Webster University	M
Wentworth Institute of Technology	M
Western Kentucky University	M
Wilfrid Laurier University	M,D

MANAGEMENT STRATEGY AND POLICY

Amberton University	M
Antioch University Santa Barbara	M
Arizona State University at the Tempe campus	M,D
Bay Path University	M
Black Hills State University	M
Boston University	M,O
Brandeis University	M
California Miramar University	M
California State University, East Bay	
Capella University	M,D
Claremont Graduate University	M,D,O
Cleary University	M,O
College of Staten Island of the City University of New York	M
Davenport University	M
Defiance College	M
DePaul University	M,D
Drexel University	M,D,O*
Duke University	M,D,O
East Tennessee State University	M
Fisher College	M
Florida State University	M,D
Freed-Hardeman University	M
Friends University	M
The George Washington University	M,D,O
Georgia State University	M,D
Grantham University	M,O
Gwynedd Mercy University	M
Harrisburg University of Science and Technology	M
Harvard University	D*
HEC Montreal	M
Hofstra University	M,O
James Madison University	D
John F. Kennedy University	M
Lawrence Technological University	M,D,O
Lenoir-Rhyne University	M
LeTourneau University	M
Lipscomb University	M,O
McGill University	M,D,O
Mercyhurst University	M,O
Messiah College	M,O
Michigan State University	M,D
Middle Tennessee State University	M
Mount Mercy University	M
Neumann University	M
New England College	M
The New School	M,O
New York University	M,D*
Niagara University	M
North Central College	M
Northwestern University	M,D
Norwich University	M
Nova Southeastern University	M
Oakland City University	M
Ohio Dominican University	M
Oklahoma Wesleyan University	M
Pace University	M
Pontificia Universidad Catolica Madre y Maestra	M
Queen's University at Kingston	M
Regent University	M,D,O
Regis University	M,O
Roberts Wesleyan College	M
Rockhurst University	M,O
St. John's University (NY)	M
Saint Mary-of-the-Woods College	M
Salve Regina University	M,D
Southeastern University (FL)	M
Southern Methodist University	M
Stevens Institute of Technology	M
Stockton University	M
Suffolk University	M
Temple University	D*
Tennessee State University	M
Tennessee Technological University	M
Thomas Jefferson University	M
Tufts University	O
Tulane University	M,D

United States International University–Africa	M
Universidad del Este	M
The University of Arizona	M,D
The University of British Columbia	D
University of Calgary	M,D
University of California, Davis	M
University of California, Los Angeles	M,D
University of Charleston	M
University of Chicago	M,O
University of Colorado Denver	M
University of Dallas	M,D
University of Detroit Mercy	M,O
University of Illinois at Urbana–Champaign	M,D,O
The University of Kansas	M,D
University of Lethbridge	M,D
The University of Manchester	M
University of Massachusetts Amherst	M,D
University of Memphis	M,O
University of Minnesota, Twin Cities Campus	D
University of New Haven	M
University of New Mexico	M
The University of North Carolina at Chapel Hill	D
University of North Texas	M,D,O
University of North Texas at Dallas	M
University of Pittsburgh	M,D*
University of Rhode Island	M,D,O
University of Rochester	M*
University of South Florida	M,D,O
The University of Texas at Dallas	M
University of Utah	M,D,O
University of Virginia	M,O
The University of Western Ontario	M,D
University of Wisconsin–Madison	M,D
University of Wisconsin–Milwaukee	M,D,O*
Valparaiso University	M,O
Vanderbilt University	M*
Villanova University	M
Walsh College of Accountancy and Business Administration	M
Wayne State University	M,D,O
Western Governors University	M
Xavier University	M*

MANUFACTURING ENGINEERING

American University of Armenia	M
Arizona State University at the Tempe campus	M
Boston University	M,D
Bradley University	M
Brigham Young University	M
Buffalo State College, State University of New York	M
California State University, Northridge	M
The Citadel, The Military College of South Carolina	M,O
Cornell University	M,D
Eastern Kentucky University	M
East Tennessee State University	M
Florida State University	M,D
Georgia Southern University	M,O
Grand Valley State University	M
Illinois Institute of Technology	M,D
Instituto Tecnológico y de Estudios Superiores de Monterrey, Campus Monterrey	M,D
Kansas State University	M,D
Kettering University	M
Lawrence Technological University	M,D
Massachusetts Institute of Technology	M,D,O
Michigan State University	M,D
Minnesota State University Mankato	M
Missouri University of Science and Technology	M
New Jersey Institute of Technology	M,D
New York University	M,D*
North Carolina State University	M
North Dakota State University	M,D
Oregon Institute of Technology	M
Oregon State University	M,D
Pittsburg State University	M
Polytechnic University of Puerto Rico	M
Rochester Institute of Technology	M
Southern Methodist University	M,D
Stevens Institute of Technology	M
Tennessee State University	M
Texas A&M University	M
Texas State University	M
Tufts University	O
Universidad Autonoma de Guadalajara	M,D
Universidad de las Américas Puebla	M
University at Buffalo, the State University of New York	M,D,O
University of Calgary	M,D
University of California, Irvine	M,D
University of California, Los Angeles	M
The University of Iowa	M,D
University of Kentucky	M
University of Manitoba	M,D
University of Maryland, College Park	M,D
University of Michigan	M,D
University of Michigan–Dearborn	M
University of Missouri	M,D
University of Nebraska–Lincoln	M,D

University of New Mexico	M
University of Puerto Rico–Mayagüez	M,D
University of St. Thomas (MN)	M,O
University of Southern California	M,D,O
The University of Texas at El Paso	M
The University of Texas at San Antonio	M,D
The University of Texas Rio Grande Valley	M
University of Toronto	M
University of Windsor	M,D
University of Wisconsin–Madison	M
University of Wisconsin–Milwaukee	M,D*
University of Wisconsin–Stout	M
Villanova University	M,O
Wayne State University	M,D,O
Western Illinois University	M
Western Michigan University	M
Western New England University	M
Wichita State University	M,D
Worcester Polytechnic Institute	M,D,O

MARINE AFFAIRS

Dalhousie University	M
Louisiana State University and Agricultural & Mechanical College	M,D
Memorial University of Newfoundland	M,D,O
Oregon State University	M
Stony Brook University, State University of New York	M
Université du Québec à Rimouski	M,O
University of Delaware	M
University of Massachusetts Dartmouth	M,D
University of Miami	M
University of Rhode Island	M,D
University of Washington	M,O

MARINE BIOLOGY

College of Charleston	M
Florida Institute of Technology	M,D
Montclair State University	M
Nicholls State University	M
Northeastern University	M,D
Nova Southeastern University	M,D
Princeton University	D
Rutgers University–New Brunswick	M,D
San Francisco State University	M
Texas A&M University	M
Texas A&M University–Corpus Christi	M,D
Texas State University	M,D
University of Alaska Fairbanks	M,D
University of California, Santa Barbara	M,D
University of Guam	M
University of Hawaii at Hilo	M
University of Hawaii at Manoa	M,D
University of Massachusetts Dartmouth	M,D
University of Miami	M,D
University of New Hampshire	M,D
The University of North Carolina Wilmington	M,D
University of Oregon	M,D
University of Rhode Island	M,D
University of Southern California	M,D
Western Illinois University	M,O
Woods Hole Oceanographic Institution	D

MARINE GEOLOGY

Cornell University	M,D
Massachusetts Institute of Technology	M,D
University of Delaware	M,D
University of Hawaii at Manoa	M,D
University of Miami	M,D
University of Rhode Island	M,D
University of Washington	M,D
Woods Hole Oceanographic Institution	D

MARINE SCIENCES

California State University, East Bay	M
California State University, Fresno	M
California State University, Monterey Bay	M
Coastal Carolina University	M,D,O
College of Charleston	M
The College of William and Mary	M,D
Cornell University	M,D
Duke University	M,D
Florida Institute of Technology	M,D
Florida State University	M,D
Hawai'i Pacific University	M
Instituto Tecnologico de Santo Domingo	M,D,O
Jacksonville University	M
Medical University of South Carolina	D
Memorial University of Newfoundland	M,O
North Carolina State University	M,D
Oregon State University	M,D
San Francisco State University	M
San Jose State University	M
Savannah State University	M
Southern Connecticut State University	M,O
Stony Brook University, State University of New York	M,D
Texas A&M University	M

M—masters degree; D—doctorate; O—other advanced degree; *—Close-Up and/or Display

Texas A&M University–Corpus Christi	M,D
University of Alaska Fairbanks	M,D
The University of British Columbia	M,D
University of California, San Diego	M
University of California, Santa Barbara	M,D
University of California, Santa Cruz	M,D
University of Delaware	M,D
University of Florida	M,D
University of Georgia	M,D
University of Hawaii at Manoa	O
University of Maine	M,D
University of Maryland, Baltimore	M,D
University of Maryland, Baltimore County	M,D
University of Maryland, College Park	M,D
University of Maryland Eastern Shore	M,D
University of Massachusetts Amherst	M,D
University of Massachusetts Boston	M,D
University of Massachusetts Dartmouth	M,D
University of Miami	M,D
University of New England	M
The University of North Carolina at Chapel Hill	M,D
The University of North Carolina Wilmington	M,D,O
University of Puerto Rico–Mayagüez	M,D
University of Rhode Island	M,D
University of South Alabama	M,D
University of South Carolina	M,D
University of Southern California	M,D
University of Southern Mississippi	M,D
University of South Florida	M,D
The University of Texas at Austin	M,D
University of the Virgin Islands	M
University of Wisconsin–La Crosse	M
University of Wisconsin–Madison	M,D
Western Washington University	M

MARKETING

Abilene Christian University	M
Adelphi University	M
American Business & Technology University	M
American College of Thessaloniki	M,O
American InterContinental University Online	M
American University	M
The American University in Dubai	M
Anderson University (SC)	M
Aquinas College (MI)	M
Argosy University, Atlanta	M,D
Argosy University, Chicago	M,D
Argosy University, Hawai'i	M,D,O
Argosy University, Los Angeles	M,D
Argosy University, Northern Virginia	M,D,O
Argosy University, Orange County	M,D,O
Argosy University, Phoenix	M,D
Argosy University, Seattle	M,D
Argosy University, Tampa	M,D
Argosy University, Twin Cities	M,D
Arizona State University at the Tempe campus	M,D
Ashworth College	M
Assumption College	M,O
Averett University	M
Azusa Pacific University	M
Baker College Center for Graduate Studies–Online	M,D
Barry University	O
Baruch College of the City University of New York	M,D*
Bayamón Central University	M
Benedictine University	M
Bentley University	M
Binghamton University, State University of New York	D
Brandeis University	M
Brandman University	M
Brigham Young University	M
Bryan College	M
California Coast University	M
California Intercontinental University	M,D
California Lutheran University	M,O
California State University, East Bay	M
California State University, Los Angeles	M
California State University, San Bernardino	M
Capella University	M,D
Cardinal Stritch University	M
Carnegie Mellon University	D
Central Michigan University	M,O
City College of the City University of New York	M
City University of Seattle	M,O
Clark University	M
Clemson University	M
Cleveland State University	D
Colorado Technical University Aurora	M
Colorado Technical University Colorado Springs	M,D
Columbia Southern University	M
Columbia University	M,D
Concordia University (Canada)	M,D,O
Concordia University Wisconsin	M
Cornell University	D
Daemen College	M
DePaul University	M,D

DEREE - The American College of Greece	M
DeSales University	M
Drexel University	M,D,O*
Duke University	M,D,O
Duquesne University	M
Eastern Michigan University	M,O
East Tennessee State University	M,O
Emory University	M,D
Fairfield University	M,O
Fairleigh Dickinson University, Florham Campus	M
Fairleigh Dickinson University, Metropolitan Campus	M,O
Fashion Institute of Technology	M
Florida Agricultural and Mechanical University	M
Florida International University	M
Florida National University	M
Florida State University	M,D
Fordham University	M,D
Franklin University	M
Full Sail University	M
Gannon University	M
Geneva College	M
George Fox University	M,D
The George Washington University	M,D
Georgia State University	M,D
Golden Gate University	M,D,O
Goldey-Beacom College	M
Grand Canyon University	M
Harvard University	D*
Hawai'i Pacific University	M
HEC Montreal	M,D
Herzing University Online	M
Hofstra University	M,O
Holy Names University	M
Hope International University	M
Howard University	M
Hult International Business School (United States)	M
Illinois Institute of Technology	M
Indiana Tech	M
Indiana University–Purdue University Indianapolis	M
Indiana University South Bend	M,O
Instituto Tecnologico de Santo Domingo	M,O
Instituto Tecnológico y de Estudios Superiores de Monterrey, Campus Central de Veracruz	M
Instituto Tecnológico y de Estudios Superiores de Monterrey, Campus Ciudad Obregón	M
Instituto Tecnológico y de Estudios Superiores de Monterrey, Campus Cuernavaca	M
Instituto Tecnológico y de Estudios Superiores de Monterrey, Campus Estado de México	M,D
Instituto Tecnológico y de Estudios Superiores de Monterrey, Campus Monterrey	M,D
Inter American University of Puerto Rico, Aguadilla Campus	M
Inter American University of Puerto Rico, Fajardo Campus	M
Inter American University of Puerto Rico, Guayama Campus	M
Inter American University of Puerto Rico, Metropolitan Campus	M
Inter American University of Puerto Rico, Ponce Campus	M
Inter American University of Puerto Rico, San Germán Campus	M,D
International University in Geneva	M,D
The International University of Monaco	M
Iona College	M,O
Jacksonville University	M
Johns Hopkins University	M*
Kansas State University	M,O
Keiser University	M,D
Kent State University	D
King University	M
Lake Forest Graduate School of Management	M
La Salle University	M,O
Lasell College	M,O
La Sierra University	M,O
Lawrence Technological University	M,D,O
Lewis University	M
Liberty University	M,D
LIM College	M
Lindenwood University	M,O
Long Island University–LIU Post	M
Louisiana Tech University	M,D
Loyola University Chicago	M
Loyola University Maryland	M
Marist College	M
Marquette University	M,O
Maryville University of Saint Louis	M,O
McGill University	M,D,O
Melbourne Business School	M,D,O
Michigan State University	M,D
Milwaukee School of Engineering	M
Mississippi State University	D
Molloy College	M,O
Monmouth University	M,O
Monroe College	M
Montclair State University	M
Morgan State University	D
Murray State University	M
National American University (TX)	M,O
National University	M,O
National University College	M
Nebraska Christian College of Hope International University	M
New England College	M
New Jersey City University	M
New York Institute of Technology	M
New York University	M,D*

Niagara University	M
Northwestern University	M,D
Northwest Missouri State University	M
Nova Southeastern University	M,O
Oakland University	M,O
Ohio Christian University	M
Oklahoma Christian University	M
Oklahoma State University	M,D
Old Dominion University	M,D
Oral Roberts University	M
Ottawa University	M
Pace University	M,D,O
Polytechnic University of Puerto Rico, Miami Campus	M
Pontifical Catholic University of Puerto Rico	M
Pontificia Universidad Catolica Madre y Maestra	M
Post University	M
Providence College	M
Purdue University Global	M
Queen's University at Kingston	M,D
Regent's University London	M
Regent University	M,D,O
Regis University	M
Roberts Wesleyan College	M
Roosevelt University	M
Rowan University	O
Rutgers University–Newark	D
Sacred Heart University	M,O
St. Bonaventure University	M
St. Catherine University	M
St. John's University (NY)	M
Saint Joseph's University	M,O
Saint Leo University	M,D
Saint Peter's University	M
St. Thomas Aquinas College	M
Saint Xavier University	M
Samford University	M
San Diego State University	M
San Francisco State University	M
San Ignacio University	M
Seton Hall University	M,O
Slippery Rock University of Pennsylvania	M
Southeastern Louisiana University	M
Southern Adventist University	M
Southern Methodist University	M
Southern New Hampshire University	M,D,O
Southwest Minnesota State University	M
State University of New York Polytechnic Institute	M
Stephen F. Austin State University	M
Stevens Institute of Technology	M,O
Stony Brook University, State University of New York	M,O
Strayer University	M
Suffolk University	M
Syracuse University	M
Tarleton State University	M
Temple University	M,D*
Texas A&M University	M
Texas A&M University–Commerce	M
Texas Tech University	M,D
Thomas Jefferson University	M
Tiffin University	M
Trident University International	M,D
United States International University–Africa	M
Universidad del Turabo	M
Universidad Iberoamericana	M,D
Universidad Metropolitana	M
Université de Sherbrooke	M
Université Laval	M,O
University at Albany, State University of New York	M
University at Buffalo, the State University of New York	M,D
The University of Akron	M
The University of Alabama	M,D
The University of Alabama at Birmingham	M
The University of Alabama in Huntsville	M,O
University of Alberta	D
The University of Arizona	M,D
University of Baltimore	M
University of Bridgeport	M
The University of British Columbia	D
University of California, Berkeley	D,O
University of California, Davis	M
University of California, Los Angeles	M,D
University of Central Missouri	M,D,O
University of Chicago	M,O
University of Cincinnati	M,D
University of Colorado Denver	M
University of Connecticut	M,D
University of Dallas	M,D
University of Dayton	M
University of Denver	M
University of Florida	M,D
University of Hawaii at Manoa	M,D
University of Houston	D
University of Houston–Victoria	M
The University of Iowa	M,D
The University of Kansas	M,D
University of La Verne	M
University of Lethbridge	M,D
The University of Manchester	M
University of Massachusetts Amherst	M,D
University of Memphis	M,D
University of Michigan–Flint	M,O
University of Minnesota, Twin Cities Campus	M,D
University of Mississippi	M,D
University of Missouri–St. Louis	M,D,O

University of Nebraska at Kearney	M
University of Nebraska–Lincoln	M,D
University of New Brunswick Fredericton	M,D
University of New Haven	M
The University of North Carolina at Chapel Hill	D
The University of North Carolina at Greensboro	M,D
University of North Texas	M,D,O
University of Notre Dame	M
University of Oregon	D
University of Pennsylvania	M,D*
University of Phoenix–Bay Area Campus	M,D
University of Phoenix–Central Valley Campus	M
University of Phoenix–Dallas Campus	M
University of Phoenix–Hawaii Campus	M
University of Phoenix–Houston Campus	M
University of Phoenix–Las Vegas Campus	M
University of Phoenix–Online Campus	M,O
University of Phoenix–Phoenix Campus	M,O
University of Phoenix–Sacramento Valley Campus	M
University of Phoenix–San Antonio Campus	M
University of Phoenix–San Diego Campus	M
University of Pittsburgh	M,D*
University of Portland	M
University of Puerto Rico–Río Piedras	M,D
University of Rhode Island	M,D
University of Rochester	M,D*
University of Saint Mary	M
University of San Francisco	M
University of Saskatchewan	M
The University of Scranton	M
University of Sioux Falls	M
University of South Africa	M,D
University of South Alabama	M,D
University of South Dakota	M,O
University of South Florida	M,D
The University of Tampa	M,O
The University of Tennessee	M,D
The University of Texas at Arlington	M
The University of Texas at Austin	M,D
The University of Texas at Dallas	M
The University of Texas at San Antonio	M,D
The University of Texas at Tyler	M
The University of Texas Rio Grande Valley	M,D
University of the Cumberlands	M,D,O
University of the Sacred Heart	M
The University of Toledo	M
University of Utah	M,D
University of Virginia	M
The University of Western Ontario	M,D
University of Wisconsin–Madison	D
University of Wisconsin–Whitewater	M
Ursuline College	M
Vancouver Island University	M
Vanderbilt University	M*
Villanova University	M
Virginia International University	M,O
Virginia Polytechnic Institute and State University	M,D
Wagner College	M
Walden University	M,D,O
Walsh University	M
Webster University	M,D,O
West Virginia University	M,D,O
Wilfrid Laurier University	M
William Paterson University of New Jersey	M,O
William Woods University	M,D,O
Wilmington University	M,D
Wingate University	M
Worcester Polytechnic Institute	M,D,O
Worcester State University	M*
Xavier University	M*
Yale University	M
Yeshiva University	M
York College of Pennsylvania	M

MARKETING RESEARCH

Hofstra University	M,O
Instituto Tecnológico y de Estudios Superiores de Monterrey, Campus Irapuato	M,D
Marquette University	M
Michigan State University	M,D
Pacific Lutheran University	M
Saint Leo University	M,D
Southern Illinois University Edwardsville	M
Towson University	M,O
Universidad Autonoma de Guadalajara	M,D
Universidad de las Americas, A.C.	
University of Missouri–St. Louis	M,D,O
University of Rochester	M*
The University of Texas at Arlington	M
University of Wisconsin–Madison	M

MARRIAGE AND FAMILY THERAPY

Abilene Christian University	M
Adler Graduate School	M
Adler University	M,D,O
Albizu University, Miami Campus	M,D

Alliant International University–Irvine	M,D
Alliant International University–Los Angeles	M,D
Alliant International University–Sacramento	M,D
Alliant International University–San Diego	M,D
Amberton University	M
Amridge University	M
Antioch University New England	M,D,O
Antioch University Seattle	M
Appalachian State University	M
Arcadia University	M
Argosy University, Atlanta	M,D,O
Argosy University, Chicago	D
Argosy University, Hawai'i	M
Argosy University, Los Angeles	M,D
Argosy University, Northern Virginia	M,D
Argosy University, Orange County	M,D
Argosy University, Tampa	M,D
Argosy University, Twin Cities	M,D,O
Arizona State University at the Tempe campus	M,D
Azusa Pacific University	D
Barry University	M,O
Bayamón Central University	M,O
Bethel Seminary	M,D,O
Brandman University	M
Briercrest Seminary	M
Brigham Young University	M,D
California Lutheran University	M,D
California State University, Chico	M
California State University, Dominguez Hills	M
California State University, East Bay	M
California State University, Fresno	M
California State University, Long Beach	M,D
California State University, Northridge	M
Cambridge College	M,O
Campbellsville University	M
Capella University	M
Central Connecticut State University	M,O
Chaminade University of Honolulu	M
Chapman University	M*
Chatham University	M,D
Chestnut Hill College	M,D,O
The Chicago School of Professional Psychology at Downtown Los Angeles	M,D
The Chicago School of Professional Psychology at Irvine	M,D
Christian Theological Seminary	M,D
The College of New Jersey	M,O
The College of New Rochelle	M
The College of William and Mary	M,D
Colorado State University	M,D
Converse College	M
Denver Seminary	M,D,O
Dominican University of California	M
Drexel University	M,D*
Duquesne University	M,D,O
East Carolina University	M,D
Eastern Nazarene College	M
Eastern University	D
East Tennessee State University	M
Evangelical Seminary	M
Fairfield University	M,O
Florida State University	M,D
Fresno Pacific University	M
Friends University	M
Fuller Theological Seminary	M
Geneva College	M
George Fox University	M,O
Gonzaga University	M,D
Hampton University	M
Hardin-Simmons University	M
Hofstra University	M,O
Hope International University	M
Houston Baptist University	M
Idaho State University	M,D,O
Indiana University South Bend	M,O
Indiana Wesleyan University	M
Instituto Tecnologico de Santo Domingo	M
Iona College	M
Jacksonville University	M
John Brown University	M,O
Kansas State University	M,D,O
Kean University	M
Lancaster Bible College	M
La Salle University	M
Lee University	M
LeTourneau University	M
Lewis & Clark College	M
Liberty University	M,D,O
Lipscomb University	M,O
Loma Linda University	M,D,O
Long Island University–Hudson	M,O
Long Island University–LIU Brooklyn	M,O
Loyola Marymount University	M
Loyola University New Orleans	M
Manhattan College	M
Maryville University of Saint Louis	M
Medaille College	M,D
Mercy College	M,O
Messiah College	M
Mid-America Christian University	M
MidAmerica Nazarene University	M
Midwest University	M,D
Mississippi College	M
Mount Mercy University	M

National University	M,D,O
Northcentral University	M,D,O
Northeastern Illinois University	M
Northern Kentucky University	M,O
Northwestern University	M
Northwest Nazarene University	M
Notre Dame de Namur University	M
Nova Southeastern University	M,D,O
Nyack College	M
Oklahoma Baptist University	M
Oral Roberts University	M,D
Ottawa University	M
Our Lady of the Lake University	M
Pacific Lutheran University	M
Pacific Oaks College	M
Palm Beach Atlantic University	M
Palo Alto University	M
Phillips Graduate University	M
Pillar College	M
Plymouth State University	M
Point Loma Nazarene University	M
Pontifical John Paul II Institute for Studies on Marriage and Family	M,D,O
Purdue University	M,D
Purdue University Fort Wayne	M,O
Purdue University Northwest	M
Reformed Theological Seminary–Jackson Campus	M,D,O
Regent University	M,D,O
Regis University	M,D,O
Richmont Graduate University	M
St. Cloud State University	M
Saint Mary's College of California	M,O
Saint Mary's University of Minnesota	M
Saint Paul University	M
St. Thomas University	M,O
San Francisco State University	M
Saybrook University	M,D
Seattle Pacific University	M,O
Seattle University	M
Seton Hall University	M
Sioux Falls Seminary	M
Southeastern University (FL)	M
Southern California Seminary	M,D
Southern Nazarene University	M
Syracuse University	M,D
Texas A&M University–Central Texas	M,O
Texas A&M University–San Antonio	M
Texas State University	M
Texas Tech University	M,D
Texas Woman's University	M,D
Thomas Jefferson University	M
Trevecca Nazarene University	M
Universidad de las Americas, A.C.	M
The University of Akron	M
The University of Alabama	M
University of Central Florida	M,O
University of Central Oklahoma	M
University of Colorado Denver	M
University of Denver	M,D,O
University of Florida	M,D,O
University of Guelph	M,D
University of Holy Cross	M,D
University of Houston–Clear Lake	M
The University of Iowa	M,D
University of La Verne	M
University of Louisiana at Monroe	M
University of Louisville	M,D,O
University of Mary Hardin-Baylor	M
University of Maryland, College Park	M,D
University of Massachusetts Boston	M
University of Miami	M,O
University of Minnesota, Twin Cities Campus	M,D
University of Mobile	M
University of Nebraska–Lincoln	M,D
University of Nevada, Las Vegas	M
University of New Hampshire	M,O
The University of North Carolina at Greensboro	M,D,O
University of Oregon	M,D
University of Phoenix–Bay Area Campus	M
University of Phoenix–Central Valley Campus	M
University of Phoenix–Las Vegas Campus	M
University of Phoenix–Phoenix campus	M
University of Rhode Island	M*
University of Rochester	M*
University of Saint Joseph	M
University of San Diego	M
University of San Francisco	M
University of Southern California	M
University of Southern Mississippi	M
University of South Florida	M,D,O
The University of Texas at Tyler	M
The University of West Alabama	M
The University of Winnipeg	M,O
University of Wisconsin–Stout	M
Utah State University	M,D
Valdosta State University	M,O
Walden University	M,D
Western Kentucky University	M
Western Seminary–Sacramento Campus	M
Western Seminary–San Jose Campus	M,O
Wheaton College	M,D

MASS COMMUNICATION

American University	M,D,O

The American University in Cairo	M,O
Arizona State University at the Tempe campus	M,D
Arkansas State University	M
Boston University	M
Brigham Young University	M
California State University, Fullerton	M
California State University, Northridge	M
Clarion University of Pennsylvania	M
Drexel University	M*
Florida International University	M
Fordham University	M
The George Washington University	M,O
Georgia State University	M,D
Grambling State University	M
Howard University	M,D
Iona College	M,O
Iowa State University of Science and Technology	M
Kansas State University	M
Kent State University	M
Lindenwood University	M
Louisiana State University and Agricultural & Mechanical College	M,D
Lynn University	M,O
Marquette University	M,O
Middle Tennessee State University	M
Murray State University	M
North Dakota State University	M,D
Oklahoma State University	M
Penn State University Park	M,D*
Point Park University	M
St. Cloud State University	M
St. John's University (NY)	M
San Jose State University	M
Southern Illinois University Carbondale	M,D
Southern Illinois University Edwardsville	M
Southern University and Agricultural and Mechanical College	M
Stephen F. Austin State University	M
Syracuse University	M,D
Texas Christian University	M
Texas State University	M
Texas Tech University	M,D
Université Laval	M,D
The University of Alabama	D
University of Arkansas at Little Rock	M
University of Colorado Boulder	M,D
University of Denver	M
University of Florida	M,D
University of Georgia	M,D
University of Houston	M
University of Iowa	M,D
University of Minnesota, Twin Cities Campus	M,D
University of Nebraska–Lincoln	M
University of Oklahoma	M,D*
University of Puerto Rico–Río Piedras	M
University of South Florida	M,O
University of Wisconsin–Madison	M,D
University of Wisconsin–Superior	M
University of Wisconsin–Whitewater	M
Virginia Commonwealth University	M

MATERIALS ENGINEERING

Alabama Agricultural and Mechanical University	M
Arizona State University at the Tempe campus	M,D
Auburn University	M,D
Binghamton University, State University of New York	M,D
Boise State University	M,D
Boston University	M,D
California State University, Northridge	M
Carleton University	M,D
Carnegie Mellon University	M,D
Case Western Reserve University	M,D
The Catholic University of America	M
Clarkson University	D
Clemson University	M,D
Colorado School of Mines	M,D
Columbia University	M,D
Cornell University	M,D
Dartmouth College	M,D
Drexel University	M,D*
Duke University	M
Florida International University	M,D
Florida State University	M,D
Georgia Institute of Technology	M,D
Illinois Institute of Technology	M,D
Instituto Tecnológico y de Estudios Superiores de Monterrey, Campus Estado de México	M,D
Iowa State University of Science and Technology	M,D
Johns Hopkins University	M,D*
Lehigh University	M,D
Massachusetts Institute of Technology	M,D,O
McGill University	M,D,O
McMaster University	M,D
Michigan State University	M,D
Michigan Technological University	M,D
Missouri University of Science and Technology	M,D
New Jersey Institute of Technology	M,D,O
New Mexico Institute of Mining and Technology	M,D

North Carolina State University	M,D
Northwestern University	M,D,O
The Ohio State University	M,D
Oklahoma State University	M,D
Penn State University Park	M,D*
Portland State University	M,D
Purdue University	M,D
Queen's University at Kingston	M,D
Rensselaer Polytechnic Institute	M,D
Rochester Institute of Technology	M
Rutgers University–New Brunswick	M,D
San Jose State University	M
South Dakota School of Mines and Technology	M,D
Stanford University	M,D,O
Stevens Institute of Technology	M,D
Stony Brook University, State University of New York	M,D
Texas A&M University	M,D
Texas State University	D
Tuskegee University	D
The University of Alabama	M,D
The University of Alabama at Birmingham	M,D
University of Alberta	M,D
The University of Arizona	M,D
The University of British Columbia	M,D
University of California, Berkeley	M,D
University of California, Davis	M,D
University of California, Irvine	M,D
University of California, Los Angeles	M,D
University of California, Riverside	M
University of California, Santa Barbara	M,D
University of Central Florida	M,D
University of Cincinnati	M,D
University of Colorado Boulder	M,D
University of Connecticut	M,D
University of Dayton	M,D
University of Delaware	M,D
University of Denver	M,D
University of Florida	M,D
University of Illinois at Chicago	M,D
University of Illinois at Urbana–Champaign	M,D
The University of Iowa	M,D
University of Kentucky	M,D
University of Maryland, College Park	M,D
University of Michigan	M,D
University of Minnesota, Twin Cities Campus	M,D
University of Nebraska–Lincoln	M,D
University of Nevada, Las Vegas	M,D,O
University of Nevada, Reno	M,D
University of New Hampshire	M,D
University of Pennsylvania	M,D*
University of Puerto Rico–Mayagüez	M,D
University of Southern California	M,D,O
University of South Florida	M,D,O
The University of Tennessee	M,D
The University of Texas at Arlington	M,D
The University of Texas at Austin	M,D
The University of Texas at Dallas	M,D
The University of Texas at El Paso	M,D
The University of Texas at San Antonio	M,D
University of Toronto	M,D
University of Utah	M,D
University of Washington	M,D
The University of Western Ontario	M,D
University of Windsor	M,D
University of Wisconsin–Madison	M,D
University of Wisconsin–Milwaukee	M,D*
Washington State University	M,D
West Virginia University	M,D
Worcester Polytechnic Institute	M,D,O
Wright State University	M

MATERIALS SCIENCES

Air Force Institute of Technology	M,D
Alabama Agricultural and Mechanical University	M,D
Alfred University	M,D
Arizona State University at the Tempe campus	M,D
Binghamton University, State University of New York	M,D
Boston University	M,D
Brown University	M,D
California Institute of Technology	M,D
Carnegie Mellon University	M,D
Case Western Reserve University	M,D
The Catholic University of America	M
Central Michigan University	D
Clarkson University	D
Clemson University	M,D
Colorado School of Mines	M,D
Colorado State University	M,D
Columbia University	M,D
Cornell University	M,D
Dartmouth College	M,D
Duke University	M,D
Florida International University	M,D
Florida State University	M,D
Georgetown University	D
The George Washington University	M,D
Harvard University	M,D*
Illinois Institute of Technology	M,D
Indiana University Bloomington	M,D

Instituto Tecnológico y de Estudios Superiores de Monterrey, Campus Estado de México — M,D
Iowa State University of Science and Technology — M,D
Jackson State University — M,D
Johns Hopkins University — M,D*
Lehigh University — M,D
Louisiana Tech University — M,D,O
Massachusetts Institute of Technology — M,D
McMaster University — M,D
Michigan State University — M,D
Missouri State University — M
Missouri University of Science and Technology — M,D
Montana Tech of The University of Montana — D
New Jersey Institute of Technology — M,D,O
Norfolk State University — M
North Carolina State University — M,D
North Dakota State University — M,D
Northwestern University — M,D,O
The Ohio State University — M,D
Oklahoma State University — M,D
Oregon State University — M,D
Penn State University Park — M,D*
Princeton University — D
Rice University — M,D
Rochester Institute of Technology — M
Rutgers University–New Brunswick — M,D
South Dakota School of Mines and Technology — M,D
Stanford University — M,D,O
State University of New York College of Environmental Science and Forestry — M,D,O
Stevens Institute of Technology — M,D
Stony Brook University, State University of New York — M,D
Texas A&M University — M,D
Texas State University — D
Trent University — M
Université du Québec, Institut National de la Recherche Scientifique — M,D
University at Buffalo, the State University of New York — M,D
The University of Alabama — D
The University of Alabama in Huntsville — M,D
The University of Arizona — M,D
University of Calgary — M,D
University of California, Berkeley — M,D
University of California, Davis — M,D
University of California, Irvine — M,D
University of California, Los Angeles — M,D
University of California, Riverside — M
University of California, San Diego — M,D
University of California, Santa Barbara — M,D
University of Central Florida — M,D
University of Cincinnati — M,D
University of Colorado Boulder — M,D
University of Connecticut — M,D
University of Delaware — M,D
University of Denver — M,D
University of Florida — M,D
University of Idaho — M,D
University of Illinois at Urbana–Champaign — M,D
University of Kentucky — M,D
The University of Manchester — M,D
University of Maryland, College Park — M,D
University of Michigan — M,D
University of Minnesota, Twin Cities Campus — M,D
University of Mississippi Medical Center — M,D
University of Nebraska–Lincoln — M,D
University of New Brunswick Fredericton — M,D
University of New Hampshire — M,D
University of Pennsylvania — M,D*
University of Pittsburgh — M,D*
University of Puerto Rico–Mayagüez — M,D
University of Rochester — M,D*
University of Southern California — M,D,O
University of South Florida — M,D,O
The University of Tennessee — M,D
The University of Texas at Arlington — M,D
The University of Texas at Austin — M,D
The University of Texas at Dallas — M,D
The University of Texas at El Paso — M,D
The University of Toledo — M,D
University of Toronto — M,D
University of Utah — M,D
University of Vermont — M,D
University of Virginia — M,D
University of Washington — M,D
Vanderbilt University — M,D*
Washington State University — M,D
Washington University in St. Louis — M,D
Wayne State University — M,D,O
West Virginia University — M,D
William Paterson University of New Jersey — M,D,O
Worcester Polytechnic Institute — M,D,O
Wright State University — M

MATERNAL AND CHILD/NEONATAL NURSING
Boston College — M,D
Case Western Reserve University — M
Creighton University — M,D
Duke University — M,D,O

Hardin-Simmons University — M
Lehman College of the City University of New York — M
Louisiana State University Health Sciences Center — M,D,O
Medical University of South Carolina — M,D
Northeastern University — M,D,O
Old Dominion University — M,D
Regis University — M,D,O
Rush University — D,O
Saint Francis Medical Center College of Nursing — M,D,O
Stony Brook University, State University of New York — M,D,O
University of Alberta — D
University of Cincinnati — M,D
University of Connecticut — M,O
University of Delaware — M,O
University of Illinois at Chicago — M,O
University of Indianapolis — M,D
University of Louisville — M,D
University of Maryland, Baltimore — M,D,O
University of Missouri–Kansas City — M,D
University of Pennsylvania — M*
University of Puerto Rico–Medical Sciences Campus — M
University of Rochester — M,D*
University of South Africa — M
The University of Texas at Austin — M,D
Wayne State University — M,D
Wright State University — M

MATERNAL AND CHILD HEALTH
Bank Street College of Education — M
Bastyr University — M,O
Columbia University — M,D
East Carolina University — M,D,O
Instituto Tecnologico de Santo Domingo — M,O
Oakland University — D,O
Troy University — M,D
The University of Alabama at Birmingham — M,D
University of California, Davis — M
University of Manitoba — M
University of Maryland, College Park — M,D
University of Minnesota, Twin Cities Campus — M,D
The University of North Carolina at Chapel Hill — M,D
University of Puerto Rico–Medical Sciences Campus — M
University of South Florida — O
The University of Texas Health Science Center at Houston — M,D,O
University of Washington — M,D

MATHEMATICAL AND COMPUTATIONAL FINANCE
Austin Peay State University — M
Boston University — M,D
Carnegie Mellon University — M,D
DePaul University — M,D
Florida State University — M,D
The George Washington University — M,D,O
Georgia Institute of Technology — M
Illinois Institute of Technology — M,D
Johns Hopkins University — M,D,O*
New Jersey Institute of Technology — M,D,O
New York University — M,D*
North Carolina State University — M
Oregon State University — M,D
Rice University — M,D
Rochester Institute of Technology — M,D
Université de Montréal — M,D,O
University of Alberta — M,D,O
University of California, Santa Barbara — M,D
University of Chicago — M
University of Connecticut — M
University of Dayton — M
The University of Manchester — M,D
University of Miami — M,D
The University of North Carolina at Charlotte — M,O
University of Notre Dame — M,D
University of Southern California — M,D
University of Toronto — M

MATHEMATICAL PHYSICS
Indiana University Bloomington — M,D
New Mexico Institute of Mining and Technology — M,D
University of Alberta — M,D,O
University of Colorado Boulder — M,D

MATHEMATICS
Acadia University — M
Alabama State University — M
American University — M,O
American University of Beirut — M,D
American University of Sharjah — M,D
Appalachian State University — M
Arizona State University at the Tempe campus — M,D,O
Arkansas State University — M
Auburn University — M,D
Augustana University — M
Aurora University — M
Ball State University — M
Baylor University — M,D
Bemidji State University — M
Binghamton University, State University of New York — M,D
Boise State University — M
Boston College — D
Boston University — M,D
Bowling Green State University — M,D
Brandeis University — M,D
Brigham Young University — M,D
Brock University — M

Brooklyn College of the City University of New York — M
Brown University — D
Bryn Mawr College — M
Bucknell University — M
Cabrini University — M,D
California Institute of Technology — D
California Polytechnic State University, San Luis Obispo — M
California State Polytechnic University, Pomona — M
California State University Channel Islands — M
California State University, East Bay — M
California State University, Fresno — M
California State University, Fullerton — M
California State University, Long Beach — M
California State University, Los Angeles — M
California State University, Northridge — M
California State University, Sacramento — M
California State University, San Bernardino — M
California State University, San Marcos — M
Carleton University — M,D
Carlow University — M
Carnegie Mellon University — M,D
Case Western Reserve University — M,D
Central Connecticut State University — M,O
Central European University — M,D
Central Michigan University — M,D
Chicago State University — M
City College of the City University of New York — M
Claremont Graduate University — M,D
Clark Atlanta University — M,D
Clarkson University — M,D
Clemson University — M,D
Cleveland State University — M
The College at Brockport, State University of New York — M
College of Charleston — M
Colorado State University — M,D
Columbia University — M,D
Columbus State University — M,O
Concordia University (Canada) — M,D
Cornell University — D
Dalhousie University — M,D
Dartmouth College — M,D
Delaware State University — M
DePaul University — M,D
Drew University — M,D,O
Drexel University — M,D*
Duke University — D
Duquesne University — M
East Carolina University — M
Eastern Illinois University — M
Eastern Kentucky University — M
Eastern Michigan University — M
East Tennessee State University — M,O
Elizabeth City State University — M
Emory University — M,D
Emporia State University — M
Fairfield University — M
Fairleigh Dickinson University, Metropolitan Campus — M
Florida Atlantic University — M,D
Florida Gulf Coast University — M
Florida International University — M
George Mason University — M,D
Georgetown University — M
The George Washington University — M,D,O
Georgia Institute of Technology — M,D
Georgia Southern University — M
Georgia State University — M,D
Governors State University — M
The Graduate Center, City University of New York — D
Harvard University — D*
Hofstra University — M,D,O
Houston Baptist University — M,D
Howard University — M,D
Hunter College of the City University of New York — M
Idaho State University — M,D
Illinois State University — M
Indiana State University — M
Indiana University Bloomington — M,D
Indiana University of Pennsylvania — M
Indiana University–Purdue University Indianapolis — M,D
Instituto Tecnologico de Santo Domingo — M,D,O
Iowa State University of Science and Technology — M,D
Jackson State University — M
Jacksonville State University — M
Jacksonville State University — M
John Carroll University — M
Johns Hopkins University — D*
Kansas State University — M
Kent State University — M,D,O
Kutztown University of Pennsylvania — M,D
Lakehead University — M
Lamar University — M
Lee University — M,O
Lehigh University — M,D
Lehman College of the City University of New York — M
Louisiana State University and Agricultural & Mechanical College — M,D
Louisiana Tech University — M,D,O
Loyola University Chicago — M
Manhattan College — M,O
Manhattanville College — M,O

Marquette University — M,D
Marshall University — M
Marygrove College — M,O
Massachusetts Institute of Technology — D
McGill University — M,D
McMaster University — M,D
McNeese State University — M
Memorial University of Newfoundland — M,D
Mercer University — M,D,O
Miami University — M,D
Michigan State University — M,D
Michigan Technological University — M,D
Middle Tennessee State University — M
Minnesota State University Mankato — M
Mississippi College — M
Mississippi State University — M,D
Missouri State University — M
Missouri University of Science and Technology — M,D
Montana State University — M,D
Montclair State University — M
Morgan State University — M,D
Murray State University — M
New Jersey Institute of Technology — M,D,O
New Mexico Institute of Mining and Technology — M,D
New York University — M,D*
North Carolina Agricultural and Technical State University — M
North Carolina Central University — M
North Carolina State University — M,D
North Dakota State University — M,D
Northeastern Illinois University — M
Northeastern University — M,D
Northern Arizona University — M,O
Northern Illinois University — M,D
Northwestern University — D
Northwest Missouri State University — M,O
Oakland University — M,D
The Ohio State University — M,D
Ohio University — M,D
Oklahoma State University — M,D
Old Dominion University — M,D
Oregon State University — M,D
Pace University — M,O
Penn State University Park — M,D*
Pittsburg State University — M
Portland State University — M,D,O
Princeton University — D
Purdue University — M,D
Purdue University Fort Wayne — M,O
Purdue University Northwest — M
Queens College of the City University of New York — M
Queen's University at Kingston — M,D
Regent University — M,D,O
Rensselaer Polytechnic Institute — M,D
Rhode Island College — M,O
Rice University — D
Rivier University — M
Rochester Institute of Technology — M,D,O
Roosevelt University — M
Rowan University — M
Royal Military College of Canada — M
Rutgers University–Camden — M
Rutgers University–Newark — D
Rutgers University–New Brunswick — M,D
St. John's University (NY) — M
Saint Joseph's University — M,O
Saint Louis University — M,D*
Salem State University — M
Sam Houston State University — M
San Diego State University — M,D
San Francisco State University — M
Simon Fraser University — M,D
Smith College — O
South Carolina State University — M
South Dakota State University — M,D
Southeast Missouri State University — M
Southern Connecticut State University — M
Southern Illinois University Carbondale — M,D
Southern Illinois University Edwardsville — M
Southern Methodist University — M,D
Southern University and Agricultural and Mechanical College — M
Stanford University — M,D
State University of New York College at Cortland — M
State University of New York College at Potsdam — M
Stephen F. Austin State University — M
Stevens Institute of Technology — M,D
Stony Brook University, State University of New York — M,D
Syracuse University — M,D
Tarleton State University — M
Temple University — M,D*
Tennessee State University — M,D
Tennessee Technological University — M
Texas A&M International University — M
Texas A&M University — M,D
Texas A&M University–Central Texas — M,O
Texas A&M University–Commerce — M,O
Texas A&M University–Corpus Christi — M
Texas A&M University–Kingsville — M
Texas Christian University — M,D
Texas Southern University — M
Texas State University — M
Texas Tech University — M,D
Texas Woman's University — M

Tufts University	M,D
Tulane University	M,D
Université de Moncton	M
Université de Montréal	M,D,O
Université de Sherbrooke	M,D
Université du Québec à Montréal	M,D
Université du Québec à Trois-Rivières	M
Université Laval	M,D
University at Albany, State University of New York	M,D
University at Buffalo, the State University of New York	M,D
The University of Akron	M
The University of Alabama	M,D
The University of Alabama at Birmingham	M
The University of Alabama in Huntsville	M,D
University of Alaska Fairbanks	M,D,O
University of Alberta	M,D,O
The University of Arizona	M,D
University of Arkansas	M,D
University of Arkansas at Little Rock	M,O
The University of British Columbia	M,D
University of Calgary	M,D
University of California, Berkeley	M,D
University of California, Davis	M,D
University of California, Irvine	M,D
University of California, Los Angeles	M,D
University of California, Riverside	M,D
University of California, San Diego	M,D
University of California, Santa Barbara	M,D
University of California, Santa Cruz	M,D
University of Central Arkansas	M
University of Central Florida	M,D,O
University of Central Missouri	M,D,O
University of Central Oklahoma	M
University of Chicago	D
University of Cincinnati	M,D
University of Colorado Boulder	M,D
University of Colorado Colorado Springs	D
University of Colorado Denver	M,D
University of Delaware	M,D
University of Denver	M,D
The University of Findlay	M,D
University of Florida	M,D
University of Georgia	M,D
University of Guelph	M,D
University of Hawaii at Manoa	M,D
University of Houston	M,D
University of Houston–Clear Lake	M
University of Idaho	M
University of Illinois at Chicago	M,D
University of Illinois at Urbana–Champaign	M,D
The University of Iowa	M,D
The University of Kansas	M,D,O
University of Kentucky	M,D
University of Lethbridge	M,D
University of Louisiana at Lafayette	M,D
University of Louisville	M,D
University of Lynchburg	M
University of Maine	M
The University of Manchester	M,D
University of Manitoba	M,D
University of Maryland, College Park	M,D
University of Massachusetts Amherst	M,D
University of Massachusetts Lowell	D
University of Memphis	M,D,O
University of Miami	M,D
University of Michigan	M,D
University of Michigan–Flint	M
University of Minnesota, Twin Cities Campus	M,D,O
University of Mississippi	M,D
University of Missouri	M,D
University of Missouri–Kansas City	M,D
University of Missouri–St. Louis	M,D
University of Montana	M,D
University of Nebraska at Omaha	M
University of Nebraska–Lincoln	M,D
University of Nevada, Las Vegas	M,D
University of Nevada, Reno	M
University of New Brunswick Fredericton	M,D
University of New Hampshire	M,D,O
University of New Mexico	M,D
University of New Orleans	M
The University of North Carolina at Chapel Hill	M,D
The University of North Carolina at Charlotte	M,D,O
The University of North Carolina at Greensboro	M,D
The University of North Carolina Wilmington	M,O
University of North Dakota	M
University of Northern British Columbia	M,D,O
University of Northern Colorado	M,D,O
University of Northern Iowa	M
University of North Florida	M
University of North Texas	M,D,O
University of Notre Dame	M,D
University of Oklahoma	M,D*

University of Oregon	M,D
University of Ottawa	M,D
University of Pennsylvania	M,D*
University of Pittsburgh	M,D*
University of Puerto Rico–Mayagüez	M
University of Puerto Rico–Río Piedras	M,D
University of Regina	M,D
University of Rhode Island	M,D
University of Rochester	D*
University of San Diego	M
University of Saskatchewan	M,D
University of South Alabama	M
University of South Carolina	M,D
University of South Dakota	M
University of Southern California	M,D
University of Southern Mississippi	M,D
University of South Florida	M,D,O
The University of Tennessee	M,D
The University of Tennessee at Chattanooga	M
The University of Texas at Arlington	M,D
The University of Texas at Austin	M,D
The University of Texas at Dallas	M,D
The University of Texas at El Paso	M
The University of Texas at San Antonio	M
The University of Texas at Tyler	M
The University of Texas Rio Grande Valley	M
University of the Incarnate Word	M
University of the Virgin Islands	M
The University of Toledo	M,D
University of Toronto	M,D
University of Tulsa	M,D
University of Utah	M,D
University of Vermont	M,D
University of Victoria	M,D
University of Virginia	M,D
University of Washington	M,D
University of Waterloo	M,D
The University of Western Ontario	M,D
University of West Florida	M
University of West Georgia	M,O
University of Windsor	M,D
University of Wisconsin–Madison	D
University of Wisconsin–Milwaukee	M,D*
University of Wyoming	M,D
Utah State University	M,D
Vanderbilt University	M,D*
Villanova University	M
Virginia Commonwealth University	M
Virginia Polytechnic Institute and State University	M,D
Virginia State University	M
Wake Forest University	M
Washington State University	M,D
Washington University in St. Louis	M,D
Wayne State University	M,D,O
Wesleyan University	M,D
West Chester University of Pennsylvania	M,O
Western Connecticut State University	M
Western Illinois University	M
Western Kentucky University	M
Western Michigan University	M,D
Western Washington University	M
West Texas A&M University	M
West Virginia University	M,D
Wichita State University	M,D
Wilfrid Laurier University	M
Wilkes University	M
Worcester Polytechnic Institute	M,D,O
Wright State University	M
Yale University	M,D
Yeshiva University	M
York University	M,D
Youngstown State University	M

MATHEMATICS EDUCATION

Adams State University	M
Alabama Agricultural and Mechanical University	M,O
Alabama State University	M,O
American University of Beirut	M,D
Appalachian State University	M
Arcadia University	M,D,O
Arizona State University at the Tempe campus	M,D,O
Arkansas State University	M
Asbury University	M
Aurora University	M
Austin Peay State University	M
Ball State University	M
Bank Street College of Education	M
Bard College	M
Bemidji State University	M
Binghamton University, State University of New York	M
Bloomsburg University of Pennsylvania	M
Bob Jones University	M,D,O
Boise State University	M
Boston College	M,D,O
Bowling Green State University	M,D
Bridgewater State University	M
Brigham Young University	M
Brooklyn College of the City University of New York	M
Buffalo State College, State University of New York	M
California State University, Chico	M
California State University, East Bay	M
California State University, Fresno	M

California State University, Fullerton	M
California State University, Long Beach	M
California State University, Northridge	M
California State University, San Bernardino	M
California University of Pennsylvania	M
Cambridge College	M,D,O
Caribbean University	M,D
Central Michigan University	M,D
Chatham University	M
The Citadel, The Military College of South Carolina	M,O
City College of the City University of New York	M,O
Clarion University of Pennsylvania	M
Clark Atlanta University	M
Clayton State University	M
Clemson University	M,D,O
Cleveland State University	M
The College at Brockport, State University of New York	M,O
College of Charleston	M
College of Staten Island of the City University of New York	M
The Colorado College	M
Columbus State University	M,O
Concordia University (United States)	M,D
Concordia University (Canada)	M,D
Converse College	M
Cornell University	M,D
Delaware State University	M
DePaul University	M,D
Drake University	M,D,O
Duquesne University	M
East Carolina University	M,O
Eastern Illinois University	M
Eastern Kentucky University	M
Eastern University	M,O
Elizabeth City State University	M
Fitchburg State University	M
Florida Agricultural and Mechanical University	M
Florida Gulf Coast University	M
Florida International University	M,D,O
Framingham State University	M
Fresno Pacific University	M
George Mason University	M
The George Washington University	M
Georgia Southwestern State University	M,O
Georgia State University	M,D,O
Gordon College	M,O
Grambling State University	M,D,O
Hampton University	M
Harding University	M,O
Harvard University	M,O*
High Point University	M,D
Hofstra University	M,D,O
Hood College	M,O
Hunter College of the City University of New York	M
Idaho State University	M,D
Illinois Institute of Technology	M,D
Illinois State University	M,D
Indiana University Bloomington	M,D,O
Indiana University of Pennsylvania	M
Indiana University–Purdue University Indianapolis	M,D
Instituto Tecnológico y de Estudios Superiores de Monterrey, Campus Ciudad Obregón	M
Inter American University of Puerto Rico, Arecibo Campus	M
Inter American University of Puerto Rico, Metropolitan Campus	M
Inter American University of Puerto Rico, Ponce Campus	M
Inter American University of Puerto Rico, San Germán Campus	M
Iona College	M
Iowa State University of Science and Technology	M,D
Jackson State University	M
James Madison University	M
Kennesaw State University	M
Kent State University	M,D
Lake Forest College	M,O
Lebanon Valley College	M,O
Lee University	M,O
Lehman College of the City University of New York	M
Lesley University	M,D,O
Longwood University	M
Loyola Marymount University	M
Manhattanville College	M,O
Marquette University	M,D
McDaniel College	M
McNeese State University	O
Metropolitan State University	M
Miami University	M
Michigan State University	M,D
Middle Tennessee State University	M,D
Millersville University of Pennsylvania	M,D
Minnesota State University Mankato	M
Minot State University	M
Mississippi College	M,D,O
Missouri State University	M
Missouri University of Science and Technology	M,D
Molloy College	M,O
Montana State University	M,D
Montclair State University	M,D,O
Morehead State University	M
Morgan State University	M,D
Mount Holyoke College	M

Murray State University	M
National Louis University	M,D,O
National University	M,O
New Jersey City University	M
New York Institute of Technology	M,O
New York University	M*
North Carolina Agricultural and Technical State University	M
North Carolina State University	M,D
North Dakota State University	D
Northeastern Illinois University	M
Northeastern State University	M
Northern Arizona University	M,O
Northwest Missouri State University	M,D,O
The Ohio State University	M,D
Oregon State University	M,D
Plymouth State University	M
Portland State University	M,D,O
Providence College	M
Purdue University	M,D,O
Purdue University Fort Wayne	M,O
Purdue University Global	M
Purdue University Northwest	M
Queens College of the City University of New York	M,O
Quinnipiac University	M
Radford University	M
Rhode Island College	M
Rowan University	M,O
Rutgers University–Camden	M
Rutgers University–New Brunswick	M,D
St. John Fisher College	M
St. John's University (NY)	D
Saint Peter's University	M,D,O
Salem State University	M
Salisbury University	M
San Diego State University	M,D
San Francisco State University	M,O
Seattle Pacific University	M
Shippensburg University of Pennsylvania	M
Simon Fraser University	M,D
Slippery Rock University of Pennsylvania	M
Smith College	M
South Carolina State University	M
Southeastern Oklahoma State University	M
Southern Illinois University Edwardsville	M
Southern University and Agricultural and Mechanical College	D
Southwestern Oklahoma State University	M
Southwest Minnesota State University	M
State University of New York at Fredonia	M,O
State University of New York at Plattsburgh	M
State University of New York College at Cortland	M
State University of New York College at Old Westbury	M
State University of New York College at Potsdam	M
Stephen F. Austin State University	M
Stevenson University	M
Stony Brook University, State University of New York	M,O
Syracuse University	M,D
Teachers College, Columbia University	M,D
Teachers College of San Joaquin	M
Temple University	M*
Tennessee Technological University	M
Texas Christian University	M
Texas State University	D
Texas Woman's University	M
Touro College	M
Towson University	M
Tufts University	M,D
Universidad Autonoma de Guadalajara	M,D
University at Buffalo, the State University of New York	M,D,O
The University of Akron	M
The University of Alabama in Huntsville	M,D,O
University of Alaska Southeast	M
The University of Arizona	M
University of Arkansas	M
University of Arkansas at Pine Bluff	M
The University of British Columbia	M,D
University of California, Berkeley	M,D
University of California, San Diego	D
University of Central Arkansas	M
University of Central Florida	M,O
University of Cincinnati	M,D
University of Colorado Denver	M,D
University of Connecticut	M,D
University of Dayton	M
University of Detroit Mercy	M,D
University of Florida	M,D,O
University of Georgia	M,D,O
University of Illinois at Chicago	M,D
University of Illinois at Urbana–Champaign	M,D
University of Indianapolis	M
The University of Iowa	M,D
University of Louisiana at Lafayette	M
University of Maryland, Baltimore County	M
University of Massachusetts Dartmouth	M,D,O

*M—masters degree; D—doctorate; O—other advanced degree; *—Close-Up and/or Display*

University of Memphis	M,D
University of Miami	D
University of Minnesota, Twin Cities Campus	M,D,O
University of Mississippi	M,D,O
University of Missouri	M,D,O
University of Montana	M,D
University of Nebraska at Kearney	M
University of Nevada, Reno	M
University of New Hampshire	M,D,O
The University of North Carolina at Chapel Hill	M
The University of North Carolina at Greensboro	M,D,O
The University of North Carolina at Pembroke	M
University of Northern Colorado	M,D
University of Northern Iowa	M
University of North Georgia	M
University of Oklahoma	M,D*
University of Phoenix–Online Campus	M,O
University of Pittsburgh	M,D*
University of Puerto Rico–Mayagüez	M
University of Puerto Rico–Río Piedras	M,D
University of St. Francis (IL)	M,D,O
University of South Africa	M,D
University of South Carolina	M,D
University of South Dakota	M
University of Southern Indiana	M
University of South Florida, St. Petersburg	M
The University of Tennessee	M,D,O
The University of Tennessee at Chattanooga	M
The University of Texas at Arlington	M,D
The University of Texas at Dallas	M
The University of Texas at San Antonio	M
University of the District of Columbia	M
University of the Incarnate Word	M
University of the Sacred Heart	M,O
University of the Virgin Islands	M
The University of Toledo	M,D,O
University of Utah	M,D
University of Victoria	M,D
University of Virginia	M,D
University of Washington	M,D
University of Washington, Tacoma	M
The University of West Alabama	M
University of Wisconsin–Milwaukee	M,D,O*
University of Wisconsin–Oshkosh	M
University of Wisconsin–River Falls	M
University of Wyoming	M,D
Utah Valley University	M
Wagner College	M
Walden University	M,D,O
Washington State University	M,D
Wayne State College	M
Wayne State University	M,D,O
Webster University	M,O
West Chester University of Pennsylvania	M
Western Governors University	M,O
Western Michigan University	M,D
Western New England University	M
Western Oregon University	M
Westfield State University	M
Widener University	M
William Jessup University	M
Wright State University	D
Youngstown State University	M

MECHANICAL ENGINEERING

Alfred University	M
The American University in Cairo	M,D,O
American University of Beirut	M,D
American University of Sharjah	M,D
Arizona State University at the Tempe campus	M,D
Arkansas Tech University	M
Auburn University	M,D
Baylor University	M,D
Binghamton University, State University of New York	M,D
Boise State University	M
Boston University	M,D
Bradley University	M
Brigham Young University	M,D
Brown University	M,D
Bucknell University	M
Buffalo State College, State University of New York	M
California Baptist University	M
California Institute of Technology	M,D,O
California Polytechnic State University, San Luis Obispo	M
California State Polytechnic University, Pomona	M
California State University, Fresno	M
California State University, Fullerton	M
California State University, Long Beach	M,D
California State University, Los Angeles	M
California State University, Northridge	M
California State University, Sacramento	M
Carleton University	M,D
Carnegie Mellon University	M,D
Case Western Reserve University	M,D
The Catholic University of America	M,D
The Citadel, The Military College of South Carolina	M,O

City College of the City University of New York	M,D
Clarkson University	M,D
Clemson University	M,D
Cleveland State University	M,D
Colorado School of Mines	M,D
Colorado State University	M,D
Columbia University	M,D
Concordia University (Canada)	M,D,O
Cooper Union for the Advancement of Science and Art	M
Cornell University	M,D
Dalhousie University	M,D
Dartmouth College	M,D
Drexel University	M,D*
Duke University	M,D
École Polytechnique de Montréal	M,D,O
Embry-Riddle Aeronautical University–Daytona	M,D
Fairfield University	M,O
Farmingdale State College	M
Florida Agricultural and Mechanical University	M,D
Florida Atlantic University	M,D
Florida Institute of Technology	M,D
Florida International University	M,D
Florida State University	M,D
Gannon University	M
The George Washington University	M,D,O
Georgia Institute of Technology	M,D
Georgia Southern University	M
Grand Valley State University	M
Harvard University	M,D*
Howard University	M,D
Idaho State University	M
Illinois Institute of Technology	M,D
Indiana University–Purdue University Indianapolis	M,D
Instituto Tecnológico y de Estudios Superiores de Monterrey, Campus Chihuahua	M,O
Instituto Tecnológico y de Estudios Superiores de Monterrey, Campus Monterrey	M,D
Inter American University of Puerto Rico, Bayamón Campus	M
Iowa State University of Science and Technology	M,D
Johns Hopkins University	M,D,O*
Kansas State University	M,D
Kennesaw State University	M
Kettering University	M
Lamar University	M,D
Lawrence Technological University	M,D
Lehigh University	M,D
Louisiana State University and Agricultural & Mechanical College	M,D
Loyola Marymount University	M
Manhattan College	M
Marquette University	M,D,O
Marshall University	M
Massachusetts Institute of Technology	M,D,O
McGill University	M,D
McMaster University	M,D
McNeese State University	M
Memorial University of Newfoundland	M,D
Mercer University	M
Merrimack College	M
Miami University	M
Michigan State University	M,D
Michigan Technological University	M,D,O
Mississippi State University	M,D
Missouri University of Science and Technology	M,D
Montana State University	M,D
Naval Postgraduate School	M,D,O
New Jersey Institute of Technology	M,D
New Mexico Institute of Mining and Technology	M
New York Institute of Technology	M
New York University	M,D*
North Carolina Agricultural and Technical State University	M,D
North Carolina State University	M,D
North Dakota State University	M,D
Northeastern University	M,D,O
Northern Arizona University	M,D
Northern Illinois University	M
Northwestern University	M,D
Oakland University	M,D
The Ohio State University	M,D
Ohio University	M,D
Oklahoma Christian University	M
Oklahoma State University	M,D
Old Dominion University	M,D
Oregon State University	M,D
Penn State Harrisburg	M,O
Penn State University Park	M,D*
Pittsburg State University	M
Polytechnic University of Puerto Rico	M
Portland State University	M,D,O
Princeton University	M,D
Purdue University	M,D,O
Purdue University Fort Wayne	M
Purdue University Northwest	M
Queen's University at Kingston	M,D
Rensselaer at Hartford	M
Rensselaer Polytechnic Institute	M,D
Rice University	M,D
Rochester Institute of Technology	M
Rose-Hulman Institute of Technology	M
Rowan University	M,D
Royal Military College of Canada	M,D
Rutgers University–New Brunswick	M,D
Saint Martin's University	M
San Diego State University	M,D
San Jose State University	M

Santa Clara University	M,D,O
Simon Fraser University	M
South Carolina State University	M
South Dakota School of Mines and Technology	M,D
South Dakota State University	M,D
Southern Illinois University Carbondale	M,D
Southern Illinois University Edwardsville	M
Southern Methodist University	M,D
Stanford University	M,D,O
Stevens Institute of Technology	M,D,O
Stony Brook University, State University of New York	M,D
Syracuse University	M,D
Temple University	M,D*
Tennessee State University	M,D
Tennessee Technological University	M
Texas A&M University	M,D
Texas A&M University–Kingsville	M
Texas State University	M
Tufts University	M,D
Tuskegee University	M
Universidad del Turabo	M
Université de Moncton	M
Université de Sherbrooke	M,D
Université Laval	M,D
University at Buffalo, the State University of New York	M,D
The University of Akron	M,D
The University of Alabama	M,D
The University of Alabama at Birmingham	M
The University of Alabama in Huntsville	M,D
University of Alaska Fairbanks	M
University of Alberta	M,D
The University of Arizona	M,D
University of Arkansas	M,D
University of Bridgeport	M,D
The University of British Columbia	M,D
University of Calgary	M,D
University of California, Berkeley	M,D
University of California, Davis	M,D,O
University of California, Irvine	M,D
University of California, Los Angeles	M,D
University of California, Merced	M,D
University of California, Riverside	M,D
University of California, San Diego	M,D
University of California, Santa Barbara	M,D
University of Central Florida	M,D
University of Central Oklahoma	M
University of Cincinnati	M,D
University of Colorado Boulder	M,D
University of Colorado Denver	M
University of Connecticut	M,D
University of Dayton	M,D
University of Delaware	M,D
University of Denver	M,D
University of Detroit Mercy	M,D
University of Florida	M,D
University of Hawaii at Manoa	M,D
University of Houston	M,D
University of Idaho	M,D
University of Illinois at Chicago	M,D
University of Illinois at Urbana–Champaign	M,D
The University of Iowa	M,D
The University of Kansas	M,D
University of Kentucky	M,D
University of Louisiana at Lafayette	M
University of Louisville	M,D
University of Maine	M,D
The University of Manchester	M,D
University of Manitoba	M,D
University of Maryland, Baltimore County	M,D
University of Maryland, College Park	M,D
University of Massachusetts Amherst	M,D
University of Massachusetts Dartmouth	M,O
University of Massachusetts Lowell	M,D
University of Memphis	M,D,O
University of Miami	M,D
University of Michigan	M,D
University of Michigan–Dearborn	M,D
University of Michigan–Flint	M
University of Minnesota, Twin Cities Campus	M,D
University of Mississippi	M,D
University of Missouri	M,D
University of Missouri–Kansas City	M,D,O
University of Nebraska–Lincoln	M,D
University of Nevada, Reno	M,D
University of New Brunswick Fredericton	M,D
University of New Hampshire	M
University of New Haven	M
University of New Mexico	M,D
University of New Orleans	M
The University of North Carolina at Charlotte	M,D
University of North Dakota	M,D
University of North Florida	M
University of North Texas	M,D,O
University of Notre Dame	M,D
University of Oklahoma	M,D*
University of Ottawa	M,D
University of Pennsylvania	M,D*
University of Pittsburgh	M,D*
University of Portland	M

University of Puerto Rico–Mayagüez	M,D
University of Rochester	M,D*
University of St. Thomas (MN)	M,O
University of Saskatchewan	M,D
University of South Alabama	M
University of South Carolina	M,D
University of Southern California	M,D,O
University of South Florida	M,D
The University of Tennessee	M,D
The University of Tennessee at Chattanooga	M
The University of Texas at Arlington	M,D
The University of Texas at Austin	M,D
The University of Texas at Dallas	M,D
The University of Texas at El Paso	M,D
The University of Texas at San Antonio	M,D
The University of Texas at Tyler	M
The University of Texas Rio Grande Valley	M
The University of Toledo	M
University of Toronto	M,D
The University of Tulsa	M,D
University of Utah	M,D
University of Vermont	M,D
University of Victoria	M,D
University of Virginia	M,D
University of Washington	M,D
University of Waterloo	M,D
The University of Western Ontario	M,D
University of Windsor	M,D
University of Wisconsin–Madison	M,D
University of Wisconsin–Milwaukee	M,D*
University of Wyoming	M,D
Utah State University	M,D
Vanderbilt University	M,D*
Villanova University	M,O
Virginia Commonwealth University	M,D
Washington State University	M,D
Washington University in St. Louis	M,D
Wayne State University	M,D
Western Michigan University	M,D
Western New England University	M
West Virginia University	M,D
Wichita State University	M,D
Widener University	M
Wilkes University	M
Worcester Polytechnic Institute	M,D,O
Wright State University	M,D
Yale University	M,D
Youngstown State University	M

MECHANICS

Brown University	M,D
California Institute of Technology	M,D
Carnegie Mellon University	M,D
Columbia University	M,D
Cornell University	M,D
Drexel University	M,D*
École Polytechnique de Montréal	M,D,O
Georgia Institute of Technology	M
Iowa State University of Science and Technology	M,D
Johns Hopkins University	M*
Lehigh University	M,D
Louisiana State University and Agricultural & Mechanical College	M,D
McGill University	M,D
Michigan State University	M,D
Michigan Technological University	M,D,O
Montana State University	M,D
New Mexico Institute of Mining and Technology	M
Northwestern University	M,D
Ohio University	M,D
Penn State University Park	M,D*
Rutgers University–New Brunswick	M,D
San Diego State University	M,D
Southern Illinois University Carbondale	M
Stanford University	M,D,O
The University of Alabama	M,D
University of Calgary	M,D
University of California, Berkeley	M,D
University of California, Merced	M,D
University of California, San Diego	M,D
University of Cincinnati	M,D
University of Colorado Denver	M
University of Dayton	M
University of Illinois at Urbana–Champaign	M,D
University of Maryland, Baltimore County	O
University of Maryland, College Park	M,D
University of Massachusetts Amherst	M,D
University of Minnesota, Twin Cities Campus	M,D
University of Nebraska–Lincoln	M,D
University of New Brunswick Fredericton	M,D
University of Pennsylvania	M,D*
University of Southern California	M,D,O
The University of Texas at Austin	M,D
University of Washington	M,D
University of Wisconsin–Madison	M,D
University of Wisconsin–Milwaukee	M,D*

MEDIA STUDIES

American University	M,D
American University of Beirut	M,D
Angelo State University	M
Arizona State University at the Tempe campus	M,D

Arkansas State University	M
Austin Peay State University	M
Boston University	M,D
Bowling Green State University	M,D
Brooklyn College of the City University of New York	M
Carnegie Mellon University	M
Central Michigan University	M
Champlain College	M
City College of the City University of New York	M
Claremont Graduate University	M,D,O
Clarion University of Pennsylvania	M
College of Staten Island of the City University of New York	M
Colorado State University	M,D
Columbia University	M
Concordia University (Canada)	M,D,O
Cornell University	M,D
Dallas Theological Seminary	M,D,O
DePaul University	M*
Drexel University	M*
Duke University	M
Fairleigh Dickinson University, Metropolitan Campus	M
Fielding Graduate University	M,D,O
Florida Atlantic University	M,O
Florida State University	M,D
Fordham University	M,D
Fordham University	M,D
Full Sail University	M
Georgetown University	M,D
Georgia State University	M,D
Howard University	M,D
Hunter College of the City University of New York	M
Indiana State University	M
Indiana University Bloomington	M,D
Indiana University of Pennsylvania	D
International University in Geneva	M,D
Johns Hopkins University	M*
Kent State University	M
La Salle University	M,O
Lindenwood University	M,O
Lindenwood University–Belleville	M
Long Island University–LIU Brooklyn	M,D,O
Louisiana State University and Agricultural & Mechanical College	M,D
Loyola University Maryland	M
Lynn University	M,O
Massachusetts College of Art and Design	M,O
Massachusetts Institute of Technology	M,D
Metropolitan College of New York	M
Michigan State University	M,D
Monmouth University	M,O
New Mexico Highlands University	M
The New School	M,O
New York University	M,D*
Norfolk State University	M
Northeastern University	M
Northern Kentucky University	M,O
Northwestern University	M,D
Ohio University	M,D
Old Dominion University	M,O
Pace University	M
Paris College of Art	M
Penn State University Park	M,D*
Pepperdine University	M
Point Park University	M
Pratt Institute	M
Purchase College, State University of New York	M
Queens College of the City University of New York	M
Rhode Island School of Design	M
Rochester Institute of Technology	O
Rowan University	M
Saginaw Valley State University	M
San Diego State University	M
San Francisco State University	M
Savannah College of Art and Design	M
Southern Illinois University Carbondale	M,D
Southern Illinois University Edwardsville	O
Stevens Institute of Technology	M
Syracuse University	M
Temple University	M*
Texas Tech University	M,D
Trinity College (United States)	M
University at Buffalo, the State University of New York	M,D,O
University of Bridgeport	M
University of California, Los Angeles	M,D
University of California, Santa Barbara	M,D
University of Chicago	M,D
University of Colorado Boulder	M,D
University of Colorado Denver	M
University of Denver	M
University of Illinois at Urbana–Champaign	M,D
The University of Iowa	M,D
The University of Kansas	M,D
University of Lethbridge	M,D
University of Maryland, College Park	M,D
University of Massachusetts Dartmouth	M
University of Michigan	M
University of Nevada, Las Vegas	M
The University of North Carolina at Chapel Hill	M,D,O
The University of North Carolina at Greensboro	M
University of Oregon	M,D

University of South Carolina	M
University of Southern California	M,D
University of South Florida	M
University of South Florida, St. Petersburg	M
The University of Texas at Austin	M,D
The University of Western Ontario	M,D
University of Wisconsin–Madison	M,D
University of Wisconsin–Milwaukee	M,D*
University of Wisconsin–Stevens Point	M
Valparaiso University	M,O
Virginia Commonwealth University	M,D
Virginia State University	M
Wagner College	M
Wayne State University	M,D,O
Webster University	M
West Virginia State University	M
West Virginia University	M,O
Wilfrid Laurier University	M

MEDICAL/SURGICAL NURSING

Case Western Reserve University	M
Daemen College	M,D,O
Eastern Virginia Medical School	M
Inter American University of Puerto Rico, Arecibo Campus	M
Inter American University of Puerto Rico, Barranquitas Campus	M
Pontifical Catholic University of Puerto Rico	M
Saint Francis Medical Center College of Nursing	M,D,O
State University of New York Downstate Medical Center	M,O
Universidad Adventista de las Antillas	M
University of South Africa	M,D
University of South Carolina	M
Ursuline College	M,D

MEDICAL ILLUSTRATION

Augusta University	M
Johns Hopkins University	M*
Rochester Institute of Technology	M
University of Illinois at Chicago	M

MEDICAL IMAGING

Boston University	M
Cedars-Sinai Medical Center	M,D
Illinois Institute of Technology	M,D
Medical University of South Carolina	D
National University of Health Sciences	M,D
Oregon State University	M,D
Rutgers University–Newark	M
Thomas Jefferson University	M
University of California, San Francisco	M
University of Cincinnati	M,D
University of Guelph	M,D,O
University of Southern California	M,D
University of Wisconsin–Milwaukee	D*
Wayne State University	M,D,O

MEDICAL INFORMATICS

Arizona State University at the Tempe campus	M,D
Brandeis University	M
Columbia University	M,D,O
Dalhousie University	M,D
Grand Valley State University	M
Middle Tennessee State University	M
Northwestern University	M,D
Nova Southeastern University	M,D,O
Oregon Health & Science University	M,D,O
Regis University	M,O
Rutgers University–Newark	M,D,O
Stanford University	M,D
University at Buffalo, the State University of New York	M,D
The University of Arizona	M,D,O
University of California, Davis	M
University of Colorado Denver	M,D
University of Illinois at Urbana–Champaign	M,D,O
The University of Kansas	M,D,O
University of Phoenix–Phoenix Campus	M,O
University of Washington	M,D
University of Wisconsin–Milwaukee	M*

MEDICAL MICROBIOLOGY

The Citadel, The Military College of South Carolina	M,O
Creighton University	M,D
HEC Montreal	D
Idaho State University	M,D
Rutgers University–New Brunswick	M,D
Université du Québec, Institut National de la Recherche Scientifique	M,D
University of Alberta	M,D
University of Hawaii at Manoa	M,D
University of Manitoba	M,D
University of Minnesota, Duluth	M,D
University of Southern California	D
University of South Florida	M,D
University of Wisconsin–La Crosse	M
University of Wisconsin–Madison	D

MEDICAL PHYSICS

Columbia University	M,D
Duke University	M,D
East Carolina University	M,D

Hampton University	M,D
Harvard University	D*
Hofstra University	M
Indiana University Bloomington	M,D
Louisiana State University and Agricultural & Mechanical College	M,D
Massachusetts Institute of Technology	M,D
McGill University	M,D
McMaster University	M,D
Oakland University	M,D
Oregon State University	M,D
Purdue University	M,D
Radiological Technologies University VT	M
Rush University	M,D
Southern Illinois University Carbondale	M
Stony Brook University, State University of New York	M,D
Thomas Jefferson University	M
University at Buffalo, the State University of New York	M,D
University of Alberta	M,D
The University of Arizona	M
University of California, Los Angeles	M,D
University of Chicago	D
University of Cincinnati	M
University of Florida	M,D,O
University of Kentucky	M
University of Minnesota, Twin Cities Campus	M,D
University of Oklahoma Health Sciences Center	M,D
University of Pennsylvania	M,D*
University of Rhode Island	M,D
University of South Florida	M,D
The University of Texas Health Science Center at Houston	M,D
The University of Texas Health Science Center at San Antonio	D
The University of Toledo	M,D
University of Utah	M,D
University of Victoria	M,D
University of Wisconsin–Madison	M,D
Virginia Commonwealth University	M,D
Wayne State University	M,D,O

MEDICINAL AND PHARMACEUTICAL CHEMISTRY

Duquesne University	M,D
Florida Agricultural and Mechanical University	M,D
Idaho State University	M,D
Medical University of South Carolina	D
New Jersey Institute of Technology	M,D,O
Rutgers University–New Brunswick	M,D
Temple University	M,D*
University at Buffalo, the State University of New York	M,D
University of California, Irvine	D
University of California, San Francisco	D
University of Connecticut	M,D
University of Florida	M,D
University of Illinois at Chicago	M,D
The University of Iowa	M,D
The University of Kansas	M,D
University of Michigan	D
University of Minnesota, Twin Cities Campus	M,D
University of Mississippi	M,D
University of Montana	M,D
University of Rhode Island	M,D
The University of Texas at Austin	M,D
University of the Sciences	M,D
The University of Toledo	M,D
University of Utah	M,D
University of Washington	D
Virginia Commonwealth University	M,D
Wayne State University	M,D

MEDIEVAL AND RENAISSANCE STUDIES

Arizona State University at the Tempe campus	M,D
The Catholic University of America	M,D,O
Central European University	M,D
Columbia University	M,D
Cornell University	M,D
Fordham University	M,O
Georgetown University	M,D
Harvard University	D*
Indiana University Bloomington	M,D
Loyola University Chicago	M,D
Rutgers University–New Brunswick	D
Southern Methodist University	M
University of California, Santa Barbara	M,D
University of Chicago	D
University of Connecticut	M,D
University of Guelph	D
University of Minnesota, Twin Cities Campus	M,D
University of Notre Dame	M,D
University of Pittsburgh	O*
University of Toronto	M,D
Yale University	M,D

METALLURGICAL ENGINEERING AND METALLURGY

Colorado School of Mines	M,D
Michigan Technological University	M,D
Missouri University of Science and Technology	M,D

Montana Tech of The University of Montana	M
The Ohio State University	M,D
Université Laval	M,D
The University of Alabama	M,D
The University of Manchester	M,D
University of Nebraska–Lincoln	M,D
University of Nevada, Reno	M,D
The University of Texas at El Paso	M,D
University of Utah	M,D

METEOROLOGY

Ball State University	M,O
Florida Institute of Technology	M
Florida State University	M,D
Iowa State University of Science and Technology	M,D
McGill University	M,D
Millersville University of Pennsylvania	M
Mississippi State University	M,D
Naval Postgraduate School	M,D
North Carolina State University	M,D
Northern Arizona University	M,D,O
Penn State University Park	M,D*
Saint Louis University	M,D*
San Jose State University	M
SIT Graduate Institute	M
Texas A&M University	M,D
Université du Québec à Montréal	M,D,O
University of California, San Diego	M
University of Hawaii at Manoa	M,D
University of Maryland, College Park	M,D
University of Miami	M,D
University of Oklahoma	M,D*
Utah State University	M,D
Yale University	D

MICROBIOLOGY

Alabama State University	M,D
Albany Medical College	M,D
Albert Einstein College of Medicine	D
American University of Beirut	M,D
Arizona State University at the Tempe campus	M,D
Baylor College of Medicine	D
Boston University	D
Brandeis University	M,D
Brigham Young University	M,D
California State University, Long Beach	M
Case Western Reserve University	D
The Catholic University of America	M,D
Central Washington University	M
Clemson University	M,D
Colorado State University	M,D
Columbia University	M,D
Cornell University	D
Dalhousie University	M,D
Dartmouth College	D
Drexel University	M,D*
Duke University	D
East Carolina University	M,D
East Tennessee State University	M,D
Emory University	D
Emporia State University	M
Georgetown University	M,D
The George Washington University	M,D,O
Georgia State University	M,D
Harvard University	D*
Howard University	M,D
Idaho State University	M,D
Illinois Institute of Technology	M,D
Illinois State University	M,D
Indiana University Bloomington	M,D
Indiana University–Purdue University Indianapolis	M,D
Inter American University of Puerto Rico, Metropolitan Campus	M
Iowa State University of Science and Technology	M,D
Johns Hopkins University	M,D*
Loma Linda University	M,D
Louisiana State University Health Sciences Center	D
Louisiana State University Health Sciences Center at Shreveport	M,D
Loyola University Chicago	M,D
Marquette University	M,D
Massachusetts Institute of Technology	D
McGill University	M,D
Medical University of South Carolina	D
Meharry Medical College	D
Miami University	M,D
Michigan State University	M,D
Montana State University	M,D
New York Medical College	M,D
New York University	M,D*
North Carolina State University	M,D
North Dakota State University	M,D
The Ohio State University	M,D
Ohio University	M,D
Oklahoma State University	M,D
Old Dominion University	M,D
Oregon Health & Science University	D
Oregon State University	M,D
Purdue University	M,D
Rosalind Franklin University of Medicine and Science	D
Rush University	M,D
Rutgers University–Newark	D
Rutgers University–New Brunswick	M,D
Saint Louis University	D*

San Diego State University	M
San Francisco State University	M
San Jose State University	M
Seton Hall University	M,D
South Dakota State University	M,D
Southern Illinois University Carbondale	M,D
Southwestern Oklahoma State University	M
Stanford University	D
State University of New York Upstate Medical University	M,D
Stony Brook University, State University of New York	D
Texas A&M University	M,D
Texas Tech University	M,D
Thomas Jefferson University	M,D
Tufts University	D
Tulane University	M
Universidad Central del Caribe	M,D
Université de Montréal	M,D
Université de Sherbrooke	M,D
Université du Québec, Institut National de la Recherche Scientifique	M,D
Université Laval	M,D
University at Buffalo, the State University of New York	M,D
The University of Alabama at Birmingham	D
University of Alberta	M,D
The University of Arizona	D
University of Arkansas for Medical Sciences	M,D,O
The University of British Columbia	M,D
University of Calgary	M,D
University of California, Berkeley	D
University of California, Davis	M,D
University of California, Irvine	M,D
University of California, Los Angeles	M,D
University of California, Riverside	M,D
University of California, Santa Cruz	M,D
University of Chicago	D
University of Cincinnati	M,D
University of Colorado Denver	D
University of Connecticut	M,D
University of Delaware	M,D
University of Florida	M,D
University of Georgia	M,D
University of Guelph	M,D
University of Hawaii at Manoa	M,D
University of Idaho	M,D
University of Illinois at Chicago	D
University of Illinois at Urbana–Champaign	M,D
The University of Iowa	M,D
The University of Kansas	M,D
University of Kentucky	D
University of Louisville	M,D
University of Maine	M,D
The University of Manchester	M,D
University of Manitoba	M,D
University of Maryland, Baltimore	D
University of Massachusetts Amherst	M,D
University of Massachusetts Medical School	M,D
University of Miami	D
University of Michigan	M,D
University of Minnesota, Twin Cities Campus	D
University of Mississippi Medical Center	D
University of Missouri	D
University of Montana	D
University of New Hampshire	M,D
University of New Mexico	M,D
The University of North Carolina at Chapel Hill	M,D
University of North Texas Health Science Center at Fort Worth	M,D
University of Oklahoma	M,D*
University of Oklahoma Health Sciences Center	M,D
University of Ottawa	M,D
University of Pennsylvania	D*
University of Pittsburgh	M,D*
University of Puerto Rico– Medical Sciences Campus	M,D
University of Rhode Island	M,D
University of Rochester	M,D*
University of Saskatchewan	M,D
University of South Dakota	M,D
University of Southern California	M
University of South Florida	M,D
The University of Tennessee	M,D
The University of Texas at Austin	D
The University of Texas Health Science Center at Houston	M,D
The University of Texas Health Science Center at San Antonio	M,D
The University of Texas Medical Branch	M,D
The University of Texas Southwestern Medical Center	D
University of Victoria	M,D
University of Virginia	D
University of Washington	D
The University of Western Ontario	M,D
University of Wisconsin–La Crosse	M
University of Wisconsin– Madison	D
University of Wisconsin– Milwaukee	M,D*
University of Wisconsin– Oshkosh	M
University of Wyoming	D
Vanderbilt University	M,D*
Virginia Commonwealth University	M,D
Wagner College	M
Wake Forest University	D
Washington University in St. Louis	D
Wayne State University	M,D,O
Wright State University	M
Yale University	D
Youngstown State University	M

MIDDLE SCHOOL EDUCATION

Alaska Pacific University	M
Albany State University	M,O
American International College	M,D,O
Appalachian State University	M
Arkansas State University	M,D,O
Augusta University	M,O
Avila University	M,O
Ball State University	M,O
Bellarmine University	M,D,O
Berry College	M
Bloomsburg University of Pennsylvania	M
Brenau University	M,O
Brooklyn College of the City University of New York	M,O
Cabrini University	M,D
California Lutheran University	M,D
Campbell University	M
Canisius College	M
Capella University	M,D
Chestnut Hill College	M
Chicago State University	M
The Citadel, The Military College of South Carolina	M,D,O
City College of the City University of New York	M,O
Clemson University	M,D,O
The College at Brockport, State University of New York	M,O
College of Mount Saint Vincent	M,O
College of Saint Elizabeth	M,O
The College of Saint Rose	M,O
College of Staten Island of the City University of New York	M
Columbus State University	M,O
Converse College	M
Daemen College	M
DePaul University	M,D
Dickinson State University	M
Drury University	M
Duquesne University	M
East Carolina University	M
Eastern Illinois University	M
Eastern Michigan University	M
Eastern Nazarene College	M,O
Eastern University	M,O
East Tennessee State University	M,O
Edinboro University of Pennsylvania	M
Emory University	M,D
Fayetteville State University	M
Fitchburg State University	M
Florida Gulf Coast University	M
Fontbonne University	M
Georgia College & State University	M
Georgia Southern University	M
Georgia Southwestern State University	M,O
Georgia State University	M,D
Gordon College	M,O
Goucher College	M,O
Grand Valley State University	M
Hampton University	M
Hebrew College	M,O
Henderson State University	M,O
Hofstra University	M,D,O
Hood College	M,O
Houston Baptist University	M
Huntington University	M,D
James Madison University	M
Kansas State University	M,D,O
Kennesaw State University	D,O
Kent State University	M,D,O
Kutztown University of Pennsylvania	M,D
LaGrange College	M,O
La Salle University	M,O
Lee University	M,O
Lehman College of the City University of New York	M
Le Moyne College	M,O
Lesley University	M,D,O
Lewis University	M
Lincoln University (MO)	M
Long Island University– Hudson	M,O
Long Island University–LIU Post	M,D,O
Longwood University	M,D
Louisiana Tech University	M,D,O
Lynn University	M,D
Manhattanville College	M,O
Mary Baldwin University	M
Marygrove College	M,O
Maryville University of Saint Louis	M,D
McNeese State University	O
Mercer University	M,D,O
Mercy College	M,O
Middle Tennessee State University	M,O
Milligan College	M,D,O
Minot State University	M
Mississippi State University	M,D,O
Morehead State University	M,O
Mount St. Joseph University	M,O
Mount Saint Mary College	M,O
Mount Saint Vincent University	M
Murray State University	M,D,O
National Louis University	M,O
Nazareth College of Rochester	M
New York Institute of Technology	M
Niagara University	M,O
Nicholls State University	M
North Carolina State University	M
Northeastern Illinois University	M

Northwestern State University of Louisiana	M
Northwest Missouri State University	M,D
Ohio University	M,D
Old Dominion University	M,O
Pacific University	M
Piedmont College	M,D,O
Point Park University	M,D
Portland State University	M,D,O
Queens College of the City University of New York	M,O
Roberts Wesleyan College	M
Roger Williams University	M,O
Rowan University	O
St. Bonaventure University	M
St. John Fisher College	M
Saint Joseph's University	M,D,O
Saint Peter's University	M,O
St. Thomas Aquinas College	M,O
Salem College	M
Salem State University	M
Salisbury University	M
Seton Hill University	M
Shippensburg University of Pennsylvania	M
Smith College	M
Southeast Missouri State University	M
Spalding University	M
State University of New York at Fredonia	M,O
State University of New York at Oswego	M
State University of New York College at Potsdam	M
Temple University	M*
Tennessee Technological University	M
Theological University of the Caribbean	M,D
Tufts University	M,D
Union College (KY)	M
University of Arkansas	M,D,O
University of Arkansas at Little Rock	M
University of Bridgeport	M,D,O
University of Central Florida	M,O
University of Dayton	M
University of Kentucky	M,D
University of Louisville	M,D,O
University of Massachusetts Dartmouth	M,D,O
University of Missouri–St. Louis	M
The University of North Carolina at Charlotte	M,D,O
The University of North Carolina at Greensboro	M,D,O
The University of North Carolina Wilmington	M
University of Northern Iowa	M
University of North Georgia	M
University of Phoenix–Online Campus	M,O
University of South Florida, St. Petersburg	M
University of the Cumberlands	M,D,O
University of the District of Columbia	M
The University of Toledo	M,D,O
University of Vermont	M
University of Washington, Bothell	M
University of West Florida	M
University of Wisconsin– Milwaukee	M*
Wagner College	M
Webster University	M,O
Western Kentucky University	M,O
Wichita State University	M
Widener University	M,D
Wilkes University	M,D
William Paterson University of New Jersey	M,O
Winston-Salem State University	M
Worcester State University	M

MILITARY AND DEFENSE STUDIES

Adler University	M
American Public University System	M,D
Austin Peay State University	M
Bellevue University	M
The Citadel, The Military College of South Carolina	M,O
East Carolina University	M
Embry-Riddle Aeronautical University–Prescott	M
George Mason University	M
The George Washington University	M
Hawai'i Pacific University	M
Henley-Putnam School of Strategic Security	M
The Institute of World Politics	M,D,O
The Judge Advocate General's School, U.S. Army	M
Liberty University	M,D
London Metropolitan University	M,D
Missouri State University	M,O
National Defense University	M
National Intelligence University	M
Naval Postgraduate School	M,D
Norwich University	M
Royal Military College of Canada	M,D
School of Advanced Air and Space Studies	M
United States Army Command and General Staff College	M
University of Calgary	M,D
University of Colorado Denver	M,D
University of Pittsburgh	M*

MINERAL/MINING ENGINEERING

Colorado School of Mines	M,D
Dalhousie University	M,D
Laurentian University	M,D

McGill University	M,D,O
Missouri University of Science and Technology	M,D
Montana Tech of The University of Montana	M
New Mexico Institute of Mining and Technology	M
Penn State University Park	M,D*
Queen's University at Kingston	M,D
South Dakota School of Mines and Technology	M
Southern Illinois University Carbondale	M,D
Université du Québec en Abitibi-Témiscamingue	M,O
Université Laval	M,D
University of Alaska Fairbanks	M,D
University of Alberta	M,D
The University of Arizona	M,D,O
The University of British Columbia	M,D
University of Kentucky	M,D
University of Nevada, Reno	M,D
The University of Texas at Austin	M,D
University of Utah	M,D
West Virginia University	M,D

MINERAL ECONOMICS

Colorado School of Mines	M,D
Michigan Technological University	M
The University of Texas at Austin	M

MINERALOGY

Cornell University	M,D
Indiana University Bloomington	M,D
Université du Québec à Chicoutimi	D
Université du Québec à Montréal	M,D,O
The University of Texas at Dallas	M,D

MISSIONS AND MISSIOLOGY

Abilene Christian University	M
Acadia University	M,D
Anderson University (IN)	M,D
Asbury Theological Seminary	M,D,O
Assemblies of God Theological Seminary	M,D
Bethel Seminary	M,D,O
Biola University	M,D,O
Boston University	M,D
Briercrest Seminary	M
Calvin Theological Seminary	M,D
Capital University	M
Catholic Theological Union	M,D,O
Cedarville University	M,D
Central Baptist Theological Seminary	M,O
Clarks Summit University	M,D
Columbia International University	M,D,O
Dallas Baptist University	M
Dallas Theological Seminary	M,D
Eastern University	M
Ecclesia College	M
Evangelical Seminary	M
Fresno Pacific University	M
Fuller Theological Seminary	M,D,O
Gardner-Webb University	M,D
Global University	M,D
Gordon-Conwell Theological Seminary	M,D
Grace Mission University	M,D
Grace Theological Seminary	M,D,O
Hope International University	M
Liberty University	M
Luther Seminary	M,D
Mid-America Baptist Theological Seminary	M,D
Midwest University	M,D,O
Milligan College	M,D,O
Missio Seminary	M,D,O
Nebraska Christian College of Hope International University	M
Northern Seminary	M
Northwest Nazarene University	M
Northwest University	M
Nyack College	M,D
Oral Roberts University	M,D
Phillips Theological Seminary	M,D
Providence University College & Theological Seminary	M,D,O
Reformed Theological Seminary–Jackson Campus	M,D,O
Regent University	M,D
Rochester College	M
Saint Paul University	M
Simpson University	M
Southeastern Baptist Theological Seminary	M,D
Southern Adventist University	M
The Southern Baptist Theological Seminary	M,D
Southern Evangelical Seminary	M,D,O
Southwestern Assemblies of God University	M
Southwestern Baptist Theological Seminary	M
Southwestern Christian University	M
Taylor College and Seminary	M,O
Theological University of the Caribbean	M,D
Trinity Bible College and Graduate School	M
Trinity International University	M,D,O
Trinity School for Ministry	M,D
Tyndale University College & Seminary	M,O
University of South Africa	M,D
Villanova University	M
Wesley Biblical Seminary	M
Westminster Theological Seminary	M,D,O
Wheaton College	M
Whitworth University	M

MODELING AND SIMULATION

Arizona State University at the Tempe campus	M,D
Carnegie Mellon University	M,D
Columbus State University	M,O
Naval Postgraduate School	M,D
Old Dominion University	M,D
Portland State University	M,D,O
Rochester Institute of Technology	D
Stevens Institute of Technology	M,D,O
Trent University	M,D
Université Laval	M,O
University at Buffalo, the State University of New York	M,D
The University of Alabama in Huntsville	M,D,O
University of California, San Diego	M,D
University of Central Florida	M,D,O
The University of Manchester	M,D
University of Pittsburgh	M,D*
University of Southern California	M,D
Worcester Polytechnic Institute	M,D,O

MOLECULAR BIOLOGY

Albany College of Pharmacy and Health Sciences	M
Albany Medical College	M,D
Albert Einstein College of Medicine	D
American University of Beirut	D
Appalachian State University	M
Arizona State University at the Tempe campus	M,D
Arkansas State University	M,D
Auburn University	M,D
Baylor College of Medicine	D
Boise State University	M,D
Boston University	M,D
Brandeis University	M,D
Brigham Young University	M,D
Brown University	M,D
California Institute of Technology	D
California State University, Sacramento	M
Carnegie Mellon University	M,D
Case Western Reserve University	D
Central Connecticut State University	M,O
Clemson University	D
Columbia University	D
Cornell University	M,D
Dartmouth College	M
Drexel University	M,D*
Duke University	D,O
East Carolina University	M,D
Emory University	D
Florida Institute of Technology	M
Florida State University	M,D
Georgetown University	M,D
Georgia State University	M,D
Grand Valley State University	M
Harvard University	D*
Howard University	D
Illinois Institute of Technology	M,D
Illinois State University	M,D
Indiana State University	M,D
Indiana University Bloomington	M,D
Indiana University–Purdue University Indianapolis	M,D
Inter American University of Puerto Rico, Metropolitan Campus	M
Iowa State University of Science and Technology	M,D
Irell & Manella Graduate School of Biological Sciences	D
Johns Hopkins University	M,D*
Kent State University	M,D
Lehigh University	M,D
Lipscomb University	M
Louisiana State University Health Sciences Center at Shreveport	M,D
Louisiana Tech University	M,D,O
Loyola University Chicago	M,D
Marquette University	M,D
Massachusetts Institute of Technology	M,D,O
Mayo Clinic Graduate School of Biomedical Sciences	M,D
McMaster University	M,D
Medical University of South Carolina	M,D
Michigan State University	M,D
Michigan Technological University	M,D,O
Middle Tennessee State University	D
Mississippi State University	M,D
Missouri State University	M
Montclair State University	M,O
New Mexico State University	M,D
New York Medical College	M,D
New York University	M,D*
North Dakota State University	M
Northeastern Illinois University	M
Northwestern University	D
The Ohio State University	M,D
Ohio University	D
Oklahoma State University	M,D
Oregon Health & Science University	M,D
Oregon State University	M,D
Pace University	M,D
Penn State University Park	M,D*
Princeton University	D
Purdue University	D
Quinnipiac University	M
Rosalind Franklin University of Medicine and Science	
Rutgers University–Newark	M,D
Rutgers University–New Brunswick	M,D
Sacred Heart University	M
Saint Louis University	D*

San Diego State University	M,D
San Francisco State University	M
San Jose State University	M
Seton Hall University	M,D
Simon Fraser University	M,D,O
Southern Illinois University Carbondale	M,D
Southern Methodist University	M,D
State University of New York Downstate Medical Center	D
State University of New York Upstate Medical University	M,D
Stony Brook University, State University of New York	M,D
Texas Woman's University	M,D
Tufts University	D
Tulane University	M,D
Uniformed Services University of the Health Sciences	M,D*
Universidad Central del Caribe	M,D
Université de Montréal	M,D
Université Laval	M,D
University at Buffalo, the State University of New York	D
The University of Alabama at Birmingham	D
University of Alberta	M,D
The University of Arizona	D
University of Arkansas	M,D
University of Arkansas for Medical Sciences	M,D,O
The University of British Columbia	M,D
University of Calgary	M,D
University of California, Berkeley	D
University of California, Davis	M,D
University of California, Irvine	M,D
University of California, Los Angeles	M,D
University of California, Riverside	M,D
University of California, San Francisco	D
University of California, Santa Barbara	
University of California, Santa Cruz	M,D
University of Chicago	D
University of Cincinnati	M,D
University of Colorado Boulder	D
University of Colorado Denver	D
University of Connecticut	M,D
University of Connecticut Health Center	D
University of Delaware	M,D
University of Denver	M,D
University of Florida	M,D
University of Georgia	M,D
University of Guelph	M,D
University of Hawaii at Manoa	M,D
University of Illinois at Chicago	D
The University of Iowa	D
The University of Kansas	D
University of Lethbridge	M,D
University of Maine	M,D
The University of Manchester	M,D
University of Maryland, Baltimore	M,D
University of Maryland, Baltimore County	
University of Maryland, College Park	M,D
University of Miami	D
University of Michigan	M,D
University of Minnesota, Duluth	M,D
University of Minnesota, Twin Cities Campus	M,D
University of Missouri–Kansas City	D
University of Montana	D
University of Nebraska Medical Center	M
University of Nevada, Reno	M,D
University of New Haven	M
University of New Mexico	M,D
The University of North Carolina at Chapel Hill	M,D
University of North Texas	M,D,O
University of Notre Dame	M,D
University of Oklahoma Health Sciences Center	M,D
University of Oregon	M,D
University of Ottawa	M,D
University of Pennsylvania	D*
University of Pittsburgh	D*
University of Puerto Rico–Río Piedras	M,D
University of Rhode Island	M,D
University of Rochester	M,D*
University of South Carolina	M,D
University of South Dakota	M,D
University of Southern California	D
University of Southern Maine	M
University of South Florida	D
The University of Texas at Austin	D
The University of Texas at Dallas	M,D
The University of Texas at San Antonio	D
University of Utah	D
University of Vermont	D
University of Washington	D
University of Wisconsin–La Crosse	M
University of Wisconsin–Madison	D
University of Wisconsin–Milwaukee	M,D*
University of Wisconsin–Parkside	M
University of Wyoming	D
Vanderbilt University	M,D*
Virginia Commonwealth University	M,D
Washington University in St. Louis	D

Wayne State University	M,D,O
Weill Cornell Medicine	M,D
Wesleyan University	D
West Virginia University	M,D
Wright State University	M
Yale University	D
Youngstown State University	M

MOLECULAR BIOPHYSICS

Baylor College of Medicine	D
California Institute of Technology	M,D
Carnegie Mellon University	D
Duke University	O
Illinois Institute of Technology	M,D
Johns Hopkins University	M,D*
Rutgers University–New Brunswick	D
University at Buffalo, the State University of New York	M,D
University of Arkansas for Medical Sciences	M,D,O
University of Chicago	D
University of Massachusetts Amherst	D
University of Pennsylvania	D*
University of Pittsburgh	D*
The University of Texas Medical Branch	D
The University of Texas Southwestern Medical Center	D
Washington University in St. Louis	D
Wesleyan University	D
Yale University	D

MOLECULAR GENETICS

Albert Einstein College of Medicine	D
Duke University	D
Emory University	D
Georgia State University	M,D
Harvard University	D*
Illinois State University	M,D
Indiana University–Purdue University Indianapolis	M,D
Iowa State University of Science and Technology	M,D
Michigan State University	M,D
New York University	M,D*
Northern Michigan University	M
The Ohio State University	M,D
Oklahoma State University	M,D
Penn State Hershey Medical Center	D
Rutgers University–Newark	D
Rutgers University–New Brunswick	M,D
Stony Brook University, State University of New York	D
University of Calgary	M,D
University of California, Irvine	M,D
University of California, Los Angeles	M,D
University of Cincinnati	M,D
University of Colorado Denver	D
University of Florida	M
University of Guelph	M,D
University of Illinois at Chicago	D
University of Louisville	M,D
The University of Manchester	M,D
University of Maryland, College Park	M,D
University of Nebraska Medical Center	M,D
University of Pittsburgh	D*
University of Rhode Island	M,D
University of Toronto	M,D
University of Virginia	D
Van Andel Institute Graduate School	D
Virginia Commonwealth University	M,D
Wake Forest University	D
Washington University in St. Louis	D
Wayne State University	M,D,O

MOLECULAR MEDICINE

Augusta University	D
Baylor College of Medicine	D
Boston University	D
Case Western Reserve University	D
Cleveland State University	M,D
Dartmouth College	
Drexel University	M*
Elmezzi Graduate School of Molecular Medicine	D
The George Washington University	D
Hofstra University	D
Johns Hopkins University	D*
Liberty University	M,D
Oregon Health & Science University	M,D
Penn State Hershey Medical Center	D
Queen's University at Kingston	M,D
Rutgers University–Newark	D
Tufts University	D
The University of Alabama at Birmingham	D
The University of Arizona	M,D
University of Cincinnati	D
University of Maryland, Baltimore	D
University of Nebraska Medical Center	D
University of Southern California	M
University of South Florida	M,D
The University of Texas Health Science Center at San Antonio	M,D
University of Washington	D
Wake Forest University	M,D
Wayne State University	M,D,O
Yale University	D

MOLECULAR PATHOGENESIS

Dartmouth College	D
Emory University	D

North Dakota State University	M,D
Washington University in St. Louis	D

MOLECULAR PATHOLOGY

Rutgers University–Newark	D
Texas Tech University Health Sciences Center	M
University of California, Los Angeles	D
University of Michigan	D
University of Pittsburgh	D*
University of Wisconsin–Madison	D

MOLECULAR PHARMACOLOGY

Albert Einstein College of Medicine	D
Brown University	M,D
Harvard University	D*
Loyola University Chicago	M,D
Mayo Clinic Graduate School of Biomedical Sciences	M,D
Medical University of South Carolina	M,D
Rosalind Franklin University of Medicine and Science	M,D
Rutgers University–New Brunswick	M,D
Thomas Jefferson University	D
University at Buffalo, the State University of New York	D
University of Maryland, Baltimore	D
University of Massachusetts Medical School	M,D
University of Nevada, Reno	D
University of Pittsburgh	D*
University of Southern California	M,D
University of South Florida	M,D

MOLECULAR PHYSIOLOGY

Baylor College of Medicine	D
Loyola University Chicago	M,D
Rutgers University–New Brunswick	M,D
Stony Brook University, State University of New York	D
University of California, Los Angeles	D
University of Illinois at Urbana–Champaign	M,D
The University of North Carolina at Chapel Hill	D
University of Pittsburgh	D*
University of Virginia	M,D
Vanderbilt University	M,D*
Yale University	D

MOLECULAR TOXICOLOGY

Massachusetts Institute of Technology	D
Oregon State University	M,D
Penn State Hershey Medical Center	D
University of California, Berkeley	D
University of California, Los Angeles	D
University of Cincinnati	M,D
University of Maryland, Baltimore	D

MULTILINGUAL AND MULTICULTURAL EDUCATION

Alliant International University–San Francisco	M,O
American College of Education	M
Bank Street College of Education	M
Boise State University	M
Brooklyn College of the City University of New York	M
Brown University	M,D
Buffalo State College, State University of New York	O
California State University, Fullerton	M
California State University, Northridge	M
California State University, Sacramento	M,D,O
California State University, Stanislaus	M
Chicago State University	M
City College of the City University of New York	M
The College at Brockport, State University of New York	M,O
College of Mount Saint Vincent	M,O
The College of New Rochelle	M,O
College of Staten Island of the City University of New York	O
Columbia International University	M,D,O
Dallas Baptist University	M
Dallas International University	M,O
DePaul University	M,D
Eastern New Mexico University	M
Eastern University	M,O
Fairfield University	M,O
Fairleigh Dickinson University, Metropolitan Campus	M
Florida Atlantic University	M,D,O
Florida International University	M,D,O
Gallaudet University	M,D,O
The George Washington University	M,D,O
Georgia Southern University	M
Heritage University	M
Hofstra University	M,D,O
Houston Baptist University	M,D
Howard University	M,D
Hunter College of the City University of New York	M
Immaculata University	M
Indiana State University	M
Indiana University Bloomington	M,D
James Madison University	M,D
Kean University	M

Institution	Degree
Langston University	M
La Salle University	M,O
Lehman College of the City University of New York	M
Long Island University–Hudson	M,O
Long Island University–LIU Brooklyn	M,O
Loyola Marymount University	M
Manhattan College	M,O
Manhattanville College	M,O
Molloy College	M,O
Mount St. Joseph University	M,O
New Jersey City University	M
New Mexico State University	M,D,O
New York University	M,D,O*
Northern Arizona University	M,O
Queens College of the City University of New York	M,O
Quincy University	M
Rider University	M
Rutgers University–New Brunswick	M,D
St. John's University (NY)	M,O
San Diego State University	M,D
Southern Connecticut State University	M
Southern Methodist University	M,D
State University of New York at New Paltz	M,O
State University of New York College at Geneseo	M
Sul Ross State University	M
Teachers College, Columbia University	M,D,O
Texas A&M University	M,D
Texas A&M University–Kingsville	M,D
Texas A&M University–San Antonio	M
Texas Southern University	M,D
Texas State University	M
Texas Tech University	M,D
University at Buffalo, the State University of New York	M,D,O
University of Alaska Fairbanks	M
University of Alberta	M
University of Calgary	M,D
University of California, Riverside	M,D,O
University of California, San Diego	M,D
University of Colorado Boulder	M,D
University of Colorado Denver	M
University of Connecticut	M,D
University of Delaware	M,D,O
University of Houston–Clear Lake	M
University of Maryland, Baltimore County	M,D
University of Massachusetts Amherst	M,D,O
University of Miami	D
University of Minnesota, Twin Cities Campus	M,D,O
University of New Mexico	M,D
The University of North Carolina at Greensboro	M,D,O
University of Northern Colorado	M,D
University of Pennsylvania	M*
University of St. Thomas (TX)	M,D
University of San Francisco	M,D
University of Southern California	D
The University of Tennessee	M,D,O
The University of Texas at Austin	M,D
The University of Texas at El Paso	M,D,O
The University of Texas at San Antonio	M,D
The University of Texas Rio Grande Valley	M
University of the Southwest	M
University of Washington	M,D
University of Wisconsin–Milwaukee	M,D,O*
Utah State University	M*
Vanderbilt University	D*
Walden University	M,D,O
Wayne State University	M,D,O
Western New Mexico University	M
Western Oregon University	M
William Paterson University of New Jersey	M,D,O
Winona State University	O
Xavier University	M*

MUSEUM EDUCATION

Institution	Degree
Bank Street College of Education	M
City College of the City University of New York	M
Eastern Michigan University	O
The George Washington University	M
Tufts University	M,D
University of Nebraska at Kearney	M
The University of the Arts	M

MUSEUM STUDIES

Institution	Degree
American Museum of Natural History–Richard Gilder Graduate School	D
Arizona State University at the Tempe campus	M,D,O
Bard College	M
Baylor University	M
Boston University	M,D,O
Buffalo State College, State University of New York	M
California College of the Arts	M
California State University, Chico	M
California State University, Fullerton	M
Caribbean University	M,D
Case Western Reserve University	M
Christie's Education	M
City College of the City University of New York	M

Institution	Degree
Claremont Graduate University	M,D,O
Cleveland State University	M
Columbia University	M,O
Eastern Michigan University	M
Fashion Institute of Technology	M
Florida International University	M,O
Florida State University	M,D
The George Washington University	M,D,O
Harvard University	M,O*
Indiana University–Purdue University Indianapolis	M,O
John F. Kennedy University	O
Johns Hopkins University	M,O*
Long Island University–LIU Post	M
Marist College	M
Maryland Institute College of Art	M
Morgan State University	M,D
New Mexico State University	M,O
The New School	M
New York University	M,O*
Penn State Harrisburg	M,D,O
St. John's University (NY)	M
San Francisco Art Institute	M
San Francisco State University	M
Seton Hall University	M
Southern Illinois University Edwardsville	O
Southern University at New Orleans	M
State University of New York College at Oneonta	M
Syracuse University	M
Texas Tech University	M,D
Trinity College (United States)	M
Tufts University	M,D,O
Université de Montréal	M
Université du Québec à Montréal	M
Université Laval	O
University at Buffalo, the State University of New York	M,D
The University of British Columbia	M,D
University of Central Oklahoma	M
University of Colorado Boulder	M
University of Denver	M
University of Florida	M,D
University of Hawaii at Manoa	O
University of Illinois at Chicago	M,D
University of Kansas	M,O
University of Louisville	M,D
The University of Manchester	D
University of Memphis	M,O
University of Michigan–Flint	M
University of Missouri–St. Louis	M,O
University of New Hampshire	M,D
The University of North Carolina at Greensboro	M,D,O
University of Oklahoma	M,O*
University of St. Thomas (MN)	M,O
University of San Francisco	M
University of South Carolina	M,O
University of South Florida	O
The University of the Arts	M
University of Toronto	M
The University of Tulsa	M
University of Washington	M
University of West Georgia	M,O
University of Wisconsin–Milwaukee	M,D,O*
Virginia Commonwealth University	M,D
Wayne State University	M,D,O
Western Illinois University	M,O

MUSIC

Institution	Degree
Academy of Art University	M
American University	M,O
Andrews University	M
Appalachian State University	M
Aquinas Institute of Theology	M,D,O
Arizona State University at the Tempe campus	M,D
Arkansas State University	M,O
Austin Peay State University	M
Azusa Pacific University	M
Ball State University	M,D,O
The Baptist College of Florida	M
Bard College	M,O
Baylor University	M,D
Bennington College	M
Berklee College of Music	M,O
Bethesda University	M
Binghamton University, State University of New York	M
Bob Jones University	M,D,O
Boise State University	M
Boston University	M,D,O
Bowling Green State University	M,D
Brandeis University	M,D
Brandon University	M
Brigham Young University	M
Brooklyn College of the City University of New York	M
Brown University	D
Butler University	M
California Baptist University	M
California Institute of the Arts	M,O
California State University, East Bay	M
California State University, Fresno	M
California State University, Fullerton	M
California State University, Long Beach	M
California State University, Los Angeles	M
California State University, Northridge	M
California State University, Sacramento	M
Campbellsville University	M
Capital University	M
Carleton University	M

Institution	Degree
Carnegie Mellon University	M
Case Western Reserve University	M,D
The Catholic University of America	M,D,O
Central Michigan University	M
Central Washington University	M
Claremont Graduate University	M,D
Cleveland Institute of Music	M,D,O
Cleveland State University	M
The Colburn School Conservatory of Music	M,O
Colorado State University	M
Columbia College Chicago	M
Columbia University	M,D
Columbus State University	M,O
Concordia University (Canada)	O
Concordia University Chicago	M
Concordia University Wisconsin	M
Conservatorio de Musica de Puerto Rico	O
Converse College	M
Cornell University	D
Curtis Institute of Music	M
Dalhousie University	M
Dartmouth College	M
DePaul University	M
Dominican University of California	M
Duke University	D
Duquesne University	M,O
East Carolina University	M,O
Eastern Illinois University	M
Eastern Kentucky University	M
Eastern Michigan University	M
Eastern University	M,O
Eastern Washington University	M
Emory University	M
Emporia State University	M
Five Towns College	M,D
Florida Atlantic University	M
Florida International University	M
Florida State University	M,D
Fuller Theological Seminary	M,D,O
Garrett-Evangelical Theological Seminary	M,D
George Mason University	M,D
Georgia Institute of Technology	M,D
Georgia Southern University	M
The Graduate Center, City University of New York	D
Hardin-Simmons University	M,O
Harvard University	M,D*
Hebrew College	M,O
Hebrew Union College–Jewish Institute of Religion (NY)	M
Hollins University	M
Holy Names University	M,O
Hope International University	M
Houghton College	M
Houston Baptist University	M,D
Howard University	M
Hunter College of the City University of New York	M
Illinois State University	M
Indiana State University	M
Indiana University Bloomington	M,D,O
Indiana University of Pennsylvania	M
Indiana University–Purdue University Indianapolis	M,D
Indiana University South Bend	M,D
Inter American University of Puerto Rico, San Germán Campus	M
Ithaca College	M
Jacksonville State University	M
James Madison University	M,D
The Jewish Theological Seminary	M
Johns Hopkins University	M,D,O*
The Juilliard School	M,D,O
Kansas State University	M
Kent State University	M,D
Lamar University	M
Lee University	M
Liberty University	M,D
Long Island University–LIU Post	M
Louisiana State University and Agricultural & Mechanical College	M
Loyola University New Orleans	M
Lynn University	M,O
Manhattan School of Music	M,D,O
Mansfield University of Pennsylvania	M
Marshall University	M
McGill University	M,D
Memorial University of Newfoundland	M,D
Mercer University	M
Messiah College	M
Miami University	M
Michigan State University	M,D
Middle Tennessee State University	M
Midwestern Baptist Theological Seminary	M,D,O
Midwest University	M,D
Mills College	M
Minnesota State University Mankato	M
Mississippi College	M
Missouri State University	M
Montclair State University	M
Morehead State University	M
Morgan State University	M
Murray State University	M
Nazareth College of Rochester	M
New England Conservatory of Music	M,D,O
New Jersey City University	M
New Mexico State University	M
New Orleans Baptist Theological Seminary	M,D
The New School	M
New York University	M,D,O*
Norfolk State University	M
North Carolina Central University	M
North Dakota State University	M
Northeastern Illinois University	M
Northern Arizona University	M,O
Northern Illinois University	M

Institution	Degree
North Park University	M
Northwestern State University of Louisiana	M
Northwestern University	M,D
Oakland University	M,D
Oberlin College	M
The Ohio State University	M,D
Ohio University	M,O
Oklahoma City University	M
Oklahoma State University	M
Old Dominion University	M
Open University	M
Park University	M
Penn State University Park	M,D,O*
Pensacola Christian College	M,D,O
Phillips Theological Seminary	M,D
Pittsburg State University	M
Point Park University	M
Portland State University	M
Pratt Institute	M
Princeton University	D
Purchase College, State University of New York	M
Queens College of the City University of New York	M,O
Radford University	M
Rice University	M,D
Rider University	M
Roosevelt University	M,O
Rowan University	M
Rutgers University–Newark	M
Rutgers University–New Brunswick	M,D,O
Saint John's University (MN)	M
Salem College	M
Samford University	M
Sam Houston State University	M
San Diego State University	M
San Francisco Conservatory of Music	M,O
San Francisco State University	M
Savannah College of Art and Design	M
Shenandoah University	M,D,O
Silver Lake College of the Holy Family	M
Southeastern Baptist Theological Seminary	M,D
Southeastern Louisiana University	M
Southern Illinois University Carbondale	M
Southern Illinois University Edwardsville	M
Southern Methodist University	M,D
Southern Oregon University	M
Southern Utah University	M
Southwestern Baptist Theological Seminary	M,D
Southwestern Oklahoma State University	M
Stanford University	M,D
State University of New York at Fredonia	M
State University of New York College at Potsdam	M
Stephen F. Austin State University	M
Stony Brook University, State University of New York	M,D
Syracuse University	M
Temple University	M,D*
Texas A&M University	M
Texas A&M University–Commerce	M,D,O
Texas A&M University–Kingsville	M
Texas Christian University	M,D
Texas Southern University	M
Texas State University	M
Texas Tech University	M,D
Texas Woman's University	M
Towson University	M
Trinity College (Canada)	M,D,O
Truman State University	M
Tufts University	M
Tulane University	M
Université de Montréal	M,D,O
Université Laval	M,D
University at Buffalo, the State University of New York	M,D,O
The University of Akron	M
The University of Alabama	M,D
University of Alberta	M,D
The University of Arizona	M,D
University of Arkansas	M
The University of British Columbia	M,D
University of Calgary	M,D
University of California, Berkeley	D
University of California, Davis	M,D
University of California, Irvine	M
University of California, Los Angeles	M,D
University of California, Riverside	M
University of California, San Diego	M,D
University of California, Santa Barbara	M,D
University of California, Santa Cruz	M,D
University of Central Arkansas	M,O
University of Central Florida	M
University of Central Missouri	M,D,O
University of Central Oklahoma	M
University of Chicago	M,D
University of Cincinnati	M,D
University of Colorado Boulder	M,D,O
University of Colorado Denver	M
University of Connecticut	M
University of Delaware	M
University of Denver	M,O
University of Florida	M,D
University of Georgia	M,D
University of Hartford	M,D,O
University of Hawaii at Manoa	M,D
University of Houston	M,D

University of Idaho	M
University of Illinois at Urbana–Champaign	M,D
The University of Iowa	M,D
The University of Kansas	M,D
University of Kentucky	M,D
University of Lethbridge	M,D
University of Louisiana at Lafayette	M
University of Louisville	M
University of Maine	M
The University of Manchester	D
University of Manitoba	M
University of Maryland, Baltimore County	O
University of Maryland, College Park	M,D
University of Massachusetts Amherst	M,D
University of Massachusetts Lowell	M
University of Memphis	M
University of Miami	M,D,O
University of Michigan	M,D,O
University of Michigan–Flint	M
University of Minnesota, Duluth	M
University of Minnesota, Twin Cities Campus	M,D
University of Mississippi	M,O
University of Missouri	M,O
University of Missouri–Kansas City	M,D
University of Mobile	M,D
University of Montana	M
University of Nebraska at Omaha	M
University of Nebraska–Lincoln	M,D
University of Nevada, Las Vegas	M,D,O
University of Nevada, Reno	M
University of New Hampshire	M
University of New Mexico	M
University of New Orleans	M
The University of North Carolina at Chapel Hill	M,D
The University of North Carolina at Charlotte	O
The University of North Carolina at Greensboro	M,D
University of North Carolina School of the Arts	M,O
University of North Dakota	M,D
University of Northern Colorado	M,D
University of Northern Iowa	M
University of North Texas	M,D,O
University of Oklahoma	M,D,O*
University of Oregon	M,D
University of Ottawa	M,O
University of Pennsylvania	M,D*
University of Pittsburgh	M,D*
University of Redlands	M
University of Regina	M
University of Rhode Island	M
University of Rochester	M,D*
University of St. Thomas (MN)	M,D
University of St. Thomas (TX)	M
University of Saskatchewan	M
University of South Africa	M
University of South Alabama	M
University of South Carolina	M,D,O
University of South Dakota	M
University of Southern California	M,D,O
University of Southern Maine	M
University of Southern Mississippi	M,D
University of South Florida	M,D
The University of Tennessee	M
The University of Tennessee at Chattanooga	M
The University of Texas at Arlington	M
The University of Texas at Austin	M,D
The University of Texas at El Paso	M
The University of Texas at San Antonio	M
The University of Texas Rio Grande Valley	M
The University of the Arts	M
University of the Pacific	M
The University of Toledo	M,O
University of Toronto	M,D
University of Valley Forge	M
University of Victoria	M,D
University of Virginia	M,D
University of Washington	M,D
The University of Western Ontario	M,D
University of West Georgia	M,O
University of Wisconsin–Madison	M,D
University of Wisconsin–Milwaukee	M,O*
University of Wyoming	M
Utah State University	M
Vermont College of Fine Arts	M
Virginia Commonwealth University	M
Washington State University	M
Washington University in St. Louis	M,D
Wayne State University	M,O
Webster University	M
Wesleyan University	M,D
West Chester University of Pennsylvania	M,O
Western Illinois University	M
Western Michigan University	M,O
Western Oregon University	M
Western Washington University	M
West Texas A&M University	M
West Virginia University	M,D
Wichita State University	M
William Paterson University of New Jersey	M
Winthrop University	M
World Mission University	M,D,O
Yale University	M,D,O

York University	M,D
Youngstown State University	M

MUSIC EDUCATION

Acadia University	M
Adams State University	M
Alabama Agricultural and Mechanical University	M
Alabama State University	M,O
Anderson University (SC)	M
Arcadia University	M,D,O
Arizona State University at the Tempe campus	M,D
Arkansas State University	M,O
Augusta University	M,O
Austin Peay State University	M
Azusa Pacific University	M
Ball State University	M,D,O
Bob Jones University	M,D,O
Boise State University	M
Boston University	M,D
Bowling Green State University	M,D
Brandon University	M
Brigham Young University	M
Brooklyn College of the City University of New York	M
Butler University	M
California Baptist University	M
California State University, Fresno	M
California State University, Fullerton	M
California State University, Los Angeles	M
California State University, Northridge	M
Campbellsville University	M
Capital University	M
Carnegie Mellon University	M
Case Western Reserve University	M,D
The Catholic University of America	M,D,O
Central Connecticut State University	M,O
Central Methodist University	M
Central Michigan University	M
Central Washington University	M
Cleveland State University	M
College of Charleston	M
The Colorado College	M
Colorado State University–Pueblo	M
Columbus State University	M,O
Conservatorio de Musica de Puerto Rico	M
Converse College	M
DePaul University	M,O
Duquesne University	M,O
East Carolina University	M,O
Eastern Illinois University	M
Eastern Kentucky University	M
Eastern Washington University	M
Five Towns College	M,D
Florida International University	M
George Mason University	M
Georgia College & State University	M
Georgia Southern University	M
Georgia State University	M
Gordon College	M
Hardin-Simmons University	M
Hebrew University	M,O
Heidelberg University	M
Hofstra University	M,D,O
Holy Names University	M,O
Howard University	M
Hunter College of the City University of New York	M
Idaho State University	M
Indiana State University	M
Indiana University of Pennsylvania	M
Inter American University of Puerto Rico, Metropolitan Campus	M
Inter American University of Puerto Rico, San Germán Campus	M
Ithaca College	M
Jackson State University	M
James Madison University	M
Kent State University	M,D
Kutztown University of Pennsylvania	M
Lake Forest College	M
Lebanon Valley College	M
Lee University	M
Lehman College of the City University of New York	M
Liberty University	M,D
Long Island University–LIU Post	M,D,O
Louisiana State University and Agricultural & Mechanical College	M,D
Loyola University Maryland	M
Manhattanville College	M,O
Marywood University	M
McGill University	M,D
McKendree University	M,D,O
McNeese State University	O
Miami University	M
Michigan State University	M,D
Minnesota State University Mankato	M
Mississippi College	M
Montclair State University	M
Morehead State University	M
Murray State University	M
Nazareth College of Rochester	M
Nebraska Christian College of Hope International University	M
New Jersey City University	M
New Mexico State University	M
New York University	M,D,O*
Norfolk State University	M
North Dakota State University	M
Northeastern Illinois University	M

Northern State University	M
Northwestern University	M,D
Oakland University	M,D
Ohio University	M,O
Oklahoma State University	M
Old Dominion University	M
Oregon State University	M
Penn State University Park	M,D,O*
Piedmont College	M,D,O
Pittsburg State University	M
Plymouth State University	M
Queens College of the City University of New York	M
Queens College of the City University of New York	M,O
Rhode Island College	M
Rider University	M
Rutgers University–New Brunswick	M,D
Saint Xavier University	M
Samford University	M
San Diego State University	M
San Francisco Conservatory of Music	M,O
San Francisco State University	M
Southern Illinois University Edwardsville	M,O
Southern Methodist University	M
Southwestern Oklahoma State University	M
State University of New York at Fredonia	M
State University of New York College at Potsdam	M
Syracuse University	M
Tarleton State University	M
Teachers College, Columbia University	M,D,O
Temple University	M,D*
Tennessee Technological University	M
Texas A&M University–Commerce	M,D,O
Texas A&M University–Kingsville	M
Texas Christian University	M
Texas State University	M
Texas Tech University	M,D
Texas Woman's University	M
Towson University	M
Union College (KY)	M
Université Laval	M,D
University at Buffalo, the State University of New York	M,D,O
The University of Akron	M
The University of Alabama	M,D,O
The University of Arizona	M,D
University of Bridgeport	M
The University of British Columbia	M,D
University of Central Arkansas	M,O
University of Central Oklahoma	M
University of Cincinnati	M
University of Colorado Boulder	M,D
University of Connecticut	M,D
University of Dayton	M
University of Delaware	M
University of Denver	M,O
University of Florida	M,D
University of Georgia	M,D
University of Hartford	M,D,O
University of Houston	M,D
University of Illinois at Urbana–Champaign	M,D
The University of Iowa	M,D
The University of Kansas	M,D
University of Kentucky	M,D
University of Louisiana at Lafayette	M
University of Louisville	M,D,O
University of Maryland, Baltimore County	M
University of Maryland, College Park	M,D
University of Massachusetts Amherst	M,D
University of Massachusetts Lowell	M
University of Memphis	M,D
University of Miami	M,D,O
University of Michigan	M,D
University of Minnesota, Duluth	M
University of Missouri	M,D,O
University of Missouri–Kansas City	M,D
University of Nebraska at Kearney	M
University of Nebraska–Lincoln	M,D
University of New Mexico	M
The University of North Carolina at Chapel Hill	M
The University of North Carolina at Greensboro	M,D
University of North Dakota	M
University of Northern Colorado	M,D
University of Northern Iowa	M
University of North Texas	M,D,O*
University of Oklahoma	M,D,O*
University of Oregon	M,D
University of Ottawa	M,D
University of Rhode Island	M
University of Rochester	M,D*
University of St. Thomas (MN)	M,D
University of South Alabama	M
University of South Carolina	M,D,O
University of South Dakota	M
University of Southern California	M,D,O
University of Southern Maine	M
University of Southern Mississippi	M,D
University of South Florida	M,D
The University of Tennessee	M
The University of Tennessee at Chattanooga	M

The University of Texas at Arlington	M
The University of Texas at Austin	M,D
The University of Texas at El Paso	M
The University of the Arts	M
University of the Pacific	M
The University of Toledo	M,O
University of Toronto	M,D
University of Utah	M,D
University of Victoria	M,D
University of Washington	M,D
University of West Georgia	M,O
University of Wisconsin–Madison	M,D
University of Wisconsin–Milwaukee	M,O*
University of Wisconsin–Stevens Point	M
University of Wyoming	M
Utah State University	M
VanderCook College of Music	M
Virginia Commonwealth University	M
Wayne State College	M
Wayne State University	M,O
Webster University	M
West Chester University of Pennsylvania	M,O
Western Connecticut State University	M
Western Kentucky University	M
Western Michigan University	M,O
West Virginia University	M,D
Wichita State University	M
Winthrop University	M
Wright State University	M
Youngstown State University	M

NANOTECHNOLOGY

The American University in Cairo	M,D,O
Arizona State University at the Tempe campus	M,D
Carnegie Mellon University	D
Cornell University	M,D
Indiana University of Pennsylvania	M*
Johns Hopkins University	M*
Louisiana Tech University	M,D,O
North Dakota State University	M,D
South Dakota School of Mines and Technology	D
State University of New York Polytechnic Institute	M,D
University at Buffalo, the State University of New York	M,D,O
University of Alberta	M,D
University of California, Riverside	M
University of California, San Diego	M,D
University of New Mexico	M,D
University of Pennsylvania	M*
University of South Florida	M,D
University of Washington	M,D
Virginia Commonwealth University	M,D

NATIONAL SECURITY

American Public University System	M,D
American University	M,D,O
Angelo State University	M
Bellevue University	M
California State University, San Bernardino	M
The Citadel, The Military College of South Carolina	M,O
Daniel Morgan Graduate School of National Security	M
George Mason University	M,D,O
The George Washington University	M,D
Henley-Putnam School of Strategic Security	D
The Institute of World Politics	M,D,O
Kansas State University	M,D
National Defense University	M
Naval Postgraduate School	M,D
Naval War College	M
New Jersey City University	M,D,O
Regent University	M,D
Trinity Washington University	M
University of Nebraska at Omaha	M,O
University of New Haven	M,O
Virginia Polytechnic Institute and State University	M,O
Western Michigan University Thomas M. Cooley Law School	M,D

NATURAL RESOURCES

American University	M,D,O
Auburn University	M,D
Ball State University	M,O
Boise State University	M,D,O
California Polytechnic State University, San Luis Obispo	M
Central Washington University	M
Colorado State University	M,D
Cornell University	M,D
Dalhousie University	M
Delaware State University	M
Duke University	M,D
Florida International University	M,D
Humboldt State University	M
Indiana University–Purdue University Indianapolis	M,D,O
Instituto Tecnologico de Santo Domingo	M,D,O
Iowa State University of Science and Technology	M,D
Kansas State University	M,D
Laurentian University	M,D
Louisiana State University and Agricultural & Mechanical College	M,D
McGill University	M,D
Michigan State University	M,D
Montana State University	M

New Mexico Highlands University	M
North Carolina Agricultural and Technical State University	M
North Carolina State University	M,D
North Dakota State University	M,D
Northeastern State University	M
The Ohio State University	M,D
Oklahoma State University	M,D
Oregon State University	M
Purdue University	M,D
State University of New York College of Environmental Science and Forestry	M,D
Sul Ross State University	M
Tarleton State University	M
Texas A&M University	M,D
Texas Tech University	M,D
Unity College	M
Universidad Metropolitana	M
Universidad Nacional Pedro Henríquez Urena	M
Université du Québec à Montréal	M,D,O
Université du Québec en Abitibi-Témiscamingue	M,D
University of Alaska Fairbanks	M,D
University of Alberta	M,D
The University of Arizona	M,D
University of Arkansas at Monticello	M
The University of British Columbia	M,D
University of California, Berkeley	M,D
University of Connecticut	M,D
University of Delaware	M
University of Florida	M,D
University of Georgia	M,D
University of Guelph	M,D
University of Hawaii at Manoa	M,D
University of Idaho	M,D
University of Illinois at Urbana–Champaign	M,D
University of Louisiana at Lafayette	M
The University of Manchester	M,D
University of Manitoba	M,D
University of Maryland, College Park	M,D
University of Michigan	M,D
University of Minnesota, Twin Cities Campus	M,D
University of Montana	M,D
University of Nebraska–Lincoln	M,D
University of New Brunswick Saint John	M
University of New Hampshire	M,D
University of New Mexico	M,D
University of Northern British Columbia	M,D,O
University of Rhode Island	M,D
University of San Francisco	M
University of South Africa	M,D
The University of Texas at Austin	M,D
University of Vermont	M,D,O
University of Washington	M,D
University of Wisconsin–Madison	M,D
University of Wisconsin–Stevens Point	M
University of Wyoming	M,D
Utah State University	M
Virginia Polytechnic Institute and State University	M,D,O
Washington State University	M,D
West Virginia University	M,D

NATUROPATHIC MEDICINE

Bastyr University	D,O
Canadian College of Naturopathic Medicine	D
Maryland University of Integrative Health	D
National University of Health Sciences	M,D
National University of Natural Medicine	M,D
Southwest College of Naturopathic Medicine and Health Sciences	D
Universidad del Turabo	D
University of Bridgeport	D

NEAR AND MIDDLE EASTERN LANGUAGES

The American University in Cairo	M,O
American University of Beirut	M,D
Bethel Seminary	M,D,O
Brandeis University	M,D
California University of Pennsylvania	M
The Catholic University of America	M,D
DePaul University	M
Georgetown University	M,O
Harvard University	M,D*
Hebrew Union College–Jewish Institute of Religion (NY)	D
Houston Baptist University	M
Indiana University Bloomington	M,D
Johns Hopkins University	D*
Kent State University	M,D
London Metropolitan University	M,D
Middlebury College	M
The Ohio State University	M,D
Oral Roberts University	M,D
University of California, Los Angeles	M,D
University of Chicago	D
University of Michigan	M,D
University of South Africa	M,D
The University of Texas at Austin	M,D
University of Utah	M,D
University of Wisconsin–Madison	M,D
Wayne State University	M,D
Yale University	M,D

NEAR AND MIDDLE EASTERN STUDIES

The American University in Cairo	M,O
American University of Beirut	M,D
The American University of Paris	M
Brandeis University	M,D
Brown University	D
California State University, Long Beach	M
The Catholic University of America	M,D,O
College of Staten Island of the City University of New York	M
Columbia University	M,D
Cornell University	M,D
George Mason University	M,O
Georgetown University	M,O
The George Washington University	M,D
Harvard University	M,D*
Johns Hopkins University	D*
McGill University	M,D,O
New York University	M,D*
Princeton University	M,D
Rice University	D
Southern Evangelical Seminary	M,D,O
Southwestern Baptist Theological Seminary	M,D
The University of Arizona	M,D,O
University of California, Berkeley	M,D
University of California, Los Angeles	M,D
University of Chicago	M,D
University of Illinois at Urbana–Champaign	M
The University of Kansas	M,O
The University of Manchester	D
University of Memphis	M,D
University of Michigan	M,D
University of Pennsylvania	M,D*
University of South Africa	M,D
The University of Texas at Austin	M,D
University of Toronto	M,D
University of Utah	M,D
University of Virginia	M
University of Washington	M,D
University of Waterloo	M
University of Wisconsin–Madison	M,D
Washington University in St. Louis	M
Wayne State University	M,D
Yale University	M,D

NEUROBIOLOGY

Boston University	M,D
Brandeis University	M,D
California Institute of Technology	D
Carnegie Mellon University	M,D
Columbia University	D
Cornell University	D
Duke University	D
Georgia State University	M,D
Harvard University	D*
Illinois State University	M,D
Indiana University–Purdue University Indianapolis	D
Louisiana State University Health Sciences Center	D
Massachusetts Institute of Technology	D
New York University	M,D*
Northwestern University	D
Penn State Hershey Medical Center	D
Purdue University	M,D
Université Laval	M,D
University of Arkansas for Medical Sciences	M,D,O
University of California, Irvine	M,D
University of California, Los Angeles	M,D
University of Chicago	D
University of Connecticut	M,D
The University of Iowa	M,D
University of Kentucky	D
University of Louisville	M,D
The University of Manchester	M,D
University of Maryland, Baltimore	D
University of Minnesota, Twin Cities Campus	M,D
The University of North Carolina at Chapel Hill	D
University of Oklahoma	M,D*
University of Rochester	D*
University of Southern California	D
The University of Texas at Austin	D
The University of Texas at San Antonio	M,D
University of Utah	D
University of Washington	D
Virginia Commonwealth University	M
Wake Forest University	D
Wesleyan University	D
Yale University	D

NEUROSCIENCE

Albany Medical College	M,D
Albert Einstein College of Medicine	D
Alliant International University–San Diego	M,D,O
American University	M,D,O
American University of Beirut	M,D
Argosy University, Chicago	D
Argosy University, Phoenix	M,D
Argosy University, Tampa	M,D
Arizona State University at the Tempe campus	M,D
Augusta University	D
Ball State University	M,D,O
Baylor College of Medicine	D
Boston University	M,D
Brandeis University	M,D
Brigham Young University	M,D
Brock University	M,D
Brown University	D
California Institute of Technology	M,D
Carleton University	M,D
Carnegie Mellon University	D

Case Western Reserve University	D
Central Michigan University	M,D
College of Staten Island of the City University of New York	M
Dalhousie University	M,D
Dartmouth College	D
Delaware State University	M,D
Drexel University	M,D*
Duke University	D,O
Emory University	D
Fielding Graduate University	O
Florida Atlantic University	D
Florida International University	M,D
Florida State University	D
Gallaudet University	M,D,O
George Mason University	M,D,O
Georgetown University	D
Georgia State University	D
The Graduate Center, City University of New York	M,D
Harvard University	D*
Icahn School of Medicine at Mount Sinai	M,D
Illinois State University	M,D
Immaculata University	M,D,O
Indiana University Bloomington	M,D
Iowa State University of Science and Technology	D
Irell & Manella Graduate School of Biological Sciences	D
Johns Hopkins University	D*
Kent State University	M,D
Louisiana State University Health Sciences Center	D
Loyola University Chicago	M,D
Marquette University	M,D
Massachusetts Institute of Technology	D
Mayo Clinic Graduate School of Biomedical Sciences	M,D
McGill University	M,D
McMaster University	M,D
Medical College of Wisconsin	D
Medical University of South Carolina	M,D
Meharry Medical College	D
Memorial University of Newfoundland	M,D
Michigan State University	M,D
Montana State University	M,D
New York University	D*
Northwestern University	D
The Ohio State University	M,D
Ohio University	M,D
Oregon Health & Science University	D
Penn State Hershey Medical Center	M,D
Princeton University	D
Purdue University	D
Queens College of the City University of New York	M
Rosalind Franklin University of Medicine and Science	D
Rush University	M,D
Rutgers University–Newark	D
Rutgers University–New Brunswick	M,D
Seton Hall University	M,D
State University of New York Downstate Medical Center	D
State University of New York Upstate Medical University	D
Stony Brook University, State University of New York	M,D
Syracuse University	M,D
Teachers College, Columbia University	M,D
Texas Christian University	M,D
Thomas Jefferson University	D
Tufts University	M,D
Tulane University	M,D
Uniformed Services University of the Health Sciences	D*
Universidad de Iberoamerica	D
Université de Montréal	M,D
University at Albany, State University of New York	M,D
University at Buffalo, the State University of New York	M,D
The University of Alabama at Birmingham	M,D
University of Alaska Fairbanks	M,D
University of Alberta	M,D
The University of Arizona	D
The University of British Columbia	M,D
University of Calgary	M,D
University of California, Berkeley	D
University of California, Davis	D
University of California, Irvine	D
University of California, Los Angeles	D
University of California, Riverside	D
University of California, San Diego	M,D
University of California, San Francisco	D
University of California, Santa Barbara	D
University of Chicago	D
University of Cincinnati	D
University of Colorado Denver	D
University of Connecticut	D
University of Connecticut Health Center	D
University of Delaware	D
University of Florida	D
University of Georgia	M,D
University of Guelph	M,D,O
University of Hartford	D
University of Illinois at Chicago	D
University of Illinois at Urbana–Champaign	D
The University of Iowa	D
The University of Kansas	M,D

University of Lethbridge	M,D
The University of Manchester	M,D
University of Maryland, Baltimore	D
University of Maryland, Baltimore County	D
University of Maryland, College Park	M,D
University of Massachusetts Amherst	M,D
University of Massachusetts Medical School	M,D
University of Miami	M,D
University of Michigan	D
University of Michigan–Flint	D,O
University of Minnesota, Twin Cities Campus	M,D
University of Mississippi Medical Center	D
University of Missouri	M,D,O
University of Missouri–St. Louis	M,D
University of Montana	M,D
University of Nebraska Medical Center	D
University of New Mexico	M,D
The University of North Carolina at Chapel Hill	D
University of North Texas Health Science Center at Fort Worth	M,D
University of Oklahoma Health Sciences Center	M,D
University of Oregon	M,D
University of Pennsylvania	D*
University of Pittsburgh	D*
University of Puerto Rico–Río Piedras	M,D
University of Rochester	D*
University of South Dakota	M,D
University of Southern California	M,D
University of South Florida	M,D,O
The University of Texas at Austin	D
The University of Texas at Dallas	M,D
The University of Texas Health Science Center at Houston	D
The University of Texas Health Science Center at San Antonio	D
The University of Texas Medical Branch	D
The University of Texas Southwestern Medical Center	D
The University of Toledo	M,D
University of Utah	D
University of Vermont	D
University of Virginia	D
University of Washington	M,D
The University of Western Ontario	M,D
University of Wisconsin–Madison	D
Virginia Commonwealth University	M,D,O
Wake Forest University	D
Washington State University	M,D
Washington University in St. Louis	D
Wayne State University	M,D,O
Weill Cornell Medicine	M,D
Wilfrid Laurier University	M,D
Wright State University	M
Yale University	D

NONPROFIT MANAGEMENT

Abilene Christian University	M
Albizu University, Miami Campus	M,D
American Jewish University	M
American University	M,D,O
Antioch University Santa Barbara	M
Arizona State University at the Tempe campus	M,D,O
Assumption College	M,O
Avila University	M
Baruch College of the City University of New York	M*
Bay Path University	M
Bradley University	M
Brandeis University	M
Brigham Young University	M
Cairn University	M,O
California State University, Northridge	O
Capella University	D
Case Western Reserve University	M,D,O
Central Michigan University	M,O
Chaminade University of Honolulu	M
Cleveland State University	M,O
The College at Brockport, State University of New York	M,O
Columbia University	M
Corban University	M
Daemen College	M
Dallas Baptist University	M
DePaul University	M
Drury University	M
Eastern Mennonite University	M
Eastern Michigan University	M,O
Eastern University	D,O
East Tennessee State University	M,O
Fairleigh Dickinson University, Metropolitan Campus	M,D
Florida Atlantic University	M,D
Fordham University	M
Geneva College	M
The George Washington University	M,O
Georgian Court University	M,O
Georgia Southern University	M,O
Georgia State University	M,D,O
Grand Valley State University	M
Gratz College	M
Hamline University	M
Hebrew Union College–Jewish Institute of Religion (NY)	M
Hope International University	M
Indiana University Bloomington	M,D,O
Indiana University Northwest	M
Indiana University of Pennsylvania	D
Indiana University–Purdue University Indianapolis	M,O

Indiana University South Bend	M,O
James Madison University	M,D
John Carroll University	M
Johns Hopkins University	M,O*
Johnson & Wales University	M
Johnson University	M,D,O
Kean University	M
La Salle University	M
Lawrence Technological University	M,D,O
Liberty University	M
Lipscomb University	M,O
Long Island University–LIU Brooklyn	M,O
Long Island University–LIU Post	M,O
Louisiana State University in Shreveport	M
Marymount University	M,O
Mercer University	M,D
Metropolitan State University	M
Minnesota State University Mankato	M,O
Mount Aloysius College	M
Murray State University	M
Nebraska Christian College of Hope International University	M
New England College	M
The New School	M
New York University	M,D,O*
North Carolina State University	M,D,O
Northeastern University	M
Northern Kentucky University	M,O
North Park University	M
Norwich University	M
Notre Dame of Maryland University	M
Oakland University	M,O
Oklahoma Christian University	M
Oklahoma State University	M,D,O
Oral Roberts University	M
Our Lady of the Lake University	M
Pace University	M,O
Park University	M,O
Penn State Harrisburg	M,D,O
Portland State University	M,D,O
Post University	M
Regent University	M,D,O
Regis University	M,O
Rockhurst University	M,O
Saint Mary-of-the-Woods College	M
Salve Regina University	M,O
San Francisco State University	M
Seton Hall University	M,O
Southern New Hampshire University	M,D,O
Suffolk University	M
Thomas Edison State University	M
Tiffin University	M
Trinity Washington University	M
Trinity Western University	M,O
Tufts University	O
University at Albany, State University of New York	M,D,O
University of Arkansas at Little Rock	O
University of California, San Diego	M
University of Central Florida	M,O
University of Central Oklahoma	M
University of Colorado Denver	M,D
University of Connecticut	M
University of Florida	M
University of Georgia	M,D,O
University of Houston–Downtown	M
University of La Verne	M,O
University of Louisville	M,D
University of Lynchburg	M
University of Maryland, Baltimore County	M,O
University of Memphis	M,O
University of Michigan–Flint	M,D,O
University of Missouri	M,D,O
University of Missouri–St. Louis	M,D,O
University of Nevada, Las Vegas	M,D,O
University of New Haven	M,O
The University of North Carolina at Charlotte	M,O
The University of North Carolina at Greensboro	M,O
University of Northern Iowa	M
University of North Florida	M,O
University of North Texas	M,D,O
University of Notre Dame	M
University of Oklahoma	M,D,O*
University of Oregon	M,O
University of Pennsylvania	M,O*
University of Pittsburgh	M*
University of Portland	M
University of San Diego	M,D,O
University of San Francisco	M
University of Southern California	M,O
University of Southern Indiana	M
University of South Florida	O
The University of Tampa	M,O
The University of Tennessee at Chattanooga	M,D
The University of Texas at Dallas	M,D
University of the Sacred Heart	M
University of the West	M
The University of Toledo	M,O
University of West Georgia	M,D,O
University of Wisconsin–Milwaukee	M,D,O*
Upper Iowa University	M
Villanova University	M,O
Virginia Commonwealth University	O
Virginia Polytechnic Institute and State University	M,O
Walden University	M,D,O
Warner Pacific University	M
Wayne State University	M,D
Webster University	M,D,O

West Chester University of Pennsylvania	M,O
Western Michigan University	M,D,O
Westfield State University	M
Worcester State University	M

NORTHERN STUDIES

University of Alaska Fairbanks	M
University of Manitoba	M

NUCLEAR ENGINEERING

Air Force Institute of Technology	M,D
Arizona State University at the Tempe campus	M,D,O
Colorado School of Mines	M,D
École Polytechnique de Montréal	M,D,O
Georgia Institute of Technology	M,D
Idaho State University	M,D
Kansas State University	M,D
Massachusetts Institute of Technology	M,D,O
McMaster University	M,D
Missouri University of Science and Technology	M,D
North Carolina State University	M,D
The Ohio State University	M,D
Oregon State University	M,D
Penn State University Park	M,D*
Purdue University	M,D
Rensselaer Polytechnic Institute	M,D
Texas A&M University	M,D
University of California, Berkeley	M,D
University of Cincinnati	M,D
University of Florida	M,D
University of Idaho	M,D
University of Illinois at Urbana–Champaign	M,D
The University of Manchester	M,D
University of Maryland, College Park	M,D
University of Massachusetts Lowell	M,D,O
University of Michigan	M,D,O
University of Nevada, Las Vegas	M,D,O
University of New Mexico	M,D
University of South Carolina	M,D
The University of Tennessee	M,D
University of Utah	M,D
University of Wisconsin–Madison	M,D
Virginia Commonwealth University	M,D
Worcester Polytechnic Institute	M,D,O

NURSE ANESTHESIA

AdventHealth University	M
Albany Medical College	M
Arkansas State University	M,D,O
Augusta University	D
Barry University	M
Baylor College of Medicine	D
Bloomsburg University of Pennsylvania	M,D
Boston College	M,D
Bryan College of Health Sciences	M
California State University, Fullerton	M,D
Case Western Reserve University	M,D
Columbia University	M,O
DeSales University	M,D,O
Drexel University	M*
Duke University	M,D
Fairfield University	M,D
Florida Gulf Coast University	M
Florida International University	M,D
Franciscan Missionaries of Our Lady University	D
Gannon University	M,O
Georgetown University	M,O
Goldfarb School of Nursing at Barnes-Jewish College	M
Inter American University of Puerto Rico, Arecibo Campus	M
Keiser University	M,D
La Roche University	M,D
La Salle University	M,D,O
Lincoln Memorial University	M
Louisiana State University Health Sciences Center	M,D,O
Lourdes University	M
Marian University (IN)	M,D
Marshall University	D
Mayo Clinic School of Health Sciences	D
Medical University of South Carolina	M
Middle Tennessee School of Anesthesia	M
Midwestern University, Glendale Campus	M
Missouri State University	D
Mount Marty College	M
Murray State University	D
National University	M,O
Newman University	M
Northeastern University	M,D,O
Oakland University	M,O
Old Dominion University	D
Oregon Health & Science University	M,D,O
Otterbein University	M,D
Quinnipiac University	D
Rosalind Franklin University of Medicine and Science	D
Rush University	D,O
Rutgers University–Newark	M,D,O
Saint Mary's University of Minnesota	M
Saint Vincent College	M,D
Samford University	M,D
Samuel Merritt University	M,D,O
Southern Illinois University Edwardsville	D

State University of New York Downstate Medical Center	M
Texas Christian University	D
Texas Wesleyan University	M,D
Uniformed Services University of the Health Sciences	M,D*
Union University	M,D,O
University at Buffalo, the State University of New York	M,D,O
The University of Alabama at Birmingham	M,D
University of Cincinnati	M,D
University of Detroit Mercy	M,D,O
The University of Kansas	D
University of Maryland, Baltimore	M,D,O
University of Miami	M,D
University of Michigan–Flint	D
University of Minnesota, Twin Cities Campus	M,D
University of New England	M,D
The University of North Carolina at Charlotte	M,D,O
The University of North Carolina at Greensboro	M,D,O
University of North Dakota	M,D,O
University of North Florida	M,D,O
University of Pennsylvania	M*
University of Saint Francis (IN)	M,D,O
The University of Scranton	M,D
University of South Carolina	M
University of Southern California	D
University of South Florida	M,D,O
The University of Tennessee at Chattanooga	M,D,O
University of Wisconsin–La Crosse	M
Villanova University	M,D,O
Virginia Commonwealth University	M,D
Wake Forest University	M
Wayne State University	M,D,O
Webster University	D
Westminster College (UT)	M
York College of Pennsylvania	M

NURSE MIDWIFERY

Bastyr University	M,O
Bethel University (MN)	M
Case Western Reserve University	M
Columbia University	M
DeSales University	M,D,O
Emory University	M
Frontier Nursing University	M,D,O*
Georgetown University	M
James Madison University	M,D
Marquette University	M,D,O
Midwives College of Utah	M
National College of Midwifery	M,D
New York University	M,D,O*
Oregon Health & Science University	M,D
Shenandoah University	M,D,O
State University of New York Downstate Medical Center	M,O
Stony Brook University, State University of New York	M,D,O
Thomas Jefferson University	M,D
University of Cincinnati	M,D
University of Colorado Denver	M,D
University of Illinois at Chicago	M,O
University of Indianapolis	M,D
The University of Kansas	M,D,O
The University of Manchester	M,D
University of Miami	M,D
University of Minnesota, Twin Cities Campus	M,D
University of Pennsylvania	M*
University of Puerto Rico–Medical Sciences Campus	M,O
University of South Africa	M,D
Wayne State University	M,D
West Virginia Wesleyan College	M,D,O

NURSING—GENERAL

Abilene Christian University	D
Adelphi University	M
Albany State University	M
Alcorn State University	M
Allen College	M,D
Alvernia University	M,D,O
Alverno College	M
American Public University System	M,D
American Sentinel University	M
American University of Beirut	M
Anderson University (SC)	M,D
Andrews University	M,D
Angelo State University	M
Arizona State University at the Tempe campus	M,D,O
Arkansas State University	M,D,O
Arkansas Tech University	M
Ashland University	D
Aspen University	M
Athabasca University	M,O
Auburn University	M
Auburn University at Montgomery	M
Augsburg University	M,D
Augusta University	D
Austin Peay State University	M
Azusa Pacific University	M,D
Ball State University	M,D,O
Barry University	M,D,O
Baylor University	M,D
Bellarmine University	M,D
Bellin College	M
Belmont University	M,D
Benedictine University	M
Bethel University (IN)	M
Binghamton University, State University of New York	M,D,O
Blessing-Rieman College of Nursing & Health Sciences	M

Bloomsburg University of Pennsylvania	M,D
Boise State University	M,D,O
Boston College	M,D
Bowie State University	M
Bradley University	M,D,O
Brandman University	D
Briar Cliff University	M,D,O
Brigham Young University	M
Brookline College	M
California Baptist University	M
California State University, Bakersfield	
California State University, Chico	M
California State University, Dominguez Hills	M
California State University, Fresno	M,D
California State University, Fullerton	M,D
California State University, Long Beach	M,D,O
California State University, Los Angeles	M,O
California State University, Sacramento	M
California State University, San Bernardino	M
California State University, San Marcos	M
California State University, Stanislaus	M
California University of Pennsylvania	M
Capella University	M,D
Capital University	M
Cardinal Stritch University	D
Carlow University	M,D
Carson-Newman University	M
The Catholic University of America	M,D,O
Cedar Crest College	M
Central Connecticut State University	M
Central Methodist University	M
Chatham University	M,D
Chicago State University	M
Clarion University of Pennsylvania	D
Clarke University	M
Clarkson College	M,O
Clayton State University	M
Clemson University	M,D
Cleveland State University	M,D
College of Mount Saint Vincent	M,O
The College of New Jersey	M,O
The College of New Rochelle	M,O
College of Saint Elizabeth	M
College of Saint Mary	M
The College of St. Scholastica	M,O
Colorado Mesa University	M,D,O
Colorado State University–Pueblo	M
Columbia College of Nursing	M
Columbia University	M,D,O
Columbus State University	M
Concordia University Irvine	M
Concordia University Wisconsin	M,D
Coppin State University	M,O
Cox College	M
Creighton University	M,D,O
Curry College	M
Daemen College	M,D,O
Dalhousie University	M,D
Delaware State University	M
Delta State University	M,D
DePaul University	M,D
DeSales University	M,D,O
Drexel University	M,D*
Duke University	D
Duquesne University	M,D,O
D'Youville College	M,D,O
East Carolina University	M,D
Eastern Kentucky University	M
Eastern Mennonite University	M,D
Eastern New Mexico University	M
East Tennessee State University	M,D,O
Edgewood College	M,D
Edinboro University of Pennsylvania	M,D
EDP University of Puerto Rico–San Sebastian	M
Elmhurst College	M
Elms College	M,D
Emmanuel College (United States)	M,O
Emory University	M,D
Endicott College	M,O
Fairfield University	M,D
Fairleigh Dickinson University, Florham Campus	
Fairleigh Dickinson University, Metropolitan Campus	M,D,O
Felician University	M,D,O
Ferris State University	M
Florida Agricultural and Mechanical University	M,D
Florida Atlantic University	M,D,O
Florida International University	M,D
Florida National University	M
Florida Southern College	M
Florida State University	D,O
Fort Hays State University	M
Framingham State University	M
Franciscan Missionaries of Our Lady University	M,D
Franciscan University of Steubenville	M
Francis Marion University	M
Fresno Pacific University	M
Frontier Nursing University	M,D,O*
Frostburg State University	M
Gannon University	D
Gardner-Webb University	M,D

*M—masters degree; D—doctorate; O—other advanced degree; *—Close-Up and/or Display*

Institution	Degrees
George Mason University	M,D,O
Georgetown University	M,D
The George Washington University	M,D,O
Georgia College & State University	M,D,O
Georgia Southern University	D
Georgia Southwestern State University	M,O
Georgia State University	M,D,O
Goldfarb School of Nursing at Barnes-Jewish College	M
Gonzaga University	M,D
Goshen College	M
Governors State University	M
Graceland University (IA)	M,D,O
The Graduate Center, City University of New York	D
Grambling State University	M,O
Grand Canyon University	M,D,O
Grand Valley State University	M,D
Grantham University	M
Gwynedd Mercy University	M,D
Hampton University	M,D
Hardin-Simmons University	M
Hawai'i Pacific University	M,D
Herzing University Online	M
Hofstra University	M
Holy Family University	M
Holy Names University	M,O
Houston Baptist University	M
Howard University	M
Hunter College of the City University of New York	M,D,O
Husson University	M,O
Idaho State University	M,D
Illinois State University	M,D,O
Immaculata University	M
Independence University	M
Indiana State University	M,D
Indiana University East	M
Indiana University Kokomo	M
Indiana University of Pennsylvania	D
Indiana University–Purdue University Indianapolis	M,D
Indiana University South Bend	M
Indiana Wesleyan University	M
Inter American University of Puerto Rico, Arecibo Campus	M
Inter American University of Puerto Rico, Barranquitas Campus	M
Jacksonville State University	M
Jacksonville University	M,D
James Madison University	M,D
Jefferson College of Health Sciences	M
Johns Hopkins University	M,D*
Kean University	M
Keiser University	M
Kennesaw State University	M,D
Kent State University	M,D
Keuka College	M
King University	M,D,O
Lamar University	M
Lander University	M
La Roche University	M,D,O
La Salle University	M,D,O
Laurentian University	M
Lehman College of the City University of New York	M
Le Moyne College	M,O
Lenoir-Rhyne University	M
Lewis University	M,D
Liberty University	M,D
Lincoln Memorial University	M
Lindenwood University	M
Loma Linda University	D
Long Island University–LIU Brooklyn	M,O
Louisiana College	M
Louisiana State University Health Sciences Center	M,D,O
Loyola University Chicago	M,D,O
Loyola University New Orleans	M,D
Madonna University	M
Malone University	M
Mansfield University of Pennsylvania	M
Marian University (IN)	M,D
Marian University (WI)	M
Marquette University	M,D,O
Marshall University	M,O
Mary Baldwin University	M
Marymount University	M,D,O
Maryville University of Saint Louis	M,D
McGill University	M,D,O
McKendree University	M
McMaster University	M,D
McMurry University	M,O
McNeese State University	M,O
MCPHS University	M
Medical University of South Carolina	D
Memorial University of Newfoundland	M,D
Mercer University	M,D,O
Mercy College	M
Mercy College of Ohio	M
Metropolitan State University	M,D
MGH Institute of Health Professions	M,D,O
Miami Regional University	M
Michigan State University	M,D
MidAmerica Nazarene University	M
Middle Tennessee State University	M,O
Midwestern State University	M
Millersville University of Pennsylvania	M,D,O
Millikin University	M,D
Minnesota State University Mankato	M,D
Minnesota State University Moorhead	M,O
Misericordia University	M,D
Mississippi University for Women	M,D,O
Missouri Southern State University	M
Missouri State University	M,D
Missouri Western State University	M,O
Molloy College	M,D,O
Monmouth University	M,D,O
Montana State University	M,D,O
Moravian College	M
Morgan State University	M,D
Morningside College	M
Mount Carmel College of Nursing	M,D
Mount Marty College	M
Mount Mercy University	M
Mount St. Joseph University	M,D
Mount Saint Mary College	M,O
Mount Saint Mary's University (CA)	M,D,O
Murray State University	D
Nebraska Methodist College	M
Nebraska Wesleyan University	M
Neumann University	M,O
New York University	M,D,O*
Nicholls State University	M
North Dakota State University	D
Northeastern University	M,D,O
Northern Arizona University	M,D,O
Northern Illinois University	M,D
Northern Kentucky University	M,D,O
Northern Michigan University	D
North Park University	M
Northwestern State University of Louisiana	M
Norwich University	M
Nova Southeastern University	M,D
Oakland University	M,D,O
The Ohio State University	M,D
Ohio University	M,D
Oklahoma Baptist University	M
Oklahoma City University	M,D
Old Dominion University	D
Olivet Nazarene University	M
Oregon Health & Science University	M,D,O
Otterbein University	M,D,O
Pace University	M,D,O
Pacific Lutheran University	M,D
Palm Beach Atlantic University	M
Penn State University Park	M,D*
Pensacola Christian College	M
Pittsburg State University	M,D
Point Loma Nazarene University	M,D,O
Pontifical Catholic University of Puerto Rico	M
Prairie View A&M University	M,D
Purdue University	M,D,O
Purdue University Fort Wayne	M,O
Purdue University Global	M
Purdue University Northwest	M
Queen's University at Kingston	M,D,O
Queens University of Charlotte	M
Quinnipiac University	D
Radford University	D
Ramapo College of New Jersey	M
Regis College (MA)	M,D,O
Research College of Nursing	M
Resurrection University	M
Rhode Island College	M
Rivier University	M,D
Robert Morris University	M,D
Roberts Wesleyan College	M
Rowan University	M
Rush University	D
Rutgers University–Camden	D
Rutgers University–Newark	M,D,O
Sacred Heart University	M,D,O
Sage Graduate School	M
Saginaw Valley State University	M
Saint Anthony College of Nursing	M
St. Catherine University	M,D
Saint Francis Medical Center College of Nursing	M,D,O
Saint Francis University	M
St. John Fisher College	M,D,O
St. Joseph's College, Long Island Campus	M
St. Joseph's College, New York	M
Saint Joseph's College of Maine	M,O
Saint Louis University	M,D,O*
Saint Mary-of-the-Woods College	M
Saint Mary's College	D
Saint Peter's University	M,D,O
Saint Xavier University	M,O
Salem State University	M
Salisbury University	M,D
Salve Regina University	D
Samford University	M,D
Samuel Merritt University	M,D,O
San Diego State University	M
San Francisco State University	M,O
San Jose State University	M,O
Seattle Pacific University	M,O
Seattle University	D
Seton Hall University	M,D
Shenandoah University	M,D,O
Simmons University	M,D
Sonoma State University	M
South Dakota State University	M,D
Southeastern Louisiana University	M,D
Southeast Missouri State University	M
Southern Adventist University	M,D
Southern Connecticut State University	M,D
Southern Illinois University Edwardsville	M,D,O
Southern Nazarene University	M
Southern New Hampshire University	M,O
Southern University and Agricultural and Mechanical College	M,D,O
South University	M
South University	M
South University (SC)	M
South University (GA)	M
South University (AL)	M
South University	M
Spalding University	M,D,O
Spring Arbor University	M
Spring Hill College	M,O
Stanbridge University	M
State University of New York College of Technology at Delhi	M
State University of New York Downstate Medical Center	M,O
State University of New York Upstate Medical University	M,O
Stephen F. Austin State University	M
Stevenson University	M
Stockton University	M
Stony Brook University, State University of New York	M,D,O
Tarleton State University	M
Temple University	D*
Tennessee State University	M,O
Tennessee Technological University	M,D
Texas A&M International University	M
Texas A&M University	M
Texas A&M University–Corpus Christi	M,D
Texas Christian University	M,D,O
Texas Tech University Health Sciences Center	M,D,O
Texas Tech University Health Sciences Center El Paso	M
Texas Woman's University	M,D
Thomas Edison State University	M,D
Thomas Jefferson University	M,D
Thomas University	O
Towson University	M
Trinity Washington University	M
Trinity Western University	M
Troy University	M,D
Tusculum University	M
Uniformed Services University of the Health Sciences	M,D*
Union University	M,D,O
Universidad Metropolitana	M,O
Université de Montréal	M,D,O
Université du Québec à Rimouski	M,O
Université du Québec à Trois-Rivières	M,O
Université du Québec en Outaouais	M,O
Université Laval	M,D,O
University at Buffalo, the State University of New York	M,D,O
The University of Akron	M,D
The University of Alabama	M,D
The University of Alabama at Birmingham	M,D
The University of Alabama in Huntsville	M,D,O
University of Alaska Anchorage	M,D,O
University of Alberta	M,D
The University of Arizona	M,D,O
University of Arkansas	M,D
University of Arkansas for Medical Sciences	D
The University of British Columbia	M,D
University of Calgary	M,D,O
University of California, Irvine	M
University of California, Los Angeles	M,D
University of California, San Francisco	M,D
University of Central Arkansas	M,O
University of Central Florida	M,D,O
University of Central Missouri	M,D,O
University of Central Oklahoma	M
University of Cincinnati	M,D
University of Colorado Colorado Springs	M,D
University of Colorado Denver	M,D
University of Connecticut	M,D,O
University of Delaware	M
University of Detroit Mercy	M,D,O
University of Florida	M,D
University of Hartford	M
University of Hawaii at Hilo	D
University of Hawaii at Manoa	M,D,O
University of Houston	M
University of Illinois at Chicago	M,D,O
University of Indianapolis	M,D
The University of Iowa	M,D
The University of Kansas	M,D,O
University of Kentucky	D
University of Louisiana at Lafayette	M,D
University of Louisville	M,D
University of Maine	M,D
The University of Manchester	M,D
University of Manitoba	M
University of Mary	M,D
University of Mary Hardin-Baylor	M,D,O
University of Maryland, Baltimore	M,D,O
University of Massachusetts Amherst	M,D
University of Massachusetts Boston	M,D
University of Massachusetts Dartmouth	M,D
University of Massachusetts Lowell	M,D
University of Massachusetts Medical School	M,D,O
University of Memphis	M,O
University of Miami	M,D
University of Michigan	M,D
University of Michigan–Flint	M,D
University of Minnesota, Twin Cities Campus	M,D
University of Mississippi Medical Center	M,D
University of Missouri	M,D
University of Missouri–Kansas City	M,D
University of Missouri–St. Louis	D,O
University of Mobile	M,D
University of Mount Olive	M
University of Nebraska Medical Center	D
University of Nevada, Las Vegas	M,D,O
University of Nevada, Reno	M,D
University of New Brunswick Fredericton	M
University of New Hampshire	M,D,O
University of New Mexico	M,D
University of North Alabama	M
The University of North Carolina at Chapel Hill	M,D,O
The University of North Carolina at Charlotte	M,D,O
The University of North Carolina at Greensboro	M,D,O
The University of North Carolina at Pembroke	M
The University of North Carolina Wilmington	M,D,O
University of North Dakota	M,D
University of Northern Colorado	M,D
University of North Florida	M,D,O
University of Oklahoma Health Sciences Center	M
University of Ottawa	M,D
University of Pennsylvania	M,D,O*
University of Phoenix–Bay Area Campus	M,D
University of Phoenix–Central Valley Campus	M
University of Phoenix–Hawaii Campus	M
University of Phoenix–Houston Campus	M
University of Phoenix–Online Campus	M,D,O
University of Phoenix–Phoenix Campus	M,O
University of Phoenix–Sacramento Valley Campus	M
University of Phoenix–San Antonio Campus	M
University of Phoenix–San Diego Campus	M
University of Portland	M,D
University of Puerto Rico–Medical Sciences Campus	M
University of Regina	M,D
University of Rhode Island	M,D,O
University of Rochester	M,D*
University of St. Augustine for Health Sciences	M,D
University of St. Francis (IL)	M,D,O
University of Saint Francis (IN)	M,D,O
University of Saint Joseph	M
University of Saint Mary	M
University of San Diego	M,D
University of San Francisco	D
University of Saskatchewan	M,D
The University of Scranton	M,D
University of South Alabama	M,D,O
University of South Carolina	M,O
University of Southern Indiana	M,D
University of Southern Maine	M,D,O
University of Southern Mississippi	M,D
University of South Florida	M,D,O
The University of Tampa	M,D
The University of Tennessee	M,D
The University of Tennessee at Chattanooga	M,D,O
The University of Tennessee Health Science Center	M,D,O
The University of Texas at Arlington	M,D
The University of Texas at Austin	M,D
The University of Texas at El Paso	M,D,O
The University of Texas at Tyler	M,D
The University of Texas Health Science Center at Houston	M,D
The University of Texas Health Science Center at San Antonio	M,D,O
The University of Texas Medical Branch	M,D
University of the Incarnate Word	M,D
The University of Toledo	M,D,O
University of Toronto	M,D
The University of Tulsa	D
University of Utah	M,D
University of Vermont	M,D,O
University of Victoria	M,D
University of Virginia	M,D
University of Washington	M,D
University of Washington, Bothell	M
University of Washington, Tacoma	M
The University of Western Ontario	M,D
University of West Florida	M
University of West Georgia	M,D,O
University of Windsor	M
University of Wisconsin–Eau Claire	M,D
University of Wisconsin–Madison	D
University of Wisconsin–Milwaukee	M,D,O*
University of Wisconsin–Oshkosh	M
University of Wyoming	M
Urbana University–A Branch Campus of Franklin University	M
Ursuline College	M,D
Utah Valley University	M
Valdosta State University	M,D,O
Valparaiso University	M,D
Vanderbilt University	M,D,O*
Vanguard University of Southern California	M
Villanova University	M,D
Virginia Commonwealth University	M,D,O
Viterbo University	D
Wagner College	M,D,O

Column 1	
Walden University	M,D,O
Walsh University	M,D
Washburn University	M,D,O
Washington Adventist University	M
Washington State University	M,D,O
Waynesburg University	M,D
Wayne State University	M,D
Weber State University	M
Webster University	M
Wesley College	M
West Chester University of Pennsylvania	M,D,O
West Coast University	M,D
Western Carolina University	M,D,O
Western Connecticut State University	M,D
Western Kentucky University	M
Western Michigan University	M
Westminster College (UT)	M
West Texas A&M University	M
West Virginia University	M,D,O
West Virginia Wesleyan College	M,D,O
Wheeling Jesuit University	M
Wichita State University	M,D,O
Widener University	M,D,O
Wilkes University	M,D
William Carey University	M
William Paterson University of New Jersey	M,D,O
Wilmington University	M,D
Wilson College	M
Winona State University	M,D
Winston-Salem State University	M,D
Wright State University	M
Xavier University	M,D,O*
Yale University	M,D,O
York College of Pennsylvania	M
York University	M
Youngstown State University	M

NURSING AND HEALTHCARE ADMINISTRATION

Abilene Christian University	D
Adelphi University	M,O
Allen College	M,D
Alvernia University	M,D,O
American International College	M,D,O
American University of Beirut	M,D,O
Anderson University (SC)	M,D
Arizona State University at the Tempe campus	M
Aspen University	M
Athabasca University	M,O
Augusta University	M,D
Austin Peay State University	M
Azusa Pacific University	M,D
Barry University	M,D,O
Bellarmine University	M,D
Blessing-Rieman College of Nursing & Health Sciences	M
Bloomsburg University of Pennsylvania	M,D
Bowie State University	M
Bradley University	M,D,O
Brenau University	M
Brookline College	M
California Baptist University	M
California State University, Fullerton	M,D
California State University, San Marcos	M
California University of Pennsylvania	M
Capella University	M
Capital University	M
Carlow University	M
Cedar Crest College	M
Central Methodist University	M
Chatham University	M,D
Clarke University	D
Clarkson College	M,O
Clarkson University	M,O
College of Mount Saint Vincent	M,O
The College of New Rochelle	M,O
Columbus State University	M
Cox College	M
Creighton University	M,D,O
Daemen College	M,D,O
DeSales University	M,D,O
Drexel University	M*
Duke University	M,D,O
Eastern Mennonite University	M,D
Eastern Michigan University	M,O
East Tennessee State University	M,D,O
Elms College	M,D
Emmanuel College (United States)	M,O
Emory University	M
Endicott College	M,O
Fairfield University	M,D
Felician University	M,D
Ferris State University	M
Florida Agricultural and Mechanical University	M,D
Florida Atlantic University	M,O
Florida National University	M
Florida Southern College	M
Framingham State University	M
Franklin Pierce University	M
Frostburg State University	M
Gannon University	M,D
George Mason University	M,D,O
The George Washington University	M,D,O
Georgia Southwestern State University	M,O
Georgia State University	M,D,O
Goldfarb School of Nursing at Barnes-Jewish College	M
Grand Valley State University	M
Grand View University	M,O
Grantham University	M
Hampton University	M,D

Column 2	
Herzing University Online	M
Hofstra University	M,D,O
Holy Family University	M
Holy Names University	M,O
Immaculata University	M
Independence University	M
Indiana State University	M,D
Indiana University Kokomo	M
Indiana University of Pennsylvania	M
Indiana University–Purdue University Indianapolis	M
Indiana Wesleyan University	M
Jacksonville University	M
James Madison University	M,D
Jefferson College of Health Sciences	M
Johns Hopkins University	M,D*
Kean University	M
Kennesaw State University	M,O
Kent State University	M,D
King University	M,D,O
Lamar University	M
La Roche University	M
La Salle University	M,D,O
Le Moyne College	M,O
Lenoir-Rhyne University	M
Lewis University	M,D
Liberty University	M,D
Loma Linda University	M
Louisiana College	M
Louisiana State University Health Sciences Center	M,D,O
Lourdes University	M
Loyola University Chicago	M,D,O
Madonna University	M
Marquette University	M
McKendree University	M
Medical University of South Carolina	M
Mercer University	M
Mercy College	M
Metropolitan State University	M
Miami Regional University	M
MidAmerica Nazarene University	M
Middle Tennessee State University	M
Milwaukee School of Engineering	M
Missouri Western State University	M
Montana State University	M,D,O
Moravian College	M
Mount Carmel College of Nursing	M
Mount Mary University	M
Mount Mercy University	M
Mount St. Joseph University	M
Mount Saint Mary College	M,O
National American University (TX)	M,D
National University	M,O
Nebraska Methodist College	M
New Mexico State University	M,D,O
New York University	M,O*
Nicholls State University	M
Northeastern State University	M
Northeastern University	M,D,O
North Park University	M
Northwest Nazarene University	M
Norwich University	M
Ohio University	M,D
Oklahoma Wesleyan University	M
Old Dominion University	M
Oregon Health & Science University	M
Otterbein University	M,D,O
Pace University	M,D,O
Palm Beach Atlantic University	M,D
Pennsylvania College of Health Sciences	M
Purdue University Fort Wayne	M,O
Purdue University Global	M
Purdue University Northwest	M
Queens University of Charlotte	M
Quinnipiac University	D
Ramapo College of New Jersey	M
Regis University	M,D,O
Research College of Nursing	M
Rivier University	M,D
Roberts Wesleyan College	M
Rush University	M
Sacred Heart University	M,D,O
Saint Francis Medical Center College of Nursing	M,D,O
Saint Francis University	M
Saint Joseph's College of Maine	M,O
Saint Peter's University	M,D,O
Salem State University	M
Salisbury University	M,D
Samford University	M,D,O
Samuel Merritt University	M,D,O
San Francisco State University	M,O
San Jose State University	M,O
Seattle Pacific University	M,O
Seton Hall University	M,D
Shenandoah University	M,D,O
Southern Illinois University Edwardsville	M,O
Southern Nazarene University	M
Southern New Hampshire University	M,O
Southern University and Agricultural and Mechanical College	M
Spalding University	M,D,O
Spring Hill College	M,O
State University of New York College of Technology at Delhi	M
Stevenson University	M
Stony Brook University, State University of New York	M,D,O
Tarleton State University	M
Teachers College, Columbia University	M,D
Tennessee Technological University	M
Texas A&M University–Corpus Christi	M,D

Column 3	
Texas Christian University	M,D,O
Texas Tech University Health Sciences Center	M,D
Texas Woman's University	M,D
Thomas Edison State University	M
Union University	M,D,O
Universidad Metropolitana	M,O
University at Buffalo, the State University of New York	M,D,O
The University of Alabama at Birmingham	M,D
University of Central Arkansas	M,O
University of Cincinnati	M,D
University of Colorado Denver	M,D
University of Delaware	M,O
University of Hawaii at Manoa	M,D,O
University of Houston	M
University of Illinois at Chicago	M,O
University of Indianapolis	M,D
University of Louisiana at Lafayette	M
University of Louisville	M
University of Mary	M,O
University of Maryland, Baltimore	M,D,O
University of Massachusetts Amherst	M,D
University of Massachusetts Medical School	M,D,O
University of Memphis	M,O
University of Minnesota, Twin Cities Campus	M,D
University of Missouri	M,D,O
University of Missouri–Kansas City	M,D
University of Mobile	M,D
The University of North Carolina at Chapel Hill	M,D,O
The University of North Carolina at Charlotte	M,D,O
The University of North Carolina at Greensboro	M,D,O
The University of North Carolina at Pembroke	M
University of Pennsylvania	M,D*
University of Phoenix–Bay Area Campus	M,D
University of Rochester	M,D*
University of St. Augustine for Health Sciences	M
University of St. Francis (IL)	M,D,O
University of Saint Mary	M
University of San Diego	M,D
The University of Scranton	M,D,O
University of South Alabama	M,D,O
University of South Carolina	M
University of Southern Indiana	M,D,O
University of Southern Maine	M,D,O
The University of Texas at Arlington	M,D
The University of Texas at Austin	M,D
The University of Texas at El Paso	M,D,O
The University of Texas at Tyler	M,D
The University of Texas Health Science Center at San Antonio	M,D
The University of Toledo	M,O
University of Victoria	M
University of Virginia	M,D
University of Washington, Tacoma	M
University of Wisconsin–Eau Claire	M,D
University of Wisconsin–Green Bay	M
Virginia Commonwealth University	M,D,O
Walden University	M,D,O
Walsh University	M,D
Washburn University	M,D,O
Washington Adventist University	M
Waynesburg University	M,D
Weber State University	M
Western Governors University	M
Western University of Health Sciences	M
West Virginia Wesleyan College	M,D,O
Wilmington University	M,D
Wilson College	M
Winona State University	M,D,O
Wright State University	M

NURSING EDUCATION

Abilene Christian University	D
Adelphi University	M,O
Albany State University	M
Allen College	M,D
Alvernia University	M,D,O
American International College	M,D,O
Anderson University (SC)	M
Angelo State University	M
Arizona State University at the Tempe campus	M,D,O
Aspen University	M
Auburn University	M
Auburn University at Montgomery	M
Austin Peay State University	M
Azusa Pacific University	M,D
Ball State University	M,D,O
Barry University	M,D
Bellarmine University	M,D
Bellin College	M
Bethel University (MN)	M,D,O
Blessing-Rieman College of Nursing & Health Sciences	M
Bowie State University	M
Bradley University	M,D,O
Brenau University	M
California Baptist University	M
California State University, Fullerton	M,D
California State University, San Marcos	M
California State University, Stanislaus	M

Column 4	
California University of Pennsylvania	M
Capella University	M,D
Carlow University	M
Carson-Newman University	M
Case Western Reserve University	M
Cedar Crest College	M
Cedarville University	M,D
Central Methodist University	M
Chatham University	M,D
Clarkson College	M,O
Cleveland State University	D
College of Mount Saint Vincent	M,O
The College of New Rochelle	M,O
Colorado Mesa University	M,D,O
Columbus State University	M
Cox College	M
Daemen College	M,D,O
Delta State University	M,D
DeSales University	M,D,O
Drexel University	M*
Duke University	M,O
Duquesne University	M,O
Eastern Michigan University	M,O
East Tennessee State University	M,D,O
Edinboro University of Pennsylvania	M,D
Elms College	M
Emmanuel College (United States)	M,O
Endicott College	M,O
Felician University	M,O
Ferris State University	M
Florida Gulf Coast University	M
Florida National University	M
Florida Southern College	M
Framingham State University	M
Francis Marion University	M
Franklin Pierce University	M,D,O
Frostburg State University	M
George Mason University	M,D
Georgetown University	M,D
Georgia Southern University	O
Georgia Southwestern State University	M,O
Graceland University (IA)	M,D,O
Grand Canyon University	M,D,O
Grand Valley State University	M,D
Grand View University	M,O
Grantham University	M
Gwynedd Mercy University	M,D
Hampton University	M,D
Hardin-Simmons University	M
Herzing University Online	M
Holy Family University	M
Howard University	M
Immaculata University	M
Indiana State University	M,D
Indiana University Kokomo	M
Indiana University of Pennsylvania	M
Indiana University–Purdue University Indianapolis	M
Indiana Wesleyan University	M
Jacksonville University	M
Jefferson College of Health Sciences	M
Kennesaw State University	M
Kent State University	M,D
Keuka College	M
King University	M,D,O
Lamar University	M
La Roche University	M
La Salle University	M,D,O
Le Moyne College	M,O
Lenoir-Rhyne University	M
Lewis University	M,D
Liberty University	M,D
Loma Linda University	M
Long Island University–LIU Brooklyn	M,O
Long Island University–LIU Post	M,O
Louisiana State University Health Sciences Center	M,D,O
Lourdes University	M
Marian University (IN)	M,D
Marian University (WI)	M
McKendree University	M
McMurry University	M
McNeese State University	M
Medical University of South Carolina	M
Mercy College	M
Messiah College	M
Metropolitan State University	M,D
MGH Institute of Health Professions	M,D,O
Miami Regional University	M
MidAmerica Nazarene University	M
Middle Tennessee State University	M
Midwestern State University	M
Millersville University of Pennsylvania	M,D,O
Minnesota State University Mankato	M,D
Missouri State University	M,D
Missouri Western State University	M,O
Molloy College	M,D,O
Montana State University	M,D,O
Moravian College	M
Mount Carmel College of Nursing	M,D
Mount Mercy University	M
Mount St. Joseph University	M
Mount Saint Mary College	M,O
National American University (TX)	M,D
Nebraska Methodist College	M
New York University	M,O*
Nicholls State University	M
Northeastern State University	M
Norwich University	M
Nova Southeastern University	M,D
Ohio University	M,D
Oklahoma Baptist University	M

Oklahoma City University	M,D
Oklahoma Wesleyan University	M
Old Dominion University	M,D
Oregon Health & Science University	M,O
Otterbein University	M,D,O
Pennsylvania College of Health Sciences	M
Pittsburg State University	M,D
Purdue University Fort Wayne	M,O
Purdue University Global	M
Queens University of Charlotte	M
Ramapo College of New Jersey	M
Regis College (MA)	M,D,O
Regis University	M,D,O
Rivier University	M,D
Roberts Wesleyan College	M
Sacred Heart University	M,D,O
Sage Graduate School	D
St. Catherine University	M,D
Saint Francis Medical Center College of Nursing	M,D,O
Saint Francis University	M
St. Joseph's College, Long Island Campus	M
St. Joseph's College, New York	M
Saint Joseph's College of Maine	M,O
Salem State University	M
Salisbury University	M
San Jose State University	M,O
Seattle Pacific University	M,O
Seton Hall University	M,D
Shenandoah University	M,D,O
Southern Adventist University	M,D
Southern Connecticut State University	M,D
Southern Illinois University Edwardsville	M,O
Southern Nazarene University	M
Southern New Hampshire University	M,O
Southern University and Agricultural and Mechanical College	M,D,O
South University	M
South University (GA)	M
Spalding University	M,D,O
State University of New York College of Technology at Delhi	M
State University of New York Empire State College	M
State University of New York Polytechnic Institute	M
Stevenson University	M
Stony Brook University, State University of New York	M,O
Tarleton State University	M
Teachers College, Columbia University	M,D,O
Tennessee Technological University	M
Texas A&M University	M
Texas A&M University–Corpus Christi	M,D
Texas Christian University	M,O
Texas Tech University Health Sciences Center	M,D,O
Texas Woman's University	M,D
Thomas Edison State University	M
Towson University	O
Union University	M,D,O
The University of Alabama in Huntsville	M,D,O
University of Central Arkansas	M,O
University of Detroit Mercy	M,D,O
University of Hartford	M
University of Houston	M
University of Indianapolis	M,D
University of Louisiana at Lafayette	M,D
University of Louisville	M,D
University of Maine	M,D
University of Mary	M,D
University of Mary Hardin-Baylor	M,D,O
University of Maryland, Baltimore	M,D,O
University of Massachusetts Medical School	M,D,O
University of Memphis	M,O
University of Missouri–Kansas City	M,D
University of Mobile	M
University of Nevada, Las Vegas	M,D,O
University of New Brunswick Fredericton	M
The University of North Carolina at Chapel Hill	M,D,O
The University of North Carolina at Charlotte	M,D,O
The University of North Carolina at Greensboro	M,D,O
The University of North Carolina at Pembroke	M
The University of North Carolina Wilmington	M,D,O
University of North Dakota	M,D,O
University of Northern Colorado	M,D
University of North Georgia	M
University of Phoenix–Bay Area Campus	M,D
University of Phoenix–Hawaii Campus	M
University of Phoenix–Online Campus	M,O
University of Phoenix–Phoenix Campus	M,O
University of Phoenix–Sacramento Valley Campus	M
University of Phoenix–San Diego Campus	M
University of Portland	M,D
University of Rhode Island	M,D,O
University of Rochester	M,D*
University of St. Augustine for Health Sciences	
University of St. Francis (IL)	M,D,O

University of Saint Joseph	M,D
University of Saint Mary	M
University of South Alabama	M,D,O
University of Southern Indiana	M,D,O
University of Southern Maine	M,D,O
University of South Florida	M,D,O
The University of Tennessee at Chattanooga	M,D,O
The University of Texas at Arlington	M,D
The University of Texas at Austin	M,D
The University of Texas at El Paso	M,D,O
The University of Texas at Tyler	M,D
The University of Texas Health Science Center at San Antonio	M,D,O
The University of Toledo	M,O
University of Victoria	M,D
University of Washington, Tacoma	M
University of West Georgia	M,O
University of Wisconsin–Eau Claire	M,D
Ursuline College	M,D
Valparaiso University	M,D,O
Villanova University	M,D,O
Virginia Commonwealth University	M,D,O
Wagner College	M,D,O
Walden University	M,D,O
Walsh University	M,D
Washington Adventist University	M
Waynesburg University	M,D
Weber State University	M
Webster University	M
West Chester University of Pennsylvania	M,D
Western Connecticut State University	D
Western Governors University	M
William Paterson University of New Jersey	M,D,O
Wilson College	M
Winona State University	M,D,O
Winston-Salem State University	M,D
Worcester State University	M

NURSING INFORMATICS

Allen College	M,D
Aspen University	M
Austin Peay State University	M
Columbus State University	M
Duke University	M,D,O
Ferris State University	M
Georgia Southwestern State University	M,O
Georgia State University	M,D,O
Grantham University	M
Holy Names University	M,O
Jacksonville University	M
Le Moyne College	M,O
Liberty University	M,D
National American University (TX)	M,D
National University	M,O
New York University	M,O*
Nova Southeastern University	M,D
Roberts Wesleyan College	M
Rutgers University–Newark	M
Samford University	M,D
Seattle Pacific University	M,O
Thomas Edison State University	M
Troy University	M,D
The University of Alabama at Birmingham	M,D
University of Maryland, Baltimore	M,D,O
University of Minnesota, Twin Cities Campus	M,D
The University of North Carolina at Chapel Hill	M,D,O
University of Phoenix–Bay Area Campus	M,D
University of Phoenix–Phoenix Campus	M,O
University of St. Augustine for Health Sciences	M
Walden University	M,D,O
Waynesburg University	M,D
Western Governors University	M

NUTRITION

Abilene Christian University	M,O
Adelphi University	M,D,O
Alabama Agricultural and Mechanical University	M
American College of Healthcare Sciences	M,O
American University	M,O
American University of Beirut	M,D
Andrews University	M,O
Appalachian State University	M
Arizona State University at the Tempe campus	M,D
Auburn University	M,D,O
Ball State University	M
Bastyr University	M,O
Baylor University	M,D
Benedictine University	M
Boston University	M,D
Bradley University	M
Brigham Young University	M
Brooklyn College of the City University of New York	M
Buffalo State College, State University of New York	M
California Polytechnic State University, San Luis Obispo	M
California State University, Chico	M
California State University, Long Beach	M
California State University, Los Angeles	M,O
California University of Pennsylvania	M
Canisius College	M,O
Case Western Reserve University	M,D
Cedar Crest College	O
Central Michigan University	M,D,O
Central Washington University	M

Chapman University	M*
Clemson University	M,D
College of Saint Elizabeth	M,O
Colorado State University	M,D
Columbia University	M,D
Cornell University	M,D
D'Youville College	M
East Carolina University	M,D
Eastern Illinois University	M
Eastern Kentucky University	M
Eastern Michigan University	M
East Tennessee State University	M
Emory University	M,D
Florida International University	M,D
Florida State University	M,D
Framingham State University	M
Franciscan Missionaries of Our Lady University	M,D
George Mason University	M,O
Georgia Southern University	O
Georgia State University	M
Grand Valley State University	M
Harvard University	D*
Howard University	M,D
Hunter College of the City University of New York	M
Huntington University of Health Sciences	M
Immaculata University	M
Indiana University Bloomington	M
Indiana University of Pennsylvania	M
Indiana University–Purdue University Indianapolis	M,D
Instituto Tecnologico de Santo Domingo	M,O
Iowa State University of Science and Technology	M,D
James Madison University	M
Johns Hopkins University	M,D*
Kansas State University	M,D
Kent State University	M
Lehman College of the City University of New York	M
Liberty University	M,D
Life University	M
Lipscomb University	M
Logan University	M,D
Loma Linda University	M,D
London Metropolitan University	M,D
Long Island University–LIU Post	M,O
Louisiana State University and Agricultural & Mechanical College	M,D
Louisiana Tech University	M,D,O
Loyola University Chicago	M,D,O
Marshall University	M,O
Maryland University of Integrative Health	M,D,O
Marywood University	M,O
McGill University	M,D,O
McMaster University	M,D
McNeese State University	M
Meredith College	M,O
Michigan State University	M,D
Mississippi State University	M,D
Missouri State University	M,D,O
Montclair State University	M,O
Mount Mary University	M
Mount Saint Vincent University	M
Murray State University	M,O
National University of Natural Medicine	M
New York Chiropractic College	M
New York Institute of Technology	M
New York University	M,D*
North Carolina Agricultural and Technical State University	M
North Carolina State University	M,D
North Dakota State University	M,D
Northeastern University	M
Northern Illinois University	M
Northwestern Health Sciences University	M
Nova Southeastern University	M,D,O
The Ohio State University	M,D
Ohio University	M,D
Oklahoma State University	M,D
Oregon Health & Science University	M,O
Oregon State University	M,D
Penn State University Park	M,D*
Purdue University	M,D
Queens College of the City University of New York	M,O
Rosalind Franklin University of Medicine and Science	M
Rush University	M
Rutgers University–Newark	M,D,O
Rutgers University–New Brunswick	M,D
Sacred Heart University	M
Sage Graduate School	M,O
Saint Louis University	M*
Samford University	M
Sam Houston State University	M
San Diego State University	M
San Jose State University	M
Saybrook University	M,D,O
Simmons University	M,D,O
South Carolina State University	M
South Dakota State University	M,D
Southern Illinois University Carbondale	M
State University of New York College at Oneonta	M
Stony Brook University, State University of New York	M,O
Syracuse University	M
Teachers College, Columbia University	M,D,O
Texas A&M University	M,D
Texas State University	M
Texas Tech University	M,D
Texas Woman's University	M,D
Tufts University	M,D,O

Tuskegee University	M
Université de Moncton	M
Université de Montréal	M,D,O
Université Laval	M,D
University at Buffalo, the State University of New York	M,D,O
The University of Alabama	M
The University of Alabama at Birmingham	M,D
The University of Arizona	M,D
University of Arkansas for Medical Sciences	M,D,O
University of Bridgeport	M
The University of British Columbia	M,D
University of California, Berkeley	M,D
University of California, Davis	M,D
University of Central Arkansas	M
University of Central Oklahoma	M
University of Chicago	D
University of Cincinnati	M
University of Connecticut	M,D
University of Delaware	M
University of Florida	M,D
University of Georgia	M,D
University of Guelph	M,D
University of Hawaii at Manoa	M
University of Houston	M,D
University of Illinois at Chicago	M,D
University of Illinois at Urbana–Champaign	M,D
The University of Kansas	M,D,O
University of Kentucky	M,D
University of Manitoba	M,D
University of Maryland, College Park	M,D
University of Massachusetts Amherst	M,D
University of Memphis	M,O
University of Miami	M
University of Michigan	M,D
University of Minnesota, Twin Cities Campus	M,D
University of Mississippi	M,D
University of Missouri	M,D
University of Nebraska–Lincoln	M,D
University of Nebraska Medical Center	O
University of Nevada, Las Vegas	M,D
University of Nevada, Reno	M
University of New England	M,D,O
University of New Hampshire	M,D
University of New Mexico	M
The University of North Carolina at Chapel Hill	M,D
The University of North Carolina at Greensboro	M,D
University of North Florida	M
University of Oklahoma Health Sciences Center	M
University of Pittsburgh	M*
University of Puerto Rico–Medical Sciences Campus	M,D,O
University of Puerto Rico–Río Piedras	M
University of Rhode Island	M
University of Saint Joseph	M
University of Saskatchewan	M,D
University of Southern Mississippi	M
University of South Florida	M,D,O
The University of Tampa	M
The University of Tennessee	M
The University of Tennessee at Martin	M
The University of Texas at Austin	M,D
The University of Texas Rio Grande Valley	M
The University of Texas Southwestern Medical Center	M
University of the District of Columbia	M
University of the Incarnate Word	M
The University of Toledo	M,O
University of Toronto	M,D
University of Utah	M,D
University of Vermont	M
University of Washington	M,D
University of Wisconsin–Madison	M,D
University of Wisconsin–Milwaukee	M,D*
University of Wisconsin–Stevens Point	M
University of Wisconsin–Stout	M
University of Wyoming	M
Utah State University	M,D
Virginia Polytechnic Institute and State University	M,D
Virginia University of Integrative Medicine	M,D,O
Washington State University	M
Wayne State University	M,D,O
West Chester University of Pennsylvania	M
West Virginia University	M,D
Winthrop University	M,O

OCCUPATIONAL HEALTH NURSING

Rutgers University–Newark	M,D,O
University of Cincinnati	M,D
University of Illinois at Chicago	M,O
University of Minnesota, Twin Cities Campus	M,D
The University of North Carolina at Chapel Hill	M,D
University of South Florida	M,D,O
University of the Sacred Heart	M

OCCUPATIONAL THERAPY

Abilene Christian University	M
AdventHealth University	M
Alabama State University	M
Allen College	M,D
Alvernia University	M

Institution	Degree
American International College	M,D,O
Arkansas State University	D
A.T. Still University	M,D,O
Augusta University	M
Baker College Center for Graduate Studies—Online	M,D
Barry University	M
Bay Path University	M,D
Belmont University	M,D
Boston University	D
Brenau University	M
Cabarrus College of Health Sciences	M
California State University, Dominguez Hills	M
Carroll University	M
Chatham University	M,D
Chicago State University	M
Clarkson University	M
Cleveland State University	M
College of Saint Mary	M
The College of St. Scholastica	M
Colorado State University	M,D
Columbia University	M,D
Concordia University Wisconsin	M
Cox College	M
Creighton University	D
Dalhousie University	M
Davenport University	M
Dominican College	M
Dominican University of California	M
Drake University	M,D
Duquesne University	M
D'Youville College	M
East Carolina University	M,D,O
Eastern Kentucky University	M
Eastern Michigan University	M
Eastern Washington University	M
Elizabethtown College	M
Elmhurst College	M
Emory & Henry College	M,D
Florida Agricultural and Mechanical University	M
Florida Gulf Coast University	M
Florida International University	M
Gannon University	M,D
Georgia State University	M
Governors State University	M
Grand Valley State University	M
Hofstra University	M,O
Howard University	M,D
Huntington University	M
Idaho State University	M
Indiana State University	M,D
Indiana University–Purdue University Indianapolis	M,D
Indiana Wesleyan University	M,D
Ithaca College	M
Jacksonville University	D
James Madison University	M
Jefferson College of Health Sciences	M
Johnson & Wales University	D
Kean University	M
Keiser University	M
Kettering College	D
Keuka College	M
Le Moyne College	M
Lenoir-Rhyne University	M
Loma Linda University	M,D
Long Island University–LIU Brooklyn	M,D,O
Louisiana State University Health Sciences Center	M
Mary Baldwin University	D
Maryville University of Saint Louis	M
McMaster University	M
Medical University of South Carolina	M
Mercy College	M
MGH Institute of Health Professions	D
Midwestern University, Downers Grove Campus	M
Midwestern University, Glendale Campus	M
Milligan College	M
Misericordia University	M
Missouri State University	M
Mount Mary University	M,D
Nebraska Methodist College	M
New England Institute of Technology	M,D
New York Institute of Technology	M
New York University	M,D*
Northeastern State University	M
Northern Arizona University	D
Nova Southeastern University	M,D
The Ohio State University	M
Pacific University	D
Queen's University at Kingston	M,D
Radford University	M
Regis College (MA)	M,D,O
Regis University	M,D,O
Rockhurst University	M
Rocky Mountain College	D
Rocky Mountain University of Health Professions	D
Rush University	D
Sacred Heart University	M
Sage Graduate School	M
Saginaw Valley State University	M
St. Ambrose University	D
St. Catherine University	M,D
Saint Francis University	M*
Saint Louis University	M*
Salem State University	M
Salus University	M,O
Samuel Merritt University	D
San Jose State University	M
Seton Hall University	M
Shawnee State University	M
Shenandoah University	M,D,O
Sonoma State University	M
South University	D
Spalding University	M
Springfield College	M
Stanbridge University	M
State University of New York Downstate Medical Center	M
Stockton University	M
Stony Brook University, State University of New York	M,D,O
Temple University	M,D*
Tennessee State University	M
Texas Tech University Health Sciences Center	M
Texas Woman's University	M,D
Thomas Jefferson University	M
Touro College	M,D
Towson University	M
Trinity Washington University	M
Tufts University	M,D,O
Tuskegee University	M
Université de Montréal	O
University at Buffalo, the State University of New York	M
The University of Alabama at Birmingham	M,O
University of Alberta	M,D
The University of British Columbia	M,D
University of Central Arkansas	M
The University of Findlay	M,D
University of Florida	M
University of Illinois at Chicago	M,D
University of Indianapolis	M,D
The University of Kansas	M
University of Louisiana at Monroe	M
University of Manitoba	M
University of Mary	M,D
University of Minnesota Rochester	M,D
University of Minnesota, Twin Cities Campus	M
University of Mississippi Medical Center	M
University of Missouri	M
University of New England	M,D
University of New Hampshire	M,O
University of New Mexico	M
The University of North Carolina at Chapel Hill	M,D
University of North Dakota	M
University of Oklahoma Health Sciences Center	M
University of Pittsburgh	M,D*
University of Puerto Rico–Medical Sciences Campus	M
University of Puget Sound	M,D
University of St. Augustine for Health Sciences	M,D
The University of Scranton	M
University of South Alabama	M
University of South Dakota	M
University of Southern California	M,D
University of Southern Indiana	M
University of Southern Maine	M
The University of Tennessee at Chattanooga	D
The University of Tennessee Health Science Center	M,D
The University of Texas at El Paso	M
The University of Texas Health Science Center at San Antonio	M,D
The University of Texas Medical Branch	M
The University of Texas Rio Grande Valley	M
University of the Sciences	M,D
The University of Toledo	M,D
University of Toronto	M
University of Utah	M,D
University of Washington	M,D
The University of Western Ontario	M
University of Wisconsin–La Crosse	M
University of Wisconsin–Madison	M,D
University of Wisconsin–Milwaukee	M*
Utica College	M
Virginia Commonwealth University	M,D
Washington University in St. Louis	M,D
Wayne State University	M
Wesley College	M
West Coast University	M,D
Western Michigan University	M
Western New England University	M
Western New Mexico University	M
West Virginia University	M
Winston-Salem State University	M
Worcester State University	M
Xavier University	M*

OCEAN ENGINEERING

Institution	Degree
Florida Atlantic University	M,D
Florida Institute of Technology	M,D
Massachusetts Institute of Technology	M,D,O
Memorial University of Newfoundland	M,D
Oregon State University	M,D
Princeton University	D
Stevens Institute of Technology	M,D
University of California, San Diego	M,D
University of Delaware	M,D
University of Florida	M,D
University of Hawaii at Manoa	M,D
University of Michigan	M,D,O
University of New Hampshire	M,D,O
University of Rhode Island	M,D
Virginia Polytechnic Institute and State University	M,O
Woods Hole Oceanographic Institution	D

OCEANOGRAPHY

Institution	Degree
Cornell University	D
Dalhousie University	M,D
Florida Institute of Technology	M,D
Florida State University	M,D
Louisiana State University and Agricultural & Mechanical College	M,D
Massachusetts Institute of Technology	M,D,O
McGill University	M,D
Memorial University of Newfoundland	M,D
Naval Postgraduate School	M,D
North Carolina State University	M,D
Nova Southeastern University	M,D
Old Dominion University	M,D
Oregon State University	M,D
Princeton University	D
Rutgers University–New Brunswick	M,D
Texas A&M University	M,D
Université du Québec à Rimouski	M,D
Université Laval	D
University of Alaska Fairbanks	M,D
The University of British Columbia	M,D
University of California, Los Angeles	M,D
University of California, San Diego	M,D
University of Colorado Boulder	M,D
University of Delaware	M,D
University of Hawaii at Manoa	M,D
University of Maryland, College Park	M,D
University of Miami	M,D
University of New Hampshire	M,D,O
University of Rhode Island	M,D
University of San Diego	M
University of Southern California	M,D
University of South Florida	M,D
The University of Texas Rio Grande Valley	M
University of Victoria	M,D
University of Washington	M,D
University of Wisconsin–Madison	M,D
Woods Hole Oceanographic Institution	D
Yale University	D

ONCOLOGY NURSING

Institution	Degree
Gwynedd Mercy University	M,D
Universidad Metropolitana	M,O
University of Delaware	M,O
University of South Florida	M,D,O

OPERATIONS RESEARCH

Institution	Degree
Air Force Institute of Technology	M,D
Bowling Green State University	M
Capella University	M
Carnegie Mellon University	D
Case Western Reserve University	M,D
Claremont Graduate University	M,D
Colorado School of Mines	M,D
Columbia University	M,D
Cornell University	M,D
École Polytechnique de Montréal	M,D,O
Florida Institute of Technology	M,D
George Mason University	M,D,O
Georgia Institute of Technology	M,D
Georgia State University	M,D
HEC Montreal	O
Idaho State University	M
Iowa State University of Science and Technology	M,D
Johns Hopkins University	M,D*
Kansas State University	M,D
Massachusetts Institute of Technology	M,D
Mississippi State University	M,D
Naval Postgraduate School	M,D
New Mexico Institute of Mining and Technology	M,D
North Carolina State University	M,D
Northeastern University	M,D,O
The Ohio State University	M
Princeton University	M,D
Purdue University Fort Wayne	M,O
Rutgers University–New Brunswick	D
Simon Fraser University	M,D
South Dakota State University	M
Southern Illinois University Edwardsville	M
Southern Methodist University	M,D
The University of Alabama in Huntsville	M,D
University of California, Berkeley	M,D
University of Colorado Denver	M,D
University of Delaware	M
University of Illinois at Chicago	M,D
The University of Iowa	M,D
University of Massachusetts Amherst	M,D
University of Michigan	M,D
The University of North Carolina at Chapel Hill	M,D
University of Southern California	M,D,O
The University of Texas at Austin	M,D
University of Waterloo	M,D

OPTICAL SCIENCES

Institution	Degree
Air Force Institute of Technology	M,D
Alabama Agricultural and Mechanical University	M,D
Delaware State University	M,D
Duke University	M
École Polytechnique de Montréal	M,D,O
Norfolk State University	M
North Carolina Agricultural and Technical State University	M,D
The Ohio State University	M,D
Rochester Institute of Technology	M,D
Rose-Hulman Institute of Technology	M
The University of Alabama in Huntsville	M,D
The University of Arizona	M,D,O
University of Central Florida	M,D
University of Dayton	M,D
University of New Mexico	M,D
The University of North Carolina at Charlotte	M,D
University of Rochester	M,D*

OPTOMETRY

Institution	Degree
Ferris State University	D
Illinois College of Optometry	D
Indiana University Bloomington	M,D
Inter American University of Puerto Rico School of Optometry	D
Marshall B. Ketchum University	M,D
MCPHS University	D
Midwestern University, Downers Grove Campus	D
Midwestern University, Glendale Campus	D
New England College of Optometry	M,D
Northeastern State University	M,D
Nova Southeastern University	M,D
The Ohio State University	M,D
Pacific University	M,D
Salus University	D
Southern College of Optometry	D
State University of New York College of Optometry	D
Université de Montréal	D
The University of Alabama at Birmingham	D
University of California, Berkeley	D,O
University of Houston	D
The University of Manchester	M,D
University of Missouri–St. Louis	D
University of Pikeville	D
University of the Incarnate Word	D
University of Waterloo	M,D
Western University of Health Sciences	D

ORAL AND DENTAL SCIENCES

Institution	Degree
American University of Beirut	M,D
A.T. Still University	M,D,O
Augusta University	M,D
Boston University	M,D
Case Western Reserve University	M,O
Columbia University	M,D,O
Dalhousie University	M,D
Harvard University	M,D,O*
Howard University	D,O
Idaho State University	O
Jacksonville University	M,O
Loma Linda University	M,O
Marquette University	M,O
McGill University	M,D,O
Metropolitan State University	M,D
New York University	M,D,O*
The Ohio State University	M,D
Oregon Health & Science University	M,D,O
Rutgers University–Newark	M,D,O
Saint Louis University	M*
Seton Hill University	M,O
Stony Brook University, State University of New York	M,D,O
Temple University	M,O*
Texas A&M University	M,D,O
Tufts University	M,O
Université de Montréal	M,O
Université Laval	M,O
University at Buffalo, the State University of New York	M,D,O
The University of Alabama at Birmingham	M
University of Alberta	M,D
The University of British Columbia	M,D
University of California, Los Angeles	M,D
University of California, San Francisco	M,D
University of Colorado Denver	D,O
University of Connecticut Health Center	M
University of Detroit Mercy	M,D,O
University of Florida	M,D,O
University of Illinois at Chicago	M,D
The University of Iowa	M,D,O
University of Kentucky	M
University of Louisville	M,D
The University of Manchester	M,D
University of Manitoba	M,D
University of Maryland, Baltimore	M,D,O
University of Michigan	M,D
University of Minnesota, Twin Cities Campus	M,D
University of Mississippi Medical Center	M,D
University of Missouri–Kansas City	M,D,O
University of Nebraska Medical Center	M,D
University of Nevada, Las Vegas	M,D,O
The University of North Carolina at Chapel Hill	M,D

M—masters degree; D—doctorate; O—other advanced degree; *—Close-Up and/or Display

University of Oklahoma Health Sciences Center	M
University of Pittsburgh	M,D,O*
University of Puerto Rico–Medical Sciences Campus	O
University of Rochester	M*
University of Southern California	M,D,O
The University of Tennessee Health Science Center	M,D
The University of Toledo	M
University of Toronto	M,D
University of Washington	M,D,O
The University of Western Ontario	M
West Virginia University	M,D

ORGANIC CHEMISTRY

Auburn University	M,D
Boston College	M,D
Brandeis University	M,D
Cleveland State University	M,D
Cornell University	D
Eastern New Mexico University	M
Florida State University	M,D
Georgetown University	D
The George Washington University	M,D
Georgia State University	M,D
Harvard University	D*
Howard University	M,D
Indiana University Bloomington	M,D
Instituto Tecnológico y de Estudios Superiores de Monterrey, Campus Monterrey	M,D
Iowa State University of Science and Technology	M,D
Laurentian University	M
Marquette University	M,D
Massachusetts Institute of Technology	M,D,O
McMaster University	M,D
Old Dominion University	M,D
Purdue University	M,D
Rice University	M,D
Rutgers University–Newark	M,D
Rutgers University–New Brunswick	M,D
Seton Hall University	M,D
Southern University and Agricultural and Mechanical College	M
State University of New York College of Environmental Science and Forestry	M,D
University of Calgary	M,D
University of Cincinnati	M,D
University of Louisville	M,D
The University of Manchester	M,D
University of Maryland, College Park	M,D
University of Massachusetts Lowell	M,D
University of Memphis	M,D
University of Miami	M,D
University of Michigan	M,D
University of Missouri–Kansas City	M,D
University of Montana	M,D
University of Nebraska–Lincoln	M,D
University of Notre Dame	M,D
University of Oklahoma	M,D*
University of Regina	M,D
University of Rochester	D*
The University of Tennessee	M,D
The University of Texas at Austin	D
The University of Toledo	M,D
Virginia Commonwealth University	M,D
Wake Forest University	M,D
Wesleyan University	D
Yale University	D
Youngstown State University	M

ORGANIZATIONAL BEHAVIOR

Argosy University, Chicago	D
Arizona State University at the Tempe campus	M,D
A.T. Still University	M,D,O
Baruch College of the City University of New York	M,D*
Benedictine University	M,D
Boston College	D
Brooklyn College of the City University of New York	M,D
California State University, East Bay	M
Carnegie Mellon University	D
Case Western Reserve University	M,D
Clemson University	M,D
Cornell University	M,D
Drexel University	M,D,O*
Fairleigh Dickinson University, Florham Campus	M,O
Florida State University	M,D
The Graduate Center, City University of New York	D
Hampton University	M
Harvard University	D*
International Institute for Restorative Practices	M,O
John Jay College of Criminal Justice of the City University of New York	M,D
Lake Forest Graduate School of Management	M
New York University	M,D*
Northwestern University	M
Phillips Graduate University	D
Purdue University	D
Queen's University at Kingston	M,D
Saybrook University	M,D
Suffolk University	M
Universidad de las Americas, A.C.	M
Université de Sherbrooke	M
University at Albany, State University of New York	M,D,O
The University of British Columbia	D

University of California, Berkeley	D
University of California, Davis	M
University of Chicago	M,O
University of Hartford	M
University of Hawaii at Manoa	M
The University of Kansas	M,D
University of New Mexico	M
The University of North Carolina at Chapel Hill	D
University of North Texas at Dallas	M
University of Oklahoma	M,D,O*
University of Pittsburgh	M,D*
The University of Texas at Austin	M
University of Utah	M,D
Wayne State University	M,D
Wilfrid Laurier University	M

ORGANIZATIONAL MANAGEMENT

Albertus Magnus College	M
Albizu University, Miami Campus	M,D
Alvernia University	D
The American College of Financial Services	M
American University	M,D,O
Anderson University (SC)	M
Antioch University Los Angeles	M
Apollos University	M,D
Aquinas College (MI)	M
Argosy University, Chicago	D
Argosy University, Hawai'i	D
Argosy University, Los Angeles	M,D
Argosy University, Northern Virginia	M,D,O
Argosy University, Orange County	D
Argosy University, Seattle	M,D
Argosy University, Tampa	M,D
Argosy University, Twin Cities	M,D
Athabasca University	M,O
Atlantic University	M
Augsburg University	M
Austin Peay State University	M
Avila University	M
Azusa Pacific University	M
Baker University	M
Bellevue University	M
Benedictine University	M,D
Bethel University (MN)	M,D,O
Binghamton University, State University of New York	D
Boise State University	M,O
Boston College	D
Boston University	M
Bowling Green State University	M
Brandman University	M
Brenau University	M
Briercrest Seminary	M
Buffalo State College, State University of New York	M
Cabrini University	M,D
Cairn University	M,O
California Baptist University	M
California Coast University	M,D
California College of the Arts	M
California Intercontinental University	M,D
California State University, Fullerton	M
Calvary University	M
Capella University	M,D
Carlow University	M,D,O
Carson-Newman University	M
Central Penn College	M
Charleston Southern University	M
Charter Oak State College	M
The Chicago School of Professional Psychology	M,D
City University of Seattle	M,O
Clarks Summit University	M,D
College of Saint Elizabeth	M
College of Saint Mary	M
The College of Saint Rose	O
Colorado State University–Global Campus	M
Columbia College (SC)	M
Columbia Southern University	M
Columbus State University	M,O
Concordia College–New York	M
Concordia University (Canada)	M,O
Concordia University Ann Arbor	M
Concordia University, St. Paul	M
Concordia University Wisconsin	M
Crandall University	M
Creighton University	M
Dallas Baptist University	M,D
Duke University	M,D,O
Duquesne University	M
Eastern Connecticut State University	M
Eastern Mennonite University	M
Eastern Michigan University	M,O
Eastern University	M,D,O
Emory & Henry College	M,D
Emory University	M,D
Endicott College	M
Evangel University	M
Fairleigh Dickinson University, Florham Campus	M,O
Fielding Graduate University	O
Gannon University	D
Gardner-Webb University	M,D,O
Geneva College	M
George Fox University	M,D
George Mason University	M
The George Washington University	M,O
Georgia State University	M,D
Gonzaga University	M,D
Graceland University (IA)	M,D
Grand Canyon University	M,D
Grand View University	M,O
Granite State College	M
Harding University	M
Hawai'i Pacific University	M
HEC Montreal	M

Hood College	M,D,O
Huntington University	M,D
Husson University	M
Immaculata University	M
Indiana Tech	M
Indiana University Bloomington	M,D,O
Indiana University–Purdue University Indianapolis	M,O
Indiana Wesleyan University	M,D,O
Instituto Tecnologico de Santo Domingo	M,O
Jacksonville University	M
James Madison University	D
Johnson & Wales University	M
Judson University	M
Juniata College	M
Keiser University	M
LaGrange College	M
Lenoir-Rhyne University	M
Lewis University	M
Lincoln Christian University	M
Lipscomb University	M,O
Lourdes University	M
Loyola University New Orleans	M
Malone University	M
Manhattan College	M
Mansfield University of Pennsylvania	M
Maranatha Baptist University	M
Marian University (WI)	M
Marlboro College	M
Medaille College	M
Mercer University	M,D
Mercy College	M
Mercyhurst University	M,O
Messiah College	M,O
Mid-America Christian University	M
Midway University	M
Midwest University	M,D
Misericordia University	M
Mount St. Joseph University	M
National University	M
Neumann University	M
New Jersey City University	M
Newman University	M
The New School	M
New York University	M,D*
Nichols College	M
Northern Kentucky University	M
Northwestern University	M,D
Northwest University	M
Norwich University	M
Nyack College	M
Oakland City University	M,D
Oakland University	M,D,O
Ohio Christian University	M
Oklahoma Christian University	M
Olivet Nazarene University	M
Omega Graduate School	M,D
Our Lady of the Lake University	M,D
Palm Beach Atlantic University	M
Peirce College	M
Penn State University Park	M,D*
Peru State College	M
Pfeiffer University	M
Point Loma Nazarene University	M
Point Park University	M
Purdue University Fort Wayne	M,O
Purdue University Global	M
Queens University of Charlotte	M
Quinnipiac University	M
Regent University	M,D,O
Regis University	M,O
Rider University	M
Robert Morris University	M,D
Rochester Institute of Technology	O
Roosevelt University	M
Rutgers University–Newark	D
Sage Graduate School	M
St. Ambrose University	M
St. Catherine University	M
St. Edward's University	M
St. Joseph's College, Long Island Campus	M
St. Joseph's College, New York	M
Saint Mary-of-the-Woods College	M
Saint Mary's College of California	M
Saint Mary's University of Minnesota	M
Salve Regina University	M,O
San Diego Christian College	M
Saybrook University	M,D
Seattle University	M,O
Shippensburg University of Pennsylvania	M
Siena Heights University	M
Simpson University	M
SIT Graduate Institute	M
Southeastern University (FL)	M,D
Southern Arkansas University–Magnolia	M
Southern New Hampshire University	M,D,O
South University	M
South University (SC)	M
South University (GA)	M
Southwest University	M
Springfield College	M
Stockton University	D
Syracuse University	O
Thomas Edison State University	M
Trevecca Nazarene University	M,D
Trine University	M
Trinity Washington University	M
Trinity Western University	M,O
Tufts University	M
Union Institute & University	M
United States International University–Africa	M
Université Laval	M
University of Alberta	D
The University of Arizona	M,D
University of Central Arkansas	D

University of Charleston	D
University of Cincinnati	M
University of Colorado Boulder	
University of Dallas	M,D
University of Denver	M,O
University of Guelph	M
University of Hawaii at Manoa	M,D
The University of Kansas	M,D,O
University of La Verne	M,D,O
University of Maryland Eastern Shore	D
University of Massachusetts Amherst	M,D
University of Michigan–Flint	M,O
University of Missouri	M,D,O
University of Nebraska at Omaha	M
University of New Haven	M,O
University of Northwestern–St. Paul	
University of Oklahoma	M,O*
University of Pennsylvania	M,O*
University of Phoenix–Bay Area Campus	M,D
University of Phoenix–Online Campus	D,O
University of Portland	M
University of Regina	M,O
University of Saint Francis (IN)	M
University of St. Thomas (MN)	D
University of San Francisco	M
University of South Dakota	M
University of Southern California	M
The University of Texas at San Antonio	D
The University of Texas at Tyler	M
University of the Incarnate Word	M,D
University of West Los Angeles	M
University of Wisconsin–Platteville	M
Upper Iowa University	M
Vanderbilt University	M*
Viterbo University	M,O
Walden University	M,D,O
Waldorf University	M
Warner Pacific University	M
Washington University in St. Louis	M
Wayland Baptist University	M,D
Waynesburg University	M,D
Wayne State College	M
Wayne State University	M,D
Western New England University	M
West Liberty University	M
Wheeling Jesuit University	M
Wilfrid Laurier University	M,D
Wilkes University	M
William Penn University	M
Williamson College	M
Wilmington University	M,D
Winona State University	M,D,O
Woodbury University	M
Worcester Polytechnic Institute	M,D,O
Worcester State University	M
Yale University	D

OSTEOPATHIC MEDICINE

Alabama College of Osteopathic Medicine	D
Arkansas Colleges of Health Education	D
A.T. Still University	M,D
Burrell College of Osteopathic Medicine	D
Campbell University	D
Des Moines University	D
Edward Via College of Osteopathic Medicine–Carolinas Campus	D
Edward Via College of Osteopathic Medicine–Virginia Campus	D
Georgia Campus–Philadelphia College of Osteopathic Medicine	D*
Kansas City University of Medicine and Biosciences	D
Lake Erie College of Osteopathic Medicine	M,D,O
Liberty University	D
Lincoln Memorial University	D
Marian University (IN)	M,D
Michigan State University	D
Midwestern University, Downers Grove Campus	D
Midwestern University, Glendale Campus	D
New York Institute of Technology	O
Nova Southeastern University	M,D,O
Ohio University	D
Oklahoma State University Center for Health Sciences	D
Pacific Northwest University of Health Sciences	D
Philadelphia College of Osteopathic Medicine	D*
Rocky Vista University	D
Rowan University	D
Touro University California	M,D
University of New England	D
University of North Texas Health Science Center at Fort Worth	D
University of Pikeville	D
University of the Incarnate Word	M,D
Western University of Health Sciences	D
West Virginia School of Osteopathic Medicine	D
William Carey University	D

PACIFIC AREA/PACIFIC RIM STUDIES

Naval Postgraduate School	M,D
University of Bridgeport	M
The University of British Columbia	M
University of Guam	M
University of Hawaii at Manoa	M,O
University of San Francisco	M
University of Victoria	M

PALEONTOLOGY

Cornell University	M,D
Duke University	D
East Tennessee State University	M,O
South Dakota School of Mines and Technology	M,D
University of Chicago	D
The University of Manchester	M,D
Yale University	M,D

PAPER AND PULP ENGINEERING

Georgia Institute of Technology	M,D
State University of New York College of Environmental Science and Forestry	M,D,O
The University of Manchester	M,D
University of Minnesota, Twin Cities Campus	
Western Michigan University	M,D

PARASITOLOGY

Illinois State University	M,D
Louisiana State University Health Sciences Center	D
McGill University	M,D,O
Oregon State University	M,D
Tulane University	M,D,O
University of Notre Dame	M,D
University of Prince Edward Island	M,D

PASTORAL MINISTRY AND COUNSELING

Abilene Christian University	M,D
Acadia University	M,D
Ambrose University	M,O
American Baptist Seminary of the West	M
Amridge University	M,D
Anabaptist Mennonite Biblical Seminary	M,O
Anderson University (SC)	M,D
Andrews University	M,D,O
Appalachian Bible College	M
Aquinas Institute of Theology	M,D,O
Asbury Theological Seminary	M,D,O
Ashland Theological Seminary	M,D
Assemblies of God Theological Seminary	M,D
Atlantic School of Theology	M,O
Atlantic University	O
Austin Presbyterian Theological Seminary	M,D
Ave Maria University	M,D
Azusa Pacific University	M
Bakke Graduate University	M,D
Baptist Bible College	M
The Baptist College of Florida	M
Barry University	M,D
Bethany Global University	M
Bethany Theological Seminary	M,O
Bethel Seminary	M,D,O
Bethel University (IN)	M
Biola University	M,D,O
Bob Jones University	M,D,O
Boston College	M,D,O
Boston University	M,D
Briercrest Seminary	M
Brite Divinity School	M,D,O
Bryan College	M
Cairn University	M
California Baptist University	M
Calvary University	M
Calvin Theological Seminary	M,D
Campbell University	M,D
Canadian Southern Baptist Seminary	M
Capital University	M
Cardinal Stritch University	M
Carolina Christian College	M
Catholic Theological Union	M,D,O
The Catholic University of America	M,D,O
Cedarville University	M,D
Chaminade University of Honolulu	M
Charlotte Christian College and Theological Seminary	M,D
Chicago Theological Seminary	M,D
Christian Theological Seminary	M,D
Christ the King Seminary	M
Cincinnati Christian University	M
City Vision University	M
Claremont Lincoln University	M
Claremont School of Theology	M,D
Clarks Summit University	M,D
College of Saint Elizabeth	M,O
Columbia International University	M,D,O
Concordia University, Nebraska	M,D,O
Corban University	M,D,O
Covenant Theological Seminary	M,D,O
Criswell University	M
Dallas Baptist University	M,D
Dallas Theological Seminary	M,D,O
Denver Seminary	M,D,O
Earlham School of Religion	M
Eastern Mennonite University	M
Ecumenical Theological Seminary	D
Emory University	M,D
Epic Bible College	M,D
Evangelical Seminary	M
Fairfield University	M,O
Faith Baptist Bible College and Theological Seminary	M
Faulkner University	M
Fordham University	M,D,O
Freed-Hardeman University	M
Fresno Pacific University	M
Fuller Theological Seminary	M,D,O
Gannon University	M,D,O
Gardner-Webb University	M,D
Garrett-Evangelical Theological Seminary	M,D
Gateway Seminary	M,D,O
The General Theological Seminary	M,D,O
Geneva College	M

George Fox University	M,D,O
Global University	M,D
Gordon-Conwell Theological Seminary	M,D
Grace Theological Seminary	M,D,O
Grand Canyon University	D
Grand Rapids Theological Seminary of Cornerstone University	M
Greenville University	M
Hampton University	M,D,O
Harding School of Theology	M,D
Harding University	M
Hardin-Simmons University	M,D
Hartford Seminary	M,D,O
Heritage Christian University	M
Holmes Institute	M
Holy Names University	M
Houston Baptist University	M
Houston Graduate School of Theology	M,D
Howard Payne University	M
Huntington University	M,D
Huntsville Bible College	M
Iliff School of Theology	M,D
Indiana Wesleyan University	M
Inter American University of Puerto Rico, Metropolitan Campus	D
Interdenominational Theological Center	M,D
International Baptist College and Seminary	M,D
Johnson University	M
Johnson University Florida	M
Judson University	M
The King's University	M,D,O
Kingswood University	M
Knox Theological Seminary	D
Lancaster Bible College	M,D,O
La Sierra University	M
Lee University	M
Liberty University	M,D,O
Lincoln Christian Seminary	M,D
Lincoln Christian University	M
Lipscomb University	M,D
Loras College	M
Loyola Marymount University	M
Loyola University Chicago	M,O
Lutheran School of Theology at Chicago	M,D
Lutheran Theological Seminary Saskatoon	M,D
Luther Rice College & Seminary	M,D
Luther Seminary	M,D
Madonna University	M
Maple Springs Baptist Bible College and Seminary	M,D,O
Maranatha Baptist University	M
Martin University	M
Marymount University	M
The Master's University	M,D
McCormick Theological Seminary	M,D,O
McMaster University	M,D,O
Meadville Lombard Theological School	M,D
Mercer University	M,D
Mesivta Torah Vodaath Rabbinical Seminary	O
Mid-America Baptist Theological Seminary	M,D
Mid-America Christian University	M
Midwestern Baptist Theological Seminary	M,D,O
Midwest University	M,D
Milligan College	M,D,O
Missio Seminary	M,O
Missouri Baptist University	M,O
Moody Bible Institute	M,O
Mount Marty College	M
Mount St. Joseph University	M
Nashotah House Theological Seminary	M,D,O
Nebraska Christian College of Hope International University	M
Neumann University	M,D,O
New Brunswick Theological Seminary	M,D
New Orleans Baptist Theological Seminary	M,D
Northern Seminary	M,D
North Greenville University	M,D
North Park Theological Seminary	M,O
Northwest Nazarene University	M
Northwest University	M
Nyack College	M,D
Oakland City University	M,D
Oakwood University	M
Oblate School of Theology	M,D,O
Ohio Christian University	M
Olivet Nazarene University	M
Oral Roberts University	M,D
Ottawa University	M
Pacific Rim Christian University	M
Pentecostal Theological Seminary	M,D
Pepperdine University	M
Phillips Theological Seminary	D
Phoenix Seminary	M,D,O
Piedmont International University	M,D
Pittsburgh Theological Seminary	M,D
Point Loma Nazarene University	M
Point University	M
Providence University College & Theological Seminary	M,D,O
Randall University	M
Reformed Theological Seminary–Charlotte Campus	M
Reformed Theological Seminary–Jackson Campus	M,D,O
Reformed Theological Seminary–Orlando Campus	M,D,O
Regent University	M,D,O
Regis College (Canada)	M,D,O
Richmont Graduate University	M,O

Sacred Heart Major Seminary	M
St. Ambrose University	M
St. Augustine's Seminary of Toronto	M,O
St. Bernard's School of Theology and Ministry	M,O
St. Catherine University	M,O
St. John's Seminary (CA)	M
Saint John's University (MN)	M
Saint Joseph's College of Maine	M
St. Joseph's Seminary	M
Saint Paul University	M,D,O
Saints Cyril and Methodius Seminary	M
St. Stephen's College	M,D
St. Thomas University	M,D,O
Saint Vincent Seminary	M
Santa Clara University	M
Seattle University	M
Selma University	M
Seton Hall University	M,O
Shasta Bible College	M
Shepherds Theological Seminary	M
Shiloh University	M,D
Simpson University	M
Sioux Falls Seminary	M
Southeastern University (FL)	M
The Southern Baptist Theological Seminary	M,D
Southern Evangelical Seminary	M,D,O
Southern Methodist University	M,D
Southern Wesleyan University	M
South University (GA)	D
Southwestern Assemblies of God University	M
Southwestern Baptist Theological Seminary	M,D,O
Southwestern Christian University	M
Spring Arbor University	M
SUM Bible College & Theological Seminary	M
Theological University of the Caribbean	M,D
Trevecca Nazarene University	M
Trinity Bible College and Graduate School	M
Trinity College (Canada)	M,D,O
Trinity International University	M,D,O
Trinity School for Ministry	M,D,O
Trinity Western University	M,D
Tyndale University College & Seminary	M,O
Union University	M,D
United Lutheran Seminary	M,D
United Lutheran Seminary	M,D,O
United Theological Seminary	M,D
United Theological Seminary of the Twin Cities	M,D,O
University of Chicago	M
University of Dallas	M
University of Dayton	M,D
University of Fort Lauderdale	M
University of Northwestern–St. Paul	M
University of Saint Mary of the Lake–Mundelein Seminary	M,D
University of St. Michael's College	M,D,O
University of St. Thomas (MN)	M,D
University of St. Thomas (TX)	M
University of South Africa	M,D
University of the Incarnate Word	M
Ursuline College	M
Virginia Beach Theological Seminary	M
Virginia University of Lynchburg	M,D
Viterbo University	M,O
Walla Walla University	M
Walsh University	M
Wayland Baptist University	M
Welch College	M
Wesley Biblical Seminary	M
Western Seminary	M,D,O
Western Seminary–Sacramento Campus	M,O
Western Seminary–San Jose Campus	M,O
Western Theological Seminary	M,D,O
Westminster Theological Seminary	M,D,O
Whitworth University	M
Wilfrid Laurier University	M,D,O
World Mission University	M,D
Xavier University	M*

PATHOBIOLOGY

Brown University	M,D
Columbia University	M,D
Drexel University	M,D*
Johns Hopkins University	D*
Kansas State University	M,D
Medical University of South Carolina	D
Michigan State University	M,D
Penn State University Park	M,D*
Purdue University	M,D
The University of Alabama at Birmingham	D
University of Cincinnati	D
University of Connecticut	M,D
University of Illinois at Urbana–Champaign	M,D
University of Missouri	M,D
University of Toronto	M,D
University of Washington	D
University of Wyoming	M

PATHOLOGY

Albert Einstein College of Medicine	D
Boston University	M,D

Case Western Reserve University	M,D
Colorado State University	M,D
Columbia University	M,D
Dalhousie University	M,D
Duke University	M,D
Harvard University	D*
Indiana University–Purdue University Indianapolis	M,D
Iowa State University of Science and Technology	M,D
Johns Hopkins University	D*
Loma Linda University	D
McGill University	M,D
Medical University of South Carolina	M,D
Michigan State University	M,D
New York Medical College	M,D
North Carolina State University	M,D
North Dakota State University	M,D
Purdue University	M,D
Queen's University at Kingston	M,D
Quinnipiac University	M
Rosalind Franklin University of Medicine and Science	M
Rutgers University–Newark	D
Saint Louis University	D*
Stony Brook University, State University of New York	M,D
Tufts University	M,D
Université de Montréal	M,D
Université Laval	O
University at Buffalo, the State University of New York	M,D
University of Alberta	M,D
The University of British Columbia	M,D
University of Calgary	M,D
University of California, Davis	M,D
University of California, Irvine	D
University of California, Los Angeles	M,D
University of Cincinnati	D
University of Georgia	M,D
University of Guelph	M,D,O
The University of Iowa	M
The University of Kansas	M,D
University of Manitoba	M
University of Maryland, Baltimore	M
University of Michigan	D
University of Mississippi Medical Center	D
University of Missouri	M,D
University of Nebraska Medical Center	M,D
University of New Mexico	M,D
The University of North Carolina at Chapel Hill	D
University of Oklahoma Health Sciences Center	D
University of Pittsburgh	D*
University of Prince Edward Island	M,D
University of Rochester	D*
University of Saskatchewan	M,D
University of Southern California	M
University of South Florida	M,D
The University of Tennessee Health Science Center	M,D
The University of Texas Medical Branch	D
The University of Toledo	M,O
University of Utah	M,D
University of Vermont	M
University of Virginia	D
University of Washington	M
The University of Western Ontario	M,D
University of Wisconsin–Madison	D
Vanderbilt University	D*
Wayne State University	M,D,O
West Virginia University	M,D
Yale University	M,D

PEDIATRIC NURSING

Augusta University	D
Azusa Pacific University	M,D
Boston College	M,D
Caribbean University	M,D
Case Western Reserve University	M
Columbia University	M,O
Creighton University	M,D,O
Drexel University	M*
Duke University	M,D,O
East Tennessee State University	M,D,O
Emory University	M
Florida International University	M,D
Georgia State University	M,D,O
Gwynedd Mercy University	M,D
Houston Baptist University	M
Indiana University–Purdue University Indianapolis	M
Johns Hopkins University	D*
Kent State University	M,D
King University	M,D,O
Lehman College of the City University of New York	M
Loma Linda University	M
Marquette University	M,D,O
Maryville University of Saint Louis	M,D
MGH Institute of Health Professions	M,D,O
Molloy College	M,D,O
New York University	M,D,O*
Northeastern University	M,D
Old Dominion University	M,D
Oregon Health & Science University	M
Point Loma Nazarene University	M
Purdue University	M,D,O
Queen's University at Kingston	M,D,O
Rush University	D,O

St. Catherine University	M,D
San Francisco State University	M,O
Seton Hall University	M,D
Spalding University	M,D,O
Stony Brook University, State University of New York	M,D,O
Texas Christian University	M,D,O
Texas Tech University Health Sciences Center	M,D,O
Texas Woman's University	M,D
The University of Alabama at Birmingham	M,D
University of Cincinnati	M,D
University of Colorado Denver	M,D
University of Delaware	M,O
University of Illinois at Chicago	M,O
University of Maryland, Baltimore	M,D,O
University of Michigan	M,D,O
University of Minnesota, Twin Cities Campus	M,D
University of Missouri	M,D,O
University of Missouri–Kansas City	M,D
University of Missouri–St. Louis	D,O
The University of North Carolina at Chapel Hill	M,D,O
University of Pennsylvania	M*
University of Puerto Rico–Medical Sciences Campus	M
University of Rochester	M,D*
University of San Diego	M,D
University of South Carolina	M
University of South Florida	M
The University of Tennessee Health Science Center	D,O
The University of Texas at Austin	M,D
The University of Texas Health Science Center at San Antonio	M,D,O
The University of Toledo	M,O
University of Wisconsin–Madison	D
Villanova University	M,D,O
Virginia Commonwealth University	M,D,O
Wayne State University	M,D
Wright State University	M

PERFUSION

Long Island University–LIU Post	M,O
Milwaukee School of Engineering	M
Quinnipiac University	M
Rush University	M
The University of Arizona	M,D
University of Nebraska Medical Center	M

PETROLEUM ENGINEERING

Colorado School of Mines	M,D
Louisiana State University and Agricultural & Mechanical College	M,D
Missouri University of Science and Technology	M,D
Montana Tech of The University of Montana	M
New Mexico Institute of Mining and Technology	M,D
Texas A&M University	M,D
Texas A&M University–Kingsville	M
University of Alaska Fairbanks	M
University of Alberta	M,D
University of Calgary	M,D
University of Houston	M,D
The University of Kansas	M,D,O
University of Louisiana at Lafayette	M
University of Oklahoma	M,D,O*
University of Pittsburgh	M,D*
University of Regina	M,D
University of Southern California	M,D,O
The University of Texas at Austin	M,D
The University of Tulsa	M,D
University of Utah	M,D
University of Wyoming	M,D
West Virginia University	M,D

PHARMACEUTICAL ADMINISTRATION

Belmont University	D
Columbia University	M
Duquesne University	M
Fairleigh Dickinson University, Metropolitan Campus	M,O
Florida Agricultural and Mechanical University	M,D
Idaho State University	M,D
New Jersey Institute of Technology	M,D
Northeast Ohio Medical University	M,D,O
The Ohio State University	M,D
Purdue University	M,D,O
Rutgers University–Newark	M
St. John's University (NY)	M
San Diego State University	M
Southwestern Oklahoma State University	M*
Temple University	M*
University of Florida	M,D
University of Georgia	D
University of Houston	M,D
University of Illinois at Chicago	M,D
University of Maryland, Baltimore	M,D
University of Michigan	D
University of Minnesota, Twin Cities Campus	M,D
University of Mississippi	M,D
The University of North Carolina at Chapel Hill	M,D
University of Pittsburgh	M*
University of Southern California	M
University of the Sciences	M
The University of Toledo	M
University of Utah	M,D
University of Wisconsin–Madison	M,D
Virginia Commonwealth University	M,D

PHARMACEUTICAL ENGINEERING

New Jersey Institute of Technology	M,D
University of Michigan	M,D

PHARMACEUTICAL SCIENCES

Albany College of Pharmacy and Health Sciences	M,D
Auburn University	M,D
Boston University	D
Butler University	M,D
Campbell University	M,D
Chapman University	M,D*
Creighton University	M,D
Drexel University	M*
Duquesne University	M,D
East Tennessee State University	D
Florida Agricultural and Mechanical University	M,D
Idaho State University	M,D
Irell & Manella Graduate School of Biological Sciences	D
Johns Hopkins University	M*
Long Island University–Hudson	M,O
Long Island University–LIU Brooklyn	M,D
MCPHS University	M,D
Memorial University of Newfoundland	M,D
Mercer University	D
Northeastern University	M,D,O
Northeast Ohio Medical University	M,D
Oregon State University	M,D
Purdue University	M,D,O
Rowan University	M
Rush University	M,D
Rutgers University–New Brunswick	M,D
St. John's University (NY)	M,D
South Dakota State University	M,D
Stevens Institute of Technology	M,O
Temple University	M,D*
Texas Southern University	M,D
Texas Tech University Health Sciences Center	M,D
Université de Montréal	M,D,O
Université Laval	M,D,O
University of Alberta	M,D
The University of Arizona	M,D
The University of British Columbia	D
University of California, Irvine	D
University of California, San Francisco	D
University of Cincinnati	M,D
University of Colorado Denver	D
University of Connecticut	M,D
University of Florida	M,D
University of Georgia	M,D
University of Hawaii at Hilo	D
University of Houston	M,D
University of Illinois at Chicago	M,D
The University of Iowa	M,D
University of Kentucky	M,D
The University of Manchester	M,D
University of Manitoba	M,D
University of Maryland, Baltimore	D
University of Maryland Eastern Shore	M,D
University of Michigan	D
University of Minnesota, Twin Cities Campus	M,D
University of Mississippi	M,D
University of Montana	M,D
University of Nebraska Medical Center	M,D
University of New Mexico	M,D
The University of North Carolina at Chapel Hill	M,D
University of North Texas Health Science Center at Fort Worth	M,D
University of Oklahoma Health Sciences Center	M,D
University of Pittsburgh	M,D*
University of Puerto Rico–Medical Sciences Campus	M,D
University of Rhode Island	M,D
University of South Carolina	M,D
University of Southern California	M,D,O
University of South Florida	M,D
The University of Tennessee Health Science Center	M,D
The University of Texas at Austin	M,D
University of the Pacific	M,D
University of the Sciences	M,D
The University of Toledo	M
University of Toronto	M,D
University of Utah	M,D
University of Washington	M,D
University of Wisconsin–Madison	M,D
Virginia Commonwealth University	M,D
Wayne State University	M,D
West Virginia University	D
York College of the City University of New York	M

PHARMACOLOGY

Albany College of Pharmacy and Health Sciences	M,D
Albany Medical College	M,D
Alliant International University–San Francisco	M
American University of Beirut	M,D
Argosy University, Hawai`i	M,O
Augusta University	D
Baylor College of Medicine	D
Boston University	M,D
Case Western Reserve University	D
The Chicago School of Professional Psychology: Online	M
Columbia University	M,D
Creighton University	M,D
Dalhousie University	M,D
Drexel University	M,D*
Duke University	D

Duquesne University	M,D
East Carolina University	M,D
East Tennessee State University	D
Emory University	D
Fairleigh Dickinson University, Florham Campus	M,O
Florida Agricultural and Mechanical University	M,D
Georgetown University	M,D
Howard University	M,D
Husson University	M,D
Idaho State University	M,D
Indiana University–Purdue University Indianapolis	M,D
Johns Hopkins University	D*
Kent State University	M,D
Loma Linda University	D
London Metropolitan University	M,D
Long Island University–LIU Brooklyn	M,D
Louisiana State University Health Sciences Center	D
Louisiana State University Health Sciences Center at Shreveport	M,D
McGill University	M,D
McMaster University	M,D
MCPHS University	M,D
Medical College of Wisconsin	D
Meharry Medical College	D
Michigan State University	M,D
Montclair State University	M
New Jersey Institute of Technology	M,D
New York Medical College	M,D
North Carolina State University	M,D
Northeastern University	M,D,O
The Ohio State University	M,D
Oregon Health & Science University	D
Purdue University	M,D
Rush University	M,D
Rutgers University–Newark	D
Saint Louis University	D*
Southern Illinois University Carbondale	M,D
State University of New York Upstate Medical University	D
Stony Brook University, State University of New York	M,D
Thomas Jefferson University	M
Tulane University	M
Universidad Central del Caribe	M,D
Université de Montréal	M,D
Université de Sherbrooke	M,D
University at Buffalo, the State University of New York	M,D
The University of Alabama at Birmingham	D
University of Alberta	M,D
The University of Arizona	M,D
University of Arkansas for Medical Sciences	M,D,O
The University of British Columbia	M,D
University of California, Davis	M,D
University of California, Los Angeles	M,D
University of California, San Francisco	D
University of Cincinnati	D
University of Colorado Denver	D
University of Connecticut	M,D
University of Florida	M,D
University of Georgia	M,D
University of Guelph	M,D
University of Hawaii at Hilo	M
University of Houston	M,D
University of Illinois at Chicago	D
The University of Iowa	M,D
The University of Kansas	M,D
University of Kentucky	D
University of Louisville	M,D
The University of Manchester	M,D
University of Manitoba	M,D
University of Maryland, Baltimore	M
University of Miami	D
University of Michigan	M,D
University of Minnesota, Duluth	M,D
University of Minnesota, Twin Cities Campus	M,D
University of Mississippi	M,D
University of Mississippi Medical Center	D
University of Missouri	M,D
University of Nebraska Medical Center	D
The University of North Carolina at Chapel Hill	D
University of North Texas Health Science Center at Fort Worth	M,D
University of Pennsylvania	D*
University of Prince Edward Island	D
University of Puerto Rico–Medical Sciences Campus	M,D
University of Rhode Island	M,D
University of Rochester	M,D*
University of Saskatchewan	M,D
University of South Dakota	M,D
The University of Tennessee Health Science Center	D
The University of Texas at Austin	M,D
The University of Texas Health Science Center at Houston	M,D
The University of Texas Health Science Center at San Antonio	D
The University of Texas Medical Branch	M,D
University of the Sciences	M,D
University of Toledo	M,D
University of Toronto	M,D
University of Utah	D
University of Vermont	M,D
University of Virginia	D
University of Washington	D
University of Wisconsin–Madison	D
Vanderbilt University	D*

Virginia Commonwealth University	M,D,O
Wake Forest University	D
Wayne State University	M,D,O
Weill Cornell Medicine	M,D
Wright State University	M
Yale University	D

PHARMACY

Albany College of Pharmacy and Health Sciences	M,D
Appalachian College of Pharmacy	D
Auburn University	D
Belmont University	D
Binghamton University, State University of New York	D
Butler University	M,D
California Health Sciences University	D
California Northstate University	D
Campbell University	M,D
Cedarville University	M,D
Chapman University	M,D*
Chicago State University	D
Concordia University Wisconsin	M,D
Creighton University	D
Drake University	M,D
Duquesne University	D
D'Youville College	D
East Tennessee State University	D
Fairleigh Dickinson University, Florham Campus	D
Ferris State University	D
Florida Agricultural and Mechanical University	D
Georgia Campus–Philadelphia College of Osteopathic Medicine	D*
Harding University	D
High Point University	D
Howard University	D
Husson University	M,D
Idaho State University	M,D
Keck Graduate Institute	D
Lake Erie College of Osteopathic Medicine	M,D,O
Lebanese American University	D
Lipscomb University	M,D
Loma Linda University	D
Long Island University–Hudson	M,O
Long Island University–LIU Brooklyn	M,D
Manchester University	D
Marshall B. Ketchum University	M,D
Marshall University	D
MCPHS University	D
Medical College of Wisconsin	D
Medical University of South Carolina	D
Mercer University	D
Midwestern University, Downers Grove Campus	D
Midwestern University, Glendale Campus	D
North Dakota State University	M,D
Northeastern University	M,D,O
Northeast Ohio Medical University	D
Notre Dame of Maryland University	D
Nova Southeastern University	D
Ohio Northern University	D
The Ohio State University	M,D
Oregon State University	D
Pacific University	D
Palm Beach Atlantic University	D
Presbyterian College	D
Purdue University	D
Regis University	M,D,O
Roosevelt University	D
Rosalind Franklin University of Medicine and Science	D
Roseman University of Health Sciences	D
Rutgers University–New Brunswick	M,D
St. John Fisher College	D
St. John's University (NY)	M,D
St. Louis College of Pharmacy	D
Samford University	D
Shenandoah University	D
South College	D
South Dakota State University	D
Southern Illinois University Edwardsville	D
South University (SC)	D
South University (GA)	D
Southwestern Oklahoma State University	D
Sullivan University	D
Temple University	M,D*
Texas A&M University	D
Texas Southern University	D
Texas Tech University Health Sciences Center	D
Thomas Jefferson University	D
Touro University California	M,D
Union University	D
Universidad de Ciencias Medicas	M,D,O
University at Buffalo, the State University of New York	D
University of Alberta	M,D
The University of Arizona	D
University of Arkansas for Medical Sciences	D
The University of British Columbia	M,D
University of California, San Diego	D
University of California, San Francisco	D
University of Charleston	D
University of Cincinnati	D
University of Colorado Denver	D
University of Connecticut	D
The University of Findlay	M,D
University of Florida	M,D
University of Georgia	M,D,O

University of Hawaii at Hilo	D
University of Houston	M,D
University of Illinois at Chicago	M,D
The University of Iowa	M,D
The University of Kansas	M,D
University of Kentucky	D
University of Louisiana at Monroe	D
The University of Manchester	M,D
University of Maryland, Baltimore	M,D
University of Maryland Eastern Shore	M,D
University of Michigan	D
University of Minnesota, Duluth	M,D
University of Minnesota, Twin Cities Campus	D
University of Mississippi	M,D
University of Missouri–Kansas City	D
University of Montana	M,D
University of Nebraska Medical Center	D
University of New England	D
University of New Mexico	D
The University of North Carolina at Chapel Hill	M,D
University of Oklahoma Health Sciences Center	D
University of Pittsburgh	D*
University of Puerto Rico–Medical Sciences Campus	M,D
University of Rhode Island	D
University of Saint Joseph	M,D
University of Saskatchewan	M,D
University of South Carolina	D
University of Southern California	D
University of South Florida	M,D,O
The University of Tennessee Health Science Center	M,D
The University of Texas at Austin	D
The University of Texas at Tyler	D
University of the Incarnate Word	D
University of the Pacific	D
University of the Sciences	D
The University of Toledo	M,D
University of Utah	D
University of Washington	M,D
University of Wisconsin–Madison	D
University of Wyoming	M,D
Virginia Commonwealth University	D
Washington State University	M,D
Wayne State University	D
West Coast University	M,D
Western New England University	D
West Virginia University	D
Wilkes University	D
William Carey University	D
Wingate University	D
Xavier University of Louisiana	D

PHILANTHROPIC STUDIES

Central Michigan University	M,O
Indiana University–Purdue University Indianapolis	M,D
Saint Mary's University of Minnesota	M
University of Denver	M,O
University of Memphis	M,O

PHILOSOPHY

Acadia University	M
American University	M,O
The American University in Cairo	M,O
American University of Beirut	M,D
Arizona State University at the Tempe campus	M,D,O
Baylor University	M,D
Binghamton University, State University of New York	M,D
Boston College	M,D
Boston University	M,D
Bowling Green State University	M
Brandeis University	M
Brock University	M
Brown University	D
California State University, Long Beach	M
California State University, Los Angeles	M
Carleton University	M
Carnegie Mellon University	M,D
The Catholic University of America	M,D,O
Central European University	M,D
Claremont Graduate University	M,O
Cleveland State University	M
Collège Dominicain de Philosophie et de Théologie	M,D
Colorado State University	M
Columbia University	M,D
Concordia University (Canada)	M
Cornell University	D
Dalhousie University	M
Dallas Theological Seminary	M,D,O
Delta State University	M
Dominican School of Philosophy and Theology	M,O
Dominican University of California	M
Duke University	D
Duquesne University	M,D
Eastern Michigan University	M
Emory University	D,O
Fordham University	M,D
Franciscan University of Steubenville	M
George Mason University	M
Georgetown University	M
The George Washington University	M
Georgia State University	M
Gonzaga University	M
The Graduate Center, City University of New York	M,D

Harrison Middleton University	M,D
Harvard University	M,D*
Houston Baptist University	M
Howard University	M
Indiana University Bloomington	M,D
Indiana University–Purdue University Indianapolis	M,D
Institute for Christian Studies	M
Institute for Doctoral Studies in the Visual Arts	D
Johns Hopkins University	M,D*
Kent State University	M
Lake Forest College	M
Lincoln Christian University	M
Louisiana State University and Agricultural & Mechanical College	M
Loyola Marymount University	M
Loyola University Chicago	M,D
Marquette University	M,D
Massachusetts Institute of Technology	D
McGill University	M,D
McMaster University	M,D
Memorial University of Newfoundland	M,D
Miami University	M
Michigan State University	M,D
Midwestern State University	M,D
Mount St. Mary's University (MD)	M
The New School	M,D
New York University	M,D*
Northern Illinois University	M
Northwestern University	D
The Ohio State University	M,D
Ohio University	M,D
Oklahoma State University	M
Old Dominion University	M,O
Open University	M
Penn State University Park	M,D*
Princeton University	D
Purdue University	M,D
Queen's University at Kingston	M,D
Regis College (Canada)	M,D,O
Rice University	M,D
Roosevelt University	M
Rutgers University–New Brunswick	D
Saint Charles Borromeo Seminary, Overbrook	M
Saint Louis University	M,D*
Saint Mary's University (Canada)	M
San Diego State University	M
San Francisco State University	M
San Jose State University	M
Simon Fraser University	M,D
Southeastern Baptist Theological Seminary	M,D
The Southern Baptist Theological Seminary	M,D
Southern Evangelical Seminary	M,D,O
Southern Illinois University Carbondale	M,D
Stanford University	M,D
Stony Brook University, State University of New York	M,D,O
Syracuse University	M,D
Teachers College, Columbia University	M,D,O
Temple University	M,D*
Texas A&M University	M,D
Texas State University	M
Texas Tech University	M
Trinity Western University	M
Tufts University	M
Tulane University	M,D
Universidad Autonoma de Guadalajara	M,D
Université de Montréal	M,D
Université de Sherbrooke	M,D,O
Université du Québec à Montréal	M,D
Université du Québec à Trois-Rivières	M,D
Université Laval	M,D
University at Albany, State University of New York	M,D
University at Buffalo, the State University of New York	M,D
University of Alberta	M,D
The University of Arizona	M,D
University of Arkansas	M,D
The University of British Columbia	M,D
University of Calgary	M,D
University of California, Berkeley	D
University of California, Davis	M,D
University of California, Irvine	M,D
University of California, Los Angeles	M,D
University of California, Riverside	M,D
University of California, San Diego	D
University of California, Santa Barbara	D
University of California, Santa Cruz	M,D
University of Chicago	M,D
University of Cincinnati	M,D
University of Colorado Boulder	M,D
University of Connecticut	M,D
University of Florida	M,D
University of Georgia	M,D
University of Guelph	M,D
University of Hawaii at Manoa	M,D
University of Houston	M
University of Idaho	M
University of Illinois at Chicago	M,D

University of Illinois at Urbana–Champaign	M,D
The University of Iowa	D
The University of Kansas	M,D
University of Kentucky	M,D
University of Lethbridge	M,D
University of Louisville	M,D
The University of Manchester	M,D
University of Manitoba	M
University of Maryland, College Park	M,D
University of Massachusetts Amherst	M,D
University of Memphis	M,D
University of Miami	M,D
University of Michigan	M,D
University of Minnesota, Twin Cities Campus	M,D
University of Mississippi	M,D
University of Missouri	M,D
University of Missouri–St. Louis	M
University of Montana	M
University of Nebraska–Lincoln	M,D
University of Nevada, Reno	M
University of New Mexico	M,D
The University of North Carolina at Chapel Hill	M,D
The University of North Carolina at Charlotte	M,O
University of North Florida	M,O
University of North Georgia	M
University of North Texas	M,D,O
University of Notre Dame	D
University of Oklahoma	M,D*
University of Oregon	M,D
University of Ottawa	M,D
University of Pennsylvania	M,D*
University of Pittsburgh	D*
University of Puerto Rico–Río Piedras	M
University of Regina	M
University of Rochester	D*
University of St. Thomas (TX)	M,D
University of Saskatchewan	M
University of South Africa	M,D
University of South Carolina	M,D
University of Southern California	M,D
University of South Florida	M,D
The University of Tennessee	M,D
The University of Texas at Austin	D
The University of Texas at El Paso	M
The University of Texas at San Antonio	M
The University of Toledo	M
University of Toronto	M,D
University of Utah	M,D
University of Victoria	M
University of Virginia	M,D
University of Washington	M,D
University of Waterloo	M
The University of Western Ontario	M,D
University of Windsor	M
University of Wisconsin–Madison	M,D
University of Wisconsin–Milwaukee	M*
University of Wyoming	M
Vanderbilt University	M,D*
Villanova University	D
Washington University in St. Louis	D
Wayne State University	M,D
West Chester University of Pennsylvania	M,O
Western Michigan University	M
Wilfrid Laurier University	M
Yale University	D
York University	M,D

PHOTOGRAPHY

Academy of Art University	M
Ball State University	M
Bard College	M
Barry University	M
Bradley University	M
Brooklyn College of the City University of New York	M
California Institute of the Arts	M,O
California State University, Fullerton	M
California State University, Los Angeles	M
Central Washington University	M
Claremont Graduate University	M
Columbia College Chicago	M
Cornell University	M,D
Cranbrook Academy of Art	M
East Carolina University	M
Ferris State University	M
The George Washington University	M,O
Georgia State University	M,D
Governors State University	M
Howard University	M
Illinois State University	M
Indiana State University	M
Indiana University–Purdue University Indianapolis	M
Inter American University of Puerto Rico, San Germán Campus	M
Ithaca College	M
James Madison University	M
Kent State University	M
Lesley University	M
Louisiana State University and Agricultural & Mechanical College	M
Louisiana Tech University	M,D,O
Maryland Institute College of Art	M
Marywood University	M
Massachusetts College of Art and Design	M,O

Mills College	M
Minneapolis College of Art and Design	M
New Hampshire Institute of Art	M
The New School	M
New York Film Academy	M
Northern Vermont University–Johnson	M
Ohio University	M
Oklahoma City University	M
Otis College of Art and Design	M
Paris College of Art	M
Rhode Island School of Design	M
Rochester Institute of Technology	M
San Diego State University	M
Savannah College of Art and Design	M
School of Visual Arts (NY)	M
Southwest University of Visual Arts	M
Syracuse University	M
Temple University	M*
Texas Woman's University	M
The University of Alabama	M
University of Alaska Fairbanks	M
University of Colorado Boulder	M
University of Illinois at Urbana–Champaign	M
University of Memphis	M,O
University of Miami	M
University of Montana	M
University of New Mexico	M,D
University of Notre Dame	M
University of Oklahoma	M,D*
University of Rochester	M*
University of South Dakota	M
University of Southern California	M
The University of Tennessee	M
University of Utah	M
University of Victoria	M
University of Washington	M
Virginia Commonwealth University	M
Wayne State University	M,D
West Virginia University	M,D
Wichita State University	M
Yale University	M

PHOTONICS

Duke University	M
Johns Hopkins University	M,O*
Lehigh University	M,D
Oklahoma State University	M,D
Princeton University	D
Queens College of the City University of New York	M
Stevens Institute of Technology	M,D,O
The University of Alabama in Huntsville	M,D
University of Arkansas	M,D
University of California, San Diego	M,D
University of California, Santa Barbara	M,D
University of Central Florida	M,D
University of Dayton	M,D
University of New Mexico	M,D

PHYSICAL CHEMISTRY

Auburn University	M,D
Binghamton University, State University of New York	M,D
Boston College	M,D
Brandeis University	M,D
Cleveland State University	M,D
Cornell University	D
Dartmouth College	M,D
Eastern New Mexico University	M
Florida State University	M,D
The George Washington University	M,D
Georgia State University	M,D
Harvard University	D*
Howard University	M,D
Indiana University Bloomington	M,D
Iowa State University of Science and Technology	M,D
Laurentian University	M
Marquette University	M,D
Massachusetts Institute of Technology	D
McMaster University	M,D
Old Dominion University	M,D
Purdue University	M,D
Rice University	M,D
Rutgers University–Newark	M,D
Rutgers University–New Brunswick	M,D
Seton Hall University	M,D
Southern University and Agricultural and Mechanical College	M
University of Calgary	M,D
University of Cincinnati	M,D
University of Louisville	M,D
The University of Manchester	M,D
University of Maryland, College Park	M,D
University of Memphis	M,D
University of Miami	M,D
University of Michigan	M,D
University of Missouri–Kansas City	M,D
University of Montana	M,D
University of Nebraska–Lincoln	M,D
University of Notre Dame	M,D
University of Oklahoma	M,D*
University of Puerto Rico–Mayagüez	M,D
University of Rochester	D*
University of Southern California	M,D
The University of Tennessee	M,D
The University of Texas at Austin	D

M—masters degree; D—doctorate; O—other advanced degree; *—Close-Up and/or Display

The University of Toledo — M,D
Virginia Commonwealth University — M,D
Wake Forest University — M,D
Yale University — D
Youngstown State University — M

PHYSICAL EDUCATION

Adams State University — M
Adelphi University — M,O
Alabama Agricultural and Mechanical University — M
Alabama State University — M
Albany State University — M,O
Alcorn State University — M
American University of Puerto Rico — M
Arizona State University at the Tempe campus — M
Arkansas State University — M,O
Auburn University — M,D,O
Auburn University at Montgomery — M
Avila University — M,O
Ball State University — M
Baylor University — M,D
Bridgewater State University — M
Brooklyn College of the City University of New York — M
California Baptist University — M
California State University, East Bay — M
California State University, Fullerton — M
California State University, Long Beach — M
California State University, Los Angeles — M,O
California State University, Sacramento — M
California State University, Stanislaus — M
Campbell University — M
Canisius College — M
Caribbean University — M,D
Central Connecticut State University — M,O
Central Washington University — M
Chicago State University — M
The Citadel, The Military College of South Carolina — M,O
Cleveland State University — M
The College at Brockport, State University of New York — M,O
Colorado State University–Pueblo — M
Columbus State University — M
Concordia University (United States) — M,D
Concordia University Irvine — M
Delta State University — M
DePaul University — M,D
East Carolina University — M,D,O
Eastern Kentucky University — M
Eastern Michigan University — M
Eastern New Mexico University — M
Eastern University — M,O
Eastern Washington University — M
East Stroudsburg University of Pennsylvania — M
Emporia State University — M
Florida Agricultural and Mechanical University — M
Florida International University — M,D,O
Fort Hays State University — M
Gardner-Webb University — M
George Mason University — M
Georgia College & State University — M
Georgia State University — M
Goucher College — M,O
Henderson State University — M
Hofstra University — M,D,O
Howard University — M
Idaho State University — M
Illinois State University — M
Indiana State University — M,D
Indiana University Bloomington — M,D
Indiana University of Pennsylvania — M
Indiana University–Purdue University Indianapolis — M,O
Inter American University of Puerto Rico, Metropolitan Campus — M
Inter American University of Puerto Rico, San Germán Campus — M
Ithaca College — M
Jackson State University — M
Jacksonville State University — M,O
James Madison University — M
Longwood University — M
Massachusetts College of Liberal Arts — M,O
McGill University — M,D,O
McNeese State University — O
Memorial University of Newfoundland — M
Meredith College — M,O
Middle Tennessee State University — M
Millersville University of Pennsylvania — M,O
Minnesota State University Mankato — M
Mississippi State University — M,D
Missouri State University — M
Montclair State University — M
Morehead State University — M
North Carolina Central University — M
Northern Illinois University — M
Northwest Missouri State University — M
The Ohio State University — M,D
Ohio University — M
Old Dominion University — M,D
Pittsburg State University — M
Purdue University — M,D
Queens College of the City University of New York — M,O
Rhode Island College — M,O
Salem State University — M

Slippery Rock University of Pennsylvania — M
Southern Connecticut State University — M
Southern Illinois University Carbondale — M
Southern Illinois University Edwardsville — M
Southwestern Oklahoma State University — M
Springfield College — M,D,O
State University of New York College at Cortland — M
Stony Brook University, State University of New York — M,O
Sul Ross State University — M
Teachers College, Columbia University — M,D
Temple University — M,D*
Tennessee State University — M
Tennessee Technological University — M
Texas Southern University — M
Union College (KY) — M
United States Sports Academy — M
Universidad del Turabo — M
Universidad Metropolitana — M,D,O
Université de Montréal — M,D,O
Université de Sherbrooke — M,O
Université du Québec à Trois-Rivières — M
The University of Akron — M
The University of Alabama — M,D
University of Alberta — M,D
University of Arkansas — M
The University of British Columbia — M,D
University of Dayton — M
University of Florida — M,D
University of Georgia — M,D
University of Houston — M,D
University of Idaho — M,D
University of Indianapolis — M
The University of Kansas — M,D
University of Kentucky — M,D
University of Louisville — M,D,O
University of Maine — M,D,O
University of Manitoba — M
University of Mary — M
University of Memphis — M,O
University of Montana — M
University of Nebraska at Kearney — M
University of New Brunswick Fredericton — M
University of New Hampshire — M,O
University of New Mexico — D
University of North Alabama — M
The University of North Carolina at Chapel Hill — M
The University of North Carolina at Pembroke — M
University of Northern Colorado — M,D
University of Northern Iowa — M
University of North Georgia — M
University of Rhode Island — M
University of Rio Grande — M
University of South Alabama — M
University of South Carolina — M,D
University of Southern Mississippi — M,D
The University of Tennessee at Chattanooga — M
The University of Tennessee at Martin — M
The University of Texas at Austin — M,D
The University of Toledo — M,D
University of Toronto — M,D
University of Victoria — M
University of Virginia — M,D
University of Washington — M,D
The University of West Alabama — M
University of West Florida — M,D
University of Wisconsin–La Crosse — M
University of Wyoming — M
Utah State University — M,D
Wayne State College — M
Wayne State University — M,D
West Chester University of Pennsylvania — M,O
Western Kentucky University — M
Western Michigan University — M
Western Washington University — M
Westfield State University — M
West Liberty University — M
West Virginia University — M,D
Wilfrid Laurier University — M
William Woods University — M,D,O
Winthrop University — M

PHYSICAL THERAPY

AdventHealth University — D
Alabama State University — D
American International College — M,D,O
Andrews University — D
Angelo State University — D
Arcadia University — D
Arkansas State University — D
A.T. Still University — M,D,O
Augusta University — D
Azusa Pacific University — D
Bellarmine University — M,D
Belmont University — M,D
Boston University — M,D
Bradley University — D
California State University, Fresno — D
California State University, Long Beach — D
California State University, Northridge — M
California State University, Sacramento — D
Campbell University — M,D
Carroll University — D
Central Michigan University — M,D
Chapman University — D*

Chatham University — D
Clarke University — D
Clarkson University — D
Cleveland State University — D
The College of St. Scholastica — D
College of Staten Island of the City University of New York — D
Columbia University — D
Concordia University, St. Paul — M,D
Concordia University Wisconsin — D
Creighton University — D
Daemen College — D,O
Dalhousie University — M
Des Moines University — D
Dominican College — M,D
Drexel University — M,D,O*
Duke University — D
Duquesne University — M,D
D'Youville College — D,O
East Carolina University — D
Eastern Washington University — D
East Tennessee State University — D
Elon University — D
Emory & Henry College — M,D
Emory University — D
Florida Agricultural and Mechanical University — D
Florida Gulf Coast University — D
Florida International University — D
Franciscan Missionaries of Our Lady University — M,D
Franklin Pierce University — M,D,O
Gannon University — D
George Fox University — D
The George Washington University — D
Georgia Campus–Philadelphia College of Osteopathic Medicine — D*
Georgia Southern University — D
Georgia State University — D
Governors State University — D
Grand Valley State University — D
Hampton University — D
Harding University — D
Hardin-Simmons University — D
High Point University — M,D
Howard University — M,D
Hunter College of the City University of New York — D
Husson University — D
Idaho State University — D
Indiana State University — M,D
Indiana University–Purdue University Indianapolis — M,D
Ithaca College — D
Kean University — D
Langston University — D
Lebanon Valley College — D
Loma Linda University — M,D
Long Island University–LIU Brooklyn — M,D,O
Louisiana State University Health Sciences Center — D
Marist College — D
Marquette University — D
Marshall University — D
Mary Baldwin University — D
Marymount University — D
Maryville University of Saint Louis — D
Mayo Clinic School of Health Sciences — D
McMaster University — M
MCPHS University — D
Medical University of South Carolina — D
Mercer University — M,D
Mercy College — D
MGH Institute of Health Professions — M,D,O
Midwestern University, Downers Grove Campus — D
Midwestern University, Glendale Campus — D
Misericordia University — D
Missouri State University — D
Mount St. Joseph University — D
Mount Saint Mary's University (CA) — M,D,O
Nazareth College of Rochester — D
Neumann University — D
New York Institute of Technology — D
New York Medical College — M,D,O
New York University — M,D,O*
Northern Arizona University — D
Northern Illinois University — D
Northwestern University — D
Nova Southeastern University — M,D
Oakland University — D,O
The Ohio State University — D
Ohio University — D
Old Dominion University — D
Pacific University — M,D
Queen's University at Kingston — M,D
Radford University — D
Regis University — M,D,O
Rockhurst University — D
Rocky Mountain University of Health Professions — D
Rosalind Franklin University of Medicine and Science — M,D
Rush University — M
Rutgers University–Camden — D
Rutgers University–Newark — D
Sacred Heart University — D
Sage Graduate School — D
St. Ambrose University — D
St. Catherine University — D
Saint Francis University — D
Saint Louis University — M,D*
Samford University — D
Samuel Merritt University — D
San Diego State University — D
San Francisco State University — D

Seton Hall University — D
Shenandoah University — M,D,O
Simmons University — M,D,O
Slippery Rock University of Pennsylvania — D
Sonoma State University — M
Southwest Baptist University — D
Springfield College — D
State University of New York Upstate Medical University — D
Stockton University — D
Stony Brook University, State University of New York — M,D,O
Tennessee State University — D
Texas State University — D
Texas Tech University Health Sciences Center — D
Texas Woman's University — D
Thomas Jefferson University — M,D
Touro College — D
Trine University — D
University at Buffalo, the State University of New York — D
The University of Alabama at Birmingham — D
University of Alberta — M,D
The University of British Columbia — M
University of California, San Francisco — D
University of Central Arkansas — D
University of Central Florida — D
University of Cincinnati — D
University of Colorado Denver — D
University of Connecticut — D
University of Dayton — D
University of Delaware — D
University of Evansville — D
The University of Findlay — M,D
University of Florida — D
University of Hartford — M,D
University of Illinois at Chicago — M,D
University of Indianapolis — M,D
The University of Iowa — M,D
University of Jamestown — D
The University of Kansas — D
University of Kentucky — D
University of Lynchburg — D
University of Manitoba — M,D
University of Mary — D
University of Mary Hardin-Baylor — D
University of Maryland, Baltimore — D
University of Maryland Eastern Shore — D
University of Massachusetts Lowell — D
University of Miami — D
University of Michigan–Flint — D,O
University of Minnesota, Twin Cities Campus — M,D
University of Mississippi Medical Center — M
University of Missouri — D
University of Montana — D
University of Mount Union — D
University of Nebraska Medical Center — D
University of Nevada, Las Vegas — D
University of New England — M,D
University of New Mexico — D
The University of North Carolina at Chapel Hill — D
University of North Dakota — D
University of North Florida — M,D
University of North Georgia — D
University of North Texas Health Science Center at Fort Worth — M,D
University of Oklahoma Health Sciences Center — M
University of Pittsburgh — M,D*
University of Puerto Rico–Medical Sciences Campus — M
University of Puget Sound — D
University of Rhode Island — D
University of St. Augustine for Health Sciences — D
University of Saint Mary — D
University of Scranton — D
University of South Alabama — D
University of South Dakota — D
University of Southern California — M,D
University of South Florida — D
The University of Tennessee at Chattanooga — D
The University of Tennessee Health Science Center — M,D
The University of Texas at El Paso — D
The University of Texas Health Science Center at San Antonio — M,D
The University of Texas Medical Branch — M,D
The University of Texas Southwestern Medical Center — D
University of the Incarnate Word — D
University of the Pacific — M,D
University of the Sciences — D
The University of Toledo — M,D
University of Toronto — M
University of Utah — D
University of Vermont — D
University of Washington — M,D
The University of Western Ontario — M,O
University of Wisconsin–La Crosse — D
University of Wisconsin–Madison — D
University of Wisconsin–Milwaukee — M,D*
Utica College — D
Virginia Commonwealth University — M,D
Walsh University — D
Washington University in St. Louis — D
Wayne State University — D
West Coast University — M,D
Western Carolina University — D
Western Kentucky University — D

West Virginia University	M,D
Wheeling Jesuit University	D
Wichita State University	D
Widener University	M,D
Wingate University	D
Winston-Salem State University	D
Youngstown State University	D

PHYSICIAN ASSISTANT STUDIES

AdventHealth University	M
Albany Medical College	M
Alderson Broaddus University	M
Arcadia University	M
A.T. Still University	M,D,O
Augsburg University	M
Augusta University	M
Baldwin Wallace University	M
Barry University	M
Baylor College of Medicine	M
Bay Path University	M
Bethel University (MN)	M,D,O
Bethel University (TN)	M
Boston University	M
Bryant University	M
Butler University	M,D
California Baptist University	M
Campbell University	M
Carroll University	M
Case Western Reserve University	M
Central Michigan University	M,D
Chapman University	M*
Chatham University	M
Christian Brothers University	M
Clarkson University	M
Cleveland State University	M
Daemen College	M
Des Moines University	M
Drexel University	M*
Duke University	M
Duquesne University	M,D
D'Youville College	M
East Carolina University	M
Eastern Michigan University	M
Eastern Virginia Medical School	M
Elon University	M
Emory & Henry College	M,D
Emory University	M
Florida Gulf Coast University	M
Florida International University	M,D
Franciscan Missionaries of Our Lady University	M,D
Francis Marion University	M
Franklin Pierce University	M,D,O
Gannon University	M
Gardner-Webb University	M
The George Washington University	M
Grand Valley State University	M
Harding University	M
Hardin-Simmons University	M,D
High Point University	M,D
Hofstra University	M
Howard University	M,D
Idaho State University	M
Indiana State University	M,D
James Madison University	M
Jefferson College of Health Sciences	M
Johnson & Wales University	M
Keiser University	M
Kettering College	M
King's College	M
Le Moyne College	M
Lenoir-Rhyne University	M
Lock Haven University of Pennsylvania	M
Loma Linda University	M
Long Island University–LIU Brooklyn	M,D,O
Louisiana State University Health Sciences Center	M
Marietta College	M
Marquette University	M
Mary Baldwin University	M
Marywood University	M
MCPHS University	M
Medical University of South Carolina	M
Mercer University	M,D
Mercy College	M
Mercyhurst University	M
Methodist University	M
MGH Institute of Health Professions	M
Midwestern University, Downers Grove Campus	M
Midwestern University, Glendale Campus	M
Milligan College	M
Missouri State University	M
New York Institute of Technology	M
Northern Arizona University	M
Nova Southeastern University	M,D
Ohio Dominican University	M
Oregon Health & Science University	M
Pace University	M
Pacific University	M
Philadelphia College of Osteopathic Medicine	M*
Quinnipiac University	M
Rocky Mountain College	M
Rocky Mountain University of Health Professions	M
Rocky Vista University	M
Rosalind Franklin University of Medicine and Science	M
Rush University	M
Rutgers University–Newark	M
Sacred Heart University	M
St. Ambrose University	M
St. Catherine University	M
Saint Francis University	M
Saint Louis University	M*
Salus University	M
Samuel Merritt University	M
Seton Hall University	M
Seton Hill University	M
Shenandoah University	M,D,O
Slippery Rock University of Pennsylvania	M
South College	M
Southern Illinois University Carbondale	M
South University	M
South University (GA)	M
Springfield College	M
Stephens College	M,O
Stony Brook University, State University of New York	M,D,O
Texas Tech University Health Sciences Center	M
Thomas Jefferson University	M
Touro College	M
Towson University	M
Trevecca Nazarene University	M
Trine University	M
Tufts University	M,D,O
Union College (NE)	M
The University of Alabama at Birmingham	M
University of Alaska Anchorage	M
University of Arkansas for Medical Sciences	M,D
University of Bridgeport	M
University of Charleston	M
University of Colorado Denver	M
University of Dayton	M
University of Detroit Mercy	M,D,O
The University of Findlay	M,D
University of Florida	M
The University of Iowa	M
University of Kentucky	M
University of Lynchburg	M
University of Mount Union	M
University of Nebraska Medical Center	M
University of New England	M,D
University of New Mexico	M
University of North Dakota	M
University of North Texas Health Science Center at Fort Worth	M,D
University of Oklahoma Health Sciences Center	M
University of Pittsburgh	M,D*
University of St. Francis (IL)	M,O
University of Saint Francis (IN)	M
University of South Alabama	M
University of South Dakota	M
University of Southern California	M
The University of Tennessee Health Science Center	M,D
The University of Texas Health Science Center at San Antonio	M
The University of Texas Medical Branch	M
The University of Texas Rio Grande Valley	M
The University of Texas Southwestern Medical Center	M
University of the Cumberlands	M
The University of Toledo	M
University of Utah	M
University of Wisconsin–La Crosse	M
University of Wisconsin–Madison	M
Valparaiso University	M,D,O
Wayne State University	M
Weill Cornell Medicine	M
Western Michigan University	M
Westfield State University	M
West Liberty University	M
Wichita State University	M
Wingate University	M
Yale University	M
York College of the City University of New York	M

PHYSICS

Alabama Agricultural and Mechanical University	M,D
The American University in Cairo	M,D,O
American University of Beirut	M,D
Arizona State University at the Tempe campus	M,D
Auburn University	M,D
Ball State University	M
Baylor University	M,D
Binghamton University, State University of New York	M,D
Boston College	M
Boston University	D
Bowling Green State University	M
Brandeis University	M,D
Brigham Young University	M,D
Brock University	M
Brooklyn College of the City University of New York	M
Brown University	M,D
Bryn Mawr College	M,D
California Institute of Technology	D
California State University, Fresno	M
California State University, Fullerton	M
California State University, Long Beach	M
California State University, Los Angeles	M
California State University, Northridge	M
Carleton University	M,D
Carnegie Mellon University	M,D
Case Western Reserve University	M,D
The Catholic University of America	M,D
Central Michigan University	M,D
Christopher Newport University	M
City College of the City University of New York	M,D
Clark Atlanta University	M
Clarkson University	M,D
Clark University	D
Clemson University	M,D
Cleveland State University	M
Colorado School of Mines	M,D
Colorado State University	M,D
Columbia University	M,D
Concordia University (Canada)	M,D
Cornell University	M,D
Creighton University	M
Dalhousie University	M,D
Dartmouth College	D
Delaware State University	M,D
DePaul University	M,D
Drexel University	M,D*
Duke University	D
East Carolina University	M,D
Eastern Michigan University	M
Emory University	D
Fisk University	M
Florida Agricultural and Mechanical University	M,D
Florida Atlantic University	M,D
Florida Institute of Technology	M,D
Florida International University	M,D
Florida State University	M,D
George Mason University	M,D
The George Washington University	M,D
Georgia Institute of Technology	M,D
Georgia State University	M,D
The Graduate Center, City University of New York	D
Hampton University	M,D
Harvard University	D*
Howard University	M,D
Hunter College of the City University of New York	M
Idaho State University	M,D
Illinois Institute of Technology	M,D
Indiana University Bloomington	M,D
Indiana University of Pennsylvania	M
Indiana University–Purdue University Indianapolis	M,D
Iowa State University of Science and Technology	M,D
Jackson State University	M,D
Johns Hopkins University	D*
Kansas State University	M,D
Kent State University	M,D
Lakehead University	M
Lehigh University	M,D
Lewis University	M
Louisiana State University and Agricultural & Mechanical College	M,D
Manhattanville College	M,O
Marshall University	M
Massachusetts Institute of Technology	M,D
McGill University	M,D
McMaster University	D
Memorial University of Newfoundland	M,D
Miami University	M
Michigan State University	M,D
Michigan Technological University	M,D
Minnesota State University Mankato	M
Mississippi State University	M,D
Missouri State University	M
Missouri University of Science and Technology	M,D
Montana State University	M,D
Morgan State University	M
Naval Postgraduate School	M,D
New Mexico Institute of Mining and Technology	M
New York University	M,D*
North Carolina Agricultural and Technical State University	M
North Carolina Central University	M
North Carolina State University	M,D
North Dakota State University	M,D
Northeastern University	M,D
Northern Arizona University	M,D
Northern Illinois University	M,D
Northwestern University	D
Oakland University	M,D
The Ohio State University	M,D
Ohio University	M,D
Oklahoma State University	M,D
Old Dominion University	M,D
Oregon State University	M,D
Pace University	M,O
Penn State University Park	M,D*
Pittsburg State University	M
Portland State University	M,D
Princeton University	D
Purdue University	M,D
Queens College of the City University of New York	M
Queen's University at Kingston	M,D
Rensselaer Polytechnic Institute	M,D
Rice University	M,D
Royal Military College of Canada	M
Rutgers University–New Brunswick	M,D
St. John Fisher College	M
San Diego State University	M
San Francisco State University	M
San Jose State University	M
Simon Fraser University	M,D
South Dakota School of Mines and Technology	M,D
South Dakota State University	M
Southern Illinois University Carbondale	M,D
Southern Methodist University	M,D
Southern University and Agricultural and Mechanical College	M
Stanford University	D
State University of New York College at Cortland	M
Stephen F. Austin State University	M,D
Stony Brook University, State University of New York	M,D
Syracuse University	M,D
Teachers College, Columbia University	M,D
Temple University	M,D*
Texas A&M University	M,D
Texas A&M University–Commerce	M,O
Texas Christian University	M,D
Texas State University	M
Texas Tech University	M,D
Trent University	M
Tufts University	M,D
Tulane University	M,D
Université de Moncton	M
Université de Montréal	M,D
Université de Sherbrooke	M,D
Université du Québec à Trois-Rivières	M,D
Université Laval	M,D
University at Albany, State University of New York	M,D
University at Buffalo, the State University of New York	M,D
The University of Alabama	M,D
The University of Alabama at Birmingham	M,D
The University of Alabama in Huntsville	M,D
University of Alaska Fairbanks	M,D
University of Alberta	M,D
The University of Arizona	M,D
University of Arkansas	M,D
The University of British Columbia	M,D
University of Calgary	M,D
University of California, Berkeley	D
University of California, Davis	M,D
University of California, Irvine	M,D
University of California, Los Angeles	M,D
University of California, Merced	M,D
University of California, Riverside	M,D
University of California, San Diego	M,D
University of California, Santa Barbara	D
University of California, Santa Cruz	M,D
University of Central Florida	M,D
University of Central Oklahoma	M
University of Chicago	M,D
University of Cincinnati	M,D
University of Colorado Boulder	M,D
University of Colorado Colorado Springs	D
University of Connecticut	M,D
University of Delaware	M,D
University of Denver	M,D
University of Florida	M,D
University of Georgia	M,D
University of Guelph	M,D
University of Hawaii at Manoa	M,D
University of Houston	M,D
University of Houston–Clear Lake	M
University of Idaho	M,D
University of Illinois at Chicago	M,D
University of Illinois at Urbana–Champaign	M,D
The University of Iowa	M,D
The University of Kansas	M,D
University of Kentucky	M,D
University of Lethbridge	M,D
University of Louisiana at Lafayette	M
University of Louisville	M,D
University of Maine	M,D
The University of Manchester	M,D
University of Manitoba	M,D
University of Maryland, Baltimore County	M,D
University of Maryland, College Park	M,D
University of Massachusetts Amherst	M,D
University of Massachusetts Dartmouth	
University of Massachusetts Lowell	M,D
University of Memphis	M
University of Miami	M,D
University of Michigan	D
University of Minnesota, Duluth	M
University of Minnesota, Twin Cities Campus	M,D
University of Mississippi	M,D
University of Missouri	M,D
University of Missouri–Kansas City	M,D
University of Missouri–St. Louis	M,D
University of Nebraska–Lincoln	M,D
University of Nevada, Las Vegas	M,D
University of Nevada, Reno	M,D
University of New Brunswick Fredericton	M,D
University of New Hampshire	M,D
University of New Mexico	M,D
University of New Orleans	M,D

*M—masters degree; D—doctorate; O—other advanced degree; *—Close-Up and/or Display*

The University of North Carolina at Chapel Hill — M,D
University of North Dakota — M,D
University of Northern Iowa — M
University of Notre Dame — M,D
University of Oklahoma — M,D*
University of Oregon — M,D
University of Ottawa — M,D
University of Pennsylvania — M,D*
University of Pittsburgh — M,D*
University of Puerto Rico–Mayagüez — M
University of Puerto Rico–Río Piedras — M,D
University of Regina — M,D
University of Rhode Island — M,D
University of Rochester — D*
University of Saskatchewan — M,D
University of South Carolina — M,D
University of South Dakota — M,D
University of Southern California — M,D
University of Southern Mississippi — M,D
University of South Florida — M,D
The University of Tennessee — M,D
The University of Texas at Arlington — M,D
The University of Texas at Austin — M,D
The University of Texas at Dallas — M,D
The University of Texas at El Paso — M
The University of Texas at San Antonio — M,D
The University of Texas Rio Grande Valley — M
The University of Toledo — M,D
University of Toronto — M,D
University of Utah — M,D
University of Vermont — M
University of Victoria — M,D
University of Virginia — M,D
University of Washington — M,D
University of Waterloo — M,D
The University of Western Ontario — M,D
University of Windsor — M,D
University of Wisconsin–Madison — M,D
University of Wisconsin–Milwaukee — M,D*
Utah State University — M,D
Vanderbilt University — M,D*
Virginia Commonwealth University — M
Virginia Polytechnic Institute and State University — M,D
Wake Forest University — M,D
Washington State University — M,D
Washington University in St. Louis — D
Wayne State University — M,D
Wesleyan University — D
Western Illinois University — M
Western Kentucky University — M
Western Michigan University — M,D,O
West Virginia University — M,D
Wichita State University — M,D
Worcester Polytechnic Institute — M,D
Wright State University — M
Yale University — D
York University — M,D

PHYSIOLOGY

Albert Einstein College of Medicine — D
American College of Healthcare Sciences — M,O
American University of Beirut — M,D
Augusta University — D
Ball State University — M
Baylor University — M,D
Boston University — M,D
Brigham Young University — M,D
Brown University — M,D
Case Western Reserve University — M,D
Central Washington University — M
Columbia University — M,D
Cornell University — M,D
Dalhousie University — M,D
East Carolina University — M,D
Eastern Michigan University — M
East Tennessee State University — D
Georgetown University — M,D
Georgia Institute of Technology — M,D
Georgia State University — M,D
Gonzaga University — M,D
Howard University — D
Illinois State University — M,D
Indiana State University — M,D
James Madison University — M
Johns Hopkins University — D*
Kansas State University — M,D
Kent State University — M,D
Loma Linda University — D
Louisiana State University Health Sciences Center — D
Louisiana State University Health Sciences Center at Shreveport — M,D
Loyola University Chicago — D
Maharishi University of Management — D
Marquette University — M,D
Mayo Clinic Graduate School of Biomedical Sciences — M,D
McGill University — M,D
McMaster University — M,D
Medical College of Wisconsin — D
Michigan State University — M,D
Montclair State University — M
New York Medical College — M,D
Northwestern University — M
Ohio University — M,D
Oregon Health & Science University — D
Oregon State University — M,D
Penn State University Park — M,D*
Purdue University — M,D
Rocky Mountain University of Health Professions — D
Rosalind Franklin University of Medicine and Science — M,D

Rush University — D
Rutgers University–Newark — D
Rutgers University–New Brunswick — M,D
Saint Louis University — D*
Salisbury University — M
San Francisco State University — M
San Jose State University — M
Southern Illinois University Carbondale — M,D
Southern Methodist University — D
Stanford University — D
State University of New York Upstate Medical University — M,D
Stony Brook University, State University of New York — D
Teachers College, Columbia University — M,D
Tulane University — M
Universidad Central del Caribe — M,D
Université de Montréal — M,D
Université de Sherbrooke — M,D
Université Laval — M,D
University at Buffalo, the State University of New York — M,D
University of Alberta — M,D
The University of Arizona — M,D
University of Arkansas for Medical Sciences — M,D,O
University of Calgary — M,D
University of California, Berkeley — M,D
University of California, Davis — M,D
University of California, Irvine — D
University of California, Los Angeles — M,D
University of Central Florida — M,O
University of Colorado Boulder — M,D
University of Connecticut — M,D
University of Delaware — M,D
University of Florida — M,D
University of Georgia — M,D
University of Guelph — M,D
University of Hawaii at Manoa — M,D
University of Illinois at Chicago — M,D
University of Illinois at Urbana–Champaign — M,D
The University of Iowa — M,D
The University of Kansas — D
University of Kentucky — D
University of Louisville — M,D
The University of Manchester — M,D
University of Manitoba — M,D
University of Massachusetts Amherst — M,D
University of Miami — D
University of Michigan — M,D
University of Minnesota, Duluth — M,D
University of Minnesota, Twin Cities Campus — D
University of Mississippi Medical Center — D
University of Missouri — M,D
University of Nebraska Medical Center — M,D
University of Nevada, Reno — D
University of New Mexico — M,D
University of North Texas Health Science Center at Fort Worth — M,D
University of Notre Dame — M,D
University of Oklahoma Health Sciences Center — M,D
University of Oregon — M,D
University of Pennsylvania — D*
University of Prince Edward Island — D
University of Puerto Rico–Medical Sciences Campus — M,D
University of Rochester — M,D*
University of Saskatchewan — M,D
University of South Dakota — M,D
University of Southern California — M
University of South Florida — M,D
The University of Tennessee — M,D
The University of Texas Medical Branch — M,D
University of Toronto — M,D
University of Utah — M,D
University of Virginia — D
University of Washington — D
The University of Western Ontario — M,D
University of Wisconsin–La Crosse — M
University of Wisconsin–Madison — M,D
University of Wyoming — M,D
Virginia Commonwealth University — M,D
Wake Forest University — D
Wayne State University — M,D,O
Weill Cornell Medicine — M,D
Western Michigan University — M
Wright State University — M
Yale University — M,D
Youngstown State University — M

PLANETARY AND SPACE SCIENCES

Air Force Institute of Technology — M,D
Alabama Agricultural and Mechanical University — M,D
Arizona State University at the Tempe campus — M,D
California Institute of Technology — M,D
Cornell University — D
Florida Institute of Technology — M,D
Hampton University — M,D
Harvard University — M,D*
Johns Hopkins University — M,D*
Massachusetts Institute of Technology — M,D
McGill University — M,D
St. Thomas University — M,D,O
The University of Arizona — M,D
University of Arkansas — M,D
University of California, Los Angeles — M,D

University of California, Santa Cruz — M,D
University of Chicago — D
University of Hawaii at Manoa — M,D
University of Houston — M,D
University of Michigan — M,D
University of New Mexico — M,D
University of North Dakota — M
Washington University in St. Louis — D
Western Connecticut State University — M
Yale University — M,D
York University — M,D

PLANT BIOLOGY

Arizona State University at the Tempe campus — M,D
Clemson University — M,D
Cornell University — M,D
Illinois State University — M,D
Indiana University Bloomington — M,D
Iowa State University of Science and Technology — M,D
Michigan State University — M,D
New York University — M,D*
North Carolina State University — M,D
Northwestern University — M,D
Ohio University — M,D
Oklahoma State University — M,D
Penn State University Park — M,D*
Rutgers University–New Brunswick — M,D
Southern Illinois University Carbondale — M,D
Université Laval — M,D
University of Alberta — M,D
University of California, Berkeley — D
University of California, Davis — M,D
University of California, Riverside — M,D
University of Florida — M,D
University of Georgia — M,D
University of Illinois at Urbana–Champaign — M,D
University of Maryland, College Park — M,D
University of Massachusetts Amherst — M,D
University of Minnesota, Twin Cities Campus — M,D
University of Missouri — M,D
University of Oklahoma — M,D*
The University of Texas at Austin — M,D
University of Vermont — M,D
Washington University in St. Louis — D
Yale University — D

PLANT MOLECULAR BIOLOGY

Cornell University — M,D
Illinois State University — M,D
Oregon State University — D
Rutgers University–New Brunswick — M,D
University of California, Riverside — M,D
University of Florida — M,D
University of Massachusetts Amherst — M,D

PLANT PATHOLOGY

Auburn University — M,D
Colorado State University — M,D
Cornell University — M,D
Dalhousie University — M
Iowa State University of Science and Technology — M,D
Kansas State University — M,D
Louisiana State University and Agricultural & Mechanical College — M,D
Michigan State University — M,D
Montana State University — M,D
North Dakota State University — M,D
The Ohio State University — M,D
Oklahoma State University — M,D
Oregon State University — M,D
Penn State University Park — M,D*
Purdue University — M,D
Rutgers University–New Brunswick — M,D
State University of New York College of Environmental Science and Forestry — M,D
Texas A&M University — M,D
The University of Arizona — M,D
University of Arkansas — M
University of California, Davis — M,D
University of California, Riverside — M,D
University of Florida — M,D
University of Georgia — M,D
University of Guelph — M,D
University of Hawaii at Manoa — M,D
University of Idaho — M,D
University of Kentucky — M,D
University of Maine — M,D
University of Minnesota, Twin Cities Campus — M,D
The University of Tennessee — M,D
University of Vermont — M,D,O
University of Wisconsin–Madison — M,D
Virginia Polytechnic Institute and State University — M,D
Washington State University — M,D
West Virginia University — M,D

PLANT PHYSIOLOGY

Cornell University — M,D
Dalhousie University — M
Oregon State University — M,D
University of Manitoba — M,D
University of Massachusetts Amherst — M,D
The University of Tennessee — M,D

Virginia Polytechnic Institute and State University — M,D

PLANT SCIENCES

Alabama Agricultural and Mechanical University — M,D
American University of Beirut — M
Brigham Young University — M,D
California State University, Fresno — M
Colorado State University — M,D
Cornell University — M,D
Delaware State University — M
Illinois State University — M,D
Iowa State University of Science and Technology — M,D
Kansas State University — M,D,O
McGill University — M,D,O
Michigan State University — M,D
Mississippi State University — M,D
Missouri State University — M
Montana State University — M,D
North Carolina Agricultural and Technical State University — M
North Dakota State University — D
The Ohio State University — D
Oklahoma State University — M,D
Penn State University Park — M,D*
Purdue University — D
South Dakota State University — M,D
Southern Illinois University Carbondale — M
State University of New York College of Environmental Science and Forestry — M,D
Tennessee State University — M,D
Texas A&M University–Kingsville — M
Texas Tech University — M,D
Tuskegee University — M
The University of Arizona — M,D
University of Arkansas — D
The University of British Columbia — M,D
University of California, Riverside — M,D
University of Connecticut — M,D
University of Delaware — D
University of Florida — M,D
University of Georgia — M,D
University of Hawaii at Manoa — M,D
University of Idaho — M,D
University of Kentucky — M,D
The University of Manchester — M,D
University of Manitoba — M,D
University of Massachusetts Amherst — M,D
University of Minnesota, Twin Cities Campus — M,D
University of Missouri — M,D
University of Saskatchewan — M,D
The University of Tennessee — M
University of Vermont — M,D,O
University of Wisconsin–Madison — M,D
Utah State University — M,D
West Texas A&M University — M
West Virginia University — M,D

PLASMA PHYSICS

Princeton University — D
University of Colorado Boulder — M,D

PODIATRIC MEDICINE

Barry University — D
Des Moines University — D
Kent State University — D
Midwestern University, Glendale Campus — D
New York College of Podiatric Medicine — D
Rosalind Franklin University of Medicine and Science — D
Samuel Merritt University — D
Temple University — D*
Western University of Health Sciences — D

POLITICAL SCIENCE

Acadia University — M
American Public University System — M
American University — M,D,O
American University of Armenia — M
American University of Beirut — M,D
Appalachian State University — M
Arizona State University at the Tempe campus — M,D
Arkansas State University — M,O
Ashland University — M
Auburn University — M,D,O
Ball State University — M
Baylor University — M,D
Binghamton University, State University of New York — M,D
Boise State University — M
Boston College — M,D
Boston University — D
Brandeis University — M
Brigham Young University — M
Brock University — M
Brooklyn College of the City University of New York — D
Brown University — D
California Polytechnic State University, San Luis Obispo — M
California State University, Chico — M
California State University, Fullerton — M
California State University, Long Beach — M
California State University, Los Angeles — M
California State University, Northridge — M
California State University, Sacramento — M

Carleton University	M,D
Case Western Reserve University	M,D
The Catholic University of America	M,D
Central European University	M,D
Central Michigan University	M,O
The Citadel, The Military College of South Carolina	M,D
Claremont Graduate University	M,D
Clark Atlanta University	M,D
Colorado State University	M,D
Columbia University	M,D
Columbus State University	M
Concordia University (Canada)	M,D
Converse College	M
Cornell University	D
Dalhousie University	M,D
Dominican University of California	M,D
Duke University	M,D
East Carolina University	M,O
Eastern Illinois University	M
Eastern Kentucky University	M
East Stroudsburg University of Pennsylvania	M
Edinboro University of Pennsylvania	M
Emory University	D
Fairleigh Dickinson University, Metropolitan Campus	M
Florida Agricultural and Mechanical University	M
Florida Atlantic University	M
Florida International University	M,D
Florida State University	M,D
Fordham University	M
George Mason University	M,D
Georgetown University	M,D
The George Washington University	M,D
Georgia State University	M,D
Governors State University	M
The Graduate Center, City University of New York	M,D
Grambling State University	M
Harvard University	M,D*
Hillsdale College	M,D
Howard University	M,D
Idaho State University	M,D
Illinois State University	M,D
Indiana University Bloomington	M,D
Indiana University–Purdue University Indianapolis	M
Institute for Christian Studies	M,D,O
The Institute of World Politics	M
Iowa State University of Science and Technology	M
Jackson State University	M
James Madison University	M
Johns Hopkins University	M,D,O*
Kansas State University	M,D
Kent State University	M,D
Lamar University	M
Lehigh University	M
Liberty University	M
Long Island University–LIU Brooklyn	M,D,O
Long Island University–LIU Post	M,O
Louisiana State University and Agricultural & Mechanical College	M,D
Loyola University Chicago	M,D
Marquette University	M
Marshall University	M
Massachusetts Institute of Technology	M,D
McGill University	M,D
McMaster University	M,D
Memorial University of Newfoundland	M
Miami University	M
Michigan State University	M,D
Middle Tennessee State University	M
Midwestern State University	M
Mississippi College	M,O
Mississippi State University	M,D
Missouri State University	M,O
Montclair State University	M,O
Murray State University	M
New Mexico Highlands University	M
The New School	M,D
New York University	M,D*
Northeastern Illinois University	M
Northeastern University	M,D
Northern Arizona University	M,D,O
Northern Illinois University	M,D
Northwestern University	D
The Ohio State University	D
Ohio University	M,D
Oklahoma State University	M,D
Penn State University Park	M,D*
Pepperdine University	M
Portland State University	M
Princeton University	D
Purdue University	M,D
Purdue University Global	M,O
Queen's University at Kingston	M,D
Regent University	M
Rice University	D
Rutgers University–Newark	M
Rutgers University–New Brunswick	M,D
St. John's University (NY)	M,O
Saint Louis University	M*
Sam Houston State University	M
San Diego State University	M
San Francisco State University	M,D
Simon Fraser University	M,D
Sonoma State University	M
Southern Connecticut State University	M
Southern Illinois University Carbondale	M,D

Southern New Hampshire University	M
Southern University and Agricultural and Mechanical College	M
Stanford University	M,D
Stony Brook University, State University of New York	M,D
Suffolk University	M,O
Sul Ross State University	M
Syracuse University	M,D,O
Tarleton State University	M
Teachers College, Columbia University	M,D
Temple University	M,D*
Texas A&M International University	M
Texas A&M University	M,D
Texas A&M University–Central Texas	M,O
Texas A&M University–Commerce	M,D,O
Texas State University	M,D
Texas Tech University	M,D
Texas Woman's University	M
Tulane University	D
Universidad Nacional Pedro Henriquez Urena	M
Université de Montréal	M,D
Université du Québec à Montréal	M,D
Université Laval	M,D
University at Albany, State University of New York	M,D
University at Buffalo, the State University of New York	M
The University of Akron	M
The University of Alabama	M,D
University of Alberta	M,D
The University of Arizona	M,D
University of Arkansas	M
The University of British Columbia	M,D
University of Calgary	M,D
University of California, Berkeley	D
University of California, Davis	M,D
University of California, Irvine	D
University of California, Los Angeles	M,D
University of California, Riverside	M,D
University of California, San Diego	M,D
University of California, Santa Barbara	M,D
University of California, Santa Cruz	D
University of Central Oklahoma	M
University of Chicago	D
University of Cincinnati	M,D
University of Colorado Boulder	M,D
University of Colorado Denver	M,D
University of Connecticut	M,D
University of Delaware	M,D
University of Florida	M,D,O
University of Georgia	M,D
University of Guelph	M
University of Hawaii at Manoa	M,D
University of Houston	M,D
University of Idaho	M,D
University of Illinois at Chicago	M,D
University of Illinois at Springfield	M
University of Illinois at Urbana–Champaign	M,D
The University of Iowa	D
The University of Kansas	M,D
University of Kentucky	M,D
University of Lethbridge	M,D
University of Louisville	M,D
The University of Manchester	M,D
University of Manitoba	M
University of Maryland, College Park	D
University of Massachusetts Amherst	M,D
University of Memphis	M
University of Miami	M,D
University of Michigan	D
University of Michigan–Flint	M
University of Minnesota, Twin Cities Campus	D
University of Mississippi	M,D
University of Missouri	M,D,O
University of Missouri–Kansas City	M
University of Missouri–St. Louis	M,D
University of Montana	M,D
University of Nebraska at Omaha	M,O
University of Nebraska–Lincoln	M,D,O
University of Nevada, Las Vegas	M,D
University of Nevada, Reno	M,D
University of New Brunswick Fredericton	M
University of New Hampshire	M,O
University of New Mexico	M,D
University of New Orleans	M
University of North Alabama	M
The University of North Carolina at Chapel Hill	M,D,O
The University of North Carolina at Greensboro	M,O
University of Northern British Columbia	M,D,O
University of North Texas	M,D,O
University of Notre Dame	D
University of Oklahoma	M,D*
University of Oregon	M,D
University of Ottawa	M,D
University of Pennsylvania	M,D,O*
University of Pittsburgh	M,D*
University of Rhode Island	M

University of Rochester	D*
University of Saskatchewan	M
University of South Africa	M,D
University of South Carolina	M,D
University of Southern California	M,D
University of Southern Mississippi	M,D
University of South Florida	M,D,O
The University of Tennessee	M,D
The University of Texas at Arlington	M
The University of Texas at Austin	M,D
The University of Texas at Dallas	M,D
The University of Texas at El Paso	M
The University of Texas at San Antonio	M
The University of Texas of the Permian Basin	M
The University of Toledo	M,D
University of Toronto	M,D
University of Utah	M,D
University of Victoria	M,D
University of Virginia	M,D
University of Washington	M,D
University of Waterloo	M,D
The University of Western Ontario	M,D
University of West Florida	M
University of Windsor	M
University of Wisconsin–Madison	D
University of Wisconsin–Milwaukee	M,D*
University of Wyoming	M
Utah State University	M
Vanderbilt University	M,D*
Villanova University	M
Virginia Commonwealth University	M,D,O
Virginia Polytechnic Institute and State University	M,O
Walden University	M,D,O
Washington State University	M,D,O
Washington University in St. Louis	D
Wayne State University	M,D
Western Illinois University	M
Western Kentucky University	M
Western Michigan University	M,D
Western Washington University	M
West Virginia University	M,D
Wilfrid Laurier University	M,D
Yale University	D
York University	M,D

POLYMER SCIENCE AND ENGINEERING

Auburn University	M,D
California Polytechnic State University, San Luis Obispo	M
Carnegie Mellon University	M
Case Western Reserve University	M,D
Cornell University	M,D
DePaul University	M,D
Eastern Michigan University	M,O
Lehigh University	M,D
North Carolina State University	M,D
North Dakota State University	M,D
Pittsburg State University	M
The University of Akron	M,D
University of Connecticut	M,D
The University of Manchester	M,D
University of Massachusetts Amherst	M,D
University of Massachusetts Lowell	M,D
University of Missouri–Kansas City	M,D
University of Southern Mississippi	M,D
Wayne State University	M,D,O

PORTUGUESE

Emory University	D,O
Harvard University	M,D*
Indiana University Bloomington	M,D
New York University	M,D*
Northwestern University	D
The Ohio State University	M,D
Princeton University	D
Tulane University	M,D
University of California, Los Angeles	M
University of California, Santa Barbara	M,D
University of Georgia	M,D
University of Illinois at Urbana–Champaign	M,D
The University of Manchester	D
University of Maryland, College Park	M,D
University of Massachusetts Amherst	M,D
University of Massachusetts Dartmouth	M,D
University of Minnesota, Twin Cities Campus	M,D
University of New Mexico	M,D
The University of North Carolina at Chapel Hill	M,D
University of South Africa	M,D
The University of Tennessee	M,D
The University of Texas at Austin	M,D
University of Toronto	M,D
University of Washington	M,D
University of Wisconsin–Madison	M,D
University of Wisconsin–Milwaukee	M*
Vanderbilt University	M,D*
Yale University	D

PROJECT MANAGEMENT

Albertus Magnus College	M
Amberton University	M
American Business & Technology University	M
American InterContinental University Online	M

American University	M,O
Ashland University	M
Aspen University	M,O
Athabasca University	M,D,O
Avila University	M
Bellevue University	M
Boston University	M,O
Brandeis University	M
Brenau University	M
California Intercontinental University	M,D
Capella University	M,D
Carlow University	M
The Catholic University of America	M,O
Christian Brothers University	M,O
The Citadel, The Military College of South Carolina	M,O
City University of Seattle	M,O
Colorado Christian University	M
Colorado State University–Global Campus	M
Colorado Technical University Aurora	M
Colorado Technical University Colorado Springs	M,D
DeSales University	M,O
DeVry University–Folsom Campus	M
Drexel University	M*
Elmhurst College	M
Embry-Riddle Aeronautical University–Worldwide	M
Everglades University	M
Ferris State University	M
Geneva College	M
George Mason University	M,D
The George Washington University	M,D,O
Golden Gate University	M,D,O
Grand Canyon University	M
Granite State College	M
Grantham University	M,O
Harrisburg University of Science and Technology	M
Herzing University Online	M
Hult International Business School (United States)	M
IGlobal University	M
Iona College	M,O
King University	M
Lakeland University	M
Lasell College	M,O
Lawrence Technological University	M,D,O
Lebanon Valley College	M
Lehigh University	M
Lewis University	M
Liberty University	M,D
Lindenwood University	M,O
Marlboro College	M
Marymount University	M,O
Maryville University of Saint Louis	M,O
Metropolitan State University	M,D,O
Mississippi State University	M,D
Missouri State University	M
Montana Tech of The University of Montana	M
Montclair State University	M
Morgan State University	M
Mount Aloysius College	M
National American University (TX)	M
New England College	M
New York University	M*
Northeastern University	M
Northwestern University	M
Northwest University	M
Norwich University	M
Oklahoma Christian University	M
Pacific States University	M,O
Point Loma Nazarene University	M
Polytechnic University of Puerto Rico, Miami Campus	M
Post University	M
Purdue University Global	M
Queen's University at Kingston	M
Regis University	M,O
Robert Morris University	M,D
Rochester Institute of Technology	O
Saint Mary's University of Minnesota	M,O
Saint Xavier University	M,O
Sam Houston State University	M
Southern Illinois University Edwardsville	M
Southern New Hampshire University	M,D,O
Stevens Institute of Technology	M,O
Stevenson University	M
Thomas Edison State University	M
Trident University International	M,D
Universidad del Turabo	M
Universidad Nacional Pedro Henriquez Urena	M
Université du Québec à Chicoutimi	M
Université du Québec à Montréal	M,O
Université du Québec à Rimouski	M
Université du Québec en Abitibi-Témiscamingue	M,O
Université du Québec en Outaouais	M,O
The University of Alabama in Huntsville	M,O
University of Calgary	M,D
University of California, Berkeley	O
University of Connecticut	M
University of Dallas	M,D
University of Denver	M,O
University of Fairfax	M,D
University of Houston	M

*M—masters degree; D—doctorate; O—other advanced degree; *—Close-Up and/or Display*

University of Houston–Downtown	M
The University of Kansas	M
University of Louisiana at Lafayette	M
University of Management and Technology	M,D,O
The University of Manchester	M
University of Mary	M
University of Michigan–Dearborn	M
University of Nebraska at Omaha	M,D,O
University of North Alabama	M
University of Oklahoma	M,D,O*
University of Ottawa	M,O
University of Phoenix–Bay Area Campus	M,D
University of Phoenix–Online Campus	M,O
University of Phoenix–Phoenix Campus	M,O
University of Regina	M,O
The University of Tennessee at Chattanooga	M,O
The University of Texas at Dallas	M,D
University of Wisconsin–Platteville	M
University of Wisconsin–Stout	M
Virginia International University	M,O
Viterbo University	M
Walden University	M,D,O
Walsh College of Accountancy and Business Administration	M
Wayland Baptist University	M,D
Western Carolina University	M,O
Wilmington University	M
Wingate University	M

PSYCHIATRIC NURSING

Allen College	M,D
Alverno College	M,D
American University of Beirut	M
Anderson University (SC)	M
Arizona State University at the Tempe campus	M,D,O
Augusta University	D
Azusa Pacific University	M,D
Binghamton University, State University of New York	M,D,O
Boston College	M,D
California State University, San Marcos	M
Case Western Reserve University	D
Clarke University	M,O
Columbia University	M,D,O
Creighton University	M*
Drexel University	M,D,O
East Tennessee State University	M,D
Fairfield University	M
Fairleigh Dickinson University, Florham Campus	M
Florida International University	M,D
Florida State University	D,O
Frontier Nursing University	M,D,O*
George Mason University	M,D,O
Georgia Southern University	M
Georgia State University	M,D,O
Hofstra University	M
Hunter College of the City University of New York	M,D,O
Husson University	M,O
Jacksonville University	M
James Madison University	M,D
Kent State University	M,D
Lincoln Memorial University	M
McNeese State University	M,O
MGH Institute of Health Professions	M,D,O
Midwestern State University	M
Molloy College	M,D,O
Montana State University	M
National University	M,O
New Mexico State University	M
New York University	M,D,O*
Nicholls State University	M
Northeastern University	M,D
Nova Southeastern University	M,D
Oregon Health & Science University	M
Pontifical Catholic University of Puerto Rico	M
Rivier University	M,D
Rush University	D
Sage Graduate School	M,O
Saint Francis Medical Center College of Nursing	M,D,O
Shenandoah University	M,D,O
Southern Adventist University	M,D
Southern Arkansas University–Magnolia	M
Stony Brook University, State University of New York	M,D,O
Tennessee Technological University	D
Uniformed Services University of the Health Sciences	M,D*
University at Buffalo, the State University of New York	M,D,O
The University of Alabama at Birmingham	M,D
University of Colorado Denver	M,D
University of Delaware	M,O
The University of Kansas	M,D
University of Louisville	M,D
University of Maryland, Baltimore	M,D,O
University of Michigan–Flint	M,D,O
University of Minnesota, Twin Cities Campus	M,D
University of Missouri	M,D,O
University of Missouri–St. Louis	D,O
University of New Hampshire	M
The University of North Carolina at Chapel Hill	M,D,O
University of North Dakota	M,D,O

University of Pennsylvania	M*
University of Puerto Rico–Medical Sciences Campus	M
University of Rochester	M,D*
University of St. Francis (IL)	M,D
University of Saint Joseph	M,D
University of San Diego	M,D
University of South Carolina	M,O
University of Southern Indiana	M,D,O
University of Southern Maine	M,D,O
The University of Tennessee Health Science Center	D,O
The University of Texas at Austin	M,D
The University of Texas Health Science Center at San Antonio	M,D,O
University of Virginia	M,D
University of Wisconsin–Madison	D
Valdosta State University	M
Virginia Commonwealth University	M,D,O
Washington State University	M,D,O
Wayne State University	M,D
West Virginia Wesleyan College	M,D,O
Wright State University	M

PSYCHOANALYSIS AND PSYCHOTHERAPY

Adler Graduate School	M
Argosy University, Chicago	D
Atlantic University	O
Boston Graduate School of Psychoanalysis	M,D,O
Immaculata University	M,D,O
Naropa University	M
The New School	M,D
New York University	M,D,O*
Prescott College	M
University of Manitoba	M

PSYCHOLOGY—GENERAL

Abilene Christian University	M
Acadia University	M
Adelphi University	M
Alabama Agricultural and Mechanical University	M,O
Albizu University	M,D
Albizu University, Miami Campus	M,D
Alliant International University–Fresno	M,D
Alliant International University–Los Angeles	M,D
Alliant International University–Sacramento	M,D
Alliant International University–San Diego	M,D
Alliant International University–San Francisco	M,D,O
American International College	M,D,O
American University	M,D,O
The American University in Cairo	M,O
American University of Beirut	M,D
Andrews University	M,D,O
Angelo State University	M
Antioch University Los Angeles	M
Appalachian State University	M
Arcadia University	M,D,O
Argosy University, Atlanta	M,D,O
Argosy University, Chicago	M,D
Argosy University, Hawai'i	M,D,O
Argosy University, Los Angeles	M,D
Argosy University, Northern Virginia	M,D
Argosy University, Orange County	M,D
Argosy University, Phoenix	M,D
Argosy University, Seattle	M,D,O
Argosy University, Tampa	M,D
Argosy University, Twin Cities	M,D,O
Arizona State University at the Tempe campus	M,D
Arkansas Tech University	M
Auburn University	M,D
Augusta University	M
Austin Peay State University	M
Avila University	M
Azusa Pacific University	M
Ball State University	M
Barry University	M,O
Binghamton University, State University of New York	D
Biola University	D
Boston College	D
Boston Graduate School of Psychoanalysis	M
Boston University	M,D
Bowling Green State University	M,D
Brandeis University	M,D
Brandman University	M
Brenau University	M
Bridgewater State University	M
Brigham Young University	D
Brock University	M,D
Brooklyn College of the City University of New York	M,D
Brown University	M,D
Bucknell University	M
California Coast University	M
California Institute of Integral Studies	M,D
California Lutheran University	M,D
California Polytechnic State University, San Luis Obispo	M
California State Polytechnic University, Pomona	M
California State University, Chico	M
California State University, Dominguez Hills	M,O
California State University, Fresno	M,O
California State University, Fullerton	M
California State University, Long Beach	M
California State University, Los Angeles	M

California State University, Northridge	M
California State University, Sacramento	M
California State University, San Bernardino	M
California State University, San Marcos	M
California State University, Stanislaus	M
Cambridge College	M,O
Cameron University	M
Capella University	M,D
Cardinal Stritch University	M
Carleton University	M,D
Carnegie Mellon University	D
Case Western Reserve University	M,D
Castleton University	M
The Catholic University of America	M,D
Central Connecticut State University	M
Central Michigan University	M,D,O
Central Washington University	M,O
Chestnut Hill College	M,D,O
The Chicago School of Professional Psychology	M,D
The Chicago School of Professional Psychology at Irvine	D
The Chicago School of Professional Psychology: Online	M,D
The Citadel, The Military College of South Carolina	M,O
City College of the City University of New York	M,D
Claremont Graduate University	M,D,O
Clayton State University	M
Cleveland State University	M,D,O
The College at Brockport, State University of New York	M
College of Saint Elizabeth	M,D
College of St. Joseph	M
Colorado State University	M,D
Columbia University	M,D
Concordia University (Canada)	D
Cornell University	D
Dalhousie University	M,D
Dartmouth College	D
DePaul University	M,D
Divine Mercy University	M
Drexel University	M,D*
Duke University	D
Duquesne University	D
East Central University	M
Eastern Illinois University	M,O
Eastern Kentucky University	M,O
Eastern Michigan University	M,D
Eastern Washington University	M,O
East Tennessee State University	D
Elizabeth City State University	M
Emory University	D
Emporia State University	M
Fairleigh Dickinson University, Florham Campus	M,O
Fairleigh Dickinson University, Metropolitan Campus	M,D,O
Fayetteville State University	M
Fielding Graduate University	M,D,O
Fisk University	M
Fitchburg State University	O
Florida Agricultural and Mechanical University	M
Florida Atlantic University	M
Florida Institute of Technology	M,D
Florida International University	M,D
Fordham University	M,D
Fort Hays State University	M,O
Francis Marion University	M,O
Frostburg State University	M
Gardner-Webb University	M
Geneva College	M
George Mason University	M,D,O
Georgetown University	D
The George Washington University	M,D,O
Georgia Institute of Technology	M,D
Georgia Southern University	M,D
Georgia State University	D
Goddard College	M
Golden Gate University	M,D,O
Governors State University	M
The Graduate Center, City University of New York	D
Grand Canyon University	M
Hampton University	M
Hardin-Simmons University	M*
Harvard University	D*
Hofstra University	M,D
Houston Baptist University	M
Howard University	M,D
Humboldt State University	M
Hunter College of the City University of New York	M,O
Idaho State University	D
Illinois Institute of Technology	M,D
Illinois State University	M,D,O
Immaculata University	M,D,O
Indiana State University	M,D
Indiana Tech	M
Indiana University Bloomington	D
Indiana University of Pennsylvania	M,D
Indiana University–Purdue University Indianapolis	M,D
Inter American University of Puerto Rico, Metropolitan Campus	M,D
Inter American University of Puerto Rico, San Germán Campus	M,D
Iona College	M,O
Iowa State University of Science and Technology	M,D
Jackson State University	D
Jacksonville State University	M
James Madison University	M
John F. Kennedy University	M,D,O
Johns Hopkins University	D*
Kansas State University	M,D

Kean University	M
Keiser University	M,D
Kent State University	M,D
Lakehead University	M,D
Lamar University	M
La Salle University	M,D
Laurentian University	M
Lehigh University	M,D
Lesley University	M,D,O
LeTourneau University	M
Liberty University	M,D,O
Lipscomb University	M,O
Loma Linda University	D
Long Island University–LIU Brooklyn	M,D,O
Long Island University–LIU Post	M,O
Louisiana State University and Agricultural & Mechanical College	M,D
Loyola University Maryland	M,D,O
Lynn University	M
Madonna University	M
Mansfield University of Pennsylvania	M
Marietta College	M
Marist College	M,O
Marquette University	D
Marshall University	M,D,O
Martin University	M
Marywood University	M
McGill University	M,D
McMaster University	M,D
McNeese State University	M,O
Medaille College	M,D
Memorial University of Newfoundland	M,D
Mercy College	M
Meredith College	M
Miami University	M,D
Michigan School of Psychology	M,D
Michigan State University	D
Middle Tennessee State University	M,D
Minnesota State University Mankato	M,D
Mississippi State University	M,D
Missouri State University	M,O
Monmouth University	M
Montana State University	M
Montana State University Billings	M
Montclair State University	M
Morehead State University	M
Morgan State University	M,D
Murray State University	M,O
Naropa University	M
National Louis University	M,D,O
New Mexico Highlands University	M
The New School	M,D
New York Medical College	M
New York University	M,D,O*
Norfolk State University	M,D
North Carolina Central University	M
North Carolina State University	D
Northcentral University	M,D,O
North Dakota State University	M,D
Northeastern State University	M
Northeastern University	M,D
Northern Arizona University	M
Northern Illinois University	M,D
Northern Michigan University	M
Northwestern State University of Louisiana	M
Northwestern University	D
Northwest University	M
Nova Southeastern University	M,D,O
The Ohio State University	D
Ohio University	D
Oklahoma State University	M,D
Old Dominion University	M,D
Oregon State University	M,D
Our Lady of the Lake University	M
Pace University	M,D
Pacifica Graduate Institute	M,D
Pacific University	M,D
Palo Alto University	M,D
Penn State Harrisburg	M,D,O
Penn State University Park	M,D*
Philadelphia College of Osteopathic Medicine	M,D,O*
Phillips Graduate University	M
Pittsburg State University	M
Pontifical Catholic University of Puerto Rico	M,D
Pontificia Universidad Catolica Madre y Maestra	M
Portland State University	M,D,O
Princeton University	D
Purdue University	D
Queens College of the City University of New York	M
Queen's University at Kingston	M,D
Radford University	M
Rhode Island College	M,O
Rice University	M,D
Rivier University	M
Roberts Wesleyan College	M,D
Rochester Institute of Technology	M,O
Roosevelt University	M,D
Rosalind Franklin University of Medicine and Science	M,D
Rowan University	M,O
Rutgers University–Camden	M
Rutgers University–Newark	D
Rutgers University–New Brunswick	D
Sage Graduate School	M,O
St. John's University (NY)	M
Saint Joseph's University	M,O
Saint Leo University	M
Saint Louis University	M,D*
Saint Mary's University (Canada)	M,D
Salem State University	M,O
Sam Houston State University	M,D
San Diego State University	M,D

San Francisco State University	M,O
San Jose State University	M
Saybrook University	M,D
The Seattle School of Theology and Psychology	M
Seattle University	M
Seton Hall University	M,D
Shippensburg University of Pennsylvania	M
Simon Fraser University	M,D
Sofia University	M,D
Southeastern Baptist Theological Seminary	M,D
Southeastern Louisiana University	M
Southern Adventist University	M
Southern California Seminary	M,D
Southern Connecticut State University	M
Southern Illinois University Carbondale	M,D
Southern Illinois University Edwardsville	M,O
Southern Methodist University	D
Southern Nazarene University	M
Southern New Hampshire University	M
Southern Oregon University	M
Southern University and Agricultural and Mechanical College	M
Southwestern College (NM)	O
Spalding University	M,D
Stanford University	D
State University of New York at Plattsburgh	M,O
Stephen F. Austin State University	M
Stony Brook University, State University of New York	M,D
Suffolk University	M,D,O
Sul Ross State University	M
Syracuse University	D
Teachers College, Columbia University	M,D
Temple University	M,D*
Tennessee State University	M
Texas A&M International University	M
Texas A&M University–Commerce	M,D,O
Texas A&M University–Corpus Christi	M
Texas A&M University–Kingsville	M
Texas A&M University–Texarkana	M
Texas Christian University	M,D
Texas Southern University	M
Texas State University	M
Texas Tech University	M,D
Texas Woman's University	M,D,O
Tiffin University	M
Towson University	M,D
Tufts University	M,D
Tulane University	M,D
Uniformed Services University of the Health Sciences	D*
Union College (KY)	M
Universidad de las Americas, A.C.	M
Universidad de las Américas Puebla	M
Université de Montréal	M
Université de Sherbrooke	M
Université du Québec à Montréal	D
Université du Québec à Trois-Rivières	D,O
Université Laval	D
University at Albany, State University of New York	M,D
University at Buffalo, the State University of New York	M,D
The University of Akron	M,D
The University of Alabama	D
The University of Alabama at Birmingham	M,D
The University of Alabama in Huntsville	M
University of Alaska Anchorage	M,D
University of Alberta	M,D
The University of Arizona	M,D
University of Arkansas	M,D
University of Arkansas at Little Rock	M
The University of British Columbia	M,D
University of Calgary	M,D
University of California, Berkeley	D
University of California, Davis	D
University of California, Irvine	D
University of California, Los Angeles	M,D
University of California, Merced	M,D
University of California, Riverside	D
University of California, San Diego	D
University of California, Santa Barbara	D
University of California, Santa Cruz	D
University of Central Arkansas	M,D,O
University of Central Florida	M,D
University of Central Missouri	M,D,O
University of Central Oklahoma	M
University of Chicago	D
University of Cincinnati	D
University of Colorado Boulder	M,D
University of Colorado Colorado Springs	M,D
University of Connecticut	D
University of Dayton	M
University of Delaware	D
University of Denver	M,D,O

University of Florida	M,D
University of Georgia	D
University of Guelph	M,D
University of Hawaii at Manoa	M,D,O
University of Houston	M,D
University of Houston–Clear Lake	M
University of Houston–Victoria	M
University of Idaho	M,D
University of Illinois at Chicago	M,D
University of Illinois at Urbana–Champaign	M,D
University of Indianapolis	M,D
The University of Iowa	M,D,O
The University of Kansas	M,D,O
University of Kentucky	M,D
University of La Verne	M,D
University of Lethbridge	M,D
University of Louisiana at Lafayette	M,D
University of Louisiana at Monroe	M
University of Louisville	D
University of Maine	M,D
The University of Manchester	M,D
University of Manitoba	M,D
University of Maryland, Baltimore County	M,D
University of Maryland, College Park	M,D
University of Massachusetts Amherst	M,D
University of Massachusetts Dartmouth	M,O
University of Massachusetts Lowell	M
University of Memphis	M,D,O
University of Miami	M,D
University of Michigan	D,O
University of Minnesota, Twin Cities Campus	D
University of Missouri	M,D,O
University of Missouri–Kansas City	M,D
University of Missouri–St. Louis	M,D,O
University of Montana	M,D,O
University of Nebraska at Omaha	M,D,O
University of Nebraska–Lincoln	M,D
University of Nevada, Las Vegas	M,D,O
University of Nevada, Reno	M,D
University of New Brunswick Fredericton	M,D
University of New Brunswick Saint John	M,D
University of New Hampshire	D
University of New Mexico	D
University of New Orleans	M,D
The University of North Carolina at Chapel Hill	D
The University of North Carolina at Charlotte	M,D,O
The University of North Carolina at Greensboro	M,D
The University of North Carolina Wilmington	M,D
University of North Dakota	M,D
University of Northern British Columbia	M,D,O
University of Northern Iowa	M
University of North Florida	M
University of North Texas	M,D,O
University of Notre Dame	D
University of Oklahoma	M,D,O*
University of Oregon	M,D
University of Ottawa	D
University of Pennsylvania	D*
University of Philosophical Research	M
University of Phoenix–Online Campus	M,O
University of Phoenix–Phoenix Campus	M
University of Pittsburgh	D*
University of Puerto Rico–Río Piedras	M,D
University of Regina	M,D
University of Rhode Island	M,D
University of Rochester	D*
University of Saint Mary	M
University of Saskatchewan	M,D
University of South Africa	M,D
University of South Alabama	M,D
University of South Carolina	M,D
University of South Dakota	M,D
University of Southern California	M,D
University of Southern Mississippi	M,D
University of South Florida	D
University of South Florida, St. Petersburg	M
The University of Tennessee	M,D
The University of Tennessee at Chattanooga	M
The University of Texas at Arlington	M,D
The University of Texas at Austin	D
The University of Texas at Dallas	M,D
The University of Texas at El Paso	M,D
The University of Texas at San Antonio	M,D
The University of Texas at Tyler	M
The University of Texas of the Permian Basin	M
The University of Texas Rio Grande Valley	M
University of the Pacific	M
University of the West	M
The University of Toledo	M
The University of Toronto	M,D
The University of Tulsa	M,D
University of Utah	D

University of Vermont	D
University of Victoria	M,D
University of Virginia	M,D
University of Washington	M,D
University of Waterloo	M,D
The University of Western Ontario	M,D
University of West Florida	M
University of West Georgia	M,D,O
University of Windsor	M,D
University of Wisconsin–Eau Claire	M,O
University of Wisconsin–La Crosse	M,O
University of Wisconsin–Madison	D
University of Wisconsin–Milwaukee	M,D*
University of Wisconsin–Oshkosh	M
University of Wisconsin–Whitewater	M,O
University of Wyoming	M,D
Utah State University	M,D
Valdosta State University	M,O
Vanderbilt University	D*
Villanova University	M
Virginia Polytechnic Institute and State University	M,D
Virginia State University	M,D
Wake Forest University	M
Walden University	M,D,O
Washburn University	M
Washington State University	M,D
Washington University in St. Louis	D
Wayne State University	M
Webster University	M
West Chester University of Pennsylvania	M,D,O
Western Carolina University	M
Western Illinois University	M,O
Western Kentucky University	M,O
Western Michigan University	M,D
Western Washington University	M
Westfield State University	M
West Texas A&M University	M
West Virginia University	M,D
Wheaton College	M,D
Wichita State University	D
Widener University	M
Wilfrid Laurier University	M,D
William Carey University	M
William James College	M,D,O
Winthrop University	M,O
Wisconsin School of Professional Psychology	M,D
The Wright Institute	D
Wright State University	M
Xavier University	M,D*
Yale University	D
Yeshiva University	M,D
York University	M,D

PUBLIC ADMINISTRATION

Adams State University	M
Adler University	M
Albany State University	M
Alfred University	M
American University	M,D,O
The American University in Cairo	M,O
American University of Beirut	M,D
Anabaptist Mennonite Biblical Seminary	M,O
Anna Maria College	M
Appalachian State University	M
Argosy University, Chicago	M,D
Argosy University, Los Angeles	M,D
Argosy University, Northern Virginia	M,D,O
Argosy University, Orange County	M,D,O
Argosy University, Phoenix	M,D
Argosy University, Seattle	M,D
Argosy University, Tampa	M,D
Argosy University, Twin Cities	M,D
Arizona State University at the Tempe campus	M,D
Arkansas State University	M,O
Auburn University	M,D,O
Ball State University	M,O
Barry University	M
Baruch College of the City University of New York	M*
Belhaven University (MS)	M
Bellevue University	M
Binghamton University, State University of New York	M
Boise State University	M,D,O
Bowie State University	M
Bowling Green State University	M
Brandman University	M
Bridgewater State University	M
Brigham Young University	M
California Baptist University	M
California State Polytechnic University, Pomona	M
California State University, Bakersfield	M
California State University, Chico	M
California State University, Dominguez Hills	M
California State University, East Bay	M
California State University, Fresno	M
California State University, Fullerton	M
California State University, Long Beach	M,O
California State University, Los Angeles	M
California State University, Northridge	M,O

California State University, Sacramento	M
California State University, San Bernardino	M
California State University, Stanislaus	M
Capella University	M,D
Carleton University	M,D
Carnegie Mellon University	M
Central European University	M,D
Central Michigan University	M
Cheyney University of Pennsylvania	M
City College of the City University of New York	M,D
Clark Atlanta University	M
Clark University	M,O
Clemson University	M,D,O
Cleveland State University	M,D,O
The College at Brockport, State University of New York	M,O
College of Charleston	M
The College of New Rochelle	M
College of Saint Elizabeth	M,O
Columbia University	M
Columbus State University	M
Concordia University (Canada)	M,D
Concordia University Wisconsin	M
Copenhagen Business School	M,D
Cumberland University	M
Dalhousie University	M,O
DePaul University	M
DeVry University–Folsom Campus	M
Drake University	M
East Carolina University	M,O
Eastern Kentucky University	M
Eastern University	D,O
Eastern Washington University	M
East Stroudsburg University of Pennsylvania	M
East Tennessee State University	M,O
The Evergreen State College	M
Fairfield University	M
Fairleigh Dickinson University, Florham Campus	M
Fairleigh Dickinson University, Metropolitan Campus	M,O
Florida Agricultural and Mechanical University	M
Florida Atlantic University	M,D
Florida Gulf Coast University	M
Florida Institute of Technology	M
Florida International University	M,D
Florida National University	M
Florida State University	M,D,O
Framingham State University	M
Gallaudet University	M,D,O
Gannon University	M
George Mason University	M
The George Washington University	M,D
Georgia College & State University	M
Georgia Southern University	M,O
Georgia State University	M,D,O
Golden Gate University	M,D,O
Governors State University	M
Grambling State University	M
Grand Valley State University	M
Hamline University	M,D
Harvard University	M*
Hawai'i Pacific University	M
Hilbert College	M
Howard University	M
Idaho State University	M
IGlobal University	M
Illinois Institute of Technology	M
Indiana State University	M
Indiana University Bloomington	M,D,O
Indiana University Kokomo	M,O
Indiana University Northwest	M,O
Indiana University–Purdue University Indianapolis	M,O
Indiana University South Bend	M,O
Institute of Public Administration	M,O
Instituto Tecnológico y de Estudios Superiores de Monterrey, Campus Ciudad Juárez	M
International University in Geneva	M,D
Iowa State University of Science and Technology	M
Jackson State University	M,D
Jacksonville State University	M
James Madison University	M
John Jay College of Criminal Justice of the City University of New York	M
Johns Hopkins University	M,O*
Kansas State University	M
Kean University	M
Kennesaw State University	M
Kent State University	M,D
Kutztown University of Pennsylvania	M
Liberty University	M
Lipscomb University	M
London Metropolitan University	M,D
Long Island University–Hudson	M,O
Long Island University–LIU Brooklyn	M
Long Island University–LIU Post	M,O
Louisiana State University and Agricultural & Mechanical College	M,D
Marist College	M
Marshall University	M
Marywood University	M
McMaster University	M
Metropolitan College of New York	M
Metropolitan State University	M
Mid-America Christian University	M

M—masters degree; D—doctorate; O—other advanced degree; *—Close-Up and/or Display

Middlebury Institute of International Studies at Monterey	M
Midwest University	M,D
Minnesota State University Mankato	M
Mississippi State University	M,D
Missouri State University	M,O
Montana State University	M
Morehead State University	M
National University	M
New Mexico State University	M
New York University	M,D,O*
North Carolina Central University	M
North Carolina State University	M,D
Northeastern University	M
Northern Arizona University	M,D,O
Northern Illinois University	M
Northern Kentucky University	M,O
Northwestern University	M
Norwich University	M
Notre Dame de Namur University	M
Nova Southeastern University	M
Oakland University	M,D
The Ohio State University	M,D
Ohio University	M,O
Old Dominion University	M,D
Pace University	M
Park University	M,O
Penn State Harrisburg	M,D,O
Pontifical Catholic University of Puerto Rico	M
Portland State University	M,D,O
Post University	M
Queen's University at Kingston	M
Regent University	M
Reinhardt University	M
Roger Williams University	M
Roosevelt University	M
Rutgers University–Camden	M
Rutgers University–Newark	M,D
Sacred Heart University	M
Saginaw Valley State University	M
St. John's University (NY)	M,O
St. Mary's University (United States)	M,O
Saint Mary's University of Minnesota	M
Saint Peter's University	M
St. Thomas University	M,O
Sam Houston State University	M
San Diego State University	M
San Francisco State University	M
San Jose State University	M
Savannah State University	M
Seattle University	M
Seton Hall University	M,O
Shippensburg University of Pennsylvania	M
Sonoma State University	M
Southeast Missouri State University	M
Southern Arkansas University–Magnolia	M
Southern Illinois University Carbondale	M
Southern Illinois University Edwardsville	M,D,O
Southern New Hampshire University	M,D,O
Southern University and Agricultural and Mechanical College	M
Southern Utah University	M
South University (GA)	M
South University (AL)	M
South University	M
Stephen F. Austin State University	M
Strayer University	M
Suffolk University	M
Syracuse University	M,D
Tennessee State University	M
Texas A&M International University	M
Texas A&M University–Corpus Christi	M
Texas Southern University	M
Texas State University	M
Texas Tech University	M,D
Thomas Edison State University	M
Trident University International	M,D
Troy University	O
Tufts University	O
Université de Moncton	M
Université de Sherbrooke	M
Université du Québec à Montréal	M
Université du Québec, École nationale d'administration publique	D,O
University at Albany, State University of New York	M,D,O
The University of Akron	M
The University of Alabama	M,D
The University of Alabama at Birmingham	M
University of Alaska Anchorage	M
University of Alaska Southeast	M
The University of Arizona	M,D,O
University of Arkansas	M
University of Arkansas at Little Rock	M
University of Baltimore	M,D
University of Central Florida	M,O
University of Central Oklahoma	M
University of Colorado Colorado Springs	M
University of Colorado Denver	M,D
University of Connecticut	M
University of Dayton	M
University of Delaware	M
University of Evansville	M
The University of Findlay	M
University of Georgia	M,D
University of Guam	M
University of Guelph	M
University of Hawaii at Manoa	M,O

University of Houston	M,D
University of Idaho	M,D
University of Illinois at Chicago	M,D
University of Illinois at Springfield	M,D,O
The University of Kansas	M,D,O
University of Kentucky	M,D,O
University of La Verne	M
University of Louisiana at Monroe	M
University of Louisville	M,D
University of Management and Technology	M,O
University of Manitoba	M
University of Maryland, College Park	M
University of Massachusetts Amherst	M
University of Massachusetts Boston	M
University of Massachusetts Dartmouth	M,O
University of Memphis	M,O
University of Michigan–Dearborn	M
University of Michigan–Flint	M
University of Missouri	M,D,O
University of Missouri–Kansas City	M,D
University of Missouri–St. Louis	M,D,O
University of Montana	M
University of Nebraska at Omaha	M,D,O
University of Nevada, Las Vegas	M,D,O
University of Nevada, Reno	M
University of New Brunswick Fredericton	M
University of New Hampshire	M,O
University of New Haven	M,O
University of New Mexico	M
University of New Orleans	M
The University of North Carolina at Chapel Hill	M
The University of North Carolina at Charlotte	M,O
The University of North Carolina at Pembroke	M
The University of North Carolina Wilmington	M
University of North Dakota	M
University of North Florida	M,O
University of North Georgia	M
University of North Texas	M,D,O
University of North Texas at Dallas	M
University of Oklahoma	M,D*
University of Oregon	M
University of Ottawa	D,O
University of Pennsylvania	M,O*
University of Phoenix–Bay Area Campus	M,D
University of Phoenix–Central Valley Campus	M
University of Phoenix–Dallas Campus	M
University of Phoenix–Hawaii Campus	M
University of Phoenix–Houston Campus	M
University of Phoenix–Las Vegas Campus	M
University of Phoenix–Online Campus	M,O
University of Phoenix–Phoenix Campus	M
University of Phoenix–Sacramento Valley Campus	M
University of Phoenix–San Antonio Campus	M
University of Phoenix–San Diego Campus	M
University of Pittsburgh	M,D*
University of Puerto Rico–Río Piedras	M
University of Regina	M,D,O
University of Rhode Island	M
University of St. Thomas (TX)	M
University of San Francisco	M
University of South Africa	M,D
University of South Alabama	M
University of South Carolina	M
University of Southern California	M,O
University of Southern Indiana	M
University of South Florida	O
The University of Tennessee	M
The University of Tennessee at Chattanooga	M,O
The University of Texas at Arlington	M,D
The University of Texas at Austin	M,D
The University of Texas at Dallas	M,D
The University of Texas at San Antonio	M
The University of Texas at Tyler	M
The University of Texas Rio Grande Valley	M
University of the District of Columbia	M
The University of Toledo	M,O
University of Utah	M,D
University of Vermont	M
University of Victoria	M,D
University of Washington	M,D
University of West Florida	M
University of West Georgia	M,D,O
The University of Winnipeg	M
University of Wisconsin–Milwaukee	M*
University of Wisconsin–Oshkosh	M
University of Wyoming	M
Upper Iowa University	M
Valdosta State University	M,D
Villanova University	M,O
Virginia Commonwealth University	M
Virginia International University	M

Virginia Polytechnic Institute and State University	M,D
Walden University	M,D,O
Waldorf University	M
Washington Adventist University	M
Wayne State University	M,D
Webster University	M,D,O
West Chester University of Pennsylvania	M,O
Western Kentucky University	M
Western Michigan University	M,D,O
Westfield State University	M
West Virginia University	M,D
Wichita State University	M
Widener University	M,D
Wilmington University	M
Wright State University	M
York University	M

PUBLIC AFFAIRS

Arizona State University at the Tempe campus	M,D
Binghamton University, State University of New York	D
Cleveland State University	D
Concordia University (Canada)	O
Cornell University	M
Drake University	M
Florida International University	M,D
George Mason University	M
The George Washington University	M,O
Indiana University Bloomington	M,D,O
Indiana University Northwest	M
Indiana University of Pennsylvania	M
Indiana University–Purdue University Indianapolis	M,O
Indiana University South Bend	M,O
The Institute of World Politics	M,D,O
Jackson State University	M,D
McMaster University	M,D
Merrimack College	M,O
Metropolitan College of New York	M
Metropolitan State University	M
New Mexico Highlands University	M
The Ohio State University	M,D
Park University	M,O
Penn State Harrisburg	M,D,O
Portland State University	M,D,O
Princeton University	M,D,O
Syracuse University	M
Texas A&M University	M,O
The University of Alabama in Huntsville	M
University of Arkansas at Little Rock	M,O
University of Baltimore	M,D
University of California, Berkeley	M
University of California, Los Angeles	M,D
University of Central Florida	D
University of Colorado Colorado Springs	M
University of Colorado Denver	M,D
University of Florida	M,D,O
University of Louisville	M,D
University of Minnesota, Twin Cities Campus	M,D
University of Missouri	M,D,O
University of Missouri–Kansas City	M,D
University of Nevada, Las Vegas	M,D,O
The University of North Carolina at Greensboro	M,O
University of South Florida	O
The University of Texas at Austin	M,D
The University of Texas Rio Grande Valley	M
University of Washington	M,D
University of Waterloo	M
University of Wisconsin–Madison	M
Virginia Commonwealth University	M,D,O
Virginia Polytechnic Institute and State University	M,D
Washington State University	M,D,O
West Chester University of Pennsylvania	M,O
Western Carolina University	M
Western Michigan University	M,D,O
York University	M

PUBLIC HEALTH—GENERAL

Adelphi University	M
Allen College	M,D
American University of Armenia	M
American University of Beirut	M,D
Andrews University	M
Arcadia University	M
Argosy University, Atlanta	M
Argosy University, Chicago	M
Argosy University, Hawai'i	M
Argosy University, Los Angeles	M
Argosy University, Northern Virginia	M
Argosy University, Orange County	M
Argosy University, Phoenix	M
Argosy University, Seattle	M
Argosy University, Tampa	M
Argosy University, Twin Cities	M
Arizona State University at the Tempe campus	M,D,O
A.T. Still University	M,D,O
Augusta University	M
Austin Peay State University	M
Azusa Pacific University	M
Baldwin Wallace University	M
Barry University	M
Baylor University	M
Belmont University	D
Benedictine University	M
Boise State University	M,D,O
Boston University	M,D
Bowling Green State University	M
Brigham Young University	M

Brooklyn College of the City University of New York	M
Brown University	M
California Baptist University	M
California State University, Fresno	M
California State University, Fullerton	M
California State University, Long Beach	M
California State University, Northridge	M
California State University, San Bernardino	M
California State University, San Marcos	M
Campbell University	M,D
Case Western Reserve University	M
Charles R. Drew University of Medicine and Science	M
Chicago State University	M
Claremont Graduate University	M,D
Clemson University	M,D,O
Cleveland State University	M
The College at Brockport, State University of New York	M
The College of New Jersey	M
College of Saint Elizabeth	M
Columbia University	M,D
Creighton University	M
Daemen College	M
Dartmouth College	M
Davenport University	M
DePaul University	M
Des Moines University	M
Drexel University	M,D,O*
East Carolina University	M,D,O
Eastern Virginia Medical School	M
Eastern Washington University	M
East Stroudsburg University of Pennsylvania	M
East Tennessee State University	M,D,O
Elmhurst College	M
Emory University	M,D
Everglades University	M
Ferris State University	M
Florida Agricultural and Mechanical University	M,D
Florida International University	M,D
Florida State University	M
Fort Valley State University	M
George Mason University	M,O
Georgetown University	M,D
The George Washington University	M,D
Georgia Southern University	M,D
Georgia State University	M,D,O
Grand Canyon University	M,D,O
Grand Valley State University	M
Harvard University	M,D*
Hawai'i Pacific University	M
Hofstra University	M,O
Howard University	M
Hunter College of the City University of New York	M
Icahn School of Medicine at Mount Sinai	M,D
Idaho State University	M
Independence University	M
Indiana University Bloomington	M,D
Indiana University–Purdue University Indianapolis	M,D,O
Indiana Wesleyan University	M,D
Jackson State University	M,D
Johns Hopkins University	M,D*
Kansas State University	M,D,O
Kent State University	M,D
La Salle University	M
Laurentian University	D
Lenoir-Rhyne University	M
Liberty University	M,D
Loma Linda University	M,D
London Metropolitan University	M,D
Long Island University–LIU Brooklyn	M,D,O
Louisiana State University Health Sciences Center	M,D
Louisiana State University in Shreveport	M
Loyola University Chicago	M,O
Marshall University	M
McGill University	M,D
MCPHS University	M,D
Medical College of Wisconsin	M,D,O
Meharry Medical College	M
Mercer University	M,D
Michigan State University	M
MidAmerica Nazarene University	M
Mississippi University for Women	M
Missouri State University	M
Monroe College	M
Montclair State University	M
Morehouse School of Medicine	M
Morgan State University	M,D
National University	M,O
New England Institute of Technology	M
New York Medical College	M,D,O
New York University	M,D*
North Dakota State University	M
Northeastern University	M,D,O
Northeast Ohio Medical University	M,D,O
Northern Illinois University	M
Northwestern University	M
Nova Southeastern University	M,D,O
Oakland University	M
The Ohio State University	M,D
Ohio University	M
Old Dominion University	M
Oregon State University	M,D
Penn State Hershey Medical Center	M,D
Philadelphia College of Osteopathic Medicine	M,D,O*
Ponce Health Sciences University	M
Portland State University	M,D

Purdue University — M,D
Queen's University at Kingston — M,D
Rivier University — M,D
Rollins College — M
Rutgers University–Camden — M,O
Rutgers University–Newark — M,O
Rutgers University–New Brunswick — M,D
Sacred Heart University — M
St. Ambrose University — M
St. Catherine University — M
St. John's University (NY) — M
Saint Louis University — M,D*
Salus University — M
Samford University — M
San Diego State University — M,D
San Francisco State University — M
San Juan Bautista School of Medicine — M,D
Sarah Lawrence College — M
Shenandoah University — M,D,O
Simmons University — M,D,O
Simon Fraser University — M,D,O
Slippery Rock University of Pennsylvania — M
Southern Connecticut State University — M
State University of New York Downstate Medical Center — M
State University of New York Upstate Medical University — M
Stony Brook University, State University of New York — M,O
Tarleton State University — M
Temple University — M,D*
Tennessee State University — M
Texas A&M University — M,D
Thomas Edison State University — M
Thomas Jefferson University — M,O
Touro University California — M
Trinity Washington University — M
Tufts University — M,D,O
Tulane University — M,D
Uniformed Services University of the Health Sciences — M,D*
Université de Montréal — M,D,O
University at Albany, State University of New York — M,D
University at Buffalo, the State University of New York — M,D
University of Alaska Anchorage — M
University of Alberta — M,D
The University of Arizona — M,D
University of Arkansas for Medical Sciences — M,D,O
The University of British Columbia — M,D
University of California, Berkeley — M,D
University of California, Irvine — M,D
University of California, Los Angeles — M,D
University of California, San Diego — D
University of Cincinnati — M,D
University of Colorado Denver — M,D
University of Connecticut Health Center — M
University of Florida — M,D,O
University of Georgia — D
University of Hawaii at Manoa — M,D,O
University of Illinois at Chicago — M,D
University of Illinois at Springfield — M,O
University of Illinois at Urbana–Champaign — M,D
University of Indianapolis — M
The University of Iowa — M,D,O
The University of Kansas — M
University of Kentucky — M,D
University of La Verne — M
University of Louisville — M,D
University of Lynchburg — M
The University of Manchester — M,D
University of Maryland, College Park — M,D
University of Massachusetts Amherst — M,D
University of Memphis — M,D
University of Michigan — M,D
University of Michigan–Flint — M
University of Minnesota, Twin Cities Campus — M,D,O
University of Missouri — M,O
University of Montana — M,O
University of Nebraska Medical Center — M
University of Nevada, Las Vegas — M,D,O
University of Nevada, Reno — M,D
University of New England — M,D,O
University of New Hampshire — M,O
University of New Mexico — M
The University of North Carolina at Chapel Hill — M,D
The University of North Carolina at Charlotte — M,D,O
University of North Dakota — M
University of Northern Colorado — M
University of North Florida — M,O
University of North Texas Health Science Center at Fort Worth — M,D,O
University of Oklahoma Health Sciences Center — M,D
University of Ottawa — D*
University of Pennsylvania — M*
University of Pittsburgh — M,D,O*
University of Rochester — M*
University of Saint Joseph — M
University of San Francisco — M
University of South Africa — M,D
University of South Carolina — M
University of South Dakota — M

University of Southern California — M
University of Southern Maine — M,O
University of Southern Mississippi — M
University of South Florida — M,D,O
The University of Tennessee — M
The University of Texas at El Paso — M,O
The University of Texas Health Science Center at Houston — M,D
The University of Texas Health Science Center at Tyler — M
The University of Texas Medical Branch — M
University of the Sciences — M
The University of Toledo — M,D,O
University of Toronto — M,D
University of Utah — M,D
University of Vermont — M,O
University of Virginia — M,D
University of Washington — M
University of Waterloo — M,D
University of West Florida — M
University of Wisconsin–La Crosse — M
University of Wisconsin–Madison — M
University of Wisconsin–Milwaukee — M,D,O*
Utah State University — M,D,O
Valparaiso University — M,D,O
Vanderbilt University — M*
Virginia Commonwealth University — M
Virginia Polytechnic Institute and State University — M,D
Walden University — M,D,O
Washington University in St. Louis — M,D
Wayne State University — M,D
West Chester University of Pennsylvania — M,O
Western Illinois University — M
Western Kentucky University — M
Westminster College (UT) — M
West Virginia University — M,D
Wright State University — M
Yale University — M,D
Youngstown State University — M

PUBLIC HISTORY

Arizona State University at the Tempe campus — M,D,O
California State University, East Bay — M
California State University, Sacramento — M,D
The College at Brockport, State University of New York — M
College of Staten Island of the City University of New York — O
Colorado State University — M
Drew University — M,D,O
Duquesne University — M
East Carolina University — M
Florida State University — M,D
Georgia Southern University — M,O
Georgia State University — M,D
Indiana University of Pennsylvania — M
Indiana University–Purdue University Indianapolis — M
James Madison University — M
La Salle University — M,O
Lehigh University — M,D
Loyola University Chicago — M,D
Middle Tennessee State University — D
New York University — M,D,O*
North Carolina State University — M
Northern Kentucky University — M
Rutgers University–Camden — M
St. John's University (NY) — M,D
Shippensburg University of Pennsylvania — M
Sonoma State University — M
Southeast Missouri State University — M,O
Texas A&M University–Commerce — M,D,O
University at Albany, State University of New York — M,D,O
University at Buffalo, the State University of New York — M,D,O
University of Arkansas at Little Rock — M
University of California, Santa Barbara — D
University of Colorado Denver — M
University of Illinois at Springfield — M
University of Louisiana at Lafayette — M
University of Louisville — M,O
University of Maryland, Baltimore County — M,D
University of North Alabama — M
University of Northern Iowa — M
University of South Carolina — M,O
The University of Texas at Austin — M,D
University of West Florida — M
University of West Georgia — M,O
Wayne State University — M,D,O

PUBLIC POLICY

Adler University — M
Albany State University — M
American Public University System — M,D
American University — M,D,O
The American University in Cairo — M,O
American University of Beirut — M,D
The American University of Paris — M
Arizona State University at the Tempe campus — M,D
Auburn University at Montgomery — M,D
Aurora University — M

Baruch College of the City University of New York — M*
Boise State University — M,D,O
Brandeis University — M
Brock University — M
Brooklyn College of the City University of New York — M
Brown University — M
California Lutheran University — M,O
California State University, East Bay — M
California State University, Long Beach — M,O
California State University, Sacramento — M
Carleton University — M
Carnegie Mellon University — M,D
The Catholic University of America — M
Central European University — M,D
Claremont Graduate University — M,D,O
Clemson University — D,O
Columbia University — M
Concordia University (Canada) — M,D
Cornell University — M,D
DePaul University — M
Duke University — M,D
Eastern Michigan University — M
Florida State University — M,D,O
Frederick S. Pardee RAND Graduate School — D
George Mason University — M,D
Georgetown University — M,D
The George Washington University — M,D
Georgia Institute of Technology — M,D
Georgia State University — M,D,O
Harvard University — M,D*
Indiana University Bloomington — M,D,O
Indiana University Kokomo — M,O
The Institute of World Politics — M,D,O
Jackson State University — M,D
Jacksonville University — M
John Jay College of Criminal Justice of the City University of New York — M,D*
Johns Hopkins University — M,D*
Liberty University — M
Lipscomb University — M
London Metropolitan University — M
Loyola University Chicago — M
McMaster University — M,D
Midwest University — M
Mills College — M
Mississippi State University — M,D
National Louis University — M,D,O
New England College — M
The New School — M,D
New York University — M*
Northeastern University — M,D,O
Northwestern University — M
Norwich University — M
The Ohio State University — M,D
Old Dominion University — D
Oregon State University — M,D
Pepperdine University — M
Portland State University — M,D,O
Princeton University — M,D
Purdue University Fort Wayne — M,O
Regent University — M
Rochester Institute of Technology — M
Rutgers University–Camden — M
Rutgers University–Newark — M,D,O
Rutgers University–New Brunswick — M,D
San Francisco State University — M
Seton Hall University — M,O
Simmons University — M,D,O
Simon Fraser University — M
Southern University and Agricultural and Mechanical College — D
State University of New York Empire State College — M
Stony Brook University, State University of New York — M
Suffolk University — M,O
Trinity College (United States) — M
Tufts University — M,D
Union Institute & University — M,D
Universidad Autonoma de Guadalajara — M,D
Universidad del Este — M
Université de Montréal — O
University at Albany, State University of New York — M,D,O
The University of Arizona — M,D,O
University of Arkansas — D
The University of British Columbia — M
University of Calgary — M
University of California, Berkeley — M,D
University of California, Los Angeles — M
University of California, Riverside — M,D
University of California, San Diego — M
University of Chicago — M
University of Delaware — M,D
University of Denver — M
University of Georgia — M
University of Guelph — M
University of Hawaii at Manoa — O
University of Houston — M
University of Kentucky — M,D,O
University of Louisville — M,D
University of Maryland, Baltimore County — M,D,O
University of Maryland, College Park — M,D
University of Massachusetts Amherst — M
University of Massachusetts Boston — M,D

University of Massachusetts Dartmouth — M,O
University of Memphis — M,O
University of Michigan — M,D
University of Minnesota, Twin Cities Campus — M,D
University of Missouri — M,D,O
University of Missouri–St. Louis — M,D,O
University of Nebraska–Lincoln — M,D,O
University of Nevada, Las Vegas — M,D,O
University of New Brunswick Fredericton — M
University of New Hampshire — M
The University of North Carolina at Chapel Hill — D
The University of North Carolina at Charlotte — M,D,O
University of Northern Iowa — M
University of Oklahoma — M,D*
University of Pennsylvania — M,D*
University of Pittsburgh — M,D*
University of Puerto Rico–Río Piedras — M
University of Regina — M,D,O
University of Rhode Island — M
University of St. Thomas (TX) — M
University of Saskatchewan — M,D
University of Southern California — M,D
University of Southern Maine — M
The University of Texas at Arlington — M,D
The University of Texas at Austin — M,D
The University of Texas at Dallas — M,D
The University of Texas Rio Grande Valley — M
University of the Pacific — M
University of Utah — M
University of Virginia — M
University of Washington — M,D
University of Washington, Bothell — M
Vanderbilt University — D*
Virginia Commonwealth University — D
Virginia Polytechnic Institute and State University — M,D
Walden University — M,D,O
Wayne State University — M,D,O
Wilfrid Laurier University — M
William Paterson University of New Jersey — M,D,O
York University — M

PUBLISHING

Arizona State University at the Tempe campus — M,D,O
Brown University — M,D
Carnegie Mellon University — M
DePaul University — M
The George Washington University — M
The Graduate Center, City University of New York — M
New York University — M*
Northwestern University — M
Pace University — M,O
Rosemont College — M
Rowan University — O
Sam Houston State University — M
Simon Fraser University — M
Stephen F. Austin State University — M
University of Baltimore — M
University of Houston–Victoria — M
Vermont College of Fine Arts — M

QUALITY MANAGEMENT

California Intercontinental University — M,D
California State University, Dominguez Hills — M
Calumet College of Saint Joseph — M
Eastern Michigan University — M,O
Hofstra University — M,O
Instituto Tecnologico de Santo Domingo — M,O
Instituto Tecnológico y de Estudios Superiores de Monterrey, Campus Ciudad de México — M,D
Instituto Tecnológico y de Estudios Superiores de Monterrey, Campus Ciudad Juárez — M
Instituto Tecnológico y de Estudios Superiores de Monterrey, Campus Estado de México — M,D
Instituto Tecnológico y de Estudios Superiores de Monterrey, Campus Irapuato — M,D
Madonna University — M
Mount Mercy University — M
New England College of Business and Finance — M
Northwestern University — M
Penn State Erie, The Behrend College — M
Rutgers University–New Brunswick — M
San Jose State University — M
Southern New Hampshire University — M,D,O
Stevens Institute of Technology — M,O
Stevenson University — M
Trident University International — M,D,O
Universidad de las Americas, A.C. — M
Universidad del Turabo — M
The University of Alabama — M
University of Massachusetts Boston — M,O
The University of Tennessee at Chattanooga — M,O
The University of Texas at Tyler — M
University of Wisconsin–Stout — M

---

*M—masters degree; D—doctorate; O—other advanced degree; *—Close-Up and/or Display*

QUANTITATIVE ANALYSIS

Baruch College of the City University of New York	M*
Columbia University	M,D
Drexel University	M,D,O*
Duke University	M,D,O
Fordham University	M,D
The Graduate Center, City University of New York	M
Harvard University	M,D*
Hofstra University	M,O
Instituto Tecnologico de Santo Domingo	M,O
Lehigh University	M
Rutgers University–Newark	M,O
San Francisco State University	M
Southern New Hampshire University	M,D,O
Stockton University	M
University at Buffalo, the State University of New York	M,D
The University of Alabama at Birmingham	M,D
The University of British Columbia	M,D
University of California, Santa Barbara	M,D
University of Connecticut	M,O
University of Florida	M,D,O
The University of Iowa	M,D,O
University of Maryland, College Park	M,D
University of Michigan	M,D
University of Minnesota, Twin Cities Campus	M,D,O
University of New Hampshire	M,O
University of New Mexico	D
University of North Texas	M,D,O
University of Oregon	M
University of Puerto Rico–Río Piedras	M,D
University of South Africa	M,D
University of Southern California	M,D
The University of Texas at Arlington	M,D
The University of Texas at Austin	M,D
The University of Texas Health Science Center at Houston	M,D
Vanderbilt University	M*
Virginia Polytechnic Institute and State University	M,O

RADIATION BIOLOGY

Georgetown University	M
Université de Sherbrooke	M,D
The University of Iowa	M
University of Oklahoma Health Sciences Center	M,D

RANGE SCIENCE

Kansas State University	M,D,O
Montana State University	M,D
Oregon State University	M,D
Sul Ross State University	M
Texas A&M University–Kingsville	M
The University of Arizona	M,D
University of California, Berkeley	M
University of Nevada, Reno	M
University of Wyoming	M,D
Utah State University	M,D

READING EDUCATION

Abilene Christian University	M
Adelphi University	M
Alabama Agricultural and Mechanical University	M,D,O
Alabama State University	M,O
Alfred University	M
Alverno College	M
American International College	M,D,O
Appalachian State University	M
Arcadia University	M,D,O
Arkansas State University	M,D,O
Asbury University	M
Augustana University	M
Aurora University	M,D
Baldwin Wallace University	M
Ball State University	M,D,O
Bank Street College of Education	M
Barry University	M,D,O
Belhaven University (MS)	M,D,O
Bellarmine University	M,D,O
Berry College	M
Binghamton University, State University of New York	M
Bloomsburg University of Pennsylvania	M
Blue Mountain College	M
Bluffton University	M
Boise State University	M
Boston College	M,D,O
Bowie State University	M
Bowling Green State University	M,O
Bridgewater State University	M,O
Buffalo State College, State University of New York	M,D
Cabrini University	M
California Baptist University	M
California State University, East Bay	M
California State University, Fresno	M
California State University, Fullerton	M
California State University, Northridge	M
California State University, Sacramento	M,D,O
California State University, San Marcos	M,D
California State University, Stanislaus	M
California University of Pennsylvania	M
Canisius College	M,O
Capella University	M,D

Cardinal Stritch University	M,D
Carthage College	M,O
Castleton University	M,O
Centenary University	M,D
Central Connecticut State University	M,O
Central Michigan University	M,D,O
Central Washington University	M
Chestnut Hill College	M
Chicago State University	M
The Citadel, The Military College of South Carolina	M,D
City College of the City University of New York	M
City University of Seattle	M,O
Clarion University of Pennsylvania	M
Clemson University	M,D,O
Coastal Carolina University	M,O
Coker College	M
The College at Brockport, State University of New York	M,O
The College of New Jersey	M,O
The College of New Rochelle	M
College of St. Joseph	M
The College of Saint Rose	M,O
Concordia University (United States)	M,D
Concordia University Chicago	M
Concordia University, Nebraska	M
Concordia University, St. Paul	M,D,O
Concordia University Wisconsin	M
Concord University	M
Converse College	O
Crandall University	M
Curry College	M,O
Dallas Baptist University	M
Delaware State University	M
DePaul University	M,D
Dickinson State University	M
Dominican University	M
Drake University	M,D,O
Drury University	M
Duquesne University	M
East Carolina University	M
Eastern Mennonite University	M
Eastern Michigan University	M,O
Eastern Nazarene College	M,O
Eastern New Mexico University	M
Eastern University	M,O
Eastern Washington University	M
East Stroudsburg University of Pennsylvania	M
East Tennessee State University	M,O
Edinboro University of Pennsylvania	M,O
Elms College	M,O
Emory & Henry College	M,D
Emporia State University	M
Endicott College	M
Evangel University	M
Fairleigh Dickinson University, Florham Campus	M,O
Fairleigh Dickinson University, Metropolitan Campus	M,O
Fairmont State University	M
Fitchburg State University	O
Florida Atlantic University	M
Florida Gulf Coast University	M
Florida International University	M,D,O
Florida Memorial University	M
Florida State University	M,D,O
Fontbonne University	M
Framingham State University	M
Fresno Pacific University	M,O
Frostburg State University	M,D
Furman University	M,O
Gannon University	M,O
George Fox University	M,O
George Mason University	M
Georgetown College	M
Georgia Southern University	M,O
Georgia State University	M,D
Gordon College	M,O
Goucher College	M,O
Governors State University	M
Graceland University (IA)	M
Grambling State University	M,D,O
Grand Canyon University	M,D,O
Grand Valley State University	M
Hamline University	M,D
Hannibal-LaGrange University	M
Harding University	M,O
Hardin-Simmons University	M
Harvard University	M*
Heritage University	M
Hofstra University	M,D,O
Holy Family University	M
Hood College	M,O
Houston Baptist University	M,D
Idaho State University	M
Illinois State University	M
Indiana University Bloomington	M,D,O
Indiana University of Pennsylvania	M,O
Indiana University–Purdue University Indianapolis	M,O
Jackson State University	M,D,O
Jacksonville State University	M
James Madison University	M
Judson University	M,D
Kansas State University	M,D,O
Kennesaw State University	M
Kent State University	M
Kutztown University of Pennsylvania	M
La Salle University	M,O
Lehman College of the City University of New York	M
Le Moyne College	M
Lesley University	M,D,O
Lewis University	M
Liberty University	M,D,O
Lipscomb University	M,D,O
Long Island University–Brentwood Campus	M,O

Long Island University–Hudson	M,O
Long Island University–LIU Post	M,D,O
Long Island University–Riverhead	M,O
Longwood University	M
Lourdes University	M
Loyola Marymount University	M
Loyola University Maryland	M
Madonna University	M
Manhattanville College	M,O
Marquette University	M,D,O
Marshall University	M
Mary Baldwin University	M
Marygrove College	M,O
Maryville University of Saint Louis	M,D
Marywood University	M
Massachusetts College of Liberal Arts	M
McDaniel College	M
McKendree University	M,D,O
McNeese State University	M
Medaille College	M
Mercy College	M,O
Meredith College	M,O
MGH Institute of Health Professions	M,O
Michigan State University	M,D
MidAmerica Nazarene University	M
Middle Tennessee State University	M,D
Midwestern State University	M
Millersville University of Pennsylvania	M
Misericordia University	M
Mississippi State University	M,D,O
Mississippi University for Women	M
Missouri State University	M,O
Monmouth University	M,D,O
Montana State University Billings	M
Montclair State University	M
Morehead State University	M,O
Mount Mercy University	M
Mount St. Joseph University	M,O
Mount Saint Mary College	M
Mount Saint Vincent University	M
National Louis University	M,D,O
Nazareth College of Rochester	M
Newman University	M
New Mexico State University	M,D,O
New York University	M*
Niagara University	M
North Carolina Agricultural and Technical State University	M
Northeastern Illinois University	M
Northeastern State University	M
Northern Michigan University	M
Northern Vermont University–Lyndon	M
Northwestern Oklahoma State University	M
Northwestern State University of Louisiana	M,O
Northwest Missouri State University	M,D,O
Notre Dame College (OH)	M,O
Oakland University	M,D,O
Ohio University	M,D
Old Dominion University	M,D
Olivet Nazarene University	M
Pace University	M,O
Park University	M,O
Penn State Harrisburg	M,D,O
Providence College	M
Purdue University	M,D,O
Purdue University Global	M
Queens College of the City University of New York	M,O
Queens University of Charlotte	M
Quincy University	M
Radford University	M
Regent University	M,D,O
Regis University	M,O
Rhode Island College	M
Rivier University	M,D,O
Roberts Wesleyan College	M
Rockford University	M
Roger Williams University	M,O
Roosevelt University	M
Rowan University	M,O
Rutgers University–New Brunswick	M,D
Sacred Heart University	O
Sage Graduate School	M
Saginaw Valley State University	M
St. Bonaventure University	M
Saint Francis University	M
St. John Fisher College	M
St. John's University (NY)	M,D,O
St. Joseph's College, New York	M
Saint Joseph's University	M,D,O
Saint Mary's University of Minnesota	M,O
Saint Michael's College	M,O
Saint Peter's University	M,O
St. Thomas Aquinas College	M,O
St. Thomas University	M,D,O
Saint Xavier University	M
Salem College	M
Salem State University	M
Salisbury University	M,D
Sam Houston State University	M,D
San Diego State University	M,D
San Francisco State University	M
San Jose State University	M,O
Seattle Pacific University	M
Shippensburg University of Pennsylvania	M
Siena Heights University	M,O
Simon Fraser University	D
Slippery Rock University of Pennsylvania	M

Sonoma State University	M,O
Southeastern Louisiana University	M
Southeastern Oklahoma State University	M
Southeastern University (FL)	M,D
Southern Adventist University	M
Southern Connecticut State University	M,O
Southern Illinois University Edwardsville	M,O
Southern Methodist University	M,D
Southern New Hampshire University	M,D,O
Southern Oregon University	M
Southwestern Adventist University	M
Southwest Minnesota State University	M
Spring Arbor University	M
State University of New York at Fredonia	M
State University of New York at New Paltz	M
State University of New York at Oswego	M
State University of New York at Plattsburgh	M
State University of New York College at Cortland	M
State University of New York College at Geneseo	M
State University of New York College at Oneonta	M
State University of New York College at Potsdam	M,O
Sul Ross State University	M,D
Syracuse University	M,D
Teachers College, Columbia University	M,D,O
Tennessee Technological University	D
Texas A&M University–Commerce	M,D,O
Texas A&M University–Corpus Christi	M,D
Texas A&M University–Kingsville	M
Texas A&M University–San Antonio	M
Texas Christian University	M
Texas State University	M
Texas Tech University	M,D
Texas Woman's University	M,D,O
Touro College	M
Towson University	M,O
Trident University International	M
Trinity Washington University	M
Union College (KY)	M
University at Albany, State University of New York	M,D,O
University at Buffalo, the State University of New York	M,D,O
The University of Akron	M
The University of Alabama at Birmingham	M
The University of Alabama in Huntsville	M,O
University of Alaska Southeast	M
The University of Arizona	M,D,O
University of Arkansas at Little Rock	M,D,O
University of Bridgeport	M,D,O
The University of British Columbia	M,D
University of Central Arkansas	M
University of Central Florida	M,O
University of Central Missouri	M,D,O
University of Central Oklahoma	M
University of Cincinnati	M,D
University of Colorado Denver	M
University of Connecticut	M,D
University of Dayton	M
The University of Findlay	M
University of Florida	M,D,O
University of Georgia	M,D
University of Guam	M
University of Houston–Clear Lake	M
University of Houston–Victoria	M,O
University of Kentucky	M,D
University of La Verne	M,O
University of Lynchburg	M
University of Maine	M,D,O
University of Mary	M,D
University of Maryland, College Park	M,D,O
University of Massachusetts Amherst	M,D,O
University of Memphis	M,D,O
University of Miami	D
University of Michigan–Flint	M,D,O
University of Minnesota, Twin Cities Campus	M,D,O
University of Mississippi	M,D,O
University of Missouri	M,D,O
University of Missouri–Kansas City	M,D,O
University of Missouri–St. Louis	M
University of Nebraska at Kearney	M
University of Nevada, Reno	M,D
University of New England	M,D,O
University of New Mexico	M,D
The University of North Carolina at Chapel Hill	M,D
The University of North Carolina at Charlotte	M,O
The University of North Carolina at Greensboro	M,D,O
The University of North Carolina at Pembroke	M
The University of North Carolina Wilmington	M
University of North Dakota	M
University of Northern Colorado	M
University of Northern Iowa	M
University of North Florida	M

University of Oklahoma	M,D*
University of Oklahoma Health Sciences Center	M,D,O
University of Pennsylvania	M*
University of Phoenix–Online Campus	M,O
University of Phoenix–Phoenix Campus	M
University of Pittsburgh	M,D*
University of Portland	M,D
University of Rhode Island	M
University of St. Francis (IL)	M,D,O
University of Saint Joseph	M
University of St. Thomas (TX)	M
University of San Diego	M
University of San Francisco	M,D
The University of Scranton	M
University of Sioux Falls	M,D
University of South Alabama	M,D
University of South Carolina	M,D
University of South Dakota	M
University of Southern Maine	M,O
University of South Florida	M,D,O
University of South Florida, St. Petersburg	M
The University of Tennessee	M,D,O
The University of Texas at Arlington	M
The University of Texas at Austin	M,D
The University of Texas at El Paso	M,D
The University of Texas at San Antonio	M
The University of Texas at Tyler	M
The University of Texas of the Permian Basin	M
The University of Texas Rio Grande Valley	M
University of the Cumberlands	M,D,O
University of Utah	M,D,O
University of Victoria	M,D
University of Virginia	M,D
University of Washington	M,D
University of West Florida	M
University of West Georgia	M,D,O
University of Wisconsin–Eau Claire	M
University of Wisconsin–La Crosse	M,O
University of Wisconsin–Milwaukee	M*
University of Wisconsin–Oshkosh	M
University of Wisconsin–River Falls	M
University of Wisconsin–Stevens Point	M
University of Wisconsin–Superior	M
Upper Iowa University	M
Utah Valley University	M
Vanderbilt University	M*
Virginia Commonwealth University	M,O
Viterbo University	M
Walden University	M,D,O
Walla Walla University	M
Walsh University	M
Washburn University	M
Washington State University	M,D
Wayne State University	M,D,O
Webster University	M,O
West Chester University of Pennsylvania	M,O
Western Connecticut State University	M,D
Western Illinois University	M
Western Kentucky University	M,O
Western Michigan University	M,D
Western New Mexico University	M
Western State Colorado University	M
Westfield State University	M
West Liberty University	M
Westminster College (PA)	M
West Texas A&M University	M
West Virginia University	M,D
Widener University	M
Wilkes University	M,D
William Paterson University of New Jersey	M,O
Wilmington College	M
Wilmington University	M,D
Worcester State University	M,O
Xavier University	M*
York College of Pennsylvania	M
Youngstown State University	M

REAL ESTATE

American University	M,O
Arizona State University at the Tempe campus	M,D
Auburn University	M
Baruch College of the City University of New York	M*
Brandeis University	M
California State University, Sacramento	M
Clemson University	M
Cleveland State University	M,O
Columbia University	M
Cornell University	M
DePaul University	M
Drexel University	M*
Emory University	M
Florida International University	M
Georgetown University	M
The George Washington University	O
Georgia State University	M,D,O
Instituto Centroamericano de Administración de Empresas	M
Johns Hopkins University	M*
Longwood University	M
Marquette University	M

Massachusetts Institute of Technology	M
Midwest University	M,D
Monmouth University	M,O
New York University	M*
Northwestern University	M,D
Pacific States University	M,O
Pontificia Universidad Catolica Madre y Maestra	M
Portland State University	M,D,O
Pratt Institute	M
Roosevelt University	M
Rutgers University–Newark	M
Southern Methodist University	M
Syracuse University	M
Thomas Jefferson University	M
Universidad Iberoamericana	M,D
University at Buffalo, the State University of New York	M,D,O
University of California, Berkeley	D
University of Central Florida	M
University of Denver	M
University of Florida	M,D,O
University of Hawaii at Manoa	M
University of Illinois at Chicago	M
University of Maryland, College Park	M
University of Memphis	M,D
University of Miami	M,D
The University of North Carolina at Charlotte	M,O
University of Pennsylvania	M,D*
University of San Diego	M
University of South Africa	M
University of Southern California	M
University of South Florida	M,D
The University of Texas at Arlington	M,D
The University of Texas at Dallas	M
University of Utah	M
University of Wisconsin–Madison	M,D
Villanova University	M
Virginia Commonwealth University	O

RECREATION AND PARK MANAGEMENT

Acadia University	M
Bowling Green State University	M
California State University, Chico	M
California State University, East Bay	M
California State University, Long Beach	M
California State University, Northridge	M,O
California State University, Sacramento	M
Central Michigan University	M,O
Clemson University	M,D,O
Colorado State University	M,D
Delta State University	M
East Carolina University	M,O
Eastern Kentucky University	M
Eastern Washington University	M
Florida International University	M,D,O
Frostburg State University	M
Hardin-Simmons University	M
Indiana State University	M,D
Indiana University Bloomington	M,D
Iona College	M,O
Kent State University	M
Lasell College	M,O
Lehman College of the City University of New York	M
Loyola Marymount University	M
Michigan State University	M,D
Middle Tennessee State University	M
Naropa University	M
New England College	M
North Carolina Central University	M
North Carolina State University	M,D
Northern Arizona University	M,O
Northwest Missouri State University	M
Ohio University	M
Old Dominion University	M
Penn State University Park	M,D*
Purdue University	M,D
San Francisco State University	M
Slippery Rock University of Pennsylvania	M
South Dakota State University	M,D
Southern Connecticut State University	M
Southern Illinois University Carbondale	M
Southern University and Agricultural and Mechanical College	M
Southwestern Oklahoma State University	M
Springfield College	M
State University of New York College at Cortland	M
Temple University	M,D*
Texas A&M University	M,D
Texas State University	M
United States Sports Academy	M
Universidad Metropolitana	M
University of Alberta	M,D
University of Arkansas	M,D
University of Florida	M,D
The University of Iowa	M
University of Louisiana at Monroe	M
University of Manitoba	M
University of Mississippi	M,D
University of Montana	M,D
University of Nebraska at Kearney	M
University of New Brunswick Fredericton	M

University of New Hampshire	M
The University of North Carolina at Greensboro	M
University of Rhode Island	M
The University of Tennessee	M,D
The University of Toledo	M,D
University of Utah	M,D
University of Waterloo	M,D
University of Wisconsin–La Crosse	M
University of Wisconsin–Milwaukee	M*
Utah State University	M,D
Virginia Commonwealth University	M
Western Illinois University	M
Western Kentucky University	M
West Virginia University	M

REHABILITATION COUNSELING

Adler University	M
Alabama Agricultural and Mechanical University	M,O
Alabama State University	M
Arkansas State University	M,O
Assumption College	M,O
Ball State University	M,D
Barry University	M,O
Bayamón Central University	M,O
California State University, Fresno	M
California State University, Los Angeles	M,D
California State University, San Bernardino	M
Cambridge College	M,O
Central Connecticut State University	M,O
Coppin State University	M
East Carolina University	M,D,O
East Central University	M
Edinboro University of Pennsylvania	M,O
Emporia State University	M
Florida International University	M,D,O
Fort Valley State University	M
The George Washington University	M
Georgia State University	M
Hofstra University	M,O
Hunter College of the City University of New York	M
Illinois Institute of Technology	M,D
Kent State University	M
Langston University	M
Louisiana State University Health Sciences Center	M
Maryville University of Saint Louis	M
Mercer University	M,D
Michigan State University	M
Minnesota State University Mankato	M
Mississippi State University	M,D,O
Montana State University Billings	M
Mount Mary University	M,O
North Carolina Agricultural and Technical State University	M,D
Northeastern Illinois University	M
Ohio University	M,D
Pontifical Catholic University of Puerto Rico	M
Rutgers University–Newark	M
St. Bonaventure University	M,O
Salve Regina University	M,O
San Diego State University	M
South Carolina State University	M
Southern University and Agricultural and Mechanical College	M
Springfield College	M
Texas Tech University Health Sciences Center	M
Thomas University	M
University at Buffalo, the State University of New York	M,D,O
The University of Arizona	M,D
University of Arkansas	M,D
University of Arkansas at Little Rock	M,O
University of Idaho	M,D
The University of Iowa	M,D
University of Kentucky	M,D
University of Maryland, College Park	M,D,O
University of Maryland Eastern Shore	M
University of Massachusetts Boston	M,D
University of Memphis	M,D
The University of North Carolina at Chapel Hill	M
University of Northern Colorado	M,D
University of North Texas	M,D,O
University of Pittsburgh	M,D*
University of Puerto Rico–Río Piedras	M
The University of Scranton	M
University of South Carolina	M,O
University of Southern Maine	M,O
University of South Florida	M,D,O
The University of Tennessee	M,O
The University of Texas at Austin	M,D
The University of Texas at El Paso	M
The University of Texas Rio Grande Valley	M,D
The University of Texas Southwestern Medical Center	M
University of the District of Columbia	M
University of Wisconsin–Madison	M,D
University of Wisconsin–Stout	M
Utah State University	M

Virginia Commonwealth University	M
Wayne State University	M,D,O
Western Oregon University	M
Western Washington University	M
West Virginia University	M,D
Wilberforce University	M
Winston-Salem State University	M
Wright State University	M

REHABILITATION SCIENCES

Alabama State University	M
Augusta University	D
Boston University	M,D
Central Michigan University	M
Clarion University of Pennsylvania	M
Concordia University Wisconsin	M
Duquesne University	M,D
East Carolina University	M,D,O
East Stroudsburg University of Pennsylvania	M
George Mason University	D,O
Indiana University–Purdue University Indianapolis	M,D
Jackson State University	M
Lasell College	M
Logan University	M,D
Loma Linda University	M,D
Marquette University	M,D
McGill University	M,D,O
McMaster University	M,D
Medical University of South Carolina	D
New York University	M,D*
Northwestern University	D
The Ohio State University	D
Old Dominion University	D
Queen's University at Kingston	M,D
Salus University	M,O
Stony Brook University, State University of New York	M,D,O
Temple University	M,D*
Texas Tech University Health Sciences Center	D
Université de Montréal	O
University at Buffalo, the State University of New York	O
The University of Alabama at Birmingham	D
University of Alberta	M,D
The University of British Columbia	M,D
University of Colorado Denver	D
University of Florida	D
University of Illinois at Urbana–Champaign	M,D
The University of Iowa	M,D
The University of Kansas	M,D
University of Kentucky	D
University of Manitoba	M,D
University of Maryland, Baltimore	D
University of Maryland Eastern Shore	M
University of Northern Colorado	M,D
University of North Texas Health Science Center at Fort Worth	M,D
University of Oklahoma Health Sciences Center	M
University of Ottawa	M
University of Pittsburgh	M,D*
University of South Carolina	M,O
University of South Florida	D
The University of Texas Medical Branch	D
University of Toronto	M,D
The University of Tulsa	M
University of Utah	D
University of Vermont	D
University of Washington	M,D
University of Wisconsin–La Crosse	M
University of Wisconsin–Milwaukee	D*
Virginia Commonwealth University	D
Washington University in St. Louis	D
Western Michigan University	M

RELIABILITY ENGINEERING

Arizona State University at the Tempe campus	M
Rutgers University–New Brunswick	M,D
University of Maryland, College Park	M,D
The University of Tennessee	M,D

RELIGION

Abilene Christian University	M
Ambrose University	M,O
The American University of Rome	M
Amridge University	M,D
Arizona State University at the Tempe campus	M,D,O
Athens State University	M
Baylor University	M,D
Bethany Theological Seminary	M,O
Bethel Seminary	M,D,O
Bethesda University	M
Beulah Heights University	M
Biola University	M,D,O
Bob Jones University	M,D,O
Boston University	M,D
Briercrest Seminary	M
Brown University	D
Bryn Athyn College of the New Church	M
Cairn University	M
California State University, Long Beach	M
Calvin Theological Seminary	M
Canadian Southern Baptist Seminary	M
Cardinal Stritch University	M
The Catholic University of America	M,D,O

M—masters degree; D—doctorate; O—other advanced degree; *—Close-Up and/or Display

Institution	Degree
Charlotte Christian College and Theological Seminary	M,D
Chicago Theological Seminary	M,D
Christian Brothers University	M
Christian Theological Seminary	M,D
Cincinnati Christian University	M
Claremont Graduate University	M,D
Claremont Lincoln University	M
Claremont School of Theology	M,D
Clarks Summit University	M,D
Columbia University	M,D
Concordia University (Canada)	M,D
Concordia University Chicago	M,D
Concordia University Irvine	M
Concordia University of Edmonton	M
Cornell University	M,D
Dallas Baptist University	M
Dallas Theological Seminary	M,D,O
Delta State University	M
Denver Seminary	M,D,O
Dominican University of California	M
Drew University	M,D,O
Duke University	M,D
Earlham School of Religion	M
Eastern Mennonite University	M,O
East Texas Baptist University	M
Elms College	M
Emory University	D
Faith Baptist Bible College and Theological Seminary	M
Florida International University	M
Fordham University	M,D,O
The General Theological Seminary	M,D,O
George Mason University	M
Georgetown University	M,D
The George Washington University	M
Georgia State University	M
Gordon-Conwell Theological Seminary	M,D
Grace College of Divinity	M
Graceland University (IA)	M
Graduate Theological Union	M,D,O
Grand Rapids Theological Seminary of Cornerstone University	M
Hardin-Simmons University	M
Harrison Middleton University	M,D
Hartford Seminary	M,D,O
Harvard University	D*
Heritage Christian University	M
Hope International University	M
Iliff School of Theology	M,D
Indiana University Bloomington	M,D
The Jewish Theological Seminary	M,D
John Carroll University	M
Kentucky Christian University	M
Knox Theological Seminary	M
Lancaster Theological Seminary	M,D,O
La Sierra University	M
Lee University	M
Liberty University	M,D
Lincoln Christian University	M
Loma Linda University	M
Louisville Presbyterian Theological Seminary	M,D
Lutheran Theological Seminary Saskatoon	M,D
Luther Rice College & Seminary	M,D
Maranatha Baptist University	M
McGill University	M,D
McMaster University	M,D
Memorial University of Newfoundland	M
Milligan College	M,D,O
Missouri State University	M,O
Moody Theological Seminary–Michigan	M,O
Mount St. Joseph University	M,O
Mount Saint Mary's University (CA)	M,D,O
Naropa University	M
Nashotah House Theological Seminary	M,D,O
New Saint Andrews College	M,O
New York University	M,O*
Northern Seminary	M,D
Northwestern University	M,D
Northwest Nazarene University	M
Nyack College	M
Oblate School of Theology	M
Olivet Nazarene University	M
Omega Graduate School	
Pacific School of Religion	M,D,O
Pepperdine University	M
Princeton Theological Seminary	M,D
Princeton University	D
Queen's University at Kingston	M
Reformed Theological Seminary–Charlotte Campus	M,D
Reformed Theological Seminary–Houston Campus	M
Reformed Theological Seminary–Jackson Campus	M,D,O
Reformed Theological Seminary–Washington D.C.	M
Regent University	M,D
Rice University	D
The Robert E. Webber Institute for Worship Studies	M,D
Rutgers University–New Brunswick	M,O
Saint John's Seminary (MA)	M
St. Joseph's Seminary	M
Saint Mary's University (Canada)	M
Salve Regina University	M
Santa Clara University	M,D,O
Seattle Pacific University	M,O
The Seattle School of Theology and Psychology	M
Selma University	M
Seton Hall University	M,O
Sioux Falls Seminary	M
Southern Adventist University	M
The Southern Baptist Theological Seminary	M,D
Southern California Seminary	M,D
Southern Evangelical Seminary	M,D,O
Southern Methodist University	M,D
Southwestern Assemblies of God University	M
Stanford University	D
SUM Bible College & Theological Seminary	M
Syracuse University	M,D
Temple University	M,D*
Trevecca Nazarene University	M
Trinity Baptist College	M
Trinity International University Florida	M,O
Trinity School for Ministry	M,D,O
Union University	M,D
United Lutheran Seminary	M,D
United Lutheran Seminary	M,D,O
United Theological Seminary of the Twin Cities	M,D,O
Université de Montréal	M,D,O
Université de Sherbrooke	M,D,O
Université du Québec à Montréal	M,D
Université Laval	M,D
The University of British Columbia	M,D
University of Calgary	M,D
University of California, Berkeley	D
University of California, Riverside	M,D
University of California, Santa Barbara	M,D
University of Chicago	M,D
University of Colorado Boulder	M
University of Denver	M,D,O
University of Florida	M
University of Georgia	M
University of Hawaii at Manoa	M
University of Illinois at Urbana–Champaign	M
The University of Iowa	M,D
The University of Kansas	M,O
University of Lethbridge	M,D
The University of Manchester	D
University of Manitoba	M,D
University of Michigan	M,D
University of Minnesota, Twin Cities Campus	M,D
University of Missouri	M
The University of North Carolina at Chapel Hill	M,D
The University of North Carolina at Charlotte	M
University of Notre Dame	M
University of Ottawa	M,D
University of Pennsylvania	D*
University of Regina	M
University of St. Thomas (MN)	M
University of St. Thomas (TX)	M
University of Saskatchewan	M
University of South Africa	M,D
University of South Carolina	M
University of South Florida	M,D
The University of Tennessee	M,D
University of the Cumberlands	M
University of the West	M,D
University of Toronto	M,D
University of Valley Forge	M
University of Virginia	M,D
University of Washington	M,D
University of Waterloo	D
The University of Winnipeg	M
Vancouver School of Theology	M,O
Vanderbilt University	M,D*
Vanguard University of Southern California	M
Virginia University of Lynchburg	M,D
Wake Forest University	M
Walla Walla University	M
Washington Adventist University	M
Washington University in St. Louis	M
Wayland Baptist University	M
Wesley Biblical Seminary	M
Western Michigan University	M,O
Western Seminary	M,O
Westminster Seminary California	M
Westminster Theological Seminary	M,D,O
Wilfrid Laurier University	M,D
Won Institute of Graduate Studies	M
Wycliffe College	M,D,O
Yale University	D
Yeshiva Derech Chaim	D

RELIGIOUS EDUCATION

Institution	Degree
Andrews University	M,D,O
Asbury Theological Seminary	M,D,O
Biola University	M,D,O
Boston College	M,D,O
Boston University	M,D
Brandeis University	M,O
Brigham Young University	M
Calvary University	M
Calvin Theological Seminary	M,D
Capital University	M
Carolina Christian College	M
Claremont School of Theology	M,D
Clarks Summit University	M,D
Columbia International University	M,D,O
Concordia University Chicago	M
Concordia University, Nebraska	M
Dallas Baptist University	M
Dallas Theological Seminary	M,D,O
Felician University	M,O
Fordham University	M,D
Gardner-Webb University	M,D
Garrett-Evangelical Theological Seminary	M,D
Global University	M,D
Gratz College	M,D
Hebrew College	M,O
Hebrew Union College–Jewish Institute of Religion (NY)	M
Houston Baptist University	M,D
Inter American University of Puerto Rico, Metropolitan Campus	D
Interdenominational Theological Center	M,D
The Jewish Theological Seminary	M,D
Lancaster Theological Seminary	M,D,O
La Sierra University	M
Liberty University	M,D
Lincoln Christian Seminary	M,D
Loyola University Chicago	M,O
Maple Springs Baptist Bible College and Seminary	M,D,O
Midwestern Baptist Theological Seminary	M,D,O
Milligan College	M,D,O
Moody Theological Seminary–Michigan	M,O
Newman Theological College	M,O
New Orleans Baptist Theological Seminary	M,D
Oral Roberts University	M,D
Palm Beach Atlantic University	M
Pfeiffer University	M
Phillips Theological Seminary	M,D
Pontifical Catholic University of Puerto Rico	M
Providence University College & Theological Seminary	M,D
Reformed Theological Seminary–Jackson Campus	M,D,O
Regent University	M
Rochester College	M
St. Augustine's Seminary of Toronto	M,O
Saint Mary's University of Minnesota	M
Saints Cyril and Methodius Seminary	M
Selma University	M
Shasta Bible College	M
Southeastern Baptist Theological Seminary	M,D
Southern Adventist University	M
Southern Evangelical Seminary	M,D,O
Southwestern Assemblies of God University	M
Southwestern Baptist Theological Seminary	M,D
Trinity International University	M,D,O
Unification Theological Seminary	M,D
Union Presbyterian Seminary	M,D
University of Detroit Mercy	M,D,O
University of St. Michael's College	M,D,O
University of St. Thomas (TX)	M,D
University of St. Thomas (MN)	M
University of San Francisco	M,D
Vancouver School of Theology	M,O
Vanguard University of Southern California	M
Walsh University	M
Wesley Biblical Seminary	M
Wheaton College	M
Xavier University	M*
Yeshiva University	M,D

REPRODUCTIVE BIOLOGY

Institution	Degree
Eastern Virginia Medical School	M
Rutgers University–New Brunswick	M,D
Tufts University	M,D
The University of British Columbia	M,D
University of Hawaii at Manoa	M,D
University of Saskatchewan	M,D
University of Wyoming	M,D

RHETORIC

Institution	Degree
Abilene Christian University	M
Arizona State University at the Tempe campus	M,D,O
Ball State University	M,D
Bob Jones University	M,D,O
Boise State University	M
Bowling Green State University	M,D
Brigham Young University	M
California State University, Dominguez Hills	M,O
California State University, Fresno	M
California State University, Northridge	M
California State University, Stanislaus	M,O
Carnegie Mellon University	M,D
The Catholic University of America	M,D,O
Clemson University	M,D
Colorado State University	M,D
DePaul University	M
Duquesne University	M,D
East Carolina University	M,D,O
Eastern Washington University	M
Florida State University	M,D
George Mason University	M,D,O
Georgia State University	M,D
Indiana University Bloomington	M,D
Iowa State University of Science and Technology	M,D
James Madison University	M
Kent State University	M,D
Michigan State University	M,D
Monmouth University	M
New Mexico Highlands University	M
New Mexico State University	M,D
North Carolina State University	M,D
North Dakota State University	M,D
Northern Arizona University	M,D,O
Northern Kentucky University	M,O
Northwestern University	M,D
Ohio University	M,D
Old Dominion University	M,D
Oregon State University	M,D
Rensselaer Polytechnic Institute	M,D
Rowan University	O
St. Cloud State University	M

Institution	Degree
San Diego State University	M
Southern Illinois University Carbondale	M,D
Syracuse University	M,D
Texas Christian University	M,D
Texas State University	M
Texas Tech University	M,D
Texas Woman's University	M,D
The University of Alabama	M
The University of Alabama at Birmingham	M
The University of Arizona	M,D
University of Arkansas at Little Rock	M
University of California, Berkeley	D
University of Central Oklahoma	M
University of Dayton	M
The University of Findlay	M,D
University of Houston–Downtown	M
The University of Iowa	M,D
University of Louisiana at Lafayette	M,D
University of Louisville	M,D
University of Massachusetts Amherst	M,D
University of Michigan–Flint	M
University of Nebraska–Lincoln	M,D
University of North Alabama	M
The University of North Carolina at Greensboro	M,D
University of Oklahoma	M,D*
University of Southern California	D
University of South Florida	M,D
The University of Tennessee at Chattanooga	M
The University of Texas at El Paso	M,D,O
University of Utah	M,D
University of Wisconsin–Madison	M,D
University of Wisconsin–Milwaukee	M,D,O*
Wayne State University	M,D
Western Carolina University	M,O

RISK MANAGEMENT

Institution	Degree
Boston University	M
Brandeis University	M
California State University, Fullerton	M
Concordia University Wisconsin	M
DePaul University	M,D
Florida State University	M,D
Georgia State University	M,D,O
Husson University	M
Iona College	M,O
Johns Hopkins University	M*
Loyola University Chicago	M
Metropolitan College of New York	M
New York University	M*
Ohio Dominican University	M
Pace University	M
Queens College of the City University of New York	M
St. John's University (NY)	M
Saint Peter's University	
Temple University	D*
University of Colorado Denver	M
University of Connecticut	M
University of Michigan	M,D
University of Pennsylvania	M,D*
University of Saint Mary	M
The University of Texas at Austin	M,D
University of Wisconsin–Madison	M,D
Yeshiva University	M

ROMANCE LANGUAGES

Institution	Degree
Boston University	M,D
Columbia University	M,D
Cornell University	M,D
Hunter College of the City University of New York	M
Johns Hopkins University	M,D*
Michigan State University	M,D
New York University	M,D*
Northern Illinois University	M
Queens College of the City University of New York	M
San Diego State University	M
Stony Brook University, State University of New York	M,D
Texas Tech University	M,D
University at Buffalo, the State University of New York	M,D
The University of Alabama	M,D
University of California, Berkeley	D
University of Chicago	M,D
University of Cincinnati	M,D
University of Illinois at Urbana–Champaign	D
University of Miami	D
University of Missouri	M,D
University of Missouri–Kansas City	M
University of New Orleans	M
The University of North Carolina at Chapel Hill	M,D
University of Notre Dame	M,D
University of Oregon	M,D
University of Pennsylvania	M,D*
University of South Africa	M,D
The University of Texas at Austin	M,D
Washington University in St. Louis	D
Wayne State University	M

RURAL PLANNING AND STUDIES

Institution	Degree
Brandon University	M,O
Dalhousie University	M,O
East Carolina University	M,O
Iowa State University of Science and Technology	D
Université Laval	O
University of Alaska Fairbanks	M

University of Guelph M,D
University of Montana M
University of Wyoming M

RURAL SOCIOLOGY
Auburn University M
Cornell University M,D
Iowa State University of Science and Technology M,D
The Ohio State University M,D
Penn State University Park M,D,O*
University of Alberta M,D
University of Missouri M,D
University of Montana M
University of Puerto Rico–Mayagüez M
University of Wisconsin–Madison M,D

RUSSIAN
American University M,O
Boston College M
Brown University M,D
Columbia University M,D
Harvard University D*
Kent State University M,D
McGill University M,D
Middlebury College M,D
New York University M*
Penn State University Park M,D*
Princeton University D
The University of Arizona M
University of California, Berkeley D
University of Missouri M
University of Oregon M
University of South Africa M,D
The University of Tennessee D
University of Washington M,D
University of Waterloo M,D
Yale University D

SAFETY ENGINEERING
Embry-Riddle Aeronautical University–Prescott M
Indiana University Bloomington M,D
Murray State University M
New Jersey Institute of Technology M,D
Rochester Institute of Technology M
The University of Alabama at Birmingham M
University of Minnesota, Duluth M
University of Southern California M,D,O
West Virginia University M,D

SCANDINAVIAN LANGUAGES
Cornell University M,D
Harvard University D*
University of California, Berkeley D
University of California, Los Angeles M
University of Massachusetts Amherst M,D
University of Minnesota, Twin Cities Campus M,D
University of Washington M,D
University of Wisconsin–Madison M,D

SCHOOL NURSING
California State University, Fullerton M,D
Cambridge College M,D,O
Eastern Mennonite University M,D
Eastern University M,O
La Salle University M,D,O
Lewis University M,D
Rowan University M,D,O
Seton Hall University M,D
University of Illinois at Chicago M,O
West Chester University of Pennsylvania M,D,O
William Paterson University of New Jersey M,D,O
Wright State University M

SCHOOL PSYCHOLOGY
Abilene Christian University O
Adelphi University M
Adler University M
Alabama Agricultural and Mechanical University M,O
Alfred University M,D,O
Alliant International University–Irvine M,D,O
Alliant International University–Los Angeles M,D,O
Alliant International University–San Diego M,D,O
Alliant International University–San Francisco M,D,O
American University of Beirut M,D
Andrews University M,O
Appalachian State University M
Argosy University, Hawai'i M
Argosy University, Phoenix M,D
Arkansas State University M,O
Assumption College M,O
Auburn University at Montgomery M,O
Augusta University M,O
Azusa Pacific University M,D
Ball State University M,D,O
Barry University M,O
Baylor University M,D,O
Brigham Young University M,D,O
Brooklyn College of the City University of New York M,O
California Baptist University M
California State University, Chico M
California State University, Dominguez Hills M
California State University, Fresno M,O

California State University, Los Angeles M,D
California State University, Northridge M
California State University, Sacramento M
California University of Pennsylvania M
Cambridge College M,O
Campbellsville University M
Canisius College M
Capella University M,D
Central Connecticut State University M,O
Central Michigan University D,O
Central Washington University O
Chaminade University of Honolulu M
Chapman University M,D,O*
The Chicago School of Professional Psychology D,O
The Chicago School of Professional Psychology at Washington DC O
The Citadel, The Military College of South Carolina M,D
The College of New Rochelle M
College of Saint Elizabeth M,D
College of St. Joseph M
The College of Saint Rose M,O
The College of William and Mary M,O
Creighton University M
DePaul University M,D
Doane University M,D,O
Duquesne University M,D
Eastern Illinois University M,O
Eastern Kentucky University M,O
Eastern University M,O
Eastern Washington University O
East Tennessee State University M
Edinboro University of Pennsylvania M,O
Emporia State University M,O
Evangel University M
Fairfield University M,O
Fairleigh Dickinson University, Metropolitan Campus M,D
Florida Gulf Coast University M
Florida International University M,D,O
Fordham University M,D
Fort Hays State University O
Francis Marion University M,O
Fresno Pacific University M
Gallaudet University M,D,O
Gardner-Webb University M
George Fox University M,O
Georgian Court University M,O
Georgia Southern University M,O
Georgia State University M,D,O
Grand Valley State University M,O
Hofstra University M,D
Hood College M
Houston Baptist University M
Howard University M,D
Humboldt State University M
Husson University M
Idaho State University M,D,O
Illinois State University M,D,O
Immaculata University M,D,O
Indiana State University M,D,O
Indiana University Bloomington M,D,O
Indiana University of Pennsylvania D,O
Indiana University South Bend M,O
Inter American University of Puerto Rico, Metropolitan Campus M,D
Inter American University of Puerto Rico, San Germán Campus M,D
Iona College M,O
Jackson State University M
James Madison University M,D,O
Kean University D,O
Kent State University M,D,O
La Sierra University M,O
Lehigh University D,O
Lesley University M,D,O
Lewis & Clark College M,O
Liberty University M,D,O
Lindenwood University M,D,O
Lipscomb University M,D,O
Long Island University–Hudson M,O
Long Island University–LIU Post M,D,O
Louisiana State University and Agricultural & Mechanical College M,D
Louisiana State University in Shreveport O
Loyola Marymount University M
Loyola University Chicago D,O
Marist College M,O
Marshall University O
McNeese State University M,O
Mercer University M,D
Mercy College M
Michigan State University M,D,O
MidAmerica Nazarene University M
Middle Tennessee State University M,O
Millersville University of Pennsylvania M
Minnesota State University Mankato M,D
Minnesota State University Moorhead M
Minot State University O
Mississippi State University M,D,O
Monmouth University M,D,O
Montana State University M,D,O
Mount Saint Vincent University M
Murray State University M,D,O
National Louis University M,D,O
National University M,O
New Mexico State University M,D,O
Niagara University M,O

Nicholls State University M,O
North Carolina State University D
North Dakota State University M,D
Northeastern University M,D,O
Northern Arizona University M,D,O
Northern Vermont University–Johnson M
Northwest Nazarene University M
Nova Southeastern University M,D,O
Old Dominion University M,D,O
Oregon State University M,D
Oregon State University–Cascades M
Ottawa University M
Our Lady of the Lake University M
Pace University M
Penn State University Park M,D,O*
Philadelphia College of Osteopathic Medicine M,D,O*
Phillips Graduate University M
Pittsburg State University O
Plymouth State University O
Purdue University Northwest M
Queens College of the City University of New York M,O
Quincy University M
Radford University O
Rhode Island College M,O
Rider University O
Roberts Wesleyan College M,D
Rochester Institute of Technology M,O
Roosevelt University M
Rowan University M,O
Rutgers University–New Brunswick M,D
St. John's University (NY) M,D
Saint Mary's College of California M,O
Sam Houston State University M,D,O
San Diego State University M
San Francisco State University M,O
Seattle University M
Seton Hall University M
Slippery Rock University of Pennsylvania M
Sonoma State University M
Southern Connecticut State University M,O
Southern Illinois University Edwardsville O
Southwestern Oklahoma State University O
State University of New York at Plattsburgh M,O
Stephen F. Austin State University M
Syracuse University M,D,O
Teachers College, Columbia University M,D,O
Temple University M,D,O*
Texas A&M University M,D
Texas A&M University–Central Texas M,O
Texas State University O
Texas Woman's University M,D,O
Towson University M
Trinity University M
Tufts University M,O
Union College (KY) M
University of Alberta M,D
The University of Arizona D,O
The University of British Columbia M,D,O
University of Calgary M,D
University of California, Riverside M,D,O
University of California, Santa Barbara M,D,O
University of Central Arkansas M,D,O
University of Central Florida O
University of Central Oklahoma M
University of Cincinnati D,O
University of Colorado Denver M,D
University of Dayton M,O
University of Delaware M,D,O
University of Denver M,D,O
University of Detroit Mercy M,D,O
University of Florida M,D,O
University of Hartford M
University of Houston–Clear Lake M
University of Houston–Victoria M
The University of Iowa M,D,O
The University of Kansas D,O
University of Kentucky M,D,O
University of La Verne M,O
University of Louisville M,D
University of Lynchburg M
University of Manitoba M,D
University of Maryland, College Park M,D,O
University of Massachusetts Amherst M,D,O
University of Massachusetts Boston M,D,O
University of Memphis M,D,O
University of Minnesota, Twin Cities Campus M,D,O
University of Missouri M,D,O
University of Missouri–St. Louis M,O
University of Montana M
University of Nebraska at Kearney M,O
University of Nebraska at Omaha M,D,O
University of Nebraska–Lincoln M,D,O
The University of North Carolina at Chapel Hill M,D,O
The University of North Carolina at Greensboro M,D,O
University of Northern Colorado O
University of Northern Iowa M,O
University of Oregon M,D

University of Phoenix–Las Vegas Campus M
University of Rhode Island M,D
University of San Diego M
University of Saskatchewan M,D
University of South Carolina D
University of South Dakota M,D,O
University of Southern Maine M,D
University of South Florida M,D,O
The University of Tennessee M,D,O
The University of Tennessee at Chattanooga M,D,O
The University of Texas at Austin M,D
The University of Texas at San Antonio M,O
The University of Texas at Tyler M
The University of Texas Rio Grande Valley M
University of the Pacific M,D,O
University of the Virgin Islands M,D,O
The University of Toledo M,D,O
University of Utah M,D,O
University of Vermont M
University of Virginia M,D
University of Washington M,D
University of Wisconsin–Eau Claire M,O
University of Wisconsin–La Crosse M,O
University of Wisconsin–Milwaukee M,D,O*
University of Wisconsin–River Falls M,O
University of Wisconsin–Stout M,O
University of Wisconsin–Superior M
University of Wisconsin–Whitewater M,O
Utah State University M,D
Valparaiso University M,O
Wayne State University M,D,O
Western Illinois University M,O
Western Kentucky University M
Wichita State University M,D,O
William James College M,D,O
Worcester State University M,O
Yeshiva University D
Youngstown State University M,D,O

SCIENCE EDUCATION
Adams State University M
Alabama Agricultural and Mechanical University M,O
Alabama State University M,O
Alverno College M
American University of Beirut M,D
American University of Puerto Rico M
Andrews University M,D,O
Antioch University New England M
Appalachian State University M
Arcadia University M,D,O
Arkansas State University M,O
Asbury University M
Athabasca University M,O
Augustana University M
Aurora University M
Austin Peay State University M
Bard College M
Binghamton University, State University of New York M
Biola University M,O
Bloomsburg University of Pennsylvania M
Blue Mountain College M
Boston College M,D,O
Bowling Green State University M
Bridgewater State University M
Brigham Young University M,D
Brooklyn College of the City University of New York M
Brown University M
Buffalo State College, State University of New York M
California Baptist University M
California State University, Bakersfield M
California State University, Long Beach M
California State University, Northridge M
California University of Pennsylvania M
Cambridge College M,D,O
Campbellsville University M
Caribbean University M,D
Carlow University M
Carthage College M,O
Catawba College M
Central Connecticut State University M,O
Central Michigan University M
Chatham University M
The Citadel, The Military College of South Carolina M,O
City College of the City University of New York M
Clarion University of Pennsylvania M
Clark Atlanta University M
Clemson University D,O
Cleveland State University M
The College at Brockport, State University of New York M,O
College of Charleston M
Columbia University M,D,O
Columbus State University M,O
Concordia University (United States) M,D
Converse College M
Delaware State University M

*M—masters degree; D—doctorate; O—other advanced degree; *—Close-Up and/or Display*

Institution	Degree
DePaul University	M,D
Drake University	M,D,O
Duquesne University	M
East Carolina University	M,D
Eastern Kentucky University	M
Eastern Michigan University	M
Eastern University	M,O
Elizabeth City State University	M
Elms College	M,O
Fairleigh Dickinson University, Metropolitan Campus	M
Fitchburg State University	M
Florida Agricultural and Mechanical University	M
Florida Atlantic University	M,D
Florida Gulf Coast University	M
Florida International University	M,D,O
Florida State University	M,D
Fresno Pacific University	M
George Mason University	M
The George Washington University	M
Georgia State University	M,D
Grambling State University	M,D,O
Grand Canyon University	M,D,O
Hamline University	M,D
Harrison Middleton University	M,D
Heritage University	M
Hofstra University	M,D,O
Hood College	M,O
Houston Baptist University	M,D
Hunter College of the City University of New York	M
Illinois Institute of Technology	M,D
Indiana State University	M,D
Indiana University Bloomington	M,D,O
Instituto Tecnológico y de Estudios Superiores de Monterrey, Campus Monterrey	M,D
Inter American University of Puerto Rico, Arecibo Campus	M
Inter American University of Puerto Rico, Metropolitan Campus	M
Inter American University of Puerto Rico, Ponce Campus	M
Inter American University of Puerto Rico, San Germán Campus	M
Iona College	M
Iowa State University of Science and Technology	M
Jackson State University	M,D
Kennesaw State University	M
Lake Forest College	M
Laurentian University	O
Lawrence Technological University	M
Lebanon Valley College	M,O
Lehman College of the City University of New York	M
Lesley University	M,D,O
Lewis University	M
Manhattanville College	M,O
McDaniel College	M,O
McNeese State University	O
Mercer University	M,D,O
Metropolitan State University	M
Michigan Technological University	M,D,O
Middle Tennessee State University	M,D
Millersville University of Pennsylvania	M,D
Minnesota State University Mankato	M
Minot State University	M
Mississippi College	M,D,O
Missouri State University	M,O
Molloy College	M,O
Montclair State University	M
Morehead State University	M
Morgan State University	M,D
National Louis University	M,D,O
New Mexico Institute of Mining and Technology	M
New York Institute of Technology	M,O
New York University	M,D,O*
North Carolina Agricultural and Technical State University	M
North Carolina State University	M,D
North Dakota State University	D
Northeastern Illinois University	M
Northeastern State University	M
Northern Arizona University	M
Northern Michigan University	M
Northern Vermont University–Lyndon	M
Northwest Missouri State University	M,O
Oregon State University	M,D
Our Lady of the Lake University	M
Pacific University	M
Portland State University	M,D,O
Purdue University	M,D,O
Purdue University Global	M
Purdue University Northwest	M
Queens College of the City University of New York	M,O
Quinnipiac University	M
Regent University	M,D,O
Rice University	M,D
Rowan University	M,O
Rutgers University–New Brunswick	M,D
St. John Fisher College	M
St. John's University (NY)	D
Saint Xavier University	M
Salem State University	M
San Diego State University	M,D
Seattle Pacific University	M
Shippensburg University of Pennsylvania	M
Slippery Rock University of Pennsylvania	M
Smith College	M
South Carolina State University	M
Southern Connecticut State University	M,O

Institution	Degree
Southern University and Agricultural and Mechanical College	D
Southwestern Oklahoma State University	M
State University of New York at New Paltz	M,O
State University of New York at Plattsburgh	M
State University of New York College at Cortland	M
State University of New York College at Old Westbury	M
State University of New York College at Potsdam	M
Stevenson University	M
Stony Brook University, State University of New York	M,D
Syracuse University	M,D
Teachers College, Columbia University	M,D
Teachers College of San Joaquin	M
Temple University	M*
Tennessee Technological University	M,O
Texas A&M University–Kingsville	M
Texas Christian University	M,D
Texas Tech University	M,D
Tufts University	M,D
Universidad Nacional Pedro Henríquez Ureña	M
University at Buffalo, the State University of New York	M,D
The University of Akron	M
The University of Alabama in Huntsville	M,D,O
University of Arkansas at Pine Bluff	M
The University of British Columbia	M,D
University of California, Berkeley	M,D
University of California, San Diego	D
University of Central Florida	M,O
University of Chicago	D
University of Colorado Denver	M,D
University of Connecticut	M,D
The University of Findlay	M,D
University of Florida	M,D,O
University of Georgia	M,D,O
University of Illinois at Chicago	D
University of Illinois at Urbana–Champaign	M,D
University of Indianapolis	M
The University of Iowa	M,D
University of Lynchburg	M
University of Maryland, Baltimore County	M
University of Massachusetts Amherst	M,D,O
University of Massachusetts Dartmouth	M,D,O
University of Memphis	M,D,O
University of Miami	D
University of Minnesota, Twin Cities Campus	M
University of Missouri	M,D,O
University of Nebraska at Kearney	M,D,O
University of Nebraska at Omaha	M,O
University of New Hampshire	M,D
University of New Mexico	O
The University of North Carolina at Chapel Hill	M
The University of North Carolina at Greensboro	M,D,O
The University of North Carolina at Pembroke	M
University of Northern Colorado	M,D
University of Northern Iowa	M
University of North Georgia	M
University of Oklahoma	M,D*
University of Pennsylvania	M,O*
University of Phoenix–Online Campus	M,O
University of Pittsburgh	M,D*
University of Puerto Rico–Río Piedras	M,D
University of St. Francis (IL)	M,D,O
University of San Diego	M
University of South Africa	M,D
University of South Alabama	M,D
University of South Carolina	M,D
University of South Dakota	M
University of South Florida, St. Petersburg	M
The University of Tennessee	M,D,O
The University of Texas at Arlington	M
The University of Texas at Dallas	M
The University of Toledo	M,D,O
University of Utah	M,D
University of Vermont	M,D
University of Victoria	M,D
University of Virginia	M,D,O
University of Washington	M,D
University of Washington, Tacoma	M
The University of West Alabama	M
University of Wisconsin–Milwaukee	M*
University of Wisconsin–River Falls	M
University of Wisconsin–Stevens Point	M
University of Wyoming	M
Wagner College	M
Walden University	M,D,O
Warner University	M
Wayland Baptist University	M
Wayne State College	M
Wayne State University	M,D,O
West Chester University of Pennsylvania	M,O
Western Governors University	M,O
Western Michigan University	M,D,O
Western Oregon University	M

Institution	Degree
Western Washington University	M
Westfield State University	M
Widener University	M,D
Wisconsin Lutheran College	M
Wright State University	M,D
Youngstown State University	M

SECONDARY EDUCATION

Institution	Degree
Acacia University	M
Adelphi University	M
Alabama Agricultural and Mechanical University	M,O
Alabama State University	M,O
Alcorn State University	M
American International College	M,D,O
American Public University System	M,O
Andrews University	M,D,O
Aquinas College (TN)	M
Arcadia University	M,D,O
Argosy University, Atlanta	M,D,O
Argosy University, Chicago	M,D,O
Argosy University, Hawai'i	M,D
Argosy University, Los Angeles	M,D
Argosy University, Northern Virginia	M,D,O
Argosy University, Orange County	M,D
Argosy University, Phoenix	M,D
Argosy University, Seattle	M,D
Argosy University, Tampa	M,D,O
Argosy University, Twin Cities	M,D,O
Arizona State University at the Tempe campus	M
Auburn University at Montgomery	M,O
Augusta University	M,O
Avila University	M,O
Ball State University	M
Bard College	M
Bellarmine University	M,D,O
Berry College	M
Bethel University (MN)	M,D,O
Binghamton University, State University of New York	M
Blue Mountain College	M
Bob Jones University	M,D,O
Boston College	M,D,O
Bowie State University	M
Brandeis University	M,O
Brandman University	M
Brenau University	M,O
Bridgewater State University	M
Brooklyn College of the City University of New York	M
Brown University	M
Cabrini University	M,D
California State University, Fullerton	M
California State University, Long Beach	M
California State University, Northridge	M
California State University, Stanislaus	M
California University of Pennsylvania	M
Campbell University	M
Canisius College	M,O
Carroll University	M
Carson-Newman University	M
The Catholic University of America	M
Centenary College of Louisiana	M
Central Connecticut State University	M,O
Central Michigan University	M,D,O
Chadron State College	M,O
Chaminade University of Honolulu	M
Chapman University	M,D,O*
Chatham University	M
Chestnut Hill College	M
Chicago State University	M
The Citadel, The Military College of South Carolina	M,O
City College of the City University of New York	M,O
Clemson University	M,D,O
Colgate University	M
The College of New Jersey	M
College of St. Joseph	M
The College of Saint Rose	M,O
College of Staten Island of the City University of New York	M
The Colorado College	M
Columbus State University	M,O
Concordia University (United States)	M,D
Concordia University Chicago	M
Concordia University, Nebraska	M
Converse College	M
Cornell University	M,D
Creighton University	M
Dakota Wesleyan University	M
Dallas Baptist University	M
Delta State University	M,D,O
DePaul University	M,D
DeSales University	M
Dominican University	M
Drew University	M,D,O
Drury University	M
Duquesne University	M
D'Youville College	M,D
Eastern Connecticut State University	M
Eastern Illinois University	M
Eastern Kentucky University	M
Eastern Michigan University	M
Eastern Nazarene College	M,O
Eastern New Mexico University	M
Eastern Oregon University	M,O
Eastern University	M
East Stroudsburg University of Pennsylvania	M,D
East Tennessee State University	M
Edinboro University of Pennsylvania	M
Elms College	M,O

Institution	Degree
Emory University	M,D
Endicott College	M
Evangel University	M
Fairfield University	M,O
Fayetteville State University	M
Florida Agricultural and Mechanical University	M
Florida Atlantic University	M
Fontbonne University	M
Frostburg State University	M,D
Gallaudet University	M,D,O
George Mason University	M
The George Washington University	M
Georgia College & State University	M
Georgia Southern University	M,O
Georgia State University	M,D
Gonzaga University	M
Gordon College	M
Goucher College	M,O
Grand Canyon University	M,D,O
Grand Valley State University	M
Greenville University	M
Harding University	M,O
Hawai'i Pacific University	M
High Point University	M,D
Hofstra University	M,D,O
Hood College	M,O
Hope International University	M
Howard University	M
Hunter College of the City University of New York	M
Idaho State University	M
Immaculata University	M,D,O
Indiana University Bloomington	M,D,O
Indiana University Northwest	M,O
Indiana University South Bend	M,O
Indiana University Southeast	M
Instituto Tecnologico de Santo Domingo	M,O
Ithaca College	M
Jacksonville State University	M
James Madison University	M
John Brown University	M
Johnson & Wales University	M
Kennesaw State University	M,D,O
Kent State University	M,D
Keuka College	M
Kutztown University of Pennsylvania	M,D
LaGrange College	M,O
Lake Forest College	M
Lancaster Bible College	M,D
La Salle University	M,O
Lee University	M,O
Lehman College of the City University of New York	M
Le Moyne College	M,O
Lenoir-Rhyne University	M
Lesley University	M,D,O
Lewis & Clark College	M
Lewis University	M
Lincoln University (MO)	M
Long Island University–LIU Post	M,D,O
Louisiana State University and Agricultural & Mechanical College	M,D,O
Louisiana Tech University	M,D,O
Loyola Marymount University	M
Loyola University Chicago	M
Loyola University Maryland	M
Loyola University New Orleans	M
Manhattanville College	M,O
Mansfield University of Pennsylvania	M
Marquette University	M,D,O
Marymount University	M
Maryville University of Saint Louis	M,D
Marywood University	M
McDaniel College	M,O
McNeese State University	M,O
Medaille College	M
Mercer University	M,D,O
Mercer University	M,D,O
Mercy College	M,O
Mercyhurst University	M
Metropolitan State University	M
Middle Tennessee State University	M,O
Milligan College	M,D,O
Mississippi College	M,D,O
Mississippi State University	M,D,O
Missouri State University	M,O
Monmouth University	M,D,O
Montana State University Billings	M
Morehead State University	M
Mount St. Joseph University	M,O
Murray State University	M,D,O
National Louis University	M,D,O
Nebraska Christian College of Hope International University	M
Neumann University	M
New Jersey City University	M
New York Institute of Technology	M
New York University	M,D,O*
Niagara University	M
Nicholls State University	M
Norfolk State University	M
North Carolina Agricultural and Technical State University	M
Northeastern Illinois University	M
Northern Arizona University	M,D,O
Northwest Christian University	M
Northwestern Oklahoma State University	M
Northwestern State University of Louisiana	M,O
Northwestern University	M
Oakland City University	M,D
Oakland University	M,D
Ohio University	M,D
Old Dominion University	M,D
Olivet Nazarene University	M
Pacific Union College	M
Pacific University	M

Piedmont College — M,D,O
Pittsburg State University — M,O
Point Park University — M,D
Prescott College — M,D
Providence College — M
Purdue University Fort Wayne — M,O
Purdue University Global — M
Queens College of the City University of New York — M,O
Quinnipiac University — M
Regis University — M,O
Rhode Island College — M
Rider University — M
Roberts Wesleyan College — M
Rochester Institute of Technology — M
Rockford University — M
Roosevelt University — M
St. Bonaventure University — M
St. John's University (NY) — M
Saint Joseph's University — M,D,O
Saint Mary's University of Minnesota — M
Saint Peter's University — M
St. Thomas Aquinas College — M,O
Saint Xavier University — M
Salem College — M
Salem State University — M
Salisbury University — M
Samford University — M
San Diego State University — M
San Francisco State University — M
Seattle Pacific University — M
Siena Heights University — M
Sierra Nevada College — M
Simpson College — M
Slippery Rock University of Pennsylvania — M
Smith College — M
South Carolina State University — M
Southeast Missouri State University — M,D,O
Southern Oregon University — M
Southern University and Agricultural and Mechanical College — M
Southwestern Assemblies of God University — M
Spalding University — M
Springfield College — M,O
Spring Hill College — M
Stanford University — M
State University of New York at Fredonia — M
State University of New York at New Paltz — M
State University of New York at Oswego — M
State University of New York at Plattsburgh — M
State University of New York College at Cortland — M
State University of New York College at Geneseo — M
State University of New York College at Potsdam — M
Stephen F. Austin State University — M,D
Sul Ross State University — M
Tarleton State University — M
Teachers College, Columbia University — M,D
Temple University — M*
Tennessee Technological University — M,O
Texas A&M University–Commerce — M,D,O
Texas A&M University–Corpus Christi — M
Texas Southern University — M
Texas State University — M
Texas Tech University — M
Towson University — M
Trevecca Nazarene University — M
Trinity Washington University — M
Troy University — M
Tufts University — M,D
Union College (KY) — M
Universidad Metropolitana — M
The University of Akron — M
The University of Alabama — M,D,O
The University of Alabama at Birmingham — M
The University of Alabama in Huntsville — M,O
University of Alaska Southeast — M
University of Alberta — M,D
The University of Arizona — M,D
University of Arkansas — M,O
University of Arkansas at Little Rock — M
University of Arkansas at Pine Bluff — M
University of Bridgeport — M,D,O
University of California, Irvine — M,D
University of Central Oklahoma — M
University of Colorado Denver — M
University of Connecticut — M,D
University of Dayton — M
University of Guam — M
University of Illinois at Chicago — M,D
University of Indianapolis — M
The University of Iowa — M,D
University of Kentucky — M
University of La Verne — M,D,O
University of Louisiana at Monroe — M
University of Louisville — M,D,O
University of Mary Hardin-Baylor — M,D
University of Maryland, College Park — M,D,O
University of Massachusetts Amherst — M
University of Massachusetts Dartmouth — M
University of Memphis — M,D,O

University of Michigan–Flint — M,D,O
University of Mississippi — M,O
University of Missouri–St. Louis — M
University of Montevallo — M
University of Nebraska at Kearney — M
University of Nebraska at Omaha — M,O
University of Nevada, Las Vegas — M,D,O
University of Nevada, Reno — M
University of New Hampshire — M,O
University of New Mexico — M
University of North Alabama — M
The University of North Carolina at Chapel Hill — M
The University of North Carolina at Charlotte — M,D,O
The University of North Carolina Wilmington — M
University of Northern Iowa — M
University of North Florida — M
University of North Georgia — M
University of Pennsylvania — M*
University of Phoenix–Bay Area Campus — M,D,O
University of Phoenix–Central Valley Campus — M
University of Phoenix–Hawaii Campus — M
University of Phoenix–Online Campus — M,O
University of Phoenix–Phoenix Campus — M
University of Phoenix–Sacramento Valley Campus — M,O
University of Phoenix–San Diego Campus — M
University of Pittsburgh — M,D*
University of Puget Sound — M
University of St. Francis (IL) — M,D,O
University of Saint Francis (IN) — M
University of Saint Joseph — M
University of St. Thomas (TX) — M,D
The University of Scranton — M
University of South Alabama — M
University of South Carolina — M,D
University of South Dakota — M
University of Southern Indiana — M
University of Southern Mississippi — M,D
University of South Florida — O
The University of Tennessee — M,D,O
The University of Tennessee at Chattanooga — M,D,O
The University of Tennessee at Martin — M
The University of Texas Rio Grande Valley — M,D
University of the Cumberlands — M,D,O
University of the District of Columbia — M
University of the Virgin Islands — M
The University of Toledo — M,D,O
University of Vermont — M
University of Washington, Bothell — M
The University of West Alabama — M
University of West Florida — M
University of West Georgia — M,D,O
University of Wisconsin–Eau Claire — M
University of Wisconsin–Milwaukee — M,D*
University of Wisconsin–Stevens Point — M
Utah State University — M
Valparaiso University — M,O
Vanderbilt University — M*
Virginia Wesleyan University — M
Wagner College — M
Wake Forest University — M
Washington State University — M,D
Washington University in St. Louis — M
Wayland Baptist University — M
Wayne State University — M,D,O
Webster University — M,O
Western Kentucky University — M,O
Western New Mexico University — M
Western Oregon University — M
Western Washington University — M
Westfield State University — M
West Virginia University — M
Wheaton College — M
Whittier College — M
Whitworth University — M
Wichita State University — M
William Carey University — M,O
William Paterson University of New Jersey — M,O
Wilmington University — M,D
Wilson College — M
Winthrop University — M
Worcester State University — M,O
Wright State University — M
Xavier University — M*

SLAVIC LANGUAGES

Brown University — M,D
Columbia University — M,D
Cornell University — M,D
Duke University — M,O
Florida State University — M
Harvard University — D*
Indiana University Bloomington — M,D
New York University — M*
Northwestern University — D
The Ohio State University — M,D
Princeton University — D
Stanford University — D
University of Alberta — M,D
University of California, Berkeley — D
University of California, Los Angeles — D
University of Chicago — M

University of Illinois at Chicago — M,D
University of Illinois at Urbana–Champaign — M,D
The University of Kansas — M,D
University of Manitoba — M
University of Michigan — M,D
The University of North Carolina at Chapel Hill — D
University of Pittsburgh — M,D*
University of Southern California — M,D
The University of Texas at Austin — M,D
University of Toronto — M,D
University of Virginia — M,D
University of Washington — M,D
University of Wisconsin–Madison — M,D
Yale University — D

SOCIAL PSYCHOLOGY

Adler University — M
Alliant International University–Los Angeles — D
Alvernia University — M
Alverno College — M
Andrews University — M
Argosy University, Atlanta — M,D,O
Argosy University, Chicago — M,D
Argosy University, Northern Virginia — M,D
Arizona State University at the Tempe campus — M,D
Ball State University — M
Becker College — M
Bowling Green State University — M,D
Brandeis University — M,D
Brock University — M,D
Brooklyn College of the City University of New York — M,D
California State University, East Bay — M
California State University, Fullerton — M
Canisius College — M
Carnegie Mellon University — D
Claremont Graduate University — M,D,O
Clark University — D
College of St. Joseph — M
Concordia University (United States) — M
Cornell University — M,D
Delaware Valley University — M
Florida Agricultural and Mechanical University — M
Florida State University — D
Future Generations University — M
The George Washington University — D
Georgia State University — D
The Graduate Center, City University of New York — D
Harvard University — D*
Hofstra University — M,D
Howard University — M,D
Humboldt State University — M
Husson University — M
Indiana University Bloomington — D
Indiana University of Pennsylvania — M
Indiana University–Purdue University Indianapolis — M,D
Indiana Wesleyan University — M
Iowa State University of Science and Technology — M,D
Lesley University — M,D,O
Loyola University Chicago — M,O
Marquette University — M,D
Martin University — M
Missouri Valley College — M
Mount Aloysius College — M
The New School — M,D
New York University — M,D,O*
Norfolk State University — M
North Carolina State University — M,D
North Dakota State University — M,D
Northwestern University — D
The Ohio State University — D
Oregon State University–Cascades — M
Penn State Harrisburg — M,D,O
Queen's University at Kingston — M,D
Rutgers University–Newark — D
Rutgers University–New Brunswick — D
Sacred Heart University — M
Sage Graduate School — M
St. Bonaventure University — M,O
Saint Martin's University — M
San Francisco State University — M,O
Southwestern College (NM) — O
Syracuse University — D
Teachers College, Columbia University — M,D
Temple University — M,D,O*
Texas Christian University — M,D
Thomas Jefferson University — M
Thomas University — M
Université du Québec à Rimouski — M
Université Laval — D
University at Albany, State University of New York — M,D
University of Alaska Anchorage — M,D
University of Alaska Fairbanks — M,O
University of Bridgeport — M,D
The University of British Columbia — M,D
University of Central Arkansas — M
University of Connecticut — M,D
University of Delaware — D
University of Denver — D
University of Guelph — M,D
University of Hawaii at Manoa — M,D

University of Houston — M,D
The University of Kansas — M,D
University of Maryland, Baltimore County — M,D
University of Maryland, College Park — M,D
University of Massachusetts Amherst — M,D
University of Massachusetts Lowell — M
University of Michigan — D
University of Minnesota, Twin Cities Campus — D
University of Missouri–Kansas City — M,D
University of Nebraska–Lincoln — M,D
University of Nevada, Reno — D
University of New Haven — M,O
The University of North Carolina at Chapel Hill — D
The University of North Carolina at Greensboro — M,D
University of Oregon — M,D
University of Phoenix–Phoenix Campus — M
University of Pittsburgh — D*
University of Puerto Rico–Río Piedras — M,D
University of Rochester — M,D*
University of South Carolina — M,D
University of Southern California — M,D
The University of Tennessee at Chattanooga — M,D,O
The University of Tennessee at Martin — M
University of Utah — D
University of Vermont — D
University of Victoria — M,D
University of Washington — M,D
University of Windsor — M,D
University of Wisconsin–Madison — D
University of Wisconsin–Superior — M
Walden University — M,D,O
Wayne State University — M,D,O
Western Illinois University — M,O
Wichita State University — D
Wilfrid Laurier University — M,D
Yale University — D

SOCIAL SCIENCES

Assumption College — O
Augusta University — M
California Institute of Technology — M,D
California State University, Chico — M
California State University, San Bernardino — M
Campbellsville University — M
Carnegie Mellon University — D
The Citadel, The Military College of South Carolina — M
Colorado School of Mines — O
Columbia University — M,D
East Carolina University — M,D,O
Eastern Michigan University — M
Elms College — M,O
Evangel University — M
Florida Agricultural and Mechanical University — M
The Graduate Center, City University of New York — M
Graduate Theological Union — M,D,O
Harrison Middleton University — M,D
Hollins University — M
Humboldt State University — M
Indiana University Bloomington — M,D,O
Indiana University–Purdue University Indianapolis — M,D,O
Massachusetts Institute of Technology — D
Mississippi College — M,O
Montclair State University — M
The New School — M,D
New York University — M,D*
Nova Southeastern University — M,D,O
The Ohio State University — M,D
Ohio University — M
Oregon State University — M,D
Southern University and Agricultural and Mechanical College — M
Syracuse University — M,D
Texas A&M International University — M
Towson University — M
Troy University — M
University at Buffalo, the State University of New York — M
University of California, Merced — M,D
University of California, Santa Barbara — D
University of California, Santa Cruz — D
University of Chicago — M,D
University of Florida — M,D,O
University of Illinois at Springfield — M,O
The University of Manchester — M,D
University of Maryland, Baltimore County — D
University of Memphis — M,D
University of Michigan — M
University of Michigan–Flint — M
University of Northern Iowa — M
University of Regina — M
University of South Florida Sarasota-Manatee — M
The University of Texas at Tyler — M
University of the Virgin Islands — M
University of Toronto — M,D
University of Washington — M,D

---

*M—masters degree; D—doctorate; O—other advanced degree; *—Close-Up and/or Display*

Wilfrid Laurier University	M
Worcester Polytechnic Institute	M,D,O
Yale University	M,D

SOCIAL SCIENCES EDUCATION

Alabama Agricultural and Mechanical University	M,O
Alabama State University	M,O
Andrews University	M,D,O
Appalachian State University	M
Arkansas State University	M,D,O
Asbury University	M
Binghamton University, State University of New York	M
Bloomsburg University of Pennsylvania	M
Bob Jones University	M,D,O
Boston College	M,D,O
Bridgewater State University	M
Brooklyn College of the City University of New York	M
Brown University	M
Buffalo State College, State University of New York	M
California State University, East Bay	M
California State University, Fresno	M
Caribbean University	M,D
Carthage College	M,O
Chadron State College	M,O
Chatham University	M
The Citadel, The Military College of South Carolina	M,O
City College of the City University of New York	M,O
The College at Brockport, State University of New York	M,O
College of St. Joseph	M
The Colorado College	M
Columbus State University	M,O
Concordia University (United States)	M,D
Converse College	M
Delta State University	M
Duquesne University	M
East Carolina University	M
Eastern Kentucky University	M
Eastern University	M,O
Fayetteville State University	M
Fitchburg State University	M
Florida Agricultural and Mechanical University	M
Florida Gulf Coast University	M
Florida International University	M,D,O
George Mason University	M
Georgia State University	M,D
Grambling State University	M
Harding University	M
Hofstra University	M,D,O
Hunter College of the City University of New York	M
Indiana University Bloomington	M,D,O
Instituto Tecnologico de Santo Domingo	M,O
Inter American University of Puerto Rico, Arecibo Campus	M
Inter American University of Puerto Rico, Metropolitan Campus	M
Inter American University of Puerto Rico, Ponce Campus	M
Iona College	M
Kent State University	M,D
Kutztown University of Pennsylvania	M,D
Lake Forest College	M
La Salle University	M,O
Lebanon Valley College	M,O
Lee University	M,O
Lehman College of the City University of New York	M
Le Moyne College	M,O
Lewis University	M
Long Island University–LIU Brooklyn	M,D,O
Manhattanville College	M,O
Metropolitan State University	M
Michigan State University	M,D
Minnesota State University Mankato	
Mississippi College	M,D,O
Missouri State University	M,O
Molloy College	M,O
Morehead State University	M,O
New York Institute of Technology	
New York University	M,D,O*
Northeastern Illinois University	M
Northwest Missouri State University	M,O
Oregon State University	M,D
Pace University	M,O
Plymouth State University	M
Portland State University	M
Purdue University	M,D,O
Queens College of the City University of New York	M,O
Quinnipiac University	M
Rhode Island College	M
Rivier University	M
Rutgers University–New Brunswick	M,D
St. John Fisher College	M
Slippery Rock University of Pennsylvania	M
Smith College	M
South Carolina State University	M
Southwestern Oklahoma State University	
State University of New York at New Paltz	M,O
State University of New York at Plattsburgh	M
State University of New York College at Geneseo	M

State University of New York College at Old Westbury	M
State University of New York College at Potsdam	M
Stony Brook University, State University of New York	M,O
Syracuse University	M
Teachers College, Columbia University	M,D,O
Temple University	M*
Texas Tech University	M
Trinity Washington University	M
University at Buffalo, the State University of New York	M,D,O
The University of Akron	M
The University of Alabama in Huntsville	M,O
University of Arkansas at Pine Bluff	M
The University of British Columbia	M,D
University of California, Santa Cruz	M
University of Central Florida	M,O
University of Connecticut	M,D
University of Florida	M,D,O
University of Illinois at Chicago	D
University of Indianapolis	M
The University of Iowa	M,D
University of Maine	M,D,O
University of Maryland, Baltimore County	M
University of Minnesota, Twin Cities Campus	M
University of Missouri	M,D,O
University of Missouri–St. Louis	M,O
The University of North Carolina at Chapel Hill	M
The University of North Carolina at Greensboro	M,D,O
The University of North Carolina at Pembroke	M
University of North Georgia	M
University of Oklahoma	M,D*
University of Pittsburgh	M,D*
University of Puerto Rico–Río Piedras	M,D
University of St. Francis (IL)	M,D,O
University of South Carolina	M,D
University of South Florida	M,D,O
The University of Tennessee	M,D,O
University of the District of Columbia	M
The University of Toledo	M,D,O
University of Victoria	M,D
University of Virginia	M,D,O
University of Washington	M,D
The University of West Alabama	M
University of Wisconsin–Milwaukee	M*
University of Wisconsin–River Falls	M
University of Wisconsin–Stevens Point	M
Virginia Polytechnic Institute and State University	M,D,O
Wagner College	M
Wayland Baptist University	M
Wayne State College	M
Wayne State University	M,D,O
Western Oregon University	M
Westfield State University	M
Widener University	M,D
William Carey University	M,O
Worcester State University	M

SOCIAL WORK

Abilene Christian University	M
Adelphi University	M,D
Alabama Agricultural and Mechanical University	M,O
Albany State University	M
American Jewish University	M
Andrews University	M
Anna Maria College	M
Appalachian State University	M
Arizona State University at the Tempe campus	M,D,O
Arkansas State University	M,O
Asbury University	M
Auburn University	M
Augsburg University	M
Aurora University	M
Austin Peay State University	M
Azusa Pacific University	M
Barry University	M,D
Baylor University	M,D
Binghamton University, State University of New York	M
Boise State University	M
Boston College	M,D
Boston University	M,D
Bowling Green State University	M
Brandman University	M
Brescia University	M
Bridgewater State University	M
Brigham Young University	M
Bryn Mawr College	M,D
California Baptist University	M
California State University, Bakersfield	M
California State University, Chico	M
California State University, Dominguez Hills	M
California State University, East Bay	M
California State University, Fresno	M
California State University, Fullerton	M
California State University, Long Beach	M
California State University, Los Angeles	M

California State University, Monterey Bay	M
California State University, Northridge	M,O
California State University, Sacramento	M
California State University, San Bernardino	M
California State University, Stanislaus	M
California University of Pennsylvania	M
Campbellsville University	M
Capella University	D
Carleton University	M
Carlow University	M
Case Western Reserve University	M,D
The Catholic University of America	M,D
Chicago State University	M
Clark Atlanta University	M,D
Clarke University	M
Cleveland State University	M
The College at Brockport, State University of New York	M,O
The College of Saint Rose	M
The College of St. Scholastica	M
College of Staten Island of the City University of New York	M
Colorado State University	M,D
Columbia University	M,D
Concordia University Wisconsin	M
Concord University	M
Cornell University	M,D
Daemen College	M
Dalhousie University	M
Delaware State University	M
DePaul University	M
Dominican University	M
East Carolina University	M,O
Eastern Michigan University	M
Eastern Washington University	M
East Tennessee State University	M
Edinboro University of Pennsylvania	M
Erikson Institute	M
Fayetteville State University	M
Ferris State University	M
Florida Agricultural and Mechanical University	
Florida Atlantic University	M
Florida Gulf Coast University	M
Florida International University	M,D
Florida State University	M,D
Fordham University	M,D
Gallaudet University	M,D,O
George Fox University	M
George Mason University	M
Georgia State University	M,O
Governors State University	M
The Graduate Center, City University of New York	D
Grambling State University	M
Grand Valley State University	M
Gratz College	M,O
Hawai'i Pacific University	M
Howard University	M,D
Humboldt State University	M
Hunter College of the City University of New York	M
Illinois State University	M
Indiana State University	M
Indiana University East	M
Indiana University Northwest	M
Indiana University–Purdue University Indianapolis	M,D,O
Indiana University South Bend	M
Institute for Clinical Social Work	D
Inter American University of Puerto Rico, Metropolitan Campus	M
Jackson State University	M,D
Jacksonville State University	M
Johnson C. Smith University	M
Kean University	M
Kennesaw State University	M
Keuka College	M
Kutztown University of Pennsylvania	M,D
Lakehead University	M
Laurentian University	M
Lehman College of the City University of New York	M
Lewis University	M
Loma Linda University	M,D
London Metropolitan University	M,D
Long Island University–Brentwood Campus	M,O
Long Island University–LIU Brooklyn	M,D,O
Long Island University–LIU Post	M,O
Louisiana State University	M
Louisiana State University and Agricultural & Mechanical College	M,D
Loyola University Chicago	M,D,O
Madonna University	M
Marshall University	M
Marywood University	M,D
McGill University	M,D,O
McMaster University	M
Memorial University of Newfoundland	M,D
Metropolitan State University of Denver	M
Michigan State University	M,D
Middle Tennessee State University	M
Millersville University of Pennsylvania	M,D
Minnesota State University Mankato	M
Missouri State University	M
Monmouth University	M,O
Morgan State University	M
Nazareth College of Rochester	M
Newman University	M
New Mexico Highlands University	M

New York University	M,D*
Norfolk State University	M,D
North Carolina Agricultural and Technical University	M
North Carolina Central University	M
North Carolina State University	M
Northeastern Illinois University	M
Northern Kentucky University	M
Northwest Nazarene University	M
Nyack College	M
The Ohio State University	M,D
The Ohio State University at Lima	M
The Ohio State University at Mansfield	M
The Ohio State University at Newark	M
Ohio University	M
Our Lady of the Lake University	M,D
Pacific University	M
Park University	M,O
Phillips Theological Seminary	M,D
Pontifical Catholic University of Puerto Rico	M
Portland State University	M,D
Quinnipiac University	M
Radford University	M
Ramapo College of New Jersey	M
Rhode Island College	M
Roberts Wesleyan College	M
Rutgers University–New Brunswick	M,D
Sacred Heart University	M
Saginaw Valley State University	M
St. Ambrose University	M
St. Catherine University	M,D
St. Cloud State University	M
Saint Leo University	M
Saint Louis University	M,D*
Salem State University	M
Salisbury University	M
Samford University	M
San Diego State University	M
San Francisco State University	M
Savannah State University	M
Seattle University	M
Seton Hall University	M
Shippensburg University of Pennsylvania	M
Simmons University	M,D
Smith College	M,D
Southeastern University (FL)	M
Southern Adventist University	M
Southern Connecticut State University	M
Southern Illinois University Carbondale	M
Southern Illinois University Edwardsville	M
Southern University at New Orleans	M
Spalding University	M
Spring Arbor University	M
Springfield College	M,O
Stephen F. Austin State University	M
Stockton University	M
Stony Brook University, State University of New York	M,D
Syracuse University	M
Tarleton State University	M
Temple University	M*
Tennessee State University	M,D
Texas A&M University–Commerce	M,D,O
Texas A&M University–Kingsville	M
Texas Christian University	M
Texas State University	M
Texas Tech University	M
Thompson Rivers University	M
Touro College	M
Troy University	M
Tulane University	M,D
Union University	M
Universidad del Este	M
Université de Moncton	M
Université de Montréal	O
Université de Sherbrooke	M
Université du Québec à Montréal	M
Université du Québec en Abitibi-Témiscamingue	M
Université du Québec en Outaouais	M
Université Laval	M,D
University at Albany, State University of New York	M,D
University at Buffalo, the State University of New York	M,D
The University of Akron	M
The University of Alabama	M,D
The University of Alabama at Birmingham	M
University of Alaska Anchorage	M,O
University of Arkansas	M
University of Arkansas at Little Rock	M
The University of British Columbia	M,D
University of Calgary	M,D,O
University of California, Berkeley	M,D
University of California, Los Angeles	M,D
University of Central Florida	M,O
University of Chicago	M,D
University of Cincinnati	M,D
University of Connecticut	M,D
University of Denver	M,D,O
University of Georgia	M,D,O
University of Guam	M
University of Hawaii at Manoa	M,D
University of Houston	M,D
University of Houston–Downtown	M
University of Illinois at Chicago	M,D,O
University of Illinois at Urbana–Champaign	M,D

University of Indianapolis — M,D
The University of Iowa — M,D
The University of Kansas — M,D
University of Kentucky — M,D
University of Louisville — M,D,O
University of Maine — M,O
The University of Manchester — M,D
University of Manitoba — M,D
University of Maryland, Baltimore — M,D
University of Maryland, College Park — M,D
University of Memphis — M
University of Michigan — M,D
University of Minnesota, Duluth — M
University of Minnesota, Twin Cities Campus — M,D
University of Mississippi — M,D
University of Missouri — M,D,O
University of Missouri–Kansas City — M
University of Missouri–St. Louis — M
University of Montana — M
University of Nebraska at Omaha — M
University of Nevada, Las Vegas — M
University of Nevada, Reno — M
University of New England — M,D,O
University of New Hampshire — M,O
The University of North Carolina at Chapel Hill — M,D
The University of North Carolina at Charlotte — M
The University of North Carolina at Greensboro — M
The University of North Carolina at Pembroke — M
The University of North Carolina Wilmington — M
University of North Dakota — M
University of Northern British Columbia — M,D,O
University of Northern Iowa — M
University of North Florida — M
University of Oklahoma — M*
University of Ottawa — M
University of Pennsylvania — M,D*
University of Pittsburgh — M,D,O*
University of Puerto Rico–Río Piedras — M,D
University of Regina — M,O
University of St. Francis (IL) — M,O
University of Saint Joseph — M
University of St. Thomas (MN) — M
University of South Africa — M
University of South Carolina — M
University of South Dakota — M
University of Southern California — M,D
University of Southern Indiana — M
University of Southern Maine — M
University of Southern Mississippi — M
University of South Florida — M,D,O
University of South Florida Sarasota-Manatee — M
The University of Tennessee — M,D
The University of Tennessee at Chattanooga — M
The University of Texas at Arlington — M,D
The University of Texas at Austin — M,D
The University of Texas at El Paso — M
The University of Texas at San Antonio — M
University of the Fraser Valley — M
The University of Toledo — M,O
University of Toronto — M,D
University of Utah — M,D
University of Vermont — M
University of Victoria — M
University of Washington — M,D
University of Washington, Tacoma — M
University of West Florida — M
University of Windsor — M
University of Wisconsin–Green Bay — M
University of Wisconsin–Madison — M,D
University of Wisconsin–Milwaukee — M,D,O*
University of Wisconsin–Oshkosh — M
University of Wyoming — M,D
Utah State University — M
Utah Valley University — M
Valdosta State University — M
Virginia Commonwealth University — M,D
Walden University — M,D
Walla Walla University — M
Washburn University — M
Washington University in St. Louis — M,D
Wayne State University — M,D,O
West Chester University of Pennsylvania — M,O
Western Carolina University — M
Western Illinois University — M
Western Kentucky University — M
Western Michigan University — M
Western New Mexico University — M
Westfield State University — M
West Texas A&M University — M
West Virginia University — M
Wichita State University — M
Widener University — M,D
Wilfrid Laurier University — M
Winthrop University — M
Yeshiva University — M,D
York University — M,D
Youngstown State University — M

SOCIOLOGY
Acadia University — M
American University — M,O

American University of Beirut — M,D
Angelo State University — M
Arizona State University at the Tempe campus — M,D
Arkansas State University — M,O
Arkansas Tech University — M
Auburn University — M
Ball State University — M
Baylor University — M,D
Binghamton University, State University of New York — M,D
Boston College — M,D
Boston University — M,D
Bowling Green State University — M,D
Brandeis University — M,D
Brigham Young University — M
Brock University — M
Brooklyn College of the City University of New York — M,D
Brown University — M,D
California State University, Bakersfield — M
California State University, Dominguez Hills — M
California State University, Fullerton — M
California State University, Los Angeles — M
California State University, Northridge — M
California State University, Sacramento — M
California State University, San Marcos — M
Carleton University — M,D
Case Western Reserve University — M,D
The Catholic University of America — M
Central European University — M
City College of the City University of New York — M
Clark Atlanta University — M
Clemson University — M
Colorado State University — M,D
Columbia University — M,D
Concordia University (Canada) — M,D
Cornell University — M,D
Dalhousie University — M
DePaul University — M
Duke University — M,D
East Carolina University — M
Eastern Michigan University — M
East Tennessee State University — M
Emory University — D
Fayetteville State University — M
Florida Atlantic University — M
Florida International University — M,D
Florida State University — M,D
George Mason University — M,D
The George Washington University — M
Georgia Southern University — M
Georgia State University — M,D
The Graduate Center, City University of New York — D
Harvard University — D*
Howard University — M,D
Humboldt State University — M
Hunter College of the City University of New York — M
Idaho State University — M
Illinois State University — M
Indiana University Bloomington — M,D
Indiana University of Pennsylvania — M
Indiana University–Purdue University Indianapolis — M
Iowa State University of Science and Technology — M,D
Jackson State University — M
Johns Hopkins University — D*
Kansas State University — M,D
Kent State University — M,D
Lakehead University — M
Laurentian University — M
Lehigh University — M
Lincoln University (MO) — M
Louisiana State University and Agricultural & Mechanical College — M,D
Loyola University Chicago — M,D
Marshall University — M
McGill University — M,D,O
McMaster University — M,D
Memorial University of Newfoundland — M,D
Michigan State University — M,D
Middle Tennessee State University — M
Minnesota State University Mankato — M
Mississippi State University — M
Morehead State University — M
Morgan State University — M
Murray State University — M
New Mexico Highlands University — M
The New School — M,D
New York University — M,D*
North Carolina State University — D
North Dakota State University — M
Northeastern University — M
Northern Arizona University — M
Northern Illinois University — M
Northwestern University — M,D
The Ohio State University — D
Ohio University — M
Oklahoma City University — M
Oklahoma State University — M,D
Old Dominion University — M
Omega Graduate School — M,D
Our Lady of the Lake University — M
Penn State University Park — M,D*
Portland State University — M,D,O
Prairie View A&M University — M
Princeton University — D,O
Purdue University — M,D

Queens College of the City University of New York — M
Queen's University at Kingston — M,D
Rice University — D
Roosevelt University — M
Rutgers University–New Brunswick — M,D
St. John's University (NY) — M
Sam Houston State University — M
San Diego State University — M
San Jose State University — M
Shippensburg University of Pennsylvania — M
Simon Fraser University — M,D
South Dakota State University — M,D
Southeastern Louisiana University — M
Southern Connecticut State University — M
Southern Illinois University Carbondale — M,D
Southern Illinois University Edwardsville — M
Stanford University — D
Stony Brook University, State University of New York — M,D
Syracuse University — M,D
Teachers College, Columbia University — M,D
Temple University — M,D*
Texas A&M International University — M
Texas A&M University — M,D
Texas A&M University–Commerce — M,D,O
Texas A&M University–Kingsville — M
Texas Southern University — M
Texas State University — M
Texas Tech University — M
Texas Woman's University — M,D
Tulane University — M
Université de Montréal — M,D
Université du Québec à Montréal — M,D
Université Laval — M,D
University at Albany, State University of New York — M,D,O
University at Buffalo, the State University of New York — M,D
The University of Alabama at Birmingham — D
University of Alberta — M,D
The University of Arizona — M,D
University of Arkansas — M
The University of British Columbia — M,D
University of Calgary — M,D
University of California, Berkeley — D
University of California, Davis — M,D
University of California, Irvine — D
University of California, Los Angeles — M,D
University of California, Merced — M,D
University of California, Riverside — M,D
University of California, San Diego — D
University of California, San Francisco — D
University of California, Santa Barbara — D
University of California, Santa Cruz — D
University of Central Florida — M,D
University of Central Missouri — M,D,O
University of Central Oklahoma — M
University of Chicago — D
University of Cincinnati — M,D
University of Colorado Boulder — D
University of Colorado Colorado Springs — M
University of Colorado Denver — M,O
University of Connecticut — M,D
University of Delaware — M,D
University of Florida — M,D
University of Georgia — M,D
University of Guelph — M,D
University of Hawaii at Manoa — M,D
University of Houston — M
University of Houston–Clear Lake — M
University of Illinois at Chicago — M,D
University of Illinois at Urbana–Champaign — M,D
University of Indianapolis — M
The University of Iowa — M,D
The University of Kansas — D
University of Kentucky — M,D
University of Lethbridge — M,D
University of Louisiana at Lafayette — M,D
University of Louisville — M,D
The University of Manchester — M,D
University of Manitoba — M,D
University of Maryland, Baltimore County — M
University of Maryland, College Park — M,D
University of Massachusetts Amherst — M,D
University of Massachusetts Boston — M,D
University of Massachusetts Lowell — M,O
University of Memphis — M
University of Miami — M,D
University of Michigan — D
University of Minnesota, Duluth — M
University of Minnesota, Twin Cities Campus — M,D
University of Missouri — M,D
University of Missouri–Kansas City — M
University of Montana — M

University of Nebraska at Omaha — M
University of Nebraska–Lincoln — M,D
University of Nevada, Las Vegas — M,D
University of Nevada, Reno — D
University of New Brunswick Fredericton — M,D
University of New Hampshire — M,D
University of New Mexico — M,D
University of New Orleans — M
The University of North Carolina at Chapel Hill — M,D
The University of North Carolina at Charlotte — M
The University of North Carolina at Greensboro — M
The University of North Carolina Wilmington — M
University of North Dakota — M
University of Northern Colorado — M
University of North Texas — M,D,O
University of Notre Dame — D
University of Oklahoma — M,D*
University of Oregon — M,D
University of Ottawa — M
University of Pennsylvania — M,D*
University of Pittsburgh — M,D*
University of Puerto Rico–Río Piedras — M
University of Regina — M
University of Saskatchewan — M,D
University of South Africa — M,D
University of South Alabama — M
University of South Carolina — M,D
University of Southern California — D
University of South Florida — M,D
The University of Tennessee — M,D
The University of Texas at Arlington — M
The University of Texas at Austin — M
The University of Texas at El Paso — M,O
The University of Texas at San Antonio — M
The University of Texas at Tyler — M
The University of Texas Rio Grande Valley — M
The University of Toledo — M
University of Toronto — M,D
University of Utah — M,D
University of Victoria — M,D
University of Virginia — M,D
University of Washington — M,D
University of Waterloo — M,D
The University of Western Ontario — M,D
University of West Georgia — M,D,O
University of Windsor — M,D
University of Wisconsin–Madison — M,D
University of Wisconsin–Milwaukee — M,D*
University of Wyoming — M
Utah State University — M
Vanderbilt University — M,D*
Virginia Commonwealth University — M
Washington State University — M,D
Wayne State University — M,D
Western Illinois University — M
Western Kentucky University — M
Western Michigan University — M
West Virginia University — M,D
Wichita State University — M
Wilfrid Laurier University — M
William Paterson University of New Jersey — M,D,O
Yale University — D
York University — M,D

SOFTWARE ENGINEERING
Arizona State University at the Tempe campus — M,D
Auburn University — M,D
Boston University — M,O
Bowling Green State University — M
Brandeis University — M
California Baptist University — M
California State University, Fullerton — M
California State University, Northridge — M
California State University, Sacramento — M
Carnegie Mellon University — M,D
Carroll University — M
Cleveland State University — M,D
College of Staten Island of the City University of New York — M
Colorado Technical University Aurora — M
Colorado Technical University Colorado Springs — M,D
Concordia University (Canada) — M,D,O
DePaul University — M,D
Drexel University — M,D,O*
East Carolina University — M
Embry-Riddle Aeronautical University–Daytona — M
Fairfield University — M,O
Florida Agricultural and Mechanical University — M
Florida Institute of Technology — M
Gannon University — M
Grand Valley State University — M
Harrisburg University of Science and Technology — M
Illinois Institute of Technology — M,D
Indiana University–Purdue University Indianapolis — M,D,O
Instituto Tecnológico de Santo Domingo — M,O
International Technological University — M

Jacksonville State University	M
Kennesaw State University	M,O
Lewis University	M
Lipscomb University	M,O
Loyola University Chicago	M
Marist College	M,O
Marymount University	M,O
McMaster University	M,D
Mercer University	M
Monmouth University	M
Naval Postgraduate School	M,D
New Jersey Institute of Technology	M,D,O
New York University	O*
North Dakota State University	M,D,O
Northern Kentucky University	M,O
Northwestern University	M
Oakland University	M,D
Oklahoma Christian University	M
Pace University	M,D,O
Penn State Great Valley	M,O
Regis University	M,O
Rochester Institute of Technology	M
Royal Military College of Canada	M,D
Saint Louis University	M*
St. Mary's University (United States)	M,O
San Jose State University	M
Santa Clara University	M,D,O
Shippensburg University of Pennsylvania	M,O
Southern Methodist University	M,D
Stevens Institute of Technology	M,O
Stratford University (VA)	M
Strayer University	M
Texas State University	M
Texas Tech University	M,D
Université Laval	O
The University of Alabama in Huntsville	M,D,O
University of Calgary	M,D
University of Colorado-Colorado Springs	M
University of Connecticut	M,D
University of Detroit Mercy	M,D
University of Houston–Clear Lake	M
University of Management and Technology	M,O
University of Massachusetts Dartmouth	M,O
University of Michigan–Dearborn	M,D
University of Minnesota, Twin Cities Campus	M
University of Missouri–Kansas City	M,D,O
University of Nebraska at Omaha	M,O
University of New Haven	M,O
University of North Florida	M
University of Regina	M,D
University of St. Thomas (MN)	M,O
The University of Scranton	M
University of South Carolina	M,D
University of Southern California	M,D
University of Southern Maine	M,O
The University of Texas at Arlington	M
The University of Texas at Dallas	M,D
The University of Texas at El Paso	M,D,O
University of Utah	M,D,O
University of Washington, Bothell	M
University of Washington, Tacoma	M
University of Waterloo	M,D
University of West Florida	M
University of Wisconsin–La Crosse	M
Vermont Technical College	M
Virginia International University	M,O
Virginia Polytechnic Institute and State University	M,O
West Virginia University	M,D
Emory University	D,O
Florida Atlantic University	M
Florida International University	M,D
Florida State University	M,D
George Mason University	M
Georgetown University	M,D
Georgia Southern University	M
Georgia State University	M,O
Harvard University	M,D*
Houston Baptist University	M
Howard University	M
Hunter College of the City University of New York	M
Illinois State University	M
Indiana State University	M,D,O
Indiana University Bloomington	M,D,O
Inter American University of Puerto Rico, Metropolitan Campus	M
Inter American University of Puerto Rico, Ponce Campus	M
Iona College	M
Johns Hopkins University	M,D*
Kansas State University	M
Kent State University	M,D
Lake Forest College	M
Lamar University	M
Lee University	M,O
Lehman College of the City University of New York	M
Loyola University Chicago	M
Manhattanville College	M,O
Marquette University	M
Michigan State University	M,D
Middlebury College	M,D
Middle Tennessee State University	M
Millersville University of Pennsylvania	M
Minnesota State University Mankato	M
Montclair State University	M
New York University	M,D,O*
North Carolina State University	M
Northern Arizona University	M
Northern Illinois University	M
Northwestern University	D
The Ohio State University	M,D
Ohio University	M
Penn State University Park	M,D*
Pontifical Catholic University of Puerto Rico	M,O
Portland State University	M
Princeton University	D
Purdue University	M,D
Queens College of the City University of New York	M
Rutgers University–New Brunswick	M,D
St. John's University (NY)	M
Saint Louis University	M*
Saint Louis University–Madrid Campus	M
Saint Xavier University	M
Salem State University	M
Sam Houston State University	M
San Diego State University	M
San Francisco State University	M
Southern Oregon University	M
Stanford University	M,D
State University of New York at New Paltz	M,O
State University of New York College at Geneseo	M
Syracuse University	M
Temple University	M,D*
Texas A&M University	M,D
Texas A&M University–Commerce	M,D,O
Texas A&M University–Kingsville	M
Texas State University	M
Texas Tech University	M,D
Tulane University	M,D
Universidad Autonoma de Guadalajara	M,D
Université de Montréal	M
Université Laval	M,D
University at Albany, State University of New York	M,D
University at Buffalo, the State University of New York	M,D,O
The University of Alabama	M,D
The University of Arizona	M,D
University of Arkansas	M
University of California, Berkeley	D
University of California, Davis	M,D
University of California, Irvine	M,D
University of California, Los Angeles	M
University of California, Riverside	M,D
University of California, Santa Barbara	M,D
University of Central Arkansas	M
University of Central Florida	M
University of Chicago	D
University of Cincinnati	M,D
University of Colorado Boulder	M,D
University of Colorado Denver	M
University of Delaware	M
University of Florida	M,D
University of Georgia	M,D
University of Hawaii at Manoa	M,D
University of Houston	M,D
University of Illinois at Chicago	M,D
University of Illinois at Urbana–Champaign	M,D
The University of Iowa	M,D
The University of Kansas	M,D
University of Lethbridge	M
University of Louisville	M,O
The University of Manchester	D
University of Maryland, College Park	M,D
University of Massachusetts Amherst	M,D
University of Memphis	M
University of Miami	M,D
University of Michigan	D
University of Minnesota, Twin Cities Campus	M,D
University of Missouri–Kansas City	M
University of Montana	M
University of Nebraska–Lincoln	M,D
University of Nevada, Reno	M
University of New Hampshire	M,O
University of New Mexico	M,D
The University of North Carolina at Chapel Hill	M,D
The University of North Carolina at Charlotte	M,O
The University of North Carolina at Greensboro	M,O
The University of North Carolina Wilmington	M,O
University of Northern Iowa	M
University of North Texas	M,D,O
University of Notre Dame	M
University of Oklahoma	M,D*
University of Oregon	M
University of Ottawa	M
University of Pennsylvania	M,D*
University of Pittsburgh	D*
University of Rhode Island	M
University of South Africa	M,D
University of South Carolina	M,D
University of Southern California	D
University of Southern Mississippi	M
University of South Florida	M,D
The University of Tennessee	M,D
The University of Texas at Arlington	M
The University of Texas at Austin	M,D
The University of Texas at El Paso	M,O
The University of Texas at San Antonio	M
The University of Texas of the Permian Basin	M
The University of Texas Rio Grande Valley	M
The University of Toledo	M
University of Toronto	M,D
University of Utah	M,D
University of Virginia	M,D
University of Washington	M
The University of Western Ontario	M,D
University of Wisconsin–Madison	M,D
University of Wisconsin–Milwaukee	M,O*
University of Wyoming	M
Vanderbilt University	M,D*
Washington University in St. Louis	D
Wayne State University	M,D
West Chester University of Pennsylvania	M,O
Western Kentucky University	M
Western Michigan University	M,D
Wichita State University	M
Worcester State University	M
Yale University	D

SPANISH

American University	M,O
Arizona State University at the Tempe campus	M,D
Asbury University	M
Auburn University	M
Bard College	M
Baylor University	M
Binghamton University, State University of New York	M
Boston College	M
Bowling Green State University	M
Brooklyn College of the City University of New York	M
California State University, Bakersfield	M
California State University, Fresno	M
California State University, Fullerton	M
California State University, Long Beach	M
California State University, Los Angeles	M
California State University, Northridge	M
California State University, San Bernardino	M
California State University, San Marcos	M
The Catholic University of America	M,D
Central Connecticut State University	M,O
Central Michigan University	M
City College of the City University of New York	M
Cleveland State University	M
Columbia University	M,D
Cornell University	D
DePaul University	M
Duke University	D
Eastern University	M,O

SPECIAL EDUCATION

Acacia University	M
Acadia University	M
Adelphi University	M,O
Alabama Agricultural and Mechanical University	M,D,O
Albany State University	M,O
Albizu University, Miami Campus	M,D
Albright College	M
Alcorn State University	M,O
Alliant International University–San Francisco	M,O
Alverno College	M
American International College	M,D,O
American University	M,O
American University of Puerto Rico	M
Andrews University	M
Antioch University New England	M,O
Appalachian State University	M
Arcadia University	M,D,O
Arizona State University at the Tempe campus	M,O
Arkansas State University	M,D,O
Arkansas Tech University	M,D,O
Asbury University	M
Assumption College	M,O
Auburn University	M,D
Auburn University at Montgomery	M,O
Augustana University	M
Augusta University	M,O
Aurora University	M,D
Averett University	M
Azusa Pacific University	M
Baldwin Wallace University	M
Ball State University	M,D,O
Bank Street College of Education	M
Barry University	M,D,O
Bayamón Central University	M,O
Baylor University	M,D,O
Bay Path University	M
Bemidji State University	M
Bethel University (MN)	M,D,O
Binghamton University, State University of New York	M
Biola University	M,O
Bloomsburg University of Pennsylvania	M,O
Bluffton University	M
Bob Jones University	M,D,O
Boise State University	M
Boston College	M,D,O
Bowie State University	M
Bowling Green State University	M
Brandman University	M,D
Brandon University	M,O
Brenau University	M,O
Bridgewater State University	M
Brooklyn College of the City University of New York	M,O
Buffalo State College, State University of New York	M
Cabrini University	M,D
Caldwell University	M,D,O
California Baptist University	M
California Lutheran University	M,D
California State University, Bakersfield	M
California State University, Chico	M
California State University, Dominguez Hills	M
California State University, East Bay	M
California State University, Fresno	M
California State University, Fullerton	M
California State University, Long Beach	M,D
California State University, Los Angeles	M,D
California State University, Northridge	M
California State University, Sacramento	M,D,O
California State University, San Marcos	M,D
California State University, Stanislaus	M
California University of Pennsylvania	M
Cambridge College	M,D,O
Campbellsville University	M
Canisius College	M,O
Capella University	M,D
Cardinal Stritch University	M,D
Caribbean University	M,D
Carlow University	M,O
Castleton University	M,O
The Catholic University of America	M,O
Centenary University	M,D
Central Connecticut State University	M,O
Central Michigan University	M,O
Chaminade University of Honolulu	M
Chapman University	M,D,O*
Chatham University	M
Chestnut Hill College	M
Cheyney University of Pennsylvania	M
Chicago State University	M
City College of the City University of New York	M,O
City University of Seattle	M,O
Claremont Graduate University	M,D,O
Clarion University of Pennsylvania	M
Clark Atlanta University	M
Clemson University	M,D,O
Cleveland State University	M
Coastal Carolina University	M,O
College of Charleston	M
The College of New Jersey	M
The College of New Rochelle	M
College of Saint Elizabeth	M,O
College of St. Joseph	M
The College of Saint Rose	M,O
College of Staten Island of the City University of New York	M,O
Colorado Christian University	M
Colorado Mesa University	M,O
Colorado State University–Pueblo	M
Columbus State University	M,O
Concordia College–New York	M
Concordia University, St. Paul	M,D,O
Concordia University Wisconsin	M
Concord University	M
Converse College	M
Coppin State University	M
Curry College	M,O
Daemen College	M
Dallas Baptist University	M
Delaware State University	M
Delta State University	M
DePaul University	M,D
DeSales University	M,O
Dominican College	M
Dominican University	M
Dominican University of California	M
Drake University	M,D,O
Drew University	M
Drexel University	M,D*
Drury University	M
Duquesne University	M,D
D'Youville College	M,D
East Carolina University	M,O
Eastern Illinois University	M
Eastern Kentucky University	M
Eastern Mennonite University	M
Eastern Michigan University	M,O
Eastern Nazarene College	M
Eastern New Mexico University	M,O
Eastern University	M,O
East Stroudsburg University of Pennsylvania	M
East Tennessee State University	M,O
Edinboro University of Pennsylvania	M
Elmhurst College	M
Elms College	M,O
Emmanuel College (United States)	M,O
Emporia State University	M
Endicott College	M,D,O
Fairfield University	M
Fairleigh Dickinson University, Metropolitan Campus	M
Fairmont State University	M
Ferris State University	M
Fitchburg State University	M
Flagler College	M
Florida Atlantic University	M,D
Florida Gulf Coast University	M

Institution	Degrees
Florida International University	M,D,O
Florida Memorial University	M
Fontbonne University	M
Fordham University	M,O
Fort Hays State University	M
Framingham State University	M
Francis Marion University	M
Franklin Pierce University	M,D,O
Freed-Hardeman University	M,O
Fresno Pacific University	M
Frostburg State University	M
Furman University	M,O
Gallaudet University	M,D,O
George Fox University	M
George Mason University	M,D,O
Georgetown College	M
The George Washington University	M,D,O
Georgia College & State University	M,O
Georgian Court University	M,O
Georgia Southern University	M,O
Georgia Southwestern State University	M,O
Georgia State University	D
Gonzaga University	M,D
Gordon College	M,O
Goucher College	M,O
Governors State University	M
Graceland University (IA)	M
Grambling State University	M
Grand Canyon University	M,D,O
Grand Valley State University	M
Greensboro College	M
Gwynedd Mercy University	M,D
Harding University	M,O
Hebrew College	M,O
Henderson State University	M,O
Heritage University	M
High Point University	M,D
Hofstra University	M,D,O
Holy Family University	M
Holy Names University	M,O
Hood College	M
Houston Baptist University	M,D
Howard University	M
Hunter College of the City University of New York	M
Idaho State University	M
Illinois State University	M,D,O
Immaculata University	M,D,O
Indiana University Bloomington	M,D,O
Indiana University of Pennsylvania	M
Indiana University–Purdue University Indianapolis	M,O
Indiana University South Bend	M,O
Inter American University of Puerto Rico, Barranquitas Campus	M
Inter American University of Puerto Rico, Fajardo Campus	M
Inter American University of Puerto Rico, Metropolitan Campus	M
Inter American University of Puerto Rico, San Germán Campus	M
Iona College	M
Iowa State University of Science and Technology	M,D
Jackson State University	M,O
Jacksonville State University	M
James Madison University	M
Johnson & Wales University	M
Kansas State University	M,D,O
Kean University	M
Kennesaw State University	M,D,O
Kent State University	M,D,O
Lamar University	M,D
Lancaster Bible College	M,D
La Salle University	M,O
Lasell College	M,O
Lee University	M,O
Lehigh University	M,D
Lehman College of the City University of New York	M
Le Moyne College	M,O
Lesley University	M,D,O
Lewis & Clark College	M
Lewis University	M
Lincoln University (PA)	M
Lipscomb University	M,D,O
London Metropolitan University	M,D
Long Island University–Brentwood Campus	M,O
Long Island University–Hudson	M,O
Long Island University–LIU Brooklyn	M,O
Long Island University–LIU Post	M,D,O
Long Island University–Riverhead	M,O
Longwood University	M
Loras College	M
Louisiana Tech University	M,D,O
Loyola Marymount University	M
Loyola University Chicago	M
Lynn University	M,D
Madonna University	M
Malone University	M
Manhattan College	M,O
Manhattanville College	M,O
Mansfield University of Pennsylvania	M
Marian University (WI)	M,D
Marshall University	M
Martin Luther College	M
Mary Baldwin University	M
Marygrove College	M,O
Marymount University	M
Marywood University	M
Massachusetts College of Liberal Arts	M,O
McDaniel College	M
McKendree University	M,D,O
McNeese State University	M,O
Medaille College	M
Mercyhurst University	M
Meredith College	M,O
Messiah College	M
Metropolitan College of New York	M
Metropolitan State University	M
Metropolitan State University of Denver	M
Michigan State University	M,D,O
Middle Tennessee State University	M
Midwestern State University	M
Millersville University of Pennsylvania	M
Milligan College	M,O
Minnesota State University Mankato	M,O
Minot State University	M
Misericordia University	M
Mississippi College	M,D,O
Mississippi State University	M,D,O
Missouri State University	M
Missouri Western State University	M
Molloy College	M,O
Monmouth University	M,D,O
Montana State University Billings	M,O
Montclair State University	M
Morehead State University	M,O
Morningside College	M
Mount Mercy University	M
Mount St. Joseph University	M,O
Mount Saint Mary College	M
Mount Saint Vincent University	M
Murray State University	M,O
National Louis University	M,D,O
National University	M,O
National University College	M
Neumann University	M
New England College	M,D
New Jersey City University	M
New Mexico Highlands University	M
New York University	M*
Niagara University	M
Norfolk State University	M
North Carolina Central University	M
North Carolina State University	M
Northeastern Illinois University	M
Northeastern State University	M
Northeastern University	M
Northern Arizona University	M,O
Northern Illinois University	M
Northern Kentucky University	M,O
Northern Michigan University	M
Northern Vermont University–Johnson	M
Northern Vermont University–Lyndon	M
Northwest Christian University	M
Northwestern State University of Louisiana	M,O
Northwest Missouri State University	M,D,O
Northwest Nazarene University	M,D,O
Notre Dame College (OH)	M,O
Notre Dame de Namur University	M
Nyack College	M
Oakland University	M,O
The Ohio State University	D
Ohio University	M,D
Old Dominion University	M,D
Ottawa University	M
Pace University	M,O
Pacific Oaks College	M
Pacific University	M
Penn State University Park	M,D,O*
Piedmont College	M,D,O
Pittsburg State University	M,O
Point Loma Nazarene University	M
Point Park University	M,D
Prescott College	M,D
Providence College	M
Purdue University Fort Wayne	M,O
Purdue University Global	M,O
Purdue University Northwest	M
Queens College of the City University of New York	M,O
Radford University	M,O
Ramapo College of New Jersey	M
Randolph College	M
Regent University	M,D,O
Regis College (MA)	M,D
Regis University	M,O
Rhode Island College	M
Rider University	M,O
Rivier University	M,D,O
Roberts Wesleyan College	M
Rochester Institute of Technology	M
Rockford University	M
Roosevelt University	M
Rowan University	M,O
Rutgers University–New Brunswick	M,D
Sage Graduate School	M
Saginaw Valley State University	M
St. Bonaventure University	M,O
St. Cloud State University	M,O
St. John Fisher College	M,O
St. John's University (NY)	M,O
St. Joseph's College, Long Island Campus	M
St. Joseph's College, New York	M
Saint Joseph's University	M,D,O
Saint Louis University	M,D*
Saint Mary's College of California	M
Saint Mary's University of Minnesota	M,O
Saint Michael's College	M,O
Saint Peter's University	M,O
St. Thomas Aquinas College	M
St. Thomas University	M,D
Saint Vincent College	M
Saint Xavier University	M
Salem College	M
Salem State University	M
Salus University	M,O
Samford University	M,D,O
Sam Houston State University	M,D
San Diego State University	M
San Francisco State University	M,D,O
San Ignacio University	M
San Jose State University	M
Seattle University	M
Seton Hall University	M
Seton Hill University	M
Shippensburg University of Pennsylvania	M,D
Siena Heights University	M,O
Simmons University	M,D,O
Slippery Rock University of Pennsylvania	M,D
Sonoma State University	M,O
South Carolina State University	M
Southeastern Louisiana University	M
Southeast Missouri State University	M
Southern Connecticut State University	M
Southern Illinois University Carbondale	M,D
Southern Illinois University Edwardsville	M,O
Southern Methodist University	M,D
Southern New Hampshire University	M,D,O
Southern Oregon University	M
Southwestern College (KS)	M,D
Southwestern Oklahoma State University	M
Southwest Minnesota State University	M
Spalding University	M
Spring Arbor University	M
Springfield College	M,O
State University of New York at New Paltz	M
State University of New York at Oswego	M
State University of New York at Plattsburgh	M
State University of New York College at Cortland	M
State University of New York College at Oneonta	M,O
State University of New York College at Potsdam	M
Stephen F. Austin State University	M
Stonehill College	M
Syracuse University	M,D
Tarleton State University	M
Teachers College, Columbia University	M,D,O
Teachers College of San Joaquin	M,D,O
Tennessee State University	M,D
Tennessee Technological University	M
Texas A&M International University	M
Texas A&M University	M,D
Texas A&M University–Commerce	M,D,O
Texas A&M University–Corpus Christi	M
Texas A&M University–Kingsville	M
Texas A&M University–San Antonio	M
Texas A&M University–Texarkana	M
Texas Christian University	M
Texas State University	M
Texas Tech University	M,D
Texas Woman's University	M,D
Touro College	M
Towson University	M,O
Trevecca Nazarene University	M,O
Trinity Baptist College	M
Trinity Christian College	M
Trinity Washington University	M
Tusculum University	M
Union College (KY)	M
Universidad del Este	M
Universidad del Turabo	M
Universidad Iberoamericana	M,D
Universidad Metropolitana	M
Université de Sherbrooke	M,O
University at Buffalo, the State University of New York	M,D,O
The University of Alabama	M,D,O
The University of Alabama at Birmingham	M
The University of Alabama in Huntsville	M,O
University of Alaska Anchorage	M,O
University of Alaska Fairbanks	M
University of Alaska Southeast	M
University of Alberta	M,D
The University of Arizona	M,D
University of Arkansas	M
University of Arkansas at Little Rock	M,O
The University of British Columbia	M,D,O
University of California, Berkeley	M,D
University of California, Los Angeles	D
University of California, Riverside	M,D,O
University of Central Arkansas	M,O
University of Central Florida	M,O
University of Central Missouri	M
University of Central Oklahoma	M
University of Cincinnati	M,D
University of Colorado Colorado Springs	M,D
University of Colorado Denver	M,D
University of Denver	M,D,O
University of Detroit Mercy	M,D,O
University of Florida	M,D,O
University of Georgia	M,D,O
University of Guam	M
University of Hawaii at Manoa	M,D
University of Houston	M,D
University of Houston–Victoria	M,O
University of Idaho	M,O
University of Illinois at Chicago	M,D
University of Illinois at Urbana–Champaign	M,D,O
The University of Iowa	M,D
The University of Kansas	M,D,O
University of Kentucky	M,D
University of La Verne	M,D,O
University of Louisiana at Lafayette	M
University of Louisiana at Monroe	M
University of Louisville	M,D,O
University of Lynchburg	M
University of Maine	M,D,O
University of Manitoba	M
University of Mary	M,D
University of Maryland Eastern Shore	M
University of Massachusetts Amherst	M
University of Massachusetts Boston	M
University of Massachusetts Dartmouth	M,O
University of Memphis	M,D,O
University of Miami	M,D,O
University of Minnesota, Twin Cities Campus	M,D
University of Mississippi	M,D,O
University of Missouri	D
University of Missouri–Kansas City	M,D,O
University of Missouri–St. Louis	M
University of Nebraska at Kearney	M,O
University of Nebraska at Omaha	M
University of Nebraska–Lincoln	M,D,O
University of Nevada, Las Vegas	M,D,O
University of Nevada, Reno	M,D
University of New Hampshire	M,O
University of New Mexico	M,D,O
University of New Orleans	M
University of North Alabama	M
The University of North Carolina at Charlotte	M,D,O
The University of North Carolina at Greensboro	M,D,O
The University of North Carolina Wilmington	M
University of North Dakota	M
University of Northern Colorado	M,D
University of Northern Iowa	M
University of North Florida	M
University of North Texas	M,D,O
University of Oklahoma	M,D*
University of Oklahoma Health Sciences Center	M,D,O
University of Oregon	M,D
University of Phoenix–Bay Area Campus	M,D,O
University of Phoenix–Hawaii Campus	M
University of Phoenix–Online Campus	M,O
University of Phoenix–Phoenix Campus	M
University of Pittsburgh	M,D*
University of Portland	M,D
University of Puerto Rico–Medical Sciences Campus	O
University of Puerto Rico–Río Piedras	M
University of Rhode Island	M,D
University of Rio Grande	M
University of St. Francis (IL)	M,D,O
University of Saint Francis (IN)	M,O
University of Saint Joseph	M,O
University of Saint Mary	M
University of St. Thomas (MN)	M,O
University of St. Thomas (TX)	M,O
University of San Diego	M,D
University of San Francisco	M,D
University of Saskatchewan	M,D
The University of Scranton	M
University of South Alabama	M,D
University of South Carolina	M,D
University of South Carolina Upstate	M
University of South Dakota	M,D,O
University of Southern Maine	M,O
University of Southern Mississippi	M,D
University of South Florida	O
The University of Tennessee	M,D,O
The University of Tennessee at Chattanooga	M,D,O
The University of Tennessee at Martin	M
The University of Texas at Austin	M,D
The University of Texas at El Paso	M
The University of Texas at San Antonio	M,D
The University of Texas at Tyler	M
The University of Texas Health Science Center at San Antonio	M,D
The University of Texas of the Permian Basin	M
The University of Texas Rio Grande Valley	M
University of the Cumberlands	M,D,O
University of the Pacific	M,D,O
University of the Southwest	M
The University of Toledo	M,D,O

M—masters degree; D—doctorate; O—other advanced degree; *—Close-Up and/or Display

University of Vermont	M
University of Victoria	M,D
University of Virginia	M,D,O
University of Washington	M,D
University of Washington, Tacoma	M
The University of West Alabama	M,O
The University of Western Ontario	M
University of West Florida	M
University of West Georgia	M,D,O
University of Wisconsin–Eau Claire	M
University of Wisconsin–La Crosse	M,O
University of Wisconsin–Madison	M,D
University of Wisconsin–Milwaukee	M,D,O*
University of Wisconsin–Oshkosh	M
University of Wisconsin–Stevens Point	M
University of Wisconsin–Superior	M
University of Wisconsin–Whitewater	M,O
University of Wyoming	M,D,O
Utah State University	M,D,O
Valdosta State University	M,D,O
Vanderbilt University	D*
Virginia Commonwealth University	M
Viterbo University	M,O
Wagner College	M
Walden University	M,D,O
Walla Walla University	M
Washburn University	M
Washington State University	M,D
Washington University in St. Louis	M,D
Wayland Baptist University	M,D
Waynesburg University	M,D
Wayne State College	M
Wayne State University	M,D,O
Webster University	M,O
West Chester University of Pennsylvania	M,O
Western Connecticut State University	M
Western Governors University	M,O
Western Illinois University	M
Western Kentucky University	M,O
Western Michigan University	M,D
Western New Mexico University	M
Western Oregon University	M
Westfield State University	M
West Liberty University	M
Westminster College (PA)	M
West Virginia University	M,D
Whitworth University	M
Wichita State University	M
Widener University	M,D
Wilkes University	M,D
William Carey University	M,O
William Paterson University of New Jersey	M,O
Wilmington College	M
Wilmington University	M,D
Wilson College	M
Winona State University	M
Winston-Salem State University	M
Winthrop University	M
Worcester State University	M,O
Wright State University	M*
Xavier University	M*
Youngstown State University	M

SPEECH AND INTERPERSONAL COMMUNICATION

Ball State University	M
Bob Jones University	M,D,O
Brooklyn College of the City University of New York	M,D
California State University, Fullerton	M
California State University, Northridge	M
Colorado State University	M,D
Georgia State University	M,D
Marquette University	M,O
New York University	M,D*
North Dakota State University	M,D
Northeastern Illinois University	M
Northwestern University	M,D
Ohio University	M,D
Old Dominion University	M,O
Portland State University	M,O
Rensselaer Polytechnic Institute	M,D
San Francisco State University	M
San Jose State University	M
Seton Hall University	M
Southern Illinois University Carbondale	M,D
Southern Illinois University Edwardsville	M
Texas Christian University	M
The University of Alabama	M
University of Arkansas at Little Rock	M
University of California, Santa Barbara	D
University of Hawaii at Manoa	M
University of Houston	M
The University of Iowa	M,D
University of Maryland, College Park	M,D
University of Nebraska–Lincoln	M,D
University of Nevada, Reno	M,D
University of South Carolina	M,D
University of Wisconsin–Madison	M,D
University of Wisconsin–Stevens Point	M
University of Wisconsin–Superior	M
Wake Forest University	M

Washington University in St. Louis	M,D

SPORT PSYCHOLOGY

Adams State University	M
Adler University	M
Argosy University, Atlanta	M,D,O
Argosy University, Orange County	M
Argosy University, Phoenix	M,D
A.T. Still University	M,D,O
Ball State University	M
Barry University	M
California State University, Fresno	M
California State University, Long Beach	M
California University of Pennsylvania	M
Capella University	M
Chatham University	M,D
John F. Kennedy University	M,O
Lock Haven University of Pennsylvania	M
Purdue University	M,D
Queen's University at Kingston	M,D
Seton Hall University	M
Southern Illinois University Edwardsville	M,D,O
Springfield College	M,D,O
University of Denver	M,D,O
University of Rhode Island	M
The University of Texas at Austin	M,D
West Virginia University	M,D

SPORTS AND ENTERTAINMENT LAW

Arizona State University at the Tempe campus	M,D
Chapman University	M,D*
Drexel University	M,D*
London Metropolitan University	M,D
New York University	M*
Southwestern Law School	M
University of New Hampshire	M,D,O

SPORTS MANAGEMENT

Adams State University	M
Adelphi University	M
Alcorn State University	M,O
American Public University System	M,D
American University	M,D
Angelo State University	M
Arkansas State University	M,O
Ashland University	M
Auburn University at Montgomery	M,O
Augustana University	M
Austin Peay State University	M
Azusa Pacific University	M
Ball State University	M
Barry University	M
Belhaven University (MS)	M
Boise State University	M
Bowling Green State University	M
Brooklyn College of the City University of New York	M
Bryan College	M
California Baptist University	M
California State University, Fresno	M
California State University, Long Beach	M
California University of Management and Sciences	M,D
California University of Pennsylvania	M
Campbellsville University	M
Canisius College	M
Cardinal Stritch University	M
Central Michigan University	M,O
Central Washington University	M
The Citadel, The Military College of South Carolina	M,O
Clayton State University	M
Clemson University	M,D,O
Coastal Carolina University	M,D,O
Coker University	M
The College at Brockport, State University of New York	M
Columbia University	M
Concordia University Irvine	M
Concordia University, St. Paul	M,D
Dallas Baptist University	M
Drexel University	M*
Duquesne University	M
East Carolina University	M,D,O
Eastern Kentucky University	M
Eastern Michigan University	M
Eastern New Mexico University	M
Eastern Washington University	M
East Stroudsburg University of Pennsylvania	M
East Tennessee State University	M,D
Endicott College	M
Fairleigh Dickinson University, Florham Campus	M
Fairleigh Dickinson University, Metropolitan Campus	M
Florida Agricultural and Mechanical University	M
Florida Atlantic University	M
Florida International University	M,D,O
Florida State University	M,D
Franklin Pierce University	M,D,O
George Mason University	M,O
Georgetown University	M,D
The George Washington University	M,O
Georgia Southern University	M
Georgia State University	M
Gonzaga University	M,D
Grambling State University	M
Grand Canyon University	M
Grand View University	M
Hampton University	M
Hardin-Simmons University	M
Henderson State University	M
Hofstra University	M,O

Houston Baptist University	M
Howard Payne University	M
Howard University	M
Husson University	M
Idaho State University	M
Indiana State University	M,D
Indiana University Bloomington	M,D
Indiana University of Pennsylvania	M
Iona College	M,O
Ithaca College	M
Jackson State University	M
Jacksonville University	M
Johnson & Wales University	M
Kansas Wesleyan University	M
Kennesaw State University	M
Kent State University	M
Lasell College	M,O
Lewis University	M
Lock Haven University of Pennsylvania	M
Marquette University	M,O
Marshall University	M
Maryville University of Saint Louis	M,O
Mercyhurst University	M,O
Messiah College	M
Midwestern State University	M
Millersville University of Pennsylvania	M
Misericordia University	M
Mississippi State University	M,O
Missouri State University	M,O
Missouri Western State University	M
Montclair State University	M
Mount St. Mary's University (MD)	M
Neumann University	M
New England College	M
New Mexico Highlands University	M
North Carolina State University	M,D
Northeastern University	M
Northern State University	M
Northwestern University	M
Ohio Dominican University	M
Ohio University	M
Old Dominion University	M
Pittsburg State University	M
Point Loma Nazarene University	M
Point Park University	M
Purdue University	M,D
Robert Morris University Illinois	M
St. John's University (NY)	M
Saint Mary's College of California	M
St. Thomas University	M,O
Sam Houston State University	M
San Diego State University	M
Seattle University	M
Seton Hall University	M,O
Sonoma State University	M
Southeastern University (FL)	M,D
Southeast Missouri State University	M
Southern Methodist University	M,D
Southern Nazarene University	M
Southern New Hampshire University	M,D,O
Southwestern Oklahoma State University	M
Springfield College	M,D,O
State University of New York College at Cortland	M
Syracuse University	M
Temple University	M,D*
Tennessee State University	M
Tennessee Technological University	M
Texas A&M University	M,D
Texas Tech University	M
Tiffin University	M
Troy University	M,D
United States Sports Academy	M
The University of Alabama	M
University of Alberta	M
University of Arkansas	M,D
University of Arkansas at Little Rock	M
University of Central Florida	M
University of Cincinnati	M
University of Colorado Denver	M
University of Connecticut	M
University of Dallas	M,D
University of Florida	M,D
University of Idaho	M,D
University of Indianapolis	M
The University of Iowa	M,D
The University of Kansas	M,D
University of Louisiana at Monroe	M
University of Louisville	M,D,O
University of Mary	M
University of Mary Hardin-Baylor	M
University of Massachusetts Amherst	M,D
University of Miami	M
University of Michigan	M,D
University of Minnesota, Twin Cities Campus	M,D
University of Nebraska at Kearney	M
University of New Brunswick Fredericton	M
University of New Haven	M,O
University of New Mexico	D
The University of North Carolina at Chapel Hill	M
The University of North Carolina at Pembroke	M
University of Northern Colorado	M,D
University of Northern Iowa	M
University of North Florida	M,D
University of Oregon	M
University of San Francisco	M
University of South Alabama	M
University of South Carolina	M
University of Southern Indiana	M
University of Southern Mississippi	M
University of South Florida	M,D

The University of Tennessee	M,D
University of the Incarnate Word	M,D
University of the Southwest	M
University of Wisconsin–Parkside	M
Upper Iowa University	M
Valparaiso University	M
Waldorf University	M
Washington State University	M,D
Wayland Baptist University	M
Wayne State College	M
Wayne State University	M,D
Webber International University	M
West Chester University of Pennsylvania	M,O
Western Illinois University	M
Western Kentucky University	M
Western Michigan University	M
Western New England University	M
West Liberty University	M
West Texas A&M University	M
West Virginia University	M,D
Wichita State University	M
Wingate University	M
Winona State University	M,O
Xavier University	M*

STATISTICS

Acadia University	M
American University	M,O
Arizona State University at the Tempe campus	M,D,O
Auburn University	M,D
Ball State University	M
Baruch College of the City University of New York	M*
Baylor University	M,D
Binghamton University, State University of New York	M,D
Bowling Green State University	M,D
Brigham Young University	M
Brock University	M
California State University, East Bay	M
Carnegie Mellon University	M,D
Central Connecticut State University	M,O
Claremont Graduate University	M,D
Clemson University	M,D
Colorado State University	M,D
Columbia University	M,D
Concordia University (Canada)	M,D
Cornell University	M,D
Dalhousie University	M,D
Duke University	M,D
East Carolina University	M
Florida Atlantic University	M,D
Florida International University	M
George Mason University	M,D,O
Georgetown University	M
The George Washington University	M,D,O
Georgia Institute of Technology	M
Georgia State University	M,D
Hampton University	M
Harvard University	M,D*
Hunter College of the City University of New York	M
Indiana University Bloomington	M,D
Indiana University–Purdue University Indianapolis	M,D
Iowa State University of Science and Technology	M,D
Jackson State University	M
Johns Hopkins University	M,D*
Kansas State University	M,D,O
Lehigh University	M,D
Louisiana State University and Agricultural & Mechanical College	M
Loyola University Chicago	M
McGill University	M,D,O
McMaster University	M
McNeese State University	M
Memorial University of Newfoundland	M,D
Miami University	M
Michigan State University	M,D
Minnesota State University Mankato	M
Mississippi State University	M,D
Missouri University of Science and Technology	M,D
Montana State University	M,D
Montclair State University	M,D
Murray State University	M
New Jersey Institute of Technology	M,D,O
New Mexico Institute of Mining and Technology	M,D
New York University	M,D*
North Carolina State University	M,D
North Dakota State University	M,D
Northern Arizona University	M,O
Northern Illinois University	M,D
Northwestern University	M,D
Oakland University	O
The Ohio State University	M,D
Oklahoma State University	M,D
Old Dominion University	M,D
Oregon State University	M,D
Penn State University Park	M,D*
Portland State University	M,D,O
Purdue University	M,D
Queen's University at Kingston	M,D
Rice University	M,D
Rochester Institute of Technology	O
Rutgers University–New Brunswick	M,D
St. John's University (NY)	M,D
Sam Houston State University	M
San Diego State University	M
Simon Fraser University	M,D
South Dakota State University	M,D
Southern Illinois University Edwardsville	M
Southern Methodist University	M,D

Stanford University	M,D
Stephen F. Austin State University	M
Stevens Institute of Technology	M,O
Stony Brook University, State University of New York	M,D,O
Temple University	M,D*
Texas A&M University	M,D
Texas A&M University–Kingsville	M
Texas Tech University	M,D
Université de Montréal	M,D,O
Université Laval	M
The University of Akron	M
University of Alaska Fairbanks	M,D,O
University of Alberta	M,D,O
The University of Arizona	M,D
University of Arkansas	M
The University of British Columbia	M,D
University of Calgary	M,D
University of California, Berkeley	M,D
University of California, Davis	M,D
University of California, Irvine	M,D
University of California, Los Angeles	M,D
University of California, Riverside	M
University of California, San Diego	M,D
University of California, Santa Barbara	M,D
University of California, Santa Cruz	M,D
University of Central Oklahoma	M
University of Chicago	M,D,O
University of Cincinnati	M,D
University of Colorado Denver	M,D
University of Connecticut	M,D
University of Delaware	M
University of Florida	M,D
University of Georgia	M,D
University of Guelph	M,D
University of Houston–Clear Lake	M
University of Idaho	M
University of Illinois at Chicago	M,D
University of Illinois at Urbana–Champaign	M,D
The University of Iowa	M,D,O
The University of Kansas	M,D,O
University of Kentucky	M,D
The University of Manchester	M,D
University of Manitoba	M,D
University of Maryland, Baltimore County	M,D
University of Maryland, College Park	M,D
University of Massachusetts Amherst	M,D
University of Memphis	M,D
University of Michigan	M,D,O
University of Minnesota, Twin Cities Campus	M,D
University of Missouri	M,D
University of Missouri–Kansas City	M,D
University of Nebraska–Lincoln	M,D
University of New Brunswick Fredericton	M,D
University of New Mexico	M,D
The University of North Carolina at Chapel Hill	M,D
The University of North Carolina Wilmington	M,O
University of North Florida	M
University of Notre Dame	M,D
University of Ottawa	M,D
University of Pennsylvania	M,D*
University of Pittsburgh	M,D*
University of Regina	M,D
University of Rhode Island	M,D,O
University of Rochester	M,D*
University of Saskatchewan	M,D
University of South Africa	M,D
University of South Carolina	M,D,O
University of Southern California	M,D
University of Southern Maine	M,O
University of South Florida	M,D
The University of Tennessee	M,D
The University of Texas at Austin	M,D
The University of Texas at Dallas	M,D
The University of Texas at El Paso	M
The University of Texas at San Antonio	M,D
The University of Toledo	M,D
University of Toronto	M,D
University of Utah	M,D,O
University of Vermont	M
University of Victoria	M,D
University of Virginia	M,D
University of Washington	M,D
University of Waterloo	M,D
The University of Western Ontario	M,D
University of Windsor	M,D
University of Wisconsin–Madison	M,D
University of Wisconsin–Milwaukee	M,D*
Utah State University	M,D
Virginia Polytechnic Institute and State University	M,D
Washington University in St. Louis	M,D
Wayne State University	M
Western Michigan University	M,D,O
West Virginia University	M,D
Yale University	M,D
York University	M,D
Youngstown State University	M

STRUCTURAL BIOLOGY

Albert Einstein College of Medicine	D
Baylor College of Medicine	D
Carnegie Mellon University	M,D
Columbia University	D
Duke University	O
Florida State University	D
Illinois State University	M,D
Iowa State University of Science and Technology	M,D
Massachusetts Institute of Technology	D
Michigan State University	D
Northwestern University	D
Stanford University	D
Stony Brook University, State University of New York	D
Tufts University	D
Tulane University	M,D
University at Buffalo, the State University of New York	M,D
The University of Alabama at Birmingham	D
University of Connecticut	M,D
The University of Manchester	M,D
University of Minnesota, Twin Cities Campus	D
University of Oklahoma	M,D*
University of Pittsburgh	D*
University of Rochester	D*
The University of Texas Health Science Center at San Antonio	M,D
The University of Texas Medical Branch	D
University of Washington	D
Weill Cornell Medicine	M,D

STRUCTURAL ENGINEERING

California State University, Northridge	M
The Citadel, The Military College of South Carolina	M,O
Clemson University	M,D
Cornell University	M,D
Drexel University	M,D*
École Polytechnique de Montréal	M,D,O
Illinois Institute of Technology	M,D
Instituto Tecnologico de Santo Domingo	M,O
Iowa State University of Science and Technology	M,D
Kansas State University	M,D
Kennesaw State University	M
Louisiana State University and Agricultural & Mechanical College	M,D
Marquette University	M,D,O
Massachusetts Institute of Technology	M,D,O
McGill University	M,D
Northwestern University	M,D
Norwich University	M
Ohio University	M,D
Old Dominion University	M
Oregon State University	M,D
Penn State Harrisburg	M,O
Pontificia Universidad Catolica Madre y Maestra	M
Southern Illinois University Edwardsville	M
Southern Methodist University	M,D
Stanford University	M,D,O
Stevens Institute of Technology	M,D,O
Tufts University	M,D
University at Buffalo, the State University of New York	M,D
The University of Alabama at Birmingham	M
University of Alberta	M,D
University of Calgary	M,D
University of California, Berkeley	M,D
University of California, San Diego	M,D
University of Central Florida	M,D,O
University of Colorado Denver	M,D
University of Dayton	M
University of Delaware	M,D
The University of Manchester	M,D
University of Massachusetts Amherst	M
University of Memphis	M,D,O
University of Michigan	M,D,O
University of New Brunswick Fredericton	M,D
University of Puerto Rico–Mayagüez	M,D
University of South Florida	M,D
The University of Texas at Tyler	M
University of Washington	M,D
University of Wisconsin–Madison	M

STUDENT AFFAIRS

Alfred University	M
Alliant International University–Los Angeles	M,D,O
Alliant International University–San Diego	M,D,O
Appalachian State University	M
Arkansas State University	M,O
Arkansas Tech University	M,D,O
Binghamton University, State University of New York	M
Bloomsburg University of Pennsylvania	M
Bob Jones University	M,D,O
Bowling Green State University	M
Bucknell University	M
California State University, Bakersfield	M

California State University, Fresno	M
California State University, Long Beach	M,O
Canisius College	M,O
Cardinal Stritch University	M,D
Carlow University	M
Central Michigan University	M,D,O
The Citadel, The Military College of South Carolina	M,O
Claremont Graduate University	M,D,O
Clemson University	M,D,O
The College of Saint Rose	M
Colorado State University	M,D
Dallas Baptist University	M
DePaul University	M,D
Eastern Illinois University	M
Eastern Michigan University	M,D,O
Fresno Pacific University	M,O
The George Washington University	M,D,O
Grambling State University	M,D,O
Hampton University	M,D,O
Illinois State University	M
Indiana State University	M,D,O
Indiana University Bloomington	M,D,O
Indiana University of Pennsylvania	M
Iowa State University of Science and Technology	M,D
Kansas State University	M,D
Kent State University	M
Lewis & Clark College	M,D,O
Lewis University	M
Manhattan College	M,O
Marquette University	M,D
Messiah College	M
Miami University	M,D
Minnesota State University Mankato	M,D
Mississippi State University	M,D,O
Missouri State University	M
Monmouth University	M,D,O
Morgan State University	M,D
New York University	M,D*
Northern Arizona University	M,D,O
Northwestern State University of Louisiana	M
Nova Southeastern University	M,D,O
Ohio University	M,D
Oregon State University	M
Providence University College & Theological Seminary	M,D,O
Purdue University Global	M
Quincy University	M
Regent University	M,D,O
Rutgers University–New Brunswick	M
St. Cloud State University	M
St. Edward's University	M
Saint Louis University	M,D,O*
San Jose State University	M
Seton Hall University	M
Shippensburg University of Pennsylvania	M,D
Slippery Rock University of Pennsylvania	M
Southern Arkansas University–Magnolia	M
Southern Illinois University Edwardsville	M
Springfield College	M,D,O
State University of New York at Plattsburgh	M,O
Syracuse University	M
Texas State University	M
University of Arkansas at Little Rock	M,D
University of Bridgeport	M
University of Central Arkansas	M
University of Central Florida	M,O
University of Central Missouri	M,D,O
University of Central Oklahoma	M
University of Dayton	M,O
University of Florida	M,D,O
University of Georgia	M,D,O
The University of Iowa	M,D
University of La Verne	M
University of Louisville	M,D
University of Maryland, College Park	M,D,O
University of Minnesota, Twin Cities Campus	M
University of Nebraska at Kearney	M,O
University of Northern Colorado	M,D
University of Northern Iowa	M
University of Rhode Island	M
University of Rochester	M*
University of St. Thomas (MN)	M
University of South Carolina	M
University of Southern California	M
University of Southern Mississippi	M,D
University of South Florida	M,D,O
The University of Tennessee	M
The University of Tennessee at Martin	M
University of the Cumberlands	M,D,O
University of Utah	M,D
University of Virginia	M,D,O
The University of West Alabama	M
University of West Florida	M
University of Wisconsin–La Crosse	M,D
University of Wyoming	M,D
Virginia Commonwealth University	M,D
Walsh University	M
West Chester University of Pennsylvania	M,O
Western Illinois University	M
Western Kentucky University	M
William James College	M,D,O

SUPPLY CHAIN MANAGEMENT

Abilene Christian University	M

Adelphi University	M
Albany State University	M
American Graduate University	M,O
Anderson University (SC)	M
Arizona State University at the Tempe campus	M,D
Ashland University	M
Athens State University	M
Binghamton University, State University of New York	D
Boston University	M
Brigham Young University	M
California Polytechnic State University, San Luis Obispo	M
California State University, East Bay	M
California State University, San Bernardino	M,D
Capella University	M,D
Case Western Reserve University	M,D
Central Connecticut State University	M,O
Clarkson University	M,O
Clayton State University	M
Clemson University	M,D
Concordia University (Canada)	M,D,O
Delaware Valley University	M
DePaul University	M,D
DeSales University	M
Duquesne University	M
Eastern Michigan University	M,O
Elmhurst College	M
Embry-Riddle Aeronautical University–Worldwide	M
Fairleigh Dickinson University, Florham Campus	M
Ferris State University	M
Fontbonne University	M
Friends University	M
Georgia Southern University	D
Golden Gate University	M,D,O
HEC Montreal	M,O
Howard University	M
Indiana University–Purdue University Indianapolis	M
Johnson & Wales University	M
Loyola University Chicago	M,O
Maine Maritime Academy	M
Marquette University	M,O
Maryville University of Saint Louis	M,O
McGill University	M,D,O
Metropolitan State University	M,D,O
Michigan State University	M,D
Moravian College	M
Naval Postgraduate School	M
New York Institute of Technology	M
Niagara University	M
North Carolina Agricultural and Technical State University	M
North Carolina State University	M
Norwich University	M
Nova Southeastern University	M
Old Dominion University	M
Penn State Harrisburg	M,O
Polytechnic University of Puerto Rico, Miami Campus	M
Portland State University	M
Purdue University Global	M
Quinnipiac University	M
Rensselaer Polytechnic Institute	M
Rutgers University–Newark	D
St. Norbert College	M
Santa Clara University	M
Seton Hall University	M,O
Shippensburg University of Pennsylvania	M,D,O
Southern Arkansas University–Magnolia	M
Southern New Hampshire University	M,D,O
Strayer University	M
Suffolk University	M
Syracuse University	M
Towson University	M,O
University at Buffalo, the State University of New York	M,D
The University of Akron	M
The University of Alabama in Huntsville	M,O
University of Dallas	M,D
University of Florida	M,D,O
University of Houston	M
University of Houston–Downtown	M
The University of Kansas	M,D
University of La Verne	M
University of Louisville	M,D,O
The University of Manchester	M
University of Memphis	M,D
University of Michigan	M,D
University of Michigan–Dearborn	M
University of Minnesota, Twin Cities Campus	M,D
University of Missouri–St. Louis	M,D,O
The University of North Carolina at Charlotte	M,O
The University of North Carolina at Greensboro	M,D,O
University of North Texas	M,D,O
University of Pittsburgh	M*
University of Rhode Island	M,O
University of St. Francis (IL)	M,O
University of South Dakota	M,O
University of Southern California	M,D,O
The University of Tennessee at Chattanooga	M
The University of Texas at Austin	M,D
The University of Texas at Dallas	M,D
University of Washington	M,D

M—masters degree; D—doctorate; O—other advanced degree; *—Close-Up and/or Display

University of Wisconsin–Madison — M
University of Wisconsin–Platteville — M
University of Wisconsin–Stout — M,D,O
Walden University — M
Washington University in St. Louis — M
Western Illinois University — M,O
Wichita State University — M
Wilfrid Laurier University — M,D
Worcester Polytechnic Institute — M,D,O
Wright State University — M
Youngstown State University — O

SURVEYING SCIENCE AND ENGINEERING
University of New Brunswick Fredericton — M,D

SURVEY METHODOLOGY
University of Maryland, College Park — M,D
University of Michigan — M,D,O
University of Nebraska–Lincoln — M,D

SUSTAINABILITY MANAGEMENT
Adler University — M
American University — M
Anaheim University — M,D,O
Antioch University New England — M
Aquinas College (MI) — M
Argosy University, Chicago — M,D
Argosy University, Hawai'i — M,D
Argosy University, Los Angeles — M,D
Argosy University, Northern Virginia — M,D,O
Argosy University, Orange County — M,D,O
Argosy University, Phoenix — M,D,O
Argosy University, Seattle — M,D
Argosy University, Tampa — M,D
Argosy University, Twin Cities — M,O
Bard College — M,O
Baruch College of the City University of New York — M,D*
Bluffton University — M
Case Western Reserve University — D
Chatham University — M
City University of Seattle — M
Clark University — M
Colorado State University — M
Columbia University — M
DePaul University — M
Duquesne University — M
Edgewood College — M
Fairleigh Dickinson University, Florham Campus — O
Franklin Pierce University — M,D,O
Goddard College — M
Illinois Institute of Technology — M
Indiana University Bloomington — M,D,O
James Madison University — M
Maastricht School of Management — M,D
Maharishi University of Management — M,D
Michigan Technological University — M,D,O
Naropa University — M
National University — M
The New School — M
Oklahoma State University — M,D,O
Oregon State University — M,D
Penn State Great Valley — M,O
Presidio Graduate School (CA) — M,O
Rochester Institute of Technology — M,O
Royal Roads University — M,O
San Francisco State University — M
Seattle Pacific University — M
SIT Graduate Institute — M
Southeastern Louisiana University — M
Southern New Hampshire University — M,D,O
South University (GA) — M
State University of New York College of Environmental Science and Forestry — M,D,O
Syracuse University — O
Tufts University — M,D
The University of British Columbia — M,D
University of California, Berkeley — O
University of California, Merced — M
University of Colorado Denver — M
University of Louisville — M,D
University of New Hampshire — M,O
University of Portland — M
University of Saint Francis (IN) — M
University of Saskatchewan — M
University of Southern Maine — M
University of South Florida — M,O
University of Vermont — M
University of Wisconsin–Green Bay — M
University of Wisconsin–Parkside — M
University of Wisconsin–Stout — M
University of Wisconsin–Superior — M

SUSTAINABLE DEVELOPMENT
American University — M,D,O
The American University in Cairo — M,D,O
Antioch University Los Angeles — M
Antioch University New England — M,O
Arizona State University at the Tempe campus — M
Baruch College of the City University of New York — M*
Binghamton University, State University of New York — M
Boston Architectural College — M
Brandeis University — M
California State University, Stanislaus — M
Carnegie Mellon University — M,D
The Catholic University of America — M,O

City College of the City University of New York — M
Clarkson University — M,D
Clark University — M
Cleveland State University — M,O
Colorado State University — M,O
Columbia University — M,D
Cornell University — M,D
Dartmouth College — D
DePaul University — M
Eastern Illinois University — M
Eastern Michigan University — M
Emory University — M
Future Generations University — M
Hawai'i Pacific University — M
HEC Montreal — O
Hofstra University — M
Hunter College of the City University of New York — M,O
Instituto Centroamericano de Administración de Empresas — M
Instituto Tecnologico de Santo Domingo — M,O
Iowa State University of Science and Technology — M,D
Johnson & Wales University — M
Judson University — M
Lehigh University — M,O
Lenoir-Rhyne University — M
Lesley University — M,D,O
Lipscomb University — M,O
Long Island University–LIU Post — M,O
Manhattanville College — M,O
Michigan State University — M,D
Minneapolis College of Art and Design — M,O
Mississippi State University — M
Montclair State University — M
New Jersey Institute of Technology — M,D,O
New York School of Interior Design — M
New York University — M*
Northern Arizona University — M
Penn State University Park — M*
Pratt Institute — M
Rochester Institute of Technology — M
St. Edward's University — M
Savannah College of Art and Design — M
Saybrook University — M,D
SIT Graduate Institute — M
Southern Illinois University Edwardsville — M
Southern Methodist University — M,D
Stanford University — M,D,O
State University of New York College of Environmental Science and Forestry — M,D,O
Texas A&M University–Kingsville — D
Texas State University — M
Texas Tech University — M,D
Thomas Jefferson University — M
Unity College — M
University at Buffalo, the State University of New York — M,D
The University of Alabama at Birmingham — M
University of Alaska Fairbanks — M
The University of British Columbia — M
University of Calgary — M,D
University of California, Berkeley — M,O
University of California, Santa Barbara — M,D
University of Colorado Denver — M,D
University of Florida — M,O
University of Georgia — M,D
University of Hawaii at Manoa — M,D,O
University of Houston — M
The University of Iowa — M,D
University of Maryland, College Park — M
University of Massachusetts Amherst — M
University of Michigan — M,D
University of New Brunswick Fredericton — M
University of North Carolina at Asheville — M,O
University of Notre Dame — M
University of Oklahoma — M,D*
University of South Dakota — M,D
University of Southern California — M,D,O
University of South Florida — M
The University of Texas at Austin — M
The University of Texas Rio Grande Valley — M
University of Vermont — M
University of Washington — M,D
The University of Western Ontario — M,D
University of Wisconsin–Madison — M
University of Wisconsin–Stevens Point — D
Walden University — M,D,O
West Chester University of Pennsylvania — M,O
Xavier University — M*

SYSTEMS BIOLOGY
Albert Einstein College of Medicine — D
George Mason University — M,D,O
The George Washington University — D
Harvard University — D*
Massachusetts Institute of Technology — D
Michigan State University — D
Northwestern University — D
Oregon State University — M,D
Purdue University — D
Rutgers University–New Brunswick — D
Stanford University — D
University of California, Irvine — D

University of California, Merced — M,D
University of California, San Diego — D
University of Chicago — D
University of Cincinnati — D
University of Colorado Denver — M,D
University of Pittsburgh — D*
University of Toronto — M,D
Virginia Commonwealth University — D
Washington University in St. Louis — D
Weill Cornell Medicine — M,D

SYSTEMS ENGINEERING
Air Force Institute of Technology — M,D
Arizona State University at the Tempe campus — M
Auburn University — M,D,O
Boston University — M,D
California Institute of Technology — M,D
California State Polytechnic University, Pomona — M
California State University, Fullerton — M
California State University, Northridge — M
Carleton University — M,D
Carnegie Mellon University — M
Case Western Reserve University — M,D
The Catholic University of America — M,O
The Citadel, The Military College of South Carolina — M,D
Clarkson University — M
Colorado State University — M,D
Colorado State University–Pueblo — M
Colorado Technical University Aurora — M
Colorado Technical University Colorado Springs — M
Concordia University (Canada) — M,D,O
Cornell University — M,D
Dartmouth College — M,D
Embry-Riddle Aeronautical University–Daytona — M
Embry-Riddle Aeronautical University–Worldwide — M
Florida Institute of Technology — M,D
George Mason University — M,D,O
Georgetown University — M,D
The George Washington University — M,D
Georgia Institute of Technology — M
Georgia Southern University — M
Harrisburg University of Science and Technology — M
Indiana University Bloomington — D
Instituto Tecnológico y de Estudios Superiores de Monterrey, Campus Chihuahua — M,O
Instituto Tecnológico y de Estudios Superiores de Monterrey, Campus Monterrey — M,D
Iowa State University of Science and Technology — M,D
Johns Hopkins University — M,O*
Kennesaw State University — M
Lehigh University — M,D,O
Loyola Marymount University — M
Massachusetts Institute of Technology — M,D
Mississippi State University — M,D
Missouri University of Science and Technology — M,D
Naval Postgraduate School — M,D,O
New Mexico Institute of Mining and Technology — M
New Mexico State University — M,D,O
North Carolina Agricultural and Technical State University — M,D
Northeastern University — M,D,O
Oakland University — M,D
The Ohio State University — M,D
Ohio University — M
Old Dominion University — M,D
Oregon State University — M,D
Penn State Great Valley — M,O
Purdue University Fort Wayne — M
Regis University — M,O
Rensselaer Polytechnic Institute — M,D
Rochester Institute of Technology — M,D
Rose-Hulman Institute of Technology — M
Rutgers University–New Brunswick — M,D
San Jose State University — M
Simon Fraser University — M,D
Southern Methodist University — M,D
Stevens Institute of Technology — M,D,O
Stony Brook University, State University of New York — M
Tennessee State University — M,D
Texas A&M University–Kingsville — D
The University of Alabama in Huntsville — M,D
University of Alberta — M,D
The University of Arizona — M,D,O
University of Arkansas at Little Rock — M,D,O
University of California, Merced — M,D
University of Colorado Colorado Springs — M,D
University of Florida — M,D,O
University of Houston–Clear Lake — M
University of Illinois at Urbana–Champaign — M,D
University of Louisiana at Lafayette — M
University of Maryland, Baltimore County — M,O
University of Maryland, College Park — M
University of Massachusetts Dartmouth — M,O

University of Michigan — M,D
University of Michigan–Dearborn — M,D
University of Nebraska at Omaha — M,O
University of New Mexico — M,D
The University of North Carolina at Charlotte — M,D,O
University of Pennsylvania — M,D*
University of Regina — M,D
University of Rhode Island — M,D
University of St. Thomas (MN) — M,O
University of South Alabama — D
University of Southern California — M,D,O
University of South Florida — O
The University of Texas at Arlington — M
The University of Texas at Dallas — M
The University of Texas at El Paso — M
The University of Texas Rio Grande Valley — M
University of Utah — M,O
University of Virginia — M,D
University of Washington — M,D
University of Waterloo — M,D
University of Wisconsin–Madison — M,D
Virginia Polytechnic Institute and State University — M,O
Wayne State University — M,D,O
Worcester Polytechnic Institute — M,D,O
Youngstown State University — M

SYSTEMS SCIENCE
Arizona State University at the Tempe campus — M
Binghamton University, State University of New York — M,D
Carleton University — M,D
Claremont Graduate University — M,D,O
Eastern Illinois University — M,O
Fairleigh Dickinson University, Metropolitan Campus — M
Harrisburg University of Science and Technology — M
Hood College — M
Louisiana State University and Agricultural & Mechanical College — M,D
Louisiana State University in Shreveport — M
Miami University — M
Oakland University — D
Portland State University — M,D,O
Rensselaer at Hartford — M
Stevens Institute of Technology — M,D
Strayer University — M
Universidad Autonoma de Guadalajara — M,D
University of Michigan — M,D,O
University of Ottawa — M,D
Worcester Polytechnic Institute — M,D,O

TAXATION
American International College — M,D,O
American University — M,O
Appalachian State University — M
Baruch College of the City University of New York — M*
Bentley University — M
Boise State University — M
Bryant University — M
California Miramar University — M
California Polytechnic State University, San Luis Obispo — M
California State University, Fullerton — M
California State University, Northridge — M,O
Capital University — M
Chapman University — M,D*
DePaul University — M,O
Fairfield University — M
Fairleigh Dickinson University, Florham Campus — M
Fairleigh Dickinson University, Metropolitan Campus — M
Florida Gulf Coast University — M
Florida State University — M,D
Fordham University — M,D
Georgetown University — M,D
Georgia State University — M
Golden Gate University — M,D,O
Goldey-Beacom College — M
Gonzaga University — M
Grand Valley State University — M
HEC Montreal — M,O
Hofstra University — M,O
Illinois Institute of Technology — M,D
Instituto Tecnologico de Santo Domingo — M,O
James Madison University — M
Liberty University — M,D
Lipscomb University — M,O
Long Island University–LIU Brooklyn — M,O
Long Island University–LIU Post — M
Loyola University Chicago — M,D,O
Metropolitan State University of Denver — M
Michigan State University — M,D
Mississippi State University — M
National Paralegal College — M
New York University — M,D,O*
Northeastern University — M
Northern Illinois University — M
Northern Kentucky University — M,O
Northwestern University — M,D
Pace University — M
Robert Morris University — M
St. John's University (NY) — M
St. Thomas University — M,D
Southern Illinois University Edwardsville — M
Southern Methodist University — M,D
Southern New Hampshire University — M,D,O

State University of New York College at Old Westbury — M
Strayer University — M
Suffolk University — M,O
Taft University System — M,D
Temple University — M,D*
Texas Christian University — M
Texas Tech University — M,D
Thomas Jefferson University — M
Université de Montréal — M,D,O
Université de Sherbrooke — M,O
The University of Akron — M
The University of Alabama — M,D
The University of Alabama in Huntsville — M
University of Baltimore — M,D
The University of British Columbia — M,D
University of Cincinnati — M
University of Colorado Denver — M
University of Denver — M
University of Florida — M,D
University of Hartford — M,O
University of Hawaii at Manoa — M
University of Houston — M
University of Miami — M,D
University of Michigan — M,D
University of Minnesota, Twin Cities Campus — M
University of Mississippi — M,D
University of Missouri — M,D,O
University of New Haven — M,D,O
University of New Mexico — M
University of New Orleans — M
University of Notre Dame — M
University of San Diego — M,D,O
University of Southern California — M
University of South Florida — M,D
The University of Texas at Arlington — M,D
University of the Sacred Heart — M
University of Washington — M,D
University of Waterloo — M,D
University of Wisconsin–Madison — M
University of Wisconsin–Milwaukee — M,O*
Villanova University — M
Wake Forest University — M
Walsh College of Accountancy and Business Administration — M
Wayne State University — M,D,O
Weber State University — M
Western Michigan University Thomas M. Cooley Law School —
Wichita State University — M
Widener University — M
Yeshiva University — M

TECHNICAL COMMUNICATION

Auburn University — M,D,O
Boise State University — M
Bowling Green State University — M,D
Drexel University — M*
East Carolina University — M,D,O
Eastern Michigan University — M,O
Eastern Washington University — M
Harvard University — M*
Indiana University–Purdue University Indianapolis — M
Lawrence Technological University — M,O
Minnesota State University Mankato — M,O
Missouri University of Science and Technology — M
Missouri Western State University — M,O
Montana Tech of The University of Montana — M
New Jersey Institute of Technology — M,D,O
Northeastern University — M
Texas State University — M
University of Houston–Downtown — M
University of Nebraska at Omaha — M,O
University of South Florida — O
University of Wisconsin–Stout — M

TECHNICAL WRITING

Carnegie Mellon University — M
Drexel University — M*
Illinois Institute of Technology — M,D
James Madison University — M
Johns Hopkins University — M,O*
Laurentian University — O
Louisiana Tech University — M,D,O
Massachusetts Institute of Technology — M
Metropolitan State University — M
Texas Tech University — M
The University of Alabama in Huntsville — M,O
University of Arkansas at Little Rock — M
University of North Alabama — M
The University of North Carolina at Charlotte — M,O
The University of North Carolina at Greensboro — M,D,O
University of the Sciences — M,O
University of Waterloo — M,O
Western Carolina University — M,O

TECHNOLOGY AND PUBLIC POLICY

Arizona State University at the Tempe campus — M
Carnegie Mellon University — M,D
Eastern Michigan University — M
The George Washington University — M,O
Massachusetts Institute of Technology — M,D
Rensselaer Polytechnic Institute — M,D
Rochester Institute of Technology — M

TELECOMMUNICATIONS

Ball State University — M
Boston University — M,O
California Miramar University — M
Claremont Graduate University — M,D,O
Drexel University — M*
Fairfield University — M,O
Florida International University — M,D
Franklin Pierce University — M,D,O
The George Washington University — M,D
Illinois Institute of Technology — M,D
Instituto Tecnologico de Santo Domingo — M,O
New Jersey Institute of Technology — M,D
Northeastern University — M,D,O
Ohio University — M
Pace University — M,D,O
Rochester Institute of Technology — M
Southern Methodist University — M,D
Stevens Institute of Technology — M,D,O
Stony Brook University, State University of New York — M,D,O
Stratford University (VA) — M,D
Universidad del Turabo — M
Université du Québec, Institut National de la Recherche Scientifique — M,D
University of Alberta — M,D
University of Arkansas — M,D
University of California, San Diego — M,D
University of Colorado Boulder — M
University of Florida — M,D
University of Hawaii at Manoa — O
University of Houston — M
University of Maryland, College Park — M
University of Massachusetts Dartmouth — M,D,O
University of Mississippi — M,D
University of Missouri–Kansas City — M,D,O
The University of North Carolina at Chapel Hill — M,D,O
University of Oklahoma — M,D*
University of Southern California — M,D,O
The University of Texas at Dallas — M,D

TELECOMMUNICATIONS MANAGEMENT

Alaska Pacific University — M
Boston University — M,O
California Miramar University — M
Capitol Technology University — M
Carnegie Mellon University — M
Concordia University (Canada) — M,D,O
East Carolina University — M,D,O
Instituto Tecnológico y de Estudios Superiores de Monterrey, Campus Ciudad de México — M
Instituto Tecnológico y de Estudios Superiores de Monterrey, Campus Ciudad Obregón — M
Instituto Tecnológico y de Estudios Superiores de Monterrey, Campus Estado de México — M,D
Instituto Tecnológico y de Estudios Superiores de Monterrey, Campus Irapuato — M
Murray State University — M
Oklahoma State University — M,D,O
San Diego State University — M
Stevens Institute of Technology — M,D,O
Strayer University — M
University of Colorado Boulder — M
University of South Africa — M,D
University of Wisconsin–Stout — M

TEXTILE DESIGN

Academy of Art University — M
Arizona State University at the Tempe campus — M,D
California State University, Los Angeles — M
Concordia University (Canada) — M
Cornell University — M,D
Cranbrook Academy of Art — M
Drexel University — M*
East Carolina University — M
Illinois State University — M
Kent State University — M
Massachusetts College of Art and Design — M,O
The New School — M
Paris College of Art — M
Rhode Island School of Design — M
Savannah College of Art and Design — M
Temple University — M*
Thomas Jefferson University — M
University of California, Davis — M
University of Cincinnati — M
The University of Kansas — M
The University of Manchester — M,D
University of Minnesota, Twin Cities Campus — M,D,O
The University of North Carolina at Greensboro — M,D
University of North Texas — M,D,O
Wayne State University — M

TEXTILE SCIENCES AND ENGINEERING

Cornell University — M,D
North Carolina State University — M,D
Thomas Jefferson University — M,D
The University of Texas at Austin — M

THANATOLOGY

Brooklyn College of the City University of New York — M
The College of New Rochelle — M,O
Marian University (WI) — M
Southwestern College (NM) — M,O
University of Maryland, Baltimore — O
Washington & Jefferson College — M,O

THEATER

Academy of Art University — M
American Conservatory Theater — M,O
Arcadia University — M,D,O
Arizona State University at the Tempe campus — M,D
Baylor University — M
Berklee College of Music — M,O
Binghamton University, State University of New York — M
Bob Jones University — M,D,O
Boston University — M,O
Bowling Green State University — M,D
Brooklyn College of the City University of New York — M,D
Brown University — M,D
California Institute of the Arts — M,O
California State University, Fullerton — M
California State University, Long Beach — M
California State University, Los Angeles — M
California State University, Northridge — M
Carnegie Mellon University — M
Case Western Reserve University — M
The Catholic University of America — M,O
Central Washington University — M
Columbia University — M,D
Columbus State University — M
Cornell University — D
Dell'Arte International School of Physical Theatre — M
DePaul University — M
Eastern Michigan University — M
Florida Atlantic University — M
Florida State University — M,D
Fontbonne University — M
Fordham University — M
The George Washington University — M,O
The Graduate Center, City University of New York — D
Hollins University — M,O
Hunter College of the City University of New York — M
Idaho State University — M
Illinois State University — M
Indiana University Bloomington — M,D
The Juilliard School — M,D,O
Kansas State University — M
Kent State University — M
Long Island University–LIU Post — M
Louisiana State University and Agricultural & Mechanical College — M,D
Mary Baldwin University — M
Miami University — M
Michigan State University — M
Minnesota State University Mankato — M
Montclair State University — M
Naropa University — M
The New School — M
New York University — M,D,O*
Northern Illinois University — M
Northern Michigan University — M,O
Northwestern University — M,D
The Ohio State University — M,D
Ohio University — M
Oklahoma State University — M
Pace University — M
Penn State University Park — M*
Pensacola Christian College — M,D,O
Point Park University — M
Portland State University — M
Purdue University — M
Regent University — M,D
Roosevelt University — M
Rowan University — M
Rutgers University–New Brunswick — M
San Diego State University — M
San Francisco State University — M
San Jose State University — M
Sarah Lawrence College — M
Savannah College of Art and Design — M
Smith College — M
Southern Illinois University Carbondale — M,D
Southern Methodist University — M
Southern Oregon University — M
Stanford University — D
Stony Brook University, State University of New York — M
Temple University — M*
Texas A&M University–Commerce — M,D,O
Texas State University — M
Texas Tech University — M
Texas Woman's University — M
Towson University — M
Tufts University — M,D
Tulane University — M
Université de Sherbrooke — M,D
Université Laval — M,D
University at Buffalo, the State University of New York — M,D
The University of Akron — M
The University of Alabama — M
University of Alberta — M
The University of Arizona — M
University of Arkansas — M

The University of British Columbia — M,D
University of California, Berkeley — D
University of California, Davis — M,D
University of California, Irvine — M,D
University of California, Los Angeles — M,D
University of California, San Diego — M,D
University of California, Santa Barbara — M,D
University of California, Santa Cruz — O
University of Central Florida — M
University of Central Missouri — M,D,O
University of Chicago — D
University of Cincinnati — M,D
University of Colorado Boulder — M,D
University of Connecticut — M
University of Delaware — M
University of Florida — M
University of Georgia — M
University of Guelph — M
University of Hawaii at Manoa — M,D
University of Houston — M
University of Idaho — M
University of Illinois at Urbana–Champaign — M,D
The University of Iowa — M
The University of Kansas — M,D
University of Lethbridge — M,D
University of Louisville — M
The University of Manchester — D
University of Maryland, Baltimore County — M
University of Maryland, College Park — M,D
University of Massachusetts Amherst — M
University of Memphis — M
University of Minnesota, Twin Cities Campus — M,D
University of Missouri — M,D
University of Missouri–Kansas City — M
University of Montana — M
University of Nebraska–Lincoln — M
University of Nevada, Las Vegas — M
University of New Mexico — M
University of New Orleans — M
The University of North Carolina at Chapel Hill — M
The University of North Carolina at Charlotte — M,D,O
The University of North Carolina at Greensboro — M
University of North Carolina School of the Arts — M
University of Oklahoma — M*
University of Oregon — M,D
University of Ottawa — M
University of Pittsburgh — M,D*
University of San Diego — M
University of Saskatchewan — M
University of South Carolina — M,D
University of South Dakota — M
University of Southern California — M
University of Southern Mississippi — M
The University of Tennessee — M
The University of Texas at Austin — M,D
The University of the Arts — M,O
University of the Cumberlands — M,D,O
University of Toronto — M,D
University of Victoria — M
University of Virginia — M
University of Washington — M,D
University of Wisconsin–Madison — M,D
University of Wisconsin–Superior — M
Utah State University — M
Villanova University — M
Virginia Commonwealth University — M
Washington University in St. Louis — M
Wayne State University — M
Western Illinois University — M
West Virginia University — M,D
Yale University — M,D,O
York University — M,D

THEOLOGY

Abilene Christian University — M
Acadia University — M,D
Ambrose University — M,O
American Baptist Seminary of the West — M
American Jewish University — M
Amridge University — M,D
Anabaptist Mennonite Biblical Seminary — M,O
Anderson University (IN) — M,D
Andrews University — M,D,O
Apex School of Theology — D
Aquinas Institute of Theology — M,D,O
Arlington Baptist University — M
Asbury Theological Seminary — M,D,O
Ashland Theological Seminary — M,D
Assemblies of God Theological Seminary — M,D
The Athenaeum of Ohio — M,O
Atlantic School of Theology — M,O
Austin Presbyterian Theological Seminary — M,D
Ave Maria University — M,D
Azusa Pacific University — M,D
Bakke Graduate University — M,D
Baptist Bible College — M
The Baptist College of Florida — M
Baptist Missionary Association Theological Seminary — M
Barclay College — M

Institution	Degree
Barry University	M,D
Baylor University	M,D
Bethany Theological Seminary	M,O
Bethel Seminary	M,D,O
Bethel University (IN)	M
Bethesda University	M
Beth HaMedrash Shaarei Yosher Institute	
Beth Hatalmud Rabbinical College	
Bethlehem College & Seminary	M
Beth Medrash Govoha	
Bethune-Cookman University	
Bexley Seabury Seminary	M,D,O
Biola University	M,D,O
Bob Jones University	M,D,O
Boston College	M,D,O
Boston University	M,D
Briercrest Seminary	
Brite Divinity School	M,D,O
Bryn Athyn College of the New Church	M
Byzantine Catholic Seminary of Saints Cyril and Methodius	M
Cairn University	M
California Lutheran University	M
Calvary University	M
Calvin Theological Seminary	M,D
Campbellsville University	M
Campbell University	M
Canadian Southern Baptist Seminary	M
Capital University	M,D
Carey Theological College	M,D
Carson-Newman University	M
Catholic Distance University	M
Catholic Theological Union	M,D,O
The Catholic University of America	M,D,O
Central Baptist Theological Seminary	M,O
Central Yeshiva Tomchei Tmimim-Lubavitch	M
Chaminade University of Honolulu	M
Charlotte Christian College and Theological Seminary	M,D
Chicago Theological Seminary	M,D
Christendom College	M
Christian Theological Seminary	M,D
Christ the King Seminary	M
Church Divinity School of the Pacific	M,D,O
Cincinnati Christian University	M
Claremont Graduate University	M,D
Claremont School of Theology	M,D
Clarks Summit University	M
Colgate Rochester Crozer Divinity School	M,D,O
Collège Dominicain de Philosophie et de Théologie	M,D,O
College of Emmanuel and St. Chad	M,D,O
College of Saint Elizabeth	M,O
Columbia International University	M,D,O
Columbia Theological Seminary	M,D
Concordia Lutheran Seminary	M,D,O
Concordia Seminary	M,D,O
Concordia Theological Seminary	M,D
Concordia University (Canada)	M
Concordia University Irvine	M
Concordia University of Edmonton	M
Corban University	M,D,O
Covenant Theological Seminary	M,D,O
Criswell College	M
Crown College	M
Dallas Baptist University	M
Dallas Theological Seminary	M,D,O
Denver Seminary	M,D,O
Dominican House of Studies, Pontifical Faculty of the Immaculate Conception	M,D,O
Dominican School of Philosophy and Theology	M,O
Drew University	M,D,O
Duke University	M,D
Duquesne University	M
Earlham School of Religion	M
Eastern Mennonite University	M,O
Eastern University	M
Ecumenical Theological Seminary	M
Eden Theological Seminary	M,D
Emory University	M,D
Erskine Theological Seminary	M
Evangelical Seminary	M
Evangelical Seminary of Puerto Rico	M,D
Faith Baptist Bible College and Theological Seminary	M
Faith International University	M,D
Faith Theological Seminary	M
Faulkner University	M
Fordham University	M,D
Franciscan School of Theology	M
Franciscan University of Steubenville	M
Freed-Hardeman University	M
Fresno Pacific University	M
Fuller Theological Seminary	M,D,O
Gannon University	M,O
Gardner-Webb University	M,D
Garrett-Evangelical Theological Seminary	M,D
Gateway Seminary	M,D,O
The General Theological Seminary	M,D,O
George Fox University	M,D,O
Georgetown University	D
Georgian Court University	M
Global University	M
Gonzaga University	M
Gordon-Conwell Theological Seminary	M,D
Graceland University (IA)	M
Grace School of Theology	M
Grace Theological Seminary	M
Graduate Theological Union	M,D,O
Grand Rapids Theological Seminary of Cornerstone University	M
Greensboro College	M
Harding School of Theology	M,D
Hardin-Simmons University	M
Hartford Seminary	M,D,O
Harvard University	M*
Hebrew College	M
Hebrew Union College–Jewish Institute of Religion (NY)	M,D
Heritage College and Seminary	M
Holy Apostles College and Seminary	M,O
Holy Cross Greek Orthodox School of Theology	M
Hood Theological Seminary	M,D
Houston Baptist University	M
Houston Graduate School of Theology	M,D
Howard Payne University	M
Howard University	M
Iliff School of Theology	M,D
Indiana Wesleyan University	M
Institute for Christian Studies	M,D
Inter American University of Puerto Rico, Metropolitan Campus	D
Interdenominational Theological Center	M,D
International Baptist College and Seminary	M
The Jewish Theological Seminary	M,D,O
John Carroll University	M
John Paul the Great Catholic University	M
Johnson University	M,D,O
Kehilath Yakov Rabbinical Seminary	
Kenrick-Glennon Seminary	M
Kentucky Christian University	M
The King's University	M,D,O
Kingswood University	M
Knox College	M,D
Knox Theological Seminary	M
Lakeland University	M
Lancaster Bible College	M,D
Lancaster Theological Seminary	M,D,O
Lee University	M
Lenoir-Rhyne University	M
Lexington Theological Seminary	M,D
Liberty University	M,D,O
Lincoln Christian Seminary	M
Lincoln Christian University	M
Lipscomb University	M,D
Logos Evangelical Seminary	M,D,O
Loras College	M
Louisville Presbyterian Theological Seminary	M,D
Lourdes University	M
Loyola Marymount University	M
Loyola University Chicago	M,D,O
Loyola University Chicago	M,D,O
Loyola University Maryland	M,D
Loyola University New Orleans	M,O
Lubbock Christian University	M
Lutheran School of Theology at Chicago	M,D
Lutheran Theological Seminary Saskatoon	M,D
Luther Rice College & Seminary	M,D
Luther Seminary	M,D
Machzikei Hadath Rabbinical College	O
Madonna University	M
Maple Springs Baptist Bible College and Seminary	M,D,O
Maranatha Baptist University	M
Marquette University	M,D
The Master's University	M,D
McCormick Theological Seminary	M,D,O
McGill University	M,D
McMaster University	M,D,O
Meadville Lombard Theological School	M,D
Memphis Theological Seminary	M,D
Mercer University	M,D
Merrimack College	M,O
Mesivta of Eastern Parkway–Yeshiva Zichron Meilech	
Mesivta Torah Vodaath Rabbinical Seminary	O
Mesivtha Tifereth Jerusalem of America	
Methodist Theological School in Ohio	M,D
Mid-America Baptist Theological Seminary	M,D
Mid-America Baptist Theological Seminary Northeast Branch	
Mid-America Reformed Seminary	M
Midwestern Baptist Theological Seminary	M,D,O
Midwest University	M,D
Milligan College	M,D,O
Mirrer Yeshiva Central Institute	
Missio Seminary	M,D,O
Moody Bible Institute	M,O
Moody Theological Seminary–Michigan	M,O
Moravian Theological Seminary	M,O
Mount Angel Seminary	M
Mount St. Joseph University	M,O
Mount St. Mary's University (MD)	M
Mount Vernon Nazarene University	M
Multnomah University	M,D
Naropa University	M
Nashotah House Theological Seminary	M,D,O
Nazarene Theological Seminary	M,D
Nebraska Christian College of Hope International University	M,D
Ner Israel Rabbinical College	M,D,O
Ner Israel Yeshiva College of Toronto	
New Brunswick Theological Seminary	M,D
Newman Theological College	M
Newman University	M
New Orleans Baptist Theological Seminary	M,D
New Saint Andrews College	M,O
New York Theological Seminary	M,D
Northeastern Seminary at Roberts Wesleyan College	M,D
Northern Seminary	M,D
North Park Theological Seminary	M,D
Northwest Nazarene University	M
Northwest University	M
Notre Dame Seminary	M
Nyack College	M,D
Oakland City University	M,D
Oblate School of Theology	M,D,O
Ohio Christian University	M
Ohio Dominican University	M
Ohr Hameir Theological Seminary	
Oklahoma Christian University	M
Oklahoma Wesleyan University	M
Olivet Nazarene University	M
Oral Roberts University	M,D
Pacific School of Religion	M,D,O
Palm Beach Atlantic University	M
Payne Theological Seminary	M
Pentecostal Theological Seminary	M,D
Pfeiffer University	M
Phillips Theological Seminary	M,D
Phoenix Seminary	M,D,O
Piedmont International University	M,D
Pittsburgh Theological Seminary	M,D
Point Loma Nazarene University	M
Pontifical Catholic University of Puerto Rico	M
Pontifical College Josephinum	M
Pontifical John Paul II Institute for Studies on Marriage and Family	M,D
Pope St. John XXIII National Seminary	M
Princeton Theological Seminary	M,D
Providence College	M
Providence University College & Theological Seminary	M,D
Rabbinical Academy Mesivta Rabbi Chaim Berlin	O
Rabbinical College Beth Shraga	
Rabbinical College Bobover Yeshiva B'nei Zion	O
Rabbinical College of Long Island	
Rabbinical Seminary of America	
Reconstructionist Rabbinical College	M,D,O
Reformed Episcopal Seminary	M
Reformed Presbyterian Theological Seminary	M,D
Reformed Theological Seminary–Atlanta Campus	M,D,O
Reformed Theological Seminary–Charlotte Campus	M,D
Reformed Theological Seminary–Dallas Campus	M
Reformed Theological Seminary–Jackson Campus	M,D,O
Reformed Theological Seminary–Orlando Campus	M,D,O
Reformed Theological Seminary–Washington D.C.	M
Reformed University	M
Regent College	M,O
Regent University	M,D
Regis College (Canada)	M,D,O
Sacred Heart Major Seminary	M
Sacred Heart Seminary and School of Theology	M,O
St. Andrew's College	M,D,O
St. Andrew's College in Winnipeg	M
St. Augustine's Seminary of Toronto	M,O
St. Bernard's School of Theology and Ministry	M,O
St. Catherine University	M,O
Saint Charles Borromeo Seminary, Overbrook	M
St. John's Seminary (CA)	M
Saint John's Seminary (MA)	M
Saint John's University (MN)	M
St. John's University (NY)	M
St. Joseph's Seminary	M
Saint Leo University	M,O
Saint Louis University	M,D*
Saint Mary Seminary and Graduate School of Theology	M,D
St. Mary's Seminary and University	M,D,O
Saint Mary's University (Canada)	M
St. Mary's University (United States)	M
Saint Meinrad School of Theology	M
St. Norbert College	M
St. Patrick's Seminary & University	M,O
Saint Paul School of Theology	M,D
Saint Paul University	M,D,O
St. Peter's Seminary	M
Saints Cyril and Methodius Seminary	M
St. Stephen's College	M,D
St. Thomas University	M,D,O
St. Tikhon's Orthodox Theological Seminary	M
St. Vincent de Paul Regional Seminary	M
Saint Vincent Seminary	M
St. Vladimir's Orthodox Theological Seminary	M,D
Samford University	M,D
San Francisco Theological Seminary	M,D
Santa Clara University	M,D,O
Seattle Pacific University	M,O
The Seattle School of Theology and Psychology	M,D
Seattle University	M,D,O
Seton Hall University	M,O
Shaw University	M
Shepherds Theological Seminary	M
Shiloh University	M,D
Sh'or Yoshuv Rabbinical College	
Sioux Falls Seminary	M,D,O
Southeastern Baptist Theological Seminary	M,D
Southeastern University (FL)	M,D
Southern Adventist University	M
The Southern Baptist Theological Seminary	M,D
Southern California Seminary	M,D
Southern Evangelical Seminary	M,D,O
Southern Methodist University	M,D
South Florida Bible College and Theological Seminary	M
Southwestern Assemblies of God University	
Southwestern Baptist Theological Seminary	M,D
Spring Arbor University	M
Spring Hill College	M,O
Starr King School for the Ministry	M
SUM Bible College & Theological Seminary	M
Talmudic University	M
Taylor College and Seminary	M,O
Toronto School of Theology	M,D
Trinity Bible College and Graduate School	M
Trinity College (Canada)	M,D,O
Trinity International University	M,D,O
Trinity School for Ministry	M,D,O
Trinity Western University	M,D
Tri-State Bible College	M
Truett McConnell University	M
Tyndale University College & Seminary	M,O
Unification Theological Seminary	M,D
Union Theological Seminary in the City of New York	M,D
United Lutheran Seminary	M,D
United Lutheran Seminary	M,D,O
United Talmudical Seminary	
United Theological Seminary	M,D
United Theological Seminary of the Twin Cities	M,D,O
Université de Montréal	M,D,O
Université de Sherbrooke	M,D,O
Université du Québec à Chicoutimi	M,D
Université Laval	M,D
University of Chicago	D
University of Dayton	M,D
University of Denver	D,O
University of Dubuque	M,D
University of Holy Cross	M,D
The University of Manchester	D
University of Mobile	M
University of Northwestern–St. Paul	M
University of Notre Dame	M,D
University of Philosophical Research	M
University of Saint Mary of the Lake–Mundelein Seminary	M,D
University of St. Michael's College	M,D,O
University of St. Thomas (MN)	M
University of St. Thomas (TX)	M
The University of Scranton	M
University of South Africa	M,D
The University of the South	M,D
University of the West	M
University of Valley Forge	M
The University of Winnipeg	M,O
Urshan Graduate School of Theology	M
Ursuline College	M
Vancouver School of Theology	M,O
Vanderbilt University	M*
Vanguard University of Southern California	
Victoria University	M,D,O
Villanova University	M,D
Virginia Baptist College	M
Virginia Beach Theological Seminary	M
Virginia Theological Seminary	M,D
Virginia Union University	M,D
Walsh University	M
Wartburg Theological Seminary	M
Wayland Baptist University	M
Welch College	M
Wesley Biblical Seminary	M
Wesley Theological Seminary	M,O
Western Seminary	M
Western Seminary–Sacramento Campus	M,O
Western Seminary–San Jose Campus	M,O
Western Theological Seminary	M,D,O
Westminster Seminary California	M
Westminster Theological Seminary	M,D,O
Wheaton College	M,D
Whitworth University	M
Wilfrid Laurier University	M,D,O
Winebrenner Theological Seminary	M,D
World Mission University	M,D
Wycliffe College	M,D,O
Xavier University	M*
Yale University	M
Yeshiva Beth Moshe	O
Yeshiva Karlin Stolin	
Yeshiva of Nitra Rabbinical College	O
Yeshiva Shaar Hatorah Talmudic Research Institute	
Yeshivath Zichron Moshe	O

THEORETICAL CHEMISTRY

Institution	Degree
Carnegie Mellon University	D
Cornell University	
Georgetown University	D
Laurentian University	M
University of Calgary	M,D

The University of Manchester	M,D
University of Regina	M,D
The University of Tennessee	M,D
Wesleyan University	D
Yale University	D

THEORETICAL PHYSICS

American University of Beirut	M,D
Cornell University	M,D
Delaware State University	D*
Harvard University	D*
Rutgers University–New Brunswick	M,D
The University of Manchester	M,D
University of Victoria	M,D

THERAPIES—DANCE, DRAMA, AND MUSIC

Antioch University New England	M,O
Antioch University Seattle	M
Appalachian State University	M
Arizona State University at the Tempe campus	M,D
California Institute of Integral Studies	M,D
Concordia University (Canada)	M
Drexel University	M,O*
East Carolina University	M,O
Florida State University	M,D
Georgia College & State University	M
Immaculata University	M
Indiana University–Purdue University Indianapolis	M,D
Lesley University	M,D,O
Loyola University New Orleans	M
Maryville University of Saint Louis	M
Michigan State University	M
Molloy College	M
Montclair State University	M,O
Naropa University	M
Nazareth College of Rochester	M
New York University	M*
Ohio University	M,O
Pratt Institute	M
Saint Mary-of-the-Woods College	M
Slippery Rock University of Pennsylvania	M
Southwestern Oklahoma State University	M
State University of New York at New Paltz	M
Temple University	M,D*
Texas Woman's University	M
The University of Kansas	M,D
University of Kentucky	M,D
University of Miami	M,D,O
University of Missouri–Kansas City	M,D
University of the Pacific	M
Western Michigan University	M,O
Wilfrid Laurier University	M

TOXICOLOGY

Clemson University	M,D
Columbia University	M,D
Cornell University	M,D
Duke University	O
East Carolina University	M,D
Florida Agricultural and Mechanical University	M,D
The George Washington University	M,O
Indiana University Bloomington	M,D,O
Indiana University–Purdue University Indianapolis	M,D
Iowa State University of Science and Technology	M,D
Long Island University–LIU Brooklyn	M,D
Louisiana State University and Agricultural & Mechanical College	M,D
Massachusetts Institute of Technology	M,D
Medical College of Wisconsin	D
Medical University of South Carolina	D
Michigan State University	M,D
Oklahoma State University Center for Health Sciences	M
Oregon State University	M,D
Purdue University	M,D
Rutgers University–New Brunswick	M,D
St. John's University (NY)	M
San Diego State University	M,D
Simon Fraser University	M,D,O
Texas Southern University	M,D
Texas Tech University	M,D
Thomas Jefferson University	M
Université de Montréal	O
University at Albany, State University of New York	M,D
University at Buffalo, the State University of New York	M,D
The University of Alabama at Birmingham	M,D
University of Arkansas for Medical Sciences	M,D,O
University of California, Davis	M,D
University of California, Irvine	M,D
University of California, Riverside	M,D
University of California, Santa Cruz	M,D
University of Colorado Denver	D
University of Connecticut	M,D
University of Florida	M,D,O
University of Guelph	M,D
University of Illinois at Chicago	M,D
The University of Iowa	M,D
The University of Kansas	M,D
University of Kentucky	M,D

University of Louisiana at Monroe	D
University of Louisville	M,D
The University of Manchester	M,D
University of Maryland, Baltimore	M,D
University of Maryland Eastern Shore	M,D
University of Michigan	M,D
University of Minnesota, Duluth	M,D
University of Minnesota, Twin Cities Campus	M,D
University of Mississippi	M,D
University of Mississippi Medical Center	D
University of Montana	M,D
University of Nebraska–Lincoln	M,D
University of Nebraska Medical Center	D
University of New Mexico	M,D
The University of North Carolina at Chapel Hill	M,D
University of Prince Edward Island	M,D
University of Puerto Rico–Medical Sciences Campus	M,D
University of Rhode Island	M,D
University of Rochester	D*
University of Saskatchewan	M,D,O
University of South Alabama	M
University of Southern California	M,D
University of South Florida	O
The University of Texas at Austin	M,D
The University of Texas Health Science Center at San Antonio	M
The University of Texas Medical Branch	M,D
University of the Sciences	M,D
University of Utah	D
University of Washington	M,D
University of Wisconsin–Madison	M,D
Utah State University	M,D
Virginia Commonwealth University	M,D,O
Wayne State University	M,D
Wright State University	M

TRANSCULTURAL NURSING

Augsburg University	M,D
Rutgers University–Newark	M,D,O

TRANSLATIONAL BIOLOGY

Baylor College of Medicine	D
Boston University	D
Cedars-Sinai Medical Center	M,D
Rutgers University–New Brunswick	M
University of California, Irvine	M
The University of Iowa	M,D
University of Massachusetts Medical School	M,D
The University of Texas at San Antonio	D
The University of Texas Medical Branch	M,D
Virginia Polytechnic Institute and State University	M,D
Wake Forest University	M,D

TRANSLATION AND INTERPRETATION

American University of Sharjah	M,D
Arizona State University at the Tempe campus	M,D,O
Babel University Professional School of Translation	M
Binghamton University, State University of New York	D,O
Columbia University	M,D
Concordia University (Canada)	M,O
East Tennessee State University	M,O
Gallaudet University	M,D,O
Georgia State University	O
Kent State University	M,D
La Salle University	M,O
London Metropolitan University	M,D
Middlebury Institute of International Studies at Monterey	M
Mills College	M,O
Montclair State University	O
New York University	M*
Rochester Institute of Technology	M
Rutgers University–New Brunswick	M,D
Texas A&M International University	M
Universidad Autonoma de Guadalajara	M,D
Université de Montréal	M,D,O
Université Laval	M,O
University of California, Santa Barbara	M,D
University of Delaware	M
University of Denver	M,O
University of Illinois at Urbana–Champaign	M
The University of Manchester	D
University of Nevada, Las Vegas	M,O
University of Northern Colorado	M
University of North Florida	M
University of Ottawa	M,D
University of Puerto Rico–Río Piedras	M,O
University of Rochester	M,O*
The University of Texas Rio Grande Valley	M
University of Wisconsin–Milwaukee	M,O*
Vermont College of Fine Arts	M
Wesley Biblical Seminary	M
York University	M

TRANSPERSONAL AND HUMANISTIC PSYCHOLOGY

Atlantic University	M
John F. Kennedy University	M

Michigan School of Psychology	M,D
Naropa University	M
Saybrook University	M,D
Seattle University	M
Sofia University	M,D

TRANSPORTATION AND HIGHWAY ENGINEERING

Arizona State University at the Tempe campus	M,D,O
ArtCenter College of Design	M
The Catholic University of America	M,D,O
The Citadel, The Military College of South Carolina	M,O
Clemson University	M,D
College for Creative Studies	M
Cornell University	M,D
École Polytechnique de Montréal	M,D,O
George Mason University	M,D
Illinois State University of Technology	M,D
Iowa State University of Science and Technology	M,D
Kansas State University	M,D
Kennesaw State University	M
Louisiana State University and Agricultural & Mechanical College	M,D
Marquette University	M,D,O
Marshall University	M
Massachusetts Institute of Technology	M,D,O
Morgan State University	M,D,O
New Jersey Institute of Technology	M,D
New York University	M,D*
North Dakota State University	D
Northwestern University	M,D
Ohio University	M,D
Old Dominion University	M
Oregon State University	M,D
Rensselaer Polytechnic Institute	M,D
South Carolina State University	M
Southern Illinois University Edwardsville	M
Southern Methodist University	M,D
Stevens Institute of Technology	M,D,O
Texas Southern University	M
University of Arkansas	M,D
University of Calgary	M,D
University of California, Berkeley	M,D
University of California, Davis	M,D
University of California, Irvine	M,D
University of Central Florida	M,D,O
University of Colorado Denver	M,D
University of Dayton	M
University of Delaware	M
The University of Iowa	M,D
University of Massachusetts Amherst	M,D
University of Memphis	M,D,O
University of Nevada, Las Vegas	M,D
University of New Brunswick Fredericton	M,D
University of Puerto Rico–Mayagüez	M,D
University of Southern California	M,D,O
University of South Florida	M,D,O
The University of Texas at Tyler	M
University of Washington	M,D
University of Wisconsin–Madison	M
Virginia Polytechnic Institute and State University	M,O
Wentworth Institute of Technology	M

TRANSPORTATION MANAGEMENT

American Public University System	M,D
California State University Maritime Academy	M
George Mason University	M
Instituto Tecnologico de Santo Domingo	M,O
Iowa State University of Science and Technology	M
Maine Maritime Academy	M
McGill University	M,D
Naval Postgraduate School	M
New Jersey Institute of Technology	M,D
North Dakota State University	M,D
Pontifical Catholic University of Puerto Rico	O
State University of New York Maritime College	M
Texas A&M University	M
Texas Southern University	M
University at Buffalo, the State University of New York	M
The University of British Columbia	D
University of California, Davis	M,D
University of California, Santa Barbara	M,D
University of Hawaii at Manoa	M,D,O
University of New Orleans	M
University of Southern Mississippi	M
The University of Tennessee	M,D
University of Washington	O

TRAVEL AND TOURISM

Arizona State University at the Tempe campus	M,D,O
Boston University	M
California State University, Chico	M
California State University, East Bay	M
California State University, Fullerton	M
California State University, Northridge	M
Clemson University	M,D,O
Colorado State University	M,D
The George Washington University	M,O
IGlobal University	M,O
Indiana University Bloomington	M,D

Johnson & Wales University	M
Kent State University	M
Lasell College	M,O
New Mexico State University	M
New York University	M*
North Carolina State University	M,D
Old Dominion University	M
Penn State University Park	M,D*
Pontificia Universidad Catolica Madre y Maestra	M
Purdue University	M,D
Rochester Institute of Technology	M
Royal Roads University	M,O
San Diego State University	M
San Francisco State University	M
San Ignacio University	M
Savannah College of Art and Design	M
Schiller International University (United States)	M
Strayer University	M
Syracuse University	M
Temple University	M,D*
Tropical Agriculture Research and Higher Education Center	M,D
Université du Québec à Trois-Rivières	M,O
University of Central Florida	M,D,O
University of Florida	M,D
University of Hawaii at Manoa	M
University of Idaho	M,D
University of Massachusetts Amherst	M,D
University of Minnesota, Twin Cities Campus	M,D
University of New Orleans	M
University of North Texas	M,D,O
University of South Africa	M
University of South Carolina	M
University of South Florida	M
The University of Tennessee	M
Western Illinois University	M
West Virginia University	M,D

URBAN AND REGIONAL PLANNING

Alabama Agricultural and Mechanical University	M
American University of Beirut	M,D
American University of Sharjah	M,D
Andrews University	M
Arizona State University at the Tempe campus	M,D,O
Auburn University	M
Ball State University	M,O
Boston University	M
California Polytechnic State University, San Luis Obispo	M
California State Polytechnic University, Pomona	M
The Catholic University of America	M,O
Clark University	M,D
Cleveland State University	M
College of Charleston	O
Columbia University	M,D
Concordia University (Canada)	O
Cornell University	M,D
Dalhousie University	M,D
Delta State University	M
East Carolina University	M,O
Eastern Kentucky University	M
Eastern Michigan University	M
Eastern University	M
East Tennessee State University	M,O
Florida Atlantic University	M
Florida State University	M,D
Future Generations University	M
Georgetown University	M,D
Georgia Institute of Technology	M,D
Georgia State University	M
Harvard University	M,D*
Hunter College of the City University of New York	M
Indiana University of Pennsylvania	M
Iowa State University of Science and Technology	M
Jackson State University	M,D
Kansas State University	M
Lesley University	M,D,O
Massachusetts Institute of Technology	M,D
McGill University	M,D
Michigan State University	M,D
Minnesota State University Mankato	M,O
Missouri State University	M,O
Morgan State University	M
New York University	M,D*
North Dakota State University	M
Northern Arizona University	M,O
Northwest University	M,D
The Ohio State University	M,D
Pratt Institute	M
Queen's University at Kingston	M
Roger Williams University	M,O
Rutgers University–New Brunswick	M,D
St. Francis Xavier University	M
Saint Louis University	M*
San Diego State University	M
Savannah State University	M
Southeastern University (FL)	M
Southern California Institute of Architecture	M
State University of New York College of Environmental Science and Forestry	M,D
Syracuse University	O
Texas A&M University	M,D
Texas Southern University	M,D
Thomas Edison State University	M
Thomas Jefferson University	M
Tufts University	M

M—masters degree; D—doctorate; O—other advanced degree; *—Close-Up and/or Display

Université de Montréal	M,D,O
Université du Québec à Rimouski	M,D,O
Université du Québec en Outaouais	M
Université Laval	M,D
University at Albany, State University of New York	M,O
The University of Arizona	M
The University of British Columbia	M,D
University of California, Berkeley	M,D
University of California, Davis	M
University of California, Irvine	M,D
University of California, Los Angeles	M,D
University of Central Arkansas	M,O
University of Central Florida	M,O
University of Central Oklahoma	M
University of Cincinnati	M,D
University of Colorado Denver	M,D
University of Detroit Mercy	M
University of Florida	M,D
University of Hawaii at Manoa	M,D,O
University of Idaho	M
University of Illinois at Chicago	M,D
University of Illinois at Urbana–Champaign	M,D
The University of Iowa	M
The University of Kansas	M
University of Louisville	M,D
University of Manitoba	M
University of Maryland, College Park	M,D
University of Massachusetts Amherst	M,D
University of Massachusetts Boston	M
University of Massachusetts Lowell	M,O
University of Memphis	M
University of Minnesota, Twin Cities Campus	M,D
University of Nebraska–Lincoln	M,D
University of New Brunswick Fredericton	M
University of New Mexico	M
University of New Orleans	M
The University of North Carolina at Chapel Hill	M,D
The University of North Carolina at Charlotte	M,O
University of Oklahoma	M,D*
University of Oregon	M
University of Pennsylvania	M,D,O*
University of Pittsburgh	M*
University of Puerto Rico–Río Piedras	M
University of Southern California	M,D,O
University of Southern Maine	M,O
University of South Florida	O
The University of Texas at Arlington	D
The University of Texas at Austin	M,D
The University of Texas at San Antonio	M
The University of Toledo	M,D,O
University of Toronto	M,D
University of Virginia	M
University of Washington	M,D
University of Waterloo	M,D
University of West Georgia	M,D,O
University of Wisconsin–Madison	M,D
University of Wisconsin–Milwaukee	M*
Utah State University	M*
Vanderbilt University	M*
Virginia Commonwealth University	M
Virginia Polytechnic Institute and State University	M,D
Wayne State University	M,O
West Chester University of Pennsylvania	M,O

URBAN DESIGN

American University of Beirut	M,D
Arizona State University at the Tempe campus	M,D
Ball State University	M
Carnegie Mellon University	M
City College of the City University of New York	M
Cornell University	M,D
DePaul University	M
Drexel University	M*
Georgia Institute of Technology	M*
Harvard University	M*
Hofstra University	M
Judson University	M
Kent State University	M
Lawrence Technological University	M,O
London Metropolitan University	M,D
The New School	M
New York Institute of Technology	M
Pratt Institute	M
Rice University	M,D
Savannah College of Art and Design	M
Southern California Institute of Architecture	M
State University of New York College of Environmental Science and Forestry	M
The University of British Columbia	M,D
University of California, Berkeley	M,D
University of California, Los Angeles	M,D
University of Colorado Denver	M,D
University of Houston	M
The University of Kansas	M,D,O
University of Miami	M
The University of North Carolina at Charlotte	M
University of Pennsylvania	M,D,O*
University of South Florida	M
The University of Texas at Austin	M

University of Toronto	M,D
University of Utah	M,D
University of Washington	M,D,O
Washington University in St. Louis	M

URBAN EDUCATION

Alvernia University	M
Bakke Graduate University	M,D
Brown University	M
Buffalo State College, State University of New York	M
Cardinal Stritch University	M,D
Cheyney University of Pennsylvania	M
Claremont Graduate University	M,D,O
Cleveland State University	D
College of Mount Saint Vincent	M,O
Eastern Michigan University	M,O
Emmanuel College (United States)	M,O
Florida International University	M,D,O
Georgia State University	M,D,O
The Graduate Center, City University of New York	D
Grand View University	M,O
Holy Names University	M,O
Langston University	M
Long Island University–LIU Brooklyn	M,O
Loyola Marymount University	M
Manhattanville College	M
Metropolitan State University	M
Morgan State University	D
New Jersey City University	M
Norfolk State University	M
Northeastern Illinois University	M
Providence College	M
Teachers College, Columbia University	M,D
Temple University	M*
University of Chicago	M
University of Houston–Downtown	M
University of Illinois at Chicago	M,D
University of Massachusetts Boston	D
University of Memphis	M,D,O
University of Michigan–Dearborn	M
University of Nebraska at Omaha	M,O
University of Pennsylvania	M*
University of San Francisco	M
University of Southern California	D
University of Wisconsin–Milwaukee	M,D,O*
Virginia Commonwealth University	D

URBAN STUDIES

Arizona State University at the Tempe campus	M,D,O
Azusa Pacific University	M
Boston University	M
Brooklyn College of the City University of New York	M
Cleveland State University	M,D,O
Columbus State University	M
Concordia University (Canada)	M,D,O
Fordham University	M
Fresno Pacific University	M
Hunter College of the City University of New York	M
Indiana University Northwest	M
Le Moyne College	M,O
Long Island University–LIU Brooklyn	M,D,O
Loyola University Chicago	M
Massachusetts Institute of Technology	M,D
Minnesota State University Mankato	M,O
Moody Bible Institute	M,O
New Jersey City University	M
New York University	M,D*
Norfolk State University	M
North Dakota State University	M,D
Northeastern University	M,D
Queens College of the City University of New York	M
Rutgers University–Newark	M,D
Savannah State University	M
Simon Fraser University	M,O
Temple University	M,D,O*
Tufts University	M
Université du Québec à Montréal	M,D
Université du Québec, École nationale d'administration publique	M
Université du Québec, Institut National de la Recherche Scientifique	M,D,O
University at Albany, State University of New York	M,D,O
University of California, Irvine	M,D
University of Delaware	M,D
University of Lethbridge	M,D
University of Louisville	M,D
University of Maryland, Baltimore County	M,D
University of New Orleans	M,D
University of San Francisco	M
University of Wisconsin–Milwaukee	M,D*
Virginia Polytechnic Institute and State University	M
Wayne State University	M,D,O

VETERINARY MEDICINE

Auburn University	D
Colorado State University	D
Cornell University	D
Iowa State University of Science and Technology	M
Kansas State University	D
Lincoln Memorial University	M
Louisiana State University and Agricultural & Mechanical College	D
Michigan State University	D

Midwestern University, Glendale Campus	D
Mississippi State University	D
Oklahoma State University	D
Oregon State University	D
Purdue University	D
Texas A&M University	M,D
Tufts University	M,D
Tuskegee University	M,D
Université de Montréal	D
University of California, Davis	D
University of Florida	D
University of Georgia	D
University of Guelph	M,D,O
University of Illinois at Urbana–Champaign	D
University of Maryland, College Park	D
University of Minnesota, Twin Cities Campus	D
University of Missouri	M,D
University of Pennsylvania	D*
University of Prince Edward Island	D
University of Saskatchewan	M,D
The University of Tennessee	D
University of Wisconsin–Madison	M,D
Virginia Polytechnic Institute and State University	M,D
Washington State University	D
Western University of Health Sciences	D

VETERINARY SCIENCES

Clemson University	M,D
Colorado State University	M,D
Drexel University	M*
Iowa State University of Science and Technology	M,D
Kansas State University	M,O
Louisiana State University and Agricultural & Mechanical College	M,D
Michigan State University	M,D
Mississippi State University	M,D
North Carolina State University	M,D
The Ohio State University	M,D
Oklahoma State University	M,D
Penn State Hershey Medical Center	M
Purdue University	M,D
South Dakota State University	M,D
Texas A&M University	M,D
Tuskegee University	M,D
Université de Montréal	M,D
University of California, Davis	M,O
University of Florida	M,D,O
University of Guelph	M,D,O
University of Idaho	M,D
University of Illinois at Urbana–Champaign	M,D
University of Kentucky	M,D
University of Maryland, College Park	M,D
University of Minnesota, Twin Cities Campus	M,D
University of Missouri	M
University of Nebraska–Lincoln	M,D
University of Prince Edward Island	M,D
University of Saskatchewan	M,D
University of Vermont	M,D
University of Washington	M
University of Wisconsin–Madison	M,D
Utah State University	M,D
Virginia Polytechnic Institute and State University	M,D
Washington State University	M,D

VIROLOGY

Baylor College of Medicine	D
Case Western Reserve University	D
Mayo Clinic Graduate School of Biomedical Sciences	D
McMaster University	M,D
Oregon State University	M,D
Penn State Hershey Medical Center	M,D
Purdue University	M,D
Rush University	M,D
Rutgers University–New Brunswick	M,D
Université de Montréal	D
Université du Québec, Institut National de la Recherche Scientifique	M,D
The University of Iowa	M,D
University of Minnesota, Twin Cities Campus	M,D
University of Pennsylvania	D*
University of Prince Edward Island	M,D
Yale University	D

VISION SCIENCES

Eastern Virginia Medical School	O
Marshall B. Ketchum University	M,D
New England College of Optometry	M,D
Pacific University	M,D
Salus University	M,O
State University of New York College of Optometry	D
Université de Montréal	M,O
The University of Alabama at Birmingham	M,D
University of Alberta	M,D
University of California, Berkeley	M,D
University of Guelph	M,D,O
University of Houston	M,D
The University of Manchester	M,D
University of Massachusetts Boston	M
University of Pittsburgh	M,D*
University of Waterloo	M,D
Western Michigan University	M

VITICULTURE AND ENOLOGY

California State University, Fresno	M

Cornell University	M,D
Oregon State University	M,D
University of California, Davis	M,D

VOCATIONAL AND TECHNICAL EDUCATION

Alcorn State University	M,O
Appalachian State University	M
Athens State University	M
Bowling Green State University	M
Buffalo State College, State University of New York	M
California Baptist University	M
California University of Pennsylvania	M
Capella University	D
Central Connecticut State University	M
Central Washington University	M
Chicago State University	M
Clarion University of Pennsylvania	M
Concordia University (United States)	M,D
East Carolina University	M,O
Eastern Kentucky University	M
Eastern New Mexico University	M
Fitchburg State University	M
Florida Agricultural and Mechanical University	O
The George Washington University	O
Indiana State University	M
Indiana University of Pennsylvania	M
Inter American University of Puerto Rico, Metropolitan Campus	M
Iowa State University of Science and Technology	M,D
Jackson State University	M,D
James Madison University	M
Kent State University	M
Louisiana State University and Agricultural & Mechanical College	M,D
Middle Tennessee State University	M
Mississippi State University	M,D,O
Montana State University	M,D,O
Morehead State University	M
Murray State University	M,O
North Carolina State University	M,D,O
Northern Arizona University	M,O
Old Dominion University	M,D
Penn State University Park	M,D,O*
Pittsburg State University	M,O
Purdue University	M,D,O
Rochester Institute of Technology	O
South Carolina State University	M
Southern Illinois University Carbondale	M,D
State University of New York at Oswego	M
Temple University	M*
Texas State University	M
University of Arkansas	M,D,O
The University of British Columbia	M,D
University of Central Florida	M,O
University of Central Missouri	M,D,O
University of Georgia	M,D,O
University of Idaho	M,O
University of Maryland Eastern Shore	M
University of Minnesota, Twin Cities Campus	M,D,O
University of Missouri	M,D,O
University of Nebraska–Lincoln	M,D,O
University of New England	M,D,O
University of Northern Iowa	M,D
University of North Texas	M,D,O
University of Phoenix–Phoenix Campus	M
University of South Africa	M,D
University of South Florida	M,D,O
The University of Toledo	M,D,O
University of Victoria	M,D
University of Wisconsin–Stout	M,D,O
Utah State University	D
Valley City State University	M
Virginia Polytechnic Institute and State University	M,D,O
Washington State University	M,D
Wayne State College	M
Western Michigan University	M
Westfield State University	M
Wilmington University	M,D

WATER RESOURCES

Albany State University	M
California State University, Monterey Bay	M
Colorado State University	M,D
Cornell University	M,D
Dalhousie University	M
Humboldt State University	M
Marquette University	M
Missouri University of Science and Technology	M,D,O
Montclair State University	M,D*
New Mexico State University	O
Old Dominion University	M,D
Oregon State University	M
Rutgers University–New Brunswick	M,D
State University of New York College of Environmental Science and Forestry	M,D
Tropical Agriculture Research and Higher Education Center	M,D
Tufts University	M,D
The University of Arizona	M,D,O
The University of British Columbia	M,D
University of Calgary	M
University of California, Riverside	M
University of Colorado Denver	M
University of Florida	M,D
University of Idaho	M,D

The University of Iowa — M,D
University of Maine — M,D
University of Massachusetts Amherst — M,D
University of Minnesota, Twin Cities Campus — M,D
University of Missouri — M,D,O
University of Nevada, Las Vegas — M
University of New Brunswick Fredericton — M,D
University of New Hampshire — M
University of New Mexico — M
University of Southern California — M,D,O
University of the District of Columbia — M
University of the Pacific — M,D
University of Wisconsin–Madison — M
University of Wisconsin–Milwaukee — M,D*
University of Wyoming — M,D
Utah State University — M,D

WATER RESOURCES ENGINEERING

American University of Beirut — M,D
Carnegie Mellon University — M,D
Clemson University — M,D
Cornell University — M,D
Indiana University Bloomington — M,D,O
Kansas State University — M,D
Kennesaw State University — M
Lawrence Technological University — M,D
Louisiana State University and Agricultural & Mechanical College — M,D
Marquette University — M,D,O
McGill University — M,D
New Mexico Institute of Mining and Technology — M
Ohio University — M,D
Oregon State University — M,D
State University of New York College of Environmental Science and Forestry — M,D
Stevens Institute of Technology — M,D,O
Tufts University — M,D
University at Buffalo, the State University of New York — M,D
University of Alberta — M,D
University of California, Berkeley — M,D
University of Dayton — M
University of Delaware — M,D
University of Guelph — M,D
University of Idaho — M,D
The University of Iowa — M,D
University of Massachusetts Amherst — M,D
University of Memphis — M,D,O
University of New Haven — M
University of South Florida — M,D,O
The University of Texas at Austin — M,D
The University of Texas at Tyler — M
University of Wisconsin–Madison — M,D
Villanova University — M,O

WESTERN EUROPEAN STUDIES

American University — M,D,O
Boston College — M,D
Brown University — M,D
Carleton University — M,O
The Catholic University of America — M,D
Central Michigan University — M,O
Claremont Graduate University — M,D,O
College of Staten Island of the City University of New York — M
Columbia University — M,D
Cornell University — M,D
Dallas Baptist University — M
Drew University — M,D,O
East Carolina University — M
Georgetown University — M
The George Washington University — M
Indiana University Bloomington — M
Indiana University–Purdue University Indianapolis — M
La Salle University — M,O
Monmouth University — M
New York University — M*
San Diego State University — M
University of Colorado Denver — M
University of Guelph — M
University of Illinois at Urbana–Champaign — M
University of Louisiana at Lafayette — M
University of Nevada, Reno — D
University of Pittsburgh — O*
University of South Florida — M,D
University of Virginia — M

WOMEN&APOSS HEALTH NURSING

Boston College — M,D
California State University, Fullerton — M,D
Carlow University — M
Case Western Reserve University — M
Drexel University — M*
Duke University — M,D,O
East Tennessee State University — M,D,O
Emory University — M
Frontier Nursing University — M,D,O*
Georgia State University — M,D,O
Loyola University Chicago — M,D,O
MGH Institute of Health Professions — M,D,O
Queen's University at Kingston — M,D,O
Rutgers University–Newark — M,D,O
San Francisco State University — M,O
Stony Brook University, State University of New York — M,D,O
Tennessee Technological University — D

Texas Woman's University — M,D
Uniformed Services University of the Health Sciences — M,D*
The University of Alabama at Birmingham — M,D
University of Cincinnati — M,D
University of Colorado Denver — M,D
University of Delaware — M,O
University of Illinois at Chicago — M,O
University of Indianapolis — M,D
University of Louisville — M,D
University of Minnesota, Twin Cities Campus — M,D
University of Missouri–Kansas City — M,D
University of Missouri–St. Louis — D,O
University of Pennsylvania — M*
University of South Carolina — M
Virginia Commonwealth University — M,D,O
Wayne State University — M,D

WOMEN&APOSS STUDIES

American University — O
The American University in Cairo — M,O
Brandeis University — M,D
Carnegie Mellon University — D
Chatham University — M
Claremont Graduate University — M,D
Cornell University — M,D
DePaul University — M
Eastern Michigan University — M,O
Emory University — D,O
Florida Atlantic University — M
George Mason University — M
The George Washington University — M,O
Georgia State University — M,O
Grace Theological Seminary — M,D,O
Inter American University of Puerto Rico, Metropolitan Campus — M
The Jewish Theological Seminary — M,D
Kansas State University — O
Lakehead University — M,D
Lesley University — M,D,O
London Metropolitan University — M,D
Loyola University Chicago — M
Middle Tennessee State University — O
Minnesota State University Mankato — M,D
Mount Saint Vincent University — M
Northern Arizona University — O
The Ohio State University — M,D
Old Dominion University — M
Oregon State University — M,D
Queen's University at Kingston — M,D
Reconstructionist Rabbinical College — M,D,O
Rutgers University–New Brunswick — M,D
Saint Mary's University (Canada) — M
San Diego State University — M
San Francisco State University — M
Sarah Lawrence College — M
Simon Fraser University — M,D
Smith College — O
Southeastern Baptist Theological Seminary — M,D
Southern Connecticut State University — M
Stony Brook University, State University of New York — O
Texas Woman's University — M,D
Towson University — M,O
United Theological Seminary of the Twin Cities — M,D,O
Université Laval — O
University at Albany, State University of New York — M
The University of Alabama — M
The University of Arizona — M,D,O
University of California, Santa Barbara — M
University of Cincinnati — M,O
University of Colorado Denver — M,O
University of Florida — M,O
University of Georgia — O
University of Hawaii at Manoa — O
The University of Iowa — O
University of Lethbridge — M,D
University of Louisville — M,O
University of Maryland, Baltimore County — O
University of Maryland, College Park — M,D
University of Michigan — D,O
University of Minnesota, Twin Cities Campus — D
University of New Hampshire — O
The University of North Carolina at Charlotte — M,D,O
The University of North Carolina at Greensboro — M,D,O
University of Northern Iowa — M*
University of Oklahoma — O*
University of Ottawa — M
University of Pittsburgh — O*
University of Regina — M
University of Rhode Island — O
University of South Carolina — O
University of South Florida — O
The University of Toledo — O
University of Toronto — M,D
University of Washington — D
University of Wisconsin–Madison — M,D
University of Wisconsin–Milwaukee — M,O*
Wayne State University — M,D,O
Western Seminary — M

Western Seminary–Sacramento Campus — O
Western Seminary–San Jose Campus — M,O
Wilson College — M
York University — M,D

WRITING

Abilene Christian University — M
Academy of Art University — M
Adelphi University — M
Agnes Scott College — M
Albertus Magnus College — M
American College Dublin — M
American University — M
Antioch University Santa Barbara — M
Arcadia University — M
Arizona State University at the Tempe campus — M,D
Asbury University — M
Ashland University — M
Auburn University at Montgomery — M
Ball State University — M,D
Bard College — M
Bay Path University — M
Bennington College — M
Binghamton University, State University of New York — M,D
Boston University — M
Bowling Green State University — M,D
Brigham Young University — M
Brooklyn College of the City University of New York — M
Brown University — M,D
California College of the Arts — M
California Institute of the Arts — M,O
California State University, Fresno — M
California State University, Long Beach — M
California State University, Northridge — M
California State University, Sacramento — M
California State University, San Bernardino — M
California State University, San Marcos — M
California State University, Stanislaus — M,O
Carlow University — M
Carnegie Mellon University — M
Cedar Crest College — M
Central Michigan University — M
Central Washington University — M
Chapman University — M*
Chatham University — M
Chicago State University — M
City College of the City University of New York — M
Claremont Graduate University — M,D
Clemson University — M,D
Cleveland State University — M
Coastal Carolina University — M
The College at Brockport, State University of New York — M,O
College of Charleston — M
Colorado State University — M
Columbia College Chicago — M
Columbia University — M
Concordia University (Canada) — M
Concordia University, St. Paul — M
Converse College — M
Cornell University — M,D
Creighton University — M
DePaul University — M
Dominican University of California — M
Drew University — M,D,O
East Carolina University — M,D,O
Eastern Kentucky University — M
Eastern Michigan University — M,O
Fairfield University — M
Fairleigh Dickinson University, Florham Campus — M
Fitchburg State University — M
Florida International University — M
Florida State University — M,D
Full Sail University — M
George Mason University — M
Georgia College & State University — M
Georgia Southern University — M,O
Georgia State University — M,D
Goddard College — M
Goucher College — M
Hamline University — M
Hofstra University — M
Hollins University — M,O
Holy Names University — M
Hunter College of the City University of New York — M
Illinois State University — M,D
Indiana State University — M
Indiana University Bloomington — M,D
Indiana University–Purdue University Indianapolis — M,O
Indiana University South Bend — M,O
Institute of American Indian Arts — M
Iowa State University of Science and Technology — M,D
Ithaca College — M
James Madison University — M
Johns Hopkins University — M,O*
Kean University — M
Kennesaw State University — M
Kent State University — M,D
Lake Forest College — M
La Sierra University — M
Lenoir-Rhyne University — M
Lesley University — M,D,O
Lindenwood University — M,O
Lipscomb University — M

London Metropolitan University — M,D
Long Island University–LIU Brooklyn — M,D,O
Louisiana State University and Agricultural & Mechanical College — M,D
Loyola Marymount University — M
Maharishi University of Management — M
Manhattanville College — M
Massachusetts Institute of Technology — M
McDaniel College — M,O
McNeese State University — M
Michigan State University — M,D
Millersville University of Pennsylvania — M,O
Mills College — M,O
Minnesota State University Mankato — M,O
Missouri State University — M,O
Missouri Western State University — M,O
Monmouth University — M
Montclair State University — O
Mount Mary University — M
Mount Saint Mary's University (CA) — M,D,O
Murray State University — M,D,O
Naropa University — M
National Louis University — M,D,O
National University — M,O
New England College — M
New Hampshire Institute of Art — M
New Mexico Highlands University — M
New Mexico State University — M,D
New Saint Andrews College — M,O
The New School — M
New York University — M*
North Carolina State University — M
North Dakota State University — M,D
Northern Arizona University — M,D,O
Northern Kentucky University — M,O
Northern Michigan University — M,O
Northwestern University — M
Oklahoma City University — M
Oklahoma State University — M,D
Old Dominion University — M
Oregon State University — M
Otis College of Art and Design — M
Our Lady of the Lake University — M
Pacific Lutheran University — M
Pacific University — M
Park University — M,O
Pepperdine University — M
Pittsburg State University — M
Portland State University — M
Pratt Institute — M
Purdue University — M,D
Queens College of the City University of New York — M
Queens University of Charlotte — M
Randolph College — M
Regent University — M,D
Regis University — M,O
Reinhardt University — M
Rhode Island College — M,O
Rivier University — M
Roosevelt University — M
Rosemont College — M
Rowan University — M,O
Rutgers University–Camden — M
Rutgers University–Newark — M
Rutgers University–New Brunswick — M
St. Cloud State University — M
St. Joseph's College, New York — M
Saint Joseph's University — M
Saint Leo University — M
Saint Mary's College of California — M
Salve Regina University — M
Sam Houston State University — M
San Diego State University — M
San Francisco State University — M
Sarah Lawrence College — M
Savannah College of Art and Design — M
School of the Art Institute of Chicago — M,O
School of Visual Arts (NY) — M
Seattle Pacific University — M
Seton Hill University — M
Shenandoah University — M,D,O
Simmons University — M,D,O
Sonoma State University — M
Southeastern Louisiana University — M
Southern Illinois University Carbondale — M
Southern Illinois University Edwardsville — M
Southern New Hampshire University — M
Spalding University — M
State University of New York at Fredonia — M,O
Stephens College — M,O
Stetson University — M
Stony Brook University, State University of New York — M,O
Syracuse University — M,D
Temple University — M,D*
Texas A&M University–Commerce — M,D,O
Texas State University — M
Tiffin University — M
Towson University — M
Trinity College (United States) — M
Union Institute & University — M
The University of Akron — M
The University of Alabama — M,D
The University of Alabama at Birmingham — M
University of Alaska Anchorage — M
University of Alaska Fairbanks — M
The University of Arizona — M

M—masters degree; D—doctorate; O—other advanced degree; *—Close-Up and/or Display

University of Arkansas	M	University of Massachusetts Dartmouth	M,O	The University of Tennessee at Chattanooga	M	Western State Colorado University	M
University of Arkansas at Little Rock	M	University of Memphis	M,D,O	The University of Texas at Austin	M,D	Westminster College (UT)	M
University of Baltimore	M	University of Miami	M,D	The University of Texas at El Paso	M,D,O	West Virginia University	M,D
The University of British Columbia	M,D	University of Michigan	M	The University of Texas Rio Grande Valley	M	West Virginia Wesleyan College	M
University of California, Berkeley	O	University of Michigan–Flint	M	University of the Sacred Heart	M,O	Wichita State University	M
University of California, Davis	M,D	University of Mississippi	M,D	The University of the South	M	Wilkes University	M
University of California, Irvine	M	University of Missouri–St. Louis	M	The University of Toledo	M,O	William Paterson University of New Jersey	M,D,O
University of California, Riverside	M	University of Montana	M	University of Toronto	M,D	Yale University	M,D,O
University of California, San Diego	M,D	University of Nebraska at Kearney	M	University of Utah	M,D		
University of California, Santa Barbara	D	University of Nebraska at Omaha	M,O	University of Victoria	M	**ZOOLOGY**	
University of California, Santa Cruz	M	University of Nebraska–Lincoln	M,D	University of Virginia	M	Auburn University	M,D
University of Central Arkansas	M	University of Nevada, Las Vegas	M,D,O	University of Washington	M	Colorado State University	M,D
University of Central Oklahoma	M	University of New Hampshire	M,D	University of Washington, Bothell	M	Emporia State University	M
University of Chicago	M	University of New Mexico	M	University of West Florida	M	Illinois State University	M,D
University of Colorado Boulder	M,D	University of New Orleans	M	University of Windsor	M	Indiana University Bloomington	M,D
University of Colorado Denver	M	University of North Alabama	M	University of Wisconsin–Eau Claire	M	Michigan State University	M,D
University of Dayton	M	The University of North Carolina at Charlotte	M,O	University of Wisconsin–Madison	M,D	North Dakota State University	M,D
University of Denver	M,D,O	The University of North Carolina at Greensboro	M	University of Wisconsin–Milwaukee	M,D*	Southern Illinois University Carbondale	M,D
The University of Findlay	M,D	The University of North Carolina Wilmington	M	University of Wyoming	M	Texas Tech University	M,D
University of Florida	M,D	University of Northern Iowa	M	Utah State University	M	Uniformed Services University of the Health Sciences	M,D*
University of Houston	M,D	University of North Florida	M	Vanderbilt University	M*	The University of British Columbia	M,D
University of Houston–Victoria	M	University of North Texas	M,D,O	Vermont College of Fine Arts	M	University of California, Davis	M
University of Idaho	M	University of Notre Dame	M	Virginia Commonwealth University	M	University of Florida	M,D
University of Illinois at Urbana–Champaign	M,D	University of Oklahoma	M,D*	Virginia Polytechnic Institute and State University	M,D,O	University of Guelph	M,D
The University of Iowa	M,D	University of Oregon	M	Warren Wilson College	M	University of Hawaii at Manoa	M,D
The University of Kansas	M,D	University of Pittsburgh	M,D*	Washington & Jefferson College	M,O	University of Illinois at Urbana–Champaign	M,D
University of King's College	M	University of Regina	M,D	Washington University in St. Louis	M	University of Maine	M,D
University of Louisiana at Lafayette	M,D	University of Rhode Island	M,D	Wayne State University	M,D	University of Manitoba	M,D
University of Louisville	M,D	University of San Francisco	M	Wesleyan University	M,O	University of Montana	M,D
The University of Manchester	D	University of South Alabama	M	West Chester University of Pennsylvania	M,O	University of North Dakota	M,D
University of Maryland, College Park	M,D	University of South Carolina	M,D	Western Carolina University	M,O	University of Wisconsin–Madison	M,D
University of Massachusetts Amherst	M,D	University of Southern California	M,D	Western Connecticut State University	M	University of Wisconsin–Oshkosh	M
University of Massachusetts Boston	M	University of Southern Maine	M	Western Kentucky University	M	University of Wyoming	M,D
		University of Southern Mississippi	M,D	Western Michigan University	M,D	Western Illinois University	M,O
		University of South Florida	M,D,O	Western New England University	M	West Liberty University	M
		The University of Tampa	M				

DIRECTORY OF INSTITUTIONS AND THEIR OFFERINGS

ABILENE CHRISTIAN UNIVERSITY

Accounting	M
Business Administration and Management—General	M
Business Analytics	M
Clinical Psychology	M
Communication Disorders	M
Communication—General	M
Conflict Resolution and Mediation/Peace Studies	M,O
Counseling Psychology	M
Education—General	M,O
Educational Leadership and Administration	M,D,O
English	M
Health Services Management and Hospital Administration	M
Higher Education	M
Human Resources Development	M
Human Services	M,O
International Business	M
Liberal Studies	M
Marketing	M
Marriage and Family Therapy	M
Missions and Missiology	M
Nonprofit Management	M
Nursing and Healthcare Administration	D
Nursing Education	D
Nursing—General	D
Nutrition	M,O
Occupational Therapy	M
Pastoral Ministry and Counseling	M,D
Psychology—General	M
Reading Education	M
Religion	M
Rhetoric	M
School Psychology	O
Social Work	M
Supply Chain Management	M
Theology	M
Writing	M

ABRAHAM LINCOLN UNIVERSITY

Law	D

ACACIA UNIVERSITY

Education—General	M
Educational Leadership and Administration	M
Elementary Education	M
English as a Second Language	M
Secondary Education	M
Special Education	M

ACADEMY FOR FIVE ELEMENT ACUPUNCTURE

Acupuncture and Oriental Medicine	M

ACADEMY FOR JEWISH RELIGION CALIFORNIA

Jewish Studies	M

ACADEMY OF ART UNIVERSITY

Advertising and Public Relations	M
Applied Arts and Design—General	M
Architecture	M
Art Education	M
Art History	M
Art/Fine Arts	M
Arts Journalism	M
Computer Art and Design	M
Film, Television, and Video Production	M
Game Design and Development	M
Graphic Design	M
Illustration	M
Industrial Design	M
Interior Design	M
Internet and Interactive Multimedia	M
Landscape Architecture	M
Music	M
Photography	M
Textile Design	M
Theater	M
Writing	M

ACADEMY OF CHINESE CULTURE AND HEALTH SCIENCES

Acupuncture and Oriental Medicine	M

ACADIA UNIVERSITY

Biological and Biomedical Sciences—General	M
Chemistry	M
Clinical Psychology	M
Computer Science	M
Counselor Education	M
Curriculum and Instruction	M
Education—General	M,D
Educational Leadership and Administration	M
English	M
Geographic Information Systems	M
Geology	M
Mathematics	M
Missions and Missiology	M,D
Music Education	M
Pastoral Ministry and Counseling	M,D
Philosophy	M
Political Science	M
Psychology—General	M
Recreation and Park Management	M
Sociology	M
Special Education	M
Statistics	M
Theology	M,D

ACUPUNCTURE & INTEGRATIVE MEDICINE COLLEGE, BERKELEY

Acupuncture and Oriental Medicine	M

ACUPUNCTURE AND MASSAGE COLLEGE

Acupuncture and Oriental Medicine	M

ADAMS STATE UNIVERSITY

Business Administration and Management—General	M
Clinical Psychology	M,D
Counselor Education	M,D
Curriculum and Instruction	M
Education—General	M
Educational Leadership and Administration	M
Exercise and Sports Science	M
History	M
Humanities	M
Mathematics Education	M
Music Education	M
Physical Education	M
Public Administration	M
Science Education	M
Sport Psychology	M
Sports Management	M

ADELPHI UNIVERSITY

Accounting	M
Adult Nursing	M
Art Education	M
Art/Fine Arts	M
Biological and Biomedical Sciences—General	M
Biotechnology	M
Business Administration and Management—General	M
Clinical Psychology	D
Communication Disorders	M,D
Community Health	M,O
Counseling Psychology	M
Education—General	M,D,O
Educational Media/Instructional Technology	M
Elementary Education	M
Emergency Management	O
English as a Second Language	M,O
Environmental Management and Policy	M
Environmental Sciences	M
Finance and Banking	M
Gerontology	M,O
Health Education	M,O
Health Informatics	M,D,O
Health Services Management and Hospital Administration	M
Human Resources Management	M,O
Management Information Systems	M
Marketing	M
Nursing and Healthcare Administration	M,O
Nursing Education	M,O
Nursing—General	D
Nutrition	M,D,O
Physical Education	M,O
Psychology—General	M
Public Health—General	M
Reading Education	M
School Psychology	M
Secondary Education	M
Social Work	M,D
Special Education	M,O
Sports Management	M
Supply Chain Management	M
Writing	M

ADLER GRADUATE SCHOOL

Addictions/Substance Abuse Counseling	M
Art Therapy	M
Clinical Psychology	M
Counseling Psychology	M
Counselor Education	M
Marriage and Family Therapy	M
Psychoanalysis and Psychotherapy	M

ADLER UNIVERSITY

Addictions/Substance Abuse Counseling	O
Applied Psychology	M
Art Therapy	M,D
Child Development	M
Clinical Psychology	M,D
Community Health	M
Counseling Psychology	M
Counselor Education	D
Criminal Justice and Criminology	M
Developmental Psychology	M
Forensic Psychology	M
Gender Studies	M
Health Promotion	M
Health Psychology	M
Industrial and Organizational Psychology	M,D
Marriage and Family Therapy	M,D,O
Military and Defense Studies	M
Public Administration	M
Public Policy	M
Rehabilitation Counseling	M
School Psychology	M
Social Psychology	M
Sport Psychology	M
Sustainability Management	M

ADRIAN COLLEGE

Accounting	M
Athletic Training and Sports Medicine	M
Criminal Justice and Criminology	M

ADVENTHEALTH UNIVERSITY

Health Services Management and Hospital Administration	M
Nurse Anesthesia	M
Occupational Therapy	M
Physical Therapy	D
Physician Assistant Studies	M

AGNES SCOTT COLLEGE

Internet and Interactive Multimedia	M
Writing	M

AIR FORCE INSTITUTE OF TECHNOLOGY

Aerospace/Aeronautical Engineering	M,D
Applied Mathematics	M,D
Applied Physics	M,D
Astrophysics	M,D
Computer Engineering	M,D
Computer Science	M,D
Electrical Engineering	M,D
Engineering and Applied Sciences—General	M,D
Engineering Management	M
Engineering Physics	M,D
Environmental Engineering	M
Environmental Management and Policy	M
Logistics	M
Management Information Systems	M
Management of Technology	M,D
Materials Sciences	M,D
Nuclear Engineering	M,D
Operations Research	M,D
Optical Sciences	M,D
Planetary and Space Sciences	M,D
Systems Engineering	M,D

ALABAMA AGRICULTURAL AND MECHANICAL UNIVERSITY

Agricultural Sciences—General	M,D
Agronomy and Soil Sciences	M,D
Art Education	M
Biological and Biomedical Sciences—General	M,D
Business Administration and Management—General	M,O
Business Education	M,O
Child and Family Studies	M
Clinical Psychology	M,O
Clothing and Textiles	M
Communication Disorders	M
Computer Science	M
Counseling Psychology	M,O
Counselor Education	M,O
Early Childhood Education	M,D,O
Education—General	M,D,O
Educational Media/Instructional Technology	M,O
Elementary Education	M,D,O
Engineering and Applied Sciences—General	M,O
English Education	M,O
Family and Consumer Sciences-General	M
Food Science and Technology	M,D
Home Economics Education	M,O
Hospitality Management	M,O
Human Development	M
Kinesiology and Movement Studies	M
Materials Engineering	M
Materials Sciences	M,D
Mathematics Education	M,O
Music Education	M
Nutrition	M
Optical Sciences	M,D
Physical Education	M
Physics	M,D
Planetary and Space Sciences	M,D
Plant Sciences	M,D
Psychology—General	M,O
Reading Education	M,D,O
Rehabilitation Counseling	M,O
School Psychology	M,O
Science Education	M,O
Secondary Education	M,O
Social Sciences Education	M,O
Social Work	M
Special Education	M,D,O
Urban and Regional Planning	M

ALABAMA COLLEGE OF OSTEOPATHIC MEDICINE

Osteopathic Medicine	D

ALABAMA STATE UNIVERSITY

Accounting	M
Allied Health—General	M,D
Biological and Biomedical Sciences—General	M,D
Business Administration and Management—General	M
Counselor Education	M,D,O
Early Childhood Education	M,O
Education—General	M,D,O
Educational Leadership and Administration	M,D,O
Educational Media/Instructional Technology	M,D,O
English Education	M,O
Forensic Sciences	M
Health Education	M
Mathematics Education	M,O
Mathematics	M
Microbiology	M,D
Music Education	M,O
Occupational Therapy	M
Physical Education	M
Physical Therapy	D
Reading Education	M,O
Rehabilitation Counseling	M
Rehabilitation Sciences	M
Science Education	M,O
Secondary Education	M,O
Social Sciences Education	M,O

ALASKA PACIFIC UNIVERSITY

Business Administration and Management—General	M
Counseling Psychology	M
Education—General	M
Elementary Education	M
Environmental Education	M
Environmental Sciences	M
Health Services Management and Hospital Administration	M
Interdisciplinary Studies	M
Investment Management	M,O
Liberal Studies	M
Middle School Education	M
Telecommunications Management	M

ALBANY COLLEGE OF PHARMACY AND HEALTH SCIENCES

Cell Biology	M
Clinical Laboratory Sciences/Medical Technology	M
Health Services Research	M,D
Molecular Biology	M
Pharmaceutical Sciences	M,D
Pharmacology	M,D
Pharmacy	M,D

ALBANY LAW SCHOOL

Law	M,D

ALBANY MEDICAL COLLEGE

Allopathic Medicine	D
Bioethics	M,D,O
Cardiovascular Sciences	M,D
Cell Biology	M,D
Immunology	M,D
Microbiology	M,D
Molecular Biology	M,D
Neuroscience	M,D
Nurse Anesthesia	M
Pharmacology	M,D
Physician Assistant Studies	M

ALBANY STATE UNIVERSITY

Accounting	M
Business Administration and Management—General	M
Counselor Education	M,O
Criminal Justice and Criminology	M
Early Childhood Education	M,O
Economic Development	M
Economics	M
Education—General	M,O
Educational Leadership and Administration	M,O
English Education	M
Family Nurse Practitioner Studies	M
Health Education	M,O
Health Services Management and Hospital Administration	M
Human Resources Management	M
Logistics	M
Middle School Education	M,O
Nursing Education	M
Nursing—General	M
Physical Education	M,O
Public Administration	M
Public Policy	M
Social Work	M
Special Education	M,O
Supply Chain Management	M
Water Resources	M

ALBERT EINSTEIN COLLEGE OF MEDICINE

Allopathic Medicine	D
Anatomy	D
Biochemistry	D
Biological and Biomedical Sciences—General	D
Biophysics	D
Cell Biology	D
Clinical Research	D
Computational Biology	D
Developmental Biology	D
Genetics	D
Genomic Sciences	D
Immunology	D
Microbiology	D
Molecular Biology	D
Molecular Genetics	D
Molecular Pharmacology	D
Neuroscience	D
Pathology	D
Physiology	D
Structural Biology	D
Systems Biology	D

ALBERTUS MAGNUS COLLEGE

Accounting	M
Art Therapy	M
Business Administration and Management—General	M
Criminal Justice and Criminology	M
Education—General	M
Health Services Management and Hospital Administration	M
Human Resources Management	M
Human Services	M
Liberal Studies	M
Organizational Management	M
Project Management	M
Writing	M

ALBIZU UNIVERSITY

Clinical Psychology	M,D
Communication Disorders	M,D
Industrial and Organizational Psychology	M
Psychology—General	M,D

ALBIZU UNIVERSITY, MIAMI CAMPUS

Business Administration and Management—General	M,D
Clinical Psychology	M,D
Communication Disorders	M,D

Counseling Psychology — M,D
Education of the Gifted — M,D
English as a Second Language — M,D
Entrepreneurship — M,D
Human Services — M,D
Industrial and Organizational
  Psychology — M,D
Marriage and Family Therapy — M,D
Nonprofit Management — M,D
Organizational Management — M,D
Psychology—General — M,D
Special Education — M,D

ALBRIGHT COLLEGE
Early Childhood Education — M
Education—General — M
Elementary Education — M
English as a Second Language — M
Special Education — M

ALCORN STATE UNIVERSITY
Agricultural Economics and
  Agribusiness — M
Agricultural Education — M,O
Agricultural Sciences—
  General — M
Agronomy and Soil Sciences — M
Animal Sciences — M
Biological and Biomedical
  Sciences—General — M
Business Administration and
  Management—General — M
Computer Science — M
Counselor Education — M,O
Education—General — M,O
Elementary Education — M,O
Health Education — M,O
Information Science — M
Nursing—General — M
Physical Education — M,O
Secondary Education — M
Special Education — M,O
Sports Management — M,O
Vocational and Technical Education — M,O

ALDERSON BROADDUS UNIVERSITY
Physician Assistant Studies — M

ALFRED UNIVERSITY
Accounting — M
Applied Arts and Design—
  General — M
Art/Fine Arts — M,D
Bioengineering — M,D
Business Administration and
  Management—General — M
Ceramic Sciences and
  Engineering — M,D
Computer Art and Design — M
Counseling Psychology — M,D,O
Counselor Education — M,D,O
Education—General — M
Electrical Engineering — M,D
Engineering and Applied
  Sciences—General — M,D
Internet and Interactive
  Multimedia — M
Materials Sciences — M,D
Mechanical Engineering — M,D
Public Administration — M
Reading Education — M
School Psychology — M,D,O
Student Affairs — M

ALLEN COLLEGE
Adult Nursing — M,D
Community Health Nursing — M,D
Family Nurse Practitioner Studies — M,D
Gerontological Nursing — M,D
Health Education — M,D
Nursing and Healthcare
  Administration — M,D
Nursing Education — M,D
Nursing Informatics — M,D
Nursing—General — M,D
Occupational Therapy — M,D
Psychiatric Nursing — M,D
Public Health—General — M,D

**ALLIANT INTERNATIONAL
UNIVERSITY–FRESNO**
Clinical Psychology — D
Forensic Psychology — D
Industrial and Organizational
  Psychology — M,D
Psychology—General — M,D

**ALLIANT INTERNATIONAL
UNIVERSITY–IRVINE**
Educational Psychology — M,D,O
Forensic Psychology — D
Forensic Sciences — D
Marriage and Family Therapy — M,D
School Psychology — M,D,O

**ALLIANT INTERNATIONAL
UNIVERSITY–LOS ANGELES**
Addictions/Substance Abuse
  Counseling — M
Business Administration and
  Management—General — D
Clinical Psychology — D
Education—General — M,O
Educational Psychology — M,D,O
Forensic Psychology — D
Gerontology — M
Health Psychology — D
Industrial and Organizational
  Psychology — M,D
Marriage and Family Therapy — M,D
Psychology—General — M,D
School Psychology — M,D,O
Social Psychology — D

Student Affairs — M,D,O

**ALLIANT INTERNATIONAL
UNIVERSITY–SACRAMENTO**
Clinical Psychology — D
Education—General — M,O
Forensic Psychology — D
Marriage and Family Therapy — M,D
Psychology—General — M,D

**ALLIANT INTERNATIONAL
UNIVERSITY–SAN DIEGO**
Business Administration and
  Management—General — M
Clinical Psychology — M,D
Education—General — M,O
Educational Leadership and
  Administration — M,D,O
Educational Psychology — M,D,O
English as a Second Language — M,D,O
Forensic Psychology — D
Higher Education — M,D,O
Industrial and Organizational
  Psychology — M,D
Marriage and Family Therapy — M,D
Neuroscience — M,D,O
Psychology—General — M,D
School Psychology — M,D,O
Student Affairs — M,D,O

**ALLIANT INTERNATIONAL
UNIVERSITY–SAN FRANCISCO**
Clinical Psychology — M,D,O
Counselor Education — M
Criminal Justice and Criminology — M
Education—General — M,O
Educational Leadership and
  Administration — M,D,O
Educational Psychology — M,D,O
English as a Second Language — M,O
Forensic Psychology — M,D
Higher Education — M,D,O
Industrial and Organizational
  Psychology — M,D
Law — D
Multilingual and Multicultural
  Education — M,O
Pharmacology — M
Psychology—General — M,D,O
School Psychology — M,D,O
Special Education — M,O

ALVERNIA UNIVERSITY
Business Administration and
  Management—General — M
Education—General — M
Family Nurse Practitioner Studies — M,D,O
Gerontological Nursing — M,D,O
Liberal Studies — M
Nursing and Healthcare
  Administration — M,D,O
Nursing Education — M,D,O
Nursing—General — M,D,O
Occupational Therapy — M
Organizational Management — D
Social Psychology — M
Urban Education — M

ALVERNO COLLEGE
Adult Education — M
Business Administration and
  Management—General — M
Education—General — M
Educational Leadership and
  Administration — M
Educational Media/Instructional
  Technology — M
Family Nurse Practitioner Studies — M,D
Nursing—General — M,D
Psychiatric Nursing — M,D
Reading Education — M
Science Education — M
Social Psychology — M
Special Education — M

AMBERTON UNIVERSITY
Business Administration and
  Management—General — M
Child and Family Studies — M
Counseling Psychology — M
Counselor Education — M
Human Resources Development — M
Human Resources Management — M
Interdisciplinary Studies — M
International Business — M
Management Strategy and Policy — M
Marriage and Family Therapy — M
Project Management — M

AMBROSE UNIVERSITY
Pastoral Ministry and Counseling — M,O
Religion — M,O
Theology — M,O

**AMERICAN ACADEMY OF
ACUPUNCTURE AND ORIENTAL
MEDICINE**
Acupuncture and Oriental Medicine — M,D

**AMERICAN BAPTIST SEMINARY OF THE
WEST**
Pastoral Ministry and Counseling — M
Theology — M

**AMERICAN BUSINESS & TECHNOLOGY
UNIVERSITY**
Accounting — M
Business Administration and
  Management—General — M
Finance and Banking — M
International Business — M
Management Information Systems — M
Marketing — M
Project Management — M

AMERICAN COLLEGE DUBLIN
Business Administration and
  Management—General — M
Energy Management and
  Policy — M
International Business — M
Writing — M

**AMERICAN COLLEGE OF
ACUPUNCTURE AND ORIENTAL
MEDICINE**
Acupuncture and Oriental Medicine — M

AMERICAN COLLEGE OF EDUCATION
Curriculum and Instruction — M
Education—General — M
Educational Leadership and
  Administration — M
Educational Media/Instructional
  Technology — M
English as a Second Language — M
Multilingual and Multicultural
  Education — M

**THE AMERICAN COLLEGE OF
FINANCIAL SERVICES**
Business Administration and
  Management—General — M
Finance and Banking — M
Organizational Management — M

**AMERICAN COLLEGE OF HEALTHCARE
SCIENCES**
Allied Health—General — M,O
Health Promotion — M,O
Nutrition — M,O
Physiology — M,O

**AMERICAN COLLEGE OF
THESSALONIKI**
Business Administration and
  Management—General — M,O
Entrepreneurship — M,O
Finance and Banking — M,O
Marketing — M,O

AMERICAN CONSERVATORY THEATER
Theater — M,O

**AMERICAN FILM INSTITUTE
CONSERVATORY**
Film, Television, and Video
  Production — M

**AMERICAN GRADUATE SCHOOL IN
PARIS**
International Affairs — M,D

AMERICAN GRADUATE UNIVERSITY
Business Administration and
  Management—General — M,O
Supply Chain Management — M,O

**AMERICAN INSTITUTE OF
ALTERNATIVE MEDICINE**
Acupuncture and Oriental Medicine — M

**AMERICAN INTERCONTINENTAL
UNIVERSITY ATLANTA**
Information Science — M
International Business — M
Management Information Systems — M

**AMERICAN INTERCONTINENTAL
UNIVERSITY HOUSTON**
Business Administration and
  Management—General — M

**AMERICAN INTERCONTINENTAL
UNIVERSITY ONLINE**
Accounting — M
Business Administration and
  Management—General — M
Computer and Information
  Systems Security — M
Curriculum and Instruction — M
Education—General — M
Educational Leadership and
  Administration — M
Educational Measurement and
  Evaluation — M
Educational Media/Instructional
  Technology — M
Finance and Banking — M
Health Services Management and
  Hospital Administration — M
Human Resources Management — M
Industrial and Manufacturing
  Management — M
Industrial and Organizational
  Psychology — M
Information Science — M
International Business — M
Marketing — M
Project Management — M

AMERICAN INTERNATIONAL COLLEGE
Accounting — M,D,O
Business Administration and
  Management—General — M,D,O
Clinical Psychology — M,D,O
Counseling Psychology — M,D
Counselor Education — M,D,O
Early Childhood Education — M,D,O
Education—General — M,D
Educational Leadership and
  Administration — M,D
Educational Psychology — M,D,O
Elementary Education — M,D,O
Exercise and Sports Science — M,D,O
Family Nurse Practitioner Studies — M,D,O
Forensic Psychology — M,D,O
Hospitality Management — M,D,O
Middle School Education — M,D,O

Nursing and Healthcare
  Administration — M,D,O
Nursing Education — M,D,O
Occupational Therapy — M,D,O
Physical Therapy — M,D,O
Psychology—General — M,D,O
Reading Education — M,D,O
Secondary Education — M,D,O
Special Education — M,D,O
Taxation — M,D,O

AMERICAN JEWISH UNIVERSITY
Business Administration and
  Management—General — M
Education—General — M
Jewish Studies — M
Nonprofit Management — M
Social Work — M
Theology — M

**AMERICAN MUSEUM OF NATURAL
HISTORY–RICHARD GILDER
GRADUATE SCHOOL**
Biological and Biomedical
  Sciences—General — D
Museum Studies — D

AMERICAN NATIONAL UNIVERSITY
Business Administration and
  Management—General — M

**AMERICAN PUBLIC UNIVERSITY
SYSTEM**
Accounting — M,D
American Studies — M
Business Administration and
  Management—General — M,D
Business Analytics — M,D
Computer and Information
  Systems Security — M,D
Conflict Resolution and
  Mediation/Peace Studies — M,D
Criminal Justice and Criminology — M,D
Educational Leadership and
  Administration — M,D
Environmental Management
  and Policy — M,D
Health Informatics — M,D
History — M,D
International Affairs — M,D
Logistics — M,D
Military and Defense Studies — M,D
National Security — M,D
Nursing—General — M,D
Political Science — M,D
Public Policy — M,D
Secondary Education — M,D
Sports Management — M,D
Transportation Management — M,D

AMERICAN SENTINEL UNIVERSITY
Business Administration and
  Management—General — M
Computer Science — M
Health Informatics — M
Health Services Management and
  Hospital Administration — M
Management Information Systems — M
Nursing—General — M

AMERICAN UNIVERSITY
Accounting — M,O
American Studies — M,D,O
Anthropology — M,D,O
Applied Social Research — M,O
Applied Statistics — M,O
Art History — M
Arts Administration — M,O
Asian Studies — O
Biological and Biomedical
  Sciences—General — M
Biopsychology — M,D,O
Biostatistics — M
Biotechnology — M
Broadcast Journalism — M
Business Administration and
  Management—General — M,O
Chemistry — M
Clinical Psychology — M,D,O
Cognitive Sciences — M,D,O
Communication—General — M,D
Comparative Literature — M
Conflict Resolution and
  Mediation/Peace Studies — M,D,O
Corporate and Organizational
  Communication — M
Criminal Justice and Criminology — M,D
Cultural Studies — M,D,O
Data Science/Data Analytics — M,O
Economics — M,D,O
Education—General — M,O
Educational Leadership and
  Administration — M,O
Educational Measurement and
  Evaluation — M,O
Educational Media/Instructional
  Technology — M,O
Educational Policy — M,O
English as a Second Language — M,O
Entrepreneurship — M,D,O
Environmental Management
  and Policy — M,D,O
Environmental Sciences — M,D,O
Ethics — M,D,O
Film, Television, and Video
  Production — M
Finance and Banking — M,O
French — M,O
Gender Studies — M,D,O
Health Promotion — M,O
Health Services Management and
  Hospital Administration — M,O
History — M,D

M—masters degree; D—doctorate; O—other advanced degree; *—Close-Up and/or Display

Human Resources Management	M,O
International Affairs	M,D,O
International and Comparative Education	M,O
International Development	M,D,O
International Economics	M,D,O
Journalism	M
Latin American Studies	M,O
Law	M,D
Management Information Systems	M,D,O
Marketing	M
Mass Communication	M,D,O
Mathematics	M,D
Media Studies	M,D
Music	M,O
National Security	M,D,O
Natural Resources	M,D,O
Neuroscience	M,D,O
Nonprofit Management	M,D,O
Nutrition	M,O
Organizational Management	M,D,O
Philosophy	M
Political Science	M,D,O
Project Management	M,O
Psychology—General	M,D,O
Public Administration	M,D,O
Public Policy	M,D,O
Real Estate	M,O
Russian	M,O
Sociology	M,O
Spanish	M,O
Special Education	M,O
Sports Management	M,O
Statistics	M,O
Sustainability Management	M
Sustainable Development	M,D,O
Taxation	M,O
Western European Studies	M,D,O
Women's Studies	O
Writing	M

AMERICAN UNIVERSITY IN BULGARIA

Business Administration and Management—General	M

THE AMERICAN UNIVERSITY IN CAIRO

Artificial Intelligence/Robotics	M,D,O
Biotechnology	M,D,O
Broadcast Journalism	M,O
Business Administration and Management—General	M,O
Chemistry	M,D,O
Communication—General	M,D,O
Comparative Literature	M,O
Computer Science	M,D,O
Construction Engineering	M,D,O
Economic Development	M,O
Economics	M,O
Education—General	M
Educational Leadership and Administration	M
Electrical Engineering	M,D,O
Engineering and Applied Sciences—General	M,D,O
English as a Second Language	M,O
English	M,O
Environmental Engineering	M,D,O
Finance and Banking	M,O
Gender Studies	M,O
Humanities	M,O
International Affairs	M,O
International and Comparative Education	M
Journalism	M,O
Law	M,O
Mass Communication	M,O
Mechanical Engineering	M,D,O
Nanotechnology	M,D,O
Near and Middle Eastern Languages	M,O
Near and Middle Eastern Studies	M,O
Philosophy	M,O
Physics	M,D,O
Psychology—General	M,O
Public Administration	M,O
Public Policy	M,O
Sustainable Development	M,D,O
Women's Studies	M

THE AMERICAN UNIVERSITY IN DUBAI

Business Administration and Management—General	M
Construction Management	M
Education—General	M
Finance and Banking	M
International Business	M
Marketing	M

AMERICAN UNIVERSITY OF ARMENIA

Business Administration and Management—General	M
Computer Science	M
Economics	M
Energy Management and Policy	M
English as a Second Language	M
Industrial/Management Engineering	M
Information Science	M
International Affairs	M
Law	M
Management Information Systems	M
Manufacturing Engineering	M
Political Science	M
Public Health—General	M

AMERICAN UNIVERSITY OF BEIRUT

Agricultural Economics and Agribusiness	M
Allopathic Medicine	M,D
Animal Sciences	M
Anthropology	M,D
Aquaculture	M
Archaeology	M,D
Art History	M,D
Biochemistry	M,D

Biological and Biomedical Sciences—General	M,D
Biomedical Engineering	M,D
Biostatistics	M,D
Business Administration and Management—General	M
Cell Biology	M,D
Chemistry	M,D
Civil Engineering	M,D
Clinical Psychology	M,D
Clinical Research	M,D
Community Health Nursing	M,D
Community Health	M,D
Computational Sciences	M,D
Computer Engineering	M,D
Computer Science	M,D
Economics	M,D
Education—General	M,D
Educational Leadership and Administration	M,D
Educational Policy	M,D
Electrical Engineering	M,D
Elementary Education	M,D
Engineering and Applied Sciences—General	M,D
Engineering Management	M,D
English as a Second Language	M,D
English	M,D
Environmental and Occupational Health	M,D
Environmental Management and Policy	M,D
Environmental Sciences	M,D
Epidemiology	M,D
Finance and Banking	M,D
Food Science and Technology	M
Geology	M,D
Gerontological Nursing	M
Health Promotion	M,D
Health Services Management and Hospital Administration	M,D
Health Services Research	M,D
History	M,D
Human Resources Management	M
Immunology	M,D
International Affairs	M,D
Mathematics Education	M,D
Mathematics	M,D
Mechanical Engineering	M,D
Media Studies	M,D
Microbiology	M,D
Molecular Biology	M,D
Near and Middle Eastern Languages	M,D
Near and Middle Eastern Studies	M,D
Neuroscience	M,D
Nursing and Healthcare Administration	M
Nursing—General	M
Nutrition	M,D
Oral and Dental Sciences	M,D
Pharmacology	M,D
Philosophy	M,D
Physics	M,D
Physiology	M,D
Plant Sciences	M
Political Science	M,D
Psychiatric Nursing	M
Psychology—General	M,D
Public Administration	M,D
Public Health—General	M,D
Public Policy	M,D
School Psychology	M,D
Science Education	M,D
Sociology	M,D
Theoretical Physics	M,D
Urban and Regional Planning	M,D
Urban Design	M,D
Water Resources Engineering	M,D

AMERICAN UNIVERSITY OF HEALTH SCIENCES

Clinical Research	M

THE AMERICAN UNIVERSITY OF PARIS

Business Administration and Management—General	M
Communication—General	M
Conflict Resolution and Mediation/Peace Studies	M
Cultural Studies	M
International Affairs	M
International Business	M
Law	M
Near and Middle Eastern Studies	M
Public Policy	M

AMERICAN UNIVERSITY OF PUERTO RICO

Art Education	M
Criminal Justice and Criminology	M
Education—General	M
Elementary Education	M
Physical Education	M
Science Education	M
Special Education	M

THE AMERICAN UNIVERSITY OF ROME

Arts Administration	M
Conflict Resolution and Mediation/Peace Studies	M
Food Science and Technology	M
Historic Preservation	M
Religion	M

AMERICAN UNIVERSITY OF SHARJAH

Accounting	M,D
Biomedical Engineering	M,D
Business Administration and Management—General	M,D
Chemical Engineering	M,D
Civil Engineering	M,D
Computer Engineering	M,D
Electrical Engineering	M,D
Engineering Management	M,D

English as a Second Language	M,D
Mathematics	M,D
Mechanical Engineering	M,D
Translation and Interpretation	M,D
Urban and Regional Planning	M,D

AMRIDGE UNIVERSITY

Counseling Psychology	M,D
Counselor Education	M,D
Human Services	M,D
Marriage and Family Therapy	M,D
Pastoral Ministry and Counseling	M,D
Religion	M,D
Theology	M,D

ANABAPTIST MENNONITE BIBLICAL SEMINARY

Conflict Resolution and Mediation/Peace Studies	M,O
Ethics	M,O
International Affairs	M,O
Pastoral Ministry and Counseling	M,O
Public Administration	M,O
Theology	M,O

ANAHEIM UNIVERSITY

Business Administration and Management—General	M,D,O
English as a Second Language	M,D,O
Entrepreneurship	M,D,O
International Business	M,D,O
Sustainability Management	M,D,O

ANDERSON UNIVERSITY (IN)

Accounting	M,D
Business Administration and Management—General	M,D
Education—General	M
Missions and Missiology	M,D
Theology	M,D

ANDERSON UNIVERSITY (SC)

Business Administration and Management—General	M
Criminal Justice and Criminology	M
Education—General	M
Educational Leadership and Administration	M
Elementary Education	M
Family Nurse Practitioner Studies	M,D
Health Services Management and Hospital Administration	M
Human Resources Management	M
Marketing	M
Music Education	M
Nursing and Healthcare Administration	M,D
Nursing Education	M,D
Nursing—General	M,D
Organizational Management	M
Pastoral Ministry and Counseling	M,D
Psychiatric Nursing	M,D
Supply Chain Management	M

ANDREWS UNIVERSITY

Accounting	M
Allied Health—General	M
Architecture	M
Biological and Biomedical Sciences—General	M
Clinical Psychology	M
Communication Disorders	M
Communication—General	M
Counseling Psychology	M,D
Curriculum and Instruction	M,D,O
Developmental Psychology	M,D
Economics	M
Education—General	M,D,O
Educational Leadership and Administration	M,D,O
Educational Psychology	M,D
Elementary Education	M,D,O
English as a Second Language	M,D,O
English Education	M,D,O
English	M
Finance and Banking	M
Foreign Languages Education	M,D,O
Higher Education	M,D,O
International and Comparative Education	M
International Development	M
Music	M
Nursing—General	M,D
Nutrition	M
Pastoral Ministry and Counseling	M,D,O
Physical Therapy	D
Psychology—General	M,D,O
Public Health—General	M,O
Religious Education	M,D,O
School Psychology	M,O
Science Education	M,D,O
Secondary Education	M,D,O
Social Psychology	M
Social Sciences Education	M,D,O
Social Work	M
Special Education	M
Theology	M,D,O
Urban and Regional Planning	M

ANGELO STATE UNIVERSITY

Accounting	M
Agricultural Sciences—General	M
Biological and Biomedical Sciences—General	M
Business Administration and Management—General	M
Communication—General	M
Counselor Education	M
Criminal Justice and Criminology	M
Curriculum and Instruction	M
Educational Leadership and Administration	M
English as a Second Language	M
English	M
Family Nurse Practitioner Studies	M

Higher Education	M
Homeland Security	M
Industrial and Organizational Psychology	M
Media Studies	M
National Security	M
Nursing Education	M
Nursing—General	M
Physical Therapy	D
Psychology—General	M
Sociology	M
Sports Management	M

ANNA MARIA COLLEGE

Art/Fine Arts	M,O
Business Administration and Management—General	M,O
Counseling Psychology	M
Criminal Justice and Criminology	M
Early Childhood Education	M,O
Education—General	M,O
Elementary Education	M,O
Emergency Management	M,O
English Education	M,O
Industrial and Organizational Psychology	M
Public Administration	M
Social Work	M

ANTIOCH UNIVERSITY LOS ANGELES

Business Administration and Management—General	M
Clinical Psychology	M
Education—General	M
Human Resources Development	M
Organizational Management	M
Psychology—General	M
Sustainable Development	M

ANTIOCH UNIVERSITY MIDWEST

Health Services Management and Hospital Administration	M

ANTIOCH UNIVERSITY NEW ENGLAND

Addictions/Substance Abuse Counseling	M
Applied Behavior Analysis	M,O
Applied Psychology	M,D,O
Business Administration and Management—General	M
Clinical Psychology	M,D
Conservation Biology	M
Counseling Psychology	M
Early Childhood Education	M
Education—General	M,O
Educational Leadership and Administration	M,O
Educational Media/Instructional Technology	M,O
Elementary Education	M,O
Environmental Education	M
Environmental Management and Policy	M,D
Environmental Sciences	M,D
Foundations and Philosophy of Education	M,O
Humanities	M
Interdisciplinary Studies	M
Marriage and Family Therapy	M,D,O
Science Education	M
Special Education	M,O
Sustainability Management	M
Sustainable Development	M,O
Therapies—Dance, Drama, and Music	M,O

ANTIOCH UNIVERSITY SANTA BARBARA

Business Administration and Management—General	M
Clinical Psychology	M,D
Education—General	M
Management Strategy and Policy	M
Nonprofit Management	M
Writing	M

ANTIOCH UNIVERSITY SEATTLE

Adult Education	M
Clinical Psychology	M,D
Counselor Education	M,D
Education—General	M
Marriage and Family Therapy	M,D
Therapies—Dance, Drama, and Music	M

AOMA GRADUATE SCHOOL OF INTEGRATIVE MEDICINE

Acupuncture and Oriental Medicine	M,D

APEX SCHOOL OF THEOLOGY

Theology	M,D

APOLLOS UNIVERSITY

Business Administration and Management—General	M,D
Organizational Management	M,D

APPALACHIAN BIBLE COLLEGE

Pastoral Ministry and Counseling	M

APPALACHIAN COLLEGE OF PHARMACY

Pharmacy	D

APPALACHIAN SCHOOL OF LAW

Law	D

APPALACHIAN STATE UNIVERSITY

Accounting	M
American Studies	M
Biological and Biomedical Sciences—General	M
Business Administration and Management—General	M
Cell Biology	M
Clinical Psychology	M
Communication Disorders	M
Computer Science	M

Counseling Psychology	M
Counselor Education	M
Cultural Studies	M
Curriculum and Instruction	M
Educational Leadership and Administration	M,O
Educational Media/Instructional Technology	M,O
Elementary Education	M
Energy and Power Engineering	M
English Education	M
English	M
Exercise and Sports Science	M
Foreign Languages Education	M
Geographic Information Systems	M
Geography	M
Health Psychology	M
Higher Education	M
History	M
Library Science	M,O
Marriage and Family Therapy	M
Mathematics Education	M
Mathematics	M
Middle School Education	M
Molecular Biology	M
Music	M
Nutrition	M
Political Science	M
Psychology—General	M
Public Administration	M
Reading Education	M
School Psychology	M
Science Education	M
Social Sciences Education	M
Social Work	M
Special Education	M
Student Affairs	M
Taxation	M
Therapies—Dance, Drama, and Music	M
Vocational and Technical Education	M

AQUINAS COLLEGE (MI)

Business Administration and Management—General	M
Education—General	M
Marketing	M
Organizational Management	M
Sustainability Management	M

AQUINAS COLLEGE (TN)

Education—General	M
Elementary Education	M
Secondary Education	M

AQUINAS INSTITUTE OF THEOLOGY

Health Services Management and Hospital Administration	M,D,O
Music	M,D,O
Pastoral Ministry and Counseling	M,D,O
Theology	M,D,O

ARCADIA UNIVERSITY

Applied Behavior Analysis	M
Art Education	M,D,O
Business Administration and Management—General	M
Computer Education	M
Conflict Resolution and Mediation/Peace Studies	M
Counseling Psychology	M
Curriculum and Instruction	M,D,O
Early Childhood Education	M,D,O
Education—General	M,D,O
Educational Leadership and Administration	M,D,O
Educational Media/Instructional Technology	M,D,O
Elementary Education	M,D,O
English Education	M,D,O
English	M
Environmental Education	M,D,O
Forensic Sciences	M
Health Education	M
Marriage and Family Therapy	M
Mathematics Education	M,D,O
Music Education	M,D,O
Physical Therapy	D
Physician Assistant Studies	M
Psychology—General	M,D,O
Public Health—General	M
Reading Education	M,D,O
Science Education	M,D,O
Secondary Education	M,D,O
Special Education	M,D,O
Theater	M
Writing	M

ARGOSY UNIVERSITY, ATLANTA

Accounting	M,D
Biopsychology	M,D,O
Business Administration and Management—General	M,D
Clinical Psychology	M,D,O
Counselor Education	M,D,O
Education—General	M,D,O
Educational Leadership and Administration	M,D,O
Educational Media/Instructional Technology	M,D,O
Elementary Education	M,D,O
Finance and Banking	M,D
Forensic Psychology	M,D,O
Health Psychology	M,D,O
Health Services Management and Hospital Administration	M,D
Higher Education	M,D,O
Industrial and Organizational Psychology	M,D,O
International Business	M,D
Management Information Systems	M,D

Marketing	M,D
Marriage and Family Therapy	M,D,O
Psychology—General	M,D,O
Public Health—General	M
Secondary Education	M,D,O
Social Psychology	M,D,O
Sport Psychology	M,D,O

ARGOSY UNIVERSITY, CHICAGO

Accounting	M,D
Adult Education	M,D,O
Business Administration and Management—General	M,D
Clinical Psychology	M,D
Community College Education	M,D,O
Counseling Psychology	D
Counselor Education	D
Education—General	M,D,O
Educational Leadership and Administration	M,D,O
Elementary Education	M,D,O
Finance and Banking	M,D
Forensic Psychology	D
Health Psychology	D
Health Services Management and Hospital Administration	M,D
Higher Education	M,D,O
Human Development	D
Industrial and Organizational Psychology	M,D
International Business	M,D
Management Information Systems	M,D
Marketing	M,D
Marriage and Family Therapy	D
Neuroscience	D
Organizational Behavior	D
Organizational Management	D
Psychoanalysis and Psychotherapy	D
Psychology—General	M,D
Public Administration	M,D
Public Health—General	M
Secondary Education	M,D,O
Social Psychology	M,D
Sustainability Management	M,D

ARGOSY UNIVERSITY, HAWAI'I

Accounting	M,D,O
Addictions/Substance Abuse Counseling	O
Adult Education	M,D
Business Administration and Management—General	M,D,O
Clinical Psychology	M,D,O
Counseling Psychology	D
Education—General	M,D
Educational Leadership and Administration	M,D
Elementary Education	M,D
Finance and Banking	M,D,O
Forensic Psychology	M
Health Services Management and Hospital Administration	M,D,O
Higher Education	M,D
International Business	M,D,O
Management Information Systems	M,D,O
Marketing	M,D,O
Marriage and Family Therapy	M
Organizational Management	D
Pharmacology	M,O
Psychology—General	M,D
Public Health—General	M
School Psychology	M
Secondary Education	M,D
Sustainability Management	M,D

ARGOSY UNIVERSITY, LOS ANGELES

Accounting	M,D
Business Administration and Management—General	M,D
Clinical Psychology	M,D
Community College Education	M,D
Counseling Psychology	M,D
Education—General	M,D
Educational Leadership and Administration	M,D
Elementary Education	M,D
Finance and Banking	M,D
Forensic Psychology	M,D
Health Services Management and Hospital Administration	M,D
Higher Education	M,D
International Business	M,D
Management Information Systems	M,D
Marketing	M,D
Marriage and Family Therapy	M,D
Organizational Management	M,D
Psychology—General	M,D
Public Administration	M,D
Public Health—General	M
Secondary Education	M,D
Sustainability Management	M,D

ARGOSY UNIVERSITY, NORTHERN VIRGINIA

Accounting	M,D,O
Business Administration and Management—General	M,D,O
Clinical Psychology	M,D
Community College Education	M,D
Counseling Psychology	M,D
Counselor Education	M,D
Education—General	M,D,O
Educational Leadership and Administration	M,D,O
Elementary Education	M,D,O
Finance and Banking	M,D,O
Forensic Psychology	M,D
Health Psychology	M,D
Health Services Management and Hospital Administration	M,D,O
Higher Education	M,D,O
International Business	M,D,O

Management Information Systems	M,D,O
Marketing	M,D,O
Marriage and Family Therapy	M,D,O
Organizational Management	M,D
Psychology—General	M,D
Public Administration	M,D,O
Public Health—General	M
Secondary Education	M,D,O
Social Psychology	M,D
Sustainability Management	M,D,O

ARGOSY UNIVERSITY, ORANGE COUNTY

Accounting	M,D,O
Business Administration and Management—General	M,D
Clinical Psychology	M,D
Community College Education	M,D
Counseling Psychology	M,D
Education—General	M,D
Educational Leadership and Administration	M,D
Educational Media/Instructional Technology	M,D
Elementary Education	M,D
Finance and Banking	M,D,O
Forensic Psychology	M
Health Services Management and Hospital Administration	M,D,O
Higher Education	M,D,O
International Business	M,D,O
Management Information Systems	M,D,O
Marketing	M,D,O
Marriage and Family Therapy	M,D
Organizational Management	D
Psychology—General	M,D
Public Administration	M,D,O
Public Health—General	M
Secondary Education	M,D
Sport Psychology	M
Sustainability Management	M,D,O

ARGOSY UNIVERSITY, PHOENIX

Accounting	M,D
Adult Education	M,D,O
Business Administration and Management—General	M,D
Clinical Psychology	M,D
Community College Education	M,D,O
Counseling Psychology	M
Education—General	M,D,O
Educational Leadership and Administration	M,D
Educational Media/Instructional Technology	M,D,O
Elementary Education	M,D,O
Finance and Banking	M,D
Forensic Psychology	M
Health Services Management and Hospital Administration	M,D
Higher Education	M,D,O
Industrial and Organizational Psychology	M
International Business	M,D
Management Information Systems	M,D
Marketing	M,D
Neuroscience	M,D
Psychology—General	M,D
Public Administration	M,D
Public Health—General	M
School Psychology	M,D
Secondary Education	M,D,O
Sport Psychology	M,D
Sustainability Management	M,D

ARGOSY UNIVERSITY, SEATTLE

Accounting	M,D
Adult Education	M,D
Business Administration and Management—General	M,D
Clinical Psychology	M,D,O
Community College Education	M,D
Counseling Psychology	M,D
Education—General	M,D
Educational Leadership and Administration	M,D
Educational Media/Instructional Technology	M,D
Elementary Education	M,D
Finance and Banking	M,D
Health Services Management and Hospital Administration	M,D
Higher Education	M,D
International Business	M,D
Management Information Systems	M,D
Marketing	M,D
Organizational Management	M,D
Psychology—General	M,D,O
Public Administration	M,D
Public Health—General	M
Secondary Education	M,D
Sustainability Management	M,D

ARGOSY UNIVERSITY, TAMPA

Accounting	M,D
Business Administration and Management—General	M,D
Clinical Psychology	M,D
Community College Education	M,D,O
Counseling Psychology	M,D
Counselor Education	M,D,O
Education—General	M,D,O
Educational Leadership and Administration	M,D,O
Elementary Education	M,D,O
Finance and Banking	M,D
Health Services Management and Hospital Administration	M,D
Higher Education	M,D,O
Industrial and Organizational Psychology	M,D
International Business	M,D

Management Information Systems	M,D
Marketing	M,D
Marriage and Family Therapy	M,D
Neuroscience	M,D
Organizational Management	M,D
Psychology—General	M,D
Public Administration	M,D
Public Health—General	M
Secondary Education	M,D,O
Sustainability Management	M,D

ARGOSY UNIVERSITY, TWIN CITIES

Accounting	M,D
Biopsychology	M,D,O
Business Administration and Management—General	M,D
Clinical Psychology	M,D,O
Education—General	M,D,O
Educational Leadership and Administration	M,D,O
Educational Media/Instructional Technology	M,D,O
Elementary Education	M,D,O
Finance and Banking	M,D
Forensic Psychology	M,D,O
Health Psychology	M,D,O
Health Services Management and Hospital Administration	M,D
Higher Education	M,D,O
Industrial and Organizational Psychology	M,D,O
International Business	M,D
Management Information Systems	M,D
Marketing	M,D
Marriage and Family Therapy	M,D,O
Organizational Management	M,D
Psychology—General	M,D,O
Public Administration	M,D
Public Health—General	M
Secondary Education	M,D,O
Sustainability Management	M,D

ARIZONA SCHOOL OF ACUPUNCTURE AND ORIENTAL MEDICINE

Acupuncture and Oriental Medicine	M

ARIZONA STATE UNIVERSITY AT THE TEMPE CAMPUS

Accounting	M,D
Aerospace/Aeronautical Engineering	M,D
African Studies	M,D,O
Agricultural Economics and Agribusiness	D
Animal Behavior	M,D
Anthropology	M,D,O
Applied Arts and Design—General	M,D
Applied Behavior Analysis	M,D
Applied Mathematics	M,D,O
Applied Psychology	M
Archaeology	M,D,O
Architectural History	D
Architecture	M,D
Art Education	M,D
Art History	M,D
Art/Fine Arts	M,D
Arts Administration	M,D
Astrophysics	M,D
Aviation Management	M
Biochemistry	M,D
Bioinformatics	M,D
Biological and Biomedical Sciences—General	M,D
Biomedical Engineering	M,D
Biotechnology	M,D
Building Science	M,D
Business Administration and Management—General	M,D
Cell Biology	M,D
Chemical Engineering	M,D
Chemistry	M,D
Child and Family Studies	M,D
Chinese	M,D
Civil Engineering	M,D
Clinical Psychology	M,D
Cognitive Sciences	M,D
Communication Disorders	M,D
Communication—General	M,D
Community Health	M,D,O
Comparative Literature	M,D,O
Computer Engineering	M,D
Computer Science	M,D
Conservation Biology	M,D
Construction Engineering	M,D
Construction Management	M,D
Counseling Psychology	D
Counselor Education	M
Criminal Justice and Criminology	M,D,O
Cultural Studies	M,D
Curriculum and Instruction	M
Dance	M
Developmental Psychology	M,D
Economics	D
Education—General	M,D,O
Educational Leadership and Administration	M,D
Educational Measurement and Evaluation	D
Educational Media/Instructional Technology	M,O
Educational Policy	D
Electrical Engineering	M,D,O
Elementary Education	M,D
Emergency Management	M,D
Energy and Power Engineering	M,D
Engineering and Applied Sciences—General	M,D,O
English as a Second Language	M,D,O
English	M,D,O
Entrepreneurship	M,D

M—masters degree; D—doctorate; O—other advanced degree; *—Close-Up and/or Display

Arizona State University at the Tempe campus (continued)

Environmental Design	D
Environmental Engineering	M,D
Environmental Management and Policy	M
Environmental Sciences	M,D,O
Ergonomics and Human Factors	M
Ethics	M,D
Evolutionary Biology	M,D
Exercise and Sports Science	M,D,O
Family Nurse Practitioner Studies	M,D,O
Film, Television, and Video Production	M
Finance and Banking	M,D
Foreign Languages Education	M,D
French	M
Gender Studies	M,D,O
Geographic Information Systems	M,D,O
Geography	M,D,O
Geological Engineering	M,D
Geology	M,D
Geosciences	M,D
German	M
Gerontological Nursing	M,D,O
Gerontology	M,D,O
Health Education	D
Health Promotion	M,D
Health Services Management and Hospital Administration	M
Higher Education	M
History of Science and Technology	M,D
History	M,D,O
Homeland Security	M,D
Human Development	M,D
Industrial/Management Engineering	M,D
Information Science	M
Interdisciplinary Studies	M
International Business	M,D
International Health	M,D,O
Japanese	M
Journalism	M,D
Landscape Architecture	M,D
Law	M,D
Legal and Justice Studies	M,D,O
Liberal Studies	M
Linguistics	M,D,O
Management Information Systems	M,D
Management of Technology	M
Management Strategy and Policy	M,D
Manufacturing Engineering	M
Marketing	M,D
Marriage and Family Therapy	M
Mass Communication	M,D
Materials Engineering	M,D
Materials Sciences	M,D
Mathematics Education	M,D,O
Mathematics	M,D,O
Mechanical Engineering	M,D
Media Studies	M,D
Medical Informatics	M,D
Medieval and Renaissance Studies	M,D,O
Microbiology	M,D
Modeling and Simulation	M,D
Molecular Biology	M,D
Museum Studies	M,D,O
Music Education	M,D
Music	M
Nanotechnology	M,D
Neuroscience	M,D
Nonprofit Management	M,D,O
Nuclear Engineering	M,D,O
Nursing and Healthcare Administration	M,D,O
Nursing Education	M,D,O
Nursing—General	M,D,O
Nutrition	M,D
Organizational Behavior	M,D
Philosophy	M,D,O
Physical Education	M
Physics	M,D
Planetary and Space Sciences	M,D
Plant Biology	M,D
Political Science	M,D
Psychiatric Nursing	M,D,O
Psychology—General	M,D
Public Administration	M,D
Public Affairs	M,D
Public Health—General	M,D,O
Public History	M,D,O
Public Policy	M,D
Publishing	M,D,O
Real Estate	M,D
Reliability Engineering	M
Religion	M,D,O
Rhetoric	M,D,O
Secondary Education	M
Social Psychology	M,D
Social Work	M,D,O
Sociology	M,D
Software Engineering	M,D
Spanish	M,D
Special Education	M,O
Sports and Entertainment Law	M,D
Statistics	M,D,O
Supply Chain Management	M,D
Sustainable Development	M,D,O
Systems Engineering	M
Systems Science	M,D
Technology and Public Policy	M
Textile Design	M,D
Theater	M,D
Therapies—Dance, Drama, and Music	M
Translation and Interpretation	M,D,O
Transportation and Highway Engineering	M,D,O
Travel and Tourism	M,D,O
Urban and Regional Planning	M,D,O
Urban Design	M,D
Urban Studies	M,D,O
Writing	M,D

ARKANSAS COLLEGES OF HEALTH EDUCATION

Biological and Biomedical Sciences—General	M
Osteopathic Medicine	D

ARKANSAS STATE UNIVERSITY

Accounting	M
Addictions/Substance Abuse Counseling	M,O
Agricultural Education	M,O
Agricultural Sciences—General	M,O
Biological and Biomedical Sciences—General	M,O
Biotechnology	M,O
Business Administration and Management—General	M
Business Education	O
Chemistry	M,O
Clinical Psychology	M,O
Communication Disorders	M,O
Communication—General	M,O
Community College Education	M,D,O
Computer Science	M
Counselor Education	M,O
Criminal Justice and Criminology	M,O
Early Childhood Education	M,D,O
Education of the Gifted	M,D,O
Education—General	M,D,O
Educational Leadership and Administration	M,D,O
Elementary Education	M,D,O
Emergency Management	M,O
Engineering and Applied Sciences—General	M
Engineering Management	M
English Education	M,O
English	M,O
Environmental Sciences	M
Exercise and Sports Science	M,O
Foundations and Philosophy of Education	M,D,O
Gerontology	M,D,O
Health Communication	M,O
Health Education	M,D,O
Health Services Management and Hospital Administration	M,D,O
History	M,O
Historic Preservation	M,D
History	M,O
Journalism	M
Management Information Systems	O
Mass Communication	M
Mathematics Education	M
Mathematics	M
Media Studies	M
Middle School Education	M,D,O
Molecular Biology	M,D
Music Education	M,O
Music	M,O
Nurse Anesthesia	M,D,O
Nursing—General	M,D,O
Occupational Therapy	D
Physical Education	M,O
Physical Therapy	D
Political Science	M,O
Public Administration	M,O
Reading Education	M,D,O
Rehabilitation Counseling	M,O
School Psychology	M,O
Science Education	M,O
Social Sciences Education	M,D,O
Social Work	M,O
Sociology	M
Special Education	M,D,O
Sports Management	M,O
Student Affairs	M,O

ARKANSAS TECH UNIVERSITY

Business Administration and Management—General	M
Counselor Education	M,D,O
Education—General	M,D,O
Educational Leadership and Administration	M,D,O
Educational Media/Instructional Technology	M,D,O
Electrical Engineering	M
Elementary Education	M,D,O
Emergency Management	M
Engineering and Applied Sciences—General	M
English as a Second Language	M
English Education	M
English	M
Fish, Game, and Wildlife Management	M
Health Informatics	M
History	M
Information Science	M
Journalism	M
Liberal Studies	M
Mechanical Engineering	M
Nursing—General	M
Psychology—General	M
Sociology	M
Special Education	M,D,O
Student Affairs	M,D,O

ARLINGTON BAPTIST UNIVERSITY

Curriculum and Instruction	M
Education—General	M
Educational Leadership and Administration	M
Theology	M

ART ACADEMY OF CINCINNATI

Art Education	M

ARTCENTER COLLEGE OF DESIGN

Art/Fine Arts	M
Computer Art and Design	M
Environmental Design	M
Film, Television, and Video Production	M
Graphic Design	M

Industrial Design	M
Transportation and Highway Engineering	M

THE ART INSTITUTE OF DALLAS, A BRANCH OF MIAMI INTERNATIONAL UNIVERSITY OF ART & DESIGN

Applied Arts and Design—General	M

ASBURY THEOLOGICAL SEMINARY

Missions and Missiology	M,D,O
Pastoral Ministry and Counseling	M,D,O
Religious Education	M,D,O
Theology	M,D,O

ASBURY UNIVERSITY

Child and Family Studies	M
Classics	M
Educational Leadership and Administration	M
English as a Second Language	M
English	M
French	M
Mathematics Education	M
Reading Education	M
Science Education	M
Social Sciences Education	M
Social Work	M
Spanish	M
Special Education	M
Writing	M

ASHLAND THEOLOGICAL SEMINARY

Clinical Psychology	M,D
Counselor Education	M,D
Pastoral Ministry and Counseling	M,D
Theology	M,D

ASHLAND UNIVERSITY

Accounting	M
Business Administration and Management—General	M
Business Analytics	M
Communication—General	M
Corporate and Organizational Communication	M
Education—General	M,D
Educational Leadership and Administration	M,D
Entrepreneurship	M
Exercise and Sports Science	M
Family Nurse Practitioner Studies	D
Finance and Banking	M
Health Services Management and Hospital Administration	M
History	M
Human Resources Management	M
International Business	M
Management Information Systems	M
Nursing—General	D
Political Science	M
Project Management	M
Sports Management	M
Supply Chain Management	M
Writing	M

ASHWORTH COLLEGE

Business Administration and Management—General	M
Criminal Justice and Criminology	M
Health Services Management and Hospital Administration	M
Human Resources Management	M
International Business	M
Marketing	M

ASPEN UNIVERSITY

Business Administration and Management—General	M,O
Finance and Banking	M,O
Forensic Nursing	M,O
Information Science	M,O
Management Information Systems	M,O
Nursing and Healthcare Administration	M
Nursing Education	M
Nursing Informatics	M
Nursing—General	M
Project Management	M,O

ASSEMBLIES OF GOD THEOLOGICAL SEMINARY

Cultural Studies	M,D
Missions and Missiology	M,D
Pastoral Ministry and Counseling	M,D
Theology	M,D

ASSUMPTION COLLEGE

Accounting	M,O
Addictions/Substance Abuse Counseling	O
Applied Behavior Analysis	M,O
Business Administration and Management—General	M,O
Child and Family Studies	M,O
Counseling Psychology	M,O
Economics	M,O
Finance and Banking	M,O
Health Services Management and Hospital Administration	M,O
Human Resources Management	M,O
International Business	M,O
Marketing	M,O
Nonprofit Management	M,O
Rehabilitation Counseling	M,O
School Psychology	M,O
Social Sciences	O
Special Education	M,O

ATHABASCA UNIVERSITY

Adult Education	M,O
Allied Health—General	M,O
Applied Psychology	M,O
Architecture	M,O
Art Therapy	M,O

Business Administration and Management—General	M,D,O
Counseling Psychology	M,O
Counselor Education	M,O
Cultural Studies	M,O
Distance Education Development	M,D,O
Education—General	M,O
Interdisciplinary Studies	M,O
International Development	M,O
Management of Technology	M,D,O
Nursing and Healthcare Administration	M,O
Nursing—General	M,O
Organizational Management	M,O
Project Management	M,D,O
Science Education	M,O

THE ATHENAEUM OF OHIO

Theology	M,O

ATHENS STATE UNIVERSITY

Logistics	M
Religion	M
Supply Chain Management	M
Vocational and Technical Education	M

ATLANTA'S JOHN MARSHALL LAW SCHOOL

Law	M,D

ATLANTIC INSTITUTE OF ORIENTAL MEDICINE

Acupuncture and Oriental Medicine	M,D

ATLANTIC SCHOOL OF THEOLOGY

Pastoral Ministry and Counseling	M,O
Theology	M,O

ATLANTIC UNIVERSITY

Organizational Management	M,O
Pastoral Ministry and Counseling	O
Psychoanalysis and Psychotherapy	O
Transpersonal and Humanistic Psychology	M

ATLANTIC UNIVERSITY COLLEGE

Graphic Design	M

ATLANTIS UNIVERSITY

Business Administration and Management—General	M,D
Computer Engineering	M
Engineering and Applied Sciences—General	M
Health Services Management and Hospital Administration	M
Management of Technology	M

A.T. STILL UNIVERSITY

Allied Health—General	M,D,O
Athletic Training and Sports Medicine	M,D,O
Biological and Biomedical Sciences—General	M,D
Communication Disorders	M,D,O
Dentistry	M
Health Services Management and Hospital Administration	M,D,O
International Health	M,D,O
Kinesiology and Movement Studies	M,D,O
Occupational Therapy	M,D,O
Oral and Dental Sciences	M,D,O
Organizational Behavior	M,D,O
Osteopathic Medicine	M,D
Physical Therapy	M,D,O
Physician Assistant Studies	M,D,O
Public Health—General	M,D,O
Sport Psychology	M,D,O

AUBURN UNIVERSITY

Accounting	M
Adult Education	M,D,O
Aerospace/Aeronautical Engineering	M,D
Agricultural Economics and Agribusiness	M
Agricultural Sciences—General	M,D
Agronomy and Soil Sciences	M,D
Analytical Chemistry	M,D
Animal Sciences	M,D
Applied Economics	M,D
Applied Mathematics	M,D
Aquaculture	M,D
Architecture	M
Biochemistry	M,D
Biological and Biomedical Sciences—General	M,D
Biosystems Engineering	M,D
Botany	M,D
Business Administration and Management—General	M,D
Cell Biology	M,D
Chemical Engineering	M,D
Chemistry	M,D
Child and Family Studies	M,D
Civil Engineering	M,D
Clothing and Textiles	M,D
Communication Disorders	M,D
Communication—General	M,D
Computer Engineering	M,D
Computer Science	M,D
Construction Engineering	M
Curriculum and Instruction	M,D,O
Economics	M,D
Education—General	M,D,O
Educational Leadership and Administration	M,D,O
Educational Media/Instructional Technology	M,D,O
Electrical Engineering	M,D
Engineering and Applied Sciences—General	M,D,O
English	M,D
Entomology	M,D
Exercise and Sports Science	M,D,O
Finance and Banking	M

Fish, Game, and Wildlife
Management M,D
Food Science and
Technology M,D,O
Forestry M,D
Geography M
Geology M
Health Education M,D,O
Higher Education M,D,O
History M,D,O
Horticulture M,D
Human Development M,D
Industrial Design M
Industrial/Management
Engineering M,D,O
Inorganic Chemistry M,D
Landscape Architecture M
Materials Engineering M,D
Mathematics M,D
Mechanical Engineering M,D
Molecular Biology M,D
Natural Resources M,D
Nursing Education M
Nursing—General M
Nutrition M,D,O
Organic Chemistry M,D
Pharmaceutical Sciences M,D
Pharmacy D
Physical Chemistry M,D
Physical Education M,D,O
Physics M,D
Plant Pathology M,D
Political Science M,D,O
Polymer Science and
Engineering M,D
Psychology—General M,D
Public Administration M,D,O
Real Estate M
Rural Sociology M
Social Work M
Sociology M
Software Engineering M
Spanish M
Special Education M,D
Statistics M,D
Systems Engineering M,D,O
Technical Communication M,D,O
Urban and Regional Planning M
Veterinary Medicine D
Zoology M,D

AUBURN UNIVERSITY AT MONTGOMERY
Accounting M
Applied Economics M
Business Administration and
Management—General M
Clinical Psychology M,O
Counselor Education M
Criminal Justice and Criminology M
Early Childhood Education M,O
Education—General M,O
Educational Leadership and
Administration M,O
Educational Media/Instructional
Technology M,O
Elementary Education M,O
Exercise and Sports Science M,O
Family Nurse Practitioner Studies M
Geographic Information Systems M
Legal and Justice Studies M
Liberal Studies M
Management Information Systems M
Nursing Education M
Nursing—General M
Physical Education M,O
Public Policy M,D
School Psychology M,O
Secondary Education M,O
Special Education M,O
Sports Management M,O
Writing M

AUGSBURG UNIVERSITY
Business Administration and
Management—General M
Education—General M
Family Nurse Practitioner Studies M,D
Nursing—General M,D
Organizational Management M
Physician Assistant Studies M
Social Work M
Transcultural Nursing M,D

AUGUSTANA UNIVERSITY
Accounting M
Education—General M
Educational Media/Instructional
Technology M
Genetic Counseling M
Mathematics M
Reading Education M
Science Education M
Special Education M
Sports Management M

AUGUSTA UNIVERSITY
Acute Care/Critical Care Nursing D
Allied Health—General D
Allopathic Medicine D
Anatomy D
Biochemistry D
Business Administration and
Management—General M
Cancer Biology/Oncology D
Cardiovascular Sciences D
Cell Biology D
Clinical Psychology M,O
Clinical Research M
Computer and Information
Systems Security M
Counselor Education M,O

Curriculum and Instruction M,O
Dentistry D
Education—General M,D,O
Educational Leadership and
Administration M,O
Educational Media/Instructional
Technology D
Elementary Education M,O
Environmental and Occupational
Health M
Family Nurse Practitioner Studies D
Foreign Languages Education M,O
Genomic Sciences D
Gerontological Nursing D
Health Informatics M
Medical Illustration M
Middle School Education M,O
Molecular Medicine D
Music Education M,O
Neuroscience D
Nurse Anesthesia D
Nursing and Healthcare
Administration D
Nursing—General D
Occupational Therapy M
Oral and Dental Sciences M,D
Pediatric Nursing D
Pharmacology D
Physical Therapy D
Physician Assistant Studies M
Physiology D
Psychiatric Nursing D
Psychology—General M
Public Health—General M
Rehabilitation Sciences D
School Psychology M,O
Secondary Education M,O
Social Sciences M
Special Education M,O

AURORA UNIVERSITY
Accounting M
Adult Education M,D
Applied Behavior Analysis M,D
Business Administration and
Management—General M
Curriculum and Instruction M,D
Education—General M,D
Educational Leadership and
Administration M,D
Educational Media/Instructional
Technology M,D
English as a Second Language M,D
Homeland Security M
Mathematics Education M
Mathematics M
Public Policy M
Reading Education M,D
Science Education M
Social Work M,D
Special Education M,D

AUSTIN COLLEGE
Education—General M

AUSTIN PEAY STATE UNIVERSITY
Biological and Biomedical
Sciences—General M
Business Administration and
Management—General M
Clinical Laboratory
Sciences/Medical Technology M
Clinical Psychology M
Communication—General M
Computer and Information
Systems Security M
Corporate and Organizational
Communication M
Counseling Psychology M
Counselor Education M
Data Science/Data Analytics M
Education—General M,O
Engineering and Applied
Sciences—General M
English M
Exercise and Sports Science M
Family Nurse Practitioner Studies M
Health Education M
Industrial and Organizational
Psychology M
Mathematical and
Computational Finance M
Mathematics Education M
Media Studies M
Military and Defense Studies M
Music Education M
Music M
Nursing and Healthcare
Administration M
Nursing Education M
Nursing Informatics M
Nursing—General M
Organizational Management M
Psychology—General M
Public Health—General M
Science Education M
Social Work M
Sports Management M

AUSTIN PRESBYTERIAN THEOLOGICAL SEMINARY
Pastoral Ministry and Counseling M,D
Theology M,D

AVE MARIA SCHOOL OF LAW
Law D

AVE MARIA UNIVERSITY
Pastoral Ministry and Counseling M,D
Theology M,D

AVERETT UNIVERSITY
Accounting M

Business Administration and
Management—General M
Curriculum and Instruction M
Education—General M
Educational Leadership and
Administration M
Human Resources Management M
Marketing M
Special Education M

AVILA UNIVERSITY
Business Administration and
Management—General M
Counseling Psychology M
Early Childhood Education M,O
Education—General M,O
Educational Media/Instructional
Technology M
Elementary Education M,O
English as a Second Language M,O
Human Resources Management M
Middle School Education M,O
Nonprofit Management M
Organizational Management M
Physical Education M,O
Project Management M
Psychology—General M
Secondary Education M,O

AZUSA PACIFIC UNIVERSITY
Accounting M
Adult Nursing M,D
Art/Fine Arts M
Athletic Training and Sports
Medicine M
Biotechnology M
Business Administration and
Management—General M
Clinical Psychology D
Counselor Education M
Curriculum and Instruction M
Data Science/Data Analytics M
Developmental Psychology M
Education—General M,D
Educational Leadership and
Administration M,D
Educational Media/Instructional
Technology M
English as a Second Language M
English M
Entrepreneurship M
Ethics M
Experimental Psychology M
Family Nurse Practitioner Studies M,D
Film, Television, and Video
Production M
Finance and Banking M
Gerontological Nursing M,D
Higher Education M,D
Industrial and Organizational
Psychology M
International Business M
Kinesiology and Movement Studies M
Marketing M
Marriage and Family Therapy D
Music Education M
Music M
Nursing and Healthcare
Administration M,D
Nursing Education M,D
Nursing—General M,D
Organizational Management M
Pastoral Ministry and Counseling M
Pediatric Nursing M,D
Physical Therapy D
Psychiatric Nursing M,D
Psychology—General M
Public Health—General M
School Psychology M,D
Social Work M
Special Education M
Sports Management M
Theology M,D
Urban Studies M

BABEL UNIVERSITY PROFESSIONAL SCHOOL OF TRANSLATION
Translation and Interpretation M

BABSON COLLEGE
Accounting M,O
Business Administration and
Management—General M,O
Business Analytics M,O
Entrepreneurship M,O
Finance and Banking M,O

BAKER COLLEGE CENTER FOR GRADUATE STUDIES—ONLINE
Accounting M,D
Business Administration and
Management—General M,D
Finance and Banking M,D
Health Services Management and
Hospital Administration M,D
Human Resources Management M,D
Management Information Systems M,D
Marketing M,D
Occupational Therapy M,D

BAKER UNIVERSITY
Business Administration and
Management—General M
Education—General M,D
Liberal Studies M
Organizational Management M

BAKKE GRADUATE UNIVERSITY
Business Administration and
Management—General M,D
Entrepreneurship M,D
Pastoral Ministry and Counseling M,D
Theology M,D

Urban Education M,D

BALDWIN WALLACE UNIVERSITY
Accounting M
Business Administration and
Management—General M
Business Analytics M
Communication Disorders M
Education—General M
Educational Leadership and
Administration M
Educational Media/Instructional
Technology M
Health Education M
Health Services Management and
Hospital Administration M
Human Resources Management M
International Business M
Physician Assistant Studies M
Public Health—General M
Reading Education M
Special Education M

BALL STATE UNIVERSITY
Accounting M
Actuarial Science M
Adult Education M,D
Advertising and Public Relations M
Anthropology M,O
Applied Behavior Analysis M
Architecture M
Art/Fine Arts M
Biological and Biomedical
Sciences—General M,D
Business Administration and
Management—General M,O
Business Education M,O
Chemistry M,D
Clinical Psychology M,D
Cognitive Sciences M
Communication Disorders M,D
Communication—General M,O
Computer Education M,D,O
Computer Science M
Counseling Psychology M,D
Counselor Education M,D
Criminal Justice and Criminology M,O
Curriculum and Instruction M,O
Economic Development M,O
Education of the Gifted M,D,O
Education—General M,D,O
Educational Leadership and
Administration M,D,O
Educational Measurement and
Evaluation M,D,O
Educational Media/Instructional
Technology M,D
Educational Policy D
Educational Psychology M,D
Elementary Education M,D,O
Emergency Management M,O
English as a Second Language M
English M,D
Environmental Education M,O
Environmental Management
and Policy M,O
Environmental Sciences D
Exercise and Sports Science M,D
Family and Consumer
Sciences—General M
Family Nurse Practitioner Studies M,D,O
Foundations and Philosophy of
Education D
Geographic Information Systems M,O
Geography M,O
Geology M,D
Geosciences M
Gerontological Nursing M,D,O
Health Promotion M
Higher Education M,D
Historic Preservation M
History M
Homeland Security M,O
Human Development M,D,O
Information Science M,O
Interior Design M
Internet and Interactive
Multimedia M
Journalism M
Kinesiology and Movement Studies M,D,O
Landscape Architecture M
Linguistics M
Management Information Systems M,O
Mathematics Education M
Mathematics M
Meteorology M,O
Middle School Education M,O
Music Education M,D,O
Music M,D,O
Natural Resources M,O
Neuroscience M,D,O
Nursing Education M,D,O
Nursing—General M,D,O
Nutrition M
Photography M
Physical Education M
Physics M
Physiology M
Political Science M
Psychology—General M
Public Administration M,O
Reading Education M,D,O
Rehabilitation Counseling M,D
Rhetoric M,D
School Psychology M,D,O
Secondary Education M
Social Psychology M
Sociology M
Special Education M,D,O
Speech and Interpersonal
Communication M

M—masters degree; D—doctorate; O—other advanced degree; *—Close-Up and/or Display

Ball State University (continued)

Sport Psychology	M
Sports Management	M
Statistics	M
Telecommunications	M
Urban and Regional Planning	M,O
Urban Design	M
Writing	M,D

BANK STREET COLLEGE OF EDUCATION

Child and Family Studies	M
Early Childhood Education	M
Education—General	M
Educational Leadership and Administration	M
Elementary Education	M
Foundations and Philosophy of Education	M
Maternal and Child Health	M
Mathematics Education	M
Multilingual and Multicultural Education	M
Museum Education	M
Reading Education	M
Special Education	M

BAPTIST BIBLE COLLEGE

Pastoral Ministry and Counseling	M
Theology	M

THE BAPTIST COLLEGE OF FLORIDA

Music	M
Pastoral Ministry and Counseling	M
Theology	M

BAPTIST MISSIONARY ASSOCIATION THEOLOGICAL SEMINARY

Theology	M

BARCLAY COLLEGE

Theology	M

BARD COLLEGE

Art/Fine Arts	M
Atmospheric Sciences	M,O
Economics	M
Education—General	M
English	M
Environmental Management and Policy	M,O
Film, Television, and Video Production	M
History	M
Mathematics Education	M
Museum Studies	M
Music	M,O
Photography	M
Science Education	M
Secondary Education	M
Spanish	M
Sustainability Management	M,O
Writing	M

BARD GRADUATE CENTER

Art History	M,D
Decorative Arts	M,D

BARRY UNIVERSITY

Accounting	M
Acute Care/Critical Care Nursing	M,O
Anatomy	M
Art/Fine Arts	M
Athletic Training and Sports Medicine	M
Biological and Biomedical Sciences—General	M
Business Administration and Management—General	M,O
Clinical Psychology	M,O
Communication Disorders	M
Counselor Education	M,D,O
Curriculum and Instruction	D,O
Distance Education Development	O
Early Childhood Education	M,D,O
Education of the Gifted	M,D,O
Education—General	M,D,O
Educational Leadership and Administration	M,D,O
Educational Media/Instructional Technology	M,D,O
Elementary Education	M,D,O
English as a Second Language	M,D,O
Exercise and Sports Science	M
Family Nurse Practitioner Studies	M,O
Finance and Banking	O
Health Informatics	O
Health Services Management and Hospital Administration	M,O
Higher Education	M,D
Human Resources Development	M,D
Human Resources Management	O
Information Science	M
International Business	O
Kinesiology and Movement Studies	M
Law	D
Liberal Studies	M
Management Information Systems	O
Marketing	O
Marriage and Family Therapy	M,O
Nurse Anesthesia	M
Nursing and Healthcare Administration	M,D,O
Nursing Education	M,O
Nursing—General	M,D,O
Occupational Therapy	M
Pastoral Ministry and Counseling	M,D
Photography	M
Physician Assistant Studies	M
Podiatric Medicine	D
Psychology—General	M,O
Public Administration	M
Public Health—General	M,D,O
Reading Education	M,D,O
Rehabilitation Counseling	M,O
School Psychology	M,O
Social Work	M
Special Education	M,D,O

BARTON COLLEGE

Elementary Education	M

BARUCH COLLEGE OF THE CITY UNIVERSITY OF NEW YORK

Accounting	M,D
Arts Administration	M
Business Administration and Management—General	M,D,O
Corporate and Organizational Communication	M
Counseling Psychology	M
Economics	M
Educational Leadership and Administration	M,O
Entrepreneurship	M,D
Finance and Banking	M,D
Financial Engineering	M
Health Services Management and Hospital Administration	M
Higher Education	M
Human Resources Management	M,D
Industrial and Labor Relations	M
Industrial and Manufacturing Management	M,D
Industrial and Organizational Psychology	M,D
International Affairs	M*
International Business	M,D
International Economics	M
International Trade Policy	M
Management Information Systems	M,D
Marketing	M,D
Nonprofit Management	M
Organizational Behavior	M
Public Administration	M
Public Policy	M
Quantitative Analysis	M
Real Estate	M
Statistics	M
Sustainability Management	M,D
Sustainable Development	M
Taxation	M

BASTYR UNIVERSITY

Acupuncture and Oriental Medicine	M,D
Counseling Psychology	M,O
Health Psychology	M,O
Maternal and Child Health	M,O
Naturopathic Medicine	D,O
Nurse Midwifery	M,O
Nutrition	M,O

BAYAMÓN CENTRAL UNIVERSITY

Accounting	M
Business Administration and Management—General	M
Counselor Education	M,O
Early Childhood Education	M,O
Education—General	M,O
Educational Leadership and Administration	M,O
Elementary Education	M,O
Finance and Banking	M
Industrial and Organizational Psychology	M
Marketing	M
Marriage and Family Therapy	M,O
Rehabilitation Counseling	M,O
Special Education	M,O

BAYLOR COLLEGE OF MEDICINE

Allopathic Medicine	D
Biochemistry	D
Bioengineering	D
Biological and Biomedical Sciences—General	M,D
Biomedical Engineering	D
Biophysics	D
Cancer Biology/Oncology	D
Cardiovascular Sciences	D
Cell Biology	D
Clinical Laboratory Sciences/Medical Technology	M,D
Computational Biology	D
Developmental Biology	D
Genetic Counseling	M
Genetics	D
Human Genetics	D
Immunology	D
Microbiology	D
Molecular Biology	D
Molecular Biophysics	D
Molecular Medicine	D
Molecular Physiology	D
Neuroscience	D
Nurse Anesthesia	M
Pharmacology	D
Physician Assistant Studies	M
Structural Biology	D
Translational Biology	D
Virology	D

BAYLOR UNIVERSITY

Accounting	M
American Studies	M
Athletic Training and Sports Medicine	M,D
Biochemistry	M,D
Biological and Biomedical Sciences—General	M,D
Biomedical Engineering	M,D
Business Administration and Management—General	M,D
Chemistry	M,D
Clinical Psychology	D
Communication Disorders	M
Communication—General	M
Community Health	M
Computer Engineering	M,D
Computer Science	M,D
Curriculum and Instruction	M,D

Baylor University (continued)

Ecology	D
Economics	M
Education—General	M,D,O
Educational Leadership and Administration	M,O
Educational Psychology	M,D,O
Electrical Engineering	M,D
English	D
Entrepreneurship	D
Environmental Management and Policy	M,D
Environmental Sciences	D
Exercise and Sports Science	M,D
Geosciences	M,D
Health Education	M,D
History	M,D
Interdisciplinary Studies	D
International Affairs	M
Journalism	M
Kinesiology and Movement Studies	M,D
Law	D
Management Information Systems	M,D
Mathematics	M,D
Mechanical Engineering	M,D
Museum Studies	M
Music	M,D
Nursing—General	M,D
Nutrition	M,D
Philosophy	M,D
Physical Education	M,D
Physics	M,D
Physiology	M,D
Political Science	M,D
Public Health—General	M
Religion	M,D
School Psychology	M,D,O
Social Work	M,D
Sociology	M,D
Spanish	M
Special Education	M,D,O
Statistics	M,D
Theater	M
Theology	M,D

BAY PATH UNIVERSITY

Accounting	M
Addictions/Substance Abuse Counseling	M
Applied Behavior Analysis	M
Applied Statistics	M
Clinical Psychology	M
Communication—General	M
Computer and Information Systems Security	M
Developmental Psychology	M
Educational Leadership and Administration	M
Educational Media/Instructional Technology	M
Entrepreneurship	M
Forensic Sciences	M
Genetic Counseling	M
Health Informatics	M
Health Services Management and Hospital Administration	M
Higher Education	M
Management Information Systems	M
Management Strategy and Policy	M
Nonprofit Management	M
Occupational Therapy	M,D
Physician Assistant Studies	M
Special Education	M
Writing	M

BECKER COLLEGE

Counseling Psychology	M
Counselor Education	M
Social Psychology	M

BELHAVEN UNIVERSITY (MS)

Business Administration and Management—General	M
Education—General	M,D,O
Educational Leadership and Administration	M,D,O
Health Services Management and Hospital Administration	M
Human Resources Management	M
Public Administration	M
Reading Education	M,D,O
Sports Management	M

BELLARMINE UNIVERSITY

Athletic Training and Sports Medicine	M,D
Business Administration and Management—General	M
Communication—General	M
Education—General	M,D,O
Educational Leadership and Administration	M,D,O
Elementary Education	M,D,O
Family Nurse Practitioner Studies	M,D
Higher Education	M,D,O
Middle School Education	M,D,O
Nursing and Healthcare Administration	M,D
Nursing Education	M,D
Nursing—General	M,D
Physical Therapy	M,D
Reading Education	M,D,O
Secondary Education	M,D,O

BELLEVUE UNIVERSITY

Business Administration and Management—General	M,D
Corporate and Organizational Communication	M
Counselor Education	M
Criminal Justice and Criminology	M
Educational Media/Instructional Technology	M
Finance and Banking	M,D
Health Services Management and Hospital Administration	M
Human Resources Management	M,D

Bellevue University (continued)

Human Services	M
Information Science	M
Management Information Systems	M
Military and Defense Studies	M
National Security	M
Organizational Management	M
Project Management	M
Public Administration	M

BELLIN COLLEGE

Family Nurse Practitioner Studies	M
Nursing Education	M
Nursing—General	M

BELMONT UNIVERSITY

Accounting	M
Allied Health—General	M,D
Business Administration and Management—General	M
Health Informatics	D
Health Services Management and Hospital Administration	M
Law	D
Nursing—General	M,D
Occupational Therapy	M
Pharmaceutical Administration	D
Pharmacy	D
Physical Therapy	M,D
Public Health—General	D

BEMIDJI STATE UNIVERSITY

Biological and Biomedical Sciences—General	M
Education—General	M
English	M
Environmental Management and Policy	M
Mathematics Education	M
Mathematics	M
Special Education	M

BENEDICTINE COLLEGE

Business Administration and Management—General	M
Education—General	M
Educational Leadership and Administration	M

BENEDICTINE UNIVERSITY

Accounting	M
Business Administration and Management—General	M,D
Clinical Psychology	M
Computer and Information Systems Security	M
Emergency Management	M
Entrepreneurship	M
Exercise and Sports Science	M
Finance and Banking	M
Health Education	M
Health Informatics	M
Health Services Management and Hospital Administration	M
Human Resources Management	M
International Business	M
Logistics	M
Management Information Systems	M
Marketing	M
Nursing—General	M
Nutrition	M
Organizational Behavior	M,D
Organizational Management	M,D
Public Health—General	M

BENNINGTON COLLEGE

Allied Health—General	O
Dance	M
Music	M
Writing	M

BENTLEY UNIVERSITY

Accounting	M,D
Business Administration and Management—General	M,D,O
Business Analytics	M,O
Ergonomics and Human Factors	M
Finance and Banking	M
Information Science	M
Marketing	M
Taxation	M

BERGIN UNIVERSITY OF CANINE STUDIES

Animal Sciences	M

BERKELEY COLLEGE–WOODLAND PARK CAMPUS

Business Administration and Management—General	M

BERKLEE COLLEGE OF MUSIC

Entertainment Management	M
Music	M,O
Theater	M,O

BERRY COLLEGE

Business Administration and Management—General	M
Curriculum and Instruction	M,O
Education—General	M,O
Educational Leadership and Administration	O
Middle School Education	M
Reading Education	M
Secondary Education	M

BETHANY COLLEGE

Education—General	M

BETHANY GLOBAL UNIVERSITY

Pastoral Ministry and Counseling	M

BETHANY THEOLOGICAL SEMINARY

Conflict Resolution and Mediation/Peace Studies	M,O
Pastoral Ministry and Counseling	M,O
Religion	M,O
Theology	M,O

BETHEL SEMINARY
Classics	M,D,O
Clinical Psychology	M,D,O
Marriage and Family Therapy	M,D,O
Missions and Missiology	M,D,O
Near and Middle Eastern Languages	M,D,O
Pastoral Ministry and Counseling	M,D,O
Religion	M,D,O
Theology	M,D,O

BETHEL UNIVERSITY (IN)
Business Administration and Management—General	M
Education—General	M
Nursing—General	M
Pastoral Ministry and Counseling	M
Theology	M

BETHEL UNIVERSITY (MN)
Business Administration and Management—General	M,D,O
Counseling Psychology	M,D,O
Education—General	M,D,O
Educational Leadership and Administration	M,D,O
Elementary Education	M,D,O
Nurse Midwifery	M,D,O
Nursing Education	M,D,O
Organizational Management	M,D,O
Physician Assistant Studies	M,D,O
Secondary Education	M,D,O
Special Education	M,D,O

BETHEL UNIVERSITY (TN)
Business Administration and Management—General	M
Conflict Resolution and Mediation/Peace Studies	M
Educational Leadership and Administration	M
Physician Assistant Studies	M

BETHESDA UNIVERSITY
Music	M
Religion	M
Theology	M

BETH HAMEDRASH SHAAREI YOSHER INSTITUTE
Theology	

BETH HATALMUD RABBINICAL COLLEGE
Theology	

BETHLEHEM COLLEGE & SEMINARY
Theology	M

BETH MEDRASH GOVOHA
Theology	

BETHUNE-COOKMAN UNIVERSITY
Theology	M

BEULAH HEIGHTS UNIVERSITY
Religion	

BEXLEY SEABURY SEMINARY
Theology	M,D,O

BINGHAMTON UNIVERSITY, STATE UNIVERSITY OF NEW YORK
Accounting	M
Analytical Chemistry	M,D
Anthropology	M,D
Applied Physics	M,D
Art History	M,D
Asian Studies	M,O
Asian-American Studies	M,O
Biological and Biomedical Sciences—General	M,D
Biomedical Engineering	M,D
Biopsychology	D
Business Administration and Management—General	M,D
Chemistry	M,D
Clinical Psychology	D
Cognitive Sciences	D
Community Health Nursing	M,D,O
Comparative Literature	M,D
Computer Science	M,D
Early Childhood Education	M
Economics	M,D
Education—General	M,D,O
Educational Leadership and Administration	M,D,O
Electrical Engineering	M,D
Engineering and Applied Sciences—General	M,D
English as a Second Language	M
English Education	M
English	M,D
Environmental Management and Policy	M,D
Family Nurse Practitioner Studies	M,D,O
Finance and Banking	D
Foreign Languages Education	M
Foundations and Philosophy of Education	D
French	M
Geography	M
Geology	M,D
Gerontological Nursing	M,D,O
Health Services Management and Hospital Administration	M,D
History	M,D
Industrial/Management Engineering	M,D
Inorganic Chemistry	M,D
Italian	M
Legal and Justice Studies	M,D
Liberal Studies	M
Management Information Systems	D
Marketing	D
Materials Engineering	M,D

Materials Sciences	M,D
Mathematics Education	M
Mathematics	M,D
Mechanical Engineering	M,D
Music	M
Nursing—General	M,D,O
Organizational Management	D
Pharmacy	D
Philosophy	M,D
Physical Chemistry	M,D
Physics	M,D
Political Science	M,D
Psychiatric Nursing	M,D,O
Psychology—General	D
Public Administration	M
Public Affairs	D
Reading Education	M
Science Education	M
Secondary Education	M
Social Sciences Education	M
Social Work	M
Sociology	M,D
Spanish	M
Special Education	M
Statistics	M,D
Student Affairs	M
Supply Chain Management	D
Sustainable Development	M
Systems Science	M,D
Theater	M
Translation and Interpretation	D,O
Writing	M,D

BIOLA UNIVERSITY
Anthropology	M,D,O
Business Administration and Management—General	M
Clinical Psychology	D
Communication Disorders	M,O
Cultural Studies	M,D,O
Curriculum and Instruction	M,O
Early Childhood Education	M,O
Education—General	M,O
English as a Second Language	M,D,O
Jewish Studies	M,D,O
Linguistics	M,D,O
Missions and Missiology	M,D,O
Pastoral Ministry and Counseling	M,D,O
Psychology—General	D
Religion	M,D,O
Religious Education	M,D,O
Science Education	M,O
Special Education	M,O
Theology	M,D,O

BISHOP'S UNIVERSITY
Education—General	M,O
English as a Second Language	M,O

BLACK HILLS STATE UNIVERSITY
Business Administration and Management—General	M
Curriculum and Instruction	M
Genomic Sciences	M
Management Strategy and Policy	M

BLESSING-RIEMAN COLLEGE OF NURSING & HEALTH SCIENCES
Nursing and Healthcare Administration	M
Nursing Education	M
Nursing—General	M

BLOOMFIELD COLLEGE
Accounting	M

BLOOMSBURG UNIVERSITY OF PENNSYLVANIA
Accounting	M
Adult Nursing	M,D
Athletic Training and Sports Medicine	M
Biological and Biomedical Sciences—General	M
Business Administration and Management—General	M,O
Business Education	M
Communication Disorders	M,D
Community Health	M,D
Counselor Education	M
Curriculum and Instruction	M
Early Childhood Education	M
Education—General	M,O
Educational Leadership and Administration	M
Educational Media/Instructional Technology	M,O
English Education	M
Exercise and Sports Science	M
Family Nurse Practitioner Studies	M,D
Mathematics Education	M
Middle School Education	M
Nurse Anesthesia	M,D
Nursing and Healthcare Administration	M,D
Nursing—General	M,D
Reading Education	M
Science Education	M
Social Sciences Education	M
Special Education	M,O
Student Affairs	M

BLUEFIELD COLLEGE
Education—General	M

BLUE MOUNTAIN COLLEGE
Elementary Education	M
Reading Education	M
Science Education	M
Secondary Education	M

BLUFFTON UNIVERSITY
Accounting	M

Business Administration and Management—General	M
Curriculum and Instruction	M
Education—General	M
Educational Leadership and Administration	M
Finance and Banking	M
Health Services Management and Hospital Administration	M
Industrial and Manufacturing Management	M
Reading Education	M
Special Education	M
Sustainability Management	M

BOB JONES UNIVERSITY
Accounting	M,D,O
Art/Fine Arts	M,D,O
Business Administration and Management—General	M,D,O
Counselor Education	M,D,O
Curriculum and Instruction	M,D,O
Educational Leadership and Administration	M,D,O
Elementary Education	M,D,O
English Education	M,D,O
English	M,D,O
Film, Television, and Video Production	M,D,O
Graphic Design	M,D,O
History	M,D,O
Illustration	M,D,O
Mathematics Education	M,D,O
Music Education	M,D,O
Music	M,D,O
Pastoral Ministry and Counseling	M,D,O
Religion	M,D,O
Rhetoric	M,D,O
Secondary Education	M,D,O
Social Sciences Education	M,D,O
Special Education	M,D,O
Speech and Interpersonal Communication	M,D,O
Student Affairs	M,D,O
Theater	M,D,O
Theology	M,D,O

BOISE STATE UNIVERSITY
Accounting	M
Animal Sciences	M,D
Anthropology	M
Art/Fine Arts	M
Biological and Biomedical Sciences—General	M,D
Business Administration and Management—General	M
Chemistry	M
Civil Engineering	M
Communication—General	M
Computer Engineering	M,D
Computer Science	M,O
Counselor Education	M,O
Criminal Justice and Criminology	M
Curriculum and Instruction	M,D,O
Distance Education Development	M,D,O
Early Childhood Education	M
Economics	M
Education—General	M,D,O
Educational Leadership and Administration	M,D,O
Educational Media/Instructional Technology	M,D,O
Electrical Engineering	M,D
Engineering and Applied Sciences—General	M,D,O
English as a Second Language	M
English Education	M
Environmental and Occupational Health	M,O
Geophysics	M,D
Geosciences	M,D
Gerontological Nursing	M,D,O
Health Promotion	M,O
History	M
Hydrology	M,D
Interdisciplinary Studies	M
Kinesiology and Movement Studies	M
Materials Engineering	M,D
Mathematics Education	M
Mathematics	M
Mechanical Engineering	M
Molecular Biology	M,D
Multilingual and Multicultural Education	M
Music Education	M
Music	M
Natural Resources	M,D,O
Nursing—General	M,D,O
Organizational Management	M,O
Political Science	M
Public Administration	M,D,O
Public Health—General	M,D,O
Public Policy	M,D,O
Reading Education	M
Rhetoric	M
Social Work	M
Special Education	M
Sports Management	M
Taxation	M
Technical Communication	M

BORICUA COLLEGE
English as a Second Language	M
Human Services	M

BOSTON ARCHITECTURAL COLLEGE
Architecture	M
Historic Preservation	M
Interior Design	M
Landscape Architecture	M
Sustainable Development	M

BOSTON COLLEGE
Accounting	M
Adult Nursing	M,D
Biochemistry	M,D
Biological and Biomedical Sciences—General	D
Business Administration and Management—General	M
Chemistry	M,D
Classics	M
Counseling Psychology	M,D,O
Curriculum and Instruction	M,D,O
Developmental Psychology	M,D
Early Childhood Education	M,D,O
East European and Russian Studies	D
Economics	D
Education—General	M,D,O
Educational Psychology	M,D
Elementary Education	M,D,O
English Education	M,D,O
English	M,D
Finance and Banking	M,D
Foreign Languages Education	M,D,O
French	M
Geology	M
Geophysics	M
Gerontological Nursing	M,D
History	M,D
Inorganic Chemistry	M,D
Italian	M
Law	D
Linguistics	M
Maternal and Child/Neonatal Nursing	M,D
Mathematics Education	M,D,O
Mathematics	D
Nurse Anesthesia	M,D
Nursing—General	M,D
Organic Chemistry	M,D
Organizational Behavior	D
Organizational Management	D
Pastoral Ministry and Counseling	M,D,O
Pediatric Nursing	M,D
Philosophy	M,D
Physical Chemistry	M,D
Physics	M,D
Political Science	M,D
Psychiatric Nursing	M,D
Psychology—General	D
Reading Education	M,D,O
Religious Education	M,D,O
Russian	M
Science Education	M,D,O
Secondary Education	M,D,O
Social Sciences Education	M,D,O
Social Work	M,D
Sociology	M,D
Spanish	M
Special Education	M,D,O
Theology	M,D,O
Western European Studies	M,D
Women's Health Nursing	M,D

BOSTON GRADUATE SCHOOL OF PSYCHOANALYSIS
Counseling Psychology	M
Developmental Psychology	O
Psychoanalysis and Psychotherapy	M,D,O
Psychology—General	M

BOSTON UNIVERSITY
Actuarial Science	M
Advertising and Public Relations	M
African-American Studies	M
Allied Health—General	M,D
Allopathic Medicine	D
American Studies	D
Anatomy	M,D
Anthropology	M,D
Archaeology	M,D
Art Education	M
Art History	M,D,O
Art/Fine Arts	M
Arts Administration	M,O
Astronomy	M,D
Athletic Training and Sports Medicine	M,D
Biochemistry	M,D
Bioinformatics	M,D
Biological and Biomedical Sciences—General	M,D
Biomedical Engineering	M,D
Biophysics	M,D
Biopsychology	M,D
Biostatistics	M,D
Business Administration and Management—General	M,D
Business Analytics	M,D
Cell Biology	M,D
Chemistry	M,D
Classics	M,D
Clinical Research	M
Communication Disorders	M,D
Communication—General	M
Community Health	M,D
Computer and Information Systems Security	M,D,O
Computer Engineering	M,D,O
Computer Science	M,D,O
Corporate and Organizational Communication	M
Counseling Psychology	M
Criminal Justice and Criminology	M
Cultural Studies	M
Data Science/Data Analytics	M,O
Dentistry	M,D,O
Economic Development	M
Economics	M
Education—General	M,D,O
Electrical Engineering	M,D
Emergency Management	M

Energy Management and Policy	M,D
Engineering and Applied Sciences—General	M,D
English	M,D
Environmental and Occupational Health	M,D
Environmental Sciences	M,D
Epidemiology	M,D
Film, Television, and Video Production	M
Finance and Banking	M
Food Science and Technology	M
Forensic Sciences	M
Genetic Counseling	M
Genetics	D
Genomic Sciences	D
Geographic Information Systems	M,D
Geosciences	M,D
Health Communication	M
Health Education	M
Health Informatics	M,O
Health Law	M,D
Health Services Management and Hospital Administration	M,D
Health Services Research	M
Hispanic and Latin American Languages	M
Historic Preservation	M
History	M,D
Hospitality Management	M
Immunology	D
International Affairs	M
International Business	M
International Health	M
Internet and Interactive Multimedia	M,O
Journalism	M
Law	M,D
Linguistics	M,D
Management Information Systems	M,D
Management of Technology	M
Management Strategy and Policy	M,O
Manufacturing Engineering	M,D
Mass Communication	M
Materials Engineering	M,D
Materials Sciences	M,D
Mathematical and Computational Finance	M,D
Mathematics	M,D
Mechanical Engineering	M,D
Media Studies	M
Medical Imaging	M
Microbiology	D
Missions and Missiology	M
Molecular Biology	M
Molecular Medicine	D
Museum Studies	M,D,O
Music Education	M
Music	M,D,O
Neurobiology	D
Neuroscience	D
Nutrition	M,D
Occupational Therapy	D
Oral and Dental Sciences	M,D
Organizational Management	M
Pastoral Ministry and Counseling	M
Pathology	M,D
Pharmaceutical Sciences	D
Pharmacology	M,D
Philosophy	M,D
Physical Therapy	M,D
Physician Assistant Studies	M
Physics	D
Physiology	M,D
Political Science	D
Project Management	M,O
Psychology—General	M,D
Public Health—General	M,D
Rehabilitation Sciences	M,D
Religion	M,D
Religious Education	M,D
Risk Management	M
Romance Languages	M,D
Social Work	M,D
Sociology	M,D
Software Engineering	M,O
Supply Chain Management	M
Systems Engineering	M,D
Telecommunications Management	M,O
Telecommunications	M,O
Theater	M,O
Theology	M,D
Translational Biology	D
Travel and Tourism	M
Urban and Regional Planning	M
Urban Studies	M
Writing	M

BOWIE STATE UNIVERSITY

Applied Mathematics	M
Business Administration and Management—General	M
Computer Science	M,D
Corporate and Organizational Communication	M,O
Counseling Psychology	M
Counselor Education	M
Education—General	M
Educational Leadership and Administration	M,D
Elementary Education	M
English	M
Family Nurse Practitioner Studies	M
Human Resources Development	M
Management Information Systems	M,O
Nursing and Healthcare Administration	M
Nursing Education	M
Nursing—General	M
Public Administration	M
Reading Education	M

Secondary Education	M
Special Education	M

BOWLING GREEN STATE UNIVERSITY

Accounting	M
American Studies	M
Applied Arts and Design—General	M
Applied Statistics	M
Art Education	M
Art History	M
Art/Fine Arts	M
Biological and Biomedical Sciences—General	M,D
Business Administration and Management—General	M
Business Education	M
Chemistry	M,D
Clinical Psychology	M,D
Communication Disorders	M,D
Communication—General	M,D
Computer Art and Design	M
Computer Science	M
Counselor Education	M
Criminal Justice and Criminology	M
Curriculum and Instruction	M
Demography and Population Studies	M
Developmental Psychology	M,D
Economics	M
Educational Leadership and Administration	M,D,O
Educational Media/Instructional Technology	M
English	M,D
Experimental Psychology	M,D
Film, Television, and Video Production	M,D
French	M
Geology	M
Geophysics	M
German	M
Graphic Design	M
Higher Education	D
History	M,D
Industrial and Organizational Psychology	M,D
Interdisciplinary Studies	M,D
International and Comparative Education	M
Kinesiology and Movement Studies	M
Leisure Studies	M
Mathematics Education	M,D
Mathematics	M
Media Studies	M,D
Music Education	M,D
Music	M,D
Operations Research	M
Organizational Management	M
Philosophy	M,D
Physics	M
Psychology—General	M,D
Public Administration	M
Public Health—General	M
Reading Education	M,O
Recreation and Park Management	M
Rhetoric	M,D
Science Education	M
Social Psychology	M,D
Social Work	M
Sociology	M,D
Software Engineering	M
Spanish	M
Special Education	M
Sports Management	M
Statistics	M,D
Student Affairs	M
Technical Communication	M,D
Theater	M
Vocational and Technical Education	M
Writing	M,D

BRADLEY UNIVERSITY

Accounting	M
Art/Fine Arts	M
Biochemistry	M
Biological and Biomedical Sciences—General	M
Business Administration and Management—General	M
Chemistry	M
Civil Engineering	M
Clinical Psychology	M
Computer Science	M
Construction Engineering	M
Counseling Psychology	M
Counselor Education	M
Curriculum and Instruction	M
Education—General	M,D,O
Educational Leadership and Administration	M
Electrical Engineering	M
Engineering and Applied Sciences—General	M
English	M
Family Nurse Practitioner Studies	M,D,O
Graphic Design	M
Health Services Management and Hospital Administration	M,D,O
Human Development	M
Industrial/Management Engineering	M
Information Science	M
Manufacturing Engineering	M
Mechanical Engineering	M
Nonprofit Management	M
Nursing and Healthcare Administration	M,D,O
Nursing Education	M,D,O
Nursing—General	M,D,O
Nutrition	M
Photography	M
Physical Therapy	D

BRANDEIS UNIVERSITY

Anthropology	M,D

Applied Economics	M
Art/Fine Arts	O
Artificial Intelligence/Robotics	M
Biochemistry	M,D
Bioinformatics	M
Biological and Biomedical Sciences—General	M,D,O
Biophysics	M,D
Biotechnology	M
Business Administration and Management—General	M
Cell Biology	M,D
Chemistry	M,D
Child and Family Studies	M,D
Chinese	M
Classics	M
Cognitive Sciences	M,D
Computer and Information Systems Security	M
Computer Science	M,D
Conflict Resolution and Mediation/Peace Studies	M,D
Cultural Anthropology	M,D
Developmental Psychology	M,D
Disability Studies	D
Distance Education Development	M
Economics	M,D
Educational Leadership and Administration	M,O
Educational Measurement and Evaluation	O
Elementary Education	M,O
English	M,D
Entrepreneurship	M
Finance and Banking	M,D
Foreign Languages Education	M,D
Gender Studies	M,D
Genetic Counseling	M
Genetics	M,D
Health Education	D
Health Informatics	M
Health Services Management and Hospital Administration	M
History	M,D
Human Services	M
Human-Computer Interaction	M
Inorganic Chemistry	M,D
International Business	M,D
International Health	M,D
Internet and Interactive Multimedia	M
Jewish Studies	M,D
Linguistics	M
Management Information Systems	M
Management Strategy and Policy	M
Marketing	M
Mathematics	M,D
Medical Informatics	M
Microbiology	M,D
Molecular Biology	M,D
Music	M,D
Near and Middle Eastern Languages	M,D
Near and Middle Eastern Studies	M,D
Neurobiology	M,D
Neuroscience	M,D
Nonprofit Management	M
Organic Chemistry	M,D
Philosophy	M
Physical Chemistry	M,D
Physics	M,D
Political Science	M,D
Project Management	M
Psychology—General	M,D
Public Policy	M
Real Estate	M
Religious Education	M,O
Risk Management	M
Secondary Education	M,O
Social Psychology	M,D
Sociology	M,D
Software Engineering	M
Sustainable Development	M
Women's Studies	M,D

BRANDMAN UNIVERSITY

Accounting	M
Business Administration and Management—General	M
Counseling Psychology	M
Counselor Education	M,D
Curriculum and Instruction	M,D
Data Science/Data Analytics	M
Early Childhood Education	M,D
Education—General	M,D
Educational Leadership and Administration	M,D
Educational Media/Instructional Technology	M,D
Elementary Education	M,D
Entrepreneurship	M
Finance and Banking	M
Health Services Management and Hospital Administration	M
Human Resources Management	M
International Business	M
Marketing	M
Marriage and Family Therapy	M
Nursing—General	D
Organizational Management	M
Psychology—General	M
Public Administration	M
Secondary Education	M,D
Social Work	M
Special Education	M

BRANDON UNIVERSITY

Counselor Education	M,O
Curriculum and Instruction	M
Education—General	M,O
Educational Leadership and Administration	M,O
Music Education	M
Music	M
Rural Planning and Studies	M,O
Special Education	M,O

BRENAU UNIVERSITY

Accounting	M
Business Administration and Management—General	M
Early Childhood Education	M,O
Education—General	M,O
Family Nurse Practitioner Studies	M
Health Services Management and Hospital Administration	M
Interior Design	M
Middle School Education	M,O
Nursing and Healthcare Administration	M
Nursing Education	M
Occupational Therapy	M
Organizational Management	M
Project Management	M
Psychology—General	M
Secondary Education	M,O
Special Education	M,O

BRESCIA UNIVERSITY

Business Administration and Management—General	M
Curriculum and Instruction	M
Social Work	M

BRIAR CLIFF UNIVERSITY

Nursing—General	M,D,O

BRIDGEWATER COLLEGE

Athletic Training and Sports Medicine	M

BRIDGEWATER STATE UNIVERSITY

Accounting	M
Art Education	M
Business Administration and Management—General	M
Communication Disorders	M
Computer Science	M
Counselor Education	M,O
Criminal Justice and Criminology	M
Early Childhood Education	M
Education—General	M,O
Educational Leadership and Administration	M,O
Educational Media/Instructional Technology	M
Elementary Education	M
English	M
Finance and Banking	M
Health Promotion	M
Mathematics Education	M
Physical Education	M
Psychology—General	M
Public Administration	M
Reading Education	M,O
Science Education	M
Secondary Education	M
Social Sciences Education	M
Social Work	M
Special Education	M

BRIERCREST SEMINARY

Business Administration and Management—General	M
Marriage and Family Therapy	M
Missions and Missiology	M
Organizational Management	M
Pastoral Ministry and Counseling	M
Religion	M
Theology	M

BRIGHAM YOUNG UNIVERSITY

Agricultural Sciences—General	M,D
Analytical Chemistry	M,D
Animal Sciences	M,D
Anthropology	M
Applied Statistics	M
Art Education	M
Astronomy	M,D
Athletic Training and Sports Medicine	M,D
Biochemistry	M,D
Biological and Biomedical Sciences—General	M,D
Biotechnology	M,D
Business Administration and Management—General	M
Chemical Engineering	M,D
Chemistry	M,D
Child and Family Studies	M,D
Civil Engineering	M,D
Clinical Psychology	D
Cognitive Sciences	D
Comparative and Interdisciplinary Arts	M
Computer Engineering	M,D
Computer Science	M,D
Construction Management	M
Developmental Biology	M,D
Education—General	M,D,O
Educational Media/Instructional Technology	M
Educational Policy	M,D
Electrical Engineering	M,D
Engineering and Applied Sciences—General	M,D
English as a Second Language	M
Entrepreneurship	M
Environmental Sciences	M,D
Exercise and Sports Science	M,D
Family Nurse Practitioner Studies	M
Finance and Banking	M
Fish, Game, and Wildlife Management	M,D
Food Science and Technology	M
Foreign Languages Education	M
Geology	M
Health Promotion	M,D
Health Services Management and Hospital Administration	M

Hispanic and Latin American
  Languages — M
Human Development — M,D
Human Resources Management — M
Information Science — M
International Affairs — M,D
Law — M,D
Linguistics — M
Manufacturing Engineering — M
Marketing — M
Marriage and Family Therapy — M,D
Mass Communication — M
Mathematics Education — M
Mathematics — M,D
Mechanical Engineering — M
Microbiology — M,D
Molecular Biology — M,D
Music Education — M
Music — M
Neuroscience — M,D
Nonprofit Management — M
Nursing—General — M
Nutrition — M
Physics — M,D
Physiology — M,D
Plant Sciences — M,D
Political Science — M
Psychology—General — D
Public Administration — M
Public Health—General — M
Religious Education — M
Rhetoric — M
School Psychology — M,D,O
Science Education — M,D
Social Work — M
Sociology — M
Statistics — M
Supply Chain Management — M
Writing — M

BRITE DIVINITY SCHOOL
Pastoral Ministry and Counseling — M,D,O
Theology — M,D,O

BROADVIEW UNIVERSITY–WEST JORDAN
Business Administration and
  Management—General — M
Health Services Management and
  Hospital Administration — M
Management Information Systems — M

BROCK UNIVERSITY
Accounting — M
Allied Health—General — M,D
Biological and Biomedical
  Sciences—General — M,D
Biotechnology — M,D
Business Administration and
  Management—General — M
Chemistry — M
Child and Family Studies — M
Classics — M
Comparative Literature — M
Computer Science — M
Cultural Studies — M
Disability Studies — M,O
Economics — M
Education—General — M,D
English as a Second Language — M
English — M
Geography — M
Geosciences — M
History — M
Human Development — M,D
International Affairs — M
Legal and Justice Studies — M
Mathematics — M
Neuroscience — M,D
Philosophy — M
Physics — M
Political Science — M
Psychology—General — M,D
Public Policy — M
Social Psychology — M
Sociology — M
Statistics — M

BROOKLINE COLLEGE
Nursing and Healthcare
  Administration — M
Nursing—General — M

BROOKLYN COLLEGE OF THE CITY UNIVERSITY OF NEW YORK
Accounting — M
Art Education — M
Art History — M
Art/Fine Arts — M
Arts Administration — M
Biological and Biomedical
  Sciences—General — M
Business Administration and
  Management—General — M
Chemistry — M,D
Communication Disorders — M,D
Community Health — M
Computer Science — M,O
Counseling Psychology — M,D,O
Counselor Education — M
Early Childhood Education — M,O
Economics — M
Education—General — M,O
Educational Leadership and
  Administration — M
Elementary Education — M,O
English Education — M
English — M
Environmental Education — M
Exercise and Sports Science — M
Experimental Psychology — M,D

Film, Television, and Video
  Production — M
Film, Television, and Video
  Theory and Criticism — M
Finance and Banking — M
Foreign Languages Education — M
French — M
Geology — M
Geosciences — M
Health Informatics — M,O
Health Services Management and
  Hospital Administration — M
History — M
Industrial and Organizational
  Psychology — M,D
Information Science — M,O
International Affairs — M
International Business — M
Internet and Interactive
  Multimedia — M
Jewish Studies — M
Kinesiology and Movement Studies — M
Liberal Studies — M
Mathematics Education — M
Mathematics — M
Media Studies — M
Middle School Education — M,O
Multilingual and Multicultural
  Education — M
Music Education — M
Music — M
Nutrition — M
Organizational Behavior — M,D
Photography — M
Physical Education — M
Physics — M
Political Science — M
Psychology—General — M,D
Public Health—General — M
Public Policy — M
School Psychology — M,O
Science Education — M
Secondary Education — M
Social Psychology — M,D
Social Sciences Education — M
Sociology — M,D
Spanish — M
Special Education — M,O
Speech and Interpersonal
  Communication — M,D
Sports Management — M
Thanatology — M
Theater — M
Urban Studies — M
Writing — M

BROOKLYN LAW SCHOOL
Law — M,D

BROWN UNIVERSITY
Allopathic Medicine — D
American Studies — M,D
Anthropology — M,D
Applied Mathematics — M,D
Archaeology — D
Art History — D
Asian Studies — D
Biochemical Engineering — M,D
Biochemistry — M,D
Biological and Biomedical
  Sciences—General — M,D
Biomedical Engineering — M,D
Biostatistics — M,D
Biotechnology — M,D
Cell Biology — M,D
Chemical Engineering — M,D
Chemistry — D
Classics — M,D
Cognitive Sciences — M,D
Community Health — M
Comparative Literature — D
Computer Engineering — M,D
Computer Science — M,D
East European and Russian Studies — M,D
Ecology — D
Economics — D
Education—General — M
Electrical Engineering — M,D
Elementary Education — M
Engineering and Applied
  Sciences—General — M,D
English as a Second Language — M,D
English Education — M
English — M,D
Epidemiology — M,D
Evolutionary Biology — D
French — D
Geosciences — D
German — D
Health Services Research — D
Hispanic Studies — D
History of Science and Technology — D
History — M,D
Italian — D
Latin American Studies — M,D
Linguistics — M,D
Materials Sciences — M,D
Mathematics — D
Mechanical Engineering — M,D
Mechanics — M,D
Molecular Biology — M,D
Molecular Pharmacology — M,D
Multilingual and Multicultural
  Education — M,D
Music — D
Near and Middle Eastern Studies — M
Neuroscience — D
Pathobiology — M,D
Philosophy — D
Physics — M,D
Physiology — M,D

Political Science — D
Psychology—General — M,D
Public Health—General — M
Public Policy — M
Publishing — D
Religion — M,D
Russian — M,D
Science Education — M
Secondary Education — M
Slavic Languages — M,D
Social Sciences Education — M
Sociology — M,D
Theater — M,D
Urban Education — M
Western European Studies — M,D
Writing — M,D

BRYAN COLLEGE
Business Administration and
  Management—General — M
Health Services Management and
  Hospital Administration — M
Human Resources Management — M
Marketing — M
Pastoral Ministry and Counseling — M
Sports Management — M

BRYAN COLLEGE OF HEALTH SCIENCES
Nurse Anesthesia — M

BRYANT UNIVERSITY
Accounting — M
Business Administration and
  Management—General — M
Communication—General — M,O
Corporate and Organizational
  Communication — M,O
Physician Assistant Studies — M
Taxation — M

BRYAN UNIVERSITY
Business Administration and
  Management—General — M

BRYN ATHYN COLLEGE OF THE NEW CHURCH
Religion — M
Theology — M

BRYN MAWR COLLEGE
Archaeology — M,D
Art History — M,D
Chemistry — M,D
Classics — M,D
Mathematics — M,D
Physics — M,D
Social Work — M,D

BUCKNELL UNIVERSITY
Animal Behavior — M
Biological and Biomedical
  Sciences—General — M
Chemical Engineering — M
Chemistry — M
Civil Engineering — M
Computer Engineering — M
Education—General — M
Electrical Engineering — M
Engineering and Applied
  Sciences—General — M
English — M
Mathematics — M
Mechanical Engineering — M
Psychology—General — M
Student Affairs — M

BUENA VISTA UNIVERSITY
Counselor Education — M
Curriculum and Instruction — M
Education—General — M
English as a Second Language — M

BUFFALO STATE COLLEGE, STATE UNIVERSITY OF NEW YORK
Adult Education — M,O
Applied Economics — M
Art Education — M
Biological and Biomedical
  Sciences—General — M
Business Education — M
Communication Disorders — M
Criminal Justice and Criminology — M
Data Science/Data Analytics — M
Early Childhood Education — M
Economics — M
Education—General — M,O
Educational Leadership and
  Administration — O
Educational Media/Instructional
  Technology — M
English Education — M
English — M
Forensic Sciences — M
Historic Preservation — M,O
History — M
Human Resources Management — M,O
Industrial/Management
  Engineering — M
Interdisciplinary Studies — M
Manufacturing Engineering — M
Mathematics Education — M
Mechanical Engineering — M
Multilingual and Multicultural
  Education — O
Museum Studies — M
Nutrition — M
Organizational Management — M
Reading Education — M
Science Education — M
Social Sciences Education — M
Special Education — M
Urban Education — M
Vocational and Technical Education — M

BURRELL COLLEGE OF OSTEOPATHIC MEDICINE
Osteopathic Medicine — D

BUTLER UNIVERSITY
Art/Fine Arts — M
Business Administration and
  Management—General — M
Education—General — M,O
Educational Leadership and
  Administration — M,O
Music Education — M
Music — M
Pharmaceutical Sciences — M,D
Pharmacy — M,D
Physician Assistant Studies — M,D

BYZANTINE CATHOLIC SEMINARY OF SAINTS CYRIL AND METHODIUS
Theology — M

CABARRUS COLLEGE OF HEALTH SCIENCES
Occupational Therapy — M

CABRINI UNIVERSITY
Accounting — M,D
Biological and Biomedical
  Sciences—General — M,D
Chemistry — M,D
Communication—General — M,D
Criminal Justice and Criminology — M,D
Curriculum and Instruction — M,D
Early Childhood Education — M,D
Educational Leadership and
  Administration — M,D
Elementary Education — M,D
English as a Second Language — M,D
English — M,D
History — M,D
Mathematics — M,D
Middle School Education — M,D
Organizational Management — M,D
Reading Education — M,D
Secondary Education — M,D
Special Education — M,D

CAIRN UNIVERSITY
Accounting — M,O
Applied Behavior Analysis — M,O
Business Administration and
  Management—General — M,O
Education—General — M,O
Educational Leadership and
  Administration — M,O
Entrepreneurship — M,O
Nonprofit Management — M,O
Organizational Management — M,O
Pastoral Ministry and Counseling — M
Religion — M
Theology — M

CALDWELL UNIVERSITY
Applied Behavior Analysis — M,D,O
Business Administration and
  Management—General — M
Counseling Psychology — M,O
Education—General — M,D,O
Educational Leadership and
  Administration — M,D,O
Special Education — M,D,O

CALIFORNIA BAPTIST UNIVERSITY
Accounting — M
Adult Education — M
Adult Nursing — M
Advertising and Public Relations — M
Applied Mathematics — M
Architecture — M
Athletic Training and Sports
  Medicine — M
Business Administration and
  Management—General — M
Civil Engineering — M
Communication Disorders — M
Communication—General — M
Construction Management — M
Counseling Psychology — M
Counselor Education — M
Curriculum and Instruction — M
Distance Education Development — M
Education of Students with
  Severe/Multiple Disabilities — M
Education—General — M
Educational Leadership and
  Administration — M
Educational Media/Instructional
  Technology — M
English as a Second Language — M
English Education — M
English — M
Exercise and Sports Science — M
Family Nurse Practitioner Studies — M
Forensic Psychology — M
Health Education — M
Health Promotion — M
Health Services Management and
  Hospital Administration — M
Higher Education — M
International and Comparative
  Education — M
Mechanical Engineering — M
Music Education — M
Music — M
Nursing and Healthcare
  Administration — M
Nursing Education — M
Nursing—General — M,D
Organizational Management — M
Pastoral Ministry and Counseling — M
Physical Education — M
Physician Assistant Studies — M
Public Administration — M

Public Health—General	M
Reading Education	M
School Psychology	M
Science Education	M
Social Work	M
Software Engineering	M
Special Education	M
Sports Management	M
Vocational and Technical Education	M

CALIFORNIA COAST UNIVERSITY

Business Administration and Management—General	M
Criminal Justice and Criminology	M
Curriculum and Instruction	M,D
Education—General	M,D
Educational Leadership and Administration	M,D
Educational Psychology	M,D
Health Services Management and Hospital Administration	M
Human Resources Management	M
Marketing	M
Organizational Management	M,D
Psychology—General	M

CALIFORNIA COLLEGE OF THE ARTS

Applied Arts and Design—General	M
Architecture	M
Art/Fine Arts	M
Computer Art and Design	M
Film, Television, and Video Production	M
Film, Television, and Video Theory and Criticism	M
Finance and Banking	M
Graphic Design	M
Illustration	M
Industrial Design	M
Museum Studies	M
Organizational Management	M
Writing	M

CALIFORNIA HEALTH SCIENCES UNIVERSITY

Pharmacy	D

CALIFORNIA INSTITUTE OF ADVANCED MANAGEMENT

Business Administration and Management—General	M
Entrepreneurship	M

CALIFORNIA INSTITUTE OF INTEGRAL STUDIES

Acupuncture and Oriental Medicine	M,D
Cultural Anthropology	M,D,O
Humanities	M,D,O
Psychology—General	M,D
Therapies—Dance, Drama, and Music	M,D

CALIFORNIA INSTITUTE OF TECHNOLOGY

Aerospace/Aeronautical Engineering	M,D,O
Applied Mathematics	M,D
Applied Physics	M,D
Astronomy	D
Biochemistry	M,D
Bioengineering	M,D
Biological and Biomedical Sciences—General	D
Biophysics	D
Cell Biology	D
Chemical Engineering	M,D
Chemistry	M,D
Civil Engineering	M,D,O
Computational Sciences	M,D
Computer Science	M,D
Developmental Biology	D
Electrical Engineering	M,D,O
Engineering and Applied Sciences—General	M,D,O
Environmental Engineering	M,D
Environmental Sciences	M,D
Genetics	D
Geochemistry	M,D
Geology	M,D
Geophysics	M,D
Immunology	D
Materials Sciences	M,D
Mathematics	D
Mechanical Engineering	M,D,O
Mechanics	M,D
Molecular Biology	D
Molecular Biophysics	D
Neurobiology	D
Neuroscience	D
Physics	D
Planetary and Space Sciences	M,D
Social Sciences	M,D
Systems Engineering	M,D

CALIFORNIA INSTITUTE OF THE ARTS

Applied Arts and Design—General	M,O
Art/Fine Arts	M,O
Dance	M,O
Film, Television, and Video Production	M,O
Graphic Design	M,O
Music	M,O
Photography	M,O
Theater	M,O
Writing	M,O

CALIFORNIA INTERCONTINENTAL UNIVERSITY

Business Administration and Management—General	M,D
Entertainment Management	M
Entrepreneurship	M
Finance and Banking	M,D

Health Services Management and Hospital Administration	M,D
Human Resources Management	M,D
International Business	M,D
Management Information Systems	M,D
Marketing	M,D
Organizational Management	M,D
Project Management	M,D
Quality Management	M,D

CALIFORNIA INTERNATIONAL BUSINESS UNIVERSITY

Business Administration and Management—General	M,D

CALIFORNIA LUTHERAN UNIVERSITY

Business Administration and Management—General	M,O
Clinical Psychology	M,D
Counselor Education	M,D
Education—General	M,D
Educational Leadership and Administration	M,D
Elementary Education	M,D
Entrepreneurship	M,O
Finance and Banking	M,D
Higher Education	M,D
International Business	M,O
Management Information Systems	M,O
Management of Technology	M,O
Marketing	M,O
Marriage and Family Therapy	M,D
Middle School Education	M,D
Psychology—General	M,D
Public Policy	M,O
Special Education	M,D
Theology	M,D,O

CALIFORNIA MIRAMAR UNIVERSITY

Business Administration and Management—General	M
Management Strategy and Policy	M
Taxation	M
Telecommunications Management	M
Telecommunications	M

CALIFORNIA NORTHSTATE UNIVERSITY

Allopathic Medicine	D
Pharmacy	D

CALIFORNIA POLYTECHNIC STATE UNIVERSITY, SAN LUIS OBISPO

Accounting	M
Aerospace/Aeronautical Engineering	M
Agricultural Education	M
Agricultural Sciences—General	M
Architectural Engineering	M
Architecture	M
Biochemistry	M
Biological and Biomedical Sciences—General	M
Biomedical Engineering	M
Business Administration and Management—General	M
Business Analytics	M
Chemistry	M
Civil Engineering	M
Computer Science	M
Economics	M
Education—General	M
Electrical Engineering	M
English	M
Environmental Engineering	M
Food Science and Technology	M
Forestry	M
History	M
Industrial/Management Engineering	M
Mathematics	M
Mechanical Engineering	M
Natural Resources	M
Nutrition	M
Political Science	M
Polymer Science and Engineering	M
Psychology—General	M
Supply Chain Management	M
Taxation	M
Urban and Regional Planning	M

CALIFORNIA STATE POLYTECHNIC UNIVERSITY, POMONA

Accounting	M
Aerospace/Aeronautical Engineering	M
Agricultural Sciences—General	M
Applied Mathematics	M
Architecture	M
Biological and Biomedical Sciences—General	M
Business Administration and Management—General	M
Chemistry	M
Civil Engineering	M
Computer Science	M
Curriculum and Instruction	M
Economics	M
Educational Leadership and Administration	D
Electrical Engineering	M
Engineering Management	M
English	M
Environmental Sciences	M
Geology	M
History	M
Hospitality Management	M
Interior Design	M
Kinesiology and Movement Studies	M
Landscape Architecture	M
Management Information Systems	M
Mathematics	M

Mechanical Engineering	M
Psychology—General	M
Public Administration	M
Systems Engineering	M
Urban and Regional Planning	M

CALIFORNIA STATE UNIVERSITY, BAKERSFIELD

Biological and Biomedical Sciences—General	M
Business Administration and Management—General	M
Counseling Psychology	M
Counselor Education	M
Education—General	M,D
Educational Leadership and Administration	M,D
English	M
Family Nurse Practitioner Studies	M
Geology	M
Health Services Management and Hospital Administration	M
History	M
Hydrology	M
Interdisciplinary Studies	M
Nursing—General	M
Public Administration	M
Science Education	M
Social Work	M
Sociology	M
Spanish	M
Special Education	M
Student Affairs	M

CALIFORNIA STATE UNIVERSITY CHANNEL ISLANDS

Bioinformatics	M
Biotechnology	M
Business Administration and Management—General	M
Computer Science	M
Mathematics	M

CALIFORNIA STATE UNIVERSITY, CHICO

Agricultural Education	M
Agricultural Sciences—General	M
Anthropology	M
Applied Psychology	M
Art History	M
Art/Fine Arts	M
Biological and Biomedical Sciences—General	M
Business Administration and Management—General	M
Communication Disorders	M
Communication—General	M
Computer Engineering	M
Computer Science	M
Construction Management	M
Curriculum and Instruction	M
Electrical Engineering	M
Engineering and Applied Sciences—General	M
English	M
Environmental Sciences	M
Geology	M
Geosciences	M
Health Services Management and Hospital Administration	M
History	M
Kinesiology and Movement Studies	M
Marriage and Family Therapy	M
Mathematics Education	M
Museum Studies	M
Nursing—General	M
Nutrition	M
Political Science	M
Psychology—General	M
Public Administration	M
Recreation and Park Management	M
School Psychology	M
Social Sciences	M
Social Work	M
Special Education	M
Travel and Tourism	M

CALIFORNIA STATE UNIVERSITY, DOMINGUEZ HILLS

Applied Social Research	M
Bioinformatics	M
Biological and Biomedical Sciences—General	M
Business Administration and Management—General	M
Clinical Psychology	M
Computer Science	M
Conflict Resolution and Mediation/Peace Studies	M
Counselor Education	M
Early Childhood Education	M
Education—General	M
English as a Second Language	M,O
English	M,O
Health Psychology	M
Humanities	M
International and Comparative Education	M
Marriage and Family Therapy	M
Nursing—General	M
Occupational Therapy	M
Psychology—General	M
Public Administration	M
Quality Management	M
Rhetoric	M,O
School Psychology	M
Social Work	M
Sociology	M
Special Education	M

CALIFORNIA STATE UNIVERSITY, EAST BAY

Accounting	M
Actuarial Science	M

Anthropology	M
Applied Statistics	M
Biochemistry	M
Biological and Biomedical Sciences—General	M
Biostatistics	M
Business Administration and Management—General	M
Business Analytics	M
Chemistry	M
Child and Family Studies	M
Communication Disorders	M
Communication—General	M
Computer Science	M
Construction Management	M
Counselor Education	M
Early Childhood Education	M
Economics	M
Education of Students with Severe/Multiple Disabilities	M
Education—General	M
Educational Leadership and Administration	M,D
Educational Media/Instructional Technology	M
Engineering and Applied Sciences—General	M
Engineering Management	M
English as a Second Language	M
English	M
Environmental Sciences	M
Finance and Banking	M
Geography	M
Geology	M
Health Services Management and Hospital Administration	M
History	M
Human Resources Management	M
Industrial and Manufacturing Management	M
Interdisciplinary Studies	M
Internet and Interactive Multimedia	M
Management Strategy and Policy	M
Marine Sciences	M
Marketing	M
Marriage and Family Therapy	M
Mathematics Education	M
Mathematics	M
Music	M
Organizational Behavior	M
Physical Education	M
Public Administration	M
Public History	M
Public Policy	M
Reading Education	M
Recreation and Park Management	M
Social Psychology	M
Social Sciences Education	M
Social Work	M
Special Education	M
Statistics	M
Supply Chain Management	M
Travel and Tourism	M

CALIFORNIA STATE UNIVERSITY, FRESNO

Animal Sciences	M
Applied Arts and Design—General	M
Applied Behavior Analysis	M,O
Art/Fine Arts	M
Biological and Biomedical Sciences—General	M
Business Administration and Management—General	M
Chemistry	M
Civil Engineering	M
Communication Disorders	M
Communication—General	M
Computer Engineering	M
Computer Science	M
Counseling Psychology	M
Counselor Education	M
Criminal Justice and Criminology	M
Curriculum and Instruction	M
Early Childhood Education	M
Education—General	M,D
Educational Leadership and Administration	M,D
Electrical Engineering	M
Engineering and Applied Sciences—General	M
English as a Second Language	M
English	M
Exercise and Sports Science	M
Experimental Psychology	M,O
Geology	M
Health Promotion	M
Health Services Management and Hospital Administration	M
History	M
Human Development	M,D
Industrial/Management Engineering	M
Kinesiology and Movement Studies	M
Linguistics	M
Marine Sciences	M
Marriage and Family Therapy	M
Mathematics Education	M
Mathematics	M
Mechanical Engineering	M
Music Education	M
Music	M
Nursing—General	M,D
Physical Therapy	D
Physics	M
Plant Sciences	M
Psychology—General	M,O
Public Administration	M
Public Health—General	M
Reading Education	M
Rehabilitation Counseling	M
Rhetoric	M

School Psychology	M,O
Social Sciences Education	M
Social Work	M
Spanish	M
Special Education	M
Sport Psychology	M
Sports Management	M
Student Affairs	M
Viticulture and Enology	M
Writing	M

CALIFORNIA STATE UNIVERSITY, FULLERTON

Accounting	M
American Studies	M
Anthropology	M
Applied Arts and Design—General	M
Applied Mathematics	M
Architectural Engineering	M
Art History	M
Art/Fine Arts	M
Biological and Biomedical Sciences—General	M
Biotechnology	M
Business Administration and Management—General	M
Business Analytics	M
Chemistry	M
Civil Engineering	M
Clinical Psychology	M
Communication Disorders	M
Communication—General	M
Computer Engineering	M
Computer Science	M
Counselor Education	M
Economics	M
Educational Leadership and Administration	M,D
Educational Media/Instructional Technology	M
Electrical Engineering	M
Electronic Commerce	M
Elementary Education	M
Engineering and Applied Sciences—General	M
English	M
Environmental and Occupational Health	M
Environmental Engineering	M
Environmental Management and Policy	M
Film, Television, and Video Production	M
Finance and Banking	M
Geography	M
Geology	M
Gerontology	M
Graphic Design	M
Health Promotion	M
History	M
Illustration	M
Information Science	M
Insurance	M
International Business	M
Linguistics	M
Management Information Systems	M
Mass Communication	M
Mathematics Education	M
Mathematics	M
Mechanical Engineering	M
Multilingual and Multicultural Education	M
Museum Studies	M
Music Education	M
Music	M
Nurse Anesthesia	M,D
Nursing and Healthcare Administration	M
Nursing Education	M,D
Nursing—General	M,D
Organizational Management	M
Photography	M
Physical Education	M
Physics	M
Political Science	M
Psychology—General	M
Public Administration	M
Public Health—General	M
Reading Education	M,D
Risk Management	M
School Nursing	M,D
Secondary Education	M
Social Psychology	M
Social Work	M
Sociology	M
Software Engineering	M
Spanish	M
Special Education	M
Speech and Interpersonal Communication	M
Systems Engineering	M
Taxation	M
Theater	M
Travel and Tourism	M
Women's Health Nursing	M,D

CALIFORNIA STATE UNIVERSITY, LONG BEACH

African Studies	M
Anthropology	M
Applied Mathematics	M,D
Applied Statistics	M
Art Education	M
Art/Fine Arts	M
Asian Studies	M
Asian-American Studies	M
Athletic Training and Sports Medicine	M
Biochemistry	M
Biological and Biomedical Sciences—General	M
Business Administration and Management—General	M
Chemistry	M
Civil Engineering	M
Communication Disorders	M
Communication—General	M
Computer Science	M
Counselor Education	M,D
Criminal Justice and Criminology	M
Dance	M
Economics	M
Education—General	M
Educational Leadership and Administration	M,D
Educational Psychology	M,D
Electrical Engineering	M
Elementary Education	M
Emergency Management	M
Engineering Management	M,D
English as a Second Language	M,O
English	M
Ergonomics and Human Factors	M
Exercise and Sports Science	M
French	M
Geography	M
Geology	M
German	M
Gerontology	M
Health Education	M
Health Services Management and Hospital Administration	M
Higher Education	M,D
History	M
Industrial and Organizational Psychology	M
Kinesiology and Movement Studies	M
Leisure Studies	M
Linguistics	M,O
Marriage and Family Therapy	M,D
Mathematics Education	M
Mathematics	M
Mechanical Engineering	M,D
Microbiology	M
Music	M
Near and Middle Eastern Studies	M
Nursing—General	M,D,O
Nutrition	M
Philosophy	M
Physical Education	M
Physical Therapy	D
Physics	M
Political Science	M
Psychology—General	M
Public Administration	M,O
Public Health—General	M
Public Policy	M,O
Recreation and Park Management	M
Religion	M
Science Education	M
Secondary Education	M
Social Work	M
Spanish	M
Special Education	M,D
Sport Psychology	M
Sports Management	M
Student Affairs	M,D
Theater	M
Writing	M

CALIFORNIA STATE UNIVERSITY, LOS ANGELES

Accounting	M
Analytical Chemistry	M
Anthropology	M
Applied Arts and Design—General	M
Applied Mathematics	M
Art Education	M
Art History	M
Art Therapy	M
Art/Fine Arts	M
Biochemistry	M
Biological and Biomedical Sciences—General	M
Business Administration and Management—General	M,O
Chemistry	M
Child and Family Studies	M
Child Development	M
Civil Engineering	M
Communication Disorders	M
Communication—General	M
Computer Science	M
Counselor Education	M,D
Criminal Justice and Criminology	M
Curriculum and Instruction	M
Economics	M
Education—General	M,D,O
Electrical Engineering	M
Elementary Education	M
Engineering and Applied Sciences—General	M
English	M,O
Finance and Banking	M
French	M
Geography	M
Geology	M
Graphic Design	M
Health Services Management and Hospital Administration	M
Hispanic Studies	M
History	M
International Business	M
Kinesiology and Movement Studies	M,O
Latin American Studies	M
Management Information Systems	M
Management of Technology	M

Marketing	M
Mathematics	M
Mechanical Engineering	M
Music Education	M
Music	M
Nursing—General	M,O
Nutrition	M,O
Philosophy	M,O
Photography	M
Physical Education	M,O
Physics	M
Political Science	M
Psychology—General	M
Public Administration	M
Rehabilitation Counseling	M,D
School Psychology	M,D
Social Work	M
Sociology	M
Spanish	M
Special Education	M,D
Textile Design	M
Theater	M

CALIFORNIA STATE UNIVERSITY MARITIME ACADEMY

Emergency Management	M
Engineering Management	M
Transportation Management	M

CALIFORNIA STATE UNIVERSITY, MONTEREY BAY

Business Administration and Management—General	M
Education—General	M
Management Information Systems	M
Marine Sciences	M
Social Work	M
Water Resources	M

CALIFORNIA STATE UNIVERSITY, NORTHRIDGE

Anthropology	M
Applied Mathematics	M
Archaeology	M
Art Education	M
Art History	M
Art/Fine Arts	M
Artificial Intelligence/Robotics	M
Biochemistry	M
Biological and Biomedical Sciences—General	M
Business Administration and Management—General	M
Chemistry	M
Civil Engineering	M
Clinical Psychology	M
Communication Disorders	M
Communication—General	M
Comparative Literature	M
Computer Science	M
Construction Management	M
Counselor Education	M
Curriculum and Instruction	M
Early Childhood Education	M
Education of Students with Severe/Multiple Disabilities	M
Education—General	M,D
Educational Leadership and Administration	M,D
Educational Media/Instructional Technology	M
Educational Psychology	M
Electrical Engineering	M
Elementary Education	M
Engineering and Applied Sciences—General	M
Engineering Management	M
English Education	M
English	M
Entertainment Management	M,O
Environmental and Occupational Health	M
Environmental Sciences	M
Epidemiology	M
Experimental Psychology	M
Family and Consumer Sciences-General	M
Film, Television, and Video Production	M
Geography	M
Geology	M
Health Education	M,O
Health Services Management and Hospital Administration	M
Hispanic Studies	M
History	M
Hospitality Management	M,O
Industrial Hygiene	M
Industrial/Management Engineering	M
Journalism	M
Kinesiology and Movement Studies	M
Linguistics	M
Manufacturing Engineering	M
Marriage and Family Therapy	M
Mass Communication	M
Materials Engineering	M
Mathematics Education	M
Mathematics	M
Mechanical Engineering	M
Multilingual and Multicultural Education	M
Music Education	M
Music	M
Nonprofit Management	O
Physical Therapy	M
Physics	M
Political Science	M
Psychology—General	M
Public Administration	M,O
Public Health—General	M

Reading Education	M
Recreation and Park Management	M,O
Rhetoric	M
School Psychology	M
Science Education	M
Secondary Education	M
Social Work	M,O
Sociology	M
Software Engineering	M
Spanish	M
Special Education	M
Speech and Interpersonal Communication	M
Structural Engineering	M
Systems Engineering	M
Taxation	M,O
Theater	M
Travel and Tourism	M
Writing	M

CALIFORNIA STATE UNIVERSITY, SACRAMENTO

Accounting	M
Anthropology	M
Applied Behavior Analysis	M
Art/Fine Arts	M
Biochemistry	M
Biological and Biomedical Sciences—General	M
Business Administration and Management—General	M
Cell Biology	M
Chemistry	M
Child Development	M,D,O
Civil Engineering	M
Communication Disorders	M
Communication—General	M
Computer Science	M
Conservation Biology	M
Counselor Education	M,D,O
Criminal Justice and Criminology	M,D,O
Curriculum and Instruction	M,D,O
Developmental Biology	M
Early Childhood Education	M
Education—General	M,D,O
Educational Leadership and Administration	M,D,O
Educational Media/Instructional Technology	M,D,O
Educational Policy	M,D,O
Electrical Engineering	M
Elementary Education	M,D,O
Engineering and Applied Sciences—General	M
English as a Second Language	M
English	M
Exercise and Sports Science	M
Foreign Languages Education	M
Higher Education	M,D,O
Human Resources Development	M
Human Resources Management	M
Human Services	M
Industrial and Organizational Psychology	M
Mathematics	M
Mechanical Engineering	M
Molecular Biology	M
Multilingual and Multicultural Education	M,D,O
Music	M
Nursing—General	M
Physical Education	M
Physical Therapy	D
Political Science	M
Psychology—General	M
Public Administration	M
Public History	M,D
Public Policy	M
Reading Education	M,D,O
Real Estate	M
Recreation and Park Management	M
School Psychology	M,D,O
Social Work	M
Sociology	M
Software Engineering	M
Special Education	M,D,O
Writing	M

CALIFORNIA STATE UNIVERSITY, SAN BERNARDINO

Accounting	M
Archaeology	M
Art/Fine Arts	M
Biological and Biomedical Sciences—General	M
Business Administration and Management—General	M
Child Development	M
Clinical Psychology	M
Communication—General	M
Community College Education	M
Computer and Information Systems Security	M
Computer Science	M
Corporate and Organizational Communication	M
Counseling Psychology	M
Counselor Education	M
Criminal Justice and Criminology	M
Education—General	M
Educational Leadership and Administration	M,D
English	M
Entrepreneurship	M
Environmental Sciences	M
Finance and Banking	M
Geosciences	M
Health Services Management and Hospital Administration	M
Industrial and Organizational Psychology	M

*M—masters degree; D—doctorate; O—other advanced degree; *—Close-Up and/or Display*

Interdisciplinary Studies	M
International Business	M
Management Information Systems	M
Marketing	M
Mathematics Education	M
Mathematics	M
National Security	M
Nursing—General	M
Psychology—General	M
Public Administration	M
Public Health—General	M
Rehabilitation Counseling	M
Social Sciences	M
Social Work	M
Spanish	M
Supply Chain Management	M
Writing	M

CALIFORNIA STATE UNIVERSITY, SAN MARCOS
Biological and Biomedical Sciences—General	M
Biotechnology	M
Communication Disorders	M
Computer and Information Systems Security	M
Computer Science	M
Education—General	M,D
Educational Leadership and Administration	M,D
English	M
Family Nurse Practitioner Studies	M
Hispanic and Latin American Languages	M
Hispanic Studies	M
History	M
Mathematics	M
Nursing and Healthcare Administration	M
Nursing Education	M
Nursing—General	M
Psychiatric Nursing	M
Psychology—General	M
Public Health—General	M
Reading Education	M,D
Sociology	M
Spanish	M
Special Education	M,D
Writing	M

CALIFORNIA STATE UNIVERSITY, STANISLAUS
Applied Behavior Analysis	M
Business Administration and Management—General	M
Community College Education	D
Conservation Biology	M
Counseling Psychology	M
Counselor Education	M
Criminal Justice and Criminology	M
Curriculum and Instruction	M
Ecology	M
Education—General	M,D
Educational Leadership and Administration	M,D
Educational Media/Instructional Technology	M
Elementary Education	M
English as a Second Language	M,O
English	M,O
Genetic Counseling	M
Gerontological Nursing	M
History	M
Interdisciplinary Studies	M
Multilingual and Multicultural Education	M
Nursing Education	M
Nursing—General	M
Physical Education	M
Psychology—General	M
Public Administration	M
Reading Education	M
Rhetoric	M,O
Secondary Education	M
Social Work	M
Special Education	M
Sustainable Development	M
Writing	M,O

CALIFORNIA UNIVERSITY OF MANAGEMENT AND SCIENCES
Business Administration and Management—General	M,D
Economics	M,D
International Business	M,D
Management Information Systems	M,D
Sports Management	M,D

CALIFORNIA UNIVERSITY OF PENNSYLVANIA
Athletic Training and Sports Medicine	M
Business Administration and Management—General	M
Business Analytics	M
Clinical Psychology	M
Communication Disorders	M
Computer and Information Systems Security	M
Conflict Resolution and Mediation/Peace Studies	M
Counseling Psychology	M
Counselor Education	M
Criminal Justice and Criminology	M
Early Childhood Education	M
Education—General	M,D
Educational Leadership and Administration	M,D
Elementary Education	M
Entrepreneurship	M
Exercise and Sports Science	M
Health Services Management and Hospital Administration	M
Legal and Justice Studies	M
Mathematics Education	M

Near and Middle Eastern Languages	M
Nursing and Healthcare Administration	M
Nursing Education	M
Nursing—General	M
Nutrition	M
Reading Education	M
School Psychology	M
Science Education	M
Secondary Education	M
Social Work	M
Special Education	M
Sport Psychology	M
Sports Management	M
Vocational and Technical Education	M

CALIFORNIA WESTERN SCHOOL OF LAW
Accounting	M,D
Law	M,D

CALUMET COLLEGE OF SAINT JOSEPH
Criminal Justice and Criminology	M
Educational Leadership and Administration	M
Quality Management	M

CALVARY UNIVERSITY
Curriculum and Instruction	M
Education—General	M
Educational Leadership and Administration	M
Elementary Education	M
Organizational Management	M
Pastoral Ministry and Counseling	M
Religious Education	M
Theology	M

CALVIN COLLEGE
Accounting	M
Communication Disorders	M
Curriculum and Instruction	M
Education—General	M

CALVIN THEOLOGICAL SEMINARY
Missions and Missiology	M,D
Pastoral Ministry and Counseling	M,D
Religion	M,D
Religious Education	M,D
Theology	M,D

CAMBRIDGE COLLEGE
Addictions/Substance Abuse Counseling	M,O
Business Administration and Management—General	M
Conflict Resolution and Mediation/Peace Studies	M
Counseling Psychology	M,O
Counselor Education	M,O
Curriculum and Instruction	M,D,O
Early Childhood Education	M,D,O
Education—General	M,D,O
Educational Leadership and Administration	M,D,O
Educational Measurement and Evaluation	M,D,O
Educational Media/Instructional Technology	M,D,O
Elementary Education	M,D,O
English as a Second Language	M,D,O
Entrepreneurship	M
Health Education	M,D,O
Health Services Management and Hospital Administration	M
Interdisciplinary Studies	M,D,O
Management of Technology	M
Marriage and Family Therapy	M,O
Mathematics Education	M,D,O
Psychology—General	M,O
Rehabilitation Counseling	M,O
School Nursing	M,O
School Psychology	M,O
Science Education	M,D,O
Special Education	M,D,O

CAMERON UNIVERSITY
Business Administration and Management—General	M
Education—General	M
Educational Leadership and Administration	M
Entrepreneurship	M
Psychology—General	M

CAMPBELLSVILLE UNIVERSITY
Business Administration and Management—General	M,D
Economics	M,D
Education—General	M
Educational Leadership and Administration	M
English Education	M
Legal and Justice Studies	M
Management of Technology	M,D
Marriage and Family Therapy	M
Music Education	M
Music	M
School Psychology	M
Science Education	M
Social Sciences	M
Social Work	M
Special Education	M
Sports Management	M
Theology	M

CAMPBELL UNIVERSITY
Athletic Training and Sports Medicine	M,D
Business Administration and Management—General	M
Counselor Education	M
Education—General	M
Educational Leadership and Administration	M
Elementary Education	M
Interdisciplinary Studies	M

Law	D
Middle School Education	D
Osteopathic Medicine	D
Pastoral Ministry and Counseling	M,D
Pharmaceutical Sciences	M,D
Pharmacy	M,D
Physical Education	M
Physical Therapy	M
Physician Assistant Studies	M,D
Public Health—General	M,D
Secondary Education	M,D
Theology	M,D

CANADIAN COLLEGE OF NATUROPATHIC MEDICINE
Naturopathic Medicine	D

CANADIAN MEMORIAL CHIROPRACTIC COLLEGE
Acupuncture and Oriental Medicine	O
Chiropractic	D,O

CANADIAN SOUTHERN BAPTIST SEMINARY
Pastoral Ministry and Counseling	M
Religion	M
Theology	M

CANISIUS COLLEGE
Accounting	M
Allied Health—General	M,O
Business Administration and Management—General	M
Business Education	M,O
Communication Disorders	M,O
Community Health	M,O
Counselor Education	M
Early Childhood Education	M,O
Education of the Gifted	M,O
Education—General	M,O
Educational Leadership and Administration	M,O
Educational Media/Instructional Technology	M,O
Elementary Education	M,O
English as a Second Language	M,O
Health Informatics	M
International Business	M
Kinesiology and Movement Studies	M
Middle School Education	M
Nutrition	M,O
Physical Education	M,O
Reading Education	M,O
School Psychology	M
Secondary Education	M,O
Social Psychology	M
Special Education	M,O
Sports Management	M
Student Affairs	M,O

CAPE BRETON UNIVERSITY
Business Administration and Management—General	M

CAPELLA UNIVERSITY
Accounting	M,D
Addictions/Substance Abuse Counseling	M,D
Adult Education	M,D
Applied Behavior Analysis	M
Business Administration and Management—General	M,D
Business Education	D
Child and Family Studies	M
Clinical Psychology	M,D
Computer and Information Systems Security	M,D
Counseling Psychology	M,D
Counselor Education	M,D
Criminal Justice and Criminology	M,D
Curriculum and Instruction	M,D
Developmental Psychology	M,D
Distance Education Development	M,D
Early Childhood Education	M,D
Education—General	M,D
Educational Leadership and Administration	M,D
Educational Media/Instructional Technology	M,D
Educational Psychology	M,D
Elementary Education	M,D
Emergency Management	M,D
Entrepreneurship	M,D
Environmental and Occupational Health	M,D
Epidemiology	D
Finance and Banking	M,D
Gerontological Nursing	M
Gerontology	M
Health Informatics	M
Health Services Management and Hospital Administration	M,D
Higher Education	M,D
Homeland Security	M
Human Resources Management	M,D
Human Services	M,D
Industrial and Organizational Psychology	M,D
Management Information Systems	M,D
Management of Technology	M,D
Management Strategy and Policy	M,D
Marketing	M,D
Marriage and Family Therapy	M,D
Middle School Education	M,D
Nonprofit Management	D
Nursing and Healthcare Administration	M
Nursing Education	M,D
Nursing—General	M,D
Operations Research	M
Organizational Management	M,D
Project Management	M,D
Psychology—General	M,D
Public Administration	M,D
Reading Education	M,D
School Psychology	M,D

Social Work	D
Special Education	M,D
Sport Psychology	M
Supply Chain Management	M,D
Vocational and Technical Education	D

CAPITAL UNIVERSITY
African-American Studies	M
Business Administration and Management—General	
Law	M,D
Legal and Justice Studies	M
Missions and Missiology	M
Music Education	M
Music	M
Nursing and Healthcare Administration	M
Nursing—General	M
Pastoral Ministry and Counseling	M
Religious Education	M
Taxation	M
Theology	M

CAPITOL TECHNOLOGY UNIVERSITY
Business Administration and Management—General	M
Computer and Information Systems Security	M
Computer Science	M
Electrical Engineering	M
Information Science	M
Management Information Systems	M
Telecommunications Management	M

CARDINAL STRITCH UNIVERSITY
Business Administration and Management—General	M
Clinical Psychology	M
Computer and Information Systems Security	M
Criminal Justice and Criminology	M
Education—General	M,D
Educational Leadership and Administration	M,D
Health Services Management and Hospital Administration	M
Higher Education	M,D
Liberal Studies	M
Marketing	M
Nursing—General	M
Pastoral Ministry and Counseling	M
Psychology—General	M
Reading Education	M,D
Religion	M
Special Education	M,D
Sports Management	M
Student Affairs	M,D
Urban Education	M,D

CAREY THEOLOGICAL COLLEGE
Theology	M,D

CARIBBEAN UNIVERSITY
Art History	M,D
Criminal Justice and Criminology	M,D
Curriculum and Instruction	M,D
Early Childhood Education	M,D
Education—General	M,D
Educational Leadership and Administration	M,D
Educational Media/Instructional Technology	M,D
Elementary Education	M,D
English Education	M,D
Foreign Languages Education	M,D
Gerontological Nursing	M,D
Human Resources Management	M,D
Mathematics Education	M,D
Museum Studies	M,D
Pediatric Nursing	M,D
Physical Education	M,D
Science Education	M,D
Social Sciences Education	M,D
Special Education	M,D

CARLETON UNIVERSITY
Aerospace/Aeronautical Engineering	M,D
Anthropology	M
Architecture	M
Art History	M
Biological and Biomedical Sciences—General	M,D
Biomedical Engineering	M
Business Administration and Management—General	M,D
Canadian Studies	M,D
Chemistry	M,D
Civil Engineering	M,D
Cognitive Sciences	D
Communication—General	M,D
Comparative Literature	D
Computer Science	M,D
Conflict Resolution and Mediation/Peace Studies	M,O
East European and Russian Studies	M,O
Economics	M,D
Electrical Engineering	M,D
Engineering and Applied Sciences—General	M,D
English	M,D
Environmental Engineering	M,D
Film, Television, and Video Production	M
French	M
Geography	M,D
Geosciences	M,D
History	M
Industrial Design	M
Information Science	M,D
International Affairs	M,D
Journalism	M,D
Legal and Justice Studies	M,O
Linguistics	M
Management of Technology	M

Materials Engineering M,D
Mathematics M,D
Mechanical Engineering M,D
Music M
Neuroscience M,D
Philosophy M
Physics M,D
Political Science M,D
Psychology—General M,D
Public Administration M,D
Public Policy M,D
Social Work M
Sociology M,D
Systems Engineering M,D
Systems Science M,D
Western European Studies M,O

CARLOW UNIVERSITY
Art/Fine Arts M
Business Administration and
    Management—General M
Counseling Psychology M,D,O
Curriculum and Instruction M
Distance Education Development M,O
Early Childhood Education M,O
Education—General M,O
Family Nurse Practitioner Studies M,O
Forensic Sciences M
Health Services Management and
    Hospital Administration M
Human Resources Management M
Mathematics M
Nursing and Healthcare
    Administration M
Nursing Education M
Nursing—General D
Organizational Management M,D,O
Project Management M
Science Education M
Social Work M
Special Education M,O
Student Affairs M
Women's Health Nursing M,O
Writing M

CARNEGIE MELLON UNIVERSITY
Accounting D
African Studies D
African-American Studies D
Applied Arts and Design—
    General M,D
Applied Physics M,D
Architectural Engineering M,D
Architecture M,D
Art/Fine Arts M
Artificial Intelligence/Robotics M,D
Arts Administration M
Atmospheric Sciences D
Biochemistry M,D
Bioengineering M,D
Biological and Biomedical
    Sciences—General M,D
Biomedical Engineering M,D
Biophysics M,D
Biopsychology D
Biotechnology M
Building Science M,D
Business Administration and
    Management—General M,D
Cell Biology M,D
Chemical Engineering M,D
Chemistry D
Civil Engineering M,D
Cognitive Sciences D
Communication—General M,D
Comparative Literature M,D
Computational Biology M,D
Computer and Information
    Systems Security M
Computer Art and Design M
Computer Engineering M,D
Computer Science M,D
Construction Management M,D
Corporate and Organizational
    Communication M
Criminal Justice and Criminology M
Cultural Studies D
Developmental Biology M,D
Developmental Psychology D
Economics D
Electrical Engineering M,D
Energy and Power
    Engineering M,D
English M,D
Entertainment Management M
Entrepreneurship D
Environmental Engineering M,D
Environmental Sciences D
Film, Television, and Video
    Production M
Finance and Banking D
Gender Studies D
Genetics M,D
Health Services Management and
    Hospital Administration M
History of Science and Technology D
History D
Human-Computer Interaction M,D
Industrial and Labor Relations D
Industrial and Manufacturing
    Management M,D
Information Science M,D
Linguistics M,D
Management Information Systems M,D
Marketing D
Materials Engineering M,D
Materials Sciences M,D
Mathematical and
    Computational Finance M,D
Mathematics M,D
Mechanical Engineering M,D

Mechanics M,D
Media Studies M,D
Modeling and Simulation M,D
Molecular Biology M,D
Molecular Biophysics D
Music Education M
Music M
Nanotechnology D
Neurobiology M,D
Neuroscience D
Operations Research D
Organizational Behavior D
Philosophy M,D
Physics M,D
Polymer Science and
    Engineering M
Psychology—General M
Public Administration M
Public Policy M
Publishing M
Rhetoric M
Social Psychology D
Social Sciences D
Software Engineering M,D
Statistics M,D
Structural Biology M,D
Sustainable Development M,D
Systems Engineering M
Technical Writing M
Technology and Public Policy M,D
Telecommunications
    Management M
Theater M
Theoretical Chemistry D
Urban Design M,D
Water Resources Engineering M,D
Women's Studies D
Writing M

CAROLINA CHRISTIAN COLLEGE
Pastoral Ministry and Counseling M
Religious Education M

CARROLL UNIVERSITY
Adult Education M
Business Administration and
    Management—General M
Early Childhood Education M
Education—General M
Educational Leadership and
    Administration M
Elementary Education M
Exercise and Sports Science M
Occupational Therapy M
Physical Therapy D
Physician Assistant Studies M
Secondary Education M
Software Engineering M

CARSON-NEWMAN UNIVERSITY
Business Administration and
    Management—General M
Counselor Education M
Curriculum and Instruction M
Education—General M
Educational Leadership and
    Administration M
Elementary Education M
English as a Second Language M
Family Nurse Practitioner Studies M
Nursing Education M
Nursing—General M
Organizational Management M
Secondary Education M
Theology M

CARTHAGE COLLEGE
Art Education M,O
Counselor Education M,O
Education of the Gifted M,O
Education—General M,O
Educational Leadership and
    Administration M,O
English Education M,O
Reading Education M,O
Science Education M,O
Social Sciences Education M,O

CASE WESTERN RESERVE UNIVERSITY
Accounting M,D
Acute Care/Critical Care Nursing M
Aerospace/Aeronautical
    Engineering M,D
Allopathic Medicine D
Anatomy M
Anesthesiologist Assistant Studies M
Anthropology M,D
Applied Mathematics M,D
Art Education M
Art History M,D
Astronomy M
Biochemistry M,D
Bioethics M
Biological and Biomedical
    Sciences—General M,D
Biomedical Engineering M,D
Biophysics M,D
Biostatistics M,D
Business Administration and
    Management—General M,D
Business Analytics M
Cancer Biology/Oncology D
Cell Biology D
Chemical Engineering M,D
Chemistry M,D
Civil Engineering M,D
Clinical Psychology D
Clinical Research M
Cognitive Sciences M
Communication Disorders M,D
Comparative Literature M
Computer Engineering M,D

Computer Science M,D
Dance M
Dentistry D
Electrical Engineering M,D
Engineering and Applied
    Sciences—General M,D
Engineering Management M
English M,D
Epidemiology D
Experimental Psychology D
Family Nurse Practitioner Studies M
Finance and Banking M
French M
Genetic Counseling M,D
Genomic Sciences M,D
Geology M,D
Geosciences M,D
Gerontological Nursing M
Health Law M,D
Health Services Management and
    Hospital Administration M
History M,D
Human Genetics M,D
Industrial and Manufacturing
    Management M,D
Information Science M,D
Intellectual Property Law M,D
Law M,D
Legal and Justice Studies M,D
Linguistics M
Logistics M,D
Materials Engineering M,D
Materials Sciences M,D
Maternal and Child/Neonatal
    Nursing M
Mathematics M,D
Mechanical Engineering M,D
Medical/Surgical Nursing M
Microbiology D
Molecular Biology D
Molecular Medicine D
Museum Studies M
Music Education M,D
Music M,D
Neuroscience D
Nonprofit Management M,D,O
Nurse Anesthesia M
Nurse Midwifery M
Nursing Education M
Nutrition M,D
Operations Research M,D
Oral and Dental Sciences M,O
Organizational Behavior M,D
Pathology M,D
Pediatric Nursing M
Pharmacology D
Physician Assistant Studies M
Physics M,D
Physiology M,D
Political Science M,D
Polymer Science and
    Engineering M,D
Psychiatric Nursing M
Psychology—General M,D
Public Health—General M
Social Work M
Sociology M,D
Supply Chain Management M,D
Sustainability Management D
Systems Engineering M,D
Theater M
Virology D
Women's Health Nursing M

CASTLETON UNIVERSITY
Curriculum and Instruction M
Education—General M,O
Educational Leadership and
    Administration M,O
Forensic Psychology M
Psychology—General M
Reading Education M,O
Special Education M,O

CATAWBA COLLEGE
Elementary Education M
Science Education M

CATHOLIC DISTANCE UNIVERSITY
Theology M

CATHOLIC THEOLOGICAL UNION
Missions and Missiology M,D,O
Pastoral Ministry and Counseling M,D,O
Theology M,D,O

**THE CATHOLIC UNIVERSITY OF
AMERICA**
Accounting M
American Studies M,D
Anthropology M
Applied Psychology M,D
Architecture M,O
Biological and Biomedical
    Sciences—General M,D
Biomedical Engineering M,D
Biotechnology M,D
Business Administration and
    Management—General M
Cell Biology M,D
Civil Engineering M,D,O
Classics M,D,O
Clinical Laboratory
    Sciences/Medical Technology M,D
Clinical Psychology M,D
Computer Science M,D
Criminal Justice and Criminology M,D
Early Childhood Education M,O
Economic Development M
Education—General M,O
Educational Leadership and
    Administration M,O

Electrical Engineering M,D
Energy and Power
    Engineering M,D
Engineering and Applied
    Sciences—General M,D,O
Engineering Management M,O
English M,D
Environmental Engineering M,D
Ergonomics and Human
    Factors M,D
Experimental Psychology M,D
Health Services Management and
    Hospital Administration M
Hispanic Studies M,D
History M,D
Human Resources Management M,O
Information Studies M,O
International Affairs M,D
Law M,D
Legal and Justice Studies M,D,O
Library Science M,O
Management Information Systems M,O
Management of Technology M,O
Materials Engineering M
Materials Sciences M
Mechanical Engineering M,D
Medieval and Renaissance Studies M,D,O
Microbiology M,D
Music Education M,D,O
Music M,D,O
Near and Middle Eastern Languages M,D
Near and Middle Eastern Studies M,D,O
Nursing—General M,D,O
Pastoral Ministry and Counseling M,D,O
Philosophy M,D,O
Physics M,D
Political Science M,D
Project Management M,O
Psychology—General M,D
Public Policy M
Religion M,D,O
Rhetoric M,D
Secondary Education M,O
Social Work M,D
Sociology M
Spanish M,D
Special Education M,O
Sustainable Development M,O
Systems Engineering M,O
Theater M,O
Theology M,D,O
Transportation and Highway
    Engineering M,D,O
Urban and Regional Planning M,O
Western European Studies M,D

CEDAR CREST COLLEGE
Art Therapy M
Business Administration and
    Management—General M
Education—General M
Forensic Sciences M
Nursing and Healthcare
    Administration M
Nursing Education M
Nursing—General M
Nutrition O
Writing M

CEDARS-SINAI MEDICAL CENTER
Biological and Biomedical
    Sciences—General M,D
Medical Imaging M,D
Translational Biology M,D

CEDARVILLE UNIVERSITY
Business Administration and
    Management—General M,D
Family Nurse Practitioner Studies M,D
Health Services Management and
    Hospital Administration M,D
Industrial and Manufacturing
    Management M,D
International Health M,D
Missions and Missiology M,D
Nursing Education M,D
Pastoral Ministry and Counseling M,D
Pharmacy M,D

CENTENARY COLLEGE OF LOUISIANA
Business Administration and
    Management—General M
Education—General M
Elementary Education M
Secondary Education M

CENTENARY UNIVERSITY
Accounting M
Business Administration and
    Management—General M
Counseling Psychology M
Education—General M,D
Educational Leadership and
    Administration M,D
Reading Education M,D
Special Education M,D

**CENTRAL BAPTIST THEOLOGICAL
SEMINARY**
Missions and Missiology M,O
Theology M,O

**CENTRAL CONNECTICUT STATE
UNIVERSITY**
Accounting M
Actuarial Science M,O
Advertising and Public Relations M,O
Art Education M,O
Biological and Biomedical
    Sciences—General M,D
Business Administration and
    Management—General M
Communication—General M,O

---

*M—masters degree; D—doctorate; O—other advanced degree; *—Close-Up and/or Display*

Computer Science — M,O
Construction Management — M,O
Counselor Education — M,O
Criminal Justice and Criminology — M,O
Early Childhood Education — M,O
Education—General — M,D,O
Educational Leadership and
  Administration — M,D,O
Elementary Education — M,O
Engineering and Applied
  Sciences—General — M
English Education — M,O
English — M,O
Exercise and Sports Science — M,O
Foreign Languages Education — M,O
French — M,O
Geography — M
German — M,O
Graphic Design — M
History — M,O
Hospice Nursing — M
Industrial and Manufacturing
  Management — M,O
Information Studies — M
International Affairs — M
Italian — M,O
Logistics — M,O
Management of Technology — M,O
Marriage and Family Therapy — M,O
Mathematics — M,O
Molecular Biology — M,O
Music Education — M,O
Nursing—General — M
Physical Education — M,O
Psychology—General — M
Reading Education — M,O
Rehabilitation Counseling — M,O
School Psychology — M,O
Science Education — M,O
Secondary Education — M,O
Spanish — M,O
Special Education — M,O
Statistics — M,O
Supply Chain Management — M,O
Vocational and Technical Education — M

CENTRAL EUROPEAN UNIVERSITY
Anthropology — M,D
Applied Mathematics — M,D
Business Administration and
  Management—General — M,D
Business Analytics — M,D
Cognitive Sciences — D
Data Science/Data Analytics — D
Economics — M,D
Environmental Management
  and Policy — M,D
Finance and Banking — M,D
Gender Studies — M,D
History — M,D
International Affairs — M,D
International Business — M,D
Law — M,D
Legal and Justice Studies — M,D
Management of Technology — M,D
Mathematics — M,D
Medieval and Renaissance Studies — M,D
Philosophy — M,D
Political Science — M,D
Public Administration — M,D
Public Policy — M,D
Sociology — M,D

CENTRAL METHODIST UNIVERSITY
Counselor Education — M
Education—General — M
Music Education — M
Nursing and Healthcare
  Administration — M
Nursing Education — M
Nursing—General — M

CENTRAL MICHIGAN UNIVERSITY
Accounting — M,O
Allopathic Medicine — D
American Indian/Native American
  Studies — M
American Studies — M,O
Applied Psychology — M,D
Biological and Biomedical
  Sciences—General — M
Business Administration and
  Management—General — M,O
Chemistry — M
Child and Family Studies — M,O
Clinical Psychology — D
Clothing and Textiles — M,O
Communication Disorders — M,D
Communication—General — M
Community College Education — M,D,O
Computer and Information
  Systems Security — O
Computer Science — M
Conservation Biology — M
Counseling Psychology — M,D,O
Counselor Education — M
Cultural Studies — M
Curriculum and Instruction — M,D,O
Early Childhood Education — M,O
Economics — M
Education—General — M,D,O
Educational Leadership and
  Administration — M,D,O
Educational Media/Instructional
  Technology — M,D,O
Elementary Education — M,D,O
Engineering and Applied
  Sciences—General — M
Engineering Management — M,O
English as a Second Language — M
English — M
Exercise and Sports Science — M,D
Experimental Psychology — M,D
Family and Consumer
  Sciences-General — M,O

Film, Television, and Video
  Production — M
Film, Television, and Video
  Theory and Criticism — M
Finance and Banking — M
Gender Studies — M
Geographic Information Systems — M
Gerontology — M,D
Health Psychology — M,D
Health Services Management and
  Hospital Administration — M,D,O
Higher Education — M,D,O
History — M,O
Human Development — M,O
Human Resources Management — M,O
Humanities — M
Industrial and Manufacturing
  Management — M
Industrial and Organizational
  Psychology — M,D
International Affairs — M,O
International Business — M,O
International Health — M,D,O
Logistics — M,O
Management Information Systems — M,O
Marketing — M,O
Materials Sciences — D
Mathematics Education — M,D
Mathematics — M,D
Media Studies — M
Music Education — M
Music — M
Neuroscience — M,D
Nonprofit Management — M,O
Nutrition — M,D,O
Philanthropic Studies — M,O
Physical Therapy — M,D
Physician Assistant Studies — M,D
Physics — M,D
Political Science — M,O
Psychology—General — M,D,O
Public Administration — M,O
Reading Education — M,D,O
Recreation and Park Management — M,O
Rehabilitation Sciences — M,D
School Psychology — D,O
Science Education — M
Secondary Education — M,D,O
Spanish — M
Special Education — M,O
Sports Management — M,O
Student Affairs — M,D,O
Western European Studies — M,O
Writing — M

CENTRAL PENN COLLEGE
Management Information Systems — M
Organizational Management — M

CENTRAL WASHINGTON UNIVERSITY
Anthropology — M
Art/Fine Arts — M
Biological and Biomedical
  Sciences—General — M
Botany — M
Chemistry — M
Child and Family Studies — M
Counseling Psychology — M
Curriculum and Instruction — M
Ecology — M
Education—General — M
Educational Leadership and
  Administration — M
English as a Second Language — M
English — M
Environmental Management
  and Policy — M
Experimental Psychology — M
Family and Consumer
  Sciences-General — M
Fish, Game, and Wildlife
  Management — M
Geography — M
Geology — M
Graphic Design — M
Health Education — M
Higher Education — M
History — M
Home Economics Education — M
Interdisciplinary Studies — M
Microbiology — M
Music Education — M
Music — M
Natural Resources — M
Nutrition — M
Photography — M
Physical Education — M
Physiology — M
Psychology—General — M,O
Reading Education — M
School Psychology — O
Sports Management — M
Theater — M
Vocational and Technical Education — M
Writing — M

CENTRAL YESHIVA TOMCHEI TMIMIM-LUBAVITCH
Jewish Studies — M
Theology — M

CENTRO DE ESTUDIOS AVANZADOS DE PUERTO RICO Y EL CARIBE
History — M,D
Latin American Studies — M,D

CHADRON STATE COLLEGE
Business Administration and
  Management—General — M
Business Education — M,O
Counselor Education — M,O
Education—General — M,O
Educational Leadership and
  Administration — M,O
Elementary Education — M,O
English Education — M,O

Secondary Education — M,O
Social Sciences Education — M,O

CHAMINADE UNIVERSITY OF HONOLULU
Accounting — M
Business Administration and
  Management—General — M
Child Development — M
Counseling Psychology — M
Criminal Justice and Criminology — M
Early Childhood Education — M
Education—General — M
Educational Leadership and
  Administration — M
Elementary Education — M
Marriage and Family Therapy — M
Nonprofit Management — M
Pastoral Ministry and Counseling — M
School Psychology — M
Secondary Education — M
Special Education — M
Theology — M

CHAMPLAIN COLLEGE
Business Administration and
  Management—General — M
Computer and Information
  Systems Security — M
Conflict Resolution and
  Mediation/Peace Studies — M
Early Childhood Education — M
Forensic Sciences — M
Health Services Management and
  Hospital Administration — M
Internet and Interactive
  Multimedia — M
Law — M
Management of Technology — M
Media Studies — M

CHAPMAN UNIVERSITY
Accounting — M
Business Administration and
  Management—General — M
Communication Disorders — M
Communication—General — M
Computational Sciences — M,D*
Counselor Education — M,D,O
Cultural Studies — M,D,O
Curriculum and Instruction — M,D,O
Disability Studies — M,D,O
Education of Students with
  Severe/Multiple Disabilities — M,D,O
Education—General — M,D,O
Educational Leadership and
  Administration — M,D,O
Educational Psychology — M,D,O
Elementary Education — M,D,O
English — M
Environmental Law — M,D
Film, Television, and Video
  Production — M
Food Science and
  Technology — M*
Holocaust and Genocide Studies — M
International Affairs — M
Law — M,D
Marriage and Family Therapy — M
Nutrition — M
Pharmaceutical Sciences — M,D
Pharmacy — M,D
Physical Therapy — D
Physician Assistant Studies — M
School Psychology — M,D,O
Secondary Education — M,D,O
Special Education — M,D,O
Sports and Entertainment Law — M,D
Taxation — M,D
Writing — M

CHARLES R. DREW UNIVERSITY OF MEDICINE AND SCIENCE
Allopathic Medicine — D
Public Health—General — M

CHARLESTON SCHOOL OF LAW
Law — M

CHARLESTON SOUTHERN UNIVERSITY
Accounting — M
Business Administration and
  Management—General — M
Criminal Justice and Criminology — M
Education—General — M
Educational Leadership and
  Administration — M
Elementary Education — M
Finance and Banking — M
Human Resources Management — M
Management Information Systems — M
Organizational Management — M

CHARLOTTE CHRISTIAN COLLEGE AND THEOLOGICAL SEMINARY
Cultural Studies — M,D
Pastoral Ministry and Counseling — M,D
Religion — M,D
Theology — M,D

CHARTER COLLEGE
Business Administration and
  Management—General — M

CHARTER OAK STATE COLLEGE
Organizational Management — M

CHATHAM UNIVERSITY
Accounting — M
Art Education — M
Biological and Biomedical
  Sciences—General — M
Business Administration and
  Management—General — M
Communication—General — M
Computer Art and Design — M
Counseling Psychology — M,D

Developmental Psychology — M,D
Early Childhood Education — M
Education—General — M
Elementary Education — M
English Education — M
Environmental Biology — M
Environmental Education — M
Film, Television, and Video
  Production — M
Health Communication — M
Health Informatics — M
Health Psychology — M,D
Industrial and Organizational
  Psychology — M,D
Interior Design — M
Marriage and Family Therapy — M,D
Mathematics Education — M
Nursing and Healthcare
  Administration — M,D
Nursing Education — M,D
Nursing—General — M,D
Occupational Therapy — M,D
Physical Therapy — D
Physician Assistant Studies — M
Science Education — M
Secondary Education — M
Social Sciences Education — M
Special Education — M
Sport Psychology — M,D
Sustainability Management — M
Women's Studies — M
Writing — M

CHESTNUT HILL COLLEGE
Clinical Psychology — M,D,O
Counseling Psychology — M,O
Early Childhood Education — M
Education—General — M
Educational Leadership and
  Administration — M
Educational Media/Instructional
  Technology — M,O
Elementary Education — M
Human Services — M,O
Marriage and Family Therapy — M,D,O
Middle School Education — M
Psychology—General — M,D,O
Reading Education — M
Secondary Education — M
Special Education — M,O

CHEYNEY UNIVERSITY OF PENNSYLVANIA
Education—General — M,O
Educational Leadership and
  Administration — M,O
Elementary Education — M
Public Administration — M
Special Education — M
Urban Education — M

THE CHICAGO SCHOOL OF PROFESSIONAL PSYCHOLOGY
Applied Behavior Analysis — M,D
Clinical Psychology — M,D
Forensic Psychology — M,D
Industrial and Organizational
  Psychology — M,D
Organizational Management — M,D
Psychology—General — M,D
School Psychology — D,O

THE CHICAGO SCHOOL OF PROFESSIONAL PSYCHOLOGY AT DOWNTOWN LOS ANGELES
Applied Behavior Analysis — M,D
Clinical Psychology — M,D
Forensic Psychology — D
Industrial and Organizational
  Psychology — M,D
Marriage and Family Therapy — M,D

THE CHICAGO SCHOOL OF PROFESSIONAL PSYCHOLOGY AT IRVINE
Clinical Psychology — D
Forensic Psychology — D
Marriage and Family Therapy — M,D
Psychology—General — D

THE CHICAGO SCHOOL OF PROFESSIONAL PSYCHOLOGY AT SAN DIEGO
Applied Behavior Analysis — M,D
Applied Psychology — M,D
Clinical Psychology — M,D
Industrial and Organizational
  Psychology — M,D

THE CHICAGO SCHOOL OF PROFESSIONAL PSYCHOLOGY AT WASHINGTON DC
School Psychology — O

THE CHICAGO SCHOOL OF PROFESSIONAL PSYCHOLOGY AT XAVIER UNIVERSITY OF LOUISIANA
Clinical Psychology — D

THE CHICAGO SCHOOL OF PROFESSIONAL PSYCHOLOGY: ONLINE
Applied Psychology — M,O
Clinical Psychology — M,O
Forensic Psychology — M,O
Health Services Management and
  Hospital Administration — M
Industrial and Organizational
  Psychology — M,D,O
Pharmacology — M
Psychology—General — M,D

CHICAGO STATE UNIVERSITY
Adult Education — M
Biological and Biomedical
  Sciences—General — M

Clinical Psychology	M
Computer Science	M
Counselor Education	M
Criminal Justice and Criminology	M
Early Childhood Education	M
Education—General	M,D
Educational Leadership and Administration	M,D
Elementary Education	M
English	M
Foundations and Philosophy of Education	M
Geographic Information Systems	M
Higher Education	M,D
History	M
Library Science	M
Mathematics	M
Middle School Education	M
Multilingual and Multicultural Education	M
Nursing—General	M
Occupational Therapy	M
Pharmacy	D
Physical Education	M
Public Health—General	M
Reading Education	M
Secondary Education	M
Social Work	M
Special Education	M
Vocational and Technical Education	M
Writing	M

CHICAGO THEOLOGICAL SEMINARY

Ethics	M,D
Pastoral Ministry and Counseling	M,D
Religion	M,D
Theology	M,D

CHOWAN UNIVERSITY

Education—General	M

CHRISTENDOM COLLEGE

Theology	M

CHRISTIAN BROTHERS UNIVERSITY

Accounting	M,O
Business Administration and Management—General	M,O
Education—General	M
Educational Leadership and Administration	M
Engineering and Applied Sciences—General	M
International Business	M,O
Physician Assistant Studies	M
Project Management	M,O
Religion	M

CHRISTIAN THEOLOGICAL SEMINARY

Marriage and Family Therapy	M,D
Pastoral Ministry and Counseling	M,D
Religion	M,D
Theology	M,D

CHRISTIE'S EDUCATION

Art History	M
Art/Fine Arts	O
Arts Administration	M,O
Museum Studies	M

CHRISTOPHER NEWPORT UNIVERSITY

Applied Physics	M
Computer Science	M
Education—General	M
Environmental Sciences	M
Physics	M

CHRIST THE KING SEMINARY

Pastoral Ministry and Counseling	M
Theology	M

CHURCH DIVINITY SCHOOL OF THE PACIFIC

Theology	M,D,O

CINCINNATI CHRISTIAN UNIVERSITY

Pastoral Ministry and Counseling	M
Religion	M
Theology	M

THE CITADEL, THE MILITARY COLLEGE OF SOUTH CAROLINA

Aerospace/Aeronautical Engineering	M,O
Biological and Biomedical Sciences—General	M,O
Business Administration and Management—General	M
Civil Engineering	M,O
Computer Engineering	M,O
Counselor Education	M,O
Early Childhood Education	M,O
Education—General	M,O
Educational Leadership and Administration	M,O
Electrical Engineering	M,O
Engineering and Applied Sciences—General	M,O
Engineering Management	M,O
English Education	M,O
English	M
Environmental Management and Policy	M,O
Exercise and Sports Science	M,O
Geotechnical Engineering	M,O
Hispanic Studies	O
History	M,O
Homeland Security	M,O
Information Science	M
Interdisciplinary Studies	M,O
Manufacturing Engineering	M,O
Mathematics Education	M,O
Mechanical Engineering	M,O
Medical Microbiology	M,O

Middle School Education	M,O
Military and Defense Studies	M,O
National Security	M,O
Physical Education	M,O
Political Science	M
Project Management	M,O
Psychology—General	M,O
Reading Education	M,O
School Psychology	M,O
Science Education	M,O
Secondary Education	M,O
Social Sciences Education	M,O
Social Sciences	M,O
Sports Management	M,O
Structural Engineering	M,O
Student Affairs	M,O
Systems Engineering	M,O
Transportation and Highway Engineering	M,O

CITY COLLEGE OF THE CITY UNIVERSITY OF NEW YORK

Architecture	M
Art History	M
Art/Fine Arts	M
Atmospheric Sciences	M
Biochemistry	M,D
Biological and Biomedical Sciences—General	M,D
Biomedical Engineering	M,D
Business Administration and Management—General	M
Chemical Engineering	M,D
Chemistry	M,D
Civil Engineering	M,D
Clinical Psychology	M,D
Computer Art and Design	M
Computer Science	M,D
Corporate and Organizational Communication	M
Early Childhood Education	M
Economics	M
Education—General	M,O
Educational Leadership and Administration	M,O
Electrical Engineering	M,D
Engineering and Applied Sciences—General	M
English as a Second Language	M,O
English Education	M,O
English	M
Geology	M
Geosciences	M
Graphic Design	M
History	M
International Affairs	M
Landscape Architecture	M
Management Information Systems	M,D
Marketing	M
Mathematics Education	M
Mathematics	M
Mechanical Engineering	M,D
Media Studies	M
Middle School Education	M,O
Multilingual and Multicultural Education	M
Museum Education	M
Museum Studies	M
Physics	M,D
Psychology—General	M,D
Public Administration	M,D
Reading Education	M
Science Education	M
Secondary Education	M,O
Social Sciences Education	M,O
Sociology	M
Spanish	M
Special Education	M
Sustainable Development	M
Urban Design	M
Writing	M

CITY UNIVERSITY OF NEW YORK SCHOOL OF LAW

Law	D

CITY UNIVERSITY OF SEATTLE

Accounting	M,O
Business Administration and Management—General	M,O
Computer and Information Systems Security	M,O
Computer Science	M,O
Counseling Psychology	M
Counselor Education	M,O
Curriculum and Instruction	M,O
Education—General	M,O
Educational Leadership and Administration	M,D,O
Elementary Education	M,O
Finance and Banking	M,O
Human Resources Management	M,O
International Business	M,O
Management Information Systems	M,O
Management of Technology	M,O
Marketing	M,O
Organizational Management	M,O
Project Management	M,O
Reading Education	M,O
Special Education	M,O
Sustainability Management	M,O

CITY VISION UNIVERSITY

Entrepreneurship	M
Pastoral Ministry and Counseling	M

CLAFLIN UNIVERSITY

Biotechnology	M
Business Administration and Management—General	M

CLAREMONT GRADUATE UNIVERSITY

African Studies	M,D,O

American Studies	M,D,O
Applied Mathematics	M,D
Archives/Archival Administration	M,D,O
Art/Fine Arts	M
Arts Administration	M,D
Botany	M,D
Business Administration and Management—General	M,D,O
Cognitive Sciences	M,D,O
Comparative Literature	M,D
Computational Biology	M,D
Computational Sciences	M,D
Computer and Information Systems Security	M,D,O
Computer Art and Design	M
Cultural Studies	M,D,O
Data Science/Data Analytics	M,D,O
Developmental Psychology	M,D,O
Economic Development	M,D,O
Economics	M,D,O
Education—General	M,D,O
Educational Leadership and Administration	M,D,O
Educational Measurement and Evaluation	M,D,O
Electronic Commerce	M,D,O
English	M,D
Ethics	M,D
Film, Television, and Video Theory and Criticism	M,D
Financial Engineering	M
Geographic Information Systems	M,D,O
Health Informatics	M,D,O
Health Promotion	M,D
Health Psychology	M,D,O
Higher Education	M,D,O
History	M,D,O
Human Development	M,D,O
Human Resources Development	M,D,O
Human Resources Management	M,D,O
Humanities	M,D,O
Industrial and Organizational Psychology	M,D,O
Information Science	M,D,O
International Affairs	M,D
International Economics	M,D,O
Management Information Systems	M,D,O
Management Strategy and Policy	M,D,O
Mathematics	M,D,O
Media Studies	M,D
Museum Studies	M,D,O
Music	M,D
Operations Research	M,D
Philosophy	M,D
Photography	M
Political Science	M,D
Psychology—General	M,D,O
Public Health—General	M,D
Public Policy	M,D,O
Religion	M,D
Social Psychology	M,D,O
Special Education	M,D,O
Statistics	M,D
Student Affairs	M,D,O
Systems Science	M,D,O
Telecommunications	M,D,O
Theology	M,D
Urban Education	M,D,O
Western European Studies	M,D,O
Women's Studies	M,D
Writing	M,D

CLAREMONT LINCOLN UNIVERSITY

Ethics	M
Pastoral Ministry and Counseling	M
Religion	M

CLAREMONT SCHOOL OF THEOLOGY

Ethics	M,D
Pastoral Ministry and Counseling	M,D
Religion	M,D
Religious Education	M,D
Theology	M,D

CLARION UNIVERSITY OF PENNSYLVANIA

Accounting	M
Business Administration and Management—General	M
Communication Disorders	M
Communication—General	M
Curriculum and Instruction	M
Data Science/Data Analytics	M
Early Childhood Education	M
Education—General	M
Educational Media/Instructional Technology	M
Entrepreneurship	M
Family Nurse Practitioner Studies	M
Finance and Banking	M
Health Services Management and Hospital Administration	M
Information Science	M
Journalism	M
Library Science	M
Mass Communication	M
Mathematics Education	M
Media Studies	M
Nursing—General	M,D
Reading Education	M
Rehabilitation Sciences	M
Science Education	M
Special Education	M
Vocational and Technical Education	M

CLARK ATLANTA UNIVERSITY

Accounting	M
African-American Studies	M,D
Biological and Biomedical Sciences—General	M,D
Business Administration and Management—General	M

Chemistry	M,D
Computer Science	M
Counselor Education	M
Criminal Justice and Criminology	M
Curriculum and Instruction	M
Economics	M
Education—General	M,D,O
Educational Leadership and Administration	M,D,O
Educational Psychology	M
English	M,D
Information Science	M
Mathematics Education	M
Mathematics	M
Physics	M
Political Science	M,D
Public Administration	M
Science Education	M
Social Work	M,D
Sociology	M
Special Education	M

CLARKE UNIVERSITY

Business Administration and Management—General	M
Education—General	M
Educational Leadership and Administration	M
Family Nurse Practitioner Studies	D
Nursing and Healthcare Administration	D
Nursing—General	D
Physical Therapy	D
Psychiatric Nursing	D
Social Work	M

CLARKSON COLLEGE

Adult Nursing	M,O
Family Nurse Practitioner Studies	M,O
Nursing and Healthcare Administration	M,O
Nursing Education	M,O
Nursing—General	M,O

CLARKSON UNIVERSITY

Bioethics	M,O
Biological and Biomedical Sciences—General	M
Biotechnology	M,D
Business Administration and Management—General	M,O
Chemical Engineering	M,D
Chemistry	M,D
Civil Engineering	M,D
Computer Science	M,D
Education—General	M
Electrical Engineering	M
Energy and Power Engineering	M
Energy Management and Policy	M,O
Engineering and Applied Sciences—General	M,D,O
Engineering Management	M
Environmental Engineering	M,D
Environmental Management and Policy	M
Environmental Sciences	M,D
Health Informatics	M
Health Services Management and Hospital Administration	M,O
Health Services Research	M
Human Resources Management	M,O
Interdisciplinary Studies	M,D
International Business	M,O
Materials Engineering	D
Materials Sciences	D
Mathematics	M,D
Mechanical Engineering	M,D
Nursing and Healthcare Administration	M,O
Occupational Therapy	M
Physical Therapy	D
Physician Assistant Studies	M
Physics	M,D
Supply Chain Management	M,O
Sustainable Development	M,D
Systems Engineering	M

CLARKS SUMMIT UNIVERSITY

Communication—General	M,D
Counselor Education	M
Curriculum and Instruction	M
Educational Leadership and Administration	M
English	M
Missions and Missiology	M,D
Organizational Management	M,D
Pastoral Ministry and Counseling	M,D
Religion	M,D
Religious Education	M,D
Theology	M,D

CLARK UNIVERSITY

Accounting	M
American Studies	D
Biochemistry	D
Biological and Biomedical Sciences—General	M,D
Business Administration and Management—General	M
Business Analytics	M
Chemistry	D
Clinical Psychology	D
Communication—General	M
Community Health	M
Developmental Psychology	D
Economics	M
Education—General	M,D
English	M
Environmental Management and Policy	M

Clark University (continued)

Environmental Sciences	M
Finance and Banking	M
Geographic Information Systems	M
Geography	D
Health Education	M
History	D
Holocaust and Genocide Studies	D
Information Science	M
International Development	M
International Health	M
Management Information Systems	M
Marketing	M
Physics	D
Public Administration	M,O
Social Psychology	D
Sustainability Management	M
Sustainable Development	M
Urban and Regional Planning	M

CLAYTON STATE UNIVERSITY

Accounting	M
Applied Psychology	M
Archives/Archival Administration	M
Biological and Biomedical Sciences—General	M
Business Administration and Management—General	M
Clinical Psychology	M
Criminal Justice and Criminology	M
Developmental Psychology	M
Education—General	M
English Education	M
Family Nurse Practitioner Studies	M
History	M
Human Resources Management	M
International Business	M
Liberal Studies	M
Mathematics Education	M
Nursing—General	M
Psychology—General	M
Sports Management	M
Supply Chain Management	M

CLEARY UNIVERSITY

Business Administration and Management—General	M,O
Business Analytics	M,O
Finance and Banking	M,O
Health Services Management and Hospital Administration	M,O
Management Strategy and Policy	M,O

CLEMSON UNIVERSITY

Accounting	M
Agricultural Education	M,D
Agricultural Sciences—General	M,D
Animal Sciences	M,D
Anthropology	M
Applied Economics	M,D
Applied Psychology	M,D
Applied Statistics	M,D
Architecture	M,D,O
Art/Fine Arts	M
Automotive Engineering	M,D,O
Bioengineering	M,D,O
Bioinformatics	M,D,O
Biological and Biomedical Sciences—General	M,D
Biomedical Engineering	M,D,O
Biosystems Engineering	M,D
Business Administration and Management—General	M,D
Business Analytics	M
Business Education	M,D
Chemical Engineering	M,D
Chemistry	M,D
Civil Engineering	M,D
Clinical Psychology	M,D,O
Clinical Research	M,D,O
Communication—General	M
Computer Engineering	M,D
Computer Science	M,D
Construction Engineering	M,D
Construction Management	M,D
Counselor Education	M,D,O
Criminal Justice and Criminology	M
Curriculum and Instruction	M,D,O
Distance Education Development	M,D,O
Early Childhood Education	M,D,O
Economics	M,D
Education—General	M,D,O
Educational Leadership and Administration	M,D,O
Educational Measurement and Evaluation	M,D,O
Electrical Engineering	M,D
Elementary Education	M,D,O
Engineering and Applied Sciences—General	M,D,O
Entomology	M,D
Entrepreneurship	M,D
Environmental and Occupational Health	M,D
Environmental Engineering	M,D
Environmental Management and Policy	M,D
Environmental Sciences	M,D
Ergonomics and Human Factors	M,D
Family and Consumer Sciences-General	D,O
Family Nurse Practitioner Studies	M,D,O
Fish, Game, and Wildlife Management	M,D
Food Science and Technology	M,D
Forestry	M,D
Genetics	M,D,O
Geotechnical Engineering	M,D
Gerontological Nursing	M,D,O
Higher Education	M,D,O
Historic Preservation	M,O
History	M
Human Resources Development	M,D,O

Hydrogeology	M,D
Industrial and Organizational Psychology	M,D
Industrial/Management Engineering	M,D
International Health	M,D,O
Management Information Systems	M,D
Marketing	M
Materials Engineering	M,D
Materials Sciences	M,D
Mathematics Education	M,D,O
Mathematics	M,D
Mechanical Engineering	M,D
Microbiology	M,D
Middle School Education	D
Molecular Biology	D
Nursing—General	M,D,O
Nutrition	M,D
Organizational Behavior	M,D
Physics	M,D
Plant Biology	M,D
Public Administration	M,D,O
Public Health—General	M,D,O
Public Policy	D,O
Reading Education	M,D,O
Real Estate	M
Recreation and Park Management	M,D,O
Rhetoric	M,D
Science Education	D,O
Secondary Education	M,D,O
Sociology	M
Special Education	M,D,O
Sports Management	M,D
Statistics	M,D
Structural Engineering	M,D
Student Affairs	M,D,O
Supply Chain Management	M,D
Toxicology	M,D
Transportation and Highway Engineering	M,D
Travel and Tourism	M,D,O
Veterinary Sciences	M,D
Water Resources Engineering	M,D
Writing	M,D

CLEVELAND INSTITUTE OF MUSIC

Music	M,D,O

CLEVELAND STATE UNIVERSITY

Accounting	M
Adult Education	M,D,O
Allied Health—General	M
Applied Statistics	M
Art Education	M
Art History	M
Bioethics	M,O
Biological and Biomedical Sciences—General	M,D
Biomedical Engineering	D
Business Administration and Management—General	M,D
Chemical Engineering	M,D
Chemistry	M,D
Civil Engineering	M,D
Communication Disorders	M
Communication—General	M,D,O
Counseling Psychology	M,D,O
Counselor Education	M,D,O
Early Childhood Education	M
Economic Development	M,O
Economics	M,O
Education of Students with Severe/Multiple Disabilities	M
Education—General	M,D,O
Educational Leadership and Administration	M,D,O
Educational Media/Instructional Technology	D
Educational Policy	D
Electrical Engineering	M,D
Engineering and Applied Sciences—General	M,D
English as a Second Language	M
English	M
Environmental Engineering	M,D
Environmental Management and Policy	M,O
Environmental Sciences	M,D
Foreign Languages Education	M
Geographic Information Systems	M,O
Health Education	M
Health Services Management and Hospital Administration	M
Higher Education	D
Historic Preservation	M,O
History	M
Human Resources Management	M
Industrial and Labor Relations	M
International Affairs	M
International Economics	M
Law	M,D,O
Management Information Systems	D
Marketing	D
Mathematics Education	M
Mathematics	M
Mechanical Engineering	M,D
Molecular Medicine	M,D
Museum Studies	M
Music Education	M
Music	M
Nonprofit Management	M,O
Nursing Education	D
Nursing—General	M,D
Occupational Therapy	M
Organic Chemistry	M,D
Philosophy	M,O
Physical Chemistry	M,D
Physical Education	M
Physical Therapy	D
Physician Assistant Studies	M
Physics	M
Psychology—General	M,D,O
Public Administration	M,D,O
Public Affairs	D
Public Health—General	M

Real Estate	M,O
Science Education	M
Social Work	M
Software Engineering	M,D
Spanish	M
Special Education	M
Sustainable Development	M,O
Urban and Regional Planning	M,O
Urban Education	M
Urban Studies	M,D,O
Writing	M

CLEVELAND UNIVERSITY–KANSAS CITY

Chiropractic	D
Health Education	M
Health Promotion	M

COASTAL CAROLINA UNIVERSITY

Accounting	M,O
Business Administration and Management—General	M,O
Computer Science	M,D,O
Distance Education Development	M,O
Education—General	M,O
Educational Leadership and Administration	M,O
Educational Media/Instructional Technology	M,O
English as a Second Language	M,O
Liberal Studies	M
Management Information Systems	M,D,O
Marine Sciences	M,D,O
Reading Education	M,O
Special Education	M,O
Sports Management	M,D,O
Writing	M

COGSWELL POLYTECHNICAL COLLEGE

Entrepreneurship	M

COKER COLLEGE

Business Administration and Management—General	M
Criminal Justice and Criminology	M
Curriculum and Instruction	M
Educational Media/Instructional Technology	M
Reading Education	M
Sports Management	M

THE COLBURN SCHOOL CONSERVATORY OF MUSIC

Music	M,O

COLD SPRING HARBOR LABORATORY

Biological and Biomedical Sciences—General	D

COLGATE ROCHESTER CROZER DIVINITY SCHOOL

Conflict Resolution and Mediation/Peace Studies	M,D,O
Theology	M,D,O

COLGATE UNIVERSITY

Secondary Education	M

THE COLLEGE AT BROCKPORT, STATE UNIVERSITY OF NEW YORK

Accounting	M,O
American Studies	M
Art/Fine Arts	M
Arts Administration	M,O
Biological and Biomedical Sciences—General	M,O
Chemistry	M,O
Communication—General	M
Community Health	M
Counseling Psychology	M,O
Counselor Education	M,O
Curriculum and Instruction	M
Dance	M
Early Childhood Education	M,O
Education—General	M,O
Educational Leadership and Administration	M,O
English Education	M,O
English	M,O
Environmental Sciences	M
Gerontology	M,O
Health Education	M
Health Services Management and Hospital Administration	M,O
History of Medicine	M,O
History	M
Liberal Studies	M
Mathematics Education	M,O
Mathematics	M
Middle School Education	M,O
Multilingual and Multicultural Education	M,O
Nonprofit Management	M,O
Physical Education	M,O
Psychology—General	M
Public Administration	M,O
Public Health—General	M
Public History	M
Reading Education	M
Science Education	M,O
Social Sciences Education	M,O
Social Work	M
Sports Management	M,O
Writing	M

COLLÈGE DOMINICAIN DE PHILOSOPHIE ET DE THÉOLOGIE

Philosophy	M,D
Theology	M,D,O

COLLEGE FOR CREATIVE STUDIES

Applied Arts and Design—General	M
Art/Fine Arts	M
Automotive Engineering	M

COLLEGE FOR FINANCIAL PLANNING

Finance and Banking	M

COLLEGE OF CHARLESTON

Accounting	M
Arts Administration	O
Business Administration and Management—General	M
Computer Science	M
Early Childhood Education	M
Education—General	M,O
Elementary Education	M
English as a Second Language	O
English	M
Environmental Sciences	M
Foreign Languages Education	M
Historic Preservation	M
History	M
Management Information Systems	M
Marine Biology	M
Marine Sciences	M
Mathematics Education	M
Mathematics	M
Music Education	M
Public Administration	M
Science Education	M
Special Education	M
Urban and Regional Planning	O
Writing	M

COLLEGE OF EMMANUEL AND ST. CHAD

Theology	M,D,O

THE COLLEGE OF IDAHO

Curriculum and Instruction	M
Education—General	M

COLLEGE OF MOUNT SAINT VINCENT

Education—General	M
Educational Media/Instructional Technology	M,O
English as a Second Language	M,O
Family Nurse Practitioner Studies	M,O
Middle School Education	M,O
Multilingual and Multicultural Education	M,O
Nursing and Healthcare Administration	M,O
Nursing Education	M,O
Nursing—General	M,O
Urban Education	M,O

THE COLLEGE OF NEW JERSEY

Addictions/Substance Abuse Counseling	M,O
Counselor Education	M
Early Childhood Education	M
Education—General	M,O
Educational Leadership and Administration	M,O
Elementary Education	M
English as a Second Language	M
English	O
Gender Studies	M
Health Communication	M
International and Comparative Education	M,O
International Health	M
Marriage and Family Therapy	M
Nursing—General	M
Public Health—General	M
Reading Education	M,O
Secondary Education	M
Special Education	M

THE COLLEGE OF NEW ROCHELLE

Acute Care/Critical Care Nursing	M,O
Art Education	M
Art Therapy	M
Communication—General	M,O
Counseling Psychology	M,O
Early Childhood Education	M
Education of the Gifted	O
Education—General	M,O
Educational Leadership and Administration	M,O
Elementary Education	M
English as a Second Language	M,O
Family Nurse Practitioner Studies	M,O
Human Resources Development	M,O
Marriage and Family Therapy	M
Multilingual and Multicultural Education	M,O
Nursing and Healthcare Administration	M,O
Nursing Education	M,O
Nursing—General	M
Public Administration	M
Reading Education	M
School Psychology	M,O
Special Education	M
Thanatology	M,O

COLLEGE OF SAINT ELIZABETH

Applied Behavior Analysis	M,O
Business Administration and Management—General	M
Computer and Information Systems Security	M,O
Counseling Psychology	M,D
Criminal Justice and Criminology	M,O
Data Science/Data Analytics	M,O
Distance Education Development	M,O
Early Childhood Education	M,O
Education—General	M,O
Educational Leadership and Administration	M,D,O
Elementary Education	M,O
English as a Second Language	M,O
Health Services Management and Hospital Administration	M
Higher Education	M,D,O
Holocaust and Genocide Studies	M,O

Human Resources Management — M
Internet and Interactive
  Multimedia — M
Middle School Education — M,O
Nursing—General — M,O
Nutrition — M
Organizational Management — M,O
Pastoral Ministry and Counseling — M,O
Psychology—General — M,D
Public Administration — M
Public Health—General — M
School Psychology — M,D
Special Education — M,O
Theology — M,O

COLLEGE OF ST. JOSEPH
Addictions/Substance Abuse
  Counseling — M
Business Administration and
  Management—General — M
Clinical Psychology — M
Counseling Psychology — M
Counselor Education — M
Education—General — M
Elementary Education — M
English Education — M
Psychology—General — M
Reading Education — M
School Psychology — M
Secondary Education — M
Social Psychology — M
Social Sciences Education — M
Special Education — M

COLLEGE OF SAINT MARY
Education—General — M
Educational Leadership and
  Administration — M
Educational Measurement and
  Evaluation — M
English as a Second Language — M
Health Education — D
Nursing—General — M
Occupational Therapy — M
Organizational Management — M

THE COLLEGE OF SAINT ROSE
Accounting — M
Business Administration and
  Management—General — M
Business Analytics — M
Communication Disorders — M
Computer Science — M,O
Counseling Psychology — M,O
Counselor Education — M,O
Curriculum and Instruction — M,O
Early Childhood Education — M,O
Education—General — M,O
Educational Leadership and
  Administration — M,O
Educational Psychology — M,O
Finance and Banking — O
Higher Education — M,O
Information Science — M,O
Middle School Education — M,O
Organizational Management — O
Reading Education — M,O
School Psychology — M,O
Secondary Education — M,O
Social Work — M
Special Education — M,O
Student Affairs — M

THE COLLEGE OF ST. SCHOLASTICA
Athletic Training and Sports
  Medicine — M
Business Administration and
  Management—General — M,O
Education—General — M,O
Exercise and Sports Science — M
Health Informatics — M,O
Management Information Systems — M,O
Nursing—General — M,O
Occupational Therapy — M
Physical Therapy — D
Social Work — M

COLLEGE OF STATEN ISLAND OF THE CITY UNIVERSITY OF NEW YORK
Accounting — M
Adult Nursing — M,O
African Studies — M
American Studies — M
Artificial Intelligence/Robotics — M
Asian Studies — M
Biological and Biomedical
  Sciences—General — M
Biotechnology — M
Business Administration and
  Management—General — M
Clinical Psychology — M
Computer and Information
  Systems Security — M
Computer Science — M
Counseling Psychology — M,O
Data Science/Data Analytics — M,O
Early Childhood Education — M,O
Education—General — M,O
Educational Leadership and
  Administration — O
Electrical Engineering — M
Elementary Education — M
English as a Second Language — M,O
English Education — M
English — M
Environmental Sciences — M
Film, Television, and Video
  Theory and Criticism — M
Gerontological Nursing — M,O
Health Services Management and
  Hospital Administration — M
History — M

Latin American Studies — M
Liberal Studies — M
Management Strategy and Policy — M
Mathematics Education — M
Media Studies — M
Middle School Education — M
Multilingual and Multicultural
  Education — O
Near and Middle Eastern Studies — M
Neuroscience — M
Physical Therapy — D
Public History — O
Secondary Education — M
Social Work — M
Software Engineering — M
Special Education — M,O
Western European Studies — M

COLLEGE OF THE ATLANTIC
Environmental Management
  and Policy — M

THE COLLEGE OF WILLIAM AND MARY
Accounting — M
Business Administration and
  Management—General — M
Business Analytics — M
Counselor Education — M,D
Curriculum and Instruction — M
Education—General — M,D,O
Educational Leadership and
  Administration — M,D
Law — M,D
Marine Sciences — M,D
Marriage and Family Therapy — M,D
School Psychology — M,D

COLORADO CHRISTIAN UNIVERSITY
Business Administration and
  Management—General — M
Business Education — M
Computer and Information
  Systems Security — M
Counseling Psychology — M
Curriculum and Instruction — M
Distance Education Development — M
Early Childhood Education — M
Education—General — M
Educational Media/Instructional
  Technology — M
Elementary Education — M
Project Management — M
Special Education — M

THE COLORADO COLLEGE
American Studies — M
Art Education — M
Education—General — M
Elementary Education — M
English Education — M
Foreign Languages Education — M
Humanities — M
Liberal Studies — M
Mathematics Education — M
Music Education — M
Science Education — M
Secondary Education — M
Social Sciences Education — M

COLORADO MESA UNIVERSITY
Business Administration and
  Management—General — M
Education of the Gifted — M,O
Education—General — M
Educational Leadership and
  Administration — M,O
English as a Second Language — M,O
Family Nurse Practitioner Studies — M,D,O
Health Informatics — M,D,O
Nursing Education — M,D,O
Nursing—General — M,D,O
Special Education — M,O

COLORADO SCHOOL OF MINES
Applied Mathematics — M,D
Applied Physics — M,D
Applied Statistics — M,D
Bioengineering — M,D
Chemical Engineering — M,D
Chemistry — M,D
Civil Engineering — M,D
Computer Science — M,D
Construction Engineering — M,D
Electrical Engineering — M,D
Electronic Materials — M,D
Energy Management and
  Policy — M,D
Engineering and Applied
  Sciences—General — M,D,O
Engineering Management — M
Environmental Engineering — M,D
Environmental Sciences — M,D
Geochemistry — M,D
Geological Engineering — M,D
Geology — M,D
Geophysics — M,D
Humanities — O
Hydrology — M,D
Management of Technology — M,D
Materials Engineering — M,D
Materials Sciences — M,D
Mechanical Engineering — M,D
Metallurgical Engineering and
  Metallurgy — M,D
Mineral Economics — M,D
Mineral/Mining Engineering — M,D
Nuclear Engineering — M,D
Operations Research — M,D
Petroleum Engineering — M,D
Physics — M,D
Social Sciences — O

COLORADO SCHOOL OF TRADITIONAL CHINESE MEDICINE
Acupuncture and Oriental Medicine — M

COLORADO STATE UNIVERSITY
Accounting — M
Adult Education — M,D
Advertising and Public Relations — M,D
Agricultural Economics and
  Agribusiness — M,D
Agricultural Education — M
Agricultural Sciences—
  General — M,D
Agronomy and Soil Sciences — M,D
Animal Sciences — M,D
Anthropology — M,D
Art History — M
Art/Fine Arts — M
Arts Administration — M
Atmospheric Sciences — M,D
Biochemistry — M,D
Bioengineering — M,D
Biological and Biomedical
  Sciences—General — M,D
Biomedical Engineering — M,D
Botany — M,D
Business Administration and
  Management—General — M
Chemical Engineering — M,D
Chemistry — M,D
Child and Family Studies — M,D
Civil Engineering — M,D
Computer Science — M,D
Conservation Biology — M,D
Construction Management — M
Consumer Economics — M
Counselor Education — M,D
Economics — M,D
Education—General — M,D
Educational Leadership and
  Administration — M,D
Electrical Engineering — M,D
Energy Management and
  Policy — M
Engineering and Applied
  Sciences—General — M,D
English — M
Entomology — M,D
Environmental and Occupational
  Health — M,D
Environmental Management
  and Policy — M,D
Epidemiology — D
Ethnic Studies — M
Exercise and Sports Science — M,D
Finance and Banking — M
Fish, Game, and Wildlife
  Management — M,D
Food Science and
  Technology — M,D
French — M
Geosciences — M,D
Higher Education — M,D
History — M,D
Horticulture — M,D
Human Development — M,D
Immunology — M,D
Interdisciplinary Studies — M,D
Landscape Architecture — M,D
Liberal Studies — M
Management Information Systems — M
Marriage and Family Therapy — M,D
Materials Sciences — M,D
Mathematics — M,D
Mechanical Engineering — M,D
Media Studies — M,D
Microbiology — M,D
Music — M
Natural Resources — M,D
Nutrition — M,D
Occupational Therapy — M,D
Pathology — M,D
Philosophy — M
Physics — M,D
Plant Pathology — M,D
Plant Sciences — M,D
Political Science — M,D
Psychology—General — M,D
Public History — M
Recreation and Park Management — M,D
Rhetoric — M
Social Work — M,D
Sociology — M,D
Speech and Interpersonal
  Communication — M,D
Statistics — M,D
Student Affairs — M,D
Sustainability Management — M
Sustainable Development — M,O
Systems Engineering — M,D
Travel and Tourism — M,D
Veterinary Medicine — D
Veterinary Sciences — M,D
Water Resources — M
Writing — M
Zoology — M,D

COLORADO STATE UNIVERSITY–GLOBAL CAMPUS
Accounting — M
Business Administration and
  Management—General — M
Criminal Justice and Criminology — M
Education—General — M
Educational Leadership and
  Administration — M
Finance and Banking — M
Health Services Management and
  Hospital Administration — M
Human Resources Management — M
International Business — M

Management Information Systems — M
Organizational Management — M
Project Management — M

COLORADO STATE UNIVERSITY–PUEBLO
Applied Science and
  Technology — M
Art Education — M
Biochemistry — M
Biological and Biomedical
  Sciences—General — M
Business Administration and
  Management—General — M
Chemistry — M
Education—General — M
Educational Media/Instructional
  Technology — M
Engineering and Applied
  Sciences—General — M
Foreign Languages Education — M
Health Education — M
Industrial/Management
  Engineering — M
Music Education — M
Nursing—General — M
Physical Education — M
Special Education — M
Systems Engineering — M

COLORADO TECHNICAL UNIVERSITY AURORA
Accounting — M
Business Administration and
  Management—General — M
Computer and Information
  Systems Security — M
Computer Engineering — M
Computer Science — M
Conflict Resolution and
  Mediation/Peace Studies — M
Criminal Justice and Criminology — M
Data Science/Data Analytics — M
Electrical Engineering — M
Finance and Banking — M
Human Resources Management — M
Industrial and Manufacturing
  Management — M
Management of Technology — M
Marketing — M
Project Management — M
Software Engineering — M
Systems Engineering — M

COLORADO TECHNICAL UNIVERSITY COLORADO SPRINGS
Accounting — M,D
Business Administration and
  Management—General — M,D
Computer and Information
  Systems Security — M,D
Computer Engineering — M
Computer Science — M,D
Conflict Resolution and
  Mediation/Peace Studies — M,D
Criminal Justice and Criminology — M
Data Science/Data Analytics — M,D
Electrical Engineering — M
Finance and Banking — M,D
Human Resources Management — M,D
Industrial and Manufacturing
  Management — M,D
Logistics — M,D
Management of Technology — M,D
Marketing — M,D
Project Management — M,D
Software Engineering — M,D
Systems Engineering — M

COLUMBIA COLLEGE (MO)
Accounting — M
Business Administration and
  Management—General — M
Criminal Justice and Criminology — M
Education—General — M
Educational Leadership and
  Administration — M
Human Resources Management — M

COLUMBIA COLLEGE (SC)
Criminal Justice and Criminology — M
Education—General — M
Educational Leadership and
  Administration — M
Elementary Education — M
Higher Education — M
Organizational Management — M

COLUMBIA COLLEGE CHICAGO
Art History — M
Art/Fine Arts — M
Business Administration and
  Management—General — M
Communication—General — M
English — M
Entertainment Management — M
Film, Television, and Video
  Production — M
Music — M
Photography — M
Writing — M

COLUMBIA COLLEGE OF NURSING
Nursing—General — M

COLUMBIA INTERNATIONAL UNIVERSITY
Counselor Education — M,D,O
Cultural Studies — M,D,O
Curriculum and Instruction — M,D,O
Early Childhood Education — M,D,O
Education—General — M,D,O

*M—masters degree; D—doctorate; O—other advanced degree; *—Close-Up and/or Display*

Educational Leadership and
   Administration — M,D,O
Elementary Education — M,D,O
English as a Second Language — M,D,O
Missions and Missiology — M,D,O
Multilingual and Multicultural
   Education — M,D,O
Pastoral Ministry and Counseling — M,D,O
Religious Education — M,D,O
Theology — M,D,O

COLUMBIA SOUTHERN UNIVERSITY

Business Administration and
   Management—General — M,D
Criminal Justice and Criminology — M
Emergency Management — M
Environmental and Occupational
   Health — M
Finance and Banking — M
Health Services Management and
   Hospital Administration — M
Human Resources Management — M
Marketing — M
Organizational Management — M

COLUMBIA THEOLOGICAL SEMINARY

Theology — M,D

COLUMBIA UNIVERSITY

Accounting — M,D
Actuarial Science — M
Acute Care/Critical Care Nursing — M,O
Adult Nursing — M,O
African Studies — M,D
African-American Studies — M,D
Allopathic Medicine — M,D
American Studies — M,D
Anatomy — M,D
Anthropology — M,D
Applied Mathematics — M,D
Applied Physics — M,D
Archaeology — M,D
Architecture — M,D
Archives/Archival Administration — M
Art History — M,D
Art/Fine Arts — M,D
Asian Studies — M,D,O
Astronomy — M,D
Atmospheric Sciences — M,D
Biochemistry — M,D
Bioethics — M
Biological and Biomedical
   Sciences—General — M,D,O
Biomedical Engineering — M,D
Biophysics — M,D
Biostatistics — M,D
Biotechnology — M,D
Business Administration and
   Management—General — M,D
Business Analytics — M
Cell Biology — M,D
Chemical Engineering — M,D
Chemical Physics — M,D
Chemistry — M,D
Civil Engineering — M,D
Classics — M,D
Communication—General — M,D
Community Health — M,D
Comparative Literature — M,D
Computer Engineering — M,D
Computer Science — M,D
Conflict Resolution and
   Mediation/Peace Studies — M
Conservation Biology — M,D
Construction Engineering — M,D
Construction Management — M,D
Corporate and Organizational
   Communication — M
Data Science/Data Analytics — M
Dentistry — D
Developmental Biology — M,D
East European and Russian Studies — M,D
Ecology — M,D
Economics — M,D
Electrical Engineering — M,D
Engineering and Applied
   Sciences—General — M,D
English — M,D
Entrepreneurship — M
Environmental and Occupational
   Health — M,D
Environmental Design — M
Environmental Engineering — M,D
Environmental Management
   and Policy — M
Environmental Sciences — M,D
Epidemiology — M,D
Ethics — M
Evolutionary Biology — M,D
Family Nurse Practitioner Studies — M,O
Film, Television, and Video
   Production — M
Film, Television, and Video
   Theory and Criticism — M
Finance and Banking — M,D
Financial Engineering — M,D
Foreign Languages Education — M,D
Foundations and Philosophy of
   Education — M,D
French — M,D
Genetics — M,D
Geosciences — M,D
German — M,D
Gerontological Nursing — M,O
Health Services Management and
   Hospital Administration — M
Hispanic Studies — M,D
Historic Preservation — M,D,O
History — M,D
Human Resources Management — M
Industrial/Management
   Engineering — M,D
Information Studies — M
International Affairs — M,D
International Business — M

Italian — M,D
Japanese — M,D
Jewish Studies — M,D
Journalism — M,D
Kinesiology and Movement Studies — M
Landscape Architecture — M
Latin American Studies — M,D
Law — M,D
Legal and Justice Studies — M,D
Management of Technology — M
Marketing — M,D
Materials Engineering — M,D
Materials Sciences — M,D
Maternal and Child Health — M,D
Mathematics — M,D
Mechanical Engineering — M,D
Mechanics — M,D
Media Studies — M
Medical Informatics — M,D,O
Medical Physics — M,D
Medieval and Renaissance Studies — M,D
Microbiology — M,D
Molecular Biology — D
Museum Studies — M,D
Music — M,D
Near and Middle Eastern Studies — M,D
Neurobiology — D
Nonprofit Management — M
Nurse Anesthesia — M,O
Nurse Midwifery — M,O
Nursing—General — M,D,O
Nutrition — M,O
Occupational Therapy — M,D
Operations Research — M,D
Oral and Dental Sciences — M,D,O
Pathobiology — M,D
Pathology — M,D
Pediatric Nursing — M,O
Pharmaceutical Administration — M
Pharmacology — M,D
Philosophy — M,D
Physical Therapy — D
Physics — M,D
Physiology — M,D
Political Science — M,D
Psychiatric Nursing — M,O
Psychology—General — M,D
Public Administration — M
Public Health—General — M
Public Policy — M,D
Quantitative Analysis — M,D
Real Estate — M
Religion — M,D
Romance Languages — M,D
Russian — M,D
Science Education — M,D,O
Slavic Languages — M,D
Social Sciences — M,D
Social Work — M,D
Sociology — M,D
Spanish — M,D
Sports Management — M
Statistics — M,D
Structural Biology — D
Sustainability Management — M
Sustainable Development — M,D
Theater — M,D
Toxicology — M,D
Translation and Interpretation — M,D
Urban and Regional Planning — M,D
Western European Studies — M,D
Writing — M,D

COLUMBUS COLLEGE OF ART & DESIGN

Art/Fine Arts — M

COLUMBUS STATE UNIVERSITY

Art Education — M
Biological and Biomedical
   Sciences—General — M
Business Administration and
   Management—General — M,O
Chemistry — M,O
Clinical Psychology — M,D,O
Computer and Information
   Systems Security — M,O
Computer Science — M,O
Counselor Education — M,D,O
Criminal Justice and Criminology — M
Curriculum and Instruction — M,D,O
Early Childhood Education — M,O
Education—General — M,D,O
Educational Leadership and
   Administration — M,D,O
English as a Second Language — O
English Education — M,O
Environmental Management
   and Policy — M
Environmental Sciences — M,O
Exercise and Sports Science — M
Family Nurse Practitioner Studies — M
Health Education — M
Health Services Management and
   Hospital Administration — M
Higher Education — M,D,O
History — M,O
Homeland Security — M
Human Resources Management — M,O
Mathematics Education — M,O
Mathematics — M,O
Middle School Education — M,O
Modeling and Simulation — M
Music Education — M,O
Music — M,O
Nursing and Healthcare
   Administration — M
Nursing Education — M
Nursing Informatics — M
Nursing—General — M
Organizational Management — M,O
Physical Education — M
Political Science — M
Public Administration — M
Science Education — M,O

Secondary Education — M,O
Social Sciences Education — M,O
Special Education — M,O
Theater — M
Urban Studies — M

CONCORDIA COLLEGE

Education—General — M
Foreign Languages Education — M

CONCORDIA COLLEGE–NEW YORK

Organizational Management — M
Special Education — M

CONCORDIA LUTHERAN SEMINARY

Theology — M,O

CONCORDIA SEMINARY

Theology — M,D,O

CONCORDIA THEOLOGICAL SEMINARY

Theology — M,D

CONCORDIA UNIVERSITY (CANADA)

Adult Education — M,O
Aerospace/Aeronautical
   Engineering — M
Anthropology — M,D
Applied Arts and Design—
   General — M,O
Art Education — M,D
Art History — M,D
Art Therapy — M
Art/Fine Arts — M
Biological and Biomedical
   Sciences—General — M,D,O
Biotechnology — M,D,O
Business Administration and
   Management—General — M,D,O
Chemistry — M,D
Child and Family Studies — M
Civil Engineering — M,D
Clinical Psychology — D,O
Communication—General — M,D,O
Computer and Information
   Systems Security — M,D,O
Computer Art and Design — M,O
Computer Engineering — M,D
Computer Science — M,D
Construction Engineering — M,D,O
Cultural Anthropology — M,D
Economic Development — O
Economics — M,D,O
Education—General — M,D
Educational Media/Instructional
   Technology — M,O
Electrical Engineering — M,D
Engineering and Applied
   Sciences—General — M,D,O
English as a Second Language — M,D
English — M,D
Environmental Engineering — M,D,O
Environmental Management
   and Policy — M,D,O
Exercise and Sports Science — M
Film, Television, and Video
   Production — M,D
Film, Television, and Video
   Theory and Criticism — M,D
Finance and Banking — M,D,O
French — M,O
Game Design and
   Development — M,D,O
Genomic Sciences — M,D,O
Geography — M,D,O
History — M,D
Humanities — D
Industrial/Management
   Engineering — M,D
Interdisciplinary Studies — M,D
Internet and Interactive
   Multimedia — M,D,O
Jewish Studies — M
Journalism — M,O
Linguistics — M,O
Marketing — M,D,O
Mathematics Education — M,D
Mathematics — M,D
Mechanical Engineering — M,D,O
Media Studies — M,D,O
Music — O
Organizational Management — M,O
Philosophy — M
Physics — M,D
Political Science — M,D
Psychology—General — M
Public Administration — M,D
Public Affairs — O
Public Policy — M
Religion — M,D
Sociology — M,D
Software Engineering — M,D,O
Statistics — M,D
Supply Chain Management — M,D,O
Systems Engineering — M,D,O
Telecommunications
   Management — M,D,O
Textile Design — M
Theology — M
Therapies—Dance, Drama, and
   Music — M
Translation and Interpretation — M,O
Urban and Regional Planning — O
Urban Studies — M,D,O
Writing — M

CONCORDIA UNIVERSITY (UNITED STATES)

Art Education — M,D
Business Administration and
   Management—General — M
Curriculum and Instruction — M,D
Early Childhood Education — M,D
Education—General — M,D
Educational Leadership and
   Administration — M,D

Educational Media/Instructional
   Technology — M,D
Elementary Education — M,D
English as a Second Language — M,D
Environmental Education — M,D
Health Education — M,D
Higher Education — M,D
Law — D
Mathematics Education — M,D
Physical Education — M,D
Reading Education — M,D
Science Education — M,D
Secondary Education — M,D
Social Psychology — M,D
Social Sciences Education — M,D
Vocational and Technical Education — M,D

CONCORDIA UNIVERSITY ANN ARBOR

Curriculum and Instruction — M
Educational Leadership and
   Administration — M
Organizational Management — M

CONCORDIA UNIVERSITY CHICAGO

Business Administration and
   Management—General — M,D
Counseling Psychology — M
Counselor Education — M
Curriculum and Instruction — M
Early Childhood Education — M
Education—General — M
Educational Leadership and
   Administration — M,D
Educational Media/Instructional
   Technology — M
Elementary Education — M
Exercise and Sports Science — M
Gerontology — M
Human Services — M
Music — M
Reading Education — M
Religion — M
Religious Education — M
Secondary Education — M

CONCORDIA UNIVERSITY IRVINE

Applied Social Research — M
Business Administration and
   Management—General — M
Counselor Education — M
Cultural Studies — M
Curriculum and Instruction — M
Education—General — M
Educational Leadership and
   Administration — M
Educational Media/Instructional
   Technology — M
Health Services Management and
   Hospital Administration — M
International Affairs — M
Nursing—General — M
Physical Education — M
Religion — M
Sports Management — M
Theology — M

CONCORDIA UNIVERSITY, NEBRASKA

Computer and Information
   Systems Security — M
Computer Science — M
Early Childhood Education — M
Education—General — M
Educational Leadership and
   Administration — M
Elementary Education — M
Pastoral Ministry and Counseling — M
Reading Education — M
Religious Education — M
Secondary Education — M

CONCORDIA UNIVERSITY OF EDMONTON

Computer and Information
   Systems Security — M
Religion — M
Theology — M

CONCORDIA UNIVERSITY, ST. PAUL

Allied Health—General — M,D
Business Administration and
   Management—General — M
Child and Family Studies — M
Computer and Information
   Systems Security — M
Corporate and Organizational
   Communication — M
Criminal Justice and Criminology — M
Curriculum and Instruction — M,D,O
Early Childhood Education — M,D,O
Education—General — M,D,O
Educational Leadership and
   Administration — M,D,O
Educational Media/Instructional
   Technology — M,D,O
Exercise and Sports Science — M,D
Health Services Management and
   Hospital Administration — M
Human Resources Management — M
Human Services — M
Organizational Management — M
Physical Therapy — M,D
Reading Education — M,D
Special Education — M,D,O
Sports Management — M
Writing — M

CONCORDIA UNIVERSITY TEXAS

Education—General — M

CONCORDIA UNIVERSITY WISCONSIN

Art Education — M
Business Administration and
   Management—General — M
Child and Family Studies — M
Corporate and Organizational
   Communication — M
Counselor Education — M

Early Childhood Education — M
Education—General — M
Educational Leadership and Administration — M
Environmental Education — M
Family Nurse Practitioner Studies — M,D
Finance and Banking — M
Health Education — M,D
Health Services Management and Hospital Administration — M
Human Resources Management — M
International Business — M
Management Information Systems — M
Marketing — M
Music — M
Nursing—General — M,D
Occupational Therapy — M
Organizational Management — M
Pharmacy — M,D
Physical Therapy — D
Public Administration — M
Reading Education — M
Rehabilitation Sciences — M
Risk Management — M
Social Work — M
Special Education — M

CONCORD LAW SCHOOL
Law — D

CONCORD UNIVERSITY
Education—General — M
Educational Leadership and Administration — M
Health Promotion — M
Reading Education — M
Social Work — M
Special Education — M

CONSERVATORIO DE MUSICA DE PUERTO RICO
Music Education — M
Music — O

CONVERSE COLLEGE
Art Education — M
Education of the Gifted — M
Educational Leadership and Administration — M,O
Elementary Education — M
English Education — M
English — M
History — M
Liberal Studies — M
Marriage and Family Therapy — M
Mathematics Education — M
Middle School Education — M
Music Education — M
Music — M
Political Science — M
Reading Education — O
Science Education — M
Secondary Education — M
Social Sciences Education — M
Special Education — M
Writing — M

THE CONWAY SCHOOL
Landscape Architecture — M

COOPER UNION FOR THE ADVANCEMENT OF SCIENCE AND ART
Architecture — M
Chemical Engineering — M
Civil Engineering — M
Electrical Engineering — M
Engineering and Applied Sciences—General — M
Mechanical Engineering — M

COPENHAGEN BUSINESS SCHOOL
Business Administration and Management—General — M,D
Economics — M,D
Health Services Management and Hospital Administration — M,D
International Business — M,D
Logistics — M,D
Management Information Systems — M,D
Public Administration — M,D

COPPIN STATE UNIVERSITY
Addictions/Substance Abuse Counseling — M
Adult Education — M
Criminal Justice and Criminology — M
Curriculum and Instruction — M
Education—General — M
Family Nurse Practitioner Studies — M,O
Human Services — M
Nursing—General — M,O
Rehabilitation Counseling — M
Special Education — M

CORBAN UNIVERSITY
Business Administration and Management—General — M
Education—General — M
Nonprofit Management — M,D,O
Pastoral Ministry and Counseling — M,D,O
Theology — M,D,O

CORNELL UNIVERSITY
Accounting — M,D
Adult Education — M,D
Aerospace/Aeronautical Engineering — M,D
African Studies — M
African-American Studies — M,D
Agricultural Economics and Agribusiness — M,D
Agricultural Education — M,D
Agricultural Engineering — M,D
Agronomy and Soil Sciences — M,D

American Studies — M,D
Analytical Chemistry — D
Animal Behavior — D
Animal Sciences — M,D
Anthropology — D
Applied Economics — M,D
Applied Mathematics — M,D
Applied Physics — M,D
Applied Statistics — M,D
Archaeology — M,D
Architectural History — M,D
Architecture — M,D
Art History — D
Art/Fine Arts — M
Artificial Intelligence/Robotics — M,D
Asian Languages — M,D
Asian Studies — M,D
Astronomy — D
Astrophysics — D
Atmospheric Sciences — M,D
Biochemical Engineering — M,D
Biochemistry — M,D
Bioengineering — M,D
Biological and Biomedical Sciences—General — D
Biological Anthropology — D
Biomedical Engineering — M,D
Biometry — M,D
Biophysics — D
Biopsychology — D
Biotechnology — M,D
Business Administration and Management—General — M,D
Cell Biology — D
Chemical Engineering — M,D
Chemical Physics — D
Chemistry — D
Child and Family Studies — M,D
Civil Engineering — M,D
Classics — D
Clothing and Textiles — M,D
Cognitive Sciences — D
Communication—General — M,D
Comparative Literature — D
Computational Biology — D
Computational Sciences — M,D
Computer Art and Design — M,D
Computer Engineering — M,D
Computer Science — M,D
Conflict Resolution and Mediation/Peace Studies — M,D
Conservation Biology — M,D
Consumer Economics — M,D
Corporate and Organizational Communication — M,D
Cultural Anthropology — D
Cultural Studies — M,D
Curriculum and Instruction — M,D
Demography and Population Studies — M,D
Developmental Biology — D
Developmental Psychology — M,D
East European and Russian Studies — M,D
Ecology — M,D
Economic Development — M,D
Economics — M,D
Education—General — M,D
Educational Policy — M,D
Electrical Engineering — M,D
Energy and Power Engineering — M,D
Engineering and Applied Sciences—General — M,D
Engineering Management — M,D
Engineering Physics — M,D
English — M,D
Entomology — M,D
Environmental Design — M
Environmental Engineering — M,D
Environmental Management and Policy — M,D
Environmental Sciences — M,D
Ergonomics and Human Factors — M
Ethnic Studies — M,D
Evolutionary Biology — D
Experimental Psychology — D
Facilities Management — M
Finance and Banking — D
Fish, Game, and Wildlife Management — M,D
Food Science and Technology — M,D
Foreign Languages Education — M,D
Forestry — M,D
French — D
Gender Studies — M,D
Genetics — D
Genomic Sciences — D
Geochemistry — M,D
Geology — M,D
Geophysics — M,D
Geosciences — M,D
Geotechnical Engineering — M,D
German — M,D
Health Communication — M,D
Health Services Management and Hospital Administration — M,D
Hispanic and Latin American Languages — D
Historic Preservation — M,D
History of Science and Technology — M,D
History — M,D
Horticulture — M,D
Hospitality Management — M,D
Human Development — M,D
Human Resources Management — M,D
Human-Computer Interaction — M,D
Hydrology — M,D
Industrial and Labor Relations — M,D
Industrial/Management Engineering — M,D

Information Science — D
Information Studies — D
Inorganic Chemistry — D
Interior Design — M
International Affairs — D
Italian — D
Jewish Studies — M,D
Landscape Architecture — M
Latin American Studies — M,D
Law — M,D
Limnology — D
Linguistics — M,D
Manufacturing Engineering — M,D
Marine Geology — M,D
Marine Sciences — M,D
Marketing — D
Materials Engineering — M,D
Materials Sciences — M,D
Mathematics Education — M,D
Mathematics — D
Mechanical Engineering — M,D
Mechanics — M,D
Media Studies — M,D
Medieval and Renaissance Studies — M,D
Microbiology — D
Mineralogy — M,D
Molecular Biology — M,D
Music — M,D
Nanotechnology — M,D
Natural Resources — M,D
Near and Middle Eastern Studies — M,D
Neurobiology — D
Nutrition — M,D
Oceanography — D
Operations Research — M,D
Organic Chemistry — D
Organizational Behavior — M,D
Paleontology — M,D
Philosophy — D
Photography — M,D
Physical Chemistry — D
Physics — M,D
Physiology — M,D
Planetary and Space Sciences — D
Plant Biology — M,D
Plant Molecular Biology — M,D
Plant Pathology — M,D
Plant Physiology — M,D
Plant Sciences — M,D
Political Science — D
Polymer Science and Engineering — M,D
Psychology—General — D
Public Affairs — M
Public Policy — M,D
Real Estate — M
Religion — M,D
Romance Languages — M,D
Rural Sociology — M,D
Scandinavian Languages — M,D
Secondary Education — M,D
Slavic Languages — M,D
Social Psychology — M,D
Social Work — M,D
Sociology — M,D
Spanish — D
Statistics — M,D
Structural Engineering — M,D
Sustainable Development — M,D
Systems Engineering — M,D
Textile Design — M,D
Textile Sciences and Engineering — M,D
Theater — D
Theoretical Chemistry — D
Theoretical Physics — M,D
Toxicology — M,D
Transportation and Highway Engineering — M,D
Urban and Regional Planning — M,D
Urban Design — M,D
Veterinary Medicine — D
Viticulture and Enology — M,D
Water Resources Engineering — M,D
Water Resources — M,D
Western European Studies — M,D
Women's Studies — M,D
Writing — M,D

CORNERSTONE UNIVERSITY
Business Administration and Management—General — M,O
Education—General — M,O
English as a Second Language — M,O

COVENANT COLLEGE
Education—General — M

COVENANT THEOLOGICAL SEMINARY
Pastoral Ministry and Counseling — M,D,O
Theology — M,D,O

COX COLLEGE
Family Nurse Practitioner Studies — M
Nursing and Healthcare Administration — M
Nursing Education — M
Nursing—General — M
Occupational Therapy — M

CRANBROOK ACADEMY OF ART
Architecture — M
Art/Fine Arts — M
Photography — M
Textile Design — M

CRANDALL UNIVERSITY
Education—General — M
Organizational Management — M
Reading Education — M

CREIGHTON UNIVERSITY
Accounting — M,D
Adult Nursing — M,D,O
Allied Health—General — M,D
Allopathic Medicine — D
Anatomy — M
Bioethics — M
Biological and Biomedical Sciences—General — M,D
Business Administration and Management—General — M,D
Business Analytics — M,D
Conflict Resolution and Mediation/Peace Studies — M,D,O
Counselor Education — M
Dentistry — D
Education—General — M
Educational Leadership and Administration — M,D
Elementary Education — M
Emergency Medical Services — M
English — M
Family Nurse Practitioner Studies — M,D,O
Finance and Banking — M,D
Gerontological Nursing — M,D,O
Health Promotion — M
Health Services Management and Hospital Administration — M,D
Immunology — M,D
Investment Management — M,D
Law — M,D,O
Maternal and Child/Neonatal Nursing — M,D,O
Medical Microbiology — M,D
Nursing and Healthcare Administration — M,D,O
Nursing—General — M,D,O
Occupational Therapy — D
Organizational Management — M
Pediatric Nursing — M,D,O
Pharmaceutical Sciences — M,D
Pharmacology — M,D
Pharmacy — D
Physical Therapy — D
Physics — M
Psychiatric Nursing — M,D,O
Public Health—General — M
School Psychology — M
Secondary Education — M
Writing — M

CRISWELL COLLEGE
Jewish Studies — M
Pastoral Ministry and Counseling — M
Theology — M

CROWN COLLEGE
Theology — M

CULVER-STOCKTON COLLEGE
Accounting — M
Business Administration and Management—General — M
Finance and Banking — M

CUMBERLAND UNIVERSITY
Business Administration and Management—General — M
Education—General — M
Public Administration — M

CUNY CRAIG NEWMARK GRADUATE SCHOOL OF JOURNALISM
Journalism — M

CURRY COLLEGE
Business Administration and Management—General — M,O
Criminal Justice and Criminology — M
Education—General — M,O
Elementary Education — M,O
Finance and Banking — M,O
Foundations and Philosophy of Education — M,O
Nursing—General — M
Reading Education — M,O
Special Education — M,O

CURTIS INSTITUTE OF MUSIC
Music — M

DAEMEN COLLEGE
Accounting — M
Adult Nursing — M,D,O
Business Administration and Management—General — M
Community Health — M
Early Childhood Education — M
Education—General — M
Epidemiology — M
Health Education — M
Health Services Management and Hospital Administration — M
International Business — M
Management Information Systems — M
Marketing — M
Medical/Surgical Nursing — M,D,O
Middle School Education — M
Nonprofit Management — M
Nursing and Healthcare Administration — M,D,O
Nursing Education — M,D,O
Nursing—General — M,D,O
Physical Therapy — D,O
Physician Assistant Studies — M
Public Health—General — M
Social Work — M
Special Education — M

DAKOTA STATE UNIVERSITY
Business Administration and Management—General — M,D,O
Business Analytics — M,D,O
Computer Science — M,D,O

M—masters degree; D—doctorate; O—other advanced degree; *—Close-Up and/or Display

Education—General — M
Educational Media/Instructional
  Technology — M
Health Informatics — M,D,O
Information Science — M,D,O
Management Information Systems — M,D,O

DAKOTA WESLEYAN UNIVERSITY
Curriculum and Instruction — M
Education—General — M
Educational Leadership and
  Administration — M
Secondary Education — M

DALHOUSIE UNIVERSITY
Agricultural Sciences—
  General — M
Agronomy and Soil Sciences — M
Allopathic Medicine — M,D
Anatomy — M
Animal Sciences — M
Anthropology — M
Applied Mathematics — M,D
Aquaculture — M
Architecture — M
Biochemistry — M,D
Bioengineering — M,D
Bioinformatics — M,D
Biological and Biomedical
  Sciences—General — M,D
Biomedical Engineering — M,D
Biophysics — M,D
Botany — M
Business Administration and
  Management—General — M,O
Chemical Engineering — M,D
Chemistry — M,D
Civil Engineering — M,D
Classics — M,D
Clinical Psychology — M,D
Communication Disorders — M,D
Community Health — M
Computer Engineering — M,D
Computer Science — M,D
Developmental Biology — M,D
Ecology — M
Economics — M,D
Electrical Engineering — M,D
Electronic Commerce — M,D
Engineering and Applied
  Sciences—General — M,D
English — M,D
Environmental Biology — M
Environmental Engineering — M,D
Environmental Management
  and Policy — M
Environmental Sciences — M
Epidemiology — M
Finance and Banking — M
Food Science and
  Technology — M,D
French — M,D
Geosciences — M,D
German — M
Health Education — M
Health Services Management and
  Hospital Administration — M,D
History — M,D
Horticulture — M
Human-Computer Interaction — M,D
Immunology — M,D
Industrial/Management
  Engineering — M,D
Information Studies — M
Interdisciplinary Studies — D
International Development — M
Internet Engineering — M,D
Kinesiology and Movement Studies — M
Law — M,D
Leisure Studies — M
Library Science — M
Management Information Systems — M
Marine Affairs — M
Mathematics — M,D
Mechanical Engineering — M,D
Medical Informatics — M,D
Microbiology — M,D
Mineral/Mining Engineering — M,D
Music — M
Natural Resources — M
Neuroscience — M,D
Nursing—General — M,D
Occupational Therapy — M
Oceanography — M,D
Oral and Dental Sciences — M
Pathology — M,D
Pharmacology — M,D
Philosophy — M,D
Physical Therapy — M
Physics — M,D
Physiology — M,D
Plant Pathology — M
Plant Physiology — M
Political Science — M,D
Psychology—General — M,D
Public Administration — M,O
Rural Planning and Studies — M
Social Work — M
Sociology — M,D
Statistics — M,D
Urban and Regional Planning — M
Water Resources — M

DALLAS BAPTIST UNIVERSITY
Accounting — M
Asian Studies — M
Business Administration and
  Management—General — M,D
Communication—General — M
Conflict Resolution and
  Mediation/Peace Studies — M
Counseling Psychology — M
Counselor Education — M
Criminal Justice and Criminology — M
Curriculum and Instruction — M

Distance Education Development — M
Early Childhood Education — M,D
Education—General — M
Educational Leadership and
  Administration — M
Educational Media/Instructional
  Technology — M
Elementary Education — M
English as a Second Language — M
Entrepreneurship — M
Finance and Banking — M
Health Services Management and
  Hospital Administration — M
Higher Education — M
Human Resources Management — M
Interdisciplinary Studies — M
International Affairs — M
International Business — M
Kinesiology and Movement Studies — M
Liberal Studies — M
Management Information Systems — M
Missions and Missiology — M
Multilingual and Multicultural
  Education — M
Nonprofit Management — M
Organizational Management — M,D
Pastoral Ministry and Counseling — M,D
Reading Education — M
Religion — M
Religious Education — M
Secondary Education — M
Special Education — M
Sports Management — M
Student Affairs — M
Theology — M
Western European Studies — M

DALLAS INTERNATIONAL UNIVERSITY
Linguistics — M,O
Multilingual and Multicultural
  Education — M,O

DALLAS THEOLOGICAL SEMINARY
Adult Education — M,D,O
Child and Family Studies — M,D,O
Educational Leadership and
  Administration — M,D,O
Jewish Studies — M,D,O
Media Studies — M,D,O
Missions and Missiology — M,D,O
Pastoral Ministry and Counseling — M,D,O
Philosophy — M,D,O
Religion — M,D,O
Religious Education — M,D,O
Theology — M,D,O

DANIEL MORGAN GRADUATE SCHOOL OF NATIONAL SECURITY
National Security — M

DAOIST TRADITIONS COLLEGE OF CHINESE MEDICAL ARTS
Acupuncture and Oriental Medicine — M,D

DARTMOUTH COLLEGE
Allopathic Medicine — D
Astronomy — D
Biochemistry — M,D
Biological and Biomedical
  Sciences—General — D
Biomedical Engineering — M,D
Biostatistics — M,D
Business Administration and
  Management—General — M
Cell Biology — D
Chemical Engineering — M,D
Chemistry — M,D
Cognitive Sciences — D
Comparative Literature — M
Computer Engineering — M,D
Computer Science — M,D
Ecology — D
Electrical Engineering — M,D
Energy and Power
  Engineering — M,D
Engineering and Applied
  Sciences—General — M,D
Engineering Management — M
Entrepreneurship — D
Environmental Biology — D
Epidemiology — M,D
Evolutionary Biology — D
Genetics — D
Geosciences — M,D
Health Informatics — M,D
Health Services Management and
  Hospital Administration — M,D
Health Services Research — M,D
Immunology — D
Liberal Studies — M
Materials Engineering — M,D
Materials Sciences — M,D
Mathematics — M,D
Mechanical Engineering — M,D
Microbiology — M,D
Molecular Biology — D
Molecular Medicine — D
Molecular Pathogenesis — D
Music — D
Neuroscience — D
Physical Chemistry — M,D
Physics — D
Psychology—General — D
Public Health—General — M
Sustainable Development — D
Systems Engineering — M,D

DAVENPORT UNIVERSITY
Accounting — M
Business Administration and
  Management—General — M
Computer and Information
  Systems Security — M
Finance and Banking — M
Health Services Management and
  Hospital Administration — M

Human Resources Management — M
Management Strategy and Policy — M
Occupational Therapy — M
Public Health—General — M

DEFIANCE COLLEGE
Business Administration and
  Management—General — M
Education—General — M
Management Strategy and Policy — M

DELAWARE STATE UNIVERSITY
Adult Education — M
Applied Mathematics — M,D
Art Education — M
Biological and Biomedical
  Sciences—General — M
Business Administration and
  Management—General — M
Chemistry — M,D
Curriculum and Instruction — M
Education—General — M,D
Educational Leadership and
  Administration — M,D
Exercise and Sports Science — M
Foreign Languages Education — M
Historic Preservation — M
Mathematics Education — M
Mathematics — M
Natural Resources — M
Neuroscience — M,D
Nursing—General — M
Optical Sciences — M,D
Physics — M,D
Plant Sciences — M
Reading Education — M
Science Education — M,D
Social Work — M
Special Education — M
Theoretical Physics — D

DELAWARE VALLEY UNIVERSITY
Accounting — M
Agricultural Economics and
  Agribusiness — M
Business Administration and
  Management—General — M
Counseling Psychology — M
Criminal Justice and Criminology — M
Curriculum and Instruction — M
Developmental Psychology — M
Educational Leadership and
  Administration — M
Educational Media/Instructional
  Technology — M
Entrepreneurship — M
Finance and Banking — M
Human Resources Management — M
International Business — M
Social Psychology — M
Supply Chain Management — M

DELL'ARTE INTERNATIONAL SCHOOL OF PHYSICAL THEATRE
Theater — M

DELTA STATE UNIVERSITY
Accounting — M
Aviation Management — M
Biological and Biomedical
  Sciences—General — M
Business Administration and
  Management—General — M
Counselor Education — M,D,O
Criminal Justice and Criminology — M
Education—General — M,D,O
Educational Leadership and
  Administration — M,D,O
Elementary Education — M,D,O
English Education — M
Exercise and Sports Science — M
Family Nurse Practitioner Studies — M,D
Gender Studies — M
Health Education — M
Health Services Management and
  Hospital Administration — M,D
Higher Education — D
Liberal Studies — M
Nursing Education — M,D
Nursing—General — M,D
Philosophy — M
Physical Education — M
Recreation and Park Management — M
Religion — M
Secondary Education — M,D,O
Social Sciences Education — M
Special Education — M
Urban and Regional Planning — M

DENVER SEMINARY
Marriage and Family Therapy — M,D,O
Pastoral Ministry and Counseling — M,D,O
Religion — M,D,O
Theology — M,D,O

DEPAUL UNIVERSITY
Accounting — M,D
Adult Education — M
Advertising and Public Relations — M
Applied Economics — M,D
Applied Mathematics — M,D
Applied Statistics — M,D
Biological and Biomedical
  Sciences—General — M,D
Business Administration and
  Management—General — M,D
Business Analytics — M,D
Chemistry — M,D
Chinese — M
Clinical Psychology — M,D
Communication—General — M
Computer and Information
  Systems Security — M,D
Computer Art and Design — M,D
Computer Science — M,D

Human Resources Management — M
Management Strategy and Policy — M
Occupational Therapy — M
Public Health—General — M

DEFIANCE COLLEGE
Business Administration and
  Management—General — M
Education—General — M
Management Strategy and Policy — M

Corporate and Organizational
  Communication — M
Counseling Psychology — M,D
Counselor Education — M,D
Curriculum and Instruction — M,D
Data Science/Data Analytics — M,D
Early Childhood Education — M,D
Economics — M,D
Education—General — M,D
Educational Leadership and
  Administration — M,D
Electronic Commerce — M,D
Elementary Education — M,D
English — M,D
Entrepreneurship — M,D
Environmental Sciences — M,D
Ethnic Studies — M
Family Nurse Practitioner Studies — M,D
Film, Television, and Video
  Production — M,D
Film, Television, and Video
  Theory and Criticism — M
Finance and Banking — M,D
Foreign Languages Education — M,D
Foundations and Philosophy of
  Education — M,D
French — M
Game Design and
  Development — M,D
Gender Studies — M
German — M
Health Communication — M
Health Informatics — M,D
Health Law — M,D
Higher Education — M,D
History — M
Hospitality Management — M
Human Resources Management — M,D
Human-Computer Interaction — M,D
Information Science — M,D
Intellectual Property Law — M,D
Interdisciplinary Studies — M
International Affairs — M
International Business — M,D
Internet and Interactive
  Multimedia — M,D
Italian — M
Japanese — M
Journalism — M
Law — M,D
Liberal Studies — M
Management Information Systems — M,D
Management Strategy and Policy — M,D
Marketing — M,D
Mathematical and
  Computational Finance — M,D
Mathematics Education — M,D
Mathematics — M,D
Media Studies — M
Middle School Education — M,D
Multilingual and Multicultural
  Education — M,D
Music Education — M,O
Music — M
Near and Middle Eastern Languages — M
Nonprofit Management — M
Nursing—General — M,D
Physical Education — M,D
Physics — M,D
Polymer Science and
  Engineering — M,D
Psychology—General — M,D
Public Administration — M
Public Health—General — M
Public Policy — M
Publishing — M
Reading Education — M,D
Real Estate — M,D
Rhetoric — M
Risk Management — M,D
School Psychology — M,D
Science Education — M,D
Secondary Education — M,D
Social Work — M
Sociology — M
Software Engineering — M,D
Spanish — M
Special Education — M,D
Student Affairs — M,D
Supply Chain Management — M
Sustainability Management — M,D
Sustainable Development — M
Taxation — M,D
Theater — M
Urban Design — M
Women's Studies — M
Writing — M

DEREE - THE AMERICAN COLLEGE OF GREECE
Applied Psychology — M
Communication—General — M
Marketing — M

DESALES UNIVERSITY
Accounting — M
Business Administration and
  Management—General — M
Computer and Information
  Systems Security — M,O
Criminal Justice and Criminology — M,O
Data Science/Data Analytics — M,O
Education—General — M,O
Educational Media/Instructional
  Technology — M,O
English as a Second Language — M,O
Family Nurse Practitioner Studies — M,D,O
Finance and Banking — M
Forensic Sciences — M,O
Gerontology — M,D,O
Health Informatics — M,O
Health Services Management and
  Hospital Administration — M
Human Resources Management — M
Management Information Systems — M,O

Marketing — M
Nurse Anesthesia — M,D,O
Nurse Midwifery — M,D,O
Nursing and Healthcare
  Administration — M,D,O
Nursing Education — M,D,O
Nursing—General — M,D,O
Project Management — M,O
Secondary Education — M,O
Special Education — M,O
Supply Chain Management — M

DES MOINES UNIVERSITY
Anatomy — M
Biological and Biomedical
  Sciences—General — M
Health Services Management and
  Hospital Administration — M
Osteopathic Medicine — D
Physical Therapy — D
Physician Assistant Studies — M
Podiatric Medicine — D
Public Health—General — M

DEVRY COLLEGE OF NEW YORK–MIDTOWN MANHATTAN CAMPUS
Business Administration and
  Management—General — M

DEVRY UNIVERSITY–ALPHARETTA CAMPUS
Business Administration and
  Management—General — M

DEVRY UNIVERSITY–ARLINGTON CAMPUS
Business Administration and
  Management—General — M

DEVRY UNIVERSITY–CHARLOTTE CAMPUS
Business Administration and
  Management—General — M

DEVRY UNIVERSITY–CHESAPEAKE CAMPUS
Business Administration and
  Management—General — M

DEVRY UNIVERSITY–CHICAGO CAMPUS
Business Administration and
  Management—General — M

DEVRY UNIVERSITY–CHICAGO LOOP CAMPUS
Business Administration and
  Management—General — M

DEVRY UNIVERSITY–CINCINNATI CAMPUS
Business Administration and
  Management—General — M

DEVRY UNIVERSITY–COLUMBUS CAMPUS
Business Administration and
  Management—General — M

DEVRY UNIVERSITY–DECATUR CAMPUS
Business Administration and
  Management—General — M

DEVRY UNIVERSITY–FOLSOM CAMPUS
Accounting — M
Business Administration and
  Management—General — M
Curriculum and Instruction — M
Educational Leadership and
  Administration — M
Educational Media/Instructional
  Technology — M
Finance and Banking — M
Higher Education — M
Human Resources Management — M
Management Information Systems — M
Project Management — M
Public Administration — M

DEVRY UNIVERSITY–FREMONT CAMPUS
Business Administration and
  Management—General — M

DEVRY UNIVERSITY–FT. WASHINGTON CAMPUS
Business Administration and
  Management—General — M

DEVRY UNIVERSITY–HENDERSON CAMPUS
Business Administration and
  Management—General — M

DEVRY UNIVERSITY–IRVING CAMPUS
Business Administration and
  Management—General — M

DEVRY UNIVERSITY–JACKSONVILLE CAMPUS
Business Administration and
  Management—General — M

DEVRY UNIVERSITY–LONG BEACH CAMPUS
Business Administration and
  Management—General — M

DEVRY UNIVERSITY–MIRAMAR CAMPUS
Business Administration and
  Management—General — M

DEVRY UNIVERSITY–MORRISVILLE CAMPUS
Business Administration and
  Management—General — M

DEVRY UNIVERSITY–NASHVILLE CAMPUS
Business Administration and
  Management—General — M

DEVRY UNIVERSITY–NORTH BRUNSWICK CAMPUS
Business Administration and
  Management—General — M

DEVRY UNIVERSITY ONLINE
Business Administration and
  Management—General — M

DEVRY UNIVERSITY–ORLANDO CAMPUS
Business Administration and
  Management—General — M

DEVRY UNIVERSITY–PHOENIX CAMPUS
Business Administration and
  Management—General — M

DEVRY UNIVERSITY–POMONA CAMPUS
Business Administration and
  Management—General — M

DEVRY UNIVERSITY–SAN DIEGO CAMPUS
Business Administration and
  Management—General — M,O

DEVRY UNIVERSITY–SEVEN HILLS CAMPUS
Business Administration and
  Management—General — M,O

DEVRY UNIVERSITY–TINLEY PARK CAMPUS
Business Administration and
  Management—General — M

DICKINSON STATE UNIVERSITY
Early Childhood Education — M
Education—General — M
Entrepreneurship — M
Middle School Education — M
Reading Education — M

DIGIPEN INSTITUTE OF TECHNOLOGY
Computer Art and Design — M
Computer Science — M

DIVINE MERCY UNIVERSITY
Clinical Psychology — M,D
Psychology—General — M

DOANE UNIVERSITY
Business Administration and
  Management—General — M
Counselor Education — M
Curriculum and Instruction — M,D,O
Education—General — M,D,O
Educational Leadership and
  Administration — M,D,O
School Psychology — M,D,O

DOMINICAN COLLEGE
Accounting — M
Allied Health—General — M,D
Business Administration and
  Management—General — M
Education—General — M
Elementary Education — M
Family Nurse Practitioner Studies — M,D
Health Services Management and
  Hospital Administration — M
Occupational Therapy — M
Physical Therapy — M,D
Special Education — M

DOMINICAN HOUSE OF STUDIES, PONTIFICAL FACULTY OF THE IMMACULATE CONCEPTION
Theology — M,D,O

DOMINICAN SCHOOL OF PHILOSOPHY AND THEOLOGY
Philosophy — M,O
Theology — M,O

DOMINICAN UNIVERSITY
Accounting — M
Business Administration and
  Management—General — M
Early Childhood Education — M
Education—General — M
Elementary Education — M
English as a Second Language — M
Information Studies — M,D,O
Management Information Systems — M,D,O
Reading Education — M
Secondary Education — M
Social Work — M
Special Education — M

DOMINICAN UNIVERSITY OF CALIFORNIA
Art History — M
Biological and Biomedical
  Sciences—General — M
Business Administration and
  Management—General — M
Clinical Laboratory
  Sciences/Medical Technology — M
Counseling Psychology — M
Education—General — M
Gender Studies — M
History — M
Humanities — M
Liberal Studies — M

Marriage and Family Therapy — M
Music — M
Occupational Therapy — M
Philosophy — M
Political Science — M
Religion — M
Special Education — M
Writing — M

DONGGUK UNIVERSITY LOS ANGELES
Acupuncture and Oriental Medicine — M

DORDT COLLEGE
Education—General — M

DRAGON RISES COLLEGE OF ORIENTAL MEDICINE
Acupuncture and Oriental Medicine — M

DRAKE UNIVERSITY
Accounting — M
Applied Behavior Analysis — M,D,O
Athletic Training and Sports
  Medicine — M,D
Business Administration and
  Management—General — M
Communication—General — M
Counselor Education — M,D,O
Education—General — M,D,O
Educational Leadership and
  Administration — M,D,O
Law — M,D
Mathematics Education — M,D,O
Occupational Therapy — M,D
Pharmacy — M,D
Public Administration — M
Public Affairs — M
Reading Education — M,D,O
Science Education — M,D,O
Special Education — M,D,O

DREW UNIVERSITY
American Studies — M,D,O
Art/Fine Arts — M,D,O
Biological and Biomedical
  Sciences—General — M,D,O
Chemistry — M,D,O
Community College Education — M,D,O
Conflict Resolution and
  Mediation/Peace Studies — M,D,O
Cultural Studies — M,D,O
Education—General — M,D,O
Elementary Education — M,D,O
English — M,D,O
Finance and Banking — M,D,O
French — M,D,O
Health Education — M,D,O
Health Services Management and
  Hospital Administration — M,D,O
History — M,D,O
Italian — M,D,O
Liberal Studies — M,D,O
Mathematics — M,D,O
Public History — M,D,O
Religion — M,D,O
Secondary Education — M,D,O
Special Education — M,D,O
Theology — M,D,O
Western European Studies — M,D,O
Writing — M,D,O

DREXEL UNIVERSITY
Accounting — M,D,O
Acute Care/Critical Care Nursing — M
Allied Health—General — M,D,O
Allopathic Medicine — D
Applied Arts and Design—
  General — M,D
Applied Behavior Analysis — M,D
Architectural Engineering — M,D
Archives/Archival Administration — M
Art Therapy — M,O
Arts Administration — M
Biochemical Engineering — M
Biochemistry — M,D
Biological and Biomedical
  Sciences—General — M,D,O
Biomedical Engineering — M,D
Biopsychology — M,D
Biostatistics — M,D,O
Business Administration and
  Management—General — M,D,O
Cell Biology — M,D
Chemical Engineering — M,D
Chemistry — M,D
Civil Engineering — M,D
Clinical Psychology — D
Clothing and Textiles — M
Communication—General — M
Computer Art and Design — M,D
Computer Engineering — M
Computer Science — M,D,O*
Construction Management — M
Corporate and Organizational
  Communication — M
Curriculum and Instruction — M,D
Economics — M,D,O
Education—General — M,D
Educational Leadership and
  Administration — M,D
Educational Media/Instructional
  Technology — M,D
Electrical Engineering — M
Emergency Management — M
Emergency Medical Services — M
Engineering and Applied
  Sciences—General — M,D,O
Engineering Management — M,O
Entrepreneurship — M
Environmental Engineering — M,D
Environmental Management
  and Policy — M

Environmental Sciences — M,D
Epidemiology — M,D,O
Family Nurse Practitioner Studies — M
Film, Television, and Video
  Production — M
Finance and Banking — M,D,O
Food Science and
  Technology — M
Forensic Psychology — D
Genetics — M,D
Geotechnical Engineering — M,D
Health Law — M,D
Health Psychology — D
Higher Education — M,D
History of Science and Technology — M
Homeland Security — M
Hospitality Management — M
Human Resources Development — M,D
Hydraulics — M,D
Hydrology — M,D
Immunology — M,D
Information Science — M,D,O
Intellectual Property Law — M,D
Interior Design — M
International and Comparative
  Education — M,D
Law — M,D
Library Science — M,D,O
Management Information Systems — M,D,O
Management Strategy and Policy — M,D,O
Marketing — M,D,O
Marriage and Family Therapy — M,D
Mass Communication — M
Materials Engineering — M,D
Mathematics — M,D
Mechanical Engineering — M,D
Mechanics — M,D
Media Studies — M
Microbiology — M,D
Molecular Biology — M,D
Molecular Medicine — M
Neuroscience — M,D
Nurse Anesthesia — M
Nursing and Healthcare
  Administration — M
Nursing Education — M
Nursing—General — M,D
Organizational Behavior — M,D,O
Pathobiology — M,D
Pediatric Nursing — M
Pharmaceutical Sciences — M
Pharmacology — M,D
Physical Therapy — M,D,O
Physician Assistant Studies — M
Physics — M,D
Project Management — M
Psychiatric Nursing — M
Psychology—General — M,D
Public Health—General — M,D,O
Quantitative Analysis — M,D,O
Real Estate — M
Software Engineering — M,D,O
Special Education — M,D
Sports and Entertainment Law — M,D
Sports Management — M
Structural Engineering — M,D
Technical Communication — M
Technical Writing — M
Telecommunications — M
Textile Design — M
Therapies—Dance, Drama, and
  Music — M,O
Urban Design — M
Veterinary Sciences — M
Women's Health Nursing — M

DRURY UNIVERSITY
Business Administration and
  Management—General — M
Communication—General — M
Computer and Information
  Systems Security — O
Curriculum and Instruction — M
Education—General — M
Educational Leadership and
  Administration — M
Educational Media/Instructional
  Technology — M
Elementary Education — M
Middle School Education — M
Nonprofit Management — M
Reading Education — M
Secondary Education — M
Special Education — M

DUKE UNIVERSITY
Accounting — D
Acute Care/Critical Care Nursing — M,D,O
Adult Nursing — M,D,O
Allopathic Medicine — D
Anatomy — D
Art History — M,D
Art/Fine Arts — M,D
Asian Studies — M,O
Biochemistry — D
Bioethics — M
Bioinformatics — D,O
Biological and Biomedical
  Sciences—General — M,D
Biological Anthropology — D
Biomedical Engineering — M,D
Biopsychology — D
Biostatistics — M
Business Administration and
  Management—General — M,D,O
Business Analytics — M
Cancer Biology/Oncology — D
Cell Biology — D,O
Chemistry — D
Civil Engineering — M,D
Classics — D

Duke University (continued)

Clinical Laboratory Sciences/Medical Technology — M
Clinical Psychology — D
Clinical Research — M
Cognitive Sciences — D
Comparative Literature — D
Computational Biology — D,O
Computational Sciences — M,D
Computer Engineering — M,D
Computer Science — M,D
Cultural Anthropology — D
Developmental Biology — O
Developmental Psychology — D
Ecology — D,O
Economics — M,D
Education—General — M
Electrical Engineering — M,D
Energy Management and Policy — M,O
Engineering and Applied Sciences—General — M
Engineering Management — M
English — D
Entrepreneurship — M,O
Environmental and Occupational Health — O
Environmental Engineering — M,D
Environmental Management and Policy — D
Environmental Sciences — M,D
Ethics — M,O
Experimental Psychology — D
Family Nurse Practitioner Studies — M,D,O
Finance and Banking — M,D,O
French — D
Genetics — D
Genomic Sciences — D
Geology — M,D
Geosciences — M,D
German — D
Gerontological Nursing — M,D,O
Gerontology — M,D,O
Health Informatics — M
Health Psychology — D
Health Services Management and Hospital Administration — M,O
History — M,D
Human Development — D
Humanities — M
Immunology — D
Industrial and Manufacturing Management — M,D,O
International Business — M,O
International Development — M
International Health — M
Italian — D
Latin American Studies — M,D
Law — M,D
Liberal Studies — M
Management of Technology — M,O
Management Strategy and Policy — M,D,O
Marine Sciences — M,D
Marketing — M,D,O
Materials Engineering — M
Materials Sciences — M,D
Maternal and Child/Neonatal Nursing — M,D,O
Mathematics — D
Mechanical Engineering — M,D
Media Studies — M
Medical Physics — M,D
Microbiology — D
Molecular Biology — D,O
Molecular Biophysics — O
Molecular Genetics — D
Music — D
Natural Resources — M,D
Neurobiology — D
Neuroscience — D,O
Nurse Anesthesia — M,D,O
Nursing and Healthcare Administration — M,D,O
Nursing Education — M,D,O
Nursing Informatics — M,D,O
Nursing—General — D
Optical Sciences — M
Organizational Management — M,D,O
Paleontology — D
Pathology — M,D
Pediatric Nursing — M,D,O
Pharmacology — D
Philosophy — D
Photonics — M
Physical Therapy — D
Physician Assistant Studies — M
Physics — D
Political Science — M,D
Psychology—General — D
Public Policy — M,D
Quantitative Analysis — M,D,O
Religion — M,D
Slavic Languages — M,O
Sociology — M,D
Spanish — D
Statistics — M,D
Structural Biology — O
Theology — M,D
Toxicology — O
Women's Health Nursing — M,D,O

DUNLAP-STONE UNIVERSITY

Law — M

DUQUESNE UNIVERSITY

Accounting — M
Allied Health—General — M,D,O
Bioethics — M,D,O
Biological and Biomedical Sciences—General — D
Biotechnology — M
Business Administration and Management—General — M
Chemistry — D
Classics — M
Clinical Psychology — M,D,O

Communication Disorders — M,D
Communication—General — M,D
Counseling Psychology — M,D,O
Counselor Education — M,D,O
Curriculum and Instruction — M,O
Early Childhood Education — M
Education—General — M,D,O
Educational Leadership and Administration — M,D,O
Educational Measurement and Evaluation — M
Educational Media/Instructional Technology — M,D,O
Elementary Education — M
English as a Second Language — M
English Education — M
English — M,D
Environmental Management and Policy — M,O
Environmental Sciences — M,O
Family Nurse Practitioner Studies — M,O
Finance and Banking — M
Foreign Languages Education — M
Forensic Nursing — M,O
Forensic Sciences — M
Foundations and Philosophy of Education — M
Health Services Management and Hospital Administration — M,D
History — M
Law — M,D
Management Information Systems — M
Marketing — M
Marriage and Family Therapy — M,D
Mathematics Education — M
Mathematics — M
Medicinal and Pharmaceutical Chemistry — M,D
Middle School Education — M
Music Education — M,O
Music — M,O
Nursing Education — M,O
Nursing—General — M,D,O
Occupational Therapy — M,D
Organizational Management — M
Pharmaceutical Administration — M
Pharmaceutical Sciences — M,D
Pharmacology — M,D
Pharmacy — D
Philosophy — M,D
Physical Therapy — M,D
Physician Assistant Studies — M,D
Psychology—General — D
Public History — M
Reading Education — M
Rehabilitation Sciences — M,D
Rhetoric — M,D
School Psychology — M,D
Science Education — M
Secondary Education — M
Social Sciences Education — M
Special Education — M,D
Sports Management — M
Supply Chain Management — M
Sustainability Management — M
Theology — M,D

D'YOUVILLE COLLEGE

Anatomy — M
Business Administration and Management—General — M
Chiropractic — D
Education—General — M,D
Educational Leadership and Administration — M,D
Elementary Education — M,D
Family Nurse Practitioner Studies — M,D,O
Health Services Management and Hospital Administration — M,D,O
International Business — M
Nursing—General — M,D,O
Nutrition — M
Occupational Therapy — M
Pharmacy — D
Physical Therapy — D,O
Physician Assistant Studies — M
Secondary Education — M,D
Special Education — M,D

EARLHAM COLLEGE

Education—General — M

EARLHAM SCHOOL OF RELIGION

Pastoral Ministry and Counseling — M
Religion — M
Theology — M

EAST CAROLINA UNIVERSITY

Accounting — M
Addictions/Substance Abuse Counseling — M,D,O
Adult Education — M,O
Allied Health—General — M,D,O
Allopathic Medicine — D
American Studies — M
Anatomy — M,D
Anthropology — M
Applied Economics — M
Applied Physics — M,D
Art Education — M
Art/Fine Arts — M
Biochemistry — M,D
Biological and Biomedical Sciences—General — M,D
Biomedical Engineering — M
Biophysics — M,D
Biotechnology — M
Business Administration and Management—General — M,D,O
Business Education — M,O
Cell Biology — M,D
Chemistry — M,D
Child and Family Studies — M,D
Child Development — M,D
Clinical Psychology — M,D,O

Communication Disorders — M,D
Community College Education — M,D,O
Comparative Literature — M,D,O
Computer and Information Systems Security — M,D,O
Computer Engineering — M,D,O
Computer Science — M,D,O
Construction Management — M,O
Corporate and Organizational Communication — M,D,O
Counselor Education — M,D,O
Criminal Justice and Criminology — M,O
Curriculum and Instruction — M,O
Dentistry — D
Distance Education Development — M,O
Early Childhood Education — M,D
Economic Development — M,O
Education—General — M,D,O
Educational Leadership and Administration — M,D,O
Educational Media/Instructional Technology — M,O
Elementary Education — M,O
English as a Second Language — M,D,O
English Education — M,D,O
English — M,D,O
Environmental and Occupational Health — M,D,O
Exercise and Sports Science — M,D,O
Geographic Information Systems — M,O
Geography — M,O
Geology — M,O
Gerontology — M,O
Graphic Design — M
Health Communication — M,O
Health Education — M
Health Informatics — M,O
Health Physics/Radiological Health — M,D
Health Promotion — M
Health Psychology — M,D,O
Health Services Management and Hospital Administration — M,O
Higher Education — M,O
History — M
Hospitality Management — M,O
Hydrogeology — M,O
Illustration — M
Immunology — M,D
Industrial and Manufacturing Management — M,D,O
Industrial and Organizational Psychology — M,D,O
International Affairs — M,O
International and Comparative Education — M,O
Kinesiology and Movement Studies — M,D,O
Leisure Studies — M,O
Library Science — M,O
Linguistics — M,D,O
Logistics — M,D,O
Management Information Systems — M,D,O
Management of Technology — M,D,O
Marriage and Family Therapy — M,D
Maternal and Child Health — M,D,O
Mathematics Education — M,O
Mathematics — M
Medical Physics — M,D
Microbiology — M,D
Middle School Education — M
Military and Defense Studies — M
Molecular Biology — M,D
Music Education — M,O
Music — M,O
Nursing—General — M,D
Nutrition — M
Occupational Therapy — M,D,O
Pharmacology — M,D
Photography — M
Physical Education — M,D,O
Physical Therapy — D
Physician Assistant Studies — M
Physics — M,D
Physiology — M,O
Political Science — M,O
Public Administration — M,O
Public Health—General — M,D,O
Public History — M
Reading Education — M
Recreation and Park Management — M,O
Rehabilitation Counseling — M,D,O
Rehabilitation Sciences — M,D,O
Rhetoric — M,D,O
Rural Planning and Studies — M,O
Science Education — M
Social Sciences Education — M
Social Sciences — M,D,O
Social Work — M,O
Sociology — M
Software Engineering — M,O
Special Education — M,O
Sports Management — M,D,O
Statistics — M
Technical Communication — M,D,O
Telecommunications Management — M,D,O
Textile Design — M
Therapies—Dance, Drama, and Music — M,O
Toxicology — M,D
Urban and Regional Planning — M,O
Vocational and Technical Education — M,O
Western European Studies — M
Writing — M,D,O

EAST CENTRAL UNIVERSITY

Accounting — M
Clinical Psychology — M
Criminal Justice and Criminology — M
Education—General — M
Human Resources Management — M
Psychology—General — M
Rehabilitation Counseling — M

EASTERN CONNECTICUT STATE UNIVERSITY

Accounting — M
Early Childhood Education — M
Education—General — M
Educational Media/Instructional Technology — M
Elementary Education — M
Organizational Management — M
Secondary Education — M

EASTERN ILLINOIS UNIVERSITY

Accounting — M
Art Education — M
Art/Fine Arts — M
Biological and Biomedical Sciences—General — M
Business Administration and Management—General — M
Chemistry — M
Clinical Psychology — M,O
Communication—General — M
Computer and Information Systems Security — M
Computer Science — M
Counselor Education — M
Curriculum and Instruction — M
Early Childhood Education — M
Economics — M
Education—General — M,O
Educational Leadership and Administration — M,O
Elementary Education — M
Energy Management and Policy — M
Engineering and Applied Sciences—General — M,O
English — M
Geographic Information Systems — M
History — M
Mathematics Education — M
Mathematics — M
Middle School Education — M
Music Education — M
Music — M
Nutrition — M
Political Science — M
Psychology—General — M,O
School Psychology — M,O
Secondary Education — M
Special Education — M
Student Affairs — M
Sustainable Development — M
Systems Science — M,O

EASTERN KENTUCKY UNIVERSITY

Agricultural Education — M
Allied Health—General — M
Art Education — M
Biological and Biomedical Sciences—General — M
Business Administration and Management—General — M
Business Education — M
Chemistry — M
Clinical Psychology — M,O
Communication Disorders — M
Community Health — M
Counselor Education — M
Criminal Justice and Criminology — M
Curriculum and Instruction — M
Ecology — M
Education—General — M
Educational Leadership and Administration — M
Elementary Education — M
English Education — M
English — M
Environmental and Occupational Health — M
Exercise and Sports Science — M
Family Nurse Practitioner Studies — M
Geology — M,D
Health Education — M
Health Promotion — M
Health Services Management and Hospital Administration — M
Higher Education — M
History — M
Home Economics Education — M
Industrial and Organizational Psychology — M,O
Industrial Hygiene — M
Industrial/Management Engineering — M
Library Science — M
Manufacturing Engineering — M
Mathematics Education — M
Mathematics — M
Music Education — M
Music — M
Nursing—General — M
Nutrition — M
Occupational Therapy — M
Physical Education — M
Political Science — M
Psychology—General — M,O
Public Administration — M
Recreation and Park Management — M
School Psychology — M,O
Science Education — M
Secondary Education — M
Social Sciences Education — M
Special Education — M
Sports Management — M
Urban and Regional Planning — M
Vocational and Technical Education — M
Writing — M

EASTERN MENNONITE UNIVERSITY

Biological and Biomedical Sciences—General — M
Business Administration and Management—General — M

Conflict Resolution and Mediation/Peace Studies	M,O
Counselor Education	M
Curriculum and Instruction	M
Education—General	M
Health Services Management and Hospital Administration	M
Nonprofit Management	M
Nursing and Healthcare Administration	M,D
Nursing—General	M,D
Organizational Management	M
Pastoral Ministry and Counseling	M,O
Reading Education	M
Religion	M
School Nursing	M,D
Special Education	M
Theology	M,O

EASTERN MICHIGAN UNIVERSITY

Accounting	M
Adult Nursing	M,O
African-American Studies	O
Art Education	M
Art/Fine Arts	M
Arts Administration	M
Athletic Training and Sports Medicine	M,O
Biological and Biomedical Sciences—General	M
Business Administration and Management—General	M,O
Chemistry	M
Clinical Psychology	M,D
Clinical Research	M
Clothing and Textiles	M
Communication Disorders	M
Communication—General	M
Community College Education	M,D,O
Computer and Information Systems Security	O
Computer Science	M,O
Construction Management	M,O
Corporate and Organizational Communication	M,O
Counselor Education	M,O
Criminal Justice and Criminology	M
Cultural Studies	O
Curriculum and Instruction	M,O
Dance	M
Distance Education Development	M
Early Childhood Education	M
Economics	M,O
Education—General	M,D,O
Educational Leadership and Administration	M,D,O
Educational Measurement and Evaluation	M,O
Educational Media/Instructional Technology	M,O
Educational Policy	M
Educational Psychology	M,O
Electronic Commerce	M,O
Engineering and Applied Sciences—General	M
Engineering Management	M
English as a Second Language	M,O
English Education	M
English	M
Entrepreneurship	M,O
Exercise and Sports Science	M
Finance and Banking	M,O
Foreign Languages Education	M,O
Foundations and Philosophy of Education	M
Gender Studies	M,O
Geographic Information Systems	M,O
Geosciences	M
Gerontology	O
Health Education	M,O
Health Promotion	M,O
Health Services Management and Hospital Administration	M,O
Higher Education	M,D,O
Historic Preservation	M,O
History	M
Hospitality Management	O
Human Resources Management	M,O
Human Services	O
Interior Design	M
International Business	M,O
Kinesiology and Movement Studies	M
Linguistics	M
Management Information Systems	M,O
Management of Technology	D
Marketing	M,O
Mathematics	M
Middle School Education	M
Museum Education	O
Museum Studies	M,O
Music	M
Nonprofit Management	M,O
Nursing and Healthcare Administration	M,O
Nursing Education	M,O
Nutrition	M
Occupational Therapy	M
Organizational Management	M,O
Philosophy	M
Physical Education	M
Physician Assistant Studies	M
Physics	M
Physiology	M
Polymer Science and Engineering	M,O
Psychology—General	M,D
Public Policy	M,O
Quality Management	M,O
Reading Education	M,O
Science Education	M
Secondary Education	M

Social Sciences	M
Social Work	M
Sociology	M
Special Education	M,O
Sports Management	M
Student Affairs	M,D,O
Supply Chain Management	M,O
Sustainable Development	M,O
Technical Communication	M,O
Technology and Public Policy	M
Theater	M
Urban and Regional Planning	M,O
Urban Education	M
Women's Studies	M,O
Writing	M,O

EASTERN NAZARENE COLLEGE

Business Administration and Management—General	M
Counseling Psychology	M
Early Childhood Education	M,O
Education—General	M,O
Educational Leadership and Administration	M,O
Elementary Education	M,O
English as a Second Language	M,O
Marriage and Family Therapy	M
Middle School Education	M,O
Reading Education	M,O
Secondary Education	M,O
Special Education	M,O

EASTERN NEW MEXICO UNIVERSITY

Analytical Chemistry	M
Anthropology	M
Biochemistry	M
Biological and Biomedical Sciences—General	M
Business Administration and Management—General	M
Chemistry	M
Communication Disorders	M
Communication—General	M
Counselor Education	M
Curriculum and Instruction	M
Early Childhood Education	M
Education of the Gifted	M
Education—General	M
Educational Leadership and Administration	M
Educational Media/Instructional Technology	M
Elementary Education	M
English as a Second Language	M
English	M
Exercise and Sports Science	M
Multilingual and Multicultural Education	M
Nursing—General	M
Organic Chemistry	M
Physical Chemistry	M
Physical Education	M
Reading Education	M
Secondary Education	M
Special Education	M
Sports Management	M
Vocational and Technical Education	M

EASTERN OREGON UNIVERSITY

Business Administration and Management—General	M
Education—General	M
Elementary Education	M
Secondary Education	M

EASTERN SCHOOL OF ACUPUNCTURE AND TRADITIONAL MEDICINE

Acupuncture and Oriental Medicine	M

EASTERN UNIVERSITY

Business Administration and Management—General	M,D,O
Child and Family Studies	D
Communication—General	M,O
Counseling Psychology	M,O
Early Childhood Education	M,O
Educational Leadership and Administration	M,D,O
Elementary Education	M,O
English as a Second Language	M,O
English Education	M,O
Foreign Languages Education	M,O
Health Education	M,O
Health Services Management and Hospital Administration	M
International Affairs	M
International Development	M
Marriage and Family Therapy	D
Mathematics Education	M,O
Middle School Education	M,O
Missions and Missiology	M
Multilingual and Multicultural Education	M,O
Music	M,O
Nonprofit Management	D,O
Organizational Management	M,D,O
Physical Education	M,O
Public Administration	D,O
Reading Education	M,O
School Nursing	M,O
School Psychology	M,O
Science Education	M,O
Secondary Education	M,O
Social Sciences Education	M,O
Spanish	M,O
Special Education	M,O
Theology	M
Urban and Regional Planning	M

EASTERN VIRGINIA MEDICAL SCHOOL

Allopathic Medicine	D
Art Therapy	M

Biological and Biomedical Sciences—General	M,D
Biotechnology	M
Clinical Psychology	D
Medical/Surgical Nursing	M
Physician Assistant Studies	M
Public Health—General	M
Reproductive Biology	M
Vision Sciences	O

EASTERN WASHINGTON UNIVERSITY

Accounting	M
Adult Education	M
Applied Psychology	M
Biological and Biomedical Sciences—General	M
Business Administration and Management—General	M
Clinical Psychology	M
Communication Disorders	M
Communication—General	M
Computer Education	M
Computer Science	M
Counseling Psychology	M
Counselor Education	M
Curriculum and Instruction	M
Dental Hygiene	M
Early Childhood Education	M
Education—General	M
Educational Leadership and Administration	M
Elementary Education	M
English as a Second Language	M
English	M
Exercise and Sports Science	M
Experimental Psychology	M
Foundations and Philosophy of Education	M
History	M
Interdisciplinary Studies	M
Liberal Studies	M
Music Education	M
Music	M
Occupational Therapy	M
Physical Education	M
Physical Therapy	D
Psychology—General	M,O
Public Administration	M
Public Health—General	M
Reading Education	M
Recreation and Park Management	M
Rhetoric	M
School Psychology	O
Social Work	M
Sports Management	M
Technical Communication	M

EAST STROUDSBURG UNIVERSITY OF PENNSYLVANIA

Athletic Training and Sports Medicine	M
Biological and Biomedical Sciences—General	M
Communication Disorders	M
Communication—General	M
Computer Science	M
Early Childhood Education	M
Education—General	M,D
Educational Media/Instructional Technology	M
Elementary Education	M
Geography	M
Health Education	M
History	M
Physical Education	M
Political Science	M
Public Administration	M
Public Health—General	M
Reading Education	M
Rehabilitation Sciences	M
Secondary Education	M,D
Special Education	M
Sports Management	M

EAST TENNESSEE STATE UNIVERSITY

Accounting	M
Allied Health—General	M
Allopathic Medicine	D
Anatomy	D
Archives/Archival Administration	M,O
Art/Fine Arts	M
Biochemistry	D
Biological and Biomedical Sciences—General	M,D
Biostatistics	M,D,O
Business Administration and Management—General	M,O
Chemistry	M
Clinical Psychology	M,D
Communication Disorders	M,D
Communication—General	M,O
Community Health	M,D,O
Computer Art and Design	M
Computer Science	M,O
Counselor Education	M,O
Criminal Justice and Criminology	M,O
Curriculum and Instruction	M,O
Developmental Education	M,O
Early Childhood Education	M,D,O
Economic Development	M,O
Education—General	M,D,O
Educational Leadership and Administration	M,D,O
Educational Media/Instructional Technology	M,O
Elementary Education	M,O
English as a Second Language	M,O
English	M,O
Entrepreneurship	M,O
Environmental and Occupational Health	M,D,O
Epidemiology	M,D,O

Exercise and Sports Science	M,D
Experimental Psychology	D
Family Nurse Practitioner Studies	M,D,O
Geographic Information Systems	M,O
Geosciences	M,D,O
Gerontological Nursing	M
Gerontology	M,D,O
Health Services Management and Hospital Administration	M,D,O
History	M,O
Human Services	M
Information Science	M,O
International Health	M
Kinesiology and Movement Studies	M,D
Liberal Studies	M,O
Library Science	M,O
Management Strategy and Policy	M,O
Manufacturing Engineering	M
Marketing	M,O
Marriage and Family Therapy	M
Mathematics	M,O
Microbiology	M,D
Middle School Education	M,O
Nonprofit Management	M,O
Nursing and Healthcare Administration	M,D,O
Nursing Education	M,D,O
Nursing—General	M,D,O
Nutrition	M
Paleontology	M,O
Pediatric Nursing	M,D,O
Pharmaceutical Sciences	D
Pharmacology	D
Pharmacy	D
Physical Therapy	D
Physiology	D
Psychiatric Nursing	M,D,O
Psychology—General	D
Public Administration	M,O
Public Health—General	M,D,O
Reading Education	M,O
School Psychology	M
Secondary Education	M,O
Social Work	M
Sociology	M
Special Education	M,O
Sports Management	M,D
Translation and Interpretation	M,O
Urban and Regional Planning	M,O
Women's Health Nursing	M,D,O

EAST TEXAS BAPTIST UNIVERSITY

Business Administration and Management—General	M
Counseling Psychology	M
Education—General	M
Kinesiology and Movement Studies	M
Religion	M

EAST WEST COLLEGE OF NATURAL MEDICINE

Acupuncture and Oriental Medicine	M

ECCLESIA COLLEGE

Missions and Missiology	M

EC-COUNCIL UNIVERSITY

Computer and Information Systems Security	M

ECOLE HÔTELIÈRE DE LAUSANNE

Hospitality Management	M

ÉCOLE POLYTECHNIQUE DE MONTRÉAL

Aerospace/Aeronautical Engineering	M,D,O
Applied Mathematics	M,D,O
Biomedical Engineering	M,D,O
Chemical Engineering	M,D,O
Civil Engineering	M,D,O
Computer Engineering	M,D,O
Computer Science	M,D,O
Electrical Engineering	M,D,O
Engineering and Applied Sciences—General	M,D,O
Engineering Physics	M,D,O
Environmental Engineering	M,D,O
Geotechnical Engineering	M,D,O
Hydraulics	M,D,O
Industrial/Management Engineering	M,D,O
Management of Technology	M,D,O
Mechanical Engineering	M,D,O
Mechanics	M,D,O
Nuclear Engineering	M,D,O
Operations Research	M,D,O
Optical Sciences	M,D,O
Structural Engineering	M,D,O
Transportation and Highway Engineering	M,D,O

ECPI UNIVERSITY

Business Administration and Management—General	M
Computer and Information Systems Security	M
Management Information Systems	M

ECUMENICAL THEOLOGICAL SEMINARY

Pastoral Ministry and Counseling	D
Theology	M

EDEN THEOLOGICAL SEMINARY

Theology	M,D

EDGEWOOD COLLEGE

Accounting	M
Business Administration and Management—General	M
Education—General	M,D,O
Nursing—General	M,D
Sustainability Management	M

M—masters degree; D—doctorate; O—other advanced degree; *—Close-Up and/or Display

EDINBORO UNIVERSITY OF PENNSYLVANIA

Anthropology	M
Art Education	M
Art Therapy	M,O
Art/Fine Arts	M
Clinical Psychology	M,O
Communication Disorders	M
Communication—General	M
Counseling Psychology	M,O
Counselor Education	M,O
Early Childhood Education	M,O
Educational Leadership and Administration	M
Educational Psychology	M,O
Family Nurse Practitioner Studies	M,D
History	M
Middle School Education	M
Nursing Education	M,D
Nursing—General	M,D
Political Science	M
Reading Education	M,O
Rehabilitation Counseling	M,O
School Psychology	M,O
Secondary Education	M
Social Work	M
Special Education	M,O

EDP UNIVERSITY OF PUERTO RICO–SAN SEBASTIAN

Nursing—General	M

EDWARD VIA COLLEGE OF OSTEOPATHIC MEDICINE–CAROLINAS CAMPUS

Osteopathic Medicine	D

EDWARD VIA COLLEGE OF OSTEOPATHIC MEDICINE–VIRGINIA CAMPUS

Osteopathic Medicine	D

ELIZABETH CITY STATE UNIVERSITY

Applied Mathematics	M
Biological and Biomedical Sciences—General	M
Community College Education	M
Computer Science	M
Education—General	M
Educational Leadership and Administration	M
Elementary Education	M
Geographic Information Systems	M
Mathematics Education	M
Mathematics	M
Psychology—General	M
Science Education	M

ELIZABETHTOWN COLLEGE

Occupational Therapy	M

ELMEZZI GRADUATE SCHOOL OF MOLECULAR MEDICINE

Molecular Medicine	D

ELMHURST COLLEGE

Business Administration and Management—General	M
Communication Disorders	M
Data Science/Data Analytics	M
Educational Leadership and Administration	M
Geographic Information Systems	M
Health Services Management and Hospital Administration	M
Industrial and Organizational Psychology	M
Management Information Systems	M
Nursing—General	M
Occupational Therapy	M
Project Management	M
Public Health—General	M
Special Education	M
Supply Chain Management	M

ELMS COLLEGE

Accounting	M,O
Acute Care/Critical Care Nursing	M,D
Applied Behavior Analysis	M,O
Biological and Biomedical Sciences—General	M
Business Administration and Management—General	M,O
Early Childhood Education	M,O
Education—General	M,O
Elementary Education	M,O
English as a Second Language	M,O
English Education	M,O
Entrepreneurship	M,O
Family Nurse Practitioner Studies	M,D
Finance and Banking	M,O
Foreign Languages Education	M,O
Gerontological Nursing	M,D
Health Services Management and Hospital Administration	M,O
Nursing and Healthcare Administration	M,D
Nursing Education	M,D
Nursing—General	M,D
Reading Education	M,O
Religion	M
Science Education	M,O
Secondary Education	M,O
Social Sciences	M,O
Special Education	M,O

ELON UNIVERSITY

Business Administration and Management—General	M
Education—General	M
Elementary Education	M
Internet and Interactive Multimedia	M
Law	D
Physical Therapy	D
Physician Assistant Studies	M

EMBRY-RIDDLE AERONAUTICAL UNIVERSITY–DAYTONA

Aerospace/Aeronautical Engineering	M,D
Aviation	M
Business Administration and Management—General	M
Civil Engineering	M
Computer and Information Systems Security	M
Electrical Engineering	M
Engineering Physics	M,D
Ergonomics and Human Factors	M,D
Finance and Banking	M
Human Resources Management	M
Mechanical Engineering	M,D
Software Engineering	M
Systems Engineering	M

EMBRY-RIDDLE AERONAUTICAL UNIVERSITY–PRESCOTT

Aviation	M
Military and Defense Studies	M
Safety Engineering	M

EMBRY-RIDDLE AERONAUTICAL UNIVERSITY–WORLDWIDE

Aerospace/Aeronautical Engineering	M
Aviation Management	M
Business Administration and Management—General	M
Computer and Information Systems Security	M
Education—General	M
Engineering Management	M
Entrepreneurship	M
Environmental and Occupational Health	M
Finance and Banking	M
Human Resources Management	M
International Affairs	M
International Business	M
Logistics	M
Management Information Systems	M
Management of Technology	M
Project Management	M
Supply Chain Management	M
Systems Engineering	M

EMILY CARR UNIVERSITY OF ART + DESIGN

Applied Arts and Design—General	M
Art/Fine Arts	M
Computer Art and Design	M

EMMANUEL COLLEGE (UNITED STATES)

Business Administration and Management—General	M,O
Education—General	M,O
Human Resources Management	M,O
Nursing and Healthcare Administration	M,O
Nursing Education	M,O
Nursing—General	M,O
Special Education	M,O
Urban Education	M,O

EMORY & HENRY COLLEGE

American Studies	M,D
Education—General	M,D
History	M,D
Occupational Therapy	M,D
Organizational Management	M,D
Physical Therapy	M,D
Physician Assistant Studies	M,D
Reading Education	M,D

EMORY UNIVERSITY

Accounting	M,D
Adult Nursing	M
Allied Health—General	D
Allopathic Medicine	D
Anesthesiologist Assistant Studies	M
Animal Behavior	D
Anthropology	D
Art History	D
Biochemistry	D
Bioethics	M
Bioinformatics	M,D
Biological and Biomedical Sciences—General	D
Biostatistics	M,D
Business Administration and Management—General	M,D
Cancer Biology/Oncology	D
Cell Biology	D
Chemistry	D
Clinical Psychology	D
Clinical Research	M
Cognitive Sciences	D
Comparative Literature	D,O
Computer Science	M,D
Developmental Biology	D
Developmental Psychology	D
Ecology	D
Economics	D
Education—General	M,D
English	D,O
Entrepreneurship	M
Environmental and Occupational Health	M,D
Epidemiology	M,D
Ethics	M,D
Evolutionary Biology	D
Family Nurse Practitioner Studies	M
Film, Television, and Video Theory and Criticism	M,D,O
Finance and Banking	M,D
French	D
Genetic Counseling	M
Genetics	D
Health Education	M,D

EMORY UNIVERSITY (continued column)

Health Informatics	M,D
Health Promotion	M
Health Services Management and Hospital Administration	M,D
Health Services Research	M,D
History	D
Human Genetics	M
Immunology	D
Industrial and Manufacturing Management	M
Interdisciplinary Studies	D
International Business	M
International Health	M
Law	M,D,O
Management Information Systems	M,D
Marketing	M,D
Mathematics	M,D
Microbiology	D
Middle School Education	M,D
Molecular Biology	D
Molecular Genetics	D
Molecular Pathogenesis	D
Music	M
Neuroscience	D
Nurse Midwifery	M
Nursing and Healthcare Administration	M
Nursing—General	M,D
Nutrition	M,D
Organizational Management	M,D
Pastoral Ministry and Counseling	M,D
Pediatric Nursing	M
Pharmacology	D
Philosophy	D,O
Physical Therapy	D
Physician Assistant Studies	M
Physics	D
Political Science	D
Portuguese	D,O
Psychology—General	D
Public Health—General	M,D
Real Estate	M
Religion	D
Secondary Education	M,D
Sociology	D
Spanish	D,O
Sustainable Development	M
Theology	M,D
Women's Health Nursing	M
Women's Studies	D,O

EMPEROR'S COLLEGE OF TRADITIONAL ORIENTAL MEDICINE

Acupuncture and Oriental Medicine	M,D

EMPIRE COLLEGE

Law	M,D

EMPORIA STATE UNIVERSITY

Accounting	M
Art Therapy	M
Biological and Biomedical Sciences—General	M
Botany	M
Business Administration and Management—General	M
Cell Biology	M
Clinical Psychology	M
Counseling Psychology	M
Counselor Education	M
Curriculum and Instruction	M,O
Distance Education Development	M,O
Early Childhood Education	M
Education of the Gifted	M
Education—General	M
Educational Leadership and Administration	M
Educational Media/Instructional Technology	M,O
Elementary Education	M
English as a Second Language	M,O
English	M
Environmental Biology	M
Forensic Sciences	M,O
Geosciences	M,O
History	M
Industrial and Organizational Psychology	M
Library Science	M,D,O
Mathematics	M
Microbiology	M
Music	M
Physical Education	M
Psychology—General	M
Reading Education	M
Rehabilitation Counseling	M
School Psychology	M,O
Special Education	M
Zoology	M

ENDICOTT COLLEGE

Applied Behavior Analysis	M,D,O
Bioinformatics	M
Business Administration and Management—General	M
Computer and Information Systems Security	M,O
Distance Education Development	M
Early Childhood Education	M
Educational Leadership and Administration	M,D
Elementary Education	M
Emergency Management	M,O
Family Nurse Practitioner Studies	M,O
Homeland Security	M,O
Interior Design	M
International Health	M,O
Management Information Systems	M
Nursing and Healthcare Administration	M,O
Nursing Education	M,O
Nursing—General	M,O
Organizational Management	M
Reading Education	M
Secondary Education	M

EPIC BIBLE COLLEGE

Special Education	M,D,O
Sports Management	M
Ethics	M,D
Pastoral Ministry and Counseling	M,D

ERIKSON INSTITUTE

Child Development	M
Developmental Psychology	M,O
Early Childhood Education	M,D
English as a Second Language	M,O
Human Development	M,O
Social Work	M

ERSKINE THEOLOGICAL SEMINARY

Theology	M,D

ESSEC BUSINESS SCHOOL

Business Administration and Management—General	M,D
Hospitality Management	M,D
International Business	M,D

EVANGELICAL SEMINARY

Marriage and Family Therapy	M
Missions and Missiology	M
Pastoral Ministry and Counseling	M
Theology	M

EVANGELICAL SEMINARY OF PUERTO RICO

Theology	M,D

EVANGEL UNIVERSITY

Clinical Psychology	M
Counseling Psychology	M
Counselor Education	M
Curriculum and Instruction	M,D
Education—General	M
Educational Leadership and Administration	M,D
Organizational Management	M
Reading Education	M
School Psychology	M
Secondary Education	M
Social Sciences	M

EVERGLADES UNIVERSITY

Accounting	M
Aviation	M
Business Administration and Management—General	M
Entrepreneurship	M
Human Resources Management	M
Industrial and Manufacturing Management	M
Project Management	M
Public Health—General	M

THE EVERGREEN STATE COLLEGE

Education—General	M
Environmental Management and Policy	M
Public Administration	M

FAIRFIELD UNIVERSITY

Accounting	M,O
Addictions/Substance Abuse Counseling	M
American Studies	M
Applied Behavior Analysis	M
Applied Psychology	M,O
Business Administration and Management—General	M,O
Business Analytics	M,O
Child and Family Studies	M,O
Clinical Psychology	M,O
Communication—General	M
Computer and Information Systems Security	M,O
Computer Engineering	M,O
Counseling Psychology	M,O
Counselor Education	M,O
Data Science/Data Analytics	M,O
Education—General	M,O
Educational Media/Instructional Technology	M,O
Electrical Engineering	M,O
Elementary Education	M,O
Engineering and Applied Sciences—General	M,O
English as a Second Language	M,O
Family Nurse Practitioner Studies	M,O
Finance and Banking	M,O
Foundations and Philosophy of Education	M,O
Health Education	M,D
Internet and Interactive Multimedia	M,O
Management Information Systems	M,O
Management of Technology	M,O
Marketing	M,O
Marriage and Family Therapy	M,O
Mathematics	M
Mechanical Engineering	M,O
Multilingual and Multicultural Education	M,O
Nurse Anesthesia	M,D
Nursing and Healthcare Administration	M,D
Nursing—General	M,D
Pastoral Ministry and Counseling	M,O
Psychiatric Nursing	M,D
Public Administration	M
School Psychology	M,O
Secondary Education	M,O
Software Engineering	M,O
Special Education	M,O
Taxation	M,O
Telecommunications	M,O
Writing	M

FAIRLEIGH DICKINSON UNIVERSITY, FLORHAM CAMPUS

Accounting	M
Biological and Biomedical Sciences—General	M

Business Administration and Management—General M,O
Chemical Engineering M
Chemistry M
Clinical Psychology M
Computer Science M
Corporate and Organizational Communication M
Counseling Psychology M,O
Early Childhood Education M,O
Education—General M,O
Educational Leadership and Administration M
Educational Media/Instructional Technology M,O
Entrepreneurship M,O
Finance and Banking M,O
Gerontological Nursing M
Health Services Management and Hospital Administration M
Hospitality Management M
Human Resources Management M
Industrial and Organizational Psychology M
International Business M,O
Management of Technology M,O
Marketing M
Nursing—General M,O
Organizational Behavior M,O
Organizational Management M,O
Pharmacology M,O
Pharmacy D
Psychiatric Nursing M
Psychology—General M,O
Public Administration M
Reading Education M,O
Sports Management M
Supply Chain Management M
Sustainability Management O
Taxation M,O
Writing M

FAIRLEIGH DICKINSON UNIVERSITY, METROPOLITAN CAMPUS
Accounting M,O
Art/Fine Arts M
Biological and Biomedical Sciences—General M
Business Administration and Management—General M,O
Chemistry M
Clinical Laboratory Sciences/Medical Technology M
Clinical Psychology M,D
Communication—General M
Comparative Literature M
Computer Engineering M
Computer Science M
Criminal Justice and Criminology M
Curriculum and Instruction M,O
Early Childhood Education M
Education—General M,O
Educational Leadership and Administration M
Educational Media/Instructional Technology M,O
Electrical Engineering M
Electronic Commerce M
Engineering and Applied Sciences—General M
English M
Entrepreneurship M,O
Experimental Psychology M,O
Finance and Banking M,O
Forensic Psychology M
Foundations and Philosophy of Education M
Health Services Management and Hospital Administration M
History M
Homeland Security M
Hospitality Management M
Human Resources Management M,O
International Affairs M
International Business M
Management Information Systems M,O
Marketing M,O
Mathematics M
Media Studies M
Multilingual and Multicultural Education M
Nonprofit Management M,O
Nursing—General M,D,O
Pharmaceutical Administration M
Political Science M
Psychology—General M,D,O
Public Administration M,O
Reading Education M,O
School Psychology M,D
Science Education M
Special Education M
Sports Management M
Systems Science M
Taxation M

FAIRMONT STATE UNIVERSITY
Business Administration and Management—General M
Criminal Justice and Criminology M
Education—General M
Educational Media/Instructional Technology M
Exercise and Sports Science M
Health Promotion M
Reading Education M
Special Education M

FAITH BAPTIST BIBLE COLLEGE AND THEOLOGICAL SEMINARY
Pastoral Ministry and Counseling M
Religion M
Theology M

FAITH INTERNATIONAL UNIVERSITY
Theology M,D

FAITH THEOLOGICAL SEMINARY
Theology M,D

FARMINGDALE STATE COLLEGE
Construction Management M
Electrical Engineering M
Management of Technology M
Mechanical Engineering M

FASHION INSTITUTE OF TECHNOLOGY
Applied Arts and Design—General M
Art History M
Arts Administration M
Business Administration and Management—General M
Clothing and Textiles M
Illustration M
Marketing M
Museum Studies M

FAULKNER UNIVERSITY
Business Administration and Management—General M
Counselor Education M
Criminal Justice and Criminology M
Curriculum and Instruction M
Education—General M
Elementary Education M
Humanities M,D
Law D
Pastoral Ministry and Counseling M,D
Theology M,D

FAYETTEVILLE STATE UNIVERSITY
Business Administration and Management—General M
Criminal Justice and Criminology M
Educational Leadership and Administration M,D
Elementary Education M
Middle School Education M
Psychology—General M
Secondary Education M
Social Sciences Education M
Social Work M
Sociology M

FELICIAN UNIVERSITY
Adult Nursing M,O
Business Administration and Management—General M,D
Counseling Psychology M,D
Education—General M,O
Educational Leadership and Administration M,O
Entrepreneurship M,D
Family Nurse Practitioner Studies M,O
Gerontological Nursing M,O
Health Services Management and Hospital Administration M
Nursing and Healthcare Administration M,D,O
Nursing Education M,O
Nursing—General M,D,O
Religious Education M,O

FERRIS STATE UNIVERSITY
Allied Health—General M
Applied Arts and Design—General M
Art/Fine Arts M
Business Administration and Management—General M
Community College Education D
Criminal Justice and Criminology M
Curriculum and Instruction M
Developmental Education M
Education—General M
Educational Leadership and Administration D
Health Services Management and Hospital Administration M
Human Services M
Management Information Systems M
Nursing and Healthcare Administration M
Nursing Education M
Nursing Informatics M
Nursing—General M
Optometry D
Pharmacy D
Photography M
Project Management M
Public Health—General M
Social Work M
Special Education M
Supply Chain Management M

FIELDING GRADUATE UNIVERSITY
Child Development M,D,O
Clinical Psychology D,O
Developmental Psychology M,D,O
Early Childhood Education M,D,O
Education—General M,D
Human Development M,D,O
Media Studies M,D,O
Neuroscience O
Organizational Management O
Psychology—General M,D,O

FISHER COLLEGE
Business Administration and Management—General M
Management Strategy and Policy M

FISK UNIVERSITY
Biological and Biomedical Sciences—General M
Chemistry M
Clinical Psychology M

Physics M
Psychology—General M

FITCHBURG STATE UNIVERSITY
Accounting M
Art Education M,O
Biological and Biomedical Sciences—General M
Business Administration and Management—General M
Communication—General M,O
Computer Science M
Counseling Psychology M
Counselor Education M,O
Curriculum and Instruction M
Data Science/Data Analytics M
Early Childhood Education M
Educational Leadership and Administration M,O
Elementary Education M,O
English Education M,O
English M,O
Forensic Nursing M,O
Higher Education M,O
History M
Human Resources Management M
Interdisciplinary Studies O
Mathematics Education M
Middle School Education M
Psychology—General O
Reading Education O
Science Education M
Social Sciences Education M
Special Education M
Vocational and Technical Education M
Writing M

FIVE BRANCHES UNIVERSITY
Acupuncture and Oriental Medicine M,D

FIVE TOWNS COLLEGE
Early Childhood Education M,D
Music Education M,D
Music M,D

FLAGLER COLLEGE
Special Education M

FLORIDA AGRICULTURAL AND MECHANICAL UNIVERSITY
Accounting M
Adult Education M,D
Allied Health—General M,D
Architecture M
Biomedical Engineering M,D
Business Administration and Management—General M
Business Education M
Chemical Engineering M,D
Chemistry M
Civil Engineering M,D
Counselor Education M,D
Criminal Justice and Criminology M
Education—General M,D
Educational Leadership and Administration M,D
Electrical Engineering M,D
Elementary Education M
Engineering and Applied Sciences—General M,D
English Education M
Environmental Sciences M,D
Finance and Banking M
Health Services Research M,D
History M
Industrial/Management Engineering M,D
Journalism M
Landscape Architecture M
Law D
Management Information Systems M
Marketing M
Mathematics Education M
Mechanical Engineering M,D
Medicinal and Pharmaceutical Chemistry M,D
Nursing and Healthcare Administration M,D
Nursing—General M,D
Occupational Therapy M
Pharmaceutical Administration M,D
Pharmaceutical Sciences M,D
Pharmacology M,D
Pharmacy D
Physical Education M
Physical Therapy D
Physics M,D
Political Science M
Psychology—General M
Public Administration M
Public Health—General M
Science Education M
Secondary Education M
Social Psychology M
Social Sciences Education M
Social Sciences M
Social Work M
Software Engineering M
Sports Management M
Toxicology M,D
Vocational and Technical Education M

FLORIDA ATLANTIC UNIVERSITY
Accounting M
Adult Education M,D,O
Allopathic Medicine M,D
Anthropology M
Applied Arts and Design—General M
Applied Mathematics M,D
Art/Fine Arts M
Bioengineering M,D

Biological and Biomedical Sciences—General M,D
Business Administration and Management—General M
Chemistry M,D
Civil Engineering M
Communication Disorders M
Communication—General M,O
Comparative and Interdisciplinary Arts D
Comparative Literature M
Computer Engineering M,D
Computer Science M,D
Counselor Education M,D
Criminal Justice and Criminology M
Curriculum and Instruction M,D,O
Early Childhood Education M,D,O
Economics M
Education—General M,D,O
Educational Leadership and Administration M,D,O
Educational Media/Instructional Technology M
Electrical Engineering M,D
Elementary Education M
Engineering and Applied Sciences—General M,D
English as a Second Language M,D,O
English M
Entrepreneurship M
Environmental Education M
Environmental Engineering M
Exercise and Sports Science M
Film, Television, and Video Production M,O
French M
Geology M,D
Geosciences M,D
Graphic Design M
Health Promotion M
Health Services Management and Hospital Administration M
Higher Education M,D,O
History M
International Business M
Linguistics M
Management Information Systems M
Mathematics M,D
Mechanical Engineering M,D
Media Studies M,O
Multilingual and Multicultural Education M,D,O
Music M
Neuroscience D
Nonprofit Management M,D
Nursing and Healthcare Administration M,D,O
Nursing—General M,D,O
Ocean Engineering M,D
Physics M,D
Political Science M
Psychology—General M
Public Administration M,D
Reading Education M
Science Education M,D
Secondary Education M
Social Work M,D
Sociology M
Spanish M
Special Education M,D
Sports Management M
Statistics M
Theater M
Urban and Regional Planning M
Women's Studies M

FLORIDA COASTAL SCHOOL OF LAW
Law D

FLORIDA COLLEGE OF INTEGRATIVE MEDICINE
Acupuncture and Oriental Medicine M

FLORIDA GULF COAST UNIVERSITY
Accounting M
Allied Health—General M,D
Business Administration and Management—General M
Clinical Psychology M
Criminal Justice and Criminology M
Curriculum and Instruction M
Education of the Gifted M
Education—General M
Educational Leadership and Administration M
Elementary Education M
English as a Second Language M
English Education M
English M
Environmental Management and Policy M
Environmental Sciences M
Forensic Sciences M
History M
Interdisciplinary Studies M
Management Information Systems M
Mathematics Education M
Mathematics M
Middle School Education M
Nurse Anesthesia M
Nursing Education M
Occupational Therapy M
Physical Therapy D
Physician Assistant Studies M
Public Administration M
Reading Education M
School Psychology M
Science Education M
Social Sciences Education M
Social Work M
Special Education M
Taxation M

---

*M—masters degree; D—doctorate; O—other advanced degree; *—Close-Up and/or Display*

FLORIDA INSTITUTE OF TECHNOLOGY

Aerospace/Aeronautical Engineering	M,D
Applied Mathematics	M,D
Aviation	M,D
Biochemistry	M
Biological and Biomedical Sciences—General	M,D
Biomedical Engineering	M,D
Biotechnology	M,D
Business Administration and Management—General	M
Cell Biology	M
Chemical Engineering	M,D
Chemistry	M,D
Civil Engineering	M,D
Computer and Information Systems Security	M
Computer Engineering	M,D
Computer Science	M,D
Conservation Biology	M
Ecology	M,D
Electrical Engineering	M,D
Engineering and Applied Sciences—General	M,D
Engineering Management	M
Environmental Management and Policy	M
Environmental Sciences	M,D
Geosciences	M
Health Services Management and Hospital Administration	M
Human Resources Management	M
Information Science	M
Interdisciplinary Studies	M
International Business	M
Logistics	M
Management Information Systems	M
Marine Biology	M,D
Marine Sciences	M,D
Mechanical Engineering	M,D
Meteorology	M
Molecular Biology	M
Ocean Engineering	M,D
Oceanography	M,D
Operations Research	M,D
Physics	M,D
Planetary and Space Sciences	M,D
Psychology—General	M,D
Public Administration	M
Software Engineering	M
Systems Engineering	M

FLORIDA INTERNATIONAL UNIVERSITY

Accounting	M
Adult Education	M,D,O
Adult Nursing	M,D
African Studies	M
Allopathic Medicine	M,D
Applied Behavior Analysis	M,D
Architecture	M
Art Education	M,D,O
Art/Fine Arts	M,O
Asian Studies	M
Athletic Training and Sports Medicine	M
Biological and Biomedical Sciences—General	M,D
Biomedical Engineering	M,D
Biostatistics	M,D
Chemistry	M,D
Civil Engineering	M,D
Clinical Psychology	M,D,O
Cognitive Sciences	M,D
Communication Disorders	M
Communication—General	M
Computer and Information Systems Security	M,D
Computer Engineering	M,D
Computer Science	M,D
Construction Management	M
Counseling Psychology	M,D,O
Counselor Education	M,D,O
Criminal Justice and Criminology	M,D
Curriculum and Instruction	M,D,O
Data Science/Data Analytics	M,D
Developmental Psychology	M,D
Early Childhood Education	M,D,O
Economics	M,D
Educational Leadership and Administration	M,D,O
Educational Media/Instructional Technology	M,D,O
Electrical Engineering	M,D
Elementary Education	M,D,O
Emergency Management	M
Engineering and Applied Sciences—General	M,D
Engineering Management	M
English as a Second Language	M,D,O
English Education	M,D,O
English	M
Environmental and Occupational Health	M,D
Environmental Engineering	M,D
Environmental Management and Policy	M,D
Epidemiology	M,D
Finance and Banking	M
Foreign Languages Education	M,D,O
Forensic Sciences	M
Geosciences	M,D
Health Promotion	M,D
Health Services Management and Hospital Administration	M,D
Higher Education	M,D,O
History	M,D
Hospitality Management	M
Human Resources Development	M,D,O
Human Resources Management	M
Industrial and Organizational Psychology	M,D
Information Science	M,D

Interior Design	M,O
International Affairs	M,D
International and Comparative Education	M,D,O
International Business	M
Journalism	M
Landscape Architecture	M
Law	M,D
Liberal Studies	M
Linguistics	M
Management Information Systems	M,D
Marketing	M
Mass Communication	M
Materials Engineering	M,D
Materials Sciences	M,D
Mathematics Education	M,D,O
Mathematics	M,D
Mechanical Engineering	M,D
Multilingual and Multicultural Education	M,D,O
Museum Studies	M,O
Music Education	M
Music	M
Natural Resources	M
Neuroscience	M,D
Nurse Anesthesia	M,D
Nursing—General	M,D
Nutrition	M,D
Occupational Therapy	M
Pediatric Nursing	M,D
Physical Education	M,D,O
Physical Therapy	D
Physician Assistant Studies	M,D
Physics	M,D
Political Science	M,D
Psychiatric Nursing	M,D
Psychology—General	M,D
Public Administration	M,D
Public Affairs	M,D
Public Health—General	M,D
Reading Education	M,D,O
Real Estate	M
Recreation and Park Management	M,D,O
Rehabilitation Counseling	M,D
Religion	M
School Psychology	M,D,O
Science Education	M,D,O
Social Sciences Education	M,D,O
Social Work	M,D
Sociology	M,D
Spanish	M
Special Education	M,D,O
Sports Management	M,D,O
Statistics	M
Telecommunications	M,D
Urban Education	M,D,O
Writing	M

FLORIDA MEMORIAL UNIVERSITY

Business Administration and Management—General	M
Education—General	M
Elementary Education	M
Reading Education	M
Special Education	M

FLORIDA NATIONAL UNIVERSITY

Accounting	M
Business Administration and Management—General	M
Family Nurse Practitioner Studies	M
Finance and Banking	M
Health Services Management and Hospital Administration	M
Marketing	M
Nursing and Healthcare Administration	M
Nursing Education	M
Nursing—General	M
Public Administration	M

FLORIDA POLYTECHNIC UNIVERSITY

Computer Science	M
Engineering and Applied Sciences—General	M

FLORIDA SOUTHERN COLLEGE

Accounting	M
Adult Nursing	M
Business Administration and Management—General	M
Education—General	M,D
Family Nurse Practitioner Studies	M,D
Gerontological Nursing	M
Nursing and Healthcare Administration	M
Nursing Education	M
Nursing—General	M

FLORIDA STATE UNIVERSITY

Accounting	M,D
Actuarial Science	M,D
Allopathic Medicine	D
American Studies	M,D
Analytical Chemistry	M,D
Applied Behavior Analysis	M
Applied Economics	M,D
Applied Mathematics	M,D
Applied Social Research	M,D
Applied Statistics	M,D
Archaeology	M,D
Architecture	M
Art Education	M,D
Art History	M,D
Art Therapy	M,D
Art/Fine Arts	M
Arts Administration	M,D
Asian Studies	M
Atmospheric Sciences	M,D
Biochemistry	M,D
Biological and Biomedical Sciences—General	M,D
Biomathematics	M,D
Biomedical Engineering	M,D
Biopsychology	M,D
Biostatistics	M,D

Business Administration and Management—General	M,D
Cell Biology	M,D
Chemical Engineering	M,D
Child and Family Studies	M,D
Civil Engineering	M,D
Clinical Psychology	D
Cognitive Sciences	D
Computational Sciences	M,D
Computer and Information Systems Security	M,D
Corporate and Organizational Communication	M,D
Criminal Justice and Criminology	M,D
Cultural Studies	M,D
Curriculum and Instruction	M,D,O
Dance	M
Demography and Population Studies	M
Developmental Psychology	D
East European and Russian Studies	M
Ecology	M,D
Economics	M,D
Education—General	M,D,O
Educational Leadership and Administration	M,D,O
Educational Measurement and Evaluation	M,D,O
Educational Media/Instructional Technology	M,D,O
Educational Policy	M,D,O
Educational Psychology	M,D,O
Electrical Engineering	M,D
Energy and Power Engineering	M,D
Engineering and Applied Sciences—General	M,D
English as a Second Language	M,D,O
English Education	M,D,O
Environmental Engineering	M,D
Environmental Law	M
Environmental Sciences	M,D
Evolutionary Biology	M,D
Exercise and Sports Science	M,D
Family and Consumer Sciences—General	M
Family Nurse Practitioner Studies	D,O
Film, Television, and Video Production	M
Finance and Banking	M,D
Food Science and Technology	M,D
Foundations and Philosophy of Education	M,D,O
French	M,D
Geographic Information Systems	M
Geography	M,D
Geology	M,D
Geosciences	M,D
German	M
Health Education	M,D
Health Law	M,D
Higher Education	M,D,O
History	M,D
Human Development	M,D
Human Resources Management	M,D
Industrial/Management Engineering	M,D
Inorganic Chemistry	M,D
Insurance	M,D
Interior Design	M
International Affairs	M
International and Comparative Education	M,D,O
Italian	M
Law	M,D
Management Information Systems	M,D,O
Management Strategy and Policy	M,D
Manufacturing Engineering	M,D
Marine Sciences	M,D
Marketing	M,D
Marriage and Family Therapy	M,D
Materials Engineering	M,D
Materials Sciences	M,D
Mathematical and Computational Finance	M,D
Mechanical Engineering	M,D
Media Studies	M,D
Meteorology	M,D
Molecular Biology	M,D
Museum Studies	M,D
Music	M,D
Neuroscience	D
Nursing—General	D,O
Nutrition	M,D
Oceanography	M,D
Organic Chemistry	M,D
Organizational Behavior	M,D
Physical Chemistry	M,D
Physics	M,D
Political Science	M,D
Psychiatric Nursing	D,O
Public Administration	M,D,O
Public Health—General	M
Public History	M,D
Public Policy	M,D,O
Reading Education	M,D,O
Rhetoric	M,D
Risk Management	M,D
Science Education	M,D
Slavic Languages	M,D
Social Psychology	D
Social Work	M,D
Sociology	M,D
Spanish	M,D
Sports Management	M,D
Structural Biology	D
Taxation	M,D
Theater	M,D
Therapies—Dance, Drama, and Music	M,D
Urban and Regional Planning	M,D
Writing	M,D

FONTBONNE UNIVERSITY

Accounting	M
Art Education	M
Art/Fine Arts	M
Business Administration and Management—General	M
Communication Disorders	M
Computer Science	M
Curriculum and Instruction	M
Early Childhood Education	M
Education—General	M
Educational Media/Instructional Technology	M
Elementary Education	M
Family and Consumer Sciences-General	M
Health Communication	M
Middle School Education	M
Reading Education	M
Secondary Education	M
Special Education	M
Supply Chain Management	M
Theater	M

FORDHAM UNIVERSITY

Accounting	M,D
Applied Psychology	M,D
Applied Statistics	M,D
Biological and Biomedical Sciences—General	M,D,O
Business Administration and Management—General	M,D
Classics	M,D
Clinical Psychology	D
Clinical Research	M
Communication—General	M,D
Computer Science	M
Conservation Biology	M,D,O
Counseling Psychology	M,D
Counselor Education	M,D
Curriculum and Instruction	M,O
Data Science/Data Analytics	M,D
Developmental Psychology	D
Early Childhood Education	M,O
Economic Development	M,O
Economics	M,D,O
Education—General	M,D,O
Educational Leadership and Administration	M,D,O
Educational Psychology	M,D
Electronic Commerce	M,D
Elementary Education	M,O
Emergency Management	M
English as a Second Language	M,O
English	M,D
Entrepreneurship	M,D
Ethics	M,O
Finance and Banking	M,D
Health Services Management and Hospital Administration	M,D
History	M,D
Intellectual Property Law	M,D
International Affairs	M,O
International Development	M,O
International Economics	M,D,O
Investment Management	M,D
Law	M,D
Management Information Systems	M,D
Marketing	M,D
Mass Communication	M
Media Studies	M,D
Medieval and Renaissance Studies	M,O
Nonprofit Management	M,D
Pastoral Ministry and Counseling	M,D,O
Philosophy	M,D
Political Science	M
Psychology—General	M,D
Quantitative Analysis	M,D
Religion	M,D,O
Religious Education	M,D,O
School Psychology	M,D
Social Work	M,D
Special Education	M,O
Taxation	M,D
Theater	M
Theology	M,D
Urban Studies	M

FORT HAYS STATE UNIVERSITY

Art/Fine Arts	M
Biological and Biomedical Sciences—General	M
Business Administration and Management—General	M
Communication Disorders	M
Communication—General	M
Counselor Education	M
Education—General	M,O
Educational Leadership and Administration	M,O
Educational Media/Instructional Technology	M
English	M
Geography	M
Geology	M
Geosciences	M
Health Education	M
History	M
Liberal Studies	M
Nursing—General	M
Physical Education	M
Psychology—General	M
School Psychology	O
Special Education	M

FORT LEWIS COLLEGE

Educational Leadership and Administration	M,O

FORT VALLEY STATE UNIVERSITY

Animal Sciences	M
Counseling Psychology	M
Counselor Education	M,O
Environmental and Occupational Health	M

Public Health—General — M
Rehabilitation Counseling — M

FRAMINGHAM STATE UNIVERSITY
Art Education — M
Business Administration and
  Management—General — M
Counseling Psychology — M
Curriculum and Instruction — M
Early Childhood Education — M
Educational Leadership and
  Administration — M
Educational Media/Instructional
  Technology — M
Elementary Education — M
English as a Second Language — M,O
English — M
Health Services Management and
  Hospital Administration — M
Human Resources Management — M
Mathematics Education — M
Nursing and Healthcare
  Administration — M
Nursing Education — M
Nursing—General — M
Nutrition — M
Public Administration — M
Reading Education — M
Special Education — M

**FRANCISCAN MISSIONARIES OF OUR
LADY UNIVERSITY**
Family Nurse Practitioner Studies — M
Health Services Management and
  Hospital Administration — M,D
Nurse Anesthesia — D
Nursing—General — M,D
Nutrition — M,D
Physical Therapy — M,D
Physician Assistant Studies — M

FRANCISCAN SCHOOL OF THEOLOGY
Theology — M

**FRANCISCAN UNIVERSITY OF
STEUBENVILLE**
Business Administration and
  Management—General — M
Clinical Psychology — M
Counseling Psychology — M
Curriculum and Instruction — M
Education—General — M
Educational Leadership and
  Administration — M
Nursing—General — M
Philosophy — M
Theology — M

FRANCIS MARION UNIVERSITY
Applied Psychology — M,O
Business Administration and
  Management—General — M
Clinical Psychology — M,O
Communication Disorders — M
Counseling Psychology — M,O
Education—General — M
Family Nurse Practitioner Studies — M
Health Services Management and
  Hospital Administration — M
Nursing Education — M
Nursing—General — M
Physician Assistant Studies — M
Psychology—General — M,O
School Psychology — M,O
Special Education — M

FRANKLIN COLLEGE
Athletic Training and Sports
  Medicine — M

FRANKLIN PIERCE UNIVERSITY
Business Administration and
  Management—General — M,D,O
Curriculum and Instruction — M,D,O
Elementary Education — M,D,O
Energy Management and
  Policy — M,D,O
Health Services Management and
  Hospital Administration — M,D,O
Human Resources Management — M,D,O
Management Information Systems — M,D,O
Nursing and Healthcare
  Administration — M,D,O
Nursing Education — M,D,O
Physical Therapy — M,D,O
Physician Assistant Studies — M,D,O
Special Education — M,D,O
Sports Management — M,D,O
Sustainability Management — M,D,O
Telecommunications — M,D,O

FRANKLIN UNIVERSITY
Accounting — M
Business Administration and
  Management—General — M
Computer Science — M
Corporate and Organizational
  Communication — M
Criminal Justice and Criminology — M
Educational Media/Instructional
  Technology — M
Marketing — M

FRANKLIN UNIVERSITY SWITZERLAND
International Business — M

**FREDERICK S. PARDEE RAND
GRADUATE SCHOOL**
Public Policy — D

FREED-HARDEMAN UNIVERSITY
Accounting — M
Business Administration and
  Management—General — M

Counselor Education — M,O
Curriculum and Instruction — M,O
Education—General — M,O
Educational Leadership and
  Administration — M,O
Ethics — M
Management Strategy and Policy — M
Pastoral Ministry and Counseling — M
Special Education — M,O
Theology — M

FRESNO PACIFIC UNIVERSITY
Business Administration and
  Management—General — M
Conflict Resolution and
  Mediation/Peace Studies — M
Counselor Education — M
Curriculum and Instruction — M
Education—General — M,O
Educational Leadership and
  Administration — M
Educational Media/Instructional
  Technology — M
English as a Second Language — M
Family Nurse Practitioner Studies — M
Interdisciplinary Studies — M
Kinesiology and Movement Studies — M
Marriage and Family Therapy — M
Mathematics Education — M
Missions and Missiology — M
Nursing—General — M
Pastoral Ministry and Counseling — M
Reading Education — M
School Psychology — M
Science Education — M
Special Education — M
Student Affairs — M,O
Theology — M
Urban Studies — M

FRIENDS UNIVERSITY
Accounting — M
Health Services Management and
  Hospital Administration — M
Law — M
Logistics — M
Management Information Systems — M
Management Strategy and Policy — M
Marriage and Family Therapy — M
Supply Chain Management — M

FRONTIER NURSING UNIVERSITY
Family Nurse Practitioner Studies — M,D,O
Nurse Midwifery — M,D,O
Nursing—General — M,D,O*
Psychiatric Nursing — M,D,O
Women's Health Nursing — M,D,O

FROSTBURG STATE UNIVERSITY
Biological and Biomedical
  Sciences—General — M
Business Administration and
  Management—General — M
Computer Science — M
Conservation Biology — M
Counseling Psychology — M
Counselor Education — M
Curriculum and Instruction — M,D
Ecology — M
Education—General — M,D
Educational Leadership and
  Administration — M,D
Educational Media/Instructional
  Technology — M,D
Elementary Education — M,D
Fish, Game, and Wildlife
  Management — M
Interdisciplinary Studies — M,D
Nursing and Healthcare
  Administration — M
Nursing Education — M
Nursing—General — M
Psychology—General — M
Reading Education — M,D
Recreation and Park Management — M
Secondary Education — M,D
Special Education — M

FULLER THEOLOGICAL SEMINARY
Clinical Psychology — M,D,O
Marriage and Family Therapy — M,D,O
Missions and Missiology — M,D,O
Music — M,D,O
Pastoral Ministry and Counseling — M,D,O
Theology — M,D,O

FULL SAIL UNIVERSITY
Art/Fine Arts — M
Business Administration and
  Management—General — M
Computer Art and Design — M
Educational Media/Instructional
  Technology — M
Entertainment Management — M
Game Design and
  Development — M
Graphic Design — M
Internet and Interactive
  Multimedia — M
Journalism — M
Marketing — M
Media Studies — M
Writing — M

FURMAN UNIVERSITY
Chemistry — M
Curriculum and Instruction — M,O
Early Childhood Education — M,O
Education—General — M,O
Educational Leadership and
  Administration — M,O
English as a Second Language — M,O
Reading Education — M,O

Special Education — M,O

FUTURE GENERATIONS UNIVERSITY
Social Psychology — M
Sustainable Development — M
Urban and Regional Planning — M

GALLAUDET UNIVERSITY
Clinical Psychology — M,D,O
Communication Disorders — M,D,O
Counseling Psychology — M,D,O
Counselor Education — M,D,O
Early Childhood Education — M,D,O
Education—General — M,D,O
Elementary Education — M,D,O
International and Comparative
  Education — M,D,O
Linguistics — M,D,O
Multilingual and Multicultural
  Education — M,D,O
Neuroscience — M,D,O
Public Administration — M,D,O
School Psychology — M,D,O
Secondary Education — M,D,O
Social Work — M,D,O
Special Education — M,D,O
Translation and Interpretation — M,D,O

GANNON UNIVERSITY
Athletic Training and Sports
  Medicine — M
Business Administration and
  Management—General — M
Clinical Psychology — M
Computer Science — M
Counseling Psychology — M
Criminal Justice and Criminology — M
Curriculum and Instruction — M,O
Education—General — M,O
Educational Leadership and
  Administration — D,O
Electrical Engineering — M
Engineering Management — M
English as a Second Language — O
English — M
Environmental and Occupational
  Health — M
Environmental Engineering — M
Environmental Sciences — M
Exercise and Sports Science — M
Family Nurse Practitioner Studies — M,O
Finance and Banking — M
Health Communication — M
Human Resources Management — M
Information Science — M
Marketing — M
Mechanical Engineering — M
Nurse Anesthesia — M,O
Nursing and Healthcare
  Administration — M
Nursing—General — D
Occupational Therapy — M,D
Organizational Management — D
Pastoral Ministry and Counseling — M,O
Physical Therapy — D
Physician Assistant Studies — M
Public Administration — M
Reading Education — M,O
Software Engineering — M
Theology — M,O

GARDNER-WEBB UNIVERSITY
Business Administration and
  Management—General — M
Counseling Psychology — M
Cultural Studies — M,D
Curriculum and Instruction — M,D,O
Education—General — M,D,O
Educational Leadership and
  Administration — M,D,O
English Education — M
English — M
Exercise and Sports Science — M
Family Nurse Practitioner Studies — M,D
Missions and Missiology — M,D
Nursing—General — M,D
Organizational Management — M,D,O
Pastoral Ministry and Counseling — M,D
Physical Education — M
Physician Assistant Studies — M
Psychology—General — M
Religious Education — M,D
School Psychology — M
Theology — M,D

**GARRETT-EVANGELICAL
THEOLOGICAL SEMINARY**
Music — M,D
Pastoral Ministry and Counseling — M,D
Religious Education — M,D
Theology — M,D

GATEWAY SEMINARY
Early Childhood Education — M,D,O
Educational Leadership and
  Administration — M,D,O
Pastoral Ministry and Counseling — M,D,O
Theology — M,D,O

**GEISINGER COMMONWEALTH SCHOOL
OF MEDICINE**
Allopathic Medicine — D
Biological and Biomedical
  Sciences—General — M

**THE GENERAL THEOLOGICAL
SEMINARY**
Pastoral Ministry and Counseling — M,D,O
Religion — M,D,O
Theology — M,D,O

GENEVA COLLEGE
Business Administration and
  Management—General — M

Clinical Psychology — M
Counseling Psychology — M
Counselor Education — M
Education—General — M
Educational Leadership and
  Administration — M
Finance and Banking — M
Higher Education — M
Marketing — M
Marriage and Family Therapy — M
Nonprofit Management — M
Organizational Management — M
Pastoral Ministry and Counseling — M
Project Management — M
Psychology—General — M

GEORGE FOX UNIVERSITY
Accounting — M,D
Business Administration and
  Management—General — M,D
Clinical Psychology — M,D,O
Counseling Psychology — M,O
Counselor Education — M,O
Cultural Studies — M,D,O
Education—General — M,D,O
Educational Leadership and
  Administration — M,D,O
Educational Media/Instructional
  Technology — M,O
English as a Second Language — M,O
Finance and Banking — M,D
Human Resources Management — M,D
Marketing — M,D
Marriage and Family Therapy — M,D
Organizational Management — M,D
Pastoral Ministry and Counseling — M,D,O
Physical Therapy — D
Reading Education — M,O
School Psychology — M,O
Social Work — M
Special Education — M,O
Theology — M,D,O

GEORGE MASON UNIVERSITY
Accounting — M
Adult Nursing — M,D,O
Anthropology — M,D
Art Education — M
Art History — M
Art/Fine Arts — M
Arts Administration — M
Astronomy — M,D
Athletic Training and Sports
  Medicine — M,O
Atmospheric Sciences — D
Biochemistry — M,D
Bioengineering — D
Bioinformatics — M,D,O
Biological and Biomedical
  Sciences—General — M,D,O
Biostatistics — M,D,O
Business Administration and
  Management—General — M
Chemistry — M,D
Civil Engineering — M,D
Clinical Psychology — M,D,O
Cognitive Sciences — M,D,O
Communication—General — M,D,O
Community Health — M,O
Computational Biology — M,D,O
Computational Sciences — M,D,O
Computer and Information
  Systems Security — M
Computer Engineering — M,D,O
Computer Science — M,D,O
Conflict Resolution and
  Mediation/Peace Studies — M,D,O
Construction Engineering — M,D
Counselor Education — M
Criminal Justice and Criminology — M,D
Cultural Studies — D
Curriculum and Instruction — M
Data Science/Data Analytics — M,D,O
Developmental Psychology — M,D,O
Early Childhood Education — M
Economics — M,D
Education of the Gifted — M
Education—General — M,D,O
Educational Leadership and
  Administration — M,O
Educational Media/Instructional
  Technology — M
Educational Psychology — M,O
Electrical Engineering — M,D,O
Elementary Education — M
Engineering and Applied
  Sciences—General — M,D,O
English as a Second Language — M
English Education — M
English — M,D,O
Environmental Management
  and Policy — M,D
Environmental Sciences — M,D
Epidemiology — M,O
Ethics — M
Exercise and Sports Science — M
Family Nurse Practitioner Studies — M,D,O
Foreign Languages Education — M
Forensic Sciences — M
French — M
Gender Studies — M
Geographic Information Systems — M,D,O
Geography — M,D,O
Geosciences — M,D,O
Gerontological Nursing — M,D,O
Graphic Design — M
Health Informatics — M,D,O
Health Promotion — M,O
Health Services Management and
  Hospital Administration — M,D,O
Health Services Research — M,D,O

Higher Education	M,D,O
History	M,D,O
Human Resources Management	M
Industrial and Organizational Psychology	M,D,O
Information Science	M,D,O
Interdisciplinary Studies	M
International Affairs	M
International Business	M,O
International Health	M,O
Law	M,D
Linguistics	M,D,O
Logistics	M
Management Information Systems	M
Management of Technology	M
Mathematics Education	M
Mathematics	M,D
Military and Defense Studies	M
Music Education	M
Music	M,D,O
National Security	M,D,O
Near and Middle Eastern Studies	M,O
Neuroscience	M,D,O
Nursing and Healthcare Administration	M,D,O
Nursing Education	M,D,O
Nursing—General	M,D,O
Nutrition	M,O
Operations Research	M,D,O
Organizational Management	M
Philosophy	M
Physical Education	M
Physics	M,D
Political Science	M,D
Project Management	M,D
Psychiatric Nursing	M,D,O
Psychology—General	M,D,O
Public Administration	M
Public Affairs	M
Public Health—General	M,O
Public Policy	M,D
Reading Education	M
Rehabilitation Sciences	D,O
Religion	M
Rhetoric	M,D,O
Science Education	M
Secondary Education	M
Social Sciences Education	M
Social Work	M,D
Sociology	M
Spanish	M
Special Education	M,O
Sports Management	M,O
Statistics	M,D,O
Systems Biology	M,D,O
Systems Engineering	M,D,O
Transportation and Highway Engineering	M,D
Transportation Management	M
Women's Studies	M
Writing	M

GEORGETOWN COLLEGE

Education—General	M
Reading Education	M
Special Education	M

GEORGETOWN UNIVERSITY

Acute Care/Critical Care Nursing	M,D
Advertising and Public Relations	M
Allopathic Medicine	D
American Studies	M,D
Analytical Chemistry	D
Asian Studies	M
Biochemistry	M,D
Bioinformatics	M,O
Biological and Biomedical Sciences—General	D
Biostatistics	M,O
Business Administration and Management—General	M
Chemistry	D
Communication—General	M
Comparative Literature	M,D
Computer Science	M,D
Conflict Resolution and Mediation/Peace Studies	M
East European and Russian Studies	M
Economic Development	D
Economics	D
Educational Measurement and Evaluation	M
Emergency Management	M,D
English	M
Environmental Law	M,D
Epidemiology	M,O
Ethics	M,D
Family Nurse Practitioner Studies	M,D
Finance and Banking	M,D
German	M,D
Health Law	M,D
Health Physics/Radiological Health	M
Health Promotion	M,D
Health Services Management and Hospital Administration	M,D
History	M,D
Hospitality Management	M,D
Human Development	M,D
Human Resources Management	M,D
Humanities	M,D
Immunology	M,D
Industrial and Labor Relations	D
Industrial and Manufacturing Management	D
Infectious Diseases	M,D
Inorganic Chemistry	D
Interdisciplinary Studies	M,D
International Affairs	M,D
International Business	M
International Development	M
International Health	M,D
Internet and Interactive Multimedia	M
Journalism	M,D
Latin American Studies	M

Law	M,D
Liberal Studies	M,D
Linguistics	M,D
Management of Technology	M,D
Materials Sciences	D
Mathematics	M
Media Studies	M,D
Medieval and Renaissance Studies	M,D
Microbiology	M,D
Molecular Biology	M,D
Near and Middle Eastern Languages	M,O
Near and Middle Eastern Studies	M,O
Neuroscience	D
Nurse Anesthesia	M,D
Nurse Midwifery	M,D
Nursing Education	M,D
Nursing—General	M,D
Organic Chemistry	D
Pharmacology	M,D
Philosophy	M,D
Physiology	M,D
Political Science	M,D
Psychology—General	D
Public Health—General	M,D
Public Policy	M,D
Radiation Biology	M
Real Estate	M,D
Religion	M,D
Spanish	M,D
Sports Management	M
Statistics	M
Systems Engineering	M,D
Taxation	M,D
Theology	D
Theoretical Chemistry	D
Urban and Regional Planning	M,D
Western European Studies	M

THE GEORGE WASHINGTON UNIVERSITY

Accounting	M
Addictions/Substance Abuse Counseling	M
Adult Education	O
Adult Nursing	M,D,O
Aerospace/Aeronautical Engineering	M,D,O
Allopathic Medicine	D
American Studies	M,D
Analytical Chemistry	M,D
Anthropology	M,D
Applied Mathematics	M,D,O
Applied Psychology	D
Art Education	M
Art History	M
Art Therapy	M,O
Art/Fine Arts	M,O
Asian Studies	M
Biochemistry	D
Biological and Biomedical Sciences—General	M,D
Biomedical Engineering	M,D
Biostatistics	M,D
Biotechnology	M,D,O
Business Administration and Management—General	M,D,O
Business Analytics	M,O
Chemistry	M,D
Civil Engineering	M,D,O
Clinical Psychology	M,D
Cognitive Sciences	D
Communication Disorders	M
Communication—General	M
Community Health	M,D
Computer and Information Systems Security	M,D,O
Computer Engineering	M,D,O
Computer Science	M,D,O
Counselor Education	M,D,O
Criminal Justice and Criminology	M,O
Curriculum and Instruction	M,D,O
Dance	M,O
Decorative Arts	M
Distance Education Development	O
Early Childhood Education	M
East European and Russian Studies	M
Economics	M,D
Education—General	M,D,O
Educational Leadership and Administration	M,D,O
Educational Media/Instructional Technology	M,O
Educational Policy	M,D,O
Electrical Engineering	M,D,O
Elementary Education	M
Emergency Management	M,D,O
Engineering and Applied Sciences—General	M,D,O
Engineering Management	M,D,O
English	M,D
Environmental and Occupational Health	D
Environmental Engineering	M,D,O
Environmental Management and Policy	M
Epidemiology	M
Exercise and Sports Science	M
Family Nurse Practitioner Studies	M,D,O
Finance and Banking	M,D
Folklore	M,D
Foreign Languages Education	M
Forensic Psychology	M,D,O
Forensic Sciences	M,O
Gender Studies	O
Geography	M,O
Health Communication	M
Health Services Management and Hospital Administration	M,D,O
Health Services Research	M,D,O
Higher Education	M,D
Historic Preservation	M,D
History	M,D
Hospitality Management	M,O
Human Development	M

Human Resources Development	M,D,O
Human Resources Management	M,O
Immunology	D
Infectious Diseases	M,D,O
Inorganic Chemistry	M,D
Interior Design	M
International Affairs	M,D
International and Comparative Education	M,D
International Business	M,D
International Development	M,D
International Health	M,D
International Trade Policy	M
Investment Management	M,D
Latin American Studies	M
Law	M,D
Legal and Justice Studies	M,D,O
Management Information Systems	M,D
Management of Technology	M,D
Management Strategy and Policy	M,D,O
Marketing	M,D
Mass Communication	M,O
Materials Sciences	M,D
Mathematical and Computational Finance	M,D,O
Mathematics Education	M
Mathematics	M,D,O
Mechanical Engineering	M,D,O
Microbiology	M,D,O
Military and Defense Studies	M
Molecular Medicine	D
Multilingual and Multicultural Education	M,D,O
Museum Education	M
Museum Studies	M,D,O
National Security	M,D
Near and Middle Eastern Studies	M
Nonprofit Management	M,O
Nursing and Healthcare Administration	M,D,O
Nursing—General	M,D,O
Organic Chemistry	M,D
Organizational Management	M,O
Philosophy	M
Photography	M,O
Physical Chemistry	M,D
Physical Therapy	D
Physician Assistant Studies	M
Physics	M,D
Political Science	M,D
Project Management	M,D,O
Psychology—General	M,D,O
Public Administration	M,D
Public Affairs	M,O
Public Health—General	M,D
Public Policy	M,D
Publishing	M
Real Estate	O
Rehabilitation Counseling	M
Religion	M
Science Education	M
Secondary Education	M
Social Psychology	D
Sociology	M
Special Education	M,D,O
Sports Management	M,O
Statistics	M,D,O
Student Affairs	M
Systems Biology	D
Systems Engineering	M,D,O
Technology and Public Policy	M,O
Telecommunications	M,D,O
Theater	M,O
Toxicology	M,O
Travel and Tourism	M,O
Vocational and Technical Education	O
Western European Studies	M
Women's Studies	M,O

GEORGIA CAMPUS–PHILADELPHIA COLLEGE OF OSTEOPATHIC MEDICINE

Osteopathic Medicine	D
Pharmacy	D*
Physical Therapy	D*

GEORGIA COLLEGE & STATE UNIVERSITY

Accounting	M
Art Therapy	M
Biological and Biomedical Sciences—General	M
Business Administration and Management—General	M
Criminal Justice and Criminology	M
Curriculum and Instruction	M
Early Childhood Education	M
Education—General	M,O
Educational Leadership and Administration	M,O
Educational Media/Instructional Technology	M
English	M
Exercise and Sports Science	M
Health Education	M
Health Promotion	M
Kinesiology and Movement Studies	M
Logistics	M
Management Information Systems	M
Middle School Education	M
Music Education	M
Nursing—General	M,D,O
Physical Education	M
Public Administration	M
Secondary Education	M
Special Education	M,O
Therapies—Dance, Drama, and Music	M
Writing	M

GEORGIA INSTITUTE OF TECHNOLOGY

Aerospace/Aeronautical Engineering	M,D
Architecture	M,D
Artificial Intelligence/Robotics	D
Atmospheric Sciences	M,D

Bioengineering	M,D
Bioinformatics	M,D
Biological and Biomedical Sciences—General	M,D
Biomedical Engineering	D
Building Science	M,D
Business Administration and Management—General	M
Chemical Engineering	M,D
Chemistry	M,D
Civil Engineering	M,D
Computational Sciences	M,D
Computer and Information Systems Security	M
Computer Art and Design	M,D
Computer Engineering	M,D
Computer Science	M,D
Economic Development	M,D
Economics	M,D
Electrical Engineering	M,D
Engineering and Applied Sciences—General	M,D
Environmental Engineering	M
Environmental Management and Policy	M,D
Ergonomics and Human Factors	M,D
Geographic Information Systems	M,D
Geosciences	M,D
Health Physics/Radiological Health	M,D
Health Services Management and Hospital Administration	M
History of Science and Technology	M,D
Human-Computer Interaction	M
Industrial Design	M
Industrial/Management Engineering	M,D
International Affairs	M
International Business	M
Internet and Interactive Multimedia	M,D
Logistics	M
Management Information Systems	M
Materials Engineering	M,D
Mathematical and Computational Finance	M
Mathematics	M,D
Mechanical Engineering	M,D
Mechanics	M
Music	M,D
Nuclear Engineering	M,D
Operations Research	M,D
Paper and Pulp Engineering	M,D
Physics	M,D
Physiology	M,D
Psychology—General	M,D
Public Policy	M,D
Statistics	M
Systems Engineering	M
Urban and Regional Planning	M,D
Urban Design	M,D

GEORGIAN COURT UNIVERSITY

Applied Behavior Analysis	M,O
Business Administration and Management—General	M,O
Clinical Psychology	M,O
Computer Art and Design	M,O
Counseling Psychology	M,O
Counselor Education	M,O
Criminal Justice and Criminology	M,O
Education—General	M,O
Educational Leadership and Administration	M,O
Educational Media/Instructional Technology	M,O
Health Psychology	M,O
Homeland Security	M,O
Legal and Justice Studies	M,O
Nonprofit Management	M,O
School Psychology	M,O
Special Education	M,O
Theology	M,O

GEORGIA SOUTHERN UNIVERSITY

Accounting	M
Allied Health—General	M,D,O
Applied Economics	M,O
Applied Physics	M
Art/Fine Arts	M
Athletic Training and Sports Medicine	M,O
Biological and Biomedical Sciences—General	M
Biostatistics	M,D
Business Administration and Management—General	M
Civil Engineering	M
Clinical Psychology	M
Communication Disorders	M
Community Health	M,D
Computer and Information Systems Security	M,O
Computer Science	M
Construction Management	M
Corporate and Organizational Communication	M,O
Counseling Psychology	M
Counselor Education	M
Criminal Justice and Criminology	M,O
Curriculum and Instruction	M
Education—General	M,D,O
Educational Leadership and Administration	M,D,O
Educational Measurement and Evaluation	M,D,O
Educational Media/Instructional Technology	M,O
Electrical Engineering	M
Elementary Education	M
Energy and Power Engineering	M
Engineering and Applied Sciences—General	M,O
Engineering Management	M,O

English	M
Environmental and Occupational Health	M,D,O
Epidemiology	M,D
Family Nurse Practitioner Studies	M
Foreign Languages Education	M
Graphic Design	M
Health Education	M,D
Health Services Management and Hospital Administration	M,D
Higher Education	M,O
History	M,O
Kinesiology and Movement Studies	M
Logistics	D
Management Information Systems	M,O
Manufacturing Engineering	M,O
Mathematics	M
Mechanical Engineering	M
Middle School Education	M,O
Multilingual and Multicultural Education	D
Music Education	M
Music	M
Nonprofit Management	M,O
Nursing Education	O
Nursing—General	O
Nutrition	O
Physical Therapy	D
Psychiatric Nursing	M
Psychology—General	M,D
Public Administration	M,D
Public Health—General	M,D
Public History	M,O
Reading Education	M,O
School Psychology	M,O
Secondary Education	M,O
Sociology	M
Spanish	M
Special Education	M,O
Sports Management	M
Supply Chain Management	D
Systems Engineering	M
Writing	M,O

GEORGIA SOUTHWESTERN STATE UNIVERSITY

Business Administration and Management—General	M
Computer Science	M,O
Early Childhood Education	M,O
Education—General	M,O
English Education	M,O
Family Nurse Practitioner Studies	M,O
Health Informatics	M,O
Management Information Systems	M,O
Mathematics Education	M,O
Middle School Education	M,O
Nursing and Healthcare Administration	M,O
Nursing Education	M,O
Nursing Informatics	M,O
Nursing—General	M,O
Special Education	M,O

GEORGIA STATE UNIVERSITY

Accounting	M
Actuarial Science	M
Adult Nursing	M,D,O
African-American Studies	M
Allied Health—General	M
Analytical Chemistry	M,D
Anthropology	M
Art Education	M
Art History	M
Art/Fine Arts	M
Astronomy	D
Athletic Training and Sports Medicine	M
Biochemistry	M,D
Bioinformatics	M,D
Biological and Biomedical Sciences—General	M,D
Biostatistics	M,D
Business Administration and Management—General	M,D
Cell Biology	M,D
Chemistry	M,D
Clinical Psychology	D
Clothing and Textiles	M
Cognitive Sciences	D
Communication Disorders	M,D
Communication—General	M,D
Computer Science	M,D
Counseling Psychology	M,O
Counselor Education	M,O
Criminal Justice and Criminology	M,D,O
Cultural Studies	M,O
Curriculum and Instruction	M,D
Developmental Psychology	D
Early Childhood Education	M,D,O
Economic Development	M,D
Economics	M,D
Education of Students with Severe/Multiple Disabilities	M,D
Education—General	M,D,O
Educational Leadership and Administration	M,D,O
Educational Measurement and Evaluation	M,D
Educational Media/Instructional Technology	M,D
Educational Policy	M,D,O
Educational Psychology	M,D
Elementary Education	M,D,O
Emergency Management	M,D,O
English Education	M,D
English	M,D
Entrepreneurship	M,D
Environmental Biology	M,D
Environmental Management and Policy	M,D,O

Exercise and Sports Science	M
Family Nurse Practitioner Studies	M,D,O
Film, Television, and Video Production	M,D
Finance and Banking	M,D,O
Foreign Languages Education	M,O
Forensic Sciences	M
Foundations and Philosophy of Education	M,D
French	M,O
Gender Studies	M,O
Geochemistry	M,D
Geographic Information Systems	O
Geography	M,D
Geology	M
Geosciences	M,D,O
German	O
Gerontology	M
Graphic Design	M
Health Education	M
Health Informatics	M,D,O
Health Services Management and Hospital Administration	M,D,O
Historic Preservation	M,D
History	M,D
Human Development	M,D,O
Human Resources Management	M,D
Human Services	M
Industrial and Labor Relations	M
Information Science	M,D,O
Insurance	M,D,O
Interior Design	M
International Business	M
Kinesiology and Movement Studies	D
Latin American Studies	M,O
Law	D
Linguistics	M,D
Management Information Systems	M,D,O
Management Strategy and Policy	M,D
Marketing	M,D
Mass Communication	M,D
Mathematics Education	M,D
Mathematics	M,D
Media Studies	M,D
Microbiology	M,D
Middle School Education	M,D
Molecular Biology	M,D
Molecular Genetics	M,D
Music Education	M,D
Neurobiology	M,D
Neuroscience	M
Nonprofit Management	M,D,O
Nursing and Healthcare Administration	M,D,O
Nursing Informatics	M,D,O
Nursing—General	M,D,O
Nutrition	M
Occupational Therapy	M
Operations Research	M,D
Organic Chemistry	M,D
Organizational Management	M,D
Pediatric Nursing	M,D,O
Philosophy	M
Photography	M
Physical Chemistry	M,D
Physical Education	M
Physical Therapy	D
Physics	M,D
Physiology	M
Political Science	M,D
Psychiatric Nursing	M,D,O
Psychology—General	D
Public Administration	M,D,O
Public Health—General	M,D,O
Public History	M,D
Public Policy	M,D
Reading Education	M,D
Real Estate	M,D,O
Rehabilitation Counseling	M
Religion	M
Rhetoric	M,D
Risk Management	M,D,O
School Psychology	M,D,O
Science Education	M,D
Secondary Education	M,D
Social Psychology	D
Social Sciences Education	M,D
Social Work	M,O
Sociology	M,D
Spanish	M,O
Special Education	D
Speech and Interpersonal Communication	M,D
Sports Management	M,D
Statistics	M,D
Taxation	M
Translation and Interpretation	O
Urban and Regional Planning	M,D,O
Urban Education	M,D
Women's Health Nursing	M,D,O
Women's Studies	M,O
Writing	M,D

GERSTNER SLOAN KETTERING GRADUATE SCHOOL OF BIOMEDICAL SCIENCES

Biological and Biomedical Sciences—General	D
Cancer Biology/Oncology	D*

GLION INSTITUTE OF HIGHER EDUCATION

Hospitality Management	M

GLOBAL UNIVERSITY

Missions and Missiology	M,D
Pastoral Ministry and Counseling	M,D
Religious Education	M,D
Theology	M,D

GODDARD COLLEGE

Art Therapy	M

Business Administration and Management—General	M
Clinical Psychology	M
Comparative and Interdisciplinary Arts	M
Education—General	M
Health Promotion	M
Interdisciplinary Studies	M
Psychology—General	M
Sustainability Management	M
Writing	M

GOLDEN GATE UNIVERSITY

Accounting	M,D,O
Business Administration and Management—General	M,D,O
Business Analytics	M,D,O
Entrepreneurship	M,D,O
Environmental Law	M,D
Finance and Banking	M,D,O
Forensic Sciences	M,O
Human Resources Management	M,D,O
Intellectual Property Law	M,D
International Business	M,D,O
Law	M,D
Legal and Justice Studies	M,D
Management Information Systems	M,D,O
Management of Technology	M,D,O
Marketing	M,D,O
Project Management	M,D,O
Psychology—General	M,D,O
Public Administration	M,D,O
Supply Chain Management	M,D,O
Taxation	M,D,O

GOLDEY-BEACOM COLLEGE

Business Administration and Management—General	M
Finance and Banking	M
Health Services Management and Hospital Administration	M
Human Resources Management	M
International Business	M
Management Information Systems	M
Marketing	M
Taxation	M

GOLDFARB SCHOOL OF NURSING AT BARNES-JEWISH COLLEGE

Acute Care/Critical Care Nursing	M
Gerontological Nursing	M
Nurse Anesthesia	M
Nursing and Healthcare Administration	M
Nursing—General	M

GONZAGA UNIVERSITY

Accounting	M
Business Administration and Management—General	M
Education—General	M,D
Educational Leadership and Administration	M,D
Elementary Education	M,D
Engineering and Applied Sciences—General	M,O
English as a Second Language	M
Law	D
Marriage and Family Therapy	M,D
Nursing—General	M,D
Organizational Management	M,D
Philosophy	M
Physiology	M,D
Secondary Education	M,D
Special Education	M,D
Sports Management	M,D
Taxation	M,D
Theology	M

GORDON COLLEGE

Early Childhood Education	M,O
Education—General	M,O
Educational Leadership and Administration	M,O
Elementary Education	M,O
English as a Second Language	M,O
Finance and Banking	M
Mathematics Education	M,O
Middle School Education	M,O
Music Education	M
Reading Education	M,O
Secondary Education	M,O
Special Education	M,O

GORDON-CONWELL THEOLOGICAL SEMINARY

Archaeology	M,D
Missions and Missiology	M,D
Pastoral Ministry and Counseling	M,D
Religion	M,D
Theology	M,D

GOSHEN COLLEGE

Environmental Education	M
Family Nurse Practitioner Studies	M
Nursing—General	M

GOUCHER COLLEGE

Arts Administration	M
Biological and Biomedical Sciences—General	O
Computer Art and Design	M
Cultural Studies	M
Education—General	M,O
Educational Leadership and Administration	M,O
Educational Media/Instructional Technology	M,O
Elementary Education	M,O
Historic Preservation	M
Middle School Education	M,O
Physical Education	M,O
Reading Education	M,O

Secondary Education	M,O
Special Education	M,O
Writing	M

GOVERNORS STATE UNIVERSITY

Accounting	M
Actuarial Science	M
Addictions/Substance Abuse Counseling	M
Analytical Chemistry	M
Art/Fine Arts	M
Business Administration and Management—General	M
Communication Disorders	M
Communication—General	M
Computer Science	M
Counseling Psychology	M
Criminal Justice and Criminology	M
Early Childhood Education	M
Education—General	M
Educational Leadership and Administration	M,D
English	M
Environmental Biology	M
Film, Television, and Video Production	M
Health Services Management and Hospital Administration	M
Human Services	M,D
Legal and Justice Studies	M
Management Information Systems	M
Mathematics	M
Nursing—General	M
Occupational Therapy	M
Photography	M
Physical Therapy	D
Political Science	M
Psychology—General	M
Public Administration	M
Reading Education	M
Social Work	M
Special Education	M

GRACE COLLEGE

Clinical Psychology	M

GRACE COLLEGE OF DIVINITY

Religion	M

GRACELAND UNIVERSITY (IA)

Curriculum and Instruction	M
Education—General	M
Educational Leadership and Administration	M
Educational Media/Instructional Technology	M
Family Nurse Practitioner Studies	M,D,O
Gerontological Nursing	M,D,O
Nursing Education	M,D,O
Nursing—General	M,D,O
Organizational Management	M,D,O
Reading Education	M
Religion	M
Special Education	M
Theology	M

GRACE MISSION UNIVERSITY

Missions and Missiology	M,D

GRACE SCHOOL OF THEOLOGY

Theology	M

GRACE THEOLOGICAL SEMINARY

Cultural Studies	M,D,O
Missions and Missiology	M,D,O
Pastoral Ministry and Counseling	M,D,O
Theology	M,D,O
Women's Studies	M,D,O

THE GRADUATE CENTER, CITY UNIVERSITY OF NEW YORK

Accounting	D
Anthropology	D
Archaeology	D
Architectural History	D
Art History	D
Biochemistry	D
Biological and Biomedical Sciences—General	D
Biopsychology	D
Business Administration and Management—General	D
Chemistry	D
Classics	M,D
Clinical Psychology	D
Cognitive Sciences	D
Communication Disorders	D
Comparative Literature	M,D
Computer Science	D
Criminal Justice and Criminology	D
Cultural Anthropology	D
Data Science/Data Analytics	M
Developmental Psychology	D
Economics	D
Educational Psychology	D
English	D
Environmental Sciences	D
Experimental Psychology	D
Finance and Banking	D
French	D
Geographic Information Systems	M
Geosciences	D
Hispanic and Latin American Languages	D
History	D
Humanities	M
Industrial and Organizational Psychology	D
Italian	M,D
Liberal Studies	M
Linguistics	M,D
Management Information Systems	D
Mathematics	D

---

*M—masters degree; D—doctorate; O—other advanced degree; *—Close-Up and/or Display*

Music	D
Neuroscience	M,D
Nursing—General	D
Organizational Behavior	D
Philosophy	M,D
Physics	D
Political Science	M,D
Psychology—General	D
Publishing	M
Quantitative Analysis	M
Social Psychology	D
Social Sciences	D
Social Work	D
Sociology	D
Theater	D
Urban Education	D

GRADUATE THEOLOGICAL UNION

Art History	M,D,O
Cultural Studies	M,D,O
Ethics	M,D,O
Jewish Studies	M,D,O
Religion	M,D,O
Social Sciences	M,D,O
Theology	M,D,O

GRAMBLING STATE UNIVERSITY

Counselor Education	M,D,O
Criminal Justice and Criminology	M
Curriculum and Instruction	M,D,O
Developmental Education	M,D,O
Education—General	M,D,O
Educational Leadership and Administration	M,D,O
Educational Media/Instructional Technology	M,D,O
English	M,D,O
Family Nurse Practitioner Studies	M,O
Health Services Management and Hospital Administration	M
Higher Education	M,D,O
Human Resources Management	M
Mass Communication	M
Mathematics Education	M,D,O
Nursing—General	M,O
Political Science	M
Public Administration	M
Reading Education	M,D,O
Science Education	M,D,O
Social Sciences Education	M
Social Work	M
Special Education	M
Sports Management	M
Student Affairs	M,D,O

GRAND CANYON UNIVERSITY

Accounting	M
Acute Care/Critical Care Nursing	M,D,O
Business Administration and Management—General	M,D
Business Analytics	M
Cognitive Sciences	D
Curriculum and Instruction	M,D,O
Data Science/Data Analytics	D
Early Childhood Education	M,D,O
Education of the Gifted	M,D,O
Education—General	M,D,O
Educational Leadership and Administration	M,D,O
Educational Media/Instructional Technology	M,D,O
Elementary Education	M,D,O
Emergency Management	M
English as a Second Language	M,D,O
Entrepreneurship	M
Family Nurse Practitioner Studies	M,D,O
Finance and Banking	M
Health Informatics	M,D,O
Health Services Management and Hospital Administration	M,D,O
Human Resources Management	M
Industrial and Organizational Psychology	D
Management of Technology	M
Marketing	M,D
Nursing Education	M,D,O
Nursing—General	M,D,O
Organizational Management	M,D
Pastoral Ministry and Counseling	D
Project Management	M
Psychology—General	D
Public Health—General	M,D,O
Reading Education	M,D,O
Science Education	M,D,O
Secondary Education	M,D,O
Special Education	M,D,O
Sports Management	M

GRAND RAPIDS THEOLOGICAL SEMINARY OF CORNERSTONE UNIVERSITY

Interdisciplinary Studies	M
Pastoral Ministry and Counseling	M
Religion	M
Theology	M

GRAND VALLEY STATE UNIVERSITY

Accounting	M
Adult Education	M
Allied Health—General	M,D
Bioinformatics	M
Biological and Biomedical Sciences—General	M
Biostatistics	M
Business Administration and Management—General	M
Cancer Biology/Oncology	M
Cell Biology	M
Communication Disorders	M
Communication—General	M
Computer Engineering	M
Computer Science	M
Criminal Justice and Criminology	M
Curriculum and Instruction	M
Early Childhood Education	M
Education—General	M
Educational Leadership and Administration	M,O
Educational Media/Instructional Technology	M
Electrical Engineering	M
Elementary Education	M
Engineering and Applied Sciences—General	M
English as a Second Language	M
English Education	M
English	M
Health Services Management and Hospital Administration	M
Higher Education	M
Information Science	M
Linguistics	M
Management Information Systems	M
Manufacturing Engineering	M
Mechanical Engineering	M
Medical Informatics	M
Middle School Education	M
Molecular Biology	M
Nonprofit Management	M
Nursing and Healthcare Administration	M,D
Nursing Education	M,D
Nursing—General	M,D
Nutrition	M
Occupational Therapy	M
Physical Therapy	D
Physician Assistant Studies	M
Public Administration	M
Public Health—General	M
Reading Education	M
School Psychology	M,O
Secondary Education	M
Social Work	M
Software Engineering	M
Special Education	M
Taxation	M

GRAND VIEW UNIVERSITY

Athletic Training and Sports Medicine	M,O
Educational Leadership and Administration	M,O
Nursing and Healthcare Administration	M,O
Nursing Education	M,O
Organizational Management	M,O
Sports Management	M,O
Urban Education	M,O

GRANITE STATE COLLEGE

Business Administration and Management—General	M
Educational Leadership and Administration	M
Organizational Management	M
Project Management	M

GRANTHAM UNIVERSITY

Business Administration and Management—General	M,O
Engineering and Applied Sciences—General	M
Health Services Management and Hospital Administration	M
Human Resources Development	M,O
Human Resources Management	M,O
Management Information Systems	M,O
Management Strategy and Policy	M,O
Nursing and Healthcare Administration	M
Nursing Education	M
Nursing Informatics	M
Nursing—General	M
Project Management	M

GRATZ COLLEGE

Education—General	M
Educational Leadership and Administration	M,D
Holocaust and Genocide Studies	M,D
Jewish Studies	M,O
Nonprofit Management	M
Religious Education	M,D
Social Work	M,O

GREENSBORO COLLEGE

Cultural Studies	M
Education—General	M
Elementary Education	M
English as a Second Language	M
Ethics	M
Special Education	M
Theology	M

GREENVILLE UNIVERSITY

Education—General	M
Elementary Education	M
Pastoral Ministry and Counseling	M
Secondary Education	M

GUILFORD COLLEGE

Criminal Justice and Criminology	M

GWYNEDD MERCY UNIVERSITY

Adult Nursing	M,D
Business Administration and Management—General	M
Counselor Education	M,D
Education—General	M,D
Educational Leadership and Administration	M
Family Nurse Practitioner Studies	M,D
Gerontological Nursing	M,D
Health Services Management and Hospital Administration	M
Management Strategy and Policy	M
Nursing Education	M,D
Nursing—General	M,D
Oncology Nursing	M,D
Pediatric Nursing	M,D
Special Education	M,D

HALLMARK UNIVERSITY

Business Administration and Management—General	M
International Business	M

HAMLINE UNIVERSITY

Business Administration and Management—General	M,D
Education—General	M,D
English as a Second Language	M,D
Environmental Education	M,D
Nonprofit Management	M,D
Public Administration	M,D
Reading Education	M,D
Science Education	M,D
Writing	M

HAMPTON UNIVERSITY

Allied Health—General	M
Applied Mathematics	M
Atmospheric Sciences	M,D
Biological and Biomedical Sciences—General	M
Business Administration and Management—General	M
Chemistry	M
Communication Disorders	M
Community Health Nursing	M,D
Computational Sciences	M
Computer and Information Systems Security	M
Computer Science	M
Counselor Education	M,D,O
Education—General	M,D,O
Educational Leadership and Administration	M,D
English Education	M
Environmental Biology	M
Family Nurse Practitioner Studies	M,D
Liberal Studies	M,D,O
Marriage and Family Therapy	M
Mathematics Education	M
Medical Physics	M,D
Middle School Education	M
Nursing and Healthcare Administration	M,D
Nursing Education	M,D
Nursing—General	M,D
Organizational Behavior	M
Pastoral Ministry and Counseling	M,D,O
Physical Therapy	D
Physics	M,D
Planetary and Space Sciences	M,D
Psychology—General	M
Sports Management	M
Statistics	M
Student Affairs	M,D,O

HANNIBAL-LAGRANGE UNIVERSITY

Education—General	M
Reading Education	M

HARDING SCHOOL OF THEOLOGY

Pastoral Ministry and Counseling	M,D
Theology	M,D

HARDING UNIVERSITY

Allied Health—General	M,D
Art Education	M,O
Business Administration and Management—General	M
Communication Disorders	M
Counselor Education	M,O
Early Childhood Education	M,O
Education—General	M,O
Educational Leadership and Administration	M,O
Elementary Education	M,O
English as a Second Language	M,O
English Education	M,O
Foreign Languages Education	M,O
Health Education	M,O
International Business	M
Mathematics Education	M,O
Organizational Management	M
Pastoral Ministry and Counseling	M
Pharmacy	D
Physical Therapy	D
Physician Assistant Studies	M
Reading Education	M,O
Secondary Education	M,O
Social Sciences Education	M,O
Special Education	M,O

HARDIN-SIMMONS UNIVERSITY

Business Administration and Management—General	M
Counseling Psychology	M
Counselor Education	M
Education of the Gifted	M
Education—General	M,D
Educational Leadership and Administration	D
Family Nurse Practitioner Studies	M
Higher Education	D
Information Science	M
Kinesiology and Movement Studies	M
Marriage and Family Therapy	M
Maternal and Child/Neonatal Nursing	M
Music Education	M
Music	M
Nursing Education	M
Nursing—General	M
Pastoral Ministry and Counseling	M,D
Physical Therapy	D
Physician Assistant Studies	M,D
Psychology—General	M
Reading Education	M
Recreation and Park Management	M
Religion	M
Sports Management	M
Theology	M

HARRISBURG UNIVERSITY OF SCIENCE AND TECHNOLOGY

Computer and Information Systems Security	M
Educational Media/Instructional Technology	M
Entrepreneurship	M
Human-Computer Interaction	M
Management Information Systems	M
Management of Technology	M
Management Strategy and Policy	M
Project Management	M
Software Engineering	M
Systems Engineering	M
Systems Science	M

HARRISON MIDDLETON UNIVERSITY

Comparative Literature	M,D
Education—General	M,D
Humanities	M,D
Interdisciplinary Studies	M,D
Legal and Justice Studies	M,D
Philosophy	M,D
Religion	M,D
Science Education	M,D
Social Sciences	M,D

HARTFORD SEMINARY

Pastoral Ministry and Counseling	M,D,O
Religion	M,D,O
Theology	M,D,O

HARVARD UNIVERSITY

Accounting	D
African Studies	D
African-American Studies	D
Allopathic Medicine	D
American Studies	D
Anthropology	M,D
Applied Mathematics	M,D
Applied Physics	M,D
Applied Science and Technology	M,O
Archaeology	M,D
Architectural History	D
Architecture	M,D
Art Education	M
Art History	M,D
Asian Languages	M,D
Asian Studies	M,D
Astronomy	D
Astrophysics	D
Biochemistry	D
Bioengineering	M,D
Biological and Biomedical Sciences—General	M,D,O
Biological Anthropology	M,D
Biomedical Engineering	D
Biophysics	D
Biopsychology	D
Biostatistics	M,D
Biotechnology	M,O
Business Administration and Management—General	M,D,O
Cell Biology	D
Celtic Languages	D
Chemical Physics	D
Chemistry	D
Chinese	D
Classics	D
Cognitive Sciences	M,D
Communication—General	M,O
Comparative Literature	D
Computational Biology	M
Computational Sciences	M,D
Computer Science	M,D
Curriculum and Instruction	M
Demography and Population Studies	M,D
Dentistry	M,D,O
Developmental Psychology	M
East European and Russian Studies	M
Economics	D
Education—General	M,D
Educational Leadership and Administration	M,D
Educational Media/Instructional Technology	M,O
Educational Policy	M
Educational Psychology	M
Electrical Engineering	M,D
Engineering and Applied Sciences—General	M,D
Engineering Design	M,D
English	M,D,O
Environmental and Occupational Health	M,D
Environmental Engineering	M,D
Environmental Management and Policy	M,D
Environmental Sciences	M,D
Epidemiology	M,D
Ergonomics and Human Factors	M,D
Evolutionary Biology	D
Experimental Psychology	D
Forestry	M
Foundations and Philosophy of Education	M,O
French	M,D
Genetics	M,D
Geosciences	D
German	D
Health Promotion	M,D
Health Services Management and Hospital Administration	M,D
History of Science and Technology	M,D
History	M
Human Development	M
Industrial and Manufacturing Management	D
Information Science	M,D,O
Inorganic Chemistry	D
International Affairs	D
International and Comparative Education	M

International Development — M
International Health — M,D
Italian — D
Japanese — D
Jewish Studies — M,O
Journalism — M,D
Landscape Architecture — M,D
Law — D
Legal and Justice Studies — D
Liberal Studies — M,O
Linguistics — D
Management of Technology — D
Management Strategy and Policy — D
Marketing — D
Materials Sciences — M,D
Mathematics Education — M,O
Mathematics — D
Mechanical Engineering — M,D
Medical Physics — D
Medieval and Renaissance Studies — D
Microbiology — D
Molecular Biology — D
Molecular Genetics — D
Molecular Pharmacology — D
Museum Studies — M,O
Music — M,D
Near and Middle Eastern Languages — M,D
Near and Middle Eastern Studies — M,D
Neurobiology — D
Neuroscience — D
Nutrition — D
Oral and Dental Sciences — M,D,O
Organic Chemistry — D
Organizational Behavior — D
Pathology — D
Philosophy — M,D
Physical Chemistry — D
Physics — D
Planetary and Space Sciences — M,D
Political Science — M,D
Portuguese — M,D
Psychology—General — D
Public Administration — M
Public Health—General — M,D*
Public Policy — M,D
Quantitative Analysis — M,D
Reading Education — M
Religion — D
Russian — D
Scandinavian Languages — D
Slavic Languages — D
Social Psychology — D
Sociology — D
Spanish — M,D
Statistics — M,D
Systems Biology — D
Technical Communication — M
Theology — M
Theoretical Physics — D
Urban and Regional Planning — M,D
Urban Design — M

HASTINGS COLLEGE
Education—General — M

HAWAI'I PACIFIC UNIVERSITY
Business Administration and Management—General — M
Clinical Psychology — M
Communication—General — M
Educational Leadership and Administration — M
Elementary Education — M
English as a Second Language — M
Finance and Banking — M
Human Resources Management — M
International Business — M
Liberal Studies — M
Management Information Systems — M
Marine Sciences — M
Marketing — M
Military and Defense Studies — M
Nursing—General — M,D
Organizational Management — M
Public Administration — M
Public Health—General — M
Secondary Education — M
Social Work — M
Sustainable Development — M

HAZELDEN BETTY FORD GRADUATE SCHOOL OF ADDICTION STUDIES
Addictions/Substance Abuse Counseling — M,O

HEBREW COLLEGE
Early Childhood Education — M,O
Education—General — M,O
Jewish Studies — M,O
Middle School Education — M,O
Music Education — M,O
Music — M,O
Religious Education — M,O
Special Education — M,O
Theology — M

HEBREW UNION COLLEGE–JEWISH INSTITUTE OF RELIGION (NY)
Education—General — M
Jewish Studies — M
Music — M
Near and Middle Eastern Languages — M
Nonprofit Management — M
Religious Education — M
Theology — M,D

HEC MONTREAL
Accounting — M,D,O
Applied Economics — M,D
Arts Administration — O
Business Administration and Management—General — M,D,O

Business Analytics — M
Corporate and Organizational Communication — O
Data Science/Data Analytics — D
Electronic Commerce — M,O
Entrepreneurship — M,O
Finance and Banking — M,D,O
Financial Engineering — M,D
Human Resources Development — O
Human Resources Management — M,D,O
Industrial and Manufacturing Management — M
International Business — M,D
Logistics — M
Management Information Systems — M
Management Strategy and Policy — M
Marketing — M,D
Medical Microbiology — D
Operations Research — O
Organizational Management — M
Supply Chain Management — M,O
Sustainable Development — O
Taxation — M,O

HEIDELBERG UNIVERSITY
Business Administration and Management—General — M
Counseling Psychology — M
Education—General — M
Music Education — M

HENDERSON STATE UNIVERSITY
Business Administration and Management—General — M
Counseling Psychology — M,O
Counselor Education — M,O
Curriculum and Instruction — M,O
Early Childhood Education — M,O
Education—General — M,O
Educational Leadership and Administration — M,O
English as a Second Language — M,O
Liberal Studies — M
Middle School Education — M,O
Physical Education — M
Special Education — M,O
Sports Management — M

HENDRIX COLLEGE
Accounting — M

HENLEY-PUTNAM SCHOOL OF STRATEGIC SECURITY
Conflict Resolution and Mediation/Peace Studies — M
Homeland Security — M
Military and Defense Studies — M
National Security — D

HERITAGE CHRISTIAN UNIVERSITY
Classics — M
Pastoral Ministry and Counseling — M
Religion — M

HERITAGE COLLEGE AND SEMINARY
Theology — M,O

HERITAGE UNIVERSITY
Counselor Education — M
Education—General — M
Educational Leadership and Administration — M
English as a Second Language — M
English — M
Multilingual and Multicultural Education — M
Reading Education — M
Science Education — M
Special Education — M

HERZING UNIVERSITY ONLINE
Accounting — M
Business Administration and Management—General — M
Health Services Management and Hospital Administration — M
Human Resources Management — M
Management of Technology — M
Marketing — M
Nursing and Healthcare Administration — M
Nursing Education — M
Nursing—General — M
Project Management — M

HIGH POINT UNIVERSITY
Athletic Training and Sports Medicine — M,D
Business Administration and Management—General — M,D
Corporate and Organizational Communication — M,D
Educational Leadership and Administration — M,D
Elementary Education — M,D
Mathematics Education — M,D
Pharmacy — M,D
Physical Therapy — M,D
Physician Assistant Studies — M,D
Secondary Education — M,D
Special Education — M,D

HIGH TECH HIGH GRADUATE SCHOOL OF EDUCATION
Educational Leadership and Administration — M

HILBERT COLLEGE
Criminal Justice and Criminology — M
Health Services Management and Hospital Administration — M
Public Administration — M

HILLSDALE COLLEGE
Political Science — M,D

HIRAM COLLEGE
Interdisciplinary Studies — M

HODGES UNIVERSITY
Accounting — M
Business Administration and Management—General — M
Clinical Psychology — M
Counseling Psychology — M
Health Services Management and Hospital Administration — M
Legal and Justice Studies — M
Management Information Systems — M

HOFSTRA UNIVERSITY
Accounting — M,O
Advertising and Public Relations — M
Allopathic Medicine — D
Applied Behavior Analysis — M,D,O
Art Education — M,D,O
Art Therapy — M,O
Bioethics — M,D,O
Biological and Biomedical Sciences—General — M
Business Administration and Management—General — M,O
Business Education — M,D,O
Clinical Psychology — M,D
Communication Disorders — M,D,O
Computer and Information Systems Security — M
Counseling Psychology — M,O
Counselor Education — M,O
Early Childhood Education — M,D,O
Education of Students with Severe/Multiple Disabilities — M,D,O
Education of the Gifted — M,D,O
Education—General — M,D,O
Educational Leadership and Administration — M,D,O
Educational Media/Instructional Technology — M,D,O
Elementary Education — M,D,O
Engineering and Applied Sciences—General — M
English as a Second Language — M,D,O
English Education — M,D,O
English — M
Entertainment Management — M,O
Exercise and Sports Science — M,O
Family and Consumer Sciences-General — M,D,O
Family Nurse Practitioner Studies — M
Finance and Banking — M,O
Foreign Languages Education — M,D,O
Gerontological Nursing — M
Health Education — M,D,O
Health Informatics — M,O
Health Law — M,D,O
Health Services Management and Hospital Administration — M
Higher Education — M,D,O
Human Resources Management — M,O
Industrial and Organizational Psychology — M,D
Intellectual Property Law — M,D,O
International Business — M,O
Investment Management — M,O
Journalism — M
Law — M,D,O
Legal and Justice Studies — M,D,O
Linguistics — M
Management Information Systems — M,O
Management Strategy and Policy — M,O
Marketing Research — M,O
Marketing — M,O
Marriage and Family Therapy — M,O
Mathematics Education — M,D,O
Mathematics — M,D,O
Medical Physics — M
Middle School Education — M,D,O
Molecular Medicine — D
Multilingual and Multicultural Education — M,D,O
Music Education — M,D,O
Nursing and Healthcare Administration — M,D,O
Nursing—General — M
Occupational Therapy — M,O
Physical Education — M,D,O
Physician Assistant Studies — M
Psychiatric Nursing — M
Psychology—General — M,D
Public Health—General — M,O
Quality Management — M,O
Quantitative Analysis — M,O
Reading Education — M,D,O
Rehabilitation Counseling — M,O
School Psychology — M,D
Science Education — M,D,O
Secondary Education — M,D,O
Social Psychology — M,D
Social Sciences Education — M,D,O
Special Education — M,D,O
Sports Management — M
Sustainable Development — M
Taxation — M,O
Urban Design — M
Writing — M

HOLLINS UNIVERSITY
Art/Fine Arts — M
Dance — M
Education—General — M
English — M,O
Film, Television, and Video Production — M
Film, Television, and Video Theory and Criticism — M
Humanities — M
Illustration — M,O
Interdisciplinary Studies — M

Liberal Studies — M
Music — M
Social Sciences — M
Theater — M,O
Writing — M,O

HOLMES INSTITUTE
Pastoral Ministry and Counseling — M

HOLY APOSTLES COLLEGE AND SEMINARY
Theology — M,O

HOLY CROSS GREEK ORTHODOX SCHOOL OF THEOLOGY
Theology — M

HOLY FAMILY UNIVERSITY
Accounting — M
Business Administration and Management—General — M
Counseling Psychology — M
Criminal Justice and Criminology — M
Early Childhood Education — M
Education—General — M,D
Educational Leadership and Administration — M,D
Elementary Education — M
English as a Second Language — M
Finance and Banking — M
Health Services Management and Hospital Administration — M
Human Resources Management — M
Management Information Systems — M
Nursing and Healthcare Administration — M
Nursing Education — M
Nursing—General — M
Reading Education — M
Special Education — M

HOLY NAMES UNIVERSITY
Business Administration and Management—General — M
Counseling Psychology — M
Education—General — M,O
Educational Psychology — M,O
Family Nurse Practitioner Studies — M
Finance and Banking — M
Forensic Psychology — M
Marketing — M
Music Education — M,O
Music — M,O
Nursing and Healthcare Administration — M,O
Nursing Informatics — M
Nursing—General — M
Pastoral Ministry and Counseling — M
Special Education — M,O
Urban Education — M,O
Writing — M

HOOD COLLEGE
Accounting — M,O
Art/Fine Arts — M,O
Bioinformatics — M,O
Biological and Biomedical Sciences—General — M
Business Administration and Management—General — M,O
Clinical Psychology — M
Computer and Information Systems Security — M,O
Computer Science — M,O
Curriculum and Instruction — M,O
Education—General — M,O
Educational Leadership and Administration — M,O
Elementary Education — M,O
Environmental Biology — M,O
Geographic Information Systems — M,O
Humanities — M,O
Information Science — M,O
Management Information Systems — M,O
Mathematics Education — M,O
Middle School Education — M,O
Organizational Management — M,D,O
Reading Education — M,O
School Psychology — M
Science Education — M,O
Secondary Education — M,O
Special Education — M,O
Systems Science — M

HOOD THEOLOGICAL SEMINARY
Theology — M,D

HOPE INTERNATIONAL UNIVERSITY
Education—General — M
Educational Leadership and Administration — M
Elementary Education — M
International Business — M
International Development — M
Marketing — M
Marriage and Family Therapy — M
Missions and Missiology — M
Music — M
Nonprofit Management — M
Religion — M
Secondary Education — M

HOUGHTON COLLEGE
Music — M

HOUSTON BAPTIST UNIVERSITY
Addictions/Substance Abuse Counseling — M
Art/Fine Arts — M
Business Administration and Management—General — M,D
Counseling Psychology — M
Counselor Education — M,D
Curriculum and Instruction — M,D

---

*M—masters degree; D—doctorate; O—other advanced degree; *—Close-Up and/or Display*

Education—General M,D
Educational Leadership and Administration M,D
Educational Measurement and Evaluation M,D
Educational Media/Instructional Technology M,D
Elementary Education M
English as a Second Language M,D
English Education M
English M,D
Family Nurse Practitioner Studies M
Higher Education M,D
Human Resources Management M
International Business M
Kinesiology and Movement Studies M
Liberal Studies M
Marriage and Family Therapy M
Mathematics M,D
Middle School Education M
Multilingual and Multicultural Education M,D
Music M
Near and Middle Eastern Languages M
Nursing—General M
Pastoral Ministry and Counseling M
Pediatric Nursing M
Philosophy M
Psychology—General M,D
Reading Education M,D
Religious Education M,D
School Psychology M
Science Education M,D
Spanish M
Special Education M
Sports Management M
Theology M

HOUSTON GRADUATE SCHOOL OF THEOLOGY
Pastoral Ministry and Counseling M,D
Theology M,D

HOWARD PAYNE UNIVERSITY
Business Administration and Management—General M
Criminal Justice and Criminology M
Educational Leadership and Administration M
Pastoral Ministry and Counseling M
Sports Management M
Theology M

HOWARD UNIVERSITY
Accounting M
African Studies M,D
Allied Health—General M,D
Allopathic Medicine D
Analytical Chemistry M,D
Anatomy M,D
Applied Arts and Design—General M
Applied Mathematics M,D
Art History M
Art/Fine Arts M
Atmospheric Sciences M,D
Biochemistry M,D
Biological and Biomedical Sciences—General M,D
Biophysics D
Biopsychology M,D
Biotechnology M,D
Business Administration and Management—General M
Chemical Engineering M
Chemistry M,D
Civil Engineering M
Clinical Psychology M,D
Communication Disorders M,D
Communication—General M,D
Computer Science M
Corporate and Organizational Communication M,D
Counseling Psychology D
Counselor Education M
Dentistry D,O
Developmental Psychology M,D
Economics M,D
Education—General M,D,O
Educational Leadership and Administration M,D,O
Educational Policy M,D,O
Educational Psychology D
Electrical Engineering M,D
Elementary Education M
Engineering and Applied Sciences—General M,D
English M,D
Environmental Sciences M,D
Exercise and Sports Science M
Experimental Psychology M,D
Family Nurse Practitioner Studies M
Film, Television, and Video Production M
Finance and Banking M
French M
Health Education M,D
History M,D
Human Resources Management M
Inorganic Chemistry M,D
International Business M,D
Law M,D
Leisure Studies M
Management Information Systems M
Marketing M
Mass Communication M,D
Mathematics M,D
Mechanical Engineering M,D
Media Studies M,D
Microbiology D
Molecular Biology M,D
Multilingual and Multicultural Education M
Music Education M
Music M

Nursing Education M
Nursing—General M
Nutrition M,D
Occupational Therapy M,D
Oral and Dental Sciences D,O
Organic Chemistry M,D
Pharmacology M,D
Pharmacy D
Philosophy M
Photography M
Physical Chemistry M,D
Physical Education M
Physical Therapy M,D
Physician Assistant Studies M
Physics M,D
Physiology D
Political Science M,D
Psychology—General M,D
Public Administration M
Public Health—General M
School Psychology M,D
Secondary Education M
Social Psychology M,D
Social Work M,D
Sociology M,D
Spanish M
Special Education M
Sports Management M
Supply Chain Management M
Theology M,D

HULT INTERNATIONAL BUSINESS SCHOOL (UNITED STATES)
Business Administration and Management—General M
Business Analytics M
Entrepreneurship M
Finance and Banking M
International Business M
Marketing M
Project Management M

HUMBOLDT STATE UNIVERSITY
Anthropology M
Biological and Biomedical Sciences—General M
Business Administration and Management—General M
Counseling Psychology M
Developmental Psychology M
Education—General M
English as a Second Language M
English M
Environmental Management and Policy M
Environmental Sciences M
Fish, Game, and Wildlife Management M
Forestry M
Geology M
Hazardous Materials Management M
Kinesiology and Movement Studies M
Natural Resources M
Psychology—General M
School Psychology M
Social Psychology M
Social Sciences M
Social Work M
Sociology M
Water Resources M

HUMPHREYS UNIVERSITY
Law D

HUNTER COLLEGE OF THE CITY UNIVERSITY OF NEW YORK
Accounting M
Adult Nursing M
Animal Behavior M,O
Anthropology M
Applied Mathematics M
Applied Social Research M
Art History M
Art/Fine Arts M
Astronomy M,D
Biochemistry M,D
Bioinformatics M
Biological and Biomedical Sciences—General M,D
Chemistry D
Chinese M
Classics M
Communication Disorders M
Community Health Nursing M
Comparative Literature M
Counselor Education M
Early Childhood Education M,D,O
Economics M
Education of Students with Severe/Multiple Disabilities M
Education—General M,D,O
Educational Leadership and Administration D,O
English as a Second Language M
English Education M
Family Nurse Practitioner Studies D
Foreign Languages Education M
French M
Geographic Information Systems M,O
Geography M,O
Geosciences M
Gerontological Nursing M,D
History M
Italian M
Mathematics Education M
Mathematics M
Media Studies M
Multilingual and Multicultural Education M
Music Education M
Music M
Nursing—General M,D,O
Nutrition M
Physical Therapy D

Physics M,D
Psychiatric Nursing M,D,O
Psychology—General M,O
Public Health—General M
Rehabilitation Counseling M
Romance Languages M
Science Education M
Secondary Education M
Social Sciences Education M
Social Work M
Sociology M
Spanish M
Special Education M
Statistics M
Sustainable Development M,O
Theater M
Urban and Regional Planning M
Urban Studies M
Writing M

HUNTINGTON UNIVERSITY
Business Administration and Management—General M,D
Elementary Education M,D
English as a Second Language M,D
Middle School Education M,D
Occupational Therapy M,D
Organizational Management M,D
Pastoral Ministry and Counseling M,D

HUNTINGTON UNIVERSITY OF HEALTH SCIENCES
Nutrition M,D

HUNTSVILLE BIBLE COLLEGE
Pastoral Ministry and Counseling M

HUSSON UNIVERSITY
Biotechnology M
Business Administration and Management—General M
Clinical Psychology M
Community Health Nursing M,O
Counseling Psychology M
Counselor Education M
Criminal Justice and Criminology M
Educational Leadership and Administration M,O
Family Nurse Practitioner Studies M,O
Health Services Management and Hospital Administration M
Hospitality Management M
Nursing—General M,O
Organizational Management M
Pharmacology M,D
Pharmacy D
Physical Therapy D
Psychiatric Nursing M,O
Risk Management M
School Psychology M
Social Psychology M
Sports Management M

HUSTON-TILLOTSON UNIVERSITY
Educational Leadership and Administration M

ICAHN SCHOOL OF MEDICINE AT MOUNT SINAI
Allopathic Medicine D
Bioethics M
Biological and Biomedical Sciences—General M,D
Clinical Research M,D
Community Health M,D
Genetic Counseling M,D
Neuroscience M,D
Public Health—General M,D

IDAHO STATE UNIVERSITY
Allied Health—General M,D,O
Anthropology M
Applied Physics M,D
Art/Fine Arts M
Athletic Training and Sports Medicine M
Biological and Biomedical Sciences—General M,D
Business Administration and Management—General M,O
Chemistry M
Civil Engineering M
Clinical Psychology D
Communication Disorders M,D
Communication—General M
Community Health O
Counseling Psychology M,D,O
Counselor Education M,D,O
Dental Hygiene M
Dentistry O
Education—General M,D,O
Educational Leadership and Administration M,D,O
Educational Media/Instructional Technology M,D
Elementary Education M
Engineering and Applied Sciences—General M,D,O
English as a Second Language M,D,O
English M,D,O
Environmental Engineering M
Environmental Management and Policy M
Environmental Sciences M,O
Experimental Psychology D
Geographic Information Systems M,O
Geology M,O
Geophysics M,O
Geosciences M,O
Health Education M
Health Physics/Radiological Health M,D
History M
Human Resources Management M
Hydrology M,O
Management Information Systems M,O
Marriage and Family Therapy M,D,O

Mathematics Education M,D
Mathematics M,D
Mechanical Engineering M
Medical Microbiology M,D
Medicinal and Pharmaceutical Chemistry M,D
Microbiology M
Music Education M
Nuclear Engineering M,D
Nursing—General M,D
Occupational Therapy M
Operations Research M
Oral and Dental Sciences O
Pharmaceutical Administration M,D
Pharmaceutical Sciences M,D
Pharmacology M,D
Pharmacy M,D
Physical Education M
Physical Therapy D
Physician Assistant Studies M
Physics M,D
Political Science M,D
Psychology—General D
Public Administration M
Public Health—General M
Reading Education M
School Psychology M,D,O
Secondary Education M
Sociology M
Special Education M
Sports Management M
Theater M

IGLOBAL UNIVERSITY
Accounting M
Business Administration and Management—General M
Data Science/Data Analytics M
Entrepreneurship M
Finance and Banking M
Health Services Management and Hospital Administration M
Hospitality Management M
Human Resources Management M
International Business M
Management Information Systems M
Project Management M
Public Administration M
Travel and Tourism M

ILIFF SCHOOL OF THEOLOGY
Pastoral Ministry and Counseling M,D
Religion M,D
Theology M,D

ILLINOIS COLLEGE
Education—General M

ILLINOIS COLLEGE OF OPTOMETRY
Optometry D

ILLINOIS INSTITUTE OF TECHNOLOGY
Aerospace/Aeronautical Engineering M,D
Agricultural Engineering M
Analytical Chemistry M,D
Applied Arts and Design—General M,D
Applied Mathematics M,D
Applied Physics M,D
Architectural Engineering M,D
Architecture M,D
Artificial Intelligence/Robotics M,D
Biochemistry M,D
Bioengineering M,D
Biological and Biomedical Sciences—General M,D
Biomedical Engineering M,D
Business Administration and Management—General M,D
Cell Biology M,D
Chemical Engineering M,D
Chemistry M,D
Civil Engineering M,D
Clinical Psychology M,D
Communication—General M,D
Computer and Information Systems Security M,D
Computer Education M,D
Computer Engineering M,D
Computer Science M,D
Construction Engineering M,D
Construction Management M,D
Corporate and Organizational Communication M
Data Science/Data Analytics M,D
Electrical Engineering M,D
Engineering and Applied Sciences—General M,D
Entrepreneurship M
Environmental Engineering M,D
Environmental Management and Policy M
Finance and Banking M,D
Food Science and Technology M
Geotechnical Engineering M,D
Health Physics/Radiological Health M,D
Human Resources Development M,D
Humanities M,D
Industrial and Manufacturing Management M
Industrial and Organizational Psychology M,D
Inorganic Chemistry M,D
Landscape Architecture M,D
Law M,D
Legal and Justice Studies M,D
Management Information Systems M,D
Manufacturing Engineering M,D
Marketing M,D
Materials Engineering M,D
Materials Sciences M,D
Mathematical and Computational Finance M,D
Mathematics Education M,D

Mechanical Engineering	M,D
Medical Imaging	M,D
Microbiology	M,D
Molecular Biology	M,D
Molecular Biophysics	M,D
Physics	M,D
Psychology—General	M,D
Public Administration	M
Rehabilitation Counseling	M,D
Science Education	M,D
Software Engineering	M,D
Structural Engineering	M,D
Sustainability Management	M
Taxation	M,D
Technical Writing	M,D
Telecommunications	M,D
Transportation and Highway Engineering	M,D

ILLINOIS STATE UNIVERSITY

Accounting	M
Agricultural Economics and Agribusiness	M
Agricultural Sciences—General	M
Animal Behavior	M,D
Archaeology	M
Art History	M
Art/Fine Arts	M
Bacteriology	M,D
Biochemistry	M,D
Biological and Biomedical Sciences—General	M,D
Biophysics	M,D
Biotechnology	M
Botany	M,D
Business Administration and Management—General	M
Cell Biology	M,D
Clinical Psychology	M,D,O
Cognitive Sciences	M,D,O
Communication Disorders	M
Communication—General	M
Conservation Biology	M,D
Counseling Psychology	M,D,O
Criminal Justice and Criminology	M
Curriculum and Instruction	M
Developmental Biology	M,D
Developmental Psychology	M,D,O
Ecology	M,D
Economics	M
Educational Leadership and Administration	M,D
Educational Policy	M,D
English	M,D
Entomology	M,D
Evolutionary Biology	M,D
Family and Consumer Sciences-General	M
Family Nurse Practitioner Studies	M,D,O
French	M
Genetics	M,D
German	M
Graphic Design	M
Health Education	M,D
Higher Education	M
History	M
Immunology	M,D
Industrial and Organizational Psychology	M,D,O
Industrial/Management Engineering	M
Management Information Systems	M
Management of Technology	M
Mathematics Education	M,D
Mathematics	M
Microbiology	M,D
Molecular Biology	M,D
Molecular Genetics	M,D
Music	M
Neurobiology	M,D
Neuroscience	M,D
Nursing—General	M,D,O
Parasitology	M,D
Photography	M
Physical Education	M
Physiology	M,D
Plant Biology	M,D
Plant Molecular Biology	M,D
Plant Sciences	M,D
Political Science	M
Psychology—General	M,D,O
Reading Education	M
School Psychology	M,D,O
Social Work	M
Sociology	M
Spanish	M
Special Education	M,D,O
Structural Biology	M,D
Student Affairs	M
Textile Design	M
Theater	M
Writing	M,D
Zoology	M,D

IMMACULATA UNIVERSITY

Clinical Psychology	M,D,O
Counseling Psychology	M,D,O
Educational Leadership and Administration	M,D,O
Educational Psychology	M,D,O
English as a Second Language	M
Forensic Psychology	M,D,O
Health Promotion	M
Multilingual and Multicultural Education	M
Neuroscience	M,D,O
Nursing and Healthcare Administration	M
Nursing Education	M
Nursing—General	M

Nutrition	M
Organizational Management	M
Psychoanalysis and Psychotherapy	M,D,O
Psychology—General	M,D,O
School Psychology	M,D,O
Secondary Education	M,D,O
Special Education	M,D,O
Therapies—Dance, Drama, and Music	M

INDEPENDENCE UNIVERSITY

Business Administration and Management—General	M
Community Health Nursing	M
Community Health	M
Gerontological Nursing	M
Health Promotion	M
Health Services Management and Hospital Administration	M
Nursing and Healthcare Administration	M
Nursing—General	M
Public Health—General	M

INDIANA STATE UNIVERSITY

Art/Fine Arts	M
Athletic Training and Sports Medicine	M,D
Biological and Biomedical Sciences—General	M,D
Business Administration and Management—General	M
Cell Biology	M,D
Clinical Psychology	M,D,O
Communication Disorders	M,D,O
Communication—General	M
Computer Engineering	M
Computer Science	M
Counselor Education	M,D,O
Criminal Justice and Criminology	M
Curriculum and Instruction	M
Ecology	M,D
Education—General	M,D,O
Educational Leadership and Administration	M,D
Educational Media/Instructional Technology	M,D
Engineering and Applied Sciences—General	M
English as a Second Language	M,D,O
English	M
Environmental and Occupational Health	M
Evolutionary Biology	M,D
Family Nurse Practitioner Studies	M,D
Foreign Languages Education	M,D
Graphic Design	M
Health Education	M
Higher Education	M,D,O
History	M
Human Resources Development	M
Linguistics	M,D,O
Management of Technology	M,D
Mathematics	M
Media Studies	M
Molecular Biology	M,D
Multilingual and Multicultural Education	M,D,O
Music Education	M
Music	M
Nursing and Healthcare Administration	M,D
Nursing Education	M,D
Nursing—General	M,D
Occupational Therapy	M,D
Photography	M
Physical Education	M,D
Physical Therapy	M,D
Physician Assistant Studies	M,D
Physiology	M,D
Psychology—General	M,D
Public Administration	M
Recreation and Park Management	M,D
School Psychology	M,D,O
Science Education	M,D
Social Work	M
Spanish	M,D,O
Sports Management	M,D
Student Affairs	M,D,O
Vocational and Technical Education	M
Writing	M

INDIANA TECH

Accounting	M
Business Administration and Management—General	M
Engineering Management	M
Health Services Management and Hospital Administration	M
Human Resources Development	M
Human Resources Management	M
International Business	D
Marketing	M
Organizational Management	M
Psychology—General	M

INDIANA UNIVERSITY BLOOMINGTON

African Studies	M
African-American Studies	M,D
Analytical Chemistry	M,D
Anthropology	M,D
Applied Arts and Design—General	M
Applied Mathematics	M,D
Applied Statistics	M,D
Archaeology	M,D
Architecture	M
Art Education	M,D,O
Art History	M,D
Art/Fine Arts	M
Artificial Intelligence/Robotics	D
Arts Administration	M

Asian Languages	M,D
Asian Studies	M,D
Astronomy	M,D
Astrophysics	M,D
Athletic Training and Sports Medicine	M,D
Atmospheric Sciences	M,D
Biochemistry	M,D
Bioinformatics	M,D,O
Biological and Biomedical Sciences—General	M,D
Biostatistics	M,D
Biotechnology	M,D
Business Administration and Management—General	M,D
Cell Biology	M,D
Chemistry	M,D
Chinese	M,D
Classics	M,D
Cognitive Sciences	D
Communication Disorders	M,D
Community Health	M,D
Comparative Literature	M,D
Computer and Information Systems Security	M,D
Computer Science	M,D,O
Counselor Education	M,D,O
Criminal Justice and Criminology	M,D
Curriculum and Instruction	M,D,O
Data Science/Data Analytics	M,O
Developmental Psychology	D
East European and Russian Studies	M,D
Ecology	M,D,O
Economic Development	M,D,O
Economics	M,D
Education—General	M,D,O
Educational Leadership and Administration	M,D
Educational Measurement and Evaluation	M,D
Educational Media/Instructional Technology	M,D
Educational Policy	M,D,O
Educational Psychology	M,D,O
Elementary Education	M,D,O
Energy Management and Policy	M,D,O
English as a Second Language	M,D
English	M,D
Environmental and Occupational Health	M,D
Environmental Management and Policy	M,D,O
Environmental Sciences	M,D,O
Epidemiology	M,D
Ergonomics and Human Factors	M,D
Evolutionary Biology	M,D
Exercise and Sports Science	M,D
Finance and Banking	M,D,O
Folklore	M,D
Foreign Languages Education	M,D
Foundations and Philosophy of Education	M,D,O
French	M,D
Gender Studies	D
Genetics	M,D
Geochemistry	M,D
Geography	D
Geophysics	M,D
Geosciences	M,D
German	M,D
Hazardous Materials Management	M,D,O
Health Education	M,D
Health Informatics	M,D
Health Promotion	M,D
Health Services Management and Hospital Administration	M,D
Higher Education	M,D,O
Hispanic and Latin American Languages	M,D
History of Medicine	M,D
History of Science and Technology	M,D
History	M,D
Human-Computer Interaction	M,D
Hydrogeology	M,D,O
Information Science	M,D,O
Inorganic Chemistry	M,D
International Affairs	M
International and Comparative Education	M,D,O
International Development	M,D,O
Italian	M,D
Japanese	M,D
Jewish Studies	M
Kinesiology and Movement Studies	M,D
Latin American Studies	M
Law	M,D,O
Leisure Studies	M,D
Library Science	M,D,O
Linguistics	M,D
Management Information Systems	M,D,O
Materials Sciences	M,D
Mathematical Physics	M,D
Mathematics Education	M,D,O
Mathematics	M,D
Media Studies	M,D
Medical Physics	M,D
Medieval and Renaissance Studies	M,D
Microbiology	M,D
Mineralogy	M,D
Molecular Biology	M,D
Multilingual and Multicultural Education	M,D
Music	M,D
Near and Middle Eastern Languages	M,D
Neuroscience	D
Nonprofit Management	M,D,O
Nutrition	M,D
Optometry	M,D

Organic Chemistry	M,D
Organizational Management	M,D,O
Philosophy	M,D
Physical Chemistry	M,D
Physical Education	M,D
Physics	M,D
Plant Biology	M,D
Political Science	M,D
Portuguese	M,D
Psychology—General	D
Public Administration	M,D,O
Public Affairs	M,D,O
Public Health—General	M,D
Public Policy	M,D,O
Reading Education	M,D,O
Recreation and Park Management	M,D
Religion	M,D
Rhetoric	M,D
Safety Engineering	M,D
School Psychology	M,D,O
Science Education	M,D,O
Secondary Education	M,D,O
Slavic Languages	M,D
Social Psychology	D
Social Sciences Education	M,D,O
Social Sciences	M,D,O
Sociology	M,D
Spanish	M,D
Special Education	M,D,O
Sports Management	M,D
Statistics	M,D
Student Affairs	M,D
Sustainability Management	M,D,O
Systems Engineering	D
Theater	M,D
Toxicology	M,D,O
Travel and Tourism	M,D
Water Resources Engineering	M,D,O
Western European Studies	M
Writing	M,D
Zoology	M,D

INDIANA UNIVERSITY EAST

Education—General	M
Nursing—General	M
Social Work	M

INDIANA UNIVERSITY KOKOMO

Accounting	M,O
Business Administration and Management—General	M,O
Family Nurse Practitioner Studies	M
Health Services Management and Hospital Administration	M,O
Nursing and Healthcare Administration	M
Nursing Education	M
Nursing—General	M
Public Administration	M,O
Public Policy	M,O

INDIANA UNIVERSITY NORTHWEST

Accounting	M,O
Addictions/Substance Abuse Counseling	M,O
Business Administration and Management—General	M,O
Counseling Psychology	M,O
Criminal Justice and Criminology	M,O
Education—General	M,O
Educational Leadership and Administration	M,O
Elementary Education	M,O
Environmental Management and Policy	M,O
Gender Studies	M,O
Health Services Management and Hospital Administration	M,O
Liberal Studies	M,O
Management Information Systems	M,O
Nonprofit Management	M,O
Public Administration	M,O
Public Affairs	M,O
Secondary Education	M,O
Social Work	M
Urban Studies	M,O

INDIANA UNIVERSITY OF PENNSYLVANIA

Adult Education	M
Applied Mathematics	M
Archaeology	M
Art/Fine Arts	M
Biological and Biomedical Sciences—General	M
Business Administration and Management—General	M
Business Education	M
Chemistry	M
Clinical Psychology	M,D
Communication Disorders	M
Communication—General	D
Counselor Education	M
Criminal Justice and Criminology	M,D
Curriculum and Instruction	D
Education—General	M,D,O
Educational Leadership and Administration	D,O
Educational Media/Instructional Technology	M,D
Educational Psychology	M,O
English as a Second Language	M,D
English Education	D
English	M,D
Environmental and Occupational Health	M,D
Environmental Management and Policy	M
Exercise and Sports Science	M
Geographic Information Systems	M,O
Geography	M,O
Health Education	M

Health Services Management and Hospital Administration	M
Higher Education	M
History	M
Human Resources Development	M
Industrial and Labor Relations	M
Mathematics Education	M
Mathematics	M
Media Studies	D
Music Education	M
Music	M
Nanotechnology	M
Nonprofit Management	D
Nursing and Healthcare Administration	M
Nursing Education	M
Nursing—General	D
Nutrition	M
Physical Education	M
Physics	M
Psychology—General	M,D
Public Affairs	M
Public History	M
Reading Education	M,O
School Psychology	D,O
Social Psychology	M
Sociology	M
Special Education	M
Sports Management	M
Student Affairs	M
Urban and Regional Planning	M
Vocational and Technical Education	M

INDIANA UNIVERSITY–PURDUE UNIVERSITY INDIANAPOLIS

Accounting	M
Acute Care/Critical Care Nursing	M
Allopathic Medicine	M,D
American Studies	M,D
Anatomy	M,D
Applied Mathematics	M,D
Applied Statistics	M,D
Art Therapy	M
Art/Fine Arts	M
Biochemistry	M,D
Bioethics	M,D,O
Bioinformatics	M,D
Biological and Biomedical Sciences—General	M,D
Biomedical Engineering	M,D
Biostatistics	M,D,O
Business Administration and Management—General	M
Cell Biology	M,D
Chemistry	M,D
Clinical Psychology	M,D
Communication—General	M,D
Community Health	M,D,O
Computer and Information Systems Security	M,D,O
Computer Art and Design	M
Computer Engineering	M,D
Computer Science	M,D,O
Counselor Education	M,O
Criminal Justice and Criminology	M,O
Curriculum and Instruction	M,O
Data Science/Data Analytics	M,D,O
Dentistry	M,O
Early Childhood Education	M,O
Economics	M
Education—General	M,O
Educational Leadership and Administration	M,O
Electrical Engineering	M,D
Emergency Management	M,O
English as a Second Language	M,O
English	M,O
Entrepreneurship	M
Environmental and Occupational Health	M,D,O
Epidemiology	M,D,O
Family Nurse Practitioner Studies	M
Finance and Banking	M
Foreign Languages Education	M,O
Forensic Sciences	M
Geographic Information Systems	M,O
Geology	M,D
Geosciences	M,D
Gerontological Nursing	M
Graphic Design	M
Health Communication	M,D
Health Education	M,D
Health Informatics	M,D
Health Law	M,D,O
Health Services Management and Hospital Administration	M,D,O
History	M
Homeland Security	M
Human-Computer Interaction	M,D
Immunology	M,D
Industrial and Organizational Psychology	M,D
Information Science	M
Intellectual Property Law	M,D,O
International Health	M,D,O
Kinesiology and Movement Studies	M
Law	M,D,O
Liberal Studies	M,D,O
Library Science	M
Management of Technology	M
Marketing	M
Mathematics Education	M,D
Mathematics	M,D
Mechanical Engineering	M,D
Microbiology	M,D
Molecular Biology	M,D
Molecular Genetics	M,D
Museum Studies	M
Music	M,D
Natural Resources	M,D,O
Neurobiology	D
Nonprofit Management	M,O
Nursing and Healthcare Administration	M,D

Nursing Education	M
Nursing—General	M,D
Nutrition	M,D
Occupational Therapy	M,D
Organizational Management	M,O
Pathology	M,D
Pediatric Nursing	M
Pharmacology	M,D
Philanthropic Studies	M,D
Philosophy	M,O
Photography	M
Physical Education	M
Physical Therapy	M,D
Physics	M,D
Political Science	M
Psychology—General	M,D
Public Administration	M,O
Public Affairs	M,O
Public Health—General	M,D,O
Public History	M
Reading Education	M,O
Rehabilitation Sciences	M,D
Social Psychology	M
Social Sciences	M,D,O
Social Work	M,D,O
Sociology	M
Software Engineering	M,D,O
Special Education	M,O
Statistics	M,D
Supply Chain Management	M
Technical Communication	M
Therapies—Dance, Drama, and Music	M,D
Toxicology	M,D
Western European Studies	M
Writing	M,O

INDIANA UNIVERSITY SOUTH BEND

Accounting	M
Addictions/Substance Abuse Counseling	M,O
Applied Mathematics	M,O
Business Administration and Management—General	M,O
Clinical Psychology	M,O
Communication—General	M,D
Computer Science	M,O
Counseling Psychology	M,O
Counselor Education	M,O
Education—General	M,O
Educational Leadership and Administration	M,O
Educational Media/Instructional Technology	M,O
Elementary Education	M,O
English	M,O
Family Nurse Practitioner Studies	M
Finance and Banking	M,O
Health Services Management and Hospital Administration	M,O
Human Resources Management	M,O
International Affairs	M,O
Legal and Justice Studies	M,O
Liberal Studies	M,O
Marketing	M,O
Marriage and Family Therapy	M,O
Music	M,D
Nonprofit Management	M,O
Nursing—General	M
Public Administration	M,O
Public Affairs	M,O
School Psychology	M,O
Secondary Education	M,O
Social Work	M
Special Education	M,O
Writing	M,O

INDIANA UNIVERSITY SOUTHEAST

Business Administration and Management—General	M
Counselor Education	M
Education—General	M
Elementary Education	M
Finance and Banking	M
Interdisciplinary Studies	M
Secondary Education	M

INDIANA WESLEYAN UNIVERSITY

Accounting	M,O
Addictions/Substance Abuse Counseling	M
Athletic Training and Sports Medicine	M,D
Business Administration and Management—General	M,O
Counseling Psychology	M
Counselor Education	M
Educational Leadership and Administration	M,O
Health Services Management and Hospital Administration	M,O
Higher Education	M
Human Resources Management	M,O
Marriage and Family Therapy	M
Nursing and Healthcare Administration	M
Nursing Education	M
Nursing—General	M
Occupational Therapy	M,D
Organizational Management	M,D,O
Pastoral Ministry and Counseling	M
Public Health—General	M,D
Social Psychology	M
Theology	M

INSTITUTE FOR CHRISTIAN STUDIES

Education—General	M,D
Philosophy	M,D
Political Science	M,D
Theology	M,D

INSTITUTE FOR CLINICAL SOCIAL WORK

Social Work	D

INSTITUTE FOR DOCTORAL STUDIES IN THE VISUAL ARTS

Art/Fine Arts	D
Philosophy	D

INSTITUTE OF AMERICAN INDIAN ARTS

Writing	M

INSTITUTE OF CLINICAL ACUPUNCTURE AND ORIENTAL MEDICINE

Acupuncture and Oriental Medicine	M

INSTITUTE OF PUBLIC ADMINISTRATION

Health Services Management and Hospital Administration	M,O
Public Administration	M,O

INSTITUTE OF TAOIST EDUCATION AND ACUPUNCTURE

Acupuncture and Oriental Medicine	M

THE INSTITUTE OF WORLD POLITICS

Computer and Information Systems Security	M,D,O
Conflict Resolution and Mediation/Peace Studies	M,D,O
Homeland Security	M,D,O
International Affairs	M,D,O
International Economics	M,D,O
Military and Defense Studies	M,D,O
National Security	M,D,O
Political Science	M,D,O
Public Affairs	M,D,O
Public Policy	M,D,O

INSTITUT FRANCO-EUROPÉEN DE CHIROPRAXIE

Chiropractic	D

INSTITUTO CENTROAMERICANO DE ADMINISTRACIÓN DE EMPRESAS

Agricultural Economics and Agribusiness	M
Business Administration and Management—General	M
Finance and Banking	M
Management of Technology	M
Real Estate	M
Sustainable Development	M

INSTITUTO TECNOLOGICO DE SANTO DOMINGO

Accounting	M,O
Adult Education	M,O
Allopathic Medicine	M,D
Bioethics	M,O
Business Administration and Management—General	M,O
Communication—General	M,O
Construction Management	M,O
Counseling Psychology	M,O
Economics	M,O
Education—General	M,O
Educational Leadership and Administration	M,O
Educational Psychology	M,O
Energy and Power Engineering	M,D,O
Energy Management and Policy	M,D,O
Engineering and Applied Sciences—General	M,O
Environmental Education	M,D,O
Environmental Engineering	M,O
Environmental Management and Policy	M,D,O
Environmental Sciences	M,D,O
Finance and Banking	M,O
Gender Studies	M,O
Health Promotion	M,O
Human Resources Management	M,O
Humanities	M,O
Industrial and Manufacturing Management	M,O
Industrial/Management Engineering	M,O
Information Science	M,O
International Affairs	M,O
International Business	M,O
Linguistics	M,O
Marine Sciences	M,D,O
Marketing	M,O
Marriage and Family Therapy	M,O
Maternal and Child Health	M,O
Mathematics	M,D,O
Natural Resources	M,D,O
Nutrition	M,O
Organizational Management	M,O
Quality Management	M,O
Quantitative Analysis	M,O
Secondary Education	M,O
Social Sciences Education	M,O
Software Engineering	M,O
Structural Engineering	M,O
Sustainable Development	M,O
Taxation	M,O
Telecommunications	M,O
Transportation Management	M,O

INSTITUTO TECNOLÓGICO Y DE ESTUDIOS SUPERIORES DE MONTERREY, CAMPUS CENTRAL DE VERACRUZ

Business Administration and Management—General	M
Computer Science	M
Education—General	M
Educational Leadership and Administration	M
Educational Media/Instructional Technology	M
Electronic Commerce	M
Finance and Banking	M
Humanities	M

INSTITUTE FOR DOCTORAL STUDIES IN THE VISUAL ARTS

International Business	M
Management Information Systems	M
Marketing	M

INSTITUTO TECNOLÓGICO Y DE ESTUDIOS SUPERIORES DE MONTERREY, CAMPUS CHIHUAHUA

Computer Engineering	M,O
Electrical Engineering	M,O
Engineering Management	M,O
Industrial/Management Engineering	M,O
International Business	M,O
Mechanical Engineering	M,O
Systems Engineering	M,O

INSTITUTO TECNOLÓGICO Y DE ESTUDIOS SUPERIORES DE MONTERREY, CAMPUS CIUDAD DE MÉXICO

Business Administration and Management—General	M,D
Computer Science	M,D
Economics	M,D
Education—General	M,D
Educational Media/Instructional Technology	M,D
Environmental Engineering	M,D
Environmental Sciences	M,D
Finance and Banking	M,D
Humanities	M,D
Industrial/Management Engineering	M,D
International Business	M,D
Law	O
Management Information Systems	M,D
Quality Management	M,D
Telecommunications Management	M

INSTITUTO TECNOLÓGICO Y DE ESTUDIOS SUPERIORES DE MONTERREY, CAMPUS CIUDAD JUÁREZ

Business Administration and Management—General	M
Education—General	M
Educational Leadership and Administration	M
Educational Media/Instructional Technology	M,D
Electronic Commerce	M
Humanities	M
Management Information Systems	M
Public Administration	M
Quality Management	M

INSTITUTO TECNOLÓGICO Y DE ESTUDIOS SUPERIORES DE MONTERREY, CAMPUS CIUDAD OBREGÓN

Business Administration and Management—General	M
Communication—General	M
Developmental Education	M
Education—General	M
Engineering and Applied Sciences—General	M
Finance and Banking	M
International Affairs	M
Management Information Systems	M
Marketing	M
Mathematics Education	M
Telecommunications Management	M

INSTITUTO TECNOLÓGICO Y DE ESTUDIOS SUPERIORES DE MONTERREY, CAMPUS CUERNAVACA

Business Administration and Management—General	M
Computer Science	M,D
Finance and Banking	M
Human Resources Management	M
Information Science	M,D
International Business	M
Management of Technology	M,D
Marketing	M

INSTITUTO TECNOLÓGICO Y DE ESTUDIOS SUPERIORES DE MONTERREY, CAMPUS ESTADO DE MÉXICO

Architecture	M,D
Business Administration and Management—General	M,D
Computer Science	M,D
Education—General	M,D
Educational Leadership and Administration	M,D
Educational Media/Instructional Technology	M,D
Electronic Commerce	M,D
Environmental Management and Policy	M,D
Finance and Banking	M,D
Humanities	M,D
Industrial and Manufacturing Management	M,D
Information Science	M,D
Management Information Systems	M,D
Marketing	M,D
Materials Engineering	M,D
Materials Sciences	M,D
Quality Management	M,D
Telecommunications Management	M,D

INSTITUTO TECNOLÓGICO Y DE ESTUDIOS SUPERIORES DE MONTERREY, CAMPUS GUADALAJARA

Business Administration and Management—General	M
Finance and Banking	M

INSTITUTO TECNOLÓGICO Y DE ESTUDIOS SUPERIORES DE MONTERREY, CAMPUS IRAPUATO

Architecture	M,D
Business Administration and Management—General	M,D
Computer Science	M,D
Education—General	M,D
Educational Leadership and Administration	M,D
Educational Media/Instructional Technology	M,D
Electronic Commerce	M,D
Environmental Management and Policy	M,D
Finance and Banking	M,D
Humanities	M,D
Industrial and Manufacturing Management	M,D
Information Science	M,D
International Business	M,D
Library Science	M,D
Management Information Systems	M,D
Management of Technology	M,D
Marketing Research	M,D
Quality Management	M,D
Telecommunications Management	M,D

INSTITUTO TECNOLÓGICO Y DE ESTUDIOS SUPERIORES DE MONTERREY, CAMPUS LAGUNA

Business Administration and Management—General	M
Industrial/Management Engineering	M
Management Information Systems	M

INSTITUTO TECNOLÓGICO Y DE ESTUDIOS SUPERIORES DE MONTERREY, CAMPUS LEÓN

Business Administration and Management—General	M

INSTITUTO TECNOLÓGICO Y DE ESTUDIOS SUPERIORES DE MONTERREY, CAMPUS MONTERREY

Agricultural Engineering	M,D
Agricultural Sciences—General	M,D
Applied Statistics	M,D
Artificial Intelligence/Robotics	M,D
Biotechnology	M,D
Business Administration and Management—General	M,D
Chemical Engineering	M,D
Chemistry	M,D
Civil Engineering	M,D
Communication—General	M,D
Computer Science	M,D
Electrical Engineering	M,D
Engineering and Applied Sciences—General	M,D
Environmental Engineering	M,D
Finance and Banking	M
Industrial/Management Engineering	M,D
Information Science	M
International Business	M
Manufacturing Engineering	M,D
Marketing	M
Mechanical Engineering	M,D
Organic Chemistry	M,D
Science Education	M,D
Systems Engineering	M,D

INSTITUTO TECNOLÓGICO Y DE ESTUDIOS SUPERIORES DE MONTERREY, CAMPUS QUERÉTARO

Business Administration and Management—General	M

INSTITUTO TECNOLÓGICO Y DE ESTUDIOS SUPERIORES DE MONTERREY, CAMPUS SONORA NORTE

Business Administration and Management—General	M
Education—General	M
Information Science	M

INSTITUTO TECNOLÓGICO Y DE ESTUDIOS SUPERIORES DE MONTERREY, CAMPUS TOLUCA

Business Administration and Management—General	M

INTER AMERICAN UNIVERSITY OF PUERTO RICO, AGUADILLA CAMPUS

Accounting	M
Business Administration and Management—General	M
Counseling Psychology	M
Criminal Justice and Criminology	M
Educational Leadership and Administration	M
Elementary Education	M
Finance and Banking	M
Human Resources Management	M
Management Information Systems	M
Marketing	M

INTER AMERICAN UNIVERSITY OF PUERTO RICO, ARECIBO CAMPUS

Accounting	M
Acute Care/Critical Care Nursing	M
Business Administration and Management—General	M
Counselor Education	M
Curriculum and Instruction	M
Education—General	M

Educational Leadership and Administration	M
Elementary Education	M
English as a Second Language	M
Finance and Banking	M
Foreign Languages Education	M
Human Resources Management	M
Mathematics Education	M
Medical/Surgical Nursing	M
Nurse Anesthesia	M
Nursing—General	M
Science Education	M
Social Sciences Education	M

INTER AMERICAN UNIVERSITY OF PUERTO RICO, BARRANQUITAS CAMPUS

Accounting	M
Acute Care/Critical Care Nursing	M
Biological and Biomedical Sciences—General	M
Biotechnology	M
Business Administration and Management—General	M
Criminal Justice and Criminology	M
Curriculum and Instruction	M
Education—General	M
Educational Leadership and Administration	M
Elementary Education	M
English as a Second Language	M
Foreign Languages Education	M
History	M
Human Resources Management	M
Library Science	M
Medical/Surgical Nursing	M
Nursing—General	M
Special Education	M

INTER AMERICAN UNIVERSITY OF PUERTO RICO, BAYAMÓN CAMPUS

Aerospace/Aeronautical Engineering	M
Biotechnology	M
Ecology	M
Electrical Engineering	M
Energy and Power Engineering	M
Human Resources Management	M
Mechanical Engineering	M

INTER AMERICAN UNIVERSITY OF PUERTO RICO, FAJARDO CAMPUS

Business Administration and Management—General	M
Computer Science	M
Educational Leadership and Administration	M
Human Resources Management	M
Management Information Systems	M
Marketing	M
Special Education	M

INTER AMERICAN UNIVERSITY OF PUERTO RICO, GUAYAMA CAMPUS

Business Administration and Management—General	M
Computer and Information Systems Security	M
Computer Science	M
Early Childhood Education	M
Elementary Education	M
Marketing	M

INTER AMERICAN UNIVERSITY OF PUERTO RICO, METROPOLITAN CAMPUS

Accounting	M
American Studies	M,D
Athletic Training and Sports Medicine	M
Business Administration and Management—General	M
Business Education	M
Clinical Laboratory Sciences/Medical Technology	M
Computer Science	M
Counseling Psychology	M,D
Counselor Education	M,D
Criminal Justice and Criminology	M
Curriculum and Instruction	M,D
Education—General	M
Educational Leadership and Administration	M,D
Educational Media/Instructional Technology	M
Elementary Education	M
English as a Second Language	M
English	M
Environmental Management and Policy	M
Exercise and Sports Science	M
Finance and Banking	M
Foreign Languages Education	M
Health Education	M
Higher Education	M
History	M,D
Human Resources Development	M
Human Resources Management	M
Industrial and Labor Relations	M,D
Industrial and Manufacturing Management	M
Industrial and Organizational Psychology	M,D
International Business	M,D
Management Information Systems	M
Marketing	M
Mathematics Education	M
Microbiology	M
Molecular Biology	M
Music Education	M
Pastoral Ministry and Counseling	D

Physical Education	M
Psychology—General	M,D
Religious Education	D
School Psychology	M,D
Science Education	M
Social Sciences Education	M
Social Work	M
Spanish	M
Special Education	M
Theology	D
Vocational and Technical Education	M
Women's Studies	M

INTER AMERICAN UNIVERSITY OF PUERTO RICO, PONCE CAMPUS

Accounting	M
Criminal Justice and Criminology	M
Elementary Education	M
English as a Second Language	M
Finance and Banking	M
Human Resources Management	M
Marketing	M
Mathematics Education	M
Science Education	M
Social Sciences Education	M
Spanish	M

INTER AMERICAN UNIVERSITY OF PUERTO RICO, SAN GERMÁN CAMPUS

Accounting	M,D
Applied Mathematics	M
Art/Fine Arts	M
Business Administration and Management—General	M,D
Business Education	M
Counseling Psychology	M,D
Counselor Education	M,D
Curriculum and Instruction	D
Elementary Education	M
English as a Second Language	M
Environmental Sciences	M
Finance and Banking	M,D
Graphic Design	M
Health Education	M
Human Resources Development	M,D
Human Resources Management	M,D
Industrial and Manufacturing Management	M,D
International Business	M
Kinesiology and Movement Studies	M
Library Science	M
Management Information Systems	M,D
Marketing	M,D
Mathematics Education	M
Music Education	M
Music	M
Photography	M
Physical Education	M
Psychology—General	M,D
School Psychology	M,D
Science Education	M,D
Special Education	M

INTER AMERICAN UNIVERSITY OF PUERTO RICO SCHOOL OF LAW

Law	D

INTER AMERICAN UNIVERSITY OF PUERTO RICO SCHOOL OF OPTOMETRY

Optometry	D

INTERDENOMINATIONAL THEOLOGICAL CENTER

Pastoral Ministry and Counseling	M,D
Religious Education	M,D
Theology	M,D

INTERIOR DESIGNERS INSTITUTE

Interior Design	M

INTERNATIONAL BAPTIST COLLEGE AND SEMINARY

Education—General	M
Pastoral Ministry and Counseling	M,D
Theology	M

INTERNATIONAL INSTITUTE FOR RESTORATIVE PRACTICES

Organizational Behavior	M,O

INTERNATIONAL TECHNOLOGICAL UNIVERSITY

Business Administration and Management—General	M,D
Computer Art and Design	M
Computer Engineering	M
Electrical Engineering	M,D
Engineering Management	M
Software Engineering	M

INTERNATIONAL UNIVERSITY IN GENEVA

Business Administration and Management—General	M,D
Communication—General	M,D
Entrepreneurship	M,D
International Affairs	M,D
International Business	M,D
Marketing	M,D
Media Studies	M,D
Public Administration	M,D

THE INTERNATIONAL UNIVERSITY OF MONACO

Business Administration and Management—General	M
Entrepreneurship	M
Finance and Banking	M
Financial Engineering	M
International Business	M
Marketing	M

IONA COLLEGE

Accounting	M,O
Advertising and Public Relations	M,O
Business Administration and Management—General	M,O
Communication Disorders	M
Computer and Information Systems Security	M,O
Computer Science	M
Counseling Psychology	M,O
Criminal Justice and Criminology	M,O
Early Childhood Education	M
Education—General	M
Educational Leadership and Administration	M
English Education	M
English	M
Experimental Psychology	M,O
Finance and Banking	M,O
Foreign Languages Education	M
Forensic Sciences	M
Game Design and Development	M
Health Services Management and Hospital Administration	M,O
History	M
Human Resources Management	M,O
Industrial and Organizational Psychology	M,O
International Business	M,O
Management Information Systems	M,O
Management of Technology	M,O
Marketing	M,O
Marriage and Family Therapy	M
Mass Communication	M,O
Mathematics Education	M
Project Management	M,O
Psychology—General	M,O
Recreation and Park Management	M,O
Risk Management	M,O
School Psychology	M,O
Science Education	M
Social Sciences Education	M
Spanish	M
Special Education	M
Sports Management	M,O

IOWA STATE UNIVERSITY OF SCIENCE AND TECHNOLOGY

Accounting	M
Aerospace/Aeronautical Engineering	M,D
Agricultural Economics and Agribusiness	M,D
Agricultural Education	M,D
Agricultural Engineering	M,D
Agricultural Sciences—General	M,D
Agronomy and Soil Sciences	M,D
Analytical Chemistry	M,D
Animal Sciences	M,D
Anthropology	M
Applied Arts and Design—General	M,D
Applied Mathematics	M,D
Applied Physics	M,D
Architecture	M
Art/Fine Arts	M
Astrophysics	M,D
Bioinformatics	M,D
Biological and Biomedical Sciences—General	M,D
Biophysics	M,D
Biostatistics	M,D
Business Administration and Management—General	M
Business Analytics	M
Cell Biology	M,D
Chemical Engineering	M,D
Chemistry	M,D
Child and Family Studies	M,D
Civil Engineering	M,D
Clothing and Textiles	M,D
Cognitive Sciences	M,D
Computational Biology	M,D
Computer Engineering	M,D
Computer Science	M,D
Condensed Matter Physics	M,D
Construction Engineering	M,D
Corporate and Organizational Communication	M,D
Counseling Psychology	M,D
Counselor Education	M,D
Curriculum and Instruction	M,D
Developmental Biology	M,D
Ecology	M,D
Economics	M,D
Education—General	M,D
Educational Leadership and Administration	M,D
Educational Measurement and Evaluation	M,D
Educational Media/Instructional Technology	M,D
Electrical Engineering	M,D
Elementary Education	M,D
English as a Second Language	M,D
English	M,D
Entomology	M,D
Environmental Engineering	M,D
Environmental Sciences	M,D
Evolutionary Biology	M,D
Exercise and Sports Science	M
Family and Consumer Sciences-General	M
Finance and Banking	M
Fish, Game, and Wildlife Management	M,D
Food Science and Technology	M,D
Forestry	M,D

Foundations and Philosophy of Education	M,D
Genetics	M,D
Geology	M,D
Geosciences	M,D
Geotechnical Engineering	M,D
Graphic Design	M
Higher Education	M,D
History	M,D
Horticulture	M,D
Human Development	M,D
Human Resources Development	M,D
Human-Computer Interaction	M,D
Immunology	M,D
Industrial Design	M
Industrial/Management Engineering	M,D
Information Science	M
Inorganic Chemistry	M,D
Interdisciplinary Studies	M
Interior Design	M
Journalism	M
Kinesiology and Movement Studies	M,D
Landscape Architecture	M
Linguistics	M
Management Information Systems	M,D
Mass Communication	M
Materials Engineering	M,D
Materials Sciences	M,D
Mathematics Education	M,D
Mathematics	M,D
Mechanical Engineering	M,D
Mechanics	M,D
Meteorology	M,D
Microbiology	M,D
Molecular Biology	M,D
Molecular Genetics	M,D
Natural Resources	M,D
Neuroscience	M,D
Nutrition	M,D
Operations Research	M,D
Organic Chemistry	M,D
Pathology	M,D
Physical Chemistry	M,D
Physics	M,D
Plant Biology	M,D
Plant Pathology	M,D
Plant Sciences	M,D
Political Science	M
Psychology—General	M,D
Public Administration	M
Rhetoric	M,D
Rural Planning and Studies	D
Rural Sociology	M,D
Science Education	M
Social Psychology	M,D
Sociology	M,D
Special Education	M,D
Statistics	M,D
Structural Biology	M,D
Structural Engineering	M,D
Student Affairs	M,D
Sustainable Development	M,D
Systems Engineering	M
Toxicology	M,D
Transportation and Highway Engineering	M,D
Transportation Management	M
Urban and Regional Planning	M
Veterinary Medicine	M
Veterinary Sciences	M,D
Vocational and Technical Education	M,D
Writing	M,D

IOWA WESLEYAN UNIVERSITY

Curriculum and Instruction	M

IRELL & MANELLA GRADUATE SCHOOL OF BIOLOGICAL SCIENCES

Biochemistry	D
Biological and Biomedical Sciences—General	D
Cancer Biology/Oncology	D
Cell Biology	D
Developmental Biology	D
Genetics	D
Immunology	D
Molecular Biology	D
Neuroscience	D
Pharmaceutical Sciences	D

ITHACA COLLEGE

Accounting	M
Agricultural Education	M
Allied Health—General	M,D
Art/Fine Arts	M
Business Administration and Management—General	M
Communication Disorders	M
Elementary Education	M
English Education	M
Exercise and Sports Science	M
Health Education	M
Internet and Interactive Multimedia	M
Music Education	M
Music	M
Occupational Therapy	M
Photography	M
Physical Education	M
Physical Therapy	D
Secondary Education	M
Sports Management	M
Writing	M

JACKSON STATE UNIVERSITY

Accounting	M
Applied Mathematics	M
Atmospheric Sciences	M
Biological and Biomedical Sciences—General	M
Business Administration and Management—General	M,D
Chemistry	M,D
Civil Engineering	M,D

Clinical Psychology	M,D
Communication Disorders	M
Computer Science	M
Counselor Education	M
Criminal Justice and Criminology	M
Early Childhood Education	M,D,O
Education—General	M,D,O
Educational Leadership and Administration	M,D,O
Elementary Education	M,D,O
English Education	M
English	M
Environmental Engineering	M,D
Environmental Sciences	M
Geosciences	M,D
Hazardous Materials Management	M,D
Health Education	M
Higher Education	M,D,O
History	M
Materials Sciences	M,D
Mathematics Education	M
Mathematics	M
Music Education	M
Physical Education	M
Physics	M,D
Political Science	M
Psychology—General	D
Public Administration	M,D
Public Affairs	M,D
Public Health—General	M,D
Public Policy	M,D
Reading Education	M,D,O
Rehabilitation Sciences	M
School Psychology	M
Science Education	M,D
Social Work	M,D
Sociology	M
Special Education	M,O
Sports Management	M
Statistics	M
Urban and Regional Planning	M
Vocational and Technical Education	M,D

JACKSONVILLE STATE UNIVERSITY

Biological and Biomedical Sciences—General	M
Business Administration and Management—General	M
Computer Science	M
Counselor Education	M
Criminal Justice and Criminology	M
Early Childhood Education	M
Education—General	M,O
Educational Leadership and Administration	M,O
Educational Media/Instructional Technology	M
Elementary Education	M
Emergency Management	M
English	M
History	M
Liberal Studies	M
Mathematics	M
Music	M
Nursing—General	M
Physical Education	M,O
Psychology—General	M
Public Administration	M
Reading Education	M
Secondary Education	M
Social Work	M
Software Engineering	M
Special Education	M

JACKSONVILLE UNIVERSITY

Accounting	M
Adult Nursing	M,D,O
Allied Health—General	M,D
Art/Fine Arts	M
Business Administration and Management—General	M,D
Communication Disorders	M
Counseling Psychology	M
Dance	M
Dentistry	M,O
Educational Leadership and Administration	M
Family Nurse Practitioner Studies	M
Finance and Banking	M
Gerontological Nursing	M,D,O
Health Informatics	M
Kinesiology and Movement Studies	M
Marine Sciences	M
Marketing	M
Marriage and Family Therapy	M
Mathematics	M
Nursing and Healthcare Administration	M
Nursing Education	M
Nursing Informatics	M
Nursing—General	M,D
Occupational Therapy	D
Oral and Dental Sciences	M,O
Organizational Management	M
Psychiatric Nursing	M
Public Policy	M
Sports Management	M

JAMES MADISON UNIVERSITY

Accounting	M
American Studies	M
Applied Behavior Analysis	M
Art Education	M
Art History	M
Art/Fine Arts	M
Biological and Biomedical Sciences—General	M
Business Administration and Management—General	M
Clinical Psychology	D
Communication Disorders	M,D
Communication—General	M
Computer and Information Systems Security	M

Computer Science	M
Counseling Psychology	D
Early Childhood Education	M
Education of the Gifted	M
Educational Leadership and Administration	M
Educational Measurement and Evaluation	M,D
Educational Media/Instructional Technology	M
Elementary Education	M
Engineering and Applied Sciences—General	M
English as a Second Language	M
English	M
Entrepreneurship	M
Environmental Management and Policy	M
Exercise and Sports Science	M
Experimental Psychology	M
Family Nurse Practitioner Studies	M,D
Foreign Languages Education	M
Forensic Sciences	M
Gerontological Nursing	M,D
Health Education	M
Higher Education	M
History	M
Human Resources Management	M
Kinesiology and Movement Studies	M
Management Information Systems	M
Management Strategy and Policy	D
Mathematics Education	M
Middle School Education	M
Multilingual and Multicultural Education	M
Music Education	M
Music	M,D
Nonprofit Management	M,D
Nurse Midwifery	M,D
Nursing and Healthcare Administration	M,D
Nursing—General	M,D
Nutrition	M
Occupational Therapy	M
Organizational Management	D
Photography	M
Physical Education	M
Physician Assistant Studies	M
Physiology	M
Political Science	M
Psychiatric Nursing	M,D
Psychology—General	M
Public Administration	M
Public History	M
Reading Education	M
Rhetoric	M
School Psychology	M,D,O
Secondary Education	M
Special Education	M
Sustainability Management	M
Taxation	M
Technical Writing	M
Vocational and Technical Education	M
Writing	M

JEFFERSON COLLEGE OF HEALTH SCIENCES

Nursing and Healthcare Administration	M
Nursing Education	M
Nursing—General	M
Occupational Therapy	M
Physician Assistant Studies	M

THE JEWISH THEOLOGICAL SEMINARY

Jewish Studies	M,D
Music	M
Religion	M,D
Religious Education	M,D
Theology	M,D,O
Women's Studies	M,D

JOHN BROWN UNIVERSITY

Business Administration and Management—General	M
Clinical Psychology	M,O
Counseling Psychology	M,O
Counselor Education	M,O
Curriculum and Instruction	M
Education—General	M
Ethics	M
International Business	M
Marriage and Family Therapy	M,O
Secondary Education	M

JOHN CABOT UNIVERSITY

Art History	M

JOHN CARROLL UNIVERSITY

Accounting	M
Biological and Biomedical Sciences—General	M
Business Administration and Management—General	M
Counseling Psychology	M,O
Counselor Education	M,O
Education—General	M
Educational Psychology	M,O
English	M
Humanities	M
Mathematics	M
Nonprofit Management	M
Religion	M
Theology	M

JOHN F. KENNEDY UNIVERSITY

Business Administration and Management—General	M
Counseling Psychology	M
Finance and Banking	M
Health Education	M
Health Psychology	M
Health Services Management and Hospital Administration	M
Human Resources Management	M
Law	D

Management of Technology	M
Management Strategy and Policy	M
Museum Studies	O
Psychology—General	M,D,O
Sport Psychology	M,O
Transpersonal and Humanistic Psychology	M

JOHN JAY COLLEGE OF CRIMINAL JUSTICE OF THE CITY UNIVERSITY OF NEW YORK

Criminal Justice and Criminology	M,D
Forensic Psychology	M,D
Forensic Sciences	M,D
Legal and Justice Studies	M,D
Organizational Behavior	M,D
Public Administration	M,D
Public Policy	M,D

THE JOHN MARSHALL LAW SCHOOL

Law	M,D

JOHN PAUL THE GREAT CATHOLIC UNIVERSITY

Theology	M

JOHNS HOPKINS UNIVERSITY

Aerospace/Aeronautical Engineering	M
Allopathic Medicine	D
Anatomy	D
Anthropology	D
Applied Economics	M
Applied Mathematics	M,D,O
Applied Physics	M,O
Archaeology	D
Art History	M,D
Artificial Intelligence/Robotics	M
Asian Studies	M,D,O
Astronomy	D
Biochemistry	M,D
Bioengineering	M,D
Bioethics	M,D
Bioinformatics	M
Biological and Biomedical Sciences—General	M,D
Biomedical Engineering	M,D,O
Biophysics	M,D
Biostatistics	M,D
Biotechnology	M
Business Administration and Management—General	M,O
Business Analytics	M
Cardiovascular Sciences	M,D
Cell Biology	D
Chemical Engineering	M,D
Chemistry	M,D
Civil Engineering	M,D,O
Classics	D
Clinical Psychology	M,D
Clinical Research	M,D
Cognitive Sciences	M,D
Communication—General	M,O
Community Health Nursing	M
Community Health	M,D
Comparative Literature	D
Computer and Information Systems Security	M,O
Computer Engineering	M,D,O
Computer Science	M,D,O
Demography and Population Studies	M,D
Developmental Biology	D
Economics	D
Education—General	M,D,O
Electrical Engineering	M,D,O
Energy Management and Policy	M,O
Engineering and Applied Sciences—General	M,D,O
Engineering Management	M
English	D
Environmental and Occupational Health	M,D
Environmental Engineering	M,D,O
Environmental Management and Policy	M,O
Environmental Sciences	M,O
Epidemiology	M,D
Evolutionary Biology	D
Family Nurse Practitioner Studies	D
Film, Television, and Video Production	M
Finance and Banking	M,D,O
French	M,D
Genetic Counseling	M,D
Genetics	M,D
Geographic Information Systems	M,O
Geosciences	M,D
German	M,D
Gerontological Nursing	D
Health Communication	M,O
Health Education	M,D
Health Services Management and Hospital Administration	M,D
History of Science and Technology	M,D
History	D
Homeland Security	M,O
Immunology	M,D
Infectious Diseases	M,D
International Affairs	M,D,O
International Development	M,D,O
International Economics	M,D,O
International Health	M,D
Investment Management	M,O
Italian	M,D
Liberal Studies	M,O
Management Information Systems	M,O
Management of Technology	M,O
Marketing	M
Materials Engineering	M,D
Materials Sciences	M,D
Mathematical and Computational Finance	M,D,O
Mathematics	M,D
Mechanical Engineering	M,D,O

Mechanics	M
Media Studies	M
Medical Illustration	M
Microbiology	M,D
Molecular Biology	M,D
Molecular Biophysics	M,D
Molecular Medicine	D
Museum Studies	M,O
Music	M,D,O
Nanotechnology	M
Near and Middle Eastern Languages	D
Near and Middle Eastern Studies	D
Neuroscience	D
Nonprofit Management	M,O
Nursing and Healthcare Administration	M,D
Nursing—General	M,D*
Nutrition	M,D
Operations Research	M,D
Pathobiology	D
Pathology	D
Pediatric Nursing	D
Pharmaceutical Sciences	M
Pharmacology	D
Philosophy	M,D
Photonics	M,O
Physics	D
Physiology	D
Planetary and Space Sciences	M,D
Political Science	M,D,O
Psychology—General	D
Public Administration	M,O
Public Health—General	M,D
Public Policy	M,D
Real Estate	M
Risk Management	M
Romance Languages	M,D
Sociology	D
Spanish	M,D
Statistics	M
Systems Engineering	M,O
Technical Writing	M,O
Writing	M,O

JOHNSON & WALES UNIVERSITY

Accounting	M
Addictions/Substance Abuse Counseling	M
Business Administration and Management—General	M
Business Education	M
Clinical Psychology	M
Computer and Information Systems Security	M
Criminal Justice and Criminology	M
Data Science/Data Analytics	M
Economic Development	M
Education—General	M
Educational Leadership and Administration	D
Elementary Education	M
Finance and Banking	M
Hospitality Management	M
Human Resources Management	M
Management Information Systems	M
Nonprofit Management	M
Occupational Therapy	D
Organizational Management	M
Physician Assistant Studies	M
Secondary Education	M
Special Education	M
Sports Management	M
Supply Chain Management	M
Sustainable Development	M
Travel and Tourism	M

JOHNSON C. SMITH UNIVERSITY

Social Work	M

JOHNSON UNIVERSITY

Clinical Psychology	M,D,O
Counselor Education	M,D,O
Cultural Studies	M,D,O
Education—General	M,D,O
Educational Media/Instructional Technology	M,D,O
Higher Education	M,D,O
Nonprofit Management	M,D,O
Pastoral Ministry and Counseling	M,D,O
Theology	M,D,O

JOHNSON UNIVERSITY FLORIDA

Pastoral Ministry and Counseling	M

JOSE MARIA VARGAS UNIVERSITY

Early Childhood Education	M

THE JUDGE ADVOCATE GENERAL'S SCHOOL, U.S. ARMY

Law	M
Military and Defense Studies	M

JUDSON UNIVERSITY

Architecture	M
Business Administration and Management—General	M
Clinical Psychology	M
Human Services	M
Organizational Management	M
Pastoral Ministry and Counseling	M
Reading Education	M,D
Sustainable Development	M
Urban Design	M

THE JUILLIARD SCHOOL

Music	M,D,O
Theater	M,D,O

JUNIATA COLLEGE

Accounting	M
Business Administration and Management—General	M
Organizational Management	M

KANSAS CITY UNIVERSITY OF MEDICINE AND BIOSCIENCES

Bioethics	M
Biological and Biomedical Sciences—General	M
Osteopathic Medicine	D

KANSAS STATE UNIVERSITY

Accounting	M
Adult Education	M,D,O
Advertising and Public Relations	M
Agricultural Economics and Agribusiness	M,D
Agricultural Education	M
Agricultural Engineering	M,D
Agricultural Sciences—General	M,D,O
Agronomy and Soil Sciences	M,D,O
Animal Sciences	M,D
Applied Science and Technology	M,O
Architectural Engineering	M
Architecture	M
Art/Fine Arts	M
Biochemistry	M,D
Bioengineering	M,D
Biological and Biomedical Sciences—General	M,D
Business Administration and Management—General	M,O
Chemical Engineering	M,D,O
Chemistry	M,D
Child and Family Studies	M,D
Child Development	M
Civil Engineering	M,D
Clothing and Textiles	M,D
Communication Disorders	M,D,O
Communication—General	M,D
Computer Engineering	M,D
Computer Science	M,D
Conflict Resolution and Mediation/Peace Studies	M,D,O
Consumer Economics	M,D,O
Counselor Education	M,D,O
Curriculum and Instruction	M,O
Data Science/Data Analytics	M,O
Distance Education Development	M,D,O
Early Childhood Education	M,D,O
Economics	M,D
Education—General	M,D,O
Educational Leadership and Administration	M,D,O
Educational Media/Instructional Technology	M,D,O
Electrical Engineering	M,D
Elementary Education	M,D,O
Energy and Power Engineering	M,D
Energy Management and Policy	M,D
Engineering and Applied Sciences—General	M,D,O
Engineering Management	M
English as a Second Language	M,D,O
English Education	M,D,O
English	M,O
Entomology	M,D
Entrepreneurship	M,O
Environmental Design	D
Environmental Engineering	M,D
Environmental Sciences	M,D,O
Family and Consumer Sciences—General	M,D,O
Finance and Banking	M,D,O
Food Science and Technology	M,D
French	M
Gender Studies	O
Genetics	M,D
Geographic Information Systems	M,D,O
Geography	M,D,O
Geology	M
Geotechnical Engineering	M,D
German	M
Gerontology	M,O
Health Communication	M
Health Education	M,D
History	M,D
Horticulture	M,D
Hospitality Management	M,D
Human Development	M,D,O
Human Services	M,D,O
Industrial/Management Engineering	M,D
Interdisciplinary Studies	M,O
Interior Design	M
Journalism	M
Kinesiology and Movement Studies	M,D
Landscape Architecture	M
Management of Technology	M
Manufacturing Engineering	M,D
Marketing	M,O
Marriage and Family Therapy	M,D,O
Mass Communication	M
Mathematics	M,D,O
Mechanical Engineering	M,D
Middle School Education	M,D,O
Music	M
National Security	M,D
Natural Resources	M
Nuclear Engineering	M,D
Nutrition	M,D
Operations Research	M,D
Pathobiology	M,D
Physics	M,D
Physiology	M,D
Plant Pathology	M,D
Plant Sciences	M,D
Political Science	M,D
Psychology—General	M,D
Public Administration	M

Public Health—General	M,D,O
Range Science	M,D,O
Reading Education	M,D,O
Sociology	M,D
Spanish	M
Special Education	M,D,O
Statistics	M,D,O
Structural Engineering	M,D
Student Affairs	M,D,O
Theater	M
Transportation and Highway Engineering	M,D
Urban and Regional Planning	M
Veterinary Medicine	D
Veterinary Sciences	M,O
Water Resources Engineering	M,D
Women's Studies	O

KANSAS WESLEYAN UNIVERSITY

Business Administration and Management—General	M
Sports Management	M

KEAN UNIVERSITY

Accounting	M
Addictions/Substance Abuse Counseling	M
Art Education	M
Biotechnology	M
Business Administration and Management—General	M
Clinical Psychology	M,D
Communication Disorders	M,D
Communication—General	M
Community Health Nursing	M
Counseling Psychology	M
Counselor Education	M
Criminal Justice and Criminology	M
Curriculum and Instruction	M
Early Childhood Education	M
Education—General	M
Educational Leadership and Administration	M,D
English as a Second Language	M
Exercise and Sports Science	M
Foreign Languages Education	M
Forensic Psychology	M
Health Services Management and Hospital Administration	M
Holocaust and Genocide Studies	M
Industrial and Organizational Psychology	M
International Business	M
Liberal Studies	M
Management Information Systems	M
Marriage and Family Therapy	M
Multilingual and Multicultural Education	M
Nonprofit Management	M
Nursing and Healthcare Administration	M
Nursing—General	M
Occupational Therapy	M
Physical Therapy	D
Psychology—General	M
Public Administration	M
School Psychology	D,O
Social Work	M
Special Education	M
Writing	M

KECK GRADUATE INSTITUTE

Biological and Biomedical Sciences—General	M,D,O
Data Science/Data Analytics	M
Pharmacy	D

KEHILATH YAKOV RABBINICAL SEMINARY

Theology	M

KEISER UNIVERSITY

Accounting	M
Business Administration and Management—General	M,D
Computer and Information Systems Security	M
Criminal Justice and Criminology	M
Distance Education Development	M
Education—General	M
Educational Leadership and Administration	M,D,O
Educational Media/Instructional Technology	D,O
Family Nurse Practitioner Studies	M
Health Education	M
Health Services Management and Hospital Administration	M
Homeland Security	M
Industrial and Organizational Psychology	M,D
International Business	M,D
Management Information Systems	M
Management of Technology	M
Marketing	M,D
Nurse Anesthesia	M,D
Nursing—General	M
Occupational Therapy	M
Organizational Management	M
Physician Assistant Studies	M
Psychology—General	M,D

KENNESAW STATE UNIVERSITY

Accounting	M
American Studies	M
Applied Statistics	M
Art Education	M
Biochemistry	M
Biological and Biomedical Sciences—General	M
Business Administration and Management—General	M,D
Chemistry	M

Civil Engineering	M
Communication—General	M
Computer and Information Systems Security	M,O
Computer Science	M
Conflict Resolution and Mediation/Peace Studies	M,D
Construction Management	M
Criminal Justice and Criminology	M
Curriculum and Instruction	O
Data Science/Data Analytics	M,D,O
Early Childhood Education	M,D,O
Education—General	M,D,O
Educational Leadership and Administration	M,D,O
Educational Media/Instructional Technology	M,D,O
Electrical Engineering	M
Engineering and Applied Sciences—General	M
Engineering Management	M
English as a Second Language	M
English Education	M
Environmental Engineering	M
Exercise and Sports Science	M
Geotechnical Engineering	M
Health Informatics	M,O
Health Services Management and Hospital Administration	M
Information Science	M,O
International Affairs	M
Management of Technology	M
Mathematics Education	M
Mechanical Engineering	M
Middle School Education	D,O
Nursing and Healthcare Administration	M
Nursing Education	M
Nursing—General	M,D
Public Administration	M
Reading Education	M
Science Education	M
Secondary Education	M,D,O
Social Work	M
Software Engineering	M,O
Special Education	M,D,O
Sports Management	M
Structural Engineering	M
Systems Engineering	M
Transportation and Highway Engineering	M
Water Resources Engineering	M
Writing	M

KENRICK-GLENNON SEMINARY

Theology	M

KENT STATE UNIVERSITY

Accounting	M,D
Adult Nursing	M,D
Advertising and Public Relations	M
Aerospace/Aeronautical Engineering	M
Anthropology	M
Applied Mathematics	M,D
Architecture	M
Art Education	M
Art History	M
Art/Fine Arts	M
Athletic Training and Sports Medicine	M,D
Biological and Biomedical Sciences—General	M,D
Biological Anthropology	M,D
Biostatistics	M,D
Botany	M,D
Broadcast Journalism	M
Business Administration and Management—General	M
Business Analytics	M
Cell Biology	M,D
Chemical Physics	M,D
Chemistry	M,D
Child and Family Studies	M
Clinical Psychology	M,D
Communication Disorders	M,D,O
Communication—General	M
Computer and Information Systems Security	M
Computer Education	M,D,O
Computer Science	M,D
Conflict Resolution and Mediation/Peace Studies	M,D
Counseling Psychology	M
Counselor Education	M,D,O
Criminal Justice and Criminology	M,D
Curriculum and Instruction	M,D,O
Early Childhood Education	M,D,O
Ecology	M,D
Economics	M
Education of the Gifted	M,D,O
Education—General	M,D,O
Educational Leadership and Administration	M,D,O
Educational Measurement and Evaluation	M,D
Educational Media/Instructional Technology	M,D,O
Educational Psychology	M
English as a Second Language	M,D
English Education	M,D
English	M,D
Environmental and Occupational Health	M,D
Environmental Design	M
Epidemiology	M,D
Exercise and Sports Science	M,D
Experimental Psychology	M,D
Family Nurse Practitioner Studies	M,D
Finance and Banking	D

Foundations and Philosophy of Education — M,D
French — M,D
Genetics — M,D
Geographic Information Systems — M,D
Geography — M,D
Geology — M,D
German — M,D
Gerontological Nursing — M,D
Gerontology — M,D
Graphic Design — M
Health Education — M,D
Health Informatics — M,D
Health Promotion — M,D
Health Services Management and Hospital Administration — M,D
Higher Education — M,D,O
History — M,D
Hospitality Management — M
Human Development — M,D
Human Services — M
Illustration — M
Information Science — M,D
Japanese — M,D
Journalism — M
Landscape Architecture — M
Liberal Studies — M
Library Science — M
Linguistics — M
Management Information Systems — D
Marketing — D
Mass Communication — M
Mathematics Education — M,D
Mathematics — M,D,O
Media Studies — M
Middle School Education — M,D,O
Molecular Biology — M,D
Music Education — M,D
Music — M
Near and Middle Eastern Languages — M,D
Neuroscience — M,D
Nursing and Healthcare Administration — M,D
Nursing Education — M,D
Nursing—General — M,D
Nutrition — M,D
Pediatric Nursing — M,D
Pharmacology — M
Philosophy — M
Photography — M
Physics — M,D
Physiology — M,D
Podiatric Medicine — D
Political Science — M,D
Psychiatric Nursing — M,D
Psychology—General — M,D
Public Administration — M,D
Public Health—General — M,D
Reading Education — M
Recreation and Park Management — M
Rehabilitation Counseling — M
Rhetoric — M,D
Russian — M,D
School Psychology — M,D,O
Secondary Education — M,D
Social Sciences Education — M,D
Sociology — M,D
Spanish — M,D
Special Education — M,D,O
Sports Management — M
Student Affairs — M
Textile Design — M
Theater — M
Translation and Interpretation — M
Travel and Tourism — M
Urban Design — M
Vocational and Technical Education — M
Writing — M,D

KENT STATE UNIVERSITY AT STARK
Business Administration and Management—General — M
Curriculum and Instruction — M
Education—General — M

KENTUCKY CHRISTIAN UNIVERSITY
Religion — M
Theology — M

KETTERING COLLEGE
Occupational Therapy — D
Physician Assistant Studies — M

KETTERING UNIVERSITY
Business Administration and Management—General — M
Electrical Engineering — M
Engineering Management — M
Manufacturing Engineering — M
Mechanical Engineering — M

KEUKA COLLEGE
Business Administration and Management—General — M
Criminal Justice and Criminology — M
Early Childhood Education — M
Elementary Education — M
Gerontological Nursing — M
Nursing Education — M
Nursing—General — M
Occupational Therapy — M
Secondary Education — M
Social Work — M

KEYSTONE COLLEGE
Business Administration and Management—General — M
Early Childhood Education — M
Educational Leadership and Administration — M

KING'S COLLEGE
Education—General — M
Health Services Management and Hospital Administration — M
Physician Assistant Studies — M

THE KING'S UNIVERSITY
Pastoral Ministry and Counseling — M,D,O
Theology — M,D,O

KINGSWOOD UNIVERSITY
Pastoral Ministry and Counseling — M
Theology — M

KING UNIVERSITY
Accounting — M
Business Administration and Management—General — M
Family Nurse Practitioner Studies — M
Finance and Banking — M
Health Services Management and Hospital Administration — M
Human Resources Management — M
Marketing — M
Nursing and Healthcare Administration — M,D,O
Nursing Education — M,D,O
Nursing—General — M,D,O
Pediatric Nursing — M,D,O
Project Management — M

KNOX COLLEGE
Theology — M,D

KNOX THEOLOGICAL SEMINARY
Classics — M
Pastoral Ministry and Counseling — D
Religion — M
Theology — M

KUTZTOWN UNIVERSITY OF PENNSYLVANIA
Art Education — M
Arts Administration — M
Biological and Biomedical Sciences—General — M,D
Business Administration and Management—General — M
Computer Science — M
Counseling Psychology — M
Counselor Education — M
Curriculum and Instruction — M,D
Education—General — M,D
Educational Leadership and Administration — M
Educational Media/Instructional Technology — M
Elementary Education — M
English Education — M,D
English — M
Internet and Interactive Multimedia — M
Library Science — M
Mathematics — M,D
Middle School Education — M,D
Music Education — M
Public Administration — M
Reading Education — M
Secondary Education — M,D
Social Sciences Education — M,D
Social Work — M,D

LAGRANGE COLLEGE
Clinical Psychology — M
Curriculum and Instruction — M,O
Education—General — M,O
Middle School Education — M,O
Organizational Management — M
Secondary Education — M,O

LAGUNA COLLEGE OF ART & DESIGN
Art/Fine Arts — M

LAKE ERIE COLLEGE
Business Administration and Management—General — M
Education—General — M
Health Services Management and Hospital Administration — M
Management Information Systems — M

LAKE ERIE COLLEGE OF OSTEOPATHIC MEDICINE
Biological and Biomedical Sciences—General — M,D,O
Health Education — M,D,O
Osteopathic Medicine — M,D,O
Pharmacy — M,D,O

LAKE FOREST COLLEGE
American Studies — M
Art Education — M
Art/Fine Arts — M
Education—General — M
Elementary Education — M
English Education — M
Environmental Management and Policy — M
Film, Television, and Video Production — M
French — M
History — M
Liberal Studies — M
Mathematics Education — M
Music Education — M
Philosophy — M
Science Education — M
Secondary Education — M
Social Sciences Education — M
Spanish — M
Writing — M

LAKE FOREST GRADUATE SCHOOL OF MANAGEMENT
Business Administration and Management—General — M
Finance and Banking — M
Health Services Management and Hospital Administration — M
International Business — M
Marketing — M
Organizational Behavior — M

LAKEHEAD UNIVERSITY
Biological and Biomedical Sciences—General — M
Chemistry — M
Clinical Psychology — M,D
Computer Engineering — M
Computer Science — M
Economics — M
Education—General — M,D
Electrical Engineering — M
Engineering and Applied Sciences—General — M
English — M
Environmental Engineering — M
Exercise and Sports Science — M
Experimental Psychology — M
Forestry — M,D
Geology — M
Gerontology — M,D
Health Services Research — M
History — M
Kinesiology and Movement Studies — M
Mathematics — M
Physics — M
Psychology—General — M,D
Social Work — M
Sociology — M
Women's Studies — M,D

LAKELAND UNIVERSITY
Accounting — M
Business Administration and Management—General — M
Counselor Education — M
Education—General — M
Finance and Banking — M
Health Services Management and Hospital Administration — M
Project Management — M
Theology — M

LAMAR UNIVERSITY
Accounting — M
Biological and Biomedical Sciences—General — M
Business Administration and Management—General — M
Chemical Engineering — M,D
Chemistry — M
Clinical Psychology — M
Communication Disorders — M,D
Computer Science — M
Counseling Psychology — M
Counselor Education — M
Criminal Justice and Criminology — M
Education—General — M,D,O
Educational Leadership and Administration — M,D
Educational Media/Instructional Technology — M
Electrical Engineering — M,D
Engineering and Applied Sciences—General — M,D
English — M
Family and Consumer Sciences-General — M
Foreign Languages Education — M
History — M
Kinesiology and Movement Studies — M
Mathematics — M
Mechanical Engineering — M,D
Music — M
Nursing and Healthcare Administration — M
Nursing Education — M
Nursing—General — M
Political Science — M
Psychology—General — M
Spanish — M
Special Education — M,D

LANCASTER BIBLE COLLEGE
Counseling Psychology — M,D
Counselor Education — M,D
Elementary Education — M,D
Marriage and Family Therapy — M,D
Pastoral Ministry and Counseling — M,D,O
Secondary Education — M,D
Special Education — M,D
Theology — M,D,O

LANCASTER THEOLOGICAL SEMINARY
Art History — M,D,O
Ethics — M,D,O
Religion — M,D,O
Religious Education — M,D,O
Theology — M,D,O

LANDER UNIVERSITY
Early Childhood Education — M
Education—General — M
Emergency Management — M
Nursing—General — M

LANGSTON UNIVERSITY
Education—General — M
Elementary Education — M
English as a Second Language — M
Multilingual and Multicultural Education — M
Physical Therapy — D
Rehabilitation Counseling — M
Urban Education — M

LA ROCHE UNIVERSITY
Accounting — M
Human Resources Management — M,O
Nurse Anesthesia — M,D
Nursing and Healthcare Administration — M
Nursing Education — M
Nursing—General — M

LA SALLE UNIVERSITY
Accounting — M,O
Adult Nursing — M,D,O
Advertising and Public Relations — M,O

American Studies — M,O
Business Administration and Management—General — M,O
Business Analytics — M,O
Clinical Psychology — M,D
Communication Disorders — M
Communication—General — M
Community Health Nursing — M,D,O
Computer Science — M,O
Corporate and Organizational Communication — M,O
Counseling Psychology — M
Developmental Psychology — M,D
Early Childhood Education — M,O
Education—General — M,O
Educational Leadership and Administration — M,O
Educational Media/Instructional Technology — M,O
English as a Second Language — M,O
English — M
Family Nurse Practitioner Studies — M,D,O
Finance and Banking — M,O
Forensic Sciences — M,O
Gerontological Nursing — M,D,O
Gerontology — M,D,O
Health Psychology — M,O
Hispanic Studies — M,O
History — M,O
Human Resources Development — M,O
Human Resources Management — M,O
Industrial and Organizational Psychology — M
International Business — M,O
Latin American Studies — M,O
Management of Technology — M,O
Marketing — M,O
Marriage and Family Therapy — M
Media Studies — M,O
Middle School Education — M,O
Multilingual and Multicultural Education — M,O
Nonprofit Management — M
Nurse Anesthesia — M,D,O
Nursing and Healthcare Administration — M,D,O
Nursing Education — M,D,O
Nursing—General — M,D,O
Psychology—General — M,D
Public Health—General — M
Public History — M,O
Reading Education — M,O
School Nursing — M,D,O
Secondary Education — M,O
Social Sciences Education — M,O
Special Education — M,O
Translation and Interpretation — M,O
Western European Studies — M,O

LASELL COLLEGE
Advertising and Public Relations — M,O
Business Administration and Management—General — M,O
Communication—General — M,O
Corporate and Organizational Communication — M,O
Criminal Justice and Criminology — M,O
Curriculum and Instruction — M,O
Education—General — M,O
Educational Leadership and Administration — M,O
Elementary Education — M,O
Emergency Management — M,O
English as a Second Language — M,O
Health Communication — M,O
Health Services Management and Hospital Administration — M,O
Homeland Security — M,O
Hospitality Management — M,O
Human Resources Management — M,O
Marketing — M,O
Project Management — M,O
Recreation and Park Management — M,O
Rehabilitation Sciences — M,O
Special Education — M,O
Sports Management — M,O
Travel and Tourism — M,O

LA SIERRA UNIVERSITY
Accounting — M
Advertising and Public Relations — M
Business Administration and Management—General — M,O
Communication—General — M
Counselor Education — M
Curriculum and Instruction — M,D,O
Education—General — M,D,O
Educational Leadership and Administration — M,D,O
Educational Psychology — M,O
English — M
Finance and Banking — M,O
Human Resources Management — M,O
Marketing — M,O
Pastoral Ministry and Counseling — M
Religion — M
Religious Education — M
School Psychology — M,O
Writing — M

LAURENTIAN UNIVERSITY
Analytical Chemistry — M
Applied Physics — M
Applied Psychology — M
Applied Social Research — M
Biochemistry — M
Biological and Biomedical Sciences—General — M,D
Business Administration and Management—General — M
Chemistry — M
Ecology — M,D
Engineering and Applied Sciences—General — M,D
Environmental Sciences — M

Experimental Psychology M
Geology M,D
History M
Human Development M
Humanities M
Mineral/Mining Engineering M,D
Natural Resources M,D
Nursing—General M
Organic Chemistry M
Physical Chemistry M
Psychology—General M
Public Health—General D
Science Education O
Social Work M
Sociology M
Technical Writing O
Theoretical Chemistry M

LAWRENCE TECHNOLOGICAL UNIVERSITY

Architectural Engineering M,D
Architecture M,O
Artificial Intelligence/Robotics M,O
Automotive Engineering M,D
Bioinformatics M,O
Biomedical Engineering M,D
Business Administration and
  Management—General M,D,O
Civil Engineering M,D
Communication—General M,O
Computer and Information
  Systems Security M,D,O
Computer Engineering M,D
Computer Science M,O
Construction Engineering M,D
Data Science/Data Analytics M,O
Educational Media/Instructional
  Technology M,O
Electrical Engineering M,D
Energy and Power
  Engineering M,D
Engineering and Applied
  Sciences—General M,D
Engineering Management M,D
Finance and Banking M,D,O
Health Services Management and
  Hospital Administration M,D,O
Human Resources Development M,O
Industrial and Manufacturing
  Management M,D
Industrial/Management
  Engineering M,D
Information Science M,D,O
Interior Design M,O
Management Strategy and Policy M,D,O
Manufacturing Engineering M,D
Marketing M,D,O
Mechanical Engineering M,D
Nonprofit Management M,D,O
Project Management M,D,O
Science Education M,O
Technical Communication M,O
Urban Design M,O
Water Resources Engineering M,D

LEBANESE AMERICAN UNIVERSITY

Business Administration and
  Management—General M
Computer Science M
International Affairs M
Pharmacy D

LEBANON VALLEY COLLEGE

Athletic Training and Sports
  Medicine M
Business Administration and
  Management—General M
Communication Disorders M
Ethics M
Health Services Management and
  Hospital Administration M
Human Resources Management M
Mathematics Education M,O
Music Education M
Physical Therapy D
Project Management M
Science Education M,O
Social Sciences Education M,O

LEE UNIVERSITY

Art/Fine Arts M,O
Biological and Biomedical
  Sciences—General M,O
Business Administration and
  Management—General M
Child Development M
Counseling Psychology M
Counselor Education M
Curriculum and Instruction M,O
Early Childhood Education M,O
Economics M,O
Education—General M,O
Educational Leadership and
  Administration M,O
Elementary Education M,O
English as a Second Language M,O
English M,O
Ethics M
Higher Education M,O
History M,O
Marriage and Family Therapy M
Mathematics Education M,O
Mathematics M,O
Middle School Education M,O
Music Education M
Music M
Pastoral Ministry and Counseling M
Religion M
Secondary Education M,O
Social Sciences Education M,O
Spanish M,O
Special Education M,O

Theology M

LEHIGH UNIVERSITY

Accounting M
African Studies M,O
American Studies M,D,O
Applied Mathematics M,D
Biochemical Engineering M,D
Biochemistry M,D
Bioengineering M,D
Biological and Biomedical
  Sciences—General M,D
Business Administration and
  Management—General M
Cell Biology M,D
Chemical Engineering M,D
Chemistry M,D
Civil Engineering M,D
Computer Engineering M,D
Computer Science M,D
Counseling Psychology M,D,O
Counselor Education M,D,O
Curriculum and Instruction M,D,O
Early Childhood Education M,D,O
Economics M,D
Education—General M,D,O
Educational Leadership and
  Administration M,D,O
Educational Media/Instructional
  Technology M,D
Electrical Engineering M,D
Elementary Education M,D
Energy and Power
  Engineering M
Engineering and Applied
  Sciences—General M,D,O
Engineering Management M,D,O
English M,D
Entrepreneurship M
Environmental and Occupational
  Health M,O
Environmental Engineering M,D
Environmental Law M,O
Environmental Management
  and Policy M,O
Environmental Sciences M,D
Finance and Banking M
Geology M,D
Geosciences M,D
Health Services Management and
  Hospital Administration M,O
History M,D
Human Services M,D,O
Industrial/Management
  Engineering M,D,O
Information Science M
Interdisciplinary Studies M,D
Materials Engineering M,D
Materials Sciences M,D
Mathematics M,D
Mechanical Engineering M,D
Mechanics M,D
Molecular Biology M,D
Photonics M,D
Physics M,D
Political Science M
Polymer Science and
  Engineering M,D
Project Management M
Psychology—General M,D
Public History M,D
Quantitative Analysis M
School Psychology D,O
Sociology M
Special Education M,D
Statistics M,D
Sustainable Development M,O
Systems Engineering M,D,O

LEHMAN COLLEGE OF THE CITY UNIVERSITY OF NEW YORK

Accounting M
Adult Nursing M
Art Education M
Art/Fine Arts M
Biological and Biomedical
  Sciences—General M
Business Administration and
  Management—General M
Communication Disorders M
Computer Science M
Counselor Education M
Early Childhood Education M
Education—General M
Elementary Education M
English as a Second Language M
English Education M
English M
Gerontological Nursing M
Health Education M
Health Promotion M
History M
Maternal and Child/Neonatal
  Nursing M
Mathematics Education M
Mathematics M
Middle School Education M
Multilingual and Multicultural
  Education M
Music Education M
Nursing—General M
Nutrition M
Pediatric Nursing M
Reading Education M
Recreation and Park Management M
Science Education M
Secondary Education M
Social Sciences Education M
Social Work M
Spanish M
Special Education M

LE MOYNE COLLEGE

Arts Administration M
Business Administration and
  Management—General M
Early Childhood Education M,O
Education—General M,O
Educational Leadership and
  Administration M,O
Elementary Education M,O
English as a Second Language M,O
English Education M,O
Family Nurse Practitioner Studies M,O
Foreign Languages Education M,O
Management Information Systems M
Middle School Education M,O
Nursing and Healthcare
  Administration M,O
Nursing Education M,O
Nursing Informatics M,O
Nursing—General M,O
Occupational Therapy M
Physician Assistant Studies M
Reading Education M,O
Secondary Education M,O
Social Sciences Education M,O
Special Education M,O
Urban Studies M,O

LENOIR-RHYNE UNIVERSITY

Accounting M
Addictions/Substance Abuse
  Counseling M
Athletic Training and Sports
  Medicine M
Business Administration and
  Management—General M
Business Analytics M
Clinical Psychology M
Community College Education M
Counseling Psychology M
Counselor Education M
Distance Education Development M
Education—General M
Educational Leadership and
  Administration M
Educational Media/Instructional
  Technology M
Entrepreneurship M
Health Services Management and
  Hospital Administration M
Human Services M
International Business M
Management Information Systems M
Management Strategy and Policy M
Nursing and Healthcare
  Administration M
Nursing Education M
Nursing—General M
Occupational Therapy M
Organizational Management M
Physician Assistant Studies M
Public Health—General M
Secondary Education M
Sustainable Development M
Theology M
Writing M

LESLEY UNIVERSITY

Adult Education M,D,O
Art Education M,D,O
Art Therapy M,D,O
Art/Fine Arts M,D,O
Clinical Psychology M,D,O
Computer Education M,D,O
Conflict Resolution and
  Mediation/Peace Studies M,D,O
Counseling Psychology M,D,O
Curriculum and Instruction M,D,O
Distance Education Development M,D,O
Early Childhood Education M,D,O
Ecology M,D,O
Education of Students with
  Severe/Multiple Disabilities M,D,O
Education—General M,D,O
Educational Leadership and
  Administration M,D,O
Educational Media/Instructional
  Technology M,D,O
Elementary Education M,D,O
English as a Second Language M,D,O
Health Psychology M,D,O
Interdisciplinary Studies M,D,O
International Affairs M,D,O
Mathematics Education M,D,O
Middle School Education M,D,O
Photography M
Psychology—General M,D,O
Reading Education M,D,O
School Psychology M,D,O
Science Education M,D,O
Secondary Education M,D,O
Social Psychology M,D,O
Special Education M,D,O
Sustainable Development M,D,O
Therapies—Dance, Drama, and
  Music M,D,O
Urban and Regional Planning M,D,O
Women's Studies M,D,O
Writing M,D,O

LES ROCHES INTERNATIONAL SCHOOL OF HOTEL MANAGEMENT

Hospitality Management M

LETOURNEAU UNIVERSITY

Business Administration and
  Management—General M
Counseling Psychology M
Curriculum and Instruction M
Educational Leadership and
  Administration M

Engineering and Applied
  Sciences—General M
Engineering Management M
Health Services Management and
  Hospital Administration M
Management Strategy and Policy M
Marriage and Family Therapy M
Psychology—General M

LEWIS & CLARK COLLEGE

Addictions/Substance Abuse
  Counseling M
Communication Disorders M
Counseling Psychology M
Curriculum and Instruction M
Educational Leadership and
  Administration M,D,O
Elementary Education M
Environmental Law M,D
Law M,D
Marriage and Family Therapy M
School Psychology M,O
Secondary Education M
Special Education M
Student Affairs M,D,O

LEWIS UNIVERSITY

Accounting M
Adult Nursing M,D
Aviation M
Bioinformatics M
Business Administration and
  Management—General M
Business Analytics M
Chemical Physics M
Chemistry M
Clinical Psychology M
Computational Biology M
Computer and Information
  Systems Security M
Computer Science M
Counseling Psychology M
Counselor Education M
Criminal Justice and Criminology M
Curriculum and Instruction M
Data Science/Data Analytics M
Early Childhood Education M
Education—General M,D
Educational Leadership and
  Administration M,D
Educational Media/Instructional
  Technology M
Electronic Commerce M
Elementary Education M
English as a Second Language M
English Education M
Environmental and Occupational
  Health M
Family Nurse Practitioner Studies M,D
Finance and Banking M
Foreign Languages Education M
Health Services Management and
  Hospital Administration M
Higher Education M
Human Resources Management M
International Business M
Management Information Systems M
Management of Technology M
Marketing M
Middle School Education M
Nursing and Healthcare
  Administration M,D
Nursing Education M,D
Nursing—General M,D
Organizational Management M
Physics M
Project Management M
Reading Education M
School Nursing M,D
Science Education M
Secondary Education M
Social Sciences Education M
Social Work M
Software Engineering M
Special Education M
Sports Management M
Student Affairs M

LEXINGTON THEOLOGICAL SEMINARY

Theology M,D

LIBERTY UNIVERSITY

Accounting M,D
Addictions/Substance Abuse
  Counseling M,D,O
Advertising and Public Relations M,D
Anatomy M,D
Applied Psychology M,D,O
Art/Fine Arts M
Biological and Biomedical
  Sciences—General M,D
Biopsychology M,D
Business Administration and
  Management—General M,D
Cell Biology M,D
Child and Family Studies M,D,O
Clinical Psychology M,D,O
Communication—General M
Computer and Information
  Systems Security M,D
Counseling Psychology M,D,O
Counselor Education M,D,O
Criminal Justice and Criminology M,D,O
Developmental Psychology M,D,O
Education—General M,D,O
Emergency Management M,D,O
English M
Epidemiology M,D
Exercise and Sports Science M,D
Facilities Management M,D
Family Nurse Practitioner Studies M,D
Finance and Banking M,D

Forensic Psychology — M
Graphic Design — M,D
Health Informatics — M,D
Health Promotion — M,D,O
History — M
Homeland Security — M
Human Services — M,D,O
Industrial and Organizational Psychology — M,D,O
International Affairs — M,D
International Business — M,D
International Health — M
Internet and Interactive Multimedia — M
Law — M
Legal and Justice Studies — M
Marketing — M,D
Marriage and Family Therapy — M,D,O
Military and Defense Studies — M,D
Missions and Missiology — M,D
Molecular Medicine — M,D
Music Education — M,D
Music — M,D
Nonprofit Management — M
Nursing and Healthcare Administration — M,D
Nursing Education — M,D
Nursing Informatics — M,D
Nursing—General — M,D
Nutrition — M,D
Osteopathic Medicine — D
Pastoral Ministry and Counseling — M,D,O
Political Science — M
Project Management — M,D
Psychology—General — M,D,O
Public Administration — M
Public Health—General — M,D
Public Policy — M
Reading Education — M,D,O
Religion — M,D
Religious Education — M,D
School Psychology — M,D
Taxation — M,D
Theology — M,D

LIFE CHIROPRACTIC COLLEGE WEST
Chiropractic — D

LIFE UNIVERSITY
Athletic Training and Sports Medicine — M
Chiropractic — D
Exercise and Sports Science — M
Nutrition — M

LIM COLLEGE
Business Administration and Management—General — M
Clothing and Textiles — M
Marketing — M

LIMESTONE COLLEGE
Business Administration and Management—General — M

LINCOLN CHRISTIAN SEMINARY
Pastoral Ministry and Counseling — M,D
Religious Education — M,D
Theology — M,D

LINCOLN CHRISTIAN UNIVERSITY
Cultural Studies — M
Organizational Management — M
Pastoral Ministry and Counseling — M
Philosophy — M
Religion — M
Theology — M

LINCOLN MEMORIAL UNIVERSITY
Business Administration and Management—General — M
Counselor Education — M,D,O
Curriculum and Instruction — M,D,O
Education—General — M,D,O
Educational Leadership and Administration — M,D,O
English Education — M,D,O
Family Nurse Practitioner Studies — M
Higher Education — M,D,O
Human Resources Development — M,D,O
Law — D
Nurse Anesthesia — M
Nursing—General — M
Osteopathic Medicine — M
Psychiatric Nursing — M
Veterinary Medicine — D

LINCOLN UNIVERSITY (CA)
Business Administration and Management—General — M,D
Finance and Banking — M,D
Human Resources Management — M,D
International Business — M,D
Investment Management — M,D
Management Information Systems — M,D

LINCOLN UNIVERSITY (MO)
Counselor Education — M
Criminal Justice and Criminology — M
Elementary Education — M
Environmental Sciences — M
Higher Education — M
History — M
Middle School Education — M
Secondary Education — M
Sociology — M

LINCOLN UNIVERSITY (PA)
Early Childhood Education — M
Educational Leadership and Administration — M
Finance and Banking — M
Human Resources Management — M
Human Services — M
Special Education — M

LINDENWOOD UNIVERSITY
Advertising and Public Relations — M

Applied Behavior Analysis — M,D,O
Art History — M
Business Administration and Management—General — M,D,O
Communication Disorders — M,D,O
Communication—General — M,O
Computer and Information Systems Security — M,O
Counseling Psychology — M,D,O
Criminal Justice and Criminology — M
Education of the Gifted — M,D,O
Education—General — M,D,O
Educational Leadership and Administration — M,D,O
Educational Media/Instructional Technology — M,D,O
English as a Second Language — M,D,O
Entrepreneurship — M
Film, Television, and Video Production — M
Health Promotion — M
Health Services Management and Hospital Administration — M,O
Human Resources Management — M,O
Internet and Interactive Multimedia — M
Journalism — M
Management Information Systems — M
Marketing — M
Mass Communication — M
Media Studies — M
Nursing—General — M
Project Management — M,O
School Psychology — M,D,O
Writing — M,O

LINDENWOOD UNIVERSITY—BELLEVILLE
Business Administration and Management—General — M
Communication—General — M
Computer Art and Design — M
Counselor Education — M
Criminal Justice and Criminology — M
Education—General — M
Educational Leadership and Administration — M
Health Services Management and Hospital Administration — M
Human Resources Management — M
Internet and Interactive Multimedia — M
Media Studies — M

LINDSEY WILSON COLLEGE
Counseling Psychology — M,D
Counselor Education — M,D
Educational Leadership and Administration — M
Human Development — M,D
Internet and Interactive Multimedia — M

LIPSCOMB UNIVERSITY
Accounting — M,O
Applied Behavior Analysis — M,D,O
Business Administration and Management—General — M,O
Clinical Laboratory Sciences/Medical Technology — M
Clinical Psychology — M,O
Computer and Information Systems Security — M
Conflict Resolution and Mediation/Peace Studies — M,O
Counseling Psychology — M,O
Data Science/Data Analytics — M,O
Education—General — M,D,O
Educational Leadership and Administration — M,D,O
Educational Media/Instructional Technology — M,D,O
English Education — M,D,O
English — M,D,O
Exercise and Sports Science — M
Film, Television, and Video Production — M
Finance and Banking — M,O
Health Informatics — M,D
Health Services Management and Hospital Administration — M,O
International Affairs — M,O
Management Information Systems — M,O
Management of Technology — M,O
Management Strategy and Policy — M,O
Marriage and Family Therapy — M,O
Molecular Biology — M
Nonprofit Management — M,O
Nutrition — M
Organizational Management — M,O
Pastoral Ministry and Counseling — M,D
Pharmacy — M,D
Psychology—General — M
Public Administration — M
Public Policy — M
Reading Education — M,D,O
School Psychology — M,O
Software Engineering — M,O
Special Education — M,D,O
Sustainable Development — M,O
Taxation — M,O
Theology — M,D
Writing — M

LOCK HAVEN UNIVERSITY OF PENNSYLVANIA
Actuarial Science — M
Athletic Training and Sports Medicine — M
Business Education — M
Clinical Psychology — M
Counseling Psychology — M
Education—General — M
Educational Leadership and Administration — M

Elementary Education — M
Health Education — M
Health Promotion — M
Health Services Management and Hospital Administration — M
Human Services — M
Information Studies — M
Physician Assistant Studies — M
Sport Psychology — M
Sports Management — M

LOGAN UNIVERSITY
Chiropractic — D
Exercise and Sports Science — M,D
Health Education — M,D
Health Informatics — M,D
Nutrition — M,D
Rehabilitation Sciences — M,D

LOGOS EVANGELICAL SEMINARY
Theology — M,D,O

LOMA LINDA UNIVERSITY
Addictions/Substance Abuse Counseling — M,D,O
Adult Nursing — M
Allied Health—General — M,D
Allopathic Medicine — M,D
Anatomy — D
Applied Social Research — M,D
Biochemistry — M,D
Bioethics — M,O
Biostatistics — M,D
Child and Family Studies — M,D,O
Clinical Psychology — D
Communication Disorders — M,D
Counselor Education — M,D
Criminal Justice and Criminology — M,D
Dentistry — M,D,O
Environmental and Occupational Health — M
Epidemiology — M,D
Gerontological Nursing — M
Gerontology — M,D
Health Education — M,D
Health Services Management and Hospital Administration — M
International Health — M
Marriage and Family Therapy — M,D,O
Microbiology — M,D
Nursing and Healthcare Administration — M
Nursing Education — M
Nursing—General — D
Nutrition — M,D
Occupational Therapy — M,D
Oral and Dental Sciences — M,O
Pathology — D
Pediatric Nursing — M
Pharmacology — D
Pharmacy — D
Physical Therapy — M,D
Physician Assistant Studies — M
Physiology — D
Psychology—General — D
Public Health—General — M,D
Rehabilitation Sciences — M,D
Religion — M
Social Work — M,D

LONDON METROPOLITAN UNIVERSITY
Applied Psychology — M,D
Architecture — M,D
Arts Administration — M,D
Athletic Training and Sports Medicine — M,D
Biological and Biomedical Sciences—General — M,D
Child and Family Studies — M,D
Clinical Psychology — M,D
Computer and Information Systems Security — M,D
Conflict Resolution and Mediation/Peace Studies — M,D
Counseling Psychology — M,D
Criminal Justice and Criminology — M,D
Data Science/Data Analytics — M,D
Early Childhood Education — M,D
Education—General — M,D
Emergency Management — M,D
English Education — M,D
Food Science and Technology — M,D
Foreign Languages Education — M,D
Forensic Psychology — M,D
Health Services Management and Hospital Administration — M,D
Higher Education — M,D
Homeland Security — M,D
Human Resources Management — M,D
Immunology — M,D
Industrial and Organizational Psychology — M,D
International Affairs — M,D
Internet and Interactive Multimedia — M,D
Law — M,D
Management Information Systems — M,D
Management of Technology — M,D
Military and Defense Studies — M,D
Near and Middle Eastern Languages — M,D
Nutrition — M,D
Pharmacology — M,D
Public Administration — M,D
Public Health—General — M,D
Public Policy — M,D
Social Work — M,D
Special Education — M,D
Sports and Entertainment Law — M,D
Translation and Interpretation — M,D
Urban Design — M,D
Women's Studies — M,D
Writing — M,D

LONG ISLAND UNIVERSITY—BRENTWOOD CAMPUS
Clinical Psychology — M,O
Counseling Psychology — M,O
Counselor Education — M,O
Criminal Justice and Criminology — M,O
Early Childhood Education — M,O
Educational Leadership and Administration — M,O
Elementary Education — M,O
Family Nurse Practitioner Studies — M,O
Health Services Management and Hospital Administration — M,O
Library Science — M,O
Reading Education — M,O
Social Work — M,O
Special Education — M,O

LONG ISLAND UNIVERSITY—HUDSON
Addictions/Substance Abuse Counseling — M,O
Counseling Psychology — M,O
Counselor Education — M,O
Early Childhood Education — M,O
Educational Leadership and Administration — M,O
Elementary Education — M,O
English as a Second Language — M,O
Health Services Management and Hospital Administration — M,O
Marriage and Family Therapy — M,O
Middle School Education — M,O
Multilingual and Multicultural Education — M,O
Pharmaceutical Sciences — M,O
Pharmacy — M,O
Public Administration — M,O
Reading Education — M,O
School Psychology — M,O
Special Education — M,O

LONG ISLAND UNIVERSITY—LIU BROOKLYN
Accounting — M,O
Adult Nursing — M,O
Applied Behavior Analysis — M,O
Athletic Training and Sports Medicine — M,D,O
Biological and Biomedical Sciences—General — M,D,O
Business Administration and Management—General — M,O
Chemistry — M,D,O
Clinical Psychology — M,D,O
Communication Disorders — M,D,O
Community Health — M,D,O
Computer Science — M,O
Counseling Psychology — M,O
Counselor Education — M,O
Early Childhood Education — M,O
Education—General — M,O
Educational Leadership and Administration — M,O
English as a Second Language — M,O
English — M,D,O
Exercise and Sports Science — M,D,O
Family Nurse Practitioner Studies — M,O
Forensic Sciences — M,D,O
Gerontology — M,O
Health Services Management and Hospital Administration — M,O
Human Resources Management — M,O
Marriage and Family Therapy — M,O
Media Studies — M,D,O
Multilingual and Multicultural Education — M,O
Nonprofit Management — M,O
Nursing Education — M,O
Nursing—General — M,O
Occupational Therapy — M,D,O
Pharmaceutical Sciences — M,D
Pharmacology — M,D
Pharmacy — M,D
Physical Therapy — M,D,O
Physician Assistant Studies — M,D,O
Political Science — M,D,O
Psychology—General — M,D,O
Public Administration — M,O
Public Health—General — M,D,O
Social Sciences Education — M,D,O
Social Work — M,D,O
Special Education — M,O
Taxation — M,O
Toxicology — M,D
Urban Education — M,O
Urban Studies — M,D,O
Writing — M,O

LONG ISLAND UNIVERSITY—LIU POST
Accounting — M
Allied Health—General — M,O
Applied Behavior Analysis — M,O
Applied Mathematics — M,O
Art Education — M,D,O
Art Therapy — M
Art/Fine Arts — M
Biological and Biomedical Sciences—General — M,O
Business Administration and Management—General — M
Clinical Psychology — M,D,O
Communication Disorders — M,D,O
Counseling Psychology — M,D,O
Criminal Justice and Criminology — M,O
Early Childhood Education — M,D,O
Education—General — M,D,O
Educational Leadership and Administration — M,D,O
Educational Media/Instructional Technology — M,D,O
Engineering Management — M
English as a Second Language — M,D,O
English — M,O
Environmental Management and Policy — M,O

Family Nurse Practitioner Studies — M,O
Finance and Banking — M
Game Design and Development — M,O
Genetic Counseling — M,O
Geosciences — M,O
Gerontology — M,O
Health Services Management and Hospital Administration — M,O
History — M,O
Interdisciplinary Studies — M,D,O
International Business — M
Internet and Interactive Multimedia — M
Library Science — M,D,O
Management Information Systems — M
Marketing — M
Middle School Education — M,D,O
Museum Studies — M
Music Education — M,D,O
Music — M
Nonprofit Management — M,O
Nursing Education — M,O
Nutrition — M,O
Perfusion — M,O
Political Science — M,O
Psychology—General — M,O
Public Administration — M,O
Reading Education — M,D,O
School Psychology — M,D,O
Secondary Education — M,D,O
Social Work — M,O
Special Education — M,D,O
Sustainable Development — M,O
Taxation — M
Theater — M

LONG ISLAND UNIVERSITY–RIVERHEAD
Applied Behavior Analysis — M,O
Computer and Information Systems Security — M,O
Early Childhood Education — M,O
Elementary Education — M,O
English as a Second Language — M,O
Homeland Security — M,O
Reading Education — M,O
Special Education — M,O

LONGWOOD UNIVERSITY
Business Administration and Management—General — M
Communication Disorders — M
Counselor Education — M
Education—General — M
Educational Media/Instructional Technology — M
Elementary Education — M
Health Education — M
Mathematics Education — M
Middle School Education — M
Physical Education — M
Reading Education — M
Real Estate — M
Special Education — M

LORAS COLLEGE
Applied Psychology — M
Educational Leadership and Administration — M
Pastoral Ministry and Counseling — M
Special Education — M
Theology — M

LOUISIANA COLLEGE
Education—General — M
Educational Leadership and Administration — M
Nursing and Healthcare Administration — M
Nursing—General — M
Social Work — M

LOUISIANA STATE UNIVERSITY AND AGRICULTURAL & MECHANICAL COLLEGE
Accounting — M,D
Agricultural Economics and Agribusiness — M,D
Agricultural Education — M,D
Agricultural Engineering — M,D
Agricultural Sciences—General — M,D
Agronomy and Soil Sciences — M,D
Animal Sciences — M,D
Anthropology — M,D
Applied Arts and Design—General — M
Applied Science and Technology — M
Applied Statistics — M
Architecture — M
Art History — M
Art/Fine Arts — M
Astronomy — M,D
Astrophysics — M,D
Biochemistry — M,D
Bioengineering — M,D
Biological and Biomedical Sciences—General — M,D
Biopsychology — M,D
Business Administration and Management—General — M,D
Business Education — M,D
Chemical Engineering — M,D
Chemistry — M,D
Civil Engineering — M,D
Clinical Psychology — M,D
Cognitive Sciences — M,D
Communication Disorders — M,D
Communication—General — M,D
Comparative Literature — M,D

Computer Engineering — M,D
Computer Science — M,D
Construction Management — M,D
Counselor Education — M,D,O
Developmental Psychology — M,D
Economics — M,D
Education—General — M,D,O
Educational Leadership and Administration — M,D,O
Educational Measurement and Evaluation — M,D,O
Educational Media/Instructional Technology — M,D,O
Electrical Engineering — M,D
Elementary Education — M,D
Engineering and Applied Sciences—General — M,D
English — M,D
Entomology — M,D
Environmental Engineering — M,D
Environmental Management and Policy — M,D
Environmental Sciences — M,D
Family and Consumer Sciences-General — M,D
Finance and Banking — M,D
Fish, Game, and Wildlife Management — M,D
Food Science and Technology — M,D
Forestry — M,D
French — M,D
Geography — M,D
Geology — M,D
Geophysics — M,D
Geotechnical Engineering — M,D
Graphic Design — M
Higher Education — M,D,O
Hispanic Studies — M
History — M,D
Home Economics Education — M,D
Horticulture — M,D
Human Resources Development — M,D
Information Studies — M
International and Comparative Education — M,D
Internet and Interactive Multimedia — M
Kinesiology and Movement Studies — M,D
Landscape Architecture — M
Law — M,D
Liberal Studies — M
Library Science — M
Management Information Systems — M,D
Marine Affairs — M,D
Mass Communication — M,D
Mathematics — M,D
Mechanical Engineering — M,D
Mechanics — M,D
Media Studies — M,D
Medical Physics — M,D
Music Education — M,D
Music — M,D
Natural Resources — M,D
Nutrition — M,D
Oceanography — M,D
Petroleum Engineering — M,D
Philosophy — M
Photography — M
Physics — M,D
Plant Pathology — M,D
Political Science — M,D
Psychology—General — M,D
Public Administration — M,D
School Psychology — M,D
Secondary Education — M,D,O
Social Work — M,D
Sociology — M,D
Statistics — M
Structural Engineering — M,D
Systems Science — M,D
Theater — M,D
Toxicology — M,D
Transportation and Highway Engineering — M,D
Veterinary Medicine — D
Veterinary Sciences — M,D
Vocational and Technical Education — M,D
Water Resources Engineering — M,D
Writing — M,D

LOUISIANA STATE UNIVERSITY HEALTH SCIENCES CENTER
Allopathic Medicine — M,D
Anatomy — D
Biological and Biomedical Sciences—General — D
Biostatistics — M,D
Cell Biology — D
Communication Disorders — M,D
Community Health Nursing — M,D,O
Community Health — M,D
Dentistry — D
Developmental Biology — D
Environmental and Occupational Health — M,D
Epidemiology — M,D
Family Nurse Practitioner Studies — M,D,O
Gerontological Nursing — M,D,O
Health Services Management and Hospital Administration — M,D
Human Genetics — D
Immunology — D
Maternal and Child/Neonatal Nursing — M,D,O
Microbiology — D
Neurobiology — D
Neuroscience — D
Nurse Anesthesia — M,D,O
Nursing and Healthcare Administration — M,D,O

Nursing Education — M,D,O
Nursing—General — M,D,O
Occupational Therapy — M
Parasitology — D
Pharmacology — D
Physical Therapy — D
Physician Assistant Studies — M
Physiology — D
Public Health—General — M,D
Rehabilitation Counseling — M

LOUISIANA STATE UNIVERSITY HEALTH SCIENCES CENTER AT SHREVEPORT
Allopathic Medicine — D
Anatomy — M,D
Biochemistry — M,D
Biological and Biomedical Sciences—General — M
Cell Biology — M,D
Immunology — M,D
Microbiology — M,D
Molecular Biology — M,D
Pharmacology — M,D
Physiology — M,D

LOUISIANA STATE UNIVERSITY IN SHREVEPORT
Biological and Biomedical Sciences—General — M
Business Administration and Management—General — M
Computer Science — M
Counselor Education — M
Curriculum and Instruction — M,D
Education—General — M,D
Educational Leadership and Administration — M,D
Health Services Management and Hospital Administration — M
Liberal Studies — M
Nonprofit Management — M
Public Health—General — M
School Psychology — O
Systems Science — M

LOUISIANA TECH UNIVERSITY
Accounting — M,D
Agricultural Sciences—General — M,D,O
Applied Physics — M,D,O
Architecture — M,D,O
Art/Fine Arts — M,D,O
Biological and Biomedical Sciences—General — M,D,O
Biomedical Engineering — M,D,O
Business Administration and Management—General — M,D,O
Chemistry — M,D,O
Clinical Psychology — M,D,O
Communication Disorders — M,D,O
Computer and Information Systems Security — M,D
Computer Science — M,D,O
Counseling Psychology — M,D,O
Curriculum and Instruction — M,D,O
Early Childhood Education — M,D,O
Education—General — M,D,O
Educational Leadership and Administration — M,D,O
Elementary Education — M,D,O
Engineering and Applied Sciences—General — M,D,O
Engineering Management — M,D,O
Engineering Physics — M,D,O
English — M,D,O
Finance and Banking — M,D
Graphic Design — M,D,O
Health Informatics — M,D,O
Higher Education — M,D,O
History — M,D,O
Human Services — M,D,O
Industrial and Organizational Psychology — M,D,O
Kinesiology and Movement Studies — M,D,O
Management Information Systems — M,D
Management of Technology — M,D,O
Marketing — M,D
Materials Sciences — M,D,O
Mathematics — M,D,O
Middle School Education — M,D,O
Molecular Biology — M,D,O
Nanotechnology — M,D,O
Nutrition — M,D,O
Photography — M,D,O
Secondary Education — M,D,O
Special Education — M,D,O
Technical Writing — M,D,O

LOUISVILLE PRESBYTERIAN THEOLOGICAL SEMINARY
Religion — M,D
Theology — M,D

LOURDES UNIVERSITY
Business Administration and Management—General — M
Curriculum and Instruction — M
Educational Leadership and Administration — M
Nurse Anesthesia — M
Nursing and Healthcare Administration — M
Nursing Education — M
Organizational Management — M
Reading Education — M
Theology — M

LOYOLA MARYMOUNT UNIVERSITY
Accounting — M
Bioethics — M

Business Administration and Management—General — M
Civil Engineering — M
Counseling Psychology — M
Counselor Education — M
Education—General — M,D
Educational Leadership and Administration — M,D
Electrical Engineering — M
Elementary Education — M
Engineering Management — M
English — M
Environmental Sciences — M
Film, Television, and Video Production — M
Higher Education — M
Law — M,D
Marriage and Family Therapy — M
Mathematics Education — M
Mechanical Engineering — M
Multilingual and Multicultural Education — M
Pastoral Ministry and Counseling — M
Philosophy — M
Reading Education — M
Recreation and Park Management — M
School Psychology — M
Secondary Education — M
Special Education — M
Systems Engineering — M
Theology — M
Urban Education — M
Writing — M

LOYOLA UNIVERSITY CHICAGO
Accounting — M
Adult Nursing — M,D,O
Applied Statistics — M
Biochemistry — M,D
Bioethics — M,D,O
Bioinformatics — M
Biological and Biomedical Sciences—General — M,D
Business Administration and Management—General — M,O
Business Analytics — M,O
Cell Biology — M,D
Chemistry — M,D
Clinical Psychology — M,D,O
Clinical Research — M
Communication—General — M
Computer Science — M
Corporate and Organizational Communication — M
Counseling Psychology — M,D,O
Counselor Education — M,O
Criminal Justice and Criminology — M
Curriculum and Instruction — M,D
Developmental Psychology — M,D
Economics — M
Education—General — M,D,O
Educational Leadership and Administration — M,D,O
Educational Measurement and Evaluation — M,D,O
Educational Policy — M,D
Elementary Education — M
English — M,D
Entrepreneurship — M
Ethics — M
Family Nurse Practitioner Studies — M,D,O
Finance and Banking — M
Gender Studies — M
Health Law — M,D,O
Health Services Management and Hospital Administration — M
Higher Education — M,D
History — M,D
Human Resources Management — M
Humanities — M
Immunology — M,D
Infectious Diseases — M,D,O
Information Science — M
International and Comparative Education — M,D
International Business — M
Law — M,D,O
Legal and Justice Studies — M,O
Management Information Systems — M,O
Marketing — M
Mathematics — M
Medieval and Renaissance Studies — M,D
Microbiology — M,D
Molecular Biology — M,D
Molecular Pharmacology — M,D
Molecular Physiology — M,D
Neuroscience — M,D
Nursing and Healthcare Administration — M,D,O
Nursing—General — M,D,O
Nutrition — M,D,O
Pastoral Ministry and Counseling — M,O
Philosophy — M,D
Physiology — M,D
Political Science — M,D
Public Health—General — M,O
Public History — M
Public Policy — M
Religious Education — M,O
Risk Management — M
School Psychology — D,O
Secondary Education — M
Social Psychology — M,O
Social Work — M,D,O
Sociology — M,D
Software Engineering — M
Spanish — M
Special Education — M
Statistics — M
Supply Chain Management — M,O
Taxation — M

---

*M—masters degree; D—doctorate; O—other advanced degree; *—Close-Up and/or Display*

Theology — M,D,O
Urban Studies — M
Women's Health Nursing — M,D,O
Women's Studies — M

LOYOLA UNIVERSITY MARYLAND
Business Administration and
  Management—General — M
Clinical Psychology — M,D,O
Communication Disorders — M
Counseling Psychology — M,D,O
Counselor Education — M,O
Curriculum and Instruction — M
Early Childhood Education — M,O
Education—General — M,O
Educational Leadership and
  Administration — M,O
Educational Media/Instructional
  Technology — M
Elementary Education — M
Finance and Banking — M
Investment Management — M
Management Information Systems — M
Marketing — M
Media Studies — M
Music Education — M
Psychology—General — M,D,O
Reading Education — M
Secondary Education — M
Theology — M

LOYOLA UNIVERSITY NEW ORLEANS
Business Administration and
  Management—General — M
Clinical Psychology — M
Criminal Justice and Criminology — M
Education—General — M
Family Nurse Practitioner Studies — M,D
Law — M,D
Marriage and Family Therapy — M
Music — M,D
Nursing—General — M,D
Organizational Management — M
Secondary Education — M
Theology — M,O
Therapies—Dance, Drama, and
  Music — M

LUBBOCK CHRISTIAN UNIVERSITY
Theology — M

LUTHERAN SCHOOL OF THEOLOGY AT CHICAGO
Pastoral Ministry and Counseling — M,D
Theology — M,D

LUTHERAN THEOLOGICAL SEMINARY SASKATOON
Ethics — M,D
Pastoral Ministry and Counseling — M,D
Religion — M,D
Theology — M,D

LUTHER RICE COLLEGE & SEMINARY
Pastoral Ministry and Counseling — M,D
Religion — M,D
Theology — M,D

LUTHER SEMINARY
Missions and Missiology — M,D
Pastoral Ministry and Counseling — M,D
Theology — M,D

LYNN UNIVERSITY
Applied Psychology — M
Business Administration and
  Management—General — M
Communication—General — M,O
Computer Art and Design — M
Counseling Psychology — M
Criminal Justice and Criminology — M
Early Childhood Education — M,D
Education of the Gifted — M
Education—General — M,D
Educational Leadership and
  Administration — M,D
Graphic Design — M,O
Internet and Interactive
  Multimedia — M,O
Mass Communication — M,O
Media Studies — M,O
Middle School Education — M,O
Music — M,O
Psychology—General — M,O
Special Education — M,D

MAASTRICHT SCHOOL OF MANAGEMENT
Business Administration and
  Management—General — M,D
Facilities Management — M,D
Sustainability Management — M

MACHZIKEI HADATH RABBINICAL COLLEGE
Theology — O

MADONNA UNIVERSITY
Adult Nursing — M
Business Administration and
  Management—General — M
Clinical Psychology — M
Criminal Justice and Criminology — M
Education—General — M
Educational Leadership and
  Administration — M
English as a Second Language — M
Health Services Management and
  Hospital Administration — M
Hospice Nursing — M
International Business — M
Liberal Studies — M
Nursing and Healthcare
  Administration — M
Nursing—General — M
Pastoral Ministry and Counseling — M
Psychology—General — M
Quality Management — M

Reading Education — M
Social Work — M
Special Education — M
Theology — M

MAHARISHI UNIVERSITY OF MANAGEMENT
Accounting — M
Asian Studies — M,D
Business Administration and
  Management—General — M,D
Computer Science — M
Physiology — D
Sustainability Management — M,D
Writing — M

MAINE COLLEGE OF ART
Art/Fine Arts — M

MAINE MARITIME ACADEMY
International Business — M
Supply Chain Management — M
Transportation Management — M

MALONE UNIVERSITY
Business Administration and
  Management—General — M
Counselor Education — M
Curriculum and Instruction — M
Education—General — M
Educational Leadership and
  Administration — M
Family Nurse Practitioner Studies — M
Nursing—General — M
Organizational Management — M
Special Education — M

MANCHESTER UNIVERSITY
Athletic Training and Sports
  Medicine — M
Genomic Sciences — M
Pharmacy — D

MANHATTAN COLLEGE
Applied Mathematics — M
Business Administration and
  Management—General — M
Chemical Engineering — M
Civil Engineering — M
Computer Engineering — M
Construction Management — M
Counseling Psychology — M,O
Counselor Education — M,O
Data Science/Data Analytics — M
Early Childhood Education — M,O
Education—General — M,O
Educational Leadership and
  Administration — M,O
Educational Media/Instructional
  Technology — M
Electrical Engineering — M
Elementary Education — M,O
Engineering and Applied
  Sciences—General — M
English — M,O
Environmental Engineering — M
Marriage and Family Therapy — M
Mathematics — M,O
Mechanical Engineering — M
Multilingual and Multicultural
  Education — M,O
Organizational Management — M
Special Education — M,O
Student Affairs — M

MANHATTAN SCHOOL OF MUSIC
Music — M,D,O

MANHATTANVILLE COLLEGE
Accounting — M,O
Art Education — M,O
Biological and Biomedical
  Sciences—General — M,O
Business Education — M,O
Chemistry — M,O
Corporate and Organizational
  Communication — M,O
Early Childhood Education — M,O
Education—General — M,D,O
Educational Leadership and
  Administration — M,D,O
Elementary Education — M,O
English as a Second Language — M,O
English Education — M,O
English — M,O
Entrepreneurship — M
Exercise and Sports Science — M,O
Finance and Banking — M,O
Foreign Languages Education — M,O
Geosciences — M,O
Health Promotion — M,O
Human Resources Management — M,O
Investment Management — M,O
Mathematics Education — M,O
Mathematics — M,O
Middle School Education — M,O
Multilingual and Multicultural
  Education — M,O
Music Education — M,O
Physics — M,O
Reading Education — M,O
Science Education — M,O
Secondary Education — M,O
Social Sciences Education — M,O
Spanish — M,O
Special Education — M,O
Sustainable Development — M,O
Urban Education — M,O
Writing — M

MANSFIELD UNIVERSITY OF PENNSYLVANIA
Art Education — M
Education—General — M
Elementary Education — M
Information Studies — M
Library Science — M

Music — M
Nursing—General — M
Organizational Management — M
Psychology—General — M
Secondary Education — M
Special Education — M

MAPLE SPRINGS BAPTIST BIBLE COLLEGE AND SEMINARY
Pastoral Ministry and Counseling — M,D,O
Religious Education — M,D,O
Theology — M,D,O

MARANATHA BAPTIST UNIVERSITY
Cultural Studies — M
Education—General — M
Organizational Management — M
Pastoral Ministry and Counseling — M,D
Religion — M
Theology — M

MARCONI INTERNATIONAL UNIVERSITY
Business Administration and
  Management—General — M,D
Educational Leadership and
  Administration — M,D
Educational Media/Instructional
  Technology — M,D
International Business — M,D

MARIAN UNIVERSITY (IN)
Counseling Psychology — M
Counselor Education — M
Education—General — M
Family Nurse Practitioner Studies — M,D
Nurse Anesthesia — M,D
Nursing Education — M,D
Nursing—General — M,D
Osteopathic Medicine — M,D

MARIAN UNIVERSITY (WI)
Adult Nursing — M
Business Administration and
  Management—General — M
Curriculum and Instruction — M,D
Education—General — M,D
Educational Leadership and
  Administration — M,D
Educational Media/Instructional
  Technology — M,D
Nursing Education — M
Nursing—General — M
Organizational Management — M
Special Education — M,D
Thanatology — M

MARIETTA COLLEGE
Physician Assistant Studies — M
Psychology—General — M

MARIST COLLEGE
Accounting — M
Business Administration and
  Management—General — M,O
Business Analytics — M,O
Communication—General — M
Computer Science — M,O
Corporate and Organizational
  Communication — M
Counseling Psychology — M,O
Education—General — M,O
Management Information Systems — M,O
Marketing — M
Museum Studies — M
Physical Therapy — D
Psychology—General — M,O
Public Administration — M
School Psychology — M,O
Software Engineering — M,O

MARLBORO COLLEGE
Business Administration and
  Management—General — M
Educational Media/Instructional
  Technology — M,O
English as a Second Language — M
Entrepreneurship — M
Legal and Justice Studies — M
Organizational Management — M
Project Management — M

MARQUETTE UNIVERSITY
Accounting — M
Acute Care/Critical Care Nursing — M,D,O
Adult Nursing — M,D,O
Advertising and Public Relations — M,O
Analytical Chemistry — M,D
Bioinformatics — M,D
Biological and Biomedical
  Sciences—General — M,D
Biomedical Engineering — M,D
Business Administration and
  Management—General — M,O
Cardiovascular Sciences — M
Cell Biology — M,D
Chemical Physics — M,D
Chemistry — M,D
Civil Engineering — M,D,O
Clinical Psychology — M,D
Communication Disorders — M,O
Communication—General — M,O
Computational Sciences — M,D
Computer Engineering — M,D,O
Computer Science — M,D
Construction Engineering — M,D,O
Construction Management — M,D,O
Counseling Psychology — M,D
Counselor Education — M,D
Curriculum and Instruction — M,D,O
Dentistry — D
Developmental Biology — M,D
Ecology — M,D
Economics — M,O
Education—General — M,D,O
Educational Leadership and
  Administration — M,D,O
Educational Policy — M,D,O

Electrical Engineering — M,D,O
Elementary Education — M
Engineering and Applied
  Sciences—General — M,D,O
Engineering Management — M,D,O
English — M,D
Entrepreneurship — M,O
Environmental Engineering — M,D,O
Ethics — M,D
Family Nurse Practitioner Studies — M,D,O
Finance and Banking — M,O
Foreign Languages Education — M
Foundations and Philosophy of
  Education — M,D,O
Genetics — M,D
Gerontological Nursing — M,D,O
Hazardous Materials
  Management — M,D,O
Health Communication — M,O
History — M,D
Human Resources Development — M
Human Resources Management — M,O
Industrial and Manufacturing
  Management — M,O
Inorganic Chemistry — M,D
Interdisciplinary Studies — D
International Affairs — M,D
International Business — M,O
Journalism — M,O
Law — D
Management Information Systems — M,O
Management of Technology — M,D
Marketing Research — M
Marketing — M,O
Mass Communication — M,O
Mathematics Education — M,D
Mathematics — M,D
Mechanical Engineering — M,D,O
Microbiology — M,D
Molecular Biology — M,D
Neuroscience — M,D
Nurse Midwifery — M,D,O
Nursing and Healthcare
  Administration — M,D,O
Nursing—General — M,D,O
Oral and Dental Sciences — M,O
Organic Chemistry — M,D
Pediatric Nursing — M,D,O
Philosophy — M,D
Physical Chemistry — M,D
Physical Therapy — D
Physician Assistant Studies — M,D
Physiology — M,D
Political Science — M
Psychology—General — D
Reading Education — M,D,O
Real Estate — M
Rehabilitation Sciences — M,D
Secondary Education — M,D,O
Social Psychology — M,D
Spanish — M
Speech and Interpersonal
  Communication — M,O
Sports Management — M,O
Structural Engineering — M,D,O
Student Affairs — M,D,O
Supply Chain Management — M,O
Theology — M,D
Transportation and Highway
  Engineering — M,D,O
Water Resources Engineering — M,D,O
Water Resources — M,D,O

MARSHALL B. KETCHUM UNIVERSITY
Optometry — M,D
Pharmacy — M,D
Vision Sciences — M,D

MARSHALL UNIVERSITY
Accounting — M
Adult Education — M
Advertising and Public Relations — M,O
Allopathic Medicine — D
Athletic Training and Sports
  Medicine — M
Biological and Biomedical
  Sciences—General — M,D
Business Administration and
  Management—General — M,O
Chemistry — M
Clinical Psychology — M,D,O
Communication Disorders — M
Communication—General — M
Computer Engineering — M
Computer Science — M
Counselor Education — M
Criminal Justice and Criminology — M
Education—General — M,D,O
Educational Leadership and
  Administration — M
Electrical Engineering — M
Engineering and Applied
  Sciences—General — M,O
Engineering Management — M
English — M,O
Environmental Engineering — M
Environmental Sciences — M
Exercise and Sports Science — M
Forensic Sciences — M,O
Geography — M,O
Health Education — M
Health Informatics — M
Health Services Management and
  Hospital Administration — M
History — M,O
Human Resources Management — M
Humanities — M,O
Information Science — M
Journalism — M,O
Management of Technology — M,O
Mathematics — M
Mechanical Engineering — M
Music — M
Nurse Anesthesia — D
Nursing—General — M,O

Nutrition	M,O
Pharmacy	D
Physical Therapy	D
Physics	M
Political Science	M
Psychology—General	M,D,O
Public Administration	M
Public Health—General	M
Reading Education	M
School Psychology	O
Social Work	M
Sociology	M
Special Education	M
Sports Management	M
Transportation and Highway Engineering	M

MARS HILL UNIVERSITY
Elementary Education	M

MARTIN LUTHER COLLEGE
Curriculum and Instruction	M
Early Childhood Education	M
Education—General	M
Educational Leadership and Administration	M
Educational Media/Instructional Technology	M
Special Education	M

MARTIN UNIVERSITY
Pastoral Ministry and Counseling	M
Psychology—General	M
Social Psychology	M

MARY BALDWIN UNIVERSITY
Applied Behavior Analysis	M
Education of the Gifted	M
Education—General	M
Educational Leadership and Administration	M
Elementary Education	M
English as a Second Language	M
English	M
Environmental Education	M
Higher Education	M
Middle School Education	M
Nursing—General	M
Occupational Therapy	D
Physical Therapy	D
Physician Assistant Studies	M
Reading Education	M
Special Education	M
Theater	M

MARYGROVE COLLEGE
Curriculum and Instruction	M,O
Early Childhood Education	M,O
Educational Leadership and Administration	M,O
Educational Media/Instructional Technology	M,O
Elementary Education	M,O
Human Resources Management	M,O
Legal and Justice Studies	M,O
Mathematics	M,O
Middle School Education	M,O
Reading Education	M,O
Special Education	M,O

MARYLAND INSTITUTE COLLEGE OF ART
Applied Arts and Design—General	M
Art Education	M
Art/Fine Arts	M,O
Business Administration and Management—General	M
Film, Television, and Video Production	M
Graphic Design	M
Illustration	M
Museum Studies	M
Photography	M

MARYLAND UNIVERSITY OF INTEGRATIVE HEALTH
Acupuncture and Oriental Medicine	M,D,O
Health Promotion	M,O
Naturopathic Medicine	D
Nutrition	M,D,O

MARYMOUNT CALIFORNIA UNIVERSITY
Business Administration and Management—General	M
International Development	M
Social Psychology	M

MARYMOUNT UNIVERSITY
Allied Health—General	M,D,O
Business Administration and Management—General	M,O
Clinical Psychology	M
Community College Education	M,O
Computer and Information Systems Security	M,D,O
Counseling Psychology	M
Counselor Education	M
Curriculum and Instruction	M
Education—General	M
Elementary Education	M
English Education	M,O
English	M,O
Family Nurse Practitioner Studies	M,D,O
Forensic Psychology	M
Health Education	M
Health Informatics	M
Health Promotion	M
Health Services Management and Hospital Administration	M
Human Resources Management	O
Interior Design	M
Management Information Systems	M,O
Nonprofit Management	M,O

Nursing—General	M,D,O
Pastoral Ministry and Counseling	M
Physical Therapy	D
Project Management	M,O
Secondary Education	M
Software Engineering	M,O
Special Education	M

MARYVILLE UNIVERSITY OF SAINT LOUIS
Accounting	M,O
Actuarial Science	M
Acute Care/Critical Care Nursing	M,D
Addictions/Substance Abuse Counseling	M
Adult Nursing	M,D
Allied Health—General	M,D,O
Business Administration and Management—General	M,O
Business Education	M,O
Communication Disorders	M
Computer and Information Systems Security	M,O
Data Science/Data Analytics	M
Early Childhood Education	M,D
Education—General	M,D
Educational Leadership and Administration	M,D
Elementary Education	M,D
Family Nurse Practitioner Studies	M,D
Finance and Banking	M,O
Gerontological Nursing	M,D
Health Services Management and Hospital Administration	M,O
Higher Education	M,D
Human Resources Management	M,O
Information Science	M,O
Logistics	M,O
Marketing	M,O
Marriage and Family Therapy	M
Middle School Education	M,D
Nursing—General	M,D
Occupational Therapy	M
Pediatric Nursing	M,D
Physical Therapy	D
Project Management	M,O
Reading Education	M,D
Rehabilitation Counseling	M
Secondary Education	M,D
Sports Management	M,O
Supply Chain Management	M,O
Therapies—Dance, Drama, and Music	M

MARYWOOD UNIVERSITY
Architecture	M
Art Education	M
Art Therapy	M,O
Art/Fine Arts	M
Biotechnology	M
Business Administration and Management—General	M
Clinical Psychology	M,D
Communication Disorders	M
Communication—General	M
Computer and Information Systems Security	M
Counseling Psychology	M
Counselor Education	M
Criminal Justice and Criminology	M
Early Childhood Education	M
Education—General	M
Educational Leadership and Administration	M,D
Elementary Education	M
Exercise and Sports Science	M
Finance and Banking	M
Gerontology	M
Graphic Design	M
Health Education	D
Health Services Management and Hospital Administration	M
Higher Education	M,D
Human Development	D
Illustration	M
Interdisciplinary Studies	D
Interior Design	M
Investment Management	M
Management Information Systems	M
Music Education	M
Nutrition	M,O
Photography	M
Physician Assistant Studies	M
Psychology—General	M
Public Administration	M
Reading Education	M
Secondary Education	M
Social Work	M,D
Special Education	M

MASSACHUSETTS COLLEGE OF ART AND DESIGN
Applied Arts and Design—General	M,O
Architecture	M
Art Education	M,O
Art/Fine Arts	M,O
Film, Television, and Video Production	M,O
Interdisciplinary Studies	M,O
Media Studies	M,O
Photography	M,O
Textile Design	M,O

MASSACHUSETTS COLLEGE OF LIBERAL ARTS
Business Administration and Management—General	M,O
Curriculum and Instruction	M,O
Education—General	M,O
Educational Leadership and Administration	M,O

Educational Media/Instructional Technology	M,O
Health Education	M,O
Physical Education	M,O
Reading Education	M,O
Special Education	M

MASSACHUSETTS INSTITUTE OF TECHNOLOGY
Aerospace/Aeronautical Engineering	M,D,O
Archaeology	M,D,O
Architectural History	M,D
Architecture	M,D
Art History	M,D
Atmospheric Sciences	M,D
Biochemistry	D
Bioengineering	M,D
Bioinformatics	M,D
Biological and Biomedical Sciences—General	M,D
Biomedical Engineering	M,D
Business Administration and Management—General	M,D
Cell Biology	D
Chemical Engineering	M,D
Chemistry	D
Civil Engineering	M,D,O
Cognitive Sciences	D
Communication Disorders	M,D
Computational Biology	D
Computational Sciences	M
Computer Engineering	M,D,O
Computer Science	M,D,O
Construction Engineering	M,D,O
Developmental Biology	D
Economics	M,D
Electrical Engineering	M,D,O
Engineering and Applied Sciences—General	M,D,O
Engineering Management	M
Environmental Biology	M,D,O
Environmental Engineering	M,D,O
Environmental Sciences	M,D,O
Genetics	D
Genomic Sciences	M,D
Geochemistry	M,D
Geology	M,D
Geophysics	M,D
Geosciences	M,D
Geotechnical Engineering	M,D,O
History of Science and Technology	D
Hydrology	M,D,O
Immunology	D
Information Science	M,D,O
Inorganic Chemistry	D
Linguistics	D
Logistics	M
Manufacturing Engineering	M,D,O
Marine Geology	M,D
Materials Engineering	M,D,O
Materials Sciences	M,D,O
Mathematics	D
Mechanical Engineering	M,D,O
Media Studies	M,D
Medical Physics	M,D
Microbiology	D
Molecular Biology	M,D,O
Molecular Toxicology	D
Neurobiology	D
Neuroscience	D
Nuclear Engineering	M,D,O
Ocean Engineering	M,D,O
Oceanography	M,D,O
Operations Research	M,D
Organic Chemistry	M,D,O
Philosophy	D
Physical Chemistry	D
Physics	M,D
Planetary and Space Sciences	M,D
Political Science	M,D
Real Estate	M
Social Sciences	D
Structural Biology	D
Structural Engineering	M,D,O
Systems Biology	D
Systems Engineering	M,D
Technical Writing	M
Technology and Public Policy	M,D
Toxicology	M,D
Transportation and Highway Engineering	M,D,O
Urban and Regional Planning	M,D
Urban Studies	M,D
Writing	M

MASSACHUSETTS MARITIME ACADEMY
Emergency Management	M
Facilities Management	M

MASSACHUSETTS SCHOOL OF LAW AT ANDOVER
Law	D

THE MASTER'S UNIVERSITY
Pastoral Ministry and Counseling	M,D
Theology	M,D

MAYO CLINIC ALIX SCHOOL OF MEDICINE
Allopathic Medicine	D

MAYO CLINIC GRADUATE SCHOOL OF BIOMEDICAL SCIENCES
Biochemistry	M,D
Biomedical Engineering	M,D
Clinical Laboratory Sciences/Medical Technology	M,D
Genetics	D
Immunology	D
Molecular Biology	M,D

Molecular Pharmacology	M,D
Neuroscience	M,D
Physiology	M,D
Virology	M,D

MAYO CLINIC SCHOOL OF HEALTH SCIENCES
Nurse Anesthesia	D
Physical Therapy	D

MCCORMICK THEOLOGICAL SEMINARY
Pastoral Ministry and Counseling	M,D,O
Theology	M,D,O

MCDANIEL COLLEGE
Counselor Education	M
Curriculum and Instruction	M
Educational Leadership and Administration	M
Educational Media/Instructional Technology	M
Elementary Education	M,O
English as a Second Language	M
Gerontology	M,O
Human Resources Development	M
Human Services	M
Kinesiology and Movement Studies	M
Liberal Studies	M,O
Library Science	M
Mathematics Education	M,O
Reading Education	M
Science Education	M,O
Secondary Education	M,O
Special Education	M
Writing	M,O

MCGILL UNIVERSITY
Accounting	M,D,O
Aerospace/Aeronautical Engineering	M,D
Agricultural Economics and Agribusiness	M
Agricultural Engineering	M,D
Agricultural Sciences—General	M,D,O
Agronomy and Soil Sciences	M,D
Allopathic Medicine	M,D
Anatomy	M,D
Animal Sciences	M,D
Anthropology	M,D
Applied Mathematics	M,D
Architecture	M,D,O
Art History	M,D
Asian Studies	M,D
Atmospheric Sciences	M,D
Biochemistry	M,D
Bioengineering	M,D
Bioethics	M,D,O
Bioinformatics	M,D
Biological and Biomedical Sciences—General	M,D
Biomedical Engineering	M,D
Biostatistics	M,D
Biotechnology	M,D,O
Business Administration and Management—General	M,D,O
Cell Biology	M,D
Chemical Engineering	M,D
Chemistry	M,D
Civil Engineering	M,D
Clinical Psychology	M,D
Communication Disorders	M,D
Communication—General	M,D
Computational Sciences	M,D
Computer Engineering	M,D
Computer Science	M,D
Counseling Psychology	M,D,O
Curriculum and Instruction	M,D,O
Dentistry	M,D,O
Developmental Psychology	M,D,O
Economics	M,D
Education—General	M,D,O
Educational Leadership and Administration	M,D,O
Educational Psychology	M,D,O
Electrical Engineering	M,D
Engineering and Applied Sciences—General	M,D,O
English	M,D
Entomology	M,D
Entrepreneurship	M,D,O
Environmental and Occupational Health	M,D
Environmental Engineering	M,D
Environmental Management and Policy	M,D
Epidemiology	M,D
Experimental Psychology	M,D
Family Nurse Practitioner Studies	M,D,O
Finance and Banking	M,D,O
Fish, Game, and Wildlife Management	M,D
Food Science and Technology	M,D
Foreign Languages Education	M,D,O
Forensic Sciences	M,D,O
Forestry	M,D
Foundations and Philosophy of Education	M,D,O
French	M,D
Genetic Counseling	M,D
Geography	M,D
Geosciences	M,D
Geotechnical Engineering	M,D
German	M,D
Hispanic Studies	M,D
History of Medicine	M,D
History	M,D
Human Genetics	M,D
Hydraulics	M,D
Immunology	M,D

Industrial and Manufacturing
  Management — M,D,O
Information Studies — M,D,O
International Business — M,D,O
International Development — M,D,O
Italian — M,D
Jewish Studies — M
Kinesiology and Movement Studies — M,D,O
Law — M,D,O
Library Science — M,D,O
Linguistics — M,D
Management Information Systems — M,D,O
Management Strategy and Policy — M,D,O
Marketing — M,D,O
Materials Engineering — M,D,O
Mathematics — M,D
Mechanical Engineering — M,D
Mechanics — M,D
Medical Physics — M,D
Meteorology — M,D
Microbiology — M,D
Mineral/Mining Engineering — M,D,O
Music Education — M,D
Music — M,D
Natural Resources — M,D
Near and Middle Eastern Studies — M,D,O
Neuroscience — M,D
Nursing—General — M,D,O
Nutrition — M,D,O
Oceanography — M,D
Oral and Dental Sciences — M,D,O
Parasitology — M,D,O
Pathology — M,D
Pharmacology — M,D
Philosophy — M,D
Physical Education — M,D
Physics — M,D
Physiology — M,D
Planetary and Space
  Sciences — M,D
Plant Sciences — M,D,O
Political Science — M,D
Psychology—General — M,D
Public Health—General — M,D
Rehabilitation Sciences — M,D,O
Religion — M,D
Russian — M,D
School Psychology — M,D,O
Social Work — M,D
Sociology — M,D,O
Statistics — M,D,O
Structural Engineering — M,D
Supply Chain Management — M,D,O
Theology — M,D
Transportation Management — M,D
Urban and Regional Planning — M,D
Water Resources Engineering — M,D

MCKENDREE UNIVERSITY

Business Administration and
  Management—General — M
Clinical Psychology — M
Counseling Psychology — M
Curriculum and Instruction — M,D,O
Education—General — M,D,O
Educational Leadership and
  Administration — M,D,O
Higher Education — M,D,O
Human Resources Management — M
International Business — M
Music Education — M,D,O
Nursing and Healthcare
  Administration — M
Nursing Education — M
Nursing—General — M
Reading Education — M,D,O
Special Education — M,D,O

MCMASTER UNIVERSITY

Analytical Chemistry — M,D
Anthropology — M,D
Applied Statistics — M
Astrophysics — D
Biochemistry — M,D
Biological and Biomedical
  Sciences—General — M,D
Business Administration and
  Management—General — M,D
Cancer Biology/Oncology — M,D
Cardiovascular Sciences — M,D
Cell Biology — M,D
Chemical Engineering — M,D
Chemical Physics — M,D
Chemistry — M,D
Civil Engineering — M,D
Classics — M,D
Computer Science — M,D
Cultural Studies — M,D
Economics — M,D
Electrical Engineering — M,D
Engineering and Applied
  Sciences—General — M,D
Engineering Physics — M,D
English — M,D
French — M
Genetics — M,D
Geochemistry — M,D
Geography — M,D
Geology — M,D
Geosciences — M,D
Health Physics/Radiological Health — M,D
Health Services Research — M,D
History — M,D
Human Resources Management — M,D
Immunology — M,D
Industrial and Labor Relations — M
Inorganic Chemistry — M,D
International Affairs — M,D
Kinesiology and Movement Studies — M,D
Management Information Systems — D
Materials Engineering — M,D
Materials Sciences — M,D
Mathematics — M,D
Mechanical Engineering — M,D
Medical Physics — M,D

Molecular Biology — M,D
Neuroscience — M,D
Nuclear Engineering — M,D
Nursing—General — M,D
Nutrition — M
Occupational Therapy — M
Organic Chemistry — M,D
Pastoral Ministry and Counseling — M,D,O
Pharmacology — M,D
Philosophy — M,D
Physical Chemistry — M,D
Physical Therapy — M
Physics — D
Physiology — M,D
Political Science — M,D
Psychology—General — M,D
Public Administration — M,D
Public Affairs — M,D
Public Policy — M,D
Rehabilitation Sciences — M,D
Religion — M,D
Social Work — M
Sociology — M,D
Software Engineering — M,D
Statistics — M
Theology — M,D,O
Virology — M,D

MCMURRY UNIVERSITY

Family Nurse Practitioner Studies — M
Nursing Education — M
Nursing—General — M

MCNEESE STATE UNIVERSITY

Agricultural Sciences—
  General — M
Applied Behavior Analysis — M,O
Art Education — O
Business Administration and
  Management—General — M
Chemical Engineering — M
Chemistry — M
Civil Engineering — M
Computer Science — M
Counseling Psychology — M,O
Counselor Education — M
Criminal Justice and Criminology — M
Curriculum and Instruction — M
Early Childhood Education — O
Education of the Gifted — M
Education—General — O
Educational Leadership and
  Administration — M,O
Educational Measurement and
  Evaluation — M,O
Educational Media/Instructional
  Technology — M,O
Electrical Engineering — M
Elementary Education — M,O
Engineering and Applied
  Sciences—General — M
Engineering Management — M
English — M
Environmental Sciences — M
Exercise and Sports Science — M
Experimental Psychology — M,O
Family Nurse Practitioner Studies — M
Health Education — O
Health Promotion — M
Library Science — O
Mathematics Education — O
Mathematics — M
Mechanical Engineering — M
Middle School Education — O
Music Education — O
Nursing Education — M
Nursing—General — M,O
Nutrition — M
Physical Education — O
Psychiatric Nursing — M,O
Psychology—General — M
Reading Education — M
School Psychology — M,O
Science Education — O
Secondary Education — M,O
Special Education — M
Statistics — M
Writing — M

MCPHERSON COLLEGE

Education—General — M

MCPHS UNIVERSITY

Acupuncture and Oriental Medicine — M
Chemistry — M,D
Health Services Management and
  Hospital Administration — M
Nursing—General — M
Optometry — D
Pharmaceutical Sciences — M,D
Pharmacology — M,D
Pharmacy — D
Physical Therapy — M
Physician Assistant Studies — M
Public Health—General — M

MEADVILLE LOMBARD THEOLOGICAL SCHOOL

Pastoral Ministry and Counseling — M,D
Theology — M,D

MEDAILLE COLLEGE

Business Administration and
  Management—General — M
Clinical Psychology — M,D
Counseling Psychology — M,D
Curriculum and Instruction — M
Education—General — M
Elementary Education — M
Marriage and Family Therapy — M,D
Organizational Management — M
Psychology—General — M
Reading Education — M
Secondary Education — M
Special Education — M

MEDICAL COLLEGE OF WISCONSIN

Allopathic Medicine — D
Anesthesiologist Assistant Studies — M
Biochemistry — D
Bioethics — M,O
Biological and Biomedical
  Sciences—General — M,D,O
Biostatistics — D
Clinical Laboratory
  Sciences/Medical Technology — M
Clinical Research — D
Community Health — D
Neuroscience — D
Pharmacology — D
Pharmacy — D
Physiology — D
Public Health—General — M,D,O
Toxicology — D

MEDICAL UNIVERSITY OF SOUTH CAROLINA

Adult Nursing — M,D
Allied Health—General — M,D
Allopathic Medicine — D
Biochemistry — M,D
Biological and Biomedical
  Sciences—General — M,D
Biostatistics — M,D
Cancer Biology/Oncology — D
Cardiovascular Sciences — D
Cell Biology — D
Clinical Research — M
Dentistry — D
Developmental Biology — D
Epidemiology — M,D
Family Nurse Practitioner Studies — M,D
Genetics — D
Gerontological Nursing — M,D
Health Services Management and
  Hospital Administration — M,D
Immunology — M,D
International Health — M
Marine Sciences — D
Maternal and Child/Neonatal
  Nursing — M,D
Medical Imaging — D
Medicinal and Pharmaceutical
  Chemistry — D
Microbiology — M,D
Molecular Biology — M,D
Molecular Pharmacology — M,D
Neuroscience — M,D
Nurse Anesthesia — M
Nursing and Healthcare
  Administration — M
Nursing Education — M
Nursing—General — D
Occupational Therapy — M
Pathobiology — D
Pathology — M,D
Pharmacy — D
Physical Therapy — D
Physician Assistant Studies — M
Rehabilitation Sciences — D
Toxicology — D

MEHARRY MEDICAL COLLEGE

Allopathic Medicine — D
Biochemistry — D
Biological and Biomedical
  Sciences—General — D
Cancer Biology/Oncology — D
Dentistry — D
Environmental and Occupational
  Health — M
Health Services Management and
  Hospital Administration — M
Immunology — D
Microbiology — D
Neuroscience — D
Pharmacology — D
Public Health—General — M

MELBOURNE BUSINESS SCHOOL

Business Administration and
  Management—General — M,D,O
Marketing — M,D,O

MEMORIAL UNIVERSITY OF NEWFOUNDLAND

Adult Education — M,D,O
Anthropology — M,D
Aquaculture — M
Archaeology — M,D
Biochemistry — M,D
Biological and Biomedical
  Sciences—General — M,D,O
Biopsychology — M,D
Business Administration and
  Management—General — M
Cancer Biology/Oncology — M,D
Cardiovascular Sciences — M,D
Chemistry — M,D
Civil Engineering — M,D
Classics — M
Clinical Psychology — M,D
Clinical Research — M,D
Community Health — M,D,O
Computational Sciences — M
Computer Engineering — M,D
Computer Science — M,D
Condensed Matter Physics — M,D
Cultural Anthropology — M,D
Curriculum and Instruction — M,D,O
Economics — M,D
Education—General — M,D,O
Educational Leadership and
  Administration — M,D,O
Educational Media/Instructional
  Technology — M,D,O
Educational Psychology — M,D,O
Electrical Engineering — M,D
Engineering and Applied
  Sciences—General — M,D
English — M,D

Environmental Engineering — M
Environmental Sciences — M,D,O
Epidemiology — M,D,O
Exercise and Sports Science — M
Experimental Psychology — M,D
Fish, Game, and Wildlife
  Management — M,O
Folklore — M,D
Food Science and
  Technology — M,D
French — M
Gender Studies — M,D
Geography — M,D
Geology — M,D
Geophysics — M,D
Geosciences — M,D
German — M,D
History — M,D
Human Genetics — M,D
Humanities — M
Immunology — M,D
Industrial and Labor Relations — M
Kinesiology and Movement Studies — M
Linguistics — M,D
Marine Affairs — M,D,O
Marine Sciences — M,O
Mathematics — M,D
Mechanical Engineering — M,D
Music — M,D
Neuroscience — M,D
Nursing—General — M,D
Ocean Engineering — M,D
Oceanography — M,D
Pharmaceutical Sciences — M,D
Philosophy — M,D
Physical Education — M
Physics — M,D
Political Science — M
Psychology—General — M,D
Religion — M
Social Work — M,D
Sociology — M,D
Statistics — M,D

MEMPHIS THEOLOGICAL SEMINARY

Theology — M,D

MERCER UNIVERSITY

Accounting — M
Allopathic Medicine — M,D
Athletic Training and Sports
  Medicine — M,D
Biomedical Engineering — M
Business Administration and
  Management—General — M
Clinical Psychology — M,D
Computer Engineering — M
Counselor Education — M,D
Criminal Justice and Criminology — M,D
Curriculum and Instruction — M,D,O
Early Childhood Education — M,D,O
Education—General — M,D,O
Educational Leadership and
  Administration — M,D,O
Electrical Engineering — M
Engineering and Applied
  Sciences—General — M
Engineering Management — M
Entrepreneurship — M
Environmental and Occupational
  Health — M,D
Environmental Engineering — M
Environmental Sciences — M
Family Nurse Practitioner Studies — M,D,O
Gerontological Nursing — M,D,O
Gerontology — M,D
Health Informatics — M,D
Higher Education — M,D,O
Human Services — M,D
Law — D
Management of Technology — M
Mathematics — M,D,O
Mechanical Engineering — M
Middle School Education — M,D,O
Music — M
Nonprofit Management — M,D
Nursing and Healthcare
  Administration — M,D
Nursing—General — M,D,O
Organizational Management — M,D
Pastoral Ministry and Counseling — M,D
Pharmaceutical Sciences — D
Pharmacy — D
Physical Therapy — M,D
Physician Assistant Studies — M,D
Public Health—General — M,D
Rehabilitation Counseling — M,D
School Psychology — M,D
Science Education — M,D,O
Secondary Education — M,D,O
Software Engineering — M
Theology — M,D

MERCY COLLEGE

Accounting — M
Allied Health—General — M,D
Business Administration and
  Management—General — M
Communication Disorders — M
Computer and Information
  Systems Security — M
Counseling Psychology — M,O
Counselor Education — M,O
Early Childhood Education — M,O
Education—General — M,O
Educational Leadership and
  Administration — M,O
Elementary Education — M
English as a Second Language — M,O
English — M
Health Services Management and
  Hospital Administration — M
Human Resources Management — M
Marriage and Family Therapy — M,O
Middle School Education — M,O

Nursing and Healthcare Administration — M
Nursing Education — M
Nursing—General — M
Occupational Therapy — M
Organizational Management — M
Physical Therapy — D
Physician Assistant Studies — M
Psychology—General — M
Reading Education — M,O
School Psychology — M
Secondary Education — M,O

MERCY COLLEGE OF OHIO

Health Services Management and Hospital Administration — M
Nursing—General — M

MERCYHURST UNIVERSITY

Accounting — M,O
Anthropology — M
Applied Behavior Analysis — M
Archaeology — M
Biological Anthropology — M
Computer and Information Systems Security — M
Criminal Justice and Criminology — M,O
Educational Leadership and Administration — M,O
Entrepreneurship — M,O
Forensic Sciences — M
Higher Education — M,O
Human Resources Management — M,O
Management Strategy and Policy — M,O
Organizational Management — M,O
Physician Assistant Studies — M
Secondary Education — M
Special Education — M
Sports Management — M,O

MEREDITH COLLEGE

Business Administration and Management—General — M
Education of the Gifted — M,O
Education—General — M,O
Elementary Education — M,O
English as a Second Language — M,O
Health Education — M,O
Industrial and Organizational Psychology — M
Nutrition — M,O
Physical Education — M,O
Psychology—General — M
Reading Education — M,O
Special Education — M,O

MERRIMACK COLLEGE

Accounting — M
Athletic Training and Sports Medicine — M
Business Administration and Management—General — M
Business Analytics — M
Civil Engineering — M
Clinical Psychology — M,O
Computer Science — M
Data Science/Data Analytics — M
Education—General — M,O
Engineering and Applied Sciences—General — M
Engineering Management — M
Exercise and Sports Science — M
Health Education — M
Health Promotion — M
Mechanical Engineering — M
Public Affairs — M,O
Theology — M,O

MESIVTA OF EASTERN PARKWAY–YESHIVA ZICHRON MEILECH

Theology

MESIVTA TORAH VODAATH RABBINICAL SEMINARY

Pastoral Ministry and Counseling — O
Theology — O

MESIVTHA TIFERETH JERUSALEM OF AMERICA

Theology

MESSIAH COLLEGE

Business Administration and Management—General — M,O
Clinical Psychology — M,O
Counseling Psychology — M,O
Counselor Education — M,O
Curriculum and Instruction — M
English as a Second Language — M
Higher Education — M
Management Strategy and Policy — M,O
Marriage and Family Therapy — M,O
Music — M
Nursing Education — M
Organizational Management — M,O
Special Education — M
Sports Management — M
Student Affairs — M

METHODIST THEOLOGICAL SCHOOL IN OHIO

Theology — M,D

METHODIST UNIVERSITY

Business Administration and Management—General — M
Criminal Justice and Criminology — M
Physician Assistant Studies — M

METROPOLITAN COLLEGE OF NEW YORK

Business Administration and Management—General — M
Elementary Education — M

Emergency Management — M
Finance and Banking — M
Media Studies — M
Public Administration — M
Public Affairs — M
Risk Management — M
Special Education — M

METROPOLITAN STATE UNIVERSITY

Addictions/Substance Abuse Counseling — M
Business Administration and Management—General — M,D,O
Business Analytics — M,D,O
Computer and Information Systems Security — M,D,O
Computer Science — M
Criminal Justice and Criminology — M
Curriculum and Instruction — M
Data Science/Data Analytics — M,D,O
English as a Second Language — M
English Education — M
Information Studies — M,D,O
Liberal Studies — M
Management Information Systems — M,D,O
Mathematics Education — M
Nonprofit Management — M
Nursing and Healthcare Administration — M,D
Nursing Education — M,D
Nursing—General — M,D
Oral and Dental Sciences — M,D
Project Management — M,D,O
Public Administration — M
Public Affairs — M
Science Education — M
Secondary Education — M
Social Sciences Education — M
Special Education — M
Supply Chain Management — M,D,O
Technical Writing — M
Urban Education — M

METROPOLITAN STATE UNIVERSITY OF DENVER

Accounting — M
Education—General — M
Elementary Education — M
Social Work — M
Special Education — M
Taxation — M

MGH INSTITUTE OF HEALTH PROFESSIONS

Communication Disorders — M,O
Gerontological Nursing — M,D,O
Nursing Education — M,D,O
Nursing—General — M,D,O
Occupational Therapy — D
Pediatric Nursing — M,D,O
Physical Therapy — M,D,O
Physician Assistant Studies — M
Psychiatric Nursing — M,D,O
Reading Education — M,O
Women's Health Nursing — M,D,O

MIAMI INTERNATIONAL UNIVERSITY OF ART & DESIGN

Applied Arts and Design—General — M
Film, Television, and Video Production — M

MIAMI REGIONAL UNIVERSITY

Nursing and Healthcare Administration — M
Nursing Education — M
Nursing—General — M

MIAMI UNIVERSITY

Accounting — M
Architecture — M
Art Education — M
Art/Fine Arts — M
Biochemistry — M,D
Biological and Biomedical Sciences—General — M,D
Business Administration and Management—General — M
Chemical Engineering — M
Chemistry — M,D
Child and Family Studies — M
Communication Disorders — M
Computer Engineering — M
Demography and Population Studies — M,D
Economics — M
Education—General — M,D,O
Educational Leadership and Administration — M,D
Educational Psychology — M,O
Electrical Engineering — M
Engineering and Applied Sciences—General — M,D
English — M
Environmental Sciences — M
Exercise and Sports Science — M
French — M
Geography — M
Geology — M,D
Gerontology — M,D
History — M
Interior Design — M
Mathematics Education — M
Mathematics — M
Mechanical Engineering — M
Microbiology — M,D
Music Education — M
Music — M
Philosophy — M
Physics — M
Political Science — M
Psychology—General — M
Statistics — M

Student Affairs — M,D
Systems Science — M
Theater — M

MICHIGAN SCHOOL OF PSYCHOLOGY

Clinical Psychology — M,D
Educational Psychology — M,D
Psychology—General — M,D
Transpersonal and Humanistic Psychology — M,D

MICHIGAN STATE UNIVERSITY

Accounting — M,D
Adult Education — M,D,O
Advertising and Public Relations — M
African Studies — M,D
African-American Studies — M,D
Agricultural Economics and Agribusiness — M,D
Agricultural Sciences—General — M,D
Agronomy and Soil Sciences — M,D
Allopathic Medicine — D
American Studies — M,D
Animal Sciences — M,D
Anthropology — M,D
Applied Mathematics — M,D
Applied Statistics — M,D
Art/Fine Arts — M
Astronomy — M,D
Astrophysics — M,D
Biochemistry — M,D
Biological and Biomedical Sciences—General — M,D
Biosystems Engineering — M,D
Business Administration and Management—General — M,D
Business Analytics — M
Cell Biology — M,D
Chemical Engineering — M,D
Chemical Physics — M,D
Chemistry — M,D
Child and Family Studies — M,D
Child Development — M,D
Civil Engineering — M,D
Clinical Laboratory Sciences/Medical Technology — M
Communication Disorders — M,D
Communication—General — M,D
Computer Science — M,D
Construction Management — M,D
Counselor Education — M,D,O
Criminal Justice and Criminology — M,D
Curriculum and Instruction — M,D,O
Ecology — D
Economics — M,D
Education—General — M,D,O
Educational Leadership and Administration — M,D,O
Educational Measurement and Evaluation — M,D,O
Educational Media/Instructional Technology — M,D,O
Educational Policy — D
Educational Psychology — M,D,O
Electrical Engineering — M,D
Engineering and Applied Sciences—General — M,D
English as a Second Language — M,D
English — M,D
Entomology — M,D
Environmental Design — M,D
Environmental Engineering — M,D
Environmental Sciences — M,D
Epidemiology — M,D
Evolutionary Biology — D
Finance and Banking — M,D
Fish, Game, and Wildlife Management — M,D
Food Science and Technology — M,D
Foreign Languages Education — D
Forensic Sciences — M,D
Forestry — M,D
French — M,D
Game Design and Development — M
Genetics — M,D
Geography — M,D
Geosciences — M,D
German — M,D
Health Communication — M
Higher Education — M,D,O
Hispanic and Latin American Languages — M,D
Hispanic Studies — M,D
History — M,D
Horticulture — M,D
Hospitality Management — M
Human Development — M,D
Human Resources Management — M,D
Industrial and Labor Relations — M,D
Interior Design — M,D
Journalism — M
Kinesiology and Movement Studies — M,D
Latin American Studies — D
Linguistics — M,D
Logistics — M,D
Management Information Systems — M,D
Management Strategy and Policy — M,D
Manufacturing Engineering — M,D
Marketing Research — M,D
Marketing — M,D
Materials Engineering — M,D
Materials Sciences — M,D
Mathematics Education — M,D
Mathematics — M,D
Mechanical Engineering — M,D
Mechanics — M,D
Media Studies — M,D
Microbiology — M,D

Molecular Biology — M,D
Molecular Genetics — M,D
Music Education — M,D
Music — M,D
Natural Resources — M,D
Neuroscience — M,D
Nursing—General — M,D
Nutrition — M,D
Osteopathic Medicine — D
Pathobiology — M,D
Pathology — M,D
Pharmacology — M,D
Philosophy — M,D
Physics — M,D
Physiology — M,D
Plant Biology — M,D
Plant Pathology — M,D
Plant Sciences — M,D
Political Science — M,D
Psychology—General — M,D
Public Health—General — M
Reading Education — M
Recreation and Park Management — M,D
Rehabilitation Counseling — M,D,O
Rhetoric — M,D
Romance Languages — M,D
School Psychology — M,D,O
Social Sciences Education — M,D
Social Work — M,D
Sociology — M,D
Spanish — M,D
Special Education — M,D,O
Statistics — M,D
Structural Biology — D
Supply Chain Management — M,D
Sustainable Development — M,D
Systems Biology — D
Taxation — M,D
Theater — M
Therapies—Dance, Drama, and Music — M,D
Toxicology — M,D
Urban and Regional Planning — M,D
Veterinary Medicine — D
Veterinary Sciences — M,D
Writing — M,D
Zoology — M,D

MICHIGAN STATE UNIVERSITY COLLEGE OF LAW

Intellectual Property Law — M,D
Law — M,D
Legal and Justice Studies — M,D

MICHIGAN TECHNOLOGICAL UNIVERSITY

Applied Physics — M,D
Biochemistry — M,D,O
Biological and Biomedical Sciences—General — M,D
Biomedical Engineering — M,D
Business Administration and Management—General — M
Chemical Engineering — M,D
Chemistry — M,D
Civil Engineering — M,D
Cognitive Sciences — M,D,O
Computational Sciences — M,D,O
Computer Engineering — M,D,O
Data Science/Data Analytics — M,D,O
Electrical Engineering — M,D,O
Engineering and Applied Sciences—General — M,D,O
Environmental Engineering — M,D
Ergonomics and Human Factors — M,D,O
Forestry — M,D
Geophysics — M,D
Interdisciplinary Studies — M,D,O
Kinesiology and Movement Studies — M,D
Materials Engineering — M,D
Mathematics — M,D
Mechanical Engineering — M,D,O
Mechanics — M,D,O
Metallurgical Engineering and Metallurgy — M,D
Mineral Economics — M
Molecular Biology — M,D,O
Physics — M,D
Science Education — M,D,O
Sustainability Management — M

MID-AMERICA BAPTIST THEOLOGICAL SEMINARY

Missions and Missiology — M,D
Pastoral Ministry and Counseling — M,D
Theology — M,D

MID-AMERICA BAPTIST THEOLOGICAL SEMINARY NORTHEAST BRANCH

Theology — M

MID-AMERICA CHRISTIAN UNIVERSITY

Business Administration and Management—General — M
Counseling Psychology — M
Marriage and Family Therapy — M
Organizational Management — M
Pastoral Ministry and Counseling — M
Public Administration — M

MIDAMERICA NAZARENE UNIVERSITY

Business Administration and Management—General — M
Clinical Psychology — M
Education—General — M
Educational Media/Instructional Technology — M
English as a Second Language — M
Marriage and Family Therapy — M
Nursing and Healthcare Administration — M

---

*M—masters degree; D—doctorate; O—other advanced degree; *—Close-Up and/or Display*

Nursing Education — M
Nursing—General — M
Public Health—General — M
Reading Education — M
School Psychology — M

MID-AMERICA REFORMED SEMINARY
Theology — M

MIDDLEBURY COLLEGE
Chinese — M
English — M
French — M,D
German — M,D
Italian — M,D
Near and Middle Eastern Languages — M
Russian — M,D
Spanish — M,D

MIDDLEBURY INSTITUTE OF INTERNATIONAL STUDIES AT MONTEREY
Conflict Resolution and Mediation/Peace Studies — M
English as a Second Language — M
Environmental Management and Policy — M
Foreign Languages Education — M
International Affairs — M
International and Comparative Education — M
International Development — M
International Trade Policy — M
Public Administration — M
Translation and Interpretation — M

MIDDLE GEORGIA STATE UNIVERSITY
Computer and Information Systems Security — M
Forensic Sciences — M
Gerontological Nursing — M
Health Informatics — M
Management Information Systems — M

MIDDLE TENNESSEE SCHOOL OF ANESTHESIA
Nurse Anesthesia — M,D

MIDDLE TENNESSEE STATE UNIVERSITY
Accounting — M
Actuarial Science — M
Aerospace/Aeronautical Engineering — M
Archives/Archival Administration — M,D,O
Aviation Management — M
Biological and Biomedical Sciences—General — M
Biostatistics — M
Biotechnology — M
Business Administration and Management—General — M
Business Education — M
Chemistry — M
Clinical Psychology — M,O
Computational Sciences — D
Computer Science — M
Counseling Psychology — M
Counselor Education — M
Criminal Justice and Criminology — M
Curriculum and Instruction — M,O
Early Childhood Education — M,O
Economics — M,D
Education—General — M,D,O
Educational Leadership and Administration — M,O
Educational Media/Instructional Technology — M,O
Elementary Education — M,O
Engineering Management — M
English as a Second Language — M,O
English — M,D
Exercise and Sports Science — M,D
Experimental Psychology — M,O
Family Nurse Practitioner Studies — M
Foreign Languages Education — M
French — M
Gender Studies — O
Geosciences — O
German — M
Gerontology — O
Health Education — O
History — M
Human Resources Management — M
Industrial and Organizational Psychology — M,O
International Affairs — M
Management Information Systems — M
Management Strategy and Policy — M
Mass Communication — M
Mathematics Education — M,D
Mathematics — M
Medical Informatics — M
Middle School Education — M,O
Molecular Biology — D
Music — M
Nursing and Healthcare Administration — M
Nursing Education — M
Nursing—General — M
Physical Education — M
Political Science — M
Psychology—General — M,O
Public History — D
Reading Education — M,D
Recreation and Park Management — M
School Psychology — M,O
Science Education — M,D
Secondary Education — M
Social Work — M
Sociology — M
Spanish — M
Special Education — M
Vocational and Technical Education — M
Women's Studies — O

MIDWAY UNIVERSITY
Business Administration and Management—General — M
Education—General — M
Organizational Management — M

MIDWEST COLLEGE OF ORIENTAL MEDICINE
Acupuncture and Oriental Medicine — M,O

MIDWESTERN BAPTIST THEOLOGICAL SEMINARY
Music — M,D,O
Pastoral Ministry and Counseling — M,D,O
Religious Education — M,D,O
Theology — M,D,O

MIDWESTERN STATE UNIVERSITY
Biological and Biomedical Sciences—General — M
Business Administration and Management—General — M
Clinical Psychology — M
Community Health — M
Computer Science — M
Counseling Psychology — M
Counselor Education — M
Criminal Justice and Criminology — M,O
Curriculum and Instruction — M
Education—General — M
Educational Leadership and Administration — M
Educational Media/Instructional Technology — M
English — M,D
Exercise and Sports Science — M
Family Nurse Practitioner Studies — M
Health Informatics — M,O
Health Physics/Radiological Health — M
Health Services Management and Hospital Administration — M,O
History — M
Human Resources Development — M
Nursing Education — M
Nursing—General — M
Philosophy — M,D
Political Science — M
Psychiatric Nursing — M
Reading Education — M
Special Education — M
Sports Management — M

MIDWESTERN UNIVERSITY, DOWNERS GROVE CAMPUS
Biological and Biomedical Sciences—General — M
Clinical Psychology — D
Communication Disorders — M
Dentistry — D
Occupational Therapy — M
Optometry — D
Osteopathic Medicine — D
Pharmacy — D
Physical Therapy — D
Physician Assistant Studies — M

MIDWESTERN UNIVERSITY, GLENDALE CAMPUS
Allied Health—General — M,D
Biological and Biomedical Sciences—General — M
Cardiovascular Sciences — M
Clinical Psychology — D
Communication Disorders — M
Dentistry — D
Nurse Anesthesia — M
Occupational Therapy — M
Optometry — D
Osteopathic Medicine — D
Pharmacy — D
Physical Therapy — D
Physician Assistant Studies — M
Podiatric Medicine — D
Veterinary Medicine — D

MIDWEST UNIVERSITY
Aviation Management — M,D
Counselor Education — M,D
Education of the Gifted — M,D
Education—General — M,D
English as a Second Language — M,D
Entrepreneurship — M,D
International Business — M,D
Investment Management — M,D
Marriage and Family Therapy — M,D
Missions and Missiology — M,D
Music — M,D
Organizational Management — M,D
Pastoral Ministry and Counseling — M,D
Public Administration — M,D
Public Policy — M,D
Real Estate — M,D
Theology — M,D

MIDWIVES COLLEGE OF UTAH
Nurse Midwifery — M

MILLENNIA ATLANTIC UNIVERSITY
Accounting — M
Business Administration and Management—General — M
Health Informatics — M
Human Resources Management — M

MILLERSVILLE UNIVERSITY OF PENNSYLVANIA
Clinical Psychology — M
Distance Education Development — M,D
Early Childhood Education — M
Education of the Gifted — M
Education—General — M,D,O
Educational Leadership and Administration — M,D
English Education — M
Environmental Management and Policy — M
Family Nurse Practitioner Studies — M,D,O

French — M
Geographic Information Systems — M
German — M
Mathematics Education — M,D
Meteorology — M
Nursing Education — M,D,O
Nursing—General — M,D,O
Physical Education — M,O
Reading Education — M
School Psychology — M
Science Education — M,D
Social Work — M,D
Spanish — M
Special Education — M
Sports Management — M,O
Writing — M,O

MILLIGAN COLLEGE
Business Administration and Management—General — M,O
Clinical Psychology — M,O
Counselor Education — M,O
Early Childhood Education — M,D,O
Education—General — M,D,O
Educational Leadership and Administration — M,D,O
Elementary Education — M
Health Services Management and Hospital Administration — M,O
Industrial and Manufacturing Management — M,O
Middle School Education — M,D,O
Missions and Missiology — M,O
Occupational Therapy — M
Pastoral Ministry and Counseling — M,D,O
Physician Assistant Studies — M
Religion — M,D,O
Religious Education — M,D,O
Secondary Education — M,O
Special Education — M,D,O
Theology — M,D,O

MILLIKIN UNIVERSITY
Business Administration and Management—General — M
Nursing—General — M,D

MILLSAPS COLLEGE
Accounting — M
Business Administration and Management—General — M

MILLS COLLEGE
Applied Economics — M
Art/Fine Arts — M
Biological and Biomedical Sciences—General — O
Business Administration and Management—General — M
Computer Science — M,O
Dance — M
Early Childhood Education — M
Education—General — M,D,O
Educational Leadership and Administration —
English — M,O
Illustration — M,O
Interdisciplinary Studies — M,O
Music — M
Photography — M
Public Policy — M
Translation and Interpretation — M,O
Writing — M,O

MILWAUKEE SCHOOL OF ENGINEERING
Architectural Engineering — M
Business Administration and Management—General — M
Business Education — M
Cardiovascular Sciences — M
Civil Engineering — M
Clinical Laboratory Sciences/Medical Technology — M
Engineering and Applied Sciences—General — M
Engineering Management — M
Health Services Management and Hospital Administration — M
Industrial and Manufacturing Management — M
International Business — M
Marketing — M
Nursing and Healthcare Administration — M
Perfusion — M

MINNEAPOLIS COLLEGE OF ART AND DESIGN
Applied Arts and Design—General — M
Art/Fine Arts — M,O
Computer Art and Design — O
Film, Television, and Video Production — M
Graphic Design — M,O
Illustration — M
Internet and Interactive Multimedia — M
Photography — M
Sustainable Development — M,O

MINNESOTA STATE UNIVERSITY MANKATO
Accounting — M
Allied Health—General — M,D,O
Anthropology — M
Applied Statistics — M
Art Education — M
Art/Fine Arts — M
Astronomy — M
Automotive Engineering — M
Biological and Biomedical Sciences—General — M
Business Administration and Management—General — M

Clinical Psychology — M,D
Communication Disorders — M
Communication—General — M,O
Community Health — M,O
Computer Science — M,O
Corporate and Organizational Communication — M,O
Counseling Psychology — M,D
Counselor Education — M,D
Criminal Justice and Criminology — M
Education—General — M,D,O
Educational Leadership and Administration — M
English as a Second Language — M,O
English — M,O
Environmental Sciences — M
Ethnic Studies — M
Family Nurse Practitioner Studies — M,D
Foreign Languages Education — M
French — M
Gender Studies — M
Geography — M
Gerontology — M
Health Education — M,O
Higher Education — M
History — M
Human Services — M
Industrial and Organizational Psychology — M,D
Information Science — M,O
Interdisciplinary Studies — M
Manufacturing Engineering — M
Mathematics Education — M
Mathematics — M
Music Education — M
Music — M
Nonprofit Management — M,O
Nursing Education — M,D
Nursing—General — M,D
Physical Education — M
Physics — M
Psychology—General — M,D
Public Administration — M
Rehabilitation Counseling — M
School Psychology — M,D
Science Education — M
Social Sciences Education — M
Social Work — M
Sociology — M
Spanish — M
Special Education — M,O
Statistics — M
Student Affairs — M,D
Technical Communication — M,O
Theater — M
Urban and Regional Planning — M,O
Urban Studies — M,O
Women's Studies — M,O
Writing — M,O

MINNESOTA STATE UNIVERSITY MOORHEAD
Business Administration and Management—General — M
Counselor Education — M,D,O
Education—General — M,D,O
Educational Leadership and Administration — M,D,O
Health Services Management and Hospital Administration — M,O
Nursing—General — M,O
School Psychology — M,O

MINOT STATE UNIVERSITY
Business Administration and Management—General — M
Communication Disorders — M
Elementary Education — M
Management Information Systems — M
Mathematics Education — M
Middle School Education — M
School Psychology — O
Science Education — M
Special Education — M

MIRRER YESHIVA CENTRAL INSTITUTE
Theology —

MISERICORDIA UNIVERSITY
Accounting — M
Allied Health—General — M,D
Business Administration and Management—General — M
Communication Disorders — M
Curriculum and Instruction — M
Education—General — M
Educational Media/Instructional Technology — M
Health Services Management and Hospital Administration — M
Human Resources Management — M
Nursing—General — M,D
Occupational Therapy — M,D
Organizational Management — M
Physical Therapy — D
Reading Education — M
Special Education — M
Sports Management — M

MISSIO SEMINARY
Missions and Missiology — M,D,O
Pastoral Ministry and Counseling — M,D,O
Theology — M,D,O

MISSISSIPPI COLLEGE
Accounting — M,O
Advertising and Public Relations — M
Art Education — M,D,O
Art/Fine Arts — M
Biochemistry — M
Biological and Biomedical Sciences—General — M
Business Administration and Management—General — M,O
Business Education — M,D,O
Chemistry — M

Communication—General | M
Computer and Information Systems Security | M
Computer Education | M,D,O
Computer Science | M
Corporate and Organizational Communication | M
Counseling Psychology | M,O
Counselor Education | M,O
Criminal Justice and Criminology | M,O
Curriculum and Instruction | M,D,O
Education—General | M,D,O
Educational Leadership and Administration | M,D,O
Elementary Education | M,D,O
English as a Second Language | M
English Education | M,D,O
English | M
Finance and Banking | M,O
Health Services Management and Hospital Administration | M
Higher Education | M,D,O
History | M
Kinesiology and Movement Studies | M
Law | D,O
Legal and Justice Studies | M,O
Liberal Studies | M
Marriage and Family Therapy | M,O
Mathematics Education | M
Mathematics | M
Music Education | M
Music | M
Political Science | M,O
Science Education | M,D,O
Secondary Education | M,D,O
Social Sciences Education | M,O
Social Sciences | M,O
Special Education | M,D,O

MISSISSIPPI STATE UNIVERSITY
Accounting | M
Aerospace/Aeronautical Engineering | M,D
Agricultural Economics and Agribusiness | M
Agricultural Education | M,D
Agricultural Sciences—General | M,D
Agronomy and Soil Sciences | M,D
Animal Sciences | M,D
Anthropology | M
Applied Psychology | M,D
Atmospheric Sciences | M,D
Biochemistry | M,D
Bioengineering | M,D
Biological and Biomedical Sciences—General | M,D
Biomedical Engineering | M,D
Business Administration and Management—General | M,D
Chemical Engineering | M,D
Chemistry | M,D
Child and Family Studies | M,D
Civil Engineering | M,D
Clinical Psychology | M,D,O
Clothing and Textiles | M,D
Cognitive Sciences | M,D
Communication—General | M,D
Community College Education | M,D,O
Computer Engineering | M,D
Computer Science | M,D
Counselor Education | M,D,O
Curriculum and Instruction | M,D,O
Early Childhood Education | M,D,O
Economics | M,D
Education—General | M,D,O
Educational Leadership and Administration | M,D,O
Educational Media/Instructional Technology | M,D,O
Educational Psychology | M,D,O
Electrical Engineering | M,D
Elementary Education | M,D,O
Engineering and Applied Sciences—General | M,D
English | M
Ergonomics and Human Factors | M,D
Exercise and Sports Science | M,D
Finance and Banking | M,D
Fish, Game, and Wildlife Management | M,D
Food Science and Technology | M,D
Foreign Languages Education | M
Forestry | M,D
Genetics | M,D
Geography | M,D
Geology | M,D
Geosciences | M,D
Higher Education | M,D,O
History | M,D
Horticulture | M,D
Human Development | M
Human Resources Development | M,D,O
Industrial and Manufacturing Management | M,D
Industrial/Management Engineering | M,D
Kinesiology and Movement Studies | M,D
Landscape Architecture | M
Management Information Systems | M,D
Marketing | D
Mathematics | M,D
Mechanical Engineering | M,D
Meteorology | M,D
Middle School Education | M,D,O
Molecular Biology | M,D
Nutrition | M,D
Operations Research | M,D
Physical Education | M,D

Physics | M,D
Plant Sciences | M,D
Political Science | M,D
Project Management | M,D
Psychology—General | M,D
Public Administration | M,D
Public Policy | M,D
Reading Education | M,D,O
Rehabilitation Counseling | M,D
School Psychology | M,D,O
Secondary Education | M,D,O
Sociology | M,D
Special Education | M,D,O
Sports Management | M,D
Statistics | M,D
Student Affairs | M,D,O
Sustainable Development | M,D
Systems Engineering | M,D
Taxation | M
Veterinary Medicine | D
Veterinary Sciences | M,D
Vocational and Technical Education | M,D,O

MISSISSIPPI UNIVERSITY FOR WOMEN
Communication Disorders | M
Curriculum and Instruction | M
Education of the Gifted | M
Education—General | M
Educational Leadership and Administration | M
Health Education | M,D,O
Nursing—General | M,D,O
Public Health—General | M,D,O
Reading Education | M

MISSISSIPPI VALLEY STATE UNIVERSITY
Criminal Justice and Criminology | M
Education—General | M
Environmental and Occupational Health | M

MISSOURI BAPTIST UNIVERSITY
Business Administration and Management—General | M,O
Counselor Education | M,O
Education—General | M,O
Educational Leadership and Administration | M,O
Pastoral Ministry and Counseling | M,O

MISSOURI SOUTHERN STATE UNIVERSITY
Business Administration and Management—General | M
Criminal Justice and Criminology | M
Dental Hygiene | M
Early Childhood Education | M
Education—General | M
Educational Media/Instructional Technology | M
Nursing—General | M

MISSOURI STATE UNIVERSITY
Accounting | M
Agricultural Sciences—General | M
Applied Behavior Analysis | M,O
Applied Science and Technology | M,O
Art/Fine Arts | M
Athletic Training and Sports Medicine | M
Biological and Biomedical Sciences—General | M
Business Administration and Management—General | M
Cell Biology | M
Chemistry | M
Child and Family Studies | M
Clinical Psychology | M,D
Communication Disorders | M,D
Communication—General | M,O
Computer Science | M
Construction Management | M
Counseling Psychology | M
Counselor Education | M
Criminal Justice and Criminology | M,O
Early Childhood Education | M
Educational Leadership and Administration | M,O
Educational Measurement and Evaluation | O
Educational Media/Instructional Technology | M
Elementary Education | M,O
English as a Second Language | M,O
English Education | M,O
English | M,O
Environmental Management and Policy | M,O
Experimental Psychology | M,D
Family Nurse Practitioner Studies | M,D
Film, Television, and Video Production | M,O
Geography | M,O
Geology | M,O
Geosciences | M
Higher Education | M
History | M,O
Homeland Security | M,O
Industrial and Organizational Psychology | M,O
International Affairs | M
Kinesiology and Movement Studies | M
Materials Sciences | M
Mathematics Education | M
Mathematics | M
Military and Defense Studies | M
Molecular Biology | M
Music | M
Nurse Anesthesia | D

Nursing Education | M,D
Nursing—General | M,D
Nutrition | M,D,O
Occupational Therapy | M
Physical Education | M
Physical Therapy | D
Physician Assistant Studies | M
Physics | M
Plant Sciences | M
Political Science | M,O
Project Management | M
Psychology—General | M,O
Public Administration | M,O
Public Health—General | M
Reading Education | M,O
Religion | M,O
Science Education | M,O
Secondary Education | M,O
Social Sciences Education | M,O
Social Work | M
Special Education | M
Sports Management | M,O
Student Affairs | M
Urban and Regional Planning | M,O
Writing | M,O

MISSOURI UNIVERSITY OF SCIENCE AND TECHNOLOGY
Aerospace/Aeronautical Engineering | M,D
Applied Mathematics | M,D
Biological and Biomedical Sciences—General | M
Business Administration and Management—General | M
Ceramic Sciences and Engineering | M,D
Chemical Engineering | M,D
Chemistry | M,D
Civil Engineering | M,D
Computer Engineering | M,D
Computer Science | M,D
Electrical Engineering | M,D
Engineering Management | M,D
Environmental Biology | M
Environmental Engineering | M,D
Geochemistry | M,D
Geological Engineering | M,D
Geology | M,D
Geophysics | M,D
Geotechnical Engineering | M
Industrial and Organizational Psychology | M
Information Science | M
Manufacturing Engineering | M,D
Materials Engineering | M,D
Materials Sciences | M,D
Mathematics Education | M,D
Mathematics | M,D
Mechanical Engineering | M,D
Metallurgical Engineering and Metallurgy | M,D
Mineral/Mining Engineering | M,D
Nuclear Engineering | M,D
Petroleum Engineering | M,D
Physics | M,D
Statistics | M,D
Systems Engineering | M,D
Technical Communication | M
Water Resources | M,D

MISSOURI VALLEY COLLEGE
Social Psychology | M

MISSOURI WESTERN STATE UNIVERSITY
Accounting | M
Animal Sciences | M
Biological and Biomedical Sciences—General | M
Business Administration and Management—General | M
Chemistry | M
Computer and Information Systems Security | M
Early Childhood Education | M,O
Educational Measurement and Evaluation | M,O
Engineering and Applied Sciences—General | M
English as a Second Language | M,O
Forensic Sciences | M,O
Nursing and Healthcare Administration | M,O
Nursing Education | M,O
Nursing—General | M,O
Special Education | M,O
Sports Management | M
Technical Communication | M,O
Writing | M,O

MITCHELL HAMLINE SCHOOL OF LAW
Law | M,D

MOLLOY COLLEGE
Accounting | M,O
Business Administration and Management—General | M,O
Clinical Psychology | M
Communication Disorders | M
Criminal Justice and Criminology | M
Early Childhood Education | M,O
Education—General | M,O
Educational Media/Instructional Technology | M,O
English as a Second Language | M,O
English Education | M,O
Family Nurse Practitioner Studies | M,D,O
Finance and Banking | M,O
Foreign Languages Education | M,O
Gerontological Nursing | M,D,O

Health Services Management and Hospital Administration | M,D,O
Marketing | M,O
Mathematics Education | M,O
Multilingual and Multicultural Education | M,O
Nursing Education | M,D,O
Nursing—General | M,D,O
Pediatric Nursing | M,D,O
Psychiatric Nursing | M,D,O
Science Education | M,O
Social Sciences Education | M,O
Special Education | M,O
Therapies—Dance, Drama, and Music | M

MONMOUTH UNIVERSITY
Accounting | M,O
Addictions/Substance Abuse Counseling | M,O
Adult Nursing | M,D,O
Advertising and Public Relations | M,O
American Studies | M
Anthropology | M
Applied Behavior Analysis | M,D,O
Business Administration and Management—General | M,O
Communication Disorders | M,D,O
Communication—General | M,O
Computer Science | M
Counseling Psychology | M,O
Criminal Justice and Criminology | M,O
Early Childhood Education | M,D,O
Education—General | M,D,O
Educational Leadership and Administration | M,D,O
Elementary Education | M,D,O
English as a Second Language | M,D,O
English | M
Finance and Banking | M,O
Forensic Nursing | M,D,O
Gerontological Nursing | M,D,O
History | M
Homeland Security | M,O
Information Studies | M
Marketing | M,O
Media Studies | M,O
Nursing—General | M,D,O
Psychology—General | M,O
Reading Education | M,D,O
Real Estate | M,O
Rhetoric | M
School Psychology | M,D,O
Secondary Education | M,D,O
Social Work | M,O
Software Engineering | M,O
Special Education | M,D,O
Student Affairs | M,D,O
Western European Studies | M
Writing | M

MONROE COLLEGE
Accounting | M
Biostatistics | M
Business Administration and Management—General | M
Community Health | M
Computer Science | M
Criminal Justice and Criminology | M
Entrepreneurship | M
Epidemiology | M
Finance and Banking | M
Health Services Management and Hospital Administration | M
Hospitality Management | M
Human Resources Management | M
Information Science | M
Marketing | M
Public Health—General | M

MONTANA STATE UNIVERSITY
Accounting | M
Adult Education | M,D,O
Agricultural Education | M
Agricultural Sciences—General | M,D
American Indian/Native American Studies | M
Animal Sciences | M,D
Architecture | M
Art History | M
Art/Fine Arts | M
Biochemistry | M,D
Biological and Biomedical Sciences—General | M,D
Chemical Engineering | M,D
Chemistry | M,D
Civil Engineering | M,D
Computer Engineering | M,D
Computer Science | M,D
Construction Engineering | M,D
Curriculum and Instruction | M,D,O
Ecology | M,D
Education—General | M,D,O
Educational Leadership and Administration | M,D,O
Electrical Engineering | M,D
Engineering and Applied Sciences—General | M,D
English | M
Environmental Engineering | M,D
Environmental Sciences | M,D
Family Nurse Practitioner Studies | M,D,O
Film, Television, and Video Production | M
Fish, Game, and Wildlife Management | M,D
Geosciences | M,D
Health Education | M
Higher Education | M,D,O
History | M,D
Home Economics Education | M

Human Development — M
Immunology — M,D
Industrial/Management Engineering — M,D
Infectious Diseases — M,D
Mathematics Education — M,D
Mathematics — M,D
Mechanical Engineering — M,D
Mechanics — M,D
Microbiology — M,D
Natural Resources — M
Neuroscience — D
Nursing and Healthcare Administration — M,D,O
Nursing Education — M,D,O
Nursing—General — M,D,O
Physics — M,D
Plant Pathology — M,D
Plant Sciences — M,D
Psychiatric Nursing — M,D,O
Psychology—General — M
Public Administration — M
Range Science — M,D
School Psychology — M,D,O
Statistics — M
Vocational and Technical Education — M,D,O

MONTANA STATE UNIVERSITY BILLINGS
Advertising and Public Relations — M
Applied Behavior Analysis — M
Athletic Training and Sports Medicine — M
Communication—General — M
Counseling Psychology — M
Counselor Education — M
Curriculum and Instruction — M
Education—General — M,O
Educational Media/Instructional Technology — M
Elementary Education — M
Health Services Management and Hospital Administration — M
Interdisciplinary Studies — M
Psychology—General — M
Reading Education — M
Rehabilitation Counseling — M
Secondary Education — M
Special Education — M

MONTANA STATE UNIVERSITY–NORTHERN
Counselor Education — M
Education—General — M

MONTANA TECH OF THE UNIVERSITY OF MONTANA
Electrical Engineering — M
Engineering and Applied Sciences—General — M
Environmental Engineering — M
Geochemistry — M
Geological Engineering — M
Geology — M
Geosciences — M
Health Informatics — O
Hydrogeology — M
Industrial Hygiene — M
Industrial/Management Engineering — M
Interdisciplinary Studies — M
Materials Sciences — D
Metallurgical Engineering and Metallurgy — M
Mineral/Mining Engineering — M
Petroleum Engineering — M
Project Management — M
Technical Communication — M

MONTCLAIR STATE UNIVERSITY
Accounting — M,O
Addictions/Substance Abuse Counseling — O
Advertising and Public Relations — M
Applied Mathematics — M
Archives/Archival Administration — M
Art Education — M
Art/Fine Arts — M
Arts Administration — M
Biochemistry — M
Biological and Biomedical Sciences—General — M
Business Administration and Management—General — M,O
Business Analytics — M
Chemistry — M
Child and Family Studies — M,D,O
Child Development — M,O
Clinical Psychology — M
Communication Disorders — M,D
Computer Science — M,O
Conflict Resolution and Mediation/Peace Studies — M,O
Corporate and Organizational Communication — M
Counselor Education — M,D
Curriculum and Instruction — M
Data Science/Data Analytics — O
Disability Studies — M
Ecology — M
Education—General — M,D,O
Educational Leadership and Administration — M,D
Educational Measurement and Evaluation — O
English as a Second Language — M,O
English Education — M,O
English — M
Environmental Education — M
Environmental Law — O
Environmental Management and Policy — M,D
Environmental Sciences — M
Evolutionary Biology — M

Exercise and Sports Science — M,O
Finance and Banking — M
Forensic Psychology — O
French — M
Geographic Information Systems — O
Geosciences — M
Health Education — M
Human Resources Management — M
Industrial and Organizational Psychology — M
Intellectual Property Law — M,O
Internet and Interactive Multimedia — M
Law — M,O
Legal and Justice Studies — O
Linguistics — M,O
Management Information Systems — M
Management of Technology — M
Marine Biology — M
Marketing — M
Mathematics Education — M,D,O
Mathematics — M
Molecular Biology — M
Music Education — M
Music — M
Nutrition — M
Pharmacology — M
Physical Education — M
Physiology — M
Political Science — M
Project Management — M
Psychology—General — M
Public Health—General — M
Reading Education — M
Science Education — M
Social Sciences — M
Spanish — M
Special Education — M
Sports Management — M
Statistics — M
Sustainable Development — M
Theater — M
Therapies—Dance, Drama, and Music — M
Translation and Interpretation — O
Water Resources — O
Writing — O

MOODY BIBLE INSTITUTE
Pastoral Ministry and Counseling — M,O
Theology — M,O
Urban Studies — M,O

MOODY THEOLOGICAL SEMINARY–MICHIGAN
Counseling Psychology — M,O
Religion — M,O
Religious Education — M,O
Theology — M,O

MOORE COLLEGE OF ART & DESIGN
Art Education — M
Art/Fine Arts — M
Arts Administration — M
Communication—General — M
Interior Design — M

MORAVIAN COLLEGE
Accounting — M
Acute Care/Critical Care Nursing — M
Athletic Training and Sports Medicine — M,D
Business Administration and Management—General — M
Communication Disorders — M,D
Curriculum and Instruction — M
Education—General — M
Health Services Management and Hospital Administration — M
Human Resources Management — M
Nursing and Healthcare Administration — M
Nursing Education — M
Nursing—General — M
Supply Chain Management — M

MORAVIAN THEOLOGICAL SEMINARY
Theology — M,O

MOREHEAD STATE UNIVERSITY
Adult Education — M,O
Agricultural Sciences—General — M
Art Education — M
Art/Fine Arts — M
Biological and Biomedical Sciences—General — M
Business Administration and Management—General — M
Business Education — M,O
Clinical Psychology — M
Communication—General — M
Counseling Psychology — M
Counselor Education — M,O
Criminal Justice and Criminology — M
Curriculum and Instruction — M,O
Education of the Gifted — M,O
Education—General — M,O
Educational Leadership and Administration — M,O
Educational Media/Instructional Technology — M,O
Elementary Education — M,O
English Education — M,O
English — M
Environmental Management and Policy — M
Experimental Psychology — M
Foreign Languages Education — M
Gerontology — M
Graphic Design — M
Health Education — M
Health Promotion — M
Higher Education — M,O
Management Information Systems — M

Mathematics Education — M
Middle School Education — M,O
Music Education — M
Music — M
Physical Education — M
Psychology—General — M
Public Administration — M
Reading Education — M,O
Science Education — M
Secondary Education — M
Social Sciences Education — M,O
Sociology — M
Special Education — M,O
Vocational and Technical Education — M

MOREHOUSE SCHOOL OF MEDICINE
Allopathic Medicine — D
Biological and Biomedical Sciences—General — M,D
Clinical Research — M
Public Health—General — M

MORGAN STATE UNIVERSITY
Accounting — M,D
African-American Studies — M,D
Architecture — M
Bioinformatics — M
Biological and Biomedical Sciences—General — M,D
Business Administration and Management—General — M,D
Chemistry — M
Civil Engineering — M,D,O
Community College Education — D
Computational Sciences — M,D
Computer Science — M
Economics — M
Education—General — M,D
Educational Leadership and Administration — M,D
Electrical Engineering — M,D,O
Elementary Education — M
Engineering and Applied Sciences—General — M,D,O
English — M,D
Environmental Biology — D
Higher Education — M,D
Historic Preservation — M,D
History — M,D
Hospitality Management — M
Industrial/Management Engineering — M,D,O
International Affairs — M
Journalism — M
Landscape Architecture — M
Management Information Systems — D
Marketing — D
Mathematics Education — M,D
Mathematics — M,D
Museum Studies — M
Music — M
Nursing—General — M,D
Physics — M
Project Management — M
Psychology—General — M,D
Public Health—General — M,D
Science Education — M,D
Social Work — M
Sociology — M
Student Affairs — M,D
Transportation and Highway Engineering — M,D,O
Urban and Regional Planning — M
Urban Education — D

MORNINGSIDE COLLEGE
Education—General — M
Family Nurse Practitioner Studies — M
Gerontological Nursing — M
Nursing—General — M
Special Education — M

MOUNT ALLISON UNIVERSITY
Biochemistry — M
Biological and Biomedical Sciences—General — M
Chemistry — M

MOUNT ALOYSIUS COLLEGE
Accounting — M
Business Administration and Management—General — M
Health Services Management and Hospital Administration — M
Nonprofit Management — M
Project Management — M
Social Psychology — M

MOUNT ANGEL SEMINARY
Theology — M

MOUNT CARMEL COLLEGE OF NURSING
Acute Care/Critical Care Nursing — M,D
Adult Nursing — M,D
Family Nurse Practitioner Studies — M,D
Gerontological Nursing — M,D
Nursing and Healthcare Administration — M,D
Nursing Education — M,D
Nursing—General — M,D

MOUNT HOLYOKE COLLEGE
Educational Leadership and Administration — M
Mathematics Education — M

MOUNT MARTY COLLEGE
Business Administration and Management—General — M
Nurse Anesthesia — M
Nursing—General — M
Pastoral Ministry and Counseling — M

MOUNT MARY UNIVERSITY
Art Therapy — M,D

Business Administration and Management—General — M
Clinical Psychology — M,O
Counseling Psychology — M,O
Counselor Education — M,O
Education—General — M
English — M
Internet and Interactive Multimedia — M
Nursing and Healthcare Administration — M
Nutrition — M
Occupational Therapy — M,D
Rehabilitation Counseling — M,O
Writing — M

MOUNT MERCY UNIVERSITY
Business Administration and Management—General — M
Criminal Justice and Criminology — M
Education—General — M
Educational Leadership and Administration — M
Human Resources Management — M
Management Strategy and Policy — M
Marriage and Family Therapy — M
Nursing and Healthcare Administration — M
Nursing Education — M
Nursing—General — M
Quality Management — M
Reading Education — M
Special Education — M

MOUNT ST. JOSEPH UNIVERSITY
Business Administration and Management—General — M
Early Childhood Education — M,O
Education—General — M,O
Health Promotion — M,O
Health Services Management and Hospital Administration — D
Middle School Education — M,O
Multilingual and Multicultural Education — M,O
Nursing and Healthcare Administration — M
Nursing Education — M
Nursing—General — M,D
Organizational Management — M
Pastoral Ministry and Counseling — M,O
Physical Therapy — D
Reading Education — M,O
Religion — M,O
Secondary Education — M,O
Special Education — M,O
Theology — M,O

MOUNT SAINT MARY COLLEGE
Adult Nursing — M,O
Business Administration and Management—General — M
Child Development — M,O
Education—General — M,O
Family Nurse Practitioner Studies — M,O
Finance and Banking — M
Health Services Management and Hospital Administration — M
Middle School Education — M,O
Nursing and Healthcare Administration — M,O
Nursing Education — M,O
Nursing—General — M,O
Reading Education — M,O
Special Education — M,O

MOUNT SAINT MARY'S UNIVERSITY (CA)
Business Administration and Management—General — M,D,O
Counseling Psychology — M,D,O
Education—General — M,D,O
English — M,D,O
Film, Television, and Video Production — M,D,O
Health Services Management and Hospital Administration — M,D,O
Humanities — M,D,O
Nursing—General — M,D,O
Physical Therapy — M,D,O
Religion — M,D,O
Writing — M,D,O

MOUNT ST. MARY'S UNIVERSITY (MD)
Biotechnology — M
Business Administration and Management—General — M
Education—General — M
Health Services Management and Hospital Administration — M
Philosophy — M
Sports Management — M
Theology — M

MOUNT SAINT VINCENT UNIVERSITY
Adult Education — M
Advertising and Public Relations — M
Child and Family Studies — M
Communication—General — M
Curriculum and Instruction — M
Education—General — M
Educational Measurement and Evaluation — M
Educational Psychology — M
Elementary Education — M
English as a Second Language — M
Foundations and Philosophy of Education — M
Gerontology — M
Middle School Education — M
Nutrition — M
Reading Education — M
School Psychology — M
Special Education — M
Women's Studies — M

MOUNT VERNON NAZARENE UNIVERSITY
Business Administration and Management—General	M
Education—General	M
Theology	M

MULTNOMAH UNIVERSITY
Education—General	M
English as a Second Language	M
Theology	M,D

MURRAY STATE UNIVERSITY
Accounting	M
Advertising and Public Relations	M
Agricultural Education	M,O
Agricultural Sciences—General	M
Biological and Biomedical Sciences—General	M
Business Administration and Management—General	M
Chemistry	M
Clinical Psychology	M,O
Communication Disorders	M,O
Computer Science	M
Corporate and Organizational Communication	M
Counselor Education	M,D,O
Early Childhood Education	M,O
Economic Development	M
Economics	M
Education of Students with Severe/Multiple Disabilities	M,O
Education—General	M,D,O
Educational Leadership and Administration	M,D,O
Educational Media/Instructional Technology	M,D,O
Elementary Education	M,O
English as a Second Language	M,D,O
English Education	M,D,O
English	M,D,O
Environmental and Occupational Health	M
Environmental Sciences	M,O
Experimental Psychology	M,O
Family Nurse Practitioner Studies	D
Finance and Banking	M
Gender Studies	M,D,O
Geosciences	M
History	M
Human Development	M,D,O
Human Resources Management	M
Human Services	M,D,O
Interdisciplinary Studies	M,O
Journalism	M
Management Information Systems	M
Marketing	M
Mass Communication	M
Mathematics Education	M
Mathematics	M
Middle School Education	M,D,O
Music Education	M
Music	M
Nonprofit Management	M,O
Nurse Anesthesia	D
Nursing—General	D
Nutrition	M,O
Political Science	M
Psychology—General	M,O
Safety Engineering	M
School Psychology	M,D,O
Secondary Education	M,D,O
Sociology	M
Special Education	M,O
Statistics	M
Telecommunications Management	M
Vocational and Technical Education	M,O
Writing	M,D,O

MUSKINGUM UNIVERSITY
Education—General	M

NAROPA UNIVERSITY
Art Therapy	M
Counseling Psychology	M
Counselor Education	M
Ecology	M
Psychoanalysis and Psychotherapy	M
Psychology—General	M
Recreation and Park Management	M
Religion	M
Sustainability Management	M
Theater	M
Theology	M
Therapies—Dance, Drama, and Music	M
Transpersonal and Humanistic Psychology	M
Writing	M

NASHOTAH HOUSE THEOLOGICAL SEMINARY
Pastoral Ministry and Counseling	M,D,O
Religion	M,D,O
Theology	M,D,O

NATIONAL AMERICAN UNIVERSITY (TX)
Accounting	M,D
Aviation Management	M,D
Business Administration and Management—General	M,D
Community College Education	M,D
Criminal Justice and Criminology	M,D
Educational Leadership and Administration	M,D
Health Services Management and Hospital Administration	M,D
Higher Education	M,D
Human Resources Management	M,D
International Business	M,D

Management Information Systems	M,D
Marketing	M,D
Nursing and Healthcare Administration	M,D
Nursing Education	M,D
Nursing Informatics	M,D
Project Management	M,D

NATIONAL COLLEGE OF MIDWIFERY
Nurse Midwifery	M,D

NATIONAL DEFENSE UNIVERSITY
Homeland Security	M
Military and Defense Studies	M
National Security	M

NATIONAL INTELLIGENCE UNIVERSITY
Military and Defense Studies	M

NATIONAL LOUIS UNIVERSITY
Adult Education	M,D,O
Business Administration and Management—General	M
Counselor Education	M,D,O
Curriculum and Instruction	M,D,O
Developmental Education	M,D,O
Early Childhood Education	M,D,O
Education—General	M,D,O
Educational Leadership and Administration	M,D,O
Educational Media/Instructional Technology	M,D,O
Educational Psychology	M,D,O
Elementary Education	M,D,O
English Education	M,D,O
Human Development	M,D,O
Human Resources Development	M
Human Resources Management	M
Human Services	M,D,O
Mathematics Education	M,D,O
Middle School Education	M,D,O
Psychology—General	M,D,O
Public Policy	M,D,O
Reading Education	M,D,O
School Psychology	M,D,O
Science Education	M,D,O
Secondary Education	M,D,O
Special Education	M,D,O
Writing	M,D,O

NATIONAL PARALEGAL COLLEGE
Legal and Justice Studies	M
Taxation	M

NATIONAL TEST PILOT SCHOOL
Aviation	M

NATIONAL UNIVERSITY
Accounting	M,O
Applied Behavior Analysis	M,O
Biological and Biomedical Sciences—General	M,O
Business Administration and Management—General	M,O
Business Analytics	M,O
Clinical Psychology	M,O
Computer and Information Systems Security	M
Computer Science	M
Counseling Psychology	M,O
Counselor Education	M,O
Criminal Justice and Criminology	M
Data Science/Data Analytics	M
Distance Education Development	M,O
Education—General	M,O
Educational Leadership and Administration	M,O
Educational Media/Instructional Technology	M,O
Electrical Engineering	M
Emergency Management	M
Engineering and Applied Sciences—General	M
Engineering Management	M
English	M,O
Family Nurse Practitioner Studies	M,O
Film, Television, and Video Production	M
Film, Television, and Video Theory and Criticism	M,O
Forensic Sciences	M,O
Health Informatics	M,O
Health Promotion	M,O
Health Services Management and Hospital Administration	M,O
Higher Education	M,O
Homeland Security	M
Human Resources Management	M,O
Human Services	M,O
International Business	M,O
Internet and Interactive Multimedia	M
Journalism	M
Legal and Justice Studies	M
Management Information Systems	M,O
Management of Technology	M
Marketing	M,O
Marriage and Family Therapy	M,O
Mathematics Education	M,O
Nurse Anesthesia	M,O
Nursing and Healthcare Administration	M,O
Nursing Informatics	M,O
Organizational Management	M,O
Psychiatric Nursing	M,O
Public Administration	M,O
Public Health—General	M,O
School Psychology	M,O
Special Education	M,O
Sustainability Management	M
Writing	M,O

NATIONAL UNIVERSITY COLLEGE
Business Administration and Management—General	M
Marketing	M
Special Education	M

NATIONAL UNIVERSITY OF HEALTH SCIENCES
Acupuncture and Oriental Medicine	M,D
Chiropractic	M,D
Medical Imaging	M,D
Naturopathic Medicine	M,D

NATIONAL UNIVERSITY OF NATURAL MEDICINE
Acupuncture and Oriental Medicine	M,D
Clinical Research	M
International Health	M
Naturopathic Medicine	M,D
Nutrition	M

NAVAJO TECHNICAL UNIVERSITY
American Indian/Native American Studies	M

NAVAL POSTGRADUATE SCHOOL
Acoustics	M,D
Aerospace/Aeronautical Engineering	M,D,O
Applied Mathematics	M,D
Applied Physics	M,D,O
Applied Science and Technology	M,D
Business Administration and Management—General	M
Computer and Information Systems Security	M,D
Computer Engineering	M,D,O
Computer Science	M,D,O
Conflict Resolution and Mediation/Peace Studies	M,D
Electrical Engineering	M,D,O
Engineering Management	M,D,O
Finance and Banking	M
Geographic Information Systems	M,D,O
Homeland Security	M,D
Information Science	M,D,O
Logistics	M
Management Information Systems	M,D,O
Mechanical Engineering	M,D,O
Meteorology	M,D
Military and Defense Studies	M,D
Modeling and Simulation	M,D
National Security	M,D
Oceanography	M,D
Operations Research	M,D
Pacific Area/Pacific Rim Studies	M,D
Physics	M,D
Software Engineering	M,D
Supply Chain Management	M
Systems Engineering	M,D,O
Transportation Management	M

NAVAL WAR COLLEGE
National Security	M

NAZARENE THEOLOGICAL SEMINARY
Cultural Studies	M,D,O
Theology	M,D,O

NAZARETH COLLEGE OF ROCHESTER
Art Education	M
Art Therapy	M
Business Administration and Management—General	M
Communication Disorders	M
Early Childhood Education	M
Education—General	M
Educational Media/Instructional Technology	M
Elementary Education	M
English as a Second Language	M
Human Resources Management	M
Middle School Education	M
Music Education	M
Music	M
Physical Therapy	D
Reading Education	M
Social Work	M
Therapies—Dance, Drama, and Music	M

NEBRASKA CHRISTIAN COLLEGE OF HOPE INTERNATIONAL UNIVERSITY
Business Administration and Management—General	M
Counseling Psychology	M
Education of the Gifted	M
Educational Leadership and Administration	M
Elementary Education	M
Entrepreneurship	M
International Business	M
Marketing	M
Missions and Missiology	M
Music Education	M
Nonprofit Management	M
Pastoral Ministry and Counseling	M
Secondary Education	M
Theology	M

NEBRASKA METHODIST COLLEGE
Health Promotion	M
Health Services Management and Hospital Administration	M
Nursing and Healthcare Administration	M
Nursing Education	M
Nursing—General	M
Occupational Therapy	M

NEBRASKA WESLEYAN UNIVERSITY
Nursing—General	M

NER ISRAEL RABBINICAL COLLEGE
Theology	M,D,O

NER ISRAEL YESHIVA COLLEGE OF TORONTO
Theology	

NEUMANN UNIVERSITY
Accounting	M
Adult Nursing	M,O
Business Administration and Management—General	M
Clinical Psychology	M,D,O
Education—General	M
Educational Leadership and Administration	M,D
Elementary Education	M
Gerontological Nursing	M,O
Management Strategy and Policy	M
Nursing—General	M,O
Organizational Management	M
Pastoral Ministry and Counseling	M,D,O
Physical Therapy	D
Secondary Education	M
Special Education	M
Sports Management	M

NEW BRUNSWICK THEOLOGICAL SEMINARY
Pastoral Ministry and Counseling	M,D
Theology	M,D

NEW CHARTER UNIVERSITY
Business Administration and Management—General	M
Finance and Banking	M
Health Services Management and Hospital Administration	M

NEW COLLEGE OF FLORIDA
Data Science/Data Analytics	M

NEW ENGLAND COLLEGE
Accounting	M
Business Administration and Management—General	M
Counseling Psychology	M
Education—General	M,D
Educational Leadership and Administration	M,D
Health Services Management and Hospital Administration	M
Higher Education	M,D
Human Services	M
International Affairs	M
Management Strategy and Policy	M
Marketing	M
Nonprofit Management	M
Project Management	M
Public Policy	M
Recreation and Park Management	M
Special Education	M,D
Sports Management	M
Writing	M

NEW ENGLAND COLLEGE OF BUSINESS AND FINANCE
Ethics	M
Finance and Banking	M
Quality Management	M

NEW ENGLAND COLLEGE OF OPTOMETRY
Optometry	M,D
Vision Sciences	M,D

NEW ENGLAND CONSERVATORY OF MUSIC
Music	M,D,O

NEW ENGLAND INSTITUTE OF TECHNOLOGY
Construction Management	M
Engineering Management	M
Management Information Systems	M
Occupational Therapy	M,D
Public Health—General	M

NEW ENGLAND LAW–BOSTON
Law	M,D

NEW HAMPSHIRE INSTITUTE OF ART
Art Education	M
Art/Fine Arts	M
Photography	M
Writing	M

NEW JERSEY CITY UNIVERSITY
Accounting	M,O
Allied Health—General	M
Art Education	M
Art/Fine Arts	M
Business Administration and Management—General	M,O
Community Health	M
Computer and Information Systems Security	M,D,O
Counselor Education	M
Criminal Justice and Criminology	M,D,O
Early Childhood Education	M
Education—General	M,D
Educational Leadership and Administration	M
Educational Media/Instructional Technology	M,D
Elementary Education	M
English as a Second Language	M
Finance and Banking	M,O
Health Education	M
Health Services Management and Hospital Administration	M
Marketing	M
Mathematics Education	M
Multilingual and Multicultural Education	M

M—masters degree; D—doctorate; O—other advanced degree; *—Close-Up and/or Display

Music Education	M
Music	M,D,O
National Security	M
Organizational Management	M
Secondary Education	M
Special Education	M
Urban Education	M
Urban Studies	M

NEW JERSEY INSTITUTE OF TECHNOLOGY

Applied Mathematics	M,D,O
Applied Physics	M,D,O
Applied Statistics	M,D,O
Architecture	M,D
Biological and Biomedical Sciences—General	M,D
Biomedical Engineering	M,D
Biostatistics	M,D,O
Business Administration and Management—General	M,D
Chemical Engineering	M,D
Chemistry	M,D,O
Computer and Information Systems Security	M,D,O
Computer Engineering	M,D,O
Computer Science	M,D,O
Data Science/Data Analytics	M,D,O
Electrical Engineering	M,D
Energy and Power Engineering	M,D
Engineering and Applied Sciences—General	M,D
Engineering Management	M
Environmental Engineering	M,D
Environmental Management and Policy	M,D,O
Environmental Sciences	M,D,O
Health Services Management and Hospital Administration	M,D
History	M,D,O
Industrial/Management Engineering	M,D
Information Science	M,D,O
Internet Engineering	M
Management Information Systems	M,D,O
Management of Technology	M,D,O
Manufacturing Engineering	M,D
Materials Engineering	M,D
Materials Sciences	M,D,O
Mathematical and Computational Finance	M,D,O
Mathematics	M,D,O
Mechanical Engineering	M,D
Medicinal and Pharmaceutical Chemistry	M,D,O
Pharmaceutical Administration	M,D
Pharmaceutical Engineering	M,D
Pharmacology	M,D
Safety Engineering	M,D
Software Engineering	M,D,O
Statistics	M,D,O
Sustainable Development	M,D,O
Technical Communication	M,D
Telecommunications	M,D
Transportation and Highway Engineering	M,D
Transportation Management	M

NEWMAN THEOLOGICAL COLLEGE

Religious Education	M,O
Theology	M

NEWMAN UNIVERSITY

Business Administration and Management—General	M
Curriculum and Instruction	M
Education—General	M
Educational Leadership and Administration	M
English as a Second Language	M
Finance and Banking	M
International Business	M
Management Information Systems	M
Nurse Anesthesia	M
Organizational Management	M
Reading Education	M
Social Work	M
Theology	M

NEW MEXICO HIGHLANDS UNIVERSITY

American Studies	M
Anthropology	M
Business Administration and Management—General	M
Chemistry	M
Clinical Psychology	M
Computer Art and Design	M
Computer Science	M
Counseling Psychology	M
Counselor Education	M
Curriculum and Instruction	M
Education—General	M
Educational Leadership and Administration	M
English	M
Exercise and Sports Science	M
Health Education	M
History	M
Human Resources Management	M
International Business	M
Internet and Interactive Multimedia	M
Media Studies	M
Natural Resources	M
Political Science	M
Psychology—General	M
Public Affairs	M
Rhetoric	M
Social Work	M
Sociology	M
Special Education	M
Sports Management	M
Writing	M

NEW MEXICO INSTITUTE OF MINING AND TECHNOLOGY

Applied Mathematics	M,D
Astrophysics	M,D
Atmospheric Sciences	M,D
Biological and Biomedical Sciences—General	M,D
Chemistry	M,D
Computer Science	M,D
Electrical Engineering	M
Engineering Management	M
Environmental Engineering	M
Geochemistry	M,D
Geological Engineering	M
Geology	M,D
Geophysics	M,D
Geosciences	M,D
Hazardous Materials Management	M
Hydrology	M,D
Materials Engineering	M,D
Mathematical Physics	M,D
Mathematics	M,D
Mechanical Engineering	M
Mechanics	M
Mineral/Mining Engineering	M
Operations Research	M
Petroleum Engineering	M,D
Physics	M,D
Science Education	M
Statistics	M,D
Systems Engineering	M
Water Resources Engineering	M

NEW MEXICO STATE UNIVERSITY

Agricultural Economics and Agribusiness	M,D
Agricultural Sciences—General	M,D
Applied Statistics	M,D,O
Art History	M
Astrophysics	M,D
Bioinformatics	M,D
Biotechnology	M,D
Business Administration and Management—General	D
Clothing and Textiles	M
Corporate and Organizational Communication	M,D
Cultural Studies	M,D,O
Early Childhood Education	M,D,O
Economic Development	M,D,O
Education—General	M,D,O
Educational Measurement and Evaluation	M,D,O
Engineering and Applied Sciences—General	M,D,O
English as a Second Language	M,D,O
English Education	M
Environmental Engineering	M,D
Family Nurse Practitioner Studies	M,D,O
Finance and Banking	M
Food Science and Technology	M
Higher Education	M,D
Hydrology	M,D
Interdisciplinary Studies	M,D
Management Information Systems	M
Molecular Biology	M,D
Multilingual and Multicultural Education	M,D,O
Museum Studies	M,O
Music Education	M
Music	M
Nursing and Healthcare Administration	M,D,O
Psychiatric Nursing	M,D,O
Public Administration	M
Reading Education	M,D,O
Rhetoric	M
School Psychology	M,D,O
Systems Engineering	M,D,O
Travel and Tourism	M
Water Resources	M,D
Writing	M

NEW ORLEANS BAPTIST THEOLOGICAL SEMINARY

Music	M,D
Pastoral Ministry and Counseling	M,D
Religious Education	M,D
Theology	M,D

NEW SAINT ANDREWS COLLEGE

Religion	M,O
Theology	M,O
Writing	M,O

THE NEW SCHOOL

Anthropology	M,D
Applied Arts and Design—General	M
Applied Social Research	M,D
Architecture	M
Art/Fine Arts	M
Clinical Psychology	M,D
Clothing and Textiles	M
Cognitive Sciences	M,D
Computer Art and Design	M
Data Science/Data Analytics	M
Economics	M,D
English as a Second Language	M
Environmental Management and Policy	M
Finance and Banking	M,D
History	M,D
Industrial Design	M
Interior Design	M
International Affairs	M
International Economics	M,D
Internet and Interactive Multimedia	M
Liberal Studies	M
Lighting Design	M
Management Strategy and Policy	M,O
Media Studies	M,O
Museum Studies	M,O
Music	M,O
Nonprofit Management	M,O
Organizational Management	M,O
Philosophy	M,D
Photography	M
Political Science	M,D
Psychoanalysis and Psychotherapy	M,D
Psychology—General	M,D
Public Policy	M,D
Social Psychology	M,D
Social Sciences	M,D
Sociology	M,D
Sustainability Management	M
Textile Design	M
Theater	M
Urban Design	M
Writing	M

NEWSCHOOL OF ARCHITECTURE AND DESIGN

Architecture	M
Construction Management	M

NEW YORK ACADEMY OF ART

Anatomy	M
Art/Fine Arts	M

NEW YORK CHIROPRACTIC COLLEGE

Acupuncture and Oriental Medicine	M
Anatomy	M
Chiropractic	D
Nutrition	M

NEW YORK COLLEGE OF HEALTH PROFESSIONS

Acupuncture and Oriental Medicine	M

NEW YORK COLLEGE OF PODIATRIC MEDICINE

Podiatric Medicine	D

NEW YORK COLLEGE OF TRADITIONAL CHINESE MEDICINE

Acupuncture and Oriental Medicine	M

NEW YORK FILM ACADEMY

Film, Television, and Video Production	M
Photography	M

NEW YORK INSTITUTE OF TECHNOLOGY

Applied Arts and Design—General	M
Architecture	M
Art/Fine Arts	M
Bioengineering	M
Business Administration and Management—General	M
Communication—General	M
Computer and Information Systems Security	M
Computer Art and Design	M
Computer Engineering	M
Computer Science	M
Counselor Education	M,O
Early Childhood Education	M
Educational Leadership and Administration	O
Educational Media/Instructional Technology	M,O
Electrical Engineering	M
Elementary Education	M
Energy and Power Engineering	O
Energy Management and Policy	O
Engineering and Applied Sciences—General	M,O
English Education	M
Environmental Engineering	M
Environmental Management and Policy	O
Finance and Banking	M
Graphic Design	M
Human Resources Management	M,O
Industrial and Labor Relations	M,O
International Health	O
Marketing	M
Mathematics Education	M,O
Mechanical Engineering	M
Middle School Education	M
Nutrition	M
Occupational Therapy	M
Osteopathic Medicine	O
Physical Therapy	D
Physician Assistant Studies	M
Science Education	M,O
Secondary Education	M
Social Sciences Education	M
Supply Chain Management	M
Urban Design	M

NEW YORK LAW SCHOOL

Law	M,D

NEW YORK MEDICAL COLLEGE

Allopathic Medicine	D
Biochemistry	M,D
Biological and Biomedical Sciences—General	M,D
Biostatistics	M,D,O
Business Administration and Management—General	M,D,O
Cell Biology	M,D
Communication Disorders	M,D,O
Emergency Management	M,D,O
Environmental and Occupational Health	M,D,O
Epidemiology	M,D,O
Health Education	M,D,O
Health Services Management and Hospital Administration	M,D,O
Immunology	M,D
Industrial Hygiene	M,D,O
International Health	M,D,O
Microbiology	M,D
Molecular Biology	M,D
Pathology	M,D
Pharmacology	M,D,O
Physical Therapy	M,D
Physiology	M,D
Psychology—General	M,D,O
Public Health—General	M,D,O

NEW YORK SCHOOL OF INTERIOR DESIGN

Interior Design	M
Lighting Design	M
Sustainable Development	M

NEW YORK STUDIO SCHOOL OF DRAWING, PAINTING AND SCULPTURE

Art/Fine Arts	M,O*

NEW YORK THEOLOGICAL SEMINARY

Theology	M,D

NEW YORK UNIVERSITY

Accounting	M,D
Acute Care/Critical Care Nursing	M,D,O
Adult Nursing	M,D,O
Advertising and Public Relations	M
African Studies	M
Allopathic Medicine	M,D
American Studies	M,D
Anthropology	M,D
Applied Arts and Design—General	M
Applied Economics	M,D,O
Applied Psychology	M,D,O
Applied Social Research	M
Applied Statistics	M
Archaeology	M,D
Architectural History	M
Archives/Archival Administration	M,D,O
Art Education	M,O
Art History	M,D
Art Therapy	M
Art/Fine Arts	M,D,O
Artificial Intelligence/Robotics	M
Arts Administration	M
Asian Studies	M,D
Bioinformatics	M,D,O
Biological and Biomedical Sciences—General	M,D
Business Administration and Management—General	M,D,O
Business Education	M,O
Cancer Biology/Oncology	M,D
Chemistry	M,D
Chinese	M,D,O
Civil Engineering	M,D
Classics	M,D,O
Clinical Research	M
Cognitive Sciences	M,D,O
Communication Disorders	M,D
Communication—General	M,D
Community Health	M,D
Comparative Literature	M,D
Computational Biology	D
Computer and Information Systems Security	M
Computer Engineering	M,D
Computer Science	M,D,O
Conflict Resolution and Mediation/Peace Studies	M
Construction Management	M
Corporate and Organizational Communication	M
Counseling Psychology	M,D,O
Counselor Education	M,D,O
Cultural Studies	M,D,O
Dance	M,D,O
Data Science/Data Analytics	M
Demography and Population Studies	M,D
Dentistry	D
Developmental Biology	M,D
Developmental Psychology	M,D
Early Childhood Education	M
Economics	M,D,O
Education—General	M,D,O
Educational Leadership and Administration	M,D,O
Educational Media/Instructional Technology	M,D,O
Educational Policy	M,D
Educational Psychology	M,D
Electrical Engineering	M,D
Elementary Education	M
Engineering and Applied Sciences—General	M,D,O
English as a Second Language	M,D,O
English Education	M,D,O
English	M,D
Environmental and Occupational Health	M,D*
Environmental Education	M
Environmental Management and Policy	M
Family Nurse Practitioner Studies	M,D,O
Film, Television, and Video Production	M
Film, Television, and Video Theory and Criticism	M,D
Finance and Banking	M,D
Food Science and Technology	M,D
Foreign Languages Education	M,D,O
Foundations and Philosophy of Education	M,D,O
French	M,D,O
Game Design and Development	M
Gender Studies	M
Genetics	M,D
German	M,D
Gerontological Nursing	M,D,O
Health Promotion	M,D,O

Health Services Management and	
Hospital Administration	M,D,O
Higher Education	M,D
Historic Preservation	M
History	M,D,O
Hospitality Management	M,D
Human Development	M,D,O
Human Resources Development	M
Human Resources Management	M,O
Humanities	M
Immunology	M,D
Industrial and Organizational	
Psychology	M,D,O
Interdisciplinary Studies	M
International Affairs	M,D
International and Comparative	
Education	M,D,O
International Business	M,D
International Health	M,D
Internet and Interactive	
Multimedia	M
Investment Management	M
Italian	M,D,O
Japanese	M,D,O
Jewish Studies	M,D
Journalism	M,D,O
Kinesiology and Movement Studies	M,D,O
Latin American Studies	M
Law	M,D,O
Legal and Justice Studies	M,D
Linguistics	M,D
Management Information Systems	M,D
Management Strategy and Policy	M,D
Manufacturing Engineering	M,D
Marketing	M,D
Mathematical and	
Computational Finance	M,D
Mathematics Education	M
Mathematics	M,D*
Mechanical Engineering	M,D
Media Studies	M,D
Microbiology	M,D
Molecular Biology	M,D
Molecular Genetics	M,D
Multilingual and Multicultural	
Education	M,D,O
Museum Studies	M,O
Music Education	M,D,O
Music	M,D
Near and Middle Eastern Studies	M,D
Neurobiology	M,D
Neuroscience	D
Nonprofit Management	M,D
Nurse Midwifery	M,D,O
Nursing and Healthcare	
Administration	M,O
Nursing Education	M,O
Nursing Informatics	M
Nursing—General	M,D,O
Nutrition	M,D
Occupational Therapy	M,D
Oral and Dental Sciences	M,D,O
Organizational Behavior	M,D
Organizational Management	M,D
Pediatric Nursing	M,D,O
Philosophy	M,D
Physical Therapy	M,D,O
Physics	M,D
Plant Biology	M,D
Political Science	M,D
Portuguese	M,D
Project Management	M
Psychiatric Nursing	M,D,O
Psychoanalysis and Psychotherapy	M,D,O
Psychology—General	M,D,O
Public Administration	M,D,O
Public Health—General	M
Public History	M,D,O
Public Policy	M
Publishing	M
Reading Education	M
Real Estate	M
Rehabilitation Sciences	M,D
Religion	M,O
Risk Management	M
Romance Languages	M,D
Russian	M
Science Education	M,D,O
Secondary Education	M,D,O
Slavic Languages	M
Social Psychology	M,D,O
Social Sciences Education	M,D,O
Social Sciences	M,D
Social Work	M,D
Sociology	M,D
Software Engineering	O
Spanish	M,D,O
Special Education	M
Speech and Interpersonal	
Communication	M,D
Sports and Entertainment Law	M
Statistics	M,D
Student Affairs	M,D
Sustainable Development	M
Taxation	M,D,O
Theater	M,D,O
Therapies—Dance, Drama, and	
Music	M
Translation and Interpretation	M
Transportation and Highway	
Engineering	M,D
Travel and Tourism	M
Urban and Regional Planning	M,D
Urban Studies	M,D
Western European Studies	M
Writing	M

NIAGARA UNIVERSITY

Accounting	M
Applied Behavior Analysis	M,D,O

Business Administration and	
Management—General	M
Computer and Information	
Systems Security	M
Counseling Psychology	M,D,O
Counselor Education	M,O
Criminal Justice and Criminology	M
Early Childhood Education	M,O
Education—General	M,D,O
Educational Leadership and	
Administration	M,D,O
Educational Policy	M,D,O
Elementary Education	M,O
English as a Second Language	M,O
Finance and Banking	M
Forensic Sciences	M
Health Services Management and	
Hospital Administration	M
Human Resources Management	M
Interdisciplinary Studies	M
International Business	M
Management Strategy and Policy	M
Marketing	M
Middle School Education	M,O
Reading Education	M
School Psychology	M
Secondary Education	M,O
Special Education	M,O
Supply Chain Management	M

NICHOLLS STATE UNIVERSITY

Business Administration and	
Management—General	M
Clinical Psychology	M,O
Counselor Education	M,O
Curriculum and Instruction	M
Education—General	M
Educational Leadership and	
Administration	M
Elementary Education	M
Environmental Biology	M
Family Nurse Practitioner Studies	M
Health Education	M
Marine Biology	M
Middle School Education	M
Nursing and Healthcare	
Administration	M
Nursing Education	M
Nursing—General	M
Psychiatric Nursing	M
School Psychology	M,O
Secondary Education	M

NICHOLS COLLEGE

Business Administration and	
Management—General	M
Homeland Security	M
Organizational Management	M

NIPISSING UNIVERSITY

Education—General	M,O

NORFOLK STATE UNIVERSITY

Art/Fine Arts	M
Clinical Psychology	M
Communication—General	M
Computer Engineering	M
Computer Science	M
Criminal Justice and Criminology	M
Early Childhood Education	M
Education of Students with	
Severe/Multiple Disabilities	M
Education—General	M
Educational Leadership and	
Administration	M
Electrical Engineering	M
Materials Sciences	M
Media Studies	M
Music Education	M
Music	M
Optical Sciences	M
Psychology—General	M,D
Secondary Education	M
Social Psychology	M
Social Work	M,D
Special Education	M
Urban Education	M
Urban Studies	M

NORTH AMERICAN UNIVERSITY

Educational Leadership and	
Administration	M

NORTH CAROLINA AGRICULTURAL AND TECHNICAL STATE UNIVERSITY

Accounting	M
Adult Education	M,D
African-American Studies	M
Agricultural Economics and	
Agribusiness	M
Agricultural Education	M
Agricultural Sciences—	
General	M
Agronomy and Soil Sciences	M
Animal Sciences	M
Applied Mathematics	M
Bioengineering	M
Biological and Biomedical	
Sciences—General	M
Business Administration and	
Management—General	M
Business Education	M
Chemical Engineering	M
Chemistry	M
Child and Family Studies	M
Child Development	M
Civil Engineering	M
Clinical Psychology	M,D
Computational Sciences	M
Computer Engineering	M,D
Computer Science	M,D
Counselor Education	M,D
Early Childhood Education	M

Education—General	M,D
Educational Leadership and	
Administration	M,D
Educational Media/Instructional	
Technology	M
Electrical Engineering	M,D
Elementary Education	M
Energy and Power	
Engineering	M,D
Engineering and Applied	
Sciences—General	M,D
English Education	M
English	M
Environmental Design	M
Environmental Sciences	M
Family and Consumer	
Sciences-General	M
Food Science and	
Technology	M
Hospitality Management	M
Human Resources Management	M
Industrial/Management	
Engineering	M,D
Mathematics Education	M
Mathematics	M
Mechanical Engineering	M,D
Natural Resources	M
Nutrition	M
Optical Sciences	M
Physics	M
Plant Sciences	M
Reading Education	M
Rehabilitation Counseling	M,D
Science Education	M
Secondary Education	M
Social Work	M
Supply Chain Management	M
Systems Engineering	M,D

NORTH CAROLINA CENTRAL UNIVERSITY

Biological and Biomedical	
Sciences—General	M
Business Administration and	
Management—General	M
Chemistry	M
Clinical Psychology	M
Communication Disorders	M
Counselor Education	M
Criminal Justice and Criminology	M
Education—General	M
Educational Leadership and	
Administration	M
Educational Media/Instructional	
Technology	M
English	M
Environmental Sciences	M
Geographic Information Systems	M
Geosciences	M
History	M
Information Studies	M
Law	D
Library Science	M
Mathematics	M
Music	M
Physical Education	M
Physics	M
Psychology—General	M
Public Administration	M
Recreation and Park Management	M
Social Work	M
Special Education	M

NORTH CAROLINA STATE UNIVERSITY

Accounting	M
Adult Education	M,D
Aerospace/Aeronautical	
Engineering	M,D
Agricultural Economics and	
Agribusiness	M,D
Agricultural Engineering	M,D,O
Agricultural Sciences—	
General	M,D,O
Agronomy and Soil Sciences	M,D
Animal Sciences	M,D
Anthropology	M
Applied Arts and Design—	
General	M
Applied Psychology	D
Architecture	M
Atmospheric Sciences	M,D
Biochemistry	D
Bioengineering	M,D,O
Biological and Biomedical	
Sciences—General	M,D,O
Business Administration and	
Management—General	M
Business Education	M
Cell Biology	M,D
Chemical Engineering	M,D
Chemistry	M,D
Civil Engineering	M,D
Clothing and Textiles	M
Cognitive Sciences	D
Communication—General	M
Community College Education	M,D
Computer Art and Design	M,D
Computer Engineering	M,D
Computer Science	M,D
Counselor Education	M,D
Curriculum and Instruction	M,D
Developmental Psychology	D
Economics	M,D
Education—General	M,D,O
Educational Leadership and	
Administration	M,D
Educational Measurement and	
Evaluation	D
Educational Media/Instructional	
Technology	M,D
Electrical Engineering	M,D

Elementary Education	M
Engineering and Applied	
Sciences—General	M,D
English	M
Entomology	M,D
Entrepreneurship	M
Epidemiology	M,D
Ergonomics and Human	
Factors	D
Financial Engineering	M
Food Science and	
Technology	M,D
Forestry	M,D
French	M
Genomic Sciences	M,D
Geographic Information Systems	M,D
Geosciences	M,D
Graphic Design	M
History	M
Horticulture	M,D,O
Human Resources Development	M
Industrial and Organizational	
Psychology	D
Industrial Design	M
Industrial/Management	
Engineering	M,D
Infectious Diseases	M,D
International Affairs	M
Landscape Architecture	M
Management of Technology	M,D
Manufacturing Engineering	M
Marine Sciences	M,D
Materials Engineering	M,D
Materials Sciences	M,D
Mathematical and	
Computational Finance	M
Mathematics Education	M,D
Mathematics	M,D
Mechanical Engineering	M,D
Meteorology	M,D
Microbiology	M,D
Middle School Education	M
Natural Resources	M,D
Nonprofit Management	M,D,O
Nuclear Engineering	M,D
Nutrition	M,D
Oceanography	M,D
Operations Research	M,D
Pathology	M,D
Pharmacology	M,D
Physics	M,D
Plant Biology	M,D
Polymer Science and	
Engineering	M,D
Psychology—General	D
Public Administration	M,D
Public History	M
Recreation and Park Management	M,D
Rhetoric	M,D
School Psychology	D
Science Education	M,D
Social Psychology	.M,D
Social Work	M
Sociology	D
Spanish	M
Special Education	M
Sports Management	M,D
Statistics	M,D
Supply Chain Management	M
Textile Sciences and	
Engineering	M,D
Travel and Tourism	M,D
Veterinary Sciences	M,D
Vocational and Technical Education	M,D,O
Writing	M

NORTH CENTRAL COLLEGE

Business Administration and	
Management—General	M
Computer Science	M
Cultural Studies	M
Education—General	M
Educational Leadership and	
Administration	M
Finance and Banking	M
Human Resources Management	M
Liberal Studies	M
Management Strategy and Policy	M

NORTHCENTRAL UNIVERSITY

Business Administration and	
Management—General	M,D,O
Computer and Information	
Systems Security	M,D,O
Computer Science	M,D,O
Data Science/Data Analytics	M,D,O
Education—General	M,D,O
Marriage and Family Therapy	M,D,O
Psychology—General	M,D,O

NORTH DAKOTA STATE UNIVERSITY

Accounting	M
Agricultural Economics and	
Agribusiness	M
Agricultural Education	M
Agricultural Engineering	M,D
Agricultural Sciences—	
General	M,D
Agronomy and Soil Sciences	M,D
Animal Sciences	M,D
Anthropology	M
Applied Mathematics	M,D
Architecture	M
Athletic Training and Sports	
Medicine	M,D
Biochemistry	M,D
Bioinformatics	M,D
Biological and Biomedical	
Sciences—General	M,D
Biosystems Engineering	M,D
Botany	M,D

Business Administration and
  Management—General   M
Cell Biology   D
Chemistry   M,D
Child and Family Studies   M,D,O
Child Development   M
Civil Engineering   M,D
Clinical Psychology   M,D
Cognitive Sciences   M,D
Communication—General   M,D
Community Health   M
Computer Engineering   M,D
Computer Science   M,D,O
Conservation Biology   M,D
Construction Management   M,O
Consumer Economics   M,O
Counseling Psychology   M,O
Counselor Education   M,O
Criminal Justice and Criminology   M,D
Developmental Psychology   D
Education—General   M,D,O
Educational Leadership and
  Administration   M,O
Electrical Engineering   M,D
Engineering and Applied
  Sciences—General   M,D,O
English   M,D
Entomology   M,D
Environmental Engineering   M,D
Environmental Sciences   M,D
Exercise and Sports Science   M,D
Family and Consumer
  Sciences-General   M
Food Science and
  Technology   M,D
Genomic Sciences   M,D
Gerontology   D,O
Health Psychology   M,D
Higher Education   O
History   M,D
Horticulture   M,D
Industrial/Management
  Engineering   M,D
Infectious Diseases   M
Landscape Architecture   M
Logistics   M,D
Manufacturing Engineering   M,D
Mass Communication   M,D
Materials Sciences   M,D
Mathematics Education   D
Mathematics   M,D
Mechanical Engineering   M,D
Microbiology   M
Molecular Biology   D
Molecular Pathogenesis   M,D
Music Education   M,D
Music   M,D
Nanotechnology   M,D
Natural Resources   M,D
Nursing—General   D
Nutrition   M,D
Pathology   M,D
Pharmacy   M,D
Physics   M,D
Plant Pathology   M,D
Plant Sciences   M,D
Polymer Science and
  Engineering   M,D
Psychology—General   M,D
Public Health—General   M
Rhetoric   M,D
School Psychology   M,D
Science Education   D
Social Psychology   M,D
Sociology   M
Software Engineering   M,D,O
Speech and Interpersonal
  Communication   M,D
Statistics   M,D
Transportation and Highway
  Engineering   D
Transportation Management   M,D
Urban and Regional Planning   M
Urban Studies   M,D
Writing   M,D
Zoology   M,D

NORTHEASTERN ILLINOIS UNIVERSITY

Accounting   M
Applied Mathematics   M
Biological and Biomedical
  Sciences—General   M
Business Administration and
  Management—General   M
Cell Biology   M
Chemistry   M
Clinical Psychology   M
Computer Science   M
Counselor Education   M
Early Childhood Education   M
Ecology   M
Education of the Gifted   M
Education—General   M
Educational Leadership and
  Administration   M
Elementary Education   M
English as a Second Language   M
English Education   M
English   M
Environmental Management
  and Policy   M,O
Exercise and Sports Science   M
Geographic Information Systems   M,O
Geography   M,O
Gerontology   M
History   M
Human Resources Development   M
Latin American Studies   M
Linguistics   M
Marriage and Family Therapy   M
Mathematics Education   M
Mathematics   M
Middle School Education   M
Molecular Biology   M

Music Education   M
Music   M
Political Science   M
Reading Education   M
Rehabilitation Counseling   M
Science Education   M
Secondary Education   M
Social Sciences Education   M
Social Work   M
Special Education   M
Speech and Interpersonal
  Communication   M
Urban Education   M

NORTHEASTERN SEMINARY AT ROBERTS WESLEYAN COLLEGE

Theology   M,D

NORTHEASTERN STATE UNIVERSITY

Accounting   M
American Indian/Native American
  Studies   M
Business Administration and
  Management—General   M
Communication Disorders   M
Communication—General   M
Criminal Justice and Criminology   M
Early Childhood Education   M
Education—General   M
Educational Leadership and
  Administration   M
Educational Media/Instructional
  Technology   M
English   M
Finance and Banking   M
Health Education   M
Kinesiology and Movement Studies   M
Mathematics Education   M
Natural Resources   M
Nursing and Healthcare
  Administration   M
Nursing Education   M
Occupational Therapy   M
Optometry   D
Psychology—General   M
Reading Education   M
Science Education   M
Special Education   M

NORTHEASTERN UNIVERSITY

Accounting   M
Acute Care/Critical Care Nursing   M,D,O
Allied Health—General   M,D,O
Applied Arts and Design—
  General   M
Applied Behavior Analysis   M,D,O
Applied Mathematics   M,D
Architecture   M
Arts Administration   M
Bioengineering   M,D,O
Bioinformatics   M,D
Biological and Biomedical
  Sciences—General   M,D
Biotechnology   M,D
Business Administration and
  Management—General   M
Chemical Engineering   M,D,O
Chemistry   M,D
Civil Engineering   M,D,O
Communication Disorders   M,D,O
Computer and Information
  Systems Security   M,D,O
Computer Engineering   M,D,O
Computer Science   M,D
Corporate and Organizational
  Communication   M
Counseling Psychology   M,D,O
Criminal Justice and Criminology   M,D
Data Science/Data Analytics   M,D
Economic Development   M
Economics   M,D
Educational Leadership and
  Administration   M
Electrical Engineering   M,D,O
Elementary Education   M
Energy and Power
  Engineering   M,D,O
Engineering and Applied
  Sciences—General   M,D,O
Engineering Management   M,D,O
English   M,D
Entrepreneurship   M
Environmental Engineering   M,D,O
Environmental Management
  and Policy   M,D
Environmental Sciences   M,D
Exercise and Sports Science   M,D,O
Family Nurse Practitioner Studies   M,D,O
Finance and Banking   M
Geographic Information Systems   M
Gerontological Nursing   M,D,O
Health Informatics   M,D
Higher Education   M
History   M,D
Homeland Security   M,D
Human Services   M
Industrial/Management
  Engineering   M,D,O
Interdisciplinary Studies   M,D,O
International Affairs   M,D
International Business   M
Internet and Interactive
  Multimedia   M
Journalism   M
Law   M,D
Legal and Justice Studies   M,D
Management Information Systems   M,D,O
Marine Biology   M,D
Maternal and Child/Neonatal
  Nursing   M,D,O
Mathematics   M,D
Mechanical Engineering   M,D,O
Media Studies   M
Nonprofit Management   M
Nurse Anesthesia   M,D,O

Nursing and Healthcare
  Administration   M,D,O
Nursing—General   M,D,O
Nutrition   M
Operations Research   M,D,O
Pediatric Nursing   M,D,O
Pharmaceutical Sciences   M,D
Pharmacology   M,D
Pharmacy   M,D,O
Physics   M,D
Political Science   M,D
Project Management   M
Psychiatric Nursing   M,D,O
Psychology—General   M,D
Public Administration   M,D
Public Health—General   M,D
Public Policy   M,D,O
School Psychology   M,D,O
Sociology   M,D
Special Education   M
Sports Management   M
Systems Engineering   M,D,O
Taxation   M
Technical Communication   M
Telecommunications   M,D,O
Urban Studies   M,D

NORTHEAST OHIO MEDICAL UNIVERSITY

Allopathic Medicine   D
Bioethics   M,D,O
Health Services Management and
  Hospital Administration   M,D,O
Humanities   M,D,O
Pharmaceutical Administration   M,D,O
Pharmaceutical Sciences   M,D,O
Pharmacy   D
Public Health—General   M,D,O

NORTHERN ARIZONA UNIVERSITY

Allied Health—General   M,D,O
American Indian/Native American
  Studies   O
Anthropology   M
Applied Physics   M,D
Applied Statistics   M,O
Athletic Training and Sports
  Medicine   M
Atmospheric Sciences   M,D,O
Bioengineering   M,D
Biological and Biomedical
  Sciences—General   M,D
Business Administration and
  Management—General   M
Chemistry   M
Civil Engineering   M
Communication Disorders   M
Communication—General   M,O
Community College Education   M,D,O
Computer Engineering   M,D
Computer Science   M,D
Counseling Psychology   M,D,O
Counselor Education   M,D,O
Criminal Justice and Criminology   M
Curriculum and Instruction   M,D
Early Childhood Education   M,D,O
Education—General   M,D,O
Educational Leadership and
  Administration   M,D,O
Educational Media/Instructional
  Technology   M,O
Educational Psychology   M,D,O
Electrical Engineering   M,D
Elementary Education   M,D
Engineering and Applied
  Sciences—General   M,D,O
English as a Second Language   M,D,O
English   M,D,O
Environmental Management
  and Policy   M,D,O
Environmental Sciences   M,D
Ethnic Studies   O
Family Nurse Practitioner Studies   M,D,O
Foreign Languages Education   M
Forestry   M,D
Foundations and Philosophy of
  Education   M,D,O
Gender Studies   O
Geographic Information Systems   M,O
Geography   M,O
Geology   M,D,O
Health Services Management and
  Hospital Administration   D
Higher Education   M,D,O
History   M
Human Development   O
International Business   M
Liberal Studies   M
Linguistics   M,D,O
Mathematics Education   M,O
Mathematics   M,O
Mechanical Engineering   M,D
Meteorology   M,D,O
Multilingual and Multicultural
  Education   M,O
Music   M,O
Nursing—General   M,D,O
Occupational Therapy   D
Physical Therapy   D
Physician Assistant Studies   M
Physics   M,D
Political Science   M,D,O
Psychology—General   M
Public Administration   M,D,O
Recreation and Park Management   M,O
Rhetoric   M,D,O
School Psychology   M,D,O
Science Education   M
Secondary Education   M,D,O
Sociology   M
Spanish   M
Special Education   M,O
Statistics   M,O
Student Affairs   M,D,O
Sustainable Development   M

Urban and Regional Planning   M,O
Vocational and Technical Education   M,O
Women's Studies   O
Writing   M,D,O

NORTHERN ILLINOIS UNIVERSITY

Accounting   M
Adult Education   M,D
Anthropology   M
Art/Fine Arts   M
Biochemistry   M,D
Biological and Biomedical
  Sciences—General   M,D
Business Administration and
  Management—General   M
Chemistry   M,D
Child and Family Studies   M
Communication Disorders   M,D
Communication—General   M
Computer Science   M
Counselor Education   M,D
Curriculum and Instruction   M,D
Dance   M
Early Childhood Education   M
Economics   M
Education—General   M,D,O
Educational Leadership and
  Administration   M,D,O
Educational Media/Instructional
  Technology   M,D
Educational Psychology   M,D,O
Electrical Engineering   M,D
Elementary Education   M
Engineering and Applied
  Sciences—General   M
English   M,D
Foundations and Philosophy of
  Education   M,D,O
French   M
Geography   M,D
Geology   M,D
Higher Education   M,D
History   M,D
Industrial and Manufacturing
  Management   M
Industrial/Management
  Engineering   M
Law   D
Management Information Systems   M
Mathematics   M,D
Mechanical Engineering   M
Music   M,O
Nursing—General   M,D
Nutrition   M
Philosophy   M
Physical Education   M
Physical Therapy   D
Physics   M,D
Political Science   M,D
Psychology—General   M,D
Public Administration   M
Public Health—General   M
Romance Languages   M
Sociology   M
Spanish   M
Special Education   M
Statistics   M
Taxation   M
Theater   M

NORTHERN KENTUCKY UNIVERSITY

Accounting   M,O
Advertising and Public Relations   M,O
Allied Health—General   M
Business Administration and
  Management—General   M,O
Clinical Psychology   M
Communication—General   M,O
Computer and Information
  Systems Security   M,O
Computer Science   M,O
Counseling Psychology   M
Counselor Education   M
Cultural Studies   M,O
Education—General   M,D,O
Educational Leadership and
  Administration   M,D,O
English   M,O
Geographic Information Systems   M,O
Health Informatics   M,O
Health Psychology   M,O
Industrial and Organizational
  Psychology   M,O
Information Science   M,O
Law   D
Liberal Studies   M
Management of Technology   M
Marriage and Family Therapy   M,O
Media Studies   M,O
Nonprofit Management   M,O
Nursing—General   M,D,O
Organizational Management   M,O
Public Administration   M,O
Public History   M,O
Rhetoric   M,O
Social Work   M
Software Engineering   M,O
Special Education   M,O
Taxation   M,O
Writing   M,O

NORTHERN MICHIGAN UNIVERSITY

Applied Behavior Analysis   M
Biological and Biomedical
  Sciences—General   M
Business Administration and
  Management—General   M
Clinical Laboratory
  Sciences/Medical Technology   M
Curriculum and Instruction   M
Education—General   M
Educational Leadership and
  Administration   M
English as a Second Language   M,O
English   M,O

Exercise and Sports Science	M
Molecular Genetics	M
Nursing—General	D
Psychology—General	M
Reading Education	M
Science Education	M
Special Education	M
Theater	M,O
Writing	M,O

NORTHERN SEMINARY

Missions and Missiology	M,D
Pastoral Ministry and Counseling	M,D
Religion	M,D
Theology	M,D

NORTHERN STATE UNIVERSITY

Clinical Psychology	M
Counseling Psychology	M
Counselor Education	M
Curriculum and Instruction	M
Education—General	M
Educational Leadership and Administration	M
Educational Media/Instructional Technology	M
Finance and Banking	M
Music Education	M
Sports Management	M

NORTHERN VERMONT UNIVERSITY–JOHNSON

Addictions/Substance Abuse Counseling	M
Applied Behavior Analysis	M
Art/Fine Arts	M
Computer Art and Design	M
Counselor Education	M
Curriculum and Instruction	M
Education—General	M
Foundations and Philosophy of Education	M
Photography	M
School Psychology	M
Special Education	M

NORTHERN VERMONT UNIVERSITY–LYNDON

Counselor Education	M
Curriculum and Instruction	M
Education—General	M
Reading Education	M
Science Education	M
Special Education	M

NORTH GREENVILLE UNIVERSITY

Education—General	M,D
Finance and Banking	M,D
Human Resources Management	M,D
Pastoral Ministry and Counseling	M,D

NORTH PARK THEOLOGICAL SEMINARY

Pastoral Ministry and Counseling	M,O
Theology	M,D

NORTH PARK UNIVERSITY

Adult Nursing	M
Business Administration and Management—General	M
Education—General	M
Music	M
Nonprofit Management	M
Nursing and Healthcare Administration	M
Nursing—General	M

NORTHWEST CHRISTIAN UNIVERSITY

Accounting	M
Business Administration and Management—General	M
Counseling Psychology	M
Counselor Education	M
Education—General	M
Elementary Education	M
English as a Second Language	M
Secondary Education	M
Special Education	M

NORTHWESTERN COLLEGE

Early Childhood Education	M,O
Education—General	M,O
Educational Leadership and Administration	M,O

NORTHWESTERN HEALTH SCIENCES UNIVERSITY

Acupuncture and Oriental Medicine	M
Chiropractic	D
Nutrition	M

NORTHWESTERN OKLAHOMA STATE UNIVERSITY

Adult Education	M
American Studies	M
Counseling Psychology	M
Counselor Education	M
Curriculum and Instruction	M
Education—General	M
Educational Leadership and Administration	M
Elementary Education	M
Reading Education	M
Secondary Education	M

NORTHWESTERN POLYTECHNIC UNIVERSITY

Business Administration and Management—General	M,D
Computer Engineering	M,D
Computer Science	M,D
Electrical Engineering	M,D
Engineering and Applied Sciences—General	M,D

NORTHWESTERN STATE UNIVERSITY OF LOUISIANA

Adult Education	M
Art/Fine Arts	M
Clinical Psychology	M
Counselor Education	M,O
Curriculum and Instruction	M
Early Childhood Education	M
Education—General	M,O
Educational Leadership and Administration	M,O
Educational Media/Instructional Technology	M,O
Elementary Education	M
English	M
Health Education	M
Health Physics/Radiological Health	M
Homeland Security	M
Middle School Education	M
Music	M
Nursing—General	M
Psychology—General	M
Reading Education	M,O
Secondary Education	M,O
Special Education	M,O
Student Affairs	M

NORTHWESTERN UNIVERSITY

Accounting	M,D
African Studies	O
African-American Studies	D
Allopathic Medicine	
American Studies	M
Anthropology	D
Applied Mathematics	M,D
Applied Physics	D
Art History	D
Art/Fine Arts	M
Artificial Intelligence/Robotics	M
Arts Administration	M
Astronomy	D
Biochemistry	D
Bioengineering	D
Biological and Biomedical Sciences—General	D
Biomedical Engineering	M,D
Biophysics	D
Biopsychology	D
Biostatistics	D
Biotechnology	M,D
Broadcast Journalism	M
Business Administration and Management—General	M,D
Business Analytics	M,D
Cell Biology	D
Chemical Engineering	M,D
Chemistry	D
Civil Engineering	M,D
Clinical Laboratory Sciences/Medical Technology	M
Clinical Psychology	D
Clinical Research	M,O
Cognitive Sciences	D
Communication Disorders	M,D
Communication—General	M,D
Comparative Literature	M,D
Computer and Information Systems Security	M
Computer Engineering	M,D
Computer Science	M,D
Corporate and Organizational Communication	M,D
Data Science/Data Analytics	M
Developmental Biology	D
Economics	D
Education—General	M,D
Educational Leadership and Administration	M
Educational Media/Instructional Technology	M,D
Electrical Engineering	M,D
Electronic Commerce	M
Elementary Education	M
Engineering and Applied Sciences—General	M,D,O
Engineering Design	M
Engineering Management	M
English	M,D
Entrepreneurship	M,D
Environmental Engineering	M,D
Epidemiology	D
Ethics	M
Film, Television, and Video Production	M,D
Finance and Banking	M,D
French	D,O
Gender Studies	O
Genetic Counseling	M
Geology	D
Geosciences	D
Geotechnical Engineering	M
German	D
Health Informatics	M,D
Health Services Management and Hospital Administration	M,D
Health Services Research	D
History	M,D
Human Development	D
Human Resources Management	M
Industrial and Manufacturing Management	M,D
Industrial/Management Engineering	M,D
Information Science	M
International Affairs	M,D,O
International Business	M
International Health	M
Internet and Interactive Multimedia	M
Italian	D,O
Journalism	M

Kinesiology and Movement Studies	D
Law	M,D
Liberal Studies	M
Linguistics	D
Management Information Systems	M
Management Strategy and Policy	M,D
Marketing	M,D
Marriage and Family Therapy	M
Materials Engineering	M,D,O
Materials Sciences	M,D,O
Mathematics	D
Mechanical Engineering	M,D
Mechanics	M,D
Media Studies	M,D
Medical Informatics	M,D
Molecular Biology	D
Music Education	M,D
Music	M,D
Neurobiology	M,D
Neuroscience	D
Organizational Behavior	M
Organizational Management	M,D
Philosophy	D
Physical Therapy	D
Physics	D
Physiology	M
Plant Biology	D
Political Science	D
Portuguese	D
Project Management	M
Psychology—General	D
Public Administration	M
Public Health—General	M
Public Policy	M,D
Publishing	M
Quality Management	M
Real Estate	M,D
Rehabilitation Sciences	D
Religion	M,D
Rhetoric	M,D
Secondary Education	M
Slavic Languages	D
Social Psychology	D
Sociology	M,D
Software Engineering	M
Spanish	D
Speech and Interpersonal Communication	M,D
Sports Management	M
Statistics	M,D
Structural Biology	D
Structural Engineering	M,D
Systems Biology	D
Taxation	M,D
Theater	M,D
Transportation and Highway Engineering	M,D
Writing	M

NORTHWEST MISSOURI STATE UNIVERSITY

Agricultural Economics and Agribusiness	M
Agricultural Education	M
Agricultural Sciences—General	M
Biological and Biomedical Sciences—General	M,O
Business Administration and Management—General	M
Business Analytics	M
Computer Science	M
Early Childhood Education	M,D,O
Education—General	M,D,O
Educational Leadership and Administration	M,D,O
Educational Media/Instructional Technology	M
Educational Policy	M,D,O
Elementary Education	M,D,O
English as a Second Language	M,D,O
English Education	M,O
English	M,O
Exercise and Sports Science	M
Geographic Information Systems	M,O
Health Education	M
Higher Education	M,D,O
Human Resources Management	M
Management Information Systems	M
Marketing	M
Mathematics Education	M,D,O
Mathematics	M,O
Middle School Education	M,D,O
Physical Education	M
Reading Education	M
Recreation and Park Management	M
Science Education	M,O
Social Sciences Education	M,O
Special Education	M,D,O

NORTHWEST NAZARENE UNIVERSITY

Addictions/Substance Abuse Counseling	M
Business Administration and Management—General	M
Clinical Psychology	M
Counselor Education	M
Curriculum and Instruction	M,D,O
Education—General	M,D,O
Educational Leadership and Administration	M,D,O
Marriage and Family Therapy	M
Missions and Missiology	M
Nursing and Healthcare Administration	M
Pastoral Ministry and Counseling	M
Religion	M
School Psychology	M
Social Work	M
Special Education	M,D,O
Theology	M

NORTHWEST UNIVERSITY

Business Administration and Management—General	M
Counseling Psychology	M,D
Cultural Studies	M
Education—General	M
International Business	M
Missions and Missiology	M
Organizational Management	M
Pastoral Ministry and Counseling	M
Project Management	M
Psychology—General	M,D
Theology	M
Urban and Regional Planning	M,D

NORTHWOOD UNIVERSITY, MICHIGAN CAMPUS

Business Administration and Management—General	M

NORWICH UNIVERSITY

Business Administration and Management—General	M
Civil Engineering	M
Computer and Information Systems Security	M
Conflict Resolution and Mediation/Peace Studies	M
Construction Management	M
Criminal Justice and Criminology	M
Emergency Management	M
Energy Management and Policy	M
Environmental Engineering	M
Finance and Banking	M
Geotechnical Engineering	M
History	M
Human Resources Management	M
International Affairs	M
International Business	M
International Development	M
Logistics	M
Management Strategy and Policy	M
Military and Defense Studies	M
Nonprofit Management	M
Nursing and Healthcare Administration	M
Nursing Education	M
Nursing—General	M
Organizational Management	M
Project Management	M
Public Administration	M
Public Policy	M
Structural Engineering	M
Supply Chain Management	M

NOTRE DAME COLLEGE (OH)

Computer Science	M,O
Homeland Security	M,O
Reading Education	M,O
Special Education	M,O

NOTRE DAME DE NAMUR UNIVERSITY

Art Therapy	M,D
Business Administration and Management—General	M
Clinical Psychology	M
Curriculum and Instruction	M
Education—General	M
Educational Leadership and Administration	M
Finance and Banking	M
Marriage and Family Therapy	M
Public Administration	M
Special Education	M

NOTRE DAME OF MARYLAND UNIVERSITY

Business Administration and Management—General	M
Communication—General	M
Education—General	M
Educational Leadership and Administration	M,D
English as a Second Language	M
Liberal Studies	M
Nonprofit Management	M
Pharmacy	D

NOTRE DAME SEMINARY

Theology	M

NOVA SOUTHEASTERN UNIVERSITY

Accounting	M
Addictions/Substance Abuse Counseling	M,D,O
Adult Nursing	M,D
Allied Health—General	M,D
Allopathic Medicine	D
Anesthesiologist Assistant Studies	M,D
Art/Fine Arts	M,D,O
Bioinformatics	M,D,O
Biological and Biomedical Sciences—General	M,D
Business Administration and Management—General	M
Business Analytics	M
Business Education	M
Clinical Psychology	M,D
Communication Disorders	M,D
Computer and Information Systems Security	M,D
Computer Science	M,D
Conflict Resolution and Mediation/Peace Studies	M,D,O
Counseling Psychology	M,D,O
Counselor Education	M,D,O
Criminal Justice and Criminology	M,D,O
Dentistry	M,D
Distance Education Development	M,D,O
Education—General	M,D,O
Educational Media/Instructional Technology	M,D,O

Emergency Management — M,D,O
Entrepreneurship — M
Experimental Psychology — M,D,O
Family Nurse Practitioner Studies — M,D
Finance and Banking — M
Forensic Psychology — M,D,O
Gerontological Nursing — M,D
Health Education — M,D,O
Health Informatics — M,D,O
Health Law — M,D
Human Resources Management — M
Humanities — M,D,O
Information Science — M,D
Interdisciplinary Studies — M,D,O
International Business — M
Law — M,D
Legal and Justice Studies — M,D
Management Information Systems — M,D
Management Strategy and Policy — M
Marine Biology — M,D
Marketing — M
Marriage and Family Therapy — M,D,O
Medical Informatics — M,D,O
Nursing Education — M,D
Nursing Informatics — M,D
Nursing—General — M,D,O
Nutrition — M,D,O
Occupational Therapy — M,D
Oceanography — M,D
Optometry — M,D
Osteopathic Medicine — M,D,O
Pharmacy — M,D
Physical Therapy — M,D
Physician Assistant Studies — M,D
Psychiatric Nursing — M
Psychology—General — M,D,O
Public Administration — M
Public Health—General — M,D
School Psychology — M,D,O
Social Sciences — M,D,O
Student Affairs — M,D,O
Supply Chain Management — M

NSCAD UNIVERSITY
Applied Arts and Design—
General — M
Art/Fine Arts — M

NYACK COLLEGE
Business Administration and
Management—General — M
Counseling Psychology — M
Counselor Education — M
Elementary Education — M
English as a Second Language — M
Marriage and Family Therapy — M
Missions and Missiology — M,D
Organizational Management — M
Pastoral Ministry and Counseling — M,D
Religion — M
Social Work — M
Special Education — M
Theology — M,D

OAKLAND CITY UNIVERSITY
Business Administration and
Management—General — M
Curriculum and Instruction — M,D
Education—General — M,D
Educational Leadership and
Administration — M,D
Elementary Education — M
Management Strategy and Policy — M
Organizational Management — M,D
Pastoral Ministry and Counseling — M,D
Secondary Education — M,D
Theology — M,D

OAKLAND UNIVERSITY
Accounting — M,O
Allied Health—General — M,D,O
Applied Behavior Analysis — M,O
Applied Mathematics — M,D
Applied Statistics — M
Biological and Biomedical
Sciences—General — M,D,O
Business Administration and
Management—General — M,O
Chemistry — M,D
Computer Engineering — M,D
Computer Science — M,D
Counseling Psychology — M,D,O
Early Childhood Education — M,D,O
Economics — M
Education—General — M,D,O
Educational Leadership and
Administration — M,D,O
Electrical Engineering — M,D
Elementary Education — M,O
Engineering and Applied
Sciences—General — M,D,O
Engineering Management — M
English as a Second Language — M,O
English — M
Entrepreneurship — M,O
Environmental and Occupational
Health — M
Environmental Sciences — M,D
Exercise and Sports Science — M,D,O
Family Nurse Practitioner Studies — M,O
Finance and Banking — M,O
Gerontological Nursing — M,O
Higher Education — M,D,O
History — M
Human Resources Management — M,O
Industrial and Manufacturing
Management — M,O
International Business — M,O
Liberal Studies — M
Linguistics — M,O
Management Information Systems — M,D,O
Marketing — M,O
Maternal and Child Health — D,O
Mathematics — M
Mechanical Engineering — M,D

Medical Physics — M,D
Music Education — M,D
Music — M,D
Nonprofit Management — M,O
Nurse Anesthesia — M,O
Nursing—General — M,D,O
Organizational Management — M,D,O
Physical Therapy — D,O
Physics — M,D
Public Administration — M,O
Public Health—General — M
Reading Education — M,D,O
Secondary Education — M,O
Software Engineering — M,D
Special Education — M,O
Statistics — O
Systems Engineering — M,D
Systems Science — M,D

OAKWOOD UNIVERSITY
Pastoral Ministry and Counseling — M

OBERLIN COLLEGE
Music — M,O

OBLATE SCHOOL OF THEOLOGY
African-American Studies — M,D,O
Pastoral Ministry and Counseling — M,D,O
Religion — M,D,O
Theology — M,D,O

OCCIDENTAL COLLEGE
Biological and Biomedical
Sciences—General — M

OGLALA LAKOTA COLLEGE
Business Administration and
Management—General — M
Educational Leadership and
Administration — M

OHIO CHRISTIAN UNIVERSITY
Accounting — M
Business Administration and
Management—General — M
Finance and Banking — M
Health Services Management and
Hospital Administration — M
Human Resources Management — M
Marketing — M
Organizational Management — M
Pastoral Ministry and Counseling — M
Theology — M

OHIO DOMINICAN UNIVERSITY
Accounting — M
Business Administration and
Management—General — M
Curriculum and Instruction — M
Data Science/Data Analytics — M
Education—General — M
Educational Leadership and
Administration — M
Engineering Design — M
English as a Second Language — M
English — M
Finance and Banking — M
Health Services Management and
Hospital Administration — M
Management Strategy and Policy — M
Physician Assistant Studies — M
Risk Management — M
Sports Management — M
Theology — M

OHIO NORTHERN UNIVERSITY
Accounting — M
Law — M,D
Pharmacy — D

THE OHIO STATE UNIVERSITY
Accounting — M
Actuarial Science — M,D
Aerospace/Aeronautical
Engineering — M,D
African Studies — M,D
African-American Studies — M,D
Agricultural Economics and
Agribusiness — M,D
Agricultural Education — M
Agricultural Engineering — M,D
Agricultural Sciences—
General — M,D
Agronomy and Soil Sciences — M,D
Allied Health—General — M
Allopathic Medicine — D
Anatomy — M,D
Animal Sciences — M,D
Anthropology — M,D
Architecture — M,D
Art Education — M,D
Art History — M,D
Art/Fine Arts — M,D
Arts Administration — M
Asian Languages — M,D
Asian Studies — M
Astronomy — M,D
Atmospheric Sciences — M,D
Biochemistry — M,D
Bioengineering — M,D
Biological and Biomedical
Sciences—General — M,D
Biomedical Engineering — M,D
Biophysics — M,D
Biostatistics — M,D
Business Administration and
Management—General — M,D
Cell Biology — M,D
Chemical Engineering — M,D
Chemical Physics — M,D
Chemistry — M,D
Child and Family Studies — M,D
Chinese — M,D
Civil Engineering — M,D
Classics — M,D
Clinical Psychology — D
Cognitive Sciences — D

Communication Disorders — M,D
Communication—General — M,D
Computational Sciences — M,D
Computer Art and Design — M
Computer Engineering — M,D
Computer Science — M,D
Dance — M,D
Dental Hygiene — M,D
Dentistry — M,D
Developmental Biology — M,D
Developmental Psychology — D
East European and Russian Studies — M,D
Ecology — M,D
Economics — M,D
Education—General — M,D,O
Educational Leadership and
Administration — M,D,O
Educational Policy — M,D,O
Electrical Engineering — M,D
Engineering and Applied
Sciences—General — M,D
English — M,D
Entomology — M,D
Environmental Management
and Policy — M,D
Environmental Sciences — M,D
Evolutionary Biology — M,D
Family and Consumer
Sciences-General — M,D
Finance and Banking — M
Fish, Game, and Wildlife
Management — M,D
Food Science and
Technology — M,D
Forestry — M,D
French — M,D
Gender Studies — M,D
Genetics — M,D
Geodetic Sciences — M,D
Geography — M,D
Geology — M,D
Geosciences — M,D
German — M,D
Health Services Management and
Hospital Administration — M,D
History — M,D
Horticulture — M,D
Human Development — M,D
Human Resources Management — M,D
Industrial and Labor Relations — M,D
Industrial Design — M
Industrial/Management
Engineering — M,D
Interdisciplinary Studies — M,D
Interior Design — M
Internet and Interactive
Multimedia — M
Italian — M,D
Japanese — M,D
Kinesiology and Movement Studies — M,D
Landscape Architecture — M,D
Latin American Studies — M
Law — M,D
Linguistics — M,D
Logistics — M
Management Information Systems — M,D
Materials Engineering — M,D
Materials Sciences — M,D
Mathematics Education — M,D
Mathematics — M,D
Mechanical Engineering — M,D
Metallurgical Engineering and
Metallurgy — M,D
Microbiology — M,D
Molecular Biology — M,D
Molecular Genetics — M,D
Music — M,D
Natural Resources — M,D
Near and Middle Eastern Languages — M,D
Neuroscience — D
Nuclear Engineering — M,D
Nursing—General — M,D
Nutrition — M,D
Occupational Therapy — M
Operations Research — M
Optical Sciences — M,D
Optometry — M,D
Oral and Dental Sciences — M,D
Pharmaceutical Administration — M,D
Pharmacology — M,D
Pharmacy — M,D
Philosophy — M,D
Physical Education — M,D
Physical Therapy — D
Physics — M,D
Plant Pathology — M,D
Plant Sciences — D
Political Science — M,D
Portuguese — M,D
Psychology—General — D
Public Administration — M,D
Public Affairs — M,D
Public Health—General — M,D
Public Policy — M,D
Rehabilitation Sciences — D
Rural Sociology — M,D
Slavic Languages — M,D
Social Psychology — D
Social Sciences — M,D
Social Work — M,D
Sociology — D
Spanish — M,D
Special Education — D
Statistics — M,D
Systems Engineering — M,D
Theater — M,D
Urban and Regional Planning — M,D
Veterinary Sciences — M,D
Women's Studies — M,D

THE OHIO STATE UNIVERSITY AT LIMA
Social Work — M

THE OHIO STATE UNIVERSITY AT MANSFIELD
Education—General — M
Social Work — M

THE OHIO STATE UNIVERSITY AT MARION
Education—General — M

THE OHIO STATE UNIVERSITY AT NEWARK
Education—General — M
Social Work — M

OHIO UNIVERSITY
African Studies — M
Applied Economics — M
Art History — M
Art/Fine Arts — M
Asian Studies — M
Astronomy — M,D
Athletic Training and Sports
Medicine — M
Biochemistry — M,D
Biological and Biomedical
Sciences—General — M,D
Biomedical Engineering — M
Business Administration and
Management—General — M
Cell Biology — M,D
Chemical Engineering — M,D
Child and Family Studies — M
Child Development — M
Civil Engineering — M,D
Clinical Psychology — D
Communication Disorders — M,D
Communication—General — M,D
Comparative and Interdisciplinary
Arts — D
Computer Education — M,D
Computer Science — M,D
Construction Engineering — M,D
Consumer Economics — M
Corporate and Organizational
Communication — M,D
Counselor Education — M,D
Curriculum and Instruction — M,D
Ecology — M,D
Economics — M
Education—General — M,D
Educational Leadership and
Administration — M,D
Educational Measurement and
Evaluation — M,D
Educational Media/Instructional
Technology — M,D
Electrical Engineering — M,D
Engineering and Applied
Sciences—General — M,D
English — M,D
Environmental Biology — M,D
Environmental Engineering — M,D
Environmental Management
and Policy — M,O
Evolutionary Biology — M,D
Exercise and Sports Science — M,D
Experimental Psychology — D
Family Nurse Practitioner Studies — M,D
Film, Television, and Video
Production — M
Film, Television, and Video
Theory and Criticism — M
Finance and Banking — M
French — M
Geochemistry — M
Geography — M
Geology — M
Geotechnical Engineering — M,D
Graphic Design — M
Health Communication — M,D
Health Services Management and
Hospital Administration — M
Higher Education — M,D
History — M,D
Industrial and Organizational
Psychology — D
Industrial/Management
Engineering — M,D
International Affairs — M
International Development — M
Internet and Interactive
Multimedia — M
Journalism — M,D
Latin American Studies — M
Linguistics — M,D
Mathematics — M,D
Mechanical Engineering — M,D
Mechanics — M,D
Media Studies — M,D
Microbiology — M,D
Middle School Education — M,D
Molecular Biology — D
Music Education — M,O
Music — M,O
Neuroscience — M,D
Nursing and Healthcare
Administration — M,D
Nursing Education — M,D
Nursing—General — M,D
Nutrition — M
Osteopathic Medicine — D
Philosophy — M
Photography — M
Physical Education — M
Physical Therapy — D
Physics — M,D
Physiology — M,D
Plant Biology — M,D
Political Science — M
Psychology—General — D
Public Administration — M,O
Public Health—General — M
Reading Education — M,D
Recreation and Park Management — M
Rehabilitation Counseling — M,D

Rhetoric M,D
Secondary Education M,D
Social Sciences M
Social Work M
Sociology M
Spanish M,D
Special Education M
Speech and Interpersonal
  Communication M,D
Sports Management M
Structural Engineering M,D
Student Affairs M,D
Systems Engineering M
Telecommunications M
Theater M
Therapies—Dance, Drama, and
  Music M,O
Transportation and Highway
  Engineering M,D
Water Resources Engineering M,D

OHIO VALLEY UNIVERSITY
Curriculum and Instruction M
Education—General M

OHR HAMEIR THEOLOGICAL SEMINARY
Theology

OKLAHOMA BAPTIST UNIVERSITY
Business Administration and
  Management—General M
Energy Management and
  Policy M
Marriage and Family Therapy M
Nursing Education M
Nursing—General M

OKLAHOMA CHRISTIAN UNIVERSITY
Accounting M
Business Administration and
  Management—General M
Computer Engineering M
Computer Science M
Electrical Engineering M
Engineering and Applied
  Sciences—General M
Engineering Management M
Finance and Banking M
Health Services Management and
  Hospital Administration M
Human Resources Management M
International Business M
Marketing M
Mechanical Engineering M
Nonprofit Management M
Organizational Management M
Project Management M
Software Engineering M
Theology M

OKLAHOMA CITY UNIVERSITY
Applied Behavior Analysis M
Business Administration and
  Management—General M
Computer Science M
Counselor Education M
Criminal Justice and Criminology M
Early Childhood Education M
Elementary Education M
Energy Management and
  Policy M
English as a Second Language M
Law M,D
Music M
Nursing Education M,D
Nursing—General M
Photography M
Sociology M
Writing M

OKLAHOMA STATE UNIVERSITY
Accounting M,D
Agricultural Economics and
  Agribusiness M,D
Agricultural Education M,D
Agricultural Engineering M,D
Agricultural Sciences—
  General M,D
Agronomy and Soil Sciences M,D
Animal Sciences M,D
Applied Arts and Design—
  General M,D
Applied Behavior Analysis M,D,O
Applied Mathematics M,D
Applied Psychology M,D,O
Art History M
Aviation M,D,O
Biochemistry M,D
Bioengineering
Biological and Biomedical
  Sciences—General M,D
Botany M,D
Business Administration and
  Management—General M,D
Chemical Engineering M,D
Chemistry M,D
Child and Family Studies M,D
Civil Engineering M,D
Clinical Psychology M,D
Clothing and Textiles M
Communication Disorders M
Computer Engineering M,D
Computer Science M,D
Consumer Economics M,D
Curriculum and Instruction M,D
Ecology M,D
Economics M,D
Education—General M,D,O
Educational Leadership and
  Administration M,D
Educational Psychology M,D,O
Electrical Engineering M,D
Emergency Management M

Engineering and Applied
  Sciences—General M,D
English M,D
Entomology M,D
Entrepreneurship M
Environmental Engineering M,D
Environmental Sciences M,D,O
Evolutionary Biology M,D
Family and Consumer
  Sciences-General M,D
Finance and Banking M,D
Fire Protection Engineering M,D
Food Science and
  Technology M,D
Forestry M,D
Geography M,D
Geology M,D
Graphic Design M
Health Education M,D,O
Health Psychology M,D,O
Higher Education M,D
History M,D
Horticulture M,D
Hospitality Management M,D
Industrial/Management
  Engineering M,D
Information Science M,D
International Affairs M,D,O
International Business M,D
Landscape Architecture M
Management Information Systems M,D
Marketing M,D
Mass Communication M
Materials Engineering M,D
Materials Sciences M,D
Mathematics M,D
Mechanical Engineering M,D
Microbiology M,D
Molecular Biology M,D
Molecular Genetics M,D
Music Education M
Music M
Natural Resources M,D
Nonprofit Management M,D,O
Nutrition M,D
Philosophy M
Photonics M,D
Physics M,D
Plant Biology M,D
Plant Pathology M,D
Plant Sciences M,D
Political Science M,D
Psychology—General M,D
Sociology M,D
Statistics M,D
Sustainability Management M,D,O
Telecommunications
  Management M,D,O
Theater M
Veterinary Medicine D
Veterinary Sciences M,D
Writing M

OKLAHOMA STATE UNIVERSITY CENTER FOR HEALTH SCIENCES
Biological and Biomedical
  Sciences—General M,D
Forensic Sciences M
Health Services Management and
  Hospital Administration M
Osteopathic Medicine D
Toxicology M

OKLAHOMA WESLEYAN UNIVERSITY
Management Strategy and Policy M
Nursing and Healthcare
  Administration M
Nursing Education M
Theology M

OLD DOMINION UNIVERSITY
Accounting M
Adult Nursing M,D
Aerospace/Aeronautical
  Engineering M,D
Allied Health—General M,D
Analytical Chemistry M,D
Applied Mathematics M,D
Applied Psychology D
Athletic Training and Sports
  Medicine M
Biochemistry M,D
Biological and Biomedical
  Sciences—General M,D
Biomedical Engineering M,D
Biostatistics M,D
Business Administration and
  Management—General M,D
Business Education M,D
Chemistry M,D
Civil Engineering M,D
Clinical Psychology D
Communication Disorders M
Communication—General M,O
Community College Education M,D
Community Health M
Computer Art and Design M
Computer Engineering M,D
Computer Science M,D
Conflict Resolution and
  Mediation/Peace Studies M,D
Counseling Psychology M,D,O
Counselor Education M,D,O
Criminal Justice and Criminology M,D
Cultural Studies M,D,O
Curriculum and Instruction M,D
Dental Hygiene M
Early Childhood Education M
Ecology D
Economics M
Education—General M,D,O

Educational Leadership and
  Administration M,D,O
Educational Measurement and
  Evaluation D
Educational Media/Instructional
  Technology M,D,O
Educational Psychology D
Electrical Engineering M,D
Elementary Education M,O
Engineering and Applied
  Sciences—General M,D
Engineering Management M,D
English as a Second Language M
English M,D
Entrepreneurship M,O
Environmental and Occupational
  Health M
Environmental Engineering M,D
Environmental Sciences M,D
Ergonomics and Human
  Factors D
Exercise and Sports Science M
Family Nurse Practitioner Studies M
Finance and Banking D
Gender Studies M,O
Geotechnical Engineering M,D
Gerontological Nursing M,D
Health Education M,D
Health Promotion M
Health Services Research D
Higher Education M,D,O
History M
Humanities M,O
Hydraulics M
Immunology M
Industrial and Organizational
  Psychology D
Industrial Hygiene M
Information Science D
Inorganic Chemistry M,D
International Affairs M,D
International Business M
International Development M,D
Kinesiology and Movement Studies M
Library Science M,O
Linguistics M
Management Information Systems M,D
Marketing M,D
Maternal and Child/Neonatal
  Nursing M,D
Mathematics M,D
Mechanical Engineering M,D
Media Studies M,O
Microbiology M
Middle School Education M,O
Modeling and Simulation M,D
Music Education M
Music M
Nurse Anesthesia D
Nursing and Healthcare
  Administration M,D
Nursing Education M,D
Nursing—General D
Oceanography M,D
Organic Chemistry M,D
Pediatric Nursing M,D
Philosophy M,O
Physical Chemistry M,D
Physical Education M,D
Physical Therapy D
Physics M,D
Psychology—General M,D
Public Administration M,D
Public Health—General M
Public Policy D
Reading Education M,D
Recreation and Park Management M
Rehabilitation Sciences D
Rhetoric M
School Psychology M,D,O
Secondary Education M
Sociology M
Special Education M,D
Speech and Interpersonal
  Communication M
Sports Management M
Statistics M
Structural Engineering M,D
Supply Chain Management M
Systems Engineering M,D
Transportation and Highway
  Engineering M
Travel and Tourism M
Vocational and Technical Education M,D
Water Resources M
Women's Studies M
Writing M

OLIVET COLLEGE
Insurance M

OLIVET NAZARENE UNIVERSITY
Business Administration and
  Management—General M
Curriculum and Instruction M
Education—General M
Educational Leadership and
  Administration M
Elementary Education M
Family Nurse Practitioner Studies M
Library Science M
Nursing—General M
Organizational Management M
Pastoral Ministry and Counseling M
Reading Education M
Religion M
Secondary Education M
Theology M

OMEGA GRADUATE SCHOOL
Child and Family Studies M,D
Organizational Management M,D

Religion M,D
Sociology M,D

OPEN UNIVERSITY
Business Administration and
  Management—General M
Education—General M
Engineering and Applied
  Sciences—General M
History M
Music M
Philosophy M

ORAL ROBERTS UNIVERSITY
Accounting M
Addictions/Substance Abuse
  Counseling M,D
Business Administration and
  Management—General M
Curriculum and Instruction M,D
Education—General M,D
Educational Leadership and
  Administration M,D
Entrepreneurship M
Finance and Banking M
Higher Education M,D
International Business M
Marketing M
Marriage and Family Therapy M,D
Missions and Missiology M,D
Near and Middle Eastern Languages M
Nonprofit Management M
Pastoral Ministry and Counseling M,D
Religious Education M,D
Theology M,D

OREGON COLLEGE OF ORIENTAL MEDICINE
Acupuncture and Oriental Medicine M,D

OREGON HEALTH & SCIENCE UNIVERSITY
Allopathic Medicine D
Biochemistry M,D
Bioinformatics M,D,O
Biological and Biomedical
  Sciences—General M,D,O
Biomedical Engineering M,D
Biopsychology D
Cancer Biology/Oncology D
Cell Biology D
Clinical Research M,O
Community Health Nursing M,O
Computational Biology M,D,O
Computer Engineering M,D
Computer Science D,O
Dentistry D,O
Developmental Biology D
Electrical Engineering M,D
Environmental Engineering M,D
Environmental Sciences M,D
Family Nurse Practitioner Studies M
Genetics D
Gerontological Nursing M
Gerontology M,O
Health Informatics M,D,O
Health Services Management and
  Hospital Administration M,O
Immunology D
Medical Informatics M,D,O
Microbiology D
Molecular Biology M,D
Molecular Medicine M,D
Neuroscience D
Nurse Anesthesia M
Nurse Midwifery M
Nursing and Healthcare
  Administration M
Nursing Education M,O
Nursing—General M,D,O
Nutrition M,O
Oral and Dental Sciences M,D,O
Pediatric Nursing M
Pharmacology D
Physician Assistant Studies M
Physiology D
Psychiatric Nursing M

OREGON INSTITUTE OF TECHNOLOGY
Manufacturing Engineering M

OREGON STATE UNIVERSITY
Accounting M,D
Actuarial Science M,D
Adult Education M,D
Agricultural Education M,D
Agricultural Engineering M,D
Agronomy and Soil Sciences M,D
Allied Health—General M,D
Analytical Chemistry M,D
Animal Sciences M
Anthropology M
Applied Economics M,D
Applied Mathematics M,D
Aquaculture M
Artificial Intelligence/Robotics M,D
Athletic Training and Sports
  Medicine M
Atmospheric Sciences M,D
Biochemistry M,D
Bioengineering M,D
Bioinformatics D
Biological and Biomedical
  Sciences—General M,D
Biophysics M,D
Biostatistics M,D
Biotechnology M,D
Botany M,D
Business Administration and
  Management—General M,D
Cell Biology M,D
Chemical Engineering M,D
Chemistry M,D

Child and Family Studies — M,D
Civil Engineering — M,D
Clinical Psychology — M,D
Cognitive Sciences — M,D
Computational Biology — M,D
Computational Sciences — M,D
Computer Engineering — M,D
Computer Science — M,D
Conservation Biology — M,D
Construction Engineering — M,D
Counselor Education — M,D
Data Science/Data Analytics — M
Ecology — M,D
Education—General — M,D
Educational Leadership and Administration — M,D
Educational Policy — M,D
Electrical Engineering — M,D
Elementary Education — M
Engineering and Applied Sciences—General — M,D
Engineering Management — M
English Education — M
English — M
Environmental and Occupational Health — M,D
Environmental Biology — M,D
Environmental Education — M,D
Environmental Engineering — M,D
Environmental Management and Policy — M,D
Environmental Sciences — M,D
Epidemiology — M,D
Ethics — M
Finance and Banking — M,D
Fish, Game, and Wildlife Management — M,D
Food Science and Technology — M,D
Forestry — M,D
Gender Studies — M
Genetics — M,D
Genomic Sciences — M,D
Geochemistry — M,D
Geographic Information Systems — M
Geography — M,D
Geology — M,D
Geophysics — M,D
Geotechnical Engineering — M,D
Health Physics/Radiological Health — M,D
Health Promotion — M,D
Health Psychology — M,D
Health Services Management and Hospital Administration — M,D
Higher Education — M,D
Hispanic Studies — M
History of Science and Technology — M,D
Horticulture — M,D
Human Development — M,D
Hydrogeology — M,D
Hydrology — M,D
Immunology — M,D
Industrial/Management Engineering — M,D
Interdisciplinary Studies — M
International Health — M,D
Kinesiology and Movement Studies — M,D
Limnology — M,D
Manufacturing Engineering — M,D
Marine Affairs — M
Marine Sciences — M
Materials Sciences — M,D
Mathematical and Computational Finance — M,D
Mathematics Education — M,D
Mathematics — M,D
Mechanical Engineering — M,D
Medical Imaging — M,D
Medical Physics — M,D
Microbiology — M,D
Molecular Biology — M,D
Molecular Toxicology — M,D
Music Education — M
Natural Resources — M
Nuclear Engineering — M,D
Nutrition — M,D
Ocean Engineering — M,D
Oceanography — M,D
Parasitology — M,D
Pharmaceutical Sciences — M,D
Pharmacy — D
Physics — M,D
Physiology — M,D
Plant Molecular Biology — D
Plant Pathology — M,D
Plant Physiology — M,D
Psychology—General — M,D
Public Health—General — M,D
Public Policy — M,D
Range Science — M,D
Rhetoric — M
School Psychology — M,D
Science Education — M,D
Social Sciences Education — M,D
Social Sciences — M,D
Statistics — M,D
Structural Engineering — M,D
Student Affairs — M
Sustainability Management — M,D
Systems Biology — M,D
Systems Engineering — M,D
Toxicology — M,D
Transportation and Highway Engineering — M,D
Veterinary Medicine — D
Virology — M,D
Viticulture and Enology — M,D
Water Resources Engineering — M,D
Water Resources — M,D
Women's Studies — M,D
Writing — M

OREGON STATE UNIVERSITY–CASCADES
Education—General — M
School Psychology — M
Social Psychology — M

OTIS COLLEGE OF ART AND DESIGN
Art/Fine Arts — M
Graphic Design — M
Photography — M
Writing — M

OTTAWA UNIVERSITY
Art Therapy — M
Business Administration and Management—General — M
Counseling Psychology — M
Counselor Education — M
Curriculum and Instruction — M
Early Childhood Education — M
Education—General — M
Educational Leadership and Administration — M
Educational Media/Instructional Technology — M
Elementary Education — M
Finance and Banking — M
Human Resources Development — M
Human Resources Management — M
Marketing — M
Marriage and Family Therapy — M
Pastoral Ministry and Counseling — M
School Psychology — M
Special Education — M

OTTERBEIN UNIVERSITY
Business Administration and Management—General — M
Education—General — M
Family Nurse Practitioner Studies — M,D,O
Nurse Anesthesia — M,D,O
Nursing and Healthcare Administration — M,D,O
Nursing Education — M,D,O
Nursing—General — M,D,O

OUR LADY OF THE LAKE UNIVERSITY
Accounting — M
Business Administration and Management—General — M
Communication Disorders — M
Computer and Information Systems Security — M
Counseling Psychology — D
Counselor Education — M
Curriculum and Instruction — M
English — M
Finance and Banking — M
Health Services Management and Hospital Administration — M
Management Information Systems — M
Marriage and Family Therapy — M
Nonprofit Management — M
Organizational Management — M,D
Psychology—General — M
School Psychology — M
Science Education — M
Social Work — M,D
Sociology — M
Writing — M

PACE UNIVERSITY
Accounting — M,O
Addictions/Substance Abuse Counseling — M,D
Biochemistry — M
Biological and Biomedical Sciences—General — M,O
Business Administration and Management—General — M,D,O
Chemistry — M,O
Clinical Psychology — M,D
Communication Disorders — M
Communication—General — M
Computer and Information Systems Security — M,D,O
Computer Science — M,D,O
Counseling Psychology — M,D
Developmental Psychology — M,D
Early Childhood Education — M,O
Economics — O
Education—General — M,O
Educational Media/Instructional Technology — M,O
Electronic Commerce — O
Elementary Education — M,O
Emergency Management — M
English — M,O
Entrepreneurship — M
Environmental Law — M,D
Environmental Management and Policy — M
Environmental Sciences — M
Family Nurse Practitioner Studies — M,D,O
Finance and Banking — M,D,O
Foreign Languages Education — M,O
Forensic Sciences — M
Geosciences — M,O
Health Services Management and Hospital Administration — M
Homeland Security — M
Human Resources Management — M
Information Science — M,D,O
International Business — M,O
International Economics — O
Internet and Interactive Multimedia — M
Investment Management — M,O
Law — M,D
Legal and Justice Studies — M,D
Management Information Systems — M,D,O
Management Strategy and Policy — M
Marketing — M,D,O
Mathematics — M,O
Media Studies — M
Molecular Biology — M

Nonprofit Management — M
Nursing and Healthcare Administration — M,D,O
Nursing—General — M,D,O
Physician Assistant Studies — M
Physics — M,O
Psychology—General — M,D
Public Administration — M
Publishing — M,O
Reading Education — M,O
Risk Management — M
School Psychology — M,D
Social Sciences Education — M,O
Software Engineering — M,D,O
Special Education — M,O
Taxation — M
Telecommunications — M,D,O
Theater — M

PACIFICA GRADUATE INSTITUTE
Clinical Psychology — M,D
Counseling Psychology — M,D
Psychology—General — M,D

PACIFIC COLLEGE OF ORIENTAL MEDICINE
Acupuncture and Oriental Medicine — M,D

PACIFIC COLLEGE OF ORIENTAL MEDICINE–CHICAGO
Acupuncture and Oriental Medicine — M

PACIFIC COLLEGE OF ORIENTAL MEDICINE-NEW YORK
Acupuncture and Oriental Medicine — M

PACIFIC LUTHERAN UNIVERSITY
Accounting — M
Business Administration and Management—General — M
Curriculum and Instruction — M
Education—General — M
Family Nurse Practitioner Studies — D
Finance and Banking — M
Marketing Research — M
Marriage and Family Therapy — M
Nursing—General — M,D
Writing — M

PACIFIC NORTHWEST COLLEGE OF ART
Applied Arts and Design—General — M
Art/Fine Arts — M
Cultural Studies — M

PACIFIC NORTHWEST UNIVERSITY OF HEALTH SCIENCES
Osteopathic Medicine — D

PACIFIC OAKS COLLEGE
Early Childhood Education — M
Education—General — M
Human Development — M
Marriage and Family Therapy — M
Special Education — M

PACIFIC RIM CHRISTIAN UNIVERSITY
Pastoral Ministry and Counseling — M

PACIFIC SCHOOL OF RELIGION
Religion — M,D,O
Theology — M,D,O

PACIFIC STATES UNIVERSITY
Accounting — M,O
Business Administration and Management—General — M,O
Computer Science — M
Finance and Banking — M,O
International Business — M,O
Management Information Systems — M,O
Management of Technology — M,O
Project Management — M,O
Real Estate — M,O

PACIFIC UNION COLLEGE
Education—General — M
Elementary Education — M
Secondary Education — M

PACIFIC UNIVERSITY
Athletic Training and Sports Medicine — M,D
Business Administration and Management—General — M
Clinical Psychology — M,D
Communication Disorders — M,D
Early Childhood Education — M
Education of the Gifted — M
Education—General — M
Elementary Education — M
English as a Second Language — M
Finance and Banking — M
Health Services Management and Hospital Administration — M
Middle School Education — M
Occupational Therapy — D
Optometry — M,D
Pharmacy — D
Physical Therapy — M,D
Physician Assistant Studies — M
Psychology—General — M,D
Science Education — M
Secondary Education — M
Social Work — M
Special Education — M
Vision Sciences — M,D
Writing — M

PALM BEACH ATLANTIC UNIVERSITY
Addictions/Substance Abuse Counseling — M
Business Administration and Management—General — M
Counseling Psychology — M
Counselor Education — M
Education—General — M
Family Nurse Practitioner Studies — M,D

Marriage and Family Therapy — M
Nursing and Healthcare Administration — M,D
Nursing—General — M,D
Organizational Management — M
Pharmacy — D
Religious Education — M
Theology — M

PALMER COLLEGE OF CHIROPRACTIC
Anatomy — M
Chiropractic — D
Clinical Research — M

PALO ALTO UNIVERSITY
Biopsychology — D
Clinical Psychology — M,D
Counseling Psychology — M
Marriage and Family Therapy — M
Psychology—General — M,D

PARIS COLLEGE OF ART
Art/Fine Arts — M
Interior Design — M
Media Studies — M
Photography — M
Textile Design — M

PARKER UNIVERSITY
Chiropractic — D

PARK UNIVERSITY
Business Administration and Management—General — M,O
Curriculum and Instruction — M,O
Education—General — M,O
Educational Leadership and Administration — M,O
Emergency Management — M,O
Finance and Banking — M,O
Health Services Management and Hospital Administration — M,O
International Business — M,O
International Health — M,O
Management Information Systems — M,O
Music — M,O
Nonprofit Management — M,O
Public Administration — M,O
Public Affairs — M,O
Reading Education — M,O
Social Work — M,O
Writing — M,O

PAYNE THEOLOGICAL SEMINARY
Theology — M

PEIRCE COLLEGE
Organizational Management — M

PENN STATE ERIE, THE BEHREND COLLEGE
Accounting — M
Applied Psychology — M
Business Administration and Management—General — M
Clinical Psychology — M
Industrial and Manufacturing Management — M
Quality Management — M

PENN STATE GREAT VALLEY
Business Administration and Management—General — M,O
Computer and Information Systems Security — M,O
Data Science/Data Analytics — M,O
Engineering and Applied Sciences—General — M,O
Engineering Management — M,O
Entrepreneurship — M,O
Finance and Banking — M,O
Health Services Management and Hospital Administration — M,O
Human Resources Development — M,O
Human Resources Management — M,O
Information Science — M,O
Software Engineering — M,O
Sustainability Management — M,O
Systems Engineering — M,O

PENN STATE HARRISBURG
Accounting — M,D,O
Adult Education — M,D,O
American Studies — M,D,O
Applied Behavior Analysis — M,D,O
Applied Psychology — M,D,O
Business Administration and Management—General — M,O
Civil Engineering — M,O
Clinical Psychology — M,D,O
Communication—General — M,D,O
Computer Science — M,O
Criminal Justice and Criminology — M,D,O
Curriculum and Instruction — M,D,O
Developmental Education — M,D,O
Education—General — M,D,O
Electrical Engineering — M,O
Engineering and Applied Sciences—General — M,O
Engineering Management — M,O
English as a Second Language — M,D,O
Environmental Engineering — M,O
Environmental Sciences — M,O
Finance and Banking — M,D,O
Folklore — M,D,O
Health Education — M,D,O
Health Psychology — M,D,O
Health Services Management and Hospital Administration — M,D,O
Historic Preservation — M,D,O
Homeland Security — M,D,O
Human Resources Management — M,D,O
Humanities — M,D,O
Management Information Systems — M,O
Mechanical Engineering — M,O
Museum Studies — M,D,O
Nonprofit Management — M,D,O

Psychology—General M,D,O
Public Administration M,D,O
Public Affairs M,D,O
Reading Education M,D,O
Social Psychology M,D,O
Structural Engineering M,O
Supply Chain Management M,O

PENN STATE HERSHEY MEDICAL CENTER
Allopathic Medicine M,D
Anatomy M,D
Biochemistry M,D
Bioinformatics M,D
Biological and Biomedical
  Sciences—General M,D
Biostatistics D
Cell Biology D
Developmental Biology D
Genomic Sciences M,D
Health Services Research M
Immunology M,D
Molecular Genetics M,D
Molecular Medicine D
Molecular Toxicology D
Neurobiology D
Neuroscience M,D
Public Health—General M,D
Veterinary Sciences M
Virology M,D

PENN STATE UNIVERSITY–DICKINSON LAW
Law M,D

PENN STATE UNIVERSITY PARK
Accounting M,D
Acoustics M,D
Adult Education M,D
Aerospace/Aeronautical
  Engineering M,D
Agricultural Economics and
  Agribusiness M,D,O
Agricultural Education M,D,O
Agricultural Engineering M,D
Agricultural Sciences—
  General M,D,O
Agronomy and Soil Sciences M,D
Animal Sciences M,D
Anthropology M,D
Applied Statistics M,D
Architectural Engineering M,D
Architecture M,D
Art Education M,D,O
Art History M,D
Art/Fine Arts M,D,O
Astronomy M,D
Astrophysics M,D
Biochemistry M,D
Bioengineering M,D
Biological and Biomedical
  Sciences—General M,D
Biopsychology M,D
Biotechnology M,D
Business Administration and
  Management—General M,D
Cell Biology M,D
Chemical Engineering M,D
Chemistry M,D
Child and Family Studies M,D
Civil Engineering M,D
Communication Disorders M,D,O
Communication—General M,D
Comparative Literature M,D
Computer Engineering M,D
Computer Science M,D*
Counselor Education M,D,O
Criminal Justice and Criminology M,D
Curriculum and Instruction M,D,O
Ecology M,D
Economics M,D
Education—General M,D,O
Educational Leadership and
  Administration M,D,O
Educational Media/Instructional
  Technology M,D,O
Educational Policy M,D,O
Educational Psychology M,D,O
Electrical Engineering M,D
Engineering and Applied
  Sciences—General M,D
Engineering Design M
English as a Second Language M
English M,D
Entomology M,D
Entrepreneurship M
Environmental Engineering M,D
Environmental Management
  and Policy M
Environmental Sciences M
Fish, Game, and Wildlife
  Management M,D
Food Science and
  Technology M,D
Forensic Sciences M
Forestry M,D
Foundations and Philosophy of
  Education M,D,O
French M,D
Geography M,D
Geosciences M,D
Geotechnical Engineering M,D
German M,D
Health Services Management and
  Hospital Administration M,D
Higher Education M,D,O
History M,D
Horticulture M,D
Hospitality Management M,D
Human Development M,D
Human Resources Development M
Human Resources Management M

Industrial and Labor Relations M
Industrial/Management
  Engineering M,D
Information Science M
International Affairs M
Kinesiology and Movement Studies M,D,O
Landscape Architecture M
Law M,D
Leisure Studies M
Linguistics M,D
Management Information Systems M,D
Mass Communication M,D
Materials Engineering M,D
Materials Sciences M,D
Mathematics M,D
Mechanical Engineering M,D
Mechanics M,D
Media Studies M,D
Meteorology M,D
Mineral/Mining Engineering M,D
Molecular Biology M,D
Music Education M,D,O
Music M,D,O
Nuclear Engineering M,D
Nursing—General M,D
Nutrition M,D
Organizational Management M,D
Pathobiology M,D
Philosophy M,D
Physics M,D
Physiology M,D
Plant Biology M,D
Plant Pathology M,D
Plant Sciences M,D
Political Science M,D
Psychology—General M,D
Recreation and Park Management M,D
Rural Sociology M,D,O
Russian M,D
School Psychology M,D,O
Sociology M,D
Spanish M,D
Special Education M,D,O
Statistics M,D
Sustainable Development M
Theater M,D
Travel and Tourism M
Vocational and Technical Education M,D,O

PENN STATE YORK
Curriculum and Instruction M,O
Education—General M,O
English as a Second Language M,O

PENNSYLVANIA ACADEMY OF THE FINE ARTS
Art/Fine Arts M,O

PENNSYLVANIA COLLEGE OF HEALTH SCIENCES
Health Education M
Health Services Management and
  Hospital Administration M
Nursing and Healthcare
  Administration M
Nursing Education M

PENSACOLA CHRISTIAN COLLEGE
Art/Fine Arts M,D,O
Business Administration and
  Management—General M,D,O
Curriculum and Instruction M,D,O
Educational Leadership and
  Administration M,D,O
Graphic Design M,D,O
Music M,D,O
Nursing—General M,D,O
Theater M,D,O

PENTECOSTAL THEOLOGICAL SEMINARY
Pastoral Ministry and Counseling M,D
Theology M,D

PEPPERDINE UNIVERSITY
Accounting M
American Studies M
Communication—General M
Economics M
Humanities M
International Affairs M
Media Studies M
Pastoral Ministry and Counseling M
Political Science M
Public Policy M
Religion M
Writing M

PERU STATE COLLEGE
Curriculum and Instruction M
Economics M
Education—General M
Entrepreneurship M
Organizational Management M

PFEIFFER UNIVERSITY
Business Administration and
  Management—General M
Elementary Education M
Health Services Management and
  Hospital Administration M
Organizational Management M
Religious Education M
Theology M

PHILADELPHIA COLLEGE OF OSTEOPATHIC MEDICINE
Applied Behavior Analysis M,D,O
Biological and Biomedical
  Sciences—General M
Biopsychology M,D,O
Clinical Psychology M,D,O
Counseling Psychology M,D,O
Educational Psychology M,D,O

Forensic Sciences M
Health Services Management and
  Hospital Administration M,D,O
Industrial and Organizational
  Psychology M,D,O
Osteopathic Medicine D
Physician Assistant Studies M
Psychology—General M,D,O*
Public Health—General M,D,O
School Psychology M,D,O

PHILLIPS GRADUATE UNIVERSITY
Art Therapy M
Counselor Education M
Marriage and Family Therapy M
Organizational Behavior D
Psychology—General M
School Psychology M

PHILLIPS THEOLOGICAL SEMINARY
Business Administration and
  Management—General M,D
Ethics M,D
Higher Education M,D
Missions and Missiology M,D
Music M,D
Pastoral Ministry and Counseling D
Religious Education M,D
Social Work M,D
Theology M,D

PHOENIX INSTITUTE OF HERBAL MEDICINE & ACUPUNCTURE
Acupuncture and Oriental Medicine M

PHOENIX SEMINARY
Counseling Psychology M,D,O
Pastoral Ministry and Counseling M,D,O
Theology M,D,O

PIEDMONT COLLEGE
Art Education M,D,O
Business Administration and
  Management—General M
Curriculum and Instruction M,D,O
Early Childhood Education M,D,O
Education—General M,D,O
Middle School Education M,D,O
Music Education M,D,O
Secondary Education M,D,O
Special Education M,D,O

PIEDMONT INTERNATIONAL UNIVERSITY
Curriculum and Instruction M,D
Educational Leadership and
  Administration M,D
Pastoral Ministry and Counseling M,D
Theology M,D

PILLAR COLLEGE
Clinical Psychology M
Marriage and Family Therapy M

PITTSBURGH THEOLOGICAL SEMINARY
Pastoral Ministry and Counseling M,D
Theology M,D

PITTSBURG STATE UNIVERSITY
Accounting M
Biological and Biomedical
  Sciences—General M
Business Administration and
  Management—General M
Chemistry M
Clinical Psychology M
Communication—General M
Construction Engineering M
Construction Management M,O
Counselor Education M
Education—General M,O
Educational Leadership and
  Administration M,O
Educational Media/Instructional
  Technology M
Electrical Engineering M
English as a Second Language M,O
English M
Exercise and Sports Science M
Graphic Design M,O
Health Education M
History M
Human Resources Development M
International Business M
Management of Technology M,O
Manufacturing Engineering M
Mathematics M
Mechanical Engineering M
Music Education M
Music M
Nursing Education M,D
Nursing—General M,D
Physical Education M
Physics M
Polymer Science and
  Engineering M
Psychology—General M
School Psychology O
Secondary Education M,O
Special Education M,O
Sports Management M
Vocational and Technical Education M,O
Writing M

PLYMOUTH STATE UNIVERSITY
Accounting M
Addictions/Substance Abuse
  Counseling M
Adult Education D
Art Education M
Athletic Training and Sports
  Medicine M

Business Administration and
  Management—General M
Clinical Psychology O
Counselor Education M
Cultural Studies M
Curriculum and Instruction D
Education—General O
Educational Leadership and
  Administration M,D,O
English Education M
Health Education M
Health Promotion M,O
Higher Education D,O
Historic Preservation M,O
Marriage and Family Therapy M
Mathematics Education M
Music Education M
School Psychology O
Social Sciences Education M

POINT LOMA NAZARENE UNIVERSITY
Acute Care/Critical Care Nursing M
Biological and Biomedical
  Sciences—General M
Business Administration and
  Management—General M
Clinical Psychology M
Counselor Education M
Education—General M
Educational Leadership and
  Administration M
Entrepreneurship M
Exercise and Sports Science M
Family Nurse Practitioner Studies M
Gerontological Nursing M
Health Services Management and
  Hospital Administration M
Kinesiology and Movement Studies M
Marriage and Family Therapy M
Nursing—General M,D,O
Organizational Management M
Pastoral Ministry and Counseling M
Pediatric Nursing M
Project Management M
Special Education M
Sports Management M
Theology M

POINT PARK UNIVERSITY
Adult Education M,D
Business Administration and
  Management—General M
Business Analytics M
Clinical Psychology M,D
Communication—General M
Criminal Justice and Criminology M
Curriculum and Instruction M,D
Education—General M,D
Educational Leadership and
  Administration M,D
Elementary Education M,D
Engineering Management M
Entertainment Management M
Environmental Management
  and Policy M
Health Services Management and
  Hospital Administration M
International Business M
Journalism M
Management Information Systems M
Mass Communication M
Media Studies M
Middle School Education M,D
Music M
Organizational Management M
Secondary Education M,D
Special Education M,D
Sports Management M
Theater M

POINT UNIVERSITY
Business Administration and
  Management—General M
Pastoral Ministry and Counseling M

POLYTECHNIC UNIVERSITY OF PUERTO RICO
Business Administration and
  Management—General M
Civil Engineering M
Computer Engineering M
Computer Science M
Electrical Engineering M
Engineering Management M
Environmental Management
  and Policy M
Industrial and Manufacturing
  Management M
International Business M
Landscape Architecture M
Management Information Systems M
Management of Technology M
Manufacturing Engineering M
Mechanical Engineering M

POLYTECHNIC UNIVERSITY OF PUERTO RICO, MIAMI CAMPUS
Accounting M
Business Administration and
  Management—General M
Construction Management M
Environmental Engineering M
Environmental Management
  and Policy M
Finance and Banking M
Human Resources Management M
Industrial and Manufacturing
  Management M
International Business M
Logistics M
Marketing M
Project Management M

M—masters degree; D—doctorate; O—other advanced degree; *—Close-Up and/or Display

Supply Chain Management — M

POLYTECHNIC UNIVERSITY OF PUERTO RICO, ORLANDO CAMPUS
Accounting — M
Business Administration and Management—General — M
Construction Management — M
Engineering Management — M
Environmental Engineering — M
Environmental Management and Policy — M
Finance and Banking — M
Human Resources Management — M
Industrial and Manufacturing Management — M
International Business — M
Management of Technology — M

PONCE HEALTH SCIENCES UNIVERSITY
Biological and Biomedical Sciences—General — D
Clinical Psychology — D
Epidemiology — M,D
Public Health—General — M,D

PONTIFICAL CATHOLIC UNIVERSITY OF PUERTO RICO
Accounting — M,O
Art/Fine Arts — M
Biological and Biomedical Sciences—General — M
Business Administration and Management—General — M,D,O
Business Education — M
Chemistry — M
Clinical Laboratory Sciences/Medical Technology — O
Clinical Psychology — D
Counselor Education — M
Criminal Justice and Criminology — M
Curriculum and Instruction — M,D
Education—General — M,D
Educational Leadership and Administration — D
Educational Psychology — M
English as a Second Language — M
Environmental Sciences — M
Finance and Banking — M
Hispanic Studies — M,O
History — M
Human Resources Management — M,O
Human Services — M,D
Industrial and Organizational Psychology — D
International Business — M
Law — D
Logistics — O
Management Information Systems — M,O
Marketing — M
Medical/Surgical Nursing — M
Nursing—General — M
Psychiatric Nursing — M
Psychology—General — M,D
Public Administration — M
Rehabilitation Counseling — M
Religious Education — M
Social Work — M
Spanish — M,O
Theology — M
Transportation Management — O

PONTIFICAL COLLEGE JOSEPHINUM
Theology — M

PONTIFICAL JOHN PAUL II INSTITUTE FOR STUDIES ON MARRIAGE AND FAMILY
Biotechnology — M,D,O
Ethics — M,D,O
Marriage and Family Therapy — M,D,O
Theology — M,D,O

PONTIFICIA UNIVERSIDAD CATOLICA MADRE Y MAESTRA
Allopathic Medicine — D
Architecture — M
Building Science — M
Business Administration and Management—General — M
Clinical Psychology — M
Criminal Justice and Criminology — M
Developmental Psychology — M
Early Childhood Education — M
Engineering and Applied Sciences—General — M
Entrepreneurship — M
Finance and Banking — M
Forensic Psychology — M
Hospitality Management — M
Human Resources Management — M
Insurance — M
Interior Design — M
International Affairs — M
International Business — M
Landscape Architecture — M
Law — M
Logistics — M
Management Strategy and Policy — M
Marketing — M
Psychology—General — M
Real Estate — M
Structural Engineering — M
Travel and Tourism — M

POPE ST. JOHN XXIII NATIONAL SEMINARY
Theology — M

PORTLAND STATE UNIVERSITY
American Studies — M
Anthropology — M,D,O
Applied Social Research — M,D
Applied Statistics — M,D,O
Architecture — M
Art/Fine Arts — M

Artificial Intelligence/Robotics — M,D,O
Biological and Biomedical Sciences—General — M,D,O
Business Administration and Management—General — M,D,O
Chemistry — M,D
Civil Engineering — M,D,O
Communication Disorders — M
Computer and Information Systems Security — M,D,O
Computer Engineering — M,D
Computer Science — M,D,O
Conflict Resolution and Mediation/Peace Studies — M
Criminal Justice and Criminology — M
Economics — M,D,O
Education—General — M,D
Electrical Engineering — M,D
Energy Management and Policy — M,D,O
Engineering and Applied Sciences—General — M,D,O
Engineering Management — M,D,O
English as a Second Language — M,O
English — M
Environmental Engineering — M,D
Environmental Management and Policy — M,D,O
Environmental Sciences — M,D,O
Finance and Banking — M
Food Science and Technology — M,D,O
Foreign Languages Education — M
French — M
Geography — M,D
Geology — M,D,O
German — M
Health Promotion — M,D
Health Services Management and Hospital Administration — M,D,O
History — M
Human Resources Management — M,D,O
Hydrology — M,D,O
International Affairs — M
International Business — M
Japanese — M
Management of Technology — M,D
Materials Engineering — M,D
Mathematics Education — M,D,O
Mathematics — M,D,O
Mechanical Engineering — M,D
Middle School Education — M
Modeling and Simulation — M,D,O
Music — M
Nonprofit Management — M,D,O
Physics — M,D
Political Science — M
Psychology—General — M,D,O
Public Administration — M,D,O
Public Affairs — M,D,O
Public Health—General — M,D
Public Policy — M,D,O
Real Estate — M,D,O
Science Education — M,D,O
Social Sciences Education — M
Social Work — M,D
Sociology — M,D,O
Spanish — M
Speech and Interpersonal Communication — M,O
Statistics — M,D,O
Supply Chain Management — M
Systems Science — M,D,O
Theater — M
Writing — M

POST UNIVERSITY
Accounting — M
Addictions/Substance Abuse Counseling — M
Business Administration and Management—General — M
Clinical Psychology — M
Curriculum and Instruction — M
Distance Education Development — M
Education—General — M
Educational Leadership and Administration — M
Educational Media/Instructional Technology — M
Emergency Management — M
English as a Second Language — M
Finance and Banking — M
Forensic Psychology — M
Health Services Management and Hospital Administration — M
Homeland Security — M
Human Services — M
Marketing — M
Nonprofit Management — M
Project Management — M
Public Administration — M

PRAIRIE VIEW A&M UNIVERSITY
Accounting — M
Agricultural Sciences—General — M
Architecture — M
Business Administration and Management—General — M
Chemistry — M
Clinical Psychology — M,D
Computer Science — M,D
Counselor Education — M,D
Curriculum and Instruction — M
Education—General — M,D
Educational Leadership and Administration — M,D
Electrical Engineering — M,D
Engineering and Applied Sciences—General — M,D
Forensic Psychology — M,D
Health Education — M
Kinesiology and Movement Studies — M
Legal and Justice Studies — M,D

Management Information Systems — M,D
Nursing—General — M,D
Sociology — M

PRATT INSTITUTE
Applied Arts and Design—General — M,O
Architecture — M
Art Education — M,O
Art Therapy — M
Art/Fine Arts — M
Arts Administration — M
Facilities Management — M
Graphic Design — M
Historic Preservation — M
Industrial Design — M
Information Studies — M,O
Interior Design — M
Internet and Interactive Multimedia — M
Library Science — M,O
Media Studies — M
Music — M
Real Estate — M
Sustainable Development — M
Therapies—Dance, Drama, and Music — M
Urban and Regional Planning — M
Urban Design — M
Writing — M

PRESBYTERIAN COLLEGE
Pharmacy — D

PRESCOTT COLLEGE
Art Therapy — M
Art/Fine Arts — M
Counseling Psychology — M
Counselor Education — M,D
Early Childhood Education — M
Education—General — M,D
Educational Leadership and Administration — M,D
Elementary Education — M,D
Environmental Education — M,D
Environmental Management and Policy — M
Health Psychology — M
Humanities — M
Legal and Justice Studies — M
Leisure Studies — M
Psychoanalysis and Psychotherapy — M
Secondary Education — M
Special Education — M,D

PRESIDIO GRADUATE SCHOOL (CA)
Business Administration and Management—General — M,O
Sustainability Management — M,O

PRINCETON THEOLOGICAL SEMINARY
Religion — M,D
Theology — M,D

PRINCETON UNIVERSITY
Aerospace/Aeronautical Engineering — M,D
Anthropology — D
Applied Mathematics — D
Archaeology — D
Architecture — M,D
Asian Studies — D
Astronomy — D
Astrophysics — D
Atmospheric Sciences — D
Bioengineering — M,D
Chemical Engineering — M,D
Chemistry — M,D
Civil Engineering — M,D
Classics — D
Comparative Literature — D
Computational Biology — D
Computational Sciences — D
Computer Science — M,D
Demography and Population Studies — D,O
Ecology — D
Economics — D,O
Electrical Engineering — M,D
Electronic Materials — D
Engineering and Applied Sciences—General — M,D
English — D
Environmental Engineering — M,D
Evolutionary Biology — D
Finance and Banking — M
Financial Engineering — M,D
French — D
Geosciences — D
German — D
History of Science and Technology — D
History — D
International Affairs — M,D
Marine Biology — D
Materials Sciences — D
Mathematics — D
Mechanical Engineering — M,D
Molecular Biology — D
Music — D
Near and Middle Eastern Studies — M,D
Neuroscience — D
Ocean Engineering — D
Oceanography — D
Operations Research — M,D
Philosophy — D
Photonics — D
Physics — D
Plasma Physics — D
Political Science — D
Portuguese — D
Psychology—General — D
Public Affairs — M,D,O
Public Policy — M,D
Religion — D
Russian — D
Slavic Languages — D
Sociology — D,O

Spanish — D

PROVIDENCE COLLEGE
Accounting — M
American Studies — M
Business Administration and Management—General — M
Counselor Education — M
Educational Leadership and Administration — M
Elementary Education — M
Finance and Banking — M
History — M
International Business — M
Marketing — M
Mathematics Education — M
Reading Education — M
Secondary Education — M
Special Education — M
Theology — M
Urban Education — M

PROVIDENCE UNIVERSITY COLLEGE & THEOLOGICAL SEMINARY
Counseling Psychology — M,D,O
English as a Second Language — M,D,O
Missions and Missiology — M,D,O
Pastoral Ministry and Counseling — M,D,O
Religious Education — M,D,O
Student Affairs — M,D,O
Theology — M,D,O

PURCHASE COLLEGE, STATE UNIVERSITY OF NEW YORK
Art History — M
Art/Fine Arts — M
Arts Administration — M
Computer Art and Design — M
Entrepreneurship — M
Media Studies — M
Music — M

PURDUE UNIVERSITY
Aerospace/Aeronautical Engineering — M,D
Agricultural Economics and Agribusiness — M,D
Agricultural Education — M,D,O
Agricultural Engineering — M,D
Agricultural Sciences—General — M,D
Agronomy and Soil Sciences — M,D
Allied Health—General — M,D
American Studies — M,D
Analytical Chemistry — M,D
Anatomy — M,D
Animal Sciences — M,D
Anthropology — M,D
Applied Arts and Design—General — M,D
Aquaculture — M,D
Art Education — M,D,O
Art/Fine Arts — M,D
Atmospheric Sciences — M,D
Aviation Management — M
Biochemistry — M,D
Biological and Biomedical Sciences—General — M,D
Biomedical Engineering — M,D
Biophysics — D
Biotechnology — D
Botany — M,D
Business Administration and Management—General — M,D
Cancer Biology/Oncology — D
Cell Biology — M,D
Chemical Engineering — M,D
Chemistry — M,D
Child and Family Studies — M,D
Child Development — M,D
Civil Engineering — M,D
Clinical Psychology — D
Cognitive Sciences — D
Communication Disorders — M,D
Communication—General — M,D
Comparative Literature — D
Computational Sciences — M
Computer and Information Systems Security — M
Computer Art and Design — M,D
Computer Engineering — M,D
Computer Science — M,D
Construction Management — M,D
Consumer Economics — M,D
Curriculum and Instruction — M,D,O
Developmental Biology — M,D
Ecology — M,D
Economics — D
Education—General — M,D,O
Educational Leadership and Administration — M,D,O
Educational Media/Instructional Technology — M,D,O
Electrical Engineering — M,D
Elementary Education — M,D,O
Engineering and Applied Sciences—General — M,D,O
English Education — M,D,O
English — M,D
Entomology — M,D
Environmental and Occupational Health — M
Environmental Engineering — M,D
Environmental Management and Policy — M,D
Epidemiology — M,D
Ergonomics and Human Factors — M
Evolutionary Biology — D
Exercise and Sports Science — M,D
Family Nurse Practitioner Studies — M,D,O
Finance and Banking — M
Fish, Game, and Wildlife Management — M,D

Food Science and Technology — M,D
Foreign Languages Education — M,D,O
Forestry — M,D
Foundations and Philosophy of Education — M,D,O
French — M,D
Genetics — M,D
Genomic Sciences — D
Geosciences — M,D
German — M,D
Gerontological Nursing — M,D,O
Health Education — M,D
Health Physics/Radiological Health — M,D
Higher Education — M,D,O
History — M,D
Home Economics Education — M,D,O
Horticulture — M,D
Hospitality Management — M,D
Human Development — M,D
Human Resources Management — M,D
Immunology — M,D
Industrial and Organizational Psychology — D
Industrial Design — M,D
Industrial/Management Engineering — M,D
Inorganic Chemistry — M,D
Interior Design — M,D
International Business — M
Japanese — M,D
Kinesiology and Movement Studies — M,D
Linguistics — M,D
Management Information Systems — M
Management of Technology — M,D
Marriage and Family Therapy — M,D
Materials Engineering — M,D
Mathematics Education — M,D
Mathematics — M,D
Mechanical Engineering — M,D,O
Medical Physics — M,D
Microbiology — M,D
Molecular Biology — D
Natural Resources — M,D
Neurobiology — M,D
Neuroscience — D
Nuclear Engineering — M,D
Nursing—General — M,D,O
Nutrition — M,D
Organic Chemistry — M,D
Organizational Behavior — D
Pathobiology — M,D
Pathology — M,D
Pediatric Nursing — M,D,O
Pharmaceutical Administration — M,D,O
Pharmaceutical Sciences — M,D,O
Pharmacology — M,D
Pharmacy — D
Philosophy — M,D
Physical Chemistry — M,D
Physical Education — M,D
Physics — M,D
Physiology — M,D
Plant Pathology — M,D
Plant Sciences — D
Political Science — M,D
Psychology—General — D
Public Health—General — M,D
Reading Education — M,D,O
Recreation and Park Management — M,D
Science Education — M,D,O
Social Sciences Education — M,D,O
Sociology — M,D
Spanish — M,D
Sport Psychology — M,D
Sports Management — M,D
Statistics — M,D
Systems Biology — D
Theater — M
Toxicology — M,D
Travel and Tourism — M,D
Veterinary Medicine — D
Veterinary Sciences — M,D
Virology — M,D
Vocational and Technical Education — M,D,O
Writing — M,D

PURDUE UNIVERSITY FORT WAYNE
Adult Nursing — M,O
Applied Mathematics — M,O
Applied Statistics — M,O
Biological and Biomedical Sciences—General — M
Business Administration and Management—General
Civil Engineering — M
Communication—General — M
Computer Engineering — M
Computer Science — M
Construction Management — M
Counselor Education — M,O
Education—General — M,O
Educational Leadership and Administration — M,O
Electrical Engineering — M
Elementary Education — M,O
Engineering and Applied Sciences—General — M,O
English as a Second Language — M,O
English Education — M,O
English — M,O
Facilities Management — M
Family Nurse Practitioner Studies — M,O
Gerontological Nursing — M,O
Industrial/Management Engineering — M
Information Science — M
Marriage and Family Therapy — M,O
Mathematics Education — M,O
Mathematics — M,O
Mechanical Engineering — M

Nursing and Healthcare Administration — M,O
Nursing Education — M,O
Nursing—General — M,O
Operations Research — M,O
Organizational Management — M,O
Public Policy — M,O
Secondary Education — M,O
Special Education — M,O
Systems Engineering — M

PURDUE UNIVERSITY GLOBAL
Business Administration and Management—General — M
Computer and Information Systems Security — M
Criminal Justice and Criminology — M
Education—General — M
Educational Leadership and Administration — M
Educational Media/Instructional Technology — M
Entrepreneurship — M
Finance and Banking — M
Health Services Management and Hospital Administration — M,O
Higher Education — M
Human Resources Management — M
International Business — M
Law — M
Legal and Justice Studies — M,O
Logistics — M
Management Information Systems — M
Marketing — M
Mathematics Education — M
Nursing and Healthcare Administration — M
Nursing Education — M
Nursing—General — M
Organizational Management — M
Political Science — M,O
Project Management — M
Reading Education — M
Science Education — M
Secondary Education — M
Special Education — M
Student Affairs — M
Supply Chain Management — M

PURDUE UNIVERSITY NORTHWEST
Accounting — M
Acute Care/Critical Care Nursing — M
Adult Nursing — M
Biological and Biomedical Sciences—General — M
Biotechnology — M
Business Administration and Management—General — M
Child and Family Studies — M
Child Development — M
Communication—General — M
Computer Engineering — M
Computer Science — M
Counseling Psychology — M
Counselor Education — M
Education—General — M
Educational Leadership and Administration — M
Educational Media/Instructional Technology — M
Electrical Engineering — M
Engineering and Applied Sciences—General — M
English — M
Family Nurse Practitioner Studies — M
History — M
Human Services — M
Marriage and Family Therapy — M
Mathematics Education — M
Mathematics — M
Mechanical Engineering — M
Nursing and Healthcare Administration — M
Nursing—General — M
School Psychology — M
Science Education — M
Special Education — M

QUEENS COLLEGE OF THE CITY UNIVERSITY OF NEW YORK
Accounting — M
Applied Behavior Analysis — M
Applied Mathematics — M
Applied Social Research — M
Archives/Archival Administration — M,O
Art Education — M,O
Art History — M
Art/Fine Arts — M
Biological and Biomedical Sciences—General — M
Chemistry — M
Child and Family Studies — M,O
Communication Disorders — M,O
Computer Science — M
Counseling Psychology — M,O
Counselor Education — M
Data Science/Data Analytics — M
Early Childhood Education — M,O
Education—General — M,O
Educational Leadership and Administration — M,O
Elementary Education — M,O
English as a Second Language — M,O
English Education — M,O
English — M
Environmental Sciences — M
Exercise and Sports Science — M,O
Family and Consumer Sciences-General — M
Finance and Banking — M
Foreign Languages Education — M,O
French — M

Geology — M
Geosciences — M
Hispanic and Latin American Languages — M
History — M
Information Studies — M,O
Italian — M
Liberal Studies — M
Library Science — M,O
Linguistics — M,O
Mathematics Education — M,O
Mathematics — M
Media Studies — M
Middle School Education — M
Multilingual and Multicultural Education — M,O
Music Education — M,O
Music — M
Neuroscience — M,O
Nutrition — M
Photonics — M
Physical Education — M,O
Physics — M
Psychology—General — M
Reading Education — M
Risk Management — M
Romance Languages — M
School Psychology — M,O
Science Education — M,O
Secondary Education — M,O
Social Sciences Education — M,O
Sociology — M
Spanish — M
Special Education — M,O
Urban Studies — M
Writing — M

QUEEN'S UNIVERSITY AT KINGSTON
Allopathic Medicine — D
Artificial Intelligence/Robotics — M,D
Astronomy — M,D
Biological and Biomedical Sciences—General — M,D
Business Administration and Management—General — M,D
Business Analytics — M,D
Canadian Studies — M,D
Chemical Engineering — M,D
Chemistry — M,D
Civil Engineering — M,D
Classics — M
Clinical Psychology — M,D
Cognitive Sciences — M,D
Communication—General — M,D
Computer Engineering — M,D
Computer Science — M,D
Developmental Psychology — M,D
Economics — M,D
Education—General — M,D
Electrical Engineering — M,D
Engineering and Applied Sciences—General — M,D
Engineering Physics — M,D
English — M,D
Entrepreneurship — M
Epidemiology — M,D
Ergonomics and Human Factors — M,D
Exercise and Sports Science — M,D
Family Nurse Practitioner Studies — M,D,O
Finance and Banking — M,D
French — M,D
Gender Studies — M,D
Geography — M,D
Geology — M,D
Health Promotion — M,D
Industrial and Labor Relations — M
Information Studies — M,D
International Affairs — M,D
International Business — M
Law — M,D
Legal and Justice Studies — M,D
Management Information Systems — M,D
Management Strategy and Policy — M,D
Marketing — M,D
Materials Engineering — M,D
Mathematics — M,D
Mechanical Engineering — M,D
Mineral/Mining Engineering — M,D
Molecular Medicine — M,D
Nursing—General — M,D,O
Occupational Therapy — M
Organizational Behavior — M,D
Pathology — M,D
Pediatric Nursing — M,D,O
Philosophy — M,D
Physical Therapy — M,D
Physics — M,D
Political Science — M
Project Management — M
Psychology—General — M,D
Public Administration — M
Public Health—General — M,D
Rehabilitation Sciences — M,D
Religion — M
Social Psychology — M,D
Sociology — M,D
Sport Psychology — M,D
Statistics — M,D
Urban and Regional Planning — M
Women's Health Nursing — M,D,O
Women's Studies — M

QUEENS UNIVERSITY OF CHARLOTTE
Business Administration and Management—General — M
Communication—General — M
Education—General — M
Educational Leadership and Administration — M
Elementary Education — M

Interior Design — M
Nursing and Healthcare Administration — M
Nursing Education — M
Nursing—General — M
Organizational Management — M
Reading Education — M
Writing — M

QUINCY UNIVERSITY
Business Administration and Management—General — M
Clinical Psychology — M
Counselor Education — M
Curriculum and Instruction — M
Education—General — M
Educational Leadership and Administration — M
English as a Second Language — M
Multilingual and Multicultural Education — M
Reading Education — M
School Psychology — M
Student Affairs — M

QUINNIPIAC UNIVERSITY
Accounting — M
Adult Nursing — D
Advertising and Public Relations — M
Allied Health—General — M
Allopathic Medicine — D
Anesthesiologist Assistant Studies — M
Biological and Biomedical Sciences—General — M
Broadcast Journalism — M
Business Administration and Management—General — M
Cardiovascular Sciences — M
Cell Biology — M
Communication—General — M
Community Health — D
Computer and Information Systems Security — M
Education—General — M,O
Educational Leadership and Administration — M,O
Educational Media/Instructional Technology — M
Elementary Education — M
English Education — D
Family Nurse Practitioner Studies — M
Film, Television, and Video Production — M
Finance and Banking — M
Foreign Languages Education — M
Health Physics/Radiological Health — M
Health Services Management and Hospital Administration — M
Internet and Interactive Multimedia — M
Journalism — M
Law — M,D
Mathematics Education — M
Molecular Biology — M
Nurse Anesthesia — D
Nursing and Healthcare Administration — D
Nursing—General — D
Organizational Management — M
Pathology — M
Perfusion — M
Physician Assistant Studies — M
Science Education — M
Secondary Education — M
Social Sciences Education — M
Social Work — M
Supply Chain Management — M

RABBINICAL ACADEMY MESIVTA RABBI CHAIM BERLIN
Theology — O

RABBINICAL COLLEGE BETH SHRAGA
Theology

RABBINICAL COLLEGE BOBOVER YESHIVA B'NEI ZION
Theology — O

RABBINICAL COLLEGE OF LONG ISLAND
Theology

RABBINICAL SEMINARY OF AMERICA
Theology

RADFORD UNIVERSITY
Art/Fine Arts — M
Business Administration and Management—General — M
Clinical Psychology — M
Communication Disorders — M
Corporate and Organizational Communication — M
Counseling Psychology — D
Counselor Education — M
Criminal Justice and Criminology — M,O
Data Science/Data Analytics — M
Early Childhood Education — M
Educational Leadership and Administration — M
English — M
Experimental Psychology — M
Industrial and Organizational Psychology — M
Management Information Systems — M
Mathematics Education — M
Music — M
Nursing—General — D
Occupational Therapy — M
Physical Therapy — D
Psychology—General — M
Reading Education — M

School Psychology	O
Social Work	M
Special Education	M,O

RADIOLOGICAL TECHNOLOGIES UNIVERSITY VT

Health Physics/Radiological Health	M
Medical Physics	M

RAMAPO COLLEGE OF NEW JERSEY

Accounting	M
Business Administration and Management—General	M
Educational Leadership and Administration	M
Educational Media/Instructional Technology	M
Family Nurse Practitioner Studies	M
Nursing and Healthcare Administration	M
Nursing Education	M
Nursing—General	M
Social Work	M
Special Education	M

RANDALL UNIVERSITY

Pastoral Ministry and Counseling	M

RANDOLPH COLLEGE

Curriculum and Instruction	M
Education—General	M
Special Education	M
Writing	M

RECONSTRUCTIONIST RABBINICAL COLLEGE

Jewish Studies	M,D,O
Theology	M,D,O
Women's Studies	M,D,O

REED COLLEGE

Liberal Studies	M

REFORMED EPISCOPAL SEMINARY

Theology	M

REFORMED PRESBYTERIAN THEOLOGICAL SEMINARY

Theology	M,D

REFORMED THEOLOGICAL SEMINARY–ATLANTA CAMPUS

Theology	M,D,O

REFORMED THEOLOGICAL SEMINARY–CHARLOTTE CAMPUS

Pastoral Ministry and Counseling	M,D
Religion	M,D
Theology	M,D

REFORMED THEOLOGICAL SEMINARY–DALLAS CAMPUS

Theology	M

REFORMED THEOLOGICAL SEMINARY–HOUSTON CAMPUS

Religion	M

REFORMED THEOLOGICAL SEMINARY–JACKSON CAMPUS

Marriage and Family Therapy	M,D,O
Missions and Missiology	M,D,O
Pastoral Ministry and Counseling	M,D,O
Religion	M,D,O
Religious Education	M,D,O
Theology	M,D,O

REFORMED THEOLOGICAL SEMINARY–ORLANDO CAMPUS

Pastoral Ministry and Counseling	M,D,O
Theology	M,D,O

REFORMED THEOLOGICAL SEMINARY–WASHINGTON D.C.

Religion	M
Theology	M

REFORMED UNIVERSITY

Business Administration and Management—General	M
Theology	M

REGENT COLLEGE

Theology	M,O

REGENT'S UNIVERSITY LONDON

Business Administration and Management—General	M
Finance and Banking	M
Human Resources Management	M
International Affairs	M
International Business	M
Management Information Systems	M
Marketing	M

REGENT UNIVERSITY

Accounting	M,D,O
Addictions/Substance Abuse Counseling	M,D,O
Adult Education	M,D,O
American Studies	M
Business Administration and Management—General	M,D,O
Business Analytics	M,D,O
Clinical Psychology	M,D,O
Communication—General	M,D
Computer and Information Systems Security	M
Conflict Resolution and Mediation/Peace Studies	M,D
Corporate and Organizational Communication	M,D
Counseling Psychology	M,D,O
Counselor Education	M,D,O
Criminal Justice and Criminology	M,D,O
Cultural Studies	M,D
Curriculum and Instruction	M,D,O
Distance Education Development	M,D,O
Early Childhood Education	M,D,O
Economics	M,D,O

Education of the Gifted	M,D,O
Education—General	M,D,O
Educational Leadership and Administration	M,D,O
Educational Media/Instructional Technology	M,D,O
Educational Psychology	M,D,O
Elementary Education	M,D,O
Emergency Management	M
English as a Second Language	M,D,O
Entrepreneurship	M,D,O
Film, Television, and Video Production	M,D
Finance and Banking	M,D,O
Health Services Management and Hospital Administration	M,D,O
Higher Education	M,D,O
Homeland Security	M
Human Resources Development	M,D,O
Human Resources Management	M,D,O
Human Services	M,D,O
Interdisciplinary Studies	M,D,O
International Affairs	M
Investment Management	M,D
Journalism	M,D
Law	M,D
Legal and Justice Studies	M,D
Management Strategy and Policy	M,D,O
Marketing	M,D,O
Marriage and Family Therapy	M,D,O
Mathematics	M,D,O
Missions and Missiology	M,D
National Security	M,D
Nonprofit Management	M,D,O
Organizational Management	M,D,O
Pastoral Ministry and Counseling	M,D,O
Political Science	M
Public Administration	M
Public Policy	M
Reading Education	M,D,O
Religion	M,D
Religious Education	M,D,O
Science Education	M,D,O
Special Education	M,D,O
Student Affairs	M,D,O
Theater	M,D
Theology	M,D
Writing	M,D

REGIS COLLEGE (CANADA)

Pastoral Ministry and Counseling	M,D,O
Philosophy	M,D,O
Theology	M,D,O

REGIS COLLEGE (MA)

Applied Behavior Analysis	M,D,O
Corporate and Organizational Communication	M
Counseling Psychology	M,D,O
Education—General	M,D
Educational Leadership and Administration	M,D
Elementary Education	M,D
Family Nurse Practitioner Studies	M,D
Health Services Management and Hospital Administration	M,D,O
Higher Education	M,D
Nursing Education	M,D,O
Nursing—General	M,D,O
Occupational Therapy	M,D,O
Special Education	M,D

REGIS UNIVERSITY

Accounting	M,O
Allied Health—General	M,D,O
Biological and Biomedical Sciences—General	M
Business Education	M,O
Computer and Information Systems Security	M,O
Computer Science	M,O
Counselor Education	M,D,O
Criminal Justice and Criminology	M,O
Curriculum and Instruction	M,O
Data Science/Data Analytics	M,O
Developmental Psychology	M,D,O
Economics	M,O
Education—General	M
Educational Leadership and Administration	M,O
Elementary Education	M,O
Environmental Biology	M
Finance and Banking	M,O
Health Informatics	M,O
Health Services Management and Hospital Administration	M,D,O
Human Resources Management	M,O
Industrial and Manufacturing Management	M,O
Information Science	M,O
Management Information Systems	M,O
Management Strategy and Policy	M,O
Marketing	M,O
Marriage and Family Therapy	M,D,O
Maternal and Child/Neonatal Nursing	M,D,O
Medical Informatics	M,O
Nonprofit Management	M,O
Nursing and Healthcare Administration	M,D,O
Nursing Education	M,D,O
Occupational Therapy	M,D,O
Organizational Management	M,O
Pharmacy	M,D,O
Physical Therapy	M,O
Project Management	M,O
Reading Education	M,O
Secondary Education	M,O
Software Engineering	M,O
Special Education	M,O
Systems Engineering	M,O
Writing	M,O

REINHARDT UNIVERSITY

Business Administration and Management—General	M
Early Childhood Education	M
Education—General	M
Public Administration	M
Writing	M

RELAY GRADUATE SCHOOL OF EDUCATION

Education—General	M

RENSSELAER AT HARTFORD

Business Administration and Management—General	M
Computer Engineering	M
Computer Science	M
Electrical Engineering	M
Engineering and Applied Sciences—General	M
Information Science	M
Mechanical Engineering	M
Systems Science	M

RENSSELAER POLYTECHNIC INSTITUTE

Acoustics	D
Aerospace/Aeronautical Engineering	M,D
Applied Mathematics	M
Architecture	M
Art/Fine Arts	D
Astronomy	M
Biochemistry	M,D
Biological and Biomedical Sciences—General	M,D
Biomedical Engineering	M,D
Biophysics	M,D
Business Administration and Management—General	M,D
Business Analytics	M
Chemical Engineering	M,D
Chemistry	M,D
Civil Engineering	M,D
Cognitive Sciences	M,D
Computer Art and Design	D
Computer Engineering	M,D
Computer Science	M,D
Electrical Engineering	M,D
Engineering and Applied Sciences—General	M,D
Engineering Physics	M,D
Entrepreneurship	M
Environmental Engineering	M,D
Financial Engineering	M
Geology	M,D
History of Science and Technology	M,D
Industrial/Management Engineering	M,D
Information Science	M
Interdisciplinary Studies	M,D
Lighting Design	M,D
Materials Engineering	M,D
Mathematics	M,D
Mechanical Engineering	M,D
Nuclear Engineering	M,D
Physics	M,D
Rhetoric	M,D
Speech and Interpersonal Communication	M,D
Supply Chain Management	M
Systems Engineering	M,D
Technology and Public Policy	M,D
Transportation and Highway Engineering	M,D

RESEARCH COLLEGE OF NURSING

Adult Nursing	M
Family Nurse Practitioner Studies	M
Gerontological Nursing	M
Nursing and Healthcare Administration	M
Nursing—General	M

RESURRECTION UNIVERSITY

Nursing—General	M

RHODE ISLAND COLLEGE

Accounting	M,O
Art Education	M
Art/Fine Arts	M
Arts Administration	M
Biological and Biomedical Sciences—General	M,O
Counseling Psychology	M,O
Counselor Education	M,O
Early Childhood Education	M
Education of Students with Severe/Multiple Disabilities	M,O
Education—General	D
Educational Leadership and Administration	M,O
Elementary Education	M
English as a Second Language	M
English Education	M
English	M,O
Finance and Banking	M,O
Foreign Languages Education	M,O
Health Education	M,O
Health Psychology	M,O
Health Services Management and Hospital Administration	M
History	M
Legal and Justice Studies	M
Mathematics Education	M
Mathematics	M,O
Music Education	M
Nursing—General	M,O
Physical Education	M
Psychology—General	M,O
Reading Education	M,O
School Psychology	M,O
Secondary Education	M
Social Sciences Education	M
Social Work	M,O
Special Education	M,O

Writing	M,O

RHODE ISLAND SCHOOL OF DESIGN

Applied Arts and Design—General	M
Architecture	M
Art Education	M
Art/Fine Arts	M
Computer Art and Design	M
Graphic Design	M
Industrial Design	M
Interior Design	M
Landscape Architecture	M
Media Studies	M
Photography	M
Textile Design	M

RHODES COLLEGE

Accounting	M

RICE UNIVERSITY

African Studies	D
American Studies	D
Anthropology	M,D
Applied Mathematics	M,D
Applied Physics	M,D
Archaeology	M,D
Architecture	M,D
Art History	D
Astronomy	M,D
Biochemistry	M,D
Bioengineering	M,D
Bioinformatics	M,D
Biomedical Engineering	M,D
Biostatistics	M,D
Business Administration and Management—General	M
Cell Biology	M,D
Chemical Engineering	M,D
Chemistry	M,D
Civil Engineering	M,D
Cognitive Sciences	M,D
Computational Sciences	M,D
Computer Engineering	M,D
Computer Science	M,D
Cultural Anthropology	M,D
Ecology	M,D
Economics	M,D
Education—General	M,D
Electrical Engineering	M,D
Energy Management and Policy	M,D
Engineering and Applied Sciences—General	M,D
English	M,D
Environmental Engineering	M,D
Environmental Management and Policy	M,D
Environmental Sciences	M,D
Evolutionary Biology	M,D
Geophysics	M
Geosciences	M,D
Health Services Management and Hospital Administration	M
History	M,D
Industrial and Organizational Psychology	M,D
Inorganic Chemistry	M,D
Jewish Studies	D
Liberal Studies	M
Linguistics	M,D
Materials Sciences	M,D
Mathematical and Computational Finance	M,D
Mathematics	D
Mechanical Engineering	M,D
Music	M,D
Near and Middle Eastern Studies	D
Organic Chemistry	M,D
Philosophy	M,D
Physical Chemistry	M,D
Physics	M,D
Political Science	D
Psychology—General	M,D
Religion	D
Science Education	M,D
Sociology	D
Statistics	M,D
Urban Design	M,D

RICHMOND, THE AMERICAN INTERNATIONAL UNIVERSITY IN LONDON

Art History	M
International Affairs	M

RICHMONT GRADUATE UNIVERSITY

Clinical Psychology	M
Counselor Education	M
Marriage and Family Therapy	M
Pastoral Ministry and Counseling	M,O

RIDER UNIVERSITY

Accounting	M,O
Arts Administration	M
Business Administration and Management—General	M
Clinical Psychology	M,O
Corporate and Organizational Communication	M
Counselor Education	M,O
Early Childhood Education	M,O
Education—General	M,O
Elementary Education	M
English as a Second Language	M
Finance and Banking	M
Foreign Languages Education	M
Health Communication	M
Homeland Security	M
Multilingual and Multicultural Education	M
Music Education	M
Music	M
Organizational Management	M
School Psychology	M,O
Secondary Education	M

Special Education — M,O

RIVIER UNIVERSITY

Business Administration and Management—General	M
Clinical Psychology	M
Computer Science	M
Counseling Psychology	M,D,O
Counselor Education	M,D,O
Curriculum and Instruction	M,D,O
Early Childhood Education	M,D,O
Education—General	M,D,O
Educational Leadership and Administration	M,D,O
Elementary Education	M,D,O
English	M
Experimental Psychology	M
Family Nurse Practitioner Studies	M,D
Foreign Languages Education	M
Management Information Systems	M
Mathematics	M
Nursing and Healthcare Administration	M,D
Nursing Education	M,D
Nursing—General	M,D
Psychiatric Nursing	M,D
Psychology—General	M
Public Health—General	M,D
Reading Education	M,D,O
Social Sciences Education	M
Special Education	M,D,O
Writing	M

THE ROBERT E. WEBBER INSTITUTE FOR WORSHIP STUDIES

Religion	M,D

ROBERT MORRIS UNIVERSITY

Business Administration and Management—General	M
Computer and Information Systems Security	M,D
Data Science/Data Analytics	M,D
Engineering and Applied Sciences—General	M
Engineering Management	M
Human Resources Management	M
Information Science	M
Management Information Systems	M,D
Nursing—General	M,D
Organizational Management	M,D
Project Management	M,D
Taxation	M

ROBERT MORRIS UNIVERSITY ILLINOIS

Accounting	M
Business Administration and Management—General	M
Business Analytics	M
Computer and Information Systems Security	M
Criminal Justice and Criminology	M
Educational Leadership and Administration	M
Finance and Banking	M
Health Services Management and Hospital Administration	M
Higher Education	M
Human Resources Management	M
Management Information Systems	M
Sports Management	M

ROBERTS WESLEYAN COLLEGE

Business Administration and Management—General	M
Child and Family Studies	M
Clinical Psychology	M,D
Counselor Education	M,D
Early Childhood Education	M
Education—General	M
Health Informatics	M
Health Services Management and Hospital Administration	M
Human Services	M
Management Strategy and Policy	M
Marketing	M
Middle School Education	M
Nursing and Healthcare Administration	M
Nursing Education	M
Nursing Informatics	M
Nursing—General	M
Psychology—General	M,D
Reading Education	M
School Psychology	M,D
Secondary Education	M
Social Work	M
Special Education	M

ROCHESTER COLLEGE

Missions and Missiology	M
Religious Education	M

ROCHESTER INSTITUTE OF TECHNOLOGY

Accounting	M
Applied Mathematics	M
Applied Statistics	M
Architecture	M
Art Education	M
Art/Fine Arts	M
Astrophysics	M,D
Bioinformatics	M
Biological and Biomedical Sciences—General	M
Business Administration and Management—General	M
Chemistry	M
Cognitive Sciences	O
Communication—General	M
Computer and Information Systems Security	M,O
Computer Art and Design	M
Computer Engineering	M
Computer Science	M,D
Criminal Justice and Criminology	O
Data Science/Data Analytics	M,D,O
Electrical Engineering	M
Engineering and Applied Sciences—General	M,D,O
Engineering Design	M
Engineering Management	M
Entrepreneurship	M
Environmental and Occupational Health	M
Environmental Sciences	M
Experimental Psychology	M
Film, Television, and Video Production	M
Finance and Banking	M
Game Design and Development	M
Graphic Design	M
Health Informatics	M
Health Services Management and Hospital Administration	M,O
Hospitality Management	M
Human Resources Development	M
Human-Computer Interaction	M
Industrial and Manufacturing Management	M
Industrial Design	M
Industrial/Management Engineering	M
Information Science	M,D
Interdisciplinary Studies	M
International Business	M
Internet and Interactive Multimedia	M
Management Information Systems	O
Manufacturing Engineering	M
Materials Engineering	M
Materials Sciences	M
Mathematical and Computational Finance	M
Mathematics	M,D,O
Mechanical Engineering	M
Media Studies	M
Medical Illustration	M
Modeling and Simulation	D
Optical Sciences	M,D
Organizational Management	O
Photography	M
Project Management	O
Psychology—General	M,O
Public Policy	M
Safety Engineering	M
School Psychology	M,O
Secondary Education	M
Software Engineering	M
Special Education	M
Statistics	O
Sustainability Management	M,D
Sustainable Development	M,D
Systems Engineering	M,D
Technology and Public Policy	M
Telecommunications	M
Translation and Interpretation	M
Travel and Tourism	M
Vocational and Technical Education	O

THE ROCKEFELLER UNIVERSITY

Biological and Biomedical Sciences—General	M,D*

ROCKFORD UNIVERSITY

Business Administration and Management—General	M
Early Childhood Education	M
Education—General	M
Educational Media/Instructional Technology	M
Elementary Education	M
Reading Education	M
Secondary Education	M
Special Education	M

ROCKHURST UNIVERSITY

Accounting	M,O
Business Administration and Management—General	M,O
Business Analytics	M,O
Communication Disorders	M
Data Science/Data Analytics	M,O
Education—General	M
Entrepreneurship	M,O
Finance and Banking	M,O
Health Services Management and Hospital Administration	M,O
Human Resources Development	M,O
International Business	M,O
Management Strategy and Policy	M,O
Nonprofit Management	M,O
Occupational Therapy	M
Physical Therapy	D

ROCKY MOUNTAIN COLLEGE

Accounting	M
Educational Leadership and Administration	M
Occupational Therapy	D
Physician Assistant Studies	M

ROCKY MOUNTAIN COLLEGE OF ART + DESIGN

Art Education	M
Arts Administration	M
Internet and Interactive Multimedia	M

ROCKY MOUNTAIN UNIVERSITY OF HEALTH PROFESSIONS

Communication Disorders	D
Family Nurse Practitioner Studies	D
Occupational Therapy	D
Physical Therapy	D

Physician Assistant Studies	M
Physiology	D

ROCKY VISTA UNIVERSITY

Biological and Biomedical Sciences—General	M
Osteopathic Medicine	D
Physician Assistant Studies	M

ROGERS STATE UNIVERSITY

Business Administration and Management—General	M

ROGER WILLIAMS UNIVERSITY

Architectural History	M,O
Architecture	M,O
Art History	M,O
Business Administration and Management—General	M
Clinical Psychology	M
Computer and Information Systems Security	M
Criminal Justice and Criminology	M
Education—General	M,O
Forensic Psychology	M
Health Services Management and Hospital Administration	M
Historic Preservation	M,O
Law	M,D
Middle School Education	M,O
Public Administration	M
Reading Education	M,O
Urban and Regional Planning	M,O

ROLLINS COLLEGE

Applied Behavior Analysis	M
Business Administration and Management—General	M
Counselor Education	M
Education—General	M
Elementary Education	M
Entrepreneurship	M
Finance and Banking	M
Human Resources Development	M
Human Resources Management	M
International Business	M
Liberal Studies	M
Public Health—General	M

ROOSEVELT UNIVERSITY

Accounting	M
Actuarial Science	M
Arts Administration	M,O
Biotechnology	M
Business Administration and Management—General	M
Chemistry	M
Clinical Psychology	M
Communication—General	M
Computer Science	M
Corporate and Organizational Communication	M
Early Childhood Education	M
Economics	M
Education—General	M
Educational Leadership and Administration	M
Elementary Education	M
History	M
Hospitality Management	M
Human Resources Development	M
Human Resources Management	M
Humanities	M
Industrial and Organizational Psychology	M,D
Marketing	M
Mathematics	M
Music	M,O
Organizational Management	M
Pharmacy	D
Philosophy	M
Psychology—General	M,D
Public Administration	M
Reading Education	M
Real Estate	M
School Psychology	M
Secondary Education	M
Sociology	M
Special Education	M
Theater	M
Writing	M

ROSALIND FRANKLIN UNIVERSITY OF MEDICINE AND SCIENCE

Allied Health—General	M,D,O
Allopathic Medicine	D
Anatomy	D
Biochemistry	D
Biological and Biomedical Sciences—General	M,D
Biophysics	M,D
Cell Biology	D
Clinical Psychology	M,D
Health Education	M
Health Promotion	M
Health Services Management and Hospital Administration	M,O
Immunology	D
Interdisciplinary Studies	D
Microbiology	D
Molecular Biology	D
Molecular Pharmacology	M,D
Neuroscience	D
Nurse Anesthesia	M
Nutrition	M
Pathology	M
Pharmacy	D
Physical Therapy	M,D
Physician Assistant Studies	M
Physiology	M,D
Podiatric Medicine	D
Psychology—General	M,D

ROSE-HULMAN INSTITUTE OF TECHNOLOGY

Biomedical Engineering	M
Chemical Engineering	M
Civil Engineering	M
Computer Engineering	M
Electrical Engineering	M
Engineering and Applied Sciences—General	M
Engineering Management	M
Environmental Engineering	M
Management Information Systems	M
Mechanical Engineering	M
Optical Sciences	M
Systems Engineering	M

ROSEMAN UNIVERSITY OF HEALTH SCIENCES

Business Administration and Management—General	M,O
Dentistry	M,D,O
Pharmacy	D

ROSEMONT COLLEGE

Business Administration and Management—General	M
Counseling Psychology	M
Counselor Education	M
Education—General	M
Elementary Education	M
Human Services	M
Publishing	M
Writing	M

ROWAN UNIVERSITY

Advertising and Public Relations	M
Allopathic Medicine	D
Applied Behavior Analysis	M,O
Arts Administration	M
Bioinformatics	M
Biological and Biomedical Sciences—General	M
Business Administration and Management—General	M,O
Chemical Engineering	M
Civil Engineering	M
Clinical Psychology	M,O
Computer and Information Systems Security	O
Computer Science	M
Corporate and Organizational Communication	O
Counselor Education	M
Criminal Justice and Criminology	M
Education—General	M,D,O
Educational Leadership and Administration	M,D,O
Educational Media/Instructional Technology	M,O
Electrical Engineering	M
Engineering and Applied Sciences—General	M
English as a Second Language	O
English Education	O
Exercise and Sports Science	M
Health Promotion	M
Higher Education	M
History	M,O
Library Science	M,D,O
Marketing	M
Mathematics Education	M,O
Mathematics	M
Mechanical Engineering	M
Media Studies	O
Middle School Education	O
Music	M
Nursing—General	M
Osteopathic Medicine	D
Pharmaceutical Sciences	M
Psychology—General	M,O
Publishing	O
Reading Education	M
Rhetoric	O
School Nursing	M,D,O
School Psychology	M,O
Science Education	M,O
Special Education	M,O
Theater	M
Writing	M,O

ROYAL MILITARY COLLEGE OF CANADA

Business Administration and Management—General	M
Chemical Engineering	M,D
Chemistry	M,D
Civil Engineering	M,D
Computer Engineering	M,D
Computer Science	M
Electrical Engineering	M,D
Engineering and Applied Sciences—General	M,D
Mathematics	M
Mechanical Engineering	M,D
Military and Defense Studies	M,D
Physics	M,D
Software Engineering	M,D

ROYAL ROADS UNIVERSITY

Conflict Resolution and Mediation/Peace Studies	M,O
Emergency Management	M,O
Environmental Education	M,O
Environmental Management and Policy	M,O
Legal and Justice Studies	M,O
Sustainability Management	M,O
Travel and Tourism	M,O

RUSH UNIVERSITY

Adult Nursing	D,O
Allopathic Medicine	D

M—masters degree; D—doctorate; O—other advanced degree; *—Close-Up and/or Display

Anatomy	M,D
Biochemistry	M,D
Cell Biology	M,D
Clinical Laboratory Sciences/Medical Technology	M
Communication Disorders	M,D
Community Health Nursing	D
Family Nurse Practitioner Studies	D
Gerontological Nursing	D,O
Health Services Management and Hospital Administration	M,D
Immunology	M,D
Maternal and Child/Neonatal Nursing	D,O
Medical Physics	M,D
Microbiology	M,D
Neuroscience	M,D
Nurse Anesthesia	D,O
Nursing and Healthcare Administration	M
Nursing—General	D
Nutrition	M
Occupational Therapy	D
Pediatric Nursing	D,O
Perfusion	M
Pharmaceutical Sciences	M,D
Pharmacology	M,D
Physical Therapy	M
Physician Assistant Studies	M
Physiology	D
Psychiatric Nursing	D
Virology	M

RUTGERS UNIVERSITY–CAMDEN

Applied Mathematics	M
Biological and Biomedical Sciences—General	M
Business Administration and Management—General	M
Chemistry	M
Child Development	M,D
Computational Biology	M,D
Computer Science	M
Criminal Justice and Criminology	M
Educational Leadership and Administration	M
Educational Policy	M
English	M
Family Nurse Practitioner Studies	M
Gerontological Nursing	D
Health Services Management and Hospital Administration	M,O
History	M
International Affairs	M
International Development	M
Law	D
Liberal Studies	M
Mathematics Education	M
Mathematics	M
Nursing—General	D
Physical Therapy	D
Psychology—General	M
Public Administration	M
Public Health—General	M,O
Public History	M
Public Policy	M
Writing	M

RUTGERS UNIVERSITY–NEWARK

Accounting	M,D
Adult Nursing	M,D,O
Allied Health—General	M,D,O
Allopathic Medicine	D
American Studies	M,D
Analytical Chemistry	M,D
Applied Physics	M,D
Biochemistry	M,D
Bioinformatics	M,D
Biological and Biomedical Sciences—General	M,D,O
Biomedical Engineering	O
Biopsychology	D
Business Administration and Management—General	M,D
Cell Biology	D
Chemistry	M,D
Clinical Laboratory Sciences/Medical Technology	M
Clothing and Textiles	M
Cognitive Sciences	D
Computational Biology	M
Criminal Justice and Criminology	M,D
Dentistry	M,D,O
Economics	M,D
English	M
Environmental Sciences	M,D
Epidemiology	M,O
Family Nurse Practitioner Studies	M,D,O
Finance and Banking	M,D
Geology	M
Health Education	D
Health Physics/Radiological Health	M
Health Services Management and Hospital Administration	M,D,O
History	M
Human Resources Management	M,D
Immunology	D
Inorganic Chemistry	M,D
International Affairs	M,D
International Business	D
Law	D
Logistics	M
Management Information Systems	M,D
Management of Technology	D
Marketing	D
Mathematics	D
Medical Imaging	M
Medical Informatics	M,D,O
Microbiology	D
Molecular Biology	M,D
Molecular Genetics	D
Molecular Medicine	D
Molecular Pathology	D
Music	M
Neuroscience	D

Nurse Anesthesia	M,D,O
Nursing Informatics	M
Nursing—General	M,D,O
Nutrition	M,D,O
Occupational Health Nursing	M,D,O
Oral and Dental Sciences	M,D,O
Organic Chemistry	M,D
Organizational Management	D
Pathology	D
Pharmaceutical Administration	M
Pharmacology	D
Physical Chemistry	M,D
Physical Therapy	D
Physician Assistant Studies	M
Physiology	D
Political Science	M
Psychology—General	D
Public Administration	M,D
Public Health—General	M,O
Public Policy	M,D,O
Quantitative Analysis	M,O
Real Estate	M
Rehabilitation Counseling	M,D
Social Psychology	D
Supply Chain Management	M
Transcultural Nursing	M,D,O
Urban Studies	M,D
Women's Health Nursing	M,D,O
Writing	M

RUTGERS UNIVERSITY–NEW BRUNSWICK

Aerospace/Aeronautical Engineering	M,D
African Studies	D
African-American Studies	D
Agricultural Economics and Agribusiness	M
Allopathic Medicine	D
Animal Sciences	M,D
Anthropology	M,D
Applied Arts and Design—General	M
Applied Mathematics	M,D
Applied Psychology	M,D
Applied Statistics	M,D
Art History	M,D,O
Art/Fine Arts	M
Asian Studies	M,D
Astronomy	M,D
Atmospheric Sciences	M,D
Biochemical Engineering	M,D
Biochemistry	M,D
Biological and Biomedical Sciences—General	M,D
Biomedical Engineering	M,D
Biopsychology	D
Biostatistics	M,D,O
Cancer Biology/Oncology	M,D
Cell Biology	M,D
Chemical Engineering	M,D
Chemistry	M,D
Civil Engineering	M,D
Classics	M,D
Clinical Laboratory Sciences/Medical Technology	M
Clinical Psychology	M,D
Cognitive Sciences	D
Communication—General	D
Comparative Literature	M,D
Computational Biology	D
Computer Engineering	M,D
Computer Science	M,D
Condensed Matter Physics	M,D
Counseling Psychology	M
Counselor Education	M
Developmental Biology	M,D
Developmental Education	M,D
Early Childhood Education	M,D
Ecology	M,D
Economics	M,D
Education—General	M,D
Educational Leadership and Administration	M,D
Educational Measurement and Evaluation	M
Educational Policy	D
Educational Psychology	M,D
Electrical Engineering	M,D
Elementary Education	M,D
Emergency Management	M,D,O
English as a Second Language	M,D
English Education	M
English	D
Entomology	M,D
Environmental and Occupational Health	M,D,O
Environmental Biology	M,D
Environmental Engineering	M,D
Environmental Sciences	M,D
Epidemiology	M,D,O
Evolutionary Biology	M,D
Food Science and Technology	M,D
Foreign Languages Education	M,D
Foundations and Philosophy of Education	M,D
French	M,D
Gender Studies	M,D
Genetics	M,D
Geography	M,D
Geology	M,D
German	M,D
Hazardous Materials Management	M,D
Health Education	M,D,O
Health Informatics	M
Health Psychology	D
Health Services Management and Hospital Administration	M,D,O
Historic Preservation	M,D,O
History of Medicine	D
History of Science and Technology	D
History	D

Horticulture	M,D
Human Resources Management	M,D
Immunology	M,D
Industrial and Labor Relations	M,D
Industrial/Management Engineering	M,D
Information Science	M
Information Studies	M,D
Inorganic Chemistry	M,D
Interdisciplinary Studies	D
International Affairs	M,D
Italian	M,D
Jewish Studies	M,O
Landscape Architecture	M
Legal and Justice Studies	M,D
Library Science	D
Linguistics	D
Marine Biology	M,D
Materials Engineering	M,D
Materials Sciences	M,D
Mathematics Education	M,D
Mathematics	M,D
Mechanical Engineering	M,D
Mechanics	M,D
Medical Microbiology	M,D
Medicinal and Pharmaceutical Chemistry	M,D
Medieval and Renaissance Studies	D
Microbiology	M,D
Molecular Biology	M,D
Molecular Biophysics	D
Molecular Genetics	M,D
Molecular Pharmacology	M,D
Molecular Physiology	M,D
Multilingual and Multicultural Education	M,D
Music Education	M,D,O
Music	M,D,O
Neuroscience	M,D
Nutrition	M,D
Oceanography	M,D
Operations Research	D
Organic Chemistry	M,D
Pharmaceutical Sciences	M,D
Pharmacy	M,D
Philosophy	D
Physical Chemistry	M,D
Physics	M,D
Physiology	M,D
Plant Biology	M,D
Plant Molecular Biology	M,D
Plant Pathology	M,D
Political Science	M,D
Psychology—General	D
Public Health—General	M,D
Public Policy	M,D
Quality Management	M,D
Reading Education	M,D
Reliability Engineering	M,D
Religion	M,O
Reproductive Biology	M,D
School Psychology	M,D
Science Education	M,D
Social Psychology	D
Social Sciences Education	M,D
Social Work	M,D
Sociology	M,D
Spanish	M,D
Special Education	M,D
Statistics	M,D
Student Affairs	M
Systems Biology	D
Systems Engineering	M,D
Theater	M
Theoretical Physics	M,D
Toxicology	M,D
Translation and Interpretation	M,D
Translational Biology	M
Urban and Regional Planning	M,D
Virology	M,D
Water Resources	M,D
Women's Studies	M,D
Writing	M

RYERSON UNIVERSITY

Arts Administration	M
Business Administration and Management—General	M
Management of Technology	M

SACRED HEART MAJOR SEMINARY

Pastoral Ministry and Counseling	M
Theology	M

SACRED HEART SEMINARY AND SCHOOL OF THEOLOGY

Theology	M,O

SACRED HEART UNIVERSITY

Accounting	M,O
Applied Psychology	M
Business Administration and Management—General	M,O
Chemistry	M
Communication Disorders	M
Communication—General	M
Computer and Information Systems Security	M
Computer Science	M
Criminal Justice and Criminology	M
Education—General	M,O
Educational Leadership and Administration	O
Exercise and Sports Science	M
Family Nurse Practitioner Studies	M,D,O
Film, Television, and Video Production	M
Finance and Banking	M,D,O
Game Design and Development	M
Health Informatics	M
Human Resources Management	M,O
Industrial and Organizational Psychology	M
Information Science	M

Investment Management	M,D,O
Journalism	M
Marketing	M,O
Molecular Biology	M
Nursing and Healthcare Administration	M,D,O
Nursing Education	M,D,O
Nursing—General	M,D,O
Nutrition	M
Occupational Therapy	M
Physical Therapy	D
Physician Assistant Studies	M
Public Administration	M
Public Health—General	M
Reading Education	O
Social Psychology	M
Social Work	M

SAGE GRADUATE SCHOOL

Applied Behavior Analysis	M,O
Business Administration and Management—General	M
Counseling Psychology	M
Counselor Education	M,O
Education—General	M,D,O
Educational Leadership and Administration	D
Elementary Education	M
Family Nurse Practitioner Studies	M
Forensic Psychology	M,O
Gerontological Nursing	M,O
Gerontology	M
Health Education	M
Health Services Management and Hospital Administration	M
Nursing Education	D
Nursing—General	M,D,O
Nutrition	M,O
Occupational Therapy	M
Organizational Management	M
Physical Therapy	D
Psychiatric Nursing	M,O
Psychology—General	M,O
Reading Education	M
Social Psychology	M
Special Education	M

SAGINAW VALLEY STATE UNIVERSITY

Business Administration and Management—General	M
Chinese	M
Communication—General	M
Computer and Information Systems Security	M
Computer Science	M
Early Childhood Education	M
Education—General	M,O
Educational Leadership and Administration	M,O
Educational Media/Instructional Technology	M
Energy and Power Engineering	M
Engineering and Applied Sciences—General	M
Family Nurse Practitioner Studies	M,D
Foreign Languages Education	M
Health Services Management and Hospital Administration	M
Media Studies	M
Nursing—General	M
Occupational Therapy	M
Public Administration	M
Reading Education	M
Social Work	M
Special Education	M

ST. AMBROSE UNIVERSITY

Accounting	M
Business Administration and Management—General	M,D
Communication Disorders	M
Criminal Justice and Criminology	M
Early Childhood Education	M
Education—General	M
Educational Leadership and Administration	M
Exercise and Sports Science	M
Health Services Management and Hospital Administration	M,D
Human Resources Management	M
Management of Technology	M
Occupational Therapy	D
Organizational Management	M
Pastoral Ministry and Counseling	M
Physical Therapy	D
Physician Assistant Studies	M
Public Health—General	M
Social Work	M

ST. ANDREW'S COLLEGE

Theology	M,D,O

ST. ANDREW'S COLLEGE IN WINNIPEG

Theology	M

SAINT ANTHONY COLLEGE OF NURSING

Nursing—General	M

ST. AUGUSTINE'S SEMINARY OF TORONTO

Pastoral Ministry and Counseling	M,O
Religious Education	M,O
Theology	M,O

ST. BERNARD'S SCHOOL OF THEOLOGY AND MINISTRY

Pastoral Ministry and Counseling	M,O
Theology	M,O

ST. BONAVENTURE UNIVERSITY

Accounting	M
Business Administration and Management—General	M
Corporate and Organizational Communication	M

Counseling Psychology	M,O
Counselor Education	M,O
Early Childhood Education	M
Education of the Gifted	M,O
Education—General	M,O
Educational Leadership and Administration	M,O
Marketing	M
Middle School Education	M
Reading Education	M
Rehabilitation Counseling	M
Secondary Education	M
Social Psychology	M
Special Education	M,O

ST. CATHERINE UNIVERSITY

Adult Nursing	M,D
Business Administration and Management—General	M
Curriculum and Instruction	M
Early Childhood Education	M
Education—General	M,O
Gerontological Nursing	M,D
Health Informatics	M
Health Services Management and Hospital Administration	M
Information Studies	M
International Health	M
Library Science	M
Marketing	M
Nursing Education	M,D
Nursing—General	M,D
Occupational Therapy	M,D
Organizational Management	M
Pastoral Ministry and Counseling	M,O
Pediatric Nursing	M,D
Physical Therapy	D
Physician Assistant Studies	M
Public Health—General	M
Social Work	M,D
Theology	M,O

SAINT CHARLES BORROMEO SEMINARY, OVERBROOK

Philosophy	M
Theology	M

ST. CLOUD STATE UNIVERSITY

Applied Behavior Analysis	M
Applied Economics	M
Archaeology	M,O
Biological and Biomedical Sciences—General	M
Biomedical Engineering	M
Business Administration and Management—General	M
Child and Family Studies	M
Communication Disorders	M
Computer and Information Systems Security	M
Computer Science	M,O
Counselor Education	M
Criminal Justice and Criminology	M
Economics	M
Education—General	M,D,O
Educational Leadership and Administration	M,D
Educational Media/Instructional Technology	M,O
Electrical Engineering	M
Engineering and Applied Sciences—General	M,O
English	M
Geography	M,O
Gerontology	M,O
Higher Education	D
Historic Preservation	M,O
History	M
Human Services	M
Industrial and Organizational Psychology	M
Marriage and Family Therapy	M
Mass Communication	M
Rhetoric	M
Social Work	M
Special Education	M,O
Student Affairs	M
Writing	M

ST. EDWARD'S UNIVERSITY

Accounting	M
Counseling Psychology	M
Education—General	M,O
Environmental Management and Policy	M
Humanities	M
Liberal Studies	M,O
Organizational Management	M
Student Affairs	M
Sustainable Development	M

ST. FRANCIS COLLEGE

Accounting	M

SAINT FRANCIS MEDICAL CENTER COLLEGE OF NURSING

Family Nurse Practitioner Studies	M,D,O
Gerontological Nursing	M,D,O
Maternal and Child/Neonatal Nursing	M,D,O
Medical/Surgical Nursing	M,D,O
Nursing and Healthcare Administration	M,D,O
Nursing Education	M,D,O
Nursing—General	M,D,O
Psychiatric Nursing	M,D,O

SAINT FRANCIS UNIVERSITY

Biological and Biomedical Sciences—General	M
Business Administration and Management—General	M
Cancer Biology/Oncology	M

Education—General	M
Educational Leadership and Administration	M
Health Education	M
Human Resources Management	M
Nursing and Healthcare Administration	M
Nursing Education	M
Nursing—General	M
Occupational Therapy	M
Physical Therapy	D
Physician Assistant Studies	M
Reading Education	M

ST. FRANCIS XAVIER UNIVERSITY

Adult Education	M
Biological and Biomedical Sciences—General	M
Chemistry	M
Computer Science	M
Cultural Studies	M
Curriculum and Instruction	M
Education—General	M
Educational Leadership and Administration	M
Geology	M
Geosciences	M
Urban and Regional Planning	M

ST. JOHN FISHER COLLEGE

Biological and Biomedical Sciences—General	M
Business Administration and Management—General	M
Chemistry	M
Counseling Psychology	M
Education—General	M,D,O
Educational Leadership and Administration	M,D
Educational Media/Instructional Technology	M
Elementary Education	M,O
English Education	M
Foreign Languages Education	M
French	M
Mathematics Education	M
Middle School Education	M
Nursing—General	M,D,O
Pharmacy	D
Physics	M
Reading Education	M
Science Education	M
Social Sciences Education	M
Special Education	M,O

ST. JOHN'S COLLEGE (MD)

Liberal Studies	M

ST. JOHN'S COLLEGE (NM)

Asian Languages	M
Asian Studies	M
Liberal Studies	M

ST. JOHN'S SEMINARY (CA)

Pastoral Ministry and Counseling	M
Theology	M

SAINT JOHN'S SEMINARY (MA)

Religion	M
Theology	M

SAINT JOHN'S UNIVERSITY (MN)

Music	M
Pastoral Ministry and Counseling	M
Theology	M

ST. JOHN'S UNIVERSITY (NY)

Accounting	M
Actuarial Science	M
Applied Mathematics	M
Asian Studies	M
Biological and Biomedical Sciences—General	M,D
Biotechnology	M
Business Administration and Management—General	M
Business Analytics	M
Chemistry	M
Clinical Psychology	M,D,O
Communication Disorders	M,D
Computational Sciences	M
Counseling Psychology	M,O
Counselor Education	M,O
Criminal Justice and Criminology	M
Curriculum and Instruction	D
Data Science/Data Analytics	M
Early Childhood Education	M,D,O
Education of the Gifted	D,O
Education—General	M,D,O
Educational Leadership and Administration	M,D,O
Elementary Education	M
English as a Second Language	M,O
English	M,D
Finance and Banking	M
History	M,D
Homeland Security	M
Information Science	M
Information Studies	M,O
Insurance	M
International and Comparative Education	D
International Business	M
Law	D
Legal and Justice Studies	M
Liberal Studies	M
Library Science	M,O
Management Information Systems	M
Management Strategy and Policy	M
Marketing	M
Mass Communication	M
Mathematics Education	D
Mathematics	M

Multilingual and Multicultural Education	M,O
Museum Studies	M
Pharmaceutical Administration	M
Pharmaceutical Sciences	M,D
Pharmacy	M,D
Political Science	M,O
Psychology—General	M
Public Administration	M,O
Public Health—General	M
Public History	M,D
Reading Education	M,D,O
Risk Management	M
School Psychology	M,D
Science Education	D
Secondary Education	M
Sociology	M
Spanish	M
Special Education	M,O
Sports Management	M
Statistics	M
Taxation	M
Theology	M
Toxicology	M

ST. JOSEPH'S COLLEGE, LONG ISLAND CAMPUS

Accounting	M
Adult Nursing	M
Business Administration and Management—General	M
Forensic Sciences	M
Gerontological Nursing	M
Health Informatics	M
Health Services Management and Hospital Administration	M
Human Resources Management	M
Human Services	M
Nursing Education	M
Nursing—General	M
Organizational Management	M
Special Education	M

ST. JOSEPH'S COLLEGE, NEW YORK

Accounting	M
Adult Nursing	M
Business Administration and Management—General	M
Education—General	M
Educational Leadership and Administration	M
Forensic Sciences	M
Gerontological Nursing	M
Health Informatics	M
Health Services Management and Hospital Administration	M
Human Resources Management	M
Human Services	M
Nursing Education	M
Nursing—General	M
Organizational Management	M
Reading Education	M
Special Education	M
Writing	M

SAINT JOSEPH'S COLLEGE OF MAINE

Accounting	M
Adult Education	M
Business Administration and Management—General	M
Education—General	M
Educational Leadership and Administration	M
Family Nurse Practitioner Studies	M,O
Health Education	M
Health Services Management and Hospital Administration	M
Nursing and Healthcare Administration	M,O
Nursing Education	M,O
Nursing—General	M,O
Pastoral Ministry and Counseling	M

ST. JOSEPH'S SEMINARY

Pastoral Ministry and Counseling	M
Religion	M
Theology	M

SAINT JOSEPH'S UNIVERSITY

Accounting	M,O
Biological and Biomedical Sciences—General	M
Business Administration and Management—General	M,O
Business Analytics	M
Communication Disorders	M,D,O
Computer Science	M,O
Criminal Justice and Criminology	M,O
Curriculum and Instruction	M,D,O
Early Childhood Education	M,D,O
Education—General	M,D,O
Educational Leadership and Administration	M,D,O
Elementary Education	M,D,O
Finance and Banking	M,O
Health Informatics	M
Health Services Management and Hospital Administration	M,O
Human Resources Management	M,O
International Business	M,O
Law	M,O
Marketing	M,O
Mathematics	M,O
Middle School Education	M,D,O
Psychology—General	M,O
Reading Education	M,D,O
Secondary Education	M,D,O
Special Education	M,D,O
Writing	M

SAINT LEO UNIVERSITY

Accounting	M,D
Agricultural Education	M,D

Business Administration and Management—General	M,D
Computer and Information Systems Security	M,D
Criminal Justice and Criminology	M,D
Education—General	M,D,O
Educational Leadership and Administration	M,D,O
Emergency Management	M,D
Forensic Sciences	M,D
Health Services Management and Hospital Administration	M,D
Human Resources Management	M,D
Human Services	M
Legal and Justice Studies	M,D
Marketing Research	M,D
Marketing	M,D
Psychology—General	M
Social Work	M
Theology	M,O
Writing	M

ST. LOUIS COLLEGE OF PHARMACY

Pharmacy	D

SAINT LOUIS UNIVERSITY

Accounting	M
Allied Health—General	M,D,O
Allopathic Medicine	D
American Studies	M,D
Anatomy	M,D
Applied Behavior Analysis	M,D
Athletic Training and Sports Medicine	M,D
Biochemistry	D
Bioethics	D,O
Bioinformatics	M
Biological and Biomedical Sciences—General	M,D*
Biomedical Engineering	M,D
Business Administration and Management—General	M
Chemistry	M,D
Clinical Psychology	M
Communication Disorders	M
Communication—General	M
Community Health	M
Computational Biology	M
Computer Science	M
Criminal Justice and Criminology	M,D
Curriculum and Instruction	M,D
Dentistry	M
Education—General	M,D
Educational Leadership and Administration	M,D,O
Emergency Management	M
English	M,D
Experimental Psychology	M,D
Finance and Banking	M
Foundations and Philosophy of Education	M,D
French	M
Geophysics	M,D
Geosciences	M,D
Health Services Management and Hospital Administration	M,D
Higher Education	M,D,O
History	M,D
Immunology	D
Industrial and Organizational Psychology	M,D
International Business	M,D
Law	M,D
Mathematics	M,D
Meteorology	M,D
Microbiology	D
Molecular Biology	D
Nursing—General	M,D,O
Nutrition	M
Occupational Therapy	M
Oral and Dental Sciences	M
Pathology	D
Pharmacology	M,D
Philosophy	M,D
Physical Therapy	M,D
Physician Assistant Studies	M
Physiology	D
Political Science	M
Psychology—General	M,D
Public Health—General	M,D
Social Work	M
Software Engineering	M
Spanish	M
Special Education	M,D
Student Affairs	M,D,O
Theology	M,D
Urban and Regional Planning	M

SAINT LOUIS UNIVERSITY–MADRID CAMPUS

English	M
Spanish	M

SAINT MARTIN'S UNIVERSITY

Business Administration and Management—General	M
Civil Engineering	M
Counseling Psychology	M
Education—General	M
Engineering Management	M
Mechanical Engineering	M
Social Psychology	M

SAINT MARY-OF-THE-WOODS COLLEGE

Art Therapy	M,O
Health Services Management and Hospital Administration	M
Management Strategy and Policy	M
Nonprofit Management	M
Nursing—General	M
Organizational Management	M

M—masters degree; D—doctorate; O—other advanced degree; *—Close-Up and/or Display

Therapies—Dance, Drama, and Music — M

SAINT MARY'S COLLEGE
Adult Nursing — D
Communication Disorders — M
Data Science/Data Analytics — M
Family Nurse Practitioner Studies — D
Gerontological Nursing — D
Nursing—General — D

SAINT MARY'S COLLEGE OF CALIFORNIA
Accounting — M
Business Administration and Management—General — M
Business Analytics — M
Conflict Resolution and Mediation/Peace Studies — M
Counselor Education — M,O
Dance — M
Early Childhood Education — M
Education—General — M,D,O
Educational Leadership and Administration — M,D,O
Exercise and Sports Science — M
Finance and Banking — M
Investment Management — M
Kinesiology and Movement Studies — M
Marriage and Family Therapy — M,O
Organizational Management — M
School Psychology — M,O
Special Education — M
Sports Management — M
Writing — M

ST. MARY'S COLLEGE OF MARYLAND
Education—General — M

SAINT MARY SEMINARY AND GRADUATE SCHOOL OF THEOLOGY
Theology — M,D

ST. MARY'S SEMINARY AND UNIVERSITY
Theology — M,D,O

SAINT MARY'S UNIVERSITY (CANADA)
Applied Psychology — M,D
Applied Science and Technology — M
Astronomy — M,D
Business Administration and Management—General — M,D
Canadian Studies — M,O
Criminal Justice and Criminology — M
Gender Studies — M
History — M
Industrial and Organizational Psychology — M,D
International Development — M,O
Philosophy — M
Psychology—General — M,D
Religion — M
Theology — M
Women's Studies — M

ST. MARY'S UNIVERSITY (UNITED STATES)
Business Administration and Management—General — M
Communication—General — M
Computer and Information Systems Security — M,O
Computer Engineering — M
Computer Science — M
Conflict Resolution and Mediation/Peace Studies — M,O
Counseling Psychology — M
Counselor Education — D
Criminal Justice and Criminology — M
Education—General — M
Educational Leadership and Administration — M
Electrical Engineering — M
Engineering Management — M
English — M
Environmental Law — M
Health Law — M
Homeland Security — M,O
Industrial and Organizational Psychology — M
Industrial/Management Engineering — M
Information Science — M
International Affairs — M,O
International Development — M,O
Law — M,D
Legal and Justice Studies — M
Public Administration — M,O
Software Engineering — M,O
Theology — M

SAINT MARY'S UNIVERSITY OF MINNESOTA
Accounting — M
Business Administration and Management—General — M,D
Computer and Information Systems Security — M
Counseling Psychology — M,D,O
Data Science/Data Analytics — M
Education—General — M,O
Educational Leadership and Administration — M,D,O
Educational Media/Instructional Technology — M
Elementary Education — M
Geographic Information Systems — M,O
Health Services Management and Hospital Administration — M
Human Development — M
Human Resources Management — M
International Development — M
Marriage and Family Therapy — M
Nurse Anesthesia — M

Organizational Management — M
Philanthropic Studies — M
Project Management — M
Public Administration — M
Reading Education — M,O
Religious Education — M
Secondary Education — M
Special Education — M,O

SAINT MEINRAD SCHOOL OF THEOLOGY
Theology — M

SAINT MICHAEL'S COLLEGE
Art Education — M,O
Clinical Psychology — M
Education—General — M,O
Educational Leadership and Administration — M,O
English as a Second Language — M,O
Reading Education — M,O
Special Education — M,O

ST. NORBERT COLLEGE
Business Administration and Management—General — M
Health Services Management and Hospital Administration — M
Liberal Studies — M
Supply Chain Management — M
Theology — M

ST. PATRICK'S SEMINARY & UNIVERSITY
Theology — M,O

SAINT PAUL SCHOOL OF THEOLOGY
Theology — M,D

SAINT PAUL UNIVERSITY
Conflict Resolution and Mediation/Peace Studies — M
Counseling Psychology — M
Marriage and Family Therapy — M
Missions and Missiology — M
Pastoral Ministry and Counseling — M,D,O
Theology — M,D,O

ST. PETER'S SEMINARY
Theology — M

SAINT PETER'S UNIVERSITY
Accounting — M
Adult Nursing — M,D,O
Applied Behavior Analysis — M,D,O
Business Administration and Management—General — M
Counselor Education — M,O
Criminal Justice and Criminology — M
Data Science/Data Analytics — M
Education—General — M,D,O
Educational Leadership and Administration — M,D
Elementary Education — M,O
Family and Consumer Sciences-General — M
Finance and Banking — M
Health Services Management and Hospital Administration — M
Higher Education — M,D
Human Resources Management — M
International Business — M
Management Information Systems — M
Marketing — M
Mathematics Education — M,D,O
Middle School Education — M,O
Nursing and Healthcare Administration — M,D,O
Nursing—General — M,D,O
Public Administration — M
Reading Education — M,O
Risk Management — M
Secondary Education — M,O
Special Education — M

SAINTS CYRIL AND METHODIUS SEMINARY
Pastoral Ministry and Counseling — M
Religious Education — M
Theology — M

ST. STEPHEN'S COLLEGE
Pastoral Ministry and Counseling — M,D
Theology — M

ST. THOMAS AQUINAS COLLEGE
Business Administration and Management—General — M
Education—General — M,O
Educational Leadership and Administration — M,O
Elementary Education — M,O
Finance and Banking — M
Marketing — M
Middle School Education — M,O
Reading Education — M,O
Secondary Education — M,O
Special Education — M,O

ST. THOMAS UNIVERSITY
Accounting — M,O
Arts Administration — M
Business Administration and Management—General — M,O
Communication—General — M,D,O
Counseling Psychology — M
Counselor Education — M,O
Criminal Justice and Criminology — M,O
Education of the Gifted — M,D,O
Education—General — M,D,O
Educational Leadership and Administration — M,D,O
Educational Media/Instructional Technology — M,D,O
Elementary Education — M,D,O
English as a Second Language — M,D,O
Film, Television, and Video Production — M

Geosciences — M,D,O
Health Services Management and Hospital Administration — M,O
Hispanic Studies — M,O
Human Resources Management — M,O
International Business — M,O
Law — M,D
Marriage and Family Therapy — M,O
Pastoral Ministry and Counseling — M,D,O
Planetary and Space Sciences — M,D,O
Public Administration — M,O
Reading Education — M,D,O
Special Education — M,D,O
Sports Management — M,O
Taxation — M,D
Theology — M,D,O

ST. TIKHON'S ORTHODOX THEOLOGICAL SEMINARY
Theology — M

SAINT VINCENT COLLEGE
Business Administration and Management—General — M
Curriculum and Instruction — M
Education—General — M
Educational Leadership and Administration — M
Educational Media/Instructional Technology — M
Nurse Anesthesia — M,D
Special Education — M

ST. VINCENT DE PAUL REGIONAL SEMINARY
Theology — M

SAINT VINCENT SEMINARY
Pastoral Ministry and Counseling — M
Theology — M

ST. VLADIMIR'S ORTHODOX THEOLOGICAL SEMINARY
Theology — M,D

SAINT XAVIER UNIVERSITY
Business Administration and Management—General — M,O
Communication Disorders — M
Computer Science — M
Counselor Education — M
Curriculum and Instruction — M
Early Childhood Education — M
Education—General — M
Educational Leadership and Administration — M
Educational Media/Instructional Technology — M
Elementary Education — M
English as a Second Language — M
Finance and Banking — M,O
Foreign Languages Education — M
Health Services Management and Hospital Administration — M,O
Marketing — M
Music Education — M
Nursing—General — M,O
Project Management — M,O
Reading Education — M
Science Education — M
Secondary Education — M
Spanish — M
Special Education — M

SALEM COLLEGE
Art Education — M
Counselor Education — M
Education—General — M
Elementary Education — M
English as a Second Language — M
Middle School Education — M
Music — M
Reading Education — M
Secondary Education — M
Special Education — M

SALEM INTERNATIONAL UNIVERSITY
Business Administration and Management—General — M
Computer and Information Systems Security — M
Curriculum and Instruction — M
Education—General — M
Educational Leadership and Administration — M
International Business — M

SALEM STATE UNIVERSITY
Art Education — M
Business Administration and Management—General — M
Counseling Psychology — M,O
Counselor Education — M
Criminal Justice and Criminology — M
Early Childhood Education — M
Educational Leadership and Administration — M
Educational Media/Instructional Technology — M
Elementary Education — M
English as a Second Language — M
English — M
Geography — M
Gerontological Nursing — M
Higher Education — M
History — M
Mathematics Education — M
Mathematics — M
Middle School Education — M
Nursing and Healthcare Administration — M
Nursing Education — M
Nursing—General — M
Occupational Therapy — M
Physical Education — M
Psychology—General — M,O

Reading Education — M
Science Education — M
Secondary Education — M
Social Work — M
Spanish — M
Special Education — M

SALISBURY UNIVERSITY
American Studies — M
Athletic Training and Sports Medicine — M
Biological and Biomedical Sciences—General — M
Business Administration and Management—General — M
Conflict Resolution and Mediation/Peace Studies — M
Curriculum and Instruction — M
Educational Leadership and Administration — M
English — M
Family Nurse Practitioner Studies — D
Geographic Information Systems — M
History — M
Mathematics Education — M
Middle School Education — M
Nursing and Healthcare Administration — M,D
Nursing Education — M
Nursing—General — M,D
Physiology — M
Reading Education — M,D
Secondary Education — M
Social Work — M

SALUS UNIVERSITY
Communication Disorders — M,D,O
Occupational Therapy — M,O
Optometry — D
Physician Assistant Studies — M
Public Health—General — M
Rehabilitation Sciences — M,O
Special Education — M,O
Vision Sciences — M,O

SALVE REGINA UNIVERSITY
Addictions/Substance Abuse Counseling — M,O
Applied Behavior Analysis — M,O
Business Administration and Management—General — M,O
Business Education — M,O
Computer and Information Systems Security — M,O
Conflict Resolution and Mediation/Peace Studies — M,D
Counseling Psychology — M,O
Criminal Justice and Criminology — M,O
Entrepreneurship — M
Forensic Sciences — M,O
Health Services Management and Hospital Administration — M,O
Homeland Security — M,O
Human Resources Management — M,O
Humanities — M,D
International Affairs — M,D,O
Management Strategy and Policy — M,O
Nonprofit Management — M,O
Nursing—General — D
Organizational Management — M,O
Rehabilitation Counseling — M,O
Religion — M,D
Writing — M

SAMFORD UNIVERSITY
Accounting — M
Athletic Training and Sports Medicine — M,D
Business Administration and Management—General — M
Communication Disorders — M,D
Education of the Gifted — M,D,O
Education—General — M,D,O
Educational Leadership and Administration — M,D,O
Educational Media/Instructional Technology — M,D,O
Elementary Education — M,D,O
Energy Management and Policy — M
Entrepreneurship — M
Environmental Management and Policy — M
Family Nurse Practitioner Studies — M,D
Finance and Banking — M
Health Informatics — M
Health Services Management and Hospital Administration — M
Law — M,D
Marketing — M
Music Education — M
Music — M
Nurse Anesthesia — M,D
Nursing and Healthcare Administration — M,D
Nursing Informatics — M,D
Nursing—General — M,D
Nutrition — M
Pharmacy — D
Physical Therapy — M,D
Public Health—General — M
Secondary Education — M,D,O
Social Work — M
Special Education — M,D,O
Theology — M

SAM HOUSTON STATE UNIVERSITY
Accounting — M
Agricultural Sciences—General — M
Allied Health—General — M
Biological and Biomedical Sciences—General — M
Business Administration and Management—General — M
Chemistry — M

Clinical Psychology — M,D,O
Communication—General — M
Computational Sciences — M,D
Computer and Information
  Systems Security — M,D
Computer Science — M,D
Counselor Education — M,D
Criminal Justice and Criminology — M,D
Curriculum and Instruction — M,D
Dance — M
Developmental Education — M,D
Education—General — M,D
Educational Leadership and
  Administration — M,D
English — M
Family and Consumer
  Sciences-General — M
Finance and Banking — M
Forensic Sciences — M,D
Geographic Information Systems — M,O
Higher Education — M,D
History — M
Homeland Security — M
Humanities — M,D,O
Information Science — M,D
Internet and Interactive
  Multimedia — M
Kinesiology and Movement Studies — M
Library Science — M
Mathematics — M
Music — M
Nutrition — M
Political Science — M
Project Management — M
Psychology—General — M,D,O
Public Administration — M
Publishing — M
Reading Education — M,D
School Psychology — M,D,O
Sociology — M
Spanish — M
Special Education — M,D
Sports Management — M
Statistics — M
Writing — M

SAMUEL MERRITT UNIVERSITY

Family Nurse Practitioner Studies — M,D,O
Nurse Anesthesia — M,D,O
Nursing and Healthcare
  Administration — M,D,O
Nursing—General — M,D,O
Occupational Therapy — D
Physical Therapy — D
Physician Assistant Studies — M
Podiatric Medicine — D

SAN DIEGO CHRISTIAN COLLEGE

Education—General — M
Organizational Management — M

SAN DIEGO STATE UNIVERSITY

Accounting — M
Advertising and Public Relations — M
Aerospace/Aeronautical
  Engineering — M,D
Anthropology — M
Applied Arts and Design—
  General — M
Applied Mathematics — M
Art/Fine Arts — M
Asian Studies — M
Astronomy — M
Biochemistry — M,D
Biological and Biomedical
  Sciences—General — M,D
Biometry — M
Biostatistics — M,D
Business Administration and
  Management—General — M
Cell Biology — M,D
Chemistry — M,D
Child and Family Studies — M
Child Development — M
Civil Engineering — M
Clinical Psychology — M,D
Communication Disorders — M,D
Communication—General — M
Computational Sciences — M,D
Computer Science — M
Counselor Education — M
Criminal Justice and Criminology — M
Curriculum and Instruction — M
Ecology — M,D
Economics — M
Education—General — M,D
Educational Leadership and
  Administration — M
Educational Media/Instructional
  Technology — M,D
Electrical Engineering — M
Elementary Education — M
Emergency Management — M,D
Emergency Medical Services — M,D
Engineering and Applied
  Sciences—General — M,D
Engineering Design — M
English as a Second Language — M,O
English — M
Entrepreneurship — M
Environmental and Occupational
  Health — M,D
Epidemiology — M,D
Exercise and Sports Science — M
Film, Television, and Video
  Production — M
Finance and Banking — M
Gender Studies — O
Geography — M
Geology — M
Gerontology — M
Graphic Design — M

Health Physics/Radiological Health — M
Health Promotion — M,D
Health Psychology — M,D
Health Services Management and
  Hospital Administration — M,D
Higher Education — M
History — M
Hospitality Management — M
Human Resources Management — M
Industrial and Organizational
  Psychology — M,D
Interdisciplinary Studies — M
Interior Design — M
International Health — M,D
Internet and Interactive
  Multimedia — M
Kinesiology and Movement Studies — M
Latin American Studies — M
Liberal Studies — M
Linguistics — M,O
Management Information Systems — M
Marketing — M
Mathematics Education — M
Mathematics — M,D
Mechanical Engineering — M,D
Mechanics — M,D
Media Studies — M
Microbiology — M
Molecular Biology — M,D
Multilingual and Multicultural
  Education — M,D
Music Education — M
Music — M
Nursing—General — M
Nutrition — M
Pharmaceutical Administration — M
Philosophy — M
Photography — M
Physical Therapy — D
Physics — M
Political Science — M
Psychology—General — M,D
Public Administration — M
Public Health—General — M,D
Reading Education — M
Rehabilitation Counseling — M
Rhetoric — M
Romance Languages — M
School Psychology — M
Science Education — M,D
Secondary Education — M
Social Work — M
Sociology — M
Spanish — M
Special Education — M
Sports Management — M
Statistics — M
Telecommunications
  Management — M
Theater — M
Toxicology — M,D
Travel and Tourism — M
Urban and Regional Planning — M
Western European Studies — M
Women's Studies — M
Writing — M

SANFORD BURNHAM PREBYS MEDICAL DISCOVERY INSTITUTE

Biological and Biomedical
  Sciences—General — D

SAN FRANCISCO ART INSTITUTE

Art History — M
Art/Fine Arts — M,O
Museum Studies — M

SAN FRANCISCO CONSERVATORY OF MUSIC

Music Education — M,O
Music — M,O

SAN FRANCISCO STATE UNIVERSITY

Accounting — M
Acute Care/Critical Care Nursing — M,O
Adult Education — M
Anthropology — M
Applied Arts and Design—
  General — M
Archaeology — M
Art/Fine Arts — M
Asian-American Studies — M
Astronomy — M
Biochemistry — M
Biological and Biomedical
  Sciences—General — M
Biological Anthropology — M
Biotechnology — M
Business Administration and
  Management—General — M
Cell Biology — M
Chemistry — M
Chinese — M
Classics — M
Clinical Psychology — M,O
Communication Disorders — M
Community Health Nursing — M,O
Community Health — M
Comparative Literature — M
Computer Science — M
Criminal Justice and Criminology — M
Cultural Anthropology — M
Cultural Studies — M
Developmental Biology — M
Developmental Psychology — M,O
Early Childhood Education — M,D,O
Ecology — M
Economics — M
Education—General — M,D,O
Educational Leadership and
  Administration — M,D,O

Educational Media/Instructional
  Technology — M
Electrical Engineering — M
Elementary Education — M
Energy and Power
  Engineering — M
Engineering and Applied
  Sciences—General — M
English as a Second Language — M
English Education — M,O
English — M
Entrepreneurship — M
Environmental Management
  and Policy — M
Ethnic Studies — M
Family and Consumer
  Sciences-General — M
Family Nurse Practitioner Studies — M,O
Film, Television, and Video
  Production — M
Film, Television, and Video
  Theory and Criticism — M
Finance and Banking — M
French — M
Geographic Information Systems — M
Geography — M
Geosciences — M
German — M
Gerontology — M
Health Education — M
Health Services Management and
  Hospital Administration — M
History — M
Hospitality Management — M
Humanities — M
Industrial and Manufacturing
  Management — M
Industrial and Organizational
  Psychology — M,O
International Affairs — M
International Business — M
Italian — M
Japanese — M
Kinesiology and Movement Studies — M
Legal and Justice Studies — M
Leisure Studies — M
Liberal Studies — M
Linguistics — M
Management Information Systems — M
Marine Biology — M
Marine Sciences — M
Marketing — M
Marriage and Family Therapy — M
Mathematics Education — M,O
Mathematics — M
Media Studies — M
Microbiology — M
Molecular Biology — M
Museum Studies — M
Music Education — M
Music — M
Nonprofit Management — M
Nursing and Healthcare
  Administration — M,O
Nursing—General — M,O
Pediatric Nursing — M,O
Philosophy — M
Physical Therapy — D
Physics — M
Physiology — M
Political Science — M
Psychology—General — M,O
Public Administration — M
Public Health—General — M
Public Policy — M
Quantitative Analysis — M
Reading Education — M,O
Recreation and Park Management — M
School Psychology — M,O
Secondary Education — M,O
Social Psychology — M,O
Social Work — M
Spanish — M
Special Education — M,D,O
Speech and Interpersonal
  Communication — M
Sustainability Management — M
Theater — M
Travel and Tourism — M
Women's Health Nursing — M,O
Women's Studies — M
Writing — M

SAN FRANCISCO THEOLOGICAL SEMINARY

Theology — M,D

SAN IGNACIO UNIVERSITY

Business Administration and
  Management—General — M
Early Childhood Education — M
Education—General — M
Educational Leadership and
  Administration — M
Hospitality Management — M
Human Resources Management — M
International Business — M
Marketing — M
Special Education — M
Travel and Tourism — M

SAN JOAQUIN COLLEGE OF LAW

Law — D

SAN JOSE STATE UNIVERSITY

Aerospace/Aeronautical
  Engineering — M
Anthropology — M
Applied Economics — M
Biological and Biomedical
  Sciences—General — M
Chemical Engineering — M

Chemistry — M
Child and Family Studies — M
Civil Engineering — M
Clinical Psychology — M
Communication Disorders — M
Communication—General — M
Computer Engineering — M
Counselor Education — M
Criminal Justice and Criminology — M
Curriculum and Instruction — M,O
Ecology — M
Economics — M
Educational Leadership and
  Administration — M,D
Electrical Engineering — M
Elementary Education — M,O
English as a Second Language — M,O
Environmental Management
  and Policy — M
Experimental Psychology — M
Film, Television, and Video
  Production — M
Geographic Information Systems — M
Geography — M,O
Geology — M
Gerontological Nursing — M,O
Higher Education — M,D
History — M
Industrial and Organizational
  Psychology — M
Industrial/Management
  Engineering — M
Kinesiology and Movement Studies — M
Linguistics — M,O
Marine Sciences — M
Mass Communication — M
Materials Engineering — M
Mechanical Engineering — M
Meteorology — M
Microbiology — M
Molecular Biology — M
Nursing and Healthcare
  Administration — M,O
Nursing Education — M,O
Nursing—General — M,O
Nutrition — M
Occupational Therapy — M
Philosophy — M
Physics — M
Physiology — M
Psychology—General — M
Public Administration — M
Quality Management — M
Reading Education — M,O
Sociology — M
Software Engineering — M
Special Education — M
Speech and Interpersonal
  Communication — M
Student Affairs — M
Systems Engineering — M
Theater — M

SAN JUAN BAUTISTA SCHOOL OF MEDICINE

Allopathic Medicine — M,D
Public Health—General — M,D

THE SANS TECHNOLOGY INSTITUTE

Computer and Information
  Systems Security — M

THE SANTA BARBARA AND VENTURA COLLEGES OF LAW–SANTA BARBARA

Law — M,D
Legal and Justice Studies — M,D

THE SANTA BARBARA AND VENTURA COLLEGES OF LAW–VENTURA

Law — M,D
Legal and Justice Studies — M,D

SANTA CLARA UNIVERSITY

Applied Mathematics — M,D,O
Bioengineering — M,D,O
Business Administration and
  Management—General — M
Business Analytics — M
Civil Engineering — M,D,O
Computer Engineering — M,D,O
Computer Science — M,D,O
Counseling Psychology — M,O
Counselor Education — M,O
Education—General — M,O
Educational Leadership and
  Administration — M,O
Electrical Engineering — M,D,O
Energy and Power
  Engineering — M,D,O
Engineering and Applied
  Sciences—General — M,D,O
Engineering Management — M,D,O
Ethics — M,D,O
Finance and Banking — M
Intellectual Property Law — M,D,O
Law — M,D,O
Management Information Systems — M
Mechanical Engineering — M,D,O
Pastoral Ministry and Counseling — M
Religion — M,D,O
Software Engineering — M,D,O
Supply Chain Management — M
Theology — M,D,O

SARAH LAWRENCE COLLEGE

Child Development — M
Dance — M
Education—General — M
Genetic Counseling — M
History — M
Human Genetics — M
Kinesiology and Movement Studies — M
Public Health—General — M

M—masters degree; D—doctorate; O—other advanced degree; *—Close-Up and/or Display

Theater — M
Women's Studies — M
Writing — M

SAVANNAH COLLEGE OF ART AND DESIGN
Advertising and Public Relations — M
Applied Arts and Design— General — M
Architectural History — M
Architecture — M
Art History — M
Art/Fine Arts — M
Arts Administration — M
Clothing and Textiles — M
Computer Art and Design — M
Film, Television, and Video Production — M
Film, Television, and Video Theory and Criticism — M
Game Design and Development — M
Graphic Design — M
Historic Preservation — M
Illustration — M
Industrial Design — M
Interior Design — M
Internet and Interactive Multimedia — M
Media Studies — M
Music — M
Photography — M
Sustainable Development — M
Textile Design — M
Theater — M
Travel and Tourism — M
Urban Design — M
Writing — M

SAVANNAH STATE UNIVERSITY
Business Administration and Management—General — M
Human Resources Management — M
Marine Sciences — M
Public Administration — M
Social Work — M
Urban and Regional Planning — M
Urban Studies — M

SAYBROOK UNIVERSITY
Clinical Psychology — M
Counseling Psychology — M,D
Health Psychology — M,D
Marriage and Family Therapy — M,D
Nutrition — M,D,O
Organizational Behavior — M,D
Organizational Management — M,D
Psychology—General — M,D
Sustainable Development — M,D
Transpersonal and Humanistic Psychology — M,D

SCHILLER INTERNATIONAL UNIVERSITY (GERMANY)
Business Administration and Management—General — M
International Business — M
Management Information Systems — M

SCHILLER INTERNATIONAL UNIVERSITY
Business Administration and Management—General — M
International Affairs — M
International Business — M

SCHILLER INTERNATIONAL UNIVERSITY (SPAIN)
Business Administration and Management—General — M
International Business — M

SCHILLER INTERNATIONAL UNIVERSITY (UNITED STATES)
Business Administration and Management—General — M
Finance and Banking — M
Hospitality Management — M
International Business — M
Management Information Systems — M
Travel and Tourism — M

SCHOOL OF ADVANCED AIR AND SPACE STUDIES
Military and Defense Studies — M

SCHOOL OF ARCHITECTURE AT TALIESIN
Architecture — M

SCHOOL OF THE ART INSTITUTE OF CHICAGO
Writing — M,O

SCHOOL OF VISUAL ARTS (NY)
Applied Arts and Design— General — M
Art Education — M
Art History — M
Art Therapy — M
Art/Fine Arts — M
Computer Art and Design — M
Cultural Studies — M
Film, Television, and Video Production — M
Graphic Design — M
Illustration — M
Internet and Interactive Multimedia — M
Photography — M
Writing — M

SCHREINER UNIVERSITY
Business Administration and Management—General — M
Education—General — M,O
Educational Leadership and Administration — M,O

Ethics — M

THE SCRIPPS RESEARCH INSTITUTE
Biological and Biomedical Sciences—General — D
Chemistry — D

SEATTLE INSTITUTE OF EAST ASIAN MEDICINE
Acupuncture and Oriental Medicine — M

SEATTLE PACIFIC UNIVERSITY
Adult Nursing — M,O
Business Administration and Management—General — M
Clinical Psychology — D
Computer and Information Systems Security — M
Counselor Education — M,D,O
Data Science/Data Analytics — M
Education—General — D
Educational Leadership and Administration — M,D,O
Educational Media/Instructional Technology — M
English as a Second Language — M
Family Nurse Practitioner Studies — M,O
Gerontological Nursing — M,O
Human Resources Management — M
Industrial and Organizational Psychology — M,D
Management Information Systems — M
Marriage and Family Therapy — M,O
Mathematics Education — M
Nursing and Healthcare Administration — M,O
Nursing Education — M,O
Nursing Informatics — M,O
Nursing—General — M
Reading Education — M
Religion — M,O
Science Education — M
Secondary Education — M
Sustainability Management — M
Theology — M,O
Writing — M

THE SEATTLE SCHOOL OF THEOLOGY AND PSYCHOLOGY
Counseling Psychology — M
Psychology—General — M
Religion — M
Theology — M

SEATTLE UNIVERSITY
Accounting — M
Adult Education — M,O
Arts Administration — M
Business Administration and Management—General — M,O
Business Analytics — M,O
Computer Science — M
Counselor Education — M,O
Criminal Justice and Criminology — M
Education—General — M,D,O
Educational Leadership and Administration — M,D,O
Engineering and Applied Sciences—General — M
English as a Second Language — M,O
Finance and Banking — M,O
Forensic Sciences — M,O
Health Law — M,D
Law — M,D
Marriage and Family Therapy — M
Nursing—General — D
Organizational Management — M,O
Pastoral Ministry and Counseling — M
Psychology—General — M
Public Administration — M
School Psychology — M,O
Social Work — M
Special Education — M,O
Sports Management — M
Theology — M,D,O
Transpersonal and Humanistic Psychology — M

SELMA UNIVERSITY
Pastoral Ministry and Counseling — M
Religion — M
Religious Education — M

SETON HALL UNIVERSITY
Accounting — M,O
Adult Nursing — M,D
Advertising and Public Relations — M
Allied Health—General — D
Allopathic Medicine — D
Analytical Chemistry — M,D
Asian Studies — M
Athletic Training and Sports Medicine — M
Biochemistry — M,D
Biological and Biomedical Sciences—General — M,D
Business Administration and Management—General — M,O
Chemistry — M,D
Communication Disorders — M
Communication—General — M
Corporate and Organizational Communication — M
Counseling Psychology — M,D
Counselor Education — M,D
Education—General — M,D,O
Educational Leadership and Administration — D,O
Educational Measurement and Evaluation — M,D,O
Educational Media/Instructional Technology — M
English — M
Entrepreneurship — M,O
Experimental Psychology — M
Finance and Banking — M,O

Gerontological Nursing — M,D
Health Law — M,D
Health Services Management and Hospital Administration — D
Higher Education — D
History — M,D
Inorganic Chemistry — M,D
International Affairs — M,O
International Business — M,O
International Health — M,O
Jewish Studies — M,O
Law — M,D
Management of Technology — M,O
Marketing — M,O
Marriage and Family Therapy — M,D
Microbiology — M,D
Molecular Biology — M,D
Museum Studies — M
Neuroscience — M,D
Nonprofit Management — M,O
Nursing and Healthcare Administration — M,D
Nursing Education — M,D
Nursing—General — M,D
Occupational Therapy — M
Organic Chemistry — M,D
Pastoral Ministry and Counseling — M,O
Pediatric Nursing — M,D
Physical Chemistry — M,D
Physical Therapy — D
Physician Assistant Studies — M
Psychology—General — M,O
Public Administration — M,O
Public Policy — M,O
Religion — M,O
School Nursing — M,D
School Psychology — M,O
Social Work — M
Special Education — M
Speech and Interpersonal Communication — M
Sport Psychology — M
Sports Management — M,O
Student Affairs — M
Supply Chain Management — M,O
Theology — M,O

SETON HILL UNIVERSITY
Accounting — M
Art Therapy — M
Business Administration and Management—General — M
Educational Media/Instructional Technology — M
Elementary Education — M
Entrepreneurship — M
Health Services Management and Hospital Administration — M
Middle School Education — M
Oral and Dental Sciences — M,O
Physician Assistant Studies — M
Special Education — M
Writing — M

SHASTA BIBLE COLLEGE
Educational Leadership and Administration — M
Pastoral Ministry and Counseling — M
Religious Education — M

SHAWNEE STATE UNIVERSITY
Curriculum and Instruction — M
Education—General — M
Occupational Therapy — M

SHAW UNIVERSITY
Curriculum and Instruction — M
Theology — M

SHENANDOAH UNIVERSITY
Adult Nursing — M,D,O
Allied Health—General — M,D,O
Applied Behavior Analysis — M
Athletic Training and Sports Medicine — M,D,O
Business Administration and Management—General — M,O
Early Childhood Education — M,D,O
Education—General — M,D,O
Family Nurse Practitioner Studies — M,D,O
Gerontological Nursing — M,D,O
Health Services Management and Hospital Administration — M,D,O
Music — M,D,O
Nurse Midwifery — M,D,O
Nursing and Healthcare Administration — M,D,O
Nursing Education — M,D,O
Nursing—General — M,D,O
Occupational Therapy — M,D,O
Pharmacy — D
Physical Therapy — M,D,O
Physician Assistant Studies — M,D,O
Psychiatric Nursing — M,D,O
Public Health—General — M,D,O
Writing — M,D,O

SHEPHERDS THEOLOGICAL SEMINARY
Pastoral Ministry and Counseling — M
Theology — M

SHEPHERD UNIVERSITY (WV)
Curriculum and Instruction — M

SHERMAN COLLEGE OF CHIROPRACTIC
Chiropractic — D

SHILOH UNIVERSITY
Pastoral Ministry and Counseling — M,D
Theology — M,D

SHIPPENSBURG UNIVERSITY OF PENNSYLVANIA
Biological and Biomedical Sciences—General — M

Business Administration and Management—General — M,D,O
Business Analytics — M,D,O
Clinical Psychology — M,D
Communication—General — M
Computer Science — M
Counselor Education — M
Criminal Justice and Criminology — M
Curriculum and Instruction — M
Early Childhood Education — M
Education—General — M,D
Educational Leadership and Administration — M,D
Elementary Education — M
Environmental Management and Policy — M
Finance and Banking — M,D,O
Foreign Languages Education — M
Geography — M
Health Services Management and Hospital Administration — M
History — M
Information Science — M
Logistics — M,D,O
Management Information Systems — M,D,O
Mathematics Education — M
Middle School Education — M
Organizational Management — M
Psychology—General — M
Public Administration — M
Public History — M
Reading Education — M
Science Education — M
Social Work — M
Sociology — M
Software Engineering — M,O
Special Education — M,D
Student Affairs — M,D
Supply Chain Management — M,D,O

SHORTER UNIVERSITY
Accounting — M
Business Administration and Management—General — M

SH'OR YOSHUV RABBINICAL COLLEGE
Theology — M

SIENA COLLEGE
Accounting — M
Business Administration and Management—General — M

SIENA HEIGHTS UNIVERSITY
Clinical Psychology — M,O
Counseling Psychology — M,O
Early Childhood Education — M,O
Education—General — M,O
Educational Leadership and Administration — M,O
Elementary Education — M,O
Health Services Management and Hospital Administration — M,O
Higher Education — M,O
Organizational Management — M,O
Reading Education — M,O
Secondary Education — M,O
Special Education — M,O

SIERRA NEVADA COLLEGE
Education—General — M
Educational Leadership and Administration — M
Elementary Education — M
Secondary Education — M

SILVER LAKE COLLEGE OF THE HOLY FAMILY
Business Administration and Management—General — M
Education—General — M
Educational Leadership and Administration — M
Music — M

SIMMONS UNIVERSITY
Applied Behavior Analysis — M,D,O
Business Administration and Management—General — M
Cultural Studies — M,D,O
Education of Students with Severe/Multiple Disabilities — M,D,O
Elementary Education — M,D,O
English — M,D,O
Family Nurse Practitioner Studies — M,D
Gender Studies — M,D,O
Health Promotion — M,D,O
Health Services Management and Hospital Administration — M,D,O
History — M,D,O
Nursing—General — M,D
Nutrition — M,D,O
Physical Therapy — M,D,O
Public Health—General — M,D,O
Public Policy — M,D,O
Social Work — M,D
Special Education — M,D,O
Writing — M,D,O

SIMON FRASER UNIVERSITY
Actuarial Science — M,D
Anthropology — M,D
Applied Mathematics — M,D
Archaeology — M,D
Art Education — M,D
Biochemistry — M,D,O
Bioinformatics — M,D,O
Biological and Biomedical Sciences—General — M,D,O
Biotechnology — M,D,O
Business Administration and Management—General — M,D,O
Chemistry — M,D
Communication—General — M,D
Comparative and Interdisciplinary Arts — M
Computational Sciences — M,D

Computer Science	M,D
Counselor Education	M,D
Criminal Justice and Criminology	M,D
Cultural Studies	D
Curriculum and Instruction	M,D
Economics	M,D
Education—General	M,D,O
Educational Leadership and Administration	M,D
Educational Media/Instructional Technology	M,D
Educational Psychology	M,D
Engineering and Applied Sciences—General	M,D
English as a Second Language	M
English Education	M,D
English	M,D
Entomology	M,D,O
Environmental Management and Policy	M,D,O
Finance and Banking	M,D,O
Fish, Game, and Wildlife Management	M,D,O
Foundations and Philosophy of Education	M,D
French	M
Gender Studies	M,D
Geography	M,D
Geosciences	M,D
Gerontology	M,D
History	M,D
Humanities	M
International Affairs	M
International Health	M,D,O
Kinesiology and Movement Studies	M,D
Latin American Studies	M,O
Legal and Justice Studies	M,D
Liberal Studies	M
Linguistics	M,D
Management of Technology	M,D,O
Mathematics Education	M,D
Mathematics	M,D
Mechanical Engineering	M,D
Molecular Biology	M,D,O
Operations Research	M,D
Philosophy	M,D
Physics	M,D
Political Science	M,D
Psychology—General	M,D
Public Health—General	M,D,O
Public Policy	M
Publishing	M
Reading Education	D
Sociology	M,D
Statistics	M,D
Systems Engineering	M,D
Toxicology	M,D,O
Urban Studies	M,O
Women's Studies	M,D

SIMPSON COLLEGE

Criminal Justice and Criminology	M
Education—General	M
Secondary Education	M

SIMPSON UNIVERSITY

Counseling Psychology	M
Curriculum and Instruction	M
Education—General	M
Educational Leadership and Administration	M
Missions and Missiology	M
Organizational Management	M
Pastoral Ministry and Counseling	M

SINTE GLESKA UNIVERSITY

Education—General	M
Elementary Education	M

SIOUX FALLS SEMINARY

Marriage and Family Therapy	M
Pastoral Ministry and Counseling	M
Religion	M
Theology	M,D,O

SIT GRADUATE INSTITUTE

Business Administration and Management—General	M
Conflict Resolution and Mediation/Peace Studies	M
Educational Leadership and Administration	M
Energy Management and Policy	M
English as a Second Language	M
Entrepreneurship	M
Environmental Management and Policy	M
International Affairs	M
International and Comparative Education	M
International Business	M
Meteorology	M
Organizational Management	M
Sustainability Management	M
Sustainable Development	M

SITTING BULL COLLEGE

Curriculum and Instruction	M
Environmental Sciences	M

SLIPPERY ROCK UNIVERSITY OF PENNSYLVANIA

Accounting	M
Business Administration and Management—General	M
Clinical Psychology	M
Counseling Psychology	M
Counselor Education	M
Criminal Justice and Criminology	M
Data Science/Data Analytics	M
Education—General	M,D

Educational Leadership and Administration	M,D
Educational Media/Instructional Technology	M,D
Elementary Education	M
English as a Second Language	M
English Education	M
English	M
Environmental Education	M
Environmental Management and Policy	M
Finance and Banking	M
Health Informatics	M
History	M
Marketing	M
Mathematics Education	M
Physical Education	M
Physical Therapy	D
Physician Assistant Studies	M
Public Health—General	M
Reading Education	M
Recreation and Park Management	M
School Psychology	M
Science Education	M
Secondary Education	M
Social Sciences Education	M
Special Education	M,D
Student Affairs	M
Therapies—Dance, Drama, and Music	M

SMITH COLLEGE

Biological and Biomedical Sciences—General	M
Chemistry	M
Dance	M
Education—General	M
Elementary Education	M
English Education	M
Exercise and Sports Science	M
History	M
Mathematics Education	M
Mathematics	O
Middle School Education	M
Science Education	M
Secondary Education	M
Social Sciences Education	M
Social Work	M,D
Theater	M
Women's Studies	O

SOFIA UNIVERSITY

Clinical Psychology	M,D
Computer Science	M,D
Counseling Psychology	M,D
Psychology—General	M,D
Transpersonal and Humanistic Psychology	M,D

SOKA UNIVERSITY OF AMERICA

Educational Leadership and Administration	M

SONOMA STATE UNIVERSITY

Anthropology	M
Biochemistry	M
Biological and Biomedical Sciences—General	M
Business Administration and Management—General	M
Clinical Psychology	M
Counseling Psychology	M
Curriculum and Instruction	M,O
Early Childhood Education	M,O
Education—General	M,O
Educational Leadership and Administration	M,O
English	M
Exercise and Sports Science	M
Family Nurse Practitioner Studies	M
Health Promotion	M
History	M
Interdisciplinary Studies	M
Kinesiology and Movement Studies	M
Nursing—General	M
Occupational Therapy	M
Physical Therapy	M
Political Science	M
Public Administration	M
Public History	M
Reading Education	M,O
School Psychology	M
Special Education	M,O
Sports Management	M
Writing	M

SOTHEBY'S INSTITUTE OF ART–LONDON

Art/Fine Arts	M
Arts Administration	M
Decorative Arts	M

SOTHEBY'S INSTITUTE OF ART–NEW YORK

Art/Fine Arts	M
Arts Administration	M
Decorative Arts	M

SOUTH BAYLO UNIVERSITY

Acupuncture and Oriental Medicine	M

SOUTH CAROLINA STATE UNIVERSITY

Agricultural Economics and Agribusiness	M
Allied Health—General	M
Biological and Biomedical Sciences—General	M
Business Administration and Management—General	M
Business Education	M
Child and Family Studies	M
Civil Engineering	M
Communication Disorders	M

Counselor Education	M
Early Childhood Education	M
Education—General	M
Elementary Education	M
English Education	M
English	M
Entrepreneurship	M
Family and Consumer Sciences-General	M
Health Services Management and Hospital Administration	M
Home Economics Education	M
Human Services	M
Mathematics Education	M
Mathematics	M
Mechanical Engineering	M
Nutrition	M
Rehabilitation Counseling	M
Science Education	M
Secondary Education	M
Social Sciences Education	M
Special Education	M
Transportation and Highway Engineering	M
Vocational and Technical Education	M

SOUTH COLLEGE

Pharmacy	D
Physician Assistant Studies	M

SOUTH DAKOTA SCHOOL OF MINES AND TECHNOLOGY

Artificial Intelligence/Robotics	M
Atmospheric Sciences	M,D
Bioengineering	D
Biomedical Engineering	M,D
Chemical Engineering	M,D
Civil Engineering	M,D
Construction Management	M
Electrical Engineering	M
Engineering and Applied Sciences—General	M,D
Engineering Management	M
Environmental Sciences	D
Geological Engineering	M,D
Geology	M,D
Management of Technology	M
Materials Engineering	M,D
Materials Sciences	M,D
Mechanical Engineering	M,D
Mineral/Mining Engineering	M,D
Nanotechnology	D
Paleontology	M,D
Physics	M,D

SOUTH DAKOTA STATE UNIVERSITY

Agricultural Education	M
Agricultural Engineering	M,D
Agricultural Sciences—General	M,D
Animal Sciences	M,D
Athletic Training and Sports Medicine	M,D
Biochemistry	M,D
Biological and Biomedical Sciences—General	M,D
Biosystems Engineering	M,D
Chemistry	M,D
Civil Engineering	M
Communication—General	M
Computational Sciences	M,D
Consumer Economics	M
Counselor Education	M
Curriculum and Instruction	M
Economics	M
Education—General	M,D
Educational Leadership and Administration	M
Electrical Engineering	M,D
Engineering and Applied Sciences—General	M,D
English	M
Exercise and Sports Science	M,D
Family and Consumer Sciences-General	M
Fish, Game, and Wildlife Management	M,D
Food Science and Technology	M,D
Geography	M
Geosciences	D
Human Resources Development	M
Industrial and Organizational Psychology	M
Journalism	M
Mathematics	M,D
Mechanical Engineering	M,D
Microbiology	M,D
Nursing—General	M,D
Nutrition	M,D
Operations Research	M
Pharmaceutical Sciences	M,D
Pharmacy	D
Physics	M
Plant Sciences	M,D
Recreation and Park Management	M,D
Sociology	M,D
Statistics	M,D
Veterinary Sciences	M,D

SOUTHEASTERN BAPTIST THEOLOGICAL SEMINARY

Ethics	M,D
Missions and Missiology	M,D
Music	M,D
Philosophy	M,D
Psychology—General	M,D
Religious Education	M,D
Theology	M,D
Women's Studies	M,D

SOUTHEASTERN LOUISIANA UNIVERSITY

Advertising and Public Relations	M
Applied Science and Technology	M
Biological and Biomedical Sciences—General	M
Business Administration and Management—General	M
Communication Disorders	M
Communication—General	M
Counselor Education	M
Curriculum and Instruction	M
Education—General	M,D
Educational Leadership and Administration	M,D
Elementary Education	M
English Education	M
English	M
Health Communication	M
Health Education	M
History	M
Industrial and Organizational Psychology	M
Journalism	M
Kinesiology and Movement Studies	M
Marketing	M
Music	M
Nursing—General	M,D
Psychology—General	M
Reading Education	M
Sociology	M
Special Education	M
Sustainability Management	M
Writing	M

SOUTHEASTERN OKLAHOMA STATE UNIVERSITY

Aviation Management	M
Aviation	M
Biotechnology	M
Business Administration and Management—General	M
Clinical Psychology	M
Counseling Psychology	M
Counselor Education	M
Education—General	M
Educational Leadership and Administration	M
Environmental and Occupational Health	M
Management Information Systems	M
Mathematics Education	M
Reading Education	M

SOUTHEASTERN UNIVERSITY (FL) *

Business Administration and Management—General	M,D
Counseling Psychology	M
Counselor Education	M
Curriculum and Instruction	M,D
Education of the Gifted	M,D
Education—General	M,D
Educational Leadership and Administration	M,D
Elementary Education	M,D
English as a Second Language	M,D
Entrepreneurship	M,D
Health Services Management and Hospital Administration	M,D
Human Services	M
International Business	M,D
Kinesiology and Movement Studies	M,D
Management Strategy and Policy	M,D
Marriage and Family Therapy	M
Organizational Management	M,D
Pastoral Ministry and Counseling	M,D
Reading Education	M,D
Social Work	M
Sports Management	M,D
Theology	M,D
Urban and Regional Planning	M

SOUTHEAST MISSOURI STATE UNIVERSITY

Accounting	M
Biological and Biomedical Sciences—General	M
Business Administration and Management—General	M
Chemistry	M
Communication Disorders	M
Counseling Psychology	M,O
Counselor Education	M,O
Criminal Justice and Criminology	M
Educational Leadership and Administration	M,D,O
Elementary Education	M,D,O
English as a Second Language	M
English	M
Entrepreneurship	M
Environmental Management and Policy	M
Environmental Sciences	M
Exercise and Sports Science	M
Finance and Banking	M
Higher Education	M,D,O
Historic Preservation	M,O
History	M,O
Leisure Studies	M
Management of Technology	M
Mathematics	M
Middle School Education	M
Nursing—General	M
Public Administration	M
Public History	M,O
Secondary Education	M,D,O
Special Education	M
Sports Management	M

SOUTHERN ADVENTIST UNIVERSITY

Accounting	M

Acute Care/Critical Care Nursing	M,D
Adult Nursing	M,D
Business Administration and Management—General	M
Computer Science	M
Counseling Psychology	M
Counselor Education	M
Education—General	M
Educational Leadership and Administration	M
Family Nurse Practitioner Studies	M,D
Finance and Banking	M
Gerontological Nursing	M,D
Health Services Management and Hospital Administration	M
Marketing	M
Missions and Missiology	M
Nursing Education	M,D
Nursing—General	M,D
Psychiatric Nursing	M,D
Psychology—General	M
Reading Education	M
Religion	M
Religious Education	M
Social Work	M
Theology	M

SOUTHERN ARKANSAS UNIVERSITY–MAGNOLIA

Adult Education	M
Agricultural Sciences—General	M
Business Administration and Management—General	M
Computer and Information Systems Security	M
Computer Science	M
Counselor Education	M
Curriculum and Instruction	M
Data Science/Data Analytics	M
Education of the Gifted	M
Education—General	M
Educational Leadership and Administration	M
Higher Education	M
Kinesiology and Movement Studies	M
Library Science	M
Organizational Management	M
Psychiatric Nursing	M
Public Administration	M
Student Affairs	M
Supply Chain Management	M

THE SOUTHERN BAPTIST THEOLOGICAL SEMINARY

Missions and Missiology	M,D
Pastoral Ministry and Counseling	M,D
Philosophy	M,D
Religion	M,D
Theology	M,D

SOUTHERN CALIFORNIA INSTITUTE OF ARCHITECTURE

Architecture	M
Urban and Regional Planning	M
Urban Design	M

SOUTHERN CALIFORNIA SEMINARY

Counseling Psychology	M,D
Marriage and Family Therapy	M,D
Psychology—General	M,D
Religion	M,D
Theology	M,D

SOUTHERN CALIFORNIA UNIVERSITY OF HEALTH SCIENCES

Acupuncture and Oriental Medicine	M,D
Chiropractic	D

SOUTHERN COLLEGE OF OPTOMETRY

Optometry	D

SOUTHERN CONNECTICUT STATE UNIVERSITY

Art Education	M
Biological and Biomedical Sciences—General	M
Business Administration and Management—General	M
Chemistry	M
Communication Disorders	M
Computer Science	M
Counselor Education	M,O
Education—General	M,D,O
Educational Leadership and Administration	M,D,O
Educational Measurement and Evaluation	M,D,O
Elementary Education	M,O
English as a Second Language	M
English	M
Environmental Education	M,O
Environmental Sciences	M,O
Exercise and Sports Science	M
Family Nurse Practitioner Studies	M,D
Foreign Languages Education	M
Health Education	M
History	M
Information Studies	M,O
Leisure Studies	M
Library Science	M,O
Marine Sciences	M,O
Mathematics	M
Multilingual and Multicultural Education	M
Nursing Education	M,D
Nursing—General	M,D
Physical Education	M
Political Science	M
Psychology—General	M
Public Health—General	M
Reading Education	M
Recreation and Park Management	M
School Psychology	M,O
Science Education	M,O
Social Work	M
Sociology	M
Special Education	M
Women's Studies	M

SOUTHERN EVANGELICAL SEMINARY

Jewish Studies	M,D,O
Missions and Missiology	M,D,O
Near and Middle Eastern Studies	M,D,O
Pastoral Ministry and Counseling	M,D,O
Philosophy	M,D,O
Religion	M,D,O
Religious Education	M,D,O
Theology	M,D,O

SOUTHERN ILLINOIS UNIVERSITY CARBONDALE

Accounting	M,D
Agricultural Economics and Agribusiness	M
Agricultural Sciences—General	M
Agronomy and Soil Sciences	M
Animal Sciences	M
Anthropology	M,D
Applied Arts and Design—General	M
Applied Physics	M
Architecture	M
Art/Fine Arts	M
Biochemistry	M,D
Biological and Biomedical Sciences—General	M,D
Biomedical Engineering	M
Business Administration and Management—General	M,D
Chemistry	M,D
Civil Engineering	M,D
Clinical Psychology	M,D
Communication Disorders	M
Communication—General	M,D
Community Health	M
Computer Engineering	M,D
Computer Science	M,D
Counseling Psychology	M,D
Criminal Justice and Criminology	M,D
Cultural Studies	M
Curriculum and Instruction	M,D
Economics	M,D
Education—General	M
Educational Leadership and Administration	M,D
Educational Psychology	M,D
Electrical Engineering	M,D
Energy and Power Engineering	D
Engineering and Applied Sciences—General	M,D
Engineering Management	M
English as a Second Language	M
English	M,D
Environmental Engineering	D
Environmental Management and Policy	M,D
Environmental Sciences	D
Experimental Psychology	M,D
Forestry	M
Geography	M,D
Geology	M,D
Geosciences	M,D
Health Education	M,D
Health Law	M
Health Services Management and Hospital Administration	M
Higher Education	M
History	M,D
Homeland Security	M
Kinesiology and Movement Studies	M
Law	M,D
Legal and Justice Studies	M
Linguistics	M
Mass Communication	M,D
Mathematics	M,D
Mechanical Engineering	M,D
Mechanics	M
Media Studies	M,D
Medical Physics	M
Microbiology	M,D
Mineral/Mining Engineering	M,D
Molecular Biology	M,D
Music	M
Nutrition	M
Pharmacology	M,D
Philosophy	M,D
Physical Education	M
Physician Assistant Studies	M
Physics	M,D
Physiology	M,D
Plant Biology	M,D
Plant Sciences	M
Political Science	M,D
Psychology—General	M,D
Public Administration	M
Recreation and Park Management	M
Rhetoric	M
Social Work	M
Sociology	M,D
Special Education	M,D
Speech and Interpersonal Communication	M,D
Theater	M,D
Vocational and Technical Education	M
Writing	M
Zoology	M,D

SOUTHERN ILLINOIS UNIVERSITY EDWARDSVILLE

Accounting	M
Advertising and Public Relations	M
Applied Mathematics	M
Art Therapy	M
Art/Fine Arts	M
Biological and Biomedical Sciences—General	M
Business Administration and Management—General	M
Business Analytics	M
Chemistry	M
Civil Engineering	M
Clinical Psychology	M
Communication Disorders	M
Computational Sciences	M
Computer Science	M
Corporate and Organizational Communication	M
Cultural Anthropology	M
Curriculum and Instruction	M
Dentistry	D
Economics	M
Education—General	M,D,O
Educational Leadership and Administration	M,D,O
Educational Media/Instructional Technology	M,O
Electrical Engineering	M
Engineering and Applied Sciences—General	M
English as a Second Language	M,O
English Education	M,O
English	M,O
Environmental Engineering	M
Environmental Management and Policy	M
Environmental Sciences	M
Exercise and Sports Science	M
Family Nurse Practitioner Studies	M,D,O
Finance and Banking	M
Foundations and Philosophy of Education	M
Geography	M
Geotechnical Engineering	M
Health Communication	M
Health Education	M,D,O
Health Informatics	M
Higher Education	M
History	M
Industrial and Organizational Psychology	M
Industrial/Management Engineering	M
Interdisciplinary Studies	M
Kinesiology and Movement Studies	M
Management Information Systems	M
Marketing Research	M
Mass Communication	M
Mathematics Education	M
Mathematics	M
Mechanical Engineering	M
Media Studies	O
Museum Studies	O
Music Education	M,O
Music	M
Nurse Anesthesia	D
Nursing and Healthcare Administration	M,O
Nursing Education	M,O
Nursing—General	M,D,O
Operations Research	M
Pharmacy	D
Physical Education	M
Project Management	M
Psychology—General	M,O
Public Administration	M
Reading Education	M,O
School Psychology	O
Social Work	M
Sociology	M
Special Education	M,O
Speech and Interpersonal Communication	M
Sport Psychology	M
Statistics	M
Structural Engineering	M
Student Affairs	M
Sustainable Development	M
Taxation	M
Transportation and Highway Engineering	M
Writing	M

SOUTHERN METHODIST UNIVERSITY

Accounting	M
Advertising and Public Relations	M
Anthropology	M,D
Applied Economics	M,D
Applied Mathematics	M,D
Applied Statistics	M,D
Archaeology	M,D
Art History	M,D
Art/Fine Arts	M
Arts Administration	M
Biological and Biomedical Sciences—General	M,D
Biostatistics	M,D
Business Administration and Management—General	M
Business Analytics	M
Cell Biology	M,D
Chemistry	M,D
Civil Engineering	M,D
Clinical Psychology	D
Computational Sciences	M,D
Computer Engineering	M,D
Computer Science	M,D
Conflict Resolution and Mediation/Peace Studies	M,O
Counselor Education	M,O
Cultural Anthropology	M,D
Data Science/Data Analytics	M,D
Economics	M,D
Education of the Gifted	M
Education—General	M,D
Educational Leadership and Administration	M,D
Electrical Engineering	M,D
Engineering and Applied Sciences—General	M,D
Engineering Management	M,D
English as a Second Language	M,D
English	M,D

SOUTHERN METHODIST UNIVERSITY (continued)

Entrepreneurship	M
Environmental Engineering	M
Finance and Banking	M
Geology	M,D
Geophysics	M,D
Geotechnical Engineering	M,D
Health Promotion	M,D
Higher Education	M,D
History	M,D
Information Science	M,D
Law	M,D
Liberal Studies	M,D
Management Information Systems	M
Management Strategy and Policy	M
Manufacturing Engineering	M,D
Marketing	M
Mathematics	M,D
Mechanical Engineering	M,D
Medieval and Renaissance Studies	M
Molecular Biology	M,D
Multilingual and Multicultural Education	M,D
Music Education	M
Music	M,D
Operations Research	M,D
Pastoral Ministry and Counseling	M,D
Physics	M,D
Physiology	M,D
Psychology—General	D
Reading Education	M,D
Real Estate	M
Religion	M,D
Software Engineering	M,D
Special Education	M,D
Sports Management	M,D
Statistics	M,D
Structural Engineering	M,D
Sustainable Development	M,D
Systems Engineering	M,D
Taxation	M,D
Telecommunications	M,D
Theater	M
Theology	M,D
Transportation and Highway Engineering	M,D

SOUTHERN NAZARENE UNIVERSITY

Business Administration and Management—General	M
Counseling Psychology	M
Health Services Management and Hospital Administration	M
Marriage and Family Therapy	M
Nursing and Healthcare Administration	M
Nursing Education	M
Nursing—General	M
Psychology—General	M
Sports Management	M

SOUTHERN NEW HAMPSHIRE UNIVERSITY

Accounting	M,D,O
Advertising and Public Relations	M,D,O
Applied Economics	M,D,O
Business Administration and Management—General	M,D,O
Business Analytics	M,D,O
Clinical Psychology	M
Computer and Information Systems Security	M
Criminal Justice and Criminology	M
Curriculum and Instruction	M,D,O
Data Science/Data Analytics	M,D,O
Early Childhood Education	M,D,O
Economic Development	M,D,O
Economics	M,D,O
Education—General	M,D,O
Educational Leadership and Administration	M,D,O
Educational Media/Instructional Technology	M,D,O
Elementary Education	M,D,O
Engineering Management	M,D,O
English as a Second Language	M,D,O
English	M
Entertainment Management	M,D,O
Entrepreneurship	M,D,O
Environmental Management and Policy	M,D,O
Finance and Banking	M,D,O
Health Informatics	M,D,O
Health Services Management and Hospital Administration	M,D,O
Higher Education	M,D,O
History	M
Human Resources Management	M,D,O
Industrial and Manufacturing Management	M,D,O
International Business	M,D,O
Internet and Interactive Multimedia	M,D,O
Investment Management	M,D,O
Legal and Justice Studies	M,D,O
Management Information Systems	M,D,O
Marketing	M,D,O
Nonprofit Management	M,D,O
Nursing and Healthcare Administration	M,O
Nursing Education	M,O
Nursing—General	M,O
Organizational Management	M,D,O
Political Science	M
Project Management	M,D,O
Psychology—General	M
Public Administration	M,D,O
Quality Management	M,D,O
Quantitative Analysis	M,D,O
Reading Education	M,D,O
Special Education	M,D,O
Sports Management	M,D,O
Supply Chain Management	M,D,O
Sustainability Management	M,D,O
Taxation	M,D,O
Writing	M

SOUTHERN OREGON UNIVERSITY

Accounting	M,O
Business Administration and Management—General	M,O
Computer Science	M
Counseling Psychology	M
Early Childhood Education	M
Education—General	M
Educational Leadership and Administration	M
Elementary Education	M
Environmental Education	M
Foreign Languages Education	M
French	M
Interdisciplinary Studies	M
International Business	M,O
Music	M
Psychology—General	M
Reading Education	M
Secondary Education	M
Spanish	M
Special Education	M
Theater	M

SOUTHERN STATES UNIVERSITY

Business Administration and Management—General	M
Information Science	M

SOUTHERN UNIVERSITY AND AGRICULTURAL AND MECHANICAL COLLEGE

Agricultural Sciences—General	M
Analytical Chemistry	M
Biochemistry	M
Biological and Biomedical Sciences—General	M
Business Administration and Management—General	M
Chemistry	M
Communication Disorders	M
Computer Science	M
Counselor Education	M
Criminal Justice and Criminology	M
Education—General	M,D
Educational Leadership and Administration	M
Educational Media/Instructional Technology	M
Elementary Education	M
Engineering and Applied Sciences—General	M
Environmental Sciences	M
Family Nurse Practitioner Studies	M,D,O
Forestry	M
Gerontological Nursing	M,D,O
History	M
Inorganic Chemistry	M
Law	D
Mass Communication	M
Mathematics Education	D
Mathematics	M
Nursing and Healthcare Administration	M,D,O
Nursing Education	M,D,O
Nursing—General	M,D,O
Organic Chemistry	M
Physical Chemistry	M
Physics	M
Political Science	M
Psychology—General	M
Public Administration	M
Public Policy	D
Recreation and Park Management	M
Rehabilitation Counseling	M
Science Education	D
Secondary Education	M
Social Sciences	M

SOUTHERN UNIVERSITY AT NEW ORLEANS

Criminal Justice and Criminology	M
Management Information Systems	M
Museum Studies	M
Social Work	M

SOUTHERN UTAH UNIVERSITY

Accounting	M
Arts Administration	M
Business Administration and Management—General	M
Communication—General	M
Computer and Information Systems Security	M
Education—General	M,O
Exercise and Sports Science	M
Interdisciplinary Studies	M
Music	M
Public Administration	M

SOUTHERN WESLEYAN UNIVERSITY

Business Administration and Management—General	M
Education—General	M
Pastoral Ministry and Counseling	M

SOUTH FLORIDA BIBLE COLLEGE AND THEOLOGICAL SEMINARY

Theology	M

SOUTH TEXAS COLLEGE OF LAW HOUSTON

Law	D

SOUTH UNIVERSITY (AL)

Business Administration and Management—General	M
Counseling Psychology	M
Criminal Justice and Criminology	M
Health Services Management and Hospital Administration	M
Management Information Systems	M

Nursing—General	M
Public Administration	M

SOUTH UNIVERSITY

Business Administration and Management—General	M
Counseling Psychology	M
Criminal Justice and Criminology	M
Family Nurse Practitioner Studies	M
Health Services Management and Hospital Administration	M
Management Information Systems	M
Nursing—General	M
Occupational Therapy	D
Public Administration	M

SOUTH UNIVERSITY

Adult Nursing	M
Business Administration and Management—General	M
Criminal Justice and Criminology	M
Family Nurse Practitioner Studies	M
Health Services Management and Hospital Administration	M
Management Information Systems	M
Nursing Education	M
Nursing—General	M
Physician Assistant Studies	M

SOUTH UNIVERSITY (GA)

Anesthesiologist Assistant Studies	M
Business Administration and Management—General	M
Counseling Psychology	M
Criminal Justice and Criminology	M
Entrepreneurship	M
Health Services Management and Hospital Administration	M
Hospitality Management	M
Nursing Education	M
Nursing—General	M
Organizational Management	M
Pastoral Ministry and Counseling	D
Pharmacy	
Physician Assistant Studies	M
Public Administration	M
Sustainability Management	M

SOUTH UNIVERSITY (SC)

Business Administration and Management—General	M
Counseling Psychology	M
Criminal Justice and Criminology	M
Health Services Management and Hospital Administration	M
Nursing—General	M
Organizational Management	M
Pharmacy	D

SOUTH UNIVERSITY (TX)

Business Administration and Management—General	M
Counseling Psychology	M
Management Information Systems	M

SOUTH UNIVERSITY

Business Administration and Management—General	M
Counseling Psychology	M
Nursing—General	M

SOUTH UNIVERSITY

Business Administration and Management—General	M
Counseling Psychology	M
Family Nurse Practitioner Studies	M
Management Information Systems	M
Nursing—General	M
Organizational Management	M

SOUTHWEST ACUPUNCTURE COLLEGE

Acupuncture and Oriental Medicine	M

SOUTHWEST BAPTIST UNIVERSITY

Business Administration and Management—General	M
Education—General	M,O
Educational Leadership and Administration	M,O
Health Services Management and Hospital Administration	M
Physical Therapy	D

SOUTHWEST COLLEGE OF NATUROPATHIC MEDICINE AND HEALTH SCIENCES

Naturopathic Medicine	D

SOUTHWESTERN ADVENTIST UNIVERSITY

Accounting	M
Business Administration and Management—General	M
Curriculum and Instruction	M
Education—General	M
Educational Leadership and Administration	M
Finance and Banking	M
Reading Education	M

SOUTHWESTERN ASSEMBLIES OF GOD UNIVERSITY

Counseling Psychology	M
Curriculum and Instruction	M
Education—General	M
Educational Leadership and Administration	M
History	M
Missions and Missiology	M
Pastoral Ministry and Counseling	M
Religion	M
Religious Education	M
Secondary Education	M
Theology	M

SOUTHWESTERN BAPTIST THEOLOGICAL SEMINARY

Missions and Missiology	M,D
Music	M,D
Near and Middle Eastern Studies	M,D
Pastoral Ministry and Counseling	M,D,O
Religious Education	M,D
Theology	M,D

SOUTHWESTERN CHRISTIAN UNIVERSITY

Missions and Missiology	M
Pastoral Ministry and Counseling	M

SOUTHWESTERN COLLEGE (KS)

Business Administration and Management—General	M
Criminal Justice and Criminology	M
Curriculum and Instruction	M,D
Early Childhood Education	M,D
Education—General	M,D
Educational Leadership and Administration	M,D
Elementary Education	M,D
Higher Education	M,D
Special Education	M,D

SOUTHWESTERN COLLEGE (NM)

Art Therapy	M
Counseling Psychology	M,O
Health Psychology	O
Psychology—General	O
Social Psychology	O
Thanatology	M,O

SOUTHWESTERN LAW SCHOOL

Law	M,D
Sports and Entertainment Law	M,D

SOUTHWESTERN OKLAHOMA STATE UNIVERSITY

Art Education	M
Business Administration and Management—General	M
Counselor Education	M
Early Childhood Education	M
Education—General	M,O
Educational Leadership and Administration	M
Educational Measurement and Evaluation	M
Elementary Education	M
Health Education	M
Kinesiology and Movement Studies	M
Mathematics Education	M
Microbiology	M
Music Education	M
Music	M
Pharmaceutical Administration	D
Pharmacy	D
Physical Education	M
Recreation and Park Management	M
School Psychology	O
Science Education	M
Social Sciences Education	M
Special Education	M
Sports Management	M
Therapies—Dance, Drama, and Music	M

SOUTHWEST MINNESOTA STATE UNIVERSITY

Business Administration and Management—General	M
Early Childhood Education	M
Education—General	M
Educational Leadership and Administration	M
English as a Second Language	M
Marketing	M
Mathematics Education	M
Reading Education	M
Special Education	M

SOUTHWEST UNIVERSITY

Business Administration and Management—General	M
Criminal Justice and Criminology	M
Organizational Management	M

SOUTHWEST UNIVERSITY OF VISUAL ARTS

Art/Fine Arts	M
Photography	M

SPALDING UNIVERSITY

Adult Nursing	M,D,O
Art Education	M
Athletic Training and Sports Medicine	M
Business Administration	M
Clinical Psychology	M,D
Corporate and Organizational Communication	M
Counselor Education	M
Education—General	M,D
Educational Leadership and Administration	M,D
Elementary Education	M
Family Nurse Practitioner Studies	M,D,O
Foreign Languages Education	M
Middle School Education	M
Nursing and Healthcare Administration	M,D,O
Nursing Education	M,D,O
Nursing—General	M,D,O
Occupational Therapy	M
Pediatric Nursing	M,D,O
Psychology—General	M
Secondary Education	M
Social Work	M
Special Education	M
Writing	M

SPERTUS INSTITUTE FOR JEWISH LEARNING AND LEADERSHIP

Jewish Studies	M,D

SPRING ARBOR UNIVERSITY

Business Administration and Management—General	M
Child and Family Studies	M
Communication—General	M
Counseling Psychology	M
Education—General	M
Nursing—General	M
Pastoral Ministry and Counseling	M
Reading Education	M
Social Work	M
Special Education	M
Theology	M

SPRINGFIELD COLLEGE

Art Therapy	M,O
Athletic Training and Sports Medicine	M
Business Administration and Management—General	M
Clinical Psychology	M,D,O
Counseling Psychology	M,D,O
Counselor Education	M,D,O
Early Childhood Education	M,O
Education—General	M,O
Educational Leadership and Administration	M,D,O
Elementary Education	M,O
Exercise and Sports Science	M,D,O
Health Promotion	M,D,O
Higher Education	M,D,O
Human Services	M
Industrial and Organizational Psychology	M,D,O
Occupational Therapy	M
Organizational Management	M
Physical Education	M,D,O
Physical Therapy	D
Physician Assistant Studies	M
Recreation and Park Management	M
Rehabilitation Counseling	M
Secondary Education	M,O
Social Work	M,O
Special Education	M,O
Sport Psychology	M,D,O
Sports Management	M,D,O
Student Affairs	M,D,O

SPRING HILL COLLEGE

Art/Fine Arts	M,O
Business Administration and Management—General	M
Early Childhood Education	M
Education—General	M
Elementary Education	M
English	M
Ethics	M,O
Foundations and Philosophy of Education	M
Liberal Studies	M,O
Nursing and Healthcare Administration	M,O
Nursing—General	M
Secondary Education	M
Theology	M,O

STANBRIDGE UNIVERSITY

Nursing—General	M
Occupational Therapy	M

STANFORD UNIVERSITY

Allopathic Medicine	D
Anthropology	M,D
Applied Arts and Design—General	M,D,O
Applied Physics	M,D
Archaeology	M,D
Art/Fine Arts	M,D
Asian Languages	M,D
Asian Studies	M
Biochemistry	D
Bioengineering	M,D
Biological and Biomedical Sciences—General	M,D
Biomedical Engineering	M,D,O
Biophysics	D
Biostatistics	M,D
Business Administration and Management—General	M,D
Chemical Engineering	M,D
Chemistry	D
Chinese	M,D
Classics	M,D
Clinical Research	M,D
Communication—General	M,D
Comparative Literature	D
Computational Sciences	M,D
Computer Science	M,D,O
Construction Engineering	M,D,O
Cultural Studies	M,D
Curriculum and Instruction	M,D
Developmental Biology	M,D
East European and Russian Studies	M
Ecology	M,D
Economics	D
Education—General	M,D
Educational Leadership and Administration	M
Educational Media/Instructional Technology	M
Educational Policy	M
Electrical Engineering	M,D
Elementary Education	M
Energy and Power Engineering	M,D,O
Engineering and Applied Sciences—General	M,D,O
Engineering Design	M,D,O

Stanford University (continued)

Program	Degree
Engineering Management	M,D
Engineering Physics	M,D
English	M,D
Environmental Law	M,D
Environmental Sciences	M,D,O
Epidemiology	M,D
Film, Television, and Video Production	M,D
French	M,D
Genetics	D
Geophysics	M,D
Geosciences	M,D,O
Geotechnical Engineering	M,D,O
German	M,D
Health Services Research	M,D
History	M,D
Hydrology	M,D,O
Immunology	D
Industrial/Management Engineering	M,D
International and Comparative Education	M,D
Italian	M,D
Japanese	M,D
Law	M,D
Legal and Justice Studies	M,D
Linguistics	M,D
Materials Engineering	M,D,O
Materials Sciences	M,D,O
Mathematics	M,D
Mechanical Engineering	M,D,O
Mechanics	M,D,O
Medical Informatics	M,D
Microbiology	D
Music	M,D
Philosophy	M,D
Physics	D
Physiology	D
Political Science	M,D
Psychology—General	D
Religion	D
Secondary Education	M
Slavic Languages	D
Sociology	D
Spanish	M,D
Statistics	M,D
Structural Biology	D
Structural Engineering	M,D,O
Sustainable Development	M,D,O
Systems Biology	D
Theater	M

STARR KING SCHOOL FOR THE MINISTRY

Program	Degree
Theology	M

STATE UNIVERSITY OF NEW YORK AT FREDONIA

Program	Degree
Biological and Biomedical Sciences—General	M,O
Communication Disorders	M
Curriculum and Instruction	M
Early Childhood Education	M
Education—General	M
English as a Second Language	M
English Education	M,O
English	M,O
Interdisciplinary Studies	M,O
Mathematics Education	M,O
Middle School Education	M,O
Music Education	M
Music	M
Reading Education	M
Secondary Education	M
Writing	M,O

STATE UNIVERSITY OF NEW YORK AT NEW PALTZ

Program	Degree
Accounting	M
Art/Fine Arts	M
Business Administration and Management—General	M
Chemistry	M,O
Clinical Psychology	M,O
Counseling Psychology	M,O
Counselor Education	M,O
Early Childhood Education	M
Education—General	M,O
Educational Leadership and Administration	M,O
Elementary Education	M
English as a Second Language	M,O
English Education	M,O
French	M,O
Geosciences	M,O
Multilingual and Multicultural Education	M,O
Reading Education	M
Science Education	M,O
Secondary Education	M
Social Sciences Education	M,O
Spanish	M,O
Special Education	M
Therapies—Dance, Drama, and Music	M

STATE UNIVERSITY OF NEW YORK AT OSWEGO

Program	Degree
Agricultural Education	M
Art Education	M
Art/Fine Arts	M
Bioinformatics	M
Business Administration and Management—General	M
Business Education	M
Chemistry	M
Child and Family Studies	M
Communication—General	M
Consumer Economics	M
Corporate and Organizational Communication	M
Counseling Psychology	M
Curriculum and Instruction	M
Early Childhood Education	M
Education—General	M,O

Program	Degree
Educational Leadership and Administration	O
Elementary Education	M
English	M
Graphic Design	M
Health Communication	M
Health Informatics	M
History	M
Human-Computer Interaction	M
Internet and Interactive Multimedia	M
Middle School Education	M
Reading Education	M
Secondary Education	M
Special Education	M
Vocational and Technical Education	M

STATE UNIVERSITY OF NEW YORK AT PLATTSBURGH

Program	Degree
Clinical Psychology	M,O
Communication Disorders	M,O
Counseling Psychology	M,O
Counselor Education	M,O
Curriculum and Instruction	M
Early Childhood Education	O
Educational Leadership and Administration	O
Elementary Education	M,O
English Education	M
Foreign Languages Education	M
Mathematics Education	M
Psychology—General	M,O
Reading Education	M
School Psychology	M,O
Science Education	M
Secondary Education	M
Social Sciences Education	M
Special Education	M
Student Affairs	M,O

STATE UNIVERSITY OF NEW YORK COLLEGE AT CORTLAND

Program	Degree
Communication Disorders	M
Community Health	M
Early Childhood Education	M
Education—General	M,O
Educational Leadership and Administration	O
English as a Second Language	M
English Education	M
English	M
Environmental Education	M
Health Education	M
History	M
Mathematics Education	M
Mathematics	M
Physical Education	M
Physics	M
Reading Education	M
Recreation and Park Management	M
Science Education	M
Secondary Education	M
Special Education	M
Sports Management	M

STATE UNIVERSITY OF NEW YORK COLLEGE AT GENESEO

Program	Degree
Accounting	M
Business Administration and Management—General	M
Education—General	M
English Education	M
French	M
Multilingual and Multicultural Education	M
Reading Education	M
Secondary Education	M
Social Sciences Education	M
Spanish	M

STATE UNIVERSITY OF NEW YORK COLLEGE AT OLD WESTBURY

Program	Degree
Accounting	M
Business Administration and Management—General	M
Counseling Psychology	M
Education—General	M
English Education	M
Foreign Languages Education	M
Liberal Studies	M
Mathematics Education	M
Science Education	M
Social Sciences Education	M
Taxation	M

STATE UNIVERSITY OF NEW YORK COLLEGE AT ONEONTA

Program	Degree
Biological and Biomedical Sciences—General	M,O
Counselor Education	M,O
Education—General	M,O
Educational Psychology	M,O
Elementary Education	M
Museum Studies	M
Nutrition	M
Reading Education	M
Special Education	M,O

STATE UNIVERSITY OF NEW YORK COLLEGE AT POTSDAM

Program	Degree
Community Health	M
Curriculum and Instruction	M
Early Childhood Education	M
Educational Media/Instructional Technology	M
Elementary Education	M
English Education	M
Mathematics Education	M
Mathematics	M
Middle School Education	M
Music Education	M
Music	M
Reading Education	M
Science Education	M
Secondary Education	M
Social Sciences Education	M

Program	Degree
Special Education	M

STATE UNIVERSITY OF NEW YORK COLLEGE OF ENVIRONMENTAL SCIENCE AND FORESTRY

Program	Degree
Biochemistry	M,D
Chemistry	M,D
Conservation Biology	M,D
Ecology	M,D
Economics	M,D
Entomology	M,D
Environmental Biology	M,D
Environmental Engineering	M,D
Environmental Management and Policy	M,D
Environmental Sciences	M,D
Fish, Game, and Wildlife Management	M,D
Forestry	M,D
Geographic Information Systems	M,D
Landscape Architecture	M,D
Materials Sciences	M,D,O
Natural Resources	M,D
Organic Chemistry	M,D
Paper and Pulp Engineering	M,D,O
Plant Pathology	M,D
Plant Sciences	M,D
Sustainability Management	M,D,O
Sustainable Development	M,D,O
Urban and Regional Planning	M,D
Urban Design	M
Water Resources Engineering	M,D
Water Resources	M,D

STATE UNIVERSITY OF NEW YORK COLLEGE OF OPTOMETRY

Program	Degree
Optometry	D
Vision Sciences	D

STATE UNIVERSITY OF NEW YORK COLLEGE OF TECHNOLOGY AT DELHI

Program	Degree
Nursing and Healthcare Administration	M
Nursing Education	M
Nursing—General	M

STATE UNIVERSITY OF NEW YORK DOWNSTATE MEDICAL CENTER

Program	Degree
Allopathic Medicine	M,D
Biological and Biomedical Sciences—General	M,D
Biomedical Engineering	M,D
Cell Biology	D
Community Health	M
Family Nurse Practitioner Studies	M,O
Medical/Surgical Nursing	M,O
Molecular Biology	D
Neuroscience	D
Nurse Anesthesia	M
Nurse Midwifery	M,O
Nursing—General	M,O
Occupational Therapy	M
Public Health—General	M

STATE UNIVERSITY OF NEW YORK EMPIRE STATE COLLEGE

Program	Degree
Adult Education	M
Business Administration and Management—General	M
Economic Development	M
Education—General	M
Educational Media/Instructional Technology	M
Industrial and Labor Relations	M
International Business	M
Liberal Studies	M
Nursing Education	M
Public Policy	M

STATE UNIVERSITY OF NEW YORK MARITIME COLLEGE

Program	Degree
Transportation Management	M

STATE UNIVERSITY OF NEW YORK POLYTECHNIC INSTITUTE

Program	Degree
Accounting	M
Business Administration and Management—General	M
Computer and Information Systems Security	M
Computer Science	M
Family Nurse Practitioner Studies	M,O
Finance and Banking	M
Human Resources Management	M
Information Science	M
Management of Technology	M
Marketing	M
Nanotechnology	M,D
Nursing Education	M

STATE UNIVERSITY OF NEW YORK UPSTATE MEDICAL UNIVERSITY

Program	Degree
Allopathic Medicine	D
Anatomy	M,D
Biochemistry	M,D
Biological and Biomedical Sciences—General	M,D
Cell Biology	M,D
Clinical Laboratory Sciences/Medical Technology	M
Family Nurse Practitioner Studies	M,O
Immunology	M,D
Microbiology	M,D
Molecular Biology	M,D
Neuroscience	D
Nursing—General	M,O
Pharmacology	D
Physical Therapy	D
Physiology	M,D
Public Health—General	M

STEPHEN F. AUSTIN STATE UNIVERSITY

Program	Degree
Accounting	M
Agricultural Sciences—General	M

Program	Degree
Special Education	M

Program	Degree
Applied Arts and Design—General	M
Art Education	M
Art/Fine Arts	M
Athletic Training and Sports Medicine	M
Biological and Biomedical Sciences—General	M
Biotechnology	M
Business Administration and Management—General	M
Chemistry	M
Communication Disorders	M
Communication—General	M
Computer and Information Systems Security	M
Counselor Education	M
Early Childhood Education	M
Education—General	M,D
Educational Leadership and Administration	M,D
Elementary Education	M
English	M
Environmental Sciences	M
Family and Consumer Sciences-General	M
Family Nurse Practitioner Studies	M
Film, Television, and Video Production	M
Forestry	M,D
Geology	M
Hispanic Studies	M
History	M
Interdisciplinary Studies	M
Kinesiology and Movement Studies	M
Marketing	M
Mass Communication	M
Mathematics Education	M
Mathematics	M
Music	M
Nursing—General	M
Physics	M,D
Psychology—General	M
Public Administration	M
Publishing	M
School Psychology	M
Secondary Education	M,D
Social Work	M
Special Education	M
Statistics	M

STEPHENS COLLEGE

Program	Degree
Addictions/Substance Abuse Counseling	M,O
Clinical Psychology	M,O
Counselor Education	M,O
Health Informatics	M,O
Physician Assistant Studies	M,O
Writing	M,O

STETSON UNIVERSITY

Program	Degree
Accounting	M
Business Administration and Management—General	M
Counselor Education	M
Education—General	M
Educational Leadership and Administration	M
Law	M,D
Writing	M

STEVENS INSTITUTE OF TECHNOLOGY

Program	Degree
Aerospace/Aeronautical Engineering	M,O
Applied Mathematics	M
Artificial Intelligence/Robotics	M,D,O
Biochemistry	M,D,O
Biomedical Engineering	M,D,O
Business Administration and Management—General	M,O
Business Analytics	M,O
Chemical Engineering	M,D,O
Chemistry	M,D,O
Civil Engineering	M,D,O
Communication—General	M,D,O
Computer and Information Systems Security	M,O
Computer Engineering	M,D,O
Computer Science	M,D,O
Construction Engineering	M,O
Construction Management	M,O
Electrical Engineering	M,D,O
Electronic Commerce	M,O
Engineering and Applied Sciences—General	M,D,O
Engineering Design	M
Engineering Management	M,D,O
Entrepreneurship	M,O
Environmental Engineering	M,D,O
Ethics	M,O
Film, Television, and Video Production	M
Finance and Banking	M,O
Financial Engineering	M,D,O
Human Resources Management	M
Hydraulics	M,D,O
Hydrology	M,D,O
Industrial and Manufacturing Management	M
Information Science	M,O
International Business	M
Management Information Systems	M,D,O
Management of Technology	M,D,O
Management Strategy and Policy	M,O
Manufacturing Engineering	M
Marketing	M,O
Materials Engineering	M,D
Materials Sciences	M,D
Mathematics	M
Mechanical Engineering	M,D,O
Media Studies	M
Modeling and Simulation	M,D,O
Ocean Engineering	M,D
Pharmaceutical Sciences	M
Photonics	M,D,O

Project Management	M,O
Quality Management	M,O
Software Engineering	M,O
Statistics	M,O
Structural Engineering	M,D,O
Systems Engineering	M,D,O
Systems Science	M,D
Telecommunications Management	M,D,O
Telecommunications	M,D,O
Transportation and Highway Engineering	M,D,O
Water Resources Engineering	M,D,O

STEVENSON UNIVERSITY

Biological and Biomedical Sciences—General	M
Chemistry	M
Communication—General	M
Computer and Information Systems Security	M
Education—General	M
Educational Leadership and Administration	M
Forensic Sciences	M
Health Services Management and Hospital Administration	M
Management of Technology	M
Mathematics Education	M
Nursing and Healthcare Administration	M
Nursing Education	M
Nursing—General	M
Project Management	M
Quality Management	M
Science Education	M

STOCKTON UNIVERSITY

American Studies	M,O
Business Administration and Management—General	M
Communication Disorders	M
Criminal Justice and Criminology	M
Data Science/Data Analytics	M
Education—General	M
Educational Media/Instructional Technology	M
Environmental Sciences	M
Holocaust and Genocide Studies	M
Management Strategy and Policy	M
Nursing—General	M
Occupational Therapy	M
Organizational Management	D
Physical Therapy	D
Quantitative Analysis	M
Social Work	M

STONEHILL COLLEGE

Internet and Interactive Multimedia	M
Special Education	M

STONY BROOK UNIVERSITY, STATE UNIVERSITY OF NEW YORK

Accounting	M,O
Addictions/Substance Abuse Counseling	M,O
Adult Nursing	M,D,O
African Studies	M,O
Allopathic Medicine	D
Anatomy	D
Anthropology	M,D
Applied Mathematics	M,D,O
Art History	M,D
Art/Fine Arts	M
Asian Studies	M
Asian-American Studies	M
Astronomy	D
Atmospheric Sciences	M,D
Biochemistry	D
Bioethics	
Bioinformatics	M,D,O
Biological and Biomedical Sciences—General	M,D,O
Biomedical Engineering	M,D,O
Biophysics	D
Business Administration and Management—General	M,O
Cell Biology	M,D
Chemistry	M,D
Civil Engineering	M,D,O
Community Health	M,D,O
Comparative Literature	M,D,O
Computer Engineering	M,D
Computer Science	M,D,O
Cultural Studies	M,D,O
Dentistry	D,O
Developmental Biology	M,D
Ecology	M,D
Economics	M,D
Educational Leadership and Administration	M,O
Electrical Engineering	M,D
Energy Management and Policy	M
Engineering and Applied Sciences—General	M,D,O
English as a Second Language	M
English	M,D,O
Entrepreneurship	M,O
Environmental Management and Policy	M,O
Evolutionary Biology	M,D
Family Nurse Practitioner Studies	M,D,O
Film, Television, and Video Production	M
Finance and Banking	M,O
Foreign Languages Education	M,O
French	M
Gender Studies	O
Genetics	D
Geographic Information Systems	O

Geosciences	M,D
Gerontological Nursing	M,D,O
Health Communication	M,O
Health Education	M,O
Health Informatics	M,O
Health Promotion	M,O
Health Services Management and Hospital Administration	M,D,O
Higher Education	M,O
Hispanic and Latin American Languages	M,D
History	M,D
Human Resources Management	M,O
Immunology	M,D
Italian	M,O
Journalism	M,O
Liberal Studies	M,O
Linguistics	M,D
Management of Technology	M,O
Marine Affairs	M
Marine Sciences	M,D
Marketing	M,O
Materials Engineering	M,D
Materials Sciences	M,D
Maternal and Child/Neonatal Nursing	M,D,O
Mathematics Education	M,O
Mathematics	M,D
Mechanical Engineering	M,D
Medical Physics	M,D
Microbiology	D
Molecular Biology	M,D
Molecular Genetics	D
Molecular Physiology	D
Music	M,D
Neuroscience	M,D
Nurse Midwifery	M,D,O
Nursing and Healthcare Administration	M,D,O
Nursing Education	M,O
Nursing—General	M,D,O
Nutrition	M,O
Occupational Therapy	M,D,O
Oral and Dental Sciences	M,D,O
Pathology	M,D
Pediatric Nursing	M,D,O
Pharmacology	M,D
Philosophy	M,D,O
Physical Education	M,O
Physical Therapy	M,D,O
Physician Assistant Studies	M,D
Physics	M,D
Physiology	D
Political Science	M,D
Psychiatric Nursing	M,D,O
Psychology—General	M,D
Public Health—General	M,O
Public Policy	M
Rehabilitation Sciences	M,D,O
Romance Languages	M
Science Education	M,D
Social Sciences Education	M,D
Social Work	M,D
Sociology	M,D
Statistics	M,D,O
Structural Biology	D
Systems Engineering	M,D
Telecommunications	M,D,O
Theater	M
Women's Health Nursing	M,D,O
Women's Studies	O
Writing	M,O

STRATFORD UNIVERSITY (MD)

Hospitality Management	M

STRATFORD UNIVERSITY (VA)

Accounting	M,D
Business Administration and Management—General	M
Computer and Information Systems Security	M,D
Computer Science	M,D
Forensic Sciences	M,D
Health Services Management and Hospital Administration	M,D
Management Information Systems	M,D
Management of Technology	M,D
Software Engineering	M,D
Telecommunications	M,D

STRAYER UNIVERSITY

Accounting	M
Business Administration and Management—General	M
Computer and Information Systems Security	M
Education—General	M
Educational Media/Instructional Technology	M
Finance and Banking	M
Health Services Management and Hospital Administration	M
Hospitality Management	M
Human Resources Management	M
Information Science	M
Management Information Systems	M
Marketing	M
Public Administration	M
Software Engineering	M
Supply Chain Management	M
Systems Science	M
Taxation	M
Telecommunications Management	M
Travel and Tourism	M

SUFFOLK UNIVERSITY

Accounting	M,O
Advertising and Public Relations	M
Applied Arts and Design—General	M

Business Administration and Management—General	M
Business Analytics	M
Clinical Psychology	M,D,O
Community Health	M
Corporate and Organizational Communication	M
Counseling Psychology	M,D,O
Counselor Education	M,D,O
Criminal Justice and Criminology	M
Data Science/Data Analytics	M
Educational Leadership and Administration	M,O
Entrepreneurship	M
Ethics	M,O
Finance and Banking	M
Graphic Design	M
Health Law	M,D
Health Services Management and Hospital Administration	M
Intellectual Property Law	M,D
Interior Design	M
International Business	M
Law	M,D
Management Information Systems	M
Management Strategy and Policy	M
Marketing	M
Nonprofit Management	M
Organizational Behavior	M
Political Science	M,O
Psychology—General	M,D,O
Public Administration	M
Public Policy	M,O
Supply Chain Management	M
Taxation	M,O

SULLIVAN UNIVERSITY

Business Administration and Management—General	M,D
Pharmacy	D

SUL ROSS STATE UNIVERSITY

Animal Sciences	M
Art Education	M
Art History	M
Art/Fine Arts	M
Biological and Biomedical Sciences—General	M
Business Administration and Management—General	M
Counselor Education	M
Criminal Justice and Criminology	M
Education—General	M,O
Educational Leadership and Administration	M
Educational Measurement and Evaluation	M,O
Elementary Education	M
Emergency Management	M
English	M
Fish, Game, and Wildlife Management	M
Geology	M
History	M
Multilingual and Multicultural Education	M
Natural Resources	M
Physical Education	M
Political Science	M
Psychology—General	M
Range Science	M
Reading Education	M,O
Secondary Education	M

SUM BIBLE COLLEGE & THEOLOGICAL SEMINARY

Pastoral Ministry and Counseling	M
Religion	M
Theology	M

SWEDISH INSTITUTE, COLLEGE OF HEALTH SCIENCES

Acupuncture and Oriental Medicine	M

SWEET BRIAR COLLEGE

Education—General	M

SYRACUSE UNIVERSITY

Accounting	M
Addictions/Substance Abuse Counseling	M,O
Advertising and Public Relations	M
Aerospace/Aeronautical Engineering	M,D
African Studies	M
African-American Studies	M
Anthropology	M,D
Applied Arts and Design—General	M
Applied Statistics	M
Architecture	M
Art Education	M
Art History	M
Art/Fine Arts	M
Arts Journalism	M
Bioengineering	M,D
Biological and Biomedical Sciences—General	M
Broadcast Journalism	M
Business Administration and Management—General	M,D
Business Analytics	M
Chemical Engineering	M,D
Chemistry	M,D
Child and Family Studies	M,D
Civil Engineering	M,D
Clinical Psychology	M,D
Cognitive Sciences	D
Communication Disorders	M,D
Communication—General	M,D
Computer and Information Systems Security	M,O
Computer Art and Design	M

Computer Engineering	M,D
Computer Science	M
Conflict Resolution and Mediation/Peace Studies	O
Counselor Education	M,D
Curriculum and Instruction	M,D,O
Data Science/Data Analytics	M,O
Disability Studies	O
Early Childhood Education	M
Economics	M,D
Education of Students with Severe/Multiple Disabilities	M
Education—General	M,D,O
Educational Leadership and Administration	M,D,O
Educational Measurement and Evaluation	M,D,O
Educational Media/Instructional Technology	M,O
Electrical Engineering	M,D
Emergency Management	O
Engineering and Applied Sciences—General	M,D,O
Engineering Management	M
English as a Second Language	M,O
English Education	M
English	M,D
Entertainment Management	M
Entrepreneurship	M
Environmental and Occupational Health	O
Environmental Engineering	M
Exercise and Sports Science	M
Film, Television, and Video Production	M
Finance and Banking	M,D
Forensic Sciences	M,O
Foundations and Philosophy of Education	M,D,O
French	M
Geography	M,D
Geology	M,D
Health Services Management and Hospital Administration	O
Higher Education	M,D
History	M,D
Hospitality Management	M,O
Human Development	M,D
Illustration	M
Information Science	M,D
Information Studies	M
International Affairs	M
International Health	M
Journalism	M
Kinesiology and Movement Studies	M,D,O
Law	M,D
Library Science	M
Linguistics	M
Management Information Systems	M,D,O
Marketing	M
Marriage and Family Therapy	M,D
Mass Communication	M,D
Mathematics Education	M,D
Mathematics	M,D
Mechanical Engineering	M,D
Media Studies	M
Museum Studies	M
Music Education	M
Music	M
Neuroscience	M,D
Nutrition	M,D
Organizational Management	O
Philosophy	M,D
Photography	M
Physics	M,D
Political Science	M,D,O
Psychology—General	D
Public Administration	M,D
Public Affairs	M
Reading Education	M,D
Real Estate	M
Religion	M,D
Rhetoric	M,D
School Psychology	M,D,O
Science Education	M,D
Social Psychology	D
Social Sciences Education	M
Social Sciences	M,D
Social Work	M
Sociology	M,D
Spanish	M
Special Education	M,D
Sports Management	M
Student Affairs	M
Supply Chain Management	M
Sustainability Management	O
Travel and Tourism	M
Urban and Regional Planning	O
Writing	M,D

TABOR COLLEGE

Accounting	M
Business Administration and Management—General	M

TAFT UNIVERSITY SYSTEM

Education—General	M
Law	M,D
Legal and Justice Studies	M,D
Taxation	M,D

TALMUDIC UNIVERSITY

Theology	M

TARLETON STATE UNIVERSITY

Accounting	M
Agricultural Sciences—General	M
Applied Psychology	M
Athletic Training and Sports Medicine	M

M—masters degree; D—doctorate; O—other advanced degree; *—Close-Up and/or Display

Biological and Biomedical
  Sciences—General | M
Business Administration and
  Management—General | M
Clinical Laboratory
  Sciences/Medical Technology | M
Communication—General | M
Counseling Psychology | M
Criminal Justice and Criminology | M
Curriculum and Instruction | M
Education—General | M,D,O
Educational Leadership and
  Administration | M,D,O
Educational Media/Instructional
  Technology | M
Elementary Education | M
Engineering Management | M
English | M
Environmental Sciences | M
Fish, Game, and Wildlife
  Management | M
History | M
Human Resources Management | M
Kinesiology and Movement Studies | M
Management Information Systems | M
Marketing | M
Mathematics | M
Music Education | M
Natural Resources | M
Nursing and Healthcare
  Administration | M
Nursing Education | M
Nursing—General | M
Political Science | M
Public Health—General | M
Secondary Education | M
Social Work | M
Special Education | M

TAYLOR COLLEGE AND SEMINARY
Cultural Studies | M,O
English as a Second Language | M,O
Missions and Missiology | M,O
Theology | M,O

TAYLOR UNIVERSITY
Higher Education | M

TEACHERS COLLEGE, COLUMBIA UNIVERSITY
Adult Education | M,D
Anthropology | M,D
Applied Behavior Analysis | M,D,O
Applied Psychology | M,D
Applied Statistics | M,D
Art Education | M,D,O
Arts Administration | M,D,O
Biological and Biomedical
  Sciences—General | M,D
Chemistry | M,D
Clinical Psychology | M,D
Communication Disorders | M,D,O
Communication—General | M,D
Community Health | M,D,O
Computer Education | M,D
Counseling Psychology | M,D
Curriculum and Instruction | M,D
Developmental Psychology | M,D
Early Childhood Education | M,D
Economics | M,D
Education of Students with
  Severe/Multiple Disabilities | M,D,O
Education of the Gifted | M,D
Education—General | M,D
Educational Leadership and
  Administration | M,D
Educational Measurement and
  Evaluation | M,D
Educational Media/Instructional
  Technology | M,D
Educational Policy | M,D
Educational Psychology | M,D,O
Elementary Education | M,D
English as a Second Language | M,D,O
English Education | M,D,O
Foundations and Philosophy of
  Education | M,D,O
Geosciences | M,D
Health Education | M,D,O
Higher Education | M,D
Industrial and Organizational
  Psychology | M,D
Interdisciplinary Studies | M,D
International Affairs | M,D,O
International and Comparative
  Education | M,D
Kinesiology and Movement Studies | M,D
Linguistics | M,D,O
Mathematics Education | M,D
Multilingual and Multicultural
  Education | M,D,O
Music Education | M,D,O
Neuroscience | M,D
Nursing and Healthcare
  Administration | M,D
Nursing Education | M,D,O
Nutrition | M,D,O
Philosophy | M,D,O
Physical Education | M,D
Physics | M,D
Physiology | M,D
Political Science | M,D
Psychology—General | M,D
Reading Education | M,D,O
School Psychology | M,D,O
Science Education | M,D
Secondary Education | M,D
Social Psychology | M,D
Social Sciences Education | M,D,O
Sociology | M,D
Special Education | M,D,O
Urban Education | M,D

TEACHERS COLLEGE OF SAN JOAQUIN
Early Childhood Education | M

Education—General | M
Educational Leadership and
  Administration | M
Educational Measurement and
  Evaluation | M
Mathematics Education | M
Science Education | M
Special Education | M

TÉLÉ-UNIVERSITÉ
Computer Science | M,D
Distance Education Development | M,D
Finance and Banking | M,D

TELSHE YESHIVA–CHICAGO
Jewish Studies | O

TEMPLE UNIVERSITY
Accounting | M,D
Actuarial Science | M
Adult Nursing | D
African-American Studies | M,D
Allied Health—General | M,D
Allopathic Medicine | D
Anthropology | D
Applied Behavior Analysis | M,D,O
Applied Mathematics | M,D
Architecture | M
Art Education | M
Art History | M,D
Art/Fine Arts | M
Artificial Intelligence/Robotics | M,D
Arts Administration | M,D
Athletic Training and Sports
  Medicine | M,D
Bioengineering | M,D
Biological and Biomedical
  Sciences—General | M,D
Biotechnology | M,D
Business Administration and
  Management—General | M,D
Business Education | M
Chemistry | M,D
Civil Engineering | M,D,O
Communication Disorders | M,D
Communication—General | M,D
Computer and Information
  Systems Security | M,D
Computer Science | M,D
Corporate and Organizational
  Communication | M,D
Counseling Psychology | M,D,O
Criminal Justice and Criminology | M,D
Dance | M,D
Dentistry | D
Economics | M,D
Education—General | M,D,O
Educational Leadership and
  Administration | M,D
Educational Psychology | M,D,O
Electrical Engineering | M,D
Engineering and Applied
  Sciences—General | D*
Engineering Management | M,O
English as a Second Language | M
English Education | M
English | M,D
Entrepreneurship | M,D
Environmental and Occupational
  Health | M,D
Environmental Engineering | M,D,O
Epidemiology | M,D
Family Nurse Practitioner Studies | D
Film, Television, and Video
  Production | M
Finance and Banking | M,D
Financial Engineering | M
Geographic Information Systems | M,D,O
Geography | M,D,O
Geology | M,D
Geosciences | M,D
Gerontology | D
Graphic Design | M
Health Informatics | M,D
Health Services Management and
  Hospital Administration | M
History | M,D
Hospitality Management | M,D
Human Resources Management | M
Hydrology | M,O
Industrial and Labor Relations | M,O
Information Science | M,D
Insurance | D
International Business | M,D
Investment Management | M,O
Journalism | M
Kinesiology and Movement Studies | M,D
Law | M,D,O
Legal and Justice Studies | M,D
Management Information Systems | M,D
Management Strategy and Policy | D
Marketing | M,D
Mathematics Education | M
Mathematics | M,D
Mechanical Engineering | M,D
Media Studies | M
Medicinal and Pharmaceutical
  Chemistry | M,D
Middle School Education | M
Music Education | M,D
Music | M,D
Nursing—General | D
Occupational Therapy | M,D
Oral and Dental Sciences | M,O
Pharmaceutical Administration | M
Pharmaceutical Sciences | M,D
Pharmacy | M,D
Philosophy | M,D
Photography | M
Physical Education | M,D
Physics | M,D
Podiatric Medicine | D
Political Science | M,D
Psychology—General | M,D
Public Health—General | M,D

Recreation and Park Management | M,D
Rehabilitation Sciences | M,D
Religion | M,D
Risk Management | D
School Psychology | M,D,O
Science Education | M
Secondary Education | M
Social Psychology | M,D,O
Social Sciences Education | M
Social Work | M
Sociology | M,D
Spanish | M,D
Sports Management | M,D
Statistics | M,D
Taxation | M,D
Textile Design | M
Theater | M
Therapies—Dance, Drama, and
  Music | M,D
Travel and Tourism | M,D
Urban Education | M
Urban Studies | M,D,O
Vocational and Technical Education | M
Writing | M,D

TENNESSEE STATE UNIVERSITY
Agricultural Education | M,D
Agricultural Sciences—
  General | M,D
Agronomy and Soil Sciences | M,D
Allied Health—General | M,D,O
Biological and Biomedical
  Sciences—General | D
Biomedical Engineering | M,D
Biotechnology | M,D
Business Administration and
  Management—General | M
Chemistry | M
Civil Engineering | M,D
Communication Disorders | M
Computer Engineering | M,D
Counseling Psychology | M
Criminal Justice and Criminology | M
Curriculum and Instruction | M
Education—General | M,D,O
Electrical Engineering | M,D
Elementary Education | M,D
Engineering and Applied
  Sciences—General | M,D
Environmental Engineering | M,D
Exercise and Sports Science | M
Family and Consumer
  Sciences-General | M,D
Family Nurse Practitioner Studies | M,O
Human Resources Management | M,D
Management Strategy and Policy | M,D
Manufacturing Engineering | M,D
Mathematics | M,D
Mechanical Engineering | M,D
Nursing—General | M,O
Occupational Therapy | M
Physical Education | M
Physical Therapy | D
Plant Sciences | M,D
Psychology—General | M
Public Administration | M,D
Public Health—General | M
Social Work | M,D
Special Education | M,D
Sports Management | M
Systems Engineering | M,D

TENNESSEE TECHNOLOGICAL UNIVERSITY
Accounting | M
Acute Care/Critical Care Nursing | D
Agricultural Sciences—
  General | D
Applied Behavior Analysis | D
Biological and Biomedical
  Sciences—General | M,D
Business Administration and
  Management—General | M
Chemical Engineering | M
Chemistry | M,D
Civil Engineering | M
Computer Science | M,D
Curriculum and Instruction | M,O
Early Childhood Education | M,O
Education of the Gifted | M,O
Education—General | M,D,O
Educational Leadership and
  Administration | M,O
Educational Measurement and
  Evaluation | D
Educational Media/Instructional
  Technology | M,O
Educational Psychology | M,O
Electrical Engineering | M
Elementary Education | M,O
Engineering and Applied
  Sciences—General | M,D
English as a Second Language | M
English | M
Environmental Management
  and Policy | M
Environmental Sciences | M
Family Nurse Practitioner Studies | M,D
Finance and Banking | M
Fish, Game, and Wildlife
  Management | M
Geosciences | D
Gerontological Nursing | D
Health Education | M
Health Promotion | M
Human Resources Management | M
International Business | M
Kinesiology and Movement Studies | M,O
Library Science | M,O
Management Information Systems | M
Management Strategy and Policy | M
Mathematics Education | M
Mathematics | M
Mechanical Engineering | M
Middle School Education | M

Music Education | M
Nursing and Healthcare
  Administration | M,D
Nursing Education | M
Nursing—General | M
Physical Education | M,D
Psychiatric Nursing | D
Reading Education | D
Science Education | M,O
Secondary Education | M,O
Special Education | M,O
Sports Management | M
Women's Health Nursing | D

TENNESSEE WESLEYAN UNIVERSITY
Accounting | M
Business Administration and
  Management—General | M

TEXAS A&M INTERNATIONAL UNIVERSITY
Accounting | M
Biological and Biomedical
  Sciences—General | M
Business Administration and
  Management—General | M,D
Counseling Psychology | M
Counselor Education | M
Criminal Justice and Criminology | M
Curriculum and Instruction | M
Education—General | M
Educational Leadership and
  Administration | M
English | M
Family Nurse Practitioner Studies | M
Finance and Banking | M
Foreign Languages Education | M
History | M
International Business | M,D
Management Information Systems | M,D
Mathematics | M
Nursing—General | M
Political Science | M
Psychology—General | M
Public Administration | M
Social Sciences | M
Sociology | M
Special Education | M
Translation and Interpretation | M

TEXAS A&M UNIVERSITY
Accounting | M
Aerospace/Aeronautical
  Engineering | M,D
Agricultural Economics and
  Agribusiness | M,D
Agricultural Education | M,D
Agricultural Engineering | M,D
Agricultural Sciences—
  General | M,D
Agronomy and Soil Sciences | M,D
Allopathic Medicine | M,D
Animal Sciences | M,D
Anthropology | M,D
Applied Physics | M,D
Architecture | M,D
Art/Fine Arts | M
Astronomy | M,D
Athletic Training and Sports
  Medicine | M,D
Biochemistry | M,D
Bioengineering | M,D
Biological and Biomedical
  Sciences—General | M,D
Biomedical Engineering | M,D
Biostatistics | M,D
Business Administration and
  Management—General | M
Chemical Engineering | M,D
Chemistry | M,D
Civil Engineering | M,D
Communication—General | M,D
Computer Engineering | M,D
Computer Science | M
Construction Management | M
Counseling Psychology | M
Cultural Studies | M
Curriculum and Instruction | M,D
Dentistry | M,D,O
Economics | M,D
Education—General | M,D
Educational Leadership and
  Administration | M,D
Educational Media/Instructional
  Technology | M,D
Educational Psychology | M,D
Electrical Engineering | M,D
Engineering Management | M,D
English | M,D
Entomology | M,D
Entrepreneurship | M
Environmental and Occupational
  Health | M,D
Epidemiology | M,D
Family Nurse Practitioner Studies | M
Finance and Banking | M
Fish, Game, and Wildlife
  Management | M,D
Food Science and
  Technology | M,D
Forensic Nursing | M
Forestry | M,D
Geography | M,D
Geology | M,D
Geophysics | M,D
Health Education | M,D
Health Services Management and
  Hospital Administration | M,D
Health Services Research | M,D
History | M,D
Horticulture | M,D
Human Resources Development | M,D
Human Resources Management | M
Industrial/Management
  Engineering | M,D

Intellectual Property Law	M,D
International Affairs	M,O
Kinesiology and Movement Studies	M,D
Landscape Architecture	M,D
Law	M,D
Management Information Systems	M
Manufacturing Engineering	M
Marine Biology	M,D
Marine Sciences	M
Marketing	M
Materials Engineering	M,D
Materials Sciences	M,D
Mathematics	M,D
Mechanical Engineering	M,D
Meteorology	M,D
Microbiology	M,D
Multilingual and Multicultural Education	M,D
Music	M
Natural Resources	M,D
Nuclear Engineering	M,D
Nursing Education	M
Nursing—General	M
Nutrition	M,D
Oceanography	M,D
Oral and Dental Sciences	M,D,O
Petroleum Engineering	M,D
Pharmacy	D
Philosophy	M,D
Physics	M,D
Plant Pathology	M,D
Political Science	M,D
Psychology—General	M,D
Public Affairs	M,D
Public Health—General	M,D
Recreation and Park Management	M,D
School Psychology	M,D
Sociology	M,D
Spanish	M,D
Special Education	M,D
Sports Management	M,D
Statistics	M,D
Transportation Management	M
Urban and Regional Planning	M,D
Veterinary Medicine	M,D
Veterinary Sciences	M,D

TEXAS A&M UNIVERSITY–CENTRAL TEXAS

Accounting	M,O
Business Administration and Management—General	M,O
Clinical Psychology	M,O
Counselor Education	M,O
Criminal Justice and Criminology	M,O
Curriculum and Instruction	M,O
Educational Leadership and Administration	M,O
Educational Psychology	M,O
Experimental Psychology	M,O
History	M,O
Human Resources Management	M,O
Liberal Studies	M,O
Management Information Systems	M,O
Marriage and Family Therapy	M,O
Mathematics	M,O
Political Science	M,O
School Psychology	M,O

TEXAS A&M UNIVERSITY–COMMERCE

Accounting	M
Agricultural Sciences—General	M
Art/Fine Arts	M,D,O
Biological and Biomedical Sciences—General	M,O
Business Administration and Management—General	M
Business Analytics	M
Chemistry	M,O
Computational Sciences	M,O
Counselor Education	M,D,O
Criminal Justice and Criminology	M,D,O
Curriculum and Instruction	M,D,O
Early Childhood Education	M,D,O
Education—General	M,D,O
Educational Leadership and Administration	M,D,O
Educational Media/Instructional Technology	M,D,O
Educational Psychology	M,D,O
Elementary Education	M,D,O
English as a Second Language	M,D,O
English	M,D,O
Environmental Sciences	M,O
Exercise and Sports Science	M,D,O
Film, Television, and Video Theory and Criticism	M,D,O
Finance and Banking	M
Higher Education	M,D,O
History	M,D,O
Holocaust and Genocide Studies	M
Homeland Security	M
Kinesiology and Movement Studies	M,D,O
Library Science	M,D,O
Linguistics	M,D,O
Management of Technology	M,O
Marketing	M
Mathematics	M,O
Music Education	M,D,O
Music	M,D,O
Physics	M,D,O
Political Science	M,D,O
Psychology—General	M,O
Public History	M,D,O
Reading Education	M,D,O
Secondary Education	M,D,O
Social Work	M,D,O
Sociology	M,D,O
Spanish	M,D,O
Special Education	M,D,O

TEXAS A&M UNIVERSITY–CORPUS CHRISTI

Accounting	M
Aquaculture	M
Art/Fine Arts	M
Biological and Biomedical Sciences—General	M,D
Business Administration and Management—General	M
Chemistry	M,D
Clinical Psychology	M
Communication—General	M
Computer Science	M
Counselor Education	M,D
Curriculum and Instruction	M,D
Early Childhood Education	M,D
Education—General	M,D
Educational Leadership and Administration	M,D
Educational Media/Instructional Technology	M,D
Elementary Education	M
English	M
Environmental Sciences	M
Family Nurse Practitioner Studies	M
Finance and Banking	M
Geographic Information Systems	M,D
Health Services Management and Hospital Administration	M,D
History	M
Human Development	M,D
International Business	M
Kinesiology and Movement Studies	M,D
Marine Biology	M,D
Marine Sciences	M,D
Mathematics	M
Nursing and Healthcare Administration	M,D
Nursing Education	M,D
Nursing—General	M,D
Psychology—General	M
Public Administration	M
Reading Education	M,D
Secondary Education	M
Special Education	M

TEXAS A&M UNIVERSITY–KINGSVILLE

Adult Education	M
Agricultural Economics and Agribusiness	M,D
Agricultural Sciences—General	M,D
Agronomy and Soil Sciences	M
Animal Sciences	M
Biological and Biomedical Sciences—General	M
Business Administration and Management—General	M
Chemical Engineering	M
Chemistry	M
Civil Engineering	M
Communication Disorders	M
Computer Science	M
Counselor Education	M
Criminal Justice and Criminology	M
Cultural Studies	M
Early Childhood Education	M
Education—General	M,D,O
Educational Leadership and Administration	M,D
Educational Media/Instructional Technology	M
Electrical Engineering	M
Energy and Power Engineering	D
Engineering and Applied Sciences—General	M,D
English as a Second Language	M,D
English	M
Environmental Engineering	M,D
Family and Consumer Sciences-General	M
Fish, Game, and Wildlife Management	M,D
Foreign Languages Education	M
Health Education	M
Hispanic Studies	D
Horticulture	M,D
Industrial and Manufacturing Management	M
Industrial/Management Engineering	M
Kinesiology and Movement Studies	M
Mathematics	M
Mechanical Engineering	M
Multilingual and Multicultural Education	M,D
Music Education	M
Music	M
Petroleum Engineering	M
Plant Sciences	M
Psychology—General	M
Range Science	M
Reading Education	M
Science Education	M
Social Work	M
Sociology	M
Spanish	M
Special Education	M
Statistics	M
Sustainable Development	D
Systems Engineering	M

TEXAS A&M UNIVERSITY–SAN ANTONIO

Accounting	M
Business Administration and Management—General	M
Clinical Psychology	M

Counselor Education	M
Early Childhood Education	M
Education—General	M
Educational Leadership and Administration	M
Educational Measurement and Evaluation	M
English	M
Kinesiology and Movement Studies	M
Marriage and Family Therapy	M
Multilingual and Multicultural Education	M
Reading Education	M
Special Education	M

TEXAS A&M UNIVERSITY–TEXARKANA

Accounting	M
Adult Education	M
Business Administration and Management—General	M
Counseling Psychology	M
Curriculum and Instruction	M
Education—General	M
Educational Leadership and Administration	M
Educational Media/Instructional Technology	M
English	M
Interdisciplinary Studies	M
Psychology—General	M
Special Education	M

TEXAS CHIROPRACTIC COLLEGE

Chiropractic	D

TEXAS CHRISTIAN UNIVERSITY

Accounting	M
Adult Nursing	M,O
Allied Health—General	M,D,O
American Studies	M,D
Applied Mathematics	M,D
Art History	M
Art/Fine Arts	M
Astrophysics	M,D
Biochemistry	M,D
Biological and Biomedical Sciences—General	M,D
Biophysics	M,D
Business Administration and Management—General	M
Chemistry	M,D
Cognitive Sciences	M,D
Communication Disorders	M
Communication—General	M
Corporate and Organizational Communication	M
Counselor Education	M,D
Criminal Justice and Criminology	M
Curriculum and Instruction	M,D
Developmental Psychology	M,D
Education—General	M,D
Educational Leadership and Administration	M,D
English	M,D
Environmental Sciences	M
Experimental Psychology	M,D
Family Nurse Practitioner Studies	D
Gerontological Nursing	M,O
Gerontology	D
History	M,D
Kinesiology and Movement Studies	M
Latin American Studies	M,D
Liberal Studies	M
Mass Communication	M
Mathematics Education	M
Mathematics	M,D
Music Education	M,D
Music	M,D
Neuroscience	M,D
Nurse Anesthesia	D
Nursing and Healthcare Administration	M,D,O
Nursing Education	M,O
Nursing—General	M,D,O
Pediatric Nursing	M,D,O
Physics	M,D
Psychology—General	M,D
Reading Education	M
Rhetoric	M,D
Science Education	M,D
Social Psychology	M,D
Social Work	M
Special Education	M
Speech and Interpersonal Communication	M
Taxation	M

TEXAS HEALTH AND SCIENCE UNIVERSITY

Acupuncture and Oriental Medicine	M,D
Business Administration and Management—General	M,D
Health Services Management and Hospital Administration	M,D

TEXAS LUTHERAN UNIVERSITY

Accounting	M

TEXAS SOUTHERN UNIVERSITY

Art/Fine Arts	M
Biological and Biomedical Sciences—General	M
Business Administration and Management—General	M
Chemistry	M
Communication—General	M
Computer Science	M
Counselor Education	M,D
Criminal Justice and Criminology	M,D
Curriculum and Instruction	M,D
Education—General	M,D
Educational Leadership and Administration	M,D

English	M
Environmental Management and Policy	M,D
Family and Consumer Sciences-General	M
Health Education	M
Health Services Management and Hospital Administration	M
Higher Education	M,D
History	M
Human Services	M
Industrial/Management Engineering	M
Law	D
Management Information Systems	M
Mathematics	M
Multilingual and Multicultural Education	M,D
Music	M
Pharmaceutical Sciences	M,D
Pharmacy	D
Physical Education	M
Psychology—General	M
Public Administration	M
Secondary Education	M,D
Sociology	M
Toxicology	M,D
Transportation and Highway Engineering	M
Transportation Management	M
Urban and Regional Planning	M,D

TEXAS STATE UNIVERSITY

Accounting	M
Adult Education	M,D
Agricultural Education	M
Allied Health—General	M,D
Anthropology	M
Applied Arts and Design—General	M
Athletic Training and Sports Medicine	M
Biochemistry	M
Biological and Biomedical Sciences—General	M
Business Administration and Management—General	M
Chemistry	M
Child and Family Studies	M
Civil Engineering	M
Clinical Psychology	M
Communication Disorders	M
Communication—General	M
Computer Art and Design	M
Computer Science	M,D
Conservation Biology	M
Counselor Education	M
Criminal Justice and Criminology	M,D
Developmental Education	M,D
Early Childhood Education	M
Education—General	M,D,O
Educational Leadership and Administration	M,D
Educational Media/Instructional Technology	M
Electrical Engineering	M
Elementary Education	M
Engineering and Applied Sciences—General	M
English	M
Ethics	M
Family and Consumer Sciences-General	M
Family Nurse Practitioner Studies	M
Fish, Game, and Wildlife Management	M
Geographic Information Systems	M,D
Geography	M,D
Gerontology	M
Graphic Design	M
Health Education	M
Health Informatics	M
Health Services Management and Hospital Administration	M
Higher Education	M
History	M
Human Resources Management	M
Industrial/Management Engineering	M
Interdisciplinary Studies	M
International Affairs	M
Legal and Justice Studies	M
Leisure Studies	M
Management Information Systems	M
Management of Technology	M
Manufacturing Engineering	M
Marine Biology	M,D
Marriage and Family Therapy	M
Mass Communication	M
Materials Engineering	D
Materials Sciences	D
Mathematics Education	D
Mathematics	M
Mechanical Engineering	M
Multilingual and Multicultural Education	M
Music Education	M
Music	M
Nutrition	M
Philosophy	M
Physical Therapy	D
Physics	M
Political Science	M
Psychology—General	M
Public Administration	M
Reading Education	M
Recreation and Park Management	M
Rhetoric	M
School Psychology	O
Secondary Education	M
Social Work	M

M—masters degree; D—doctorate; O—other advanced degree; *—Close-Up and/or Display

Sociology	M
Software Engineering	M
Spanish	M
Special Education	M
Student Affairs	M
Sustainable Development	M
Technical Communication	M
Theater	M
Vocational and Technical Education	M
Writing	M

TEXAS TECH UNIVERSITY

Accounting	M,D
Agricultural Economics and Agribusiness	M,D
Agricultural Education	M,D
Agricultural Sciences—General	M,D
Agronomy and Soil Sciences	M,D
Animal Sciences	M,D
Anthropology	M
Applied Economics	M,D
Architecture	M,D
Art Education	M
Art History	M
Art/Fine Arts	M,D
Astronomy	M,D
Atmospheric Sciences	M,D
Biological and Biomedical Sciences—General	M,D
Biotechnology	M,D
Business Administration and Management—General	M,D
Chemistry	M,D
Child and Family Studies	M,D
Clinical Psychology	M,D
Communication—General	M
Consumer Economics	M,D
Counseling Psychology	M,D
Counselor Education	M,D
Cultural Studies	M,D
Curriculum and Instruction	M,D
Data Science/Data Analytics	M,D
Economics	M,D
Education—General	M,D
Educational Leadership and Administration	M,D
Educational Media/Instructional Technology	M,D
Educational Psychology	M,D
Elementary Education	M,D
Energy and Power Engineering	M,D
Engineering and Applied Sciences—General	M,D
Engineering Management	M,D
English	M,D
Environmental Design	M,D
Environmental Management and Policy	M,D
Environmental Sciences	M,D
Exercise and Sports Science	M
Experimental Psychology	M,D
Finance and Banking	M,D
Fish, Game, and Wildlife Management	M,D
Food Science and Technology	M,D
Geography	M,D
Geosciences	M,D
Gerontology	M,D
Health Services Management and Hospital Administration	M,D
Higher Education	M,D
History	M,D
Home Economics Education	M,D
Horticulture	M,D
Hospitality Management	M,D
Human Development	M,D
Interdisciplinary Studies	M,D
Interior Design	M,D
Kinesiology and Movement Studies	M,D
Landscape Architecture	M
Law	M,D
Legal and Justice Studies	M,D
Management Information Systems	M,D
Marketing	M,D
Marriage and Family Therapy	M,D
Mass Communication	M,D
Mathematics	M,D
Media Studies	M,D
Microbiology	M,D
Multilingual and Multicultural Education	M,D
Museum Studies	M,D
Music Education	M,D
Music	M,D
Natural Resources	M,D
Nutrition	M,D
Philosophy	M
Physics	M,D
Plant Sciences	M,D
Political Science	M,D
Psychology—General	M,D
Public Administration	M,D
Reading Education	M,D
Rhetoric	M,D
Romance Languages	M,D
Science Education	M,D
Secondary Education	M,D
Social Sciences Education	M,D
Social Work	M
Sociology	M
Software Engineering	M,D
Spanish	M,D
Special Education	M,D
Sports Management	M,D
Statistics	M,D
Sustainable Development	M,D
Taxation	M,D
Technical Writing	M,D
Theater	M
Toxicology	M,D
Zoology	M,D

TEXAS TECH UNIVERSITY HEALTH SCIENCES CENTER

Acute Care/Critical Care Nursing	M,D,O
Addictions/Substance Abuse Counseling	M
Allopathic Medicine	D
Athletic Training and Sports Medicine	M
Biological and Biomedical Sciences—General	M,D
Biotechnology	M
Cell Biology	M,D
Clinical Psychology	M
Communication Disorders	M,D
Family Nurse Practitioner Studies	M,D,O
Gerontological Nursing	M,D,O
Health Services Management and Hospital Administration	M
Molecular Pathology	M
Nursing and Healthcare Administration	M,D,O
Nursing Education	M,D,O
Nursing—General	M,D,O
Occupational Therapy	M
Pediatric Nursing	M,D,O
Pharmaceutical Sciences	M,D
Pharmacy	D
Physical Therapy	D
Physician Assistant Studies	M
Rehabilitation Counseling	M
Rehabilitation Sciences	D

TEXAS TECH UNIVERSITY HEALTH SCIENCES CENTER EL PASO

Allopathic Medicine	D
Biological and Biomedical Sciences—General	M
Nursing—General	M

TEXAS WESLEYAN UNIVERSITY

Business Administration and Management—General	M
Education—General	M,D
Nurse Anesthesia	M

TEXAS WOMAN'S UNIVERSITY

Accounting	M
Acute Care/Critical Care Nursing	M,D
Adult Nursing	M,D
Allied Health—General	M,D
Art Education	M
Art History	M
Art/Fine Arts	M
Biological and Biomedical Sciences—General	M,D
Business Administration and Management—General	M
Business Analytics	M
Chemistry	M
Child and Family Studies	M,D
Child Development	M,D
Communication Disorders	M
Counseling Psychology	M,D,O
Counselor Education	M,D
Curriculum and Instruction	M,D
Dance	M,D
Dental Hygiene	M,D
Early Childhood Education	M,D
Education—General	M,D,O
Educational Leadership and Administration	M,D
English Education	M,D
English	M,D
Exercise and Sports Science	M,D
Family Nurse Practitioner Studies	M,D
Food Science and Technology	M,D
Gender Studies	M,D
Gerontological Nursing	M,D
Graphic Design	M
Health Education	M,D
Health Services Management and Hospital Administration	M
History	M
Human Resources Management	M
Information Science	M
Internet and Interactive Multimedia	M
Library Science	M
Marriage and Family Therapy	M,D
Mathematics Education	M
Mathematics	M
Molecular Biology	M
Music Education	M
Music	M
Nursing and Healthcare Administration	M,D
Nursing Education	M,D
Nursing—General	M,D
Nutrition	M,D
Occupational Therapy	M,D
Pediatric Nursing	M,D
Photography	M
Physical Therapy	D
Political Science	M
Psychology—General	M,D,O
Reading Education	M,D,O
Rhetoric	M
School Psychology	M,D,O
Sociology	M,D
Special Education	M,D
Theater	M
Therapies—Dance, Drama, and Music	M
Women's Health Nursing	M,D
Women's Studies	M,D

THEOLOGICAL UNIVERSITY OF THE CARIBBEAN

Early Childhood Education	M,D
Middle School Education	M,D
Missions and Missiology	M,D
Pastoral Ministry and Counseling	M,D

THOMAS COLLEGE

Business Administration and Management—General	M
Business Education	M
Computer Education	M
Human Resources Management	M

THOMAS EDISON STATE UNIVERSITY

Accounting	M
Applied Science and Technology	M,O
Business Administration and Management—General	M
Computer and Information Systems Security	M,O
Distance Education Development	M,O
Economic Development	M
Educational Leadership and Administration	M,O
Educational Media/Instructional Technology	M,O
Environmental Management and Policy	M
Finance and Banking	M
Homeland Security	M
Hospitality Management	M
Human Resources Management	M
Industrial and Organizational Psychology	M,O
Information Science	M
International Business	M
Liberal Studies	M,O
Nonprofit Management	M
Nursing and Healthcare Administration	M
Nursing Education	M
Nursing Informatics	M
Nursing—General	M,D
Organizational Management	M
Project Management	M
Public Administration	M
Public Health—General	M
Urban and Regional Planning	M

THOMAS JEFFERSON SCHOOL OF LAW

Law	D

THOMAS JEFFERSON UNIVERSITY

Allopathic Medicine	D
Applied Economics	M,D,O
Architecture	M
Art/Fine Arts	M
Athletic Training and Sports Medicine	M
Biochemistry	D
Biological and Biomedical Sciences—General	M,D,O
Biotechnology	M
Business Administration and Management—General	M
Business Analytics	M
Cancer Biology/Oncology	D
Cell Biology	M,D
Clinical Laboratory Sciences/Medical Technology	M
Clinical Research	M,O
Clothing and Textiles	M
Construction Management	M
Developmental Biology	M
Emergency Management	M
Genetic Counseling	M
Genetics	D
Genomic Sciences	D
Geography	M
Health Education	M,D,O
Health Physics/Radiological Health	M
Health Services Management and Hospital Administration	M,D,O
Health Services Research	M,D,O
Human Genetics	M
Immunology	D
Industrial Design	M
Infectious Diseases	O
Interior Design	M
Internet and Interactive Multimedia	M
Management Strategy and Policy	M,D
Marketing	M
Marriage and Family Therapy	M
Medical Imaging	M
Medical Physics	M
Microbiology	M,D
Molecular Pharmacology	D
Neuroscience	D
Nurse Midwifery	M
Nursing—General	M,D
Occupational Therapy	M
Pharmacology	M
Pharmacy	D
Physical Therapy	D
Physician Assistant Studies	M
Public Health—General	M,O
Real Estate	M
Social Psychology	M
Sustainable Development	M
Taxation	M
Textile Design	M
Textile Sciences and Engineering	M,D
Toxicology	M
Urban and Regional Planning	M

THOMAS MORE UNIVERSITY

Business Administration and Management—General	M
Education—General	M
Educational Leadership and Administration	M

THOMAS UNIVERSITY

Business Administration and Management—General	M
Education—General	M
Human Services	M
Nursing—General	M
Rehabilitation Counseling	M

Social Psychology	M

THOMPSON RIVERS UNIVERSITY

Business Administration and Management—General	M
Education—General	M
Environmental Sciences	M
Social Work	M

TIFFIN UNIVERSITY

Art/Fine Arts	M
Business Administration and Management—General	M
Communication—General	M
Criminal Justice and Criminology	M
Education—General	M
Educational Leadership and Administration	M
Educational Media/Instructional Technology	M
English	M
Film, Television, and Video Theory and Criticism	M
Finance and Banking	M
Forensic Psychology	M
Health Services Management and Hospital Administration	M
Higher Education	M
Homeland Security	M
Human Resources Management	M
Humanities	M
International Business	M
Marketing	M
Nonprofit Management	M
Psychology—General	M
Sports Management	M
Writing	M

TORONTO SCHOOL OF THEOLOGY

Theology	M,D

TOURO COLLEGE

Communication Disorders	M,D
Counseling Psychology	M,D
Education—General	M
Educational Leadership and Administration	M
Educational Media/Instructional Technology	M
English as a Second Language	M
Industrial and Organizational Psychology	M,D
Internet and Interactive Multimedia	M
Jewish Studies	M
Law	M,D
Legal and Justice Studies	M,D
Management Information Systems	M
Mathematics Education	M
Occupational Therapy	M,D
Physical Therapy	M,D
Physician Assistant Studies	M
Reading Education	M
Social Work	M
Special Education	M

TOURO UNIVERSITY CALIFORNIA

Education—General	M,D
Osteopathic Medicine	M,D
Pharmacy	M,D
Public Health—General	M,D

TOWSON UNIVERSITY

Accounting	M
Allied Health—General	M
Applied Mathematics	M
Applied Physics	M
Art Education	M,O
Art History	M
Art/Fine Arts	M
Biological and Biomedical Sciences—General	M
Child and Family Studies	M,O
Communication Disorders	M,D
Communication—General	M
Computer Science	M
Corporate and Organizational Communication	M
Counseling Psychology	M
Early Childhood Education	M,O
Education—General	M
Educational Leadership and Administration	M,O
Educational Media/Instructional Technology	M
Electronic Commerce	M,O
Elementary Education	M
Environmental and Occupational Health	D
Environmental Management and Policy	M
Environmental Sciences	M,O
Experimental Psychology	M
Forensic Sciences	M
Geography	M
Health Services Management and Hospital Administration	M,O
Homeland Security	M,O
Human Resources Development	M
Human Resources Management	M
Humanities	M
Information Science	M,D,O
Internet and Interactive Multimedia	M,O
Jewish Studies	M,O
Liberal Studies	M
Management of Technology	M,O
Marketing Research	M
Mathematics Education	M
Music Education	M
Music	M
Nursing Education	O
Nursing—General	M
Occupational Therapy	M
Physician Assistant Studies	M
Psychology—General	M

Reading Education — M,O
School Psychology — M
Secondary Education — M
Social Sciences — M
Special Education — M,O
Supply Chain Management — M,O
Theater — M
Women's Studies — M
Writing — M

TOYOTA TECHNOLOGICAL INSTITUTE AT CHICAGO
Computer Science — D

TRENT UNIVERSITY
American Indian/Native American Studies — M,D
Anthropology — M
Biological and Biomedical Sciences—General — M,D
Canadian Studies — M,D
Chemistry — M,D
Computer Science — M
Cultural Studies — D
Environmental Management and Policy — M,D
Geography — M,D
Materials Sciences — M
Modeling and Simulation — M,D
Physics — M

TREVECCA NAZARENE UNIVERSITY
Business Administration and Management—General — M
Counselor Education — M,D
Curriculum and Instruction — M,O
Education—General — M,D
Educational Leadership and Administration — M,D,O
Educational Media/Instructional Technology — M
Elementary Education — M,O
English as a Second Language — M,O
Health Services Management and Hospital Administration — M
Information Science — M,O
Library Science — M,O
Marriage and Family Therapy — M,D
Organizational Management — M
Pastoral Ministry and Counseling — M
Physician Assistant Studies — M
Religion — M
Secondary Education — M,O
Special Education — M,O

TRIDENT UNIVERSITY INTERNATIONAL
Adult Education — M
Business Administration and Management—General — M,D
Clinical Research — M,D,O
Computer and Information Systems Security — M,D
Conflict Resolution and Mediation/Peace Studies — M,D
Criminal Justice and Criminology — M,D
Early Childhood Education — M
Education—General — M,D
Educational Leadership and Administration — M,D
Educational Media/Instructional Technology — M,D
Emergency Management — M,D,O
Environmental and Occupational Health — M,D,O
Finance and Banking — M,D
Health Education — M,D,O
Health Informatics — M,D,O
Health Services Management and Hospital Administration — M,D,O
Higher Education — M,D
Human Resources Management — M,D
International Business — M,D
International Health — M,D,O
Legal and Justice Studies — M,D,O
Logistics — M,D
Management Information Systems — M,D,O
Marketing — M,D
Project Management — M,D
Public Administration — M,D
Quality Management — M,D,O
Reading Education — M

TRINE UNIVERSITY
Business Administration and Management—General — M
Criminal Justice and Criminology — M
Emergency Management — M
Engineering Management — M
Management Information Systems — M
Organizational Management — M
Physical Therapy — D
Physician Assistant Studies — M

TRINITY BAPTIST COLLEGE
Curriculum and Instruction — M
Educational Leadership and Administration — M
Religion — M
Special Education — M

TRINITY BIBLE COLLEGE AND GRADUATE SCHOOL
Missions and Missiology — M
Pastoral Ministry and Counseling — M
Theology — M

TRINITY CHRISTIAN COLLEGE
Counseling Psychology — M
Special Education — M

TRINITY COLLEGE (CANADA)
Music — M,D,O
Pastoral Ministry and Counseling — M,O
Theology — M,D,O

TRINITY COLLEGE (UNITED STATES)
American Studies — M
Cultural Studies — M
English — M
Media Studies — M
Museum Studies — M
Public Policy — M
Writing — M

TRINITY INTERNATIONAL UNIVERSITY
Archaeology — M,D,O
Athletic Training and Sports Medicine — M
Bioethics — M,D
Business Administration and Management—General — M,D,O
Counseling Psychology — M,D,O
Education—General — M
Human Resources Management — M,D
Law — M,D
Missions and Missiology — M,D,O
Pastoral Ministry and Counseling — M,D,O
Religious Education — M,D,O
Theology — M,D,O

TRINITY INTERNATIONAL UNIVERSITY FLORIDA
Counseling Psychology — M
Religion — M,O

TRINITY SCHOOL FOR MINISTRY
Missions and Missiology — M,D,O
Pastoral Ministry and Counseling — M,D,O
Religion — M,D,O
Theology — M,D,O

TRINITY UNIVERSITY
Accounting — M
Business Administration and Management—General — M
Education—General — M
Educational Leadership and Administration — M
Health Services Management and Hospital Administration — M
School Psychology — M

TRINITY WASHINGTON UNIVERSITY
Business Administration and Management—General — M
Clinical Psychology — M
Communication—General — M
Counseling Psychology — M
Counselor Education — M
Curriculum and Instruction — M
Early Childhood Education — M
Education—General — M
Educational Leadership and Administration — M
Elementary Education — M
English Education — M
Human Resources Management — M
National Security — M
Nonprofit Management — M
Nursing—General — M
Occupational Therapy — M
Organizational Management — M
Public Health—General — M
Reading Education — M
Secondary Education — M
Social Sciences Education — M
Special Education — M

TRINITY WESTERN UNIVERSITY
Business Administration and Management—General — M
Counseling Psychology — M
Educational Leadership and Administration — M,O
English as a Second Language — M
English — M
Health Services Management and Hospital Administration — M,O
History — M
Humanities — M
Interdisciplinary Studies — M
International Business — M
Linguistics — M
Nonprofit Management — M,O
Nursing—General — M
Organizational Management — M,O
Pastoral Ministry and Counseling — M,D
Philosophy — M
Theology — M,D

TRI-STATE BIBLE COLLEGE
Theology — M

TROPICAL AGRICULTURE RESEARCH AND HIGHER EDUCATION CENTER
Agricultural Economics and Agribusiness — M,D
Agricultural Sciences—General — M,D
Conservation Biology — M,D
Environmental Management and Policy — M,D
Forestry — M,D
Travel and Tourism — M,D
Water Resources — M,D

TROY UNIVERSITY
Accounting — M
Adult Education — M
Adult Nursing — M,D
Biological and Biomedical Sciences—General — M,O
Business Administration and Management—General — M
Communication—General — M
Computer Science — M
Corporate and Organizational Communication — M
Counselor Education — M,O

Criminal Justice and Criminology — M
Early Childhood Education — M,O
Economic Development — M
Economics — M
Education—General — M,O
Educational Leadership and Administration — M,O
Elementary Education — M,O
English as a Second Language — M
Environmental Management and Policy — M
Family Nurse Practitioner Studies — M
Finance and Banking — M
Health Services Management and Hospital Administration — M
History — M
Human Resources Management — M
International Affairs — M
Management Information Systems — M
Maternal and Child Health — M,D
Nursing Informatics — M,D
Nursing—General — M,D
Public Administration — M
Secondary Education — M
Social Sciences — M
Social Work — M
Sports Management — M

TRUETT MCCONNELL UNIVERSITY
Biological and Biomedical Sciences—General — M
Business Administration and Management—General — M
Counseling Psychology — M
Theology — M

TRUMAN STATE UNIVERSITY
Accounting — M
Communication Disorders — M
Education—General — M
English — M
Music — M

TUFTS UNIVERSITY
Allopathic Medicine — D
Animal Sciences — M
Art Education — M,D,O
Art History — M,O
Art/Fine Arts — M
Artificial Intelligence/Robotics — M,D
Astrophysics — M,D
Biochemistry — D
Bioengineering — M,D,O
Bioinformatics — M,D
Biological and Biomedical Sciences—General — M,D,O
Biomedical Engineering — M,D
Biostatistics — M,D,O
Biotechnology — M,D,O
Cancer Biology/Oncology — D
Cell Biology — D
Chemical Engineering — M,D
Chemical Physics — M,D
Chemistry — M,D
Child and Family Studies — M,D
Child Development — M,D
Civil Engineering — M,D
Classics — M
Clinical Laboratory Sciences/Medical Technology — M,D,O
Cognitive Sciences — M,D
Computer Science — M,D,O
Data Science/Data Analytics — M,D
Dentistry — D
Developmental Biology — D
Economics — M,D
Education—General — M,D,O
Electrical Engineering — M,D,O
Elementary Education — M,D
Engineering and Applied Sciences—General — M,D
Engineering Management — M
English — M,D
Entrepreneurship — M
Environmental and Occupational Health — M,D
Environmental Engineering — M,D
Environmental Management and Policy — M,D,O
Epidemiology — M,D,O
Ergonomics and Human Factors — M,D
Family and Consumer Sciences—General — M,D
French — M
Genetics — D
Geotechnical Engineering — M,D
German — M
Health Communication — M,D,O
Health Services Management and Hospital Administration — M,D,O
History — M,D
Human Development — M,D
Human-Computer Interaction — O
Immunology — D
Infectious Diseases — M,D
Interdisciplinary Studies — D
International Affairs — M,D
International Business — M
International Development — M
Law — M,D
Management Strategy and Policy — O
Manufacturing Engineering — O
Mathematics Education — M,D
Mathematics — M,D
Mechanical Engineering — M,D
Microbiology — D
Middle School Education — M,D
Molecular Biology — D
Molecular Medicine — D
Museum Education — M,D
Museum Studies — M,D,O

Music — M
Neuroscience — M,D
Nonprofit Management — O
Nutrition — M,D,O
Occupational Therapy — M,D,O
Oral and Dental Sciences — M,O
Organizational Management — M
Pathology — M,D
Philosophy — M
Physician Assistant Studies — M,D,O
Physics — M,D
Psychology—General — M,D
Public Administration — O
Public Health—General — M,D,O
Public Policy — M,D
Reproductive Biology — M,D
School Psychology — M,O
Science Education — M,D
Secondary Education — M,D
Structural Biology — D
Structural Engineering — M,D
Sustainability Management — M,D
Theater — M,D
Urban and Regional Planning — M
Urban Studies — M
Veterinary Medicine — M,D
Water Resources Engineering — M,D
Water Resources — M,D

TULANE UNIVERSITY
Accounting — M,D
Allopathic Medicine — D
Anthropology — D
Architecture — M
Art History — M
Art/Fine Arts — M
Biochemistry — M
Biological and Biomedical Sciences—General — M,D
Biomedical Engineering — M,D
Biostatistics — M,D
Business Administration and Management—General — M,D
Business Analytics — M,D
Cell Biology — M,D
Chemical Engineering — M,D
Chemistry — M,D
Classics — M
Community Health — M,D
Dance — M
Ecology — M,D
Economics — M,D
Emergency Management — M,D
Energy Management and Policy — M,D
English — M
Entrepreneurship — M,D
Environmental and Occupational Health — M,D
Epidemiology — M,D
Evolutionary Biology — M,D
Finance and Banking — M,D
French — M,D
Health Promotion — M
Health Services Management and Hospital Administration — M,D
History — M,D
Homeland Security — M
Human Genetics — M
Immunology — M
Interdisciplinary Studies — D
International Business — M,D
International Development — M,D
International Health — M,D
Latin American Studies — M,D
Law — M,D
Liberal Studies — M
Management Information Systems — M
Management Strategy and Policy — M,D
Mathematics — M,D
Microbiology — M
Molecular Biology — M,D
Music — M
Neuroscience — M,D
Parasitology — M,D,O
Pharmacology — M
Philosophy — M,D
Physics — M,D
Physiology — M
Political Science — D
Portuguese — M,D
Psychology—General — M,D
Public Health—General — M,D
Social Work — M,D
Sociology — M,D
Spanish — M,D
Structural Biology — M,D
Theater — M

TUSCULUM UNIVERSITY
Business Administration and Management—General — M
Curriculum and Instruction — M
Education—General — M
Family Nurse Practitioner Studies — M
Human Resources Development — M
Nursing—General — M
Special Education — M

TUSKEGEE UNIVERSITY
Agricultural Economics and Agribusiness — M
Agronomy and Soil Sciences — M
Animal Sciences — M
Biological and Biomedical Sciences—General — M,D
Chemistry — M
Computer and Information Systems Security — M
Electrical Engineering — M
Engineering and Applied Sciences—General — M,D

M—masters degree; D—doctorate; O—other advanced degree; *—Close-Up and/or Display

Environmental Sciences — M
Food Science and Technology — M
Management Information Systems — M
Materials Engineering — D
Mechanical Engineering — M
Nutrition — M
Occupational Therapy — M
Plant Sciences — M
Veterinary Medicine — M,D
Veterinary Sciences — M,D

TYNDALE UNIVERSITY COLLEGE & SEMINARY
Missions and Missiology — M,O
Pastoral Ministry and Counseling — M,O
Theology — M,O

UNIFICATION THEOLOGICAL SEMINARY
Religious Education — M,D
Theology — M,D

UNIFORMED SERVICES UNIVERSITY OF THE HEALTH SCIENCES
Allopathic Medicine — M,D
Biological and Biomedical Sciences—General — M,D
Cell Biology — M,D
Clinical Psychology — D
Environmental and Occupational Health — M,D
Family Nurse Practitioner Studies — M,D
Gerontological Nursing — M,D
Health Services Management and Hospital Administration — M,D
Immunology — D
Infectious Diseases — D*
International Health — M,D
Molecular Biology — M,D*
Neuroscience — D*
Nurse Anesthesia — M,D
Nursing—General — M,D
Psychiatric Nursing — M,D
Psychology—General — D
Public Health—General — M,D
Women's Health Nursing — M,D
Zoology — M,D

UNION COLLEGE (KY)
Clinical Psychology — M
Counseling Psychology — M
Education—General — M
Educational Leadership and Administration — M
Elementary Education — M
Health Education — M
Middle School Education — M
Music Education — M
Physical Education — M
Psychology—General — M
Reading Education — M
School Psychology — M
Secondary Education — M
Special Education — M

UNION COLLEGE (NE)
Physician Assistant Studies — M

UNION INSTITUTE & UNIVERSITY
Clinical Psychology — M
Cultural Studies — M,D
Education—General — D
Health Promotion — M
Health Services Management and Hospital Administration — M
History — M
Humanities — D
Interdisciplinary Studies — D
Organizational Management — M
Public Policy — M,D
Writing — M

UNION PRESBYTERIAN SEMINARY
Religious Education — M,D

UNION THEOLOGICAL SEMINARY IN THE CITY OF NEW YORK
Theology — M,D

UNION UNIVERSITY
Accounting — M
Business Administration and Management—General — M
Cultural Studies — M
Education—General — M,D,O
Educational Leadership and Administration — M,D,O
Family Nurse Practitioner Studies — M,D,O
Higher Education — M,D,O
Nurse Anesthesia — M,D,O
Nursing and Healthcare Administration — M,D,O
Nursing Education — M,D,O
Nursing—General — M,D,O
Pastoral Ministry and Counseling — M,D
Pharmacy — D
Religion — M,D
Social Work — M

UNITED LUTHERAN SEMINARY
Pastoral Ministry and Counseling — M,D
Religion — M,D
Theology — M,D

UNITED LUTHERAN SEMINARY
Pastoral Ministry and Counseling — M,D,O
Religion — M,O
Theology — M,D,O

UNITED STATES ARMY COMMAND AND GENERAL STAFF COLLEGE
Military and Defense Studies — M

UNITED STATES INTERNATIONAL UNIVERSITY–AFRICA
Addictions/Substance Abuse Counseling — M

Business Administration and Management—General — M
Conflict Resolution and Mediation/Peace Studies — M
Counseling Psychology — M
Entrepreneurship — M
Finance and Banking — M
Health Psychology — M
Human Resources Management — M
International Affairs — M
International Business — M
Management Information Systems — M
Management Strategy and Policy — M
Marketing — M
Organizational Management — M

UNITED STATES MERCHANT MARINE ACADEMY
Civil Engineering — M

UNITED STATES SPORTS ACADEMY
Exercise and Sports Science — M
Physical Education — M
Recreation and Park Management — M
Sports Management — M,D

UNITED STATES UNIVERSITY
Family Nurse Practitioner Studies — M

UNITED TALMUDICAL SEMINARY
Theology — M

UNITED THEOLOGICAL SEMINARY
Pastoral Ministry and Counseling — M,D
Theology — M,D

UNITED THEOLOGICAL SEMINARY OF THE TWIN CITIES
Art/Fine Arts — M,D,O
Asian Studies — M,D,O
Conflict Resolution and Mediation/Peace Studies — M,D,O
Ethnic Studies — M,D,O
Humanities — M,D,O
Pastoral Ministry and Counseling — M,D,O
Religion — M,D,O
Theology — M,D,O
Women's Studies — M,D,O

UNITY COLLEGE
Natural Resources — M
Sustainable Development — M

UNIVERSIDAD ADVENTISTA DE LAS ANTILLAS
Curriculum and Instruction — M
Educational Leadership and Administration — M
Medical/Surgical Nursing — M

UNIVERSIDAD AUTONOMA DE GUADALAJARA
Advertising and Public Relations — M,D
Allopathic Medicine — D
Architecture — M,D
Business Administration and Management—General — M,D
Computer Art and Design — M,D
Computer Science — M,D
Corporate and Organizational Communication — M,D
Education—General — M,D
Energy and Power Engineering — M,D
Entertainment Management — M,D
Environmental and Occupational Health — M,D
Environmental Management and Policy — M,D
Film, Television, and Video Production — M,D
International Business — M,D
Internet and Interactive Multimedia — M,D
Law — M,D
Legal and Justice Studies — M,D
Manufacturing Engineering — M,D
Marketing Research — M,D
Mathematics Education — M,D
Philosophy — M,D
Public Policy — M,D
Spanish — M,D
Systems Science — M,D
Translation and Interpretation — M,D

UNIVERSIDAD CENTRAL DEL CARIBE
Addictions/Substance Abuse Counseling — M
Allopathic Medicine — M,D
Anatomy — M,D
Biochemistry — M,D
Biological and Biomedical Sciences—General — M,D
Cell Biology — M,D
Immunology — M,D
Microbiology — M,D
Molecular Biology — M,D
Pharmacology — M,D
Physiology — M,D

UNIVERSIDAD CENTRAL DEL ESTE
Allopathic Medicine — D
Dentistry — D
Environmental Engineering — M
Finance and Banking — M
Higher Education — M
Human Resources Development — M
Law — D

UNIVERSIDAD DE CIENCIAS MEDICAS
Allopathic Medicine — M,D,O
Anatomy — M,D,O
Biological and Biomedical Sciences—General — M,D,O
Community Health — M,D,O
Environmental and Occupational Health — M,D,O

Health Services Management and Hospital Administration — M,D,O
Pharmacy — M,D,O

UNIVERSIDAD DE IBEROAMERICA
Acute Care/Critical Care Nursing — M,D
Allopathic Medicine — M,D
Clinical Psychology — M,D
Educational Psychology — M,D
Forensic Psychology — M,D
Health Services Management and Hospital Administration — M,D
Neuroscience — M,D

UNIVERSIDAD DE LAS AMERICAS, A.C.
Business Administration and Management—General — M
Education—General — M
Finance and Banking — M
International Affairs — M
Marketing Research — M
Marriage and Family Therapy — M
Organizational Behavior — M
Psychology—General — M
Quality Management — M

UNIVERSIDAD DE LAS AMÉRICAS PUEBLA
American Studies — M
Anthropology — M
Archaeology — M
Biotechnology — M
Business Administration and Management—General — M
Chemical Engineering — M
Clinical Laboratory Sciences/Medical Technology — M
Computer Art and Design — M
Computer Science — M
Construction Management — M
Economics — M
Education—General — M
Electrical Engineering — M
Engineering and Applied Sciences—General — M,D
English — M
Finance and Banking — M
Food Science and Technology — M
Industrial and Manufacturing Management — M
Industrial/Management Engineering — M
Linguistics — M
Manufacturing Engineering — M
Psychology—General — M

UNIVERSIDAD DEL ESTE
Accounting — M
Adult Education — M
Agricultural Economics and Agribusiness — M
Business Administration and Management—General — M
Computer and Information Systems Security — M
Criminal Justice and Criminology — M
Electronic Commerce — M
Elementary Education — M
English as a Second Language — M
Foreign Languages Education — M
Human Resources Management — M
Management Information Systems — M
Management Strategy and Policy — M
Public Policy — M
Social Work — M
Special Education — M

UNIVERSIDAD DEL TURABO
Accounting — M
Adult Nursing — M,O
Art/Fine Arts — M
Arts Administration — M
Athletic Training and Sports Medicine — M
Business Administration and Management—General — M,D
Chemistry — M,D
Communication Disorders — M
Computer Engineering — M
Conflict Resolution and Mediation/Peace Studies — M
Counseling Psychology — M,D,O
Counselor Education — M
Criminal Justice and Criminology — M
Curriculum and Instruction — M,D
Early Childhood Education — M
Education—General — M,D
Educational Leadership and Administration — M,D
Electrical Engineering — M
Engineering and Applied Sciences—General — M
English as a Second Language — M
Environmental Biology — M,D
Environmental Management and Policy — M,D
Environmental Sciences — M,D
Family Nurse Practitioner Studies — M,O
Forensic Psychology — M,D,O
Forensic Sciences — M
Health Promotion — M
Human Resources Management — M
Human Services — M
Information Studies — M
Library Science — M
Logistics — M
Management Information Systems — D
Marketing — M
Mechanical Engineering — M
Naturopathic Medicine — D
Physical Education — M
Project Management — M
Quality Management — M
Special Education — M
Telecommunications — M

UNIVERSIDAD IBEROAMERICANA
Allopathic Medicine — D
Business Administration and Management—General — M,D
Corporate and Organizational Communication — M,D
Dentistry — M,D
Educational Leadership and Administration — M,D
Human Resources Development — M,D
Law — M,D
Marketing — M,D
Real Estate — M,D
Special Education — M,D

UNIVERSIDAD METROPOLITANA
Accounting — M
Adult Education — M
Business Administration and Management—General — M
Counseling Psychology — M
Curriculum and Instruction — M
Education—General — M
Educational Leadership and Administration — M
Elementary Education — M
Environmental Management and Policy — M
Finance and Banking — M
Human Resources Management — M
International Business — M
Leisure Studies — M
Management Information Systems — M
Marketing — M
Natural Resources — M
Nursing and Healthcare Administration — M,O
Nursing—General — M,O
Oncology Nursing — M,O
Physical Education — M
Recreation and Park Management — M
Secondary Education — M
Special Education — M

UNIVERSIDAD NACIONAL PEDRO HENRIQUEZ URENA
Agricultural Sciences—General — M
Allopathic Medicine — D
Animal Sciences — M
Architecture — M
Dentistry — D
Ecology — M
Environmental Engineering — M
Environmental Sciences — M
Historic Preservation — M
Horticulture — M
International Affairs — M
Natural Resources — M
Political Science — M
Project Management — M
Science Education — M

UNIVERSITÉ DE MONCTON
Astronomy — M
Biochemistry — M
Biological and Biomedical Sciences—General — M
Business Administration and Management—General — M
Chemistry — M
Civil Engineering — M
Computer Science — M,O
Counselor Education — M
Economics — M
Education—General — M
Educational Leadership and Administration — M
Educational Psychology — M
Electrical Engineering — M
Engineering and Applied Sciences—General — M
Food Science and Technology — M
French — M,D
History — M
Industrial/Management Engineering — M
Mathematics — M
Mechanical Engineering — M
Nutrition — M
Physics — M
Public Administration — M
Social Work — M

UNIVERSITÉ DE MONTRÉAL
Allopathic Medicine — D
Anthropology — M,D
Art History — M,D
Biochemistry — M,D,O
Bioethics — M,D,O
Bioinformatics — M,D
Biological and Biomedical Sciences—General — M,D
Biomedical Engineering — M,D,O
Cell Biology — M,D
Chemistry — M,D
Classics — M,D
Communication Disorders — M,O
Communication—General — M,D
Community Health — M,D,O
Comparative Literature — M,D
Computer Science — M,D
Criminal Justice and Criminology — M,D
Curriculum and Instruction — M,D,O
Demography and Population Studies — M,D
Dental Hygiene — O
Developmental Psychology — M,D
Economics — M,D,O
Education—General — M,D,O
Educational Leadership and Administration — M,D,O
Educational Psychology — M,D,O
Electronic Commerce — M,D
Emergency Management — O

English	M,D
Environmental and Occupational Health	M
Environmental Design	M,D,O
Environmental Management and Policy	O
Ergonomics and Human Factors	O
Film, Television, and Video Theory and Criticism	M,D
French	M,D
Genetic Counseling	O
Genetics	O
Geography	M,D,O
German	M
Health Services Management and Hospital Administration	M,O
Hispanic and Latin American Languages	M,D
History	M,D
Human Services	D
Immunology	M,D
Industrial and Labor Relations	M,D
Information Studies	M,D
International Affairs	M,O
Kinesiology and Movement Studies	M,D,O
Law	M,D,O
Library Science	M
Linguistics	M,D,O
Mathematical and Computational Finance	M,D,O
Mathematics	M,D
Microbiology	M,D
Molecular Biology	M,D
Museum Studies	M
Music	M,D,O
Neuroscience	M,D
Nursing—General	M,D,O
Nutrition	M,D,O
Occupational Therapy	O
Optometry	D
Oral and Dental Sciences	M,O
Pathology	M,D
Pharmaceutical Sciences	M,D,O
Pharmacology	M,D
Philosophy	M,D
Physical Education	M,D,O
Physics	M,D
Physiology	M,D
Political Science	M,D
Psychology—General	M,D
Public Health—General	M,D,O
Public Policy	O
Rehabilitation Sciences	M,D
Religion	M,D,O
Social Work	O
Sociology	M,D
Spanish	M
Statistics	M,D,O
Taxation	M,D,O
Theology	M,D,O
Toxicology	O
Translation and Interpretation	M,D,O
Urban and Regional Planning	M,D,O
Veterinary Medicine	D
Veterinary Sciences	M,D
Virology	D
Vision Sciences	M,O

UNIVERSITÉ DE SAINT-BONIFACE

Canadian Studies	M
Education—General	M

UNIVERSITÉ DE SHERBROOKE

Accounting	M
Allopathic Medicine	D
Biochemistry	M,D
Biological and Biomedical Sciences—General	M,D,O
Biophysics	M,D
Business Administration and Management—General	M,D,O
Canadian Studies	M,D
Cell Biology	M,D
Chemical Engineering	M,D
Chemistry	M,D,O
Civil Engineering	M,D
Clinical Laboratory Sciences/Medical Technology	M,D
Comparative Literature	M,D
Computer and Information Systems Security	M
Conflict Resolution and Mediation/Peace Studies	M,D,O
Corporate and Organizational Communication	M
Economic Development	D
Economics	M
Education—General	M,O
Educational Leadership and Administration	M
Electrical Engineering	M,D
Electronic Commerce	M
Elementary Education	M,O
Engineering and Applied Sciences—General	M,D,O
Engineering Management	M
Environmental Engineering	M
Environmental Sciences	M,O
Ethics	M,D,O
Finance and Banking	M,D
French	M,D
Geography	M,D
Gerontology	M
Health Law	M,D,O
Higher Education	M,O
History	M,D
Immunology	M,D
Information Science	M
International Business	M
Kinesiology and Movement Studies	M,O

Law	M,D,O
Linguistics	M,D
Management Information Systems	M,O
Marketing	M
Mathematics	M,D
Mechanical Engineering	M,D
Microbiology	M,D
Organizational Behavior	M
Pharmacology	M,D
Philosophy	M,D,O
Physical Education	M,O
Physics	M,D
Physiology	M,D
Psychology—General	M
Public Administration	M
Radiation Biology	M,D
Religion	M,D
Social Work	M
Special Education	M
Taxation	M,O
Theater	M
Theology	M,D,O

UNIVERSITÉ DU QUÉBEC À CHICOUTIMI

Art/Fine Arts	M
Business Administration and Management—General	M
Canadian Studies	M
Comparative Literature	M
Education—General	M,D
Engineering and Applied Sciences—General	M,D
Environmental Management and Policy	M
Ethics	O
French	O
Genetics	M
Geosciences	M
Linguistics	M
Mineralogy	D
Project Management	M
Theology	M,D

UNIVERSITÉ DU QUÉBEC À MONTRÉAL

Accounting	M,O
Actuarial Science	O
Art History	M,D
Art/Fine Arts	M
Atmospheric Sciences	M,D,O
Biological and Biomedical Sciences—General	M,D
Business Administration and Management—General	M,D,O
Chemistry	M,D
Communication—General	M,D
Comparative Literature	M,D
Dance	M
Economics	M,D
Education—General	M,D,O
Environmental and Occupational Health	O
Environmental Education	M,D,O
Environmental Sciences	M,D,O
Ergonomics and Human Factors	O
Finance and Banking	O
Geographic Information Systems	O
Geography	M
Geology	M,D,O
Geosciences	M,D,O
History	M,D
Kinesiology and Movement Studies	M,D
Law	O
Linguistics	M,D
Management Information Systems	M
Mathematics	M,D,O
Meteorology	M,D
Mineralogy	M,D,O
Museum Studies	M
Natural Resources	M,D,O
Philosophy	M,D
Political Science	M,D
Project Management	M,O
Psychology—General	D
Public Administration	M,D
Religion	M,D
Social Work	M
Sociology	M,D
Urban Studies	M,D

UNIVERSITÉ DU QUÉBEC À RIMOUSKI

Business Administration and Management—General	M,O
Comparative Literature	M
Education—General	M,D,O
Engineering and Applied Sciences—General	M
Ethics	M,O
Fish, Game, and Wildlife Management	M,D,O
Marine Affairs	M,O
Nursing—General	M,O
Oceanography	M,D
Project Management	M,O
Social Psychology	M
Urban and Regional Planning	M

UNIVERSITÉ DU QUÉBEC À TROIS-RIVIÈRES

Accounting	M
Biophysics	M,D
Business Administration and Management—General	M,D
Chemistry	M,D
Chiropractic	D
Communication—General	M
Comparative Literature	M
Computer Science	M
Education—General	M,D
Educational Leadership and Administration	M

Educational Psychology	M,D
Electrical Engineering	M,D
Environmental Sciences	M,D
Finance and Banking	O
Industrial and Labor Relations	O
Industrial/Management Engineering	M,O
Leisure Studies	M,O
Mathematics	M
Nursing—General	M,O
Philosophy	M,D
Physical Education	M
Physics	M,D
Psychology—General	D,O
Travel and Tourism	M,D

UNIVERSITÉ DU QUÉBEC, ÉCOLE DE TECHNOLOGIE SUPÉRIEURE

Engineering and Applied Sciences—General	M,D,O

UNIVERSITÉ DU QUÉBEC, ÉCOLE NATIONALE D'ADMINISTRATION PUBLIQUE

International Business	M,O
Public Administration	D,O
Urban Studies	M,O

UNIVERSITÉ DU QUÉBEC EN ABITIBI-TÉMISCAMINGUE

Biological and Biomedical Sciences—General	M,D
Business Administration and Management—General	M
Education—General	M,D,O
Engineering and Applied Sciences—General	M,O
Environmental Sciences	M,D
Forestry	M,D
Mineral/Mining Engineering	M,O
Natural Resources	M,O
Project Management	M,O
Social Work	M

UNIVERSITÉ DU QUÉBEC EN OUTAOUAIS

Accounting	M,O
Computer Science	M,D,O
Education—General	M,D,O
Educational Psychology	M
Finance and Banking	M,O
Foreign Languages Education	O
Industrial and Labor Relations	M,D,O
Nursing—General	M,O
Project Management	M,O
Social Work	M
Urban and Regional Planning	M

UNIVERSITÉ DU QUÉBEC, INSTITUT NATIONAL DE LA RECHERCHE SCIENTIFIQUE

Biological and Biomedical Sciences—General	M,D
Demography and Population Studies	M,D,O
Energy Management and Policy	M,D
Environmental Management and Policy	M,D
Geosciences	M,D
Hydrology	M,D
Immunology	M,D
Materials Sciences	M,D
Medical Microbiology	M,D
Microbiology	M,D
Telecommunications	M,D
Urban Studies	M,D,O
Virology	M,D

UNIVERSITÉ LAVAL

Accounting	M,O
Advertising and Public Relations	O
Aerospace/Aeronautical Engineering	M
Agricultural Economics and Agribusiness	M
Agricultural Engineering	M
Agricultural Sciences—General	M,D,O
Agronomy and Soil Sciences	M,D
Allopathic Medicine	D,O
Anatomy	O
Anesthesiologist Assistant Studies	O
Animal Sciences	M,D
Anthropology	M,D
Archaeology	M,D
Architecture	M
Art History	M,D
Art/Fine Arts	M
Biochemistry	M,D,O
Biological and Biomedical Sciences—General	M,D,O
Business Administration and Management—General	M,D,O
Cancer Biology/Oncology	O
Cardiovascular Sciences	O
Cell Biology	M,D
Chemical Engineering	M,D
Chemistry	M,D
Civil Engineering	M,D,O
Clinical Psychology	D
Communication Disorders	M
Community Health	M,D,O
Comparative Literature	M,D
Computer Science	M,D
Consumer Economics	O
Counselor Education	M,D
Curriculum and Instruction	M,D
Dentistry	D
Economics	M,D
Education—General	M,D,O
Educational Leadership and Administration	M,D,O

Educational Measurement and Evaluation	M,D,O
Educational Media/Instructional Technology	M,D
Educational Psychology	M,D
Electrical Engineering	M,D
Electronic Commerce	M,O
Emergency Medical Services	O
Engineering and Applied Sciences—General	M,D,O
English	M,D
Entrepreneurship	M,O
Environmental and Occupational Health	O
Environmental Engineering	M,D
Environmental Management and Policy	M,D
Environmental Sciences	M,D
Epidemiology	M,D
Ethics	O
Ethnic Studies	M,D
Facilities Management	M,O
Film, Television, and Video Theory and Criticism	M,D
Finance and Banking	M,O
Food Science and Technology	M,D
Forestry	M,D
Geodetic Sciences	M,D
Geographic Information Systems	M,O
Geography	M,D
Geology	M,D
Geosciences	M,D
Gerontology	O
Graphic Design	M
Health Physics/Radiological Health	M,D
History	M,D
Immunology	M,D
Industrial and Labor Relations	M,D
Industrial/Management Engineering	O
Infectious Diseases	O
International Affairs	M,D
International Business	M,O
Journalism	O
Kinesiology and Movement Studies	M,D
Law	M,D,O
Legal and Justice Studies	O
Linguistics	M,D
Management Information Systems	M,O
Marketing	M,O
Mass Communication	M,D
Mathematics	M,D
Mechanical Engineering	M,D
Metallurgical Engineering and Metallurgy	M,D
Microbiology	M,D
Mineral/Mining Engineering	M,D
Modeling and Simulation	M,O
Molecular Biology	M,D
Museum Studies	O
Music Education	M,D
Music	M,D
Neurobiology	M,D
Nursing—General	M,D,O
Nutrition	M,D
Oceanography	D
Oral and Dental Sciences	M,O
Organizational Management	M,O
Pathology	O
Pharmaceutical Sciences	M,D,O
Philosophy	M,D
Physics	M,D
Physiology	M,D
Plant Biology	M,D
Political Science	M,D
Psychology—General	D
Religion	M,D
Rural Planning and Studies	O
Social Psychology	D
Social Work	M,D
Sociology	M,D
Software Engineering	O
Spanish	M,D
Statistics	M
Theater	M,D
Theology	M,D
Translation and Interpretation	M,O
Urban and Regional Planning	M,D
Women's Studies	O

UNIVERSITÉ SAINTE-ANNE

Education—General	M

UNIVERSITY AT ALBANY, STATE UNIVERSITY OF NEW YORK

African Studies	M
African-American Studies	M
Anthropology	M,D
Art/Fine Arts	M
Atmospheric Sciences	M,D
Biological and Biomedical Sciences—General	M,D
Biostatistics	M,D
Business Administration and Management—General	M
Business Analytics	M
Chemistry	M,D
Clinical Psychology	M,D
Cognitive Sciences	M,D
Communication—General	M,D
Computer and Information Systems Security	M,D,O
Computer Science	M,D
Counseling Psychology	M,D,O
Criminal Justice and Criminology	M,D
Curriculum and Instruction	M,D
Demography and Population Studies	M,D,O
Economics	M,D,O
Education—General	M,D,O

Educational Leadership and Administration — M,D,O
Educational Media/Instructional Technology — M,D,O
Educational Policy — M,D,O
Emergency Management — M,D,O
Engineering and Applied Sciences—General — M,D,O
English — M,D
Entrepreneurship — M
Environmental and Occupational Health — M,D
Epidemiology — M,D
Finance and Banking — M,D,O
Forensic Sciences — M
Gender Studies — M
Geographic Information Systems — M,O
Geography — M,O
Health Services Management and Hospital Administration — M,D,O
Higher Education — M,D,O
History — M,D,O
Homeland Security — M,D,O
Human Resources Management — M,D,O
Industrial and Organizational Psychology — M,D
Information Science — M,D
International and Comparative Education — M,D,O
Latin American Studies — M,D,O
Liberal Studies — M
Management Information Systems — M,D,O
Marketing — M
Mathematics — M,D
Neuroscience — M,D
Nonprofit Management — M,D,O
Organizational Behavior — M,D,O
Philosophy — M,D
Physics — M,D
Political Science — M,D
Psychology—General — M,D
Public Administration — M,D,O
Public Health—General — M,D
Public History — M,D,O
Public Policy — M,D,O
Reading Education — M,D,O
Social Psychology — M,D
Social Work — M,D
Sociology — M,D,O
Spanish — M,D
Toxicology — M,D
Urban and Regional Planning — M,O
Urban Studies — M
Women's Studies — M

UNIVERSITY AT BUFFALO, THE STATE UNIVERSITY OF NEW YORK

Accounting — M,D
Adult Nursing — M,D,O
Aerospace/Aeronautical Engineering — M,D
Allied Health—General — M,D,O
Allopathic Medicine — D
American Studies — M,D
Anatomy — M,D
Anthropology — M,D
Art History — M,D
Art/Fine Arts — M
Arts Administration — M
Biochemistry — M,D
Bioengineering — M,D,O
Bioinformatics — M,D
Biological and Biomedical Sciences—General — M,D
Biomedical Engineering — M,D
Biophysics — M,D
Biostatistics — M,D
Biotechnology — M
Business Administration and Management—General — M,D
Business Analytics — M,D
Canadian Studies — M,D
Cancer Biology/Oncology — M
Cell Biology — M,D
Chemical Engineering — M,D,O
Chemistry — M,D
Civil Engineering — M,D
Classics — M,D,O
Clinical Laboratory Sciences/Medical Technology — M
Communication Disorders — M,D
Communication—General — M,D
Community Health — M,D,O
Comparative Literature — M,D
Computational Sciences — D,O
Computer Science — M,D,O
Counseling Psychology — M,D,O
Counselor Education — M,D,O
Curriculum and Instruction — M,D,O
Dance — M,D
Data Science/Data Analytics — M,D
Distance Education Development — M,D,O
Early Childhood Education — M,D,O
Ecology — M,D,O
Economic Development — M,D,O
Economics — M,D
Education of the Gifted — M,D,O
Education—General — M,D,O
Educational Leadership and Administration — M,D,O
Educational Media/Instructional Technology — M,D,O
Educational Psychology — M,D,O
Electrical Engineering — M,D,O
Electronic Commerce — M,D,O
Elementary Education — M,D,O
Energy and Power Engineering — M,D
Engineering and Applied Sciences—General — M,D,O
Engineering Management — M,D,O
English as a Second Language — M,D,O
English Education — M,D,O
English — M,D,O

Environmental Engineering — M,D
Environmental Law — M,D
Environmental Sciences — M,D
Epidemiology — M,D
Evolutionary Biology — M,D,O
Exercise and Sports Science — M,D,O
Family Nurse Practitioner Studies — M,D,O
Film, Television, and Video Theory and Criticism — M,D,O
Finance and Banking — M,D
Food Science and Technology — M,D,O
Foreign Languages Education — M,D,O
Foundations and Philosophy of Education — M,D,O
French — M,D,O
Gender Studies — M,D
Genetics — M,D
Genomic Sciences — M,D
Geographic Information Systems — M,D
Geography — M,D
Geology — M,D
Geosciences — M,D
German — M,D,O
Gerontological Nursing — M,D,O
Health Services Management and Hospital Administration — M,D
Higher Education — M,D,O
Historic Preservation — M,D,O
History — M,D,O
Human Resources Management — M,D,O
Humanities — M
Immunology — M,D
Industrial/Management Engineering — M,D,O
Information Studies — M,O
Interdisciplinary Studies — M
International Business — M,D
International Trade Policy — M,D
Law — M,D
Legal and Justice Studies — M,D
Library Science — M,O
Linguistics — M,D
Logistics — M,D
Management Information Systems — M,D,O
Manufacturing Engineering — M,D,O
Marketing — M,D
Materials Sciences — M,D
Mathematics Education — M,D,O
Mathematics — M,D
Mechanical Engineering — M,D
Media Studies — M,D,O
Medical Informatics — M,D
Medical Physics — M,D
Medicinal and Pharmaceutical Chemistry — M,D
Microbiology — M,D
Modeling and Simulation — M,D
Molecular Biology — D
Molecular Biophysics — M,D
Molecular Pharmacology — D
Multilingual and Multicultural Education — M,D,O
Museum Studies — M,D
Music Education — M,D,O
Music — M,D,O
Nanotechnology — M,D,O
Neuroscience — M,D
Nurse Anesthesia — M,D,O
Nursing and Healthcare Administration — M,D,O
Nursing—General — M,D,O
Nutrition — M,D,O
Occupational Therapy — M
Oral and Dental Sciences — M,D,O
Pathology — M,D
Pharmacology — D
Pharmacy — D
Philosophy — M,D
Physical Therapy — D
Physics — M,D
Physiology — M,D
Political Science — M,D
Psychiatric Nursing — M,D,O
Psychology—General — M,D
Public Health—General — M,D
Public History — M,D,O
Quantitative Analysis — M,D
Reading Education — M,D,O
Real Estate — M,D,O
Rehabilitation Counseling — M,D,O
Rehabilitation Sciences — O
Romance Languages — M,D
Science Education — M,D,O
Social Sciences Education — M,D,O
Social Sciences — M
Social Work — M,D
Sociology — M,D,O
Spanish — M,D,O
Special Education — M,D,O
Structural Biology — M,D
Structural Engineering — M,D
Supply Chain Management — M,D
Sustainable Development — M,D
Theater — M,D
Toxicology — M,D
Transportation Management — M
Water Resources Engineering — M,D

UNIVERSITY OF ADVANCING TECHNOLOGY

Computer and Information Systems Security — M
Computer Science — M
Game Design and Development — M
Internet and Interactive Multimedia — M
Management of Technology — M

THE UNIVERSITY OF AKRON

Accounting — M
Applied Mathematics — M
Art Education — M
Arts Administration — M

Biological and Biomedical Sciences—General — M,D
Biomedical Engineering — M,D
Business Administration and Management—General — M
Chemical Engineering — M,D
Chemistry — M,D
Child and Family Studies — M
Child Development — M
Civil Engineering — M,D
Clinical Psychology — M
Clothing and Textiles — M
Communication Disorders — M,D
Communication—General — M
Computer Engineering — M,D
Computer Science — M
Counseling Psychology — M,D
Counselor Education — M,D
Curriculum and Instruction — M
Economics — M
Education—General — M
Educational Leadership and Administration — M,O
Electrical Engineering — M,D
Electronic Commerce — M
Elementary Education — M
Engineering and Applied Sciences—General — M,D
English Education — M
English — M
Exercise and Sports Science — M,D
Finance and Banking — M
Geological Engineering — M
Geology — M
Geosciences — M
Gerontology — D
History — M,D
Industrial and Organizational Psychology — M,D
Law — M,D
Management Information Systems — M
Marketing — M
Marriage and Family Therapy — M
Mathematics Education — M
Mathematics — M
Mechanical Engineering — M,D
Music Education — M
Music — M
Nursing—General — M,D
Physical Education — M
Political Science — M
Polymer Science and Engineering — M,D
Psychology—General — M,D
Public Administration — M
Reading Education — M
Science Education — M
Secondary Education — M
Social Sciences Education — M
Social Work — M
Statistics — M
Supply Chain Management — M
Taxation — M
Theater — M
Writing — M

THE UNIVERSITY OF ALABAMA

Accounting — M,D
Advertising and Public Relations — M
Aerospace/Aeronautical Engineering — M,D
American Studies — M
Anthropology — M,D
Applied Mathematics — M,D
Applied Statistics — M,D
Art History — M
Art/Fine Arts — M
Astronomy — M,D
Biological and Biomedical Sciences—General — M,D
Business Administration and Management—General — M,D
Chemical Engineering — M,D
Chemistry — M,D
Child and Family Studies — M
Civil Engineering — M,D
Clinical Psychology — D
Clothing and Textiles — M
Communication Disorders — M
Communication—General — M,D
Community Health — M
Computer Engineering — M,D
Computer Science — M,D
Construction Engineering — M,D
Consumer Economics — M
Counselor Education — M,D,O
Criminal Justice and Criminology — M
Economics — M,D
Education of the Gifted — M,D,O
Educational Leadership and Administration — M,D,O
Electrical Engineering — M,D
Elementary Education — M,D,O
Engineering and Applied Sciences—General — M,D
English as a Second Language — M,D
English — M,D
Environmental Engineering — M,D
Ergonomics and Human Factors — M
Exercise and Sports Science — M,D
Experimental Psychology — D
Family and Consumer Sciences—General — M,D
Finance and Banking — M,D
French — M,D
Geographic Information Systems — M
Geography — M,D
Geology — M,D
Geosciences — M,D
German — M
Health Education — M,D
Health Promotion — M,D
Higher Education — M,D

History — M,D
Hospitality Management — M
Human Development — M
Industrial and Manufacturing Management — M,D
Information Studies — M
Interdisciplinary Studies — D
Journalism — M
Kinesiology and Movement Studies — M,D
Law — M,D
Library Science — M,D
Marketing — M,D
Marriage and Family Therapy — M
Mass Communication — D
Materials Engineering — M
Materials Sciences — D
Mathematics — M,D
Mechanical Engineering — M,D
Mechanics — M,D
Metallurgical Engineering and Metallurgy — M
Music Education — M,D,O
Music — M,D
Nursing—General — M,D
Nutrition — M
Photography — M
Physical Education — M,D
Physics — M,D
Political Science — M
Psychology—General — D
Public Administration — M,D
Quality Management — M
Rhetoric — M
Romance Languages — M
Secondary Education — M,D,O
Social Work — M,D
Spanish — M,D
Special Education — M,D,O
Speech and Interpersonal Communication — M
Sports Management — M
Taxation — M,D
Theater — M
Women's Studies — M
Writing — M,D

THE UNIVERSITY OF ALABAMA AT BIRMINGHAM

Accounting — M
Adult Nursing — M,D
Allied Health—General — M,D,O
Allopathic Medicine — D
Anthropology — M
Applied Mathematics — D
Art Education — M
Art History — M
Biochemistry — D
Bioinformatics — D
Biological and Biomedical Sciences—General — M,D
Biomedical Engineering — M,D
Biostatistics — M,D
Biotechnology — M
Business Administration and Management—General — M
Cancer Biology/Oncology — D
Cell Biology — D
Chemistry — M,D
Civil Engineering — M,D
Clinical Laboratory Sciences/Medical Technology — M,D
Clinical Psychology — M
Communication—General — M
Community Health — M
Computational Sciences — D
Computer and Information Systems Security — M
Computer Engineering — M,D
Computer Science — M,D
Construction Engineering — M
Construction Management — M
Counselor Education — M
Criminal Justice and Criminology — M
Curriculum and Instruction — O
Dentistry — D
Developmental Biology — D
Developmental Psychology — M,D
Early Childhood Education — M,D
Education—General — M,D,O
Educational Leadership and Administration — M,D,O
Electrical Engineering — M,D
Elementary Education — M
Engineering and Applied Sciences—General — D
Engineering Design — M
Engineering Management — M
English as a Second Language — M,O
English — M
Environmental and Occupational Health — M,D
Epidemiology — M,D
Family Nurse Practitioner Studies — M,D
Finance and Banking — M
Forensic Sciences — M
Genetic Counseling — M
Genetics — D
Genomic Sciences — D
Gerontological Nursing — M,D
Health Informatics — M
Health Psychology — M,D
Health Services Management and Hospital Administration — M,D
Health Services Research — M
History — M
Immunology — D
Industrial Hygiene — M,D
Information Science — M
Management Information Systems — M
Marketing — M
Materials Engineering — M,D
Maternal and Child Health — M,D
Mathematics — M
Mechanical Engineering — M

Microbiology	D
Molecular Biology	D
Molecular Medicine	D
Neuroscience	M,D
Nurse Anesthesia	M,D
Nursing and Healthcare Administration	M,D
Nursing Informatics	M,D
Nursing—General	M,D
Nutrition	M,D
Occupational Therapy	M,O
Optometry	D
Oral and Dental Sciences	M
Pathobiology	D
Pediatric Nursing	M,D
Pharmacology	D
Physical Therapy	D
Physician Assistant Studies	M,D
Physics	M,D
Psychiatric Nursing	M,D
Psychology—General	M,D
Public Administration	M
Quantitative Analysis	M,D
Reading Education	M
Rehabilitation Sciences	D
Rhetoric	M
Safety Engineering	M
Secondary Education	M
Social Work	M
Sociology	D
Special Education	M
Structural Biology	D
Structural Engineering	M
Sustainable Development	M
Toxicology	M,D
Vision Sciences	M,D
Women's Health Nursing	M,D
Writing	M

THE UNIVERSITY OF ALABAMA IN HUNTSVILLE

Accounting	M,O
Acute Care/Critical Care Nursing	M,D,O
Aerospace/Aeronautical Engineering	M,D
Applied Mathematics	M,D
Astronomy	M,D
Atmospheric Sciences	M,D
Biological and Biomedical Sciences—General	M,D
Biotechnology	M,D
Business Administration and Management—General	M,O
Business Analytics	M,O
Chemical Engineering	M,D
Chemistry	M,D
Civil Engineering	M,D
Computer and Information Systems Security	M,D,O
Computer Engineering	M,D
Computer Science	M,D,O
Electrical Engineering	M,D
Engineering and Applied Sciences—General	M,D
English as a Second Language	M,O
English Education	M,O
English	M,O
Entrepreneurship	M,O
Environmental Engineering	M,D
Family Nurse Practitioner Studies	M,D,O
Finance and Banking	M,O
Geosciences	M,D
Gerontological Nursing	M,D,O
Health Services Management and Hospital Administration	M,D,O
History	M
Human Resources Management	M,O
Industrial and Organizational Psychology	M
Industrial/Management Engineering	M,D
Logistics	M,O
Management Information Systems	M,O
Management of Technology	M,O
Marketing	M,O
Materials Sciences	M,D
Mathematics Education	M,D,O
Mathematics	M,D
Mechanical Engineering	M,D
Modeling and Simulation	M,D,O
Nursing Education	M,D,O
Nursing—General	M,D,O
Operations Research	M,D
Optical Sciences	M,D
Photonics	M,D
Physics	M,D
Project Management	M
Psychology—General	M
Public Affairs	M
Reading Education	M,O
Science Education	M,D,O
Secondary Education	M,O
Social Sciences Education	M,O
Software Engineering	M,D,O
Special Education	M,O
Supply Chain Management	M,O
Systems Engineering	M,D
Taxation	M
Technical Writing	M,O

UNIVERSITY OF ALASKA ANCHORAGE

Anthropology	M
Biological and Biomedical Sciences—General	M
Business Administration and Management—General	M
Clinical Psychology	M,D
Early Childhood Education	M,D
Education—General	M,O
Educational Leadership and Administration	M,O

English	M
Logistics	M
Nursing—General	M,D,O
Physician Assistant Studies	M
Psychology—General	M
Public Administration	M
Public Health—General	M
Social Psychology	M,D
Social Work	M,O
Special Education	M,O
Writing	M

UNIVERSITY OF ALASKA FAIRBANKS

Anthropology	M,D
Art/Fine Arts	M
Astrophysics	M,D
Atmospheric Sciences	M,D
Biochemistry	M,D
Biological and Biomedical Sciences—General	M,D,O
Business Administration and Management—General	M
Chemistry	M,D
Civil Engineering	M,D,O
Communication—General	M
Computational Sciences	M,D
Computer Art and Design	M
Computer Science	M
Construction Management	M
Corporate and Organizational Communication	M
Counselor Education	M,O
Criminal Justice and Criminology	M
Cultural Studies	M
Education—General	M,O
Electrical Engineering	M
Emergency Management	M
Engineering and Applied Sciences—General	D
English	M
Environmental Engineering	M,D,O
Environmental Management and Policy	M
Finance and Banking	M
Fish, Game, and Wildlife Management	M,D,O
Geographic Information Systems	M
Geological Engineering	M
Geophysics	M
History	M
Homeland Security	M
Interdisciplinary Studies	M,D
Limnology	M,D
Linguistics	M
Marine Biology	M,D
Marine Sciences	M,D
Mathematics	M,D,O
Mechanical Engineering	M
Mineral/Mining Engineering	M
Multilingual and Multicultural Education	M
Natural Resources	M,D
Neuroscience	M,D
Northern Studies	M
Oceanography	M,D
Petroleum Engineering	M
Photography	M
Physics	M,D
Rural Planning and Studies	M
Social Psychology	M,O
Special Education	M
Statistics	M,D
Sustainable Development	M,D
Writing	M

UNIVERSITY OF ALASKA SOUTHEAST

Education—General	M
Educational Leadership and Administration	M
Educational Media/Instructional Technology	M
Elementary Education	M
Mathematics Education	M
Public Administration	M
Reading Education	M
Secondary Education	M
Special Education	M

UNIVERSITY OF ALBERTA

Accounting	D
Adult Education	M,D,O
Agricultural Economics and Agribusiness	M,D
Agricultural Sciences—General	M,D
Agronomy and Soil Sciences	M,D
Allopathic Medicine	D
Anthropology	M,D
Applied Arts and Design—General	M
Applied Mathematics	M,D,O
Archaeology	M,D
Art History	M
Art/Fine Arts	M
Asian Studies	M
Astrophysics	M,D
Biochemistry	M,D
Biological and Biomedical Sciences—General	M,D
Biostatistics	M,D,O
Biotechnology	M,D
Business Administration and Management—General	M,D
Cancer Biology/Oncology	M,D
Cell Biology	M,D
Chemical Engineering	M,D
Chemistry	M,D
Chinese	M
Civil Engineering	M,D
Classics	M,D

Clinical Laboratory Sciences/Medical Technology	M,D
Clothing and Textiles	M,D
Communication Disorders	M
Communication—General	M
Community Health	M,D
Computer Engineering	M,D
Computer Science	M,D
Condensed Matter Physics	M,D
Conservation Biology	M,D
Construction Engineering	M,D
Counseling Psychology	M,D
Counselor Education	M,D
Criminal Justice and Criminology	M,D
Demography and Population Studies	M,D
Dental Hygiene	O
Dentistry	D
East European and Russian Studies	M,D
Ecology	M,D
Economics	M,D
Educational Leadership and Administration	M,D,O
Educational Media/Instructional Technology	M,D
Educational Policy	M,D,O
Educational Psychology	M,D
Electrical Engineering	M,D
Elementary Education	M,D
Energy and Power Engineering	M,D
Engineering Management	M,D
English as a Second Language	M,D
English	M,D
Environmental and Occupational Health	M,D
Environmental Biology	M,D
Environmental Engineering	M,D
Environmental Management and Policy	M,D
Environmental Sciences	M,D
Epidemiology	M,D
Evolutionary Biology	M,D
Exercise and Sports Science	M,D
Family and Consumer Sciences—General	M,D
Finance and Banking	M,D
Folklore	M,D
Forestry	M,D
French	M,D
Genetics	M,D
Geophysics	M,D
Geosciences	M,D
Geotechnical Engineering	M,D
German	M,D
Health Physics/Radiological Health	M,D
Health Promotion	M,O
Health Services Management and Hospital Administration	M,D
Health Services Research	M,D
Hispanic Studies	M,D
History	M,D
Immunology	M,D
Industrial and Labor Relations	D
Information Studies	M
International Business	M
International Health	M,D
Italian	M,D
Japanese	M
Kinesiology and Movement Studies	M,D
Law	M,D
Library Science	M
Linguistics	M,D
Marketing	D
Materials Engineering	M,D
Maternal and Child/Neonatal Nursing	D
Mathematical and Computational Finance	M,D,O
Mathematical Physics	M,D,O
Mathematics	M,D,O
Mechanical Engineering	M,D
Medical Microbiology	M,D
Medical Physics	M,D
Microbiology	M,D
Mineral/Mining Engineering	M,D
Molecular Biology	M,D
Multilingual and Multicultural Education	M
Music	M,D
Nanotechnology	M,D
Natural Resources	M,D
Neuroscience	M,D
Nursing—General	M,D
Occupational Therapy	M,D
Oral and Dental Sciences	M,D
Organizational Management	D
Pathology	M,D
Petroleum Engineering	M,D
Pharmaceutical Sciences	M,D
Pharmacology	M,D
Pharmacy	M,D
Philosophy	M,D
Physical Education	M,D
Physical Therapy	M,D
Physics	M,D
Physiology	M,D
Plant Biology	M,D
Political Science	M,D
Psychology—General	M,D
Public Health—General	M,D
Recreation and Park Management	M,D
Rehabilitation Sciences	M,D
Rural Sociology	M,D
School Psychology	M,D
Secondary Education	M,D
Slavic Languages	M,D
Sociology	M,D
Special Education	M,D
Sports Management	M
Statistics	M,D,O
Structural Engineering	M,D

Systems Engineering	M,D
Telecommunications	M,D
Theater	M
Vision Sciences	M,D
Water Resources Engineering	M,D

UNIVERSITY OF ANTELOPE VALLEY

Business Administration and Management—General	M
Criminal Justice and Criminology	M

THE UNIVERSITY OF ARIZONA

Accounting	M
Aerospace/Aeronautical Engineering	M,D,O
African Studies	M
Agricultural Economics and Agribusiness	M
Agricultural Education	M,O
Agricultural Engineering	M,D
Agricultural Sciences—General	M,D,O
Agronomy and Soil Sciences	M,D,O
Allopathic Medicine	M,D
American Indian/Native American Studies	M,D
Animal Sciences	M,D
Anthropology	M,D,O
Applied Economics	M
Applied Mathematics	M,D
Architecture	M
Art Education	M,D
Art History	M,D
Art/Fine Arts	M
Asian Studies	M,D
Astronomy	D
Atmospheric Sciences	M,D
Biochemistry	M,D
Biological and Biomedical Sciences—General	M,D
Biomedical Engineering	M,D
Biostatistics	M,D
Biosystems Engineering	M,D
Business Administration and Management—General	M,D,O
Cancer Biology/Oncology	D
Cell Biology	D
Chemical Engineering	M,D
Chemistry	M,D
Child and Family Studies	M,D,O
Classics	M
Communication Disorders	M,D,O
Communication—General	M,D
Computer Engineering	M,D
Computer Science	M,D
Counseling Psychology	M
Counselor Education	M
Dance	M
Data Science/Data Analytics	M
Ecology	M,D
Economics	M,D
Education of Students with Severe/Multiple Disabilities	M,D,O
Education—General	M,D,O
Educational Leadership and Administration	M,D,O
Educational Psychology	M,D,O
Electrical Engineering	M,D
Elementary Education	M,D
Engineering and Applied Sciences—General	M,D,O
Engineering Management	M,D
English as a Second Language	M,D
English Education	M,D
English	M,D
Entomology	M,D
Environmental Engineering	M,D
Environmental Management and Policy	M,D
Environmental Sciences	M,D,O
Epidemiology	M,D
Evolutionary Biology	M,D
Family and Consumer Sciences—General	D
Family Nurse Practitioner Studies	M,D,O
Film, Television, and Video Theory and Criticism	M
Finance and Banking	M
Forestry	M,D
French	M,D
Gender Studies	M,D,O
Genetics	M,D
Geographic Information Systems	M,D,O
Geography	M,D
Geological Engineering	M,D,O
Geosciences	M,D
German	M,D
Higher Education	M,D
History	M,D,O
Human Development	M,D,O
Hydrology	D,O
Immunology	D
Industrial/Management Engineering	M,D,O
Information Studies	M,D
Interdisciplinary Studies	M,D
Journalism	M
Landscape Architecture	M
Latin American Studies	M
Law	M,D
Library Science	M,D
Linguistics	M,D
Management Information Systems	M,O
Management Strategy and Policy	M,D
Marketing	M,D
Materials Engineering	M,D
Materials Sciences	M,D
Mathematics Education	M
Mathematics	M,D
Mechanical Engineering	M,D
Medical Informatics	M,D,O

Medical Physics	M
Microbiology	D
Mineral/Mining Engineering	M,D,O
Molecular Biology	D
Molecular Medicine	M,D
Music Education	M,D
Music	M,D
Natural Resources	M,D
Near and Middle Eastern Studies	M,D,O
Neuroscience	D
Nursing—General	M,D,O
Nutrition	M,D
Optical Sciences	M,D,O
Organizational Management	M,D
Perfusion	M,D
Pharmaceutical Sciences	M,D
Pharmacology	M,D
Pharmacy	D
Philosophy	M,D
Physics	M,D
Physiology	M,D
Planetary and Space Sciences	M,D
Plant Pathology	M,D
Plant Sciences	M,D
Political Science	M,D
Psychology—General	M,D
Public Administration	M,D,O
Public Health—General	M,D
Public Policy	M,D,O
Range Science	M,D
Reading Education	M,D,O
Rehabilitation Counseling	M,D
Rhetoric	M,D
Russian	M
School Psychology	D,O
Secondary Education	M,D
Sociology	M,D
Spanish	M,D
Special Education	M,D
Statistics	M,D
Systems Engineering	M,D,O
Theater	M
Urban and Regional Planning	M
Water Resources	M,D,O
Women's Studies	M,D,O
Writing	M

UNIVERSITY OF ARKANSAS

Accounting	M
Adult Education	M,D
Agricultural Economics and Agribusiness	M
Agricultural Education	M
Agricultural Engineering	M,D
Agricultural Sciences—General	M,D
Agronomy and Soil Sciences	M,D
Animal Sciences	M,D
Anthropology	M,D
Applied Physics	M,D
Art/Fine Arts	M
Athletic Training and Sports Medicine	M
Bioengineering	M
Biological and Biomedical Sciences—General	M,D
Biomedical Engineering	M
Business Administration and Management—General	M,D
Cell Biology	M,D
Chemical Engineering	M,D
Chemistry	M,D
Civil Engineering	M,D
Communication Disorders	M,D
Communication—General	M
Community Health	M,D
Comparative Literature	M,D
Computer Engineering	M,D
Computer Science	M,D
Counselor Education	M,D
Cultural Studies	M,D
Curriculum and Instruction	M,D,O
Early Childhood Education	M
Economics	M,D
Education—General	M,D,O
Educational Leadership and Administration	M,D,O
Educational Measurement and Evaluation	M
Educational Media/Instructional Technology	M
Educational Policy	D
Electrical Engineering	M,D
Electronic Materials	M,D
Engineering and Applied Sciences—General	M,D
English	M,D
Entomology	M,D
Environmental Engineering	M,D
Family and Consumer Sciences-General	M
Food Science and Technology	M,D
French	M
Geography	M
Geology	M
German	M
Health Education	M,D
Health Promotion	M,D
Higher Education	M,D,O
History	M,D
Horticulture	M,D
Human Resources Development	M,D,O
Industrial and Manufacturing Management	M
Industrial/Management Engineering	M,D
Journalism	M
Kinesiology and Movement Studies	M,D
Law	M,D
Management Information Systems	M
Mathematics Education	M
Mathematics	M,D

Mechanical Engineering	M,D
Middle School Education	M,D,O
Molecular Biology	D
Music	M
Nursing—General	M
Philosophy	M,D
Photonics	M,D
Physical Education	M
Physics	M,D
Planetary and Space Sciences	M,D
Plant Pathology	M
Plant Sciences	D
Political Science	M
Psychology—General	M,D
Public Administration	M
Public Policy	D
Recreation and Park Management	M,D
Rehabilitation Counseling	M,D
Secondary Education	M,O
Social Work	M
Sociology	M
Spanish	M
Special Education	M
Sports Management	M,D
Statistics	M
Telecommunications	M,D
Theater	M
Transportation and Highway Engineering	M,D
Vocational and Technical Education	M,D,O
Writing	M

UNIVERSITY OF ARKANSAS AT LITTLE ROCK

Adult Education	M
Applied Mathematics	M,O
Applied Psychology	M
Applied Science and Technology	M,D
Applied Statistics	M,O
Art Education	M
Art History	M
Art/Fine Arts	M
Bioinformatics	M,D
Biological and Biomedical Sciences—General	M
Business Administration and Management—General	M,O
Chemistry	M
Community College Education	M,D
Computer Science	M,D
Conflict Resolution and Mediation/Peace Studies	O
Construction Management	M
Counselor Education	M
Criminal Justice and Criminology	M,D
Curriculum and Instruction	M
Education of the Gifted	M,O
Education—General	M,D,O
Educational Leadership and Administration	M,D,O
Educational Media/Instructional Technology	M
English as a Second Language	M
Entrepreneurship	O
Exercise and Sports Science	M
Foreign Languages Education	M
Geosciences	O
Gerontology	O
Health Education	M,D
Higher Education	M,D
Information Science	M,D,O
Interdisciplinary Studies	M
Law	D
Management Information Systems	M,O
Mass Communication	M
Mathematics	M,O
Middle School Education	M
Nonprofit Management	O
Psychology—General	M
Public Administration	M
Public Affairs	M,O
Public History	M
Reading Education	M,D,O
Rehabilitation Counseling	M,O
Rhetoric	M
Secondary Education	M
Social Work	M
Special Education	M,O
Speech and Interpersonal Communication	M
Sports Management	M
Student Affairs	M,D
Systems Engineering	M,D,O
Technical Writing	M
Writing	M

UNIVERSITY OF ARKANSAS AT MONTICELLO

Education—General	M
Educational Leadership and Administration	M
Forestry	M
Natural Resources	M

UNIVERSITY OF ARKANSAS AT PINE BLUFF

Aquaculture	M,D
Education—General	M
Elementary Education	M
English Education	M
Fish, Game, and Wildlife Management	M,D
Mathematics Education	M
Science Education	M
Secondary Education	M
Social Sciences Education	M

UNIVERSITY OF ARKANSAS FOR MEDICAL SCIENCES

Allopathic Medicine	D
Biochemistry	M,D,O
Bioinformatics	M,D,O

Biological and Biomedical Sciences—General	M,D,O
Biostatistics	M,D,O
Communication Disorders	M,D
Environmental and Occupational Health	M,D,O
Epidemiology	M,D,O
Genetic Counseling	M
Health Education	M,D,O
Health Physics/Radiological Health	M,D
Health Promotion	M,D,O
Health Services Management and Hospital Administration	M,D,O
Health Services Research	M,D,O
Immunology	M,D,O
Microbiology	M,D,O
Molecular Biology	M,D,O
Molecular Biophysics	M,D,O
Neurobiology	M,D,O
Nursing—General	D
Nutrition	M,D,O
Pharmacology	M,D,O
Pharmacy	M,D
Physician Assistant Studies	M,D
Physiology	M,D,O
Public Health—General	M,D
Toxicology	M,D,O

UNIVERSITY OF ARKANSAS–FORT SMITH

Health Services Management and Hospital Administration	M

UNIVERSITY OF BALTIMORE

Accounting	M,O
Applied Arts and Design—General	M
Applied Psychology	M
Business Administration and Management—General	M,O
Conflict Resolution and Mediation/Peace Studies	M
Counseling Psychology	M
Criminal Justice and Criminology	M
Entrepreneurship	M
Finance and Banking	M
Graphic Design	D
Health Services Management and Hospital Administration	M
Human Services	M
Human-Computer Interaction	M
Intellectual Property Law	M,D
International Business	M
Law	M,D
Legal and Justice Studies	M
Management Information Systems	M,O
Marketing	M
Public Administration	M,D
Public Affairs	M,D
Publishing	M
Taxation	M,D
Writing	M

UNIVERSITY OF BRIDGEPORT

Accounting	M
Acupuncture and Oriental Medicine	M
Applied Arts and Design—General	M
Asian Studies	M
Biomedical Engineering	M
Business Administration and Management—General	M
Chiropractic	D
Clinical Psychology	M
Communication—General	M
Computer Education	M,D,O
Computer Engineering	M,D
Computer Science	M,D
Conflict Resolution and Mediation/Peace Studies	M
Counseling Psychology	M
Dental Hygiene	M
Early Childhood Education	M,D,O
Education—General	M,D,O
Educational Leadership and Administration	M,D,O
Electrical Engineering	M
Elementary Education	M,D,O
Engineering and Applied Sciences—General	M,D
Entrepreneurship	M
Finance and Banking	M
Human Resources Development	M
Human Resources Management	M
Human Services	M
Industrial and Manufacturing Management	M
International Affairs	M
International and Comparative Education	M,D,O
International Business	M
Management Information Systems	M
Management of Technology	M,D
Marketing	M
Mechanical Engineering	M
Media Studies	M
Middle School Education	M,D,O
Music Education	M,D,O
Naturopathic Medicine	D
Nutrition	M
Pacific Area/Pacific Rim Studies	M
Physician Assistant Studies	M
Reading Education	M,D,O
Secondary Education	M,D,O
Social Psychology	M
Student Affairs	M

THE UNIVERSITY OF BRITISH COLUMBIA

Accounting	D
Adult Education	M,D
Agricultural Economics and Agribusiness	M
Agricultural Sciences—General	M,D

Agronomy and Soil Sciences	M,D
Allopathic Medicine	M,D
Animal Sciences	M,D
Anthropology	M,D
Archaeology	M
Architecture	M,D
Archives/Archival Administration	M,D
Art Education	M,D
Art History	M,D
Art/Fine Arts	M,D
Asian Studies	M,D
Astronomy	M,D
Atmospheric Sciences	M,D
Biochemistry	M,D
Bioengineering	M,D
Bioinformatics	M,D
Biomedical Engineering	M,D
Biopsychology	M,D
Botany	M,D
Business Administration and Management—General	M,D
Business Analytics	M
Cell Biology	M,D
Chemical Engineering	M,D
Chemistry	M,D
Civil Engineering	M,D
Classics	M,D
Clinical Psychology	M,D
Cognitive Sciences	M,D
Communication Disorders	M,D
Computer Engineering	M,D
Computer Science	M,D
Counseling Psychology	M,D,O
Curriculum and Instruction	M,D
Dentistry	D
Developmental Biology	M,D
Developmental Psychology	M,D
East European and Russian Studies	M,D
Economics	M,D
Education—General	M,D,O
Educational Leadership and Administration	M,D
Educational Measurement and Evaluation	M,D,O
Educational Policy	M,D
Electrical Engineering	M,D
Energy and Power Engineering	M
Engineering and Applied Sciences—General	M,D
English as a Second Language	M,D
English	M,D
Environmental Management and Policy	M,D
Ethnic Studies	M
Film, Television, and Video Production	M
Film, Television, and Video Theory and Criticism	M
Finance and Banking	D
Food Science and Technology	M,D
Forestry	M,D
Foundations and Philosophy of Education	M,D
French	M,D
Gender Studies	M,D
Genetic Counseling	M
Genetics	M,D
Geography	M,D
Geological Engineering	M,D
Geology	M,D
Geophysics	M,D
German	M,D
Health Psychology	M,D
Health Services Management and Hospital Administration	M,D
Higher Education	M,D
Hispanic Studies	M,D
History	M,D
Home Economics Education	M,D
Human Development	M,D,O
Immunology	M,D
Infectious Diseases	M,D
Information Studies	M,D
International Affairs	M
Internet and Interactive Multimedia	M
Journalism	M
Kinesiology and Movement Studies	M,D
Landscape Architecture	M
Law	M,D
Library Science	M,D
Linguistics	M,D
Management Information Systems	D
Management Strategy and Policy	D
Marine Sciences	M,D
Marketing	D
Materials Engineering	M,D
Mathematics Education	M,D
Mathematics	M,D
Mechanical Engineering	M,D
Microbiology	M,D
Mineral/Mining Engineering	M,D
Molecular Biology	M,D
Museum Studies	M,D
Music Education	M,D
Music	M,D
Natural Resources	M,D
Neuroscience	M,D
Nursing—General	M,D
Nutrition	M,D
Occupational Therapy	M
Oceanography	M,D
Oral and Dental Sciences	M,D
Organizational Behavior	D
Pacific Area/Pacific Rim Studies	M
Pathology	M,D
Pharmaceutical Sciences	M,D
Pharmacology	M,D
Pharmacy	M,D
Philosophy	M,D
Physical Education	M,D
Physical Therapy	M

Physics	M,D
Plant Sciences	M,D
Political Science	M,D
Psychology—General	M,D
Public Health—General	M,D
Public Policy	M
Quantitative Analysis	M,D
Reading Education	M,D
Rehabilitation Sciences	M,D
Religion	M,D
Reproductive Biology	M,D
School Psychology	M,D,O
Science Education	M,D
Social Psychology	M,D
Social Sciences Education	M,D
Social Work	M,D
Sociology	M,D,O
Special Education	M,D
Statistics	M,D
Sustainability Management	M
Sustainable Development	M,D
Taxation	M,D
Theater	M,D
Transportation Management	D
Urban and Regional Planning	M,D
Urban Design	M
Vocational and Technical Education	M,D
Water Resources	M
Writing	M,D
Zoology	M,D

UNIVERSITY OF CALGARY

Adult Education	M,D
Allopathic Medicine	D
Analytical Chemistry	M,D
Applied Psychology	M,D
Architecture	M,D
Astronomy	M,D
Biochemistry	M,D
Biological and Biomedical Sciences—General	M,D
Biomedical Engineering	M,D
Biotechnology	M
Business Administration and Management—General	M,D
Cancer Biology/Oncology	M,D
Cardiovascular Sciences	M,D
Chemical Engineering	M,D
Chemistry	M,D
Civil Engineering	M,D
Classics	M,D
Clinical Psychology	M,D
Community Health	M,D
Computer Engineering	M,D
Computer Science	M,D
Counseling Psychology	M,D
Curriculum and Instruction	M,D
Educational Leadership and Administration	M,D
Educational Measurement and Evaluation	M,D
Electrical Engineering	M,D
Energy and Power Engineering	M,D
Energy Management and Policy	M,D
Engineering and Applied Sciences—General	M,D
Environmental Design	M,D
Environmental Engineering	M,D
Environmental Law	M,O
Environmental Management and Policy	M,D,O
Genetics	M,D
Geography	M,D
Geology	M,D
Geophysics	M,D
Geosciences	M,D
Geotechnical Engineering	M,D
German	M,D
History	M,D
Hydrology	M,D
Immunology	M,D
Infectious Diseases	M,D
Inorganic Chemistry	M,D
Kinesiology and Movement Studies	M,D
Landscape Architecture	M,D,O
Law	M,D,O
Legal and Justice Studies	M,O
Linguistics	M,D
Management Strategy and Policy	M,D
Manufacturing Engineering	M,D
Materials Sciences	M,D
Mathematics	M,D
Mechanical Engineering	M,D
Mechanics	M,D
Microbiology	M,D
Military and Defense Studies	M,D
Molecular Biology	M,D
Molecular Genetics	M,D
Multilingual and Multicultural Education	M,D
Music	M,D
Neuroscience	M,D
Nursing—General	M,D,O
Organic Chemistry	M,D
Pathology	M,D
Petroleum Engineering	M,D
Philosophy	M,D
Physical Chemistry	M,D
Physics	M,D
Physiology	M,D
Political Science	M,D
Project Management	M,D
Psychology—General	M,D
Public Policy	M
Religion	M,D
School Psychology	M,D
Social Work	M,D,O
Sociology	M,D
Software Engineering	M,D

Statistics	M,D
Structural Engineering	M,D
Sustainable Development	M,D
Theoretical Chemistry	M,D
Transportation and Highway Engineering	M,D
Water Resources	M,D

UNIVERSITY OF CALIFORNIA, BERKELEY

Accounting	D,O
Addictions/Substance Abuse Counseling	O
African-American Studies	D
Agricultural Economics and Agribusiness	D
Allopathic Medicine	M
Anthropology	D
Applied Arts and Design—General	O
Applied Mathematics	M,D
Applied Science and Technology	D
Archaeology	M,D
Architectural History	M,D
Architecture	M,D
Art History	D
Art/Fine Arts	M,O
Asian Languages	M,D
Asian Studies	M,D
Astrophysics	D
Biochemistry	D
Bioengineering	M,D
Biological and Biomedical Sciences—General	D
Biophysics	D
Biostatistics	M,D
Building Science	M,D
Business Administration and Management—General	M,D,O
Cell Biology	D
Chemical Engineering	M,D
Chemistry	D
Chinese	D
Civil Engineering	M,D
Classics	M,D
Clinical Research	O
Comparative Literature	D
Computer Science	M,D
Construction Management	O
Counseling Psychology	O
Data Science/Data Analytics	M
Demography and Population Studies	M,D
Economics	D
Education—General	M,D,O
Educational Leadership and Administration	M,D
Electrical Engineering	M,D
Energy Management and Policy	M,D
Engineering and Applied Sciences—General	M,D,O
Engineering Management	M,D
English as a Second Language	O
English	D
Environmental and Occupational Health	M,D
Environmental Design	M,D
Environmental Engineering	M,D
Environmental Management and Policy	M,D,O
Environmental Sciences	M,D
Epidemiology	M,D
Ethnic Studies	D
Facilities Management	O
Film, Television, and Video Theory and Criticism	D
Finance and Banking	D,O
Financial Engineering	M
Folklore	M
Forestry	M,D
French	D
Geography	D
Geology	M,D
Geophysics	M,D
Geotechnical Engineering	M,D
German	D
Health Services Management and Hospital Administration	D
Hispanic and Latin American Languages	D
History of Science and Technology	M,D
History	M,D
Human Development	M,D
Human Resources Management	O
Immunology	D
Industrial and Labor Relations	D
Industrial/Management Engineering	M,D
Infectious Diseases	M,D
Information Studies	M,D
Interior Design	O
International Affairs	M
International Business	O
Italian	D
Japanese	D
Journalism	M
Landscape Architecture	M,D,O
Law	M,D
Legal and Justice Studies	D
Linguistics	D
Management Information Systems	M,D,O
Marketing	D,O
Materials Engineering	M,D
Materials Sciences	M,D
Mathematics Education	M,D
Mathematics	D
Mechanical Engineering	M,D
Mechanics	M,D
Microbiology	D
Molecular Biology	D

Molecular Toxicology	D
Music	M,D
Natural Resources	M,D
Near and Middle Eastern Studies	M,D
Neuroscience	D
Nuclear Engineering	M,D
Nutrition	D
Operations Research	M,D
Optometry	D,O
Organizational Behavior	D
Philosophy	D
Physics	D
Physiology	M,D
Plant Biology	D
Political Science	D
Project Management	O
Psychology—General	D
Public Affairs	M
Public Health—General	M,D
Public Policy	M,D
Range Science	M
Real Estate	D
Religion	D
Rhetoric	D
Romance Languages	D
Russian	D
Scandinavian Languages	D
Science Education	M,D
Slavic Languages	D
Social Work	M,D
Sociology	D
Spanish	D
Special Education	M,D
Statistics	M,D
Structural Engineering	M,D
Sustainability Management	O
Sustainable Development	M,O
Theater	D
Transportation and Highway Engineering	M,D
Urban and Regional Planning	M,D
Urban Design	M,D
Vision Sciences	M,D
Water Resources Engineering	M,D
Writing	O

UNIVERSITY OF CALIFORNIA, DAVIS

Accounting	M
Aerospace/Aeronautical Engineering	M,D,O
Agricultural Economics and Agribusiness	M,D
Agricultural Sciences—General	M
Agronomy and Soil Sciences	M,D
Allopathic Medicine	D
American Indian/Native American Studies	M,D
Animal Behavior	D
Animal Sciences	M,D
Anthropology	M,D
Applied Mathematics	M,D
Applied Science and Technology	M,D
Art History	M
Art/Fine Arts	M
Atmospheric Sciences	M,D
Biochemistry	M,D
Bioengineering	M,D
Biomedical Engineering	M,D
Biophysics	M,D
Biostatistics	M,D
Business Administration and Management—General	M
Business Analytics	M
Cell Biology	M,D
Chemical Engineering	M,D
Chemistry	M,D
Child Development	M
Civil Engineering	M,D,O
Clinical Research	M
Clothing and Textiles	M
Communication—General	M
Comparative Literature	D
Computer Engineering	M,D
Computer Science	M,D
Cultural Studies	M,D
Curriculum and Instruction	M,D
Developmental Biology	M,D
Ecology	M,D
Economics	M,D
Education—General	M,D
Educational Psychology	M,D
Electrical Engineering	M,D
Engineering and Applied Sciences—General	M,D,O
English	M,D
Entomology	M,D
Entrepreneurship	M
Environmental Engineering	M,D,O
Environmental Sciences	M,D
Epidemiology	M,D
Evolutionary Biology	D
Exercise and Sports Science	M
Finance and Banking	M
Food Science and Technology	M,D
Forensic Sciences	M
French	D
Genetics	M,D
Geography	M,D
Geology	M,D
German	M,D
History	M,D
Horticulture	M
Human Development	D
Hydrology	M,D
Immunology	M,D
Law	D
Linguistics	M,D
Management Strategy and Policy	M

Marketing	M
Materials Engineering	M,D
Materials Sciences	M,D
Maternal and Child Health	M
Mathematics	M,D
Mechanical Engineering	M,D,O
Medical Informatics	M
Microbiology	M,D
Molecular Biology	M,D
Music	D
Neuroscience	M,D
Nutrition	M,D
Organizational Behavior	M
Pathology	M,D
Pharmacology	M,D
Philosophy	M,D
Physics	M,D
Physiology	M,D
Plant Biology	M,D
Plant Pathology	M,D
Political Science	M,D
Psychology—General	D
Sociology	M,D
Spanish	M,D
Statistics	M,D
Textile Design	M
Theater	M,D
Toxicology	M,D
Transportation and Highway Engineering	M,D
Transportation Management	M,D
Urban and Regional Planning	M
Veterinary Medicine	D
Veterinary Sciences	M,O
Viticulture and Enology	M,D
Writing	M,D
Zoology	M

UNIVERSITY OF CALIFORNIA, HASTINGS COLLEGE OF THE LAW

Law	M,D

UNIVERSITY OF CALIFORNIA, IRVINE

Accounting	
Aerospace/Aeronautical Engineering	M,D
Allopathic Medicine	D
Anatomy	M,D
Anthropology	M,D
Applied Mathematics	M,D
Art/Fine Arts	M,D
Asian Languages	M,D
Biochemical Engineering	M,D
Biochemistry	M,D
Biological and Biomedical Sciences—General	M,D
Biomedical Engineering	M,D
Biophysics	D
Biotechnology	M
Business Administration and Management—General	M,D
Business Analytics	M
Cell Biology	M,D
Chemical Engineering	M,D
Chemistry	M,D
Chinese	M,D
Civil Engineering	M,D
Classics	M,D
Comparative Literature	M,D
Computational Biology	D
Computer Science	M,D
Criminal Justice and Criminology	M,D
Cultural Studies	D
Dance	M
Demography and Population Studies	M,D
Developmental Biology	M,D
Ecology	M,D
Economics	M,D
Education—General	M,D
Educational Leadership and Administration	M,D
Electrical Engineering	M,D
Elementary Education	M,D
Engineering and Applied Sciences—General	M,D
Engineering Management	M
English	M,D
Environmental and Occupational Health	M,D
Environmental Design	D
Environmental Engineering	M,D
Epidemiology	M,D
Evolutionary Biology	M,D
Foreign Languages Education	M,D
French	M,D
Genetic Counseling	M
Genetics	D
Geosciences	M,D
German	M,D
Health Services Management and Hospital Administration	M
History	M,D
Information Science	M,D
Japanese	M,D
Law	D
Manufacturing Engineering	M,D
Materials Engineering	M,D
Materials Sciences	M,D
Mathematics	M,D
Mechanical Engineering	M,D
Medicinal and Pharmaceutical Chemistry	D
Microbiology	M,D
Molecular Biology	M,D
Molecular Genetics	M,D
Music	M
Neurobiology	M,D
Neuroscience	D
Nursing—General	M
Pathology	D
Pharmaceutical Sciences	D

M—masters degree; D—doctorate; O—other advanced degree; *—Close-Up and/or Display

Philosophy | M,D
Physics | M,D
Physiology | D
Political Science | D
Psychology—General | D
Public Health—General | M,D
Secondary Education | M,D
Sociology | D
Spanish | M,D
Statistics | M,D
Systems Biology | D
Theater | M,D
Toxicology | M,D
Translational Biology | M
Transportation and Highway Engineering | M,D
Urban and Regional Planning | M,D
Urban Studies | M
Writing | M

UNIVERSITY OF CALIFORNIA, LOS ANGELES

Accounting | M,D
Aerospace/Aeronautical Engineering | M,D
African Studies | M
African-American Studies | M
Allopathic Medicine | D
American Indian/Native American Studies | M
Anatomy | M,D
Anthropology | M,D
Applied Arts and Design—General | M
Applied Economics | M,D
Archaeology | M,D
Architecture | M,D
Archives/Archival Administration | M,D,O
Art History | M,D
Art/Fine Arts | M
Asian Languages | M,D
Asian Studies | M,D
Asian-American Studies | M
Astronomy | M,D
Astrophysics | M,D
Atmospheric Sciences | M,D
Biochemistry | M,D
Bioengineering | M,D
Bioinformatics | M,D
Biological and Biomedical Sciences—General | M,D
Biomathematics | M,D
Biomedical Engineering | M,D
Biostatistics | M,D
Business Administration and Management—General | M,D
Business Analytics | M,D
Cell Biology | M,D
Chemical Engineering | M,D
Chemistry | M,D
Civil Engineering | M,D
Classics | M,D
Clinical Research | M
Community Health | M,D
Comparative Literature | M,D
Computer Engineering | M,D
Computer Science | M,D
Dance | M,D
Dentistry | D,O
Developmental Biology | M,D
Ecology | M,D
Economics | D
Education—General | M,D
Educational Leadership and Administration | D
Electrical Engineering | M,D
Engineering and Applied Sciences—General | M,D
English as a Second Language | M,D,O
English | M,D
Environmental and Occupational Health | M,D
Environmental Engineering | M,D
Environmental Sciences | M,D
Epidemiology | M,D
Evolutionary Biology | M,D
Film, Television, and Video Production | M,D
Finance and Banking | M,D
Financial Engineering | M,D
French | M,D
Gender Studies | M,D
Geochemistry | M,D
Geography | M,D
Geology | M,D
Geophysics | M,D
Geosciences | M,D
German | M,D
Health Services Management and Hospital Administration | M,D
Hispanic and Latin American Languages | D
Historic Preservation | M
History | M,D
Human Genetics | M,D
Immunology | M,D
Information Studies | M,D,O
Italian | M,D
Latin American Studies | M
Law | M,D
Library Science | M,D,O
Linguistics | M,D
Management of Technology | M,D
Management Strategy and Policy | M,D
Manufacturing Engineering | M
Marketing | M,D
Materials Engineering | M,D
Materials Sciences | M,D
Mathematics | M,D
Mechanical Engineering | M,D
Media Studies | M,D
Medical Physics | M,D
Microbiology | M,D

Molecular Biology | M,D
Molecular Genetics | M,D
Molecular Pathology | D
Molecular Physiology | D
Molecular Toxicology | D
Music | M,D
Near and Middle Eastern Languages | M,D
Near and Middle Eastern Studies | M,D
Neurobiology | M,D
Neuroscience | D
Nursing—General | M,D
Oceanography | M,D
Oral and Dental Sciences | M,D
Pathology | M,D
Pharmacology | M,D
Philosophy | M,D
Physics | M,D
Physiology | M,D
Planetary and Space Sciences | M,D
Political Science | M,D
Portuguese | M
Psychology—General | M,D
Public Affairs | M,D
Public Health—General | M,D
Public Policy | M
Scandinavian Languages | M
Slavic Languages | M,D
Social Work | M,D
Sociology | M,D
Spanish | M
Special Education | D
Statistics | M,D
Theater | M,D
Urban and Regional Planning | M,D
Urban Design | M,D

UNIVERSITY OF CALIFORNIA, MERCED

Applied Mathematics | M,D
Biochemistry | M,D
Bioengineering | M,D
Biological and Biomedical Sciences—General | M,D
Chemistry | M,D
Cognitive Sciences | M,D
Computer Science | M,D
Electrical Engineering | M,D
Engineering and Applied Sciences—General | M,D
Entrepreneurship | M,D
Environmental Engineering | M,D
Humanities | M,D
Information Science | M,D
Mechanical Engineering | M,D
Mechanics | M,D
Physics | M,D
Psychology—General | M,D
Social Sciences | M,D
Sociology | M,D
Sustainability Management | M,D
Systems Biology | M,D
Systems Engineering | M,D

UNIVERSITY OF CALIFORNIA, RIVERSIDE

Accounting | M,D
Agronomy and Soil Sciences | M,D
Allopathic Medicine | D
Anthropology | M,D
Applied Behavior Analysis | M,D,O
Archives/Archival Administration | M,D
Art History | M,D
Art/Fine Arts | M
Artificial Intelligence/Robotics | M,D
Asian Studies | M
Biochemistry | M,D
Bioengineering | M,D
Bioinformatics | D
Biological and Biomedical Sciences—General | M,D
Botany | M,D
Business Administration and Management—General | M,D
Cell Biology | M,D
Chemical Engineering | M,D
Chemistry | M,D
Classics | D
Comparative Literature | M,D
Computer Engineering | M
Computer Science | M,D
Cultural Studies | D
Dance | M
Developmental Biology | M,D
Economics | M,D
Education—General | M,D,O
Educational Leadership and Administration | M,D,O
Educational Measurement and Evaluation | M,D,O
Educational Policy | M,D,O
Educational Psychology | M,D,O
Electrical Engineering | M,D
English as a Second Language | M,D,O
English | M,D
Entomology | M,D
Environmental Engineering | M,D
Environmental Sciences | M
Ethnic Studies | D
Evolutionary Biology | M,D
Finance and Banking | M,D
Foundations and Philosophy of Education | M,D,O
Genetics | D
Genomic Sciences | D
Geology | M,D
Higher Education | M,D,O
Hispanic Studies | M,D
History | M,D
International Health | M,D
Materials Engineering | M,D
Materials Sciences | M
Mathematics | M,D
Mechanical Engineering | M,D
Microbiology | M,D

Molecular Biology | M,D
Multilingual and Multicultural Education | M,D,O
Music | M,D
Nanotechnology | M
Neuroscience | D
Philosophy | M,D
Physics | M,D
Plant Biology | M,D
Plant Molecular Biology | M,D
Plant Pathology | M,D
Plant Sciences | M,D
Political Science | M,D
Psychology—General | D
Public Policy | M,D
Religion | M,D
School Psychology | M,D,O
Sociology | M,D
Spanish | M,D
Special Education | M,D,O
Statistics | M,D
Toxicology | M,D
Water Resources | M,D
Writing | M

UNIVERSITY OF CALIFORNIA, SAN DIEGO

Aerospace/Aeronautical Engineering | M,D
Allopathic Medicine | D
Anthropology | D
Applied Mathematics | M,D
Applied Physics | M,D
Architectural Engineering | M
Art History | M,D
Art/Fine Arts | M,D
Artificial Intelligence/Robotics | M,D
Biochemistry | M,D
Bioengineering | M,D
Bioinformatics | D
Biological and Biomedical Sciences—General | M,D
Biophysics | M,D
Biostatistics | D
Business Administration and Management—General | M,D
Business Analytics | M,D
Chemical Engineering | M,D
Chemistry | M,D
Clinical Laboratory Sciences/Medical Technology | M,D
Clinical Psychology | D
Clinical Research | M
Cognitive Sciences | D
Communication Disorders | D
Communication—General | D
Computational Sciences | M,D
Computer Engineering | M,D
Computer Science | M,D
Curriculum and Instruction | M,D
Dance | M,D
Data Science/Data Analytics | M
Economics | D
Education—General | M,D
Educational Leadership and Administration | M,D
Electrical Engineering | M,D
Energy Management and Policy | M
Engineering Physics | M,D
English | M,D
Environmental Management and Policy | M
Epidemiology | D
Ethnic Studies | D
Finance and Banking | M,D
Geophysics | M,D
Geosciences | M,D
Health Services Management and Hospital Administration | M
History of Science and Technology | D
History | M,D
International Affairs | M,D
International Business | M
International Development | M
International Economics | M
International Health | M
Jewish Studies | M,D
Latin American Studies | M
Linguistics | D
Marine Sciences | M
Materials Sciences | M,D
Mathematics Education | D
Mathematics | M,D
Mechanical Engineering | M,D
Mechanics | M,D
Meteorology | M
Modeling and Simulation | M,D
Multilingual and Multicultural Education | M,D
Music | M,D
Nanotechnology | M,D
Neuroscience | M,D
Nonprofit Management | M
Ocean Engineering | M,D
Oceanography | M,D
Pharmacy | D
Philosophy | M,D
Photonics | M,D
Physics | M,D
Political Science | M,D
Psychology—General | D
Public Health—General | M,D
Public Policy | M
Science Education | D
Sociology | D
Statistics | M,D
Structural Engineering | M,D
Systems Biology | M,D
Telecommunications | M,D
Theater | M,D
Writing | M,D

UNIVERSITY OF CALIFORNIA, SAN FRANCISCO

Allopathic Medicine | D
Anthropology | D
Biochemistry | D
Bioengineering | D
Bioinformatics | D
Biological and Biomedical Sciences—General | D
Biophysics | D
Cell Biology | D
Chemistry | D
Dentistry | D
Developmental Biology | D
Genetics | D
Genomic Sciences | D
Health Law | M
History of Science and Technology | M,D
Medical Imaging | M
Medicinal and Pharmaceutical Chemistry | D
Molecular Biology | D
Neuroscience | D
Nursing—General | M,D
Oral and Dental Sciences | M,D
Pharmaceutical Sciences | D
Pharmacology | D
Pharmacy | D
Physical Therapy | D
Sociology | D

UNIVERSITY OF CALIFORNIA, SANTA BARBARA

African-American Studies | D
Agricultural Economics and Agribusiness | M,D
Anthropology | M,D
Applied Mathematics | M,D
Applied Statistics | M,D
Art History | D
Art/Fine Arts | M
Asian Languages | M,D
Asian Studies | M,D
Biochemistry | M,D
Bioengineering | M,D
Biophysics | D
Cell Biology | M,D
Chemical Engineering | M,D
Chemistry | M,D
Classics | M,D
Clinical Psychology | M,D,O
Cognitive Sciences | M,D
Communication—General | D
Comparative Literature | D
Computational Sciences | M,D
Computer Engineering | M,D
Computer Science | M,D
Counseling Psychology | M,D,O
Cultural Anthropology | M,D
Cultural Studies | M,D
Developmental Biology | M,D
Ecology | M,D
Economics | M,D
Education—General | M,D,O
Electrical Engineering | M,D
Engineering and Applied Sciences—General | M,D
English | D
Environmental Management and Policy | M,D
Environmental Sciences | M,D
Evolutionary Biology | M,D
Film, Television, and Video Production | D
Finance and Banking | M,D
French | D
Geography | M,D
Geosciences | M,D
Hispanic and Latin American Languages | M,D
Hispanic Studies | M,D
History | M,D
Interdisciplinary Studies | D
International Affairs | M,D
Latin American Studies | M
Linguistics | M,D
Management of Technology | M
Marine Biology | M,D
Marine Sciences | M,D
Materials Engineering | M,D
Materials Sciences | M,D
Mathematical and Computational Finance | M,D
Mathematics | M,D
Mechanical Engineering | M,D
Media Studies | M,D
Medieval and Renaissance Studies | M,D
Molecular Biology | M,D
Music | M,D
Neuroscience | D
Philosophy | D
Photonics | M,D
Physics | D
Political Science | M,D
Portuguese | M,D
Psychology—General | D
Public History | D
Quantitative Analysis | M,D
Religion | M,D
School Psychology | M,D,O
Social Sciences | D
Sociology | D
Spanish | M,D
Speech and Interpersonal Communication | D
Statistics | M,D
Sustainable Development | M,D
Theater | M,D
Translation and Interpretation | M,D
Transportation Management | M,D
Women's Studies | D
Writing | D

UNIVERSITY OF CALIFORNIA, SANTA CRUZ

Anthropology	D
Applied Economics	M
Applied Mathematics	M,D
Art/Fine Arts	M,D
Astronomy	D
Astrophysics	D
Biochemistry	M,D
Bioinformatics	M,D
Cell Biology	M,D
Chemistry	M,D
Communication—General	O
Comparative Literature	M,D
Computer Art and Design	M,D
Computer Engineering	M,D
Computer Science	M,D
Cultural Anthropology	D
Developmental Biology	M,D
Ecology	M,D
Economics	D
Education—General	M,D
Electrical Engineering	M,D
Engineering and Applied Sciences—General	M,D
English	M,D
Environmental Biology	M,D
Environmental Management and Policy	D
Evolutionary Biology	M,D
Film, Television, and Video Theory and Criticism	D
Finance and Banking	M
Game Design and Development	M,D
Geosciences	M,D
History	M,D
Humanities	D
Interdisciplinary Studies	M,D
International Affairs	D
Internet and Interactive Multimedia	M,D
Linguistics	M,D
Marine Sciences	M,D
Mathematics	M,D
Microbiology	M,D
Molecular Biology	M,D
Music	M,D
Philosophy	M,D
Physics	M,D
Planetary and Space Sciences	M,D
Political Science	D
Psychology—General	D
Social Sciences Education	M
Social Sciences	D
Sociology	D
Statistics	M,D
Theater	O
Toxicology	M,D
Writing	M

UNIVERSITY OF CENTRAL ARKANSAS

Accounting	M
Adult Education	M,O
Adult Nursing	M,O
Applied Mathematics	M
Biological and Biomedical Sciences—General	M
Business Administration and Management—General	M
Communication Disorders	M,D
Computer Art and Design	M
Computer Science	M
Counseling Psychology	M
Counselor Education	M
Curriculum and Instruction	M,O
Economic Development	M,O
Education of the Gifted	M,O
Education—General	M,O
Educational Leadership and Administration	M,O
Educational Media/Instructional Technology	M
English	M
Family and Consumer Sciences-General	M
Family Nurse Practitioner Studies	M,O
Film, Television, and Video Production	M
Geographic Information Systems	M,O
Geography	M,O
Health Education	M
History	M
Kinesiology and Movement Studies	M
Library Science	M
Mathematics Education	M
Mathematics	M
Music Education	M,O
Music	M
Nursing and Healthcare Administration	M,O
Nursing Education	M,O
Nursing—General	M,O
Nutrition	M
Occupational Therapy	M
Organizational Management	D
Physical Therapy	D
Psychology—General	M,D,O
Reading Education	M
School Psychology	M,D,O
Social Psychology	M
Spanish	M
Special Education	M,O
Student Affairs	M
Urban and Regional Planning	M
Writing	M

UNIVERSITY OF CENTRAL FLORIDA

Accounting	M
Aerospace/Aeronautical Engineering	M
Allopathic Medicine	M,D
Anthropology	M
Art Education	M,O
Art/Fine Arts	M
Athletic Training and Sports Medicine	M
Biological and Biomedical Sciences—General	M,D,O
Business Administration and Management—General	M,D,O
Chemistry	M,D,O
Civil Engineering	M,D,O
Clinical Psychology	M,D
Communication Disorders	M,O
Community College Education	M,O
Computer Art and Design	M
Computer Engineering	M,D
Computer Science	M,D
Conservation Biology	M,D,O
Counselor Education	M,O
Criminal Justice and Criminology	M,O
Curriculum and Instruction	M,O
Educational Leadership and Administration	M,O
Educational Media/Instructional Technology	M,O
Electrical Engineering	M,D
Elementary Education	M
Emergency Management	M,O
Engineering and Applied Sciences—General	M,D,O
English as a Second Language	M,O
English Education	M,O
English	M,O
Entrepreneurship	M,O
Environmental Engineering	M,D
Exercise and Sports Science	M,O
Film, Television, and Video Production	M
Foreign Languages Education	M,O
Health Informatics	M,O
Health Services Management and Hospital Administration	M,O
Higher Education	M,O
History	M,O
Homeland Security	M,O
Hospitality Management	M,D,O
Industrial/Management Engineering	M,D
Kinesiology and Movement Studies	M
Marriage and Family Therapy	M,O
Materials Engineering	M,D
Materials Sciences	M,D
Mathematics Education	M,D,O
Mathematics	M,D,O
Mechanical Engineering	M,D
Middle School Education	M,O
Modeling and Simulation	M,D,O
Music	M
Nonprofit Management	M,O
Nursing—General	M,D,O
Optical Sciences	M,D
Photonics	M,D
Physical Therapy	D
Physics	M,D
Physiology	M,O
Psychology—General	M,D
Public Administration	M,O
Public Affairs	D
Reading Education	M,O
Real Estate	M
School Psychology	O
Science Education	M,O
Social Sciences Education	M,O
Social Work	M
Sociology	M,D
Spanish	M
Special Education	M,O
Sports Management	M
Structural Engineering	M,D,O
Student Affairs	M,O
Theater	M
Transportation and Highway Engineering	M,D,O
Travel and Tourism	M,D,O
Urban and Regional Planning	M,O
Vocational and Technical Education	M,O

UNIVERSITY OF CENTRAL MISSOURI

Accounting	M,D,O
Aerospace/Aeronautical Engineering	M,D,O
Applied Mathematics	M,D,O
Biological and Biomedical Sciences—General	M,D,O
Business Administration and Management—General	M,D,O
Communication Disorders	M,D,O
Communication—General	M,D,O
Computer Science	M,D,O
Counseling Psychology	M,D,O
Counselor Education	M,D,O
Criminal Justice and Criminology	M,D,O
Early Childhood Education	M,D,O
Education—General	M,D,O
Educational Leadership and Administration	M,D,O
Educational Media/Instructional Technology	M,D,O
Elementary Education	M,D,O
English as a Second Language	M,D,O
English	M,D,O
Environmental and Occupational Health	M,D,O
Environmental Management and Policy	M,D,O
Finance and Banking	M,D,O
Gerontology	M,D,O
History	M,D,O

Human Services	M,D,O
Industrial and Manufacturing Management	M,D,O
Industrial Hygiene	M,D,O
Information Science	M,D,O
Kinesiology and Movement Studies	M,D,O
Library Science	M,D,O
Management Information Systems	M,D,O
Management of Technology	M,D,O
Marketing	M,D,O
Mathematics	M,D,O
Music	M,D,O
Nursing—General	M,D,O
Psychology—General	M,D,O
Reading Education	M,D,O
Sociology	M,D,O
Special Education	M,D,O
Student Affairs	M,D,O
Theater	M,D,O
Vocational and Technical Education	M,D,O

UNIVERSITY OF CENTRAL OKLAHOMA

Addictions/Substance Abuse Counseling	M
Adult Education	M
Applied Arts and Design— General	M
Applied Mathematics	M
Athletic Training and Sports Medicine	M
Biological and Biomedical Sciences—General	M
Biomedical Engineering	M
Business Analytics	M
Child and Family Studies	M
Communication Disorders	M
Computational Sciences	M
Computer Science	M
Counseling Psychology	M
Counselor Education	M
Criminal Justice and Criminology	M
Early Childhood Education	M
Education of Students with Severe/Multiple Disabilities	M
Education—General	M
Educational Leadership and Administration	M
Educational Media/Instructional Technology	M
Electrical Engineering	M
Elementary Education	M
Engineering and Applied Sciences—General	M
Engineering Physics	M
English as a Second Language	M
English	M
Exercise and Sports Science	M
Experimental Psychology	M
Family and Consumer Sciences-General	M
Forensic Psychology	M
Forensic Sciences	M
Foundations and Philosophy of Education	M
Gerontology	M
Health Promotion	M
History	M
Human Development	M
Interdisciplinary Studies	M
Liberal Studies	M
Library Science	M
Marriage and Family Therapy	M
Mathematics	M
Mechanical Engineering	M
Museum Studies	M
Music Education	M
Music	M
Nonprofit Management	M
Nursing—General	M
Nutrition	M
Physics	M
Political Science	M
Psychology—General	M
Public Administration	M
Reading Education	M
Rhetoric	M
School Psychology	M
Secondary Education	M
Sociology	M
Special Education	M
Statistics	M
Student Affairs	M
Urban and Regional Planning	M
Writing	M

UNIVERSITY OF CHARLESTON

Accounting	M
Business Administration and Management—General	M
Forensic Sciences	M
Legal and Justice Studies	M
Management Strategy and Policy	M
Organizational Management	D
Pharmacy	D
Physician Assistant Studies	M

UNIVERSITY OF CHICAGO

Accounting	M,O
Allopathic Medicine	D
Anatomy	D
Anthropology	D
Applied Mathematics	D
Applied Statistics	M
Archaeology	D
Art History	M,D
Art/Fine Arts	M
Asian Languages	D
Asian Studies	M,D
Astronomy	D
Astrophysics	D
Atmospheric Sciences	D
Bioengineering	D

Bioinformatics	M
Biological and Biomedical Sciences—General	D
Biophysics	D
Business Administration and Management—General	M,D,O
Cancer Biology/Oncology	D
Cell Biology	D
Chemistry	D
Classics	M,D
Comparative Literature	M,D
Computational Sciences	M
Computer Science	M,D
Developmental Biology	D
Ecology	D
Economics	M,D,O
Emergency Management	M
English	M,D
Entrepreneurship	M,O
Environmental Management and Policy	M
Environmental Sciences	M
Ethics	D
Evolutionary Biology	D
Film, Television, and Video Theory and Criticism	D
Finance and Banking	M,O
French	D
Gender Studies	M
Genetics	D
Genomic Sciences	D
Geophysics	D
Geosciences	D
German	M,D
Health Promotion	M,D
Health Services Management and Hospital Administration	M,O
History	D
Human Development	D
Human Genetics	D
Humanities	M
Immunology	D
Industrial and Manufacturing Management	M,O
International Affairs	M
International Business	M,O
Internet and Interactive Multimedia	M
Italian	D
Latin American Studies	M
Law	M,D
Liberal Studies	M
Linguistics	M,D
Management Strategy and Policy	M,O
Marketing	M,O
Mathematical and Computational Finance	M
Mathematics	D
Media Studies	M,D
Medical Physics	D
Medieval and Renaissance Studies	D
Microbiology	D
Molecular Biology	D
Molecular Biophysics	D
Music	M,D
Near and Middle Eastern Languages	D
Near and Middle Eastern Studies	M,D
Neurobiology	D
Neuroscience	D
Nutrition	D
Organizational Behavior	M,O
Paleontology	D
Pastoral Ministry and Counseling	M
Philosophy	M,D
Physics	M,D
Planetary and Space Sciences	D
Political Science	D
Psychology—General	D
Public Policy	M,D
Religion	M,D
Romance Languages	M,D
Science Education	D
Slavic Languages	M
Social Sciences	M,D
Social Work	M,D
Sociology	D
Spanish	D
Statistics	M,D,O
Systems Biology	D
Theater	M
Theology	D
Urban Education	M
Writing	M

UNIVERSITY OF CINCINNATI

Accounting	M,D
Acute Care/Critical Care Nursing	M,D
Addictions/Substance Abuse Counseling	M,D,O
Adult Nursing	M,D
Aerospace/Aeronautical Engineering	M,D
Allopathic Medicine	D
Analytical Chemistry	M,D
Anthropology	M
Applied Arts and Design— General	M
Applied Economics	M
Applied Mathematics	M
Architecture	M
Art Education	M
Art History	M
Art/Fine Arts	M
Arts Administration	M,D
Biochemistry	M,D
Bioinformatics	D,O
Biological and Biomedical Sciences—General	M,D,O
Biomedical Engineering	M,D
Biophysics	M

Biostatistics	M,D
Business Administration and Management—General	M,D
Business Analytics	M,D
Cancer Biology/Oncology	D
Cell Biology	D
Chemical Engineering	M,D
Chemistry	M,D
Civil Engineering	M,D
Classics	M
Clinical Psychology	D
Communication Disorders	M,D
Communication—General	M
Computer Engineering	M,D
Computer Science	M,D
Counselor Education	M,D,O
Criminal Justice and Criminology	M,D
Curriculum and Instruction	M,D
Developmental Biology	D
Economics	M
Education—General	M,D,O
Educational Leadership and Administration	M,D,O
Electrical Engineering	M,D
Engineering and Applied Sciences—General	M,D
English as a Second Language	M,D
English	M,D
Environmental and Occupational Health	M,D
Environmental Engineering	M,D
Environmental Sciences	M,D
Epidemiology	M,D
Ergonomics and Human Factors	M,D
Experimental Psychology	D
Finance and Banking	M,D
Foundations and Philosophy of Education	M,D
French	M,D
Genetic Counseling	M
Genomic Sciences	M,D
Geography	M,D
Geology	M,D
German	M,D
Gerontological Nursing	M,D
Graphic Design	M
Health Education	M
Health Informatics	M
Health Physics/Radiological Health	M,D
Health Promotion	M,D
Health Services Research	M
History	M,D
Human Resources Management	M
Immunology	M,D
Industrial and Labor Relations	M
Industrial and Manufacturing Management	D
Industrial Design	M
Industrial Hygiene	M,D
Industrial/Management Engineering	M,D
Information Science	M,O
Inorganic Chemistry	M,D
Interdisciplinary Studies	D
Interior Design	M
Law	M
Management Information Systems	M,D
Marketing	M,D
Materials Engineering	M,D
Materials Sciences	M,D
Maternal and Child/Neonatal Nursing	M,D
Mathematics Education	M,D
Mathematics	M,D
Mechanical Engineering	M,D
Mechanics	M,D
Medical Imaging	M,D
Medical Physics	M
Microbiology	M,D
Molecular Biology	M,D
Molecular Genetics	M,D
Molecular Medicine	D
Molecular Toxicology	M,D
Music Education	M
Music	M,D,O
Neuroscience	D
Nuclear Engineering	M,D
Nurse Anesthesia	M,D
Nurse Midwifery	M,D
Nursing and Healthcare Administration	M,D
Nursing—General	M,D
Nutrition	M
Occupational Health Nursing	M,D
Organic Chemistry	M,D
Organizational Management	M
Pathobiology	D
Pathology	D
Pediatric Nursing	M,D
Pharmaceutical Sciences	M,D
Pharmacology	D
Pharmacy	D
Philosophy	M,D
Physical Chemistry	M,D
Physical Therapy	D
Physics	M,D
Political Science	M,D
Psychology—General	D
Public Health—General	M,D
Reading Education	M
Romance Languages	M,D
School Psychology	D,O
Social Work	M
Sociology	M,D
Spanish	M,D
Special Education	M,D
Sports Management	M
Statistics	M,D
Systems Biology	D
Taxation	M
Textile Design	M
Theater	M
Urban and Regional Planning	M

UNIVERSITY OF COLORADO BOULDER

Advertising and Public Relations	M,D
Aerospace/Aeronautical Engineering	M,D
Anthropology	M,D
Applied Mathematics	M,D
Architectural Engineering	M,D
Art History	M
Art/Fine Arts	M
Asian Studies	M,D
Astrophysics	M,D
Atmospheric Sciences	M,D
Biochemistry	M,D
Business Administration and Management—General	M,D
Cell Biology	M,D
Chemical Engineering	M,D
Chemistry	M,D
Chinese	M,D
Civil Engineering	M,D
Classics	M,D
Communication Disorders	M,D
Communication—General	M,D
Computer Engineering	M,D
Computer Science	M,D
Curriculum and Instruction	M,D
Dance	M,D
Developmental Biology	M,D
East European and Russian Studies	M
Ecology	M,D
Economics	M,D
Education—General	M,D
Educational Measurement and Evaluation	D
Educational Policy	M,D
Educational Psychology	M,D
Electrical Engineering	M,D
Engineering and Applied Sciences—General	M,D
Engineering Management	M
English	M,D
Environmental Engineering	M,D
Environmental Management and Policy	M,D
Ethnic Studies	D
Evolutionary Biology	M,D
Film, Television, and Video Production	M
French	M,D
Geography	M,D
Geology	M,D
Geophysics	M,D
German	M
Hispanic and Latin American Languages	M,D
History	M,D
Information Science	D
Internet and Interactive Multimedia	D
Japanese	M,D
Journalism	M,D
Kinesiology and Movement Studies	M,D
Law	D
Linguistics	M,D
Mass Communication	M,D
Materials Engineering	M,D
Materials Sciences	M,D
Mathematical Physics	M,D
Mathematics	M,D
Mechanical Engineering	M,D
Media Studies	M,D
Molecular Biology	M,D
Multilingual and Multicultural Education	M,D
Museum Studies	M
Music Education	M,D
Music	M,D
Oceanography	M,D
Organizational Management	
Philosophy	M,D
Photography	M
Physics	M,D
Physiology	M,D
Plasma Physics	M,D
Political Science	M,D
Psychology—General	M,D
Religion	M
Sociology	D
Spanish	M,D
Telecommunications Management	M
Telecommunications	M
Theater	M,D
Writing	M,D

UNIVERSITY OF COLORADO COLORADO SPRINGS

Adult Nursing	M,D
Aerospace/Aeronautical Engineering	M,D
Applied Mathematics	M
Business Administration and Management—General	M
Communication—General	M
Computer and Information Systems Security	M,D
Counselor Education	M,D
Criminal Justice and Criminology	M
Curriculum and Instruction	M,D
Education—General	M,D
Educational Leadership and Administration	M,D
Energy and Power Engineering	M,D
Engineering and Applied Sciences—General	M,D
English as a Second Language	M,D
Environmental Sciences	M
Geography	M
Gerontological Nursing	M,D
History	M
Human Services	M,D

Interdisciplinary Studies	M
Mathematics	D
Nursing—General	M,D
Physics	D
Psychology—General	M,D
Public Administration	M
Public Affairs	M
Sociology	M
Software Engineering	M,D
Special Education	M,D
Systems Engineering	M,D

UNIVERSITY OF COLORADO DENVER

Accounting	M
Adult Education	M
Adult Nursing	M,D
Allopathic Medicine	D
American Studies	M
Anatomy	M,D
Anesthesiologist Assistant Studies	M
Anthropology	M
Applied Mathematics	M,D
Applied Science and Technology	M
Applied Statistics	M,D
Archaeology	M
Architectural History	D
Architecture	M
Art/Fine Arts	M,O
Biochemistry	M
Bioengineering	M,D
Bioinformatics	D
Biological and Biomedical Sciences—General	M,D
Biological Anthropology	M
Biophysics	M
Biostatistics	M,D
Business Administration and Management—General	M
Cancer Biology/Oncology	D
Cell Biology	M,D
Chemistry	M
Child and Family Studies	M,D
Civil Engineering	M,D
Clinical Laboratory Sciences/Medical Technology	M
Clinical Psychology	M,D
Clinical Research	M,D
Communication—General	M
Community Health	M,D,O
Computational Biology	M
Computational Sciences	M
Computer Science	M,D
Corporate and Organizational Communication	M
Counseling Psychology	M
Counselor Education	M
Criminal Justice and Criminology	M,D
Data Science/Data Analytics	M
Demography and Population Studies	D
Dentistry	D,O
Developmental Biology	M,D
Distance Education Development	M
Early Childhood Education	M,D
Ecology	M
Economic Development	M
Economics	M
Education—General	M,D,O
Educational Leadership and Administration	M,D,O
Educational Measurement and Evaluation	M,D
Educational Media/Instructional Technology	M
Educational Policy	M,D,O
Electrical Engineering	M,D
Elementary Education	M
Emergency Management	M,D
Energy Management and Policy	M
Engineering and Applied Sciences—General	M
English Education	M
English	M
Entertainment Management	M
Entrepreneurship	M
Environmental and Occupational Health	M
Environmental Engineering	M,D
Environmental Law	M,D
Environmental Management and Policy	M,D,O
Environmental Sciences	M
Epidemiology	M,D
Ethnic Studies	M,O
Family and Consumer Sciences-General	M,D
Family Nurse Practitioner Studies	M,D
Finance and Banking	M
Forensic Sciences	M
Gender Studies	M,O
Genetic Counseling	M
Genetics	D
Genomic Sciences	D
Geographic Information Systems	M,D
Geotechnical Engineering	M,D
Hazardous Materials Management	M
Health Education	M,D
Health Informatics	M
Health Psychology	D
Health Services Management and Hospital Administration	M
Health Services Research	M,D
Historic Preservation	M
History	M,D
Homeland Security	M,D
Human Development	M,D
Human Resources Management	M
Humanities	M,O
Hydraulics	M,D
Hydrology	M,D
Immunology	D
Information Science	M,D

Insurance	M
International Affairs	M,O
International Business	M
International Health	M
Landscape Architecture	M
Linguistics	M
Management Information Systems	M,D
Management of Technology	M
Management Strategy and Policy	M
Marketing	M
Marriage and Family Therapy	M
Mathematics Education	M,D
Mathematics	M,D
Mechanical Engineering	M
Mechanics	M
Media Studies	M
Medical Informatics	D
Military and Defense Studies	M,D
Molecular Biology	D
Molecular Genetics	D
Multilingual and Multicultural Education	M
Music	M
Neuroscience	D
Nonprofit Management	M,D
Nurse Midwifery	M,D
Nursing and Healthcare Administration	M,D
Nursing—General	M,D
Operations Research	M,D
Oral and Dental Sciences	D,O
Pediatric Nursing	M,D
Pharmaceutical Sciences	D
Pharmacology	D
Pharmacy	D
Physical Therapy	D
Physician Assistant Studies	M
Political Science	M,D
Psychiatric Nursing	M,D
Public Administration	M,D
Public Affairs	M
Public Health—General	M,D
Public History	M
Reading Education	M
Rehabilitation Sciences	D
Risk Management	M
School Psychology	M,D
Science Education	M,D
Secondary Education	M
Sociology	M,O
Spanish	M
Special Education	M,D
Sports Management	M
Statistics	M,D
Structural Engineering	M,D
Sustainability Management	M
Sustainable Development	M,D
Systems Biology	M,D
Taxation	M
Toxicology	D
Transportation and Highway Engineering	M,D
Urban and Regional Planning	M,D
Urban Design	M,D
Water Resources	M
Western European Studies	M
Women's Health Nursing	M,D
Women's Studies	M,O
Writing	M

UNIVERSITY OF CONNECTICUT

Accounting	M,D
Adult Education	M,O
Agricultural Economics and Agribusiness	M,D
Agricultural Education	M,D
Agricultural Sciences—General	M,D
Agronomy and Soil Sciences	M,D
Animal Sciences	M,D
Anthropology	M,D
Applied Arts and Design—General	M
Applied Mathematics	M
Biochemical Engineering	M,D
Biomedical Engineering	M,D
Biophysics	M,D
Biopsychology	M,D
Botany	M,D
Business Administration and Management—General	M,D
Business Analytics	M,D
Cell Biology	M,D
Chemical Engineering	M,D
Chemistry	M,D
Child and Family Studies	M,D
Civil Engineering	M,D
Clinical Psychology	M,D
Cognitive Sciences	M,D
Communication Disorders	M,D
Communication—General	M,D
Computer Engineering	M,D
Computer Science	M,D
Counseling Psychology	M,D
Counselor Education	M,D
Curriculum and Instruction	M,D
Developmental Biology	M,D
Developmental Psychology	M,D
Ecology	M,D
Economics	M,D
Education of the Gifted	O
Education—General	M,D
Educational Leadership and Administration	M
Educational Media/Instructional Technology	M,D
Educational Psychology	M,D,O
Electrical Engineering	M,D
Elementary Education	M,D
Engineering and Applied Sciences—General	M,D
English Education	M,D
English	M,D

Women's Health Nursing — M,D
Women's Studies — M,O

Environmental and Occupational Health — O
Environmental Engineering — M,D
Exercise and Sports Science — M,D
Experimental Psychology — M,D
Family Nurse Practitioner Studies — M
Finance and Banking — M,D,O
Foreign Languages Education — M,D
Genetics — M,D
Genomic Sciences — M,D
Geography — M,D
Geology — M,D
Gerontological Nursing — M,O
Health Services Management and Hospital Administration — M,D
Higher Education — M
History — M,D
Human Development — M,D
Human Resources Management — M,D
Industrial and Organizational Psychology — M,D
International Affairs — M
Jewish Studies — M,D
Landscape Architecture — M,D
Latin American Studies — M
Law — D
Linguistics — M
Management Information Systems — M,D
Marketing — M,D
Materials Engineering — M
Materials Sciences — M,D
Maternal and Child/Neonatal Nursing — M,O
Mathematical and Computational Finance — M
Mathematics Education — M
Mechanical Engineering — M,D
Medicinal and Pharmaceutical Chemistry — M,D
Medieval and Renaissance Studies — M,D
Microbiology — M,D
Molecular Biology — M,D
Multilingual and Multicultural Education — M,D
Music Education — M,D
Music — M,D
Natural Resources — M,D
Neurobiology — M,D
Neuroscience — M,D
Nonprofit Management — M,O
Nursing—General — M,D,O
Nutrition — M,D
Pathobiology — M,D
Pharmaceutical Sciences — M,D
Pharmacology — M,D
Pharmacy — D
Philosophy — M,D
Physical Therapy — D
Physics — M,D
Physiology — M,D
Plant Sciences — M,D
Political Science — M,D
Polymer Science and Engineering — M,D
Project Management — M,D
Psychology—General — M,D
Public Administration — M
Quantitative Analysis — M,O
Reading Education — M,D
Risk Management — M,D
Science Education — M,D
Secondary Education — M,D
Social Psychology — M,D
Social Sciences Education — M,D
Social Work — M,D
Sociology — M,D
Software Engineering — M,D
Sports Management — M,D
Statistics — M,D
Structural Biology — M
Theater — M
Toxicology — M,D

UNIVERSITY OF CONNECTICUT HEALTH CENTER
Allopathic Medicine — D
Anatomy — D
Biochemistry — D
Biological and Biomedical Sciences—General — D
Cell Biology — M
Clinical Research — M
Dentistry — D,O
Developmental Biology — D
Genetics — D
Immunology — D
Molecular Biology — D
Neuroscience — D
Oral and Dental Sciences — M
Public Health—General — M

UNIVERSITY OF DALLAS
Accounting — M,D
Business Administration and Management—General — M,D
Business Analytics — M,D
Computer and Information Systems Security — M,D
Entertainment Management — M,D
Finance and Banking — M,D
Health Services Management and Hospital Administration — M,D
Human Resources Management — M,D
International Business — M,D
Logistics — M,D
Management Information Systems — M,D
Management of Technology — M,D
Management Strategy and Policy — M,D
Marketing — M,D
Organizational Management — M,D
Pastoral Ministry and Counseling — M

Project Management — M,D
Sports Management — M,D
Supply Chain Management — M,D

UNIVERSITY OF DAYTON
Accounting — M
Aerospace/Aeronautical Engineering — M,D
Applied Mathematics — M
Art/Fine Arts — M
Biochemistry — M
Bioengineering — M
Biological and Biomedical Sciences—General — M,D
Business Administration and Management—General — M
Chemical Engineering — M
Chemistry — M
Civil Engineering — M
Clinical Psychology — M,O
Communication—General — M
Computer and Information Systems Security — M
Computer Engineering — M,D
Computer Science — M
Counseling Psychology — M,O
Counselor Education — M,O
Cultural Studies — M
Early Childhood Education — M
Educational Leadership and Administration — M,D,O
Educational Media/Instructional Technology — M
Electrical Engineering — M,D
Elementary Education — M
Engineering Management — M
English as a Second Language — M
English — M
Environmental Engineering — M
Environmental Management and Policy — M,D
Exercise and Sports Science — M
Finance and Banking — M
Foreign Languages Education — M
Geotechnical Engineering — M
Human Development — M,O
Interdisciplinary Studies — M
Law — M,D
Marketing — M
Materials Engineering — M,D
Mathematical and Computational Finance — M
Mathematics Education — M
Mechanical Engineering — M,D
Mechanics — M
Middle School Education — M
Music Education — M
Optical Sciences — M,D
Pastoral Ministry and Counseling — M,D
Photonics — M,D
Physical Education — M
Physical Therapy — D
Physician Assistant Studies — M
Psychology—General — M
Public Administration — M
Reading Education — M
Rhetoric — M
School Psychology — M,O
Secondary Education — M
Structural Engineering — M
Student Affairs — M,O
Theology — M,D
Transportation and Highway Engineering — M
Water Resources Engineering — M
Writing — M

UNIVERSITY OF DELAWARE
Accounting — M
Adult Nursing — M,O
Agricultural Economics and Agribusiness — M
Agricultural Education — M
Agricultural Sciences—General — M,D
Agronomy and Soil Sciences — M,D
American Studies — M
Animal Sciences — M,D
Applied Arts and Design—General — M
Applied Mathematics — M,D
Art History — M
Art/Fine Arts — M
Astronomy — M,D
Biochemistry — M,D
Biological and Biomedical Sciences—General — M,D
Biotechnology — M,D
Business Administration and Management—General — M,D
Business Education — M,D
Cancer Biology/Oncology — M,D
Cell Biology — M,D
Chemical Engineering — M,D
Chemistry — M,D
Child and Family Studies — M,D
Chinese — M
Civil Engineering — M,D
Clinical Psychology — D
Clothing and Textiles — M,D
Cognitive Sciences — M
Communication Disorders — M
Communication—General — M,D
Computer Engineering — M,D
Computer Science — M,D
Criminal Justice and Criminology — M,D
Curriculum and Instruction — M,D,O
Developmental Biology — M,D
Ecology — M,D
Economics — M
Education—General — M,D,O

Educational Leadership and Administration — M,D,O
Electrical Engineering — M,D
Emergency Management — M,D
Energy Management and Policy — M,D
Engineering and Applied Sciences—General — M,D
English as a Second Language — M,D,O
English — M,D
Entomology — M,D
Entrepreneurship — M,D
Environmental Engineering — M,D
Environmental Management and Policy — M,D
Evolutionary Biology — M,D
Family Nurse Practitioner Studies — M,O
Finance and Banking — M
Fish, Game, and Wildlife Management — M,D
Food Science and Technology — M,D
Foreign Languages Education — M
French — M
Genetics — M,D
Geography — M,D
Geology — M,D
Geotechnical Engineering — M,D
German — M
Gerontological Nursing — M,O
Health Promotion — M
Higher Education — M,D,O
Historic Preservation — M
History of Science and Technology — M,D
History — M,D
HIV/AIDS Nursing — M,O
Horticulture — M
Hospitality Management — M
Human Development — M,D
Information Science — M,D
International Affairs — M,D
Kinesiology and Movement Studies — M,D
Liberal Studies — M
Linguistics — M,D
Management Information Systems — M,D
Management of Technology — M
Marine Affairs — M,D
Marine Geology — M,D
Marine Sciences — M,D
Materials Engineering — M,D
Materials Sciences — M,D
Maternal and Child/Neonatal Nursing — M,O
Mathematics — M,D
Mechanical Engineering — M,D
Microbiology — M,D
Molecular Biology — M,D
Multilingual and Multicultural Education — M,D,O
Music Education — M
Music — M
Natural Resources — M
Neuroscience — D
Nursing and Healthcare Administration — M,O
Nursing—General — M,O
Nutrition — M
Ocean Engineering — M,D
Oceanography — M,D
Oncology Nursing — M,O
Operations Research — M
Pediatric Nursing — M,O
Physical Therapy — D
Physics — M,D
Physiology — M,D
Plant Sciences — M,D
Political Science — M,D
Psychiatric Nursing — M,O
Psychology—General — D
Public Administration — M
Public Policy — M,D
School Psychology — M,D,O
Social Psychology — D
Sociology — M,D
Spanish — M
Statistics — M,D
Structural Engineering — M,D
Theater — M
Translation and Interpretation — M
Transportation and Highway Engineering — M,D
Urban Studies — M,D
Water Resources Engineering — M,D
Women's Health Nursing — M,O

UNIVERSITY OF DENVER
Accounting — M
Anthropology — M
Archaeology — M
Art Education — M,O
Art History — M
Art/Fine Arts — M
Bioengineering — M,D
Biological and Biomedical Sciences—General — M,D
Business Administration and Management—General — M
Business Analytics — M
Cell Biology — M,D
Chemistry — M,D
Child and Family Studies — M,D,O
Clinical Psychology — M,D,O
Communication—General — M,O
Computer and Information Systems Security — M,D
Computer Art and Design — M
Computer Engineering — M,D
Computer Science — M,D
Conflict Resolution and Mediation/Peace Studies — M,D,O
Construction Management — M

Counseling Psychology — M,D
Criminal Justice and Criminology — M,O
Cultural Anthropology — M
Cultural Studies — M,D,O
Curriculum and Instruction — M,D,O
Data Science/Data Analytics — M
Developmental Psychology — D
Early Childhood Education — M,D,O
Ecology — M,D
Economics — M
Education—General — M,D,O
Educational Leadership and Administration — M,D,O
Educational Measurement and Evaluation — M,D,O
Educational Policy — M,D,O
Electrical Engineering — M,D
Emergency Management — M,O
Engineering and Applied Sciences—General — M,D
Engineering Management — M,D
English — M,D
Environmental Management and Policy — M,O
Evolutionary Biology — M,D
Finance and Banking — M,D
Forensic Psychology — M,D,O
Geographic Information Systems — M,D,O
Geography — M,D
Health Services Management and Hospital Administration — M,O
Higher Education — M,D,O
History — M,O
Homeland Security — M,D,O
Human Resources Management — M,O
Information Science — M,O
International Affairs — M,D,O
International Development — M,D,O
International Health — M,D,O
Law — M,D,O
Legal and Justice Studies — M,O
Library Science — M,D,O
Marketing — M
Marriage and Family Therapy — M,D
Mass Communication — M
Materials Engineering — M,D
Materials Sciences — M,D
Mathematics — M,D
Mechanical Engineering — M,D
Media Studies — M
Molecular Biology — M,D
Museum Studies — M
Music Education — M,O
Music — M,O
Organizational Management — M,O
Philanthropic Studies — M,O
Physics — M,O
Project Management — M,O
Psychology—General — M,D,O
Public Policy — M
Real Estate — M
Religion — M,D,O
School Psychology — M,D,O
Social Psychology — D
Social Work — M,D,O
Special Education — M,D,O
Sport Psychology — M,D,O
Taxation — M
Theology — D,O
Translation and Interpretation — M,O
Writing — M,D,O

UNIVERSITY OF DETROIT MERCY
Accounting — M,O
Addictions/Substance Abuse Counseling — M,D,O
Allied Health—General — M,D,O
Architectural Engineering — M
Business Administration and Management—General — M,O
Chemistry — M,D
Civil Engineering — M,D
Clinical Psychology — M,D,O
Computer and Information Systems Security — M,D,O
Computer Engineering — M,D
Computer Science — M,D,O
Criminal Justice and Criminology — M,D,O
Curriculum and Instruction — M,D,O
Dentistry — M,D,O
Economics — M,D,O
Educational Leadership and Administration — M,D,O
Electrical Engineering — M,D
Engineering and Applied Sciences—General — M,D
Engineering Management — M,D
Environmental Engineering — M,D
Ethics — M,O
Family Nurse Practitioner Studies — M,D,O
Finance and Banking — M,D,O
Forensic Sciences — M,O
Health Services Management and Hospital Administration — M,D,O
Industrial and Organizational Psychology — M,D,O
Industrial Design — M,D
Law — D
Liberal Studies — M,D,O
Management Information Systems — M,D,O
Management Strategy and Policy — M,O
Mathematics Education — M,D
Mechanical Engineering — M,D
Nurse Anesthesia — M,D,O
Nursing Education — M,D,O
Nursing—General — M,D,O
Oral and Dental Sciences — M,D,O
Physician Assistant Studies — M,D,O
Religious Education — M,D,O
School Psychology — M,D,O
Software Engineering — M,D

*M—masters degree; D—doctorate; O—other advanced degree; *—Close-Up and/or Display*

Special Education	M,D,O
Urban and Regional Planning	M

UNIVERSITY OF DUBUQUE

Business Administration and Management—General	M
Communication—General	M
Theology	M,D

UNIVERSITY OF EAST-WEST MEDICINE

Acupuncture and Oriental Medicine	M,D

UNIVERSITY OF EVANSVILLE

Athletic Training and Sports Medicine	M
Health Services Management and Hospital Administration	M
Physical Therapy	D
Public Administration	M

UNIVERSITY OF FAIRFAX

Business Administration and Management—General	M,D
Computer and Information Systems Security	M,D
Computer Science	M,D
Information Science	M,D
Project Management	M,D

THE UNIVERSITY OF FINDLAY

Accounting	M,D
Athletic Training and Sports Medicine	M,D
Business Administration and Management—General	M,D
Education—General	M,D
Educational Leadership and Administration	M,D
Educational Media/Instructional Technology	M,D
English as a Second Language	M,D
Environmental Management and Policy	M,D
Health Informatics	M,D
Health Services Management and Hospital Administration	M,D
Hospitality Management	M,D
Linguistics	M,D
Mathematics	M,D
Occupational Therapy	M,D
Pharmacy	M,D
Physical Therapy	M,D
Physician Assistant Studies	M,D
Public Administration	M,D
Reading Education	M,D
Rhetoric	M,D
Science Education	M,D
Writing	M,D

UNIVERSITY OF FLORIDA

Accounting	M,D
Advertising and Public Relations	M,D
Aerospace/Aeronautical Engineering	M,D
Agricultural Economics and Agribusiness	M,D
Agricultural Education	M,D
Agricultural Engineering	M,D,O
Agricultural Sciences—General	M,D,O
Agronomy and Soil Sciences	M,D
Allied Health—General	M,D,O
Allopathic Medicine	D
Animal Sciences	M,D
Anthropology	M,D
Aquaculture	M,D
Architecture	M,D
Art Education	M,D
Art History	M,D
Art/Fine Arts	M,D
Astronomy	M,D
Athletic Training and Sports Medicine	M,D
Biochemistry	D
Bioengineering	M,D,O
Biological and Biomedical Sciences—General	M,D
Biomedical Engineering	M,D,O
Biostatistics	M,D,O
Botany	M,D
Business Administration and Management—General	M,D
Cell Biology	M,D
Chemical Engineering	M,D,O
Chemistry	M,D
Child Development	M
Civil Engineering	M,D
Classics	M,D
Clinical Laboratory Sciences/Medical Technology	M,D
Clinical Psychology	M,D
Clinical Research	M,D,O
Communication Disorders	M,D
Communication—General	M,D
Computer Art and Design	M,D
Computer Engineering	M,D
Computer Science	M,D
Construction Management	M,D
Counseling Psychology	M,D
Counselor Education	M,D,O
Criminal Justice and Criminology	M,D
Curriculum and Instruction	M,D,O
Dentistry	D,O
Early Childhood Education	M,D,O
Ecology	M,D,O
Economics	M,D
Education—General	M,D,O
Educational Leadership and Administration	M,D,O
Educational Measurement and Evaluation	M,D,O
Educational Policy	M,D,O
Electrical Engineering	M,D
Elementary Education	M,D,O
Emergency Management	M

Engineering and Applied Sciences—General	M,D,O
English as a Second Language	M,D,O
English Education	M,D,O
English	M,D,O
Entrepreneurship	M,D,O
Environmental and Occupational Health	M,D,O
Environmental Education	M,D,O
Environmental Engineering	M,D,O
Environmental Law	M,D
Epidemiology	M,D,O
Exercise and Sports Science	M,D
Family and Consumer Sciences-General	M
Finance and Banking	M,D,O
Fish, Game, and Wildlife Management	M,D,O
Food Science and Technology	M,D
Foreign Languages Education	M,D
Forensic Sciences	M,O
Forestry	M,D
French	M,D
Gender Studies	M,O
Genetics	D
Geographic Information Systems	M,D
Geography	M,D
Geology	M,D
Geosciences	M,D
German	M,D
Health Communication	M,D,O
Health Education	M,D,O
Health Psychology	M,D
Health Services Management and Hospital Administration	M,D
Health Services Research	M,D
Higher Education	M,D,O
Historic Preservation	M,D
History	M,D
Horticulture	M,D
Human Resources Management	M,D
Hydrology	D
Immunology	M,D
Industrial/Management Engineering	M,D,O
Information Science	M,D
Insurance	M,D,O
Interdisciplinary Studies	M,D
Interior Design	M,D
International Affairs	M
International Business	M,D
International Development	M,D,O
International Health	M,D
Jewish Studies	M,D
Journalism	M,D
Kinesiology and Movement Studies	M,D
Landscape Architecture	M,D
Latin American Studies	M,O
Law	M,D
Limnology	M,D
Linguistics	M,D,O
Management Information Systems	M,D,O
Marine Sciences	M,D
Marketing	M,D
Marriage and Family Therapy	M,D,O
Mass Communication	M,D
Materials Engineering	M,D
Materials Sciences	M,D
Mathematics Education	M,D,O
Mathematics	M,D
Mechanical Engineering	M,D
Medical Physics	M,D,O
Medicinal and Pharmaceutical Chemistry	M,D
Microbiology	M,D
Molecular Biology	M,D
Molecular Genetics	M
Museum Studies	M,D
Music Education	M,D
Music	M,D
Natural Resources	M,D
Neuroscience	D
Nonprofit Management	M
Nuclear Engineering	M,D
Nursing—General	M,D
Nutrition	M,D
Occupational Therapy	M
Ocean Engineering	M,D
Oral and Dental Sciences	M,D,O
Pharmaceutical Administration	M,D
Pharmaceutical Sciences	M,D
Pharmacology	M,D
Pharmacy	M,D
Philosophy	M,D
Physical Education	M,D
Physical Therapy	D
Physician Assistant Studies	M
Physics	M,D
Physiology	M,D
Plant Biology	M,D
Plant Molecular Biology	M,D
Plant Pathology	M,D
Plant Sciences	D
Political Science	M,D,O
Psychology—General	M,D
Public Affairs	M,D,O
Public Health—General	M,D,O
Quantitative Analysis	M,D,O
Reading Education	M,D,O
Real Estate	M,D,O
Recreation and Park Management	M,D
Rehabilitation Sciences	D
Religion	M,D
School Psychology	M,D,O
Science Education	M,D,O
Social Sciences Education	M,D
Social Sciences	M,D
Sociology	M,D
Spanish	M,D
Special Education	M,D,O
Sports Management	M,D
Statistics	M,D
Student Affairs	M,D,O

Supply Chain Management	M,D,O
Sustainable Development	M,O
Systems Engineering	M,D,O
Taxation	M,D
Telecommunications	M,D
Theater	M
Toxicology	M,D,O
Travel and Tourism	M,D
Urban and Regional Planning	M,D
Veterinary Medicine	D
Veterinary Sciences	M,D,O
Water Resources	M,D
Women's Studies	M,O
Writing	M,D
Zoology	M,D

UNIVERSITY OF FORT LAUDERDALE

Pastoral Ministry and Counseling	M

UNIVERSITY OF GEORGIA

Accounting	M
Adult Education	D,O
Agricultural Economics and Agribusiness	M,D
Agricultural Sciences—General	M,D
Agronomy and Soil Sciences	M,D
Analytical Chemistry	M,D
Animal Sciences	M,D
Anthropology	M,D
Applied Economics	M,D
Applied Mathematics	M,D
Art History	M,D
Art/Fine Arts	M,D
Artificial Intelligence/Robotics	M
Biochemical Engineering	M
Biochemistry	M,D
Bioinformatics	M,D
Biological and Biomedical Sciences—General	D
Business Administration and Management—General	M
Business Analytics	M
Business Education	M,D,O
Cell Biology	M,D
Chemistry	M,D
Child and Family Studies	M
Classics	M
Clothing and Textiles	M,D
Communication Disorders	M,D,O
Communication—General	M,D
Comparative Literature	M,D
Computer Science	M,D
Counselor Education	M,D,O
Ecology	M,D
Economics	M,D
Education—General	M,D,O
Educational Leadership and Administration	D,O
Educational Media/Instructional Technology	M,D,O
Educational Policy	D,O
Educational Psychology	O
English Education	M,D
English	M,D
Entomology	M,D
Environmental and Occupational Health	M,D
Environmental Design	M
Environmental Engineering	M
Family and Consumer Sciences-General	M,D
Food Science and Technology	M,D
Forestry	M,D
French	M,D
Genetics	M,D
Genomic Sciences	M,D
Geography	M,D
Geology	M,D
German	M
Gerontology	O
Health Education	M,D
Health Promotion	M,D
Higher Education	M,D
Historic Preservation	M
History	M,D
Horticulture	M,D
Infectious Diseases	D
Interior Design	M,D
International Affairs	M,D
Italian	M,D
Journalism	M,D
Kinesiology and Movement Studies	M,D
Landscape Architecture	M
Law	M,D
Linguistics	M,D
Marine Sciences	M,D
Mass Communication	M,D
Mathematics Education	M,D,O
Mathematics	M,D
Microbiology	M,D
Molecular Biology	M,D
Music Education	M,D
Music	M,D
Natural Resources	M,D
Neuroscience	D
Nonprofit Management	M,D,O
Nutrition	M,D
Pathology	M,D
Pharmaceutical Administration	D
Pharmaceutical Sciences	M,D
Pharmacology	M,D
Pharmacy	M,D,O
Philosophy	M,D
Physical Education	M,D
Physics	M,D
Physiology	M,D
Plant Biology	M,D
Plant Pathology	M,D
Plant Sciences	M,D
Political Science	M,D
Portuguese	M
Psychology—General	D
Public Administration	M,D

Public Health—General	D
Public Policy	M,D
Reading Education	M,D
Religion	M
Science Education	M,D,O
Social Work	M,D,O
Sociology	M,D
Spanish	M,D
Special Education	M,D,O
Statistics	M,D
Student Affairs	M,D,O
Sustainable Development	M,D
Theater	M,D
Veterinary Medicine	M,D
Vocational and Technical Education	M,D,O
Women's Studies	O

UNIVERSITY OF GUAM

Art/Fine Arts	M
Biological and Biomedical Sciences—General	M
Business Administration and Management—General	M
Counselor Education	M
Education—General	M
Educational Leadership and Administration	M
English as a Second Language	M
English	M
Environmental Sciences	M
Graphic Design	M
Marine Biology	M
Pacific Area/Pacific Rim Studies	M
Public Administration	M
Reading Education	M
Secondary Education	M
Social Work	M
Special Education	M

UNIVERSITY OF GUELPH

Acute Care/Critical Care Nursing	M,D,O
Agricultural Economics and Agribusiness	M,D
Agricultural Sciences—General	M,D,O
Agronomy and Soil Sciences	M,D
Anatomy	M,D
Anesthesiologist Assistant Studies	M,D,O
Animal Sciences	M,D
Anthropology	M,D
Applied Mathematics	M,D
Applied Psychology	M,D
Applied Statistics	M,D
Aquaculture	M
Art/Fine Arts	M
Atmospheric Sciences	M,D
Biochemistry	M,D
Bioengineering	M,D
Biological and Biomedical Sciences—General	M,D
Biophysics	M,D
Biotechnology	M,D
Botany	M,D
Business Administration and Management—General	M,D
Cardiovascular Sciences	M,D,O
Cell Biology	M,D
Chemistry	M,D
Child and Family Studies	M,D
Clinical Psychology	M,D
Cognitive Sciences	M,D
Comparative Literature	D
Computer Science	M
Consumer Economics	M,D
Criminal Justice and Criminology	M,D
Demography and Population Studies	M,D
Ecology	M,D
Economics	M,D
Emergency Medical Services	M,D,O
Engineering and Applied Sciences—General	M,D
English	M
Entomology	M,D
Environmental Biology	M,D
Environmental Engineering	M,D
Environmental Management and Policy	M,D
Environmental Sciences	M,D
Epidemiology	M,D
Evolutionary Biology	M,D
Food Science and Technology	M,D
French	M
Geography	M,D
History	M,D
Horticulture	M,D
Hospitality Management	M
Human Development	M,D
Immunology	M,D,O
Industrial and Organizational Psychology	M,D
Infectious Diseases	M,D,O
International Development	M,D
Landscape Architecture	M
Marriage and Family Therapy	M,D
Mathematics	M,D
Medical Imaging	M,D,O
Medieval and Renaissance Studies	D
Microbiology	M,D
Molecular Biology	M,D
Molecular Genetics	M,D
Natural Resources	M,D
Neuroscience	M,D,O
Nutrition	M,D
Organizational Management	M
Pathology	M,D,O
Pharmacology	M,D
Philosophy	M,D
Physics	M,D
Physiology	M,D
Plant Pathology	M,D
Political Science	M
Psychology—General	M,D
Public Administration	M
Public Policy	M

Rural Planning and Studies — M,D
Social Psychology — M,D
Sociology — M,D
Statistics — M,D
Theater — M
Toxicology — M,D
Veterinary Medicine — M,D,O
Veterinary Sciences — M,D,O
Vision Sciences — M,D,O
Water Resources Engineering — M,D
Western European Studies — M
Zoology — M,D

UNIVERSITY OF HARTFORD
Accounting — M,O
Architecture — M
Art/Fine Arts — M
Business Administration and Management—General — M
Clinical Psychology — M,D
Communication—General — M
Community Health Nursing — M
Early Childhood Education — M
Education—General — M,D,O
Educational Leadership and Administration — D
Elementary Education — M
Engineering and Applied Sciences—General — M
Music Education — M,D,O
Music — M,D,O
Neuroscience — M
Nursing Education — M
Nursing—General — M
Organizational Behavior — M
Physical Therapy — M,D
School Psychology — M
Taxation — M,O

UNIVERSITY OF HAWAII AT HILO
Conservation Biology — M
Counseling Psychology — M
Cultural Studies — M,D
Education—General — M
Environmental Sciences — M
Foreign Languages Education — M,D
Marine Biology — M
Nursing—General — D
Pharmaceutical Sciences — D
Pharmacology — M
Pharmacy — D

UNIVERSITY OF HAWAII AT MANOA
Accounting — M,D
Adult Nursing — M,D,O
Agricultural Sciences—General — M,D
Allopathic Medicine — D
American Studies — M,D,O
Animal Sciences — M
Anthropology — M,D
Architecture — D
Art History — M
Art/Fine Arts — M
Asian Languages — M,D
Asian Studies — O
Astronomy — M,D
Bioengineering — M
Biological and Biomedical Sciences—General — M,D
Botany — M,D
Business Administration and Management—General — M
Chemistry — M,D
Chinese — M,D,O
Civil Engineering — M,D
Clinical Psychology — M,D,O
Communication Disorders — M
Communication—General — M,O
Community Health Nursing — M,D,O
Computer Science — M,D,O
Conflict Resolution and Mediation/Peace Studies — M,O
Cultural Studies — O
Curriculum and Instruction — M,D
Dance — M,D
Demography and Population Studies — O
Developmental Biology — M,D
Disability Studies — O
Early Childhood Education — M
Economics — M,D
Education—General — M,D,O
Educational Leadership and Administration — M,D
Educational Media/Instructional Technology — M,D
Educational Policy — D
Educational Psychology — M,D
Electrical Engineering — M,D
Emergency Management — O
Engineering and Applied Sciences—General — M,D
English as a Second Language — M,D,O
English — M,D
Entomology — M,D
Entrepreneurship — M,D
Environmental Engineering — M,D
Environmental Management and Policy — M,D,O
Epidemiology — D
Family Nurse Practitioner Studies — M,D,O
Finance and Banking — M,D
Food Science and Technology — M
Foreign Languages Education — M,D,O
Foundations and Philosophy of Education — M
French — M
Genetics — M,D
Geochemistry — M,D
Geography — M,D,O
Geological Engineering — M,D

Geology — M,D
Geophysics — M,D
Historic Preservation — O
History — M,D
Horticulture — M,D
Human Resources Management — M
Hydrogeology — M,D
Information Science — M,D
Information Studies — M,O
International Affairs — O
International Business — M,D
International Development — M,D,O
Japanese — M,D,O
Kinesiology and Movement Studies — M,D,O
Law — M,D,O
Library Science — M,O
Linguistics — M,D
Management Information Systems — M,D,O
Marine Biology — M,D
Marine Geology — M,D
Marine Sciences — O
Marketing — M,D
Mathematics — M,D
Mechanical Engineering — M,D
Medical Microbiology — M,D
Meteorology — M,D
Microbiology — M,D
Molecular Biology — M,D
Museum Studies — O
Music — M,D
Natural Resources — M,D
Nursing and Healthcare Administration — M,D,O
Nursing—General — M,D,O
Nutrition — M,D
Ocean Engineering — M,D
Oceanography — M,D
Organizational Behavior — M
Organizational Management — M,D
Pacific Area/Pacific Rim Studies — M,D
Philosophy — M,D
Physics — M,D
Physiology — M,D
Planetary and Space Sciences — M,D
Plant Pathology — M,D
Plant Sciences — M,D
Political Science — M,D
Psychology—General — M,D,O
Public Administration — M,O
Public Health—General — M,D,O
Public Policy — O
Real Estate — M
Religion — M
Reproductive Biology — M,D
Social Psychology — M,D,O
Social Work — M,D
Sociology — M,D
Spanish — M
Special Education — M,D
Speech and Interpersonal Communication — M
Sustainable Development — M,D,O
Taxation — M
Telecommunications — O
Theater — M,D
Transportation Management — M,D,O
Travel and Tourism — M
Urban and Regional Planning — M,D,O
Women's Studies — O
Zoology — M,D

UNIVERSITY OF HOLY CROSS
Biological and Biomedical Sciences—General — M,D
Business Administration and Management—General — M,D
Counselor Education — M,D
Education—General — M,D
Educational Leadership and Administration — M,D
Health Services Management and Hospital Administration — M,D
Marriage and Family Therapy — M,D
Theology — M,D

UNIVERSITY OF HOUSTON
Accounting — M,D
Advertising and Public Relations — M
Anthropology — M
Applied Economics — M,D
Applied Mathematics — M,D
Architecture — M
Art History — M
Art/Fine Arts — M
Atmospheric Sciences — M,D
Biochemistry — M,D
Biological and Biomedical Sciences—General — M,D
Biomedical Engineering — D
Business Administration and Management—General — M,D
Chemical Engineering — M,D
Chemistry — M,D
Civil Engineering — M,D
Clinical Psychology — M,D
Communication Disorders — M
Communication—General — M
Comparative Literature — M
Computer and Information Systems Security — M
Computer Science — M,D
Construction Management — M
Counseling Psychology — M,D
Cultural Studies — M
Developmental Psychology — M,D
Economics — M,D
Education—General — M,D
Educational Leadership and Administration — M,D
Electrical Engineering — M,D

Engineering and Applied Sciences—General — M,D
Environmental Law — M,D
Exercise and Sports Science — M,D
Family and Consumer Sciences-General — M
Family Nurse Practitioner Studies — M
Finance and Banking — M
Geology — M,D
Geophysics — M,D
Health Communication — M
Health Education — M,D
Health Law — M,D
Higher Education — M,D
Hispanic Studies — M,D
History — M,D
Hospitality Management — M
Human Resources Development — M
Industrial and Organizational Psychology — M,D
Industrial/Management Engineering — M,D
Information Science — M,D
Intellectual Property Law — M,D
Kinesiology and Movement Studies — M,D
Law — M,D
Linguistics — M,D
Logistics — M
Marketing — D
Mass Communication — M
Mathematics — M,D
Mechanical Engineering — M,D
Music Education — M,D
Music — M,D
Nursing and Healthcare Administration — M
Nursing Education — M
Nursing—General — M
Nutrition — M,D
Optometry — D
Petroleum Engineering — M,D
Pharmaceutical Administration — M,D
Pharmaceutical Sciences — M,D
Pharmacology — M,D
Pharmacy — M,D
Philosophy — M
Physical Education — M,D
Physics — M,D
Planetary and Space Sciences — M,D
Political Science — M,D
Project Management — M
Psychology—General — M,D
Public Administration — M,D
Public Policy — M
Social Psychology — M,D
Social Work — M,D
Sociology — M,D
Spanish — M
Special Education — M,D
Speech and Interpersonal Communication — M
Supply Chain Management — M
Sustainable Development — M
Taxation — M,D
Telecommunications — M
Theater — M
Urban Design — M
Vision Sciences — M,D
Writing — M,D

UNIVERSITY OF HOUSTON—CLEAR LAKE
Accounting — M
Biological and Biomedical Sciences—General — M
Biotechnology — M
Business Administration and Management—General — M
Chemistry — M
Clinical Psychology — M
Computer Engineering — M
Computer Science — M
Counselor Education — M
Criminal Justice and Criminology — M
Cultural Studies — M
Curriculum and Instruction — M
Early Childhood Education — M
Education—General — M,D
Educational Leadership and Administration — M,D
Educational Media/Instructional Technology — M
English — M
Environmental Management and Policy — M
Environmental Sciences — M
Exercise and Sports Science — M
Finance and Banking — M
Foundations and Philosophy of Education — M
Health Services Management and Hospital Administration — M
History — M
Human Resources Management — M
Humanities — M
Information Science — M
Library Science — M
Management Information Systems — M
Marriage and Family Therapy — M
Mathematics — M
Multilingual and Multicultural Education — M
Physics — M
Psychology—General — M
Reading Education — M
School Psychology — M
Sociology — M
Software Engineering — M
Statistics — M
Systems Engineering — M

UNIVERSITY OF HOUSTON—DOWNTOWN
Accounting — M
Business Administration and Management—General — M
Criminal Justice and Criminology — M
Curriculum and Instruction — M
Data Science/Data Analytics — M
English — M
Finance and Banking — M
Human Resources Management — M
International Business — M
Investment Management — M
Nonprofit Management — M
Project Management — M
Rhetoric — M
Social Work — M
Supply Chain Management — M
Technical Communication — M
Urban Education — M

UNIVERSITY OF HOUSTON—VICTORIA
Accounting — M
Adult Education — M,O
Biological and Biomedical Sciences—General — M
Business Administration and Management—General — M
Computer Science — M
Counseling Psychology — M
Counselor Education — M,O
Curriculum and Instruction — M,O
Economic Development — M
Education—General — M,O
Educational Leadership and Administration — M,O
Educational Media/Instructional Technology — M,O
Entrepreneurship — M
Finance and Banking — M
Forensic Psychology — M
Forensic Sciences — M
Higher Education — M,O
Interdisciplinary Studies — M
International Business — M
Management Information Systems — M
Marketing — M
Psychology—General — M
Publishing — M
Reading Education — M,O
School Psychology — M
Special Education — M,O
Writing — M

UNIVERSITY OF IDAHO
Accounting — M
Agricultural Economics and Agribusiness — M
Agronomy and Soil Sciences — M,D
Animal Sciences — M,D
Anthropology — M
Architecture — M
Art/Fine Arts — M
Athletic Training and Sports Medicine — M,D
Biochemistry — M,D
Bioengineering — M,D
Bioinformatics — M,D
Biological and Biomedical Sciences—General — M,D
Business Administration and Management—General — M
Chemical Engineering — M,D
Chemistry — M,D
Civil Engineering — M,D
Computational Biology — M,D
Computer Science — M,D
Consumer Economics — M
Counselor Education — M,O
Curriculum and Instruction — M,O
Education—General — M,D,O
Educational Leadership and Administration — M,O
Electrical Engineering — M,D
Engineering and Applied Sciences—General — M
Entomology — M,D
Environmental Sciences — M,D
Exercise and Sports Science — M,D
Experimental Psychology — M,D
Food Science and Technology — M,D
Geography — M,D
Geological Engineering — M,D
Geology — M,D
History — M
Human Services — M,O
Interdisciplinary Studies — M
Kinesiology and Movement Studies — M,D
Landscape Architecture — M
Law — M,D
Materials Sciences — M,D
Mathematics — M,D
Mechanical Engineering — M,D
Microbiology — M,D
Music — M
Natural Resources — M,D
Nuclear Engineering — M,D
Philosophy — M,D
Physical Education — M,D
Physics — M,D
Plant Pathology — M,D
Plant Sciences — M,D
Political Science — M,D
Psychology—General — M,D
Public Administration — M,D
Rehabilitation Counseling — M,O
Special Education — M
Sports Management — M,D
Statistics — M
Theater — M

*M—masters degree; D—doctorate; O—other advanced degree; *—Close-Up and/or Display*

Travel and Tourism	M,D
Urban and Regional Planning	M,D
Veterinary Sciences	M,D
Vocational and Technical Education	M,O
Water Resources Engineering	M,D
Water Resources	M,D
Writing	M

UNIVERSITY OF ILLINOIS AT CHICAGO

Accounting	M
Acute Care/Critical Care Nursing	M,O
Adult Nursing	M,O
Allied Health—General	M,D,O
Allopathic Medicine	D
Anatomy	M
Anthropology	M,D
Applied Arts and Design— General	M
Architecture	M
Art History	M,D
Art/Fine Arts	M,D
Biochemistry	D
Bioengineering	M,D
Bioinformatics	M,D
Biological and Biomedical Sciences—General	M,D
Biophysics	M,D
Biostatistics	M,D
Business Administration and Management—General	M,D
Cell Biology	M,D
Chemical Engineering	M,D
Chemistry	M,D
Civil Engineering	M,D
Communication—General	M,D
Community Health Nursing	M,O
Community Health	M,D
Computer Education	D
Computer Engineering	M,D
Computer Science	M,D
Criminal Justice and Criminology	M,D
Curriculum and Instruction	M,D
Dentistry	D
Developmental Psychology	M,D
Disability Studies	M,D
Early Childhood Education	M,D
East European and Russian Studies	M,D
Economics	M,D
Education—General	M,D
Educational Leadership and Administration	M,D
Educational Measurement and Evaluation	M,D
Educational Policy	M,D
Educational Psychology	M,D
Electrical Engineering	M,D
Elementary Education	M,D
Engineering and Applied Sciences—General	M,D
English as a Second Language	M,D
English	M,D
Environmental and Occupational Health	M,D
Epidemiology	M,D
Family Nurse Practitioner Studies	M,O
Finance and Banking	M
Foreign Languages Education	M,D
Forensic Sciences	M
French	M,D
Genetics	D
Geography	M,D
Geology	M,D
Geosciences	M,D
German	M,D
Gerontological Nursing	M,O
Graphic Design	M
Health Education	M
Health Informatics	M,O
Health Services Management and Hospital Administration	M,D
Health Services Research	M,D
Hispanic and Latin American Languages	M,D
Hispanic Studies	M,D
History	M,D
Human Development	M
Immunology	D
Industrial/Management Engineering	M,D
Interdisciplinary Studies	D
Kinesiology and Movement Studies	M,D
Latin American Studies	M
Linguistics	M,D
Management Information Systems	M,D
Materials Engineering	M,D
Maternal and Child/Neonatal Nursing	M,O
Mathematics Education	M,D
Mathematics	M,D
Mechanical Engineering	M,D
Medical Illustration	M
Medicinal and Pharmaceutical Chemistry	M,D
Microbiology	D
Molecular Biology	D
Molecular Genetics	D
Museum Studies	M
Neuroscience	M,D
Nurse Midwifery	M,O
Nursing and Healthcare Administration	M,O
Nursing—General	M,D,O
Nutrition	M,D
Occupational Health Nursing	M,O
Occupational Therapy	M,D
Operations Research	M,D
Oral and Dental Sciences	M,D
Pediatric Nursing	M,O
Pharmaceutical Administration	M,D
Pharmaceutical Sciences	M,D
Pharmacology	D
Pharmacy	D
Philosophy	M,D
Physical Therapy	M,D

Physics	M,D
Physiology	M,D
Political Science	M,D
Psychology—General	M,D
Public Administration	M,D
Public Health—General	M
Real Estate	M
School Nursing	M,O
Science Education	D
Secondary Education	M,D
Slavic Languages	M,D
Social Sciences Education	D
Social Work	M,D,O
Sociology	M,D
Spanish	M,D
Special Education	M,D
Statistics	M,D
Toxicology	M,D
Urban and Regional Planning	M,D
Urban Education	M,D
Women's Health Nursing	M,O

UNIVERSITY OF ILLINOIS AT SPRINGFIELD

Accounting	M
Addictions/Substance Abuse Counseling	M,O
Biological and Biomedical Sciences—General	M
Business Administration and Management—General	M
Child and Family Studies	M,O
Communication—General	M
Community Health	M,O
Computer Science	M
Data Science/Data Analytics	M
Education—General	M,O
Educational Leadership and Administration	M,O
Emergency Management	M,O
English	M,O
Environmental and Occupational Health	M,O
Environmental Management and Policy	M
Environmental Sciences	M
Epidemiology	M,O
Gerontology	M,O
Health Education	M,O
History	M
Homeland Security	M,O
Human Development	M
Human Services	M,O
Interdisciplinary Studies	M
Journalism	M
Legal and Justice Studies	M
Management Information Systems	M
Political Science	M
Public Administration	M,D,O
Public Health—General	M,O
Public History	M
Social Sciences	M,O

UNIVERSITY OF ILLINOIS AT URBANA–CHAMPAIGN

Accounting	M,D
Actuarial Science	M,D
Advertising and Public Relations	M
Aerospace/Aeronautical Engineering	M,D
African Studies	M
Agricultural Economics and Agribusiness	M,D
Agricultural Education	M
Agricultural Engineering	M,D
Agricultural Sciences— General	M
Agronomy and Soil Sciences	M,D
Animal Sciences	M,D
Anthropology	M,D
Applied Arts and Design— General	M,D
Applied Economics	M,D
Applied Mathematics	M,D
Applied Statistics	M,D
Architecture	M,D
Art Education	M,D
Art History	M,D
Art/Fine Arts	M
Asian Languages	M,D
Asian Studies	M,D
Astronomy	M,D
Atmospheric Sciences	M,D
Biochemistry	M,D
Bioengineering	M,D
Bioinformatics	M,D,O
Biological and Biomedical Sciences—General	M,D
Biophysics	M,D
Business Administration and Management—General	M,D
Cell Biology	D
Chemical Engineering	M,D
Chemical Physics	M,D
Chemistry	M,D
Civil Engineering	M,D
Classics	M,D
Communication Disorders	M,D
Communication—General	M,D
Community Health	M,D
Comparative Literature	M,D
Computational Biology	M,D
Computer Engineering	M,D
Computer Science	M,D
Conservation Biology	M,D
Consumer Economics	M,D
Corporate and Organizational Communication	M
Counselor Education	M,D,O
Curriculum and Instruction	M,D,O
Dance	M
Developmental Biology	D
East European and Russian Studies	M
Ecology	M,D

Economics	M,D
Education of Students with Severe/Multiple Disabilities	M,D,O
Education—General	M,D,O
Educational Leadership and Administration	M,D,O
Educational Policy	M,D,O
Educational Psychology	M,D,O
Electrical Engineering	M,D
Energy and Power Engineering	M,D
Energy Management and Policy	M
Engineering and Applied Sciences—General	M,D
English as a Second Language	M,D
English	M,D
Entomology	M,D
Environmental Engineering	M,D
Environmental Sciences	M,D
Evolutionary Biology	M,D
Finance and Banking	M,D
Financial Engineering	M
Food Science and Technology	M,D
Foreign Languages Education	M,D
French	M,D
Geography	M,D
Geology	M,D
Geosciences	M,D
German	M,D
Graphic Design	M
Health Informatics	M,D,O
Health Services Management and Hospital Administration	M,D
History	M,D
Human Development	M,D
Human Resources Management	M,D,O
Human Services	M,D
Human-Computer Interaction	M,D,O
Industrial and Labor Relations	M,D
Industrial Design	M
Industrial/Management Engineering	M,D
Information Science	M,D,O
Information Studies	M,D,O
Interdisciplinary Studies	D
Italian	M,D
Journalism	M
Kinesiology and Movement Studies	M,D
Landscape Architecture	M,D
Latin American Studies	M
Law	M,D
Leisure Studies	M,D
Library Science	M,D,O
Linguistics	M,D
Management Information Systems	M,D,O
Management of Technology	M,D
Management Strategy and Policy	M,D
Materials Engineering	M,D
Materials Sciences	M,D
Mathematics Education	M,D
Mathematics	M,D
Mechanical Engineering	M,D
Mechanics	M,D
Media Studies	M,D
Medical Informatics	M,D,O
Microbiology	M,D
Molecular Physiology	M,D
Music Education	M,D
Music	M,D
Natural Resources	M,D
Near and Middle Eastern Studies	M
Neuroscience	D
Nuclear Engineering	M,D
Nutrition	M,D
Pathobiology	M,D
Philosophy	M,D
Photography	M
Physics	M,D
Physiology	M,D
Plant Biology	M,D
Political Science	M,D
Portuguese	M,D
Psychology—General	M,D
Public Health—General	M,D
Rehabilitation Sciences	M,D
Religion	M
Romance Languages	D
Science Education	M,D
Slavic Languages	M,D
Social Work	M,D
Sociology	M,D
Spanish	M,D
Special Education	M,D,O
Statistics	M,D
Systems Engineering	M,D
Theater	M
Translation and Interpretation	M
Urban and Regional Planning	M,D
Veterinary Medicine	D
Veterinary Sciences	M,D
Western European Studies	M
Writing	M,D
Zoology	M,D

UNIVERSITY OF INDIANAPOLIS

Addictions/Substance Abuse Counseling	M,D
Anthropology	M
Art Education	M
Art/Fine Arts	M
Biological and Biomedical Sciences—General	M
Business Administration and Management—General	M,O
Clinical Psychology	M,D
Counseling Psychology	M,D
Curriculum and Instruction	M
Education—General	M
Educational Leadership and Administration	M
Elementary Education	M
English Education	M

English	M
Family Nurse Practitioner Studies	M
Foreign Languages Education	M
Gerontology	M,D,O
History	M
International Affairs	M
Maternal and Child/Neonatal Nursing	M,D
Mathematics Education	M
Nurse Midwifery	M,D
Nursing and Healthcare Administration	M,D
Nursing Education	M,D
Nursing—General	M,D
Occupational Therapy	M,D
Physical Education	M
Physical Therapy	M,D
Psychology—General	M,D
Public Health—General	M
Science Education	M
Secondary Education	M
Social Sciences Education	M
Social Work	M
Sociology	M
Sports Management	M
Women's Health Nursing	M,D

THE UNIVERSITY OF IOWA

Accounting	M,D
Actuarial Science	M,D
Agricultural Sciences— General	M,D,O
Allopathic Medicine	D
American Studies	M,D
Anatomy	D
Anthropology	M,D
Applied Mathematics	D
Art Education	M,D
Art History	M,D
Art/Fine Arts	M
Asian Languages	M
Asian Studies	M
Astronomy	M
Athletic Training and Sports Medicine	M,D
Bacteriology	M,D
Biochemical Engineering	M,D
Biochemistry	M,D
Bioinformatics	M,D,O
Biological and Biomedical Sciences—General	M,D
Biomedical Engineering	M,D
Biophysics	M,D
Biostatistics	M,D,O
Business Administration and Management—General	M,D
Business Analytics	M
Cell Biology	M,D
Chemical Engineering	M,D
Chemistry	D
Chinese	M
Civil Engineering	M,D
Classics	M,D
Clinical Research	M,D
Communication Disorders	M,D
Communication—General	M,D
Community Health	M,D
Computational Biology	M,D,O
Computational Sciences	D
Computer Engineering	M,D
Computer Science	M,D
Counseling Psychology	M,D,O
Counselor Education	M,D
Dance	M
Dentistry	M,D,O
Developmental Education	M,D
Economics	D
Education—General	M,D,O
Educational Leadership and Administration	M,D,O
Educational Measurement and Evaluation	M,D,O
Educational Policy	M,D,O
Educational Psychology	M,D,O
Electrical Engineering	M,D
Elementary Education	M,D
Energy and Power Engineering	M,D
Engineering and Applied Sciences—General	M,D
English as a Second Language	M,D
English Education	M,D
English	M,D
Environmental and Occupational Health	M,D,O
Environmental Engineering	M,D
Epidemiology	M,D
Ergonomics and Human Factors	M,D,O
Evolutionary Biology	M,D
Exercise and Sports Science	M,D
Film, Television, and Video Production	M
Film, Television, and Video Theory and Criticism	M,D
Finance and Banking	M,D
Foreign Languages Education	M,D
Foundations and Philosophy of Education	M,D,O
French	M,D
Genetics	M,D
Geographic Information Systems	M,D,O
Geography	M,D,O
Geosciences	M,D
Health Informatics	M,D,O
Health Services Management and Hospital Administration	M,D
Higher Education	M,D
History	M,D
Hydraulics	M,D
Immunology	M,D
Industrial Hygiene	M,D,O
Industrial/Management Engineering	M,D

Information Science	M,D,O
Information Studies	M,D
Journalism	M,D
Law	M,D
Leisure Studies	M,D
Library Science	M,D
Linguistics	M,D
Manufacturing Engineering	M,D
Marketing	M,D
Marriage and Family Therapy	M,D
Mass Communication	M,D
Materials Engineering	M,D
Mathematics Education	M,D
Mathematics	M,D
Mechanical Engineering	M,D
Media Studies	M,D
Medicinal and Pharmaceutical Chemistry	M,D
Microbiology	M,D
Molecular Biology	D
Music Education	M,D
Music	M,D
Neurobiology	M,D
Neuroscience	D
Nursing—General	M,D
Operations Research	M,D
Oral and Dental Sciences	M,D,O
Pathology	M
Pharmaceutical Sciences	M,D
Pharmacology	M,D
Pharmacy	M,D
Philosophy	D
Physical Therapy	M,D
Physician Assistant Studies	M
Physics	M,D
Physiology	M,D
Political Science	D
Psychology—General	M,D,O
Public Health—General	M,D,O
Quantitative Analysis	M,D,O
Radiation Biology	M
Recreation and Park Management	M,D
Rehabilitation Counseling	M,D
Rehabilitation Sciences	M,D
Religion	M,D
Rhetoric	M,D
School Psychology	M,D,O
Science Education	M,D
Secondary Education	M,D
Social Sciences Education	M,D
Social Work	M,D
Sociology	M,D
Spanish	M,D
Special Education	M,D
Speech and Interpersonal Communication	M,D
Sports Management	M,D
Statistics	M,D,O
Student Affairs	M,D
Sustainable Development	M,D
Theater	M
Toxicology	M,D
Translational Biology	M,D
Transportation and Highway Engineering	M,D
Urban and Regional Planning	M
Virology	M,D
Water Resources Engineering	M,D
Water Resources	M,D
Women's Studies	O
Writing	M,D

UNIVERSITY OF JAMESTOWN

Curriculum and Instruction	M
Education—General	M
Physical Therapy	D

THE UNIVERSITY OF KANSAS

Accounting	M
Acoustics	M,D,O
Adult Nursing	M,D,O
Aerospace/Aeronautical Engineering	M,D
African Studies	M,O
African-American Studies	M,O
Allied Health—General	M,D,O
Allopathic Medicine	D
American Indian/Native American Studies	M,O
American Studies	M,D
Anatomy	M,D
Anthropology	M,D
Applied Arts and Design—General	M
Applied Behavior Analysis	M,D,O
Applied Mathematics	M,D,O
Applied Statistics	M,D,O
Architectural Engineering	M
Architecture	M,D,O
Art Education	M
Art History	M,D
Art/Fine Arts	M,D
Asian Languages	M,O
Asian Studies	M,O
Astronomy	M,D
Atmospheric Sciences	M,D
Biochemistry	D
Bioengineering	M,D
Biological and Biomedical Sciences—General	D
Biophysics	D
Biostatistics	M,D,O
Biotechnology	M
Business Administration and Management—General	M,D
Cancer Biology/Oncology	M,D
Cell Biology	M,D
Chemical Engineering	M,D,O
Chemistry	M,D
Civil Engineering	M,D
Classics	M

Clinical Psychology	M,D
Clinical Research	M
Cognitive Sciences	M,D
Communication Disorders	M,D
Communication—General	M,D,O
Community Health Nursing	M,D,O
Community Health	M,D,O
Computational Biology	D
Computer Engineering	M
Computer Science	M,D
Construction Management	M
Counseling Psychology	M,D
Cultural Studies	M,D
Curriculum and Instruction	M,D
Developmental Biology	D
Developmental Psychology	M,D
Early Childhood Education	M,D,O
East European and Russian Studies	M,O
Ecology	M,D
Economics	M,D
Education—General	M,D,O
Educational Leadership and Administration	M,D
Educational Measurement and Evaluation	M,D
Educational Media/Instructional Technology	M,D
Educational Policy	M,D
Educational Psychology	M,D
Electrical Engineering	M,D
Engineering and Applied Sciences—General	M,D,O
Engineering Management	M,O
English	M,D
Environmental Engineering	M,D
Environmental Sciences	M,D
Epidemiology	M
Evolutionary Biology	M,D
Exercise and Sports Science	M,D
Film, Television, and Video Theory and Criticism	M,D
Finance and Banking	M,D
French	M,D
Geographic Information Systems	M,D,O
Geography	M,D,O
Geology	M,D
Gerontological Nursing	M,D,O
Gerontology	D
Health Education	M,D,O
Health Informatics	M,O
Health Promotion	M,D,O
Health Services Management and Hospital Administration	M,D
Higher Education	M,D
Historic Preservation	M,D,O
History	M,D
Human Resources Management	M,D
Interdisciplinary Studies	D
International Affairs	M
Journalism	M,D
Latin American Studies	M,O
Law	D
Linguistics	M,D
Logistics	M
Management Information Systems	M
Management Strategy and Policy	M,D
Marketing	M,D
Mathematics	M,D,O
Mechanical Engineering	M,D
Media Studies	M,D
Medical Informatics	M,D,O
Medicinal and Pharmaceutical Chemistry	M,D
Microbiology	M,D
Molecular Biology	D
Museum Studies	M,O
Music Education	M,D
Music	M,D
Near and Middle Eastern Studies	M,O
Neuroscience	M,D
Nurse Anesthesia	D
Nurse Midwifery	M,D,O
Nursing—General	M,D,O
Nutrition	M,D,O
Occupational Therapy	M,D
Organizational Behavior	M,D
Organizational Management	M,D,O
Pathology	M,D
Petroleum Engineering	M,D,O
Pharmacology	M,D
Pharmacy	M,D
Philosophy	M,D
Physical Education	M,D
Physical Therapy	D
Physics	M,D
Physiology	D
Political Science	M,D
Project Management	M
Psychiatric Nursing	M,D,O
Psychology—General	M,D,O
Public Administration	M,D,O
Public Health—General	M
Rehabilitation Sciences	M,D
Religion	M,O
School Psychology	D,O
Slavic Languages	M,D
Social Psychology	M,D
Social Work	M,D
Sociology	D
Spanish	M,D
Special Education	M,D,O
Sports Management	M,D,O
Statistics	M,D,O
Supply Chain Management	M,D
Textile Design	M
Theater	M,D
Therapies—Dance, Drama, and Music	M,D
Toxicology	M,D
Urban and Regional Planning	M
Urban Design	M,D,O

Writing	M,D

UNIVERSITY OF KENTUCKY

Accounting	M
Agricultural Economics and Agribusiness	M,D
Agricultural Engineering	M,D
Agricultural Sciences—General	M,D
Agronomy and Soil Sciences	M,D
Allied Health—General	M,D
Allopathic Medicine	D
Anatomy	D
Animal Sciences	M,D
Anthropology	M,D
Applied Arts and Design—General	M
Applied Mathematics	M,D
Architecture	M
Art Education	M
Art History	M
Art/Fine Arts	M
Arts Administration	M
Astronomy	M,D
Athletic Training and Sports Medicine	M
Biochemistry	D
Biological and Biomedical Sciences—General	M,D
Biomedical Engineering	M,D
Biostatistics	D
Business Administration and Management—General	M,D
Chemical Engineering	M,D
Chemistry	M,D
Child and Family Studies	M,D
Civil Engineering	M,D
Classics	M
Clinical Research	M
Communication Disorders	M
Computer Science	M,D
Counseling Psychology	M,D,O
Curriculum and Instruction	M,D
Dentistry	D
Early Childhood Education	M,D
Economics	M,D
Education—General	M,D,O
Educational Leadership and Administration	M,D,O
Educational Measurement and Evaluation	M,D
Educational Media/Instructional Technology	M,D
Educational Policy	M,D
Educational Psychology	M,D,O
Electrical Engineering	M,D
Elementary Education	M,D
Engineering and Applied Sciences—General	M,D
English	M,D
Entomology	M,D
Epidemiology	D
Exercise and Sports Science	M,D
Food Science and Technology	M
Foreign Languages Education	M
Forestry	M
Geography	M,D
Geology	M,D
German	M,D
Gerontology	D,O
Health Physics/Radiological Health	M
Health Promotion	M,D
Health Services Management and Hospital Administration	M
Higher Education	M,D
Hispanic Studies	M,D
Historic Preservation	M,D
History	M,D
Hospitality Management	M
Immunology	D
Information Science	M,D
Interior Design	M
International Affairs	M
International Business	M
Kinesiology and Movement Studies	M,D
Law	D
Library Science	M
Manufacturing Engineering	M
Materials Engineering	M,D
Materials Sciences	M,D
Mathematics	M,D
Mechanical Engineering	M,D
Medical Physics	M
Microbiology	D
Middle School Education	M,D
Mineral/Mining Engineering	M,D
Music Education	M,D
Music	M,D
Neurobiology	D
Nursing—General	D
Nutrition	M,D
Oral and Dental Sciences	M
Pharmaceutical Sciences	M,D
Pharmacology	D
Pharmacy	D
Philosophy	M,D
Physical Education	M,D
Physical Therapy	D
Physician Assistant Studies	M
Physics	M,D
Physiology	D
Plant Pathology	M,D
Plant Sciences	M,D
Political Science	M,D
Psychology—General	M,D
Public Administration	M,D,O
Public Health—General	M,D
Public Policy	M,D,O
Reading Education	M,D
Rehabilitation Counseling	M,D

Rehabilitation Sciences	D
School Psychology	M,D,O
Secondary Education	M,D
Social Work	M,D
Sociology	M,D
Special Education	M,D
Statistics	M,D
Therapies—Dance, Drama, and Music	M,D
Toxicology	M,D
Veterinary Sciences	M,D

UNIVERSITY OF KING'S COLLEGE

Journalism	M
Writing	M

UNIVERSITY OF LA VERNE

Accounting	M
Business Administration and Management—General	M,D,O
Child and Family Studies	M
Child Development	M
Clinical Psychology	D
Counselor Education	M,D,O
Education—General	M,O
Educational Leadership and Administration	M,D,O
Elementary Education	M,D,O
English	M,O
Finance and Banking	M
Gerontology	M,O
Health Services Management and Hospital Administration	M,D,O
Health Services Research	M
Higher Education	M
Human Resources Management	M,O
International Business	M
Law	D
Management Information Systems	M
Marketing	M
Marriage and Family Therapy	M,O
Nonprofit Management	M
Organizational Management	M,D,O
Psychology—General	M,D
Public Administration	M,D
Public Health—General	M
Reading Education	M,O
School Psychology	M,O
Secondary Education	M,D,O
Special Education	M,D,O
Student Affairs	M
Supply Chain Management	M

UNIVERSITY OF LETHBRIDGE

Accounting	M,D
Addictions/Substance Abuse Counseling	M,D
Agricultural Sciences—General	M,D
American Indian/Native American Studies	M,D
Anthropology	M,D
Archaeology	M,D
Art/Fine Arts	M,D
Biochemistry	M,D
Biological and Biomedical Sciences—General	M,D
Business Administration and Management—General	M,D
Canadian Studies	M,D
Chemistry	M,D
Computational Sciences	M,D
Computer Science	M,D
Counseling Psychology	M,D
Counselor Education	M,D
Economics	M,D
Education—General	M,D
Educational Leadership and Administration	M,D
English	M,D
Environmental Sciences	M,D
Exercise and Sports Science	M,D
Finance and Banking	M,D
French	M,D
Gender Studies	M,D
Geographic Information Systems	M,D
Geography	M,D
German	M,D
Human Resources Management	M,D
International Business	M,D
Kinesiology and Movement Studies	M,D
Management Information Systems	M,D
Management Strategy and Policy	M,D
Marketing	M,D
Mathematics	M,D
Media Studies	M,D
Molecular Biology	M,D
Music	M,D
Neuroscience	M,D
Nursing—General	M,D
Philosophy	M,D
Physics	M,D
Political Science	M,D
Psychology—General	M,D
Religion	M,D
Sociology	M,D
Spanish	M,D
Theater	M,D
Urban Studies	M,D
Women's Studies	M,D

UNIVERSITY OF LOUISIANA AT LAFAYETTE

Accounting	M
American Studies	M
Architectural Engineering	M
Biological and Biomedical Sciences—General	M,D
Business Administration and Management—General	M
Chemical Engineering	M
Civil Engineering	M

M—masters degree; D—doctorate; O—other advanced degree; *—Close-Up and/or Display

Communication Disorders — M,D
Communication—General — M,D
Counselor Education — M
Cultural Studies — M
Curriculum and Instruction — M
Early Childhood Education — M
Education of the Gifted — M
Education—General — M,D
Educational Leadership and Administration — M,D
Educational Media/Instructional Technology
Electrical Engineering — M,D
English as a Second Language — M,D
English — M
Entrepreneurship — M
Environmental Biology — M,D
Environmental Sciences — M
Evolutionary Biology — M,D
Family Nurse Practitioner Studies — M
Finance and Banking — M
Folklore — M,D
French — M,D
Geosciences — M
History — M,D
Hospitality Management — M
Human Resources Management — M
International Business — M
Latin American Studies — M
Mathematics Education — M
Mathematics — M
Mechanical Engineering — M
Music Education — M
Music — M
Natural Resources — M
Nursing and Healthcare Administration
Nursing Education — M,D
Nursing—General — M,D
Petroleum Engineering — M
Physics — M
Project Management — M
Psychology—General — M
Public History — M
Rhetoric — M,D
Sociology — M
Special Education — M
Systems Engineering — M,D
Western European Studies — M
Writing — M

UNIVERSITY OF LOUISIANA AT MONROE
Biological and Biomedical Sciences—General — M
Business Administration and Management—General — M,O
Clinical Psychology — M
Communication Disorders — M
Communication—General — M
Counseling Psychology — M
Counselor Education — M
Criminal Justice and Criminology — M
Curriculum and Instruction — M,D
Education—General — M,D
Elementary Education — M
English — M
Exercise and Sports Science — M
Forensic Psychology — M
Gerontology — M,O
History — M
Marriage and Family Therapy — M,D
Occupational Therapy — M
Pharmacy — D
Psychology—General — M
Public Administration — M
Recreation and Park Management — M
Secondary Education — M
Special Education — M
Sports Management — M
Toxicology — D

UNIVERSITY OF LOUISVILLE
Accounting — M
Addictions/Substance Abuse Counseling — M,D,O
African Studies — M
African-American Studies — M
Allopathic Medicine — D
Analytical Chemistry — M,D
Anatomy — M,D
Anthropology — M
Applied Arts and Design—General — M,D
Applied Behavior Analysis — M,D,O
Applied Mathematics — M,D
Art Education — M,D,O
Art History — M,D
Art Therapy — M,D
Biochemistry — M,D
Bioengineering — M,D
Bioethics — M,D
Bioinformatics — M,D
Biological and Biomedical Sciences—General — M,D
Business Administration and Management—General — M
Chemical Engineering — M,D
Chemical Physics — M,D
Chemistry — M,D
Civil Engineering — M,D
Clinical Psychology — D
Cognitive Sciences — D
Communication Disorders — M,D
Communication—General — M
Community Health — M
Computer and Information Systems Security — M,D,O
Computer Engineering — M,D,O
Computer Science — M,D,O
Counseling Psychology — M,D
Counselor Education — M,D
Criminal Justice and Criminology — M,D
Cultural Studies — M,D
Curriculum and Instruction — M,D,O

Data Science/Data Analytics — M,D,O
Dentistry — M,D
Developmental Psychology — D
Early Childhood Education — M,D,O
Education—General — M,D,O
Educational Leadership and Administration — M,D,O
Educational Measurement and Evaluation — M,D
Educational Psychology — M,D
Electrical Engineering — M,D
Elementary Education — M,D,O
Engineering and Applied Sciences—General — M,D,O
Engineering Management — M,D,O
English — M,D
Entrepreneurship — M,D
Environmental Biology — M,D
Exercise and Sports Science — M,D,O
Experimental Psychology — D
Family Nurse Practitioner Studies — M,D
French — M,O
Geography — M
Gerontological Nursing — M,D
Gerontology — M,D,O
Health Education — M,D,O
Health Services Management and Hospital Administration — M
Higher Education — M,D,O
History — M,O
Human Resources Development — M,D,O
Human Resources Management — M,D,O
Humanities — M,D
Immunology — M,D
Industrial/Management Engineering — M,D,O
Inorganic Chemistry — M,D
Interdisciplinary Studies — M,D
International Business — M
Law — D
Linguistics — M,D
Logistics — M,D,O
Marriage and Family Therapy — M,D,O
Maternal and Child/Neonatal Nursing — M,D
Mathematics — M,D
Mechanical Engineering — M,D
Microbiology — M,D
Middle School Education — M,D,O
Molecular Genetics — M,D
Museum Studies — M,D
Music Education — M,D,O
Music — M
Neurobiology — M,D
Nonprofit Management — M,D
Nursing and Healthcare Administration — M,D
Nursing Education — M,D
Nursing—General — M,D
Oral and Dental Sciences — M,D
Organic Chemistry — M,D
Pharmacology — M,D
Philosophy — M,D
Physical Chemistry — M,D
Physical Education — M,D,O
Physics — M,D
Physiology — M,D
Political Science — M
Psychiatric Nursing — M,D
Psychology—General — D
Public Administration — M,D
Public Affairs — M,D
Public Health—General — M,D
Public History — M,O
Public Policy — M,D
Rhetoric — M,D
School Psychology — M,D
Secondary Education — M,D,O
Social Work — M,D,O
Sociology — M,D
Spanish — M,O
Special Education — M,D,O
Sports Management — M,D,O
Student Affairs — M,D
Supply Chain Management — M,D,O
Sustainability Management — M,D
Theater — M
Toxicology — M,D
Urban and Regional Planning — M,D
Urban Studies — M,D
Women's Health Nursing — M,D
Women's Studies — M,O
Writing — M,D

UNIVERSITY OF LYNCHBURG
Allopathic Medicine — D
Athletic Training and Sports Medicine — M
Business Administration and Management—General — M
Clinical Psychology — M
Counseling Psychology — M
Counselor Education — M
Criminal Justice and Criminology — M
Curriculum and Instruction — M
Educational Leadership and Administration — M,D
Geosciences — M
Health Informatics — O
Health Promotion — M
Higher Education — M
Mathematics — M
Nonprofit Management — M
Physical Therapy — D
Physician Assistant Studies — M
Public Health—General — M
Reading Education — M
School Psychology — M
Science Education — M
Special Education — M

UNIVERSITY OF MAINE
Agricultural Economics and Agribusiness — M

Agricultural Sciences—General — M,D,O
Anthropology — D
Art/Fine Arts — M
Bioinformatics — M,D
Biological and Biomedical Sciences—General — M,D
Biomedical Engineering — M,D
Botany — M,D
Business Administration and Management—General — M,O
Chemical Engineering — M,D
Chemistry — M,D
Civil Engineering — M,D
Communication Disorders — M
Communication—General — M,D
Computer Engineering — M,D
Computer Science — M,D,O
Early Childhood Education — M,D,O
Economics — M
Education—General — M,D,O
Educational Leadership and Administration — M,D,O
Educational Media/Instructional Technology — M,D,O
Electrical Engineering — M,D
Engineering and Applied Sciences—General — M,D
English — M
Entomology — M,D
Environmental Management and Policy — D
Exercise and Sports Science — M,D,O
Family Nurse Practitioner Studies — M,O
Finance and Banking — M
Fish, Game, and Wildlife Management — M,D
Foreign Languages Education — M
Forestry — M,D
French — M
Geology — M,O
Geosciences — M,D
Higher Education — M,D,O
History — M,D
Horticulture — M,D,O
Human Development — M,D,O
Information Science — M,D,O
Interdisciplinary Studies — M,D
International Affairs — M
Kinesiology and Movement Studies — M,D,O
Law — D
Marine Sciences — M,D
Mathematics — M
Mechanical Engineering — M,D
Microbiology — M,D
Molecular Biology — M,D
Music — M
Nursing Education — M,O
Nursing—General — M,O
Physical Education — M,D,O
Physics — M,D
Plant Pathology — M,D
Psychology—General — M,D
Reading Education — M,D,O
Social Sciences Education — M,D,O
Social Work — M,O
Special Education — M,D,O
Water Resources — M,D
Zoology — M,D

UNIVERSITY OF MAINE AT FARMINGTON
Early Childhood Education — M
Education—General — M
Educational Leadership and Administration — M
Educational Media/Instructional Technology — M

UNIVERSITY OF MANAGEMENT AND TECHNOLOGY
Business Administration and Management—General — M,D,O
Computer Science — M,O
Criminal Justice and Criminology — M,O
Engineering Management — M
Health Services Management and Hospital Administration — M
Homeland Security — M
Management Information Systems — M,O
Project Management — M,D,O
Public Administration — M,O
Software Engineering — M,O

THE UNIVERSITY OF MANCHESTER
Accounting — M
Actuarial Science — M,D
Aerospace/Aeronautical Engineering — M,D
Analytical Chemistry — M,D
Anthropology — M,D
Applied Mathematics — M,D
Archaeology — D
Architecture — M,D
Art History — D
Art/Fine Arts — M,D
Arts Administration — D
Asian Studies — D
Astronomy — M,D
Astrophysics — M,D
Atmospheric Sciences — M,D
Biochemical Engineering — M,D
Biochemistry — M,D
Bioinformatics — M,D
Biological and Biomedical Sciences—General — M,D
Biophysics — M,D
Biotechnology — M,D
Business Administration and Management—General — M
Business Analytics — M
Cancer Biology/Oncology — M,D
Cell Biology — M,D
Chemical Engineering — M,D
Chemistry — M,D

Chinese — D
Civil Engineering — M,D
Classics — D
Clinical Psychology — M,D
Clothing and Textiles — M,D
Communication Disorders — M,D
Computer Science — M,D
Condensed Matter Physics — M,D
Conflict Resolution and Mediation/Peace Studies — D
Counseling Psychology — M,D
Criminal Justice and Criminology — M,D
Cultural Studies — M,D
Dentistry — M,D
Developmental Biology — M,D
Developmental Psychology — M,D
East European and Russian Studies — D
Ecology — M,D
Education—General — M,D
Educational Psychology — M,D
Electrical Engineering — M,D
Engineering Management — M,D
English — D
Entrepreneurship — M
Environmental Biology — M,D
Environmental Design — M,D
Environmental Engineering — M,D
Environmental Management and Policy — M,D
Environmental Sciences — M,D
Evolutionary Biology — M,D
Finance and Banking — M
French — D
Genetics — M,D
Geochemistry — M,D
Geography — M,D
Geosciences — M,D
German — D
Hazardous Materials Management — M,D
Health Law — M,D
History of Medicine — M,D
History of Science and Technology — M,D
History — D
Human Resources Management — M
Immunology — M,D
Industrial and Labor Relations — M
Industrial and Manufacturing Management — M,D
Industrial and Organizational Psychology — M
Inorganic Chemistry — M,D
International Affairs — D
International Business — M
International Development — M,D
Japanese — D
Landscape Architecture — M,D
Latin American Studies — D
Law — M,D
Linguistics — D
Management Strategy and Policy — M
Marketing — M
Materials Sciences — M,D
Mathematical and Computational Finance — M,D
Mathematics — M,D
Mechanical Engineering — M,D
Metallurgical Engineering and Metallurgy — M,D
Microbiology — M,D
Modeling and Simulation — M,D
Molecular Biology — M,D
Molecular Genetics — M,D
Museum Studies — D
Music — M
Natural Resources — M,D
Near and Middle Eastern Studies — D
Neurobiology — M,D
Neuroscience — M,D
Nuclear Engineering — M,D
Nurse Midwifery — M,D
Nursing—General — M,D
Optometry — M,D
Oral and Dental Sciences — M,D
Organic Chemistry — M,D
Paleontology — M,D
Paper and Pulp Engineering — M,D
Pharmaceutical Sciences — M,D
Pharmacology — M,D
Pharmacy — M,D
Philosophy — M,D
Physical Chemistry — M,D
Physics — M,D
Physiology — M,D
Plant Sciences — M,D
Political Science — M,D
Polymer Science and Engineering — M,D
Portuguese — M
Project Management — M
Psychology—General — M,D
Public Health—General — M,D
Religion — D
Social Sciences — M,D
Social Work — M,D
Sociology — M,D
Spanish — D
Statistics — M,D
Structural Biology — M,D
Structural Engineering — M,D
Supply Chain Management — M
Textile Design — M,D
Theater — D
Theology — D
Theoretical Chemistry — M,D
Theoretical Physics — M,D
Toxicology — M,D
Translation and Interpretation — D
Vision Sciences — M,D
Writing — D

UNIVERSITY OF MANITOBA
Adult Education — M

Agricultural Economics and Agribusiness — M,D
Agricultural Sciences—General — M,D
Agronomy and Soil Sciences — M,D
Allopathic Medicine — M
American Indian/Native American Studies — M
Anatomy — M,D
Animal Sciences — M,D
Anthropology — M,D
Architecture — M
Archives/Archival Administration — M,D
Biochemistry — M,D
Biological and Biomedical Sciences—General — M,D,O
Biosystems Engineering — M,D
Botany — M,D
Business Administration and Management—General — M,D
Canadian Studies — M
Cancer Biology/Oncology — M
Chemistry — M,D
Civil Engineering — M,D
Classics — M
Clinical Psychology — M,D
Community Health — M,D,O
Computational Sciences — M
Computer Engineering — M,D
Computer Science — M,D
Counselor Education — M
Curriculum and Instruction — M
Dentistry — D
Disability Studies — M
Ecology — M,D
Economics — M,D
Education—General — M,D
Educational Leadership and Administration — M
Educational Psychology — M
Electrical Engineering — M,D
Engineering and Applied Sciences—General — M,D
English as a Second Language — M
English Education — M
English — M,D
Entomology — M,D
Environmental Sciences — M,D
Food Science and Technology — M,D
Foundations and Philosophy of Education — M
French — M,D
Genetic Counseling — M,D
Geography — M,D
Geology — M,D
Geophysics — M,D
German — M
Higher Education — M,D
History — M,D
Horticulture — M,D
Human Genetics — M,D
Immunology — M,D
Industrial/Management Engineering — M,D
Infectious Diseases — M,D
Interdisciplinary Studies — M,D
Interior Design — M
Kinesiology and Movement Studies — M
Landscape Architecture — M
Law — M
Linguistics — M,D
Manufacturing Engineering — M,D
Maternal and Child Health — M
Mathematics — M,D
Mechanical Engineering — M,D
Medical Microbiology — M,D
Microbiology — M,D
Music — M
Natural Resources — M,D
Northern Studies — M
Nursing—General — M,D
Nutrition — M,D
Occupational Therapy — M,D
Oral and Dental Sciences — M
Pathology — M
Pharmaceutical Sciences — M,D
Pharmacology — M,D
Philosophy — M,D
Physical Education — M
Physical Therapy — M,D
Physics — M,D
Physiology — M,D
Plant Physiology — M,D
Plant Sciences — M,D
Political Science — M
Psychoanalysis and Psychotherapy — M
Psychology—General — M,D
Public Administration — M
Recreation and Park Management — M,D
Rehabilitation Sciences — M,D
Religion — M
School Psychology — M,D
Slavic Languages — M
Social Work — M,D
Sociology — M,D
Special Education — M
Statistics — M,D
Urban and Regional Planning — M
Zoology — M,D

UNIVERSITY OF MARY

Bioethics — M
Business Administration and Management—General — M
Cardiovascular Sciences — M
Communication Disorders — M
Curriculum and Instruction — M,D
Education—General — M,D
Educational Leadership and Administration — M,D

Energy Management and Policy — M
Exercise and Sports Science — M
Family Nurse Practitioner Studies — M
Health Services Management and Hospital Administration — M
Human Resources Management — M
Kinesiology and Movement Studies — M
Nursing and Healthcare Administration — M,D
Nursing Education — M,D
Nursing—General — M,D
Occupational Therapy — M
Physical Education — M
Physical Therapy — D
Project Management — M
Reading Education — M
Special Education — M,D
Sports Management — M

UNIVERSITY OF MARY HARDIN-BAYLOR

Accounting — M
Business Administration and Management—General — M
Clinical Psychology — M
Counseling Psychology — M
Counselor Education — M
Curriculum and Instruction — M
Education—General — M,D
Educational Leadership and Administration — M
Elementary Education — M,D
Exercise and Sports Science — M
Family Nurse Practitioner Studies — M,D,O
Higher Education — M,D
International Business — M
Management Information Systems — M
Marriage and Family Therapy — M
Nursing Education — M,D,O
Nursing—General — M,D,O
Physical Therapy — D
Secondary Education — M,D
Sports Management — M

UNIVERSITY OF MARYLAND, BALTIMORE

Allied Health—General — M
Allopathic Medicine — D
Biochemistry — M,D
Biological and Biomedical Sciences—General — M,D,O
Biostatistics — M,D
Cancer Biology/Oncology — D
Cell Biology — M,D
Clinical Laboratory Sciences/Medical Technology — M
Clinical Research — M,D,O
Community Health Nursing — M,D,O
Dentistry — D,O
Environmental Sciences — M,D
Epidemiology — M,D,O
Ethics — O
Family Nurse Practitioner Studies — M,D,O
Forensic Sciences — M
Genetic Counseling — M
Genomic Sciences — M,D
Gerontological Nursing — M,D,O
Gerontology — M,D
Health Services Research — M,D
Human Genetics — M,D
Immunology — D
International Health — M,D,O
Law — M,D
Marine Sciences — M,D
Maternal and Child/Neonatal Nursing — M,D,O
Microbiology — D
Molecular Biology — M,D
Molecular Medicine — D
Molecular Pharmacology — D
Molecular Toxicology — D
Neurobiology — D
Neuroscience — D
Nurse Anesthesia — M,D,O
Nursing and Healthcare Administration — M,D,O
Nursing Education — M,D,O
Nursing Informatics — M,D,O
Nursing—General — M,D,O
Oral and Dental Sciences — M
Pathology — M
Pediatric Nursing — M,D,O
Pharmaceutical Administration — M,D
Pharmaceutical Sciences — D
Pharmacology — M
Pharmacy — M,D
Physical Therapy — D
Psychiatric Nursing — M,D,O
Rehabilitation Sciences — D
Social Work — M,D
Thanatology — O
Toxicology — M,D

UNIVERSITY OF MARYLAND, BALTIMORE COUNTY

Applied Mathematics — M,D
Applied Psychology — D
Art Education — M
Atmospheric Sciences — M,D
Biochemical Engineering — M,D,O
Biological and Biomedical Sciences—General — M,D
Biostatistics — M,D
Biotechnology — M,O
Cell Biology — D
Chemical Engineering — M,D
Chemistry — M,D,O
Clinical Psychology — M,D
Cognitive Sciences — D
Communication—General — M
Computer and Information Systems Security — M,O

Computer Art and Design — M,D
Computer Engineering — M,D
Computer Science — M,D
Dance — M
Data Science/Data Analytics — M
Developmental Psychology — D
Distance Education Development — M,O
Early Childhood Education — M
Economics — M,D
Education—General — M,O
Educational Media/Instructional Technology — M,O
Educational Policy — M,D
Electrical Engineering — M,D
Elementary Education — M
Emergency Management — M,D,O
Engineering and Applied Sciences—General — M,D,O
Engineering Management — M,O
English as a Second Language — M,O
English Education — M
English — M
Environmental Engineering — M,D
Environmental Management and Policy — M,D
Environmental Sciences — M,D
Epidemiology — M,D,O
Foreign Languages Education — M
Gender Studies — O
Geographic Information Systems — M,O
Geography — M,D
Gerontology — M,D
Health Informatics — M
Health Services Management and Hospital Administration — M,D,O
History — M
Human Services — M,D
Industrial and Organizational Psychology — M
Information Science — M,D
Linguistics — M
Management of Technology — M
Marine Sciences — M,D
Mathematics Education — M
Mechanical Engineering — M,D
Mechanics — O
Molecular Biology — M,D
Multilingual and Multicultural Education — M,D
Music Education — M
Music — O
Neuroscience — D
Nonprofit Management — M,O
Physics — M,D
Psychology—General — M,D
Public History — M,D
Public Policy — M,D,O
Science Education — M
Social Psychology — M,D
Social Sciences Education — M
Social Sciences — D
Sociology — M
Statistics — M,D
Systems Engineering — M,O
Theater — M
Urban Studies — M,D
Women's Studies — O

UNIVERSITY OF MARYLAND, COLLEGE PARK

Advertising and Public Relations — M,D
Aerospace/Aeronautical Engineering — M,D
Agricultural Economics and Agribusiness — M,D
Agricultural Sciences—General — M,D
American Studies — M,D
Analytical Chemistry — M,D
Animal Sciences — M,D
Anthropology — M
Applied Mathematics — M,D
Architecture — M
Art History — M,D
Art Therapy — M,D,O
Art/Fine Arts — M
Astronomy — M,D
Biochemistry — M,D
Bioengineering — M,D
Bioinformatics — D
Biological and Biomedical Sciences—General — M,D
Biophysics — D
Biostatistics — M,D
Broadcast Journalism — M,D
Business Administration and Management—General — M,D
Cell Biology — M,D
Chemical Engineering — M,D
Chemical Physics — M,D
Chemistry — M,D
Child and Family Studies — M,D
Civil Engineering — M,D
Classics — M
Clinical Psychology — M,D
Cognitive Sciences — D
Communication Disorders — M,D
Communication—General — M,D
Comparative Literature — M,D
Computational Biology — D
Computer Engineering — M,D
Computer Science — M,D
Conservation Biology — M
Counseling Psychology — M,D,O
Counselor Education — M,D,O
Criminal Justice and Criminology — M,D
Curriculum and Instruction — M,D,O
Dance — M
Developmental Psychology — M,D
Ecology — M,D
Economics — M,D

Education—General — M,D,O
Educational Leadership and Administration — M,D,O
Educational Measurement and Evaluation — M,D
Educational Media/Instructional Technology — M,D,O
Electrical Engineering — M,D
Engineering and Applied Sciences—General — M
English as a Second Language — M,D,O
English — M,D
Entomology — M,D
Environmental and Occupational Health — M
Environmental Engineering — M,D
Environmental Sciences — M,D
Epidemiology — M,D
Evolutionary Biology — M,D
Experimental Psychology — M,D
Family and Consumer Sciences-General — M,D
Fire Protection Engineering — M
Food Science and Technology — M,D
Foreign Languages Education — D
Foundations and Philosophy of Education — M,D,O
French — M,D
Genomic Sciences — D
Geography — M,D
Geology — M,D
German — M,D
Health Education — M,D
Health Services Management and Hospital Administration — M,D
Historic Preservation — M,O
History — M,D
Horticulture — M,D
Human Development — M,D
Industrial and Organizational Psychology — M,D
Information Studies — M,D
Inorganic Chemistry — M,D
Jewish Studies — M,D
Journalism — M,D
Kinesiology and Movement Studies — M,D
Landscape Architecture — M
Law —
Library Science —
Linguistics — M,D
Manufacturing Engineering — M,D
Marine Sciences — M,D
Marriage and Family Therapy — M,D
Materials Engineering — M,D
Materials Sciences — M,D
Maternal and Child Health — M,D
Mathematics — M,D
Mechanical Engineering — M,D
Mechanics — M,D
Media Studies — M,D
Meteorology — M,D
Molecular Biology — D
Molecular Genetics — M,D
Music Education — M,D
Music — M,D
Natural Resources — M,D
Neuroscience — M,D
Nuclear Engineering — M,D
Nutrition — M,D
Oceanography — M,D
Organic Chemistry — M,D
Philosophy — M,D
Physical Chemistry — M,D
Physics — M,D
Plant Biology — M,D
Political Science — D
Portuguese — M,D
Psychology—General — M,D
Public Administration — M
Public Health—General — M,D
Public Policy — M,D
Quantitative Analysis — M,D
Reading Education — M,D,O
Real Estate —
Rehabilitation Counseling — M,D,O
Reliability Engineering — M,D
School Psychology — M,D,O
Secondary Education — M,D,O
Social Psychology — M,D
Social Work —
Sociology — M,D
Spanish — M,D
Speech and Interpersonal Communication — M,D
Statistics — M,D
Student Affairs — M,D,O
Survey Methodology — M,D
Sustainable Development — M
Systems Engineering — M
Telecommunications — M
Theater — M
Urban and Regional Planning — M,D
Veterinary Medicine — D
Veterinary Sciences — M,D
Women's Studies — M,D
Writing — M,D

UNIVERSITY OF MARYLAND EASTERN SHORE

Agricultural Sciences—General — M
Chemistry — M,D
Computer Science — M
Counselor Education — M
Criminal Justice and Criminology — M
Education—General — M
Educational Leadership and Administration — D
Environmental Management and Policy — M,D

---

*M—masters degree; D—doctorate; O—other advanced degree; *—Close-Up and/or Display*

Environmental Sciences — M,D
Fish, Game, and Wildlife
  Management — M,D
Food Science and
  Technology — M,D
Marine Sciences — M,D
Organizational Management — D
Pharmaceutical Sciences — M,D
Pharmacy — M,D
Physical Therapy — D
Rehabilitation Counseling — M
Rehabilitation Sciences — M
Special Education — M
Toxicology — M
Vocational and Technical Education — M

UNIVERSITY OF MARYLAND UNIVERSITY COLLEGE

Accounting — M,O
Biotechnology — M,O
Business Administration and
  Management—General — M,D,O
Computer and Information
  Systems Security — M,O
Data Science/Data Analytics — M,O
Distance Education Development — M
Education—General — M
Educational Media/Instructional
  Technology — M
Environmental Management
  and Policy — M
Finance and Banking — M
Health Informatics — M
Health Services Management and
  Hospital Administration — M
Information Science — M
Management Information Systems — M,O

UNIVERSITY OF MARY WASHINGTON

Business Administration and
  Management—General — M
Education—General — M
Elementary Education — M

UNIVERSITY OF MASSACHUSETTS AMHERST

Accounting — M,D
Adult Nursing — M,D
African-American Studies — M,D
Agricultural Economics and
  Agribusiness — M,D
American Studies — M,D
Animal Behavior — M,D
Animal Sciences — M,D
Anthropology — M,D
Applied Mathematics — M,D
Architectural Engineering — M,D
Architecture — M
Art Education — M
Art History — M
Art/Fine Arts — M
Astronomy — M
Biochemistry — M,D
Biological and Biomedical
  Sciences—General — M,D
Biostatistics — M,D
Biotechnology — M,D
Business Administration and
  Management—General — M,D
Cell Biology — M,D
Chemical Engineering — M,D
Chemistry — M,D
Child and Family Studies — M,D,O
Chinese — M
Civil Engineering — M,D
Classics — M
Clinical Psychology — M,D
Cognitive Sciences — M,D
Communication Disorders — M,D
Communication—General — M,D
Community Health Nursing — M,D
Community Health — M,D
Comparative Literature — M,D
Computer Engineering — M,D
Computer Science — M,D
Conflict Resolution and
  Mediation/Peace Studies — M,D
Counselor Education — M,D,O
Developmental Biology — D
Developmental Psychology — M,D
Early Childhood Education — M,D,O
Economics — M,D
Education—General — M,D,O
Educational Leadership and
  Administration — M,D,O
Educational Measurement and
  Evaluation — M,D,O
Educational Media/Instructional
  Technology — M,D,O
Educational Policy — M,D,O
Electrical Engineering — M,D
Elementary Education — M,D,O
Engineering and Applied
  Sciences—General — M,D
English as a Second Language — M,D,O
English — M,D
Entertainment Management
Entrepreneurship — M,D
Environmental and Occupational
  Health — M,D
Environmental Biology — M,D
Environmental Engineering — M,D
Environmental Management
  and Policy — M,D
Epidemiology — M,D
Evolutionary Biology — M,D
Family Nurse Practitioner Studies — M,D
Finance and Banking — M,D
Fish, Game, and Wildlife
  Management — M,D
Food Science and
  Technology — M,D
Foreign Languages Education — M
Forestry — M,D
French — M

Genetics — M,D
Geography — M
Geosciences — M,D
Geotechnical Engineering — M,D
German — M
Gerontological Nursing — M,D
Health Education — M,D
Health Services Management and
  Hospital Administration — M,D
Higher Education — M,D,O
Hispanic and Latin American
  Languages — M,D
Historic Preservation — M
History — M,D
Hospitality Management — M,D
Industrial and Labor Relations — M
Industrial/Management
  Engineering — M,D
Interior Design — M
International and Comparative
  Education — M,D,O
Italian — M
Japanese — M
Kinesiology and Movement Studies — M,D
Landscape Architecture — M
Linguistics — M,D
Management Strategy and Policy — M,D
Marine Sciences — M,D
Marketing — M,D
Mathematics — M,D
Mechanical Engineering — M,D
Mechanics — M,D
Microbiology — M,D
Molecular Biophysics — D
Multilingual and Multicultural
  Education — M,D,O
Music Education — M,D
Music — M,D
Neuroscience — M,D
Nursing and Healthcare
  Administration — M,D
Nursing—General — M,D
Nutrition — M,D
Operations Research — M,D
Organizational Management — M,D
Philosophy — M,D
Physics — M,D
Physiology — M,D
Plant Biology — M,D
Plant Molecular Biology — M,D
Plant Physiology — M,D
Plant Sciences — M,D
Political Science — M,D
Polymer Science and
  Engineering — M,D
Portuguese — M,D
Psychology—General — M,D
Public Administration — M
Public Health—General — M,D
Public Policy — M
Reading Education — M,D,O
Rhetoric — M,D
Scandinavian Languages — M,D
School Psychology — M,D,O
Science Education — M,D,O
Secondary Education — M,D,O
Social Psychology — M,D
Sociology — M,D
Spanish — M,D
Special Education — M,D,O
Sports Management — M,D
Statistics — M,D
Structural Engineering — M,D
Sustainable Development — M,D
Theater — M
Transportation and Highway
  Engineering — M,D
Travel and Tourism — M,D
Urban and Regional Planning — M,D
Water Resources Engineering — M,D
Water Resources — M,D
Writing — M,D

UNIVERSITY OF MASSACHUSETTS BOSTON

Accounting — M
American Studies — M
Applied Economics — M
Applied Physics — M
Archaeology — M
Archives/Archival Administration — M
Biological and Biomedical
  Sciences—General — M,D
Biomedical Engineering — D
Biotechnology — M,D
Business Administration and
  Management—General — M
Business Analytics — M
Chemistry — M,D
Classics — M
Clinical Psychology — D
Cognitive Sciences — M
Computational Sciences — D
Computer Science — M,D
Conflict Resolution and
  Mediation/Peace Studies — M,O
Counseling Psychology — M,D
Counselor Education — M
Cultural Studies — M
Early Childhood Education — D
Education—General — M,D,O
Educational Leadership and
  Administration — M,D,O
Educational Media/Instructional
  Technology — M,O
Educational Policy — M
English — M
Environmental Sciences — M,D
Exercise and Sports Science — M,D
Finance and Banking — M
Gerontology — M,D,O
Higher Education — D
History — M
Human Services — M

International Affairs — M
International Business — M
International Development — M,D
Linguistics — M
Management Information Systems — M
Marine Sciences — M,D
Marriage and Family Therapy — M
Nursing—General — M,D
Public Administration — M
Public Policy — M,D
Quality Management — M,O
Rehabilitation Counseling — M
School Psychology — M,D
Sociology — M,D
Special Education — M
Urban and Regional Planning — M
Urban Education — D
Vision Sciences — M
Writing — M

UNIVERSITY OF MASSACHUSETTS DARTMOUTH

Accounting — M,O
Applied Behavior Analysis — M,O
Art Education — M
Art History — M
Art/Fine Arts — M,O
Biochemistry — M,D
Biological and Biomedical
  Sciences—General — M,D
Biomedical Engineering — D
Biotechnology — D
Business Administration and
  Management—General — M,O
Chemistry — M,D
Civil Engineering — M
Clinical Psychology — M,O
Community Health Nursing — M,D
Computer Engineering — M,D,O
Computer Science — M,O
Data Science/Data Analytics — M
Education—General — M,D,O
Educational Leadership and
  Administration — D
Educational Policy — M,D,O
Electrical Engineering — M,D,O
Engineering and Applied
  Sciences—General — D
English as a Second Language — M,D,O
Environmental Management
  and Policy — M,O
Experimental Psychology — M,O
Finance and Banking — M,O
Health Services Management and
  Hospital Administration — M
Industrial/Management
  Engineering — M,O
Latin American Studies — M,D
Law — D
Management of Technology — M
Marine Affairs — M,D
Marine Biology — M,D
Marine Sciences — M,D
Mathematics Education — M,D,O
Mechanical Engineering — M,O
Media Studies — M
Middle School Education — M,D,O
Nursing—General — M,D
Physics — M
Portuguese — M,D
Psychology—General — M,O
Public Administration — M,O
Public Policy — M,O
Science Education — M,D,O
Secondary Education — M,D,O
Software Engineering — M,O
Special Education — M,O
Systems Engineering — M,O
Telecommunications — M,D,O
Writing — M,O

UNIVERSITY OF MASSACHUSETTS LOWELL

Allied Health—General — M,D
Analytical Chemistry — M,D
Biochemistry — M,D
Biological and Biomedical
  Sciences—General — M
Business Administration and
  Management—General — M,D
Chemical Engineering — M,D
Chemistry — M,D
Civil Engineering — M,D
Clinical Laboratory
  Sciences/Medical Technology — M
Computer Engineering — M,D
Computer Science — M,D
Conflict Resolution and
  Mediation/Peace Studies — M
Criminal Justice and Criminology — M
Curriculum and Instruction — M
Economic Development — M,O
Economics — M,O
Education—General — M,D,O
Electrical Engineering — M,D
Energy and Power
  Engineering — M,D
Engineering and Applied
  Sciences—General — M,D
Entrepreneurship — M,D
Environmental Engineering — M,D
Environmental Sciences — M,D
Family Nurse Practitioner Studies — M
Gerontological Nursing — M
Health Physics/Radiological Health — M
Health Promotion — M
Industrial/Management
  Engineering — D
Inorganic Chemistry — M,D
Legal and Justice Studies — M
Mathematics — M,D
Mechanical Engineering — M,D
Music Education — M
Music — M

Nuclear Engineering — M,D
Nursing—General — M,D
Organic Chemistry — M,D
Physical Therapy — D
Physics — M,D
Polymer Science and
  Engineering — M,D
Psychology—General — M
Social Psychology — M
Sociology — M,O
Urban and Regional Planning — M,O

UNIVERSITY OF MASSACHUSETTS MEDICAL SCHOOL

Adult Nursing — M,D,O
Allopathic Medicine — D
Biochemistry — M,D
Bioinformatics — M,D
Biological and Biomedical
  Sciences—General — M,D
Cancer Biology/Oncology — M,D
Clinical Research — M,D
Computational Biology — M,D
Family Nurse Practitioner Studies — M,D,O
Gerontological Nursing — M,D,O
Health Services Research — M,D
Immunology — M,D
Interdisciplinary Studies — M,D
Microbiology — M,D
Molecular Pharmacology — M,D
Neuroscience — M,D
Nursing and Healthcare
  Administration — M,D,O
Nursing Education — M,D,O
Nursing—General — M,D,O
Translational Biology — M,D

UNIVERSITY OF MEMPHIS

Accounting — M,D
Adult Education — M,D,O
African-American Studies — M,D,O
Allied Health—General — M,O
Analytical Chemistry — M,D
Anthropology — M
Applied Behavior Analysis — M,D,O
Applied Mathematics — M,D
Applied Statistics — M,D
Archaeology — M,D,O
Architecture — M
Art History — M,O
Art/Fine Arts — M,O
Bioinformatics — M,D
Biological and Biomedical
  Sciences—General — M,D
Biomedical Engineering — M,D
Biostatistics — M,D
Business Administration and
  Management—General — M,D
Chemistry — M,D
Civil Engineering — M,D,O
Clinical Psychology — M,D,O
Communication Disorders — M,D
Communication—General — M,D
Community College Education — M,D,O
Comparative Literature — M,D,O
Computational Sciences — M
Computer Engineering — M,D,O
Computer Science — M,D
Counseling Psychology — M,D
Counselor Education — M,D
Criminal Justice and Criminology — M
Curriculum and Instruction — M,D,O
Early Childhood Education — M,D,O
Economics — M,D
Education—General — M,D
Educational Leadership and
  Administration — M,D,O
Educational Measurement and
  Evaluation — M,D
Educational Media/Instructional
  Technology — M,D,O
Educational Psychology — M,D
Electrical Engineering — M,D,O
Electronic Materials — M,O
Elementary Education — M,D,O
Energy and Power
  Engineering — M,D,O
Engineering and Applied
  Sciences—General — M,D,O
English as a Second Language — M,D,O
English — M,D,O
Environmental and Occupational
  Health — M,D
Environmental Engineering — M,D,O
Epidemiology — M,D
Exercise and Sports Science — M,O
Experimental Psychology — M,D,O
Family Nurse Practitioner Studies — M,O
Film, Television, and Video
  Production — M,D
Finance and Banking — M,D
French — M
Gender Studies — O
Geographic Information Systems — M,D,O
Geography — M,D,O
Geology — M,D,O
Geophysics — M,D,O
Geotechnical Engineering — M,D,O
Graphic Design — M,O
Health Promotion — M,O
Health Services Management and
  Hospital Administration — M,D
Higher Education — M,D,O
History — M,D
Hospitality Management — M,O
Human Resources Management — M,O
Inorganic Chemistry — M,D
Interdisciplinary Studies — M,D,O
Journalism — M,O
Law — D
Liberal Studies — M,O
Linguistics — M,D,O
Management Information Systems — M,D,O
Management Strategy and Policy — M,O
Marketing — M,D

Mathematics Education	M,D
Mathematics	M,D,O
Mechanical Engineering	M,D,O
Museum Studies	M,O
Music Education	M,D
Music	M,D
Near and Middle Eastern Studies	M,D
Nonprofit Management	M,O
Nursing and Healthcare Administration	M,O
Nursing Education	M,O
Nursing—General	M,O
Nutrition	M,D
Organic Chemistry	M,D
Philanthropic Studies	M,O
Philosophy	M,D
Photography	M,O
Physical Chemistry	M,D
Physical Education	M,O
Physics	M
Political Science	M
Psychology—General	M,D,O
Public Administration	M,O
Public Health—General	M,D
Public Policy	M,D
Reading Education	M,D,O
Real Estate	M,D
Rehabilitation Counseling	M,D
School Psychology	M,D,O
Science Education	M,D,O
Secondary Education	M,D
Social Sciences	M,D
Social Work	M
Sociology	M
Spanish	M
Special Education	M,D,O
Statistics	M,D
Structural Engineering	M,D,O
Supply Chain Management	M,D
Theater	M
Transportation and Highway Engineering	M,D,O
Urban and Regional Planning	M
Urban Education	M,D
Water Resources Engineering	M,D,O
Writing	M,D,O

UNIVERSITY OF MIAMI

Accounting	M,D
Acute Care/Critical Care Nursing	M,D
Adult Nursing	M,D
Advertising and Public Relations	M,D
Aerospace/Aeronautical Engineering	M,D
Allopathic Medicine	D
Architectural Engineering	M,D
Architecture	M
Art History	M
Art/Fine Arts	M
Athletic Training and Sports Medicine	M,D
Biochemistry	D
Biological and Biomedical Sciences—General	M,D
Biomedical Engineering	M,D
Biophysics	D
Biostatistics	M,D
Broadcast Journalism	M,D
Business Administration and Management—General	M,D
Business Analytics	M,D
Cancer Biology/Oncology	D
Cell Biology	D
Chemistry	M,D
Civil Engineering	M,D
Clinical Psychology	D
Communication—General	M,D
Community Health	M,D
Computer Engineering	M,D
Computer Science	M,D
Counseling Psychology	D
Counselor Education	M,O
Developmental Biology	D
Developmental Psychology	D
Early Childhood Education	M,O
Economics	M,D
Education—General	M,D,O
Educational Measurement and Evaluation	M,D
Electrical Engineering	M,D
Engineering and Applied Sciences—General	M,D
English	M,D
Environmental and Occupational Health	M
Ergonomics and Human Factors	M
Evolutionary Biology	M,D
Exercise and Sports Science	M,D
Family Nurse Practitioner Studies	M,D
Film, Television, and Video Production	M,D
Film, Television, and Video Theory and Criticism	M,D
Finance and Banking	M,D
Fish, Game, and Wildlife Management	M,D
French	D
Genetics	M,D
Geography	M
Geophysics	M,D
Graphic Design	M
Health Services Management and Hospital Administration	M,D
Higher Education	M,D,O
History	M,D
Immunology	D
Industrial/Management Engineering	M,D
Inorganic Chemistry	M,D
International Affairs	M,D

International Business	M,D
Internet and Interactive Multimedia	M
Journalism	M,D
Latin American Studies	M
Law	M,D
Liberal Studies	M
Management of Technology	M
Marine Affairs	M
Marine Biology	M,D
Marine Geology	M,D
Marine Sciences	M,D
Marriage and Family Therapy	M,O
Mathematical and Computational Finance	M,D
Mathematics Education	D
Mathematics	M,D
Mechanical Engineering	M,D
Meteorology	M,D
Microbiology	D
Molecular Biology	D
Multilingual and Multicultural Education	D
Music Education	M,D
Music	M,D,O
Neuroscience	M,D
Nurse Anesthesia	M,D
Nurse Midwifery	M,D
Nursing—General	M,D
Nutrition	M
Oceanography	M,D
Organic Chemistry	M,D
Pharmacology	D
Philosophy	M,D
Photography	M
Physical Chemistry	M,D
Physical Therapy	D
Physics	M,D
Physiology	D
Political Science	M
Psychology—General	M,D
Reading Education	D
Real Estate	M,D
Romance Languages	D
Science Education	D
Sociology	M,D
Spanish	M,D
Special Education	M,D,O
Sports Management	M
Taxation	M,D
Therapies—Dance, Drama, and Music	M,D,O
Urban Design	M
Writing	M,D

UNIVERSITY OF MICHIGAN

Accounting	M,D
Aerospace/Aeronautical Engineering	M,D
African Studies	M
Allopathic Medicine	D
American Studies	M,D
Analytical Chemistry	M,D
Anthropology	D
Applied Arts and Design—General	M,D
Applied Economics	M
Applied Physics	D
Applied Statistics	M,D
Archaeology	M,D
Architecture	M,D
Art History	M,D
Art/Fine Arts	M
Artificial Intelligence/Robotics	M,D
Asian Languages	D
Asian Studies	M,D,O
Astronomy	D
Astrophysics	D
Atmospheric Sciences	M,D
Automotive Engineering	M,D
Biochemistry	M,D
Bioinformatics	M,D
Biological and Biomedical Sciences—General	M,D
Biological Anthropology	D
Biomedical Engineering	M,D
Biophysics	D
Biopsychology	D
Biostatistics	M,D
Business Administration and Management—General	M,D
Cancer Biology/Oncology	M,D
Cell Biology	M,D
Chemical Engineering	M,D,O
Chemistry	M,D
Civil Engineering	M,D,O
Classics	M,D,O
Clinical Psychology	D
Clinical Research	M
Cognitive Sciences	D
Communication—General	D
Comparative Literature	D
Computer Engineering	M,D
Computer Science	M,D
Construction Engineering	M,D,O
Cultural Anthropology	D
Dance	M
Data Science/Data Analytics	M,D,O
Dental Hygiene	M
Dentistry	D
Developmental Biology	M,D
Developmental Psychology	D
East European and Russian Studies	M,O
Ecology	M,D
Economics	M,D
Education—General	M,D
Electrical Engineering	M,D
Energy and Power Engineering	M,D
Engineering and Applied Sciences—General	M,D,O

Engineering Design	M,D
English Education	D
English	M,D,O
Environmental and Occupational Health	M,D
Environmental Engineering	M,D,O
Environmental Management and Policy	M,D
Environmental Sciences	M,D
Epidemiology	M,D
Evolutionary Biology	M,D
Film, Television, and Video Theory and Criticism	D,O
Foreign Languages Education	M,D
French	D
Genetic Counseling	M,D
Geosciences	M,D
German	M,D,O
Health Education	M,D
Health Informatics	M,D
Health Physics/Radiological Health	M,D,O
Health Promotion	M,D
Health Services Management and Hospital Administration	M,D
History	D,O
Human Genetics	M,D
Immunology	M,D
Industrial Hygiene	M,D
Industrial/Management Engineering	M,D
Information Science	M,D
Information Studies	M,D
Inorganic Chemistry	M,D
International Health	M,D
Italian	D
Jewish Studies	M,D,O
Kinesiology and Movement Studies	M,D
Landscape Architecture	M
Law	M,D
Linguistics	D
Manufacturing Engineering	M,D
Materials Engineering	M,D
Materials Sciences	M,D
Mathematics	M,D
Mechanical Engineering	M,D
Media Studies	M
Medicinal and Pharmaceutical Chemistry	D
Microbiology	M,D
Molecular Biology	M,D
Molecular Pathology	D
Music Education	M,D,O
Music	M,D,O
Natural Resources	M,D
Near and Middle Eastern Languages	M,D
Near and Middle Eastern Studies	M,D
Neuroscience	D
Nuclear Engineering	M,D,O
Nursing—General	M,D,O
Nutrition	M,D
Ocean Engineering	M,D,O
Operations Research	M,D
Oral and Dental Sciences	M,D
Organic Chemistry	M,D
Pathology	D
Pediatric Nursing	M,D,O
Pharmaceutical Administration	D
Pharmaceutical Engineering	M,D
Pharmaceutical Sciences	D
Pharmacology	M,D
Pharmacy	D
Philosophy	M,D
Physical Chemistry	M,D
Physics	D
Physiology	M,D
Planetary and Space Sciences	M,D
Political Science	D
Psychology—General	D,O
Public Health—General	M,D
Public Policy	M,D
Quantitative Analysis	M,D
Religion	M,D
Risk Management	M,D
Slavic Languages	M,D
Social Psychology	D
Social Sciences	D
Social Work	M
Sociology	D
Spanish	D
Sports Management	M,D
Statistics	M,D,O
Structural Engineering	M,D,O
Supply Chain Management	M,D
Survey Methodology	M,D,O
Sustainable Development	M,D
Systems Engineering	M,D
Systems Science	M,D
Taxation	M,D
Toxicology	M,D
Women's Studies	D,O
Writing	M,D

UNIVERSITY OF MICHIGAN–DEARBORN

Accounting	M
Applied Behavior Analysis	M
Applied Mathematics	M
Automotive Engineering	M
Bioengineering	M
Business Administration and Management—General	M
Business Analytics	M
Clinical Psychology	M
Computational Sciences	M
Computer and Information Systems Security	D
Computer Engineering	M,D
Computer Science	D
Criminal Justice and Criminology	M
Curriculum and Instruction	D,O
Data Science/Data Analytics	M,D

Early Childhood Education	M
Education—General	M
Educational Leadership and Administration	M,D,O
Educational Measurement and Evaluation	M
Educational Media/Instructional Technology	M,D
Electrical Engineering	M,D
Energy and Power Engineering	M
Engineering and Applied Sciences—General	M,D
Engineering Management	M
Environmental Sciences	M
Finance and Banking	M
Health Informatics	M
Health Psychology	M
Industrial/Management Engineering	M,D
Information Science	M,D
Management Information Systems	M
Manufacturing Engineering	M
Mechanical Engineering	M,D
Project Management	M
Public Administration	M
Software Engineering	M,D
Supply Chain Management	M
Systems Engineering	M,D
Urban Education	M,D

UNIVERSITY OF MICHIGAN–FLINT

Accounting	M,O
American Studies	M
Art/Fine Arts	M
Arts Administration	M
Biological and Biomedical Sciences—General	M
Business Administration and Management—General	M,O
Communication—General	M
Computer Science	M
Criminal Justice and Criminology	M
Curriculum and Instruction	M,D,O
Early Childhood Education	M,D,O
Education—General	M,D,O
Educational Leadership and Administration	M,D,O
Educational Media/Instructional Technology	M
English	M
Family Nurse Practitioner Studies	M,D,O
Finance and Banking	M,O
Gender Studies	M
Gerontology	M,D,O
Health Education	M
Health Informatics	M
Health Services Management and Hospital Administration	M,O
Industrial and Manufacturing Management	M,O
Information Science	M
International Affairs	M
International Business	M,O
Liberal Studies	M
Management Information Systems	M,O
Marketing	M,O
Mathematics	M
Mechanical Engineering	M
Museum Studies	M
Music	M
Neuroscience	D,O
Nonprofit Management	M
Nurse Anesthesia	D
Nursing—General	M,D,O
Organizational Management	M,O
Physical Therapy	D,O
Political Science	M
Psychiatric Nursing	M,D,O
Public Administration	M
Public Health—General	M
Reading Education	M,D,O
Rhetoric	M
Secondary Education	M,D,O
Social Sciences	M
Writing	M

UNIVERSITY OF MINNESOTA, DULUTH

Allopathic Medicine	D
Anthropology	M
Applied Mathematics	M
Art/Fine Arts	M
Biochemistry	M,D
Biological and Biomedical Sciences—General	M
Biophysics	M,D
Business Administration and Management—General	M
Chemistry	M
Communication Disorders	M
Computational Sciences	M
Computer Engineering	M
Computer Science	M
Criminal Justice and Criminology	M
Education—General	M,D
Electrical Engineering	M
Engineering Management	M
English	M
Geology	M,D
Graphic Design	M
Immunology	M,D
Liberal Studies	M
Medical Microbiology	M,D
Molecular Biology	M,D
Music Education	M
Music	M
Pharmacology	M,D
Pharmacy	M,D
Physics	M
Physiology	M,D
Safety Engineering	M

M—masters degree; D—doctorate; O—other advanced degree; *—Close-Up and/or Display

Social Work — M
Sociology — M
Toxicology — M,D

UNIVERSITY OF MINNESOTA ROCHESTER
Bioinformatics — M,D
Business Administration and Management—General — M,D
Computational Biology — M,D
Occupational Therapy — M,D

UNIVERSITY OF MINNESOTA, TWIN CITIES CAMPUS
Accounting — M,D
Adult Education — M,D,O
Aerospace/Aeronautical Engineering — M,D
Agricultural Sciences—General — M,D
Agronomy and Soil Sciences — M,D
Allopathic Medicine — M,D
American Studies — D
Animal Behavior — M,D
Animal Sciences — M,D
Anthropology — M,D
Applied Arts and Design—General — M,D,O
Applied Economics — M,D
Archaeology — M,D
Architecture — M
Art Education — M
Art History — M,D
Art/Fine Arts — M
Asian Languages — M,D
Asian Studies — D
Astrophysics — M,D
Biochemistry — D
Biological and Biomedical Sciences—General — M
Biomedical Engineering — M,D
Biophysics — M,D
Biopsychology — D
Biostatistics — M,D
Biosystems Engineering — M,D
Biotechnology — M
Business Administration and Management—General — M,D
Cancer Biology/Oncology — D
Cell Biology — M,D
Chemical Engineering — M,D
Chemical Physics — M,D
Chemistry — M,D
Child and Family Studies — M,D
Child Development — M,D
Civil Engineering — M,D,O
Classics — M,D
Clinical Laboratory Sciences/Medical Technology — M
Clinical Psychology — D
Clinical Research — M
Clothing and Textiles — M,D,O
Cognitive Sciences — D
Communication Disorders — M,D
Communication—General — M,D,O
Community Health — M
Comparative Literature — D
Computational Sciences — M,D
Computer and Information Systems Security — M
Computer Engineering — M,D
Computer Science — M,D
Conservation Biology — M,D
Counseling Psychology — D
Counselor Education — M
Cultural Studies — D
Curriculum and Instruction — M,D
Data Science/Data Analytics — M
Dentistry — D
Developmental Biology — M,D
Early Childhood Education — M,D,O
Ecology — M,D
Economics — M,D
Education of the Gifted — M,D,O
Education—General — M,D,O
Educational Leadership and Administration — M,D
Educational Measurement and Evaluation — M,D
Educational Media/Instructional Technology — M,D,O
Educational Policy — M,D
Educational Psychology — M,D,O
Electrical Engineering — M,D
Elementary Education — M
Engineering and Applied Sciences—General — M,D,O
English as a Second Language — M,D,O
English Education — M
English — M,D
Entomology — D
Entrepreneurship — M
Environmental and Occupational Health — M,D,O
Environmental Management and Policy — M,D
Epidemiology — M,D
Evolutionary Biology — M,D
Exercise and Sports Science — M,D
Family Nurse Practitioner Studies — M,D
Finance and Banking — M,D
Food Science and Technology — M,D
Foreign Languages Education — M
Forestry — M,D
Foundations and Philosophy of Education — M,D
French — M,D
Genetic Counseling — M,D
Genetics — M,D
Geographic Information Systems — M,D
Geography — M,D
Geological Engineering — M,D,O
Geology — M,D

Geophysics — M,D
German — M,D
Gerontological Nursing — M,D
Health Informatics — M,D
Health Services Management and Hospital Administration — M,D
Health Services Research — M,D
Higher Education — M,D
Hispanic and Latin American Languages — M,D
History of Medicine — M,D
History of Science and Technology — M,D
History — M,D,O
Human Resources Development — M
Human Resources Management — M
Hydrology — M,D
Immunology — D
Industrial and Labor Relations — M
Industrial and Organizational Psychology — D
Industrial Hygiene — M,D
Industrial/Management Engineering — M,D
Infectious Diseases — M,D
Interdisciplinary Studies — D
Interior Design — M,D,O
International and Comparative Education — M,D
International Development — M
International Health — M,D
Kinesiology and Movement Studies — M,D
Landscape Architecture — M
Law — M,D
Linguistics — M,D
Management Information Systems — M,D
Management of Technology — M
Management Strategy and Policy — D
Marketing — M,D
Marriage and Family Therapy — M,D
Mass Communication — M,D
Materials Engineering — M,D
Materials Sciences — M,D
Maternal and Child Health — M
Mathematics Education — M,D,O
Mathematics — M,D
Mechanical Engineering — M,D
Mechanics — M,D
Medical Physics — M,D
Medicinal and Pharmaceutical Chemistry — M,D
Medieval and Renaissance Studies — M,D
Microbiology — D
Molecular Biology — M,D
Multilingual and Multicultural Education — M,D,O
Music — M,D
Natural Resources — M,D
Neurobiology — M,D
Neuroscience — M,D
Nurse Anesthesia — M,D
Nurse Midwifery — M,D
Nursing and Healthcare Administration — M,D
Nursing Informatics — M,D
Nursing—General — M,D
Nutrition — M,D
Occupational Health Nursing — M,D
Occupational Therapy — M
Oral and Dental Sciences — M,D,O
Paper and Pulp Engineering — M,D
Pediatric Nursing — M,D
Pharmaceutical Administration — M,D
Pharmaceutical Sciences — M,D
Pharmacology — M,D
Pharmacy — D
Philosophy — M,D
Physical Therapy — M,D
Physics — M,D
Physiology — D
Plant Biology — M,D
Plant Pathology — M,D
Plant Sciences — M,D
Political Science — D
Portuguese — M,D
Psychiatric Nursing — M,D
Psychology—General — D
Public Affairs — M
Public Health—General — M,D,O
Public Policy — M,D
Quantitative Analysis — M,D,O
Reading Education — M,D,O
Religion — M,D
Scandinavian Languages — M,D
School Psychology — M,D,O
Science Education — M
Social Psychology — D
Social Sciences Education — M
Social Work — M,D
Sociology — M,D
Software Engineering — M
Spanish — M,D
Special Education — M,D
Sports Management — M,D
Statistics — M,D
Structural Biology — D
Student Affairs — M
Supply Chain Management — M,D
Taxation — M
Technology and Public Policy — M
Textile Design — M,D,O
Theater — M,D
Toxicology — M,D
Travel and Tourism — M,D
Urban and Regional Planning — M,D
Veterinary Medicine — D
Veterinary Sciences — M,D
Virology — D
Vocational and Technical Education — M,D,O
Water Resources — M,D
Women's Health Nursing — M,D
Women's Studies — D

UNIVERSITY OF MISSISSIPPI
Accounting — M,D

Anthropology — M,D
Applied Science and Technology — M,D
Art/Fine Arts — M
Biological and Biomedical Sciences—General — M,D
Business Administration and Management—General — M,D
Chemical Engineering — M,D
Chemistry — M,D
Civil Engineering — M,D
Communication Disorders — M,D
Computer Science — M,D
Counselor Education — M,D,O
Criminal Justice and Criminology — M,D
Data Science/Data Analytics — M,D
Early Childhood Education — M,D,O
Economics — M,D
Education—General — M,D,O
Educational Leadership and Administration — M,D,O
Electrical Engineering — M,D
Elementary Education — M,D,O
Engineering and Applied Sciences—General — M,D
English — M,D
Environmental Engineering — M,D
Exercise and Sports Science — M,D
Experimental Psychology — M,D
Film, Television, and Video Production — M,D
Finance and Banking — M,D
Food Science and Technology — M,D
Foreign Languages Education — M,D
Geological Engineering — M,D
Geology — M,D
Health Promotion — M,D
Higher Education — M,D,O
History — M,D
Hospitality Management — M,D
Hydrology — M,D
Journalism — M
Kinesiology and Movement Studies — M,D
Law — M,D
Management Information Systems — M,D
Marketing — M,D
Mathematics Education — M,D,O
Mathematics — M,D
Mechanical Engineering — M,D
Medicinal and Pharmaceutical Chemistry — M,D
Music — M,D
Nutrition — M,D
Pharmaceutical Administration — M,D
Pharmaceutical Sciences — M,D
Pharmacology — M,D
Pharmacy — M,D
Philosophy — M,D
Physics — M,D
Political Science — M,D
Reading Education — M,D,O
Recreation and Park Management — M,D
Secondary Education — M,D,O
Social Work — M,D
Special Education — M,D,O
Taxation — M,D
Telecommunications — M,D
Toxicology — M,D
Writing — M,D

UNIVERSITY OF MISSISSIPPI MEDICAL CENTER
Allied Health—General — M
Allopathic Medicine — D
Anatomy — M,D
Biochemistry — D
Biological and Biomedical Sciences—General — M,D
Biophysics — D
Dentistry — M,D
Materials Sciences — M,D
Microbiology — D
Neuroscience — D
Nursing—General — M,D
Occupational Therapy — M
Oral and Dental Sciences — M,D
Pathology — D
Pharmacology — D
Physical Therapy — M
Physiology — D
Toxicology — D

UNIVERSITY OF MISSOURI
Accounting — M,D,O
Adult Education — M,D,O
Adult Nursing — M,D,O
Aerospace/Aeronautical Engineering — M,D
Agricultural Economics and Agribusiness — M,D
Agricultural Education — M,D,O
Agricultural Sciences—General — M,D
Agronomy and Soil Sciences — M,D,O
Allopathic Medicine — D
Analytical Chemistry — D
Anatomy — M,D
Animal Sciences — M,D
Anthropology — M,D
Applied Mathematics — M,D
Archaeology — M,D
Architecture — M,D
Art Education — M,D,O
Art History — M,D
Art/Fine Arts — M
Astronomy — M,D
Biochemistry — M,D
Bioengineering — M,D
Bioinformatics — M
Biological and Biomedical Sciences—General — M,D
Business Administration and Management—General — M,D
Business Education — M,D,O

Chemical Engineering — M,D
Chemistry — D
Child and Family Studies — M,D
Civil Engineering — M,D
Classics — M,D
Clothing and Textiles — M,D
Communication Disorders — M,D
Communication—General — M,D
Computer Engineering — M,D
Computer Science — M,D
Conflict Resolution and Mediation/Peace Studies — M,D
Conservation Biology — M,D,O
Consumer Economics — D
Counseling Psychology — M,D,O
Curriculum and Instruction — M,D,O
Early Childhood Education — M,D,O
Ecology — M,D
Economics — M,D
Education—General — M,D,O
Educational Leadership and Administration — M,D,O
Educational Media/Instructional Technology — D
Educational Psychology — M,D,O
Electrical Engineering — M,D
Elementary Education — M,D,O
Engineering and Applied Sciences—General — M,D,O
English Education — M,D,O
English — M,D
Entomology — M,D
Environmental Engineering — M,D
Environmental Sciences — M,D,O
Evolutionary Biology — M,D
Family and Consumer Sciences—General — M,D,O
Family Nurse Practitioner Studies — M,D,O
Finance and Banking — M,D
Fish, Game, and Wildlife Management — M,D,O
Food Science and Technology — M,D
Foreign Languages Education — M,D,O
Forestry — M,D,O
French — M,D
Geographic Information Systems — M,D,O
Geography — M,O
Geology — M,D
German — M
Gerontological Nursing — M,D,O
Health Communication — M,D
Health Education — M,D,O
Health Informatics — M,O
Health Physics/Radiological Health — M
Health Promotion — M,O
Health Services Management and Hospital Administration — M,O
Higher Education — M,D,O
History — M,D
Horticulture — M,D
Hospitality Management — M,D
Human Development — M,D
Immunology — D
Industrial/Management Engineering — M,D
Information Studies — D
International Health — M,O
Journalism — M,D
Law — M,D
Library Science — M,D
Manufacturing Engineering — M,D
Mathematics Education — M,D,O
Mathematics — M,D
Mechanical Engineering — M,D
Microbiology — D
Music Education — M,D,O
Music — M,O
Neuroscience — M,D,O
Nonprofit Management — M,D,O
Nursing and Healthcare Administration — M,D,O
Nursing—General — M,D,O
Nutrition — M
Occupational Therapy — M
Organizational Management — M,D,O
Pathobiology — M,D
Pathology — M,D
Pediatric Nursing — M,D,O
Pharmacology — M,D
Philosophy — M,D
Physical Therapy — D
Physics — M,D
Physiology — M,D
Plant Biology — M,D
Plant Sciences — M,D
Political Science — M,D,O
Psychiatric Nursing — M,D,O
Psychology—General — M,D,O
Public Administration — M,D,O
Public Affairs — M,D,O
Public Health—General — M,O
Public Policy — M,D,O
Reading Education — M,D,O
Religion — M
Romance Languages — M,D
Rural Sociology — M,D
Russian — M
School Psychology — M,D,O
Science Education — M,D,O
Social Sciences Education — M,D,O
Social Work — M,D,O
Sociology — M,D
Special Education — D
Statistics — M,D
Taxation — M,D,O
Theater — M,D
Veterinary Medicine — M,D
Veterinary Sciences — M,D
Vocational and Technical Education — M,D,O
Water Resources — M,D,O

UNIVERSITY OF MISSOURI–KANSAS CITY

Accounting	M,D
Adult Nursing	M,D
Allopathic Medicine	M,D
Analytical Chemistry	M,D
Art/Fine Arts	M,D
Biochemistry	D
Bioinformatics	M,D,O
Biological and Biomedical Sciences—General	M,D
Biophysics	D
Business Administration and Management—General	M,D
Cell Biology	D
Chemistry	M,D
Civil Engineering	M,D,O
Computer Engineering	M,D,O
Computer Science	M,D,O
Construction Engineering	M,D,O
Counseling Psychology	M,D,O
Counselor Education	M,D,O
Criminal Justice and Criminology	M
Curriculum and Instruction	M,D,O
Dental Hygiene	M,D,O
Dentistry	M,D,O
Economics	M,D
Education—General	M,D,O
Educational Leadership and Administration	M,D,O
Electrical Engineering	M,D,O
Engineering and Applied Sciences—General	M,D,O
Engineering Management	M,D,O
English	M,D
Family Nurse Practitioner Studies	M,D
Finance and Banking	M,D
French	M
Geosciences	M,D
Gerontological Nursing	M,D
Health Education	M,D
Higher Education	M,D,O
History	M,D
Inorganic Chemistry	M,D
Interdisciplinary Studies	D
Law	M,D
Maternal and Child/Neonatal Nursing	M,D
Mathematics	M,D
Mechanical Engineering	M,D,O
Molecular Biology	D
Music Education	M,D
Music	M,D
Nursing and Healthcare Administration	M,D
Nursing Education	M,D
Nursing—General	M,D
Oral and Dental Sciences	M,D,O
Organic Chemistry	M,D
Pediatric Nursing	M,D
Pharmacy	D
Physical Chemistry	M,D
Physics	M,D
Political Science	M
Polymer Science and Engineering	M,D
Psychology—General	M,D
Public Administration	M,D
Public Affairs	M,D
Reading Education	M,D,O
Romance Languages	M
Social Psychology	M,D
Social Work	M
Sociology	M
Software Engineering	M,D,O
Spanish	M
Special Education	M,D,O
Statistics	M,D
Telecommunications	M,D,O
Theater	M
Therapies—Dance, Drama, and Music	M,D
Women's Health Nursing	M,D

UNIVERSITY OF MISSOURI–ST. LOUIS

Accounting	M,D,O
Adult Education	M,O
Adult Nursing	D,O
American Studies	M,D
Applied Physics	M,D
Astrophysics	M,D
Biochemistry	M,D
Biological and Biomedical Sciences—General	M,D,O
Biotechnology	M,D
Business Administration and Management—General	M,D,O
Chemistry	M,D
Clinical Psychology	M,D,O
Communication—General	M
Computer and Information Systems Security	M,D,O
Computer Science	M,D
Counselor Education	D
Criminal Justice and Criminology	M,D
Curriculum and Instruction	M
Early Childhood Education	M
Economics	M
Education—General	M,D,O
Educational Leadership and Administration	D
Educational Measurement and Evaluation	M,O
Educational Policy	D
Educational Psychology	D
Elementary Education	M
English as a Second Language	M
English	M
Family Nurse Practitioner Studies	D,O
Gerontological Nursing	D,O
Higher Education	M,O

UNIVERSITY OF MOBILE

Business Administration and Management—General	M
Education—General	M
Educational Leadership and Administration	M
Educational Policy	M
Marriage and Family Therapy	M
Music	M,D
Nursing and Healthcare Administration	M,D
Nursing Education	M,D
Nursing—General	M,D
Theology	M

UNIVERSITY OF MONTANA

Accounting	M
Analytical Chemistry	M,D
Animal Behavior	M,D,O
Anthropology	M,D
Art Education	M
Art History	M
Art/Fine Arts	M
Biochemistry	D
Biological and Biomedical Sciences—General	M,D
Business Administration and Management—General	M
Cell Biology	D
Chemistry	M,D
Child and Family Studies	M,D,O
Clinical Psychology	M,D,O
Communication Disorders	M,O
Communication—General	M
Community Health	M
Computer Art and Design	M
Computer Science	M
Counseling Psychology	M,D,O
Counselor Education	M,D,O
Criminal Justice and Criminology	M
Cultural Studies	M,D,O
Curriculum and Instruction	M,D
Developmental Biology	D
Developmental Psychology	M,D,O
Early Childhood Education	M,D
Ecology	M,D
Economics	M
Education—General	M,D,O
Educational Leadership and Administration	M,D,O
English Education	M
English	M
Environmental Management and Policy	M
Environmental Sciences	M
Exercise and Sports Science	M
Experimental Psychology	M,D,O
Film, Television, and Video Production	M
Fish, Game, and Wildlife Management	M,D
Forestry	M,D
French	M
Geography	M,D
Geology	M,D
Geosciences	M,D
German	M
Health Education	M
History	M,D
Immunology	D
Inorganic Chemistry	M,D
Interdisciplinary Studies	M,D
Internet and Interactive Multimedia	M
Journalism	D
Law	D
Legal and Justice Studies	M
Linguistics	M,D
Mathematics Education	M,D
Mathematics	M,D
Medicinal and Pharmaceutical Chemistry	M,D
Microbiology	D
Molecular Biology	D
Music	M
Natural Resources	M,D
Neuroscience	M,D
Organic Chemistry	M,D
Pharmaceutical Sciences	M,D
Pharmacy	M,D

UNIVERSITY OF MONTEVALLO

Business Administration and Management—General	M
Communication Disorders	M
Counselor Education	M
Education—General	M,O
Educational Leadership and Administration	M,O
Elementary Education	M
English	M
Secondary Education	M

UNIVERSITY OF MOUNT OLIVE

Business Administration and Management—General	M
Nursing—General	M

UNIVERSITY OF MOUNT UNION

Educational Leadership and Administration	M
Physical Therapy	D
Physician Assistant Studies	M

UNIVERSITY OF NEBRASKA AT KEARNEY

Accounting	M
Art Education	M
Biological and Biomedical Sciences—General	M
Business Administration and Management—General	M
Communication Disorders	M
Counseling Psychology	M,O
Counselor Education	M,O
Curriculum and Instruction	M
Early Childhood Education	M
Education of the Gifted	M
Education—General	M,O
Educational Leadership and Administration	M,O
Educational Media/Instructional Technology	M
Elementary Education	M
English as a Second Language	M
English	M
Exercise and Sports Science	M
Foreign Languages Education	M
History	M
Human Resources Management	M
Human Services	M
Leisure Studies	M
Library Science	M
Management Information Systems	M
Marketing	M
Mathematics Education	M
Museum Education	M
Music Education	M
Physical Education	M
Reading Education	M
Recreation and Park Management	M
School Psychology	M,O
Science Education	M
Secondary Education	M
Special Education	M,O
Sports Management	M
Student Affairs	M,O
Writing	M

UNIVERSITY OF NEBRASKA AT OMAHA

Accounting	M
Applied Behavior Analysis	M,D,O
Art/Fine Arts	M
Artificial Intelligence/Robotics	M,O
Athletic Training and Sports Medicine	M,D
Bioinformatics	M,D
Biological and Biomedical Sciences—General	M,O
Business Administration and Management—General	M,O
Communication Disorders	M
Communication—General	M,O
Computer and Information Systems Security	M,D,O
Computer Science	M,D
Counselor Education	M
Criminal Justice and Criminology	M,D,O
Data Science/Data Analytics	M,D,O
Economics	M
Education—General	M,D,O
Educational Leadership and Administration	M,D,O
Elementary Education	M
English as a Second Language	M
English	M,O
Exercise and Sports Science	M
Foreign Languages Education	M
Geographic Information Systems	M
Geography	M,O
Gerontology	M,D,O
Health Education	M,D

UNIVERSITY OF NEBRASKA–LINCOLN

Philosophy	M
Photography	M
Physical Chemistry	M,D
Physical Education	M
Physical Therapy	D
Political Science	M
Psychology—General	M,D,O
Public Administration	M
Public Health—General	M,O
Recreation and Park Management	M
Rural Planning and Studies	M
Rural Sociology	M
School Psychology	M,D,O
Social Work	M
Sociology	M
Spanish	M
Theater	M
Toxicology	M,D
Writing	M
Zoology	M,D

History	M
Human Resources Development	M,D,O
Industrial and Organizational Psychology	M,D,O
Information Science	M,D,O
Kinesiology and Movement Studies	M,D
Management Information Systems	M,D,O
Mathematics	M
Music	M
National Security	M
Organizational Management	M
Political Science	M,O
Project Management	M,D,O
Psychology—General	M,D,O
Public Administration	M
School Psychology	M,D,O
Science Education	M,O
Secondary Education	M
Social Work	M
Sociology	M
Software Engineering	M,O
Special Education	M
Systems Engineering	M
Technical Communication	M,O
Urban Education	M
Writing	M,O

Accounting	M,D
Actuarial Science	M
Adult Education	M,D,O
Advertising and Public Relations	M,D
Agricultural Economics and Agribusiness	M,D
Agricultural Education	M
Agricultural Engineering	M,D
Agricultural Sciences—General	M,D
Agronomy and Soil Sciences	M,D
Analytical Chemistry	M,D
Animal Sciences	M,D
Anthropology	M
Archaeology	M
Architectural Engineering	M,D
Architecture	M,D
Art History	M
Art/Fine Arts	M
Astronomy	M,D
Biochemistry	M,D
Bioengineering	M,D
Bioinformatics	M,D
Biological and Biomedical Sciences—General	M,D
Biomedical Engineering	M,D
Biopsychology	M,D
Business Administration and Management—General	M,D
Chemical Engineering	M,D
Chemistry	M,D
Child and Family Studies	M,D
Child Development	M,D
Civil Engineering	M,D
Classics	M
Clinical Psychology	M,D
Clothing and Textiles	M,D
Cognitive Sciences	M,D,O
Communication Disorders	M,D
Communication—General	M,D
Comparative Literature	M,D
Computer Engineering	M,D
Computer Science	M,D
Consumer Economics	M,D
Corporate and Organizational Communication	M,D
Counseling Psychology	M,D,O
Curriculum and Instruction	M,D,O
Developmental Psychology	M,D,O
Early Childhood Education	M,D
Economics	M,D
Educational Leadership and Administration	M,D,O
Educational Measurement and Evaluation	M,D,O
Educational Psychology	M,D,O
Electrical Engineering	M,D
Engineering and Applied Sciences—General	M,D
Engineering Management	M,D
English	M,D
Entomology	M,D
Environmental Engineering	M,D
Exercise and Sports Science	M,D
Family and Consumer Sciences—General	M,D
Finance and Banking	M,D
Food Science and Technology	M,D
French	M,D
Geography	M,D
Geosciences	M,D
German	M,D
Gerontology	M,D
Health Promotion	M,D
History	M,D
Home Economics Education	M,D
Horticulture	M,D
Human Development	M,D,O
Industrial/Management Engineering	M,D
Information Science	M,D
Inorganic Chemistry	M,D
Interior Design	M,D
Journalism	M
Law	M
Legal and Justice Studies	M
Management Information Systems	M,D
Manufacturing Engineering	M,D
Marketing	M
Marriage and Family Therapy	M,D
Mass Communication	M,D
Materials Engineering	M,D

---

*M—masters degree; D—doctorate; O—other advanced degree; *—Close-Up and/or Display*

Materials Sciences — M,D
Mathematics — M,D
Mechanical Engineering — M,D
Mechanics — M,D
Metallurgical Engineering and Metallurgy — M,D
Music Education — M,D
Music — M,D
Natural Resources — M,D
Nutrition — M,D
Organic Chemistry — M,D
Philosophy — M,D
Physical Chemistry — M,D
Physics — M,D
Political Science — M,D,O
Psychology—General — M,D
Public Policy — M,D,O
Rhetoric — M,D
School Psychology — M,D,O
Social Psychology — M,D
Sociology — M,D
Spanish — M,D
Special Education — M,D,O
Speech and Interpersonal Communication — M,D
Statistics — M,D
Survey Methodology — M,D
Theater — M
Toxicology — M,D
Urban and Regional Planning — M,D
Veterinary Sciences — M,D
Vocational and Technical Education — M,D,O
Writing — M,D

UNIVERSITY OF NEBRASKA MEDICAL CENTER
Allied Health—General — M,D,O
Allopathic Medicine — D,O
Applied Behavior Analysis — M,D
Biochemistry — M
Bioinformatics — M,D
Biological and Biomedical Sciences—General — M,D
Biostatistics — D
Cancer Biology/Oncology — D
Clinical Laboratory Sciences/Medical Technology — M,O
Dentistry — M,D,O
Emergency Management — M
Environmental and Occupational Health — D
Epidemiology — D
Health Promotion — D
Health Services Management and Hospital Administration — M,D
Health Services Research — M,D
Immunology — M,D
Infectious Diseases — M,D
Molecular Biology — M
Molecular Genetics — M,D
Molecular Medicine — D
Neuroscience — D
Nursing—General — D
Nutrition — O
Oral and Dental Sciences — M,D
Pathology — M,D
Perfusion — M
Pharmaceutical Sciences — M,D
Pharmacology — D
Pharmacy — D
Physical Therapy — D
Physician Assistant Studies — M
Physiology — D
Public Health—General — M
Toxicology — M

UNIVERSITY OF NEVADA, LAS VEGAS
Accounting — M,O
Addictions/Substance Abuse Counseling — M,D,O
Aerospace/Aeronautical Engineering — M,D,O
Allied Health—General — M,D,O
Anthropology — M,D
Applied Economics — M,O
Architecture — M,O
Art/Fine Arts — M
Astronomy — M,D
Biochemistry — M,D
Biological and Biomedical Sciences—General — M,D
Biomedical Engineering — M,D,O
Business Administration and Management—General — M,O
Chemistry — M,D
Clinical Psychology — M,D,O
Communication—General — M
Community Health — M,D,O
Computer and Information Systems Security — M,D,O
Counseling Psychology — M,D,O
Counselor Education — M,D,O
Criminal Justice and Criminology — M,D
Curriculum and Instruction — M,D,O
Data Science/Data Analytics — M,O
Dentistry — M,D,O
Distance Education Development — M,D,O
Early Childhood Education — M,D,O
Economics — M
Education—General — M,D,O
Educational Leadership and Administration — M,D,O
Educational Media/Instructional Technology — M,D,O
Elementary Education — M,D,O
Emergency Management — M,D,O
Engineering and Applied Sciences—General — M,D,O
English as a Second Language — M,D,O
English — M,D
Environmental Sciences — M,D,O
Exercise and Sports Science — M,D
Family Nurse Practitioner Studies — M,D,O
Film, Television, and Video Production — M,O

Geosciences — M,D
Health Physics/Radiological Health — M,D,O
Health Services Management and Hospital Administration — M
Higher Education — M,D,O
Hispanic Studies — M,O
History — M,D
Hospitality Management — M,D
Journalism — M
Kinesiology and Movement Studies — M,D
Law — M,D
Management Information Systems — M,O
Marriage and Family Therapy — M
Materials Engineering — M,D
Mathematics — M,D
Media Studies — M
Music — M,D,O
Nonprofit Management — M,D,O
Nuclear Engineering — M,D,O
Nursing Education — M,D,O
Nursing—General — M,D,O
Nutrition — M,D
Oral and Dental Sciences — M,D,O
Physical Therapy — D
Physics — M,D
Political Science — M,D
Psychology—General — M,D,O
Public Administration — M,D,O
Public Affairs — M
Public Health—General — M,D,O
Public Policy — M,D,O
Secondary Education — M,D,O
Social Work — M
Sociology — M,D
Special Education — M,D,O
Theater — M
Translation and Interpretation — M,O
Transportation and Highway Engineering — M,D
Water Resources — M
Writing — M,D,O

UNIVERSITY OF NEVADA, RENO
Accounting — M
Agricultural Sciences—General — M,D
Allopathic Medicine — D
Animal Sciences — M
Anthropology — M,D
Applied Behavior Analysis — M,D
Art/Fine Arts — M
Atmospheric Sciences — M,D
Biochemistry — M,D
Biological and Biomedical Sciences—General — M
Biomedical Engineering — M,D
Biotechnology — M
Business Administration and Management—General — M
Cell Biology — M,D
Chemical Engineering — M,D
Chemical Physics — D
Chemistry — M,D
Child and Family Studies — M
Civil Engineering — M,D
Clinical Psychology — D
Cognitive Sciences — M,D
Communication Disorders — M,D
Computer Engineering — M,D
Computer Science — M,D
Conservation Biology — D
Counselor Education — M,D,O
Criminal Justice and Criminology — M
Curriculum and Instruction — D
Ecology — D
Economics — M
Education—General — M,D,O
Educational Leadership and Administration — M,D,O
Educational Psychology — M,D,O
Electrical Engineering — M,D
Elementary Education — M
Engineering and Applied Sciences—General — M,D
English as a Second Language — M
English — M,D
Environmental and Occupational Health — M,D
Environmental Management and Policy — M
Environmental Sciences — M,D
Evolutionary Biology — D
Finance and Banking — M
Geochemistry — M,D
Geography — M,D
Geological Engineering — M,D
Geology — M,D
Geophysics — M,D
History — M,D
Human Development — M
Hydrogeology — M,D
Hydrology — M
Journalism — M
Legal and Justice Studies — M
Management Information Systems — M
Materials Engineering — M,D
Mathematics Education — M
Mathematics — M
Mechanical Engineering — M,D
Metallurgical Engineering and Metallurgy — M,D
Mineral/Mining Engineering — M,D
Molecular Biology — M,D
Molecular Pharmacology — D
Music — M
Nursing—General — M
Nutrition — M
Philosophy — M
Physics — M,D
Physiology — D
Political Science — M,D
Psychology—General — M,D
Public Administration — M
Public Health—General — M,D

Range Science — M
Reading Education — M,D
Secondary Education — M
Social Psychology — D
Social Work — M
Sociology — M
Spanish — M
Special Education — M,D
Speech and Interpersonal Communication — M
Western European Studies — D

UNIVERSITY OF NEW BRUNSWICK FREDERICTON
Anthropology — M
Applied Economics — M
Biological and Biomedical Sciences—General — M,D
Business Administration and Management—General — M
Chemical Engineering — M,D
Chemistry — M,D
Civil Engineering — M,D
Classics — M
Computer Engineering — M,D
Computer Science — M,D
Conflict Resolution and Mediation/Peace Studies — M
Construction Engineering — M,D
Economics — M
Education—General — M,D
Electrical Engineering — M,D
Engineering and Applied Sciences—General — M,D,O
Engineering Management — M
English — M,D
Entrepreneurship — M
Environmental Engineering — M,D
Environmental Management and Policy — M
Exercise and Sports Science — M
Forestry — M,D
Geodetic Sciences — M,D
Geology — M,D
Geotechnical Engineering — M,D
Health Services Research — M
History — M,D
Hydrology — M,D
Interdisciplinary Studies — M,D
International Development — M
Marketing — M,D
Materials Sciences — M,D
Mathematics — M,D
Mechanical Engineering — M,D
Mechanics — M,D
Nursing Education — M
Nursing—General — M
Physical Education — M
Physics — M,D
Political Science — M
Psychology—General — M,D
Public Administration — M
Public Policy — M
Recreation and Park Management — M
Sociology — M,D
Sports Management — M
Statistics — M,D
Structural Engineering — M,D
Surveying Science and Engineering — M,D
Sustainable Development — M
Transportation and Highway Engineering — M,D
Urban and Regional Planning — M
Water Resources — M,D

UNIVERSITY OF NEW BRUNSWICK SAINT JOHN
Biological and Biomedical Sciences—General — M,D
Business Administration and Management—General — M
Clinical Psychology — M,D
Electronic Commerce — M
Experimental Psychology — M,D
International Business — M
Natural Resources — M
Psychology—General — M,D

UNIVERSITY OF NEW ENGLAND
Biological and Biomedical Sciences—General — M
Curriculum and Instruction — M,D,O
Dentistry — D
Early Childhood Education — M,D,O
Education—General — M,D,O
Educational Leadership and Administration — M,D,O
Health Informatics — M,D,O
Health Services Management and Hospital Administration — M,D,O
Marine Sciences — M
Nurse Anesthesia — M,D
Nutrition — M,D,O
Occupational Therapy — M,D
Osteopathic Medicine — D
Pharmacy — D
Physical Therapy — M,D
Physician Assistant Studies — M,D
Public Health—General — M,D,O
Reading Education — M,D,O
Social Work — M,D,O
Vocational and Technical Education — M,D,O

UNIVERSITY OF NEW HAMPSHIRE
Accounting — M
Addictions/Substance Abuse Counseling — M,O
Agricultural Sciences—General — M,D
Animal Sciences — M,D
Applied Mathematics — M,D,O
Biochemistry — M,D
Biological and Biomedical Sciences—General — M,D

Business Administration and Management—General — M,O
Chemical Engineering — M,D
Chemistry — M,D
Child and Family Studies — M
Civil Engineering — M,D
Communication Disorders — M
Computer and Information Systems Security — M
Computer Science — M,D
Conservation Biology — M
Curriculum and Instruction — D,O
Early Childhood Education — M
Economic Development — M
Economics — M,D
Education—General — M,D,O
Educational Leadership and Administration — M,O
Educational Media/Instructional Technology — M,O
Electrical Engineering — M,D,O
Elementary Education — M,D
English — M,D
Environmental Engineering — M,D
Environmental Management and Policy — M
Evolutionary Biology — D
Family Nurse Practitioner Studies — M,D,O
Fish, Game, and Wildlife Management — M
Forestry — M
Genetics — M,D
Geographic Information Systems — O
Geology — M
Geosciences — M
Higher Education — O
History — M,D
Hydrology — M
Intellectual Property Law — M,D,O
Kinesiology and Movement Studies — M,O
Law — M,D,O
Legal and Justice Studies — M,D,O
Liberal Studies — M
Linguistics — M,D
Management Information Systems — M,O
Marine Biology — M,D
Marriage and Family Therapy — M,O
Materials Engineering — M,D
Materials Sciences — M,D
Mathematics Education — M,D,O
Mathematics — M,D,O
Mechanical Engineering — M,D
Microbiology — M,D
Museum Studies — M
Music — M
Natural Resources — M
Nursing—General — M,D,O
Nutrition — M,D
Occupational Therapy — M,D
Ocean Engineering — M,D,O
Oceanography — M,D,O
Physical Education — M,D
Physics — M,D
Political Science — M
Psychiatric Nursing — M,D,O
Psychology—General — D
Public Administration — M,O
Public Health—General — M,O
Public Policy — M
Quantitative Analysis — M,O
Recreation and Park Management — M
Science Education — M,D
Secondary Education — M,O
Social Work — M,O
Sociology — M,D
Spanish — M,O
Special Education — M,O
Sports and Entertainment Law — M,D,O
Sustainability Management — M
Water Resources — M,O
Women's Studies — O
Writing — M,D

UNIVERSITY OF NEW HAVEN
Accounting — M,O
Biomedical Engineering — M
Business Administration and Management—General — M
Cell Biology — M
Civil Engineering — M
Computer and Information Systems Security — M
Computer Engineering — M
Computer Science — M,O
Conflict Resolution and Mediation/Peace Studies — M,O
Criminal Justice and Criminology — M,D,O
Ecology — M
Electrical Engineering — M
Emergency Management — M,O
Engineering and Applied Sciences—General — M,O
Engineering Management — M,O
Environmental and Occupational Health — M
Environmental Engineering — M
Environmental Management and Policy — M
Environmental Sciences — M,O
Facilities Management — M,O
Finance and Banking — M,O
Fire Protection Engineering — M,O
Forensic Psychology — M,O
Forensic Sciences — M,O
Geographic Information Systems — M
Geosciences — M
Hazardous Materials Management — M
Human Resources Management — M,O
Industrial and Manufacturing Management — M,O
Industrial and Organizational Psychology — M,O

Industrial/Management Engineering	M,O
International Business	M
Management Strategy and Policy	M
Marketing	M
Mechanical Engineering	M
Molecular Biology	M
National Security	M,O
Nonprofit Management	M,O
Organizational Management	M,O
Public Administration	M,O
Social Psychology	M,O
Software Engineering	M,O
Sports Management	M,O
Taxation	M,O
Water Resources Engineering	M

UNIVERSITY OF NEW MEXICO

Allied Health—General	M,D,O
Allopathic Medicine	D
American Indian/Native American Studies	M,D
American Studies	M,D
Anthropology	M,D
Archaeology	M,D
Architecture	M,D
Art Education	M
Art History	M,D
Art/Fine Arts	M
Biochemistry	M,D
Biological and Biomedical Sciences—General	M,D
Biomedical Engineering	M,D
Business Administration and Management—General	M
Cell Biology	M,D
Chemical Engineering	M,D
Chemistry	M,D
Child and Family Studies	M,D
Civil Engineering	M,D
Clinical Laboratory Sciences/Medical Technology	M,O
Clinical Psychology	D
Cognitive Sciences	D
Communication Disorders	M
Communication—General	M
Community Health	M
Comparative Literature	M,D
Computer and Information Systems Security	M
Computer Engineering	M,D
Computer Science	M,D
Construction Management	M,D
Counselor Education	M,D
Cultural Studies	M
Dance	M
Dental Hygiene	M
Developmental Psychology	D
Early Childhood Education	D
Economics	M,D
Education of Students with Severe/Multiple Disabilities	M,D,O
Education—General	M,D,O
Educational Leadership and Administration	M,D,O
Educational Media/Instructional Technology	M,D,O
Educational Psychology	M,D
Electrical Engineering	M,D
Elementary Education	M
Engineering and Applied Sciences—General	M,D
English as a Second Language	M,D
English Education	M,D
English	M,D
Entrepreneurship	M
Environmental Management and Policy	M
Epidemiology	M
Ethnic Studies	M
Exercise and Sports Science	D
Foundations and Philosophy of Education	M,D
French	M,D
Genetics	M,D
Geography	M
Geosciences	M,D
German	M,D
Health Education	M
Health Psychology	D
Health Services Management and Hospital Administration	M
Higher Education	O
Historic Preservation	O
History	M,D
Human Development	M,D
Human Resources Management	M
International Business	M
International Development	M,D
International Economics	M,D
Landscape Architecture	M
Latin American Studies	M,D
Law	D
Linguistics	M,D
Management of Technology	M
Management Strategy and Policy	M
Manufacturing Engineering	M
Mathematics	M,D
Mechanical Engineering	M,D
Microbiology	M,D
Molecular Biology	M,D
Multilingual and Multicultural Education	M,D
Music Education	M
Music	M
Nanotechnology	M,D
Natural Resources	M,D
Neuroscience	M,D
Nuclear Engineering	M,D
Nursing—General	M,D
Nutrition	M

Occupational Therapy	M
Optical Sciences	M,D
Organizational Behavior	M
Pathology	M,D
Pharmaceutical Sciences	M,D
Pharmacy	D
Philosophy	M,D
Photography	M,D
Photonics	M,D
Physical Education	M
Physical Therapy	D
Physician Assistant Studies	M
Physics	M,D
Physiology	M
Planetary and Space Sciences	M
Political Science	M,D
Portuguese	M,D
Psychology—General	D
Public Administration	M
Public Health—General	M
Quantitative Analysis	D
Reading Education	M,D
Science Education	O
Secondary Education	M
Sociology	M,D
Spanish	M,D
Special Education	M,D,O
Sports Management	D
Statistics	M,D
Systems Engineering	M,D
Taxation	M
Theater	M
Toxicology	M
Urban and Regional Planning	M
Water Resources	M
Writing	M

UNIVERSITY OF NEW ORLEANS

Accounting	M
Art/Fine Arts	M
Arts Administration	M
Biological and Biomedical Sciences—General	M
Business Administration and Management—General	M
Chemistry	M,D
Civil Engineering	M,D
Computer Science	M,D
Counselor Education	M
Curriculum and Instruction	M
Economics	D
Educational Leadership and Administration	M
Electrical Engineering	M
Engineering and Applied Sciences—General	M,D
Engineering Management	M
English	M
Environmental Sciences	M,D
Film, Television, and Video Production	M
Finance and Banking	M
Geosciences	M,D
Health Services Management and Hospital Administration	M
Higher Education	M
History	M
Hospitality Management	M
Mathematics	M
Mechanical Engineering	M
Music	M
Physics	M,D
Political Science	M
Psychology—General	M,D
Public Administration	M
Romance Languages	M
Sociology	M
Special Education	M
Taxation	M
Theater	M
Transportation Management	M
Travel and Tourism	M
Urban and Regional Planning	M
Urban Studies	M,D
Writing	M

UNIVERSITY OF NORTH ALABAMA

Accounting	M
Business Administration and Management—General	M
Child and Family Studies	M
Clinical Psychology	M
Counselor Education	M
Criminal Justice and Criminology	M
Economic Development	M
Education—General	M,O
Educational Leadership and Administration	M
Elementary Education	M,O
English	M
Exercise and Sports Science	M
Finance and Banking	M
Geographic Information Systems	M
Health Promotion	M
Health Services Management and Hospital Administration	M
Higher Education	M
Historic Preservation	M
History	M
Information Science	M
Interdisciplinary Studies	M
International Business	M
Kinesiology and Movement Studies	M
Law	M
Management Information Systems	M
Nursing—General	M
Physical Education	M
Political Science	M
Project Management	M
Public History	M

Rhetoric	M
Secondary Education	M
Special Education	M
Technical Writing	M
Writing	M

UNIVERSITY OF NORTH CAROLINA AT ASHEVILLE

Cultural Studies	M,O
Liberal Studies	M,O
Sustainable Development	M,O

THE UNIVERSITY OF NORTH CAROLINA AT CHAPEL HILL

Accounting	M,D
Adult Nursing	M,D,O
Allied Health—General	M,D
Allopathic Medicine	D
Anthropology	M,D
Archaeology	M,D
Art History	M,D
Art/Fine Arts	M
Astronomy	M,D
Astrophysics	M,D
Athletic Training and Sports Medicine	M
Biochemistry	M,D
Bioinformatics	D
Biological and Biomedical Sciences—General	M,D
Biomedical Engineering	M,D
Biophysics	M,D
Biopsychology	D
Biostatistics	M,D
Botany	M,D
Business Administration and Management—General	M,D
Cell Biology	M,D
Chemistry	M,D
Classics	M,D
Clinical Psychology	D
Clinical Research	M,D
Cognitive Sciences	D
Communication Disorders	M,D
Communication—General	M,D,O
Computational Biology	D
Computer Science	M,D
Counselor Education	M
Curriculum and Instruction	M,D
Dental Hygiene	M,D
Dentistry	D
Developmental Biology	M,D
Developmental Psychology	D
Early Childhood Education	M,D
East European and Russian Studies	M
Ecology	M,D
Economics	M,D
Education—General	M,D
Educational Leadership and Administration	M,D
Educational Measurement and Evaluation	M,D
Educational Psychology	M,D
English as a Second Language	M
English Education	M
English	M,D
Environmental and Occupational Health	M,D
Environmental Engineering	M,D
Environmental Sciences	M,D
Epidemiology	M,D
Evolutionary Biology	M,D
Exercise and Sports Science	M
Family Nurse Practitioner Studies	M,D,O
Finance and Banking	D
Folklore	M
Foreign Languages Education	M
French	M,D
Genetics	M,D
Geography	M,D
Geology	M,D
German	D
Gerontological Nursing	M,D,O
Health Communication	M,D,O
Health Promotion	M
Health Psychology	M,D
Health Services Management and Hospital Administration	M,D
History	M,D
Immunology	M,D
Information Studies	M,D,O
International Affairs	M
Italian	M,D
Journalism	M,D,O
Kinesiology and Movement Studies	D
Latin American Studies	M,D,O
Law	M,D
Library Science	M,D,O
Linguistics	M,D
Management Information Systems	D
Management Strategy and Policy	M,D
Marine Sciences	M,D
Marketing	M
Maternal and Child Health	M,D
Mathematics Education	M
Mathematics	M,D
Media Studies	M,D,O
Microbiology	M,D
Molecular Biology	M,D
Molecular Physiology	D
Music Education	M
Music	M,D
Neurobiology	D
Neuroscience	D
Nursing and Healthcare Administration	M,D,O
Nursing Education	M,D,O
Nursing Informatics	M,D,O
Nursing—General	M,D,O
Nutrition	M,D
Occupational Health Nursing	M

Occupational Therapy	M,D
Operations Research	M,D
Oral and Dental Sciences	M,D
Organizational Behavior	D
Pathology	D
Pediatric Nursing	M,D,O
Pharmaceutical Administration	M,D
Pharmaceutical Sciences	M,D
Pharmacology	D
Pharmacy	M,D
Philosophy	M,D
Physical Education	M
Physical Therapy	D
Physics	M,D,O
Political Science	M,D
Portuguese	M,D
Psychiatric Nursing	M,D,O
Psychology—General	D
Public Administration	M
Public Health—General	M,D
Public Policy	D
Reading Education	M,D
Rehabilitation Counseling	M
Religion	M,D
Romance Languages	M,D
School Psychology	M,D
Science Education	M
Secondary Education	M
Slavic Languages	D
Social Psychology	D
Social Sciences Education	M
Social Work	M,D
Sociology	M,D
Spanish	M,D
Sports Management	M
Statistics	M,D
Telecommunications	M,D,O
Theater	M
Toxicology	M,D
Urban and Regional Planning	M,D

THE UNIVERSITY OF NORTH CAROLINA AT CHARLOTTE

Accounting	M
Acute Care/Critical Care Nursing	M,D,O
Addictions/Substance Abuse Counseling	M,D,O
African Studies	O
Anthropology	M
Applied Economics	M,O
Applied Mathematics	M,D
Applied Physics	M,D
Architecture	M
Art Education	M,D,O
Arts Administration	M,O
Bioinformatics	M,D,O
Biological and Biomedical Sciences—General	M,D
Business Administration and Management—General	M,D,O
Business Analytics	M,D,O
Business Education	D
Chemistry	M,D
Child and Family Studies	M,D,O
Child Development	M,D,O
Civil Engineering	M,D
Cognitive Sciences	M,D,O
Communication—General	M
Community Health	M,D,O
Computer and Information Systems Security	M,D,O
Computer Engineering	M,D
Computer Science	M,D
Construction Management	M,O
Counselor Education	M,D,O
Criminal Justice and Criminology	M
Cultural Studies	M,O
Curriculum and Instruction	M,D,O
Data Science/Data Analytics	M,O
Early Childhood Education	M,D,O
Economics	M,O
Education of the Gifted	M,D,O
Education—General	M,D,O
Educational Leadership and Administration	M,D,O
Educational Media/Instructional Technology	M,D,O
Electrical Engineering	M,D
Elementary Education	M,O
Emergency Management	M,O
Energy and Power Engineering	M,O
Engineering and Applied Sciences—General	M,D,O
Engineering Management	M,O
English as a Second Language	M,D,O
English	M,O
Environmental Engineering	M,D
Ethics	M,O
Facilities Management	M,O
Family Nurse Practitioner Studies	M,D,O
Finance and Banking	M,D
Fire Protection Engineering	M,O
Foreign Languages Education	M,D,O
Game Design and Development	M,O
Gender Studies	M,D,O
Geographic Information Systems	M,D,O
Geography	M,D
Geosciences	M,D
Gerontological Nursing	M,D,O
Gerontology	M,O
Health Informatics	M,O
Health Psychology	M,D,O
Health Services Management and Hospital Administration	M,D,O
Health Services Research	D
History	M
Industrial and Manufacturing Management	M,D,O

---

*M—masters degree; D—doctorate; O—other advanced degree; *—Close-Up and/or Display*

Industrial and Organizational
  Psychology — M,D,O
Information Science — M,O
Interdisciplinary Studies — M,D,O
Kinesiology and Movement Studies — M
Latin American Studies — M,D,O
Liberal Studies — M,D,O
Linguistics — M,O
Logistics — M,O
Management Information Systems — M,O
Mathematical and
  Computational Finance — M,O
Mathematics — M,D,O
Mechanical Engineering — M,D
Middle School Education — M,D,O
Music — O
Nonprofit Management — M,O
Nurse Anesthesia — M,D,O
Nursing and Healthcare
  Administration — M,D,O
Nursing Education — M,D,O
Nursing—General — M,D,O
Optical Sciences — M,O
Philosophy — M,O
Psychology—General — M,D,O
Public Administration — M,O
Public Health—General — M,D,O
Public Policy — M,D,O
Reading Education — M,O
Real Estate — M,O
Religion — M
Secondary Education — M,D,O
Social Work — M
Sociology — M
Spanish — M,O
Special Education — M,D,O
Supply Chain Management — M,O
Systems Engineering — M,D,O
Technical Writing — M,O
Theater — M,D,O
Urban and Regional Planning — M,O
Urban Design — M
Women's Studies — M,D,O
Writing — M,O

**THE UNIVERSITY OF NORTH CAROLINA
AT GREENSBORO**

Accounting — M,O
Adult Education — M,D,O
Adult Nursing — M,D,O
Applied Economics — M
Architecture — M,O
Art/Fine Arts — M
Athletic Training and Sports
  Medicine — M,D
Biochemistry — M
Biological and Biomedical
  Sciences—General — M
Business Administration and
  Management—General — M,O
Chemistry — M
Child and Family Studies — M,D
Classics — M
Clinical Psychology — M,D
Cognitive Sciences — M
Communication Disorders — M,D
Communication—General — M
Community Health — M,D
Computer Science — M
Conflict Resolution and
  Mediation/Peace Studies — M,O
Counseling Psychology — M,D,O
Counselor Education — M,D,O
Criminal Justice and Criminology — M
Curriculum and Instruction — M,D,O
Dance — M
Developmental Psychology — M,D
Early Childhood Education — M,D,O
Economic Development — M,D,O
Economics — D
Education—General — M,D,O
Educational Leadership and
  Administration — M,D,O
Educational Measurement and
  Evaluation — D
Educational Media/Instructional
  Technology — M,D,O
Elementary Education — D
English as a Second Language — M,D,O
English Education — M,D
English — M,D
Film, Television, and Video
  Production — M
Finance and Banking — M,O
Foreign Languages Education — M,D,O
French — M
Gender Studies — M
Genetic Counseling — M
Geographic Information Systems — M,D,O
Geography — M,D,O
Gerontological Nursing — M,D,O
Gerontology — M
Higher Education — D
Hispanic and Latin American
  Languages — M,O
Hispanic Studies — M,O
Historic Preservation — M,O
History — M,D,O
Human Development — M,D
Information Studies — M
Interior Design — M,O
Kinesiology and Movement Studies — M,D
Liberal Studies — M
Library Science — M
Management Information Systems — M,D,O
Marketing — M,D
Marriage and Family Therapy — M,D,O
Mathematics Education — M,D
Mathematics — M,D
Media Studies — M
Middle School Education — M,D,O
Multilingual and Multicultural
  Education — M,D,O
Museum Studies — M,D,O

Music Education — M,D
Music — M,D
Nonprofit Management — M,O
Nurse Anesthesia — M,D,O
Nursing and Healthcare
  Administration — M,D,O
Nursing Education — M,D,O
Nursing—General — M,D,O
Nutrition — M,D
Political Science — M,O
Psychology—General — M,D
Public Affairs — M,O
Reading Education — M,D,O
Recreation and Park Management — M
Rhetoric — M,D
School Psychology — M,D,O
Science Education — M,D,O
Social Psychology — M,D
Social Sciences Education — M,D,O
Social Work — M
Sociology — M
Spanish — M,O
Special Education — M,D,O
Supply Chain Management — M,O
Technical Writing — M,D,O
Textile Design — M,D
Theater — M
Women's Studies — M,D,O
Writing — M

**THE UNIVERSITY OF NORTH CAROLINA
AT PEMBROKE**

Art Education — M
Business Administration and
  Management—General — M
Counseling Psychology — M
Counselor Education — M
Criminal Justice and Criminology — M
Education—General — M
Educational Leadership and
  Administration — M
Elementary Education — M
Emergency Management — M
English Education — M
Exercise and Sports Science — M
Health Education — M
Health Services Management and
  Hospital Administration — M
Mathematics Education — M
Nursing and Healthcare
  Administration — M
Nursing Education — M
Nursing—General — M
Physical Education — M
Public Administration — M
Reading Education — M
Science Education — M
Social Sciences Education — M
Social Work — M
Sports Management — M

**UNIVERSITY OF NORTH CAROLINA
SCHOOL OF THE ARTS**

Film, Television, and Video
  Production — M
Music — M,O
Theater — M

**THE UNIVERSITY OF NORTH CAROLINA
WILMINGTON**

Accounting — M
Applied Behavior Analysis — M,D
Applied Statistics — M,O
Biological and Biomedical
  Sciences—General — M,D
Business Administration and
  Management—General — M
Chemistry — M
Clinical Psychology — M,D
Clinical Research — M,D,O
Computer Science — M
Conflict Resolution and
  Mediation/Peace Studies — M
Criminal Justice and Criminology — M
Curriculum and Instruction — M,D
Data Science/Data Analytics — M
Early Childhood Education — M
Education—General — M,D
Educational Leadership and
  Administration — M,D,O
Educational Media/Instructional
  Technology — M
Educational Policy — M
Elementary Education — M
English as a Second Language — M
English — M
Environmental Management
  and Policy — M
Environmental Sciences — M
Family Nurse Practitioner Studies — M,D,O
Geographic Information Systems — M,O
Geosciences — M,O
Gerontology — M
Higher Education — M,D
Hispanic Studies — M,O
History — M
International Business — M
Liberal Studies — M
Management Information Systems — M
Marine Biology — M,D
Marine Sciences — M,D,O
Mathematics — M,O
Middle School Education — M
Nursing Education — M,D,O
Nursing—General — M,D,O
Psychology—General — M,D
Public Administration — M
Reading Education — M
Secondary Education — M
Social Work — M
Sociology — M
Spanish — M,O
Special Education — M
Statistics — M,O
Writing — M

UNIVERSITY OF NORTH DAKOTA

Applied Economics — M
Art/Fine Arts — M
Astrophysics — M,D
Atmospheric Sciences — M,D
Aviation — M
Biological and Biomedical
  Sciences—General — M,D
Business Administration and
  Management—General — M
Chemical Engineering — M
Chemistry — M,D
Civil Engineering — M,D
Clinical Laboratory
  Sciences/Medical Technology — M
Clinical Psychology — M,D
Communication Disorders — M
Communication—General — D
Community Health Nursing — M,D,O
Computer Science — M
Counseling Psychology — M,D
Criminal Justice and Criminology — D
Early Childhood Education — M
Education—General — M,D,O
Educational Leadership and
  Administration — M,D,O
Educational Media/Instructional
  Technology — M
Electrical Engineering — M,D
Elementary Education — M
Engineering and Applied
  Sciences—General — D
English — M,D
Environmental Engineering — M,D
Family Nurse Practitioner Studies — M,D,O
Fish, Game, and Wildlife
  Management — M,D
Forensic Psychology — M,D
Genetics — M,D
Geographic Information Systems — M
Geography — M
Geological Engineering — M
Geology — M,D
Geosciences — M,D
Gerontological Nursing — M,D,O
History — M,D
Kinesiology and Movement Studies — M
Law — D
Linguistics — M
Mathematics — M
Mechanical Engineering — M,D
Music Education — M,D
Music — M,D
Nurse Anesthesia — M,D,O
Nursing Education — M,D,O
Nursing—General — M,D,O
Occupational Therapy — M
Physical Therapy — D
Physician Assistant Studies — M
Physics — M,D
Planetary and Space
  Sciences — M
Psychiatric Nursing — M,D,O
Psychology—General — M,D
Public Administration — M
Public Health—General — M
Reading Education — M
Social Work — M
Sociology — M
Special Education — M
Zoology — M,D

**UNIVERSITY OF NORTHERN BRITISH
COLUMBIA**

Community Health — M,D,O
Computer Science — M,D,O
Disability Studies — M,D,O
Education—General — M,D,O
Environmental Management
  and Policy — M,D,O
Gender Studies — M,D,O
History — M,D,O
Interdisciplinary Studies — M,D,O
International Affairs — M,D,O
Mathematics — M,D,O
Natural Resources — M,D,O
Political Science — M,D,O
Psychology—General — M,D,O
Social Work — M,D,O

**UNIVERSITY OF NORTHERN
COLORADO**

Accounting — M
Acute Care/Critical Care Nursing — M,D
Applied Statistics — M,D
Art Education — M
Art History — M
Art/Fine Arts — M
Biological and Biomedical
  Sciences—General — M
Business Administration and
  Management—General — M
Chemistry — M,D
Clinical Psychology — M
Communication Disorders — M,D
Communication—General — M
Community Health — M
Counseling Psychology — D
Counselor Education — M,D
Criminal Justice and Criminology — M
Curriculum and Instruction — M,D
Education of the Gifted — M,D
Education—General — M,D,O
Educational Leadership and
  Administration — M,D,O
Educational Measurement and
  Evaluation — M,D
Educational Policy — M,D,O
Educational Psychology — M,D
Elementary Education — M
English as a Second Language — M,D
English Education — M,D
English — M
Exercise and Sports Science — M,D

Family Nurse Practitioner Studies — M,D
Foreign Languages Education — M,D
Geosciences — M
Gerontology — M,D
Health Education — M
Health Services Management and
  Hospital Administration — M
Higher Education — M,D
History — M
Human Resources Management — M
International Health — M
Mathematics Education — M,D
Mathematics — M,D
Multilingual and Multicultural
  Education — M,D
Music Education — M,D
Music — M,D
Nursing Education — M,D
Nursing—General — M,D
Physical Education — M,D
Public Health—General — M
Reading Education — M
Rehabilitation Counseling — M
Rehabilitation Sciences — M,D
School Psychology — O
Science Education — M,D
Sociology — M
Special Education — M,D
Sports Management — M,D
Student Affairs — M,D
Translation and Interpretation — M

UNIVERSITY OF NORTHERN IOWA

Accounting — M
Allied Health—General — M,D
Applied Mathematics — M
Art Education — M
Art/Fine Arts — M
Athletic Training and Sports
  Medicine — M
Biological and Biomedical
  Sciences—General — M
Business Administration and
  Management—General — M
Communication Disorders — M
Communication—General — M
Community College Education — M
Community Health — M
Counseling Psychology — M
Counselor Education — M
Curriculum and Instruction — D
Early Childhood Education — M
Education—General — M,D,O
Educational Leadership and
  Administration — M,D
Educational Measurement and
  Evaluation — M
Educational Media/Instructional
  Technology — M
Educational Psychology — M
Elementary Education — M
English as a Second Language — M
English Education — M
English — M
Foreign Languages Education — M
Gender Studies — M
Geography — M
Geosciences — M
Health Education — M
Health Promotion — M
Higher Education — M
History — M
Human Services — M
Kinesiology and Movement Studies — M
Mathematics Education — M
Mathematics — M
Middle School Education — M
Music Education — M
Music — M
Nonprofit Management — M
Physical Education — M
Physics — M
Psychology—General — M
Public History — M
Public Policy — M
Reading Education — M
School Psychology — M,O
Science Education — M
Secondary Education — M
Social Sciences — M
Social Work — M
Spanish — M
Special Education — M
Sports Management — M
Student Affairs — M
Vocational and Technical Education — M,D
Women's Studies — M
Writing — M

UNIVERSITY OF NORTH FLORIDA

Accounting — M
Adult Education — M
Allied Health—General — M,D,O
Applied Behavior Analysis — M
Biological and Biomedical
  Sciences—General — M
Business Administration and
  Management—General — M
Civil Engineering — M
Communication Disorders — M
Community Health — M
Computer Science — M
Construction Management — M
Counseling Psychology — M
Counselor Education — M,D
Criminal Justice and Criminology — M
Economics — M
Education—General — M,D
Educational Leadership and
  Administration — M,D
Educational Media/Instructional
  Technology — M,D
Electrical Engineering — M
Electronic Commerce — M
Elementary Education — M

English as a Second Language	M
English	M,O
Ethics	M,O
Exercise and Sports Science	M,D
Family Nurse Practitioner Studies	M
Finance and Banking	M
Health Services Management and Hospital Administration	M
History	M
Human Resources Management	M
International Business	M
Logistics	M
Management Information Systems	M
Mathematics	M
Mechanical Engineering	M
Nonprofit Management	M,O
Nurse Anesthesia	M,D,O
Nursing—General	M,D,O
Nutrition	M
Philosophy	M,O
Physical Therapy	M
Psychology—General	M
Public Administration	M
Public Health—General	M,O
Reading Education	M
Secondary Education	M
Social Work	M
Software Engineering	M
Special Education	M
Sports Management	M,D
Statistics	M
Translation and Interpretation	M
Writing	M

UNIVERSITY OF NORTH GEORGIA

Anthropology	M
Athletic Training and Sports Medicine	M
Business Administration and Management—General	M
Counseling Psychology	M
Criminal Justice and Criminology	M
Curriculum and Instruction	M
Early Childhood Education	M
Education—General	M
Educational Leadership and Administration	D,O
English Education	M
Family Nurse Practitioner Studies	M,O
Higher Education	D
History	M
Human Services	M
International Affairs	M
Kinesiology and Movement Studies	M
Mathematics Education	M
Middle School Education	M
Nursing Education	M
Philosophy	M
Physical Education	M
Physical Therapy	D
Public Administration	M
Science Education	M
Secondary Education	M
Social Sciences Education	M

UNIVERSITY OF NORTH TEXAS

Accounting	M,D,O
Advertising and Public Relations	M,D,O
Anthropology	M,D,O
Applied Arts and Design—General	M,D,O
Applied Behavior Analysis	M,D,O
Art Education	M,D,O
Art History	M,D,O
Art/Fine Arts	M,D,O
Biochemistry	M,D,O
Biological and Biomedical Sciences—General	M,D,O
Biomedical Engineering	M,D,O
Business Administration and Management—General	M,D,O
Chemistry	M,D,O
Child and Family Studies	M,D,O
Clinical Psychology	M,D,O
Communication Disorders	M,D,O
Communication—General	M,D,O
Computer Engineering	M,D,O
Computer Science	M,D,O
Counseling Psychology	M,D,O
Counselor Education	M,D,O
Criminal Justice and Criminology	M,D,O
Curriculum and Instruction	M,D,O
Early Childhood Education	M,D,O
Economics	M,D,O
Education of the Gifted	M,D,O
Education—General	M,D,O
Educational Leadership and Administration	M,D,O
Educational Measurement and Evaluation	M,D,O
Educational Psychology	M,D,O
Electrical Engineering	M,D,O
Emergency Management	M,D,O
Energy and Power Engineering	M,D,O
Engineering and Applied Sciences—General	M,D,O
English as a Second Language	M,D,O
English	M,D,O
Environmental Sciences	M,D,O
Film, Television, and Video Production	M,D,O
Finance and Banking	M,D,O
French	M,D,O
Geography	M,D,O
Gerontology	M,D,O
Health Services Management and Hospital Administration	M,D,O
Higher Education	M,D,O
History	M,D,O
Hospitality Management	M,D,O

Human Development	M,D,O
Human Resources Management	M,D,O
Industrial and Manufacturing Management	M,D,O
Information Science	M,D,O
Interdisciplinary Studies	M,D,O
Interior Design	M,D,O
International Affairs	M,D,O
Internet and Interactive Multimedia	M,D,O
Journalism	M,D,O
Kinesiology and Movement Studies	M,D,O
Linguistics	M,D,O
Logistics	M,D,O
Management Information Systems	M,D,O
Management Strategy and Policy	M,D,O
Marketing	M,D,O
Mathematics	M,D,O
Mechanical Engineering	M,D,O
Molecular Biology	M,D,O
Music Education	M,D,O
Music	M,D,O
Nonprofit Management	M,D,O
Philosophy	M,D,O
Political Science	M,D,O
Psychology—General	M,D,O
Public Administration	M,D,O
Quantitative Analysis	M,D,O
Rehabilitation Counseling	M,D,O
Sociology	M,D,O
Spanish	M,D,O
Special Education	M,D,O
Supply Chain Management	M,D,O
Textile Design	M,D,O
Travel and Tourism	M,D,O
Vocational and Technical Education	M,D,O
Writing	M,D,O

UNIVERSITY OF NORTH TEXAS AT DALLAS

Accounting	M
Business Administration and Management—General	M
Clinical Psychology	M
Counselor Education	M
Criminal Justice and Criminology	M
Curriculum and Instruction	M
Educational Leadership and Administration	M
Human Resources Management	M
Law	D
Management Strategy and Policy	M
Organizational Behavior	M
Public Administration	M

UNIVERSITY OF NORTH TEXAS HEALTH SCIENCE CENTER AT FORT WORTH

Anatomy	M,D
Biochemistry	M,D
Biological and Biomedical Sciences—General	M,D
Biostatistics	M,D,O
Biotechnology	M,D
Cancer Biology/Oncology	M,D
Epidemiology	M,D,O
Forensic Sciences	M,D
Genetics	M,D
Geographic Information Systems	M,D,O
Health Services Management and Hospital Administration	M,D,O
Health Services Research	M,D,O
Immunology	M,D
International Health	M,D,O
Microbiology	M,D
Neuroscience	M,D
Osteopathic Medicine	D
Pharmaceutical Sciences	M,D
Pharmacology	M,D
Physical Therapy	M,D
Physician Assistant Studies	M
Physiology	M,D
Public Health—General	M,D,O
Rehabilitation Sciences	M,D

UNIVERSITY OF NORTHWESTERN OHIO

Business Administration and Management—General	M

UNIVERSITY OF NORTHWESTERN–ST. PAUL

Business Administration and Management—General	M
Education—General	M
Human Services	M
Organizational Management	M
Pastoral Ministry and Counseling	M
Theology	M

UNIVERSITY OF NOTRE DAME

Accounting	M
Aerospace/Aeronautical Engineering	M,D
Applied Arts and Design—General	M
Applied Mathematics	M,D
Applied Statistics	M,D
Architecture	M
Art History	M
Art/Fine Arts	M
Biochemistry	M,D
Bioengineering	M,D
Biological and Biomedical Sciences—General	M,D
Business Administration and Management—General	M
Business Analytics	M
Cell Biology	M,D
Chemical Engineering	M,D
Chemistry	M,D
Civil Engineering	M,D
Cognitive Sciences	D
Comparative Literature	D

Computational Sciences	M,D
Computer Engineering	M,D
Computer Science	M,D
Conflict Resolution and Mediation/Peace Studies	M,D
Counseling Psychology	D
Developmental Psychology	D
Ecology	M,D
Economics	D
Education—General	M
Electrical Engineering	M,D
Engineering and Applied Sciences—General	M,D
English	M,D
Entrepreneurship	M
Environmental Engineering	M,D
Evolutionary Biology	M,D
Finance and Banking	M
French	M
Genetics	M,D
Geosciences	M,D
Graphic Design	M
History of Science and Technology	M,D
History	M,D
Industrial Design	M
Inorganic Chemistry	M,D
International Affairs	M
Investment Management	M
Italian	M
Latin American Studies	M
Law	M,D
Marketing	M
Mathematical and Computational Finance	M,D
Mathematics	M,D
Mechanical Engineering	M,D
Medieval and Renaissance Studies	M,D
Molecular Biology	M,D
Nonprofit Management	M
Organic Chemistry	M,D
Parasitology	M,D
Philosophy	D
Photography	M
Physical Chemistry	M,D
Physics	M,D
Physiology	M,D
Political Science	D
Psychology—General	D
Religion	M
Romance Languages	M
Sociology	D
Spanish	M
Statistics	M,D
Sustainable Development	M
Taxation	M
Theology	M,D
Writing	M

UNIVERSITY OF OKLAHOMA

Accounting	M
Adult Education	M,D
Aerospace/Aeronautical Engineering	M,D
American Indian/Native American Studies	M
Analytical Chemistry	M,D
Anthropology	M,D
Applied Arts and Design—General	M,D
Applied Behavior Analysis	M,D
Applied Economics	M,D
Archaeology	M,D
Archives/Archival Administration	M,D,O
Art History	M,D
Art/Fine Arts	M,D
Biochemistry	M,D
Business Administration and Management—General	M,D,O
Business Analytics	M,O
Chemistry	M,D
Civil Engineering	M,D
Clinical Psychology	M,O
Communication—General	M,D
Computer Engineering	M,D
Corporate and Organizational Communication	M,D
Criminal Justice and Criminology	M,O
Cultural Studies	M,D
Curriculum and Instruction	M,D
Dance	M
Early Childhood Education	M,D
Ecology	M,D
Economics	M,D
Education—General	M,D,O
Educational Leadership and Administration	M,D
Educational Media/Instructional Technology	M,D,O
Educational Psychology	M,D
Electrical Engineering	M,D
Elementary Education	M,D
Engineering Physics	M,D
English Education	M,D
English	M,D
Entrepreneurship	M,D,O
Environmental Engineering	M,D
Environmental Sciences	M,D
Evolutionary Biology	M,D
Exercise and Sports Science	M,D
Film, Television, and Video Theory and Criticism	M,D
Foreign Languages Education	M,D
French	M,D
Gender Studies	O
Geography	M,D
Geological Engineering	M,D,O
Geology	M,D
Geophysics	M,D
German	M,D
Health Communication	M,D
Health Promotion	M,D

Health Services Management and Hospital Administration	M,O
Higher Education	M,D
History of Science and Technology	M,D
History	M,D
Human Resources Management	M,D,O
Human Services	M,O
Information Studies	M,D,O
Inorganic Chemistry	M,D
International Affairs	M
Law	M,D
Library Science	M,D,O
Management Information Systems	M,D,O
Mass Communication	M,D
Mathematics Education	M,D
Mathematics	M,D*
Mechanical Engineering	M,D
Meteorology	M,D
Microbiology	M,D
Museum Studies	M,O
Music Education	M,D,O
Music	M,D,O
Neurobiology	M,D
Nonprofit Management	M,D,O
Organic Chemistry	M,D
Organizational Behavior	M,D,O
Organizational Management	M,O
Petroleum Engineering	M,D,O
Philosophy	M,D
Photography	M,D
Physical Chemistry	M,D
Physics	M,D
Plant Biology	M,D
Political Science	M,D
Project Management	M,D,O
Psychology—General	M,D,O
Public Administration	M,D
Public Policy	M,D
Reading Education	M,D
Rhetoric	M,D
Science Education	M,D
Social Sciences Education	M,D
Social Work	M
Sociology	M,D
Spanish	M,D
Special Education	M,D
Structural Biology	M,D
Sustainable Development	M,D
Telecommunications	M,D
Theater	M
Urban and Regional Planning	M,D
Women's Studies	O
Writing	M,D

UNIVERSITY OF OKLAHOMA HEALTH SCIENCES CENTER

Allied Health—General	M,D,O
Allopathic Medicine	D
Biochemistry	M,D
Biological and Biomedical Sciences—General	M,D
Biopsychology	M,D
Biostatistics	M,D
Cell Biology	M,D
Communication Disorders	M,D,O
Dentistry	D,O
Environmental and Occupational Health	M,D
Epidemiology	M,D
Genetic Counseling	M
Health Education	D
Health Physics/Radiological Health	M
Health Promotion	M,D
Health Services Management and Hospital Administration	M,D
Homeland Security	M
Immunology	M,D
Medical Physics	M,D
Microbiology	M,D
Molecular Biology	M,D
Neuroscience	M,D
Nursing—General	M
Nutrition	M
Occupational Therapy	M
Oral and Dental Sciences	M,D
Pathology	D
Pharmaceutical Sciences	M,D
Pharmacy	D
Physical Therapy	M
Physician Assistant Studies	M
Physiology	M,D
Public Health—General	M,D
Radiation Biology	M,D
Reading Education	M,D,O
Rehabilitation Sciences	M
Special Education	M,D,O

UNIVERSITY OF OREGON

Accounting	M,D
Anthropology	M,D
Applied Arts and Design—General	M
Architecture	M
Art History	M,D
Art/Fine Arts	M
Asian Languages	M,D
Asian Studies	M
Biochemistry	M,D
Biological and Biomedical Sciences—General	M,D
Biopsychology	M,D
Business Administration and Management—General	M,D
Chemistry	M,D
Chinese	M,D
Classics	M
Clinical Psychology	D
Cognitive Sciences	M,D
Communication Disorders	M,D
Communication—General	M,D
Comparative Literature	M,D

---

*M—masters degree; D—doctorate; O—other advanced degree; *—Close-Up and/or Display*

Computer Science — M,D
Counseling Psychology — M,D
Curriculum and Instruction — M,D
Dance — M
Developmental Psychology — M,D
Ecology — M,D
Economics — M,D
Education—General — M,D
Educational Leadership and Administration — M,D
English — M,D
Environmental Management and Policy — M,D
Evolutionary Biology — M,D
Finance and Banking — D
Folklore — M
French — M
Genetics — M,D
Geography — M,D
Geology — M,D
German — M,D
Historic Preservation — M
History — M,D
Information Science — M,D
Interdisciplinary Studies — M
Interior Design — M
International Affairs — M
Italian — M
Japanese — M,D
Journalism — M,D
Landscape Architecture — M
Law — M,D
Linguistics — M,D
Management Information Systems — M
Marine Biology — M,D
Marketing — D
Marriage and Family Therapy — M,D
Mathematics — M,D
Media Studies — M,D
Molecular Biology — M,D
Music Education — M,D
Music — M,D
Neuroscience — M,D
Nonprofit Management — M,O
Philosophy — M,D
Physics — M,D
Physiology — M,D
Political Science — M,D
Psychology—General — M,D
Public Administration — M
Quantitative Analysis — M
Romance Languages — M
Russian — M
School Psychology — M,D
Social Psychology — M,D
Sociology — M,D
Spanish — M,D
Special Education — M,D
Sports Management — M
Theater — M,D
Urban and Regional Planning — M
Writing — M

UNIVERSITY OF OTTAWA

Aerospace/Aeronautical Engineering — M,D
Allopathic Medicine — M,D
Anthropology — M
Biochemistry — M,D
Bioengineering — M,D
Biological and Biomedical Sciences—General — M,D
Biomedical Engineering — M
Business Administration and Management—General — M
Canadian Studies — D
Cell Biology — M,D
Chemical Engineering — M,D
Chemistry — M,D
Civil Engineering — M,D
Classics — M,D
Communication Disorders — M
Communication—General — M
Community Health — D,O
Computer Engineering — M,D
Computer Science — M,D
Criminal Justice and Criminology — M,D
Economics — M,D
Education—General — M,D,O
Electrical Engineering — M,D
Electronic Commerce — M,D,O
Engineering and Applied Sciences—General — M,D,O
Engineering Management — M,O
English — M,D
Epidemiology — M
Finance and Banking — D,O
French — M,D
Geography — M,D
Geosciences — M,D
Health Services Management and Hospital Administration — M
Health Services Research — D,O
History — M,D
Immunology — M,D
Information Science — M,O
Interdisciplinary Studies — D,O
International Development — M
Kinesiology and Movement Studies — M
Law — M,D
Linguistics — M,D
Mathematics — M,D
Mechanical Engineering — M,D
Microbiology — M,D
Molecular Biology — M,D
Music Education — M,O
Music — M,O
Nursing—General — M,D,O
Philosophy — M,D
Physics — M,D
Political Science — M,D
Project Management — M,O
Psychology—General — D
Public Administration — D,O

Public Health—General — D
Rehabilitation Sciences — M
Religion — M,D
Social Work — M
Sociology — M
Spanish — M,D
Statistics — M,D
Systems Science — M,D,O
Theater — M
Translation and Interpretation — M,D
Women's Studies — M

UNIVERSITY OF PENNSYLVANIA

Accounting — M
Acute Care/Critical Care Nursing — M
Adult Nursing — M
African Studies — M,D
Allopathic Medicine — D
Anthropology — M,D
Applied Economics — D
Applied Mathematics — D
Applied Psychology — M
Archaeology — M,D
Architecture — M,D,O
Art History — M,D
Art/Fine Arts — M,O
Artificial Intelligence/Robotics — M,D
Asian Studies — M,D
Biochemistry — D
Bioengineering — M,D
Bioethics — M
Biological and Biomedical Sciences—General — M,D
Biostatistics — M,D
Biotechnology — M
Business Administration and Management—General — M,D
Cancer Biology/Oncology — D
Cell Biology — D
Chemical Engineering — M,D
Chemistry — M,D
Classics — M,D
Clinical Laboratory Sciences/Medical Technology — M
Communication—General — D
Comparative Literature — M,D
Computational Biology — D
Computational Sciences — M,D
Computer Art and Design — M,D
Computer Science — M,D
Counseling Psychology — M
Counselor Education — M
Criminal Justice and Criminology — M,D
Data Science/Data Analytics — M
Demography and Population Studies — M,D
Dentistry — M,D
Developmental Biology — D
Economic Development — M,O
Economics — M,D
Education—General — M,D,O
Educational Leadership and Administration — M,D
Educational Measurement and Evaluation — M,D
Educational Media/Instructional Technology — M
Educational Policy — M,D
Electrical Engineering — M,D
Elementary Education — M
Engineering and Applied Sciences—General — M,D*
English as a Second Language — M
English Education — M,D
English — M
Entrepreneurship — M
Environmental and Occupational Health — M
Environmental Management and Policy — M
Environmental Sciences — M,D
Epidemiology — M
Ethics — M,D
Family Nurse Practitioner Studies — M,O
Finance and Banking — M,D
Foundations and Philosophy of Education — M,D
French — M,D
Game Design and Development — M,D
Genetics — D
Genomic Sciences — D
Geographic Information Systems — M,D,O
Geosciences — M,D
German — M,D
Gerontological Nursing — M
Graphic Design — M,O
Health Services Management and Hospital Administration — M,D
Health Services Research — M
Higher Education — M,D
Historic Preservation — M
History of Science and Technology — M,D
History — M,D
Human Development — M,D
Human Genetics — D
Immunology — D
Information Science — M,D
Insurance — M,D
International Affairs — M
International and Comparative Education — M
International Business — M
International Health — M
Internet and Interactive Multimedia — M,O
Italian — M,D
Landscape Architecture — M,D
Law — M,D
Legal and Justice Studies — M,D
Liberal Studies — M
Linguistics — M,D
Management Information Systems — M,D
Marketing — M,D
Materials Engineering — M,D

Materials Sciences — M,D
Maternal and Child/Neonatal Nursing — M
Mathematics — M,D
Mechanical Engineering — M,D
Mechanics — M,D
Medical Physics — M,D
Microbiology — D
Molecular Biology — D
Molecular Biophysics — D
Multilingual and Multicultural Education — M
Music — M,D
Nanotechnology — M,D
Near and Middle Eastern Studies — M,D
Neuroscience — D
Nonprofit Management — M,O
Nurse Anesthesia — M
Nurse Midwifery — M
Nursing and Healthcare Administration — M,D
Nursing—General — M,D,O
Organizational Management — M,O
Pediatric Nursing — M
Pharmacology — D
Philosophy — M,D
Physics — M,D
Physiology — D
Political Science — M,D,O
Psychiatric Nursing — M
Psychology—General — D
Public Administration — M,O
Public Health—General — M
Public Policy — M,D
Reading Education — M
Real Estate — M,D
Religion — D
Risk Management — M,D
Romance Languages — M,D
Science Education — M,O
Secondary Education — M
Social Work — M
Sociology — M,D
Spanish — M,D
Statistics — M,D
Systems Engineering — M,D
Urban and Regional Planning — M,D,O
Urban Design — M,D,O
Urban Education — M
Veterinary Medicine — D
Virology — D
Women's Health Nursing — M

UNIVERSITY OF PHILOSOPHICAL RESEARCH

Psychology—General — M
Theology — M

UNIVERSITY OF PHOENIX–BAY AREA CAMPUS

Accounting — M,D
Adult Education — M,D,O
Business Administration and Management—General — M,D
Criminal Justice and Criminology — M
Early Childhood Education — M,D,O
Education—General — M,D,O
Educational Leadership and Administration — M,D,O
Elementary Education — M,D,O
Energy Management and Policy — M,D
Gerontological Nursing — M,D
Health Services Management and Hospital Administration — M,D
Higher Education — M,D,O
Human Resources Management — M,D
International Business — M,D
Management Information Systems — M,D
Management of Technology — M,D
Marketing — M,D
Marriage and Family Therapy — M
Nursing and Healthcare Administration — M,D
Nursing Education — M,D
Nursing Informatics — M,D
Nursing—General — M,D
Organizational Management — M,D
Project Management — M,D
Public Administration — M,D
Secondary Education — M,D,O
Special Education — M,D,O

UNIVERSITY OF PHOENIX–CENTRAL VALLEY CAMPUS

Accounting — M
Business Administration and Management—General — M
Community Health — M
Computer Education — M
Curriculum and Instruction — M
Education—General — M
Elementary Education — M
Gerontology — M
Health Services Management and Hospital Administration — M
Human Resources Management — M
International Business — M
Management Information Systems — M
Management of Technology — M
Marketing — M
Marriage and Family Therapy — M
Nursing—General — M
Public Administration — M
Secondary Education — M

UNIVERSITY OF PHOENIX–DALLAS CAMPUS

Accounting — M
Business Administration and Management—General — M
Criminal Justice and Criminology — M
Curriculum and Instruction — M
Education—General — M
Electronic Commerce — M

Human Resources Management — M
International Business — M
Management Information Systems — M
Management of Technology — M
Marketing — M
Public Administration — M

UNIVERSITY OF PHOENIX–HAWAII CAMPUS

Accounting — M
Business Administration and Management—General — M
Community Health — M
Curriculum and Instruction — M
Education—General — M
Educational Leadership and Administration — M
Elementary Education — M
Family Nurse Practitioner Studies — M
Gerontology — M
Health Services Management and Hospital Administration — M
Human Resources Management — M
International Business — M
Management Information Systems — M
Management of Technology — M
Marketing — M
Nursing Education — M
Nursing—General — M
Public Administration — M
Secondary Education — M
Special Education — M

UNIVERSITY OF PHOENIX–HOUSTON CAMPUS

Accounting — M
Business Administration and Management—General — M
Curriculum and Instruction — M
Education—General — M
Electronic Commerce — M
Health Services Management and Hospital Administration — M
Human Resources Management — M
International Business — M
Management Information Systems — M
Management of Technology — M
Marketing — M
Nursing—General — M
Public Administration — M

UNIVERSITY OF PHOENIX–LAS VEGAS CAMPUS

Accounting — M
Allied Health—General — M
Business Administration and Management—General — M
Counseling Psychology — M
Counselor Education — M
Curriculum and Instruction — M
Education—General — M
Educational Leadership and Administration — M
Elementary Education — M
Human Resources Management — M
International Business — M
Management Information Systems — M
Management of Technology — M
Marketing — M
Marriage and Family Therapy — M
Public Administration — M
School Psychology — M

UNIVERSITY OF PHOENIX–ONLINE CAMPUS

Accounting — M,O
Adult Education — M,O
Business Administration and Management—General — M,D,O
Computer Education — M,O
Conflict Resolution and Mediation/Peace Studies — M,O
Criminal Justice and Criminology — M
Curriculum and Instruction — M,D,O
Early Childhood Education — M,O
Education—General — M,O
Educational Leadership and Administration — M,D,O
Educational Media/Instructional Technology — D,O
Elementary Education — M,O
Energy Management and Policy — M,O
English as a Second Language — M,O
English Education — M,O
Family Nurse Practitioner Studies — M,O
Health Education — M,O
Health Informatics — M,O
Health Services Management and Hospital Administration — M,D,O
Higher Education — D,O
Homeland Security — M
Human Resources Management — M,O
Industrial and Organizational Psychology — M,D,O
International Business — M,O
Management Information Systems — M
Management of Technology — M,O
Marketing — M,O
Mathematics Education — M,O
Middle School Education — M,O
Nursing Education — M,O
Nursing—General — M,D,O
Organizational Management — D,O
Project Management — M,O
Psychology—General — M,O
Public Administration — M,O
Reading Education — M,O
Science Education — M,O
Secondary Education — M,O
Special Education — M,O

UNIVERSITY OF PHOENIX–PHOENIX CAMPUS

Accounting — M,O

Adult Education	M
Business Administration and Management—General	M,O
Clinical Psychology	M
Counseling Psychology	M
Counselor Education	M
Criminal Justice and Criminology	M
Curriculum and Instruction	M
Early Childhood Education	M
Education—General	M
Educational Leadership and Administration	M
Elementary Education	M
Energy Management and Policy	M,O
Family Nurse Practitioner Studies	M,O
Gerontological Nursing	M,O
Health Services Management and Hospital Administration	M,O
Homeland Security	M
Human Resources Management	M,O
International Business	M,O
Management of Technology	M,O
Marketing	M,O
Marriage and Family Therapy	M
Medical Informatics	M,O
Nursing Education	M,O
Nursing Informatics	M,O
Nursing—General	M,O
Project Management	M,O
Psychology—General	M
Public Administration	M
Reading Education	M
Secondary Education	M
Social Psychology	M
Special Education	M
Vocational and Technical Education	M

UNIVERSITY OF PHOENIX–SACRAMENTO VALLEY CAMPUS

Accounting	M
Adult Education	M,O
Business Administration and Management—General	M
Curriculum and Instruction	M,O
Education—General	M,O
Elementary Education	M,O
Family Nurse Practitioner Studies	M
Health Services Management and Hospital Administration	M
Human Resources Management	M
International Business	M
Management Information Systems	M
Management of Technology	M
Marketing	M
Nursing Education	M
Nursing—General	M
Public Administration	M
Secondary Education	M,O

UNIVERSITY OF PHOENIX–SAN ANTONIO CAMPUS

Accounting	M
Business Administration and Management—General	M
Criminal Justice and Criminology	M
Curriculum and Instruction	M
Electronic Commerce	M
Health Services Management and Hospital Administration	M
Human Resources Management	M
International Business	M
Management Information Systems	M
Management of Technology	M
Marketing	M
Nursing—General	M
Public Administration	M

UNIVERSITY OF PHOENIX–SAN DIEGO CAMPUS

Accounting	M
Business Administration and Management—General	M
Computer Education	M
Curriculum and Instruction	M
Education—General	M
Elementary Education	M
English as a Second Language	M
Human Resources Management	M
International Business	M
Management Information Systems	M
Management of Technology	M
Marketing	M
Nursing Education	M
Nursing—General	M
Public Administration	M
Secondary Education	M

UNIVERSITY OF PIKEVILLE

Business Administration and Management—General	M
Education—General	M
Educational Leadership and Administration	M
Entrepreneurship	M
Health Services Management and Hospital Administration	M
Optometry	D
Osteopathic Medicine	D

UNIVERSITY OF PITTSBURGH

Accounting	M,D
African Studies	O
Allopathic Medicine	D
Anthropology	M,D
Applied Behavior Analysis	M,D
Applied Mathematics	M,D
Applied Psychology	M,D
Applied Statistics	M,D
Architectural History	M,D
Art History	M,D

Artificial Intelligence/Robotics	M,D
Asian Studies	M,O
Athletic Training and Sports Medicine	M
Bioengineering	M,D
Bioethics	M
Bioinformatics	M,D,O
Biological and Biomedical Sciences—General	M,D
Biostatistics	M,D
Business Administration and Management—General	M,D
Business Analytics	D
Cell Biology	D
Chemical Engineering	M,D
Chemistry	M,D
Chinese	M
Civil Engineering	M,D
Clinical Laboratory Sciences/Medical Technology	D
Clinical Psychology	M,D
Clinical Research	M,D
Communication Disorders	M,D
Communication—General	M,D,O
Community Health	M
Computational Biology	D
Computational Sciences	M,D,O
Computer Engineering	M,D
Computer Science	M,D
Criminal Justice and Criminology	M
Cultural Studies	O
Data Science/Data Analytics	M,D,O
Dentistry	M,D,O
Developmental Biology	D
Developmental Psychology	M,D
Disability Studies	O
Early Childhood Education	M
East European and Russian Studies	O
Ecology	D
Economics	M,D
Education—General	M,D
Educational Leadership and Administration	M,D
Educational Measurement and Evaluation	M,D
Educational Policy	D
Electrical Engineering	M,D
Elementary Education	M
Energy Management and Policy	M
Engineering and Applied Sciences—General	M,D
English as a Second Language	D,O
English Education	M
English	M,D
Environmental and Occupational Health	M,D
Environmental Engineering	M
Environmental Law	M
Environmental Sciences	M
Epidemiology	M,D
Evolutionary Biology	D
Exercise and Sports Science	M,D
Film, Television, and Video Theory and Criticism	M,D,O
Finance and Banking	M,D
Foreign Languages Education	M,D
Foundations and Philosophy of Education	M,D
French	M,D,O
Genetic Counseling	M,D,O
Geographic Information Systems	M,D
Geology	M,D
Gerontological Nursing	D
Health Education	M,D
Health Informatics	M
Health Law	M
Health Psychology	D
Health Services Management and Hospital Administration	M,D,O
Health Services Research	M
Higher Education	M,D
History of Science and Technology	D
History	M,D
Human Genetics	M,D,O
Human Resources Management	M,D
Immunology	D
Industrial and Manufacturing Management	M
Industrial/Management Engineering	M,D
Infectious Diseases	M,D
Information Science	M,D,O
Intellectual Property Law	M
Interdisciplinary Studies	D
International Affairs	M,D,O
International and Comparative Education	M,D
International Business	O
International Development	M
International Health	M,D,O
Italian	M
Japanese	M
Latin American Studies	O
Law	M
Legal and Justice Studies	M,D
Library Science	M,D
Linguistics	M,D
Management Information Systems	M,D
Management Strategy and Policy	M,D
Marketing	M,D
Materials Sciences	M,D
Mathematics Education	M,D
Mathematics	M,D
Mechanical Engineering	M,D
Medieval and Renaissance Studies	O
Microbiology	M,D
Military and Defense Studies	M,D
Modeling and Simulation	M,D
Molecular Biology	D
Molecular Biophysics	D

Molecular Genetics	D
Molecular Pathology	D
Molecular Pharmacology	D
Molecular Physiology	D
Music	M,D
Neuroscience	D
Nonprofit Management	M
Nutrition	M,D
Occupational Therapy	M,D
Oral and Dental Sciences	M,D,O
Organizational Behavior	M,D
Pathology	D
Petroleum Engineering	M
Pharmaceutical Administration	M
Pharmaceutical Sciences	M,D
Pharmacy	D
Philosophy	D
Physical Therapy	M,D
Physician Assistant Studies	M
Physics	M,D*
Political Science	D
Psychology—General	D
Public Administration	M
Public Health—General	M,D,O
Public Policy	M,D
Reading Education	M,D
Rehabilitation Counseling	M,D
Rehabilitation Sciences	M,D
Science Education	M,D
Secondary Education	M
Slavic Languages	M,D
Social Psychology	D
Social Sciences Education	M,D
Social Work	M,D,O
Sociology	M,D
Spanish	D
Special Education	M,D
Statistics	M,D
Structural Biology	D
Supply Chain Management	M
Systems Biology	D
Theater	M,D
Urban and Regional Planning	M
Vision Sciences	M,D
Western European Studies	O
Women's Studies	O
Writing	M,D

UNIVERSITY OF PORTLAND

Biomedical Engineering	M
Business Administration and Management—General	M
Civil Engineering	M
Communication—General	M
Computer Science	M
Corporate and Organizational Communication	M
Education—General	M,D
Educational Leadership and Administration	M,D
Electrical Engineering	M
Engineering and Applied Sciences—General	M
English as a Second Language	M,D
Entrepreneurship	M
Family Nurse Practitioner Studies	M,D
Finance and Banking	M
Health Services Management and Hospital Administration	M
Industrial and Manufacturing Management	M
Management of Technology	M
Marketing	M
Mechanical Engineering	M
Nonprofit Management	M
Nursing Education	M,D
Nursing—General	M,D
Organizational Management	M,D
Reading Education	M,D
Special Education	M,D
Sustainability Management	M

UNIVERSITY OF PRINCE EDWARD ISLAND

Anatomy	M,D
Bacteriology	M,D
Biological and Biomedical Sciences—General	M,D
Chemistry	M,D
Education—General	M,D
Educational Leadership and Administration	M,D
Environmental Sciences	M,D
Epidemiology	M,D
Geography	M,D
Immunology	M,D
Parasitology	M,D
Pathology	M,D
Pharmacology	M,D
Physiology	M,D
Toxicology	M,D
Veterinary Medicine	D
Veterinary Sciences	M,D
Virology	M,D

UNIVERSITY OF PROVIDENCE

Counseling Psychology	M
Criminal Justice and Criminology	M
Human Services	M

UNIVERSITY OF PUERTO RICO–MAYAGÜEZ

Aerospace/Aeronautical Engineering	M,D
Agricultural Economics and Agribusiness	M
Agricultural Sciences—General	M
Agronomy and Soil Sciences	M
Animal Sciences	M
Applied Mathematics	M

Bioengineering	M,D
Biological and Biomedical Sciences—General	M
Business Administration and Management—General	M
Chemical Engineering	M,D
Chemistry	M,D
Civil Engineering	M,D
Computational Sciences	M,D
Computer Engineering	M,D
Computer Science	M,D
Construction Engineering	M,D
Electrical Engineering	M,D
Energy and Power Engineering	M,D
Engineering and Applied Sciences—General	M,D
Engineering Management	M,D
English Education	M
English	M
Environmental Engineering	M,D
Environmental Sciences	M,D
Exercise and Sports Science	M
Finance and Banking	M
Food Science and Technology	M
Geology	M
Geotechnical Engineering	M,D
Higher Education	M
Hispanic Studies	M
Horticulture	M
Human Resources Management	M
Industrial and Manufacturing Management	M
Industrial/Management Engineering	M
Information Science	M,D
Kinesiology and Movement Studies	M,D
Manufacturing Engineering	M,D
Marine Sciences	M,D
Materials Engineering	M,D
Materials Sciences	M,D
Mathematics Education	M
Mathematics	M
Mechanical Engineering	M,D
Physical Chemistry	M,D
Physics	M
Rural Sociology	M
Structural Engineering	M,D
Transportation and Highway Engineering	M,D

UNIVERSITY OF PUERTO RICO–MEDICAL SCIENCES CAMPUS

Acute Care/Critical Care Nursing	M
Adult Nursing	M
Allied Health—General	M,D,O
Allopathic Medicine	D
Anatomy	M,D
Biochemistry	M,D
Biological and Biomedical Sciences—General	M,D
Biostatistics	M
Clinical Laboratory Sciences/Medical Technology	M,O
Clinical Research	M,O
Communication Disorders	M,D
Community Health Nursing	M
Demography and Population Studies	M
Dentistry	D
Environmental and Occupational Health	M,D
Epidemiology	M
Family Nurse Practitioner Studies	M
Gerontological Nursing	M
Gerontology	M,O
Health Education	M
Health Informatics	M
Health Promotion	O
Health Services Management and Hospital Administration	M
Health Services Research	M
Industrial Hygiene	M
Maternal and Child Health	M
Maternal and Child/Neonatal Nursing	M
Microbiology	M,D
Nurse Midwifery	M,O
Nursing—General	M
Nutrition	M,D,O
Occupational Therapy	M
Oral and Dental Sciences	O
Pediatric Nursing	M
Pharmaceutical Sciences	M,D
Pharmacology	M,D
Pharmacy	M,D
Physical Therapy	M
Physiology	M,D
Psychiatric Nursing	M
Special Education	O
Toxicology	M,D

UNIVERSITY OF PUERTO RICO–RÍO PIEDRAS

Accounting	M,D
Architecture	M
Biological and Biomedical Sciences—General	M,D
Business Administration and Management—General	M,D
Cell Biology	M,D
Chemistry	M,D
Clinical Psychology	M,D
Communication—General	M
Comparative Literature	M
Counselor Education	M
Curriculum and Instruction	M,D
Early Childhood Education	M
Ecology	M,D
Economic Development	M
Economics	M

Education—General | M,D
Educational Leadership and Administration | M,D
Educational Measurement and Evaluation | M
English as a Second Language | M
English | M,D
Environmental Management and Policy | M
Environmental Sciences | M,D
Evolutionary Biology | M,D
Exercise and Sports Science | M
Family and Consumer Sciences-General | M
Finance and Banking | M,D
Foreign Languages Education | M,D
Genetics | M,D
Hispanic Studies | M,D
History | M,D
Human Resources Management | M,D
Industrial and Manufacturing Management | M,D
Industrial and Organizational Psychology | M,D
Information Science | M,O
Information Studies | M,O
International Business | M,D
Journalism | M
Law | M,D
Library Science | M,O
Linguistics | M,D
Marketing | M,D
Mass Communication | M
Mathematics Education | M,D
Mathematics | M,D
Molecular Biology | M,D
Neuroscience | M,D
Nutrition | M
Philosophy | M
Physics | M,D
Psychology—General | M,D
Public Administration | M
Public Policy | M
Quantitative Analysis | M
Rehabilitation Counseling | M
Science Education | M,D
Social Psychology | M,D
Social Sciences Education | M,D
Social Work | M,D
Sociology | M
Special Education | M
Translation and Interpretation | M,O
Urban and Regional Planning | M

UNIVERSITY OF PUGET SOUND
Counseling Psychology | M
Counselor Education | M
Education—General | M
Elementary Education | M
Occupational Therapy | M,D
Physical Therapy | D
Secondary Education | M

UNIVERSITY OF REDLANDS
Business Administration and Management—General | M
Communication Disorders | M
Education—General | M,D,O
Geographic Information Systems | M
Management Information Systems | M
Music | M

UNIVERSITY OF REGINA
Adult Education | M
Analytical Chemistry | M,D
Anthropology | M
Applied Psychology | M,D
Art/Fine Arts | M
Biochemistry | M,D
Biological and Biomedical Sciences—General | M,D
Biophysics | M,D
Business Administration and Management—General | M,O
Cancer Biology/Oncology | M,D
Chemistry | M,D
Clinical Psychology | M,D
Computer Engineering | M,D
Computer Science | M,D
Criminal Justice and Criminology | M
Curriculum and Instruction | M
Economics | M,D,O
Education—General | M,D,O
Educational Leadership and Administration | M
Educational Psychology | M
Engineering and Applied Sciences—General | M,D
Engineering Management | M,O
English | M,D
Environmental Engineering | M,D
Experimental Psychology | M,D
Film, Television, and Video Production | M
French | M
Geography | M,D
Geology | M,D
Gerontology | M
Health Services Management and Hospital Administration | M,D,O
History | M
Human Resources Development | M
Human Resources Management | M,O
Industrial/Management Engineering | M,D
Inorganic Chemistry | M,D
Interdisciplinary Studies | M
International Business | M,O
Journalism | M,D
Kinesiology and Movement Studies | M,D
Mathematics | M
Music | M
Nursing—General | M
Organic Chemistry | M,D
Organizational Management | M,O

Petroleum Engineering | M,D
Philosophy | M
Physics | M,D
Project Management | M,O
Psychology—General | M,D,O
Public Administration | M,D,O
Public Policy | M,D,O
Religion | M
Social Sciences | M
Social Work | M,D
Sociology | M
Software Engineering | M,D
Statistics | M,D
Systems Engineering | M,D
Theoretical Chemistry | M,D
Women's Studies | M
Writing | M,D

UNIVERSITY OF RHODE ISLAND
Accounting | M
Acute Care/Critical Care Nursing | M,D,O
Adult Nursing | M,D,O
Animal Sciences | M,D
Anthropology | M
Applied Mathematics | M,D
Aquaculture | M,D
Archaeology | M
Biochemistry | M,D
Biological and Biomedical Sciences—General | M,D
Biomedical Engineering | M,D
Biotechnology | M,D
Business Administration and Management—General | M,D
Cell Biology | M,D
Chemical Engineering | M,D,O
Chemistry | M,D
Child and Family Studies | M,D
Civil Engineering | M,D
Clinical Laboratory Sciences/Medical Technology | M,D
Clinical Psychology | M,D
Clothing and Textiles | M,O
Communication Disorders | M
Communication—General | M
Computer and Information Systems Security | M,D,O
Computer Art and Design | M
Computer Engineering | M,D
Computer Science | M,D,O
Counseling Psychology | M
Ecology | M,D
Economics | M,D
Education—General | M,D
Electrical Engineering | M,D
Engineering and Applied Sciences—General | M,D,O
English | M,D
Entrepreneurship | M,D,O
Environmental Engineering | M,D
Environmental Management and Policy | M,D
Environmental Sciences | M,D
Evolutionary Biology | M,D
Exercise and Sports Science | M
Family Nurse Practitioner Studies | M,D,O
Film, Television, and Video Production | M,D
Finance and Banking | M,D
Fish, Game, and Wildlife Management | M,D
Food Science and Technology | M,D
Forensic Sciences | M,D,O
Gender Studies | M,D,O
Geophysics | M,D
Geosciences | M,D,O
Geotechnical Engineering | M,D
Gerontological Nursing | M,D,O
Health Education | M
Health Services Management and Hospital Administration | M,D,O
History | M
Human Development | M
Human Resources Management | M,O
Hydrology | M,D,O
Industrial and Labor Relations | M,O
Industrial/Management Engineering | M,D
Information Studies | M
Library Science | M
Management Strategy and Policy | M,D,O
Marine Affairs | M,D
Marine Biology | M,D
Marine Geology | M,D
Marine Sciences | M,D
Marketing | M,D
Marriage and Family Therapy | M
Mathematics | M,D
Medical Physics | M,D
Medicinal and Pharmaceutical Chemistry | M,D
Microbiology | M,D
Molecular Biology | M,D
Molecular Genetics | M,D
Music Education | M
Music | M
Natural Resources | M,D
Nursing Education | M,D,O
Nursing—General | M,D,O
Nutrition | M
Ocean Engineering | M,D
Oceanography | M,D
Pharmaceutical Sciences | M,D
Pharmacology | M,D
Pharmacy | D
Physical Education | M
Physical Therapy | D
Physics | M,D
Political Science | M
Psychology—General | M,D
Public Administration | M
Public Policy | M
Reading Education | M,D

Recreation and Park Management | M
School Psychology | M,D
Spanish | M
Special Education | M,D
Sport Psychology | M
Statistics | M,D,O
Student Affairs | M
Supply Chain Management | M,D
Systems Engineering | M,D
Toxicology | M,D
Women's Studies | O
Writing | M,D

UNIVERSITY OF RICHMOND
Business Administration and Management—General | M
Law | D

UNIVERSITY OF RIO GRANDE
Art Education | M
Education—General | M
Educational Leadership and Administration | M
Physical Education | M
Special Education | M

UNIVERSITY OF ROCHESTER
Accounting | M,D
Acute Care/Critical Care Nursing | M,D
Adult Nursing | M,D
Allopathic Medicine | D
Anatomy | D
Archives/Archival Administration | M
Art History | D
Art/Fine Arts | D
Artificial Intelligence/Robotics | M,D
Astronomy | D
Biochemistry | D
Bioinformatics | M,D
Biological and Biomedical Sciences—General | M,D
Biomedical Engineering | M,D
Biophysics | D
Biostatistics | M
Business Administration and Management—General | M,D
Chemical Engineering | M,D*
Chemistry | M,D
Clinical Psychology | D
Clinical Research | M
Cognitive Sciences | D
Computational Biology | M,D
Computer Engineering | M,D
Computer Science | M,D
Counselor Education | M,D
Curriculum and Instruction | M,D
Data Science/Data Analytics | M
Developmental Psychology | D
Ecology | M,D
Economics | D
Education—General | M,D
Educational Leadership and Administration | M,D
Educational Policy | M,D
Electrical Engineering | M,D
Engineering and Applied Sciences—General | M,D
English | M,D
Entrepreneurship | M
Epidemiology | D
Family Nurse Practitioner Studies | M,D
Finance and Banking | M,D
Foundations and Philosophy of Education | D
Genetics | M,D
Genomic Sciences | D
Geology | M,D
Geosciences | M,D
Gerontological Nursing | M,D
Health Services Management and Hospital Administration | M,D
Health Services Research | D
Higher Education | M,D
Historic Preservation | M
History | M,D
Human Development | M,D
Human-Computer Interaction | M,D
Immunology | M,D
Industrial and Manufacturing Management | D
Inorganic Chemistry | D
Linguistics | M
Management Information Systems | M,D
Management Strategy and Policy | M
Marketing Research | M
Marketing | M,D
Marriage and Family Therapy | M
Materials Sciences | M,D
Maternal and Child/Neonatal Nursing | M,D
Mathematics | D
Mechanical Engineering | M,D
Microbiology | M,D
Molecular Biology | M,D
Music Education | M,D
Music | M,D
Neurobiology | D
Neuroscience | D
Nursing and Healthcare Administration | M,D
Nursing Education | M,D
Nursing—General | M,D
Optical Sciences | M,D
Oral and Dental Sciences | M,D
Organic Chemistry | D
Pathology | D
Pediatric Nursing | M,D
Pharmacology | M,D
Philosophy | D
Photography | M
Physical Chemistry | D
Physics | M,D
Physiology | M,D
Political Science | D
Psychiatric Nursing | M,D

Psychology—General | D
Public Health—General | M
Social Psychology | M,D
Statistics | M,D
Structural Biology | D
Student Affairs | M
Toxicology | D
Translation and Interpretation | M,O

UNIVERSITY OF ST. AUGUSTINE FOR HEALTH SCIENCES
Athletic Training and Sports Medicine | M
Health Education | M,D
Health Informatics | M
Health Services Management and Hospital Administration | M
Nursing and Healthcare Administration | M
Nursing Education | M
Nursing Informatics | M
Nursing—General | M,D
Occupational Therapy | M
Physical Therapy | D

UNIVERSITY OF ST. FRANCIS (IL)
Accounting | M
Art Education | M,D,O
Business Administration and Management—General | M,O
Business Analytics | M,O
Curriculum and Instruction | M,D,O
Education—General | M,D,O
Educational Leadership and Administration | M,D,O
Elementary Education | M,D,O
English as a Second Language | M,D,O
English Education | M,D,O
Family Nurse Practitioner Studies | M,D,O
Finance and Banking | M,O
Forensic Sciences | M,O
Health Services Management and Hospital Administration | M,O
Human Resources Management | M,O
Logistics | M,O
Mathematics Education | M,D,O
Nursing and Healthcare Administration | M,D,O
Nursing Education | M,D,O
Nursing—General | M,D,O
Physician Assistant Studies | M
Psychiatric Nursing | M,D,O
Reading Education | M,D,O
Science Education | M,D,O
Secondary Education | M,D,O
Social Sciences Education | M,D,O
Social Work | M,O
Special Education | M,D,O
Supply Chain Management | M,O

UNIVERSITY OF SAINT FRANCIS (IN)
Art/Fine Arts | M
Business Administration and Management—General | M
Clinical Psychology | M,O
Counseling Psychology | M,O
Counselor Education | M,O
Education—General | M
Environmental and Occupational Health | M
Family Nurse Practitioner Studies | M,D,O
Health Services Management and Hospital Administration | M
Nurse Anesthesia | M,D,O
Nursing—General | M,D,O
Organizational Management | M
Physician Assistant Studies | M
Secondary Education | M
Special Education | M
Sustainability Management | M

UNIVERSITY OF SAINT JOSEPH
Biochemistry | M
Biological and Biomedical Sciences—General | M
Business Administration and Management—General | M
Chemistry | M
Clinical Psychology | M
Counseling Psychology | M
Counselor Education | M
Curriculum and Instruction | M
Education—General | M
Educational Media/Instructional Technology | M
Elementary Education | M
English as a Second Language | M
Family Nurse Practitioner Studies | M,D
Marriage and Family Therapy | M
Nursing Education | M,D
Nursing—General | M,D
Nutrition | M
Pharmacy | D
Psychiatric Nursing | M,D
Public Health—General | M
Reading Education | M
Secondary Education | M
Social Work | M
Special Education | M,O

UNIVERSITY OF SAINT MARY
Advertising and Public Relations | M
Business Administration and Management—General | M
Counseling Psychology | M
Education—General | M
Elementary Education | M
Finance and Banking | M
Health Services Management and Hospital Administration | M
Human Resources Management | M
Marketing | M
Nursing and Healthcare Administration | M
Nursing Education | M
Nursing—General | M

Physical Therapy	D
Psychology—General	M
Risk Management	M
Special Education	M

UNIVERSITY OF SAINT MARY OF THE LAKE–MUNDELEIN SEMINARY
Pastoral Ministry and Counseling	M,D
Theology	M,D

UNIVERSITY OF ST. MICHAEL'S COLLEGE
Jewish Studies	M,D,O
Pastoral Ministry and Counseling	M,D,O
Religious Education	M,D,O
Theology	M,D,O

UNIVERSITY OF ST. THOMAS (MN)
Accounting	M
Art History	M,O
Business Administration and Management—General	M
Business Analytics	M
Counseling Psychology	M,D
Data Science/Data Analytics	M,O
Education—General	M,D,O
Educational Leadership and Administration	M,D,O
Electrical Engineering	M,O
Engineering and Applied Sciences—General	M,O
Engineering Management	M,O
English	M,D
Ethics	M,D
Health Communication	M
Health Services Management and Hospital Administration	M
Human Development	D
Information Science	M,O
Law	M
Management of Technology	M,O
Manufacturing Engineering	M,O
Mechanical Engineering	M,O
Museum Studies	M,O
Music Education	M,D
Music	M,D
Organizational Management	D
Pastoral Ministry and Counseling	M
Religion	M
Religious Education	M
Social Work	M
Software Engineering	M
Special Education	M,O
Student Affairs	M,D,O
Systems Engineering	M,O
Theology	M

UNIVERSITY OF ST. THOMAS (TX)
Accounting	M
Business Administration and Management—General	M
Counselor Education	M,D
Curriculum and Instruction	M,D
Education—General	M,D
Educational Leadership and Administration	M,D
Educational Measurement and Evaluation	M,D
Elementary Education	M,D
English as a Second Language	M,D
Finance and Banking	M
International Business	M
Liberal Studies	M
Multilingual and Multicultural Education	M,D
Music	M
Pastoral Ministry and Counseling	M
Philosophy	M,D
Public Administration	M
Public Policy	M
Reading Education	M,D
Religion	M
Religious Education	M,D
Secondary Education	M,D
Special Education	M,D
Theology	M

UNIVERSITY OF SAN DIEGO
Adult Nursing	M,D
Business Administration and Management—General	M
Computer and Information Systems Security	M
Computer Engineering	M
Conflict Resolution and Mediation/Peace Studies	M
Counseling Psychology	M
Counselor Education	M
Criminal Justice and Criminology	M
Curriculum and Instruction	M
Education—General	M,D,O
Educational Leadership and Administration	M,D,O
English as a Second Language	M
Environmental Sciences	M
Family Nurse Practitioner Studies	M,D
Gerontological Nursing	M,D
Health Informatics	M,D
Higher Education	M,D,O
International Affairs	M
Law	M,D,O
Legal and Justice Studies	M,D,O
Marriage and Family Therapy	M
Mathematics	M
Nonprofit Management	M,D,O
Nursing and Healthcare Administration	M,D
Nursing—General	M,D
Oceanography	M,D
Pediatric Nursing	M,D
Psychiatric Nursing	M,D
Reading Education	M

Real Estate	M
School Psychology	M
Science Education	M
Special Education	M
Taxation	M,D,O
Theater	M

UNIVERSITY OF SAN FRANCISCO
Asian Studies	M
Biological and Biomedical Sciences—General	M
Biotechnology	M
Business Administration and Management—General	M
Chemistry	M
Clinical Psychology	D
Communication—General	M
Computer Science	M
Counseling Psychology	M
Counselor Education	M
Curriculum and Instruction	M,D
Data Science/Data Analytics	M
Economics	M,D
Education—General	M,D
Educational Leadership and Administration	M,D
Educational Media/Instructional Technology	M,D
Energy Management and Policy	M
Entrepreneurship	M
Finance and Banking	M
Health Informatics	M
Health Services Management and Hospital Administration	M
Intellectual Property Law	M
International Affairs	M
International and Comparative Education	M,D
International Business	M
International Development	M
Law	D
Management Information Systems	M
Marketing	M
Marriage and Family Therapy	M
Multilingual and Multicultural Education	M,D
Museum Studies	M
Natural Resources	M
Nonprofit Management	M
Nursing—General	D
Organizational Management	M
Pacific Area/Pacific Rim Studies	M
Public Administration	M
Public Health—General	M
Reading Education	M,D
Religious Education	M,D
Special Education	M,D
Sports Management	M
Urban Education	M
Urban Studies	M
Writing	M

UNIVERSITY OF SASKATCHEWAN
Accounting	M
Agricultural Economics and Agribusiness	M,D,O
Agricultural Sciences—General	M,D,O
Agronomy and Soil Sciences	M,D
Allopathic Medicine	D
Anatomy	M,D
Animal Sciences	M,D
Anthropology	M
Archaeology	M
Art/Fine Arts	M
Biochemistry	M,D
Bioengineering	M,D
Biological and Biomedical Sciences—General	M,D
Biomedical Engineering	M,D,O
Business Administration and Management—General	M,D
Canadian Studies	M
Cell Biology	M,D
Chemical Engineering	M,D
Chemistry	M,D
Civil Engineering	M,D
Community Health	M
Computer Science	M,D
Counseling Psychology	M
Cultural Studies	M
Curriculum and Instruction	M,D,O
Dentistry	D
Economics	M,O
Education—General	M,D,O
Educational Leadership and Administration	M,D,O
Educational Measurement and Evaluation	M,D
Educational Psychology	M,D,O
Electrical Engineering	M,D,O
Engineering and Applied Sciences—General	M,D,O
Engineering Physics	M,D
English as a Second Language	M,D
English	M,D
Environmental Sciences	M,D
Epidemiology	M,D
Finance and Banking	M,D
Food Science and Technology	M,D
Foundations and Philosophy of Education	M,D,O
French	M
Geography	M,D
Geological Engineering	M,D
Geology	M,D,O
History	M,D
Immunology	M,D
Kinesiology and Movement Studies	M,D

Law	M,D
Linguistics	M
Marketing	M
Mathematics	M,D
Mechanical Engineering	M,D
Microbiology	M,D
Music	M
Nursing—General	M,D
Nutrition	M,D
Pathology	M,D
Pharmacology	M,D
Pharmacy	M,D
Philosophy	M
Physics	M,D
Physiology	M,D
Plant Sciences	M,D
Political Science	M
Psychology—General	M,D
Public Policy	M,D
Religion	M
Reproductive Biology	M,D
School Psychology	M,D
Sociology	M,D
Special Education	M,D
Statistics	M,D
Sustainability Management	M,D
Theater	M,D
Toxicology	M,D,O
Veterinary Medicine	M,D
Veterinary Sciences	M,D

THE UNIVERSITY OF SCRANTON
Accounting	M
Art/Fine Arts	M
Biochemistry	M
Business Administration and Management—General	M
Chemistry	M
Clinical Psychology	M
Counseling Psychology	M
Counselor Education	M
Curriculum and Instruction	M
Education—General	M
Educational Leadership and Administration	M
Family Nurse Practitioner Studies	M,D,O
Finance and Banking	M
Health Services Management and Hospital Administration	M
Human Resources Development	M
International Business	M
Management Information Systems	M
Marketing	M
Nurse Anesthesia	M,D,O
Nursing and Healthcare Administration	M,D,O
Nursing—General	M,D,O
Occupational Therapy	M
Physical Therapy	D
Reading Education	M
Rehabilitation Counseling	M
Secondary Education	M
Software Engineering	M
Special Education	M
Theology	M

UNIVERSITY OF SIOUX FALLS
Business Administration and Management—General	M
Education—General	M,O
Educational Leadership and Administration	M,O
Educational Media/Instructional Technology	M,O
Entrepreneurship	M
Health Services Management and Hospital Administration	M
Marketing	M
Reading Education	M,O

UNIVERSITY OF SOUTH AFRICA
Accounting	M,D
Acute Care/Critical Care Nursing	M,D
Adult Education	M,D
Agricultural Sciences—General	M,D
Anthropology	M,D
Archaeology	M,D
Art History	M,D
Business Administration and Management—General	M,D
Chemical Engineering	M
Classics	M,D
Clinical Psychology	M,D
Communication—General	M,D
Counseling Psychology	M,D
Counselor Education	M,D
Criminal Justice and Criminology	M,D
Curriculum and Instruction	M,D
Economics	M,D
Education—General	M,D
Educational Leadership and Administration	M,D
Educational Media/Instructional Technology	M,D
Educational Psychology	M,D
Engineering and Applied Sciences—General	M
English as a Second Language	M,D
English	M,D
Environmental Education	M,D
Environmental Management and Policy	M,D
Environmental Sciences	M,D
Ethics	M,D
Family and Consumer Sciences—General	M,D
Foundations and Philosophy of Education	M,D
French	M,D
Geography	M,D
German	M,D

Health Education	M,D
Health Services Management and Hospital Administration	M,D
History	M,D
Horticulture	M,D
Human Development	M,D
Human Resources Development	M,D
Industrial and Organizational Psychology	M,D
Information Science	M,D
International and Comparative Education	M,D
Italian	M,D
Law	M,D
Linguistics	M,D
Logistics	M,D
Management Information Systems	M
Marketing	M,D
Maternal and Child/Neonatal Nursing	M,D
Mathematics Education	M,D
Medical/Surgical Nursing	M,D
Missions and Missiology	M,D
Music	M,D
Natural Resources	M,D
Near and Middle Eastern Languages	M,D
Near and Middle Eastern Studies	M,D
Nurse Midwifery	M,D
Pastoral Ministry and Counseling	M,D
Philosophy	M,D
Political Science	M,D
Portuguese	M,D
Psychology—General	M,D
Public Administration	M,D
Public Health—General	M,D
Quantitative Analysis	M,D
Real Estate	M,D
Religion	M,D
Romance Languages	M,D
Russian	M,D
Science Education	M,D
Social Work	M,D
Sociology	M,D
Spanish	M,D
Statistics	M,D
Technology and Public Policy	M,D
Telecommunications Management	M,D
Theology	M,D
Travel and Tourism	M,D
Vocational and Technical Education	M,D

UNIVERSITY OF SOUTH ALABAMA
Accounting	M
Allied Health—General	M,D
Allopathic Medicine	D
Art Education	M,D
Art/Fine Arts	M
Biological and Biomedical Sciences—General	M,D
Business Administration and Management—General	M,D
Chemical Engineering	M
Chemistry	M
Civil Engineering	M
Clinical Psychology	M,D,O
Communication Disorders	M,D
Communication—General	M
Computer Engineering	M
Computer Science	M,D
Counseling Psychology	M,D,O
Counselor Education	M,D,O
Early Childhood Education	M,D
Education—General	M,D,O
Educational Leadership and Administration	M,D
Educational Media/Instructional Technology	M,D,O
Electrical Engineering	M
Elementary Education	M,D
Engineering and Applied Sciences—General	M,D
English	M
Environmental and Occupational Health	M
Environmental Engineering	M
Environmental Management and Policy	M,D
Exercise and Sports Science	M
Health Education	M
History	M
Kinesiology and Movement Studies	M
Management Information Systems	M,D
Marine Sciences	M,D
Marketing	M,D
Mathematics	M
Mechanical Engineering	M
Music Education	M
Music	M
Nursing and Healthcare Administration	M,D,O
Nursing Education	M,D,O
Nursing—General	M,D,O
Occupational Therapy	M
Physical Education	M
Physical Therapy	D
Physician Assistant Studies	M
Psychology—General	M
Public Administration	M
Reading Education	M,D
Science Education	M,D
Secondary Education	M,D
Sociology	M
Special Education	M,D
Sports Management	M
Systems Engineering	D
Toxicology	M
Writing	M

UNIVERSITY OF SOUTH CAROLINA
Accounting	M

*M—masters degree; D—doctorate; O—other advanced degree; *—Close-Up and/or Display*

Acute Care/Critical Care Nursing	M,O
Adult Nursing	M
Allopathic Medicine	D
Anthropology	M,D
Applied Statistics	M,D,O
Archives/Archival Administration	M,O
Art Education	M,D
Art History	M
Art/Fine Arts	M
Astronomy	M,D
Biochemistry	M,D
Biological and Biomedical Sciences—General	M,D,O
Biostatistics	M,D
Business Administration and Management—General	M,D
Business Education	M,D
Cell Biology	M,D
Chemical Engineering	M,D
Chemistry	M,D
Civil Engineering	M,D
Clinical Psychology	M,D
Communication Disorders	M,D
Community Health Nursing	M
Comparative Literature	M,D
Computer Engineering	M,D
Computer Science	M,D
Consumer Economics	M
Counselor Education	D,O
Criminal Justice and Criminology	M,D
Curriculum and Instruction	D
Developmental Biology	M,D
Early Childhood Education	M,D
Ecology	M,D
Economics	M,D
Education—General	M,D,O
Educational Leadership and Administration	M,D,O
Educational Measurement and Evaluation	M,D
Educational Media/Instructional Technology	M
Educational Psychology	M,D
Electrical Engineering	M,D
Elementary Education	M,D
Engineering and Applied Sciences—General	M,D
English as a Second Language	M,D,O
English Education	M,D
English	M,D
Entertainment Management	M
Environmental and Occupational Health	M,D
Environmental Management and Policy	M
Epidemiology	M,D
Evolutionary Biology	M,D
Exercise and Sports Science	M,D
Experimental Psychology	M,D
Family Nurse Practitioner Studies	M
Foreign Languages Education	M,D
Foundations and Philosophy of Education	D
French	M,D
Genetic Counseling	M
Geography	M,D
Geology	M,D
Geosciences	M,D
German	M,D
Gerontology	O
Hazardous Materials Management	M,D
Health Education	M,D,O
Health Promotion	M,D,O
Health Services Management and Hospital Administration	M,D
Higher Education	M
Historic Preservation	M,O
History	M,D,O
Hospitality Management	M
Human Resources Management	M
Industrial Hygiene	M,D
Information Studies	M,D,O
International Affairs	M,D
International Business	M
Journalism	M,D
Law	D
Library Science	M,D,O
Linguistics	M,D,O
Marine Sciences	M,D
Mathematics Education	M,D
Mathematics	M,D
Mechanical Engineering	M,D
Media Studies	M
Medical/Surgical Nursing	M
Molecular Biology	M,D
Museum Studies	M,O
Music Education	M,D,O
Music	M,D,O
Nuclear Engineering	M,D
Nurse Anesthesia	M
Nursing and Healthcare Administration	M
Nursing—General	M,O
Pediatric Nursing	M
Pharmaceutical Sciences	M,D
Pharmacy	D
Philosophy	M,D
Physical Education	M,D
Physics	M,D
Political Science	M,D
Psychiatric Nursing	M,O
Psychology—General	M,D
Public Administration	M
Public Health—General	M
Public History	M,O
Reading Education	M,D
Rehabilitation Counseling	M
Rehabilitation Sciences	M,O
Religion	M
School Psychology	D
Science Education	M,D
Secondary Education	M,D
Social Psychology	M,D
Social Sciences Education	M,D
Social Work	M,D
Sociology	M,D
Software Engineering	M,D
Spanish	M,D
Special Education	M,D
Speech and Interpersonal Communication	M,D
Sports Management	M
Statistics	M,D,O
Student Affairs	M
Theater	M,D
Travel and Tourism	M
Women's Health Nursing	M
Women's Studies	O
Writing	M,D

UNIVERSITY OF SOUTH CAROLINA AIKEN

Applied Psychology	M
Business Administration and Management—General	M
Clinical Psychology	M
Educational Media/Instructional Technology	M

UNIVERSITY OF SOUTH CAROLINA UPSTATE

Early Childhood Education	M
Education—General	M
Elementary Education	M
Health Informatics	M
Information Science	M
Special Education	M

UNIVERSITY OF SOUTH DAKOTA

Accounting	M
Addictions/Substance Abuse Counseling	M
Adult Education	M,D,O
Allied Health—General	M,D,O
Allopathic Medicine	D,O
American Indian/Native American Studies	M,D,O
Art Education	M
Art/Fine Arts	M
Bioethics	D,O
Biological and Biomedical Sciences—General	M,D
Business Administration and Management—General	M,O
Business Analytics	M,O
Cardiovascular Sciences	M,D
Cell Biology	M,D
Chemistry	M,D
Clinical Psychology	M,D
Communication Disorders	M,D
Communication—General	M
Computer Science	M
Counseling Psychology	M,D,O
Counselor Education	M,D,O
Criminal Justice and Criminology	M
Curriculum and Instruction	M,D,O
Early Childhood Education	M,D,O
Education—General	M,D,O
Educational Leadership and Administration	M,D,O
Educational Media/Instructional Technology	M
Educational Psychology	M,D,O
Elementary Education	M
English as a Second Language	M
English	M,D
Exercise and Sports Science	M
Graphic Design	M
Health Services Management and Hospital Administration	M,O
Higher Education	M,D,O
History	M
Human Development	M,D,O
Human Resources Management	M
Immunology	M,D
Interdisciplinary Studies	M
Kinesiology and Movement Studies	M
Law	D
Marketing	M,O
Mathematics Education	M
Mathematics	M
Microbiology	M,D
Molecular Biology	M,D
Music Education	M
Music	M
Neuroscience	M,D
Occupational Therapy	M
Organizational Management	M
Pharmacology	M,D
Photography	M
Physical Therapy	D
Physician Assistant Studies	M
Physics	M,D
Physiology	M,D
Psychology—General	M,D
Public Health—General	M
Reading Education	M
School Psychology	M,D,O
Science Education	M
Secondary Education	M
Social Work	M
Special Education	M,D,O
Supply Chain Management	M,O
Sustainable Development	M,D
Theater	M

UNIVERSITY OF SOUTHERN CALIFORNIA

Accounting	M
Advertising and Public Relations	M
Aerospace/Aeronautical Engineering	M,D,O
Allopathic Medicine	D
American Studies	D
Applied Mathematics	M
Architecture	M
Art History	M,D
Art/Fine Arts	M,D,O
Artificial Intelligence/Robotics	M,D
Arts Administration	M
Asian Languages	M,D
Asian Studies	M
Biochemistry	M
Bioinformatics	D
Biological and Biomedical Sciences—General	M,D,O
Biomedical Engineering	M,D
Biophysics	M,D
Biostatistics	M,D
Biotechnology	M
Business Administration and Management—General	M,D
Cancer Biology/Oncology	D
Cell Biology	M,D
Chemical Engineering	M,D,O
Chemistry	D
Child and Family Studies	M,D
Civil Engineering	M,D,O
Classics	M,D
Clinical Psychology	M,D
Clinical Research	M
Cognitive Sciences	M,D
Communication—General	M,D
Comparative Literature	D
Computational Biology	M
Computer and Information Systems Security	M,D
Computer Art and Design	M
Computer Engineering	M,D,O
Computer Science	M,D
Construction Management	M,D,O
Corporate and Organizational Communication	M
Counselor Education	M
Cultural Studies	D
Dentistry	D
Developmental Biology	D
Developmental Psychology	M,D
Economic Development	M,D
Economics	M,D
Education—General	M,D
Educational Leadership and Administration	D
Educational Policy	D
Educational Psychology	D
Electrical Engineering	M,D,O
Engineering and Applied Sciences—General	M,D,O
Engineering Management	M,D,O
English as a Second Language	M
English	M,D
Entrepreneurship	M
Environmental and Occupational Health	M
Environmental Biology	M,D
Environmental Engineering	M,D,O
Epidemiology	M,D
Evolutionary Biology	D
Film, Television, and Video Production	M
Film, Television, and Video Theory and Criticism	M,D
Food Science and Technology	M,D,O
Game Design and Development	M,D
Genomic Sciences	D
Geographic Information Systems	M,O
Geography	M,O
Geosciences	M,D
Geotechnical Engineering	M,D,O
Gerontology	M,D,O
Hazardous Materials Management	M,D,O
Health Communication	M,D
Health Education	M
Health Promotion	M
Health Services Management and Hospital Administration	M,O
Health Services Research	D
Higher Education	D
Historic Preservation	M
History	D
Homeland Security	M,O
Immunology	M
Industrial/Management Engineering	M,D,O
International Affairs	M,D
International Health	M,O
Internet and Interactive Multimedia	M,D,O
Journalism	M
Kinesiology and Movement Studies	M,D
Landscape Architecture	M
Latin American Studies	D
Law	M,D
Linguistics	M,D
Manufacturing Engineering	M,D,O
Marine Biology	M,D
Marine Sciences	M,D
Marriage and Family Therapy	M
Materials Engineering	M,D,O
Materials Sciences	M,D,O
Mathematical and Computational Finance	M,D
Mathematics	M,D
Mechanical Engineering	M,D,O
Mechanics	M,D,O
Media Studies	M
Medical Imaging	M,D
Medical Microbiology	D
Microbiology	M
Modeling and Simulation	M,D
Molecular Biology	M,D
Molecular Medicine	D
Molecular Pharmacology	M,D
Multilingual and Multicultural Education	D
Music Education	M,D,O
Music	M,D,O
Neurobiology	D
Neuroscience	M,D

Nonprofit Management	M,O
Nurse Anesthesia	D
Occupational Therapy	M,D
Oceanography	M,D
Operations Research	M,D,O
Oral and Dental Sciences	M,D,O
Organizational Management	M
Pathology	M
Petroleum Engineering	M,D,O
Pharmaceutical Administration	M
Pharmaceutical Sciences	M,D,O
Pharmacy	D
Philosophy	M,D
Photography	M
Physical Chemistry	D
Physical Therapy	M,D
Physician Assistant Studies	M
Physics	M,D
Physiology	M
Political Science	M,D
Psychology—General	M,D
Public Administration	M,O
Public Health—General	M
Public Policy	M,D,O
Quantitative Analysis	M,D
Real Estate	M
Rhetoric	D
Safety Engineering	M,D,O
Slavic Languages	M,D
Social Psychology	M,D
Social Work	M,D
Sociology	D
Software Engineering	M,D
Spanish	D
Statistics	M,D
Student Affairs	M
Supply Chain Management	M,D,O
Sustainable Development	M,D,O
Systems Engineering	M,D,O
Taxation	M
Telecommunications	M,D,O
Theater	M
Toxicology	M,D
Transportation and Highway Engineering	M,D,O
Urban and Regional Planning	M,D,O
Urban Education	D
Water Resources	M,D,O
Writing	M

UNIVERSITY OF SOUTHERN INDIANA

Accounting	M
Business Administration and Management—General	M
Communication—General	M
Cultural Studies	M
Data Science/Data Analytics	M
Education—General	M,D
Educational Leadership and Administration	M,D
Elementary Education	M
Engineering and Applied Sciences—General	M,D
Engineering Management	M
English as a Second Language	M
English	M
Family Nurse Practitioner Studies	M,D,O
Gerontology	M,D,O
Health Services Management and Hospital Administration	M
Human Resources Management	M
Industrial and Manufacturing Management	M
Liberal Studies	M
Mathematics Education	M
Nonprofit Management	M
Nursing and Healthcare Administration	M,D,O
Nursing Education	M,D,O
Nursing—General	M,D,O
Occupational Therapy	M
Psychiatric Nursing	M,D,O
Public Administration	M
Secondary Education	M
Social Work	M
Sports Management	M

UNIVERSITY OF SOUTHERN MAINE

Accounting	M
Addictions/Substance Abuse Counseling	M,O
Adult Education	M,O
Adult Nursing	M,D,O
American Studies	M,O
Applied Behavior Analysis	M,O
Biological and Biomedical Sciences—General	M
Business Administration and Management—General	M,O
Computer Science	M,O
Counseling Psychology	M,O
Counselor Education	M,O
Cultural Studies	M,O
Education of the Gifted	M,O
Education—General	M,D,O
Educational Leadership and Administration	M,O
Educational Psychology	M,O
English as a Second Language	M,O
Family Nurse Practitioner Studies	M,D,O
Finance and Banking	M
Gerontological Nursing	M,D,O
Health Services Management and Hospital Administration	M
Higher Education	M,O
Immunology	M
Molecular Biology	M
Music Education	M
Music	M
Nursing and Healthcare Administration	M,D,O
Nursing Education	M,D,O
Nursing—General	M,D,O
Occupational Therapy	M
Psychiatric Nursing	M,D,O

Public Health—General M,O
Public Policy M
Reading Education M,O
Rehabilitation Counseling M,O
School Psychology M,D
Social Work M
Software Engineering M,O
Special Education M,O
Statistics M,O
Sustainability Management M
Urban and Regional Planning M,O
Writing M

UNIVERSITY OF SOUTHERN MISSISSIPPI

Accounting M
Advertising and Public Relations M
Anthropology M
Biochemistry M,D
Biological and Biomedical
  Sciences—General M,D
Biostatistics M
Business Administration and
  Management—General M
Chemistry M,D
Child and Family Studies M
Clinical Laboratory
  Sciences/Medical Technology M
Communication Disorders M,D
Communication—General M,D
Computational Sciences M,D
Computer Science M,D
Construction Engineering M
Counselor Education M,D
Criminal Justice and Criminology M,D
Curriculum and Instruction M,D
Economic Development M
Education—General M,D,O
Educational Leadership and
  Administration M,D,O
Educational Measurement and
  Evaluation M,D,O
Educational Media/Instructional
  Technology M,D
Elementary Education M,D
English as a Second Language M
English Education M,D
English M,D
Epidemiology M
Food Science and
  Technology M,D
Foreign Languages Education M
Forensic Sciences M,D
French M
Geography M
Geology M,D
Health Services Management and
  Hospital Administration M
Higher Education M,D,O
History M,D
Hydrology M,D
Information Science M,D
International Development M,D
Library Science M
Logistics M
Marine Sciences M,D
Marriage and Family Therapy M
Mathematics M,D
Music Education M,D
Music M
Nursing—General M,D,O
Nutrition M
Physical Education M,D
Physics M,D
Political Science M,D
Polymer Science and
  Engineering M,D
Psychology—General M,D
Public Health—General M,D
Secondary Education M,D
Social Work M
Spanish M
Special Education M,D
Sports Management M
Student Affairs M,D,O
Theater M
Transportation Management M
Writing M,D

UNIVERSITY OF SOUTH FLORIDA

Accounting M,D
Acute Care/Critical Care Nursing M,D,O
Addictions/Substance Abuse
  Counseling M,D
Adult Education M,D,O
Adult Nursing M,D,O
African Studies M,D,O
Allopathic Medicine M,D
American Studies M,D
Anatomy M,D
Anthropology M,D,O
Applied Behavior Analysis M,D
Applied Mathematics M,D
Applied Physics M,D
Archaeology M,D,O
Architecture M
Art History M
Art/Fine Arts M
Athletic Training and Sports
  Medicine M,D
Bioethics O
Bioinformatics M,D,O
Biological and Biomedical
  Sciences—General M,D
Biomedical Engineering M,D,O
Biostatistics O
Biotechnology M,D
Business Administration and
  Management—General M
Cancer Biology/Oncology M,D
Cardiovascular Sciences O

Cell Biology M,D
Chemical Engineering M,D,O
Chemistry M,D
Child and Family Studies M,D,O
Civil Engineering M,D,O
Clinical Psychology D
Clinical Research M,D,O
Cognitive Sciences D
Communication Disorders M,D,O
Communication—General M,D
Community College Education M,D,O
Community Health O
Comparative Literature O
Computational Biology M,D
Computer and Information
  Systems Security M,D
Computer Engineering M,D
Computer Science M,D
Corporate and Organizational
  Communication M,O
Counseling Psychology M,D,O
Counselor Education M,D,O
Criminal Justice and Criminology M,D,O
Data Science/Data Analytics M,D,O
Distance Education Development O
Early Childhood Education M,D,O
Ecology M,D
Economics M,D
Education of Students with
  Severe/Multiple Disabilities O
Education—General M,D,O
Educational Leadership and
  Administration M,D,O
Educational Measurement and
  Evaluation O
Educational Media/Instructional
  Technology O
Educational Psychology M,D,O
Electrical Engineering M,D
Elementary Education M,D,O
Emergency Management O
Engineering and Applied
  Sciences—General M,D,O
Engineering Management M,D
English as a Second Language M,D,O
English M,D,O
Entrepreneurship M,O
Environmental and Occupational
  Health O
Environmental Biology M,D
Environmental Engineering M,D
Environmental Management
  and Policy M,D,O
Environmental Sciences M,D
Epidemiology O
Evolutionary Biology M,D
Family Nurse Practitioner Studies M,D,O
Film, Television, and Video
  Theory and Criticism M
Finance and Banking M,D
Foreign Languages Education O
Forensic Sciences M,D,O
French M,D
Gender Studies O
Geographic Information Systems M,D,O
Geography O
Geology M,D,O
Geosciences M,D
Geotechnical Engineering M,D
Gerontological Nursing M,D,O
Gerontology M,D,O
Health Education M,D
Health Informatics M,D,O
Health Services Management and
  Hospital Administration O
Higher Education M,D
History M,D
Holocaust and Genocide Studies O
Human Resources Development O
Human Resources Management M
Humanities M
Hydrogeology O
Immunology M,D
Industrial and Organizational
  Psychology D
Industrial/Management
  Engineering M,D,O
Infectious Diseases M,D
Information Science M
Information Studies M,O
Interdisciplinary Studies M,D
International Affairs O
International Health O
Internet and Interactive
  Multimedia M,O
Journalism M,O
Latin American Studies M,D,O
Legal and Justice Studies O
Liberal Studies M,D
Library Science M
Linguistics M,D
Management Information Systems M,D,O
Management of Technology O
Management Strategy and Policy M,D,O
Marine Sciences M,D
Marketing M
Marriage and Family Therapy M,D,O
Mass Communication M,D
Materials Engineering M,D,O
Materials Sciences M,D,O
Maternal and Child Health O
Mathematics M,D
Mechanical Engineering M,D
Media Studies M
Medical Microbiology M,D
Medical Physics M,D
Microbiology M,D
Molecular Biology M,D
Molecular Medicine M,D
Molecular Pharmacology M,D
Museum Studies O

Music Education M,D
Music M,D
Nanotechnology M,D
Neuroscience M,D,O
Nonprofit Management O
Nurse Anesthesia M,D,O
Nursing Education M,D,O
Nursing—General M,D,O
Nutrition M,D,O
Occupational Health Nursing M,D,O
Oceanography M,D
Oncology Nursing M,D,O
Pathology M,D
Pediatric Nursing M,D,O
Pharmaceutical Sciences M,D
Pharmacy M,D,O
Philosophy M,D
Physical Therapy D
Physics M,D
Physiology M,D
Political Science D
Psychology—General D
Public Administration O
Public Affairs O
Public Health—General M,D,O
Reading Education M,D,O
Real Estate M
Rehabilitation Counseling M,D,O
Rehabilitation Sciences D
Religion M,D
Rhetoric M,D
School Psychology M,D,O
Secondary Education O
Social Sciences Education M,D,O
Social Work M,D,O
Sociology M,D
Spanish M,D
Special Education O
Sports Management M,D
Statistics M,D
Structural Engineering M,D
Student Affairs O
Sustainability Management M,O
Sustainable Development O
Systems Engineering O
Taxation M,D
Technical Communication O
Toxicology O
Transportation and Highway
  Engineering M,D,O
Travel and Tourism M,O
Urban and Regional Planning O
Urban Design M
Vocational and Technical Education M,D,O
Water Resources Engineering M,D,O
Western European Studies M,D
Women's Studies M
Writing M,D,O

UNIVERSITY OF SOUTH FLORIDA, ST. PETERSBURG

Business Administration and
  Management—General M
Computer Art and Design M
Education—General M
Educational Leadership and
  Administration M
Elementary Education M
English Education M
Environmental Management
  and Policy M
Environmental Sciences M
Journalism M
Liberal Studies M
Mathematics Education M
Media Studies M
Middle School Education M
Psychology—General M
Reading Education M
Science Education M

UNIVERSITY OF SOUTH FLORIDA SARASOTA-MANATEE

Business Administration and
  Management—General M
Criminal Justice and Criminology M
Curriculum and Instruction M
Educational Leadership and
  Administration M
Elementary Education M
English Education M
Hospitality Management M
Liberal Studies M
Social Sciences M
Social Work M

THE UNIVERSITY OF TAMPA

Accounting M,O
Adult Nursing M
Business Administration and
  Management—General M,O
Business Analytics M,O
Computer and Information
  Systems Security M,O
Criminal Justice and Criminology M
Curriculum and Instruction M
Education—General M
Educational Leadership and
  Administration M
Educational Media/Instructional
  Technology M
Entrepreneurship M,O
Exercise and Sports Science M
Family Nurse Practitioner Studies M
Finance and Banking M,O
International Business M,O
Management Information Systems M,O
Marketing M,O
Nonprofit Management M,O
Nursing—General M
Nutrition M
Writing M

THE UNIVERSITY OF TENNESSEE

Accounting M,D
Adult Education M
Advertising and Public Relations M,D
Aerospace/Aeronautical
  Engineering M,D
Agricultural Education M
Agricultural Engineering M
Agricultural Sciences—
  General M,D
Analytical Chemistry M,D
Anatomy M,D
Animal Behavior M,D
Animal Sciences M,D
Anthropology M,D
Applied Mathematics M,D
Applied Psychology M,D
Archaeology M,D
Architecture M
Art Education M,D,O
Art/Fine Arts M
Athletic Training and Sports
  Medicine M,D
Aviation M
Biochemistry M,D
Bioethics M,D
Biological and Biomedical
  Sciences—General M,D
Biological Anthropology M,D
Biomedical Engineering M,D
Biosystems Engineering M,D
Business Administration and
  Management—General M,D
Chemical Engineering M,D
Chemical Physics M,D
Chemistry M,D
Child and Family Studies M,D
Civil Engineering M,D
Clinical Psychology M,D
Clothing and Textiles M,D
Communication Disorders M,D,O
Communication—General M,D
Community Health M,D
Computer Engineering M,D
Computer Science M,D
Consumer Economics M,D
Counseling Psychology M,D
Counselor Education M,D,O
Criminal Justice and Criminology M,D
Cultural Anthropology M,D
Curriculum and Instruction M,D,O
Data Science/Data Analytics D
Early Childhood Education M,D,O
Ecology M,D
Economics M,D
Education—General M,D,O
Educational Leadership and
  Administration M,D,O
Educational Measurement and
  Evaluation M,D,O
Educational Media/Instructional
  Technology M,D,O
Educational Psychology M,D,O
Electrical Engineering M,D
Elementary Education M,D,O
Energy and Power
  Engineering D
Engineering and Applied
  Sciences—General M,D
Engineering Management M,D
English as a Second Language M,D,O
English Education M,D,O
English M,D
Entomology M,D
Environmental Engineering M
Environmental Management
  and Policy M,D
Evolutionary Biology M,D
Exercise and Sports Science M,D,O
Experimental Psychology M,D
Family and Consumer
  Sciences-General D
Finance and Banking M,D
Fish, Game, and Wildlife
  Management M
Food Science and
  Technology M,D
Foreign Languages Education M,D,O
Forestry M
Foundations and Philosophy of
  Education M,D,O
French M,D
Genetics M,D
Genomic Sciences M,D
Geography M,D
Geology M,D
German M
Gerontology M
Graphic Design M
Health Education M
Health Promotion M
Health Services Management and
  Hospital Administration M
History M,D
Hospitality Management M
Human Resources Development M
Industrial and Manufacturing
  Management M,D
Industrial and Organizational
  Psychology D
Industrial/Management
  Engineering M,D
Information Science M,D
Inorganic Chemistry M,D
Internet and Interactive
  Multimedia M,D
Italian D
Journalism M,D
Kinesiology and Movement Studies M,D
Landscape Architecture M
Law D

M—masters degree; D—doctorate; O—other advanced degree; *—Close-Up and/or Display

Program	Degree
Leisure Studies	M,D
Linguistics	D
Logistics	M,D
Marketing	M,D
Materials Engineering	M,D
Materials Sciences	M,D
Mathematics Education	M,D,O
Mathematics	M,D
Mechanical Engineering	M,D
Microbiology	M,D
Multilingual and Multicultural Education	M,D,O
Music Education	M
Music	M
Nuclear Engineering	M,D
Nursing—General	M,D
Nutrition	M
Organic Chemistry	M,D
Philosophy	M,D
Photography	M
Physical Chemistry	M,D
Physics	M,D
Physiology	M,D
Plant Pathology	M,D
Plant Physiology	M,D
Plant Sciences	M
Political Science	M,D
Portuguese	D
Psychology—General	M,D
Public Administration	M
Public Health—General	M
Reading Education	M,D,O
Recreation and Park Management	M,D
Rehabilitation Counseling	M,D
Reliability Engineering	M,D
Religion	M,D
Russian	D
School Psychology	M,D,O
Science Education	M,D,O
Secondary Education	M,D,O
Social Sciences Education	M,D,O
Social Work	M,D
Sociology	M,D
Spanish	M,D
Special Education	M,D,O
Sports Management	M,D
Statistics	M,D
Student Affairs	M
Theater	M
Theoretical Chemistry	M,D
Transportation Management	M,D
Travel and Tourism	M
Veterinary Medicine	D

THE UNIVERSITY OF TENNESSEE AT CHATTANOOGA

Program	Degree
Accounting	M
Applied Mathematics	M
Applied Statistics	M
Athletic Training and Sports Medicine	M
Automotive Engineering	M
Bioinformatics	M,O
Business Administration and Management—General	M
Chemical Engineering	M
Civil Engineering	M
Computational Sciences	D
Computer Science	M,O
Construction Management	M,O
Counselor Education	M,D,O
Criminal Justice and Criminology	M
Education—General	M,D,O
Educational Leadership and Administration	M,D,O
Electrical Engineering	M
Elementary Education	M,D,O
Energy and Power Engineering	M,O
Engineering Management	M,O
English	M
Environmental Sciences	M
Ethics	M,O
Experimental Psychology	M
Family Nurse Practitioner Studies	M,D,O
Gerontological Nursing	M,D,O
Industrial and Organizational Psychology	M
Interior Design	M
Logistics	M,O
Mathematics Education	M
Mathematics	M
Mechanical Engineering	M
Music Education	M
Music	M
Nonprofit Management	M,O
Nurse Anesthesia	M,D,O
Nursing Education	M,D,O
Nursing—General	M,D,O
Occupational Therapy	D
Physical Education	M
Physical Therapy	D
Project Management	M,O
Psychology—General	M
Public Administration	M,O
Quality Management	M,O
Rhetoric	M
School Psychology	M,D,O
Secondary Education	M,D,O
Social Psychology	M,D,O
Social Work	M
Special Education	M,D,O
Supply Chain Management	M,O
Writing	M

THE UNIVERSITY OF TENNESSEE AT MARTIN

Program	Degree
Addictions/Substance Abuse Counseling	M
Agricultural Economics and Agribusiness	M
Agricultural Sciences—General	M

Program	Degree
Business Administration and Management—General	M
Child and Family Studies	M
Child Development	M
Communication—General	M
Counselor Education	M
Curriculum and Instruction	M
Education—General	M
Educational Leadership and Administration	M
Elementary Education	M
Family and Consumer Sciences-General	M
Finance and Banking	M
Food Science and Technology	M
Interdisciplinary Studies	M
Nutrition	M
Physical Education	M
Secondary Education	M
Social Psychology	M
Special Education	M
Student Affairs	M

THE UNIVERSITY OF TENNESSEE HEALTH SCIENCE CENTER

Program	Degree
Allied Health—General	M,D
Allopathic Medicine	D
Biological and Biomedical Sciences—General	M,D
Biomedical Engineering	M,D
Clinical Laboratory Sciences/Medical Technology	M,D
Communication Disorders	M,D
Dentistry	D
Epidemiology	M,D
Family Nurse Practitioner Studies	D,O
Gerontological Nursing	D,O
Health Informatics	M,D
Health Services Research	M,D
Nursing—General	M,D,O
Occupational Therapy	M,D
Oral and Dental Sciences	M,D
Pathology	M,D
Pediatric Nursing	D,O
Pharmaceutical Sciences	M,D
Pharmacology	M,D
Pharmacy	M,D
Physical Therapy	M,D
Physician Assistant Studies	M,D
Psychiatric Nursing	M,D

THE UNIVERSITY OF TENNESSEE—OAK RIDGE NATIONAL LABORATORY

Program	Degree
Biological and Biomedical Sciences—General	M,D
Genomic Sciences	M,D

THE UNIVERSITY OF TEXAS AT ARLINGTON

Program	Degree
Accounting	M,D
Aerospace/Aeronautical Engineering	M,D
Anthropology	M
Applied Mathematics	M,D
Architecture	M
Art/Fine Arts	M
Athletic Training and Sports Medicine	M,D
Bioengineering	M,D
Biological and Biomedical Sciences—General	M,D
Chemistry	M,D
Civil Engineering	M,D
Communication—General	M
Computer Engineering	M,D
Computer Science	M,D
Construction Management	M,D
Criminal Justice and Criminology	M
Curriculum and Instruction	M
Economics	M
Education—General	M,D
Educational Leadership and Administration	M,D
Educational Policy	M,D
Electrical Engineering	M,D
Engineering and Applied Sciences—General	M,D
Engineering Management	M
English as a Second Language	M
English	M,D
Environmental Sciences	M,D
Exercise and Sports Science	M,D
Experimental Psychology	M,D
Family Nurse Practitioner Studies	M,D
Film, Television, and Video Production	M
Finance and Banking	M,D
French	M
Geology	M,D
Health Psychology	M,D
Health Services Management and Hospital Administration	M
Higher Education	M,D
History	M,D
Human Resources Management	M
Industrial and Organizational Psychology	M,D
Industrial/Management Engineering	M,D
Kinesiology and Movement Studies	M,D
Landscape Architecture	M
Linguistics	M,D
Logistics	M
Management Information Systems	M,D
Marketing Research	M
Marketing	M
Materials Engineering	M,D
Materials Sciences	M,D
Mathematics Education	M,D
Mathematics	M,D
Mechanical Engineering	M,D
Music Education	M
Music	M

Program	Degree
Nursing and Healthcare Administration	M,D
Nursing Education	M,D
Nursing—General	M,D
Physics	M,D
Political Science	M
Psychology—General	M,D
Public Administration	M,D
Public Policy	M,D
Quantitative Analysis	M,D
Reading Education	M
Real Estate	M
Science Education	M
Social Work	M,D
Sociology	M
Software Engineering	M
Spanish	M
Systems Engineering	M
Taxation	M
Urban and Regional Planning	D

THE UNIVERSITY OF TEXAS AT AUSTIN

Program	Degree
Accounting	M,D
Actuarial Science	M,D
Adult Nursing	M,D
Advertising and Public Relations	M,D
Aerospace/Aeronautical Engineering	M,D
African Studies	M,D
Allopathic Medicine	D
American Studies	M,D
Analytical Chemistry	D
Animal Behavior	D
Anthropology	M,D
Applied Arts and Design—General	M
Applied Mathematics	M,D
Applied Physics	M,D
Archaeology	M,D
Architectural Engineering	M
Architectural History	M,D
Architecture	M,D
Art Education	M
Art History	M,D
Art/Fine Arts	M
Asian Languages	M,D
Asian Studies	M,D
Astronomy	M,D
Biochemistry	D
Biological and Biomedical Sciences—General	M,D
Biomedical Engineering	M,D
Biopsychology	D
Business Administration and Management—General	M,D
Cell Biology	D
Chemical Engineering	M,D
Chemistry	D
Child and Family Studies	M,D
Child Development	D
Civil Engineering	M,D
Classics	M,D
Clinical Laboratory Sciences/Medical Technology	M,D
Clinical Psychology	D
Communication Disorders	M,D
Communication—General	M,D
Community Health Nursing	M,D
Comparative Literature	M,D
Computational Sciences	M,D
Computer and Information Systems Security	M,D
Computer Engineering	M,D
Computer Science	M,D
Counseling Psychology	M,D
Counselor Education	M,D
Cultural Studies	M,D
Curriculum and Instruction	M,D
Dance	M,D
Developmental Psychology	D
Early Childhood Education	M,D
East European and Russian Studies	M
Ecology	D
Economics	M,D
Education—General	M,D
Educational Leadership and Administration	M,D
Educational Media/Instructional Technology	M,D
Educational Psychology	M,D
Electrical Engineering	M,D
Engineering and Applied Sciences—General	M,D
English	M,D
Entrepreneurship	M
Environmental Engineering	M,D
Environmental Management and Policy	M,D
Evolutionary Biology	D
Exercise and Sports Science	M,D
Family and Consumer Sciences-General	M,D
Family Nurse Practitioner Studies	M,D
Film, Television, and Video Production	M,D
Finance and Banking	M,D
Folklore	M,D
French	M,D
Geography	M,D
Geology	M,D
Geosciences	M,D
Geotechnical Engineering	M,D
German	M,D
Gerontological Nursing	M,D
Health Education	M,D
Hispanic and Latin American Languages	M,D
Hispanic Studies	M,D
Historic Preservation	M
History	M,D
Human Development	M,D
Industrial and Manufacturing Management	M,D

Program	Degree
Industrial/Management Engineering	M,D
Information Studies	D
Inorganic Chemistry	D
Interior Design	M
Italian	M,D
Journalism	M,D
Kinesiology and Movement Studies	M,D
Landscape Architecture	M
Latin American Studies	M
Law	M,D
Linguistics	M,D
Management Information Systems	M,D
Marine Sciences	M,D
Marketing	M,D
Materials Engineering	M,D
Materials Sciences	M,D
Maternal and Child/Neonatal Nursing	M,D
Mathematics	M,D
Mechanical Engineering	M,D
Mechanics	M,D
Media Studies	M,D
Medicinal and Pharmaceutical Chemistry	M,D
Microbiology	D
Mineral Economics	M
Mineral/Mining Engineering	M
Molecular Biology	D
Multilingual and Multicultural Education	M,D
Music Education	M,D
Music	M,D
Natural Resources	M
Near and Middle Eastern Languages	M,D
Near and Middle Eastern Studies	M,D
Neurobiology	D
Neuroscience	D
Nursing and Healthcare Administration	M,D
Nursing Education	M,D
Nursing—General	M,D
Nutrition	M,D
Operations Research	M,D
Organic Chemistry	D
Organizational Behavior	M
Pediatric Nursing	M,D
Petroleum Engineering	M,D
Pharmaceutical Sciences	M,D
Pharmacology	M,D
Pharmacy	D
Philosophy	D
Physical Chemistry	D
Physical Education	M,D
Physics	M,D
Plant Biology	M,D
Political Science	M,D
Portuguese	M,D
Psychiatric Nursing	M,D
Psychology—General	D
Public Administration	M,D
Public Affairs	M,D
Public History	M,D
Public Policy	M,D
Quantitative Analysis	M,D
Reading Education	M,D
Rehabilitation Counseling	M,D
Risk Management	M,D
Romance Languages	M,D
School Psychology	M,D
Slavic Languages	M,D
Social Work	M,D
Sociology	M,D
Spanish	M,D
Special Education	M,D
Sport Psychology	M,D
Statistics	M,D
Supply Chain Management	M,D
Sustainable Development	M
Technology and Public Policy	M
Textile Sciences and Engineering	M
Theater	M,D
Toxicology	M,D
Urban and Regional Planning	M,D
Urban Design	M
Water Resources Engineering	M,D
Writing	M,D

THE UNIVERSITY OF TEXAS AT DALLAS

Program	Degree
Accounting	M
Actuarial Science	M,D
Applied Mathematics	M,D
Art History	M,D
Biochemistry	M,D
Biological and Biomedical Sciences—General	M,D
Biomedical Engineering	M,D
Biotechnology	M,D
Business Administration and Management—General	M,D
Cell Biology	M,D
Chemistry	M,D
Child and Family Studies	M,D
Cognitive Sciences	M,D
Communication Disorders	M,D
Communication—General	M,D
Comparative Literature	M,D
Computer Engineering	M,D
Computer Science	M,D
Criminal Justice and Criminology	M,D
Data Science/Data Analytics	M,D
Economics	M,D
Electrical Engineering	M,D
Engineering and Applied Sciences—General	M,D
Entrepreneurship	M
Finance and Banking	M
Geographic Information Systems	M,D
Geography	M,D
Geosciences	M,D
Health Services Management and Hospital Administration	M,D
History	M,D

Humanities	M,D
Industrial and Manufacturing Management	M,D
Interdisciplinary Studies	M
International Business	M,D
Internet and Interactive Multimedia	M,D
Latin American Studies	M,D
Law	M,D
Management Information Systems	M
Management of Technology	M
Management Strategy and Policy	M
Marketing	M
Materials Engineering	M,D
Materials Sciences	M,D
Mathematics Education	M
Mathematics	M,D
Mechanical Engineering	M,D
Mineralogy	M,D
Molecular Biology	M,D
Neuroscience	M,D
Nonprofit Management	M
Physics	M,D
Political Science	M,D
Project Management	M,D
Psychology—General	M,D
Public Administration	M,D
Public Policy	M,D
Real Estate	M
Science Education	M
Software Engineering	M,D
Statistics	M
Supply Chain Management	M
Systems Engineering	M
Telecommunications	M,D

THE UNIVERSITY OF TEXAS AT EL PASO

Accounting	M
Allied Health—General	D
Anthropology	M,O
Applied Psychology	M,O
Art Education	M
Art/Fine Arts	M
Biochemistry	M,D
Bioinformatics	M,D
Biological and Biomedical Sciences—General	M,D
Business Administration and Management—General	M,D,O
Chemistry	M,D
Civil Engineering	M,D,O
Clinical Psychology	M,D
Communication Disorders	M
Communication—General	M
Computer and Information Systems Security	M,D,O
Computer Engineering	M,D,O
Computer Science	M,D,O
Construction Management	M,D,O
Counselor Education	M
Curriculum and Instruction	M,D
Economics	M
Education—General	M,D
Educational Leadership and Administration	M,D
Educational Measurement and Evaluation	M
Educational Psychology	M
Electrical Engineering	M,D,O
Energy and Power Engineering	M,D,O
Engineering and Applied Sciences—General	M,D,O
English as a Second Language	M,O
English Education	M,D,O
English	M,D,O
Environmental Engineering	M,D,O
Environmental Sciences	M,D
Experimental Psychology	M,D
Family Nurse Practitioner Studies	M,D,O
Geology	M,D
Geophysics	M,D
Health Services Management and Hospital Administration	M,D,O
History	M,D
Industrial/Management Engineering	M
Information Science	M,D,O
Interdisciplinary Studies	M
International Business	M,D,O
Kinesiology and Movement Studies	M
Liberal Studies	M
Linguistics	M,O
Manufacturing Engineering	M
Materials Engineering	M,D
Materials Sciences	M,D
Mathematics	M
Mechanical Engineering	M,D
Metallurgical Engineering and Metallurgy	M,D
Multilingual and Multicultural Education	M,D,O
Music Education	M
Music	M
Nursing and Healthcare Administration	M,D,O
Nursing Education	M,D,O
Nursing—General	M,D,O
Occupational Therapy	M
Philosophy	M
Physical Therapy	D
Physics	M
Political Science	M
Psychology—General	M,D
Public Health—General	M,O
Reading Education	M
Rehabilitation Counseling	M
Rhetoric	M,D,O
Social Work	M
Sociology	M,O
Software Engineering	M,D,O
Spanish	M,O
Special Education	M
Statistics	M
Systems Engineering	M
Writing	M,D,O

THE UNIVERSITY OF TEXAS AT SAN ANTONIO

Accounting	M,D
Anthropology	M,O
Applied Behavior Analysis	M,O
Applied Mathematics	M
Applied Statistics	M
Architecture	M
Art History	M
Art/Fine Arts	M
Biological and Biomedical Sciences—General	M,D
Biomedical Engineering	M,D
Biotechnology	M,D
Business Administration and Management—General	M,D,O
Cell Biology	M,D
Chemistry	M,D
Civil Engineering	M,D
Communication—General	M
Computer and Information Systems Security	M,D,O
Computer Engineering	M,D
Computer Science	M,D
Counselor Education	M,D
Criminal Justice and Criminology	M,D
Cultural Studies	M,D
Curriculum and Instruction	M,D
Demography and Population Studies	D
Early Childhood Education	M,D
Ecology	M
Economics	M
Educational Leadership and Administration	M,D
Educational Measurement and Evaluation	M,O
Educational Media/Instructional Technology	M
Educational Psychology	M,O
Electrical Engineering	M,D
Engineering and Applied Sciences—General	M,D,O
English as a Second Language	M,D,O
English	M,D
Environmental Engineering	M,D
Environmental Sciences	M,D
Finance and Banking	M
Geology	M
Health Education	M
Higher Education	M,D
History	M,D
Information Science	M,D,O
Interdisciplinary Studies	M,D
Kinesiology and Movement Studies	M
Management of Technology	M,D,O
Manufacturing Engineering	M,D
Marketing	M
Materials Engineering	M,D
Mathematics Education	M
Mathematics	M
Mechanical Engineering	M,D
Molecular Biology	M
Multilingual and Multicultural Education	M,D
Music	M
Neurobiology	M,D
Organizational Management	D
Philosophy	M
Physics	M,D
Political Science	M
Psychology—General	M,D
Public Administration	M
Reading Education	M,D
School Psychology	M,O
Social Work	M
Sociology	M
Spanish	M,D
Special Education	M,D
Statistics	M,D
Translational Biology	D
Urban and Regional Planning	M

THE UNIVERSITY OF TEXAS AT TYLER

Accounting	M
Art History	M
Art/Fine Arts	M
Biological and Biomedical Sciences—General	M
Business Administration and Management—General	M
Civil Engineering	M
Clinical Psychology	M
Communication—General	M
Computer and Information Systems Security	M
Computer Science	M
Counseling Psychology	M
Criminal Justice and Criminology	M
Early Childhood Education	M
Electrical Engineering	M
Energy Management and Policy	M
Engineering Management	M
English	M
Environmental and Occupational Health	M
Environmental Engineering	M
Family Nurse Practitioner Studies	M,D
Health Education	M
Health Services Management and Hospital Administration	M
History	M,D
Human Resources Development	M,D

Industrial and Manufacturing Management	M
Interdisciplinary Studies	M
Kinesiology and Movement Studies	M
Marketing	M
Marriage and Family Therapy	M
Mathematics	M
Mechanical Engineering	M
Nursing and Healthcare Administration	M,D
Nursing Education	M,D
Nursing—General	M,D
Organizational Management	M
Pharmacy	D
Psychology—General	M
Public Administration	M
Quality Management	M
Reading Education	M
School Psychology	M
Social Sciences	M
Sociology	M
Special Education	M
Structural Engineering	M
Transportation and Highway Engineering	M
Water Resources Engineering	M

THE UNIVERSITY OF TEXAS HEALTH SCIENCE CENTER AT HOUSTON

Allopathic Medicine	D
Biochemistry	M,D
Bioinformatics	M,D,O
Biological and Biomedical Sciences—General	M,D
Biostatistics	M,D,O
Cancer Biology/Oncology	M,D
Cell Biology	M,D
Community Health	M
Data Science/Data Analytics	M,D,O
Dentistry	M,D
Environmental and Occupational Health	M,D,O
Epidemiology	M,D
Genetic Counseling	M,D
Genetics	M,D
Genomic Sciences	M,D,O
Health Informatics	M,D,O
Health Promotion	M,D,O
Health Services Management and Hospital Administration	M,D,O
Immunology	M,D
Infectious Diseases	M,D
Maternal and Child Health	M,D,O
Medical Physics	M,D
Microbiology	M,D
Neuroscience	M,D
Nursing—General	M,D
Pharmacology	M,D
Public Health—General	M,D,O
Quantitative Analysis	M,D

THE UNIVERSITY OF TEXAS HEALTH SCIENCE CENTER AT SAN ANTONIO

Acute Care/Critical Care Nursing	M
Allopathic Medicine	M,D
Biochemistry	M,D
Biological and Biomedical Sciences—General	D
Biomedical Engineering	M,D
Cell Biology	M,D
Clinical Laboratory Sciences/Medical Technology	D
Clinical Research	M
Communication Disorders	M,D
Community Health Nursing	M,D,O
Dentistry	M,D,O
Family Nurse Practitioner Studies	M,D,O
Gerontological Nursing	M,D,O
Immunology	M,D
Interdisciplinary Studies	D
Medical Physics	D
Microbiology	M,D
Molecular Medicine	M,D
Neuroscience	D
Nursing and Healthcare Administration	M,D,O
Nursing Education	M,D,O
Nursing—General	M,D,O
Occupational Therapy	M,D
Pediatric Nursing	M,D,O
Pharmacology	D
Physical Therapy	M,D
Physician Assistant Studies	M,D
Psychiatric Nursing	M,D
Special Education	M
Structural Biology	M,D
Toxicology	M,D

THE UNIVERSITY OF TEXAS HEALTH SCIENCE CENTER AT TYLER

Biotechnology	M
Health Services Management and Hospital Administration	M
Public Health—General	M

THE UNIVERSITY OF TEXAS MD ANDERSON CANCER CENTER

Genetics	M

THE UNIVERSITY OF TEXAS MEDICAL BRANCH

Allied Health—General	M,D
Allopathic Medicine	D
Biochemistry	D
Bioinformatics	D
Biological and Biomedical Sciences—General	M,D
Biophysics	D
Cell Biology	M,D
Clinical Laboratory Sciences/Medical Technology	M,D
Computational Biology	M
Demography and Population Studies	D
Humanities	M,D
Immunology	M,D
Microbiology	M,D
Molecular Biophysics	D
Neuroscience	D
Nursing—General	M,D
Occupational Therapy	M
Pathology	D
Pharmacology	M,D
Physical Therapy	M,D
Physician Assistant Studies	M
Physiology	M,D
Public Health—General	M
Rehabilitation Sciences	D
Structural Biology	D
Toxicology	M,D
Translational Biology	M,D

THE UNIVERSITY OF TEXAS OF THE PERMIAN BASIN

Accounting	M
Biological and Biomedical Sciences—General	M
Business Administration and Management—General	M
Clinical Psychology	M
Computer Science	M
Counselor Education	M
Criminal Justice and Criminology	M
Early Childhood Education	M
Education—General	M
Educational Leadership and Administration	M
English as a Second Language	M
English	M
Experimental Psychology	M
Foundations and Philosophy of Education	M
Geology	M
History	M
Kinesiology and Movement Studies	M
Political Science	M
Psychology—General	M
Reading Education	M
Spanish	M
Special Education	M

THE UNIVERSITY OF TEXAS RIO GRANDE VALLEY

Accounting	M
Agricultural Sciences—General	M
Allopathic Medicine	D
Art/Fine Arts	M
Biological and Biomedical Sciences—General	M
Business Administration and Management—General	M,D
Chemistry	M
Clinical Laboratory Sciences/Medical Technology	M
Clinical Psychology	M
Communication Disorders	M
Communication—General	M
Computer Science	M
Counselor Education	M
Criminal Justice and Criminology	M
Curriculum and Instruction	M,D
Early Childhood Education	M
Education—General	M,D
Educational Leadership and Administration	M,D
Educational Media/Instructional Technology	M,D
Educational Psychology	M
Electrical Engineering	M
Elementary Education	M,D
Emergency Management	M
Engineering Management	M
English as a Second Language	M
English	M
Environmental Sciences	M
Exercise and Sports Science	M
Experimental Psychology	M
Finance and Banking	M
Geosciences	M
Health Services Management and Hospital Administration	M
History	M
Interdisciplinary Studies	M
Kinesiology and Movement Studies	M
Management Information Systems	M
Manufacturing Engineering	M
Marketing	M,D
Mathematics	M
Mechanical Engineering	M
Multilingual and Multicultural Education	M
Music	M
Nutrition	M
Occupational Therapy	M
Oceanography	M
Physician Assistant Studies	M
Physics	M
Psychology—General	M
Public Administration	M
Public Affairs	M
Public Policy	M
Reading Education	M
Rehabilitation Counseling	M,D
School Psychology	M
Secondary Education	M
Sociology	M
Spanish	M
Special Education	M
Sustainable Development	M
Systems Engineering	M
Translation and Interpretation	M
Writing	M

M—masters degree; D—doctorate; O—other advanced degree; *—Close-Up and/or Display

THE UNIVERSITY OF TEXAS SOUTHWESTERN MEDICAL CENTER

Allopathic Medicine	D
Biochemistry	D
Biological and Biomedical Sciences—General	M,D
Biomedical Engineering	M,D
Cancer Biology/Oncology	D
Cell Biology	D
Clinical Psychology	D
Developmental Biology	D
Genetics	D
Immunology	D
Microbiology	D
Molecular Biophysics	D
Neuroscience	D
Nutrition	M
Physical Therapy	D
Physician Assistant Studies	M
Rehabilitation Counseling	M

THE UNIVERSITY OF THE ARTS

Art Education	M
Art/Fine Arts	M
Dance	M
Industrial Design	M
Museum Education	M
Museum Studies	M
Music Education	M
Music	M
Theater	M,O

UNIVERSITY OF THE CUMBERLANDS

Accounting	M
Business Administration and Management—General	M
Business Education	M,D,O
Clinical Psychology	D
Counseling Psychology	M
Counselor Education	M,D,O
Education—General	M,D,O
Educational Leadership and Administration	M,D,O
Elementary Education	M,D,O
Marketing	M,D,O
Middle School Education	M,D,O
Physician Assistant Studies	M
Reading Education	M,D,O
Religion	M
Secondary Education	M,D,O
Special Education	M,D,O
Student Affairs	M,D,O
Theater	M,D,O

UNIVERSITY OF THE DISTRICT OF COLUMBIA

Adult Education	O
Architecture	M
Business Administration and Management—General	M
Cancer Biology/Oncology	M
Communication Disorders	M
Computer Science	M
Counseling Psychology	M
Early Childhood Education	M
Electrical Engineering	M
Elementary Education	M
Engineering and Applied Sciences—General	M
English Education	M
Homeland Security	M
Law	M,D
Legal and Justice Studies	M,D
Mathematics Education	M
Middle School Education	M
Nutrition	M
Public Administration	M
Rehabilitation Counseling	M
Secondary Education	M
Social Sciences Education	M
Water Resources	M

UNIVERSITY OF THE FRASER VALLEY

Criminal Justice and Criminology	M
Social Work	M

UNIVERSITY OF THE INCARNATE WORD

Accounting	M
Applied Statistics	M
Biological and Biomedical Sciences—General	M
Business Administration and Management—General	M,D
Clothing and Textiles	M
Communication—General	M,D
Education—General	M,D
Health Services Management and Hospital Administration	M,D
Industrial and Organizational Psychology	M,D
Kinesiology and Movement Studies	M,D
Mathematics Education	M
Mathematics	M
Nursing—General	M,D
Nutrition	M
Optometry	D
Organizational Management	M,D
Osteopathic Medicine	M,D
Pastoral Ministry and Counseling	M
Pharmacy	D
Physical Therapy	D
Sports Management	M,D

UNIVERSITY OF THE PACIFIC

Biological and Biomedical Sciences—General	M
Business Administration and Management—General	M
Communication Disorders	M,D
Communication—General	M
Curriculum and Instruction	M,D,O
Dentistry	M,D,O
Education—General	M,D,O
Educational Leadership and Administration	M,D,O
Educational Psychology	M,D,O

Engineering and Applied Sciences—General	M
Exercise and Sports Science	M
Hospitality Management	M
International Affairs	M,D
Law	M,D
Music Education	M
Music	M
Pharmaceutical Sciences	M,D
Pharmacy	D
Physical Therapy	M,D
Psychology—General	M
Public Policy	M,D
School Psychology	M,D,O
Special Education	M,D,O
Therapies—Dance, Drama, and Music	M
Water Resources	M,D

UNIVERSITY OF THE PEOPLE

Business Administration and Management—General	M

UNIVERSITY OF THE POTOMAC

Business Administration and Management—General	M

UNIVERSITY OF THE SACRED HEART

Accounting	M,O
Advertising and Public Relations	M
Broadcast Journalism	M,O
Business Administration and Management—General	M,O
Communication—General	M,O
Conflict Resolution and Mediation/Peace Studies	M
Cultural Studies	M
Early Childhood Education	M,O
Education—General	M,O
Educational Media/Instructional Technology	M
English Education	M,O
Environmental and Occupational Health	M
Film, Television, and Video Production	M,O
Foreign Languages Education	M,O
Human Resources Management	M
Information Science	O
Internet and Interactive Multimedia	M,O
Legal and Justice Studies	M
Management Information Systems	M
Marketing	M
Mathematics Education	M,O
Nonprofit Management	M
Occupational Health Nursing	M
Taxation	M
Writing	M,O

UNIVERSITY OF THE SCIENCES

Biochemistry	M,D
Bioinformatics	M
Biotechnology	M
Cell Biology	M
Chemistry	M,D
Health Psychology	M
Health Services Management and Hospital Administration	M,D
Medicinal and Pharmaceutical Chemistry	M,D
Occupational Therapy	M,D
Pharmaceutical Administration	M
Pharmaceutical Sciences	M,D
Pharmacology	D
Pharmacy	D
Physical Therapy	D
Public Health—General	M
Technical Writing	M,O
Toxicology	M,D

THE UNIVERSITY OF THE SOUTH

English	M
Theology	M,D
Writing	M

UNIVERSITY OF THE SOUTHWEST

Business Administration and Management—General	M
Counseling Psychology	M
Counselor Education	M
Curriculum and Instruction	M
Early Childhood Education	M
Education—General	M
Educational Leadership and Administration	M
English as a Second Language	M
Multilingual and Multicultural Education	M
Special Education	M
Sports Management	M

UNIVERSITY OF THE VIRGIN ISLANDS

Business Administration and Management—General	M
Education—General	M,D,O
Educational Leadership and Administration	M,D,O
Environmental Sciences	M
Liberal Studies	M
Marine Sciences	M
Mathematics Education	M
Mathematics	M
School Psychology	M,D,O
Secondary Education	M
Social Sciences	M

UNIVERSITY OF THE WEST

Business Administration and Management—General	M
Finance and Banking	M
International Business	M
Management Information Systems	M
Nonprofit Management	M
Psychology—General	M
Religion	M,D
Theology	M

THE UNIVERSITY OF TOLEDO

Accounting	M
Allopathic Medicine	M,D,O
Analytical Chemistry	M,D
Applied Mathematics	M,D
Art Education	M,D,O
Astrophysics	M,D
Athletic Training and Sports Medicine	M,D
Biochemistry	M,D
Bioengineering	M,D
Bioinformatics	M,O
Biological and Biomedical Sciences—General	M,D,O
Biomedical Engineering	D
Biostatistics	M,O
Business Administration and Management—General	M
Business Education	M,D,O
Cancer Biology/Oncology	M,D
Cardiovascular Sciences	M,D
Chemical Engineering	M,D
Chemistry	M,D
Civil Engineering	M,D
Clinical Psychology	M,D
Communication Disorders	M,D,O
Communication—General	O
Community Health Nursing	M
Computer Science	M,D
Counselor Education	M,D,O
Criminal Justice and Criminology	M,O
Curriculum and Instruction	M,D,O
Early Childhood Education	M,D,O
Ecology	M,D
Economics	M,D,O
Education of the Gifted	M,D,O
Education—General	M,D,O
Educational Leadership and Administration	M,D,O
Educational Measurement and Evaluation	M,D,O
Educational Media/Instructional Technology	M,D,O
Educational Psychology	M,D,O
Electrical Engineering	M,D
Elementary Education	M,D,O
Emergency Management	M,O
Engineering and Applied Sciences—General	M
English as a Second Language	M,D,O
English Education	M,D,O
English	M,O
Environmental and Occupational Health	M,D,O
Environmental Sciences	M,D
Epidemiology	M,O
Exercise and Sports Science	M,D
Experimental Psychology	M,D
Family Nurse Practitioner Studies	M,O
Finance and Banking	M
Foreign Languages Education	M,D,O
Foundations and Philosophy of Education	M,D,O
French	M
Gender Studies	O
Genomic Sciences	M,O
Geographic Information Systems	M,D,O
Geography	M,D,O
Geology	M,D
German	M
Gerontology	M,O
Health Education	M,D,O
Health Promotion	M,D,O
Health Services Management and Hospital Administration	M,O
Higher Education	M,D,O
History	M,D
Immunology	M,D
Industrial Hygiene	M,D,O
Industrial/Management Engineering	M,D
Inorganic Chemistry	M,D
International Business	M
International Health	M,O
Law	M,D,O
Leisure Studies	M,D
Liberal Studies	M
Marketing	M
Materials Sciences	M,D
Mathematics Education	M,D,O
Mathematics	M,D
Mechanical Engineering	M,D
Medical Physics	M,D
Medicinal and Pharmaceutical Chemistry	M,D
Middle School Education	M,D,O
Music Education	M,O
Music	M,O
Neuroscience	M,D
Nonprofit Management	M,O
Nursing and Healthcare Administration	M,O
Nursing Education	M,O
Nursing—General	M,D,O
Nutrition	M,O
Occupational Therapy	M,D
Oral and Dental Sciences	M,D
Organic Chemistry	M,D
Pathology	M,O
Pediatric Nursing	M,O
Pharmaceutical Administration	M
Pharmaceutical Sciences	M
Pharmacology	M,D
Pharmacy	M,D
Philosophy	M
Physical Chemistry	M,D
Physical Education	M,D
Physical Therapy	M,D
Physician Assistant Studies	M
Physics	M,D
Political Science	M,O
Psychology—General	M,O
Public Administration	M,O
Public Health—General	M,D,O

Recreation and Park Management	M,D
School Psychology	M,D,O
Science Education	M,D,O
Secondary Education	M,D,O
Social Sciences Education	M,D,O
Social Work	M,O
Sociology	M
Spanish	M
Special Education	M,D,O
Statistics	M
Urban and Regional Planning	M,D,O
Vocational and Technical Education	M,D,O
Women's Studies	O
Writing	M,O

UNIVERSITY OF TORONTO

Aerospace/Aeronautical Engineering	M,D
Allopathic Medicine	M,D
Anthropology	M,D
Architecture	M
Art History	M,D
Asian Studies	M,D
Astronomy	M,D
Astrophysics	M,D
Biochemistry	M,D
Bioethics	M
Biomedical Engineering	M,D
Biophysics	M,D
Biostatistics	M,D
Biotechnology	M
Business Administration and Management—General	M,D
Cell Biology	M,D
Chemical Engineering	M,D
Chemistry	M,D
Civil Engineering	M,D
Classics	M,D
Communication Disorders	M,D
Community Health	M,D
Comparative Literature	M,D
Computer Engineering	M,D
Computer Science	M,D
Criminal Justice and Criminology	M,D
Dentistry	D
East European and Russian Studies	M
Ecology	M,D
Economics	M,D
Education—General	M,D
Electrical Engineering	M,D
Engineering and Applied Sciences—General	M,D
English	M,D
Environmental and Occupational Health	M,D
Environmental Sciences	M,D
Epidemiology	M,D
Evolutionary Biology	M,D
Film, Television, and Video Theory and Criticism	M,D
Finance and Banking	M
Forestry	M,D
French	M,D
Gender Studies	M,D
Genetic Counseling	M,D
Geography	M,D
Geology	M,D
German	M,D
Health Informatics	M
Health Physics/Radiological Health	M,D
Health Promotion	M,D
Health Services Management and Hospital Administration	M
History of Science and Technology	M,D
History	M,D
Human Resources Management	M,D
Immunology	M,D
Industrial and Labor Relations	M,D
Industrial/Management Engineering	M,D
Information Studies	M,D
International Affairs	M
Italian	M,D
Kinesiology and Movement Studies	M,D
Landscape Architecture	M
Law	M
Linguistics	M,D
Management of Technology	M
Manufacturing Engineering	M
Materials Engineering	M,D
Materials Sciences	M,D
Mathematical and Computational Finance	M
Mathematics	M,D
Mechanical Engineering	M,D
Medieval and Renaissance Studies	M,D
Molecular Genetics	M,D
Museum Studies	M,D
Music Education	M,D
Music	M,D
Near and Middle Eastern Studies	M,D
Nursing—General	M,D
Nutrition	M,D
Occupational Therapy	M
Oral and Dental Sciences	M,D
Pathobiology	M,D
Pharmaceutical Sciences	M,D
Pharmacology	M,D
Philosophy	M,D
Physical Education	M,D
Physical Therapy	M,D
Physics	M,D
Physiology	M,D
Political Science	M,D
Portuguese	M,D
Psychology—General	M,D
Public Health—General	M,D
Rehabilitation Sciences	M,D
Religion	M,D
Slavic Languages	M,D
Social Sciences	M,D
Social Work	M,D
Sociology	M,D
Spanish	M,D

Statistics M,D
Systems Biology M,D
Theater M,D
Urban and Regional Planning M,D
Urban Design M,D
Women's Studies M,D
Writing M,D

THE UNIVERSITY OF TULSA

Accounting M
American Indian/Native American
Studies M,D,O
Anthropology M
Biological and Biomedical
Sciences—General M,D
Business Administration and
Management—General M
Business Analytics M
Chemical Engineering M,D
Clinical Psychology M,D
Communication Disorders M
Computer and Information
Systems Security M,D
Computer Science M,D
Electrical Engineering M,D
Energy Management and
Policy M
Engineering and Applied
Sciences—General M,D
English M,D
Environmental Law M,D,O
Family Nurse Practitioner Studies D
Geophysics M,D
Geosciences M,D
Gerontological Nursing D
Health Law M,D,O
Industrial and Organizational
Psychology M,D
Kinesiology and Movement Studies M
Law M,D,O
Mathematics M,D
Mechanical Engineering M,D
Museum Studies M
Nursing—General D
Petroleum Engineering M,D
Psychology—General M
Rehabilitation Sciences M

UNIVERSITY OF UTAH

Accounting M,D
Allopathic Medicine D
American Studies M,D
Anatomy D
Anthropology M,D
Applied Behavior Analysis M,D
Art Education M
Art History M
Art/Fine Arts M
Asian Studies M
Atmospheric Sciences M,D
Biochemistry M,D
Bioengineering M,D
Bioinformatics M,D,O
Biological and Biomedical
Sciences—General M,D,O
Biostatistics M,D
Biotechnology M
Business Administration and
Management—General M,D,O
Cancer Biology/Oncology M,D
Chemical Engineering M,D
Chemical Physics M,D
Chemistry M,D
Child and Family Studies M
Civil Engineering M,D
Clinical Laboratory
Sciences/Medical Technology M
Clinical Psychology M,D,O
Communication Disorders M
Communication—General M,D
Comparative Literature M,D
Computational Sciences M
Computer and Information
Systems Security M,O
Computer Engineering M,D
Computer Science M,D
Counseling Psychology M,D
Counselor Education M,D,O
Cultural Studies M
Dentistry D
Developmental Psychology D
Early Childhood Education M,D
Economics M,D
Education of Students with
Severe/Multiple Disabilities M
Education—General M,D,O
Educational Media/Instructional
Technology M,D,O
Electrical Engineering M,D
Elementary Education M,D,O
Engineering and Applied
Sciences—General M,D
English M,D
Environmental Engineering M,D
Environmental Sciences M
Finance and Banking M,D
French M,D
Game Design and
Development M
Geographic Information Systems M,D
Geography M,D
Geological Engineering M,D
Geology M,D
Geophysics M,D
Gerontological Nursing M,O
Gerontology M
Graphic Design M
Health Education M,D
Health Promotion M
Health Services Management and
Hospital Administration M,D

Health Services Research M,D
Higher Education M,D
History M,D
Human Development M,D
Human Genetics M,D
Humanities M
Industrial and Manufacturing
Management M,D,O
International Affairs M,D
Internet and Interactive
Multimedia M,D
Kinesiology and Movement Studies M,D
Latin American Studies M
Law M,D
Leisure Studies M,D
Linguistics M,D
Management Information Systems M,D,O
Management Strategy and Policy M,D,O
Marketing M,D
Materials Engineering M,D
Materials Sciences M,D
Mathematics Education M,D
Mathematics M,D
Mechanical Engineering M,D
Medical Physics M,D
Medicinal and Pharmaceutical
Chemistry M,D
Metallurgical Engineering and
Metallurgy M,D
Mineral/Mining Engineering M,D
Molecular Biology D
Music Education M,D
Near and Middle Eastern Languages M,D
Near and Middle Eastern Studies M,D
Neurobiology D
Neuroscience M,D
Nuclear Engineering M,D
Nursing—General M,D
Nutrition M,D
Occupational Therapy M,D
Organizational Behavior M,D
Pathology M,D
Petroleum Engineering M,D
Pharmaceutical Administration M,D
Pharmaceutical Sciences M,D
Pharmacology D
Pharmacy D
Philosophy M,D
Photography M
Physical Therapy D
Physician Assistant Studies M
Physics M,D
Physiology M,D
Political Science M,D
Psychology—General D
Public Administration M,D
Public Health—General M,D
Public Policy M
Reading Education M,D,O
Real Estate M
Recreation and Park Management M,D
Rehabilitation Sciences D
Rhetoric M,D
School Psychology M,D,O
Science Education M,D,O
Social Psychology D
Social Work M,D
Sociology M,D
Software Engineering M,D,O
Spanish M,D
Statistics M,D,O
Student Affairs M,D
Systems Engineering M,O
Toxicology D
Urban Design M,D
Writing M,D

UNIVERSITY OF VALLEY FORGE

Music M
Religion M
Theology M

UNIVERSITY OF VERMONT

Accounting M
Agricultural Economics and
Agribusiness M
Agricultural Sciences—
General M,D,O
Agronomy and Soil Sciences M,D,O
Allied Health—General M,D,O
Allopathic Medicine M,D,O
Animal Sciences M,D
Applied Economics M,D
Biochemistry M,D
Bioengineering D
Biological and Biomedical
Sciences—General M,D
Biomedical Engineering M
Biostatistics M
Business Administration and
Management—General M
Cell Biology D
Chemistry M,D
Civil Engineering M,D
Classics M,O
Clinical Laboratory
Sciences/Medical Technology M,D,O
Clinical Psychology M,D
Communication Disorders M
Community Health M
Computer Science M,D
Counseling Psychology M
Counselor Education M
Curriculum and Instruction M
Data Science/Data Analytics M,D
Developmental Psychology M,D
Early Childhood Education M
Economics M,D,O
Education—General M,D
Educational Leadership and
Administration M,D

Educational Policy D
Electrical Engineering M,D
Elementary Education M
Engineering and Applied
Sciences—General M,D
Engineering Management M
English M
Entomology M,D,O
Environmental and Occupational
Health M,D
Environmental Engineering M,D
Environmental Sciences M
Epidemiology M,O
Experimental Psychology D
Food Science and
Technology M,D
Foreign Languages Education M,O
Forestry M,D,O
Geology M
German M
Health Promotion M
Health Services Management and
Hospital Administration M,O
Higher Education M
Historic Preservation M
History M
Horticulture M,D,O
Interdisciplinary Studies M
International Health M,O
Materials Sciences M,D
Mathematics M,D
Mechanical Engineering M,D
Middle School Education M
Molecular Biology D
Natural Resources M,D,O
Neuroscience D
Nursing—General M,D,O
Nutrition M,D
Pathology M
Pharmacology M,D
Physical Therapy D
Physics M
Plant Biology M,D
Plant Pathology M,D,O
Plant Sciences M,D,O
Psychology—General D
Public Administration M
Public Health—General M,O
Rehabilitation Sciences D
School Psychology M
Science Education M,D
Secondary Education M
Social Psychology D
Social Work M
Special Education M
Statistics M
Sustainability Management M
Sustainable Development M
Veterinary Sciences M,D

UNIVERSITY OF VICTORIA

Anthropology M
Art Education M,D
Art History M,D
Art/Fine Arts M
Asian Studies M
Astronomy M,D
Astrophysics M,D
Biochemistry M,D
Biological and Biomedical
Sciences—General M,D
Business Administration and
Management—General M
Chemistry M,D
Child and Family Studies M,D
Classics M,D
Clinical Psychology M,D
Computer Art and Design M
Computer Engineering M,D
Computer Science M,D
Condensed Matter Physics M,D
Conflict Resolution and
Mediation/Peace Studies M,D
Counseling Psychology M,D
Counselor Education M,D
Curriculum and Instruction M,D
Developmental Psychology M,D
Early Childhood Education M,D
Economics M,D
Education—General M,D
Educational Leadership and
Administration M,D
Educational Measurement and
Evaluation M,D
Educational Psychology M,D
Electrical Engineering M,D
Engineering and Applied
Sciences—General M,D
English Education M,D
English M,D
Environmental Education M,D
Experimental Psychology M,D
Family Nurse Practitioner Studies M,D
Film, Television, and Video
Production M
Foreign Languages Education M
Foundations and Philosophy of
Education M,D
French M
Geography M,D
Geosciences M,D
German M
Health Informatics M
Hispanic Studies M
History M,D
Human Development M,D
Italian M
Kinesiology and Movement Studies M,D
Law M,D
Leisure Studies M
Linguistics M,D

Mathematics Education M,D
Mathematics M,D
Mechanical Engineering M,D
Medical Physics M,D
Microbiology M,D
Music Education M,D
Music M,D
Nursing and Healthcare
Administration M,D
Nursing Education M,D
Nursing—General M,D
Oceanography M,D
Pacific Area/Pacific Rim Studies M
Philosophy M
Photography M
Physical Education M
Physics M,D
Political Science M,D
Psychology—General M,D
Public Administration M,D
Reading Education M,D
Science Education M,D
Social Psychology M,D
Social Sciences Education M,D
Social Work M
Sociology M,D
Special Education M,D
Statistics M,D
Theater M,D
Theoretical Physics M,D
Vocational and Technical Education M,D
Writing M

UNIVERSITY OF VIRGINIA

Accounting M
Acute Care/Critical Care Nursing M,D
Aerospace/Aeronautical
Engineering M,D
Allopathic Medicine M,D
Anthropology M,D
Architectural History M,D
Architecture M
Art History M,D
Asian Studies M
Astronomy M,D
Biochemistry D
Biological and Biomedical
Sciences—General M,D
Biomedical Engineering M,D
Biophysics M,D
Business Administration and
Management—General M,D,O
Cell Biology D
Chemical Engineering M,D
Chemistry M,D
Civil Engineering M,D
Classics M,D
Clinical Psychology D
Clinical Research M
Communication Disorders M,D
Community Health M,D
Computer Engineering M,D
Computer Science M,D
Construction Engineering D
Counselor Education M,D,O
Curriculum and Instruction M,D,O
Data Science/Data Analytics M
Early Childhood Education M,D
Economics M,D
Education of the Gifted M,D,O
Education—General M,D,O
Educational Leadership and
Administration M,D,O
Educational Measurement and
Evaluation M,D,O
Educational Media/Instructional
Technology M,D,O
Educational Policy D
Educational Psychology M,D,O
Electrical Engineering M,D
Elementary Education M,D,O
Engineering and Applied
Sciences—General M,D
Engineering Physics M,D
English Education M,D,O
English M,D
Environmental Sciences M,D
Finance and Banking M
Foreign Languages Education M,D
French M,D
German M
Health Informatics M
Health Services Management and
Hospital Administration M
Health Services Research M
Higher Education M,D,O
History M,D
Interdisciplinary Studies M,D
International Affairs M,O
International Business M
Kinesiology and Movement Studies M,D
Landscape Architecture M
Law M,D
Linguistics M
Management of Technology M
Management Strategy and Policy M,O
Marketing M
Materials Sciences M,D
Mathematics Education M,D,O
Mathematics M,D
Mechanical Engineering M,D
Microbiology D
Molecular Genetics D
Molecular Physiology M,D
Music M,D
Near and Middle Eastern Studies M
Neuroscience D
Nursing and Healthcare
Administration M,D
Nursing—General M,D
Pathology D

Pharmacology	D
Philosophy	M,D
Physical Education	M,D
Physics	M,D
Physiology	D
Political Science	M,D
Psychiatric Nursing	M,D
Psychology—General	M,D
Public Health—General	M,D
Public Policy	M
Reading Education	M,D
Religion	M,D
School Psychology	M,D
Science Education	M,D,O
Slavic Languages	M,D
Social Sciences Education	M,D,O
Sociology	M,D
Spanish	M,D
Special Education	M,D,O
Statistics	M,D
Student Affairs	M,D,O
Systems Engineering	M,D
Theater	M
Urban and Regional Planning	M
Western European Studies	M
Writing	M

UNIVERSITY OF WASHINGTON

Accounting	M,D
Aerospace/Aeronautical Engineering	M,D
Allopathic Medicine	D
Animal Behavior	M,D
Anthropology	M,D
Applied Arts and Design—General	M
Applied Mathematics	M,D
Applied Physics	M,D
Architecture	M,D,O
Art History	M,D
Art/Fine Arts	M
Asian Languages	M,D
Asian Studies	M,D
Astronomy	M,D
Atmospheric Sciences	M,D
Biochemistry	D
Bioengineering	M,D
Bioethics	M
Bioinformatics	M,D
Biological and Biomedical Sciences—General	M,D
Biophysics	D
Biostatistics	M,D
Biotechnology	D
Business Administration and Management—General	M,D
Cell Biology	D
Chemical Engineering	M,D
Chemistry	M,D
Chinese	M,D
Civil Engineering	M,D
Classics	M,D
Clinical Laboratory Sciences/Medical Technology	M
Clinical Psychology	M,D
Clinical Research	M,D
Cognitive Sciences	M,D
Communication Disorders	M,D
Communication—General	M,D
Community Health	M,D
Comparative Literature	M,D
Computational Sciences	M,D
Computer and Information Systems Security	M,D
Computer Engineering	M,D
Computer Science	M,D
Construction Engineering	M,D
Construction Management	M
Curriculum and Instruction	M,D
Dance	M
Data Science/Data Analytics	M
Dentistry	M,D,O
Developmental Psychology	M,D
East European and Russian Studies	M
Ecology	M,D
Economics	D
Education of Students with Severe/Multiple Disabilities	M,D
Education—General	M,D
Educational Leadership and Administration	M,D
Educational Measurement and Evaluation	M,D
Educational Media/Instructional Technology	M,D
Educational Policy	M,D
Educational Psychology	M,D
Electrical Engineering	M,D
Engineering and Applied Sciences—General	M,D,O
English as a Second Language	M,D
English Education	M,D
English	M,D
Entrepreneurship	M,D
Environmental and Occupational Health	M
Environmental Engineering	M,D
Environmental Management and Policy	M,D
Epidemiology	M,D
Fish, Game, and Wildlife Management	M,D
Forestry	M,D
Foundations and Philosophy of Education	M,D
French	M,D
Genetics	M,D,O
Genomic Sciences	D
Geography	M,D
Geology	M,D
Geophysics	M,D
Geotechnical Engineering	M,D
German	M,D
Health Informatics	M,D

Health Services Management and Hospital Administration	M
Health Services Research	M,D
Higher Education	M,D
Hispanic and Latin American Languages	M
Historic Preservation	O
History	M,D
Horticulture	M,D
Human Development	M,D
Human-Computer Interaction	M,D,O
Hydrology	M,D
Immunology	D
Industrial Design	M
Industrial/Management Engineering	M,D
Infectious Diseases	D
Information Science	M,D
Intellectual Property Law	M,D
International Affairs	M,D
International Business	M,D,O
International Health	M,D
Italian	M,D
Japanese	M,D
Landscape Architecture	M
Law	M,D
Legal and Justice Studies	M,D
Library Science	M,D
Lighting Design	M,D,O
Linguistics	M,D
Logistics	O
Management Information Systems	M,D
Management of Technology	M,D
Marine Affairs	M,O
Marine Geology	M,D
Materials Engineering	M,D
Materials Sciences	M,D
Maternal and Child Health	M,D
Mathematics Education	M,D
Mathematics	M,D
Mechanical Engineering	M,D
Mechanics	M,D
Medical Informatics	M,D
Medicinal and Pharmaceutical Chemistry	D
Microbiology	D
Molecular Biology	D
Molecular Medicine	D
Multilingual and Multicultural Education	M,D
Museum Studies	M
Music Education	M,D
Music	M,D
Nanotechnology	M,D
Natural Resources	M,D
Near and Middle Eastern Studies	M,D
Neurobiology	D
Neuroscience	M,D
Nursing—General	M,D,O
Nutrition	M,D
Occupational Therapy	M,D
Oceanography	M,D
Oral and Dental Sciences	M,D,O
Pathobiology	M
Pathology	D
Pharmaceutical Sciences	M,D
Pharmacology	D
Pharmacy	M,D
Philosophy	M,D
Photography	M
Physical Education	M,D
Physical Therapy	M,D
Physics	M,D
Physiology	D
Political Science	M,D
Portuguese	M
Psychology—General	M,D
Public Administration	M,D
Public Affairs	M,D
Public Health—General	M
Public Policy	M,D
Reading Education	M,D
Rehabilitation Sciences	M,D
Religion	M,D
Russian	M,D
Scandinavian Languages	M,D
School Psychology	M,D
Science Education	M,D
Slavic Languages	M,D
Social Psychology	M,D
Social Sciences Education	M,D
Social Sciences	M,D
Social Work	M,D
Sociology	M,D
Spanish	M
Special Education	M,D
Statistics	M,D
Structural Biology	D
Structural Engineering	M,D
Supply Chain Management	M,D
Sustainable Development	M,D
Systems Engineering	M,D
Taxation	M,D
Theater	M,D
Toxicology	M,D
Transportation and Highway Engineering	M,D
Transportation Management	O
Urban and Regional Planning	M,D
Urban Design	M,D,O
Veterinary Sciences	D
Women's Studies	M
Writing	M

UNIVERSITY OF WASHINGTON, BOTHELL

Business Administration and Management—General	M
Computer Engineering	M
Cultural Studies	M
Education—General	M
Educational Leadership and Administration	M
Middle School Education	M

Nursing—General	M
Public Policy	M
Secondary Education	M
Software Engineering	M
Writing	M

UNIVERSITY OF WASHINGTON, TACOMA

Accounting	M
Business Administration and Management—General	M
Community Health Nursing	M
Computer Engineering	M
Education—General	M
Educational Leadership and Administration	M
Elementary Education	M
Finance and Banking	M
Interdisciplinary Studies	M
Mathematics Education	M
Nursing and Healthcare Administration	M
Nursing Education	M
Nursing—General	M
Science Education	M
Social Work	M
Software Engineering	M
Special Education	M

UNIVERSITY OF WATERLOO

Accounting	M,D
Actuarial Science	M,D
Anthropology	M,D
Applied Mathematics	M,D
Architecture	M
Art/Fine Arts	M
Biochemistry	M,D
Biological and Biomedical Sciences—General	M,D
Biostatistics	M,D
Business Administration and Management—General	M
Chemical Engineering	M,D
Chemistry	M,D
Civil Engineering	M,D
Computer Engineering	M,D
Computer Science	M,D
Economics	M,D
Electrical Engineering	M,D
Engineering and Applied Sciences—General	M,D
Engineering Management	M,D
English	M,D
Entrepreneurship	M
Environmental Engineering	M,D
Environmental Management and Policy	M,D
Environmental Sciences	M,D
Finance and Banking	M,D
French	M,D
Geography	M,D
Geosciences	M,D
German	M,D
Health Education	M,D
Health Informatics	M,D
History	M,D
Information Science	M,D
International Affairs	M,D
Kinesiology and Movement Studies	M,D
Leisure Studies	M,D
Management of Technology	M,D
Mathematics	M,D
Mechanical Engineering	M,D
Near and Middle Eastern Studies	M
Operations Research	M,D
Optometry	M,D
Philosophy	M,D
Physics	M,D
Political Science	M,D
Psychology—General	M
Public Affairs	M
Public Health—General	M,D
Recreation and Park Management	M,D
Religion	D
Russian	M,D
Sociology	M,D
Software Engineering	M,D
Statistics	M,D
Systems Engineering	M,D
Taxation	M,D
Technical Writing	M,D
Urban and Regional Planning	M,D
Vision Sciences	M,D

THE UNIVERSITY OF WEST ALABAMA

Adult Education	M
Business Administration and Management—General	M
Child Development	M,O
Clinical Psychology	M
Conservation Biology	M
Counselor Education	M,O
Early Childhood Education	M,O
Education—General	M,O
Educational Leadership and Administration	M,O
Educational Media/Instructional Technology	M,O
Elementary Education	M,O
English Education	M
Experimental Psychology	M
Finance and Banking	M
Higher Education	M
History	M
Marriage and Family Therapy	M
Mathematics Education	M
Physical Education	M
Science Education	M
Secondary Education	M
Social Sciences Education	M
Special Education	M,O
Student Affairs	M

THE UNIVERSITY OF WESTERN ONTARIO

Allopathic Medicine	M,D
Anatomy	M,D
Anthropology	M,D
Applied Mathematics	M,D
Astronomy	M,D
Biochemical Engineering	M,D
Biochemistry	M,D
Biological and Biomedical Sciences—General	M,D
Biophysics	M,D
Biostatistics	M,D
Business Administration and Management—General	M,D
Cell Biology	M,D
Chemical Engineering	M,D
Chemistry	M,D
Civil Engineering	M,D
Classics	M
Communication Disorders	M
Comparative Literature	M,D
Computer Engineering	M,D
Computer Science	M,D
Counseling Psychology	M
Curriculum and Instruction	M
Dentistry	D
Economics	M,D
Education—General	M,D
Educational Policy	M
Educational Psychology	M,D
Electrical Engineering	M,D
Engineering and Applied Sciences—General	M,D
English	M,D
Entrepreneurship	M,D
Environmental Engineering	M,D
Environmental Sciences	M,D
Epidemiology	M,D
Finance and Banking	M,D
French	M,D
Geography	M,D
Geology	M,D
Geophysics	M,D
Geosciences	M,D
Health Services Management and Hospital Administration	M,D
History	M,D
Immunology	M,D
Information Studies	M,D
Interdisciplinary Studies	M,D
International Business	M,D
Journalism	M
Kinesiology and Movement Studies	M,D
Law	M,D,O
Library Science	M,D
Management Strategy and Policy	M,D
Marketing	M,D
Materials Engineering	M,D
Mathematics	M,D
Mechanical Engineering	M,D
Media Studies	M,D
Microbiology	M,D
Music	M,D
Neuroscience	M,D
Nursing—General	M,D
Occupational Therapy	M
Oral and Dental Sciences	M
Pathology	M,D
Philosophy	M,D
Physical Therapy	M,O
Physics	M,D
Physiology	M,D
Political Science	M,D
Psychology—General	M,D
Sociology	M,D
Spanish	M,D
Special Education	M,D
Statistics	M,D
Sustainable Development	M,D

UNIVERSITY OF WESTERN STATES

Chiropractic	D

UNIVERSITY OF WEST FLORIDA

Accounting	M
American Studies	M
Anthropology	M
Applied Behavior Analysis	M
Applied Psychology	M
Archaeology	M
Biological and Biomedical Sciences—General	M
Business Administration and Management—General	M
Communication—General	M
Computer and Information Systems Security	M
Computer Science	M
Counseling Psychology	M
Criminal Justice and Criminology	M
Curriculum and Instruction	M,O
Data Science/Data Analytics	M
Educational Leadership and Administration	M,D
Educational Media/Instructional Technology	M,D
Elementary Education	M
English	M
Environmental Sciences	M
Exercise and Sports Science	M
Experimental Psychology	M
Geographic Information Systems	M
Health Promotion	M
Health Services Management and Hospital Administration	M
History	M
Industrial and Organizational Psychology	M
Leisure Studies	M
Mathematics	M
Middle School Education	M
Nursing—General	M
Physical Education	M,D

Political Science	M
Psychology—General	M
Public Administration	M
Public Health—General	M
Public History	M
Reading Education	M
Secondary Education	M
Social Work	M
Software Engineering	M
Special Education	M
Student Affairs	M
Writing	M

UNIVERSITY OF WEST GEORGIA

Accounting	M
Biological and Biomedical Sciences—General	M,O
Business Administration and Management—General	M
Business Education	M,D,O
Communication Disorders	M,D,O
Computer Science	M,O
Counselor Education	M,D,O
Criminal Justice and Criminology	M,D,O
Early Childhood Education	M,D,O
Education—General	M,D,O
Educational Leadership and Administration	M,D,O
Educational Media/Instructional Technology	M,D,O
English	M,O
Geographic Information Systems	M,O
Health Services Management and Hospital Administration	M,D,O
History	M,O
Mathematics	M,O
Museum Studies	M,O
Music Education	M,O
Music	M,O
Nonprofit Management	M,D,O
Nursing Education	M,D,O
Nursing—General	M,D,O
Psychology—General	M,D,O
Public Administration	M,O
Public History	M,O
Reading Education	M,D,O
Secondary Education	M,D,O
Sociology	M,D,O
Special Education	M,D,O
Urban and Regional Planning	M,D,O

UNIVERSITY OF WEST LOS ANGELES

Business Administration and Management—General	M
Entrepreneurship	M
Law	D
Organizational Management	M

UNIVERSITY OF WINDSOR

Applied Psychology	M,D
Art/Fine Arts	M
Biochemistry	M,D
Biological and Biomedical Sciences—General	M,D
Biopsychology	M,D
Business Administration and Management—General	M
Chemistry	M,D
Civil Engineering	M,D
Clinical Psychology	M,D
Communication—General	M
Computer Science	M,D
Criminal Justice and Criminology	M,D
Economics	M
Education—General	M,D
Electrical Engineering	M,D
Engineering and Applied Sciences—General	M,D
English	M,D
Environmental Engineering	M,D
Environmental Sciences	M,D
Geosciences	M,D
History	M
Industrial/Management Engineering	M,D
Kinesiology and Movement Studies	M
Legal and Justice Studies	M
Manufacturing Engineering	M,D
Materials Engineering	M,D
Mathematics	M,D
Mechanical Engineering	M,D
Nursing—General	M
Philosophy	M
Physics	M
Political Science	M
Psychology—General	M,D
Social Psychology	M,D
Social Work	M
Sociology	M,D
Statistics	M,D
Writing	M

THE UNIVERSITY OF WINNIPEG

History	M
Marriage and Family Therapy	M,O
Public Administration	M
Religion	M
Theology	M,O

UNIVERSITY OF WISCONSIN–EAU CLAIRE

Adult Nursing	M,D
Business Administration and Management—General	M
Communication Disorders	M
Education—General	M
English	M
Family Nurse Practitioner Studies	M,D
Gerontological Nursing	M
History	M
Library Science	M

Nursing and Healthcare Administration	M,D
Nursing Education	M,D
Nursing—General	M,D
Psychology—General	M,O
Reading Education	M
School Psychology	M
Secondary Education	M
Special Education	M
Writing	M

UNIVERSITY OF WISCONSIN–GREEN BAY

Business Administration and Management—General	M
Education—General	M
Environmental Management and Policy	M
Environmental Sciences	M
Nursing and Healthcare Administration	M
Social Work	M
Sustainability Management	M

UNIVERSITY OF WISCONSIN–LA CROSSE

Athletic Training and Sports Medicine	M
Biological and Biomedical Sciences—General	M
Cancer Biology/Oncology	M
Cell Biology	M
Community Health	M
Data Science/Data Analytics	M
Education—General	M,O
English Education	M,O
Exercise and Sports Science	M
Health Education	M
Higher Education	M,D
Marine Sciences	M
Medical Microbiology	M
Microbiology	M
Molecular Biology	M
Nurse Anesthesia	M
Occupational Therapy	M
Physical Education	M
Physical Therapy	D
Physician Assistant Studies	M
Physiology	M
Psychology—General	M,O
Public Health—General	M
Reading Education	M,O
Recreation and Park Management	M
Rehabilitation Sciences	M
School Psychology	M,O
Software Engineering	M
Special Education	M,O
Student Affairs	M,D

UNIVERSITY OF WISCONSIN–MADISON

Accounting	M,D
Actuarial Science	D
Adult Nursing	D
African Studies	M,D
African-American Studies	M
Agricultural Economics and Agribusiness	M,D
Agricultural Engineering	M,D
Agricultural Sciences—General	M,D
Agronomy and Soil Sciences	M,D
Allopathic Medicine	D
American Studies	M,D
Animal Sciences	M,D
Anthropology	D
Applied Arts and Design—General	M,D
Applied Economics	M,D
Archaeology	D
Art History	M,D
Art/Fine Arts	M
Arts Administration	M
Asian Languages	M,D
Asian Studies	M,D
Astronomy	D
Atmospheric Sciences	M,D
Automotive Engineering	M,D
Bacteriology	M
Biochemistry	M,D
Bioinformatics	M,D
Biological and Biomedical Sciences—General	M,D
Biological Anthropology	D
Biomedical Engineering	M,D
Biometry	M
Biophysics	D
Biopsychology	M,D
Botany	M,D
Business Administration and Management—General	M
Cancer Biology/Oncology	M,D
Cell Biology	D
Chemical Engineering	M,D
Chemistry	M,D
Child and Family Studies	M,D
Chinese	M,D
Civil Engineering	M,D
Classics	M,D
Clinical Psychology	M,D
Clinical Research	M,D
Cognitive Sciences	D
Communication Disorders	M,D
Communication—General	M,D
Comparative Literature	M,D
Computer and Information Systems Security	M
Computer Science	M,D
Conservation Biology	M
Construction Engineering	M
Consumer Economics	M,D
Counseling Psychology	D
Counselor Education	M

Cultural Anthropology	D
Curriculum and Instruction	M,D
Demography and Population Studies	D
Developmental Psychology	D
Ecology	M
Economics	D
Education—General	M,D,O
Educational Leadership and Administration	M,D,O
Educational Policy	M,D
Educational Psychology	M,D
Electrical Engineering	M,D
Engineering and Applied Sciences—General	M,D
Engineering Physics	M,D
English as a Second Language	M,D
English	M,D
Entomology	M,D
Environmental Biology	M,D
Environmental Engineering	M
Environmental Sciences	M
Epidemiology	M,D
Ergonomics and Human Factors	M,D
Family and Consumer Sciences-General	M,D
Film, Television, and Video Theory and Criticism	M,D
Finance and Banking	M,D
Fish, Game, and Wildlife Management	M,D
Folklore	M,D
Food Science and Technology	M,D
Forestry	M,D
French	M,D,O
Genetic Counseling	M
Genetics	M,D
Geographic Information Systems	M,D,O
Geography	M,D,O
Geological Engineering	M,D
Geology	M,D
Geophysics	M,D
Geotechnical Engineering	M
German	M,D
Gerontological Nursing	D
Higher Education	M,D,O
History of Medicine	M,D
History of Science and Technology	M,D
History	M,D
Horticulture	M,D
Human Development	M,D
Human Resources Management	M,D
Industrial/Management Engineering	M,D
Information Studies	M,D
Insurance	M,D
International and Comparative Education	M,D,O
Investment Management	D
Italian	M,D
Japanese	M,D
Jewish Studies	M,D
Journalism	M,D
Kinesiology and Movement Studies	M,D
Landscape Architecture	M,D
Latin American Studies	M,D
Law	M,D
Library Science	M,D
Linguistics	M,D
Management Information Systems	D
Management of Technology	M
Management Strategy and Policy	M,D
Manufacturing Engineering	M
Marine Sciences	M,D
Marketing Research	M
Marketing	D
Mass Communication	M,D
Materials Engineering	M,D
Mathematics	D
Mechanical Engineering	M,D
Mechanics	M,D
Media Studies	M,D
Medical Microbiology	D
Medical Physics	M,D
Microbiology	D
Molecular Biology	D
Molecular Pathology	D
Music Education	M,D
Music	M,D
Natural Resources	M,D
Near and Middle Eastern Languages	M,D
Near and Middle Eastern Studies	M,D
Neuroscience	D
Nursing—General	D
Nutrition	M,D
Occupational Therapy	M,D
Oceanography	M,D
Pathology	D
Pediatric Nursing	D
Pharmaceutical Administration	M,D
Pharmaceutical Sciences	M,D
Pharmacology	D
Pharmacy	D
Philosophy	M,D
Physical Therapy	D
Physician Assistant Studies	M
Physics	M,D
Physiology	M,D
Plant Pathology	M,D
Plant Sciences	M,D
Political Science	D
Portuguese	M
Psychiatric Nursing	D
Psychology—General	D
Public Affairs	M
Public Health—General	M
Real Estate	M,D
Rehabilitation Counseling	M,D
Rhetoric	M,D

Risk Management	M,D
Rural Sociology	M,D
Scandinavian Languages	M,D
Slavic Languages	M,D
Social Psychology	D
Social Work	M,D
Sociology	M,D
Spanish	M,D
Special Education	M,D
Speech and Interpersonal Communication	M,D
Statistics	M,D
Structural Engineering	M
Supply Chain Management	M
Sustainable Development	M
Systems Engineering	M,D
Taxation	M
Theater	M,D
Toxicology	M,D
Transportation and Highway Engineering	M
Urban and Regional Planning	M,D
Veterinary Medicine	M,D
Veterinary Sciences	M,D
Water Resources Engineering	M
Water Resources	M,D
Women's Studies	M,D
Writing	M,D
Zoology	M,D

UNIVERSITY OF WISCONSIN–MILWAUKEE

Actuarial Science	M,D
Adult Education	M,D,O
African Studies	D
Allied Health—General	M,D,O
Anthropology	M,D,O
Applied Arts and Design—General	M
Applied Mathematics	M,D
Architecture	M,D,O
Art Education	M,D,O
Art History	M
Art/Fine Arts	M,O
Athletic Training and Sports Medicine	M,D
Atmospheric Sciences	M,D
Biochemistry	M,D
Biological and Biomedical Sciences—General	M,D
Biomedical Engineering	M,D
Biostatistics	M,D,O
Business Administration and Management—General	M,D,O
Business Analytics	M,O
Cell Biology	M,D
Chemistry	M,D
Civil Engineering	M,D
Classics	M,O
Communication Disorders	M
Communication—General	M,D,O
Community Health	D
Comparative Literature	M,O
Computer Art and Design	M,O
Computer Engineering	M,D
Computer Science	M,D
Conflict Resolution and Mediation/Peace Studies	M,D,O
Counseling Psychology	M,D,O
Criminal Justice and Criminology	M,O
Curriculum and Instruction	M,D,O
Dance	M,O
Developmental Psychology	M,D,O
Early Childhood Education	M
Economics	M,D
Education—General	M,D,O
Educational Leadership and Administration	M,D,O
Educational Measurement and Evaluation	M,D,O
Educational Media/Instructional Technology	M
Educational Policy	M,O
Educational Psychology	M,D,O
Electrical Engineering	M,D
Elementary Education	M
Engineering and Applied Sciences—General	M,D
English as a Second Language	M,D
English Education	M,D
English	M,D
Entrepreneurship	M,D,O
Environmental and Occupational Health	M,D,O
Environmental Sciences	M,D
Epidemiology	M,D,O
Ergonomics and Human Factors	M
Exercise and Sports Science	M,D
Family Nurse Practitioner Studies	M,D,O
Film, Television, and Video Production	M,O
Film, Television, and Video Theory and Criticism	M,D
Foreign Languages Education	M,O
Foundations and Philosophy of Education	M,D,O
French	M,O
Gender Studies	M,O
Geographic Information Systems	M,D,O
Geography	M,D
Geology	M,O
German	M,O
Gerontology	M,D,O
Health Informatics	M,D
Health Promotion	M,D,O
Health Services Management and Hospital Administration	M,D
Higher Education	M,O
History	M,D
Human Resources Management	M,O

Industrial and Labor Relations	M,O
Industrial/Management Engineering	M,D
Information Studies	M,D,O
Investment Management	M,O
Kinesiology and Movement Studies	M,O
Latin American Studies	M,O
Liberal Studies	M
Library Science	M,D,O
Linguistics	M,D,O
Management of Technology	M,O
Management Strategy and Policy	M,D,O
Manufacturing Engineering	M,D
Materials Engineering	M,D
Mathematics Education	M,D,O
Mathematics	M,D
Mechanical Engineering	M,D
Mechanics	M,D
Media Studies	M,D
Medical Imaging	D
Medical Informatics	M
Microbiology	M,D
Middle School Education	M
Molecular Biology	M,D
Multilingual and Multicultural Education	M,D,O
Museum Studies	M,O
Music Education	M,O
Music	M,O
Nonprofit Management	M,D,O
Nursing—General	M,D,O*
Nutrition	M,D
Occupational Therapy	M
Philosophy	M
Physical Therapy	M,D
Physics	M,D
Political Science	M,D
Portuguese	M
Psychology—General	M,D
Public Administration	M
Public Health—General	M,D,O
Reading Education	M
Recreation and Park Management	M
Rehabilitation Sciences	D
Rhetoric	M,D,O
School Psychology	M,D,O
Science Education	M
Secondary Education	M,D
Social Sciences Education	M
Social Work	M,D,O
Sociology	M,D
Spanish	M,O
Special Education	M,D,O
Statistics	M,D
Taxation	M,O
Translation and Interpretation	M,O
Urban and Regional Planning	M
Urban Education	M,D,O
Urban Studies	M,D
Water Resources	M,D
Women's Studies	M,O
Writing	M

UNIVERSITY OF WISCONSIN–OSHKOSH

Adult Nursing	M
Biological and Biomedical Sciences—General	M
Botany	M
Business Administration and Management—General	M
Counselor Education	M
Curriculum and Instruction	M
Early Childhood Education	M
Education—General	M
Educational Leadership and Administration	M
English	M
Experimental Psychology	M
Family Nurse Practitioner Studies	M
Health Services Management and Hospital Administration	M
Industrial and Organizational Psychology	M
International Business	M
Mathematics Education	M
Microbiology	M
Nursing—General	M
Psychology—General	M
Public Administration	M
Reading Education	M
Social Work	M
Special Education	M
Zoology	M

UNIVERSITY OF WISCONSIN–PARKSIDE

Business Administration and Management—General	M
Clinical Psychology	M
Computer Science	M
Health Promotion	M
Information Science	M
Molecular Biology	M
Sports Management	M
Sustainability Management	M

UNIVERSITY OF WISCONSIN–PLATTEVILLE

Adult Education	M
Computer Science	M
Criminal Justice and Criminology	M
Education—General	M
Engineering and Applied Sciences—General	M
Organizational Management	M
Project Management	M
Supply Chain Management	M

UNIVERSITY OF WISCONSIN–RIVER FALLS

Agricultural Education	M
Agricultural Sciences—General	M
Art/Fine Arts	M
Business Administration and Management—General	M

Communication Disorders	M
Counselor Education	M,O
Education—General	M
Elementary Education	M
English as a Second Language	M
Mathematics Education	M
Reading Education	M
School Psychology	M,O
Science Education	M
Social Sciences Education	M

UNIVERSITY OF WISCONSIN–STEVENS POINT

Advertising and Public Relations	M
Athletic Training and Sports Medicine	M
Communication Disorders	M,D
Communication—General	M
Corporate and Organizational Communication	M
Data Science/Data Analytics	M
Education—General	M,D
Educational Leadership and Administration	M,D
Elementary Education	M
English Education	M
Family and Consumer Sciences-General	O
Health Promotion	M
Media Studies	M
Music Education	M
Natural Resources	M
Nutrition	M
Reading Education	M
Science Education	M
Secondary Education	M
Social Sciences Education	M
Special Education	M
Speech and Interpersonal Communication	M
Sustainable Development	D

UNIVERSITY OF WISCONSIN–STOUT

Applied Mathematics	M
Applied Psychology	M
Art/Fine Arts	M
Clinical Psychology	M
Conservation Biology	M
Construction Management	M
Counseling Psychology	M
Education—General	M,D,O
Food Science and Technology	M
Human Resources Development	M
Industrial Hygiene	M
Industrial/Management Engineering	M
Information Science	M
Manufacturing Engineering	M
Marriage and Family Therapy	M
Nutrition	M
Project Management	M
Quality Management	M
Rehabilitation Counseling	M
School Psychology	M,O
Supply Chain Management	M
Sustainability Management	M
Technical Communication	M
Telecommunications Management	M
Vocational and Technical Education	M,D,O

UNIVERSITY OF WISCONSIN–SUPERIOR

Art Education	M
Art History	M
Art Therapy	M
Art/Fine Arts	M
Communication—General	M
Counselor Education	M
Curriculum and Instruction	M
Education—General	M
Educational Leadership and Administration	M,O
Mass Communication	M
Reading Education	M
School Psychology	M
Social Psychology	M
Special Education	M
Speech and Interpersonal Communication	M
Sustainability Management	M
Theater	M

UNIVERSITY OF WISCONSIN–WHITEWATER

Accounting	M
Business Administration and Management—General	M
Business Education	M
Communication Disorders	M
Communication—General	M
Corporate and Organizational Communication	M
Education—General	M,O
Educational Leadership and Administration	M
Environmental and Occupational Health	M
Finance and Banking	M
Marketing	M
Mass Communication	M
Psychology—General	M,O
School Psychology	M,O
Special Education	M,O

UNIVERSITY OF WYOMING

Accounting	M
Agricultural Economics and Agribusiness	M
Agricultural Sciences—General	M,D
Agronomy and Soil Sciences	M,D
American Studies	M
Animal Sciences	M,D
Anthropology	M,D
Applied Economics	M

Applied Statistics	M,D
Architectural Engineering	M,D
Atmospheric Sciences	M,D
Biotechnology	D
Botany	M,D
Business Administration and Management—General	M
Cell Biology	D
Chemical Engineering	M,D
Chemistry	M,D
Child Development	M
Civil Engineering	M,D
Communication Disorders	M
Communication—General	M
Community Health	M
Computational Biology	D
Computer Science	M,D
Consumer Economics	M
Counselor Education	M,D
Curriculum and Instruction	M,D
Ecology	M,D
Economics	M,D
Educational Leadership and Administration	M,D,O
Educational Media/Instructional Technology	M,D
Electrical Engineering	M,D
Engineering and Applied Sciences—General	M,D
English	M,D
Entomology	M,D
Environmental Engineering	M
Exercise and Sports Science	M
Finance and Banking	M
Food Science and Technology	M
French	M
Genetics	D
Geography	M
Geology	M,D
Geophysics	M,D
German	M
Health Education	M
Health Promotion	M
Health Services Management and Hospital Administration	M,D
History	M
International Affairs	M
Kinesiology and Movement Studies	M
Law	D
Mathematics Education	M,D
Mathematics	M,D
Mechanical Engineering	M,D
Microbiology	D
Molecular Biology	M,D
Music Education	M
Music	M
Natural Resources	M,D
Nursing—General	M
Nutrition	M
Pathobiology	M
Petroleum Engineering	M,D
Pharmacy	M
Philosophy	M
Physical Education	M
Physiology	M,D
Political Science	M
Psychology—General	M,D
Public Administration	M
Range Science	M,D
Reproductive Biology	M,D
Rural Planning and Studies	M
Science Education	M
Social Work	M
Sociology	M
Spanish	M
Special Education	M,D,O
Student Affairs	M,D
Water Resources	M,D
Writing	M
Zoology	M,D

UPPER IOWA UNIVERSITY

Accounting	M
Business Administration and Management—General	M
Early Childhood Education	M
Education—General	M
Educational Leadership and Administration	M
Emergency Management	M
English as a Second Language	M
Finance and Banking	M
Higher Education	M
Homeland Security	M
Human Resources Management	M
Human Services	M
Nonprofit Management	M
Organizational Management	M
Public Administration	M
Reading Education	M
Sports Management	M

URBANA UNIVERSITY–A BRANCH CAMPUS OF FRANKLIN UNIVERSITY

Business Administration and Management—General	M
Criminal Justice and Criminology	M
Education—General	M
Nursing—General	M

URSHAN GRADUATE SCHOOL OF THEOLOGY

Theology	M

URSULINE COLLEGE

Accounting	M
Adult Nursing	M,D
Art Therapy	M
Business Administration and Management—General	M
Educational Leadership and Administration	M
Entrepreneurship	M
Family Nurse Practitioner Studies	M,D

Finance and Banking	M
Gerontological Nursing	M,D
Health Services Management and Hospital Administration	M
Historic Preservation	M
Marketing	M
Medical/Surgical Nursing	M,D
Nursing Education	M,D
Nursing—General	M,D
Pastoral Ministry and Counseling	M
Theology	M

UTAH STATE UNIVERSITY

Accounting	M
Aerospace/Aeronautical Engineering	M,D
Agricultural Economics and Agribusiness	M,D
Agricultural Education	M
Agricultural Sciences—General	M,D
Agronomy and Soil Sciences	M,D
American Studies	M
Animal Sciences	M,D
Anthropology	M,D
Applied Economics	M,D
Applied Mathematics	M,D
Art/Fine Arts	M
Biochemistry	M,D
Bioengineering	M,D
Biological and Biomedical Sciences—General	M,D
Business Administration and Management—General	M
Business Education	D
Chemistry	M,D
Child and Family Studies	M,D
Civil Engineering	M,D,O
Clinical Psychology	M,D
Communication Disorders	M,D,O
Communication—General	M
Computer Science	M,D
Consumer Economics	M
Counseling Psychology	M,D
Counselor Education	M,D
Curriculum and Instruction	D
Disability Studies	M,D,O
Ecology	M,D
Economics	M
Education—General	M,D,O
Educational Measurement and Evaluation	M,D
Educational Media/Instructional Technology	M,D,O
Electrical Engineering	M,D
Elementary Education	M
Engineering and Applied Sciences—General	M,D,O
English	M
Environmental Engineering	M,D,O
Environmental Management and Policy	M,D
Family and Consumer Sciences-General	M,D
Finance and Banking	M
Fish, Game, and Wildlife Management	M,D
Folklore	M
Food Science and Technology	M,D
Forestry	M,D
Geography	M,D
Geology	M
Health Education	M,D
Health Promotion	M,D
History	M
Home Economics Education	M,D
Horticulture	M,D
Human Development	M,D
Human Resources Management	M
Kinesiology and Movement Studies	M,D
Landscape Architecture	M
Management Information Systems	M
Marriage and Family Therapy	M,D
Mathematics	M,D
Mechanical Engineering	M,D
Meteorology	M,D
Multilingual and Multicultural Education	M
Music Education	M
Music	M
Natural Resources	M
Nutrition	M,D
Physical Education	M,D
Physics	M,D
Plant Sciences	M,D
Political Science	M
Psychology—General	M,D
Public Health—General	M,D
Range Science	M,D
Recreation and Park Management	M,D
Rehabilitation Counseling	M
School Psychology	M,D
Secondary Education	M
Social Work	M,D
Sociology	M,D
Special Education	M,D,O
Statistics	M,D
Theater	M,D
Toxicology	M,D
Urban and Regional Planning	M,D
Veterinary Sciences	D
Vocational and Technical Education	D
Water Resources	M,D
Writing	M

UTAH VALLEY UNIVERSITY

Accounting	M
Business Administration and Management—General	M
Computer and Information Systems Security	O
Education—General	M
Educational Leadership and Administration	M

Educational Media/Instructional
  Technology — M
Elementary Education — M
English as a Second Language — M
Mathematics Education — M
Nursing—General — M
Reading Education — M
Social Work — M

UTICA COLLEGE
Accounting — M
Computer and Information
  Systems Security — M
Criminal Justice and Criminology — M
Education—General — M,O
Health Services Management and
  Hospital Administration — M
Occupational Therapy — M
Physical Therapy — D

VALDOSTA STATE UNIVERSITY
Accounting — M
Business Administration and
  Management—General — M
Communication Disorders — M,D,O
Counselor Education — M,O
Educational Leadership and
  Administration — M,D,O
Elementary Education — M
English Education — M
English — M
Exercise and Sports Science — M
Family Nurse Practitioner Studies — M
Gerontological Nursing — M
Health Services Management and
  Hospital Administration — M
Industrial and Organizational
  Psychology — M,O
Information Studies — M
Library Science — M
Marriage and Family Therapy — M
Nursing—General — M
Psychiatric Nursing — M
Psychology—General — M,O
Public Administration — M,D
Social Work — M
Special Education — M,D,O

VALLEY CITY STATE UNIVERSITY
Education—General — M
Educational Media/Instructional
  Technology — M
Elementary Education — M
English as a Second Language — M
English Education — M
Library Science — M
Vocational and Technical Education — M

VALPARAISO UNIVERSITY
Arts Administration — M
Business Administration and
  Management—General — M,O
Clinical Psychology — M
Communication—General — M,O
Computational Sciences — M
Computer and Information
  Systems Security — M
Education—General — M,O
Educational Leadership and
  Administration — M,O
Elementary Education — M,O
Engineering Management — M,O
English as a Second Language — M,O
English — M
Entertainment Management — M
Ethics — M,O
Finance and Banking — M,O
Health Services Management and
  Hospital Administration — M
International Economics — M
International Trade Policy — M
Management Information Systems — M
Management Strategy and Policy — M,O
Media Studies — M,O
Nursing Education — M,D,O
Nursing—General — M,D,O
Physician Assistant Studies — M,D,O
Public Health—General — M,D,O
School Psychology — M,O
Secondary Education — M,O
Sports Management — M

VAN ANDEL INSTITUTE GRADUATE SCHOOL
Genetics — D
Molecular Genetics — D

VANCOUVER ISLAND UNIVERSITY
Business Administration and
  Management—General — M
Finance and Banking — M
International Business — M
Marketing — M

VANCOUVER SCHOOL OF THEOLOGY
Religion — M,O
Religious Education — M,O
Theology — M,O

VANDERBILT UNIVERSITY
Accounting — M
Allopathic Medicine — M,D
Anthropology — M,D
Biochemistry — M,D
Bioinformatics — M,D
Biological and Biomedical
  Sciences—General — M,D
Biomedical Engineering — M,D
Biophysics — M,D
Business Administration and
  Management—General — M
Cell Biology — M,D
Chemical Engineering — M,D

Chemistry — M,D
Civil Engineering — M,D
Communication Disorders — M,D
Computer and Information
  Systems Security — M
Computer Science — M,D
Developmental Biology — M,D
Economic Development — M,D
Economics — M,D
Education—General — M,D*
Educational Leadership and
  Administration — D
Electrical Engineering — M,D
Elementary Education — M
Engineering and Applied
  Sciences—General — M,D
English Education — M
English — M,D
Environmental Engineering — M,D
Environmental Management
  and Policy — M,D
Environmental Sciences — M
Finance and Banking — M
Foreign Languages Education — M,D
French — M,D
Geology — M
German — M,D
Health Services Management and
  Hospital Administration — M
History — M,D
Human Genetics — D
Immunology — M,D
Latin American Studies — M
Law — M,D
Liberal Studies — M
Management Strategy and Policy — M
Marketing — M
Materials Sciences — M,D
Mathematics — M,D
Mechanical Engineering — M,D
Microbiology — M,D
Molecular Biology — M,D
Molecular Physiology — M,D
Multilingual and Multicultural
  Education — D
Nursing—General — M,D,O
Organizational Management — M
Pathology — D
Pharmacology — D
Philosophy — M,D
Physics — M,D
Political Science — M,D
Portuguese — M,D
Psychology—General — D
Public Health—General — M
Public Policy — D
Quantitative Analysis — M
Reading Education — M
Religion — M,D
Secondary Education — M
Sociology — M,D
Spanish — M,D
Special Education — D
Theology — M
Urban and Regional Planning — M
Writing — M

VANDERCOOK COLLEGE OF MUSIC
Music Education — M

VANGUARD UNIVERSITY OF SOUTHERN CALIFORNIA
Clinical Psychology — M
Curriculum and Instruction — M
Education—General — M
Educational Leadership and
  Administration — M
Industrial and Organizational
  Psychology — M
Nursing—General — M
Religion — M
Religious Education — M
Theology — M

VAUGHN COLLEGE OF AERONAUTICS AND TECHNOLOGY
Aviation Management — M

VERMONT COLLEGE OF FINE ARTS
Art Education — M
Art/Fine Arts — M
Film, Television, and Video
  Production — M
Graphic Design — M
Music — M
Publishing — M
Translation and Interpretation — M
Writing — M

VERMONT LAW SCHOOL
Energy Management and
  Policy — M
Environmental Law — M
Environmental Management
  and Policy — M
Law — D
Legal and Justice Studies — M

VERMONT TECHNICAL COLLEGE
Software Engineering — M

VICTORIA UNIVERSITY
Theology — M,D,O

VILLANOVA UNIVERSITY
Accounting — M
Adult Nursing — M,D,O
Applied Statistics — M
Artificial Intelligence/Robotics — M,O
Biochemical Engineering — M,O
Biological and Biomedical
  Sciences—General — M

Business Administration and
  Management—General — M
Business Analytics — M
Chemical Engineering — M,O
Chemistry — M
Civil Engineering — M
Classics — M
Communication—General — M
Computer Engineering — M,O
Computer Science — M,O
Counselor Education — M
Education—General — M
Educational Leadership and
  Administration — M
Electrical Engineering — M,O
Engineering and Applied
  Sciences—General — M,D,O
English — M
Environmental Engineering — M,O
Family Nurse Practitioner Studies — M,D,O
Finance and Banking — M
Gerontological Nursing — M,D,O
Health Services Management and
  Hospital Administration — M
Hispanic Studies — M
History — M
Human Resources Development — M
International Business — M
Law — D
Liberal Studies — M
Management Strategy and Policy — M
Manufacturing Engineering — M,O
Marketing — M
Mathematics — M
Mechanical Engineering — M,O
Missions and Missiology — M
Nonprofit Management — M,O
Nurse Anesthesia — M,D,O
Nursing Education — M,D,O
Nursing—General — M,D,O
Pediatric Nursing — M,D,O
Philosophy — D
Political Science — M
Psychology—General — M
Public Administration — M
Real Estate — M
Taxation — M
Theater — M
Theology — M,D
Water Resources Engineering — M,O

VIRGINIA BAPTIST COLLEGE
Theology — M

VIRGINIA BEACH THEOLOGICAL SEMINARY
Pastoral Ministry and Counseling — M
Theology — M

VIRGINIA COMMONWEALTH UNIVERSITY
Accounting — M
Adult Education — M
Adult Nursing — M,D,O
Advertising and Public Relations — M
Allied Health—General — D
Allopathic Medicine — D
Analytical Chemistry — M,D
Anatomy — M
Applied Mathematics — M
Applied Physics — M
Art Education — M,D
Art History — M,D
Art/Fine Arts — M,D
Biochemistry — M,D
Biological and Biomedical
  Sciences—General — M,D,O
Biomedical Engineering — M,D
Biostatistics — M,D
Business Administration and
  Management—General — M,D
Chemical Physics — M,D
Chemistry — M,D
Clinical Laboratory
  Sciences/Medical Technology — M,D
Clinical Psychology — D
Communication—General — D
Community Health — M,D
Computer Science — M,D
Counseling Psychology — M,D
Counselor Education — M,D
Criminal Justice and Criminology — M,O
Curriculum and Instruction — D
Dentistry — M,D
Early Childhood Education — M
Economics — M
Education—General — M,D,O
Educational Leadership and
  Administration — M,D
Educational Measurement and
  Evaluation — D
Educational Media/Instructional
  Technology — M
Educational Psychology — D
Elementary Education — M
Emergency Management — M,O
Engineering and Applied
  Sciences—General — M,D
English — M
Environmental Management
  and Policy — M
Epidemiology — M,D
Exercise and Sports Science — M
Family Nurse Practitioner Studies — M
Film, Television, and Video
  Production — M
Finance and Banking — M
Forensic Sciences — M
Geographic Information Systems — O
Gerontology — M
Health Physics/Radiological Health — D
Health Psychology — D

Health Services Management and
  Hospital Administration — M,D
Health Services Research — D
History — M
Homeland Security — M
Human Genetics — M,D
Human Resources Development — M
Human Resources Management — M
Immunology — M,D
Inorganic Chemistry — M,D
Interdisciplinary Studies — M
Interior Design — M,D
Journalism — M
Management Information Systems — M
Mass Communication — M
Mathematics — M
Mechanical Engineering — M,D
Media Studies — M,D
Medical Physics — M,D
Medicinal and Pharmaceutical
  Chemistry — M,D
Microbiology — M,D
Molecular Biology — M,D
Molecular Genetics — M,D
Museum Studies — M,D
Music Education — M
Music — M
Nanotechnology — M,D
Neurobiology — M
Neuroscience — M,D,O
Nonprofit Management — O
Nuclear Engineering — M,D
Nurse Anesthesia — M,D
Nursing and Healthcare
  Administration — M,D,O
Nursing Education — M,D,O
Nursing—General — M,D,O
Occupational Therapy — M,D
Organic Chemistry — M,D
Pediatric Nursing — M,D,O
Pharmaceutical Administration — M,D
Pharmaceutical Sciences — M,D
Pharmacology — M,D,O
Pharmacy — D
Photography — M,D
Physical Chemistry — M,D
Physical Therapy — M,D
Physics — M
Physiology — M
Political Science — M,D,O
Psychiatric Nursing — M,D,O
Public Administration — M
Public Affairs — M,D,O
Public Health—General — M,D
Public Policy — D
Reading Education — M,O
Real Estate — O
Recreation and Park Management — M
Rehabilitation Counseling — M
Rehabilitation Sciences — D
Social Work — M,D
Sociology — M
Special Education — M,D
Student Affairs — M
Systems Biology — D
Theater — M
Toxicology — M,D,O
Urban and Regional Planning — M
Urban Education — D
Women's Health Nursing — M,D,O
Writing — M

VIRGINIA INTERNATIONAL UNIVERSITY
Accounting — M,O
Advertising and Public Relations — M,O
Business Administration and
  Management—General — M,O
Computer and Information
  Systems Security — M,O
Computer Art and Design — M,O
Computer Science — M,O
Data Science/Data Analytics — M,O
Education—General — M
English as a Second Language — M
Entrepreneurship — M,O
Finance and Banking — M,O
Game Design and
  Development — M,O
Health Informatics — M,O
Health Services Management and
  Hospital Administration — M,O
Hospitality Management — M,O
Human Resources Management — M,O
International Affairs — M,O
International Business — M,O
Linguistics — M
Logistics — M,O
Management Information Systems — M,O
Marketing — M,O
Project Management — M,O
Public Administration — M
Software Engineering — M,O

VIRGINIA POLYTECHNIC INSTITUTE AND STATE UNIVERSITY
Accounting — M,D
Aerospace/Aeronautical
  Engineering — M,D,O
Agricultural Economics and
  Agribusiness — M,D
Agricultural Engineering — M,D
Agricultural Sciences—
  General — M,D,O
Agronomy and Soil Sciences — M,D
Allopathic Medicine — D
Animal Sciences — M,D
Applied Economics — M,D
Applied Statistics — M,D
Biochemistry — M,D
Bioengineering — M,D
Bioinformatics — M,D

Biological and Biomedical
  Sciences—General — M,D
Biomedical Engineering — M,D
Biotechnology — M,D
Business Administration and
  Management—General — M,D
Business Analytics — M,D
Chemical Engineering — M,D
Chemistry — M,D
Civil Engineering — M,D,O
Communication—General — M,D,O
Computer and Information
  Systems Security — M,O
Computer Engineering — M,D,O
Computer Science — M,D,O
Counselor Education — M,D,O
Curriculum and Instruction — M,D,O
Distance Education Development — M,O
Economics — M,D
Education—General — M,O
Educational Leadership and
  Administration — M,D,O
Educational Measurement and
  Evaluation — M,D,O
Educational Media/Instructional
  Technology — M,O
Educational Policy — M,D,O
Electrical Engineering — M,D,O
Engineering and Applied
  Sciences—General — M,D
Engineering Management — M,O
English — M,D,O
Entomology — M,D
Environmental Design — M,D
Environmental Engineering — M,O
Environmental Management
  and Policy — M,D,O
Environmental Sciences — M,O
Exercise and Sports Science — M,D
Finance and Banking — M,D
Fish, Game, and Wildlife
  Management — M,D
Forestry — M,D
Genetics — M,D
Geography — M,D
Geosciences — M,D
Horticulture — M,D
Humanities — M,D,O
Industrial/Management
  Engineering — M,O
Interdisciplinary Studies — M,D
International Affairs — M,D
Internet and Interactive
  Multimedia — M,D
Landscape Architecture — M,D
Liberal Studies — M,O
Management Information Systems — M,D,O
Marketing — M,D
Mathematics — M,D
National Security — M,O
Natural Resources — M,D,O
Nonprofit Management — M,O
Nutrition — M,D
Ocean Engineering — M,O
Physics — M,D
Plant Pathology — M,D
Plant Physiology — M,D
Political Science — M,O
Psychology—General — M,D
Public Administration — M,D
Public Affairs — M,D
Public Health—General — M,D
Public Policy — M,D
Quantitative Analysis — M,O
Social Sciences Education — M,D,O
Software Engineering — M,O
Statistics — M,D
Systems Engineering — M,O
Translational Biology — M,D
Transportation and Highway
  Engineering — M,O
Urban and Regional Planning — M,D
Urban Studies — M,D
Veterinary Medicine — M,D
Veterinary Sciences — M,D
Vocational and Technical Education — M,D,O
Writing — M,D,O

VIRGINIA STATE UNIVERSITY
Biological and Biomedical
  Sciences—General — M
Clinical Psychology — M,D
Community Health — M,D
Counselor Education — M
Criminal Justice and Criminology — M
Economics — M
Education—General — M,D
Educational Leadership and
  Administration — M
Health Education — M,D
Health Psychology — M,D
Interdisciplinary Studies — M
Mathematics — M
Media Studies — M
Psychology—General — M,D

VIRGINIA THEOLOGICAL SEMINARY
Educational Leadership and
  Administration — M,D
Theology — M,D

VIRGINIA UNION UNIVERSITY
Curriculum and Instruction — M
Education—General — M
Theology — M,D

VIRGINIA UNIVERSITY OF INTEGRATIVE MEDICINE
Acupuncture and Oriental Medicine — M
Nutrition — M,D,O

VIRGINIA UNIVERSITY OF LYNCHBURG
Pastoral Ministry and Counseling — M,D
Religion — M,D

VIRGINIA WESLEYAN UNIVERSITY
Business Administration and
  Management—General — M
Education—General — M
Secondary Education — M

VITERBO UNIVERSITY
Addictions/Substance Abuse
  Counseling — M
Business Administration and
  Management—General — M
Counseling Psychology — M
Developmental Psychology — M
Early Childhood Education — M,O
Education of the Gifted — M,O
Education—General — M,O
Educational Leadership and
  Administration — M,O
Ethics — M,O
Health Psychology — M
Health Services Management and
  Hospital Administration — M
International Business — M
Nursing—General — D
Organizational Management — M,O
Pastoral Ministry and Counseling — M,O
Project Management — M
Reading Education — M,O
Special Education — M,O

WAGNER COLLEGE
Accounting — M
Business Administration and
  Management—General — M
Early Childhood Education — M
Education—General — M
Elementary Education — M
English Education — M
Family Nurse Practitioner Studies — M,D,O
Finance and Banking — M
Foreign Languages Education — M
Higher Education — M
Marketing — M
Mathematics Education — M
Media Studies — M
Microbiology — M
Middle School Education — M
Nursing Education — M,D,O
Nursing—General — M,D,O
Science Education — M
Secondary Education — M
Social Sciences Education — M
Special Education — M

WAKE FOREST UNIVERSITY
Accounting — M
Allopathic Medicine — D
Analytical Chemistry — M,D
Anatomy — D
Biochemistry — D
Biological and Biomedical
  Sciences—General — M,D
Biomedical Engineering — M,D
Business Administration and
  Management—General — M
Business Analytics — M
Cancer Biology/Oncology — D
Chemistry — M,D
Clinical Laboratory
  Sciences/Medical Technology — M
Communication—General — M
Computer Science — M
Counselor Education — M
Education—General — M
English — M
Exercise and Sports Science — M
Genomic Sciences — D
Immunology — D
Inorganic Chemistry — M,D
Law — M,D
Liberal Studies — M
Mathematics — M
Microbiology — D
Molecular Genetics — D
Molecular Medicine — M,D
Neurobiology — D
Neuroscience — D
Nurse Anesthesia — M
Organic Chemistry — M,D
Pharmacology — D
Physical Chemistry — M,D
Physics — M,D
Physiology — D
Psychology—General — M
Religion — M
Secondary Education — M
Speech and Interpersonal
  Communication — M
Taxation — M
Translational Biology — M,D

WALDEN UNIVERSITY
Accounting — M,D,O
Addictions/Substance Abuse
  Counseling — M,D
Adult Education — M,D,O
Adult Nursing — M,D,O
Applied Psychology — M,D,O
Business Administration and
  Management—General — M,D,O
Child and Family Studies — M,D
Clinical Psychology — M,D,O
Clinical Research — M,D,O
Communication—General — M,D,O
Community Health — M,D,O
Computer and Information
  Systems Security — M,D,O
Conflict Resolution and
  Mediation/Peace Studies — M,D,O
Counseling Psychology — M,D,O
Counselor Education — M,D
Criminal Justice and Criminology — M,D,O
Curriculum and Instruction — M,D,O
Developmental Education — M,D,O
Distance Education Development — M,D,O

Early Childhood Education — M,D,O
Education—General — M,D,O
Educational Leadership and
  Administration — M,D,O
Educational Measurement and
  Evaluation — M,D,O
Educational Media/Instructional
  Technology — M,D,O
Educational Psychology — M,D,O
Elementary Education — M,D,O
Emergency Management — M,D,O
English as a Second Language — M,D,O
Entrepreneurship — M,D,O
Epidemiology — M,D,O
Family Nurse Practitioner Studies — M,D,O
Finance and Banking — M,D,O
Forensic Psychology — M,D,O
Gerontological Nursing — M,D,O
Gerontology — M,D
Health Education — M,D,O
Health Informatics — M,D,O
Health Promotion — M,D,O
Health Psychology — M,D,O
Health Services Management and
  Hospital Administration — M,D,O
Higher Education — M,D,O
Homeland Security — M,D,O
Human Resources Management — M,D,O
Human Services — M,D
Industrial and Organizational
  Psychology — M,D,O
Interdisciplinary Studies — M,D,O
International Affairs — M,D,O
International and Comparative
  Education — M,D,O
International Business — M,D,O
International Development — M,D,O
International Health — M,D,O
Law — M,D,O
Management Information Systems — M,D,O
Marketing — M,D,O
Marriage and Family Therapy — M,D
Mathematics Education — M,D,O
Multilingual and Multicultural
  Education — M,D,O
Nonprofit Management — M,D,O
Nursing and Healthcare
  Administration — M,D,O
Nursing Education — M,D,O
Nursing Informatics — M,D,O
Nursing—General — M,D,O
Organizational Management — M,D,O
Political Science — M,D,O
Project Management — M,D,O
Psychology—General — M,D,O
Public Administration — M,D,O
Public Health—General — M,D,O
Public Policy — M,D,O
Reading Education — M,D,O
Science Education — M,D,O
Social Psychology — M,D,O
Social Work — M,D
Special Education — M,D,O
Supply Chain Management — M,D,O
Sustainable Development — M,D,O

WALDORF UNIVERSITY
Criminal Justice and Criminology — M
Educational Leadership and
  Administration — M
Emergency Management — M
Human Resources Development — M
Organizational Management — M
Public Administration — M
Sports Management — M

WALLA WALLA UNIVERSITY
Biological and Biomedical
  Sciences—General — M
Communication—General — M
Curriculum and Instruction — M
Education—General — M
Educational Leadership and
  Administration — M
Film, Television, and Video
  Theory and Criticism — M
Internet and Interactive
  Multimedia — M
Pastoral Ministry and Counseling — M
Reading Education — M
Religion — M
Social Work — M
Special Education — M

WALSH COLLEGE OF ACCOUNTANCY AND BUSINESS ADMINISTRATION
Business Administration and
  Management—General — M
Business Analytics — M
Computer and Information
  Systems Security — M
Data Science/Data Analytics — M
Finance and Banking — M
Human Resources Management — M
International Business — M
Investment Management — M
Management Strategy and Policy — M
Project Management — M
Taxation — M

WALSH UNIVERSITY
Adult Nursing — M,D
Business Administration and
  Management—General — M
Counseling Psychology — M
Counselor Education — M
Education—General — M
Health Services Management and
  Hospital Administration — M
Higher Education — M
Marketing — M
Nursing and Healthcare
  Administration — M,D
Nursing Education — M,D
Nursing—General — M,D

Pastoral Ministry and Counseling — M
Physical Therapy — D
Reading Education — M
Religious Education — M
Student Affairs — M
Theology — M

WARNER PACIFIC UNIVERSITY
Education—General — M
Human Services — M
Nonprofit Management — M
Organizational Management — M

WARNER UNIVERSITY
Accounting — M
Business Administration and
  Management—General — M
Curriculum and Instruction — M
Education—General — M
Educational Media/Instructional
  Technology — M
Elementary Education — M
Human Resources Management — M
International Business — M
Science Education — M

WARREN WILSON COLLEGE
Art/Fine Arts — M
Writing — M

WARTBURG THEOLOGICAL SEMINARY
Theology — M

WASHBURN UNIVERSITY
Accounting — M
Addictions/Substance Abuse
  Counseling — M
Business Administration and
  Management—General — M
Clinical Psychology — M
Criminal Justice and Criminology — M
Curriculum and Instruction — M
Education—General — M
Educational Leadership and
  Administration — M
Health Education — M
Human Services — M
Law — M,D
Legal and Justice Studies — M,D
Liberal Studies — M
Nursing and Healthcare
  Administration — M,D,O
Nursing—General — M,D,O
Psychology—General — M
Reading Education — M
Social Work — M
Special Education — M

WASHINGTON ADVENTIST UNIVERSITY
Business Administration and
  Management—General — M
Counseling Psychology — M
Health Services Management and
  Hospital Administration — M
Nursing and Healthcare
  Administration — M
Nursing Education — M
Nursing—General — M
Public Administration — M
Religion — M

WASHINGTON & JEFFERSON COLLEGE
Accounting — M,O
Applied Economics — M,O
Thanatology — M,O
Writing — M,O

WASHINGTON AND LEE UNIVERSITY
Law — D

WASHINGTON STATE UNIVERSITY
Accounting — M
Agricultural Economics and
  Agribusiness — M,D,O
Agricultural Engineering — M,D
Agronomy and Soil Sciences — M,D,O
Allopathic Medicine — M,D
American Studies — M,D
Animal Sciences — M,D
Anthropology — M,D
Applied Mathematics — M,D
Archaeology — M,D
Architecture — M
Art/Fine Arts — M
Biochemistry — M,D
Bioengineering — M,D
Bioethics — M,D,O
Biological and Biomedical
  Sciences—General — M,D
Biophysics — M,D
Business Administration and
  Management—General — M,D
Business Education — M,D
Chemical Engineering — M,D
Chemistry — M,D
Civil Engineering — M,D
Clinical Psychology — M
Clothing and Textiles — M
Communication Disorders — M
Communication—General — M,D
Community Health — M,D,O
Computer Engineering — M,D
Computer Science — M,D
Corporate and Organizational
  Communication — M,D
Counseling Psychology — M,D
Criminal Justice and Criminology — M,D
Cultural Anthropology — M,D
Cultural Studies — M,D
Curriculum and Instruction — M,D
Economics — M,D,O
Education—General — M,D
Educational Leadership and
  Administration — M,D
Educational Psychology — M,D
Electrical Engineering — M,D
Elementary Education — M,D

Energy and Power
  Engineering M,D
Engineering and Applied
  Sciences—General M,D,O
Engineering Management M,D
English as a Second Language M,D
English M,D
Entomology M,D
Environmental Engineering M,D
Environmental Sciences M,D
Exercise and Sports Science M
Experimental Psychology M,D
Family Nurse Practitioner Studies M,D,O
Food Science and
  Technology M,D
Foreign Languages Education M
Genetics M,D
Geology M,D
Health Services Management and
  Hospital Administration M
History M,D
Horticulture M,D
Human Development D
Immunology M,D
Infectious Diseases M,D
Interdisciplinary Studies D
Interior Design M
Landscape Architecture M
Management of Technology M,O
Materials Engineering M,D
Materials Sciences M,D
Mathematics Education M,D
Mathematics M,D
Mechanical Engineering M,D
Music M
Natural Resources M,D
Neuroscience M,D
Nursing—General M,D,O
Nutrition M,D
Pharmacy M,D
Physics M,D
Plant Pathology M,D
Political Science M,D,O
Psychiatric Nursing M,D,O
Psychology—General M,D
Public Affairs M,D,O
Reading Education M,D
Secondary Education M,D
Sociology M,D
Special Education M,D
Sports Management M,D
Veterinary Medicine D
Veterinary Sciences M,D
Vocational and Technical Education M,D

WASHINGTON UNIVERSITY IN ST. LOUIS

Accounting M
Aerospace/Aeronautical
  Engineering M,D
Allopathic Medicine D
Anthropology M
Archaeology M,D
Architecture M
Art History M,D
Art/Fine Arts M
Asian Languages M,D
Asian Studies M,D
Biochemistry D
Bioethics M
Biological and Biomedical
  Sciences—General D
Biomedical Engineering M,D
Biostatistics M,D,O
Business Administration and
  Management—General M,D
Cell Biology D
Chemical Engineering M,D
Chemistry D
Child and Family Studies M,D
Chinese M,D
Classics M,D
Clinical Research M
Communication Disorders M,D
Comparative Literature M,D
Computational Biology D
Computer Engineering M,D
Computer Science M,D
Dance M
Data Science/Data Analytics M
Developmental Biology D
Developmental Psychology D
Ecology D
Economics M,D
Education—General M,D
Educational Measurement and
  Evaluation D
Elementary Education M
Engineering and Applied
  Sciences—General M,D
English M,D
Entrepreneurship M
Environmental Biology D
Environmental Engineering M,D
Epidemiology M,D
Evolutionary Biology D
Finance and Banking M,D
French D
Genetics M,D
Genomic Sciences M
Geosciences D
German D
Gerontology M,O
Health Services Research M,O
History D
Human Genetics D
Immunology D
International Health M,D
Japanese M,D
Jewish Studies M
Kinesiology and Movement Studies D

Landscape Architecture M
Law M,D
Materials Sciences M,D
Mathematics M,D
Mechanical Engineering M,D
Microbiology D
Molecular Biology D
Molecular Biophysics D
Molecular Genetics D
Molecular Pathogenesis D
Music M
Near and Middle Eastern Studies M
Neuroscience D
Occupational Therapy M
Organizational Management M,D
Philosophy D
Physical Therapy M
Physics D
Planetary and Space
  Sciences D
Plant Biology D
Political Science D
Psychology—General D
Public Health—General M,D
Rehabilitation Sciences D
Religion M
Romance Languages D
Secondary Education M
Social Work M,D
Spanish D
Special Education M,D
Speech and Interpersonal
  Communication M,D
Statistics M,D
Supply Chain Management M
Systems Biology D
Theater M
Urban Design M
Writing M

WATKINS COLLEGE OF ART, DESIGN, & FILM

Film, Television, and Video
  Production M

WAYLAND BAPTIST UNIVERSITY

Accounting M,D
Business Administration and
  Management—General M,D
Counseling Psychology M
Criminal Justice and Criminology M
Education—General M
Educational Leadership and
  Administration M
Educational Measurement and
  Evaluation M
Educational Media/Instructional
  Technology M
Elementary Education M
English as a Second Language M
English Education M
Health Services Management and
  Hospital Administration M,D
Higher Education M
History M
Homeland Security M
Human Resources Management M,D
Humanities M
International Business M,D
Management Information Systems M,D
Organizational Management M,D
Pastoral Ministry and Counseling M,D
Project Management M,D
Religion M
Science Education M
Secondary Education M
Social Sciences Education M
Special Education M
Sports Management M
Theology M

WAYNESBURG UNIVERSITY

Addictions/Substance Abuse
  Counseling M,D
Business Administration and
  Management—General M,D
Clinical Psychology M,D
Counseling Psychology M,D
Counselor Education M,D
Criminal Justice and Criminology M,D
Curriculum and Instruction M,D
Distance Education Development M,D
Educational Leadership and
  Administration M,D
Educational Media/Instructional
  Technology M,D
Energy Management and
  Policy M,D
Finance and Banking M,D
Health Services Management and
  Hospital Administration M,D
Human Resources Management M,D
Nursing and Healthcare
  Administration M,D
Nursing Education M,D
Nursing Informatics M,D
Nursing—General M,D
Organizational Management M,D
Special Education M,D

WAYNE STATE COLLEGE

Business Administration and
  Management—General M
Business Education M
Communication—General M
Counselor Education M
Curriculum and Instruction M
Early Childhood Education M
Education—General M,O
Educational Leadership and
  Administration M,O
Elementary Education M

English as a Second Language M
English Education M
Exercise and Sports Science M
Home Economics Education M
Mathematics Education M
Music Education M
Organizational Management M
Physical Education M
Science Education M
Social Sciences Education M
Special Education M
Sports Management M
Vocational and Technical Education M

WAYNE STATE UNIVERSITY

Accounting M,D,O
Acute Care/Critical Care Nursing M,D
Adult Nursing M,D
Advertising and Public Relations M,D,O
African-American Studies M,D,O
Analytical Chemistry M,D
Anatomy M,D
Anthropology M,D
Applied Behavior Analysis M,D,O
Applied Mathematics M,D
Archives/Archival Administration M,O
Art Education M,D,O
Art History M
Art/Fine Arts M
Athletic Training and Sports
  Medicine M,D
Automotive Engineering M,O
Biochemistry M,D
Bioinformatics M,D
Biological and Biomedical
  Sciences—General M,D
Biomedical Engineering M,D,O
Biopsychology M,D,O
Business Administration and
  Management—General M,D
Cancer Biology/Oncology M,D,O
Cell Biology M,D,O
Chemical Engineering M,D
Chemistry M,D
Civil Engineering M,D
Clinical Psychology M,D
Clothing and Textiles M
Cognitive Sciences M,D
Communication Disorders M,D
Communication—General M,D
Community Health Nursing M,D
Computational Biology M,D
Computer Engineering M,D
Computer Science M,D
Conflict Resolution and
  Mediation/Peace Studies M,D,O
Counseling Psychology M,D,O
Counselor Education M,D,O
Criminal Justice and Criminology M
Cultural Studies M,D
Curriculum and Instruction M,D,O
Dance M,D,O
Data Science/Data Analytics M,D,O
Distance Education Development M,D,O
Early Childhood Education M,D,O
Economic Development M,D,O
Economics M,D,O
Education—General M,D,O
Educational Leadership and
  Administration M,D,O
Educational Measurement and
  Evaluation M,D,O
Educational Media/Instructional
  Technology M,D,O
Educational Policy M,D,O
Educational Psychology M,D,O
Electrical Engineering M,D
Electronic Materials M
Elementary Education M,D,O
Energy and Power
  Engineering M,O
Engineering and Applied
  Sciences—General M,D,O
Engineering Management M,D,O
English as a Second Language M,D,O
English Education M,D
English M,D
Entrepreneurship M,D
Exercise and Sports Science M,D
Film, Television, and Video
  Theory and Criticism M,D
Finance and Banking M,D
Food Science and
  Technology M,D,O
Foreign Languages Education M,D,O
Foundations and Philosophy of
  Education M,D
French M,D
Gender Studies M,D,O
Genetic Counseling M,D
Genomic Sciences M,D
Geology M,D
German M,D
Gerontological Nursing M,D
Gerontology M,D
Graphic Design M
Health Communication M,D,O
Health Education M,D,O
Health Services Management and
  Hospital Administration M,D
Health Services Research M,D
History M,D,O
Human Resources Management M,D
Immunology M,D,O
Industrial and Labor Relations M,D
Industrial and Manufacturing
  Management M,D
Industrial and Organizational
  Psychology M,D
Industrial Design M

Industrial/Management
  Engineering M,D,O
Information Studies M,D,O
Interior Design M
International Economics M,D
Italian M
Journalism M,D,O
Kinesiology and Movement Studies M
Law M,O
Library Science M
Linguistics M
Management Information Systems M,D,O
Management Strategy and Policy M,D,O
Manufacturing Engineering M,D,O
Materials Sciences M,D,O
Maternal and Child/Neonatal
  Nursing M,D
Mathematics Education M,D
Mathematics M,D
Mechanical Engineering M,D,O
Media Studies M,D,O
Medical Imaging M,D,O
Medical Physics M,D,O
Medicinal and Pharmaceutical
  Chemistry M,D
Microbiology M,D,O
Molecular Biology M,D,O
Molecular Genetics M,D
Molecular Medicine M,D,O
Multilingual and Multicultural
  Education M,D,O
Museum Studies M,D,O
Music Education M,O
Music M,O
Near and Middle Eastern Languages M,D
Near and Middle Eastern Studies M,D
Neuroscience M,D
Nonprofit Management M,D
Nurse Anesthesia M,D,O
Nurse Midwifery M,D
Nursing—General M,D,O
Nutrition M,D,O
Occupational Therapy M
Organizational Behavior M
Organizational Management M,D
Pathology M,D,O
Pediatric Nursing M,D,O
Pharmaceutical Sciences M,D
Pharmacology M,D,O
Pharmacy D
Philosophy M,D
Photography M
Physical Education M,D
Physical Therapy D
Physician Assistant Studies M
Physics M,D
Physiology M,D,O
Political Science M,D
Polymer Science and
  Engineering M,D,O
Psychiatric Nursing M,D
Psychology—General M,D
Public Administration M,D
Public Health—General M,D,O
Public History M,D,O
Public Policy M,D,O
Reading Education M,D,O
Rehabilitation Counseling M,D,O
Rhetoric M,D
Romance Languages M,D
School Psychology M,D,O
Science Education M,D,O
Secondary Education M,D,O
Social Psychology M,D,O
Social Sciences Education M,D,O
Social Work M,D,O
Sociology M,D
Spanish M,D
Special Education M,D,O
Sports Management M,D
Statistics M,D
Systems Engineering M,D,O
Taxation M,D,O
Textile Design M
Theater M
Toxicology M,D
Urban and Regional Planning M
Urban Studies M,D,O
Women's Health Nursing M,D
Women's Studies M,D,O
Writing M,D

WEBBER INTERNATIONAL UNIVERSITY

Accounting M
Business Administration and
  Management—General M
Criminal Justice and Criminology M
International Business M
Sports Management M

WEBER STATE UNIVERSITY

Accounting M
Athletic Training and Sports
  Medicine M
Business Administration and
  Management—General M,O
Communication—General M
Computer Engineering M
Curriculum and Instruction M
Education—General M
English M
Health Physics/Radiological Health M
Health Services Management and
  Hospital Administration M
Legal and Justice Studies M
Nursing and Healthcare
  Administration M
Nursing Education M
Nursing—General M
Taxation M

M—masters degree; D—doctorate; O—other advanced degree; *—Close-Up and/or Display

WEBSTER UNIVERSITY

Accounting	M
Advertising and Public Relations	M
Aerospace/Aeronautical Engineering	M,D,O
Art History	M
Art/Fine Arts	M
Business Administration and Management—General	M,D,O
Communication Disorders	M
Communication—General	M
Computer and Information Systems Security	M
Computer Science	M
Corporate and Organizational Communication	M
Counseling Psychology	M
Criminal Justice and Criminology	M,D,O
Early Childhood Education	M,O
Education—General	M,O
Educational Media/Instructional Technology	M,O
Educational Psychology	M,O
Elementary Education	M,O
English as a Second Language	M,O
Environmental Management and Policy	M
Finance and Banking	M
Forensic Sciences	M
Gerontology	M
Health Services Management and Hospital Administration	M,D,O
Human Resources Development	M,D,O
Human Resources Management	M,D,O
Human Services	M
International Affairs	M
International Business	M
Internet and Interactive Multimedia	M
Legal and Justice Studies	M,O
Management Information Systems	M,D,O
Management of Technology	M,D,O
Marketing	M,D,O
Mathematics Education	M,O
Media Studies	M
Middle School Education	M,O
Music Education	M
Music	M
Nonprofit Management	M,D,O
Nurse Anesthesia	D
Nursing Education	M
Nursing—General	M
Psychology—General	M
Public Administration	M,D,O
Reading Education	M,O
Secondary Education	M,O
Special Education	M,O

WEILL CORNELL MEDICINE

Biochemistry	M,D
Biological and Biomedical Sciences—General	M,D
Biophysics	M,D
Biostatistics	M
Cell Biology	M,D
Computational Biology	D
Data Science/Data Analytics	M
Epidemiology	M
Health Informatics	M
Health Services Management and Hospital Administration	M
Health Services Research	M
Immunology	M,D
Molecular Biology	M,D
Neuroscience	M,D
Pharmacology	M,D
Physician Assistant Studies	M
Physiology	M,D
Structural Biology	M,D
Systems Biology	M,D

WELCH COLLEGE

Pastoral Ministry and Counseling	M
Theology	M

WENTWORTH INSTITUTE OF TECHNOLOGY

Architecture	M
Civil Engineering	M
Computer Science	M
Construction Engineering	M
Construction Management	M
Facilities Management	M
Management of Technology	M
Transportation and Highway Engineering	M

WESLEYAN COLLEGE

Business Administration and Management—General	M
Early Childhood Education	M
Education—General	M

WESLEYAN UNIVERSITY

Astronomy	M
Biochemistry	D
Bioinformatics	D
Biological and Biomedical Sciences—General	D
Cell Biology	D
Chemical Physics	D
Chemistry	D
Computer Science	M,D
Developmental Biology	D
Ecology	D
Environmental Sciences	M
Evolutionary Biology	D
Genetics	D
Genomic Sciences	D
Geosciences	M
Inorganic Chemistry	D
Liberal Studies	M,O
Mathematics	M,D
Molecular Biology	D
Molecular Biophysics	D
Music	M,D

Neurobiology	D
Organic Chemistry	D
Physics	D
Theoretical Chemistry	D
Writing	M,O

WESLEY BIBLICAL SEMINARY

Linguistics	M
Missions and Missiology	M
Pastoral Ministry and Counseling	M
Religion	M
Religious Education	M
Theology	M
Translation and Interpretation	M

WESLEY COLLEGE

Business Administration and Management—General	M
Education—General	M
Environmental Management and Policy	M
Nursing—General	M
Occupational Therapy	M

WESLEY THEOLOGICAL SEMINARY

Theology	M,D

WEST CHESTER UNIVERSITY OF PENNSYLVANIA

Applied Mathematics	M,O
Applied Statistics	M,O
Astronomy	M,O
Athletic Training and Sports Medicine	M,O
Biological and Biomedical Sciences—General	M,O
Business Administration and Management—General	M,O
Business Analytics	M,O
Business Education	M,O
Chemistry	O
Clinical Psychology	M,D,O
Communication Disorders	M
Communication—General	M
Computer and Information Systems Security	M,O
Computer Science	M,O
Counselor Education	M,O
Criminal Justice and Criminology	M
Cultural Studies	M,O
Early Childhood Education	M,O
Education—General	M,D,O
Educational Leadership and Administration	M,D,O
Educational Media/Instructional Technology	M,O
Educational Policy	M,D,O
English as a Second Language	M,O
English Education	M,O
English	M,O
Ethics	M,O
Exercise and Sports Science	M,O
Foreign Languages Education	M,O
Foundations and Philosophy of Education	M,O
French	M,O
Geographic Information Systems	M,O
Geography	M,O
Geosciences	M,O
German	M,O
Gerontological Nursing	M,D,O
Gerontology	M,O
Health Services Management and Hospital Administration	M,O
Higher Education	M,O
History	M
Holocaust and Genocide Studies	M,O
Human Resources Management	M,O
Industrial and Organizational Psychology	M,D,O
Kinesiology and Movement Studies	M,O
Management Information Systems	M,O
Mathematics Education	M,O
Mathematics	M,O
Music Education	M,O
Music	M,O
Nonprofit Management	M,O
Nursing Education	M,D,O
Nursing—General	M,D,O
Nutrition	M
Philosophy	M,O
Physical Education	M,O
Psychology—General	M,D,O
Public Administration	M,O
Public Affairs	M,O
Public Health—General	M,O
Reading Education	M,O
School Nursing	M,D,O
Science Education	M,O
Social Work	M,O
Spanish	M,O
Special Education	M,O
Sports Management	M,O
Student Affairs	M,O
Sustainable Development	M,O
Urban and Regional Planning	M,O
Writing	M,O

WESTCLIFF UNIVERSITY

Business Administration and Management—General	M,D
Education—General	M
English as a Second Language	M

WEST COAST UNIVERSITY

Family Nurse Practitioner Studies	M,D
Health Services Management and Hospital Administration	M,D
Nursing—General	M,D
Occupational Therapy	M,D
Pharmacy	M,D
Physical Therapy	M,D

WESTERN CAROLINA UNIVERSITY

Accounting	M

Applied Arts and Design—General	M
Art/Fine Arts	M
Biological and Biomedical Sciences—General	M
Business Administration and Management—General	M
Chemistry	M
Communication Disorders	M
Construction Management	M
Education—General	M
English as a Second Language	M,O
English	M,O
Entrepreneurship	M
Health Services Management and Hospital Administration	M
History	M
Industrial/Management Engineering	M
Nursing—General	M,D,O
Physical Therapy	D
Project Management	M,O
Psychology—General	M
Public Affairs	M
Rhetoric	M,O
Social Work	M
Technical Writing	M,O
Writing	M,O

WESTERN CONNECTICUT STATE UNIVERSITY

Accounting	M
Adult Nursing	M,D
Art/Fine Arts	M
Business Administration and Management—General	M,O
Clinical Psychology	M
Counselor Education	M
Curriculum and Instruction	M
Education—General	M,D
Educational Leadership and Administration	D
Educational Media/Instructional Technology	M
English	M
Geosciences	M
Gerontological Nursing	M,D
Health Services Management and Hospital Administration	M
History	M
Illustration	M
Mathematics	M
Music Education	M
Nursing Education	D
Nursing—General	M,D
Planetary and Space Sciences	M
Reading Education	M,D
Special Education	M
Writing	M

WESTERN GOVERNORS UNIVERSITY

Accounting	M
Business Administration and Management—General	M
Computer and Information Systems Security	M
Data Science/Data Analytics	M
Education—General	M,O
Educational Leadership and Administration	M,O
Educational Media/Instructional Technology	M,O
Elementary Education	M,O
English Education	M,O
Health Services Management and Hospital Administration	M
Information Science	M
Management Information Systems	M
Management Strategy and Policy	M
Mathematics Education	M,O
Nursing and Healthcare Administration	M
Nursing Education	M
Nursing Informatics	M
Science Education	M,O
Special Education	M,O

WESTERN ILLINOIS UNIVERSITY

Accounting	M
Applied Statistics	M
Biological and Biomedical Sciences—General	M,O
Business Administration and Management—General	M,O
Chemistry	M
Clinical Psychology	M,O
Communication Disorders	M
Communication—General	M
Computer Science	M
Counselor Education	M
Criminal Justice and Criminology	M,O
Curriculum and Instruction	M
Distance Education Development	M,O
Ecology	D
Economic Development	M
Economics	M
Education—General	M,D,O
Educational Leadership and Administration	M,D,O
Educational Media/Instructional Technology	M,O
English as a Second Language	M,O
English	M,O
Environmental Sciences	D
Experimental Psychology	M,O
Foundations and Philosophy of Education	M,O
Geographic Information Systems	M,O
Geography	M,O
Health Education	M
Higher Education	M
History	M
Kinesiology and Movement Studies	M
Liberal Studies	M

Manufacturing Engineering	M
Marine Biology	M,O
Mathematics	M,O
Museum Studies	M,O
Music	M
Physics	M
Political Science	M
Psychology—General	M,O
Public Health—General	M
Reading Education	M
Recreation and Park Management	M
School Psychology	M,O
Social Psychology	M,O
Social Work	M
Sociology	M
Special Education	M
Sports Management	M
Student Affairs	M
Supply Chain Management	M,O
Theater	M
Travel and Tourism	M
Zoology	M,O

WESTERN KENTUCKY UNIVERSITY

Adult Education	M,D,O
Agricultural Sciences—General	M
Anthropology	M
Applied Economics	M
Art Education	M
Biological and Biomedical Sciences—General	M
Business Administration and Management—General	M
Chemistry	M
Clinical Psychology	M,O
Communication Disorders	M
Communication—General	M
Comparative Literature	M
Computer Science	M
Corporate and Organizational Communication	M,O
Counseling Psychology	M
Counselor Education	M
Criminal Justice and Criminology	M
Early Childhood Education	M,O
Education of Students with Severe/Multiple Disabilities	M,O
Educational Leadership and Administration	M,D,O
Educational Media/Instructional Technology	M,O
Elementary Education	M,O
English as a Second Language	M
English Education	M
English	M
Experimental Psychology	M,O
Foreign Languages Education	M
French	M
Geology	M
Geosciences	M
German	M
Health Services Management and Hospital Administration	M
Higher Education	M
History	M
Homeland Security	M
Industrial and Organizational Psychology	M,O
Interdisciplinary Studies	M,O
Management of Technology	M
Marriage and Family Therapy	M
Mathematics	M
Middle School Education	M,O
Music Education	M
Nursing—General	M
Physical Education	M
Physical Therapy	D
Physics	M
Political Science	M
Psychology—General	M,O
Public Administration	M
Public Health—General	M
Reading Education	M,O
Recreation and Park Management	M
School Psychology	M,O
Secondary Education	M,O
Social Work	M
Sociology	M
Spanish	M
Special Education	M,O
Sports Management	M
Student Affairs	M
Writing	M

WESTERN MICHIGAN UNIVERSITY

Accounting	M
Aerospace/Aeronautical Engineering	M,D
Anthropology	M
Applied Arts and Design—General	M
Applied Economics	M,D
Applied Mathematics	M,D
Art Education	M
Athletic Training and Sports Medicine	M
Biological and Biomedical Sciences—General	M,D,O
Business Administration and Management—General	M
Chemical Engineering	M,D
Chemistry	M,D,O
Civil Engineering	M
Clinical Psychology	M,D
Communication Disorders	M,D
Communication—General	M
Computational Sciences	M,D
Computer Engineering	M,D
Computer Science	M,D
Counseling Psychology	M,D
Counselor Education	M,D
Economics	M,D
Education—General	M,D,O

Educational Leadership and Administration — M,D,O
Educational Measurement and Evaluation — M,D,O
Educational Media/Instructional Technology — M,D,O
Electrical Engineering — M,D
Engineering and Applied Sciences—General — M,D
Engineering Management — M,D
English Education — M,D
English — M,D
Exercise and Sports Science — M
Family and Consumer Sciences-General — M
Geographic Information Systems — M,O
Geography — M,D,O
Geosciences — M,D,O
Health Education — D,O
Health Services Management and Hospital Administration — M,D,O
Higher Education — M,D
History — M,D
Human Services — D,O
Industrial and Organizational Psychology — M,D
Industrial/Management Engineering — M,D
International Affairs — M,D
Manufacturing Engineering — M
Mathematics Education — M,D
Mathematics — M,D
Mechanical Engineering — M,D
Music Education — M,O
Music — M,O
Nonprofit Management — M,D,O
Nursing—General — M
Occupational Therapy — M
Paper and Pulp Engineering — M,D
Philosophy — M
Physical Education — M
Physician Assistant Studies — M
Physics — M,D,O
Physiology — M
Political Science — M,D
Psychology—General — M,D
Public Administration — M,D,O
Public Affairs — M,D,O
Reading Education — M,D
Rehabilitation Sciences — M
Religion — M,O
Science Education — M,D,O
Social Work — M
Sociology — M,D
Spanish — M,D
Special Education — M,D
Sports Management — M
Statistics — M,D,O
Therapies—Dance, Drama, and Music — M,O
Vision Sciences — M
Vocational and Technical Education — M
Writing — M,D

WESTERN MICHIGAN UNIVERSITY HOMER STRYKER MD SCHOOL OF MEDICINE
Allopathic Medicine — D

WESTERN MICHIGAN UNIVERSITY THOMAS M. COOLEY LAW SCHOOL
Environmental Law — M,D
Finance and Banking — M,D
Homeland Security — M,D
Insurance — M,D
Intellectual Property Law — M,D
Law — M,D
Legal and Justice Studies — M,D
National Security — M,D
Taxation — M,D

WESTERN NEW ENGLAND UNIVERSITY
Accounting — M
Advertising and Public Relations — M
Applied Behavior Analysis — M,D
Business Administration and Management—General — M
Civil Engineering — M
Communication—General — M
Curriculum and Instruction — M
Electrical Engineering — M
Engineering and Applied Sciences—General — M,D
Engineering Management — M,D
English Education — M
Industrial/Management Engineering — M
Law — M,D
Manufacturing Engineering — M
Mathematics Education — M
Mechanical Engineering — M
Occupational Therapy — D
Organizational Management — M
Pharmacy — D
Sports Management — M
Writing — M

WESTERN NEW MEXICO UNIVERSITY
Business Administration and Management—General — M
Education—General — M
Educational Leadership and Administration — M
Elementary Education — M
English as a Second Language — M
Interdisciplinary Studies — M
Multilingual and Multicultural Education — M
Occupational Therapy — M
Reading Education — M
Secondary Education — M
Social Work — M

Special Education — M

WESTERN OREGON UNIVERSITY
Criminal Justice and Criminology — M
Early Childhood Education — M
Education—General — M
Educational Media/Instructional Technology — M
Health Education — M
Mathematics Education — M
Multilingual and Multicultural Education — M
Music — M
Rehabilitation Counseling — M
Science Education — M
Secondary Education — M
Social Sciences Education — M
Special Education — M

WESTERN SEMINARY
Human Resources Development — M
Pastoral Ministry and Counseling — M,D,O
Religion — M,O
Theology — M,O
Women's Studies — M

WESTERN SEMINARY–SACRAMENTO CAMPUS
Marriage and Family Therapy — M
Pastoral Ministry and Counseling — M,O
Theology — M,O
Women's Studies — O

WESTERN SEMINARY–SAN JOSE CAMPUS
Marriage and Family Therapy — M,O
Pastoral Ministry and Counseling — M,O
Theology — M,O
Women's Studies — M,O

WESTERN STATE COLLEGE OF LAW AT ARGOSY UNIVERSITY
Law — D

WESTERN STATE COLORADO UNIVERSITY
Education—General — M
Educational Leadership and Administration — M
Environmental Management and Policy — M
Film, Television, and Video Production — M
Reading Education — M
Writing — M

WESTERN THEOLOGICAL SEMINARY
Pastoral Ministry and Counseling — M,D,O
Theology — M,D,O

WESTERN UNIVERSITY OF HEALTH SCIENCES
Allied Health—General — M,D
Biological and Biomedical Sciences—General — M
Dentistry — D
Health Education — M
Nursing and Healthcare Administration — M
Optometry — D
Osteopathic Medicine — D
Podiatric Medicine — D
Veterinary Medicine — D

WESTERN WASHINGTON UNIVERSITY
Adult Education — M
Anthropology — M
Biological and Biomedical Sciences—General — M
Business Administration and Management—General — M
Chemistry — M
Communication Disorders — M
Computer Science — M
Counseling Psychology — M
Counselor Education — M
Education of the Gifted — M
Education—General — M
Educational Leadership and Administration — M
Elementary Education — M
English — M
Environmental Education — M
Environmental Sciences — M
Exercise and Sports Science — M
Experimental Psychology — M
Geography — M
Geology — M
Higher Education — M
History — M
Marine Sciences — M
Mathematics — M
Music — M
Physical Education — M
Political Science — M
Psychology—General — M
Rehabilitation Counseling — M
Science Education — M
Secondary Education — M

WESTFIELD STATE UNIVERSITY
Accounting — M
Applied Behavior Analysis — M
Counseling Psychology — M
Counselor Education — M
Criminal Justice and Criminology — M
Early Childhood Education — M
Education—General — M
Elementary Education — M
English — M
Forensic Psychology — M
Mathematics Education — M
Nonprofit Management — M
Physical Education — M

Physician Assistant Studies — M
Psychology—General — M
Public Administration — M
Reading Education — M
Science Education — M
Secondary Education — M
Social Sciences Education — M
Social Work — M
Special Education — M
Vocational and Technical Education — M

WEST LIBERTY UNIVERSITY
Accounting — M
Biological and Biomedical Sciences—General — M
Business Administration and Management—General — M
Education of Students with Severe/Multiple Disabilities — M
Education—General — M
Educational Leadership and Administration — M
Organizational Management — M
Physical Education — M
Physician Assistant Studies — M
Reading Education — M
Special Education — M
Sports Management — M
Zoology — M

WESTMINSTER COLLEGE (PA)
Clinical Psychology — M
Counselor Education — M
Early Childhood Education — M
Educational Leadership and Administration — M
Reading Education — M
Special Education — M

WESTMINSTER COLLEGE (UT)
Accounting — M,O
Business Administration and Management—General — M,O
Communication—General — M
Counseling Psychology — M
Education—General — M
Family Nurse Practitioner Studies — M
Nurse Anesthesia — M
Nursing—General — M
Public Health—General — M
Writing — M

WESTMINSTER SEMINARY CALIFORNIA
Religion — M
Theology — M

WESTMINSTER THEOLOGICAL SEMINARY
Missions and Missiology — M,D,O
Pastoral Ministry and Counseling — M,D,O
Religion — M,D,O
Theology — M,D,O

WEST TEXAS A&M UNIVERSITY
Accounting — M
Agricultural Economics and Agribusiness — M
Agricultural Sciences—General — M,D
Animal Sciences — M
Art/Fine Arts — M
Biological and Biomedical Sciences—General — M
Business Administration and Management—General — M
Communication Disorders — M
Communication—General — M
Counselor Education — M
Criminal Justice and Criminology — M
Curriculum and Instruction — M
Economics — M
Education—General — M
Educational Leadership and Administration — M
Educational Measurement and Evaluation — M
Educational Media/Instructional Technology — M
Engineering and Applied Sciences—General — M
English — M
Environmental Sciences — M
Exercise and Sports Science — M
Family Nurse Practitioner Studies — M
Finance and Banking — M
History — M
Interdisciplinary Studies — M
Mathematics — M
Music — M
Nursing—General — M
Plant Sciences — M
Psychology—General — M
Reading Education — M
Social Work — M
Sports Management — M

WEST VIRGINIA SCHOOL OF OSTEOPATHIC MEDICINE
Osteopathic Medicine — D

WEST VIRGINIA STATE UNIVERSITY
Biotechnology — M
Criminal Justice and Criminology — M
Media Studies — M

WEST VIRGINIA UNIVERSITY
Accounting — M,D,O
Aerospace/Aeronautical Engineering — M,D
Agricultural Education — M
Agricultural Sciences—General — M,D
Agronomy and Soil Sciences — M,D

Allopathic Medicine — M,D
Animal Sciences — M,D
Art Education — M,D
Art History — M,D
Art/Fine Arts — M,D
Athletic Training and Sports Medicine — M,D
Biochemistry — M,D
Biological and Biomedical Sciences—General — M,D
Biostatistics — M,D
Business Administration and Management—General — M,D,O
Business Analytics — M,D,O
Cancer Biology/Oncology — M,D
Chemical Engineering — M,D
Chemistry — M,D
Civil Engineering — M,D
Clinical Psychology — M,D
Communication Disorders — M,D
Communication—General — M,D
Computer and Information Systems Security — M,D,O
Computer Engineering — M,D
Computer Science — M,D
Corporate and Organizational Communication — M,O
Counseling Psychology — M,D
Counselor Education — M,D
Curriculum and Instruction — M,D
Dental Hygiene — M,D
Dentistry — M,D
Developmental Biology — M,D
Early Childhood Education — M,D
Economics — M,D,O
Education of the Gifted — M,D
Education—General — M,D
Educational Leadership and Administration — M,D
Educational Media/Instructional Technology — M,D
Educational Psychology — M,D
Electrical Engineering — M,D
Elementary Education — M,D
Energy and Power Engineering — M,D
Engineering and Applied Sciences—General — M,D
English Education — M,D
English — M,D
Entomology — M,D
Environmental and Occupational Health — M,D
Epidemiology — M,D
Exercise and Sports Science — M,D
Finance and Banking — M,D,O
Fish, Game, and Wildlife Management — M,D
Food Science and Technology — M,D
Forensic Sciences — M,D
Forestry — M,D
Genetics — M,D
Geography — M,D
Geology — M,D
Graphic Design — M,D
Higher Education — M,D
History — M,D
Horticulture — M,D
Human Services — M,D
Immunology — M,D
Industrial and Labor Relations — M,D,O
Industrial Hygiene — M,D
Industrial/Management Engineering — M,D
Journalism — M,O
Landscape Architecture — M,D
Law — M,D
Legal and Justice Studies — M,D
Marketing — M,D,O
Materials Engineering — M,D
Materials Sciences — M,D
Mathematics — M,D
Mechanical Engineering — M,D
Media Studies — M,O
Mineral/Mining Engineering — M,D
Molecular Biology — M,D
Music Education — M,D
Music — M,D
Natural Resources — M,D
Nursing—General — M,D,O
Nutrition — M,D
Occupational Therapy — M,D
Oral and Dental Sciences — M,D
Pathology — M,D
Petroleum Engineering — M,D
Pharmaceutical Sciences — D
Pharmacy — D
Photography — M,D
Physical Education — M,D
Physical Therapy — M,D
Physics — M,D
Plant Pathology — M,D
Plant Sciences — M,D
Political Science — M,D
Psychology—General — M,D
Public Administration — M,D
Public Health—General — M,D
Reading Education — M,D
Recreation and Park Management — M,D
Rehabilitation Counseling — M,D
Safety Engineering — M,D
Secondary Education — M,D
Social Work — M,D
Sociology — M,D
Software Engineering — M,D
Special Education — M,D
Sport Psychology — M,D
Sports Management — M,D
Statistics — M,D
Theater — M,D

Travel and Tourism — M,D
Writing — M,D

WEST VIRGINIA WESLEYAN COLLEGE
Athletic Training and Sports Medicine — M
Business Administration and Management—General — M
Family Nurse Practitioner Studies — M,D,O
Nurse Midwifery — M,D,O
Nursing and Healthcare Administration — M,D,O
Nursing—General — M,D,O
Psychiatric Nursing — M,D,O
Writing — M

WHEATON COLLEGE
Archaeology — M,D
Clinical Psychology — M,D
Counseling Psychology — M,D
Education—General — M
Elementary Education — M
Emergency Management — M
Marriage and Family Therapy — M,D
Missions and Missiology — M
Psychology—General — M,D
Religious Education — M
Secondary Education — M
Theology — M,D

WHEELING JESUIT UNIVERSITY
Accounting — M
Business Administration and Management—General — M
Educational Leadership and Administration — M
Nursing—General — M
Organizational Management — M
Physical Therapy — D

WHITTIER COLLEGE
Child Development — M
Education—General — M
Educational Leadership and Administration — M
Elementary Education — M
Secondary Education — M

WHITWORTH UNIVERSITY
Business Administration and Management—General — M
Counselor Education — M
Education of the Gifted — M
Education—General — M
Educational Leadership and Administration — M
Elementary Education — M
Missions and Missiology — M
Pastoral Ministry and Counseling — M
Secondary Education — M
Special Education — M
Theology — M

WHU - OTTO BEISHEIM SCHOOL OF MANAGEMENT
Business Administration and Management—General — M

WICHITA STATE UNIVERSITY
Accounting — M
Aerospace/Aeronautical Engineering — M,D
Allied Health—General — M,D
Anthropology — M
Applied Mathematics — M,D
Art/Fine Arts — M
Biological and Biomedical Sciences—General — M
Biomedical Engineering — M
Business Administration and Management—General — M
Chemistry — M,D
Clinical Psychology — D
Communication Disorders — M,D
Communication—General — M
Computer Engineering — M,D
Computer Science — M,D
Counselor Education — M,D,O
Criminal Justice and Criminology — M
Curriculum and Instruction — M
Early Childhood Education — M
Economics — M
Education of the Gifted — M
Education—General — M,D,O
Educational Leadership and Administration — M,D,O
Educational Psychology — M,D,O
Electrical Engineering — M,D
Engineering and Applied Sciences—General — M,D
Engineering Management — M,D
English — M
Entrepreneurship — M
Environmental Sciences — M
Exercise and Sports Science — M
Geology — M
Gerontology — M
History — M
Human Services — M
Industrial/Management Engineering — M,D
International Economics — M
Liberal Studies — M
Management Information Systems — M
Manufacturing Engineering — M,D
Mathematics — M,D
Mechanical Engineering — M,D
Middle School Education — M
Music Education — M
Music — M
Nursing—General — M,D
Photography — M
Physical Therapy — D
Physician Assistant Studies — M
Physics — M,D
Psychology—General — D

Public Administration — M
School Psychology — M,D,O
Secondary Education — M
Social Psychology — D
Social Work — M
Sociology — M
Spanish — M
Special Education — M
Sports Management — M
Supply Chain Management — M
Taxation — M
Writing — M

WIDENER UNIVERSITY
Adult Education — M,D
Biomedical Engineering — M
Business Administration and Management—General — M
Chemical Engineering — M
Civil Engineering — M
Clinical Psychology — D
Counselor Education — M
Criminal Justice and Criminology — M
Early Childhood Education — M,D
Education—General — M,D
Educational Leadership and Administration — M,D
Educational Media/Instructional Technology — M,D
Educational Psychology — M,D
Electrical Engineering — M
Elementary Education — M,D
Engineering and Applied Sciences—General — M
Engineering Management — M
English Education — M,D
Foundations and Philosophy of Education — M,D
Health Education — M,D
Health Law — M,D
Health Services Management and Hospital Administration — M
Law — M,D
Mathematics Education — M,D
Mechanical Engineering — M
Middle School Education — M,D
Nursing—General — M,D,O
Physical Therapy — M,D
Psychology—General — M
Public Administration — M
Reading Education — M,D
Science Education — M,D
Social Sciences Education — M,D
Social Work — M,D
Special Education — M,D
Taxation — M

WILBERFORCE UNIVERSITY
Rehabilitation Counseling — M

WILFRID LAURIER UNIVERSITY
Accounting — M,D
American Studies — M,D
Biological and Biomedical Sciences—General — M
Business Administration and Management—General — M,D
Canadian Studies — M,D
Chemistry — M
Cognitive Sciences — M,D
Communication—General — M
Conflict Resolution and Mediation/Peace Studies — D
Criminal Justice and Criminology — M
Cultural Studies — M
Developmental Psychology — M,D
Economics — M,D
English — M,D
Environmental Management and Policy — M,D
Environmental Sciences — M,D
Film, Television, and Video Theory and Criticism — M,D
Finance and Banking — M,D
Gender Studies — M
Geography — M,D
Health Promotion — M
History — M,D
Human Resources Management — M,D
International Affairs — M,D
International Economics — M
Kinesiology and Movement Studies — M
Legal and Justice Studies — D
Management of Technology — M,D
Marketing — M
Mathematics — M
Media Studies — M,D
Neuroscience — M,D
Organizational Behavior — M,D
Organizational Management — M,D
Pastoral Ministry and Counseling — M,D,O
Philosophy — M
Physical Education — M
Political Science — M,D
Psychology—General — M,D
Public Policy — M
Religion — M,D
Social Psychology — M,D
Social Sciences — M
Social Work — M,D
Sociology — M
Supply Chain Management — M,D
Theology — M,D,O
Therapies—Dance, Drama, and Music — M

WILKES UNIVERSITY
Accounting — M
Bioengineering — M
Business Administration and Management—General — M
Distance Education Development — M,D
Education—General — M
Educational Leadership and Administration — M,D

Educational Measurement and Evaluation — M,D
Educational Media/Instructional Technology — M,D
Electrical Engineering — M
Engineering and Applied Sciences—General — M
Engineering Management — M
English as a Second Language — M,D
Entrepreneurship — M
Finance and Banking — M
Health Services Management and Hospital Administration — M
Human Resources Management — M
Industrial and Manufacturing Management — M
International and Comparative Education — M,D
International Business — M
Mathematics — M
Mechanical Engineering — M
Middle School Education — M,D
Nursing—General — M,D
Organizational Management — M
Pharmacy — D
Reading Education — M,D
Special Education — M,D
Writing — M

WILLAMETTE UNIVERSITY
Business Administration and Management—General — M
Conflict Resolution and Mediation/Peace Studies — M,D
Law — M,D

WILLIAM CAREY UNIVERSITY
Art Education — M,O
Business Administration and Management—General — M
Counseling Psychology — M
Education of the Gifted — M,O
Education—General — M,O
Elementary Education — M,O
English Education — M,O
Nursing—General — M
Osteopathic Medicine — D
Pharmacy — M
Psychology—General — M
Secondary Education — M,O
Social Sciences Education — M,O
Special Education — M,O

WILLIAM JAMES COLLEGE
Applied Psychology — M,D,O
Clinical Psychology — M,D,O
Community Health — M,D,O
Counseling Psychology — M,D,O
Forensic Psychology — M,D,O
Industrial and Organizational Psychology — M,D,O
International Health — M
Psychology—General — M,D,O
School Psychology — M,D,O
Student Affairs — M,D,O

WILLIAM JESSUP UNIVERSITY
Education—General — M
English Education — M
Mathematics Education — M

WILLIAM JEWELL COLLEGE
Education—General — M

WILLIAM PATERSON UNIVERSITY OF NEW JERSEY
Accounting — M,O
Adult Nursing — M,D,O
Biological and Biomedical Sciences—General — M,D,O
Biotechnology — M,D,O
Business Administration and Management—General — M,O
Business Analytics — M
Clinical Psychology — M,D,O
Communication Disorders — M,D,O
Counseling Psychology — M,O
Counselor Education — M,O
Early Childhood Education — M,O
Education—General — M,O
Educational Leadership and Administration — M,O
Educational Media/Instructional Technology — M,O
Elementary Education — M,O
English as a Second Language — M,D,O
English — M,O
Entertainment Management — M,O
Entrepreneurship — M,O
Exercise and Sports Science — M,D,O
Finance and Banking — M,O
Foundations and Philosophy of Education — M,O
Gerontological Nursing — M,D,O
Higher Education — M,O
History — M,D,O
Human Resources Management — M,O
Marketing — M,O
Materials Sciences — M,D,O
Middle School Education — M,O
Multilingual and Multicultural Education — M,D,O
Music — M
Nursing Education — M,D,O
Nursing—General — M,D,O
Public Policy — M,O
Reading Education — M,O
School Nursing — M,D,O
Secondary Education — M,O
Sociology — M,D,O
Special Education — M,O
Writing — M,O

WILLIAM PENN UNIVERSITY
Organizational Management — M

WILLIAMS BAPTIST COLLEGE
Education—General — M

WILLIAMS COLLEGE
Art History — M
Economic Development — M

WILLIAMSON COLLEGE
Organizational Management — M

WILLIAM WOODS UNIVERSITY
Advertising and Public Relations — M,D,O
Business Administration and Management—General — M,D,O
Curriculum and Instruction — M,D,O
Educational Leadership and Administration — M,D,O
Educational Media/Instructional Technology — M,D,O
Health Services Management and Hospital Administration — M,D,O
Human Resources Development — M,D,O
Marketing — M,D,O
Physical Education — M,D,O

WILMINGTON COLLEGE
Education—General — M
Reading Education — M
Special Education — M

WILMINGTON UNIVERSITY
Accounting — M
Adult Nursing — M,D
Business Administration and Management—General — M,D
Clinical Psychology — M
Computer and Information Systems Security — M
Counseling Psychology — M,D
Counselor Education — M,D
Criminal Justice and Criminology — M,D
Education of the Gifted — M
Education—General — M,D
Educational Leadership and Administration — M,D
Educational Media/Instructional Technology — M
Elementary Education — M,D
English as a Second Language — M,D
Environmental Management and Policy — M,D
Family Nurse Practitioner Studies — M,D
Finance and Banking — M,D
Gerontological Nursing — M,D
Health Services Management and Hospital Administration — M,D
Higher Education — M,D
Homeland Security — M
Human Resources Management — M,D
Human Services — M
Internet and Interactive Multimedia — M
Internet Engineering — M
Management Information Systems — M,D
Marketing — M,D
Nursing and Healthcare Administration — M,D
Nursing—General — M,D
Organizational Management — M
Project Management — M
Public Administration — M,D
Reading Education — M,D
Secondary Education — M,D
Special Education — M,D
Vocational and Technical Education — M,D

WILSON COLLEGE
Accounting — M
Art/Fine Arts — M
Business Administration and Management—General — M
Cultural Studies — M
Dance — M
Education—General — M
Educational Media/Instructional Technology — M
Elementary Education — M
English — M
Health Services Management and Hospital Administration — M
Humanities — M
Nursing and Healthcare Administration — M
Nursing Education — M
Nursing—General — M
Secondary Education — M
Special Education — M
Women's Studies — M

WINEBRENNER THEOLOGICAL SEMINARY
Counseling Psychology — M,D
Theology — M,D

WINGATE UNIVERSITY
Accounting — M
Business Administration and Management—General — M
Community College Education — M,D,O
Education—General — M,D,O
Educational Leadership and Administration — M,D,O
Elementary Education — M,D,O
Entrepreneurship — M
Finance and Banking — M
Health Services Management and Hospital Administration — M
Marketing — M
Pharmacy — D
Physical Therapy — D
Physician Assistant Studies — M
Project Management — M
Sports Management — M

WINONA STATE UNIVERSITY
Acute Care/Critical Care Nursing — M,D,O

Addictions/Substance Abuse
  Counseling — M,O
Adult Nursing — M,O
Clinical Psychology — M,O
Counselor Education — M,O
Education—General — O
Educational Leadership and
  Administration — M,O
English as a Second Language — M
English — M
Family Nurse Practitioner Studies — M,D,O
Gerontological Nursing — M,D,O
Human Services — M,O
Multilingual and Multicultural
  Education — O
Nursing and Healthcare
  Administration — M,D,O
Nursing Education — M,D,O
Nursing—General — M,D,O
Organizational Management — M,D,O
Special Education — M
Sports Management — M,O

WINSTON-SALEM STATE UNIVERSITY
Business Administration and
  Management—General — M
Computer Science — M
Education—General — M
Family Nurse Practitioner Studies — M,D
Health Services Management and
  Hospital Administration — M
Management Information Systems — M
Middle School Education — M
Nursing Education — M,D
Nursing—General — M,D
Occupational Therapy — M
Physical Therapy — D
Rehabilitation Counseling — M
Special Education — M

WINTHROP UNIVERSITY
Art Education — M
Art/Fine Arts — M
Arts Administration — M
Biological and Biomedical
  Sciences—General — M
Business Administration and
  Management—General — M
Counselor Education — M
Education—General — M
Educational Leadership and
  Administration — M
English — M
History — M
Liberal Studies — M
Music Education — M
Music — M
Nutrition — M,O
Physical Education — M
Psychology—General — M,O
Secondary Education — M
Social Work — M
Special Education — M

WISCONSIN LUTHERAN COLLEGE
Curriculum and Instruction — M
Educational Leadership and
  Administration — ·
Educational Media/Instructional
  Technology — M
Science Education — M

WISCONSIN SCHOOL OF PROFESSIONAL PSYCHOLOGY
Clinical Psychology — M,D
Psychology—General — M,D

WITTENBERG UNIVERSITY
Education—General — M

WONGU UNIVERSITY OF ORIENTAL MEDICINE
Acupuncture and Oriental Medicine — M

WON INSTITUTE OF GRADUATE STUDIES
Acupuncture and Oriental Medicine — M,O
Religion — M

WOODBURY UNIVERSITY
Architecture — M
Business Administration and
  Management—General — M
Organizational Management — M

WOODS HOLE OCEANOGRAPHIC INSTITUTION
Marine Biology — D
Marine Geology — D
Ocean Engineering — D
Oceanography — D

WORCESTER POLYTECHNIC INSTITUTE
Aerospace/Aeronautical
  Engineering — M,D
Applied Mathematics — M,D,O
Applied Statistics — M,D,O
Artificial Intelligence/Robotics — M,D
Biochemistry — M,D
Bioinformatics — M,D
Biological and Biomedical
  Sciences—General — M,D
Biomedical Engineering — M,D,O
Biotechnology — M,D
Business Administration and
  Management—General — M,D,O
Chemical Engineering — M,D
Chemistry — M,D
Civil Engineering — M,D,O
Computational Biology — M,D
Computer Engineering — M,D,O
Computer Science — M,D,O
Data Science/Data Analytics — M,D,O

Educational Media/Instructional
  Technology — M,D
Electrical Engineering — M,D,O
Energy and Power
  Engineering — M,D,O
Engineering and Applied
  Sciences—General — M,D,O
Engineering Design — M,D,O
Environmental Engineering — M,D,O
Fire Protection Engineering — M,D,O
Game Design and
  Development — M
Interdisciplinary Studies — M,D,O
Internet and Interactive
  Multimedia — M
Management Information Systems — M,D,O
Manufacturing Engineering — M,D,O
Marketing — M,D,O
Materials Engineering — M,D,O
Materials Sciences — M,D,O
Mathematics — M,D,O
Mechanical Engineering — M,D,O
Modeling and Simulation — M,D,O
Nuclear Engineering — M,D,O
Organizational Management — M,D,O
Physics — M,D
Social Sciences — M,D,O
Supply Chain Management — M,D,O
Systems Engineering — M,D,O
Systems Science — M,D,O

WORCESTER STATE UNIVERSITY
Accounting — M
Biotechnology — M
Business Administration and
  Management—General — M
Communication Disorders — M
Community Health Nursing — M
Curriculum and Instruction — M,O
Early Childhood Education — M,O
Education—General — M,O
Educational Leadership and
  Administration — M,O
Elementary Education — M,O
English as a Second Language — M,O
English Education — M
Foreign Languages Education — M
Health Education — M,O
Health Services Management and
  Hospital Administration — M
History — M
Marketing — M
Middle School Education — M
Nonprofit Management — M
Nursing Education — M
Occupational Therapy — M
Organizational Management — M
Reading Education — M,O
School Psychology — M,O
Secondary Education — M,O
Social Sciences Education — M
Spanish — M
Special Education — M,O

WORLD MISSION UNIVERSITY
Music — M,D
Pastoral Ministry and Counseling — M,D
Theology — M,D

WRIGHT GRADUATE UNIVERSITY FOR THE REALIZATION OF HUMAN POTENTIAL
Human Development — M,D,O

THE WRIGHT INSTITUTE
Clinical Psychology — D
Counseling Psychology — M
Psychology—General — D

WRIGHT STATE UNIVERSITY
Accounting — M
Acute Care/Critical Care Nursing — M
Adult Nursing — M
Aerospace/Aeronautical
  Engineering — M
Allopathic Medicine — D
Anatomy — M
Applied Behavior Analysis — M
Applied Economics — M
Applied Mathematics — M
Applied Statistics — M
Biochemistry — M
Biological and Biomedical
  Sciences—General — M,D
Biomedical Engineering — M
Business Administration and
  Management—General — M
Chemistry — M
Clinical Psychology — D
Computer Engineering — M,D
Computer Science — M,D
Counselor Education — M
Criminal Justice and Criminology — M
Curriculum and Instruction — O
Economics — M
Education—General — M,O
Educational Leadership and
  Administration — O
Electrical Engineering — M
Elementary Education — M
Engineering and Applied
  Sciences—General — M,D
English — M
Environmental Sciences — D
Ergonomics and Human
  Factors — M,D
Family Nurse Practitioner Studies — M
Geology — O
Geophysics — M
Gerontological Nursing — M
Health Education — M
Health Promotion — M

History — M
Humanities — M
Immunology — M
Industrial and Organizational
  Psychology — M,D
Industrial/Management
  Engineering — M
Logistics — M
Management Information Systems — M
Materials Engineering — M
Materials Sciences — M
Maternal and Child/Neonatal
  Nursing — M
Mathematics Education — D
Mathematics — M
Mechanical Engineering — M
Microbiology — M
Molecular Biology — M
Music Education — M
Neuroscience — M
Nursing and Healthcare
  Administration — M
Nursing—General — M
Pediatric Nursing — M
Pharmacology — M
Physics — M
Physiology — M
Psychiatric Nursing — M
Psychology—General — M,D
Public Administration — M
Public Health—General — M
Rehabilitation Counseling — M
School Nursing — M
Science Education — M
Secondary Education — M
Special Education — M
Supply Chain Management — M
Toxicology — M

WYCLIFFE COLLEGE
Religion — M,D,O
Theology — M,D,O

XAVIER UNIVERSITY
Accounting — M
Athletic Training and Sports
  Medicine — M
Business Administration and
  Management—General — M
Clinical Psychology — M,D
Counseling Psychology — M
Counselor Education — M
Criminal Justice and Criminology — M
Early Childhood Education — M
Education—General — M,D
Educational Leadership and
  Administration — M,D
Elementary Education — M
English — M
Ethics — M
Finance and Banking — M
Health Services Management and
  Hospital Administration — M*
Human Resources Development — M,D
Industrial and Organizational
  Psychology — M,D
International Business — M
Management Strategy and Policy — M
Marketing — M
Multilingual and Multicultural
  Education — M
Nursing—General — M,D,O
Occupational Therapy — M
Pastoral Ministry and Counseling — M
Psychology—General — M,D
Reading Education — M
Religious Education — M
Secondary Education — M
Special Education — M
Sports Management — M
Sustainable Development — M
Theology — M

XAVIER UNIVERSITY OF LOUISIANA
Counselor Education — M
Curriculum and Instruction — M
Educational Leadership and
  Administration — M
Pharmacy — D

YALE UNIVERSITY
Accounting — D
African Studies — M
African-American Studies — D
Allopathic Medicine — D
American Studies — D
Anthropology — M,D
Applied Arts and Design—
  General — M
Applied Mathematics — M,D
Applied Physics — M,D
Archaeology — M
Architecture — M,D
Art History — D
Art/Fine Arts — M
Asian Languages — D
Asian Studies — M
Astronomy — M,D
Astrophysics — M,D
Atmospheric Sciences — D
Biochemistry — D
Bioinformatics — D
Biological and Biomedical
  Sciences—General — D
Biomedical Engineering — D
Biophysics — D
Biostatistics — M,D
Business Administration and
  Management—General — M,D
Cell Biology — D
Chemical Engineering — M,D
Chemistry — D

Classics — M,D
Clinical Psychology — D
Cognitive Sciences — D
Comparative Literature — D
Computational Biology — D
Computer Science — M,D
Developmental Biology — D
Developmental Psychology — D
East European and Russian Studies — M,D
Ecology — D
Economic Development — D
Economics — M,D
Electrical Engineering — D
Engineering and Applied
  Sciences—General — M,D
Engineering Physics — M,D
English — M,D
Environmental and Occupational
  Health — D
Environmental Design — M,D
Environmental Engineering — M,D
Environmental Management
  and Policy — M,D
Environmental Sciences — M,D
Epidemiology — M,D
Evolutionary Biology — D
Film, Television, and Video
  Theory and Criticism — D
Finance and Banking — D
Forestry — M,D
French — M,D
Genetics — D
Genomic Sciences — D
Geochemistry — D
Geology — D
Geophysics — D
Geosciences — D
German — D
Graphic Design — M
Health Services Management and
  Hospital Administration — M,D
History of Medicine — M,D
History of Science and Technology — M,D
History — M,D
Immunology — D
Infectious Diseases — D
Inorganic Chemistry — D
International Affairs — M
International Economics — M
International Health — M,D
Italian — D
Latin American Studies — D
Law — M,D
Linguistics — D
Marketing — D
Mathematics — M,D
Mechanical Engineering — M,D
Medieval and Renaissance Studies — D
Meteorology — D
Microbiology — D
Molecular Biology — D
Molecular Biophysics — D
Molecular Medicine — D
Molecular Physiology — D
Music — M,D,O
Near and Middle Eastern Languages — M,D
Near and Middle Eastern Studies — M,D
Neurobiology — D
Neuroscience — D
Nursing—General — M,D,O
Oceanography — D
Organic Chemistry — D
Organizational Management — D
Paleontology — D
Pathology — M,D
Pharmacology — D
Philosophy — D
Photography — M
Physical Chemistry — D
Physician Assistant Studies — M
Physics — D
Physiology — D
Planetary and Space
  Sciences — M,D
Plant Biology — D
Political Science — D
Portuguese — D
Psychology—General — D
Public Health—General — M,D
Religion — D
Russian — D
Slavic Languages — D
Social Psychology — D
Social Sciences — M,D
Sociology — D
Spanish — D
Statistics — M,D
Theater — M,D,O
Theology — M
Theoretical Chemistry — D
Virology — D
Writing — M,D,O

YESHIVA BETH MOSHE
Theology — O

YESHIVA DERECH CHAIM
Religion — D

YESHIVA KARLIN STOLIN
Theology — O

YESHIVA OF NITRA RABBINICAL COLLEGE
Theology — O

YESHIVA SHAAR HATORAH TALMUDIC RESEARCH INSTITUTE
Theology

YESHIVATH ZICHRON MOSHE
Theology

M—masters degree; D—doctorate; O—other advanced degree; *—Close-Up and/or Display

YESHIVA UNIVERSITY

Accounting	M
Biotechnology	M
Business Administration and Management—General	M
Clinical Psychology	D
Communication Disorders	M
Conflict Resolution and Mediation/Peace Studies	M,D
Counseling Psychology	M
Data Science/Data Analytics	M
Economics	M
Educational Leadership and Administration	M,D,O
Health Psychology	D
Intellectual Property Law	M,D
Jewish Studies	M,D
Law	M,D
Marketing	M
Mathematics	M
Psychology—General	M,D
Religious Education	M,D,O
Risk Management	M
School Psychology	D
Social Work	M,D
Taxation	M

YORK COLLEGE OF PENNSYLVANIA

Accounting	M
Business Administration and Management—General	M
Education—General	M
Educational Leadership and Administration	M
Educational Media/Instructional Technology	M
Finance and Banking	M
Gerontological Nursing	M
Health Services Management and Hospital Administration	M
Marketing	M
Nurse Anesthesia	M
Nursing—General	M
Reading Education	M

YORK COLLEGE OF THE CITY UNIVERSITY OF NEW YORK

Pharmaceutical Sciences	M
Physician Assistant Studies	M

YORK UNIVERSITY

Accounting	M,D
Anthropology	M,D
Applied Arts and Design—General	M
Applied Mathematics	M,D
Art History	M,D
Art/Fine Arts	M,D
Astronomy	M,D
Biological and Biomedical Sciences—General	M,D
Business Administration and Management—General	M,D
Business Analytics	M,D
Chemistry	M,D
Communication—General	M,D
Computer Science	M,D
Dance	M,D
Disability Studies	M,D
Economics	M,D
Education—General	M,D
Emergency Management	M
English	M,D
Environmental Management and Policy	M,D
Film, Television, and Video Production	M,D
Finance and Banking	M,D
French	M,D
Gender Studies	M,D
Geography	M,D
Geosciences	M,D
History	M,D
Human Resources Management	M,D
Humanities	M,D
Interdisciplinary Studies	M
International Affairs	M
International Business	M,D
Kinesiology and Movement Studies	M,D
Law	M,D
Linguistics	M,D
Mathematics	M,D
Music	M,D
Nursing—General	M
Philosophy	M,D
Physics	M,D
Planetary and Space Sciences	M,D
Political Science	M,D
Psychology—General	M,D
Public Administration	M
Public Affairs	M
Public Policy	M
Social Work	M,D
Sociology	M,D
Statistics	M,D
Theater	M,D
Translation and Interpretation	M
Women's Studies	M,D

YO SAN UNIVERSITY OF TRADITIONAL CHINESE MEDICINE

Acupuncture and Oriental Medicine	M

YOUNGSTOWN STATE UNIVERSITY

Accounting	M
Actuarial Science	M
American Studies	M
Analytical Chemistry	M
Anatomy	M
Applied Mathematics	M
Athletic Training and Sports Medicine	M
Biochemistry	M
Biological and Biomedical Sciences—General	M
Business Administration and Management—General	M
Chemistry	M
Civil Engineering	M
Computer Engineering	M
Computer Science	M
Counselor Education	M,D,O
Criminal Justice and Criminology	M
Curriculum and Instruction	M
Economics	M
Education—General	M,D,O
Educational Leadership and Administration	M,D,O
Electrical Engineering	M
Engineering and Applied Sciences—General	M,O
English	M
Environmental Biology	M
Environmental Engineering	M
Environmental Management and Policy	M,O
Finance and Banking	M
Gerontology	M
Health Services Management and Hospital Administration	M
History	M
Human Services	M
Industrial/Management Engineering	M
Information Science	M
Inorganic Chemistry	M
Mathematics Education	M
Mathematics	M
Mechanical Engineering	M
Microbiology	M
Molecular Biology	M
Music Education	M
Music	M
Nursing—General	M
Organic Chemistry	M
Physical Chemistry	M
Physical Therapy	D
Physiology	M
Public Health—General	M
Reading Education	M
School Psychology	M,D,O
Science Education	M
Social Work	M
Special Education	M
Statistics	M
Supply Chain Management	O
Systems Engineering	M

PROFILES OF INSTITUTIONS OFFERING GRADUATE AND PROFESSIONAL WORK

ABILENE CHRISTIAN UNIVERSITY, Abilene, TX 79699

General Information Independent-religious, coed, university. CGS member. *Enrollment by degree level:* 970 master's, 426 doctoral, 17 other advanced degrees. *Graduate housing:* On-campus housing not available. *Student services:* Campus employment opportunities, campus safety program, career counseling, exercise/wellness program, grant writing training, international student services, low-cost health insurance, multicultural affairs office, services for students with disabilities, teacher training, writing training. *Library facilities:* Brown Library. *Collection:* Books: 406,890 (physical), 347,095 (digital/electronic); Serial titles: 20,683 (physical), 52,058 (digital/electronic); Databases: 109. Weekly public service hours: 97; students can reserve study rooms.

Computer facilities: Computer purchase and lease plans are available. 466 computers available on campus for general student use. A campuswide network can be accessed from student residence rooms and from off campus. Online class registration is available.
Website: http://www.acu.edu/

General Application Contact: Graduate Admissions, 325-674-6911, Fax: 325-674-6717, E-mail: gradinfo@acu.edu.

GRADUATE UNITS

College of Graduate and Professional Studies Students: 790 full-time (544 women), 382 part-time (263 women); includes 595 minority (326 Black or African American, non-Hispanic/Latino; 6 American Indian or Alaska Native, non-Hispanic/Latino; 18 Asian, non-Hispanic/Latino; 202 Hispanic/Latino; 1 Native Hawaiian or other Pacific Islander, non-Hispanic/Latino; 42 Two or more races, non-Hispanic/Latino), 18 international. 389 applicants, 89% accepted, 281 enrolled. *Faculty:* 32 full-time (16 women), 44 part-time/adjunct (21 women). Expenses: Contact institution. *Financial support:* In 2018–19, 128 students received support. Scholarships/grants available. Support available to part-time students. Financial award application deadline: 7/1; financial award applicants required to submit FAFSA. In 2018, 112 master's, 2 doctorates, 17 other advanced degrees awarded. *Program availability:* Part-time, online only, 100% online, blended/hybrid learning. Offers advanced practice nurse (DNP); business analytics (MBA); child and adolescent therapy (MMFT); conflict management (M Ed, Certificate); conflict management and resolution (MA); enrollment management (M Ed); executive nursing leadership (DNP); general management (MBA); healthcare administration (MBA); international business (MBA); learning with emerging technologies (M Ed, Certificate); management: business analytics (MS); management: healthcare administration (MS); management: international business (MS); management: marketing (MS); management: operations and supply chain management (MS); marketing (MBA); medical family therapy (MMFT); nonprofit leadership (MBA); nursing education (DNP); organizational development (MS); organizational leadership (Ed D); therapy with military families (MMFT); treatment of trauma (MMFT). *Application deadline:* For fall admission, 10/7 for domestic students; for winter admission, 12/20 for domestic students; for spring admission, 2/24 for domestic students; for summer admission, 4/20 for domestic students. Applications are processed on a rolling basis. *Application fee:* $50. *Application Contact:* Graduate Advisor, 855-219-7300, E-mail: onlineadmissions@acu.edu. *Dean,* Dr. Joe Cope, 214-305-9508, E-mail: copej@acu.edu.

Graduate Programs Students: 308 full-time (253 women), 195 part-time (90 women); includes 129 minority (45 Black or African American, non-Hispanic/Latino; 1 American Indian or Alaska Native, non-Hispanic/Latino; 5 Asian, non-Hispanic/Latino; 60 Hispanic/Latino; 1 Native Hawaiian or other Pacific Islander, non-Hispanic/Latino; 17 Two or more races, non-Hispanic/Latino), 17 international. 911 applicants, 45% accepted, 225 enrolled. *Faculty:* 20 full-time (9 women), 89 part-time/adjunct (42 women). Expenses: Contact institution. *Financial support:* In 2018–19, 246 received support, including 67 research assistantships with partial tuition reimbursements available, 12 teaching assistantships with partial tuition reimbursements available; career-related internships or fieldwork, Federal Work-Study, and scholarships/grants also available. Support available to part-time students. Financial award application deadline: 4/1; financial award applicants required to submit FAFSA. In 2018, 185 master's, 5 doctorates, 12 other advanced degrees awarded. *Program availability:* Part-time, evening/weekend, online learning. *Application deadline:* For fall admission, 4/1 priority date for domestic students; for spring admission, 11/1 priority date for domestic students. Applications are processed on a rolling basis. *Application fee:* $65. Electronic applications accepted. *Application Contact:* Graduate Admissions, 325-674-6911, E-mail: gradinfo@acu.edu. *Assistant Provost for Graduate Programs,* Dr. Donnie Snider, 325-674-2223, E-mail: gradinfo@acu.edu.

College of Arts and Sciences Students: 45 full-time (36 women), 13 part-time (11 women); includes 16 minority (7 Black or African American, non-Hispanic/Latino; 6 Hispanic/Latino; 4 Two or more races, non-Hispanic/Latino), 6 international. 102 applicants, 35% accepted, 17 enrolled. *Faculty:* 31 part-time/adjunct (11 women). Expenses: Contact institution. *Financial support:* In 2018–19, 48 students received support, including 32 research assistantships with partial tuition reimbursements available, 8 teaching assistantships with partial tuition reimbursements available; career-related internships or fieldwork, Federal Work-Study, and scholarships/grants also available. Support available to part-time students. Financial award application deadline: 4/1; financial award applicants required to submit FAFSA. In 2018, 22 master's awarded. *Program availability:* Part-time, online learning. Offers arts and sciences (MA, MLA, MS, Specialist); clinical psychology (MS); composition/rhetoric (MA); corporate communication (MA); counseling psychology (MS); liberal arts (MLA); literature (MA); psychology (MS, Specialist); school psychology (Specialist); writing (MA). *Application deadline:* For fall admission, 4/1 priority date for domestic students; for spring admission, 11/1 for domestic students. Applications are processed on a rolling basis. *Application fee:* $65. Electronic applications accepted. *Application Contact:* Graduate Admissions, 325-674-6911, E-mail: gradinfo@acu.edu. *Dean,* Dr. Greg Straughn, 325-674-2209, Fax: 325-674-6800, E-mail: cas@acu.edu.

College of Biblical Studies Students: 51 full-time (23 women), 133 part-time (40 women); includes 49 minority (26 Black or African American, non-Hispanic/Latino; 19 Hispanic/Latino; 4 Two or more races, non-Hispanic/Latino), 7 international. 135 applicants, 61% accepted, 53 enrolled. *Faculty:* 15 full-time (5 women), 15 part-time/adjunct (4 women). Expenses: Contact institution. *Financial support:* In 2018–19, 65 students received support, including 18 research assistantships with partial tuition reimbursements available; career-related internships or fieldwork, Federal Work-Study, and scholarships/grants also available. Support available to part-time students. Financial award application deadline: 4/1; financial award applicants required to submit FAFSA. In 2018, 38 master's, 5 doctorates awarded. *Program availability:* Part-time, evening/weekend, blended/hybrid learning. Offers ancient and Oriental Christianity (MA); Biblical studies (M Div, MA, MACM, MMFT, D Min); Christian ministry (MACM); Christian spiritual formation (D Min); divinity (M Div); global service (MA); leadership for missional renewal (D Min); marriage and family therapy (MMFT); ministry (M Div, D Min); missions (M Div); modern and American Christianity (MA); New Testament (MA); Old Testament (MA); preaching for community transformation (D Min); theology (M Div, MA, MACM, D Min). *Application deadline:* For fall admission, 2/15 priority date for domestic students; for spring admission, 11/1 for domestic students. Applications are processed on a rolling basis.

Application fee: $65. Electronic applications accepted. *Application Contact:* Graduate Admissions, 325-674-6911, E-mail: gradinfo@acu.edu. *Dean,* Dr. Ken Cukrowski, 325-674-3700, Fax: 325-674-3776, E-mail: cukrowski@bible.acu.edu.

College of Business Administration Students: 14 full-time (2 women), 3 part-time (2 women); includes 2 minority (both Hispanic/Latino), 1 international. 35 applicants, 26% accepted, 9 enrolled. *Faculty:* 7 part-time/adjunct (0 women). Expenses: Contact institution. *Financial support:* In 2018–19, 15 students received support. Federal Work-Study and scholarships/grants available. Support available to part-time students. Financial award application deadline: 4/1; financial award applicants required to submit FAFSA. In 2018, 33 master's awarded. *Program availability:* Part-time, online learning. Offers accountancy (M Acc); business administration (M Acc). *Application deadline:* For fall admission, 8/10 for domestic students; for spring admission, 11/1 for domestic students. Applications are processed on a rolling basis. *Application fee:* $65. Electronic applications accepted. *Application Contact:* Graduate Admissions, 325-674-6911, E-mail: gradinfo@acu.edu. *Dean,* Dr. Brad Crisp, 325-674-2245, Fax: 325-674-2564, E-mail: coba@acu.edu.

College of Education and Human Services Students: 198 full-time (192 women), 46 part-time (37 women); includes 61 minority (12 Black or African American, non-Hispanic/Latino; 1 American Indian or Alaska Native, non-Hispanic/Latino; 5 Asian, non-Hispanic/Latino; 33 Hispanic/Latino; 1 Native Hawaiian or other Pacific Islander, non-Hispanic/Latino; 9 Two or more races, non-Hispanic/Latino), 3 international. 639 applicants, 45% accepted, 146 enrolled. *Faculty:* 5 full-time (4 women), 36 part-time/adjunct (27 women). Expenses: Contact institution. *Financial support:* In 2018–19, 118 students received support. Career-related internships or fieldwork, Federal Work-Study, institutionally sponsored loans, and scholarships/grants available. Support available to part-time students. Financial award application deadline: 4/1; financial award applicants required to submit FAFSA. In 2018, 92 master's, 12 other advanced degrees awarded. Offers communication sciences and disorders (MS); dietetic internship (Certificate); education and human services (M Ed, MS, MSSW, Certificate); initial certification (M Ed); nutrition (MS); occupational therapy (MS); reading teacher (M Ed); social work (MSSW). *Application deadline:* For fall admission, 8/15 priority date for domestic students; for winter admission, 10/1 priority date for domestic students; for spring admission, 12/15 priority date for domestic students; for summer admission, 4/15 for domestic students. Applications are processed on a rolling basis. *Application fee:* $65. Electronic applications accepted. *Application Contact:* Graduate Admission, 325-674-6911, E-mail: gradinfo@acu.edu. *Dean,* Dr. Jennifer Shewmaker, 325-674-2700, Fax: 325-674-3707, E-mail: cehs@acu.edu.

ABRAHAM LINCOLN UNIVERSITY, Los Angeles, CA 90010

General Information Proprietary, coed, comprehensive institution.

GRADUATE UNITS

School of Law Offers law (JD).

ACACIA UNIVERSITY, Tempe, AZ 85284

General Information Private, coed, graduate-only institution.

GRADUATE UNITS

American Graduate School of Education Offers educational administration (M Ed); elementary education (MA); English as a second language (M Ed); secondary education (MA); special education (M Ed).

ACADEMY FOR FIVE ELEMENT ACUPUNCTURE, Gainesville, FL 32601

General Information Independent, coed, graduate-only institution.

GRADUATE UNITS

Graduate Program Offers acupuncture (M Ac).

ACADEMY FOR JEWISH RELIGION CALIFORNIA, Los Angeles, CA 90024

General Information Independent-religious, coed, graduate-only institution. *Graduate housing:* On-campus housing not available.

GRADUATE UNITS

Graduate Programs Offers Jewish studies (MJS).

ACADEMY OF ART UNIVERSITY, San Francisco, CA 94105-3410

General Information Proprietary, coed, comprehensive institution. *Graduate housing:* Room and/or apartments guaranteed to single students; on-campus housing not available to married students.

GRADUATE UNITS

Graduate Programs *Program availability:* Part-time, 100% online. Offers costume design (MA, MFA); fashion journalism (MA). Electronic applications accepted.

School of Acting *Program availability:* Part-time. Offers acting (MA, MFA). Electronic applications accepted.

School of Advertising *Program availability:* Part-time, 100% online. Offers advertising (MFA); advertising and branded media technology (MA). Electronic applications accepted.

School of Animation and Visual Effects *Program availability:* Part-time, 100% online. Offers 3D animation (MFA). Electronic applications accepted.

School of Architecture *Program availability:* Part-time, 100% online. Offers advanced architectural design (MA); architecture (M Arch). Electronic applications accepted.

School of Art Education *Program availability:* Part-time, 100% online. Offers art education (MA, MAT). Electronic applications accepted.

School of Art History *Program availability:* Part-time, 100% online. Offers art history (MA). Electronic applications accepted.

School of Communications and Media Technologies *Program availability:* Part-time, 100% online. Offers communications and media technologies (MA). Electronic applications accepted.

School of Fashion *Program availability:* Part-time, 100% online. Offers fashion (MA, MFA); fashion merchandising (MA); fashion merchandising and management (MFA); fashion product development (MFA); knitwear design (MFA); textile design (MFA). Electronic applications accepted.

School of Fine Art *Program availability:* Part-time, 100% online. Offers figurative painting (MFA). Electronic applications accepted.

School of Game Development *Program availability:* Part-time, 100% online. Offers game development (MA, MFA). Electronic applications accepted.

School of Graphic Design *Program availability:* Part-time, 100% online. Offers graphic design (MFA); graphic design and digital media (MA). Electronic applications accepted.

School of Illustration *Program availability:* Part-time, 100% online. Offers illustration (MA, MFA). Electronic applications accepted.

School of Industrial Design *Program availability:* Part-time, 100% online. Offers industrial design (MA, MFA). Electronic applications accepted.

School of Interior Architecture and Design *Program availability:* Part-time, 100% online. Offers interior architecture and design (MA, MFA). Electronic applications accepted.

School of Jewelry and Metal Arts *Program availability:* Part-time, 100% online. Offers jewelry and metal arts (MA, MFA). Electronic applications accepted.

School of Landscape Architecture *Program availability:* Part-time, 100% online. Offers landscape architecture (MA, MFA). Electronic applications accepted.

School of Motion Pictures and Television *Program availability:* Part-time, 100% online. Offers motion pictures and television (MFA); writing and directing for film (MA). Electronic applications accepted.

School of Music Production and Sound Design for Visual Media *Program availability:* Part-time, 100% online. Offers music scoring and composition (MA, MFA); sound design (MA, MFA). Electronic applications accepted.

School of Photography *Program availability:* Part-time, 100% online. Offers photography (MA, MFA). Electronic applications accepted.

School of Visual Development *Program availability:* Part-time, 100% online. Offers visual development (MA, MFA). Electronic applications accepted.

School of Web Design and New Media *Program availability:* Part-time, 100% online. Offers Web design and new media (MA, MFA). Electronic applications accepted.

School of Writing for Film, Television and Digital Media *Program availability:* Part-time, 100% online. Offers writing for film, television and digital media (MFA). Electronic applications accepted.

ACADEMY OF CHINESE CULTURE AND HEALTH SCIENCES, Oakland, CA 94612

General Information Private, coed, graduate-only institution. *Graduate housing:* On-campus housing not available.

GRADUATE UNITS

Program in Traditional Chinese Medicine *Program availability:* Part-time, evening/weekend. Offers traditional Chinese medicine (MS).

ACADIA UNIVERSITY, Wolfville, NS B4P 2R6, Canada

General Information Province-supported, coed, comprehensive institution. *Graduate housing:* Room and/or apartments available on a first-come, first-served basis to single students; on-campus housing not available to married students. Housing application deadline: 5/31. *Research affiliation:* Atlantic Research Laboratory.

GRADUATE UNITS

Divinity College *Program availability:* Part-time. Offers divinity (M Div); ministry (D Min); theology (MA).

Faculty of Arts Offers arts (MA); English (MA); political science (MA); social and political thought (MA); sociology (MA).

Faculty of Professional Studies Offers educational studies (PhD).

School of Education Offers counseling (M Ed); curriculum studies (M Ed); inclusive education (M Ed); interprofessional health practice (M Ed); leadership (M Ed); music education (M Ed).

School of Recreation Management and Community Development Offers recreation management (MR).

Faculty of Pure and Applied Science Offers applied geomatics (M Sc); applied mathematics and statistics (M Sc); biology (M Sc); chemistry (M Sc); clinical psychology (M Sc); geology (M Sc); pure and applied science (M Sc).

Jodrey School of Computer Science Offers computer science (M Sc).

ACUPUNCTURE & INTEGRATIVE MEDICINE COLLEGE, BERKELEY, Berkeley, CA 94704

General Information Independent, coed, graduate-only institution. *Graduate housing:* On-campus housing not available.

GRADUATE UNITS

Master of Science in Oriental Medicine Program *Program availability:* Part-time. Offers Oriental medicine (MS). Electronic applications accepted.

ACUPUNCTURE AND MASSAGE COLLEGE, Miami, FL 33176

General Information Proprietary, coed, graduate-only institution.

GRADUATE UNITS

Program in Oriental Medicine Offers Oriental medicine (MOM).

ADAMS STATE UNIVERSITY, Alamosa, CO 81101

General Information State-supported, coed, comprehensive institution. CGS member. *Graduate housing:* Rooms and/or apartments available on a first-come, first-served basis to single and married students. *Research affiliation:* Sandia National Laboratories (science education).

GRADUATE UNITS

Office of Graduate Studies Expenses: Contact institution. *Financial support:* In 2018–19, teaching assistantships with partial tuition reimbursements (averaging $4,000 per year) were awarded; fellowships with partial tuition reimbursements, career-related internships or fieldwork, Federal Work-Study, institutionally sponsored loans, and scholarships/grants also available. Financial award application deadline: 3/1; financial award applicants required to submit FAFSA. *Program availability:* Part-time, 100% online, summer residency. Offers counselor education (MA); counselor education and supervision (PhD); human performance and physical education (MA, MS); humanities (MA); music education (MA); teacher education (MA). *Application deadline:* Applications are processed on a rolling basis. *Application fee:* $30. Electronic applications accepted. *Application Contact:* Information Contact, 719-587-8152, Fax: 719-587-8222, E-mail: graduatestudies@adams.edu. *Interim Assistant Vice President of Graduate Studies,* Dr. Teri McCartney, 719-587-8413, Fax: 719-587-8222, E-mail: pennysanders@adams.edu.

School of Business Offers business (MBA).

ADELPHI UNIVERSITY, Garden City, NY 11530-0701

General Information Independent, coed, university. *Enrollment:* 8,149 graduate, professional, and undergraduate students; 1,483 full-time matriculated graduate/professional students (1,055 women), 1,098 part-time matriculated graduate/professional students (815 women). *Enrollment by degree level:* 2,327 master's, 254 doctoral. *Graduate faculty:* 340 full-time (182 women), 720 part-time/adjunct (495 women). *Graduate housing:* Room and/or apartments available on a first-come, first-served basis to single students; on-campus housing not available to married students. Housing application deadline: 5/1. *Student services:* Campus employment opportunities, campus safety program, career counseling, child daycare facilities, exercise/wellness program, free psychological counseling, international student

services, low-cost health insurance, multicultural affairs office, services for students with disabilities, teacher training, writing training. *Library facilities:* Swirbul Library. *Collection:* Books: 537,868 (physical), 240,988 (digital/electronic); Serial titles: 430 (physical), 87,949 (digital/electronic); Databases: 249. Students can reserve study rooms.

Computer facilities: Computer purchase and lease plans are available. 667 computers available on campus for general student use. A campuswide network can be accessed from student residence rooms and from off campus. Online class registration, payment, drop/add classes, check application status are available. Website: http://www.adelphi.edu/

General Application Contact: Kristen Capezza, Vice President for Enrollment Management, 516-877-3050, Fax: 516-877-3039, E-mail: graduateadmissions@adelphi.edu.

GRADUATE UNITS

College of Arts and Sciences Students: 55 full-time (33 women), 23 part-time (16 women); includes 24 minority (10 Black or African American, non-Hispanic/Latino; 6 Asian, non-Hispanic/Latino; 7 Hispanic/Latino; 1 Two or more races, non-Hispanic/Latino), 28 international. Average age 27. 313 applicants, 36% accepted, 45 enrolled. *Faculty:* 125 full-time (57 women), 200 part-time/adjunct (96 women). Expenses: Contact institution. *Financial support:* In 2018–19, 38 research assistantships with full and partial tuition reimbursements (averaging $14,269 per year) were awarded; fellowships, teaching assistantships, career-related internships or fieldwork, Federal Work-Study, scholarships/grants, traineeships, tuition waivers (partial), unspecified assistantships, and tuition remission for employees also available. Support available to part-time students. Financial award application deadline: 1/1; financial award applicants required to submit FAFSA. In 2018, 38 master's awarded. *Program availability:* Part-time. Offers arts and sciences (MA, MFA, MS); biology (MS); biotechnology (MS); creative writing (MFA); environmental studies (MS); studio art (MA). *Application deadline:* For fall admission, 5/1 priority date for international students; for spring admission, 11/1 priority date for international students. Applications are processed on a rolling basis. *Application fee:* $50. Electronic applications accepted. *Application Contact:* Kristen Capezza, Vice President for Enrollment Management, 516-877-3050, Fax: 516-877-3039, E-mail: graduateadmissions@adelphi.edu. *Dean,* Dr. Vincent Wang, 516-877-4125, E-mail: vwang@adelphi.edu.

College of Education & Health Sciences Students: 460 full-time (369 women), 259 part-time (160 women); includes 197 minority (57 Black or African American, non-Hispanic/Latino; 1 American Indian or Alaska Native, non-Hispanic/Latino; 26 Asian, non-Hispanic/Latino; 106 Hispanic/Latino; 1 Native Hawaiian or other Pacific Islander, non-Hispanic/Latino; 6 Two or more races, non-Hispanic/Latino), 34 international. Average age 27. 1,256 applicants, 59% accepted, 288 enrolled. *Faculty:* 69 full-time (45 women), 88 part-time/adjunct (61 women). Expenses: Contact institution. *Financial support:* Fellowships, research assistantships, teaching assistantships, career-related internships or fieldwork, Federal Work-Study, scholarships/grants, traineeships, tuition waivers (full and partial), unspecified assistantships, and tuition remission for employees available. Support available to part-time students. Financial award application deadline: 1/1; financial award applicants required to submit FAFSA. In 2018, 299 master's, 8 doctorates, 83 other advanced degrees awarded. *Program availability:* Part-time, evening/weekend. Offers adolescent education (MA); aging (Certificate); art education (MA); audiology (MS, DA); birth-grade 12 (MS); birth-grade 6 (MS); childhood education (MA); community health education (MA, Certificate); education (MA, MS, DA, Certificate); educational technology (MA); grades 5-12 (MS); p - 12 (MA); physical/educational human performance science (MA); school health education (MA); special education (MS, Certificate); speech-language pathology (MS, DA). *Application deadline:* For fall admission, 3/1 for international students; for spring admission, 11/1 for international students. Applications are processed on a rolling basis. *Application fee:* $50. Electronic applications accepted. *Application Contact:* Kristen Capezza, Vice President for Enrollment Management, 516-877-3021, Fax: 516-877-3039, E-mail: graduateadmissions@adelphi.edu. *Dean,* Dr. Xiao-Lei Wang, 516-877-4065, E-mail: xlwang@adelphi.edu.

College of Nursing and Public Health Students: 35 full-time (27 women), 387 part-time (323 women); includes 260 minority (131 Black or African American, non-Hispanic/Latino; 1 American Indian or Alaska Native, non-Hispanic/Latino; 90 Asian, non-Hispanic/Latino; 29 Hispanic/Latino; 9 Two or more races, non-Hispanic/Latino), 11 international. Average age 36. 510 applicants, 48% accepted, 123 enrolled. *Faculty:* 45 full-time (35 women), 228 part-time/adjunct (208 women). Expenses: Contact institution. *Financial support:* Fellowships, research assistantships, teaching assistantships with full and partial tuition reimbursements, career-related internships or fieldwork, Federal Work-Study, scholarships/grants, traineeships, tuition waivers, unspecified assistantships, and tuition remission for employees available. Support available to part-time students. Financial award application deadline: 1/1; financial award applicants required to submit FAFSA. In 2018, 112 master's, 4 doctorates, 3 other advanced degrees awarded. *Program availability:* Part-time, evening/weekend. Offers adult gerontology primary care nurse practitioner (Advanced Certificate); adult health nurse (MS); health information technology (MS, Advanced Certificate); nurse practitioner in adult health nursing (Certificate); nursing (PhD); nursing administration (MS); nursing education (MS, Certificate); nutrition (MS); public health (MPH). *Application deadline:* Applications are processed on a rolling basis. *Application fee:* $50. Electronic applications accepted. *Application Contact:* Kristen Capezza, Vice President for Enrollment Management, 516-877-3021, Fax: 516-877-3039, E-mail: graduateadmissions@adelphi.edu. *Dean,* Dr. Elaine Smith, 516-833-8181, E-mail: elsmith@adelphi.edu.

College of Professional and Continuing Studies Students: 3 full-time (all women), 14 part-time (7 women); includes 7 minority (5 Black or African American, non-Hispanic/Latino; 2 Hispanic/Latino). Average age 36. 28 applicants, 50% accepted, 11 enrolled. *Faculty:* 23 part-time/adjunct (10 women). Expenses: Contact institution. *Financial support:* Fellowships, research assistantships, teaching assistantships with full and partial tuition reimbursements, career-related internships or fieldwork, Federal Work-Study, scholarships/grants, traineeships, tuition waivers (full and partial), unspecified assistantships, and tuition remission for employees available. Support available to part-time students. In 2018, 3 Certificates awarded. Offers emergency management (Certificate). *Application deadline:* For fall admission, 5/1 for international students; for spring admission, 12/1 for international students. *Application fee:* $50. *Application Contact:* Kristen Capezza, Vice President for Enrollment Management, 516-877-3021, Fax: 516-877-3039, E-mail: graduateadmissions@adelphi.edu. *Dean,* Andy Atzert, 516-877-3404, E-mail: aatzert@adelphi.edu.

Gordon F. Derner School of Psychology Students: 237 full-time (190 women), 66 part-time (51 women); includes 102 minority (29 Black or African American, non-Hispanic/Latino; 2 American Indian or Alaska Native, non-Hispanic/Latino; 17 Asian, non-Hispanic/Latino; 44 Hispanic/Latino; 10 Two or more races, non-Hispanic/Latino), 22 international. Average age 28. 578 applicants, 44% accepted, 119 enrolled. *Faculty:*

26 full-time (13 women), 63 part-time/adjunct (40 women). Expenses: Contact institution. *Financial support:* Fellowships, research assistantships, teaching assistantships, career-related internships or fieldwork, Federal Work-Study, scholarships/grants, traineeships, unspecified assistantships, and tuition remission for employees available. Support available to part-time students. Financial award application deadline: 1/1; financial award applicants required to submit FAFSA. In 2018, 91 master's, 21 doctorates awarded. *Program availability:* Part-time. Offers clinical psychology (PhD); general psychology (MA); mental health counseling (MA); psychology (MA, PhD); school psychology (MA). *Application deadline:* For fall admission, 4/1 priority date for domestic students, 5/1 priority date for international students; for spring admission, 11/1 priority date for international students. *Application fee:* $50. Electronic applications accepted. *Application Contact:* Kristen Capezza, Vice President for Enrollment Management, 516-877-3021, Fax: 516-877-3039, E-mail: graduateadmissions@adelphi.edu. *Dean,* Dr. Jacques P. Barber, 516-877-4807, E-mail: jbarber@adelphi.edu.

Robert B. Willumstad School of Business Students: 363 full-time (140 women), 109 part-time (60 women); includes 83 minority (24 Black or African American, non-Hispanic/Latino; 2 American Indian or Alaska Native, non-Hispanic/Latino; 23 Asian, non-Hispanic/Latino; 25 Hispanic/Latino; 1 Native Hawaiian or other Pacific Islander, non-Hispanic/Latino; 8 Two or more races, non-Hispanic/Latino), 283 international. Average age 29. 434 applicants, 57% accepted, 195 enrolled. *Faculty:* 44 full-time (13 women), 25 part-time/adjunct (8 women). Expenses: Contact institution. *Financial support:* Fellowships, research assistantships, teaching assistantships with full and partial tuition reimbursements, career-related internships or fieldwork, Federal Work-Study, scholarships/grants, traineeships, tuition waivers (full and partial), unspecified assistantships, and tuition remission for employees available. Support available to part-time students. Financial award application deadline: 3/1. In 2018, 171 master's, 15 other advanced degrees awarded. *Program availability:* Part-time, evening/weekend. Offers accounting (MBA); business (MBA, MS, Certificate); finance (MBA); health services administration (MBA); human resource management (Certificate); management (MBA); management information systems (MBA); marketing (MBA); sport management (MBA); supply chain management (MS). *Application deadline:* For fall admission, 3/1 for international students; for spring admission, 11/1 for international students. Applications are processed on a rolling basis. *Application fee:* $50. Electronic applications accepted. *Application Contact:* Kristen Capezza, Vice President for Enrollment Management, 516-877-3021, Fax: 516-877-3039, E-mail: graduateadmissions@adelphi.edu. *Dean,* Dr. Rajib Sanyal, 516-877-4690, E-mail: rsanyal@adelphi.edu.

School of Social Work Students: 322 full-time (285 women), 145 part-time (195 women); includes 307 minority (153 Black or African American, non-Hispanic/Latino; 2 American Indian or Alaska Native, non-Hispanic/Latino; 21 Asian, non-Hispanic/Latino; 116 Hispanic/Latino; 15 Two or more races, non-Hispanic/Latino), 4 international. Average age 33. 699 applicants, 57% accepted, 192 enrolled. *Faculty:* 25 full-time (16 women), 92 part-time/adjunct (71 women). Expenses: Contact institution. *Financial support:* Fellowships, research assistantships, teaching assistantships with full and partial tuition reimbursements, career-related internships or fieldwork, Federal Work-Study, scholarships/grants, traineeships, tuition waivers (full and partial), unspecified assistantships, and tuition remission for employees available. Support available to part-time students. Financial award application deadline: 1/1. In 2018, 263 master's, 3 doctorates awarded. *Program availability:* Part-time, evening/weekend. Offers social welfare (DSW); social work (MSW, DSW, PhD). *Application deadline:* For fall admission, 7/15 priority date for domestic students, 3/1 for international students; for spring admission, 12/1 priority date for domestic students, 11/1 for international students. Applications are processed on a rolling basis. *Application fee:* $50. Electronic applications accepted. *Application Contact:* Kristen Capezza, Vice President for Enrollment Management, 516-877-3021, Fax: 516-877-3039, E-mail: graduateadmissions@adelphi.edu. *Interim Dean,* Dr. Diann Cameron Kelly, 516-877-4354, E-mail: kelly5@adelphi.edu.

ADLER GRADUATE SCHOOL, Richfield, MN 55423
General Information Independent, coed, graduate-only institution. *Graduate housing:* On-campus housing not available.

GRADUATE UNITS
Program in Adlerian Counseling and Psychotherapy *Program availability:* Part-time, evening/weekend. Offers Adlerian studies (MA); art therapy (MA); clinical mental health counseling (MA); co-occurring substance use and mental health disorders (MA); marriage and family therapy (MA); school counseling (MA). Electronic applications accepted.

ADLER UNIVERSITY, Chicago, IL 60602
General Information Independent, coed, graduate-only institution. *Graduate housing:* On-campus housing not available. *Research affiliation:* LGBTQ Mental Health and Inclusion Center, Adler Child Guidance Center, Adler Institute on Social Exclusion, Adler Institute on Public Safety and Social Justice.

GRADUATE UNITS
Graduate Programs *Program availability:* Part-time, evening/weekend, online learning. Offers advanced Adlerian psychotherapy (Psy D); art therapy (MAC, MCP, PhD); child and adolescent clinical psychology (Psy D); child and adolescent development (MA); clinical mental health counseling (MAC); community health (MPP); counseling psychology (MACP, MCP); counseling psychology: school and youth (MACP, MCP); counselor education and supervision (PhD); couple and family therapy (MA, PhD); criminal justice (MPA); crisis management (MA); forensic psychology (MAC); gender and sexuality studies (MA); health and wellness (MPP); human rights advocacy (MPP); industrial and organizational psychology (MA, PhD); military clinical psychology (Psy D); military psychology (MA); organizational psychology (MA); primary care psychology and behavioral medicine (Psy D); psychology (MA, MAC, MACP, MCP, MPA, MPP, MPPA, PhD, Psy D, Certificate); rehabilitation counseling (MAC); social change leadership (MPPA); sport and health psychology (MAC); substance abuse treatment (Psy D); sustainable communities (MPA); traumatic stress psychology (Psy D). Electronic applications accepted.

ADRIAN COLLEGE, Adrian, MI 49221-2575
General Information Independent-religious, coed, comprehensive institution. *Graduate housing:* On-campus housing not available.

GRADUATE UNITS
Graduate Programs Offers accounting (MS); athletic training (MS); criminal justice (MA).

ADVENTHEALTH UNIVERSITY, Orlando, FL 32803
General Information Independent, coed, comprehensive institution.

GRADUATE UNITS
Program in Healthcare Administration Offers healthcare administration (MHA).
Program in Nurse Anesthesia Offers nurse anesthesia (MS).
Program in Occupational Therapy Offers occupational therapy (MOT).
Program in Physical Therapy Offers physical therapy (DPT).
Program in Physician Assistant Studies Offers physician assistant studies (MS).

AGNES SCOTT COLLEGE, Decatur, GA 30030-3797
General Information Independent-religious, women only, comprehensive institution. *Enrollment:* 1,030 graduate, professional, and undergraduate students; 7 full-time matriculated graduate/professional students (all women). *Enrollment by degree level:* 7 master's. *Graduate faculty:* 2 full-time (both women), 1 (woman) part-time/adjunct. *Tuition:* Full-time $16,200; part-time $2700 per course. *Graduate housing:* On-campus housing not available. *Student services:* Campus safety program, career counseling, low-cost health insurance, multicultural affairs office, services for students with disabilities, teacher training, writing training. *Library facilities:* McCain Library. *Collection:* Books: 240,240 (physical), 57,182 (digital/electronic); Databases: 474. Study areas open 24 hours, 5–7 days a week.

Computer facilities: 450 computers available on campus for general student use. A campuswide network can be accessed from student residence rooms and from off campus. Online class registration is available.
Website: http://www.agnesscott.edu/

General Application Contact: Michelle Lacoss, Senior Director of Graduate Admission, 404-471-5377, E-mail: mlacoss@agnesscott.edu.

GRADUATE UNITS
Program in Writing and Digital Communication Offers writing and digital communication (MA).

AIR FORCE INSTITUTE OF TECHNOLOGY, Dayton, OH 45433-7765
General Information Federally supported, coed, primarily men, graduate-only institution. *Graduate housing:* On-campus housing not available. *Research affiliation:* U.S. Air Force Office of Scientific Research, U.S. Air Force Research Laboratory (AFRL), Dayton Area Graduate Studies Institute (aerospace), U.S. Department of Energy, National Security Agency.

GRADUATE UNITS
Graduate School of Engineering and Management *Program availability:* Part-time. Offers aeronautical engineering (MS, PhD); applied mathematics (MS, PhD); applied physics (MS, PhD); astronautical engineering (MS, PhD); computer engineering (MS, PhD); computer systems/science (MS); cost analysis (MS); electrical engineering (MS, PhD); electro-optics (MS, PhD); engineering and management (MS, PhD); environmental and engineering management (MS); environmental engineering science (MS); information resource/systems management (MS); logistics management (MS); materials science (MS, PhD); nuclear engineering (MS, PhD); operations research (MS, PhD); space operations (MS); space physics (MS); systems engineering (MS, PhD).

ALABAMA AGRICULTURAL AND MECHANICAL UNIVERSITY, Huntsville, AL 35811
General Information State-supported, coed, university. CGS member. *Graduate housing:* Rooms and/or apartments available on a first-come, first-served basis to single and married students. Housing application deadline: 5/5. *Research affiliation:* NASA (utilization of space resources), Boeing Defense and Space Group (plant science), Lawrence Livermore National Laboratory (chemistry, physics), Alabama Supercomputer Network (computer services), Nichols Research Corporation (computer science), Hughes Aircraft Corporation (physics).

GRADUATE UNITS
School of Graduate Studies Electronic applications accepted.

College of Agricultural, Life and Natural Sciences *Program availability:* Part-time, evening/weekend. Offers agricultural, life and natural sciences (MS, MURP, PhD); apparel, merchandising and design (MS); biology (MS); family and consumer sciences (MS); food science (MS, PhD); human development and family studies (MS); nutrition and hospitality management (MS); plant and soil science (MS, PhD); urban and regional planning (MURP). Electronic applications accepted.

College of Business and Public Affairs *Program availability:* Part-time, evening/weekend. Offers business and public affairs (MBA). Electronic applications accepted.

College of Education, Humanities, and Behavioral Sciences *Program availability:* Part-time, evening/weekend. Offers art education (MS); biology (M Ed); business/marketing education (M Ed, Ed S); chemistry (M Ed); collaborative teacher secondary education (M Ed, Ed S); early childhood education (MS Ed, Ed S); education (M Ed, Ed S); education, humanities, and behavioral sciences (M Ed, MS, MS Ed, PhD, Ed S); elementary education (MS Ed, Ed S); English language arts (M Ed); family/consumer science education (M Ed, Ed S); general science (M Ed); general social science (M Ed); kinesiology (MS); mathematics (M Ed, Ed S); music education (M Ed); physical education (MS); physics (M Ed, Ed S); psychology and counseling (MS, Ed S); reading/literacy (PhD); social work (MSW); special education collaborative teacher training (MS Ed, Ed S); speech-language pathology (MS); technology education (M Ed). Electronic applications accepted.

College of Engineering, Technology, and Physical Sciences *Program availability:* Part-time, evening/weekend. Offers computer science (MS); engineering, technology, and physical sciences (M Eng, MS, PhD); material engineering (M Eng); physics (MS, PhD). Electronic applications accepted.

ALABAMA COLLEGE OF OSTEOPATHIC MEDICINE, Dothan, AL 36303
General Information Independent, coed, graduate-only institution.

GRADUATE UNITS
Graduate Program Offers osteopathic medicine (DO).

ALABAMA STATE UNIVERSITY, Montgomery, AL 36101-0271
General Information State-supported, coed, university. CGS member. *Enrollment:* 4,413 graduate, professional, and undergraduate students; 291 full-time matriculated graduate/professional students (207 women), 219 part-time matriculated graduate/professional students (154 women). *Enrollment by degree level:* 355 master's, 145 doctoral, 6 other advanced degrees. *Graduate housing:* On-campus housing not available. *Student services:* Campus employment opportunities, campus safety program, career counseling, child daycare facilities, exercise/wellness program, free psychological counseling, international student services, low-cost health insurance,

services for students with disabilities, teacher training, writing training. *Library facilities:* Levi Watkins Learning Center plus 1 other. *Collection:* Books: 437,312 (physical), 69,796 (digital/electronic); Serial titles: 1,607 (physical), 6,084 (digital/electronic); Databases: 192. Weekly public service hours: 78; study areas open 24 hours, 5–7 days a week; students can reserve study rooms.

Computer facilities: 805 computers available on campus for general student use. A campuswide network can be accessed from student residence rooms and from off campus. Online class registration is available.
Website: http://www.alasu.edu/

General Application Contact: Dr. Ed Brown, Dean of Graduate Studies, 334-229-4753, Fax: 334-229-4928, E-mail: ebrown@alasu.edu.

GRADUATE UNITS

College of Business Administration Students: 16 full-time (6 women), 1 (woman) part-time; includes 14 minority (all Black or African American, non-Hispanic/Latino), 3 international. Average age 29. 14 applicants, 29% accepted, 3 enrolled. *Faculty:* 4 full-time (1 woman), 1 part-time/adjunct (0 women). Expenses: Contact institution. *Financial support:* Fellowships, teaching assistantships, career-related internships or fieldwork, scholarships/grants, tuition waivers (partial), and unspecified assistantships available. Financial award application deadline: 6/30; financial award applicants required to submit FAFSA. In 2018, 8 master's awarded. *Program availability:* Part-time. Offers accountancy (M Acc); business administration (M Acc). *Application deadline:* For fall admission, 4/15 for domestic and international students; for spring admission, 11/15 for domestic students, 11/1 for international students; for summer admission, 3/15 for domestic and international students. *Application fee:* $25. Electronic applications accepted. *Application Contact:* Dr. Ed Brown, Dean of Graduate Studies, 334-229-4274, Fax: 334-229-4928, E-mail: ebrown@alasu.edu. *Director, Master of Accountancy,* Dr. Dave Thompson, 334-229-6809, E-mail: dthompson@alasu.edu.

College of Education Students: 62 full-time (42 women), 189 part-time (140 women); includes 235 minority (234 Black or African American, non-Hispanic/Latino; 1 Hispanic/Latino), 5 international. Average age 41. 71 applicants, 79% accepted, 21 enrolled. *Faculty:* 7 full-time (4 women), 7 part-time/adjunct (4 women). Expenses: Contact institution. *Financial support:* Fellowships, teaching assistantships, career-related internships or fieldwork, scholarships/grants, tuition waivers (partial), and unspecified assistantships available. Financial award application deadline: 6/30; financial award applicants required to submit FAFSA. In 2018, 76 master's, 4 doctorates, 17 other advanced degrees awarded. *Program availability:* Part-time. Offers counselor education (M Ed, MS, Ed S); early childhood education (Ed S); education (M Ed, MS, Ed D, PhD, Ed S); educational administration (M Ed); educational leadership, policy and law (PhD); health education (M Ed); library education media (Ed S); physical education (M Ed); secondary education (M Ed). *Application deadline:* For fall admission, 4/15 for domestic and international students; for spring admission, 11/15 for domestic and international students; for summer admission, 3/15 for domestic and international students. Applications are processed on a rolling basis. *Application fee:* $25. Electronic applications accepted. *Application Contact:* Dr. Ed Brown, Dean of Graduate Studies, 334-229-4274, Fax: 334-229-4928, E-mail: ebrown@alasu.edu. *Dean,* Dr. Alethea Hampton, 334-229-4250, E-mail: ahampton@alasu.edu.

College of Health Sciences Students: 169 full-time (121 women), 3 part-time (0 women); includes 73 minority (60 Black or African American, non-Hispanic/Latino; 5 Asian, non-Hispanic/Latino; 4 Two or more races, non-Hispanic/Latino), 2 international. Average age 28. 171 applicants, 39% accepted, 64 enrolled. *Faculty:* 19 full-time (16 women), 19 part-time/adjunct (10 women). Expenses: Contact institution. *Financial support:* In 2018–19, 3 students received support. Research assistantships, Federal Work-Study, scholarships/grants, tuition waivers (partial), and unspecified assistantships available. Financial award application deadline: 6/30; financial award applicants required to submit FAFSA. In 2018, 42 master's, 24 doctorates awarded. *Program availability:* Part-time. Offers health sciences (MRC, MS, DPT); occupational therapy (MS); physical therapy (DPT); prosthetics and orthotics (MS); rehabilitation counseling (MRC). *Application deadline:* For fall admission, 4/15 for domestic and international students; for spring admission, 11/15 for domestic and international students; for summer admission, 3/15 for domestic and international students. Applications are processed on a rolling basis. *Application fee:* $25. Electronic applications accepted. *Application Contact:* Dr. Ed Brown, Dean of Graduate Studies, 334-229-4274, Fax: 334-229-4928, E-mail: ebrown@alasu.edu. *Dean, College of Health Sciences,* Dr. Charlene Portee, 334-229-5053, E-mail: cportee@alasu.edu.

College of Liberal Arts and Social Sciences Students: 25 full-time (21 women), 3 part-time (1 woman); includes 26 minority (all Black or African American, non-Hispanic/Latino), 1 international. Average age 33. 34 applicants, 38% accepted, 8 enrolled. *Faculty:* 16 full-time (4 women). Expenses: Contact institution. *Financial support:* Fellowships, research assistantships, scholarships/grants, tuition waivers (partial), and unspecified assistantships available. Financial award application deadline: 6/30. In 2018, 26 master's awarded. *Program availability:* Part-time. Offers history (MA); social work (MSW). *Application deadline:* For fall admission, 7/15 for domestic students; for spring admission, 12/15 for domestic students. Applications are processed on a rolling basis. *Application fee:* $25. *Application Contact:* Dr. Ed Brown, Dean of Graduate Studies, 334-229-4274, Fax: 334-229-4928, E-mail: ebrown@alasu.edu. *Associate Dean,* Dr. Kathaleen Amende, 334-229-5149, E-mail: kamende@alasu.edu.

College of Science, Mathematics and Technology Students: 19 full-time (17 women), 19 part-time (10 women); includes 32 minority (30 Black or African American, non-Hispanic/Latino; 1 Asian, non-Hispanic/Latino; 1 Hispanic/Latino), 6 international. Average age 31. 39 applicants, 33% accepted, 9 enrolled. *Faculty:* 11 full-time (4 women). Expenses: Contact institution. *Financial support:* In 2018–19, 22 students received support. Research assistantships, Federal Work-Study, scholarships/grants, tuition waivers (partial), and unspecified assistantships available. Financial award application deadline: 6/30; financial award applicants required to submit CSS PROFILE or FAFSA. In 2018, 4 master's, 2 doctorates awarded. Offers biology (MS); mathematics (MS); microbiology (MS); physical sciences (MS); science, mathematics and technology (MS, PhD). *Application deadline:* For fall admission, 4/15 for domestic and international students; for spring admission, 11/15 for domestic and international students; for summer admission, 3/15 for domestic and international students. Applications are processed on a rolling basis. *Application fee:* $25. Electronic applications accepted. *Application Contact:* Dr. Ed Brown, Dean of Graduate Studies, 334-229-4274, Fax: 334-229-4928, E-mail: ebrown@alasu.edu. *Dean,* Dr. Kennedy Weskesa, 334-229-4316, Fax: 334-229-4916, E-mail: weskesa@alasu.edu.

ALASKA PACIFIC UNIVERSITY, Anchorage, AK 99508-4672
General Information Independent, coed, comprehensive institution. *Graduate housing:* Room and/or apartments available on a first-come, first-served basis to single students; on-campus housing not available to married students. Housing application deadline: 8/15.

GRADUATE UNITS
Graduate Programs *Program availability:* Part-time, evening/weekend. Offers business administration (MBA); counseling psychology (MSCP); environmental science (MSES, MSOEE); health services administration (MBA); information and communication technology (MBAICT); investment (CGS); outdoor and environmental education (MSOEE); self-designed study (MA); teaching (MAT); teaching (K-8) (MAT). Electronic applications accepted.

ALBANY COLLEGE OF PHARMACY AND HEALTH SCIENCES, Albany, NY 12208
General Information Independent, coed, comprehensive institution. *Graduate housing:* Room and/or apartments available on a first-come, first-served basis to single students; on-campus housing not available to married students. Housing application deadline: 7/1.

GRADUATE UNITS
School of Arts and Sciences Offers clinical laboratory sciences (MS); cytotechnology and molecular cytology (MS); health outcomes research (MS); molecular biosciences (MS). Electronic applications accepted.

School of Pharmacy and Pharmaceutical Sciences Offers health outcomes research (MS); pharmaceutical sciences (MS); pharmacy (Pharm D). Electronic applications accepted.

ALBANY LAW SCHOOL, Albany, NY 12208-3494
General Information Independent, coed, graduate-only institution. *Graduate housing:* On-campus housing not available.

GRADUATE UNITS
Professional Program *Program availability:* Part-time. Offers law (LL M, JD). JD/MBA offered jointly with The College of Saint Rose, The Sage Colleges, Union Graduate College, and University at Albany, State University of New York; JD/MPA, JD/MRP, and JD/MSW offered jointly with University at Albany, State University of New York.

ALBANY MEDICAL COLLEGE, Albany, NY 12208-3479
General Information Independent, coed, graduate-only institution. *Graduate housing:* On-campus housing not available. *Research affiliation:* X-Ray Optical Systems (diagnostic equipment), Integrated Tissue Dynamics INTIGYN (integrated tissue dynamics), Regenerative Research Foundation (biomedical research), Wadsworth Center for Laboratories and Research (biomedical research), ORDWAY Research Institute (biomedical research), General Electric Company (GE) (imaging).

GRADUATE UNITS
Alden March Bioethics Institute *Program availability:* Part-time, evening/weekend, online learning. Offers bioethics (MS, DPS); clinical ethics (Certificate); clinical ethics consultation (Certificate). Electronic applications accepted.

Center for Cardiovascular Sciences *Program availability:* Part-time. Offers cardiovascular sciences (MS, PhD).

Center for Cell Biology and Cancer Research *Program availability:* Part-time. Offers cell biology and cancer research (MS, PhD).

Center for Immunology and Microbial Disease *Program availability:* Part-time. Offers immunology and microbial disease (MS, PhD).

Center for Neuropharmacology and Neuroscience Offers neuropharmacology and neuroscience (MS, PhD).

Center for Nurse Anesthesiology Offers anesthesia (MS). Electronic applications accepted.

Center for Physician Assistant Studies Offers physician assistant studies (MS). Electronic applications accepted.

Professional Program Offers medicine (MD). Electronic applications accepted.

ALBANY STATE UNIVERSITY, Albany, GA 31705-2717
General Information State-supported, coed, comprehensive institution. *Graduate housing:* Room and/or apartments available on a first-come, first-served basis to single students; on-campus housing not available to married students. Housing application deadline: 6/30.

GRADUATE UNITS
College of Arts and Humanities *Program availability:* Part-time. Offers criminal justice (MS); English education (M Ed); public administration (MPA); social work (MSW). Electronic applications accepted.

College of Business *Program availability:* Part-time, evening/weekend. Offers accounting (MBA); general business administration (MBA); healthcare (MBA); public administration (MBA); supply chain and logistics (MBA). Electronic applications accepted.

College of Education *Program availability:* Part-time, evening/weekend, online learning. Offers early childhood education (M Ed); educational leadership (Ed S); health and physical education (M Ed); middle grades education (M Ed); school counseling (M Ed); special education (M Ed). Electronic applications accepted.

Darton College of Health Professions *Program availability:* Part-time, evening/weekend, online learning. Offers nursing (MSN). Electronic applications accepted.

ALBERT EINSTEIN COLLEGE OF MEDICINE, Bronx, NY 10461
General Information Independent, coed, graduate-only institution. CGS member. *Graduate housing:* Room and/or apartments guaranteed to single students.

GRADUATE UNITS
Graduate Programs in the Biomedical Sciences Offers anatomy (PhD); biochemistry (PhD); biomedical sciences (PhD); cell biology (PhD); clinical investigation (PhD); computational genetics (PhD); developmental and molecular biology (PhD); microbiology and immunology (PhD); molecular genetics (PhD); molecular pharmacology (PhD); neuroscience (PhD); pathology (PhD); physiology and biophysics (PhD); systems and computational biology (PhD); translational genetics (PhD). Electronic applications accepted.

Medical Scientist Training Program

Professional Program in Medicine Offers medicine (MD).

ALBERTUS MAGNUS COLLEGE, New Haven, CT 06511-1189
General Information Independent-religious, coed, comprehensive institution. *Enrollment:* 242 full-time matriculated graduate/professional students (200 women), 98 part-time matriculated graduate/professional students (68 women). *Enrollment by degree level:* 340 master's. *Graduate faculty:* 37 full-time (17 women), 68 part-time/adjunct (32 women). *Tuition:* Full-time $20,112; part-time $838 per credit. *Required fees:* $184; $112 per unit. One-time fee: $150. Tuition and fees vary according to course load and program. *Graduate housing:* On-campus housing not available. *Student*

services: Campus employment opportunities, career counseling, free psychological counseling, international student services, services for students with disabilities, teacher training, writing training. *Library facilities:* Rosary Hall. *Collection:* Books: 38,339 (physical), 148,500 (digital/electronic); Databases: 88.

Computer facilities: 117 computers available on campus for general student use. A campuswide network can be accessed from student residence rooms and from off campus. Online class registration, online class sessions are available. Website: http://www.albertus.edu/

General Application Contact: Annette Bosley-Boyce, Dean- Division of Professional and Graduate Studies, 203-672-6685 Ext. 6685, E-mail: abosleboyce@albertus.edu.

GRADUATE UNITS

Master of Arts in Art Therapy and Counseling Program *Program availability:* Part-time. Offers art therapy and counseling (MA). Electronic applications accepted.

Master of Arts in Liberal Studies Program *Program availability:* Part-time, evening/weekend, blended/hybrid learning. Offers liberal studies (MALS). Electronic applications accepted.

Master of Business Administration Program *Program availability:* Part-time, evening/weekend, 100% online, blended/hybrid learning. Offers accounting (MBA); general management (MBA); health care management (MBA); human resource management (MBA); leadership (MBA); project management (MBA). Program also offered in East Hartford, CT. Electronic applications accepted.

Master of Fine Arts in Writing Program *Program availability:* Part-time, evening/weekend, 100% online, blended/hybrid learning. Offers writing (MFA). Electronic applications accepted.

Master of Science in Accounting Program *Program availability:* Part-time, evening/weekend, 100% online, blended/hybrid learning. Offers accounting (MSA). Electronic applications accepted.

Master of Science in Criminal Justice Program *Program availability:* Part-time, evening/weekend, 100% online, blended/hybrid learning. Offers corrections administration (MS); juvenile justice (MS).

Master of Science in Education Program *Program availability:* Part-time, evening/weekend, blended/hybrid learning. Offers education (MS Ed).

Master of Science in Human Services Program *Program availability:* Part-time, evening/weekend, blended/hybrid learning. Offers human services (MS). Electronic applications accepted.

Master of Science in Management and Organizational Leadership Program *Program availability:* Part-time, evening/weekend, blended/hybrid learning. Offers management and organizational leadership (MS). Electronic applications accepted.

Masters of Public Administration Program

ALBIZU UNIVERSITY, San Juan, PR 00901

General Information Independent, coed, university. *Graduate housing:* On-campus housing not available.

GRADUATE UNITS

Graduate Programs *Program availability:* Part-time, evening/weekend. Offers clinical psychology (MS, PhD, Psy D); general psychology (PhD); industrial/organizational psychology (MS, PhD); speech and language pathology (MS).

ALBIZU UNIVERSITY, MIAMI CAMPUS, Miami, FL 33172-2209

General Information Independent, coed, comprehensive institution. *Enrollment:* 479 full-time matriculated graduate/professional students (410 women), 146 part-time matriculated graduate/professional students (126 women). *Enrollment by degree level:* 421 master's, 204 doctoral. *Graduate faculty:* 32 full-time (24 women), 27 part-time/adjunct (15 women). *Tuition:* Full-time $11,160; part-time $5580 per year. *Required fees:* $322 per term. Tuition and fees vary according to course load, degree level and program. *Graduate housing:* On-campus housing not available. *Student services:* Campus employment opportunities, campus safety program, career counseling, international student services, services for students with disabilities, teacher training, writing training. *Library facilities:* Albizu Library. *Collection:* Books: 27,760 (physical), 22,900 (digital/electronic); Serial titles: 295 (physical), 17,034 (digital/electronic); Databases: 73. Weekly public service hours: 66.

Computer facilities: 268 computers available on campus for general student use. A campuswide network can be accessed from off campus. Online class registration, campus portal, virtual library, 24/7 support, Cloud computing, learning center are available. Website: http://www.albizu.edu/

General Application Contact: Nancy Alvarez, Director of Enrollment Management, 305-593-1223 Ext. 3136, Fax: 305-593-1854, E-mail: nalvarez@albizu.edu.

GRADUATE UNITS

Graduate Programs Students: 479 full-time (410 women), 146 part-time (126 women); includes 539 minority (42 Black or African American, non-Hispanic/Latino; 2 Asian, non-Hispanic/Latino; 490 Hispanic/Latino; 5 Two or more races, non-Hispanic/Latino), 22 international. Average age 33. 314 applicants, 45% accepted, 92 enrolled. *Faculty:* 32 full-time (24 women), 27 part-time/adjunct (15 women). Expenses: Contact institution. *Financial support:* In 2018–19, 141 students received support. Federal Work-Study, scholarships/grants, unspecified assistantships, and tuition discounts available. Financial award application deadline: 6/1; financial award applicants required to submit FAFSA. In 2018, 101 master's, 64 doctorates awarded. *Program availability:* Part-time, evening/weekend, 100% online, blended/hybrid learning. Offers clinical psychology (PhD, Psy D); entrepreneurship (MBA); exceptional student education (MS); human services (PhD); industrial/organizational psychology (MS); marriage and family therapy (MS); mental health counseling (MS); nonprofit management (MBA); organizational management (MBA); school counseling (MS); speech and language pathology (MS); teaching English for speakers of other languages (MS). *Application deadline:* For fall admission, 4/1 priority date for domestic students, 5/1 priority date for international students; for spring admission, 11/1 priority date for domestic students, 9/1 priority date for international students. Applications are processed on a rolling basis. *Application fee:* $50. Electronic applications accepted. *Application Contact:* Nancy Alvarez, Director of Enrollment Management, 305-593-1223 Ext. 3136, Fax: 305-593-1854, E-mail: nalvarez@albizu.edu. *President,* Dr. Jose Pons-Madera, PhD, 305-593-1223 Ext. 3120, Fax: 305-477-8983, E-mail: jpons@albizu.edu.

ALBRIGHT COLLEGE, Reading, PA 19612-5234

General Information Independent-religious, coed, comprehensive institution. *Graduate housing:* On-campus housing not available.

GRADUATE UNITS

Graduate Division *Program availability:* Part-time, evening/weekend. Offers early childhood education (MS); elementary education (MS); English as a second language (MA); general education (MA); special education (MS). Electronic applications accepted.

ALCORN STATE UNIVERSITY, Lorman, MS 39096-7500

General Information State-supported, coed, comprehensive institution. CGS member. *Graduate housing:* Room and/or apartments available on a first-come, first-served basis to single students; on-campus housing not available to married students.

GRADUATE UNITS

School of Graduate Studies *Program availability:* Part-time. Electronic applications accepted.

School of Agriculture and Applied Sciences Offers agricultural economics (MS Ag); agronomy (MS Ag); animal science (MS Ag); workforce education leadership (MS).

School of Arts and Sciences Offers arts and sciences (MS); biological sciences (MS); computer and information science (MS).

School of Business Offers business (MBA).

School of Education and Psychology Offers agricultural education (MS Ed); elementary education (MAT, MS Ed, Ed S); guidance and counseling (MS Ed); industrial education (MS Ed); secondary education (MAT, MS Ed); special education (MS Ed).

School of Nursing Offers rural nursing (MSN).

ALDERSON BROADDUS UNIVERSITY, Philippi, WV 26416

General Information Independent-religious, coed, comprehensive institution. *Graduate housing:* Rooms and/or apartments available on a first-come, first-served basis to single and married students. Housing application deadline: 8/21.

GRADUATE UNITS

Program in Physician Assistant Studies Offers physician assistant studies (MPAS). Electronic applications accepted.

ALFRED UNIVERSITY, Alfred, NY 14802-1205

General Information Independent, coed, university. *Graduate housing:* Room and/or apartments available on a first-come, first-served basis to single students; on-campus housing not available to married students. Housing application deadline: 5/1. *Research affiliation:* Center for High Temperature Characterization (materials science), New York State Center for Advanced Ceramic Technology (ceramic engineering and materials science), Center for Glass Research (glass engineering and science), National Science Foundation Industry-University Center for Glass Research, Whitewares Research Center (whitewares processing, traditional ceramics), National Science Foundation Industry-University Center for Biosurfaces (bioceramics).

GRADUATE UNITS

Graduate School *Program availability:* Part-time. Offers mental health counseling (MS Ed); public administration (MPA); school counseling (MS Ed, CAS); school psychology (MA, Psy D, CAS). Electronic applications accepted.

College of Ceramics Offers biomaterials engineering (MS); ceramic art (MFA); ceramic engineering (MS); ceramics (MFA, MS, PhD); electrical engineering (MS); electronic integrated arts (MFA); glass science (MS, PhD); materials science and engineering (MS, PhD); mechanical engineering (MS); painting (MFA); sculpture/dimensional studies (MFA). Electronic applications accepted.

Division of Education *Program availability:* Part-time. Offers college student development (MS Ed); literacy (MS Ed). Electronic applications accepted.

School of Business *Program availability:* Part-time. Offers accounting (MBA); business administration (MBA). Electronic applications accepted.

ALLEN COLLEGE, Waterloo, IA 50703

General Information Independent, coed, primarily women, comprehensive institution. *Enrollment:* 682 graduate, professional, and undergraduate students; 103 full-time matriculated graduate/professional students (89 women), 183 part-time matriculated graduate/professional students (162 women). *Enrollment by degree level:* 268 master's, 18 doctoral. *Graduate faculty:* 30 full-time (29 women), 7 part-time/adjunct (6 women). *Tuition:* Full-time $16,740; part-time $8370 per credit. *Required fees:* $1290; $645 per credit. $322 per semester. Tuition and fees vary according to course load. *Graduate housing:* On-campus housing not available. *Student services:* Campus safety program, career counseling, free psychological counseling. *Library facilities:* Barrett Library plus 1 other. *Collection:* Books: 13,280 (physical), 9,138 (digital/electronic); Serial titles: 208 (physical), 3,610 (digital/electronic); Databases: 47. Weekly public service hours: 50; study areas open 24 hours, 5–7 days a week; students can reserve study rooms.

Computer facilities: 32 computers available on campus for general student use. A campuswide network can be accessed from off campus. Online proctoring exams available. Website: http://www.allencollege.edu/

General Application Contact: Molly Quinn, Director of Admissions, 319-226-2001, Fax: 319-226-2010, E-mail: molly.quinn@allencollege.edu.

GRADUATE UNITS

Graduate Programs Students: 106 full-time (91 women), 187 part-time (164 women); includes 22 minority (12 Black or African American, non-Hispanic/Latino; 1 American Indian or Alaska Native, non-Hispanic/Latino; 2 Asian, non-Hispanic/Latino; 3 Hispanic/Latino; 4 Two or more races, non-Hispanic/Latino), 2 international. Average age 33. 352 applicants, 56% accepted, 131 enrolled. *Faculty:* 24 full-time (all women), 8 part-time/adjunct (7 women). Expenses: Contact institution. *Financial support:* In 2018–19, 97 students received support. Federal Work-Study, institutionally sponsored loans, scholarships/grants, and traineeships available. Support available to part-time students. Financial award application deadline: 8/1; financial award applicants required to submit FAFSA. In 2018, 73 master's, 2 doctorates awarded. *Program availability:* Part-time, 100% online, blended/hybrid learning. Offers adult-gerontology acute care nurse practitioner (MSN); community/public health nursing (MSN); education (MSN); family nurse practitioner (MSN); health sciences (Ed D); leadership in health care delivery (MSN); leadership in health care informatics (MSN); nursing (DNP); occupational therapy (MS); psychiatric mental health nurse practitioner (MSN). MSN in leadership in healthcare informatics offered in partnership with University of Minnesota. *Application deadline:* For fall admission, 2/1 priority date for domestic students; for spring admission, 9/1 priority date for domestic students. Applications are processed on a rolling basis. *Application fee:* $50. Electronic applications accepted. *Application Contact:* Molly Quinn, Director of Admissions, 319-226-2001, Fax: 319-226-2010, E-mail: molly.quinn@allencollege.edu. *Provost,* Dr. Bob Loch, 319-226-2040, Fax: 319-226-2070, E-mail: bob.loch@allencollege.edu.

ALLIANT INTERNATIONAL UNIVERSITY–FRESNO, Fresno, CA 93727

General Information Independent, coed, graduate-only institution. *Graduate housing:* On-campus housing not available.

GRADUATE UNITS

California School of Forensic Studies Offers clinical forensic psychology (PhD, Psy D); forensic studies (PhD, Psy D); victimology (Psy D). Electronic applications accepted.

California School of Professional Psychology Offers clinical psychology (PhD, Psy D); organizational behavior (MA); organizational development (Psy D); professional psychology (MA, PhD, Psy D). Electronic applications accepted.

ALLIANT INTERNATIONAL UNIVERSITY–IRVINE, Irvine, CA 92606

General Information Independent, coed, graduate-only institution. *Graduate housing:* On-campus housing not available.

GRADUATE UNITS

California School of Forensic Studies Offers forensic studies (Psy D). Electronic applications accepted.

California School of Professional Psychology *Program availability:* Part-time. Offers couple and family therapy (MA, Psy D); professional psychology (MA, Psy D). Electronic applications accepted.

Shirley M. Hufstedler School of Education *Program availability:* Part-time, evening/weekend, online learning. Offers education (MA, Psy D, Certificate, Credential); educational psychology (Psy D); pupil personnel services (Credential); school psychology (MA). Electronic applications accepted.

ALLIANT INTERNATIONAL UNIVERSITY–LOS ANGELES, Alhambra, CA 91803

General Information Independent, coed, graduate-only institution. *Graduate housing:* Room and/or apartments available to single students; on-campus housing not available to married students.

GRADUATE UNITS

California School of Forensic Studies Offers forensic psychology (Psy D).

California School of Professional Psychology Offers chemical dependency (MA); clinical health psychology (Psy D); clinical psychology (PhD, Psy D); family/child and couple clinical psychology (Psy D); gerontology (MA); Latin American family therapy (MA); multi-interest option (Psy D); multicultural community-clinical psychology (Psy D); professional psychology (MA, PhD, Psy D). Electronic applications accepted.

Organizational Psychology Division *Program availability:* Part-time. Offers organizational psychology (MA, PhD). Electronic applications accepted.

Marshall Goldsmith School of Management Offers management (DBA).

Business Division Offers business (DBA).

Shirley M. Hufstedler School of Education *Program availability:* Part-time, evening/weekend, online learning. Offers education (MA, Psy D, Credential); educational psychology (Psy D); pupil personnel services (Credential); school psychology (MA); teaching (MA, Credential). Electronic applications accepted.

ALLIANT INTERNATIONAL UNIVERSITY–SACRAMENTO, Sacramento, CA 95833

General Information Independent, coed, graduate-only institution. *Graduate housing:* On-campus housing not available.

GRADUATE UNITS

California School of Forensic Studies Offers clinical forensic psychology (Psy D); forensic studies (Psy D). Electronic applications accepted.

California School of Professional Psychology *Program availability:* Part-time. Offers clinical psychology (Psy D); couple and family therapy (MA, Psy D); professional psychology (MA, Psy D). Electronic applications accepted.

Shirley M. Hufstedler School of Education Offers education (MA, Credential); teaching (MA, Credential). Electronic applications accepted.

ALLIANT INTERNATIONAL UNIVERSITY–SAN DIEGO, San Diego, CA 92131

General Information Independent, coed, university. *Graduate housing:* Room and/or apartments available on a first-come, first-served basis to single students; on-campus housing not available to married students.

GRADUATE UNITS

Alliant School of Management *Program availability:* Part-time, evening/weekend. Offers management (MA, MBA). Electronic applications accepted.

Business and Management Division *Program availability:* Part-time, evening/weekend. Offers business administration (MBA). Electronic applications accepted.

California School of Forensic Studies Offers clinical forensic psychology (Psy D); forensic studies (Psy D).

California School of Professional Psychology *Program availability:* Part-time. Offers clinical psychology (PhD, Psy D); marital and family therapy (MA, Psy D); professional psychology (MA, MS, PhD, Psy D).

Organizational Psychology Division *Program availability:* Part-time, evening/weekend. Offers clinical/industrial organizational psychology (PhD); consulting psychology (PhD); industrial/organizational psychology (MA, MS, PhD); leadership (PhD). Electronic applications accepted.

Shirley M. Hufstedler School of Education *Program availability:* Part-time, evening/weekend, online learning. Offers education (MA, Ed D, Psy D, Certificate, Credential); educational administration (MA); educational leadership and management (K-12) (Ed D); educational psychology (Psy D); higher education (Ed D, Certificate); preliminary administrative services (Credential); preliminary single subject (Credential); professional clear multiple subject (Credential); professional clear single subject (Credential); pupil personnel services (Credential); school neuropsychology (Certificate); school psychology (MA); school-based mental health (Certificate); teacher education (MA); teaching English to speakers of other languages (MA, Ed D, Certificate). Electronic applications accepted.

ALLIANT INTERNATIONAL UNIVERSITY–SAN FRANCISCO, San Francisco, CA 94133

General Information Independent, coed, graduate-only institution. *Graduate housing:* On-campus housing not available.

GRADUATE UNITS

California School of Forensic Studies Offers applied criminology (MS); clinical forensic psychology (PhD, Psy D); victimology (MS).

California School of Professional Psychology Offers clinical counseling (MA); clinical psychology (PhD, Psy D, Certificate); professional psychology (MA, Post-Doctoral MS, PhD, Psy D, Certificate); psychopharmacology (Post-Doctoral MS). Electronic applications accepted.

Organizational Psychology Division *Program availability:* Part-time, evening/weekend. Offers organizational psychology (MA, PhD). Electronic applications accepted.

San Francisco Law School *Program availability:* Part-time, evening/weekend. Offers law (JD). Electronic applications accepted.

Shirley M. Hufstedler School of Education *Program availability:* Part-time, evening/weekend, online learning. Offers auditory oral education (Certificate); CLAD (Certificate); community college administration (Ed D); education (MA, Ed D, Psy D, Certificate, Credential); education specialist: mild/moderate disabilities (Credential); educational administration (MA); educational leadership and management (K-12) (Ed D); educational psychology (Psy D); higher education (Ed D); preliminary administrative services (Credential); preliminary multiple subject (Credential); preliminary single subject (Credential); professional clear multiple subject (Credential); professional clear single subject (Credential); pupil personnel services (Credential); school psychology (MA); special education (MA); teaching (MA); TESOL (Certificate). Electronic applications accepted.

ALVERNIA UNIVERSITY, Reading, PA 19607-1799

General Information Independent-religious, coed, comprehensive institution. *Graduate housing:* On-campus housing not available.

GRADUATE UNITS

School of Graduate Studies *Program availability:* Part-time, evening/weekend. Offers adult gerontology nurse practitioner (DNP); business (MBA); community counseling (MA); family nurse practitioner (DNP); leadership (PhD); liberal studies (MALS); nursing education (MSN); nursing leadership (Graduate Certificate); nursing leadership and healthcare administration (MSN); occupational therapy (MSOT); urban education (M Ed). Electronic applications accepted.

ALVERNO COLLEGE, Milwaukee, WI 53234-3922

General Information Independent-religious, Undergraduate: women only; graduate: coed, comprehensive institution. *Graduate housing:* On-campus housing not available.

GRADUATE UNITS

JoAnn McGrath School of Nursing and Health Professions *Program availability:* Part-time, evening/weekend. Offers clinical nurse specialist (MSN); family nurse practitioner (MSN); nursing practice (DNP); psychiatric mental health nurse practitioner (MSN). Electronic applications accepted.

School of Arts and Sciences *Program availability:* Part-time, evening/weekend. Offers community-based research and consultation (MSCP); professional counselor (MSCP). Electronic applications accepted.

School of Professional Studies - Business Division *Program availability:* Part-time, evening/weekend. Offers business (MBA). Electronic applications accepted.

School of Professional Studies - Education Division *Program availability:* Part-time, evening/weekend. Offers adaptive education (MA); administrative leadership (MA); adult education and organizational development (MA); adult educational and instructional design (MA); adult educational and instructional technology (MA); global connections in the humanities (MA); instructional leadership (MA); instructional technology for K-12 settings (MA); professional development (MA); reading education (MA); reading education with adaptive education (MA); science education (MA); special education (MA); teaching in alternative schools (MA). Electronic applications accepted.

AMBERTON UNIVERSITY, Garland, TX 75041-5595

General Information Independent-religious, coed, upper-level institution. *Graduate housing:* On-campus housing not available.

GRADUATE UNITS

Graduate School *Program availability:* Part-time, evening/weekend. Offers agile project management (MS); family studies (MS); general business (MBA); human relations and business (MS); human resources training and development (MS); international business (MBA); management (MBA); managerial science (MS); marriage and family therapy (MA); professional counseling (MA); professional development (MS); project management (MBA); school counseling (MA); strategic leadership (MBA).

AMBROSE UNIVERSITY, Calgary, AB T3H 0L5, Canada

General Information Independent-religious, coed, comprehensive institution. *Graduate housing:* Room and/or apartments available on a first-come, first-served basis to single students; on-campus housing not available to married students. Housing application deadline: 6/15.

GRADUATE UNITS

Ambrose Seminary *Program availability:* Part-time, blended/hybrid learning. Offers Biblical/theological studies (MA); Christian studies (MCS, Diploma); intercultural ministries (M Div, MA); leadership (Certificate); leadership and ministry (MA); pastoral ministry (M Div). Electronic applications accepted.

AMERICAN ACADEMY OF ACUPUNCTURE AND ORIENTAL MEDICINE, Roseville, MN 55113

General Information Proprietary, coed, graduate-only institution.

GRADUATE UNITS

Graduate Programs Offers acupuncture and Oriental medicine (MAOM, DAOM).

AMERICAN BAPTIST SEMINARY OF THE WEST, Berkeley, CA 94704-3029

General Information Independent-religious, coed, graduate-only institution. *Graduate housing:* Rooms and/or apartments available on a first-come, first-served basis to single and married students. Housing application deadline: 5/1.

GRADUATE UNITS

Graduate and Professional Programs *Program availability:* Part-time, evening/weekend, online learning. Offers community leadership (MA); theology (M Div, MA). MA program in theology offered jointly with Graduate Theological Union. Electronic applications accepted.

AMERICAN BUSINESS & TECHNOLOGY UNIVERSITY, Saint Joseph, MO 64506

General Information Proprietary, coed, comprehensive institution.

GRADUATE UNITS

Programs in Business Administration *Program availability:* Online learning. Offers business administration (MBA); financial management (MBA); global business management (MBA); information systems management (MBA); marketing and social media (MBA); project and operations management (MBA); public accounting (MBA).

AMERICAN COLLEGE DUBLIN, Dublin 2, Ireland

General Information Independent, coed, comprehensive institution.

GRADUATE UNITS

Graduate Programs

AMERICAN COLLEGE OF ACUPUNCTURE AND ORIENTAL MEDICINE, Houston, TX 77063

General Information Proprietary, coed, graduate-only institution. *Research affiliation:* Montrose Clinic (HIV/AIDS research and treatment), Rice University Wellness Center (student and staff care), Baylor College of Medicine (acupuncture for osteoarthritis of the knee), Memorial Herman Healthcare System, Tianjing Hospital, China (traditional Chinese medicine).

GRADUATE UNITS

Graduate Studies *Program availability:* Part-time.

AMERICAN COLLEGE OF EDUCATION, Indianapolis, IN 46204

General Information Proprietary, coed, graduate-only institution.

GRADUATE UNITS

Graduate Programs Offers curriculum and instruction (M Ed); educational leadership (M Ed); educational technology (M Ed).

THE AMERICAN COLLEGE OF FINANCIAL SERVICES, Bryn Mawr, PA 19010-2105

General Information Independent, coed, graduate-only institution. *Graduate housing:* On-campus housing not available.

GRADUATE UNITS

Graduate Programs *Program availability:* Part-time, evening/weekend, online learning. Offers financial services (MSFS); leadership (MSM). Electronic applications accepted.

AMERICAN COLLEGE OF HEALTHCARE SCIENCES, Portland, OR 97239-3719

General Information Independent, coed, comprehensive institution. *Graduate housing:* On-campus housing not available.

GRADUATE UNITS

Graduate Programs *Program availability:* Part-time, evening/weekend, online learning. Offers anatomy and physiology (Graduate Certificate); aromatherapy (MS, Graduate Certificate); botanical safety (Graduate Certificate); complementary alternative medicine (MS, Graduate Certificate); health and wellness (MS); herbal medicine (MS, Graduate Certificate); holistic nutrition (MS, Graduate Certificate); wellness coaching (Graduate Certificate).

AMERICAN COLLEGE OF THESSALONIKI, 55535 Pylaia, Greece

General Information Independent, coed, comprehensive institution.

GRADUATE UNITS

Department of Business Administration *Program availability:* Part-time, evening/weekend. Offers banking and finance (MBA); entrepreneurship (MBA, Certificate); finance (Certificate); management (MBA, Certificate); marketing (MBA, Certificate). Electronic applications accepted.

AMERICAN CONSERVATORY THEATER, San Francisco, CA 94108-5800

General Information Independent, coed, graduate-only institution. *Graduate housing:* On-campus housing not available.

GRADUATE UNITS

Program in Acting Offers acting (MFA, Certificate).

AMERICAN FILM INSTITUTE CONSERVATORY, Los Angeles, CA 90027-1657

General Information Independent, coed, graduate-only institution. *Graduate housing:* On-campus housing not available.

GRADUATE UNITS

Graduate Program Offers cinematography (MFA); directing (MFA); editing (MFA); producing (MFA); production design (MFA); screenwriting (MFA). Electronic applications accepted.

AMERICAN GRADUATE SCHOOL IN PARIS, F-75006 Paris, France

General Information Independent, coed, graduate-only institution.

GRADUATE UNITS

Program in International Relations and Diplomacy Offers international relations and diplomacy (MA, PhD).

AMERICAN GRADUATE UNIVERSITY, Covina, CA 91724

General Information Proprietary, coed, graduate-only institution. *Graduate housing:* On-campus housing not available. *Research affiliation:* Library and Information Resources Network.

GRADUATE UNITS

Program in Acquisition Management *Program availability:* Part-time, online learning. Offers acquisition management (MAM, Certificate). Electronic applications accepted.

Program in Business Administration *Program availability:* Part-time, online learning. Offers acquisition and contracting (MBA); supply chain management (MBA). Electronic applications accepted.

Program in Contract Management *Program availability:* Part-time, online learning. Offers contract management (MCM, Certificate). Electronic applications accepted.

Program in Supply Chain Management *Program availability:* Part-time, online learning. Offers supply chain management (MSCM, Certificate).

AMERICAN INSTITUTE OF ALTERNATIVE MEDICINE, Columbus, OH 43229

General Information Proprietary, coed.

GRADUATE UNITS

School of Acupuncture Offers acupuncture (M Ac).

AMERICAN INTERCONTINENTAL UNIVERSITY ATLANTA, Atlanta, GA 30328

General Information Proprietary, coed, comprehensive institution. *Graduate housing:* On-campus housing not available.

GRADUATE UNITS

Program in Global Technology Management *Program availability:* Part-time, evening/weekend, online learning. Offers global technology management (MBA). Electronic applications accepted.

Program in Information Technology *Program availability:* Part-time, evening/weekend. Offers information technology (MIT). Electronic applications accepted.

AMERICAN INTERCONTINENTAL UNIVERSITY HOUSTON, Houston, TX 77042

General Information Proprietary, coed, comprehensive institution.

GRADUATE UNITS

School of Business Offers management (MBA).

AMERICAN INTERCONTINENTAL UNIVERSITY ONLINE, Schaumburg, IL 60173

General Information Proprietary, coed, comprehensive institution.

GRADUATE UNITS

Program in Business Administration *Program availability:* Evening/weekend, online learning. Offers accounting and finance (MBA); finance (MBA); healthcare management (MBA); human resource management (MBA); international business (MBA); management (MBA); marketing (MBA); operations management (MBA); organizational psychology and development (MBA); project management (MBA). Electronic applications accepted.

Program in Education *Program availability:* Evening/weekend, online learning. Offers curriculum and instruction (M Ed); educational assessment and evaluation (M Ed); instructional technology (M Ed); leadership of educational organizations (M Ed). Electronic applications accepted.

Program in Information Technology *Program availability:* Evening/weekend, online learning. Offers Internet security (MIT); IT project management (MIT). Electronic applications accepted.

AMERICAN INTERNATIONAL COLLEGE, Springfield, MA 01109-3189

General Information Independent, coed, comprehensive institution. *Graduate housing:* Room and/or apartments available on a first-come, first-served basis to single students; on-campus housing not available to married students. Housing application deadline: 8/15.

GRADUATE UNITS

School of Business, Arts and Sciences *Program availability:* Part-time, evening/weekend. Offers accounting and taxation (MS); business administration (MBA); clinical psychology (MA); educational psychology (Ed D); forensic psychology (MS); general psychology (MA, CAGS); management (CAGS); resort and casino management (MBA, CAGS).

School of Education *Program availability:* Evening/weekend. Offers early childhood education (M Ed, CAGS); education (MA, Ed D); elementary education (M Ed, CAGS); middle education/secondary education (M Ed, CAGS); moderate disabilities (M Ed, CAGS); reading specialist (M Ed, CAGS); school adjustment counseling (MAEP, CAGS); school guidance counseling (MAEP, CAGS); school leadership (M Ed, CAGS). Electronic applications accepted.

Low Residency Programs *Program availability:* Evening/weekend. Offers counseling psychology (MA); educational leadership and supervision (Ed D); professional counseling and supervision (Ed D); teaching and learning (Ed D).

School of Health Sciences *Program availability:* Part-time, 100% online. Offers exercise science (MS); family nurse practitioner (MSN, Post-Master's Certificate); nursing administrator (MSN); nursing educator (MSN); occupational therapy (MSOT, OTD); physical therapy (DPT). Electronic applications accepted.

AMERICAN JEWISH UNIVERSITY, Bel Air, CA 90077-1599

General Information Independent-religious, coed, graduate-only institution. *Graduate housing:* Rooms and/or apartments available on a first-come, first-served basis to single and married students. Housing application deadline: 6/1.

GRADUATE UNITS

Graduate School of Education Offers education (MA Ed); education for working professionals (MA Ed).

Graduate School of Nonprofit Management *Program availability:* Part-time, evening/weekend. Offers general nonprofit administration (MBA); Jewish communal studies (MAJCS); Jewish nonprofit administration (MBA); nonprofit management (MAJCS, MBA).

Ziegler School of Rabbinic Studies Offers rabbinic studies (MARS).

AMERICAN MUSEUM OF NATURAL HISTORY–RICHARD GILDER GRADUATE SCHOOL, New York, NY 10024

General Information Independent, coed, graduate-only institution.

GRADUATE UNITS

Program in Comparative Biology Offers comparative biology (PhD).

AMERICAN NATIONAL UNIVERSITY, Salem, VA 24153

General Information Proprietary, coed, comprehensive institution.

GRADUATE UNITS

Program in Business Administration Offers business administration (MBA).

AMERICAN PUBLIC UNIVERSITY SYSTEM, Charles Town, WV 25414

General Information Proprietary, coed, comprehensive institution. CGS member. *Enrollment:* 46,088 graduate, professional, and undergraduate students; 406 full-time matriculated graduate/professional students (180 women), 7,826 part-time matriculated graduate/professional students (3,329 women). *Enrollment by degree level:* 7,818 master's, 49 doctoral, 365 other advanced degrees. *Graduate housing:* On-campus housing not available. *Student services:* Career counseling, international student services, services for students with disabilities. *Library facilities:* APUS Online Library.

Computer facilities: Online class registration is available.
Website: http://www.apus.edu/

General Application Contact: Yoci Deal, Associate Vice President, Graduate and International Admissions, 877-468-6268, Fax: 304-724-3780, E-mail: info@apus.edu.

GRADUATE UNITS

AMU/APU Graduate Programs Students: 406 full-time (180 women), 7,826 part-time (3,329 women); includes 2,781 minority (1,438 Black or African American, non-Hispanic/Latino; 44 American Indian or Alaska Native, non-Hispanic/Latino; 193 Asian, non-Hispanic/Latino; 747 Hispanic/Latino; 53 Native Hawaiian or other Pacific Islander, non-Hispanic/Latino; 306 Two or more races, non-Hispanic/Latino), 121 international. Average age 38. Expenses: Contact institution. *Financial support:* Scholarships/grants available. Financial award applicants required to submit FAFSA. In 2018, 2,717 master's awarded. *Program availability:* Part-time, evening/weekend, online only, 100% online. Offers accounting (MS); applied business analytics (MS); business administration (MBA); criminal justice (MA); cybersecurity studies (MS); educational leadership (M Ed); environmental policy and management (MS); global security (DGS); health information management (MS); history (MA); information technology (MS); international relations and conflict resolution (MA); national security studies (MA); nursing (MSN); political science (MA); public policy (MPP); reverse logistics management (MA); space studies (MS); sports management (MS); strategic intelligence (DSI); teaching (M Ed); transportation and logistics management (MA). *Application deadline:* Applications are processed on a rolling basis. *Application fee:* $0. Electronic applications accepted. *Application Contact:* Yoci Deal, Associate Vice President, Graduate and International Admissions, 877-468-6268, Fax: 304-724-3764, E-mail: info@apus.edu. *President,* Dr. Wallace Boston, 877-468-6268, Fax: 304-728-2348, E-mail: president@apus.edu.

AMERICAN SENTINEL UNIVERSITY, Aurora, CO 80014
General Information Proprietary, coed, comprehensive institution.

GRADUATE UNITS

Graduate Programs *Program availability:* Part-time, evening/weekend, online learning. Electronic applications accepted.

AMERICAN UNIVERSITY, Washington, DC 20016-8001
General Information Independent-religious, coed, university. CGS member. *Enrollment:* 14,311 graduate, professional, and undergraduate students; 3,314 full-time matriculated graduate/professional students (2,080 women), 2,487 part-time matriculated graduate/professional students (1,497 women). *Enrollment by degree level:* 4,002 master's, 1,710 doctoral, 89 other advanced degrees. *Graduate faculty:* 853 full-time (417 women), 700 part-time/adjunct (317 women). *Tuition:* Full-time $30,744; part-time $1642 per credit hour. *Required fees:* $702; $200 per semester. Tuition and fees vary according to course load, degree level and program. *Graduate housing:* On-campus housing not available. *Student services:* Campus employment opportunities, campus safety program, career counseling, child daycare facilities, exercise/wellness program, free psychological counseling, grant writing training, international student services, multicultural affairs office, services for students with disabilities, teacher training, writing training. *Library facilities:* Bender Library plus 1 other. *Collection:* Books: 700,000 (physical), 800,000 (digital/electronic); Serial titles: 650 (physical), 145,000 (digital/electronic); Databases: 500. Study areas open 24 hours, 5–7 days a week; students can reserve study rooms.

Computer facilities: 700 computers available on campus for general student use. A campuswide network can be accessed from student residence rooms and from off campus. Online class registration, online e-support through learning management system are available.
Website: http://www.american.edu/

General Application Contact: Dr. Wendy Boland, Interim Dean of Graduate Studies, 202-885-3753, E-mail: gradstudies@american.edu.

GRADUATE UNITS

College of Arts and Sciences Students: 488 full-time (325 women), 344 part-time (233 women); includes 211 minority (66 Black or African American, non-Hispanic/Latino; 2 American Indian or Alaska Native, non-Hispanic/Latino; 66 Asian, non-Hispanic/Latino; 57 Hispanic/Latino; 20 Two or more races, non-Hispanic/Latino), 120 international. Average age 31. 1,416 applicants, 58% accepted, 305 enrolled. *Faculty:* 385 full-time (206 women), 219 part-time/adjunct (120 women). Expenses: Contact institution. *Financial support:* Research assistantships, teaching assistantships, institutionally sponsored loans, scholarships/grants, and unspecified assistantships available. Financial award applicants required to submit FAFSA. In 2018, 276 master's, 29 doctorates, 27 other advanced degrees awarded. *Program availability:* Part-time, evening/weekend, 100% online, blended/hybrid learning. Offers addiction and addictive behavior (Certificate); anthropology (PhD, Certificate); applied microeconomics (Certificate); applied statistics (Certificate); art history (MA); art management (MA); arts and sciences (MA, MAT, MFA, MS, PhD, Certificate, Graduate Certificate); audio production (Certificate); audio technology (MA); behavior, cognition, and neuroscience (PhD); biology (MS); biostatistics (MS); biotechnology (MA); chemistry (MS); clinical psychology (PhD); creative writing (MFA); data science (Certificate); economics (MA, PhD); environmental assessment (Graduate Certificate); environmental science (MS); ethics, peace, and global affairs (MA); gender analysis in economics (Certificate); health promotion management (MS); history (MA, PhD); international arts management (Certificate); international economic relations (Certificate); international economics (MA); literature (MA); mathematics (MA); nutrition education (MS, Certificate); philosophy (MA); professional science: environmental assessment (MS); professional science: quantitative analysis (MS); psychobiology of healing (Certificate); psychology (MA); public anthropology (MA); public sociology (Certificate); social research (Certificate); sociology (MA); Spanish: Latin American studies (MA); statistics (MS); studio art (MFA); teaching English as a foreign language (MA); teaching English to speakers of other languages (MA, Certificate); technology in arts management (Certificate); translation: French (Certificate); translation: Russian (Certificate); translation: Spanish (Certificate). *Application fee:* $55. Electronic applications accepted. *Application Contact:* Jonathan Harper, Assistant Director, Graduate Recruitment, 202-885-3622, E-mail: casgrad@american.edu. *Dean,* Dr. Peter Starr, 202-885-2446, Fax: 202-885-2429, E-mail: pstarr@american.edu.

Critical Race, Gender, and Culture Studies Students: 2 part-time (1 woman); both minorities (1 Asian, non-Hispanic/Latino; 1 Two or more races, non-Hispanic/Latino). Average age 27. 8 applicants, 75% accepted, 1 enrolled. *Faculty:* 6 full-time (all women), 16 part-time/adjunct (10 women). Expenses: Contact institution. In 2018, 3 Graduate Certificates awarded. Offers Asian studies (Graduate Certificate); women's,

gender, and sexuality studies (Graduate Certificate). *Application deadline:* Applications are processed on a rolling basis. *Application Contact:* Jonathan Harper, Associate Director, Graduate Recruitment, 202-885-3620, E-mail: casgrad@american.edu. *Dean,* Dr. Peter Starr, 202-885-2446, E-mail: collegedeansoffice@american.edu.

Kogod School of Business Students: 591 full-time (318 women), 446 part-time (205 women); includes 443 minority (220 Black or African American, non-Hispanic/Latino; 2 American Indian or Alaska Native, non-Hispanic/Latino; 80 Asian, non-Hispanic/Latino; 99 Hispanic/Latino; 3 Native Hawaiian or other Pacific Islander, non-Hispanic/Latino; 39 Two or more races, non-Hispanic/Latino), 190 international. Average age 31. 1,081 applicants, 73% accepted, 373 enrolled. *Faculty:* 82 full-time (29 women), 90 part-time/adjunct (37 women). Expenses: Contact institution. *Financial support:* Research assistantships, teaching assistantships, institutionally sponsored loans, scholarships/grants, and unspecified assistantships available. Financial award applicants required to submit FAFSA. In 2018, 284 master's, 20 other advanced degrees awarded. *Program availability:* Part-time, evening/weekend, 100% online, blended/hybrid learning. Offers accounting (MS, Certificate); analytics (MS); business (MBA, MS, Certificate); business administration (MBA, Certificate); finance (MS, Certificate); marketing (MS); real estate (MS, Certificate); sustainability management (MS); taxation (MS, Certificate). *Application fee:* $100. Electronic applications accepted. *Application Contact:* Jason Garner, Director of Admissions, 202-885-1926, E-mail: jgarner@american.edu. *Dean,* John T. Delaney, 202-885-1900, E-mail: kogodgrad@american.edu.

School of Communication Students: 175 full-time (116 women), 197 part-time (143 women); includes 132 minority (77 Black or African American, non-Hispanic/Latino; 1 American Indian or Alaska Native, non-Hispanic/Latino; 13 Asian, non-Hispanic/Latino; 29 Hispanic/Latino; 12 Two or more races, non-Hispanic/Latino), 22 international. 887 applicants, 44% accepted, 184 enrolled. *Faculty:* 58 full-time (33 women), 23 part-time/adjunct (8 women). Expenses: Contact institution. *Financial support:* In 2018–19, 83 students received support, including 3 fellowships with partial tuition reimbursements available (averaging $20,000 per year), 36 research assistantships with partial tuition reimbursements available (averaging $4,575 per year), 36 teaching assistantships with partial tuition reimbursements available (averaging $4,575 per year); career-related internships or fieldwork, Federal Work-Study, institutionally sponsored loans, scholarships/grants, health care benefits, tuition waivers (partial), and unspecified assistantships also available. Support available to part-time students. Financial award application deadline: 2/1; financial award applicants required to submit FAFSA. In 2018, 159 master's, 4 doctorates awarded. *Program availability:* Part-time, evening/weekend, 100% online. Offers communication (MA, MFA, PhD). *Application deadline:* For fall admission, 2/1 priority date for domestic and international students; for spring admission, 10/15 for domestic and international students. Applications are processed on a rolling basis. *Application fee:* $55. Electronic applications accepted. *Application Contact:* Christine Rials, Director of Enrollment, 202-885-2040, Fax: 202-885-2019, E-mail: gradcomm@american.edu. *Interim Dean,* Dr. Laura DeNardis, 202-885-2058, Fax: 202-885-2099, E-mail: denardis@american.edu.

Division of Communication Studies Students: 26 full-time (17 women), 2 part-time (1 woman); includes 7 minority (2 Black or African American, non-Hispanic/Latino; 5 Hispanic/Latino), 8 international. 49 applicants, 18% accepted, 4 enrolled. *Faculty:* 6 full-time (3 women), 2 part-time/adjunct (1 woman). Expenses: Contact institution. *Financial support:* In 2018–19, 5 students received support, including 15 research assistantships with full tuition reimbursements available (averaging $52,000 per year); scholarships/grants, health care benefits, and unspecified assistantships also available. Financial award application deadline: 12/15; financial award applicants required to submit FAFSA. In 2018, 2 doctorates awarded. Offers media industries and institutions (PhD); media, public issues, and engagement (PhD); media, technology, and culture (PhD). *Application deadline:* For fall admission, 12/15 priority date for domestic and international students. Applications are processed on a rolling basis. *Application fee:* $55. Electronic applications accepted. *Application Contact:* Leila Hernandez, Recruitment Coordinator, Graduate Programs, 202-885-2040, Fax: 202-885-2019, E-mail: leila@american.edu. *University Professor, PhD Program Director,* Prof. Patricia Aufderheide, 202-885-2680, Fax: 202-885-2069, E-mail: paufder@american.edu.

Division of Journalism Students: 30 full-time (20 women), 19 part-time (17 women); includes 29 minority (15 Black or African American, non-Hispanic/Latino; 4 Asian, non-Hispanic/Latino; 7 Hispanic/Latino; 3 Two or more races, non-Hispanic/Latino), 2 international. 201 applicants, 59% accepted, 36 enrolled. *Faculty:* 14 full-time (7 women), 4 part-time/adjunct (3 women). Expenses: Contact institution. *Financial support:* In 2018–19, 3 fellowships with tuition reimbursements (averaging $27,000 per year), research assistantships with partial tuition reimbursements (averaging $10,000 per year), teaching assistantships with partial tuition reimbursements (averaging $10,000 per year) were awarded; career-related internships or fieldwork, Federal Work-Study, institutionally sponsored loans, scholarships/grants, tuition waivers (partial), and unspecified assistantships also available. Financial award application deadline: 2/1; financial award applicants required to submit FAFSA. In 2018, 32 master's awarded. *Program availability:* Part-time, evening/weekend. Offers broadcast journalism (MA); international journalism (MA); investigative journalism (MA); journalism and digital storytelling (MA). *Application deadline:* For fall admission, 2/1 priority date for domestic and international students. Applications are processed on a rolling basis. *Application fee:* $55. Electronic applications accepted. *Application Contact:* Christine Rials, Director of Enrollment, 202-885-2040, Fax: 202-885-2019, E-mail: crials@american.edu. *Division Director,* Prof. Amy Eisman, 202-885-2106, E-mail: aeisman@american.edu.

Division of Public Communication Students: 52 full-time (39 women), 113 part-time (90 women); includes 43 minority (26 Black or African American, non-Hispanic/Latino; 1 American Indian or Alaska Native, non-Hispanic/Latino; 2 Asian, non-Hispanic/Latino; 8 Hispanic/Latino; 6 Two or more races, non-Hispanic/Latino), 4 international. 241 applicants, 60% accepted, 65 enrolled. *Faculty:* 23 full-time (15 women), 18 part-time/adjunct (10 women). Expenses: Contact institution. *Financial support:* In 2018–19, research assistantships with partial tuition reimbursements (averaging $13,000 per year), teaching assistantships with partial tuition reimbursements (averaging $13,000 per year) were awarded; career-related internships or fieldwork, Federal Work-Study, institutionally sponsored loans, scholarships/grants, tuition waivers (partial), and unspecified assistantships also available. Financial award application deadline: 2/1; financial award applicants required to submit FAFSA. In 2018, 74 master's awarded. *Program availability:* Part-time, evening/weekend, 100% online. Offers advocacy and social impact (MA); corporate communication and reputation management (MA); political communication (MA); strategic communication (MA). *Application deadline:* For fall admission, 2/1 priority date for domestic and international students. Applications are processed on a rolling basis. *Application fee:* $55. Electronic applications accepted. *Application*

Contact: Christine Rials, Director of Enrollment, 202-885-2040, Fax: 202-885-2019, E-mail: gradcomm@american.edu. *Public Communication Division Director,* Pallavi Kumar, 202-885-2047, E-mail: kumar@american.edu.

Film and Media Arts Division Students: 99 full-time (64 women), 63 part-time (36 women); includes 71 minority (45 Black or African American, non-Hispanic/Latino; 1 American Indian or Alaska Native, non-Hispanic/Latino; 8 Asian, non-Hispanic/Latino; 13 Hispanic/Latino; 4 Two or more races, non-Hispanic/Latino), 11 international. 198 applicants, 55% accepted, 53 enrolled. *Faculty:* 16 full-time (6 women), 9 part-time/adjunct (5 women). Expenses: Contact institution. *Financial support:* In 2018–19, teaching assistantships with partial tuition reimbursements (averaging $10,000 per year) were awarded; career-related internships or fieldwork, Federal Work-Study, institutionally sponsored loans, scholarships/grants, tuition waivers (partial), and unspecified assistantships also available. Support available to part-time students. Financial award application deadline: 2/1; financial award applicants required to submit FAFSA. In 2018, 41 master's awarded. *Program availability:* Part-time, evening/weekend. Offers art in entertainment (MFA); environmental and wildlife filmmaking (MFA); film and media arts (MFA); game design (MA); games and interactive media (MFA); games and interactivity (MFA); political, cultural, and social impact (MFA); producing film, television and video (MA). *Application deadline:* For fall admission, 2/1 priority date for domestic and international students. Applications are processed on a rolling basis. *Application fee:* $55. Electronic applications accepted. *Application Contact:* Leila Hernandez, Recruitment Coordinator, Graduate Programs, 202-885-2040, Fax: 202-885-2019, E-mail: leila@american.edu. *Director, Film and Media Arts Division,* Prof. Brigid Maher, 202-885-2664, Fax: 202-885-2019, E-mail: bmaher@american.edu.

School of Education Students: 53 full-time (46 women), 246 part-time (191 women); includes 139 minority (97 Black or African American, non-Hispanic/Latino; 13 Asian, non-Hispanic/Latino; 23 Hispanic/Latino; 6 Two or more races, non-Hispanic/Latino), 5 international. Average age 29. 361 applicants, 88% accepted, 161 enrolled. *Faculty:* 17 full-time (13 women), 33 part-time/adjunct (23 women). Expenses: Contact institution. *Financial support:* Research assistantships, teaching assistantships, institutionally sponsored loans, scholarships/grants, and unspecified assistantships available. Financial award application deadline: 2/1; financial award applicants required to submit FAFSA. In 2018, 73 master's, 2 other advanced degrees awarded. *Program availability:* Part-time, evening/weekend, 100% online. Offers education (Certificate); education policy and leadership (M Ed); international training and education (MA); special education (MA); teacher education (MAT). *Application fee:* $55. Electronic applications accepted. *Application Contact:* Ashleigh Huseth, Senior Coordinator, Admissions & Onboarding, E-mail: ahuseth@american.edu. *Dean,* Dr. Cheryl Holcomb-McCoy, 202-885-3720, E-mail: educate@american.edu.

School of International Service Students: 496 full-time (320 women), 477 part-time (242 women); includes 410 minority (83 Black or African American, non-Hispanic/Latino; 2 American Indian or Alaska Native, non-Hispanic/Latino; 51 Asian, non-Hispanic/Latino; 242 Hispanic/Latino; 32 Two or more races, non-Hispanic/Latino), 93 international. Average age 30. 1,280 applicants, 82% accepted, 356 enrolled. *Faculty:* 115 full-time (48 women), 50 part-time/adjunct (22 women). Expenses: Contact institution. *Financial support:* Research assistantships, teaching assistantships, institutionally sponsored loans, scholarships/grants, and unspecified assistantships available. Financial award applicants required to submit FAFSA. In 2018, 400 master's, 3 doctorates, 8 other advanced degrees awarded. *Program availability:* Part-time, evening/weekend, 100% online, blended/hybrid learning. Offers comparative and regional studies (Certificate); cross-cultural communication (Certificate); development management (MS); ethics, peace, and global affairs (MA); European studies (Certificate); global environmental policy (MA, Certificate); global information technology (Certificate); global media (MA); international affairs (MA); international arts management (Certificate); international communication (MA, Certificate); international development (MA); international economic policy (Certificate); international economic relations (Certificate); international economics (MA); international peace and conflict resolution (MA, Certificate); international politics (Certificate); international relations (MA, PhD); international service (MIS); peacebuilding (Certificate); social enterprise (MA); the Americas (Certificate); United States foreign policy (Certificate). *Application fee:* $55. Electronic applications accepted. *Application Contact:* Jia Jiang, Director, Graduate Enrollment Management, 202-885-1689, E-mail: jiang@american.edu.

School of Professional and Extended Studies Students: 2 full-time (both women), 113 part-time (68 women); includes 6 minority (4 Black or African American, non-Hispanic/Latino; 1 Asian, non-Hispanic/Latino; 1 Hispanic/Latino). Average age 31. 156 applicants, 93% accepted, 66 enrolled. *Faculty:* 27 full-time (14 women), 33 part-time/adjunct (20 women). Expenses: Contact institution. *Financial support:* Applicants required to submit FAFSA. In 2018, 1 master's, 6 other advanced degrees awarded. *Program availability:* Part-time, evening/weekend, 100% online, blended/hybrid learning. Offers agile project management (MS); healthcare management (MS, Graduate Certificate); human resource analytics and management (MS, Graduate Certificate); instructional design and learning analytics (MS); measurement and evaluation (MS); project monitoring and evaluation (Graduate Certificate); sports analytics and management (MS, Graduate Certificate). *Application deadline:* Applications are processed on a rolling basis. *Application fee:* $55. Electronic applications accepted. *Application Contact:* Emily Emily, Assistant Director for Recruitment and Admission, 202-885-4910, E-mail: aronoff@american.edu. *Dean,* Jill Klein, 202-895-4900, E-mail: spexs@american.edu.

School of Public Affairs Students: 401 full-time (253 women), 317 part-time (212 women); includes 179 minority (83 Black or African American, non-Hispanic/Latino; 4 American Indian or Alaska Native, non-Hispanic/Latino; 34 Asian, non-Hispanic/Latino; 37 Hispanic/Latino; 1 Native Hawaiian or other Pacific Islander, non-Hispanic/Latino; 20 Two or more races, non-Hispanic/Latino), 51 international. Average age 30. 1,049 applicants, 72% accepted, 269 enrolled. *Faculty:* 95 full-time (37 women), 95 part-time/adjunct (29 women). Expenses: Contact institution. *Financial support:* Research assistantships, teaching assistantships, institutionally sponsored loans, and scholarships/grants available. Financial award applicants required to submit FAFSA. In 2018, 267 master's, 10 doctorates, 5 other advanced degrees awarded. *Program availability:* Part-time, evening/weekend, 100% online, blended/hybrid learning. Offers justice, law and criminology (MS, PhD); organization development (MSOD, Certificate); political communication (MA); political science (MA, PhD); public administration (MPA, PhD, Certificate); public administration and policy (MPAP); public affairs (MA, MPA, MPAP, MPP, MS, MSOD, PhD, Certificate); public policy (MPP, Certificate); terrorism, homeland security and policy (MS); women, policy and political leadership (Certificate). *Application fee:* $55. Electronic applications accepted. *Application Contact:* Jennifer Forney, Assistant Dean, Graduate Enrollment, 202-885-2940, E-mail: spagrad@american.edu. *Dean,* Dr. Vicky Wilkins, 202-885-2940, E-mail: spa@american.edu.

Washington College of Law Students: 1,108 full-time (700 women), 349 part-time (205 women); includes 489 minority (113 Black or African American, non-Hispanic/Latino; 2

American Indian or Alaska Native, non-Hispanic/Latino; 94 Asian, non-Hispanic/Latino; 209 Hispanic/Latino; 1 Native Hawaiian or other Pacific Islander, non-Hispanic/Latino; 70 Two or more races, non-Hispanic/Latino), 109 international. Average age 28. 5,120 applicants, 52% accepted, 561 enrolled. *Faculty:* 72 full-time (39 women), 112 part-time/adjunct (37 women). Expenses: Contact institution. *Financial support:* Institutionally sponsored loans and scholarships/grants available. Financial award applicants required to submit FAFSA. In 2018, 115 master's, 376 doctorates awarded. *Program availability:* Part-time, evening/weekend, 100% online, blended/hybrid learning. Offers law (LL M, JD, SJD). *Application fee:* $70. Electronic applications accepted. *Application Contact:* Akira Shiroma, Asst. Dean of Admissions, 202-274-4101. *Dean,* Camille A. Nelson, 202-274 4000.

AMERICAN UNIVERSITY IN BULGARIA, Blagoevgrad 2700, Bulgaria

General Information Independent, coed, comprehensive institution.

GRADUATE UNITS

Executive MBA Program Offers business administration (EMBA).

THE AMERICAN UNIVERSITY IN CAIRO, 11835 New Cairo, Egypt

General Information Independent, coed, comprehensive institution. CGS member. *Graduate housing:* Room and/or apartments available on a first-come, first-served basis to single students; on-campus housing not available to married students.

GRADUATE UNITS

Graduate School of Education *Program availability:* Part-time, evening/weekend. Offers educational leadership (MA); international and comparative education (MA). Electronic applications accepted.

School of Business *Program availability:* Part-time, evening/weekend. Offers business administration (MBA); economics (MA); economics in international development (MA, Diploma); finance (MS). Electronic applications accepted.

School of Global Affairs and Public Policy *Program availability:* Part-time, evening/weekend. Offers gender and women's studies (MA); global affairs (MGA); international and comparative law (LL M); international human rights law (MA); journalism and mass communication (MA); Middle East studies (MA); migration and refugee studies (MA, Diploma); public administration (MPA); public policy (MPP); television and digital journalism (MA). Electronic applications accepted.

School of Humanities and Social Sciences *Program availability:* Part-time, evening/weekend. Offers Arab and Islamic civilizations (Graduate Diploma); Arabic studies (MA); comparative literary studies (Graduate Diploma); Egyptology and Coptology (MA); English and comparative literature (MA); humanities and social sciences (Graduate Diploma); philosophy (MA); psychology (MA); sociology and anthropology (MA); teaching Arabic as a foreign language (MA); teaching English to speakers of other languages (MA). Electronic applications accepted.

School of Sciences and Engineering *Program availability:* Part-time, evening/weekend. Offers biotechnology (MS); chemistry (MS); computer science (MS); computing (M Comp); construction engineering (M Eng, MS); electronics and communications engineering (M Eng); environmental engineering (MS); environmental system design (M Eng); mechanical engineering (M Eng, MS); nanotechnology (MS); physics (MS); robotics, control and smart systems (MS); sciences and engineering (PhD); sustainable development (MS, Graduate Diploma). Electronic applications accepted.

THE AMERICAN UNIVERSITY IN DUBAI, Dubai, United Arab Emirates

General Information Proprietary, coed, comprehensive institution. *Graduate housing:* Room and/or apartments available on a first-come, first-served basis to single students; on-campus housing not available to married students. Housing application deadline: 7/31.

GRADUATE UNITS

Graduate Programs *Program availability:* Part-time, evening/weekend. Offers construction management (MS); education (M Ed); finance (MBA); generalist (MBA); marketing (MBA). Electronic applications accepted.

AMERICAN UNIVERSITY OF ARMENIA, Yerevan 3750198, Armenia

General Information Independent, coed, graduate-only institution. *Research affiliation:* Samsung (cryptography), Volkswagen Foundation (cryptography), Mentor Graphics (data compression algorithms), IBM (big data and data analytics), Johns Hopkins University Bloomberg School of Public Health (public health), Institut de Medecine Sociale et Preventive, Universite de Genève (Geneva, Switzerland) (tobacco control/health education).

GRADUATE UNITS

Graduate Programs *Program availability:* Part-time, evening/weekend. Offers business administration (MBA); computer and information science (MS); economics (MS); industrial engineering and systems management (ME); law (LL M); political science and international affairs (MPSIA); public health (MPH); teaching English as a foreign language (MA).

AMERICAN UNIVERSITY OF BEIRUT, 107 2020 Beirut, Lebanon

General Information Independent, coed, university. CGS member. *Enrollment:* 9,404 graduate, professional, and undergraduate students; 1,312 full-time matriculated graduate/professional students (799 women), 724 part-time matriculated graduate/professional students (481 women). *Enrollment by degree level:* 1,471 master's, 166 doctoral, 399 other advanced degrees. *Graduate faculty:* 530 full-time (219 women), 79 part-time/adjunct (33 women). *Tuition:* Full-time $17,748; part-time $986 per credit. *Required fees:* $762. Tuition and fees vary according to course load and program. *Graduate housing:* Room and/or apartments available on a first-come, first-served basis to single students; on-campus housing not available to married students. Typical cost: $2986 per year. Housing application deadline: 6/30. *Student services:* Campus employment opportunities, campus safety program, career counseling, exercise/wellness program, free psychological counseling, grant writing training, international student services, low-cost health insurance, services for students with disabilities, teacher training, writing training. *Library facilities:* Jafet Library plus 3 others. *Collection:* Books: 400,000 (physical), 1 million (digital/electronic); Serial titles: 500 (physical), 130,000 (digital/electronic); Databases: 350. Weekly public service hours: 107; study areas open 24 hours, 5–7 days a week; students can reserve study rooms.

Computer facilities Computer purchase and lease plans are available. 1,760 computers available on campus for general student use. A campuswide network can be accessed from student residence rooms and from off campus. Online class registration is available.

Website: http://www.aub.edu.lb/

General Application Contact: Dr. Salim Kanaan, Director, Admissions Office, 961-1-350000 Ext. 2594, Fax: 961-1-750775, E-mail: sk00@aub.edu.lb.

GRADUATE UNITS

Graduate Programs Students: 1,312 full-time (799 women), 724 part-time (481 women). Average age 27. 2,559 applicants, 49% accepted, 583 enrolled. *Faculty:* 530 full-time (219 women), 79 part-time/adjunct (33 women). Expenses: Contact institution. *Financial support:* In 2018–19, 420 students received support, including 1,387 research assistantships (averaging $6,067 per year); career-related internships or fieldwork, institutionally sponsored loans, scholarships/grants, health care benefits, and unspecified assistantships also available. Financial award application deadline: 12/20; financial award applicants required to submit CSS PROFILE. In 2018, 439 master's, 119 doctorates awarded. *Program availability:* Part-time, evening/weekend. *Application deadline:* For fall admission, 3/18 for domestic and international students; for spring admission, 11/1 for domestic and international students; for summer admission, 3/18 for domestic and international students. *Application fee:* $50. Electronic applications accepted. *Application Contact:* Dr. Salim Kanaan, Director, Admissions Office, 961-1-350000 Ext. 2594, Fax: 961-1-750775, E-mail: sk00@aub.edu.lb. *Graduate Council Chairperson,* Prof. Zaher Dawy, 961-1-374374 Ext. 4386, E-mail: zd03@aub.edu.lb.

Faculty of Agricultural and Food Sciences Students: 30 full-time (22 women), 90 part-time (69 women); includes 9 minority (all Black or African American, non-Hispanic/Latino). Average age 25. 238 applicants, 77% accepted, 37 enrolled. *Faculty:* 24 full-time (4 women). Expenses: Contact institution. *Financial support:* In 2018–19, 2 fellowships with full and partial tuition reimbursements (averaging $11,637 per year), 12 research assistantships with full and partial tuition reimbursements (averaging $3,840 per year), 73 teaching assistantships with full and partial tuition reimbursements were awarded; scholarships/grants, health care benefits, and unspecified assistantships also available. Financial award application deadline: 2/2. In 2018, 19 master's awarded. *Program availability:* Part-time. Offers agricultural economics (MS); animal science (MS); ecosystem management (MSES); food safety (MS); food security (MS); food technology (MS); irrigation (MS); nutrition (MS); plant protection (MS); plant science (MS); poultry science (MS); public health nutrition (MS); rural community development (MS). *Application deadline:* For fall admission, 2/10 for domestic and international students; for spring admission, 11/2 for domestic and international students. *Application fee:* $50. Electronic applications accepted. *Application Contact:* Prof. Zaher Dawy, Associate Provost, 961-1-374374 Ext. 4386, Fax: 961-1-374374, E-mail: graduate.council@aub.edu.lb. *Dean of Faculty of Agricultural and Food Sciences,* Prof. Rabi Hassan Mohtar, 961-1-350000 Ext. 4400, Fax: 961-1-744460, E-mail: mohtar@aub.edu.lb.

Faculty of Arts and Sciences Students: 292 full-time (215 women), 216 part-time (148 women). Average age 27. 422 applicants, 64% accepted, 124 enrolled. *Faculty:* 187 full-time (64 women), 27 part-time/adjunct (15 women). Expenses: Contact institution. *Financial support:* In 2018–19, 227 fellowships with full tuition reimbursements, 17 research assistantships with full tuition reimbursements, 83 teaching assistantships with full tuition reimbursements were awarded; scholarships/grants, tuition waivers (full and partial), and unspecified assistantships also available. Financial award application deadline: 3/18. In 2018, 90 master's, 3 doctorates awarded. *Program availability:* Part-time. Offers anthropology (MA); Arab and Middle Eastern history (PhD); Arabic language and literature (MA, PhD); archaeology (MA); art history and curating (MA); biology (MA); cell and molecular biology (PhD); chemistry (MS); clinical psychology (MA); computational sciences (MS); computer science (MS); economics (MA); education (MA); English language (MA); English literature (MA); environmental policy planning (MS); financial economics (MAFE); general psychology (MA); geology (MS); history (MA); Islamic studies (MA); mathematics (MS); media studies (MA); Middle East studies (MA); philosophy (MA); physics (MS); political studies (MA); public administration (MA); public policy and international affairs (MA); sociology (MA); theoretical physics (PhD). *Application deadline:* For fall admission, 3/18 for domestic students; for spring admission, 11/5 for domestic students. *Application fee:* $50. Electronic applications accepted. *Application Contact:* Adriana Michelle Zanaty, Curriculum and Graduate Studies Officer, 961-1-350000 Ext. 3833, Fax: 961-1-744461, E-mail: az48@aub.edu.lb. *Dean, Faculty of Arts and Sciences,* Dr. Nadia Maria El Cheikh, 961-1-350000 Ext. 3800, Fax: 961-1-744461, E-mail: nmcheikh@aub.edu.lb.

Faculty of Health Sciences Students: 65 full-time (56 women), 84 part-time (77 women). Average age 26. 391 applicants, 42% accepted, 64 enrolled. *Faculty:* 33 full-time (20 women), 10 part-time/adjunct (5 women). Expenses: Contact institution. *Financial support:* In 2018–19, 50 students received support, including 3 fellowships with full and partial tuition reimbursements available (averaging $14,400 per year), 9 research assistantships with full and partial tuition reimbursements available (averaging $6,816 per year), 6 teaching assistantships with full and partial tuition reimbursements available (averaging $3,808 per year); scholarships/grants and unspecified assistantships also available. Financial award application deadline: 4/4. In 2018, 136 master's awarded. *Program availability:* Part-time, evening/weekend. Offers environmental sciences (MS); epidemiology (MS, PhD); epidemiology and biostatistics (MPH); health care leadership (EMHCL); health management and policy (MPH); health promotion and community health (MPH); health research (MS); public health nutrition (MS). *Application deadline:* For fall admission, 4/4 for domestic and international students; for spring admission, 11/5 for domestic and international students. *Application fee:* $50. Electronic applications accepted. *Application Contact:* Lama El Kadi, Administrative Coordinator, 961-1-350000 Ext. 4687, E-mail: le19@aub.edu.lb. *Dean/Professor,* Prof. Iman Adel Nuwayhid, 961-1-759683 Ext. 4600, Fax: 961-1-744470, E-mail: nuwayhid@aub.edu.lb.

Faculty of Medicine Students: 556 full-time (304 women). 463 applicants, 51% accepted, 165 enrolled. *Faculty:* 346 full-time (128 women), 44 part-time/adjunct (5 women). Expenses: Contact institution. *Financial support:* Fellowships, research assistantships, teaching assistantships, and tuition waivers available. In 2018, 23 master's, 101 doctorates awarded. *Program availability:* Part-time. Offers biochemistry (MS); biomedical engineering (MS); biomedical sciences (PhD); health research (MS); human morphology (MS); medicine (MD); microbiology and immunology (MS); neuroscience (MS); orthodontics (clinical) (MS); pharmacology and therapeutics (MS); physiology (MS). *Application deadline:* Applications are processed on a rolling basis. *Application fee:* $75. Electronic applications accepted. *Application Contact:* Dr. Salim Kanaan, Director, Admission's Office, 961-1-350000 Ext. 2594, Fax: 961-1-750775, E-mail: sk00@aub.edu.lb. *Dean,* Dr. Mohamed Sayegh, 961-1-135000 Ext. 4700, Fax: 961-1-744489, E-mail: msayegh@aub.edu.lb.

Maroun Semaan Faculty of Engineering and Architecture Students: 380 full-time (186 women), 100 part-time (38 women). Average age 27. 489 applicants, 64% accepted, 127 enrolled. *Faculty:* 105 full-time (25 women), 102 part-time/adjunct (33 women). Expenses: Contact institution. *Financial support:* In 2018–19, 15 students received support, including 92 fellowships with full tuition reimbursements available (averaging $14,400 per year), 80 research assistantships with full and partial tuition reimbursements available (averaging $5,300 per year), 162 teaching assistantships with full and partial tuition reimbursements available (averaging $1,400 per year); scholarships/grants, tuition waivers (full and partial), and unspecified assistantships also available. Financial award application deadline: 4/4. In 2018, 109 master's, 14 doctorates awarded. *Program availability:* Part-time, 100% online. Offers applied energy (ME); civil engineering (PhD); electrical and computer engineering (PhD); energy studies (MS); engineering management (MEM); environmental and water resources (ME); environmental technology (MSES); mechanical engineering (ME, PhD); urban design (MUD); urban planning and policy (MUPP). For progreen diploma: LAU/AUC. *Application deadline:* For fall admission, 4/4 for domestic and international students; for spring admission, 11/3 for domestic and international students; for summer admission, 4/4 for domestic and international students. *Application fee:* $50. *Application Contact:* Dr. Salim Kanaan, Director, Admissions Office, 961-1-374374 Ext. 2590, Fax: 961-1-750775, E-mail: sk00@aub.edu.lb. *Dean,* Prof. Alan Shihade, 961-1-374374 Ext. 3400, Fax: 961-1-744462, E-mail: as20@aub.edu.lb.

Rafic Hariri School of Nursing Students: 6 full-time (5 women), 45 part-time (39 women). Average age 27. 30 applicants, 77% accepted, 17 enrolled. *Faculty:* 13 full-time (12 women), 23 part-time/adjunct (18 women). Expenses: Contact institution. *Financial support:* In 2018–19, 6 students received support. Fellowships, research assistantships, teaching assistantships, scholarships/grants, tuition waivers (full and partial), and unspecified assistantships available. Financial award application deadline: 4/3. In 2018, 12 master's awarded. *Program availability:* Part-time. Offers adult gerontology clinical nurse specialist (MSN); community and public health nursing (MSN); nursing administration and management (MSN); psychiatric mental health clinical nurse specialist (MSN). *Application deadline:* For fall admission, 3/18 for domestic students. Applications are processed on a rolling basis. *Application fee:* $50. Electronic applications accepted. *Application Contact:* Nisreen Ghalayini, Administrative Assistant, 961-1-350000 Ext. 5951, Fax: 961-1-744476, E-mail: ng28@aub.edu.lb. *Dean,* Dr. Huda Abu-Saad Huijer, 961-1-350000 Ext. 5953, Fax: 961-1-744476, E-mail: hh35@aub.edu.lb.

Suliman S. Olayan School of Business Students: 109 (64 women). Average age 29. 362 applicants, 62% accepted, 109 enrolled. Expenses: Contact institution. *Financial support:* In 2018–19, 33 research assistantships with partial tuition reimbursements (averaging $22,050 per year) were awarded; fellowships, teaching assistantships, and tuition waivers also available. In 2018, 79 master's awarded. *Program availability:* Part-time, online learning. Offers business (M Fin, MBA, MHRM); business administration (MBA); executive business administration (EMBA); finance (M Fin); human resource management (MHRM). *Application fee:* $50. Electronic applications accepted. *Application Contact:* Maya El Helou, Director of Graduate Programs, 961-1-350000 Ext. 3955, E-mail: helou@aub.edu.lb. *Dean,* Dr. Steve Harvey, 961-1-350000 Ext. 3934, E-mail: sh146@aub.edu.lb.

AMERICAN UNIVERSITY OF HEALTH SCIENCES, Signal Hill, CA 90755

General Information Proprietary, coed, comprehensive institution.

GRADUATE UNITS

School of Clinical Research Offers clinical research (MSCR).

THE AMERICAN UNIVERSITY OF PARIS, 75007 Paris, France

General Information Independent, coed, comprehensive institution. *Graduate housing:* Room and/or apartments available on a first-come, first-served basis to single students; on-campus housing not available to married students.

GRADUATE UNITS

Graduate Programs Offers cross-cultural and sustainable business management (MA); cultural translation (MA); global communications (MA); global communications and civil society (MA); international affairs (MA); international affairs, conflict resolution and civil society development (MA); Middle East and Islamic studies (MA); Middle East and Islamic studies and international affairs (MA); public policy and international affairs (MA); public policy and international law (MA). Electronic applications accepted.

AMERICAN UNIVERSITY OF PUERTO RICO, Bayamon, PR 00960-2037

General Information Independent, coed, comprehensive institution. *Graduate housing:* On-campus housing not available.

GRADUATE UNITS

Program in Criminal Justice *Program availability:* Part-time, evening/weekend. Offers criminal justice (MA).

Program in Education *Program availability:* Part-time, evening/weekend. Offers art education (M Ed); elementary education 4-6 (M Ed); elementary education K-3 (M Ed); general science education (M Ed); physical education (M Ed); special education (M Ed).

THE AMERICAN UNIVERSITY OF ROME, 00153 Rome, Italy

General Information Independent, coed, comprehensive institution. *Research affiliation:* ARCA - Association for Research into Crimes against Art (art crime prevention), ENFSI - European Network of Forensic Science Institutes (forensic archaeology), Conservation Science in Cultural Heritage.

GRADUATE UNITS

Graduate School Offers arts management (MA); food studies (MA); peace studies (MA); sustainable cultural heritage (MA). Electronic applications accepted.

AMERICAN UNIVERSITY OF SHARJAH, Sharjah, United Arab Emirates

General Information Independent, coed, comprehensive institution. *Graduate housing:* Room and/or apartments available on a first-come, first-served basis to single students; on-campus housing not available to married students. Housing application deadline: 8/16. *Research affiliation:* Emirates Foundation (philanthropy), International Atomic Energy Agency (energy), National Research Foundation, Mohammed Bin Rashid Space Center (space), Advanced Technology Investment Company (technology and investment), Qatar National Research Foundation.

GRADUATE UNITS

Graduate Programs *Program availability:* Part-time, evening/weekend. Offers accounting (MS); biomedical engineering (MSBME); business administration (MBA); chemical engineering (MS Ch E); civil engineering (MSCE); computer engineering (MS); electrical engineering (MSEE); engineering systems management (MS, PhD); mathematics (MS); mechanical engineering (MSME); mechatronics engineering (MS); teaching English to speakers of other languages (MA); translation and interpreting (MA); urban planning (MUP). Electronic applications accepted.

AMRIDGE UNIVERSITY, Montgomery, AL 36117

General Information Independent-religious, coed, university. *Graduate housing:* On-campus housing not available.

GRADUATE UNITS

Graduate and Professional Programs *Program availability:* Part-time, evening/weekend, online learning. Offers Biblical studies (MA, PhD); Christian ministry (MS); family therapy (D Min); human services (MS); leadership and management (MS); marriage and family therapy (M Div, MA, PhD); ministerial leadership (M Div, MS); New Testament studies (MA); Old Testament studies (MA); professional counseling (M Div, MA, PhD); theology (M Div, D Min). Electronic applications accepted.

ANABAPTIST MENNONITE BIBLICAL SEMINARY, Elkhart, IN 46517-1999

General Information Independent-religious, coed, graduate-only institution. *Enrollment by degree level:* 94 master's, 4 other advanced degrees. *Graduate faculty:* 14 full-time (6 women), 17 part-time/adjunct (8 women). *Tuition:* Full-time $14,000; part-time $500 per credit hour. *Required fees:* $20; $20 per credit hour. *Graduate housing:* Rooms and/or apartments available on a first-come, first-served basis to single and married students. Typical cost: $3396 per year for single students; $7020 per year for married students. Room charges vary according to housing facility selected. Housing application deadline: 8/1. *Student services:* Campus employment opportunities, campus safety program, exercise/wellness program, free psychological counseling, international student services, low-cost health insurance, multicultural affairs office, services for students with disabilities, writing training. *Library facilities:* AMBS Library. *Collection:* Books: 100,160 (physical), 129,600 (digital/electronic); Serial titles: 1,465 (physical), 7,415 (digital/electronic); Databases: 3. Weekly public service hours: 60; students can reserve study rooms.

Computer facilities: 8 computers available on campus for general student use. A campuswide network can be accessed from student residence rooms and from off campus. Online class registration is available.
Website: http://www.ambs.edu/

General Application Contact: Daniel Grimes, Director of Admissions, 574-295-3726 Ext. 266, Fax: 574-295-0092, E-mail: admissions@ambs.edu.

GRADUATE UNITS

Graduate and Professional Programs *Program availability:* Part-time, 100% online, blended/hybrid learning. Offers chaplaincy (M Div); Christian faith formation (M Div); Christian formation (MA); Christian spiritual formation (Certificate); divinity (M Div); pastoral ministry (M Div); pastoral theology for financial professionals (Certificate); peace studies (M Div); theological studies (M Div, Certificate); theology and peace studies (MA); United Methodist leadership (M Div). Conflict transformation and environmental sustainability leadership concentrations offered in cooperation with Goshen College; international development administration offered in cooperation with Andrews University. Electronic applications accepted.

ANAHEIM UNIVERSITY, Anaheim, CA 92806-5150

General Information Proprietary, coed, graduate-only institution. *Library facilities:* Anaheim University Library plus 1 other. *Collection:* Study areas open 24 hours, 5–7 days a week.
Website: http://www.anaheim.edu/

General Application Contact: Elizabeth Mays, Director of Admissions and Student Services, 714-772-3330, E-mail: ausupport@anaheim.edu.

GRADUATE UNITS

Master of Fine Arts in Digital Film Making

Program in Teaching English to Speakers of Other Languages Expenses: Contact institution. In 2018, 1 master's, 1 doctorate awarded. *Program availability:* Part-time, evening/weekend, online only, 100% online. Offers teaching English to speakers of other languages (MA, Ed D, Certificate, Diploma). *Application deadline:* Applications are processed on a rolling basis. Electronic applications accepted. *Application Contact:* Dr. Hayo Reinders, Director, Doctor of Education in TESOL Program, 714-772-3330, Fax: 714-772-3331, E-mail: admissions@anaheim.edu. *Director, Doctor of Education in TESOL Program,* Dr. Hayo Reinders, 714-772-3330, Fax: 714-772-3331, E-mail: admissions@anaheim.edu.

Programs in Business Administration Expenses: Contact institution. In 2018, 3 master's, 4 doctorates awarded. *Program availability:* Part-time, evening/weekend, online only, 100% online. Offers entrepreneurship (ME, DBA); global sustainable management (MBA); international business (MBA, DBA, Certificate, Diploma); management (DBA); sustainable management (DBA, Certificate, Diploma). *Application deadline:* Applications are processed on a rolling basis. Electronic applications accepted. *Application Contact:* Dr. Robert Robertson, Dean, Graduate School of Business, 714-772-3330, Fax: 714-772-3331, E-mail: admissions@anaheim.edu. *Dean, Graduate School of Business,* Dr. Robert Robertson, 714-772-3330, Fax: 714-772-3331, E-mail: admissions@anaheim.edu.

ANDERSON UNIVERSITY, Anderson, IN 46012-3495

General Information Independent-religious, coed, comprehensive institution. *Graduate housing:* Room or apartments available to single students; on-campus housing not available to married students. Housing application deadline: 6/1.

GRADUATE UNITS

Falls School of Business Offers accountancy (MA); business administration (MBA, DBA).

School of Education Offers education (M Ed).

School of Theology *Program availability:* Part-time. Offers missions (MA); theology (M Div, MTS, D Min).

ANDERSON UNIVERSITY, Anderson, SC 29621-4035

General Information Independent-religious, coed, comprehensive institution. *Enrollment:* 455 full-time matriculated graduate/professional students (248 women), 97 part-time matriculated graduate/professional students (44 women). *Enrollment by degree level:* 486 master's, 66 doctoral. *Tuition:* Full-time $400; part-time $400 per credit. *Required fees:* $200; $200 per semester. Tuition and fees vary according to course load. *Graduate housing:* Room and/or apartments available on a first-come, first-served basis to single students; on-campus housing not available to married students. Housing application deadline: 5/1. *Student services:* Campus employment opportunities, campus safety program, career counseling, exercise/wellness program, multicultural affairs office, teacher training, writing training. *Library facilities:* Thrift Library. *Collection:* Books: 90,729 (physical), 99,204 (digital/electronic); Serial titles: 14,268 (physical), 174,052 (digital/electronic); Databases: 200. Weekly public service hours: 88; students can reserve study rooms.

Computer facilities: 192 computers available on campus for general student use. A campuswide network can be accessed from student residence rooms and from off campus. Online class registration is available.
Website: http://www.andersonuniversity.edu/

General Application Contact: Chesley Tench, Director of Post-Traditional Admission, 864-231-5000, E-mail: ctench@andersonuniversity.edu.

GRADUATE UNITS

Clamp Divinity School Expenses: Contact institution. *Financial support:* Scholarships/grants and tuition waivers available. Financial award application deadline: 3/1; financial award applicants required to submit FAFSA. *Program availability:* Part-time, online only, 100% online, blended/hybrid learning. Offers 21st-century ministry (D Min); ministry (M Min); youth ministry (M Div). *Application Contact:* Dr. Ben Brammer, Senior Recruiter, 864-2312039, E-mail: bbrammer@andersonuniversity.edu. *Dean,* Dr. Michael Duduit, 864-328-1809, E-mail: ministry@andersonuniversity.edu.

College of Business Expenses: Contact institution. *Financial support:* Scholarships/grants and tuition waivers available. Financial award application deadline: 3/1; financial award applicants required to submit FAFSA. Offers business administration (MBA); healthcare leadership (MBA); human resources (MBA); marketing (MBA); organizational leadership (MOL); supply chain management (MBA). *Application deadline:* Applications are processed on a rolling basis. Electronic applications accepted. *Application Contact:* Sharon Vargo, Graduate Admission Counselor, 864-231-2000, E-mail: svargo@andersonuniversity.edu. *Dean,* Steve Nail, 864-MBA-6000.

College of Education Expenses: Contact institution. *Financial support:* Scholarships/grants and tuition waivers available. Financial award application deadline: 3/1; financial award applicants required to submit FAFSA. *Program availability:* 100% online. Offers administration and supervision (M Ed); education (M Ed); elementary education (MAT). *Application Contact:* Dr. Mark Butler, Dean, 864-231-2042. *Dean,* Dr. Mark Butler, 864-231-2042.

College of Health Professions Expenses: Contact institution. *Financial support:* Scholarships/grants available. *Program availability:* Online learning. Offers advanced practice (DNP); executive leadership (MSN, DNP); family nurse practitioner (MSN, DNP); nurse educator (MSN); psychiatric mental health nurse practitioner (MSN, DNP). *Application deadline:* Applications are processed on a rolling basis. Electronic applications accepted. *Application Contact:* Dr. Donald M. Peace, Dean, 864-231-5513, E-mail: dpeace@andersonuniversity.edu. *Dean,* Dr. Donald M. Peace, 864-231-5513, E-mail: dpeace@andersonuniversity.edu.

Command College of South Carolina Expenses: Contact institution. *Financial support:* Scholarships/grants available. Financial award application deadline: 3/1; financial award applicants required to submit FAFSA. *Program availability:* Blended/hybrid learning. Offers criminal justice (MCJ). *Application deadline:* Applications are processed on a rolling basis. Electronic applications accepted.

South Carolina School of the Arts Expenses: Contact institution. *Financial support:* Scholarships/grants available. *Program availability:* Online learning. Offers music education (MM). *Application Contact:* David Larson, Dean, 864-231-2002, E-mail: dlarson@andersonuniversity.edu. *Dean,* David Larson, 864-231-2002, E-mail: dlarson@andersonuniversity.edu.

ANDREWS UNIVERSITY, Berrien Springs, MI 49104

General Information Independent-religious, coed, university. CGS member. *Graduate housing:* Rooms and/or apartments available on a first-come, first-served basis to single and married students. *Research affiliation:* RAND Corporation (drug abuse), Argonne National Laboratory (physics), Deutches Electronen Synchroton (physics).

GRADUATE UNITS

School of Graduate Studies *Program availability:* Part-time, evening/weekend, online learning.

College of Arts and Sciences *Program availability:* Part-time, evening/weekend. Offers arts and sciences (M Mus, MA, MAT, MS, MSA, MSCID, MSW); biology (MAT, MS); communication (MA); community and international development (MSCID); English (MA, MAT); international development (MSCID); music (M Mus, MA); social work (MSW).

School of Architecture, Art and Design Offers architecture, art and design (M Arch). Electronic applications accepted.

School of Business *Program availability:* Part-time. Offers business (MBA, MSA).

School of Education *Program availability:* Part-time. Offers clinical mental health counseling (MA); community counseling (MA); counseling psychology (MA, PhD); curriculum and instruction (MA, Ed D, PhD, Ed S); education (MA, MAT, MS, Ed D, PhD, Ed S); educational administration and leadership (MA, Ed D, PhD, Ed S); educational and developmental psychology (MA, Ed D, PhD); educational psychology (Ed D, PhD); elementary education (MAT); higher education administration (MA, Ed D, PhD, Ed S); leadership (MA, Ed D, PhD, Ed S); school counseling (MA); school psychology (Ed S); secondary education (MAT); special education (MS); teacher education (MAT).

Seventh-day Adventist Theological Seminary Offers ministry (M Div, D Min); pastoral ministry (MA); religious education (MA, Ed D, PhD, Ed S); theology (M Th, Th D); youth ministry (MA).

School of Health Professions Offers health professions (MPH, MS, MSMLS, DNP, DPT, Dr Sc PT, TDPT, Certificate); medical laboratory sciences (MSMLS); nursing (MS, DNP); nutrition (MS); nutrition and dietetics (Certificate); orthopedic manual therapy (Dr Sc PT); physical therapy (DPT, Dr Sc PT, TDPT); public health (MPH); speech-language pathology (MS).

ANGELO STATE UNIVERSITY, San Angelo, TX 76909

General Information State-supported, coed, comprehensive institution. *Enrollment:* 10,387 graduate, professional, and undergraduate students; 750 full-time matriculated graduate/professional students (524 women), 885 part-time matriculated graduate/professional students (589 women). *Enrollment by degree level:* 1,557 master's, 78 doctoral. *Graduate faculty:* 144 full-time (65 women). *International tuition:* $11,434 full-time. *Tuition, area resident:* Full-time $3964; part-time $220 per credit hour. Tuition, state resident: full-time $3964; part-time $220 per credit hour. Tuition, nonresident: full-time $11,434; part-time $635 per credit hour. *Graduate housing:* Room and/or apartments available on a first-come, first-served basis to single students; on-campus housing not available to married students. Typical cost: $9130 (including board). Room and board charges vary according to board plan, campus/location and housing facility selected. *Student services:* Campus employment opportunities, campus safety program, career counseling, free psychological counseling, grant writing training, international student services, low-cost health insurance, multicultural affairs office, services for students with disabilities, writing training. *Library facilities:* Porter Henderson Library. *Collection:* Books: 309,338 (physical), 100,539 (digital/electronic); Serial titles:

105 (physical), 54,329 (digital/electronic); Databases: 243. Weekly public service hours: 137; study areas open 24 hours, 5–7 days a week; students can reserve study rooms.

Computer facilities: Computer purchase and lease plans are available. 750 computers available on campus for general student use. A campuswide network can be accessed from student residence rooms and from off campus. Online class registration, online courses, tuition payments, book purchase, parking permits, university calendar, discounted hardware and software are available.
Website: http://www.angelo.edu/

General Application Contact: Graduate Admissions Coordinator, 325-942-2169, Fax: 325-942-2194, E-mail: graduate.studies@angelo.edu.

GRADUATE UNITS

College of Graduate Studies and Research Students: 522 full-time (296 women), 1,113 part-time (589 women); includes 603 minority (150 Black or African American, non-Hispanic/Latino; 5 American Indian or Alaska Native, non-Hispanic/Latino; 26 Asian, non-Hispanic/Latino; 377 Hispanic/Latino; 2 Native Hawaiian or other Pacific Islander, non-Hispanic/Latino; 43 Two or more races, non-Hispanic/Latino), 26 international. Average age 33. Expenses: Contact institution. *Financial support:* Research assistantships, teaching assistantships, career-related internships or fieldwork, Federal Work-Study, scholarships/grants, and unspecified assistantships available. Support available to part-time students. Financial award application deadline: 3/1. *Program availability:* Part-time, evening/weekend, online learning. *Application deadline:* For fall admission, 7/15 priority date for domestic students, 6/10 for international students; for spring admission, 12/1 priority date for domestic students, 11/1 for international students. Applications are processed on a rolling basis. *Application fee:* $40 ($50 for international students). Electronic applications accepted. *Application Contact:* Amanda Martinez, Graduate Admissions Coordinator, 325-942-2169, Fax: 325-942-2194, E-mail: graduate.studies@angelo.edu. *Dean,* Dr. Micheal W Salisbury, 325-942-2169, Fax: 325-942-2194, E-mail: micheal.salisbury@angelo.edu.

Archer College of Health and Human Services Students: 206 full-time (126 women), 149 part-time (113 women); includes 118 minority (20 Black or African American, non-Hispanic/Latino; 10 Asian, non-Hispanic/Latino; 75 Hispanic/Latino; 13 Two or more races, non-Hispanic/Latino), 9 international. Average age 30. Expenses: Contact institution. Offers family nurse practitioner (MSN); health and human services (M Ed, MS, MSN, DPT); industrial-organizational psychology (MS); kinesiology (M Ed); nurse educator (MSN); physical therapy (DPT). *Application deadline:* For fall admission, 7/15 priority date for domestic students, 6/10 for international students; for spring admission, 12/1 priority date for domestic students, 11/1 for international students. *Application fee:* $40 ($50 for international students). *Application Contact:* Dr. Leslie M. Mayrand, Dean, 325-486-6258, Fax: 325-942-2631, E-mail: leslie.mayrand@angelo.edu. *Dean,* Dr. Leslie M. Mayrand, 325-486-6258, Fax: 325-942-2631, E-mail: leslie.mayrand@angelo.edu.

College of Arts and Humanities Students: 70 full-time (31 women), 172 part-time (65 women); includes 93 minority (25 Black or African American, non-Hispanic/Latino; 1 American Indian or Alaska Native, non-Hispanic/Latino; 7 Asian, non-Hispanic/Latino; 48 Hispanic/Latino; 12 Two or more races, non-Hispanic/Latino), 6 international. Average age 31. Expenses: Contact institution. *Financial support:* Research assistantships, teaching assistantships, career-related internships or fieldwork, Federal Work-Study, scholarships/grants, and unspecified assistantships available. Support available to part-time students. Financial award application deadline: 3/1; financial award applicants required to submit FAFSA. *Program availability:* Part-time, evening/weekend. Offers arts and humanities (MA, MS, MSS); communication (MA); criminal justice (MS); English (MA); homeland security (MS); intelligence, security studies, and analysis (MSS); security studies (MSS); TESOL (MA). *Application deadline:* For fall admission, 7/15 priority date for domestic students, 6/10 for international students; for spring admission, 12/1 priority date for domestic students, 11/1 for international students. Applications are processed on a rolling basis. *Application fee:* $40 ($50 for international students). Electronic applications accepted. *Application Contact:* Dr. John Klingemann, Dean, 325-942-2162, E-mail: john.klingemann@angelo.edu. *Dean,* Dr. John Klingemann, 325-942-2162, E-mail: john.klingemann@angelo.edu.

College of Education Students: 360 full-time (307 women), 456 part-time (364 women); includes 312 minority (93 Black or African American, non-Hispanic/Latino; 3 American Indian or Alaska Native, non-Hispanic/Latino; 7 Asian, non-Hispanic/Latino; 193 Hispanic/Latino; 1 Native Hawaiian or other Pacific Islander, non-Hispanic/Latino; 15 Two or more races, non-Hispanic/Latino). Average age 35. Expenses: Contact institution. *Financial support:* Career-related internships or fieldwork, Federal Work-Study, scholarships/grants, and unspecified assistantships available. Support available to part-time students. Financial award application deadline: 3/1; financial award applicants required to submit FAFSA. *Program availability:* Part-time, evening/weekend. Offers curriculum and instruction (MA); education (M Ed, MA); educational administration (M Ed); guidance and counseling (M Ed); student development and leadership in higher education (M Ed). *Application deadline:* For fall admission, 7/15 priority date for domestic students, 6/10 for international students; for spring admission, 12/1 priority date for domestic students, 11/1 for international students. Applications are processed on a rolling basis. *Application fee:* $40 ($50 for international students). Electronic applications accepted. *Application Contact:* Dr. Scarlet Clouse, Dean, 325-942-2212, E-mail: scarlet.clouse@angelo.edu. *Dean,* Dr. Scarlet Clouse, 325-942-2212, E-mail: scarlet.clouse@angelo.edu.

College of Science and Engineering Students: 19 full-time (12 women), 13 part-time (8 women); includes 6 minority (1 Black or African American, non-Hispanic/Latino; 1 Asian, non-Hispanic/Latino; 4 Hispanic/Latino). Average age 26. Expenses: Contact institution. *Financial support:* Research assistantships, teaching assistantships, career-related internships or fieldwork, Federal Work-Study, scholarships/grants, and unspecified assistantships available. Support available to part-time students. Financial award application deadline: 8/1; financial award applicants required to submit FAFSA. *Program availability:* Part-time, evening/weekend. Offers agriculture (M Ag); biology (MS); science and engineering (M Ag, MS). *Application deadline:* For fall admission, 7/15 priority date for domestic students, 6/10 for international students; for spring admission, 12/1 priority date for domestic students, 11/1 for international students. Applications are processed on a rolling basis. *Application fee:* $40 ($50 for international students). Electronic applications accepted. *Application Contact:* Dr. Paul K. Swets, Dean, 325-942-2470, Fax: 325-942-2340, E-mail: paul.swets@angelo.edu. *Dean,* Dr. Paul K. Swets, 325-942-2470, Fax: 325-942-2340, E-mail: paul.swets@angelo.edu.

Norris-Vincent College of Business Students: 95 full-time (48 women), 95 part-time (39 women); includes 74 minority (11 Black or African American, non-Hispanic/Latino; 1 American Indian or Alaska Native, non-Hispanic/Latino; 1 Asian, non-Hispanic/Latino; 57 Hispanic/Latino; 1 Native Hawaiian or other Pacific Islander, non-Hispanic/Latino; 3 Two or more races, non-Hispanic/Latino), 11 international. Average

age 30. Expenses: Contact institution. *Financial support:* Career-related internships or fieldwork, Federal Work-Study, and scholarships/grants available. Support available to part-time students. Financial award application deadline: 3/1; financial award applicants required to submit FAFSA. *Program availability:* Part-time, evening/weekend. Offers business (MBA, MPAC); business administration (MBA); professional accountancy (MPAC). *Application deadline:* Applications are processed on a rolling basis. *Application fee:* $40 ($50 for international students). Electronic applications accepted. *Application Contact:* Dr. Clifton T. Jones, Dean, 325-942-2337, Fax: 325-942-2718, E-mail: clifton.jones@angelo.edu. *Dean,* Dr. Clifton T. Jones, 325-942-2337, Fax: 325-942-2718, E-mail: clifton.jones@angelo.edu.

ANNA MARIA COLLEGE, Paxton, MA 01612

General Information Independent-religious, coed, comprehensive institution. *Graduate housing:* On-campus housing not available.

GRADUATE UNITS

Graduate Division *Program availability:* Part-time, evening/weekend. Offers business administration (MBA, AC); counseling psychology (MA); criminal justice (MS); early childhood education (M Ed); education (CAGS); elementary education (M Ed); English language arts (M Ed); health emergency management (MS, Graduate Certificate); industrial/organizational psychology (MS); public administration (MPA); social work (MSW); visual arts (M Ed). Electronic applications accepted.

ANTIOCH UNIVERSITY LOS ANGELES, Culver City, CA 90230

General Information Independent, coed, upper-level institution. *Graduate housing:* On-campus housing not available.

GRADUATE UNITS

Program in Education *Program availability:* Evening/weekend. Offers education (MA).

Program in Leadership, Management and Business *Program availability:* Part-time, evening/weekend. Offers human resource development (MA); leadership (MA); organizational development (MA).

Program in Psychology *Program availability:* Part-time. Offers clinical psychology (MA); psychology (MA).

Program in Urban Sustainability Offers urban sustainability (MA).

ANTIOCH UNIVERSITY MIDWEST, Yellow Springs, OH 45387-1609

General Information Independent, coed, upper-level institution. *Graduate housing:* On-campus housing not available.

GRADUATE UNITS

MBA Program in Healthcare Leadership *Program availability:* Part-time, evening/weekend, online learning. Offers healthcare leadership (MBA). Electronic applications accepted.

ANTIOCH UNIVERSITY NEW ENGLAND, Keene, NH 03431-3552

General Information Independent, coed, graduate-only institution. *Graduate housing:* On-campus housing not available. *Research affiliation:* Cheshire Medical Center Cardiac Rehabilitation Program (clinical psychology), Northeast Foundation for Children (education), Pine Hill Waldorf School (education), Harris Center for Conservation Education (environmental studies).

GRADUATE UNITS

Graduate School *Program availability:* Evening/weekend. Offers advocacy for social justice and sustainability (MS); applied behavior analysis (Certificate); applied behavior analysis internship (Certificate); autism spectrum disorders (Certificate); clinical mental health counseling (MA); clinical psychology (Psy D); conservation biology (MS); dance/movement therapy and counseling (M Ed, MA, PMC); early childhood education (M Ed); elementary education (M Ed, Certificate); environmental education (MS); environmental studies (PhD); foundations of education (M Ed); integrated learning (M Ed); marriage and family therapy (MA, PhD, Certificate); principal certification (PMC); resource management and conservation (MS); science teacher certification (MS); self-designed studies (MS); special education (M Ed); substance abuse counseling (MA); sustainability (MBA); sustainable development and climate change (MS); teaching (M Ed, PMC); Waldorf teacher training (M Ed, Certificate). Electronic applications accepted.

ANTIOCH UNIVERSITY SANTA BARBARA, Santa Barbara, CA 93101-1581

General Information Independent, coed, upper-level institution. *Graduate housing:* On-campus housing not available.

GRADUATE UNITS

Program in Business Administration Offers non-profit management (MBA); social business (MBA); strategic leadership (MBA).

Program in Clinical Psychology Offers clinical psychology (MA, Psy D). Electronic applications accepted.

Program in Education/Teacher Credentialing *Program availability:* Part-time. Offers education/teacher credentialing (M Ed, MA). Electronic applications accepted.

Program in Writing and Contemporary Media *Program availability:* Part-time. Offers writing and contemporary media (MFA).

ANTIOCH UNIVERSITY SEATTLE, Seattle, WA 98121

General Information Independent, coed, university. *Graduate housing:* On-campus housing not available.

GRADUATE UNITS

Program in Clinical Psychology *Program availability:* Part-time, evening/weekend. Offers psychology (Psy D). Electronic applications accepted.

Program in Counseling, Therapy and Wellness Offers clinical mental health counseling (MA); counselor education and supervision (PhD); couple and family therapy (MA).

Program in Education *Program availability:* Part-time, evening/weekend. Offers adult education (MA); drama therapy (MA); individualized studies (MA); leadership in edible education (MA); teaching (MAT); urban environmental education (MA).

AOMA GRADUATE SCHOOL OF INTEGRATIVE MEDICINE, Austin, TX 78757

General Information Proprietary, coed, graduate-only institution. *Graduate housing:* On-campus housing not available.

GRADUATE UNITS

Doctor of Acupuncture and Oriental Medicine Program Offers acupuncture and Oriental medicine (DAOM). Electronic applications accepted.

Master of Acupuncture and Oriental Medicine Program Offers acupuncture and Oriental medicine (MAcOM). Electronic applications accepted.

APEX SCHOOL OF THEOLOGY, Durham, NC 27703
General Information Independent-religious, coed, comprehensive institution. *Graduate housing:* On-campus housing not available.

GRADUATE UNITS
Graduate Programs

APOLLOS UNIVERSITY, Great Falls, MT 59401
General Information Proprietary, coed, comprehensive institution.

GRADUATE UNITS
School of Business and Management Offers business administration (MBA, DBA); organizational management (MS).

APPALACHIAN BIBLE COLLEGE, Mount Hope, WV 25880
General Information Independent-religious, coed, comprehensive institution. *Enrollment:* 11 matriculated graduate/professional students. *Graduate faculty:* 5 part-time/adjunct. *Tuition:* Part-time $450 per credit hour. *Graduate housing:* Rooms and/or apartments available on a first-come, first-served basis to single and married students. Housing application deadline: 1/1. *Library facilities:* John Van Pufflen Library.

Computer facilities: 15 computers available on campus for general student use. A campuswide network can be accessed from student residence rooms and from off campus.
Website: http://www.abc.edu/

General Application Contact: Benjamin Cale, Director of Admissions, 304-877-6428 Ext. 311, Fax: 304-877-5082, E-mail: admissions@abc.edu.

GRADUATE UNITS
Graduate Program *Program availability:* Part-time, online learning. Offers ministry (MA). Electronic applications accepted.

APPALACHIAN COLLEGE OF PHARMACY, Oakwood, VA 24631
General Information Independent, coed, graduate-only institution.

GRADUATE UNITS
Doctor of Pharmacy Program Offers pharmacy (Pharm D).

APPALACHIAN SCHOOL OF LAW, Grundy, VA 24614
General Information Independent, coed, graduate-only institution. *Enrollment by degree level:* 146 doctoral. *Graduate faculty:* 12 full-time (2 women), 9 part-time/adjunct (4 women). *Tuition:* Full-time $35,000. *Required fees:* $525. *Graduate housing:* On-campus housing not available. *Student services:* Campus employment opportunities, campus safety program, career counseling, international student services, services for students with disabilities, writing training. *Library facilities:* ASL Library. *Collection:* Students can reserve study rooms.

Computer facilities: 32 computers available on campus for general student use. Online class registration is available.
Website: http://www.asl.edu/

General Application Contact: Kelsea Wagner, Director of Admissions, 276-244-1245, Fax: 276-244-1298, E-mail: kwagner@asl.edu.

GRADUATE UNITS
Professional Program in Law Students: 146 full-time (75 women); includes 39 minority (18 Black or African American, non-Hispanic/Latino; 7 American Indian or Alaska Native, non-Hispanic/Latino; 8 Asian, non-Hispanic/Latino; 6 Hispanic/Latino). 409 applicants, 63% accepted, 61 enrolled. *Faculty:* 12 full-time (2 women), 9 part-time/adjunct (4 women). Expenses: Contact institution. *Financial support:* In 2018–19, 83 students received support. Research assistantships, teaching assistantships, career-related internships or fieldwork, Federal Work-Study, institutionally sponsored loans, scholarships/grants, and tuition waivers (full and partial) available. Financial award application deadline: 7/25; financial award applicants required to submit FAFSA. In 2018, 34 doctorates awarded. Offers law (JD). *Application deadline:* For fall admission, 7/25 for domestic students; for winter admission, 12/27 for domestic students. Applications are processed on a rolling basis. *Application fee:* $0. Electronic applications accepted. *Application Contact:* Kelsea Wagner, Director of Admissions, 276-244-1245, Fax: 276-935-8496, E-mail: kwagner@asl.edu. *Dean,* Sandra Keen McGlothlin, 276-935-4349 Ext. 1265, Fax: 276-935-8261, E-mail: smcglothlin@asl.edu.

APPALACHIAN STATE UNIVERSITY, Boone, NC 28608
General Information State-supported, coed, comprehensive institution. CGS member. *Enrollment:* 19,108 graduate, professional, and undergraduate students; 861 full-time matriculated graduate/professional students (570 women), 827 part-time matriculated graduate/professional students (595 women). *Enrollment by degree level:* 1,390 master's, 80 doctoral, 218 other advanced degrees. *Graduate faculty:* 538 full-time, 211 part-time/adjunct. *Tuition, area resident:* Full-time $4839; part-time $237 per credit hour. Tuition, state resident: full-time $4839; part-time $237 per credit hour. Tuition, nonresident: full-time $18,271; part-time $895.50 per credit hour. *Graduate housing:* On-campus housing not available. *Student services:* Campus employment opportunities, campus safety program, career counseling, child daycare facilities, exercise/wellness program, free psychological counseling, grant writing training, international student services, low-cost health insurance, multicultural affairs office, services for students with disabilities, teacher training, writing training. *Library facilities:* Carol Grotnes Belk Library plus 1 other. *Collection:* Books: 666,451 (physical), 831,648 (digital/electronic); Serial titles: 12,785 (physical), 161,860 (digital/electronic); Databases: 447. Weekly public service hours: 137; students can reserve study rooms.

Computer facilities: Computer purchase and lease plans are available. 2,280 computers available on campus for general student use. A campuswide network can be accessed from student residence rooms and from off campus. Online class registration is available.
Website: http://www.appstate.edu/

General Application Contact: Dontrell Parson, Director of Graduate Admissions and Recruiting, 828-262-2130, Fax: 828-262-2709, E-mail: parsondo@appstate.edu.

GRADUATE UNITS
Cratis D. Williams School of Graduate Studies Students: 861 full-time (570 women), 827 part-time (595 women); includes 118 minority (64 Black or African American, non-Hispanic/Latino; 1 American Indian or Alaska Native, non-Hispanic/Latino; 13 Asian, non-Hispanic/Latino; 16 Hispanic/Latino; 24 Two or more races, non-Hispanic/Latino), 5 international. Expenses: Contact institution. *Financial support:* Fellowships, research assistantships, career-related internships or fieldwork, Federal Work-Study, institutionally sponsored loans, scholarships/grants, and unspecified assistantships

available. Financial award application deadline: 4/1; financial award applicants required to submit FAFSA. *Program availability:* Part-time, evening/weekend, 100% online, blended/hybrid learning. Offers appropriate technology (MS); cell and molecular biology (MS); clinical health psychology (MA); clinical mental health counseling (MA); college student development (MA); computer science (MS); curriculum specialist (MA); educational administration (Ed S); educational media (MA); elementary education (MA); English (MA); exercise science (MS); general history (MA); general management (MBA); geography (MA); higher education (MA, Ed S); library science (MLS); marriage and family therapy (MA); mathematics (MA); middle grades education (MA); nutrition (MS); political science (MA); public administration (MPA); reading education (MA); renewable energy engineering (MS); romance languages (MA); school administration (MSA); school counseling (MA); social work (MSW); special education (MA); speech-language pathology (MS); taxation (MS). *Application deadline:* For fall admission, 2/1 for international students; for spring admission, 7/1 for international students. Applications are processed on a rolling basis. *Application fee:* $65. Electronic applications accepted. *Application Contact:* Dontrell Parson, Director of Admissions and Recruiting, 828-262-2130, Fax: 828-262-2709, E-mail: parsondo@appstate.edu. *Dean,* Dr. Mike McKenzie, 828-262-2130, E-mail: mckenziemj@appstate.edu.

Center for Appalachian Studies *Program availability:* Part-time. Offers culture (MA). Electronic applications accepted.

School of Music *Program availability:* Part-time. Offers music performance (MM); music therapy (MMT). Electronic applications accepted.

AQUINAS COLLEGE, Grand Rapids, MI 49506
General Information Independent-religious, coed, comprehensive institution. *Enrollment:* 32 full-time matriculated graduate/professional students (20 women), 143 part-time matriculated graduate/professional students (113 women). *Enrollment by degree level:* 175 master's. *Graduate faculty:* 11 full-time (7 women), 29 part-time/adjunct (18 women). *Tuition:* Part-time $593 per credit hour. *Required fees:* $120. *Graduate housing:* On-campus housing not available. *Student services:* Campus employment opportunities, campus safety program, career counseling, exercise/wellness program, free psychological counseling, multicultural affairs office, services for students with disabilities, teacher training, writing training. *Library facilities:* Grace Hauenstein Library plus 1 other. *Collection:* Books: 85,348 (physical), 196,003 (digital/electronic); Serial titles: 231 (physical); Databases: 85. Weekly public service hours: 90; students can reserve study rooms.

Computer facilities: Computer purchase and lease plans are available. 210 computers available on campus for general student use. A campuswide network can be accessed from student residence rooms and from off campus. Online class registration is available.
Website: http://www.aquinas.edu/

General Application Contact: Lynn Atkins-Rykert, Graduate Programs Coordinator, 616-632-2924, Fax: 616-732-4465, E-mail: atkinlyn@aquinas.edu.

GRADUATE UNITS
School of Education Students: 4 full-time (all women), 108 part-time (91 women); includes 10 minority (1 Black or African American, non-Hispanic/Latino; 1 Asian, non-Hispanic/Latino; 8 Hispanic/Latino). Average age 36. *Faculty:* 4 full-time (all women), 20 part-time/adjunct (16 women). Expenses: Contact institution. *Financial support:* Scholarships/grants available. Support available to part-time students. Financial award application deadline: 3/15. In 2018, 8 master's awarded. *Program availability:* Part-time, evening/weekend. Offers education (M Ed, MAT). *Application deadline:* Applications are processed on a rolling basis. *Application fee:* $0. *Application Contact:* Michele Mazurek, Certification Officer, Data Records Specialist, 616-632-2427, E-mail: michele.mazurek@aquinas.edu. *Dean,* Dr. Susan English, 616-632-2800, Fax: 616-732-4465, E-mail: englisus@aquinas.edu.

School of Management Students: 12 full-time (4 women), 32 part-time (19 women); includes 3 minority (1 Black or African American, non-Hispanic/Latino; 1 Asian, non-Hispanic/Latino; 1 Hispanic/Latino), 2 international. Average age 31. *Faculty:* 4 full-time (1 woman), 5 part-time/adjunct (0 women). Expenses: Contact institution. *Financial support:* Scholarships/grants available. Support available to part-time students. Financial award application deadline: 3/15; financial award applicants required to submit FAFSA. In 2018, 19 master's awarded. *Program availability:* Part-time, evening/weekend. Offers marketing management (MM); organizational leadership (MM); sustainable business (MM). *Application deadline:* Applications are processed on a rolling basis. *Application fee:* $0. *Application Contact:* Lynn Atkins-Rykert, Program Coordinator, 616-632-2925, Fax: 616-732-4489, E-mail: atkinlyn@aquinas.edu. *Interim Dean of Business Division,* Dr. Linda Hagan, 616-632-2193, Fax: 616-732-4489, E-mail: lmh010@aquinas.edu.

AQUINAS COLLEGE, Nashville, TN 37205-2005
General Information Independent-religious, coed, comprehensive institution. *Graduate housing:* On-campus housing not available.

GRADUATE UNITS
School of Education Offers elementary education (MAT); secondary education (MAT); teaching and learning (M Ed).

AQUINAS INSTITUTE OF THEOLOGY, St. Louis, MO 63108
General Information Independent-religious, coed, graduate-only institution. *Graduate housing:* On-campus housing not available.

GRADUATE UNITS
Graduate and Professional Programs *Program availability:* Part-time, evening/weekend, online learning. Offers biblical studies (Certificate); church music (MM); health care mission (MAHCM); ministry (M Div); pastoral care (Certificate); pastoral ministry (MAPM); pastoral studies (MAPS); preaching (D Min); spiritual direction (Certificate); theology (M Div, MA); Thomistic studies (Certificate).

ARCADIA UNIVERSITY, Glenside, PA 19038-3295
General Information Independent-religious, coed, comprehensive institution. CGS member. *Enrollment:* 471 full-time matriculated graduate/professional students (360 women), 899 part-time matriculated graduate/professional students (660 women). *Enrollment by degree level:* 662 master's, 632 doctoral, 76 other advanced degrees. *Graduate housing:* On-campus housing not available. *Student services:* Campus safety program, career counseling, international student services, low-cost health insurance, multicultural affairs office, services for students with disabilities, writing training. *Library facilities:* Bette E. Landman Library. *Collection:* Students can reserve study rooms.

Computer facilities: A campuswide network can be accessed from student residence rooms and from off campus. Online class registration is available.
Website: http://www.arcadia.edu/

General Application Contact: Information Contact, 215-572-2910, Fax: 215-572-4049, E-mail: admiss@arcadia.edu.

GRADUATE UNITS

College of Arts and Sciences Students: 91 full-time (75 women), 84 part-time (62 women); includes 41 minority (27 Black or African American, non-Hispanic/Latino; 4 Asian, non-Hispanic/Latino; 7 Hispanic/Latino; 3 Two or more races, non-Hispanic/Latino), 2 international. Expenses: Contact institution. In 2018, 80 master's awarded. Offers applied behavior analysis (MAC); arts and sciences (MA, MAC, MAH, MFA, MSFS); autism (MAC); child/family therapy (MAC); community public health (MAC); counseling/international peace and conflict resolution dual degree (MAC); creative writing (MFA); English (MA); forensic science (MSFS); international peace and conflict resolution (MA); mental health counseling (MAC); trauma (MAC). *Application Contact:* Information Contact, 215-572-2910, Fax: 215-572-4049, E-mail: admiss@arcadia.edu. *Dean, College of Arts & Sciences*, Rebecca Kohn, 215-572-2108.

College of Health Sciences Students: 341 full-time (258 women), 491 part-time (340 women); includes 186 minority (11 Black or African American, non-Hispanic/Latino; 2 American Indian or Alaska Native, non-Hispanic/Latino; 152 Asian, non-Hispanic/Latino; 13 Hispanic/Latino; 2 Native Hawaiian or other Pacific Islander, non-Hispanic/Latino; 6 Two or more races, non-Hispanic/Latino), 142 international. Expenses: Contact institution. In 2018, 152 master's, 190 doctorates awarded. Offers health education (MSHE); health sciences (MMS, MPH, MSGC, MSHE, DPT); physical therapy (DPT); physician assistant (MMS); public health (MPH, MSHE). *Application Contact:* Information Contact, 215-572-2910, Fax: 215-572-4049, E-mail: admiss@arcadia.edu. *Dean*, Rebecca Craik, 215-572-2143, E-mail: craikr@arcadia.edu.

Program in Business Administration Students: 4 full-time (3 women), 25 part-time (15 women); includes 10 minority (6 Black or African American, non-Hispanic/Latino; 1 Asian, non-Hispanic/Latino; 2 Hispanic/Latino; 1 Two or more races, non-Hispanic/Latino), 3 international. *Faculty:* 9 full-time (5 women), 14 part-time/adjunct (5 women). Expenses: Contact institution. In 2018, 18 master's awarded. *Program availability:* Part-time, evening/weekend. Offers business administration (MBA). *Application fee:* $25. *Application Contact:* Office of Enrollment Management, 215-572-2910, Fax: 215-572-4049, E-mail: admiss@arcadia.edu. *Executive Director*, Dr. Thomas M. Brinker, 215-572-4039.

School of Education Students: 35 full-time (24 women), 299 part-time (243 women); includes 72 minority (49 Black or African American, non-Hispanic/Latino; 1 American Indian or Alaska Native, non-Hispanic/Latino; 12 Asian, non-Hispanic/Latino; 8 Hispanic/Latino; 2 Two or more races, non-Hispanic/Latino), 5 international. *Faculty:* 14 full-time (10 women). Expenses: Contact institution. *Financial support:* Career-related internships or fieldwork, tuition waivers (partial), and unspecified assistantships available. In 2018, 152 master's, 8 doctorates awarded. *Program availability:* Part-time, evening/weekend, online learning. Offers art education (M Ed); computer education (CAS); curriculum (CAS); curriculum studies (M Ed); early childhood education (M Ed); educational leadership (M Ed, Ed D, CAS); elementary education (M Ed); English education (MA Ed); environmental education (MA Ed); instructional technology (M Ed); language arts (M Ed); library science (M Ed); mathematics education (M Ed, MA Ed); music education (MA Ed); psychology (MA Ed); reading (M Ed, CAS); science education (M Ed, CAS); secondary education (M Ed, CAS); special education (M Ed, Ed D, CAS); theater arts (MA Ed); written communication (MA Ed). *Application deadline:* Applications are processed on a rolling basis. *Application fee:* $25. Electronic applications accepted. *Application Contact:* 215-572-2925, Fax: 215-572-2126, E-mail: grad@arcadia.edu. *Chair*, Kimberly Dean, 215-572-8629.

ARGOSY UNIVERSITY, ATLANTA, Atlanta, GA 30328
General Information Proprietary, coed, university.

GRADUATE UNITS

College of Business Offers accounting (DBA); corporate compliance (MBA); customized professional concentration (MBA, DBA); finance (MBA); healthcare administration (MBA); information systems (DBA); information systems management (MBA); international business (MBA, DBA); management (MBA, MSM, DBA); marketing (MBA, DBA).

College of Education Offers educational leadership (MAEd, Ed D, Ed S); teaching and learning (MAEd, Ed D, Ed S).

College of Health Sciences Offers public health (MPH).

Georgia School of Professional Psychology Offers clinical psychology (MA, Psy D, Postdoctoral Respecialization Certificate); community counseling (MA); counselor education and supervision (Ed D); forensic psychology (MA); industrial organizational psychology (MA); marriage and family therapy (Certificate); sport-exercise psychology (MA).

ARGOSY UNIVERSITY, CHICAGO, Chicago, IL 60601
General Information Proprietary, coed, university.

GRADUATE UNITS

College of Business *Program availability:* Online learning. Offers accounting (DBA); customized professional concentration (MBA, DBA); finance (MBA); fraud examination (MBA); global business sustainability (DBA); healthcare administration (MBA); information systems (DBA); information systems management (MBA); international business (MBA, DBA); management (MBA, MSM, DBA); marketing (MBA, DBA); organizational leadership (Ed D); public administration (MBA); sustainable management (MBA).

College of Education *Program availability:* Online learning. Offers adult education and training (MA Ed); community college executive leadership (Ed D); educational leadership (MA Ed, Ed D, Ed S); instructional leadership (Ed D, Ed S).

College of Health Sciences Offers public health (MPH).

Illinois School of Professional Psychology *Program availability:* Online learning. Offers child and adolescent psychology (Psy D); client-centered and experiential psychotherapies (Psy D); clinical psychology (MA, Psy D); community counseling (MA); counseling psychology (Ed D); counselor education and supervision (Ed D); diversity and multicultural psychology (Psy D); family psychology (Psy D); forensic psychology (Psy D); health psychology (Psy D); industrial organizational psychology (MA); neuropsychology (Psy D); organizational consulting (Psy D); psychoanalytic psychology (Psy D); psychology and spirituality (Psy D).

ARGOSY UNIVERSITY, HAWAI`I, Honolulu, HI 96813
General Information Proprietary, coed, university.

GRADUATE UNITS

College of Business Offers accounting (DBA); corporate compliance (MBA); customized professional concentration (MBA, DBA); finance (MBA, Certificate); fraud examination (MBA); global business sustainability (DBA); healthcare administration (MBA, Certificate); information systems (DBA); information systems management (MBA,

Certificate); international business (MBA, DBA, Certificate); management (MBA, MSM, DBA); marketing (MBA, DBA, Certificate); organizational leadership (Ed D); public administration (MBA); sustainable management (MBA).

College of Education Offers adult education and training (MAEd); educational leadership (Ed D); instructional leadership (Ed D); school psychology (MA).

College of Health Sciences Offers public health (MPH).

Hawai`i School of Professional Psychology Offers clinical psychology (MA, Psy D, Postdoctoral Respecialization Certificate); counseling psychology (Ed D); forensic psychology (MA); marriage and family therapy (MA); professional psychology (MA, MS, Ed D, Psy D, Certificate, Postdoctoral Respecialization Certificate); psychopharmacology (MS, Certificate); substance abuse counseling (Certificate).

ARGOSY UNIVERSITY, LOS ANGELES, Los Angeles, CA 90045
General Information Proprietary, coed, university.

GRADUATE UNITS

College of Business Offers accounting (DBA); corporate compliance (MBA); customized professional concentration (MBA, DBA); finance (MBA); fraud examination (MBA); global business sustainability (DBA); healthcare administration (MBA); information systems (DBA); information systems management (MBA); international business (MBA, DBA); management (MBA, MSM, DBA); marketing (MBA, DBA); organizational leadership (Ed D); public administration (MBA); sustainable management (MBA).

College of Education Offers community college executive leadership (Ed D); educational leadership (MA Ed, Ed D); instructional leadership (MA Ed, Ed D).

College of Health Sciences Offers public health (MPH).

College of Psychology and Behavioral Sciences Offers clinical psychology/marriage and family therapy (MA); counseling psychology (Ed D); counseling psychology/marriage and family therapy (MA); forensic psychology (MA).

ARGOSY UNIVERSITY, NORTHERN VIRGINIA, Arlington, VA 22209
General Information Proprietary, coed, university.

GRADUATE UNITS

American School of Professional Psychology Offers clinical psychology (MA, Psy D); community counseling (MA); counseling psychology (Ed D); counselor education and supervision (Ed D); forensic psychology (MA).

College of Business Offers accounting (DBA); customized professional concentration (MBA, DBA); finance (MBA); fraud examination (MBA); global business sustainability (DBA); healthcare administration (MBA); information systems (DBA); information systems management (MBA); international business (MBA, DBA, Certificate); management (MBA, MSM, DBA); marketing (MBA, DBA, Certificate); organizational leadership (Ed D); public administration (MBA); sustainable management (MBA).

College of Education Offers community college executive leadership (Ed D); educational leadership (MA Ed, Ed D, Ed S); instructional leadership (MA Ed, Ed D, Ed S).

College of Health Sciences Offers public health (MPH).

ARGOSY UNIVERSITY, ORANGE COUNTY, Orange, CA 92868
General Information Proprietary, coed, university.

GRADUATE UNITS

American School of Professional Psychology *Program availability:* Part-time, evening/weekend. Offers child and adolescent psychology (Psy D); counseling psychology (Ed D); forensic psychology (MA); marriage and family therapy (MA); professional psychology (MA, Ed D, Psy D); sport-exercise psychology (MA). Electronic applications accepted.

College of Business Offers accounting (DBA, Adv C); corporate compliance (MBA); customized professional concentration (MBA, DBA); finance (MBA, Certificate); fraud examination (MBA); global business sustainability (DBA); healthcare administration (MBA, Certificate); information systems (DBA, Adv C, Certificate); information systems management (MBA); international business (MBA, DBA, Adv C, Certificate); management (MBA, MSM, DBA, Adv C); marketing (MBA, DBA, Adv C, Certificate); organizational leadership (Ed D); public administration (MBA, Certificate); sustainable management (MBA).

College of Education Offers community college executive leadership (Ed D); educational leadership (MA Ed, Ed D); instructional leadership (MA Ed, Ed D).

College of Health Sciences Offers public health (MPH).

ARGOSY UNIVERSITY, PHOENIX, Phoenix, AZ 85021
General Information Proprietary, coed, university.

GRADUATE UNITS

Arizona School of Professional Psychology Offers clinical psychology (MA); forensic psychology (MA); industrial organizational psychology (MA); mental health counseling (MA); neuropsychology (Psy D); professional psychology (MA, Psy D); sport-exercise psychology (MA); sports-exercise psychology (Psy D).

College of Business Offers accounting (DBA); corporate compliance (MBA); customized professional concentration (MBA, DBA); finance (MBA); fraud examination (MBA); global business sustainability (DBA); healthcare administration (MBA); information systems (DBA); information systems management (MBA); international business (MBA, DBA); management (MBA, DBA); marketing (MBA, DBA); public administration (MBA); sustainable management (MBA).

College of Education Offers adult education and training (MA Ed); advanced educational administration (Ed D, Ed S); community college executive leadership (Ed D); educational administration (MA Ed); educational leadership (MA Ed, Ed D, Ed S); higher and postsecondary education (MA Ed); initial educational administration (Ed D, Ed S); school psychology (MA, Psy D); teaching and learning (MA Ed, Ed D, Ed S).

College of Health Sciences Offers public health (MPH).

ARGOSY UNIVERSITY, SEATTLE, Seattle, WA 98121
General Information Proprietary, coed, university.

GRADUATE UNITS

College of Business Offers accounting (DBA); corporate compliance (MBA); customized professional concentration (MBA, DBA); finance (MBA); fraud examination (MBA); global business sustainability (DBA); healthcare administration (MBA); information systems (DBA); information systems management (MBA); international business (MBA, DBA); management (MBA, MSM, DBA); marketing (MBA, DBA); organizational leadership (Ed D); public administration (MBA); sustainable management (MBA).

College of Education Offers adult education and training (MA Ed); community college executive leadership (Ed D); educational leadership (MA Ed, Ed D); higher and postsecondary education (MA Ed); instructional leadership (MA Ed, Ed D).

College of Health Sciences Offers public health (MPH).

College of Psychology and Behavioral Sciences Offers clinical psychology (MA, Psy D, Postdoctoral Respecialization Certificate); counseling psychology (MA, Ed D); psychology and behavioral sciences (MA, Ed D, Psy D, Postdoctoral Respecialization Certificate).

ARGOSY UNIVERSITY, TAMPA, Tampa, FL 33607

General Information Proprietary, coed, university.

GRADUATE UNITS

College of Business Offers accounting (DBA); corporate compliance (MBA); customized professional concentration (MBA, DBA); finance (MBA); fraud examination (MBA); global business sustainability (DBA); healthcare administration (MBA); information systems (DBA); information systems management (MBA); international business (MBA, DBA); management (MBA, MSM, DBA); marketing (MBA, DBA); organizational leadership (Ed D); public administration (MBA); sustainable management (MBA).

College of Education Offers community college executive leadership (Ed D); educational leadership (MA Ed, Ed D, Ed S); school counseling (MA); teaching and learning (MA Ed, Ed D, Ed S).

College of Health Sciences Offers public health (MPH).

Florida School of Professional Psychology Offers clinical psychology (MA, Psy D); counselor education and supervision (Ed D); industrial organizational psychology (MA); marriage and family therapy (MA); mental health counseling (MA).

ARGOSY UNIVERSITY, TWIN CITIES, Eagan, MN 55121

General Information Proprietary, coed, university.

GRADUATE UNITS

College of Business Offers accounting (DBA); customized professional concentration (MBA, DBA); finance (MBA); fraud examination (MBA); global business sustainability (DBA); healthcare administration (MBA); information systems (DBA); information systems management (MBA); international business (MBA, DBA); management (MBA, MSM, DBA); marketing (MBA, DBA); organizational leadership (Ed D); public administration (MBA); sustainable management (MBA).

College of Education Offers advanced educational administration (Ed D, Ed S); educational leadership (MA Ed, Ed D, Ed S); higher and postsecondary education (MA Ed); initial educational administration (Ed D, Ed S); instructional leadership (MA Ed, Ed D, Ed S).

College of Health Sciences Offers health services management (MS); public health (MPH).

Minnesota School of Professional Psychology Offers clinical psychology (MA, Psy D); forensic counseling (Post-Graduate Certificate); forensic psychology (MA); industrial organizational psychology (MA); marriage and family therapy (MA, DMFT).

ARIZONA SCHOOL OF ACUPUNCTURE AND ORIENTAL MEDICINE, Tucson, AZ 85712

General Information Proprietary, coed, graduate-only institution.

GRADUATE UNITS

Graduate Programs Offers acupuncture (M Ac, M Ac OM).

ARIZONA STATE UNIVERSITY AT THE TEMPE CAMPUS, Tempe, AZ 85287

General Information State-supported, coed, university. CGS member. *Graduate housing:* Room and/or apartments available to single students; on-campus housing not available to married students. *Research affiliation:* Arizona Public Service (electrical, computer and energy engineering), Banner Health (health, biomedical, and life sciences), Honeywell (mechanical and aerospace engineering), Mayo Clinic (healthcare, biomedical informatics), Raytheon Corporation (computer science and engineering), Translational Genomics Research Institute (TGen) (biomedicine).

GRADUATE UNITS

College of Health Solutions Offers audiology (Au D); behavioral health (DBH); biomedical informatics (MS, PhD); communication disorders (MS); health solutions (MS, Au D, DBH, PhD); speech and hearing science (PhD).

School of Nutrition and Health Promotion Offers clinical exercise physiology (MS); exercise and wellness (MS); nutrition (MS); obesity prevention and management (MS); physical activity, nutrition and wellness (PhD).

College of Liberal Arts and Sciences *Program availability:* Part-time, online learning. Offers American media and popular culture (MAS); applied behavior analysis (MS); applied linguistics (PhD); behavioral neuroscience (PhD); biochemistry (MS, PhD); chemistry (MS, PhD); clinical psychology (PhD); cognitive science (PhD); creative writing (MFA); developmental psychology (PhD); English (MA, PhD); film and media studies (MAS); liberal arts and sciences (MA, MAS, MFA, MLS, MNS, MS, MTESOL, MUEP, PSM, PSM, PhD, Graduate Certificate); liberal studies (MLS); linguistics (Graduate Certificate); nanoscience (PSM, PSM); physics (MNS, PhD); quantitative psychology (PhD); science and technology policy (MS); social psychology (PhD); teaching English to speakers of other languages (MTESOL); translation studies (Graduate Certificate). Electronic applications accepted.

Hugh Downs School of Human Communication *Program availability:* Evening/weekend. Offers communication (PhD). Electronic applications accepted.

School of Earth and Space Exploration Offers astrophysics (MS, PhD); exploration systems design (PhD); geological sciences (MS, PhD). PhD in exploration systems design is offered in collaboration with the Ira A. Fulton School of Engineering. Electronic applications accepted.

School of Geographical Sciences and Urban Planning Offers geographic information systems (MAS); geographical information science (Graduate Certificate); geography (MA, PhD); transportation systems (Graduate Certificate); urban and environmental planning (MUEP); urban planning (PhD). Electronic applications accepted.

School of Historical, Philosophical and Religious Studies *Program availability:* Part-time. Offers European history (MA, PhD); medieval studies (Graduate Certificate); North American history (MA, PhD); philosophy (MA, PhD); public history (MA); religious studies (MA, PhD); Renaissance studies (Graduate Certificate); scholarly publishing (Graduate Certificate). Electronic applications accepted.

School of Human Evolution and Social Change Offers anthropology (MA, PhD); applied mathematics for the life and social sciences (PhD); environmental social science (PhD); global health (MA, PhD); immigration studies (Graduate Certificate). Electronic applications accepted.

School of International Letters and Cultures Offers Asian languages and civilizations: Chinese (MA); Asian languages and civilizations: Japanese (MA); Chinese (MA, PhD); comparative literature (MA); cultural studies (PhD); French (MA); German (MA); Japanese (MA); language and culture (MA); linguistics (MA); literature (MA, PhD); literature and culture (MA); Spanish (MA, PhD). Electronic applications accepted.

School of Life Sciences Offers animal behavior (PhD); applied ethics (biomedical and health ethics) (MA); biology (MS, PhD); environmental life sciences (PhD); evolutionary biology (PhD); history and philosophy of science (PhD); human and social dimensions of science and technology (PhD); microbiology (PhD); molecular and cellular biology (PhD); neuroscience (PhD). Electronic applications accepted.

School of Mathematical and Statistical Sciences *Program availability:* Part-time. Offers applied mathematics (PhD); mathematics (MA, PhD); mathematics education (PhD); statistics (MS, PhD, Graduate Certificate). Electronic applications accepted.

School of Politics and Global Studies *Program availability:* Part-time. Offers political science (MA, PhD). Electronic applications accepted.

School of Social and Family Dynamics Offers family and human development (MS, PhD); infant-family practice (MAS); marriage and family therapy (MAS); sociology (MA, PhD). Electronic applications accepted.

School of Social Transformation *Program availability:* Part-time. Offers African studies (Graduate Certificate); gender studies (PhD, Graduate Certificate); justice studies (MS, PhD); social and cultural pedagogy (MA); socio-economic justice (Graduate Certificate). Electronic applications accepted.

College of Nursing and Health Innovation *Program availability:* Online learning. Offers advanced nursing practice (DNP); clinical research management (MS); community and public health practice (Graduate Certificate); family mental health nurse practitioner (Graduate Certificate); family nurse practitioner (Graduate Certificate); geriatric nursing (Graduate Certificate); healthcare innovation (MHI); nurse education in academic and practice settings (Graduate Certificate); nurse educator (MS); nursing and healthcare innovation (PhD). Electronic applications accepted.

College of Public Programs *Program availability:* Part-time, evening/weekend, online learning. Electronic applications accepted.

School of Community Resources and Development *Program availability:* Part-time, evening/weekend. Offers community resources and development (MS, PhD); nonprofit leadership and management (Graduate Certificate); nonprofit studies (MNpS); sustainable tourism (MAS). Electronic applications accepted.

School of Criminology and Criminal Justice *Program availability:* Part-time, evening/weekend, online learning. Offers corrections management (Graduate Certificate); criminal justice (MA); criminology and criminal justice (MS, PhD); law enforcement administration (Graduate Certificate). Electronic applications accepted.

School of Public Affairs *Program availability:* Part-time, evening/weekend. Offers emergency management and homeland security (MA); program evaluation (MS); public administration (MPA, PhD); public policy (MPP). Electronic applications accepted.

School of Social Work *Program availability:* Part-time. Offers advanced direct practice (MSW); assessment of integrative health modalities (Graduate Certificate); gerontology (Graduate Certificate); Latino cultural competency (Graduate Certificate); planning, administration and community practice (MSW); social work (PhD); trauma and bereavement (Graduate Certificate). Electronic applications accepted.

Graduate College *Program availability:* Part-time, evening/weekend, online learning. Offers human and social dimensions of science and technology (PhD); neuroscience (PhD). Electronic applications accepted.

Herberger Institute for Design and the Arts Offers design and the arts (M Arch, MA, MFA, MLA, MM, MS, MSD, MUD, DMA, PhD). Electronic applications accepted.

The Design School Offers architecture (M Arch); building design/built environment (MS); design (MSD); design, environment and the arts (PhD); digital culture (PhD); healthcare and healing environments (PhD); history, theory, and criticism (PhD); landscape architecture (MLA); urban design (MUD). Electronic applications accepted.

School of Art Offers art education (MA); art history (MA); ceramics (MFA); design, environment and the arts (PhD); drawing (MFA); fibers (MFA); intermedia (MFA); metals (MFA); museum studies (MFA); painting (MFA); printmaking (MFA); sculpture (MFA); wood (MFA). Electronic applications accepted.

School of Arts, Media and Engineering Offers media arts and sciences (PhD). Electronic applications accepted.

School of Film, Dance and Theatre Offers dance (MFA); interdisciplinary digital media and performance (MFA); theatre (MA, MFA, PhD). Electronic applications accepted.

School of Music Offers composition (MM, DMA); conducting (DMA); ethnomusicology (MA); interdisciplinary digital media/performance (DMA); music education (MM, PhD); music history and literature (MA); music therapy (MM); performance (MM, DMA). Electronic applications accepted.

Ira A. Fulton Schools of Engineering *Program availability:* Part-time, evening/weekend, online learning. Offers aerospace engineering (MS, PhD); chemical engineering (MS, PhD); construction (MS); embedded systems (M Eng); engineering (M Eng, MA, MCS, MS, MSE, PSM, PhD, Graduate Certificate); enterprise systems innovation and management (MSE); materials science and engineering (MS, PhD); mechanical engineering (MS, PhD); modeling and simulation (M Eng); quality and reliability engineering (M Eng); software engineering (MSE); solar energy engineering and commercialization (PSM); systems engineering (M Eng). Electronic applications accepted.

The Polytechnic School *Program availability:* Part-time, evening/weekend. Offers applied psychology (MS); aviation management and human factors (MS); environmental technology management (MS); global technology and development (MS); graphic information technology (MS); management of technology (MS); manufacturing engineering technology (MS); simulation, modeling, and applied cognitive science (PhD); technology and innovation (MS, PhD). Electronic applications accepted.

School of Biological and Health Systems Engineering *Program availability:* Part-time, evening/weekend. Offers biological design (PhD); biomedical engineering (MS, PhD). Electronic applications accepted.

School of Computing, Informatics, and Decision Systems Engineering *Program availability:* Part-time, evening/weekend, online learning. Offers computer engineering (MS, PhD); computer science (MCS, MS, PhD); industrial engineering (MS, PhD); software engineering (MS). Electronic applications accepted.

School of Electrical, Computer and Energy Engineering *Program availability:* Part-time, evening/weekend, online learning. Offers electrical engineering (MS, MSE, PhD); nuclear power generation (Graduate Certificate). Electronic applications accepted.

School of Sustainable Engineering and the Built Environment *Program availability:* Part-time, evening/weekend, online learning. Offers civil, environmental and sustainable engineering (MS, MSE, PhD); construction engineering (MSE); construction management (MS, PhD). Electronic applications accepted.

Mary Lou Fulton Teachers College *Program availability:* Part-time, evening/weekend, online learning. Offers autism spectrum disorder (Graduate Certificate); curriculum and instruction (M Ed, MA); education (M Ed, MA, MC, MPE, Ed D, PhD, Graduate Certificate); educational leadership (M Ed); educational policy and evaluation (PhD); educational technology (M Ed); elementary education (M Ed); higher and post-secondary education (M Ed); instructional design and performance improvement (Graduate Certificate); leadership and innovation (Ed D); online teaching for grades K-12 (Graduate Certificate); physical education (MPE); secondary education (M Ed); special education (M Ed). Electronic applications accepted.

New College of Interdisciplinary Arts and Sciences *Program availability:* Part-time, evening/weekend. Offers applied ethics and the professions (MA); communication studies (MA); interdisciplinary studies (MA); psychology (MS); social justice and human rights (MA). Electronic applications accepted.

Sandra Day O'Connor College of Law Students: 812 full-time (372 women); includes 201 minority (16 Black or African American, non-Hispanic/Latino; 15 American Indian or Alaska Native, non-Hispanic/Latino; 37 Asian, non-Hispanic/Latino; 97 Hispanic/Latino; 3 Native Hawaiian or other Pacific Islander, non-Hispanic/Latino; 33 Two or more races, non-Hispanic/Latino), 16 international. Average age 28. 3,363 applicants, 34% accepted, 271 enrolled. *Faculty:* 62 full-time (26 women), 146 part-time/adjunct (40 women). Expenses: Contact institution. *Financial support:* In 2018–19, 579 students received support. Institutionally sponsored loans and scholarships/grants available. Financial award application deadline: 3/15; financial award applicants required to submit FAFSA. In 2018, 131 master's, 276 doctorates awarded. *Program availability:* 100% online. Offers biotechnology and genomics (LL M); law (JD); legal studies (MLS); patent practice (MLS); sports law and business (MSLB); tribal policy, law and government (LL M). JD/MD offered jointly with Mayo Medical School. *Application deadline:* For fall admission, 3/1 priority date for domestic and international students. Applications are processed on a rolling basis. *Application fee:* $0. Electronic applications accepted. *Application Contact:* Chitra Damania, Director, 480-965-1474, Fax: 480-727-7930, E-mail: law.admissions@asu.edu. *Dean/Professor,* Douglas Sylvester, 480-965-6188, Fax: 480-965-6521, E-mail: douglas.sylvester@asu.edu.

School of Letters and Sciences *Program availability:* Part-time, evening/weekend, online learning. Offers biomedical and health ethics (MA); counseling (MC); counseling psychology (PhD); ethics and emerging technologies (MA); letters and sciences (MA, MC, PhD); public administration, policy and ethics (MA); science, technology and ethics (MA). Electronic applications accepted.

School of Sustainability *Program availability:* Part-time, evening/weekend. Offers sustainability (MA, MS, PhD); sustainable technology and management (Graduate Certificate). Electronic applications accepted.

Thunderbird School of Global Management *Program availability:* Online learning. Offers global affairs and management (MA); global management (MGM).

Walter Cronkite School of Journalism and Mass Communication Offers journalism and mass communication (PhD); mass communication (MMC). Electronic applications accepted.

W. P. Carey School of Business *Program availability:* Part-time, evening/weekend, online learning. Offers business (M Acc, M Tax, MBA, MRED, MS, PhD, Graduate Certificate); business administration (PhD); economics (PhD); entrepreneurship (MBA); finance (MBA); health sector management (MBA); information management (MS); international business (MBA); leadership (MBA); marketing (MBA); organizational behavior (PhD); real estate development (MRED); strategic management (PhD); supply chain management (MBA, PhD). Electronic applications accepted.

Morrison School of Agribusiness *Program availability:* Part-time, evening/weekend. Offers agribusiness (PhD). Electronic applications accepted.

School of Accountancy *Program availability:* Part-time, evening/weekend. Offers accountancy (M Acc, M Tax); business administration (PhD). Electronic applications accepted.

ARKANSAS COLLEGES OF HEALTH EDUCATION, Fort Smith, AR 72916

General Information Independent, coed, graduate-only institution.

GRADUATE UNITS

Arkansas College of Osteopathic Medicine Offers osteopathic medicine (DO).

Program in Biomedicine Offers biomedicine (MS).

ARKANSAS STATE UNIVERSITY, State University, AR 72467

General Information State-supported, coed, comprehensive institution. CGS member. *Graduate housing:* Rooms and/or apartments available on a first-come, first-served basis to single and married students. *Research affiliation:* Oak Ridge Associated Universities (scientific research and education development), Applied Biotechnologies Institute (recombinant proteins), Biostrategies, LLC (biotechnology), Infinite Enzymes (plant biotechnology), Nature West (physical, engineering, and life sciences), GeneCoMe (biotechnology).

GRADUATE UNITS

Graduate School *Program availability:* Part-time, online learning. Electronic applications accepted.

College of Agriculture and Technology *Program availability:* Part-time. Offers agricultural education (SCCT); agriculture (MSA); vocational-technical administration (SCCT). Electronic applications accepted.

College of Business *Program availability:* Part-time, evening/weekend. Offers accountancy (M Acc); business (M Acc, MBA, SCCT); business administration (MBA); business administration education (SCCT); business technology education (SCCT). Electronic applications accepted.

College of Education and Behavioral Science *Program availability:* Part-time, online learning. Offers clinical mental health counseling (Graduate Certificate); college student personnel services (MS); community college administration (SCCT); curriculum and instruction (MSE); dyslexia therapy (Graduate Certificate); early childhood education (MSE); early childhood services (MS); education and behavioral science (MAT, MRC, MS, MSE, Ed D, Ed S, Graduate Certificate, SCCT); educational leadership (MSE, Ed D, Ed S); educational theory and practice (MSE); exercise science (MS); middle level education (MAT, MSE); physical education (MSE, SCCT); psychological science (MS); psychology and counseling (Ed S); reading (MSE, Ed S); rehabilitation counseling (MRC); school counseling (MSE); special education - gifted, talented, and creative (MSE); special education - instructional specialist grades 4-12 (MSE); special education - instructional specialist grades P-4 (MSE); special

education, K-12 (MSE); sports administration (MS); student affairs (Graduate Certificate). Electronic applications accepted.

College of Engineering *Program availability:* Part-time. Offers engineering (MS Eng); engineering management (MEM). Electronic applications accepted.

College of Fine Arts *Program availability:* Part-time. Offers fine arts (MM, MME, SCCT); music education (MME, SCCT); music performance (MM). Electronic applications accepted.

College of Humanities and Social Sciences *Program availability:* Part-time. Offers criminal justice (MA); English (MA); English education (MSE, SCCT); heritage studies (MA, PhD); history (MA); history education (SCCT); humanities and social sciences (MA, MPA, MSE, PhD, SCCT); political science (MA); political science education (SCCT); public administration (MPA); social science education (MSE); sociology (MA); sociology education (SCCT). Electronic applications accepted.

College of Media and Communication *Program availability:* Part-time. Offers communication studies (MA, SCCT); health communications (Graduate Certificate); mass communications (MSMC); media and communication (MA, MSMC, Graduate Certificate, SCCT). Electronic applications accepted.

College of Nursing and Health Professions *Program availability:* Part-time. Offers addiction studies (Graduate Certificate); aging studies (Graduate Certificate); communication disorders (MCD); disaster preparedness and emergency management (MS); dyslexia therapy (Graduate Certificate); health care management (Graduate Certificate); health sciences (MS); health sciences education (Graduate Certificate); healthcare emergency management (Graduate Certificate); nurse anesthesia (MSN); nursing (MSN); nursing and health professions (MCD, MS, MSN, MSW, DNP, DOT, DPT, Graduate Certificate); nursing practice (DNP); occupational therapy (DOT); physical therapy (DPT); social work (MSW). Electronic applications accepted.

College of Sciences and Mathematics *Program availability:* Part-time. Offers biological sciences (MA); biology (MS); biology education (MSE, SCCT); biotechnology (PSM); chemistry (MS); chemistry education (MSE, SCCT); computer science (MS); environmental sciences (MS, PhD); mathematics (MS); mathematics education (MSE); molecular biosciences (MS, PhD); sciences and mathematics (MA, MS, MSE, PSM, PhD, SCCT). Electronic applications accepted.

ARKANSAS TECH UNIVERSITY, Russellville, AR 72801

General Information State-supported, coed, comprehensive institution. CGS member. *Enrollment:* 12,101 graduate, professional, and undergraduate students; 187 full-time matriculated graduate/professional students (98 women), 728 part-time matriculated graduate/professional students (542 women). *Enrollment by degree level:* 836 master's, 39 doctoral, 40 other advanced degrees. *Graduate faculty:* 84 full-time (35 women), 15 part-time/adjunct (11 women). *International tuition:* $13,632 full-time. *Tuition, area resident:* Full-time $6816; part-time $284 per credit hour. Tuition, state resident: full-time $6816; part-time $284 per credit hour. Tuition, nonresident: full-time $13,632; part-time $568 per credit hour. *Required fees:* $457.50 per semester. Tuition and fees vary according to course load and degree level. *Graduate housing:* Room and/or apartments available on a first-come, first-served basis to single students; on-campus housing not available to married students. *Typical cost:* $7870 (including board). Room and board charges vary according to board plan and housing facility selected. Housing application deadline: 8/1. *Student services:* Campus employment opportunities, campus safety program, career counseling, exercise/wellness program, free psychological counseling, international student services, low-cost health insurance, multicultural affairs office, services for students with disabilities, teacher training. *Library facilities:* Ross Pendergraft Library and Technology Center. *Collection:* Books: 154,336 (physical), 386,793 (digital/electronic); Serial titles: 5,478 (physical), 73,489 (digital/electronic); Databases: 279. Students can reserve study rooms.

Computer facilities: Computer purchase and lease plans are available. 1,190 computers available on campus for general student use. A campuswide network can be accessed from student residence rooms and from off campus. Online class registration is available.
Website: http://www.atu.edu/

General Application Contact: Dr. Jeff Robertson, Interim Dean of Graduate College, 479-968-0398, Fax: 479-964-0542, E-mail: gradcollege@atu.edu.

GRADUATE UNITS

College of Arts and Humanities Students: 34 full-time (21 women), 150 part-time (108 women); includes 38 minority (10 Black or African American, non-Hispanic/Latino; 4 Asian, non-Hispanic/Latino; 20 Hispanic/Latino; 4 Two or more races, non-Hispanic/Latino), 11 international. Average age 34. Expenses: Contact institution. *Financial support:* In 2018–19, research assistantships with full and partial tuition reimbursements (averaging $4,800 per year), teaching assistantships with full and partial tuition reimbursements (averaging $4,800 per year) were awarded; career-related internships or fieldwork, Federal Work-Study, scholarships/grants, health care benefits, and unspecified assistantships also available. Support available to part-time students. Financial award application deadline: 4/15; financial award applicants required to submit FAFSA. In 2018, 75 master's awarded. *Program availability:* Part-time, 100% online, blended/hybrid learning. Offers applied sociology (MS); English (M Ed, MA); history (MA); liberal arts (MLA); multi-media journalism (MA); psychology (MA); teaching English as a second language (MA). *Application deadline:* For fall admission, 3/1 priority date for domestic students, 5/1 priority date for international students; for spring admission, 10/1 priority date for domestic and international students. Applications are processed on a rolling basis. *Application fee:* $40 ($90 for international students). Electronic applications accepted. *Application Contact:* Dr. Jeff Robertson, Interim Dean of Graduate College, 479-968-0398, Fax: 479-964-0542, E-mail: gradcollege@atu.edu. *Dean,* Dr. Wayne Powell, 479-968-0274, Fax: 479-964-0812, E-mail: wpowell4@atu.edu.

College of Business Students: 6 full-time (1 woman), 43 part-time (29 women); includes 7 minority (3 Black or African American, non-Hispanic/Latino; 1 Asian, non-Hispanic/Latino; 1 Hispanic/Latino; 2 Two or more races, non-Hispanic/Latino). Average age 32. Expenses: Contact institution. *Financial support:* In 2018–19, research assistantships with full and partial tuition reimbursements (averaging $4,800 per year), teaching assistantships with full and partial tuition reimbursements (averaging $4,800 per year) were awarded; career-related internships or fieldwork, Federal Work-Study, scholarships/grants, health care benefits, and unspecified assistantships also available. Support available to part-time students. Financial award application deadline: 4/15; financial award applicants required to submit FAFSA. In 2018, 8 master's awarded. *Program availability:* Part-time, evening/weekend, 100% online, blended/hybrid learning. Offers business (MBA). *Application deadline:* For fall admission, 3/1 priority date for domestic students, 5/1 priority date for international students; for spring admission, 10/1 priority date for domestic and international students. Applications are processed on a rolling basis. *Application fee:* $40 ($90 for international students). Electronic applications accepted. *Application Contact:* Dr. Jeff Robertson, Interim Dean of Graduate College, 479-968-0398, Fax: 479-964-0542, E-mail: gradcollege@atu.edu. *Interim Dean,* Dr. Kevin Mason, 479-968-0498, E-mail: kmason@atu.edu.

College of Education Students: 90 full-time (52 women), 450 part-time (359 women); includes 100 minority (63 Black or African American, non-Hispanic/Latino; 6 American Indian or Alaska Native, non-Hispanic/Latino; 1 Asian, non-Hispanic/Latino; 15 Hispanic/Latino; 15 Two or more races, non-Hispanic/Latino), 4 international. Average age 34. Expenses: Contact institution. *Financial support:* In 2018–19, research assistantships with full and partial tuition reimbursements (averaging $4,800 per year), teaching assistantships with full and partial tuition reimbursements (averaging $4,800 per year) were awarded; career-related internships or fieldwork, Federal Work-Study, scholarships/grants, health care benefits, and unspecified assistantships also available. Support available to part-time students. Financial award application deadline: 4/15; financial award applicants required to submit FAFSA. In 2018, 130 master's, 14 doctorates, 1 other advanced degree awarded. *Program availability:* Part-time, evening/weekend, 100% online, blended/hybrid learning. Offers college student personnel (MS); educational leadership (M Ed, Ed S); instructional technology (M Ed); school counseling and leadership (M Ed); school leadership (Ed D); special education K-12 (M Ed); strength and conditioning studies (MS); teaching (MAT); teaching, learning, and leadership (M Ed). *Application deadline:* For fall admission, 3/1 priority date for domestic students, 5/1 priority date for international students; for spring admission, 10/1 priority date for domestic and international students. Applications are processed on a rolling basis. *Application fee:* $40 ($90 for international students). Electronic applications accepted. *Application Contact:* Dr. Jeff Robertson, Interim Dean of Graduate College, 479-968-0398, Fax: 479-964-0542, E-mail: gradcollege@atu.edu. *Dean,* Dr. Linda Bean, 479-964-3217, E-mail: lbean@atu.edu.

College of Engineering and Applied Sciences Students: 46 full-time (17 women), 39 part-time (16 women); includes 12 minority (7 Black or African American, non-Hispanic/Latino; 1 American Indian or Alaska Native, non-Hispanic/Latino; 1 Asian, non-Hispanic/Latino; 2 Hispanic/Latino; 1 Two or more races, non-Hispanic/Latino), 29 international. Average age 31. Expenses: Contact institution. *Financial support:* In 2018–19, research assistantships with full and partial tuition reimbursements (averaging $4,800 per year), teaching assistantships with full and partial tuition reimbursements (averaging $4,800 per year) were awarded; career-related internships or fieldwork, Federal Work-Study, scholarships/grants, health care benefits, and unspecified assistantships also available. Support available to part-time students. Financial award application deadline: 4/15; financial award applicants required to submit FAFSA. In 2018, 54 master's awarded. *Program availability:* Part-time, evening/weekend, 100% online, blended/hybrid learning. Offers electrical engineering (M Engr); emergency management (MS); information technology (MS); mechanical engineering (M Engr). *Application deadline:* For fall admission, 3/1 priority date for domestic students, 5/1 priority date for international students; for spring admission, 10/1 priority date for domestic and international students. Applications are processed on a rolling basis. *Application fee:* $40 ($90 for international students). Electronic applications accepted. *Application Contact:* Dr. Jeff Robertson, Interim Dean of Graduate College, 479-968-0398, Fax: 479-964-0542, E-mail: gradcollege@atu.edu. *Dean,* Dr. Judy Cezeaux, 479-968-0353, E-mail: jcezeaux@atu.edu.

College of Natural and Health Sciences Students: 11 full-time (7 women), 46 part-time (30 women); includes 10 minority (9 Black or African American, non-Hispanic/Latino; 1 Asian, non-Hispanic/Latino), 1 international. Average age 35. Expenses: Contact institution. *Financial support:* In 2018–19, research assistantships with full and partial tuition reimbursements (averaging $4,800 per year), teaching assistantships with full and partial tuition reimbursements (averaging $4,800 per year) were awarded; career-related internships or fieldwork, Federal Work-Study, scholarships/grants, health care benefits, and unspecified assistantships also available. Support available to part-time students. Financial award application deadline: 4/15; financial award applicants required to submit FAFSA. In 2018, 22 master's awarded. *Program availability:* Part-time, evening/weekend, 100% online, blended/hybrid learning. Offers fisheries and wildlife biology (MS); health informatics (MS); nursing (MSN). *Application deadline:* For fall admission, 3/1 priority date for domestic students, 5/1 priority date for international students; for spring admission, 10/1 priority date for domestic and international students. Applications are processed on a rolling basis. *Application fee:* $40 ($90 for international students). Electronic applications accepted. *Application Contact:* Dr. Jeff Robertson, Interim Dean of Graduate College, 479-968-0398, Fax: 479-964-0542, E-mail: gradcollege@atu.edu. *Dean,* Dr. Jeff Robertson, 479-968-0498, E-mail: jrobertson@atu.edu.

ARLINGTON BAPTIST UNIVERSITY, Arlington, TX 76012-3425

General Information Independent-religious, coed, comprehensive institution.

GRADUATE UNITS

Program in Biblical and Theological Studies Offers Biblical and theological studies (MA). Electronic applications accepted.

Program in Education Offers curriculum and instruction (M Ed); educational leadership (M Ed).

ART ACADEMY OF CINCINNATI, Cincinnati, OH 45202

General Information Independent, coed, comprehensive institution. *Graduate housing:* Rooms and/or apartments available on a first-come, first-served basis to single and married students. Housing application deadline: 5/1.

GRADUATE UNITS

Program in Art Education *Program availability:* Part-time. Offers art education (MAAE). Offered during summer only. Electronic applications accepted.

ARTCENTER COLLEGE OF DESIGN, Pasadena, CA 91103

General Information Independent, coed, comprehensive institution. *Graduate housing:* On-campus housing not available.

GRADUATE UNITS

Graduate Art Program Offers art (MFA).

Graduate Environmental Design Program Offers furniture and fixtures (MS); spatial experience (MS).

Graduate Film Program Offers film (MFA).

Graduate Graphic Design Program Offers graphic design (MFA).

Graduate Industrial Design Program Offers industrial design (MS).

Graduate Media Design Practices Program Offers media design practices (MFA).

Graduate Transportation Systems and Design Program Offers transportation systems (MS).

THE ART INSTITUTE OF DALLAS, A BRANCH OF MIAMI INTERNATIONAL UNIVERSITY OF ART & DESIGN, Dallas, TX 75231-5993

General Information Proprietary, coed, comprehensive institution.

GRADUATE UNITS

Program in Design and Media Management Offers design and media management (MA).

ASBURY THEOLOGICAL SEMINARY, Wilmore, KY 40390-1199

General Information Independent-religious, coed, primarily men, graduate-only institution. *Graduate housing:* Rooms and/or apartments available on a first-come, first-served basis to single and married students. Housing application deadline: 8/15.

GRADUATE UNITS

Graduate and Professional Programs *Program availability:* Part-time, online learning. Offers theology (M Div, MA, MAAS, MACE, MACL, MACM, MACP, MAMFC, MAMHC, MAPC, MASF, MAYM, Th M, D Min, PhD, Certificate). Electronic applications accepted.

ASBURY UNIVERSITY, Wilmore, KY 40390-1198

General Information Independent-religious, coed, comprehensive institution. *Graduate housing:* On-campus housing not available.

GRADUATE UNITS

School of Graduate and Professional Studies *Program availability:* Part-time. Offers biology: alternative certificate (MA Ed); chemistry: alternative certificate (MA Ed); child and family services (MSW); English (MA Ed); English as a second language (MA Ed); ESL (MA Ed); French (MA Ed); Latin: alternative certificate (MA Ed); mathematics: alternative certificate (MA Ed); reading/writing endorsement (MA Ed); social studies (MA Ed); social work (MSW); Spanish (MA Ed); special education (MA Ed); special education: alternative certificate (MA Ed); teacher as leader endorsement (MA Ed). Electronic applications accepted.

ASHLAND THEOLOGICAL SEMINARY, Ashland, OH 44805

General Information Independent-religious, coed, graduate-only institution. *Graduate housing:* Rooms and/or apartments available on a first-come, first-served basis to single and married students. Housing application deadline: 8/30. *Research affiliation:* Tel Gezer Excavation and Publication Program (archaeological studies), Tyndale House, Cambridge England (faculty study and research).

GRADUATE UNITS

Graduate Programs *Program availability:* Part-time. Offers Biblical studies (MA); Christian ministries (MACM); clinical mental health counseling (MA); counseling (MAC); historical and theological studies (MA); ministry (D Min); pastoral ministry (M Div). MAC program offered in Detroit, MI. Electronic applications accepted.

ASHLAND UNIVERSITY, Ashland, OH 44805-3702

General Information Independent-religious, coed, comprehensive institution. *Enrollment:* 1,111 full-time matriculated graduate/professional students (634 women), 880 part-time matriculated graduate/professional students (531 women). *Enrollment by degree level:* 1,520 master's, 116 doctoral, 355 other advanced degrees. *Graduate faculty:* 53 full-time (29 women), 133 part-time/adjunct (67 women). *Tuition:* Full-time $6660; part-time $3330 per credit hour. *Required fees:* $360; $180 per credit hour. Tuition and fees vary according to program. *Graduate housing:* Room and/or apartments available on a first-come, first-served basis to single students; on-campus housing not available to married students. Typical cost: $6432 per year ($11,162 including board). Room and board charges vary according to board plan, campus/location and housing facility selected. Housing application deadline: 9/5. *Student services:* Campus employment opportunities, campus safety program, career counseling, exercise/wellness program, free psychological counseling, international student services, low-cost health insurance, multicultural affairs office, services for students with disabilities, teacher training, writing training. *Library facilities:* Ashland University Library plus 2 others. *Collection:* Books: 223,607 (physical), 255,789 (digital/electronic); Serial titles: 1,070 (physical), 114,001 (digital/electronic); Databases: 200. Weekly public service hours: 102; students can reserve study rooms.

Computer facilities: Computer purchase and lease plans are available. 760 computers available on campus for general student use. A campuswide network can be accessed from student residence rooms and from off campus. Online class registration is available.
Website: http://www.ashland.edu/

General Application Contact: Bernie Bannin, Director, Graduate, Online, and Adult Admissions, 419-289-5291, E-mail: grad-admissions@ashland.edu.

GRADUATE UNITS

College of Arts and Sciences Offers American history and government (MAHG); arts and sciences (MA, MAHG, MFA); communication (MA); creative writing (MFA). Electronic applications accepted.

Dauch College of Business and Economics *Program availability:* Part-time, evening/weekend, 100% online, blended/hybrid learning. Offers accounting (MBA); business analytics (MBA); entrepreneurship (MBA); financial management (MBA); global management (MBA); health care management and leadership (MBA); human resource management (MBA); human resources (MBA); management information systems (MBA); project management (MBA); sport management (MBA); supply chain management (MBA). Electronic applications accepted.

Dwight Schar College of Education *Program availability:* Part-time. Offers education (M Ed, Ed D); educational leadership and administration (M Ed); executive leadership studies (Ed D); leadership studies (Ed D). Electronic applications accepted.

Dwight Schar College of Nursing and Health Sciences *Program availability:* 100% online, blended/hybrid learning. Offers applied exercise science (MS); family nurse practitioner (DNP); nursing and health sciences (MS, DNP). Electronic applications accepted.

ASHWORTH COLLEGE, Norcross, GA 30092

General Information Proprietary, coed, comprehensive institution.

GRADUATE UNITS

Graduate Programs Offers business administration (MBA); criminal justice (MS); health care administration (MBA, MS); human resource management (MBA, MS); international business (MBA); management (MS); marketing (MBA, MS).

ASPEN UNIVERSITY, Denver, CO 80246-1930

General Information Independent, coed, comprehensive institution. *Graduate housing:* On-campus housing not available.

GRADUATE UNITS

Program in Business Administration Students: 556 part-time. Average age 37. *Faculty:* 16 full-time (15 women), 240 part-time/adjunct (120 women). Expenses: Contact institution. *Financial support:* Applicants required to submit FAFSA. *Program availability:* Part-time, evening/weekend, online only, 100% online. Offers business administration (MBA); finance (MBA); information management (MBA); project management (MBA, Certificate). *Application deadline:* Applications are processed on a rolling basis. *Application fee:* $0. Electronic applications accepted. *Application Contact:* Enrollment Advisor, 800-373-7814. *Provost,* Dr. Kevin Thrasher, 602-5706708, E-mail: kevin.thrasher@aspen.edu.

Program in Information Technology Average age 37. *Faculty:* 10 part-time/adjunct (5 women). Expenses: Contact institution. *Financial support:* Applicants required to submit FAFSA. *Program availability:* Part-time, evening/weekend, online only, 100% online. Offers information technology (MS, Certificate). *Application deadline:* Applications are processed on a rolling basis. *Application fee:* $0. Electronic applications accepted. *Application Contact:* Enrollment Advisor, 800-373-7814. *Provost,* Kevin Thrasher, 602-5706708, E-mail: kevin.thrasher@aspen.edu.

Program in Nursing *Faculty:* 15 full-time (all women), 240 part-time/adjunct (120 women). Expenses: Contact institution. *Financial support:* Applicants required to submit FAFSA. *Program availability:* Part-time, evening/weekend, online only, 100% online. Offers forensic nursing (MSN); informatics (MSN); nursing (MSN); nursing administration and management (MSN); nursing education (MSN); public health (MSN). *Application deadline:* Applications are processed on a rolling basis. *Application fee:* $0. Electronic applications accepted. *Application Contact:* Enrollment Advisor, 800-373-7814.

Programs in Information Management Students: 27 part-time. Average age 37. *Faculty:* 10 part-time/adjunct (5 women). Expenses: Contact institution. *Financial support:* Applicants required to submit FAFSA. In 2018, 6 master's awarded. *Program availability:* Part-time, evening/weekend, online only, 100% online. Offers information management (MS); information systems (Certificate). *Application deadline:* Applications are processed on a rolling basis. *Application fee:* $0. Electronic applications accepted. *Application Contact:* Enrollment Advisor, 800-373-7814, E-mail: kevin.thrasher@aspen.edu.

ASSEMBLIES OF GOD THEOLOGICAL SEMINARY, Springfield, MO 65802

General Information Independent-religious, coed, graduate-only institution. *Graduate housing:* On-campus housing not available.

GRADUATE UNITS

Graduate and Professional Programs *Program availability:* Part-time, evening/weekend, 100% online. Offers Biblical interpretation and theology (PhD); Christian ministries (MA); divinity (M Div); intercultural studies (MA, PhD); leadership and ministry (MLM); ministry (D Min); missiology (DAIS); pastoral studies (MPL); theological studies (MA, Th M). Electronic applications accepted.

ASSUMPTION COLLEGE, Worcester, MA 01609-1296

General Information Independent-religious, coed, comprehensive institution. *Graduate housing:* On-campus housing not available.

GRADUATE UNITS

Addiction Counseling Program *Program availability:* Part-time, evening/weekend. Offers addiction counseling (CGS). Electronic applications accepted.

Applied Behavior Analysis Program *Program availability:* Part-time, evening/weekend. Offers applied behavior analysis (MA, CAGS). Electronic applications accepted.

Business Studies Program *Program availability:* Part-time, evening/weekend. Offers accounting (MBA); business studies (CAGS); finance/economics (MBA); human resources (MBA); international business (MBA); management (MBA); marketing (MBA); nonprofit leadership (MBA). Electronic applications accepted.

Clinical Counseling Psychology Program *Program availability:* Part-time, evening/weekend. Offers child and family interventions (MA); clinical counseling psychology (CAGS); cognitive-behavioral therapies (MA). Electronic applications accepted.

Health Advocacy Program *Program availability:* Part-time, evening/weekend, online only, 100% online. Offers health advocacy (MA, Professional Certificate). Electronic applications accepted.

Healthcare Management Program *Program availability:* Part-time, evening/weekend, online only, 100% online, blended/hybrid learning. Offers healthcare management (MBA, CAGS, CGS). Electronic applications accepted.

Rehabilitation Counseling Program *Program availability:* Part-time, evening/weekend, blended/hybrid learning. Offers rehabilitation counseling (MA, CAGS). Electronic applications accepted.

Resiliency in the Helping Professions Program *Program availability:* Part-time, evening/weekend. Offers resiliency in the helping professions (CAGS, CGS).

School Counseling Program *Program availability:* Part-time, evening/weekend. Offers school counseling (MA, CAGS). Electronic applications accepted.

Special Education Program *Program availability:* Part-time, evening/weekend. Offers positive behavior support (CAGS); special education (MA). Electronic applications accepted.

Special Ops: Service Members, Veterans, and their Families Program

ATHABASCA UNIVERSITY, Athabasca, AB T9S 3A3, Canada

General Information Province-supported, coed, comprehensive institution. *Enrollment:* 4,527 part-time matriculated graduate/professional students (3,397 women). *Enrollment by degree level:* 3,754 master's, 84 doctoral, 689 other advanced degrees. *Graduate faculty:* 184 full-time (83 women), 66 part-time/adjunct (40 women). *Graduate housing:* On-campus housing not available. *Student services:* International student services, services for students with disabilities, writing training. *Library facilities:* Athabasca University Library.

Computer facilities: Computer purchase and lease plans are available. 28 computers available on campus for general student use. A campuswide network can be accessed. Online class registration is available.
Website: http://www.athabascau.ca/

General Application Contact: Information Contact, 800-788-9041, Fax: 780-675-6437.

GRADUATE UNITS

Centre for Distance Education *Program availability:* Part-time, online learning. Offers distance education (MDE, Ed D); distance education technology (Advanced Diploma). Electronic applications accepted.

Centre for Interdisciplinary Studies *Program availability:* Part-time, evening/weekend, online learning. Offers adult education (MA); community studies (MA); cultural studies (MA); educational studies (MA); global change (MA); heritage resource management (Postbaccalaureate Certificate); legislative drafting (Postbaccalaureate Certificate); work, organization, and leadership (MA). Electronic applications accepted.

Faculty of Business *Program availability:* Part-time, evening/weekend, online learning. Offers business administration (MBA); information technology management (MBA); innovative management (DBA); management (GDM); project management (MBA, GDM). Electronic applications accepted.

Faculty of Health Disciplines *Program availability:* Part-time, online learning. Offers advanced nursing practice (MN, Advanced Diploma); generalist (MN); health studies (MHS). Electronic applications accepted.

Faculty of Science and Technology *Program availability:* Part-time, online learning. Offers architecture (Postgraduate Diploma); information systems (M Sc). Electronic applications accepted.

Program in Counseling Offers applied psychology (Post Master's Certificate); art therapy (MC); career counseling (MC); counseling (Advanced Certificate); counseling psychology (MC); school counseling (MC).

THE ATHENAEUM OF OHIO, Cincinnati, OH 45230-5900

General Information Independent-religious, coed, graduate-only institution. *Graduate housing:* On-campus housing not available.

GRADUATE UNITS

Graduate Programs *Program availability:* Part-time, evening/weekend. Offers theology (M Div, MA, MA Th, MABS, Certificate).

ATHENS STATE UNIVERSITY, Athens, AL 35611

General Information State-supported, coed, upper-level institution. *Graduate housing:* On-campus housing not available.

GRADUATE UNITS

Graduate Programs Offers career and technical education (M Ed); global logistics and supply chain management (MS); religious studies (MA).

ATLANTA'S JOHN MARSHALL LAW SCHOOL, Atlanta, GA 30309

General Information Private, coed, graduate-only institution.

GRADUATE UNITS

JD and LL M Programs *Program availability:* Part-time, evening/weekend, online learning. Offers American legal studies (LL M); employment law (LL M); law (JD). Electronic applications accepted.

ATLANTIC INSTITUTE OF ORIENTAL MEDICINE, Fort Lauderdale, FL 33301

General Information Independent, coed, graduate-only institution. *Graduate housing:* On-campus housing not available.

GRADUATE UNITS

Graduate Program *Program availability:* Evening/weekend. Offers Oriental medicine (MS, DAOM).

ATLANTIC SCHOOL OF THEOLOGY, Halifax, NS B3H 3B5, Canada

General Information Independent, coed, graduate-only institution. *Graduate housing:* Rooms and/or apartments available on a first-come, first-served basis to single and married students. Housing application deadline: 6/1.

GRADUATE UNITS

Graduate and Professional Programs *Program availability:* Part-time, online learning. Offers ministry (M Div); theological studies (Graduate Certificate).

ATLANTIC UNIVERSITY, Virginia Beach, VA 23451-2061

General Information Independent, coed, primarily women, graduate-only institution. *Graduate housing:* On-campus housing not available.

GRADUATE UNITS

Program in Integrated Imagery: Regression Hypnosis *Program availability:* Blended/hybrid learning. Offers integrated imagery: regression hypnosis (Graduate Certificate). Electronic applications accepted.

Program in Mindful Leadership *Program availability:* Online learning. Offers global leadership (MA).

Program in Transpersonal Psychology *Program availability:* Part-time, evening/weekend, online learning. Offers applied spirituality (MA); consciousness (MA); creativity (MA); general studies (MA); leadership and conflict transformation (MA). Electronic applications accepted.

Spiritual Guidance Mentor Program *Program availability:* Online learning. Offers spiritual guidance mentor (Certificate). Electronic applications accepted.

ATLANTIC UNIVERSITY COLLEGE, Guaynabo, PR 00970

General Information Independent, coed, comprehensive institution.

GRADUATE UNITS

Program in Graphic Arts *Program availability:* Part-time. Offers digital graphic design (MGD).

ATLANTIS UNIVERSITY, Miami, FL 33132

General Information Proprietary, coed, comprehensive institution.

GRADUATE UNITS

School of Business Offers business (MBA, DBA).

School of Computer Science and Information Technology Offers information technology (MIT).

School of Engineering Offers computer engineering (MS).

School of Health Care Offers healthcare management (MS).

A.T. STILL UNIVERSITY, Kirksville, MO 63501

General Information Independent, coed, graduate-only institution. *Enrollment by degree level:* 829 master's, 2,740 doctoral, 148 other advanced degrees. *Graduate faculty:* 791 full-time (517 women), 615 part-time/adjunct (283 women). *Graduate housing:* Rooms and/or apartments available on a first-come, first-served basis to single and married students. Typical cost: $5460 per year for single students; $5460 per year for married students. Housing application deadline: 4/1. *Student services:* Campus employment opportunities, campus safety program, career counseling, exercise/wellness program, free psychological counseling, multicultural affairs office, services for students with disabilities, writing training. *Library facilities:* A.T. Still Memorial Library plus 1 other. *Collection:* Books: 13,285 (physical), 307,890 (digital/electronic); Serial titles: 1,281 (physical), 25,393 (digital/electronic); Databases: 84. Weekly public service hours: 156.

Computer facilities: 45 computers available on campus for general student use. A campuswide network can be accessed from off campus. X available. Website: http://www.atsu.edu/

General Application Contact: Donna Sparks, Director, Admissions Processing, 660-626-2117, Fax: 660-626-2969, E-mail: admissions@atsu.edu.

GRADUATE UNITS

Arizona School of Dentistry & Oral Health Students: 312 full-time (161 women); includes 155 minority (7 Black or African American, non-Hispanic/Latino; 5 American Indian or Alaska Native, non-Hispanic/Latino; 98 Asian, non-Hispanic/Latino; 22 Hispanic/Latino; 23 Two or more races, non-Hispanic/Latino), 3 international. Average age 28. 2,236 applicants, 7% accepted, 76 enrolled. *Faculty:* 128 full-time (91 women), 99 part-time/adjunct (31 women). Expenses: Contact institution. *Financial support:* In 2018–19, 54 students received support. Federal Work-Study and scholarships/grants available. Financial award application deadline: 6/1; financial award applicants required to submit FAFSA. In 2018, 73 doctorates, 5 other advanced degrees awarded. Offers dental medicine (DMD); orthodontics (MS, Certificate). *Application deadline:* For fall admission, 11/15 for domestic and international students; for summer admission, 11/15 for domestic and international students. Applications are processed on a rolling basis. *Application fee:* $70. Electronic applications accepted. *Application Contact:* Donna Sparks, Director, Admissions Processing, 660-626-2117, Fax: 660-626-2969, E-mail: admissions@atsu.edu. *Dean,* Dr. Robert Trombly, 480-248-8105, Fax: 623-223-7063, E-mail: rtrombly@atsu.edu.

Arizona School of Health Sciences Students: 627 full-time (429 women), 349 part-time (228 women); includes 302 minority (46 Black or African American, non-Hispanic/Latino; 6 American Indian or Alaska Native, non-Hispanic/Latino; 99 Asian, non-Hispanic/Latino; 108 Hispanic/Latino; 43 Two or more races, non-Hispanic/Latino), 88 international. Average age 32. 5,235 applicants, 13% accepted, 431 enrolled. *Faculty:* 88 full-time (65 women), 215 part-time/adjunct (157 women). Expenses: Contact institution. *Financial support:* In 2018–19, 161 students received support. Federal Work-Study and scholarships/grants available. Financial award application deadline: 6/1; financial award applicants required to submit FAFSA. In 2018, 140 master's, 310 doctorates, 1 other advanced degree awarded. *Program availability:* Part-time, 100% online. Offers advanced occupational therapy (MS); advanced physician assistant studies (MS); athletic training (MS, DAT); audiology (Au D); clinical decision making in athletic training (Graduate Certificate); occupational therapy (MS, OTD); orthopedic rehabilitation (Graduate Certificate); physical therapy (DPT); physician assistant studies (MS); post-professional audiology (Au D); post-professional physical therapy (DPT). *Application deadline:* For fall admission, 7/7 for domestic and international students; for winter admission, 10/3 for domestic and international students; for spring admission, 1/16 for domestic and international students; for summer admission, 4/17 for domestic and international students. Applications are processed on a rolling basis. *Application fee:* $70. Electronic applications accepted. *Application Contact:* Donna Sparks, Director, Admissions Processing, 660-626-2117, Fax: 660-626-2969, E-mail: admissions@atsu.edu. *Dean,* Dr. Ann Lee Burch, 480-219-6061, E-mail: aburch@atsu.edu.

College of Graduate Health Studies Students: 600 full-time (388 women), 512 part-time (306 women); includes 448 minority (185 Black or African American, non-Hispanic/Latino; 14 American Indian or Alaska Native, non-Hispanic/Latino; 108 Asian, non-Hispanic/Latino; 111 Hispanic/Latino; 1 Native Hawaiian or other Pacific Islander, non-Hispanic/Latino; 29 Two or more races, non-Hispanic/Latino), 31 international. Average age 35. 386 applicants, 82% accepted, 279 enrolled. *Faculty:* 50 full-time (38 women), 95 part-time/adjunct (57 women). Expenses: Contact institution. *Financial support:* In 2018–19, 8 students received support. Scholarships/grants available. Financial award applicants required to submit FAFSA. In 2018, 141 master's, 111 doctorates, 112 other advanced degrees awarded. *Program availability:* Part-time, evening/weekend, online only, 100% online, blended/hybrid learning. Offers dental public health (MPH); exercise and sport psychology (Certificate); fundamentals of education (Certificate); geriatric exercise science (Certificate); global health (Certificate); health administration (MHA, DHA); health professions (Ed D); health sciences (DH Sc); kinesiology (MS); leadership and organizational behavior (Certificate); public health (MPH); sports conditioning (Certificate). *Application deadline:* For fall admission, 6/25 for domestic and international students; for winter admission, 9/10 for domestic and international students; for spring admission, 12/10 for domestic and international students; for summer admission, 3/4 for domestic and international students. Applications are processed on a rolling basis. *Application fee:* $70. Electronic applications accepted. *Application Contact:* Amie Waldemer, Associate Director, Online Admissions, 480-219-6146, E-mail: awaldemer@atsu.edu. *Dean,* Dr. Donald Altman, 480-219-6008, Fax: 660-626-2826, E-mail: daltman@atsu.edu.

Kirksville College of Osteopathic Medicine Students: 716 full-time (298 women), 6 part-time (3 women); includes 134 minority (17 Black or African American, non-Hispanic/Latino; 41 Asian, non-Hispanic/Latino; 34 Hispanic/Latino; 1 Native Hawaiian or other Pacific Islander, non-Hispanic/Latino; 41 Two or more races, non-Hispanic/Latino). Average age 27. 4,388 applicants, 9% accepted, 185 enrolled. *Faculty:* 121 full-time (80 women), 77 part-time/adjunct (27 women). Expenses: Contact institution. *Financial support:* In 2018–19, 201 students received support, including 17 fellowships with full tuition reimbursements available (averaging $56,358 per year); Federal Work-Study and scholarships/grants also available. Financial award application deadline: 6/1; financial award applicants required to submit FAFSA. In 2018, 11 master's, 168 doctorates awarded. Offers biomedical sciences (MS); osteopathic medicine (DO). *Application deadline:* For fall admission, 2/1 for domestic students; for summer admission, 2/1 for domestic students. Applications are processed on a rolling basis. *Application fee:* $70. Electronic applications accepted. *Application Contact:* Donna Sparks, Director, Admissions Processing, 660-626-2117, Fax: 660-626-2969, E-mail: admissions@atsu.edu. *Dean,* Dr. Margaret Wilson, 660-626-2354, Fax: 660-626-2080, E-mail: mwilson@atsu.edu.

Missouri School of Dentistry & Oral Health Students: 167 full-time (83 women); includes 52 minority (1 American Indian or Alaska Native, non-Hispanic/Latino; 35 Asian, non-Hispanic/Latino; 11 Hispanic/Latino; 5 Two or more races, non-Hispanic/Latino). Average age 27. 1,257 applicants, 9% accepted, 42 enrolled. *Faculty:* 42 full-time (22 women), 39 part-time/adjunct (10 women). Expenses: Contact institution. *Financial support:* In 2018–19, 36 students received support. Federal Work-Study and scholarships/grants available. Financial award application deadline: 6/1; financial award applicants required to submit FAFSA. In 2018, 41 doctorates awarded. Offers dental medicine (DMD). *Application deadline:* For fall admission, 12/1 for domestic students; for summer admission, 12/1 for domestic students. Applications are processed on a rolling basis. *Application fee:* $70. Electronic applications accepted. *Application Contact:* Donna Sparks, Director, Admissions Processing, 660-626-2237, Fax: 660-626-2969, E-mail: admissions@atsu.edu. *Dean,* Dr. Dwight McLeod, 660-626-2842, Fax: 660-626-2969, E-mail: dmcleod@atsu.edu.

School of Osteopathic Medicine in Arizona Students: 427 full-time (238 women), 1 (woman) part-time; includes 224 minority (10 Black or African American, non-Hispanic/Latino; 142 Asian, non-Hispanic/Latino; 32 Hispanic/Latino; 2 Native Hawaiian or other Pacific Islander, non-Hispanic/Latino; 38 Two or more races, non-Hispanic/Latino). Average age 27. 5,642 applicants, 5% accepted, 108 enrolled. *Faculty:* 69 full-time (43 women), 48 part-time/adjunct (25 women). Expenses: Contact institution. *Financial support:* In 2018–19, 48 students received support, including 2 fellowships with full tuition reimbursements available (averaging $57,818 per year); Federal Work-Study and scholarships/grants also available. Financial award application deadline: 6/1; financial award applicants required to submit FAFSA. In 2018, 106 doctorates awarded. Offers osteopathic medicine (DO). *Application deadline:* For fall admission, 3/1 for domestic students; for summer admission, 3/1 for domestic students. Applications are processed on a rolling basis. *Application fee:* $70. Electronic applications accepted. *Application Contact:* Donna Sparks, Director, Admissions Processing, 660-626-2117, Fax: 660-626-2969, E-mail: admissions@atsu.edu. *Dean,* Dr. Jeffrey Morgan, 480-265-8017, Fax: 480-219-6159, E-mail: jeffreymorgan@atsu.edu.

AUBURN UNIVERSITY, Auburn University, AL 36849

General Information State-supported, coed, university. *Enrollment:* 30,440 graduate, professional, and undergraduate students; 3,342 full-time matriculated graduate/professional students (1,894 women), 2,374 part-time matriculated graduate/professional students (1,155 women). *Enrollment by degree level:* 2,670 master's, 2,887 doctoral, 159 other advanced degrees. *Graduate faculty:* 1,287 full-time (514 women), 161 part-time/adjunct (67 women). Tuition, state resident: full-time $11,282; part-time $535 per credit hour. Tuition, nonresident: full-time $30,542; part-time $1605 per credit hour. *Required fees:* $826 per semester. Tuition and fees vary according to degree level and program. *Graduate housing:* Rooms and/or apartments available on a first-come, first-served basis to single and married students. Typical cost: $7860 per year ($13,332 including board) for single students; $7860 per year ($13,332 including board) for married students. *Student services:* Campus employment opportunities, campus safety program, career counseling, exercise/wellness program, free psychological counseling, international student services, low-cost health insurance, multicultural affairs office, services for students with disabilities, teacher training, writing training. *Library facilities:* R. B. Draughon Library plus 3 others. *Collection:* Books: 4.6 million (physical), 1 million (digital/electronic); Serial titles: 76,345 (physical), 94,890 (digital/electronic); Databases: 245. Study areas open 24 hours, 5–7 days a week.

Computer facilities: Computer purchase and lease plans are available. 1,722 computers available on campus for general student use. A campuswide network can be accessed. Online class registration, bursar payments, course materials are available. Website: http://www.auburn.edu/

General Application Contact: Dr. George Flowers, Dean of the Graduate School, 334-844-2125, E-mail: flowegt@auburn.edu.

GRADUATE UNITS

College of Veterinary Medicine *Program availability:* Part-time. Offers veterinary medicine (MS, DVM, PhD).

Graduate School *Program availability:* Part-time, evening/weekend. Offers applied economics (PhD); cell and molecular biology (PhD); real estate development (MRED); sociology and rural sociology (MA, MS).

College of Agriculture *Program availability:* Part-time. Offers agricultural economics (M Ag); agriculture (M Ag, M Aq, MS, PhD); agronomy and soils (M Ag, MS, PhD); animal sciences (M Ag, MS, PhD); entomology (M Ag, MS); fisheries and allied aquacultures (M Aq, MS, PhD); horticulture (M Ag, MS, PhD); plant pathology (M Ag, MS, PhD); poultry science (M Ag, MS, PhD). Electronic applications accepted.

College of Architecture, Design, and Construction *Program availability:* Part-time. Offers architecture, design, and construction (MBC, MCP, MID, ML Arch); building science (MBC); community planning (MCP); industrial design (MID); landscape architecture (ML Arch). Electronic applications accepted.

College of Business *Program availability:* Part-time. Offers accountancy (M Acc); business (M Acc, MBA, MRED, MS, PhD); business administration (MBA); finance (MS); management (PhD). Electronic applications accepted.

College of Education *Program availability:* Part-time. Offers adult education (PhD, Ed S); curriculum and instruction (M Ed, MS, Ed S); curriculum supervision (M Ed, PhD); education (M Ed, MS, Ed D, PhD, Ed S, Graduate Certificate); exercise science (M Ed); higher education administration (PhD); library media (Ed S); school administration (M Ed, PhD); special education, rehabilitation, and counseling (M Ed, MS, PhD). Electronic applications accepted.

College of Human Sciences *Program availability:* Part-time. Offers consumer affairs (MS, PhD); human development and family studies (MS, PhD); human sciences (MS, PhD, Graduate Certificate); nutrition and food science (MS, PhD, Graduate Certificate). Electronic applications accepted.

College of Liberal Arts *Program availability:* Part-time. Offers applied economics (PhD); audiology (MCD, Au D); communication and journalism (MA, Graduate Certificate); economics (MS); English (MA, MTPC, PhD, Graduate Certificate); foreign languages and literatures (MA, MHS); history (MA, PhD, Graduate Certificate); liberal arts (MA, MCD, MHS, MPA, MS, MSW, MTPC, Au D, PhD, Graduate Certificate); psychology (MS, PhD); public administration (MPA, PhD, Graduate Certificate); social work (MSW). Electronic applications accepted.

College of Sciences and Mathematics *Program availability:* Part-time. Offers analytical chemistry (MS, PhD); applied mathematics (MAM, MS); biochemistry (MS, PhD); botany (MS); geology and geography (MS); inorganic chemistry (MS); mathematics (MS, PhD); organic chemistry (PhD); physical chemistry (MS, PhD); physics (MS, PhD); probability and statistics (M Prob S); sciences and mathematics (M Prob S, MAM, MS, PhD); statistics (MS); zoology (MS).

Ginn College of Engineering *Program availability:* Part-time. Offers aerospace engineering (MAE, MS, PhD); biosystems engineering (MS, PhD); chemical engineering (M Ch E, MS, PhD); civil engineering (MCE, MS, PhD); computer science and software engineering (MS, MSWE, PhD); electrical and computer engineering (MEE, MS, PhD); engineering (M Ch E, M Mtl E, MAE, MCE, MEE, MISE, MME, MS, MSWE, PhD, Graduate Certificate); industrial and systems engineering (MISE, MS, PhD, Graduate Certificate); materials engineering (M Mtl E, MS, PhD); mechanical engineering (M Mtl E, MME, MS, PhD); polymer and fiber engineering (MS, PhD). Electronic applications accepted.

School of Forestry and Wildlife Sciences *Program availability:* Part-time. Offers forestry (MS); natural resource conservation (MNR); wildlife sciences (MS, PhD). Electronic applications accepted.

School of Nursing Offers nursing educator (MSN); primary care practitioner (MSN).

Harrison School of Pharmacy *Program availability:* Part-time. Offers pharmacal sciences (MS, PhD); pharmaceutical sciences (PhD); pharmacy (MS, PhD, Pharm D); pharmacy care systems (MS, PhD). Electronic applications accepted.

AUBURN UNIVERSITY AT MONTGOMERY, Montgomery, AL 36124-4023

General Information State-supported, coed, comprehensive institution. *Enrollment:* 5,211 graduate, professional, and undergraduate students; 221 full-time matriculated graduate/professional students (142 women), 358 part-time matriculated graduate/professional students (245 women). *Enrollment by degree level:* 520 master's, 9 doctoral, 45 other advanced degrees. *Graduate faculty:* 91 full-time (36 women), 16 part-time/adjunct (9 women). *International tuition:* $16,056 full-time. *Tuition, area resident:* Full-time $7146; part-time $4764 per credit hour. Tuition, state resident: full-time $7146; part-time $4764 per credit hour. Tuition, nonresident: full-time $16,056; part-time $10,704 per credit hour. *Required fees:* $766. One-time fee: $25 full-time. *Graduate housing:* Rooms and/or apartments available on a first-come, first-served basis to single and married students. Typical cost: $4580 per year ($6980 including board) for single students; $4580 per year ($6980 including board) for married students. Room and board charges vary according to housing facility selected. Housing application deadline: 5/1. *Student services:* Campus employment opportunities, campus safety program, career counseling, exercise/wellness program, free psychological counseling, international student services, low-cost health insurance, multicultural affairs office, services for students with disabilities. *Library facilities:* Auburn University at Montgomery Library. *Collection:* Books: 340,819 (physical), 1.2 million (digital/electronic). Weekly public service hours: 84; students can reserve study rooms.

Computer facilities: 500 computers available on campus for general student use. A campuswide network can be accessed from student residence rooms. Online class registration is available.
Website: http://www.aum.edu/

General Application Contact: Ashley Warren, Administrative Coordinator, Provost's Office, 334-244-3623, Fax: 334-244-3947, E-mail: awarren3@aum.edu.

GRADUATE UNITS

College of Business Students: 47 full-time (24 women), 58 part-time (32 women); includes 29 minority (21 Black or African American, non-Hispanic/Latino; 1 American Indian or Alaska Native, non-Hispanic/Latino; 5 Asian, non-Hispanic/Latino; 1 Hispanic/Latino; 1 Two or more races, non-Hispanic/Latino), 15 international. Average age 29. 129 applicants, 77% accepted, 65 enrolled. *Faculty:* 11 full-time (3 women), 1 part-time/adjunct (0 women). Expenses: Contact institution. *Financial support:* Research assistantships, career-related internships or fieldwork, and scholarships/grants available. Support available to part-time students. Financial award application deadline: 3/1; financial award applicants required to submit FAFSA. In 2018, 67 master's awarded. *Program availability:* Part-time, evening/weekend. Offers business (M Acc, MBA, MS); business and management (MBA); information systems management (MS). *Application deadline:* For fall admission, 7/15 for international students; for spring admission, 11/15 for international students; for summer admission, 4/15 for international students. Applications are processed on a rolling basis. *Application fee:* $25 ($0 for international students). Electronic applications accepted. *Application Contact:* Jennifer Taylor, Assistant Director of Graduate Programs, 334-244-3587, Fax: 334-244-3137, E-mail: jtaylor5@aum.edu. *Dean,* Dr. Rhea Ingram, 334-244-3476, Fax: 334-244-3792, E-mail: wingram4@aum.edu.
School of Accountancy Average age 28. 34 applicants, 85% accepted, 23 enrolled. Expenses: Contact institution. *Financial support:* Scholarships/grants available. Financial award applicants required to submit FAFSA. In 2018, 10 master's awarded. *Program availability:* Part-time. Offers accountancy (M Acc). *Application deadline:* Applications are processed on a rolling basis. *Application fee:* $25 ($0 for international students). Electronic applications accepted. *Application Contact:* Rhonda Seay, Graduate Advisor, 334-244-3115, E-mail: rseay@aum.edu.

College of Education Students: 82 full-time (66 women), 156 part-time (127 women); includes 91 minority (87 Black or African American, non-Hispanic/Latino; 4 Hispanic/Latino), 2 international. Average age 33. 198 applicants, 71% accepted, 73 enrolled. *Faculty:* 26 full-time (15 women), 11 part-time/adjunct (all women). Expenses: Contact institution. *Financial support:* Teaching assistantships, career-related internships or fieldwork, and scholarships/grants available. Support available to part-time students. Financial award application deadline: 3/1; financial award applicants required to submit FAFSA. In 2018, 102 master's awarded. *Program availability:* Part-time, evening/weekend. Offers counselor education (M Ed, Ed S); early childhood special education (M Ed); education (M Ed, Ed S); elementary education (M Ed, Ed S); exercise science (M Ed); instructional leadership (M Ed, Ed S); instructional technology (Ed S); physical education (Ed S); secondary education (M Ed); special education/collaborative teacher (M Ed, Ed S); sport management (M Ed). *Application deadline:* For fall admission, 7/1 for international students; for spring admission, 11/1 for international students; for summer admission, 4/15 for international students. Applications are processed on a rolling basis. *Application fee:* $25. Electronic applications accepted. *Application Contact:* Dr. Rhonda Morton, Associate Dean/Graduate Coordinator, 334-224-3287, Fax: 334-244-3978, E-mail: rmorton@aum.edu. *Dean,* Dr. Sheila Austin, 334-244-3425, Fax: 334-244-3102, E-mail: saustin1@aum.edu.

College of Liberal Arts & Social Sciences Offers applied economics (MS); political science (MPS); public administration (MPA); public administration and public policy (PhD).

College of Liberal Arts & Social Sciences Students: 35 full-time (20 women), 65 part-time (43 women); includes 26 minority (25 Black or African American, non-Hispanic/Latino; 1 Asian, non-Hispanic/Latino), 16 international. Average age 32. 71 applicants, 85% accepted, 29 enrolled. *Faculty:* 32 full-time (15 women), 2 part-time/adjunct (1 woman). Expenses: Contact institution. *Financial support:* Teaching assistantships, career-related internships or fieldwork, and scholarships/grants available. Support available to part-time students. Financial award application deadline: 3/1; financial award applicants required to submit FAFSA. In 2018, 34 master's awarded. *Program availability:* Part-time, evening/weekend. Offers arts and sciences (MLA, MS, MTW); liberal arts (MLA); teaching writing (MTW). *Application deadline:* For fall admission, 7/15 for international students; for spring admission, 11/15 for international students; for summer admission, 4/15 for international students. Applications are processed on a rolling basis. *Application fee:* $25 ($0 for international students). Electronic applications accepted. *Application Contact:* Ashley Warren, Graduate Admissions Coordinator, 334-244-3623, E-mail: awarren3@aum.edu. *Associate Provost for Graduate Studies and Faculty Services/Acting Dean, College of Arts and Sciences,* Dr. Matthew Ragland, 334-244-3138, E-mail: mragland@aum.edu.

College of Nursing and Health Sciences Students: 23 full-time (14 women), 19 part-time (9 women); includes 10 minority (9 Black or African American, non-Hispanic/Latino;

1 Hispanic/Latino), 2 international. Expenses: Contact institution. Offers family nurse practitioner (MSN); nurse educator for interprofessional practice (MSN). Programs offered jointly with Auburn University. *Application deadline:* For fall admission, 7/1 for domestic students; for spring admission, 10/1 for domestic students; for summer admission, 3/1 for domestic students. Applications are processed on a rolling basis. *Application fee:* $25 ($0 for international students). Electronic applications accepted. *Application Contact:* Dr. Barbara Wilder, Graduate Program Director, 334-844-6766, E-mail: wildebf@auburn.edu. *Dean,* Dr. Jean Leuner, 334-244-3658, E-mail: jleuner@aum.edu.

College of Public Policy and Justice Students: 36 full-time (17 women), 65 part-time (40 women); includes 49 minority (46 Black or African American, non-Hispanic/Latino; 2 Asian, non-Hispanic/Latino; 1 Two or more races, non-Hispanic/Latino), 8 international. Average age 31. 71 applicants, 83% accepted, 35 enrolled. *Faculty:* 19 full-time (3 women), 2 part-time/adjunct (1 woman). Expenses: Contact institution. *Financial support:* Teaching assistantships, career-related internships or fieldwork, and scholarships/grants available. Support available to part-time students. Financial award application deadline: 3/1; financial award applicants required to submit FAFSA. In 2018, 29 master's awarded. *Program availability:* Part-time, evening/weekend. Offers criminal studies (MSJPS); geographic information systems (MS); public policy and justice (MPA, MPS, MS, MSJPS, PhD). *Application deadline:* For fall admission, 7/15 for international students; for spring admission, 11/15 for international students; for summer admission, 4/15 for international students. Applications are processed on a rolling basis. *Application fee:* $25. Electronic applications accepted.

College of Sciences Offers psychology (MS).
Department of Mathematics and Computer Science Average age 26. 29 applicants, 76% accepted, 6 enrolled. Expenses: Contact institution. *Financial support:* Teaching assistantships available. Financial award application deadline: 3/1; financial award applicants required to submit FAFSA. In 2018, 10 master's awarded. Offers mathematics and computer science (MS). *Application deadline:* For fall admission, 7/15 for international students; for spring admission, 11/15 for international students; for summer admission, 4/15 for international students. Applications are processed on a rolling basis. *Application fee:* $25 ($0 for international students). Electronic applications accepted. *Application Contact:* Dr. Luis Cueva-Parra, Associate Dean, 334-244-3321, Fax: 334-244-3826, E-mail: lcuevapa@aum.edu. *Chair,* Dr. Yi Wang, 334-244-3318, Fax: 334-244-3826, E-mail: ywang2@aum.edu.

AUGSBURG UNIVERSITY, Minneapolis, MN 55454-1351

General Information Independent-religious, coed, comprehensive institution. *Graduate housing:* On-campus housing not available.

GRADUATE UNITS

Program in Business Administration *Program availability:* Evening/weekend. Offers business administration (MBA). Electronic applications accepted.

Program in Education *Program availability:* Part-time, evening/weekend. Offers education (MAE). Electronic applications accepted.

Program in Leadership *Program availability:* Part-time, evening/weekend. Offers leadership (MA).

Program in Physician Assistant Studies Offers physician assistant studies (MS).

Program in Social Work *Program availability:* Part-time, evening/weekend. Offers social work (MSW).

Programs in Nursing Offers nursing (MA, DNP).

AUGUSTANA UNIVERSITY, Sioux Falls, SD 57197

General Information Independent-religious, coed, comprehensive institution. *Enrollment:* 37 full-time matriculated graduate/professional students (22 women), 289 part-time matriculated graduate/professional students (240 women). *Enrollment by degree level:* 326 master's. *Graduate faculty:* 18 full-time (9 women), 8 part-time/adjunct (6 women). *Tuition:* Full-time $34,000; part-time $490 per credit. *Required fees:* $530. Tuition and fees vary according to course load and program. *Graduate housing:* Rooms and/or apartments available on a first-come, first-served basis to single and married students. Housing application deadline: 9/1. *Student services:* Campus employment opportunities, campus safety program, career counseling, exercise/wellness program, international student services, low-cost health insurance, multicultural affairs office, services for students with disabilities, teacher training, writing training. *Library facilities:* Mikkelsen Library. *Collection:* Students can reserve study rooms.

Computer facilities: Computer purchase and lease plans are available. 295 computers available on campus for general student use. A campuswide network can be accessed from student residence rooms and from off campus. Online class registration is available.
Website: http://www.augie.edu/

General Application Contact: Julia Paluch, Administrative Assistant, Graduate Education, 605-274-4043, Fax: 605-274-4450, E-mail: julia.paluch@augie.edu.

GRADUATE UNITS

Augustana-Sanford Genetic Counseling Program Offers genetic counseling (MS). Program offered in collaboration with Sanford Health. Electronic applications accepted.

MA in Education Program *Program availability:* Part-time-only, evening/weekend, online only, 100% online. Offers instructional strategies (MA); reading (MA); special populations (MA); STEM (MA); technology (MA). Electronic applications accepted.

Master of Professional Accountancy Program *Program availability:* Part-time. Offers professional accountancy (MPA). Electronic applications accepted.

Sports Administration and Leadership Program *Program availability:* Part-time. Offers sports administration and leadership (MA). Electronic applications accepted.

AUGUSTA UNIVERSITY, Augusta, GA 30912

General Information State-supported, coed, university. CGS member. *Graduate housing:* Rooms and/or apartments available on a first-come, first-served basis to single and married students. *Research affiliation:* Georgia Cancer Coalition (cancer research programs), Advanced Technology Development Center (biotechnology transfer), Medical College of Georgia Research Institute, Inc. (biomedical research), Georgia Center of Innovation for Life Sciences (research commercialization and economic development), Georgia Research Alliance (science and technology development).

GRADUATE UNITS

College of Allied Health Sciences *Program availability:* Online learning. Offers allied health sciences (MHS, MPA, MPH, MS, DPT, PhD); clinical laboratory sciences (MHS); diagnostic sciences (PhD); environmental health (MPH); health care outcomes (PhD); health informatics (MPH); health management (MPH); medical illustration (MS); occupational therapy (MHS); physical therapy (DPT); physician assistant (MPA); rehabilitation science (PhD); social and behavioral sciences (MPH).

College of Education *Program availability:* Part-time, evening/weekend. Offers counselor education (M Ed, Ed S); curriculum and instruction (Ed S); education (M Ed, MAT, Ed D, Ed S); educational innovation (Ed D); elementary education (MAT); foreign language education (MAT); instruction (M Ed); leadership (Ed S); middle grades education (MAT); music education (MAT); school administration (M Ed); secondary education (MAT); special education (MAT); teacher leadership (M Ed).

College of Nursing Offers adult gerontology acute care nurse practitioner (DNP); clinical nurse leader (MSN); family nurse practitioner (DNP); nurse executive (DNP); nursing (DNP); nursing anesthesia (DNP); pediatric nurse practitioner (DNP); psychiatric mental health nurse practitioner (DNP).

College of Science and Mathematics Offers psychological sciences (MS); science and mathematics (MS).

The Dental College of Georgia Offers dentistry (DMD). Electronic applications accepted.

Hull College of Business *Program availability:* Part-time, evening/weekend. Offers business administration (MBA); information security management (MS).

Medical College of Georgia Offers medicine (MD).

Program in Biochemistry and Cancer Biology Offers biochemistry and cancer biology (PhD). Electronic applications accepted.

Program in Cellular Biology and Anatomy Offers cellular biology and anatomy (PhD). Electronic applications accepted.

Program in Genomic Medicine Offers genomic medicine (PhD). Electronic applications accepted.

Program in Molecular Medicine Offers molecular medicine (PhD). Electronic applications accepted.

Program in Neuroscience Offers neuroscience (PhD). Electronic applications accepted.

Program in Oral Biology *Program availability:* Part-time. Offers oral biology (MS, PhD). Electronic applications accepted.

Program in Pharmacology Offers pharmacology (PhD). Electronic applications accepted.

Program in Physiology Offers physiology (PhD). Electronic applications accepted.

Program in Vascular Biology Offers vascular biology (PhD).

AURORA UNIVERSITY, Aurora, IL 60506-4892

General Information Independent, coed, comprehensive institution. *Enrollment:* 6,005 graduate, professional, and undergraduate students; 830 full-time matriculated graduate/professional students (702 women), 1,155 part-time matriculated graduate/professional students (836 women). *Enrollment by degree level:* 1,692 master's, 279 doctoral, 14 other advanced degrees. *Graduate faculty:* 38 full-time (17 women), 170 part-time/adjunct (129 women). *Tuition:* Full-time $12,600; part-time $600 per credit hour. Tuition and fees vary according to degree level, campus/location and program. *Graduate housing:* On-campus housing not available. *Student services:* Campus employment opportunities, campus safety program, career counseling, exercise/wellness program, free psychological counseling, international student services, multicultural affairs office, services for students with disabilities, teacher training, writing training. *Library facilities:* Charles B. Phillips Library plus 1 other. *Collection:* Books: 24,587 (physical), 178,780 (digital/electronic); Serial titles: 2 (physical), 71,529 (digital/electronic); Databases: 63. Weekly public service hours: 96; students can reserve study rooms.

Computer facilities: 193 computers available on campus for general student use. A campuswide network can be accessed from student residence rooms and from off campus. Online class registration, learning management system are available. Website: http://www.aurora.edu/

General Application Contact: Luke Kerber, Director of Graduate Enrollment, 630-947-8904, E-mail: lkerber@aurora.edu.

GRADUATE UNITS

Dunham School of Business and Public Policy Students: 152 full-time (106 women), 180 part-time (112 women); includes 133 minority (51 Black or African American, non-Hispanic/Latino; 10 Asian, non-Hispanic/Latino; 63 Hispanic/Latino; 1 Native Hawaiian or other Pacific Islander, non-Hispanic/Latino; 8 Two or more races, non-Hispanic/Latino), 2 international. Average age 31. 253 applicants, 99% accepted, 156 enrolled. *Faculty:* 8 full-time (2 women), 28 part-time/adjunct (13 women). Expenses: Contact institution. *Financial support:* In 2018–19, 94 students received support. Federal Work-Study, scholarships/grants, and unspecified assistantships available. Financial award applicants required to submit FAFSA. In 2018, 117 master's awarded. *Program availability:* Part-time, evening/weekend, 100% online, blended/hybrid learning. Offers accountancy (MS); business (MBA). *Application deadline:* For fall admission, 6/1 for international students; for spring admission, 10/1 for international students. Applications are processed on a rolling basis. *Application fee:* $0. Electronic applications accepted. *Application Contact:* Center for Graduate Studies, 630-947-8955, E-mail: AUadmission@aurora.edu. *Dean, School of Business and Policy,* Dr. Toby Arquette, 630-844-5614, E-mail: tarquett@aurora.edu.

School of Arts and Sciences Students: 9 full-time (4 women), 76 part-time (52 women); includes 13 minority (6 Black or African American, non-Hispanic/Latino; 1 Asian, non-Hispanic/Latino; 5 Hispanic/Latino; 1 Two or more races, non-Hispanic/Latino). Average age 36. 54 applicants, 98% accepted, 24 enrolled. *Faculty:* 3 full-time (1 woman), 10 part-time/adjunct (4 women). Expenses: Contact institution. *Financial support:* In 2018–19, 2 students received support. Federal Work-Study, scholarships/grants, and unspecified assistantships available. Financial award applicants required to submit FAFSA. In 2018, 6 master's awarded. *Program availability:* Part-time, evening/weekend, 100% online. Offers homeland security (MS); mathematics (MS); mathematics and science education for elementary teachers (MA); mathematics education (MA); science education (MA). *Application deadline:* For fall admission, 6/1 for international students; for spring admission, 10/1 for international students. Applications are processed on a rolling basis. *Application fee:* $0. Electronic applications accepted. *Application Contact:* Center for Graduate Studies, 630-947-8955, E-mail: AUadmission@aurora.edu. *Vice President for Academic Affairs,* Dr. Frank Buscher, 630-844-5252, E-mail: fbuscher@aurora.edu.

School of Education and Human Performance Students: 28 full-time (25 women), 537 part-time (359 women); includes 101 minority (25 Black or African American, non-Hispanic/Latino; 8 Asian, non-Hispanic/Latino; 58 Hispanic/Latino; 2 Native Hawaiian or other Pacific Islander, non-Hispanic/Latino; 8 Two or more races, non-Hispanic/Latino), 2 international. Average age 38. 191 applicants, 98% accepted, 133 enrolled. *Faculty:* 14 full-time (6 women), 32 part-time/adjunct (17 women). Expenses: Contact institution. *Financial support:* In 2018–19, 31 students received support. Federal Work-Study, scholarships/grants, and unspecified assistantships available. Financial award applicants required to submit FAFSA. In 2018, 213 master's, 16 doctorates awarded. *Program availability:* Part-time, evening/weekend, 100% online. Offers applied

behavioral analysis (MS); bilingual-ESL education (MA); educational leadership with principal endorsement (MA); educational technology (MA); leadership in adult learning higher education (Ed D); leadership in curriculum and instruction (Ed D); leadership in educational administration (Ed D); reading instruction (MA); special education (MA). *Application deadline:* For fall admission, 6/1 for international students; for spring admission, 10/1 for international students. Applications are processed on a rolling basis. *Application fee:* $0. Electronic applications accepted. *Application Contact:* Center for Graduate Studies, 630-947-8955, E-mail: AUadmission@aurora.edu. *Dean, School of Education and Human Performance,* Dr. Jen Buckley, 630-844-1542, Fax: 630-844-6155, E-mail: jbuckley@aurora.edu.

School of Social Work Students: 640 full-time (566 women), 360 part-time (311 women); includes 325 minority (149 Black or African American, non-Hispanic/Latino; 1 American Indian or Alaska Native, non-Hispanic/Latino; 19 Asian, non-Hispanic/Latino; 135 Hispanic/Latino; 21 Two or more races, non-Hispanic/Latino). Average age 31. 652 applicants, 98% accepted, 421 enrolled. *Faculty:* 13 full-time (8 women), 100 part-time/adjunct (95 women). Expenses: Contact institution. *Financial support:* In 2018–19, 432 students received support. Federal Work-Study, scholarships/grants, and unspecified assistantships available. Financial award applicants required to submit FAFSA. In 2018, 414 master's, 6 doctorates awarded. *Program availability:* Part-time, evening/weekend, 100% online, blended/hybrid learning. Offers social work (MSW, DSW). *Application deadline:* For fall admission, 6/1 for international students; for spring admission, 10/1 for international students. Applications are processed on a rolling basis. *Application fee:* $0. Electronic applications accepted. *Application Contact:* Center for Graduate Studies, 630-947-8955, E-mail: AUadmission@aurora.edu. *Dean, School of Social Work,* Dr. Brenda Barnwell, 630-947-8933, E-mail: bbarnwel@aurora.edu.

AUSTIN COLLEGE, Sherman, TX 75090-4400

General Information Independent-religious, coed, comprehensive institution. *Graduate housing:* Room and/or apartments available on a first-come, first-served basis to single students; on-campus housing not available to married students. Housing application deadline: 5/1.

GRADUATE UNITS

Austin Teacher Program Students: 19 full-time (11 women); includes 7 minority (1 Asian, non-Hispanic/Latino; 5 Hispanic/Latino; 1 Two or more races, non-Hispanic/Latino). Average age 23. *Faculty:* 3 full-time (all women), 4 part-time/adjunct (3 women). Expenses: Contact institution. *Financial support:* Career-related internships or fieldwork, Federal Work-Study, scholarships/grants, and unspecified assistantships available. Support available to part-time students. Financial award application deadline: 4/1; financial award applicants required to submit FAFSA. In 2018, 13 master's awarded. *Program availability:* Part-time. Offers teaching (MAT). *Application deadline:* For fall admission, 5/1 priority date for domestic students; for spring admission, 1/15 priority date for domestic students. Applications are processed on a rolling basis. *Application fee:* $35. Electronic applications accepted. *Application Contact:* Administrative Assistant, 903-813-2327. *Department Chair,* Julia Shahid, 903-813-2457, E-mail: jshahid@austincollege.edu.

AUSTIN GRADUATE SCHOOL OF THEOLOGY, Austin, TX 78752

General Information Independent-religious, coed, upper-level institution. *Enrollment:* 6 full-time matriculated graduate/professional students (1 woman), 8 part-time matriculated graduate/professional students (4 women). *Enrollment by degree level:* 14 master's. *Graduate faculty:* 5 full-time (0 women), 4 part-time/adjunct (0 women). *Tuition:* Full-time $7650; part-time $5100 per credit hour. *Required fees:* $350; $350 per semester. $175 per semester. *Graduate housing:* On-campus housing not available. *Student services:* Campus employment opportunities, international student services, services for students with disabilities. *Library facilities:* David Worley Library.

Computer facilities: 6 computers available on campus for general student use. A campuswide network can be accessed. Website: http://www.austingrad.edu/

General Application Contact: Lindi Parshall, Director of Admissions/Registrar, 512-476-2772 Ext. 103, Fax: 512-476-3919, E-mail: lparshall@austingrad.edu.

AUSTIN PEAY STATE UNIVERSITY, Clarksville, TN 37044

General Information State-supported, coed, comprehensive institution. CGS member. *Enrollment:* 10,954 graduate, professional, and undergraduate students; 330 full-time matriculated graduate/professional students (204 women), 728 part-time matriculated graduate/professional students (504 women). *Enrollment by degree level:* 1,047 master's, 11 other advanced degrees. *Graduate faculty:* 131 full-time (62 women), 23 part-time/adjunct (19 women). *Tuition, area resident:* Part-time $450 per credit hour. Tuition, state resident: full-time $5987; part-time $450 per credit hour. Tuition, nonresident: full-time $8757; part-time $806 per credit hour. *Required fees:* $1583; $79.15 per credit hour. *Graduate housing:* Rooms and/or apartments available on a first-come, first-served basis to single and married students. Typical cost: $6700 per year ($10,614 including board) for single students; $6700 per year ($10,614 including board) for married students. Room and board charges vary according to board plan, campus/location and housing facility selected. *Student services:* Campus employment opportunities, campus safety program, career counseling, child daycare facilities, exercise/wellness program, free psychological counseling, grant writing training, international student services, multicultural affairs office, services for students with disabilities, teacher training, writing training. *Library facilities:* Felix G. Woodward Library. *Collection:* Books: 196,384 (physical), 397,836 (digital/electronic); Serial titles: 53,295 (physical), 59,165 (digital/electronic); Databases: 299. Weekly public service hours: 109.

Computer facilities: Computer purchase and lease plans are available. 1,400 computers available on campus for general student use. A campuswide network can be accessed from student residence rooms and from off campus. Online class registration is available. Website: http://www.apsu.edu/

General Application Contact: Megan Mitchell, Coordinator of Graduate Admissions and Recruitment, 800-859-4723, Fax: 931-221-7641, E-mail: gradadmissions@apsu.edu.

GRADUATE UNITS

College of Graduate Studies Students: 330 full-time (204 women), 728 part-time (504 women); includes 241 minority (138 Black or African American, non-Hispanic/Latino; 3 American Indian or Alaska Native, non-Hispanic/Latino; 15 Asian, non-Hispanic/Latino; 42 Hispanic/Latino; 3 Native Hawaiian or other Pacific Islander, non-Hispanic/Latino; 40 Two or more races, non-Hispanic/Latino), 49 international. Average age 33. 597 applicants, 85% accepted, 407 enrolled. *Faculty:* 135 full-time (63 women), 23 part-time/adjunct (22 women). Expenses: Contact institution. *Financial support:* In 2018–19, 136 students received support, including 136 research assistantships with full tuition reimbursements available (averaging $5,184 per year); career-related internships or fieldwork, Federal Work-Study, institutionally sponsored loans, scholarships/grants, and unspecified assistantships also available. Support available to part-time students. Financial award application deadline: 7/1; financial award applicants required to submit FAFSA. In 2018, 303 master's, 13 other advanced degrees awarded. *Program availability:* Part-time, evening/weekend, online learning. *Application deadline:* For fall admission, 8/21 priority date for domestic students. Applications are processed on a rolling basis. *Application fee:* $45 ($55 for international students). Electronic applications accepted. *Application Contact:* Megan Mitchell, Director of Graduate Admissions and Recruitment, 931-221-6189, Fax: 931-221-7641, E-mail: mitchellm@apsu.edu. *Associate Provost of Research and Dean of the College of Graduate Studies,* Dr. Chad Brooks, 931-221-7415, Fax: 931-221-7641, E-mail: brooksc@apsu.edu.

College of Arts and Letters Students: 50 full-time (23 women), 84 part-time (51 women); includes 27 minority (15 Black or African American, non-Hispanic/Latino; 5 Hispanic/Latino; 7 Two or more races, non-Hispanic/Latino), 2 international. Average age 31. 68 applicants, 84% accepted, 49 enrolled. *Faculty:* 44 full-time (17 women), 5 part-time/adjunct (3 women). Expenses: Contact institution. *Financial support:* Research assistantships with full tuition reimbursements, teaching assistantships, career-related internships or fieldwork, Federal Work-Study, institutionally sponsored loans, scholarships/grants, and unspecified assistantships available. Support available to part-time students. Financial award application deadline: 7/1; financial award applicants required to submit FAFSA. In 2018, 45 master's awarded. *Program availability:* Part-time, evening/weekend, online learning. Offers arts and letters (M Mu, MA); English (MA); marketing communication (MA); media management (MA); military history (MA); music education (M Mu); music performance (M Mu). *Application deadline:* For fall admission, 8/21 priority date for domestic students. Applications are processed on a rolling basis. *Application fee:* $45 ($55 for international students). Electronic applications accepted. *Application Contact:* Megan Mitchell, Coordinator of Graduate Admissions, 931-221-6189, Fax: 931-221-7641, E-mail: mitchellm@apsu.edu. *Interim Dean,* Dr. Barry Jones, 931-221-7330, Fax: 931-221-1024, E-mail: jonesb@apsu.edu.

College of Behavioral and Health Sciences Students: 121 full-time (93 women), 314 part-time (244 women); includes 124 minority (76 Black or African American, non-Hispanic/Latino; 3 American Indian or Alaska Native, non-Hispanic/Latino; 4 Asian, non-Hispanic/Latino; 22 Hispanic/Latino; 2 Native Hawaiian or other Pacific Islander, non-Hispanic/Latino; 17 Two or more races, non-Hispanic/Latino), 2 international. Average age 34. 256 applicants, 82% accepted, 190 enrolled. *Faculty:* 37 full-time (25 women), 13 part-time/adjunct (all women). Expenses: Contact institution. *Financial support:* Research assistantships with full tuition reimbursements, career-related internships or fieldwork, Federal Work-Study, institutionally sponsored loans, scholarships/grants, and unspecified assistantships available. Support available to part-time students. Financial award application deadline: 7/1; financial award applicants required to submit FAFSA. In 2018, 126 master's awarded. *Program availability:* Part-time, evening/weekend, online learning. Offers behavioral and health sciences (MA, MPS, MS, MSN, MSW); family nurse practitioner (MSN); industrial-organizational psychology (MS); mental health counseling (MS); nursing administration (MSN); nursing education (MSN); nursing informatics (MSN); public health education (MS); school counseling (MS); social work (MSW); sports and wellness leadership (MS); strategic leadership (MPS). *Application deadline:* For fall admission, 8/21 priority date for domestic students. Applications are processed on a rolling basis. *Application fee:* $45 ($55 for international students). Electronic applications accepted. *Application Contact:* Megan Mitchell, Coordinator of Graduate Admissions, 931-221-6189, Fax: 931-221-7641, E-mail: mitchellm@apsu.edu. *Interim Dean,* Dr. Rebecca Corvey, 931-221-1040, Fax: 931-221-6382, E-mail: corveyr@apsu.edu.

College of Business Students: 19 full-time (8 women), 47 part-time (23 women); includes 16 minority (9 Black or African American, non-Hispanic/Latino; 3 Asian, non-Hispanic/Latino; 1 Hispanic/Latino; 1 Native Hawaiian or other Pacific Islander, non-Hispanic/Latino; 2 Two or more races, non-Hispanic/Latino). Average age 35. 43 applicants, 93% accepted, 27 enrolled. *Faculty:* 8 full-time (4 women). Expenses: Contact institution. *Financial support:* Research assistantships with full tuition reimbursements, career-related internships or fieldwork, Federal Work-Study, institutionally sponsored loans, scholarships/grants, and unspecified assistantships available. Support available to part-time students. Financial award application deadline: 7/1; financial award applicants required to submit FAFSA. In 2018, 30 master's awarded. *Program availability:* Part-time, evening/weekend, online learning. Offers management (MS). *Application deadline:* For fall admission, 8/21 priority date for domestic students. Applications are processed on a rolling basis. *Application fee:* $45 ($55 for international students). Electronic applications accepted. *Application Contact:* Megan Mitchell, Coordinator of Graduate Admissions, 931-221-6189, Fax: 931-221-7641, E-mail: mitchellm@apsu.edu. *Dean,* Dr. Mickey Hepner, 931-221-7675, Fax: 931-221-7355, E-mail: hepnerm@apsu.edu.

College of Education Students: 86 full-time (66 women), 181 part-time (141 women); includes 48 minority (29 Black or African American, non-Hispanic/Latino; 3 Asian, non-Hispanic/Latino; 7 Hispanic/Latino; 9 Two or more races, non-Hispanic/Latino), 1 international. Average age 33. 128 applicants, 89% accepted, 98 enrolled. *Faculty:* 17 full-time (12 women), 9 part-time/adjunct (5 women). Expenses: Contact institution. *Financial support:* Research assistantships with full tuition reimbursements, career-related internships or fieldwork, Federal Work-Study, institutionally sponsored loans, scholarships/grants, and unspecified assistantships available. Support available to part-time students. Financial award application deadline: 7/1; financial award applicants required to submit FAFSA. In 2018, 72 master's, 13 Ed Ss awarded. *Program availability:* Part-time, evening/weekend, online learning. Offers education (MA Ed, Ed S). *Application deadline:* For fall admission, 8/21 priority date for domestic students. Applications are processed on a rolling basis. *Application fee:* $45 ($55 for international students). Electronic applications accepted. *Application Contact:* Megan Mitchell, Coordinator of Graduate Admissions, 931-221-6189, Fax: 931-221-7641, E-mail: mitchellm@apsu.edu. *Dean,* Dr. Prentice Chandler, 931-221-7511, Fax: 931-221-1292, E-mail: chandlerp@apsu.edu.

College of Science, Technology, Engineering and Mathematics Students: 54 full-time (14 women), 102 part-time (45 women); includes 26 minority (9 Black or African American, non-Hispanic/Latino; 5 Asian, non-Hispanic/Latino; 7 Hispanic/Latino; 5 Two or more races, non-Hispanic/Latino), 44 international. Average age 31. 102 applicants, 87% accepted, 59 enrolled. *Faculty:* 29 full-time (5 women), 3 part-time/adjunct (1 woman). Expenses: Contact institution. *Financial support:* Research assistantships with full tuition reimbursements, career-related internships or fieldwork, Federal Work-Study, institutionally sponsored loans, scholarships/grants, and unspecified assistantships available. Support available to part-time students. Financial award application deadline: 7/1; financial award applicants required to submit FAFSA. In 2018, 28 master's awarded. *Program availability:* Part-time, online learning. Offers clinical laboratory science (MS); data management and analysis (MS,

PSM); engineering technology (MS); information assurance and security (MS, PSM); mathematical finance (MS, PSM); mathematics instruction (MS); predictive analytics (MS, PSM); science, technology, engineering and mathematics (MS, PSM). *Application deadline:* For fall admission, 8/21 priority date for domestic students. Applications are processed on a rolling basis. *Application fee:* $45 ($55 for international students). Electronic applications accepted. *Application Contact:* Megan Mitchell, Coordinator of Graduate Admissions, 931-221-6189, Fax: 931-221-7641, E-mail: mitchellm@apsu.edu. *Interim Dean,* Dr. Karen Meisch, 931-221-7780, Fax: 931-221-7984, E-mail: meischk@apsu.edu.

AUSTIN PRESBYTERIAN THEOLOGICAL SEMINARY, Austin, TX 78705-5797

General Information Independent-religious, coed, graduate-only institution. *Enrollment by degree level:* 122 master's, 37 doctoral. *Graduate faculty:* 21 full-time (6 women), 7 part-time/adjunct (1 woman). *Tuition:* Full-time $13,800; part-time $230 per credit. *Required fees:* $145; $145 $25. One-time fee: $120. *Graduate housing:* Rooms and/or apartments available on a first-come, first-served basis to single and married students. Typical cost: $2250 per year ($2300 including board) for single students; $6750 per year ($6800 including board) for married students. Room and board charges vary according to housing facility selected. Housing application deadline: 5/31. *Student services:* Campus employment opportunities, campus safety program, career counseling, free psychological counseling, international student services, services for students with disabilities, writing training. *Library facilities:* Stitt Library. *Collection:* Books: 109,766 (physical), 312,522 (digital/electronic); Serial titles: 1,007 (physical), 47,945 (digital/electronic); Databases: 97. Weekly public service hours: 37; students can reserve study rooms.

Computer facilities: 20 computers available on campus for general student use. A campuswide network can be accessed from off campus.
Website: http://www.austinseminary.edu/

General Application Contact: Rev. JD Herrera, Vice President for Enrollment Management, 512-404-4827, Fax: 512-472-7089, E-mail: admissions@austinseminary.edu.

GRADUATE UNITS

Graduate and Professional Programs Offers divinity (M Div); ministry (D Min); ministry practice (MA); theological studies (MA); youth ministry (MA). M Div/MSSW offered in collaboration with The University of Texas at Austin School of Social Work. Electronic applications accepted.

AVE MARIA SCHOOL OF LAW, Naples, FL 34119

General Information Independent-religious, coed, graduate-only institution. *Enrollment by degree level:* 241 doctoral. *Tuition:* Full-time $39,450. *Required fees:* $2256. *Graduate housing:* Rooms and/or apartments available on a first-come, first-served basis to single and married students. Housing application deadline: 4/15. *Student services:* Campus employment opportunities, campus safety program, career counseling, exercise/wellness program, international student services, services for students with disabilities, writing training. *Library facilities:* Veterans Memorial Law Library. *Collection:* Books: 53,471 (physical), 48,624 (digital/electronic); Serial titles: 2,330 (physical), 29,769 (digital/electronic); Databases: 206. Weekly public service hours: 168; study areas open 24 hours, 5–7 days a week; students can reserve study rooms.

Computer facilities: 20 computers available on campus for general student use. Online class registration is available.
Website: http://www.avemarialaw.edu/

General Application Contact: Claire T. O'Keefe, Associate Dean of Admissions and Student Engagement, 239-687-5423, Fax: 239-352-2890, E-mail: info@avemarialaw.edu.

GRADUATE UNITS

Professional Program Students: 241 full-time (132 women); includes 67 minority (13 Black or African American, non-Hispanic/Latino; 1 American Indian or Alaska Native, non-Hispanic/Latino; 1 Asian, non-Hispanic/Latino; 52 Hispanic/Latino), 7 international. Average age 26. 568 applicants, 55% accepted, 97 enrolled. *Faculty:* 22 full-time (7 women), 18 part-time/adjunct (7 women). Expenses: Contact institution. *Financial support:* In 2018–19, 182 students received support. Research assistantships, career-related internships or fieldwork, Federal Work-Study, and scholarships/grants available. Financial award application deadline: 6/30; financial award applicants required to submit FAFSA. In 2018, 81 doctorates awarded. Offers law (JD). *Application deadline:* For fall admission, 7/15 priority date for domestic and international students. Applications are processed on a rolling basis. *Application fee:* $0. Electronic applications accepted. *Application Contact:* Claire T. O'Keefe, Associate Dean of Admissions and Student Engagement, 239-687-5423, Fax: 239-352-2890, E-mail: info@avemarialaw.edu. *President/Dean,* Kevin Cieply, 239-687-5300, E-mail: kcieply@avemarialaw.edu.

AVE MARIA UNIVERSITY, Ave Maria, FL 34142

General Information Independent-religious, coed, comprehensive institution. *Graduate housing:* Room and/or apartments available on a first-come, first-served basis to single students; on-campus housing not available to married students. Housing application deadline: 7/15.

GRADUATE UNITS
Graduate Programs

AVERETT UNIVERSITY, Danville, VA 24541-3692

General Information Independent-religious, coed, comprehensive institution. *Enrollment:* 965 graduate, professional, and undergraduate students; 311 full-time matriculated graduate/professional students (211 women), 10 part-time matriculated graduate/professional students (7 women). *Enrollment by degree level:* 321 master's. *Graduate faculty:* 10 full-time (4 women), 26 part-time/adjunct (14 women). *Graduate housing:* On-campus housing not available. *Student services:* Campus employment opportunities, campus safety program, career counseling, free psychological counseling, services for students with disabilities, teacher training, writing training. *Library facilities:* Mary B. Blount Library. *Collection:* Books: 86,432 (physical), 313,632 (digital/electronic); Serial titles: 98 (physical), 35,069 (digital/electronic); Databases: 160. Weekly public service hours: 81; students can reserve study rooms.

Computer facilities: 150 computers available on campus for general student use. A campuswide network can be accessed from student residence rooms. Online class registration is available.
Website: http://www.averett.edu/

General Application Contact: Christy Davis, Assistant Director of Admissions, 434-791-7133, E-mail: cdavis@averett.edu.

GRADUATE UNITS

Master in Education Program Students: 141 full-time (108 women), 4 part-time (2 women); includes 31 minority (30 Black or African American, non-Hispanic/Latino; 1 Hispanic/Latino). Average age 37. 106 applicants, 58% accepted, 52 enrolled. *Faculty:* 2 full-time (both women), 14 part-time/adjunct (11 women). Expenses: Contact institution. *Financial support:* Application deadline: 3/1; applicants required to submit FAFSA. In 2018, 52 master's awarded. *Program availability:* Part-time, online only, 100% online. Offers administration and supervision (M Ed); curriculum and instruction (M Ed); special education with endorsement (M Ed); special education with licensure (M Ed). *Application deadline:* Applications are processed on a rolling basis. Electronic applications accepted. *Application Contact:* Christy Davis, Assistant Director of Admissions, 434-791-7133, E-mail: cdavis@averett.edu. *Chair of the Education Department; Director of Teacher Education,* Dr. Nancy Riddell, 434-791-5741, Fax: 434-791-5020, E-mail: nriddell@averett.edu.

Master of Accountancy Program Students: 6 full-time (5 women), 2 part-time (both women). Average age 31. 5 applicants, 80% accepted, 4 enrolled. *Faculty:* 2 full-time (1 woman). Expenses: Contact institution. *Financial support:* In 2018–19, 1 student received support. Application deadline: 3/1; applicants required to submit FAFSA. In 2018, 2 master's awarded. *Program availability:* Part-time. Offers accountancy (M Acc). *Application deadline:* Applications are processed on a rolling basis. Electronic applications accepted. *Application Contact:* Christy Davis, Assistant Director of Admissions, 434-791-7133, E-mail: cdavis@averett.edu. *Director of the Master in Accountancy Program,* Dr. Peggy C. Wright, 434-791-7118, E-mail: pwright@averett.edu.

Master of Business Administration Program Students: 156 full-time (93 women), 2 part-time (1 woman); includes 61 minority (51 Black or African American, non-Hispanic/Latino; 2 American Indian or Alaska Native, non-Hispanic/Latino; 3 Asian, non-Hispanic/Latino; 3 Hispanic/Latino; 2 Two or more races, non-Hispanic/Latino), 2 international. Average age 35. 61 applicants, 70% accepted, 35 enrolled. *Faculty:* 7 full-time (1 woman), 10 part-time/adjunct (2 women). Expenses: Contact institution. *Financial support:* Application deadline: 3/1; applicants required to submit FAFSA. In 2018, 62 master's awarded. *Program availability:* Part-time. Offers business administration (MBA); human resources management (MBA); leadership (MBA); marketing (MBA). *Application deadline:* Applications are processed on a rolling basis. Electronic applications accepted. *Application Contact:* Christy Davis, Assistant Director of Admissions, 434-791-7133, E-mail: cdavis@averett.edu. *Chair, Business Department,* Dr. Peggy C. Wright, 434-791-7118, E-mail: pwright@averett.edu.

Master of Science in Applied Data Analytics Program

Master of Science in Criminal Justice Leadership and Administration Program

AVILA UNIVERSITY, Kansas City, MO 64145-1698

General Information Independent-religious, coed, comprehensive institution. *Enrollment:* 1,671 graduate, professional, and undergraduate students; 320 full-time matriculated graduate/professional students (242 women), 186 part-time matriculated graduate/professional students (149 women). *Enrollment by degree level:* 354 master's, 47 other advanced degrees. *Graduate faculty:* 19 full-time (13 women), 33 part-time/adjunct (19 women). *Tuition:* Full-time $7200; part-time $600 per credit hour. Tuition and fees vary according to program. *Graduate housing:* Room and/or apartments available on a first-come, first-served basis to single students; on-campus housing not available to married students. Typical cost: $3300 per year ($7200 including board). Room and board charges vary according to board plan and housing facility selected. *Student services:* Campus employment opportunities, campus safety program, career counseling, child daycare facilities, exercise/wellness program, free psychological counseling, international student services, low-cost health insurance, multicultural affairs office, services for students with disabilities, teacher training, writing training. *Library facilities:* Hooley-Bundshu Library plus 1 other. *Collection:* Books: 39,963 (physical), 309,288 (digital/electronic); Serial titles: 205 (physical), 389,497 (digital/electronic); Databases: 72. Weekly public service hours: 91; students can reserve study rooms.

Computer facilities: 141 computers available on campus for general student use. A campuswide network can be accessed from student residence rooms and from off campus. Online class registration, laptop checkout through library are available. Website: http://www.avila.edu/

General Application Contact: Jesse Reinert, Admission Representative, 816-501-2483, E-mail: jessie.reinert@avila.edu.

GRADUATE UNITS

Department of Psychology Students: 67 full-time (58 women), 15 part-time (all women); includes 27 minority (16 Black or African American, non-Hispanic/Latino; 2 American Indian or Alaska Native, non-Hispanic/Latino; 2 Asian, non-Hispanic/Latino; 4 Hispanic/Latino; 3 Two or more races, non-Hispanic/Latino), 2 international. Average age 33. 69 applicants, 65% accepted, 34 enrolled. *Faculty:* 7 full-time (6 women), 4 part-time/adjunct (1 woman). Expenses: Contact institution. *Financial support:* In 2018–19, 12 students received support, including 4 research assistantships with partial tuition reimbursements available; career-related internships or fieldwork, scholarships/grants, and unspecified assistantships also available. Support available to part-time students. Financial award applicants required to submit FAFSA. In 2018, 21 master's awarded. *Program availability:* Part-time. Offers counseling psychology (MS); psychology (MS). *Application deadline:* Applications are processed on a rolling basis. *Application fee:* $0. Electronic applications accepted. *Application Contact:* Tamika Doolin, Graduate Admissions Advisor, 816-501-3661, Fax: 816-501-2455, E-mail: gradpsych@avila.edu. *Director of Graduate Psychology Enrollment Management,* Phil Gebauer, 816-501-0419, Fax: 816-501-2455, E-mail: philip.gebauer@avila.edu.

School of Business Students: 49 full-time (28 women), 26 part-time (14 women); includes 20 minority (13 Black or African American, non-Hispanic/Latino; 1 Asian, non-Hispanic/Latino; 4 Hispanic/Latino; 2 Two or more races, non-Hispanic/Latino), 17 international. Average age 37. 51 applicants, 47% accepted, 20 enrolled. *Faculty:* 6 full-time (2 women), 6 part-time/adjunct (2 women). Expenses: Contact institution. *Financial support:* In 2018–19, 15 students received support. Career-related internships or fieldwork and scholarships/grants available. Support available to part-time students. Financial award applicants required to submit FAFSA. In 2018, 22 master's awarded. *Program availability:* Part-time, evening/weekend. Offers business (MBA). *Application deadline:* For fall admission, 7/30 priority date for domestic and international students; for winter admission, 11/30 priority date for domestic and international students; for spring admission, 2/28 priority date for domestic and international students; for summer admission, 6/1 priority date for domestic and international students. Applications are processed on a rolling basis. *Application fee:* $0. Electronic applications accepted. *Application Contact:* Brandon Black, MBA Admission Advisor, 816-501-3601, Fax: 816-501-2463, E-mail: brandon.black@avila.edu. *Interim Dean,* Dr. Wendy L. Acker, 816-501-3720, Fax: 816-501-2463, E-mail: wendy.acker@avila.edu.

School of Education Students: 83 full-time (71 women), 84 part-time (69 women); includes 13 minority (6 Black or African American, non-Hispanic/Latino; 2 Asian, non-Hispanic/Latino; 4 Hispanic/Latino; 1 Two or more races, non-Hispanic/Latino), 2 international. Average age 40. 92 applicants, 62% accepted, 40 enrolled. *Faculty:* 6 full-time (5 women), 9 part-time/adjunct (8 women). Expenses: Contact institution. *Financial support:* In 2018–19, 12 students received support. Unspecified assistantships available. Financial award applicants required to submit FAFSA. In 2018, 21 master's awarded. *Program availability:* Part-time, evening/weekend, online learning. Offers advanced classroom management (MA); elementary education (Teaching Certificate); English language learners (Advanced Certificate); middle school (Teaching Certificate); physical education K-12 (Teaching Certificate); secondary education (Teaching Certificate). *Application deadline:* Applications are processed on a rolling basis. Electronic applications accepted. *Application Contact:* Cory Roup, Graduate Education Enrollment and Academic Advisor, 816-501-2464, E-mail: cory.roup@avila.edu. *Director of Graduate Education,* Dr. Stacy Keith, 816-501-2446, Fax: 816-501-2915, E-mail: stacy.keith@avila.edu.

School of Professional Studies Students: 69 full-time (49 women), 48 part-time (42 women); includes 45 minority (38 Black or African American, non-Hispanic/Latino; 5 Hispanic/Latino; 2 Two or more races, non-Hispanic/Latino), 5 international. Average age 39. 63 applicants, 60% accepted, 29 enrolled. *Faculty:* 14 part-time/adjunct (8 women). Expenses: Contact institution. *Financial support:* In 2018–19, 12 students received support. Unspecified assistantships available. Support available to part-time students. Financial award applicants required to submit FAFSA. In 2018, 34 master's awarded. *Program availability:* Part-time-only, evening/weekend, 100% online, blended/hybrid learning. Offers executive leadership (MS); fundraising (MA); instructional design and technology (MA, MS); leadership coaching (MS); project management (MA); strategic human resources (MS). *Application deadline:* Applications are processed on a rolling basis. *Application fee:* $0. Electronic applications accepted. *Application Contact:* Jessica Burson, Graduate Admission Advisor, 816-501-2482, Fax: 816-941-4650, E-mail: advantage@avila.edu. *Coordinator,* Sarah Sullivan, 816-501-0429, Fax: 816-941-4650, E-mail: advantage@avila.edu.

AZUSA PACIFIC UNIVERSITY, Azusa, CA 91702-7000

General Information Independent-religious, coed, university. CGS member. *Graduate housing:* On-campus housing not available.

GRADUATE UNITS

Azusa Pacific Seminary *Program availability:* Part-time, evening/weekend. Offers Biblical studies (M Div, MA); church leadership and development (MAPS); ministry (D Min); theology (M Div, MA, MAPS, D Min); theology and ethics (MA); urban studies (MAPS).

College of Liberal Arts and Sciences *Program availability:* Part-time, evening/weekend, online learning. Offers biotechnology (MS); English (MA); liberal arts and sciences (MA, MS); teaching English to speakers of other languages (MA).

Haggard Graduate School of Theology Offers theology (MA).

College of Music and the Arts *Program availability:* Part-time, evening/weekend. Offers composition (M Mus); conducting (M Mus); education (M Mus); modern art history, theory, and criticism (MA); music entrepreneurial studies (MA); performance (M Mus); screenwriting (MA); visual art (MFA).

School of Behavioral and Applied Sciences Offers athletic training (MS); behavioral and applied sciences (MA, MS, MSW, DPT, Ed D, PhD, Psy D); child life (MS); college counseling and student development (MS); executive leadership (MA); family psychology (Psy D); higher education (PhD); higher education leadership (Ed D); leadership (MA); leadership development (MA); leadership studies (MA); organizational psychology (MS); physical education (MA, MS); physical therapy (DPT); research psychology and data analytics (MS); social work (MSW); sport management (MA).

School of Business and Management *Program availability:* Part-time, evening/weekend. Offers accounting (MBA); business administration (MBA); entrepreneurship (MBA); finance (MBA); international business (MBA); marketing (MBA); organizational science (MBA); professional accountancy (M Acc); sport management (MBA).

School of Education *Program availability:* Part-time, evening/weekend. Offers education (M Ed, MA, MA Ed, Ed D); educational counseling (MA Ed); educational leadership (MA, Ed D); educational psychology (MA Ed); educational technology (MA); learning and technology (MA Ed); special education (MA Ed); teaching (MA Ed).

School of Nursing *Program availability:* Part-time, evening/weekend. Offers adult clinical nurse specialist (MSN); adult-gerontology nurse practitioner (MSN); family nurse practitioner (MSN); healthcare administration and leadership (MSN); nursing (MSN, DNP, PhD); nursing education (MSN); parent-child clinical nurse specialist (MSN); psychiatric mental health nurse practitioner (MSN).

University College *Program availability:* Online learning. Offers leadership and organizational studies (MA); public health (MPH).

BABEL UNIVERSITY PROFESSIONAL SCHOOL OF TRANSLATION, Honolulu, HI 96815

General Information Proprietary, coed, primarily women, graduate-only institution. *Graduate housing:* On-campus housing not available.

GRADUATE UNITS

Program in Translation *Program availability:* Part-time, evening/weekend, online learning. Offers translation (MS).

BABSON COLLEGE, Babson Park, MA 02457-0310

General Information Independent, coed, comprehensive institution. *Graduate housing:* Rooms and/or apartments available on a first-come, first-served basis to single and married students. Housing application deadline: 5/1.

GRADUATE UNITS

F. W. Olin Graduate School of Business *Program availability:* Part-time, evening/weekend, online learning. Offers accounting (MSA); advanced management (Certificate); business administration (MBA); business analytics (MS); finance (MS); global entrepreneurship (MS); technological entrepreneurship (MS). Electronic applications accepted.

BAKER COLLEGE CENTER FOR GRADUATE STUDIES—ONLINE, Flint, MI 48507

General Information Independent, coed, graduate-only institution. *Graduate housing:* On-campus housing not available.

GRADUATE UNITS

Graduate Programs *Program availability:* Part-time, evening/weekend, online learning. Offers accounting (MBA); business administration (DBA); finance (MBA); general business (MBA); health care management (MBA); human resources management (MBA); information management (MBA); leadership studies (MBA); management information systems (MSIS); marketing (MBA); occupational therapy (MOT). Electronic applications accepted.

BAKER UNIVERSITY, Baldwin City, KS 66006-0065
General Information Independent-religious, coed, comprehensive institution. *Graduate housing:* On-campus housing not available.

GRADUATE UNITS

School of Education *Program availability:* Part-time, evening/weekend, 100% online. Offers education (MA Ed, MSSE, MSSL, Ed D). Master's-level programs also offered in Wichita, KS. Electronic applications accepted.

School of Professional and Graduate Studies *Program availability:* Part-time, evening/weekend, 100% online. Offers business (MAOL, MBA, MSM, MSSM); liberal arts (MLA).

BAKKE GRADUATE UNIVERSITY, Dallas, TX 75243-7039
General Information Independent-religious, coed, primarily men, graduate-only institution. *Graduate housing:* On-campus housing not available.

GRADUATE UNITS

Programs in Pastoral Ministry and Business *Program availability:* Part-time, online learning. Offers business administration (MBA); church and ministry multiplication (D Min); global urban leadership (MA); leadership (D Min); ministry in complex contexts (D Min); social and civic entrepreneurship (MA); theology of work (D Min); theology reflection (D Min); transformational leadership (DTL); urban youth ministry (D Min). Electronic applications accepted.

BALDWIN WALLACE UNIVERSITY, Berea, OH 44017-2088
General Information Independent-religious, coed, comprehensive institution. *Enrollment:* 3,741 graduate, professional, and undergraduate students; 359 full-time matriculated graduate/professional students (244 women), 209 part-time matriculated graduate/professional students (139 women). *Enrollment by degree level:* 568 master's. *Graduate faculty:* 59 full-time (29 women), 35 part-time/adjunct (13 women). *Graduate housing:* On-campus housing not available. *Student services:* Campus employment opportunities, campus safety program, career counseling, free psychological counseling, international student services, multicultural affairs office, services for students with disabilities, teacher training, writing training. *Library facilities:* Ritter Library plus 2 others. *Collection:* Books: 106,091 (physical), 451,472 (digital/electronic); Serial titles: 148 (physical), 86,238 (digital/electronic); Databases: 265. Weekly public service hours: 90; study areas open 24 hours, 5–7 days a week; students can reserve study rooms.

Computer facilities: 457 computers available on campus for general student use. A campuswide network can be accessed from student residence rooms. Online class registration is available.
Website: http://www.bw.edu/

General Application Contact: Winnie W. Gerhardt, Director of Transfer, Adult and Graduate Admission, 440-826-2222, Fax: 440-826-3830, E-mail: admission@bw.edu.

GRADUATE UNITS

Graduate Programs Students: 359 full-time (244 women), 209 part-time (139 women); includes 100 minority (50 Black or African American, non-Hispanic/Latino; 18 Asian, non-Hispanic/Latino; 14 Hispanic/Latino; 1 Native Hawaiian or other Pacific Islander, non-Hispanic/Latino; 17 Two or more races, non-Hispanic/Latino), 7 international. Average age 32. *Faculty:* 59 full-time (29 women), 35 part-time/adjunct (13 women). Expenses: Contact institution. In 2018, 255 master's awarded. *Program availability:* Part-time, evening/weekend, 100% online, blended/hybrid learning. Offers health education and disease prevention (MPH); physician assistant (MMS); population health leadership and management (MPH); speech-language pathology (MS). *Application deadline:* Applications are processed on a rolling basis. *Application fee:* $25. Electronic applications accepted. *Application Contact:* Winnie W. Gerhardt, Director of Transfer, Adult and Graduate Admission, 440-826-2222, Fax: 440-826-3830, E-mail: admission@bw.edu. *Provost, Academic Affairs,* Stephen D. Stahl, 440-826-2251, Fax: 440-826-2329, E-mail: sstahl@bw.edu.

School of Business Students: 155 full-time (83 women), 118 part-time (64 women); includes 56 minority (31 Black or African American, non-Hispanic/Latino; 9 Asian, non-Hispanic/Latino; 9 Hispanic/Latino; 1 Native Hawaiian or other Pacific Islander, non-Hispanic/Latino; 6 Two or more races, non-Hispanic/Latino), 4 international. Average age 35. 130 applicants, 56% accepted, 50 enrolled. *Faculty:* 32 full-time (11 women), 18 part-time/adjunct (5 women). Expenses: Contact institution. *Financial support:* In 2018–19, 20 students received support. Scholarships/grants and tuition discounts available. Financial award applicants required to submit FAFSA. In 2018, 148 master's awarded. *Program availability:* Part-time, evening/weekend, blended/hybrid learning. Offers accounting (MBA); business (MAM, MBA); business analytics (MBA); health care (MBA); human resources (MBA); international management (MAM, MBA); management (MAM, MBA). *Application deadline:* For fall admission, 7/25 priority date for domestic students, 4/30 priority date for international students; for spring admission, 12/15 priority date for domestic students, 9/30 priority date for international students; for summer admission, 4/15 for domestic students. Applications are processed on a rolling basis. *Application fee:* $0. Electronic applications accepted. *Application Contact:* Laura Spencer, Graduate Business Admission Specialist, 440-826-2191, Fax: 440-826-3868, E-mail: lspencer@bw.edu. *Dean of School of Business,* Dr. Frank C. Braun, 440-826-3566, Fax: 440-826-3868, E-mail: fbraun@bw.edu.

School of Education Students: 81 full-time (60 women), 80 part-time (66 women); includes 22 minority (14 Black or African American, non-Hispanic/Latino; 1 Asian, non-Hispanic/Latino; 1 Hispanic/Latino; 6 Two or more races, non-Hispanic/Latino). Average age 32. 108 applicants, 52% accepted, 45 enrolled. *Faculty:* 10 full-time (6 women), 8 part-time/adjunct (2 women). Expenses: Contact institution. *Financial support:* Career-related internships or fieldwork available. Financial award applicants required to submit FAFSA. In 2018, 62 master's awarded. *Program availability:* Part-time, evening/weekend, 100% online, blended/hybrid learning. Offers leadership in higher education (MA Ed); leadership in technology for teaching and learning (MA Ed); literacy (MA Ed); mild/moderate educational needs (MA Ed); school leadership (MA Ed). *Application deadline:* For fall admission, 8/15 priority date for domestic students; for spring admission, 12/15 priority date for domestic students. Applications are processed on a rolling basis. *Application fee:* $25. Electronic applications accepted. *Application Contact:* Amiyra Alveranga, Admission Counselor, 440-826-8005, Fax: 440-826-3830, E-mail: aalveran@bw.edu. *Interim Dean of EDU/HSC/HPE,* Michael J Smith, 440-826-3137, Fax: 440-826-3779, E-mail: mjsmith@bw.edu.

BALL STATE UNIVERSITY, Muncie, IN 47306
General Information State-supported, coed, university. CGS member. *Enrollment:* 1,187 full-time matriculated graduate/professional students (801 women), 4,343 part-time matriculated graduate/professional students (3,519 women). *Graduate faculty:* 456 full-time (224 women), 121 part-time/adjunct (77 women). *Graduate housing:* Rooms and/or apartments available on a first-come, first-served basis to single and married students. Housing application deadline: 6/1. *Student services:* Campus employment opportunities, campus safety program, career counseling, child daycare facilities, exercise/wellness program, free psychological counseling, grant writing training, international student services, low-cost health insurance, multicultural affairs office, services for students with disabilities, teacher training, writing training. *Library facilities:* Bracken Library plus 2 others. *Collection:* Books: 822,983 (physical), 15,244 (digital/electronic); Serial titles: 13,599 (physical), 103,640 (digital/electronic); Databases: 296. Weekly public service hours: 123; students can reserve study rooms.

Computer facilities: Computer purchase and lease plans are available. 578 computers available on campus for general student use. A campuswide network can be accessed from student residence rooms and from off campus. Online class registration, room reservations, testing and test results, manage and pay tuition, order/buy textbooks, request room repairs, order transcripts, manage meal plan, manage and prepay long distance service, undergraduate degree progress report are available.
Website: http://www.bsu.edu/

General Application Contact: Dr. Adam Beach, Dean of the Graduate School, 765-285-1300, Fax: 765-285-1994, E-mail: arbeach@bsu.edu.

GRADUATE UNITS

Graduate School *Program availability:* Part-time, evening/weekend, 100% online, blended/hybrid learning. Electronic applications accepted.

College of Architecture and Planning *Program availability:* Part-time. Offers architecture (M Arch, M Arch II); architecture and planning (M Arch, M Arch II, MLA, MS, MUD, MURP, Certificate); digital fabrication (Certificate); historic preservation (MS); landscape architecture (MLA); urban and regional planning (MURP); urban design (MUD). Electronic applications accepted.

College of Communication, Information, and Media *Program availability:* Part-time, 100% online, blended/hybrid learning. Offers communication studies (MA); communication, information, and media (MA, MS, Certificate); emerging media and visual reporting (Certificate); emerging media design and development (MA); information and communication sciences (MS); information and communication technologies (Certificate); journalism (MA); literary journalism (Certificate); public relations (MA); telecommunications (MA). Electronic applications accepted.

College of Fine Arts *Program availability:* Part-time. Offers fine arts (MFA); music (MA, MM, DA, Artist Diploma); visual arts studio (MA). Electronic applications accepted.

College of Health *Program availability:* Part-time, evening/weekend, 100% online. Offers adult/gerontology nurse practitioner (Post Master's Certificate); athletic coaching education (Certificate); audiology (Au D); counseling (MA); counseling psychology (MA, PhD); evidence-based clinical practice (Postbaccalaureate Certificate); exercise science (MA, MS); family nurse practitioner (Post Master's Certificate); health (MA, MS, Au D, DNP, PhD, Certificate, Post Master's Certificate, Postbaccalaureate Certificate); human bioenergetics (PhD); identity and leadership development for counselors (Certificate); nurse educator (Post Master's Certificate); nursing (MS); nursing education (Postbaccalaureate Certificate); nursing practice (DNP); physical education (MS); physical education and sport (MA, MS); social psychology (MA); social psychology and clinical mental health counseling (MA); speech-language pathology (MA); wellness management (MA, MS). Electronic applications accepted.

College of Sciences and Humanities *Program availability:* Part-time, 100% online, blended/hybrid learning. Offers actuarial science (MA); anthropology (MA); biology (MA, MS); chemistry (MA, MS); clinical psychology (MA); cognitive and social processes (MA); computer science (MA, MS); elementary mathematics teacher leadership (Certificate); emergency management and homeland security (Certificate); English (MA, PhD); environmental science (PhD); geographic information systems (Certificate); geography (MS); geology (MA, MS); history (MA); interpretive ethnography (Certificate); linguistics (MA); mathematics (MA, MS); mathematics education (MA); middle school mathematics education (Certificate); natural resources and environmental management (MA, MS); physics (MA, MAE, MS); physiology (MA, MS); political science (MA, Certificate); post-secondary foundational mathematics teaching (MA, Certificate); professional meteorology and climatology (Certificate); public administration (MPA, Certificate); sciences and humanities (MA, MAE, MPA, MS, PhD, Certificate); sociology (MA); statistical modeling (Certificate); statistics (MA, MS); teaching English to speakers of other languages (TESOL) and linguistics (MA). Electronic applications accepted.

Miller College of Business *Program availability:* Part-time, evening/weekend, 100% online, blended/hybrid learning. Offers accounting (MS); business administration (MBA, Certificate, Graduate Certificate); business education (MA); business essentials (Graduate Certificate); community and economic development (Certificate); health economics, policy and administration (Certificate); information systems and operations management (MA, Certificate); information systems security management (Certificate); selling and sales management (Certificate). Electronic applications accepted.

Teachers College *Program availability:* Part-time, evening/weekend, 100% online, blended/hybrid learning. Offers adult and community education (MA); adult education (MA, Ed D, Certificate); adult, higher and community education (Ed D); applied behavior analysis (MA, Certificate); autism (Certificate); charter school leadership (Certificate); college and university teaching (Certificate); community college leadership (Certificate); community education (Certificate); computer education (Certificate); curriculum and educational technology (MA); diversity studies (Certificate); early childhood administration (Certificate); education (MA, MAE, MS, Ed D, PhD, Certificate, Ed S); educational administration and supervision (MA, Ed D); educational psychology (MA, MS, PhD, Certificate, Ed S); educational psychology (PhD); educational studies (PhD); elementary education (MAE, Ed D, PhD); enhanced teaching practices for elementary teachers (Certificate); executive development for public service (MA); family and consumer science (MS); family and consumer sciences (MA); gifted and talented education (Certificate); human development and learning (Certificate); instructional design and assessment (Certificate); literacy instruction (Certificate); middle-level education (Certificate); neuropsychology (Certificate); nutrition and dietetics (MA, MS); qualitative research in education (Certificate); quantitative psychology (MS); response to intervention (Certificate); school psychology (MA, PhD, Ed S); school psychology (Ed S); school superintendency (Ed S); secondary education (MA, MAE, Ed D); special education (MA, MAE, Ed D); student affairs administration in higher education (MA). Electronic applications accepted.

BANK STREET COLLEGE OF EDUCATION, New York, NY 10025

General Information Independent, coed, graduate-only institution. *Research affiliation:* Annenberg Institute (education), Stanford University (education), Educational Development Center (education), Mathematica Policy Research, Inc. (education), Center for Teaching Quality (education).

GRADUATE UNITS

Graduate School Offers advanced literacy specialization (Ed M); bilingual childhood special education (Ed M); bilingual early childhood general education (MS Ed); bilingual early childhood special and general education (MS Ed); bilingual early childhood special education (Ed M, MS Ed); bilingual elementary/childhood general education (MS Ed); bilingual elementary/childhood special and general education (MS Ed); bilingual elementary/childhood special education (MS Ed); child life (MS); early childhood and elementary/childhood education (MS Ed); early childhood education (MS Ed); early childhood leadership (MS Ed); early childhood special and general education (MS Ed); early childhood special education (Ed M, MS Ed); education (Ed M, MS, MS Ed); educational leadership (MS Ed); elementary/childhood education (MS Ed); elementary/childhood special and general education (MS Ed); elementary/childhood special education (MS Ed); elementary/childhood special education certification (Ed M); infant and family development (MS Ed); infant and family early childhood special and general education (MS Ed); infant and family/early childhood special education (Ed M); leadership for educational change (Ed M, MS Ed); leadership in community-based learning (MS Ed); leadership in mathematics education (MS Ed); leadership in museum education (MS Ed); leadership in the arts: creative writing (MS Ed); leadership in the arts: visual arts (MS Ed); museum education (MS Ed); museum education: elementary education certification (MS Ed); reading and literacy (MS Ed); teaching literacy (MS Ed); teaching literacy and childhood general education (MS Ed). Electronic applications accepted.

BAPTIST BIBLE COLLEGE, Springfield, MO 65803-3498

General Information Independent-religious, coed, comprehensive institution. *Enrollment:* 3 full-time matriculated graduate/professional students, 16 part-time matriculated graduate/professional students (1 woman). *Enrollment by degree level:* 19 master's. *Graduate faculty:* 1 full-time (0 women), 6 part-time/adjunct (0 women). *Tuition:* Full-time $8100; part-time $450 per credit. *Required fees:* $400; $200 $100. *Graduate housing:* Rooms and/or apartments available on a first-come, first-served basis to single and married students. *Student services:* Campus employment opportunities, campus safety program, free psychological counseling, international student services. *Library facilities:* G. B. Vick Memorial Library plus 1 other.

Computer facilities: 50 computers available on campus for general student use. Website: http://www.gobbc.edu/

General Application Contact: Terry Allcorn, Registrar, 417-268-6003, Fax: 800-819-8330, E-mail: tallcorn@gobbc.edu.

GRADUATE UNITS

Graduate and Professional Programs *Program availability:* Part-time. Offers biblical counseling (MA); church ministry (MA); theology (M Div). Electronic applications accepted.

THE BAPTIST COLLEGE OF FLORIDA, Graceville, FL 32440

General Information Independent-religious, coed, comprehensive institution. *Enrollment:* 33 full-time matriculated graduate/professional students (6 women). *Enrollment by degree level:* 33 master's. *Graduate faculty:* 12 full-time (0 women). *Tuition:* Full-time $4320; part-time $2160 per semester hour. *Required fees:* $360; $30 per semester hour. *Graduate housing:* Rooms and/or apartments available on a first-come, first-served basis to single and married students. Typical cost: $4612 (including board) for single students; $3500 per year for married students. Room and board charges vary according to board plan and housing facility selected. Housing application deadline: 8/12. *Student services:* Campus employment opportunities, campus safety program, exercise/wellness program, free psychological counseling, services for students with disabilities, writing training. *Library facilities:* Ida J. MacMillan Library plus 1 other. *Collection:* Books: 90,006 (physical), 88,931 (digital/electronic); Serial titles: 5,602 (physical), 5,602 (digital/electronic); Databases: 16. Weekly public service hours: 66.

Computer facilities: 25 computers available on campus for general student use. A campuswide network can be accessed from student residence rooms. Online class registration is available. Website: http://www.baptistcollege.edu/

General Application Contact: Sandra Richards, Director of Student Life and Marketing, 850-263-3261 Ext. 415, E-mail: skrichards@baptistcollege.edu.

GRADUATE UNITS

Graduate Programs Students: 33 full-time (6 women); includes 2 minority (1 Black or African American, non-Hispanic/Latino; 1 Hispanic/Latino). Average age 28. 10 applicants, 100% accepted, 10 enrolled. *Faculty:* 12 full-time (0 women). Expenses: Contact institution. *Financial support:* In 2018–19, 2 students received support. In 2018, 3 master's awarded. *Program availability:* Part-time, 100% online, blended/hybrid learning. Offers Christian studies (MA); music and worship leadership (MA). *Application deadline:* For fall admission, 8/12 for domestic and international students; for spring admission, 1/15 for domestic and international students. Applications are processed on a rolling basis. *Application fee:* $25. Electronic applications accepted. *Application Contact:* Sandra Richards, Director of Student Life and Marketing, 850-263-3261 Ext. 415, Fax: 850-263-9026, E-mail: skrichards@baptistcollege.edu. *Academic Dean:* Dr. Robin Jumper, 850-263-3261 Ext. 425, Fax: 850-263-2141, E-mail: grjumper@baptistcollege.edu.

BAPTIST MISSIONARY ASSOCIATION THEOLOGICAL SEMINARY, Jacksonville, TX 75766-5407

General Information Independent-religious, coed, primarily men, comprehensive institution. *Graduate housing:* Rooms and/or apartments available on a first-come, first-served basis to single and married students. Housing application deadline: 6/1.

GRADUATE UNITS

Graduate and Professional Programs *Program availability:* Part-time. Offers theology (M Div, MAR). Electronic applications accepted.

BARCLAY COLLEGE, Haviland, KS 67059-0288

General Information Independent-religious, coed, comprehensive institution.

GRADUATE UNITS

Master of Arts Program *Program availability:* Online learning. Offers transformational leadership (MA). Electronic applications accepted.

BARD COLLEGE, Annandale-on-Hudson, NY 12504

General Information Independent, coed, comprehensive institution. *Graduate housing:* On-campus housing not available.

GRADUATE UNITS

Bard Center for Environmental Policy *Program availability:* Part-time. Offers climate science and policy (MS, Professional Certificate); environmental policy (MS, Professional Certificate); sustainability (MBA). Electronic applications accepted.

Center for Curatorial Studies Offers curatorial studies (MA). Electronic applications accepted.

Conservatory of Music Offers music (MM); vocal arts (MM).

The Conductors Institute Offers choral conducting (MM); orchestral conducting (MM).

International Center of Photography Offers advanced photographic studies (MFA).

Levy Economics Institute Offers economic theory and policy (MS).

Longy School of Music *Program availability:* Part-time. Offers chamber music (Artist Diploma); collaborative piano (MM, Artist Diploma, GPD); composition (MM); opera (MM, GPD); organ (MM, Artist Diploma, GPD); piano (MM, Artist Diploma, GPD); voice (MM, Artist Diploma, GPD). MAT offered in partnership with the Los Angeles Philharmonic at the Los Angeles campus only. Electronic applications accepted.

Master of Arts in Teaching Program *Program availability:* Part-time. Offers secondary education (MAT). Electronic applications accepted.

Milton Avery Graduate School of the Arts Offers film/video (MFA); music/sound (MFA); painting (MFA); photography (MFA); sculpture (MFA); writing (MFA). Electronic applications accepted.

BARD GRADUATE CENTER, New York, NY 10024-3602

General Information Independent, coed, primarily women, graduate-only institution. *Graduate housing:* Rooms and/or apartments available on a first-come, first-served basis to single and married students. Housing application deadline: 4/1. *Research affiliation:* Association of Research Institutes in Art History, Metropolitan Museum of Art, Brooklyn Museum, American Museum of Natural History, Museum of Arts and Design, The Frick Collection.

GRADUATE UNITS

Graduate Studies *Program availability:* Part-time. Offers decorative arts, design history, and material culture (MA, PhD).

BARRY UNIVERSITY, Miami Shores, FL 33161-6695

General Information Independent-religious, coed, university. *Graduate housing:* On-campus housing not available. *Research affiliation:* Baxter Corporation (immunology, diagnostics), Coulter Corporation (immunology, cytology), Cordis Corporation (cardiac product development), Diamedix (immunological diagnostics), Noven Pharmaceutical, Sano Pharmaceuticals.

GRADUATE UNITS

Andreas School of Business *Program availability:* Part-time, evening/weekend. Offers accounting (MSA); business (MBA, MSA, MSM, Certificate); business administration (MBA); finance (Certificate); health services administration (Certificate); international business (Certificate); management (MSM); management information systems (Certificate); marketing (Certificate). Electronic applications accepted.

College of Arts and Sciences *Program availability:* Part-time, evening/weekend. Offers arts and sciences (MA, MFA, MS, D Min, Certificate, SSP); clinical psychology (MS); liberal studies (MA); ministry (D Min); pastoral ministry for Hispanics (MA); pastoral theology (MA); photography (MA, MFA); practical theology (MA); school psychology (MS, SSP). Electronic applications accepted.

College of Health Sciences *Program availability:* Part-time, evening/weekend. Offers anesthesiology (MS); biology (MS); biomedical sciences (MS); health care leadership (Certificate); health care planning and informatics (Certificate); health sciences (MS, Certificate); health services administration (MS); histotechnology (Certificate); long term care management (Certificate); medical group practice management (Certificate); occupational therapy (MS); quality improvement and outcomes management (Certificate). Electronic applications accepted.

Dwayne O. Andreas School of Law Offers law (JD).

Ellen Whiteside McDonnell School of Social Work *Program availability:* Part-time, evening/weekend. Offers social work (MSW, PhD). Electronic applications accepted.

Physician Assistant Program Offers physician assistant (MCMS). Electronic applications accepted.

School of Adult and Continuing Education *Program availability:* Part-time, evening/weekend. Offers administrative studies (MA); adult and continuing education (MA, MPA, MS, MSN, PhD, Certificate); information technology (MS); public administration (MPA). Electronic applications accepted.

Division of Nursing *Program availability:* Part-time, evening/weekend. Offers acute care nurse practitioner (MSN); family nurse practitioner (MSN); nurse practitioner (Certificate); nursing (MSN, PhD, Certificate); nursing administration (MSN, PhD, Certificate); nursing education (MSN, Certificate). Electronic applications accepted.

School of Education *Program availability:* Part-time, evening/weekend, online learning. Offers accomplished teacher (Ed S); advanced teaching and learning with technology (Certificate); counseling (MS, PhD, Ed S); culture, language and literacy (TESOL) (PhD); curriculum evaluation and research (PhD); distance education (Certificate); early childhood (Ed S); early childhood education (PhD); education (MS, Ed D, PhD, Certificate, Ed S); education for teachers of students with hearing impairments (MS); educational computing and technology (MS, Ed S); educational leadership (MS, Ed D, Certificate, Ed S); educational technology (PhD); elementary (Ed S); elementary education (MS, PhD); elementary education/ESOL (MS); ESOL (Ed S); exceptional student education (PhD); gifted (Ed S); higher education administration (PhD); higher education technology integration (Certificate); human resource development (PhD); human resource development and administration (MS); human resources: not for profit and religious organizations (Certificate); K-12 technology integration (Certificate); leadership (PhD); marital, couple and family counseling/therapy (MS, Ed S); mental health counseling (MS, Ed S); Montessori (Ed S); Montessori education (MS, Ed S); PKP/elementary (Ed S); pre-k/primary (MS); pre-k/primary/ESOL (MS); reading (Ed S); reading, language and cognition (PhD); rehabilitation counseling (MS, Ed S); school counseling (MS, Ed S); technology and TESOL (MS, Ed S); TESOL (MS); TESOL international (MS). Electronic applications accepted.

School of Human Performance and Leisure Sciences *Program availability:* Part-time, evening/weekend. Offers athletic training (MS); biomechanics (MS); exercise science (MS); general movement science (MS); human performance and leisure sciences (MS); sport and exercise psychology (MS); sport management (MS). Electronic applications accepted.

School of Podiatric Medicine Offers anatomy (MS); podiatric medicine (MS, DPM); podiatric medicine and surgery (DPM). Electronic applications accepted.

BARTON COLLEGE, Wilson, NC 27893-7000

General Information Independent-religious, coed, comprehensive institution. *Enrollment:* 1,059 graduate, professional, and undergraduate students; 41 full-time matriculated graduate/professional students (27 women), 42 part-time matriculated graduate/professional students (36 women). *Enrollment by degree level:* 59 master's, 24 other advanced degrees. *Graduate faculty:* 6 full-time (4 women), 1 part-time/adjunct (0 women). Tuition and fees vary according to program. *Graduate housing:* Room and/or apartments available on a first-come, first-served basis to single students; on-campus housing not available to married students. *Student services:* Campus employment opportunities, career counseling, exercise/wellness program, free psychological counseling, services for students with disabilities. *Library facilities:* Willis N. Hackney Library. *Collection:* Books: 121,046 (physical), 421,508 (digital/electronic); Serial titles: 88,792 (digital/electronic); Databases: 160. Weekly public service hours: 96; students can reserve study rooms.

Computer facilities: A campuswide network can be accessed from student residence rooms and from off campus. Online class registration is available.
Website: http://www.barton.edu/

GRADUATE UNITS
Program in Business Administration in Strategic Leadership
Program in Criminology and Criminal Justice Sciences
Program in Elementary Education Offers elementary education (M Ed). Electronic applications accepted.
Program in Nursing
Program in School Administration

BARUCH COLLEGE OF THE CITY UNIVERSITY OF NEW YORK, New York, NY 10010-5585

General Information State and locally supported, coed, comprehensive institution. *Graduate housing:* On-campus housing not available.

GRADUATE UNITS
Austin W. Marxe School of Public and International Affairs *Program availability:* Part-time, evening/weekend. Offers educational leadership (MS Ed); general public administration (MPA); health care policy (MPA); higher education administration (MS Ed); international nongovernmental organizations (MIA); nonprofit administration (MPA); policy analysis and evaluation (MPA); public and international affairs (MIA, MPA, MS Ed, Advanced Certificate); public management (MPA); school building leadership (Advanced Certificate); school district leadership (Advanced Certificate); trade policy and global economic governance (MIA); urban development and sustainability (MPA); Western Hemisphere affairs (MIA). Electronic applications accepted.
Weissman School of Arts and Sciences *Program availability:* Part-time, evening/weekend. Offers arts administration (MA); arts and sciences (MA, MS); corporate communication (MA); financial engineering (MS); industrial/organizational psychology (MS); mental health counseling (MA). Electronic applications accepted.
Zicklin School of Business *Program availability:* Part-time, evening/weekend. Offers accounting (MBA, MS, PhD); business (MBA, MS, PhD, Certificate); business administration (MBA); decision sciences (MBA); economics (MBA); entrepreneurship (MBA, MS); finance (MBA, MS, PhD); general business administration (MBA); health care administration (MBA); industrial and labor relations (MS); industrial and organizational psychology (MBA, MS, PhD); information systems (MBA, MS, PhD); international business (MBA); management (PhD); marketing (MBA, MS, PhD); operations management (MBA); organizational behavior/human resources management (MBA); quantitative methods and modeling (MBA, MS); real estate (MBA, MS); statistics (MBA, MS); sustainable business (MBA); taxation (MBA, MS). JD/MBA offered jointly with Brooklyn Law School and New York Law School. Electronic applications accepted.

BASTYR UNIVERSITY, Kenmore, WA 98028-4966

General Information Independent, coed, upper-level institution. *Graduate housing:* Room and/or apartments available on a first-come, first-served basis to single students; on-campus housing not available to married students. Housing application deadline: 5/1. *Research affiliation:* University of Washington (health), Fred Hutchinson Cancer Research Center (oncology), Seattle Cancer Care Alliance (oncology), Benaroya Research Institute at Virginia Mason (health).

GRADUATE UNITS
School of Natural Health Arts and Sciences *Program availability:* Part-time. Offers counseling psychology (MA); maternal-child health systems (MA); midwifery (MS); nutrition (Certificate); nutrition and clinical health psychology (MS); nutrition and wellness (MS).
School of Naturopathic Medicine *Program availability:* Part-time. Offers naturopathic medicine (ND, Postbaccalaureate Certificate). Electronic applications accepted.
School of Traditional World Medicines *Program availability:* Evening/weekend. Offers acupuncture and Oriental medicine (MS, DAOM); Ayurvedic sciences (MS). Electronic applications accepted.

BAYAMÓN CENTRAL UNIVERSITY, Bayamón, PR 00960-1725

General Information Independent-religious, coed, comprehensive institution. *Graduate housing:* On-campus housing not available.

GRADUATE UNITS
Graduate Programs *Program availability:* Part-time, evening/weekend. Offers accounting (MBA); administration and supervision (MA Ed); commercial education (MA Ed); elementary education (K–3) (MA Ed); family counseling (Graduate Certificate); finance (MBA); general business (MBA); guidance and counseling (MA Ed); management (MBA); marketing (MBA); organizational psychology (MA); pre-elementary teacher (MA Ed); rehabilitation counseling (MA Ed); special education (MA Ed).

BAYLOR COLLEGE OF MEDICINE, Houston, TX 77030-3498

General Information Independent, coed, graduate-only institution. CGS member. *Graduate housing:* On-campus housing not available. *Research affiliation:* Veterans Affairs Medical Center (biomedical research), Texas Children's Hospital (pediatric biomedical research), St. Luke's Episcopal Hospital (biomedical research), National Space Biomedical Research Institute (biomedical research), Harris Health System (biomedical research), Children's Nutrition Research Center (pediatric nutrition).

GRADUATE UNITS
Graduate School of Biomedical Sciences Offers biochemistry (PhD); biochemistry and molecular biology (PhD); biomedical sciences (MS, PhD); cardiovascular sciences (PhD); cell and molecular biology (PhD); clinical scientist training (MS, PhD); developmental biology (PhD); genetics (PhD); human genetics (PhD); immunology (PhD); microbiology (PhD); molecular and cellular biology (PhD); molecular and human genetics (PhD); molecular physiology and biophysics (PhD); molecular virology and microbiology (PhD); neuroscience (PhD); pharmacology (PhD); structural and computational biology and molecular biophysics (PhD); translational biology and molecular medicine (PhD); virology (PhD). Electronic applications accepted.
Medical School Offers medicine (MD). Electronic applications accepted.
School of Health Professions Offers genetic counseling (MS); health professions (MS, DNP); nurse anesthesia (DNP); physician assistant (MS). Electronic applications accepted.

BAYLOR UNIVERSITY, Waco, TX 76798

General Information Independent-religious, coed, university. CGS member. *Enrollment:* 17,217 graduate, professional, and undergraduate students; 2,597 full-time matriculated graduate/professional students (1,318 women), 566 part-time matriculated graduate/professional students (268 women). *Enrollment by degree level:* 1,654 master's, 1,494 doctoral, 15 other advanced degrees. *Graduate faculty:* 789. *Graduate housing:* Rooms and/or apartments available to single and married students. *Student services:* Campus employment opportunities, campus safety program, career counseling, exercise/wellness program, free psychological counseling, international student services, low-cost health insurance, multicultural affairs office, services for students with disabilities. *Library facilities:* Moody Memorial Library plus 8 others.

Computer facilities: Computer purchase and lease plans are available. A campuswide network can be accessed from student residence rooms and from off campus. Online class registration is available.
Website: http://www.baylor.edu/

General Application Contact: Tosah Hendrickson, Admissions Coordinator, 254-710-3588, Fax: 254-710-3870.

GRADUATE UNITS
Diana R. Garland School of Social Work Students: 123 full-time (115 women), 11 part-time (10 women); includes 46 minority (19 Black or African American, non-Hispanic/Latino; 1 American Indian or Alaska Native, non-Hispanic/Latino; 4 Asian, non-Hispanic/Latino; 16 Hispanic/Latino; 6 Two or more races, non-Hispanic/Latino), 6 international. Average age 27. 190 applicants, 72% accepted, 71 enrolled. *Faculty:* 11 full-time (5 women), 13 part-time/adjunct (7 women). Expenses: Contact institution. *Financial support:* In 2018–19, 138 students received support, including 12 research assistantships with tuition reimbursements available (averaging $6,800 per year); career-related internships or fieldwork, Federal Work-Study, institutionally sponsored loans, scholarships/grants, traineeships, tuition waivers (full and partial), and unspecified assistantships also available. Support available to part-time students. Financial award application deadline: 2/15; financial award applicants required to submit FAFSA. In 2018, 69 master's awarded. *Program availability:* Part-time, blended/hybrid learning. Offers social work (MSW, PhD). *Application deadline:* For spring admission, 3/15 for domestic and international students. Applications are processed on a rolling basis. *Application fee:* $45. Electronic applications accepted. *Application Contact:* Dr. Crystal Diaz-Espinoza, Director of Recruitment and Career Services, 254-710-4479, Fax: 254-710-6455, E-mail: crystal_diaz-espinoza@baylor.edu. *Associate Dean for Academic Affairs,* Melody Zuniga, 254-710-3702, Fax: 254-710-7412, E-mail: melody_zuniga@baylor.edu.
George W. Truett Theological Seminary Students: 248 full-time (97 women), 69 part-time (24 women); includes 82 minority (37 Black or African American, non-Hispanic/Latino; 7 Asian, non-Hispanic/Latino; 22 Hispanic/Latino; 16 Two or more races, non-Hispanic/Latino), 18 international. Average age 30. 129 applicants, 95% accepted, 91 enrolled. *Faculty:* 21 full-time (2 women), 14 part-time/adjunct (4 women). Expenses: Contact institution. *Financial support:* In 2018–19, 342 students received support, including 38 research assistantships with partial tuition reimbursements available (averaging $5,130 per year); career-related internships or fieldwork, Federal Work-Study, scholarships/grants, and unspecified assistantships also available. Support available to part-time students. Financial award application deadline: 8/1; financial award applicants required to submit FAFSA. In 2018, 67 master's, 7 doctorates awarded. *Program availability:* Part-time. Offers theology (M Div, MACM, MTS, D Min). *Application deadline:* For fall admission, 5/1 priority date for domestic students, 6/10 for international students; for spring admission, 11/15 for domestic students, 10/10 for international students; for summer admission, 4/1 for domestic students, 3/10 for international students. Applications are processed on a rolling basis. *Application fee:* $35. Electronic applications accepted. *Application Contact:* Carley Lund, Administrative Associate, Admission Services, 254-710-7334, Fax: 254-710-7233, E-mail: carley_lund@baylor.edu. *Dean,* Dr. Todd D. Still, 254-710-6080, Fax: 254-710-7234, E-mail: todd_still@baylor.edu.
Graduate School Students: 1,810 full-time (913 women), 485 part-time (236 women); includes 514 minority (110 Black or African American, non-Hispanic/Latino; 8 American Indian or Alaska Native, non-Hispanic/Latino; 87 Asian, non-Hispanic/Latino; 213 Hispanic/Latino; 1 Native Hawaiian or other Pacific Islander, non-Hispanic/Latino; 95 Two or more races, non-Hispanic/Latino), 206 international. 1,692 applicants. *Faculty:* 789. Expenses: Contact institution. *Financial support:* Fellowships, research assistantships with tuition reimbursements, teaching assistantships with tuition reimbursements, career-related internships or fieldwork, Federal Work-Study, institutionally sponsored loans, scholarships/grants, health care benefits, tuition waivers (full and partial), and unspecified assistantships available. Support available to part-time students. Financial award applicants required to submit FAFSA. In 2018, 680 master's, 136 doctorates, 7 other advanced degrees awarded. *Program availability:* Part-time, evening/weekend, 100% online, blended/hybrid learning. *Application deadline:* For fall admission, 2/15 for domestic students; for spring admission, 12/1 for domestic students; for summer admission, 5/1 for domestic students. Applications are processed on a rolling basis. *Application fee:* $50. Electronic applications accepted. *Application Contact:* Tosha Hendrickson, Graduate Admissions Coordinator, 254-710-3588, Fax: 254-710-3870, E-mail: tosha_hendrickson@baylor.edu. *Dean,* Dr. Larry Lyon, 254-710-3588, Fax: 254-710-3870, E-mail: larry_lyon@baylor.edu.
College of Arts and Sciences Students: 578 full-time (262 women), 78 part-time (36 women); includes 97 minority (14 Black or African American, non-Hispanic/Latino; 1 American Indian or Alaska Native, non-Hispanic/Latino; 16 Asian, non-Hispanic/Latino; 40 Hispanic/Latino; 26 Two or more races, non-Hispanic/Latino), 97 international. Expenses: Contact institution. *Financial support:* Fellowships, research assistantships with partial tuition reimbursements, teaching assistantships, career-related internships or fieldwork, Federal Work-Study, institutionally sponsored loans, scholarships/grants, tuition waivers (full and partial), and laboratory assistantships, practicum stipends available. Support available to part-time students. In 2018, 104 master's, 66 doctorates awarded. *Program availability:* Part-time, evening/weekend. Offers American studies (MA); arts and sciences (IMES, MA, MES, MFA, MIJ, MPPA,

MS, MSCSD, MSW, PhD, Psy D); biochemistry (MS, PhD); biology (MA, MS, PhD); chemistry (MS, PhD); clinical psychology (Psy D); communication (MA); community analytics (PhD); ecological, earth and environmental sciences (PhD); english (MA); environmental science (MES, MS, PhD); geosciences (MS, PhD); health and society (PhD); history (MA, PhD); journalism, public relations, advertising, photography (MIJ); mathematics (MS, PhD); museum studies (MA); news editorial, public relations, advertising, photography (MA); philosophy (MA, PhD); physics (MA, MS, PhD); political science (MA, MPPA, PhD); psychology and neuroscience (MA, MSCP, PhD, Psy D); religion (MA, PhD); social, general experimental, behavioral neuroscience (PhD); sociology (MA); sociology of religion (PhD); Spanish (MA); statistical science (MA, PhD); theatre arts (MA, MFA). *Application deadline:* Applications are processed on a rolling basis. *Application fee:* $50. Electronic applications accepted. *Application Contact:* Dr. Larry Lyon, Dean, 254-710-3588, Fax: 254-710-3870, E-mail: larry_lyon@baylor.edu. *Dean,* Dr. Larry Lyon, 254-710-3588, Fax: 254-710-3870, E-mail: larry_lyon@baylor.edu.

Hankamer School of Business Students: 464 full-time (188 women), 216 part-time (72 women); includes 177 minority (35 Black or African American, non-Hispanic/Latino; 1 American Indian or Alaska Native, non-Hispanic/Latino; 38 Asian, non-Hispanic/Latino; 71 Hispanic/Latino; 1 Native Hawaiian or other Pacific Islander, non-Hispanic/Latino; 31 Two or more races, non-Hispanic/Latino), 38 international. Expenses: Contact institution. *Financial support:* Research assistantships, teaching assistantships, career-related internships or fieldwork, Federal Work-Study, and institutionally sponsored loans available. In 2018, 383 master's, 5 doctorates awarded. *Program availability:* Part-time. Offers accounting and business law (M Acc, MT); business (M Acc, MBA, MS Eco, MSIS, MT, PhD); business administration (MBA); economics (MS Eco); entrepreneurship (PhD); health care administration (MHA); information systems (PhD); information systems management (MBA). *Application deadline:* Applications are processed on a rolling basis. *Application fee:* $50. *Application Contact:* Laurie Wilson, Director, Graduate Business Programs, 254-710-4163, Fax: 254-710-1066, E-mail: laurie_wilson@baylor.edu. *Associate Dean,* Dr. Gary Carini, 254-710-3718, Fax: 254-710-1092, E-mail: gary_carini@baylor.edu.

Institute of Biomedical Studies Students: 16 full-time (7 women); includes 3 minority (1 Black or African American, non-Hispanic/Latino; 2 Hispanic/Latino), 7 international. Average age 24. 69 applicants, 10% accepted, 5 enrolled. Expenses: Contact institution. *Financial support:* In 2018–19, 22 students received support. Research assistantships, teaching assistantships, and tuition waivers available. In 2018, 4 master's, 4 doctorates awarded. Offers biomedical studies (MS, PhD). *Application deadline:* For spring admission, 2/15 for domestic and international students. Applications are processed on a rolling basis. *Application fee:* $25. Electronic applications accepted. *Application Contact:* Rhonda Bellert, Administrative Associate, 254-710-2514, Fax: 254-710-2199, E-mail: rhonda_bellert@baylor.edu. *Acting Graduate Program Director,* Dr. Bob Kane, 254-710-4556, Fax: 254-710-2199, E-mail: bob_kane@baylor.edu.

Louise Herrington School of Nursing Students: 111 full-time (86 women), 17 part-time (15 women); includes 36 minority (12 Black or African American, non-Hispanic/Latino; 1 American Indian or Alaska Native, non-Hispanic/Latino; 7 Asian, non-Hispanic/Latino; 12 Hispanic/Latino; 4 Two or more races, non-Hispanic/Latino). Average age 35. 61 applicants, 66% accepted, 19 enrolled. *Faculty:* 23 full-time (22 women), 8 part-time/adjunct (all women). Expenses: Contact institution. *Financial support:* In 2018–19, 66 students received support, including 6 teaching assistantships (averaging $2,235 per year); research assistantships, Federal Work-Study, scholarships/grants, and unspecified assistantships also available. Support available to part-time students. Financial award application deadline: 6/30; financial award applicants required to submit FAFSA. In 2018, 13 master's, 4 doctorates awarded. *Program availability:* Part-time, online only, Online with on campus immersions. Offers nursing practice (MSN). *Application deadline:* Applications are processed on a rolling basis. *Application fee:* $50. Electronic applications accepted. *Application Contact:* Elaine Lark, Coordinator of Recruitment and Enrollment, 972-576-9216, Fax: 972-576-9081, E-mail: elaine_lark@baylor.edu. *Associate Dean for Online Graduate Programs,* Dr. Kristi Feutz, 972-576-9116, Fax: 972-576-9082, E-mail: Kristi_Feutz@baylor.edu.

Robbins College of Health and Human Sciences Students: 376 full-time (235 women), 22 part-time (16 women); includes 95 minority (14 Black or African American, non-Hispanic/Latino; 3 American Indian or Alaska Native, non-Hispanic/Latino; 13 Asian, non-Hispanic/Latino; 49 Hispanic/Latino; 16 Two or more races, non-Hispanic/Latino), 11 international. Expenses: Contact institution. In 2018, 98 master's, 53 doctorates awarded. Offers athletic training (MS); communication sciences and disorders (MS); community health (MPH); exercise physiology (MS); health and human sciences (MA, MPH, MS, MS Ed, PhD); kinesiology, exercise nutrition, and health promotion (PhD); nutrition (MS); nutrition sciences (MS); sport pedagogy (MS). *Application Contact:* Lori McNamara, Graduate Admissions Coordinator, 254-710-3588, Fax: 254-710-3870, E-mail: lori_mcnamara@baylor.edu. *Dean,* Dr. Rodney G. Bowden, 254-710-6111, Fax: 254-710-3699, E-mail: rodney_bowden@baylor.edu.

School of Education Students: 163 full-time (113 women), 96 part-time (74 women); includes 81 minority (30 Black or African American, non-Hispanic/Latino; 1 American Indian or Alaska Native, non-Hispanic/Latino; 7 Asian, non-Hispanic/Latino; 30 Hispanic/Latino; 13 Two or more races, non-Hispanic/Latino), 9 international. 248 applicants, 35% accepted, 28 enrolled. *Faculty:* 42 full-time (26 women), 10 part-time/adjunct (6 women). Expenses: Contact institution. *Financial support:* In 2018–19, 181 students received support, including 38 research assistantships (averaging $12,050 per year), 68 teaching assistantships (averaging $12,050 per year); career-related internships or fieldwork, Federal Work-Study, institutionally sponsored loans, scholarships/grants, health care benefits, tuition waivers (partial), unspecified assistantships, and stipends also available. Support available to part-time students. Financial award application deadline: 2/1; financial award applicants required to submit FAFSA. In 2018, 52 master's, 4 doctorates, 9 other advanced degrees awarded. *Program availability:* Part-time. Offers curriculum and instruction (MA, MS Ed, Ed D, PhD); education (MA, MS Ed, Ed D, PhD, Ed S); educational leadership (MS Ed, Ed S); educational psychology (MS Ed); exceptionalities (PhD); learning and development (PhD); quantitative methods (MA); school psychology (Ed S). *Application deadline:* For fall admission, 2/1 priority date for domestic and international students. Applications are processed on a rolling basis. *Application fee:* $50. Electronic applications accepted. *Application Contact:* Dr. Terrill F. Saxon, Interim Dean/Associate Dean of Graduate Programs, 254-710-3111, Fax: 254-710-3987, E-mail: terrill_saxon@baylor.edu. *Interim Dean/Associate Dean of Graduate Programs,* Dr. Terrill F. Saxon, 254-710-3111, Fax: 254-710-3987, E-mail: terrill_saxon@baylor.edu.

School of Engineering and Computer Science Students: 89 full-time (15 women), 11 part-time (0 women); includes 15 minority (2 Black or African American, non-

Hispanic/Latino; 1 American Indian or Alaska Native, non-Hispanic/Latino; 6 Asian, non-Hispanic/Latino; 4 Hispanic/Latino; 2 Two or more races, non-Hispanic/Latino), 43 international. Expenses: Contact institution. *Financial support:* Research assistantships and teaching assistantships available. Financial award application deadline: 3/15. In 2018, 29 master's, 8 doctorates awarded. *Program availability:* Part-time. Offers biomedical engineering (MSBME); computer science (MS, PhD); electrical and computer engineering (MSECE, PhD); engineering (ME); engineering and computer science (ME, MS, MSBME, PhD); mechanical engineering (MS, MSME, PhD). *Application deadline:* Applications are processed on a rolling basis. *Application fee:* $50. *Application Contact:* Dr. Dennis L. O'Neal, Dean, 254-710-3871, Fax: 254-710-3839, E-mail: dennis_oneal@baylor.edu. *Dean,* Dr. Dennis L. O'Neal, 254-710-3871, Fax: 254-710-3839, E-mail: dennis_oneal@baylor.edu.

School of Music Students: 20 full-time (7 women), 40 part-time (18 women); includes 11 minority (2 Black or African American, non-Hispanic/Latino; 6 Hispanic/Latino; 3 Two or more races, non-Hispanic/Latino), 8 international. Average age 25. 91 applicants, 48% accepted, 26 enrolled. *Faculty:* 40 full-time (15 women). Expenses: Contact institution. *Financial support:* In 2018–19, 55 students received support, including 51 teaching assistantships with full tuition reimbursements available (averaging $7,500 per year); Federal Work-Study, institutionally sponsored loans, and scholarships/grants also available. Financial award application deadline: 2/15. In 2018, 31 master's, 2 doctorates awarded. Offers church music (MM, DMA); conducting (MM); musicology (MM). Truett Seminary for MDiv/MM degree. *Application deadline:* For fall admission, 2/1 for domestic and international students; for spring admission, 10/15 for domestic and international students. *Application fee:* $50. Electronic applications accepted. *Application Contact:* Melinda Coats, Administrative Assistant, 254-710-2360, Fax: 254-710-1491, E-mail: melinda_coats@baylor.edu. *Graduate Program Director,* Dr. Timothy McKinney, 254-710-6498, Fax: 254-710-1191, E-mail: Timothy_McKinney@baylor.edu.

School of Law Students: 431 full-time (203 women); includes 108 minority (11 Black or African American, non-Hispanic/Latino; 8 American Indian or Alaska Native, non-Hispanic/Latino; 20 Asian, non-Hispanic/Latino; 58 Hispanic/Latino; 1 Native Hawaiian or other Pacific Islander, non-Hispanic/Latino; 10 Two or more races, non-Hispanic/Latino), 3 international. Average age 24. 1,559 applicants, 50% accepted, 86 enrolled. *Faculty:* 32 full-time (11 women), 55 part-time/adjunct (14 women). Expenses: Contact institution. *Financial support:* In 2018–19, 325 students received support. Federal Work-Study and scholarships/grants available. Financial award application deadline: 2/1; financial award applicants required to submit FAFSA. In 2018, 118 doctorates awarded. Offers law (JD). *Application deadline:* For fall admission, 3/16 for domestic and international students; for spring admission, 11/15 for domestic and international students; for summer admission, 3/16 for domestic and international students. Applications are processed on a rolling basis. *Application fee:* $0. Electronic applications accepted. *Application Contact:* Jenny Branson, Assistant Dean of Admissions and Financial Aid, 254-710-1911, Fax: 254-710-2316, E-mail: jenny_branson@baylor.edu. *Dean,* Bradley J. B. Toben, 254-710-1911, Fax: 254-710-2316.

BAY PATH UNIVERSITY, Longmeadow, MA 01106-2292

General Information Independent, Undergraduate: women only; graduate: coed, comprehensive institution. *Enrollment:* 591 full-time matriculated graduate/professional students (513 women), 930 part-time matriculated graduate/professional students (817 women). *Enrollment by degree level:* 1,384 master's, 23 doctoral, 92 other advanced degrees. *Graduate faculty:* 35 full-time (30 women), 137 part-time/adjunct (105 women). *Graduate housing:* Room and/or apartments available on a first-come, first-served basis to single students; on-campus housing not available to married students. Housing application deadline: 7/2. *Student services:* Campus employment opportunities, campus safety program, career counseling, exercise/wellness program, free psychological counseling, international student services, low-cost health insurance, multicultural affairs office, services for students with disabilities. *Library facilities:* Hatch Library. *Collection:* Books: 52,565 (physical), 408,000 (digital/electronic); Serial titles: 80 (physical), 55,000 (digital/electronic); Databases: 110. Weekly public service hours: 86; students can reserve study rooms.

Computer facilities: 235 computers available on campus for general student use. A campuswide network can be accessed from student residence rooms and from off campus. Online class registration is available.
Website: http://www.baypath.edu/

General Application Contact: Sheryl Kosakowski, Executive Director of Graduate Admissions, 413-565-1075, Fax: 413-565-1250, E-mail: skosakowski@baypath.edu.

GRADUATE UNITS
Doctorate Program in Nursing Practice
Doctorate Program in Occupational Therapy

Program in Accounting Students: 1 (woman) full-time, 16 part-time (all women); includes 2 minority (1 Black or African American, non-Hispanic/Latino; 1 Asian, non-Hispanic/Latino). Average age 34. Expenses: Contact institution. *Financial support:* In 2018–19, 2 students received support. Scholarships/grants and unspecified assistantships available. Financial award applicants required to submit FAFSA. In 2018, 3 master's awarded. *Program availability:* Part-time, online only, 100% online. Offers forensic accounting (MS); private accounting (MS); public accounting (tax and audit) (MS). *Application deadline:* Applications are processed on a rolling basis. Electronic applications accepted. *Application Contact:* Sheryl Kosakowski, Executive Director of Graduate Admissions, 413-565-1075, Fax: 413-565-1250, E-mail: skosakowski@baypath.edu. *Director of Finance and Accounting Programs,* Kara Stevens, 413-565-1344, E-mail: kastevens@baypath.edu.

Program in Applied Behavior Analysis Students: 6 full-time (all women), 191 part-time (175 women); includes 24 minority (8 Black or African American, non-Hispanic/Latino; 4 Asian, non-Hispanic/Latino; 9 Hispanic/Latino; 3 Two or more races, non-Hispanic/Latino), 2 international. Average age 28. Expenses: Contact institution. *Financial support:* Unspecified assistantships available. Financial award applicants required to submit FAFSA. *Program availability:* Part-time, blended/hybrid learning. Offers applied behavior analysis (MS); autism spectrum disorders (MS). *Application deadline:* Applications are processed on a rolling basis. Electronic applications accepted. *Application Contact:* Katie Manning, Director of Graduate Admissions, 413-565-1337, Fax: 413-565-1250, E-mail: kmanning@baypath.edu. *DIRECTOR OF GRADUATE PROGRAM IN APPLIED BEHAVIOR ANALYSIS,* Susan Ainsleigh, 413-565-6873, E-mail: sainsleigh@baypath.edu.

Program in Applied Data Science Students: 5 full-time (2 women), 12 part-time (6 women); includes 8 minority (4 Black or African American, non-Hispanic/Latino; 2 Asian, non-Hispanic/Latino). Average age 37. Expenses: Contact institution. *Financial support:* Applicants required to submit FAFSA. *Program availability:* Part-time, 100% online. Offers applied data science (MS). *Application deadline:* Applications are processed on a rolling basis. Electronic applications accepted. *Application Contact:* Elise Carrier, Assistant Director of Graduate Admissions, 413-565-1621, Fax: 413-565-1250, E-mail: ecarrier@baypath.edu. *DIRECTOR, MS APPLIED DATA SCIENCE*, Ning Jia, E-mail: njia@baypath.edu.

Program in Applied Laboratory Science and Operations Students: 13 full-time (12 women), 1 (woman) part-time; includes 4 minority (1 Asian, non-Hispanic/Latino; 2 Hispanic/Latino; 1 Two or more races, non-Hispanic/Latino). Average age 29. Expenses: Contact institution. *Financial support:* Unspecified assistantships available. Financial award applicants required to submit FAFSA. *Program availability:* Part-time, evening/weekend. Offers applied laboratory science and operations (MS). *Application deadline:* Applications are processed on a rolling basis. Electronic applications accepted. *Application Contact:* Jennifer Palma, Director of Graduate Admissions, 413-565-1181, Fax: 413-565-1250, E-mail: jpalma@baypath.edu. *DIRECTOR OF THE APPLIED LABORATORY SCIENCE & OPERATIONS GRADUATE PROGRAM*, Dr. Thomas Mennella, 413-565-1318, E-mail: tmennella@baypath.edu.

Program in Clinical Mental Health Counseling Students: 75 full-time (66 women), 83 part-time (75 women); includes 37 minority (21 Black or African American, non-Hispanic/Latino; 1 American Indian or Alaska Native, non-Hispanic/Latino; 14 Hispanic/Latino; 1 Two or more races, non-Hispanic/Latino). Average age 34. Expenses: Contact institution. *Financial support:* Unspecified assistantships available. Financial award applicants required to submit FAFSA. *Program availability:* Part-time, blended/hybrid learning. Offers clinical mental health counseling (MS). Program also offered in Sturbridge and Burlington, MA. *Application deadline:* Applications are processed on a rolling basis. Electronic applications accepted. *Application Contact:* Anastasia Spremulli, Assistant Director of Graduate Admissions, 413-565-140, Fax: 413-565-1250, E-mail: aspremulli@baypath.edu. *Director*, Dr. Mark Benander, 413-565-1332, E-mail: mbenander@baypath.edu.

Program in Communications *Program availability:* Part-time, evening/weekend, 100% online, blended/hybrid learning. Offers communications (MS). Electronic applications accepted.

Program in Communications and Information Management Students: 7 full-time (all women), 8 part-time (6 women); includes 4 minority (all Hispanic/Latino), 1 international. Average age 35. Expenses: Contact institution. *Financial support:* Unspecified assistantships available. Financial award applicants required to submit FAFSA. *Program availability:* Part-time, evening/weekend, 100% online. Offers communications and information management (MS). *Application deadline:* Applications are processed on a rolling basis. Electronic applications accepted. *Application Contact:* Elise Carrier, Assistant Director of Graduate Admissions, 413-565-1621, Fax: 413-565-1250, E-mail: ecarrier@baypath.edu. *Program Director*, Robin Saunders, 413-565-1009, E-mail: rsaunders@baypath.edu.

Program in Creative Nonfiction Students: 2 full-time (both women), 40 part-time (35 women); includes 5 minority (2 Black or African American, non-Hispanic/Latino; 1 Hispanic/Latino; 2 Two or more races, non-Hispanic/Latino). Average age 46. Expenses: Contact institution. *Financial support:* Applicants required to submit FAFSA. *Program availability:* Part-time, evening/weekend, online only, 100% online. Offers creative nonfiction (MFA). *Application deadline:* Applications are processed on a rolling basis. Electronic applications accepted. *Application Contact:* Jennifer Palma, Director of Graduate Admissions, 413-565-1181, Fax: 413-565-1250, E-mail: jpalma@baypath.edu. *Director*, Leanne James Blackwell, 413-565-1232, E-mail: ljblackwell@baypath.edu.

Program in Cybersecurity Management Students: 9 full-time (6 women), 20 part-time (11 women); includes 14 minority (2 Black or African American, non-Hispanic/Latino; 1 Asian, non-Hispanic/Latino; 8 Hispanic/Latino; 3 Two or more races, non-Hispanic/Latino). Average age 36. Expenses: Contact institution. *Financial support:* Unspecified assistantships available. Financial award applicants required to submit FAFSA. *Program availability:* Part-time, evening/weekend, online only, 100% online. Offers cybersecurity management (MS). *Application deadline:* Applications are processed on a rolling basis. Electronic applications accepted. *Application Contact:* Sheryl Kosakowski, Executive Director of Graduate Admissions, 413-565-1075, Fax: 413-565-1250, E-mail: skosakowski@baypath.edu. *DIRECTOR OF COMPUTER SCIENCE & CYBERSECURITY PROGRAMS*, Dr. Matthew J. Smith, 413-565-6828, E-mail: matsmith@baypath.edu.

Program in Developmental Psychology Students: 4 full-time (all women), 12 part-time (11 women); includes 6 minority (4 Black or African American, non-Hispanic/Latino; 1 Hispanic/Latino; 1 Two or more races, non-Hispanic/Latino). Average age 31. Expenses: Contact institution. *Financial support:* Unspecified assistantships available. Financial award applicants required to submit FAFSA. *Program availability:* Part-time, 100% online. Offers developmental psychology (MS). *Application deadline:* Applications are processed on a rolling basis. Electronic applications accepted. *Application Contact:* Carol Lombardi, Director of Graduate Admissions, 413-565-6851, Fax: 413-565-1250, E-mail: clombardi@baypath.edu. *Program Director*, Dr. Mark Benander, 413-5651196, E-mail: mbenander@baypath.edu.

Program in Education Students: 55 full-time (50 women), 168 part-time (149 women); includes 22 minority (6 Black or African American, non-Hispanic/Latino; 3 Asian, non-Hispanic/Latino; 11 Hispanic/Latino; 2 Two or more races, non-Hispanic/Latino). Average age 31. Expenses: Contact institution. *Financial support:* Unspecified assistantships available. Financial award applicants required to submit FAFSA. *Program availability:* Part-time, 100% online. Offers education. *Application deadline:* Applications are processed on a rolling basis. Electronic applications accepted. *Application Contact:* Katie Manning, Director of Graduate Admissions, 413-565-1337, Fax: 413-565-1250, E-mail: kmanning@baypath.edu. *Program Coordinator*, Dr. Ellen Rustico, E-mail: erustico@baypath.edu.

Program in Entrepreneurial Thinking and Innovative Practices Students: 21 full-time (17 women), 51 part-time (43 women); includes 31 minority (17 Black or African American, non-Hispanic/Latino; 2 Asian, non-Hispanic/Latino; 11 Hispanic/Latino; 1 Two or more races, non-Hispanic/Latino). Average age 34. Expenses: Contact institution. *Financial support:* Unspecified assistantships available. Financial award applicants required to submit FAFSA. *Program availability:* Part-time, 100% online. Offers entrepreneurial thinking and innovative practices (MBA). *Application deadline:* Applications are processed on a rolling basis. Electronic applications accepted. *Application Contact:* Sheryl Kosakowski, Executive Director of Graduate Admissions, 413-565-1075, Fax: 413-565-1250, E-mail: skosakowski@baypath.edu. *Program Director*, Mo Sattar, 413-5651228, E-mail: msattar@baypath.edu.

Program in Genetic Counseling Students: 24 full-time (23 women), 1 international. Average age 28. Expenses: Contact institution. *Financial support:* Scholarships/grants available. Financial award applicants required to submit FAFSA. *Program availability:* Evening/weekend, blended/hybrid learning. Offers genetic counseling (MS). *Application deadline:* Applications are processed on a rolling basis. Electronic applications accepted. *Application Contact:* Anastasia Spremulli, Assistant Director of Graduate Admissions, 413-565-1340, Fax: 413-565-1250, E-mail: aspremulli@baypath.edu. *Program Director*, Janice Berliner, 413-5651454, E-mail: jberliner@baypath.edu.

Program in Healthcare Management Students: 34 part-time (25 women); includes 11 minority (4 Black or African American, non-Hispanic/Latino; 1 Asian, non-Hispanic/Latino; 4 Hispanic/Latino; 2 Two or more races, non-Hispanic/Latino). Average age 39. Expenses: Contact institution. *Program availability:* Part-time, online only, 100% online. Offers health informatics (MS); organizational excellence (MS). *Application deadline:* Applications are processed on a rolling basis. Electronic applications accepted. *Application Contact:* Anastasia Spremulli, Assistant Director of Graduate Admissions, 413-565-1340, Fax: 413-565-1250, E-mail: aspremulli@baypath.edu. *Coordinator*, Dr. Terry DeVito, E-mail: tdevito@baypath.edu.

Program in Higher Education Administration Students: 2 full-time (both women), 34 part-time (25 women); includes 11 minority (6 Black or African American, non-Hispanic/Latino; 1 Asian, non-Hispanic/Latino; 3 Hispanic/Latino; 1 Two or more races, non-Hispanic/Latino). Average age 34. Expenses: Contact institution. *Financial support:* Unspecified assistantships available. Financial award applicants required to submit FAFSA. *Program availability:* Part-time, online only, 100% online. Offers enrollment management (MS); general administration (MS); institutional advancement (MS); online teaching and program administration (MS). *Application deadline:* Applications are processed on a rolling basis. Electronic applications accepted. *Application Contact:* Jennifer Palma, Director of Graduate Admissions, 413-565-1181, Fax: 413-565-1250, E-mail: jpalma@baypath.edu. *Program Director*, Dr. Lauren Way, 413-565-1193, E-mail: lway@baypath.edu.

Program in Higher Education Leadership and Organizational Studies

Program in Information Management Students: 1 (woman) full-time, 4 part-time (2 women); includes 1 minority (Hispanic/Latino). Average age 36. Expenses: Contact institution. *Financial support:* Unspecified assistantships available. Financial award applicants required to submit FAFSA. *Program availability:* Part-time, 100% online. Offers information management (MS). *Application deadline:* Applications are processed on a rolling basis. Electronic applications accepted. *Application Contact:* Elise Carrier, Assistant Director of Graduate Admissions, 413-565-1621, Fax: 413-565-1250, E-mail: ecarrier@baypath.edu. *Director*, Robin Saunders, 413-565-1009, E-mail: rsaunders@baypath.edu.

Program in Leadership and Negotiation Students: 4 full-time (3 women), 26 part-time (25 women); includes 9 minority (7 Black or African American, non-Hispanic/Latino; 1 Asian, non-Hispanic/Latino; 1 Hispanic/Latino). Average age 38. Expenses: Contact institution. *Financial support:* Unspecified assistantships available. Financial award applicants required to submit FAFSA. *Program availability:* Part-time, 100% online, blended/hybrid learning. Offers leadership and negotiation (MS). *Application deadline:* Applications are processed on a rolling basis. Electronic applications accepted. *Application Contact:* Elise Carrier, Assistant Dean of Graduate Director, 413-565-1621, Fax: 413-565-1250, E-mail: ecarrier@baypath.edu. *Director*, Dr. Joshua Weiss, E-mail: joweiss@baypath.edu.

Program in Nonprofit Management and Philanthropy Students: 4 full-time (all women), 31 part-time (28 women); includes 16 minority (9 Black or African American, non-Hispanic/Latino; 1 Asian, non-Hispanic/Latino; 4 Hispanic/Latino; 2 Two or more races, non-Hispanic/Latino). Average age 36. Expenses: Contact institution. *Financial support:* Unspecified assistantships available. Financial award applicants required to submit FAFSA. *Program availability:* Part-time, 100% online. Offers nonprofit management and philanthropy (MS). *Application deadline:* Applications are processed on a rolling basis. Electronic applications accepted. *Application Contact:* Jennifer Palma, Director of Graduate Admissions, 413-565-1181, Fax: 413-565-1250, E-mail: jpamla@baypath.edu. *Program Director*, Silvia de Haas-Phillips, E-mail: sdphillips@baypath.edu.

Program in Nursing

Program in Occupational Therapy Students: 271 full-time (241 women), 49 part-time (42 women); includes 74 minority (24 Black or African American, non-Hispanic/Latino; 1 American Indian or Alaska Native, non-Hispanic/Latino; 21 Asian, non-Hispanic/Latino; 21 Hispanic/Latino; 7 Two or more races, non-Hispanic/Latino). Average age 26. Expenses: Contact institution. *Financial support:* Unspecified assistantships available. Financial award applicants required to submit FAFSA. *Program availability:* Part-time. Offers occupational therapy (MOT, OTD). *Application deadline:* Applications are processed on a rolling basis. Electronic applications accepted. *Application Contact:* Maggie Pereiras, Director of Graduate Admissions Health Sciences, 413-565-1167, Fax: 413-565-1250, E-mail: mpereiras@baypath.edu. *Program Director*, Dr. Beverly St. Pierre, E-mail: bstpierre@baypath.edu.

Program in Physician Assistant Studies Students: 60 full-time (40 women); includes 15 minority (3 Black or African American, non-Hispanic/Latino; 1 American Indian or Alaska Native, non-Hispanic/Latino; 4 Asian, non-Hispanic/Latino; 7 Hispanic/Latino). Average age 29. Expenses: Contact institution. *Financial support:* Unspecified assistantships available. Financial award applicants required to submit FAFSA. Offers physician assistant studies (MS). *Application deadline:* Applications are processed on a rolling basis. Electronic applications accepted. *Application Contact:* Lisa Adams, Executive Program Manager Physician Assistant Program, 413-565-1317, Fax: 413-565-1250, E-mail: paprogram@baypath.edu. *Director*, Theresa Riethle, 413-565-1206, E-mail: triethle@baypath.edu.

Program in Public Health

Program in Strategic Fundraising and Philanthropy Students: 10 part-time (9 women); includes 1 minority (Black or African American, non-Hispanic/Latino). Average age 41. Expenses: Contact institution. *Financial support:* Unspecified assistantships available. Financial award applicants required to submit FAFSA. In 2018, 4 master's awarded. *Program availability:* Part-time, 100% online. Offers higher education fundraising (MS); nonprofit fundraising (MS). *Application deadline:* Applications are processed on a rolling basis. Electronic applications accepted. *Application Contact:* Jennifer Palma, Director of Graduate Admissions, 413-565-1181, Fax: 413-565-1250, E-mail: jpalma@baypath.edu. *Program Director*, Silvia de Haas-Phillips, E-mail: sdphillips@baypath.edu.

BECKER COLLEGE, Worcester, MA 01609
General Information Independent, coed, comprehensive institution.
GRADUATE UNITS
Program in Mental Health Counseling Offers community mental health (MA); school consultation (MA). Electronic applications accepted.

BELHAVEN UNIVERSITY, Jackson, MS 39202-1789
General Information Independent-religious, coed, comprehensive institution. *Enrollment:* 33 full-time matriculated graduate/professional students (22 women), 1,864 part-time matriculated graduate/professional students (1,386 women). *Enrollment by degree level:* 1,804 master's, 93 doctoral. *Graduate faculty:* 37 full-time (18 women), 107 part-time/adjunct (50 women). *Tuition:* Full-time $9900; part-time $550 per credit. *Required fees:* $450; $75 per course. *Graduate housing:* On-campus housing not

available. *Student services:* Career counseling, free psychological counseling. *Library facilities:* Warren A. Hood Library plus 1 other. *Collection:* Books: 42,425 (physical), 106,114 (digital/electronic); Serial titles: 160 (physical), 75,718 (digital/electronic); Databases: 96. Weekly public service hours: 104.

Computer facilities: 36 computers available on campus for general student use. A campuswide network can be accessed from student residence rooms and from off campus. Online class registration is available.
Website: http://www.belhaven.edu/

General Application Contact: Suzanne Sullivan, Assistant Vice President for Jackson and Online, 601-968-5940, E-mail: ssullivan@belhaven.edu.

GRADUATE UNITS

School of Business Average age 35. 574 applicants, 75% accepted, 306 enrolled. Expenses: Contact institution. *Financial support:* Applicants required to submit FAFSA. In 2018, 326 master's awarded. *Program availability:* Part-time, evening/weekend, 100% online. Offers business administration (MBA); health administration (MBA, MHA); human resources (MBA, MSL); leadership (MBA); public administration (MPA); sports administration (MBA, MSA). *Application deadline:* Applications are processed on a rolling basis. *Application fee:* $25. Electronic applications accepted. *Application Contact:* Dr. Audrey Kelleher, Vice President of Adult and Graduate Marketing and Development, 407-804-1424, Fax: 407-620-5210, E-mail: akelleher@belhaven.edu. *Dean,* Dr. Ralph Mason, 601-968-8949, Fax: 601-968-8951, E-mail: cmason@belhaven.edu.

School of Education Students: 11 full-time (7 women), 452 part-time (360 women); includes 262 minority (244 Black or African American, non-Hispanic/Latino; 1 American Indian or Alaska Native, non-Hispanic/Latino; 3 Asian, non-Hispanic/Latino; 3 Hispanic/Latino; 11 Two or more races, non-Hispanic/Latino; 1 international. Average age 36. 299 applicants, 49% accepted, 103 enrolled. *Faculty:* 8 full-time (6 women), 24 part-time/adjunct (20 women). Expenses: Contact institution. *Financial support:* Applicants required to submit FAFSA. In 2018, 65 master's, 5 other advanced degrees awarded. *Program availability:* Part-time, evening/weekend, 100% online, blended/hybrid learning. Offers education (M Ed, MAT); educational leadership (Ed D, Ed S); reading literacy (M Ed). *Application deadline:* Applications are processed on a rolling basis. *Application fee:* $25. Electronic applications accepted. *Application Contact:* Sean Kirnan, Assistant Vice President for Adult and Graduate Enrollment and Student Services, 601-968-8727, Fax: 601-968-5953, E-mail: gradadmission@belhaven.edu. *Dean,* Dr. David Hand, 601-965-7020, E-mail: dhand@belhaven.edu.

BELLARMINE UNIVERSITY, Louisville, KY 40205

General Information Independent-religious, coed, comprehensive institution. *Enrollment:* 3,369 graduate, professional, and undergraduate students; 354 full-time matriculated graduate/professional students (207 women), 377 part-time matriculated graduate/professional students (273 women). *Enrollment by degree level:* 412 master's, 311 doctoral, 8 other advanced degrees. *Graduate faculty:* 61 full-time (40 women), 58 part-time/adjunct (35 women). Tuition and fees vary according to class time, degree level and program. *Graduate housing:* Rooms and/or apartments available on a first-come, first-served basis to single and married students. Typical cost: $4800 per year ($9420 including board) for single students. Room and board charges vary according to housing facility selected. Housing application deadline: 5/1. *Student services:* Campus employment opportunities, campus safety program, career counseling, exercise/wellness program, free psychological counseling, international student services, multicultural affairs office, services for students with disabilities, teacher training, writing training. *Library facilities:* W. L. Lyons Brown Library. *Collection:* Books: 130,534 (physical), 288,828 (digital/electronic); Serial titles: 189 (physical), 88,144 (digital/electronic); Databases: 145. Weekly public service hours: 140; study areas open 24 hours, 5–7 days a week.

Computer facilities: 440 computers available on campus for general student use. A campuswide network can be accessed from student residence rooms and from off campus. Online class registration, mobile app are available.
Website: http://www.bellarmine.edu/

General Application Contact: Dr. Sara Pettingill, Dean of Graduate Admission, 502-272-8401, Fax: 502-272-8002, E-mail: spettingill@bellarmine.edu.

GRADUATE UNITS

Annsley Frazier Thornton School of Education Students: 27 full-time (19 women), 205 part-time (156 women); includes 74 minority (53 Black or African American, non-Hispanic/Latino; 6 Asian, non-Hispanic/Latino; 7 Hispanic/Latino; 8 Two or more races, non-Hispanic/Latino. Average age 34. 155 applicants, 71% accepted, 95 enrolled. *Faculty:* 14 full-time (7 women), 17 part-time/adjunct (11 women). Expenses: Contact institution. *Financial support:* Scholarships/grants available. Financial award applicants required to submit FAFSA. In 2018, 69 master's, 10 doctorates, 30 other advanced degrees awarded. *Program availability:* Part-time, evening/weekend. Offers education and district leadership (Ed D); education and social change (PhD); elementary education (MA Ed, MAT); leadership in higher education (PhD); middle school education (MA Ed, MAT); principalship (Ed S); reading and writing (MA Ed); secondary education (MAT); teacher leadership (MA Ed). *Application deadline:* For fall admission, 8/1 priority date for domestic and international students; for spring admission, 12/1 priority date for domestic and international students; for summer admission, 4/10 priority date for domestic and international students. Applications are processed on a rolling basis. *Application fee:* $40. Electronic applications accepted. *Application Contact:* Sarah Schuble, Assistant Director of Graduate Student Enrollment, 502-272-8271, Fax: 502-272-8002, E-mail: sschuble@bellarmine.edu. *Dean,* Dr. Elizabeth Dinkins, 502-272-7958, Fax: 502-272-8189, E-mail: edinkins@bellarmine.edu.

College of Health Professions Students: 1 (woman) full-time, 19 part-time (17 women); includes 3 minority (all Black or African American, non-Hispanic/Latino). Average age 32. 12 applicants, 67% accepted, 6 enrolled. *Faculty:* 4 full-time (3 women). Expenses: Contact institution. *Financial support:* Career-related internships or fieldwork, scholarships/grants, and unspecified assistantships available. Support available to part-time students. Financial award applicants required to submit FAFSA. *Program availability:* Part-time, evening/weekend. Offers health professions (MHS, MSAT, MSN, DNP, DPT). *Application deadline:* Applications are processed on a rolling basis. *Application fee:* $40. Electronic applications accepted. *Application Contact:* Dr. Sara Pettingill, Dean of Graduate Admission, 502-272-8401, Fax: 502-272-8002, E-mail: spettingill@bellarmine.edu. *Vice Provost,* Dr. Mark Wiegand, 502-272-8001, E-mail: mwiegand@bellarmine.edu.

Donna and Allan Lansing School of Nursing and Clinical Sciences Students: 20 full-time (14 women), 82 part-time (68 women); includes 13 minority (5 Black or African American, non-Hispanic/Latino; 5 Asian, non-Hispanic/Latino; 2 Hispanic/Latino; 1 Two or more races, non-Hispanic/Latino), 6 international. Average age 32. 61 applicants, 84% accepted, 37 enrolled. *Faculty:* 10 full-time (8 women), 4 part-time/adjunct (all women). Expenses: Contact institution. *Financial support:* Career-

related internships or fieldwork and scholarships/grants available. Financial award applicants required to submit FAFSA. In 2018, 32 master's, 3 doctorates awarded. *Program availability:* Part-time, evening/weekend. Offers family nurse practitioner (MSN); health science (MHS); nursing administration (MSN); nursing education (MSN); nursing practice (DNP). *Application deadline:* Applications are processed on a rolling basis. *Application fee:* $40. Electronic applications accepted. *Application Contact:* Julie Armstrong-Binnix, Health Science Recruiter, 800-274-4723 Ext. 8364, E-mail: julieab@bellarmine.edu. *Dean,* Dr. Nancy York, 502-272-8639, E-mail: nyork@bellarmine.edu.

School of Movement and Rehabilitation Sciences Students: 213 full-time (136 women), 1 (woman) part-time; includes 17 minority (3 Black or African American, non-Hispanic/Latino; 3 Asian, non-Hispanic/Latino; 3 Hispanic/Latino; 8 Two or more races, non-Hispanic/Latino), 1 international. Average age 24. 663 applicants, 18% accepted, 81 enrolled. *Faculty:* 20 full-time (14 women), 30 part-time/adjunct (17 women). Expenses: Contact institution. *Financial support:* Applicants required to submit FAFSA. In 2018, 76 doctorates awarded. *Program availability:* Part-time. Offers athletic training (MSAT); physical therapy (DPT). *Application deadline:* Applications are processed on a rolling basis. *Application fee:* $40. Electronic applications accepted. *Application Contact:* Dr. Sara Pettingill, Dean of Graduate Admission, 502-272-8401, Fax: 502-272-8002, E-mail: spettingill@bellarmine.edu. *Dean,* Dr. Tony Brosky, 502-272-8375, E-mail: jbrosky@bellarmine.edu.

School of Communication Students: 7 full-time (5 women), 28 part-time (20 women); includes 4 minority (3 Black or African American, non-Hispanic/Latino; 1 Asian, non-Hispanic/Latino), 9 international. Average age 25. 21 applicants, 62% accepted, 6 enrolled. *Faculty:* 3 full-time (1 woman), 3 part-time/adjunct (2 women). Expenses: Contact institution. *Financial support:* Applicants required to submit FAFSA. In 2018, 12 master's awarded. *Program availability:* Part-time, evening/weekend. Offers communication (MA, MSDM). *Application deadline:* Applications are processed on a rolling basis. *Application fee:* $40. Electronic applications accepted. *Application Contact:* Dr. Sara Pettingill, Dean of Graduate Admission, 502-272-8401, Fax: 502-272-8002, E-mail: spettingill@bellarmine.edu. *Dean,* Dr. Lara Needham, 502-272-7965, E-mail: lneedham@bellarmine.edu.

W. Fielding Rubel School of Business Students: 84 full-time (30 women), 44 part-time (13 women); includes 19 minority (6 Black or African American, non-Hispanic/Latino; 7 Asian, non-Hispanic/Latino; 3 Hispanic/Latino; 3 Two or more races, non-Hispanic/Latino), 1 international. Average age 27. 81 applicants, 70% accepted, 40 enrolled. *Faculty:* 11 full-time (5 women), 2 part-time/adjunct (0 women). Expenses: Contact institution. *Financial support:* Career-related internships or fieldwork, scholarships/grants, and unspecified assistantships available. Support available to part-time students. Financial award applicants required to submit FAFSA. In 2018, 65 master's awarded. *Program availability:* Part-time, evening/weekend. Offers business (MBA). *Application deadline:* Applications are processed on a rolling basis. *Application fee:* $40. Electronic applications accepted. *Application Contact:* Dr. Sara Pettingill, Dean of Graduate Admission, 800-274-4723 Ext. 8258, Fax: 502-272-8002, E-mail: spettingill@bellarmine.edu. *Interim Dean,* Dr. Frank Raymond, 502-272-8487, Fax: 502-272-7443, E-mail: fraymond@bellarmine.edu.

BELLEVUE UNIVERSITY, Bellevue, NE 68005-3098

General Information Independent, coed, comprehensive institution. *Graduate housing:* Room and/or apartments available on a first-come, first-served basis to single students; on-campus housing not available to married students.

GRADUATE UNITS

Graduate School *Program availability:* Part-time, evening/weekend, online learning.

College of Arts and Sciences *Program availability:* Online learning. Offers clinical counseling (MS); healthcare administration (MHA); human services (MA); international security and intelligence studies (MS); managerial communication (MA).

College of Business Offers acquisition and contract management (MS); business administration (MBA); finance (MS); human capital management (PhD); management (MSM).

College of Information Technology Offers computer information systems (MS); cybersecurity (MS); management of information systems (MS); project management (MPM).

College of Professional Studies

BELLIN COLLEGE, Green Bay, WI 54305

General Information Independent, coed, primarily women, comprehensive institution. *Graduate housing:* On-campus housing not available.

GRADUATE UNITS

School of Nursing Offers family nurse practitioner (MSN); nurse educator (MSN).

BELMONT UNIVERSITY, Nashville, TN 37212

General Information Independent-religious, coed, university. *Enrollment:* 1,484 full-time matriculated graduate/professional students (990 women), 110 part-time matriculated graduate/professional students (63 women). *Enrollment by degree level:* 676 master's, 915 doctoral. *Graduate faculty:* 164 full-time (85 women), 67 part-time/adjunct (30 women). *Graduate housing:* On-campus housing not available. *Student services:* Campus employment opportunities, campus safety program, career counseling, exercise/wellness program, free psychological counseling, international student services, low-cost health insurance, multicultural affairs office, services for students with disabilities. *Library facilities:* Lila D. Bunch Library plus 1 other. *Collection:* Books: 184,352 (physical), 224,292 (digital/electronic); Serial titles: 1,033 (physical), 94,560 (digital/electronic); Databases: 288. Weekly public service hours: 127; students can reserve study rooms.

Computer facilities: Computer purchase and lease plans are available. 500 computers available on campus for general student use. A campuswide network can be accessed from student residence rooms and from off campus. Online class registration, individual student information via course management system are available.
Website: http://www.belmont.edu/

General Application Contact: David Mee, Dean of Enrollment Services, 615-460-6785, Fax: 615-460-5434, E-mail: david.mee@belmont.edu.

GRADUATE UNITS

College of Health Sciences Average age 26. *Faculty:* 29 full-time (25 women), 16 part-time/adjunct (11 women). Expenses: Contact institution. *Financial support:* Teaching assistantships with full tuition reimbursements, career-related internships or fieldwork, scholarships/grants, and traineeships available. Financial award application deadline: 3/1; financial award applicants required to submit FAFSA. In 2018, 52 master's, 79 doctorates awarded. *Program availability:* Part-time, blended/hybrid learning. Offers nursing (MSN, DNP); occupational therapy (MSOT, OTD); physical therapy (DPT). *Application deadline:* Applications are processed on a rolling basis. *Application fee:* $50.

Electronic applications accepted. *Application Contact:* Bill Nichols, Director of Enrollment Services, 615-460-6107, E-mail: bill.nichols@belmont.edu. *Dean*, Dr. Cathy Taylor, 615-460-6916, Fax: 615-460-6750.

College of Law Average age 26. 760 applicants, 47% accepted, 113 enrolled. *Faculty:* 18 full-time (8 women), 9 part-time/adjunct (3 women). Expenses: Contact institution. *Financial support:* In 2018–19, 180 students received support. Career-related internships or fieldwork and scholarships/grants available. Financial award application deadline: 12/1; financial award applicants required to submit FAFSA. In 2018, 82 doctorates awarded. Offers law (JD). *Application deadline:* For fall admission, 7/15 priority date for domestic and international students. Applications are processed on a rolling basis. *Application fee:* $50. Electronic applications accepted. *Application Contact:* Drew Ford, Recruiting Coordinator, 615-460-8250, Fax: 615-460-8250, E-mail: drew.ford@belmont.edu. *Dean*, Judge Alberto R. Gonzales, 615-460-8259, E-mail: alberto.gonzales@belmont.edu.

College of Pharmacy Average age 25. 638 applicants, 34% accepted, 94 enrolled. *Faculty:* 25 full-time (16 women), 3 part-time/adjunct (2 women). Expenses: Contact institution. *Financial support:* In 2018–19, 112 students received support. Career-related internships or fieldwork and scholarships/grants available. Financial award application deadline: 12/1; financial award applicants required to submit FAFSA. In 2018, 65 doctorates awarded. Offers advanced pharmacotherapy (Pharm D); health care informatics (Pharm D); management (Pharm D); missions/public health (Pharm D). PharmD/MBA offered in collaboration with Jack C. Massey Graduate School of Business. *Application deadline:* For fall admission, 8/31 priority date for domestic students; for spring admission, 3/1 for domestic students. Applications are processed on a rolling basis. *Application fee:* $50. Electronic applications accepted. *Application Contact:* Dr. David Gregory, Dean, 615-460-6746, Fax: 615-460-6741, E-mail: david.gregory@belmont.edu. *Dean*, Dr. David Gregory, 615-460-6746, Fax: 615-460-6741, E-mail: david.gregory@belmont.edu.

Jack C. Massey Graduate School of Business Students: 163 full-time (72 women), 42 part-time (19 women); includes 36 minority (13 Black or African American, non-Hispanic/Latino; 9 Asian, non-Hispanic/Latino; 5 Hispanic/Latino; 9 Two or more races, non-Hispanic/Latino), 10 international. Average age 30. 135 applicants, 96% accepted, 102 enrolled. *Faculty:* 29 full-time (9 women), 7 part-time/adjunct (3 women). Expenses: Contact institution. *Financial support:* In 2018–19, 86 students received support. Scholarships/grants, tuition waivers (partial), and unspecified assistantships available. Financial award application deadline: 7/1; financial award applicants required to submit FAFSA. In 2018, 110 master's awarded. *Program availability:* Part-time, evening/weekend. Offers accounting (M Acc); business (AMBA, PMBA); healthcare (MBA). *Application deadline:* For fall admission, 7/1 for domestic and international students; for spring admission, 11/1 for domestic and international students. Applications are processed on a rolling basis. *Application fee:* $50. Electronic applications accepted. *Application Contact:* Dr. Patrick Raines, Dean, 615-460-6480, Fax: 615-460-6455, E-mail: pat.raines@belmont.edu. *Dean*, Dr. Patrick Raines, 615-460-6480, Fax: 615-460-6455, E-mail: pat.raines@belmont.edu.

Program in Audio Engineering Technology

Program in Education

Program in Music

BEMIDJI STATE UNIVERSITY, Bemidji, MN 56601-2699

General Information State-supported, coed, comprehensive institution. CGS member. *Graduate housing:* Room and/or apartments available on a first-come, first-served basis to single students; on-campus housing not available to married students. Housing application deadline: 8/1. *Research affiliation:* National Interscholastic Athletic Administrators Association, Sanford Research, Mossy Oak, Bass Pro Shops.

GRADUATE UNITS

School of Graduate Studies *Program availability:* Part-time, online learning. Offers biology (MS); education (MS); English (MA, MS); environmental studies (MS); mathematics (MS); mathematics (elementary and middle level education) (MS); special education (M Sp Ed). Electronic applications accepted.

BENEDICTINE COLLEGE, Atchison, KS 66002-1499

General Information Independent-religious, coed, comprehensive institution. *Graduate housing:* Room and/or apartments available on a first-come, first-served basis to single students; on-campus housing not available to married students.

GRADUATE UNITS

Master of Arts in Education Program *Program availability:* Part-time, evening/weekend. Offers education (MA). Electronic applications accepted.

Master of Arts in School Leadership Program *Program availability:* Part-time, evening/weekend. Offers school leadership (MA). Electronic applications accepted.

Master of Business Administration Program *Program availability:* Part-time, evening/weekend. Offers business administration (MBA). Electronic applications accepted.

BENEDICTINE UNIVERSITY, Lisle, IL 60532

General Information Independent-religious, coed, comprehensive institution. *Enrollment:* 4,940 graduate, professional, and undergraduate students; 360 full-time matriculated graduate/professional students (264 women), 1,792 part-time matriculated graduate/professional students (1,309 women). *Enrollment by degree level:* 2,029 master's, 79 doctoral, 44 other advanced degrees. *Graduate faculty:* 43 full-time (26 women), 114 part-time/adjunct (60 women). *Graduate housing:* On-campus housing not available. *Student services:* Campus employment opportunities, campus safety program, career counseling, free psychological counseling, international student services, services for students with disabilities, writing training. *Library facilities:* Benedictine Library. *Collection:* Books: 90,762 (physical), 187,960 (digital/electronic); Serial titles: 1,498 (physical), 51,758 (digital/electronic); Databases: 61. Students can reserve study rooms.

Computer facilities: 275 computers available on campus for general student use. A campuswide network can be accessed from student residence rooms and from off campus. Online class registration is available.

Website: http://www.ben.edu/

GRADUATE UNITS

Graduate Programs *Program availability:* Part-time, evening/weekend, online learning. Offers accountancy (MS); accounting (MBA); administration of health care institutions (MPH); clinical exercise physiology (MS); clinical psychology (MS); dietetics (MPH); disaster management (MPH); entrepreneurship and managing innovation (MBA); financial management (MBA); health administration (MBA); health education (MPH); health information systems (MPH); human resource management (MBA); information systems security (MBA); international business (MBA); management and organizational behavior (MS, PhD); management consulting (MBA); management information systems (MS); marketing management (MBA); nursing (MSN); operations management and logistics (MBA); organization development (PhD); organizational leadership (MBA); values-driven leadership (DBA, PhD). Electronic applications accepted.

BENNINGTON COLLEGE, Bennington, VT 05201

General Information Independent, coed, comprehensive institution. *Graduate housing:* Room and/or apartments available on a first-come, first-served basis to single students; on-campus housing not available to married students.

GRADUATE UNITS

Graduate Programs *Program availability:* Part-time, online learning. Offers allied and health sciences (Certificate); dance (MFA); music (MFA); writing (MFA).

BENTLEY UNIVERSITY, Waltham, MA 02452-4705

General Information Independent, coed, comprehensive institution. *Enrollment:* 5,460 graduate, professional, and undergraduate students; 694 full-time matriculated graduate/professional students (400 women), 513 part-time matriculated graduate/professional students (280 women). *Enrollment by degree level:* 1,169 master's, 24 doctoral, 10 other advanced degrees. *Graduate faculty:* 118 full-time (38 women), 25 part-time/adjunct (4 women). *Graduate housing:* Room and/or apartments available on a first-come, first-served basis to single students; on-campus housing not available to married students. *Student services:* Campus employment opportunities, campus safety program, career counseling, exercise/wellness program, free psychological counseling, international student services, low-cost health insurance, multicultural affairs office, services for students with disabilities. *Library facilities:* Bentley Library. *Collection:* Books: 184,868 (physical), 217,175 (digital/electronic); Serial titles: 2,781 (physical), 116,336 (digital/electronic); Databases: 144. Weekly public service hours: 110; students can reserve study rooms.

Computer facilities: Computer purchase and lease plans are available. 4,620 computers available on campus for general student use. A campuswide network can be accessed from student residence rooms and from off campus. Online class registration, grade checking; online admission; blackboard; resume review; student employment; interlibary loan; free software are available.

Website: http://www.bentley.edu/

General Application Contact: Office of Graduate Admissions, 781-891-2108, E-mail: applygrad@bentley.edu.

GRADUATE UNITS

McCallum Graduate School of Business Students: 694 full-time (400 women), 513 part-time (280 women); includes 167 minority (33 Black or African American, non-Hispanic/Latino; 1 American Indian or Alaska Native, non-Hispanic/Latino; 94 Asian, non-Hispanic/Latino; 26 Hispanic/Latino; 13 Two or more races, non-Hispanic/Latino), 485 international. Average age 28. 1,551 applicants, 76% accepted, 472 enrolled. *Faculty:* 118 full-time (38 women), 25 part-time/adjunct (4 women). Expenses: Contact institution. *Financial support:* In 2018–19, 638 students received support. Scholarships/grants, tuition waivers (partial), and unspecified assistantships available. Financial award application deadline: 6/1; financial award applicants required to submit FAFSA. In 2018, 569 master's, 4 doctorates, 73 other advanced degrees awarded. *Program availability:* Part-time, evening/weekend, 100% online, blended/hybrid learning. Offers accountancy (PhD); accounting (MS); audit analytics (MS); business (MBA, MS, MSA, MSF, MSFP, MSHFID, MSIT, MSMA, MST, PhD, Certificate, GBC, GSS); business administration (MBA); business analytics (GBC); business ethics (GBC); finance (MSF); financial planning (GBC); fraud and forensic accounting (GBC); human factors (MSHFID); information technology (MSIT); marketing analytics (MSMA); taxation (GBC). *Application deadline:* For fall admission, 7/31 for domestic students, 6/30 for international students; for spring admission, 1/1 for domestic students, 11/1 for international students. Applications are processed on a rolling basis. *Application fee:* $150. Electronic applications accepted. *Application Contact:* Office of Graduate Admissions, 781-891-2108, E-mail: applygrad@bentley.edu. *Dean of Business and Professor*, Michael Johnson-Cramer, 781-891-2921, E-mail: mjohnsoncramer@bentley.edu.

BERGIN UNIVERSITY OF CANINE STUDIES, Rohnert Park, CA 94928

General Information Independent, coed, comprehensive institution. *Graduate housing:* On-campus housing not available.

GRADUATE UNITS

Program in Canine Life Sciences *Program availability:* Online learning. Offers canine life sciences (MS).

BERKELEY COLLEGE–WOODLAND PARK CAMPUS, Woodland Park, NJ 07424

General Information Proprietary, coed, comprehensive institution.

GRADUATE UNITS

MBA Program Offers management (MBA).

BERKLEE COLLEGE OF MUSIC, Boston, MA 02215-3693

General Information Independent, coed, comprehensive institution. *Enrollment:* 497 full-time matriculated graduate/professional students (241 women), 66 part-time matriculated graduate/professional students (31 women). *Enrollment by degree level:* 487 master's, 76 other advanced degrees. *Graduate faculty:* 77 full-time (25 women), 88 part-time/adjunct (26 women). *Tuition:* Full-time $49,050. *Required fees:* $1295. Tuition and fees vary according to campus/location and program. *Graduate housing:* On-campus housing not available. *Student services:* Campus employment opportunities, campus safety program, career counseling, exercise/wellness program, free psychological counseling, grant writing training, international student services, low-cost health insurance, multicultural affairs office, services for students with disabilities, teacher training, writing training. *Library facilities:* The Stan Getz Media Center and Library.

Computer facilities: Computer purchase and lease plans are available. A campuswide network can be accessed from student residence rooms. Online class registration is available.

Website: http://www.berklee.edu/

GRADUATE UNITS

Berklee Graduate Programs Students: 222 full-time (92 women), 7 part-time (all women); includes 44 minority (13 Black or African American, non-Hispanic/Latino; 5 Asian, non-Hispanic/Latino; 19 Hispanic/Latino; 7 Two or more races, non-Hispanic/Latino), 118 international. Average age 26. 736 applicants, 36% accepted, 171 enrolled. *Faculty:* 42 full-time (10 women), 53 part-time/adjunct (13 women). Expenses: Contact institution. *Financial support:* In 2018–19, fellowships with full and partial tuition reimbursements (averaging $12,453 per year), 21 research assistantships (averaging

$4,332 per year) were awarded; career-related internships or fieldwork, scholarships/grants, and tuition waivers (full and partial) also available. Support available to part-time students. Financial award application deadline: 1/15; financial award applicants required to submit CSS PROFILE or FAFSA. In 2018, 170 master's awarded. *Program availability:* Part-time, blended/hybrid learning. Offers contemporary performance (MM); global entertainment and music business (MA); music production, technology, and innovation (MM); scoring for film, television, and video games (MM). Contemporary performance - production concentration; global entertainment and music business; music production, technology, and innovation; and scoring for film, television, and video games programs offered at Valencia, Spain campus. *Application deadline:* For fall admission, 1/15 for domestic and international students. *Application fee:* $150. Electronic applications accepted. *Application Contact:* Office of Admissions, 617-747-2221, E-mail: admissions@berklee.edu. *Associate Vice President for Academic Affairs,* Rob Lagueux, PhD, 617-747-6908, E-mail: rlagueux@berklee.edu.

The Boston Conservatory at Berklee Students: 229 full-time (136 women), 16 part-time (11 women); includes 39 minority (7 Black or African American, non-Hispanic/Latino; 6 Asian, non-Hispanic/Latino; 13 Hispanic/Latino; 13 Two or more races, non-Hispanic/Latino), 83 international. Average age 25. 750 applicants, 41% accepted, 109 enrolled. *Faculty:* 30 full-time (13 women), 21 part-time/adjunct (11 women). Expenses: Contact institution. *Financial support:* In 2018–19, 232 students received support. Research assistantships, teaching assistantships, and scholarships/grants available. Financial award application deadline: 12/1; financial award applicants required to submit FAFSA. In 2018, 85 master's, 33 other advanced degrees awarded. *Program availability:* Part-time. Offers bassoon performance (MM); cello performance (MM); choral conducting (MM); clarinet performance (MM); collaborative piano (MM); composition (MM); contemporary music performance (MM); double bass performance (MM); flute performance (MM); harp performance (MM); horn performance (MM); marimba performance (MM); music and autism (Certificate); music education (MM); music education and autism (MM); music performance (ADP); musical theater (MFA); oboe performance (MM); opera performance (MM); orchestral conducting (MM); percussion performance (MM); piano performance (MM); saxophone performance (MM); trombone performance (MM); trumpet performance (MM). *Application deadline:* For fall admission, 12/1 for domestic and international students. *Application fee:* $150. Electronic applications accepted. *Application Contact:* Director of Admissions, 617-912-9153, Fax: 617-912-9217, E-mail: admissions@bostonconservatory.edu. *Associate Vice President, Academic Affairs,* Robert Lagueux, PhD, 617-747-6908, E-mail: rlagueux@berklee.edu.

BERRY COLLEGE, Mount Berry, GA 30149

General Information Independent-religious, coed, comprehensive institution. *Enrollment by degree level:* 30 master's, 102 other advanced degrees. *Graduate housing:* On-campus housing not available. *Student services:* Campus employment opportunities, campus safety program, career counseling, child daycare facilities, exercise/wellness program, free psychological counseling, international student services, low-cost health insurance, multicultural affairs office, services for students with disabilities, teacher training, writing training. *Library facilities:* Memorial Library plus 1 other. *Collection:* Books: 246,222 (physical), 664,520 (digital/electronic); Serial titles: 7,978 (physical), 44,764 (digital/electronic); Databases: 224. Weekly public service hours: 106; students can reserve study rooms.

Computer facilities: 200 computers available on campus for general student use. A campuswide network can be accessed from student residence rooms and from off campus. Online class registration is available. Website: http://www.berry.edu/

General Application Contact: Brett Kennedy, Assistant Vice President of Enrollment Management, 706-236-2215, Fax: 706-290-2178, E-mail: admissions@berry.edu.

GRADUATE UNITS

Graduate Programs Students: 32 full-time (27 women), 46 part-time (21 women); includes 11 minority (6 Black or African American, non-Hispanic/Latino; 1 Asian, non-Hispanic/Latino; 4 Hispanic/Latino). Average age 36. *Faculty:* 1 full-time (0 women), 8 part-time/adjunct (3 women). Expenses: Contact institution. *Financial support:* In 2018–19, 25 students received support, including 9 research assistantships with full tuition reimbursements available (averaging $8,890 per year); scholarships/grants, tuition waivers (partial), and unspecified assistantships also available. Support available to part-time students. Financial award application deadline: 3/1; financial award applicants required to submit FAFSA. In 2018, 20 master's, 48 other advanced degrees awarded. *Program availability:* Part-time, evening/weekend. Offers curriculum and instruction (M Ed, Ed S); early childhood education (M Ed, MAT); educational leadership (Ed S); middle grades education (MAT); middle-grades education (M Ed); middle-grades education and reading (M Ed, MAT); reading (M Ed); secondary education (MAT). *Application deadline:* For fall admission, 7/26 for domestic students, 5/1 for international students; for spring admission, 12/1 for domestic students, 2/1 for international students. Applications are processed on a rolling basis. *Application fee:* $25 ($30 for international students). Electronic applications accepted. *Application Contact:* Admissions, 706-236-2215, Fax: 706-290-2178, E-mail: admissions@berry.edu. *Provost,* Dr. Mary K Boyd, 706-236-2216, Fax: 706-290-2179, E-mail: provostoffice@berry.edu.

Campbell School of Business Students: 3 full-time (2 women), 38 part-time (14 women); includes 4 minority (3 Black or African American, non-Hispanic/Latino; 1 Asian, non-Hispanic/Latino). Average age 33. *Faculty:* 4 part-time/adjunct (1 woman). Expenses: Contact institution. *Financial support:* In 2018–19, 22 students received support, including 9 research assistantships with full tuition reimbursements available (averaging $8,890 per year); scholarships/grants, tuition waivers (partial), and unspecified assistantships also available. Support available to part-time students. Financial award application deadline: 3/1; financial award applicants required to submit FAFSA. In 2018, 16 master's awarded. *Program availability:* Part-time, evening/weekend. Offers business (MBA). *Application deadline:* For fall admission, 7/26 for domestic students; for spring admission, 12/1 for domestic students. Applications are processed on a rolling basis. *Application fee:* $25 ($30 for international students). Electronic applications accepted. *Application Contact:* Admissions, 706-236-2215, Fax: 706-290-2178, E-mail: admissions@berry.edu. *Dean,* Dr. Joyce Heames, 706-236-2233, Fax: 706-802-6728, E-mail: jheames@berry.edu.

BETHANY COLLEGE, Bethany, WV 26032

General Information Independent-religious, coed, comprehensive institution. *Graduate housing:* Room and/or apartments available on a first-come, first-served basis to single students; on-campus housing not available to married students.

GRADUATE UNITS

Master of Arts in Teaching Program *Program availability:* Part-time. Offers teaching (MAT). Electronic applications accepted.

BETHANY GLOBAL UNIVERSITY, Bloomington, MN 55438

General Information Independent-religious, coed, comprehensive institution. *Graduate housing:* On-campus housing not available.

GRADUATE UNITS

Graduate Programs *Program availability:* Part-time, evening/weekend, online only, 100% online. Offers intercultural ministry education (MA); intercultural ministry leadership (MA); intercultural ministry studies (MA). Electronic applications accepted.

BETHANY THEOLOGICAL SEMINARY, Richmond, IN 47374-4019

General Information Independent-religious, coed, graduate-only institution. *Graduate housing:* On-campus housing not available.

GRADUATE UNITS

Graduate and Professional Programs *Program availability:* Part-time, online learning. Offers biblical studies (MA Th); ministry studies (M Div); peace studies (M Div, MA Th); theological studies (MA Th, CATS); youth ministry (M Div).

BETHEL SEMINARY, St. Paul, MN 55112-6998

General Information Independent-religious, coed, graduate-only institution. *Graduate housing:* On-campus housing not available.

GRADUATE UNITS

Graduate and Professional Programs *Program availability:* Part-time, evening/weekend, 100% online, blended/hybrid learning. Offers Anglican studies (Certificate); children's and family ministry (MA); Christian studies (Certificate); Christian thought (MA); church planting (Certificate); Greek and Hebrew language (M Div); Greek language (M Div); Hebrew language (M Div); marriage and family therapy (MA, Certificate); mental health counseling (MA); ministry (MA, D Min); ministry practice (Certificate); theological studies (MA, Certificate); transformational leadership (MA); young life youth ministry (Certificate). Electronic applications accepted.

BETHEL UNIVERSITY, Mishawaka, IN 46545-5591

General Information Independent-religious, coed, comprehensive institution. *Graduate housing:* On-campus housing not available.

GRADUATE UNITS

Adult and Graduate Programs *Program availability:* Part-time, evening/weekend, 100% online, blended/hybrid learning. Offers business administration (MBA); education (M Ed, MAT); ministries (M Min); nursing (MSN); theological studies (MATS). Electronic applications accepted.

BETHEL UNIVERSITY, St. Paul, MN 55112-6999

General Information Independent-religious, coed, comprehensive institution. *Graduate housing:* On-campus housing not available.

GRADUATE UNITS

Graduate School Students: 586 full-time (426 women), 372 part-time (244 women); includes 141 minority (49 Black or African American, non-Hispanic/Latino; 6 American Indian or Alaska Native, non-Hispanic/Latino; 19 Asian, non-Hispanic/Latino; 40 Hispanic/Latino; 2 Native Hawaiian or other Pacific Islander, non-Hispanic/Latino; 25 Two or more races, non-Hispanic/Latino), 25 international. Average age 35. 642 applicants, 39% accepted, 194 enrolled. *Faculty:* 23 full-time (17 women), 73 part-time/adjunct (45 women). Expenses: Contact institution. *Financial support:* Teaching assistantships, career-related internships or fieldwork, and scholarships/grants available. Support available to part-time students. Financial award applicants required to submit FAFSA. In 2018, 312 master's, 28 doctorates, 134 other advanced degrees awarded. *Program availability:* Part-time, evening/weekend, 100% online, blended/hybrid learning. Offers business administration (MBA); classroom management (Certificate); counseling (MA); K-12 education (MA); leadership (Ed D); leadership foundations (Certificate); nurse educator (MS, Certificate); nurse-midwifery (MS); physician assistant (MS); special education (MA); strategic leadership (MA); teaching (MA); teaching and learning (Certificate). *Application deadline:* Applications are processed on a rolling basis. *Application fee:* $0. Electronic applications accepted. *Application Contact:* Director of Admissions, 651-635-8004, E-mail: gs@bethel.edu. *Associate Provost,* Dr. Randy Bergen, 651-635-8000, Fax: 651-635-8004, E-mail: r-bergen@bethel.edu.

BETHEL UNIVERSITY, McKenzie, TN 38201

General Information Independent-religious, coed, comprehensive institution. *Graduate housing:* Room and/or apartments available on a first-come, first-served basis to single students; on-campus housing not available to married students. Housing application deadline: 7/31.

GRADUATE UNITS

Graduate Programs *Program availability:* Part-time, evening/weekend. Offers administration and supervision (MA Ed); business administration (MBA); conflict resolution (MA); physician assistant studies (MS).

BETHESDA UNIVERSITY, Anaheim, CA 92801

General Information Independent-religious, coed, comprehensive institution.

GRADUATE UNITS

Graduate and Professional Programs Offers biblical studies (MA); music (MA); theology (M Div).

BETH HAMEDRASH SHAAREI YOSHER INSTITUTE, Brooklyn, NY 11204

General Information Independent-religious, men only, comprehensive institution.

GRADUATE UNITS
Graduate Programs

BETH HATALMUD RABBINICAL COLLEGE, Brooklyn, NY 11214

General Information Independent-religious, men only, comprehensive institution.

GRADUATE UNITS
Graduate Programs

BETHLEHEM COLLEGE & SEMINARY, Minneapolis, MN 55415

General Information Independent-religious, coed, comprehensive institution. *Graduate housing:* On-campus housing not available.

GRADUATE UNITS

Graduate and Professional Programs Offers church planting and revitalization (M Div); exegesis and theology (MA); theology (Th M); worship pastor (M Div).

BETH MEDRASH GOVOHA, Lakewood, NJ 08701-2797

General Information Independent-religious, men only, comprehensive institution.

GRADUATE UNITS
Graduate Programs

BETHUNE-COOKMAN UNIVERSITY, Daytona Beach, FL 32114-3099

General Information Independent-religious, coed, comprehensive institution.

GRADUATE UNITS
School of Graduate Studies *Program availability:* Online learning. Offers transformative leadership (MS). Electronic applications accepted.

BEULAH HEIGHTS UNIVERSITY, Atlanta, GA 30316

General Information Independent-religious, coed, comprehensive institution.

GRADUATE UNITS
Graduate School Offers biblical studies (MA); leadership studies (MA). Electronic applications accepted.

BEXLEY SEABURY SEMINARY, Chicago, IL 60637

General Information Independent-religious, coed, graduate-only institution. *Enrollment by degree level:* 28 doctoral, 17 other advanced degrees. *Graduate faculty:* 2 full-time (1 woman), 10 part-time/adjunct (3 women). *Tuition:* Full-time $11,160. Tuition and fees vary according to class time, course level, course load, degree level, program, reciprocity agreements and student level. *Graduate housing:* On-campus housing not available. *Student services:* Career counseling, low-cost health insurance. *Library facilities:* United Library.

Computer facilities: A campuswide network can be accessed. Online class registration is available.
Website: http://www.bexleyseabury.edu.

General Application Contact: Jaime Briceno, Recruiter and Digital Missioner, 773-380-7045, Fax: 773-380-6788, E-mail: jbriceno@bexleyseabury.edu.

GRADUATE UNITS
Graduate Programs *Program availability:* Part-time. Offers Anglican studies (Diploma); congregational development (D Min); preaching (D Min); theology (M Div).

BINGHAMTON UNIVERSITY, STATE UNIVERSITY OF NEW YORK, Binghamton, NY 13902-6000

General Information State-supported, coed, university. CGS member. *Graduate housing:* Room and/or apartments available on a first-come, first-served basis to single students; on-campus housing not available to married students. *Research affiliation:* United Health Services Hospitals (health care, engineering), Mount Sinai Hospital (health care, engineering), Lockheed Martin Corporation (engineering, management, mathematics), Matco Company (engineering), IBM (engineering), Universal Instruments (engineering).

GRADUATE UNITS
Graduate School *Program availability:* Part-time, evening/weekend, online learning. Offers materials science and engineering (MS, PhD); sustainable communities (MA, MS). Electronic applications accepted.

College of Community and Public Affairs *Program availability:* Part-time, evening/weekend. Offers adolescence education (MAT, MS Ed); biology education (MAT, MS Ed); chemistry education (MAT, MS Ed); childhood and early childhood education (MS Ed); community and public affairs (MA, MAT, MPA, MS, MS Ed, MSW, Ed D, PhD, Certificate); community research and action (PhD); earth science education (MAT, MS Ed); educational leadership (Certificate); educational studies (MS); educational theory and practice (Ed D); English education (MAT, MS Ed); French education (MAT, MS Ed); literacy education (MS Ed); mathematical sciences education (MAT, MS Ed); physics (MAT, MS Ed); public administration (MPA); social studies (MAT, MS Ed); social work (MSW); Spanish education (MAT, MS Ed); special education (MS Ed); student affairs administration (MS); TESOL education (MA, MS Ed). Electronic applications accepted.

Decker School of Nursing *Program availability:* Part-time, evening/weekend. Offers adult-gerontological nursing (MS, DNP, Certificate); community health nursing (MS, DNP, Certificate); family health nursing (MS, DNP, Certificate); family psychiatric mental health nursing (MS, DNP, Certificate); nursing (PhD). Electronic applications accepted.

Harpur College of Arts and Sciences *Program availability:* Part-time, evening/weekend. Offers analytical chemistry (PhD); anthropology (MA, PhD); applied liberal studies (MA); art history (MA, PhD); arts and sciences (MA, MM, MS, PhD, Certificate); Asian and Asian American studies (MA, Certificate); biological sciences (MA, MS, PhD); biomedical anthropology (MS); chemistry (MA, MS); comparative literature (MA, PhD); creative writing (MA); economics (MA, PhD); English (PhD); English/American literature (MA); environmental studies (MS); French (MA); geography (MA); geological sciences (MS, PhD); history (MA, PhD); inorganic chemistry (PhD); Italian (MA); mathematical sciences (MA, PhD); music (MM); philosophy (MA, PhD); physical chemistry (PhD); physics, applied physics, and astronomy (MS, PhD); political science (MA, PhD); psychology - behavioral neuroscience (PhD); psychology - clinical psychology (PhD); psychology - cognitive and behavioral science (PhD); social, political, ethical and legal philosophy (MA, PhD); sociology (MA, PhD); Spanish (MA); statistics (MA); theatre (MA); translation (Certificate); translation studies (PhD). Electronic applications accepted.

School of Management *Program availability:* Part-time, evening/weekend. Offers accounting (MS); business administration (MBA); corporate executive (MBA); executive business administration (MBA); finance (PhD); health care professional executive (MBA); management (MBA, MS, PhD); management information systems (PhD); marketing (PhD); organizational studies (PhD); professional business administration (MBA); supply chain management (PhD). Electronic applications accepted.

School of Pharmacy and Pharmaceutical Sciences Offers pharmacy (Pharm D).

Thomas J. Watson School of Engineering and Applied Science *Program availability:* Part-time, evening/weekend, online learning. Offers biomedical engineering (MS, PhD); computer science (MS, PhD); electrical and computer engineering (MS, PhD); engineering and applied science (M Eng, MS, PhD); executive health systems (MS); industrial and systems engineering (M Eng); mechanical engineering (M Eng, MS, PhD); systems science and industrial engineering (MS, PhD). Electronic applications accepted.

BIOLA UNIVERSITY, La Mirada, CA 90639-0001

General Information Independent-religious, coed, university. *Graduate housing:* Rooms and/or apartments available on a first-come, first-served basis to single and married students.

GRADUATE UNITS
Cook School of Intercultural Studies *Program availability:* Part-time, 100% online. Offers anthropology (MA); applied linguistics (MA); intercultural education (PhD); intercultural studies (MA, PhD); linguistics (Certificate); linguistics and Biblical languages (MA); missiology (D Miss); missions (MA); teaching English to speakers of other languages (MA, Certificate). Electronic applications accepted.

Crowell School of Business *Program availability:* Part-time, evening/weekend. Offers business (MBA, MP Acc). Electronic applications accepted.

Rosemead School of Psychology Offers clinical psychology (PhD, Psy D). Electronic applications accepted.

School of Arts and Sciences *Program availability:* Part-time, evening/weekend, online learning. Offers Christian apologetics (MA, Certificate); science and religion (MA); speech language pathology (MA). Electronic applications accepted.

School of Education *Program availability:* Part-time, evening/weekend, online learning. Offers curriculum and instruction (Certificate); early childhood (MA Ed, MAT); multiple subject (MAT); single subject (MAT); special education (MA Ed, MAT, Certificate). Electronic applications accepted.

Talbot School of Theology *Program availability:* Part-time, evening/weekend. Offers adult/family ministry (MACE); Bible exposition (MA, Th M); Biblical and theological studies (Certificate); children's ministry (MACE); Christian education (M Div); cross-cultural education ministry (MACE); educational studies (Ed D, PhD); evangelism and discipleship (M Div); general Christian education (MACE); Messianic Jewish studies (M Div, Certificate); missions and intercultural studies (M Div); New Testament (MA, Th M); Old Testament (MA); Old Testament and Semitics (Th M); pastoral and general ministry (M Div); pastoral care and counseling (M Div, MACML); philosophy (MA); preaching and pastoral ministry (MACML); spiritual formation (M Div, Certificate); spiritual formation and soul care (MA); sports ministry (MACML); theology (MA, Th M, D Min, Certificate); youth ministry (MACE). Electronic applications accepted.

BISHOP'S UNIVERSITY, Sherbrooke, QC J1M 1Z7, Canada

General Information Province-supported, coed, comprehensive institution. *Graduate housing:* Room and/or apartments available on a first-come, first-served basis to single students; on-campus housing not available to married students. Housing application deadline: 7/1.

GRADUATE UNITS
School of Education *Program availability:* Part-time, online learning. Offers advanced studies in education (Diploma); education (M Ed, MA); teaching English as a second language (Certificate).

BLACK HILLS STATE UNIVERSITY, Spearfish, SD 57799

General Information State-supported, coed, comprehensive institution. *Graduate housing:* Room and/or apartments available on a first-come, first-served basis to single students; on-campus housing not available to married students. Housing application deadline: 4/1.

GRADUATE UNITS
Graduate Studies *Program availability:* Part-time, evening/weekend, online learning. Offers business administration (MBA); curriculum and instruction (MS); integrative genomics (MS); strategic leadership (MS). Electronic applications accepted.

BLESSING-RIEMAN COLLEGE OF NURSING & HEALTH SCIENCES, Quincy, IL 62305-7005

General Information Independent, coed, primarily women, comprehensive institution. *Graduate housing:* On-campus housing not available.

GRADUATE UNITS
Master of Science in Nursing Program *Program availability:* Part-time-only, evening/weekend, online only, 100% online. Offers nursing education (MSN); nursing leadership (MSN). Electronic applications accepted.

BLOOMFIELD COLLEGE, Bloomfield, NJ 07003-9981

General Information Independent-religious, coed, comprehensive institution.

GRADUATE UNITS
Program in Accounting Offers accounting (MS).

BLOOMSBURG UNIVERSITY OF PENNSYLVANIA, Bloomsburg, PA 17815-1301

General Information State-supported, coed, comprehensive institution. *Graduate housing:* Room and/or apartments available on a first-come, first-served basis to single students; on-campus housing not available to married students. *Research affiliation:* Marine Science Consortium (biology), Consortium of Big Ten Universities Research and Training Reactors (physics), Melanoma Research Fund (biology), Merck & Company, Inc. (biology).

GRADUATE UNITS
School of Graduate Studies *Program availability:* Part-time, evening/weekend. Electronic applications accepted.

College of Education *Program availability:* Part-time. Offers college student affairs (M Ed); curriculum and instruction (M Ed, Certificate); early childhood education (M Ed); education (M Ed, MS, Certificate); education of the deaf/hard of hearing (MS); educational leadership (M Ed); language arts (M Ed); math (M Ed); middle level education grades 4-8 (M Ed); PreK-12 curriculum and instruction (M Ed); PreK-12 school counseling (M Ed); PreK-12 school principal (M Ed); reading (M Ed); school principal (Certificate); science (M Ed); social studies (M Ed); special education (M Ed, MS, Certificate). Electronic applications accepted.

College of Science and Technology Offers adult and family nurse practitioner (MSN); audiology (Au D); biology (MS); clinical athletic training (MS); community health (MSN); corporate instructional technology (MS); eLearning developer (Certificate); exercise science (MS); intraoperative neurophysiological monitoring (Certificate); nurse anesthesia (MSN); nursing (MSN, DNP); nursing administration (MSN); science and technology (M Ed, MS, MSN, Au D, Certificate); speech pathology (MS); speech-language pathology (MS). Electronic applications accepted.

Zeigler College of Business *Program availability:* Part-time, evening/weekend. Offers accounting (M Acc); business (M Acc, M Ed, MBA, Certificate); business administration (MBA); business education (M Ed); management (Certificate). Electronic applications accepted.

BLUEFIELD COLLEGE, Bluefield, VA 24605-1799

General Information Independent-religious, coed, comprehensive institution. *Graduate housing:* On-campus housing not available.

GRADUATE UNITS

School of Education *Program availability:* Part-time, online only, 100% online. Offers education (MA Ed). Electronic applications accepted.

BLUE MOUNTAIN COLLEGE, Blue Mountain, MS 38610

General Information Independent-religious, coed, comprehensive institution. *Graduate housing:* Room and/or apartments available on a first-come, first-served basis to single students; on-campus housing not available to married students. Housing application deadline: 7/1.

GRADUATE UNITS

Program in Elementary Education *Program availability:* Part-time, evening/weekend. Offers elementary education (M Ed). Electronic applications accepted.

Program in Literacy/Reading (K-12) *Program availability:* Part-time, evening/weekend. Offers literacy/reading (K-12) (M Ed). Electronic applications accepted.

Program in Secondary Education - Biology *Program availability:* Part-time, evening/weekend. Offers secondary education - biology (M Ed). Electronic applications accepted.

BLUFFTON UNIVERSITY, Bluffton, OH 45817

General Information Independent-religious, coed, comprehensive institution. *Enrollment:* 52 full-time matriculated graduate/professional students (29 women), 8 part-time matriculated graduate/professional students (7 women). *Enrollment by degree level:* 60 master's. *Graduate faculty:* 6 full-time (4 women), 7 part-time/adjunct (2 women). *Graduate housing:* Room and/or apartments available on a first-come, first-served basis to single students; on-campus housing not available to married students. *Student services:* Campus employment opportunities, career counseling, exercise/wellness program, free psychological counseling, international student services, multicultural affairs office, services for students with disabilities, writing training. *Library facilities:* Musselman Library plus 1 other. *Collection:* Books: 73,648 (physical), 283,031 (digital/electronic); Serial titles: 1,001 (physical), 46,672 (digital/electronic); Databases: 258. Weekly public service hours: 74; students can reserve study rooms.

Computer facilities: 175 computers available on campus for general student use. A campuswide network can be accessed from student residence rooms and from off campus. Online class registration is available. Website: http://www.bluffton.edu/.

General Application Contact: Shelby Koenig, Enrollment Counselor for Graduate Program, 419-358-3684, E-mail: admissions@bluffton.edu.

GRADUATE UNITS

Graduate Programs in Business Students: 38 full-time (22 women), 1 part-time (0 women); includes 11 minority (6 Black or African American, non-Hispanic/Latino; 3 Hispanic/Latino; 2 Two or more races, non-Hispanic/Latino). Average age 33. *Faculty:* 4 full-time (2 women), 5 part-time/adjunct (1 woman). Expenses: Contact institution. *Financial support:* Unspecified assistantships and faculty/staff grants available. Financial award applicants required to submit FAFSA. In 2018, 25 master's awarded. *Program availability:* Evening/weekend, blended/hybrid learning, videoconference. Offers accounting and financial management (MBA); health care management (MBA); leadership (MAOM, MBA); production and operations management (MBA); sustainability management (MBA). *Application deadline:* For fall admission, 7/31 priority date for domestic and international students. Applications are processed on a rolling basis. Electronic applications accepted. *Application Contact:* Shelby Koenig, Enrollment Counselor for Graduate Program, 419-3583684, E-mail: koenigs@bluffton.edu. *Director of Graduate Programs in Business,* Dr. Melissa Green, 419-358-3447, E-mail: greenm@bluffton.edu.

Programs in Education Students: 14 full-time (7 women), 7 part-time (all women). Average age 31. *Faculty:* 2 full-time (both women), 2 part-time/adjunct (1 woman). Expenses: Contact institution. *Financial support:* Unspecified assistantships available. Financial award application deadline: 9/15; financial award applicants required to submit FAFSA. In 2018, 8 master's awarded. *Program availability:* Part-time, 100% online, blended/hybrid learning, videoconference. Offers intervention specialist (MA Ed); leadership (MA Ed); reading (MA Ed). *Application deadline:* For fall admission, 8/15 priority date for domestic students, 6/15 priority date for international students; for spring admission, 12/15 priority date for domestic students, 9/15 priority date for international students. Applications are processed on a rolling basis. Electronic applications accepted. *Application Contact:* Shelby Koenig, Enrollment Counselor for Graduate Program, 419-358-3022, E-mail: koenigs@bluffton.edu. *Director of Graduate Programs in Education,* Dr. Amy K. Mullins, 419-358-3457, E-mail: mullinsa@bluffton.edu.

BOB JONES UNIVERSITY, Greenville, SC 29614

General Information Independent-religious, coed, university.

GRADUATE UNITS
Graduate Programs

BOISE STATE UNIVERSITY, Boise, ID 83725-0399

General Information State-supported, coed, university. CGS member. *Graduate housing:* Rooms and/or apartments available on a first-come, first-served basis to single and married students. Housing application deadline: 6/1. *Research affiliation:* Federal Aviation Administration (airliner cabin environment research), Lee Pesky Learning Center (elementary mathematics education), Prewitt & Associates, Inc. (C-130 drop zones), Bechtel BWXT Idaho, LLC (energy policy analysis), Argonne National Laboratory (energy policy analysis), American Chemical Society (petroleum research).

GRADUATE UNITS

College of Arts and Sciences *Program availability:* Part-time. Offers anthropology (MA); applied anthropology (MAA); applied historical research (MAHR); arts and sciences (M E Sci, MA, MAA, MAHR, MFA, MM, MS, PhD); biology (MA, MS); biomolecular sciences (PhD); chemistry (MS); communication (MA); earth science (M E Sci); English literature (MA); English, rhetoric and composition (MA); geophysics (MS, PhD); geoscience (MS); geosciences (PhD); history (MA); hydrologic sciences (MS); interdisciplinary studies (MA, MS); mathematics (MS); mathematics education (MS); music education (MM); music performance (MM); raptor biology (MS); teaching English language (MA); technical communication (MA); visual arts (MFA). Electronic applications accepted.

College of Business and Economics *Program availability:* Part-time, online learning. Offers accountancy (MSA); accountancy taxation (MSAT); business administration (MBA); business and economics (M Ec, MBA, MSA, MSAT, MSE); economics (M Ec, MSE). Electronic applications accepted.

College of Education *Program availability:* Part-time, 100% online, blended/hybrid learning. Offers bilingual education (M Ed); counselor education (MA, Graduate Certificate); curriculum and instruction (MA Ed, Ed D); early and special education (M Ed); education (M Ed, MA, MET, MPE, MS, MS Ed, Ed D, Ed S, Graduate Certificate); educational leadership (M Ed); educational technology (MET, MS, Ed D); English as a new language (M Ed); executive educational leadership (Ed S); literacy (MA); online teaching (Graduate Certificate); school technology coordination (Graduate Certificate); technology integration (Graduate Certificate). Electronic applications accepted.

College of Engineering *Program availability:* Part-time, online learning. Offers civil engineering (M Engr, MS); computer science (MS); computer science teacher endorsement (Graduate Certificate); electrical and computer engineering (M Engr, MS, PhD); engineering (M Engr, MS, PhD, Graduate Certificate); mechanical engineering (M Engr, MS); organizational performance and workplace learning (MS); STEM education (MS); workplace e-learning and performance support (Graduate Certificate); workplace instructional design (Graduate Certificate); workplace performance improvement (Graduate Certificate). Electronic applications accepted.

Micron School of Materials Science and Engineering Offers materials science and engineering (M Engr, MS, PhD). Electronic applications accepted.

College of Health Sciences *Program availability:* Part-time, 100% online. Offers athletic leadership (MAL); community and environmental health (MHS); health science (MHS); health sciences (MAL, MHS, MK, MS, MSN, MSW, DNP, Graduate Certificate); health services leadership (Graduate Certificate); kinesiology (MK, MS). Electronic applications accepted.

School of Nursing Offers acute care adult gerontology (Graduate Certificate); adult gerontology acute care (MSN); adult gerontology primary care (MSN); healthcare simulation (Graduate Certificate); nursing practice (DNP); primary care adult gerontology (Graduate Certificate). Electronic applications accepted.

School of Social Work *Program availability:* Part-time, 100% online. Offers social work (MSW). Electronic applications accepted.

School of Public Service *Program availability:* Part-time. Offers criminal justice (MA); political science (MA); public policy and administration (MPA, PhD, Graduate Certificate); public service (MA, MPA, PhD, Graduate Certificate). Electronic applications accepted.

BORICUA COLLEGE, New York, NY 10032-1560

General Information Independent, coed, comprehensive institution. *Enrollment:* 92 full-time matriculated graduate/professional students (78 women). *Enrollment by degree level:* 92 master's. *Graduate faculty:* 4 full-time (1 woman), 4 part-time/adjunct (all women). *Tuition:* Full-time $15,000. One-time fee: $100 full-time. *Student services:* Career counseling, teacher training. *Library facilities:* Boricua College Library plus 1 other.

Computer facilities: 120 computers available on campus for general student use. Website: http://www.boricuacollege.edu/

General Application Contact: Teofilo Santiago, Director of Admissions, 347-964-8680 Ext. 364, E-mail: tsantiago@boricuacollege.edu.

GRADUATE UNITS

Program in Human Services Students: 33 full-time (26 women); includes 31 minority (5 Black or African American, non-Hispanic/Latino; 26 Hispanic/Latino). Average age 39. 73 applicants, 75% accepted, 33 enrolled. *Faculty:* 2 full-time (1 woman), 2 part-time/adjunct (both women). Expenses: Contact institution. *Financial support:* Career-related internships or fieldwork and Federal Work-Study available. Financial award applicants required to submit FAFSA. In 2018, 33 master's awarded. *Program availability:* Evening/weekend. Offers human services (MS). Program offered in Brooklyn Campus and Bronx Campus. *Application deadline:* Applications are processed on a rolling basis. *Application fee:* $100 ($500 for international students). *Application Contact:* Teofilo Santiago, Director of Admissions, 347-964-8600 Ext. 364, E-mail: tsantiago@boricuacollege.edu. *Chairperson,* Esteban Galvan, 347-964-8600 Ext. 419, E-mail: egalvan@boricuacollege.edu.

Program in TESOL Education (K-12) Students: 59 full-time (52 women); includes 55 minority (9 Black or African American, non-Hispanic/Latino; 46 Hispanic/Latino). Average age 34. 92 applicants, 76% accepted, 59 enrolled. *Faculty:* 2 full-time (0 women), 2 part-time/adjunct (both women). Expenses: Contact institution. *Financial support:* Career-related internships or fieldwork and Federal Work-Study available. Financial award applicants required to submit FAFSA. In 2018, 53 master's awarded. *Program availability:* Evening/weekend. Offers TESOL education (MS). Program offered in Brooklyn Campus and Bronx Campus. *Application deadline:* Applications are processed on a rolling basis. *Application fee:* $100 ($500 for international students). *Application Contact:* Dr. Shivaji Sengupta, Vice President, 212-694-1000 Ext. 650, Fax: 212-694-1015, E-mail: ssengupta@boricuacollege.edu. *Co-Chairperson,* Dr. Joseph H. Gaines, 347-964-8600 Ext. 451, E-mail: jgaines@boricuacollege.edu.

BOSTON ARCHITECTURAL COLLEGE, Boston, MA 02115-2795

General Information Independent, coed, comprehensive institution.

GRADUATE UNITS

Graduate Programs Offers architecture (M Arch); historic preservation (MDS); interior design (MID); landscape architecture (MLA); sustainable design (MDS). Electronic applications accepted.

BOSTON COLLEGE, Chestnut Hill, MA 02467-3800

General Information Independent-religious, coed, university. CGS member. *Graduate housing:* On-campus housing not available.

GRADUATE UNITS

Carroll School of Management *Program availability:* Part-time, evening/weekend. Offers accounting (MSA); business administration (MBA); finance (MSF, PhD); management (MBA, MSA, MSF, PhD); management and organization (PhD). Electronic applications accepted.

Law School Offers law (JD). Electronic applications accepted.

Lynch School of Education and Human Development Students: 523 full-time (382 women), 290 part-time (223 women); includes 187 minority (57 Black or African American, non-Hispanic/Latino; 1 American Indian or Alaska Native, non-Hispanic/Latino; 30 Asian, non-Hispanic/Latino; 73 Hispanic/Latino; 26 Two or more races, non-Hispanic/Latino), 129 international. Average age 29. 1,416 applicants, 342 enrolled. *Faculty:* 67 full-time (43 women). Expenses: Contact institution. *Financial support:* Fellowships with tuition reimbursements, research assistantships with tuition reimbursements, teaching assistantships with tuition reimbursements, career-related internships or fieldwork, Federal Work-Study, institutionally sponsored loans, scholarships/grants, traineeships, health care benefits, tuition waivers (full and partial), and unspecified assistantships available. Support available to part-time students.

Financial award applicants required to submit FAFSA. In 2018, 267 master's, 29 doctorates, 2 other advanced degrees awarded. *Program availability:* Part-time, 100% online. Offers applied developmental and education psychology (MA, PhD); counseling psychology (PhD); curriculum and instruction (M Ed, PhD, CAES); early childhood education (M Ed); education (M Ed, MA, MAT, MS, MST, Ed D, PhD, CAES); elementary education (M Ed); law and curriculum and instruction (M Ed, MAT, MST, PhD, CAES); mental health counseling (MA); reading specialist (M Ed, CAES); religious education (M Ed, CAES); school counseling (MA); secondary education (M Ed, MAT, MST); special needs: moderate disabilities (M Ed, CAES); special needs: severe disabilities (M Ed); theology and ministry and counseling (MA, PhD). *Application deadline:* For fall admission, 1/9 priority date for domestic and international students; for spring admission, 11/1 for domestic and international students. Applications are processed on a rolling basis. *Application fee:* $75. Electronic applications accepted. *Application Contact:* Jessica Rivers, Assistant Dean for Graduate Admissions and Financial Aid, 617-552-4214, Fax: 617-552-0398, E-mail: riversja@bc.edu. *Dean,* Dr. Stanton Wortham, 617-552-4200, Fax: 617-552-0812.

Morrissey Graduate School of Arts and Sciences Students: 734 full-time (304 women), 40 part-time (24 women). 1,617 applicants, 30% accepted, 189 enrolled. *Faculty:* 497 full-time (167 women). Expenses: Contact institution. *Financial support:* In 2018–19, fellowships with full and partial tuition reimbursements (averaging $22,600 per year), research assistantships with full and partial tuition reimbursements (averaging $22,600 per year), teaching assistantships with full and partial tuition reimbursements (averaging $22,600 per year) were awarded; career-related internships or fieldwork, Federal Work-Study, scholarships/grants, health care benefits, tuition waivers (full and partial), and unspecified assistantships also available. Support available to part-time students. Financial award application deadline: 3/1; financial award applicants required to submit FAFSA. In 2018, 120 master's, 90 doctorates awarded. *Program availability:* Part-time. Offers arts and sciences (MA, MS, MST, PhD); biochemistry (PhD); biology (PhD); classics (MA); earth and environmental sciences (MS); economics (PhD); English (MA, PhD); European national studies (MA); French (MA); Greek (MA); history (MA, PhD); inorganic chemistry (PhD); Irish studies (MA, PhD); Italian (MA); Latin (MA); linguistics (MA); mathematics (PhD); medieval studies (MA); organic chemistry (PhD); philosophy (MA, PhD); philosophy and theology (MA); physical chemistry (PhD); physics (MS, PhD); political science (MA, PhD); psychology (PhD); Russian (MA); science education (MST); Slavic studies (MA); sociology (MA, PhD); Spanish (MA); theology (PhD). *Application deadline:* For fall admission, 1/2 priority date for domestic and international students. *Application fee:* $75. Electronic applications accepted. *Application Contact:* Robert V. Howe, Associate Dean, 617-552-3265, Fax: 617-552-3700, E-mail: hower@bc.edu. *Dean,* Dr. Gregory Kalscheur, 617-552-6850, E-mail: gregory.kalscheur@bc.edu.

School of Social Work *Program availability:* Part-time. Offers social work (MSW, PhD). Electronic applications accepted.

School of Theology and Ministry *Program availability:* Part-time. Offers church leadership (MA); divinity (M Div); pastoral ministry (MA); religious education (MA, PhD); sacred theology (STD, STL); social justice/social ministry (MA); spiritual direction (MA); theological studies (MTS); theology (Th M, PhD); youth ministry (MA). Electronic applications accepted.

William F. Connell School of Nursing Students: 201 full-time (176 women), 80 part-time (73 women); includes 46 minority (7 Black or African American, non-Hispanic/Latino; 14 Asian, non-Hispanic/Latino; 17 Hispanic/Latino; 8 Two or more races, non-Hispanic/Latino), 6 international. Average age 28. 360 applicants, 56% accepted, 93 enrolled. Expenses: Contact institution. *Financial support:* In 2018–19, 135 students received support, including 12 fellowships with full tuition reimbursements available (averaging $24,504 per year), 29 teaching assistantships (averaging $4,380 per year); scholarships/grants, health care benefits, tuition waivers (partial), and unspecified assistantships also available. Support available to part-time students. Financial award application deadline: 4/18; financial award applicants required to submit FAFSA. In 2018, 95 master's, 3 doctorates awarded. *Program availability:* Part-time. Offers adult-gerontology primary care nurse practitioner (MS); family health nursing (MS); nurse anesthesia (MS); nursing (PhD); pediatric primary care nurse practitioner (MS); psychiatric-mental health nursing (MS); women's health nursing (MS). *Application deadline:* For fall admission, 9/30 for domestic and international students; for winter admission, 1/15 for domestic and international students; for spring admission, 3/15 for domestic and international students. *Application fee:* $40. Electronic applications accepted. *Application Contact:* Sean Sendall, Assistant Dean, Graduate Enrollment and Data Analytics, 617-552-4745, Fax: 617-552-2121, E-mail: sean.sendall@bc.edu. *Dean,* Dr. Susan Gennaro, 617-552-4251, Fax: 617-552-0931, E-mail: susan.gennaro@bc.edu.

BOSTON GRADUATE SCHOOL OF PSYCHOANALYSIS, Brookline, MA 02446-4602

General Information Independent, coed, graduate-only institution. *Graduate housing:* On-campus housing not available. *Research affiliation:* Boston Institute for Psychotherapy (psychotherapy).

GRADUATE UNITS

BGSP-New Jersey Offers psychoanalysis (MA); psychoanalytic counseling (MA). Programs offered in conjunction with Academic of Clinical and Applied Psychoanalysis in Livingston, NJ.

CAGS and Certificate Programs *Program availability:* Part-time. Offers child and adolescent intervention (CAGS); psychoanalysis (Certificate); psychoanalytic psychotherapy (CAGS).

Doctoral Programs *Program availability:* Part-time. Offers psychoanalysis (Psya D); psychoanalysis, society and culture (Psya D).

Master's Programs *Program availability:* Part-time. Offers mental health counseling (MA); psychoanalysis (MA); psychoanalysis, society and culture (MA).

New York Graduate School of Psychoanalysis *Program availability:* Part-time. Offers psychoanalysis (MA).

BOSTON UNIVERSITY, Boston, MA 02215

General Information Independent, coed, university. CGS member. *Enrollment:* 34,657 graduate, professional, and undergraduate students; 10,221 full-time matriculated graduate/professional students (5,784 women), 5,017 part-time matriculated graduate/professional students (2,757 women). *Enrollment by degree level:* 9,948 master's, 5,110 doctoral, 180 other advanced degrees. *Graduate housing:* On-campus housing not available. *Student services:* Campus employment opportunities, campus safety program, career counseling, child daycare facilities, exercise/wellness program, free psychological counseling, international student services, low-cost health insurance, services for students with disabilities, writing training. *Library facilities:* Mugar Memorial Library plus 20 others. *Collection:* Books: 1.2 million (physical), 2.1 million (digital/electronic); Serial titles: 248,885 (physical), 111,406 (digital/electronic); Databases: 721. Weekly public service hours: 123; students can reserve study rooms.

Computer facilities: Computer purchase and lease plans are available. 250 computers available on campus for general student use. A campuswide network can be accessed from student residence rooms and from off campus. Online class registration, research and educational networks are available.
Website: http://www.bu.edu/

GRADUATE UNITS

College of Communication Students: 394 full-time (322 women), 36 part-time (23 women); includes 51 minority (17 Black or African American, non-Hispanic/Latino; 8 Asian, non-Hispanic/Latino; 19 Hispanic/Latino; 7 Two or more races, non-Hispanic/Latino), 257 international. Average age 24. 1,285 applicants, 55% accepted, 237 enrolled. *Faculty:* 67 full-time, 73 part-time/adjunct. Expenses: Contact institution. *Financial support:* In 2018–19, 175 students received support, including 35 research assistantships (averaging $12,000 per year), 99 teaching assistantships (averaging $12,000 per year); career-related internships or fieldwork, Federal Work-Study, institutionally sponsored loans, scholarships/grants, health care benefits, and unspecified assistantships also available. Support available to part-time students. Financial award application deadline: 5/1; financial award applicants required to submit FAFSA. In 2018, 245 master's awarded. *Program availability:* Part-time. Offers advertising (MS); communication (MA, MFA, MS, PhD); film and television (MFA, MS); journalism (MS); mass communication (MS); public relations (MS). *Application deadline:* For fall admission, 5/1 for domestic and international students. Applications are processed on a rolling basis. *Application fee:* $95. Electronic applications accepted. *Application Contact:* Kayla Ring, Assistant Director, Graduate Affairs, 617-353-3481, E-mail: comgrad@bu.edu. *Dean,* Mariette DiChristina, 617-353-3450, Fax: 617-358-0399, E-mail: comdean@bu.edu.

Division of Emerging Media Studies Students: 37 full-time (30 women), 10 part-time (7 women); includes 3 minority (1 Asian, non-Hispanic/Latino; 2 Hispanic/Latino), 32 international. Average age 24. 194 applicants, 40% accepted, 24 enrolled. *Faculty:* 4 full-time (1 woman). Expenses: Contact institution. *Financial support:* In 2018–19, 3 fellowships with full tuition reimbursements were awarded; research assistantships, teaching assistantships, career-related internships or fieldwork, Federal Work-Study, scholarships/grants, health care benefits, and unspecified assistantships also available. Financial award application deadline: 5/1; financial award applicants required to submit FAFSA. In 2018, 21 master's awarded. *Program availability:* Part-time. Offers emerging media studies (MA, PhD). *Application deadline:* For fall admission, 5/1 for domestic and international students. Applications are processed on a rolling basis. *Application fee:* $95. Electronic applications accepted. *Application Contact:* Jackie Cummings, Admission and Financial Aid Counselor, 617-353-3481, E-mail: comgrad@bu.edu. *Professor of Emerging Media/Chair of the Division of Emerging Media Studies,* Dr. James Katz, 617-353-7733, E-mail: dems@bu.edu.

College of Engineering Students: 872 full-time (279 women), 174 part-time (48 women); includes 125 minority (11 Black or African American, non-Hispanic/Latino; 72 Asian, non-Hispanic/Latino; 24 Hispanic/Latino; 18 Two or more races, non-Hispanic/Latino), 602 international. Average age 24. 3,733 applicants, 40% accepted, 389 enrolled. *Faculty:* 112 full-time (12 women), 9 part-time/adjunct (1 woman). Expenses: Contact institution. *Financial support:* In 2018–19, 458 students received support, including 115 fellowships with full tuition reimbursements available (averaging $33,000 per year), 246 research assistantships with full tuition reimbursements available (averaging $33,000 per year), 7 teaching assistantships with full tuition reimbursements available (averaging $22,000 per year); scholarships/grants and unspecified assistantships also available. Support available to part-time students. Financial award application deadline: 1/15; financial award applicants required to submit FAFSA. In 2018, 322 master's, 55 doctorates awarded. *Program availability:* Part-time, blended/hybrid learning. Offers biomedical engineering (M Eng, MS, PhD); computer engineering (M Eng, MS, PhD); engineering (M Eng, MS, PhD); manufacturing engineering (MS); materials science and engineering (M Eng, MS, PhD); mechanical engineering (PhD); systems engineering (M Eng, MS, PhD). *Application deadline:* For fall admission, 12/15 for domestic and international students; for spring admission, 10/1 for domestic and international students. *Application fee:* $95. Electronic applications accepted. *Application Contact:* Andrew Butler, Assistant Director, Enrollment Operations, 617-353-9760, E-mail: enggrad@bu.edu. *Dean,* Dr. Kenneth R. Lutchen, 617-353-2800, Fax: 617-358-3468, E-mail: klutch@bu.edu.

College of Fine Arts Students: 834 full-time (518 women), 16 part-time (6 women); includes 116 minority (29 Black or African American, non-Hispanic/Latino; 28 Asian, non-Hispanic/Latino; 40 Hispanic/Latino; 1 Native Hawaiian or other Pacific Islander, non-Hispanic/Latino; 18 Two or more races, non-Hispanic/Latino), 189 international. Average age 31. 2,276 applicants, 22% accepted, 161 enrolled. Expenses: Contact institution. *Financial support:* In 2018–19, 213 students received support. Fellowships, teaching assistantships, Federal Work-Study, and scholarships/grants available. Support available to part-time students. Financial award application deadline: 1/1. In 2018, 262 master's, 72 doctorates, 5 other advanced degrees awarded. *Program availability:* Part-time. Offers ethnomusicology (PhD); fine arts (MA, MFA, MM, DMA, PhD, CAS, Certificate, Performance Diploma); historical musicology (PhD); musicology (MA). *Application deadline:* For fall admission, 1/15 for domestic and international students. *Application fee:* $95. Electronic applications accepted. *Application Contact:* Mark Krone, Assistant Director of Graduate Affairs, 617-353-3350, E-mail: arts@bu.edu. *Dean,* Harvey Young, 617-353-3350.

School of Music Students: 301 full-time (175 women), 8 part-time (4 women); includes 36 minority (3 Black or African American, non-Hispanic/Latino; 14 Asian, non-Hispanic/Latino; 10 Hispanic/Latino; 9 Two or more races, non-Hispanic/Latino), 151 international. Average age 27. 1,590 applicants, 21% accepted, 101 enrolled. *Faculty:* 36 full-time, 21 part-time/adjunct. Expenses: Contact institution. *Financial support:* In 2018–19, 175 teaching assistantships (averaging $3,500 per year) were awarded; fellowships, scholarships/grants, and unspecified assistantships also available. Financial award application deadline: 12/1. In 2018, 128 master's, 57 doctorates, 10 other advanced degrees awarded. *Program availability:* Part-time. Offers choral conducting (MM); composition and theory (DMA); conducting (Performance Diploma); music education (MM, DMA); musicology (MA, PhD). *Application deadline:* For fall admission, 12/1 priority date for domestic and international students. *Application fee:* $95. Electronic applications accepted. *Application Contact:* Katie Luellen, Director of Admissions, 617-353-3341, E-mail: arts@bu.edu. *Director,* Shiela Kibbe, 617-353-3341, Fax: 617-353-7455, E-mail: cfamusic@bu.edu.

School of Theatre Students: 50 full-time (35 women), 3 part-time (0 women); includes 5 minority (3 Asian, non-Hispanic/Latino; 1 Hispanic/Latino; 1 Two or more races, non-Hispanic/Latino), 2 international. Average age 28. 212 applicants, 14% accepted, 17 enrolled. *Faculty:* 16 full-time, 9 part-time/adjunct. Expenses: Contact institution. *Financial support:* In 2018–19, 16 students received support, including 16 teaching assistantships (averaging $3,000 per year); scholarships/grants, unspecified assistantships, and stipends also available. Financial award application deadline: 2/1. In 2018, 17 master's awarded. *Program availability:* Part-time. Offers design (MFA); lighting crafts (Certificate); management (MFA); production (MFA); scenic painting (Certificate). *Application deadline:* For fall admission, 2/1 priority date for domestic and international students. *Application fee:* $95. Electronic applications accepted. *Application Contact:* Mark Krone, Assistant Director of Graduate Affairs, 617-353-3350, E-mail: krone@bu.edu. *Director,* Susan Mickey, 617-353-3390.

School of Visual Arts Students: 155 full-time (133 women), 3 part-time (all women); includes 19 minority (3 Black or African American, non-Hispanic/Latino; 5 Asian, non-Hispanic/Latino; 10 Hispanic/Latino; 1 Two or more races, non-Hispanic/Latino), 41 international. Average age 30. 365 applicants, 27% accepted, 21 enrolled. *Faculty:* 17 full-time, 4 part-time/adjunct. Expenses: Contact institution. *Financial support:* In 2018–19, 36 students received support. Fellowships, teaching assistantships, scholarships/grants, and unspecified assistantships available. Financial award application deadline: 2/1. In 2018, 89 master's awarded. Offers sculpture (MFA); studio teaching (MA). *Application deadline:* For fall admission, 2/1 for domestic and international students. Applications are processed on a rolling basis. *Application fee:* $95. *Application Contact:* Jessica Caccamo, Assistant Director of Admissions, 617-353-3371, E-mail: visuarts@bu.edu. *Director,* Lynne Allen, 617-353-3371.

College of Health and Rehabilitation Sciences: Sargent College Students: 417 full-time (331 women), 95 part-time (86 women); includes 106 minority (10 Black or African American, non-Hispanic/Latino; 52 Asian, non-Hispanic/Latino; 32 Hispanic/Latino; 12 Two or more races, non-Hispanic/Latino), 41 international. Average age 26. 1,698 applicants, 28% accepted, 145 enrolled. *Faculty:* 58 full-time (48 women), 31 part-time/adjunct (26 women). Expenses: Contact institution. *Financial support:* In 2018–19, 300 students received support, including 30 research assistantships with full tuition reimbursements available (averaging $22,000 per year), 18 teaching assistantships (averaging $2,500 per year); career-related internships or fieldwork, Federal Work-Study, institutionally sponsored loans, scholarships/grants, and health care benefits also available. Support available to part-time students. Financial award application deadline: 1/1; financial award applicants required to submit FAFSA. In 2018, 143 master's, 93 doctorates awarded. *Program availability:* Blended/hybrid learning. Offers athletic training (MS); health and rehabilitation sciences (MS, DPT, OTD, PhD); human physiology (MS, PhD); nutrition (MS); occupational therapy (OTD); physical therapy (DPT); rehabilitation sciences (PhD); speech, language and hearing sciences (PhD); speech-language pathology (MS). *Application deadline:* For fall admission, 1/1 priority date for domestic and international students. Applications are processed on a rolling basis. *Application fee:* $95. Electronic applications accepted. *Application Contact:* Sharon Sankey, Assistant Dean, Student Services, 617-353-2713, Fax: 617-353-7500, E-mail: ssankey@bu.edu. *Dean,* Dr. Christopher Moore, 617-353-2705, Fax: 617-353-7500, E-mail: mooreca@bu.edu.

Graduate School of Arts and Sciences Students: 1,851 full-time (896 women), 194 part-time (100 women); includes 230 minority (28 Black or African American, non-Hispanic/Latino; 87 Asian, non-Hispanic/Latino; 87 Hispanic/Latino; 1 Native Hawaiian or other Pacific Islander, non-Hispanic/Latino; 27 Two or more races, non-Hispanic/Latino), 970 international. Average age 25. 9,328 applicants, 29% accepted, 692 enrolled. Expenses: Contact institution. *Financial support:* In 2018–19, 1,335 students received support, including 220 fellowships with full tuition reimbursements available (averaging $22,660 per year), 415 research assistantships with full tuition reimbursements available (averaging $22,660 per year), 500 teaching assistantships with full tuition reimbursements available (averaging $22,660 per year); career-related internships or fieldwork, Federal Work-Study, scholarships/grants, traineeships, health care benefits, and unspecified assistantships also available. In 2018, 495 master's, 174 doctorates awarded. Offers African American studies (MA); American and New England studies (PhD); anthropology (PhD); applied anthropology (MA); archaeology (MA, PhD); arts and sciences (MA, MAEP, MFA, MS, PhD, Certificate); astronomy (MA, PhD); bioinformatics (MS, PhD); biology (MA, PhD); biostatistics (MA, PhD); chemistry (MA, PhD); classical studies (MA, PhD); computer science (MS, PhD); creative writing (MFA); cyber security (MS); data-centric computing (MS); earth and environment (MA, PhD); economics (MA, MAEP); energy and environment (MA); English (MA, PhD); Hispanic language and literature (MA, PhD); history (MA, PhD); history of art and architecture (MA, PhD); linguistics (MA, PhD); mathematics and statistics (MA, MS, PhD); molecular biology, cell biology, and biochemistry (MA, PhD); museum studies (Certificate); philosophy (MA, PhD); physics (PhD); playwriting (MFA); political science (PhD); preservation studies (MA); psychological and brain sciences (MA, PhD); religion (MA, PhD); remote sensing and geospatial sciences (MA); sociology (MA, PhD). *Application deadline:* For fall admission, 1/15 priority date for domestic and international students; for spring admission, 10/15 priority date for domestic and international students. *Application fee:* $95. Electronic applications accepted. *Application Contact:* Martin Gastmann, Assistant Director of Admissions and Financial Aid, 617-353-2696, Fax: 617-358-5492, E-mail: grs@bu.edu. *Associate Dean,* Dr. Emily Barman, 617-353-2696, Fax: 617-358-5492.

Editorial Institute Students: 9 full-time (6 women), 3 part-time (1 woman); includes 2 minority (1 Hispanic/Latino; 1 Two or more races, non-Hispanic/Latino). Average age 33. Expenses: Contact institution. *Financial support:* In 2018–19, 8 students received support, including 1 fellowship with full tuition reimbursement available (averaging $22,660 per year), 3 research assistantships with full tuition reimbursements available (averaging $22,660 per year), 2 teaching assistantships with full tuition reimbursements available (averaging $22,660 per year); Federal Work-Study, scholarships/grants, and health care benefits also available. Offers editorial studies (MA). *Application fee:* $95. *Application Contact:* Ellen Wrigley, Administrative Assistant, 617-353-6631, Fax: 617-353-6917, E-mail: ellen@bu.edu. *Director,* Archie Burnett, 617-353-6631, E-mail: burnetta@bu.edu.

Frederick S. Pardee School of Global Studies Students: 79 full-time (53 women), 16 part-time (10 women); includes 16 minority (2 Black or African American, non-Hispanic/Latino; 4 Asian, non-Hispanic/Latino; 8 Hispanic/Latino; 2 Two or more races, non-Hispanic/Latino), 36 international. Average age 24. 261 applicants, 77% accepted, 29 enrolled. *Faculty:* 33 full-time (8 women), 10 part-time/adjunct (4 women). Expenses: Contact institution. *Financial support:* In 2018–19, 49 students received support. Federal Work-Study, scholarships/grants, and unspecified assistantships available. Financial award application deadline: 1/18. In 2018, 51 master's awarded. Offers global studies (MA). *Application deadline:* For fall admission, 1/18 priority date for domestic and international students; for spring admission, 12/15 for domestic and international students. Applications are processed on a rolling basis. *Application fee:* $95. Electronic applications accepted. *Application Contact:* Megan Kerin, Graduate Student Affairs Administrator, 617-358-9349, Fax: 617-353-9290, E-mail: psgsgrad@bu.edu. *Dean,* Adil Najam, 617-358-0988, Fax: 617-353-9290, E-mail: anajam@bu.edu.

Henry M. Goldman School of Dental Medicine Students: 826 full-time (428 women); includes 244 minority (19 Black or African American, non-Hispanic/Latino; 1 American Indian or Alaska Native, non-Hispanic/Latino; 153 Asian, non-Hispanic/Latino; 54 Hispanic/Latino; 17 Two or more races, non-Hispanic/Latino), 250 international. Average age 28. 5,077 applicants, 11% accepted, 260 enrolled. *Faculty:* 116 full-time (41 women), 123 part-time/adjunct (57 women). Expenses: Contact institution. *Financial support:* In 2018–19, 117 students received support. Institutionally sponsored loans, scholarships/grants, and stipends (for oral surgery residents) available. Financial award application deadline: 4/15; financial award applicants required to submit FAFSA. In 2018, 22 master's, 211 doctorates, 32 other advanced degrees awarded. Offers dental medicine (MS, MSD, D Sc, D Sc D, DMD, CAGS). *Application deadline:* For fall admission, 12/15 for domestic and international students. Applications are processed on a rolling basis. *Application fee:* $75. Electronic applications accepted. *Application Contact:* Admissions Representative, 617-358-6827, Fax: 617-638-4798, E-mail: applydmd@bu.edu. *Dean,* Dr. Jeffrey W. Hutter, 617-358-6621, E-mail: jhutter@bu.edu.

Metropolitan College Students: 936 full-time (469 women), 1,984 part-time (836 women); includes 614 minority (154 Black or African American, non-Hispanic/Latino; 7 American Indian or Alaska Native, non-Hispanic/Latino; 239 Asian, non-Hispanic/Latino; 176 Hispanic/Latino; 1 Native Hawaiian or other Pacific Islander, non-Hispanic/Latino; 37 Two or more races, non-Hispanic/Latino), 1,214 international. Average age 29. 3,868 applicants, 75% accepted, 1049 enrolled. *Faculty:* 52 full-time (15 women), 107 part-time/adjunct (46 women). Expenses: Contact institution. *Financial support:* In 2018–19, 44 research assistantships (averaging $8,400 per year), 36 teaching assistantships (averaging $5,000 per year) were awarded; career-related internships or fieldwork, scholarships/grants, and unspecified assistantships also available. Support available to part-time students. Financial award applicants required to submit FAFSA. In 2018, 1,193 master's awarded. *Program availability:* Part-time, evening/weekend, 100% online, blended/hybrid learning. Offers actuarial science (MS); advertising (MS); applied business analytics (MS); arts administration (MS, Graduate Certificate); city planning (MCP); communications (MLA); computer information systems (MS); computer networks (Certificate); computer science (MS); cybercrime investigation and cybersecurity (MCJ); data analytics (Certificate); digital forensics (Certificate); economic development and tourism management (MSAS); enterprise risk management (MS); financial management (MS); fundraising management (Graduate Certificate); global marketing management (MS); health communication (MS); health informatics (Certificate); history and culture (MLA); information technology project management (Certificate); innovation and technology (MSAS); insurance management (MS); leadership (MS); project management (MS); software development (MS); software engineering in health care systems (Certificate); strategic management (MCJ); supply chain management (MS); telecommunications (MS); urban affairs (MUA). *Application deadline:* For fall admission, 8/1 priority date for domestic students, 6/1 priority date for international students; for spring admission, 12/1 priority date for domestic students, 11/15 priority date for international students; for summer admission, 4/1 priority date for domestic students, 3/1 priority date for international students. Applications are processed on a rolling basis. *Application fee:* $85. Electronic applications accepted. *Application Contact:* Enrollment Services, 617-353-6000, E-mail: met@bu.edu. *Dean,* Dr. Tanya Zlateva, 617-353-3010, Fax: 617-353-6066, E-mail: met@bu.edu.

Questrom School of Business Students: 724 full-time (322 women), 636 part-time (286 women); includes 225 minority (43 Black or African American, non-Hispanic/Latino; 1 American Indian or Alaska Native, non-Hispanic/Latino; 104 Asian, non-Hispanic/Latino; 57 Hispanic/Latino; 20 Two or more races, non-Hispanic/Latino), 451 international. Average age 28. 1,069 applicants, 40% accepted, 164 enrolled. *Faculty:* 85 full-time (23 women), 28 part-time/adjunct (10 women). Expenses: Contact institution. *Financial support:* Career-related internships or fieldwork, Federal Work-Study, institutionally sponsored loans, scholarships/grants, and tuition waivers (partial) available. Support available to part-time students. Financial award applicants required to submit FAFSA. In 2018, 585 master's, 11 doctorates awarded. *Program availability:* Part-time, evening/weekend. Offers business (EMBA, MBA); business analytics (MS); management (PhD); management studies (MSMS); mathematical finance (MS, PhD). *Application deadline:* For fall admission, 3/18 for domestic and international students; for spring admission, 11/7 for domestic and international students. *Application fee:* $125. Electronic applications accepted. *Application Contact:* Meredith C. Siegel, Assistant Dean, Graduate Admissions Office, 617-353-2670, Fax: 617-353-7368, E-mail: mba@bu.edu. *Professor/Dean,* Kenneth W. Freeman, 617-353-9720, Fax: 617-353-5581, E-mail: kfreeman@bu.edu.

School of Hospitality Administration Students: 45 full-time (37 women), 8 part-time (6 women); includes 8 minority (3 Asian, non-Hispanic/Latino; 5 Hispanic/Latino), 28 international. Average age 26. *Faculty:* 9 full-time, 17 part-time/adjunct. Expenses: Contact institution. *Financial support:* In 2018–19, 43 students received support. Scholarships/grants and unspecified assistantships available. Financial award application deadline: 2/1; financial award applicants required to submit FAFSA. In 2018, 29 master's awarded. *Program availability:* Part-time. Offers hospitality administration (MMH). *Application deadline:* For fall admission, 2/1 priority date for domestic and international students. Applications are processed on a rolling basis. *Application fee:* $95. Electronic applications accepted. *Application Contact:* Micah Sieber, Director of Graduate Affairs, 617-353-1011, E-mail: shagrad@bu.edu. *Dean,* Dr. Arun Upneja, 617-353-3261, E-mail: aupneja@bu.edu.

School of Law Students: 983 full-time (588 women), 101 part-time (53 women); includes 218 minority (38 Black or African American, non-Hispanic/Latino; 1 American Indian or Alaska Native, non-Hispanic/Latino; 54 Asian, non-Hispanic/Latino; 93 Hispanic/Latino; 1 Native Hawaiian or other Pacific Islander, non-Hispanic/Latino; 31 Two or more races, non-Hispanic/Latino), 252 international. Average age 26. 5,450 applicants, 29% accepted, 233 enrolled. Expenses: Contact institution. *Financial support:* In 2018–19, 650 students received support. Career-related internships or fieldwork, Federal Work-Study, institutionally sponsored loans, scholarships/grants, and resident assistantships available. Financial award application deadline: 3/1; financial award applicants required to submit FAFSA. In 2018, 262 master's, 227 doctorates awarded. *Program availability:* 100% online, blended/hybrid learning. Offers law (LL M, JD). MD/JD offered jointly with the School of Medicine. *Application deadline:* For fall admission, 4/1 for domestic and international students. Applications are processed on a rolling basis. *Application fee:* $85. Electronic applications accepted. *Application Contact:* Alissa Leonard, Director of Admissions and Financial Aid, 617-353-3100, Fax: 617-353-0578, E-mail: bulawadm@bu.edu. *Dean,* Maureen A. O'Rourke, 617-353-3112, Fax: 617-358-4706, E-mail: lawdean@bu.edu.

School of Medicine Students: 1,611 full-time (921 women), 120 part-time (67 women); includes 680 minority (71 Black or African American, non-Hispanic/Latino; 369 Asian, non-Hispanic/Latino; 170 Hispanic/Latino; 5 Native Hawaiian or other Pacific Islander, non-Hispanic/Latino; 65 Two or more races, non-Hispanic/Latino), 142 international. Average age 25. Expenses: Contact institution. *Financial support:* In 2018–19, 388 students received support. Fellowships, teaching assistantships, career-related internships or fieldwork, Federal Work-Study, institutionally sponsored loans, and scholarships/grants available. Support available to part-time students. Financial award application deadline: 2/15; financial award applicants required to submit CSS PROFILE or FAFSA. In 2018, 366 master's, 178 doctorates awarded. *Program availability:* Part-time, evening/weekend. Offers medicine (MA, MS, MD, PhD). *Application Contact:* Dr. Kristen Goodell, Associate Dean/Director of Admissions, 617-414-4465, E-mail: kgoodell@bu.edu. *Dean,* Dr. Karen H. Antman, 617-638-5300.

Graduate Medical Sciences Students: 911 full-time (560 women), 91 part-time (50 women); includes 336 minority (41 Black or African American, non-Hispanic/Latino; 179 Asian, non-Hispanic/Latino; 82 Hispanic/Latino; 2 Native Hawaiian or other Pacific Islander, non-Hispanic/Latino; 32 Two or more races, non-Hispanic/Latino), 96 international. Average age 25. *Faculty:* 287 full-time (130 women), 31 part-time/adjunct (13 women). Expenses: Contact institution. *Financial support:* Fellowships, research assistantships, teaching assistantships, Federal Work-Study, scholarships/grants, and traineeships available. Financial award applicants required to submit FAFSA. In 2018, 366 master's, 34 doctorates awarded. *Program availability:* Part-time. Offers anatomy and neurobiology (MA, PhD); behavioral neuroscience (PhD); biochemistry (MA, PhD); bioimaging (MS); biomedical forensic sciences (MS); biomedical sciences (PhD); cell and molecular biology (PhD); clinical research (MA); forensic anthropology (MS); genetic counseling (MS); genetics and genomics (PhD); health sciences education (MS); healthcare emergency management (MS); immunology (PhD); medical anthropology and cross cultural practice (MS); medical sciences (MA, MS, PhD); mental health counseling and behavioral medicine (MA); microbiology (PhD); molecular and translational medicine (PhD); neuroscience (PhD); nutrition and metabolism (MS, PhD); oral biology (PhD); oral health sciences (MS); pathology and laboratory medicine (MS, PhD); pharmacology and experimental therapeutics (PhD); physician assistant (MS); physiology and biophysics (MA, PhD). *Application deadline:* For fall admission, 1/31 for domestic and international students; for spring admission, 10/15 for domestic and international students. *Application fee:* $95. Electronic applications accepted. *Application Contact:* GMS Admissions Office, 617-638-5255, Fax: 617-638-5740, E-mail: askgms@bu.edu. *Associate Provost,* Dr. Linda Hyman, 617-638-5255, Fax: 617-638-5740.

School of Public Health Students: 706 full-time (572 women), 369 part-time (309 women); includes 347 minority (85 Black or African American, non-Hispanic/Latino; 1 American Indian or Alaska Native, non-Hispanic/Latino; 143 Asian, non-Hispanic/Latino; 91 Hispanic/Latino; 27 Two or more races, non-Hispanic/Latino), 127 international. Average age 26. 2,914 applicants, 60% accepted, 387 enrolled. *Faculty:* 115 full-time, 190 part-time/adjunct. Expenses: Contact institution. *Financial support:* In 2018–19, 318 students received support. Federal Work-Study, institutionally sponsored loans, scholarships/grants, and stipends available. Support available to part-time students. Financial award application deadline: 5/31; financial award applicants required to submit FAFSA. In 2018, 411 master's, 23 doctorates awarded. *Program availability:* Part-time, evening/weekend. Offers biostatistics (MA, MPH, PhD); community health sciences (MPH, Dr PH); environmental health (MPH, MS, PhD); epidemiology (MPH, MS, PhD); global health (MPH, Dr PH); health law, policy and management (MPH); health services and systems research (MS); health services research (PhD); public health (MA, MPH, MS, Dr PH, PhD). *Application deadline:* For fall admission, 1/1 priority date for domestic and international students; for spring admission, 10/1 priority date for domestic and international students. Applications are processed on a rolling basis. *Application fee:* $120. Electronic applications accepted. *Application Contact:* Faetitia Desamours, Assistant Director of Admissions, 617-353-3185, Fax: 617-358-3248, E-mail: asksph@bu.edu. *Dean,* Dr. Sandro Galea, 617-358-3301, E-mail: asksph@bu.edu.

School of Social Work Students: 241 full-time (216 women), 695 part-time (624 women); includes 256 minority (72 Black or African American, non-Hispanic/Latino; 1 American Indian or Alaska Native, non-Hispanic/Latino; 46 Asian, non-Hispanic/Latino; 113 Hispanic/Latino; 2 Native Hawaiian or other Pacific Islander, non-Hispanic/Latino; 22 Two or more races, non-Hispanic/Latino), 13 international. Average age 30. 985 applicants, 74% accepted, 248 enrolled. *Faculty:* 33 full-time (23 women), 42 part-time/adjunct (33 women). Expenses: Contact institution. *Financial support:* In 2018–19, 183 students received support. Career-related internships or fieldwork, Federal Work-Study, scholarships/grants, and stipends available. Support available to part-time students. Financial award application deadline: 3/1; financial award applicants required to submit FAFSA. In 2018, 229 master's, 2 doctorates awarded. *Program availability:* Part-time, evening/weekend, 100% online. Offers social work (MSW, PhD). *Application deadline:* For fall admission, 2/10 for domestic students, 1/10 for international students. *Application fee:* $95. Electronic applications accepted. *Application Contact:* Julie Billings, Graduate Admissions Specialist, 617-353-1212, Fax: 617-353-5612, E-mail: jbilling@bu.edu. *Dean,* Dr. Jorge Delva, 617-353-3760, Fax: 617-353-5612.

School of Theology Students: 250 full-time (120 women), 90 part-time (41 women); includes 76 minority (36 Black or African American, non-Hispanic/Latino; 1 American Indian or Alaska Native, non-Hispanic/Latino; 11 Asian, non-Hispanic/Latino; 22 Hispanic/Latino; 6 Two or more races, non-Hispanic/Latino), 61 international. Average age 34. 334 applicants, 69% accepted, 106 enrolled. *Faculty:* 39 full-time (17 women), 11 part-time/adjunct (5 women). Expenses: Contact institution. *Financial support:* In 2018–19, 236 students received support, including 102 fellowships with full tuition reimbursements available (averaging $7,500 per year), 11 research assistantships with full tuition reimbursements available (averaging $22,000 per year), 12 teaching assistantships with full tuition reimbursements available (averaging $22,000 per year); career-related internships or fieldwork, Federal Work-Study, scholarships/grants, and health care benefits also available. Support available to part-time students. Financial award application deadline: 7/15. In 2018, 77 master's, 20 doctorates awarded. *Program availability:* Part-time, blended/hybrid learning. Offers chaplaincy (M Div); choral conducting (MSM); church and the arts (M Div); community and global engagement (M Div); organ (MSM); pastoral ministry (M Div); practical theology (PhD); religion and the academy (M Div); transformational leadership (D Min). PhD in mission studies offered in collaboration with Gordon-Conwell Theological Seminary. *Application deadline:* For fall admission, 1/15 priority date for domestic and international students; for spring admission, 10/15 priority date for domestic and international students. Applications are processed on a rolling basis. *Application fee:* $95. Electronic applications accepted. *Application Contact:* Rev. Dr. Anastasia Kidd, Director of Enrollment, 617-353-3036, Fax: 617-358-0140, E-mail: sthadmis@bu.edu. *Dean,* Rev. Dr. Mary Elizabeth Moore, 617-353-3050, Fax: 617-353-3061, E-mail: memoore@bu.edu.

Wheelock College of Education and Human Development Students: 234 full-time (183 women), 444 part-time (331 women); includes 168 minority (38 Black or African American, non-Hispanic/Latino; 46 Asian, non-Hispanic/Latino; 63 Hispanic/Latino; 1 Native Hawaiian or other Pacific Islander, non-Hispanic/Latino; 20 Two or more races, non-Hispanic/Latino), 53 international. Average age 27. 1,303 applicants, 65% accepted, 346 enrolled. *Faculty:* 85 full-time (59 women), 87 part-time/adjunct (67 women). Expenses: Contact institution. *Financial support:* In 2018–19, 450 students received support, including 36 fellowships with full tuition reimbursements available (averaging $22,660 per year), 25 research assistantships (averaging $10,000 per year),

32 teaching assistantships with partial tuition reimbursements available (averaging $8,000 per year); career-related internships or fieldwork, Federal Work-Study, and scholarships/grants also available. Support available to part-time students. Financial award applicants required to submit FAFSA. In 2018, 286 master's, 26 doctorates, 6 other advanced degrees awarded. *Program availability:* Part-time, evening/weekend. Offers education and human development (Ed M, MAT, Ed D, PhD, CAGS). *Application deadline:* For fall admission, 1/15 priority date for domestic and international students; for spring admission, 9/15 priority date for domestic and international students. Applications are processed on a rolling basis. *Application fee:* $95. Electronic applications accepted. *Application Contact:* Julia Cocca, Director of Graduate Enrollment, 617-353-4237, E-mail: whegrad@bu.edu. *Interim Dean,* Dr. David J. Chard, 617-353-3213.

BOWIE STATE UNIVERSITY, Bowie, MD 20715-9465

General Information State-supported, coed, comprehensive institution. CGS member. *Graduate housing:* Room and/or apartments available on a first-come, first-served basis to single students; on-campus housing not available to married students. Housing application deadline: 8/1.

GRADUATE UNITS

Graduate Programs *Program availability:* Part-time, evening/weekend. Offers administration of nursing services (MS); applied and computational mathematics (MS); business administration (MBA); computer science (MS, App Sc D); counseling psychology (MA); educational leadership (Ed D); elementary and secondary school administration (M Ed); elementary education (M Ed); English (MA); family nurse practitioner (MS); guidance and counseling (M Ed); human resource development (MA); information systems analyst (Certificate); management information systems (MS); mental health counseling (MA); nursing education (MS); organizational communication (MA, Certificate); public administration (MPA); reading education (M Ed); school administration and supervision (M Ed); secondary education (M Ed); special education (M Ed); teaching (MAT). Electronic applications accepted.

BOWLING GREEN STATE UNIVERSITY, Bowling Green, OH 43403

General Information State-supported, coed, university. CGS member. *Graduate housing:* Rooms and/or apartments available to single and married students. *Research affiliation:* Spectra Group, Inc. (photoscience).

GRADUATE UNITS

Graduate College *Program availability:* Part-time, evening/weekend. Electronic applications accepted.

College of Arts and Sciences *Program availability:* Part-time. Offers 2-D studio art (MA, MFA); 3-D studio art (MA, MFA); American culture studies (MA, PhD); applied philosophy (PhD); art education (MA); art history (MA); arts and sciences (MA, MAT, MFA, MPA, MS, PhD); biological sciences (MS, PhD); chemistry (MS, PhD); clinical psychology (MA, PhD); computer art (MA); computer science (MS); creative writing (MFA); demography and population studies (MA); design (MFA); developmental psychology (MA, PhD); digital arts (MFA); English (MA, PhD); experimental psychology (MA, PhD); fiction (MFA); French (MA); geology (MS); geophysics (MS); German (MA); graphics (MFA); history (MA, MAT, PhD); industrial/organizational psychology (MA, PhD); institutional theory and history (PhD); literature (MA); mathematics (MA, MAT, PhD); media and communication (MA, PhD); philosophy (MA); photochemical sciences (PhD); physics (MAT, MS); poetry (MFA); popular culture (MA); public administration (MPA); public history (MA); quantitative psychology (MA, PhD); rhetoric and writing (PhD); scientific and technical communication (MA); social psychology (MA); sociology (MA, PhD); Spanish (MA); statistics (PhD); strategic communication (MA); theatre and film (MA, PhD). Electronic applications accepted.

College of Business *Program availability:* Part-time, evening/weekend. Offers accountancy (M Acc); applied statistics (MS); business (M Acc, MA, MBA, MOD, MS); business administration (MBA); financial economics (MA); organization development (MOD). Electronic applications accepted.

College of Education and Human Development *Program availability:* Part-time, evening/weekend. Offers assistive technology (M Ed); autism spectrum disorders (M Ed); classroom technology (M Ed); clinical mental health counseling (M Ed, MA); college student personnel (MA); cross-cultural and international education (MA); curriculum and teaching (M Ed); developmental kinesiology (M Ed); education and human development (M Ed, MA, Ed D, PhD, Ed S); educational administration and supervision (M Ed, Ed D, Ed S); educational leadership (M Ed, Ed S); general special education (M Ed); higher education administration (PhD); intervention specialist: mild/moderate disabilities (M Ed); intervention specialist: moderate/intensive disabilities (M Ed); leadership studies (Ed D); reading (M Ed, Ed S); recreation and leisure (M Ed); school counseling (M Ed); secondary transition/transition-to-work (M Ed); special education (M Ed); sport administration (M Ed); workforce education and development (M Ed). Electronic applications accepted.

College of Health and Human Services *Program availability:* Part-time, evening/weekend. Offers communication disorders (PhD); criminal justice (MSCJ); health and human services (MPH, MS, MSCJ, MSW, PhD); public health (MPH); social work (MSW); speech-language pathology (MS). Electronic applications accepted.

College of Musical Arts *Program availability:* Part-time. Offers composition (MM); contemporary music (DMA); ethnomusicology (MM); music education (MM); music history (MM); music theory (MM); performance (MM). Electronic applications accepted.

College of Technology *Program availability:* Part-time. Offers career and technology education (M Ed); technology (M Ed). Electronic applications accepted.

Interdisciplinary Studies *Program availability:* Part-time. Offers interdisciplinary studies (M Ed, MA, MS, PhD). Electronic applications accepted.

BRADLEY UNIVERSITY, Peoria, IL 61625-0002

General Information Independent, coed, comprehensive institution. CGS member. *Enrollment:* 5,882 graduate, professional, and undergraduate students; 377 full-time matriculated graduate/professional students (237 women), 882 part-time matriculated graduate/professional students (730 women). *Enrollment by degree level:* 802 master's, 368 doctoral, 89 other advanced degrees. *Graduate faculty:* 199 full-time (85 women), 48 part-time/adjunct (36 women). *Tuition:* Part-time $890 per credit. *Required fees:* $50 per unit. *Graduate housing:* On-campus housing not available. *Student services:* Campus employment opportunities, campus safety program, career counseling, exercise/wellness program, free psychological counseling, international student services, low-cost health insurance, multicultural affairs office, services for students with disabilities, teacher training. *Library facilities:* Cullom-Davis Library. *Collection:* Books: 545,721 (physical), 5,632 (digital/electronic); Serial titles: 1,557 (physical), 54,082 (digital/electronic); Databases: 54. Weekly public service hours: 129; students can reserve study rooms.

Computer facilities: Computer purchase and lease plans are available. 80 computers available on campus for general student use. A campuswide network can be accessed from student residence rooms and from off campus. Online class registration, Online directory, catalog, library materials and other resources are available. Website: http://www.bradley.edu/

General Application Contact: Rachel Webb, Director of On-Campus Graduate Admissions & International Student and Scholar Services, 309-677-2375, Fax: 309-677-3343, E-mail: rkwebb@bradley.edu.

GRADUATE UNITS

The Graduate School Students: 377 full-time (237 women), 882 part-time (730 women); includes 321 minority (161 Black or African American, non-Hispanic/Latino; 9 American Indian or Alaska Native, non-Hispanic/Latino; 55 Asian, non-Hispanic/Latino; 69 Hispanic/Latino; 1 Native Hawaiian or other Pacific Islander, non-Hispanic/Latino; 26 Two or more races, non-Hispanic/Latino; 107 international. Average age 34. 1,237 applicants, 93% accepted, 314 enrolled. *Faculty:* 199 full-time (85 women), 48 part-time/adjunct (36 women). Expenses: Contact institution. *Financial support:* In 2018–19, 235 students received support, including 5 fellowships with full tuition reimbursements available (averaging $13,350 per year), 78 research assistantships with full and partial tuition reimbursements available (averaging $8,073 per year); career-related internships or fieldwork, institutionally sponsored loans, scholarships/grants, tuition waivers (full and partial), and unspecified assistantships also available. Support available to part-time students. Financial award application deadline: 4/1. In 2018, 228 master's, 43 doctorates, 6 other advanced degrees awarded. *Program availability:* Part-time, evening/weekend, online learning. *Application deadline:* For fall admission, 5/15 priority date for domestic and international students; for spring admission, 10/15 priority date for domestic and international students. Applications are processed on a rolling basis. *Application fee:* $40 ($50 for international students). Electronic applications accepted. *Application Contact:* Rachel Webb, Director of On-Campus Graduate Admissions & International Student and Scholar Services, 309-677-2375, E-mail: rkwebb@bradley.edu. *Dean,* Dr. Jeffrey Bakken, 309-677-2375, E-mail: jbakken@bradley.edu.

Caterpillar College of Engineering and Technology Students: 44 full-time (6 women), 21 part-time (5 women); includes 3 minority (2 Black or African American, non-Hispanic/Latino; 1 Hispanic/Latino); 53 international. Average age 26. 195 applicants, 85% accepted, 14 enrolled. *Faculty:* 45 full-time (6 women), 1 part-time/adjunct (0 women). Expenses: Contact institution. *Financial support:* In 2018–19, 66 students received support, including 26 research assistantships with full and partial tuition reimbursements available (averaging $5,032 per year); teaching assistantships, institutionally sponsored loans, scholarships/grants, tuition waivers (partial), and unspecified assistantships also available. Support available to part-time students. Financial award application deadline: 4/1. In 2018, 34 master's awarded. *Program availability:* Part-time, evening/weekend. Offers construction management, structural engineering, geo-environmental engineering (MSCE); electrical and computer engineering (MSEE); engineering and technology (MS, MSCE, MSEE, MSME); industrial engineering (MS); manufacturing engineering (MS); mechanical engineering (MSME). *Application deadline:* For fall admission, 5/15 priority date for domestic and international students; for spring admission, 10/15 priority date for domestic and international students. Applications are processed on a rolling basis. *Application fee:* $40 ($50 for international students). Electronic applications accepted. *Application Contact:* Rachel Webb, Director of On-Campus Graduate Admissions & International Student and Scholar Services, 309-677-2375, E-mail: rkwebb@bradley.edu. *Dean,* Lex Akers, 309-677-2721, E-mail: lakers@bradley.edu.

College of Education and Health Sciences Students: 271 full-time (207 women), 814 part-time (706 women); includes 307 minority (156 Black or African American, non-Hispanic/Latino; 8 American Indian or Alaska Native, non-Hispanic/Latino; 52 Asian, non-Hispanic/Latino; 65 Hispanic/Latino; 1 Native Hawaiian or other Pacific Islander, non-Hispanic/Latino; 25 Two or more races, non-Hispanic/Latino), 22 international. Average age 35. 767 applicants, 95% accepted, 234 enrolled. *Faculty:* 54 full-time (40 women), 42 part-time/adjunct (34 women). Expenses: Contact institution. *Financial support:* In 2018–19, 78 students received support, including 1 fellowship with full tuition reimbursement available (averaging $16,020 per year), 23 research assistantships with full and partial tuition reimbursements available (averaging $12,382 per year); career-related internships or fieldwork, institutionally sponsored loans, scholarships/grants, tuition waivers (partial), and unspecified assistantships also available. Support available to part-time students. Financial award application deadline: 4/1. In 2018, 124 master's, 43 doctorates awarded. *Program availability:* Part-time, evening/weekend, 100% online, blended/hybrid learning. Offers counseling (MA); curriculum and instruction (MS); dietetic internship (MS); education and health sciences (MA, MS, MSN, DNP, DPT, Certificate); family nurse practitioner (MSN, DNP, Certificate); leadership (DNP); leadership in educational administration (MA); nonprofit leadership (MA); nursing administration (MSN); nursing education (MSN, Certificate); physical therapy (DPT). *Application deadline:* For fall admission, 5/15 priority date for domestic students, 5/15 for international students; for spring admission, 10/15 priority date for domestic students, 10/15 for international students. Applications are processed on a rolling basis. *Application fee:* $40 ($50 for international students). Electronic applications accepted. *Application Contact:* Rachel Webb, Director of On-Campus Graduate Admissions & International Student and Scholar Services, 309-677-2375, E-mail: rkwebb@bradley.edu. *Interim Dean,* Dr. Molly Cluskey, 309-677-3181, E-mail: mcluskey@bradley.edu.

College of Liberal Arts and Sciences Students: 32 full-time (11 women), 19 part-time (12 women); includes 5 minority (1 Black or African American, non-Hispanic/Latino; 1 Asian, non-Hispanic/Latino; 3 Hispanic/Latino), 21 international. Average age 27. 143 applicants, 94% accepted, 23 enrolled. *Faculty:* 53 full-time (24 women), 1 part-time/adjunct. Expenses: Contact institution. *Financial support:* In 2018–19, 40 students received support, including 2 fellowships with full tuition reimbursements available (averaging $8,010 per year), 21 research assistantships with full and partial tuition reimbursements available (averaging $6,506 per year); teaching assistantships, career-related internships or fieldwork, institutionally sponsored loans, scholarships/grants, tuition waivers (partial), and unspecified assistantships also available. Support available to part-time students. Financial award application deadline: 4/1. In 2018, 19 master's awarded. *Program availability:* Part-time, evening/weekend. Offers biochemistry (MS); biology (MS); chemistry (MS); computer information systems (MS); computer science (MS); English (MA); liberal arts and sciences (MA, MS). *Application deadline:* For fall admission, 5/15 priority date for domestic and international students; for spring admission, 10/15 priority date for domestic and international students. Applications are processed on a rolling basis. *Application fee:* $40 ($50 for international students). Electronic applications accepted. *Application Contact:* Rachel Webb, Director of On-Campus Graduate Admissions & International Student and Scholar Services, 309-677-2375, E-mail: rkwebb@bradley.edu. *Dean,* Dr. Christopher Jones, 309-677-2380, E-mail: cmjones@bradley.edu.

Foster College of Business Students: 23 full-time (10 women), 26 part-time (5 women); includes 5 minority (2 Black or African American, non-Hispanic/Latino; 2 Asian, non-Hispanic/Latino; 1 Two or more races, non-Hispanic/Latino), 11 international. Average age 29. 59 applicants, 98% accepted, 17 enrolled. *Faculty:* 34 full-time (10 women), 4 part-time/adjunct (2 women). Expenses: Contact institution. *Financial support:* In 2018–19, 43 students received support, including 2 fellowships with full tuition reimbursements available (averaging $17,355 per year), 8 research assistantships with full tuition reimbursements available (averaging $9,679 per year); teaching assistantships with full and partial tuition reimbursements available, career-related internships or fieldwork, scholarships/grants, tuition waivers (partial), and unspecified assistantships also available. Support available to part-time students. Financial award application deadline: 4/1. In 2018, 45 master's awarded. *Program availability:* Part-time, evening/weekend. Offers accounting (MSA); business (MBA, MSA); business administration (MBA). *Application deadline:* For fall admission, 5/15 priority date for domestic and international students; for spring admission, 10/15 priority date for domestic and international students. Applications are processed on a rolling basis. *Application fee:* $40 ($50 for international students). Electronic applications accepted. *Application Contact:* Rachel Webb, Director of On-Campus Graduate Admissions & International Student and Scholar Services, 309-677-2375, E-mail: rkwebb@bradley.edu. *Interim Dean and Associate Professor, Marketing,* Dr. Matthew O'Brien, 309-677-2255, E-mail: mobrien@bradley.edu.

Slane College of Communications and Fine Arts Students: 7 full-time (3 women), 2 part-time (both women); includes 1 minority (American Indian or Alaska Native, non-Hispanic/Latino). Average age 32. 12 applicants, 83% accepted, 1 enrolled. *Faculty:* 13 full-time (5 women). Expenses: Contact institution. *Financial support:* In 2018–19, 8 students received support, including 5 teaching assistantships with full and partial tuition reimbursements available (averaging $15,486 per year); scholarships/grants, tuition waivers (partial), and unspecified assistantships also available. Support available to part-time students. Financial award application deadline: 4/1. In 2018, 6 master's awarded. *Program availability:* Part-time, evening/weekend. Offers ceramics (MA, MFA); communications and fine arts (MA, MFA); drawing (MA, MFA); graphic design (MA, MFA); painting (MA, MFA); photography (MA, MFA); printmaking (MA, MFA); sculpture (MA, MFA). *Application deadline:* For fall admission, 4/1 priority date for domestic students, 4/11 priority date for international students; for spring admission, 11/1 priority date for domestic and international students. Applications are processed on a rolling basis. *Application fee:* $40 ($50 for international students). Electronic applications accepted. *Application Contact:* Rachel Webb, Director of On-Campus Graduate Admissions & International Student and Scholar Services, 309-677-2375, E-mail: rkwebb@bradley.edu. *Dean,* Dr. Jeffrey Huberman, 309-677-2360.

BRANDEIS UNIVERSITY, Waltham, MA 02454-9110

General Information Independent, coed, university. CGS member. *Enrollment:* 5,801 graduate, professional, and undergraduate students; 1,494 full-time matriculated graduate/professional students (841 women), 487 part-time matriculated graduate/professional students (286 women). *Enrollment by degree level:* 1,367 master's, 580 doctoral, 34 other advanced degrees. *Graduate faculty:* 361 full-time (156 women), 208 part-time/adjunct (88 women). *Graduate housing:* On-campus housing not available. *Student services:* Campus employment opportunities, career counseling, exercise/wellness program, free psychological counseling, grant writing training, international student services, low-cost health insurance, multicultural affairs office, services for students with disabilities, teacher training, writing training. *Library facilities:* Brandeis Library plus 1 other. *Collection:* Books: 1 million (physical), 1.1 million (digital/electronic); Serial titles: 11,941 (physical), 37,330 (digital/electronic); Databases: 445. Students can reserve study rooms.

Computer facilities: Computer purchase and lease plans are available. 130 computers available on campus for general student use. A campuswide network can be accessed from student residence rooms and from off campus. Online class registration, educational software are available. Website: http://www.brandeis.edu/

General Application Contact: Emily Goldberg, Department Coordinator, 781-736-3410, E-mail: gradschool@brandeis.edu.

GRADUATE UNITS

Graduate School of Arts and Sciences Students: 768 full-time (397 women), 54 part-time (46 women); includes 130 minority (15 Black or African American, non-Hispanic/Latino; 2 American Indian or Alaska Native, non-Hispanic/Latino; 41 Asian, non-Hispanic/Latino; 50 Hispanic/Latino; 2 Two or more races, non-Hispanic/Latino), 260 international. Average age 28. 2,689 applicants, 35% accepted, 329 enrolled. *Faculty:* 316 full-time (145 women), 94 part-time/adjunct (50 women). Expenses: Contact institution. *Financial support:* In 2018–19, 298 fellowships with tuition reimbursements, 108 research assistantships with tuition reimbursements, 162 teaching assistantships with partial tuition reimbursements were awarded; scholarships/grants, health care benefits, tuition waivers (full and partial), and unspecified assistantships also available. Support available to part-time students. In 2018, 332 master's, 67 doctorates, 28 other advanced degrees awarded. *Program availability:* Part-time, blended/hybrid learning. Offers ancient Greek and Roman studies (classical studies) (MA); anthropology/women's, gender, and sexuality studies (MA); arts and sciences (Ed M, MA, MAT, MFA, MS, PSM, PhD, AGC, Postbaccalaureate Certificate); biochemistry and biophysics (MS, PhD); biotechnology (PSM); brain, body and behavior (PhD); cognitive neuroscience (PhD); composition and theory (MA, MFA, PhD); computational linguistics (MS); computer science (PhD); English (MA, PhD); English/women's, gender, and sexuality studies (MA); general psychology (MA); genetic counseling (MS); genetics (PhD); history (MA, PhD); inorganic chemistry (MA, MS, PhD); Jewish day schools (MAT); jewish professional leadership and business administration jewish professional leadership and near eastern and judaic studies jewish professional leadership and public policy mathematics (MA, PhD); Mesoamerican archaeology (MA, PhD); microbiology (PhD); molecular and cell biology (MS, PhD); molecular biology (PhD); musicology (MA, MFA, PhD); Near Eastern and Judaic studies (MA); near Eastern and Judaic studies /women's, gender, and sexuality studies (MA); near Eastern and Judaic studies/conflict resolution and coexistence (MA); near Eastern and Judaic studies/Jewish professional leadership (MA); near Eastern and Judaic studies/women's, gender, and sexuality studies (MA); neurobiology (PhD); neuroscience (MS, PhD); organic chemistry (MA, MS, PhD); philosophy (MA); physical chemistry (MS, PhD); physics (MS, PhD); politics (MA, PhD); premedical studies (Postbaccalaureate Certificate); public elementary education (MAT); public policy/women's, gender, and sexuality studies (MA); quantitative biology (PhD); secondary education (MAT); social policy and sociology (PhD); social/developmental psychology (PhD); sociocultural anthropology (MA, PhD); sociology (PhD); sociology/women's, gender, and sexuality studies (MA); studio art (Postbaccalaureate Certificate); sustainable international development/women's, gender, and sexuality studies (MA); teacher leadership (Ed M, AGC); teaching Chinese language and culture (MA); teaching of Hebrew (MAT); the bible and ancient near east

(PhD); women's, gender, and sexuality studies (MA). Offered jointly with The Heller School of Social Policy and Management. *Application deadline:* For fall admission, 1/15 priority date for domestic and international students; for spring admission, 11/1 priority date for domestic and international students. Applications are processed on a rolling basis. *Application fee:* $75. Electronic applications accepted. *Application Contact:* Emily Goldberg, Department Coordinator, 781-736-3410, Fax: 781-736-3412, E-mail: gradschool@brandeis.edu. *Dean,* Dr. Eric Chasalow, 781-736-3410, Fax: 781-736-3412, E-mail: gradschool@brandeis.edu.

The Heller School for Social Policy and Management *Program availability:* Part-time. Offers aging (MPP); assets and inequalities (PhD); behavioral health (MPP); child, youth, and family management (MBA); children, youth and families (MPP, PhD); coexistence and conflict (MA); general social policy (MPP); global health and development (PhD); health (MPP); health and behavioral health (PhD); health care management (MBA); international development (MA); international health policy and management (MS); poverty alleviation and development (MPP); social impact management (MBA); social policy and management (MBA); sustainable development (MBA). Electronic applications accepted.

International Business School (IBS) Offers advanced macroeconomics (PhD); applied economic analysis (PhD); applied microeconomics (PhD); asset management (MSF); corporate finance (MSF); data analytics (MBA); finance (MBA); international business (MA, MBA, MSF, PhD); marketing (MBA); real estate (MSF); risk management (MSF). Electronic applications accepted.

Rabb School of Continuing Studies, Division of Graduate Professional Studies *Program availability:* Part-time-only. Offers bioinformatics (MS); digital innovation for finance technology (MS); digital marketing and design (MS); health and medical informatics (MS); information security leadership (MS); instructional design and technology (MS); learning analytics (Graduate Certificate); project and program management (MS); robotic software engineering (MS); software engineering (MSE); strategic analytics (MS); technology management (MS); user-centered design (MS). Electronic applications accepted.

BRANDMAN UNIVERSITY, Irvine, CA 92618

General Information Independent, coed, comprehensive institution.

GRADUATE UNITS

Marybelle and S. Paul Musco School of Nursing and Health Professions Offers nursing (DNP).

School of Arts and Sciences Offers psychology (MA); social work (MSW).

School of Business and Professional Studies Offers accounting (MBA); business administration (MBA); business intelligence and data analytics (MBA); e-business strategic management (MBA); entrepreneurship (MBA); finance (MBA); health administration (MBA); human resources (MBA, MS); international business (MBA); marketing (MBA); organizational leadership (MA, MBA, MPA); public administration (MPA).

School of Education Offers curriculum and instruction (MAE); educational administration (MAE); educational leadership (MAE); educational leadership and administration (MAT); elementary education (MAT); instructional technology: teaching the 21st century learner (MAE); leadership in early childhood education (MAE); organizational leadership (Ed D); school counseling (MA); secondary education (MAT); special education (MA); teaching and learning (MAE).

BRANDON UNIVERSITY, Brandon, MB R7A 6A9, Canada

General Information Province-supported, coed, comprehensive institution. *Graduate housing:* Room and/or apartments available on a first-come, first-served basis to single students; on-campus housing not available to married students.

GRADUATE UNITS

Department of Rural Development Offers rural development (MRD, Diploma). Electronic applications accepted.

Faculty of Education Offers curriculum and instruction (M Ed, Diploma); educational administration (M Ed, Diploma); guidance and counseling (M Ed, Diploma); special education (M Ed, Diploma).

School of Music *Program availability:* Part-time. Offers composition (M Mus); music education (M Mus); performance and literature (M Mus). Electronic applications accepted.

BRENAU UNIVERSITY, Gainesville, GA 30501

General Information Independent, coed, primarily women, comprehensive institution. *Enrollment:* 2,842 graduate, professional, and undergraduate students; 438 full-time matriculated graduate/professional students (355 women), 649 part-time matriculated graduate/professional students (546 women). *Enrollment by degree level:* 911 master's, 132 doctoral, 44 other advanced degrees. *Graduate faculty:* 38 full-time (29 women), 42 part-time/adjunct (32 women). *Tuition:* Full-time $11,641; part-time $4061 per credit hour. *Required fees:* $200; $200. Tuition and fees vary according to course load, degree level and program. *Graduate housing:* Room and/or apartments available on a first-come, first-served basis; on-campus housing not available to married students. *Student services:* Child daycare facilities, exercise/wellness program, services for students with disabilities. *Library facilities:* Brenau Trustee Library. *Collection:* Books: 83,560 (physical), 431,102 (digital/electronic); Serial titles: 190 (physical), 64,642 (digital/electronic); Databases: 155. Weekly public service hours: 76; students can reserve study rooms.

Computer facilities: 157 computers available on campus for general student use. A campuswide network can be accessed from student residence rooms and from off campus. Online class registration is available.
Website: http://www.brenau.edu/

General Application Contact: Gale Starich, Dean of Graduate Admissions, 678-707-5016, E-mail: gstarich@brenau.edu.

GRADUATE UNITS

Sydney O. Smith Graduate School *Program availability:* Part-time, evening/weekend, online learning. Electronic applications accepted.

College of Business and Mass Communication *Program availability:* Part-time, evening/weekend, online learning. Offers accounting (MBA); business administration (MBA); healthcare management (MBA); organizational leadership (MS); project management (MBA). Electronic applications accepted.

College of Education *Program availability:* Part-time, evening/weekend, online learning. Offers early childhood (Ed S); early childhood education (M Ed, MAT); middle grades (Ed S); middle grades education (M Ed, MAT); secondary education (MAT); special education (M Ed, MAT). Electronic applications accepted.

College of Fine Arts and Humanities *Program availability:* Part-time. Offers interior design (MID). Electronic applications accepted.

College of Health Sciences *Program availability:* Part-time, evening/weekend. Offers family nurse practitioner (MSN); nurse educator (MSN); nursing management (MSN); occupational therapy (MS); psychology (MS). Electronic applications accepted.

BRESCIA UNIVERSITY, Owensboro, KY 42301-3023

General Information Independent-religious, coed, comprehensive institution. *Graduate housing:* Room and/or apartments available on a first-come, first-served basis to single students; on-campus housing not available to married students.

GRADUATE UNITS

Program in Business Administration *Program availability:* Part-time, evening/weekend. Offers business administration (MBA). Electronic applications accepted.

Program in Management *Program availability:* Part-time, evening/weekend. Offers management (MSM).

Program in Social Work *Program availability:* Online learning. Offers social work (MSW). Electronic applications accepted.

Program in Teacher Leadership *Program availability:* Part-time, evening/weekend. Offers teacher leadership (MSTL). Electronic applications accepted.

BRIAR CLIFF UNIVERSITY, Sioux City, IA 51104-0100

General Information Independent-religious, coed, comprehensive institution. *Graduate housing:* Room and/or apartments available on a first-come, first-served basis to single students; on-campus housing not available to married students. Housing application deadline: 6/1.

GRADUATE UNITS

Graduate Nursing Programs *Program availability:* Part-time, online only, 100% online, blended/hybrid learning. Offers nursing (MSN, DNP, Post-Master's Certificate). Electronic applications accepted.

BRIDGEWATER COLLEGE, Bridgewater, VA 22812-1599

General Information Independent-religious, coed, comprehensive institution.

GRADUATE UNITS

Program in Athletic Training Offers athletic training (MS). Electronic applications accepted.

BRIDGEWATER STATE UNIVERSITY, Bridgewater, MA 02325

General Information State-supported, coed, comprehensive institution. CGS member. *Graduate housing:* On-campus housing not available.

GRADUATE UNITS

College of Graduate Studies *Program availability:* Part-time, evening/weekend.

Bartlett College of Science and Mathematics Offers biology (MAT); computer science (MS); mathematics (MAT); physics (MAT); science and mathematics (MAT, MS).

College of Education and Allied Studies *Program availability:* Part-time, evening/weekend. Offers counseling (M Ed, CAGS); early childhood education (M Ed); education and allied studies (M Ed, MAT, MS, CAGS); educational leadership (M Ed, CAGS); elementary education (M Ed); health promotion (M Ed); instructional technology (M Ed); physical education (MS); reading (M Ed, CAGS); secondary education (MAT); special education (M Ed); speech/language pathology (MS).

College of Humanities and Social Sciences *Program availability:* Part-time, evening/weekend. Offers art (MAT); criminal justice (MS); English (MA, MAT); history (MAT); humanities and social sciences (MA, MAT, MPA, MS, MSW); physical sciences (MAT); psychology (MA); public administration (MPA); social work (MSW).

Ricciardi College of Business *Program availability:* Part-time, evening/weekend. Offers accounting and finance (MSM); business (MSM); management (MSM).

BRIERCREST SEMINARY, Caronport, SK S0H 0S0, Canada

General Information Independent-religious, coed, graduate-only institution. *Graduate housing:* Rooms and/or apartments guaranteed to single students and available on a first-come, first-served basis to married students.

GRADUATE UNITS

Graduate Programs *Program availability:* Part-time. Offers Biblical studies (M Div); leadership (MA); leadership and management (M Div); marriage and family counseling (MA); missions (MA); New Testament (MATS); Old Testament (MATS); organizational leadership (MA); pastoral counseling (M Div, MA); pastoral ministry (M Div); theological studies (M Div); theology (MATS); worship (M Div, MA); youth and family ministry (M Div, MA).

BRIGHAM YOUNG UNIVERSITY, Provo, UT 84602-1001

General Information Independent-religious, coed, university. CGS member. *Enrollment:* 2,044 full-time matriculated graduate/professional students (833 women), 1,049 part-time matriculated graduate/professional students (383 women). *Enrollment by degree level:* 2,110 master's, 935 doctoral, 48 other advanced degrees. *Graduate faculty:* 1,042 full-time (188 women), 6 part-time/adjunct (1 woman). *Graduate housing:* Rooms and/or apartments available on a first-come, first-served basis to single and married students. Housing application deadline: 2/1. *Student services:* Campus employment opportunities, campus safety program, career counseling, exercise/wellness program, free psychological counseling, grant writing training, international student services, low-cost health insurance, multicultural affairs office, services for students with disabilities, teacher training, writing training. *Library facilities:* Harold B. Lee Library plus 2 others.

Computer facilities: Computer purchase and lease plans are available. A campuswide network can be accessed from student residence rooms and from off campus. Online class registration is available.
Website: http://www.byu.edu/

General Application Contact: Graduate Studies, 801-422-4091, Fax: 801-422-0270, E-mail: gradstudies@byu.edu.

GRADUATE UNITS

Graduate Studies Students: 2,044 full-time (833 women), 1,049 part-time (383 women); includes 359 minority (14 Black or African American, non-Hispanic/Latino; 6 American Indian or Alaska Native, non-Hispanic/Latino; 60 Asian, non-Hispanic/Latino; 165 Hispanic/Latino; 16 Native Hawaiian or other Pacific Islander, non-Hispanic/Latino; 98 Two or more races, non-Hispanic/Latino), 307 international. Average age 31. 2,171 applicants, 51% accepted, 1069 enrolled. *Faculty:* 1,042 full-time (188 women), 6 part-time/adjunct (1 woman). *Expenses:* Contact institution. *Financial support:* Fellowships, research assistantships, teaching assistantships, career-related internships or fieldwork, institutionally sponsored loans, scholarships/grants, health care benefits, and tuition waivers (full and partial) available. Support available to part-time students. Financial award applicants required to submit FAFSA. *Program availability:* Part-time, evening/weekend. *Application deadline:* For fall admission, 12/1 priority date for domestic and international students; for winter admission, 6/30 priority date for domestic and international students; for spring admission, 1/15 priority date for domestic and international students; for summer admission, 2/1 for domestic and international students. Applications are processed on a rolling basis. *Application fee:* $50. Electronic applications accepted. *Application Contact:* Logan Gillette, Director of Graduate Admissions and Recruitment, 801-422-7308, E-mail: logangillette@byu.edu. *Dean,* Dr. John S.K. Kauwe, 801-422-4465, Fax: 801-422-0089, E-mail: gradstudies@byu.edu.

BYU Marriott School of Business *Program availability:* Part-time, evening/weekend. Offers business (EMBA, MBA, MPA); business administration (MBA); entrepreneurship (MBA); finance (MBA); global supply chain management (MBA); healthcare (MPA); local government (MPA); marketing (MBA); nonprofit management (MPA); public administration (MPA); state and federal government (MPA); strategic human resources (MBA). Electronic applications accepted.

College of Family, Home, and Social Sciences Offers anthropology (MA); clinical psychology (PhD); cognitive and behavioral neuroscience (PhD); family, home, and social sciences (MA, MS, MSW, PhD); marriage and family therapy (MS, PhD); marriage, family and human development (MS, PhD); social work (MSW); sociology (MS). Electronic applications accepted.

College of Fine Arts and Communications Students: 76 full-time (46 women), 33 part-time (19 women); includes 22 minority (1 American Indian or Alaska Native, non-Hispanic/Latino; 11 Asian, non-Hispanic/Latino; 9 Hispanic/Latino; 1 Native Hawaiian or other Pacific Islander, non-Hispanic/Latino), 3 international. Average age 30. 93 applicants, 49% accepted, 37 enrolled. *Faculty:* 100 full-time (20 women), 61 part-time/adjunct (39 women). Expenses: Contact institution. *Financial support:* In 2018–19, 80 students received support, including 65 research assistantships (averaging $3,170 per year), 58 teaching assistantships with full and partial tuition reimbursements available (averaging $3,585 per year); career-related internships or fieldwork, institutionally sponsored loans, scholarships/grants, tuition waivers (partial), unspecified assistantships, and supplementary awards also available. Support available to part-time students. Financial award applicants required to submit FAFSA. In 2018, 35 master's awarded. Offers art education (MA); composition (MM); conducting, choral (MM); mass communications (MA); media and performance studies (MA); music education (MA, MM); performance (MM); studio arts (MFA). *Application deadline:* Applications are processed on a rolling basis. *Application fee:* $50. Electronic applications accepted. *Application Contact:* Logan Gillette, Director of Graduate Admissions and Recruitment, 801-422-7308, E-mail: logangillette@byu.edu. *Dean,* Edward E. Adams, 801-422-8271, Fax: 801-422-0253, E-mail: francie_jenson@byu.edu.

College of Humanities Students: 166 full-time (111 women), 34 part-time (17 women); includes 64 minority (17 Black or African American, non-Hispanic/Latino; 1 American Indian or Alaska Native, non-Hispanic/Latino; 13 Asian, non-Hispanic/Latino; 32 Hispanic/Latino; 1 Native Hawaiian or other Pacific Islander, non-Hispanic/Latino). Average age 30. 132 applicants, 65% accepted, 86 enrolled. *Faculty:* 166 full-time (41 women), 3 part-time/adjunct (1 woman). Expenses: Contact institution. *Financial support:* In 2018–19, 181 students received support, including 7 fellowships (averaging $7,200 per year), 35 research assistantships (averaging $2,855 per year), 169 teaching assistantships (averaging $5,033 per year); career-related internships or fieldwork, institutionally sponsored loans, scholarships/grants, and student instructorships, travel money for conference presentations also available. Financial award application deadline: 2/1. In 2018, 83 master's awarded. Offers comparative studies (MA); creative writing (MFA); linguistics (MA); literature (MA); Portuguese (MA); rhetoric/composition (MA); second language teaching (MA); Spanish (MA); teaching English as a second language (MA). *Application deadline:* For fall admission, 1/15 for domestic and international students. *Application fee:* $50. Electronic applications accepted. *Application Contact:* Adviser, 801-422-4541, Fax: 801-378-5238, E-mail: gradstudies@byu.edu. *Dean,* Scott J. Miller, 801-422-2779, Fax: 801-422-0308, E-mail: scott_miller@byu.edu.

College of Life Sciences Offers athletic training (MS); biological science education (MS); biology (MS, PhD); environmental science (MS); exercise physiology (MS, PhD); exercise sciences (MS); food science (MS); genetics and biotechnology (MS); health promotion (MS, PhD); life sciences (MPH, MS, PhD); microbiology and molecular biology (MS, PhD); neuroscience (MS); nutrition (MS); physical medicine and rehabilitation (PhD); physiology and developmental biology (MS, PhD); public health (MPH); wildlife and wildlands conservation (MS, PhD). Electronic applications accepted.

College of Nursing Offers family nurse practitioner (MS). Electronic applications accepted.

College of Physical and Mathematical Sciences *Program availability:* Part-time. Offers applied statistics (MS); biochemistry (MS, PhD); chemistry (MS, PhD); computer science (MS, PhD); geological sciences (MS); mathematics (MS, PhD); mathematics education (MA); physical and mathematical sciences (MA, MS, PhD); physics (MS, PhD); physics and astronomy (PhD). Electronic applications accepted.

College of Religious Education Offers religious education (MA). Electronic applications accepted.

David O. McKay School of Education Students: 159 full-time (106 women), 157 part-time (91 women); includes 31 minority (3 Black or African American, non-Hispanic/Latino; 4 American Indian or Alaska Native, non-Hispanic/Latino; 8 Asian, non-Hispanic/Latino; 12 Hispanic/Latino; 4 Native Hawaiian or other Pacific Islander, non-Hispanic/Latino), 10 international. Average age 34. 264 applicants, 48% accepted, 109 enrolled. *Faculty:* 74 full-time (23 women), 10 part-time/adjunct (3 women). Expenses: Contact institution. *Financial support:* In 2018–19, 245 students received support. Research assistantships, teaching assistantships, career-related internships or fieldwork, institutionally sponsored loans, scholarships/grants, health care benefits, tuition waivers, and unspecified assistantships available. Support available to part-time students. Financial award applicants required to submit FAFSA. In 2018, 57 master's, 15 doctorates, 9 other advanced degrees awarded. Offers counseling psychology (PhD); doctorate of education (Ed D); education policy studies (M Ed); educational research, measurement, and evaluation (PhD); instructional psychology and technology (PhD); school leadership (M Ed); school psychology (Ed S); special education (MS); speech language pathology (MS); teacher education (MA). *Application fee:* $50. Electronic applications accepted. *Application Contact:* Brandan Beerli, Director, Education Student Services, 801-422-9199, Fax: 801-422-0195. *Dean,* Dr. Mary Anne Prater, 801-422-1592, Fax: 801-422-0200, E-mail: prater@byu.edu.

Ira A. Fulton College of Engineering Students: 354 full-time (44 women); includes 28 minority (7 Asian, non-Hispanic/Latino; 4 Hispanic/Latino; 1 Native Hawaiian or other Pacific Islander, non-Hispanic/Latino; 16 Two or more races, non-Hispanic/Latino), 58 international. Average age 28. 155 applicants, 48% accepted, 73 enrolled. *Faculty:* 113 full-time (4 women), 8 part-time/adjunct (2 women). Expenses: Contact institution. *Financial support:* In 2018–19, 337 students received support, including 14 fellowships with full and partial tuition reimbursements available (averaging $19,559 per year), 364 research assistantships with full and partial tuition reimbursements available (averaging $14,564 per year), 152 teaching assistantships with full and partial tuition reimbursements available (averaging $11,021 per year); scholarships/grants and health care benefits also available. Financial award application deadline: 1/1; financial award applicants required to submit FAFSA. In 2018, 121 master's, 17 doctorates awarded. Offers chemical engineering (MS); civil engineering (MS, PhD); construction management (MS); electrical & computer engineering (PhD); engineering and technology (MS, PhD); information technology (MS); manufacturing engineering technology (MS); mechanical engineering (PhD); technology and engineering education (MS). *Application deadline:* For fall admission, 1/15 for domestic and international students; for winter admission, 6/15 for domestic and international students; for spring admission, 2/5 for domestic and international students; for summer admission, 2/5 for domestic and international students. *Application fee:* $50. Electronic applications accepted. *Application Contact:* Claire A. DeWitt, Adviser, 801-422-4541, Fax: 801-422-0270, E-mail: gradstudies@byu.edu. *Dean,* Dr. Michael A. Jensen, 801-422-5736, Fax: 801-422-0218, E-mail: college@et.byu.edu.

J. Reuben Clark Law School Students: 356 full-time (144 women); includes 60 minority (3 Black or African American, non-Hispanic/Latino; 2 American Indian or Alaska Native, non-Hispanic/Latino; 5 Asian, non-Hispanic/Latino; 26 Hispanic/Latino; 5 Native Hawaiian or other Pacific Islander, non-Hispanic/Latino; 19 Two or more races, non-Hispanic/Latino), 6 international. Average age 28. 451 applicants, 38% accepted, 104 enrolled. *Faculty:* 37 full-time (13 women), 35 part-time/adjunct (7 women). Expenses: Contact institution. *Financial support:* In 2018–19, 227 students received support, including 20 fellowships (averaging $40,000 per year); career-related internships or fieldwork, institutionally sponsored loans, scholarships/grants, unspecified assistantships, and Student employment also available. Financial award application deadline: 6/1; financial award applicants required to submit FAFSA. In 2018, 5 master's, 138 doctorates awarded. Offers law (LL M, JD). *Application deadline:* For fall admission, 3/1 for domestic and international students. Applications are processed on a rolling basis. *Application fee:* $0. Electronic applications accepted. *Application Contact:* Jillyn Comstock, Admissions Coordinator, 801-422-4356, Fax: 801-422-0389, E-mail: comstockj@law.byu.edu. *Dean,* D. Gordon Smith, 801-422-6383, Fax: 801-422-0389, E-mail: smithg@law.byu.edu.

BRITE DIVINITY SCHOOL, Fort Worth, TX 76109

General Information Independent-religious, coed, graduate-only institution. *Graduate housing:* Rooms and/or apartments available on a first-come, first-served basis to single and married students. Housing application deadline: 4/1.

GRADUATE UNITS

Graduate and Professional Programs *Program availability:* Part-time, evening/weekend. Offers Biblical interpretation (PhD); divinity (M Div); ministry (D Min); pastoral theology (PhD); theological studies (MTS, CTS); theology (Th M); theology and ministry (MA).

BROADVIEW UNIVERSITY–WEST JORDAN, West Jordan, UT 84088

General Information Proprietary, coed, comprehensive institution.

GRADUATE UNITS
Graduate Programs

BROCK UNIVERSITY, St. Catharines, ON L2S 3A1, Canada

General Information Province-supported, coed, university. *Graduate housing:* Room and/or apartments available on a first-come, first-served basis to single students; on-campus housing not available to married students. *Research affiliation:* Registered Nurses Association of Ontario (nursing best practices), Canadian Honey Council (agriculture, therapeutic product development), Fly Fishing Canada/Trout Unlimited Canada (fisheries management), Henry Ford Health Centre (cancer epidemiology).

GRADUATE UNITS

Faculty of Graduate Studies *Program availability:* Part-time, evening/weekend. Electronic applications accepted.

Faculty of Applied Health Sciences Offers applied health sciences (M Sc, MA, PhD). Electronic applications accepted.

Faculty of Business *Program availability:* Part-time. Offers accountancy (M Acc); business (M Acc, M Sc, MBA); business administration (MBA); management (M Sc). Electronic applications accepted.

Faculty of Education *Program availability:* Part-time, evening/weekend. Offers education (M Ed, PhD). Electronic applications accepted.

Faculty of Humanities *Program availability:* Part-time. Offers applied linguistics (MA); classics (MA); English (MA); history (MA); humanities (MA); philosophy (MA); studies in comparative literatures and arts (MA). Electronic applications accepted.

Faculty of Mathematics and Science *Program availability:* Part-time. Offers biological sciences (M Sc, PhD); biotechnology (M Sc, PhD); chemistry (M Sc, PhD); computer science (M Sc); earth sciences (M Sc); mathematics and science (M Sc, PhD); mathematics and statistics (M Sc); physics (M Sc). Electronic applications accepted.

Faculty of Social Sciences *Program availability:* Part-time. Offers applied disability studies (MA, MADS, Diploma); behavioral neuroscience (MA, PhD); business economics (MBE); Canadian politics (MA); child and youth studies (MA); comparative politics (MA); critical sociology (MA); geography (MA); international relations (MA); life span development (MA, PhD); political theory or philosophy (MA); popular culture (MA); public policy (MA); social justice and equity studies (MA); social personality (MA, PhD); social sciences (MA, MADS, MBE, PhD, Diploma). Electronic applications accepted.

BROOKLINE COLLEGE, Phoenix, AZ 85021

General Information Proprietary, coed, comprehensive institution.

GRADUATE UNITS

Nursing Programs *Program availability:* Part-time, online learning. Offers health systems administration (MSN); nursing (MSN).

BROOKLYN COLLEGE OF THE CITY UNIVERSITY OF NEW YORK, Brooklyn, NY 11210-2889

General Information State and locally supported, coed, comprehensive institution. *Graduate housing:* Room and/or apartments available on a first-come, first-served basis to single students; on-campus housing not available to married students. *Research affiliation:* Biothera Inc. (biology), Silicon Valley Community Foundation (computer and information science), Jessie Smith Noyes Foundation (sustainability), Sloan-Kettering Memorial Cancer Center (health/biology), Community Health Care Association of New York State (health and nutrition sciences), Welfare Research Inc. (education).

GRADUATE UNITS

School of Business *Program availability:* Part-time, evening/weekend. Offers accounting (MS); business administration (MS). Electronic applications accepted.

School of Education *Program availability:* Part-time, evening/weekend. Offers adolescence science education (MAT); art teacher (K-12) (MA); autism spectrum disorders (AC); bilingual education (MS Ed); biology (MA); biology teacher (7-12) (MA); birth-grade 2 (MS Ed); chemistry (MA); chemistry teacher (7-12) (MA); earth science (MA); earth science teacher (7-12) (MAT); education (MA, MAT, MS Ed, AC); English teacher (7-12) (MA); French teacher (7-12) (MA); general science (MA); liberal arts (MS Ed); mathematics (MA); mathematics teacher (7-12) (MA); middle childhood mathematics education (MS Ed); music teacher (MA); physics (MA); physics teacher (7-12) (MA); play therapy (AC); school building leader (MS Ed); school counseling (MS Ed); school district leader (MS Ed); school psychologist (MS Ed); science and environmental education (MS Ed); social studies teacher (7-12) (MA); Spanish teacher (7-12) (MA); teacher of students with disabilities (MS Ed). Electronic applications accepted.

School of Humanities and Social Sciences *Program availability:* Part-time, evening/weekend. Offers audiology (Au D); creative writing (MFA); English (MA); French (MA); history (MA); humanities and social sciences (MA, MFA, MS, Au D, PhD); international affairs (MA); Judaic studies (MA); political science (MA); sociology (MA, PhD); Spanish (MA); speech (MA); speech-language pathology (MS); urban policy and administration (MA). Electronic applications accepted.

School of Natural and Behavioral Sciences *Program availability:* Part-time, evening/weekend. Offers biology (MA); chemistry (MA, MS, PhD); community health (MA); community health education (MA); computer science (MA); earth and environmental sciences (MA, PhD); exercise and sports science (MS); experimental psychology (MA); general public health (MPH); grief counseling (CAS); health care policy and administration (MPH); health informatics (MS); industrial and organizational psychology (MA); information systems (MS); mathematics (MS); mental health counseling (MA); natural and behavioral sciences (MA, MPH, MS, PhD, AC, Advanced Certificate); nutrition (MS); parallel and distributed computing (Advanced Certificate); physical education teacher (MS); physics (MA); psychology (PhD); public health (MPH); sport management (MS); thanatology (MA). Electronic applications accepted.

School of Visual, Media and Performing Arts *Program availability:* Part-time, evening/weekend. Offers acting (MFA); art history (MA); cinema arts (MFA); cinema studies (MA); design and technical theater (MFA); digital art (MFA); directing (MFA); drawing and painting (MFA); media studies (MS); performance and interactive media arts (MFA); performing arts management (MFA); photography (MFA); printmaking (MFA); sculpture (MFA); television production (MFA); theater history and criticism (MA); visual, media and performing arts (M Mus, MA, MFA, MS). Electronic applications accepted.

Conservatory of Music *Program availability:* Part-time. Offers composition (MM); music teacher (MA); musicology (MA); performance (MM). Electronic applications accepted.

BROOKLYN LAW SCHOOL, Brooklyn, NY 11201-3798

General Information Independent, coed, graduate-only institution. *Graduate housing:* Rooms and/or apartments available to single students and guaranteed to married students. Housing application deadline: 5/1.

GRADUATE UNITS

Graduate and Professional Programs *Program availability:* Part-time, evening/weekend. Offers law (LL M, JD). JD/MBA offered jointly with Bernard M. Baruch College of the City University of New York; JD/MS with Pratt Institute; JD/MUP with Hunter College of the City University of New York; and JD/MA with Brooklyn College of the City University of New York. Electronic applications accepted.

BROWN UNIVERSITY, Providence, RI 02912

General Information Independent, coed, university. CGS member. *Graduate housing:* Room and/or apartments available to single students; on-campus housing not available to married students. *Research affiliation:* Woods Hole Oceanographic Institution-Marine Biological Laboratory, Rhode Island Reactor, International Center for Numismatic Studies, Meeting Street School.

GRADUATE UNITS

Graduate School *Program availability:* Part-time. Offers acting and directing (MFA); American studies (PhD); American studies for international students (MA); ancient western Asian studies (PhD); anthropology (MA, PhD); Asian religious traditions (PhD); Brazilian studies (AM); chemistry (PhD); classics (MA, PhD); cognitive science (Sc M, PhD); comparative literature (PhD); computer music and multimedia (PhD); computer science (Sc M, PhD); earth, environmental and planetary sciences (PhD); economics (PhD); Egyptology (PhD); elementary education (MAT); English (MAT, PhD); English as a second language and cross-cultural studies (AM); ethnomusicology (PhD); French studies (PhD); German (PhD); Hispanic studies (PhD); history (MA, PhD); history of art and architecture (PhD); history of the exact sciences in antiquity (PhD); history/social studies (MAT); Islam, society and culture (PhD); Italian studies (PhD); linguistics (AM, PhD); literary arts (MFA); mathematics (PhD); philosophy (PhD); physics (Sc M, PhD); playwriting (MFA); political science (PhD); Portuguese and Brazilian studies (AM, PhD); Portuguese bilingual education and cross-cultural studies (AM); psychology (PhD); public humanities (MA); religion and critical thought (PhD); religions of the ancient Mediterranean (PhD); Russian language and literature (AM); science (MAT); secondary education (MAT); Slavic linguistics (AM); Slavic studies (PhD); sociology (MA, PhD); teaching (MAT); theatre and performance studies (PhD); urban education policy (AM).

A. Alfred Taubman Center for Public Policy and American Institutions Offers public policy and American institutions (MPA, MPP).

Division of Applied Mathematics Offers applied mathematics (Sc M, PhD).

Division of Biology and Medicine *Program availability:* Part-time. Offers behavioral and social sciences intervention (M Sc); biology and medicine (AM, M Sc, MA, MPH, Sc M, MD, PhD); biomedical engineering (Sc M, PhD); biostatistics (AM, Sc M, PhD); biotechnology (PhD); ecology and evolutionary biology (PhD); epidemiology (Sc M, PhD); health services, policy and practice (PhD); medicine (MD); molecular biology, cell biology, and biochemistry (MA, PhD); molecular pharmacology and physiology (PhD); neuroscience (PhD); pathology and laboratory medicine (Sc M, PhD); public health (MPH). Electronic applications accepted.

Joukowsky Institute for Archaeology and the Ancient World Offers archaeology and the ancient world (PhD).

School of Engineering Offers biomedical engineering (Sc M, PhD); chemical and biochemical engineering (Sc M, PhD); electrical sciences and computer engineering (Sc M, PhD); fluid and thermal sciences (Sc M, PhD); materials science and engineering (Sc M, PhD); mechanics of solids and structures (Sc M, PhD).

National Institutes of Health Sponsored Programs Offers neuroscience (PhD).

BRYAN COLLEGE, Dayton, TN 37321

General Information Independent-religious, coed, comprehensive institution. *Graduate housing:* On-campus housing not available.

GRADUATE UNITS

MBA Program *Program availability:* Online only, 100% online. Offers business administration (MBA); healthcare administration (MBA); human resources (MBA); marketing (MBA); ministry (MBA); sports management (MBA). Electronic applications accepted.

BRYAN COLLEGE OF HEALTH SCIENCES, Lincoln, NE 68506

General Information Independent, coed, comprehensive institution. CGS member.

GRADUATE UNITS

School of Nurse Anesthesia Offers nurse anesthesia (MS).

BRYANT UNIVERSITY, Smithfield, RI 02917

General Information Independent, coed, comprehensive institution. *Enrollment:* 3,788 graduate, professional, and undergraduate students; 169 full-time matriculated graduate/professional students (95 women), 118 part-time matriculated graduate/professional students (53 women). *Enrollment by degree level:* 287 master's. *Graduate faculty:* 37 full-time (10 women), 19 part-time/adjunct (8 women). *Tuition:* Full-time $40,248; part-time $1118 per credit hour. Part-time tuition and fees vary according to course load, degree level and program. *Graduate housing:* Room and/or apartments available on a first-come, first-served basis to single students; on-campus housing not available to married students. Typical cost: $11,212 per year ($17,392 including board). Room and board charges vary according to board plan and housing facility selected. Housing application deadline: 8/1. *Student services:* Campus employment opportunities, campus safety program, career counseling, exercise/wellness program, free psychological counseling, international student services, low-cost health insurance, multicultural affairs office, services for students with disabilities, teacher training, writing training. *Library facilities:* Douglas and Judith Krupp Library plus 1 other. *Collection:* Books: 121,623 (physical), 16,854 (digital/electronic); Serial titles: 3,183 (physical), 299 (digital/electronic); Databases: 80. Weekly public service hours: 110; students can reserve study rooms.

Computer facilities: Computer purchase and lease plans are available. 526 computers available on campus for general student use. A campuswide network can be accessed from student residence rooms and from off campus. Online class registration, e-mail, online library, student Web hosts are available. Website: http://www.bryant.edu/

General Application Contact: Jamie Grenon, Director, Graduate Programs, 401-232-6707, E-mail: graduateprograms@bryant.edu.

GRADUATE UNITS

College of Arts and Sciences Students: 5 full-time (1 woman), 12 part-time (7 women); includes 3 minority (all Black or African American, non-Hispanic/Latino), 2 international. Average age 28. 15 applicants, 60% accepted, 9 enrolled. *Faculty:* 6 full-time (3 women), 1 (woman) part-time/adjunct. *Expenses:* Contact institution. *Financial support:* Scholarships/grants and unspecified assistantships available. Financial award applicants required to submit FAFSA. In 2018, 5 master's, 1 other advanced degree awarded. *Program availability:* Part-time, evening/weekend. Offers communication (MA, Graduate Certificate); organizational communication (Graduate Certificate). *Application deadline:* For fall admission, 8/15 for domestic and international students; for spring admission, 1/14 for domestic students, 1/15 for international students; for summer admission, 5/15 for domestic and international students. Applications are processed on a rolling basis. *Application fee:* $80. Electronic applications accepted. *Application Contact:* Mary Robins, M.S., Department of Communication, Lecturer and Graduate Programs Faculty Representative, 401-232-6596, E-mail: mrobins@bryant.edu. *Graduate Program Director,* Associate Professor, College of Arts and Sciences, Dr. Christopher Morse, Ph.D., 401-232-6582, E-mail: cmorse2@bryant.edu.

Graduate School of Business Students: 77 full-time (31 women), 106 part-time (46 women); includes 32 minority (7 Black or African American, non-Hispanic/Latino; 1 American Indian or Alaska Native, non-Hispanic/Latino; 9 Asian, non-Hispanic/Latino; 8 Hispanic/Latino; 7 Two or more races, non-Hispanic/Latino), 8 international. Average age 28. 215 applicants, 66% accepted, 96 enrolled. *Faculty:* 31 full-time (8 women), 6 part-time/adjunct (2 women). *Expenses:* Contact institution. *Financial support:* In 2018–19, 95 fellowships with full and partial tuition reimbursements (averaging $9,825 per year), 9 research assistantships with full and partial tuition reimbursements (averaging $7,100 per year) were awarded; scholarships/grants and unspecified assistantships also available. Support available to part-time students. Financial award application deadline: 2/15; financial award applicants required to submit FAFSA. In 2018, 134 master's awarded. *Program availability:* Part-time, evening/weekend, 100% online. Offers accounting (MPAC); business administration (MBA); taxation (MST). *Application deadline:* For fall admission, 7/15 for domestic and international students; for spring admission, 11/15 for domestic and international students; for summer admission, 4/15 for domestic and international students. Applications are processed on a rolling basis. *Application fee:* $80. Electronic applications accepted. *Application Contact:* Jeanne Creighton, Senior Admissions Assistant, 401-232-6123, Fax: 401-232-6494, E-mail: graduateprograms@bryant.edu. *Director, Graduate Programs Office,* Jamie R Grenon, 401-232-6707, E-mail: jgrenon@bryant.edu.

School of Health Sciences Students: 88 full-time (64 women); includes 15 minority (2 Black or African American, non-Hispanic/Latino; 2 American Indian or Alaska Native, non-Hispanic/Latino; 5 Asian, non-Hispanic/Latino; 2 Hispanic/Latino; 2 Native Hawaiian or other Pacific Islander, non-Hispanic/Latino; 2 Two or more races, non-Hispanic/Latino), 1 international. Average age 25. 910 applicants, 6% accepted, 48 enrolled. *Faculty:* 5 full-time (2 women), 12 part-time/adjunct (6 women). *Expenses:* Contact institution. *Financial support:* Fund for a Healthy Rhode Island awards available. Financial award application deadline: 10/1; financial award applicants required to submit FAFSA. In 2018, 41 master's awarded. Offers physician assistant studies (MPAS). *Application deadline:* For winter admission, 10/1 for domestic and international students. Applications are processed on a rolling basis. *Application fee:* $50. Electronic applications accepted. *Application Contact:* Kayla Cetrone, Director, Physician Assistant Admissions, 401-232-6404, E-mail: kcetrone@bryant.edu. *Program Director,* Robert Jay Amrien, 401-232-6556, E-mail: jamrien@bryant.edu.

BRYAN UNIVERSITY, Springfield, MO 65804

General Information Proprietary, coed, comprehensive institution.

GRADUATE UNITS

Program in Business Administration *Program availability:* Online learning. Offers business administration (MBA).

BRYN ATHYN COLLEGE OF THE NEW CHURCH, Bryn Athyn, PA 19009-0717

General Information Independent-religious, coed, comprehensive institution. *Graduate housing:* Room and/or apartments available on a first-come, first-served basis to single students; on-campus housing not available to married students. Housing application deadline: 1/31.

GRADUATE UNITS

Academy of the New Church Theological School *Program availability:* Part-time, online learning. Offers divinity (M Div); religious studies (M Div).

BRYN MAWR COLLEGE, Bryn Mawr, PA 19010-2899

General Information Independent, Undergraduate: women only; graduate: coed, comprehensive institution. CGS member. *Graduate housing:* On-campus housing not available.

GRADUATE UNITS

Graduate School of Arts and Sciences *Program availability:* Part-time. Offers arts and sciences (MA, PhD); chemistry (MA, PhD); classical and Near Eastern archaeology (MA, PhD); Greek, Latin, and classical studies (MA, PhD); history of art (MA, PhD); mathematics (MA, PhD); physics (MA, PhD). Electronic applications accepted.

Graduate School of Social Work and Social Research *Program availability:* Part-time, evening/weekend. Offers social work and social research (MSS, PhD). Electronic applications accepted.

BUCKNELL UNIVERSITY, Lewisburg, PA 17837

General Information Independent, coed, comprehensive institution. CGS member. *Graduate housing:* On-campus housing not available.

GRADUATE UNITS

Graduate Studies *Program availability:* Part-time.

College of Arts and Sciences *Program availability:* Part-time. Offers animal behavior (MS); arts and sciences (MA, MS, MS Ed); biology (MS); chemistry (MA, MS); college student personnel (MS Ed); English (MA); mathematics (MA, MS); psychology (MS).

College of Engineering *Program availability:* Part-time. Offers chemical engineering (MS Ch E); civil and environmental engineering (MSCE, MSEV); electrical and computer engineering (MSEE); engineering (MS Ch E, MSCE, MSEE, MSEV, MSME); mechanical engineering (MSME).

BUENA VISTA UNIVERSITY, Storm Lake, IA 50588

General Information Independent-religious, coed, comprehensive institution. *Graduate housing:* Room and/or apartments available on a first-come, first-served basis to single students; on-campus housing not available to married students. Housing application deadline: 5/1.

GRADUATE UNITS

School of Education *Program availability:* Part-time, evening/weekend, online learning. Offers curriculum and instruction (M Ed); school guidance and counseling (MS Ed). Program offered in summer only. Electronic applications accepted.

BUFFALO STATE COLLEGE, STATE UNIVERSITY OF NEW YORK, Buffalo, NY 14222-1095

General Information State-supported, coed, comprehensive institution. CGS member. *Graduate housing:* Room and/or apartments available on a first-come, first-served basis to single students; on-campus housing not available to married students. Housing application deadline: 8/15. *Research affiliation:* Friends of Buffalo River, Research Institute on Addictions at the University of Buffalo, Roswell Park Memorial Institute, Hauptman-Woodward Medical Research Institute, Ecology and Environment Corporation, Phillip Morris Foundation.

GRADUATE UNITS

The Graduate School *Program availability:* Part-time, evening/weekend, online learning. Offers data science and analytics (MS); individualized studies (MA, MS); nutrition (MS).

School of Arts and Humanities *Program availability:* Part-time, evening/weekend. Offers art conservation (CAS); art education (MS Ed); arts and humanities (MA, MS Ed, CAS); conservation of historic works and art works (MA); English (MA); secondary education (MS Ed).

School of Education *Program availability:* Part-time, evening/weekend, online learning. Offers adult education (MS, Certificate); business and marketing education (MS Ed); career and technical education (MS Ed); childhood education (MS Ed); childhood education (grades 1-6) (MS Ed); early childhood and childhood curriculum and instruction (MS Ed); early childhood education (birth-grade 2) (MS Ed); education (MS, MS Ed, CAS, Certificate, Graduate Certificate); educational leadership (CAS); human resource development (Certificate); literacy specialist (MS Ed); literacy specialist (birth-grade 12) (MS Ed); special education (MS Ed); special education: childhood (MS Ed); special education: early childhood (MS Ed); teaching bilingual exceptional individuals (Graduate Certificate); technology education (MS Ed); urban education (MS).

School of Natural and Social Sciences *Program availability:* Part-time, evening/weekend. Offers applied economics (MA); biology (MA); forensic science (MS); history (MA); mathematics education (MS Ed); museum studies (MA); natural and social sciences (MA, MS, MS Ed); physics education (7-12) (MS Ed); science education (MS Ed); secondary education (MS Ed).

School of the Professions Offers creative studies (MS); criminal justice (MS); industrial technology (MS); mechanical and manufacturing technology (MS); speech-language pathology (MS Ed).

BURRELL COLLEGE OF OSTEOPATHIC MEDICINE, Las Cruces, NM 88001

General Information Proprietary, coed, graduate-only institution.

GRADUATE UNITS

Graduate Program Offers osteopathic medicine (DO).

BUTLER UNIVERSITY, Indianapolis, IN 46208-3485

General Information Independent, coed, comprehensive institution. *Enrollment:* 5,506 graduate, professional, and undergraduate students; 435 full-time matriculated graduate/professional students (304 women), 362 part-time matriculated graduate/professional students (221 women). *Enrollment by degree level:* 534 master's, 206 doctoral, 57 other advanced degrees. *Graduate faculty:* 138 full-time (71 women), 38 part-time/adjunct (21 women). *Tuition:* Full-time $10,440; part-time $8960 per credit hour. Tuition and fees vary according to course level, program and student level. *Graduate housing:* Room and/or apartments available on a first-come, first-served basis to single students; on-campus housing not available to married students. Typical cost: $8300 per year ($15,540 including board). Room and board charges vary according to board plan, campus/location and housing facility selected. Housing application deadline: 8/1. *Student services:* Campus safety program, career counseling, exercise/wellness program, free psychological counseling, international student services, low-cost health insurance, multicultural affairs office, services for students with disabilities. *Library facilities:* Irwin Library plus 2 others. *Collection:* Books: 195,698 (physical), 821,771 (digital/electronic); Serial titles: 13,168 (physical), 99,038 (digital/electronic); Databases: 323. Weekly public service hours: 106; students can reserve study rooms.

Computer facilities: Computer purchase and lease plans are available. 490 computers available on campus for general student use. A campuswide network can be accessed from student residence rooms and from off campus. Online class registration is available.

Website: http://www.butler.edu/

General Application Contact: Diane Dubord, Graduate Student Services Specialist, 317-940-8107, Fax: 317-940-8250, E-mail: ddubord@butler.edu.

GRADUATE UNITS

College of Education Students: 11 full-time (8 women), 169 part-time (140 women); includes 27 minority (11 Black or African American, non-Hispanic/Latino; 3 Asian, non-Hispanic/Latino; 7 Hispanic/Latino; 6 Two or more races, non-Hispanic/Latino). Average age 34. 74 applicants, 85% accepted, 63 enrolled. *Faculty:* 12 full-time (8 women), 12 part-time/adjunct (all women). Expenses: Contact institution. *Financial support:* In 2018–19, 64 students received support. Scholarships/grants, tuition waivers (full and partial), and unspecified assistantships available. Financial award application deadline: 7/15; financial award applicants required to submit FAFSA. In 2018, 51 master's, 32 other advanced degrees awarded. *Program availability:* Part-time. Offers educational administration (MS). *Application deadline:* For fall admission, 2/1 for domestic and international students; for spring admission, 11/1 for domestic and international students; for summer admission, 4/1 for domestic and international students. Applications are processed on a rolling basis. *Application fee:* $0. Electronic applications accepted. *Application Contact:* Diane Dubord, Graduate Student Services Specialist, 317-940-8100, Fax: 317-940-8250, E-mail: ddubord@butler.edu. *Dean,* Dr. Ena Shelley, 317-940-9752, Fax: 317-940-6481.

College of Liberal Arts and Sciences Students: 7 full-time (3 women), 40 part-time (22 women); includes 6 minority (2 Black or African American, non-Hispanic/Latino; 3 Hispanic/Latino; 3 Two or more races, non-Hispanic/Latino). Average age 48. 64 applicants, 75% accepted, 19 enrolled. *Faculty:* 20 full-time (9 women). Expenses: Contact institution. *Financial support:* In 2018–19, 20 students received support. Scholarships/grants, tuition waivers (full and partial), and unspecified assistantships available. Financial award application deadline: 7/15; financial award applicants required to submit FAFSA. In 2018, 20 master's awarded. *Program availability:* Part-time, evening/weekend. Offers liberal arts and sciences (MA, MFA). *Application deadline:* For fall admission, 2/15 for domestic and international students; for spring admission, 9/15 for domestic and international students. Applications are processed on a rolling basis. *Application fee:* $0. Electronic applications accepted. *Application Contact:* Diane Dubord, Graduate Student Services Specialist, 317-940-8107, Fax: 317-940-8250, E-mail: ddubord@butler.edu. *Dean,* Dr. Jay Howard, 317-940-9874, E-mail: jrhoward@butler.edu.

College of Pharmacy and Health Sciences Students: 359 full-time (271 women), 5 part-time (3 women); includes 40 minority (3 Black or African American, non-Hispanic/Latino; 22 Asian, non-Hispanic/Latino; 8 Hispanic/Latino; 7 Two or more races, non-Hispanic/Latino), 5 international. Average age 24. 522 applicants, 26% accepted, 78 enrolled. *Faculty:* 62 full-time (42 women). Expenses: Contact institution. *Financial support:* In 2018–19, 9 students received support. Scholarships/grants, tuition waivers (full and partial), and unspecified assistantships available. Financial award application deadline: 7/15; financial award applicants required to submit FAFSA. In 2018, 71 master's, 136 doctorates awarded. Offers pharmaceutical science (MS); pharmacy (Pharm D); physician assistant studies (MS). *Application deadline:* For fall admission, 4/1 for domestic and international students. *Application fee:* $0. Electronic applications accepted. *Application Contact:* Diane Dubord, Graduate Student Services Specialist, 317-940-8107, E-mail: ddubord@butler.edu. *Dean,* Dr. Robert Soltis, 317-940-8056, E-mail: rsoltis@butler.edu.

Jordan College of the Arts Students: 19 full-time (8 women), 22 part-time (9 women); includes 9 minority (3 Black or African American, non-Hispanic/Latino; 1 Asian, non-Hispanic/Latino; 3 Hispanic/Latino; 2 Two or more races, non-Hispanic/Latino), 2 international. Average age 27. 48 applicants, 79% accepted, 18 enrolled. *Faculty:* 21 full-time (4 women), 7 part-time/adjunct (4 women). Expenses: Contact institution. *Financial support:* In 2018–19, 20 students received support. Scholarships/grants, tuition waivers (full and partial), and unspecified assistantships available. Financial award application deadline: 7/15; financial award applicants required to submit FAFSA. In 2018, 12 master's awarded. *Program availability:* Part-time. Offers composition (MM); conducting (MM); music education (MM); musicology (MA); performance (MM); piano pedagogy (MM). *Application deadline:* For fall admission, 2/1 for domestic and international students; for spring admission, 12/15 for domestic and international students; for summer admission, 4/15 for domestic and international students. Applications are processed on a rolling basis. *Application fee:* $0. Electronic applications accepted. *Application Contact:* Diane Dubord, Graduate Student Services Specialist, 317-940-8107, E-mail: ddubord@butler.edu. *Associate Dean,* Wendy Meaden, 317-940-9229, E-mail: wmeaden@butler.edu.

Lacy School of Business Students: 39 full-time (14 women), 126 part-time (47 women); includes 18 minority (2 Black or African American, non-Hispanic/Latino; 5 Asian, non-Hispanic/Latino; 8 Hispanic/Latino; 3 Two or more races, non-Hispanic/Latino), 10 international. Average age 29. 144 applicants, 83% accepted, 56 enrolled. *Faculty:* 23 full-time (8 women), 19 part-time/adjunct (5 women). Expenses: Contact institution. *Financial support:* In 2018–19, 17 students received support. Scholarships/grants, tuition waivers (full and partial), and unspecified assistantships available. Financial award application deadline: 7/15; financial award applicants required to submit FAFSA. In 2018, 70 master's awarded. *Program availability:* Part-time. Offers business (MBA, MP Acc). *Application deadline:* For fall admission, 8/1 for domestic and international students; for spring admission, 12/1 for domestic and international students; for summer admission, 4/1 for domestic and international students. Applications are processed on a rolling basis. *Application fee:* $0. Electronic applications accepted. *Application Contact:* Diane Dubord, Graduate Student Service Specialist, 317-940-8107, Fax: 317-940-8250, E-mail: ddubord@butler.edu. *Dean,* Dr. Stephen Standifird, 317-940-6307.

BYZANTINE CATHOLIC SEMINARY OF SAINTS CYRIL AND METHODIUS, Pittsburgh, PA 15214

General Information Independent-religious, coed, graduate-only institution.

GRADUATE UNITS

Graduate and Professional Programs Offers theology (M Div, MAT).

CABARRUS COLLEGE OF HEALTH SCIENCES, Concord, NC 28025

General Information Independent, coed, primarily women, comprehensive institution.

GRADUATE UNITS

Program in Occupational Therapy Offers occupational therapy (MOT).

CABRINI UNIVERSITY, Radnor, PA 19087

General Information Independent-religious, coed, comprehensive institution. *Graduate housing:* On-campus housing not available.

GRADUATE UNITS

Academic Affairs *Program availability:* Part-time, evening/weekend. Offers accounting (M Acc); autism spectrum disorder (M Ed); biological sciences (MS); criminology and criminal justice (MA); curriculum, instruction, and assessment (M Ed); educational leadership (M Ed, Ed D); English as a second language (M Ed); organizational leadership (DBA, PhD); preK to 4 (M Ed); reading specialist (M Ed); secondary education (M Ed); special education grades 7-12 (M Ed); special education preK-8 (M Ed); teaching and learning (M Ed). Electronic applications accepted.

CAIRN UNIVERSITY, Langhorne, PA 19047-2990

General Information Independent-religious, coed, comprehensive institution. *Graduate housing:* Rooms and/or apartments available on a first-come, first-served basis to single and married students.

GRADUATE UNITS

Department of Counseling *Program availability:* Part-time, evening/weekend. Offers counseling (MS). Electronic applications accepted.

School of Business *Program availability:* Part-time, evening/weekend, 100% online, blended/hybrid learning. Offers accounting (MBA); business administration (MBA); international entrepreneurship (MBA); nonprofit leadership (MBA); organizational leadership (MSOL, Postbaccalaureate Certificate). Electronic applications accepted.

School of Divinity *Program availability:* Part-time, evening/weekend, 100% online, blended/hybrid learning. Offers divinity (M Div); religion (MA); theology (Th M). Electronic applications accepted.

School of Education *Program availability:* Part-time, evening/weekend, 100% online, blended/hybrid learning. Offers applied behavior analysis (MS Sp Ed, Certificate); educational leadership and administration (MS El); instruction (MS Sp Ed); teacher education (MS Ed). Electronic applications accepted.

CALDWELL UNIVERSITY, Caldwell, NJ 07006-6195

General Information Independent-religious, coed, comprehensive institution. CGS member. *Enrollment:* 2,176 graduate, professional, and undergraduate students; 144 full-time matriculated graduate/professional students (121 women), 386 part-time matriculated graduate/professional students (305 women). *Enrollment by degree level:* 372 master's, 60 doctoral, 97 other advanced degrees. *Graduate faculty:* 28 full-time (19 women), 39 part-time/adjunct (20 women). *Tuition:* Full-time $11,940; part-time $995 per credit. *Required fees:* $460; $460 per unit. *Graduate housing:* Room and/or apartments available on a first-come, first-served basis to single students; on-campus housing not available to married students. Housing application deadline: 5/1. *Student services:* Campus employment opportunities, campus safety program, career counseling, free psychological counseling, international student services, services for students with disabilities, teacher training, writing training. *Library facilities:* Jennings Library plus 1 other. *Collection:* Books: 142,662 (physical), 166,014 (digital/electronic); Serial titles: 88 (physical), 66,812 (digital/electronic); Databases: 66. Students can reserve study rooms.

Computer facilities: 52 computers available on campus for general student use. A campuswide network can be accessed from student residence rooms. Online class registration is available. Website: http://www.caldwell.edu/

General Application Contact: Tom Disch, Senior Graduate Admissions Counselor, 973-618-3544, Fax: 973-618-3640, E-mail: graduate@caldwell.edu.

GRADUATE UNITS

Department of Applied Behavior Analysis Students: 8 full-time (7 women), 68 part-time (57 women); includes 21 minority (2 Black or African American, non-Hispanic/Latino; 3 Asian, non-Hispanic/Latino; 14 Hispanic/Latino; 2 Two or more races, non-Hispanic/Latino). Average age 28. 42 applicants, 98% accepted, 13 enrolled. *Faculty:* 6 full-time (4 women), 1 part-time/adjunct (0 women). Expenses: Contact institution. *Financial support:* In 2018–19, 4 fellowships (averaging $35,000 per year) were awarded; 10 clinical assistantships (averaging $23,000 annually) also available. Financial award applicants required to submit FAFSA. In 2018, 11 master's, 5 doctorates awarded. *Program availability:* Part-time. Offers applied behavior analysis (MA, PhD, Post-Master's Certificate). *Application deadline:* For fall admission, 6/1 for domestic students; for spring admission, 12/1 for domestic students; for summer admission, 4/1 for domestic students. *Application fee:* $50. Electronic applications accepted. *Application Contact:* Tom Disch, Senior Graduate Admissions Counselor, 973-618-3544, E-mail: graduate@caldwell.edu. *Department Chair,* Dr. Tina Sidener, 973-618-3539, E-mail: TSidener@caldwell.edu.

School of Business and Computer Science Students: 29 full-time (18 women), 55 part-time (35 women); includes 27 minority (7 Black or African American, non-Hispanic/Latino; 3 Asian, non-Hispanic/Latino; 15 Hispanic/Latino; 2 Two or more races, non-Hispanic/Latino), 9 international. Average age 30. 34 applicants, 85% accepted, 19 enrolled. *Faculty:* 7 full-time (4 women), 9 part-time/adjunct (2 women). Expenses: Contact institution. *Financial support:* Unspecified assistantships available. In 2018, 23 master's awarded. *Program availability:* Part-time. Offers business and computer information systems (MBA, MS). *Application deadline:* Applications are processed on a rolling basis. *Application fee:* $50. Electronic applications accepted. *Application Contact:* Tom Disch, Senior Admissions Counselor, 973-618-3544, E-mail: graduate@caldwell.edu. *Associate Dean,* Virginia Rich, 973-618-3516, Fax: 973-618-3355, E-mail: vrich@caldwell.edu.

School of Education Students: 35 full-time (29 women), 170 part-time (125 women); includes 45 minority (22 Black or African American, non-Hispanic/Latino; 1 American Indian or Alaska Native, non-Hispanic/Latino; 5 Asian, non-Hispanic/Latino; 14 Hispanic/Latino; 3 Two or more races, non-Hispanic/Latino). Average age 36. 75 applicants, 93% accepted, 42 enrolled. *Faculty:* 9 full-time (6 women), 18 part-time/adjunct (10 women). Expenses: Contact institution. *Financial support:* Unspecified assistantships available. Financial award applicants required to submit FAFSA. In 2018, 40 master's, 8 doctorates awarded. *Program availability:* Part-time, evening/weekend. Offers elementary, secondary or preschool endorsement, special ed, ESL

(Postbaccalaureate Certificate). *Application deadline:* For fall admission, 7/15 for domestic students. Applications are processed on a rolling basis. *Application fee:* $50. Electronic applications accepted. *Application Contact:* Tom Disch, Senior Admissions Counselor, 973-618-3544, E-mail: graduate@caldwell.edu. *Associate Dean,* Dr. Joan Moriarity, 973-618-3626, E-mail: jmoriarity@caldwell.edu.

School of Psychology and Counseling Students: 72 full-time (67 women), 92 part-time (87 women); includes 39 minority (12 Black or African American, non-Hispanic/Latino; 5 Asian, non-Hispanic/Latino; 18 Hispanic/Latino; 4 Two or more races, non-Hispanic/Latino), 1 international. Average age 28. 87 applicants, 92% accepted, 32 enrolled. *Faculty:* 6 full-time (5 women), 11 part-time/adjunct (8 women). Expenses: Contact institution. *Financial support:* Unspecified assistantships available. Financial award applicants required to submit FAFSA. In 2018, 34 master's awarded. *Program availability:* Part-time. Offers psychology and counseling (MA, Post-Master's Certificate). *Application deadline:* For fall admission, 6/1 for domestic students, 7/1 for international students; for spring admission, 12/1 for domestic and international students; for summer admission, 4/1 for domestic and international students. Applications are processed on a rolling basis. *Application fee:* $50. Electronic applications accepted. *Application Contact:* Tom Disch, Senior Graduate Admissions Counselor, 973-618-3544, E-mail: graduate@caldwell.edu. *Associate Dean,* Dr. Thomson Ling, 973-618-3596, E-mail: tling@caldwell.edu.

CALIFORNIA BAPTIST UNIVERSITY, Riverside, CA 92504-3206

General Information Independent-religious, coed, comprehensive institution. *Enrollment:* 1,501 full-time matriculated graduate/professional students (1,093 women), 1,130 part-time matriculated graduate/professional students (802 women). *Enrollment by degree level:* 2,522 master's, 109 doctoral. *Graduate faculty:* 199 full-time (103 women), 126 part-time/adjunct (72 women). *Tuition:* Full-time $14,130. *Required fees:* $710; $710. *Graduate housing:* Room and/or apartments available on a first-come, first-served basis to single students; on-campus housing not available to married students. Typical cost: $8780 per year ($14,220 including board). Housing application deadline: 8/1. *Student services:* Campus employment opportunities, campus safety program, career counseling, exercise/wellness program, free psychological counseling, international student services, low-cost health insurance, services for students with disabilities, teacher training, writing training. *Library facilities:* Annie Gabriel Library. *Collection:* Books: 130,837 (physical), 190,918 (digital/electronic); Serial titles: 59,915 (physical), 21,548 (digital/electronic); Databases: 83. Weekly public service hours: 101; students can reserve study rooms.

Computer facilities: Computer purchase and lease plans are available. 279 computers available on campus for general student use. A campuswide network can be accessed from student residence rooms and from off campus. Online class registration, online course evaluations are available.
Website: http://www.calbaptist.edu/

General Application Contact: Alma Salazar, Director of Graduate Admissions, 951-552-8086, Fax: 951-552-8700, E-mail: graduateadmissions@calbaptist.edu.

GRADUATE UNITS

Doctor of Nursing Practice Program Students: 8 part-time (5 women); includes 6 minority (5 Black or African American, non-Hispanic/Latino; 1 Two or more races, non-Hispanic/Latino). Average age 49. 1 applicant, 100% accepted, 2 enrolled. *Faculty:* 6 full-time (5 women). Expenses: Contact institution. *Financial support:* In 2018–19, 11 students received support. Federal Work-Study and scholarships/grants available. Financial award applicants required to submit CSS PROFILE or FAFSA. In 2018, 1 doctorate awarded. *Program availability:* Part-time. Offers nursing (DNP). *Application deadline:* For fall admission, 8/1 priority date for domestic students, 7/1 priority date for international students; for spring admission, 12/1 priority date for domestic students, 11/1 priority date for international students. Applications are processed on a rolling basis. *Application fee:* $45. Electronic applications accepted. *Application Contact:* Dr. Lisa Bursch, DNP Program Director, 951-343-4940, E-mail: lbursch@calbaptist.edu. *Dean, School of Nursing,* Dr. Karen Bradley, 951-552-8913, E-mail: kbradley@calbaptist.edu.

Program in Accounting Students: 12 full-time (5 women), 15 part-time (8 women); includes 11 minority (2 Black or African American, non-Hispanic/Latino; 2 Asian, non-Hispanic/Latino; 5 Hispanic/Latino; 1 Native Hawaiian or other Pacific Islander, non-Hispanic/Latino; 1 Two or more races, non-Hispanic/Latino). Average age 32. 25 applicants, 44% accepted, 10 enrolled. *Faculty:* 4 full-time (2 women), 1 part-time/adjunct (0 women). Expenses: Contact institution. *Financial support:* In 2018–19, 9 students received support. Federal Work-Study and scholarships/grants available. Financial award applicants required to submit CSS PROFILE or FAFSA. In 2018, 10 master's awarded. *Program availability:* Part-time, evening/weekend, online only, 100% online. Offers accounting (MS). *Application deadline:* For fall admission, 8/1 priority date for domestic students, 7/1 priority date for international students; for spring admission, 12/1 priority date for domestic students, 11/1 priority date for international students. Applications are processed on a rolling basis. *Application fee:* $45. Electronic applications accepted. *Application Contact:* Dr. Julianna Browning, Program Director, Accounting, 951-343-3972, E-mail: jbrowning@calbaptist.edu. *Vice President, Online and Professional Studies,* Pamela Daly, 951-343-3901, E-mail: pdaly@calbaptist.edu.

Program in Applied Mathematics Students: 3 full-time (2 women), 7 part-time (5 women); includes 5 minority (all Hispanic/Latino). Average age 28. 2 applicants, 100% accepted, 2 enrolled. *Faculty:* 6 full-time (2 women). Expenses: Contact institution. *Financial support:* In 2018–19, 3 students received support. Federal Work-Study, scholarships/grants, and unspecified assistantships available. Financial award applicants required to submit CSS PROFILE or FAFSA. In 2018, 9 master's awarded. *Program availability:* Part-time. Offers applied mathematics (MS). *Application deadline:* For fall admission, 8/1 priority date for domestic students, 7/1 priority date for international students; for spring admission, 12/1 priority date for domestic students, 11/1 priority date for international students. Applications are processed on a rolling basis. *Application fee:* $45. Electronic applications accepted. *Application Contact:* Dr. Linn Carothers, Department Chair, Mathematical Sciences, 951-343-4961, E-mail: lcarothers@calbaptist.edu. *Dean, College of Arts and Science,* Dr. Lisa Hernandez, 951-343-4767, E-mail: lihernandez@calbaptist.edu.

Program in Architecture Students: 10 full-time (3 women); includes 5 minority (4 Hispanic/Latino; 1 Native Hawaiian or other Pacific Islander, non-Hispanic/Latino). Average age 25. 12 applicants, 100% accepted, 10 enrolled. *Faculty:* 4 full-time. Expenses: Contact institution. *Financial support:* In 2018–19, 9 students received support. Federal Work-Study and scholarships/grants available. Financial award applicants required to submit CSS PROFILE or FAFSA. In 2018, 10 master's awarded. Offers architecture (M Arch). *Application deadline:* For fall admission, 8/1 priority date for domestic students, 7/1 for international students; for spring admission, 12/1 priority date for domestic students, 11/1 for international students. Applications are processed on a rolling basis. *Application fee:* $45. Electronic applications accepted. *Application Contact:* Keelan Kaiser, Program Director, Architecture, 951-552-8149, E-mail: kkaiser@

California Baptist University

calbaptist.edu. *Dean, College of Architecture, Visual Arts and Design*, Mark Roberson, 951-552-8652, E-mail: maroberson@calbaptist.edu.

Program in Athletic Training Students: 43 full-time (23 women); includes 31 minority (4 Black or African American, non-Hispanic/Latino; 6 Asian, non-Hispanic/Latino; 20 Hispanic/Latino; 1 Two or more races, non-Hispanic/Latino). Average age 27. 1 applicant, 0% accepted, 0 enrolled. *Faculty:* 5 full-time (3 women). Expenses: Contact institution. *Financial support:* In 2018–19, 1 student received support. Federal Work-Study, scholarships/grants, and unspecified assistantships available. Financial award applicants required to submit CSS PROFILE or FAFSA. In 2018, 18 master's awarded. *Program availability:* Part-time. Offers athletic training (MS). *Application deadline:* For fall admission, 8/1 priority date for domestic students, 7/1 for international students; for spring admission, 12/1 priority date for domestic students, 11/1 for international students. Applications are processed on a rolling basis. *Application fee:* $45. Electronic applications accepted. *Application Contact:* Dr. Nicole MacDonald, Director, Athletic Training Program, 951-343-4379, E-mail: nmacdona@calbaptist.edu. *Dean of the College of Health Science*, Dr. David Pearson, 951-343-4298, E-mail: dpearson@calbaptist.edu.

Program in Business Administration Students: 124 full-time (65 women), 71 part-time (38 women); includes 108 minority (16 Black or African American, non-Hispanic/Latino; 11 Asian, non-Hispanic/Latino; 74 Hispanic/Latino; 1 Native Hawaiian or other Pacific Islander, non-Hispanic/Latino; 6 Two or more races, non-Hispanic/Latino), 21 international. Average age 36. 71 applicants, 77% accepted, 55 enrolled. *Faculty:* 22 full-time (7 women), 14 part-time/adjunct (3 women). Expenses: Contact institution. *Financial support:* In 2018–19, 70 students received support. Federal Work-Study and scholarships/grants available. Financial award applicants required to submit CSS PROFILE or FAFSA. In 2018, 131 master's awarded. *Program availability:* Part-time, evening/weekend, 100% online, blended/hybrid learning. Offers accounting (MBA); construction management (MBA); healthcare management (MBA); management (MBA). *Application deadline:* For fall admission, 8/1 priority date for domestic students, 7/1 for international students; for spring admission, 12/1 priority date for domestic students, 11/1 for international students. Applications are processed on a rolling basis. *Application fee:* $45. Electronic applications accepted. *Application Contact:* Dr. Scott Dunbar, Program Director, Online Masters in Business Administration, 951-343-2193, E-mail: sdunbar@calbaptist.edu. *Dean, School of Business*, Dr. Andrea Scott, 951-343-4701, E-mail: ascott@calbaptist.edu.

Program in Civil Engineering Students: 7 full-time (1 woman), 1 part-time (0 women); includes 3 minority (all Hispanic/Latino), 3 international. Average age 28. 3 applicants, 100% accepted, 1 enrolled. *Faculty:* 7 full-time (1 woman), 1 part-time/adjunct (0 women). Expenses: Contact institution. *Financial support:* In 2018–19, 1 student received support. Federal Work-Study and scholarships/grants available. Financial award applicants required to submit CSS PROFILE or FAFSA. In 2018, 4 master's awarded. *Program availability:* Part-time. Offers civil engineering (MS). *Application deadline:* For fall admission, 8/1 priority date for domestic students, 7/1 for international students; for spring admission, 12/1 priority date for domestic students, 11/1 priority date for international students. Applications are processed on a rolling basis. *Application fee:* $45. Electronic applications accepted. *Application Contact:* Dr. Jong-Wha Bai, Department Chair, Civil Engineering and Construction Management, 951-343-4935, E-mail: jbai@calbaptist.edu. *Dean, College of Engineering*, Dr. Anthony Donaldson, 951-343-4841, E-mail: adonaldson@calbaptist.edu.

Program in Communication Students: 10 full-time (9 women), 4 part-time (3 women); includes 12 minority (4 Black or African American, non-Hispanic/Latino; 6 Hispanic/Latino; 2 Two or more races, non-Hispanic/Latino). Average age 32. 11 applicants, 55% accepted, 6 enrolled. *Faculty:* 1 (woman) full-time, 3 part-time/adjunct (all women). Expenses: Contact institution. *Financial support:* In 2018–19, 7 students received support. Federal Work-Study and scholarships/grants available. Financial award applicants required to submit CSS PROFILE or FAFSA. In 2018, 6 master's awarded. *Program availability:* Part-time, evening/weekend, online only, 100% online, blended/hybrid learning. Offers communication (MA). *Application deadline:* For fall admission, 8/1 priority date for domestic students, 7/1 for international students; for spring admission, 12/1 priority date for domestic students, 11/1 priority date for international students. Applications are processed on a rolling basis. *Application fee:* $45. Electronic applications accepted. *Application Contact:* Dr. Sandra Romo, Program Director, M.A. in Communication, 951-343-2173, E-mail: sromo@calbaptist.edu. *Vice President, Online and Professional Studies*, Pamela Daly, 951-343-3901, E-mail: pdaly@calbaptist.edu.

Program in Counseling Ministry Students: 8 full-time (6 women), 1 (woman) part-time; includes 6 minority (1 Black or African American, non-Hispanic/Latino; 5 Hispanic/Latino), 1 international. Average age 33. 2 applicants, 100% accepted, 1 enrolled. *Faculty:* 8 full-time (4 women), 4 part-time/adjunct (2 women). Expenses: Contact institution. *Financial support:* In 2018–19, 4 students received support. Federal Work-Study and scholarships/grants available. Financial award applicants required to submit CSS PROFILE or FAFSA. In 2018, 4 master's awarded. *Program availability:* Part-time. Offers professional ministry (MA); research in counseling ministry (MA). *Application deadline:* For fall admission, 8/1 priority date for domestic students, 7/1 for international students; for spring admission, 12/1 priority date for domestic students, 11/1 for international students. Applications are processed on a rolling basis. *Application fee:* $45. Electronic applications accepted. *Application Contact:* Dr. Nathan Lewis, Program Director, Counseling Ministry, 951-342-4348, E-mail: nlewis@calbaptist.edu. *Dean, College of Behavioral and Social Sciences*, Dr. Jacqueline Gustafson, 951-552-8372, E-mail: jgustafson@calbaptist.edu.

Program in Counseling Ministry and Counseling Psychology (Dual Master's) Students: 8 full-time (5 women), 2 part-time (both women); includes 8 minority (3 Black or African American, non-Hispanic/Latino; 5 Hispanic/Latino). Average age 37. 2 applicants, 100% accepted, 2 enrolled. *Faculty:* 18 full-time (10 women), 18 part-time/adjunct (13 women). Expenses: Contact institution. *Financial support:* In 2018–19, 6 students received support. Federal Work-Study and scholarships/grants available. Financial award applicants required to submit CSS PROFILE or FAFSA. *Program availability:* Part-time. *Application deadline:* For fall admission, 8/1 priority date for domestic students, 7/1 for international students; for spring admission, 12/1 priority date for domestic students, 11/1 for international students. Applications are processed on a rolling basis. *Application fee:* $45. Electronic applications accepted. *Application Contact:* Dr. Jay Burke, Program Director, Counseling Psychology, 951-552-8190, E-mail: jburke@calbaptist.edu. *Dean, School of Behavioral Sciences*, Dr. Jacqueline Gustafson, 951-552-8372, E-mail: jgustafson@calbaptist.edu.

Program in Counseling Psychology Students: 229 full-time (193 women), 80 part-time (65 women); includes 215 minority (55 Black or African American, non-Hispanic/Latino; 3 American Indian or Alaska Native, non-Hispanic/Latino; 11 Asian, non-Hispanic/Latino; 137 Hispanic/Latino; 1 Native Hawaiian or other Pacific Islander, non-Hispanic/Latino; 8 Two or more races, non-Hispanic/Latino), 1 international. Average age 39. 83 applicants, 77% accepted, 64 enrolled. *Faculty:* 20 full-time (11

women), 19 part-time/adjunct (13 women). Expenses: Contact institution. *Financial support:* In 2018–19, 89 students received support. Federal Work-Study and scholarships/grants available. Financial award applicants required to submit CSS PROFILE or FAFSA. In 2018, 145 master's awarded. *Program availability:* Part-time, evening/weekend, 100% online, blended/hybrid learning. Offers counseling psychology (MS); forensic psychology (MS); professional clinical counseling (MS). *Application deadline:* For fall admission, 8/1 priority date for domestic students, 7/1 for international students; for spring admission, 12/1 priority date for domestic students, 11/1 for international students. Applications are processed on a rolling basis. *Application fee:* $45. Electronic applications accepted. *Application Contact:* Dr. Thomas Frederick, Program Director, Online Counseling Psychology, 951-343-2191, E-mail: tfrederick@calbaptist.edu. *Dean, College of Behavioral and Social Sciences*, Dr. Jacqueline Gustafson, 951-552-8372, E-mail: jgustafson@calbaptist.edu.

Program in Education Students: 201 full-time (164 women), 265 part-time (209 women); includes 226 minority (23 Black or African American, non-Hispanic/Latino; 4 American Indian or Alaska Native, non-Hispanic/Latino; 7 Asian, non-Hispanic/Latino; 169 Hispanic/Latino; 6 Native Hawaiian or other Pacific Islander, non-Hispanic/Latino; 17 Two or more races, non-Hispanic/Latino), 2 international. Average age 39. 145 applicants, 97% accepted, 141 enrolled. *Faculty:* 26 full-time (13 women), 28 part-time/adjunct (21 women). Expenses: Contact institution. *Financial support:* In 2018–19, 312 students received support. Federal Work-Study and scholarships/grants available. Financial award applicants required to submit CSS PROFILE or FAFSA. In 2018, 253 master's awarded. *Program availability:* Part-time, evening/weekend, 100% online, blended/hybrid learning. Offers educational leadership (MS); educational leadership for faith-based institutions (MS); educational leadership for public institutions (MS); educational technology (MS); instructional computer applications (MS); international education (MS); leadership and adult learning (MS); leadership and organizational studies (MS); online teaching and learning (MS); reading (MS); science education (MA); special education in mild/moderate disabilities (MS); special education in moderate/severe disabilities (MS); teacher leadership (MS); teaching (MS); teaching and learning (MS). *Application deadline:* For fall admission, 8/1 priority date for domestic students, 7/1 for international students; for spring admission, 12/1 priority date for domestic students, 11/1 for international students. Applications are processed on a rolling basis. *Application fee:* $45. Electronic applications accepted. *Application Contact:* Dr. Shari Farris, Program Director, Online MS in Education, 951-343-2455, E-mail: sfarris@calbaptist.edu. *Dean, School of Education*, Dr. Robin Duncan, 951-552-8948, E-mail: rduncan@calbaptist.edu.

Program in English Students: 1 (woman) full-time, 19 part-time (12 women); includes 14 minority (8 Black or African American, non-Hispanic/Latino; 6 Hispanic/Latino). Average age 33. 2 applicants, 100% accepted, 2 enrolled. *Faculty:* 17 full-time (11 women). *Financial support:* In 2018–19, 9 students received support. Federal Work-Study and scholarships/grants available. Financial award applicants required to submit CSS PROFILE or FAFSA. In 2018, 6 master's awarded. *Program availability:* Part-time. Offers English pedagogy (MA); literature (MA); teaching English to speakers of other languages (TESOL) (MA). *Application deadline:* For fall admission, 8/1 priority date for domestic students, 7/1 for international students; for spring admission, 12/1 priority date for domestic students, 11/1 for international students. Applications are processed on a rolling basis. *Application fee:* $45. Electronic applications accepted. *Application Contact:* Dr. Laura Veltman, Director, MA in English, 951-343-4649, E-mail: lveltman@calbaptist.edu. *Dean, College of Arts and Sciences*, Dr. Lisa Hernandez, 951-343-4767, E-mail: lihernandez@calbaptist.edu.

Program in Forensic Psychology Students: 62 full-time (56 women), 7 part-time (6 women); includes 37 minority (8 Black or African American, non-Hispanic/Latino; 1 Asian, non-Hispanic/Latino; 23 Hispanic/Latino; 2 Native Hawaiian or other Pacific Islander, non-Hispanic/Latino; 3 Two or more races, non-Hispanic/Latino), 1 international. Average age 27. 9 applicants, 100% accepted, 9 enrolled. *Faculty:* 5 full-time (4 women), 2 part-time/adjunct (1 woman). Expenses: Contact institution. *Financial support:* In 2018–19, 17 students received support. Federal Work-Study and scholarships/grants available. Financial award applicants required to submit CSS PROFILE or FAFSA. In 2018, 20 master's awarded. *Program availability:* Part-time. Offers forensic psychology (MA). *Application deadline:* For fall admission, 8/1 priority date for domestic students, 7/1 for international students; for spring admission, 12/1 priority date for domestic students, 11/1 for international students. Applications are processed on a rolling basis. *Application fee:* $45. Electronic applications accepted. *Application Contact:* Dr. Erica Roth, Program Director, Forensic Psychology, 951-552-8146, E-mail: eroth@calbaptist.edu. *Dean, College of Behavioral and Social Sciences*, Dr. Jacqueline Gustafson, 951-552-8372, E-mail: jgustafson@calbaptist.edu.

Program in Higher Education Leadership and Student Development Students: 11 full-time (10 women), 5 part-time (all women); includes 8 minority (3 Black or African American, non-Hispanic/Latino; 5 Hispanic/Latino). Average age 31. 18 applicants, 100% accepted, 18 enrolled. *Faculty:* 8 full-time (3 women), 3 part-time/adjunct (1 woman). Expenses: Contact institution. *Financial support:* In 2018–19, 11 students received support. Federal Work-Study and scholarships/grants available. Financial award applicants required to submit CSS PROFILE or FAFSA. In 2018, 14 master's awarded. *Program availability:* Part-time. Offers higher education leadership and student development (MS). *Application deadline:* For fall admission, 8/1 priority date for domestic students, 7/1 for international students; for spring admission, 12/1 priority date for domestic students, 11/1 for international students. Applications are processed on a rolling basis. *Application fee:* $45. Electronic applications accepted. *Application Contact:* Dr. Robin Duncan, Dean, School of Education, 951-552-8948, E-mail: rduncan@calbaptist.edu. *Dean, School of Education*, Dr. Robin Duncan, 951-552-8948, E-mail: rduncan@calbaptist.edu.

Program in Kinesiology Students: 75 full-time (40 women), 77 part-time (37 women); includes 79 minority (10 Black or African American, non-Hispanic/Latino; 1 American Indian or Alaska Native, non-Hispanic/Latino; 6 Asian, non-Hispanic/Latino; 50 Hispanic/Latino; 2 Native Hawaiian or other Pacific Islander, non-Hispanic/Latino; 10 Two or more races, non-Hispanic/Latino), 13 international. Average age 35. 71 applicants, 79% accepted, 56 enrolled. *Faculty:* 13 full-time (3 women), 5 part-time/adjunct (1 woman). Expenses: Contact institution. *Financial support:* In 2018–19, 21 students received support. Federal Work-Study, scholarships/grants, and unspecified assistantships available. Financial award applicants required to submit CSS PROFILE or FAFSA. In 2018, 77 master's awarded. *Program availability:* Part-time, evening/weekend, 100% online, blended/hybrid learning. Offers exercise science (MS); physical education (MS); sport management (MS). *Application deadline:* For fall admission, 8/1 priority date for domestic students, 7/1 for international students; for spring admission, 12/1 priority date for domestic students, 11/1 for international students. Applications are processed on a rolling basis. *Application fee:* $45. Electronic applications accepted. *Application Contact:* Dr. Dominick Sturz, Assistant, Health and Human Services, 951-343-2192, E-mail: dsturz@calbaptist.edu. *Dean, College of Health Science*, Dr. David Pearson, 951-343-4298, E-mail: dpearson@calbaptist.edu.

Program in Leadership and Organizational Studies Students: 1 full-time (0 women), 16 part-time (10 women); includes 12 minority (3 Black or African American, non-Hispanic/Latino; 1 Asian, non-Hispanic/Latino; 7 Hispanic/Latino; 1 Two or more races, non-Hispanic/Latino), 1 international. Average age 37. 5 applicants, 100% accepted, 5 enrolled. *Faculty:* 3 full-time (0 women), 2 part-time/adjunct (0 women). Expenses: Contact institution. *Financial support:* In 2018–19, 10 students received support. Federal Work-Study and scholarships/grants available. Financial award applicants required to submit CSS PROFILE or FAFSA. In 2018, 12 master's awarded. *Program availability:* Part-time. Offers leadership and organizational studies (MA). *Application deadline:* For fall admission, 8/1 priority date for domestic students, 7/1 for international students; for spring admission, 11/1 priority date for domestic students, 11/1 for international students. Applications are processed on a rolling basis. *Application fee:* $45. Electronic applications accepted. *Application Contact:* Dr. John Shoup, Director, Leadership Institute, 951-343-4205, E-mail: jshoup@calbaptist.edu. *Dean, School of Education,* Dr. Robin Duncan, 951-552-8948, E-mail: rduncan@calbaptist.edu.

Program in Mechanical Engineering Students: 9 full-time (0 women), 4 part-time (1 woman); includes 3 minority (1 Black or African American, non-Hispanic/Latino; 2 Two or more races, non-Hispanic/Latino), 10 international. Average age 25. 1 applicant, 100% accepted, 1 enrolled. *Faculty:* 10 full-time (3 women). Expenses: Contact institution. *Financial support:* In 2018–19, 4 students received support. Federal Work-Study and scholarships/grants available. Financial award applicants required to submit CSS PROFILE or FAFSA. In 2018, 6 master's awarded. *Program availability:* Part-time. Offers mechanical engineering (MS). *Application deadline:* For fall admission, 8/1 priority date for domestic students, 7/1 priority date for international students; for spring admission, 12/1 priority date for domestic students, 11/1 priority date for international students. Applications are processed on a rolling basis. *Application fee:* $45. Electronic applications accepted. *Application Contact:* Dr. Xiuhua "April" Si, Department Chair, Aerospace, Industrial, and Mechanical Engineering, 951-552-8479, E-mail: asi@calbaptist.edu. *Dean, College of Engineering,* Dr. Anthony Donaldson, 951-343-4841, E-mail: adonaldson@calbaptist.edu.

Program in Music Students: 18 full-time (6 women), 3 part-time (1 woman); includes 9 minority (5 Black or African American, non-Hispanic/Latino; 4 Hispanic/Latino), 8 international. Average age 31. 2 applicants, 100% accepted, 2 enrolled. *Faculty:* 16 full-time (3 women), 11 part-time/adjunct (5 women). Expenses: Contact institution. *Financial support:* In 2018–19, 9 students received support. Federal Work-Study and scholarships/grants available. Financial award applicants required to submit CSS PROFILE or FAFSA. In 2018, 5 master's awarded. *Program availability:* Part-time. Offers conducting (MM); music education (MM); performance (MM). *Application deadline:* For fall admission, 8/1 priority date for domestic students, 7/1 for international students; for spring admission, 12/1 priority date for domestic students, 11/1 for international students. Applications are processed on a rolling basis. *Application fee:* $45. Electronic applications accepted. *Application Contact:* Dr. Lance Beaumont, Associate Dean for Graduate Studies and Program Development, 951-552-8162, E-mail: lbeaumont@calbaptist.edu. *Dean, School of Music,* Dr. Joseph Bolin, 951-343-4714, Fax: 951-343-4570, E-mail: jbolin@calbaptist.edu.

Program in Nursing Students: 72 full-time (58 women), 146 part-time (121 women); includes 134 minority (24 Black or African American, non-Hispanic/Latino; 2 American Indian or Alaska Native, non-Hispanic/Latino; 41 Asian, non-Hispanic/Latino; 58 Hispanic/Latino; 2 Native Hawaiian or other Pacific Islander, non-Hispanic/Latino; 7 Two or more races, non-Hispanic/Latino), 15 international. Average age 39. 27 applicants, 59% accepted, 15 enrolled. *Faculty:* 15 full-time (14 women), 13 part-time/adjunct (11 women). Expenses: Contact institution. *Financial support:* In 2018–19, 40 students received support. Federal Work-Study and scholarships/grants available. Financial award applicants required to submit CSS PROFILE or FAFSA. In 2018, 75 master's awarded. *Program availability:* Part-time. Offers clinical nurse specialist (MSN); family nurse practitioner (MSN); healthcare systems management (MSN); teaching-learning (MSN). *Application deadline:* For fall admission, 8/1 priority date for domestic students, 7/1 for international students; for spring admission, 12/1 priority date for domestic students, 11/1 for international students. Applications are processed on a rolling basis. *Application fee:* $45. Electronic applications accepted. *Application Contact:* Dr. Karen Bradley, Dean, College of Nursing, 951-552-8913, E-mail: kbradley@calbaptist.edu. *Dean, College of Nursing,* Dr. Karen Bradley, 951-552-8913, E-mail: kbradley@calbaptist.edu.

Program in Organizational Leadership Students: 52 full-time (33 women), 31 part-time (21 women); includes 45 minority (8 Black or African American, non-Hispanic/Latino; 4 Asian, non-Hispanic/Latino; 28 Hispanic/Latino; 1 Native Hawaiian or other Pacific Islander, non-Hispanic/Latino; 4 Two or more races, non-Hispanic/Latino). Average age 38. 62 applicants, 73% accepted, 38 enrolled. *Faculty:* 3 full-time (1 woman), 3 part-time/adjunct (2 women). Expenses: Contact institution. *Financial support:* In 2018–19, 37 students received support. Federal Work-Study and scholarships/grants available. Financial award applicants required to submit CSS PROFILE or FAFSA. In 2018, 54 master's awarded. *Program availability:* Part-time, evening/weekend, 100% online, blended/hybrid learning. Offers organizational leadership (MA). *Application deadline:* For fall admission, 8/1 priority date for domestic students, 7/1 for international students; for spring admission, 12/1 priority date for domestic students, 11/1 for international students. Applications are processed on a rolling basis. *Application fee:* $45. Electronic applications accepted. *Application Contact:* Dr. Jeannette Guignard, Program, MA in Organizational Leadership, 951-343-2458, E-mail: jguignard@calbaptist.edu. *Vice President, Online and Professional Studies,* Pamela Daly, 951-343-3901, E-mail: pdaly@calbaptist.edu.

Program in Physician Assistant Studies Students: 61 full-time (45 women); includes 28 minority (3 Black or African American, non-Hispanic/Latino; 12 Asian, non-Hispanic/Latino; 11 Hispanic/Latino; 2 Two or more races, non-Hispanic/Latino). Average age 29. 43 applicants, 65% accepted, 28 enrolled. *Faculty:* 9 full-time (3 women). Expenses: Contact institution. *Financial support:* In 2018–19, 4 students received support. Federal Work-Study and scholarships/grants available. Financial award applicants required to submit CSS PROFILE or FAFSA. In 2018, 30 master's awarded. *Program availability:* Part-time. Offers physician assistant studies (MS). *Application deadline:* For fall admission, 12/1 priority date for domestic students, 11/1 priority date for international students; for spring admission, 8/1 priority date for domestic students, 7/1 priority date for international students. Applications are processed on a rolling basis. *Application fee:* $45. Electronic applications accepted. *Application Contact:* Dr. Allan Bedashi, Department Chair, Physician Assistant Studies, 951-552-8838, E-mail: abedashi@calbaptist.edu. *Dean, College of Health Science,* Dr. David Pearson, 951-343-4298, E-mail: dpearson@calbaptist.edu.

Program in Public Administration Students: 40 full-time (27 women), 22 part-time (11 women); includes 40 minority (5 Black or African American, non-Hispanic/Latino; 1 American Indian or Alaska Native, non-Hispanic/Latino; 3 Asian, non-Hispanic/Latino; 30 Hispanic/Latino; 1 Two or more races, non-Hispanic/Latino). Average age 37. 38 applicants, 53% accepted, 19 enrolled. *Faculty:* 5 full-time (all women), 1 part-time/adjunct (0 women). Expenses: Contact institution. *Financial support:* In 2018–19, 40 students received support. Federal Work-Study and scholarships/grants available. Financial award applicants required to submit CSS PROFILE or FAFSA. In 2018, 32 master's awarded. *Program availability:* Part-time, evening/weekend, online only, 100% online, blended/hybrid learning. Offers public administration (MPA). *Application deadline:* For fall admission, 8/1 priority date for domestic students, 7/1 for international students; for spring admission, 12/1 priority date for domestic students, 11/1 for international students. Applications are processed on a rolling basis. *Application fee:* $45. Electronic applications accepted. *Application Contact:* Dr. Linda-Marie Sundstrom, Program Director, Masters in Public Administration, 951-343-2172, E-mail: lsundstrom@calbaptist.edu. *Vice President, Online and Professional Studies,* Pamela Daly, 951-343-3901, E-mail: pdaly@calbaptist.edu.

Program in Public Health Students: 44 full-time (37 women), 34 part-time (28 women); includes 61 minority (12 Black or African American, non-Hispanic/Latino; 9 Asian, non-Hispanic/Latino; 35 Hispanic/Latino; 5 Two or more races, non-Hispanic/Latino), 4 international. Average age 33. 33 applicants, 61% accepted, 20 enrolled. *Faculty:* 10 full-time (7 women), 3 part-time/adjunct (1 woman). Expenses: Contact institution. *Financial support:* In 2018–19, 23 students received support. Federal Work-Study and scholarships/grants available. Financial award applicants required to submit CSS PROFILE or FAFSA. In 2018, 22 master's awarded. *Program availability:* Part-time, evening/weekend, 100% online, blended/hybrid learning. Offers health education and promotion (MPH); health policy and administration (MPH). *Application deadline:* For fall admission, 8/1 priority date for domestic students, 7/1 for international students; for spring admission, 12/1 priority date for domestic students, 11/1 for international students. Applications are processed on a rolling basis. *Application fee:* $45. Electronic applications accepted. *Application Contact:* Dr. Bochi McKinney, Program Director, Online MPH, 951-343-2177, E-mail: omckinney@calbaptist.edu. *Dean, College of Health Science,* Dr. David Pearson, 951-343-4298, E-mail: dpearson@calbaptist.edu.

Program in Public Relations Students: 11 full-time (7 women), 9 part-time (all women); includes 12 minority (2 Black or African American, non-Hispanic/Latino; 1 Asian, non-Hispanic/Latino; 9 Hispanic/Latino). Average age 34. 17 applicants, 47% accepted, 8 enrolled. *Faculty:* 1 (woman) full-time, 2 part-time/adjunct (both women). Expenses: Contact institution. *Financial support:* In 2018–19, 5 students received support. Federal Work-Study and scholarships/grants available. Financial award applicants required to submit CSS PROFILE or FAFSA. In 2018, 15 master's awarded. *Program availability:* Part-time, evening/weekend, online only, 100% online, blended/hybrid learning. Offers public relations (MA). *Application deadline:* For fall admission, 8/1 priority date for domestic students, 7/1 for international students; for spring admission, 12/1 priority date for domestic students, 11/1 priority date for international students. Applications are processed on a rolling basis. *Application fee:* $45. Electronic applications accepted. *Application Contact:* Dr. Cammy Purper, Assistant Dean, Arts and Sciences, 951-343-3935, E-mail: cpurper@calbaptist.edu. *Vice President, Online and Professional Studies,* Pamela Daly, 951-343-3901, E-mail: pdaly@calbaptist.edu.

Program in School Counseling Students: 2 full-time (1 woman), 59 part-time (46 women); includes 35 minority (1 Black or African American, non-Hispanic/Latino; 1 Asian, non-Hispanic/Latino; 30 Hispanic/Latino; 3 Two or more races, non-Hispanic/Latino). Average age 34. 23 applicants, 87% accepted, 20 enrolled. *Faculty:* 2 full-time (both women), 10 part-time/adjunct (5 women). Expenses: Contact institution. *Financial support:* In 2018–19, 30 students received support. Federal Work-Study and scholarships/grants available. Financial award applicants required to submit CSS PROFILE or FAFSA. In 2018, 18 master's awarded. *Program availability:* Part-time. Offers school counseling (MS). *Application deadline:* For fall admission, 8/1 priority date for domestic students, 7/7 priority date for international students; for spring admission, 12/1 priority date for domestic students, 11/1 priority date for international students. Applications are processed on a rolling basis. *Application fee:* $45. Electronic applications accepted. *Application Contact:* Daniel Robinson, Program Director, School Counseling, 951-552-8351, E-mail: darobinson@calbaptist.edu. *Dean, School of Education,* Dr. Robin Duncan, 951-552-8048, E-mail: rduncan@calbaptist.edu.

Program in School Psychology Students: 30 full-time (28 women), 53 part-time (48 women); includes 49 minority (4 Black or African American, non-Hispanic/Latino; 4 Asian, non-Hispanic/Latino; 39 Hispanic/Latino; 2 Two or more races, non-Hispanic/Latino). Average age 32. 21 applicants, 67% accepted, 7 enrolled. *Faculty:* 2 full-time (both women), 8 part-time/adjunct (4 women). Expenses: Contact institution. *Financial support:* In 2018–19, 36 students received support. Federal Work-Study and scholarships/grants available. Financial award applicants required to submit CSS PROFILE or FAFSA. In 2018, 24 master's awarded. *Program availability:* Part-time. Offers school psychology (MS). *Application deadline:* For fall admission, 7/1 priority date for domestic and international students; for spring admission, 12/1 priority date for domestic students, 11/1 priority date for international students. Applications are processed on a rolling basis. *Application fee:* $45. Electronic applications accepted. *Application Contact:* Dr. Karen Cross, Program Coordinator, School Psychology, 951-552-8356, E-mail: kcross@calbaptist.edu. *Dean, School of Education,* Dr. Robin Duncan, 951-552-8948, E-mail: rduncan@calbaptist.edu.

Program in Social Work Students: 158 full-time (141 women); includes 126 minority (28 Black or African American, non-Hispanic/Latino; 1 Asian, non-Hispanic/Latino; 87 Hispanic/Latino; 10 Two or more races, non-Hispanic/Latino), 1 international. Average age 37. 92 applicants, 100% accepted, 92 enrolled. *Faculty:* 11 full-time (9 women), 7 part-time/adjunct (6 women). Expenses: Contact institution. *Financial support:* In 2018–19, 64 students received support. Federal Work-Study and scholarships/grants available. In 2018, 76 master's awarded. *Program availability:* Part-time. Offers clinical social work (MSW); community social work practice (MSW). *Application deadline:* For fall admission, 8/1 priority date for domestic students, 7/1 for international students; for spring admission, 12/1 priority date for domestic students, 11/1 for international students. Applications are processed on a rolling basis. *Application fee:* $45. Electronic applications accepted. *Application Contact:* Dr. Charles Lee-Johnson, Program Director, Social Work, 951-552-8081, E-mail: cleejohnson@calbaptist.edu. *Dean, College of Behavioral and Social Sciences,* Dr. Jacqueline Gustafson, 951-552-8372, E-mail: jgustafson@calbaptist.edu.

Program in Software Engineering Students: 13 full-time (6 women), 5 part-time (2 women); includes 2 minority (1 Asian, non-Hispanic/Latino; 1 Two or more races, non-Hispanic/Latino), 14 international. Average age 27. 2 applicants, 100% accepted, 2 enrolled. *Faculty:* 4 full-time (1 woman), 2 part-time/adjunct (0 women). Expenses: Contact institution. *Financial support:* In 2018–19, 1 student received support. Federal Work-Study and scholarships/grants available. Financial award applicants required to submit CSS PROFILE or FAFSA. In 2018, 11 master's awarded. *Program availability:* Part-time. Offers software engineering (MS). *Application deadline:* For fall admission, 8/1 priority date for domestic students, 7/1 priority date for international students; for spring admission, 12/1 priority date for domestic students, 11/1 priority date for international students. Applications are processed on a rolling basis. *Application fee:* $45. Electronic applications accepted. *Application Contact:* Larry Clement, Interim Department Chair,

Computing, Software, and Data Sciences, 951-343-4471, E-mail: lclement@calbaptist.edu. *Dean, College of Engineering*, Dr. Anthony Donaldson, 951-343-4841, E-mail: adonaldson@calbaptist.edu.

Program in Speech Language Pathology Students: 48 full-time (46 women); includes 16 minority (4 Asian, non-Hispanic/Latino; 11 Hispanic/Latino; 1 Two or more races, non-Hispanic/Latino). Average age 30. 23 applicants, 100% accepted, 23 enrolled. *Faculty:* 6 full-time (5 women), 1 part-time/adjunct (0 women). Expenses: Contact institution. *Financial support:* In 2018–19, 3 students received support. Federal Work-Study and scholarships/grants available. Financial award applicants required to submit CSS PROFILE or FAFSA. In 2018, 24 master's awarded. *Program availability:* Part-time. Offers speech language pathology (MS). *Application deadline:* For fall admission, 12/1 priority date for domestic students, 11/1 priority date for international students; for spring admission, 8/1 priority date for domestic students, 7/1 priority date for international students. Applications are processed on a rolling basis. *Application fee:* $45. Electronic applications accepted. *Application Contact:* Dr. Candace Vickers, Program Director, Speech Language Pathology, 951-552-8129, E-mail: cvickers@calbaptist.edu. *Dean, College of Health Science*, Dr. David Pearson, 951-343-4298, E-mail: dpearson@calbaptist.edu.

CALIFORNIA COAST UNIVERSITY, Santa Ana, CA 92701
General Information Proprietary, coed, comprehensive institution.

GRADUATE UNITS
School of Administration and Management *Program availability:* Online learning. Offers business marketing (MBA); health care management (MBA); human resource management (MBA); management (MBA, MS). Electronic applications accepted.

School of Behavioral Science *Program availability:* Online learning. Offers psychology (MS).

School of Criminal Justice Offers criminal justice (MS).

School of Education *Program availability:* Online learning. Offers administration (M Ed); curriculum and instruction (M Ed); educational administration (Ed D); educational psychology (Ed D); organizational leadership (Ed D).

CALIFORNIA COLLEGE OF THE ARTS, San Francisco, CA 94107
General Information Independent, coed, comprehensive institution. *Enrollment:* 380 full-time matriculated graduate/professional students (244 women), 33 part-time matriculated graduate/professional students (20 women). *Enrollment by degree level:* 413 master's. *Graduate faculty:* 51 full-time (26 women), 106 part-time/adjunct (46 women). *Tuition:* Full-time $51,210; part-time $1707 per unit. *Required fees:* $490; $490. Tuition and fees vary according to program. *Graduate housing:* Room and/or apartments available on a first-come, first-served basis to single students; on-campus housing not available to married students. Typical cost: $8416 per year. Room charges vary according to housing facility selected. Housing application deadline: 5/15. *Student services:* Campus employment opportunities, campus safety program, career counseling, exercise/wellness program, free psychological counseling, grant writing training, international student services, low-cost health insurance, multicultural affairs office, services for students with disabilities, writing training. *Library facilities:* Meyer Library plus 1 other.

Computer facilities: Computer purchase and lease plans are available. 400 computers available on campus for general student use. A campuswide network can be accessed from student residence rooms and from off campus. Online class registration, online course evaluations, learning management system, media applications, software training, print payments are available. Website: http://www.cca.edu/

General Application Contact: David Murray, Director of Graduate Admissions, 415-703-9533, Fax: 415-703-9539, E-mail: graduateprograms@cca.edu.

GRADUATE UNITS
Graduate Programs Students: 380 full-time (244 women), 33 part-time (20 women); includes 103 minority (13 Black or African American, non-Hispanic/Latino; 40 Asian, non-Hispanic/Latino; 49 Hispanic/Latino; 1 Native Hawaiian or other Pacific Islander, non-Hispanic/Latino; 177 international. Average age 28. 1,138 applicants, 56% accepted, 194 enrolled. *Faculty:* 51 full-time (26 women), 106 part-time/adjunct (46 women). Expenses: Contact institution. *Financial support:* Teaching assistantships, Federal Work-Study, scholarships/grants, and unspecified assistantships available. Financial award applicants required to submit FAFSA. In 2018, 184 master's awarded. *Program availability:* Part-time. Offers advanced architecture design (MAAD); architecture (M Arch); comics (MFA); creative non-fiction (MFA); curatorial practice (MA); design strategy (MBA); fiction (MFA); film (MFA); fine arts (MFA); graphic design (MFA); industrial design (MFA); interaction design (MFA); poetry (MFA); visual and critical studies (MA). *Application deadline:* For fall admission, 1/31 priority date for domestic and international students. Applications are processed on a rolling basis. *Application fee:* $70. Electronic applications accepted. *Application Contact:* Emmitt Smith, Senior Counselor for Graduate Admissions, 415-703-9525, Fax: 415-703-9539, E-mail: emmittsmith@cca.edu. *Director of Graduate Admissions*, David Murray, 415-703-9533, Fax: 415-703-9539, E-mail: dmurray@cca.edu.

CALIFORNIA HEALTH SCIENCES UNIVERSITY, Clovis, CA 93612
General Information Proprietary, coed, graduate-only institution.

GRADUATE UNITS
College of Pharmacy Offers pharmacy (Pharm D).

CALIFORNIA INSTITUTE OF ADVANCED MANAGEMENT, El Monte, CA 91731
General Information Private, coed, graduate-only institution.

GRADUATE UNITS
The MBA Program Offers executive management and entrepreneurship (MBA).

CALIFORNIA INSTITUTE OF INTEGRAL STUDIES, San Francisco, CA 94103
General Information Independent, coed, upper-level institution. CGS member. *Enrollment:* 1,073 full-time matriculated graduate/professional students (793 women), 343 part-time matriculated graduate/professional students (252 women). *Enrollment by degree level:* 729 master's, 687 doctoral. *Graduate housing:* On-campus housing not available. *Student services:* Campus employment opportunities, campus safety program, career counseling, grant writing training, international student services, low-cost health insurance, multicultural affairs office, services for students with disabilities, writing training. *Library facilities:* The Laurance S. Rockefeller Library plus 1 other.

Computer facilities: 25 computers available on campus for general student use. A campuswide network can be accessed from off campus. Online class registration is available. Website: http://www.ciis.edu/

General Application Contact: Ellen Durst, Director of Admissions, 415-575-6153, Fax: 415-575-1264, E-mail: admissions@ciis.edu.

GRADUATE UNITS
American College of Traditional Chinese Medicine Students: 149 full-time (114 women), 53 part-time (39 women); includes 81 minority (3 Black or African American, non-Hispanic/Latino; 3 American Indian or Alaska Native, non-Hispanic/Latino; 45 Asian, non-Hispanic/Latino; 15 Hispanic/Latino; 5 Native Hawaiian or other Pacific Islander, non-Hispanic/Latino; 10 Two or more races, non-Hispanic/Latino), 9 international. Average age 37. 67 applicants, 93% accepted, 47 enrolled. Expenses: Contact institution. In 2018, 22 master's, 47 doctorates awarded. Offers acupuncture and Chinese medicine (DACM, tDACM); acupuncture and Oriental medicine (DAOM); traditional Chinese medicine (MSTCM). *Application deadline:* For fall admission, 8/1 priority date for domestic students; for spring admission, 12/1 priority date for domestic students; for summer admission, 4/1 priority date for domestic students. *Application fee:* $65. Electronic applications accepted. *Application Contact:* Yuwen Chiu, Associate Director of Admissions, 415-828-7600, E-mail: yuwenchiu@actcm.edu. *Academic Dean,* Dr. Carla Wilson, 415-828-7600, E-mail: cwilson@ciis.edu.

School of Consciousness and Transformation Average age 43. 212 applicants, 96% accepted, 153 enrolled. Expenses: Contact institution. *Financial support:* Fellowships, research assistantships, teaching assistantships, career-related internships or fieldwork, Federal Work-Study, and scholarships/grants available. Support available to part-time students. Financial award application deadline: 4/15; financial award applicants required to submit FAFSA. In 2018, 49 master's, 36 doctorates awarded. *Program availability:* Part-time, evening/weekend, 100% online, blended/hybrid learning. Offers anthropology and social change (PhD); transformative studies (PhD). *Application deadline:* For fall admission, 2/1 priority date for domestic and international students; for spring admission, 10/15 priority date for domestic and international students. Applications are processed on a rolling basis. *Application fee:* $65. Electronic applications accepted. *Application Contact:* Ellen Durst, Director of Admissions, 415-575-6100, Fax: 415-575-1268, E-mail: admissions@ciis.edu. *Academic Dean,* Kathy Littles, 415-575-6100, E-mail: klittles@ciis.edu.

School of Professional Psychology and Health Students: 537 full-time (419 women), 109 part-time (86 women); includes 189 minority (35 Black or African American, non-Hispanic/Latino; 1 American Indian or Alaska Native, non-Hispanic/Latino; 35 Asian, non-Hispanic/Latino; 72 Hispanic/Latino; 4 Native Hawaiian or other Pacific Islander, non-Hispanic/Latino; 42 Two or more races, non-Hispanic/Latino), 50 international. Average age 34. 358 applicants, 87% accepted, 199 enrolled. Expenses: Contact institution. *Financial support:* Research assistantships with tuition reimbursements, teaching assistantships with tuition reimbursements, career-related internships or fieldwork, Federal Work-Study, scholarships/grants, and institutional work-study available. Support available to part-time students. Financial award application deadline: 4/15; financial award applicants required to submit FAFSA. In 2018, 158 master's, 12 doctorates awarded. *Program availability:* Part-time, evening/weekend, 100% online, blended/hybrid learning. Offers clinical psychology (Psy D); drama therapy (MA); psychological studies (MA). *Application deadline:* For fall admission, 2/1 priority date for domestic and international students; for spring admission, 10/15 priority date for domestic and international students. Applications are processed on a rolling basis. *Application fee:* $65. Electronic applications accepted. *Application Contact:* Ellen Durst, Director of Admissions, 415-575-6100, Fax: 415-575-1268, E-mail: admissions@ciis.edu. *Provost,* Liz Beaven, 415-575-5577, E-mail: ebeaven@ciis.edu.

CALIFORNIA INSTITUTE OF TECHNOLOGY, Pasadena, CA 91125-0001
General Information Independent, coed, university. CGS member. *Graduate housing:* Rooms and/or apartments available on a first-come, first-served basis to single students and available to married students. Housing application deadline: 5/1. *Research affiliation:* Scripps Institute of Oceanography, Stanford Linear Accelerator Center (high-energy physics), European Center for Nuclear Research (high-energy physics), National Science Foundation Center for Research in Parallel Computing, Cosmic Gravitational Waves Observatory (laser interferometer gravitational waves).

GRADUATE UNITS
Division of Biology and Biological Engineering Offers biochemistry and molecular biophysics (PhD); cell biology and biophysics (PhD); developmental biology (PhD); genetics (PhD); immunology (PhD); molecular biology (PhD); neurobiology (PhD). Electronic applications accepted.

Division of Chemistry and Chemical Engineering Offers biochemistry and molecular biophysics (MS, PhD); chemical engineering (MS, PhD); chemistry (MS, PhD). Electronic applications accepted.

Division of Engineering and Applied Science Offers aeronautics (MS, PhD, Engr); applied and computational mathematics (MS, PhD); applied mechanics (MS, PhD); applied physics (MS, PhD); bioengineering (MS, PhD); civil engineering (MS, PhD, Engr); computation and neural systems (MS, PhD); computer science (MS, PhD); control and dynamical systems (MS, PhD); electrical engineering (MS, PhD, Engr); environmental science and engineering (MS, PhD); materials science (MS, PhD); mechanical engineering (MS, PhD, Engr). Electronic applications accepted.

Division of Geological and Planetary Sciences Offers environmental science and engineering (MS, PhD); geobiology (MS, PhD); geochemistry (MS, PhD); geology (MS, PhD); geophysics (MS, PhD); planetary science (MS, PhD). Electronic applications accepted.

Division of Physics, Mathematics and Astronomy Offers astronomy (PhD); mathematics (PhD); physics (PhD).

Division of the Humanities and Social Sciences Offers humanities and social sciences (MS, PhD); social science (MS, PhD). Electronic applications accepted.

CALIFORNIA INSTITUTE OF THE ARTS, Valencia, CA 91355-2340
General Information Independent, coed, comprehensive institution. *Graduate housing:* Room and/or apartments available on a first-come, first-served basis to single students; on-campus housing not available to married students. Housing application deadline: 7/1.

GRADUATE UNITS
The Herb Alpert School of Music *Program availability:* Part-time. Offers African music (MFA, Adv C); composition (MFA, Adv C); composition/new media (MFA, Adv C); Indonesian music (MFA, Adv C); jazz (MFA, Adv C); North Indian music (MFA, Adv C); performance (MFA, Adv C); performer/composer (MFA, Adv C); voice (MFA, Adv C); world music performance (MFA). Electronic applications accepted.

School of Art Offers art (MFA, Adv C); graphic design (MFA, Adv C); photography (MFA, Adv C). Electronic applications accepted.

School of Critical Studies Offers writing (MFA, Adv C).

School of Film/Video Offers experimental animation (MFA); film directing (MFA, Adv C); film/video (Adv C). Electronic applications accepted.

School of Theater Offers acting (MFA, Adv C); creative producing and management (MFA); design and production (MFA); design and technology (Adv C); directing (MFA); theater management (Adv C). Electronic applications accepted.

The Sharon Disney Lund School of Dance Offers dance (MFA, Adv C).

CALIFORNIA INTERCONTINENTAL UNIVERSITY, Irvine, CA 92614

General Information Proprietary, coed, comprehensive institution.

GRADUATE UNITS

Hollywood College of the Entertainment Industry Offers Hollywood and entertainment management (MBA).

School of Business Offers banking and finance (MBA); entrepreneurship and business management (DBA); global business leadership (DBA); international management and marketing (MBA); organizational management and human resource management (MBA).

School of Healthcare Offers healthcare management and leadership (MBA, DBA).

School of Information Technology Offers information systems and enterprise resource management (DBA); information systems and knowledge management (MBA); project and quality management (MBA).

CALIFORNIA INTERNATIONAL BUSINESS UNIVERSITY, San Diego, CA 92101

General Information Independent, coed, graduate-only institution.

GRADUATE UNITS

Graduate Programs Offers business (MBA, MSIM, DBA).

CALIFORNIA LUTHERAN UNIVERSITY, Thousand Oaks, CA 91360-2787

General Information Independent-religious, coed, comprehensive institution. CGS member. *Graduate housing:* Room and/or apartments available on a first-come, first-served basis to single students; on-campus housing not available to married students.

GRADUATE UNITS

Graduate Studies *Program availability:* Part-time, evening/weekend. Offers clinical psychology (MS, Psy D); marital and family therapy (MS). Electronic applications accepted.

Graduate School of Education *Program availability:* Part-time, evening/weekend. Offers counseling and guidance (MS); educational leadership (MA, Ed D); special education (MS); teacher leadership (M Ed); teaching (M Ed). Electronic applications accepted.

Pacific Lutheran Theological Seminary *Program availability:* Part-time. Offers theology (M Div, MA, MCM, MTS, PhD, Th D, Certificate). MA, Th D, PhD offered jointly with Graduate Theological Union; PhD with University of California, Berkeley. Electronic applications accepted.

School of Management *Program availability:* Part-time, evening/weekend, 100% online, blended/hybrid learning. Offers business (IMBA); entrepreneurship (MBA, Certificate); finance (MBA, MS, Certificate); financial planning (MBA, MS, Certificate); human capital management (MBA, Certificate); information technology (MS); information technology management (MBA, Certificate); international business (MBA, Certificate); management (MS); marketing (MBA, Certificate); public policy and administration (MPPA); quantitative economics (MS). Electronic applications accepted.

CALIFORNIA MIRAMAR UNIVERSITY, San Diego, CA 92108

General Information Proprietary, coed, comprehensive institution.

GRADUATE UNITS

Program in Business Administration Offers business administration (MBA).

Program in Strategic Leadership Offers strategic leadership (MS).

Program in Taxation and Trade for Executives Offers taxation and trade for executives (MT).

Program in Telecommunications Management Offers telecommunications management (MST).

CALIFORNIA NORTHSTATE UNIVERSITY, Elk Grove, CA 95757

General Information Proprietary, coed, comprehensive institution.

GRADUATE UNITS

College of Medicine Offers medicine (MD).

College of Pharmacy Offers pharmacy (Pharm D).

CALIFORNIA POLYTECHNIC STATE UNIVERSITY, SAN LUIS OBISPO, San Luis Obispo, CA 93407

General Information State-supported, coed, comprehensive institution. CGS member. *Enrollment:* 21,812 graduate, professional, and undergraduate students; 538 full-time matriculated graduate/professional students (246 women), 189 part-time matriculated graduate/professional students (79 women). *Enrollment by degree level:* 727 master's. *Graduate faculty:* 171 full-time (51 women), 20 part-time/adjunct (9 women). *Tuition, area resident:* Full-time $7176; part-time $4164 per year. Tuition, state resident: full-time $10,965. Tuition, nonresident: full-time $10,965. *Required fees:* $6336; $3711. *Graduate housing:* Room and/or apartments available on a first-come, first-served basis to single students; on-campus housing not available to married students. *Student services:* Campus employment opportunities, campus safety program, career counseling, child daycare facilities, exercise/wellness program, free psychological counseling, grant writing training, international student services, low-cost health insurance, multicultural affairs office, services for students with disabilities, teacher training, writing training. *Library facilities:* Robert E. Kennedy Library.

Computer facilities: A campuswide network can be accessed from student residence rooms and from off campus. Online class registration is available. Website: http://www.calpoly.edu/

General Application Contact: Dr. James Maraviglia, Associate Vice Provost for Marketing and Enrollment Development, 805-756-2311, Fax: 805-756-5400, E-mail: admissions@calpoly.edu.

GRADUATE UNITS

College of Agriculture, Food and Environmental Sciences Students: 58 full-time (41 women), 24 part-time (13 women); includes 25 minority (8 Asian, non-Hispanic/Latino; 14 Hispanic/Latino; 3 Two or more races, non-Hispanic/Latino), 1 international. Average age 27. 82 applicants, 56% accepted, 37 enrolled. *Faculty:* 27 full-time (10 women), 1 (woman) part-time/adjunct. Expenses: Contact institution. *Financial support:* Fellowships, research assistantships, teaching assistantships, career-related internships or fieldwork, institutionally sponsored loans, scholarships/grants, health care benefits, and unspecified assistantships available. Financial award application deadline: 3/2; financial award applicants required to submit FAFSA. In 2018, 60 master's awarded. *Program availability:* Part-time. Offers agricultural education and communication (MAE); agriculture (MS); agriculture, food and environmental sciences (MAE, MS); food science (MS); forestry sciences (MS); nutrition (MS). *Application deadline:* For fall admission, 4/1 for domestic and international students; for winter admission, 10/1 for domestic students; for spring admission, 2/1 for domestic students, 1/1 for international students. Applications are processed on a rolling basis. *Application fee:* $55. Electronic applications accepted. *Application Contact:* Dr. Jim Prince, Associate Dean, Research and Graduate Programs, 805-756-5104, E-mail: jpprince@calpoly.edu. *Dean,* Dr. Andrew Thulin, 805-756-2161, Fax: 805-756-6577, E-mail: athulin@calpoly.edu.

College of Architecture and Environmental Design Students: 42 full-time (17 women), 6 part-time (2 women); includes 19 minority (5 Asian, non-Hispanic/Latino; 8 Hispanic/Latino; 6 Two or more races, non-Hispanic/Latino), 3 international. Average age 25. 76 applicants, 63% accepted, 29 enrolled. *Faculty:* 9 full-time (3 women), 2 part-time/adjunct (1 woman). Expenses: Contact institution. *Financial support:* Research assistantships, teaching assistantships, career-related internships or fieldwork, and institutionally sponsored loans available. Financial award application deadline: 3/2; financial award applicants required to submit FAFSA. In 2018, 24 master's awarded. *Program availability:* Part-time. Offers architectural engineering (MS); architecture (MS); architecture and environmental design (MCRP, MS); city and regional planning (MCRP). *Application deadline:* For fall admission, 6/1 for domestic students, 11/30 for international students; for winter admission, 11/1 for domestic students, 6/30 for international students. Applications are processed on a rolling basis. *Application fee:* $55. Electronic applications accepted. *Application Contact:* Dr. Mark Cabrinha, Associate Dean, 805-756-5988. *Dean,* Dr. Christine Theodoropoulos, E-mail: theo@calpoly.edu.

College of Engineering Students: 181 full-time (51 women), 97 part-time (21 women); includes 87 minority (1 American Indian or Alaska Native, non-Hispanic/Latino; 39 Asian, non-Hispanic/Latino; 27 Hispanic/Latino; 1 Native Hawaiian or other Pacific Islander, non-Hispanic/Latino; 19 Two or more races, non-Hispanic/Latino), 14 international. Average age 26. 476 applicants, 42% accepted, 107 enrolled. *Faculty:* 60 full-time (13 women), 6 part-time/adjunct (1 woman). Expenses: Contact institution. *Financial support:* Fellowships, research assistantships, teaching assistantships, career-related internships or fieldwork, institutionally sponsored loans, and unspecified assistantships available. Financial award application deadline: 3/2; financial award applicants required to submit FAFSA. In 2018, 227 master's awarded. *Program availability:* Part-time. Offers aerospace engineering (MS); biomedical engineering (MS); civil and environmental engineering (MS); computer science (MS); electrical engineering (MS); engineering (MS); industrial engineering (MS); mechanical engineering (MS). *Application deadline:* For fall admission, 1/1 for domestic and international students. Applications are processed on a rolling basis. *Application fee:* $55. Electronic applications accepted. *Application Contact:* Dr. Robert Crockett, Associate Dean, 805-756-6403, E-mail: rcrocket@calpoly.edu. *Associate Dean,* Dr. Robert Crockett, 805-756-6403, E-mail: rcrocket@calpoly.edu.

College of Liberal Arts Students: 41 full-time (33 women), 50 part-time (34 women); includes 28 minority (1 Black or African American, non-Hispanic/Latino; 2 Asian, non-Hispanic/Latino; 20 Hispanic/Latino; 5 Two or more races, non-Hispanic/Latino). Average age 28. 139 applicants, 54% accepted, 46 enrolled. *Faculty:* 14 full-time (6 women), 5 part-time/adjunct (1 woman). Expenses: Contact institution. *Financial support:* Fellowships, teaching assistantships, career-related internships or fieldwork, Federal Work-Study, institutionally sponsored loans, scholarships/grants, and tutorships; writing laboratory assistantships available. Support available to part-time students. Financial award application deadline: 3/2; financial award applicants required to submit FAFSA. In 2018, 40 master's awarded. *Program availability:* Part-time. Offers English (MA); history (MA); liberal arts (MA, MPP, MS); political science (MPP); psychology (MS). *Application deadline:* For fall admission, 4/1 for domestic students, 3/1 for international students. *Application fee:* $55. *Application Contact:* Dr. Debra Valencia-Laver, Associate Dean, 805-756-2706, Fax: 805-756-5748, E-mail: dlvalenc@calpoly.edu. *Associate Dean,* Dr. Debra Valencia-Laver, 805-756-2706, Fax: 805-756-5748, E-mail: dlvalenc@calpoly.edu.

College of Science and Mathematics Students: 107 full-time (68 women), 43 part-time (33 women); includes 56 minority (3 Black or African American, non-Hispanic/Latino; 8 Asian, non-Hispanic/Latino; 37 Hispanic/Latino; 1 Native Hawaiian or other Pacific Islander, non-Hispanic/Latino; 7 Two or more races, non-Hispanic/Latino), 5 international. Average age 28. 223 applicants, 55% accepted, 96 enrolled. *Faculty:* 37 full-time (11 women), 9 part-time/adjunct (6 women). Expenses: Contact institution. *Financial support:* Fellowships, research assistantships, teaching assistantships, career-related internships or fieldwork, and Federal Work-Study available. Support available to part-time students. Financial award application deadline: 3/2; financial award applicants required to submit FAFSA. In 2018, 123 master's awarded. *Program availability:* Part-time. Offers biological sciences (MS); mathematics (MS); polymers and coating science (MS); science and mathematics (MA, MS). *Application deadline:* For fall admission, 2/1 for domestic and international students. Applications are processed on a rolling basis. *Application fee:* $55. Electronic applications accepted. *Application Contact:* Dr. Kellie G. Hall, Associate Dean, 805-756-2226, Fax: 805-756-1670, E-mail: kghall@calpoly.edu. *Associate Dean,* Dr. Kellie G. Hall, 805-756-2226, Fax: 805-756-1670, E-mail: kghall@calpoly.edu.

School of Education Students: 68 full-time (49 women), 22 part-time (20 women); includes 11 minority (1 Black or African American, non-Hispanic/Latino; 1 Asian, non-Hispanic/Latino; 9 Hispanic/Latino). Average age 30. 143 applicants, 59% accepted, 72 enrolled. *Faculty:* 8 full-time (5 women), 8 part-time/adjunct (5 women). Expenses: Contact institution. *Financial support:* Fellowships, research assistantships, career-related internships or fieldwork, Federal Work-Study, and institutionally sponsored loans available. Support available to part-time students. Financial award application deadline: 3/2; financial award applicants required to submit FAFSA. In 2018, 95 master's awarded. *Program availability:* Part-time, evening/weekend. Offers education (MA). *Application deadline:* For fall admission, 4/1 for domestic and international students. Applications are processed on a rolling basis. *Application fee:* $55. Electronic applications accepted. *Application Contact:* Dr. Kevin Taylor, Director, 805-756-1503, E-mail: jktaylor@calpoly.edu. *Director,* Dr. Kevin Taylor, 805-756-1503, E-mail: jktaylor@calpoly.edu.

Orfalea College of Business Students: 101 full-time (47 women), 18 part-time (8 women); includes 40 minority (12 Asian, non-Hispanic/Latino; 23 Hispanic/Latino; 1 Native Hawaiian or other Pacific Islander, non-Hispanic/Latino; 4 Two or more races, non-Hispanic/Latino), 11 international. Average age 24. 50 applicants, 74% accepted, 25 enrolled. *Faculty:* 5 full-time (1 woman), 1 part-time/adjunct (0 women). Expenses: Contact institution. *Financial support:* Fellowships, career-related internships or fieldwork, Federal Work-Study, institutionally sponsored loans, scholarships/grants, and unspecified assistantships available. Support available to part-time students. Financial award application deadline: 3/2; financial award applicants required to submit FAFSA. In 2018, 118 master's awarded. Offers accounting (MS); business (MBA, MS); business administration (MBA); business analytics (MS); economics (MS); packaging value chain (MS); taxation (MS). *Application deadline:* For fall admission, 4/1 for domestic and international students. Applications are processed on a rolling basis. *Application fee:* $55. Electronic applications accepted. *Application Contact:* Dr. Beena Khurana, Director, 805-756-1771, E-mail: bkhurana@calpoly.edu. *Associate Dean,* Dr. Jean-Francois Coget, 805-756-5308, E-mail: jcoget@calpoly.edu.

CALIFORNIA STATE POLYTECHNIC UNIVERSITY, POMONA, Pomona, CA 91768-2557

General Information State-supported, coed, comprehensive institution. *Enrollment:* 552 full-time matriculated graduate/professional students (255 women), 791 part-time matriculated graduate/professional students (348 women). *Enrollment by degree level:* 1,299 master's, 44 doctoral. *Graduate faculty:* 620 full-time (260 women), 691 part-time/adjunct (294 women). *Graduate housing:* Room and/or apartments available on a first-come, first-served basis to single students; on-campus housing not available to married students. Housing application deadline: 5/1. *Student services:* Campus employment opportunities, campus safety program, career counseling, child daycare facilities, free psychological counseling, international student services, low-cost health insurance, multicultural affairs office, services for students with disabilities. *Library facilities:* University Library. *Collection:* Books: 576,734 (physical), 246,874 (digital/electronic); Serial titles: 278,011 (physical), 13,335 (digital/electronic); Databases: 143. Weekly public service hours: 92; study areas open 24 hours, 5–7 days a week; students can reserve study rooms.

Computer facilities: Computer purchase and lease plans are available. 2,117 computers available on campus for general student use. A campuswide network can be accessed from student residence rooms and from off campus. Website: http://www.cpp.edu/

General Application Contact: Deborah L. Brandon, Executive Director of Admissions and Enrollment Planning, 909-869-3427, Fax: 909-869-5315, E-mail: dlbrandon@cpp.edu.

GRADUATE UNITS

Ed D Program in Educational Leadership Students: 2 full-time (0 women), 42 part-time (31 women); includes 29 minority (8 Black or African American, non-Hispanic/Latino; 4 Asian, non-Hispanic/Latino; 16 Hispanic/Latino; 1 Two or more races, non-Hispanic/Latino), 3 international. Average age 43. 2 applicants, 100% accepted, 2 enrolled. Expenses: Contact institution. *Financial support:* Applicants required to submit FAFSA. In 2018, 18 doctorates awarded. *Program availability:* Part-time, evening/weekend. Offers educational leadership (Ed D). *Application deadline:* Applications are processed on a rolling basis. *Application fee:* $55. Electronic applications accepted. *Application Contact:* Dr. Betty T Alford, Professor/Doctoral Program Co-Director, 909-869-5369, Fax: 909-869-4822, E-mail: btalford@cpp.edu. *Professor/Doctoral Program Co-Director,* Dr. Betty T Alford, 909-869-5369, Fax: 909-869-4822, E-mail: btalford@cpp.edu.

John T. Lyle Center for Regenerative Studies Students: 11 full-time (5 women), 9 part-time (5 women); includes 10 minority (2 Black or African American, non-Hispanic/Latino; 2 Asian, non-Hispanic/Latino; 5 Hispanic/Latino; 1 Two or more races, non-Hispanic/Latino), 1 international. Average age 32. 18 applicants, 100% accepted, 13 enrolled. Expenses: Contact institution. *Financial support:* Application deadline: 3/2; applicants required to submit FAFSA. In 2018, 6 master's awarded. *Program availability:* Part-time. Offers regenerative studies (MS). *Application deadline:* Applications are processed on a rolling basis. *Application fee:* $55. Electronic applications accepted. *Application Contact:* Dr. Pablo La Roche, Interim Director/Graduate Coordinator, 909-869-2700, Fax: 909-869-4331, E-mail: pmlaroche@cpp.edu. *Interim Director/Graduate Coordinator,* Dr. Pablo La Roche, 909-869-2700, Fax: 909-869-4331, E-mail: pmlaroche@cpp.edu.

Master of Science in Business Administration Program Students: 15 full-time (5 women), 9 part-time (3 women); includes 11 minority (1 Black or African American, non-Hispanic/Latino; 6 Asian, non-Hispanic/Latino; 4 Hispanic/Latino), 3 international. Average age 31. 39 applicants, 67% accepted, 18 enrolled. Expenses: Contact institution. *Financial support:* Application deadline: 3/2; applicants required to submit FAFSA. *Program availability:* Part-time, evening/weekend. Offers business administration (MS). *Application deadline:* Applications are processed on a rolling basis. *Application fee:* $55. Electronic applications accepted. *Application Contact:* Dr. Tarique Hossain, Associate Professor/Director of Graduate Programs, 909-869-2362, Fax: 909-869-4559, E-mail: tmhossain@cpp.edu. *Associate Professor/Director of Graduate Programs,* Dr. Tarique Hossain, 909-869-2362, Fax: 909-869-4559, E-mail: tmhossain@cpp.edu.

Master's Programs in Education Students: 34 full-time (20 women), 73 part-time (48 women); includes 75 minority (7 Black or African American, non-Hispanic/Latino; 13 Asian, non-Hispanic/Latino; 52 Hispanic/Latino; 1 Native Hawaiian or other Pacific Islander, non-Hispanic/Latino; 2 Two or more races, non-Hispanic/Latino), 3 international. Average age 34. 35 applicants, 54% accepted, 11 enrolled. Expenses: Contact institution. *Financial support:* Application deadline: 3/2; applicants required to submit FAFSA. In 2018, 39 master's awarded. *Program availability:* Part-time, evening/weekend. Offers education (MA). *Application deadline:* Applications are processed on a rolling basis. *Application fee:* $55. Electronic applications accepted. *Application Contact:* Dr. Richard A. Navarro, Professor/Graduate Coordinator, 909-869-2081, Fax: 909-869-4822, E-mail: ranavarro@cpp.edu. *Professor/Graduate Coordinator,* Dr. Richard A. Navarro, 909-869-2081, Fax: 909-869-4822, E-mail: ranavarro@cpp.edu.

MBA Program Students: 43 full-time (14 women), 29 part-time (10 women); includes 42 minority (4 Black or African American, non-Hispanic/Latino; 1 American Indian or Alaska Native, non-Hispanic/Latino; 13 Asian, non-Hispanic/Latino; 23 Hispanic/Latino; 1 Two or more races, non-Hispanic/Latino), 4 international. Average age 31. 154 applicants, 54% accepted, 51 enrolled. Expenses: Contact institution. *Financial support:* Application deadline: 3/2; applicants required to submit FAFSA. In 2018, 24 master's awarded. *Program availability:* Part-time, evening/weekend. Offers business administration (MBA). *Application deadline:* Applications are processed on a rolling basis. *Application fee:* $55. Electronic applications accepted. *Application Contact:* Dr. Tarique Hossain, Associate Professor/Director of Graduate Programs, 909-869-2362, Fax: 909-869-4559, E-mail: tmhossain@cpp.edu. *Associate Professor/Director of Graduate Programs,* Dr. Tarique Hossain, 909-869-2362, Fax: 909-869-4559, E-mail: tmhossain@cpp.edu.

Program in Accountancy Students: 18 full-time (7 women), 7 part-time (4 women); includes 13 minority (7 Asian, non-Hispanic/Latino; 6 Hispanic/Latino), 5 international. Average age 26. 65 applicants, 55% accepted, 21 enrolled. Expenses: Contact institution. *Financial support:* Application deadline: 3/2; applicants required to submit

FAFSA. In 2018, 12 master's awarded. *Program availability:* Part-time, evening/weekend. Offers accountancy (MS). *Application deadline:* Applications are processed on a rolling basis. *Application fee:* $55. Electronic applications accepted. *Application Contact:* Dr. Meihua Koo, Assistant Professor/MSA Coordinator, 909-869-4531, Fax: 909-869-4511, E-mail: mkoo@cpp.edu. *Assistant Professor/MSA Coordinator,* Dr. Meihua Koo, 909-869-4531, Fax: 909-869-4511, E-mail: mkoo@cpp.edu.

Program in Agriculture Students: 28 full-time (16 women), 28 part-time (14 women); includes 36 minority (3 Black or African American, non-Hispanic/Latino; 8 Asian, non-Hispanic/Latino; 21 Hispanic/Latino; 4 Two or more races, non-Hispanic/Latino), 3 international. Average age 31. 48 applicants, 71% accepted, 26 enrolled. Expenses: Contact institution. *Financial support:* Application deadline: 3/2; applicants required to submit FAFSA. In 2018, 11 master's awarded. *Program availability:* Part-time, evening/weekend. Offers agriculture (MS). *Application deadline:* Applications are processed on a rolling basis. *Application fee:* $55. Electronic applications accepted. *Application Contact:* Dr. Harmit Singh, Associate Professor/Director of Research and Graduate Studies, 909-869-3023, Fax: 909-869-5078, E-mail: harmitsingh@cpp.edu. *Associate Professor/Director of Research and Graduate Studies,* Dr. Harmit Singh, 909-869-3023, Fax: 909-869-5078, E-mail: harmitsingh@cpp.edu.

Program in Architecture Students: 33 full-time (16 women), 4 part-time (1 woman); includes 23 minority (1 Black or African American, non-Hispanic/Latino; 7 Asian, non-Hispanic/Latino; 14 Hispanic/Latino; 1 Two or more races, non-Hispanic/Latino), 1 international. Average age 31. 58 applicants, 53% accepted, 8 enrolled. Expenses: Contact institution. *Financial support:* Application deadline: 3/2; applicants required to submit FAFSA. In 2018, 14 master's awarded. *Program availability:* Part-time, evening/weekend. Offers architecture (M Arch). *Application deadline:* Applications are processed on a rolling basis. *Application fee:* $55. Electronic applications accepted. *Application Contact:* Prof. Kip A. Dickson, Professor/Graduate Coordinator, 909-869-2682, Fax: 909-869-4331, E-mail: kadickson@cpp.edu. *Professor/Graduate Coordinator,* Prof. Kip A. Dickson, 909-869-2682, Fax: 909-869-4331, E-mail: kadickson@cpp.edu.

Program in Biological Sciences Students: 38 full-time (20 women), 49 part-time (23 women); includes 56 minority (3 Black or African American, non-Hispanic/Latino; 13 Asian, non-Hispanic/Latino; 35 Hispanic/Latino; 5 Two or more races, non-Hispanic/Latino), 7 international. Average age 27. 57 applicants, 46% accepted, 23 enrolled. Expenses: Contact institution. *Financial support:* Application deadline: 3/2; applicants required to submit FAFSA. In 2018, 25 master's awarded. *Program availability:* Part-time, evening/weekend. Offers biological science (MS). *Application deadline:* Applications are processed on a rolling basis. *Application fee:* $55. Electronic applications accepted. *Application Contact:* Dr. Robert J. Talmadge, Professor/Graduate Coordinator, 909-869-3025, Fax: 909-869-4078, E-mail: rjtalmadge@cpp.edu. *Professor/Graduate Coordinator,* Dr. Robert J. Talmadge, 909-869-3025, Fax: 909-869-4078, E-mail: rjtalmadge@cpp.edu.

Program in Chemistry Students: 9 full-time (3 women), 11 part-time (3 women); includes 9 minority (1 Black or African American, non-Hispanic/Latino; 7 Asian, non-Hispanic/Latino; 1 Hispanic/Latino), 3 international. Average age 28. 16 applicants, 44% accepted, 5 enrolled. Expenses: Contact institution. *Financial support:* Application deadline: 3/2; applicants required to submit FAFSA. In 2018, 6 master's awarded. *Program availability:* Part-time, evening/weekend. Offers chemistry (MS). *Application deadline:* Applications are processed on a rolling basis. *Application fee:* $55. Electronic applications accepted. *Application Contact:* Dr. Gregory Barding, Graduate Coordinator, 909-869-3681, Fax: 909-869-4344, E-mail: gabarding@cpp.edu. *Graduate Coordinator,* Dr. Gregory Barding, 909-869-3681, Fax: 909-869-4344, E-mail: gabarding@cpp.edu.

Program in Civil Engineering Students: 34 full-time (11 women), 63 part-time (15 women); includes 62 minority (3 Black or African American, non-Hispanic/Latino; 25 Asian, non-Hispanic/Latino; 32 Hispanic/Latino; 2 Two or more races, non-Hispanic/Latino), 20 international. Average age 28. 116 applicants, 66% accepted, 45 enrolled. Expenses: Contact institution. *Financial support:* Application deadline: 3/2; applicants required to submit FAFSA. In 2018, 51 master's awarded. *Program availability:* Part-time, evening/weekend. Offers civil engineering (MS). *Application deadline:* Applications are processed on a rolling basis. *Application fee:* $55. Electronic applications accepted. *Application Contact:* Dr. Lisa Wang, Professor/Graduate Coordinator, 909-869-4641, Fax: 909-869-4342, E-mail: ylwang@cpp.edu. *Professor/Graduate Coordinator,* Dr. Lisa Wang, 909-869-4641, Fax: 909-869-4342, E-mail: ylwang@cpp.edu.

Program in Computer Science Students: 25 full-time (7 women), 45 part-time (6 women); includes 37 minority (1 Black or African American, non-Hispanic/Latino; 28 Asian, non-Hispanic/Latino; 7 Hispanic/Latino; 1 Two or more races, non-Hispanic/Latino), 22 international. Average age 28. 184 applicants, 38% accepted, 22 enrolled. Expenses: Contact institution. *Financial support:* Application deadline: 3/2; applicants required to submit FAFSA. In 2018, 39 master's awarded. *Program availability:* Part-time, evening/weekend. Offers computer science (MS). *Application deadline:* Applications are processed on a rolling basis. *Application fee:* $55. Electronic applications accepted. *Application Contact:* Dr. Gilbert S. Young, Professor/Graduate Coordinator, 909-869-4413, Fax: 909-869-4733, E-mail: gsyoung@cpp.edu. *Professor/Graduate Coordinator,* Dr. Gilbert S. Young, 909-869-4413, Fax: 909-869-4733, E-mail: gsyoung@cpp.edu.

Program in Economics Students: 23 full-time (11 women), 12 part-time (5 women); includes 15 minority (1 Black or African American, non-Hispanic/Latino; 5 Asian, non-Hispanic/Latino; 6 Hispanic/Latino; 3 Two or more races, non-Hispanic/Latino), 13 international. Average age 28. 35 applicants, 74% accepted, 10 enrolled. Expenses: Contact institution. *Financial support:* Application deadline: 3/2; applicants required to submit FAFSA. In 2018, 17 master's awarded. *Program availability:* Part-time, evening/weekend. Offers economics (MS). *Application deadline:* Applications are processed on a rolling basis. *Application fee:* $55. Electronic applications accepted. *Application Contact:* Dr. Carsten Lange, Professor/Graduate Coordinator, 909-869-3843, Fax: 909-869-6987, E-mail: clange@cpp.edu. *Professor/Graduate Coordinator,* Dr. Carsten Lange, 909-869-3843, Fax: 909-869-6987, E-mail: clange@cpp.edu.

Program in Electrical Engineering Students: 13 full-time (2 women), 42 part-time (7 women); includes 32 minority (18 Asian, non-Hispanic/Latino; 12 Hispanic/Latino; 2 Two or more races, non-Hispanic/Latino), 5 international. Average age 28. 93 applicants, 48% accepted, 23 enrolled. Expenses: Contact institution. *Financial support:* Application deadline: 3/2; applicants required to submit FAFSA. In 2018, 25 master's awarded. *Program availability:* Part-time, evening/weekend. Offers communication systems (MSEE). *Application deadline:* Applications are processed on a rolling basis. *Application fee:* $55. Electronic applications accepted. *Application Contact:* Dr. Thomas Ketseoglou, Professor/Graduate Program Coordinator, 909-869-3977, Fax: 909-869-4687, E-mail: tketseoglou@cpp.edu. *Professor/Graduate Program Coordinator,* Dr. Thomas Ketseoglou, 909-869-3977, Fax: 909-869-4687, E-mail: tketseoglou@cpp.edu.

Program in Engineering Students: 1 full-time (0 women), 43 part-time (9 women); includes 24 minority (1 Black or African American, non-Hispanic/Latino; 11 Asian, non-Hispanic/Latino; 10 Hispanic/Latino; 2 Two or more races, non-Hispanic/Latino), 4 international. Average age 27. 61 applicants, 34% accepted, 15 enrolled. Expenses: Contact institution. *Financial support:* Application deadline: 3/2; applicants required to submit FAFSA. In 2018, 1 master's awarded. *Program availability:* Part-time, evening/weekend. Offers engineering (MSE). *Application deadline:* Applications are processed on a rolling basis. *Application fee:* $55. Electronic applications accepted. *Application Contact:* Dr. Ali R. Ahmadi, Department Chair/Professor, 909-869-2470, Fax: 909-869-6920, E-mail: arahmadi@cpp.edu. *Department Chair/Professor,* Dr. Ali R. Ahmadi, 909-869-2470, Fax: 909-869-6920, E-mail: arahmadi@cpp.edu.

Program in Engineering Management Students: 11 full-time (3 women), 12 part-time (2 women); includes 11 minority (2 Asian, non-Hispanic/Latino; 7 Hispanic/Latino; 2 Two or more races, non-Hispanic/Latino), 7 international. Average age 30. 39 applicants, 54% accepted, 9 enrolled. Expenses: Contact institution. *Financial support:* Application deadline: 3/2; applicants required to submit FAFSA. In 2018, 24 master's awarded. *Program availability:* Part-time, evening/weekend. Offers engineering management (MS). *Application deadline:* Applications are processed on a rolling basis. *Application fee:* $55. Electronic applications accepted. *Application Contact:* Dr. Kamran Abedini, Chair/Graduate Coordinator, 909-869-2569, Fax: 909-869-2564, E-mail: kabedini@cpp.edu. *Chair/Graduate Coordinator,* Dr. Kamran Abedini, 909-869-2569, Fax: 909-869-2564, E-mail: kabedini@cpp.edu.

Program in English Students: 30 full-time (23 women), 52 part-time (28 women); includes 51 minority (2 Black or African American, non-Hispanic/Latino; 10 Asian, non-Hispanic/Latino; 37 Hispanic/Latino; 2 Two or more races, non-Hispanic/Latino), 2 international. Average age 29. 59 applicants, 80% accepted, 32 enrolled. Expenses: Contact institution. *Financial support:* Application deadline: 3/2; applicants required to submit FAFSA. In 2018, 26 master's awarded. *Program availability:* Part-time, evening/weekend. Offers English (MA). *Application deadline:* Applications are processed on a rolling basis. *Application fee:* $55. Electronic applications accepted. *Application Contact:* Dr. Lise-Helene V. Smith, Associate Professor/Graduate Coordinator, 909-869-3979, Fax: 909-869-4896, E-mail: lvtrouilloud@cpp.edu. *Associate Professor/Graduate Coordinator,* Dr. Lise-Helene V. Smith, 909-869-3979, Fax: 909-869-4896, E-mail: lvtrouilloud@cpp.edu.

Program in Geology Students: 7 full-time (3 women), 22 part-time (10 women); includes 13 minority (2 Black or African American, non-Hispanic/Latino; 2 Asian, non-Hispanic/Latino; 8 Hispanic/Latino; 1 Two or more races, non-Hispanic/Latino). Average age 29. 10 applicants, 100% accepted, 8 enrolled. Expenses: Contact institution. *Financial support:* Application deadline: 3/2; applicants required to submit FAFSA. In 2018, 6 master's awarded. *Program availability:* Part-time, evening/weekend. Offers geology (MS). *Application deadline:* Applications are processed on a rolling basis. Electronic applications accepted. *Application Contact:* Dr. Jonathan A. Nourse, Department Chair/Coordinator, 909-869-3460, Fax: 909-869-2920, E-mail: janourse@cpp.edu. *Department Chair/Coordinator,* Dr. Jonathan A. Nourse, 909-869-3460, Fax: 909-869-2920, E-mail: janourse@cpp.edu.

Program in History Students: 4 full-time (2 women), 11 part-time (4 women); includes 8 minority (3 Asian, non-Hispanic/Latino; 4 Hispanic/Latino; 1 Two or more races, non-Hispanic/Latino). Average age 33. 23 applicants, 39% accepted, 8 enrolled. Expenses: Contact institution. *Financial support:* Application deadline: 3/2; applicants required to submit FAFSA. In 2018, 9 master's awarded. *Program availability:* Part-time, evening/weekend. Offers history (MA). *Application deadline:* Applications are processed on a rolling basis. *Application fee:* $55. Electronic applications accepted. *Application Contact:* Dr. Amanda H. Podany, Professor/Graduate Coordinator, 909-869-3875, Fax: 909-869-4724, E-mail: ahpodany@cpp.edu. *Professor/Graduate Coordinator,* Dr. Amanda H. Podany, 909-869-3875, Fax: 909-869-4724, E-mail: ahpodany@cpp.edu.

Program in Hospitality Management Students: 21 full-time (11 women), 20 part-time (12 women); includes 16 minority (4 Black or African American, non-Hispanic/Latino; 9 Asian, non-Hispanic/Latino; 2 Hispanic/Latino; 1 Two or more races, non-Hispanic/Latino), 20 international. Average age 29. 29 applicants, 72% accepted, 15 enrolled. Expenses: Contact institution. *Financial support:* Application deadline: 3/2; applicants required to submit FAFSA. In 2018, 17 master's awarded. *Program availability:* Part-time, evening/weekend. Offers hospitality management (MS). *Application deadline:* Applications are processed on a rolling basis. *Application fee:* $55. Electronic applications accepted. *Application Contact:* Dr. Neha Singh, Associate Professor/MSHM Program Director, 909-869-4565, Fax: 909-869-4805, E-mail: nsingh@cpp.edu. *Associate Professor/MSHM Program Director,* Dr. Neha Singh, 909-869-4565, Fax: 909-869-4805, E-mail: nsingh@cpp.edu.

Program in Interior Architecture Students: 2 full-time (1 woman), 54 part-time (50 women); includes 16 minority (10 Asian, non-Hispanic/Latino; 2 Hispanic/Latino; 4 Two or more races, non-Hispanic/Latino), 22 international. Average age 30. 53 applicants, 57% accepted, 21 enrolled. Expenses: Contact institution. *Financial support:* Application deadline: 3/2; applicants required to submit FAFSA. In 2018, 21 master's awarded. *Program availability:* Part-time, evening/weekend. Offers interior architecture (MIA). Program offered in partnership with UCLA Extension. *Application deadline:* Applications are processed on a rolling basis. *Application fee:* $55. Electronic applications accepted. *Application Contact:* Prof. Irma Ramirez, Professor/Coordinator, 909-869-5355, Fax: 909-869-4331, E-mail: ieramirez@cpp.edu. *Professor/Coordinator,* Prof. Irma Ramirez, 909-869-5355, Fax: 909-869-4331, E-mail: ieramirez@cpp.edu.

Program in Kinesiology Students: 8 full-time (4 women), 4 part-time (3 women); includes 4 minority (1 Asian, non-Hispanic/Latino; 2 Hispanic/Latino; 1 Two or more races, non-Hispanic/Latino), 1 international. Average age 25. 21 applicants, 43% accepted, 6 enrolled. Expenses: Contact institution. *Financial support:* Application deadline: 3/2; applicants required to submit FAFSA. In 2018, 7 master's awarded. *Program availability:* Part-time, evening/weekend. Offers kinesiology (MS). *Application deadline:* Applications are processed on a rolling basis. *Application fee:* $55. Electronic applications accepted. *Application Contact:* Dr. Ken Hansen, Professor/Graduate Coordinator, 909-869-4638, Fax: 909-869-4797, E-mail: kahansen@cpp.edu. *Professor/Graduate Coordinator,* Dr. Ken Hansen, 909-869-4638, Fax: 909-869-4797, E-mail: kahansen@cpp.edu.

Program in Landscape Architecture Students: 33 full-time (19 women), 4 part-time (3 women); includes 14 minority (5 Asian, non-Hispanic/Latino; 9 Hispanic/Latino), 3 international. Average age 32. 45 applicants, 69% accepted, 14 enrolled. Expenses: Contact institution. *Financial support:* Application deadline: 3/2; applicants required to submit FAFSA. In 2018, 4 master's awarded. *Program availability:* Part-time, evening/weekend. Offers landscape architecture (M Land Arch). *Application deadline:* Applications are processed on a rolling basis. *Application fee:* $55. Electronic applications accepted. *Application Contact:* Dr. Weimin Li, Associate Professor/Graduate Coordinator, 909-869-2715, Fax: 909-869-2580, E-mail: wli@cpp.edu. *Associate Professor/Graduate Coordinator,* Dr. Weimin Li, 909-869-2715, Fax: 909-869-2580, E-mail: wli@cpp.edu.

Program in Mathematics Students: 14 full-time (5 women), 42 part-time (14 women); includes 33 minority (2 Black or African American, non-Hispanic/Latino; 9 Asian, non-Hispanic/Latino; 19 Hispanic/Latino; 3 Two or more races, non-Hispanic/Latino), 7 international. Average age 27. 67 applicants, 58% accepted, 25 enrolled. Expenses: Contact institution. *Financial support:* Application deadline: 3/2; applicants required to submit FAFSA. In 2018, 14 master's awarded. *Program availability:* Part-time, evening/weekend. Offers mathematics (MS). *Application deadline:* Applications are processed on a rolling basis. *Application fee:* $55. Electronic applications accepted. *Application Contact:* Dr. Adam King, Assistant Professor/Graduate Coordinator, 909-979-5595, Fax: 909-869-4904, E-mail: king@cpp.edu. *Assistant Professor/Graduate Coordinator,* Dr. Adam King, 909-979-5595, Fax: 909-869-4904, E-mail: king@cpp.edu.

Program in Mechanical Engineering Students: 11 full-time (5 women), 54 part-time (9 women); includes 35 minority (2 Black or African American, non-Hispanic/Latino; 17 Asian, non-Hispanic/Latino; 15 Hispanic/Latino; 1 Two or more races, non-Hispanic/Latino), 8 international. Average age 28. 79 applicants, 54% accepted, 13 enrolled. Expenses: Contact institution. *Financial support:* Application deadline: 3/2; applicants required to submit FAFSA. In 2018, 28 master's awarded. *Program availability:* Part-time, evening/weekend. Offers mechanical engineering (MS). *Application deadline:* Applications are processed on a rolling basis. *Application fee:* $55. Electronic applications accepted. *Application Contact:* Dr. Henry Xue, Graduate Coordinator, 909-869-4304, Fax: 909-869-4341, E-mail: hxue@cpp.edu. *Graduate Coordinator,* Dr. Henry Xue, 909-869-4304, Fax: 909-869-4341, E-mail: hxue@cpp.edu.

Program in Psychology Students: 29 full-time (21 women), 2 part-time (1 woman); includes 21 minority (2 Asian, non-Hispanic/Latino; 15 Hispanic/Latino; 4 Two or more races, non-Hispanic/Latino). Average age 27. 91 applicants, 15% accepted, 13 enrolled. Expenses: Contact institution. *Financial support:* Application deadline: 3/2; applicants required to submit FAFSA. In 2018, 13 master's awarded. *Program availability:* Part-time, evening/weekend. Offers psychology (MS). *Application deadline:* Applications are processed on a rolling basis. *Application fee:* $55. Electronic applications accepted. *Application Contact:* Dr. Jeffery Mio, Director of Graduate Studies, 909-869-3899, Fax: 909-869-4930, E-mail: jsmio@cpp.edu. *Director of Graduate Studies,* Dr. Jeffery Mio, 909-869-3899, Fax: 909-869-4930, E-mail: jsmio@cpp.edu.

Program in Public Administration Average age 33. 29 applicants, 52% accepted, 11 enrolled. Expenses: Contact institution. *Financial support:* Application deadline: 3/2; applicants required to submit FAFSA. In 2018, 11 master's awarded. *Program availability:* Part-time, evening/weekend. Offers public administration (MPA). *Application deadline:* Applications are processed on a rolling basis. *Application fee:* $55. Electronic applications accepted. *Application Contact:* Deborah L. Brandon, Executive Director of Admissions and Enrollment Planning, 909-869-3427, Fax: 909-869-5315, E-mail: dlbrandon@cpp.edu. *Professor/MPA Coordinator,* Dr. Sandra M. Emerson, 909-869-3879, Fax: 909-869-6995, E-mail: smemerson@cpp.edu.

Program in Systems Engineering Students: 8 full-time (0 women), 1 (woman) part-time; includes 3 minority (1 Asian, non-Hispanic/Latino; 2 Hispanic/Latino), 3 international. Average age 26. 3 applicants, 33% accepted, 0 enrolled. Expenses: Contact institution. *Financial support:* Application deadline: 3/2. In 2018, 5 master's awarded. *Program availability:* Part-time, evening/weekend. Offers systems engineering (MS). *Application deadline:* Applications are processed on a rolling basis. *Application fee:* $55. Electronic applications accepted. *Application Contact:* Dr. Kamran Abedini, Professor/MSSE Coordinator, 909-869-2569, Fax: 909-869-2564, E-mail: kabedini@cpp.edu. *Professor/MSSE Coordinator,* Dr. Kamran Abedini, 909-869-2569, Fax: 909-869-2564, E-mail: kabedini@cpp.edu.

Program in Urban and Regional Planning Students: 33 full-time (15 women), 17 part-time (8 women); includes 34 minority (2 Black or African American, non-Hispanic/Latino; 9 Asian, non-Hispanic/Latino; 23 Hispanic/Latino), 2 international. Average age 29. 67 applicants, 69% accepted, 24 enrolled. Expenses: Contact institution. *Financial support:* Application deadline: 3/2; applicants required to submit FAFSA. In 2018, 13 master's awarded. *Program availability:* Part-time, evening/weekend. Offers urban and regional planning (MURP). *Application deadline:* Applications are processed on a rolling basis. *Application fee:* $55. Electronic applications accepted. *Application Contact:* Dr. Dina Abdul Karim, Assistant Professor/Graduate Coordinator, 909-869-3658, Fax: 909-869-4688, E-mail: dabdulkarim@cpp.edu. *Assistant Professor/Graduate Coordinator,* Dr. Dina Abdul Karim, 909-869-3658, Fax: 909-869-4688, E-mail: dabdulkarim@cpp.edu.

CALIFORNIA STATE UNIVERSITY, BAKERSFIELD, Bakersfield, CA 93311

General Information State-supported, coed, comprehensive institution. *Enrollment:* 10,493 graduate, professional, and undergraduate students. *Graduate housing:* Room and/or apartments available on a first-come, first-served basis to single students; on-campus housing not available to married students. Housing application deadline: 7/15. *Student services:* Campus employment opportunities, campus safety program, career counseling, child daycare facilities, exercise/wellness program, free psychological counseling, grant writing training, international student services, multicultural affairs office, services for students with disabilities, teacher training, writing training. *Library facilities:* Walter W. Stiern Library.

Computer facilities: A campuswide network can be accessed from student residence rooms and from off campus. Online class registration is available. Website: http://www.csub.edu/

General Application Contact: Dr., Director, Graduate Programs, 661-654-.

GRADUATE UNITS

Division of Graduate Studies *Program availability:* Part-time, evening/weekend, online learning. Offers administration (MSA); interdisciplinary studies (MA).

School of Arts and Humanities *Program availability:* Part-time, evening/weekend. Offers arts and humanities (MA); English (MA); history (MA); Spanish (MA).

School of Business and Public Administration Offers business administration (MBA); business and public administration (MBA, MPA, MS); health care administration (MS); public administration (MPA).

School of Natural Sciences, Mathematics, and Engineering Offers biology (MS); family nurse practitioner (MSN); geological sciences (MS); hydrogeology (MS); natural sciences, mathematics, and engineering (MA, MS, MSN); petroleum geology (MS); science education (MS).

School of Social Sciences and Education Offers counseling psychology (MS); educational administration (MA); educational leadership (Ed D); school counseling (MS); social sciences and education (MA, MS, MSW, Ed D); social work (MSW); sociology (MA); special education (MA); student affairs (MS).

CALIFORNIA STATE UNIVERSITY CHANNEL ISLANDS, Camarillo, CA 93012

General Information State-supported, coed, comprehensive institution. *Graduate housing:* Room and/or apartments available on a first-come, first-served basis to single students; on-campus housing not available to married students. Housing application deadline: 6/1.

California State University Channel Islands

GRADUATE UNITS

Extended University and International Programs Students: 197 full-time (66 women); includes 110 minority (2 Black or African American, non-Hispanic/Latino; 1 American Indian or Alaska Native, non-Hispanic/Latino; 62 Asian, non-Hispanic/Latino; 33 Hispanic/Latino; 2 Native Hawaiian or other Pacific Islander, non-Hispanic/Latino; 10 Two or more races, non-Hispanic/Latino). Expenses: Contact institution. *Financial support:* Applicants required to submit FAFSA. *Program availability:* Part-time, evening/weekend. Offers biotechnology and bioinformatics (MS); business administration (MBA); computer science (MS); mathematics (MS). *Application deadline:* For fall admission, 5/1 for domestic students; for spring admission, 11/1 for domestic students. *Application fee:* $55. Electronic applications accepted. *Application Contact:* Andrew Conley, Graduate Programs Recruiter, 805-437-2652, E-mail: andrew.conley@csuci.edu. *Associate Director of Enrollment & Outreach*, Daniel Banyai, 805-437-2651, E-mail: daniel.banyai@csuci.edu.

CALIFORNIA STATE UNIVERSITY, CHICO, Chico, CA 95929-0722

General Information State-supported, coed, comprehensive institution. CGS member. *Enrollment:* 18,073 graduate, professional, and undergraduate students; 764 full-time matriculated graduate/professional students (551 women), 304 part-time matriculated graduate/professional students (204 women). *Enrollment by degree level:* 1,068 master's. *Graduate faculty:* 151 full-time (89 women), 68 part-time/adjunct (52 women). *Tuition, area resident:* Full-time $4622; part-time $3116 per unit. Tuition, state resident: full-time $4622; part-time $3116 per unit. Tuition, nonresident: full-time $10,634. *Required fees:* $2160; $1620 per year. Tuition and fees vary according to class time and program. *Graduate housing:* Room and/or apartments available on a first-come, first-served basis to single students; on-campus housing not available to married students. *Student services:* Campus employment opportunities, campus safety program, career counseling, child daycare facilities, exercise/wellness program, free psychological counseling, grant writing training, international student services, low-cost health insurance, multicultural affairs office, services for students with disabilities, teacher training, writing training. *Library facilities:* Meriam Library plus 1 other. *Collection:* Books: 544,345 (physical), 306,440 (digital/electronic); Serial titles: 72,555 (physical). Study areas open 24 hours, 5–7 days a week; students can reserve study rooms.

Computer facilities: Computer purchase and lease plans are available. 1,328 computers available on campus for general student use. A campuswide network can be accessed from student residence rooms and from off campus. Online class registration, student account information, calendar, transcripts are available. Website: http://www.csuchico.edu/

General Application Contact: Micah Lehner, Admissions Counselor, 530-898-6880, Fax: 530-898-3342, E-mail: graduatestudies@csuchico.edu.

GRADUATE UNITS

Office of Graduate Studies Students: 764 full-time (551 women), 304 part-time (204 women); includes 348 minority (18 Black or African American, non-Hispanic/Latino; 9 American Indian or Alaska Native, non-Hispanic/Latino; 63 Asian, non-Hispanic/Latino; 219 Hispanic/Latino; 1 Native Hawaiian or other Pacific Islander, non-Hispanic/Latino; 38 Two or more races, non-Hispanic/Latino). Average age 29. 1,236 applicants, 51% accepted, 467 enrolled. *Faculty:* 151 full-time (89 women), 68 part-time/adjunct (52 women). Expenses: Contact institution. *Financial support:* Fellowships, research assistantships, teaching assistantships, career-related internships or fieldwork, Federal Work-Study, scholarships/grants, traineeships, health care benefits, unspecified assistantships, and stipends available. Support available to part-time students. Financial award application deadline: 3/2; financial award applicants required to submit FAFSA. In 2018, 276 master's awarded. *Program availability:* Part-time, 100% online, blended/hybrid learning. *Application deadline:* For fall admission, 3/1 priority date for domestic students, 3/1 for international students; for spring admission, 9/15 priority date for domestic students, 9/15 for international students. *Application fee:* $55. Electronic applications accepted. *Application Contact:* Micah Lehner, Graduate Admissions Coordinator, 530-898-5416, Fax: 530-898-3342, E-mail: mlehner@csuchico.edu. *Office of Graduate Studies*, Dr. Sharon Barrios, 530-898-6880, Fax: 530-898-3342, E-mail: sbarrios@csuchico.edu.

College of Agriculture Students: 1 full-time (0 women). 3 applicants, 67% accepted, 0 enrolled. Expenses: Contact institution. *Financial support:* Fellowships, research assistantships, teaching assistantships, career-related internships or fieldwork, Federal Work-Study, scholarships/grants, traineeships, health care benefits, unspecified assistantships, and stipends available. Support available to part-time students. Financial award application deadline: 3/2; financial award applicants required to submit FAFSA. In 2018, 10 master's awarded. Offers agricultural education (MS). *Application deadline:* For fall admission, 6/1 priority date for domestic students, 7/1 priority date for international students. *Application fee:* $55. Electronic applications accepted. *Application Contact:* Micah Lehner, Graduate Admissions Coordinator, 530-898-5416, Fax: 530-898-3342, E-mail: mlehner@csuchico.edu. *MS Education Coordinator*, Mollie Aschenbrener, 530-898-4568, Fax: 530-898-5844, E-mail: maschenbrener@csuchico.edu.

College of Behavioral and Social Sciences Students: 473 full-time (346 women), 134 part-time (96 women); includes 116 minority (16 Black or African American, non-Hispanic/Latino; 7 American Indian or Alaska Native, non-Hispanic/Latino; 22 Asian, non-Hispanic/Latino; 52 Hispanic/Latino; 1 Native Hawaiian or other Pacific Islander, non-Hispanic/Latino; 18 Two or more races, non-Hispanic/Latino). 593 applicants, 70% accepted, 311 enrolled. *Faculty:* 43 full-time (22 women), 28 part-time/adjunct (26 women). Expenses: Contact institution. *Financial support:* Fellowships, research assistantships, teaching assistantships, career-related internships or fieldwork, Federal Work-Study, scholarships/grants, traineeships, health care benefits, unspecified assistantships, and stipends available. Support available to part-time students. Financial award application deadline: 3/2; financial award applicants required to submit FAFSA. In 2018, 142 master's awarded. Offers anthropology (MA); applied/school psychology (MA); behavioral and social sciences (MA, MPA, MS, MSW); health administration (MPA); local government management (MPA); marriage and family therapy (MS); museum studies (MA); political science (MA); psychological science (MA); public administration (MPA); social science (MA); social work (MSW). *Application deadline:* For fall admission, 3/2 priority date for domestic and international students; for spring admission, 9/16 priority date for domestic and international students. *Application fee:* $55. Electronic applications accepted. *Application Contact:* Micah Lehner, Graduate Admissions Coordinator, 530-898-5416, Fax: 530-898-3342, E-mail: mlehner@csuchico.edu. *Dean*, Dr. Eddie Vela, 530-898-6171, Fax: 530-898-5986, E-mail: bss@csuchico.edu.

College of Business Students: 32 full-time (10 women), 27 part-time (13 women); includes 28 minority (1 American Indian or Alaska Native, non-Hispanic/Latino; 18 Asian, non-Hispanic/Latino; 8 Hispanic/Latino; 1 Two or more races, non-Hispanic/Latino). 36 applicants, 67% accepted, 16 enrolled. *Faculty:* 10 full-time (2 women), 1 part-time/adjunct (0 women). Expenses: Contact institution. *Financial support:* Fellowships, research assistantships, teaching assistantships, career-related internships or fieldwork, Federal Work-Study, scholarships/grants, traineeships, health care benefits, unspecified assistantships, and stipends available. Support available to part-time students. Financial award application deadline: 3/2; financial award applicants required to submit FAFSA. In 2018, 33 master's awarded. *Program availability:* Part-time. Offers business (MBA). *Application deadline:* For fall admission, 3/2 priority date for domestic and international students; for spring admission, 9/16 priority date for domestic and international students. *Application fee:* $55. Electronic applications accepted. *Application Contact:* Micah Lehner, Graduate Admissions Coordinator, 530-898-5416, Fax: 530-898-3342, E-mail: mlehner@csuchico.edu. *Dean*, Dr. Terrence Lau, 530-898-6272, Fax: 530-898-4584, E-mail: tjlau@csuchico.edu.

College of Communication and Education Students: 103 full-time (79 women), 35 part-time (26 women); includes 47 minority (2 Black or African American, non-Hispanic/Latino; 1 American Indian or Alaska Native, non-Hispanic/Latino; 6 Asian, non-Hispanic/Latino; 31 Hispanic/Latino; 7 Two or more races, non-Hispanic/Latino). 220 applicants, 30% accepted, 56 enrolled. *Faculty:* 25 full-time (19 women), 19 part-time/adjunct (15 women). Expenses: Contact institution. *Financial support:* Fellowships, research assistantships, teaching assistantships, career-related internships or fieldwork, Federal Work-Study, scholarships/grants, traineeships, health care benefits, unspecified assistantships, and stipends available. Support available to part-time students. Financial award application deadline: 3/2; financial award applicants required to submit FAFSA. In 2018, 83 master's awarded. *Program availability:* Part-time. Offers communication and education (MA, MS); communication sciences and disorders (MA); communication studies (MA); curriculum and instruction (MA); kinesiology (MA); recreation, parks, and tourism (MS); teaching English learners and special education advising patterns (MA). *Application deadline:* For fall admission, 3/1 priority date for domestic and international students; for spring admission, 9/15 priority date for domestic and international students. *Application fee:* $55. Electronic applications accepted. *Application Contact:* Micah Lehner, Graduate Admission Coordinator, 530-898-5416, Fax: 530-898-3342, E-mail: mlehner@csuchico.edu. *Dean*, Dr. Angela Trethewey, 530-898-4015, Fax: 530-898-4345, E-mail: cme@csuchico.edu.

College of Engineering, Computer Science, and Construction Management Students: 1 full-time (0 women), 4 part-time (0 women); includes 3 minority (2 Asian, non-Hispanic/Latino; 1 Hispanic/Latino). 21 applicants, 0% accepted, 0 enrolled. *Faculty:* 7 full-time (1 woman), 3 part-time/adjunct (1 woman). Expenses: Contact institution. *Financial support:* Fellowships, research assistantships, teaching assistantships, career-related internships or fieldwork, Federal Work-Study, scholarships/grants, traineeships, health care benefits, unspecified assistantships, and stipends available. Support available to part-time students. Financial award application deadline: 3/2; financial award applicants required to submit FAFSA. In 2018, 20 master's awarded. *Program availability:* Part-time, online learning. Offers computer engineering (MS); computer science (MS); electronic engineering (MS); electronics engineering (MS); engineering, computer science, and construction management (MS). *Application deadline:* For fall admission, 4/1 priority date for domestic and international students. *Application fee:* $55. Electronic applications accepted. *Application Contact:* Micah Lehner, Graduate Admissions Counselor, 530-898-5416, Fax: 530-898-3342, E-mail: mlehner@csuchico.edu. *Interim Dean*, Melody Stapleton, 530-898-5963, Fax: 530-898-4070, E-mail: ecc@csuchico.edu.

College of Humanities and Fine Arts Students: 32 full-time (24 women), 23 part-time (17 women); includes 13 minority (4 Asian, non-Hispanic/Latino; 8 Hispanic/Latino; 1 Two or more races, non-Hispanic/Latino). 47 applicants, 57% accepted, 18 enrolled. *Faculty:* 30 full-time (20 women), 8 part-time/adjunct (5 women). Expenses: Contact institution. *Financial support:* Fellowships, research assistantships, teaching assistantships, career-related internships or fieldwork, Federal Work-Study, scholarships/grants, traineeships, health care benefits, unspecified assistantships, and stipends available. Support available to part-time students. Financial award application deadline: 3/2; financial award applicants required to submit FAFSA. In 2018, 15 master's awarded. Offers art history (MA); art studio (MFA); English (MA); fine arts (MFA); history (MA); humanities and fine arts (MA, MFA). *Application deadline:* For fall admission, 3/1 priority date for domestic and international students; for spring admission, 9/15 priority date for domestic and international students. *Application fee:* $55. Electronic applications accepted. *Application Contact:* Micah Lehner, Graduate Admissions Coordinator, 530-898-5416, Fax: 530-898-3342, E-mail: mlehner@csuchico.edu. *Interim Dean*, Dr. Tracy Butts, 530-898-5351, Fax: 530-898-5581, E-mail: hfa@csuchico.edu.

College of Natural Sciences Students: 40 full-time (30 women), 37 part-time (21 women); includes 18 minority (5 Asian, non-Hispanic/Latino; 10 Hispanic/Latino; 1 Native Hawaiian or other Pacific Islander, non-Hispanic/Latino; 2 Two or more races, non-Hispanic/Latino). 160 applicants, 24% accepted, 28 enrolled. *Faculty:* 32 full-time (23 women), 7 part-time/adjunct (4 women). Expenses: Contact institution. *Financial support:* Fellowships, research assistantships, teaching assistantships, career-related internships or fieldwork, Federal Work-Study, scholarships/grants, traineeships, health care benefits, unspecified assistantships, and stipends available. Support available to part-time students. Financial award application deadline: 3/2; financial award applicants required to submit FAFSA. In 2018, 21 master's awarded. *Program availability:* Part-time. Offers biological sciences (MS); environmental science (MS, PSM); general nutritional science (MS); geosciences (MS); mathematics in education (MS); natural sciences (MS, MSN, PSM); nursing (MSN); nutrition education (MS). *Application deadline:* For fall admission, 3/2 priority date for domestic and international students; for spring admission, 10/1 priority date for domestic and international students. *Application fee:* $55. Electronic applications accepted. *Application Contact:* Micah Lehner, Graduate Admissions Coordinator, 530-898-5416, Fax: 530-898-3342, E-mail: mlehner@csuchico.edu. *Dean*, Dr. David Hassenzahl, 530-898-6121, Fax: 530-898-4363, E-mail: ns@csuchico.edu.

CALIFORNIA STATE UNIVERSITY, DOMINGUEZ HILLS, Carson, CA 90747-0001

General Information State-supported, coed, comprehensive institution. CGS member. *Graduate housing:* Rooms and/or apartments available on a first-come, first-served basis to single and married students. Housing application deadline: 4/15. *Research affiliation:* Los Angeles Biomedical Research Institute at Harbor UCLA Medical Center (biomedical science), Hewlett Packard (catalyst initiative grants).

GRADUATE UNITS

College of Arts and Humanities *Program availability:* Part-time, evening/weekend, 100% online. Offers arts and humanities (MA, Certificate); English literature (MA); negotiation, conflict resolution and peacebuilding (MA); rhetoric and composition (Certificate); teaching English as a second language (MA, Certificate).

College of Business Administration and Public Policy *Program availability:* Part-time, evening/weekend, online learning. Offers business administration (MBA); business administration and public policy (MBA, MPA); public administration (MPA).

College of Education *Program availability:* Part-time, evening/weekend. Offers education (MA, MS).

Division of Graduate Education *Program availability:* Part-time, evening/weekend. Offers college counseling (MS); counseling (MS); school counseling (MS).

Division of Teacher Education *Program availability:* Part-time, evening/weekend. Offers early childhood special education (MA); special education (MA).

College of Extended and International Education *Program availability:* Part-time, evening/weekend, online learning. Offers extended and international education (MA, MS); humanities (MA); quality assurance (MS). Electronic applications accepted.

College of Health, Human Services and Nursing Offers health, human services and nursing (MS, MSN, MSW); marital and family therapy (MS); nursing (MSN); occupational therapy (MS); social work (MSW). Electronic applications accepted.

College of Natural and Behavioral Sciences Offers biology (MS); clinical psychology (MA); computer science (MS); health psychology (MA); natural and behavioral sciences (MA, MS, Certificate); social research (MA); sociology (MA).

CALIFORNIA STATE UNIVERSITY, EAST BAY, Hayward, CA 94542-3000

General Information State-supported, coed, comprehensive institution. *Graduate housing:* On-campus housing not available. *Research affiliation:* Bayer USA Foundation (STEM), Chevron (STEM), Hearst Foundation (STEM), NASA (earth and environmental sciences), Irvine Foundation (education: teacher preparation), Carnegie Foundation (statistics for non-STEM majors).

GRADUATE UNITS

Office of Graduate Studies *Program availability:* Part-time, evening/weekend, online learning. Offers interdisciplinary studies (MA, MS). Electronic applications accepted.

College of Business and Economics *Program availability:* Part-time, evening/weekend, online learning. Offers accountancy (MS); business analytics (MS); business and economics (MA, MBA, MS); economics (MA); finance (MBA); human resources and organizational behavior (MBA); marketing management (MBA); operations and supply chain management (MBA); strategy and innovation (MBA). Electronic applications accepted.

College of Education and Allied Studies *Program availability:* Part-time, evening/weekend, online learning. Offers counseling (MS); education (MS); education and allied studies (MS, Ed D); educational leadership (MS, Ed D); kinesiology (MS); mild-moderate disabilities (MS); moderate-severe disabilities (MS); recreation and tourism (MS); special education (MS). Electronic applications accepted.

College of Letters, Arts, and Social Sciences *Program availability:* Part-time, evening/weekend, online learning. Offers anthropology (MA); children, youth, and family services (MSW); communication (MA); community mental health services (MSW); English (MA); geography (MA); health care administration (MPA, MS); history (MA); letters, arts, and social sciences (MA, MPA, MS, MSW); management and change in health care (MS); multimedia (MA); music (MA); public administration (MPA); public history (MA); public management and policy analysis (MPA); speech-language pathology (MS); teaching (MA); teaching English to speaker of other languages (MA). Electronic applications accepted.

College of Science *Program availability:* Part-time, evening/weekend. Offers actuarial science (MS); applied statistics (MS); biochemistry (MS); biostatistics (MS); computational statistics (MS); computer networks (MS); computer science (MS); construction management (MS); engineering management (MS); geology (MS); marine science (MA, MS); mathematical statistics (MS); mathematics teaching (MS); pure mathematics (MS); science (MA, MS); statistics (MS). Electronic applications accepted.

CALIFORNIA STATE UNIVERSITY, FRESNO, Fresno, CA 93740-8027

General Information State-supported, coed, comprehensive institution. CGS member. *Graduate housing:* Room and/or apartments available on a first-come, first-served basis to single students; on-campus housing not available to married students. Housing application deadline: 4/1. *Research affiliation:* Coleman Foundation (administration), Starburst Foundation (engineering), Garabedian Foundation (agribusiness), California Endowment (arts and humanities).

GRADUATE UNITS

Division of Research and Graduate Studies *Program availability:* Part-time, evening/weekend. Electronic applications accepted.

College of Arts and Humanities *Program availability:* Part-time, evening/weekend. Offers art (MA); arts and humanities (MA, MFA); communication (MA); creative writing (MFA); linguistics (MA); literature (MA); music (MA); music education (MA); performance (MA); rhetoric and writing studies (MA); Spanish (MA). Electronic applications accepted.

College of Health and Human Services *Program availability:* Part-time, evening/weekend. Offers communicative disorders (MA); exercise science (MA); general kinesiology (MA); health and human services (MA, MPH, MS, MSW, DNP, DPT); health policy and management (MPH); health promotion (MPH); nursing (MS, DNP); physical therapy (DPT); social work education (MSW); sport administration (MA); sport psychology (MA). Electronic applications accepted.

College of Science and Mathematics *Program availability:* Part-time, evening/weekend. Offers applied behavior analysis (MA); biology (MS); biotechnology (MBT); chemistry (MS); computer science (MS); general/experimental psychology (MA); geology (MS); marine science (MS); mathematics (MA); mathematics teaching (MA); physics (MS); school psychology (Ed S); science and mathematics (MA, MBT, MS, Ed S). Electronic applications accepted.

College of Social Sciences *Program availability:* Part-time, evening/weekend. Offers criminology (MS); history (MA); history teaching (MA); public administration (MPA); social sciences (MA, MPA, MS). Electronic applications accepted.

Craig School of Business *Program availability:* Part-time, blended/hybrid learning. Offers business (MBA). Electronic applications accepted.

Jordan College of Agricultural Sciences and Technology *Program availability:* Part-time, evening/weekend. Offers agricultural sciences and technology (MS); animal science (MS); industrial technology (MS); plant science (MS); viticulture and enology (MS). Electronic applications accepted.

Kremen School of Education and Human Development *Program availability:* Part-time, evening/weekend. Offers clinical rehabilitation and mental health counseling (MS); clinical rehabilitation and mental health counseling (MS); education (MA); education and human development (MA, MS, Ed D); educational leadership (MA,

Ed D); marriage, family and child counseling (MS); special education (MA); student affairs and college counseling (MS). Electronic applications accepted.

Lyles College of Engineering *Program availability:* Part-time, evening/weekend. Offers civil and geomatics engineering (MS); computer engineering (MSE); electrical engineering (MSE); engineering (MS, MSE); mechanical engineering (MS). Electronic applications accepted.

CALIFORNIA STATE UNIVERSITY, FULLERTON, Fullerton, CA 92831-3599

General Information State-supported, coed, comprehensive institution. CGS member. *Graduate housing:* Rooms and/or apartments available on a first-come, first-served basis to single and married students. Housing application deadline: 6/30. *Research affiliation:* U.S. Department of Interior (desert studies), County of Orange (demographic research), Department of Literacy and Reading Education, SchoolsFirst Federal Credit Union (creativity and critical thinking), California Office of Historic Preservation and the State Historic Resources Commission (South Central coastal information).

GRADUATE UNITS

Graduate Studies *Program availability:* Part-time, evening/weekend, online learning. Electronic applications accepted.

College of Business and Economics *Program availability:* Part-time. Offers accounting (MBA, MS); business administration (MBA); business analytics (MBA); business and economics (MA, MBA, MS); decision science (MBA); economics (MA, MBA); finance (MBA); information systems (MBA, MS); information systems and decision sciences (MS); information systems and e-commerce (MS); information technology (MS); international business (MBA); organizational leadership (MBA); risk management and insurance (MBA). Electronic applications accepted.

College of Communications *Program availability:* Part-time. Offers communication studies (MA); communications (MA, MFA); communications in tourism and entertainment (MA); communicative disorders (MA); mass communications research and theory (MA); professional communications (MA); screenwriting (MFA).

College of Education Offers bilingual/bicultural education (MS); education (MS, Ed D); educational administration (MS); educational leadership (Ed D); educational technology (MS); elementary curriculum and instruction (MS); instructional design and technology (MS); literacy and reading education (MS); special education (MS); teacher instruction (MS); teaching foundational mathematics (MS).

College of Engineering and Computer Science *Program availability:* Part-time. Offers civil engineering (MS); computer engineering (MS); computer science (MS); electrical engineering (MS); engineering and computer science (MS); mechanical engineering (MS); software engineering (MS); systems engineering (MS).

College of Health and Human Development *Program availability:* Part-time. Offers aging (MS); child welfare (MSW); community mental health (MSW); counseling (MS); environmental and occupational health and safety (MPH); gerontological health (MPH); health and human development (MPH, MS, MSW, DNP); health promotion and disease (MPH); kinesiology (MS); leadership (MS); nurse anesthesia (MS); nurse educator (MS); nursing (DNP); school nursing (MS); women's health care (MS).

College of Humanities and Social Sciences *Program availability:* Part-time. Offers American studies (MA); anthropology (MA); clinical psychology (MS); English (MA); environmental studies (MS); geography (MA); gerontology (MS); history (MA); humanities and social sciences (MA, MPA, MS); linguistics (MA); political science (MA); psychology (MA); public administration (MPA); sociology (MA); Spanish (MA).

College of Natural Science and Mathematics *Program availability:* Part-time. Offers applied mathematics (MA); biology (MS); biotechnology (MBT); chemistry (MA, MS); geological sciences (MS); mathematics education (MA); natural science and mathematics (MA, MBT, MS); physics (MS).

College of the Arts *Program availability:* Part-time. Offers art (MA, MFA); arts (MA, MFA, MM); music education (MA); performance (MM); theatre arts (MFA).

CALIFORNIA STATE UNIVERSITY, LONG BEACH, Long Beach, CA 90840

General Information State-supported, coed, comprehensive institution. *Enrollment:* 36,846 graduate, professional, and undergraduate students; 3,302 full-time matriculated graduate/professional students (2,203 women), 2,097 part-time matriculated graduate/professional students (1,302 women). *Required fees:* $2628 per term. Tuition and fees vary according to class time, course level, course load, degree level, campus/location and program. *Graduate housing:* Room and/or apartments available on a first-come, first-served basis to single students; on-campus housing not available to married students. Typical cost: $8994 per year. Room charges vary according to board plan. Housing application deadline: 5/1. *Student services:* Campus employment opportunities, campus safety program, career counseling, child daycare facilities, exercise/wellness program, free psychological counseling, grant writing training, international student services, low-cost health insurance, multicultural affairs office, services for students with disabilities, teacher training, writing training. *Library facilities:* CSULB University Library. *Collection:* Books: 681,649 (physical), 1 million (digital/electronic); Serial titles: 16,851 (physical), 105,038 (digital/electronic); Databases: 227. Weekly public service hours: 97.

Computer facilities: 2,000 computers available on campus for general student use. A campuswide network can be accessed from student residence rooms and from off campus. Online class registration is available.
Website: http://www.csulb.edu/

General Application Contact: Michelle Ramirez, Assistant to the Vice Provost, 562-985-8225, Fax: 562-985-1680, E-mail: michelle.ramirez@csulb.edu.

GRADUATE UNITS

Graduate Studies Expenses: Contact institution. *Financial support:* Fellowships, research assistantships, teaching assistantships, career-related internships or fieldwork, Federal Work-Study, institutionally sponsored loans, scholarships/grants, traineeships, tuition waivers (partial), and unspecified assistantships available. Financial award application deadline: 3/2; financial award applicants required to submit FAFSA. *Program availability:* Part-time, evening/weekend, online learning. *Application deadline:* For fall admission, 7/1 for domestic and international students; for spring admission, 12/1 for domestic and international students. Applications are processed on a rolling basis. *Application fee:* $55. Electronic applications accepted. *Application Contact:* Michelle Ramirez, Assistant to Vice Provost for Academic Programs and Dean of Graduate Studies, 562-985-8225, Fax: 562-985-7786, E-mail: michelle.ramirez@csulb.edu. *Vice Provost for Academic Programs and Dean of Graduate Studies,* Dr. Jody Cormack, 562-985-8225, Fax: 562-985-1680, E-mail: AA-Grad@csulb.edu.

College of Business Students: 74 full-time (29 women), 112 part-time (53 women); includes 105 minority (9 Black or African American, non-Hispanic/Latino; 34 Asian, non-Hispanic/Latino; 53 Hispanic/Latino; 2 Native Hawaiian or other Pacific Islander, non-Hispanic/Latino; 7 Two or more races, non-Hispanic/Latino), 21 international. Average age 32. Expenses: Contact institution. *Financial support:* Career-related internships or fieldwork and scholarships/grants available. Financial award application deadline: 3/2; financial award applicants required to submit FAFSA. *Program availability:* Part-time, evening/weekend. Offers business administration (MS). *Application deadline:* For fall admission, 6/1 for domestic students. Applications are processed on a rolling basis. *Application fee:* $55. Electronic applications accepted. *Application Contact:* Dr. Ingrid Martin, Director, Graduate Business Programs, 562-985-5565, Fax: 562-985-5742, E-mail: Ingrid.Martin@csulb.edu. *Dean,* Dr. Michael E. Solt, 562-985-5307, E-mail: Michael.Solt@csulb.edu.

College of Education Students: 1,287 full-time (897 women), 694 part-time (518 women); includes 1,236 minority (99 Black or African American, non-Hispanic/Latino; 3 American Indian or Alaska Native, non-Hispanic/Latino; 223 Asian, non-Hispanic/Latino; 825 Hispanic/Latino; 6 Native Hawaiian or other Pacific Islander, non-Hispanic/Latino; 80 Two or more races, non-Hispanic/Latino), 51 international. Average age 30. Expenses: Contact institution. *Financial support:* Federal Work-Study, institutionally sponsored loans, and scholarships/grants available. Financial award application deadline: 3/2; financial award applicants required to submit FAFSA. *Program availability:* Part-time, evening/weekend. Offers counseling (MS); education (MA, Ed D); educational administration (MA, Ed D); educational psychology (MA); elementary education (MA); secondary education (MA); special education (MS). *Application deadline:* Applications are processed on a rolling basis. *Application fee:* $55. Electronic applications accepted. *Application Contact:* Megan Duggan, Program Support Specialist, 562-985-5238, Fax: 562-985-7786, E-mail: megan.duggan@csulb.edu. *Dean,* Shireen Pavri, 562-985-4513, Fax: 562-985-4951.

College of Engineering Students: 211 full-time (53 women), 249 part-time (51 women); includes 200 minority (4 Black or African American, non-Hispanic/Latino; 79 Asian, non-Hispanic/Latino; 105 Hispanic/Latino; 12 Two or more races, non-Hispanic/Latino), 173 international. Average age 26. Expenses: Contact institution. *Financial support:* Research assistantships, teaching assistantships, career-related internships or fieldwork, Federal Work-Study, institutionally sponsored loans, scholarships/grants, and unspecified assistantships available. Financial award application deadline: 3/2; financial award applicants required to submit FAFSA. *Program availability:* Part-time, evening/weekend. Offers aerospace engineering (MSAE); civil engineering (MSCE); computer engineering (MSCS); computer science (MSCS); electrical engineering (MSEE); engineering (MS, MSAE, MSCE, MSCS, MSE, MSEE, MSME, PhD); engineering and industrial applied mathematics (PhD); interdisciplinary engineering (MSE); management engineering (MSE); mechanical engineering (MSME). *Application fee:* $55. Electronic applications accepted. *Application Contact:* Dr. Fieke Leij, Graduate Programs Coordinator, 562-437-5119, E-mail: feike.leij@csulb.edu. *Dean,* Dr. Forouzan Golshani, 562-985-5123, Fax: 562-985-7561, E-mail: coe-dean@csulb.edu.

College of Health and Human Services Students: 1,168 full-time (904 women), 480 part-time (387 women); includes 1,114 minority (89 Black or African American, non-Hispanic/Latino; 3 American Indian or Alaska Native, non-Hispanic/Latino; 289 Asian, non-Hispanic/Latino; 672 Hispanic/Latino; 7 Native Hawaiian or other Pacific Islander, non-Hispanic/Latino; 54 Two or more races, non-Hispanic/Latino), 53 international. Average age 30. Expenses: Contact institution. *Financial support:* Fellowships, research assistantships, teaching assistantships, career-related internships or fieldwork, Federal Work-Study, institutionally sponsored loans, and scholarships/grants available. Financial award application deadline: 3/2; financial award applicants required to submit FAFSA. *Program availability:* Part-time, evening/weekend, online learning. Offers adapted physical education (MA); coaching and student athlete development (MA); criminal justice (MS); emergency services administration (MS); exercise physiology and nutrition (MS); gerontology (MS); health and human services (MA, MPA, MPH, MS, MSN, MSW, DNP, DPT, Graduate Certificate); health care administration (MS); health science (MPH); individualized studies (MA); kinesiology (MA); nursing (MSN, DNP, Graduate Certificate); pedagogical studies (MA); physical therapy (DPT); public policy and administration (MPA, Graduate Certificate); recreation administration (MS); social work (MSW); speech-language pathology (MA); sport and exercise psychology (MS); sport management (MA); sports medicine and injury studies (MS). *Application deadline:* Applications are processed on a rolling basis. *Application fee:* $55. Electronic applications accepted. *Application Contact:* Monica Lounsbery, Dean, 562-985-5381, E-mail: Monica.Lounsbery@csulb.edu. *Dean,* Monica Lounsbery, 562-985-5381, E-mail: Monica.Lounsbery@csulb.edu.

College of Liberal Arts Students: 241 full-time (148 women), 236 part-time (141 women); includes 252 minority (20 Black or African American, non-Hispanic/Latino; 2 American Indian or Alaska Native, non-Hispanic/Latino; 46 Asian, non-Hispanic/Latino; 162 Hispanic/Latino; 2 Native Hawaiian or other Pacific Islander, non-Hispanic/Latino; 20 Two or more races, non-Hispanic/Latino), 31 international. Average age 29. Expenses: Contact institution. *Financial support:* Research assistantships, teaching assistantships, career-related internships or fieldwork, Federal Work-Study, institutionally sponsored loans, and scholarships/grants available. Financial award application deadline: 3/2; financial award applicants required to submit FAFSA. *Program availability:* Part-time, evening/weekend. Offers Africa and the Middle East (MA); anthropology (MA); applied anthropology (MA); Asian studies (MA); communication studies (MA); creative writing (MFA); economics (MA); English (MA); French and Francophone studies (MA); general linguistics (MA); geography (MA, MS); German (MA); human factors (MS); industrial/organizational psychology (MS); language and culture (MA); liberal arts (MA, MFA, MS, Graduate Certificate); philosophy (MA); political science (MA); psychology (MA); religious studies (MA); Spanish (MA); special concentration (MA); teaching English to speakers of other languages (MA, Graduate Certificate). *Application deadline:* For spring admission, 12/1 for international students. Applications are processed on a rolling basis. *Application fee:* $55. Electronic applications accepted. *Application Contact:* David Wallace, Dean, 562-985-5381, Fax: 562-985-2463. *Dean,* David Wallace, 562-985-5381, Fax: 562-985-2463.

College of Natural Sciences and Mathematics Students: 245 full-time (112 women), 107 part-time (41 women); includes 198 minority (14 Black or African American, non-Hispanic/Latino; 1 American Indian or Alaska Native, non-Hispanic/Latino; 71 Asian, non-Hispanic/Latino; 100 Hispanic/Latino; 12 Two or more races, non-Hispanic/Latino), 25 international. Average age 28. Expenses: Contact institution. *Financial support:* Research assistantships, teaching assistantships, Federal Work-Study, institutionally sponsored loans, scholarships/grants, traineeships, and unspecified assistantships available. Financial award application deadline: 3/2; financial award applicants required to submit FAFSA. *Program availability:* Part-time. Offers biochemistry (MS); biology (MS); chemistry (MS); geology (MS); mathematics (MS); microbiology (MS); natural sciences and mathematics (MS); physics (MS); science education (MS). *Application deadline:* Applications are processed on a rolling

basis. *Application fee:* $55. Electronic applications accepted. *Application Contact:* Babette Benken, Director for Graduate Studies, 562-985-4798, E-mail: babette.benken@csulb.edu. *Dean,* Dr. Curtis Bennett, 562-985-4707, Fax: 562-985-2315, E-mail: cnsm@csulb.edu.

College of the Arts Students: 39 full-time (19 women), 128 part-time (90 women); includes 71 minority (3 Black or African American, non-Hispanic/Latino; 19 Asian, non-Hispanic/Latino; 39 Hispanic/Latino; 10 Two or more races, non-Hispanic/Latino), 28 international. Average age 30. Expenses: Contact institution. *Financial support:* Research assistantships, teaching assistantships, Federal Work-Study, institutionally sponsored loans, scholarships/grants, and traineeships available. Financial award application deadline: 3/2; financial award applicants required to submit FAFSA. *Program availability:* Part-time. Offers acting (MFA); art education (MA); arts (MA, MFA, MM); composition (MM); dance (MA, MFA); music (MA); studio art (MFA). *Application deadline:* Applications are processed on a rolling basis. *Application fee:* $55. Electronic applications accepted. *Application Contact:* Margaret Black, Interim Dean, 562-985-4364, Fax: 562-985-7883, E-mail: cota@csulb.edu. *Interim Dean,* Margaret Black, 562-985-4364, Fax: 562-985-7883, E-mail: cota@csulb.edu.

CALIFORNIA STATE UNIVERSITY, LOS ANGELES, Los Angeles, CA 90032-8530

General Information State-supported, coed, comprehensive institution. CGS member. *Graduate housing:* Room and/or apartments available on a first-come, first-served basis to single students; on-campus housing not available to married students. *Research affiliation:* NASA (engineering), General Motors (engineering).

GRADUATE UNITS

Graduate Studies *Program availability:* Part-time, evening/weekend. Electronic applications accepted.

Charter College of Education *Program availability:* Part-time, evening/weekend. Offers applied and advanced studies in education (Graduate Certificate); counseling (MS); education (MA, MS, Ed D, PhD, Graduate Certificate); elementary teaching (MA); special education (MA, PhD). Electronic applications accepted.

College of Arts and Letters *Program availability:* Part-time, evening/weekend. Offers art (MA); arts and letters (MA, MFA, MM, Certificate, Graduate Certificate); communication studies (MA, MFA); English (MA, Certificate); fine arts (MFA); French (MA); music composition (MM); music education (MA); musicology (MA); performance (MM); philosophy (MA, Graduate Certificate); Spanish (MA); theater arts (MA). Electronic applications accepted.

College of Business and Economics *Program availability:* Part-time, evening/weekend. Offers accounting (MBA); business and economics (MA, MBA, MS, Postbaccalaureate Certificate); finance and banking (MBA, MS); financial economics (MA); global economics (MA); health care management (MS); international business (MBA, MS); management (MA, MBA, MS). Electronic applications accepted.

College of Engineering, Computer Science, and Technology *Program availability:* Part-time, evening/weekend. Offers civil engineering (MS); computer science (MS); electrical engineering (MS); engineering, computer science, and technology (MA, MS); industrial and technical studies (MA); mechanical engineering (MS). Electronic applications accepted.

College of Health and Human Services *Program availability:* Part-time, evening/weekend. Offers child development (MA); criminal justice (MS); criminalistics (MS); health and human services (MA, MS, MSW, Certificate, Post Master's Certificate); nursing (MS, Post Master's Certificate); nutritional science (MS); physical education and kinesiology (MA); social work (MSW); speech and hearing (MS); speech-language pathology (MA). Electronic applications accepted.

College of Natural and Social Sciences *Program availability:* Part-time, evening/weekend. Offers analytical chemistry (MS); anthropology (MA); biology (MS); geography (MA); geological sciences (MS); history (MA); Latin American studies (MA); mathematics (MS); Mexican-American studies (MA); natural and social sciences (MA, MS); physics (MS); political science (MA); psychology (MA, MS); public administration (MS); sociology (MA).

CALIFORNIA STATE UNIVERSITY MARITIME ACADEMY, Vallejo, CA 94590

General Information State-supported, coed, comprehensive institution. *Enrollment:* 34 full-time matriculated graduate/professional students (6 women). *Enrollment by degree level:* 34 master's. *Graduate faculty:* 13 part-time/adjunct (2 women). *Graduate housing:* On-campus housing not available. *Student services:* Campus employment opportunities, career counseling, services for students with disabilities, writing training.

Computer facilities: A campuswide network can be accessed. Online class registration is available.
Website: http://www.csum.edu/

General Application Contact: Kathy Arnold, Graduate Program Coordinator, 707-654-1271, Fax: 707-654-1158, E-mail: karnold@csum.edu.

GRADUATE UNITS

Graduate Studies Students: 34 full-time (6 women); includes 10 minority (2 Black or African American, non-Hispanic/Latino; 4 Asian, non-Hispanic/Latino; 4 Hispanic/Latino), 2 international. Average age 38. 21 applicants, 86% accepted, 16 enrolled. *Faculty:* 13 part-time/adjunct (2 women). Expenses: Contact institution. *Financial support:* Applicants required to submit FAFSA. In 2018, 19 master's awarded. *Program availability:* Evening/weekend, online only, 100% online. Offers transportation and engineering management (MS). *Application deadline:* Applications are processed on a rolling basis. *Application fee:* $55. Electronic applications accepted. *Application Contact:* Kathy Arnold, Program Coordinator, 707-654-1271, Fax: 707-654-1158, E-mail: karnold@csum.edu. *Associate Vice President, Academic Affairs,* Dr. Graham Benton, 707-654-1147, E-mail: gbenton@csum.edu.

CALIFORNIA STATE UNIVERSITY, MONTEREY BAY, Seaside, CA 93955-8001

General Information State-supported, coed, comprehensive institution. *Graduate housing:* Rooms and/or apartments available on a first-come, first-served basis to single and married students.

GRADUATE UNITS

College of Business *Program availability:* Part-time, evening/weekend, online learning. Offers business (MBA). Electronic applications accepted.

College of Education *Program availability:* Part-time, evening/weekend. Offers education (MAE). Electronic applications accepted.

College of Health Sciences and Human Services *Program availability:* Part-time. Offers social work (MSW). Electronic applications accepted.

College of Science *Program availability:* Part-time. Offers applied marine and watershed science (MS); marine science (MS); science (MS, MSMIT). Electronic applications accepted.

School of Computing and Design Offers computing and design (MS, MSMIT). MSMIT offered in conjunction with College of Business. Electronic applications accepted.

CALIFORNIA STATE UNIVERSITY, NORTHRIDGE, Northridge, CA 91330

General Information State-supported, coed, comprehensive institution. *Graduate housing:* Room and/or apartments available to single students; on-campus housing not available to married students. *Research affiliation:* Haagen Company (archaeology), Northridge Hospital (biology), Warner Center Institute (child care), Jet Propulsion Laboratory (engineering), Hughes Aircraft Corporation (engineering), California Institute of Technology (science).

GRADUATE UNITS

Graduate Studies *Program availability:* Part-time, evening/weekend. Electronic applications accepted.

College of Engineering and Computer Science *Program availability:* Part-time, evening/weekend. Offers computer science (MS); electrical engineering (MS); engineering (MS); engineering and computer science (MS); engineering automation (MS); engineering management (MS); manufacturing systems engineering (MS); materials engineering (MS); mechanical engineering (MS); software engineering (MS).

College of Health and Human Development *Program availability:* Part-time, evening/weekend. Offers audiology (MS); environmental and occupational health (MS); family and consumer sciences (MS); health administration (MS); health and human development (MPH, MPT, MS); hospitality and tourism (MS); industrial hygiene (MS); kinesiology (MS); physical therapy (MPT); public health (MPH); recreational sport management/campus recreation (MS); speech language pathology (MS).

College of Humanities *Program availability:* Part-time, evening/weekend. Offers Chicana and Chicano studies (MA); creative writing (MA); humanities (MA); linguistics (MA); literature (MA); rhetoric and composition theory (MA); Spanish (MA).

College of Science and Mathematics *Program availability:* Part-time, evening/weekend. Offers applied mathematics (MS); biochemistry (MS); biology (MS); chemistry (MS); geology (MS); mathematics (MS); physics (MS); science and mathematics (MS).

College of Social and Behavioral Sciences *Program availability:* Part-time, evening/weekend. Offers clinical psychology (MA); general anthropology (MA); general experimental psychology (MA); geography (MA); history (MA); political science (MA); public archaeology (MA); social and behavioral sciences (MA, MSW); social work (MSW); sociology (MA).

David Nazarian College of Business and Economics *Program availability:* Part-time. Offers business and economics (MBA).

Michael D. Eisner College of Education *Program availability:* Part-time, evening/weekend. Offers counseling (MS); curriculum and instruction (MA); early childhood special education (MA); education (MA, MA Ed, MS, Ed D); education of the deaf and hard of hearing (MA); educational administration (MA); educational leadership (Ed D); educational psychology (MA Ed); educational technology (MA); educational therapy (MA); English education (MA); language and literacy (MA); mathematics education (MA); mild/moderate disabilities (MA); moderate/severe disabilities (MA); multilingual/multicultural education (MA); secondary science education (MA); teaching and learning (MA).

Mike Curb College of Arts, Media, and Communication *Program availability:* Part-time, evening/weekend. Offers art education (MA); art history (MA); arts, media, and communication (MA, MFA, MM); communication studies (MA); composition (MM); conducting (MM); mass communication (MA); music education (MM); performance (MM); screenwriting (MA); studio art (MA, MFA); theatre (MA); visual communications (MA, MFA).

Tseng College Offers business administration (Graduate Certificate); health administration (MPA); health education (MPH); knowledge management (MKM); music industry administration (MA); nonprofit-sector management (Graduate Certificate); public administration (MPA); public sector management and leadership (MPA); social work (MSW); taxation (MS); tourism, hospitality and recreation management (MS).

CALIFORNIA STATE UNIVERSITY, SACRAMENTO, Sacramento, CA 95819

General Information State-supported, coed, comprehensive institution. CGS member. *Graduate housing:* Room and/or apartments available on a first-come, first-served basis to single students; on-campus housing not available to married students.

GRADUATE UNITS

College of Arts and Letters *Program availability:* Part-time, evening/weekend. Offers arts and letters (MA, MM, PhD); communication studies (MA); composition (MA, MM); conducting (MM); creative writing (MA); history (MA); literature (MA); performance (MM); public historical studies (PhD); public history (MA); studio art (MA); teaching English to speakers of other languages (MA); world languages and literatures (MA). Electronic applications accepted.

College of Business Administration *Program availability:* Part-time, evening/weekend, 100% online, blended/hybrid learning. Offers accountancy (MS); business administration (IMBA, MBA); human resources (MBA); urban land development (MBA). Electronic applications accepted.

College of Education *Program availability:* Part-time, evening/weekend, blended/hybrid learning. Offers behavioral science and gender equity (MA); child development (MA); counseling (MS); curriculum and instruction (MA); education (MA, MS, Ed D, Ed S); education leadership and policy studies (MA); education specialist (Ed S); educational technology (MA); language and literacy (MA); multicultural education (MA); school psychology (MA); special education (MA); workforce development advocacy (MA). Electronic applications accepted.

College of Engineering and Computer Science *Program availability:* Part-time, evening/weekend. Offers civil engineering (MS); computer science (MS); electrical and electronic engineering (MS); engineering and computer science (MS); mechanical engineering (MS); software engineering (MS). Electronic applications accepted.

College of Health and Human Services *Program availability:* Part-time, evening/weekend. Offers communication sciences and disorders (MS); exercise science (MS); health and human services (MS, MSW, DPT); movement studies (MS); physical therapy (DPT); recreation, parks and tourism administration (MS). Electronic applications accepted.

Division of Criminal Justice *Program availability:* Part-time. Offers criminal justice (MS). Electronic applications accepted.

Division of Social Work *Program availability:* Part-time, evening/weekend. Offers family and children's services (MSW). Electronic applications accepted.

School of Nursing *Program availability:* Part-time. Offers nursing (MS). Electronic applications accepted.

College of Natural Sciences and Mathematics *Program availability:* Part-time. Offers biochemistry (MS); biological conservation (MS); chemistry (MS); mathematics (MA); molecular and cellular biology (MS); natural sciences and mathematics (MA, MS); stem cell (MA). Electronic applications accepted.

College of Social Sciences and Interdisciplinary Studies *Program availability:* Part-time. Offers anthropology (MA); applied behavior analysis (MA); government (MA); industrial/organizational psychology (MA); public policy and administration (MPPA); social sciences and interdisciplinary studies (MA, MPPA); sociology (MA). Electronic applications accepted.

CALIFORNIA STATE UNIVERSITY, SAN BERNARDINO, San Bernardino, CA 92407

General Information State-supported, coed, comprehensive institution. CGS member. *Enrollment:* 19,973 graduate, professional, and undergraduate students; 721 full-time matriculated graduate/professional students (508 women), 1,035 part-time matriculated graduate/professional students (661 women). *Enrollment by degree level:* 1,688 master's, 68 doctoral. *Graduate faculty:* 134 full-time (68 women), 81 part-time/adjunct (50 women). *Graduate housing:* Room and/or apartments available on a first-come, first-served basis to single students; on-campus housing not available to married students. *Student services:* Campus employment opportunities, campus safety program, career counseling, child daycare facilities, exercise/wellness program, free psychological counseling, international student services, low-cost health insurance, multicultural affairs office, services for students with disabilities, teacher training. *Library facilities:* Pfau Library.

Computer facilities: Computer purchase and lease plans are available. A campuswide network can be accessed from student residence rooms and from off campus. Online class registration is available.
Website: http://www.csusb.edu/

General Application Contact: Dr. Dorota Huizinga, Dean of Graduate Studies, 909-537-5058, Fax: 909-537-5078, E-mail: dorota.huizinga@csusb.edu.

GRADUATE UNITS

Graduate Studies Students: 721 full-time (508 women), 1,035 part-time (661 women); includes 1,082 minority (129 Black or African American, non-Hispanic/Latino; 1 American Indian or Alaska Native, non-Hispanic/Latino; 85 Asian, non-Hispanic/Latino; 811 Hispanic/Latino; 4 Native Hawaiian or other Pacific Islander, non-Hispanic/Latino; 52 Two or more races, non-Hispanic/Latino), 164 international. Average age 32. 1,791 applicants, 49% accepted, 622 enrolled. *Faculty:* 134 full-time (68 women), 81 part-time/adjunct (50 women). *Expenses:* Contact institution. In 2018, 744 master's, 12 doctorates awarded. *Program availability:* Part-time, evening/weekend. Offers integrative studies (MA). *Application deadline:* For fall admission, 7/17 for domestic students. *Application fee:* $55. *Application Contact:* Olivia Rosas, Director of Admissions, 909-537-7577, Fax: 909-537-7034, E-mail: orosas@csusb.edu. *Dean,* Dr. Dorota Huizinga, 909-537-5058, Fax: 909-537-5078, E-mail: dorota.huizinga@csusb.edu.

College of Arts and Letters Students: 26 full-time (17 women), 98 part-time (66 women); includes 73 minority (12 Black or African American, non-Hispanic/Latino; 5 Asian, non-Hispanic/Latino; 52 Hispanic/Latino; 4 Two or more races, non-Hispanic/Latino), 7 international. Average age 33. 71 applicants, 58% accepted, 27 enrolled. *Faculty:* 19 full-time (14 women), 1 part-time/adjunct (0 women). Expenses: Contact institution. *Financial support:* Application deadline: 3/1. In 2018, 37 master's awarded. *Program availability:* Part-time, evening/weekend. Offers arts and letters (MA, MFA); communication studies (MA); creative writing (MFA); English composition (MA); integrated marketing communication (MA); Spanish (MA); studio art (MA). *Application deadline:* For fall admission, 7/17 priority date for domestic students. Applications are processed on a rolling basis. *Application fee:* $55. Electronic applications accepted. *Application Contact:* Dr. Dorota Huizinga, Dean of Graduate Studies, 909-537-3064, Fax: 909-537-5078, E-mail: rchuang@csusb.edu. *Interim Dean,* Dr. Rueyling Chuang, 909-537-5800, E-mail: rchuang@csusb.edu.

College of Business and Public Administration Students: 103 full-time (49 women), 386 part-time (199 women); includes 273 minority (32 Black or African American, non-Hispanic/Latino; 29 Asian, non-Hispanic/Latino; 195 Hispanic/Latino; 2 Native Hawaiian or other Pacific Islander, non-Hispanic/Latino; 15 Two or more races, non-Hispanic/Latino), 84 international. Average age 32. 541 applicants, 58% accepted, 189 enrolled. *Faculty:* 19 full-time (5 women), 16 part-time/adjunct (4 women). Expenses: Contact institution. *Financial support:* Application deadline: 3/1. In 2018, 214 master's awarded. *Program availability:* Part-time, evening/weekend. Offers accountancy (MSA); accounting (MBA); business and public administration (MBA, MPA, MSA); entrepreneurship (MBA); finance (MBA); global business (MBA); information management (MBA); information security (MBA); management (MBA); public administration (MPA); supply chain management (MBA). *Application deadline:* For fall admission, 7/17 for domestic students. Applications are processed on a rolling basis. *Application fee:* $55. *Application Contact:* Dr. Dorota Huizinga, Dean of Graduate Studies, 909-537-3064, Fax: 909-537-5078, E-mail: dorota.huizinga@csusb.edu. *Dean,* Dr. Lawrence C. Rose, 909-537-3703, E-mail: lrose@csusb.edu.

College of Education Students: 289 full-time (217 women), 299 part-time (227 women); includes 370 minority (46 Black or African American, non-Hispanic/Latino; 1 American Indian or Alaska Native, non-Hispanic/Latino; 28 Asian, non-Hispanic/Latino; 282 Hispanic/Latino; 1 Native Hawaiian or other Pacific Islander, non-Hispanic/Latino; 12 Two or more races, non-Hispanic/Latino), 45 international. Average age 35. 335 applicants, 68% accepted, 184 enrolled. *Faculty:* 32 full-time (19 women), 41 part-time/adjunct (30 women). Expenses: Contact institution. In 2018, 244 master's, 12 doctorates awarded. *Program availability:* Part-time, evening/weekend. Offers counseling and guidance (MS); education (MA, MS, Ed D); educational administration (MA); educational leadership: community college (MA); educational leadership: P-12 (Ed D); rehabilitation counseling (MA). *Application deadline:* For fall admission, 7/17 for domestic students. *Application fee:* $55. *Application Contact:* Dr. Dorota Huizinga, Dean of Graduate Studies, 909-537-3604, E-mail: dorota.huizinga@csusb.edu. *Dean,* Dr. Chinaka DomNwachukwu, 909-537-5645, E-mail: Chinaka.domnwachukwu@csusb.edu.

College of Natural Sciences Students: 63 full-time (39 women), 115 part-time (70 women); includes 111 minority (11 Black or African American, non-Hispanic/Latino; 11 Asian, non-Hispanic/Latino; 82 Hispanic/Latino; 1 Native Hawaiian or other Pacific Islander, non-Hispanic/Latino; 6 Two or more races, non-Hispanic/Latino), 22 international. Average age 29. 277 applicants, 34% accepted, 66 enrolled. *Faculty:* 24

California State University, San Bernardino

full-time (10 women), 5 part-time/adjunct (1 woman). Expenses: Contact institution. *Financial support:* Fellowships, research assistantships, and teaching assistantships available. In 2018, 81 master's awarded. *Program availability:* Part-time. Offers biology (MS); computer science (MS); earth and environmental sciences (MS); health services administration (MS); mathematics (MA); natural sciences (MA, MAT, MPH, MS, MSN); nursing (MSN); public health (MPH); teaching mathematics (MAT). *Application fee:* $55. *Application Contact:* Dr. Dorota Huizinga, Dean of Graduate Studies, 909-537-3064, Interim Dean, Dr. Sally McGill, 909-537-3304, Fax: 909-537-7005, E-mail: smcgill@csusb.edu.

College of Social and Behavioral Sciences Students: 237 full-time (185 women), 134 part-time (96 women); includes 252 minority (27 Black or African American, non-Hispanic/Latino; 12 Asian, non-Hispanic/Latino; 198 Hispanic/Latino; 15 Two or more races, non-Hispanic/Latino), 6 international. Average age 29. 563 applicants, 37% accepted, 139 enrolled. *Faculty:* 40 full-time (20 women), 18 part-time/adjunct (15 women). Expenses: Contact institution. *Financial support:* Career-related internships or fieldwork, Federal Work-Study, institutionally sponsored loans, and unspecified assistantships available. Support available to part-time students. In 2018, 166 master's awarded. *Program availability:* Part-time, evening/weekend. Offers child development (MA); clinical psychology (MS); clinical/counseling psychology (MS); criminal justice (MA); industrial/organizational psychology (MS); national cyber security studies (MA); national security studies (MA); psychological science (MA); psychology-life span (MA); social and behavioral sciences (MA, MS, MSW); social sciences and globalization (MA); social work (MSW). *Application deadline:* For fall admission, 7/17 for domestic students. *Application fee:* $55. *Application Contact:* Dr. Dorota Huizinga, Dean of Graduate Studies, 909-537-3064, E-mail: dorota.huizinga@csusb.edu. *Dean,* Dr. Rafik Mohamed, 909-537-7500, Fax: 909-537-7107, E-mail: rafik.mohamed@csusb.edu.

CALIFORNIA STATE UNIVERSITY, SAN MARCOS, San Marcos, CA 92096-0001

General Information State-supported, coed, comprehensive institution. *Enrollment:* 14,504 graduate, professional, and undergraduate students; 395 full-time matriculated graduate/professional students (265 women), 147 part-time matriculated graduate/professional students (90 women). *Enrollment by degree level:* 571 master's. *Graduate housing:* Room and/or apartments available on a first-come, first-served basis to single students; on-campus housing not available to married students. Housing application deadline: 10/1. *Student services:* Campus employment opportunities, campus safety program, career counseling, child daycare facilities, exercise/wellness program, free psychological counseling, international student services, low-cost health insurance, multicultural affairs office, services for students with disabilities, teacher training, writing training. *Library facilities:* Kellogg Library. *Collection:* 215,402 (physical), 268,189 (digital/electronic); Serial titles: 3,130 (physical), 81,643 (digital/electronic); Databases: 100. Weekly public service hours: 100; students can reserve study rooms.

Computer facilities: A campuswide network can be accessed from student residence rooms and from off campus. Online class registration is available. Website: http://www.csusm.edu/

General Application Contact: Dr. Wesley Schultz, Dean of Office of Graduate Studies and Research, 760-750-8045, Fax: 760-750-8045, E-mail: apply@csusm.edu.

GRADUATE UNITS

School of Education Expenses: Contact institution. *Financial support:* Applicants required to submit FAFSA. *Program availability:* Part-time, evening/weekend. Offers education (MA); educational administration (MA); educational leadership (Ed D); literacy education (MA); special education (MA). *Application deadline:* For fall admission, 2/1 priority date for domestic students. Applications are processed on a rolling basis. *Application fee:* $55. *Application Contact:* Dr. Wesley Schultz, Dean of Office of Graduate Studies and Research, 760-750-8045, Fax: 760-750-8045, E-mail: apply@csusm.edu. *Director,* Pat Stall, 760-750-4386, E-mail: pstall@csusm.edu.

School of Nursing Expenses: Contact institution. Offers advanced practice nursing (MSN); clinical nurse leader (MSN); nursing education (MSN). *Application Contact:* Dr. Wesley Schultz, Dean of Office of Graduate Studies and Research, 760-750-8045, Fax: 760-750-8045, E-mail: apply@csusm.edu. *Director,* Lorna Kendrick, 760-750-7580, E-mail: lkendrick@csusm.edu.

College of Humanities, Arts, Behavioral and Social Sciences Expenses: Contact institution. *Program availability:* Part-time, evening/weekend. Offers Hispanic cultures and society (MA); Hispanic language and linguistics (MA); Hispanic literatures and literary theory (MA); history (MA); humanities, arts, behavioral and social sciences (MA); literature and writing studies (MA); psychological science (MA); sociological practice (MA). *Application deadline:* For fall admission, 11/30 priority date for domestic students; for spring admission, 8/31 priority date for domestic students. Applications are processed on a rolling basis. *Application fee:* $55. Electronic applications accepted. *Application Contact:* Dr. Wesley Schultz, Dean of Office of Graduate Studies and Research, 760-750-8045, Fax: 760-750-8045, E-mail: apply@csusm.edu. *Dean,* Dr. Julia Johnson, 760-750-4195, E-mail: jjohnson@csusm.edu.

College of Science and Mathematics Expenses: Contact institution. Offers biology (MS); computer science (MS); cybersecurity (MS); mathematics (MS); science and mathematics (MS). *Application Contact:* Dr. Wesley Schultz, Dean of Office of Graduate Studies and Research, 760-750-8045, Fax: 760-750-8045, E-mail: apply@csusm.edu. *Dean,* Dr. Katherine Kantardjieff, 760-750-7240, E-mail: kkantard@csusm.edu.

Program in Biotechnology Expenses: Contact institution. Offers biotechnology (PSM). *Application Contact:* JoAnne Mendez, Coordinator, 760-750-8797, E-mail: jmendez@csusm.edu. *Director,* Dr. Betsy Read, 760-750-4129, E-mail: bread@csusm.edu.

CALIFORNIA STATE UNIVERSITY, STANISLAUS, Turlock, CA 95382

General Information State-supported, coed, comprehensive institution. CGS member. *Graduate housing:* Room and/or apartments available on a first-come, first-served basis to single students; on-campus housing not available to married students. Housing application deadline: 7/15. *Research affiliation:* Mathematical Association of America (mathematics), Kaiser Permanente (health care), California Campus Compact-Carnegie Fellowship Program (teaching development for faculty), Valley Mountain Regional Center (development disability), Friends of Turlock Library, EDAW, Inc. (environmental sustainable development).

GRADUATE UNITS

College of Business Administration *Program availability:* Part-time, evening/weekend. Offers business administration (EMBA, MBA).

College of Education, Kinesiology and Social Work *Program availability:* Part-time, evening/weekend. Offers community college leadership (Ed D); curriculum and instruction (MA); education, kinesiology and social work (MA, MSW, Ed D); P-12 leadership (Ed D); school administration (MA); school counseling (MA); social work (MSW).

College of Natural Sciences Offers ecological conservation (MS); genetic counseling (MS); natural sciences (MS).

College of Science Offers behavior analysis (MA, MS); counseling psychology (MS); general psychology (MA); gerontological nursing (MS); nursing education (MS); science (MA, MS).

College of the Arts, Humanities and Social Sciences Offers arts, humanities and social sciences (MA, MPA, MS, Certificate); criminal justice (MA); history (MA); interdisciplinary studies (MA, MS); literature (Certificate); public administration (MPA); rhetoric and teaching writing (MA); teaching English to speakers of other languages (MA).

CALIFORNIA UNIVERSITY OF MANAGEMENT AND SCIENCES, Anaheim, CA 92801

General Information Independent, coed, comprehensive institution.

GRADUATE UNITS

Graduate Programs Offers business administration (MBA, DBA); computer information systems (MS); economics (MS); international business (MS); sports management (MS).

CALIFORNIA UNIVERSITY OF PENNSYLVANIA, California, PA 15419-1394

General Information State-supported, coed, comprehensive institution. CGS member. *Graduate housing:* Room and/or apartments available on a first-come, first-served basis to single students; on-campus housing not available to married students. *Research affiliation:* The Center for Rural Pennsylvania (agriculture), The Technology Collaborative (robotics), International Technical Education Association (curricular development), National Collegiate Athletic Association (NCAA) (tobacco use), Gettysburg Travel Council (travel and tourism), NASA.

GRADUATE UNITS

School of Graduate Studies and Research *Program availability:* Part-time, evening/weekend, 100% online. Electronic applications accepted.

College of Education and Human Services *Program availability:* Part-time, evening/weekend, online learning. Offers advanced studies in secondary education and teacher leadership (M Ed); applied sport science (MS); athletic training (MS); autism (M Ed); clinical mental health counseling (MS); communication disorders (MS); early childhood education (M Ed); education administration and leadership (Ed D); education and human services (M Ed, MAT, MS, MSW, Ed D); educational leadership (M Ed); elementary education (M Ed); exercise science (MS); general special education (M Ed); group fitness leadership (MS); nutrition (MS); reading specialist (M Ed); school counseling (M Ed); secondary education (MAT); social work (MSW); sport management studies (MS); STEM education (M Ed); strategic sport analysis (MS); technology education (M Ed); wellness coaching (MS). Electronic applications accepted.

College of Liberal Arts *Program availability:* Part-time, evening/weekend. Offers conflict resolution (MA); criminal justice studies (MA); legal studies (MS); liberal arts (MA, MS); school psychology (MS); social science (MA). Electronic applications accepted.

Eberly College of Science and Technology *Program availability:* Part-time, evening/weekend, online learning. Offers business analytics (MBA); cybersecurity (PSM); entrepreneurship (MBA); healthcare management (MBA); nursing administration and leadership (MSN); nursing education (MSN); science and technology (MBA, MSN, PSM). Electronic applications accepted.

CALIFORNIA WESTERN SCHOOL OF LAW, San Diego, CA 92101-3090

General Information Independent, coed, graduate-only institution. *Graduate housing:* On-campus housing not available.

GRADUATE UNITS

Graduate and Professional Programs *Program availability:* Part-time. Offers law (JD); Spanish language in trial advocacy (LL M). JD/MSW and JD/MBA offered jointly with San Diego State University. Electronic applications accepted.

CALUMET COLLEGE OF SAINT JOSEPH, Whiting, IN 46394-2195

General Information Independent-religious, coed, comprehensive institution.

GRADUATE UNITS

Program in Leadership in Teaching Offers leadership in teaching (MS Ed).
Program in Public Safety Administration Offers public safety administration (MS).
Program in Quality Assurance Offers quality assurance (MS).

CALVARY UNIVERSITY, Kansas City, MO 64147

General Information Independent-religious, coed, comprehensive institution. *Graduate housing:* Rooms and/or apartments available on a first-come, first-served basis to single and married students.

GRADUATE UNITS

Graduate School and Seminary *Program availability:* Part-time, evening/weekend. Offers Bible and theology (MS); Biblical counseling (MA); education (MS); organizational development (MS); pastoral studies (M Div); worship arts (MS). Electronic applications accepted.

CALVIN COLLEGE, Grand Rapids, MI 49546-4388

General Information Independent-religious, coed, comprehensive institution. *Graduate housing:* Room and/or apartments available on a first-come, first-served basis to single students; on-campus housing not available to married students. Housing application deadline: 4/1.

GRADUATE UNITS

Graduate Programs in Education *Program availability:* Part-time. Offers curriculum and instruction (M Ed). Electronic applications accepted.
Program in Accounting *Program availability:* Part-time. Offers accounting (M Acc).
Program in Speech Pathology Offers speech pathology (MA).

CALVIN THEOLOGICAL SEMINARY, Grand Rapids, MI 49546-4387

General Information Independent-religious, coed, graduate-only institution. *Graduate housing:* Rooms and/or apartments available on a first-come, first-served basis to single and married students. Housing application deadline: 4/1.

GRADUATE UNITS

Graduate and Professional Programs *Program availability:* Part-time. Offers Bible and theology (MA); divinity (M Div); educational ministry (MA); historical theology (PhD); missions and evangelism (MA); pastoral care (MA); philosophical and moral theology (PhD); systematic theology (PhD); theological studies (MTS); theology (Th M); worship (MA); youth and family ministries (MA). Electronic applications accepted.

CAMBRIDGE COLLEGE, Boston, MA 02129

General Information Independent, coed, comprehensive institution. *Enrollment:* 698 full-time matriculated graduate/professional students (549 women), 806 part-time matriculated graduate/professional students (629 women). *Graduate housing:* On-campus housing not available. *Student services:* Career counseling, international student services, services for students with disabilities, writing training. *Library facilities:* Cambridge College Online Library.

Computer facilities: Computer purchase and lease plans are available. A campuswide network can be accessed from off campus. Online class registration is available. Website: http://www.cambridgecollege.edu/

General Application Contact: Salvadore Liberto, Interim Assistant Vice President of Enrollment, 800-877-4723, E-mail: admissions@cambridgecollege.edu.

GRADUATE UNITS

School of Education Expenses: Contact institution. *Financial support:* Career-related internships or fieldwork, Federal Work-Study, and scholarships/grants available. Financial award applicants required to submit FAFSA. *Program availability:* Part-time, evening/weekend, online learning. Offers autism specialist (M Ed); autism/behavior analyst (M Ed); behavior analyst (Post-Master's Certificate); curriculum and instruction (CAGS); early childhood teacher (M Ed); educational leadership (M Ed, Ed D); elementary teacher (M Ed); English as a second language (M Ed, Certificate); general science (M Ed); health education (Post-Master's Certificate); interdisciplinary studies (M Ed); library teacher (M Ed); mathematics education (M Ed); mathematics specialist (Certificate); school administration (M Ed, CAGS); school nurse education (M Ed); teacher of students with moderate disabilities (M Ed); teaching skills and methodologies (M Ed). *Application deadline:* Applications are processed on a rolling basis. *Application fee:* $30. Electronic applications accepted. *Application Contact:* Salvadore Liberto, Interim Assistant Vice President of Enrollment, 800-877-4723, E-mail: admissions@cambridgecollege.edu. *Interim Dean,* Dr. Mary Garrity, 617-873-0168, E-mail: mary.garrity@cambridgecollege.edu.

School of Management Expenses: Contact institution. *Financial support:* Career-related internships or fieldwork, Federal Work-Study, and scholarships/grants available. Financial award applicants required to submit FAFSA. *Program availability:* Part-time, evening/weekend, 100% online, blended/hybrid learning. Offers business administration (MBA); business negotiation and conflict resolution (M Mgt); general business (M Mgt); health care (MBA); health care management (M Mgt); small business development (M Mgt); technology management (M Mgt). *Application deadline:* Applications are processed on a rolling basis. *Application fee:* $50 ($100 for international students). Electronic applications accepted. *Application Contact:* Salvadore Liberto, Interim Assistant Vice President of Enrollment, 800-877-4723, E-mail: admissions@cambridgecollege.edu. *Interim Dean,* Joseph Miglio, E-mail: joseph.miglio@cambridgecollege.edu.

School of Psychology and Counseling Expenses: Contact institution. *Financial support:* Career-related internships or fieldwork, Federal Work-Study, and scholarships/grants available. Financial award applicants required to submit FAFSA. *Program availability:* Part-time, evening/weekend. Offers alcohol and drug counseling (Certificate); behavioral health care management (CAGS); marriage and family therapy (M Ed); mental health and school counseling (M Ed); mental health counseling (M Ed); psychological studies (M Ed); rehabilitation counseling (Certificate); school adjustment and mental health counseling (M Ed); school adjustment counseling for mental health counselors (Certificate); school counseling (M Ed); trauma studies (Certificate). *Application deadline:* Applications are processed on a rolling basis. *Application fee:* $50 ($100 for international students). Electronic applications accepted. *Application Contact:* Salvadore Liberto, Interim Assistant Vice President of Enrollment, 800-877-4723, E-mail: admissions@cambridgecollege.edu. *Dean,* Dr. Niti Seth, 617-873-0208, Fax: 617-349-3561, E-mail: niti.seth@cambridgecollege.edu.

CAMERON UNIVERSITY, Lawton, OK 73505-6377

General Information State-supported, coed, comprehensive institution. *Graduate housing:* Room and/or apartments available on a first-come, first-served basis to single students; on-campus housing not available to married students. *Research affiliation:* Telos OK, LLC (simulations), Army Research Institute (human factors), Advanced Systems Technology, Inc. (informational systems), Dynamics Research Corporation (multimedia systems), Eagle Systems, Inc. (multimedia systems), Halliburton (energy systems).

GRADUATE UNITS

Office of Graduate Studies *Program availability:* Part-time, evening/weekend, online learning. Offers behavioral sciences (MS); business administration (MBA); education (M Ed); educational leadership (MS); entrepreneurial studies (MS); teaching (MAT). Electronic applications accepted.

CAMPBELLSVILLE UNIVERSITY, Campbellsville, KY 42718-2799

General Information Independent-religious, coed, comprehensive institution. *Enrollment:* 12,629 graduate, professional, and undergraduate students; 7,216 full-time matriculated graduate/professional students (2,060 women), 274 part-time matriculated graduate/professional students (142 women). *Enrollment by degree level:* 7,477 master's, 13 doctoral. *Graduate faculty:* 94 full-time (41 women), 109 part-time/adjunct (75 women). *Tuition:* Full-time $408; part-time $408 per credit hour. *Required fees:* $75 per term. Tuition and fees vary according to degree level, campus/location and program. *Graduate housing:* Room and/or apartments available on a first-come, first-served basis to single students; on-campus housing not available to married students. Housing application deadline: 6/30. *Student services:* Campus employment opportunities, campus safety program, career counseling, exercise/wellness program, international student services, services for students with disabilities, teacher training, writing training. *Library facilities:* Montgomery Library. *Collection:* Books: 125,057 (physical), 351,230 (digital/electronic); Serial titles: 7,762 (digital/electronic); Databases: 94. Weekly public service hours: 77; students can reserve study rooms.

Computer facilities: 220 computers available on campus for general student use. A campuswide network can be accessed from student residence rooms and from off campus. Online class registration is available. Website: http://www.campbellsville.edu/

General Application Contact: Monica Bamwine, Assistant Director of Graduate Admissions, 270-789-5221, Fax: 270-789-5071, E-mail: mkbamwine@campbellsville.edu.

GRADUATE UNITS

Carver School of Social Work Students: 390 full-time (355 women), 56 part-time (49 women); includes 91 minority (83 Black or African American, non-Hispanic/Latino; 6 Hispanic/Latino; 1 Native Hawaiian or other Pacific Islander, non-Hispanic/Latino; 1 Two or more races, non-Hispanic/Latino), 1 international. Average age 33. 380 applicants, 60% accepted, 154 enrolled. *Faculty:* 15 full-time (13 women), 34 part-time/adjunct (32 women). Expenses: Contact institution. *Financial support:* Unspecified assistantships available. Financial award applicants required to submit FAFSA. In 2018, 129 master's awarded. *Program availability:* Part-time, evening/weekend, 100% online, blended/hybrid learning. Offers foundation or advanced tracks (MSW). *Application deadline:* Applications are processed on a rolling basis. *Application fee:* $25. Electronic applications accepted. *Application Contact:* Monica Bamwine, Director of Graduate Admissions, 270-789-5221, Fax: 270-789-5071, E-mail: mkbamwine@campbellsville.edu. *Dean of the Carver School of Social Work,* Dr. Helen K. Mudd, 270-789-5045, Fax: 270-789-5542, E-mail: hkmudd@campbellsville.edu.

College of Arts and Sciences Students: 51 full-time (28 women), 10 part-time (6 women); includes 12 minority (11 Black or African American, non-Hispanic/Latino; 1 Asian, non-Hispanic/Latino), 6 international. Average age 30. 65 applicants, 37% accepted, 21 enrolled. *Faculty:* 16 full-time (7 women), 4 part-time/adjunct (2 women). Expenses: Contact institution. *Financial support:* Unspecified assistantships available. Financial award application deadline: 6/1; financial award applicants required to submit FAFSA. In 2018, 26 master's awarded. *Program availability:* Part-time, evening/weekend, 100% online, blended/hybrid learning. Offers justice studies (MA); sport management (MA). *Application deadline:* Applications are processed on a rolling basis. *Application fee:* $25. Electronic applications accepted. *Application Contact:* Monica Bamwine, Director of Graduate Admissions, 270-789-5221, Fax: 270-789-5071, E-mail: mkbamwine@campbellsville.edu. *Dean of the College of Arts and Sciences,* Dr. Mike Page, 270-789-5394.

School of Business, Economics, and Technology Students: 6,515 full-time (1,494 women), 134 part-time (35 women); includes 19 minority (16 Black or African American, non-Hispanic/Latino; 1 American Indian or Alaska Native, non-Hispanic/Latino; 1 Asian, non-Hispanic/Latino; 1 Hispanic/Latino), 6,524 international. Average age 28. 3,512 applicants, 85% accepted, 2026 enrolled. *Faculty:* 62 full-time (29 women), 28 part-time/adjunct (14 women). Expenses: Contact institution. *Financial support:* Unspecified assistantships available. Financial award application deadline: 6/1; financial award applicants required to submit FAFSA. In 2018, 1,102 master's awarded. *Program availability:* Part-time, evening/weekend, 100% online, blended/hybrid learning. Offers business administration (MBA, Professional MBA); information technology management (MS); management (PhD); management and leadership (MML). *Application deadline:* Applications are processed on a rolling basis. *Application fee:* $25. Electronic applications accepted. *Application Contact:* Monica Bamwine, Director of Graduate Admissions, 270-789-5221, Fax: 270-789-5071, E-mail: mkbamwine@campbellsville.edu. *Dean of School of Business, Economics, and Technology,* Dr. Patricia H. Cowherd, 270-789-5553, Fax: 270-789-5066, E-mail: phcowherd@campbellsville.edu.

School of Education Students: 154 full-time (122 women), 44 part-time (36 women); includes 18 minority (16 Black or African American, non-Hispanic/Latino; 1 Hispanic/Latino; 1 Two or more races, non-Hispanic/Latino), 1 international. Average age 34. 280 applicants, 30% accepted, 72 enrolled. *Faculty:* 16 full-time (10 women), 13 part-time/adjunct (7 women). Expenses: Contact institution. *Financial support:* Unspecified assistantships available. Financial award applicants required to submit FAFSA. In 2018, 66 master's awarded. *Program availability:* Part-time, evening/weekend, 100% online, blended/hybrid learning. Offers education (MA); school counseling (MA); school improvement (MA); special education (MASE); special education-teacher leader (MA); teacher leader (MA); teaching (MAT). *Application deadline:* Applications are processed on a rolling basis. *Application fee:* $25. Electronic applications accepted. *Application Contact:* Monica Bamwine, Director of Graduate Admissions, 270-789-5221, Fax: 270-789-5071, E-mail: mkbamwine@campbellsville.edu. *Dean of School of Education,* Dr. Lisa Allen, 270-789-5344, Fax: 270-789-5206, E-mail: lsallen@campbellsville.edu.

School of Music Students: 16 full-time (10 women), 4 part-time (1 woman); includes 1 minority (Black or African American, non-Hispanic/Latino), 4 international. Average age 29. 22 applicants, 59% accepted, 6 enrolled. *Faculty:* 12 full-time (5 women), 8 part-time/adjunct (5 women). Expenses: Contact institution. *Financial support:* Unspecified assistantships available. Financial award application deadline: 6/1; financial award applicants required to submit FAFSA. In 2018, 6 master's awarded. *Program availability:* Part-time, 100% online, blended/hybrid learning. Offers music (MA); music education (MM); musicology (MA); worship (MA). *Application deadline:* Applications are processed on a rolling basis. *Application fee:* $25. Electronic applications accepted. *Application Contact:* Monica Bamwine, Director of Graduate Admissions, 270-789-5221, Fax: 270-789-5071, E-mail: mkbamwine@campbellsville.edu. *Dean of School of Music,* Dr. Tony Cunha, 270-789-5240, Fax: 270-789-5524, E-mail: aocunha@campbellsville.edu.

School of Theology Students: 86 full-time (48 women), 19 part-time (11 women); includes 32 minority (all Black or African American, non-Hispanic/Latino), 1 international. Average age 43. 36 applicants, 69% accepted, 20 enrolled. *Faculty:* 12 full-time (2 women). Expenses: Contact institution. *Financial support:* Unspecified assistantships available. Financial award application deadline: 6/1; financial award applicants required to submit FAFSA. In 2018, 30 master's awarded. *Program availability:* Part-time, evening/weekend, 100% online, blended/hybrid learning. Offers marriage and family therapy (MMFT); theology (M Th). *Application deadline:* Applications are processed on a rolling basis. *Application fee:* $25. Electronic applications accepted. *Application Contact:* Monica Bamwine, Director of Graduate Admissions, 270-789-5221, Fax: 270-789-5071, E-mail: mkbamwine@campbellsville.edu. *Dean of School of Theology,* Dr. John E. Hurtgen, 270-789-5077, Fax: 270-789-5050, E-mail: jehurtgen@campbellsville.edu.

CAMPBELL UNIVERSITY, Buies Creek, NC 27506

General Information Independent-religious, coed, university. *Graduate housing:* Rooms and/or apartments available on a first-come, first-served basis to single and married students. Housing application deadline: 6/2.

GRADUATE UNITS

Graduate and Professional Programs *Program availability:* Part-time, evening/weekend.

College of Pharmacy and Health Sciences *Program availability:* Part-time, evening/weekend. Offers athletic training (MAT); clinical research (MS); pharmaceutical sciences (MS); pharmacy (Pharm D); physical therapy (DPT); physician assistant (MPAP); public health (MS). Electronic applications accepted.

Divinity School Offers Christian ministry (MA); divinity (M Div); ministry (D Min).

Jerry M. Wallace School of Osteopathic Medicine Offers osteopathic medicine (DO).

Lundy-Fetterman School of Business *Program availability:* Part-time, evening/weekend. Offers business (MBA, MTWM).

Norman Adrian Wiggins School of Law Offers law (JD). JD/MPA offered in partnership with North Carolina State University. Electronic applications accepted.

School of Education *Program availability:* Part-time, evening/weekend. Offers elementary education (M Ed); interdisciplinary studies (M Ed); middle grades education (M Ed); physical education (M Ed); school administration (MSA); school counseling (M Ed); secondary education (M Ed).

CANADIAN COLLEGE OF NATUROPATHIC MEDICINE, Toronto, ON M2K 1E2, Canada

General Information Independent, coed, primarily women, graduate-only institution. *Graduate housing:* Room and/or apartments available on a first-come, first-served basis to single students; on-campus housing not available to married students. Housing application deadline: 4/30. *Research affiliation:* Ottawa Regional Cancer Centre, McMaster University, University of Oxford, Hospital for Sick Children, Mayo Clinic, Johns Hopkins University.

GRADUATE UNITS

Doctor of Naturopathy Program Offers naturopathy (ND). Electronic applications accepted.

CANADIAN MEMORIAL CHIROPRACTIC COLLEGE, Toronto, ON M2H 3J1, Canada

General Information Independent, coed, graduate-only institution. *Graduate housing:* On-campus housing not available. *Research affiliation:* University of Waterloo, University of Calgary, University of Toronto.

GRADUATE UNITS

Certificate Programs Offers chiropractic clinical sciences (Certificate); chiropractic radiology (Certificate); chiropractic sports sciences (Certificate); clinical acupuncture (Certificate).

Professional Program Offers chiropractic (DC).

CANADIAN SOUTHERN BAPTIST SEMINARY, Cochrane, AB T4C 2G1, Canada

General Information Independent-religious, coed, graduate-only institution. *Graduate housing:* Rooms and/or apartments available on a first-come, first-served basis to single and married students. Housing application deadline: 7/1.

GRADUATE UNITS

Graduate Programs *Program availability:* Part-time, 100% online, blended/hybrid learning. Offers Biblical studies (MBS); Christian ministry (MCMin); Christian studies (MCS); ministry (M Div).

CANISIUS COLLEGE, Buffalo, NY 14208-1098

General Information Independent-religious, coed, comprehensive institution. *Enrollment:* 3,464 graduate, professional, and undergraduate students; 474 full-time matriculated graduate/professional students (288 women), 514 part-time matriculated graduate/professional students (297 women). *Enrollment by degree level:* 973 master's, 15 other advanced degrees. *Graduate faculty:* 57 full-time (25 women), 78 part-time/adjunct (47 women). *Tuition:* Part-time $820 per credit hour. *Required fees:* $25 per semester. One-time fee: $65 part-time. Tuition and fees vary according to program. *Graduate housing:* Room and/or apartments available on a first-come, first-served basis to single students; on-campus housing not available to married students. Typical cost: $7744 per year ($13,280 including board). Room and board charges vary according to board plan and housing facility selected. Housing application deadline: 5/1. *Student services:* Campus employment opportunities, campus safety program, career counseling, exercise/wellness program, free psychological counseling, international student services, multicultural affairs office, services for students with disabilities, teacher training. *Library facilities:* Andrew L. Bouwhuis Library plus 1 other. *Collection:* Books: 222,252 (physical), 1.7 million (digital/electronic); Serial titles: 1,143 (physical), 303,210 (digital/electronic); Databases: 108. Weekly public service hours: 110; students can reserve study rooms.

Computer facilities: Computer purchase and lease plans are available. 700 computers available on campus for general student use. A campuswide network can be accessed from student residence rooms and from off campus. Online class registration, online accounts are available.
Website: http://www.canisius.edu/

General Application Contact: Lauren M. Kicak, Associate Director of Graduate Admissions, 716-888-2109, Fax: 716-888-3290, E-mail: kicakl@canisius.edu.

GRADUATE UNITS

Graduate Division Students: 474 full-time (288 women), 514 part-time (297 women); includes 152 minority (82 Black or African American, non-Hispanic/Latino; 2 American Indian or Alaska Native, non-Hispanic/Latino; 12 Asian, non-Hispanic/Latino; 33 Hispanic/Latino; 23 Two or more races, non-Hispanic/Latino), 33 international. Average age 29. 712 applicants, 83% accepted, 379 enrolled. *Faculty:* 47 full-time (29 women), 92 part-time/adjunct (45 women). Expenses: Contact institution. *Financial support:* In 2018–19, 767 students received support. Career-related internships or fieldwork, Federal Work-Study, scholarships/grants, tuition waivers (partial), and unspecified assistantships available. Support available to part-time students. Financial award application deadline: 4/30; financial award applicants required to submit FAFSA. In 2018, 493 master's awarded. *Program availability:* Part-time, evening/weekend, 100% online, blended/hybrid learning. *Application deadline:* Applications are processed on a rolling basis. *Application fee:* $0. Electronic applications accepted. *Application Contact:* Lauren M. Kicak, Associate Director of Graduate Admissions, 716-888-2109, Fax: 716-888-3290, E-mail: kicakl@canisius.edu. *Vice President for Academic Affairs,* Dr. Sara R. Morris, 716-888-2121, Fax: 716-888-2125, E-mail: morriss@canisius.edu.

College of Arts and Sciences Students: 35 full-time (28 women), 40 part-time (28 women); includes 12 minority (3 Black or African American, non-Hispanic/Latino; 2 Asian, non-Hispanic/Latino; 3 Hispanic/Latino; 4 Two or more races, non-Hispanic/Latino). Average age 34. 62 applicants, 45% accepted, 20 enrolled. *Faculty:* 15 full-time (5 women), 6 part-time/adjunct (3 women). Expenses: Contact institution. *Financial support:* In 2018–19, 41 students received support. Career-related internships or fieldwork, Federal Work-Study, scholarships/grants, tuition waivers (partial), and unspecified assistantships available. Financial award application deadline: 4/30; financial award applicants required to submit FAFSA. In 2018, 30 master's awarded. *Program availability:* Part-time, evening/weekend, 100% online, blended/hybrid learning. Offers anthrozoology (MS). *Application deadline:* Applications are processed on a rolling basis. *Application fee:* $0. Electronic applications accepted. *Application Contact:* Dr. Thomas A. Chambers, Dean of the College of Arts & Sciences, 716-888-2150, Fax: 716-888-3211, E-mail: chambe27@canisius.edu. *Dean of the College of Arts & Sciences,* Dr. Thomas A. Chambers, 716-888-2150, Fax: 716-888-3211, E-mail: chambe27@canisius.edu.

Richard J. Wehle School of Business Students: 118 full-time (47 women), 136 part-time (46 women); includes 20 minority (10 Black or African American, non-Hispanic/Latino; 1 American Indian or Alaska Native, non-Hispanic/Latino; 2 Asian, non-Hispanic/Latino; 2 Hispanic/Latino; 5 Two or more races, non-Hispanic/Latino), 21 international. Average age 28. 174 applicants, 89% accepted, 102 enrolled. *Faculty:* 37 full-time (8 women), 22 part-time/adjunct (3 women). Expenses: Contact institution. *Financial support:* In 2018–19, 155 students received support. Career-related internships or fieldwork, Federal Work-Study, scholarships/grants, tuition waivers (partial), and unspecified assistantships available. Support available to part-time students. Financial award application deadline: 4/30; financial award applicants required to submit FAFSA. In 2018, 148 master's awarded. *Program availability:* Part-time, evening/weekend. Offers accounting (MBA); business (MBA, MS); business administration (MBA); forensic accounting (MS); international business (MS); professional accounting (MBA). *Application deadline:* For fall admission, 7/1 priority date for domestic students; for spring admission, 11/1 priority date for domestic students. Applications are processed on a rolling basis. *Application fee:* $0. Electronic applications accepted. *Application Contact:* Dr. Denise M. Rotondo, Dean, 716-888-2164, Fax: 716-888-2145, E-mail: rotondod@canisius.edu. *Dean,* Dr. Denise M. Rotondo, 716-888-2164, Fax: 716-888-2145, E-mail: rotondod@canisius.edu.

School of Education and Human Services Students: 319 full-time (213 women), 323 part-time (212 women); includes 117 minority (68 Black or African American, non-Hispanic/Latino; 1 American Indian or Alaska Native, non-Hispanic/Latino; 7 Asian, non-Hispanic/Latino; 27 Hispanic/Latino; 14 Two or more races, non-Hispanic/Latino), 12 international. Average age 28. 411 applicants, 87% accepted, 236 enrolled. *Faculty:* 26 full-time (15 women), 58 part-time/adjunct (39 women). Expenses: Contact institution. *Financial support:* In 2018–19, 590 students received support. Career-related internships or fieldwork, Federal Work-Study, scholarships/grants, tuition waivers (partial), and unspecified assistantships available. Support available to part-time students. Financial award application deadline: 4/30; financial award applicants required to submit FAFSA. In 2018, 363 master's awarded. *Program availability:* Part-time, evening/weekend, 100% online, blended/hybrid learning. Offers adolescence education (MS Ed); applied nutrition (MS, Certificate); business and marketing education (MS Ed); childhood education (MS Ed); college student personnel (MS Ed); community and school health (MS); community mental health counseling (MS); counseling and human services (MS); deaf education (MS Ed); deaf/adolescent education, grades 7-12 (MS Ed); deaf/childhood education, grades 1-6 (MS Ed); differentiated instruction (MS Ed); education administration (MS); education and human services (MS, MS Ed, MSA, Certificate); educational administration (MS Ed); educational technologies (Certificate); general education (MS Ed); gifted education extension (Certificate); health and human performance (MS); health information technology (MS); literacy (MS Ed); physical education (MS Ed); physical education birth - 12 (MS Ed); reading (Certificate); respiratory care (MS); school agency counseling (MS); school building leadership (MS Ed, Certificate); school district leadership (Certificate); special education (MS); sport administration (MSA); teacher leader (Certificate); TESOL (MS Ed). *Application deadline:* Applications are processed on a rolling basis. *Application fee:* $0. Electronic applications accepted. *Application Contact:* Lauren M Kicak, Associate Director of Graduate Admissions, 716-888-2109, Fax: 716-888-3290, E-mail: kicakl@canisius.edu. *Dean,* Dr. Nancy V. Wallace, 716-888-3205, Fax: 716-888-3164, E-mail: wallacen@canisius.edu.

CAPE BRETON UNIVERSITY, Sydney, NS B1P 6L2, Canada

General Information Province-supported, coed, comprehensive institution. *Graduate housing:* Room and/or apartments available on a first-come, first-served basis to single students; on-campus housing not available to married students. Housing application deadline: 3/31. *Research affiliation:* Hyperspectral Data International (marine remote sensing), Sable Offshore Energy, Inc. (petroleum resources), Fortress Louisbourg National Historic Park (museum/heritage projects), Dynagen Industrial Mine Technology (mining industry equipment), Atlantic Geomatics (computer networking and software development), Advanced Glazing, Limited (transparent insulation).

GRADUATE UNITS

Shannon School of Business *Program availability:* Part-time. Offers business (MBA). Electronic applications accepted.

CAPELLA UNIVERSITY, Minneapolis, MN 55402

General Information Proprietary, coed, upper-level institution. CGS member.

GRADUATE UNITS

Harold Abel School of Social and Behavioral Science *Program availability:* Part-time, evening/weekend, online learning. Offers addiction psychology (PhD); applied behavior analysis (MS); child and adolescent development (MS); clinical psychology (MS, Psy D); counseling psychology (MS); educational psychology (MS, PhD); evaluation, research, and measurement (MS); general addiction counseling (MS); general advanced studies in human behavior (MS, PhD); general counselor education and supervision (PhD); general marriage and family counseling/therapy (MS); general mental health counseling (MS); general psychology (MS, PhD); general school counseling (MS); general social work (DSW); industrial/organizational psychology (MS, PhD); leadership coaching psychology (MS); school psychology (MS, Psy D); social and behavioral science (MS, PhD, Psy D); sport psychology (MS). Electronic applications accepted.

School of Business and Technology *Program availability:* Part-time, evening/weekend, online learning. Offers accounting (MBA, DBA, PhD); business analysis (MS); business and technology (MBA, MS, DBA, PhD); business intelligence (MBA, DBA); enterprise software architecture (MS); entrepreneurship (MBA); finance (MBA, DBA, PhD); general business administration (MBA); general business management (PhD); general human resource management (MS); general information systems and technology management (MS); general information technology (PhD); general leadership (MS); global operations and supply chain management (MBA, DBA); health care management (MBA); human resource management (MBA, DBA, PhD); information assurance and security (MS, PhD); information technology education (PhD); information technology management (MBA, DBA, PhD); leadership (DBA, PhD); management education (PhD); marketing (MBA, DBA, PhD); network management (MS); project management (MBA, MS, DBA, PhD); strategy and innovation (DBA, PhD). Electronic applications accepted.

School of Education *Program availability:* Part-time, evening/weekend, online learning. Offers adult education (MS); curriculum and instruction (MS, PhD); early childhood education (MS); education (MS, Ed D, PhD); educational leadership and management (Ed D); enrollment management (MS); higher education leadership and management

(MS); instructional design for online learning (MS, PhD); integrative studies (MS); K-12 studies in education (MS, PhD); leadership for higher education (PhD); leadership in educational administration (MS, PhD); postsecondary and adult education (PhD); professional studies in education (PhD); reading and literacy (MS, Ed D); special education leadership (PhD); special education teaching (MS); training and performance improvement (PhD). Electronic applications accepted.

School of Public Service Leadership Offers criminal justice (MS, PhD); diabetes nursing (MSN); emergency management (MS, PhD); epidemiology (Dr PH); general health administration (DHA); general nursing (MSN); general public administration (DPA); general public health (MPH); gerontology (MS); gerontology nursing (MSN); health administration (MHA); health advocacy and leadership (Dr PH); health care administration (PhD); health care leadership (DHA); health care operations (MHA); health information management (MS); health management policy (MPH); health policy (MHA); health policy advocacy (DHA); homeland security (MS); multidisciplinary human services (MS, PhD); nonprofit management and leadership (MS); nurse educator (MSN); nursing education (PhD); nursing leadership and administration (MSN); nursing practice (DNP); public administration (MPA); public safety leadership (MS, PhD); public service leadership (MHA, MPA, MPH, MS, DHA, DPA, Dr PH, PhD); social and community services (MS, PhD); social behavioral sciences (MPH).

CAPITAL UNIVERSITY, Columbus, OH 43209-2394

General Information Independent-religious, coed, comprehensive institution. *Graduate housing:* On-campus housing not available.

GRADUATE UNITS

Conservatory of Music *Program availability:* Part-time. Offers music education (MM). Program offered only in summer. Electronic applications accepted.

Law School *Program availability:* Part-time, evening/weekend. Offers business (LL M); business and taxation (LL M); law (LL M, MT, JD); taxation (LL M, MT). Electronic applications accepted.

School of Management *Program availability:* Part-time, evening/weekend. Offers leadership (MBA). Electronic applications accepted.

School of Nursing *Program availability:* Part-time, evening/weekend. Offers administration (MSN); legal studies (MSN); theological studies (MSN).

Trinity Lutheran Seminary *Program availability:* Part-time. Offers African American studies (MTS); Biblical studies (MTS, STM); Christian education (MA); Christian spirituality (STM); church in the world (MTS); church music (MA); divinity (M Div); general theological studies (MTS); mission and evangelism (STM); pastoral leadership and practice (STM); youth and family ministry (MA). Electronic applications accepted.

CAPITOL TECHNOLOGY UNIVERSITY, Laurel, MD 20708-9759

General Information Independent, coed, comprehensive institution. *Graduate housing:* On-campus housing not available.

GRADUATE UNITS

Graduate Programs *Program availability:* Part-time, evening/weekend, online learning. Offers business administration (MBA); computer science (MS); electrical engineering (MS); information and telecommunications systems management (MS); information architecture (MS); network security (MS). Electronic applications accepted.

CARDINAL STRITCH UNIVERSITY, Milwaukee, WI 53217-3985

General Information Independent-religious, coed, university. *Graduate housing:* Room and/or apartments available on a first-come, first-served basis to single students; on-campus housing not available to married students.

GRADUATE UNITS

College of Arts and Sciences *Program availability:* Part-time, evening/weekend. Offers arts and sciences (MA, MS); clinical psychology (MA); ministry (MA); religious studies (MA); sport management (MS). Electronic applications accepted.

College of Business and Management *Program availability:* Part-time, evening/weekend, 100% online, blended/hybrid learning. Offers cyber security (MBA); healthcare management (MBA); justice administration (MBA); marketing (MBA). Electronic applications accepted.

College of Education and Leadership *Program availability:* Part-time, evening/weekend, 100% online. Offers education and leadership (MA, MS, Ed D, PhD); educational leadership (MS); higher education student affairs leadership (MS); language and literacy (MA, PhD); leadership for the advancement of learning and service (Ed D, PhD); leadership for the advancement of learning and service in higher education (Ed D, PhD); special education (PhD); teaching (MAT); urban education (MA); urban special education (MA). Electronic applications accepted.

Ruth S. Coleman College of Nursing and Health Sciences *Program availability:* Part-time, evening/weekend. Offers nursing and health sciences (MSN). Electronic applications accepted.

CAREY THEOLOGICAL COLLEGE, Vancouver, BC V6T 1J6, Canada

General Information Independent-religious, coed, graduate-only institution. *Graduate housing:* Rooms and/or apartments available on a first-come, first-served basis to single and married students. Housing application deadline: 5/31.

GRADUATE UNITS

Graduate Programs *Program availability:* Part-time. Offers theology (M Div, MASF, D Min). Electronic applications accepted.

CARIBBEAN UNIVERSITY, Bayamón, PR 00960-0493

General Information Independent, coed, comprehensive institution.

GRADUATE UNITS
Graduate School

CARLETON UNIVERSITY, Ottawa, ON K1S 5B6, Canada

General Information Province-supported, coed, university. *Graduate housing:* Room and/or apartments guaranteed to single students; on-campus housing not available to married students. Housing application deadline: 5/31.

GRADUATE UNITS

Faculty of Graduate Studies *Program availability:* Part-time, evening/weekend. Electronic applications accepted.

Faculty of Arts and Social Sciences *Program availability:* Part-time, evening/weekend. Offers anthropology (MA); applied language studies (MA); art history; art and its institutions (MA); arts and social sciences (M Sc, MA, PhD); Canadian studies (MA, PhD); cognitive science (MA); cultural mediations (PhD); English (MA, PhD); film studies (MA); French (MA); geography (M Sc, MA, PhD); history (MA, PhD); music and culture (MA); neuroscience (M Sc); philosophy (MA); psychology (MA, PhD); sociology (MA, PhD).

Faculty of Business Offers business (MBA, PhD); business administration (MBA); management (PhD).

Faculty of Engineering and Design Offers aerospace engineering (M Eng, MA Sc, PhD); biomedical engineering (MA Sc); civil and environmental engineering (M Eng, MA Sc, PhD); design studies (M Arch); electrical engineering (M Eng, M Sc, MA Sc, PhD); engineering and design (M Arch, M Des, M Eng, M Sc, MA Sc, PhD); industrial design (M Des); information and systems science (M Sc); materials engineering (M Eng, MA Sc); mechanical engineering (M Eng, MA Sc, PhD); technology innovation management (M Eng, MA Sc).

Faculty of Public Affairs and Management *Program availability:* Part-time. Offers communication (MA, PhD); conflict resolution (Certificate); economics (MA, PhD); European and European Union studies (MA); European integration studies (Diploma); international affairs (MA, PhD); journalism (MJ); legal studies (MA); political economy (MA, PhD); political science (MA, PhD); public administration (MA, DPA); public affairs and management (MA, MJ, MSW, DPA, PhD, Certificate, Diploma); public policy (PhD); Russian, EurAsian and transition studies (MA); social work (MSW).

Faculty of Science *Program availability:* Part-time, evening/weekend. Offers biology (M Sc, PhD); chemistry (M Sc, PhD); computer science (MCS, PhD); earth sciences (M Sc, PhD); information and system science (M Sc); information and systems science (M Sc); mathematics (M Sc, PhD); physics (M Sc, PhD); science (M Sc, MCS, PhD).

CARLOW UNIVERSITY, Pittsburgh, PA 15213-3165

General Information Independent-religious, coed, primarily women, comprehensive institution. *Enrollment:* 537 full-time matriculated graduate/professional students (454 women), 206 part-time matriculated graduate/professional students (177 women). *Enrollment by degree level:* 633 master's, 79 doctoral, 31 other advanced degrees. *Graduate faculty:* 31 full-time, 80 part-time/adjunct. *Tuition:* Full-time $13,090; part-time $5100 per semester. *Required fees:* $215; $84. Tuition and fees vary according to course load, degree level and program. *Graduate housing:* Room and/or apartments available on a first-come, first-served basis to single students; on-campus housing not available to married students. *Student services:* Campus employment opportunities, campus safety program, career counseling, exercise/wellness program, free psychological counseling, international student services, multicultural affairs office, services for students with disabilities, teacher training, writing training. *Library facilities:* Grace Library.

Computer facilities: A campuswide network can be accessed. Online class registration is available.
Website: http://www.carlow.edu/

General Application Contact: Wendy Phillips, Director, Graduate Admissions, 412-578-8861, Fax: 412-578-6321, E-mail: gradstudies@carlow.edu.

GRADUATE UNITS

College of Health and Wellness Students: 216 full-time (198 women), 95 part-time (88 women); includes 26 minority (13 Black or African American, non-Hispanic/Latino; 6 Asian, non-Hispanic/Latino; 3 Hispanic/Latino; 4 Two or more races, non-Hispanic/Latino). Average age 29. 98 applicants, 100% accepted, 72 enrolled. Expenses: Contact institution. *Financial support:* Application deadline: 4/1; applicants required to submit FAFSA. In 2018, 107 master's, 10 doctorates, 4 other advanced degrees awarded. *Program availability:* Part-time, evening/weekend, 100% online, blended/hybrid learning, low-residency. Offers family nurse practitioner (MSN, Certificate); health and wellness (MSN, DNP, Certificate); nursing leadership and education (MSN); nursing practice (DNP); women's health nurse practitioner (MSN, Certificate). *Application deadline:* For fall admission, 6/15 priority date for domestic and international students; for spring admission, 11/15 priority date for domestic and international students. Applications are processed on a rolling basis. Electronic applications accepted. *Application Contact:* Dr. Lynn George, Dean, 412-578-6115, Fax: 412-578-6114. *Dean,* Dr. Lynn George, 412-578-6115, Fax: 412-578-6114.

College of Leadership and Social Change Students: 269 full-time (217 women), 74 part-time (55 women); includes 98 minority (78 Black or African American, non-Hispanic/Latino; 3 Asian, non-Hispanic/Latino; 7 Hispanic/Latino; 10 Two or more races, non-Hispanic/Latino), 1 international. Average age 29. 169 applicants, 97% accepted, 110 enrolled. Expenses: Contact institution. *Financial support:* Application deadline: 4/1; applicants required to submit FAFSA. In 2018, 109 master's, 5 doctorates, 13 other advanced degrees awarded. *Program availability:* Part-time, evening/weekend, 100% online, blended/hybrid learning. Offers child and family (MS); counseling psychology (Psy D); fraud and forensics (MBA); healthcare management (MBA); human resource management (MBA); leadership and management (MBA); leadership and social change (MA, MBA, MS, MSW, Psy D, Certificate); project management (MBA); social work (MSW); student affairs (MA). *Application deadline:* For fall admission, 6/15 priority date for domestic and international students; for spring admission, 11/15 priority date for domestic and international students. Applications are processed on a rolling basis. *Application fee:* $0. Electronic applications accepted. *Application Contact:* Dr. Stephanie A. Wilsey, Dean, 412-578-6346, Fax: 412-578-8722, E-mail: sawilsey@carlow.edu. *Dean,* Dr. Stephanie A. Wilsey, 412-578-6346, Fax: 412-578-8722, E-mail: sawilsey@carlow.edu.

College of Learning and Innovation Students: 52 full-time (39 women), 37 part-time (34 women); includes 15 minority (12 Black or African American, non-Hispanic/Latino; 1 Asian, non-Hispanic/Latino; 2 Two or more races, non-Hispanic/Latino), 1 international. Average age 32. 42 applicants, 93% accepted, 26 enrolled. Expenses: Contact institution. *Financial support:* Application deadline: 4/1; applicants required to submit FAFSA. In 2018, 34 master's, 6 other advanced degrees awarded. *Program availability:* Part-time, evening/weekend, 100% online, blended/hybrid learning, low-residency. Offers art (MA); autism (M Ed); early childhood education (M Ed); early childhood leadership (M Ed); education (M Ed); fiction (MFA); learning and innovation (M Ed, MA, MFA, Certificate, Graduate Certificate); non-fiction (MFA); online instructional design and technology (Certificate); online learning instructional design (M Ed); poetry (MFA); special education (M Ed); STEM (M Ed). *Application deadline:* Applications are processed on a rolling basis. *Application fee:* $0. Electronic applications accepted. *Application Contact:* Dr. Matthew Gordley, Dean, 412-578-6262, E-mail: megordley@carlow.edu. *Dean,* Dr. Matthew Gordley, 412-578-6262, E-mail: megordley@carlow.edu.

CARNEGIE MELLON UNIVERSITY, Pittsburgh, PA 15213-3891

General Information Independent, coed, university. CGS member. *Graduate housing:* On-campus housing not available. *Research affiliation:* National Census Data Research Center (public policy), Robotics Engineering Consortium (computer science and engineering), Software Engineering Institute (computer science and engineering), Carnegie Bosch Institute for Applied Studies in International Management (business and management), Pittsburgh Supercomputer Center.

GRADUATE UNITS

Carnegie Institute of Technology *Program availability:* Part-time, evening/weekend. Offers advanced infrastructure systems (MS, PhD); advanced infrastructure systems technology development and application (MS); air quality engineering and science (MS); bioengineering (MS, PhD); chemical engineering (M Ch E, MS, PhD); civil and environmental engineering (MS, PhD); civil and environmental engineering/engineering and public policy (PhD); civil engineering (MS, PhD); colloids, polymers and surfaces (MS); computational mechanics (MS, PhD); computational modeling and monitoring for resilient structural and material systems (MS); electrical and computer engineering (MS, PhD); energy infrastructure systems (MS); engineering and public policy (PhD); environmental engineering (MS, PhD); environmental management and science (MS, PhD); IT-based sustainable global infrastructure and construction management (MS); materials science and engineering (MS, PhD); mechanical engineering (MS, PhD); product development (MPD); sustainability and green design (MS); technology (M Ch E, MPD, MS, PhD); water quality engineering and science (MS).

Information Networking Institute Offers information networking (MS); information security (MS); information technology - information security (MS); information technology - mobility (MS); information technology - software management (MS).

Center for the Neural Basis of Cognition Offers neural basis of cognition (PhD).

College of Fine Arts *Program availability:* Part-time. Offers fine arts (M Des, M Sc, MAM, MET, MFA, MM, MPD, MS, MSA, MTID, MUD, D Des, PhD). Electronic applications accepted.

School of Architecture Offers architecture (MSA); architecture, engineering, and construction management (PhD); building performance and diagnostics (MS, PhD); computational design (MS, PhD); engineering construction management (MSA); tangible interaction design (MTID); urban design (MUD).

School of Art Offers art (MFA).

School of Design Offers design (M Des, MA, MPD, D Des, PhD); design for interaction (M Des); design for interactions (M Des); design theory (PhD); new product development (PhD); product development (MPD); typography and information design (PhD).

School of Drama Offers design (MFA); directing (MFA); dramatic writing (MFA); production technology and management (MFA); video and media design (MFA).

School of Music *Program availability:* Part-time. Offers collaborative piano (MM); composition (MM); instrumental performance (MM); music and technology (MS); music education (MM); vocal performance (MM).

Dietrich College of Humanities and Social Sciences *Program availability:* Part-time. Offers African and African-American diaspora (PhD); behavioral decision research (PhD); cognitive neuroscience (PhD); cognitive psychology (PhD); communication planning and design (M Des); culture and power (PhD); developmental psychology (PhD); editing and publishing (MAPW); humanities and social sciences (M Des, MA, MAPW, MS, PhD); labor, politics and social movements (PhD); literary and cultural studies (MA, PhD); logic, computation and methodology (MS, PhD); machine learning and statistics (PhD); mathematical finance (PhD); philosophy (MA, PhD); policy and non-profit communication (MAPW); professional writing (MAPW); public and media relations/corporate communications (MAPW); pure and applied logic (PhD); rhetoric (MA, PhD); science or healthcare communication (MAPW); second language acquisition (MA, PhD); social and decision science (PhD); social/personality/health psychology (PhD); statistics (MS, PhD); statistics and public policy (PhD); strategy, entrepreneurship, and technological change (PhD); technical writing (MAPW); technology, environment, science and health (PhD); women, gender and the family (PhD); writing for new media (MAPW); writing for print media (MAPW). Electronic applications accepted.

Heinz College *Program availability:* Part-time, evening/weekend. Offers information systems, public policy, and management (MAM, MEIM, MISM, MMM, MPM, MSBTM, MSHCPM, MSISPM, MSIT, MSPPM, PhD). Electronic applications accepted.

Heinz College Australia Offers information technology (MSIT); public policy and management (MS).

School of Information Systems and Management Offers information security policy and management (MSISPM); information systems and management (MISM, MSISPM, MSIT); information systems management (MISM); information technology (MSIT).

School of Public Policy and Management Offers arts management (MAM); biotechnology and management (MS); entertainment industry management (MEIM); health care policy and management (MSHCPM); medical management (MMM); public management (MPM); public policy and management (MMM, MPM, MS, MSHCPM, PhD).

Joint CMU-Pitt PhD Program in Computational Biology Offers computational biology (PhD).

Mellon College of Science *Program availability:* Part-time. Offers algorithms, combinatorics, and optimization (PhD); applied physics (PhD); atmospheric chemistry (PhD); biochemistry (PhD); bioinorganic chemistry (PhD); bioorganic chemistry and chemical biology (PhD); biophysical chemistry (PhD); biophysics (PhD); catalysis (PhD); cell and developmental biology (PhD); computational biology (MS, PhD); computational finance (MS); genetics (PhD); green and environmental chemistry (PhD); materials and nanoscience (PhD); mathematical finance (PhD); mathematical sciences (DA, PhD); molecular biology (PhD); molecular biophysics and structural biology (PhD); neuroscience (PhD); physics (MS, PhD); pure and applied logic (PhD); renewable energy (PhD); science (MS, DA, PhD); sensors, probes, and imaging (PhD); spectroscopy and single molecule analysis (PhD); structural biology (PhD); theoretical and computational chemistry (PhD). Electronic applications accepted.

School of Computer Science Offers algorithms, combinatorics, and optimization (PhD); automated science: biological experimentation (MS); computer science (MS, PhD); entertainment technology (MET); human-computer interaction (MHCI, PhD); machine learning (MS, PhD); pure and applied logic (PhD); software engineering (MSE, PhD).

Language Technologies Institute Offers language technologies (MLT, MS, PhD).

Robotics Institute Offers computer vision (MS); robotic systems development (MS); robotics (MS, PhD); robotics technology (MS).

Tepper School of Business *Program availability:* Part-time. Offers accounting (PhD); business management and software engineering (MBMSE); business technologies (PhD); civil engineering and industrial management (MS); computational finance (MSCF); economics (PhD); environmental engineering and management (MEEM); financial economics (PhD); industrial administration (MBA); marketing (PhD); mathematical finance (PhD); operations management (PhD); operations research (PhD); organizational behavior and theory (PhD); production and operations management (PhD); public policy and management (MS, MSED); software engineering and business management (MS). JD/MSIA offered jointly with University of Pittsburgh.

CAROLINA CHRISTIAN COLLEGE, Winston-Salem, NC 27102-0777

General Information Independent-religious, coed, comprehensive institution.

GRADUATE UNITS

Program in Religious Education Offers Christian education (MRE); pastoral care (MRE).

CARROLL UNIVERSITY, Waukesha, WI 53186-5593

General Information Independent-religious, coed, comprehensive institution. *Graduate housing:* On-campus housing not available.

GRADUATE UNITS

Graduate Programs in Education *Program availability:* Part-time, evening/weekend. Offers adult and continuing education (M Ed); educational leadership (MS); PK-12 (M Ed). Electronic applications accepted.

Program in Business Administration *Program availability:* Part-time. Offers business administration (MBA). Electronic applications accepted.

Program in Exercise Physiology Offers exercise physiology (MS).

Program in Occupational Therapy Offers occupational therapy (MOT).

Program in Physical Therapy Offers physical therapy (DPT).

Program in Physician Assistant Studies Offers physician assistant studies (MS).

Program in Software Engineering *Program availability:* Part-time, evening/weekend. Offers software engineering (MSE). Electronic applications accepted.

CARSON-NEWMAN UNIVERSITY, Jefferson City, TN 37760

General Information Independent-religious, coed, comprehensive institution. *Enrollment:* 2,560 graduate, professional, and undergraduate students; 178 full-time matriculated graduate/professional students (97 women), 586 part-time matriculated graduate/professional students (431 women). *Enrollment by degree level:* 582 master's, 163 doctoral, 19 other advanced degrees. *Graduate faculty:* 110 full-time (55 women), 61 part-time/adjunct (33 women). *Tuition:* Full-time $9036; part-time $502 per credit hour. *Required fees:* $900; $25 per credit hour. $300 per semester. One-time fee: $150. *Graduate housing:* Rooms and/or apartments available on a first-come, first-served basis to single students and available to married students. Housing application deadline: 7/15. *Student services:* Campus employment opportunities, campus safety program, career counseling, free psychological counseling, international student services, low-cost health insurance, services for students with disabilities. *Library facilities:* Stephens-Burnett Library plus 3 others. *Collection:* Study areas open 24 hours, 5–7 days a week; students can reserve study rooms.

Computer facilities: 200 computers available on campus for general student use. A campuswide network can be accessed from student residence rooms and from off campus. Online class registration is available. Website: http://www.cn.edu/

General Application Contact: Nilma Stewart, Graduate Admissions and Services Adviser, 865-471-3230, Fax: 865-471-3875, E-mail: adults@cn.edu.

GRADUATE UNITS

Department of Nursing Students: 7 full-time (3 women), 51 part-time (47 women); includes 3 minority (2 Black or African American, non-Hispanic/Latino; 1 Hispanic/Latino), 2 international. Average age 35. 29 applicants, 100% accepted, 26 enrolled. *Faculty:* 4 full-time (3 women). Expenses: Contact institution. *Financial support:* Federal Work-Study and tuition waivers (full and partial) available. Financial award applicants required to submit FAFSA. In 2018, 14 master's awarded. *Program availability:* Part-time. Offers family nurse practitioner (MSN); nurse educator (MSN). *Application deadline:* For fall admission, 3/15 for domestic students; for spring admission, 10/15 for domestic students. Applications are processed on a rolling basis. *Application fee:* $50. *Application Contact:* Nilma Stewart, Graduate Admissions and Services Adviser, 865-471-3230, Fax: 865-471-3875, E-mail: adults@cn.edu. *Director,* Dr. Kimberly Bolton, 865-471-4056, E-mail: kbolton@cn.edu.

Graduate Program in Education Students: 14 full-time (8 women), 401 part-time (294 women); includes 45 minority (34 Black or African American, non-Hispanic/Latino; 1 American Indian or Alaska Native, non-Hispanic/Latino; 4 Hispanic/Latino; 1 Native Hawaiian or other Pacific Islander, non-Hispanic/Latino; 5 Two or more races, non-Hispanic/Latino). Average age 36. 223 applicants, 100% accepted, 199 enrolled. *Faculty:* 20 full-time (11 women), 16 part-time/adjunct (13 women). Expenses: Contact institution. *Financial support:* Federal Work-Study and unspecified assistantships available. Financial award applicants required to submit FAFSA. In 2018, 211 master's awarded. *Program availability:* Part-time, evening/weekend, 100% online, blended/hybrid learning. Offers curriculum and instruction (M Ed); educational leadership (M Ed); elementary education (MAT); school counseling (MS); secondary education (MAT); teaching English as a second language (MATESL). *Application deadline:* For fall admission, 7/15 priority date for domestic students. Applications are processed on a rolling basis. *Application fee:* $50. *Application Contact:* Nilma Stewart, Graduate Admissions and Services Adviser, 865-471-3230, Fax: 865-471-3875, E-mail: adults@cn.edu. *Chair,* Dr. Kim Hawkins, 865-471-3314, E-mail: khawkins@cn.edu.

Program in Applied Theology Students: 8 part-time (5 women); includes 2 minority (1 Black or African American, non-Hispanic/Latino; 1 Hispanic/Latino). Average age 47. 4 applicants, 100% accepted, 4 enrolled. *Faculty:* 2 full-time (0 women). Expenses: Contact institution. *Financial support:* Federal Work-Study and tuition waivers (full and partial) available. Financial award applicants required to submit FAFSA. In 2018, 1 master's awarded. *Program availability:* Part-time, evening/weekend. Offers applied theology (MAAT). *Application deadline:* For fall admission, 7/15 priority date for domestic students. Applications are processed on a rolling basis. *Application fee:* $50. *Application Contact:* Nilma Stewart, Graduate Admissions and Services Adviser, 865-471-3230, Fax: 865-471-3875, E-mail: adults@cn.edu. *Dean, School of Religion,* Dr. David E. Crutchley, 865-471-3277, E-mail: dcruthley@cn.edu.

Program in Business Administration Students: 93 full-time (39 women), 39 part-time (19 women); includes 18 minority (12 Black or African American, non-Hispanic/Latino; 2 Asian, non-Hispanic/Latino; 3 Hispanic/Latino; 1 Two or more races, non-Hispanic/Latino), 20 international. Average age 31. 70 applicants, 100% accepted, 53 enrolled. *Faculty:* 4 full-time (2 women), 6 part-time/adjunct (1 woman). Expenses: Contact institution. *Financial support:* Federal Work-Study and tuition waivers (full and partial) available. Financial award applicants required to submit FAFSA. In 2018, 34 master's awarded. *Program availability:* Part-time, evening/weekend, 100% online, blended/hybrid learning. Offers business administration (MBA). *Application deadline:* For fall admission, 7/15 priority date for domestic students. Applications are processed on a rolling basis. *Application fee:* $50. *Application Contact:* Nilma Stewart, Graduate Admissions and Services Adviser, 865-471-3230, Fax: 865-471-3875, E-mail: adults@cn.edu. *Director,* Dr. Kyle J. Kaplan, 865-471-7124, E-mail: kkaplan@cn.edu.

Program in Counseling Students: 33 full-time (29 women), 22 part-time (21 women); includes 3 minority (2 Black or African American, non-Hispanic/Latino; 1

Hispanic/Latino), 2 international. Average age 30. 13 applicants, 100% accepted, 11 enrolled. *Faculty:* 3 full-time (2 women), 1 part-time/adjunct (0 women). Expenses: Contact institution. *Financial support:* Federal Work-Study and tuition waivers (full and partial) available. Financial award applicants required to submit FAFSA. In 2018, 18 master's awarded. *Program availability:* Part-time, evening/weekend. Offers counseling (MSC). *Application deadline:* Applications are processed on a rolling basis. *Application fee:* $50. *Application Contact:* Nilma Stewart, Graduate Admissions and Services Adviser, 865-471-3230, Fax: 865-471-3875, E-mail: adults@cn.edu. *Director,* Dr. Michael L. Bundy, 865-471-2087, E-mail: mbundy@cn.edu.

Program in Social Entrepreneurship Students: 6 part-time (4 women); includes 1 minority (Two or more races, non-Hispanic/Latino), 1 international. Average age 27. 5 applicants, 100% accepted, 5 enrolled. *Faculty:* 1 part-time/adjunct (0 women). Expenses: Contact institution. *Financial support:* Federal Work-Study and tuition waivers (full and partial) available. Financial award applicants required to submit FAFSA. In 2018, 3 master's awarded. *Program availability:* Part-time, evening/weekend, 100% online, blended/hybrid learning. Offers social entrepreneurship (MAASJ). *Application deadline:* For fall admission, 7/15 for domestic students. Applications are processed on a rolling basis. *Application fee:* $50. *Application Contact:* Nilma Stewart, Graduate Admissions and Services Adviser, 865-471-3223, Fax: 865-471-3875, E-mail: adults@cn.edu. *Department Chair,* Dr. Laura Wadlington, 865-471-3270.

CARTHAGE COLLEGE, Kenosha, WI 53140

General Information Independent-religious, coed, comprehensive institution. *Graduate housing:* On-campus housing not available.

GRADUATE UNITS

Division of Teacher Education *Program availability:* Part-time, evening/weekend. Offers classroom guidance and counseling (M Ed); creative arts (M Ed); gifted and talented children (M Ed); language arts (M Ed); modern language (M Ed); natural sciences (M Ed); reading (M Ed, Certificate); social sciences (M Ed); teacher leadership (M Ed).

CASE WESTERN RESERVE UNIVERSITY, Cleveland, OH 44106

General Information Independent, coed, university. CGS member. *Enrollment:* 5,567 full-time matriculated graduate/professional students (3,040 women), 1,062 part-time matriculated graduate/professional students (677 women). *Enrollment by degree level:* 3,492 master's, 3,071 doctoral, 43 other advanced degrees. *Graduate faculty:* 3,501 full-time (1,326 women). *Tuition:* Full-time $45,168; part-time $1939 per credit hour. *Required fees:* $36; $18 per semester. $18 per semester. *Graduate housing:* On-campus housing not available. *Student services:* Campus employment opportunities, campus safety program, career counseling, exercise/wellness program, free psychological counseling, grant writing training, international student services, low-cost health insurance, multicultural affairs office, services for students with disabilities, teacher training, writing training. *Library facilities:* Kelvin Smith Library plus 6 others. *Collection:* Books: 3.4 million (physical); Serial titles: 196,361 (physical); Databases: 470. Students can reserve study rooms.

Computer facilities: Computer purchase and lease plans are available. 357 computers available on campus for general student use. A campuswide network can be accessed from student residence rooms and from off campus. Online class registration, software library, online reference databases, electronic books and journals, research computing, training are available.
Website: http://www.case.edu/

GRADUATE UNITS

Frances Payne Bolton School of Nursing Students: 270 full-time (225 women), 225 part-time (187 women); includes 116 minority (49 Black or African American, non-Hispanic/Latino; 35 Asian, non-Hispanic/Latino; 20 Hispanic/Latino; 2 Native Hawaiian or other Pacific Islander, non-Hispanic/Latino; 10 Two or more races, non-Hispanic/Latino), 41 international. Average age 37. 329 applicants, 71% accepted, 159 enrolled. *Faculty:* 97 full-time (86 women), 25 part-time/adjunct (21 women). Expenses: Contact institution. *Financial support:* In 2018–19, 314 students received support, including 6 fellowships with full tuition reimbursements available (averaging $24,054 per year), 25 research assistantships with partial tuition reimbursements available (averaging $16,938 per year), 45 teaching assistantships with partial tuition reimbursements available (averaging $16,938 per year); scholarships/grants, traineeships, and nurse faculty loan program also available. Financial award application deadline: 5/15; financial award applicants required to submit FAFSA. In 2018, 124 master's, 48 doctorates awarded. *Program availability:* Part-time. Offers acute care pediatric nurse practitioner (MSN); acute care/cardiovascular nursing (MSN); adult gerontology acute care nurse practitioner (MSN); adult gerontology primary care nurse practitioner (MSN); educational leadership (DNP); family nurse practitioner (MSN); family systems psychiatric mental health nursing (MSN); leadership (DNP); neonatal nurse practitioner (MSN); nurse anesthesia (MSN); nurse education (MSN); nurse midwifery (MSN); nurse practitioner (MSN); nursing (MN); palliative care (MSN); pediatric nurse practitioner in acute care (MSN); pediatric primary care nurse practitioner (MSN); practice leadership (DNP); women's health nurse practitioner (MSN). *Application deadline:* For fall admission, 3/1 for domestic and international students; for spring admission, 10/1 for domestic and international students; for summer admission, 3/1 for domestic and international students. Applications are processed on a rolling basis. *Application fee:* $75. Electronic applications accepted. *Application Contact:* Jackie Tepale, Admissions Coordinator, Graduate Programs, 216-368-5253, Fax: 216-368-3542, E-mail: yyd@case.edu. *Dean/Professor,* Dr. Carol M Musil, 216-368-2545, Fax: 216-368-3542, E-mail: cmm4@case.edu.

Jack, Joseph and Morton Mandel School of Applied Social Sciences *Program availability:* Part-time, evening/weekend, 100% online. Offers nonprofit management (MNO); social welfare (PhD); social work (MSSA). Electronic applications accepted.

School of Dental Medicine Offers advanced general dentistry (Certificate); dental medicine (MSD, DMD, Certificate); dentistry (MSD, DMD, Certificate); endodontics (MSD, Certificate); oral surgery (Certificate); orthodontics (MSD, Certificate); pedodontics (MSD, Certificate); periodontics (MSD, Certificate). Electronic applications accepted.

School of Graduate Studies Students: 2,178 full-time (1,072 women), 422 part-time (229 women); includes 666 minority (155 Black or African American, non-Hispanic/Latino; 1 American Indian or Alaska Native, non-Hispanic/Latino; 300 Asian, non-Hispanic/Latino; 145 Hispanic/Latino; 65 Two or more races, non-Hispanic/Latino), 754 international. Average age 28. 4,616 applicants, 41% accepted, 902 enrolled. *Faculty:* 3,501 full-time (1,326 women). Expenses: Contact institution. *Financial support:* Fellowships with tuition reimbursements, research assistantships with tuition reimbursements, teaching assistantships with tuition reimbursements, career-related internships or fieldwork, Federal Work-Study, institutionally sponsored loans, scholarships/grants, traineeships, health care benefits, tuition waivers (full and partial),

and unspecified assistantships available. Support available to part-time students. Financial award applicants required to submit CSS PROFILE or FAFSA. In 2018, 682 master's, 192 doctorates awarded. *Program availability:* Part-time, evening/weekend, online learning. Offers acting (MFA); anthropology (MA, PhD); applied mathematics (MS, PhD); art education (MA); art history (MA, PhD); art history and museum studies (MA); astronomy (MS, PhD); biology (MS, PhD); chemistry (MS, PhD); clinical psychology (PhD); cognitive linguistics (MA); communication sciences (MA, PhD); dance (MA, MFA); early music (MA, D Mus A); earth, environmental, and planetary sciences (MS, PhD); English (MA, PhD); experimental psychology (PhD); French (MA); historical musicology (MA, PhD); historical performance practice (MA, DMA, PhD); history (MA, PhD); mathematics (MS, PhD); music education (MA, PhD); music history (MA); physics (MS, PhD); political science (MA, PhD); sociology (MA, PhD); speech-language pathology (MA, PhD); theater (MA); world literature (MA). *Application deadline:* For fall admission, 3/1 for domestic students; for spring admission, 11/1 for domestic students. *Application fee:* $50. Electronic applications accepted. *Application Contact:* Dr. Charles E. Rozek, Vice Provost for Graduate Education & Academic & Faculty Affairs, 216-368-4390, Fax: 216-368-4250, E-mail: charles.rozek@case.edu. *Vice Provost for Graduate Education & Academic & Faculty Affairs,* Dr. Charles E. Rozek, 216-368-4390, Fax: 216-368-4250, E-mail: charles.rozek@case.edu.

Case School of Engineering Students: 628 full-time (178 women), 43 part-time (9 women); includes 96 minority (5 Black or African American, non-Hispanic/Latino; 66 Asian, non-Hispanic/Latino; 18 Hispanic/Latino; 7 Two or more races, non-Hispanic/Latino), 410 international. 1,280 applicants, 40% accepted, 119 enrolled. *Faculty:* 110 full-time (17 women). Expenses: Contact institution. *Financial support:* In 2018–19, 333 students received support, including 36 fellowships with tuition reimbursements available, 252 research assistantships with tuition reimbursements available, 45 teaching assistantships; career-related internships or fieldwork, Federal Work-Study, and institutionally sponsored loans also available. Support available to part-time students. Financial award applicants required to submit FAFSA. In 2018, 169 master's, 60 doctorates awarded. *Program availability:* Part-time, evening/weekend, 100% online, blended/hybrid learning. Offers biomedical engineering (MS, PhD); chemical and biomolecular engineering (MS, PhD); civil engineering (MS, PhD); computer engineering (MS, PhD); computing and information sciences (MS, PhD); electrical engineering (MS, PhD); engineering (ME, MEM, MS, PhD); macromolecular science and engineering (MS, PhD); management and engineering (MEM); materials science and engineering (MS, PhD); mechanical and aerospace engineering (MS, PhD); systems and control engineering (MS, PhD). *Application deadline:* Applications are processed on a rolling basis. *Application fee:* $50. Electronic applications accepted. *Application Contact:* Dr. Marc Buchner, Associate Dean, Academics, 216-368-4096, Fax: 216-368-6939, E-mail: marc.buchner@case.edu. *Charles H. Phipps Dean,* Venkataramanan "Ragu" Balakrishnan, 216-368-4436, Fax: 216-368-6939, E-mail: ragu@case.edu.

School of Law Students: 433 full-time (238 women); includes 91 minority (37 Black or African American, non-Hispanic/Latino; 1 American Indian or Alaska Native, non-Hispanic/Latino; 19 Asian, non-Hispanic/Latino; 26 Hispanic/Latino; 8 Two or more races, non-Hispanic/Latino), 30 international. Average age 24. 1,415 applicants, 50% accepted, 157 enrolled. *Faculty:* 47 full-time (16 women), 63 part-time/adjunct (16 women). Expenses: Contact institution. *Financial support:* In 2018–19, 394 students received support. Career-related internships or fieldwork, Federal Work-Study, institutionally sponsored loans, and scholarships/grants available. Financial award application deadline: 5/1; financial award applicants required to submit FAFSA. In 2018, 126 master's awarded. Offers financial integrity (MA); health law (SJD); intellectual property law (LL M, ML); international business law (LL M, ML); international criminal law (LL M); law (JD, SJD); patent practice (MA); U.S. and global legal studies (LL M, ML). *Application deadline:* For fall admission, 4/1 priority date for domestic and international students. Applications are processed on a rolling basis. *Application fee:* $40. Electronic applications accepted. *Application Contact:* Kelli Curtis, Associate Dean for Admissions, 216-368-3600, Fax: 216-368-0185, E-mail: lawadmissions@case.edu. *Co-Dean,* Jessica Berg, 216-368-3283.

School of Medicine *Program availability:* Part-time. Offers clinical research (MS, PhD); medicine (MA, MPH, MS, MD, PhD); physician assistant (MS).

Graduate Programs in Medicine *Program availability:* Part-time. Offers anesthesiologist assistant (MS); applied anatomy (MS); biochemistry (MS, PhD); bioethics (MA); biostatistics (MS); cancer biology (PhD); cell biology (PhD); dietetics (MS); epidemiology and biostatistics (PhD); genetic counseling (MS); genetics and genome sciences (PhD); medical physiology (MS); medicine (MA, MPH, MS, PhD); molecular and cellular basis of disease (PhD); molecular biology (PhD); molecular medicine (PhD); molecular nutrition (MS); molecular virology (PhD); neuroscience (PhD); nutrition (MS, PhD); nutritional biochemistry and metabolism (MS); pathology (MS); pharmacology (PhD); physiology and biophysics (PhD); public health (MPH); public health nutrition (MS). Electronic applications accepted.

Weatherhead School of Management *Program availability:* Part-time, evening/weekend. Offers accountancy (M Acc, PhD); business administration (EMBA, MBA); business analytics (MSM); designing sustainable systems (PhD); finance (MSM); healthcare (MSM); management (EMBA, M Acc, MBA, MNO, MPOD, MS, MSM, EDM, PhD, CNM); operations and supply chain management (MSM); operations research (PhD); organizational behavior (PhD); positive organization development and change (MS). Electronic applications accepted.

Mandel Center for Nonprofit Organizations Offers nonprofit management (MNO, CNM).

CASTLETON UNIVERSITY, Castleton, VT 05735

General Information State-supported, coed, comprehensive institution. *Graduate housing:* Room and/or apartments available on a first-come, first-served basis to single students; on-campus housing not available to married students. Housing application deadline: 5/19.

GRADUATE UNITS

Division of Graduate Studies *Program availability:* Part-time, evening/weekend. Offers curriculum and instruction (MA Ed); educational leadership (MA Ed, CAGS); forensic psychology (MA); language arts and reading (MA Ed, CAGS); special education (MA Ed, CAGS).

CATAWBA COLLEGE, Salisbury, NC 28144-2488

General Information Independent-religious, coed, comprehensive institution. *Graduate housing:* On-campus housing not available.

GRADUATE UNITS

Department of Teacher Education *Program availability:* Part-time-only. Offers STEM education (M Ed). Electronic applications accepted.

CATHOLIC DISTANCE UNIVERSITY, Charles Town, WV 25414

General Information Independent-religious, coed, graduate-only institution. *Graduate housing:* On-campus housing not available.

GRADUATE UNITS

Graduate Programs *Program availability:* Part-time, evening/weekend, online learning. Offers religious studies (MRS); theology (MA).

CATHOLIC THEOLOGICAL UNION, Chicago, IL 60615-5698

General Information Independent-religious, coed, graduate-only institution. *Graduate housing:* Rooms and/or apartments available on a first-come, first-served basis to single and married students. Housing application deadline: 7/1.

GRADUATE UNITS

Graduate and Professional Programs *Program availability:* Part-time, evening/weekend. Offers biblical spirituality (Certificate); cross-cultural ministries (D Min); cross-cultural missions (Certificate); divinity (M Div); liturgical studies (Certificate); liturgy (D Min); pastoral studies (MAPS, Certificate); spiritual formation (Certificate); spirituality (D Min); theology (MA). M Div/PhD offered jointly with University of Chicago; M Div/MSW with Loyola University Chicago and University of Chicago.

THE CATHOLIC UNIVERSITY OF AMERICA, Washington, DC 20064

General Information Independent-religious, coed, university. CGS member. *Enrollment:* 5,956 graduate, professional, and undergraduate students; 1,059 full-time matriculated graduate/professional students (552 women), 1,565 part-time matriculated graduate/professional students (932 women). *Enrollment by degree level:* 1,331 master's, 1,188 doctoral, 105 other advanced degrees. *Graduate faculty:* 377 full-time (142 women), 416 part-time/adjunct (165 women). *Tuition:* Full-time $46,180; part-time $1840 per credit hour. *Required fees:* $150; $150 per unit. $155 per term. One-time fee: $440. *Graduate housing:* Room and/or apartments available on a first-come, first-served basis to single students; on-campus housing not available to married students. Housing application deadline: 5/15. *Student services:* Campus employment opportunities, campus safety program, career counseling, free psychological counseling, international student services, low-cost health insurance, multicultural affairs office, services for students with disabilities, teacher training, writing training. *Library facilities:* Mullen Library plus 1 other. *Collection:* Books: 734,247 (physical), 390,119 (digital/electronic); Serial titles: 342,482 (physical), 135,001 (digital/electronic); Databases: 482. Weekly public service hours: 102.

Computer facilities: 542 computers available on campus for general student use. A campuswide network can be accessed from student residence rooms and from off campus. Online class registration is available.
Website: http://www.catholic.edu/

General Application Contact: Dr. Steven Brown, Vice Provost and Dean of Graduate Studies, 202-319-5057, Fax: 202-319-6533, E-mail: cua-admissions@cua.edu.

GRADUATE UNITS

Benjamin T. Rome School of Music Students: 40 full-time (29 women), 90 part-time (55 women); includes 36 minority (10 Black or African American, non-Hispanic/Latino; 13 Asian, non-Hispanic/Latino; 8 Hispanic/Latino; 5 Two or more races, non-Hispanic/Latino), 28 international. Average age 33. 137 applicants, 61% accepted, 49 enrolled. *Faculty:* 17 full-time (4 women), 46 part-time/adjunct (17 women). Expenses: Contact institution. *Financial support:* Fellowships, research assistantships, teaching assistantships, Federal Work-Study, scholarships/grants, tuition waivers (full and partial), and unspecified assistantships available. Financial award application deadline: 2/1; financial award applicants required to submit FAFSA. In 2018, 12 master's, 10 doctorates awarded. *Program availability:* Part-time. Offers cello (Artist Diploma); chamber music (piano) (MM, DMA); composition (MM, DMA); music (MAT); musicology (MA, PhD); orchestral conducting (MM, DMA, Artist Diploma); orchestral instruments/guitar (MM, DMA); piano (Artist Diploma); piano pedagogy (MM, DMA); piano performance (MM, DMA); sacred music (MMSM, DMA); violin (Artist Diploma); vocal accompanying (MM, DMA); vocal pedagogy (MM, DMA); vocal performance (MM, DMA); voice (Artist Diploma). MA/MSLIS offered in partnership with Department of Library and Information Science. *Application deadline:* For fall admission, 7/15 priority date for domestic students, 7/1 for international students; for spring admission, 11/15 priority date for domestic students, 11/1 for international students. Applications are processed on a rolling basis. *Application fee:* $55. Electronic applications accepted. *Application Contact:* Dr. Steven Brown, Director of Graduate Admissions, 202-319-5247, Fax: 202-319-6174, E-mail: cua-graduatestudies@cua.edu. *Dean*, Jacqueline Leary-Warsaw, 202-319-5417, Fax: 202-319-6280, E-mail: cua-music@cua.edu.

Busch School of Business and Economics Students: 57 full-time (11 women), 1 (woman) part-time; includes 24 minority (3 Black or African American, non-Hispanic/Latino; 1 American Indian or Alaska Native, non-Hispanic/Latino; 8 Asian, non-Hispanic/Latino; 7 Two or more races, non-Hispanic/Latino), 1 international. Average age 33. 96 applicants, 79% accepted, 56 enrolled. *Faculty:* 38 full-time (8 women), 21 part-time/adjunct (9 women). Expenses: Contact institution. *Financial support:* Fellowships, research assistantships, teaching assistantships, Federal Work-Study, scholarships/grants, tuition waivers (full and partial), and unspecified assistantships available. Financial award application deadline: 2/1; financial award applicants required to submit FAFSA. In 2018, 58 master's awarded. *Program availability:* Part-time. Offers accounting (MS); business analysis (MSBA); integral economic development management (MA); integral economic development policy (MA); management (MS). *Application deadline:* For fall admission, 7/15 priority date for domestic students, 7/1 for international students; for spring admission, 11/15 priority date for domestic students, 11/1 for international students. Applications are processed on a rolling basis. *Application fee:* $55. Electronic applications accepted. *Application Contact:* Dr. Steven Brown, Director of Graduate Admissions, 202-319-5057, Fax: 202-319-6533, E-mail: cua-admissions@cua.edu. *Dean*, Dr. Andrew Abela, 202-319-6130, E-mail: DeanAbela@cua.edu.

Columbus School of Law *Program availability:* Part-time, evening/weekend. Offers law (MLS, JD). Electronic applications accepted.

Metropolitan School of Professional Studies Students: 39 full-time (24 women), 62 part-time (32 women); includes 44 minority (29 Black or African American, non-Hispanic/Latino; 2 Asian, non-Hispanic/Latino; 8 Hispanic/Latino; 5 Two or more races, non-Hispanic/Latino), 26 international. Average age 34. 91 applicants, 87% accepted, 55 enrolled. *Faculty:* 40 part-time/adjunct (15 women). Expenses: Contact institution. *Financial support:* Scholarships/grants available. Financial award application deadline: 3/15; financial award applicants required to submit FAFSA. In 2018, 32 master's awarded. *Program availability:* Part-time, evening/weekend, 100% online. Offers emergency service administration (MS); health administration (MHA); social service administration (MS). *Application deadline:* For fall admission, 7/15 priority date for domestic students, 7/1 for international students; for spring admission, 11/15 priority

date for domestic students, 11/1 for international students. Applications are processed on a rolling basis. *Application fee:* $55. Electronic applications accepted. *Application Contact:* Dr. Steven Brown, Director of Graduate Admissions, 202-319-5057, Fax: 202-319-6533, E-mail: cua-admissions@cua.edu. *Dean*, Dr. Vince Kiernan, 202-319-5256, Fax: 202-319-6260, E-mail: kiernan@cua.edu.

National Catholic School of Social Service Students: 141 full-time (118 women), 346 part-time (296 women); includes 250 minority (153 Black or African American, non-Hispanic/Latino; 11 Asian, non-Hispanic/Latino; 49 Hispanic/Latino; 1 Native Hawaiian or other Pacific Islander, non-Hispanic/Latino; 36 Two or more races, non-Hispanic/Latino), 8 international. Average age 35. 272 applicants, 81% accepted, 123 enrolled. *Faculty:* 15 full-time (13 women), 36 part-time/adjunct (31 women). Expenses: Contact institution. *Financial support:* Fellowships, research assistantships, teaching assistantships, Federal Work-Study, scholarships/grants, tuition waivers (full and partial), and unspecified assistantships available. Financial award application deadline: 3/15; financial award applicants required to submit FAFSA. In 2018, 166 master's, 5 doctorates awarded. *Program availability:* Part-time, 100% online. Offers clinical (MSW); combined (clinical and social change) (MSW); social change (MSW); social work (PhD). MSW/JD offered with Columbus School of Law. *Application deadline:* For fall admission, 7/15 priority date for domestic students, 7/1 for international students; for spring admission, 11/15 priority date for domestic students, 11/1 for international students. Applications are processed on a rolling basis. *Application fee:* $60. Electronic applications accepted. *Application Contact:* Dr. Steven Brown, Director of Graduate Admissions, 202-319-5057, Fax: 202-319-6533, E-mail: cua-admissions@cua.edu. *Dean*, Dr. Marie Raber, 202-319-5472, Fax: 202-319-5093, E-mail: raber@cua.edu.

School of Architecture and Planning Students: 49 full-time (25 women), 17 part-time (4 women); includes 25 minority (10 Black or African American, non-Hispanic/Latino; 1 American Indian or Alaska Native, non-Hispanic/Latino; 1 Asian, non-Hispanic/Latino; 8 Hispanic/Latino; 5 Two or more races, non-Hispanic/Latino), 7 international. Average age 29. 67 applicants, 76% accepted, 15 enrolled. *Faculty:* 14 full-time (5 women), 13 part-time/adjunct (5 women). Expenses: Contact institution. *Financial support:* Fellowships, research assistantships, teaching assistantships, Federal Work-Study, scholarships/grants, tuition waivers (full and partial), and unspecified assistantships available. Financial award application deadline: 2/1; financial award applicants required to submit FAFSA. In 2018, 24 master's awarded. *Program availability:* Part-time. Offers architecture and planning (M Arch, MS Arch St); city and regional planning (M Arch); facilities management (MS Arch); regional development (Certificate); sustainable design (M Arch, Certificate). *Application deadline:* For fall admission, 1/15 priority date for domestic students, 7/1 for international students; for spring admission, 10/15 priority date for domestic students, 11/1 for international students. Applications are processed on a rolling basis. *Application fee:* $55. Electronic applications accepted. *Application Contact:* Dr. Steven Brown, Director of Graduate Admissions, 202-319-5057, Fax: 202-319-6533, E-mail: cua-admissions@cua.edu. *Dean*, Randall Ott, 202-319-5784, Fax: 202-319-2023, E-mail: ott@cua.edu.

School of Arts and Sciences Students: 157 full-time (109 women), 340 part-time (195 women); includes 100 minority (29 Black or African American, non-Hispanic/Latino; 12 Asian, non-Hispanic/Latino; 21 Hispanic/Latino; 38 Two or more races, non-Hispanic/Latino), 107 international. Average age 32. 484 applicants, 55% accepted, 105 enrolled. *Faculty:* 115 full-time (56 women), 73 part-time/adjunct (31 women). Expenses: Contact institution. *Financial support:* Fellowships, research assistantships, teaching assistantships, Federal Work-Study, scholarships/grants, tuition waivers (full and partial), and unspecified assistantships available. Financial award application deadline: 2/1; financial award applicants required to submit FAFSA. In 2018, 118 master's, 32 doctorates awarded. *Program availability:* Part-time. Offers acting (MFA); American government (MA, PhD); ancient Near East (Biblical Hebrew/Aramaic) (MA, PhD); anthropology (MA); applied experimental psychology (PhD); Arabic (PhD); arts and sciences (MA, MFA, MS, MSBA, MSLS, PhD, Certificate); biotechnology (MS); Byzantine and Orthodox studies (MA); Catholic school leadership (MA); cell and microbial biology (MS, PhD); Christian Near East (Biblical Hebrew/Aramaic) (MA); clinical laboratory science (MS, PhD); clinical psychology (PhD); Congressional and Presidential studies (MA); Coptic (MA, PhD); creative teaching through drama (Certificate); crime and justice studies (MA); directing (MFA); early Christian studies (MA, PhD); education (Certificate); English (MA, PhD); general psychology (MA); global and comparative sociology (MA); Greek (MA, Certificate); Greek and Latin (MA, PhD, Certificate); Hispanic studies (MA, PhD); history (MA, PhD); human development psychology (PhD); human factors (MA); international affairs (MA); international political economics (MA); Latin (MA, Certificate); library and information science (MSLS, Certificate); Medieval and Byzantine studies (PhD, Certificate); nuclear environmental protection (MS); physics (MS, PhD); playwriting (MFA); political theory (MA, PhD); public policy (MA); religion and society in the late medieval and early modern world (MA); rhetoric (Certificate); secondary education (MA); special education (MA); Syriac (MA, PhD); the Islamic world (MA); the Medieval West (MA); theatre education (MA); theatre history and criticism (MA); world politics (MA, PhD). *Application deadline:* For fall admission, 2/1 priority date for domestic students, 7/1 for international students; for spring admission, 11/15 priority date for domestic students, 11/1 for international students. Applications are processed on a rolling basis. *Application fee:* $55. Electronic applications accepted. *Application Contact:* Dr. Steven Brown, Director of Graduate Admissions, 202-319-5057, Fax: 202-319-6533, E-mail: cua-admissions@cua.edu. *Dean*, Dr. David Walsh, 202-319-5115, Fax: 202-319-4463, E-mail: artsandsciences@cua.edu.

School of Canon Law Students: 30 full-time (6 women), 48 part-time (8 women); includes 12 minority (4 Black or African American, non-Hispanic/Latino; 4 Asian, non-Hispanic/Latino; 2 Hispanic/Latino; 2 Two or more races, non-Hispanic/Latino), 9 international. Average age 38. 46 applicants, 80% accepted, 23 enrolled. *Faculty:* 6 full-time (1 woman), 1 part-time/adjunct (0 women). Expenses: Contact institution. *Financial support:* Fellowships, research assistantships, teaching assistantships, Federal Work-Study, scholarships/grants, tuition waivers (full and partial), and unspecified assistantships available. Financial award application deadline: 2/1; financial award applicants required to submit FAFSA. In 2018, 13 master's, 2 doctorates awarded. *Program availability:* Part-time. Offers Canon law (JCD, JCL); church administration (MCA). JD/JCL offered jointly with Columbus School of Law. *Application deadline:* For fall admission, 7/15 priority date for domestic students, 7/1 for international students; for spring admission, 11/15 priority date for domestic students, 11/1 for international students. Applications are processed on a rolling basis. *Application fee:* $55. Electronic applications accepted. *Application Contact:* Dr. Steven Brown, Director of Graduate Admissions, 202-319-5057, Fax: 202-319-6533, E-mail: cua-admissions@cua.edu. *Dean*, Msgr. Ronny Jenkins, 202-319-5492, Fax: 202-319-4187, E-mail: cua-canonlaw@cua.edu.

School of Engineering Students: 72 full-time (26 women), 147 part-time (45 women); includes 37 minority (9 Black or African American, non-Hispanic/Latino; 5 Asian, non-Hispanic/Latino; 8 Hispanic/Latino; 15 Two or more races, non-Hispanic/Latino), 104 international. Average age 31. 176 applicants, 81% accepted, 67 enrolled. *Faculty:* 31 full-time (2 women), 34 part-time/adjunct (3 women). Expenses: Contact institution. *Financial support:* Fellowships, research assistantships, teaching assistantships, Federal Work-Study, scholarships/grants, tuition waivers (full and partial), and unspecified assistantships available. Financial award application deadline: 2/1; financial award applicants required to submit FAFSA. In 2018, 71 master's, 14 doctorates awarded. *Program availability:* Part-time. Offers biomedical engineering (MBE, PhD); civil engineering (MS, PhD); computer science (MSCS, PhD); electrical engineering (MEE, PhD); energy and environment (MME); engineering (MBE, MCE, MEE, MME, MS, MSCS, MSE, PhD, Certificate); engineering management (MSE, Certificate); general (MME); materials science and engineering (MS); mechanical engineering (MSE, PhD); program management (Certificate); systems engineering and management of information technology (Certificate); transportation and infrastructure systems (Certificate). *Application deadline:* For fall admission, 7/15 priority date for domestic students, 7/1 for international students; for spring admission, 11/15 priority date for domestic students, 11/1 for international students. Applications are processed on a rolling basis. *Application fee:* $55. Electronic applications accepted. *Application Contact:* Dr. Steven Brown, Director of Graduate Admissions, 202-319-5057, Fax: 202-319-6533, E-mail: cua-admissions@cua.edu. *Dean,* Dr. John Judge, 202-319-5127, Fax: 202-319-4499, E-mail: judge@cua.edu.

School of Nursing Students: 22 full-time (19 women), 143 part-time (133 women); includes 53 minority (28 Black or African American, non-Hispanic/Latino; 6 Asian, non-Hispanic/Latino; 7 Hispanic/Latino; 12 Two or more races, non-Hispanic/Latino), 7 international. Average age 43. 103 applicants, 72% accepted, 31 enrolled. *Faculty:* 22 full-time (all women), 43 part-time/adjunct (33 women). Expenses: Contact institution. *Financial support:* Fellowships, research assistantships, teaching assistantships, Federal Work-Study, scholarships/grants, tuition waivers (full and partial), and unspecified assistantships available. Financial award application deadline: 2/1; financial award applicants required to submit FAFSA. In 2018, 28 master's, 7 doctorates, 6 other advanced degrees awarded. *Program availability:* Part-time, 100% online. Offers nursing (MSN, DNP, PhD, Certificate). *Application deadline:* For fall admission, 7/15 priority date for domestic students, 7/1 for international students; for spring admission, 11/15 priority date for domestic students, 11/1 for international students. Applications are processed on a rolling basis. *Application fee:* $55. Electronic applications accepted. *Application Contact:* Dr. Steven Brown, Director of Graduate Admissions, 202-319-5057, Fax: 202-319-6533, E-mail: cua-admissions@cua.edu. *Dean,* Dr. Patricia McMullen, 202-319-5403, Fax: 202-319-6485, E-mail: mcmullep@cua.edu.

School of Philosophy Students: 50 full-time (9 women), 54 part-time (22 women); includes 14 minority (4 Asian, non-Hispanic/Latino; 5 Hispanic/Latino; 5 Two or more races, non-Hispanic/Latino), 7 international. Average age 31. 69 applicants, 55% accepted, 31 enrolled. *Faculty:* 23 full-time (5 women), 5 part-time/adjunct (1 woman). Expenses: Contact institution. *Financial support:* Fellowships, research assistantships, teaching assistantships, Federal Work-Study, scholarships/grants, tuition waivers (full and partial), and unspecified assistantships available. Financial award application deadline: 2/1; financial award applicants required to submit FAFSA. In 2018, 14 master's, 9 doctorates awarded. *Program availability:* Part-time. Offers philosophy (MA, PhD, Ph L). MA/JD offered in combination with Columbus School of Law. *Application deadline:* For fall admission, 7/15 priority date for domestic students, 7/1 for international students; for spring admission, 11/15 priority date for domestic students, 11/1 for international students. Applications are processed on a rolling basis. *Application fee:* $55. Electronic applications accepted. *Application Contact:* Dr. Steven Brown, Director of Graduate Admissions, 202-319-5057, Fax: 202-319-6533, E-mail: cua-admissions@cua.edu. *Dean,* Dr. John McCarthy, 202-319-6649, Fax: 202-319-4731, E-mail: mccartjc@cua.edu.

School of Theology and Religious Studies Students: 143 full-time (21 women), 179 part-time (68 women); includes 75 minority (10 Black or African American, non-Hispanic/Latino; 1 American Indian or Alaska Native, non-Hispanic/Latino; 15 Asian, non-Hispanic/Latino; 25 Hispanic/Latino; 24 Two or more races, non-Hispanic/Latino), 51 international. Average age 36. 208 applicants, 60% accepted, 61 enrolled. *Faculty:* 44 full-time (3 women), 17 part-time/adjunct (0 women). Expenses: Contact institution. *Financial support:* Fellowships, research assistantships, teaching assistantships, Federal Work-Study, scholarships/grants, tuition waivers (full and partial), and unspecified assistantships available. Financial award application deadline: 2/1; financial award applicants required to submit FAFSA. In 2018, 52 master's, 29 doctorates awarded. *Program availability:* Part-time. Offers theology and religious studies (M Cat, M Div, MA, D Min, PhD, STD, Certificate, STB, STL). MSLA/MA offered in conjunction with Department of Library and Information Science. *Application deadline:* For fall admission, 7/15 priority date for domestic students, 7/1 for international students; for spring admission, 11/15 priority date for domestic students, 11/1 for international students. Applications are processed on a rolling basis. *Application fee:* $55. Electronic applications accepted. *Application Contact:* Dr. Steven Brown, Director of Graduate Admissions, 202-319-5057, Fax: 202-319-6533, E-mail: cua-admissions@cua.edu. *Dean,* Very Rev. Mark Morozowich, 202-319-5684, Fax: 202-319-4967, E-mail: morozowich@cua.edu.

CEDAR CREST COLLEGE, Allentown, PA 18104-6196

General Information Independent-religious, coed, primarily women, comprehensive institution. *Enrollment:* 89 full-time matriculated graduate/professional students (74 women), 184 part-time matriculated graduate/professional students (149 women). *Enrollment by degree level:* 200 master's, 31 other advanced degrees. *Graduate faculty:* 27 full-time (21 women), 43 part-time/adjunct (24 women). *Tuition:* Full-time $13,998; part-time $778 per credit. *Required fees:* $240; $240 per unit. Tuition and fees vary according to program. *Graduate housing:* On-campus housing not available. *Student services:* Campus employment opportunities, campus safety program, career counseling, exercise/wellness program, free psychological counseling, international student services, multicultural affairs office, services for students with disabilities, teacher training. *Library facilities:* Frank M. Cressman Library.

Computer facilities: Computer purchase and lease plans are available. A campuswide network can be accessed from student residence rooms and from off campus. Online class registration is available.
Website: http://www.cedarcrest.edu/

General Application Contact: Nancy Wunderly, Director of School of Adult and Graduate Education, 610-437-4471, E-mail: sage@cedarcrest.edu.

GRADUATE UNITS

Department of Education Students: 11 full-time (all women), 60 part-time (49 women); includes 11 minority (1 Black or African American, non-Hispanic/Latino; 2 Asian, non-Hispanic/Latino; 7 Hispanic/Latino; 1 Two or more races, non-Hispanic/Latino). Average age 34. 14 applicants, 79% accepted, 8 enrolled. *Faculty:* 4 full-time (all women), 13 part-time/adjunct (8 women). Expenses: Contact institution. *Financial support:* In 2018–19, 60 students received support. Available to part-time students. Applicants required to submit FAFSA. In 2018, 21 master's awarded. *Program availability:* Part-time, evening/weekend, 100% online, blended/hybrid learning. Offers education (M Ed). *Application deadline:* For fall admission, 8/7 priority date for domestic and international students; for winter admission, 11/7 priority date for domestic and international students; for spring admission, 1/8 priority date for domestic and international students. Applications are processed on a rolling basis. Electronic applications accepted. *Application Contact:* Nancy Wunderly, Director of School of Adult and Graduate Education, 610-606-4666, E-mail: sage@cedarcrest.edu. *Department Chair,* Dr. Jill Purdy, 610-606-4666 Ext. 3419, E-mail: jepurdy@cedarcrest.edu.

Dietetic Internship Certificate Program Students: 17 full-time (15 women), 11 part-time (all women). Average age 26. 28 applicants, 100% accepted, 28 enrolled. *Faculty:* 1 (woman) full-time, 2 part-time/adjunct (1 woman). Expenses: Contact institution. In 2018, 25 Graduate Certificates awarded. *Program availability:* Part-time, evening/weekend, blended/hybrid learning. Offers dietetic internship (Graduate Certificate). *Application deadline:* Applications are processed on a rolling basis. Electronic applications accepted. *Application Contact:* Nancy Wunderly, Director of School of Adult and Graduate Education, 610-437-4471, E-mail: sage@cedarcrest.edu. *Director,* Marilou Wieder, 610-606-4666 Ext. 3445, E-mail: mwieder@cedarcrest.edu.

Program in Art Therapy Students: 11 full-time (all women), 6 part-time (all women). Average age 30. 10 applicants, 30% accepted, 2 enrolled. *Faculty:* 2 full-time (both women), 6 part-time/adjunct (1 woman). Expenses: Contact institution. In 2018, 5 master's awarded. *Program availability:* Part-time, evening/weekend, blended/hybrid learning. Offers art therapy (MA). *Application deadline:* Applications are processed on a rolling basis. Electronic applications accepted. *Application Contact:* Nancy Wunderly, Director of School of Adult and Graduate Education, 610-437-4471, E-mail: sage@cedarcrest.edu. *Director,* Michelle Dean, 610-437-4471 Ext. 3594, E-mail: michelle.dean@cedarcrest.edu.

Program in Business Administration Students: 18 full-time (15 women), 24 part-time (14 women); includes 8 minority (3 Black or African American, non-Hispanic/Latino; 2 Asian, non-Hispanic/Latino; 3 Hispanic/Latino), 1 international. Average age 36. 27 applicants, 81% accepted, 20 enrolled. *Faculty:* 2 full-time (1 woman), 10 part-time/adjunct (3 women). Expenses: Contact institution. In 2018, 13 master's awarded. *Program availability:* Part-time, evening/weekend, blended/hybrid learning. Offers business administration (MBA). *Application deadline:* Applications are processed on a rolling basis. Electronic applications accepted. *Application Contact:* Nancy Wunderly, Director of School of Adult and Graduate Education, 610-437-4471, E-mail: sage@cedarcrest.edu. *Program Director MBA,* Michael Zalot, 610-437-4471 Ext. 4453, E-mail: michael.zalot@cedarcrest.edu.

Program in Creative Writing Students: 6 part-time (5 women). Average age 33. *Faculty:* 1 (woman) full-time, 3 part-time/adjunct (1 woman). Expenses: Contact institution. In 2018, 6 master's awarded. *Program availability:* Part-time, evening/weekend, blended/hybrid learning. Offers creative writing (MFA). *Application deadline:* Applications are processed on a rolling basis. Electronic applications accepted. *Application Contact:* Nancy Wunderly, Director of School of Adult and Graduate Education, 610-437-4471, E-mail: sage@cedarcrest.edu. *Director of Writing Program,* Allison Wellford, 610-606-4666 Ext. 3474, E-mail: acwellfo@cedarcrest.edu.

Program in Forensic Science Students: 16 full-time (15 women), 8 part-time (3 women); includes 4 minority (1 American Indian or Alaska Native, non-Hispanic/Latino; 3 Asian, non-Hispanic/Latino), 1 international. Average age 25. 16 applicants, 88% accepted, 7 enrolled. *Faculty:* 4 full-time (2 women), 1 (woman) part-time/adjunct. Expenses: Contact institution. *Financial support:* In 2018–19, 4 students received support. Unspecified assistantships available. In 2018, 4 master's awarded. Offers forensic science (MS). *Application deadline:* For fall admission, 1/2 priority date for domestic students. Applications are processed on a rolling basis. Electronic applications accepted. *Application Contact:* Nancy Wunderly, Director of School of Adult and Graduate Education, 610-606-4666, E-mail: sage@cedarcrest.edu. *Director and Associate Professor,* Dr. Lawrence A. Quarino, 610-606-4666 Ext. 3507, Fax: 610-740-3787, E-mail: laquarin@cedarcrest.edu.

School of Nursing Students: 10 full-time (2 women), 34 part-time (29 women); includes 9 minority (3 Black or African American, non-Hispanic/Latino; 2 Asian, non-Hispanic/Latino; 4 Hispanic/Latino), 1 international. Average age 36. 59 applicants, 58% accepted, 29 enrolled. *Faculty:* 9 full-time (6 women), 6 part-time/adjunct (5 women). Expenses: Contact institution. In 2018, 1 master's awarded. *Program availability:* Part-time. Offers nursing administration (MS); nursing education (MS). *Application deadline:* Applications are processed on a rolling basis. Electronic applications accepted. *Application Contact:* Nancy Wunderly, Director of School of Adult and Graduate Education, 610-606-4666, E-mail: sage@cedarcrest.edu. *Dean,* Dr. Wendy Robb, 610-606-4666, E-mail: wjrobb@cedarcrest.edu.

CEDARS-SINAI MEDICAL CENTER, Los Angeles, CA 90048

General Information Independent, coed, graduate-only institution. *Graduate housing:* On-campus housing not available.

GRADUATE UNITS

Graduate Programs Offers biomedical and translational sciences (PhD); magnetic resonance in medicine (MS). Electronic applications accepted.

CEDARVILLE UNIVERSITY, Cedarville, OH 45314

General Information Independent-religious, coed, comprehensive institution. *Enrollment:* 4,160 graduate, professional, and undergraduate students; 342 full-time matriculated graduate/professional students (202 women), 59 part-time matriculated graduate/professional students (40 women). *Enrollment by degree level:* 231 master's, 180 doctoral, 6 other advanced degrees. *Graduate faculty:* 55 full-time (19 women), 18 part-time/adjunct (8 women). *Tuition:* Full-time $12,594; part-time $566 per credit. One-time fee: $100 full-time. Tuition and fees vary according to degree level and program. *Graduate housing:* On-campus housing not available. *Student services:* Campus employment opportunities, campus safety program, career counseling, exercise/wellness program, free psychological counseling, international student services, low-cost health insurance, services for students with disabilities, writing training. *Library facilities:* Centennial Library. *Collection:* Books: 182,596 (physical), 132,747 (digital/electronic); Serial titles: 737 (physical), 27,560 (digital/electronic); Databases: 200. Weekly public service hours: 91; students can reserve study rooms.

Computer facilities: 1,500 computers available on campus for general student use. A campuswide network can be accessed from student residence rooms and from off campus. Online class registration, over 70 software packages are available.
Website: http://www.cedarville.edu/

General Application Contact: Jim Amstutz, Director of Graduate Admissions, 937-766-8000, Fax: 937-766-7575, E-mail: gradadmissions@cedarville.edu.

GRADUATE UNITS

Graduate Programs Students: 341 full-time (201 women), 60 part-time (41 women); includes 88 minority (51 Black or African American, non-Hispanic/Latino; 2 American Indian or Alaska Native, non-Hispanic/Latino; 22 Asian, non-Hispanic/Latino; 2 Hispanic/Latino; 11 Two or more races, non-Hispanic/Latino), 3 international. Average age 26. 354 applicants, 38% accepted, 113 enrolled. *Faculty:* 55 full-time (19 women), 18 part-time/adjunct (8 women). *Expenses:* Contact institution. *Financial support:* Scholarships/grants and unspecified assistantships available. Support available to part-time students. Financial award application deadline: 1/30; financial award applicants required to submit FAFSA. In 2018, 65 master's, 34 doctorates awarded. *Program availability:* Part-time, evening/weekend, 100% online, blended/hybrid learning. Offers business administration (MBA); family nurse practitioner (MSN); global ministry (M Div); global public health nursing (MSN); healthcare administration (MBA); ministry (M Min); nurse educator (MSN); operations management (MBA); pharmacy (Pharm D). *Application deadline:* For fall admission, 5/1 priority date for domestic and international students; for spring admission, 11/1 priority date for domestic and international students. Applications are processed on a rolling basis. *Application fee:* $0. Electronic applications accepted. *Application Contact:* Alexis McKay, Director of Graduate Admissions, 937-766-7878, Fax: 937-766-7700, E-mail: amckay@cedarville.edu. *Dean of Graduate Studies,* Dr. Janice Supplee, 937-766-7700, E-mail: suppleej@cedarville.edu.

CENTENARY COLLEGE OF LOUISIANA, Shreveport, LA 71104

General Information Independent-religious, coed, comprehensive institution. *Graduate housing:* Room and/or apartments available on a first-come, first-served basis to single students; on-campus housing not available to married students.

GRADUATE UNITS

Graduate Programs *Program availability:* Part-time, evening/weekend. Offers elementary education (MAT); secondary education (MAT).

Frost School of Business *Program availability:* Part-time, evening/weekend. Offers business (MBA).

CENTENARY UNIVERSITY, Hackettstown, NJ 07840-2100

General Information Independent-religious, coed, comprehensive institution. *Graduate housing:* Room and/or apartments available on a first-come, first-served basis to single students; on-campus housing not available to married students. Housing application deadline: 6/1.

GRADUATE UNITS

Program in Business Administration *Program availability:* Part-time, evening/weekend, online learning. Offers business administration (MBA).

Program in Counseling Psychology *Program availability:* Part-time, evening/weekend, online learning. Offers counseling (MA); counseling psychology (MA).

Program in Education *Program availability:* Part-time, evening/weekend, online learning. Offers education practice (M Ed); educational leadership (MA, Ed D); instructional leadership (MA); reading (M Ed); special education (MA).

Program in Professional Accounting *Program availability:* Part-time, evening/weekend, online learning. Offers professional accounting (MS).

CENTRAL BAPTIST THEOLOGICAL SEMINARY, Shawnee, KS 66226

General Information Independent-religious, coed, graduate-only institution. *Graduate housing:* On-campus housing not available.

GRADUATE UNITS

Graduate and Professional Programs *Program availability:* Part-time. Offers missional church studies (MA); theological studies (MA); theology (M Div, Diploma). Electronic applications accepted.

CENTRAL CONNECTICUT STATE UNIVERSITY, New Britain, CT 06050-4010

General Information State-supported, coed, comprehensive institution. *Enrollment:* 11,822 graduate, professional, and undergraduate students; 588 full-time matriculated graduate/professional students (379 women), 1,530 part-time matriculated graduate/professional students (995 women). *Enrollment by degree level:* 1,606 master's, 110 doctoral, 402 other advanced degrees. *Graduate faculty:* 177 full-time (82 women), 87 part-time/adjunct (54 women). *International tuition:* $18,102 full-time. *Tuition, area resident:* Full-time $7027; part-time $388 per credit. Tuition, state resident: full-time $9750; part-time $388 per credit. Tuition, nonresident: full-time $18,102; part-time $388 per credit. *Required fees:* $266 per semester. *Graduate housing:* Room and/or apartments available on a first-come, first-served basis to single students; on-campus housing not available to married students. Typical cost: $7004 per year ($12,176 including board). Room and board charges vary according to board plan, campus/location and housing facility selected. Housing application deadline: 5/1. *Student services:* Campus employment opportunities, campus safety program, career counseling, child daycare facilities, exercise/wellness program, free psychological counseling, international student services, low-cost health insurance, multicultural affairs office, services for students with disabilities, teacher training, writing training. *Library facilities:* Elihu Burritt Library plus 1 other. *Collection:* Books: 449,293 (physical), 199,200 (digital/electronic); Serial titles: 6,833 (physical), 89,498 (digital/electronic); Databases: 151. Weekly public service hours: 84.

Computer facilities: 450 computers available on campus for general student use. A campuswide network can be accessed from student residence rooms and from off campus. Online class registration is available. Website: http://www.ccsu.edu/

General Application Contact: Patricia Gardner, Associate Director of Graduate Studies, 860-832-2350, Fax: 860-832-2362.

GRADUATE UNITS

School of Graduate Studies Students: 588 full-time (379 women), 1,530 part-time (995 women); includes 551 minority (192 Black or African American, non-Hispanic/Latino; 3 American Indian or Alaska Native, non-Hispanic/Latino; 76 Asian, non-Hispanic/Latino; 230 Hispanic/Latino; 2 Native Hawaiian or other Pacific Islander, non-Hispanic/Latino; 48 Two or more races, non-Hispanic/Latino), 24 international. Average age 32. 1,111 applicants, 72% accepted, 541 enrolled. *Faculty:* 177 full-time (82 women), 87 part-time/adjunct (54 women). *Expenses:* Contact institution. *Financial support:* In 2018–19, 302 students received support. Career-related internships or fieldwork, Federal Work-Study, scholarships/grants, and unspecified assistantships available. Support available to part-time students. Financial award application deadline: 3/1; financial award applicants required to submit FAFSA. In 2018, 568 master's, 6 doctorates, 128 other advanced degrees awarded. *Program availability:* Part-time, evening/weekend, 100%

online. *Application deadline:* For fall admission, 6/1 for domestic students, 5/1 for international students; for spring admission, 11/1 for domestic and international students. Applications are processed on a rolling basis. *Application fee:* $50. Electronic applications accepted. *Application Contact:* Patricia Gardner, Associate Director of Graduate Studies, 860-832-2350, Fax: 860-832-2362. *Associate Director of Graduate Studies,* Patricia Gardner, 860-832-2350, Fax: 860-832-2362.

College of Liberal Arts and Social Sciences Students: 103 full-time (61 women), 183 part-time (124 women); includes 78 minority (26 Black or African American, non-Hispanic/Latino; 1 American Indian or Alaska Native, non-Hispanic/Latino; 8 Asian, non-Hispanic/Latino; 36 Hispanic/Latino; 7 Two or more races, non-Hispanic/Latino), 1 international. Average age 32. 211 applicants, 69% accepted, 91 enrolled. *Faculty:* 68 full-time (34 women), 5 part-time/adjunct (3 women). *Expenses:* Contact institution. *Financial support:* In 2018–19, 66 students received support. Career-related internships or fieldwork, Federal Work-Study, scholarships/grants, and unspecified assistantships available. Support available to part-time students. Financial award application deadline: 3/1; financial award applicants required to submit FAFSA. In 2018, 108 master's, 18 other advanced degrees awarded. *Program availability:* Part-time, evening/weekend. Offers art education (MS, Certificate); communication (MS); criminal justice (MS); English (MA); English education (MAT); geography (MS); history (MA, Certificate); information design (MA); international studies (MS); liberal arts and social sciences (MA, MAT, MS, Certificate); modern language (MA, Certificate); music education (MS, Certificate); psychological science (MA); public relations/promotions (Certificate); Spanish (MS, Certificate). *Application deadline:* For fall admission, 6/1 for domestic students, 5/1 for international students; for spring admission, 11/1 for domestic and international students. Applications are processed on a rolling basis. *Application fee:* $50. Electronic applications accepted. *Application Contact:* Patricia Gardner, Associate Director of Graduate Studies, 860-832-2350, Fax: 860-832-2362. *Dean,* Dr. Robert Wolff, 860-832-2604, E-mail: wolffr@ccsu.edu.

School of Business Students: 42 full-time (20 women), 264 part-time (124 women); includes 101 minority (34 Black or African American, non-Hispanic/Latino; 25 Asian, non-Hispanic/Latino; 36 Hispanic/Latino; 6 Two or more races, non-Hispanic/Latino), 2 international. Average age 31. 165 applicants, 79% accepted, 98 enrolled. *Faculty:* 18 full-time (8 women), 5 part-time/adjunct (1 woman). *Expenses:* Contact institution. *Financial support:* In 2018–19, 29 students received support. Career-related internships or fieldwork, Federal Work-Study, scholarships/grants, and unspecified assistantships available. Support available to part-time students. Financial award application deadline: 3/1; financial award applicants required to submit FAFSA. In 2018, 75 master's awarded. *Program availability:* Part-time, evening/weekend. Offers accounting (MSA); business (MBA, MSA); business administration (MBA). *Application deadline:* For fall admission, 6/1 for domestic students, 5/1 for international students; for spring admission, 11/1 for domestic and international students. Applications are processed on a rolling basis. *Application fee:* $50. Electronic applications accepted. *Application Contact:* Patricia Gardner, Associate Director of Graduate Admissions, 860-832-2350, Fax: 860-832-2362. *Interim Dean,* Dr. Joseph Farhat, 860-832-3209, E-mail: josephfarhat@ccsu.edu.

School of Education and Professional Studies Students: 260 full-time (200 women), 831 part-time (641 women); includes 255 minority (90 Black or African American, non-Hispanic/Latino; 2 American Indian or Alaska Native, non-Hispanic/Latino; 14 Asian, non-Hispanic/Latino; 127 Hispanic/Latino; 1 Native Hawaiian or other Pacific Islander, non-Hispanic/Latino; 21 Two or more races, non-Hispanic/Latino), 2 international. Average age 33. 429 applicants, 69% accepted, 207 enrolled. *Faculty:* 44 full-time (26 women), 64 part-time/adjunct (42 women). *Expenses:* Contact institution. *Financial support:* In 2018–19, 129 students received support. Career-related internships or fieldwork, Federal Work-Study, scholarships/grants, and unspecified assistantships available. Support available to part-time students. Financial award application deadline: 3/1; financial award applicants required to submit FAFSA. In 2018, 229 master's, 6 doctorates, 99 other advanced degrees awarded. *Program availability:* Part-time, evening/weekend. Offers education and professional studies (MAT, MS, MSN, Ed D, AC, Certificate, Sixth Year Certificate); educational leadership, policy and instructional technology (MS, Ed D, AC, Sixth Year Certificate); hospice and palliative care (MSN); literacy, elementary, and early childhood education (MS, AC, Sixth Year Certificate); marriage and family therapy (MS); physical education (MS); professional counseling (MS, AC, Certificate); school counseling (MS); special education and interventions (MA, AC, Certificate); student development in higher education (MS). *Application deadline:* For fall admission, 6/1 for domestic students, 5/1 for international students; for spring admission, 11/1 for domestic and international students. Applications are processed on a rolling basis. *Application fee:* $50. Electronic applications accepted. *Application Contact:* Patricia Gardner, Associate Director of Graduate Studies, 860-832-2350, Fax: 860-832-2362. *Dean,* Dr. Kimberly Kostelis, 860-832-2101, E-mail: kimberly.kostelis@ccsu.edu.

School of Engineering, Science and Technology Students: 183 full-time (98 women), 252 part-time (106 women); includes 117 minority (42 Black or African American, non-Hispanic/Latino; 29 Asian, non-Hispanic/Latino; 31 Hispanic/Latino; 1 Native Hawaiian or other Pacific Islander, non-Hispanic/Latino; 14 Two or more races, non-Hispanic/Latino), 19 international. Average age 32. 306 applicants, 74% accepted, 145 enrolled. *Faculty:* 47 full-time (14 women), 13 part-time/adjunct (8 women). *Expenses:* Contact institution. *Financial support:* In 2018–19, 78 students received support. Career-related internships or fieldwork, Federal Work-Study, scholarships/grants, and unspecified assistantships available. Support available to part-time students. Financial award application deadline: 3/1; financial award applicants required to submit FAFSA. In 2018, 156 master's, 11 other advanced degrees awarded. *Program availability:* Part-time, evening/weekend, 100% online. Offers biology (MA, DNP-A); biomolecular sciences (MS, Certificate); computer information technology (MS); construction management (MS, Certificate); data mining (MS, Certificate); engineering (MS); engineering, science and technology (MA, MS, DNP-A, Certificate, Sixth Year Certificate); lean manufacturing and Six Sigma (Certificate); mathematics (MA, MS); mathematics education leadership (Sixth Year Certificate); mathematics for secondary education (Certificate); science education (Certificate); STEM education (MS); supply chain and logistics (Certificate); technology and engineering education (MS); technology management (MS). *Application deadline:* For fall admission, 6/1 for domestic students, 5/1 for international students; for spring admission, 11/1 for domestic and international students. Applications are processed on a rolling basis. *Application fee:* $50. Electronic applications accepted. *Application Contact:* Patricia Gardner, Associate Director of Graduate Studies, 860-832-2350, Fax: 860-832-2362. *Dean,* Dr. Ju Kim, 860-832-1800, E-mail: jhkim@ccsu.edu.

CENTRAL EUROPEAN UNIVERSITY, H-1051 Budapest, Hungary

General Information Independent, coed, graduate-only institution. CGS member. *Graduate housing:* Room and/or apartments guaranteed to single students; on-campus housing not available to married students. Housing application deadline: 2/4. *Research affiliation:* Institute of Human Sciences Vienna (social sciences), Open Society Institute (social sciences), Alfréd Rényi Institute of Mathematics.

GRADUATE UNITS

Center for Network Science Offers network science (PhD). Electronic applications accepted.

Department of Cognitive Science Offers cognitive science (PhD). Electronic applications accepted.

Department of Economics *Program availability:* Part-time. Offers business administration (PhD); business analytics (M Sc); economic policy in global markets (MA); economics (MA, PhD); finance (MS); global economic relations (MA); technology management and innovation (MS). Electronic applications accepted.

Department of Environmental Sciences and Policy *Program availability:* Part-time. Offers environmental sciences and policy (MS, PhD). Electronic applications accepted.

Department of Gender Studies Offers gender studies (MA, PhD). Electronic applications accepted.

Department of History Offers history (MA, PhD). Electronic applications accepted.

Department of International Relations Offers global economic relations (MA); international relations (MA, PhD). Electronic applications accepted.

Department of Legal Studies Offers comparative Constitutional law (LL M); human rights (LL M, MA); international business law (LL M); juridical sciences (SJD). Electronic applications accepted.

Department of Mathematics and its Applications Offers mathematics and its applications (MS, PhD). Electronic applications accepted.

Department of Medieval Studies Offers comparative history: interdisciplinary Medieval studies (MA); cultural heritage studies (MA); Medieval studies (MA, PhD). Electronic applications accepted.

Department of Philosophy Offers philosophy (MA, PhD). Electronic applications accepted.

Department of Political Science Offers political science (MA, PhD). Electronic applications accepted.

Department of Sociology and Social Anthropology Offers sociology and social anthropology (MA, PhD). Electronic applications accepted.

Nationalism Studies Program Offers nationalism studies (MA). Electronic applications accepted.

School of Public Policy Offers public administration (MPA); public policy (MA, PhD). Electronic applications accepted.

CENTRAL METHODIST UNIVERSITY, Fayette, MO 65248-1198

General Information Independent-religious, coed, comprehensive institution. *Graduate housing:* Rooms and/or apartments available on a first-come, first-served basis to single and married students.

GRADUATE UNITS

College of Graduate and Extended Studies *Program availability:* Part-time, evening/weekend, online learning. Offers clinical counseling (MS); clinical nurse leader (MSN); education (M Ed); music education (MME); nurse educator (MSN). Electronic applications accepted.

CENTRAL MICHIGAN UNIVERSITY, Mount Pleasant, MI 48859

General Information State-supported, coed, university. CGS member. *Graduate housing:* Rooms and/or apartments available on a first-come, first-served basis to single and married students. *Research affiliation:* IBM (information technology), Dendritic Nanotechnologies, Inc. (chemistry, physics), Dow Corning Corporation (silicon-based technology), Dow Chemical Company (chemicals and plastics), SAS Business Analytics (business analysis), SAP (information technology).

GRADUATE UNITS

Central Michigan University Global Campus *Program availability:* Part-time, evening/weekend, online learning. Offers acquisitions administration (MSA, Certificate); college teaching (Graduate Certificate); community college (MA); curriculum and instruction (MA); cybersecurity (Certificate); educational technology (MA, DET); engineering management administration (MSA, Certificate); enterprise resource planning (MBA, Certificate); general administration (MSA, Certificate); general public administration (MPA); health administration (DHA); health services administration (MSA, Certificate); human resource management (MBA); human resources administration (MSA, Certificate); information resource management (MSA); information resource management administration (Certificate); international administration (MSA, Certificate); international health (Certificate); K-12 leadership (Ed D); leadership (MSA, Certificate); logistics management (MBA, Certificate); marketing (MBA); nutrition and dietetics (MS); philanthropy and fundraising administration (MSA, Certificate); professional counseling (MA); public administration (MSA, Certificate); public management (MPA); reading and literacy K-12 (MA); recreation and park administration (MSA); research administration (MSA, Certificate); school counseling (MA); school principalship (MA); state and local government (MPA); training and development (MA); value-driven organization (MBA). Electronic applications accepted.

College of Graduate Studies *Program availability:* Part-time, evening/weekend, online learning. Offers acquisitions administration (MSA, Graduate Certificate); general administration (MSA, Graduate Certificate); health services administration (MSA, Graduate Certificate); human resource administration (Graduate Certificate); human resources administration (MSA); information resource management (MSA, Graduate Certificate); international administration (MSA, Graduate Certificate); leadership (MSA, Graduate Certificate); public administration (MSA, Graduate Certificate); research administration (Graduate Certificate); sport administration (MSA). Electronic applications accepted.

College of Business Administration *Program availability:* Part-time, evening/weekend. Offers accounting (MBA); business administration (MA, MBA, MS, Graduate Certificate); business computing (Graduate Certificate); business economics (MA); consulting (MBA); economics (MA); finance (MBA); general business (MBA); human resource management (MBA); information systems (MBA, MS); international business (MBA); logistics management (MBA); marketing (MBA); value-driven organization (MBA). Electronic applications accepted.

College of Education and Human Services *Program availability:* Part-time, evening/weekend. Offers apparel product development and merchandising technology (MS); autism (Graduate Certificate); counseling (MA); education and human services (MA, MS, Ed D, Ed S, Graduate Certificate); educational leadership (Ed D); educational technology (MA, Graduate Certificate); elementary education (MA); general educational administration (Ed S); gerontology (Graduate Certificate); human development and family studies (MA); nutrition and dietetics (MS); reading and literacy K-12 (MA); school principalship (MA); secondary education (MA); special education (MA, Graduate Certificate); student affairs administration (MA); teacher leadership (MA). Electronic applications accepted.

College of Liberal Arts and Social Sciences *Program availability:* Part-time, evening/weekend. Offers American politics (MA); applied experimental psychology (PhD); clinical psychology (PhD); English composition and communication (MA); English language and literature (MA); European history (Graduate Certificate); experimental psychology (MS, PhD); history (MA); humanities (MA); industrial and organizational psychology (MA, PhD); liberal arts and social sciences (MA, MPA, MS, PhD, Graduate Certificate, S Psy S); modern history (Graduate Certificate); neuroscience (MS, PhD); occupational health psychology (PhD); political science (MA); professional development in public administration (Graduate Certificate); public administration (MPA, Graduate Certificate); public management (MPA); school psychology (PhD, S Psy S); Spanish (MA); state and local government (MPA); TESOL: teaching English to speakers of other languages (MA); United States history (Graduate Certificate). Electronic applications accepted.

College of Medicine Offers medicine (MD).

College of Science and Engineering *Program availability:* Part-time, evening/weekend. Offers biology (MS); chemistry (MS); computer science (MS); conservation biology (MS); geographic information sciences (MS); industrial management and technology (MA); mathematics (MA, PhD); physics (MS); science and engineering (MA, MAT, MS, PhD, Graduate Certificate); science of advanced materials (PhD); teaching chemistry (MA). Electronic applications accepted.

College of the Arts and Media *Program availability:* Part-time. Offers arts and media (MA, MM); communication (MA); composition (MM); conducting (MM); electronic media management (MA); electronic media production (MA); electronic media studies (MA); film theory and criticism (MA); music education (MM); performance (MM). Electronic applications accepted.

The Herbert H. and Grace A. Dow College of Health Professions *Program availability:* Part-time. Offers audiology (Au D); exercise science (MA); health administration (DHA); health professions (MA, MS, Au D, DHA, DPT, Graduate Certificate); physical therapy (DPT); physician assistant (MS); speech-language pathology (MA); sport administration (MA). Electronic applications accepted.

CENTRAL PENN COLLEGE, Summerdale, PA 17093-0309

General Information Proprietary, coed, comprehensive institution.

GRADUATE UNITS

Graduate Programs *Program availability:* Evening/weekend. Offers information systems management (MPS); organizational development (MPS). Programs offered in Harrisburg, PA.

CENTRAL WASHINGTON UNIVERSITY, Ellensburg, WA 98926

General Information State-supported, coed, comprehensive institution. CGS member. *Graduate housing:* Rooms and/or apartments available on a first-come, first-served basis to single and married students. *Research affiliation:* Associated Western Universities (science and engineering), East-West Center (Pacific area studies), Jet Propulsion Laboratory (engineering).

GRADUATE UNITS

School of Graduate Studies and Research *Program availability:* Part-time, evening/weekend. Offers individual studies (M Ed, MA, MFA, MS). Electronic applications accepted.

College of Arts and Humanities *Program availability:* Part-time. Offers arts and humanities (MA, MFA, MM); ceramics (MFA); composition (MM); computer arts (MFA); conducting (MM); history (MA); jewelry and metalsmithing (MFA); literature (MA); music education (MM); painting and drawing (MFA); pedagogy (MM); performance (MM); photography (MFA); professional and creative writing (MA); sculpture (MFA); teaching English to speakers of other languages (MA); theatre production (MA); theatre studies (MA). Electronic applications accepted.

College of Education and Professional Studies *Program availability:* Part-time. Offers athletic administration (MS); career and technical education (MS); education and professional studies (M Ed, MS); family and child life (MS); family and consumer sciences education (MS); health and physical education (MS); higher education (M Ed); integrative human physiology (MS); literacy (M Ed); master teacher (M Ed); nutrition (MS). Electronic applications accepted.

College of the Sciences *Program availability:* Part-time, evening/weekend. Offers active and regional tectonics (MS); anthropology (MS); botany (MS); chemistry (MS); continental dynamics and seismology (MS); environmental geochemistry (MS); experimental psychology (MS); geography (MS); geomorphology (MS); geomorphology and climate change (MS); mental health counseling (MS); microbiology and parasitology (MS); paleohydrology and volcanology (MS); school psychology (Ed S); sciences (MS, Ed S); stream ecology and fisheries (MS); terrestrial ecology (MS). Electronic applications accepted.

CENTRAL YESHIVA TOMCHEI TMIMIM-LUBAVITCH, Brooklyn, NY 11230

General Information Independent-religious, men only, comprehensive institution.

GRADUATE UNITS

Graduate Programs Offers Jewish/Judaic studies (MA); Talmudic studies (MA).

CENTRO DE ESTUDIOS AVANZADOS DE PUERTO RICO Y EL CARIBE, Old San Juan, PR 00902-3970

General Information Independent, coed, graduate-only institution. *Graduate housing:* On-campus housing not available. *Research affiliation:* Museo de las Americas, Museo Hombre Dominicano, Archivo General, Museo Universidad del Turabo.

GRADUATE UNITS

Graduate Program in Puerto Rican and Caribbean Studies *Program availability:* Part-time, evening/weekend. Offers Puerto Rican and Caribbean history (MA, PhD); Puerto Rican and Caribbean literature (MA, PhD); Puerto Rican studies (MA).

CHADRON STATE COLLEGE, Chadron, NE 69337

General Information State-supported, coed, comprehensive institution. *Graduate housing:* Rooms and/or apartments available on a first-come, first-served basis to single and married students. Housing application deadline: 6/1.

GRADUATE UNITS

School of Professional and Graduate Studies *Program availability:* Part-time, evening/weekend, online learning. Offers business (MA Ed); business and economics (MBA); community counseling (MA Ed); educational administration (MS Ed, Sp Ed); elementary education (MS Ed); history (MA Ed); language and literature (MA Ed); secondary administration (MS Ed); secondary education (MS Ed). Electronic applications accepted.

CHAMINADE UNIVERSITY OF HONOLULU, Honolulu, HI 96816-1578

General Information Independent-religious, coed, comprehensive institution. *Enrollment:* 314 full-time matriculated graduate/professional students (204 women), 191 part-time matriculated graduate/professional students (142 women). *Enrollment by degree level:* 505 master's. *Graduate faculty:* 25 full-time (10 women), 35 part-time/adjunct (19 women). *Tuition:* Full-time $22,680; part-time $945 per credit hour. Tuition and fees vary according to course load, campus/location and program. *Graduate housing:* On-campus housing not available. *Student services:* Campus safety program, career counseling, free psychological counseling, international student services, services for students with disabilities, teacher training, writing training. *Library facilities:* Sullivan Library. *Collection:* Books: 47,508 (physical), 133,757 (digital/electronic); Serial titles: 142 (physical), 36,441 (digital/electronic); Databases: 99.

Computer facilities: 200 computers available on campus for general student use. A campuswide network can be accessed from student residence rooms and from off campus. Online class registration is available.
Website: http://www.chaminade.edu/

GRADUATE UNITS

Graduate Students: 314 full-time (204 women), 191 part-time (142 women); includes 347 minority (26 Black or African American, non-Hispanic/Latino; 9 American Indian or Alaska Native, non-Hispanic/Latino; 161 Asian, non-Hispanic/Latino; 28 Hispanic/Latino; 120 Native Hawaiian or other Pacific Islander, non-Hispanic/Latino; 3 Two or more races, non-Hispanic/Latino), 10 international. Average age 33. 140 applicants, 79% accepted, 88 enrolled. *Faculty:* 25 full-time (10 women), 35 part-time/adjunct (19 women). Expenses: Contact institution. *Financial support:* Applicants required to submit FAFSA. In 2018, 232 master's awarded. *Program availability:* Part-time, evening/weekend, 100% online, blended/hybrid learning. Offers accounting (MBA); business (MBA); child development (M Ed); correctional (MSCJA); criminal justice (MSCJA); diaconate education (MPT); early childhood education (Montessori) (MAT); early childhood education (PK-3) (MAT); educational leadership (M Ed); elementary education (MAT); instructional leadership (M Ed); island business (MBA); law enforcement (MSCJA); marriage and family counseling (MSCP); mental health counseling (MSCP); Montessori (M Ed); not-for-profit (MBA); pastoral counseling and spiritual direction (MPT); school counseling (MSCP); secondary education (MAT); special education (MAT); teacher leader (M Ed). *Application deadline:* Applications are processed on a rolling basis. *Application fee:* $40. Electronic applications accepted.

CHAMPLAIN COLLEGE, Burlington, VT 05402-0670

General Information Independent, coed, comprehensive institution. *Graduate housing:* Rooms and/or apartments available on a first-come, first-served basis to single and married students.

GRADUATE UNITS

Graduate Studies *Program availability:* Part-time, online learning. Offers business (MBA); digital forensic science (MS); early childhood education (M Ed); emergent media (MFA, MS); executive leadership (MS); health care administration (MS); information security operations (MS); law (MS); mediation and applied conflict studies (MS). MS in emergent media program held in Shanghai. Electronic applications accepted.

CHAPMAN UNIVERSITY, Orange, CA 92866

General Information Independent-religious, coed, comprehensive institution. CGS member. *Graduate housing:* Rooms and/or apartments available on a first-come, first-served basis to single and married students. Housing application deadline: 6/1. *Research affiliation:* National Science Foundation (science, engineering), National Endowment for the Arts (NEA) (art), U.S. Department of Education (DOE) (education), U.S. Geological Survey (USGS) (earth sciences), U.S. Department of Agriculture (USDA) (agriculture, food, nutrition).

GRADUATE UNITS

Crean College of Health and Behavioral Sciences Offers communication sciences and disorders (MS); health and behavioral sciences (MA, MMS, MS, DPT, TDPT); marriage and family therapy (MA); physical therapy (DPT, TDPT); physician assistant studies (MMS). Electronic applications accepted.

Dale E. Fowler School of Law *Program availability:* Part-time. Offers advocacy and dispute resolution (JD); business law (LL M, JD); criminal law (JD); entertainment and media law (LL M); entertainment law (JD); environmental, land use, and real estate law (JD); international and comparative law (LL M); international law (JD); law (JD); prosecutorial science (LL M); tax law (LL M); taxation (LL M); trial advocacy (LL M). Electronic applications accepted.

Dodge College of Film and Media Arts Offers documentary filmmaking (MFA); film and television producing (MFA); film production (MFA); film studies (MA); production design (MFA); screenwriting (MFA); television writing and producing (MFA). Electronic applications accepted.

Donna Ford Attallah College of Educational Studies *Program availability:* Part-time, evening/weekend. Offers counseling (MA); curriculum and instruction (MA); education (PhD); educational psychology (MA); leadership development (MA); multiple subjects (Credential); pupil personnel services (Credential); school psychology (Ed S); single subject (Credential); special education (MA, Credential); teaching (MA). Electronic applications accepted.

The George L. Argyros School of Business and Economics *Program availability:* Part-time, evening/weekend. Offers accounting (MS); behavioral and computational economics (MS); business administration (Exec MBA, MBA). Electronic applications accepted.

Schmid College of Science and Technology *Program availability:* Part-time, evening/weekend. Offers computational and data sciences (MS, PhD); food science (MS); science and technology (MS, PhD). Electronic applications accepted.

School of Communication *Program availability:* Evening/weekend. Offers communication (MS). Electronic applications accepted.

School of Pharmacy Offers pharmaceutical sciences (MS, PhD); pharmacy (Pharm D). Electronic applications accepted.

Wilkinson College of Arts, Humanities, and Social Sciences *Program availability:* Part-time, evening/weekend. Offers arts, humanities, and social sciences (MA, MFA); creative writing (MFA); English (MA); international studies (MA); war and society (MA). Electronic applications accepted.

CHARLES R. DREW UNIVERSITY OF MEDICINE AND SCIENCE, Los Angeles, CA 90059

General Information Independent, coed, comprehensive institution. *Graduate housing:* On-campus housing not available.

GRADUATE UNITS

College of Science and Health
Professional Program in Medicine Offers medicine (MD).

CHARLESTON SCHOOL OF LAW, Charleston, SC 29403

General Information Proprietary, coed, graduate-only institution. *Enrollment by degree level:* 627 doctoral. *Graduate faculty:* 23 full-time (10 women), 56 part-time/adjunct (22 women). *Tuition:* Full-time $40,596; part-time $32,618 per year. *Required fees:* $1034; $1034 per unit. Tuition and fees vary according to student level. *Graduate housing:* On-campus housing not available. *Student services:* Campus employment opportunities, campus safety program, career counseling, free psychological counseling, services for students with disabilities, writing training. *Library facilities:* Sol Blatt Jr. Law Library. *Collection:* Books: 7,229 (physical), 310,572 (digital/electronic). Weekly public service hours: 105; students can reserve study rooms.

Computer facilities: A campuswide network can be accessed. Online class registration is available.
Website: http://www.charlestonlaw.edu/

General Application Contact: Jacqueline B. Bell, Associate Dean of Admission and Financial Aid, 843-377-2143, Fax: 843-329-4091, E-mail: info@charlestonlaw.edu.

GRADUATE UNITS

Graduate and Professional Programs Offers law (JD). Electronic applications accepted.

CHARLESTON SOUTHERN UNIVERSITY, Charleston, SC 29423-8087

General Information Independent-religious, coed, comprehensive institution. *Graduate housing:* On-campus housing not available. *Research affiliation:* Waccamaw Regional Planning and Development Council (economic forecasting), Metro Charleston Chamber of Commerce (economic forecasting), Santee Lynches Council of Governments (economic forecasting).

GRADUATE UNITS

College of Business *Program availability:* Part-time, evening/weekend. Offers accounting (MBA); finance (MBA); general management (MBA); human resource management (MS); leadership (MBA); management information systems (MBA); organizational leadership (MA). Electronic applications accepted.

College of Education *Program availability:* Part-time, evening/weekend. Offers elementary administration and supervision (M Ed); elementary education (M Ed); secondary administration and supervision (M Ed). Electronic applications accepted.

Department of Criminal Justice *Program availability:* Part-time, evening/weekend, online learning. Offers criminal justice (MSCJ). Electronic applications accepted.

CHARLOTTE CHRISTIAN COLLEGE AND THEOLOGICAL SEMINARY, Charlotte, NC 28205

General Information Independent-religious, coed, comprehensive institution. *Graduate housing:* On-campus housing not available.

GRADUATE UNITS

Graduate Program *Program availability:* Part-time, evening/weekend. Offers Biblical studies (MA); chaplaincy (M Div); general pastoral studies (M Div); ministry (D Min); pastoral counseling (M Div); urban Christian ministry (MA). Electronic applications accepted.

CHARTER COLLEGE, Vancouver, WA 98683

General Information Proprietary, coed, comprehensive institution.

GRADUATE UNITS

Program in Business Administration *Program availability:* Online learning. Offers business administration (MBA).

CHARTER OAK STATE COLLEGE, New Britain, CT 06053-2142

General Information State-supported, coed, comprehensive institution. *Enrollment:* 7 full-time matriculated graduate/professional students (4 women), 85 part-time matriculated graduate/professional students (54 women). *Enrollment by degree level:* 92 master's. *Graduate faculty:* 9 part-time/adjunct (5 women). Tuition, state resident: full-time $12,144; part-time $506 per credit. Tuition, nonresident: full-time $12,696; part-time $529 per credit. *Required fees:* $403 per semester. Tuition and fees vary according to course load. *Graduate housing:* On-campus housing not available. *Student services:* Services for students with disabilities.

Computer facilities: A campuswide network can be accessed from off campus. Online class registration is available.
Website: http://www.charteroak.edu/

General Application Contact: Dr. Thomas Barron, Director of Organizational Effectiveness and Leadership Program, 860-515-3838, E-mail: tbarron@charteroak.edu.

GRADUATE UNITS

Program in Organizational Effectiveness and Leadership Expenses: Contact institution. *Financial support:* Scholarships/grants available. Financial award applicants required to submit FAFSA. *Program availability:* Part-time, evening/weekend, online only, 100% online. Offers organizational effectiveness and leadership (MS). *Application deadline:* Applications are processed on a rolling basis. *Application fee:* $50. Electronic applications accepted. *Application Contact:* Dr. Thomas Barron, Director of Organizational Effectiveness and Leadership Program, 860-515-3838, E-mail: tbarron@charteroak.edu. *Director of Organizational Effectiveness and Leadership Program*, Dr. Thomas Barron, 860-515-3838, E-mail: tbarron@charteroak.edu.

CHATHAM UNIVERSITY, Pittsburgh, PA 15232-2826

General Information Independent, coed, primarily women, university. CGS member. *Graduate housing:* Rooms and/or apartments available on a first-come, first-served basis to single and married students. Housing application deadline: 3/26.

GRADUATE UNITS

Nursing Programs *Program availability:* Online learning. Offers education/leadership (MSN); nursing (DNP). Electronic applications accepted.

Program in Accounting *Program availability:* Part-time, evening/weekend. Offers accounting (M Acc, MAC). Electronic applications accepted.

Program in Biology *Program availability:* Part-time. Offers environmental biology (MS); human biology (MS). Electronic applications accepted.

Program in Business Administration *Program availability:* Part-time, evening/weekend. Offers business administration (MBA); healthcare management (MBA); sustainability (MBA); women's leadership (MBA). Electronic applications accepted.

Program in Communication *Program availability:* Part-time, online learning. Offers environmental communication (M Comm); health communication (M Comm); strategic communication (M Comm). Electronic applications accepted.

Program in Counseling Psychology *Program availability:* Part-time, evening/weekend. Offers child, adolescent and family (MSCP); counseling psychology (Psy D); health and holistic (MSCP); organization and supervision (MSCP); sport and exercise (MSCP). Electronic applications accepted.

Program in Education Offers early childhood education (MAT); elementary education (MAT); environmental education (K-12) (MAT); secondary art (MAT); secondary biology education (MAT); secondary chemistry education (MAT); secondary English education (MAT); secondary math education (MAT); secondary physics education (MAT); secondary social studies education (MAT); special education (MAT). Electronic applications accepted.

Program in Film and Digital Technology *Program availability:* Part-time, evening/weekend. Offers film and digital technology (MFA). Electronic applications accepted.

Program in Healthcare Informatics *Program availability:* Online learning. Offers healthcare informatics (MHI).

Program in Interior Architecture *Program availability:* Part-time, evening/weekend, online learning. Offers interior architecture (MIA). Electronic applications accepted.

Program in Occupational Therapy Offers occupational therapy (MOT, OTD). Electronic applications accepted.

Program in Physical Therapy Offers physical therapy (DPT, TDPT). Electronic applications accepted.

Program in Physician Assistant Studies Offers physician assistant studies (MPAS). Electronic applications accepted.

Program in Writing *Program availability:* Part-time, evening/weekend, online learning. Offers children's writing (MFA); fiction (MFA); non-fiction (MFA); poetry (MFA); professional writing (MPW); screenwriting (MFA). Electronic applications accepted.

CHESTNUT HILL COLLEGE, Philadelphia, PA 19118-2693
General Information Independent-religious, coed, comprehensive institution. *Graduate housing:* On-campus housing not available.

GRADUATE UNITS
School of Graduate Studies *Program availability:* Part-time, evening/weekend. Offers administration of human services (MS, CAS); early education (M Ed); educational leadership (M Ed); elementary/middle education (M Ed); instructional technology (MS, CAS); reading (M Ed); reading specialist (M Ed); secondary education (M Ed); special education (M Ed). Electronic applications accepted.

Division of Psychology *Program availability:* Part-time, evening/weekend. Offers clinical and counseling psychology (MS, CAS); clinical psychology (Psy D).

CHEYNEY UNIVERSITY OF PENNSYLVANIA, Cheyney, PA 19319
General Information State-supported, coed, comprehensive institution. *Graduate housing:* On-campus housing not available.

GRADUATE UNITS
Graduate Programs *Program availability:* Part-time, evening/weekend. Offers educational leadership (M Ed, Certificate); elementary education (M Ed); principal certification (Certificate); public administration (MPA); special education (M Ed); urban education (M Ed). Electronic applications accepted.

THE CHICAGO SCHOOL OF PROFESSIONAL PSYCHOLOGY, Chicago, IL 60610
General Information Independent, coed, primarily women, graduate-only institution. CGS member. *Graduate housing:* On-campus housing not available.

GRADUATE UNITS
Program in Applied Behavior Analysis Offers applied behavior analysis (MS, PhD).

Program in Business Psychology Offers business psychology (PhD); industrial and organizational business psychology (Psy D); industrial and organizational psychology (MA); organizational leadership (MA, PhD).

Program in Clinical Forensic Psychology Offers clinical forensic psychology (Psy D).

Program in Clinical Mental Health Counseling *Program availability:* Part-time. Offers clinical mental health counseling (MA).

Program in Clinical Psychology Offers clinical psychology (Psy D). Electronic applications accepted.

Program in Forensic Psychology Offers forensic psychology (MA).

Program in Industrial and Organizational Psychology *Program availability:* Part-time, evening/weekend. Offers business psychology (Psy D); industrial and organizational psychology (MA).

Program in School Psychology *Program availability:* Part-time. Offers school psychology (Ed D, Psy D, Ed S).

THE CHICAGO SCHOOL OF PROFESSIONAL PSYCHOLOGY AT DOWNTOWN LOS ANGELES, Los Angeles, CA 90017
General Information Independent, coed, graduate-only institution.

GRADUATE UNITS
Program in Applied Behavior Analysis Offers applied behavior analysis (Psy D).

Program in Clinical Forensic Psychology Offers clinical forensic psychology (Psy D).

Program in Clinical Psychology Offers applied behavior analysis (MA); clinical psychology (Psy D); marital and family therapy (MA).

Program in Industrial and Organizational Psychology Offers industrial and organizational psychology (MA).

THE CHICAGO SCHOOL OF PROFESSIONAL PSYCHOLOGY AT IRVINE, Irvine, CA 92612
General Information Independent, coed, graduate-only institution.

GRADUATE UNITS
Program in Clinical Forensic Psychology Offers clinical forensic psychology (Psy D).

Program in Marital and Family Therapy Offers clinical psychology (MA); management practice (Psy D); psychodynamic psychotherapy (Psy D).

Program in Psychology Offers generalist (Psy D); psychodynamic psychotherapy (Psy D).

THE CHICAGO SCHOOL OF PROFESSIONAL PSYCHOLOGY AT SAN DIEGO, San Diego, CA 92101
General Information Independent, coed, graduate-only institution.

GRADUATE UNITS
Graduate Programs Offers applied behavior analysis (MS, PhD); applied clinical psychology (Psy D); clinical psychology (MA); industrial and organizational psychology (MA).

THE CHICAGO SCHOOL OF PROFESSIONAL PSYCHOLOGY AT WASHINGTON DC, Washington, DC 20005
General Information Independent, coed.

GRADUATE UNITS
Program in School Psychology *Program availability:* Part-time. Offers school psychology (Ed S).

THE CHICAGO SCHOOL OF PROFESSIONAL PSYCHOLOGY AT XAVIER UNIVERSITY OF LOUISIANA, New Orleans, LA 70125
General Information Independent, coed, graduate-only institution.

GRADUATE UNITS
Graduate Program Offers clinical psychology (Psy D).

THE CHICAGO SCHOOL OF PROFESSIONAL PSYCHOLOGY: ONLINE, Chicago, IL 60654
General Information Independent, coed, graduate-only institution. *Graduate housing:* On-campus housing not available.

GRADUATE UNITS
PhD Program in Organizational Leadership Offers organizational leadership (PhD).

Program in Applied Industrial and Organizational Psychology Offers applied industrial and organizational psychology (MA, Certificate).

Program in Clinical Psychopharmacology *Program availability:* Online learning. Offers clinical psychopharmacology (MS).

Program in Forensic Psychology Offers forensic psychology (MA, Certificate).

Program in Health Services Administration *Program availability:* Online learning. Offers health services administration (MHSA).

Program in International Psychology Offers international psychology (PhD).

Program in Psychology Offers child and adolescent psychology (MA); generalist (MA); gerontology (MA); international psychology (MA); organizational leadership (MA); sport and exercise psychology (MA).

CHICAGO STATE UNIVERSITY, Chicago, IL 60628
General Information State-supported, coed, comprehensive institution. *Graduate housing:* Room and/or apartments available on a first-come, first-served basis to single students; on-campus housing not available to married students.

GRADUATE UNITS
College of Pharmacy Offers pharmacy (Pharm D).

School of Graduate and Professional Studies *Program availability:* Part-time, evening/weekend. Electronic applications accepted.

College of Arts and Sciences *Program availability:* Part-time, evening/weekend. Offers arts and sciences (MA, MFA, MS, MSW); biological sciences (MS); computer science (MS); counseling (MA); creative writing (MFA); criminal justice (MS); English (MA); geographic information systems (MA); history (MA); mathematics (MS); social work (MSW).

College of Education *Program availability:* Part-time. Offers bilingual education (MS Ed); curriculum and instruction (MS Ed); early childhood education (MAT, MS Ed); education (M Ed, MA, MAT, MS Ed, Ed D); educational leadership (MA, Ed D); elementary education (MAT); higher education administration (MA); instructional foundations (MS Ed); library science (MS); middle school education (MAT); physical education (MS Ed); principal preparation (MA); reading (MS Ed); special education (MS Ed); teaching of reading (MS Ed); technology and performance improvement studies (MS).

College of Health Sciences Offers health sciences (MOT, MPH, MSN); nursing (MSN); occupational therapy (MOT); public health (MPH).

CHICAGO THEOLOGICAL SEMINARY, Chicago, IL 60637-1507
General Information Independent-religious, coed, graduate-only institution. *Graduate housing:* On-campus housing not available.

GRADUATE UNITS
Graduate and Professional Programs *Program availability:* Part-time. Offers Bible, culture and hermeneutics (PhD); preaching (D Min); religion and health (D Min); religious studies (MA); spirituality and spiritual direction (D Min); theology (M Div); theology, ethics and the human sciences (PhD).

CHOWAN UNIVERSITY, Murfreesboro, NC 27855
General Information Independent-religious, coed, comprehensive institution. *Graduate housing:* Room and/or apartments available to single students; on-campus housing not available to married students.

GRADUATE UNITS
School of Graduate Studies Offers education (M Ed). Electronic applications accepted.

CHRISTENDOM COLLEGE, Front Royal, VA 22630-5103
General Information Independent-religious, coed, comprehensive institution. *Graduate housing:* On-campus housing not available.

GRADUATE UNITS
Graduate School of Theology *Program availability:* Part-time, evening/weekend, 100% online, blended/hybrid learning. Offers theological studies (MA). Electronic applications accepted.

CHRISTIAN BROTHERS UNIVERSITY, Memphis, TN 38104-5581
General Information Independent-religious, coed, comprehensive institution. *Graduate housing:* On-campus housing not available.

GRADUATE UNITS
School of Arts *Program availability:* Part-time, evening/weekend. Offers Catholic studies (MACS); educational leadership (MSEL); teacher-leadership (M Ed); teaching (MAT).

School of Business *Program availability:* Part-time, evening/weekend. Offers accountancy (M Acc); business (MBA); international business (MIB); project management (Certificate).

School of Engineering *Program availability:* Part-time, evening/weekend, online learning. Offers engineering (MEM, MSEM).

School of Sciences Offers physician assistant studies (MS).

CHRISTIAN THEOLOGICAL SEMINARY, Indianapolis, IN 46208-3301

General Information Independent-religious, coed, graduate-only institution. *Graduate housing:* Rooms and/or apartments available on a first-come, first-served basis to single and married students.

GRADUATE UNITS

Graduate and Professional Programs *Program availability:* Part-time. Offers educational and arts ministries (MA); marriage and family therapy (MA); pastoral care and counseling (D Min); psychotherapy and faith (MA); theological studies (MTS); theology (M Div). Electronic applications accepted.

CHRISTIE'S EDUCATION, New York, NY 10020

General Information Proprietary, coed, primarily women, graduate-only institution. *Graduate housing:* On-campus housing not available.

GRADUATE UNITS

Certificate Program in Art Business Offers art business (Certificate). Electronic applications accepted.

Certificate Program in Modern and Contemporary Art in New York *Program availability:* Part-time. Offers modern and contemporary art (Certificate).

MA Program in Art, Law and Business Offers art, law and business (MA).

MA Program in Modern and Contemporary Art and the Market *Program availability:* Part-time. Offers modern and contemporary art and the market (MA).

CHRISTOPHER NEWPORT UNIVERSITY, Newport News, VA 23606-3072

General Information State-supported, coed, comprehensive institution. *Graduate housing:* On-campus housing not available. *Research affiliation:* Thomas Jefferson National Accelerator Facility (instrument and nuclear physics), Langley Research Center, Center for Distance Learning (flow visualization), National Science Foundation (science).

GRADUATE UNITS

Graduate Studies *Program availability:* Part-time. Offers applied physics and computer science (MS); environmental science (MS); teacher preparation (MAT). Electronic applications accepted.

CHRIST THE KING SEMINARY, East Aurora, NY 14052

General Information Independent-religious, coed, graduate-only institution. *Graduate housing:* On-campus housing not available.

GRADUATE UNITS

Graduate and Professional Programs *Program availability:* Part-time, evening/weekend. Offers divinity (M Div); pastoral ministry (MA); theology (MA).

CHURCH DIVINITY SCHOOL OF THE PACIFIC, Berkeley, CA 94709-1217

General Information Independent-religious, coed, graduate-only institution. *Graduate housing:* Rooms and/or apartments available on a first-come, first-served basis to single and married students. Housing application deadline: 5/1.

GRADUATE UNITS

Graduate and Professional Programs *Program availability:* Part-time. Offers theology (M Div, MA, MTS, D Min, Certificate). MA program offered jointly with Graduate Theological Union. Electronic applications accepted.

CINCINNATI CHRISTIAN UNIVERSITY, Cincinnati, OH 45204-3200

General Information Independent-religious, coed, comprehensive institution. *Graduate housing:* On-campus housing not available.

GRADUATE UNITS

Graduate School *Program availability:* Part-time. Offers biblical studies (MA); church history (MA); counseling (MAC); divinity (M Div); ministry (M Min); practical ministries (MA); theological studies (MA). Electronic applications accepted.

THE CITADEL, THE MILITARY COLLEGE OF SOUTH CAROLINA, Charleston, SC 29409

General Information State-supported, coed, primarily men, comprehensive institution. *Enrollment:* 176 full-time matriculated graduate/professional students (97 women), 676 part-time matriculated graduate/professional students (347 women). *Enrollment by degree level:* 807 master's, 45 other advanced degrees. *Graduate faculty:* 80 full-time (28 women), 22 part-time/adjunct (11 women). Tuition, state resident: part-time $595 per credit hour. Tuition, nonresident: part-time $1020 per credit hour. *Required fees:* $90 per term. *Graduate housing:* On-campus housing not available. *Student services:* Campus employment opportunities, career counseling, exercise/wellness program, free psychological counseling, international student services, low-cost health insurance, multicultural affairs office, services for students with disabilities, teacher training, writing training. *Library facilities:* Daniel Library. *Collection:* Books: 182,744 (physical), 225,852 (digital/electronic); Serial titles: 97 (physical); Databases: 250. Students can reserve study rooms.

Computer facilities: 350 computers available on campus for general student use. A campuswide network can be accessed from student residence rooms and from off campus. Online class registration is available. Website: http://www.citadel.edu/

General Application Contact: Dr. Kelly A. Brennan, Associate Provost of Enrollment Management, 843-953-5089, E-mail: cgc@citadel.edu.

GRADUATE UNITS

Citadel Graduate College *Program availability:* Part-time, evening/weekend, 100% online, blended/hybrid learning. Offers leadership studies (MS, Graduate Certificate). Electronic applications accepted.

School of Engineering *Program availability:* Part-time, evening/weekend. Offers aeronautical engineering (Graduate Certificate); built environment and public health (Graduate Certificate); civil engineering (MS); composites engineering (Graduate Certificate); computer engineering (Graduate Certificate); electrical engineering (MS); engineering (MS, Graduate Certificate); geotechnical engineering (Graduate Certificate); manufacturing engineering (Graduate Certificate); mechanical engineering (MS); mechatronics engineering (Graduate Certificate); power and energy (Graduate Certificate); project management (MS); structural engineering (Graduate Certificate); systems engineering management (Graduate Certificate); technical program management (Graduate Certificate); technical project management (Graduate Certificate); transportation engineering (Graduate Certificate). Electronic applications accepted.

School of Humanities and Social Sciences *Program availability:* Part-time, evening/weekend, 100% online, blended/hybrid learning. Offers English (MA); Hispanic studies (Graduate Certificate); history (MA); history and teaching content (Graduate Certificate); homeland security (Graduate Certificate); humanities and social sciences (MA, Ed S, Graduate Certificate); intelligence analysis (Graduate Certificate); intelligence and security studies (MA); international politics and military affairs (MA); psychology (MA); school psychology (Ed S); social science (MA). Electronic applications accepted.

School of Science and Mathematics *Program availability:* Part-time, evening/weekend. Offers biology (MA); computer and information sciences (MS); environmental studies (Graduate Certificate); health, exercise, and sport science (MS); science and mathematics (MA, MA Ed, MAT, MS, Graduate Certificate); sport management (MA, Graduate Certificate). Electronic applications accepted.

Tommy and Victoria Baker School of Business *Program availability:* Part-time, evening/weekend, 100% online, blended/hybrid learning. Offers business (MBA). Electronic applications accepted.

Zucker Family School of Education *Program availability:* Part-time, evening/weekend, 100% online, blended/hybrid learning. Offers elementary/secondary school administration and supervision (M Ed); elementary/secondary school counseling (M Ed); interdisciplinary STEM education (M Ed); literacy education (M Ed, Graduate Certificate); middle grades (MAT); physical education (grades K-12) (MAT); school superintendency (Ed S); secondary education (MAT); student affairs (Graduate Certificate); student affairs and college counseling (M Ed). Electronic applications accepted.

CITY COLLEGE OF THE CITY UNIVERSITY OF NEW YORK, New York, NY 10031-9198

General Information State and locally supported, coed, comprehensive institution. CGS member. *Graduate housing:* Room and/or apartments available on a first-come, first-served basis to single students; on-campus housing not available to married students. *Research affiliation:* New York Center for Biological Structures, Lucent Laboratories (engineering), Hospital for Joint Diseases (biomedical engineering), Museum of Natural History.

GRADUATE UNITS

Graduate School *Program availability:* Part-time, evening/weekend. Offers sustainability in the urban environment (MS).

The Bernard and Anne Spitzer School of Architecture *Program availability:* Part-time. Offers architecture (M Arch); landscape architecture (MLA); urban design (MUP).

Colin Powell School for Civic and Global Leadership *Program availability:* Part-time. Offers clinical psychology (PhD); economics (MA); economics and business (MA); general psychology (MA); international relations (MA); mental health counseling (MA); psychology (MA, PhD); public service management (MPA); sociology (MA). Electronic applications accepted.

Division of Humanities and the Arts *Program availability:* Part-time. Offers advertising design (MFA); art history (MA); art history and museum studies (MA); art museum education (MA); branding and integrated communications (MPS); ceramic design (MFA); creative writing (MFA); digital and interdisciplinary art practice (MFA); film (MFA); fine arts (MFA); history (MA); humanities and the arts (MA, MFA, MPS); language and literacy (MA); literature (MA); museum studies (MA); painting (MFA); printmaking (MFA); sculpture (MFA); Spanish (MA); wood and metal design (MFA). Electronic applications accepted.

Division of Science *Program availability:* Part-time. Offers biochemistry (MS, PhD); biology (MS, PhD); chemistry (MS, PhD); geology (MS); mathematics (MS); physics (MS, PhD); science (MS, PhD). Electronic applications accepted.

Grove School of Engineering *Program availability:* Part-time. Offers biomedical engineering (MS, PhD); chemical engineering (ME, PhD); civil engineering (ME, MS, PhD); computer science (MS, PhD); electrical engineering (ME, MS, PhD); engineering (ME, MIS, MS, PhD); information systems (MIS); mechanical engineering (ME, MS, PhD).

School of Education *Program availability:* Part-time, evening/weekend. Offers adolescent mathematics education (MA, AC); bilingual education (MS); childhood education (MS); early childhood education (MS); education (MA, MS, MS Ed, AC); educational leadership (MS, AC); educational theatre (MS); English education (MA); literacy (MS); middle school mathematics education (MS); science education (MA); social studies education (AC); teacher of students with disabilities in adolescent education (MS Ed); teacher of students with disabilities in childhood education (MS Ed); TESOL (MS).

CITY UNIVERSITY OF NEW YORK SCHOOL OF LAW, Long Island City, NY 11101-4356

General Information State and locally supported, coed, graduate-only institution. *Enrollment by degree level:* 578 doctoral. *Graduate faculty:* 51 full-time (37 women), 28 part-time/adjunct (14 women). *Tuition, area resident:* Full-time $15,000; part-time $10,300 per year. Tuition, state resident: full-time $15,000. Tuition, nonresident: full-time $24,900; part-time $17,120 per year. *Required fees:* $562.90; $347.90 per unit. Tuition and fees vary according to program. *Graduate housing:* On-campus housing not available. *Student services:* Campus employment opportunities, campus safety program, career counseling, exercise/wellness program, free psychological counseling, services for students with disabilities, writing training. *Library facilities:* CUNY School of Law Library. *Collection:* Books: 61,908 (physical), 611,977 (digital/electronic); Serial titles: 1,931 (physical), 105,425 (digital/electronic); Databases: 334. Weekly public service hours: 61; study areas open 24 hours, 5–7 days a week.

Computer facilities: 105 computers available on campus for general student use. Online class registration is available. Website: http://www.law.cuny.edu/

General Application Contact: Degna P. Levister, Assistant Dean of Admissions and Enrollment Management, 718-340-4210, Fax: 718-340-4435, E-mail: admissions@law.cuny.edu.

GRADUATE UNITS

Professional Program Students: 417 full-time (254 women), 161 part-time (94 women); includes 297 minority (68 Black or African American, non-Hispanic/Latino; 54 Asian, non-Hispanic/Latino; 135 Hispanic/Latino; 1 Native Hawaiian or other Pacific Islander, non-Hispanic/Latino; 39 Two or more races, non-Hispanic/Latino), 16 international. Average age 29. 1,606 applicants, 38% accepted, 205 enrolled. *Faculty:* 51 full-time (37 women), 28 part-time/adjunct (14 women). Expenses: Contact institution. *Financial support:* In 2018–19, 148 students received support, including 50 fellowships (averaging $15,488 per year), 33 research assistantships (averaging $1,194 per year); Federal Work-Study, scholarships/grants, tuition waivers (full and partial), and unspecified assistantships also available. Support available to part-time students. Financial award application deadline: 7/15; financial award applicants required to submit FAFSA. In 2018, 165 doctorates awarded. *Program availability:* Part-time, evening/weekend. Offers law (JD). *Application deadline:* For fall admission, 5/15 priority date for domestic students. Applications are processed on a rolling basis. *Application fee:* $60. Electronic applications accepted. *Application Contact:* Degna P. Levister, Assistant Dean of Admissions and Enrollment Management, 718-340-4210, Fax: 718-340-4435, E-mail: admissions@law.cuny.edu. *Dean/Professor of Law,* Mary Lu Bilek, 718-340-4201, Fax: 718-340-4482.

CITY UNIVERSITY OF SEATTLE, Seattle, WA 98121

General Information Independent, coed, comprehensive institution. *Graduate housing:* Room and/or apartments available on a first-come, first-served basis to single students; on-campus housing not available to married students.

GRADUATE UNITS

Graduate Division *Program availability:* Part-time, evening/weekend, online learning. Electronic applications accepted.

Albright School of Education *Program availability:* Part-time, evening/weekend, online learning. Offers administrator certification (Certificate); curriculum and instruction (M Ed); elementary education (MIT); guidance and counseling (M Ed); leadership (M Ed); reading and literacy (M Ed); school counseling (M Ed); special education (MIT); superintendent certification (Certificate). Electronic applications accepted.

Division of Arts and Sciences *Program availability:* Part-time, evening/weekend, online learning. Offers counseling psychology (MA). Electronic applications accepted.

Division of Doctoral Studies *Program availability:* Online learning. Offers leadership (Ed D).

School of Management *Program availability:* Part-time, evening/weekend, online learning. Offers accounting (Certificate); change leadership (MBA, Certificate); computer systems (MS); finance (Certificate); financial management (MBA); general management (MBA); general management-Europe (MBA); global marketing (MBA); human resources management (Certificate); individualized study (MBA); information security (MS); information systems (MBA); leadership (MA); marketing (MBA, Certificate); project management (MBA, MS, Certificate); sustainable business (Certificate); technology management (MBA, Certificate). Electronic applications accepted.

CITY VISION UNIVERSITY, Kansas City, MO 64109-1845

General Information Independent-religious, coed, comprehensive institution.

GRADUATE UNITS

Program in Technology and Ministry *Program availability:* Online learning. Offers technology and ministry (MS).

CLAFLIN UNIVERSITY, Orangeburg, SC 29115

General Information Independent-religious, coed, comprehensive institution. *Graduate housing:* Room and/or apartments available on a first-come, first-served basis to single students; on-campus housing not available to married students. Housing application deadline: 4/15.

GRADUATE UNITS

Graduate Programs *Program availability:* Part-time. Offers biotechnology (MS); business administration (MBA).

CLAREMONT GRADUATE UNIVERSITY, Claremont, CA 91711-6160

General Information Independent, coed, graduate-only institution. CGS member. *Graduate housing:* Rooms and/or apartments available on a first-come, first-served basis to single and married students. Housing application deadline: 5/15. *Research affiliation:* Claremont School of Theology (religion), Rancho Santa Ana Botanic Garden (botany, native plants).

GRADUATE UNITS

Graduate Programs *Program availability:* Part-time, evening/weekend. Offers arts management (MA); botany (MS, PhD); financial engineering (MSFE). Electronic applications accepted.

Center for Information Systems and Technology *Program availability:* Part-time. Offers cybersecurity and networking (MS); data science and analytics (MS); electronic commerce (PhD); geographic information systems (MS); health informatics (MS); information systems (Certificate); IT strategy and innovation (MS); knowledge management (PhD); systems development (PhD); telecommunications and networking (PhD). Electronic applications accepted.

Institute of Mathematical Sciences *Program availability:* Part-time. Offers computational and systems biology (PhD); computational mathematics and numerical analysis (MA, MS); computational science (PhD); engineering and industrial applied mathematics (PhD); mathematics (PhD); operations research and statistics (MA, MS); physical applied mathematics (MA, MS); pure mathematics (MA, MS); scientific computing (MA, MS); systems and control theory (MA, MS). PhD programs offered jointly with San Diego State University and California State University, Long Beach. Electronic applications accepted.

Peter F. Drucker and Masatoshi Ito Graduate School of Management *Program availability:* Part-time. Offers advanced management (MS); art business (MA); executive management (EMBA); leadership (Certificate); management (EMBA, MA, MBA, MS, PhD, Certificate); strategy (Certificate). Electronic applications accepted.

School of Arts and Humanities *Program availability:* Part-time. Offers Africana history (Certificate); Africana studies (Certificate); American studies (MA, PhD); American studies and U.S. history (MA, PhD); applied women's studies (MA); archival studies (MA); arts and humanities (M Phil, MA, MFA, DCM, DMA, PhD, Certificate); church music (MA, DCM); composition (MA, DMA); critical theory (MA, PhD); cultural studies (MA, PhD); digital media (MFA); drawing (MFA); early modern studies (PhD); English (M Phil, MA, PhD); European studies (MA, PhD); Hebrew Bible (MA, PhD); historical performance practices (MA, DMA); history of Christianity and religions of North America (MA, PhD); installation (MFA); literary theory (PhD); literature (MA, PhD); literature and creative writing (MA); literature and film (MA); media studies (MA, PhD); museum studies (MA); musicology (MA, PhD); New Testament (MA, PhD); oral history (MA, PhD); painting (MFA); performance (MA, MFA, DMA); philosophy (MA, PhD); philosophy of religion and theology (MA, PhD); photography (MFA); sculpture (MFA); studio (MFA); theology, ethics and culture (MA, PhD); women's studies in religion (MA, PhD). Electronic applications accepted.

School of Community and Global Health Offers health promotion science (PhD); public health (MPH). Electronic applications accepted.

School of Educational Studies *Program availability:* Part-time. Offers Africana education (Certificate); education and policy (MA, PhD); higher education/student affairs (MA, PhD); human development (MA, PhD); public school administration (MA, PhD); quantitative evaluation (MA, PhD); special education (MA, PhD); teacher education (MA); teaching and learning (MA, PhD); urban leadership (PhD). PhD program offered jointly with San Diego State University. Electronic applications accepted.

School of Social Science, Policy and Evaluation Offers advanced study in evaluation (Certificate); American politics (MA, PhD); behavioral economics and neuroeconomics (PhD); business and financial economics (MA, PhD); cognitive psychology (MA, PhD); comparative politics (PhD); developmental psychology (MA, PhD); economic development (Certificate); evaluation and applied research methods (MA, PhD); health behavior research and evaluation (MA, PhD); human resource development and evaluation (MA); human resource management (MS); industrial/organizational psychology (MA, PhD); international economic and development policy (PhD); international economics policy and development (MA); international money and finance (PhD); international political economy (MA); international studies (MA); organizational behavior (MA, PhD); organizational psychology (MA, PhD); political economy and public economics (PhD); political economy and public policy (MA); political philosophy (PhD); political science (PhD); politics, economics and business (MA); politics, economics, and business (MA); public policy (MA, PhD); public policy and evaluation (MA); social psychology (MA, PhD); social science, policy and evaluation (MA, MS, PhD, Certificate); world politics (PhD).

CLAREMONT LINCOLN UNIVERSITY, Claremont, CA 91711

General Information Independent, coed, graduate-only institution.

GRADUATE UNITS

Graduate Programs Offers ethical leadership (MA); interfaith action (MA); social impact (MA).

CLAREMONT SCHOOL OF THEOLOGY, Claremont, CA 91711-3199

General Information Independent-religious, coed, graduate-only institution. *Graduate housing:* Rooms and/or apartments available on a first-come, first-served basis to single students and guaranteed to married students. Housing application deadline: 5/1. *Research affiliation:* Moore Multicultural Resource and Research Center, Institute for Antiquity and Christianity, Center for Process Studies, National United Methodist Native American Center, Center for Pacific and Asian-American Ministries, Ancient Biblical Manuscript Center.

GRADUATE UNITS

Graduate and Professional Programs *Program availability:* Part-time. Offers interfaith chaplaincy (M Div); Islamic chaplaincy (M Div); ministerial leadership (M Div); practical theology (PhD); practical theology of conflict, healing and transformation in Korean contexts (D Min); religion (MA, PhD); spiritual renewal, contemplative practice, and strategic leadership (D Min). Electronic applications accepted.

CLARION UNIVERSITY OF PENNSYLVANIA, Clarion, PA 16214

General Information State-supported, coed, comprehensive institution. *Enrollment:* 4,869 graduate, professional, and undergraduate students; 282 full-time matriculated graduate/professional students (231 women), 630 part-time matriculated graduate/professional students (497 women). *Enrollment by degree level:* 900 master's, 12 doctoral. *Graduate faculty:* 63 full-time (34 women), 21 part-time/adjunct (14 women). *Tuition, area resident:* Part-time $516 per credit hour. Tuition, state resident: part-time $516 per credit hour. Tuition, nonresident: part-time $774 per credit hour. *Required fees:* $159 per credit hour. One-time fee: $50 part-time. Tuition and fees vary according to degree level, campus/location and program. *Graduate housing:* Room and/or apartments available on a first-come, first-served basis to single students; on-campus housing not available to married students. Typical cost: $12,668 (including board). Room and board charges vary according to board plan, campus/location and housing facility selected. *Student services:* Campus employment opportunities, campus safety program, career counseling, exercise/wellness program, free psychological counseling, international student services, multicultural affairs office, services for students with disabilities, teacher training, writing training. *Library facilities:* Carlson Library plus 1 other. *Collection:* Books: 444,818 (physical), 348,037 (digital/electronic); Serial titles: 179 (physical), 57,405 (digital/electronic); Databases: 102. Weekly public service hours: 94; students can reserve study rooms.

Computer facilities: 950 computers available on campus for general student use. A campuswide network can be accessed from student residence rooms and from off campus. Online class registration, Online Learning Management System, web-based personal disk space, other online student services (financial aid, billing etc.) are available.
Website: http://www.clarion.edu/

General Application Contact: Susan Staub, Graduate Admissions Counselor, 814-393-2337, Fax: 814-393-2722, E-mail: gradstudies@clarion.edu.

GRADUATE UNITS

College of Arts, Education and Sciences Students: 28 full-time (22 women), 97 part-time (81 women); includes 6 minority (5 Black or African American, non-Hispanic/Latino; 1 Two or more races, non-Hispanic/Latino). Average age 30. 90 applicants, 61% accepted, 46 enrolled. *Faculty:* 22 full-time (12 women), 9 part-time/adjunct (6 women). Expenses: Contact institution. *Financial support:* Application deadline: 3/1; applicants required to submit FAFSA. In 2018, 72 master's awarded. Offers arts, education and sciences (M Ed, MS, Certificate); curriculum and instruction (M Ed); early childhood (M Ed); mass media arts and journalism (MS); math education (M Ed); reading (M Ed); science education (M Ed); special education (MS); technology (M Ed). *Application deadline:* Applications are processed on a rolling basis. *Application fee:* $40. Electronic applications accepted. *Application Contact:* Susan Staub, Graduate Admissions Counselor, 814-393-2337, Fax: 814-393-2722, E-mail: gradstudies@clarion.edu. *Dean,* Dr. Laura Delbrugge, 814-393-2328, E-mail: delbrugge@clarion.edu.

College of Business Administration and Information Sciences Students: 148 full-time (112 women), 366 part-time (268 women); includes 74 minority (31 Black or African American, non-Hispanic/Latino; 1 American Indian or Alaska Native, non-Hispanic/Latino; 10 Asian, non-Hispanic/Latino; 25 Hispanic/Latino; 7 Two or more races, non-Hispanic/Latino), 4 international. Average age 33. 390 applicants, 58% accepted, 206 enrolled. *Faculty:* 20 full-time (5 women), 7 part-time/adjunct (4 women). Expenses: Contact institution. *Financial support:* Federal Work-Study, institutionally sponsored loans, and scholarships/grants available. Financial award application deadline: 3/1; financial award applicants required to submit FAFSA. In 2018, 185 master's awarded. Offers accounting (MS); applied data analytics (MS); business administration and information sciences (MBA, MS, MSLS, Certificate); finance (MBA);

health care administration (MBA); information and library science (MSLS); innovation and entrepreneurship (MBA); non-profit business (MBA); school library media (MSLS). *Application deadline:* Applications are processed on a rolling basis. *Application fee:* $40. Electronic applications accepted. *Application Contact:* Susan Staub, Graduate Admissions Counselor, 814-393-2337, Fax: 814-393-2722, E-mail: gradstudies@clarion.edu. *Dean,* Dr. Phillip Frese, 814-393-2600, E-mail: pfrese@clarion.edu.

College of Health Sciences & Human Services Students: 106 full-time (97 women), 167 part-time (148 women); includes 22 minority (8 Black or African American, non-Hispanic/Latino; 1 American Indian or Alaska Native, non-Hispanic/Latino; 4 Asian, non-Hispanic/Latino; 5 Hispanic/Latino; 4 Two or more races, non-Hispanic/Latino). Average age 30. 341 applicants, 36% accepted, 115 enrolled. *Faculty:* 21 full-time (17 women), 5 part-time/adjunct (4 women). Expenses: Contact institution. *Financial support:* Federal Work-Study, institutionally sponsored loans, and scholarships/grants available. Financial award application deadline: 3/1; financial award applicants required to submit FAFSA. In 2018, 101 master's, 2 doctorates awarded. Offers clinical mental health counseling (MS); family nurse practitioner (MSN); health and human services (MS, MSN, DNP); nursing (MSN, DNP); speech language pathology (MS). *Application deadline:* Applications are processed on a rolling basis. *Application fee:* $40. Electronic applications accepted. *Application Contact:* Susan Staub, Graduate Admissions Counselor, 814-393-2337, Fax: 814-393-2722, E-mail: gradstudies@clarion.edu. *Dean,* Dr. Jeffery Allen, 814-393-2163.

CLARK ATLANTA UNIVERSITY, Atlanta, GA 30314

General Information Independent-religious, coed, university. CGS member. *Graduate housing:* Room and/or apartments available on a first-come, first-served basis to single students; on-campus housing not available to married students. Housing application deadline: 6/1.

GRADUATE UNITS

School of Arts and Sciences *Program availability:* Part-time. Offers African American studies, Africana women's studies, and history (MA, PhD); arts and sciences (MA, MPA, MS, PhD); biology (MS, PhD); chemistry (MS, PhD); computer and information science (MS); English and modern languages (MA); mathematical sciences (MS); physics (MS); political science (MA, PhD); public administration (MPA); sociology (MA).

School of Business Administration *Program availability:* Part-time. Offers accounting (MA); business administration (MA, MBA); economics (MA). Electronic applications accepted.

School of Education *Program availability:* Part-time, evening/weekend. Offers counseling and psychological studies (MA); education (MA, MAT, Ed D, Ed S); educational leadership (MA, Ed D, Ed S); special education general curriculum (MA); teaching math and science (MAT). Electronic applications accepted.

School of Social Work *Program availability:* Part-time. Offers social work (MSW, PhD). Electronic applications accepted.

CLARKE UNIVERSITY, Dubuque, IA 52001-3198

General Information Independent-religious, coed, comprehensive institution. *Graduate housing:* On-campus housing not available.

GRADUATE UNITS

Department of Nursing and Health *Program availability:* Part-time. Offers family nurse practitioner (DNP); health leadership and practice (DNP); psychiatric mental health nurse practitioner (DNP). Electronic applications accepted.

Department of Social Work *Program availability:* Part-time, evening/weekend. Offers social work (MSW). Electronic applications accepted.

Graduate Business Programs *Program availability:* Part-time, evening/weekend, blended/hybrid learning. Offers business (MBA, MOL). Electronic applications accepted.

Physical Therapy Program Offers physical therapy (DPT). Electronic applications accepted.

Program in Education *Program availability:* Part-time, 100% online, blended/hybrid learning. Offers instructional leadership (MAE). Electronic applications accepted.

CLARKSON COLLEGE, Omaha, NE 68131-2739

General Information Independent, coed, primarily women, comprehensive institution. *Graduate housing:* Room and/or apartments available on a first-come, first-served basis to single students; on-campus housing not available to married students. Housing application deadline: 6/30.

GRADUATE UNITS

Master of Science in Nursing Program *Program availability:* Part-time, evening/weekend, online learning. Offers adult nurse practitioner (MSN, Post-Master's Certificate); family nurse practitioner (MSN, Post-Master's Certificate); nursing education (MSN, Post-Master's Certificate); nursing health care leadership (MSN, Post-Master's Certificate). Electronic applications accepted.

Program in Health Care Administration *Program availability:* Part-time, evening/weekend, online learning. Offers health care administration (MHCA). Electronic applications accepted.

CLARKSON UNIVERSITY, Potsdam, NY 13699

General Information Independent, coed, university. CGS member. *Enrollment:* 4,274 graduate, professional, and undergraduate students; 602 full-time matriculated graduate/professional students (298 women), 487 part-time matriculated graduate/professional students (152 women). *Enrollment by degree level:* 823 master's, 254 doctoral, 12 other advanced degrees. *Graduate faculty:* 241 full-time (79 women), 129 part-time/adjunct (38 women). *Tuition:* Full-time $24,984; part-time $1388 per credit hour. *Required fees:* $225. Tuition and fees vary according to campus/location and program. *Graduate housing:* On-campus housing not available. *Student services:* Campus employment opportunities, campus safety program, career counseling, free psychological counseling, international student services, low-cost health insurance, multicultural affairs office, services for students with disabilities, teacher training. *Library facilities:* Harriet Call Burnap Memorial Library plus 1 other. *Collection:* Books: 116,048 (physical), 208,608 (digital/electronic); Serial titles: 9,525 (physical), 50,689 (digital/electronic); Databases: 134. Weekly public service hours: 97; students can reserve study rooms.

Computer facilities: 350 computers available on campus for general student use. A campuswide network can be accessed from student residence rooms and from off campus. Online class registration is available. Website: http://www.clarkson.edu/

General Application Contact: Dan Capogna, Director of Graduate Admissions & Recruitment, 518-631-9910, E-mail: graduate@clarkson.edu.

GRADUATE UNITS

David D. Reh School of Business Students: 104 full-time (56 women), 90 part-time (40 women); includes 27 minority (8 Black or African American, non-Hispanic/Latino; 2 American Indian or Alaska Native, non-Hispanic/Latino; 9 Asian, non-Hispanic/Latino; 4 Hispanic/Latino; 4 Two or more races, non-Hispanic/Latino), 14 international. *Faculty:* 65 full-time (16 women), 25 part-time/adjunct (4 women). Expenses: Contact institution. In 2018, 119 master's, 3 other advanced degrees awarded. Offers business (MBA, MS, Advanced Certificate); business administration (MBA); business fundamentals (Advanced Certificate); clinical leadership in healthcare management (MS); global supply chain management (Advanced Certificate); healthcare data analytics (MS); healthcare management (MBA, Advanced Certificate); human resource management (Advanced Certificate); management and leadership (Advanced Certificate). *Application Contact:* Dan Capogna, Director of Graduate Admissions & Recruitment, 518-631-9910, E-mail: graduate@clarkson.edu. *Interim Dean of School Business,* Dr. Augustine Lado, 315-268-2300, E-mail: alado@clarkson.edu.

Department of Bioethics Students: 8 full-time (6 women), 33 part-time (27 women); includes 5 minority (2 Black or African American, non-Hispanic/Latino; 1 Asian, non-Hispanic/Latino; 2 Hispanic/Latino), 21 international. 28 applicants, 93% accepted, 19 enrolled. *Faculty:* 1 full-time (0 women), 4 part-time/adjunct (2 women). Expenses: Contact institution. *Financial support:* Scholarships/grants available. In 2018, 11 master's, 3 other advanced degrees awarded. *Program availability:* Part-time, evening/weekend, 100% online, blended/hybrid learning. Offers bioethics (MS, Advanced Certificate). Offered jointly with Icahn School of Medicine at Mount Sinai. *Application deadline:* Applications are processed on a rolling basis. *Application fee:* $50. Electronic applications accepted. *Application Contact:* Dan Capogna, Director of Graduate Admissions & Recruitment, 518-631-9910, E-mail: dcapogna@clarkson.edu. *Chair of Bioethics,* Dr. Sean Philpott, 518-631-9863, E-mail: sphilpott@clarkson.edu.

Division of Health Sciences Students: 177 full-time (133 women); includes 26 minority (5 Black or African American, non-Hispanic/Latino; 1 American Indian or Alaska Native, non-Hispanic/Latino; 13 Asian, non-Hispanic/Latino; 4 Hispanic/Latino; 3 Two or more races, non-Hispanic/Latino), 1 international. *Faculty:* 20 full-time (16 women), 18 part-time/adjunct (11 women). Expenses: Contact institution. In 2018, 43 master's, 22 doctorates awarded. Offers health sciences (MS, DPT); occupational therapy (MS); physical therapy (DPT); physician assistant studies (MS). *Application Contact:* Amy Thompson, Graduate Admissions Coordinator, 315-268-2161, E-mail: athompso@clarkson.edu. *Dean of the School of Arts and Sciences,* Dr. Chuck Thorpe, 315-268-4090, E-mail: cthorpe@clarkson.edu.

Institute for a Sustainable Environment Students: 19 full-time (10 women), 10 international. *Faculty:* 1 full-time (0 women), 6 part-time/adjunct (3 women). Expenses: Contact institution. In 2018, 1 master's, 3 doctorates awarded. Offers environmental politics and governance (MS); environmental science and engineering (MS, PhD); sustainable environment (MS, PhD). *Application Contact:* Dan Capogna, Director of Graduate Admissions & Recruitment, 518-631-9910, E-mail: graduate@clarkson.edu. *Director of the Institute for a Sustainable Environment/Associate Director of Sustainability,* Dr. Susan Powers, 315-268-6542, E-mail: spowers@clarkson.edu.

Program in Data Analytics Students: 12 full-time (4 women), 16 part-time (4 women); includes 1 minority (Asian, non-Hispanic/Latino), 7 international. 57 applicants, 70% accepted, 18 enrolled. Expenses: Contact institution. *Financial support:* Scholarships/grants and unspecified assistantships available. In 2018, 20 master's awarded. *Program availability:* Part-time, evening/weekend, 100% online. Offers data analytics (MS). *Application deadline:* Applications are processed on a rolling basis. *Application fee:* $50. Electronic applications accepted. *Application Contact:* Dan Capogna, Director of Graduate Admissions, 518-631-9910, E-mail: graduate@clarkson.edu. *Director of Business Analytics,* Dr. Boris Jukic, 315-268-3884, E-mail: bjukic@clarkson.edu.

Program in Education Students: 31 full-time (21 women), 22 part-time (19 women); includes 11 minority (2 Black or African American, non-Hispanic/Latino; 4 Asian, non-Hispanic/Latino; 4 Hispanic/Latino; 1 Two or more races, non-Hispanic/Latino), 10 international. 48 applicants, 88% accepted, 38 enrolled. *Faculty:* 5 full-time (all women), 7 part-time/adjunct (2 women). Expenses: Contact institution. *Financial support:* Scholarships/grants available. In 2018, 23 master's awarded. Offers education (MAT). *Application deadline:* Applications are processed on a rolling basis. *Application fee:* $50. Electronic applications accepted. *Application Contact:* Dan Capogna, Director of Graduate Admissions & Recruitment, 518-631-9910, E-mail: graduate@clarkson.edu. *Chair of Education,* Dr. Catherine Snyder, 518-631-9870, E-mail: csnyder@clarkson.edu.

Program in Engineering Management Students: 2 full-time (0 women), 199 part-time (46 women); includes 35 minority (10 Black or African American, non-Hispanic/Latino; 14 Asian, non-Hispanic/Latino; 11 Hispanic/Latino), 19 international. 82 applicants, 95% accepted, 78 enrolled. *Faculty:* 10 part-time/adjunct (0 women). Expenses: Contact institution. *Financial support:* Scholarships/grants available. In 2018, 80 master's awarded. *Program availability:* Part-time-only, evening/weekend, blended/hybrid learning. Offers engineering management (MS). *Application deadline:* Applications are processed on a rolling basis. *Application fee:* $50. Electronic applications accepted. *Application Contact:* Dan Capogna, Director of Graduate Admissions & Recruitment, 518-631-9910, E-mail: graduate@clarkson.edu. *Associate Dean of Engineering,* Hugo Irizarry-Quinones, 518-631-9881, E-mail: hirizarr@clarkson.edu.

School of Arts and Sciences Students: 97 full-time (35 women), 8 part-time (1 woman); includes 9 minority (3 Black or African American, non-Hispanic/Latino; 3 Asian, non-Hispanic/Latino; 2 Hispanic/Latino; 1 Two or more races, non-Hispanic/Latino), 52 international. *Faculty:* 52 full-time (16 women), 11 part-time/adjunct (4 women). Expenses: Contact institution. In 2018, 22 master's, 12 doctorates awarded. Offers arts and sciences (MS, DPT, PhD); basic science (MS); chemistry and biomolecular science (MS, PhD); computer science (MS, PhD); interdisciplinary bioscience and biotechnology (MS, PhD); mathematics (MS, PhD); physics (MS, PhD). *Application Contact:* Dan Capogna, Director of Graduate Admissions & Recruitment, 518-631-9910, E-mail: graduate@clarkson.edu. *Interim Dean of Arts and Sciences,* Dr. Charles Thorpe, 315-268-6544, E-mail: cthorpe@clarkson.edu.

Wallace H. Coulter School of Engineering Students: 152 full-time (33 women), 119 part-time (15 women); includes 25 minority (4 Black or African American, non-Hispanic/Latino; 10 Asian, non-Hispanic/Latino; 9 Hispanic/Latino; 2 Two or more races, non-Hispanic/Latino), 90 international. *Faculty:* 73 full-time (15 women), 34 part-time/adjunct (5 women). Expenses: Contact institution. In 2018, 72 master's, 31 doctorates, 4 other advanced degrees awarded. Offers business of energy (MS, Advanced Certificate); chemical engineering (ME); civil and environmental engineering (ME, MS, PhD); electrical and computer engineering (ME, MS, PhD); electrical engineering (ME); energy systems (MS); engineering (ME, MS, PhD, Advanced Certificate); engineering and management systems (MS); interdisciplinary engineering science (MS, PhD); materials science and engineering (PhD); mechanical engineering (ME, MS, PhD). *Application Contact:* Dan Capogna, Director of Graduate Admissions & Recruitment, 518-631-9910, E-mail: graduate@clarkson.edu. *Dean of Engineering,* Dr. William Jemison, 315-268-6446, E-mail: wjemison@clarkson.edu.

CLARKS SUMMIT UNIVERSITY, South Abington Township, PA 18411

General Information Independent-religious, coed, comprehensive institution. *Graduate housing:* Room and/or apartments available on a first-come, first-served basis to single students; on-campus housing not available to married students.

GRADUATE UNITS

Baptist Bible Seminary *Program availability:* Part-time, evening/weekend, online learning. Offers Biblical apologetics (MA); Biblical studies (MA); church education (M Min); church planting (M Div, M Min); communication (D Min); counseling and spiritual development (D Min); global ministry (M Min, D Min); ministry (PhD); missions (M Min); organizational leadership (M Min); outreach pastor (M Min); pastoral counseling (M Min); pastoral leadership (M Div, M Min); pastoral ministry (D Min); theological studies (D Min); theology (Th M); youth pastor (M Min). M Min in missions available only for Association of Baptists for World Evangelism missionary personnel. Electronic applications accepted.

Online Master's Programs *Program availability:* Part-time, evening/weekend, online learning. Offers Bible (MA); counseling (MA, MS); curriculum and instruction (M Ed); educational administration (M Ed); literature (MA); organizational leadership (MA).

CLARK UNIVERSITY, Worcester, MA 01610-1477

General Information Independent, coed, university. CGS member. *Enrollment:* 3,122 graduate, professional, and undergraduate students; 760 full-time matriculated graduate/professional students (437 women), 218 part-time matriculated graduate/professional students (116 women). *Enrollment by degree level:* 769 master's, 207 doctoral, 2 other advanced degrees. *Graduate faculty:* 209 full-time (93 women), 142 part-time/adjunct (65 women). *Tuition:* Full-time $34,110. *Required fees:* $40. Tuition and fees vary according to course load and program. *Graduate housing:* Rooms and/or apartments available on a first-come, first-served basis to single and married students. *Student services:* Campus employment opportunities, campus safety program, career counseling, exercise/wellness program, free psychological counseling, grant writing training, international student services, low-cost health insurance, multicultural affairs office, services for students with disabilities, teacher training, writing training. *Library facilities:* Robert Hutchings Goddard Library plus 8 others. *Collection:* Students can reserve study rooms.

Computer facilities: A campuswide network can be accessed from student residence rooms and from off campus. Online class registration, online course support are available.
Website: http://www.clarku.edu/

General Application Contact: Jeremiah Czub, Director of Graduate Admissions, 508-793-7676, Fax: 508-793-8834, E-mail: jczub@clarku.edu.

GRADUATE UNITS

Graduate School Average age 28. 2,048 applicants, 72% accepted, 388 enrolled. *Faculty:* 209 full-time (93 women), 142 part-time/adjunct (65 women). Expenses: Contact institution. *Financial support:* In 2018–19, 10 fellowships with tuition reimbursements (averaging $17,000 per year), 39 research assistantships with tuition reimbursements (averaging $17,000 per year), 84 teaching assistantships with tuition reimbursements (averaging $17,000 per year) were awarded; career-related internships or fieldwork, Federal Work-Study, institutionally sponsored loans, scholarships/grants, and tuition waivers (full and partial) also available. Support available to part-time students. In 2018, 491 master's, 38 doctorates awarded. *Program availability:* Part-time, evening/weekend. Offers biology (MA, PhD); community and global health (MHS); community development and planning (MA); economics (PhD); English (MA); environmental science and policy (MS); genocide studies (PhD); geographic information science for development and environment (MS); history of the Atlantic world (PhD); history of the Holocaust (PhD); history of the United States (PhD); Holocaust history and genocide studies (PhD); international development and social change (MA); physics (PhD); United States and Atlantic history (PhD). *Application deadline:* Applications are processed on a rolling basis. *Application fee:* $75. Electronic applications accepted. *Application Contact:* Jerry Czub, Director of Graduate Admission, 508-793-7373, E-mail: gradadmissions@clarku.edu. *Associate Provost and Dean of Graduate Studies,* Dr. Yuko Aoyama, 508-793-7403.

Adam Institute for Urban Teaching and School Practice Offers urban teaching and school practice (MAT, PhD). Electronic applications accepted.

Graduate School of Management Students: 244 full-time (129 women), 49 part-time (29 women); includes 22 minority (11 Black or African American, non-Hispanic/Latino; 7 Asian, non-Hispanic/Latino; 4 Hispanic/Latino), 193 international. Average age 27. 1,183 applicants, 79% accepted, 183 enrolled. *Faculty:* 25 full-time (11 women), 17 part-time/adjunct (6 women). Expenses: Contact institution. *Financial support:* Fellowships, research assistantships, teaching assistantships, career-related internships or fieldwork, Federal Work-Study, institutionally sponsored loans, and tuition waivers (partial) available. Support available to part-time students. In 2018, 202 master's awarded. *Program availability:* Part-time, evening/weekend. Offers accounting (MSA); business analytics (MSBA); finance (MBA); information management and business analytics (MBA); management (MBA); marketing (MBA); social change (MBA); sustainability (MBA). *Application deadline:* For fall admission, 6/1 priority date for domestic students; for spring admission, 12/1 priority date for domestic students. Applications are processed on a rolling basis. *Application fee:* $75. Electronic applications accepted. *Application Contact:* Jeremiah Czub, Director of Graduate Enrollment Management, 508-793-7559, E-mail: graduateadmissions@clarku.edu. *Dean,* Dr. Priscilla Elsass, 508-793-7633, Fax: 508-793-8822, E-mail: pelsass@clarku.edu.

Gustav H. Carlson School of Chemistry Offers biochemistry (PhD); chemistry (PhD). Electronic applications accepted.

Hiatt School of Psychology Offers clinical psychology (PhD); developmental psychology (PhD); social psychology (PhD). Electronic applications accepted.

School of Geography Offers geography (PhD). Electronic applications accepted.

School of Professional Studies Students: 109 full-time (67 women), 31 part-time (16 women); includes 14 minority (3 Black or African American, non-Hispanic/Latino; 2 Asian, non-Hispanic/Latino; 9 Hispanic/Latino), 78 international. Average age 29. 245 applicants, 80% accepted, 82 enrolled. *Faculty:* 46 part-time/adjunct (16 women). Expenses: Contact institution. *Financial support:* Career-related internships or fieldwork available. Support available to part-time students. In 2018, 86 master's awarded. *Program availability:* Part-time, evening/weekend. Offers information technology (MSIT); professional communication (MSPC); public administration (MPA, Certificate). *Application deadline:* Applications are processed on a rolling basis. *Application fee:* $75. Electronic applications accepted. *Application Contact:* John LaBrie, Dean, 508-793-7623, E-mail: JLaBrie@clarku.edu. *Dean,* John LaBrie, 508-793-7623, E-mail: JLaBrie@clarku.edu.

CLAYTON STATE UNIVERSITY, Morrow, GA 30260-0285

General Information State-supported, coed, comprehensive institution. *Enrollment:* 143 full-time matriculated graduate/professional students (102 women), 298 part-time matriculated graduate/professional students (225 women). *Enrollment by degree level:* 441 master's. *Graduate faculty:* 69 full-time (33 women), 5 part-time/adjunct (4 women). *International tuition:* $13,176 full-time. *Tuition, area resident:* Full-time $3528; part-time $2352 per year. Tuition, state resident: full-time $3528; part-time $2352 per year. Tuition, nonresident: full-time $13,176; part-time $8784 per year. *Required fees:* $1474; $1474 per unit. Tuition and fees vary according to campus/location and program. *Graduate housing:* On-campus housing not available. *Student services:* Campus employment opportunities, career counseling, exercise/wellness program, free psychological counseling, international student services, low-cost health insurance, multicultural affairs office, services for students with disabilities. *Library facilities:* Clayton State University Library.

Computer facilities: 3,500 computers available on campus for general student use. A campuswide network can be accessed from student residence rooms and from off campus. Online class registration is available.
Website: http://www.clayton.edu/

General Application Contact: Ira Bizzell, Graduate Enrollment Services, 678-466-4117, Fax: 678-466-4119, E-mail: IraBizzell@clayton.edu.

GRADUATE UNITS

School of Graduate Studies Electronic applications accepted.

College of Arts and Sciences Offers administration of justice (MS); applied developmental psychology (MS); arts and sciences (MA, MAT, MS); biology (MAT); clinical/counseling psychology (MS); criminology, law, and society (MS); English (MAT); history (MAT); liberal studies (MA); mathematics (MAT).

College of Business Offers accounting (MBA); business (MBA); human resource leadership (MBA); international business (MBA); sports and entertainment management (MBA); supply chain management (MBA).

College of Health Offers family nurse practitioner (MSN); health (MHA, MSN).

College of Information and Mathematical Sciences Offers archival studies (MAS); information and mathematical sciences (MAS).

CLEARY UNIVERSITY, Howell, MI 48843

General Information Independent, coed, comprehensive institution. *Graduate housing:* On-campus housing not available.

GRADUATE UNITS

Online Program in Business Administration *Program availability:* Part-time, evening/weekend, online learning. Offers analytics, technology, and innovation (MBA, Graduate Certificate); financial planning (Graduate Certificate); global leadership (MBA, Graduate Certificate); health care leadership (MBA, Graduate Certificate). Electronic applications accepted.

CLEMSON UNIVERSITY, Clemson, SC 29634

General Information State-supported, coed, university. CGS member. *Enrollment:* 2,969 full-time matriculated graduate/professional students (1,256 women), 2,313 part-time matriculated graduate/professional students (1,378 women). *Enrollment by degree level:* 3,821 master's, 1,723 doctoral, 116 other advanced degrees. *Graduate faculty:* 1,268 full-time (481 women), 116 part-time/adjunct (44 women). *International tuition:* $23,246 full-time. *Tuition, area resident:* Full-time $11,270; part-time $8688 per credit hour. Tuition, state resident: full-time $11,796. Tuition, nonresident: full-time $23,802; part-time $17,412 per credit hour. *Required fees:* $1196; $497 per semester. Tuition and fees vary according to course load, degree level, campus/location and program. *Graduate housing:* On-campus housing not available. *Student services:* Campus employment opportunities, campus safety program, career counseling, exercise/wellness program, free psychological counseling, grant writing training, international student services, low-cost health insurance, multicultural affairs office, services for students with disabilities, teacher training, writing training. *Library facilities:* Robert Muldrow Cooper Library plus 1 other. *Collection:* Study areas open 24 hours, 5–7 days a week; students can reserve study rooms.

Computer facilities: Computer purchase and lease plans are available. 1,250 computers available on campus for general student use. A campuswide network can be accessed. Online class registration is available.
Website: http://www.clemson.edu/

General Application Contact: Kathleen Costello, Director of Admissions and Recruitment, 864-656-2561, E-mail: kcostel@clemson.edu.

GRADUATE UNITS

Graduate School Students: 2,953 full-time (1,248 women), 2,044 part-time (1,148 women); includes 622 minority (279 Black or African American, non-Hispanic/Latino; 10 American Indian or Alaska Native, non-Hispanic/Latino; 79 Asian, non-Hispanic/Latino; 159 Hispanic/Latino; 8 Native Hawaiian or other Pacific Islander, non-Hispanic/Latino; 87 Two or more races, non-Hispanic/Latino), 1,266 international. Average age 30. 7,269 applicants, 64% accepted, 2679 enrolled. *Faculty:* 1,427 full-time (562 women), 120 part-time/adjunct (46 women). Expenses: Contact institution. *Financial support:* In 2018–19, 2,172 students received support, including 223 fellowships with partial tuition reimbursements available (averaging $3,546 per year), 649 research assistantships with partial tuition reimbursements available (averaging $17,404 per year), 809 teaching assistantships with partial tuition reimbursements available (averaging $17,447 per year); career-related internships or fieldwork and unspecified assistantships also available. Support available to part-time students. In 2018, 1,418 master's, 239 doctorates, 153 other advanced degrees awarded. *Program availability:* Part-time, evening/weekend, 100% online, blended/hybrid learning. *Application deadline:* For fall admission, 4/15 for international students; for spring admission, 10/15 for international students. Applications are processed on a rolling basis. *Application fee:* $80 ($90 for international students). Electronic applications accepted. *Application Contact:* Kathleen Costello, Director of Graduate Admissions and Recruitment, 864-656-2561, E-mail: kcostel@clemson.edu. *Interim Dean,* Dr. David Fleming, 864-656-2878, E-mail: dflemin@clemson.edu.

College of Agriculture, Forestry and Life Sciences Students: 226 full-time (101 women), 97 part-time (41 women); includes 19 minority (8 Black or African American, non-Hispanic/Latino; 11 Two or more races, non-Hispanic/Latino), 62 international. Average age 29. 315 applicants, 66% accepted, 169 enrolled. *Faculty:* 139 full-time (54 women), 2 part-time/adjunct (1 woman). Expenses: Contact institution. *Financial support:* In 2018–19, 173 students received support, including 20 fellowships with partial tuition reimbursements available (averaging $4,325 per year), 98 research assistantships with partial tuition reimbursements available (averaging $15,374 per year), 44 teaching assistantships with partial tuition reimbursements available (averaging $12,880 per year); career-related internships or fieldwork and unspecified assistantships also available. In 2018, 66 master's, 20 doctorates awarded. *Program availability:* 100% online, blended/hybrid learning. Offers agricultural education (M Ag Ed); agriculture, forestry and life sciences (M Ag Ed, MFR, MS, PhD); animal and veterinary sciences (MS, PhD); applied economics (PhD); applied economics and statistics (MS); entomology (MS, PhD); food technology (PhD); food, nutrition and culinary sciences (MS); forest resources (MFR, MS, PhD); packaging science (MS); plant and environmental sciences (MS, PhD); wildlife and fisheries biology (MS, PhD). *Application deadline:* For fall admission, 4/15 for international students; for winter admission, 10/15 for international students. Applications are processed on a rolling basis. *Application fee:* $80 ($90 for international students). Electronic applications accepted. *Application Contact:* Dr. Paula Agudelo, Associate Dean for Research and Graduate Studies, 864-656-2810, E-mail: pagudel@clemson.edu. *Dean,* Dr. Keith Belli, 864-656-3013, E-mail: caflsdean-l@clemson.edu.

College of Architecture, Arts, and Humanities Students: 309 full-time (163 women), 33 part-time (17 women); includes 38 minority (14 Black or African American, non-Hispanic/Latino; 6 Asian, non-Hispanic/Latino; 16 Hispanic/Latino; 2 Two or more races, non-Hispanic/Latino; 56 international. Average age 29. 478 applicants, 78% accepted, 173 enrolled. *Faculty:* 271 full-time (126 women), 39 part-time/adjunct (17 women). Expenses: Contact institution. *Financial support:* In 2018–19, 273 students received support, including 64 fellowships with partial tuition reimbursements available (averaging $2,015 per year), 29 research assistantships with partial tuition reimbursements available (averaging $4,415 per year), 77 teaching assistantships with partial tuition reimbursements available (averaging $16,393 per year); career-related internships or fieldwork and unspecified assistantships also available. In 2018, 148 master's, 11 doctorates, 9 other advanced degrees awarded. *Program availability:* Part-time, 100% online. Offers architecture (M Arch, MS, Certificate); architecture and health (M Arch); architecture, arts, and humanities (M Arch, MA, MCSM, MFA, MLA, MRED, MRUD, MS, PhD, Certificate); construction science and management (MCSM); digital ecologies (Certificate); English (MA); historic preservation (MS, Certificate); history (MA); integrated project delivery (Certificate); planning, design and the built environment (PhD); real estate development (MRED); resilient urban design (MRUD); rhetoric, communication and information design (PhD); visual arts (MFA); writing, rhetoric and media (MA). *Application deadline:* For fall admission, 4/15 for international students; for spring admission, 10/15 for international students. Applications are processed on a rolling basis. *Application fee:* $80 ($90 for international students). Electronic applications accepted. *Application Contact:* Dr. James Spencer, Associate Dean for Research and Graduate Studies, 864-656-0377, E-mail: jhspenc@clemson.edu. *Dean,* Dr. Richard Goodstein, 864-656-3084, E-mail: regst@clemson.edu.

College of Behavioral, Social and Health Sciences Students: 249 full-time (174 women), 371 part-time (254 women); includes 101 minority (62 Black or African American, non-Hispanic/Latino; 8 Asian, non-Hispanic/Latino; 23 Hispanic/Latino; 8 Two or more races, non-Hispanic/Latino, 55 international. Average age 32. 739 applicants, 56% accepted, 279 enrolled. *Faculty:* 215 full-time (124 women), 13 part-time/adjunct (6 women). Expenses: Contact institution. *Financial support:* In 2018–19, 182 students received support, including 9 fellowships with partial tuition reimbursements available (averaging $5,058 per year), 28 research assistantships with partial tuition reimbursements available (averaging $15,778 per year), 133 teaching assistantships with partial tuition reimbursements available (averaging $10,605 per year); unspecified assistantships also available. In 2018, 147 master's, 29 doctorates, 46 other advanced degrees awarded. *Program availability:* Part-time, evening/weekend, 100% online, blended/hybrid learning. Offers applied health research and evaluation (MS, PhD); applied psychology (MS); applied sociology (MS); behavioral, social and health sciences (MA, MPA, MS, DNP, PhD, Certificate); biomedical data science and informatics (PhD); clinical and translational research (PhD, Certificate); communication, technology and society (MA); global health (Certificate); healthcare genetics (PhD); human factors psychology (PhD); industrial-organizational psychology (PhD); international family and community studies (PhD, Certificate); international parks and tourism (Certificate); nursing (MS, DNP); parks, recreation and tourism management (MS, PhD); policy studies (PhD, Certificate); public administration (MPA, Certificate); recreational therapy (MS); youth development leadership (MS, Certificate). *Application deadline:* For fall admission, 4/15 for international students; for spring admission, 10/15 for international students. Applications are processed on a rolling basis. *Application fee:* $80 ($90 for international students). Electronic applications accepted. *Application Contact:* Dr. Eric Muth, Associate Dean for Research and Graduate Programs, 864-656-6741, E-mail: muth@clemson.edu. *Dean,* Dr. Leslie Hossfeld, 864-656-7640, E-mail: lhossfe@clemson.edu.

College of Business Students: 317 full-time (151 women), 442 part-time (152 women); includes 117 minority (49 Black or African American, non-Hispanic/Latino; 6 American Indian or Alaska Native, non-Hispanic/Latino; 19 Asian, non-Hispanic/Latino; 28 Hispanic/Latino; 2 Native Hawaiian or other Pacific Islander, non-Hispanic/Latino; 13 Two or more races, non-Hispanic/Latino), 75 international. Average age 31. 873 applicants, 80% accepted, 440 enrolled. *Faculty:* 156 full-time (53 women), 27 part-time/adjunct (6 women). Expenses: Contact institution. *Financial support:* In 2018–19, 128 students received support, including 17 fellowships with partial tuition reimbursements available (averaging $4,118 per year), 8 research assistantships with partial tuition reimbursements available (averaging $20,790 per year), 31 teaching assistantships with partial tuition reimbursements available (averaging $19,975 per year); career-related internships or fieldwork and unspecified assistantships also available. In 2018, 333 master's, 16 doctorates awarded. *Program availability:* Part-time, evening/weekend, 100% online. Offers accounting (MP Acc); applied economics (PhD); applied economics and statistics (MS); business (MA, MBA, MP Acc, MS, PhD); business administration (MBA, PhD); business analytics (MBA); economics (MA, PhD); entrepreneurship and innovation (MBA); graphic communications (MS); management (MS); marketing (MS). *Application deadline:* For fall admission, 4/15 for international students; for spring admission, 10/15 for international students. Applications are processed on a rolling basis. *Application fee:* $80 ($90 for international students). Electronic applications accepted. *Application Contact:* Dr. Gregory Pickett, Senior Associate Dean, 864-656-3975, E-mail: pgregor@clemson.edu. *Dean,* Wendy York, 864-656-3178, E-mail: BIZDEAN@clemson.edu.

College of Education Students: 489 full-time (378 women), 509 part-time (394 women); includes 232 minority (143 Black or African American, non-Hispanic/Latino; 2 American Indian or Alaska Native, non-Hispanic/Latino; 8 Asian, non-Hispanic/Latino; 43 Hispanic/Latino; 36 Two or more races, non-Hispanic/Latino), 11 international. Average age 32. 1,357 applicants, 81% accepted, 870 enrolled. *Faculty:* 78 full-time (56 women). Expenses: Contact institution. *Financial support:* In 2018–19, 144 students received support, including 10 fellowships with full and partial tuition reimbursements available (averaging $4,620 per year), 6 research assistantships with full and partial tuition reimbursements available (averaging $12,500 per year), 31 teaching assistantships with full and partial tuition reimbursements available

(averaging $17,241 per year); career-related internships or fieldwork and unspecified assistantships also available. In 2018, 182 master's, 25 doctorates, 62 other advanced degrees awarded. *Program availability:* Part-time, evening/weekend, 100% online. Offers administration and supervision (M Ed, Ed S); athletic leadership (MS, Certificate); counselor education (M Ed, Ed S); curriculum and instruction (PhD); education (M Ed, MAT, MHRD, MS, Ed D, PhD, Certificate, Ed S); education systems improvement science (Ed D); educational leadership (PhD); human resource development (MHRD); leadership (Certificate); learning sciences (PhD); literacy (M Ed); literacy, language and culture (PhD); middle level education (MAT); secondary math and science (MAT); special education (M Ed, MAT, PhD); STEAM education (Certificate); student affairs (M Ed); teaching and learning (M Ed). *Application deadline:* For fall admission, 4/15 for international students; for spring admission, 10/15 for international students. Applications are processed on a rolling basis. *Application fee:* $80 ($90 for international students). Electronic applications accepted. *Application Contact:* Dr. Jeff Marshall, Interim Associate Dean, Academic Affairs & Research, 864-656-2059, E-mail: marsha9@clemson.edu. *Founding Dean,* Dr. George J. Petersen, 864-656-4444, E-mail: soedean@clemson.edu.

College of Engineering, Computing and Applied Sciences Students: 1,221 full-time (298 women), 291 part-time (66 women); includes 118 minority (39 Black or African American, non-Hispanic/Latino; 2 American Indian or Alaska Native, non-Hispanic/Latino; 30 Asian, non-Hispanic/Latino; 28 Hispanic/Latino; 2 Native Hawaiian or other Pacific Islander, non-Hispanic/Latino; 17 Two or more races, non-Hispanic/Latino, 853 international. Average age 27. 2,871 applicants, 52% accepted, 593 enrolled. *Faculty:* 273 full-time (62 women), 15 part-time/adjunct (5 women). Expenses: Contact institution. *Financial support:* In 2018–19, 866 students received support, including 80 fellowships with full and partial tuition reimbursements available (averaging $4,130 per year), 398 research assistantships with full and partial tuition reimbursements available (averaging $18,301 per year), 198 teaching assistantships with full and partial tuition reimbursements available (averaging $18,423 per year); career-related internships or fieldwork and unspecified assistantships also available. In 2018, 399 master's, 87 doctorates, 36 other advanced degrees awarded. *Program availability:* Part-time, 100% online. Offers automotive engineering (MS, PhD, Certificate); bioengineering (MS, PhD); biomedical engineering (M Engr); biosystems engineering (MS, PhD); chemical engineering (MS, PhD); civil engineering (MS, PhD); computer engineering (MS, PhD); computer science (MS, PhD); digital production arts (MFA); electrical engineering (M Engr, MS, PhD); engineering and science education (PhD, Certificate); engineering, computing and applied sciences (M Engr, MFA, MS, PhD, Certificate); environmental engineering and science (MS, PhD); environmental health physics (MS); human centered computing (PhD); hydrogeology (MS); industrial engineering (M Engr, MS, PhD); materials science and engineering (MS, PhD); mechanical engineering (MS, PhD); medical device recycling and reprocessing (Certificate). *Application deadline:* For fall admission, 4/15 for international students; for spring admission, 10/15 for international students. Applications are processed on a rolling basis. *Application fee:* $80 ($90 for international students). Electronic applications accepted. *Application Contact:* Dr. Douglas Hirt, Associate Dean for Research and Graduate Studies, 864-656-3201, E-mail: hirtd@clemson.edu. *Dean,* Dr. Anand Gramopadhye, 864-656-3200, E-mail: agrampo@clemson.edu.

College of Science Students: 391 full-time (175 women), 253 part-time (169 women); includes 70 minority (14 Black or African American, non-Hispanic/Latino; 4 American Indian or Alaska Native, non-Hispanic/Latino; 12 Asian, non-Hispanic/Latino; 22 Hispanic/Latino; 2 Native Hawaiian or other Pacific Islander, non-Hispanic/Latino; 16 Two or more races, non-Hispanic/Latino), 155 international. Average age 32. 619 applicants, 59% accepted, 213 enrolled. *Faculty:* 144 full-time (35 women), 8 part-time/adjunct (0 women). Expenses: Contact institution. *Financial support:* In 2018–19, 397 students received support, including 16 fellowships with full and partial tuition reimbursements available (averaging $3,901 per year), 78 research assistantships with full and partial tuition reimbursements available (averaging $20,596 per year), 293 teaching assistantships with full and partial tuition reimbursements available (averaging $20,683 per year); career-related internships or fieldwork and unspecified assistantships also available. In 2018, 143 master's, 51 doctorates awarded. *Program availability:* Part-time, 100% online. Offers biochemistry and molecular biology (PhD); biological sciences (MS, PhD); biological sciences for science educators (MBS); chemistry (MS, PhD); environmental toxicology (MS, PhD); genetics (PhD); mathematical sciences (MS, PhD); microbiology (MS, PhD); physics (MS, PhD); science (MBS, MS, PhD). *Application deadline:* For fall admission, 4/15 for international students; for spring admission, 10/15 for international students. Applications are processed on a rolling basis. *Application fee:* $80 ($90 for international students). Electronic applications accepted. *Application Contact:* Dr. Julia Frugoli, Associate Dean for Inclusive Excellence and Graduate Education, 864-656-1859, E-mail: jfrugol@clemson.edu. *Founding Dean,* Dr. Cynthia Young, 864-656-3642, E-mail: sciencedean@clemson.edu.

CLEVELAND INSTITUTE OF MUSIC, Cleveland, OH 44106-1776

General Information Independent, coed, comprehensive institution. *Graduate housing:* Room and/or apartments available on a first-come, first-served basis to single students; on-campus housing not available to married students. Housing application deadline: 5/30.

GRADUATE UNITS

Graduate Programs Offers performance (MM, DMA, AD, CPS). DMA and MM programs offered jointly with Case Western Reserve University. Electronic applications accepted.

CLEVELAND STATE UNIVERSITY, Cleveland, OH 44115

General Information State-supported, coed, university. CGS member. *Enrollment:* 1,920 full-time matriculated graduate/professional students (1,179 women), 2,159 part-time matriculated graduate/professional students (1,326 women). *Enrollment by degree level:* 2,607 master's, 823 doctoral, 416 other advanced degrees. *Graduate faculty:* 273 full-time (125 women), 316 part-time/adjunct (162 women). *International tuition:* $18,914 full-time. Tuition, state resident: full-time $7232.55; part-time $6676 per credit hour. Tuition, nonresident: full-time $12,375. *Required fees:* $80; $80 $40. Tuition and fees vary according to program. *Graduate housing:* Room and/or apartments available on a first-come, first-served basis to single students; on-campus housing not available to married students. Typical cost: $8790 per year ($12,882 including board). Room and board charges vary according to board plan and housing facility selected. Housing application deadline: 7/15. *Student services:* Campus employment opportunities, campus safety program, career counseling, exercise/wellness program, international student services, low-cost health insurance, multicultural affairs office, services for students with disabilities, teacher training, writing training. *Library facilities:* Michael Schwartz Library plus 1 other. *Collection:* Books: 524,556 (physical), 228,146 (digital/electronic); Serial titles: 6,155 (physical), 194 (digital/electronic); Databases: 733. Students can reserve study rooms.

Computer facilities: Computer purchase and lease plans are available. 736 computers available on campus for general student use. A campuswide network can be accessed from student residence rooms and from off campus. Online class registration, each general purpose computer lab has a scanner and printer, students are allowed free black and white printing up to 2,000 pages per semester are available. Website: http://www.csuohio.edu/

General Application Contact: Tonita May, Coordinator, Graduate Student Services, 216-687-3625, Fax: 216-875-9933, E-mail: t.l.may59@csuohio.edu.

GRADUATE UNITS

Cleveland-Marshall College of Law Students: 258 full-time (120 women), 132 part-time (77 women); includes 72 minority (44 Black or African American, non-Hispanic/Latino; 10 Asian, non-Hispanic/Latino; 13 Hispanic/Latino; 5 Two or more races, non-Hispanic/Latino), 4 international. Average age 28. 711 applicants, 44% accepted, 118 enrolled. *Faculty:* 34 full-time (17 women), 61 part-time/adjunct (16 women). Expenses: Contact institution. *Financial support:* In 2018–19, 198 students received support, including 17 fellowships (averaging $2,500 per year), 34 research assistantships, 7 teaching assistantships with partial tuition reimbursements available (averaging $6,700 per year); career-related internships or fieldwork, Federal Work-Study, scholarships/grants, and unspecified assistantships also available. Support available to part-time students. Financial award application deadline: 5/1; financial award applicants required to submit FAFSA. In 2018, 11 master's, 88 doctorates, 2 Certificates awarded. *Program availability:* Part-time, evening/weekend. Offers law (LL M, MLS, JD, Certificate). *Application deadline:* For fall admission, 5/1 for domestic and international students. Applications are processed on a rolling basis. *Application fee:* $0. Electronic applications accepted. *Application Contact:* Christopher Lucak, Assistant Dean for Admission and Financial Aid, 216-687-4692, Fax: 216-687-6881, E-mail: law.admissions@csuohio.edu. *Dean,* Lee Fisher, 216-687-2300, Fax: 216-687-6881, E-mail: lee.fisher@csuohio.edu.

College of Graduate Studies Students: 1,662 full-time (1,059 women), 2,027 part-time (1,249 women); includes 831 minority (519 Black or African American, non-Hispanic/Latino; 6 American Indian or Alaska Native, non-Hispanic/Latino; 98 Asian, non-Hispanic/Latino; 136 Hispanic/Latino; 1 Native Hawaiian or other Pacific Islander, non-Hispanic/Latino; 71 Two or more races, non-Hispanic/Latino), 483 international. Average age 30. 4,931 applicants, 46% accepted, 966 enrolled. Expenses: Contact institution. *Financial support:* In 2018–19, 306 research assistantships with tuition reimbursements (averaging $3,480 per year), 123 teaching assistantships with tuition reimbursements (averaging $3,480 per year) were awarded; career-related internships or fieldwork, scholarships/grants, tuition waivers (full and partial), and unspecified assistantships also available. Financial award applicants required to submit FAFSA. In 2018, 1,259 master's, 80 doctorates, 12 other advanced degrees awarded. *Program availability:* Part-time, evening/weekend, 100% online, blended/hybrid learning. *Application deadline:* For fall admission, 7/1 priority date for domestic students; 5/15 priority date for international students; for spring admission, 11/15 priority date for domestic students, 11/1 priority date for international students; for summer admission, 4/1 for domestic students, 3/15 for international students. Applications are processed on a rolling basis. *Application fee:* $30. Electronic applications accepted. *Application Contact:* Dianne C. Oloff, Graduate Student Services Specialist, 216-523-7572, Fax: 216-875-9933, E-mail: d.oloff@csuohio.edu. *Dean, College of Graduate Studies,* Dr. Jianping Zhu, 216-687-3595, Fax: 216-875-9933, E-mail: j.zhu94@csuohio.edu.

College of Education and Human Services Students: 261 full-time (205 women), 773 part-time (593 women); includes 323 minority (233 Black or African American, non-Hispanic/Latino; 3 American Indian or Alaska Native, non-Hispanic/Latino; 11 Asian, non-Hispanic/Latino; 41 Hispanic/Latino; 1 Native Hawaiian or other Pacific Islander, non-Hispanic/Latino; 34 Two or more races, non-Hispanic/Latino), 33 international. Average age 34. 487 applicants, 58% accepted, 178 enrolled. *Faculty:* 86 full-time (60 women), 106 part-time/adjunct (81 women). Expenses: Contact institution. *Financial support:* In 2018–19, 64 students received support, including 38 research assistantships with full tuition reimbursements available (averaging $6,960 per year), 2 teaching assistantships with full tuition reimbursements available (averaging $7,800 per year); career-related internships or fieldwork, Federal Work-Study, scholarships/grants, tuition waivers (partial), and unspecified assistantships also available. Support available to part-time students. Financial award application deadline: 8/1; financial award applicants required to submit FAFSA. In 2018, 266 master's, 12 doctorates, 1 other advanced degree awarded. *Program availability:* Part-time, evening/weekend, 100% online, blended/hybrid learning. Offers adult learning and development (M Ed); adult, continuing, and higher education (PhD); art education (M Ed); counseling psychology (PhD); counselor education (PhD); early childhood education (M Ed); early childhood mental health counseling (Certificate); education and human services (M Ed, MPH, PhD, Certificate, Ed S); educational administration and supervision (M Ed); foreign language education (M Ed); learning and development (PhD); middle childhood mathematics and science education (M Ed); nursing education (PhD); physical education pedagogy (M Ed); policy studies (PhD); public health (MPH); school administration (PhD); special education (M Ed); teaching English to speakers of other languages (M Ed); urban education (PhD). *Application deadline:* For fall admission, 7/1 priority date for domestic students, 5/15 for international students; for spring admission, 11/15 priority date for domestic students, 11/1 for international students; for summer admission, 4/1 for domestic students, 3/15 for international students. Applications are processed on a rolling basis. *Application fee:* $30. Electronic applications accepted. *Application Contact:* Patricia Sokolowski, Office Coordinator/Assistant to the Dean, 216-523-7143, Fax: 216-687-5415, E-mail: p.sokolowski@csuohio.edu. *Dean,* Dr. Sajit Zachariah, 216-523-7143, Fax: 216-687-5415, E-mail: sajit.zachariah@csuohio.edu.

College of Liberal Arts and Social Sciences Students: 207 full-time (162 women), 154 part-time (99 women); includes 118 minority (85 Black or African American, non-Hispanic/Latino; 3 Asian, non-Hispanic/Latino; 20 Hispanic/Latino; 10 Two or more races, non-Hispanic/Latino), 13 international. Average age 32. 499 applicants, 46% accepted, 123 enrolled. *Faculty:* 156 full-time (64 women), 184 part-time/adjunct (79 women). Expenses: Contact institution. *Financial support:* Fellowships, research assistantships, teaching assistantships, career-related internships or fieldwork, Federal Work-Study, institutionally sponsored loans, tuition waivers (full and partial), and unspecified assistantships available. Support available to part-time students. Financial award applicants required to submit FAFSA. In 2018, 139 master's awarded. *Program availability:* Part-time, evening/weekend. Offers applied communication theory and methodology (MA); art history (MA); bioethics (MA, Certificate); composition (MM); creative writing (MFA); economics (MA); global interactions (MA); liberal arts and social sciences (M Ed, MA, MFA, MM, MSW, Certificate); museum studies (MA); music education (MM); philosophy (MA); social work (MSW); Spanish (MA). *Application deadline:* Applications are processed on a rolling basis. *Application fee:* $30. Electronic applications accepted. *Application Contact:* Deborah L. Brown,

Interim Assistant Director, Graduate Admissions, 216-523-7572, Fax: 216-687-5400, E-mail: d.l.brown@csuohio.edu. *Dean,* Dr. Gregory M. Sadlek, 216-687-3660.

College of Sciences and Health Professions Students: 579 full-time (425 women), 151 part-time (102 women); includes 105 minority (55 Black or African American, non-Hispanic/Latino; 1 American Indian or Alaska Native, non-Hispanic/Latino; 16 Asian, non-Hispanic/Latino; 21 Hispanic/Latino; 12 Two or more races, non-Hispanic/Latino), 87 international. Average age 27. 912 applicants, 34% accepted, 204 enrolled. *Faculty:* 107 full-time (35 women), 76 part-time/adjunct (43 women). Expenses: Contact institution. *Financial support:* In 2018–19, 174 students received support, including 47 research assistantships with full tuition reimbursements available (averaging $17,000 per year), 127 teaching assistantships with tuition reimbursements available (averaging $10,700 per year); unspecified assistantships also available. Financial award applicants required to submit FAFSA. In 2018, 205 master's, 54 doctorates, 11 other advanced degrees awarded. *Program availability:* Part-time, evening/weekend, online learning. Offers applied statistics (MS); biological, geological, and environmental sciences (MS, PhD); clinical chemistry (PhD); health sciences (MS); mathematics (MS); occupational therapy (MOT); organic chemistry (MS); physical chemistry (MS); physical therapy (DPT); physician assistant science (MS); physics (MS); psychology (MA, PhD, Psy S); sciences and health professions (MA, MOT, MS, DPT, PhD, Psy S); speech-language pathology (MA). *Application deadline:* For fall admission, 7/1 priority date for domestic students, 5/15 priority date for international students; for spring admission, 11/15 priority date for domestic students, 11/1 priority date for international students; for summer admission, 4/1 for domestic students, 3/15 for international students. Applications are processed on a rolling basis. *Application fee:* $30. Electronic applications accepted. *Application Contact:* Dianne C. Oloff, Graduate Student Services Specialist, 216-687-5230, Fax: 216-875-9933, E-mail: d.oloff@csuohio.edu. *Dean of the College of Graduate Studies,* Dr. Jianping Zhu, 216-687-3595, Fax: 216-875-9933, E-mail: j.zhu94@csuohio.edu.

Fenn College of Engineering Students: 200 full-time (61 women), 179 part-time (41 women); includes 39 minority (6 Black or African American, non-Hispanic/Latino; 20 Asian, non-Hispanic/Latino; 8 Hispanic/Latino; 5 Two or more races, non-Hispanic/Latino), 197 international. Average age 26. 1,037 applicants, 48% accepted, 143 enrolled. *Faculty:* 54 full-time (5 women), 12 part-time/adjunct (0 women). Expenses: Contact institution. *Financial support:* In 2018–19, 93 students received support. Fellowships, research assistantships, teaching assistantships, career-related internships or fieldwork, institutionally sponsored loans, scholarships/grants, tuition waivers (full and partial), and unspecified assistantships available. Support available to part-time students. Financial award application deadline: 3/30; financial award applicants required to submit FAFSA. In 2018, 245 master's, 9 doctorates awarded. *Program availability:* Part-time, evening/weekend. Offers applied biomedical engineering (D Eng); chemical and biomedical engineering (MS, D Eng); civil and environmental engineering (MS, D Eng); electrical engineering (MS, D Eng); engineering (MS, D Eng); mechanical engineering (MS, D Eng); software engineering (MS). *Application deadline:* Applications are processed on a rolling basis. *Application fee:* $30. Electronic applications accepted. *Application Contact:* Deborah L. Brown, Interim Assistant Director, Graduate Admissions, 216-523-7572, Fax: 216-687-9214, E-mail: d.l.brown@csuohio.edu. *Associate Dean,* Dr. Paul P. Lin, 216-687-2556, Fax: 216-687-9280, E-mail: p.lin@csuohio.edu.

Maxine Goodman Levin College of Urban Affairs Students: 72 full-time (40 women), 135 part-time (80 women); includes 53 minority (43 Black or African American, non-Hispanic/Latino; 2 Asian, non-Hispanic/Latino; 5 Hispanic/Latino; 3 Two or more races, non-Hispanic/Latino), 7 international. Average age 33. 195 applicants, 47% accepted, 38 enrolled. *Faculty:* 22 full-time (9 women), 8 part-time/adjunct (4 women). Expenses: Contact institution. *Financial support:* In 2018–19, 60 students received support, including 40 research assistantships with full tuition reimbursements available (averaging $8,000 per year), 15 teaching assistantships with tuition reimbursements available (averaging $7,000 per year); career-related internships or fieldwork, Federal Work-Study, institutionally sponsored loans, scholarships/grants, and unspecified assistantships also available. Support available to part-time students. Financial award application deadline: 3/1; financial award applicants required to submit FAFSA. In 2018, 53 master's, 3 doctorates awarded. *Program availability:* Part-time, evening/weekend. Offers communication (PhD); economic development (MPA, MUPD); environmental nonprofit management (MAES); environmental planning (MAES); environmental sustainability (MUPD); historic preservation (MUPD); housing and neighborhood development (MUPD); local and urban management (Certificate); non-profit management (MPA); nonprofit administration and leadership (MNAL); nonprofit management (Certificate); policy and administration (MAES); public administration (PhD); public management (MPA); real estate development and finance (MUPD); sustainable economic development (MAES); urban affairs (MAES, MNAL, MPA, MS, MUPD, PhD, Certificate); urban economic development (Certificate); urban geographic information systems (MUPD); urban policy and development (PhD); urban studies (MS, Certificate). *Application deadline:* For fall admission, 7/1 priority date for domestic students, 5/15 for international students; for spring admission, 11/15 for domestic students, 11/1 for international students; for summer admission, 4/1 for domestic students, 3/15 for international students. Applications are processed on a rolling basis. *Application fee:* $30. Electronic applications accepted. *Application Contact:* Graduate Program Coordinator, 216-523-7522, Fax: 216-687-5398, E-mail: urbanprograms@csuohio.edu. *Dean,* Dr. Roland V. Anglin, 216-687-2135, E-mail: r.anglin@csuohio.edu.

Monte Ahuja College of Business Students: 336 full-time (161 women), 543 part-time (257 women); includes 179 minority (90 Black or African American, non-Hispanic/Latino; 2 American Indian or Alaska Native, non-Hispanic/Latino; 45 Asian, non-Hispanic/Latino; 36 Hispanic/Latino; 6 Two or more races, non-Hispanic/Latino), 146 international. Average age 29. 1,052 applicants, 46% accepted, 258 enrolled. *Faculty:* 48 full-time (16 women), 33 part-time/adjunct (12 women). Expenses: Contact institution. *Financial support:* In 2018–19, 110 students received support, including 45 research assistantships with full tuition reimbursements available (averaging $6,960 per year), 1 teaching assistantship with full tuition reimbursement available (averaging $7,800 per year); career-related internships or fieldwork, scholarships/grants, tuition waivers (full), and unspecified assistantships also available. Financial award application deadline: 5/15; financial award applicants required to submit FAFSA. In 2018, 336 master's, 2 doctorates awarded. *Program availability:* Part-time, evening/weekend. Offers business (AMBA, EMBA, M Acc, MBA, MLRHR, DBA); business administration (AMBA, EMBA, MBA, DBA); financial accounting/audit (M Acc); health care administration (MBA); information systems (DBA); labor relations and human resources (MLRHR); marketing (DBA). *Application deadline:* For fall admission, 7/1 priority date for domestic students, 5/15 for international students; for spring admission, 11/15 priority date for domestic students, 11/1 for international students; for summer admission, 4/1 for domestic students, 3/15 for international students. Applications are processed on a rolling basis. *Application fee:* $30. Electronic applications accepted. *Application Contact:* Kenneth Dippong, Director, Student Services, 216-523-7545, Fax: 216-687-9354, E-mail: k.dippong@csuohio.edu. *Dean,* Dr. Sanjay Putrevu, 216-687-3786, Fax: 216-687-9354, E-mail: s.putrevu@csuohio.edu.

School of Nursing Students: 7 full-time (5 women), 74 part-time (68 women); includes 11 minority (6 Black or African American, non-Hispanic/Latino; 1 Asian, non-Hispanic/Latino; 4 Hispanic/Latino). Average age 37. 60 applicants, 62% accepted, 26 enrolled. *Faculty:* 7 full-time (all women). Expenses: Contact institution. *Financial support:* Tuition waivers (full) and unspecified assistantships available. Financial award application deadline: 5/1; financial award applicants required to submit FAFSA. In 2018, 15 master's awarded. *Program availability:* Part-time, 100% online. Offers nursing (MSN, PhD). *Application deadline:* For fall admission, 3/1 priority date for domestic and international students. *Application fee:* $55. Electronic applications accepted. *Application Contact:* Maureen Mitchell, Assistant Professor and Graduate Program Director, 216-523-7128, Fax: 216-687-3556, E-mail: m.m.mitchell1@csuohio.edu. *Dean,* Dr. Vida Lock, 216-523-7237, Fax: 216-687-3556, E-mail: v.lock@csuohio.edu.

CLEVELAND UNIVERSITY–KANSAS CITY, Overland Park, KS 66210
General Information Independent, coed, comprehensive institution. *Graduate housing:* On-campus housing not available.

GRADUATE UNITS
Doctor of Chiropractic Program *Program availability:* Part-time. Offers chiropractic (DC). Electronic applications accepted.
Program in Health Education and Promotion *Program availability:* Part-time. Offers health education and promotion (MS). Electronic applications accepted.

COASTAL CAROLINA UNIVERSITY, Conway, SC 29528-6054
General Information State-supported, coed, comprehensive institution. *Graduate housing:* Room and/or apartments available on a first-come, first-served basis to single students; on-campus housing not available to married students. Housing application deadline: 5/1.

GRADUATE UNITS
College of Science *Program availability:* Part-time, evening/weekend, 100% online. Offers applied computing and information systems (Certificate); coastal marine and wetland studies (MS); information systems technology (MS); marine science (PhD); sports management (MS). Electronic applications accepted.
E. Craig Wall, Sr. College of Business Administration *Program availability:* Part-time, evening/weekend, 100% online, blended/hybrid learning. Offers accounting (M Acc); business administration (MBA); business foundations (Certificate); fraud examination (Certificate). Electronic applications accepted.
Spadoni College of Education *Program availability:* Part-time, evening/weekend, 100% online, blended/hybrid learning. Offers education (MAT); educational leadership (M Ed, Ed S); English for speakers of other languages (Certificate); instructional technology (M Ed, Ed S); language, literacy and culture (M Ed); learning and teaching (M Ed); online teaching and training (Certificate); special education (M Ed). Electronic applications accepted.
Thomas W. and Robin W. Edwards College of Humanities and Fine Arts *Program availability:* Part-time, evening/weekend. Offers liberal studies (MA); writing (MA). Electronic applications accepted.

COGSWELL POLYTECHNICAL COLLEGE, San Jose, CA 95134
General Information Proprietary, coed, comprehensive institution.

GRADUATE UNITS
Program in Entrepreneurship and Innovation Offers entrepreneurship and innovation (MA).

COKER COLLEGE, Hartsville, SC 29550
General Information Independent, coed, comprehensive institution. *Graduate housing:* On-campus housing not available.

GRADUATE UNITS
Graduate Programs Students: 144 full-time (100 women), 6 part-time (2 women); includes 42 minority (33 Black or African American, non-Hispanic/Latino; 1 Asian, non-Hispanic/Latino; 4 Hispanic/Latino; 4 Two or more races, non-Hispanic/Latino). Average age 33. 120 applicants, 61% accepted, 65 enrolled. *Faculty:* 15 full-time (7 women), 7 part-time/adjunct (3 women). Expenses: Contact institution. *Financial support:* Unspecified assistantships available. Financial award application deadline: 6/30; financial award applicants required to submit FAFSA. In 2018, 92 master's awarded. *Program availability:* Part-time, 100% online. Offers college athletic administration (MS); criminal and social justice policy (MS); curriculum and instructional technology (M Ed); literacy studies (M Ed); management and leadership (MS). *Application deadline:* Applications are processed on a rolling basis. *Application fee:* $0. Electronic applications accepted. *Application Contact:* Lacey Rice-Serafin, Director of Graduate Programs, 843-857-4128, E-mail: lriceserafin@coker.edu. *Dean of Graduate and Professional Programs,* Dr. Kathryn Flaherty, 843-857-4227, E-mail: kflaherty@coker.edu.

THE COLBURN SCHOOL CONSERVATORY OF MUSIC, Los Angeles, CA 90012
General Information Independent, coed, comprehensive institution.

GRADUATE UNITS
Graduate Programs Offers music (AD); performance (MM).

COLD SPRING HARBOR LABORATORY, Cold Spring Harbor, NY 11724
General Information Independent, coed, graduate-only institution. *Graduate housing:* Rooms and/or apartments guaranteed to single students and available on a first-come, first-served basis to married students. Housing application deadline: 8/1.

GRADUATE UNITS
Watson School of Biological Sciences Offers biological sciences (PhD). Electronic applications accepted.

COLGATE ROCHESTER CROZER DIVINITY SCHOOL, Rochester, NY 14620-2530
General Information Independent-religious, coed, graduate-only institution. *Graduate housing:* On-campus housing not available.

GRADUATE UNITS
Graduate and Professional Programs *Program availability:* Part-time, evening/weekend. Offers divinity (M Div, MA, Certificate); peace building and interfaith dialogue (D Min); prophetic preaching (D Min); transformative leadership (D Min). Electronic applications accepted.

COLGATE UNIVERSITY, Hamilton, NY 13346-1386
General Information Independent, coed, comprehensive institution. *Graduate housing:* On-campus housing not available.

GRADUATE UNITS
Master of Arts in Teaching Program Offers teaching (MAT).

THE COLLEGE AT BROCKPORT, STATE UNIVERSITY OF NEW YORK, Brockport, NY 14420-2997
General Information State-supported, coed, comprehensive institution. CGS member. *Enrollment:* 8,287 graduate, professional, and undergraduate students; 298 full-time matriculated graduate/professional students (191 women), 896 part-time matriculated graduate/professional students (557 women). *Enrollment by degree level:* 1,194 master's. *Graduate faculty:* 140 full-time (73 women), 53 part-time/adjunct (29 women). Tuition, state resident: part-time $471 per credit. Tuition, nonresident: part-time $963 per credit. *Graduate housing:* On-campus housing not available. *Student services:* Campus employment opportunities, campus safety program, career counseling, child daycare facilities, exercise/wellness program, free psychological counseling, grant writing training, international student services, low-cost health insurance, multicultural affairs office, services for students with disabilities, teacher training, writing training. *Library facilities:* Drake Memorial Library plus 1 other. *Collection:* Books: 500,461 (physical), 185,000 (digital/electronic); Serial titles: 4,747 (physical), 113,396 (digital/electronic); Databases: 270. Weekly public service hours: 93; students can reserve study rooms.

Computer facilities: 1,000 computers available on campus for general student use. A campuswide network can be accessed from student residence rooms and from off campus. Online class registration is available. Website: http://www.brockport.edu/

General Application Contact: Danielle A. Welch, Graduate Admissions Counselor, 585-395-2525, Fax: 585-395-2515, E-mail: dwelch@brockport.edu.

GRADUATE UNITS
School of Arts and Sciences Students: 77 full-time (53 women), 159 part-time (92 women); includes 16 minority (12 Black or African American, non-Hispanic/Latino; 3 Hispanic/Latino; 1 Native Hawaiian or other Pacific Islander, non-Hispanic/Latino). 133 applicants, 68% accepted, 68 enrolled. *Faculty:* 38 full-time (6 women). Expenses: Contact institution. *Financial support:* Research assistantships, teaching assistantships, Federal Work-Study, scholarships/grants, and unspecified assistantships available. Support available to part-time students. Financial award applicants required to submit FAFSA. In 2018, 100 master's, 1 other advanced degree awarded. *Program availability:* Part-time. Offers arts and sciences (MA, MFA, MS, PSM, AGC); biology (MS, PSM); clinical psychology (with applied emphasis) (MA); clinical psychology (with research emphasis) (MA); communication (MA); creative writing (AGC); dance (MA, MFA); English (MA); environmental science and biology (MS); general psychology (MA); history (MA); liberal studies (MA); mathematics (MA); visual studies (MFA). *Application Contact:* Danielle A. Welch, Graduate Admissions Counselor, 585-395-2525, Fax: 585-395-2515. *Dean,* Dr. Jose Maliekal, 585-395-5806, E-mail: jmalieka@brockport.edu.
School of Business and Management Students: 64 full-time (39 women), 164 part-time (99 women); includes 24 minority (18 Black or African American, non-Hispanic/Latino; 2 Asian, non-Hispanic/Latino; 4 Hispanic/Latino). 160 applicants, 79% accepted, 96 enrolled. *Faculty:* 9 full-time (5 women), 8 part-time/adjunct (2 women). Expenses: Contact institution. *Financial support:* Career-related internships or fieldwork, Federal Work-Study, scholarships/grants, and unspecified assistantships available. Financial award application deadline: 3/15; financial award applicants required to submit FAFSA. In 2018, 124 master's, 15 other advanced degrees awarded. *Program availability:* Part-time. Offers accounting (MS); arts administration (AGC); nonprofit management (AGC); public administration (MPA, AGC). *Application deadline:* For fall admission, 7/1 priority date for domestic and international students; for spring admission, 12/1 priority date for domestic and international students. *Application fee:* $50. Electronic applications accepted. *Application Contact:* Danielle A. Welch, Graduate Admissions Counselor, 585-395-5430, Fax: 585-395-2515, E-mail: dwelch@brockport.edu. *Interim Associate Dean,* Dr. Lerong He, 585-395-5781, Fax: 585-395-2542, E-mail: lhe@brockport.edu.
School of Education, Health, and Human Services Students: 179 full-time (118 women), 825 part-time (579 women); includes 56 minority (30 Black or African American, non-Hispanic/Latino; 5 Asian, non-Hispanic/Latino; 21 Hispanic/Latino). 543 applicants, 69% accepted, 250 enrolled. *Faculty:* 40 full-time (23 women), 34 part-time/adjunct (22 women). Expenses: Contact institution. *Financial support:* In 2018–19, 3 teaching assistantships with full tuition reimbursements (averaging $3,000 per year) were awarded; institutionally sponsored loans, scholarships/grants, and unspecified assistantships also available. Financial award applicants required to submit FAFSA. In 2018, 352 master's, 88 other advanced degrees awarded. *Program availability:* Part-time, 100% online. Offers adapted physical education (AGC); adolescence education (MS Ed); bilingual education (MS Ed, AGC); childhood curriculum specialist (MS Ed); college counseling (MS Ed, CAS); community health education (MS Ed); education, health, and human services (MPA, MS, MS Ed, MSW, AGC, Advanced Certificate, CAS, Graduate Certificate); family and community practice (MSW); gerontology (AGC); health education (MS Ed); inclusive generalist education (MS Ed, AGC, Advanced Certificate); interdisciplinary health practice (MSW); literacy education B-12 (MS Ed); mental health counseling (MS, CAS); physical education (MS Ed); school building leader (CAS); school building leader/school district leader (CAS); school counseling (MS Ed, CAS); school counselor supervision (CAS); school district business leader (CAS); school district leader (CAS); teacher leadership (Graduate Certificate). *Application Contact:* Danielle A. Welch, Graduate Admissions Counselor, 585-395-2525, Fax: 585-395-2515. *Dean,* Dr. Thomas Hernandez, 585-395-2510, Fax: 585-395-2172, E-mail: thernandez@brockport.edu.

COLLÈGE DOMINICAIN DE PHILOSOPHIE ET DE THÉOLOGIE, Ottawa, ON K1R 7G3, Canada
General Information Independent-religious, coed, university. *Graduate housing:* Room and/or apartments available on a first-come, first-served basis to single students; on-campus housing not available to married students.

GRADUATE UNITS
Graduate Programs *Program availability:* Part-time, evening/weekend.
Faculty of Philosophy Offers philosophy (MA Ph, PhD).
Faculty of Theology *Program availability:* Part-time, evening/weekend. Offers theology (M Th, MA Th, PhD, Th D, L Th).

COLLEGE FOR CREATIVE STUDIES, Detroit, MI 48202-4034
General Information Independent, coed, comprehensive institution.
GRADUATE UNITS
Graduate Programs

COLLEGE FOR FINANCIAL PLANNING, Centennial, CO 80112
General Information Proprietary, coed, primarily men, graduate-only institution. *Enrollment by degree level:* 250 master's, 4,750 other advanced degrees. *Graduate faculty:* 9 full-time (2 women), 24 part-time/adjunct (4 women). *Graduate housing:* On-campus housing not available. *Student services:* Services for students with disabilities. *Library facilities:* Kaplan Library. *Collection:* Books: 190,000 (digital/electronic); Databases: 7. Study areas open 24 hours, 5–7 days a week.
Computer facilities: Online class registration is available.
Website: http://www.cffp.edu/
General Application Contact: Alicia Christensen, Director of Enrollment, 303-220-4835, Fax: 303-220-1810, E-mail: alicia.mead@cffp.edu.
GRADUATE UNITS
Graduate Programs *Program availability:* Part-time, evening/weekend, online only, 100% online. Offers finance (MSF); personal financial planning (MS). Electronic applications accepted.

COLLEGE OF CHARLESTON, Charleston, SC 29424-0001
General Information State-supported, coed, comprehensive institution. CGS member. *Graduate housing:* On-campus housing not available. *Research affiliation:* Oak Ridge Associated Universities (science), South Carolina Department of Natural Resources, Marine Resources Division (marine biology, environmental studies), National Institute of Standards and Technology (NIST) (marine biology, environmental studies), National Oceanic and Atmospheric Administration (NOAA) (marine biology, environmental studies), U.S. Department of Agriculture (USDA) (environmental studies), South Carolina Aquarium (marine biology, environmental studies).
GRADUATE UNITS
Graduate School *Program availability:* Part-time, evening/weekend. Electronic applications accepted.
School of Business Offers accountancy (MS); business (MBA, MS); business administration (MBA). Electronic applications accepted.
School of Education, Health, and Human Performance *Program availability:* Part-time, evening/weekend. Offers early childhood education (MAT); education, health, and human performance (M Ed, MAT, Certificate); elementary education (MAT); English to speakers of other languages (Certificate); languages (M Ed); performing arts education (MAT); science and mathematics for teachers (M Ed); special education (MAT); teaching, learning and advocacy (M Ed). Electronic applications accepted.
School of Humanities and Social Sciences *Program availability:* Part-time, evening/weekend. Offers creative writing (MFA); English (MA); history (MA); humanities and social sciences (MA, MFA, MPA, Certificate); public administration (MPA); urban and regional planning (Certificate). Electronic applications accepted.
School of Sciences and Mathematics *Program availability:* Part-time, evening/weekend. Offers computer and information sciences (MS); environmental studies (MS); marine biology (MS); mathematics (MS); sciences and mathematics (MS). Electronic applications accepted.
School of the Arts Offers arts (MS, Certificate); arts management (Certificate); historic preservation (MS).

COLLEGE OF EMMANUEL AND ST. CHAD, Saskatoon, SK S7N 0W6, Canada
General Information Independent-religious, coed, graduate-only institution. *Graduate housing:* Room and/or apartments available to single students; on-campus housing not available to married students. Housing application deadline: 6/15.
GRADUATE UNITS
Bachelor of Theology Program *Program availability:* Part-time, online learning. Offers theology (B Th).
Graduate Programs *Program availability:* Part-time. Offers theology (M Div, MTS, STM, D Min, L Th). STM and D Min programs offered jointly with Lutheran Theological Seminary and St. Andrew's College.

THE COLLEGE OF IDAHO, Caldwell, ID 83605
General Information Independent, coed, comprehensive institution. *Graduate housing:* Room and/or apartments available on a first-come, first-served basis to single students; on-campus housing not available to married students. Housing application deadline: 5/1.
GRADUATE UNITS
Department of Education Offers curriculum and instruction (M Ed); teaching (MAT).

COLLEGE OF MOUNT SAINT VINCENT, Riverdale, NY 10471-1093
General Information Independent, coed, comprehensive institution. *Graduate housing:* On-campus housing not available.
GRADUATE UNITS
School of Professional and Graduate Studies Offers family nurse practitioner (MSN, PMC); instructional technology and global perspectives (Certificate); middle level education (Certificate); multicultural studies (Certificate); nurse educator (PMC); nursing administration (MSN); nursing education (MSN); teaching English to speakers of other languages (MS Ed); urban and multicultural education (MS Ed).

THE COLLEGE OF NEW JERSEY, Ewing, NJ 08628
General Information State-supported, coed, comprehensive institution. CGS member. *Enrollment:* 170 full-time matriculated graduate/professional students (155 women), 464 part-time matriculated graduate/professional students (375 women). *Student services:* Campus employment opportunities, campus safety program, career counseling, exercise/wellness program, free psychological counseling, international student services, low-cost health insurance, services for students with disabilities, teacher training. *Library facilities:* The College of New Jersey Library. *Collection:* Books: 694,461 (physical), 6,455 (digital/electronic); Serial titles: 44,898 (physical), 8,859 (digital/electronic); Databases: 114. Weekly public service hours: 98; students can reserve study rooms.
Computer facilities: Computer purchase and lease plans are available. 631 computers available on campus for general student use. A campuswide network can be accessed from student residence rooms and from off campus. Online class registration is available.
Website: http://www.tcnj.edu/

General Application Contact: Susan L. Hydro, Director of Graduate and Intersession Programs, 609-771-2300, Fax: 609-637-5105, E-mail: graduate@tcnj.edu.
GRADUATE UNITS
Office of Graduate and Advancing Education Students: 348 full-time (272 women), 841 part-time (673 women); includes 207 minority (64 Black or African American, non-Hispanic/Latino; 3 American Indian or Alaska Native, non-Hispanic/Latino; 63 Asian, non-Hispanic/Latino; 71 Hispanic/Latino; 2 Native Hawaiian or other Pacific Islander, non-Hispanic/Latino; 4 Two or more races, non-Hispanic/Latino). 541 applicants, 82% accepted, 411 enrolled. Expenses: Contact institution. *Financial support:* Tuition waivers (partial) and unspecified assistantships available. Financial award application deadline: 5/1; financial award applicants required to submit FAFSA. In 2018, 375 master's, 129 other advanced degrees awarded. *Program availability:* Part-time, evening/weekend. Offers overseas education (M Ed, Certificate). *Application deadline:* For fall admission, 2/1 priority date for domestic students; for spring admission, 10/1 priority date for domestic students. *Application fee:* $75. Electronic applications accepted. *Application Contact:* Deidre Queen, Program Assistant, 609-771-2300, Fax: 609-637-5105, E-mail: graduate@tcnj.edu. *Assistant Director, Office of Graduate and Advancing Education,* Michael Ellard, 609-771-3121, E-mail: ellardm@tcnj.edu.
School of Education Students: 149 full-time (136 women), 208 part-time (167 women); includes 69 minority (17 Black or African American, non-Hispanic/Latino; 3 American Indian or Alaska Native, non-Hispanic/Latino; 14 Asian, non-Hispanic/Latino; 31 Hispanic/Latino; 4 Native Hawaiian or other Pacific Islander, non-Hispanic/Latino), 2 international. 297 applicants, 84% accepted, 202 enrolled. Expenses: Contact institution. *Financial support:* Tuition waivers (partial) and unspecified assistantships available. Financial award application deadline: 5/1; financial award applicants required to submit FAFSA. In 2018, 282 master's, 47 other advanced degrees awarded. *Program availability:* Part-time, evening/weekend. Offers community counseling: human services (MA); community counseling: substance abuse and addiction (MA, Certificate); developmental reading (M Ed); early childhood education (MAT); education (M Ed, MA, MAT, Certificate, Ed S); educational leadership (M Ed, Certificate); elementary education (M Ed, MAT); elementary teaching (MAT); English as a second language (M Ed); marriage and family therapy (Ed S); reading certification (Certificate); school counseling (MA); school personnel: preschool-grade 3 (M Ed); secondary education (MAT); special education (M Ed, MAT); special education with learning disabilities (Certificate); teaching English as a second language (M Ed, Certificate). *Application deadline:* For fall admission, 2/1 priority date for domestic students; for spring admission, 10/1 priority date for domestic students. *Application fee:* $75. Electronic applications accepted. *Application Contact:* Susan L. Hydro, Director of Graduate and Intersession Programs, 609-771-2300, Fax: 609-637-5105, E-mail: graduate@tcnj.edu. *Dean,* Dr. Jeff Passe, 609-771-3177, Fax: 609-637-5117, E-mail: passej@tcnj.edu.
School of Humanities and Social Sciences Students: 10 full-time (8 women), 20 part-time (14 women); includes 3 minority (2 Asian, non-Hispanic/Latino; 1 Hispanic/Latino). 16 applicants, 94% accepted, 15 enrolled. Expenses: Contact institution. *Financial support:* Tuition waivers (partial) and unspecified assistantships available. Financial award application deadline: 5/1; financial award applicants required to submit FAFSA. In 2018, 11 master's awarded. *Program availability:* Part-time. Offers English (MA); gender studies (Certificate); humanities and social sciences (MA, Certificate). *Application deadline:* For fall admission, 2/1 priority date for domestic students; for spring admission, 10/1 priority date for domestic students. *Application fee:* $75. Electronic applications accepted. *Application Contact:* Susan L. Hydro, Director of Graduate and Intersession Programs, 609-771-2300, Fax: 609-637-5105, E-mail: graduate@tcnj.edu. *Dean,* Dr. John Sisko, 609-771-3434, Fax: 609-637-5173, E-mail: sisko@tcnj.edu.
School of Nursing, Health, and Exercise Science Students: 10 full-time (all women), 61 part-time (58 women); includes 20 minority (6 Black or African American, non-Hispanic/Latino; 12 Asian, non-Hispanic/Latino; 2 Hispanic/Latino). 53 applicants, 75% accepted, 34 enrolled. Expenses: Contact institution. *Financial support:* Tuition waivers (partial) and unspecified assistantships available. Financial award application deadline: 5/1; financial award applicants required to submit FAFSA. In 2018, 9 master's awarded. *Program availability:* Part-time. Offers global health (MPH); health communications (MS); nursing (MSN, Certificate); nursing, health, and exercise science (M Ed, MAT, MPH, MSN, Certificate); precision health (MPH). *Application deadline:* For fall admission, 2/1 priority date for domestic students; for spring admission, 10/1 priority date for domestic students. *Application fee:* $75. Electronic applications accepted. *Application Contact:* Susan L. Hydro, Director of Graduate and Intersession Programs, 609-771-2300, Fax: 609-637-5105, E-mail: graduate@tcnj.edu. *Dean,* Dr. Carole Kenner, 609-771-2591, Fax: 609-637-5159, E-mail: kennerc@tcnj.edu.
School of Engineering
See Display on the next page and Close-Up on page 737.

THE COLLEGE OF NEW ROCHELLE, New Rochelle, NY 10805-2308
General Information Independent, coed, comprehensive institution. *Graduate housing:* On-campus housing not available.
GRADUATE UNITS
Graduate School *Program availability:* Part-time, evening/weekend. Offers acute care nurse practitioner (MS, Certificate); clinical specialist in holistic nursing (MS, Certificate); family nurse practitioner (MS, Certificate); nursing and health care management (MS); nursing education (Certificate). Electronic applications accepted.
Division of Art and Communication Studies *Program availability:* Part-time, evening/weekend. Offers art therapy (MS); art therapy/counseling (MS); communication studies (MS, Certificate).
Division of Education *Program availability:* Part-time, evening/weekend. Offers art education (MS); bilingual education (Certificate); childhood education (MS Ed); childhood education/early childhood education (MS Ed); early childhood education (MS Ed); educational leadership (MS, Advanced Certificate, Advanced Diploma); gifted education (Certificate); literacy education (MS Ed); multilingual/multicultural education (MS Ed, Certificate); school building leader (MS, Advanced Certificate); school district leader (MS, Advanced Diploma); special education (MS Ed); teaching English to speakers of other languages (MS Ed, Certificate). Electronic applications accepted.
Division of Human Services *Program availability:* Part-time, evening/weekend. Offers career development (MS, Advanced Certificate); guidance and counseling (MS, Advanced Certificate); long term care administration (MPA); marriage and family therapy (MMFT); mental health counseling (MS, Certificate); public administration (MPA); school psychology (MS); thanatology (Certificate). Electronic applications accepted.

COLLEGE OF SAINT ELIZABETH, Morristown, NJ 07960-6989

General Information Independent-religious, coed, comprehensive institution. *Graduate housing:* Room and/or apartments available on a first-come, first-served basis to single students; on-campus housing not available to married students. Housing application deadline: 7/1. *Research affiliation:* National Figure Skating Association (sports nutrition), National Institute of Mental Health (NIMH) (mental health service), Cornell University/The University of Texas at Houston (food biotechnology (attitude research)).

GRADUATE UNITS

Department of Business Administration and Management *Program availability:* Part-time. Offers human resource management (MS); organizational change (MS). Electronic applications accepted.

Department of Educational Leadership *Program availability:* Part-time. Offers educational leadership (MA, Ed D); supervisor (Certificate). Electronic applications accepted.

Department of Foods and Nutrition *Program availability:* Part-time, blended/hybrid learning. Offers dietetics verification (Certificate); nutrition (MS); nutrition/dietetic internship (MS). Electronic applications accepted.

Department of Nursing *Program availability:* Part-time. Offers nursing (MSN). Electronic applications accepted.

Department of Psychology *Program availability:* Part-time. Offers counseling psychology (MA, Psy D). Electronic applications accepted.

Department of Theology and Philosophy *Program availability:* Part-time. Offers Catholic studies (Certificate); pastoral care (Certificate); spirituality (Certificate); theology (MA). Electronic applications accepted.

Health Administration Program *Program availability:* Part-time. Offers health administration (MS). Electronic applications accepted.

Program in Applied Behavior Analysis *Program availability:* Part-time. Offers applied behavior analysis (MA, Certificate). Electronic applications accepted.

Program in Data Analytics *Program availability:* Part-time. Offers data analytics (MS). Electronic applications accepted.

Program in Education *Program availability:* Part-time. Offers assistive technology (Certificate); education (MA); ESL (Certificate); Holocaust/genocide education (Certificate); middle school science (Certificate); online teaching in the 21st century (Certificate); teaching (Certificate). Electronic applications accepted.

Program in Justice Administration and Public Service *Program availability:* Part-time, 100% online, blended/hybrid learning. Offers counter terrorism (Certificate); cyber security investigation (Certificate); justice administration and public service (MA); leadership in community policing (Certificate). Electronic applications accepted.

Program in Public Health *Program availability:* Part-time. Offers public health (MPH). Electronic applications accepted.

Program in Social Media Design and Management *Program availability:* Part-time. Offers social media design and management (MA). Electronic applications accepted.

COLLEGE OF ST. JOSEPH, Rutland, VT 05701-3899

General Information Independent-religious, coed, comprehensive institution. *Graduate housing:* Room and/or apartments guaranteed to single students; on-campus housing not available to married students. Housing application deadline: 7/1.

GRADUATE UNITS

Graduate Programs *Program availability:* Part-time, evening/weekend. Electronic applications accepted.

Division of Business *Program availability:* Part-time, evening/weekend. Offers business administration (MBA). Electronic applications accepted.

Division of Education *Program availability:* Part-time, evening/weekend. Offers elementary education (M Ed); English (M Ed); general education (M Ed); reading (M Ed); secondary education (M Ed); social studies (M Ed); special education (M Ed). Electronic applications accepted.

Division of Psychology and Human Services *Program availability:* Part-time, evening/weekend. Offers alcohol and substance abuse counseling (MS); clinical mental health counseling (MS); clinical psychology (MS); community counseling (MS); school guidance counseling (MS). Electronic applications accepted.

COLLEGE OF SAINT MARY, Omaha, NE 68106

General Information Independent-religious, women only, comprehensive institution.

GRADUATE UNITS

Program in Education *Program availability:* Part-time. Offers assessment leadership (MSE); English as a second language (MSE).

Program in Health Professions Education *Program availability:* Part-time. Offers health professions education (Ed D).

Program in Nursing *Program availability:* Part-time. Offers nursing (MSN).

Program in Occupational Therapy Offers occupational therapy (MOT).

Program in Organizational Leadership *Program availability:* Part-time, evening/weekend. Offers organizational leadership (MOL). Electronic applications accepted.

Program in Teaching *Program availability:* Evening/weekend. Offers teaching (MAT).

THE COLLEGE OF SAINT ROSE, Albany, NY 12203-1419

General Information Independent, coed, comprehensive institution. CGS member. *Enrollment:* 3,992 graduate, professional, and undergraduate students; 429 full-time matriculated graduate/professional students (345 women), 1,065 part-time matriculated graduate/professional students (824 women). *Enrollment by degree level:* 634 master's, 860 other advanced degrees. *Graduate faculty:* 60 full-time (36 women), 87 part-time/adjunct (44 women). *Tuition:* Full-time $14,382; part-time $799 per credit hour. *Required fees:* $924; $408 per credit. $286. *Graduate housing:* Room and/or apartments available on a first-come, first-served basis to single students; on-campus housing not available to married students. Typical cost: $6816 per year ($12,684 including board). Room and board charges vary according to board plan. Housing application deadline: 5/15. *Student services:* Campus employment opportunities, campus safety program, career counseling, child daycare facilities, exercise/wellness program, free psychological counseling, international student services, multicultural affairs office, services for students with disabilities, teacher training, writing training. *Library facilities:* Neil Hellman Library plus 2 others. *Collection:* Books: 241,000 (physical), 116,500 (digital/electronic); Serial titles: 1,201 (physical), 10 (digital/electronic); Databases: 104. Weekly public service hours: 73; students can reserve study rooms.

Computer facilities: 801 computers available on campus for general student use. A campuswide network can be accessed from student residence rooms and from off campus. Online class registration is available.
Website: http://www.strose.edu/

General Application Contact: Daniel Gallagher, Assistant Vice President for Graduate Recruitment and Enrollment, 518-485-3390, Fax: 518-458-5479, E-mail: grad@strose.edu.

GRADUATE UNITS

Graduate Studies Students: 429 full-time (345 women), 1,065 part-time (824 women); includes 445 minority (181 Black or African American, non-Hispanic/Latino; 2 American Indian or Alaska Native, non-Hispanic/Latino; 38 Asian, non-Hispanic/Latino; 123 Hispanic/Latino; 101 Two or more races, non-Hispanic/Latino), 46 international. Average age 33. 1,068 applicants, 68% accepted, 466 enrolled. *Faculty:* 60 full-time (36 women), 87 part-time/adjunct (44 women). Expenses: Contact institution. *Financial support:* In 2018–19, 244 students received support. Career-related internships or fieldwork, scholarships/grants, tuition waivers (partial), and unspecified assistantships available. Support available to part-time students. Financial award application deadline: 4/15. In 2018, 405 master's, 753 other advanced degrees awarded. *Program availability:* Part-time, evening/weekend, 100% online, blended/hybrid learning. University of Albany Law School joint JD/MBA. *Application deadline:* For fall admission, 4/1 priority date for domestic and international students; for spring admission, 10/15 priority date for domestic and international students; for summer admission, 3/15 priority date for domestic and international students. Applications are processed on a rolling basis. *Application fee:* $40. Electronic applications accepted. *Application Contact:* Daniel Gallagher, Assistant Vice President for Recruitment and Enrollment, 518-485-3390, Fax: 518-458-5479, E-mail: grad@strose.edu.

Huether School of Business Students: 69 full-time (31 women), 53 part-time (32 women); includes 21 minority (10 Black or African American, non-Hispanic/Latino; 1 American Indian or Alaska Native, non-Hispanic/Latino; 3 Asian, non-Hispanic/Latino; 3 Hispanic/Latino; 4 Two or more races, non-Hispanic/Latino), 16 international. Average age 29. 91 applicants, 77% accepted, 40 enrolled. *Faculty:* 11 full-time (4 women), 6 part-time/adjunct (1 woman). Expenses: Contact institution. *Financial support:* Career-related internships or fieldwork, scholarships/grants, tuition waivers (partial), and unspecified assistantships available. Support available to part-time students. Financial award application deadline: 4/15. In 2018, 76 master's, 9 other advanced degrees awarded. *Program availability:* Part-time, evening/weekend. Offers accounting (MS); business administration (MBA); business analytics (MS); financial planning (Advanced Certificate); organizational leadership and change management (Advanced Certificate). *Application deadline:* For fall admission, 4/1 priority date for domestic and international students; for spring admission, 10/15 priority date for domestic and international students; for summer admission, 3/15 priority date for domestic and international students. Applications are processed on a rolling basis. *Application fee:* $40. Electronic applications accepted. *Application Contact:* Daniel Gallagher, Assistant Vice President for Graduate Recruitment and Enrollment, 518-485-3390, Fax: 518-458-5479, E-mail: grad@strose.edu. *Dean,* Rajarshi Aroskar, 518-454-5272, E-mail: aroskarr@strose.edu.

School of Mathematics and Sciences Students: 44 full-time (36 women), 34 part-time (16 women); includes 15 minority (7 Black or African American, non-Hispanic/Latino; 4 Asian, non-Hispanic/Latino; 2 Hispanic/Latino; 2 Two or more races, non-Hispanic/Latino), 24 international. Average age 30. 127 applicants, 79% accepted, 36 enrolled. *Faculty:* 15 full-time (10 women), 4 part-time/adjunct (1 woman). Expenses: Contact institution. *Financial support:* Career-related internships or fieldwork, scholarships/grants, tuition waivers (partial), and unspecified assistantships available. Support available to part-time students. Financial award application deadline: 4/15. In 2018, 42 master's, 4 other advanced degrees awarded. *Program availability:* Part-time, evening/weekend, blended/hybrid learning. Offers computer information systems (MS, Advanced Certificate); mathematics and sciences (MS, MSSW, Advanced Certificate); social work (MSSW). *Application deadline:* For fall admission, 4/1 priority date for domestic and international students; for spring admission, 10/15 priority date for domestic and international students; for summer admission, 3/15 priority date for domestic and international students. Applications are processed on a rolling basis. *Application fee:* $40. Electronic applications accepted. *Application Contact:* Daniel Gallagher, Assistant Vice President for Graduate Recruitment and Enrollment, 518-485-3390, Fax: 518-458-5479, E-mail: grad@strose.edu. *Dean,* Dr. Ian MacDonald, 518-458-5396, E-mail: macdonai@strose.edu.

Thelma P. Lally School of Education Students: 315 full-time (277 women), 975 part-time (773 women); includes 407 minority (164 Black or African American, non-Hispanic/Latino; 1 American Indian or Alaska Native, non-Hispanic/Latino; 31 Asian, non-Hispanic/Latino; 118 Hispanic/Latino; 93 Two or more races, non-Hispanic/Latino), 6 international. Average age 33. 834 applicants, 66% accepted, 390 enrolled. *Faculty:* 32 full-time (21 women), 72 part-time/adjunct (39 women). Expenses: Contact institution. *Financial support:* Career-related internships or fieldwork, scholarships/grants, tuition waivers (partial), and unspecified assistantships available. Support available to part-time students. Financial award application deadline: 4/15. In 2018, 285 master's, 754 other advanced degrees awarded. *Program availability:* Part-time, evening/weekend, 100% online. Offers adolescence education (MS Ed, Advanced Certificate); adolescence education/special education (MS Ed, Advanced Certificate); childhood education (MS Ed); childhood education/special education (MS Ed); childhood special education (MS Ed); clinical mental health counseling (Certificate); college student services administration (MS Ed); communication sciences and disorders (MS Ed); curriculum and instruction (MS Ed); early childhood education (MS Ed); early childhood special education (MS Ed); education (MS, MS Ed, Advanced Certificate, Certificate); educational leadership (MS Ed); educational psychology (MS Ed, Certificate); higher education leadership and administration (MS Ed, Advanced Certificate); literacy: birth-grade 6 (MS Ed, Advanced Certificate); literacy: grades 5-12 (MS Ed, Advanced Certificate); school building leader (Certificate); school counseling (MS Ed, Certificate); school district business leader (Certificate); school district leader (Certificate); school psychology (MS Ed); special education (Certificate); special education professional (MS Ed). *Application deadline:* For fall admission, 4/1 priority date for domestic and international students; for spring admission, 10/15 priority date for domestic and international students; for summer admission, 3/15 priority date for domestic and international students. Applications are processed on a rolling basis. *Application fee:* $40. Electronic applications accepted. *Application Contact:* Daniel Gallagher, Assistant Vice President for Graduate Recruitment and Enrollment, 518-454-5136, Fax: 518-458-5479, E-mail: grad@strose.edu. *Interim Dean,* Dr. Theresa Ward, 518-454-5125.

THE COLLEGE OF ST. SCHOLASTICA, Duluth, MN 55811-4199

General Information Independent-religious, coed, comprehensive institution. *Graduate housing:* On-campus housing not available.

GRADUATE UNITS

Graduate Studies *Program availability:* Part-time, evening/weekend, online learning. Offers athletic training (MS); computer information systems (MA, Certificate); education

(M Ed, MS, Certificate); exe[...]
Certificate); management [...]
(MA); physical therapy (DPT)[...]

COLLEGE OF STATEN IS[...] NEW YORK, Staten Island[...]

General Information State and lo[...] Enrollment: 13,247 graduate, profes[...] matriculated graduate/professional stu[...] graduate/professional students (488 wo[...] 67 doctoral, 59 other advanced degrees.[...] part-time/adjunct (41 women). Internation[...] *resident:* Full-time $10,770; part-time $455[...] $10,770; part-time $455 per credit. Tuition,[...] $830 per credit. *Required fees:* $559.20; $18[...] according to program. *Graduate housing:* Room[...] come, first-served basis to single students; on-ca[...] students. Typical cost: $14,315 per year ($18,26[...] charges vary according to housing facility se[...] counseling, child daycare facilities, international st[...] College of Staten Island Library. *Collection:* Book[...] (digital/electronic); Serial titles: 1,842 (physical), 110,94[...] 161. Weekly public service hours: 98; students can reserv[...]

Computer facilities: 1,700 computers available on campu[...] campuswide network can be accessed from off campus.[...] MyInfo app are available.
Website: http://www.csi.cuny.edu/

General Application Contact: Sasha Spence, Associate D[...] Recruitment and Admissions, 718-982-2019, Fax: 718-[...] sasha.spence@csi.cuny.edu.

GRADUATE UNITS

Graduate Programs Expenses: Contact institution. *Application Contact[...] Associate Director for Graduate Admissions, 718-982-2019, Fax: 718-982[...] sasha.spence@csi.cuny.edu. *Provost/Senior Vice President for Academic [...] Michael Parrish, 718-982-2440, Fax: 718-982-2442, E-mail: provost@csi.[...]

Division of Humanities and Social Sciences Students: 162. 307 applican[...] accepted, 91 enrolled. Expenses: Contact institution. In 2018, 49 master's [...] advanced degrees awarded. Offers autism spectrum disorders (Ac[...] Certificate); cinema and media studies (MA); clinical mental health counselin[...] English (MA); history (MA); liberal studies (MA); public history (Advanced Cer[...] *Application Contact:* Sasha Spence, Associate Director for Graduate Admis[...] 718-982-2019, Fax: 718-982-2500, E-mail: sasha.spence@csi.cuny.edu. De[...] *Humanities and Social Sciences,* Dr. Gerry Milligan, 718-982-2315, Fax: 718[...] 2316, E-mail: gerry.milligan@csi.cuny.edu.

Division of Science and Technology Students: 118. Expenses: Contact institutio[...] 2018, 39 master's awarded. Offers biology (MS); computer science (MS); elect[...] engineering (ME); environmental science (MS); neuroscience and developme[...] disabilities (MS). *Application Contact:* Sasha Spence, Associate Director for Gradu[...] Admissions, 718-982-2019, Fax: 718-982-2500, E-mail: sasha.spence@csi.cuny.e[...] *Dean,* Dr. Vivian Incera, 718-982-2430, E-mail: vivian.incera@csi.cuny.edu.

School of Business Expenses: Contact institution. Offers accounting (MS); busines[...] (MS, Advanced Certificate); business analytics of large-scale data (Advance[...] Certificate); healthcare management (MS); large scale data analysis (MS); strategi[...] management (MS). *Application Contact:* Sasha Spence, Associate Director for[...] Graduate Admissions, 718-982-2019, Fax: 718-982-2500, E-mail: sasha.spence@[...] csi.cuny.edu. *Dean of School of Business,* Dr. Susan L. Holak, 718-982-2920, Fax:[...] 718-982-3183, E-mail: susan.holak@csi.cuny.edu.

School of Education Expenses: Contact institution. Offers adolescence education[...] (MS Ed); bilingual education (Advanced Certificate); childhood (MS Ed); education[...] (MS Ed, Advanced Certificate, Post-Master's Certificate); leadership in education[...] (Post-Master's Certificate); special education (MS Ed); teaching of English to[...] speakers of other languages (MS Ed, Advanced Certificate). *Application Contact:*[...] Sasha Spence, Associate Director for Graduate Admissions, 718-982-2019, Fax: 718-[...] 982-2500, E-mail: sasha.spence@csi.cuny.edu. *Dean of School of Education,* Dr.[...] Kenneth Gold, 718-982-3737, Fax: 718-982-3743, E-mail: kenneth.gold@[...] csi.cuny.edu.

School of Health Sciences Expenses: Contact institution. Offers adult-gerontological[...] nursing (MS, Post Master's Certificate); health sciences (MS, MSW, DNP, DPT, Post[...] Master's Certificate); physical therapy (DPT); social work (MSW). *Application Contact:*[...] Sasha Spence, Associate Director for Graduate Admissions, 718-982-2019, Fax: 718-[...] 982-2500, E-mail: sasha.spence@csi.cuny.edu. *Dean of School of Health Sciences,*[...] Dr. Marcus C. Tye, 718-982-3690, E-mail: marcus.tye@csi.cuny.edu.

See Display on the next page and Close-Up on page 739.

COLLEGE OF THE ATLANTIC, Bar Harbor, ME 04609-1198

General Information Independent, coed, comprehensive institution. *Graduate housing:* Room and/or apartments available to single students; on-campus housing not available to married students. Housing application deadline: 6/1. *Research affiliation:* Acadia National Park, National Park Service (research management, environmental education), Mount Desert Island Biological Laboratory, Jackson Laboratory (genetics), Society for Human Ecology (ecological decision making in society).

GRADUATE UNITS

Program in Human Ecology Offers human ecology (M Phil).

THE COLLEGE OF WILLIAM AND MARY, Williamsburg, VA 23187-8795

General Information State-supported, coed, university. CGS member. *Enrollment:* 8,817 graduate, professional, and undergraduate students; 1,684 full-time matriculated graduate/professional students (875 women), 647 part-time matriculated graduate/professional students (322 women). *Enrollment by degree level:* 1,281 master's, 1,028 doctoral, 22 other advanced degrees. *Graduate faculty:* 713 full-time (295 women), 182 part-time/adjunct (79 women). *Graduate housing:* Room and/or apartments available on a first-come, first-served basis to single students; on-campus housing not available to married students. Housing application deadline: 2/14. *Student services:* Campus employment opportunities, campus safety program, career counseling, child daycare facilities, exercise/wellness program, free psychological counseling, grant writing training, international student services, low-cost health insurance, multicultural affairs office, services for students with disabilities, teacher

Mary

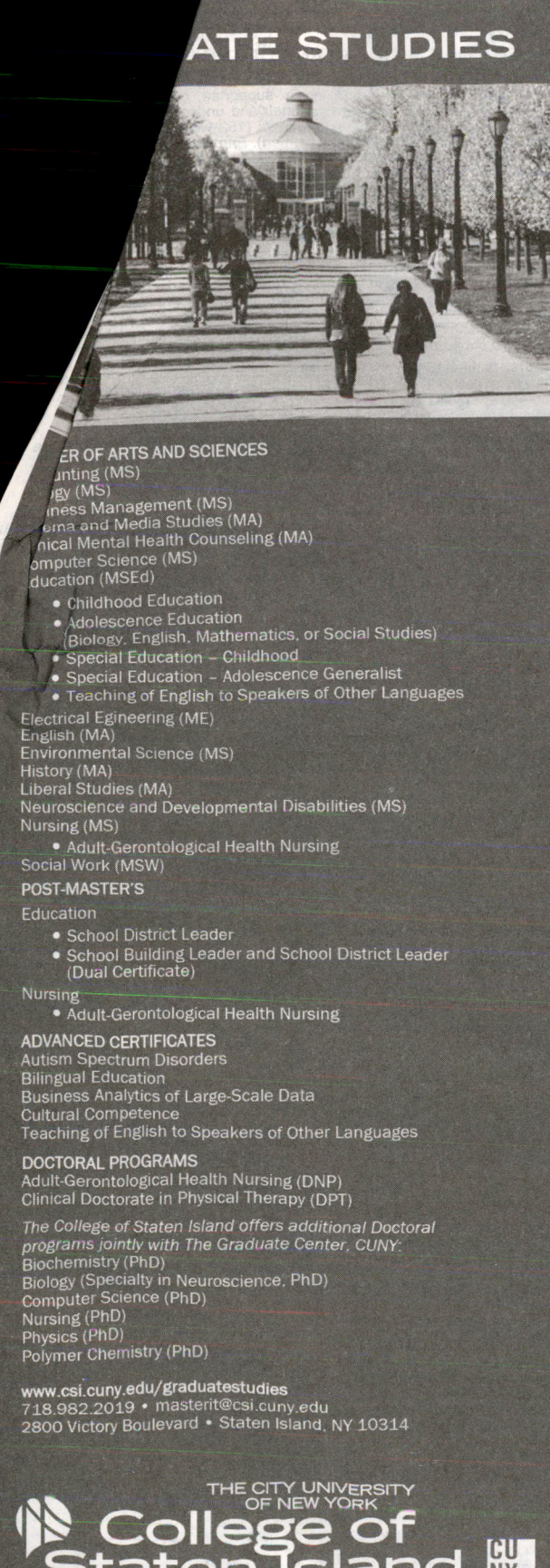

training, writing training. *Library facilities:* Earl Gregg Swem Library plus 7 others. *Collection:* Books: 1.1 million (physical), 2.2 million (digital/electronic); Serial titles: 40,428 (physical), 153,205 (digital/electronic); Databases: 540. Weekly public service hours: 110; study areas open 24 hours, 5–7 days a week; students can reserve study rooms.

Computer facilities: Computer purchase and lease plans are available. 400 computers available on campus for general student use. A campuswide network can be accessed from student residence rooms. Online class registration is available.
Website: http://www.wm.edu/

GRADUATE UNITS

Raymond A. Mason School of Business Students: 451 full-time (163 women), 407 part-time (152 women); includes 207 minority (84 Black or African American, non-Hispanic/Latino; 3 American Indian or Alaska Native, non-Hispanic/Latino; 45 Asian, non-Hispanic/Latino; 45 Hispanic/Latino; 2 Native Hawaiian or other Pacific Islander, non-Hispanic/Latino; 28 Two or more races, non-Hispanic/Latino), 148 international. Average age 32. 1,328 applicants, 60% accepted, 406 enrolled. *Faculty:* 62 full-time (22 women), 7 part-time/adjunct (3 women). Expenses: Contact institution. *Financial support:* Scholarships/grants and unspecified assistantships available. Financial award applicants required to submit FAFSA. In 2018, 487 master's awarded. *Program availability:* Part-time, evening/weekend, 100% online. Offers accounting (M Acc); business (EMBA, M Acc, MBA, MS); business analytics (MS). *Application deadline:* For fall admission, 11/16 for domestic and international students; for winter admission, 1/18 for domestic and international students; for spring admission, 5/16 for domestic and international students; for summer admission, 7/15 for domestic students. *Application fee:* $100. Electronic applications accepted. *Application Contact:* Amanda K. Barth, Director, Full-time MBA Admissions, 757-221-2944, Fax: 757-221-2958, E-mail: amanda.barth@mason.wm.edu. *Dean,* Dr. Lawrence Pulley, 757-221-2891, Fax: 757-221-2937, E-mail: larry.pulley@mason.wm.edu.

School of Education Students: 209 full-time (157 women), 269 part-time (193 women); includes 114 minority (50 Black or African American, non-Hispanic/Latino; 1 American Indian or Alaska Native, non-Hispanic/Latino; 9 Asian, non-Hispanic/Latino; 40 Hispanic/Latino; 14 Two or more races, non-Hispanic/Latino), 16 international. Average age 35. 520 applicants, 64% accepted, 220 enrolled. *Faculty:* 47 full-time (25 women), 81 part-time/adjunct (41 women). Expenses: Contact institution. *Financial support:* In 2018–19, 132 students received support, including 1 fellowship with full tuition reimbursement available (averaging $20,000 per year), 92 research assistantships with full tuition reimbursements available (averaging $17,382 per year); scholarships/grants and unspecified assistantships also available. Financial award application deadline: 1/15; financial award applicants required to submit FAFSA. In 2018, 165 master's, 40 doctorates, 10 other advanced degrees awarded. *Program availability:* Part-time, evening/weekend, Coursework is online with required residencies. Offers curriculum and instruction (MA Ed); education (M Ed, MA Ed, Ed D, PhD, Ed S); education policy, planning, and leadership (M Ed, Ed D, PhD); family counseling (M Ed); school counseling (M Ed); school psychology (M Ed, Ed S). *Application deadline:* For fall admission, 1/15 for domestic and international students; for spring admission, 10/1 for domestic and international students. *Application fee:* $50. Electronic applications accepted. *Application Contact:* Dorothy Smith Osborne, Assistant Dean for Academic Programs and Student Services, 757-221-2317, E-mail: dsosbo@wm.edu. *Dean,* Dr. Spencer G. Niles, 757-221-2317, E-mail: sgniles@wm.edu.

Virginia Institute of Marine Science Students: 73 full-time (48 women), 1 part-time (0 women); includes 8 minority (1 Asian, non-Hispanic/Latino; 3 Hispanic/Latino; 4 Two or more races, non-Hispanic/Latino), 14 international. Average age 27. 84 applicants, 31% accepted, 14 enrolled. *Faculty:* 49 full-time (14 women), 1 part-time/adjunct (0 women). Expenses: Contact institution. *Financial support:* In 2018–19, 64 students received support, including research assistantships with full tuition reimbursements available (averaging $20,452 per year), teaching assistantships with full tuition reimbursements available (averaging $20,452 per year). Financial award application deadline: 1/5. In 2018, 8 master's, 12 doctorates awarded. Offers marine science (MS, PhD). *Application deadline:* For fall admission, 1/5 for domestic students, 1/6 for international students. *Application fee:* $50. Electronic applications accepted. *Application Contact:* Dr. Linda C. Schaffner, Associate Dean of Academic Studies, 804-684-7105, Fax: 804-684-7881, E-mail: admissions@vims.edu. *Dean/Director,* Dr. John T. Wells, 804-684-7103, Fax: 804-684-7009, E-mail: wells@vims.edu.

William & Mary Law School Students: 643 full-time (359 women), 6 part-time (4 women); includes 111 minority (40 Black or African American, non-Hispanic/Latino; 2 American Indian or Alaska Native, non-Hispanic/Latino; 24 Asian, non-Hispanic/Latino; 27 Hispanic/Latino; 18 Two or more races, non-Hispanic/Latino), 50 international. Average age 25. 3,747 applicants, 38% accepted, 224 enrolled. *Faculty:* 44 full-time (19 women), 61 part-time/adjunct (17 women). Expenses: Contact institution. *Financial support:* In 2018–19, 597 students received support, including 15 fellowships with partial tuition reimbursements available (averaging $4,000 per year), 185 research assistantships (averaging $1,854 per year), 41 teaching assistantships (averaging $4,012 per year); career-related internships or fieldwork, scholarships/grants, and tuition waivers also available. Financial award application deadline: 2/15; financial award applicants required to submit FAFSA. In 2018, 38 master's, 187 doctorates awarded. Offers law (LL M, JD). *Application deadline:* For fall admission, 3/1 priority date for domestic and international students. Applications are processed on a rolling basis. *Application fee:* $0. Electronic applications accepted. *Application Contact:* Dexter A. Smith, Associate Dean for Admissions, 757-221-3785, Fax: 757-221-3261, E-mail: dsmith05@wm.edu. *Dean/Professor,* Davison M. Douglas, 757-221-3790, Fax: 757-221-3261, E-mail: dmdoug@wm.edu.

COLORADO CHRISTIAN UNIVERSITY, Lakewood, CO 80226

General Information Independent-religious, coed, comprehensive institution. *Graduate housing:* On-campus housing not available.

GRADUATE UNITS

Program in Business Administration *Program availability:* Part-time, evening/weekend, online learning. Offers corporate training (MBA); information security (MA); leadership (MBA); project management (MBA). Electronic applications accepted.

Program in Counseling *Program availability:* Part-time, evening/weekend. Offers counseling (MAC). Electronic applications accepted.

Program in Curriculum and Instruction *Program availability:* Part-time, evening/weekend. Offers corporate education (MACI); early childhood educator (MACI); elementary educator (MACI); instructional technology (MACI); master educator (MACI); online course developer (MACI); online teaching and learning (MACI); special education generalist (MACI). Electronic applications accepted.

THE COLORADO COLLEGE, Colorado Springs, CO 80903-3294

General Information Independent, coed, comprehensive institution. *Graduate housing:* On-campus housing not available.

GRADUATE UNITS

Education Department Offers art teaching (K-12) (MAT); arts and humanities (MAT); elementary education (MAT); elementary school teaching (MAT); English teaching (MAT); foreign language teaching (MAT); integrated natural sciences (MAT); liberal arts (MAT); mathematics teaching (MAT); music teaching (MAT); science teaching (MAT); secondary education (MAT); social studies teaching (MAT); Southwest studies (MAT); teaching (MAT). Electronic applications accepted.

COLORADO MESA UNIVERSITY, Grand Junction, CO 81501-3122

General Information State-supported, coed, comprehensive institution. *Graduate housing:* Room and/or apartments available on a first-come, first-served basis to single students; on-campus housing not available to married students. Housing application deadline: 8/1.

GRADUATE UNITS

Center for Teacher Education *Program availability:* Part-time. Offers educational leadership (MAEd); English for speakers of other languages (MAEd); exceptional learner/special education (MAEd); teacher education (Graduate Certificate); teacher leader (MAEd). Electronic applications accepted.

Department of Business *Program availability:* Part-time, evening/weekend. Offers business (MBA). Electronic applications accepted.

Department of Health Sciences *Program availability:* Part-time, evening/weekend, 100% online, blended/hybrid learning. Offers advanced nursing practice (MSN); family nurse practitioner (DNP); health information technology systems (Graduate Certificate); nursing education (MSN). Electronic applications accepted.

COLORADO SCHOOL OF MINES, Golden, CO 80401-1887

General Information State-supported, coed, university. CGS member. *Enrollment:* 6,268 graduate, professional, and undergraduate students; 1,115 full-time matriculated graduate/professional students (325 women), 171 part-time matriculated graduate/professional students (40 women). *Enrollment by degree level:* 702 master's, 584 doctoral. *Graduate faculty:* 426 full-time (135 women), 181 part-time/adjunct (64 women). *International tuition:* $36,270 full-time. Tuition, state resident: full-time $16,650; part-time $925 per contact hour. Tuition, nonresident: full-time $36,270; part-time $2015 per contact hour. *Required fees:* $2314; $2314 per semester. *Graduate housing:* Rooms and/or apartments available on a first-come, first-served basis to single and married students. Housing application deadline: 5/1. *Student services:* Campus employment opportunities, campus safety program, career counseling, exercise/wellness program, free psychological counseling, international student services, low-cost health insurance, multicultural affairs office, services for students with disabilities, teacher training, writing training. *Library facilities:* Arthur Lakes Library. *Collection:* Books: 369,304 (physical), 732,071 (digital/electronic); Serial titles: 527 (physical), 197,641 (digital/electronic); Databases: 162. Weekly public service hours: 107; students can reserve study rooms.

Computer facilities: Computer purchase and lease plans are available. 1,000 computers available on campus for general student use. A campuswide network can be accessed from student residence rooms and from off campus. Online class registration is available.

Website: http://www.mines.edu/

General Application Contact: Angel Dotson, Graduate Admissions Coordinator, 303-273-3348, E-mail: grad-app@mines.edu.

GRADUATE UNITS

Office of Graduate Studies Students: 1,115 full-time (325 women), 171 part-time (40 women); includes 159 minority (14 Black or African American, non-Hispanic/Latino; 3 American Indian or Alaska Native, non-Hispanic/Latino; 36 Asian, non-Hispanic/Latino; 70 Hispanic/Latino; 1 Native Hawaiian or other Pacific Islander, non-Hispanic/Latino; 35 Two or more races, non-Hispanic/Latino), 398 international. Average age 28. 2,016 applicants, 52% accepted, 425 enrolled. *Faculty:* 426 full-time (135 women), 181 part-time/adjunct (64 women). Expenses: Contact institution. *Financial support:* In 2018–19, 439 research assistantships with full tuition reimbursements, 194 teaching assistantships with full tuition reimbursements were awarded; fellowships, career-related internships or fieldwork, Federal Work-Study, institutionally sponsored loans, scholarships/grants, health care benefits, and unspecified assistantships also available. Financial award application deadline: 12/15; financial award applicants required to submit FAFSA. In 2018, 296 master's, 86 doctorates awarded. *Program availability:* Part-time. Offers applied physics (MS, PhD); chemical engineering (MS, PhD); chemistry (MS, PhD); civil and environmental engineering (MS, PhD); computational and applied mathematics (MS, PhD); electrical engineering (MS, PhD); engineering and technology management (MS); environmental engineering science (MS, PhD); environmental geochemistry (PMS); geochemistry (MS, PhD); geological engineering (ME, MS, PhD); geology (MS, PhD); geophysical engineering (ME, MS, PhD); geophysics (MS, PhD); hydrologic science and engineering (MS, PhD); hydrology (MS, PhD); international political economy (Graduate Certificate); materials science (MS, PhD); mechanical engineering (MS, PhD); metallurgical and materials engineering (ME, MS, PhD); mineral and energy economics (MS, PhD); mineral exploration (PMS); mineral exploration and mining geosciences (PMS); mining and earth systems engineering (MS); mining engineering (PhD); nuclear engineering (ME, MS, PhD); operations research and engineering (PhD); petroleum economics and management with mineral and energy economics (MS); petroleum engineering (ME, MS, PhD); petroleum reservoir systems (PMS); science and technology policy (Graduate Certificate); statistics (MS, PhD); underground construction and tunneling (MS, PhD). *Application deadline:* For fall admission, 12/15 priority date for domestic and international students; for spring admission, 9/1 priority date for domestic and international students. *Application fee:* $60 ($80 for international students). Electronic applications accepted. *Application Contact:* Kim Medina, Executive Director, Admissions, 303-273-3000, E-mail: admit@mines.edu. *Dean of Graduate Studies,* Dr. Wendy Zhou, 303-384-2181, E-mail: wzhou@mines.edu.

COLORADO SCHOOL OF TRADITIONAL CHINESE MEDICINE, Denver, CO 80206-2127

General Information Independent, coed, graduate-only institution. *Enrollment by degree level:* 99 master's. *Graduate faculty:* 52 part-time/adjunct (28 women). *Graduate housing:* On-campus housing not available. *Student services:* Campus employment opportunities, exercise/wellness program. *Library facilities:* CSTCM Library plus 1 other. *Collection:* Books: 8,000 (physical), 200 (digital/electronic).

Computer facilities: 4 computers available on campus for general student use. Online class registration is available.

Website: http://www.cstcm.edu/

General Application Contact: Chris Duxbury-Edwards, Recruiting Director, 303-329-6355 Ext. 21, Fax: 303-388-8165, E-mail: recruiting@cstcm.edu.

GRADUATE UNITS

Graduate Programs Offers acupuncture (MS); traditional Chinese medicine (MS).

COLORADO STATE UNIVERSITY, Fort Collins, CO 80523

General Information State-supported, coed, university. CGS member. *Enrollment:* 33,694 graduate, professional, and undergraduate students; 2,781 full-time matriculated graduate/professional students (1,712 women), 4,207 part-time matriculated graduate/professional students (2,041 women). *Enrollment by degree level:* 4,466 master's, 2,305 doctoral, 217 other advanced degrees. *Graduate faculty:* 1,089 full-time (438 women), 231 part-time/adjunct (101 women). *International tuition:* $25,791 full-time. Tuition, state resident: full-time $10,520; part-time $4675 per credit hour. Tuition, nonresident: full-time $25,791; part-time $11,462 per credit hour. *Required fees:* $2392; $576 $288. Tuition and fees vary according to course level, course load, degree level, program and student level. *Graduate housing:* Rooms and/or apartments available on a first-come, first-served basis to single and married students. Typical cost: $5976 per year ($12,430 including board) for single students; $7560 per year for married students. Room and board charges vary according to board plan and housing facility selected. *Student services:* Campus employment opportunities, campus safety program, career counseling, child daycare facilities, exercise/wellness program, free psychological counseling, grant writing training, international student services, low-cost health insurance, multicultural affairs office, services for students with disabilities, teacher training, writing training. *Library facilities:* William E. Morgan Library plus 1 other. *Collection:* Books: 1.2 million (physical), 1.1 million (digital/electronic); Serial titles: 45,581 (physical), 104,097 (digital/electronic); Databases: 345. Weekly public service hours: 108; study areas open 24 hours, 5–7 days a week; students can reserve study rooms.

Computer facilities: Computer purchase and lease plans are available. 1,700 computers available on campus for general student use. A campuswide network can be accessed from student residence rooms and from off campus. Online class registration, personalized portal services including transcripts and financials (billing, financial aid) are available.

Website: http://www.colostate.edu/

General Application Contact: Sandra Dailey, Academic Progress and Special Admissions Coordinator, Graduate School, 970-491-6817, Fax: 970-491-2194, E-mail: gradschool@colostate.edu.

GRADUATE UNITS

College of Agricultural Sciences *Program availability:* Part-time, evening/weekend, 100% online, blended/hybrid learning. Offers agricultural and resource economics (MS, PhD); agricultural sciences (M Agr, M Ext Ed, MAEE, MLA, MS, PhD); animal sciences (MS, PhD); entomology (MS, PhD); extension education (M Ext Ed); horticulture and landscape architecture (MLA, MS, PhD); pest management (MS); plant pathology (MS, PhD); soil and crop sciences (MS, PhD); weed science (MS, PhD). Electronic applications accepted.

College of Business *Program availability:* Part-time, evening/weekend, 100% online, blended/hybrid learning. Offers accounting (M Acc); business (M Acc, M Fin, MBA, MCIS, MS); business administration (MBA); computer information systems (MCIS); finance (M Fin). Electronic applications accepted.

College of Health and Human Sciences *Program availability:* Part-time, evening/weekend, 100% online, blended/hybrid learning. Offers apparel and merchandising (MS); applied developmental science (PhD); construction management (MS); dietetics (MS); exercise science and nutrition (MS); family and developmental studies (MS); food science and human nutrition (PhD); food science and nutrition (MS); health and human sciences (M Ed, MA, MOT, MS, MSW, PhD); human bioenergetics (PhD); marriage and family therapy (MS); nutrition and exercise science (MS); occupational therapy (MOT, MS, PhD). Electronic applications accepted.

School of Education *Program availability:* Part-time, online only, 100% online, blended/hybrid learning. Offers adult education and training (M Ed); counseling and career development (MA); education and human resources (M Ed); education, equity, and transformation (PhD); higher education leadership (PhD); organizational learning, performance, and change (M Ed, PhD); student affairs in higher education (MS). Electronic applications accepted.

School of Social Work *Program availability:* Part-time, evening/weekend, 100% online, blended/hybrid learning. Offers social work (MSW, PhD). Electronic applications accepted.

College of Liberal Arts *Program availability:* Part-time. Offers anthropology (MA, PhD); communication (PhD); communication studies (MA); communications and media management (MCMM); creative writing (MFA); economics (MA, PhD); environmental politics and policy (PhD); ethnic studies (MA); French (MA); liberal arts (MA); philosophy (MA); political science (MA); public communication and technology (MS, PhD); public history (MA); rhetoric and composition (MA); sociology (MA, PhD); studio art (MFA). Electronic applications accepted.

LEAP Institute for the Arts *Program availability:* Part-time, evening/weekend, 100% online. Offers arts leadership and cultural management (MALCM). Electronic applications accepted.

School of Music, Theatre and Dance *Program availability:* Part-time. Offers collaborative piano (MM). Electronic applications accepted.

College of Natural Sciences *Program availability:* Part-time, 100% online, blended/hybrid learning. Offers biochemistry and molecular biology (MS, PhD); botany (MS, PhD); chemistry (MS, PhD); computer science (MCS, MS, PhD); material science and engineering (PhD); mathematics (MS, PhD); natural science education (MNSE); natural sciences (MAC, MAIOP, MAS, MCS, MNSE, MS, PhD); physics (MS, PhD); psychology (PhD); statistics (MAS, MS, PhD); zoo, aquarium, and animal shelter management (MS). Electronic applications accepted.

College of Veterinary Medicine and Biomedical Sciences Offers biomedical sciences (PhD); clinical sciences (MS, PhD); environmental health (MS, PhD); microbiology, immunology and pathology (MS, PhD); pathology (PhD); reproductive technology (MS); veterinary medicine (DVM); veterinary medicine and biomedical sciences (MS, DVM, PhD). Electronic applications accepted.

Interdisciplinary College Electronic applications accepted.

School of Global Environmental Sustainability *Program availability:* Part-time-only, online only, 100% online. Offers applied global stability: agriculture (Graduate Certificate). Electronic applications accepted.

Walter Scott, Jr. College of Engineering *Program availability:* Part-time, evening/weekend, 100% online, blended/hybrid learning. Offers atmospheric science (MS, PhD); chemical and biological engineering (MS, PhD); civil and environmental engineering (MS, PhD); computer engineering (ME, PhD); electrical engineering (MS); engineering (ME, MS, PhD); engineering education (ME); mechanical engineering (MS, PhD). Electronic applications accepted.

School of Biomedical Engineering *Program availability:* Part-time, online learning. Offers bioengineering (MS, PhD). Electronic applications accepted.

Warner College of Natural Resources *Program availability:* Part-time, evening/weekend, 100% online, blended/hybrid learning. Offers earth sciences (PhD); ecological restoration (MNRS); fish, wildlife, and conservation biology (MFWCB, MS, PhD); forest sciences (MS); greenhouse gas management and accounting (MGMA); human dimensions of natural resources (MS, PhD); natural resources (MFWCB, MGMA, MNRS, MS, MTM, PhD); rangeland ecosystem science (PhD); tourism management (MTM); watershed science (MS). Electronic applications accepted.

COLORADO STATE UNIVERSITY–GLOBAL CAMPUS, Greenwood Village, CO 80111
General Information State-supported, coed, comprehensive institution.

GRADUATE UNITS

Graduate Programs *Program availability:* Online learning.

COLORADO STATE UNIVERSITY–PUEBLO, Pueblo, CO 81001-4901
General Information State-supported, coed, comprehensive institution. *Graduate housing:* Room and/or apartments available on a first-come, first-served basis to single students; on-campus housing not available to married students. Housing application deadline: 8/1.

GRADUATE UNITS

College of Education, Engineering and Professional Studies *Program availability:* Part-time, evening/weekend. Offers art education (M Ed); education, engineering and professional studies (M Ed, MS); foreign language education (M Ed); health and physical education (M Ed); industrial and systems engineering (MS); instructional technology (M Ed); linguistically diverse education (M Ed); music education (M Ed); nursing (MS); special education (M Ed). Electronic applications accepted.

College of Science and Mathematics *Program availability:* Part-time, evening/weekend. Offers applied natural science (MS).

Malik and Seeme Hasan School of Business *Program availability:* Part-time, evening/weekend. Offers business (MBA).

COLORADO TECHNICAL UNIVERSITY AURORA, Aurora, CO 80014
General Information Proprietary, coed, comprehensive institution. *Graduate housing:* On-campus housing not available.

GRADUATE UNITS

Program in Computer Engineering Offers computer engineering (MS).

Program in Computer Science *Program availability:* Part-time, evening/weekend. Offers computer systems security (MSCS); database systems (MSCS); software engineering (MSCS).

Program in Electrical Engineering Offers electrical engineering (MS).

Program in Information Science Offers information systems security (MSM).

Program in Systems Engineering Offers systems engineering (MS).

Programs in Business Administration and Management *Program availability:* Part-time, evening/weekend. Offers accounting (MBA); business administration (MBA); business administration and management (EMBA); finance (MBA); human resource management (MBA); marketing (MBA); mediation and dispute resolution (MBA); operations management (MBA); project management (MBA); technology management (MBA).

COLORADO TECHNICAL UNIVERSITY COLORADO SPRINGS, Colorado Springs, CO 80907
General Information Proprietary, coed, university. *Graduate housing:* On-campus housing not available.

GRADUATE UNITS

Graduate Studies *Program availability:* Part-time, evening/weekend. Offers accounting (MBA, MSA); business administration (MBA); computer engineering (MSCE); computer science (DCS); computer systems security (MSCS); criminal justice (MBA); database systems (MSCS); electrical engineering (MSEE); finance (MBA); human resources management (MBA); information systems security (MSM); logistics/supply chain management (MBA); management (DM); marketing (MBA); mediation and dispute resolution (MBA); operations management (MBA); project management (MBA); software engineering (MSCS); systems engineering (MS); technology management (MBA).

COLUMBIA COLLEGE, Columbia, MO 65216-0002
General Information Independent-religious, coed, comprehensive institution. *Enrollment:* 1,152 graduate, professional, and undergraduate students; 100 full-time matriculated graduate/professional students (64 women), 563 part-time matriculated graduate/professional students (350 women). *Enrollment by degree level:* 663 master's. *Graduate faculty:* 9 full-time (3 women), 87 part-time/adjunct (38 women). *Tuition:* Full-time $13,230; part-time $490 per credit hour. Tuition and fees vary according to reciprocity agreements. *Graduate housing:* Room and/or apartments available on a first-come, first-served basis to single students; on-campus housing not available to married students. *Typical cost:* $6174 per year ($9308 including board). Room and board charges vary according to board plan and housing facility selected. Housing application deadline: 7/6. *Student services:* Campus employment opportunities, campus safety program, career counseling, exercise/wellness program, free psychological counseling, international student services, low-cost health insurance, services for students with disabilities, teacher training, writing training. *Library facilities:* J. W. and Lois Stafford Library. *Collection:* Books: 61,752 (physical), 225,968 (digital/electronic); Serial titles: 104 (physical), 63,429 (digital/electronic); Databases: 70. Weekly public service hours: 94; students can reserve study rooms.

Computer facilities: Computer purchase and lease plans are available. 220 computers available on campus for general student use. A campuswide network can be accessed from student residence rooms and from off campus. Online class registration is available. Website: http://www.ccis.edu/

General Application Contact: Stephanie Johnson, Associate Vice President for Recruiting & Admissions Division, 573-875-7352, Fax: 573-875-7506, E-mail: sjohnson@ccis.edu.

GRADUATE UNITS

Master of Arts in Teaching Program Students: 5 full-time (4 women), 96 part-time (76 women); includes 21 minority (12 Black or African American, non-Hispanic/Latino; 1 Asian, non-Hispanic/Latino; 2 Hispanic/Latino; 6 Two or more races, non-Hispanic/Latino), 3 international. Average age 35. 107 applicants, 82% accepted, 45 enrolled. *Faculty:* 5 full-time (3 women), 18 part-time/adjunct (12 women). Expenses:

Contact institution. *Financial support:* In 2018–19, 34 students received support. Scholarships/grants, tuition waivers (full and partial), and unspecified assistantships available. Financial award application deadline: 3/15; financial award applicants required to submit FAFSA. In 2018, 45 master's awarded. *Program availability:* Part-time, evening/weekend, 100% online, blended/hybrid learning. Offers teaching (MAT). *Application deadline:* For fall admission, 8/9 priority date for domestic and international students; for spring admission, 12/27 priority date for domestic and international students. Applications are processed on a rolling basis. *Application fee:* $0. Electronic applications accepted. *Application Contact:* Stephanie Johnson, Associate Vice President of Recruitment & Admissions Division, 573-875-7352, Fax: 573-875-7506, E-mail: sjohnson@ccis.edu. *Dean of School of Humanities, Arts and Social Sciences*, Dr. Lisa Ford-Brown, 573-875-7570, E-mail: labrown@ccis.edu.

Master of Business Administration Program Students: 60 full-time (32 women), 335 part-time (201 women); includes 121 minority (67 Black or African American, non-Hispanic/Latino; 1 American Indian or Alaska Native, non-Hispanic/Latino; 6 Asian, non-Hispanic/Latino; 24 Hispanic/Latino; 1 Native Hawaiian or other Pacific Islander, non-Hispanic/Latino; 22 Two or more races, non-Hispanic/Latino), 31 international. Average age 37. 443 applicants, 92% accepted, 127 enrolled. *Faculty:* 1 full-time (0 women), 55 part-time/adjunct (16 women). Expenses: Contact institution. *Financial support:* In 2018–19, 54 students received support. Scholarships/grants, tuition waivers (full and partial), and unspecified assistantships available. Financial award application deadline: 3/1; financial award applicants required to submit FAFSA. In 2018, 195 master's awarded. *Program availability:* Part-time, evening/weekend, 100% online, blended/hybrid learning. Offers accounting (MBA); business administration (MBA); human resources (MBA). *Application deadline:* For fall admission, 8/9 priority date for domestic and international students; for spring admission, 12/27 priority date for domestic and international students. Applications are processed on a rolling basis. *Application fee:* $0. Electronic applications accepted. *Application Contact:* Stephanie Johnson, Associate Vice President for Recruiting & Admissions Division, 573-875-7352, Fax: 573-875-7506, E-mail: sjohnson@ccis.edu.

Master of Education in Educational Leadership Program Students: 5 full-time (all women), 36 part-time (27 women); includes 8 minority (5 Black or African American, non-Hispanic/Latino; 2 Hispanic/Latino; 1 Two or more races, non-Hispanic/Latino). Average age 38. 29 applicants, 90% accepted, 17 enrolled. *Faculty:* 5 full-time (3 women), 18 part-time/adjunct (12 women). Expenses: Contact institution. *Financial support:* In 2018–19, 30 students received support. Scholarships/grants, tuition waivers (full and partial), and unspecified assistantships available. Financial award application deadline: 3/1; financial award applicants required to submit FAFSA. In 2018, 25 master's awarded. *Program availability:* Part-time, evening/weekend, 100% online, blended/hybrid learning. Offers educational leadership (M Ed). *Application deadline:* For fall admission, 8/9 priority date for domestic and international students; for spring admission, 12/27 priority date for domestic and international students. Applications are processed on a rolling basis. *Application fee:* $0. Electronic applications accepted. *Application Contact:* Stephanie Johnson, Associate Vice President for Recruiting & Admissions Division, 573-875-7352, Fax: 573-875-7506, E-mail: sjohnson@ccis.edu. *Dean of the School of Humanities, Arts and Social Sciences*, Dr. Lisa Ford-Brown, 573-875-7570, E-mail: labrown@ccis.edu.

Master of Science in Criminal Justice Program Students: 10 full-time (6 women), 93 part-time (53 women); includes 39 minority (23 Black or African American, non-Hispanic/Latino; 1 American Indian or Alaska Native, non-Hispanic/Latino; 10 Hispanic/Latino; 5 Two or more races, non-Hispanic/Latino). Average age 39. 81 applicants, 86% accepted, 32 enrolled. *Faculty:* 2 full-time (0 women), 21 part-time/adjunct (12 women). Expenses: Contact institution. *Financial support:* In 2018–19, 5 students received support. Scholarships/grants, tuition waivers (full and partial), and unspecified assistantships available. Financial award application deadline: 3/1; financial award applicants required to submit FAFSA. In 2018, 42 master's awarded. *Program availability:* Part-time, evening/weekend, 100% online, blended/hybrid learning. Offers criminal justice (MSCJ). *Application deadline:* For fall admission, 8/9 priority date for domestic and international students; for spring admission, 12/27 priority date for domestic and international students. Applications are processed on a rolling basis. *Application fee:* $0. Electronic applications accepted. *Application Contact:* Stephanie Johnson, Associate Vice President for Recruiting & Admissions Division, 573-875-7352, Fax: 573-875-7506, E-mail: sgjohnson@ccis.edu. *Dean of the School of Humanities, Arts and Social Sciences*, Dr. Lisa Ford-Brown, 573-875-7570, E-mail: labrown@ccis.edu.

COLUMBIA COLLEGE, Columbia, SC 29203-5998
General Information Independent-religious, coed, primarily women, comprehensive institution. *Graduate housing:* On-campus housing not available.

GRADUATE UNITS

Graduate Programs *Program availability:* Part-time, evening/weekend. Offers criminal justice (MA); organizational change and leadership (MA). Electronic applications accepted.

Education Division *Program availability:* Part-time, evening/weekend, online learning. Offers divergent learning (M Ed); higher education administration (M Ed). Electronic applications accepted.

COLUMBIA COLLEGE CHICAGO, Chicago, IL 60605-1996
General Information Independent, coed, comprehensive institution. CGS member. *Graduate housing:* Room and/or apartments available on a first-come, first-served basis to single students; on-campus housing not available to married students. Housing application deadline: 5/1.

GRADUATE UNITS

School of Graduate Studies *Program availability:* Part-time, evening/weekend. Offers arts, entertainment and media management (MAM); cinema directing (MFA); civic media (MA); creative producing (MFA); fiction (MFA); fine arts (MFA); music (MFA); nonfiction (MFA); photography (MFA); poetry (MFA). Electronic applications accepted.

COLUMBIA COLLEGE OF NURSING, Glendale, WI 53212
General Information Independent, coed, primarily women, upper-level institution.

GRADUATE UNITS

Graduate Program Offers nursing (MSN).

COLUMBIA INTERNATIONAL UNIVERSITY, Columbia, SC 29203
General Information Independent-religious, coed, university. *Graduate housing:* Rooms and/or apartments available on a first-come, first-served basis to single and married students. Housing application deadline: 8/1.

GRADUATE UNITS

Columbia Graduate School *Program availability:* Part-time, evening/weekend, online learning. Offers Bible teaching (MABT); counseling (MACN); early childhood and elementary education (MAT); educational administration (M Ed); educational leadership (PhD); instruction and learning (M Ed); teaching English as a foreign language (Certificate); teaching English as a foreign language and intercultural studies (MATF). Electronic applications accepted.

Seminary and School of Ministry *Program availability:* Part-time, evening/weekend. Offers academic ministries (M Div); Bible and theology (Certificate); bible exposition (M Div, MABE); Biblical ministry (Certificate); chaplaincy (D Div); intercultural studies (MAIS); leadership (D Min); member care (D Min); missions (D Min); preaching (D Min); theological studies (MA). Electronic applications accepted.

COLUMBIA SOUTHERN UNIVERSITY, Orange Beach, AL 36561

General Information Proprietary, coed, comprehensive institution. *Graduate housing:* On-campus housing not available.

GRADUATE UNITS

College of Safety and Emergency Services *Program availability:* Part-time, evening/weekend, online learning. Offers criminal justice administration (MS); emergency services management (MS); occupational safety and health (MS). Electronic applications accepted.

DBA Program *Program availability:* Part-time, evening/weekend, online learning. Offers business administration (DBA). Electronic applications accepted.

MBA Program *Program availability:* Part-time, evening/weekend, online learning. Offers finance (MBA); health care management (MBA); human resource management (MBA); marketing (MBA); project management (MBA); public administration (MBA). Electronic applications accepted.

Program in Organizational Leadership Offers organizational leadership (MS).

COLUMBIA THEOLOGICAL SEMINARY, Decatur, GA 30031-0520

General Information Independent-religious, coed, graduate-only institution. *Graduate housing:* Rooms and/or apartments available on a first-come, first-served basis to single students and available to married students. Housing application deadline: 4/30.

GRADUATE UNITS

Graduate and Professional Programs Offers theology (M Div, MATS, Th M, D Min, Th D). Th D program offered jointly with Emory University; D Min with Interdenominational Theological Center.

COLUMBIA UNIVERSITY, New York, NY 10027

General Information Independent, coed, university. CGS member. *Graduate housing:* Rooms and/or apartments available to single and married students. Housing application deadline: 10/15. *Research affiliation:* Long Island Biological Laboratory, Brookhaven National Laboratory, New York Botanical Gardens, American Museum of Natural History, Marine Biological Laboratory, Goddard Space Flight Center.

GRADUATE UNITS

College of Dental Medicine Offers advanced education in general dentistry (Certificate); biomedical informatics (MA, PhD); dental and oral surgery (DDS); dental medicine (MA, MS, DDS, PhD, Certificate); endodontics (Certificate); orthodontics (MS, Certificate); periodontics (MS, Certificate); prosthodontics (MS, Certificate); science education (MA).

College of Physicians and Surgeons *Program availability:* Part-time. Offers anatomy (M Phil, MA, PhD); anatomy and cell biology (PhD); biochemistry and molecular biophysics (M Phil, PhD); biomedical informatics (M Phil, MA, PhD); biomedical sciences (M Phil, MA, PhD); biophysics (PhD); cellular, molecular, structural and genetic studies (PhD); genetics (M Phil, MA, PhD); medicine (M Phil, MA, MS, DN Sc, DPT, Ed D, MD, OTD, PhD, Adv C); movement science (Ed D); neurobiology and behavior (PhD); occupational therapy (MS); occupational therapy and cognition (OTD); pathobiology (M Phil, MA, PhD); pharmacology (M Phil, MA, PhD); pharmacology-toxicology (M Phil, MA, PhD); physical therapy (DPT); physiology and cellular biophysics (M Phil, MA, PhD).

Institute of Human Nutrition *Program availability:* Part-time. Offers nutrition (MS, PhD). Electronic applications accepted.

Columbia School of Social Work *Program availability:* 100% online, blended/hybrid learning. Offers advanced clinical practice (MSSW); advanced generalist practice and programming (MSSW); policy practice (MSSW); social enterprise administration (MSSW). Electronic applications accepted.

Columbia University Mailman School of Public Health *Program availability:* Part-time, evening/weekend. Offers biostatistics (MPH, MS, Dr PH, PhD); environmental health sciences (MPH, MS, Dr PH, PhD); epidemiology (MPH, MS, Dr PH, PhD); health policy and management (Exec MHA, Exec MPH, MHA, MPH); population and family health (MPH, Dr PH); public health (Exec MHA, Exec MPH, MHA, MPH, MS, Dr PH, PhD); radiological sciences (MS); sociomedical sciences (MPH, MS, Dr PH, PhD); toxicology (MS). PhD offered in cooperation with the Graduate School of Arts and Sciences. Electronic applications accepted.

Fu Foundation School of Engineering and Applied Science *Program availability:* Part-time, 100% online. Offers applied mathematics (MS, Eng Sc D, PhD); applied physics (MS, Eng Sc D, PhD); biomedical engineering (MS, Eng Sc D, PhD); business analytics (MS); chemical engineering (MS, PhD); civil engineering (MS, Eng Sc D, PhD); computer engineering (MS); computer science (MS, Eng Sc D, PhD); construction engineering and management (MS); earth and environmental engineering (Eng Sc D, PhD); earth resources engineering (MS); electrical engineering (MS, PhD); engineering and applied science (MS, Eng Sc D, PhD); engineering mechanics (MS, Eng Sc D, PhD); financial engineering (MS); industrial engineering (MS); industrial engineering and operations research (PhD); management science and engineering (MS); materials science and engineering (MS, Eng Sc D, PhD); mechanical engineering (MS, Eng Sc D, PhD); medical physics (MS); operations research (MS). Electronic applications accepted.

Data Science Institute *Program availability:* Part-time. Offers data science (MS).

Graduate School of Architecture, Planning, and Preservation Offers advanced architectural design (MS); architecture (M Arch, PhD); architecture, planning, and preservation (M Arch, MS, PhD, Certificate); historic preservation (MS, PhD, Certificate); real estate development (MS); urban planning (MS, PhD).

Graduate School of Arts and Sciences *Program availability:* Part-time. Offers African-American studies (MA); American studies (MA); anthropology (MA, PhD); art history and archaeology (MA, PhD); astronomy (PhD); biological sciences (PhD); biotechnology (MA); chemical physics (PhD); chemistry (PhD); classical studies (MA, PhD); classics (MA, PhD); climate and society (MA); conservation biology (MA); earth and environmental sciences (PhD); East Asia: regional studies (MA); East Asian languages and cultures (MA, PhD); ecology, evolution and environmental biology (MA); ecology, evolution, and environmental biology (PhD); economics (MA, PhD); English and comparative literature (MA, PhD); French and Romance philology (MA, PhD); Germanic languages (MA, PhD); global French studies (MA); global thought (MA); Hispanic cultural studies (MA); history (PhD); history and literature (MA); human rights studies (MA); Islamic studies (MA); Italian (MA, PhD); Japanese pedagogy (MA); Jewish studies (MA); Latin America and the Caribbean: regional studies (MA); Latin American and Iberian cultures (PhD); mathematics (MA, PhD); medieval and Renaissance studies (MA); Middle Eastern, South Asian, and African studies (MA, PhD); modern art: critical and curatorial studies (MA); modern European studies (MA); museum anthropology (MA); music (DMA, PhD); oral history (MA); philosophical foundations of physics (MA); philosophy (MA, PhD); physics (PhD); political science (MA, PhD); psychology (PhD); quantitative methods in the social sciences (MA); religion (MA, PhD); Russia, Eurasia and East Europe: regional studies (MA); Russian translation (MA); Slavic cultures (MA); Slavic languages (MA, PhD); sociology (MA, PhD); South Asian studies (MA); statistics (MA, PhD); theatre (PhD). Dual-degree programs require admission to both Graduate School of Arts and Sciences and another Columbia school. Electronic applications accepted.

Graduate School of Business Offers accounting (MBA); business (EMBA, MBA, PhD); business administration (EMBA, MBA); decision, risk, and operations (MBA); entrepreneurship (MBA); finance and economics (MBA); global business administration (EMBA); healthcare and pharmaceutical management (MBA); human resource management (MBA); international business (MBA); leadership and ethics (MBA); management (MBA); marketing (MBA); media (MBA); private equity (MBA); real estate (MBA); social enterprise (MBA); value investing (MBA). Electronic applications accepted.

Graduate School of Journalism *Program availability:* Part-time. Offers journalism (MA, MS, PhD).

School of International and Public Affairs *Program availability:* Part-time, evening/weekend. Offers development practice (MPA); environmental science and policy (MPA); international affairs (MIA); international and public affairs (MA, MIA, MPA, Certificate); public policy and administration (MPA). Electronic applications accepted.

School of Law Offers law (LL M, JD, JSD). Electronic applications accepted.

School of Nursing Offers adult-gerontology acute care nurse practitioner (MS, Adv C); adult-gerontology primary care nurse practitioner (MS, Adv C); family nurse practitioner (MS, Adv C); nurse anesthesia (MS, Adv C); nurse midwifery (MS); nursing (MS, DNP, PhD, Adv C); pediatric nurse practitioner (MS, Adv C); psychiatric mental health nursing (MS, Adv C). Electronic applications accepted.

School of Professional Studies *Program availability:* Part-time, evening/weekend. Offers actuarial science (MS); bioethics (MS); communications practice (MS); construction administration (MS); fundraising management (MS); information and archive management (MS); landscape design (MS); narrative medicine (MS); negotiation and conflict resolution (MS); sports management (MS); strategic communications (MS); sustainability management (MS); technology management (Exec MS). Electronic applications accepted.

School of the Arts Students: 866 full-time (494 women), 11 part-time (all women); includes 222 minority (51 Black or African American, non-Hispanic/Latino; 3 American Indian or Alaska Native, non-Hispanic/Latino; 52 Asian, non-Hispanic/Latino; 77 Hispanic/Latino; 39 Two or more races, non-Hispanic/Latino), 231 international. Average age 28. 2,290 applicants, 21% accepted, 306 enrolled. *Faculty:* 82 full-time (32 women), 283 part-time/adjunct (151 women). Expenses: Contact institution. *Financial support:* In 2018–19, 610 students received support, including 498 fellowships with full and partial tuition reimbursements available, 142 teaching assistantships with partial tuition reimbursements available; research assistantships, career-related internships or fieldwork, Federal Work-Study, and scholarships/grants also available. Financial award application deadline: 2/4; financial award applicants required to submit FAFSA. In 2018, 289 master's awarded. *Program availability:* Part-time. Offers arts (MA, MFA); film (MFA); film and media studies (MA); new genres (MFA); sound art (MFA); theatre (MFA); writing (MFA). JD/MFA offered in cooperation with Columbia Law School. *Application fee:* $110. Electronic applications accepted. *Application Contact:* Kenny Wong, Director of Admissions and Financial Aid, 212-854-2134, E-mail: soaadmissions@columbia.edu. *Dean,* Carol Becker, 212-854-9847.

South Asia Institute *Program availability:* Part-time. Offers South Asian studies (MA, Certificate). Students must be enrolled in a separate graduate degree program at Columbia University. Electronic applications accepted.

COLUMBUS COLLEGE OF ART & DESIGN, Columbus, OH 43215-1758

General Information Independent, coed, comprehensive institution. *Graduate housing:* Rooms and/or apartments available on a first-come, first-served basis to single and married students. Housing application deadline: 5/1.

GRADUATE UNITS

Graduate Programs *Program availability:* Part-time. Offers integrative design (M Des); visual arts (MFA). Electronic applications accepted.

COLUMBUS STATE UNIVERSITY, Columbus, GA 31907-5645

General Information State-supported, coed, comprehensive institution. CGS member. *Enrollment:* 450 full-time matriculated graduate/professional students (259 women), 922 part-time matriculated graduate/professional students (580 women). *Enrollment by degree level:* 1,137 master's, 175 doctoral, 60 other advanced degrees. *Graduate faculty:* 106 full-time (48 women), 92 part-time/adjunct (37 women). *International tuition:* $19,218 full-time. *Tuition, area resident:* Full-time $4924; part-time $618 per credit hour. Tuition, state resident: full-time $4924; part-time $618 per credit hour. Tuition, nonresident: full-time $19,218; part-time $2403 per credit hour. *Required fees:* $1870; $802. Tuition and fees vary according to course load, degree level and program. *Graduate housing:* Rooms and/or apartments available on a first-come, first-served basis to single and married students. Typical cost: $5720 (including board) for single students. Room and board charges vary according to housing facility selected. Housing application deadline: 6/30. *Student services:* Campus employment opportunities, campus safety program, career counseling, exercise/wellness program, free psychological counseling, international student services, low-cost health insurance, multicultural affairs office, services for students with disabilities, teacher training, writing training. *Library facilities:* Simon Schwob Memorial Library plus 1 other. *Collection:* Books: 379,660 (physical); Serial titles: 1,103 (physical).

Computer facilities: 3,053 computers available on campus for general student use. A campuswide network can be accessed from student residence rooms and from off campus. Online class registration is available.
Website: http://www.columbusstate.edu/

General Application Contact: Catrina Smith-Edmond, Assistant Director for Graduate and Global Admission, 706-507-8824, Fax: 706-568-5091, E-mail: smithedmond_catrina@columbusstate.edu.

GRADUATE UNITS

Graduate Studies Students: 450 full-time (259 women), 922 part-time (580 women); includes 537 minority (416 Black or African American, non-Hispanic/Latino; 3 American

Indian or Alaska Native, non-Hispanic/Latino; 34 Asian, non-Hispanic/Latino; 54 Hispanic/Latino; 2 Native Hawaiian or other Pacific Islander, non-Hispanic/Latino; 28 Two or more races, non-Hispanic/Latino; 50 international. Average age 35. 1,185 applicants, 44% accepted, 346 enrolled. *Faculty:* 117 full-time (53 women), 61 part-time/adjunct (31 women). Expenses: Contact institution. *Financial support:* In 2018–19, 145 students received support, including 96 research assistantships with partial tuition reimbursements available (averaging $3,000 per year); career-related internships or fieldwork, Federal Work-Study, institutionally sponsored loans, scholarships/grants, tuition waivers (partial), and unspecified assistantships also available. Support available to part-time students. Financial award application deadline: 5/1; financial award applicants required to submit FAFSA. In 2018, 479 master's, 25 doctorates, 166 other advanced degrees awarded. *Program availability:* Part-time, evening/weekend, 100% online, blended/hybrid learning. *Application deadline:* For fall admission, 6/30 for domestic and international students; for spring admission, 11/1 for domestic and international students; for summer admission, 5/1 for domestic and international students. Applications are processed on a rolling basis. *Application fee:* $50. Electronic applications accepted. *Application Contact:* Catrina Smith-Edmund, Assistant Director for Graduate and Global Admission, 706-507-8824, Fax: 706-568-5091, E-mail: smithedmond_catrina@columbusstate.edu. *Assistant Vice President for Academic Affairs*, Dr. Margie Yates, 706-507-8573, Fax: 706-569-3168, E-mail: yates_helen@columbusstate.edu.

College of Education and Health Professions Students: 193 full-time (141 women), 366 part-time (281 women); includes 263 minority (228 Black or African American, non-Hispanic/Latino; 6 Asian, non-Hispanic/Latino; 17 Hispanic/Latino; 12 Two or more races, non-Hispanic/Latino; 1 international. Average age 36. 338 applicants, 53% accepted, 128 enrolled. *Faculty:* 46 full-time (27 women), 42 part-time/adjunct (28 women). Expenses: Contact institution. *Financial support:* In 2018–19, 63 students received support, including 20 research assistantships with partial tuition reimbursements available (averaging $3,000 per year); career-related internships or fieldwork, Federal Work-Study, institutionally sponsored loans, scholarships/grants, tuition waivers (partial), and unspecified assistantships also available. Support available to part-time students. Financial award application deadline: 5/1; financial award applicants required to submit FAFSA. In 2018, 168 master's, 25 doctorates, 140 other advanced degrees awarded. *Program availability:* Part-time, evening/weekend, 100% online, blended/hybrid learning. Offers clinical mental health counseling (MS); curriculum and instruction in accomplished teaching (M Ed); curriculum and leadership (Ed D); early childhood education (M Ed, MAT, Ed S); education and health professions (M Ed, MAT, MS, MSN, Ed D, Ed S); educational leadership (M Ed, Ed S); exercise science (MS); family nurse practitioner (MSN); health and physical education (M Ed, MAT); middle grades education (M Ed, MAT, Ed S); nursing (MSN); school counseling (M Ed, Ed S); secondary education (M Ed, MAT, Ed S); special education (M Ed, MAT, Ed S); teacher leadership (M Ed). *Application deadline:* For fall admission, 6/30 for domestic students, 5/1 for international students; for spring admission, 11/1 for domestic and international students; for summer admission, 3/1 for domestic and international students. Applications are processed on a rolling basis. *Application fee:* $50. Electronic applications accepted. *Application Contact:* Catrina Smith-Edmond, Assistant Director for Graduate and Global Admission, 706-507-8824, Fax: 706-568-5091, E-mail: smithedmond_catrina@columbusstate.edu. *Dean*, Dr. Deirdre Greer, 706-507-8505, Fax: 706-569-3134, E-mail: greer_deirdre@columbusstate.edu.

College of Letters and Sciences Students: 81 full-time (29 women), 190 part-time (56 women); includes 78 minority (64 Black or African American, non-Hispanic/Latino; 2 American Indian or Alaska Native, non-Hispanic/Latino; 2 Asian, non-Hispanic/Latino; 7 Hispanic/Latino; 3 Two or more races, non-Hispanic/Latino; 6 international. Average age 39. 116 applicants, 59% accepted, 57 enrolled. *Faculty:* 8 full-time (2 women), 17 part-time/adjunct (3 women). Expenses: Contact institution. *Financial support:* In 2018–19, 6 students received support, including 25 research assistantships with partial tuition reimbursements available (averaging $3,000 per year); fellowships, career-related internships or fieldwork, Federal Work-Study, institutionally sponsored loans, scholarships/grants, tuition waivers (partial), and unspecified assistantships also available. Support available to part-time students. Financial award application deadline: 5/1; financial award applicants required to submit FAFSA. In 2018, 121 master's awarded. *Program availability:* Part-time, evening/weekend, 100% online, blended/hybrid learning. Offers history (MA); letters and sciences (MA, MPA, MPSA, MS, Certificate); natural sciences (MS); public administration (MPA); public safety administration (MPSA); teaching English to speakers of other languages (Certificate). *Application deadline:* For fall admission, 6/30 for domestic students, 5/1 for international students; for spring admission, 11/1 for domestic students, 10/1 for international students; for summer admission, 3/1 for domestic and international students. Applications are processed on a rolling basis. *Application fee:* $50. Electronic applications accepted. *Application Contact:* Catrina Smith-Edmond, Assistant Director for Graduate and Global Admission, 706-507-8824, Fax: 706-568-5091, E-mail: smithedmond_catrina@columbusstate.edu. *Dean*, Dr. Dennis Rome, 706-568-2056, E-mail: rome_dennis@columbusstate.edu.

College of the Arts Students: 46 full-time (18 women), 29 part-time (18 women); includes 19 minority (7 Black or African American, non-Hispanic/Latino; 5 Asian, non-Hispanic/Latino; 6 Hispanic/Latino; 1 Native Hawaiian or other Pacific Islander, non-Hispanic/Latino; 16 international. Average age 27. 78 applicants, 55% accepted, 32 enrolled. *Faculty:* 25 full-time (10 women), 5 part-time/adjunct (3 women). Expenses: Contact institution. *Financial support:* In 2018–19, 46 students received support, including 31 research assistantships with partial tuition reimbursements available (averaging $3,000 per year); career-related internships or fieldwork, Federal Work-Study, institutionally sponsored loans, scholarships/grants, tuition waivers (partial), and unspecified assistantships also available. Support available to part-time students. Financial award application deadline: 5/1; financial award applicants required to submit FAFSA. In 2018, 19 master's, 15 other advanced degrees awarded. *Program availability:* Part-time, evening/weekend. Offers art education (M Ed, MAT); arts (M Ed, MAT, MM, Artist Diploma); music (Artist Diploma); music education (MM); music performance (MM); theatre education (M Ed, MAT). *Application deadline:* For fall admission, 6/30 for domestic students, 5/1 for international students; for spring admission, 11/1 for domestic and international students; for summer admission, 3/1 for domestic and international students. Applications are processed on a rolling basis. *Application fee:* $50. Electronic applications accepted. *Application Contact:* Catrina Smith-Edmond, Assistant Director for Graduate and Global Admission, 706-507-8824, Fax: 706-568-5091, E-mail: smithedmond_catrina@columbusstate.edu. *Dean*, Dr. Larry Dooley, 706-507-8402, E-mail: dooley_larry@columbusstate.edu.

Turner College of Business Students: 79 full-time (24 women), 136 part-time (47 women); includes 73 minority (40 Black or African American, non-Hispanic/Latino; 1 American Indian or Alaska Native, non-Hispanic/Latino; 8 Asian, non-Hispanic/Latino; 15 Hispanic/Latino; 9 Two or more races, non-Hispanic/Latino; 27 international.

Average age 31. 237 applicants, 51% accepted, 64 enrolled. *Faculty:* 10 full-time (3 women), 1 part-time/adjunct (0 women). Expenses: Contact institution. *Financial support:* In 2018–19, 18 students received support, including 20 research assistantships (averaging $3,000 per year); Federal Work-Study also available. Financial award application deadline: 5/1; financial award applicants required to submit FAFSA. In 2018, 113 master's, 10 other advanced degrees awarded. *Program availability:* Part-time, evening/weekend, 100% online, blended/hybrid learning. Offers applied computer science (MS); business administration (MBA); cyber security (MS); human resource management (Certificate); information systems security (Certificate); modeling and simulation (Certificate); organizational leadership (MS); servant leadership (Certificate). *Application deadline:* For fall admission, 6/30 for domestic students, 5/1 for international students; for spring admission, 11/1 for domestic and international students; for summer admission, 3/1 for domestic and international students. Applications are processed on a rolling basis. *Application fee:* $50. Electronic applications accepted. *Application Contact:* Catrina Smith-Edmond, Assistant Director for Graduate and Global Admission, 706-507-8824, Fax: 706-568-5091, E-mail: smithedmond_catrina@columbusstate.edu. *Dean*, Dr. Linda U. Hadley, 706-507-8153, Fax: 706-568-2184, E-mail: hadley_linda@columbusstate.edu.

CONCORDIA COLLEGE, Moorhead, MN 56562
General Information Independent-religious, coed, comprehensive institution.
GRADUATE UNITS
Program in Education Offers world language instruction (M Ed).

CONCORDIA COLLEGE–NEW YORK, Bronxville, NY 10708-1998
General Information Independent-religious, coed, comprehensive institution.
GRADUATE UNITS
Program in Business Leadership Offers business leadership (MS).
Program in Childhood Special Education Offers childhood special education (MS Ed).

CONCORDIA LUTHERAN SEMINARY, Edmonton, AB T5B 4E3, Canada
General Information Independent-religious, coed, primarily men, graduate-only institution. *Graduate housing:* On-campus housing not available.
GRADUATE UNITS
Graduate and Professional Programs *Program availability:* Part-time. Offers theology (M Div, Graduate Certificate).

CONCORDIA SEMINARY, St. Louis, MO 63105-3199
General Information Independent-religious, coed, primarily men, graduate-only institution. *Graduate housing:* Rooms or apartments guaranteed to single students and available to married students. Housing application deadline: 3/4. *Research affiliation:* Center for Reformation Research, Concordia Historical Institute.
GRADUATE UNITS
Graduate Programs Offers theology (M Div, MA, STM, D Min, PhD, Certificate).

CONCORDIA THEOLOGICAL SEMINARY, Fort Wayne, IN 46825-4996
General Information Independent-religious, coed, primarily men, graduate-only institution. *Graduate housing:* Room and/or apartments available to single students; on-campus housing not available to married students.
GRADUATE UNITS
Graduate and Professional Programs *Program availability:* Part-time. Offers theology (M Div, MA, STM, D Min, PhD).

CONCORDIA UNIVERSITY, Montréal, QC H3G 1M8, Canada
General Information Province-supported, coed, university. CGS member. *Graduate housing:* Room and/or apartments available on a first-come, first-served basis to single students; on-campus housing not available to married students. *Research affiliation:* Canadian Rural Revitalization Foundation (sociology), Blue Metropolis Literary Series (English), Canadian Journalism Project (journalism), Centre de Recherche en Plasturgie et Composites (CREPEC) (mechanical and industrial engineering), Centre de Recherche Informatique de Montreal (CRIM) (computer science), Center d'experise et de services en application Multimedia (multimedia).
GRADUATE UNITS
School of Graduate Studies *Program availability:* Part-time, evening/weekend. Offers individualized research (M Sc, MA, PhD).

Faculty of Arts and Science Offers adult education (Certificate, Diploma); Anglais-Français en langue et techniques de localization (Certificate); applied linguistics (MA, Certificate); arts and science (M Env, M Sc, MA, MTM, PhD, Certificate, Diploma, Graduate Diploma); biology (M Sc, PhD); biotechnology and genomics (Diploma); chemistry (M Sc, PhD); child studies (MA); communication (PhD); communication studies (Diploma); community economic development (Diploma); creative writing (MA); economics (MA, PhD, Diploma); educational studies (MA); educational technology (MA); English literature (MA, PhD); environmental assessment (M Env, Diploma); exercise science (M Sc); geography, urban and environmental studies (M Sc, PhD); history (MA, PhD); human systems intervention (MA); humanities (PhD); instructional technology (Diploma); journalism (Graduate Diploma); journalism studies (MA); Judaic studies (MA); littératures Francophones et résonances médiatiques (MA); mathematics (PhD); mathematics and statistics (M Sc, MA); media studies (MA); philosophy (MA); physics (M Sc, PhD); political science (PhD); psychology (MA, PhD, Certificate); public policy and public administration (MA); religion (MA, PhD); social and cultural analysis (PhD); social and cultural anthropology (MA); sociology (MA); teaching English as a second language (Certificate); teaching of mathematics (MTM); theological studies (MA); translation (MA); translation studies (MA); visual journalism (Diploma); youth work (Graduate Diploma).

Faculty of Engineering and Computer Science Offers 3D graphics and game development (Certificate); aerospace engineering (M Eng); building engineering (M Eng, MA Sc, PhD, Certificate); civil engineering (M Eng, MA Sc, PhD); computer science (M App Comp Sc, M Comp Sc, PhD, Diploma); electrical and computer engineering (M Eng, MA Sc, PhD); engineering and computer science (M App Comp Sc, M Comp Sc, M Eng, MA Sc, PhD, Certificate, Diploma); environmental engineering (Certificate); industrial engineering (M Eng, MA Sc, PhD); information and systems engineering (PhD); information systems security (M Eng, MA Sc); mechanical engineering (M Eng, MA Sc, PhD, Certificate); quality systems engineering (M Eng, MA Sc); service engineering and network management (Certificate); software engineering (M Eng, MA Sc).

Faculty of Fine Arts *Program availability:* Part-time. Offers advanced music performance studies (Diploma); art education (MA, PhD); art history (MA, PhD); art therapy (MA); design (M Des); digital technologies in design art practice (Certificate); drama therapy (MA); film and moving image studies (PhD); film production (MFA); film studies (MA); fine arts (M Des, MA, MFA, PhD, Certificate, Diploma); music therapy (MA); studio arts (MFA).

John Molson School of Business *Program availability:* Part-time, evening/weekend. Offers administration (M Sc); business administration (MBA, PhD, Certificate, Diploma); executive business administration (EMBA); supply chain management (MSCM). PhD program offered jointly with HEC Montreal, McGill University, and Université du Québec à Montréal. Electronic applications accepted.

CONCORDIA UNIVERSITY, Portland, OR 97211-6099

General Information Independent-religious, coed, comprehensive institution. *Graduate housing:* Room and/or apartments available on a first-come, first-served basis to single students; on-campus housing not available to married students. Housing application deadline: 8/1.

GRADUATE UNITS

College of Arts and Sciences Offers community psychology (MA); teaching English to speakers of other languages (MA).

College of Education *Program availability:* Part-time, online learning. Offers administrative leadership (Ed D); career and technical education (M Ed); curriculum and instruction (M Ed); educational administration (M Ed); educational leadership (M Ed); elementary education (MAT); higher education (Ed D); instructional leadership (Ed D); professional leadership, inquiry, and transformation (Ed D); secondary education (MAT); transformational leadership (Ed D). Electronic applications accepted.

School of Law Offers law (JD). Electronic applications accepted.

School of Management *Program availability:* Evening/weekend. Offers management (MBA).

CONCORDIA UNIVERSITY ANN ARBOR, Ann Arbor, MI 48105-2797

General Information Independent-religious, coed, comprehensive institution. *Graduate housing:* On-campus housing not available.

GRADUATE UNITS

Graduate Programs *Program availability:* Part-time, evening/weekend. Offers curriculum and instruction (MS); educational leadership (MS); organizational leadership and administration (MS). Electronic applications accepted.

CONCORDIA UNIVERSITY CHICAGO, River Forest, IL 60305-1499

General Information Independent-religious, coed, comprehensive institution. CGS member. *Graduate housing:* Rooms and/or apartments available on a first-come, first-served basis to single and married students.

GRADUATE UNITS

College of Graduate Studies Offers Christian education (MA); church music (MCM); clinical mental health counseling (MA); curriculum and instruction (MA); early childhood education (MA); educational administration (MA); elementary education (MAT); gerontology (MA); human services (MA); leadership (MA, Ed D, PhD); music (MA); reading education (MA); religion (MA); school counseling (MA); secondary education (MAT); teacher leadership (MA).

College of Business *Program availability:* Part-time, evening/weekend, online learning. Offers business (MBA, DBA).

CONCORDIA UNIVERSITY IRVINE, Irvine, CA 92612-3299

General Information Independent-religious, coed, comprehensive institution. *Graduate housing:* Room and/or apartments available on a first-come, first-served basis to single students; on-campus housing not available to married students. Housing application deadline: 6/1.

GRADUATE UNITS

School of Arts and Sciences *Program availability:* Part-time, evening/weekend, online learning. Offers coaching and athletic administration (MA). Electronic applications accepted.

School of Business *Program availability:* Part-time, evening/weekend. Offers business administration (MBA). Electronic applications accepted.

School of Education *Program availability:* Part-time, evening/weekend, online learning. Offers curriculum and instruction (MA); education and preliminary teaching credential (M Ed); educational administration and preliminary administrative services credential (MA); educational technology (MA); school counseling with pupil personnel services credential (MA). Electronic applications accepted.

School of Professional Studies

School of Theology *Program availability:* Part-time, evening/weekend. Offers Christian leadership (MA); research in theology (MA); theology and culture (MA). Electronic applications accepted.

CONCORDIA UNIVERSITY, NEBRASKA, Seward, NE 68434

General Information Independent-religious, coed, comprehensive institution. *Graduate housing:* Rooms and/or apartments available on a first-come, first-served basis to single and married students.

GRADUATE UNITS

Graduate Programs in Education *Program availability:* Part-time, evening/weekend. Offers early childhood education (M Ed); education (M Ed, MPE, MS); elementary and secondary education (M Ed); elementary education (M Ed); family life ministry (MS); parish education (MPE); reading education (M Ed); secondary education (M Ed). Electronic applications accepted.

Program in Computer Science *Program availability:* Online learning. Offers cyber operations (MS).

CONCORDIA UNIVERSITY OF EDMONTON, Edmonton, AB T5B 4E4, Canada

General Information Independent-religious, coed, comprehensive institution.

GRADUATE UNITS

Program in Biblical and Christian Studies Offers Biblical and Christian studies (MA).
Program in Information Systems Security Management Offers information systems security management (MA).

CONCORDIA UNIVERSITY, ST. PAUL, St. Paul, MN 55104-5494

General Information Independent-religious, coed, comprehensive institution. CGS member. *Enrollment:* 1,833 full-time matriculated graduate/professional students (1,295

women), 111 part-time matriculated graduate/professional students (62 women). *Enrollment by degree level:* 1,693 master's, 145 doctoral, 106 other advanced degrees. *Graduate faculty:* 47 full-time (27 women), 145 part-time/adjunct (83 women). *Tuition:* Full-time $5700; part-time $475 per credit. Tuition and fees vary according to degree level and program. *Graduate housing:* Rooms and/or apartments available on a first-come, first-served basis to single and married students. Housing application deadline: 6/1. *Student services:* Campus employment opportunities, campus safety program, career counseling, exercise/wellness program, international student services, multicultural affairs office, services for students with disabilities, teacher training, writing training. *Library facilities:* Library Technology Center. *Collection:* Books: 108,345 (physical), 226,902 (digital/electronic); Serial titles: 917 (physical), 98,931 (digital/electronic); Databases: 178. Weekly public service hours: 74; students can reserve study rooms.

Computer facilities: 10 computers available on campus for general student use. A campuswide network can be accessed from student residence rooms and from off campus. Online class registration is available.
Website: http://www.csp.edu/

General Application Contact: Amber Faletti, Director of Enrollment Management, 651-641-8230, Fax: 651-603-6320, E-mail: faletti@csp.edu.

GRADUATE UNITS

College of Business and Technology Students: 448 full-time (289 women), 30 part-time (17 women); includes 135 minority (58 Black or African American, non-Hispanic/Latino; 2 American Indian or Alaska Native, non-Hispanic/Latino; 46 Asian, non-Hispanic/Latino; 13 Hispanic/Latino; 16 Two or more races, non-Hispanic/Latino), 40 international. Average age 32. 328 applicants, 96% accepted, 149 enrolled. *Faculty:* 12 full-time (5 women), 28 part-time/adjunct (14 women). Expenses: Contact institution. *Financial support:* In 2018–19, 267 students received support. Federal Work-Study, scholarships/grants, and unspecified assistantships available. Financial award applicants required to submit FAFSA. In 2018, 205 master's awarded. *Program availability:* Part-time, evening/weekend, 100% online, blended/hybrid learning. Offers business administration (MBA); health care management (MBA); human resource management (MBA); information technology (MBA); leadership and management (MA); strategic communication management (MA). *Application deadline:* For fall admission, 8/1 for domestic and international students; for spring admission, 12/1 for domestic and international students; for summer admission, 5/1 for domestic and international students. Applications are processed on a rolling basis. *Application fee:* $0. Electronic applications accepted. *Application Contact:* Amber Faletti, Director of Enrollment Management, 651-641-8838, Fax: 651-603-6320, E-mail: faletti@csp.edu. *Dean,* Dr. Kevin Hall, 651-603-6165, Fax: 651-641-8807, E-mail: khall@csp.edu.

College of Education Students: 979 full-time (748 women), 40 part-time (28 women); includes 124 minority (49 Black or African American, non-Hispanic/Latino; 6 American Indian or Alaska Native, non-Hispanic/Latino; 34 Asian, non-Hispanic/Latino; 22 Hispanic/Latino; 1 Native Hawaiian or other Pacific Islander, non-Hispanic/Latino; 12 Two or more races, non-Hispanic/Latino), 11 international. Average age 34. 423 applicants, 99% accepted, 335 enrolled. *Faculty:* 13 full-time (9 women), 82 part-time/adjunct (51 women). Expenses: Contact institution. *Financial support:* In 2018–19, 163 students received support. Federal Work-Study, scholarships/grants, and unspecified assistantships available. Financial award applicants required to submit FAFSA. In 2018, 358 master's, 3 doctorates, 119 other advanced degrees awarded. *Program availability:* Part-time, evening/weekend, 100% online, blended/hybrid learning. Offers classroom instruction (MA Ed); differentiated instruction (MA Ed); early childhood education (MA Ed); education (Ed D); educational leadership (MA Ed); educational technology (MA Ed, Certificate); K-12 principal licensure (Ed S); special education (MA Ed); superintendent (Ed S); teaching (MAT). *Application deadline:* For fall admission, 8/1 for domestic and international students; for spring admission, 12/1 for domestic and international students; for summer admission, 5/1 for domestic and international students. Applications are processed on a rolling basis. *Application fee:* $0. Electronic applications accepted. *Application Contact:* Amber Faletti, Director of Enrollment Management, 651-641-8838, Fax: 651-603-6320, E-mail: faletti@csp.edu. *Dean,* Lonn Maly, 651-641-8203, E-mail: maly@csp.edu.

College of Health and Science Students: 247 full-time (132 women), 27 part-time (9 women); includes 43 minority (18 Black or African American, non-Hispanic/Latino; 1 American Indian or Alaska Native, non-Hispanic/Latino; 4 Asian, non-Hispanic/Latino; 12 Hispanic/Latino; 8 Two or more races, non-Hispanic/Latino), 5 international. Average age 28. 241 applicants, 47% accepted, 86 enrolled. *Faculty:* 16 full-time (9 women), 15 part-time/adjunct (8 women). Expenses: Contact institution. *Financial support:* In 2018–19, 74 students received support. Federal Work-Study, scholarships/grants, and unspecified assistantships available. Financial award applicants required to submit FAFSA. In 2018, 79 master's, 26 doctorates awarded. *Program availability:* Part-time, evening/weekend, 100% online, blended/hybrid learning. Offers exercise science (MS); orthotics and prosthetics (MS); physical therapy (DPT); sports management (MA). *Application deadline:* For fall admission, 4/1 for domestic students. Applications are processed on a rolling basis. *Application fee:* $0. Electronic applications accepted. *Application Contact:* Amber Faletti, Director of Enrollment Management, 651-641-8838, Fax: 651-603-6320, E-mail: faletti@csp.edu. *Dean,* Dr. Katie Fischer, 651-641-8735, E-mail: fischer@csp.edu.

College of Humanities and Social Sciences Students: 159 full-time (126 women), 14 part-time (7 women); includes 56 minority (27 Black or African American, non-Hispanic/Latino; 2 American Indian or Alaska Native, non-Hispanic/Latino; 10 Asian, non-Hispanic/Latino; 8 Hispanic/Latino; 9 Two or more races, non-Hispanic/Latino), 1 international. Average age 35. 82 applicants, 95% accepted, 64 enrolled. *Faculty:* 8 full-time (5 women), 19 part-time/adjunct (10 women). Expenses: Contact institution. *Financial support:* In 2018–19, 83 students received support. Federal Work-Study and scholarships/grants available. Financial award applicants required to submit FAFSA. In 2018, 36 master's awarded. *Program availability:* Part-time, evening/weekend, 100% online, blended/hybrid learning. Offers creative writing (MFA); criminal justice leadership (MA); family science (MA); human services (MA). *Application deadline:* For fall admission, 8/1 for domestic students, 7/1 for international students; for spring admission, 12/1 for domestic students, 11/1 for international students. Applications are processed on a rolling basis. *Application fee:* $0. Electronic applications accepted. *Application Contact:* Amber Faletti, Director of Enrollment Management, 651-641-8838, Fax: 651-603-6320, E-mail: faletti@csp.edu. *Dean,* Dr. Paul Hillmer, 651-641-8215, E-mail: hillmer@csp.edu.

CONCORDIA UNIVERSITY TEXAS, Austin, TX 78726

General Information Independent-religious, coed, comprehensive institution.

GRADUATE UNITS

College of Education *Program availability:* Part-time, evening/weekend. Offers education (M Ed).

CONCORDIA UNIVERSITY WISCONSIN, Mequon, WI 53097-2402

General Information Independent-religious, coed, comprehensive institution. *Graduate housing:* Room and/or apartments available to single students; on-campus housing not available to married students. Housing application deadline: 8/1.

GRADUATE UNITS

Graduate Programs *Program availability:* Part-time, evening/weekend, online learning. Electronic applications accepted.

Batterman School of Business Offers business (MBA, MS); finance (MBA); health care administration (MBA); human resource management (MBA); international business (MBA); international business-bilingual English/Chinese (MBA); management (MBA); management information systems (MBA); managerial communications (MBA); marketing (MBA); organizational leadership administration (MS); public administration (MBA); risk management (MBA).

School of Arts and Sciences Offers arts and sciences (MCM); church music (MCM).

School of Education *Program availability:* Part-time, evening/weekend, online learning. Offers art education (MS Ed); early childhood (MS Ed); educational administration (MS Ed); environmental education (MS Ed); family studies (MS Ed); literacy (MS Ed); school counseling (MS Ed); special education (MS Ed).

School of Health Professions Offers health professions (MOT, MSRS, MSW, DPT); occupational therapy (MOT); physical therapy (DPT); rehabilitation science (MSRS); social work (MSW).

School of Nursing *Program availability:* Online learning. Offers family nurse practitioner (MSN).

School of Pharmacy Offers pharmaceutical/chemical product development (MPD); pharmacy (Pharm D).

CONCORD LAW SCHOOL, Los Angeles, CA 90024

General Information Proprietary, coed, graduate-only institution.

GRADUATE UNITS

Program in Law *Program availability:* Part-time, evening/weekend, online learning. Offers law (EJD, JD). Electronic applications accepted.

CONCORD UNIVERSITY, Athens, WV 24712-1000

General Information State-supported, coed, comprehensive institution. *Graduate housing:* Room and/or apartments available on a first-come, first-served basis to single students; on-campus housing not available to married students.

GRADUATE UNITS

Graduate Studies *Program availability:* Part-time, evening/weekend, 100% online. Offers educational leadership and supervision (M Ed); health promotion (MA); reading specialist (M Ed); social work (MSW); special education (M Ed); teaching (MAT). Electronic applications accepted.

CONSERVATORIO DE MUSICA DE PUERTO RICO, San Juan, PR 00907

General Information Commonwealth-supported, coed, comprehensive institution.

GRADUATE UNITS

Program in Musical Performance Offers guitar (Diploma); orchestral instruments (Diploma); piano (Diploma); vocal performance (Diploma).

Program in Music Education Offers music education (MM Ed).

CONVERSE COLLEGE, Spartanburg, SC 29302

General Information Independent, Undergraduate: women only; graduate: coed, comprehensive institution. *Graduate housing:* Room and/or apartments available to single students; on-campus housing not available to married students.

GRADUATE UNITS

Education Specialist Program *Program availability:* Part-time. Offers administration and leadership (Ed S); administration and supervision (Ed S); literacy (Ed S). Electronic applications accepted.

Petrie School of Music *Program availability:* Part-time, evening/weekend. Offers music education (M Mus); performance (M Mus). Electronic applications accepted.

Program in Art Education Offers art education (M Ed, MAT).

Program in Creative Writing Offers creative writing (MFA).

Program in Educational Administration and Supervision Offers administration and supervision (M Ed). Electronic applications accepted.

Program in Elementary Education *Program availability:* Part-time. Offers elementary education (M Ed, MAT). Electronic applications accepted.

Program in Gifted Education *Program availability:* Part-time. Offers gifted education (M Ed). Electronic applications accepted.

Program in Liberal Arts Offers English (MLA); history (MLA); political science (MLA).

Program in Marriage and Family Therapy Offers marriage and family therapy (MMFT).

Program in Middle Level Education Offers language arts/English (MAT); mathematics (MAT); middle level education (M Ed); science (MAT); social studies (MAT).

Program in Secondary Education *Program availability:* Part-time. Offers biology (MAT); chemistry (MAT); English (M Ed, MAT); mathematics (M Ed, MAT); natural sciences (M Ed); social sciences (M Ed, MAT). Electronic applications accepted.

Program in Special Education *Program availability:* Part-time. Offers intellectual disabilities (MAT); learning disabilities (MAT); special education (M Ed). Electronic applications accepted.

THE CONWAY SCHOOL, Conway, MA 01341-0179

General Information Independent, coed, graduate-only institution. *Graduate housing:* On-campus housing not available.

GRADUATE UNITS

Program in Ecological Design Offers ecological design (MS).

COOPER UNION FOR THE ADVANCEMENT OF SCIENCE AND ART, New York, NY 10003-7120

General Information Independent, coed, comprehensive institution. *Graduate housing:* On-campus housing not available. *Research affiliation:* National Science Foundation, National Institutes of Health, Defense Advanced Research Projects Agency, Naval Postgraduate School, U.S. Department of Homeland Security, U.S. Department of Defense.

GRADUATE UNITS

Albert Nerken School of Engineering *Program availability:* Part-time. Offers chemical engineering (ME); civil engineering (ME); electrical engineering (ME); mechanical engineering (ME). Electronic applications accepted.

Irwin S. Chanin School of Architecture Offers architecture (M Arch II). Electronic applications accepted.

COPPIN STATE UNIVERSITY, Baltimore, MD 21216-3698

General Information State-supported, coed, comprehensive institution. CGS member. *Graduate housing:* On-campus housing not available.

GRADUATE UNITS

School of Graduate Studies *Program availability:* Part-time, evening/weekend, online learning.

College of Behavioral and Social Sciences *Program availability:* Part-time, evening/weekend. Offers alcohol and substance abuse counseling (MS); behavioral and social sciences (M Ed, MA, MS); criminal justice (MS); human services administration (MS); rehabilitation counseling (M Ed).

Helene Fuld School of Nursing *Program availability:* Part-time, evening/weekend. Offers family nurse practitioner (PMC); nursing (MSN).

School of Education *Program availability:* Part-time, evening/weekend, online learning. Offers adult and continuing education (MS); curriculum and instruction (M Ed); education (M Ed, MAT, MS); special education (M Ed); teaching (MAT).

CORBAN UNIVERSITY, Salem, OR 97301-9392

General Information Independent-religious, coed, comprehensive institution.

GRADUATE UNITS

Graduate School Offers counseling (MA); education (MS Ed); management (MBA); non-profit management (MBA).

School of Ministry *Program availability:* Part-time, evening/weekend. Offers Biblical languages (M Div); Biblical leadership (Certificate); Christian leadership (MA); Church ministry (M Div); ministry (D Min).

CORNELL UNIVERSITY, Ithaca, NY 14853

General Information Independent, coed, university. CGS member. *Graduate housing:* Rooms and/or apartments available on a first-come, first-served basis to single and married students. Housing application deadline: 7/1. *Research affiliation:* Brookhaven National Laboratory (physics, biology, medicine, chemistry, energy, engineering, environmental science), Fermi National Accelerator Laboratory, Boyce Thompson Institute for Plant Research (plant research).

GRADUATE UNITS

College of Veterinary Medicine Students: 434 full-time (343 women); includes 115 minority (16 Black or African American, non-Hispanic/Latino; 3 American Indian or Alaska Native, non-Hispanic/Latino; 44 Asian, non-Hispanic/Latino; 45 Hispanic/Latino; 2 Native Hawaiian or other Pacific Islander, non-Hispanic/Latino; 5 Two or more races, non-Hispanic/Latino), 4 international. Average age 26. 1,136 applicants, 15% accepted, 115 enrolled. *Faculty:* 203 full-time (95 women). Expenses: Contact institution. *Financial support:* In 2018–19, 287 students received support. Federal Work-Study, institutionally sponsored loans, and scholarships/grants available. Financial award application deadline: 2/1; financial award applicants required to submit CSS PROFILE or FAFSA. In 2018, 97 doctorates awarded. Offers veterinary medicine (DVM). *Application deadline:* For fall admission, 9/15 for domestic and international students. Electronic applications accepted. *Application Contact:* Jennifer A. Mailey, Director of Admissions, 607-253-3700, Fax: 607-253-3709, E-mail: jam333@cornell.edu. *Dean,* Dr. Lorin Warnick, 607-253-3771, Fax: 607-253-3701.

Cornell Law School Offers law (LL M, JD, JSD). JD/MLLP offered jointly with Humboldt University, Berlin; JD/DESS offered jointly with Institut d'etudes Politiques de Paris ("Sciences Po") and Paris I. Electronic applications accepted.

Graduate School Offers 19th century art (PhD); acarology (MS, PhD); adult and extension education (MPS, MS, PhD); advanced composites and structures (M Eng); advanced materials processing (M Eng, MS, PhD); aerospace engineering (M Eng, MS, PhD); African history (MA, PhD); African studies (MPS); African, African American and African diaspora (PhD); African-American literature (PhD); African-American studies (MPS); Africana studies (PhD); agricultural finance (MS, PhD); agriculture and life sciences (M Eng, MFS, MLA, MPS, MS, PhD); agronomy (MS, PhD); algorithms (M Eng, PhD); American art (PhD); American history (MA, PhD); American literature after 1865 (PhD); American literature to 1865 (PhD); American politics (PhD); American studies (PhD); analytical chemistry (PhD); ancient art and archaeology (PhD); ancient Greek history (PhD); ancient history (MA, PhD); ancient Near Eastern studies (MA, PhD); ancient philosophy (PhD); ancient Roman history (PhD); animal genetics (MPS, MS, PhD); animal genomics (MPS, MS, PhD); animal nutrition (MPS, MS, PhD); animal science (MPS, MS); apiculture (MS, PhD); apparel design (MA, MPS); applied econometrics and qualitative analysis (MS, PhD); applied economics (PhD); applied entomology (MS, PhD); applied linguistics (MA, PhD); applied logic and automated reasoning (M Eng, PhD); applied mathematics (PhD); applied mathematics and computational methods (M Eng, MS, PhD); applied physics (PhD); applied probability and statistics (PhD); applied research in human-environment relations (MS); applied statistics (MPS); aquatic entomology (MS, PhD); Arabic and Islamic studies (MA, PhD); archaeological anthropology (PhD); architectural design (M Arch); architectural science (MS); architecture, art and planning (M Arch, MA, MFA, MPS, MRP, MS, PhD); artificial intelligence (M Eng, PhD); arts and sciences (MA, MFA, MPA, MPS, MS, DMA, PhD); Asian American art (PhD); Asian religions (MA, PhD); astronomy (PhD); astrophysics (PhD); atmospheric science (MS, PhD); Baroque art (PhD); basic analytical economics (PhD); behavioral biology (PhD); biblical studies (MA, PhD); bio-organic chemistry (PhD); biochemical engineering (M Eng, MS, PhD); biochemistry (PhD); bioenergy and integrated energy systems (M Eng, MPS, MS, PhD); biological anthropology (PhD); biological control (MS, PhD); biological engineering (M Eng, MPS, MS, PhD); biomechanical engineering (M Eng, MS, PhD); biomedical and biological sciences (PhD); biomedical engineering (M Eng, MS, PhD); biometry (MS, PhD); biophysical chemistry (PhD); biophysics (PhD); bioprocess engineering (M Eng, MPS, MS, PhD); biopsychology (PhD); breeding of horticultural crops (MPS); cell biology (PhD); cellular and molecular toxicology (MS, PhD); chemical biology (PhD); chemical physics (PhD); chemical reaction engineering (M Eng, MS, PhD); Chinese philosophy (PhD); city and regional planning (MRP, PhD); classical and statistical thermodynamics (M Eng, MS, PhD); classical archaeology (PhD); classical Chinese literature (PhD); classical Japanese literature (PhD); classical literature and philology (PhD); classical myth (PhD); classical rhetoric (PhD); cognition (PhD); collective bargaining, labor law and labor history (MILR, MPS, MS, PhD); colonial and postcolonial literatures (PhD); combustion (M Eng, MS, PhD); communication (MS, PhD); community nutrition (MPS, PhD); community-based natural resources management (MS, PhD); comparative literature (PhD); Comparative Modernities (PhD); comparative politics (PhD); composition (DMA); computational behavioral biology (PhD); computational biology (PhD); computational cell biology (PhD); computational ecology (PhD); computational genetics (PhD); computational macromolecular biology (PhD); computational organismal biology (PhD);

computer engineering (M Eng, PhD); computer graphics (M Eng, MS, PhD); computer science (M Eng, PhD); computer vision (M Eng, PhD); concurrency and distributed computing (M Eng, PhD); conservation biology (MS, PhD); consumer policy (PhD); creative visual arts (MFA); creative writing (MFA); cultural studies (PhD); cytology (MS, PhD); dairy science (MPS, MS, PhD); decision theory (MS, PhD); development policy (MPS); developmental biology (PhD); developmental psychology (MA, PhD); digital art (PhD); drama and the theatre (PhD); dramatic literature (PhD); dynamics and space mechanics (MS, PhD); early modern European history (MA, PhD); East Asian art (PhD); East Asian linguistics (MA, PhD); East Asian literature and culture (PhD); East Asian studies (MA); ecohydrology (M Eng, MPS, MS, PhD); ecology (PhD); econometrics and economic statistics (PhD); economic and social statistics (MILR, MS, PhD); economic development and planning (PhD); economic geology (M Eng, MS, PhD); economic theory (PhD); economics of development (PhD); economy and society (MA, PhD); ecosystem biology and biogeochemistry (MPS, MS, PhD); ecotoxicology and environmental chemistry (MS, PhD); electrical engineering (M Eng, PhD); electrical systems (M Eng, PhD); electrophysics (M Eng, PhD); energy and power systems (M Eng, MS, PhD); engineering (M Eng, MPS, MS, PhD); engineering geology (M Eng, MS, PhD); engineering management (M Eng, MS, PhD); engineering physics (M Eng); engineering statistics (MS, PhD); English history (MA, PhD); English linguistics (MA, PhD); English poetry (PhD); English Renaissance to 1660 (PhD); enology (MS, PhD); environmental archaeology (MA); environmental economics (MS, PhD); environmental engineering (M Eng, MPS, MS, PhD); environmental fluid mechanics and hydrology (M Eng, MS, PhD); environmental geophysics (M Eng, MS, PhD); environmental information science (MS, PhD); environmental management (MPS); environmental planning and design (MRP, PhD); environmental studies (MA, MS, PhD); environmental systems engineering (M Eng, MS, PhD); evolutionary biology (PhD); experimental design (MS, PhD); experimental physics (MS, PhD); facilities planning and management (MS); family and social welfare policy (PhD); farm management and production economics (MS, PhD); fiber science (MS, PhD); field crop science (MS, PhD); fishery and aquatic science (MPS, MS, PhD); fluid dynamics, rheology and biorheology (M Eng, MS, PhD); fluid mechanics (M Eng, MS, PhD); food chemistry (MPS, MS, PhD); food engineering (M Eng, MPS, MS, PhD); food microbiology (MPS, MS, PhD); food processing waste technology (MPS, MS, PhD); food science (MFS, MPS, MS, PhD); forest science (MPS, MS, PhD); French history (MA, PhD); French linguistics (PhD); French literature (PhD); fungal and oomycete biology (MPS, MS, PhD); gender and life course (MA, PhD); general geology (M Eng, MS, PhD); general linguistics (MA, PhD); general space sciences (PhD); genetics (PhD); genomics (PhD); geobiology (M Eng, MS, PhD); geochemistry and isotope geology (M Eng, MS, PhD); geohydrology (M Eng, MS, PhD); geomorphology (M Eng, MS, PhD); geophysics (M Eng, MS, PhD); geotechnical engineering (M Eng, MS, PhD); geotectonics (M Eng, MS, PhD); German area studies (MA, PhD); German history (MA, PhD); German intellectual history (MA, PhD); Germanic linguistics (MA, PhD); Germanic literature (MA, PhD); Greek and Latin language and linguistics (PhD); health administration (MHA); health management and policy (PhD); heat and mass transfer (M Eng, MS, PhD); heat transfer (M Eng, MS, PhD); Hebrew and Judaic studies (MA, PhD); Hispanic literature (PhD); historic preservation planning (MA); historical archaeology (MA); history and philosophy of science and technology (MA, PhD); history of architecture (MA, PhD); history of photography (PhD); history of science (MA, PhD); history of urban development (MA, PhD); horticultural crop management systems (MPS); housing and design (MS); human computer interaction (PhD); human development and family studies (MA, PhD); human dimensions of natural resources management (MPS, MS, PhD); human ecology (MA, MHA, MPA, MPS, MS, PhD); human experimental psychology (PhD); human factors and ergonomics (MS); human nutrition (MPS, PhD); human resource studies (MILR, MPS, MS, PhD); human-computer interaction (MS, PhD); human-environment relations (MS); human-plant interactions (MPS, PhD); Indo-European linguistics (MA, PhD); industrial and labor relations problems (MILR, MPS, MS, PhD); industrial biotechnology (M Eng, MPS, MS, PhD); industrial organization and control (PhD); information organization and retrieval (M Eng, PhD); information science (PhD); information systems (PhD); infrared astronomy (PhD); inorganic chemistry (PhD); insect behavior (MS, PhD); insect biochemistry (MS, PhD); insect ecology (MS, PhD); insect genetics (MS, PhD); insect morphology (MS, PhD); insect pathology (MS, PhD); insect physiology (MS, PhD); insect systematics (MS, PhD); insect toxicology and insecticide chemistry (MS, PhD); integrated pest management (MS, PhD); interior design (MA, MPS); international agriculture and development (MPS); international and comparative labor (MILR, MPS, MS, PhD); international development (MPS); international development planning (MRP, PhD); international economics (PhD); international food science (MPS, MS, PhD); international nutrition (MPS, PhD); international planning (MPS); international population (MPS); international relations (PhD); international spatial problems (MA, MS, PhD); Islamic art (PhD); Italian linguistics (PhD); Italian literature (PhD); kinetics and catalysis (M Eng, MS, PhD); Korean history (PhD); Korean literature (PhD); labor economics (MILR, MPS, MS, PhD); landscape architecture (MLA, MPS); language and communication (MS, PhD); Latin American archaeology (MA); Latin American art (PhD); Latin American history (MA, PhD); learning, teaching, and social policy (MPS, MS, PhD); lesbian, bisexual, and gay literary studies (PhD); literary criticism and theory (PhD); location theory (MS, PhD); manufacturing systems engineering (PhD); marine geology (MS, PhD); marketing and food distribution (MS, PhD); materials and manufacturing engineering (M Eng, MS, PhD); materials chemistry (PhD); materials engineering (M Eng, PhD); materials science (M Eng, PhD); mathematical programming (PhD); mathematical statistics (MS, PhD); mathematics (PhD); mathematics 7–12 (MS); mechanical systems and design (M Eng, MS, PhD); mechanics of materials (MS, PhD); media communication and society (MS, PhD); medical and veterinary entomology (MS, PhD); medieval and Renaissance Latin literature (PhD); medieval archaeology (MA, PhD); medieval art (PhD); medieval Chinese history (MA, PhD); medieval history (MA, PhD); medieval literature (PhD); medieval music (PhD); medieval philology and linguistics (PhD); medieval philosophy (PhD); Mediterranean and Near Eastern archaeology (MA); methodology (MA, PhD); microbiology (PhD); mineralogy (M Eng, MS, PhD); modern art (PhD); modern Chinese history (MA, PhD); modern Chinese literature (PhD); modern European history (MA, PhD); modern Japanese history (MA, PhD); modern Japanese literature (PhD); modern Middle Eastern history (PhD); molecular biochemistry (MPS, PhD); molecular biology (PhD); monetary and macro economics (MA, PhD); multiphase flows (M Eng, MS, PhD); multiregional economic analysis (MA, MS, PhD); musicology (PhD); nanobiotechnology (M Eng, MPS, MS, PhD); neurobiology (PhD); nutritional and food toxicology (MS, PhD); Old and Middle English (PhD); old Norse (MA, PhD); operating systems (M Eng, PhD); operations research and industrial engineering (M Eng); organic chemistry (PhD); organizational behavior (MILR, MPS, MS, PhD); organizational communication (MS, PhD); organizations (MA, PhD); organometallic chemistry (PhD); paleobotany (PhD); paleontology (M Eng, MS, PhD); parallel computing (M Eng, PhD); peace science (MA, MS, PhD); performance practice (DMA); personality and social psychology (PhD); petroleum geology (M Eng, MS, PhD); petrology (M Eng, MS, PhD); philosophy (PhD); phonetics (MA, PhD);

phonological theory (MA, PhD); physical chemistry (PhD); physics (MS, PhD); physiology and ecology of horticultural crops (MPS, MS, PhD); physiology of reproduction (MPS, MS, PhD); planetary geology (M Eng, MS, PhD); planetary studies (PhD); planning methods (MA, MS, PhD); planning theory and systems analysis (MRP, PhD); plant biochemistry (MS, PhD); plant breeding (MPS, MS, PhD); plant cell biology (MS, PhD); plant ecology (MS, PhD); plant genetics (MPS, MS, PhD); plant microbe pathology (MPS, MS, PhD); plant molecular biology (MS, PhD); plant morphology, anatomy and biomechanics (MS, PhD); plant pathology (MPS, MS, PhD); plant physiology (MS, PhD); plant protection (MPS); policy analysis (MA, PhD); policy and institutional analysis (PhD); political methodology (PhD); political sociology/social movements (MA, PhD); political thought (PhD); polymer chemistry (PhD); polymer science (MS, PhD); polymers (M Eng, MS, PhD); population and development (MS, PhD); Precambrian geology (M Eng, MS, PhD); premodern Islamic history (MA, PhD); premodern Japanese history (MA, PhD); probability (MS, PhD); program development and evaluation (MPS, MS, PhD); programming environments (M Eng, PhD); programming languages and methodology (M Eng, PhD); prose fiction (PhD); public affairs (MPA); public finance (PhD); public policy (PhD); public policy analysis (MS, PhD); quantitative ecology (MS, PhD); Quaternary geology (M Eng, MS, PhD); racial and ethnic relations (MA, PhD); radio astronomy (PhD); radiophysics (PhD); real estate (MPS); regional economics and development planning (MRP, PhD); regional science (MRP, PhD); remote sensing (M Eng, MS, PhD); Renaissance art (PhD); Renaissance history (MA, PhD); resource economics (PhD); Restoration and the eighteenth-century (PhD); risk assessment, management and public policy (MS, PhD); robotics (M Eng, PhD); rock mechanics (M Eng, MS, PhD); Romance linguistics (MA, PhD); rural and environmental sociology (MS, PhD); Russian history (MA, PhD); sampling (MS, PhD); science and technology policy (MPS); science, environment and health communication (MS, PhD); scientific computing (M Eng, PhD); second language acquisition (MA, PhD); sedimentology (M Eng, MS, PhD); seismology (M Eng, MS, PhD); semantics (MA, PhD); sensory evaluation (MPS, MS, PhD); Slavic linguistics (MA, PhD); social and health systems planning (MRP, PhD); social aspects of information (PhD); social networks (MA, PhD); social psychology (MA, PhD); social psychology of communication (MS, PhD); social stratification (MA, PhD); social studies of science and technology (MA, PhD); sociocultural anthropology (PhD); sociolinguistics (MA, PhD); soil science (MS, PhD); solid mechanics (MS, PhD); South Asian history (PhD); South Asian linguistics (MA, PhD); South Asian literature and culture (PhD); South Asian studies (MA); Southeast Asian art (PhD); Southeast Asian history (MA, PhD); Southeast Asian linguistics (MA, PhD); Southeast Asian literature and culture (PhD); Southeast Asian studies (MA); Spanish linguistics (PhD); state, economy, and society (MS, PhD); statistical computing (MS, PhD); stochastic processes (MS, PhD); Stone Age archaeology (MA); stratigraphy (M Eng, MS, PhD); structural engineering (M Eng, MS, PhD); structural geology (M Eng, MS, PhD); structural mechanics (M Eng, MS); surface science (M Eng, MS, PhD); sustainable systems (M Eng, MPS, MS, PhD); syntactic theory (MA, PhD); synthetic biology (MS); syntheticbiology (M Eng, MPS, PhD); systematic botany (PhD); systems engineering (M Eng, PhD); textile science (MS, PhD); the nineteenth century (PhD); the twentieth century (PhD); theatre history (PhD); theatre theory and aesthetics (PhD); theoretical astrophysics (PhD); theoretical chemistry (PhD); theoretical physics (MS, PhD); theory and criticism (PhD); theory and criticism of architecture (M Arch); theory of computation (M Eng, PhD); theory of music (MA); transportation engineering (MS, PhD); transportation systems engineering (M Eng); urban and regional economics (MA, MS, PhD); urban and regional theory (MRP, PhD); urban design (M Arch); urban planning history (MRP, PhD); visual studies (PhD); water resource systems (M Eng, MS, PhD); wildlife science (MPS, MS, PhD); women's literature (PhD). Electronic applications accepted.

Field of Hotel Administration Offers hospitality management (MMH); hotel administration (MS, PhD). Electronic applications accepted.

Graduate Field in the Law School Offers law (JSD). Electronic applications accepted.

Graduate Field of Management Offers accounting (PhD); finance (PhD); marketing (PhD); organizational behavior (PhD); production and operations management (PhD). Electronic applications accepted.

Samuel Curtis Johnson Graduate School of Management Students: 573 full-time (172 women); includes 122 minority (24 Black or African American, non-Hispanic/Latino; 2 American Indian or Alaska Native, non-Hispanic/Latino; 74 Asian, non-Hispanic/Latino; 12 Hispanic/Latino; 10 Two or more races, non-Hispanic/Latino), 168 international. Average age 28. 1,600 applicants, 33% accepted, 280 enrolled. *Faculty:* 71 full-time (18 women). Expenses: Contact institution. *Financial support:* Fellowships, institutionally sponsored loans, and scholarships/grants available. Financial award applicants required to submit FAFSA. In 2018, 283 master's awarded. Offers business administration (Exec MBA); management (MBA, PhD); management - accounting (MPS). *Application deadline:* For fall admission, 10/8 for domestic and international students; for winter admission, 11/5 for domestic and international students; for spring admission, 1/8 for domestic and international students; for summer admission, 4/8 for domestic and international students. *Application fee:* $200. Electronic applications accepted. *Application Contact:* Admissions Office, 800-847-2082, Fax: 607-255-0065, E-mail: mba@johnson.cornell.edu. *Dean,* Dr. Mark Nelson, 607-255-6418, E-mail: dean@johnson.cornell.edu.

CORNERSTONE UNIVERSITY, Grand Rapids, MI 49525-5897

General Information Independent-religious, coed, comprehensive institution. *Graduate housing:* Rooms and/or apartments available on a first-come, first-served basis to single and married students.

GRADUATE UNITS

Graduate Programs *Program availability:* Part-time, online learning. Offers business administration (MBA); education (MA Ed); management (MSM); teaching English to speakers of other languages (MA, Graduate Certificate). Programs also offered at Holland, Kalamazoo, and Troy, MI campuses. Electronic applications accepted.

COVENANT COLLEGE, Lookout Mountain, GA 30750

General Information Independent-religious, coed, comprehensive institution. *Graduate housing:* Room and/or apartments available on a first-come, first-served basis to single students; on-campus housing not available to married students. Housing application deadline: 5/1.

GRADUATE UNITS

Program in Education *Program availability:* Part-time. Offers education (M Ed, MAT).

COVENANT THEOLOGICAL SEMINARY, St. Louis, MO 63141-8697

General Information Independent-religious, coed, graduate-only institution. *Graduate housing:* Rooms and/or apartments available on a first-come, first-served basis to single and married students.

GRADUATE UNITS
Graduate and Professional Programs *Program availability:* Part-time, evening/weekend, online learning. Offers theology (M Div, MA, MAC, MAEM, Th M, D Min, Certificate). Electronic applications accepted.

COX COLLEGE, Springfield, MO 65802
General Information Independent, coed, primarily women, comprehensive institution.
GRADUATE UNITS
Program in Occupational Therapy Offers occupational therapy (MSOT).
Programs in Nursing Offers clinical nurse leader (MSN); family nurse practitioner (MSN); nurse educator (MSN). Electronic applications accepted.

CRANBROOK ACADEMY OF ART, Bloomfield Hills, MI 48303-0801
General Information Independent, coed, graduate-only institution. *Graduate housing:* Room and/or apartments available on a first-come, first-served basis to single students; on-campus housing not available to married students. Housing application deadline: 4/1.
GRADUATE UNITS
Program in Architecture Offers architecture (M Arch). Electronic applications accepted.
Program in Fine Arts Offers 2d design (MFA); 3d design (MFA); ceramics (MFA); fiber (MFA); metalsmithing (MFA); painting (MFA); photography (MFA); print media (MFA); sculpture (MFA). Electronic applications accepted.

CRANDALL UNIVERSITY, Moncton, NB E1C 9L7, Canada
General Information Independent-religious, coed, comprehensive institution.
GRADUATE UNITS
Graduate Programs

CREIGHTON UNIVERSITY, Omaha, NE 68178-0001
General Information Independent-religious, coed, university. CGS member. *Graduate housing:* Rooms and/or apartments available on a first-come, first-served basis to single and married students. Housing application deadline: 5/1. *Research affiliation:* U.S. Department of Education (DOE) (student support services), National Institutes of Health (asthma), U.S. Department of Commerce (atmospheric science), National Science Foundation (business and education).
GRADUATE UNITS
College of Nursing *Program availability:* Part-time, blended/hybrid learning. Offers adult gerontology acute care nurse practitioner (DNP, Post-Master's Certificate); adult gerontology primary care nurse practitioner (DNP); clinical nurse leader (MSN, Post-Graduate Certificate); clinical systems administration (MSN, DNP); family nurse practitioner (DNP, Post-Master's Certificate); neonatal nurse practitioner (DNP, Post-Master's Certificate); nursing (Post-Graduate Certificate); pediatric acute care nurse practitioner (DNP, Post-Master's Certificate); psychiatric mental health nurse practitioner (DNP). Electronic applications accepted.
Graduate School *Program availability:* Part-time, evening/weekend, 100% online, blended/hybrid learning. Offers emergency medical services (MS); health and wellness coaching (MS); health care ethics (MS); healthcare management (MHM); leadership (Ed D); negotiation and conflict resolution (MS); organizational leadership (MS); public health (MPH). Electronic applications accepted.
College of Arts and Sciences Students: 55 full-time (42 women), 189 part-time (138 women); includes 15 minority (3 Black or African American, non-Hispanic/Latino; 2 American Indian or Alaska Native, non-Hispanic/Latino; 4 Asian, non-Hispanic/Latino; 3 Hispanic/Latino; 2 Native Hawaiian or other Pacific Islander, non-Hispanic/Latino; 1 Two or more races, non-Hispanic/Latino), 8 international. Average age 32. 26 applicants, 77% accepted, 10 enrolled. *Faculty:* 119 full-time (37 women). Expenses: Contact institution. *Financial support:* In 2018–19, 8 fellowships with full and partial tuition reimbursements (averaging $12,000 per year), 4 teaching assistantships with full and partial tuition reimbursements (averaging $12,000 per year) were awarded; scholarships/grants and tuition waivers (partial) also available. Financial award applicants required to submit FAFSA. In 2018, 98 master's awarded. *Program availability:* Part-time, 100% online, blended/hybrid learning. Offers arts and sciences (M Ed, MA, MFA, MS); creative writing (MA, MFA); educational leadership (MS); elementary school guidance (MS); elementary teaching (M Ed); physics (MS); school counseling and preventive mental health (MS); secondary school guidance (MS); secondary teaching (M Ed); teaching (M Ed). *Application deadline:* For fall admission, 3/1 for domestic and international students; for winter admission, 10/1 for domestic students, 7/1 for international students; for spring admission, 4/1 for domestic students, 10/1 for international students. Applications are processed on a rolling basis. *Application fee:* $50. Electronic applications accepted. *Application Contact:* Lindsay Johnson, Director of Graduate and Adult Recruitment, 402-280-2703, Fax: 402-280-2423, E-mail: gradschool@creighton.edu. *Dean,* Dr. Bridget M. Keegan, 402-280-4015, E-mail: bridgetkeegan@creighton.edu.
Heider College of Business *Program availability:* Part-time, evening/weekend, 100% online, blended/hybrid learning. Offers accounting (MAC); business administration (MBA, DBA); business intelligence and analytics (MS); finance (M Fin); investment management and financial analysis (MIMFA). Electronic applications accepted.
School of Dentistry Offers dentistry (DDS).
School of Law *Program availability:* Part-time. Offers law (MS, JD, Certificate); negotiation and conflict resolution (MS, Certificate). Electronic applications accepted.
School of Medicine Offers biomedical sciences (MS, PhD); clinical anatomy (MS); medical microbiology and immunology (MS, PhD); medicine (MS, MD, PhD); pharmaceutical sciences (MS); pharmacology (MS, PhD). Electronic applications accepted.
School of Pharmacy and Health Professions *Program availability:* Online learning. Offers occupational therapy (OTD); pharmaceutical sciences (MS); pharmacy (Pharm D); pharmacy and health professions (MS, DPT, OTD, Pharm D); physical therapy (DPT). Electronic applications accepted.

CRISWELL COLLEGE, Dallas, TX 75246-1537
General Information Independent-religious, coed, comprehensive institution. *Graduate housing:* On-campus housing not available.
GRADUATE UNITS
Graduate School of the Bible *Program availability:* Part-time. Offers biblical studies (M Div); Christian leadership (MA); counseling (MA); Jewish studies (MA); ministry (MA); theological and biblical studies (MA). Electronic applications accepted.

CROWN COLLEGE, St. Bonifacius, MN 55375-9001
General Information Independent-religious, coed, comprehensive institution. *Graduate housing:* Room and/or apartments available on a first-come, first-served basis to married students; on-campus housing not available to single students. Housing application deadline: 7/1.

GRADUATE UNITS
Adult and Graduate Studies *Program availability:* Part-time, evening/weekend, online learning. Offers Christian studies (MA); instructional leadership (MA); international leadership (MA); ministry leadership (MA); organizational leadership (MA). Electronic applications accepted.

CULVER-STOCKTON COLLEGE, Canton, MO 63435-1299
General Information Independent-religious, coed, comprehensive institution.
GRADUATE UNITS
MBA Program Offers accounting and finance (MBA).

CUMBERLAND UNIVERSITY, Lebanon, TN 37087
General Information Independent, coed, comprehensive institution. *Graduate housing:* Room and/or apartments available on a first-come, first-served basis; on-campus housing not available to married students.
GRADUATE UNITS
Program in Business Administration *Program availability:* Part-time, evening/weekend. Offers business administration (MBA).
Program in Education *Program availability:* Part-time, evening/weekend, online learning. Offers education (MAE).
Program in Public Service Administration *Program availability:* Part-time, evening/weekend. Offers public service administration (MS).

CUNY CRAIG NEWMARK GRADUATE SCHOOL OF JOURNALISM, New York, NY 10018
General Information City-supported, coed, graduate-only institution.
GRADUATE UNITS
Graduate Program Offers entrepreneurial journalism (MA); journalism (MA); social journalism (MA). Electronic applications accepted.

CURRY COLLEGE, Milton, MA 02186-9984
General Information Independent, coed, comprehensive institution. *Graduate housing:* On-campus housing not available. *Research affiliation:* Literacy Centers/GED Programs.
GRADUATE UNITS
Graduate Studies *Program availability:* Part-time, evening/weekend. Offers business administration (MBA); criminal justice (MA); elementary education (M Ed); finance (Certificate); foundations (non-license) (M Ed); nursing (MSN); reading (M Ed, Certificate); special education (M Ed).

CURTIS INSTITUTE OF MUSIC, Philadelphia, PA 19103-6107
General Information Independent, coed, comprehensive institution. *Graduate housing:* On-campus housing not available.
GRADUATE UNITS
Graduate Studies Offers opera (MM).

DAEMEN COLLEGE, Amherst, NY 14226-3592
General Information Independent, coed, comprehensive institution. *Enrollment:* 551 full-time matriculated graduate/professional students (441 women), 240 part-time matriculated graduate/professional students (201 women). *Enrollment by degree level:* 643 master's, 124 doctoral, 25 other advanced degrees. *Graduate faculty:* 74 full-time (53 women), 78 part-time/adjunct (46 women). *Tuition:* Part-time $977 per credit hour. *Required fees:* $125; $14 per credit hour. *Graduate housing:* Room and/or apartments available on a first-come, first-served basis to single students; on-campus housing not available to married students. Typical cost: $9850 per year ($13,315 including board). Room and board charges vary according to board plan, campus/location and housing facility selected. Housing application deadline: 8/31. *Student services:* Campus employment opportunities, campus safety program, career counseling, exercise/wellness program, free psychological counseling, international student services, low-cost health insurance, multicultural affairs office, services for students with disabilities. *Library facilities:* Research and Information Commons. *Collection:* Books: 85,205 (physical), 138,085 (digital/electronic); Serial titles: 488 (physical); Databases: 38. Weekly public service hours: 117; students can reserve study rooms.

Computer facilities: 163 computers available on campus for general student use. A campuswide network can be accessed from student residence rooms and from off campus. Online class registration is available.
Website: http://www.daemen.edu/

General Application Contact: Megan Beardi, Senior Assistant Director of Graduate Admissions, 716-566-7861, Fax: 716-839-8229, E-mail: mbeardi@daemen.edu.

GRADUATE UNITS
Applied Behavior Analysis Programs
Athletic Training Programs
Education Programs Students: 233 full-time (210 women), 21 part-time (18 women); includes 4 minority (1 Black or African American, non-Hispanic/Latino; 3 Hispanic/Latino), 1 international. Average age 22. 76 applicants, 93% accepted, 68 enrolled. *Faculty:* 16 full-time (12 women), 19 part-time/adjunct (14 women). Expenses: Contact institution. *Financial support:* Scholarships/grants and unspecified assistantships available. Support available to part-time students. Financial award applicants required to submit FAFSA. In 2018, 204 master's awarded. *Program availability:* Part-time. Offers adolescence education (MS); childhood education (MS); childhood special education (MS); childhood special-alternative certification (MS); early childhood special-alternative certification (MS). *Application deadline:* Applications are processed on a rolling basis. *Application fee:* $25. Electronic applications accepted. *Application Contact:* Megan Beardi, Senior Assistant Director of Graduate Admissions, 716-566-7861, Fax: 716-839-8229, E-mail: mbeardi@daemen.edu. *Department Chair,* Dr. Elizabeth Heilman, 716-839-8553, E-mail: eheilman@daemen.edu.
International Business Program Students: 4 full-time (2 women), 5 part-time (3 women); includes 1 minority (Black or African American, non-Hispanic/Latino), 2 international. Average age 34. 7 applicants, 57% accepted, 2 enrolled. *Faculty:* 3 full-time (2 women), 3 part-time/adjunct (1 woman). Expenses: Contact institution. *Financial support:* Scholarships/grants and unspecified assistantships available. Support available to part-time students. Financial award applicants required to submit FAFSA. In 2018, 4 master's awarded. *Program availability:* Part-time, evening/weekend. Offers global business (MS). *Application deadline:* Applications are processed on a rolling basis. *Application fee:* $25. Electronic applications accepted. *Application Contact:* Megan Beardi, Senior Assistant Director of Graduate Admissions, 716-566-7861, Fax: 716-839-8229, E-mail: mbeardi@daemen.edu. *Director of International Business Program,* Dr. Torsten Doering, 716-839-8239, E-mail: tdoering@daemen.edu.

Leadership and Innovation Programs Students: 21 part-time (15 women); includes 3 minority (2 Black or African American, non-Hispanic/Latino; 1 Hispanic/Latino). Average age 38. 10 applicants, 70% accepted, 6 enrolled. *Faculty:* 1 (woman) full-time, 8 part-time/adjunct (4 women). Expenses: Contact institution. *Financial support:* Scholarships/grants and unspecified assistantships available. Support available to part-time students. Financial award applicants required to submit FAFSA. In 2018, 8 master's awarded. *Program availability:* Part-time-only, evening/weekend. Offers business (MS); health professions (MS); not-for-profit organizations (MS). *Application deadline:* Applications are processed on a rolling basis. *Application fee:* $25. Electronic applications accepted. *Application Contact:* Megan Beardi, Senior Assistant Director of Graduate Admissions, 716-566-7861, Fax: 716-839-8229, E-mail: mbeardi@daemen.edu. *Director,* Christina Coyle-Lenz, 716-839-8342, E-mail: ccoyle@daemen.edu.

Nursing Programs Students: 4 full-time (2 women), 87 part-time (75 women); includes 21 minority (15 Black or African American, non-Hispanic/Latino; 1 Asian, non-Hispanic/Latino; 4 Hispanic/Latino; 1 Two or more races, non-Hispanic/Latino), 2 international. Average age 37. 53 applicants, 81% accepted, 28 enrolled. *Faculty:* 7 full-time (all women), 9 part-time/adjunct (all women). Expenses: Contact institution. *Financial support:* Scholarships/grants and unspecified assistantships available. Support available to part-time students. Financial award applicants required to submit FAFSA. In 2018, 41 master's awarded. *Program availability:* Part-time. Offers adult nurse practitioner (MS, Post Master's Certificate); nurse executive leadership (Post Master's Certificate); nursing education (MS, Post Master's Certificate); nursing executive leadership (MS); nursing practice (DNP); palliative care nursing (Post Master's Certificate). *Application deadline:* Applications are processed on a rolling basis. *Application fee:* $25. Electronic applications accepted. *Application Contact:* Megan Beardi, Senior Assistant Director of Graduate Admissions, 716-566-7861, Fax: 716-839-8229, E-mail: mbeardi@daemen.edu. *Department Chair,* Dr. Cheryl Nosek, 716-839-8273, E-mail: cnosek@daemen.edu.

Paralegal Certificate Programs

Physical Therapy Programs Students: 124 full-time (78 women), 9 part-time (2 women); includes 17 minority (3 Black or African American, non-Hispanic/Latino; 7 Asian, non-Hispanic/Latino; 7 Hispanic/Latino). Average age 24. 293 applicants. *Faculty:* 20 full-time (13 women), 25 part-time/adjunct (10 women). Expenses: Contact institution. *Financial support:* Scholarships/grants and unspecified assistantships available. Financial award applicants required to submit FAFSA. In 2018, 67 doctorates awarded. Offers orthopedic manual physical therapy (Advanced Certificate); physical therapy-direct entry (DPT); transitional (DPT). *Application deadline:* For fall admission, 1/15 for domestic and international students. *Application fee:* $25. Electronic applications accepted. *Application Contact:* Megan Beardi, Senior Assistant Director of Graduate Admissions, 716-566-7861, Fax: 716-839-8229, E-mail: mbeardi@daemen.edu. *Department Chair,* Dr. Gregory Ford, 716-839-8547, E-mail: gford@daemen.edu.

Physician Assistant Programs Students: 96 full-time (76 women); includes 6 minority (2 Black or African American, non-Hispanic/Latino; 1 Asian, non-Hispanic/Latino; 3 Hispanic/Latino). Average age 24. 1,146 applicants, 1% accepted, 11 enrolled. *Faculty:* 9 full-time (4 women), 1 part-time/adjunct (0 women). Expenses: Contact institution. *Financial support:* Scholarships/grants and unspecified assistantships available. Financial award applicants required to submit FAFSA. In 2018, 55 master's awarded. Offers physician assistant (MS). *Application deadline:* For fall admission, 1/15 for domestic and international students. *Application fee:* $25. Electronic applications accepted. *Application Contact:* Megan Beardi, Senior Assistant Director of Graduate Admissions, 716-566-7861, Fax: 716-839-8229, E-mail: mbeardi@daemen.edu. *Program Director & Department Chair,* Dr. Gregg Shutts, 716-839-8316, E-mail: gshutts@daemen.edu.

Public Health Programs Students: 17 full-time (15 women), 4 part-time (3 women); includes 8 minority (6 Black or African American, non-Hispanic/Latino; 1 Asian, non-Hispanic/Latino; 1 Two or more races, non-Hispanic/Latino), 1 international. Average age 26. 18 applicants, 61% accepted, 9 enrolled. *Faculty:* 4 full-time (2 women), 6 part-time/adjunct (4 women). Expenses: Contact institution. *Financial support:* Scholarships/grants and unspecified assistantships available. Support available to part-time students. Financial award applicants required to submit FAFSA. In 2018, 8 master's awarded. *Program availability:* Part-time, evening/weekend. Offers community health education (MPH); epidemiology (MPH); generalist (MPH). *Application deadline:* Applications are processed on a rolling basis. *Application fee:* $25. Electronic applications accepted. *Application Contact:* Megan Beardi, Senior Assistant Director of Graduate Admissions, 716-566-7861, Fax: 716-839-8229, E-mail: mbeardi@daemen.edu. *Director of Masters in Public Health,* Dr. Brian Wrotniak, 716-839-8298, E-mail: bwrotnia@daemen.edu.

Social Work Programs Students: 46 full-time (40 women), 2 part-time (1 woman); includes 11 minority (7 Black or African American, non-Hispanic/Latino; 3 Hispanic/Latino; 1 Two or more races, non-Hispanic/Latino). Average age 28. 68 applicants, 69% accepted, 36 enrolled. *Faculty:* 6 full-time (4 women). Expenses: Contact institution. *Financial support:* Scholarships/grants and unspecified assistantships available. Support available to part-time students. Financial award applicants required to submit FAFSA. In 2018, 12 master's awarded. *Program availability:* Part-time, 100% online, blended/hybrid learning. Offers social work (MSW). *Application deadline:* Applications are processed on a rolling basis. *Application fee:* $25. Electronic applications accepted. *Application Contact:* Megan Beardi, Senior Assistant Director of Graduate Admissions, 716-566-7861, Fax: 716-839-8229, E-mail: mbeardi@daemen.edu. *MSW Program Director,* Dr. Diane Bessel-Matteson, 716-566-7876, E-mail: dbessel@daemen.edu.

DAKOTA STATE UNIVERSITY, Madison, SD 57042-1799

General Information State-supported, coed, comprehensive institution. CGS member. *Enrollment:* 3,382 graduate, professional, and undergraduate students; 69 full-time matriculated graduate/professional students (16 women), 284 part-time matriculated graduate/professional students (88 women). *Enrollment by degree level:* 226 master's, 114 doctoral, 13 other advanced degrees. *Graduate faculty:* 39 full-time (11 women). *International tuition:* $14,311 full-time. *Tuition, area resident:* Full-time $7666. *Tuition, state resident:* Full-time $7666. Tuition, nonresident: full-time $14,311. *Required fees:* $953. *Graduate housing:* Room and/or apartments available on a first-come, first-served basis to single students; on-campus housing not available to married students. *Student services:* Campus employment opportunities, campus safety program, career counseling, exercise/wellness program, free psychological counseling, grant writing training, international student services, low-cost health insurance, multicultural affairs office, services for students with disabilities, teacher training, writing training. *Library facilities:* Karl E. Mundt Library plus 1 other. *Collection:* Books: 49,261 (physical), 218,951 (digital/electronic); Serial titles: 200 (physical), 120 (digital/electronic); Databases: 140. Weekly public service hours: 85. *Research affiliation:* East River

Electric (Computer Science), Raven Industries (Information Security), South Dakota Networks (SDN) (Information Security), SD Attorney General (Digital Forensics), SD Dept of Health (Healthcare), NSF EPSCoR (Data Science).

Computer facilities: 110 computers available on campus for general student use. A campuswide network can be accessed from student residence rooms and from off campus. Online class registration is available. Website: http://www.dsu.edu/

General Application Contact: Erin Blankespoor, Senior Secretary, Office of Graduate Studies and Research, 605-256-5799, E-mail: erin.blankespoor@dsu.edu.

GRADUATE UNITS

Beacom College of Computer and Cyber Sciences Students: 30 full-time (6 women), 101 part-time (14 women); includes 27 minority (7 Black or African American, non-Hispanic/Latino; 3 American Indian or Alaska Native, non-Hispanic/Latino; 8 Asian, non-Hispanic/Latino; 5 Hispanic/Latino; 2 Native Hawaiian or other Pacific Islander, non-Hispanic/Latino; 2 Two or more races, non-Hispanic/Latino), 8 international. Average age 35. 188 applicants, 36% accepted, 40 enrolled. *Faculty:* 15 full-time (3 women). Expenses: Contact institution. *Financial support:* In 2018–19, 4 students received support. Research assistantships with partial tuition reimbursements available, teaching assistantships with partial tuition reimbursements available, career-related internships or fieldwork, Federal Work-Study, scholarships/grants, unspecified assistantships, and administrative Assistantships available. Support available to part-time students. Financial award applicants required to submit FAFSA. In 2018, 38 master's, 4 other advanced degrees awarded. *Program availability:* Part-time, evening/weekend, online learning. Offers applied computer science (MSACS); banking security (Graduate Certificate); cyber security (D Sc); ethical hacking (Graduate Certificate); information assurance and computer security (MSIA). *Application deadline:* For fall admission, 6/15 for domestic students, 4/15 for international students; for spring admission, 11/15 for domestic students, 9/15 priority date for international students; for summer admission, 4/15 for domestic and international students. Applications are processed on a rolling basis. *Application fee:* $35. Electronic applications accepted. *Application Contact:* Erin Blankespoor, Senior Secretary, Office of Graduate Studies and Research, 605-256-5799, E-mail: erin.blankespoor@dsu.edu. *Dean, Beacom College of Computer and Cyber Science,* Dr. Richard Hanson, 605-256-5838, E-mail: richard.hanson@dsu.edu.

College of Business and Information Systems Students: 40 full-time (11 women), 165 part-time (60 women); includes 56 minority (21 Black or African American, non-Hispanic/Latino; 4 American Indian or Alaska Native, non-Hispanic/Latino; 19 Asian, non-Hispanic/Latino; 10 Hispanic/Latino; 1 Native Hawaiian or other Pacific Islander, non-Hispanic/Latino; 1 Two or more races, non-Hispanic/Latino), 38 international. Average age 38. 246 applicants, 47% accepted, 63 enrolled. *Faculty:* 27 full-time (10 women). Expenses: Contact institution. *Financial support:* In 2018–19, 20 students received support. Research assistantships with partial tuition reimbursements available, teaching assistantships with partial tuition reimbursements available, career-related internships or fieldwork, Federal Work-Study, scholarships/grants, and unspecified assistantships available. Support available to part-time students. Financial award applicants required to submit FAFSA. In 2018, 62 master's, 7 doctorates, 9 other advanced degrees awarded. *Program availability:* Part-time, evening/weekend, 100% online, blended/hybrid learning. Offers analytics (MSA); business analytics (Graduate Certificate); general management (MBA); health informatics (MSHI); information systems (MSIS, D Sc IS); information technology (Graduate Certificate). *Application deadline:* For fall admission, 6/15 for domestic students, 4/15 for international students; for spring admission, 11/15 for domestic students, 9/15 priority date for international students; for summer admission, 4/15 for domestic and international students. Applications are processed on a rolling basis. *Application fee:* $35. Electronic applications accepted. *Application Contact:* Erin Blankespoor, Senior Secretary, Office of Graduate Studies and Research, 605-256-5799, E-mail: erin.blankespoor@dsu.edu. *Dean of College of Business and Information Systems,* Dr. Dorine Bennett, 605-256-5176, E-mail: dorine.bennett@dsu.edu.

College of Education Students: 20 part-time (15 women); includes 1 minority (American Indian or Alaska Native, non-Hispanic/Latino). Average age 34. 12 applicants, 100% accepted, 10 enrolled. *Faculty:* 4 full-time (0 women). Expenses: Contact institution. *Financial support:* In 2018–19, 3 students received support. Career-related internships or fieldwork, Federal Work-Study, scholarships/grants, unspecified assistantships, and administrative assistantships available. Support available to part-time students. Financial award applicants required to submit FAFSA. In 2018, 8 master's awarded. *Program availability:* Part-time-only, evening/weekend, online only, 100% online. Offers educational technology (MSET). *Application deadline:* For fall admission, 6/15 for domestic students; for spring admission, 11/15 for domestic students; for summer admission, 4/15 for domestic students. Applications are processed on a rolling basis. *Application fee:* $35. Electronic applications accepted. *Application Contact:* Dr. Kevin Smith, MSET Program Coordinator, 605-256-5175, Fax: 605-256-7300, E-mail: kevin.smith@dsu.edu. *Dean of College of Education,* Dr. Crystal Pauli, 605-256-5799.

DAKOTA WESLEYAN UNIVERSITY, Mitchell, SD 57301-4398

General Information Independent-religious, coed, comprehensive institution. *Enrollment:* 56 full-time matriculated graduate/professional students (21 women), 30 part-time matriculated graduate/professional students (13 women). *Enrollment by degree level:* 61 master's, 25 other advanced degrees. *Graduate faculty:* 14 part-time/adjunct (8 women). *Tuition:* Full-time $7200; part-time $3600 per credit hour. Tuition and fees vary according to course load and program. *Graduate housing:* On-campus housing not available. *Student services:* Campus employment opportunities, career counseling, services for students with disabilities, teacher training, writing training. *Library facilities:* George and Eleanor McGovern Library plus 1 other.

Computer facilities: 100 computers available on campus for general student use. A campuswide network can be accessed from student residence rooms and from off campus. Online class registration, portal, course management system are available. Website: http://www.dwu.edu/

General Application Contact: Stacy Mock, Coordinator of Graduate Admissions, 605-995-2650, Fax: 605-995-2699, E-mail: admissions@dwv.edu.

GRADUATE UNITS

Program in Education Students: 20 full-time (6 women), 4 part-time (1 woman); includes 8 minority (4 Black or African American, non-Hispanic/Latino; 3 Hispanic/Latino; 1 Two or more races, non-Hispanic/Latino). Average age 26. 12 applicants, 83% accepted, 8 enrolled. *Faculty:* 5 part-time/adjunct (2 women). Expenses: Contact institution. *Financial support:* Applicants required to submit FAFSA. In 2018, 13 master's awarded. *Program availability:* Part-time, evening/weekend, online only, 100% online. Offers curriculum and instruction (MA Ed); educational policy and administration (MA Ed); preK-12 principal certification (MA Ed); secondary certification (MA Ed). *Application deadline:* For fall admission, 8/1 priority date for domestic and international students; for winter admission, 12/1 priority date for domestic students; for spring admission, 4/1 priority date for domestic students, 12/1 priority date for international students. Applications are processed on a rolling basis. *Application fee:* $0. Electronic applications accepted. *Application Contact:* Stacy Mock, Coordinator of Adult and Online Admissions, 605-995-2650, Fax: 605-995-2699, E-mail: admissions@dwu.edu. *Director of Graduate Studies,* Dr. Melissa Weber, 605-995-2630, Fax: 605-995-2609, E-mail: melissa.weber@dwu.edu.

DALHOUSIE UNIVERSITY, Halifax, NS B3H 4R2, Canada

General Information Province-supported, coed, university. *Graduate housing:* Rooms and/or apartments available on a first-come, first-served basis to single and married students. Housing application deadline: 8/1.

GRADUATE UNITS

Faculty of Agriculture *Program availability:* Part-time. Offers agriculture (M Sc).

Faculty of Architecture and Planning Offers architecture and planning (M Arch, M Eng, M Plan, MEDS, MPS). Electronic applications accepted.

School of Planning Offers planning (M Eng, M Plan, MPS). Electronic applications accepted.

Faculty of Arts and Social Sciences *Program availability:* Part-time. Offers arts and social sciences (MA, PhD); classics (MA, PhD); English (MA, PhD); French (MA, PhD); German (MA); history (MA, PhD); international development studies (MA); philosophy (MA, PhD); political science (MA, PhD); social anthropology (MA, PhD); sociology (MA, PhD). Electronic applications accepted.

Fountain School of Performing Arts Offers musicology (MA). Electronic applications accepted.

Faculty of Computer Science Offers computational biology and bioinformatics (M Sc); computer science (MA Sc, MC Sc, PhD); electronic commerce (MEC); health informatics (MHI). Electronic applications accepted.

Faculty of Dentistry Offers dentistryoral and maxillofacial surgery.

Faculty of Engineering Offers biological engineering (M Eng, MA Sc, PhD); chemical engineering (M Eng, MA Sc, PhD); civil engineering (M Eng, MA Sc, PhD); electrical and computer engineering (M Eng, MA Sc, PhD); engineering (M Eng, M Sc, MA Sc, PhD); engineering mathematics (M Sc, PhD); environmental engineering (M Eng, MA Sc); food science (M Sc, PhD); industrial engineering (M Eng, MA Sc, PhD); internetworking (M Eng); mechanical engineering (M Eng, MA Sc, PhD); mineral resource engineering (M Eng, MA Sc, PhD).

School of Biomedical Engineering Offers biomedical engineering (MA Sc, PhD). Electronic applications accepted.

Faculty of Graduate Studies *Program availability:* Part-time, online learning. Offers anatomy and neuroscience (M Sc, PhD); interdisciplinary studies (PhD); medicine (M Sc, PhD); pathology (M Sc, PhD); pharmacology (M Sc, PhD). Electronic applications accepted.

Schulich School of Law *Program availability:* Part-time. Offers law (LL M, JSD). Electronic applications accepted.

Faculty of Health *Program availability:* Part-time, online learning. Offers health (M Sc, MA, MAHSR, MHA, MN, MPH, MSW, PhD).

School of Communication Sciences and Disorders Offers audiology (M Sc); speech-language pathology (M Sc). Electronic applications accepted.

School of Health Administration *Program availability:* Part-time, online learning. Offers health administration (MAHSR, MHA, MPH, PhD). Electronic applications accepted.

School of Health and Human Performance *Program availability:* Part-time. Offers health and human performance (M Sc, MA); health promotion (MA); kinesiology (M Sc); leisure studies (MA). Electronic applications accepted.

School of Nursing *Program availability:* Part-time, online learning. Offers nursing (MN, PhD). Electronic applications accepted.

School of Occupational Therapy *Program availability:* Part-time, evening/weekend, online learning. Offers occupational therapy (entry to profession) (M Sc); occupational therapy (post-professional) (M Sc). Electronic applications accepted.

School of Physiotherapy Offers physiotherapy (entry to profession) (M Sc); physiotherapy (rehabilitation research) (M Sc). Electronic applications accepted.

School of Social Work *Program availability:* Part-time, online learning. Offers social work (MSW). Electronic applications accepted.

Faculty of Management *Program availability:* Part-time. Offers management (MBA, MEC, MES, MIM, MLIS, MMM, MPA, MREM, GDPA); marine affairs (MMM). Electronic applications accepted.

Centre for Advanced Management Education *Program availability:* Part-time, online learning. Offers financial services (MBA); information management (MIM); management (MPA); natural resources (MBA). Electronic applications accepted.

Rowe School of Business *Program availability:* Part-time. Offers business administration (MBA); financial services (MBA). Electronic applications accepted.

School for Resource and Environmental Studies *Program availability:* Part-time. Offers resource and environmental studies (MES, MREM). Electronic applications accepted.

School of Information Management *Program availability:* Part-time. Offers information management (MIM, MLIS). Electronic applications accepted.

School of Public Administration *Program availability:* Part-time. Offers management (MPA); public administration (MPA, GDPA). Electronic applications accepted.

Faculty of Medicine Offers biochemistry and molecular biology (M Sc, PhD); community health and epidemiology (M Sc); medicine (M Sc, MD, PhD); microbiology and immunology (M Sc, PhD); physiology and biophysics (M Sc, PhD). Electronic applications accepted.

Faculty of Science Offers biology (M Sc, PhD); chemistry (M Sc, PhD); clinical psychology (PhD); earth sciences (M Sc, PhD); economics (MA, MDE, PhD); mathematics (M Sc, PhD); oceanography (M Sc, PhD); physics and atmospheric science (M Sc, PhD); psychology (M Sc, PhD); psychology/neuroscience (M Sc, PhD); science (M Sc, MA, MDE, PhD); statistics (M Sc, PhD). Electronic applications accepted.

DALLAS BAPTIST UNIVERSITY, Dallas, TX 75211-9299

General Information Independent-religious, coed, comprehensive institution. *Enrollment:* 4,766 graduate, professional, and undergraduate students; 713 full-time matriculated graduate/professional students (452 women), 1,039 part-time matriculated graduate/professional students (665 women). *Enrollment by degree level:* 1,470 master's, 282 doctoral. *Graduate faculty:* 80 full-time (30 women), 204 part-time/adjunct (81 women). *Tuition:* Full-time $17,262; part-time $959 per credit hour. *Required fees:* $1000; $500 per semester. Tuition and fees vary according to course load and degree level. *Graduate housing:* Room and/or apartments available on a first-come, first-served basis to single students; on-campus housing not available to married students. Typical

cost: $3915 per year ($7992 including board). Room and board charges vary according to board plan and housing facility selected. *Student services:* Campus employment opportunities, campus safety program, career counseling, free psychological counseling, international student services, low-cost health insurance, services for students with disabilities, writing training. *Library facilities:* Vance Memorial Library plus 3 others. *Collection:* Books: 247,606 (physical), 153,056 (digital/electronic); Serial titles: 561 (physical), 46,112 (digital/electronic); Databases: 203. Weekly public service hours: 108.

Computer facilities: 214 computers available on campus for general student use. A campuswide network can be accessed from student residence rooms and from off campus. Online class registration is available.
Website: http://www.dbu.edu/

General Application Contact: Richard Nassar, Director of Admissions, 214-333-6801, Fax: 214-333-5579, E-mail: graduate@dbu.edu.

GRADUATE UNITS

College of Business Expenses: Contact institution. *Program availability:* Part-time, evening/weekend, online learning. Offers business (MA, MBA, MS); conflict resolution management (MA); general management (MA, MS); health care management (MA, MBA); human resource management (MA); international business (MBA); management information systems (MBA); professional sales and management optimization (MA). *Application deadline:* Applications are processed on a rolling basis. *Application fee:* $25. Electronic applications accepted. *Application Contact:* Dr. Sandra Reid, Chair of Graduate Business Programs, 214-333-6860, E-mail: sandra@dbu.edu. *Dean,* Dr. Jeff Johnson, 214-333-5759, E-mail: graduate@dbu.edu.

College of Fine Arts Expenses: Contact institution. *Program availability:* Part-time, evening/weekend. Offers communication (MA). *Application deadline:* Applications are processed on a rolling basis. *Application fee:* $25. Electronic applications accepted. *Application Contact:* Carter Willis, Program Director, 214-333-5867, E-mail: carterw@dbu.edu. *Dean,* Dr. Ronald Bowles, 214-333-5316, E-mail: ronb@dbu.edu.

College of Humanities and Social Sciences Expenses: Contact institution. Offers professional counseling (MA). *Application Contact:* Dr. Mary Becerril, Program Director, 214-333-5265, Fax: 214-333-6819, E-mail: maryb@dbu.edu. *Dean,* Dr. Rob Sullivan, 214-333-5238.

Dorothy M. Bush College of Education Expenses: Contact institution. *Program availability:* Part-time, evening/weekend, online learning. Offers bilingual education (M Ed); charter school administration (M Ed); Christian school administration (M Ed); diagnostician (M Ed); distance learning (M Ed, MAT); early childhood through grade 6 certification (MAT); early childhood-12 (MAT); education (M Ed, MA, MAT, MS, Ed D); educational leadership (M Ed); educational leadership K-12 (Ed D); elementary (MAT); English as a second language (M Ed, MAT); instructional technology (M Ed); kinesiology (M Ed); Montessori (MAT); multisensory (MAT); professional life coaching (M Ed); reading and English as a second language (M Ed); school counseling (M Ed); secondary (MAT); special education (M Ed); sport management (MA); supervision (M Ed). *Application deadline:* Applications are processed on a rolling basis. *Application fee:* $25. Electronic applications accepted. *Application Contact:* Dr. Neil Dugger, Dean, 214-333-5413, E-mail: graduate@dbu.edu. *Dean,* Dr. Neil Dugger, 214-333-5413, E-mail: graduate@dbu.edu.

Gary Cook School of Leadership Expenses: Contact institution. *Program availability:* Part-time, evening/weekend, 100% online, blended/hybrid learning. Offers East Asian studies (MA); European studies (MA); general international studies (MA); global business (MA); higher education leadership (Ed D); international immersion (MA); international ministry (MA); international relations (MA); leadership (M Ed, MA, Ed D, PhD); leadership studies (M Ed, PhD); student affairs leadership (M Ed). *Application deadline:* Applications are processed on a rolling basis. *Application fee:* $25. Electronic applications accepted. *Application Contact:* Richard Nassar, Director of Admissions, 214-333-5242, Fax: 214-333-5447, E-mail: richardn@dbu.edu. *Dean,* Dr. Jack Goodyear, 214-333-5595, Fax: 214-333-6955, E-mail: jackg@dbu.edu.

Graduate School of Ministry Expenses: Contact institution. *Program availability:* Part-time, evening/weekend, online learning. Offers chaplaincy (MA); Christian counseling (MA); Christian heritage (MA); Christian ministry (MA); Christian scriptures (MA); church planting (MA); counseling ministry (MA); discipleship for the family (MA); discipleship through communications (MA); East Asian Studies (MA); English as a second language (MA); family ministry (MA); general (MA); general ministry (MA); general studies (MA); global communication (MA); global studies (MA); international business (MA); leadership (MA); leading the nonprofit organization (MA); local church discipleship (MA); ministry (MA); ministry leadership (MA); missions (MA); professional life coaching (MA); small group ministry (MA); special needs children ministry (MA); special needs family ministry (MA); student ministry (MA); urban ministry (MA); worship leadership (MA); worship theology (MA). *Application deadline:* Applications are processed on a rolling basis. *Application fee:* $25. Electronic applications accepted. *Application Contact:* Richard Nassar, Director of Admissions, 214-333-5242, Fax: 214-333-5447, E-mail: richardn@dbu.edu. *Dean,* Dr. Robert R. Brooks, 214-333-5390, Fax: 214-333-5673, E-mail: bobb@dbu.edu.

Liberal Arts Program Expenses: Contact institution. *Program availability:* Part-time, evening/weekend, online learning. Offers art (MLA); Christian studies (MLA); commercial art (MLA); East Asian studies (MLA); English (MLA); English as a second language (MLA); history (MLA); missions (MLA); political science (MLA). *Application deadline:* Applications are processed on a rolling basis. *Application fee:* $25. Electronic applications accepted. *Application Contact:* Jared Ingram, Director, 214-333-5584, E-mail: jaredi@dbu.edu. *Director,* Jared Ingram, 214-333-5584, E-mail: jaredi@dbu.edu.

Professional Development Program Expenses: Contact institution. *Program availability:* Part-time, evening/weekend, online learning. Offers accounting (MA); church leadership (MA); communication (MA); counseling (MA); criminal justice (MA); English as a second language (MA); finance (MA); higher education (MA); leadership studies (MA); management (MA). *Application deadline:* Applications are processed on a rolling basis. *Application fee:* $25. Electronic applications accepted. *Application Contact:* Jared Ingram, Program Director, 214-333-5584, E-mail: jaredi@dbu.edu. *Program Director,* Jared Ingram, 214-333-5584, E-mail: jaredi@dbu.edu.

DALLAS INTERNATIONAL UNIVERSITY, Dallas, TX 75236

General Information Independent, coed, comprehensive institution.

GRADUATE UNITS

Graduate Programs *Program availability:* Part-time. Offers applied linguistics (MA, Certificate); language development (MA). Electronic applications accepted.

DALLAS THEOLOGICAL SEMINARY, Dallas, TX 75204-6499

General Information Independent, coed, graduate-only institution. *Graduate housing:* Rooms and/or apartments available on a first-come, first-served basis to single and married students.

GRADUATE UNITS

Graduate Programs *Program availability:* Part-time, online learning. Offers adult education (Th M); apologetics (Th M); Bible backgrounds (Th M); Bible translation (Th M); Biblical and theological studies (Certificate); biblical counseling (MA); biblical exegesis and linguistics (MA); biblical exposition (PhD); biblical studies (MA); Biblical theology (Th M); children's education (Th M); Christian education (MA, D Min); Christian leadership (MA); cross-cultural ministries (MA); educational administration (Th M); educational leadership (MA); evangelism and discipleship (Th M); exposition of Biblical books (Th M); family life education (Th M); general studies (Th M); Hebrew and cognate studies (Th M); hermeneutics (Th M); historical theology (Th M); homiletics (Th M); intercultural ministries (Th M); Jesus studies (Th M); leadership studies (Th M); media and communication (MA); media arts (Th M); ministry (D Min); ministry with women (Th M); New Testament studies (Th M, PhD); Old Testament studies (Th M, PhD); parachurch ministries (Th M); pastoral care and counseling (Th M); pastoral theology and practice (Th M); philosophy (Th M); sacred theology (STM); spiritual formation (Th M); systematic theology (Th M); teaching in Christian institutions (Th M); theological studies (PhD); urban ministries (Th M); worship studies (Th M); youth education (Th M). Electronic applications accepted.

DANIEL MORGAN GRADUATE SCHOOL OF NATIONAL SECURITY, Washington, DC 20036

General Information Independent, coed, graduate-only institution.

GRADUATE UNITS

Graduate Programs Offers integrated risk value communications (MA); national security (MA).

DAOIST TRADITIONS COLLEGE OF CHINESE MEDICAL ARTS, Asheville, NC 28801

General Information Proprietary, coed, graduate-only institution.

GRADUATE UNITS
Graduate Programs

DARTMOUTH COLLEGE, Hanover, NH 03755

General Information Independent, coed, university. CGS member. *Enrollment:* 6,571 graduate, professional, and undergraduate students; 1,973 full-time matriculated graduate/professional students (929 women), 106 part-time matriculated graduate/professional students (63 women). *Graduate faculty:* 452 full-time (139 women), 132 part-time/adjunct (45 women). *Graduate housing:* Rooms and/or apartments available on a first-come, first-served basis to single and married students. Housing application deadline: 5/15. *Student services:* Campus employment opportunities, campus safety program, career counseling, free psychological counseling, international student services, low-cost health insurance, services for students with disabilities, teacher training, writing training. *Library facilities:* Baker-Berry Library plus 8 others. *Collection:* Books: 2.5 million (physical), 991,009 (digital/electronic); Serial titles: 15,595 (physical). Study areas open 24 hours, 5–7 days a week; students can reserve study rooms.

Computer facilities: Computer purchase and lease plans are available. 200 computers available on campus for general student use. A campuswide network can be accessed from student residence rooms and from off campus. Online class registration is available.

Website: http://www.dartmouth.edu/

General Application Contact: Jane Seibel, Assistant Dean of Recruiting and Diversity, School of Graduate and Advanced Studies, 603-646-6578, Fax: 603-646-3488, E-mail: jane.b.seibel@dartmouth.edu.

GRADUATE UNITS

The Dartmouth Institute Students: 85 full-time (58 women), 58 part-time (34 women); includes 41 minority (7 Black or African American, non-Hispanic/Latino; 2 American Indian or Alaska Native, non-Hispanic/Latino; 18 Asian, non-Hispanic/Latino; 7 Hispanic/Latino; 7 Two or more races, non-Hispanic/Latino; 10 international. Average age 32. 470 applicants, 67% accepted, 136 enrolled. *Faculty:* 30 full-time (16 women), 14 part-time/adjunct (5 women). Expenses: Contact institution. *Financial support:* In 2018–19, fellowships with full tuition reimbursements (averaging $28,200 per year) were awarded; scholarships/grants also available. *Program availability:* Part-time. Offers evaluative clinical sciences (MS, PhD); public health (MPH). *Application deadline:* For fall admission, 1/15 for domestic students. *Application fee:* $135. *Application Contact:* Michelle Ficke, Admissions Manager, 603-650-1540, E-mail: Dartmouth.Institute.Admissions@dartmouth.edu. *Interim Director,* Anna Tosteson, 603-653-0802.

Geisel School of Medicine Students: 399 full-time (231 women), 5 part-time (3 women); includes 169 minority (24 Black or African American, non-Hispanic/Latino; 4 American Indian or Alaska Native, non-Hispanic/Latino; 80 Asian, non-Hispanic/Latino; 47 Hispanic/Latino; 14 Two or more races, non-Hispanic/Latino; 30 international. Average age 27. 6,506 applicants, 4% accepted, 92 enrolled. *Faculty:* 136 full-time (48 women), 37 part-time/adjunct (12 women). Expenses: Contact institution. *Financial support:* Institutionally sponsored loans and scholarships/grants available. In 2018, 72 doctorates awarded. Offers medicine (MD). *Application deadline:* For fall admission, 11/1 for domestic students. *Application fee:* $130. Electronic applications accepted. *Application Contact:* Rand S. Swenson, Chair, Geisel Admissions Committee, 603-650-1505, Fax: 603-650-1560, E-mail: geisel.admissions@dartmouth.edu. *Dean of the Geisel School of Medicine,* Duane Compton, 603-650-1200, E-mail: geisel.administration@dartmouth.edu.

Graduate Program in Molecular and Cellular Biology Students: 76 full-time (37 women); includes 17 minority (3 Asian, non-Hispanic/Latino; 13 Hispanic/Latino; 1 Two or more races, non-Hispanic/Latino; 27 international. Average age 26. 199 applicants, 36% accepted, 22 enrolled. *Faculty:* 72 full-time (17 women), 8 part-time/adjunct (4 women). Expenses: Contact institution. *Financial support:* Fellowships and health care benefits available. In 2018, 9 doctorates awarded. Offers biochemistry (PhD); biological sciences (PhD); genetics (PhD); immunology (PhD); microbiology and molecular pathogenesis (PhD); molecular and cellular biology (PhD). *Application deadline:* For fall admission, 12/1 for domestic students. Applications are processed on a rolling basis. *Application fee:* $0. Electronic applications accepted. *Application Contact:* Janet Cheney, Program Coordinator, 603-650-1612, E-mail: mcb@dartmouth.edu. *Vice Chair,* Dr. Patrick J. Dolph, 603-650-1092, E-mail: mcb@dartmouth.edu.

Guarini School of Graduate and Advanced Studies Students: 564 full-time (238 women), 32 part-time (20 women); includes 93 minority (11 Black or African American, non-Hispanic/Latino; 4 American Indian or Alaska Native, non-Hispanic/Latino; 40 Asian, non-Hispanic/Latino; 25 Hispanic/Latino; 13 Two or more races, non-Hispanic/Latino; 195 international. Average age 30. 1,544 applicants, 31% accepted, 237 enrolled. *Faculty:* 178 full-time (58 women), 68 part-time/adjunct (24 women).

Expenses: Contact institution. *Financial support:* Fellowships, research assistantships, teaching assistantships, career-related internships or fieldwork, institutionally sponsored loans, scholarships/grants, traineeships, tuition waivers (full and partial), and unspecified assistantships available. Support available to part-time students. Financial award application deadline: 4/1; financial award applicants required to submit CSS PROFILE or FAFSA. In 2018, 120 master's, 72 doctorates awarded. Offers biophysical chemistry (MS); chemistry (PhD); cognitive neuroscience (PhD); comparative literature (MA); computer science (MS, PhD); creative writing (MALS); earth sciences (MS, PhD); ecology and evolutionary biology (PhD); mathematics (AM, PhD); music (MA); physics and astronomy (PhD); psychology (PhD); sustainability, ecosystems, and environment (PhD). *Application deadline:* For fall admission, 1/15 for domestic students. Electronic applications accepted. *Application Contact:* Gary Hutchins, Assistant Dean, School of Graduate and Advanced Studies, 603-646-2107, Fax: 603-646-3488, E-mail: g.hutchins@dartmouth.edu. *Dean of Graduate Studies,* Dr. Jon Kull, 603-646-1552, E-mail: f.jon.kull@dartmouth.edu.

Institute for Quantitative Biomedical Sciences Students: 57 full-time (30 women); includes 10 minority (2 Black or African American, non-Hispanic/Latino; 5 Asian, non-Hispanic/Latino; 2 Hispanic/Latino; 1 Two or more races, non-Hispanic/Latino; 27 international. Average age 26. 155 applicants, 35% accepted, 29 enrolled. Expenses: Contact institution. *Financial support:* Fellowships available. In 2018, 1 doctorate awarded. Offers epidemiology (MS); health data science (MS); quantitative biomedical sciences (PhD). PhD offered in collaboration with the Department of Genetics and the Department of Community and Family Medicine. *Application deadline:* For fall admission, 3/1 for domestic students. Applications are processed on a rolling basis. *Application fee:* $75. Electronic applications accepted. *Application Contact:* Gary Hutchins, Assistant Dean, School of Arts and Sciences, 603-646-2107, Fax: 603-646-3488, E-mail: g.hutchins@dartmouth.edu. *Director,* Dr. Micheal Whitfield, 603-650-1109.

Program in Experimental and Molecular Medicine Students: 48 full-time (32 women); includes 9 minority (4 Asian, non-Hispanic/Latino; 3 Hispanic/Latino; 2 Two or more races, non-Hispanic/Latino; 5 international. Average age 27. 87 applicants, 26% accepted, 10 enrolled. *Faculty:* 39 full-time (6 women), 23 part-time/adjunct (10 women). Expenses: Contact institution. *Financial support:* Fellowships and health care benefits available. Offers experimental and molecular medicine. *Application deadline:* For fall admission, 1/1 for domestic and international students. *Application fee:* $75. Electronic applications accepted. *Application Contact:* Gail Egner, Program Administrator, 603-650-4933, Fax: 603-650-4932, E-mail: gail.p.egner@dartmouth.edu. *Director,* Dr. Michael Spinella, 603-650-1126, Fax: 603-650-4932.

Thayer School of Engineering Students: 221 full-time (79 women); includes 29 minority (3 Black or African American, non-Hispanic/Latino; 22 Asian, non-Hispanic/Latino; 2 Hispanic/Latino; 2 Two or more races, non-Hispanic/Latino; 120 international. Average age 24. 606 applicants, 28% accepted, 92 enrolled. *Faculty:* 59 full-time (10 women), 1 part-time/adjunct (0 women). Expenses: Contact institution. *Financial support:* In 2018–19, 200 students received support, including 25 fellowships with full tuition reimbursements available (averaging $27,720 per year), 98 research assistantships with full tuition reimbursements available (averaging $27,720 per year), 27 teaching assistantships with partial tuition reimbursements available (averaging $8,640 per year); career-related internships or fieldwork, institutionally sponsored loans, scholarships/grants, and tuition waivers (full and partial) also available. Financial award application deadline: 2/15; financial award applicants required to submit CSS PROFILE. In 2018, 65 master's, 22 doctorates awarded. Offers biological and chemical engineering (MS, PhD); electrical and computer engineering (MS, PhD); energy engineering (MS, PhD); engineering (M Eng, MEM, MS, PhD); engineering in medicine/biomedical engineering (M Eng, MS, PhD); engineering management (MEM); innovation (PhD); materials sciences and engineering (MS, PhD); mechanical and systems engineering (MS, PhD). *Application deadline:* For fall admission, 1/1 priority date for domestic and international students. Applications are processed on a rolling basis. *Application fee:* $45. Electronic applications accepted. *Application Contact:* Candace S. Potter, Graduate Admissions & Financial Aid Administrator, 603-646-3844, Fax: 603-646-1620, E-mail: candace.s.potter@dartmouth.edu. *Dean,* Dr. Alexis R. Abramson, 603-646-2238, Fax: 603-646-2580, E-mail: Alexis.R.Abramson@Dartmouth.edu.

Tuck School of Business at Dartmouth Students: 582 full-time (259 women); includes 118 minority (27 Black or African American, non-Hispanic/Latino; 1 American Indian or Alaska Native, non-Hispanic/Latino; 52 Asian, non-Hispanic/Latino; 30 Hispanic/Latino; 1 Native Hawaiian or other Pacific Islander, non-Hispanic/Latino; 7 Two or more races, non-Hispanic/Latino; 172 international. Average age 28. 2,610 applicants, 23% accepted, 293 enrolled. *Faculty:* 53 full-time (11 women). Expenses: Contact institution. *Financial support:* Institutionally sponsored loans and scholarships/grants available. Financial award application deadline: 4/1; financial award applicants required to submit FAFSA. In 2018, 282 master's awarded. Offers business (MBA). *Application deadline:* For fall admission, 10/1 for domestic and international students; for winter admission, 1/1 for domestic and international students; for spring admission, 4/1 for domestic and international students. *Application fee:* $250. Electronic applications accepted. *Application Contact:* Luke Anthony Pena, Executive Director of Admissions and Financial Aid, 603-646-3162, Fax: 603-646-1441, E-mail: tuck.admissions@tuck.dartmouth.edu. *Dean,* Matthew J. Slaughter, 603-646-2460, E-mail: tuck.public.relations@tuck.dartmouth.edu.

DAVENPORT UNIVERSITY, Grand Rapids, MI 49512

General Information Independent, coed, comprehensive institution. *Graduate housing:* Room and/or apartments available on a first-come, first-served basis to single students; on-campus housing not available to married students. *Research affiliation:* Human Synergistic Center for Applied Research, Inc. (leadership, organizational culture, strategy).

GRADUATE UNITS

Sneden Graduate School *Program availability:* Evening/weekend. Offers accounting (MBA); business administration (EMBA); finance (MBA); health care management (MBA); human resources (MBA); information assurance (MS); occupational therapy (MSOT); public health (MPH); strategic management (MBA). Electronic applications accepted.

DEFIANCE COLLEGE, Defiance, OH 43512-1610

General Information Independent-religious, coed, comprehensive institution. *Graduate housing:* On-campus housing not available.

GRADUATE UNITS

Program in Business Administration *Program availability:* Part-time, evening/weekend. Offers leadership (MBA). Electronic applications accepted.

Program in Education *Program availability:* Part-time-only. Offers education (MAE); sport coaching (MAE). Electronic applications accepted.

DELAWARE STATE UNIVERSITY, Dover, DE 19901-2277

General Information State-supported, coed, university. *Graduate housing:* Room and/or apartments available on a first-come, first-served basis to single students; on-campus housing not available to married students.

GRADUATE UNITS

Graduate Programs *Program availability:* Part-time, evening/weekend. Offers applied chemistry (MS, PhD); applied mathematics (MS); applied mathematics and theoretical physics (PhD); applied optics (MS); biological sciences (MA, MS, PhD); biology education (MS); chemistry (MS); French (MA); historic preservation (MA); mathematics (MS); mathematics education (MS); molecular and cellular neuroscience (MS); natural resources (MS); neuroscience (PhD); optics (PhD); physics (MS); physics teaching (MS); plant science (MS); Spanish (MA).

College of Business *Program availability:* Part-time, evening/weekend. Offers business administration (MBA). Electronic applications accepted.

College of Education, Health and Public Policy *Program availability:* Part-time, evening/weekend. Offers adult literacy and basic education (MA); art education (MA); curriculum and instruction (MA); education, health and public policy (MA, MS, MSW, Ed D); educational leadership (MA, Ed D); nursing (MS); science education (MA); social work (MSW); special education (MA); sport administration (MS); teaching (MA). Electronic applications accepted.

DELAWARE VALLEY UNIVERSITY, Doylestown, PA 18901-2697

General Information Independent, coed, comprehensive institution. *Graduate housing:* On-campus housing not available.

GRADUATE UNITS

MBA Program *Program availability:* Part-time, evening/weekend, online learning. Offers accounting (MBA); ·entrepreneurship (MBA); finance (MBA); food and agribusiness (MBA); general business (MBA); global executive leadership (MBA); human resource management (MBA); supply chain management (MBA). Electronic applications accepted.

Program in Counseling Psychology Offers child and adolescent therapy (MA); social justice community counseling (MA).

Program in Criminal Justice Offers criminal justice (MA).

Program in Educational Leadership *Program availability:* Part-time, evening/weekend. Offers instruction, curriculum and technology (MS); school administration and leadership (MS).

DELL'ARTE INTERNATIONAL SCHOOL OF PHYSICAL THEATRE, Blue Lake, CA 95525

General Information Independent, coed, graduate-only institution. *Graduate housing:* Rooms and/or apartments available on a first-come, first-served basis to single and married students.

GRADUATE UNITS

MFA Program Offers ensemble based physical theatre (MFA). Electronic applications accepted.

DELTA STATE UNIVERSITY, Cleveland, MS 38733-0001

General Information State-supported, coed, comprehensive institution. *Enrollment:* 3,715 graduate, professional, and undergraduate students; 270 full-time matriculated graduate/professional students (179 women), 356 part-time matriculated graduate/professional students (263 women). *Enrollment by degree level:* 556 master's, 69 doctoral, 1 other advanced degree. *Graduate faculty:* 68 full-time (39 women), 25 part-time/adjunct (14 women). *International tuition:* $7076 full-time. *Tuition, area resident:* Full-time $7076; part-time $393 per credit hour. Tuition, state resident: full-time $7076; part-time $393 per credit hour. Tuition, nonresident: full-time $7076; part-time $393 per credit hour. *Required fees:* $170; $18.90 per credit hour. $9.45 per semester. Part-time tuition and fees vary according to program. *Graduate housing:* Rooms and/or apartments available on a first-come, first-served basis to single and married students. Typical cost: $4442 per year ($7722 including board) for single students; $5110 (including board) for married students. Room and board charges vary according to board plan and housing facility selected. *Student services:* Campus employment opportunities, campus safety program, career counseling, exercise/wellness program, free psychological counseling, grant writing training, international student services, services for students with disabilities, teacher training, writing training. *Library facilities:* Roberts-LaForge Library plus 1 other. *Collection:* Books: 326,317 (physical), 72,046 (digital/electronic); Serial titles: 1,174 (physical), 25,014 (digital/electronic); Databases: 83. Weekly public service hours: 75.

Computer facilities: Computer purchase and lease plans are available. A campuswide network can be accessed from student residence rooms. Online class registration is available.

Website: http://www.deltastate.edu/

General Application Contact: Cayce Friesenhahn, Coordinator of Graduate Admissions, 662-846-4875, Fax: 662-846-4313, E-mail: cfriesenhahn@deltastate.edu.

GRADUATE UNITS

Graduate Programs Students: 270 full-time (179 women), 356 part-time (263 women); includes 247 minority (227 Black or African American, non-Hispanic/Latino; 1 American Indian or Alaska Native, non-Hispanic/Latino; 5 Asian, non-Hispanic/Latino; 9 Hispanic/Latino; 5 Two or more races, non-Hispanic/Latino), 31 international. Average age 33. 527 applicants, 61% accepted, 219 enrolled. *Faculty:* 68 full-time (39 women), 25 part-time/adjunct (14 women). Expenses: Contact institution. *Financial support:* Fellowships, research assistantships, career-related internships or fieldwork, Federal Work-Study, scholarships/grants, tuition waivers (full and partial), and unspecified assistantships available. Support available to part-time students. Financial award application deadline: 6/30; financial award applicants required to submit FAFSA. In 2018, 336 master's, 18 doctorates, 1 other advanced degree awarded. *Program availability:* Part-time, evening/weekend, 100% online, blended/hybrid learning. Offers business administration (MBA); commercial aviation (MCA); community development (MS); counseling (Ed S); liberal studies (MALS); natural sciences (MSNS); nursing (MSN); nursing practice (DNP); professional studies (Ed D); social justice and criminology (MSJC); teaching (alternate route) (MAT). *Application deadline:* For fall admission, 8/1 priority date for domestic students, 6/1 for international students; for spring admission, 12/1 priority date for domestic students, 10/15 for international students. Applications are processed on a rolling basis. *Application fee:* $30. Electronic applications accepted. *Application Contact:* Cayce Friesenhahn, Graduate Studies Admissions Coordinator, 662-846-4875, E-mail: cfriesenhahn@deltastate.edu. *Dean of Graduate and Continuing Studies,* Dr. Beverly Moon, 662-846-4700, E-mail: bmoon@deltastate.edu.

College of Arts and Sciences *Program availability:* Part-time. Offers arts and sciences (M Ed, MALS, MSCD, MSCJ, MSJC, MSNS); community development (MS); evolving human voices (MALS); gender and diversity studies (MALS); globalization studies (MALS); Mississippi Delta studies (MALS); natural sciences (MSNS); philosophy (MALS); religious studies (MALS); secondary education (M Ed); social justice and criminology (MSJC); social science secondary education (M Ed).

College of Business *Program availability:* Part-time, evening/weekend, online learning. Offers accountancy (MPA); business (MBA, MCA, MPA); business administration (MBA); commercial aviation (MCA).

College of Education *Program availability:* Part-time, evening/weekend. Offers counseling (M Ed); counselor education (Ed D); education (M Ed, MAT, MS, Ed D, Ed S); educational administration and supervision (M Ed, Ed S); elementary education (M Ed, MAT, Ed S); health, physical education, and recreation (M Ed); higher education (Ed D); professional studies (Ed D); secondary education (MAT); special education (M Ed); sport and human performance (MS).

Robert E. Smith School of Nursing *Program availability:* Part-time. Offers family nurse practitioner (MSN); nurse administrator (MSN); nurse educator (MSN). Electronic applications accepted.

DENVER SEMINARY, Littleton, CO 80120

General Information Independent-religious, coed, graduate-only institution. *Graduate housing:* Rooms and/or apartments available on a first-come, first-served basis to single and married students. Housing application deadline: 6/1.

GRADUATE UNITS

Graduate and Professional Programs *Program availability:* Part-time, evening/weekend, online learning. Offers apologetics (Certificate); biblical studies (MA); Christian formation and soul care (MA, Certificate); Christian studies (MA, Certificate); church and parachurch leadership (D Min); counseling licensure (MA); counseling ministry (MA); intercultural ministry (Certificate); leadership (MA, Certificate); marriage and family counseling (D Min); pastoral ministry (D Min); philosophy of religion (MA); spiritual guidance (Certificate); theology (M Div, Certificate); worship (Certificate); youth and family ministry (MA). Electronic applications accepted.

DEPAUL UNIVERSITY, Chicago, IL 60604-2287

General Information Independent-religious, coed, university. CGS member. *Graduate housing:* Room and/or apartments available on a first-come, first-served basis to single students; on-campus housing not available to married students. *Research affiliation:* Civic Federation (public services), Metro Chicago Information Center (public services), International Institute of Higher Studies in the Criminal Sciences (law).

GRADUATE UNITS

College of Communication *Program availability:* Part-time, evening/weekend. Offers digital communication and media arts (MA); health communication (MA); journalism (MA); media and cinema studies (MA); multicultural communication (MA); organizational communication (MA); public relations and advertising (MA); relational communication (MA). Electronic applications accepted.

College of Computing and Digital Media *Program availability:* Part-time, evening/weekend, online learning. Offers animation (MA, MFA); applied technology (MS); business information technology (MS); computational finance (MS); computer and information sciences (PhD); computer science (MS); creative producing (MFA); cybersecurity (MS); data science (MS); digital communication and media arts (MA); documentary (MFA); e-commerce technology (MS); experience design (MA); film and television (MS); film and television directing (MFA); game design (MFA); game programming (MS); health informatics (MS); human centered design (PhD); human-computer interaction (MS); information systems (MS); network engineering and security (MS); product innovation and computing (MS); screenwriting (MFA); software engineering (MS). Electronic applications accepted.

College of Education *Program availability:* Part-time, evening/weekend, online learning. Offers bilingual-bicultural education (M Ed, MA); counseling (M Ed, MA); curriculum studies (M Ed, MA, Ed D); early childhood education (M Ed, MA, Ed D); educational leadership (M Ed, MA, Ed D); elementary education (M Ed, MA); middle grades education (M Ed); middle school mathematics education (MS); reading specialist (M Ed, MA); secondary education (M Ed, MA); social and cultural foundations in education (M Ed, MA); special education (M Ed); sport, fitness and recreation leadership (MS); value-creating education for global citizenship (M Ed); world languages education (M Ed, MA). Electronic applications accepted.

College of Law *Program availability:* Part-time, evening/weekend. Offers business law and taxation (MJ); criminal law (MJ); health and intellectual property law (MJ); health care compliance (MJ); health law (LL M, MJ); intellectual property law (LL M); international and comparative law (MJ); international law (LL M); law (JD); public interest law (MJ); taxation (LL M); U.S. legal studies (LL M). Electronic applications accepted.

College of Liberal Arts and Social Sciences *Program availability:* Part-time, evening/weekend, online learning. Offers Arabic (MA); Chinese (MA); critical ethnic studies (MA); English (MA); French (MA); German (MA); history (MA); interdisciplinary studies (MA, MS); international public service (MS); international studies (MA); Italian (MA); Japanese (MA); liberal studies (MA); nonprofit management (MNM); public administration (MPA); public health (MPH); public policy (MPP); public service management (MS); refugee and forced migration studies (MS); social work (MSW); sociology (MA); Spanish (MA); sustainable urban development (MA); women's and gender studies (MA); writing and publishing (MA); writing, rhetoric and discourse (MA). Electronic applications accepted.

College of Science and Health Offers applied mathematics (MS); applied statistics (MS); biological sciences (MA, MS); chemistry (MS); environmental science (MS); mathematics education (MA); mathematics for teaching (MS); nursing (MS); nursing practice (DNP); physics (MS); polymer and coatings science (MS); psychology (MS); pure mathematics (MS); science education (MS). Electronic applications accepted.

Kellstadt Graduate School of Business *Program availability:* Part-time, evening/weekend, online learning. Offers accountancy (MBA, MSA); applied economics (MBA); audit and advisory services (MS); business administration (DBA); business analytics (MS); business strategy and decision-making (MBA); computational finance (MS); economics and policy analysis (MS); enterprise risk management (MS); entrepreneurship (MBA, MS); finance (MBA, MS); general business (MBA); hospitality leadership (MBA); hospitality leadership and operational performance (MS); human resources (MS); international business (MBA); management (MBA, MS); management information systems (MBA); marketing (MBA, MS); marketing analysis (MS); marketing strategy and planning (MBA); real estate (MS); real estate finance and investment (MBA); strategy, execution and valuation (MBA); supply chain management (MS); sustainable management (MS); taxation (MS). Electronic applications accepted.

School for New Learning *Program availability:* Part-time, evening/weekend. Offers applied professional studies (MA); applied technology (MS); educating adults (MA). Electronic applications accepted.

School of Music *Program availability:* Part-time, evening/weekend. Offers composition (MM); jazz studies (MM); music education (MM); music performance (MM); performance (Certificate). Electronic applications accepted.

The Theatre School Offers acting (MFA); arts leadership (MFA); directing (MFA). Electronic applications accepted.

DEREE - THE AMERICAN COLLEGE OF GREECE, GR-153-42 Aghia Paraskevi, Athens, Greece

General Information Independent, coed, comprehensive institution.

GRADUATE UNITS

Graduate Programs

DESALES UNIVERSITY, Center Valley, PA 18034-9568

General Information Independent-religious, coed, comprehensive institution. *Graduate housing:* Room and/or apartments available on a first-come, first-served basis to single students; on-campus housing not available to married students. Housing application deadline: 3/15.

GRADUATE UNITS

Division of Business *Program availability:* Part-time, evening/weekend, 100% online, blended/hybrid learning. Offers accounting (MBA); computer information systems (MBA); finance (MBA); health care systems management (MBA); human resources management (MBA); management (MBA); marketing (MBA); project management (MBA); self-design (MBA); supply chain management (MBA). Electronic applications accepted.

Division of Healthcare *Program availability:* Part-time. Offers adult-gerontology acute care (Post Master's Certificate); adult-gerontology acute care nurse practitioner (MSN); adult-gerontology acute certified nurse practitioner (Post Master's Certificate); adult-gerontology clinical nurse specialist (MSN, Post Master's Certificate); clinical leadership (DNP); family nurse practitioner (MSN, Post Master's Certificate); general nursing practice (DNP); nurse anesthetist (MSN); nurse educator (Post Master's Certificate, Postbaccalaureate Certificate); nurse midwife (MSN); nurse practitioner (MSN); psychiatric-mental health nurse practitioner (MSN, Post Master's Certificate). Electronic applications accepted.

Division of Liberal Arts and Social Sciences *Program availability:* Part-time, 100% online, blended/hybrid learning. Offers criminal justice (MCJ); digital forensics (MCJ, Postbaccalaureate Certificate); education (M Ed); investigative forensics (MCJ, Postbaccalaureate Certificate). Electronic applications accepted.

Division of Science and Mathematics *Program availability:* Part-time, evening/weekend, 100% online, blended/hybrid learning. Offers cyber security (Postbaccalaureate Certificate); data analytics (Postbaccalaureate Certificate); information systems (MS). Electronic applications accepted.

DES MOINES UNIVERSITY, Des Moines, IA 50312-4104

General Information Independent, coed, graduate-only institution. *Graduate housing:* On-campus housing not available.

GRADUATE UNITS

College of Health Sciences *Program availability:* Part-time, evening/weekend. Offers health sciences (MHA, MPH, MS, DPT); healthcare administration (MHA); physical therapy (DPT); physician assistant (MS); public health (MPH). Electronic applications accepted.

College of Osteopathic Medicine Offers anatomy (MS); biomedical sciences (MS); osteopathic medicine (DO). Electronic applications accepted.

College of Podiatric Medicine and Surgery Offers podiatric medicine and surgery (DPM). Electronic applications accepted.

DEVRY COLLEGE OF NEW YORK–MIDTOWN MANHATTAN CAMPUS, New York, NY 10016

General Information Proprietary, coed, comprehensive institution.

GRADUATE UNITS

Keller Graduate School of Management Offers management (M Acc, MAFM, MBA, MHRM, MISM, MNCM, MPA, MPM).

DEVRY UNIVERSITY–ALPHARETTA CAMPUS, Alpharetta, GA 30009

General Information Proprietary, coed, comprehensive institution.

GRADUATE UNITS

Keller Graduate School of Management Offers management (MAFM, MBA, MHRM, MISM, MNCM, MPA, MPM).

DEVRY UNIVERSITY–ARLINGTON CAMPUS, Arlington, VA 22202

General Information Proprietary, coed, comprehensive institution.

GRADUATE UNITS

Keller Graduate School of Management Offers management (M Acc, MAFM, MBA, MHRM, MISM, MPM).

DEVRY UNIVERSITY–CHARLOTTE CAMPUS, Charlotte, NC 28273

General Information Proprietary, coed, comprehensive institution.

GRADUATE UNITS

Keller Graduate School of Management Offers management (MAFM, MBA, MHRM, MISM, MNCM, MPA, MPM).

DEVRY UNIVERSITY–CHESAPEAKE CAMPUS, Chesapeake, VA 23320

General Information Proprietary, coed, comprehensive institution.

GRADUATE UNITS

Keller Graduate School of Management Offers management (MAFM, MBA, MHRM, MISM, MNCM, MPA, MPM).

DEVRY UNIVERSITY–CHICAGO CAMPUS, Chicago, IL 60618

General Information Proprietary, coed, comprehensive institution.

GRADUATE UNITS

Keller Graduate School of Management Offers management (M Acc, MAFM, MBA, MHRM, MISM, MPM).

DEVRY UNIVERSITY–CHICAGO LOOP CAMPUS, Chicago, IL 60606

General Information Proprietary, coed, comprehensive institution.

GRADUATE UNITS

Keller Graduate School of Management Offers management (MAFM, MBA, MHRM, MISM, MNCM, MPM).

DEVRY UNIVERSITY–CINCINNATI CAMPUS, Cincinnati, OH 45249

General Information Proprietary, coed, comprehensive institution.

GRADUATE UNITS

Keller Graduate School of Management Offers management (MAFM, MBA, MHRM, MISM, MNCM, MPA, MPM).

DEVRY UNIVERSITY–COLUMBUS CAMPUS, Columbus, OH 43209

General Information Proprietary, coed, comprehensive institution.

GRADUATE UNITS

Keller Graduate School of Management Offers management (MAFM, MBA, MHRM, MISM, MPM).

DEVRY UNIVERSITY–DECATUR CAMPUS, Decatur, GA 30030

General Information Proprietary, coed, comprehensive institution.

GRADUATE UNITS

Keller Graduate School of Management Offers management (MAFM, MBA, MHRM, MISM, MNCM, MPA, MPM, MSA).

DEVRY UNIVERSITY–FOLSOM CAMPUS, Folsom, CA 95630

General Information Proprietary, coed, comprehensive institution.

GRADUATE UNITS

Graduate Programs

DEVRY UNIVERSITY–FREMONT CAMPUS, Fremont, CA 94555

General Information Proprietary, coed, comprehensive institution.

GRADUATE UNITS

Keller Graduate School of Management Offers management (MAFM, MBA, MHRM, MISM, MNCM, MPA, MPM).

DEVRY UNIVERSITY–FT. WASHINGTON CAMPUS, Fort Washington, PA 19034

General Information Proprietary, coed, comprehensive institution.

GRADUATE UNITS

Keller Graduate School of Management Offers management (MAFM, MBA, MHRM, MISM, MNCM, MPA, MPM).

DEVRY UNIVERSITY–HENDERSON CAMPUS, Henderson, NV 89074

General Information Proprietary, coed, comprehensive institution.

GRADUATE UNITS

Keller Graduate School of Management Offers management (MAFM, MBA, MHRM, MISM, MNCM, MPA, MPM).

DEVRY UNIVERSITY–IRVING CAMPUS, Irving, TX 75063

General Information Proprietary, coed, comprehensive institution.

GRADUATE UNITS

Keller Graduate School of Management Offers management (M Acc, MAFM, MBA, MHRM, MISM, MPM).

DEVRY UNIVERSITY–JACKSONVILLE CAMPUS, Jacksonville, FL 32256

General Information Proprietary, coed, comprehensive institution.

GRADUATE UNITS

Keller Graduate School of Management Offers management (MAFM, MBA, MHRM, MISM, MNCM, MPA, MPM).

DEVRY UNIVERSITY–LONG BEACH CAMPUS, Long Beach, CA 90806

General Information Proprietary, coed, comprehensive institution.

GRADUATE UNITS

Keller Graduate School of Management Offers management (MAFM, MBA, MHRM, MISM, MNCM, MPA, MPM).

DEVRY UNIVERSITY–MIRAMAR CAMPUS, Miramar, FL 33027

General Information Proprietary, coed, comprehensive institution.

GRADUATE UNITS

Keller Graduate School of Management Offers management (MAFM, MBA, MHRM, MISM, MPM, MSA).

DEVRY UNIVERSITY–MORRISVILLE CAMPUS, Morrisville, NC 27560

General Information Proprietary, coed, comprehensive institution.

GRADUATE UNITS

Keller Graduate School of Management Offers management (MBA, MHRM, MISM, MNCM, MPA, MPM).

DEVRY UNIVERSITY–NASHVILLE CAMPUS, Nashville, TN 37211

General Information Proprietary, coed, comprehensive institution.

GRADUATE UNITS

Keller Graduate School of Management Offers management (MAFM, MBA, MHRM, MISM, MNCM, MPA, MPM).

DEVRY UNIVERSITY–NORTH BRUNSWICK CAMPUS, North Brunswick, NJ 08902

General Information Proprietary, coed, comprehensive institution.

GRADUATE UNITS

Keller Graduate School of Management Offers management (MBA).

DEVRY UNIVERSITY ONLINE, Addison, IL 60101
General Information Proprietary, coed, comprehensive institution.
GRADUATE UNITS
Keller Graduate School of Management

DEVRY UNIVERSITY–ORLANDO CAMPUS, Orlando, FL 32819
General Information Proprietary, coed, comprehensive institution.
GRADUATE UNITS
Keller Graduate School of Management Offers management (MAFM, MBA, MHRM, MISM, MPA, MPM, MSA).

DEVRY UNIVERSITY–PHOENIX CAMPUS, Phoenix, AZ 85021
General Information Proprietary, coed, comprehensive institution.
GRADUATE UNITS
Keller Graduate School of Management Offers management (MAFM, MBA, MISM, MPM, MSA).

DEVRY UNIVERSITY–POMONA CAMPUS, Pomona, CA 91768
General Information Proprietary, coed, comprehensive institution.
GRADUATE UNITS
Keller Graduate School of Management Offers management (MAFM, MBA, MHRM, MISM, MPM, MSA).

DEVRY UNIVERSITY–SAN DIEGO CAMPUS, San Diego, CA 92108
General Information Proprietary, coed, comprehensive institution.
GRADUATE UNITS
Keller Graduate School of Management Offers management (MAFM, MBA, MHRM, MISM, MNCM, MPA, MPM, Graduate Certificate).

DEVRY UNIVERSITY–SEVEN HILLS CAMPUS, Seven Hills, OH 44131
General Information Proprietary, coed, comprehensive institution.
GRADUATE UNITS
Keller Graduate School of Management Offers management (MAFM, MBA, MHRM, MISM, MNCM, MPA, MPM, Graduate Certificate).

DEVRY UNIVERSITY–TINLEY PARK CAMPUS, Tinley Park, IL 60477
General Information Proprietary, coed, comprehensive institution.
GRADUATE UNITS
Keller Graduate School of Management Offers management (MAFM, MBA, MHRM, MISM, MNCM, MPA, MPM).

DICKINSON STATE UNIVERSITY, Dickinson, ND 58601-4896
General Information State-supported, coed, comprehensive institution. *Enrollment:* 2 full-time matriculated graduate/professional students (1 woman), 15 part-time matriculated graduate/professional students (9 women). *Enrollment by degree level:* 16 master's, 1 other advanced degree. *Graduate faculty:* 1 (woman) full-time, 1 (woman) part-time/adjunct. *Tuition, area resident:* Full-time $3735; part-time $311 per credit hour. Tuition, state resident: full-time $3735; part-time $311 per credit hour. Tuition, nonresident: full-time $3735; part-time $311 per credit hour. *Required fees:* $138; $138 per credit hour. *Graduate housing:* Room and/or apartments guaranteed to single students; on-campus housing not available to married students. Typical cost: $3300 per year ($7268 including board). Room and board charges vary according to board plan, campus/location and housing facility selected. Housing application deadline: 7/1. *Student services:* Campus employment opportunities, campus safety program, career counseling, exercise/wellness program, grant writing training, international student services, multicultural affairs office, services for students with disabilities, writing training. *Library facilities:* Stoxen Library plus 1 other. *Collection:* Books: 73,571 (physical), 23,355 (digital/electronic); Serial titles: 119 (physical), 107,800 (digital/electronic); Databases: 71. Weekly public service hours: 56.
Computer facilities: 250 computers available on campus for general student use. A campuswide network can be accessed from student residence rooms and from off campus. Online class registration is available.
Website: http://www.dickinsonstate.edu/
General Application Contact: Heidi Kippenhan, Director of Student Recruitment and Admissions, 701-483-2566, E-mail: Heidi.Kippenhan@dickinsonstate.edu.
GRADUATE UNITS
Department of Teacher Education Students: 2 full-time (1 woman), 15 part-time (9 women); includes 1 minority (Hispanic/Latino). Average age 36. 8 applicants, 100% accepted, 8 enrolled. *Faculty:* 2 full-time (both women). Expenses: Contact institution. *Financial support:* Application deadline: 12/1; applicants required to submit FAFSA. *Program availability:* Part-time, blended/hybrid learning. Offers master of arts in teaching (MAT); master of entrepreneurship (ME); middle school education (MAT); reading (MAT). *Application deadline:* For fall admission, 8/1 for domestic students, 7/1 for international students; for spring admission, 12/1 for domestic students, 11/15 for international students. Applications are processed on a rolling basis. *Application fee:* $35. Electronic applications accepted. *Application Contact:* Pamela Krueger, Graduate Studies Coordinator, 701-483-5631, E-mail: Pamela.j.krueger@dickinsonstate.edu. *Chair, Department of Teacher Education,* Dr. Deborah Secord, 701-483-2178, E-mail: Deborah.Secord@dickinsonstate.edu.

DIGIPEN INSTITUTE OF TECHNOLOGY, Redmond, WA 98052
General Information Proprietary, coed, comprehensive institution. *Enrollment:* 1,166 graduate, professional, and undergraduate students; 77 full-time matriculated graduate/professional students (17 women), 25 part-time matriculated graduate/professional students (5 women). *Enrollment by degree level:* 102 master's. *Graduate housing:* Room and/or apartments available on a first-come, first-served basis to single students; on-campus housing not available to married students. Housing application deadline: 7/15. *Student services:* Campus employment opportunities, career counseling, free psychological counseling, international student services, multicultural affairs office, services for students with disabilities. *Library facilities:* DigiPen Library. *Collection:* Books: 5,946 (physical), 196,396 (digital/electronic); Serial titles: 36 (physical), 6,756 (digital/electronic); Databases: 11. Weekly public service hours: 84.
Computer facilities: 1,040 computers available on campus for general student use. A campuswide network can be accessed from student residence rooms and from off campus. Online class registration is available.
Website: http://www.digipen.edu/

General Application Contact: Emily Kirby, Director of Admissions, 425-629-4862, Fax: 425-558-0378, E-mail: ekirby@digipen.edu.
GRADUATE UNITS
Graduate Programs *Program availability:* Part-time. Offers computer science (MS); digital art and animation (MFA). Electronic applications accepted.

DIVINE MERCY UNIVERSITY, Arlington, VA 30327
General Information Independent-religious, coed, graduate-only institution.
GRADUATE UNITS
Institute for the Psychological Sciences *Program availability:* Part-time. Offers clinical psychology (Psy D).
School of Counseling *Program availability:* Online learning. Offers clinical mental health counseling (MS); psychology (MS).

DOANE UNIVERSITY, Crete, NE 68333-2430
General Information Independent-religious, coed, comprehensive institution. *Enrollment:* 513 full-time matriculated graduate/professional students (383 women), 523 part-time matriculated graduate/professional students (394 women). *Enrollment by degree level:* 923 master's, 75 doctoral, 39 other advanced degrees. *Graduate faculty:* 15 full-time (10 women), 102 part-time/adjunct (70 women). *Graduate housing:* On-campus housing not available. *Student services:* Career counseling, teacher training. *Library facilities:* Perkins Library plus 1 other. *Collection:* Study areas open 24 hours, 5–7 days a week; students can reserve study rooms.
Computer facilities: Computer purchase and lease plans are available. 250 computers available on campus for general student use. A campuswide network can be accessed from student residence rooms and from off campus. Online class registration is available.
Website: http://www.doane.edu/
GRADUATE UNITS
Program in Counseling Students: 47 full-time (39 women), 17 part-time (14 women); includes 9 minority (2 Black or African American, non-Hispanic/Latino; 1 American Indian or Alaska Native, non-Hispanic/Latino; 4 Hispanic/Latino; 2 Two or more races, non-Hispanic/Latino). Average age 34. *Faculty:* 2 full-time (1 woman), 15 part-time/adjunct (11 women). Expenses: Contact institution. *Financial support:* Unspecified assistantships available. Financial award application deadline: 6/1; financial award applicants required to submit FAFSA. In 2018, 21 master's awarded. *Program availability:* Evening/weekend. Offers counseling (MAC). *Application deadline:* Applications are processed on a rolling basis. *Application fee:* $25. Electronic applications accepted. *Application Contact:* Jean Kilnoski, Assistant Dean, 402-466-4774, Fax: 404-466-4228, E-mail: jean.kilnoski@doane.edu. *Associate Dean/Director of the Counseling Program,* 402-466-4774, Fax: 402-466-4228.
Program in Education Students: 287 full-time (235 women), 474 part-time (363 women); includes 57 minority (20 Black or African American, non-Hispanic/Latino; 1 American Indian or Alaska Native, non-Hispanic/Latino; 5 Asian, non-Hispanic/Latino; 22 Hispanic/Latino; 1 Native Hawaiian or other Pacific Islander, non-Hispanic/Latino; 8 Two or more races, non-Hispanic/Latino), 6 international. Average age 34. *Faculty:* 10 full-time (7 women), 66 part-time/adjunct (50 women). Expenses: Contact institution. *Financial support:* Applicants required to submit FAFSA. In 2018, 247 master's, 9 doctorates, 33 other advanced degrees awarded. *Program availability:* Part-time, evening/weekend. Offers curriculum and instruction (M Ed); education (Ed D); education specialist (Ed S); educational leadership (M Ed); school counseling (M Ed). *Application deadline:* Applications are processed on a rolling basis. Electronic applications accepted. *Application Contact:* Leah Schaber, Assistant Dean, 402-464-1223, Fax: 402-466-4228, E-mail: leah.schaber@doane.edu. *Dean,* Dr. Lyn C. Forester, 402-826-8604, Fax: 402-826-8278.
Program in Management Students: 174 full-time (105 women), 32 part-time (17 women); includes 44 minority (16 Black or African American, non-Hispanic/Latino; 7 Asian, non-Hispanic/Latino; 11 Hispanic/Latino; 10 Two or more races, non-Hispanic/Latino), 7 international. Average age 36. *Faculty:* 3 full-time (2 women), 21 part-time/adjunct (9 women). Expenses: Contact institution. *Financial support:* Application deadline: 6/1; applicants required to submit FAFSA. In 2018, 68 master's awarded. *Program availability:* Part-time, evening/weekend. Offers management (MA, MBA). *Application deadline:* Applications are processed on a rolling basis. *Application fee:* $25. Electronic applications accepted. *Application Contact:* Cathy Dillon, Director of Academic Advising, 402-466-4774, Fax: 404-466-4228, E-mail: cathy.dillon@doane.edu. *Director of Graduate Business Program,* Dr. Debora Sepich, 880-333-6263, E-mail: deb.sepich@doane.edu.

DOMINICAN COLLEGE, Orangeburg, NY 10962-1210
General Information Independent, coed, comprehensive institution. *Enrollment:* 198 full-time matriculated graduate/professional students (145 women), 308 part-time matriculated graduate/professional students (223 women). *Enrollment by degree level:* 269 master's, 237 doctoral. *Graduate faculty:* 14 full-time (6 women), 26 part-time/adjunct (18 women). *Tuition:* Part-time $965 per credit. *Required fees:* $200 per semester. One-time fee: $200. Tuition and fees vary according to course load, degree level and program. *Graduate housing:* Room and/or apartments available on a first-come, first-served basis to single students; on-campus housing not available to married students. Housing application deadline: 5/1. *Student services:* Campus employment opportunities, campus safety program, career counseling, free psychological counseling, services for students with disabilities, teacher training. *Library facilities:* Sullivan Library plus 1 other. *Collection:* Books: 74,226 (physical), 117,187 (digital/electronic); Serial titles: 610 (physical), 75,067 (digital/electronic); Databases: 85. Weekly public service hours: 89; students can reserve study rooms.
Computer facilities: 150 computers available on campus for general student use. A campuswide network can be accessed from student residence rooms and from off campus. Online class registration, Web portal, learning management system are available.
Website: http://www.dc.edu/
General Application Contact: Heather Karsenty, Assistant Director of Graduate Admissions, 845-848-7908, Fax: 845-365-3150, E-mail: graduate.admissions@dc.edu.
GRADUATE UNITS
Division of Allied Health Students: 158 full-time (114 women), 154 part-time (92 women); includes 111 minority (6 Black or African American, non-Hispanic/Latino; 1 American Indian or Alaska Native, non-Hispanic/Latino; 74 Asian, non-Hispanic/Latino; 22 Hispanic/Latino; 1 Native Hawaiian or other Pacific Islander, non-Hispanic/Latino; 7 Two or more races, non-Hispanic/Latino), 33 international. Average age 37. *Faculty:* 11 full-time (5 women), 29 part-time/adjunct (18 women). Expenses: Contact institution. *Financial support:* Scholarships/grants available. Financial award application deadline: 3/15; financial award applicants required to submit FAFSA. In 2018, 54 master's, 112

doctorates awarded. *Program availability:* Part-time, evening/weekend, online learning. Offers allied health (MS, DPT); occupational therapy (MS); physical therapy (MS, DPT). *Application deadline:* For fall admission, 8/1 for domestic students, 6/1 for international students; for spring admission, 12/1 for domestic students; for summer admission, 5/1 for domestic students. Applications are processed on a rolling basis. *Application fee:* $50. Electronic applications accepted. *Application Contact:* Heather Karsenty, Assistant Director of Graduate Admissions, 845-848-7908, Fax: 845-365-3150, E-mail: graduate.admissions@dc.edu. *Assistant Program Director & Coordinator of Graduate Academics,* Pamela Story, 845-848-6039, Fax: 845-398-4893, E-mail: pamela.story@dc.edu.

Division of Nursing Students: 33 full-time (27 women), 89 part-time (82 women); includes 65 minority (26 Black or African American, non-Hispanic/Latino; 17 Asian, non-Hispanic/Latino; 20 Hispanic/Latino; 1 Native Hawaiian or other Pacific Islander, non-Hispanic/Latino; 1 Two or more races, non-Hispanic/Latino), 1 international. Average age 37. *Faculty:* 15 full-time (all women), 46 part-time/adjunct (41 women). Expenses: Contact institution. *Financial support:* Scholarships/grants available. Financial award application deadline: 2/1; financial award applicants required to submit FAFSA. In 2018, 36 master's, 10 doctorates awarded. *Program availability:* Part-time, evening/weekend. Offers nursing (MSN, DNP). *Application deadline:* For fall admission, 3/1 for domestic students. Applications are processed on a rolling basis. *Application fee:* $50. Electronic applications accepted. *Application Contact:* Heather Karsenty, Assistant Director of Graduate Admissions, 845-848-7908, Fax: 845-365-3150, E-mail: admissions@dc.edu. *Director,* Dr. Nancy DiDona, 845-848-6051, Fax: 845-398-4891, E-mail: nancy.didona@dc.edu.

Division of Teacher Education Students: 4 full-time (all women), 52 part-time (40 women); includes 11 minority (1 Black or African American, non-Hispanic/Latino; 2 Asian, non-Hispanic/Latino; 8 Hispanic/Latino). Average age 33. *Faculty:* 5 part-time/adjunct (all women). Expenses: Contact institution. *Financial support:* Application deadline: 2/1; applicants required to submit FAFSA. In 2018, 24 master's awarded. *Program availability:* Part-time, evening/weekend, online learning. Offers education/teaching of individuals with multiple disabilities (MS Ed). *Application deadline:* For fall admission, 8/1 for domestic students, 6/1 for international students. Applications are processed on a rolling basis. *Application fee:* $50. Electronic applications accepted. *Application Contact:* Heather Karsenty, Assistant Director of Graduate Admissions, 845-848-7908 Ext. 15, Fax: 845-365-3150, E-mail: admissions@dc.edu. *Director,* Dr. Mike Kelly, 845-848-4090, Fax: 845-359-7802, E-mail: mike.kelly@dc.edu.

MBA Program *Program availability:* Part-time, evening/weekend. Offers accounting (MBA); healthcare management (MBA); management (MBA). Electronic applications accepted.

DOMINICAN HOUSE OF STUDIES, PONTIFICAL FACULTY OF THE IMMACULATE CONCEPTION, Washington, DC 20017-1585

General Information Independent-religious, coed, primarily men, graduate-only institution. Enrollment by degree level: 90 master's. *Graduate faculty:* 19 full-time (1 woman), 2 part-time/adjunct (1 woman). *Tuition:* Full-time $16,080; part-time $8040 per credit hour. *Required fees:* $280; $280 $140. One-time fee: $200 full-time. Part-time tuition and fees vary according to course load. *Graduate housing:* On-campus housing not available. *Student services:* Campus employment opportunities, career counseling, international student services. *Library facilities:* Dominican Theological Library. *Collection:* Books: 77,000 (physical); Serial titles: 219 (physical), 18 (digital/electronic); Databases: 6. Weekly public service hours: 61; students can reserve study rooms.

Computer facilities: 8 computers available on campus for general student use. A campuswide network can be accessed.
Website: http://www.dhs.edu/

General Application Contact: Audrey Quade, Registrar and Accreditation Liaison, 202-495-3836, Fax: 202-495-3873, E-mail: registrar@dhs.edu.

GRADUATE UNITS
Graduate and Professional Programs in Theology *Program availability:* Part-time. Offers moral theology (STL); sacred scripture (STL); systematic theology (STL); theology (M Div, MA, STB); Thomistic studies (MA, STD, STL). Electronic applications accepted.

DOMINICAN SCHOOL OF PHILOSOPHY AND THEOLOGY, Berkeley, CA 94708

General Information Independent-religious, coed, graduate-only institution. *Graduate housing:* Rooms and/or apartments available on a first-come, first-served basis to single and married students. Housing application deadline: 5/1.

GRADUATE UNITS
Graduate Programs *Program availability:* Part-time. Offers philosophy (MA); theology (M Div, MA, MTS, Certificate). Electronic applications accepted.

DOMINICAN UNIVERSITY, River Forest, IL 60305-1099

General Information Independent-religious, coed, comprehensive institution. *Graduate housing:* Room and/or apartments available on a first-come, first-served basis to single students; on-campus housing not available to married students. Housing application deadline: 7/1.

GRADUATE UNITS
Brennan School of Business *Program availability:* Part-time, evening/weekend, 100% online, blended/hybrid learning. Offers business (MBA, MSA). JD/MBA offered jointly with John Marshall Law School. Electronic applications accepted.

School of Education *Program availability:* Part-time, evening/weekend, 100% online, blended/hybrid learning. Offers child life studies (MS); early childhood education (MS); education (MAT); elementary education (MA Ed); English as a second language (MA Ed); reading (MA Ed); secondary education (MAT); special education (MS).

School of Information Studies *Program availability:* Part-time, evening/weekend, 100% online, blended/hybrid learning. Offers information management (MSIM); knowledge management (Certificate); library and information science (MLIS, MPS, PhD); special studies (CSS). MLIS/M Div offered jointly with McCormick Theological Seminary, MLIS/MA with Loyola University Chicago, MLIS/MM with Northwestern University.

School of Social Work *Program availability:* Part-time. Offers social work (MSW). Electronic applications accepted.

DOMINICAN UNIVERSITY OF CALIFORNIA, San Rafael, CA 94901-2298

General Information Independent-religious, coed, comprehensive institution. *Graduate housing:* Room and/or apartments available on a first-come, first-served basis to single

students; on-campus housing not available to married students. Housing application deadline: 5/1.

GRADUATE UNITS
Barowsky School of Business *Program availability:* Part-time, evening/weekend. Offers business (MBA); healthcare leadership (MBA). MBA in healthcare leadership offered jointly with School of Health and Natural Sciences. Electronic applications accepted.

Programs in Education plus Teacher Preparation *Program availability:* Part-time, evening/weekend. Offers multiple subject (MS); single subject (MS). Electronic applications accepted.

School of Health and Natural Sciences Offers biological sciences (MS); clinical laboratory sciences (MS); general (MS); health and natural sciences (MS); marriage and family therapy (MS); occupational therapy (MS). Electronic applications accepted.

School of Liberal Arts and Education *Program availability:* Part-time, evening/weekend. Offers applied music (MA); art history (MA); creative writing (MA); gender studies (MA); history (MA); liberal arts and education (MA); philosophy (MA); political theory (MA); religion (MA). Electronic applications accepted.

DONGGUK UNIVERSITY LOS ANGELES, Los Angeles, CA 90020

General Information Independent, coed, graduate-only institution. *Graduate housing:* On-campus housing not available.

GRADUATE UNITS
Program in Oriental Medicine *Program availability:* Part-time, evening/weekend. Offers Oriental medicine (MS).

DORDT COLLEGE, Sioux Center, IA 51250-1697

General Information Independent-religious, coed, comprehensive institution. *Graduate housing:* Rooms and/or apartments available to single and married students.

GRADUATE UNITS
Program in Education *Program availability:* Part-time, online learning. Offers education (M Ed). Electronic applications accepted.

DRAGON RISES COLLEGE OF ORIENTAL MEDICINE, Gainesville, FL 32601

General Information Proprietary, coed, graduate-only institution.

GRADUATE UNITS
Graduate Program Offers Oriental medicine (MAOM). Electronic applications accepted.

DRAKE UNIVERSITY, Des Moines, IA 50311-4516

General Information Independent, coed, university. Enrollment: 4,869 graduate, professional, and undergraduate students; 926 full-time matriculated graduate/professional students (599 women), 928 part-time matriculated graduate/professional students (661 women). Enrollment by degree level: 824 master's, 923 doctoral, 107 other advanced degrees. *Graduate faculty:* 107 full-time (60 women), 70 part-time/adjunct (43 women). *Graduate housing:* Room and/or apartments available on a first-come, first-served basis to single students; on-campus housing not available to married students. Housing application deadline: 8/1. *Student services:* Campus employment opportunities, campus safety program, career counseling, exercise/wellness program, free psychological counseling, international student services, low-cost health insurance, services for students with disabilities, teacher training, writing training. *Library facilities:* Cowles Library plus 1 other. *Collection:* Study areas open 24 hours, 5–7 days a week; students can reserve study rooms.

Computer facilities: A campuswide network can be accessed from student residence rooms and from off campus. Online class registration is available.
Website: http://www.drake.edu/

General Application Contact: Jennifer Reitano, Director, Graduate Student Programs, 515-271-2188, Fax: 515-271-2831, E-mail: jennifer.reitano@drake.edu.

GRADUATE UNITS
College of Business and Public Administration Students: 31 full-time (15 women), 173 part-time (89 women); includes 19 minority (4 Black or African American, non-Hispanic/Latino; 1 American Indian or Alaska Native, non-Hispanic/Latino; 3 Asian, non-Hispanic/Latino; 9 Hispanic/Latino; 2 Two or more races, non-Hispanic/Latino), 11 international. Average age 31. Expenses: Contact institution. *Financial support:* Fellowships with tuition reimbursements, teaching assistantships, career-related internships or fieldwork, and institutionally sponsored loans available. Support available to part-time students. Financial award application deadline: 3/1; financial award applicants required to submit FAFSA. In 2018, 121 master's awarded. *Program availability:* Part-time, evening/weekend, 100% online, blended/hybrid learning. Offers accounting (M Acc); business administration (MBA); public administration (MPA). *Application deadline:* For fall admission, 8/15 priority date for domestic students; for winter admission, 12/20 priority date for domestic students; for spring admission, 12/1 priority date for domestic students. Applications are processed on a rolling basis. *Application fee:* $25. Electronic applications accepted. *Application Contact:* Danette Kenne, Assistant Dean, 515-271-2188, Fax: 515-271-4518, E-mail: cbpa.gradprograms@drake.edu. *Dean,* Dr. Daniel J. Connolly, 515-271-2872, Fax: 515-271-4518, E-mail: daniel.connolly@drake.edu.

College of Pharmacy and Health Sciences Students: 486 full-time (351 women), 2 part-time (0 women); includes 75 minority (2 Black or African American, non-Hispanic/Latino; 51 Asian, non-Hispanic/Latino; 16 Hispanic/Latino; 6 Two or more races, non-Hispanic/Latino), 5 international. Average age 23. Expenses: Contact institution. *Financial support:* Teaching assistantships, career-related internships or fieldwork, Federal Work-Study, institutionally sponsored loans, and scholarships/grants available. Support available to part-time students. Financial award application deadline: 3/1; financial award applicants required to submit FAFSA. In 2018, 104 doctorates awarded. Offers athletic training (MAT); occupational therapy (OTD); pharmacy (Pharm D). *Application deadline:* For fall admission, 2/1 priority date for domestic students. *Application fee:* $135. Electronic applications accepted. *Application Contact:* Dr. Renae Chesnut, Dean, 515-271-3018, Fax: 515-271-4171, E-mail: renae.chesnut@drake.edu. *Dean,* Dr. Renae Chesnut, 515-271-3018, Fax: 515-271-4171, E-mail: renae.chesnut@drake.edu.

Law School Students: 307 full-time (153 women), 33 part-time (17 women); includes 51 minority (16 Black or African American, non-Hispanic/Latino; 6 Asian, non-Hispanic/Latino; 17 Hispanic/Latino; 12 Two or more races, non-Hispanic/Latino), 5 international. Average age 27. Expenses: Contact institution. *Financial support:* Research assistantships, teaching assistantships, career-related internships or fieldwork, Federal Work-Study, institutionally sponsored loans, scholarships/grants, and tuition waivers (full and partial) available. Support available to part-time students. Financial award application deadline: 3/1; financial award applicants required to submit

FAFSA. In 2018, 5 master's, 101 doctorates awarded. *Program availability:* Part-time. Offers law (LL M, MJ, JD). *Application deadline:* For fall admission, 4/1 priority date for domestic and international students. Applications are processed on a rolling basis. *Application fee:* $40. Electronic applications accepted. *Application Contact:* Kara Blanchard, Assistant Dean for Admission and Financial Aid, 515-271-2953, Fax: 515-271-2530, E-mail: kara.blanchard@drake.edu. *Dean,* Jerry Anderson, 515-271-2658, Fax: 515-271-4118, E-mail: jerry.anderson@drake.edu.

School of Education Students: 90 full-time (74 women), 690 part-time (532 women); includes 69 minority (30 Black or African American, non-Hispanic/Latino; 1 American Indian or Alaska Native, non-Hispanic/Latino; 9 Asian, non-Hispanic/Latino; 16 Hispanic/Latino; 13 Two or more races, non-Hispanic/Latino). Average age 34. Expenses: Contact institution. *Financial support:* Research assistantships, career-related internships or fieldwork, and unspecified assistantships available. Support available to part-time students. In 2018, 253 master's, 30 doctorates awarded. *Program availability:* Part-time, evening/weekend, 100% online, blended/hybrid learning. Offers applied behavior analysis (MS); counseling (MS); education (PhD); education administration (Ed D); educational leadership (MSE, Ed D); effective teaching (MSE); leadership development (MSE); literacy (Ed S); literacy education (MSE); rehabilitation administration (MS); rehabilitation placement (MS); special education (MSE); STEM education (MSE); teacher education (5-12) (MAT); teacher education (K-8) (MST); teacher effectiveness and professional development (MSE). *Application deadline:* For fall admission, 7/1 priority date for domestic students, 6/1 priority date for international students; for spring admission, 11/1 priority date for domestic students, 10/1 priority date for international students. Applications are processed on a rolling basis. *Application fee:* $25. Electronic applications accepted. *Application Contact:* Dr. Janet McMahill, Dean, 515-271-3829, E-mail: janet.mcmahill@drake.edu. *Dean,* Dr. Janet McMahill, 515-271-3829, E-mail: janet.mcmahill@drake.edu.

School of Journalism and Mass Communication Students: 12 full-time (6 women), 29 part-time (22 women); includes 7 minority (3 Black or African American, non-Hispanic/Latino; 1 Asian, non-Hispanic/Latino; 3 Hispanic/Latino), 1 international. Average age 31. Expenses: Contact institution. In 2018, 5 master's awarded. *Program availability:* Part-time, evening/weekend, 100% online, blended/hybrid learning. Offers brand communication (MCL); communication leadership (MCL); public affairs and advocacy (MCL). *Application Contact:* Dr. Kathleen Richardson, Dean, 515-271-2295, Fax: 515-271-4518, E-mail: kathleen.richardson@drake.edu. *Dean,* Dr. Kathleen Richardson, 515-271-2295, Fax: 515-271-4518, E-mail: kathleen.richardson@drake.edu.

DREW UNIVERSITY, Madison, NJ 07940-1493

General Information Independent-religious, coed, university. CGS member. *Enrollment:* 2,246 graduate, professional, and undergraduate students; 248 full-time matriculated graduate/professional students (126 women), 336 part-time matriculated graduate/professional students (194 women). *Enrollment by degree level:* 279 master's, 305 doctoral. *Graduate faculty:* 27 full-time (14 women), 49 part-time/adjunct (22 women). *Graduate housing:* Rooms and/or apartments available on a first-come, first-served basis to single and married students. Housing application deadline: 7/1. *Student services:* Campus employment opportunities, campus safety program, career counseling, child daycare facilities, exercise/wellness program, free psychological counseling, international student services, low-cost health insurance, multicultural affairs office, services for students with disabilities, teacher training, writing training. *Library facilities:* Rose Memorial Library plus 1 other. *Collection:* Books: 446,142 (physical), 224,692 (digital/electronic); Serial titles: 7,192 (physical), 164,691 (digital/electronic); Databases: 196. Weekly public service hours: 108; students can reserve study rooms.

Computer facilities: Computer purchase and lease plans are available. 95 computers available on campus for general student use. A campuswide network can be accessed from student residence rooms and from off campus. Online class registration is available.
Website: http://www.drew.edu/

General Application Contact: Amo-Augustus Kubeyinje, Associate Vice President for Graduate Enrollment, 973-408-3111, E-mail: akubeyinje@drew.edu.

GRADUATE UNITS

Caspersen School of Graduate Studies Students: 66 full-time (38 women), 179 part-time (117 women); includes 37 minority (15 Black or African American, non-Hispanic/Latino; 2 Asian, non-Hispanic/Latino; 15 Hispanic/Latino; 5 Two or more races, non-Hispanic/Latino), 14 international. Average age 42. 157 applicants, 82% accepted, 57 enrolled. *Faculty:* 3 full-time (2 women), 27 part-time/adjunct (13 women). Expenses: Contact institution. *Financial support:* Fellowships, research assistantships, teaching assistantships, career-related internships or fieldwork, Federal Work-Study, scholarships/grants, and unspecified assistantships available. Support available to part-time students. Financial award applicants required to submit FAFSA. In 2018, 34 master's, 24 doctorates, 17 other advanced degrees awarded. *Program availability:* Part-time, evening/weekend. Offers conflict resolution and leadership (Certificate); education (M Ed); finance (MA); history and culture (MA, PhD); K-12 education (MAT); liberal studies (M Litt, D Litt); medical humanities (MMH, DMH, CMH); poetry (MFA). *Application deadline:* For fall admission, 8/1 for domestic students, 6/1 for international students; for spring admission, 12/1 for domestic students, 10/1 for international students. Applications are processed on a rolling basis. *Application fee:* $35. Electronic applications accepted. *Application Contact:* Amo-Augustus Kubeyinje, Associate Vice President for Graduate Enrollment, 973-408-3111, E-mail: akubeyinje@drew.edu. *Provost and Dean of the College of Liberal Arts & Caspersen School of Graduate Studies,* Dr. Debra Liebowitz, 973-4083139, E-mail: dliebowi@drew.edu.

Theological School Students: 182 full-time (88 women), 157 part-time (77 women); includes 125 minority (92 Black or African American, non-Hispanic/Latino; 2 American Indian or Alaska Native, non-Hispanic/Latino; 13 Asian, non-Hispanic/Latino; 12 Hispanic/Latino; 1 Native Hawaiian or other Pacific Islander, non-Hispanic/Latino; 5 Two or more races, non-Hispanic/Latino), 91 international. Average age 42. 269 applicants, 72% accepted, 113 enrolled. *Faculty:* 24 full-time (11 women), 23 part-time/adjunct (10 women). Expenses: Contact institution. *Financial support:* Fellowships, career-related internships or fieldwork, Federal Work-Study, institutionally sponsored loans, and scholarships/grants available. Support available to part-time students. Financial award application deadline: 2/15; financial award applicants required to submit FAFSA. In 2018, 58 master's, 33 doctorates awarded. *Program availability:* Part-time, blended/hybrid learning. Offers (M Div, MA, MA Min, STM, D Min, PhD, Certificate). *Application deadline:* For fall admission, 8/1 for domestic students, 4/1 for international students; for spring admission, 12/1 for domestic students, 10/1 for international students. Applications are processed on a rolling basis. *Application fee:* $35. Electronic applications accepted. *Application Contact:* Rev. Dr. Kevin D. Miller, Director of Theological Admissions, 973-408-3111, E-mail: kmiller@drew.edu. *Dean of the Theological School,* Dr. Javier Viera, 973-408-3418, E-mail: jviera@drew.edu.

DREXEL UNIVERSITY, Philadelphia, PA 19104-2875

General Information Independent, coed, university. CGS member. *Graduate housing:* Room and/or apartments available on a first-come, first-served basis to single students; on-campus housing not available to married students. Housing application deadline: 1/9.

GRADUATE UNITS

College of Arts and Sciences *Program availability:* Part-time, evening/weekend. Offers arts and sciences (MA, MS, PhD); biological sciences (MS, PhD); chemistry (MS, PhD); clinical psychology (PhD); communication (MS); environmental policy (MS); environmental science (MS, PhD); forensic psychology (PhD); health psychology (PhD); law-psychologymathematics (MS, PhD); neuropsychology (PhD); physics (MS, PhD); psychology (MS); public communication (MS); science communication (MS); science, technology and society (MS); technical communication (MS). Electronic applications accepted.

College of Computing and Informatics Students: 222 full-time (113 women), 296 part-time (160 women); includes 108 minority (33 Black or African American, non-Hispanic/Latino; 32 Asian, non-Hispanic/Latino; 22 Hispanic/Latino; 21 Two or more races, non-Hispanic/Latino), 109 international. Average age 32. 1,012 applicants, 40% accepted, 206 enrolled. *Faculty:* 51 full-time (16 women), 22 part-time/adjunct (9 women). Expenses: Contact institution. *Financial support:* Fellowships, research assistantships, teaching assistantships, career-related internships or fieldwork, institutionally sponsored loans, scholarships/grants, health care benefits, and tuition waivers (partial) available. Support available to part-time students. Financial award application deadline: 3/1; financial award applicants required to submit FAFSA. In 2018, 187 master's, 15 doctorates, 19 other advanced degrees awarded. *Program availability:* Part-time, evening/weekend, 100% online. Offers computer science (MS, PhD, Postbaccalaureate Certificate); computing and informatics (MS, PhD, Post-Master's Certificate, Postbaccalaureate Certificate); health informatics (MS); information science (PhD, Post-Master's Certificate, Postbaccalaureate Certificate); information systems (MS); library and information science (MS); software engineering (MS). *Application deadline:* For fall admission, 8/15 for domestic students, 7/15 for international students; for spring admission, 3/1 for domestic students, 2/1 for international students. Applications are processed on a rolling basis. *Application fee:* $65. Electronic applications accepted. *Application Contact:* Matthew Lechtenberg, Director, Recruitment, 215-895-2474, Fax: 215-895-2303, E-mail: cciinfo@drexel.edu. *Dean/Professor,* Dr. Yi Deng, 215-895-2475, Fax: 215-895-2494, E-mail: yd362@drexel.edu.

College of Engineering *Program availability:* Part-time, evening/weekend. Offers architectural/building systems engineering (MS, PhD); biochemical engineering (MS); chemical engineering (MS, PhD); civil engineering (MS, PhD); computer engineering (MS); electrical and computer engineering (PhD); electrical engineering (MSEE); engineering (MS, MSEE, MSSE, PhD, Certificate); engineering management (MS, Certificate); environmental engineering (MS, PhD); geotechnical, geoenvironmental and geosynthetics engineering (MS, PhD); hydraulics, hydrology and water resources engineering (MS, PhD); materials engineering (MS, PhD); mechanical engineering (MS, PhD); software engineering (MSSE); structures (MS); telecommunications engineering (MSEE). Electronic applications accepted.

College of Medicine *Program availability:* Part-time. Offers medicine (MLAS, MMS, MS, MD, PhD, Certificate). Electronic applications accepted.

Biomedical Graduate Programs *Program availability:* Part-time. Offers biochemistry (MS, PhD); biomedical sciences (MLAS, MMS, MS, PhD, Certificate); drug discovery and development (MS); laboratory animal science (MLAS); medical science (MMS, Certificate); microbiology and immunology (MS, PhD); molecular and cell biology and genetics (MS, PhD); molecular medicine (MS); molecular pathobiology (MS, PhD); neuroscience (MS, PhD); pharmacology and physiology (MS, PhD). Electronic applications accepted.

College of Nursing and Health Professions *Program availability:* Part-time, evening/weekend. Offers art therapy (MA, PMC); clinical biomechanics and orthopedics (PhD); couple and family therapy (MFT, PhD); creative arts therapies (PhD); dance/movement therapy (MA, PMC); emergency and public safety services (MS); hand and upper quarter rehabilitation (Certificate); hand therapy (MHS, PPDPT); music therapy (MA, PMC); nurse anesthesia (MSN); nursing and health professions (MA, MFT, MHS, MS, MSN, DPT, Dr NP, PPDPT, PhD, Certificate, PMC); nursing studies (Dr NP); orthopedics (MHS, PPDPT); pediatric rehabilitation (Certificate); pediatrics (MHS, PPDPT, PhD); physical therapy (DPT); physician assistant (MHS). Electronic applications accepted.

Division of Graduate Nursing Offers adult acute care (MSN); adult psychiatric/mental health (MSN); advanced practice nursing (MSN); clinical trials research (MSN); family nurse practitioner (MSN); leadership in health systems management (MSN); nursing education (MSN); pediatric primary care (MSN); women's health (MSN). Electronic applications accepted.

Dornsife School of Public Health Offers biostatistics (MS); epidemiology (PhD); epidemiology and biostatistics (Certificate); public health (MPH, MS, PhD, Certificate). Electronic applications accepted.

Goodwin College of Professional Studies

School of Education *Program availability:* Part-time, evening/weekend, online learning. Offers applied behavior analysis (MS); creativity and innovation (MS); education improvement and transformation (MS); educational administration (MS); educational leadership and management (Ed D); educational leadership development and learning technologies (PhD); global and international education (MS); higher education (MS); human resources development (MS); learning technologies (MS); mathematics, learning and teaching (MS); special education (MS); teaching, learning and curriculum (MS). Electronic applications accepted.

School of Technology and Professional Studies *Program availability:* Part-time, evening/weekend. Offers construction management (MS); creativity and innovation (MS); engineering technology (MS); food science (MS); hospitality management (MS); professional studies: creativity studies (MS); professional studies: e-learning leadership (MS); professional studies: homeland security management (MS); project management (MS); property management (MS); sport management (MS). Electronic applications accepted.

LeBow College of Business *Program availability:* Part-time, evening/weekend. Offers accounting (MS); business (MBA, MS, PhD, APC); business administration (MBA, PhD, APC); finance (MS). Electronic applications accepted.

School of Biomedical Engineering, Science and Health Systems Offers biomedical engineering (MS, PhD); biomedical science (MS, PhD); biostatistics (MS); clinical/rehabilitation engineering (MS). Electronic applications accepted.

Thomas R. Kline School of Law Offers business and entrepreneurship law (JD); criminal law (MLS, JD); cybersecurity and information privacy compliance (MLS); entrepreneurship and law (MLS); financial regulatory compliance (MLS); health care compliance (MLS); health law (JD); higher education compliance (MLS); human resources compliance (MLS); intellectual property law (JD); NCAA compliance and sports law (MLS).

Westphal College of Media Arts and Design *Program availability:* Part-time, evening/weekend. Offers arts administration (MS); design research (MS); digital media (MS, PhD); fashion design (MS); interior architecture and design (MS); museum leadership (MS); retail and merchandising (MS); television management (MS); urban strategy (MS). Electronic applications accepted.

DRURY UNIVERSITY, Springfield, MO 65802

General Information Independent, coed, comprehensive institution. *Enrollment:* 1,728 graduate, professional, and undergraduate students; 240 full-time matriculated graduate/professional students (182 women). *Enrollment by degree level:* 239 master's, 1 other advanced degree. *Graduate faculty:* 18 full-time (10 women), 10 part-time/adjunct (6 women). *Graduate housing:* On-campus housing not available. *Student services:* Campus employment opportunities, campus safety program, career counseling, grant writing training, international student services, multicultural affairs office, services for students with disabilities, teacher training, writing training. *Library facilities:* F. W. Olin Library plus 1 other. *Collection:* Books: 154,247 (physical), 234,110 (digital/electronic); Serial titles: 354 (digital/electronic); Databases: 44. Weekly public service hours: 92; students can reserve study rooms.

Computer facilities: 385 computers available on campus for general student use. A campuswide network can be accessed from student residence rooms and from off campus. Online class registration, digital imaging lab, online bill payment/student information are available.
Website: http://www.drury.edu/

General Application Contact: Regina Waters, Associate Provost of Adult, Online, and Graduate Education, 417-873-7530, E-mail: grad@drury.edu.

GRADUATE UNITS

Cybersecurity Leadership Certificate Program Students: 1 full-time (0 women). Average age 43. 1 applicant, 100% accepted, 1 enrolled. *Faculty:* 1 full-time (0 women), 2 part-time/adjunct (1 woman). Expenses: Contact institution. *Financial support:* Career-related Internships or fieldwork available. Financial award application deadline: 6/30; financial award applicants required to submit FAFSA. *Program availability:* Part-time, evening/weekend. Offers cybersecurity leadership (Certificate). *Application deadline:* For fall admission, 8/4 for domestic and international students; for spring admission, 1/5 for domestic and international students; for summer admission, 5/26 for domestic and international students. Applications are processed on a rolling basis. *Application fee:* $25. Electronic applications accepted. *Application Contact:* Dr. Robin Soster, Director, 417-873-7612, E-mail: rsoster@drury.edu. *Director,* Dr. Robin Soster, 417-873-7612, E-mail: rsoster@drury.edu.

Master in Business Administration Students: 28 full-time (10 women). Average age 26. 13 applicants, 100% accepted, 12 enrolled. *Faculty:* 5 full-time (3 women). Expenses: Contact institution. *Financial support:* In 2018–19, 1 student received support. Career-related internships or fieldwork, scholarships/grants, and unspecified assistantships available. Financial award application deadline: 6/30; financial award applicants required to submit FAFSA. In 2018, 29 master's awarded. *Program availability:* Part-time, evening/weekend, 100% online. Offers business administration (MBA). *Application deadline:* For fall admission, 8/4 priority date for domestic and international students; for spring admission, 1/6 priority date for domestic and international students; for summer admission, 5/26 priority date for domestic and international students. Applications are processed on a rolling basis. *Application fee:* $25. Electronic applications accepted. *Application Contact:* Dr. Robin Soster, Director, MBA Program, 417-873-7612, E-mail: rsoster@drury.edu. *Director, MBA Program,* Dr. Robin Soster, 417-873-7612, E-mail: rsoster@drury.edu.

Master in Education Program Students: 167 full-time (133 women). Average age 32. 92 applicants, 92% accepted, 69 enrolled. *Faculty:* 10 full-time (6 women), 8 part-time/adjunct (6 women). Expenses: Contact institution. *Financial support:* In 2018–19, 5 students received support. Career-related internships or fieldwork, scholarships/grants, and unspecified assistantships available. Financial award application deadline: 6/30; financial award applicants required to submit FAFSA. In 2018, 44 master's awarded. *Program availability:* Part-time, evening/weekend, 100% online, blended/hybrid learning. Offers curriculum and instruction (M Ed); instructional leadership (M Ed); instructional technology (M Ed); integrated learning (M Ed); special education (M Ed); special reading (M Ed). *Application deadline:* For fall admission, 8/4 priority date for domestic and international students; for spring admission, 1/5 priority date for domestic and international students; for summer admission, 5/26 priority date for domestic and international students. Applications are processed on a rolling basis. *Application fee:* $25. Electronic applications accepted. *Application Contact:* Dr. Asikaa Cosgrove, Director, Master in Education Program, 417-873-7806, E-mail: acosgrov@drury.edu. *Director, Master in Education Program,* Dr. Asikaa Cosgrove, 417-873-7806, E-mail: acosgrov@drury.edu.

Master of Arts in Communication Program Students: 45 full-time (39 women). Average age 27. 10 applicants, 90% accepted, 7 enrolled. *Faculty:* 3 full-time (1 woman), 2 part-time/adjunct (0 women). Expenses: Contact institution. *Financial support:* Career-related internships or fieldwork, scholarships/grants, and unspecified assistantships available. Financial award application deadline: 6/30; financial award applicants required to submit FAFSA. In 2018, 7 master's awarded. *Program availability:* Part-time, evening/weekend. Offers integrated communication (MAC); organizational leadership and change (MAC). *Application deadline:* For fall admission, 8/4 priority date for domestic and international students; for spring admission, 1/5 priority date for domestic and international students; for summer admission, 5/26 priority date for domestic and international students. Applications are processed on a rolling basis. *Application fee:* $25. Electronic applications accepted. *Application Contact:* Dr. Charles Taylor, Director, Master of Arts in Communication Program, 417-873-7391, E-mail: ctaylor@drury.edu. *Director, Master of Arts in Communication Program,* Dr. Charles Taylor, 417-873-7391, E-mail: ctaylor@drury.edu.

Master of Nonprofit and Civic Leadership Program Students: 19 full-time (16 women). Average age 27. 9 applicants, 100% accepted, 8 enrolled. *Faculty:* 3 full-time (1 woman), 2 part-time/adjunct (0 women). Expenses: Contact institution. *Financial support:* Career-related internships or fieldwork, institutionally sponsored loans, scholarships/grants, and unspecified assistantships available. Financial award application deadline: 6/30; financial award applicants required to submit FAFSA. In 2018, 9 master's awarded. *Program availability:* Part-time, evening/weekend. Offers nonprofit and civic leadership (MNCL). *Application deadline:* For fall admission, 8/4 for domestic and international students; for spring admission, 1/6 for domestic and international students; for summer admission, 5/24 for domestic and international students. Applications are processed on a rolling basis. *Application fee:* $25. Electronic applications accepted. *Application Contact:* Dr. Charles Taylor, Director, 417-873-7391,

E-mail: ctaylor@drury.edu. *Director,* Dr. Charles Taylor, 417-873-7391, E-mail: ctaylor@drury.edu.

DUKE UNIVERSITY, Durham, NC 27708

General Information Independent-religious, coed, university. CGS member. *Graduate housing:* Rooms and/or apartments available on a first-come, first-served basis to single and married students. Housing application deadline: 5/8. *Research affiliation:* Highlands Biological Station, U.S. Forest Sciences Laboratory, Organization for Tropical Studies.

GRADUATE UNITS

Divinity School *Program availability:* Part-time, online learning. Offers theology (M Div, MACP, MACS, MTS, Th M, D Min, Th D). Electronic applications accepted.

The Fuqua School of Business Students: 1,620 full-time (614 women); includes 359 minority (77 Black or African American, non-Hispanic/Latino; 6 American Indian or Alaska Native, non-Hispanic/Latino; 194 Asian, non-Hispanic/Latino; 66 Hispanic/Latino; 3 Native Hawaiian or other Pacific Islander, non-Hispanic/Latino; 13 Two or more races, non-Hispanic/Latino; 579 international. Average age 29. *Faculty:* 100 full-time (21 women), 55 part-time/adjunct (12 women). Expenses: Contact institution. In 2018, 1,025 master's, 14 doctorates awarded. Offers academic excellence in finance (Certificate); accounting (PhD); business (EMBA, GEMBA, MBA, MMS, MQM, WEMBA, PhD, Certificate); business administration (MBA); decision sciences (MBA, PhD); energy and environment (MBA); energy finance (MBA); entrepreneurship and innovation (MBA); finance (MBA, MQM, PhD); financial analysis (MBA); forensics (MQM); foundations of business (MMS); health analytics (MQM); health sector management (Certificate); leadership and ethics (MBA); management (MBA); management and organizations (PhD); management science and technology management (Certificate); management studies (MMS); marketing (MBA, MQM, PhD); operations management (MBA, PhD); social entrepreneurship (MBA); strategy (MBA, MQM, PhD). Electronic applications accepted. *Application Contact:* Shari Hubert, Associate Dean, Office of Admissions, Fax: 919-681-8026, E-mail: admissions-info@fuqua.duke.edu. *Dean,* William Boulding, 919-660-7822.

Graduate School *Program availability:* Part-time, evening/weekend. Offers bioethics and science policy (MA); biological psychology (PhD); biology (PhD); business administration (PhD); cell and molecular biology (Certificate); cell biology (PhD); cellular and molecular biology (PhD); chemistry (PhD); classical studies (PhD); clinical psychology (PhD); cognitive neuroscience (PhD, Certificate); cognitive psychology (PhD); computational biology and bioinformatics (PhD, Certificate); computer science (MS, PhD); crystallography of macromolecules (PhD); developmental and stem cell biology (Certificate); developmental psychology (PhD); East Asian studies (AM, Certificate); ecology (PhD, Certificate); econometrics (MS); economics (AM, PhD); economics and computation (MS); English (PhD); environment (PhD); environmental policy (PhD); enzyme mechanisms (PhD); experimental and documentary arts (MFA); experimental psychology (PhD); financial economics (MS); French (PhD); genetics and genomics (PhD); German studies (PhD); gross anatomy and physical anthropology (PhD); health psychology (PhD); historical and cultural visualization (MA); history (AM, PhD); history of art (PhD); human social development (PhD); humanities (AM); immunology (PhD); integrated toxicology and environmental health (Certificate); Italian (PhD); Latin American studies (AM); liberal studies (AM); lipid biochemistry (PhD); literature (PhD); marine science and conservation (PhD); mathematics (PhD); medical physics (MS, PhD); membrane structure and function (PhD); molecular cancer biology (PhD); molecular genetics (PhD); molecular genetics and microbiology (PhD); music composition (PhD); musicology (PhD); neuroanatomy (PhD); neurobiology (PhD); neurochemistry (PhD); nucleic acid structure and function (PhD); pathology (PhD); performance practice (PhD); pharmacology (PhD); philosophy (PhD); physical anthropology (PhD); physics (PhD); political science (AM, PhD); protein structure and function (PhD); public policy (PhD); religion (MA, PhD); Slavic and Eurasian studies (AM, Certificate); social/cultural anthropology (PhD); sociology (AM, PhD); Spanish (PhD); statistical science (MSS, PhD); structural biology and biophysics (Certificate); teaching (MAT). Electronic applications accepted.

Division of Earth and Ocean Sciences *Program availability:* Part-time. Offers earth and ocean sciences (MS, PhD). Electronic applications accepted.

Duke Global Health Institute Offers global health (MS).

Pratt School of Engineering *Program availability:* Part-time, online learning. Offers biomedical engineering (M Eng, MS, PhD); civil and environmental engineering (MS, PhD); civil engineering (M Eng); computational mechanics and scientific computing (M Eng); electrical and computer engineering (M Eng, MS, PhD); engineering (M Eng, MEM, MS, PhD); engineering management (MEM); environmental engineering (M Eng, MS, PhD); materials science (M Eng, MS, PhD); materials science and engineering (M Eng); mechanical engineering (M Eng, MS, PhD); photonics and optical sciences (M Eng); risk engineering (M Eng).

Nicholas School of the Environment Students: 365 full-time (243 women); includes 67 minority (7 Black or African American, non-Hispanic/Latino; 4 American Indian or Alaska Native, non-Hispanic/Latino; 36 Asian, non-Hispanic/Latino; 20 Hispanic/Latino), 93 international. Average age 27. 428 applicants, 83% accepted, 151 enrolled. *Faculty:* 50. Expenses: Contact institution. *Financial support:* Research assistantships, career-related internships or fieldwork, Federal Work-Study, institutionally sponsored loans, scholarships/grants, and unspecified assistantships available. Financial award application deadline: 12/15; financial award applicants required to submit CSS PROFILE or FAFSA. In 2018, 181 master's awarded. Offers earth and ocean sciences (PhD); environment (MEM, MF, PhD); marine science and conservation (PhD). *Application deadline:* For fall admission, 12/15 priority date for domestic and international students. *Application fee:* $400. Electronic applications accepted. *Application Contact:* Benjamin Spain, Associate Director of Enrollment Services, 919-684-1155, E-mail: admissions@nicholas.duke.edu. *Associate Dean, Student Services,* Sherri Nevius, 919-613-8063, E-mail: sherri.nevius@duke.edu.

Sanford School of Public Policy Average age 29. 704 applicants, 126 enrolled. Expenses: Contact institution. *Financial support:* Fellowships, research assistantships, teaching assistantships, career-related internships or fieldwork, Federal Work-Study, scholarships/grants, and unspecified assistantships available. Financial award application deadline: 1/5; financial award applicants required to submit FAFSA. In 2018, 113 master's awarded. Offers international development policy (MIDP); public policy (MIDP, MPP). *Application deadline:* For fall admission, 1/5 for domestic and international students. *Application fee:* $80. Electronic applications accepted. *Application Contact:* Jessica Pan, Director of Admissions, 919-613-9244, E-mail: jessica.pan@duke.edu. *Dean, Sanford School of Public Policy,* Judith Kelley, 919-613-7401.

School of Law Students: 682; includes 167 minority (47 Black or African American, non-Hispanic/Latino; 1 American Indian or Alaska Native, non-Hispanic/Latino; 56 Asian, non-Hispanic/Latino; 53 Hispanic/Latino; 10 Two or more races, non-Hispanic/Latino), 52 international. Average age 24. 5,558 applicants, 20% accepted, 230 enrolled. *Faculty:* 95 full-time (41 women), 86 part-time/adjunct (23 women). Expenses: Contact institution. *Financial support:* Institutionally sponsored loans, scholarships/grants, and unspecified assistantships available. Financial award application deadline: 3/15; financial award applicants required to submit FAFSA. Offers American law (LL M); bioethics and science policy (LL M, MJS, JD, SJD); international and comparative law or law and entrepreneurship (LL M, MJS, JD, SJD); judicial studies (MJS); law (JD, SJD); law and entrepreneurship (LL M). Sanford School of Public Policy, Fuqua School of Business, Nicholas School of the Environment, Duke Divinity School, Institut d'Etudes Politiques de Paris. *Application deadline:* For fall admission, 2/15 for domestic and international students. Applications are processed on a rolling basis. *Application fee:* $70. Electronic applications accepted. *Application Contact:* William J. Hoye, Associate Dean for Admissions and Student Affairs, 919-613-7020, Fax: 919-613-7257, E-mail: hoye@law.duke.edu. *Dean/Professor of Law,* Kerry Abrams, 919-613-7001, Fax: 919-613-7158.

School of Medicine Students: 1,067 full-time (649 women), 89 part-time (51 women); includes 459 minority (111 Black or African American, non-Hispanic/Latino; 20 American Indian or Alaska Native, non-Hispanic/Latino; 253 Asian, non-Hispanic/Latino; 69 Hispanic/Latino; 6 Native Hawaiian or other Pacific Islander, non-Hispanic/Latino; 37 international. Expenses: Contact institution. *Financial support:* In 2018–19, 438 students received support. Institutionally sponsored loans and scholarships/grants available. Financial award application deadline: 4/15; financial award applicants required to submit FAFSA. In 2018, 291 master's, 184 doctorates awarded. Offers biomedical sciences (MS); biostatistics (MS); clinical informatics (MS); clinical leadership (MHS); clinical research (MHS); medicine (MHS, MS, DPT, MD); pathologists' assistant (MHS); physician assistant (MHS). *Application Contact:* Andrea Liu, Director of Admissions, 919-684-2985, Fax: 919-684-8893, E-mail: medadm@mc.duke.edu. *Vice Dean, Medical Education,* Dr. Edward G. Buckley, 919-668-3381, Fax: 919-660-7040, E-mail: buckl002@mc.duke.edu.

Physical Therapy Division Students: 231 full-time (153 women); includes 54 minority (16 Black or African American, non-Hispanic/Latino; 1 American Indian or Alaska Native, non-Hispanic/Latino; 20 Asian, non-Hispanic/Latino; 13 Hispanic/Latino; 4 Native Hawaiian or other Pacific Islander, non-Hispanic/Latino), 1,157 applicants, 9% accepted, 83 enrolled. *Faculty:* 19 full-time (8 women), 3 part-time/adjunct (1 woman). Expenses: Contact institution. *Financial support:* In 2018–19, 22 students received support. Scholarships/grants and VA Benefits & outside scholarships available. Financial award application deadline: 4/15; financial award applicants required to submit FAFSA. In 2018, 76 doctorates awarded. Offers physical therapy (DPT). *Application deadline:* For fall admission, 11/1 priority date for domestic and international students. Applications are processed on a rolling basis. *Application fee:* $50. Electronic applications accepted. *Application Contact:* Stephanie Halpin, Assistant Director, Admissions, 919-660-1957, Fax: 919-668-1957, E-mail: stephanie.halpin@duke.edu. *Program Director,* Dr. Chad Cook, 919-684-8905, Fax: 919-684-1846, E-mail: chad.cook@duke.edu.

School of Nursing Students: 645 full-time (586 women), 172 part-time (148 women); includes 189 minority (61 Black or African American, non-Hispanic/Latino; 2 American Indian or Alaska Native, non-Hispanic/Latino; 52 Asian, non-Hispanic/Latino; 45 Hispanic/Latino; 1 Native Hawaiian or other Pacific Islander, non-Hispanic/Latino; 28 Two or more races, non-Hispanic/Latino), 10 international. Average age 33. 660 applicants, 48% accepted, 209 enrolled. *Faculty:* 71 full-time (60 women). Expenses: Contact institution. *Financial support:* Institutionally sponsored loans, scholarships/grants, and traineeships available. Support available to part-time students. Financial award applicants required to submit FAFSA. In 2018, 213 master's, 74 doctorates, 18 other advanced degrees awarded. *Program availability:* Part-time, evening/weekend, online with on-campus intensives. Offers acute care pediatric nurse practitioner (MSN, Post-Graduate Certificate); adult-gerontology nurse practitioner (MSN, Post-Graduate Certificate); family nurse practitioner (MSN, Post-Graduate Certificate); neonatal nurse practitioner (MSN, Post-Graduate Certificate); nurse anesthesia (DNP); nurse practitioner (DNP); nursing (MSN, DNP, PhD, Post-Graduate Certificate); nursing and health care leadership (MSN, Post-Graduate Certificate); nursing education (MSN, Post-Graduate Certificate); nursing informatics (MSN, Post-Graduate Certificate); pediatric nurse practitioner (MSN, Post-Graduate Certificate); psychiatric mental health nurse practitioner (MSN, Post-Graduate Certificate); women's health nurse practitioner (MSN, Post-Graduate Certificate). *Application deadline:* For fall admission, 12/1 for domestic and international students; for spring admission, 5/1 for domestic and international students. *Application fee:* $50. Electronic applications accepted. *Application Contact:* Dr. Ernie Rushing, Director of Admissions and Recruitment, 919-668-6274, Fax: 919-668-4693, E-mail: ernie.rushing@dm.duke.edu. *Dean/Vice Chancellor for Nursing Affairs/Associate Vice President for Academic Affairs for Nursing,* Dr. Marion E. Broome, 919-684-9446, Fax: 919-684-9414, E-mail: marion.broome@duke.edu.

DUNLAP-STONE UNIVERSITY, Phoenix, AZ 85024

General Information Proprietary, coed, comprehensive institution.

GRADUATE UNITS

Graduate Law Center Offers regulatory trade compliance (M Sc); U.S. regulatory trade law (LL M).

DUQUESNE UNIVERSITY, Pittsburgh, PA 15282-0001

General Information Independent-religious, coed, university. CGS member. *Enrollment:* 9,274 graduate, professional, and undergraduate students; 2,962 full-time matriculated graduate/professional students (1,882 women), 281 part-time matriculated graduate/professional students (194 women). *Enrollment by degree level:* 1,295 master's, 1,886 doctoral, 62 other advanced degrees. *Graduate faculty:* 457 full-time (217 women), 339 part-time/adjunct (162 women). *Tuition:* Full-time $23,112; part-time $1284 per credit. Tuition and fees vary according to program. *Graduate housing:* Rooms and/or apartments available on a first-come, first-served basis to single and married students. Typical cost: $6918 per year ($12,586 including board) for single students; $6918 per year ($12,586 including board) for married students. Room and board charges vary according to board plan and housing facility selected. Housing application deadline: 5/1. *Student services:* Campus employment opportunities, campus safety program, career counseling, child daycare facilities, exercise/wellness program, free psychological counseling, international student services, low-cost health insurance, multicultural affairs office, services for students with disabilities, teacher training, writing training. *Library facilities:* Gumberg Library plus 1 other. *Collection:* Books: 562,314 (physical), 342,710 (digital/electronic); Serial titles: 123 (physical), 99,402 (digital/electronic); Databases: 227. Weekly public service hours: 112; students can reserve study rooms.

Computer facilities: Computer purchase and lease plans are available. 1,000 computers available on campus for general student use. A campuswide network can be accessed from student residence rooms and from off campus. Online class registration is available.
Website: http://www.duq.edu/

General Application Contact: Todd Eicker, Director, Graduate Enrollment Services, 412-396-6219, E-mail: eickert@duq.edu.

GRADUATE UNITS

Bayer School of Natural and Environmental Sciences Students: 111 full-time (61 women), 16 part-time (12 women); includes 14 minority (3 Black or African American, non-Hispanic/Latino; 3 Asian, non-Hispanic/Latino; 5 Hispanic/Latino; 3 Two or more races, non-Hispanic/Latino), 15 international. Average age 26. 82 applicants, 77% accepted, 26 enrolled. *Faculty:* 39 full-time (12 women), 29 part-time/adjunct (11 women). Expenses: Contact institution. *Financial support:* In 2018–19, 119 students received support, including 3 fellowships with full tuition reimbursements available, 18 research assistantships with full tuition reimbursements available, 54 teaching assistantships with full tuition reimbursements available; career-related internships or fieldwork, scholarships/grants, tuition waivers (partial), and unspecified assistantships also available. Financial award application deadline: 5/31. In 2018, 50 master's, 7 doctorates awarded. *Program availability:* Part-time. Offers biological sciences (PhD); biotechnology (MS); chemistry (PhD); environmental science and management (MS, Certificate); forensic science and law (MS); natural and environmental sciences (MS, PhD, Certificate). *Application deadline:* For fall admission, 2/15 priority date for domestic students, 2/15 for international students; for spring admission, 10/1 priority date for domestic students, 10/1 for international students. Applications are processed on a rolling basis. *Application fee:* $0. Electronic applications accepted. *Application Contact:* Heather Costello, Senior Graduate Academic Advisor, 412-396-6339, Fax: 412-396-4881, E-mail: costelloh@duq.edu. *Dean,* Dr. Philip Reeder, 412-396-4877, Fax: 412-396-4881, E-mail: reederp@duq.edu.

Biomedical Engineering Program

Graduate School of Liberal Arts Students: 382 full-time (182 women), 51 part-time (30 women); includes 58 minority (31 Black or African American, non-Hispanic/Latino; 4 Asian, non-Hispanic/Latino; 16 Hispanic/Latino; 7 Two or more races, non-Hispanic/Latino), 88 international. Average age 33. 397 applicants, 56% accepted, 116 enrolled. *Faculty:* 124 full-time (45 women), 36 part-time/adjunct (17 women). Expenses: Contact institution. *Financial support:* In 2018–19, 212 students received support, including 11 research assistantships with full tuition reimbursements available (averaging $11,000 per year), 127 teaching assistantships with full tuition reimbursements available (averaging $17,500 per year); career-related internships or fieldwork, Federal Work-Study, institutionally sponsored loans, scholarships/grants, and tuition waivers (full and partial) also available. Support available to part-time students. Financial award application deadline: 5/1. In 2018, 139 master's, 47 doctorates awarded. *Program availability:* Part-time, evening/weekend, 100% online, blended/hybrid learning. Offers clinical psychology (PhD); communication (MA); computational mathematics (MS); English (MA, PhD); historical studies (MA); leadership (MS); liberal arts (MA, MS, DHCE, PhD, Certificate); media (MS, Certificate); pastoral ministry (MA); philosophy (MA, PhD); public history (MA); religious education (MA); rhetoric (PhD); systematic theology (PhD); theology (MA). *Application deadline:* For fall admission, 8/1 for domestic students, 5/1 for international students; for spring admission, 11/1 for domestic students, 9/1 for international students. Applications are processed on a rolling basis. *Application fee:* $0. Electronic applications accepted. *Application Contact:* Linda Rendulic, Assistant to the Dean, 412-396-6400, Fax: 412-396-5265, E-mail: rendulic@duq.edu. *Dean,* Dr. Kristine Blair, 412-396-6400.

Center for Healthcare Ethics Students: 43 full-time (27 women), 1 (woman) part-time; includes 13 minority (7 Black or African American, non-Hispanic/Latino; 3 Asian, non-Hispanic/Latino; 2 Hispanic/Latino; 1 Two or more races, non-Hispanic/Latino), 16 international. Average age 36. 26 applicants, 96% accepted, 15 enrolled. *Faculty:* 3 full-time (0 women). Expenses: Contact institution. *Financial support:* In 2018–19, 7 students received support, including 5 teaching assistantships with full and partial tuition reimbursements available (averaging $18,000 per year); Federal Work-Study and tuition waivers (full and partial) also available. Support available to part-time students. Financial award application deadline: 5/1. In 2018, 5 master's, 15 doctorates awarded. *Program availability:* Part-time, 100% online. Offers healthcare ethics (MA, DHCE, PhD, Certificate). *Application deadline:* For fall admission, 8/1 for domestic students, 5/1 for international students. *Application fee:* $0. Electronic applications accepted. *Application Contact:* Linda Rendulic, Assistant to the Dean, 412-396-6400, Fax: 412-396-5265, E-mail: rendulic@duq.edu. *Director,* Dr. Joris Gielen, 412-396-2616, E-mail: gielenj@duq.edu.

John G. Rangos, Sr. School of Health Sciences Students: 243 full-time (195 women), 8 part-time (5 women); includes 10 minority (1 Black or African American, non-Hispanic/Latino; 4 Asian, non-Hispanic/Latino; 4 Hispanic/Latino; 1 Two or more races, non-Hispanic/Latino), 44 international. Average age 23. 465 applicants, 26% accepted, 47 enrolled. *Faculty:* 51 full-time (38 women), 33 part-time/adjunct (17 women). Expenses: Contact institution. *Financial support:* Federal Work-Study available. Financial award applicants required to submit FAFSA. In 2018, 137 master's, 38 doctorates awarded. *Program availability:* Part-time, minimal on-campus study. Offers health management systems (MHMS); occupational therapy (MS, OTD); physical therapy (DPT); physician assistant studies (MPAS); rehabilitation science (MS, PhD); speech-language pathology (MS). *Application deadline:* For fall admission, 2/1 for domestic and international students; for spring admission, 7/1 for domestic and international students. Applications are processed on a rolling basis. *Application fee:* $0. Electronic applications accepted. *Application Contact:* Christopher R. Hilf, Director of Enrollment Management, 412-396-5653, Fax: 412-396-5554, E-mail: hilfc@duq.edu. *Dean,* Dr. Fevzi Akinci, 412-396-5303, Fax: 412-396-5554, E-mail: akincif@duq.edu.

Mary Pappert School of Music Students: 67 full-time (32 women), 6 part-time (4 women); includes 6 minority (1 Black or African American, non-Hispanic/Latino; 2 Asian, non-Hispanic/Latino; 3 Hispanic/Latino), 36 international. Average age 27. 68 applicants, 99% accepted, 32 enrolled. *Faculty:* 26 full-time (9 women), 77 part-time/adjunct (22 women). Expenses: Contact institution. *Financial support:* In 2018–19, 64 students received support. Scholarships/grants and unspecified assistantships available. Financial award application deadline: 4/1. In 2018, 23 master's, 4 ADs awarded. *Program availability:* Part-time. Offers music education (MM). *Application deadline:* For fall admission, 7/1 for domestic and international students; for spring admission, 12/1 for domestic and international students. Applications are processed on a rolling basis. *Application fee:* $50. Electronic applications accepted. *Application Contact:* Thomas Carsecka, Director of Music Admissions, 412-396-5983, Fax: 412-396-5719, E-mail: carseckat@duq.edu. *Dean/Professor,* Dr. Seth Beckman, 412-396-6082, Fax: 412-396-1524, E-mail: beckmans@duq.edu.

Palumbo-Donahue School of Business Students: 214 full-time (74 women), 42 part-time (20 women); includes 39 minority (12 Black or African American, non-Hispanic/Latino; 13 Asian, non-Hispanic/Latino; 8 Hispanic/Latino; 6 Two or more races, non-Hispanic/Latino), 123 international. Average age 29. 228 applicants, 88% accepted, 118 enrolled. *Faculty:* 59 full-time (23 women), 25 part-time/adjunct (6 women). Expenses: Contact institution. *Financial support:* In 2018–19, 174 students received support, including 6 fellowships with partial tuition reimbursements available (averaging

$24,750 per year); career-related internships or fieldwork, scholarships/grants, and unspecified assistantships also available. Support available to part-time students. Financial award application deadline: 7/1; financial award applicants required to submit FAFSA. In 2018, 149 master's awarded. *Program availability:* Part-time, evening/weekend, 100% online, blended/hybrid learning. Offers accounting (M Acc); finance (MBA); information systems management (MSISM); management (MBA, MS); marketing (MBA); sports business (MS); supply chain management (MS); sustainability (MBA). *Application deadline:* For fall admission, 7/1 priority date for domestic and international students; for spring admission, 12/1 for domestic and international students; for summer admission, 4/1 for domestic and international students. Applications are processed on a rolling basis. *Application fee:* $0. Electronic applications accepted. *Application Contact:* Chris Rouhier, Director of Graduate Admissions, 412-396-6244, Fax: 412-396-1726, E-mail: rouhierc@duq.edu. *Associate Dean of Graduate Programs and Executive Education,* Dr. Karen Donovan, 412-396-5788, Fax: 412-396-1726, E-mail: donovan6@duq.edu.

Post-Baccalaureate Pre-Medical and Health Professions Program Students: 8 full-time (6 women); includes 2 minority (1 Asian, non-Hispanic/Latino; 1 Hispanic/Latino). Average age 23. 39 applicants, 56% accepted, 8 enrolled. *Faculty:* 1 (woman) full-time. Expenses: Contact institution. *Financial support:* Applicants required to submit FAFSA. In 2018, 5 Postbaccalaureate Certificates awarded. Offers pre-medical studies and health professions (Postbaccalaureate Certificate). *Application deadline:* For fall admission, 5/1 for domestic students. Applications are processed on a rolling basis. *Application fee:* $0. Electronic applications accepted. *Application Contact:* Todd Eicker, Director of Graduate Admission, 412-396-6219, E-mail: eickert@duq.edu. *Director,* Dr. Paula Sammarone-Turocy, 412-396-6335, Fax: 412-396-5587, E-mail: turocyp@duq.edu.

School of Education Students: 490 full-time (368 women), 44 part-time (32 women); includes 93 minority (48 Black or African American, non-Hispanic/Latino; 1 American Indian or Alaska Native, non-Hispanic/Latino; 12 Asian, non-Hispanic/Latino; 16 Hispanic/Latino; 16 Two or more races, non-Hispanic/Latino), 63 international. Average age 30. 437 applicants, 85% accepted, 178 enrolled. *Faculty:* 52 full-time (31 women), 83 part-time/adjunct (63 women). Expenses: Contact institution. *Financial support:* In 2018–19, 53 research assistantships with full and partial tuition reimbursements (averaging $3,603 per year) were awarded; teaching assistantships, career-related internships or fieldwork, Federal Work-Study, institutionally sponsored loans, and tuition waivers also available. Support available to part-time students. Financial award applicants required to submit FAFSA. In 2018, 142 master's, 52 doctorates, 7 other advanced degrees awarded. *Program availability:* Part-time, evening/weekend, 100% online, blended/hybrid learning. Offers biology (MS Ed); chemistry (MS Ed); child psychology (MS Ed); clinical mental health counseling (MS Ed, Post-Master's Certificate); cognitive, behavior, physical/health disabilities (MS Ed); community and special education support (MS Ed); counselor education (MS Ed, Ed D, Post-Master's Certificate); counselor education and supervision (Ed D); counselor licensure (Post-Master's Certificate); curriculum and instruction (Post-Master's Certificate); early level (PreK-4) education (MS Ed); education (MS Ed, Ed D, PhD, Psy D, Post-Master's Certificate); educational leadership (Ed D); educational studies (MS Ed); English (MS Ed); English as a second language (MS Ed); instructional technology (MS Ed, Ed D, Post-Master's Certificate); K-12 education (MS Ed); marriage and family counseling (MS Ed); mathematics (MS Ed); middle level (4-8) education (MS Ed); physics (MS Ed); program evaluation (MS Ed); reading and language arts (MS Ed); school administration and supervision (MS Ed, Post-Master's Certificate); school administration K-12 (MS Ed, Post-Master's Certificate); school counseling (MS Ed); school psychology (MS Ed, PhD, Psy D); school supervision (MS Ed); secondary education (MS Ed); social studies (MS Ed); special education (MS Ed, PhD); special education 7-12 (MS Ed); special education PreK-8 (MS Ed). *Application deadline:* For fall admission, 3/1 for domestic students; for spring admission, 9/1 for domestic students. Applications are processed on a rolling basis. *Application fee:* $0. Electronic applications accepted. *Application Contact:* Kelly McGinley, Graduate Admissions Assistant, 412-396-1559, Fax: 412-296-5585, E-mail: mcginleyk@duq.edu. *Dean,* Dr. Cindy Walker, 412-396-6102, Fax: 412-396-5585.

School of Law Students: 436 full-time (236 women); includes 41 minority (16 Black or African American, non-Hispanic/Latino; 1 American Indian or Alaska Native, non-Hispanic/Latino; 7 Asian, non-Hispanic/Latino; 14 Hispanic/Latino; 3 Two or more races, non-Hispanic/Latino), 4 international. Average age 26. 759 applicants, 63% accepted, 171 enrolled. *Faculty:* 30 full-time (16 women), 35 part-time/adjunct (9 women). Expenses: Contact institution. *Financial support:* In 2018–19, 338 students received support, including 25 research assistantships with partial tuition reimbursements available (averaging $2,500 per year), 20 teaching assistantships with partial tuition reimbursements available (averaging $2,500 per year); career-related internships or fieldwork, scholarships/grants, tuition waivers (partial), and library assistants also available. Support available to part-time students. Financial award application deadline: 5/1; financial award applicants required to submit FAFSA. In 2018, 1 master's, 119 doctorates awarded. *Program availability:* Part-time, evening/weekend. Offers American law for foreign lawyers (LL M); law (JD). JD/M Div offered jointly with Pittsburgh Theological Seminary. *Application deadline:* For fall admission, 3/1 priority date for domestic and international students. Applications are processed on a rolling basis. *Application fee:* $0. Electronic applications accepted. *Application Contact:* Office of Admissions, 412-396-6296, Fax: 412-396-6659, E-mail: lawadmissions@duq.edu. *Dean,* Maureen Lally-Green, 412-396-6280, Fax: 412-396-6283, E-mail: lallygreen@duq.edu.

School of Nursing Students: 280 full-time (261 women), 90 part-time (79 women); includes 77 minority (33 Black or African American, non-Hispanic/Latino; 2 American Indian or Alaska Native, non-Hispanic/Latino; 17 Asian, non-Hispanic/Latino; 18 Hispanic/Latino; 1 Native Hawaiian or other Pacific Islander, non-Hispanic/Latino; 6 Two or more races, non-Hispanic/Latino), 3 international. Average age 36. 278 applicants, 80% accepted, 142 enrolled. *Faculty:* 26 full-time (21 women), 18 part-time/adjunct (17 women). Expenses: Contact institution. *Financial support:* In 2018–19, 30 students received support, including 30 teaching assistantships with partial tuition reimbursements available (averaging $4,841 per year); institutionally sponsored loans, scholarships/grants, traineeships, tuition waivers (partial), and unspecified assistantships also available. Support available to part-time students. Financial award application deadline: 5/1; financial award applicants required to submit FAFSA. In 2018, 51 master's, 12 doctorates, 5 other advanced degrees awarded. *Program availability:* Part-time, evening/weekend, online only, 100% online. Offers family (individual across the life span) nurse practitioner (MSN, Post-Master's Certificate); forensic nursing (MSN, Post-Master's Certificate); nursing (MSN, DNP, PhD, Post-Master's Certificate); nursing education and faculty role (MSN, Post-Master's Certificate); nursing ethics (PhD); nursing practice (DNP). *Application deadline:* For fall admission, 7/15 for domestic and international students; for spring admission, 12/3 for domestic and international students; for summer admission, 3/30 for domestic and international students.

Application fee: $0. Electronic applications accepted. *Application Contact:* Scott Copley, Director of Admissions, 412-396-4661, Fax: 412-396-6346, E-mail: copley@duq.edu. *Dean/Professor,* Dr. Mary Ellen Glasgow, 412-396-6554, Fax: 412-396-5974, E-mail: glasgowm@duq.edu.

School of Pharmacy Students: 720 full-time (462 women), 20 part-time (10 women); includes 112 minority (31 Black or African American, non-Hispanic/Latino; 42 Asian, non-Hispanic/Latino; 26 Hispanic/Latino; 13 Two or more races, non-Hispanic/Latino), 45 international. Average age 23. 418 applicants, 63% accepted, 207 enrolled. *Faculty:* 49 full-time (21 women), 3 part-time/adjunct (0 women). Expenses: Contact institution. *Financial support:* In 2018–19, 113 students received support. Federal Work-Study and scholarships/grants available. Financial award application deadline: 6/1; financial award applicants required to submit FAFSA. In 2018, 6 master's, 185 doctorates awarded. *Program availability:* Evening/weekend. Offers pharmacy (MS, PhD, Pharm D). *Application deadline:* For fall admission, 2/1 for domestic and international students; for spring admission, 12/1 for domestic and international students. Applications are processed on a rolling basis. *Application fee:* $50. Electronic applications accepted. *Application Contact:* Tammie Suppo, Coordinator for Recruitment and Admissions, 412-396-6393, Fax: 412-396-5130, E-mail: pharmadmission@duq.edu. *Dean,* Dr. J. Douglas Bricker, 412-396-6377, Fax: 412-396-5130.

Graduate School of Pharmaceutical Sciences Students: 47 full-time (24 women), 1 part-time (0 women); includes 3 minority (2 Asian, non-Hispanic/Latino; 1 Hispanic/Latino), 36 international. Average age 27. 39 applicants, 23% accepted, 5 enrolled. *Faculty:* 22 full-time (7 women). Expenses: Contact institution. *Financial support:* In 2018–19, 57 students received support, including 13 research assistantships with full tuition reimbursements available, 44 teaching assistantships with full tuition reimbursements available; unspecified assistantships also available. In 2018, 6 master's, 7 doctorates awarded. Offers medicinal chemistry (MS, PhD); pharmaceutics (MS, PhD); pharmacology (MS, PhD); pharmacy administration (MS). *Application deadline:* For fall admission, 12/1 priority date for domestic and international students; for spring admission, 10/1 priority date for domestic and international students. Applications are processed on a rolling basis. Electronic applications accepted. *Application Contact:* Information Contact, 412-396-1172, E-mail: gsps-adm@duq.edu. *Associate Dean for Research and Graduate Programs,* Dr. James K. Drennen, III, 412-396-5520.

D'YOUVILLE COLLEGE, Buffalo, NY 14201-1084

General Information Independent, coed, comprehensive institution. *Graduate housing:* Room and/or apartments available on a first-come, first-served basis to single students. Housing application deadline: 8/1.

GRADUATE UNITS

Department of Business *Program availability:* Part-time, evening/weekend. Offers business administration (MBA); international business (MS). Electronic applications accepted.

Department of Chiropractic Offers chiropractic (DC). Electronic applications accepted.

Department of Dietetics Offers dietetics (MS). Five-year program begins at freshman entry. Electronic applications accepted.

Department of Education *Program availability:* Part-time, evening/weekend. Offers educational leadership (Ed D); elementary education (MS Ed); secondary education (MS Ed); special education (MS Ed). Electronic applications accepted.

Department of Health Services Administration *Program availability:* Part-time, evening/weekend. Offers clinical research associate (Certificate); health administration (Ed D); health services administration (MS, Certificate); long term care administration (Certificate). Electronic applications accepted.

Department of Physical Therapy *Program availability:* Part-time, online learning. Offers advanced orthopedic physical therapy (Certificate); manual physical therapy (Certificate); physical therapy (DPT). Electronic applications accepted.

Occupational Therapy Department Offers occupational therapy (MS). Electronic applications accepted.

Physician Assistant Department Offers physician assistant (MS). Electronic applications accepted.

Program in Anatomy Offers anatomy (MS).

School of Nursing *Program availability:* Part-time. Offers advanced practice nursing (DNP); family nurse practitioner (MSN, Certificate); nursing and health-related professions education (Certificate). Electronic applications accepted.

School of Pharmacy Offers pharmacy (Pharm D). Electronic applications accepted.

EARLHAM COLLEGE, Richmond, IN 47374-4095

General Information Independent-religious, coed, comprehensive institution. *Graduate housing:* On-campus housing not available.

GRADUATE UNITS

Graduate Programs Offers education (M Ed, MAT).

EARLHAM SCHOOL OF RELIGION, Richmond, IN 47374-5360

General Information Independent-religious, coed, graduate-only institution. *Graduate housing:* On-campus housing not available.

GRADUATE UNITS

Graduate Programs *Program availability:* Part-time, online learning. Offers ministry (M Min); religion (MA); theology (M Div). Electronic applications accepted.

EAST CAROLINA UNIVERSITY, Greenville, NC 27858-4353

General Information State-supported, coed, university. CGS member. *Enrollment:* 28,718 graduate, professional, and undergraduate students; 2,517 full-time matriculated graduate/professional students (1,650 women), 2,884 part-time matriculated graduate/professional students (1,923 women). *Enrollment by degree level:* 3,753 master's, 1,287 doctoral, 361 other advanced degrees. *Graduate faculty:* 1,026 full-time (472 women), 80 part-time/adjunct (45 women). *International tuition:* $17,898 full-time. *Tuition, area resident:* Full-time $4749. Tuition, state resident: full-time $4749. Tuition, nonresident: full-time $17,898. *Required fees:* $2787. Part-time tuition and fees vary according to course load and program. *Graduate housing:* Room and/or apartments available on a first-come, first-served basis to single students; on-campus housing not available to married students. Typical cost: $5520 per year ($9712 including board). Housing application deadline: 5/1. *Student services:* Campus employment opportunities, campus safety program, career counseling, exercise/wellness program, free psychological counseling, grant writing training, international student services, low-cost health insurance, multicultural affairs office, services for students with disabilities, teacher training, writing training. *Library facilities:* Joyner Library plus 2 others. *Collection:* Books: 1 million (physical), 873,203 (digital/electronic); Serial titles: 8,238 (physical), 109,576 (digital/electronic); Databases: 456. Weekly public service hours: 142; study areas open 24 hours, 5–7 days a week; students can reserve study rooms.

Computer facilities: Computer purchase and lease plans are available. 2,760 computers available on campus for general student use. A campuswide network can be accessed from student residence rooms and from off campus. Online class registration is available.
Website: http://www.ecu.edu/

General Application Contact: Dr. Heidi Terry, Assistant Dean for Graduate Admissions, 252-328-5400, Fax: 252-328-6071, E-mail: gradschool@ecu.edu.

GRADUATE UNITS

Brody School of Medicine Expenses: Contact institution. *Financial support:* Fellowships, institutionally sponsored loans, and unspecified assistantships available. Financial award application deadline: 6/1. *Program availability:* Part-time, online learning. Offers medicine (MPH, MS, Dr PH, MD, PhD); pharmacology and toxicology (PhD); public health (Dr PH). *Application Contact:* Graduate School Admissions, 252-328-6012, Fax: 252-328-6071, E-mail: gradschool@ecu.edu.

Office of Research and Graduate Studies Students: 102 full-time (44 women), 1 part-time (0 women); includes 16 minority (4 Black or African American, non-Hispanic/Latino; 7 Asian, non-Hispanic/Latino; 4 Hispanic/Latino; 1 Two or more races, non-Hispanic/Latino), 13 international. Average age 28. 83 applicants, 40% accepted, 20 enrolled. Expenses: Contact institution. *Financial support:* Fellowships available. Financial award application deadline: 6/1. In 2018, 3 master's, 10 doctorates awarded. Offers anatomy and cell biology (PhD); biochemistry and molecular biology (PhD); biomedical science (MS); microbiology and immunology (PhD); pharmacology and toxicology (PhD); physiology (PhD). *Application deadline:* For fall admission, 8/15 for domestic students; for spring admission, 12/20 for domestic students. Applications are processed on a rolling basis. *Application fee:* $75. Electronic applications accepted. *Application Contact:* Dr. Russ Price, Associate Dean, 252-744-9346, E-mail: pricest17@ecu.edu. *Associate Dean,* Dr. Russ Price, 252-744-9346, E-mail: pricest17@ecu.edu.

Graduate School Expenses: Contact institution. *Financial support:* Application deadline: 3/1; applicants required to submit FAFSA. *Program availability:* Part-time, evening/weekend, online learning. *Application deadline:* For fall admission, 8/15 for domestic students, 2/1 for international students; for spring admission, 12/20 for domestic students, 10/1 for international students; for summer admission, 5/5 for domestic students. *Application Contact:* Graduate School Admissions, 252-328-6012, Fax: 252-328-6071, E-mail: gradschool@ecu.edu. *Dean,* Dr. Paul Gemperline, 252-328-6073, E-mail: gemperlinep@ecu.edu.

College of Allied Health Sciences Expenses: Contact institution. *Financial support:* Application deadline: 3/1. *Program availability:* Part-time, evening/weekend, online learning. Offers allied health sciences (MS, MSOT, Au D, DPT, PhD, Certificate); clinical counseling (MS); communication sciences and disorders (MS, Au D, PhD); health care administration (Certificate); health care management (Certificate); health informatics (Certificate); health informatics and information management (MS); health information management (Certificate); military and trauma counseling (Certificate); nutrition science (MS); occupational therapy (MSOT); physical therapy (DPT); physician assistant studies (MS); rehabilitation and career counseling (MS); rehabilitation counseling (Certificate); rehabilitation counseling and administration (PhD); substance abuse counseling (Certificate); vocational evaluation (Certificate). *Application deadline:* For fall admission, 2/1 for domestic and international students; for spring admission, 9/1 for domestic students, 10/1 for international students. *Application Contact:* Graduate School Admissions, 252-328-6012, Fax: 252-328-6071, E-mail: gradschool@ecu.edu. *Dean,* Dr. Robert F Orlikoff, 252-744-6010.

College of Business Expenses: Contact institution. *Financial support:* Application deadline: 3/1. *Program availability:* Part-time, evening/weekend. Offers accounting (MSA); business (MBA, MS, MSA, Postbaccalaureate Certificate); business administration (MBA); hospitality management (Postbaccalaureate Certificate); sustainable tourism and hospitality (MS). *Application deadline:* For fall admission, 6/1 priority date for domestic students, 2/1 for international students; for spring admission, 11/15 for domestic students, 10/1 for international students; for summer admission, 3/15 for domestic students. *Application Contact:* Graduate School Admissions, 252-328-6012, Fax: 252-328-6071, E-mail: gradschool@ecu.edu. *Dean,* Dr. Paul Schwager, 252-328-6966, E-mail: schwagerp@ecu.edu.

College of Education Expenses: Contact institution. *Financial support:* Application deadline: 6/1. *Program availability:* Part-time, evening/weekend, online learning. Offers adult education (MA Ed); assistive technology (Certificate); autism (Certificate); business and marketing education (MA Ed); community college instruction (Certificate); counselor education (MS); curriculum and instruction (MA Ed); distance learning and administration (Certificate); education (MA, MA Ed, MAT, MLS, MS, MSA, Ed D, Certificate, Ed S); education in the healthcare professions (Ed S); educational administration and supervision (Ed S); educational leadership (Ed D); elementary education (MA Ed, MAT); elementary mathematics education (Certificate); English education (MAT); history education (MAT); instructional technology (MA Ed, MS); library science (MLS); mathematics education (MA Ed); middle grades education (MA Ed, MAT); reading education (MA Ed); school administration (MSA); science education (MA Ed, MAT); special education (MA Ed, MAT); special endorsement in computer education (Certificate); student affairs in higher education (Certificate); vocational education (MS). *Application deadline:* For fall admission, 8/15 for domestic students, 2/1 for international students; for spring admission, 12/20 for domestic students, 10/1 for international students. *Application Contact:* Graduate School Admissions, 252-328-6012, Fax: 252-328-6071, E-mail: gradschool@ecu.edu. *Dean,* Dr. B Grant Hayes, 252-328-4260, Fax: 252-328-4219, E-mail: hayesb15@ecu.edu.

College of Engineering and Technology Expenses: Contact institution. *Financial support:* Application deadline: 6/1. *Program availability:* Part-time, evening/weekend, online learning. Offers biomedical engineering (MS); computer network professional (Certificate); computer science (MS); construction management (MCM); cyber security professional (Certificate); engineering and technology (MCM, MS, PhD, Certificate); information assurance (Certificate); Lean Six Sigma Black Belt (Certificate); network technology (MS); occupational safety (MS); residential construction management (Certificate); software engineering (MS); technology management (MS, PhD); Website developer (Certificate). *Application deadline:* For fall admission, 6/1 priority date for domestic students. *Application Contact:* Graduate School Admissions, 252-328-6012, Fax: 252-328-6071, E-mail: gradschool@ecu.edu. *Dean,* Dr. Harry Ploehn, 252-328-9600, E-mail: ploehnh17@ecu.edu.

College of Fine Arts and Communication Expenses: Contact institution. Offers advanced performance studies (Certificate); art education (MA Ed); ceramics (MFA); communication (MA); composition (MM); fine arts and communication (MA, MA Ed, MFA, MM, Certificate); graphic design (MFA); health communication (Certificate); illustration (MFA); metal design (MFA); music education (MM); music therapy (MM); painting and drawing (MFA); photography (MFA); printmaking (MFA); sculpture (MFA);

Suzuki pedagogy (Certificate); textile design (MFA); theory (MM); wood design (MFA); woodwind specialist (MM). *Application Contact:* Graduate School Admissions, 252-328-6012, Fax: 252-328-6071, E-mail: gradschool@ecu.edu. *Dean,* J. Christopher Buddo, 252-328-1282, E-mail: buddoj@ecu.edu.

College of Health and Human Performance Expenses: Contact institution. *Financial support:* Application deadline: 6/1. *Program availability:* Part-time, evening/weekend. Offers adapted physical education (MS); aquatic therapy (Certificate); bioenergetics and exercise science (PhD); biofeedback (Certificate); biomechanics and motor control (MS); birth through kindergarten education (MA Ed); environmental health (MS); exercise physiology (MS); gerontology (Certificate); health and human performance (MA, MA Ed, MAT, MS, MSEH, MSW, PhD, Certificate); health education (MA Ed); health education and promotion (MA); human development and family science (MS); marriage and family therapy (MS); medical family therapy (PhD); physical activity promotion (MS); physical education (MA Ed, MAT); physical education clinical supervision (Certificate); physical education pedagogy (MS); recreation services and interventions (MS); social work (MSW); sport and exercise psychology (MS); sport management (MS, Certificate); substance abuse (Certificate). *Application deadline:* For fall admission, 6/1 priority date for domestic students. *Application Contact:* Graduate School Admissions, 252-328-6012, Fax: 252-328-6071, E-mail: gradschool@ecu.edu. *Dean,* Dr. Ansia Zvonkovic, 252-328-4630, E-mail: zvonkovic@ecu.edu.

College of Nursing Expenses: Contact institution. *Financial support:* Application deadline: 6/1. *Program availability:* Part-time. Offers nursing (MSN, DNP, PhD). *Application deadline:* For fall admission, 3/15 priority date for domestic students; for spring admission, 10/15 priority date for domestic students. *Application Contact:* Graduate School Admissions, 252-328-6012, Fax: 252-328-6071, E-mail: gradschool@ecu.edu. *Dean,* Dr. Sylvia T Brown, 252-744-6372, E-mail: brownsy@ecu.edu.

Thomas Harriot College of Arts and Sciences Expenses: Contact institution. *Financial support:* Application deadline: 3/1. *Program availability:* Part-time, evening/weekend, online learning. Offers American history (MA); anthropology (MA); applied physics (MS); arts and sciences (MA, MPA, MS, PhD, Certificate); Atlantic world (MA); biology (MS); biomedical physics (PhD); chemistry (MS); creative writing (MA); criminal justice (MS); criminal justice education (Certificate); development and environmental planning (Certificate); economic development (Certificate); English studies (MA); European history (MA); geographic information science and technology (Certificate); geography (MA); geology (MS); health physics (MS); health psychology (PhD); hydrogeology and environmental geology (Certificate); industrial and organizational psychology (MA); international studies (MA); international teaching (Certificate); linguistics (MA); literature (MA); maritime studies (MA); mathematics (MA); medical physics (MS); military history (MA); molecular biology and biotechnology (MS); multicultural and transnational literatures (MA, Certificate); professional communication (Certificate); public administration (MPA); public history (MA); quantitative economics and econometrics (MS); quantitative methods for the social and behavioral sciences (Certificate); rhetoric and composition (MA); rhetoric, writing, and professional communication (PhD); security studies (MS, Certificate); sociology (MA); teaching English in the two-year college (Certificate); teaching English to speakers of other languages (MA, Certificate); technical and professional communication (MA). *Application deadline:* For fall admission, 8/15 priority date for domestic students, 2/1 priority date for international students; for spring admission, 12/20 priority date for domestic students, 10/1 priority date for international students. *Application Contact:* Graduate School Admissions, 252-328-6012, Fax: 252-328-6071, E-mail: gradschool@ecu.edu. *interim Dean,* Dr. Allison S Danell, 252-328-6249, E-mail: danella@ecu.edu.

School of Dental Medicine Expenses: Contact institution. Offers dental medicine (DMD). *Application deadline:* For fall admission, 6/30 for domestic students. *Application Contact:* Graduate School Admissions, 252-328-6012, Fax: 252-328-6071, E-mail: gradschool@ecu.edu. *Dean,* Dr. Greg Chadwick, 252-737-7703.

EAST CENTRAL UNIVERSITY, Ada, OK 74820

General Information State-supported, coed, comprehensive institution. *Graduate housing:* On-campus housing not available.

GRADUATE UNITS

School of Graduate Studies *Program availability:* Part-time, evening/weekend. Offers accounting (MS); clinical rehabilitation and clinical mental health counseling (MSHR); criminal justice (MSHR); education (M Ed); human resources (MSHR); psychology (MSPS). Electronic applications accepted.

EASTERN CONNECTICUT STATE UNIVERSITY, Willimantic, CT 06226-2295

General Information State-supported, coed, comprehensive institution. *Graduate housing:* Room and/or apartments available on a first-come, first-served basis to single students; on-campus housing not available to married students. Housing application deadline: 4/3. *Research affiliation:* Spencer Foundation (early childhood education), CEEDAR Center (early childhood, physical education, elementary education, secondary education).

GRADUATE UNITS

School of Education and Professional Studies/Graduate Division *Program availability:* Part-time, evening/weekend. Offers accounting (MS); early childhood education (MS); education and professional studies (MS); educational technology (MS); elementary education (MS); organizational management (MS); secondary education (MS). Electronic applications accepted.

EASTERN ILLINOIS UNIVERSITY, Charleston, IL 61920

General Information State-supported, coed, comprehensive institution. CGS member. *Enrollment:* 7,526 graduate, professional, and undergraduate students; 1,485 matriculated graduate/professional students (983 women). *Graduate faculty:* 310. Tuition, state resident: part-time $299 per credit hour. Tuition, nonresident: part-time $718 per credit hour. *Required fees:* $214.50 per credit hour. *Graduate housing:* Rooms and/or apartments available on a first-come, first-served basis to single and married students. *Student services:* Campus employment opportunities, campus safety program, career counseling, exercise/wellness program, free psychological counseling, international student services, low-cost health insurance, multicultural affairs office, services for students with disabilities, teacher training, writing training. *Library facilities:* Booth Library. *Collection:* Books: 1 million (physical), 1.3 million (digital/electronic); Serial titles: 55 (physical), 55,520 (digital/electronic); Databases: 217. Weekly public service hours: 98.

Computer facilities: Computer purchase and lease plans are available. 900 computers available on campus for general student use. A campuswide network can be accessed from student residence rooms and from off campus. Online class registration is available.
Website: http://www.eiu.edu/

General Application Contact: Dr. Ryan Hendrickson, Dean of Graduate School, 217-581-2220, Fax: 217-581-6020, E-mail: graduate@eiu.edu.

GRADUATE UNITS

Graduate School Expenses: Contact institution. *Financial support:* Fellowships with full tuition reimbursements, research assistantships with full tuition reimbursements, teaching assistantships with full tuition reimbursements, career-related internships or fieldwork, Federal Work-Study, scholarships/grants, and unspecified assistantships available. Support available to part-time students. Financial award application deadline: 3/1; financial award applicants required to submit FAFSA. *Program availability:* Part-time, evening/weekend, 100% online, blended/hybrid learning. *Application deadline:* For fall admission, 5/15 for domestic and international students; for spring admission, 10/15 for domestic and international students. Applications are processed on a rolling basis. *Application fee:* $30. Electronic applications accepted. *Application Contact:* Tracey S. Hutchison, Admissions Officer, 217-581-7488, Fax: 217-581-6020, E-mail: tshutchison@eiu.edu. *Dean,* Dr. Ryan Hendrickson, 217-581-2220, Fax: 217-581-6020, E-mail: rchendrickson@eiu.edu.

College of Education Expenses: Contact institution. *Financial support:* Research assistantships with full tuition reimbursements, teaching assistantships with full tuition reimbursements, career-related internships or fieldwork, Federal Work-Study, scholarships/grants, and unspecified assistantships available. Support available to part-time students. Financial award application deadline: 3/1; financial award applicants required to submit FAFSA. *Program availability:* Part-time, evening/weekend. Offers college student affairs (MS); counseling (MS); curriculum and instruction (MS Ed); education and professional studies (MS, MS Ed, Ed S); educational administration (Ed S); educational leadership (MS Ed); special education (MS Ed). *Application deadline:* For fall admission, 5/15 for domestic and international students; for spring admission, 10/15 for domestic and international students. Applications are processed on a rolling basis. *Application fee:* $30. Electronic applications accepted. *Application Contact:* Douglas J. Bower, Ph.D., Dean, 217-581-2200, Fax: 217-581-2518, E-mail: djbower@eiu.edu. *Dean,* Douglas J. Bower, Ph.D., 217-581-2200, Fax: 217-581-2518, E-mail: djbower@eiu.edu.

College of Health and Human Services Expenses: Contact institution. *Financial support:* Research assistantships with tuition reimbursements, teaching assistantships with tuition reimbursements, career-related internships or fieldwork, scholarships/grants, and unspecified assistantships available. Financial award applicants required to submit FAFSA. *Program availability:* Part-time, online learning. Offers aging studies (MA); communication disorders and sciences (MS); human service program administration (MS); human services program development (MHS); kinesiology and sports studies (MS); nutrition and dietetics (MS). *Application deadline:* For fall admission, 3/31 priority date for domestic students. Applications are processed on a rolling basis. *Application fee:* $30. *Application Contact:* Ozlem Ersin, Ph.D., Dean, 217-581-6025, E-mail: oersin@eiu.edu. *Dean,* Ozlem Ersin, Ph.D., 217-581-6025, E-mail: oersin@eiu.edu.

College of Liberal Arts and Sciences *Program availability:* Part-time, evening/weekend, 100% online, blended/hybrid learning. Offers art (MA); art education (MA); biological sciences (MS); chemistry (MS); clinical psychology (MA); communication pedagogy (MA); community arts (MA); composition (MA); conducting (MA); economics (MA); elementary/middle school mathematics education (MA); English (MA); geographic information sciences (PSM); history (MA); liberal arts and sciences (MA, MS, PSM, SSP); mathematics (MA); music education (MA); performance (MA); political science (MA); school psychology (SSP); secondary mathematics education (MA). Electronic applications accepted.

Lumpkin College of Business and Technology *Program availability:* Part-time, evening/weekend, online learning. Offers accountancy (MBA); applied management (MBA); business and technology (MA, MBA, MS, Certificate); computer technology (Certificate); cybersecurity (MS); geographic information systems (MBA); quality systems (Certificate); research (MBA); sustainable energy (MS); technology (MS, Certificate); technology security (Certificate); work performance improvement (Certificate). Electronic applications accepted.

EASTERN KENTUCKY UNIVERSITY, Richmond, KY 40475-3102

General Information State-supported, coed, comprehensive institution. CGS member. *Graduate housing:* Rooms and/or apartments guaranteed to single students and available to married students.

GRADUATE UNITS

The Graduate School *Program availability:* Part-time, evening/weekend, online learning. Electronic applications accepted.

College of Arts and Sciences *Program availability:* Part-time, evening/weekend. Offers arts and sciences (MA, MFA, MM, MPA, MS, PhD, Psy S); biological sciences (MS); chemistry (MS); choral conducting (MM); clinical psychology (MS); community development (MPA); community health administration (MPA); creative writing (MFA); ecology (MS); English (MA); general public administration (MPA); geology (MS, PhD); history (MA); industrial/organizational psychology (MS); mathematical sciences (MS); performance (MM); political science (MA); school psychology (Psy S); theory/composition (MM).

College of Business and Technology *Program availability:* Part-time. Offers business administration (MBA); business and technology (MBA, MS); industrial education (MS); industrial technology (MS); occupational training and development (MS); technical administration (MS); technology education (MS).

College of Education *Program availability:* Part-time, online learning. Offers communication disorders (MA Ed); education (MA, MA Ed, MAT); elementary education (MA Ed); human services (MA); instructional leadership (MA Ed); library science (MA Ed); mental health counseling (MA); music education (MA Ed); school counseling (MA Ed); secondary and higher education (MA Ed); secondary education (MA Ed); teaching (MAT).

College of Health Sciences *Program availability:* Part-time. Offers community health education (MPH); environmental health science (MPH); exercise and sport science (MS); exercise and wellness (MS); family and consumer sciences (M Ed); health sciences (MPH, MS, MSN); industrial hygiene (MPH); occupational therapy (MS); public health nutrition (MPH); recreation and park administration (MS); rural community health care (MSN); rural health family nurse practitioner (MSN); sports administration (MS).

College of Justice and Safety *Program availability:* Part-time. Offers correctional and juvenile justice studies (MS); criminal justice (MS); criminal justice education (MS); justice and safety (MS); loss prevention and safety (MS); police studies (MS).

EASTERN MENNONITE UNIVERSITY, Harrisonburg, VA 22802-2462

General Information Independent-religious, coed, comprehensive institution. *Graduate housing:* Rooms and/or apartments available on a first-come, first-served basis to single and married students. Housing application deadline: 4/15.

GRADUATE UNITS

Eastern Mennonite Seminary *Program availability:* Part-time. Offers Christian leadership (MA); divinity (M Div); ministry studies (Certificate); religion (MA); theological studies (Certificate).

Master of Arts in Counseling Program *Program availability:* Part-time. Offers counseling (MA). Electronic applications accepted.

Program in Biomedicine Offers biomedicine (MA). Electronic applications accepted.

Program in Business Administration *Program availability:* Part-time, evening/weekend. Offers general management (MBA); health services administration (MBA); non-profit leadership (MBA). Electronic applications accepted.

Program in Conflict Transformation *Program availability:* Part-time. Offers conflict transformation (MA, Graduate Certificate). Electronic applications accepted.

Program in Nursing *Program availability:* Part-time, online learning. Offers leadership and management (MSN); leadership and school nursing (MSN); nursing management (DNP).

Program in Organizational Leadership Offers organizational leadership (MA).

Program in Teacher Education *Program availability:* Part-time. Offers curriculum and instruction (MA Ed); diverse needs (MA Ed); literacy (MA Ed); restorative justice in education (MA Ed). Electronic applications accepted.

EASTERN MICHIGAN UNIVERSITY, Ypsilanti, MI 48197

General Information State-supported, coed, comprehensive institution. CGS member. *Enrollment:* 929 full-time matriculated graduate/professional students (640 women), 2,144 part-time matriculated graduate/professional students (1,397 women). *Enrollment by degree level:* 2,538 master's, 215 doctoral, 320 other advanced degrees. *Graduate faculty:* 664 full-time (334 women). *Graduate housing:* Rooms and/or apartments available on a first-come, first-served basis to single and married students. *Student services:* Campus employment opportunities, campus safety program, career counseling, child daycare facilities, exercise/wellness program, free psychological counseling, grant writing training, international student services, low-cost health insurance, multicultural affairs office, services for students with disabilities, teacher training, writing training. *Library facilities:* Bruce T. Halle Library.

Computer facilities: 1,600 computers available on campus for general student use. A campuswide network can be accessed from student residence rooms. Online class registration is available.
Website: http://www.emich.edu/

General Application Contact: Graduate Admissions, 734-487-2400, Fax: 734-487-6559, E-mail: graduate.admissions@emich.edu.

GRADUATE UNITS

Graduate School Students: 929 full-time (640 women), 2,144 part-time (1,397 women); includes 779 minority (402 Black or African American, non-Hispanic/Latino; 8 American Indian or Alaska Native, non-Hispanic/Latino; 107 Asian, non-Hispanic/Latino; 164 Hispanic/Latino; 1 Native Hawaiian or other Pacific Islander, non-Hispanic/Latino; 97 Two or more races, non-Hispanic/Latino); 238 international. Average age 32. 2,826 applicants, 57% accepted, 830 enrolled. *Faculty:* 664 full-time (334 women). Expenses: Contact institution. *Financial support:* Fellowships, research assistantships with full tuition reimbursements, teaching assistantships with full tuition reimbursements, career-related internships or fieldwork, Federal Work-Study, institutionally sponsored loans, scholarships/grants, tuition waivers (partial), and unspecified assistantships available. Support available to part-time students. Financial award applicants required to submit FAFSA. In 2018, 1,125 master's, 42 doctorates, 129 other advanced degrees awarded. *Program availability:* Part-time, evening/weekend, online learning. *Application deadline:* For fall admission, 5/15 priority date for domestic students, 2/15 priority date for international students; for winter admission, 10/15 priority date for domestic students, 9/1 priority date for international students; for summer admission, 3/15 priority date for domestic students, 3/1 priority date for international students. Applications are processed on a rolling basis. *Application fee:* $45. Electronic applications accepted. *Application Contact:* Graduate Admissions, 734-487-2400, Fax: 734-487-6559, E-mail: graduate.admissions@emich.edu. *Interim Dean, Graduate School,* Dr. Wade Tornquist, 734-487-0042, Fax: 734-487-0050, E-mail: wade.tornquist@emich.edu.

Academic and Student Affairs Division Students: 1 part-time (0 women). Average age 33. 40 applicants, 90% accepted, 13 enrolled. *Faculty:* 1 full-time (0 women). Expenses: Contact institution. In 2018, 1 master's awarded. Offers individualized studies (MA, MS); integrated marketing communications (MS). *Application fee:* $45. *Application Contact:* Graduate Admissions, 734-487-2400, Fax: 734-487-6559, E-mail: graduate.admissions@emich.edu. *Interim Dean,* Dr. Wade Tornquist, 734-487-0042, Fax: 734-487-0050, E-mail: wade.tornquist@emich.edu.

College of Arts and Sciences Students: 237 full-time (156 women), 491 part-time (309 women); includes 167 minority (63 Black or African American, non-Hispanic/Latino; 2 American Indian or Alaska Native, non-Hispanic/Latino; 25 Asian, non-Hispanic/Latino; 49 Hispanic/Latino; 28 Two or more races, non-Hispanic/Latino; 76 international. Average age 31. 899 applicants, 52% accepted, 224 enrolled. *Faculty:* 352 full-time (155 women). Expenses: Contact institution. *Financial support:* Fellowships, research assistantships with full tuition reimbursements, teaching assistantships with full tuition reimbursements, career-related internships or fieldwork, Federal Work-Study, institutionally sponsored loans, and tuition waivers (partial) available. Support available to part-time students. Financial award applicants required to submit FAFSA. In 2018, 254 master's, 8 doctorates, 8 other advanced degrees awarded. *Program availability:* Part-time, evening/weekend. Offers Africology and African-American studies (Graduate Certificate); applied drama/theatre for the young (MFA); arts administration (MA); arts and sciences (MA, MFA, MLS, MM, MPA, MS, PhD, Graduate Certificate); chemistry (MS); children's literature (MA); clinical behavioral psychology (MS); clinical psychology (PhD); communication (MA); community college biology teaching (MS); computer science (MS, Graduate Certificate); creative writing (MA); criminology and criminal justice (MA); cultural museum studies (Graduate Certificate); earth science education (MS); economics (MA, Graduate Certificate); English linguistics (MA); English studies for teachers (MA); general biology (MS); general clinical psychology (MS); general experimental psychology (MS); general public management (Graduate Certificate); geographic information systems (MS, Graduate Certificate); geographic information systems for educators (Graduate Certificate); geographic information systems for professionals (Graduate Certificate); heritage interpretation and museum practice (MS); historic preservation (MS, Graduate Certificate); history (MA); interpretation/performance studies (MA); language and international trade (MA); literature (MA); local government management (Graduate Certificate); management of public healthcare services (Graduate Certificate); mathematics (MA); music and dance (MM); nonprofit management (Graduate Certificate); philosophy (MA); physics (MS); political science (MPA, Graduate Certificate); preservation planning and administration (MS); public administration (MPA); public budget management (Graduate Certificate); public land planning and development management (Graduate Certificate); public personnel management (Graduate Certificate); public policy analysis (Graduate Certificate); recording, documentation and digital cultural heritage (MS); schools, society and violence (MA); social science (MA); sociology (MA); sociology - applied research specialty (MA); studio art (MA, MFA); teaching English to speakers of other languages (MA, Graduate Certificate); technical communication (Graduate Certificate); theatre arts (MA); transportation planning and modeling (Graduate Certificate); urban and regional planning (MS, Graduate Certificate); visual art education (MA); women's and gender studies (MA, Graduate Certificate); world languages (MA, Graduate Certificate); written communication (MA, Graduate Certificate). *Application deadline:* Applications are processed on a rolling basis. *Application fee:* $45. *Application Contact:* Dr. Dana Heller, Dean, 734-487-4344, Fax: 734-485-9592, E-mail: dheller@emich.edu. *Dean,* Dr. Dana Heller, 734-487-4344, Fax: 734-485-9592, E-mail: dheller@emich.edu.

College of Business Students: 163 full-time (101 women), 417 part-time (245 women); includes 184 minority (105 Black or African American, non-Hispanic/Latino; 2 American Indian or Alaska Native, non-Hispanic/Latino; 30 Asian, non-Hispanic/Latino; 33 Hispanic/Latino; 14 Two or more races, non-Hispanic/Latino; 50 international. Average age 31. 391 applicants, 73% accepted, 151 enrolled. *Faculty:* 74 full-time (30 women). Expenses: Contact institution. *Financial support:* Fellowships, research assistantships with full tuition reimbursements, teaching assistantships with full tuition reimbursements, career-related internships or fieldwork, Federal Work-Study, institutionally sponsored loans, traineeships, tuition waivers (partial), and unspecified assistantships available. Support available to part-time students. Financial award applicants required to submit FAFSA. In 2018, 228 master's, 52 other advanced degrees awarded. *Program availability:* Part-time, evening/weekend, online learning. Offers accounting (MS); accounting information systems (MS); business (MBA, MS, MSHROD, Graduate Certificate, Postbaccalaureate Certificate); business administration (MBA, Graduate Certificate); computer information systems (Graduate Certificate); e-business (MBA, Graduate Certificate); enterprise business intelligence (MBA); entrepreneurship (MBA, Graduate Certificate, Postbaccalaureate Certificate); finance (MBA, Graduate Certificate); human resources (MBA); human resources management (Graduate Certificate); human resources management and organizational development (MSHROD); information systems (MBA); integrated marketing communications (MS, Postbaccalaureate Certificate); internal auditing (MBA); international business (MBA, Graduate Certificate); marketing management (MBA, Graduate Certificate); nonprofit management (MBA); organizational development (Graduate Certificate); supply chain management (MBA, Graduate Certificate). *Application deadline:* Applications are processed on a rolling basis. *Application fee:* $45. *Application Contact:* K. Michelle Henry, Director, Graduate Business Programs, 734-487-4444, Fax: 734-483-1316, E-mail: cob.graduate@emich.edu. *Dean,* Dr. Kenneth Lord, 734-487-4140, Fax: 734-487-7099, E-mail: cob_dean@emich.edu.

College of Education Students: 195 full-time (159 women), 658 part-time (499 women); includes 207 minority (123 Black or African American, non-Hispanic/Latino; 12 Asian, non-Hispanic/Latino; 40 Hispanic/Latino; 32 Two or more races, non-Hispanic/Latino), 19 international. Average age 33. 618 applicants, 56% accepted, 215 enrolled. *Faculty:* 66 full-time (46 women). Expenses: Contact institution. *Financial support:* Fellowships, research assistantships with full tuition reimbursements, teaching assistantships with full tuition reimbursements, career-related internships or fieldwork, Federal Work-Study, institutionally sponsored loans, scholarships/grants, tuition waivers (partial), and unspecified assistantships available. Support available to part-time students. Financial award applicants required to submit FAFSA. In 2018, 253 master's, 19 doctorates, 49 other advanced degrees awarded. *Program availability:* Part-time, evening/weekend, online learning. Offers advanced teaching and learning (MA); autism spectrum disorders (MA); clinical mental health counseling (MA); cognitive impairment (M Ed); college counseling (MA); community college leadership (Graduate Certificate); counseling (MA, Graduate Certificate, Post Master's Certificate); curriculum and instruction (MA, Certificate, Graduate Certificate); early childhood education (MA); early literacy instruction (Graduate Certificate); education (M Ed, MA, Ed D, PhD, Graduate Certificate, Post Master's Certificate, SPA); educational assessment (Graduate Certificate); educational leadership (MA, Ed D, Graduate Certificate, Post Master's Certificate, SPA); educational media and technology (MA); educational psychology and assessment (Graduate Certificate); educational studies (PhD); emotional impairment (M Ed); helping interventions in a multicultural society (Graduate Certificate); higher education/general administration (MA); higher education/student affairs (MA); instructional leadership (MA); K-12 administration (MA); K-12 basic administration (Post Master's Certificate); K-12 education (MA); learning disabilities (MA); learning technology and design (MA, Graduate Certificate); learning, motivation and creativity (Graduate Certificate); literacy coaching (Graduate Certificate); middle school education (MA); online teaching (Certificate); physical/other health impairment (M Ed); reading (MA); school counseling (MA); school counselor licensure (Post Master's Certificate); secondary literacy instruction (Graduate Certificate); secondary school education (MA); social foundations (MA); special education (M Ed, MA, SPA); speech-language pathology (MA); urban and diversity education (MA); urban/diversity education (MA); visual impairment (M Ed). *Application deadline:* Applications are processed on a rolling basis. *Application fee:* $45. *Application Contact:* Dr. Michael Sayler, Dean, 734-487-1414, Fax: 734-484-6471, E-mail: msayler@emich.edu. *Dean,* Dr. Michael Sayler, 734-487-1414, Fax: 734-484-6471, E-mail: msayler@emich.edu.

College of Engineering and Technology Students: 71 full-time (27 women), 234 part-time (75 women); includes 63 minority (35 Black or African American, non-Hispanic/Latino; 2 American Indian or Alaska Native, non-Hispanic/Latino; 11 Asian, non-Hispanic/Latino; 8 Hispanic/Latino; 7 Two or more races, non-Hispanic/Latino), 76 international. Average age 35. 281 applicants, 53% accepted, 60 enrolled. *Faculty:* 52 full-time (15 women). Expenses: Contact institution. *Financial support:* Fellowships, research assistantships with full tuition reimbursements, teaching assistantships with full tuition reimbursements, career-related internships or fieldwork, Federal Work-Study, institutionally sponsored loans, scholarships/grants, tuition waivers (partial), and unspecified assistantships available. Support available to part-time students. Financial award applicants required to submit FAFSA. In 2018, 120 master's, 15 doctorates, 1 other advanced degree awarded. *Program availability:* Part-time, evening/weekend, online learning. Offers apparel textiles and merchandising (MS); CAD/CAM (MS); computer aided engineering (MS); computer-aided technology (MS); construction (Certificate); construction management (MS, Certificate);

engineering management (MS); hotel and restaurant management (Graduate Certificate); information assurance (Graduate Certificate); interior design (MS); polymers and coatings technology (MS, Postbaccalaureate Certificate); project leadership (Certificate); quality management (MS, Graduate Certificate); sustainable construction (Certificate); technology (MLS, MS, PhD, Graduate Certificate); technology studies (MS). *Application deadline:* For fall admission, 5/15 priority date for domestic students, 2/15 priority date for international students; for winter admission, 10/15 priority date for domestic students, 9/1 priority date for international students; for summer admission, 3/15 priority date for domestic students, 3/1 priority date for international students. Applications are processed on a rolling basis. *Application fee:* $45. *Application Contact:* Dr. Mohamad Qatu, Dean, 734-487-0354, Fax: 734-487-0843, E-mail: mqatu@emich.edu. *Dean,* Dr. Mohamad Qatu, 734-487-0354, Fax: 734-487-0843, E-mail: mqatu@emich.edu.

College of Health and Human Services Students: 263 full-time (197 women), 343 part-time (269 women); includes 158 minority (76 Black or African American, non-Hispanic/Latino; 2 American Indian or Alaska Native, non-Hispanic/Latino; 29 Asian, non-Hispanic/Latino; 34 Hispanic/Latino; 1 Native Hawaiian or other Pacific Islander, non-Hispanic/Latino; 16 Two or more races, non-Hispanic/Latino), 17 international. Average age 31. 597 applicants, 53% accepted, 167 enrolled. *Faculty:* 119 full-time (88 women). Expenses: Contact institution. *Financial support:* Fellowships, research assistantships with full tuition reimbursements, teaching assistantships with full tuition reimbursements, career-related internships or fieldwork, Federal Work-Study, institutionally sponsored loans, scholarships/grants, tuition waivers (partial), and unspecified assistantships available. Support available to part-time students. Financial award applicants required to submit FAFSA. In 2018, 269 master's, 19 other advanced degrees awarded. *Program availability:* Part-time, evening/weekend, online learning. Offers adapted physical education (MS); clinical research administration (MS, Graduate Certificate); dementia (Graduate Certificate); dietetics (MS); exercise physiology (MS); gerontology (Graduate Certificate); health administration (MHA, MS, Graduate Certificate); health and human services (MHA, MOT, MS, MSN, MSW, Graduate Certificate); health education (MS, Graduate Certificate); health promotion and human performance (MS, Graduate Certificate); health sciences (MHA, MOT, MS, Graduate Certificate); human nutrition (MS); non-profit management (Graduate Certificate); nursing (MSN); occupational therapy (MOT, MS); orthotics and prosthetics (MS, Graduate Certificate); physical education pedagogy (MS); physician assistant studies (MS); social work (MSW); sports management (MS); sports medicine-biomechanics (MS); sports medicine-corporate adult fitness (MS); sports medicine-exercise physiology (MS); teaching in health care systems (MSN, Graduate Certificate). *Application deadline:* For fall admission, 5/15 priority date for domestic students, 2/15 priority date for international students; for winter admission, 10/15 priority date for domestic students, 9/1 priority date for international students; for summer admission, 3/15 priority date for domestic students, 3/1 priority date for international students. Applications are processed on a rolling basis. *Application fee:* $45. *Application Contact:* Dr. Murali Nair, Dean, 734-487-0077, Fax: 734-487-8536, E-mail: mnair@emich.edu. *Dean,* Dr. Murali Nair, 734-487-0077, Fax: 734-487-8536, E-mail: mnair@emich.edu.

EASTERN NAZARENE COLLEGE, Quincy, MA 02170

General Information Independent-religious, coed, comprehensive institution. *Graduate housing:* Rooms and/or apartments available to single students and available on a first-come, first-served basis to married students.

GRADUATE UNITS

Adult and Graduate Studies *Program availability:* Part-time, evening/weekend. Offers management (MSM); marriage and family therapy (MS).

Division of Teacher Education *Program availability:* Part-time, evening/weekend. Offers administration (M Ed); early childhood education (M Ed, Certificate); elementary education (M Ed, Certificate); English as a second language (Certificate); instructional enrichment and development (Certificate); middle school education (M Ed, Certificate); moderate special needs education (Certificate); principal (Certificate); program development and supervision (Certificate); secondary education (M Ed, Certificate); special education administrator (Certificate); special needs (M Ed); supervisor (Certificate); teacher of reading (M Ed, Certificate). M Ed also available through weekend program for administration, special needs, and teacher of reading only.

EASTERN NEW MEXICO UNIVERSITY, Portales, NM 88130

General Information State-supported, coed, comprehensive institution. *Enrollment:* 315 full-time matriculated graduate/professional students (233 women), 994 part-time matriculated graduate/professional students (713 women). *Enrollment by degree level:* 983 master's, 326 other advanced degrees. *Graduate faculty:* 71 full-time (27 women), 4 part-time/adjunct (3 women). *Tuition, area resident:* Full-time $6776. Tuition, state resident: full-time $6776; part-time $282 per credit hour. Tuition, nonresident: full-time $8986; part-time $374 per credit hour. *Required fees:* $60 per semester. One-time fee: $25. *Graduate housing:* Rooms and/or apartments available on a first-come, first-served basis to single and married students. Typical cost: $3566 per year ($7300 including board) for single students; $3566 per year ($7300 including board) for married students. Housing application deadline: 8/1. *Student services:* Campus employment opportunities, campus safety program, career counseling, child daycare facilities, exercise/wellness program, free psychological counseling, international student services, low-cost health insurance, multicultural affairs office, services for students with disabilities, writing training. *Library facilities:* Golden Library plus 2 others.

Computer facilities: 453 computers available on campus for general student use. A campuswide network can be accessed. Online class registration is available. Website: http://www.enmu.edu/

General Application Contact: Dr. John Montgomery, Dean, Graduate School, 575-562-2147, Fax: 575-562-2500, E-mail: john.montgomery@enmu.edu.

GRADUATE UNITS

Graduate School Expenses: Contact institution. *Financial support:* Application deadline: 7/1; applicants required to submit FAFSA. *Program availability:* Part-time, evening/weekend, online learning. *Application deadline:* For fall admission, 7/20 priority date for domestic students, 6/20 priority date for international students; for spring admission, 12/15 priority date for domestic students, 11/15 priority date for international students. Applications are processed on a rolling basis. *Application fee:* $10. Electronic applications accepted. *Application Contact:* Jessica David, Receptionist/Records Clerk, 575-562-2147, Fax: 575-562-2500, E-mail: jessica.david@enmu.edu. *Dean,* Dr. John Montgomery, 575-562-2147, Fax: 575-562-2500, E-mail: linda.weems@enmu.edu.

College of Business *Program availability:* Part-time, evening/weekend, online learning. Offers business (MBA). Electronic applications accepted.

College of Education and Technology *Program availability:* Part-time, online learning. Offers alternative licensure in elementary education (M Ed); bilingual education (M Ed); career and technical education (M Ed); counseling (MA); early childhood special education (M Sp Ed); education (M Ed); education and technology (M Ed, M Sp Ed, MA, MS); educational technology (M Ed); elementary education (M Ed); English as a second language (M Ed); general special education (M Sp Ed); gifted education pedagogy (M Ed); pedagogy and learning (M Ed); reading/literacy (M Ed); school counseling (M Ed); special education (M Ed, M Sp Ed); special education pedagogy (M Ed); sport administration (MS). Electronic applications accepted.

College of Fine Arts *Program availability:* Part-time, online learning. Offers communication (MA). Electronic applications accepted.

College of Liberal Arts and Sciences *Program availability:* Part-time, evening/weekend, online learning. Offers anthropology (MA); biology (MS); chemistry (MS); communicative disorders (MS); English (MA); liberal arts and sciences (MA, MS, MSN); nursing (MSN). Electronic applications accepted.

EASTERN OREGON UNIVERSITY, La Grande, OR 97850-2899

General Information State-supported, coed, comprehensive institution. *Enrollment:* 2,978 graduate, professional, and undergraduate students; 78 full-time matriculated graduate/professional students (37 women), 123 part-time matriculated graduate/professional students (89 women). *Enrollment by degree level:* 201 master's. *Graduate faculty:* 21 full-time (13 women), 12 part-time/adjunct (7 women). *International tuition:* $17,118 full-time. *Tuition, area resident:* Full-time $13,572; part-time $377 per quarter hour. Tuition, state resident: full-time $13,572; part-time $377 per quarter hour. Tuition, nonresident: full-time $17,118; part-time $475.50 per quarter hour. *Required fees:* $1585.50; $340 per quarter. $340 per quarter. Tuition and fees vary according to course load and program. *Graduate housing:* Room and/or apartments available on a first-come, first-served basis to single students; on-campus housing not available to married students. Typical cost: $5800 per year ($9590 including board). Room and board charges vary according to board plan and housing facility selected. *Student services:* Campus employment opportunities, campus safety program, career counseling, exercise/wellness program, free psychological counseling, international student services, multicultural affairs office, services for students with disabilities, writing training. *Library facilities:* Pierce Library. *Collection:* Books: 356,951 (physical), 66,379 (digital/electronic); Serial titles: 392 (physical), 145 (digital/electronic); Databases: 139. Weekly public service hours: 90; students can reserve study rooms.

Computer facilities: Computer purchase and lease plans are available. A campuswide network can be accessed from student residence rooms and from off campus. Online class registration is available.
Website: http://www.eou.edu/

General Application Contact: Janet Frye, Administrative Program Assistant, 541-962-3772, Fax: 541-962-3701, E-mail: jfrye@eou.edu.

GRADUATE UNITS

Master of Arts in Teaching Program Students: 48 full-time (26 women), 3 part-time (all women); includes 4 minority (1 Asian, non-Hispanic/Latino; 2 Hispanic/Latino; 1 Two or more races, non-Hispanic/Latino). Average age 32. *Faculty:* 10 full-time (6 women), 5 part-time/adjunct (2 women). Expenses: Contact institution. *Financial support:* In 2018–19, 23 students received support. Federal Work-Study, scholarships/grants, and tuition waivers (full and partial) available. Support available to part-time students. In 2018, 47 master's awarded. Offers elementary education (MAT); secondary education (MAT). *Application deadline:* For fall admission, 3/1 for domestic students. Applications are processed on a rolling basis. Electronic applications accepted. *Application Contact:* Janet Frye, Administrative Support, MAT/MS Graduate Admission, 541-962-3772, Fax: 541-962-3701, E-mail: jfrye@eou.edu. *Dean of College of Business and Education,* Dr. Matt Seimears, 541-962-3399, Fax: 541-962-3701, E-mail: mseimears@eou.edu.

Master of Science Program Students: 4 full-time (2 women), 52 part-time (43 women); includes 7 minority (1 American Indian or Alaska Native, non-Hispanic/Latino; 1 Asian, non-Hispanic/Latino; 4 Hispanic/Latino; 1 Native Hawaiian or other Pacific Islander, non-Hispanic/Latino). Average age 37. *Faculty:* 9 full-time (5 women), 3 part-time/adjunct (1 woman). Expenses: Contact institution. *Financial support:* In 2018–19, 12 students received support. Federal Work-Study, scholarships/grants, and tuition waivers (full and partial) available. Support available to part-time students. In 2018, 15 master's awarded. *Program availability:* Part-time, online only, 100% online. Offers education (MS). *Application deadline:* Applications are processed on a rolling basis. Electronic applications accepted. *Application Contact:* Janet Frye, Administrative Support, MAT/MS Graduate Admission, 541-962-3772, Fax: 541-962-3701, E-mail: jfrye@eou.edu. *Dean of College of Business and Education,* Dr. Matt Seimears, 541-962-3399, Fax: 541-962-3701, E-mail: mseimears@eou.edu.

Program in Business Administration Students: 24 full-time (9 women), 57 part-time (36 women); includes 19 minority (2 American Indian or Alaska Native, non-Hispanic/Latino; 4 Asian, non-Hispanic/Latino; 9 Hispanic/Latino; 4 Two or more races, non-Hispanic/Latino), 5 international. Average age 34. *Faculty:* 6 full-time (2 women), 1 part-time/adjunct (0 women). Expenses: Contact institution. *Financial support:* In 2018–19, 14 students received support. Federal Work-Study, scholarships/grants, and tuition waivers (full and partial) available. Support available to part-time students. In 2018, 44 master's awarded. *Program availability:* Part-time, online only, 100% online. Offers business administration (MBA). *Application deadline:* For fall admission, 5/15 priority date for domestic students. Applications are processed on a rolling basis. Electronic applications accepted. *Application Contact:* Kristin Johnson, MAT Advisor/Recruiter, 541-962-3529, Fax: 541-962-3701, E-mail: kristin.johnson@eou.edu. *Chair of Curriculum/Business Faculty,* Laura Gow-Hogge, 541-962-3721, E-mail: lgow@eou.edu.

EASTERN SCHOOL OF ACUPUNCTURE AND TRADITIONAL MEDICINE, Montclair, NJ 07042-3551

General Information Proprietary, graduate-only institution.

GRADUATE UNITS

Acupuncture Program Offers acupuncture (MSAC).

EASTERN UNIVERSITY, St. Davids, PA 19087-3696

General Information Independent-religious, coed, university. *Graduate housing:* Room and/or apartments available on a first-come, first-served basis to single students; on-campus housing not available to married students.

GRADUATE UNITS

Department of Counseling Psychology *Program availability:* Part-time. Offers applied behavior analysis (Certificate); counseling (MA); professional counseling (Certificate). Electronic applications accepted.

Department of Global Studies and Mission Offers international development (MA); theological and cultural anthropology (MA). Electronic applications accepted.

Department of Marriage and Family Therapy *Program availability:* Evening/weekend, online learning. Offers marriage and family therapy (PhD); marriage and family therapy studies (DA). Electronic applications accepted.

Department of Nursing Offers nursing (MSN); school health services (M Ed); school health supervisor (K-12) (Certificate); school nurse (K-12) (Certificate). Electronic applications accepted.

Department of Social Transformation Offers urban studies (MA). Electronic applications accepted.

Graduate Education Programs *Program availability:* Part-time, evening/weekend, online learning. Offers ESL program specialist (K-12) (Certificate); general supervisor (PreK-12) (Certificate); health and physical education (K-12) (Certificate); middle level (4-8) (Certificate); multicultural education (M Ed); music (K-12) (Certificate); Pre K-4 (Certificate); Pre K-4 with special education (Certificate); reading (M Ed); reading specialist (K-12) (Certificate); reading supervisor (K-12) (Certificate); school counseling (MA, CAGS); school principalship (preK-12) (Certificate); school psychology (MS, CAGS); secondary biology education (7-12) (Certificate); secondary chemistry education (7-12) (Certificate); secondary communication education (7-12) (Certificate); secondary English education (7-12) (Certificate); secondary math education (7-12) (Certificate); secondary social studies education (7-12) (Certificate); special education (M Ed); special education (7-12) (Certificate); special education (Pre K-8) (Certificate); special education supervisor (K-12) (Certificate); TESOL (M Ed); world language (Certificate). Electronic applications accepted.

Graduate Programs in Business and Leadership *Program availability:* Part-time, evening/weekend, online learning. Offers health administration (MBA); health services management (MS); management (MBA); organizational leadership (MA); social impact (MBA). Electronic applications accepted.

Palmer Theological Seminary *Program availability:* Part-time, online learning. Offers divinity (M Div); theological studies (MTS). Electronic applications accepted.

Program in Organizational Leadership Offers leadership studies (CAGS); organizational leadership (PhD). Electronic applications accepted.

EASTERN VIRGINIA MEDICAL SCHOOL, Norfolk, VA 23501-1980

General Information Independent, coed, graduate-only institution. *Graduate housing:* On-campus housing not available.

GRADUATE UNITS

Biotechnology Program Offers biotechnology (MS). Electronic applications accepted.

Doctoral Program in Biomedical Sciences Offers biomedical sciences (PhD). Electronic applications accepted.

Graduate Art Therapy and Counseling Program Offers art therapy and counseling (MS). Electronic applications accepted.

Master of Physician Assistant Program Offers physician assistant (MPA). Electronic applications accepted.

Master of Public Health Program *Program availability:* Evening/weekend. Offers public health (MPH). Program offered jointly with Old Dominion University. Electronic applications accepted.

Master of Surgical Assisting Program Offers surgical assisting (MSA). Electronic applications accepted.

Master's Program in Biomedical Sciences Research Offers biomedical sciences research (MS). Electronic applications accepted.

Master's Program in Clinical Embryology and Andrology *Program availability:* Online learning. Offers clinical embryology and andrology (MS). Electronic applications accepted.

Medical Master's Program in Biomedical Sciences Offers biomedical sciences (MS). Electronic applications accepted.

Ophthalmic Technology Program Offers ophthalmic technology (Certificate). Electronic applications accepted.

Professional Program in Medicine Offers medicine (MD). Electronic applications accepted.

The Virginia Consortium Program in Clinical Psychology Offers clinical psychology (Psy D). Program offered jointly with The College of William and Mary, Norfolk State University, and Old Dominion University.

EASTERN WASHINGTON UNIVERSITY, Cheney, WA 99004-2431

General Information State-supported, coed, comprehensive institution. CGS member. *Graduate housing:* Rooms and/or apartments available on a first-come, first-served basis to single and married students. Housing application deadline: 5/1.

GRADUATE UNITS

Graduate Studies *Program availability:* Part-time, evening/weekend. Offers interdisciplinary studies (MA, MS). Electronic applications accepted.

College of Arts, Letters and Education *Program availability:* Part-time. Offers adult education (M Ed); arts, letters and education (M Ed, MA, MFA, MS); composition (MA); curriculum development (M Ed); early childhood education (M Ed); educational foundations (M Ed); educational leadership (M Ed); exercise science (MS); instrumental/vocal performance (MA); jazz pedagogy (MA); liberal arts (MA); literacy (M Ed); literature (MA); music education (MA); rhetoric, composition, and technical communication (MA); sports and recreation administration (MS); teaching English as a second language (MA); teaching K-8 (M Ed). Electronic applications accepted.

College of Business and Public Administration *Program availability:* Part-time, evening/weekend. Offers business administration (MBA); business and public administration (MBA, MCR, MPA); professional accounting (MP Acc); public administration (MPA). Electronic applications accepted.

College of Health Science and Public Health *Program availability:* Part-time. Offers communication sciences and disorders (MS); dental hygiene (MS); health science and public health (MOT, MPH, MS, DPT); occupational therapy (MOT); physical therapy (DPT); public health (MPH). Electronic applications accepted.

College of Science, Technology, Engineering and Mathematics *Program availability:* Part-time. Offers biology (MS); computer science (MS); science, technology, engineering and mathematics (MS). Electronic applications accepted.

College of Social Sciences *Program availability:* Part-time, evening/weekend. Offers applied psychology (MS); clinical psychology (MS); communication studies (MSC); experimental psychology (MS); history (MA); mental health counseling (MS); school counseling (MS); school psychology respecialization (Ed S); social sciences (MA, MS, MSC, MSW, Ed S); social work (MSW). Electronic applications accepted.

EAST STROUDSBURG UNIVERSITY OF PENNSYLVANIA, East Stroudsburg, PA 18301-2999

General Information State-supported, coed, comprehensive institution. *Enrollment:* 6,425 graduate, professional, and undergraduate students; 302 full-time matriculated graduate/professional students (188 women), 375 part-time matriculated graduate/professional students (279 women). *Enrollment by degree level:* 563 master's, 76 doctoral, 38 other advanced degrees. *Graduate faculty:* 88 full-time (47 women), 14 part-time/adjunct (10 women). *International tuition:* $13,932 full-time. *Tuition, area resident:* Full-time $9288; part-time $516 per credit. Tuition, state resident: full-time $9288. Tuition, nonresident: full-time $13,932; part-time $774 per credit. *Required fees:* $2059; $114 per credit. Tuition and fees vary according to course load and degree level. *Graduate housing:* Room and/or apartments available on a first-come, first-served basis to single students; on-campus housing not available to married students. Typical cost: $8800 per year ($11,570 including board). Room and board charges vary according to board plan and housing facility selected. Housing application deadline: 6/1. *Student services:* Campus employment opportunities, campus safety program, career counseling, child daycare facilities, exercise/wellness program, free psychological counseling, international student services, low-cost health insurance, multicultural affairs office, services for students with disabilities. *Library facilities:* Kemp Library. *Collection:* Books: 227,237 (physical), 411,580 (digital/electronic); Serial titles: 3,143 (physical), 76,680 (digital/electronic); Databases: 107. Weekly public service hours: 99.

Computer facilities: 500 computers available on campus for general student use. A campuswide network can be accessed. Online class registration, online classes are available.
Website: http://www.esu.edu/

General Application Contact: Kevin Quintero, Associate Director, Graduate and Extended Studies, 570-422-3890, Fax: 570-422-3711, E-mail: kquintero@esu.edu.

GRADUATE UNITS

Graduate and Extended Studies Students: 302 full-time (188 women), 375 part-time (279 women); includes 96 minority (27 Black or African American, non-Hispanic/Latino; 12 Asian, non-Hispanic/Latino; 38 Hispanic/Latino; 1 Native Hawaiian or other Pacific Islander, non-Hispanic/Latino; 18 Two or more races, non-Hispanic/Latino), 24 international. Average age 31. 513 applicants, 63% accepted, 198 enrolled. *Faculty:* 82 full-time (41 women), 12 part-time/adjunct (7 women). Expenses: Contact institution. *Financial support:* Research assistantships with tuition reimbursements, teaching assistantships, career-related internships or fieldwork, Federal Work-Study, and unspecified assistantships available. Support available to part-time students. Financial award application deadline: 6/30; financial award applicants required to submit FAFSA. In 2018, 253 master's, 5 doctorates awarded. *Program availability:* Part-time, evening/weekend, 100% online, blended/hybrid learning. *Application deadline:* For fall admission, 6/1 priority date for domestic students, 6/30 priority date for international students; for spring admission, 10/1 priority date for domestic students, 10/31 priority date for international students. Applications are processed on a rolling basis. *Application fee:* $50. Electronic applications accepted. *Application Contact:* Kevin Quintero, Associate Director, Graduate and Extended Studies, 570-422-3890, Fax: 570-422-3711, E-mail: kquintero@esu.edu. *Director, Graduate and Extended Studies,* Dr. William Bajor, 570-422-3536, Fax: 570-422-3711, E-mail: wbajor@esu.edu.

College of Arts and Sciences Students: 53 full-time (27 women), 31 part-time (17 women); includes 13 minority (4 Black or African American, non-Hispanic/Latino; 1 Asian, non-Hispanic/Latino; 5 Hispanic/Latino; 3 Two or more races, non-Hispanic/Latino), 13 international. Average age 30. 62 applicants, 58% accepted, 25 enrolled. *Faculty:* 34 full-time (13 women), 1 (woman) part-time/adjunct. Expenses: Contact institution. *Financial support:* Research assistantships with tuition reimbursements, career-related internships or fieldwork, Federal Work-Study, and unspecified assistantships available. Support available to part-time students. Financial award application deadline: 3/1; financial award applicants required to submit FAFSA. In 2018, 32 master's awarded. *Program availability:* Part-time, evening/weekend. Offers arts and sciences (M Ed, MA, MS); biology (MS); communication (MA); computer science (MS); history and geography (M Ed, MA); management and leadership in public administration (MS); political science (MA). *Application deadline:* For fall admission, 7/31 for domestic students, 6/30 priority date for international students; for spring admission, 11/30 for domestic students, 10/31 for international students. Applications are processed on a rolling basis. *Application fee:* $50. Electronic applications accepted. *Application Contact:* Kevin Quintero, Associate Director, Graduate and Extended Studies, 570-422-3890, Fax: 570-422-3711, E-mail: kquintero@esu.edu. *Dean of Arts and Sciences,* Dr. Andra Basu, 570-422-3494, Fax: 570-422-3949, E-mail: abasu1@esu.edu.

College of Business and Management Students: 32 full-time (15 women), 34 part-time (21 women); includes 12 minority (5 Black or African American, non-Hispanic/Latino; 2 Hispanic/Latino; 5 Two or more races, non-Hispanic/Latino), 7 international. Average age 30. 55 applicants, 82% accepted, 26 enrolled. *Faculty:* 8 full-time (2 women), 3 part-time/adjunct (1 woman). Expenses: Contact institution. *Financial support:* Research assistantships, career-related internships or fieldwork, Federal Work-Study, and unspecified assistantships available. Support available to part-time students. Financial award application deadline: 3/1; financial award applicants required to submit FAFSA. In 2018, 38 master's awarded. *Program availability:* Part-time, evening/weekend, online learning. Offers business and management (MS); sport management (MS). *Application deadline:* For fall admission, 7/31 for domestic students, 6/30 priority date for international students; for spring admission, 11/30 for domestic students, 10/31 for international students. Applications are processed on a rolling basis. *Application fee:* $50. Electronic applications accepted. *Application Contact:* Kevin Quintero, Associate Director, Graduate and Extended Studies, 570-422-3890, Fax: 570-422-2711, E-mail: kquintero@esu.edu. *Dean,* Sylvester Williams, 570-422-3589, Fax: 570-422-2704, E-mail: swilliams@esu.edu.

College of Education Students: 44 full-time (33 women), 281 part-time (222 women); includes 43 minority (14 Black or African American, non-Hispanic/Latino; 5 Asian, non-Hispanic/Latino; 19 Hispanic/Latino; 5 Two or more races, non-Hispanic/Latino), 1 international. Average age 36. 133 applicants, 81% accepted, 989 enrolled. *Faculty:* 14 full-time (10 women), 6 part-time/adjunct (3 women). Expenses: Contact institution. *Financial support:* Research assistantships with tuition reimbursements, career-related internships or fieldwork, Federal Work-Study, and unspecified assistantships available. Support available to part-time students. Financial award application deadline: 3/1; financial award applicants required to submit FAFSA. In 2018, 45 master's, 5 doctorates awarded. *Program availability:* Part-time, evening/weekend, online learning. Offers digital media technologies (M Ed); early childhood and elementary education (M Ed); education (M Ed, Ed D); professional and secondary education (Ed D); reading (M Ed); secondary education (M Ed); special education (M Ed). *Application deadline:* For fall admission, 7/31 priority date

for domestic students, 6/30 priority date for international students; for spring admission, 11/30 for domestic students, 10/31 for international students. Applications are processed on a rolling basis. *Application fee:* $50. Electronic applications accepted. *Application Contact:* Kevin Quintero, Associate Director, Graduate and Extended Studies, 570-422-3890, Fax: 570-422-3711, E-mail: kquintero@esu.edu. *Dean,* Dr. Terry Barry, 570-422-3377, Fax: 570-422-3506, E-mail: tbarry1@esu.edu.

College of Health Sciences Students: 173 full-time (113 women), 29 part-time (19 women); includes 28 minority (4 Black or African American, non-Hispanic/Latino; 6 Asian, non-Hispanic/Latino; 12 Hispanic/Latino; 1 Native Hawaiian or other Pacific Islander, non-Hispanic/Latino; 5 Two or more races, non-Hispanic/Latino), 3 international. Average age 25. 242 applicants, 47% accepted, 42 enrolled. *Faculty:* 26 full-time (16 women), 2 part-time/adjunct (both women). Expenses: Contact institution. *Financial support:* Research assistantships with tuition reimbursements, career-related internships or fieldwork, Federal Work-Study, and institutionally sponsored loans available. Financial award application deadline: 3/1; financial award applicants required to submit FAFSA. In 2018, 138 master's awarded. *Program availability:* Part-time, evening/weekend, online learning. Offers athletic training (MS); communication sciences and disorders (MS); exercise science (MS); health sciences (MPH, MS); health studies (MPH, MS). *Application deadline:* For fall admission, 7/31 priority date for domestic students, 6/30 priority date for international students; for spring admission, 11/30 for domestic students, 10/31 for international students. Applications are processed on a rolling basis. *Application fee:* $50. Electronic applications accepted. *Application Contact:* Kevin Quintero, Associate Director, Graduate and Extended Studies, 570-422-3890, Fax: 570-422-2711, E-mail: kquintero@esu.edu. *Dean,* Dr. Denise Seigart, 570-422-3425, Fax: 570-422-3347, E-mail: dseigart@esu.edu.

EAST TENNESSEE STATE UNIVERSITY, Johnson City, TN 37614

General Information State-supported, coed, university. CGS member. *Graduate housing:* Rooms and/or apartments available on a first-come, first-served basis to single and married students. Housing application deadline: 8/1. *Research affiliation:* Puckett Institute (education), Cyberonics (biomedical science), Mountain Home VA Medical Center (clinical and biomedical science), Mountain States Health Alliance; Wellmont Health System; State of Franklin Healthcare Associates (clinical, nursing, and biomedical science), Oak Ridge National Laboratory (biomedical physical science and computer science), Frontier Health, Inc./Cherokee Health Systems (clinical and education).

GRADUATE UNITS

Bill Gatton College of Pharmacy *Program availability:* Part-time. Offers pharmacy (Pharm D). Electronic applications accepted.

Quillen College of Medicine *Program availability:* Part-time. Offers anatomy (PhD); biochemistry (PhD); medicine (MD, PhD); microbiology (PhD); pharmaceutical sciences (PhD); pharmacology (PhD); physiology (PhD); quantitative biosciences (PhD). Electronic applications accepted.

School of Graduate Studies Offers global sport leadership (Ed D). Electronic applications accepted.

College of Arts and Sciences Offers Appalachian communities (MA); Appalachian heritage and culture (MA); Appalachian studies (Postbaccalaureate Certificate); applied sociology (MA); arts and sciences (MA, MFA, MPA, MS, PhD, Postbaccalaureate Certificate); biology (MS); biomedical sciences (MS); chemistry (MS); clinical psychology (PhD); communication and storytelling studies (MA); criminal justice and criminology (MA); economic development (Postbaccalaureate Certificate); economic development and planning (MPA); experimental psychology (PhD); forensic document examination (Postbaccalaureate Certificate); general sociology (MA); geographic information systems (Postbaccalaureate Certificate); geospatial analysis (MS); healthcare translation and interpreting (Postbaccalaureate Certificate); history (MA); literature (MA); local government management (MPA); mathematical modeling in bioscience (Postbaccalaureate Certificate); mathematical sciences (MS); microbiology (MS); nonprofit and public financial management (MPA); paleontology (MS); storytelling (Postbaccalaureate Certificate); studio art (MFA); teaching English to speakers of other languages (Postbaccalaureate Certificate); urban planning (Postbaccalaureate Certificate). Electronic applications accepted.

College of Business and Technology Offers accountancy (M Acc); applied computer science (MS); business administration (MBA, Postbaccalaureate Certificate); business and technology (M Acc, MBA, MS, Postbaccalaureate Certificate); digital marketing (MS); emerging technologies (Postbaccalaureate Certificate); entrepreneurial leadership (Postbaccalaureate Certificate); health care management (Postbaccalaureate Certificate); information technology (MS); technology (MS). Electronic applications accepted.

College of Clinical and Rehabilitative Health Sciences Offers allied health (MSAH); audiology (Au D); clinical and rehabilitative health sciences (MS, MSAH, MSW, Au D, DPT); clinical nutrition (MS); physical therapy (DPT); social work (MSW); speech-language pathology (MS). Electronic applications accepted.

College of Education Offers administrative endorsement (Ed D, Ed S); advanced studies in teaching and learning (M Ed); classroom leadership (Ed D); clinical mental health counseling (MA); college counseling/student affairs higher education (MA); community college leadership (Postbaccalaureate Certificate); community leadership (Post-Master's Certificate); counselor leadership (Ed S); couples and family therapy (MA); early childhood education (MA, PhD); early childhood education emergent inquiry (Postbaccalaureate Certificate); education (M Ed, MA, MAT, MS, Ed D, PhD, Ed S, Post-Master's Certificate, Postbaccalaureate Certificate); educational technology (M Ed); elementary education (M Ed); human services (MS); postsecondary and private sector leadership (Ed D); reading (M Ed, MA); response to intervention (Post-Master's Certificate); school and administrator leadership (M Ed); school counseling (MA); school library professional (Post-Master's Certificate); school system leadership (Ed D, Ed S); secondary education (M Ed); special education (M Ed, Post-Master's Certificate); sport management (MS); sport physiology and performance (PhD); sport science and coach education (MS); STEAM K-12 education (Postbaccalaureate Certificate); storytelling (Postbaccalaureate Certificate); student personnel leadership (M Ed); teacher education (MAT); teacher leadership (M Ed, Ed S). Electronic applications accepted.

College of Nursing *Program availability:* Part-time, evening/weekend, online learning. Offers acute care nurse practitioner (DNP); adult-gerontology primary care nurse practitioner (DNP); adult/gerontological nurse practitioner (Postbaccalaureate Certificate); executive leadership in nursing (DNP, Postbaccalaureate Certificate); family nurse practitioner (MSN, DNP, Post-Master's Certificate, Postbaccalaureate Certificate); nursing (PhD); nursing administration (MSN); nursing education (MSN); pediatric primary care nurse practitioner (DNP); psychiatric mental health nurse practitioner (Postbaccalaureate Certificate); psychiatric/mental health nurse practitioner (MSN, DNP, Post-Master's Certificate); women's health care nurse practitioner (DNP). Electronic applications accepted.

College of Public Health *Program availability:* Part-time, online learning. Offers biostatistics (MPH, Postbaccalaureate Certificate); community health (MPH, DPH); environmental health (MSEH, PhD); epidemiology (MPH, DPH, Postbaccalaureate Certificate); gerontology (Postbaccalaureate Certificate); global health (Postbaccalaureate Certificate); health care management (Postbaccalaureate Certificate); health management and policy (DPH); public health (Postbaccalaureate Certificate); public health services administration (MPH); rural health (Postbaccalaureate Certificate). Electronic applications accepted.

School of Continuing Studies and Academic Outreach *Program availability:* Part-time, online learning. Offers archival studies (Postbaccalaureate Certificate); liberal studies (MALS); reinforcing education through artistic learning (Postbaccalaureate Certificate); strategic leadership (MPS); training and development (MPS). Electronic applications accepted.

EAST TEXAS BAPTIST UNIVERSITY, Marshall, TX 75670-1498

General Information Independent-religious, coed, comprehensive institution. *Enrollment:* 1,613 graduate, professional, and undergraduate students; 31 full-time matriculated graduate/professional students (20 women), 97 part-time matriculated graduate/professional students (53 women). *Enrollment by degree level:* 128 master's. *Graduate faculty:* 10 full-time (4 women), 11 part-time/adjunct (6 women). *Graduate housing:* Rooms and/or apartments available on a first-come, first-served basis to single and married students. *Student services:* Campus employment opportunities, campus safety program, career counseling, free psychological counseling, international student services, services for students with disabilities, teacher training, writing training. *Library facilities:* Mamye Jarrett Library. *Collection:* Books: 89,001 (physical), 520,411 (digital/electronic); Serial titles: 1,119 (physical), 81,485 (digital/electronic); Databases: 184. Weekly public service hours: 88.

Computer facilities: 301 computers available on campus for general student use. A campuswide network can be accessed from student residence rooms. Online class registration is available.
Website: http://www.etbu.edu/

General Application Contact: Den Murley, Director of Graduate Admissions, 903-923-2079, Fax: 903-934-8115, E-mail: gradadmissions@etbu.edu.

GRADUATE UNITS

Master of Arts in Clinical Mental Health Counseling Students: 8 full-time (7 women), 18 part-time (17 women); includes 18 minority (13 Black or African American, non-Hispanic/Latino; 1 American Indian or Alaska Native, non-Hispanic/Latino; 4 Hispanic/Latino). Average age 34. 36 applicants, 33% accepted, 7 enrolled. *Faculty:* 3 full-time (2 women). Expenses: Contact institution. *Financial support:* In 2018–19, 5 students received support. Scholarships/grants, unspecified assistantships, and staff grants available. Financial award applicants required to submit FAFSA. In 2018, 5 master's awarded. *Program availability:* Part-time, evening/weekend. Offers counseling (MA). *Application deadline:* For fall admission, 8/15 for domestic students; for spring admission, 1/9 for domestic students. Applications are processed on a rolling basis. *Application fee:* $50. Electronic applications accepted. *Application Contact:* Den Murley, Director of Graduate Admissions, 903-923-2079, Fax: 903-934-8115, E-mail: gradadmissions@etbu.edu. *Director,* Dr. Allen Appiah-Boateng, 903-923-2318, E-mail: gradadmissions@etbu.edu.

Master of Business Administration Program Students: 15 full-time (8 women), 22 part-time (10 women); includes 15 minority (13 Black or African American, non-Hispanic/Latino; 2 Hispanic/Latino). Average age 27. 34 applicants, 65% accepted, 22 enrolled. *Faculty:* 1 (woman) full-time, 3 part-time/adjunct (0 women). Expenses: Contact institution. *Financial support:* In 2018–19, 18 students received support. Federal Work-Study, scholarships/grants, unspecified assistantships, and staff grants available. Financial award applicants required to submit FAFSA. In 2018, 13 master's awarded. *Program availability:* Part-time, evening/weekend, 100% online. Offers business administration (MBA). *Application deadline:* For fall admission, 8/15 for domestic students; for spring admission, 1/9 for domestic students; for summer admission, 5/11 for domestic students. Applications are processed on a rolling basis. *Application fee:* $50. Electronic applications accepted. *Application Contact:* Den Murley, Director of Graduate Admissions, 903-923-2079, Fax: 903-934-8115, E-mail: dmurley@etbu.edu. *Director of Graduate Admissions,* Den Murley, 903-923-2079, Fax: 903-934-8115, E-mail: dmurley@etbu.edu.

Master of Education Program Students: 34 part-time (18 women); includes 14 minority (10 Black or African American, non-Hispanic/Latino; 1 American Indian or Alaska Native, non-Hispanic/Latino; 1 Hispanic/Latino; 2 Two or more races, non-Hispanic/Latino). Average age 29. 50 applicants, 50% accepted, 19 enrolled. *Faculty:* 2 full-time (1 woman), 5 part-time/adjunct (4 women). Expenses: Contact institution. *Financial support:* In 2018–19, 12 students received support. Federal Work-Study, scholarships/grants, unspecified assistantships, and staff grants available. Financial award applicants required to submit FAFSA. In 2018, 18 master's awarded. *Program availability:* Part-time, evening/weekend, 100% online, blended/hybrid learning. Offers education (M Ed). *Application deadline:* For fall admission, 8/15 for domestic students; for spring admission, 1/9 for domestic students; for summer admission, 5/11 for domestic students. Applications are processed on a rolling basis. *Application fee:* $50. Electronic applications accepted. *Application Contact:* Den Murley, Director of Graduate Admissions, 903-923-2079, Fax: 903-934-8115, E-mail: gradadmissions@etbu.edu. *Director,* Dr. PJ Winters, 903-923-2276, Fax: 903-935-4318, E-mail: med@etbu.edu.

Master of Science in Kinesiology Program Students: 11 part-time (4 women); includes 1 minority (Black or African American, non-Hispanic/Latino). Average age 23. 14 applicants, 50% accepted, 7 enrolled. *Faculty:* 2 full-time (0 women). Expenses: Contact institution. *Financial support:* In 2018–19, 10 students received support. Federal Work-Study, scholarships/grants, unspecified assistantships, and staff grants available. Financial award applicants required to submit FAFSA. In 2018, 6 master's awarded. *Program availability:* Part-time, evening/weekend. Offers kinesiology (MS). *Application deadline:* For fall admission, 8/15 for domestic students; for spring admission, 1/2 for domestic students; for summer admission, 5/11 for domestic students. Applications are processed on a rolling basis. *Application fee:* $50. Electronic applications accepted. *Application Contact:* Den Murley, Director of Graduate Admissions, 903-923-2079, Fax: 903-934-8115, E-mail: gradadmissions@etbu.edu. *Dean, Frank S. Groner School of Professional Studies,* Dr. Joseph D. Brown, 903-923-2270, Fax: 903-935-4318, E-mail: jbrown@etbu.edu.

School of Christian Studies Students: 8 full-time (5 women), 12 part-time (4 women); includes 6 minority (2 Black or African American, non-Hispanic/Latino; 2 Hispanic/Latino; 2 Two or more races, non-Hispanic/Latino). Average age 24. 12 applicants, 83% accepted, 10 enrolled. *Faculty:* 2 full-time (0 women), 3 part-time/adjunct (2 women). Expenses: Contact institution. *Financial support:* In 2018–19, 17 students received support. Federal Work-Study, scholarships/grants, unspecified assistantships, and staff grants available. Financial award applicants required to submit FAFSA. In 2018, 7 master's awarded. *Program availability:* Part-time, evening/weekend, blended/hybrid learning. Offers Christian studies (MA, MACM). *Application deadline:* For fall admission, 8/15 for domestic students; for spring admission, 1/9 for domestic students; for summer admission, 5/11 for domestic students. Applications are processed on a rolling basis. *Application fee:* $50. Electronic applications accepted. *Application Contact:* Den Murley, Director of Graduate Admissions, 903-923-2079, Fax: 903-934-8115, E-mail: gradadmissions@etbu.edu. *Director,* Dr. Scott Stevens, 903-923-2178, Fax: 903-923-2077, E-mail: sstevens@etbu.edu.

EAST WEST COLLEGE OF NATURAL MEDICINE, Sarasota, FL 34234

General Information Proprietary, coed, graduate-only institution.

GRADUATE UNITS
Graduate Programs Offers Oriental medicine (MSOM).

ECCLESIA COLLEGE, Springdale, AR 72762
General Information Independent-religious, coed, comprehensive institution.

GRADUATE UNITS
Graduate School *Program availability:* Online learning.

EC-COUNCIL UNIVERSITY, Albuquerque, NM 87109
General Information Proprietary, coed, upper-level institution. *Graduate housing:* On-campus housing not available.

GRADUATE UNITS
Master of Science in Cyber Security Program *Program availability:* Part-time, online only, 100% online. Offers information assurance management (MSCS). Electronic applications accepted.

ECOLE HÔTELIÈRE DE LAUSANNE, CH-1000 Lausanne 25, Switzerland
General Information Independent, coed, comprehensive institution.

GRADUATE UNITS
Program in Hospitality Administration Offers hospitality administration (MHA).

ÉCOLE POLYTECHNIQUE DE MONTRÉAL, Montréal, QC H3C 3A7, Canada
General Information Province-supported, coed, university. *Graduate housing:* Room and/or apartments available on a first-come, first-served basis to single students; on-campus housing not available to married students. Housing application deadline: 2/1. *Research affiliation:* Hydro-Quebec (energy), Bell Canada (telecommunications), Bombardier, Inc. (aircraft and aviation), IBM (computer research), Pratt and Whitney (aircraft and aviation), Ubisoft (video games).

GRADUATE UNITS
Graduate Programs *Program availability:* Part-time, evening/weekend. Offers aerothermics (M Eng, M Sc A, PhD); applied mechanics (M Eng, M Sc A, PhD); automation (M Eng, M Sc A, PhD); chemical engineering (M Eng, M Sc A, PhD, DESS); civil, geological and mining engineering (DESS); computer science (M Eng, M Sc A, PhD); electrical engineering (DESS); electrotechnology (M Eng, M Sc A, PhD); environmental engineering (M Eng, M Sc A, PhD); ergonomy (M Eng, M Sc A, DESS); geotechnical engineering (M Eng, M Sc A, PhD); hydraulics engineering (M Eng, M Sc A, PhD); mathematical method in CA engineering (M Eng, M Sc A, PhD); microelectronics (M Eng, M Sc A, PhD); microwave technology (M Eng, M Sc A, PhD); operational research (M Eng, M Sc A, PhD); optical engineering (M Eng, M Sc A, PhD); production (M Eng, M Sc A); solid-state physics and engineering (M Eng, M Sc A, PhD); structural engineering (M Eng, M Sc A, PhD); technology management (M Eng, M Sc A); tool design (M Eng, M Sc A, PhD); transportation engineering (M Eng, M Sc A, PhD). Electronic applications accepted.

Institute of Biomedical Engineering *Program availability:* Part-time. Offers biomedical engineering (M Sc A, PhD, DESS). M Sc A and PhD programs offered jointly with Université de Montréal.

Institute of Nuclear Engineering Offers nuclear engineering (M Eng, PhD, DESS); nuclear engineering, socio-economics of energy (M Sc A).

ECPI UNIVERSITY, Virginia Beach, VA 23462
General Information Proprietary, coed, comprehensive institution.

GRADUATE UNITS
Graduate Programs

ECUMENICAL THEOLOGICAL SEMINARY, Detroit, MI 48201
General Information Independent-religious, coed, graduate-only institution. *Graduate housing:* On-campus housing not available.

GRADUATE UNITS
Professional Program Offers theology (M Div).
Program in Ministry Offers ministry (D Min).

EDEN THEOLOGICAL SEMINARY, St. Louis, MO 63119-3192
General Information Independent-religious, coed, graduate-only institution. *Graduate housing:* Rooms and/or apartments available on a first-come, first-served basis to single and married students. Housing application deadline: 7/30.

GRADUATE UNITS
Graduate and Professional Programs Offers theology (M Div, MAPS, MTS, D Min). Electronic applications accepted.

EDGEWOOD COLLEGE, Madison, WI 53711-1997
General Information Independent-religious, coed, comprehensive institution. *Enrollment:* 401 full-time matriculated graduate/professional students (285 women), 215 part-time matriculated graduate/professional students (151 women). *Enrollment by degree level:* 479 master's, 137 doctoral. *Tuition:* Part-time $963 per credit. *Graduate housing:* On-campus housing not available. *Student services:* Campus employment opportunities, campus safety program, career counseling, exercise/wellness program, free psychological counseling, international student services, low-cost health insurance, multicultural affairs office, services for students with disabilities, teacher training, writing training. *Library facilities:* Oscar Rennebohm Library. *Collection:* Books: 82,008 (physical), 140,319 (digital/electronic); Serial titles: 219 (physical), 38,116 (digital/electronic); Databases: 90. Weekly public service hours: 98; students can reserve study rooms.

Computer facilities: Computer purchase and lease plans are available. 180 computers available on campus for general student use. A campuswide network can be accessed

from student residence rooms and from off campus. Online class registration is available.
Website: http://www.edgewood.edu/

General Application Contact: Joann Eastman, Admissions Counselor, 608-663-3297, Fax: 608-663-2214, E-mail: gps@edgewood.edu.

GRADUATE UNITS

Henry Predolin School of Nursing Offers nursing (MSN, DNP). Electronic applications accepted.

Program in Business Students: 74 full-time (34 women), 47 part-time (28 women); includes 19 minority (5 Black or African American, non-Hispanic/Latino; 2 American Indian or Alaska Native, non-Hispanic/Latino; 1 Asian, non-Hispanic/Latino; 8 Hispanic/Latino; 1 Native Hawaiian or other Pacific Islander, non-Hispanic/Latino; 2 Two or more races, non-Hispanic/Latino), 5 international. Average age 28. Expenses: Contact institution. *Financial support:* Career-related internships or fieldwork and scholarships/grants available. In 2018, 43 master's awarded. *Program availability:* Part-time, evening/weekend. Offers accountancy (MS); sustainability leadership (MBA). *Application deadline:* For fall admission, 8/15 for domestic students, 5/1 for international students; for spring admission, 1/8 for domestic students, 11/1 for international students. Applications are processed on a rolling basis. *Application fee:* $30. Electronic applications accepted. *Application Contact:* Joann Eastman, Admissions Counselor, 608-663-3250, Fax: 608-663-2214, E-mail: gps@edgewood.edu. *Dean,* 608-663-2224, Fax: 608-663-3291.

Program in Social Innovation and Sustainability Leadership Students: 10 full-time (6 women), 7 part-time (4 women); includes 1 minority (Black or African American, non-Hispanic/Latino). Average age 36. 15 applicants, 100% accepted, 12 enrolled. *Faculty:* 1 full-time (0 women), 2 part-time/adjunct (1 woman). Expenses: Contact institution. *Financial support:* In 2018–19, 14 students received support. Scholarships/grants available. Support available to part-time students. Financial award application deadline: 5/1; financial award applicants required to submit FAFSA. In 2018, 4 master's awarded. *Program availability:* Part-time, evening/weekend. Offers social innovation and sustainability leadership (MA). *Application deadline:* For fall admission, 7/1 for domestic students. *Application fee:* $30. *Application Contact:* Joann Eastman, Assistant Director of Graduate Admissions, 608-663-3250, E-mail: jeastman@edgewood.edu. *Director,* Dr. Stephan Gilchrist, 608-663-6991, E-mail: sgilchrist@edgewood.edu.

School of Business

School of Education Students: 201 full-time (141 women), 141 part-time (97 women); includes 71 minority (24 Black or African American, non-Hispanic/Latino; 8 Asian, non-Hispanic/Latino; 31 Hispanic/Latino; 1 Native Hawaiian or other Pacific Islander, non-Hispanic/Latino; 7 Two or more races, non-Hispanic/Latino), 23 international. Average age 37. *Faculty:* 13 full-time (9 women), 15 part-time/adjunct (10 women). Expenses: Contact institution. *Financial support:* Applicants required to submit FAFSA. In 2018, 70 master's, 28 doctorates awarded. *Program availability:* Part-time, evening/weekend. Offers education (MA Ed, Ed D, Certificate). *Application deadline:* For fall admission, 8/15 for domestic students, 5/1 for international students; for spring admission, 1/8 for domestic students, 11/1 for international students. Applications are processed on a rolling basis. *Application fee:* $30. Electronic applications accepted. *Application Contact:* Joann Eastman, Admissions Counselor, 608-663-3250, Fax: 608-663-2214, E-mail: gps@edgewood.edu. *Dean,* Dr. Timothy D. Slekar, 608-663-2293, E-mail: tslekar@edgewood.edu.

EDINBORO UNIVERSITY OF PENNSYLVANIA, Edinboro, PA 16444

General Information State-supported, coed, comprehensive institution. *Graduate housing:* Room and/or apartments available on a first-come, first-served basis to single students; on-campus housing not available to married students. Housing application deadline: 4/3. *Research affiliation:* Arts Erie (art), State Higher Education Executive Officers Association (education and learning), Preventative Aftercare, Inc. (social work), CampusEAI (computing), Northwest Institute of Research (training and education), College Board (disability education).

GRADUATE UNITS

Department of Art *Program availability:* Evening/weekend. Offers art education (MA); fine arts (MFA); studio art (MA). Electronic applications accepted.

Department of Communication Sciences and Disorders *Program availability:* Part-time, evening/weekend. Offers speech language pathology (MA). Electronic applications accepted.

Department of Communication Studies *Program availability:* Part-time, evening/weekend. Offers communication studies (MA). Electronic applications accepted.

Department of Counseling, School Psychology and Special Education *Program availability:* Part-time, evening/weekend. Offers counseling (MA); educational psychology (M Ed); school psychology (Ed S); special education (M Ed). Electronic applications accepted.

Department of Early Childhood and Reading *Program availability:* Part-time, evening/weekend. Offers arts infusion (Graduate Certificate); early childhood education (M Ed); reading (M Ed); reading specialist (Graduate Certificate). Electronic applications accepted.

Department of History, Politics, Languages and Cultures *Program availability:* Part-time, evening/weekend. Offers social sciences (MA). Electronic applications accepted.

Department of Middle and Secondary Education and Educational Leadership *Program availability:* Part-time, evening/weekend. Offers educational leadership (M Ed); middle and secondary instruction (M Ed). Electronic applications accepted.

Department of Nursing *Program availability:* Part-time, evening/weekend. Offers advanced practice nursing (DNP); family nurse practitioner (MSN); nurse educator (MSN). Electronic applications accepted.

Department of Social Work *Program availability:* Evening/weekend. Offers social work (MSW). Electronic applications accepted.

EDP UNIVERSITY OF PUERTO RICO–SAN SEBASTIAN, San Sebastian, PR 00685

General Information Independent, coed, comprehensive institution.

GRADUATE UNITS

Graduate School

EDWARD VIA COLLEGE OF OSTEOPATHIC MEDICINE–CAROLINAS CAMPUS, Spartanburg, SC 29303

General Information Independent, coed, graduate-only institution.

GRADUATE UNITS

Graduate Program Offers osteopathic medicine (DO).

EDWARD VIA COLLEGE OF OSTEOPATHIC MEDICINE–VIRGINIA CAMPUS, Blacksburg, VA 24060

General Information Independent, coed, graduate-only institution. *Research affiliation:* Virginia Polytechnic Institute and State University (biomedical research).

GRADUATE UNITS

Graduate Program Offers osteopathic medicine (DO).

ELIZABETH CITY STATE UNIVERSITY, Elizabeth City, NC 27909-7806

General Information State-supported, coed, comprehensive institution. CGS member. *Graduate housing:* Room and/or apartments available on a first-come, first-served basis to single students; on-campus housing not available to married students. Housing application deadline: 5/31.

GRADUATE UNITS

Department of Education, Psychology and Health *Program availability:* Part-time, evening/weekend. Offers education, psychology and health (M Ed, MSA); elementary education (M Ed); school administration (MSA). Electronic applications accepted.

Department of Mathematics and Computer Science *Program availability:* Part-time, evening/weekend. Offers applied mathematics (MS); community college teaching (MS); mathematics (MS); mathematics education (MS); remote sensing (MS). Electronic applications accepted.

Master of Science in Biology Program *Program availability:* Part-time, evening/weekend. Offers biological sciences (MS); biology education (MS). Electronic applications accepted.

ELIZABETHTOWN COLLEGE, Elizabethtown, PA 17022-2298

General Information Independent-religious, coed, comprehensive institution.

GRADUATE UNITS

Department of Occupational Therapy Offers occupational therapy (MS).

ELMEZZI GRADUATE SCHOOL OF MOLECULAR MEDICINE, Manhasset, NY 11030

General Information Independent, coed, graduate-only institution. *Graduate housing:* On-campus housing not available. *Research affiliation:* Feinstein Institute for Medical Research (biomedical research), North Shore Long Island Jewish Health System (medicine).

GRADUATE UNITS

Graduate Program Offers molecular medicine (PhD).

ELMHURST COLLEGE, Elmhurst, IL 60126-3296

General Information Independent-religious, coed, comprehensive institution. *Enrollment:* 161 full-time matriculated graduate/professional students (140 women), 417 part-time matriculated graduate/professional students (246 women). *Enrollment by degree level:* 578 master's. *Graduate faculty:* 40 full-time (29 women), 42 part-time/adjunct (20 women). *Required fees:* $150 per term. *Graduate housing:* On-campus housing not available. *Student services:* Campus employment opportunities, campus safety program, career counseling, exercise/wellness program, free psychological counseling, international student services, low-cost health insurance, multicultural affairs office, services for students with disabilities, teacher training, writing training. *Library facilities:* Buehler Library.

Computer facilities: 800 computers available on campus for general student use. A campuswide network can be accessed. Online class registration is available.
Website: http://www.elmhurst.edu/

General Application Contact: Timothy J. Panfil, Senior Director, Graduate Admission and Enrollment Management, 630-617-3400 Ext. 3256, Fax: 630-617-6471, E-mail: panfilt@elmhurst.edu.

GRADUATE UNITS

Graduate Programs Students: 161 full-time (140 women), 417 part-time (246 women); includes 128 minority (27 Black or African American, non-Hispanic/Latino; 1 American Indian or Alaska Native, non-Hispanic/Latino; 30 Asian, non-Hispanic/Latino; 64 Hispanic/Latino; 2 Native Hawaiian or other Pacific Islander, non-Hispanic/Latino; 4 Two or more races, non-Hispanic/Latino), 11 international. Average age 29. 1,319 applicants, 33% accepted, 276 enrolled. *Faculty:* 40 full-time (29 women), 42 part-time/adjunct (20 women). Expenses: Contact institution. *Financial support:* In 2018–19, 296 students received support. Fellowships, scholarships/grants, and unspecified assistantships available. Support available to part-time students. Financial award applicants required to submit FAFSA. In 2018, 244 master's awarded. *Program availability:* Part-time, evening/weekend, 100% online, blended/hybrid learning. Offers business administration (MBA); communication sciences and disorders (MS); computer information systems (MS); data science (MS); early childhood special education (M Ed); geographic information systems (MS); health care management and administration (MHCA); industrial/organizational psychology (MA); nursing (MS, MSN); occupational therapy (MOT); project management (MPM); public health (MPH); special education (MS Ed); supply chain management (MS); teacher leadership (M Ed). *Application deadline:* For fall admission, 7/1 priority date for domestic and international students; for spring admission, 12/1 priority date for domestic students; for summer admission, 4/1 priority date for domestic students. Applications are processed on a rolling basis. *Application fee:* $0. Electronic applications accepted. *Application Contact:* Timothy J. Panfil, Senior Director of Graduate Admission and Enrollment Management, 630-617-3300 Ext. 3256, Fax: 630-617-6471, E-mail: panfilt@elmhurst.edu. *Vice President for Admission,* Dr. Timothy Ricordati, 630-617-3089, E-mail: timothy.ricordati@elmhurst.edu.

ELMS COLLEGE, Chicopee, MA 01013-2839

General Information Independent-religious, coed, comprehensive institution. *Enrollment:* 108 full-time matriculated graduate/professional students (80 women), 254 part-time matriculated graduate/professional students (197 women). *Enrollment by degree level:* 228 master's, 59 doctoral, 75 other advanced degrees. *Graduate faculty:* 26 full-time (20 women), 33 part-time/adjunct (23 women). *Tuition:* Full-time $14,328; part-time $796 per credit. *Required fees:* $200. Tuition and fees vary according to degree level and program. *Graduate housing:* On-campus housing not available. *Student services:* Career counseling, low-cost health insurance. *Library facilities:* Alumnae Library.

Computer facilities: 175 computers available on campus for general student use. A campuswide network can be accessed from student residence rooms and from off campus. Online class registration is available.
Website: http://www.elms.edu/

General Application Contact: Nancy Davis, Director, Office of Graduate and Continuing Education Admissions, 413-265-2239, E-mail: davisn@elms.edu.

GRADUATE UNITS

Division of Business Students: 36 part-time (22 women); includes 9 minority (5 Black or African American, non-Hispanic/Latino; 4 Hispanic/Latino), 1 international. Average age 35. 13 applicants, 85% accepted, 9 enrolled. *Faculty:* 4 full-time (all women), 5 part-time/adjunct (3 women). Expenses: Contact institution. In 2018, 29 master's awarded. *Program availability:* Part-time, evening/weekend. Offers accounting (MBA); accounting and finance (MS); financial planning (MBA, Certificate); healthcare leadership (MBA); lean entrepreneurship (MBA); management (MBA). *Application deadline:* Applications are processed on a rolling basis. *Application fee:* $30. Electronic applications accepted. *Application Contact:* MBA Program Coordinator, 413-265-2592, E-mail: mba@elms.edu. *MBA Program Director*, Kim Kenney-Rockwal, 413-265-2572, E-mail: kenneyrockwalk@elms.edu.

Division of Education Students: 3 full-time (all women), 117 part-time (94 women); includes 12 minority (1 Black or African American, non-Hispanic/Latino; 2 Asian, non-Hispanic/Latino; 9 Hispanic/Latino). Average age 34. 27 applicants, 96% accepted, 23 enrolled. *Faculty:* 5 full-time (all women), 6 part-time/adjunct (5 women). Expenses: Contact institution. *Financial support:* In 2018–19, 2 teaching assistantships with partial tuition reimbursements were awarded. Financial award applicants required to submit FAFSA. In 2018, 34 master's, 3 other advanced degrees awarded. *Program availability:* Part-time, evening/weekend. Offers early childhood education (MAT); education (M Ed, CAGS); elementary education (MAT); English as a second language (MAT); reading (MAT); secondary education (MAT); special education (MAT). *Application deadline:* For fall admission, 7/1 priority date for domestic students; for spring admission, 11/1 priority date for domestic students. Applications are processed on a rolling basis. *Application fee:* $30. *Application Contact:* Nancy Davis, Director, Office of Graduate and Continuing Education Admissions, 413-265-2239, E-mail: davisn@elms.edu. *Chair, Division of Education*, Dr. Mary Janeczek, 413-594-2761, Fax: 413-592-4871, E-mail: janeczeke@elms.edu.

Division of Natural Sciences, Mathematics and Technology Students: 29 full-time (19 women); includes 12 minority (8 Black or African American, non-Hispanic/Latino; 2 Asian, non-Hispanic/Latino; 2 Hispanic/Latino). Average age 26. 35 applicants, 91% accepted, 19 enrolled. *Faculty:* 5 full-time (3 women), 4 part-time/adjunct (3 women). Expenses: Contact institution. *Financial support:* Applicants required to submit FAFSA. In 2018, 16 master's awarded. Offers biomedical sciences (MS). *Application deadline:* Applications are processed on a rolling basis. *Application fee:* $30. *Application Contact:* Nancy Davis, Director, Office of Graduate and Continuing Education Admissions, 413-265-2239, E-mail: davisn@elms.edu. *Co-Chair, Division of Natural Sciences and Mathematics*, Dr. Beryl Hoffman, 413-265-2216, E-mail: hoffmanb@elms.edu.

Division of Social Sciences Students: 1 (woman) full-time, 16 part-time (12 women); includes 1 minority (Hispanic/Latino). Average age 30. 12 applicants, 75% accepted, 4 enrolled. *Faculty:* 1 (woman) full-time, 3 part-time/adjunct (2 women). Expenses: Contact institution. *Financial support:* Applicants required to submit FAFSA. In 2018, 12 master's, 4 other advanced degrees awarded. *Program availability:* Part-time. Offers applied behavior analysis (MS); autism spectrum disorders (MS, CAGS); communication sciences and disorders (CAGS). *Application deadline:* Applications are processed on a rolling basis. *Application fee:* $30. Electronic applications accepted. *Application Contact:* Nancy Davis, Director, Office of Graduate and Continuing Education Admissions, 413-265-2239, E-mail: davisn@elms.edu. *Chair, Division of Social Sciences*, Dr. Jennifer Rivers, 413-265-2422, E-mail: riversj@elms.edu.

Religious Studies Department Students: 7 part-time (3 women). Average age 54. 2 applicants, 100% accepted, 2 enrolled. *Faculty:* 2 full-time (0 women), 3 part-time/adjunct (1 woman). Expenses: Contact institution. *Financial support:* Applicants required to submit FAFSA. In 2018, 2 master's awarded. *Program availability:* Part-time, evening/weekend. Offers religious studies (MAAT). *Application deadline:* For fall admission, 7/1 priority date for domestic students; for spring admission, 11/1 priority date for domestic students. Applications are processed on a rolling basis. *Application fee:* $30. *Application Contact:* Nancy Davis, Director, Office of Graduate and Continuing Education Admissions, 413-265-2239, E-mail: davisn@elms.edu. *Chair, Division of Humanities and Fine Arts*, Dr. Tom Cerasulo, 413-265-2345, E-mail: cerasulot@elms.edu.

School of Nursing Students: 16 full-time (15 women), 75 part-time (64 women); includes 11 minority (3 Black or African American, non-Hispanic/Latino; 1 American Indian or Alaska Native, non-Hispanic/Latino; 7 Hispanic/Latino). Average age 38. 34 applicants, 94% accepted, 26 enrolled. *Faculty:* 6 full-time (all women), 10 part-time/adjunct (8 women). Expenses: Contact institution. *Financial support:* Applicants required to submit FAFSA. In 2018, 21 master's, 22 doctorates awarded. *Program availability:* Part-time, evening/weekend. Offers adult-gerontology acute care nurse practitioner (DNP); family nurse practitioner (DNP); health systems innovation and leadership (DNP); nursing and health services management (MSN); nursing education (MSN). *Application deadline:* For fall admission, 7/1 priority date for domestic students; for spring admission, 11/1 priority date for domestic students. Applications are processed on a rolling basis. *Application fee:* $30. *Application Contact:* Nancy Davis, Director, Office of Graduate and Continuing Education Admissions, 413-265-2239, E-mail: davisn@elms.edu. *Dean, School of Nursing*, Dr. Kathleen Scoble, 413-265-2204, E-mail: scoblek@elms.edu.

ELON UNIVERSITY, Elon, NC 27244-2010

General Information Independent-religious, coed, comprehensive institution. *Enrollment:* 674 full-time matriculated graduate/professional students (424 women), 121 part-time matriculated graduate/professional students (75 women). *Enrollment by degree level:* 296 master's, 499 doctoral. *Graduate faculty:* 85 full-time (41 women), 54 part-time/adjunct (30 women). *Graduate housing:* On-campus housing not available. *Student services:* Campus employment opportunities, campus safety program, career counseling, exercise/wellness program, free psychological counseling, international student services, low-cost health insurance, multicultural affairs office, services for students with disabilities, teacher training, writing training. *Library facilities:* Carol Grotnes Belk. *Collection:* Books: 401,760 (physical), 1.3 million (digital/electronic); Serial titles: 217 (physical), 64,848 (digital/electronic); Databases: 179. Weekly public service hours: 143; study areas open 24 hours, 5–7 days a week; students can reserve study rooms.

Computer facilities: Computer purchase and lease plans are available. 1,200 computers available on campus for general student use. A campuswide network can be accessed from student residence rooms and from off campus. Online class registration is available. Website: http://www.elon.edu/

General Application Contact: Art Fadde, Director of Graduate Admissions, 800-334-8448 Ext. 3, Fax: 336-278-7699, E-mail: afadde@elon.edu.

GRADUATE UNITS

Master in Higher Education Program Students: 15 full-time (10 women); includes 5 minority (3 Black or African American, non-Hispanic/Latino; 1 Hispanic/Latino; 1 Two or more races, non-Hispanic/Latino). Average age 23. 84 applicants, 24% accepted, 15 enrolled. *Faculty:* 1 (woman) full-time, 13 part-time/adjunct (4 women). Expenses: Contact institution. *Application deadline:* For fall admission, 1/4 for domestic students. *Application fee:* $60. *Application Contact:* Art Fadde, Director of Graduate Admissions, 800-334-8448 Ext. 3, Fax: 336-278-7699, E-mail: afadde@elon.edu. *Dean of the School of Education*, Dr. Ann Bullock, 336-278-5900, E-mail: abullock9@elon.edu.

Program in Business Administration Students: 55 full-time (30 women), 72 part-time (32 women); includes 25 minority (17 Black or African American, non-Hispanic/Latino; 3 Asian, non-Hispanic/Latino; 4 Hispanic/Latino; 1 Two or more races, non-Hispanic/Latino), 5 international. Average age 33. 111 applicants, 68% accepted, 57 enrolled. *Faculty:* 19 full-time (4 women), 11 part-time/adjunct (8 women). Expenses: Contact institution. *Financial support:* Federal Work-Study and scholarships/grants available. Support available to part-time students. Financial award application deadline: 3/15; financial award applicants required to submit FAFSA. In 2018, 50 master's awarded. *Program availability:* Part-time, evening/weekend. Offers business (MBA); management (M Sc). *Application deadline:* For fall admission, 8/15 priority date for domestic students; for spring admission, 2/15 priority date for domestic students. Applications are processed on a rolling basis. *Application fee:* $50. Electronic applications accepted. *Application Contact:* Art Fadde, Director of Graduate Admissions, 800-334-8448 Ext. 3, Fax: 336-278-7699, E-mail: afadde@elon.edu. *Associate Dean of the Love School of Business/Associate Professor of Economics*, Dr. Jen Platania, 336-278-5938, E-mail: jplatania@elon.edu.

Program in Education Students: 49 part-time (43 women); includes 20 minority (6 Black or African American, non-Hispanic/Latino; 2 Asian, non-Hispanic/Latino; 10 Hispanic/Latino; 2 Two or more races, non-Hispanic/Latino), 1 international. Average age 34. 51 applicants, 90% accepted, 37 enrolled. *Faculty:* 7 full-time (4 women), 4 part-time/adjunct (all women). Expenses: Contact institution. *Financial support:* Federal Work-Study and scholarships/grants available. Support available to part-time students. Financial award application deadline: 6/1; financial award applicants required to submit FAFSA. In 2018, 10 master's awarded. *Program availability:* Part-time. Offers elementary education (M Ed). *Application deadline:* For fall admission, 5/1 for domestic students. Applications are processed on a rolling basis. *Application fee:* $50. Electronic applications accepted. *Application Contact:* Art Fadde, Director of Graduate Admissions, 800-334-8448 Ext. 3, Fax: 336-278-7699, E-mail: afadde@elon.edu. *Dean of the School of Education/Professor*, Dr. Ann Bullock, 336-278-5900, E-mail: abullock9@elon.edu.

Program in Interactive Media Students: 30 full-time (17 women); includes 18 minority (12 Black or African American, non-Hispanic/Latino; 1 Asian, non-Hispanic/Latino; 4 Hispanic/Latino; 1 Two or more races, non-Hispanic/Latino). Average age 24. 45 applicants, 87% accepted, 30 enrolled. *Faculty:* 9 full-time (2 women), 1 part-time/adjunct (0 women). Expenses: Contact institution. *Financial support:* Federal Work-Study and scholarships/grants available. Support available to part-time students. Financial award application deadline: 3/15; financial award applicants required to submit FAFSA. In 2018, 26 master's awarded. Offers interactive media (MA). *Application deadline:* For fall admission, 5/1 priority date for domestic students. Applications are processed on a rolling basis. *Application fee:* $50. Electronic applications accepted. *Application Contact:* Art Fadde, Director of Graduate Admissions, 800-334-8448 Ext. 3, Fax: 336-278-7699, E-mail: afadde@elon.edu. *Dean of the School of Communications*, Dr. Rochelle Ford, 336-278-5724, E-mail: rford9@elon.edu.

Program in Law Students: 360 full-time (211 women); includes 80 minority (56 Black or African American, non-Hispanic/Latino; 5 American Indian or Alaska Native, non-Hispanic/Latino; 18 Hispanic/Latino; 1 Two or more races, non-Hispanic/Latino), 1 international. Average age 25. 1,018 applicants, 36% accepted, 146 enrolled. *Faculty:* 27 full-time (14 women), 12 part-time/adjunct (4 women). Expenses: Contact institution. *Financial support:* Scholarships/grants available. Financial award applicants required to submit FAFSA. In 2018, 111 doctorates awarded. Offers law (JD). *Application deadline:* For fall admission, 7/15 for domestic students. Applications are processed on a rolling basis. *Application fee:* $0. Electronic applications accepted. *Application Contact:* Alan Woodlief, Associate Dean of School of Law/Director of Law School Admissions, 336-279-9203, E-mail: awoodlief@elon.edu. *Dean*, Dr. Luke Bierman, 336-279-9201, E-mail: lbierman@elon.edu.

Program in Physical Therapy Students: 139 full-time (98 women); includes 18 minority (6 Black or African American, non-Hispanic/Latino; 3 Asian, non-Hispanic/Latino; 3 Hispanic/Latino; 6 Two or more races, non-Hispanic/Latino), 3 international. Average age 25. 881 applicants, 9% accepted, 46 enrolled. *Faculty:* 14 full-time (9 women), 12 part-time/adjunct (9 women). Expenses: Contact institution. *Financial support:* Federal Work-Study and scholarships/grants available. Financial award application deadline: 10/1; financial award applicants required to submit FAFSA. In 2018, 48 doctorates awarded. Offers physical therapy (DPT). *Application deadline:* For fall admission, 11/1 for domestic students. Applications are processed on a rolling basis. *Application fee:* $50. Electronic applications accepted. *Application Contact:* Art Fadde, Director of Graduate Admissions, 800-334-8448 Ext. 3, Fax: 336-278-7699, E-mail: afadde@elon.edu. *Dean of the School of Health Sciences*, Dr. Becky Neiduski, 336-278-6350, E-mail: bneiduski@elon.edu.

Program in Physician Assistant Studies Students: 75 full-time (58 women); includes 17 minority (4 Black or African American, non-Hispanic/Latino; 1 American Indian or Alaska Native, non-Hispanic/Latino; 6 Asian, non-Hispanic/Latino; 4 Hispanic/Latino; 2 Two or more races, non-Hispanic/Latino). Average age 28. 1,353 applicants, 5% accepted, 38 enrolled. *Faculty:* 8 full-time (7 women), 1 (woman) part-time/adjunct. Expenses: Contact institution. *Financial support:* Federal Work-Study and scholarships/grants available. Financial award application deadline: 10/1; financial award applicants required to submit FAFSA. In 2018, 38 master's awarded. Offers physician assistant studies (MS). *Application deadline:* For spring admission, 11/1 for domestic students. Applications are processed on a rolling basis. *Application fee:* $50. Electronic applications accepted. *Application Contact:* Art Fadde, Director of Graduate Admissions, 800-334-8448 Ext. 3, Fax: 336-278-7699, E-mail: afadde@elon.edu. *Dean of the School of Health Sciences*, Dr. Becky Neiduski, 336-278-6350, E-mail: bneiduski@elon.edu.

EMBRY-RIDDLE AERONAUTICAL UNIVERSITY–DAYTONA, Daytona Beach, FL 32114-3900

General Information Independent, coed, university. *Graduate housing:* On-campus housing not available. *Research affiliation:* United Space Alliance, SpaceX, The Boeing Company, Honeywell, Virgin Galactic, NASA.

GRADUATE UNITS

College of Business Offers airline management (MBA); airport management (MBA); aviation finance (MSAF); aviation human resources (MBA); aviation management (MBA-AM); aviation system management (MBA); finance (MBA). Electronic applications accepted.

Department of Aerospace Engineering Offers aerodynamics and propulsion (MS, PhD); dynamics and control (MS, PhD); structures and materials (MS, PhD). Electronic applications accepted.

Department of Civil Engineering Offers civil engineering (MS). Electronic applications accepted.

Department of Electrical, Computer, Software and Systems Engineering Offers cybersecurity engineering (MS); electrical and computer engineering (MSECE); software engineering (MSSE); systems engineering (MS). Electronic applications accepted.

Department of Human Factors and Behavioral Neurobiology Offers human factors (PhD). Electronic applications accepted.

Department of Mechanical Engineering Offers high performance vehicles (MSME); mechanical engineering (PhD); mechanical systems (MSME). Electronic applications accepted.

Department of Physical Sciences Offers engineering physics (MS, PhD). Electronic applications accepted.

Program in Unmanned and Autonomous Systems Engineering Offers systems engineering (MSUASE); technical (MSUASE); unmanned aircraft systems (MSUASE). Electronic applications accepted.

School of Graduate Studies Offers aeronautics (MSA); aviation (PhD). Application fee for PhD is $100. Electronic applications accepted.

EMBRY-RIDDLE AERONAUTICAL UNIVERSITY–PRESCOTT, Prescott, AZ 86301-3720

General Information Independent, coed, comprehensive institution. *Graduate housing:* On-campus housing not available. *Research affiliation:* Boeing/Intelligent Light/Pointwise (CFD analysis on aerospace vehicles and energy systems), University of Alaska, Anchorage (development of field deployed multi-spectral computer vision systems), NASA (optimization ideas for aircraft design), Federal Aviation Administration (human factors, air traffic control interoperability, air traffic management, low-altitude operations, wake separation and noise reduction), NATO Modelling & Simulation Centre of Excellence (operational requirements, training and interoperability), Flight Research Inc. (production of world-class training and curriculum programs for aircraft loss-of-control situations).

GRADUATE UNITS

Behavioral and Safety Sciences Department Offers aviation safety (MSSS). Electronic applications accepted.

Security and Intelligence Program Offers security and intelligence studies (MSSIS). Electronic applications accepted.

EMBRY-RIDDLE AERONAUTICAL UNIVERSITY–WORLDWIDE, Daytona Beach, FL 32114-3900

General Information Independent, coed, comprehensive institution. *Enrollment:* 15,549 graduate, professional, and undergraduate students; 1,788 full-time matriculated graduate/professional students (482 women), 2,022 part-time matriculated graduate/professional students (510 women). *Enrollment by degree level:* 3,810 master's. *Graduate faculty:* 60 full-time (25 women), 287 part-time/adjunct (67 women). *Tuition:* Full-time $7980; part-time $665 per credit hour. Tuition and fees vary according to course load, degree level and program. *Graduate housing:* On-campus housing not available. *Student services:* Career counseling, services for students with disabilities. *Library facilities:* Jack R. Hunt Memorial Library located in Daytona Beach. *Collection:* Books: 53,116 (physical), 122,788 (digital/electronic); Serial titles: 456 (physical), 78,964 (digital/electronic); Databases: 172.

Computer facilities: Online class registration. ERAU Worldwide does not have a physical campus; courses are offered online and at military bases worldwide. Worldwide students may use residential campus facilities. are available.
Website: http://www.worldwide.erau.edu/

General Application Contact: Worldwide Campus, 800-522-6787, E-mail: worldwide@erau.edu.

GRADUATE UNITS

Department of Aeronautics, Graduate Studies Students: 663 full-time (149 women), 877 part-time (191 women); includes 420 minority (144 Black or African American, non-Hispanic/Latino; 6 American Indian or Alaska Native, non-Hispanic/Latino; 58 Asian, non-Hispanic/Latino; 168 Hispanic/Latino; 3 Native Hawaiian or other Pacific Islander, non-Hispanic/Latino; 41 Two or more races, non-Hispanic/Latino), 126 international. Average age 37. 602 applicants, 71% accepted, 272 enrolled. *Faculty:* 30 full-time (11 women), 124 part-time/adjunct (19 women). Expenses: Contact institution. *Financial support:* Career-related internships or fieldwork and scholarships/grants available. Financial award applicants required to submit FAFSA. In 2018, 499 master's awarded. *Program availability:* Part-time, evening/weekend, 100% online. Offers aeronautics (MSA); aeronautics and design (MS); aviation & aerospace sustainability (MS); aviation maintenance (MAM); aviation/aerospace research (MS); education (MS); human factors (MSHFS); occupational safety management (MS); operations (MS); safety/emergency response (MS); space systems (MS); unmanned systems (MS). *Application deadline:* Applications are processed on a rolling basis. *Application fee:* $50. Electronic applications accepted. *Application Contact:* Worldwide Campus, 800-522-6787, E-mail: worldwide@erau.edu. *Associate Professor and Dean, College of Aeronautics, Kenneth Witcher, PhD, E-mail: kenneth.witcher@erau.edu.

Department of Business Administration *Program availability:* Part-time, evening/weekend, online only, EagleVision Classroom (between classrooms), EagleVision Home (faculty and students at home), and a blend of Classroom or Home. Offers aviation (MBAA). Electronic applications accepted.

Department of Decision Sciences *Program availability:* Part-time, evening/weekend, EagleVision Classroom (between classrooms), EagleVision Home (faculty and students at home), and a blend of Classroom or Home. Offers aviation and aerospace (MSPM); aviation/aerospace management (MSEM); financial management (MSEM, MSPM); general management (MSPM); global management (MSPM); human resources management (MSPM); information systems (MSPM); leadership (MSEM, MSPM); logistics and supply chain management (MSEM, MSLSCM, MSPM); management (MSEM, MSPM); project management (MSEM); systems engineering (MSEM, MSPM); technical management (MSPM). Electronic applications accepted.

Department of Engineering and Technology *Program availability:* Part-time, evening/weekend, 100% online, blended/hybrid learning. Offers aerospace engineering (MS); entrepreneurship in technology (MS); systems engineering (M Sys E). Electronic applications accepted.

Department of Security and Emergency Services *Program availability:* Part-time, evening/weekend, EagleVision Classroom (between classrooms), EagleVision Home (faculty and students at home), and a blend of Classroom or Home. Offers cybersecurity

management and policy (MSCMP); human security and resilience (MSHSR). Electronic applications accepted.

Department of Technology Management *Program availability:* Part-time, evening/weekend, EagleVision Classroom (between classrooms), EagleVision Home (faculty and students at home), and a blend of Classroom or Home. Offers information and security assurance (MS); management information systems (MS). Electronic applications accepted.

EMERSON COLLEGE, Boston, MA 02116-4624

General Information Independent, coed, comprehensive institution. *Graduate housing:* On-campus housing not available.

GRADUATE UNITS

Graduate Studies Students: 628 full-time (469 women), 90 part-time (69 women); includes 134 minority (34 Black or African American, non-Hispanic/Latino; 3 American Indian or Alaska Native, non-Hispanic/Latino; 22 Asian, non-Hispanic/Latino; 53 Hispanic/Latino; 22 Two or more races, non-Hispanic/Latino), 139 international. Average age 27. 1,577 applicants, 56% accepted, 337 enrolled. *Faculty:* 206 full-time (92 women), 253 part-time/adjunct (134 women). Expenses: Contact institution. *Financial support:* Fellowships with partial tuition reimbursements, research assistantships with partial tuition reimbursements, Federal Work-Study, scholarships/grants, and unspecified assistantships available. Financial award application deadline: 3/1; financial award applicants required to submit FAFSA. In 2018, 265 master's awarded. *Program availability:* Part-time, evening/weekend. *Application deadline:* Applications are processed on a rolling basis. *Application fee:* $60 ($75 for international students). Electronic applications accepted. *Application Contact:* Leanda Ferland, Director of Graduate Admission, 617-824-8610, Fax: 617-824-8614, E-mail: gradadmission@emerson.edu.

EMILY CARR UNIVERSITY OF ART + DESIGN, Vancouver, BC V6H 3R9, Canada

General Information Province-supported, coed, comprehensive institution. *Graduate housing:* On-campus housing not available. *Research affiliation:* Children's Hospital, Vancouver BC (health care research), Aldrich Pears and Associates (experience design), Kodak Communications Group (interaction design), Donat Group (e-learning), Paperny Films (television and film production), Fuel Cell Research Centre, National Research Council (clean technology).

GRADUATE UNITS

Program in Applied Arts Offers design (M Des); media arts (MAA); visual arts (MAA). Electronic applications accepted.

Program in Digital Media Offers digital media (MDM). Electronic applications accepted.

EMMANUEL COLLEGE, Boston, MA 02115

General Information Independent-religious, coed, comprehensive institution. *Enrollment:* 2,209 graduate, professional, and undergraduate students; 7 full-time matriculated graduate/professional students (5 women), 108 part-time matriculated graduate/professional students (81 women). *Enrollment by degree level:* 111 master's, 4 other advanced degrees. *Graduate faculty:* 3 full-time (all women), 23 part-time/adjunct (15 women). *Graduate housing:* On-campus housing not available. *Student services:* Campus safety program, career counseling, exercise/wellness program, multicultural affairs office, services for students with disabilities, writing training. *Library facilities:* Cardinal Cushing Library/Learning Commons. *Collection:* Books: 63,542 (physical), 191,776 (digital/electronic); Serial titles: 70 (physical), 2,855 (digital/electronic); Databases: 61. Weekly public service hours: 108; students can reserve study rooms.

Computer facilities: 284 computers available on campus for general student use. A campuswide network can be accessed from student residence rooms. Online class registration is available.
Website: http://www.emmanuel.edu/

General Application Contact: Helen Muterperl, Director of Graduate and Professional Programs, 617-735-9700, Fax: 617-507-0434, E-mail: gpp@emmanuel.edu.

GRADUATE UNITS

Graduate and Professional Programs *Program availability:* Part-time, evening/weekend, blended/hybrid learning. Offers education (MSN, Graduate Certificate); human resource management (MS, Graduate Certificate); management (MSM, MSN, Graduate Certificate); management and leadership (Graduate Certificate); moderate learning disabilities (Certificate); research administration (MSM, Graduate Certificate); urban education (M Ed). Electronic applications accepted.

EMORY & HENRY COLLEGE, Emory, VA 24327-0947

General Information Independent-religious, coed, comprehensive institution. *Graduate housing:* Room and/or apartments available on a first-come, first-served basis to single students; on-campus housing not available to married students.

GRADUATE UNITS

Graduate Programs *Program availability:* Part-time. Offers American history (MA Ed); education professional studies (M Ed); occupational therapy (MOT); organizational leadership (MCOL); physical therapy (DPT); physician assistant studies (MPAS); reading specialist (MA Ed). Electronic applications accepted.

EMORY UNIVERSITY, Atlanta, GA 30322-1100

General Information Independent-religious, coed, university. CGS member. *Graduate housing:* Rooms and/or apartments available on a first-come, first-served basis to single and married students. *Research affiliation:* Bill and Melinda Gates Foundation, Children's Pediatric Research Trust, International AIDS Vaccine Initiative, Garden City Group, Georgia Cancer Coalition, The Wistar Institute.

GRADUATE UNITS

Candler School of Theology Students: 318 full-time (172 women), 135 part-time (60 women); includes 177 minority (139 Black or African American, non-Hispanic/Latino; 1 American Indian or Alaska Native, non-Hispanic/Latino; 17 Asian, non-Hispanic/Latino; 4 Hispanic/Latino; 1 Native Hawaiian or other Pacific Islander, non-Hispanic/Latino; 15 Two or more races, non-Hispanic/Latino), 30 international. Average age 35. 440 applicants, 85% accepted, 179 enrolled. *Faculty:* 41 full-time, 56 part-time/adjunct. Expenses: Contact institution. *Financial support:* In 2018–19, 422 students received support, including 123 fellowships (averaging $8,467 per year); career-related internships or fieldwork, Federal Work-Study, institutionally sponsored loans, scholarships/grants, and student employment also available. Support available to part-time students. Financial award application deadline: 1/15; financial award applicants required to submit FAFSA. In 2018, 126 master's, 27 doctorates awarded. *Program availability:* Part-time. Offers catholic studies (M Div); formation and witness (M Div); history, scripture and tradition (MTS); leadership in church and community (M Div); modern religious thought and experience (MTS); pastoral counseling (Th D); religion and race (M Div); religion, health and science (M Div); scripture and interpretation (M Div); society and personality (M Div); theology (Th M); theology and ethics (M Div); theology and the arts (M Div); traditions of the church (M Div). *Application deadline:* For fall admission, 7/1 for domestic and international students; for spring admission, 11/1 for domestic and international students. Applications are processed on a rolling basis. *Application fee:* $50. Electronic applications accepted. *Application Contact:* Sam Martinez, Assistant Dean of Admissions and Financial Aid, 404-727-6326, Fax: 404-727-2915, E-mail: candleradmissions@emory.edu. *Registrar,* Shelly E. Hart, 404-727-0792, Fax: 404-727-4373, E-mail: shart@emory.edu.

Goizueta Business School *Program availability:* Part-time, evening/weekend. Offers accounting (MBA, PhD); alternative investments (MBA); business (MBA, PhD); business administration (MBA); business process consulting (MBA); business technology management (MBA); capital markets (MBA); corporate finance (MBA); customer relationship management (MBA); decision analytics (MBA); entrepreneurship (MBA); finance (MBA, PhD); global management (MBA); information systems and operations management (PhD); investment banking (MBA); management consulting (MBA); marketing (MBA, PhD); marketing analytics (MBA); marketing consulting (MBA); operations management (MBA); organization and management (MBA, PhD); product and brand management (MBA); real estate (MBA); social enterprise (MBA); strategy consulting (MBA). Electronic applications accepted.

Laney Graduate School Offers anthropology (PhD); art history (PhD); chemistry (PhD); choral conducting (MM, MSM); clinical psychology (PhD); clinical research (MS); cognition and development (PhD); comparative literature (PhD, Certificate); computer science (MS); computer science and informatics (PhD); development practice (MDP); economics (PhD); English (PhD, Graduate Certificate); film studies (Certificate); French (PhD); French and educational studies (PhD); history (PhD); mathematics (MS, PhD); neuroscience and animal behavior (PhD); nursing (PhD); organ performance (MM, MSM); philosophy (PhD); physics (PhD); political science (PhD); psychoanalytic studies (PhD); sociology (PhD); Spanish (PhD); women's studies (Certificate); women's, gender, and sexuality studies (PhD). Electronic applications accepted.

Division of Biological and Biomedical Sciences Offers biochemistry, cell and developmental biology (PhD); biological and biomedical sciences (PhD); cancer biology (PhD); genetics and molecular biology (PhD); immunology and molecular pathogenesis (PhD); microbiology and molecular genetics (PhD); molecular and systems pharmacology (PhD); neuroscience (PhD); nutrition and health sciences (PhD); population biology, ecology and evolution (PhD). Electronic applications accepted.

Division of Educational Studies Offers educational studies (MA, PhD); middle grades teaching (MAT); secondary teaching (MAT). Electronic applications accepted.

Division of Religion Offers religion (PhD). Electronic applications accepted.

Emory Center for Ethics Offers bioethics (MA). Electronic applications accepted.

Graduate Institute of the Liberal Arts Offers liberal arts (PhD). Electronic applications accepted.

Nell Hodgson Woodruff School of Nursing *Program availability:* Part-time. Offers adult nurse practitioner (MSN); emergency nurse practitioner (MSN); family nurse practitioner (MSN); family nurse-midwife (MSN); health systems leadership (MSN); nurse-midwifery (MSN); pediatric nurse practitioner acute and primary care (MSN); women's health care (Title X) (MSN); women's health nurse practitioner (MSN). Electronic applications accepted.

Rollins School of Public Health *Program availability:* Part-time, evening/weekend, online learning. Offers applied epidemiology (MPH); applied public health informatics (MPH); behavioral sciences and health education (MPH, PhD); bioinformatics (PhD); biostatistics (MPH, MSPH); environmental health (MPH); environmental health and epidemiology (MSPH); environmental health sciences (PhD); epidemiology (MPH, MSPH, PhD); global environmental health (MPH); global health (MPH); health policy (MPH); health policy research (MSPH); health services management (MPH); health services research and health policy (PhD); prevention science (MPH); public health (MPH, MSPH, PhD); public health informatics (MSPH); public nutrition (MSPH). Electronic applications accepted.

School of Law Offers law (LL M, JD, Certificate). Electronic applications accepted.

School of Medicine Offers anesthesiology assistant (MM Sc); genetic counseling (MM Sc); medicine (MM Sc, DPT, MD); physical therapy (DPT); physician assistant (MM Sc). Electronic applications accepted.

EMPEROR'S COLLEGE OF TRADITIONAL ORIENTAL MEDICINE, Santa Monica, CA 90403

General Information Private, coed, graduate-only institution. *Graduate housing:* On-campus housing not available. *Research affiliation:* Lotus Herbs (herbs), LA Free Clinic (herbs), UCLA Ashe Center (student health).

GRADUATE UNITS

Graduate Programs *Program availability:* Part-time, evening/weekend. Offers oriental medicine (MTOM, DAOM).

EMPIRE COLLEGE, Santa Rosa, CA 95403

General Information Proprietary, coed.

GRADUATE UNITS

School of Law Offers law (MLS, JD).

EMPORIA STATE UNIVERSITY, Emporia, KS 66801-5415

General Information State-supported, coed, comprehensive institution. CGS member. *Graduate housing:* Room and/or apartments available on a first-come, first-served basis to single students; on-campus housing not available to married students. Housing application deadline: 8/1.

GRADUATE UNITS

Department of Biological Sciences *Program availability:* Part-time. Offers botany (MS); environmental biology (MS); forensic science (MS); general biology (MS); microbial and cellular biology (MS); zoology (MS). Electronic applications accepted.

Department of Health, Physical Education and Recreation *Program availability:* Part-time, 100% online. Offers health, physical education and recreation (MS). Electronic applications accepted.

Department of Instructional Design and Technology *Program availability:* Part-time, online only, 100% online. Offers elearning/online teaching (Certificate); teaching with technology (Certificate). Electronic applications accepted.

Department of Mathematics and Economics *Program availability:* Part-time, evening/weekend, online only, 100% online. Offers mathematics (MS). Electronic applications accepted.

Department of Music *Program availability:* Part-time. Offers music (MM). Electronic applications accepted.

Department of Physical Sciences *Program availability:* Part-time, online learning. Offers forensic science (MS); geospatial analysis (Postbaccalaureate Certificate); physical science (MS). Electronic applications accepted.

Program in Accountancy *Program availability:* Part-time, 100% online, blended/hybrid learning. Offers accountancy (M Acc). Electronic applications accepted.

Program in Art Therapy *Program availability:* Part-time. Offers art therapy (MS). Electronic applications accepted.

Program in Business Administration *Program availability:* Part-time, evening/weekend, blended/hybrid learning. Offers business administration (MBA). Electronic applications accepted.

Program in Clinical Counseling *Program availability:* Part-time. Offers clinical counseling (MS). Electronic applications accepted.

Program in Clinical Psychology *Program availability:* Part-time. Offers clinical psychology (MS). Electronic applications accepted.

Program in Curriculum and Instruction *Program availability:* Part-time, online only, 100% online. Offers curriculum leadership (MS); effective practitioner (MS); national board certification (MS). Electronic applications accepted.

Program in Early Childhood Education *Program availability:* Part-time, online learning. Offers early childhood education (MS). Electronic applications accepted.

Program in Educational Administration *Program availability:* Part-time. Offers elementary administration (MS); elementary/secondary administration (MS); secondary administration (MS). Electronic applications accepted.

Program in English *Program availability:* Part-time. Offers English (MA).

Program in Forensic Science *Program availability:* Part-time. Offers forensic science (MS). Electronic applications accepted.

Program in History *Program availability:* Part-time. Offers American history (MA); world history (MA). Electronic applications accepted.

Program in Instructional Specialist *Program availability:* Part-time. Offers elementary subject matter (MS); reading (MS). Electronic applications accepted.

Program in Psychology *Program availability:* Part-time. Offers general psychology (MS); industrial/organizational psychology (MS). Electronic applications accepted.

Program in Rehabilitation Counseling *Program availability:* Part-time. Offers rehabilitation counseling (MS). Electronic applications accepted.

Program in School Counseling *Program availability:* Part-time. Offers school counseling (MS). Electronic applications accepted.

Program in School Psychology *Program availability:* Part-time. Offers school psychology (MS, Ed S). Electronic applications accepted.

Program in Special Education *Program availability:* Part-time. Offers behavior disorders (MS); gifted, talented, and creative (MS); interrelated special education (MS). Electronic applications accepted.

Program in Teaching *Program availability:* Part-time, online learning. Offers teaching (M Ed).

Program in Teaching English to Speakers of Other Languages *Program availability:* Part-time. Offers TESOL (Certificate). Electronic applications accepted.

School of Library and Information Management *Program availability:* Part-time, evening/weekend, online learning. Offers archives studies (Certificate); information technology and science literacy (Certificate); library and information management (MLS, PhD). Electronic applications accepted.

ENDICOTT COLLEGE, Beverly, MA 01915-2096

General Information Independent, coed, comprehensive institution. *Graduate housing:* Room and/or apartments available on a first-come, first-served basis to single students; on-campus housing not available to married students. Housing application deadline: 5/1. *Research affiliation:* Peabody Essex Museum (history), North Shore Consortium (special needs).

GRADUATE UNITS

Van Loan School of Graduate and Professional Studies *Program availability:* Part-time, evening/weekend, 100% online, blended/hybrid learning. Offers administrative leadership (M Ed); applied behavior analysis (M Ed, PhD, Post-Master's Certificate); athletic administration (M Ed); autism (Certificate); autism and applied behavior analysis (M Ed); bioinformatics (MS); business administration (MBA); cybersecurity (MS, Postbaccalaureate Certificate); early childhood and elementary education (M Ed); early childhood education (M Ed); educational leadership (Ed D); elementary education (M Ed); emergency management (MS); family nurse practitioner (MSN, Post-Master's Certificate); global health (MSN); information technology (MSIT); integrative education (M Ed); interior architecture (MA, MFA); nursing administration (MSN); nursing administrator (Post-Master's Certificate); nursing educator (MSN, Post-Master's Certificate); organizational leadership (MBA); organizational management (M Ed); reading and literacy (M Ed); secondary education (M Ed); special education (M Ed). Electronic applications accepted.

EPIC BIBLE COLLEGE, Sacramento, CA 95841

General Information Independent-religious, coed, comprehensive institution.

GRADUATE UNITS

Graduate School

ERIKSON INSTITUTE, Chicago, IL 60654

General Information Independent, coed, primarily women, graduate-only institution.

GRADUATE UNITS

Academic Programs *Program availability:* Part-time, evening/weekend. Offers administration (Certificate); bilingual/ESL (Certificate); child development (MS); early childhood education (MS); infant mental health (Certificate); infant studies (Certificate); social work (MSW). MS/MSW offered jointly with Loyola University Chicago.

ERSKINE THEOLOGICAL SEMINARY, Due West, SC 29639-0668

General Information Independent-religious, coed, graduate-only institution. *Graduate housing:* Room and/or apartments available on a first-come, first-served basis to single students; on-campus housing not available to married students. Housing application deadline: 6/1.

GRADUATE UNITS

Graduate and Professional Programs *Program availability:* Part-time, evening/weekend. Offers theology (M Div, MAPM, MATS, Th M, D Min). Electronic applications accepted.

EVANGELICAL SEMINARY, Myerstown, PA 17067-1212

General Information Independent-religious, coed, graduate-only institution. *Graduate housing:* Rooms and/or apartments available on a first-come, first-served basis to single and married students. Housing application deadline: 6/1.

GRADUATE UNITS

Graduate and Professional Programs *Program availability:* Part-time, online learning. Offers Biblical studies (MAR); congregational ministry (M Div); global and contextual studies (M Div, MAR); historical and theological studies (MAR); interdisciplinary studies (MAR); marriage and family counseling (M Div); marriage and family therapy (MA); New Testament (MAR); Old Testament (MAR); spiritual formation (MAR); teaching ministry (M Div); youth ministry (M Div).

EVANGELICAL SEMINARY OF PUERTO RICO, San Juan, PR 00925-2207

General Information Independent-religious, coed, graduate-only institution. *Graduate housing:* Rooms and/or apartments available on a first-come, first-served basis to single and married students. Housing application deadline: 12/15.

GRADUATE UNITS

Graduate and Professional Programs *Program availability:* Part-time. Offers theology (M Div, MAR, D Min).

EVANGEL UNIVERSITY, Springfield, MO 65802

General Information Independent-religious, coed, comprehensive institution. *Graduate housing:* Room and/or apartments available on a first-come, first-served basis to single students; on-campus housing not available to married students.

GRADUATE UNITS

Department of Behavioral and Social Sciences *Program availability:* Part-time. Offers clinical mental health counseling (MS). Electronic applications accepted.

Department of Education *Program availability:* Part-time, evening/weekend, 100% online, blended/hybrid learning. Offers curriculum and instruction (M Ed); educational leadership (M Ed); literacy (M Ed); secondary teaching (M Ed). Electronic applications accepted.

Doctor of Education in Educational Leadership, Curriculum, and Instruction Program *Program availability:* Part-time, evening/weekend. Offers educational leadership, curriculum, and instruction (Ed D). Electronic applications accepted.

Organizational Leadership Program *Program availability:* Part-time, evening/weekend, 100% online, blended/hybrid learning. Offers organizational leadership (MOL). Electronic applications accepted.

School Counseling Program *Program availability:* Part-time, evening/weekend. Offers school counseling (MS). Electronic applications accepted.

EVERGLADES UNIVERSITY, Boca Raton, FL 33431

General Information Independent, coed, comprehensive institution. *Graduate housing:* On-campus housing not available.

GRADUATE UNITS

Graduate Programs *Program availability:* Part-time, evening/weekend, 100% online. Offers accounting for managers (MBA); aviation management (MBA); aviation operations management (MSA); aviation security (MSA); business administration (MSA); complementary and alternative medicine (MPH); entrepreneurship (MS); human resource management (MBA); project management (MBA). Electronic applications accepted.

THE EVERGREEN STATE COLLEGE, Olympia, WA 98505

General Information State-supported, coed, comprehensive institution. *Enrollment:* 3,327 graduate, professional, and undergraduate students; 192 full-time matriculated graduate/professional students (126 women), 117 part-time matriculated graduate/professional students (85 women). *Enrollment by degree level:* 309 master's. *Graduate faculty:* 16 full-time (12 women), 13 part-time/adjunct (6 women). *Tuition, area resident:* Full-time $10,530; part-time $351 per credit. Tuition, state resident: full-time $10,530; part-time $351 per credit. Tuition, nonresident: full-time $24,381; part-time $812 per credit. *Required fees:* $740; $9 per credit. $145 per quarter. Tuition and fees vary according to course load. *Graduate housing:* Rooms and/or apartments available on a first-come, first-served basis to single and married students. Typical cost: $8046 per year ($11,346 including board) for single students; $8046 per year ($11,346 including board) for married students. Housing application deadline: 5/1. *Student services:* Campus employment opportunities, campus safety program, career counseling, child daycare facilities, exercise/wellness program, free psychological counseling, grant writing training, international student services, multicultural affairs office, services for students with disabilities, teacher training, writing training. *Library facilities:* Daniel J. Evans Library. *Collection:* Books: 377,812 (physical), 216,358 (digital/electronic); Serial titles: 69 (physical), 73,705 (digital/electronic); Databases: 103. Weekly public service hours: 77; students can reserve study rooms.

Computer facilities: 556 computers available on campus for general student use. A campuswide network can be accessed from student residence rooms and from off campus. Online class registration, online payment, student accounts history, financial aid records, academic history, housing application, evaluations are available. Website: http://www.evergreen.edu/

General Application Contact: Admissions, 360-867-6170, E-mail: admissions@evergreen.edu.

GRADUATE UNITS

Graduate Programs Students: 192 full-time (126 women), 103 part-time (76 women); includes 96 minority (16 Black or African American, non-Hispanic/Latino; 17 American Indian or Alaska Native, non-Hispanic/Latino; 7 Asian, non-Hispanic/Latino; 34 Hispanic/Latino; 1 Native Hawaiian or other Pacific Islander, non-Hispanic/Latino; 21 Two or more races, non-Hispanic/Latino), 1 international. Average age 33. 223 applicants, 93% accepted, 154 enrolled. *Faculty:* 16 full-time (12 women), 13 part-time/adjunct (6 women). Expenses: Contact institution. *Financial support:* In 2018–19, 150 students received support, including 46 fellowships with partial tuition reimbursements available (averaging $1,595 per year); career-related internships or fieldwork, Federal Work-Study, institutionally sponsored loans, scholarships/grants, health care benefits, and tuition waivers (partial) also available. Support available to part-time students. Financial award application deadline: 2/1; financial award applicants required to submit FAFSA. In 2018, 122 master's awarded. *Program availability:* Part-time, evening/weekend. Offers environmental studies (MES); public administration (MPA); teaching (MIT). *Application deadline:* For fall admission, 2/1 priority date for domestic and international students. Applications are processed on a rolling basis. *Application fee:* $50. Electronic applications accepted. *Application Contact:* Amanda Mobbs, Graduate Admission Coordinator, 360-867-6856, E-mail: graduateadmissions@

evergreen.edu. *Vice President and Provost*, Dr. Jennifer Drake, 360-867-6400, Fax: 360-867-6745, E-mail: drakej@evergreen.edu.

EXCELSIOR COLLEGE, Albany, NY 12203-5159

General Information Independent, coed, comprehensive institution. *Enrollment:* 28,031 graduate, professional, and undergraduate students; 2,608 part-time matriculated graduate/professional students (1,143 women). *Enrollment by degree level:* 2,601 master's, 7 other advanced degrees. *Graduate faculty:* 54 part-time/adjunct (31 women). *Tuition:* Part-time $645 per credit. *Required fees:* $265 per unit. *Student services:* Career counseling, services for students with disabilities, writing training. *Library facilities:* Excelsior College Library.

Computer facilities: A campuswide network can be accessed from off campus. Online class registration is available.
Website: http://www.excelsior.edu/

General Application Contact: Admissions Counselor, 518-464-8500, Fax: 518-464-8777, E-mail: admissions@excelsior.edu.

FAIRFIELD UNIVERSITY, Fairfield, CT 06824

General Information Independent-religious, coed, comprehensive institution. *Graduate housing:* Room and/or apartments available on a first-come, first-served basis to single students; on-campus housing not available to married students.

GRADUATE UNITS

College of Arts and Sciences *Program availability:* Part-time, evening/weekend, online learning. Offers American studies (MA); communication (MA); creative writing (MFA); mathematics (MS); public administration (MPA). Electronic applications accepted.

Dolan School of Business *Program availability:* Part-time, evening/weekend. Offers accounting (MBA, MS, CAS); business analytics (MS); finance (MBA, MS, CAS); information systems and business analytics (MBA); management (MBA, CAS); marketing (MBA, CAS); taxation (CAS). Electronic applications accepted.

Graduate School of Education and Allied Professions *Program availability:* Part-time, evening/weekend. Offers applied behavior analysis (ATC); applied psychology (MA); clinical mental health counseling (MA, CAS); educational technology (MA); elementary education (MA, CAS); family studies (MA); integration of spirituality and religion in counseling (ATC); marriage and family therapy (MA); reading and language development (Sixth Year Certificate); school counseling (MA, CAS); school psychology (MA, CAS); school-based marriage and family therapy (ATC); secondary education (MA); special education (MA, CAS); substance abuse counseling (ATC); teaching (Certificate); teaching and foundations (MA, CAS); TESOL, world languages, and bilingual education (MA, CAS). Electronic applications accepted.

Marion Peckham Egan School of Nursing and Health Studies *Program availability:* Part-time, evening/weekend. Offers advanced practice (DNP); family nurse practitioner (MSN, DNP); nurse anesthesia (DNP); nursing leadership (MSN); psychiatric nurse practitioner (MSN, DNP). Electronic applications accepted.

School of Engineering *Program availability:* Part-time, evening/weekend. Offers database management (CAS); electrical and computer engineering (MS); information security (CAS); management of technology (MS); mechanical engineering (MS); network technology (CAS); software engineering (MS); Web application development (CAS). Electronic applications accepted.

FAIRLEIGH DICKINSON UNIVERSITY, FLORHAM CAMPUS, Madison, NJ 07940-1099

General Information Independent, coed, comprehensive institution. *Graduate housing:* Room and/or apartments available on a first-come, first-served basis to single students; on-campus housing not available to married students. Housing application deadline: 5/1.

GRADUATE UNITS

Anthony J. Petrocelli College of Continuing Studies Offers continuing studies (MAS, MPA, MS, MSA); sports administration (MSA).

International School of Hospitality and Tourism Management Offers hospitality management studies (MS).

Public Administration Institute Offers public administration (MPA).

School of Administrative Science Offers administrative science (MAS).

Maxwell Becton College of Arts and Sciences Offers arts and sciences (MA, MFA, MS, Certificate); biology (MS); chemistry (MS); clinical mental health counseling (MA); computer science (MS); corporate and organizational communication (MA); counseling (MA); creative nonfiction (MFA); creative writing (MFA); creative writing and literature for educators (MA); fiction (MFA); industrial/organizational psychology (MA); literary translation (MFA); organizational behavior (MA, Certificate); organizational leadership (Certificate); poetry (MFA); writing for young adults (MFA).

School of Pharmacy Offers pharmacy (Pharm D).

Silberman College of Business *Program availability:* Part-time, evening/weekend. Offers accounting (MS); business (EMBA, MBA, MS, Certificate); business administration (MBA); entrepreneurial studies (MBA, Certificate); evolving technology (Certificate); finance (MBA, Certificate); health care and life sciences (EMBA); international business (MBA, Certificate); international taxation (Certificate); management (EMBA, MBA, Certificate); managing sustainability (Certificate); marketing (MBA, Certificate); pharmaceutical studies (MBA, Certificate); supply chain management (MS); taxation (MS, Certificate).

Center for Human Resource Management Studies Offers human resource management (MBA); human resource management studies (MBA).

University College: Arts, Sciences, and Professional Studies Offers arts, sciences, and professional studies (MA, MAT, MSN, Certificate).

The Henry P. Becton School of Nursing and Allied Health *Program availability:* Part-time, evening/weekend. Offers adult gerontology primary care nurse practitioner (MSN); family psychiatric/mental health nurse practitioner (MSN).

Peter Sammartino School of Education Offers education for certified teachers (MA, Certificate); educational leadership (MA); instructional technology (Certificate); literacy/reading (Certificate); PreK - 3 certification (MA, MAT); teaching (MAT).

FAIRLEIGH DICKINSON UNIVERSITY, METROPOLITAN CAMPUS, Teaneck, NJ 07666-1914

General Information Independent, coed, university. *Graduate housing:* Room and/or apartments available on a first-come, first-served basis to single students; on-campus housing not available to married students. Housing application deadline: 5/1.

GRADUATE UNITS

Anthony J. Petrocelli College of Continuing Studies Offers continuing studies (MAS, MPA, MS, MSA, MSHS, Certificate); sports administration (MSA).

International School of Hospitality and Tourism Management Offers hospitality management (MS).

Public Administration Institute Offers public administration (MPA, Certificate); public non-profit management (Certificate).

School of Administrative Science Offers administrative science (MAS, MSHS, Certificate); homeland security (MSHS).

Silberman College of Business Offers accounting (MBA, MS, Certificate); business (EMBA, MBA, MS, Certificate); business administration (MBA); chemical studies (Certificate); entrepreneurial studies (MBA, Certificate); executive management (EMBA); finance (MBA, Certificate); healthcare and life sciences (EMBA); international business (MBA); management (MBA, Certificate); management information systems (Certificate); marketing (MBA, Certificate); pharmaceutical studies (MBA, Certificate); taxation (MS).

Center for Human Resources Management Studies Offers human resource management (MBA, Certificate).

University College: Arts, Sciences, and Professional Studies Offers arts, sciences, and professional studies (MA, MAT, MS, MSEE, MSN, DNP, PhD, Psy D, Certificate); English and literature (MA); systems science (MS).

Henry P. Becton School of Nursing and Allied Health Offers medical technology (MS); nursing (MSN, Certificate); nursing practice (DNP).

Peter Sammartino School of Education *Program availability:* Part-time. Offers dyslexia specialist (Certificate); education for certified teachers (MA); educational leadership (MA); instructional technology (Certificate); learning disabilities (MA); literacy/reading (Certificate); multilingual education (MA); PreK - 3 certification (MA, MAT); teacher of the handicapped (Certificate); teaching (MAT).

School of Art and Media Studies Offers art and media studies (MA); media and communications (MA).

School of Computer Sciences and Engineering Offers computer engineering (MS); computer science (MS); e-commerce (MS); electrical engineering (MSEE); management information systems (MS); mathematical foundation (MS).

School of Criminal Justice and Legal Studies Offers criminal justice (MA).

School of History, Political and International Studies Offers history (MA); international studies (MA); political science (MA).

School of Natural Sciences Offers biology (MS); chemistry (MS); cosmetic science (MS); science (MA).

School of Psychology Offers clinical psychology (MA, PhD); clinical psychopharmacology (MA); forensic psychology (MA); general-theoretical psychology (MA, Certificate); school psychology (MA, Psy D).

FAIRMONT STATE UNIVERSITY, Fairmont, WV 26554

General Information State-supported, coed, comprehensive institution. CGS member. *Graduate housing:* Room and/or apartments available on a first-come, first-served basis to single students; on-campus housing not available to married students.

GRADUATE UNITS
Program in Business Administration *Program availability:* Part-time, evening/weekend. Offers business administration (MBA). Electronic applications accepted.

Program in Criminal Justice *Program availability:* Part-time, evening/weekend, 100% online. Offers criminal justice (MS). Electronic applications accepted.

Programs in Education *Program availability:* Part-time, evening/weekend, 100% online. Offers digital media, new literacies and learning (M Ed); education (MAT); exercise science, fitness and wellness (M Ed); professional studies (M Ed); reading (M Ed); special education (M Ed). Electronic applications accepted.

FAITH BAPTIST BIBLE COLLEGE AND THEOLOGICAL SEMINARY, Ankeny, IA 50023

General Information Independent-religious, coed, comprehensive institution. *Graduate housing:* Rooms and/or apartments available on a first-come, first-served basis to single and married students. Housing application deadline: 8/1.

GRADUATE UNITS
Graduate Program *Program availability:* Part-time. Offers Biblical studies (MA); pastoral studies (M Div); pastoral training (MA); religion (MA); theological studies (MA). Electronic applications accepted.

FAITH INTERNATIONAL UNIVERSITY, Tacoma, WA 98407

General Information Independent-religious, coed, comprehensive institution.

GRADUATE UNITS
Graduate and Professional Programs *Program availability:* Part-time, evening/weekend, online learning. Offers theology (M Div, MACM, MTS, D Min).

FAITH THEOLOGICAL SEMINARY, Baltimore, MD 21212

General Information Independent-religious, coed, comprehensive institution.

GRADUATE UNITS
Graduate Programs Offers theology (M Div, D Min, Th D).

FARMINGDALE STATE COLLEGE, Farmingdale, NY 11735

General Information State-supported, coed, comprehensive institution.

GRADUATE UNITS
Program in Technology Management Offers construction management (MS); electrical and mechanical engineering (MS).

FASHION INSTITUTE OF TECHNOLOGY, New York, NY 10001-5992

General Information State and locally supported, coed, primarily women, comprehensive institution. *Graduate housing:* Room and/or apartments available on a first-come, first-served basis to single students; on-campus housing not available to married students. *Research affiliation:* Grove Dictionary of Art, Oxford University Press (costume history), Exhibition Designers and Producers Association (exhibition design), Society for Environmental Graphic Design (exhibition design), Lolita S. A. (global fashion management), IDEO (design and management innovation).

GRADUATE UNITS
School of Graduate Studies *Program availability:* Part-time, evening/weekend. Offers art market studies (MA); cosmetics and fragrance marketing and management (MPS); exhibition and experience design (MA); fashion and textile studies: history, theory, museum practice (MA); fashion design (MFA); global fashion management (MPS); illustration (MFA). Electronic applications accepted.

FAULKNER UNIVERSITY, Montgomery, AL 36109-3398

General Information Independent-religious, coed, university. *Graduate housing:* On-campus housing not available.

GRADUATE UNITS
Alabama Christian College of Arts and Sciences *Program availability:* Part-time, evening/weekend, 100% online, blended/hybrid learning. Offers arts and sciences (MA, MJA, PhD); humanities (MA, PhD); justice administration (MJA). Electronic applications accepted.

College of Biblical Studies *Program availability:* Part-time, evening/weekend, 100% online, blended/hybrid learning, synchronous online/on-ground. Offers Biblical studies (MA, MDiv); Christian counseling and family ministry (MA); Christian ministry (MA). Electronic applications accepted.

College of Education *Program availability:* Part-time, evening/weekend, 100% online, blended/hybrid learning. Offers counseling (MS); curriculum and instruction (M Ed); elementary education (M Ed); school counseling (M Ed). Electronic applications accepted.

Harris College of Business and Executive Education *Program availability:* Part-time, evening/weekend, 100% online, blended/hybrid learning. Offers business administration (MBA); management (MSM). Electronic applications accepted.

Thomas Goode Jones School of Law Offers law (JD). Electronic applications accepted.

FAYETTEVILLE STATE UNIVERSITY, Fayetteville, NC 28301-4298

General Information State-supported, coed, comprehensive institution. *Enrollment:* 6,318 graduate, professional, and undergraduate students; 398 full-time matriculated graduate/professional students (263 women), 447 part-time matriculated graduate/professional students (273 women). *Enrollment by degree level:* 590 master's, 85 doctoral, 170 other advanced degrees. *Graduate faculty:* 54 full-time (26 women), 21 part-time/adjunct (11 women). *Graduate housing:* On-campus housing not available. *Student services:* Campus employment opportunities, career counseling, child daycare facilities, free psychological counseling, low-cost health insurance, services for students with disabilities. *Library facilities:* Charles W. Chestnut Library. *Collection:* Books: 223,687 (physical), 224,581 (digital/electronic); Serial titles: 314 (physical), 30,747 (digital/electronic); Databases: 442. Weekly public service hours: 97; students can reserve study rooms.

Computer facilities: Computer purchase and lease plans are available. 600 computers available on campus for general student use. A campuswide network can be accessed from student residence rooms and from off campus. Online class registration is available.
Website: http://www.uncfsu.edu/

General Application Contact: Melissa Wells, Assistant Director of Admissions, 910-672-1412, Fax: 910-672-2600, E-mail: mwells@uncfsu.edu.

GRADUATE UNITS
Graduate School Students: 398 full-time (263 women), 447 part-time (273 women); includes 523 minority (421 Black or African American, non-Hispanic/Latino; 8 American Indian or Alaska Native, non-Hispanic/Latino; 27 Asian, non-Hispanic/Latino; 56 Hispanic/Latino; 1 Native Hawaiian or other Pacific Islander, non-Hispanic/Latino; 10 Two or more races, non-Hispanic/Latino), 19 international. Average age 37. 480 applicants, 90% accepted, 353 enrolled. *Faculty:* 54 full-time (26 women), 21 part-time/adjunct (11 women). *Expenses:* Contact institution. *Financial support:* Research assistantships, institutionally sponsored loans, and unspecified assistantships available. Support available to part-time students. Financial award application deadline: 3/1; financial award applicants required to submit FAFSA. In 2018, 160 master's, 8 doctorates awarded. *Program availability:* Part-time, evening/weekend. Offers business administration (MBA); criminal justice (MA); middle grades (MA Ed); psychology (MA); school administration (MSA); social work (MSW); sociology (MA Ed); special education (MA Ed). *Application deadline:* For fall admission, 4/1 for domestic students, 3/1 for international students; for spring admission, 10/15 for domestic students. Applications are processed on a rolling basis. *Application fee:* $40. Electronic applications accepted. *Application Contact:* Melissa Wells, Assistant Director of Admissions, 910-672-1412, Fax: 910-672-2600, E-mail: mwells@uncfsu.edu. *Office of Admissions,* Ulisa Bowles, 910-672-1371, Fax: 910-672-2600.

FELICIAN UNIVERSITY, Lodi, NJ 07644-2117

General Information Independent-religious, coed, comprehensive institution. *Graduate housing:* Room and/or apartments available on a first-come, first-served basis to single students; on-campus housing not available to married students. Housing application deadline: 5/1.

GRADUATE UNITS
Doctor of Nursing Practice Program *Program availability:* Evening/weekend, online only, 100% online, blended/hybrid learning. Offers advanced practice (DNP); executive leadership (DNP). Electronic applications accepted.

Master of Science in Nursing Program *Program availability:* Evening/weekend, online only, 100% online, blended/hybrid learning. Offers adult-gerontology nurse practitioner (MSN, PMC); executive leadership (MSN, PMC); family nurse practitioner (MSN, PMC); nursing education (MSN, PMC). Electronic applications accepted.

Program in Business *Program availability:* Part-time-only, evening/weekend, online learning. Offers business administration (DBA); innovation and entrepreneurial leadership (MBA). Electronic applications accepted.

Program in Counseling Psychology *Program availability:* Part-time, evening/weekend. Offers counseling psychology (MA, Psy D). Electronic applications accepted.

Program in Education *Program availability:* Part-time, evening/weekend. Offers education (MA); educational leadership (principal/supervision) (MA); educational supervision (PMC); principal (PMC). Electronic applications accepted.

Program in Health Care Administration *Program availability:* Part-time, evening/weekend. Offers health care administration (MSHA). Electronic applications accepted.

Program in Religious Education *Program availability:* Part-time, evening/weekend, online only, 100% online. Offers religious education (MA, Certificate). Electronic applications accepted.

FERRIS STATE UNIVERSITY, Big Rapids, MI 49307

General Information State-supported, coed, comprehensive institution. CGS member. *Enrollment:* 955 full-time matriculated graduate/professional students (555 women), 388 part-time matriculated graduate/professional students (281 women). *Enrollment by degree level:* 498 master's, 724 doctoral, 121 other advanced degrees. *Graduate faculty:* 127 full-time (74 women), 159 part-time/adjunct (80 women). *Graduate housing:* Rooms and/or apartments available on a first-come, first-served basis to single and married students. *Student services:* Campus employment opportunities, campus safety program, career counseling, child daycare facilities, exercise/wellness program, free psychological counseling, international student services, low-cost health insurance, multicultural affairs office, services for students with disabilities, teacher training. *Library facilities:* Ferris Library for Information, Technology and Education. *Collection:* Books: 267,897 (physical), 214,655 (digital/electronic); Serial titles: 161 (physical), 160,936 (digital/electronic); Databases: 183. Weekly public service hours: 93; study areas open 24 hours, 5–7 days a week; students can reserve study rooms.

Computer facilities: 1,723 computers available on campus for general student use. A campuswide network can be accessed from student residence rooms and from off campus. Online class registration is available.
Website: http://www.ferris.edu/

General Application Contact: Dr. Kristen Salomonson, Dean, Enrollment Services/Director, Admissions and Records, 231-591-2100, Fax: 231-591-3944, E-mail: admissions@ferris.edu.

GRADUATE UNITS

College of Arts and Sciences Students: 36 full-time (30 women), 40 part-time (36 women); includes 11 minority (5 Black or African American, non-Hispanic/Latino; 5 Hispanic/Latino; 1 Two or more races, non-Hispanic/Latino). Average age 31. 71 applicants, 86% accepted, 47 enrolled. *Faculty:* 7 full-time (all women), 5 part-time/adjunct (4 women). Expenses: Contact institution. *Financial support:* In 2018–19, 10 students received support. Federal Work-Study available. Financial award applicants required to submit FAFSA. In 2018, 37 master's awarded. *Program availability:* Part-time, evening/weekend. Offers social work (MSW). *Application deadline:* For fall admission, 10/1 for domestic students. *Application fee:* $0 ($30 for international students). Electronic applications accepted. *Application Contact:* Dr. Janet Vizina-Roubal, MSW Coordinator, 231-357-2816, E-mail: janetvizinaroubal@ferris.edu. *Director of Social Work Program,* Dr. Wendy Samuels, 231-591-5896, E-mail: wendysamuels@ferris.edu.

College of Business Students: 14 full-time (9 women), 96 part-time (51 women); includes 12 minority (4 Black or African American, non-Hispanic/Latino; 1 American Indian or Alaska Native, non-Hispanic/Latino; 3 Asian, non-Hispanic/Latino; 2 Hispanic/Latino; 2 Two or more races, non-Hispanic/Latino), 8 international. Average age 33. 48 applicants, 88% accepted, 32 enrolled. *Faculty:* 20 full-time (7 women). Expenses: Contact institution. *Financial support:* In 2018–19, 17 students received support. Career-related internships or fieldwork, Federal Work-Study, scholarships/grants, and unspecified assistantships available. Support available to part-time students. Financial award applicants required to submit FAFSA. In 2018, 39 master's awarded. *Program availability:* Part-time, evening/weekend, 100% online, blended/hybrid learning. Offers design and innovation management (MBA); lean systems and leadership (MBA); project management (MBA); supply chain management and lean logistics (MBA). *Application deadline:* For fall admission, 7/1 priority date for domestic students, 6/15 for international students; for winter admission, 11/1 priority date for domestic students, 10/15 for international students; for spring admission, 3/1 priority date for domestic students, 2/15 for international students. Applications are processed on a rolling basis. *Application fee:* $0 ($30 for international students). Electronic applications accepted. *Application Contact:* Dr. Greg Gogolin, Professor, 231-591-3159, Fax: 231-591-3521, E-mail: greggogolin@ferris.edu. *College of Business Dean,* Dr. David Nicol, 231-591-2168, Fax: 231-591-3521, E-mail: davidnicol@ferris.edu.

College of Education and Human Services Students: 10 full-time (7 women), 78 part-time (45 women); includes 20 minority (12 Black or African American, non-Hispanic/Latino; 5 Hispanic/Latino; 3 Two or more races, non-Hispanic/Latino), 2 international. Average age 35. 35 applicants, 97% accepted, 25 enrolled. *Faculty:* 15 full-time (6 women), 1 (woman) part-time/adjunct. Expenses: Contact institution. *Financial support:* In 2018–19, 9 students received support, including 2 research assistantships (averaging $5,490 per year); career-related internships or fieldwork, Federal Work-Study, scholarships/grants, and unspecified assistantships also available. Support available to part-time students. Financial award applicants required to submit FAFSA. In 2018, 37 master's awarded. *Program availability:* Part-time, evening/weekend, blended/hybrid learning. Offers education and human services (M Ed, MS, MSCJ, MSCTE). *Application deadline:* For fall admission, 7/1 priority date for domestic and international students; for winter admission, 12/15 priority date for domestic and international students; for spring admission, 11/1 priority date for domestic and international students; for summer admission, 3/1 priority date for domestic and international students. Applications are processed on a rolling basis. *Application fee:* $0 ($30 for international students). Electronic applications accepted. *Application Contact:* Dr. Kristen Salomonson, Dean, Enrollment Services/Director, Admissions and Records, 231-591-2100, Fax: 231-591-3944, E-mail: admissions@ferris.edu. *Interim Dean,* Leonard Johnson, 231-591-3648, Fax: 231-592-3792, E-mail: LeonardJohnson@ferris.edu.

School of Criminal Justice Students: 6 full-time (4 women), 39 part-time (22 women); includes 13 minority (9 Black or African American, non-Hispanic/Latino; 3 Hispanic/Latino; 1 Two or more races, non-Hispanic/Latino). Average age 31. 3 applicants, 100% accepted, 18 enrolled. *Faculty:* 8 full-time (2 women). Expenses: Contact institution. *Financial support:* In 2018–19, 2 students received support, including 2 research assistantships (averaging $5,490 per year); Federal Work-Study and unspecified assistantships also available. Support available to part-time students. Financial award applicants required to submit FAFSA. In 2018, 19 master's awarded. *Program availability:* Part-time, evening/weekend. Offers criminal justice administration (MSCJ). *Application deadline:* For fall admission, 8/15 for domestic students; for winter admission, 12/15 for domestic students; for spring admission, 3/15 for domestic students. Applications are processed on a rolling basis. *Application fee:* $0 ($30 for international students). Electronic applications accepted. *Application Contact:* Sara P. Rasmussen, Secretary, 231-591-3652, Fax: 231-591-3792, E-mail: sararasmussen@ferris.edu. *Professor/Graduate Program Coordinator,* Dr. Nancy L. Hogan, 231-591-2664, Fax: 231-591-3792, E-mail: hogann@ferris.edu.

School of Education Students: 4 full-time (3 women), 39 part-time (23 women); includes 7 minority (3 Black or African American, non-Hispanic/Latino; 2 Hispanic/Latino; 2 Two or more races, non-Hispanic/Latino), 2 international. Average age 38. 14 applicants, 93% accepted, 7 enrolled. *Faculty:* 7 full-time (4 women), 1 (woman) part-time/adjunct. Expenses: Contact institution. *Financial support:* In 2018–19, 7 students received support. Career-related internships or fieldwork and scholarships/grants available. Support available to part-time students. Financial award applicants required to submit FAFSA. In 2018, 18 master's awarded. *Program availability:* Part-time, evening/weekend, blended/hybrid learning. Offers curriculum and instruction (M Ed); training and development (MSCTE). *Application deadline:* For fall admission, 7/1 priority date for domestic and international students; for spring admission, 11/1 priority date for domestic and international students; for summer

admission, 3/1 priority date for domestic and international students. Applications are processed on a rolling basis. *Application fee:* $0 ($30 for international students). Electronic applications accepted. *Application Contact:* Liza Ing, Graduate Program Coordinator, 231-591-5362, Fax: 231-591-2043, E-mail: lizaIng@ferris.edu. *Interim Dean,* Leonard Johnson, 231-591-3648, Fax: 231-591-2043, E-mail: LeonardJohnson@ferris.edu.

College of Health Professions Students: 34 full-time (29 women), 137 part-time (127 women); includes 31 minority (8 Black or African American, non-Hispanic/Latino; 6 American Indian or Alaska Native, non-Hispanic/Latino; 9 Asian, non-Hispanic/Latino; 2 Hispanic/Latino; 6 Two or more races, non-Hispanic/Latino). Average age 34. 53 applicants, 91% accepted, 45 enrolled. *Faculty:* 16 full-time (13 women). Expenses: Contact institution. *Financial support:* In 2018–19, 10 students received support. Career-related internships or fieldwork and scholarships/grants available. Financial award applicants required to submit FAFSA. In 2018, 26 master's awarded. *Program availability:* Part-time, evening/weekend, 100% online. Offers health professions (MHA, MPH, MSN); healthcare administration (MHA); public health (MPH). *Application deadline:* For fall admission, 4/15 priority date for domestic students; for spring admission, 10/15 for domestic students; for summer admission, 4/1 for domestic and international students. Applications are processed on a rolling basis. *Application fee:* $0 ($30 for international students). Electronic applications accepted. *Application Contact:* Dr. Kristen Salomonson, Dean of Enrollment Services and Director of Admissions and Records, 231-591-3963, Fax: 231-591-3179, E-mail: kristensalomonson@ferris.edu. *Interim Dean,* Dr. Lincoln Gibbs, 231-591-2273, E-mail: LincolnGibbs@ferris.edu.

School of Nursing Students: 4 full-time (3 women), 105 part-time (100 women); includes 12 minority (2 Black or African American, non-Hispanic/Latino; 4 American Indian or Alaska Native, non-Hispanic/Latino; 2 Asian, non-Hispanic/Latino; 2 Hispanic/Latino; 2 Two or more races, non-Hispanic/Latino). Average age 39. 29 applicants, 7% accepted, 25 enrolled. *Faculty:* 7 full-time (all women), 1 (woman) part-time/adjunct. Expenses: Contact institution. *Financial support:* In 2018–19, 8 students received support. Career-related internships or fieldwork and scholarships/grants available. Financial award application deadline: 4/15; financial award applicants required to submit FAFSA. In 2018, 22 master's awarded. *Program availability:* Part-time, evening/weekend, online only, 100% online. Offers nursing (MSN); nursing administration (MSN); nursing education (MSN); nursing informatics (MSN). *Application deadline:* For fall admission, 4/15 priority date for domestic and international students; for spring admission, 10/15 for domestic and international students. *Application fee:* $0. Electronic applications accepted. *Application Contact:* Dr. Sharon Colley, MSN Program Coordinator, 231-591-2288, Fax: 231-591-2325, E-mail: colleys@ferris.edu. *Chair, School of Nursing,* Dr. Wendy Lenon, 231-591-2267, Fax: 231-591-2325, E-mail: WendyLenon@ferris.edu.

College of Pharmacy Students: 553 full-time (295 women), 23 part-time (11 women); includes 46 minority (3 Black or African American, non-Hispanic/Latino; 3 American Indian or Alaska Native, non-Hispanic/Latino; 18 Asian, non-Hispanic/Latino; 14 Hispanic/Latino; 8 Two or more races, non-Hispanic/Latino), 12 international. Average age 24. 377 applicants, 46% accepted, 142 enrolled. *Faculty:* 35 full-time (24 women), 4 part-time/adjunct (2 women). Expenses: Contact institution. *Financial support:* In 2018–19, 177 students received support. Career-related internships or fieldwork, Federal Work-Study, institutionally sponsored loans, and scholarships/grants available. Financial award application deadline: 4/15; financial award applicants required to submit FAFSA. In 2018, 126 doctorates awarded. *Program availability:* Part-time, evening/weekend, online learning. Offers pharmacy (Pharm D). *Application deadline:* For fall admission, 2/1 for domestic and international students. *Application fee:* $150. *Application Contact:* Tara M. Lee, Director of Admissions, 231-591-2249, Fax: 231-591-3829, E-mail: leet@ferris.edu. *Dean,* Dr. Stephen Durst, 231-591-2254, Fax: 231-591-3829, E-mail: dursts@ferris.edu.

Extended and International Operations Students: 119 full-time (79 women), 2 part-time (1 woman); includes 46 minority (31 Black or African American, non-Hispanic/Latino; 1 American Indian or Alaska Native, non-Hispanic/Latino; 1 Asian, non-Hispanic/Latino; 12 Hispanic/Latino; 1 Two or more races, non-Hispanic/Latino). Average age 45. 40 applicants, 75% accepted, 26 enrolled. *Faculty:* 27 part-time/adjunct (18 women). Expenses: Contact institution. *Financial support:* In 2018–19, 15 students received support, including 6 teaching assistantships (averaging $690 per year). Financial award applicants required to submit FAFSA. In 2018, 17 doctorates awarded. *Program availability:* Evening/weekend, blended/hybrid learning. Offers community college leadership (Ed D). *Application deadline:* For spring admission, 10/31 for domestic and international students; for summer admission, 4/15 for domestic and international students. Applications are processed on a rolling basis. *Application fee:* $0. Electronic applications accepted. *Application Contact:* Megan Biller, Coordinator, 231-591-2710, Fax: 231-591-3539, E-mail: meganbiller@ferris.edu. *Director,* Dr. Roberta Teahen, 231-591-3805, E-mail: robertateahen@ferris.edu.

Kendall College of Art and Design Students: 41 full-time (22 women), 12 part-time (10 women); includes 10 minority (3 Black or African American, non-Hispanic/Latino; 1 American Indian or Alaska Native, non-Hispanic/Latino; 1 Asian, non-Hispanic/Latino; 5 Hispanic/Latino), 6 international. Average age 32. 52 applicants, 60% accepted, 18 enrolled. *Faculty:* 15 full-time (8 women), 6 part-time/adjunct (2 women). Expenses: Contact institution. *Financial support:* In 2018–19, 10 students received support, including 15 fellowships (averaging $9,762 per year); scholarships/grants and unspecified assistantships also available. Financial award application deadline: 2/1; financial award applicants required to submit FAFSA. In 2018, 10 master's awarded. *Program availability:* Part-time. Offers design (MA); painting (MFA); photography (MFA); printmaking (MFA); visual and critical studies (MA). *Application deadline:* For fall admission, 2/1 priority date for domestic and international students; for spring admission, 11/1 priority date for domestic and international students. Applications are processed on a rolling basis. *Application fee:* $0 ($30 for international students). Electronic applications accepted. *Application Contact:* Thomas Post, Graduate Recruitment Specialist, 616-451-2787, Fax: 616-831-9689, E-mail: thomaspost@ferris.edu. *President,* Tara McCrackin, 616-451-2787.

Michigan College of Optometry Students: 148 full-time (84 women); includes 4 minority (2 Asian, non-Hispanic/Latino; 2 Hispanic/Latino), 8 international. Average age 24. 194 applicants, 27% accepted, 37 enrolled. *Faculty:* 19 full-time (9 women), 115 part-time/adjunct (52 women). Expenses: Contact institution. *Financial support:* In 2018–19, 12 students received support. Career-related internships or fieldwork, Federal Work-Study, and scholarships/grants available. Financial award applicants required to submit FAFSA. In 2018, 36 doctorates awarded. Offers optometry (OD). *Application deadline:* For fall admission, 2/1 for domestic and international students. Applications are processed on a rolling basis. *Application fee:* $170. Electronic applications accepted. *Application Contact:* Amy Parks, Health College Administrative Specialist, 231-591-3703, Fax: 231-591-2394, E-mail: amyparks@ferris.edu. *Dean,* Dr. David Damari, 231-591-3706, Fax: 231-591-2394, E-mail: damarid@ferris.edu.

FIELDING GRADUATE UNIVERSITY, Santa Barbara, CA 93105-3814

General Information Independent, coed, graduate-only institution. CGS member. *Graduate housing:* On-campus housing not available.

GRADUATE UNITS

Graduate Programs Students: 825 full-time (637 women), 163 part-time (115 women); includes 383 minority (165 Black or African American, non-Hispanic/Latino; 19 American Indian or Alaska Native, non-Hispanic/Latino; 36 Asian, non-Hispanic/Latino; 109 Hispanic/Latino; 1 Native Hawaiian or other Pacific Islander, non-Hispanic/Latino; 53 Two or more races, non-Hispanic/Latino), 11 international. Average age 44. 471 applicants, 53% accepted, 165 enrolled. *Faculty:* 55 full-time (34 women), 82 part-time/adjunct (49 women). Expenses: Contact institution. *Financial support:* In 2018–19, 177 students received support, including 1 research assistantship (averaging $4,927 per year), 20 teaching assistantships (averaging $2,195 per year); scholarships/grants also available. Support available to part-time students. Financial award applicants required to submit FAFSA. In 2018, 29 master's, 99 doctorates, 76 other advanced degrees awarded. *Program availability:* Part-time, evening/weekend, 100% online, blended/hybrid learning. *Application deadline:* For fall admission, 7/15 for domestic and international students; for spring admission, 11/1 for domestic and international students; for summer admission, 3/1 for domestic and international students. *Application fee:* $75. Electronic applications accepted. *Application Contact:* Enrollment Coordinator, 800-340-1099 Ext. 4098, Fax: 805-687-9793, E-mail: admissions@fielding.edu. *President,* Dr. Katrina Rogers, 805-898-2924, Fax: 805-687-9793, E-mail: krogers@fielding.edu.

School of Leadership Studies Students: 371 full-time (283 women), 77 part-time (57 women); includes 180 minority (94 Black or African American, non-Hispanic/Latino; 17 American Indian or Alaska Native, non-Hispanic/Latino; 13 Asian, non-Hispanic/Latino; 35 Hispanic/Latino; 1 Native Hawaiian or other Pacific Islander, non-Hispanic/Latino; 20 Two or more races, non-Hispanic/Latino), 5 international. Average age 49. 106 applicants, 80% accepted, 60 enrolled. *Faculty:* 22 full-time (13 women), 56 part-time/adjunct (34 women). Expenses: Contact institution. *Financial support:* In 2018–19, 96 students received support. Research assistantships, teaching assistantships, and scholarships/grants available. Support available to part-time students. Financial award applicants required to submit FAFSA. In 2018, 21 master's, 56 doctorates, 25 other advanced degrees awarded. *Program availability:* Part-time, evening/weekend, 100% online, blended/hybrid learning. Offers comprehensive evidence based coaching (Graduate Certificate); digital teaching and learning (MA); evidence based coaching for organizational leadership (Graduate Certificate); human development (PhD); infant and early childhood development (MA, PhD, Graduate Certificate); leadership for change (Ed D); leadership studies (MA, Ed D, PhD, Graduate Certificate); organizational consulting (Graduate Certificate); organizational development and change (PhD); organizational development and leadership (MA, Graduate Certificate). *Application deadline:* For fall admission, 7/15 for domestic and international students; for spring admission, 10/24 for domestic and international students; for summer admission, 2/18 for domestic and international students. *Application fee:* $75. Electronic applications accepted. *Application Contact:* Enrollment Coordinator, 800-340-1099 Ext. 4098, Fax: 805-687-9793, E-mail: admissions@fielding.edu.

School of Psychology Students: 454 full-time (354 women), 86 part-time (58 women); includes 203 minority (71 Black or African American, non-Hispanic/Latino; 2 American Indian or Alaska Native, non-Hispanic/Latino; 23 Asian, non-Hispanic/Latino; 74 Hispanic/Latino; 33 Two or more races, non-Hispanic/Latino), 6 international. Average age 41. 365 applicants, 45% accepted, 105 enrolled. *Faculty:* 33 full-time (21 women), 26 part-time/adjunct (15 women). Expenses: Contact institution. *Financial support:* In 2018–19, 81 students received support, including 1 research assistantship (averaging $4,927 per year), 20 teaching assistantships (averaging $2,195 per year); scholarships/grants also available. Support available to part-time students. Financial award applicants required to submit FAFSA. In 2018, 8 master's, 43 doctorates, 51 other advanced degrees awarded. *Program availability:* Part-time, evening/weekend, 100% online, blended/hybrid learning. Offers clinical psychology (PhD, Postbaccalaureate Certificate); media psychology (MA, PhD, Graduate Certificate); neuropsychology (Post-Doctoral Certificate); psychology (MA, PhD, Graduate Certificate, Post-Doctoral Certificate, Postbaccalaureate Certificate); respecialization in clinical psychology (Post-Doctoral Certificate). *Application deadline:* For fall admission, 7/16 for domestic and international students; for spring admission, 10/24 for domestic and international students; for summer admission, 2/18 for domestic and international students. *Application fee:* $75. Electronic applications accepted. *Application Contact:* Enrollment Coordinator, 800-340-1099 Ext. 4098, Fax: 805-687-9793, E-mail: psyadmission@fielding.edu.

FISHER COLLEGE, Boston, MA 02116-1500

General Information Independent, coed, comprehensive institution. *Graduate housing:* Room and/or apartments available on a first-come, first-served basis to single students; on-campus housing not available to married students. Housing application deadline: 8/1.

GRADUATE UNITS

Master of Business Administration Program *Program availability:* Part-time, evening/weekend, online only, 100% online. Offers strategic leadership (MBA). Electronic applications accepted.

FISK UNIVERSITY, Nashville, TN 37208-3051

General Information Independent-religious, coed, comprehensive institution. *Graduate housing:* Rooms and/or apartments available on a first-come, first-served basis to single and married students. Housing application deadline: 4/6. *Research affiliation:* Oak Ridge Associated Universities (physics).

GRADUATE UNITS

Division of Graduate Studies *Program availability:* Part-time. Offers biology (MA); chemistry (MA); clinical psychology (MA); physics (MA); psychology (MA). Electronic applications accepted.

FITCHBURG STATE UNIVERSITY, Fitchburg, MA 01420-2697

General Information State-supported, coed, comprehensive institution. *Graduate housing:* On-campus housing not available.

GRADUATE UNITS

Division of Graduate and Continuing Education *Program availability:* Part-time, evening/weekend, online learning. Offers accounting (MBA); applied communication studies (MS); applied communications (CAGS); arts education (M Ed); biology (MA); clinical mental health counseling (MS); computer science (MS); counseling/psychology (CAGS); curriculum and teaching (M Ed); data science (MS); early childhood education (M Ed); education technology (Certificate); educational leadership and management (M Ed, CAGS); elementary education (M Ed); English (M Ed); English and teaching English (secondary level) (MA, MAT, Certificate); fine arts director (Certificate); forensic nursing (MS, Certificate); general science (M Ed); guided studies: dyslexia specialist (M Ed); guided studies: individualized (M Ed); guided studies: professional (M Ed); higher education administration (CAGS); history (M Ed); history and teaching history (secondary level) (MA); human resources management (MBA); individualized track (CAGS); management (MBA); math (M Ed); moderate disabilities: initial licensure (5-12) (M Ed); moderate disabilities: initial licensure (PK-8) (M Ed); occupational education (M Ed); reading specialist (CAGS); school guidance counseling (MS); school principal (M Ed, CAGS); science education (M Ed); supervisor/director (M Ed, CAGS); teacher of students with severe disabilities (M Ed); technical and professional writing (MS); technology education (M Ed). Electronic applications accepted.

FIVE BRANCHES UNIVERSITY, Santa Cruz, CA 95062

General Information Independent, coed, graduate-only institution. *Enrollment by degree level:* 25 master's, 340 doctoral. *Graduate faculty:* 10 full-time (5 women), 130 part-time/adjunct (65 women). *Tuition:* Full-time $15,000. *Required fees:* $300. Full-time tuition and fees vary according to class time, course level, course load, degree level, campus/location, program, reciprocity agreements and student level. *Graduate housing:* On-campus housing not available. *Student services:* Campus employment opportunities, campus safety program, career counseling, international student services. *Library facilities:* Five Branches University Library plus 1 other. *Collection:* Books: 8,000 (physical); Serial titles: 8,000 (physical); Databases: 3. Weekly public service hours: 40.

Computer facilities: 4 computers available on campus for general student use. A campuswide network can be accessed from off campus. Online class registration is available.

Website: http://www.fivebranches.edu/

General Application Contact: Eleonor Mendelson, Admissions Director, 831-476-9424, Fax: 831-476-8928, E-mail: admissions@fivebranches.com.

GRADUATE UNITS

Graduate School of Traditional Chinese Medicine Offers acupuncture (M Ac); acupuncture and Oriental medicine (DAOM); traditional Chinese medicine (MTCM, PhD). Electronic applications accepted.

FIVE TOWNS COLLEGE, Dix Hills, NY 11746-6055

General Information Independent, coed, comprehensive institution. *Graduate housing:* Room and/or apartments available on a first-come, first-served basis to single students; on-campus housing not available to married students.

GRADUATE UNITS

Graduate Programs *Program availability:* Part-time. Offers childhood education (MS Ed); composition and arranging (DMA); jazz/commercial music (MM); music education (MM, DMA); music history and literature (DMA); music performance (DMA). Electronic applications accepted.

FLAGLER COLLEGE, St. Augustine, FL 32085-1027

General Information Independent, coed, comprehensive institution.

GRADUATE UNITS

Program in Deaf Education Offers deaf education (MA).

FLORIDA AGRICULTURAL AND MECHANICAL UNIVERSITY, Tallahassee, FL 32307-3200

General Information State-supported, coed, university. CGS member. *Graduate housing:* Rooms and/or apartments available on a first-come, first-served basis to single and married students. Housing application deadline: 6/1. *Research affiliation:* Boeing (aerospace science), Minority Health Professions Foundation (health science), Pfizer, Inc.

GRADUATE UNITS

College of Law *Program availability:* Part-time, evening/weekend. Offers law (JD).

Division of Graduate Studies, Research, and Continuing Education *Program availability:* Part-time, evening/weekend.

College of Education *Program availability:* Part-time, evening/weekend. Offers administration and supervision (M Ed, MS, PhD); adult education (M Ed, MS); biology (M Ed); business education (MBE); chemistry (MS Ed); education (M Ed, MBE, MS, MS Ed, PhD); educational leadership (PhD); elementary education (M Ed, MS); English (MS Ed); guidance and counseling (M Ed, MS); history (MS Ed); industrial education (MS Ed); math (MS Ed); physics (MS Ed); sport management (MS); technology education (M Ed).

College of Pharmacy and Pharmaceutical Sciences Offers environmental toxicology (PhD); health outcomes research and pharmacoeconomics (PhD); medicinal chemistry (MS, PhD); pharmaceutics (MS, PhD); pharmacology/toxicology (MS, PhD); pharmacy administration (MS); pharmacy and pharmaceutical sciences (MPH, MS, DPH, PhD, Pharm D); public health (MPH, DPH).

College of Science and Technology Offers chemistry (MS); physics (MS, PhD); science and technology (MS, PhD); software engineering (MS).

College of Social Sciences, Arts and Humanities *Program availability:* Part-time. Offers community psychology (MS); criminal justice (MASS); history (MASS); history and political science (MASS, MSW); political science (MASS); public administration (MASS); social sciences, arts and humanities (MASS, MS, MSW); social work (MSW).

FAMU-FSU College of Engineering Offers biomedical engineering (MS, PhD); chemical engineering (MS, PhD); civil engineering (M Eng, MS, PhD); electrical engineering (MS, PhD); engineering (M Eng, MS, PhD); industrial engineering (MS, PhD); mechanical engineering (MS, PhD). College administered jointly by Florida State University.

School of Allied Health Sciences Offers health administration (MS); occupational therapy (MOT); physical therapy (DPT).

School of Architecture *Program availability:* Part-time. Offers architectural studies (MS Arch); architecture (professional) (M Arch); landscape architecture (MLA).

School of Business and Industry Offers accounting (MBA); finance (MBA); management information systems (MBA); marketing (MBA).

School of Journalism and Graphic Communication Offers journalism (MS).

School of Nursing Offers nursing (MSN, PhD).

School of the Environment Offers the environment (MS, PhD). Electronic applications accepted.

FLORIDA ATLANTIC UNIVERSITY, Boca Raton, FL 33431-0991

General Information State-supported, coed, university. CGS member. *Enrollment:* 29,772 graduate, professional, and undergraduate students; 2,074 full-time matriculated graduate/professional students (1,225 women), 2,794 part-time matriculated

Florida Atlantic University

graduate/professional students (1,721 women). *Enrollment by degree level:* 3,632 master's, 1,191 doctoral, 45 other advanced degrees. *Graduate faculty:* 677 full-time (272 women), 75 part-time/adjunct (39 women). *Tuition, area resident:* Full-time $7400; part-time $369.82 per credit. Tuition, state resident: full-time $7400; part-time $369.82 per credit. Tuition, nonresident: full-time $20,496; part-time $1024.81 per credit. *Graduate housing:* Room and/or apartments available on a first-come, first-served basis to single students; on-campus housing not available to married students. Typical cost: $9200 per year. Room charges vary according to board plan, campus/location and housing facility selected. *Student services:* Campus employment opportunities, campus safety program, career counseling, exercise/wellness program, free psychological counseling, international student services, low-cost health insurance, multicultural affairs office, services for students with disabilities, teacher training, writing training. *Library facilities:* S. E. Wimberly Library plus 2 others. *Collection:* Books: 907,932 (physical), 1.3 million (digital/electronic); Serial titles: 31,489 (physical), 194,584 (digital/electronic); Databases: 628. Study areas open 24 hours, 5–7 days a week.

Computer facilities: 1,350 computers available on campus for general student use. A campuswide network can be accessed from student residence rooms and from off campus. Online class registration is available.
Website: http://www.fau.edu/

General Application Contact: Jordan Hession, Assistant Director, Graduate Orientation and Admissions, 561-297-1213, Fax: 561-297-1212, E-mail: jhession@fau.edu.

GRADUATE UNITS

Charles E. Schmidt College of Medicine Students: 268 full-time (130 women), 30 part-time (17 women); includes 122 minority (31 Black or African American, non-Hispanic/Latino; 38 Asian, non-Hispanic/Latino; 47 Hispanic/Latino; 6 Two or more races, non-Hispanic/Latino), 3 international. Average age 25. 3,431 applicants, 3% accepted, 88 enrolled. *Faculty:* 2 full-time (1 woman), 1 part-time/adjunct (0 women). Expenses: Contact institution. *Financial support:* Fellowships and research assistantships available. Financial award applicants required to submit FAFSA. In 2018, 23 master's, 64 doctorates awarded. *Program availability:* Part-time. Offers biomedical science (MS); medicine (MD). *Application deadline:* For fall admission, 5/1 for domestic students, 3/15 for international students; for spring admission, 10/1 for domestic and international students. *Application fee:* $30. Electronic applications accepted. *Application Contact:* Deborah Roski, Director of Faculty & Staff Affairs, 561-297-2142, E-mail: dsalerno@health.fau.edu. *Director of Faculty & Staff Affairs,* Deborah Roski, 561-297-2142, E-mail: dsalerno@health.fau.edu.

Charles E. Schmidt College of Science Students: 222 full-time (119 women), 214 part-time (86 women); includes 115 minority (18 Black or African American, non-Hispanic/Latino; 18 Asian, non-Hispanic/Latino; 59 Hispanic/Latino; 20 Two or more races, non-Hispanic/Latino), 88 international. Average age 29. 339 applicants, 33% accepted, 104 enrolled. *Faculty:* 174 full-time (52 women), 11 part-time/adjunct (2 women). Expenses: Contact institution. *Financial support:* Fellowships with partial tuition reimbursements, research assistantships with partial tuition reimbursements, teaching assistantships with partial tuition reimbursements, career-related internships or fieldwork, Federal Work-Study, institutionally sponsored loans, scholarships/grants, tuition waivers (partial), and unspecified assistantships available. Financial award applicants required to submit FAFSA. In 2018, 89 master's, 31 doctorates awarded. *Program availability:* Part-time. Offers applied mathematics and statistics (MS); biology (MS, MST); chemistry (MS, MST, PhD); exercise science and health promotion (MS); geology (MS); geosciences (PhD); mathematics (MST, PhD); physics (MS, MST, PhD); psychology (MA); science (MA, MS, MSMP, MST, PhD). *Application deadline:* For fall admission, 6/1 for domestic students, 2/15 for international students; for spring admission, 11/1 for domestic students, 8/15 for international students. Applications are processed on a rolling basis. *Application fee:* $30. Electronic applications accepted. *Application Contact:* Ata Sarejedini, Dean, 561-297-3301, E-mail: ata@fau.edu. *Dean,* Ata Sarejedini, 561-297-3301, E-mail: ata@fau.edu.

Center for Complex Systems and Brain Sciences Students: 9 full-time (3 women), 5 part-time (2 women); includes 4 minority (1 Black or African American, non-Hispanic/Latino; 1 Hispanic/Latino; 2 Two or more races, non-Hispanic/Latino), 3 international. Average age 30. 13 applicants, 15% accepted, 2 enrolled. *Faculty:* 1 full-time (0 women). Expenses: Contact institution. *Financial support:* Fellowships with full tuition reimbursements, research assistantships with partial tuition reimbursements, teaching assistantships with partial tuition reimbursements, Federal Work-Study, and traineeships available. In 2018, 1 doctorate awarded. Offers complex systems and brain sciences (PhD). *Application deadline:* For fall admission, 1/15 priority date for domestic and international students. *Application fee:* $30. *Application Contact:* Keyla Thamsten, Assistant Director, Academic Support Services, 561-297-2231, E-mail: thamsten@fau.edu. *Assistant Director, Academic Support Services,* Keyla Thamsten, 561-297-2231, E-mail: thamsten@fau.edu.

Christine E. Lynn College of Nursing Students: 76 full-time (71 women), 423 part-time (385 women); includes 269 minority (140 Black or African American, non-Hispanic/Latino; 31 Asian, non-Hispanic/Latino; 81 Hispanic/Latino; 17 Two or more races, non-Hispanic/Latino), 10 international. Average age 37. 600 applicants, 28% accepted, 138 enrolled. *Faculty:* 37 full-time (36 women), 16 part-time/adjunct (14 women). Expenses: Contact institution. *Financial support:* Research assistantships with partial tuition reimbursements, teaching assistantships with partial tuition reimbursements, career-related internships or fieldwork, Federal Work-Study, institutionally sponsored loans, scholarships/grants, and traineeships available. Support available to part-time students. In 2018, 138 master's, 28 doctorates awarded. *Program availability:* Part-time. Offers administrative and clinical leadership in nursing and health care (Post Master's Certificate); nursing (MSN, PhD); nursing practice (DNP). *Application deadline:* For fall admission, 6/1 for domestic students, 2/15 for international students; for spring admission, 10/1 for domestic students, 7/15 for international students. Applications are processed on a rolling basis. *Application fee:* $30. *Application Contact:* Safiya A George Damida, Dean, 561-297-3206, E-mail: sgeorge@health.fau.edu. *Dean,* Safiya A George Damida, 561-297-3206, E-mail: sgeorge@health.fau.edu.

College for Design and Social Inquiry Students: 197 full-time (164 women), 223 part-time (164 women); includes 204 minority (105 Black or African American, non-Hispanic/Latino; 11 Asian, non-Hispanic/Latino; 71 Hispanic/Latino; 17 Two or more races, non-Hispanic/Latino), 12 international. Average age 31. 486 applicants, 45% accepted, 186 enrolled. *Faculty:* 46 full-time (15 women), 2 part-time/adjunct (1 woman). Expenses: Contact institution. *Financial support:* Fellowships with partial tuition reimbursements, research assistantships with partial tuition reimbursements, teaching assistantships with partial tuition reimbursements, career-related internships or fieldwork, Federal Work-Study, and institutionally sponsored loans available. Support available to part-time students. Financial award application deadline: 4/1. In 2018, 193 master's, 2 doctorates awarded. *Program availability:* Part-time, evening/weekend.

Offers design and social inquiry (MNM, MPA, MS, MSW, MURP, DSW, PhD). *Application deadline:* For fall admission, 5/1 for domestic students, 2/15 for international students; for spring admission, 11/1 for domestic students, 7/15 for international students. Applications are processed on a rolling basis. *Application fee:* $30. *Application Contact:* Dr. Naelys Luna, Interim Dean, 561-297-2056, E-mail: ndiaz10@fau.edu. *Interim Dean,* Dr. Naelys Luna, 561-297-2056, E-mail: ndiaz10@fau.edu.

Phyllis and Harvey Sandler School of Social Work Students: 154 full-time (133 women), 120 part-time (103 women); includes 129 minority (61 Black or African American, non-Hispanic/Latino; 1 American Indian or Alaska Native, non-Hispanic/Latino; 5 Asian, non-Hispanic/Latino; 50 Hispanic/Latino; 12 Two or more races, non-Hispanic/Latino), 2 international. Average age 31. 349 applicants, 47% accepted, 145 enrolled. *Faculty:* 12 full-time (7 women), 1 (woman) part-time/adjunct. Expenses: Contact institution. *Financial support:* Fellowships, research assistantships, career-related internships or fieldwork, Federal Work-Study, institutionally sponsored loans, and tuition waivers (partial) available. Financial award application deadline: 4/1. In 2018, 110 master's awarded. *Program availability:* Part-time, evening/weekend. Offers social work (MSW, DSW). *Application deadline:* For fall admission, 5/1 priority date for domestic students, 2/15 for international students. Applications are processed on a rolling basis. *Application fee:* $30. *Application Contact:* Joy McClellan, Program Coordinator, 561-297-3234, E-mail: jmcclel2@fau.edu. *Program Coordinator,* Joy McClellan, 561-297-3234, E-mail: jmcclel2@fau.edu.

School of Criminology and Criminal Justice Students: 10 full-time (all women), 22 part-time (20 women); includes 23 minority (15 Black or African American, non-Hispanic/Latino; 1 Asian, non-Hispanic/Latino; 4 Hispanic/Latino; 3 Two or more races, non-Hispanic/Latino). Average age 27. 54 applicants, 31% accepted, 13 enrolled. *Faculty:* 9 full-time (2 women). Expenses: Contact institution. *Financial support:* Research assistantships, institutionally sponsored loans, scholarships/grants, and unspecified assistantships available. Financial award application deadline: 4/1. In 2018, 30 master's awarded. *Program availability:* Part-time, evening/weekend, online learning. Offers criminology and criminal justice (MS). *Application deadline:* For fall admission, 5/1 priority date for domestic students, 2/15 for international students; for spring admission, 11/1 priority date for domestic students, 7/15 for international students. Applications are processed on a rolling basis. *Application fee:* $30. Electronic applications accepted. *Application Contact:* Dawn Lynette Rothe, Director, 561-297-3173, E-mail: rothed@fau.edu. *Director,* Dawn Lynette Rothe, 561-297-3173, E-mail: rothed@fau.edu.

School of Public Administration Students: 20 full-time (13 women), 65 part-time (37 women); includes 36 minority (19 Black or African American, non-Hispanic/Latino; 4 Asian, non-Hispanic/Latino; 11 Hispanic/Latino; 2 Two or more races, non-Hispanic/Latino), 8 international. Average age 35. 46 applicants, 43% accepted, 16 enrolled. *Faculty:* 11 full-time (4 women), 1 part-time/adjunct (0 women). Expenses: Contact institution. *Financial support:* Fellowships with full tuition reimbursements, research assistantships with partial tuition reimbursements, teaching assistantships with partial tuition reimbursements, career-related internships or fieldwork, Federal Work-Study, institutionally sponsored loans, and tuition waivers (partial) available. Support available to part-time students. Financial award application deadline: 4/1. In 2018, 42 master's, 2 doctorates awarded. *Program availability:* Part-time, evening/weekend. Offers public administration (MPA, PhD). *Application deadline:* For fall admission, 5/1 priority date for domestic students, 2/15 for international students; for spring admission, 11/1 for domestic students, 7/15 for international students. Applications are processed on a rolling basis. *Application fee:* $30. *Application Contact:* Leslie Leip, Program Coordinator, 561-297-4153, E-mail: lleip@fau.edu. *Program Coordinator,* Leslie Leip, 561-297-4153, E-mail: lleip@fau.edu.

School of Urban and Regional Planning Students: 13 full-time (8 women), 16 part-time (4 women); includes 17 minority (10 Black or African American, non-Hispanic/Latino; 1 Asian, non-Hispanic/Latino; 6 Hispanic/Latino), 2 international. Average age 27. 37 applicants, 43% accepted, 12 enrolled. *Faculty:* 5 full-time (1 woman). Expenses: Contact institution. *Financial support:* Fellowships with full tuition reimbursements, research assistantships, career-related internships or fieldwork, Federal Work-Study, institutionally sponsored loans, and tuition waivers (partial) available. Financial award application deadline: 4/1. In 2018, 11 master's awarded. *Program availability:* Part-time, evening/weekend. Offers urban and regional planning (MURP). *Application deadline:* For fall admission, 5/1 priority date for domestic students, 2/15 for international students; for spring admission, 11/1 priority date for domestic students, 7/15 for international students. Applications are processed on a rolling basis. *Application fee:* $30.

College of Business Students: 627 full-time (331 women), 1,077 part-time (579 women); includes 816 minority (268 Black or African American, non-Hispanic/Latino; 5 American Indian or Alaska Native, non-Hispanic/Latino; 81 Asian, non-Hispanic/Latino; 402 Hispanic/Latino; 2 Native Hawaiian or other Pacific Islander, non-Hispanic/Latino; 58 Two or more races, non-Hispanic/Latino), 95 international. Average age 32. 1,189 applicants, 66% accepted, 605 enrolled. *Faculty:* 104 full-time (36 women), 2 part-time/adjunct (1 woman). Expenses: Contact institution. *Financial support:* Fellowships with partial tuition reimbursements, research assistantships with partial tuition reimbursements, teaching assistantships with full tuition reimbursements, career-related internships or fieldwork, Federal Work-Study, institutionally sponsored loans, tuition waivers (full and partial), and unspecified assistantships available. Support available to part-time students. Financial award application deadline: 3/1. In 2018, 687 master's, 10 doctorates awarded. *Program availability:* Part-time, evening/weekend, online learning. Offers business (M Tax, MAC, MBA, MHA, MS, PhD); business administration (MBA); economics (MS); entrepreneurship (MBA); health administration (MBA); information technology management (MS); international business (MBA); sport management (MBA). *Application deadline:* For fall admission, 5/1 priority date for domestic students, 2/15 priority date for international students; for spring admission, 4/1 priority date for domestic students, 1/15 priority date for international students. Applications are processed on a rolling basis. *Application fee:* $30. *Application Contact:* Daniel Gropper, Dean, 561-297-3635, E-mail: dgropper@fau.edu. *Dean,* Daniel Gropper, 561-297-3635, E-mail: dgropper@fau.edu.

School of Accounting Students: 88 full-time (51 women), 472 part-time (261 women); includes 276 minority (54 Black or African American, non-Hispanic/Latino; 1 American Indian or Alaska Native, non-Hispanic/Latino; 31 Asian, non-Hispanic/Latino; 169 Hispanic/Latino; 21 Two or more races, non-Hispanic/Latino), 12 international. Average age 32. 408 applicants, 59% accepted, 203 enrolled. *Faculty:* 15 full-time (5 women), 2 part-time/adjunct (1 woman). Expenses: Contact institution. *Financial support:* Fellowships, research assistantships with partial tuition reimbursements, teaching assistantships, career-related internships or fieldwork, Federal Work-Study, institutionally sponsored loans, scholarships/grants, and tuition waivers (partial) available. Support available to part-time students. Financial award application deadline: 3/1. In 2018, 227 master's awarded. *Program availability:* Part-time, evening/weekend, online learning. Offers accounting (MAC). *Application deadline:* For fall admission, 7/1 priority date for domestic students, 2/15 priority date for international students; for spring admission, 11/1 priority date for domestic students, 7/15 priority date for international students. Applications are processed on a rolling basis. *Application fee:* $30. *Application Contact:* George Young, Director, 561-297-3638, E-mail: soa@fau.edu. *Director,* George Young, 561-297-3638, E-mail: soa@fau.edu.

College of Education Students: 315 full-time (236 women), 500 part-time (376 women); includes 353 minority (180 Black or African American, non-Hispanic/Latino; 15 Asian, non-Hispanic/Latino; 139 Hispanic/Latino; 19 Two or more races, non-Hispanic/Latino), 21 international. Average age 34. 927 applicants, 40% accepted, 288 enrolled. *Faculty:* 85 full-time (50 women), 30 part-time/adjunct (15 women). Expenses: Contact institution. *Financial support:* Fellowships with partial tuition reimbursements, research assistantships with partial tuition reimbursements, teaching assistantships with partial tuition reimbursements, career-related internships or fieldwork, Federal Work-Study, and unspecified assistantships available. In 2018, 224 master's, 44 doctorates, 12 other advanced degrees awarded. *Program availability:* Part-time, evening/weekend. Offers adult and community education (M Ed, PhD, Ed S); counselor education (MS, PhD); curriculum and instruction (M Ed, PhD, Ed S); early childhood education (M Ed); education (M Ed, MA, MS, Ed D, PhD, Ed S); educational leadership (M Ed, PhD, Ed S); elementary education (M Ed); environmental education (M Ed); exceptional student education (M Ed, Ed D); higher education (M Ed, PhD); instructional technology (M Ed); K-12 school leadership (M Ed, PhD, Ed S); multicultural education (M Ed); reading education (M Ed); secondary education (M Ed); speech-language pathology (MS); TESOL and bilingual education (MA). *Application deadline:* For fall admission, 5/1 for domestic students. Applications are processed on a rolling basis. *Application fee:* $30. Electronic applications accepted. *Application Contact:* Dr. Valerie Bristor, Dean, 561-297-3357, E-mail: bristor@fau.edu. *Dean,* Dr. Valerie Bristor, 561-297-3357, E-mail: bristor@fau.edu.

College of Engineering and Computer Science Students: 140 full-time (31 women), 222 part-time (47 women); includes 6,506 minority (31 Black or African American, non-Hispanic/Latino; 20 Asian, non-Hispanic/Latino; 6,447 Hispanic/Latino; 8 Two or more races, non-Hispanic/Latino), 121 international. Average age 31. 288 applicants, 47% accepted, 107 enrolled. *Faculty:* 73 full-time (8 women), 4 part-time/adjunct (0 women). Expenses: Contact institution. *Financial support:* Fellowships with partial tuition reimbursements, research assistantships with partial tuition reimbursements, teaching assistantships with partial tuition reimbursements, career-related internships or fieldwork, Federal Work-Study, and unspecified assistantships available. Support available to part-time students. Financial award applicants required to submit FAFSA. In 2018, 133 master's, 15 doctorates awarded. *Program availability:* Part-time, evening/weekend, online learning. Offers bioengineering (MS); civil engineering (MS); computer engineering (MS, PhD); computer science (MS, PhD); electrical engineering (MS, PhD); engineering and computer science (MS, PhD); environmental engineering (MS); mechanical engineering (MS, PhD). *Application deadline:* For fall admission, 7/1 for domestic students, 2/15 for international students; for spring admission, 11/1 for domestic students, 7/15 for international students. Applications are processed on a rolling basis. *Application fee:* $30. *Application Contact:* Dr. Stella Batalama, Dean, 561-297-3426, E-mail: sbatalama@fau.edu. *Dean,* Dr. Stella Batalama, 561-297-3426, E-mail: sbatalama@fau.edu.

Dorothy F. Schmidt College of Arts and Letters Students: 229 full-time (143 women), 105 part-time (67 women); includes 121 minority (36 Black or African American, non-Hispanic/Latino; 1 American Indian or Alaska Native, non-Hispanic/Latino; 4 Asian, non-Hispanic/Latino; 71 Hispanic/Latino; 9 Two or more races, non-Hispanic/Latino), 29 international. Average age 33. 271 applicants, 59% accepted, 116 enrolled. *Faculty:* 156 full-time (74 women), 9 part-time/adjunct (6 women). Expenses: Contact institution. *Financial support:* Fellowships with partial tuition reimbursements, research assistantships, teaching assistantships, career-related internships or fieldwork, Federal Work-Study, institutionally sponsored loans, and tuition waivers (partial) available. Support available to part-time students. In 2018, 103 master's, 3 doctorates awarded. *Program availability:* Part-time. Offers acting (MFA); American literature (MA); anthropology (MA, MAT); arts and letters (MA, MAT, MFA, MM, PhD, Certificate); comparative literature (MA); comparative studies (PhD); design and technology (MFA); French (MA); history (MA); linguistics (MA); music (MM); political science (MA); sociology (MA); Spanish (MA); visual art (MFA). *Application deadline:* For fall admission, 6/1 priority date for domestic students. Applications are processed on a rolling basis. *Application fee:* $30. Electronic applications accepted. *Application Contact:* Michael Horswell, Dean, 561-297-3803, E-mail: horswell@fau.edu. *Dean,* Michael Horswell, 561-297-3803, E-mail: horswell@fau.edu.

Center for Women, Gender and Sexuality Studies Students: 10 full-time (7 women), 2 part-time (both women); includes 7 minority (2 Black or African American, non-Hispanic/Latino; 5 Hispanic/Latino). Average age 29. 7 applicants, 57% accepted, 4 enrolled. *Faculty:* 2 full-time (both women). Expenses: Contact institution. *Financial support:* Fellowships, teaching assistantships, career-related internships or fieldwork, Federal Work-Study, institutionally sponsored loans, scholarships/grants, and unspecified assistantships available. Support available to part-time students. Financial award applicants required to submit FAFSA. In 2018, 3 master's awarded. *Program availability:* Part-time. Offers women, gender and sexuality studies (MA). *Application deadline:* For fall admission, 7/1 for domestic students, 2/15 for international students; for spring admission, 11/1 for domestic students, 7/15 for international students. Applications are processed on a rolling basis. *Application fee:* $30. Electronic applications accepted. *Application Contact:* Barclay Barrios, Associate Dean/Director, 561-297-4573, E-mail: bbarrios@fau.edu. *Associate Dean/Director,* Barclay Barrios, 561-297-4573, E-mail: bbarrios@fau.edu.

School of Communication and Multimedia Studies Students: 24 full-time (18 women), 13 part-time (6 women); includes 18 minority (10 Black or African American, non-Hispanic/Latino; 1 Asian, non-Hispanic/Latino; 5 Hispanic/Latino; 2 Two or more races, non-Hispanic/Latino), 2 international. Average age 32. 18 applicants, 78% accepted, 8 enrolled. *Faculty:* 23 full-time (9 women). Expenses: Contact institution. *Financial support:* Teaching assistantships with partial tuition reimbursements, Federal Work-Study, institutionally sponsored loans, scholarships/grants, and unspecified assistantships available. Support available to part-time students. Financial award application deadline: 3/1; financial award applicants required to submit FAFSA. In 2018, 6 master's awarded. *Program availability:* Part-time. Offers communication studies (MA); film and video (Certificate); media, technology and entertainment (MFA). *Application deadline:* For fall admission, 7/1 priority date for domestic students, 4/1 for international students; for spring admission, 11/1 for domestic students, 10/1 for international students. Applications are processed on a rolling basis. *Application fee:* $30. Electronic applications accepted. *Application Contact:* Dr. Stephen Charbonneau, Graduate Director, 561-297-3856, Fax: 561-297-

2615, E-mail: scharbo1@fau.edu. *Director,* Dr. Carol Bishop Mills, 561-297-0042, Fax: 561-297-2615, E-mail: millsc@fau.edu.

FLORIDA COASTAL SCHOOL OF LAW, Jacksonville, FL 32256

General Information Proprietary, coed, graduate-only institution.

GRADUATE UNITS

Professional Program *Program availability:* Part-time. Offers law (JD). Electronic applications accepted.

FLORIDA COLLEGE OF INTEGRATIVE MEDICINE, Orlando, FL 32809

General Information Proprietary, coed, graduate-only institution. *Graduate housing:* On-campus housing not available.

GRADUATE UNITS

Graduate Program *Program availability:* Evening/weekend. Offers Oriental medicine (MSOM). Electronic applications accepted.

FLORIDA GULF COAST UNIVERSITY, Fort Myers, FL 33965-6565

General Information State-supported, coed, comprehensive institution. CGS member. *Graduate housing:* Room and/or apartments available on a first-come, first-served basis to single students; on-campus housing not available to married students. Housing application deadline: 4/1. *Research affiliation:* Department of Education (education), Small Business Administration (business), Department of Commerce, U.S. Fish and Wildlife Service (biological sciences), Florida Department of Environmental Protection (biological sciences), National Institute of Standards and Technology.

GRADUATE UNITS

College of Arts and Sciences *Program availability:* Part-time, blended/hybrid learning. Offers arts and sciences (MA, MPA, MS); criminal justice (MS); English (MA); environmental policy (MPA); environmental science (MS); environmental studies (MA); forensic studies (MS); history (MA); management (MPA); mathematics (MS). Electronic applications accepted.

College of Education *Program availability:* Part-time, evening/weekend, online learning. Offers behavior disorders (M Ed); education (M Ed, MA); educational leadership (M Ed, MA); elementary education (M Ed); English education (M Ed); English speakers of other languages endorsement (M Ed); gifted education (M Ed); mathematics education (M Ed); mental retardation (M Ed); middle school education (M Ed); reading education (M Ed); science education (M Ed); social science education (M Ed); special education (M Ed); specific learning disabilities (M Ed); varying exceptionalities (M Ed). Electronic applications accepted.

Elaine Nicpon Marieb College of Health and Human Services *Program availability:* Part-time, evening/weekend, online learning. Offers clinical mental health counseling (MA); health and human services (MA, MPAS, MS, MSN, MSW, DNP, DPT); health science (MS); nurse anesthesia (MSN); nurse educator (MSN); occupational therapy (MS); physical therapy (DPT); physician assistant studies (MPAS); school counseling (MA); social work (MSW). Electronic applications accepted.

Lutgert College of Business *Program availability:* Part-time, evening/weekend. Offers accounting and taxation (MS); business (MBA, MS); business administration (MBA); information systems and analytics (MS). Electronic applications accepted.

FLORIDA INSTITUTE OF TECHNOLOGY, Melbourne, FL 32901-6975

General Information Independent, coed, university. *Enrollment:* 1,203 full-time matriculated graduate/professional students (618 women), 911 part-time matriculated graduate/professional students (304 women). *Enrollment by degree level:* 1,531 master's, 578 doctoral, 5 other advanced degrees. *Graduate faculty:* 236 full-time (41 women), 130 part-time/adjunct (31 women). *Tuition:* Full-time $22,338; part-time $1241 per credit hour. Tuition and fees vary according to degree level, campus/location and program. *Graduate housing:* Room and/or apartments available on a first-come, first-served basis to single students; on-campus housing not available to married students. Typical cost: $7000 per year ($12,880 including board). Room and board charges vary according to board plan and housing facility selected. Housing application deadline: 6/1. *Student services:* Campus employment opportunities, campus safety program, career counseling, exercise/wellness program, free psychological counseling, international student services, low-cost health insurance, multicultural affairs office, services for students with disabilities, writing training. *Library facilities:* Evans Library. Collection: Books: 131,564 (physical), 728,454 (digital/electronic); Serial titles: 1,605 (physical), 56,994 (digital/electronic); Databases: 161. Weekly public service hours: 96; students can reserve study rooms.

Computer facilities: 254 computers available on campus for general student use. A campuswide network can be accessed from student residence rooms and from off campus. Online class registration is available. Website: http://www.fit.edu/

General Application Contact: Mike Perry, Executive Director of Admissions, 321-674-7127, Fax: 321-723-9468, E-mail: perrymj@fit.edu.

GRADUATE UNITS

Aberdeen Education Center (Maryland) Students: 21 part-time (9 women); includes 7 minority (3 Black or African American, non-Hispanic/Latino; 1 Asian, non-Hispanic/Latino; 2 Hispanic/Latino; 1 Two or more races, non-Hispanic/Latino). Average age 40. 3 applicants, 100% accepted, 1 enrolled. *Faculty:* 1 full-time (0 women), 6 part-time/adjunct (4 women). Expenses: Contact institution. *Financial support:* Applicants required to submit FAFSA. *Program availability:* Part-time, evening/weekend. Offers acquisition and contract management (MS, PMBA); business administration (MS, PMBA); contracts management (PMBA); financial management (MPA); global management (PMBA); health management (MS); human resources management (MS, PMBA); information systems (PMBA); logistics management (MS); management (MS); materials acquisition management (MS); operations research (MS); public administration (MPA); research (PMBA); space systems (MS); space systems management (MS). *Application deadline:* Applications are processed on a rolling basis. *Application fee:* $50. Electronic applications accepted. *Application Contact:* Cheryl A. Brown, Associate Director of Graduate Admissions, 321-674-7581, Fax: 321-723-9468, E-mail: cbrown@fit.edu.

Aberdeen Education Center (Maryland)
College of Aeronautics Students: 46 full-time (17 women), 5 part-time (0 women); includes 7 minority (1 Black or African American, non-Hispanic/Latino; 2 Asian, non-Hispanic/Latino; 2 Hispanic/Latino; 2 Two or more races, non-Hispanic/Latino), 35 international. 25 applicants, 96% accepted, 14 enrolled. *Faculty:* 20 full-time (7 women), 13 part-time/adjunct (2 women). Expenses: Contact institution. *Financial support:* In 2018–19, 7 students received support, including 7 research assistantships with partial

tuition reimbursements available; teaching assistantships with partial tuition reimbursements available, career-related internships or fieldwork, institutionally sponsored loans, tuition waivers (partial), and tuition remissions also available. Financial award application deadline: 3/1; financial award applicants required to submit FAFSA. In 2018, 18 master's awarded. *Program availability:* Part-time, evening/weekend, 100% online. Offers airport development and mangement (MSA); applied aviation safety (MSA); aviation human factors (MS); aviation safety, applied (MSA); aviation science (PhD); aviation sciences (PhD). *Application deadline:* Applications are processed on a rolling basis. *Application fee:* $50. Electronic applications accepted. *Application Contact:* Cheryl A. Brown, Associate Director of Graduate Admissions, 321-674-7581, Fax: 321-723-9468, E-mail: cbrown@fit.edu. *Interim Dean,* Dr. Ulreen Jones, 321-674-7472, Fax: 321-674-7368, E-mail: ujones@fit.edu.

College of Engineering and Science Students: 638 full-time (226 women), 310 part-time (69 women); includes 103 minority (24 Black or African American, non-Hispanic/Latino; 2 American Indian or Alaska Native, non-Hispanic/Latino; 22 Asian, non-Hispanic/Latino; 44 Hispanic/Latino; 1 Native Hawaiian or other Pacific Islander, non-Hispanic/Latino; 10 Two or more races, non-Hispanic/Latino), 498 international. Average age 28. 601 applicants, 70% accepted, 150 enrolled. *Faculty:* 169 full-time (18 women), 42 part-time/adjunct (3 women). Expenses: Contact institution. *Financial support:* In 2018–19, 109 research assistantships with partial tuition reimbursements, 129 teaching assistantships with partial tuition reimbursements were awarded; career-related internships or fieldwork, institutionally sponsored loans, unspecified assistantships, and tuition remissions also available. Support available to part-time students. Financial award application deadline: 3/1; financial award applicants required to submit FAFSA. In 2018, 290 master's, 74 doctorates awarded. *Program availability:* Part-time. Offers aerospace engineering (MS, PhD); applied mathematics (MS, PhD); biochemistry (MS); biological oceanography (MS); biological sciences (PhD); biomedical engineering (MS, PhD); biotechnology (MS); cell and molecular biology (MS); chemical engineering (MS, PhD); chemistry (MS, PhD); civil engineering (MS, PhD); coastal management (MS); computer engineering (MS, PhD); computer information systems (MS); computer science (MS, PhD); conservation technology (MS); earth remote sensing (MS); ecology (MS); electrical engineering (MS, PhD); engineering (MS, PhD); engineering management (MS); environmental resource management (MS); environmental science (MS, PhD); information assurance and cybersecurity (MS); interdisciplinary science (MS); marine biology (MS); mechanical engineering (MS, PhD); meteorology (MS); ocean engineering (MS, PhD); operations research (MS, PhD); physics (MS, PhD); software engineering (MS); space sciences (MS, PhD); systems engineering (MS, PhD). *Application deadline:* For fall admission, 4/1 for international students; for spring admission, 9/30 for international students. Applications are processed on a rolling basis. *Application fee:* $50. Electronic applications accepted. *Application Contact:* Mike Perry, Executive Director of Admissions, 321-674-7127, E-mail: perrymj@fit.edu. *Dean,* Dr. Marco Carvalho, 321-674-7150, E-mail: mcarvalho@fit.edu.

College of Psychology and Liberal Arts Students: 416 full-time (333 women), 19 part-time (16 women); includes 122 minority (18 Black or African American, non-Hispanic/Latino; 15 Asian, non-Hispanic/Latino; 64 Hispanic/Latino; 3 Native Hawaiian or other Pacific Islander, non-Hispanic/Latino; 22 Two or more races, non-Hispanic/Latino), 50 international. Average age 28. 445 applicants, 61% accepted, 137 enrolled. *Faculty:* 76 full-time (37 women), 40 part-time/adjunct (26 women). Expenses: Contact institution. *Financial support:* In 2018–19, 85 students received support, including 78 research assistantships with partial tuition reimbursements available, 7 teaching assistantships with partial tuition reimbursements available (averaging $8,002 per year); fellowships, career-related internships or fieldwork, institutionally sponsored loans, tuition waivers (partial), unspecified assistantships, and tuition remissions also available. Support available to part-time students. Financial award application deadline: 3/1; financial award applicants required to submit FAFSA. In 2018, 196 master's, 28 doctorates awarded. *Program availability:* Part-time, evening/weekend, 100% online. Offers applied behavior analysis (MS, PhD); applied behavior analysis and organizational behavior management (MS); clinical psychology (Psy D); global strategic communication (MS); industrial/organizational psychology (MS); organizational behavior management (MS); professional behavior analysis (MA). *Application deadline:* For fall admission, 4/1 for international students; for spring admission, 9/30 for international students. Applications are processed on a rolling basis. *Application fee:* $50. Electronic applications accepted. *Application Contact:* Mike Perry, Executive Director of Admissions, 321-674-7127, E-mail: lsteelma@fit.edu. *Dean,* Dr. Lisa Steelman, 321-674-8142, E-mail: lsteelma@fit.edu.

Eglin Education Center (Florida) Students: 2 full-time (0 women), 28 part-time (3 women); includes 19 minority (6 Black or African American, non-Hispanic/Latino; 10 Hispanic/Latino; 3 Two or more races, non-Hispanic/Latino). Average age 36. 7 applicants, 86% accepted, 5 enrolled. *Faculty:* 1 full-time (0 women), 2 part-time/adjunct (0 women). Expenses: Contact institution. *Financial support:* Applicants required to submit FAFSA. *Program availability:* Part-time, evening/weekend. Offers flight test engineering (MS). *Application deadline:* Applications are processed on a rolling basis. Electronic applications accepted. *Application Contact:* Online Learnng and Off-Campus Programs Admissions, 321-674-8263, E-mail: gradadm-olocp@fit.edu. *Director, Eglin Education Center,* Dr. Jeffrey Cerny, 800-398-5958, E-mail: eglin@fit.edu.

Fort Lee Education Center (Virginia) Students: 23 part-time (2 women); includes 15 minority (8 Black or African American, non-Hispanic/Latino; 3 Asian, non-Hispanic/Latino; 3 Hispanic/Latino; 1 Two or more races, non-Hispanic/Latino). Average age 33. 2 applicants, 100% accepted, 1 enrolled. *Faculty:* 1 full-time (0 women), 4 part-time/adjunct (1 woman). Expenses: Contact institution. *Financial support:* Applicants required to submit FAFSA. *Program availability:* Part-time, evening/weekend. *Application deadline:* Applications are processed on a rolling basis. Electronic applications accepted. *Application Contact:* Online Learning and Off-Campus Programs Admissions, 321-674-8263, E-mail: gradadm-olocp@fit.edu. *Director, Fort Lee Education Center,* Dr. Darrell Burrell, 804-765-4665, E-mail: fotlee@fit.edu.

Hampton Roads Education Center (Virginia) Offers financial management (MPA); public administration (MPA).

Nathan M. Bisk College of Business Students: 62 full-time (22 women), 108 part-time (38 women); includes 47 minority (24 Black or African American, non-Hispanic/Latino; 4 Asian, non-Hispanic/Latino; 14 Hispanic/Latino; 5 Two or more races, non-Hispanic/Latino), 35 international. 85 applicants, 92% accepted, 57 enrolled. *Faculty:* 22 full-time (6 women), 15 part-time/adjunct (6 women). Expenses: Contact institution. *Financial support:* In 2018–19, 5 students received support, including 4 research assistantships with partial tuition reimbursements available, 1 teaching assistantship with partial tuition reimbursement available; career-related internships or fieldwork, institutionally sponsored loans, and unspecified assistantships also available. Support available to part-time students. Financial award application deadline: 3/1; financial award applicants required to submit FAFSA. In 2018, 36 master's awarded. *Program availability:* Part-time. Offers accounting and financial forensics (MS); business

administration (MBA); healthcare management (MBA). *Application deadline:* For fall admission, 4/1 for international students; for spring admission, 9/30 for international students. Applications are processed on a rolling basis. *Application fee:* $50. Electronic applications accepted. *Application Contact:* Mike Perry, Executive Director of Admissions, 321-674-7127, Fax: 321-723-9468, E-mail: perrymj@fit.edu. *Dean,* Dr. Theodore R. Richardson, III, 321-674-8123, Fax: 321-674-7597, E-mail: trichardson@fit.edu.

National Capital Region (Quantico) Education Center (Virginia)

Orlando Education Center (Florida) Students: 22 full-time (10 women), 118 part-time (54 women); includes 49 minority (19 Black or African American, non-Hispanic/Latino; 3 Asian, non-Hispanic/Latino; 21 Hispanic/Latino; 6 Two or more races, non-Hispanic/Latino), 9 international. Average age 29. 60 applicants, 85% accepted, 33 enrolled. *Faculty:* 1 full-time (0 women), 13 part-time/adjunct (3 women). Expenses: Contact institution. *Financial support:* Applicants required to submit FAFSA. *Program availability:* Part-time, evening/weekend. *Application deadline:* Applications are processed on a rolling basis. Electronic applications accepted. *Application Contact:* Online Learning and Off-Campus Programs Admissions, 321-671-8263, E-mail: gradadm-olocp@fit.edu. *Director, Orlando Education Center,* Dr. Nick Daher, 407-629-7132, E-mail: gradadm-olocp@fit.edu.

Redstone/Huntsville Education Center (Alabama) Students: 8 full-time (7 women), 72 part-time (38 women); includes 43 minority (35 Black or African American, non-Hispanic/Latino; 1 Asian, non-Hispanic/Latino; 1 Hispanic/Latino; 6 Two or more races, non-Hispanic/Latino). Average age 37. 32 applicants, 88% accepted, 17 enrolled. *Faculty:* 1 full-time (0 women), 8 part-time/adjunct (3 women). Expenses: Contact institution. *Financial support:* Applicants required to submit FAFSA. *Program availability:* Part-time, evening/weekend. *Application deadline:* Applications are processed on a rolling basis. Electronic applications accepted. *Application Contact:* Online Learning and Off-Campus Programs Admissions, 321-674-8263, E-mail: gradadm-olocp@fit.edu. *Director, Huntsville Education Center,* Dr. Vicky Knerly, 256-971-9353, E-mail: huntsville@fit.edu.

Southern Maryland Education Center Students: 1 full-time (0 women), 36 part-time (13 women); includes 11 minority (4 Black or African American, non-Hispanic/Latino; 1 American Indian or Alaska Native, non-Hispanic/Latino; 2 Asian, non-Hispanic/Latino; 3 Hispanic/Latino; 1 Two or more races, non-Hispanic/Latino). Average age 42. 1 applicant, 100% accepted, 1 enrolled. *Faculty:* 4 full-time (1 woman), 10 part-time/adjunct (1 woman). Expenses: Contact institution. *Financial support:* Applicants required to submit FAFSA. *Program availability:* Part-time, evening/weekend. *Application deadline:* Applications are processed on a rolling basis. Electronic applications accepted. *Application Contact:* Mike Perry, Executive Director of Admissions, 321-674-7127, E-mail: perrymj@fit.edu. *Director, Southern Maryland Education Center,* Dr. Robert Schaller, Sr, 301-737-2500 Ext. 214, Fax: 301-737-2542, E-mail: somd@fit.edu.

Spaceport Education Center (Florida) Students: 5 full-time (2 women), 111 part-time (44 women); includes 24 minority (7 Black or African American, non-Hispanic/Latino; 1 American Indian or Alaska Native, non-Hispanic/Latino; 2 Asian, non-Hispanic/Latino; 9 Hispanic/Latino; 5 Two or more races, non-Hispanic/Latino). Average age 36. 17 applicants, 94% accepted, 10 enrolled. *Faculty:* 1 full-time (0 women), 10 part-time/adjunct (2 women). Expenses: Contact institution. *Financial support:* Applicants required to submit FAFSA. *Program availability:* Part-time, evening/weekend. *Application deadline:* Applications are processed on a rolling basis. Electronic applications accepted. *Application Contact:* Online Learning and Off-Campus Programs Admissions, 321-674-8263, E-mail: gradadm-olocp@fit.edu. *Director, Spaceport Education Center,* Dr. Don Platt, 321-674-8520, E-mail: spaceport-admin@fit.edu.

FLORIDA INTERNATIONAL UNIVERSITY, Miami, FL 33199

General Information State-supported, coed, university. CGS member. Enrollment by degree level: 5,980 master's, 2,720 doctoral. *Graduate housing:* Rooms and/or apartments available on a first-come, first-served basis to single and married students. *Student services:* Campus employment opportunities, campus safety program, career counseling, child daycare facilities, exercise/wellness program, free psychological counseling, international student services, low-cost health insurance, multicultural affairs office, services for students with disabilities, writing training. *Library facilities:* Steven and Dorothea Green Library plus 4 others. *Collection:* Books: 1.5 million (physical), 443,863 (digital/electronic); Serial titles: 63,945 (physical), 111,662 (digital/electronic); Databases: 808. Weekly public service hours: 112; students can reserve study rooms.

Computer facilities: A campuswide network can be accessed from student residence rooms and from off campus. Online class registration, online financial and cashier's information; financial, campus maps information available on cell phones are available. Website: http://www.fiu.edu/

General Application Contact: Nanett Rojas, Assistant Director of Graduate Admissions, 305-348-7442, Fax: 305-348-7441, E-mail: gradadm@fiu.edu.

GRADUATE UNITS

Chaplin School of Hospitality and Tourism Management Students: 183 full-time (119 women), 92 part-time (65 women); includes 105 minority (24 Black or African American, non-Hispanic/Latino; 7 Asian, non-Hispanic/Latino; 69 Hispanic/Latino; 5 Two or more races, non-Hispanic/Latino), 134 international. Average age 27. 214 applicants, 78% accepted, 109 enrolled. *Faculty:* 25 full-time (6 women), 38 part-time/adjunct (12 women). Expenses: Contact institution. *Financial support:* Institutionally sponsored loans and scholarships/grants available. Financial award application deadline: 3/1; financial award applicants required to submit FAFSA. In 2018, 140 master's awarded. *Program availability:* Part-time, evening/weekend, online learning. Offers hospitality and tourism management (MS). *Application deadline:* For fall admission, 6/1 for domestic students, 4/1 for international students; for spring admission, 10/1 for domestic students, 9/1 for international students. Applications are processed on a rolling basis. *Application fee:* $30. Electronic applications accepted. *Application Contact:* Nanett Rojas, Manager, Admissions Operations, 305-348-7464, Fax: 305-348-7441, E-mail: gradadm@fiu.edu. *Interim Dean,* Dr. Michael Cheng, 305-919-4506, E-mail: michael.cheng@fiu.edu.

Chapman Graduate School of Business Students: 1,413 full-time (818 women), 660 part-time (340 women); includes 1,579 minority (314 Black or African American, non-Hispanic/Latino; 2 American Indian or Alaska Native, non-Hispanic/Latino; 62 Asian, non-Hispanic/Latino; 1,161 Hispanic/Latino; 4 Native Hawaiian or other Pacific Islander, non-Hispanic/Latino; 36 Two or more races, non-Hispanic/Latino), 229 international. Average age 32. 2,564 applicants, 51% accepted, 934 enrolled. *Faculty:* 132 full-time (48 women), 90 part-time/adjunct (25 women). Expenses: Contact institution. *Financial support:* Institutionally sponsored loans and scholarships/grants available. Financial award application deadline: 3/1; financial award applicants required to submit FAFSA. In 2018, 1,256 master's, 6 doctorates awarded. *Program availability:* Part-time, evening/weekend. Offers business (EMBA, IMBA, M Acc, MBA, MIB, MS, MSF, MSHRM, MST, PhD); decision sciences and information systems (PhD); finance (MSF); health information management systems (MS); human resources management (MSHRM);

international business (MIB); management and international business (EMBA, IMBA, MBA, PhD); marketing (MS); systems management (MS). *Application deadline:* For fall admission, 6/1 for domestic students, 4/1 for international students; for spring admission, 10/1 for domestic students, 9/1 for international students. Applications are processed on a rolling basis. *Application fee:* $30. Electronic applications accepted. *Application Contact:* Nanett Rojas, Manager, Admissions Operations, 305-348-7464, Fax: 305-348-7441, E-mail: gradadm@fiu.edu. *Dean,* Dr. Joanne Li, 305-348-2751, Fax: 305-919-5478, E-mail: joanne.li@fiu.edu.

Hollo School of Real Estate Students: 75 full-time (31 women), 9 part-time (6 women); includes 51 minority (18 Black or African American, non-Hispanic/Latino; 3 Asian, non-Hispanic/Latino; 29 Hispanic/Latino; 1 Two or more races, non-Hispanic/Latino), 11 international. Average age 36. 157 applicants, 64% accepted, 58 enrolled. *Faculty:* 5 full-time (1 woman), 3 part-time/adjunct (2 women). Expenses: Contact institution. *Financial support:* Institutionally sponsored loans and scholarships/grants available. Financial award application deadline: 3/1; financial award applicants required to submit FAFSA. In 2018, 75 master's awarded. *Program availability:* Part-time, evening/weekend. Offers international real estate (MS). *Application deadline:* For fall admission, 4/1 for domestic and international students. *Application fee:* $30. Electronic applications accepted. *Application Contact:* Nanett Rojas, Manager, Admissions Operations, 305-348-7464, Fax: 305-348-7441, E-mail: gradadm@fiu.edu. *Director,* Eli Beracha, 305-779-7898, E-mail: eli.beracha@fiu.edu.

School of Accounting Students: 94 full-time (53 women), 18 part-time (8 women); includes 101 minority (6 Black or African American, non-Hispanic/Latino; 4 Asian, non-Hispanic/Latino; 89 Hispanic/Latino; 2 Two or more races, non-Hispanic/Latino), 2 international. Average age 27. 200 applicants, 53% accepted, 90 enrolled. *Faculty:* 24 full-time (11 women), 11 part-time/adjunct (1 woman). Expenses: Contact institution. *Financial support:* Institutionally sponsored loans and scholarships/grants available. Financial award application deadline: 3/1; financial award applicants required to submit FAFSA. In 2018, 115 master's awarded. *Program availability:* Part-time, evening/weekend. Offers accounting (M Acc). *Application deadline:* For fall admission, 6/1 for domestic students, 4/1 for international students; for spring admission, 10/1 for domestic students, 9/1 for international students. Applications are processed on a rolling basis. *Application fee:* $30. Electronic applications accepted. *Application Contact:* Nanett Rojas, Manager, Admissions Operations, 305-348-7464, Fax: 305-348-7441, E-mail: gradadm@fiu.edu. *Director,* Clark Wheatley, 305-348-4209, Fax: 305-348-2914, E-mail: Clark.Wheatley@fiu.edu.

College of Arts, Sciences, and Education Students: 1,047 full-time (688 women), 442 part-time (329 women); includes 962 minority (211 Black or African American, non-Hispanic/Latino; 30 Asian, non-Hispanic/Latino; 686 Hispanic/Latino; 35 Two or more races, non-Hispanic/Latino), 169 international. Average age 30. 1,357 applicants, 41% accepted, 411 enrolled. *Faculty:* 400 full-time (183 women), 303 part-time/adjunct (180 women). Expenses: Contact institution. *Financial support:* Career-related internships or fieldwork, Federal Work-Study, institutionally sponsored loans, and scholarships/grants available. Financial award application deadline: 3/1; financial award applicants required to submit FAFSA. In 2018, 450 master's, 84 doctorates awarded. *Program availability:* Part-time, evening/weekend. Offers adult education and human resource development (MS, Ed D); art education (MA, MS); arts, sciences, and education (MA, MFA, MS, PSM, Ed D, PhD, Certificate, Ed S); behavioral analysis (MS); biological sciences (MS, PhD); chemistry (MS, PhD); clinical science (PhD); cognitive neuroscience (PhD); counseling (MS); counseling psychology (MS); counselor education (MS); creative writing (MFA); curriculum and instruction (MS, Ed D, PhD, Ed S); developmental science (MS, PhD); early childhood education (MS); earth science (PhD); educational administration and supervision (Ed D); educational leadership (MS, Certificate, Ed S); English (MA); environmental studies (MS); exceptional student education (Ed D); foreign language education (MS); forensic science (MS, PSM, PhD); geosciences (MS, PhD); higher education (Ed D); higher education administration (MS); international and comparative education (MS); language, literacy and culture (PhD); legal psychology (MS, PhD); liberal studies (MA); linguistics (MA); mathematical sciences (MS); mathematics, science, and learning technologies (PhD); natural resources management and policy (PSM); organizational psychology (MS, PhD); physical education (MS); physics (MS, PhD); reading education (MS); recreation and sport management (MS); school psychology (Ed S); statistics (MS); urban education (MS). *Application deadline:* For fall admission, 6/1 for domestic students, 4/1 for international students; for spring admission, 10/1 for domestic students, 9/1 for international students. Applications are processed on a rolling basis. *Application fee:* $30. Electronic applications accepted. *Application Contact:* Nanett Rojas, Manager, Admissions Operations, 305-348-7464, Fax: 305-348-7441, E-mail: gradadm@fiu.edu. *Dean,* Dr. Michael Heithaus, 305-348-2866, Fax: 305-348-4172, E-mail: casdean@fiu.edu.

College of Communication, Architecture and The Arts Students: 362 full-time (232 women), 109 part-time (65 women); includes 329 minority (56 Black or African American, non-Hispanic/Latino; 5 Asian, non-Hispanic/Latino; 258 Hispanic/Latino; 10 Two or more races, non-Hispanic/Latino), 75 international. Average age 28. 313 applicants, 60% accepted, 124 enrolled. *Faculty:* 103 full-time (47 women), 149 part-time/adjunct (69 women). Expenses: Contact institution. *Financial support:* Institutionally sponsored loans and scholarships/grants available. Financial award application deadline: 3/1; financial award applicants required to submit FAFSA. In 2018, 235 master's awarded. *Program availability:* Part-time, evening/weekend. Offers architecture (M Arch, MA, MFA, MIA, MLA, MM, MS, Certificate, Graduate Certificate); interior architecture (MA, MIA, Certificate); landscape architecture (MLA); museum studies (Graduate Certificate); studio art (MFA). *Application deadline:* For fall admission, 6/1 for domestic students, 4/1 for international students; for spring admission, 10/1 for domestic students, 9/1 for international students. Applications are processed on a rolling basis. *Application fee:* $30. Electronic applications accepted. *Application Contact:* Nanett Rojas, Manager, Admissions Operations, 305-348-7464, Fax: 305-348-7441, E-mail: gradadm@fiu.edu. *Dean,* Dr. Brian Schriner, 305-348-3176, Fax: 305-348-6716, E-mail: schriner@fiu.edu.

School of Communication and Journalism Students: 102 full-time (77 women), 60 part-time (41 women); includes 112 minority (29 Black or African American, non-Hispanic/Latino; 3 Asian, non-Hispanic/Latino; 76 Hispanic/Latino; 4 Two or more races, non-Hispanic/Latino), 30 international. Average age 29. 115 applicants, 79% accepted, 72 enrolled. *Faculty:* 32 full-time (24 women), 67 part-time/adjunct (36 women). Expenses: Contact institution. *Financial support:* Institutionally sponsored loans and scholarships/grants available. Financial award application deadline: 3/1; financial award applicants required to submit FAFSA. In 2018, 80 master's awarded. *Program availability:* Part-time, evening/weekend. Offers mass communication (MS). *Application deadline:* For fall admission, 6/1 for domestic students, 4/1 for international students; for spring admission, 10/1 for domestic students, 9/1 for international students. Applications are processed on a rolling basis. *Application fee:* $30. Electronic applications accepted. *Application Contact:* Nanett Rojas, Manager,

Admissions Operations, 305-348-7464, Fax: 305-348-7441, E-mail: gradadm@fiu.edu. *Chair,* Dr. Aileen Izquierdo, 305-919-5795, E-mail: aileen.izquierdo@fiu.edu.

School of Music Students: 28 full-time (13 women), 15 part-time (5 women); includes 32 minority (6 Black or African American, non-Hispanic/Latino; 25 Hispanic/Latino; 1 Two or more races, non-Hispanic/Latino), 4 international. Average age 32. 38 applicants, 74% accepted, 18 enrolled. *Faculty:* 27 full-time (6 women), 30 part-time/adjunct (10 women). Expenses: Contact institution. *Financial support:* Institutionally sponsored loans and scholarships/grants available. Financial award application deadline: 3/1; financial award applicants required to submit FAFSA. In 2018, 12 master's awarded. *Program availability:* Part-time, evening/weekend. Offers music (MM); music education (MS). *Application deadline:* For fall admission, 6/1 for domestic students, 4/1 for international students; for spring admission, 10/1 for domestic students, 9/1 for international students. Applications are processed on a rolling basis. *Application fee:* $30. Electronic applications accepted. *Application Contact:* Nanett Rojas, Manager, Admissions Operations, 305-348-7464, Fax: 305-348-7441, E-mail: gradadm@fiu.edu. *Program Director,* Joel Galand, 305-348-7078, E-mail: Joel.Galand@fiu.edu.

College of Engineering and Computing Students: 642 full-time (197 women), 295 part-time (76 women); includes 418 minority (47 Black or African American, non-Hispanic/Latino; 1 American Indian or Alaska Native, non-Hispanic/Latino; 30 Asian, non-Hispanic/Latino; 324 Hispanic/Latino; 16 Two or more races, non-Hispanic/Latino), 443 international. Average age 30. 1,138 applicants, 47% accepted, 267 enrolled. *Faculty:* 149 full-time (30 women), 81 part-time/adjunct (13 women). Expenses: Contact institution. *Financial support:* Career-related internships or fieldwork, Federal Work-Study, institutionally sponsored loans, scholarships/grants, and unspecified assistantships available. Financial award application deadline: 3/1; financial award applicants required to submit FAFSA. In 2018, 288 master's, 50 doctorates awarded. *Program availability:* Part-time, evening/weekend, online learning. Offers biomedical engineering (MS, PhD); civil engineering (MS, PhD); computer engineering (MS); electrical engineering (MS, PhD); engineering and computing (MS, PMS, PhD); engineering management (MS); environmental engineering (MS); materials science and engineering (MS, PhD); mechanical engineering (MS, PhD). *Application deadline:* For fall admission, 6/1 for domestic students, 4/1 for international students; for spring admission, 10/1 for domestic students, 9/1 for international students. Applications are processed on a rolling basis. *Application fee:* $30. Electronic applications accepted. *Application Contact:* Nanett Rojas, Manager, Admissions Operations, 305-348-7464, Fax: 305-348-7441, E-mail: gradadm@fiu.edu. *Dean,* Dr. John Volakis, 305-348-0273, Fax: 305-348-0217, E-mail: grad_eng@fiu.edu.

School of Computing and Information Sciences Students: 182 full-time (53 women), 132 part-time (28 women); includes 168 minority (13 Black or African American, non-Hispanic/Latino; 1 American Indian or Alaska Native, non-Hispanic/Latino; 10 Asian, non-Hispanic/Latino; 137 Hispanic/Latino; 7 Two or more races, non-Hispanic/Latino), 123 international. Average age 30. 393 applicants, 47% accepted, 92 enrolled. *Faculty:* 49 full-time (13 women), 31 part-time/adjunct (7 women). Expenses: Contact institution. *Financial support:* Research assistantships, teaching assistantships, institutionally sponsored loans, scholarships/grants, and unspecified assistantships available. Financial award application deadline: 3/1; financial award applicants required to submit FAFSA. In 2018, 81 master's, 9 doctorates awarded. *Program availability:* Part-time, evening/weekend. Offers computer science (MS, PhD); cybersecurity (MS); data science (MS); information technology (MS); telecommunications and networking (MS). *Application deadline:* For fall admission, 6/1 for domestic students, 4/1 for international students; for spring admission, 10/1 for domestic students, 9/1 for international students. Applications are processed on a rolling basis. *Application fee:* $30. Electronic applications accepted. *Application Contact:* Nanett Rojas, Manager, Admissions Operations, 305-348-7464, Fax: 305-348-7441, E-mail: gradadm@fiu.edu. *Director,* Dr. Sundararaj S. Iyengar, 305-348-3947, Fax: 305-348-3549, E-mail: sundararaj.iyengar@fiu.edu.

School of Construction Students: 23 full-time (8 women), 32 part-time (9 women); includes 26 minority (4 Black or African American, non-Hispanic/Latino; 2 Asian, non-Hispanic/Latino; 20 Hispanic/Latino), 19 international. Average age 31. 102 applicants, 30% accepted, 11 enrolled. *Faculty:* 9 full-time (1 woman), 8 part-time/adjunct (0 women). Expenses: Contact institution. *Financial support:* In 2018–19, 5 students received support. Institutionally sponsored loans, scholarships/grants, and unspecified assistantships available. Financial award application deadline: 3/1; financial award applicants required to submit FAFSA. In 2018, 37 master's awarded. *Program availability:* Part-time, evening/weekend. Offers construction management (MS, PMS). *Application deadline:* For fall admission, 6/1 for domestic students, 4/1 for international students; for spring admission, 10/1 for domestic students, 9/1 for international students. Applications are processed on a rolling basis. *Application fee:* $30. Electronic applications accepted. *Application Contact:* Nanett Rojas, Manager, Admissions Operations, 305-348-7464, Fax: 305-348-7441, E-mail: gradadm@fiu.edu. *Director,* Dr. Irtishad Ahmad, 305-348-3172, Fax: 305-348-6255, E-mail: ahmadi@fiu.edu.

College of Law Average age 27. 1,778 applicants, 32% accepted, 204 enrolled. Expenses: Contact institution. *Financial support:* Application deadline: 3/1; applicants required to submit FAFSA. In 2018, 14 master's, 154 doctorates awarded. *Program availability:* Part-time, evening/weekend. Offers American law for foreign lawyers (LL M); law (JD). *Application deadline:* For fall admission, 5/1 for domestic and international students. Applications are processed on a rolling basis. *Application fee:* $20. Electronic applications accepted. *Application Contact:* Tawia B Ansah, Acting Dean, 305-348-1118, Fax: 305-348-1159, E-mail: tawia.ansah@fiu.edu. *Acting Dean,* Tawia B Ansah, 305-348-1118, Fax: 305-348-1159, E-mail: tawia.ansah@fiu.edu.

Herbert Wertheim College of Medicine Average age 26. 5,410 applicants, 7% accepted, 170 enrolled. Expenses: Contact institution. *Financial support:* Institutionally sponsored loans and scholarships/grants available. Financial award application deadline: 3/1; financial award applicants required to submit FAFSA. In 2018, 115 doctorates awarded. Offers biomedical sciences (PhD); medicine (MD); physician assistant studies (MPAS). *Application deadline:* For fall admission, 12/15 for domestic students. *Application fee:* $160. Electronic applications accepted. *Application Contact:* Cristina M. Arabatzis, Assistant Director of Admissions, 305-348-0639, Fax: 305-348-0650, E-mail: carabatz@fiu.edu. *Dean,* Dr. John Rock, 305-348-0570, E-mail: med.admissions@fiu.edu.

Nicole Wertheim College of Nursing and Health Sciences Students: 893 full-time (681 women), 156 part-time (120 women); includes 808 minority (186 Black or African American, non-Hispanic/Latino; 1 American Indian or Alaska Native, non-Hispanic/Latino; 59 Asian, non-Hispanic/Latino; 536 Hispanic/Latino; 4 Native Hawaiian or other Pacific Islander, non-Hispanic/Latino; 22 Two or more races, non-Hispanic/Latino), 22 international. Average age 29. 1,411 applicants, 29% accepted, 346 enrolled. *Faculty:* 73 full-time (55 women), 152 part-time/adjunct (104 women). Expenses: Contact institution. *Financial support:* Career-related internships or fieldwork, Federal Work-Study, institutionally sponsored loans, and scholarships/grants available. Financial award application deadline: 3/1; financial award applicants required to submit FAFSA. In 2018, 283 master's, 94 doctorates awarded. *Program availability:* Part-time, evening/weekend. Offers adult health nursing (MSN); athletic training (MS); family health (MSN); health services administration (MHSA); nurse anesthetist (MSN); nursing and health sciences (MHSA, MS, MSN, MSOT, DNP, DPT, PhD); nursing practice (DNP); nursing science research (PhD); occupational therapy (MSOT); pediatric nurse (MSN); physical therapy (DPT); psychiatric and mental health nursing (MSN); registered nurse (MSN); speech-language pathology (MS). *Application fee:* $30. Electronic applications accepted. *Application Contact:* Nanett Rojas, Manager, Admissions Operations, 305-348-7464, Fax: 305-348-7441, E-mail: gradadm@fiu.edu. *Dean,* Dr. Ora Strickland, 305-348-0407, E-mail: olstrick@fiu.edu.

Robert Stempel College of Public Health and Social Work Students: 419 full-time (311 women), 150 part-time (126 women); includes 417 minority (122 Black or African American, non-Hispanic/Latino; 1 American Indian or Alaska Native, non-Hispanic/Latino; 27 Asian, non-Hispanic/Latino; 251 Hispanic/Latino; 16 Two or more races, non-Hispanic/Latino; 50 international. Average age 30. 604 applicants, 63% accepted, 203 enrolled. *Faculty:* 63 full-time (37 women), 37 part-time/adjunct (25 women). Expenses: Contact institution. *Financial support:* Institutionally sponsored loans, scholarships/grants, and unspecified assistantships available. Financial award application deadline: 3/1; financial award applicants required to submit FAFSA. In 2018, 207 master's, 19 doctorates awarded. *Program availability:* Part-time, evening/weekend, online learning. Offers biostatistics (MPH); dietetics and nutrition (MS, PhD); environmental and occupational health (MPH, PhD); epidemiology (MPH, PhD); health policy and management (MPH); health promotion and disease prevention (MPH, PhD); public health and social work (MPH, MS, MSW, PhD). *Application deadline:* For fall admission, 6/1 for domestic students, 4/1 for international students; for spring admission, 10/1 for domestic students, 9/1 for international students. Applications are processed on a rolling basis. *Application fee:* $30. Electronic applications accepted. *Application Contact:* Nanett Rojas, Manager, Admissions Operations, 305-348-7464, Fax: 305-348-7441, E-mail: gradadm@fiu.edu. *Dean,* Dr. Tomas Guilarte, 305-348-1158, Fax: 305-348-1691, E-mail: tomas.guilarte@fiu.edu.

School of Social Work Students: 142 full-time (117 women), 44 part-time (40 women); includes 155 minority (44 Black or African American, non-Hispanic/Latino; 2 Asian, non-Hispanic/Latino; 102 Hispanic/Latino; 7 Two or more races, non-Hispanic/Latino; 3 international. Average age 30. 123 applicants, 44% accepted, 45 enrolled. *Faculty:* 17 full-time (11 women), 14 part-time/adjunct (10 women). Expenses: Contact institution. *Financial support:* Institutionally sponsored loans and scholarships/grants available. Financial award application deadline: 3/1; financial award applicants required to submit FAFSA. In 2018, 85 master's, 6 doctorates awarded. *Program availability:* Part-time, evening/weekend. Offers social welfare (PhD); social work (MSW). *Application deadline:* For fall admission, 6/1 for domestic students, 4/1 for international students; for spring admission, 10/1 for domestic students, 9/1 for international students. Applications are processed on a rolling basis. *Application fee:* $30. Electronic applications accepted. *Application Contact:* Nanett Rojas, Manager, Admissions Operations, 305-348-7464, Fax: 305-348-7441, E-mail: gradadm@fiu.edu. *Director,* Dr. Shann Burke, 305-348-7462, E-mail: shanna.burke@fiu.edu.

Steven J. Green School of International and Public Affairs Students: 509 full-time (270 women), 261 part-time (163 women); includes 528 minority (111 Black or African American, non-Hispanic/Latino; 2 American Indian or Alaska Native, non-Hispanic/Latino; 14 Asian, non-Hispanic/Latino; 381 Hispanic/Latino; 20 Two or more races, non-Hispanic/Latino; 112 international. Average age 32. 601 applicants, 55% accepted, 226 enrolled. *Faculty:* 165 full-time (68 women), 185 part-time/adjunct (89 women). Expenses: Contact institution. *Financial support:* Career-related internships or fieldwork, Federal Work-Study, institutionally sponsored loans, and scholarships/grants available. Financial award application deadline: 3/1; financial award applicants required to submit FAFSA. In 2018, 241 master's, 34 doctorates awarded. *Program availability:* Part-time, evening/weekend. Offers African and African diaspora studies (MA); Asian studies (MA); Atlantic history (PhD); criminal justice (MS); disaster management (MA); economics (MA, PhD); global and sociocultural studies (MA, PhD); history (MA); international and public affairs (MA, MPA, MS, PhD); international crime and justice (PhD); international relations (MA, PhD); political science (MA, PhD); public administration (MPA); public affairs (PhD); religious studies (MA); Spanish (MA, PhD). *Application deadline:* For fall admission, 6/1 for domestic students, 4/1 for international students; for winter admission, 10/1 for domestic students, 9/1 for international students. Applications are processed on a rolling basis. *Application fee:* $30. Electronic applications accepted. *Application Contact:* Nanett Rojas, Manager, Admissions Operations, 305-348-7464, Fax: 305-348-7441, E-mail: gradadm@fiu.edu. *Dean,* Dr. John F. Stack, Jr., 305-348-7266, Fax: 305-348-1013, E-mail: john.stack@fiu.edu.

FLORIDA MEMORIAL UNIVERSITY, Miami-Dade, FL 33054

General Information Independent-religious, coed, comprehensive institution.

GRADUATE UNITS

School of Business *Program availability:* Part-time. Offers business (MBA).

School of Education Offers elementary education (MS); exceptional student education (MS); reading (MS).

FLORIDA NATIONAL UNIVERSITY, Hialeah, FL 33012

General Information Proprietary, coed, comprehensive institution. *Enrollment:* 38 full-time matriculated graduate/professional students (21 women), 188 part-time matriculated graduate/professional students (131 women). *Enrollment by degree level:* 226 master's. *Graduate faculty:* 12 full-time (6 women), 13 part-time/adjunct (8 women). *Tuition:* Full-time $16,200. *Required fees:* $488. *Student services:* Campus employment opportunities, campus safety program, career counseling, child daycare facilities, international student services. *Library facilities:* Hialeah Campus Library plus 1 other. *Collection:* Books: 21,521 (physical), 144,218 (digital/electronic); Serial titles: 55 (physical), 196,357 (digital/electronic); Databases: 32. Weekly public service hours: 69; students can reserve study rooms.

Computer facilities: 300 computers available on campus for general student use. A campuswide network can be accessed from off campus. Online class registration is available.
Website: http://www.fnu.edu/

General Application Contact: Virginia Rabelo, Admissions Supervisor, 305-821-3333 Ext. 1016, Fax: 305-362-0595, E-mail: vrabelo@fnu.edu.

GRADUATE UNITS

Program in Business Administration Students: 15 full-time (5 women), 15 part-time (6 women); all minorities (7 Black or African American, non-Hispanic/Latino; 21 Hispanic/Latino; 2 Two or more races, non-Hispanic/Latino; 1 international. Average age 35. 8 applicants, 88% accepted, 7 enrolled. *Faculty:* 3 full-time (1 woman), 4 part-

time/adjunct (2 women). Expenses: Contact institution. *Financial support:* Federal Work-Study, institutionally sponsored loans, scholarships/grants, and tuition waivers (full and partial) available. Financial award applicants required to submit FAFSA. In 2018, 27 master's awarded. *Program availability:* Part-time, blended/hybrid learning. Offers accounting (MBA); finance (MBA); general management (MBA); health services administration (MBA); marketing (MBA); public management and leadership (MBA). *Application deadline:* Applications are processed on a rolling basis. Electronic applications accepted. *Application Contact:* Dr. Ernesto Gonzalez, Business and Economics Department Head, 305-821-3333 Ext. 1070, Fax: 305-362-0595, E-mail: egonzalez@fnu.edu. *Business and Economics Department Head,* Dr. Ernesto Gonzalez, 305-821-3333 Ext. 1070, Fax: 305-362-0595, E-mail: egonzalez@fnu.edu.

Program in Health Services Administration Students: 9 full-time (6 women), 11 part-time (6 women); includes 19 minority (2 Black or African American, non-Hispanic/Latino; 15 Hispanic/Latino; 2 Two or more races, non-Hispanic/Latino. Average age 35. 5 applicants, 80% accepted, 4 enrolled. *Faculty:* 3 full-time (1 woman), 1 (woman) part-time/adjunct. Expenses: Contact institution. *Financial support:* Scholarships/grants available. Financial award applicants required to submit FAFSA. In 2018, 14 master's awarded. *Program availability:* Part-time, evening/weekend, 100% online, blended/hybrid learning. Offers health services administration (MHSA). *Application deadline:* Applications are processed on a rolling basis. Electronic applications accepted. *Application Contact:* Dr. Loreto Almonte, Allied Health Division Head, 305-821-3333 Ext. 1074, Fax: 305-362-0595, E-mail: lalmonte@fnu.edu. *Allied Health Division Head,* Dr. Loreto Almonte, 305-821-3333 Ext. 1074, Fax: 305-362-0595, E-mail: lalmonte@fnu.edu.

Program in Nursing Students: 14 full-time (10 women), 162 part-time (119 women); includes 174 minority (12 Black or African American, non-Hispanic/Latino; 160 Hispanic/Latino; 2 Two or more races, non-Hispanic/Latino. Average age 45. *Faculty:* 6 full-time (4 women), 8 part-time/adjunct (5 women). Expenses: Contact institution. *Financial support:* Scholarships/grants available. In 2018, 53 master's awarded. *Program availability:* 100% online, blended/hybrid learning. Offers family nurse practitioner (MSN); nurse educator (MSN); nurse leadership and management (MSN). *Application Contact:* Dr. Lydie Janvier, Master of Science in Nursing Program Director, 305-821-3333 Ext. 1056, Fax: 305-362-0595, E-mail: ljanvier@fnu.edu. *Master of Science in Nursing Program Director,* Dr. Lydie Janvier, 305-821-3333 Ext. 1056, Fax: 305-362-0595, E-mail: ljanvier@fnu.edu.

FLORIDA POLYTECHNIC UNIVERSITY, Lakeland, FL 33805

General Information State-supported, coed, comprehensive institution.

GRADUATE UNITS
Graduate Programs

FLORIDA SOUTHERN COLLEGE, Lakeland, FL 33801-5698

General Information Independent-religious, coed, comprehensive institution. *Enrollment:* 3,190 graduate, professional, and undergraduate students; 322 full-time matriculated graduate/professional students (239 women), 109 part-time matriculated graduate/professional students (86 women). *Enrollment by degree level:* 274 master's, 150 doctoral, 7 other advanced degrees. *Graduate faculty:* 26 full-time (16 women), 25 part-time/adjunct (17 women). *Tuition:* Full-time $13,572; part-time $6786 per year. *Required fees:* $300; $150 per unit. $50 per semester. *Graduate housing:* On-campus housing not available. *Student services:* Campus employment opportunities, campus safety program, career counseling, exercise/wellness program, free psychological counseling, international student services, multicultural affairs office, services for students with disabilities, teacher training. *Library facilities:* Roux Library plus 1 other. *Collection:* Books: 160,667 (physical), 167,731 (digital/electronic); Serial titles: 22 (physical), 97,772 (digital/electronic); Databases: 118. Weekly public service hours: 104; students can reserve study rooms.

Computer facilities: Computer purchase and lease plans are available. 490 computers available on campus for general student use. A campuswide network can be accessed from student residence rooms. Online class registration, campus portal are available. Website: http://www.flsouthern.edu/

General Application Contact: Kristen Pinner, Director, Adult and Graduate Admission, 863-680-3912, Fax: 863-680-3872, E-mail: kpinner@flsouthern.edu.

GRADUATE UNITS

Program in Accounting Students: 10 full-time (6 women), 9 part-time (4 women); includes 7 minority (2 Black or African American, non-Hispanic/Latino; 1 Asian, non-Hispanic/Latino; 4 Hispanic/Latino). Average age 32. 23 applicants, 74% accepted, 15 enrolled. *Faculty:* 5 full-time (2 women). Expenses: Contact institution. *Financial support:* In 2018–19, 1 student received support. Federal Work-Study, unspecified assistantships, and employee tuition grants, athletic scholarships for students still eligible available. Financial award application deadline: 8/21; financial award applicants required to submit FAFSA. In 2018, 10 master's awarded. *Program availability:* Part-time, evening/weekend, blended/hybrid learning. Offers accounting (M Acc). *Application deadline:* For fall admission, 6/1 priority date for domestic and international students; for spring admission, 11/1 priority date for domestic and international students. Applications are processed on a rolling basis. *Application fee:* $30. Electronic applications accepted. *Application Contact:* Kamalie Dodson, Associate Director, Adult and Graduate Admission (MBA MAcc), 863-680-5022, Fax: 863-680-3872, E-mail: kdodson2@flsouthern.edu. *MAcc Director,* Dr. William Quilliam, 863-680-4279, E-mail: wquilliam@flsouthern.edu.

Program in Business Administration Students: 63 full-time (27 women), 6 part-time (3 women); includes 17 minority (5 Black or African American, non-Hispanic/Latino; 4 Asian, non-Hispanic/Latino; 8 Hispanic/Latino), 4 international. Average age 30. 93 applicants, 60% accepted, 50 enrolled. *Faculty:* 7 full-time (3 women). Expenses: Contact institution. *Financial support:* In 2018–19, 12 students received support. Scholarships/grants, unspecified assistantships, and employee tuition grants, athletic scholarships for students still eligible available. Financial award application deadline: 8/21; financial award applicants required to submit FAFSA. In 2018, 33 master's awarded. *Program availability:* Part-time, 100% online, blended/hybrid learning. Offers business administration (MBA). *Application deadline:* For fall admission, 6/1 priority date for domestic and international students; for spring admission, 11/1 priority date for domestic and international students. Applications are processed on a rolling basis. *Application fee:* $0. Electronic applications accepted. *Application Contact:* Kamalie Dodson, Associate Director of Adult and Graduate Admission, 863-680-5022, Fax: 863-680-3872, E-mail: kdodson2@flsouthern.edu. *Program Director,* Krista Lewellyn, 863-680-4285, Fax: 863-680-4355, E-mail: klewellyn@flsouthern.edu.

Program in Physical Therapy

School of Education Students: 127 full-time (96 women), 88 part-time (75 women); includes 67 minority (34 Black or African American, non-Hispanic/Latino; 1 American Indian or Alaska Native, non-Hispanic/Latino; 28 Hispanic/Latino; 2 Native Hawaiian or other Pacific Islander, non-Hispanic/Latino; 2 Two or more races, non-Hispanic/Latino), 1 international. Average age 41. 50 applicants, 100% accepted, 31 enrolled. *Faculty:* 11 full-time (8 women), 13 part-time/adjunct (8 women). Expenses: Contact institution. *Financial support:* In 2018–19, 4 students received support. Application deadline: 8/21; applicants required to submit FAFSA. In 2018, 36 master's, 10 doctorates awarded. *Program availability:* Part-time, evening/weekend, 100% online, blended/hybrid learning. Offers teaching (M Ed, MAT, Ed D). *Application deadline:* For fall admission, 8/15 priority date for domestic and international students; for spring admission, 12/1 priority date for domestic and international students; for summer admission, 4/1 priority date for domestic and international students. Applications are processed on a rolling basis. Electronic applications accepted. *Application Contact:* Kristen Pinner, Director of Adult and Graduate Admission, 863-680-3912, Fax: 863-680-3872, E-mail: kpinner@flsouthern.edu. *Dean,* Dr. Tracey Tedder, 863-680-4177, Fax: 863-680-4102, E-mail: ttedder@flsouthern.edu.

School of Nursing and Health Sciences Students: 122 full-time (110 women), 6 part-time (4 women); includes 60 minority (25 Black or African American, non-Hispanic/Latino; 11 Asian, non-Hispanic/Latino; 19 Hispanic/Latino; 5 Two or more races, non-Hispanic/Latino). Average age 39. 87 applicants, 57% accepted, 43 enrolled. *Faculty:* 5 full-time (all women), 11 part-time/adjunct (8 women). Expenses: Contact institution. *Financial support:* In 2018–19, 1 student received support. Employee tuition grants, athletic scholarships for students still eligible available. Financial award application deadline: 8/21; financial award applicants required to submit FAFSA. In 2018, 85 master's awarded. *Program availability:* Part-time. Offers adult gerontology clinical nurse specialist (MSN); adult gerontology primary care nurse practitioner (MSN); family nurse practitioner (MSN); nurse educator (MSN); nursing administration (MSN). *Application deadline:* For fall admission, 6/1 for domestic and international students; for spring admission, 10/1 for domestic and international students. Electronic applications accepted. *Application Contact:* Kristen Pinner, Director of Adult and Graduate Admission, 863-680-3912, Fax: 863-680-3872, E-mail: kpinner@flsouthern.edu. *Dean,* Dr. Linda Comer, 863-680-3951, Fax: 863-680-3872, E-mail: lcomer@flsouthern.edu.

FLORIDA STATE UNIVERSITY, Tallahassee, FL 32306

General Information State-supported, coed, university. CGS member. *Enrollment:* 5,649 full-time matriculated graduate/professional students (3,046 women), 2,409 part-time matriculated graduate/professional students (1,509 women). Enrollment by degree level: 4,213 master's, 3,737 doctoral, 108 other advanced degrees. *Graduate faculty:* 2,056 full-time (868 women), 63 part-time/adjunct (32 women). *Tuition, area resident:* Part-time $479.32 per credit hour. Tuition and fees vary according to campus/location and program. *Graduate housing:* Room and/or apartments available on a first-come, first-served basis to single students; on-campus housing not available to married students. Housing application deadline: 5/1. *Student services:* Campus employment opportunities, campus safety program, career counseling, child daycare facilities, exercise/wellness program, free psychological counseling, grant writing training, international student services, low-cost health insurance, multicultural affairs office, services for students with disabilities, teacher training, writing training. *Library facilities:* Robert Manning Strozier Library plus 8 others. *Collection:* Books: 2.3 million (physical), 1.6 million (digital/electronic); Serial titles: 125,007 (digital/electronic); Databases: 1,144. Weekly online service hours: 134; study areas open 24 hours, 5–7 days a week; students can reserve study rooms.

Computer facilities: 1,100 computers available on campus for general student use. A campuswide network can be accessed from student residence rooms and from off campus. Online class registration, course home pages, course search, online fee payment are available.
Website: http://www.fsu.edu/

General Application Contact: Jermaine Williams, Associate Director for Graduate Admissions, 850-644-7145, Fax: 850-644-0197, E-mail: jawilliams@fsu.edu.

GRADUATE UNITS

College of Law Average age 26. 1,805 applicants, 36% accepted, 225 enrolled. Expenses: Contact institution. *Financial support:* In 2018–19, 400 students received support, including 2 fellowships with full tuition reimbursements available (averaging $20,683 per year), 30 research assistantships (averaging $1,205 per year), 10 teaching assistantships (averaging $1,354 per year); career-related internships or fieldwork, scholarships/grants, and unspecified assistantships also available. Financial award application deadline: 3/1; financial award applicants required to submit FAFSA. In 2018, 18 master's, 218 doctorates awarded. *Program availability:* Part-time, 100% online. Offers American law for foreign lawyers (LL M); business law (LL M); environmental law and policy (LL M); financial regulation and compliance (JM); health law compliance (JM); law (JM, JD); legal risk management and HR compliance (JM). *Application deadline:* For fall admission, 6/30 for domestic and international students; for spring admission, 12/1 for domestic students; for summer admission, 4/15 for domestic students. Applications are processed on a rolling basis. *Application fee:* $30. Electronic applications accepted. *Application Contact:* Jennifer L. Kessinger, Director of Admissions and Records, 850-644-3787, Fax: 850-644-7284, E-mail: jkessing@law.fsu.edu. *Dean,* Erin O'Hara O'Connor, 850-644-3400, Fax: 850-644-5487, E-mail: eoconnor@law.fsu.edu.

College of Medicine Students: 491 full-time (266 women); includes 201 minority (52 Black or African American, non-Hispanic/Latino; 59 Asian, non-Hispanic/Latino; 78 Hispanic/Latino; 12 Two or more races, non-Hispanic/Latino), 2 international. Average age 26. 5,866 applicants, 3% accepted, 120 enrolled. *Faculty:* 178 full-time (94 women), 70 part-time/adjunct (29 women). Expenses: Contact institution. *Financial support:* In 2018–19, 129 students received support. Scholarships/grants and tuition waivers (partial) available. Financial award application deadline: 6/30; financial award applicants required to submit FAFSA. Offers medicine (MD, PhD). *Application deadline:* Applications are processed on a rolling basis. Electronic applications accepted. *Application Contact:* Dana Auvil, Assistant Director, Office of Admissions, 850-644-7904, Fax: 850-645-2846, E-mail: medadmissions@med.fsu.edu. *Dean,* Dr. John Patrick Fogarty, MD, 850-644-1346, Fax: 850-645-1420, E-mail: john.fogarty@med.fsu.edu.

Division of Research and Graduate Programs Students: 45 full-time (30 women); includes 9 minority (3 Black or African American, non-Hispanic/Latino; 1 Asian, non-Hispanic/Latino; 3 Hispanic/Latino; 2 Two or more races, non-Hispanic/Latino), 8 international. Average age 27. 30 applicants, 50% accepted, 7 enrolled. *Faculty:* 27 full-time (8 women). Expenses: Contact institution. *Financial support:* In 2018–19, 32 students received support, including 32 research assistantships with full tuition reimbursements available (averaging $30,485 per year); tuition waivers (full) also available. Financial award application deadline: 12/1. In 2018, 4 doctorates awarded. Offers biomedical sciences (PhD); neuroscience (PhD). *Application deadline:* For fall admission, 12/1 for domestic and international students. *Application fee:* $30. Electronic applications accepted. *Application Contact:* Robin Ryan, Academic Program Specialist, 850-645-6420, Fax: 850-644-5781, E-mail: robin.ryan@med.fsu.edu. *Senior Associate Dean for Research and Graduate Programs,* Dr.

Jeffrey N. Joyce, 850-644-2190, Fax: 850-644-9399, E-mail: jeffrey.joyce@med.fsu.edu.

The Graduate School Students: 5,176 full-time (2,791 women), 2,406 part-time (1,507 women); includes 1,808 minority (645 Black or African American, non-Hispanic/Latino; 11 American Indian or Alaska Native, non-Hispanic/Latino; 192 Asian, non-Hispanic/Latino; 751 Hispanic/Latino; 11 Native Hawaiian or other Pacific Islander, non-Hispanic/Latino; 198 Two or more races, non-Hispanic/Latino), 1,144 international. Average age 30. 10,144 applicants, 37% accepted, 2031 enrolled. *Faculty:* 2,056 full-time (868 women), 63 part-time/adjunct (32 women). Expenses: Contact institution. *Financial support:* In 2018–19, 40 fellowships with full tuition reimbursements (averaging $10,000 per year), 2,042 research assistantships with full tuition reimbursements (averaging $15,500 per year), 4,502 teaching assistantships with full tuition reimbursements (averaging $15,500 per year) were awarded; career-related internships or fieldwork, Federal Work-Study, institutionally sponsored loans, scholarships/grants, traineeships, health care benefits, tuition waivers (full and partial), and unspecified assistantships also available. Support available to part-time students. Financial award applicants required to submit FAFSA. In 2018, 1,957 master's, 444 doctorates, 327 other advanced degrees awarded. *Program availability:* Part-time, evening/weekend, 100% online, blended/hybrid learning. Offers materials science and engineering (MS, PhD). *Application deadline:* For fall admission, 7/1 for domestic and international students; for spring admission, 11/1 for domestic and international students. *Application fee:* $35. Electronic applications accepted. *Application Contact:* Jermaine Williams, Associate Director for Graduate Admissions, 850-644-7145, Fax: 850-644-0197, E-mail: jawilliams@fsu.edu. *Dean,* Dr. Mark Riley, 850-644-3501, Fax: 850-644-2969, E-mail: mriley@admin.fsu.edu.

College of Business Average age 31. 300 applicants, 61% accepted, 133 enrolled. Expenses: Contact institution. *Financial support:* In 2018–19, 146 students received support, including 26 fellowships (averaging $1,500 per year), 77 research assistantships with full tuition reimbursements available (averaging $20,000 per year), 43 teaching assistantships with full tuition reimbursements available (averaging $20,000 per year); career-related internships or fieldwork, scholarships/grants, health care benefits, tuition waivers (full and partial), and unspecified assistantships also available. Support available to part-time students. Financial award application deadline: 1/1; financial award applicants required to submit FAFSA. In 2018, 268 master's, 9 doctorates awarded. *Program availability:* Part-time, 100% online. Offers accounting (M Acc); business administration (MBA, PhD); finance (MS); management information systems (MS); risk management and insurance (MS). *Application deadline:* For fall admission, 6/1 for domestic and international students; for spring admission, 10/1 for domestic and international students; for summer admission, 3/1 for domestic and international students. Applications are processed on a rolling basis. *Application fee:* $30. Electronic applications accepted. *Application Contact:* Jennifer Clark, Director, 850-644-6458, E-mail: gradprograms@business.fsu.edu. *Dean,* Dr. Michael Hartline, 850-644-4405, Fax: 850-644-0915, E-mail: mhartline@business.fsu.edu.

College of Communication and Information Students: 221 full-time (170 women), 502 part-time (374 women); includes 274 minority (73 Black or African American, non-Hispanic/Latino; 44 Asian, non-Hispanic/Latino; 102 Hispanic/Latino; 2 Native Hawaiian or other Pacific Islander, non-Hispanic/Latino; 53 Two or more races, non-Hispanic/Latino), 20 international. Average age 31. 842 applicants, 47% accepted, 242 enrolled. *Faculty:* 54 full-time (28 women), 14 part-time/adjunct (8 women). Expenses: Contact institution. *Financial support:* In 2018–19, 298 students received support, including 63 research assistantships with full tuition reimbursements available (averaging $11,562 per year), 126 teaching assistantships with full tuition reimbursements available (averaging $11,968 per year); fellowships, career-related internships or fieldwork, Federal Work-Study, institutionally sponsored loans, scholarships/grants, health care benefits, tuition waivers (full and partial), and unspecified assistantships also available. Financial award application deadline: 1/1; financial award applicants required to submit FAFSA. In 2018, 245 master's, 5 doctorates, 2 other advanced degrees awarded. *Program availability:* Part-time, evening/weekend, 100% online, blended/hybrid learning. Offers communication theory and research (PhD); information (MA, MS, PhD, Specialist); information technology (MS); integrated marketing communication (MA, MS); media and communication studies (MA, MS); public interest media and communication (MA, MS); speech-language pathology (PhD). *Application deadline:* For fall admission, 7/1 for domestic students, 5/1 for international students; for spring admission, 11/1 for domestic and international students; for summer admission, 3/1 for domestic and international students. Applications are processed on a rolling basis. *Application fee:* $30. Electronic applications accepted. *Application Contact:* Betsy Crawford, Development and Recruiting Coordinator, 850-645-9661, Fax: 850-644-0611, E-mail: betsy.crawford@cci.fsu.edu. *Dean,* Dr. Lawrence C. Dennis, 850-644-9698, Fax: 850-644-0611, E-mail: larry.dennis@cci.fsu.edu.

College of Criminology and Criminal Justice 202 applicants, 56% accepted, 59 enrolled. *Faculty:* 20 full-time (8 women). Expenses: Contact institution. *Financial support:* In 2018–19, 45 students received support, including fellowships with full tuition reimbursements available (averaging $12,000 per year), research assistantships with full tuition reimbursements available (averaging $17,100 per year), teaching assistantships with full tuition reimbursements available (averaging $16,000 per year); career-related internships or fieldwork, institutionally sponsored loans, scholarships/grants, health care benefits, tuition waivers (full), and unspecified assistantships also available. Financial award application deadline: 1/15; financial award applicants required to submit FAFSA. In 2018, 62 master's, 13 doctorates awarded. *Program availability:* Part-time, 100% online. Offers criminology and criminal justice (MA, MSC, PhD). *Application deadline:* For fall admission, 7/1 for domestic and international students; for spring admission, 11/1 for domestic and international students; for summer admission, 3/1 for domestic and international students. Applications are processed on a rolling basis. *Application fee:* $30. Electronic applications accepted. *Application Contact:* Margarita Frankeberger, Program Director, 850-644-7373, Fax: 850-644-9614, E-mail: crimgradprogram@fsu.edu. *Dean,* Dr. Thomas G. Blomberg, 850-644-7365, Fax: 850-644-9614.

College of Education *Program availability:* Part-time, evening/weekend, blended/hybrid learning, asynchronous, minimal on-campus study. Offers counseling and human systems (PhD); curriculum and instruction (MS, PhD, Ed S); education (MS, Ed D, PhD, Certificate, Ed S); educational leadership and administration (Certificate); educational leadership and policy (MS, Ed D, PhD, Ed S); educational psychology (MS, PhD); foundations of education (MS, PhD); higher education (MS, PhD); human performance and technology (Certificate); institutional research (Certificate); instructional systems and learning technologies (MS, PhD); measurement and statistics (MS, PhD, Certificate); online instructional development (Certificate); program evaluation (Certificate); sport management (MS, PhD); teaching English to speakers of other languages (Certificate). Electronic applications accepted.

Florida State University

College of Fine Arts Students: 258 full-time (201 women), 35 part-time (25 women); includes 98 minority (22 Black or African American, non-Hispanic/Latino; 1 American Indian or Alaska Native, non-Hispanic/Latino; 11 Asian, non-Hispanic/Latino; 43 Hispanic/Latino; 21 Two or more races, non-Hispanic/Latino), 9 international. Average age 27. 387 applicants, 89% accepted. *Faculty:* 67 full-time (40 women), 17 part-time/adjunct (12 women). Expenses: Contact institution. *Financial support:* In 2018–19, 265 students received support, including 5 fellowships with partial tuition reimbursements available (averaging $18,000 per year), 90 research assistantships with partial tuition reimbursements available (averaging $4,957 per year), 78 teaching assistantships with partial tuition reimbursements available (averaging $8,001 per year); career-related internships or fieldwork, Federal Work-Study, institutionally sponsored loans, scholarships/grants, and unspecified assistantships also available. Support available to part-time students. Financial award application deadline: 4/15; financial award applicants required to submit FAFSA. In 2018, 91 master's, 14 doctorates awarded. *Program availability:* Part-time. Offers acting (MFA); art (MFA); art education (MA, MS, Ed D, PhD); art therapy (PhD); arts administration (PhD); costume design (MFA); dance (MA, MFA); directing (MFA); fine arts (MA, MFA, MS, Ed D, PhD, Graduate Certificate); history and criticism of art (MA, PhD); interior architecture and design (MFA, MS); technical production (MFA); theatre (MA, PhD); theatre management (MFA). *Application deadline:* For fall admission, 7/1 priority date for domestic students; for spring admission, 11/1 priority date for domestic students. Applications are processed on a rolling basis. *Application fee:* $30. Electronic applications accepted. *Application Contact:* Jermaine Williams, Assistant Director for Graduate Admissions, 850-644-7145, Fax: 850-644-0197, E-mail: jawilliams@fsu.edu. *Dean,* James Frazier, 850-664-5244, Fax: 850-644-2604, E-mail: jfrazier@fsu.edu.

College of Human Sciences Students: 101 full-time (71 women), 16 part-time (8 women); includes 26 minority (9 Black or African American, non-Hispanic/Latino; 3 Asian, non-Hispanic/Latino; 2 Hispanic/Latino; 12 Two or more races, non-Hispanic/Latino), 14 international. 157 applicants, 51% accepted, 37 enrolled. *Faculty:* 43 full-time (23 women). Expenses: Contact institution. *Financial support:* In 2018–19, 77 students received support, including 14 research assistantships with full tuition reimbursements available (averaging $23,054 per year), 60 teaching assistantships with full tuition reimbursements available (averaging $23,054 per year); career-related internships or fieldwork, Federal Work-Study, scholarships/grants, and unspecified assistantships also available. Financial award application deadline: 1/15; financial award applicants required to submit FAFSA. In 2018, 24 master's, 9 doctorates awarded. *Program availability:* Part-time. Offers exercise physiology (MS, PhD); family and child sciences (MS); human development and family sciences (PhD); human sciences (MS, PhD); marriage and family therapy (PhD); nutrition and food science (MS, PhD); sports nutrition (MS); sports sciences (MS). *Application deadline:* For fall admission, 4/1 for domestic and international students; for spring admission, 10/1 for domestic and international students. Applications are processed on a rolling basis. *Application fee:* $30. Electronic applications accepted. *Application Contact:* Tara L. Hartman, Academic Program Specialist, 850-644-7221, Fax: 850-644-0700, E-mail: thartman@fsu.edu. *Dean,* Dr. Michael D. Delp, 850-644-1281, Fax: 850-644-0700, E-mail: mdelp@fsu.edu.

College of Motion Picture Arts Students: 62 full-time (26 women); includes 20 minority (10 Black or African American, non-Hispanic/Latino; 1 American Indian or Alaska Native, non-Hispanic/Latino; 4 Asian, non-Hispanic/Latino; 3 Hispanic/Latino; 2 Two or more races, non-Hispanic/Latino), 14 international. Average age 25. 217 applicants, 15% accepted, 32 enrolled. *Faculty:* 28 full-time (8 women), 3 part-time/adjunct (1 woman). Expenses: Contact institution. *Financial support:* In 2018–19, 20 students received support, including 20 teaching assistantships with partial tuition reimbursements available (averaging $5,500 per year); institutionally sponsored loans and unspecified assistantships also available. Financial award application deadline: 12/1; financial award applicants required to submit FAFSA. In 2018, 28 master's awarded. Offers film production (MFA); screenwriting (MFA). *Application deadline:* For fall admission, 12/1 for domestic and international students. *Application fee:* $30. Electronic applications accepted. *Application Contact:* Paige Roberts, Staff Director of Recruitment and Admissions, 850-644-8524, Fax: 850-644-2626, E-mail: proberts@fsu.edu. *Dean,* Reb Braddock, 850-644-8712, Fax: 850-644-2626.

College of Music Students: 332 full-time (168 women); includes 94 minority (23 Black or African American, non-Hispanic/Latino; 35 Asian, non-Hispanic/Latino; 33 Hispanic/Latino; 3 Native Hawaiian or other Pacific Islander, non-Hispanic/Latino). Average age 26. 710 applicants, 47% accepted, 164 enrolled. *Faculty:* 74 full-time (28 women). Expenses: Contact institution. *Financial support:* In 2018–19, 235 students received support, including 2 fellowships with full tuition reimbursements available (averaging $15,000 per year), 14 research assistantships with full and partial tuition reimbursements available (averaging $6,923 per year), 201 teaching assistantships with full and partial tuition reimbursements available (averaging $6,923 per year); career-related internships or fieldwork, scholarships/grants, tuition waivers (full and partial), and unspecified assistantships also available. Support available to part-time students. Financial award application deadline: 2/28; financial award applicants required to submit FAFSA. In 2018, 98 master's, 37 doctorates awarded. *Program availability:* Part-time. Offers accompanying (MM); arts administration (MA); choral conducting (MM); composition (MM, DM); ethnomusicology (MM); general music (MA); historical musicology (PhD); instrumental accompanying (MM); instrumental conducting (MM); jazz studies (MM); music theory (MM, PhD); music therapy (MM); musicology (MM); opera (MM); performance (MM, DM); piano pedagogy (MM); piano technology (MA); vocal accompanying (MM). *Application deadline:* For fall admission, 7/1 for domestic and international students; for spring admission, 11/1 for domestic and international students; for summer admission, 3/1 for domestic students. Applications are processed on a rolling basis. *Application fee:* $30. Electronic applications accepted. *Application Contact:* Kris Watson, Director of Admissions, 850-645-2126, Fax: 850-644-2033, E-mail: krwatson@fsu.edu. *Dean,* Dr. Patricia Flowers, 850-644-4361, Fax: 850-644-2033, E-mail: pjflowers@fsu.edu.

College of Nursing Students: 61 full-time (56 women), 72 part-time (64 women); includes 54 minority (30 Black or African American, non-Hispanic/Latino; 1 American Indian or Alaska Native, non-Hispanic/Latino; 6 Asian, non-Hispanic/Latino; 10 Hispanic/Latino; 1 Native Hawaiian or other Pacific Islander, non-Hispanic/Latino; 6 Two or more races, non-Hispanic/Latino). Average age 40. 104 applicants, 42% accepted, 37 enrolled. *Faculty:* 24 full-time (21 women), 9 part-time/adjunct (all women). Expenses: Contact institution. *Financial support:* In 2018–19, fellowships with partial tuition reimbursements (averaging $6,300 per year), research assistantships with partial tuition reimbursements (averaging $3,000 per year), 3 teaching assistantships with partial tuition reimbursements (averaging $3,000 per year) were awarded; career-related internships or fieldwork, Federal Work-Study, institutionally sponsored loans, scholarships/grants, traineeships, and tuition waivers

(partial) also available. Financial award application deadline: 4/1; financial award applicants required to submit FAFSA. In 2018, 24 doctorates awarded. *Program availability:* Part-time, 100% online. Offers family nurse practitioner (DNP); psychiatric mental health (Certificate). *Application deadline:* For fall admission, 3/1 for domestic and international students. *Application fee:* $30. Electronic applications accepted. *Application Contact:* Carlos Urrutia, Assistant Director for Student Services, 850-644-5638, Fax: 850-645-7249, E-mail: currutia@fsu.edu. *Interim Dean,* Dr. Laurie Grubbs, 850-644-6846, Fax: 850-644-7660, E-mail: lgrubbs@fsu.edu.

College of Social Sciences and Public Policy Students: 443 full-time (216 women), 183 part-time (95 women); includes 145 minority (66 Black or African American, non-Hispanic/Latino; 29 Asian, non-Hispanic/Latino; 32 Hispanic/Latino; 18 Two or more races, non-Hispanic/Latino), 100 international. Average age 26. 743 applicants, 64% accepted, 225 enrolled. *Faculty:* 134 full-time (47 women), 44 part-time/adjunct (7 women). Expenses: Contact institution. *Financial support:* In 2018–19, 273 students received support, including 33 fellowships with full tuition reimbursements available (averaging $21,828 per year), 85 research assistantships with full tuition reimbursements available (averaging $13,487 per year), 126 teaching assistantships with full tuition reimbursements available (averaging $18,710 per year); career-related internships or fieldwork, Federal Work-Study, institutionally sponsored loans, scholarships/grants, health care benefits, tuition waivers (full and partial), and unspecified assistantships also available. Support available to part-time students. Financial award application deadline: 1/15; financial award applicants required to submit FAFSA. In 2018, 294 master's, 31 doctorates awarded. *Program availability:* Part-time, evening/weekend. Offers applied American politics and policy (MS); applied economics (MS); applied social research (MS); Asian studies (MA); demography (MS); economics (PhD); geographic information science (MS); geography (MA, MS, PhD); international affairs (MA); planning (MSP); political science (MS, PhD); public administration (MPA, PhD); public administration and policy (Certificate); public health (MPH); Russian and East European studies (MA); social sciences and public policy (MA, MPA, MPH, MS, MSP, PhD, Certificate); sociology (MS, PhD); sociology of health and aging (MS); urban and regional planning (PhD). *Application deadline:* For fall admission, 7/1 priority date for domestic and international students; for spring admission, 11/1 priority date for domestic and international students; for summer admission, 3/1 priority date for domestic and international students. Applications are processed on a rolling basis. *Application fee:* $30. Electronic applications accepted. *Application Contact:* Jermaine Williams, Assistant Director for Graduate Admissions, 850-644-7145, Fax: 850-644-0197, E-mail: jawilliams@fsu.edu. *Dean,* Dr. Timothy Chapin, 850-644-5488, Fax: 850-645-4923, E-mail: tchapin@fsu.edu.

College of Social Work Students: 198 full-time (160 women), 447 part-time (404 women); includes 252 minority (139 Black or African American, non-Hispanic/Latino; 1 American Indian or Alaska Native, non-Hispanic/Latino; 7 Asian, non-Hispanic/Latino; 77 Hispanic/Latino; 1 Native Hawaiian or other Pacific Islander, non-Hispanic/Latino; 27 Two or more races, non-Hispanic/Latino), 1 international. Average age 31. 324 applicants, 70% accepted, 197 enrolled. *Faculty:* 34 full-time (24 women), 8 part-time/adjunct (4 women). Expenses: Contact institution. *Financial support:* In 2018–19, 82 students received support, including 28 research assistantships with full tuition reimbursements available, 6 teaching assistantships with full tuition reimbursements available; fellowships with full tuition reimbursements available, career-related internships or fieldwork, scholarships/grants, health care benefits, tuition waivers (full and partial), and unspecified assistantships also available. Financial award application deadline: 5/1; financial award applicants required to submit FAFSA. In 2018, 215 master's, 3 doctorates awarded. *Program availability:* Part-time, 100% online coursework with face to face internship requirements. Offers clinical social work (MSW); criminology (MSW, PhD); social leadership (MSW); social work (PhD). *Application deadline:* For fall admission, 5/1 for domestic and international students; for spring admission, 10/1 for domestic and international students; for summer admission, 3/1 for domestic and international students. Applications are processed on a rolling basis. *Application fee:* $30. Electronic applications accepted. *Application Contact:* Dana DeBoer, Coordinator of MSW Admissions, 800-378-9550, Fax: 850-644-9591, E-mail: ddeboer2@admin.fsu.edu. *Dean,* Dr. James Clark, 850-644-4752, Fax: 850-644-9750, E-mail: jclark5@fsu.edu.

Department of Anthropology Students: 1,644 full-time (942 women), 153 part-time (76 women); includes 248 minority (39 Black or African American, non-Hispanic/Latino; 53 Asian, non-Hispanic/Latino; 113 Hispanic/Latino; 1 Native Hawaiian or other Pacific Islander, non-Hispanic/Latino; 42 Two or more races, non-Hispanic/Latino), 578 international. Average age 29. 27 applicants, 48% accepted, 12 enrolled. *Faculty:* 588 full-time, 8 part-time/adjunct. Expenses: Contact institution. *Financial support:* In 2018–19, 18 students received support, including 2 research assistantships with full tuition reimbursements available (averaging $14,500 per year), 16 teaching assistantships with full tuition reimbursements available (averaging $14,500 per year); fellowships, career-related internships or fieldwork, institutionally sponsored loans, scholarships/grants, traineeships, health care benefits, and unspecified assistantships also available. Support available to part-time students. Financial award application deadline: 1/15; financial award applicants required to submit FAFSA. In 2018, 292 master's, 181 doctorates awarded. *Program availability:* Part-time. Offers analytical chemistry (MS, PhD); ancient history (MA); anthropology (MA, MS); applied and computational mathematics (MS, PhD); applied behavior analysis (MS); applied statistics (MS); aquatic environmental science (MS, PSM); biochemistry (MS, PhD); biomathematics (MS, PhD); biostatistics (MS, PhD); cell and molecular biology (MS, PhD); classical archaeology (MA); classical civilization (MA); classics (PhD); clinical psychology (PhD); cognitive psychology (PhD); computational science (MS, PhD); computational sciences (PhD); computer network and system administration (MS); computer science (MS, PhD); cyber criminology (MS); cyber security (MS); developmental psychology (PhD); ecology and evolutionary biology (MS, PhD); English (MA, MFA, PhD); financial mathematics (MS, PhD); French (MA, PhD); geological sciences (MS, PhD); German (MA); Greek (MA); Greek and Latin (MA); history (MA, MS, PhD); history and philosophy of science (MA); humanities (PhD); inorganic chemistry (MS, PhD); Italian (MA); Italian studies (MA); Latin (MA); materials chemistry (PhD); mathematical statistics (MS, PhD); meteorology (MS, PhD); neuroscience (PhD); oceanography (MS, PSM, PhD); organic chemistry (MS, PhD); philosophy (MA, PhD); physical chemistry (MS, PhD); physics (MS, PhD); psychobiology (MS); public history (MA); pure mathematics (MS, PhD); religion (MA, PhD); science teaching (MST); Slavic languages and literatures (MA); Slavic languages/Russian (MA); social psychology (PhD); Spanish (MA, PhD); statistical data science (MS); stem teaching (MST); structural biology (PhD). *Application deadline:* For fall admission, 1/15 for domestic and international students. Applications are processed on a rolling basis. *Application fee:* $30. Electronic applications accepted. *Application Contact:* Scott McLemore, MAI, Academic Program Specialist, 850-644-4281, E-mail: smclemore@fsu.edu. *Dean,* Dr. Sam Huckaba, 850-644-1081.

FAMU-FSU College of Engineering *Program availability:* Part-time. Offers biomedical engineering (MS, PhD); chemical engineering (MS, PhD); civil and environmental engineering (M Eng, MS, PhD); electrical engineering (MS, PhD); engineering (M Eng, MS, PhD); industrial engineering (MS, PhD); mechanical engineering (MS, PhD); sustainable energy (MS). Electronic applications accepted.

FONTBONNE UNIVERSITY, St. Louis, MO 63105-3098

General Information Independent-religious, coed, comprehensive institution. *Graduate housing:* Room and/or apartments available on a first-come, first-served basis to single students; on-campus housing not available to married students. Housing application deadline: 5/1.

GRADUATE UNITS

Graduate Programs *Program availability:* Part-time, evening/weekend, online learning. Offers accounting (MBA, MS); art (MA); art (K-12) (MAT); business (MBA); computer science (MS); deaf education (MA); early intervention in deaf education (MA); education (MA); elementary education (MAT); family and consumer sciences (MA); fine arts (MFA); instructional design and technology (MS); management and leadership (MM); middle school education (MAT); secondary education (MAT); special education (MAT); speech-language pathology (MS); supply chain management (MS); theatre (MA). Electronic applications accepted.

FORDHAM UNIVERSITY, New York, NY 10458

General Information Independent-religious, coed, university. CGS member. *Enrollment:* 16,515 graduate, professional, and undergraduate students; 647 full-time matriculated graduate/professional students (326 women), 236 part-time matriculated graduate/professional students (106 women). *Enrollment by degree level:* 514 master's, 349 doctoral, 20 other advanced degrees. *Graduate faculty:* 617 full-time (257 women), 922 part-time/adjunct (447 women). *Graduate housing:* Room and/or apartments available on a first-come, first-served basis to single students; on-campus housing not available to married students. Housing application deadline: 4/10. *Student services:* Campus employment opportunities, campus safety program, career counseling, free psychological counseling, international student services, low-cost health insurance, services for students with disabilities, teacher training, writing training. *Library facilities:* Walsh Library plus 3 others. *Collection:* Books: 1.5 million (physical), 992,000 (digital/electronic); Serial titles: 16,353 (physical), 94,307 (digital/electronic); Databases: 444. Weekly public service hours: 105; study areas open 24 hours, 5–7 days a week.

Computer facilities: Computer purchase and lease plans are available. 2,600 computers available on campus for general student use. A campuswide network can be accessed from student residence rooms and from off campus. Online class registration, Video Streaming; IP TV Channels; Mobile Apps for University Services; Maker Spaces; University Supplied Software, WebEX Video Conferencing are available. Website: http://www.fordham.edu/

General Application Contact: Office of Admission, 718-817-1000.

GRADUATE UNITS

Gabelli School of Business *Program availability:* Part-time, evening/weekend. Offers accounting (MBA, MS); applied statistics and decision-making (MS); business economics (DPS); capital markets (DPS); communications and media management (MBA); electronic business (MBA); entrepreneurship (MBA); finance (MBA, PhD); global finance (MBA); global sustainability (MBA); health administration (MS); healthcare management (MBA); information systems (MBA, MS); investor relations (MS); management (EMBA, MBA, MS, PhD); marketing (MBA); marketing intelligence (MS); media management (MS); nonprofit leadership (MS); quantitative finance (MS); strategy and decision-making (DPS); taxation (MS). Electronic applications accepted.

Graduate School of Arts and Sciences Students: 609 full-time (298 women), 190 part-time (88 women); includes 167 minority (45 Black or African American, non-Hispanic/Latino; 4 American Indian or Alaska Native, non-Hispanic/Latino; 46 Asian, non-Hispanic/Latino; 71 Hispanic/Latino; 1 Native Hawaiian or other Pacific Islander, non-Hispanic/Latino), 181 international. Average age 31. 2,197 applicants, 36% accepted, 296 enrolled. *Faculty:* 249 full-time (81 women). Expenses: Contact institution. *Financial support:* In 2018–19, 29 fellowships with tuition reimbursements (averaging $22,844 per year), 106 research assistantships with tuition reimbursements (averaging $16,516 per year), 280 teaching assistantships with tuition reimbursements (averaging $19,927 per year) were awarded; career-related internships or fieldwork, Federal Work-Study, institutionally sponsored loans, scholarships/grants, health care benefits, tuition waivers (full and partial), and unspecified assistantships also available. Support available to part-time students. Financial award application deadline: 1/4; financial award applicants required to submit FAFSA. In 2018, 205 master's, 56 doctorates, 58 other advanced degrees awarded. *Program availability:* Part-time, evening/weekend. Offers applied developmental psychology (PhD); applied psychological methods (MS); arts and sciences (MA, MFA, MS, PhD, Advanced Certificate, Certificate, Graduate Certificate); biological sciences (MS, PhD); classical languages and literatures (MA, PhD); clinical psychology (PhD); clinical research methods (MS); computer science (MS); conservation biology (Graduate Certificate); data analytics (MS); economics (MA, PhD); elections and campaign management (MA); English language and literature (MA, PhD); history (MA, PhD); international humanitarian action (MA); international political economy and development (MA, Certificate); philosophy (MA, PhD); playwriting (MFA); psychometrics and quantitative psychology (PhD); public media (MA); theology (MA, PhD); urban studies (MA). *Application deadline:* For fall admission, 1/4 priority date for domestic and international students; for spring admission, 10/31 for domestic and international students. Applications are processed on a rolling basis. *Application fee:* $70. Electronic applications accepted. *Application Contact:* Garrett Marino, Director of Graduate Admissions, 718-817-4419, Fax: 718-817-3566, E-mail: gmarino10@fordham.edu. *Dean,* Dr. Melissa Labonte, 718-817-4400, Fax: 718-817-4474, E-mail: labonte@fordham.edu.

Program in Ethics and Society Students: 14 full-time (9 women), 8 part-time (4 women); includes 4 minority (1 Black or African American, non-Hispanic/Latino; 2 Asian, non-Hispanic/Latino; 1 Hispanic/Latino), 2 international. Average age 34. 30 applicants, 87% accepted, 10 enrolled. Expenses: Contact institution. *Financial support:* In 2018–19, 1 student received support. Teaching assistantships, Federal Work-Study, institutionally sponsored loans, scholarships/grants, tuition waivers (partial), and unspecified assistantships available. Financial award application deadline: 1/4. In 2018, 7 master's awarded. *Program availability:* Part-time. Offers ethics and society (MA); health care ethics (Certificate). *Application deadline:* For fall admission, 1/4 priority date for domestic students; for spring admission, 10/31 for domestic students. Applications are processed on a rolling basis. *Application fee:* $70. Electronic applications accepted. *Application Contact:* Garrett Marino, Director of Graduate Admissions, 718-817-4419, Fax: 718-817-3566, E-mail: gmarino10@fordham.edu. *Interim Director of Academic Programs, Fordham University Center for Ethics Education,* Rimah Jaber, 718-817-0927, E-mail: rjaber@fordham.edu.

Program in Medieval Studies Students: 4 full-time (2 women), 11 part-time (7 women). Average age 27. 17 applicants, 82% accepted, 3 enrolled. Expenses: Contact institution. *Financial support:* In 2018–19, 4 students received support. Institutionally sponsored loans, tuition waivers (full and partial), and unspecified assistantships available. Financial award application deadline: 1/4; financial award applicants required to submit FAFSA. In 2018, 6 master's awarded. *Program availability:* Part-time, evening/weekend. Offers medieval studies (MA, Certificate). *Application deadline:* For fall admission, 1/4 priority date for domestic students; for spring admission, 11/1 for domestic students. Applications are processed on a rolling basis. *Application fee:* $70. Electronic applications accepted. *Application Contact:* Garrett Marino, Director of Graduate Admissions, 718-817-4419, Fax: 718-817-3566, E-mail: gmarino10@fordham.edu. *Director,* Dr. Susanne Hafner, 718-817-4655, E-mail: hafner@fordham.edu.

Graduate School of Education *Program availability:* Part-time, evening/weekend. Offers education (MSE, MST, Ed D, PhD, Adv C). Electronic applications accepted.

Division of Curriculum and Teaching *Program availability:* Part-time, evening/weekend. Offers curriculum and teaching (MSE); early childhood education (MSE); elementary education (MST); special education (MSE, Adv C); teaching English as a second language (MSE). Electronic applications accepted.

Division of Educational Leadership, Administration and Policy *Program availability:* Part-time, evening/weekend. Offers administration and supervision (MSE, Adv C); administration and supervision for church leaders (PhD); educational administration and supervision (Ed D, PhD). Electronic applications accepted.

Division of Psychological and Educational Services *Program availability:* Part-time, evening/weekend. Offers counseling and personnel services (MSE); counseling psychology (PhD); school psychology (PhD). Electronic applications accepted.

Graduate School of Religion and Religious Education *Program availability:* Part-time. Offers pastoral counseling and spiritual care (MA); pastoral ministry/spirituality/pastoral counseling (D Min); religion and religious education (MA); religious education (MS, PhD, PD); spiritual direction (Certificate). Electronic applications accepted.

Graduate School of Social Service *Program availability:* Part-time, evening/weekend, 100% online, blended/hybrid learning. Offers nonprofit leadership (MS); social work (MSW, PhD). MS program jointly sponsored with Graduate School of Business and conducted through the Fordham Center for Nonprofit Leaders; MSW/MPH offered with Ichan School of Public Health at Mount Sinai. Electronic applications accepted.

School of Law *Program availability:* Part-time, evening/weekend. Offers banking, corporate and finance law (LL M); corporate compliance (MSL); fashion law (MSL); intellectual property and information law (LL M); international business and trade law (LL M); law (JD). Electronic applications accepted.

FORT HAYS STATE UNIVERSITY, Hays, KS 67601-4099

General Information State-supported, coed, comprehensive institution. CGS member. *Graduate housing:* Rooms and/or apartments available to single and married students. Housing application deadline: 8/1.

GRADUATE UNITS

Graduate School *Program availability:* Part-time. Electronic applications accepted.

College of Arts, Humanities, and Social Sciences *Program availability:* Part-time. Offers arts, humanities, and social sciences (MA, MFA, MLS, MS); communication (MS); English (MA); history (MA); liberal studies (MLS); studio art (MFA). Electronic applications accepted.

College of Education *Program availability:* Part-time. Offers counseling (MS); education (MS, MSE, Ed S); educational administration (MS, Ed S); instructional technology (MS); special education (MS). Electronic applications accepted.

College of Health and Behavioral Sciences *Program availability:* Part-time. Offers health and behavioral sciences (MS, MSN, Ed S); health and human performance (MS); nursing (MSN); psychology (MS); school psychology (Ed S); speech-language pathology (MS). Electronic applications accepted.

Peter Werth College of Science, Technology and Mathematics Offers biology (MS); geography (MS); geology (MS); geosciences (MS); science, technology and mathematics (MS).

W.R. and Yvonne Robbins College of Business and Entrepreneurship *Program availability:* Part-time. Offers business and entrepreneurship (MBA); management (MBA). Electronic applications accepted.

FORT LEWIS COLLEGE, Durango, CO 81301-3999

General Information State-supported, coed, comprehensive institution.

GRADUATE UNITS

Program in Teacher Leadership Offers teacher leadership (MA, Certificate).

FORT VALLEY STATE UNIVERSITY, Fort Valley, GA 31030

General Information State-supported, coed, comprehensive institution. *Graduate housing:* Room and/or apartments available on a first-come, first-served basis to single students; on-campus housing not available to married students. Housing application deadline: 7/1.

GRADUATE UNITS

College of Graduate Studies and Extended Education *Program availability:* Part-time. Offers animal science (MS); environmental health (MPH); guidance and counseling (Ed S); mental health counseling (MS); rehabilitation counseling (MS).

FRAMINGHAM STATE UNIVERSITY, Framingham, MA 01701-9101

General Information State-supported, coed, comprehensive institution. *Graduate housing:* On-campus housing not available.

GRADUATE UNITS

Graduate Studies *Program availability:* Part-time, evening/weekend, online learning. Offers art (M Ed); biotechnology operations (MBA); counseling psychology (MA); curriculum and instructional technology (M Ed); dietetics (MS); early childhood education (M Ed); educational leadership (MA); elementary education (M Ed); English (MA); healthcare administration (MHA); human resource management (MHR); literacy and language (M Ed); management (MBA); mathematics (M Ed); nursing education (MSN); nursing leadership (MSN); nutrition science and informatics (MS); public administration (MPA); special education (M Ed); teaching of English as a second language (M Ed, Graduate Certificate).

FRANCISCAN MISSIONARIES OF OUR LADY UNIVERSITY, Baton Rouge, LA 70808

General Information Independent-religious, coed, comprehensive institution. *Graduate housing:* On-campus housing not available.

GRADUATE UNITS

School of Health Professions Offers health administration (MHA); nutritional sciences (MS); physical therapy (DPT); physician assistant studies (MMS).

School of Nursing Offers family nurse practitioner (MSN); nurse anesthesia (DNP); nursing (MSN, DNP).

FRANCISCAN SCHOOL OF THEOLOGY, Oceanside, CA 92057

General Information Independent-religious, coed, graduate-only institution. *Graduate housing:* Rooms and/or apartments available on a first-come, first-served basis to single and married students. Housing application deadline: 5/15.

GRADUATE UNITS

Graduate and Professional Programs *Program availability:* Part-time. Offers theology (M Div, MA, MAMC, MTS).

FRANCISCAN UNIVERSITY OF STEUBENVILLE, Steubenville, OH 43952-1763

General Information Independent-religious, coed, comprehensive institution. *Graduate housing:* On-campus housing not available.

GRADUATE UNITS

Graduate Programs *Program availability:* Part-time, evening/weekend, online learning. Offers administration (MS Ed); business (MBA); clinical mental health counseling (MA); nursing (MSN); philosophy (MA); teaching (MS Ed); theology and Christian ministry (MA). Electronic applications accepted.

FRANCIS MARION UNIVERSITY, Florence, SC 29502-0547

General Information State-supported, coed, comprehensive institution. *Graduate housing:* Room and/or apartments available on a first-come, first-served basis to single students; on-campus housing not available to married students. Housing application deadline: 5/1.

GRADUATE UNITS

Graduate Programs *Program availability:* Part-time, evening/weekend. Offers applied psychology (MS); family nurse practitioner (MSN); family nurse practitioner with nurse educator certificate (MSN); nurse educator (MSN); physician assistant (MPAS); school psychology (SSP); speech-language pathology (MSLP). Electronic applications accepted.

School of Business *Program availability:* Part-time, evening/weekend. Offers business (MBA); health executive management (MBA).

School of Education *Program availability:* Part-time. Offers learning disabilities (M Ed, MAT).

FRANKLIN COLLEGE, Franklin, IN 46131

General Information Independent-religious, coed, comprehensive institution.

GRADUATE UNITS

Program in Athletic Training Offers athletic training (MSAT).

FRANKLIN PIERCE UNIVERSITY, Rindge, NH 03461-0060

General Information Independent, coed, comprehensive institution. *Graduate housing:* On-campus housing not available.

GRADUATE UNITS

Graduate and Professional Studies *Program availability:* Part-time, 100% online, blended/hybrid learning. Offers curriculum and instruction (M Ed); elementary education (MS Ed); emerging network technologies (Graduate Certificate); energy and sustainability studies (MBA, Graduate Certificate); health administration (MBA, Graduate Certificate); human resource management (MBA, Graduate Certificate); information technology (MBA); leadership (MBA); nursing education (MS); nursing leadership (MS); physical therapy (DPT); physician assistant studies (MPAS); special education (M Ed); sports management (MBA). Electronic applications accepted.

FRANKLIN UNIVERSITY, Columbus, OH 43215-5399

General Information Independent, coed, comprehensive institution. *Graduate housing:* On-campus housing not available.

GRADUATE UNITS

Accounting Program *Program availability:* Online learning. Offers accounting (MSA).

Computer Science Program *Program availability:* Part-time, evening/weekend. Offers computer science (MS). Electronic applications accepted.

Criminal Justice Administration Program Offers criminal justice administration (MA).

Instructional Design and Learning Technology Program Offers instructional design and learning technology (MS).

Marketing and Communication Program *Program availability:* Part-time, evening/weekend. Offers marketing and communication (MS). Electronic applications accepted.

MBA Program *Program availability:* Part-time, evening/weekend, online learning. Offers business administration (MBA). Electronic applications accepted.

FRANKLIN UNIVERSITY SWITZERLAND, CH-6924 Sorengo, Switzerland

General Information Independent, coed, comprehensive institution.

GRADUATE UNITS

The Taylor Institute for Global Enterprise Management Offers international management (MS).

FREDERICK S. PARDEE RAND GRADUATE SCHOOL, Santa Monica, CA 90407-2138

General Information Independent, coed, graduate-only institution. *Graduate housing:* On-campus housing not available. *Research affiliation:* RAND Corporation (not-for-profit research).

GRADUATE UNITS

Program in Policy Analysis Offers policy analysis (PhD). Electronic applications accepted.

FREED-HARDEMAN UNIVERSITY, Henderson, TN 38340-2399

General Information Independent-religious, coed, comprehensive institution. *Graduate housing:* Room and/or apartments available on a first-come, first-served basis to single students; on-campus housing not available to married students. Housing application deadline: 8/22.

GRADUATE UNITS

Program in Business Administration *Program availability:* Part-time, evening/weekend, online learning. Offers accounting (MBA); corporate responsibility (MBA); leadership (MBA).

Program in Counseling *Program availability:* Part-time, evening/weekend. Offers counseling (MS).

Program in Education *Program availability:* Part-time, evening/weekend. Offers curriculum and instruction (M Ed); school counseling (M Ed); school leadership (Ed S).

School of Biblical Studies *Program availability:* Part-time. Offers biblical studies (M Div, M Min, MA); divinity (M Div); ministry (M Min); New Testament (MA).

FRESNO PACIFIC UNIVERSITY, Fresno, CA 93702-4709

General Information Independent-religious, coed, comprehensive institution. *Graduate housing:* Rooms and/or apartments available on a first-come, first-served basis to single and married students. Housing application deadline: 4/20.

GRADUATE UNITS

Biblical Seminary *Program availability:* Part-time, online learning. Offers Christian ministry (MA); community leadership and transformation (MA); divinity (M Div); marriage and family therapy (MA); New Testament (MA); Old Testament (MA); theology (MA); urban mission (MA).

Graduate Programs *Program availability:* Part-time, evening/weekend. Offers business administration (MBA); church conflict and peacemaking (Certificate); family nurse practitioner (MSN); individualized study (MA); kinesiology (MA); leadership and organizational studies (MA); mediation (Certificate); peacemaking and conflict studies (MA); restorative justice (Certificate). Electronic applications accepted.

School of Education *Program availability:* Part-time, evening/weekend. Offers administrative services (MA); board certified associate behavior analyst (Certificate); curriculum and teaching (MA); education (MA, MA Ed, Certificate); educational technology (MA); reading (Certificate); reading/English as a second language (MA Ed); reading/language arts (MA Ed); school counseling (MA); school library and information technology (MA Ed); school psychology (MA); special education (MA); STEM education (MA Ed). Electronic applications accepted.

FRIENDS UNIVERSITY, Wichita, KS 67213

General Information Independent-religious, coed, comprehensive institution.

GRADUATE UNITS

Graduate School *Program availability:* Part-time, evening/weekend, online learning. Offers family therapy (MSFT); global business administration (MBA); health care leadership (MHCL); management information systems (MMIS); professional business administration (MBA). Electronic applications accepted.

FRONTIER NURSING UNIVERSITY, Hyden, KY 41749

General Information Independent, coed, primarily women, graduate-only institution.

GRADUATE UNITS

Graduate Programs Offers family nurse practitioner (MSN, DNP, Post Master's Certificate); nurse-midwife (MSN, DNP, Post Master's Certificate); psychiatric-mental health nurse practitioner (MSN, DNP, Post Master's Certificate); women's health care nurse practitioner (MSN, DNP, Post Master's Certificate).

FROSTBURG STATE UNIVERSITY, Frostburg, MD 21532-1099

General Information State-supported, coed, comprehensive institution. *Graduate housing:* Room and/or apartments available to single students; on-campus housing not available to married students. Housing application deadline: 6/1.

GRADUATE UNITS

College of Business Students: 39 full-time (19 women), 135 part-time (75 women); includes 41 minority (19 Black or African American, non-Hispanic/Latino; 9 Asian, non-Hispanic/Latino; 6 Hispanic/Latino; 7 Two or more races, non-Hispanic/Latino), 1 international. Average age 32. 86 applicants, 84% accepted, 46 enrolled. *Faculty:* 10 full-time (3 women), 3 part-time/adjunct (1 woman). Expenses: Contact institution. *Financial support:* In 2018–19, 8 research assistantships with full tuition reimbursements (averaging $5,000 per year) were awarded; career-related internships or fieldwork and Federal Work-Study also available. Financial award application deadline: 4/1; financial award applicants required to submit FAFSA. In 2018, 80 master's awarded. *Program availability:* Part-time, evening/weekend. Offers business (MBA); business administration (MBA). *Application deadline:* For fall admission, 7/15 priority date for domestic students. Applications are processed on a rolling basis. *Application fee:* $45. Electronic applications accepted. *Application Contact:* Vickie Mazer, Director, Graduate Services, 301-687-7053, Fax: 301-687-4597, E-mail: vmmazer@frostburg.edu. *Dean*, Dr. Sudhir Singh, 301-687-4019, E-mail: ssingh@frostburg.edu.

College of Education Students: 90 full-time (62 women), 175 part-time (125 women); includes 30 minority (19 Black or African American, non-Hispanic/Latino; 2 Asian, non-Hispanic/Latino; 5 Hispanic/Latino; 4 Two or more races, non-Hispanic/Latino), 1 international. Average age 30. 164 applicants, 81% accepted, 100 enrolled. *Faculty:* 14 full-time (8 women), 29 part-time/adjunct (22 women). Expenses: Contact institution. *Financial support:* In 2018–19, 29 research assistantships with full tuition reimbursements (averaging $5,000 per year) were awarded; career-related internships or fieldwork and Federal Work-Study also available. Financial award application deadline: 4/1; financial award applicants required to submit FAFSA. In 2018, 98 master's, 7 doctorates awarded. *Program availability:* Part-time, evening/weekend. Offers curriculum and instruction (M Ed, Ed D); education (M Ed, MAT, MS, Ed D); educational administration and supervision (M Ed, Ed D); educational technology (M Ed); elementary (M Ed); elementary education (MAT); elementary teaching (MAT); interdisciplinary education (M Ed, Ed D); parks and recreational management (MS); reading (M Ed, Ed D); school counseling (M Ed); secondary (M Ed); secondary education (M Ed); secondary teaching (MAT); special education (M Ed). *Application deadline:* For fall admission, 7/15 priority date for domestic students. Applications are processed on a rolling basis. *Application fee:* $45. Electronic applications accepted. *Application Contact:* Vickie Mazer, Director, Graduate Services, 301-687-7053, Fax: 301-687-4597, E-mail: vmmazer@frostburg.edu. *Interim Dean*, Dr. Boyce Williams, 301-687-4759, E-mail: bcwilliams@frostburg.edu.

College of Liberal Arts and Sciences *Program availability:* Part-time, evening/weekend. Offers applied computer science (MS); applied ecology and conservation biology (MS); counseling psychology (MS); fisheries and wildlife management (MS); liberal arts and sciences (MS, MSN); nursing administration (MSN); nursing education (MSN). Electronic applications accepted.

FULLER THEOLOGICAL SEMINARY, Pasadena, CA 91182

General Information Independent-religious, coed, graduate-only institution. *Graduate housing:* Rooms and/or apartments available on a first-come, first-served basis to single and married students.

GRADUATE UNITS

Graduate Programs Offers Christian leadership (MACL); clinical psychology (PhD, Psy D); family studies (MA); global leadership (MA); global ministries (D Min); global ministries (Korean language) (D Min); intercultural studies (MA, Th M, PhD); intercultural studies (Korean language) (MA); marital and family therapy (MS); marriage and family enrichment (Certificate); ministry (M Div, D Min); missiology (D Miss); missiology (Korean language) (Th M); theology (MA, Th M, PhD); theology and ministry (MA).

FULL SAIL UNIVERSITY, Winter Park, FL 32792-7437

General Information Proprietary, coed, primarily men, comprehensive institution. *Graduate housing:* On-campus housing not available.

GRADUATE UNITS

Creative Writing Master of Fine Arts Program - Online *Program availability:* Online learning. Offers creative writing (MFA).

Education Media Design and Technology Master of Science Program - Online *Program availability:* Online learning. Offers education media design and technology (MS).

Entertainment Business Master of Science Program - Campus Offers entertainment business (MS).

Entertainment Business Master of Science Program - Online *Program availability:* Online learning. Offers entertainment business (MS).

Game Design Master of Science Program - Campus Offers game design (MS).

Internet Marketing Master of Science Program - Online *Program availability:* Online learning. Offers Internet marketing (MS).

Media Design Master of Fine Arts Program - Online *Program availability:* Online learning. Offers media design (MFA).

New Media Journalism Master of Arts Program - Online Offers new media journalism (MA).

FURMAN UNIVERSITY, Greenville, SC 29613

General Information Independent, coed, comprehensive institution. CGS member. *Enrollment:* 2,947 graduate, professional, and undergraduate students; 17 full-time matriculated graduate/professional students (15 women), 100 part-time matriculated graduate/professional students (83 women). *Enrollment by degree level:* 87 master's, 30 other advanced degrees. *Graduate faculty:* 14 full-time (11 women), 6 part-time/adjunct (all women). *Tuition:* Full-time $27,500; part-time $7290 per credit. Tuition and fees vary according to program. *Graduate housing:* On-campus housing not available. *Student services:* Campus employment opportunities, campus safety program, career counseling, child daycare facilities, exercise/wellness program, free psychological counseling, international student services, multicultural affairs office, services for students with disabilities, teacher training. *Library facilities:* James Buchanan Duke Library plus 3 others. *Collection:* Books: 601,063 (physical), 921,761 (digital/electronic); Serial titles: 704,239 (physical). Study areas open 24 hours, 5–7 days a week.

Computer facilities: Computer purchase and lease plans are available. 500 computers available on campus for general student use. A campuswide network can be accessed from student residence rooms and from off campus. Online class registration is available. Website: http://www.furman.edu/

General Application Contact: Dr. Troy M. Terry, Executive Director of Graduate and Evening Studies, 864-294-2213, Fax: 864-294-3579, E-mail: troy.terry@furman.edu.

GRADUATE UNITS

Graduate Division *Program availability:* Part-time, online learning. Offers chemistry (MS); curriculum and instruction (MA); early childhood education (MA); educational leadership (Ed S); English as a second language (MA); literacy (MA); school leadership (MA); special education (MA).

FUTURE GENERATIONS UNIVERSITY, Franklin, WV 26807

General Information Independent, coed, graduate-only institution. *Graduate housing:* On-campus housing not available.

GRADUATE UNITS

Program in Applied Community Change *Program availability:* Blended/hybrid learning. Offers conservation (MA). Electronic applications accepted.

GALLAUDET UNIVERSITY, Washington, DC 20002-3625

General Information Independent, coed, university. CGS member. *Graduate housing:* Rooms and/or apartments available on a first-come, first-served basis to single and married students. Housing application deadline: 4/1. *Research affiliation:* Spencer Foundation (deaf legal discourse), National Science Foundation/Howard University (linguistics, visual language and visual learning, integrated quantum materials), Maryland Sea Grant/University of Maryland/National Oceanic and Atmospheric Administration (NOAA) (advanced recruitment and retention in geosciences), U.S. Department of Education/Vcom3D Inc. (signing math dictionaries with mouth morphemes; accessibility and usability technologies for deaf and hard of hearing), University of Wisconsin-Madison/U.S. Department of Education (DOE) (telecommunications access), University of California Los Angeles/National Institutes of Health (cancer genetics).

GRADUATE UNITS

The Graduate School *Program availability:* Part-time. Offers American Sign Language/English bilingual early childhood deaf education: birth to 5 (Certificate); audiology (Au D); clinical psychology (PhD); deaf and hard of hearing infants, toddlers, and their families (Certificate); deaf education (MA, Ed S); deaf history (Certificate); deaf studies (Certificate); educating deaf students with disabilities (Certificate); education: teacher preparation (MA); educational neuroscience (PhD); hearing, speech and language sciences (MS, PhD); international development (MA); interpretation (MA, PhD); linguistics (MA, PhD); mental health counseling (MA); peer mentoring (Certificate); public administration (MPA); school counseling (MA); school psychology (Psy S); sign language teaching (MA); social work (MSW); speech-language pathology (MS). Electronic applications accepted.

GANNON UNIVERSITY, Erie, PA 16541-0001

General Information Independent-religious, coed, university. *Graduate housing:* Rooms and/or apartments available on a first-come, first-served basis to single and married students. *Research affiliation:* GE Global Research (nanotechnology), LifeLink Technologies (postural stability of flooring), Erie Insurance, Precision Rehabilitation Manufacturing (software development), AirBorn (PPS software enhancer).

GRADUATE UNITS

School of Graduate Studies *Program availability:* Part-time, evening/weekend, 100% online, blended/hybrid learning. Electronic applications accepted.

College of Engineering and Business *Program availability:* Part-time, evening/weekend, 100% online, blended/hybrid learning. Offers business administration (MBA, MPA); computer and information science (MSCIS); electrical and computer engineering (MSEE, MSES); engineering and business (MBA, MPA, MS, MSCIS, MSEE, MSEH, MSEM, MSES, MSME, Certificate); engineering management (MSEM); environmental health (MSEH); environmental health and engineering (MS); environmental science and engineering (MS, MSEH); finance (MBA); human resources management (MBA); information analytics (MSCIS, MSCIS); marketing (MBA); mechanical engineering (MSME); public administration (MPA); software engineering (MSCIS). Electronic applications accepted.

College of Humanities, Education, and Social Sciences *Program availability:* Part-time, evening/weekend, 100% online, blended/hybrid learning. Offers clinical mental health counseling (MS); criminalistics (MSC); curriculum and instruction (M Ed); curriculum supervisor (Certificate); English (MA); English as a second language (Certificate); health communication (MA); humanities, education, and social sciences (M Ed, MA, MS, MSC, PhD, Certificate); organizational learning and leadership (PhD); pastoral studies (MA, Certificate); principal certification (Certificate); reading (M Ed); reading specialist (Certificate); superintendent letter of eligibility (Certificate); theological studies (Certificate). Electronic applications accepted.

Morosky College of Health Professions and Sciences *Program availability:* Part-time, evening/weekend, 100% online. Offers athletic training (MAT); family nurse practitioner (MSN, Certificate); health professions and sciences (MAT, MPAS, MS, MSN, DNP, DPT, OTD, Certificate); human performance (MS); nurse anesthesia (MSN, Certificate); nursing administration (MSN); nursing practice (DNP); occupational therapy (MS, OTD); physical therapy (DPT); physician assistant science (MPAS); sport and exercise science (MS). Electronic applications accepted.

GARDNER-WEBB UNIVERSITY, Boiling Springs, NC 28017

General Information Independent-religious, coed, university. *Graduate housing:* Room and/or apartments available on a first-come, first-served basis to single students; on-campus housing not available to married students.

GRADUATE UNITS

Graduate School *Program availability:* Part-time, evening/weekend. Offers English (MA); English education (MA); physician assistant studies (MPAS); sport science and pedagogy (MA). Electronic applications accepted.

Graduate School of Business *Program availability:* Part-time, evening/weekend, online learning. Offers business (IMBA, M Acc, MBA). Electronic applications accepted.

School of Education *Program availability:* Part-time, evening/weekend. Offers curriculum and instruction (Ed D); educational leadership (Ed D); executive leadership studies (MA, Ed S); organizational leadership (Ed D); school administration (MA). Electronic applications accepted.

School of Nursing *Program availability:* Part-time, online learning. Offers family nurse practitioner (MSN, DNP).

School of Psychology *Program availability:* Part-time, evening/weekend. Offers mental health counseling (MA); school counseling (MA). Electronic applications accepted.

School of Divinity *Program availability:* Part-time. Offers biblical studies (M Div); Christian education and formation (M Div); intercultural studies (M Div); ministry (D Min); missiology (M Div); pastoral care and counseling (M Div); pastoral care and counseling/member care for missionaries (D Min); pastoral studies (M Div). Electronic applications accepted.

GARRETT-EVANGELICAL THEOLOGICAL SEMINARY, Evanston, IL 60201-3298

General Information Independent-religious, coed, graduate-only institution. *Graduate housing:* Rooms and/or apartments guaranteed to single students and available to married students. Housing application deadline: 4/1.

GRADUATE UNITS

Graduate and Professional Programs *Program availability:* Part-time. Offers Bible and culture (PhD); Christian education (MA); Christian education and congregational studies (PhD); contemporary theology and culture (PhD); divinity (M Div); ethics, church, and society (MA); liturgical studies (PhD); ministry (D Min); music ministry (MA); pastoral care and counseling (MA); pastoral theology, personality, and culture (PhD); spiritual formation and evangelism (MA); theological studies (MTS). M Div/MSW offered jointly with Loyola University Chicago. Electronic applications accepted.

GATEWAY SEMINARY, Ontario, CA 91761-8642

General Information Independent-religious, coed, graduate-only institution. *Graduate housing:* Rooms and/or apartments available on a first-come, first-served basis to single and married students. Housing application deadline: 6/15.

GRADUATE UNITS

Graduate and Professional Programs *Program availability:* Part-time, evening/weekend. Offers divinity (M Div); early childhood education (Certificate); education leadership (MAEL, Diploma); ministry (D Min); theological studies (MTS); theology (Th M); youth ministry (Certificate). Electronic applications accepted.

GEISINGER COMMONWEALTH SCHOOL OF MEDICINE, Scranton, PA 18509

General Information Independent, coed, graduate-only institution.

GRADUATE UNITS

Graduate Programs in Medicine *Program availability:* Part-time, evening/weekend. Offers biomedical sciences (MBS). Electronic applications accepted.

Professional Program in Medicine Offers medicine (MD).

THE GENERAL THEOLOGICAL SEMINARY, New York, NY 10011-4977

General Information Independent-religious, coed, graduate-only institution. *Graduate housing:* Rooms and/or apartments available to single and married students. Housing application deadline: 6/1.

GRADUATE UNITS

Graduate and Professional Programs *Program availability:* Part-time, evening/weekend. Offers Anglican studies (STM, Th D, Certificate); ascetical theology (Certificate); biblical studies (Certificate); congregational development (Certificate); divinity (M Div); historical and theological studies (Certificate); spiritual direction (MASD, STM, Certificate); theology (MA).

GENEVA COLLEGE, Beaver Falls, PA 15010-3599

General Information Independent-religious, coed, comprehensive institution. *Graduate housing:* On-campus housing not available. *Research affiliation:* INOVA Fairfax Hospital (cardiovascular science).

GRADUATE UNITS

Master of Arts in Counseling Program *Program availability:* Part-time, evening/weekend. Offers clinical mental health counseling (MA); marriage and family counseling (MA); school counseling (MA). Electronic applications accepted.

Master of Arts in Higher Education Program *Program availability:* Part-time, evening/weekend, blended/hybrid learning. Offers campus ministry (MA); college teaching (MA); educational leadership (MA); student affairs administration (MA). Electronic applications accepted.

Masters Program in Cybersecurity

Masters Program in Cybersecurity

Program in Business Administration *Program availability:* Part-time, evening/weekend. Offers business administration (MBA); finance (MBA); marketing (MBA); operations (MBA). Electronic applications accepted.

Program in Leadership Studies *Program availability:* Online only, 100% online. Offers business management (MS); ministry leadership (MS); non-profit leadership (MS); organizational management (MS); project management (MS). Electronic applications accepted.

GEORGE FOX UNIVERSITY, Newberg, OR 97132-2697

General Information Independent-religious, coed, university. *Graduate housing:* On-campus housing not available.

GRADUATE UNITS

College of Business *Program availability:* Part-time, evening/weekend, online learning. Offers accounting (DBA); finance (MBA); management (DBA); management and leadership (MBA); marketing (DBA); organizational strategy (MBA); strategic human resource management (MBA). MBA offered in Newberg, OR and in Portland, OR. Electronic applications accepted.

College of Education Offers administrative leadership (Ed S); clinical mental health counseling (MA); continuing administrator license (Certificate); education (M Ed, MA, MAT, Ed D, Certificate, Ed S); educational leadership (M Ed); educational technology (M Ed); English for speakers of other languages (M Ed); ESOL (Certificate); initial administrator license (Certificate); marriage, couple and family counseling (MA, Certificate); reading (M Ed, Certificate); school counseling (MA, Certificate); school psychology (Ed S); special education (M Ed); teaching (MAT).

Portland Seminary *Program availability:* Part-time, evening/weekend, online learning. Offers Biblical studies (M Div, MA); chaplaincy (M Div); Christian history and theology (M Div, MA); creation care (M Div, MA); intercultural studies (M Div, MA); leadership (M Div, MA); leadership and global perspectives (D Min); leadership and spiritual formation (D Min); semiotics and future studies (D Min); spiritual direction (MA, Certificate); spiritual direction supervision (M Div, MA, Certificate); spiritual formation and discipleship (M Div, MA, Certificate). Electronic applications accepted.

Program in Clinical Psychology Offers clinical psychology (Psy D). Electronic applications accepted.

Program in Physical Therapy Offers physical therapy (DPT). Electronic applications accepted.

School of Social Work Offers social work (MSW).

GEORGE MASON UNIVERSITY, Fairfax, VA 22030

General Information State-supported, coed, university. CGS member. *Enrollment:* 37,316 graduate, professional, and undergraduate students. *Enrollment by degree level:* 6,883 master's, 2,707 doctoral, 495 other advanced degrees. *Graduate housing:* Room and/or apartments available on a first-come, first-served basis to single students; on-campus housing not available to married students. Housing application deadline: 5/1. *Student services:* Campus employment opportunities, campus safety program, career counseling, child daycare facilities, exercise/wellness program, free psychological counseling, grant writing training, international student services, low-cost health insurance, multicultural affairs office, services for students with disabilities, teacher training, writing training. *Library facilities:* Fenwick Library plus 3 others. *Collection:* Books: 1.1 million (physical), 1.4 million (digital/electronic); Serial titles: 1,049 (physical), 127,898 (digital/electronic); Databases: 772. Weekly public service hours: 100; study areas open 24 hours, 5–7 days a week; students can reserve study rooms.

Computer facilities: Computer purchase and lease plans are available. 622 computers available on campus for general student use. A campuswide network can be accessed from student residence rooms and from off campus. Online class registration is available.
Website: http://www.gmu.edu/

General Application Contact: Graduate Admissions Office, 703-993-9700, Fax: 703-993-2392, E-mail: masongrad@gmu.edu.

GRADUATE UNITS

Antonin Scalia Law School Students: 457 full-time (228 women), 141 part-time (57 women); includes 158 minority (18 Black or African American, non-Hispanic/Latino; 1 American Indian or Alaska Native, non-Hispanic/Latino; 61 Asian, non-Hispanic/Latino; 51 Hispanic/Latino; 27 Two or more races, non-Hispanic/Latino), 49 international. Average age 29. 2,452 applicants, 25% accepted, 175 enrolled. *Faculty:* 44 full-time (9 women), 157 part-time/adjunct (41 women). Expenses: Contact institution. *Financial support:* In 2018–19, 451 students received support, including 2 fellowships with full tuition reimbursements available; research assistantships, career-related internships or fieldwork, scholarships/grants, and tuition waivers (full and partial) also available. Support available to part-time students. Financial award applicants required to submit FAFSA. In 2018, 169 doctorates awarded. *Program availability:* Part-time, evening/weekend. Offers global antitrust law and economics (LL M); intellectual property (LL M); law (JD); law and economics (LL M); U.S. law (LL M). *Application deadline:* For fall admission, 6/15 for domestic and international students. Applications are processed on a rolling basis. *Application fee:* $0. Electronic applications accepted. *Application Contact:* Sabrina A. Huffman, Director of Admissions, 703-993-8010, Fax: 703-993-8088, E-mail: lawadmit@gmu.edu. *Dean,* Henry N. Butler, 703-993-8644, Fax: 703-993-8088.

College of Education and Human Development Students: 486 full-time (379 women), 2,256 part-time (1,819 women); includes 804 minority (296 Black or African American, non-Hispanic/Latino; 4 American Indian or Alaska Native, non-Hispanic/Latino; 222 Asian, non-Hispanic/Latino; 226 Hispanic/Latino; 9 Native Hawaiian or other Pacific Islander, non-Hispanic/Latino; 47 Two or more races, non-Hispanic/Latino), 111 international. Average age 34. 1,402 applicants, 86% accepted, 884 enrolled. *Faculty:* 129 full-time (91 women), 201 part-time/adjunct (133 women). Expenses: Contact institution. *Financial support:* In 2018–19, 97 students received support, including 2 fellowships, 71 research assistantships with tuition reimbursements available (averaging $13,398 per year), 34 teaching assistantships with tuition reimbursements available (averaging $5,666 per year); career-related internships or fieldwork, Federal Work-Study, scholarships/grants, unspecified assistantships, and health care benefits (for full-time research or teaching assistantship recipients) also available. Support available to part-time students. Financial award application deadline: 3/1; financial award applicants required to submit FAFSA. In 2018, 843 master's, 46 doctorates, 288 other advanced degrees awarded. *Program availability:* Part-time, evening/weekend, 100% online, blended/hybrid learning. Offers assessment, evaluation, and testing (MS); assistive technology (M Ed); athletic training (MS); counseling and development (M Ed); designing digital learning in schools (M Ed); early childhood education (M Ed); early childhood education for diverse learners (M Ed); education and human development (M Ed, MS, PhD, Certificate); education leadership (M Ed, Certificate); elementary education (M Ed); English as a second language (M Ed); exercise, fitness, and health promotion (MS); gifted child education (M Ed); higher education (PhD); international sport management (Certificate); learning and decision-making in leadership (MS); learning, cognition, and motivation (MS); literacy (M Ed); literacy leadership for diverse schools (M Ed); physical education (M Ed); recreation, health and tourism (Certificate); science K-12 (M Ed); secondary education (M Ed); special education (M Ed, Certificate); sport management (MS); teacher leadership (M Ed); teacher preparation (MS); transformative teaching (M Ed). *Application deadline:* For fall admission, 4/2 for domestic and international students; for spring admission, 11/1 for domestic and international students. *Application fee:* $75 ($80 for international students). Electronic applications accepted. *Application Contact:* Nicole Mariam, Graduate Admissions Coordinator, 703-993-3832, Fax: 703-993-2020, E-mail: nwhite5@gmu.edu. *Dean,* Mark Ginsberg, 703-993-2004, Fax: 703-993-2001, E-mail: mginsber@gmu.edu.

College of Health and Human Services Students: 453 full-time (376 women), 481 part-time (408 women); includes 424 minority (185 Black or African American, non-Hispanic/Latino; 133 Asian, non-Hispanic/Latino; 88 Hispanic/Latino; 18 Two or more races, non-Hispanic/Latino), 81 international. Average age 32. 876 applicants, 80% accepted, 338 enrolled. *Faculty:* 80 full-time (58 women), 140 part-time/adjunct (105 women). Expenses: Contact institution. *Financial support:* In 2018–19, 64 students received support, including 52 research assistantships with tuition reimbursements available (averaging $16,512 per year), 15 teaching assistantships with tuition reimbursements available (averaging $7,662 per year); career-related internships or fieldwork, Federal Work-Study, scholarships/grants, unspecified assistantships, and health care benefits (for full-time research or teaching assistantship recipients) also available. Support available to part-time students. Financial award application deadline: 3/1; financial award applicants required to submit FAFSA. In 2018, 229 master's, 31 doctorates, 19 other advanced degrees awarded. *Program availability:* Part-time, evening/weekend, 100% online, blended/hybrid learning. Offers food security (Certificate); global and community health (Certificate); global health (MS); health and human services (MHA, MPH, MS, MSN, MSW, DNP, PhD, Certificate); health and medical policy (MS); health informatics (MS); health informatics and data analytics (Certificate); health services research (PhD); health systems management (MHA); nutrition (MS); public health (MPH, Certificate); quality improvement and outcomes management in health care systems (Certificate); rehabilitation science (PhD); social work (MSW). *Application fee:* $75 ($80 for international students). Electronic applications accepted. *Application Contact:* Kelly Benedicto, Administrative Office Specialist, Graduate Admissions, 703-993-8246, Fax: 703-993-3606, E-mail: kbenedi2@gmu.edu. *Dean,* Dr. Thomas Prohaska, 703-993-1918, Fax: 703-993-1943, E-mail: tprohask@gmu.edu.

School of Nursing Students: 66 full-time (59 women), 178 part-time (159 women); includes 117 minority (54 Black or African American, non-Hispanic/Latino; 43 Asian, non-Hispanic/Latino; 16 Hispanic/Latino; 4 Two or more races, non-Hispanic/Latino), 8 international. Average age 37. 135 applicants, 82% accepted, 58 enrolled. *Faculty:* 21 full-time (20 women), 47 part-time/adjunct (44 women). Expenses: Contact institution. *Financial support:* In 2018–19, 8 students received support, including 5 research assistantships with tuition reimbursements available (averaging $24,071 per year), 3 teaching assistantships (averaging $3,050 per year); career-related internships or fieldwork, Federal Work-Study, scholarships/grants, unspecified assistantships, and health care benefits (for full-time research or teaching assistantship recipients) also available. Financial award application deadline: 3/1; financial award applicants required to submit FAFSA. In 2018, 39 master's, 28 doctorates, 4 other advanced degrees awarded. *Program availability:* Part-time, evening/weekend, blended/hybrid learning. Offers adult gerontology (DNP); adult/gerontological nurse practitioner (MSN); family nurse practitioner (MSN, DNP); nurse educator (MSN); nursing (PhD); nursing administration (MSN, DNP); nursing education (Certificate); psychiatric mental health (DNP). *Application deadline:* For fall admission, 2/1 for domestic and international students. *Application fee:* $75 ($80 for international students). Electronic applications accepted. *Application Contact:* Susan Eckis, Office Manager, 703-993-1938, Fax: 703-993-1949, E-mail: seckis@gmu.edu. *Director,* Carol Urban, 703-993-2991, Fax: 703-993-1949, E-mail: curban@gmu.edu.

College of Humanities and Social Sciences Students: 712 full-time (443 women), 637 part-time (366 women); includes 301 minority (88 Black or African American, non-Hispanic/Latino; 6 American Indian or Alaska Native, non-Hispanic/Latino; 71 Asian, non-Hispanic/Latino; 95 Hispanic/Latino; 2 Native Hawaiian or other Pacific Islander, non-Hispanic/Latino; 39 Two or more races, non-Hispanic/Latino), 105 international. Average age 31. 1,531 applicants, 56% accepted, 402 enrolled. *Faculty:* 363 full-time (176 women), 221 part-time/adjunct (112 women). Expenses: Contact institution. *Financial support:* In 2018–19, 427 students received support, including 27 fellowships (averaging $3,309 per year), 180 research assistantships with tuition reimbursements available (averaging $15,915 per year), 281 teaching assistantships with tuition reimbursements available (averaging $12,219 per year); career-related internships or fieldwork, Federal Work-Study, scholarships/grants, unspecified assistantships, and health care benefits (for full-time research or teaching assistantship recipients) also available. Support available to part-time students. Financial award application deadline: 3/1; financial award applicants required to submit FAFSA. In 2018, 345 master's, 71 doctorates, 47 other advanced degrees awarded. *Program availability:* Part-time, evening/weekend. Offers anthropology (MA); applied developmental psychology (MA, PhD); art history (MA); clinical psychology (PhD); cognitive and behavioral neuroscience (MA, PhD); cognitive neuroscience (Certificate); college teaching (Certificate); communication (MA, PhD, Certificate); computational social science (MAIS); creative writing (MFA); criminal justice (MS); criminology, law, and society (MA, PhD); cultural studies (PhD); digital public humanities (Certificate); economics (MA, PhD); energy and sustainability (MAIS); English (MA); English pedagogy (Certificate); ethics and public affairs (MA); fiction (MFA); folklore studies (MAIS, Certificate); foreign languages (MA); global affairs (MA); higher education (MAIS); history (MA, PhD, Certificate); human factors/applied cognition (MA, PhD, Certificate); humanities and social sciences (MA, MAIS, MFA, MS, PhD, Certificate); individualized studies (MAIS);

industrial/organizational psychology (MA, PhD); linguistics (PhD); Middle East and Islamic studies (MA, Certificate); nonfiction writing (MFA); philosophy and cultural theory (MA); poetry (MFA); religion, culture, and values (MAIS); science communication (Certificate); social entrepreneurship (MAIS); social justice and human rights (MAIS); sociology (MA, PhD); war and the military in society (MAIS); women and gender studies (MAIS); writing and rhetoric (PhD). *Application fee:* $75 ($80 for international students). Electronic applications accepted. *Application Contact:* Stephanie Hinnenkamp, Graduate Admissions Coordinator, 703-993-2409, E-mail: shinnenk@gmu.edu. *Dean*, Deborah A. Boehm-Davis, 703-993-8715, Fax: 703-993-8714, E-mail: dbdavis@gmu.edu.

College of Science Students: 536 full-time (292 women), 448 part-time (204 women); includes 310 minority (103 Black or African American, non-Hispanic/Latino; 2 American Indian or Alaska Native, non-Hispanic/Latino; 122 Asian, non-Hispanic/Latino; 56 Hispanic/Latino; 3 Native Hawaiian or other Pacific Islander, non-Hispanic/Latino; 24 Two or more races, non-Hispanic/Latino), 144 international. Average age 32. 906 applicants, 76% accepted, 337 enrolled. *Faculty:* 211 full-time (75 women), 84 part-time/adjunct (31 women). Expenses: Contact institution. *Financial support:* In 2018–19, 255 students received support, including 3 fellowships (averaging $15,548 per year), 109 research assistantships with tuition reimbursements available (averaging $18,192 per year), 145 teaching assistantships with tuition reimbursements available (averaging $17,308 per year); career-related internships or fieldwork, Federal Work-Study, scholarships/grants, and health care benefits (for full-time research or teaching assistantship recipients) also available. Support available to part-time students. Financial award application deadline: 3/1; financial award applicants required to submit FAFSA. In 2018, 137 master's, 70 doctorates, 105 other advanced degrees awarded. *Program availability:* Part-time, evening/weekend, 100% online. Offers chemistry and biochemistry (MS, PhD); climate dynamics (PhD); computational science (MS); computational sciences and informatics (PhD); computational social science (PhD, Certificate); data science (Certificate); earth system science (MS); earth systems and geoinformation sciences (PhD); environmental geoinformation science and biodiversity conservation (Certificate); environmental science and policy (MS, PhD); forensic science (MS); geography and geoinformation science (Certificate); mathematical sciences (MS, PhD); neuroscience (PhD); physics and astronomy (MS, PhD); science (MS, PSM, PhD, Certificate). *Application fee:* $75 ($80 for international students). Electronic applications accepted. *Application Contact:* Melissa C. Hayes, Graduate Programs Director, 703-993-3430, Fax: 703-993-9033, E-mail: mhayes5@gmu.edu. *Dean*, Peggy Agouris, 703-993-1362, Fax: 703-993-9614, E-mail: pagouris@gmu.edu.

School of Systems Biology Students: 124 full-time (65 women), 91 part-time (46 women); includes 72 minority (16 Black or African American, non-Hispanic/Latino; 1 American Indian or Alaska Native, non-Hispanic/Latino; 29 Asian, non-Hispanic/Latino; 17 Hispanic/Latino; 9 Two or more races, non-Hispanic/Latino), 35 international. Average age 32. 150 applicants, 87% accepted, 84 enrolled. *Faculty:* 10 full-time (3 women), 1 part-time/adjunct (0 women). Expenses: Contact institution. *Financial support:* In 2018–19, 56 students received support, including 13 research assistantships with tuition reimbursements available (averaging $17,533 per year), 43 teaching assistantships with tuition reimbursements available (averaging $16,983 per year); career-related internships or fieldwork, Federal Work-Study, scholarships/grants, unspecified assistantships, and health care benefits (for full-time research or teaching assistantship recipients) also available. Support available to part-time students. Financial award application deadline: 3/1; financial award applicants required to submit FAFSA. In 2018, 39 master's, 13 doctorates, 1 other advanced degree awarded. Offers bioinformatics and computational biology (MS, PhD, Certificate); bioinformatics management (MS); biology (MS); biosciences (PhD). *Application fee:* $75 ($80 for international students). Electronic applications accepted. *Application Contact:* Diane St. Germain, Graduate Student Services Coordinator, 703-993-4263, Fax: 703-993-8976, E-mail: dstgerma@gmu.edu. *Director*, Dr. Iosif Vaisman, 703-993-8431, Fax: 703-993-8976, E-mail: ivaisman@gmu.edu.

College of Visual and Performing Arts Students: 121 full-time (82 women), 148 part-time (99 women); includes 58 minority (17 Black or African American, non-Hispanic/Latino; 21 Asian, non-Hispanic/Latino; 14 Hispanic/Latino; 1 Native Hawaiian or other Pacific Islander, non-Hispanic/Latino; 5 Two or more races, non-Hispanic/Latino), 80 international. Average age 30. 164 applicants, 70% accepted, 65 enrolled. *Faculty:* 80 full-time (35 women), 167 part-time/adjunct (75 women). Expenses: Contact institution. *Financial support:* In 2018–19, 20 students received support, including 1 research assistantship with tuition reimbursement available, 19 teaching assistantships with tuition reimbursements available (averaging $3,530 per year); career-related internships or fieldwork, Federal Work-Study, scholarships/grants, unspecified assistantships, and health care benefits (for full-time research or teaching assistantship recipients) also available. Support available to part-time students. Financial award application deadline: 3/1; financial award applicants required to submit FAFSA. In 2018, 57 master's, 3 doctorates, 3 other advanced degrees awarded. *Program availability:* Part-time, evening/weekend. Offers art education (MAT); arts management (MA); graphic design (MA); visual and performing arts (MA, MAT, MFA, MM, DMA, PhD, Certificate). *Application fee:* $75 ($80 for international students). Electronic applications accepted. *Application Contact:* Stevie Otto, Assistant Director, Graduate Admissions and Recruitment, 703-993-5576, Fax: 703-993-9037, E-mail: sotto2@gmu.edu. *Dean*, Rick Davis, 703-993-8624, Fax: 703-993-8883, E-mail: rdavi4@gmu.edu.

School of Music Students: 46 full-time (20 women), 52 part-time (21 women); includes 26 minority (7 Black or African American, non-Hispanic/Latino; 12 Asian, non-Hispanic/Latino; 4 Hispanic/Latino; 3 Two or more races, non-Hispanic/Latino), 10 international. Average age 32. 69 applicants, 77% accepted, 32 enrolled. *Faculty:* 24 full-time (11 women), 54 part-time/adjunct (18 women). Expenses: Contact institution. *Financial support:* In 2018–19, 15 students received support, including 1 research assistantship, 14 teaching assistantships with tuition reimbursements available (averaging $3,577 per year); career-related internships or fieldwork, Federal Work-Study, scholarships/grants, unspecified assistantships, and health care benefits (for full-time research or teaching assistantship recipients) also available. Support available to part-time students. Financial award application deadline: 3/1; financial award applicants required to submit FAFSA. In 2018, 19 master's, 3 doctorates, 2 other advanced degrees awarded. Offers composition (MM, DMA); conducting (MM, DMA); instrumental performance artist (Certificate); jazz studies (MM); music (MM); music education (MM, PhD); musical arts (DMA); pedagogy (MM); performance (MM, DMA). *Application fee:* $75 ($80 for international students). Electronic applications accepted. *Application Contact:* Dr. Lisa A. Billingham, Director of Graduate Studies, 703-993-3778, Fax: 703-993-1394, E-mail: lbillin1@gmu.edu. *Managing Director*, Dr. Linda Apple Monson, 703-993-3580, Fax: 703-993-1394, E-mail: lmonson@gmu.edu.

Schar School of Policy and Government Students: 302 full-time (159 women), 619 part-time (324 women); includes 281 minority (112 Black or African American, non-Hispanic/Latino; 62 Asian, non-Hispanic/Latino; 78 Hispanic/Latino; 29 Two or more races, non-Hispanic/Latino), 76 international. Average age 32. 631 applicants, 84% accepted, 239 enrolled. *Faculty:* 70 full-time (22 women), 51 part-time/adjunct (16 women). Expenses: Contact institution. *Financial support:* In 2018–19, 55 students received support, including 38 research assistantships with tuition reimbursements available (averaging $17,425 per year), 18 teaching assistantships (averaging $15,287 per year); career-related internships or fieldwork, Federal Work-Study, scholarships/grants, unspecified assistantships, and health care benefits (for full-time research or teaching assistantship recipients) also available. Support available to part-time students. Financial award application deadline: 3/1; financial award applicants required to submit FAFSA. In 2018, 347 master's, 15 doctorates, 29 other advanced degrees awarded. *Program availability:* Part-time, evening/weekend, 100% online. Offers biodefense (MS, PhD, Certificate); international commerce and policy (MA); international security (MA); organization development and knowledge management (MS); policy and government (MA, MPA, MPP, MS, PhD, Certificate); political science (MA, PhD); public administration (MPA); public policy (MPP, PhD); transportation policy, operations and logistics (MA). *Application fee:* $75 ($80 for international students). Electronic applications accepted. *Application Contact:* Travis Major, Director of Graduate Admissions, 703-993-3183, Fax: 703-993-4876, E-mail: tmajor@gmu.edu. *Dean*, Mark Rozell, 703-993-8171, Fax: 703-993-8215, E-mail: mrozell@gmu.edu.

School for Conflict Analysis and Resolution Students: 98 full-time (52 women), 146 part-time (91 women); includes 63 minority (32 Black or African American, non-Hispanic/Latino; 9 Asian, non-Hispanic/Latino; 14 Hispanic/Latino; 8 Two or more races, non-Hispanic/Latino), 35 international. Average age 36. 393 applicants, 60% accepted, 69 enrolled. *Faculty:* 19 full-time (10 women), 20 part-time/adjunct (10 women). Expenses: Contact institution. *Financial support:* In 2018–19, 37 students received support, including 21 research assistantships with tuition reimbursements available (averaging $13,856 per year), 16 teaching assistantships with tuition reimbursements available (averaging $8,343 per year); career-related internships or fieldwork, Federal Work-Study, scholarships/grants, unspecified assistantships, and health care benefits (for full-time research or teaching assistantship recipients) also available. Support available to part-time students. Financial award application deadline: 3/1; financial award applicants required to submit FAFSA. In 2018, 66 master's, 13 doctorates, 5 other advanced degrees awarded. *Program availability:* Part-time, evening/weekend, blended/hybrid learning. Offers conflict analysis and resolution (MS, PhD, Certificate). *Application fee:* $75 ($80 for international students). Electronic applications accepted. *Application Contact:* Monique Barner, Assistant Director for Graduate Admissions, 703-993-1300, Fax: 703-993-1302, E-mail: mwilli43@gmu.edu. *Dean*, Kevin Avruch, 703-993-3607, Fax: 703-993-1302, E-mail: kavruch@gmu.edu.

School of Business Students: 333 full-time (143 women), 212 part-time (93 women); includes 180 minority (66 Black or African American, non-Hispanic/Latino; 63 Asian, non-Hispanic/Latino; 39 Hispanic/Latino; 2 Native Hawaiian or other Pacific Islander, non-Hispanic/Latino; 10 Two or more races, non-Hispanic/Latino), 70 international. Average age 32. 484 applicants, 86% accepted, 238 enrolled. *Faculty:* 111 full-time (41 women), 92 part-time/adjunct (27 women). Expenses: Contact institution. *Financial support:* In 2018–19, 14 students received support, including 8 research assistantships with tuition reimbursements available (averaging $5,227 per year), 7 teaching assistantships with tuition reimbursements available (averaging $7,176 per year); career-related internships or fieldwork, Federal Work-Study, scholarships/grants, unspecified assistantships, and health care benefits (for full-time research or teaching assistantship recipients) also available. Support available to part-time students. Financial award application deadline: 3/1; financial award applicants required to submit FAFSA. In 2018, 275 master's awarded. *Program availability:* Part-time, evening/weekend, 100% online. Offers accounting (MS); business (EMBA, MBA, MS); business administration (MBA); management (MS); management of secure information systems (MS); technology management (MS). *Application fee:* $75 ($80 for international students). Electronic applications accepted. *Application Contact:* Paige Wolf, Senior Assistant Dean of Graduate Programs, 703-993-1758, Fax: 703-993-1870, E-mail: pwolf1@gmu.edu. *Interim Dean*, Anne Magro, 703-993-1765, Fax: 703-993-2472, E-mail: amagro@gmu.edu.

Volgenau School of Engineering Students: 816 full-time (323 women), 923 part-time (242 women); includes 454 minority (92 Black or African American, non-Hispanic/Latino; 1 American Indian or Alaska Native, non-Hispanic/Latino; 256 Asian, non-Hispanic/Latino; 86 Hispanic/Latino; 19 Two or more races, non-Hispanic/Latino), 674 international. Average age 30. 1,684 applicants, 71% accepted, 462 enrolled. *Faculty:* 194 full-time (52 women), 177 part-time/adjunct (30 women). Expenses: Contact institution. *Financial support:* In 2018–19, 382 students received support, including 6 fellowships (averaging $12,267 per year), 148 research assistantships with tuition reimbursements available (averaging $18,707 per year), 232 teaching assistantships with tuition reimbursements available (averaging $12,405 per year); career-related internships or fieldwork, Federal Work-Study, scholarships/grants, unspecified assistantships, and health care benefits (for full-time research or teaching assistantship recipients) also available. Support available to part-time students. Financial award application deadline: 3/1; financial award applicants required to submit FAFSA. In 2018, 575 master's, 51 doctorates, 89 other advanced degrees awarded. *Program availability:* Part-time, evening/weekend, 100% online. Offers applied information technology (MS); bioengineering (PhD); biostatistics (MS); computer engineering (MS); computer science (MS, PhD, Certificate); construction project management (MS); data analytics engineering (MS); electrical and computer engineering (PhD, Certificate); engineering (MS, PhD, Certificate); information sciences and technology (Certificate); information technology (PhD); operations research (MS); statistical science (MS, PhD); statistics (Certificate); systems engineering and operations research (PhD, Certificate); transportation engineering (PhD). *Application fee:* $75 ($80 for international students). Electronic applications accepted. *Application Contact:* Suddaf Ismail, Director, Graduate Admissions and Recruitment, 703-993-9115, Fax: 703-993-1242, E-mail: sismail@gmu.edu. *Dean*, Kenneth S. Ball, 703-993-1498, Fax: 703-993-1734, E-mail: vsdean@gmu.edu.

GEORGETOWN COLLEGE, Georgetown, KY 40324-1696

General Information Independent-religious, coed, comprehensive institution. *Graduate housing:* On-campus housing not available.

GRADUATE UNITS

Department of Education *Program availability:* Part-time. Offers reading and writing (MA Ed); special education (MA Ed); teaching (MA Ed).

GEORGETOWN UNIVERSITY, Washington, DC 20057

General Information Independent-religious, coed, university. CGS member. *Graduate housing:* On-campus housing not available.

GRADUATE UNITS

Graduate School of Arts and Sciences Offers American government (MA); analytical chemistry (PhD); arts and sciences (EMBA, EML, EMPL, GEMBA, MA, MAE, MALS,

MAT, MBA, MDSPP, MIPM, MPM, MPP, MPS, MS, DLS, DNP, PhD, Certificate); biochemistry (PhD); biochemistry and molecular and cellular biology (MS, PhD); bioethics (MA); biohazardous threat agents and emerging infectious diseases (MS); biology (PhD); biomedical science policy and advocacy (MS); biostatistics (MS, Certificate); British and American literature (MA); communication, culture, and technology (MA); computational chemistry (PhD); computer science (MS, PhD); conflict resolution (MA); democracy and governance (MA); development, management and policy (MA); econometrics (PhD); economic development (PhD); economic theory (PhD); epidemiology (Certificate); general microbiology and immunology (MS); German (MA, PhD); global history (MA); global infectious diseases (PhD); global, international and comparative history (MA); government (PhD); health physics (MS); history (MA, PhD); human development and public policy (PhD); industrial organization (PhD); inorganic chemistry (PhD); international macro and finance (PhD); international trade (PhD); labor economics (PhD); language and communication (PhD); lifespan cognitive neuroscience (PhD); linguistics (PhD, MS); macroeconomics (PhD); materials chemistry (PhD); mathematics (MS); microbiology and immunology (PhD); neuroscience (PhD); nuclear nonproliferation (MS); organic chemistry (PhD); pharmacology (MS, PhD); philosophy (PhD); physiology (MS); public economics and political economy (PhD); Spanish (MS, PhD); statistics (MS); theology (PhD); theoretical chemistry (PhD).

McDonough School of Business Offers business administration (EMBA, GEMBA, MBA); finance (MS); leadership (EML).

School of Continuing Studies Offers American studies (MALS); applied intelligence (MPS); Catholic studies (MALS); classical civilizations (MALS); emergency and disaster management (MPS); ethics and the professions (MALS); global strategic communications (MPS); hospitality management (MPS); human resources management (MPS); humanities (MALS); individualized study (MALS); integrated marketing communications (MPS); international affairs (MALS); Islam and Muslim-Christian relations (MALS); journalism (MPS); liberal studies (DLS); literature and society (MALS); medieval and early modern European studies (MALS); public relations and corporate communications (MPS); real estate (MPS); religious studies (MALS); social and public policy (MALS); sports industry management (MPS); systems engineering management (MPS); technology management (MPS); the theory and practice of American democracy (MALS); urban and regional planning (MPS); visual culture (MALS). MPS in systems engineering management offered jointly with Stevens Institute of Technology.

School of Nursing and Health Studies Offers acute care nurse practitioner (MS); clinical nurse specialist (MS); family nurse practitioner (MS); health systems administration (MS); nurse anesthesia (MS); nurse-midwifery (MS); nursing (DNP); nursing education (MS).

Walsh School of Foreign Service Offers Asian studies (MA); contemporary Arab studies (MA, Certificate); Eurasian, Russian and East European studies (MA); foreign service (MA, MS, Certificate); German and European studies (MA); global business and finance (MS); global human development (MA); global politics and security (MS); international development (MS); Latin American studies (MA); security studies (MA); self-designed studies (MS).

Law Center *Program availability:* Part-time, evening/weekend. Offers environmental law (LL M); global health law (LL M); global health law and international institutions (LL M); individualized study (LL M); international business and economic law (LL M); law (JD, SJD); national security law (LL M); securities and financial regulation (LL M); taxation (LL M).

Master of Arts in Learning and Design Program *Program availability:* Part-time, evening/weekend. Offers learning and design (MA). Electronic applications accepted.

McCourt School of Public Policy Expenses: Contact institution. *Financial support:* Research assistantships, teaching assistantships, career-related internships or fieldwork, scholarships/grants, and unspecified assistantships available. Financial award application deadline: 2/1; financial award applicants required to submit FAFSA. *Program availability:* Part-time. Offers data science for public policy (MDSPP); international development policy (MIDP); policy leadership (EMPL); policy management (MPM); public policy (MPP). *Application deadline:* For fall admission, 1/15 priority date for domestic students. Applications are processed on a rolling basis. *Application fee:* $90. Electronic applications accepted. *Application Contact:* Julie Ito, Director of Admissions, 202-687-0678, E-mail: mccourtadmissions@georgetown.edu. *Dean, McCourt School of Public Policy,* Dr. Maria Cancian, 202-687-6163, E-mail: mcancian@georgetown.edu.

School of Medicine Offers medicine (MD).

THE GEORGE WASHINGTON UNIVERSITY, Washington, DC 20052

General Information Independent, coed, university. CGS member. *Enrollment:* 7,745 full-time matriculated graduate/professional students (4,357 women), 7,766 part-time matriculated graduate/professional students (4,845 women). *Enrollment by degree level:* 10,790 master's, 4,205 doctoral, 516 other advanced degrees. *Graduate faculty:* 1,332 full-time (623 women), 1,320 part-time/adjunct (618 women). *Graduate housing:* Room and/or apartments available on a first-come, first-served basis to single students; on-campus housing not available to married students. *Student services:* Campus employment opportunities, campus safety program, career counseling, exercise/wellness program, free psychological counseling, international student services, low-cost health insurance, multicultural affairs office, services for students with disabilities, teacher training, writing training. *Library facilities:* Gelman Library.

Computer facilities A campuswide network can be accessed from student residence rooms and from off campus. Website: http://www.gwu.edu/

General Application Contact: Jeanne Fiander, Executive Director, Graduate Enrollment Management, 202-994-5136, Fax: 202-994-0371, E-mail: jfian@gwu.edu.

GRADUATE UNITS

College of Professional Studies Students: 278 full-time (108 women), 661 part-time (394 women); includes 354 minority (144 Black or African American, non-Hispanic/Latino; 7 American Indian or Alaska Native, non-Hispanic/Latino; 42 Asian, non-Hispanic/Latino; 140 Hispanic/Latino; 2 Native Hawaiian or other Pacific Islander, non-Hispanic/Latino; 19 Two or more races, non-Hispanic/Latino), 35 international. Average age 34. 755 applicants, 88% accepted, 382 enrolled. *Faculty:* 26 full-time (9 women), 89 part-time/adjunct (27 women). Expenses: Contact institution. In 2018, 415 master's, 66 other advanced degrees awarded. Offers healthcare corporate compliance (Graduate Certificate); law firm management (MPS, Graduate Certificate); paralegal studies (MPS, Graduate Certificate); publishing (MPS). *Application Contact:* Kristin Williams, Associate Provost, Graduate Enrollment, 202-994-0467, Fax: 202-994-0371, E-mail: ksw@gwu.edu. *Dean,* Christopher J. Deering, 571-553-5004.

Graduate School of Political Management Students: 34 full-time (12 women), 216 part-time (100 women); includes 105 minority (27 Black or African American, non-Hispanic/Latino; 4 American Indian or Alaska Native, non-Hispanic/Latino; 5 Asian, non-Hispanic/Latino; 63 Hispanic/Latino; 1 Native Hawaiian or other Pacific Islander,

non-Hispanic/Latino; 5 Two or more races, non-Hispanic/Latino), 13 international. Average age 32. 167 applicants, 90% accepted, 85 enrolled. *Faculty:* 8 full-time (2 women), 6 part-time/adjunct (1 woman). Expenses: Contact institution. *Financial support:* In 2018–19, 18 students received support. Fellowships with tuition reimbursements available, scholarships/grants, and tuition waivers available. Financial award application deadline: 2/1. In 2018, 103 master's, 6 other advanced degrees awarded. Offers community advocacy (Graduate Certificate); legislative affairs (MPS); PACs and political management (Graduate Certificate); political management (MPS). *Application deadline:* For fall admission, 6/15 priority date for domestic students, 4/1 priority date for international students; for spring admission, 11/15 priority date for domestic students, 10/1 priority date for international students. Applications are processed on a rolling basis. *Application fee:* $75. Electronic applications accepted. *Application Contact:* Information Contact, 202-994-6000, Fax: 202-994-6006. *Director,* Lara M. Brown, 202-994-4545.

Columbian College of Arts and Sciences Students: 1,620 full-time (1,051 women), 1,035 part-time (621 women); includes 613 minority (190 Black or African American, non-Hispanic/Latino; 4 American Indian or Alaska Native, non-Hispanic/Latino; 163 Asian, non-Hispanic/Latino; 194 Hispanic/Latino; 5 Native Hawaiian or other Pacific Islander, non-Hispanic/Latino; 57 Two or more races, non-Hispanic/Latino), 673 international. Average age 28. 7,006 applicants, 45% accepted, 962 enrolled. Expenses: Contact institution. *Financial support:* Fellowships, research assistantships, teaching assistantships, career-related internships or fieldwork, Federal Work-Study, scholarships/grants, tuition waivers, and unspecified assistantships available. Support available to part-time students. Financial award application deadline: 2/1. In 2018, 931 master's, 125 doctorates, 98 other advanced degrees awarded. *Program availability:* Part-time, evening/weekend. Offers American studies (PhD); analytical chemistry (MS, PhD); anthropology (MA, PhD); applied mathematics (MS); applied social psychology (PhD); art and the book (MA); art education (MA, MAT); art history (MA); art therapy (MA, Graduate Certificate); arts and sciences (MA, MAT, MFA, MFS, MPA, MPP, MS, PhD, Psy D, Certificate, Graduate Certificate); biological sciences (MS, PhD); biostatistics (MS, PhD); ceramics (MFA); classical acting (MFA); clinical psychology (PhD); cognitive neuroscience (PhD); crime scene investigation (MFS); criminology (MA); dance (MFA); decorative arts and design history (MA); drawing/painting (MFA); economics (MA, PhD); English (MA, PhD); environmental and resource policy (MA); exhibit design (Graduate Certificate); exhibition design (MA); financial mathematics (Graduate Certificate); folk life (MA); forensic chemistry (MFS); forensic molecular biology (MFS); forensic toxicology (MFS); geography (MA, Graduate Certificate); high-technology crime investigation (MS); historic preservation (MA); history (MA, PhD); human resources management (MA); inorganic chemistry (MS, PhD); interior design (MA, MFA); international development (MA); Islam (MA); legal institutions and theory (MA); material culture (MA); materials science (MS, PhD); mathematics (MA, PhD, Graduate Certificate); medical anthropology (MA); museum collections management and care (Graduate Certificate); museum studies (MA); museum training (MA); new media (MFA); new media photojournalism (MA); non-profit management (Graduate Certificate); organic chemistry (MS, PhD); organizational management (Graduate Certificate); philosophy and social policy (MA); photography (MFA); physical chemistry (MS, PhD); physics (MA, PhD); political science (MA); production design (MFA); professional psychology (MA, Psy D, Graduate Certificate); sculpture (MFA); security management (MFS); sociology (MA); speech-language pathology (MA); statistics (MS, PhD); survey design and data analysis (Graduate Certificate); women's studies (MA, Certificate). *Application deadline:* For fall admission, 1/15 priority date for domestic and international students; for spring admission, 10/1 priority date for domestic and international students. Applications are processed on a rolling basis. *Application fee:* $75. Electronic applications accepted. *Application Contact:* Linda Wilkerson, Executive Assistant, 202-994-6210, Fax: 202-994-6213, E-mail: askccas@gwu.edu. *Dean,* Ben Vinson, III, 202-994-6130, E-mail: bvinson3@gwu.edu.

Institute for Biomedical Sciences Average age 25. Expenses: Contact institution. *Financial support:* In 2018–19, 24 students received support. Fellowships with full tuition reimbursements available, Federal Work-Study, institutionally sponsored loans, and tuition waivers available. *Program availability:* Part-time, evening/weekend. Offers biochemistry and systems biology (PhD); microbiology and immunology (PhD); molecular and cellular oncology (PhD); molecular medicine (PhD); neurosciences (PhD); pharmacology and physiology (PhD). *Application deadline:* For fall admission, 12/15 priority date for domestic and international students. Applications are processed on a rolling basis. *Application fee:* $60. Electronic applications accepted. *Application Contact:* 202-994-2179, Fax: 202-994-0967, E-mail: gwibs@gwu.edu. *Director,* Dr. Linda L. Werling, 202-994-2918, Fax: 202-994-0967, E-mail: lwerling@gwu.edu.

School of Media and Public Affairs Students: 28 full-time (15 women), 16 part-time (12 women); includes 6 minority (2 Black or African American, non-Hispanic/Latino; 1 Asian, non-Hispanic/Latino; 4 Hispanic/Latino; 1 Two or more races, non-Hispanic/Latino), 5 international. Average age 26. 108 applicants, 60% accepted, 23 enrolled. Expenses: Contact institution. *Financial support:* In 2018–19, fellowships with tuition reimbursements (averaging $10,000 per year), teaching assistantships with tuition reimbursements (averaging $5,000 per year) were awarded. Financial award application deadline: 1/15. In 2018, 30 master's, 15 other advanced degrees awarded. Offers media and public affairs (MA, Graduate Certificate). *Application deadline:* For fall admission, 4/1 priority date for domestic students, 1/15 priority date for international students; for spring admission, 10/1 priority date for domestic students, 9/1 priority date for international students. Applications are processed on a rolling basis. *Application fee:* $75. Electronic applications accepted. *Application Contact:* Information Contact, 202-994-6227, Fax: 202-994-5806, E-mail: smpa@gwu.edu. *Director,* Frank Sesno, 202-994-9553, E-mail: sesno@gwu.edu.

Trachtenberg School of Public Policy and Public Administration *Program availability:* Part-time, evening/weekend, online learning. Offers environmental resource policy (MA); public administration (MPA); public policy (MPP); public policy and administration (PhD). Electronic applications accepted.

Elliott School of International Affairs Students: 565 full-time (300 women), 221 part-time (124 women); includes 219 minority (54 Black or African American, non-Hispanic/Latino; 1 American Indian or Alaska Native, non-Hispanic/Latino; 49 Asian, non-Hispanic/Latino; 86 Hispanic/Latino; 29 Two or more races, non-Hispanic/Latino), 107 international. Average age 27. 1,643 applicants, 81% accepted, 357 enrolled. Expenses: Contact institution. *Financial support:* In 2018–19, 155 students received support. Fellowships with partial tuition reimbursements available and Federal Work-Study available. Financial award application deadline: 1/15; financial award applicants required to submit FAFSA. In 2018, 355 master's, 3 other advanced degrees awarded. *Program availability:* Part-time. Offers Asian studies (MA); European and Eurasian studies (MA); global communication (MA); global gender policy (Graduate Certificate); international affairs (MA, MIPP, MIS, Graduate Certificate); international development studies (MA); international policy and practice (MIPP); international science and technology policy (MA, Graduate Certificate); international studies (MIS); international trade and investment policy (MA); Latin American and hemispheric studies (MA); Middle East studies (MA); security policy studies (MA). *Application deadline:* For fall admission, 1/15 priority date for domestic students, 1/15 for international students; for spring admission, 10/1 for domestic and international students. *Application fee:* $75. Electronic applications accepted. *Application Contact:* Nicole A. Campbell, Director of Graduate Admissions, 202-994-7050, Fax: 202-994-9537, E-mail: esiagrad@gwu.edu. *Dean,* Rueben E. Brigety, 202-994-6240, Fax: 202-994-0335, E-mail: esiadean@gwu.edu.

Graduate School of Education and Human Development Students: 384 full-time (312 women), 1,060 part-time (797 women); includes 497 minority (253 Black or African American, non-Hispanic/Latino; 5 American Indian or Alaska Native, non-Hispanic/Latino; 66 Asian, non-Hispanic/Latino; 126 Hispanic/Latino; 1 Native Hawaiian or other Pacific Islander, non-Hispanic/Latino; 46 Two or more races, non-Hispanic/Latino), 88 international. Average age 36. 1,625 applicants, 69% accepted, 567 enrolled. Expenses: Contact institution. *Financial support:* In 2018–19, 279 students received support. Fellowships, research assistantships, teaching assistantships, career-related internships or fieldwork, Federal Work-Study, and tuition waivers (full and partial) available. Support available to part-time students. Financial award application deadline: 1/15. In 2018, 390 master's, 74 doctorates, 104 other advanced degrees awarded. *Program availability:* Part-time, evening/weekend, online learning. Offers adolescents with emotional and behavioral disabilities (MA Ed/HD); adolescents with learning disabilities (MA Ed/HD); Arabic (M Ed); art education (MA); autism spectrum disorder (MA Ed/HD); bilingual special education (MA Ed, Certificate); brain injury special education (MA Ed/HD); brain injury specialist (MA Ed/HD); clinical mental health counseling (MA); college teaching and academic leadership (MA Ed/HD, Ed S); counseling (PhD, Ed S); counseling culturally and linguistically diverse persons (MA Ed/HD, Certificate); curriculum and instruction (MA Ed, Ed D, Ed S, Graduate Certificate); design and assessment of adult learning (Graduate Certificate); e-learning (Graduate Certificate); early childhood special education (MA Ed/HD); education and human development (M Ed, MA, MA Ed, MA Ed/HD, MAT, Ed D, PhD, Certificate, Ed S, Graduate Certificate, Teaching Certificate); education policy (Ed D); education policy studies (MA Ed); educational administration (Ed D); educational administration and policy studies (Ed D); educational leadership and administration (MA Ed, Certificate, Ed S); educational technology leadership (MA Ed); elementary education (MA Ed/HD); forensic rehabilitation counseling (Graduate Certificate); general administration (MA Ed/HD, Ed S); higher education administration (MA Ed/HD, Ed D, Ed S); higher education finance (MA Ed/HD, Ed S); human and organizational learning (Ed D, Ed S); human resource development (MA); infant special education (MA Ed/HD); instructional design (Graduate Certificate); integrating technology into education (Graduate Certificate); interdisciplinary transition services (MA Ed/HD); international education (MA Ed, MA Ed/HD, Ed S); Italian (M Ed); job development and placement (Graduate Certificate); leadership development (Graduate Certificate); leadership in educational technology (Graduate Certificate); math (M Ed); multimedia development (Graduate Certificate); museum education (MAT); organizational learning and change (Graduate Certificate); physics (MA Ed/HD, Ed S); policy (MA Ed/HD, Ed S); rehabilitation counseling (MA Ed/HD); Russian (M Ed); school counseling (MA Ed, Graduate Certificate); secondary education (M Ed); secondary special education and transition services (MA Ed/HD); special education (Ed D, Ed S); special education and transition services (Certificate); special education for children with emotional and behavioral disabilities (MA Ed/HD); special education for culturally and linguistically diverse persons (MA Ed/HD, Certificate); student affairs administration (MA Ed/HD, Ed S); substance abuse and psychiatric disabilities (MA Ed/HD); training and educational technology (Graduate Certificate); transition special education (Teaching Certificate); traumatic brain injury (MA Ed/HD). *Application deadline:* For fall admission, 1/15 priority date for domestic students; for spring admission, 10/1 for domestic students. Applications are processed on a rolling basis. *Application fee:* $75. Electronic applications accepted. *Application Contact:* Sarah Lang, Director of Graduate Admissions, 202-994-1447, Fax: 202-994-7207, E-mail: slang@gwu.edu. *Dean,* Michael Feuer, 202-994-6161, Fax: 202-994-7207, E-mail: mjfeuer@gwu.edu.

Law School Students: 1,499 full-time (777 women), 234 part-time (107 women); includes 387 minority (137 Black or African American, non-Hispanic/Latino; 11 American Indian or Alaska Native, non-Hispanic/Latino; 191 Asian, non-Hispanic/Latino; 35 Hispanic/Latino; 4 Native Hawaiian or other Pacific Islander, non-Hispanic/Latino; 9 Two or more races, non-Hispanic/Latino), 173 international. Average age 27. 173 applicants, 100% accepted, 125 enrolled. *Faculty:* 84 full-time (33 women), 233 part-time/adjunct (65 women). Expenses: Contact institution. *Financial support:* Research assistantships, career-related internships or fieldwork, Federal Work-Study, institutionally sponsored loans, scholarships/grants, and tuition waivers (full and partial) available. Support available to part-time students. Financial award application deadline: 3/1; financial award applicants required to submit CSS PROFILE or FAFSA. In 2018, 151 master's, 2 doctorates awarded. *Program availability:* Part-time, evening/weekend. Offers law (SJD); national security and U.S. foreign relations (LL M). *Application deadline:* For fall admission, 3/1 for domestic students. Applications are processed on a rolling basis. *Application fee:* $75. *Application Contact:* Sophia Sim, Assistant Dean of Admissions and Financial Aid, 202-994-7235, Fax: 202-739-0624, E-mail: ssim@law.gwu.edu. *Dean,* Blake D. Morant, E-mail: bmorant@law.gwu.edu.

Milken Institute School of Public Health Students: 582 full-time (473 women), 1,535 part-time (1,174 women); includes 1,005 minority (388 Black or African American, non-Hispanic/Latino; 8 American Indian or Alaska Native, non-Hispanic/Latino; 350 Asian, non-Hispanic/Latino; 181 Hispanic/Latino; 5 Native Hawaiian or other Pacific Islander, non-Hispanic/Latino; 73 Two or more races, non-Hispanic/Latino), 50 international. Average age 31. 3,418 applicants, 66% accepted, 681 enrolled. Expenses: Contact institution. *Financial support:* In 2018–19, 71 students received support. Career-related internships or fieldwork, Federal Work-Study, institutionally sponsored loans, scholarships/grants, and tuition waivers (partial) available. Support available to part-time students. Financial award application deadline: 2/15. In 2018, 718 master's, 14 doctorates, 4 other advanced degrees awarded. *Program availability:* Part-time, evening/weekend. Offers biostatistics (MPH); environ-occupational health (Dr PH); epidemiology (MPH); exercise and nutrition sciences (MS); global health (Dr PH); global health communication (MPH); health policy and management (EMHA, MHA, MPH, MS, Graduate Certificate); microbiology and emerging infectious diseases (MSPH); prevention and community health (MPH, Dr PH); public health (EMHA, MHA, MPH, MS, MSPH, Dr PH, Graduate Certificate). *Application deadline:* For fall admission, 2/15 priority date for domestic students, 2/15 for international students. Applications are processed on a rolling basis. *Application Contact:* Director of Admissions, 202-994-2160, Fax: 202-994-1860, E-mail: sphhsinfo@gwumc.edu. *Dean,* Dr. Lynn Goldman, 202-994-5179, E-mail: goldmanl@gwu.edu.

School of Business Students: 822 full-time (407 women), 805 part-time (423 women); includes 492 minority (190 Black or African American, non-Hispanic/Latino; 3 American Indian or Alaska Native, non-Hispanic/Latino; 149 Asian, non-Hispanic/Latino; 107 Hispanic/Latino; 4 Native Hawaiian or other Pacific Islander, non-Hispanic/Latino; 39 Two or more races, non-Hispanic/Latino), 584 international. Average age 32. 3,792 applicants, 55% accepted, 568 enrolled. Expenses: Contact institution. *Financial support:* In 2018–19, 194 students received support. Fellowships, teaching assistantships, career-related internships or fieldwork, Federal Work-Study, institutionally sponsored loans, and tuition waivers (partial) available. Financial award application deadline: 4/1. In 2018, 745 master's, 2 doctorates, 169 other advanced degrees awarded. *Program availability:* Part-time, evening/weekend, online learning. Offers accountancy (M Accy); business (M Accy, MBA, MS, MSF, MSIST, MTA, PMBA, PhD, Certificate, Professional Certificate); business administration (MBA); business analytics (MS, Certificate); destination management (Professional Certificate); event and meeting management (MTA); event management (Professional Certificate); finance (MSF, PhD); finance and investments (MBA); government contracts (MS); hospitality management (MTA); individualized studies (MTA); information and decision systems (PhD); information systems (MSIST); information systems development (MSIST); information systems management (MBA); information systems project management (MSIST); international business (PhD); management information systems (MSIST); management of science, technology, and innovation (MBA, PhD); marketing (MBA, PhD); project management (MS); sport management (MTA); strategic management and public policy (MBA, PhD); sustainable tourism destination management (MTA); tourism and hospitality management (MBA); walkable urban real estate development (Professional Certificate). PMBA also offered in Alexandria and Ashburn, VA. *Application deadline:* For fall admission, 4/1 priority date for domestic students; for spring admission, 10/1 for domestic students. Applications are processed on a rolling basis. *Application fee:* $75. Electronic applications accepted. *Application Contact:* Christopher Storer, Executive Director, Graduate Admissions, 202-994-1212, E-mail: gwmba@gwu.edu. *Dean,* Dr. Vivek Choudhury, 202-994-6380, E-mail: vchoudhury@gwu.edu.

School of Engineering and Applied Science Students: 919 full-time (217 women), 1,149 part-time (318 women); includes 408 minority (194 Black or African American, non-Hispanic/Latino; 8 American Indian or Alaska Native, non-Hispanic/Latino; 145 Asian, non-Hispanic/Latino; 40 Hispanic/Latino; 2 Native Hawaiian or other Pacific Islander, non-Hispanic/Latino; 19 Two or more races, non-Hispanic/Latino), 838 international. Average age 32. 3,123 applicants, 74% accepted, 678 enrolled. Expenses: Contact institution. *Financial support:* In 2018–19, 216 students received support. Fellowships, research assistantships, teaching assistantships, career-related internships or fieldwork, Federal Work-Study, institutionally sponsored loans, and tuition waivers (full and partial) available. Financial award application deadline: 3/1; financial award applicants required to submit FAFSA. In 2018, 609 master's, 165 doctorates, 50 other advanced degrees awarded. *Program availability:* Part-time, evening/weekend. Offers biomedical engineering (MS, PhD); civil and environmental engineering (MS, PhD, App Sc, Engr, Graduate Certificate); computer science (M, D Sc); cybersecurity (MS); electrical engineering (MS, PhD); engineering and applied science (MS, D Sc, PhD, App Sc, Engr, Graduate Certificate); mechanical and aerospace engineering (MS, PhD, App Sc, Engr, Graduate Certificate); regulatory biomedical engineering (MS); system engineering (PhD); telecommunication and computers (MS). *Application deadline:* For fall admission, 3/1 for domestic students; for spring admission, 10/1 for domestic students. Applications are processed on a rolling basis. *Application fee:* $75. *Application Contact:* Adina Lav, Marketing, Recruiting and Admissions, 202-994-5827, Fax: 202-994-0909, E-mail: engineering@gwu.edu. *Dean,* David S. Dolling, 202-994-6080, E-mail: dolling@gwu.edu.

School of Medicine and Health Sciences Students: 1,025 full-time (667 women), 513 part-time (392 women); includes 679 minority (171 Black or African American, non-Hispanic/Latino; 5 American Indian or Alaska Native, non-Hispanic/Latino; 314 Asian, non-Hispanic/Latino; 142 Hispanic/Latino; 6 Native Hawaiian or other Pacific Islander, non-Hispanic/Latino; 41 Two or more races, non-Hispanic/Latino), 31 international. Average age 30. 3,035 applicants, 16% accepted, 307 enrolled. Expenses: Contact institution. *Financial support:* Career-related internships or fieldwork, Federal Work-Study, and institutionally sponsored loans available. In 2018, 228 master's, 43 doctorates, 183 other advanced degrees awarded. Offers clinical practice management (MSHS); clinical research administration (MSHS); emergency services management (MSHS); end-of-life care (MSHS); immunohematology (MSHS); immunohematology and biotechnology (MSHS); medicine (MD); medicine and health sciences (MSHS, DPT, MD, OTD, Graduate Certificate); physical therapy (DPT); physician assistant (MSHS). *Application deadline:* Applications are processed on a rolling basis. *Application fee:* $75. *Application Contact:* Admissions, 202-994-3748, Fax: 202-994-1753, E-mail: medadmit@gwu.edu. *Dean,* Dr. Jeffrey Akman, 202-994-3727, E-mail: akman@gwu.edu.

School of Nursing Students: 51 full-time (45 women), 552 part-time (494 women); includes 210 minority (86 Black or African American, non-Hispanic/Latino; 2 American Indian or Alaska Native, non-Hispanic/Latino; 72 Asian, non-Hispanic/Latino; 40 Hispanic/Latino; 1 Native Hawaiian or other Pacific Islander, non-Hispanic/Latino; 9 Two or more races, non-Hispanic/Latino). Average age 35. 541 applicants, 73% accepted, 186 enrolled. Expenses: Contact institution. In 2018, 168 master's, 37 doctorates, 5 other advanced degrees awarded. Offers adult nurse practitioner (MSN, DNP, Post-Master's Certificate); clinical research administration (MSN); family nurse practitioner (MSN, Post-Master's Certificate); health care quality (MSN, Post-Master's Certificate); nursing leadership and management (MSN); nursing practice (DNP); palliative care nurse practitioner (Post-Master's Certificate). *Application Contact:* Kristin Williams, Associate Provost for Graduate Enrollment Management, 202-994-0467, Fax: 202-994-0371, E-mail: ksw@gwu.edu. *Dean,* Pamela R. Jeffries, 202-994-3725, E-mail: pjeffries@gwu.edu.

GEORGIA CAMPUS–PHILADELPHIA COLLEGE OF OSTEOPATHIC MEDICINE, Suwanee, GA 30024

General Information Independent, coed, graduate-only institution. *Graduate housing:* On-campus housing not available.

GRADUATE UNITS

Doctor of Osteopathic Medicine Program Offers osteopathic medicine (DO). Electronic applications accepted.

Doctor of Physical Therapy Program Offers physical therapy (DPT).

School of Pharmacy Offers pharmacy (Pharm D). Electronic applications accepted.

GEORGIA COLLEGE & STATE UNIVERSITY, Milledgeville, GA 31061

General Information State-supported, coed, comprehensive institution. *Graduate housing:* Room and/or apartments available on a first-come, first-served basis to single students; on-campus housing not available to married students. Housing application deadline: 5/1.

GRADUATE UNITS

Graduate School *Program availability:* Part-time, evening/weekend, 100% online, blended/hybrid learning. Electronic applications accepted.

College of Arts and Sciences *Program availability:* Part-time, evening/weekend, 100% online. Offers arts and sciences (MA, MFA, MM Ed, MPA, MS, MSCJ); biology (MS); creative writing (MFA); criminal justice (MSCJ); English (MA, MFA); music (MM Ed); public administration (MPA). Electronic applications accepted.

College of Health Sciences *Program availability:* Part-time, evening/weekend. Offers art therapy (MA); health and human performance (MS); health sciences (M Ed, MA, MAT, MMT, MS, MSN, DNP, Post-MSN Certificate); kinesiology/health education (MAT); music therapy (MMT); nursing (MSN, Post-MSN Certificate); nursing practice (DNP). Electronic applications accepted.

The John H. Lounsbury College of Education *Program availability:* Evening/weekend, 100% online, blended/hybrid learning. Offers curriculum and instruction (M Ed); early childhood education (M Ed); education (M Ed, MAT, Ed S); educational leadership (M Ed, Ed S); instructional technology (M Ed); library media (M Ed); middle grades education (M Ed, MAT); secondary education (MAT); special education (M Ed, MAT, Ed S); teacher education (Ed S). Electronic applications accepted.

The J. Whitney Bunting School of Business *Program availability:* Part-time, evening/weekend, 100% online, blended/hybrid learning. Offers accounting (M Acc); business (M Acc, MBA, MLSCM, MMIS); business administration (MBA); logistics (MLSCM); management information systems (MMIS). Electronic applications accepted.

GEORGIA INSTITUTE OF TECHNOLOGY, Atlanta, GA 30332-0001

General Information State-supported, coed, university. CGS member. *Graduate housing:* Rooms and/or apartments available on a first-come, first-served basis to single and married students. Housing application deadline: 6/1. *Research affiliation:* Oak Ridge National Laboratory (energy, health, environment), Children's Healthcare of Atlanta (pediatric biomedical and device research), Georgia State University (brain imaging), Southeastern Universities Research Association (high-energy physics), Emory University Medical School (biomedical engineering), Zoo Atlanta (environmental design, environmental psychology).

GRADUATE UNITS

Graduate Studies *Program availability:* Part-time, evening/weekend, 100% online. Offers algorithms, combinatorics, and optimization (PhD); analytics (MS); bioengineering (MS, PhD); bioinformatics (MS, PhD); computational science and engineering (MS, PhD); human computer interaction (MS); paper science and engineering (MS, PhD); quantitative and computational finance (MS); statistics (MS). Electronic applications accepted.

College of Computing *Program availability:* Part-time, online learning. Offers computer science (MS, PhD); computing (MS, PhD); human-centered computing (MS, PhD); information security (MS); robotics (PhD). Electronic applications accepted.

College of Design Offers architecture (M Arch, MS, PhD); building construction (PhD); city and regional planning (PhD); design (M Arch, MCRP, MS, PhD); economic development (MCRP); environmental planning and management (MCRP); geographic information systems (MCRP); industrial design (MID); integrated facility and property management (MS); integrated project delivery systems (MS); land and community development (MCRP); land use planning (MCRP); music technology (MS, PhD); program management (MS); residential construction development (MS); transportation (MCRP); urban design (MCRP). Electronic applications accepted.

College of Engineering *Program availability:* Part-time, online learning. Offers aerospace engineering (MS, PhD); applied systems engineering (PMS); biomedical engineering (PhD); chemical engineering (MS, PhD); civil engineering (MS, PhD); electrical and computer engineering (MS, PhD); engineering (MS, MSMP, MSNE, PhD); engineering science and mechanics (MS, PhD); environmental engineering (MS); health systems (MS); industrial and systems engineering (MS, PhD); industrial engineering (MS, PhD); international logistics (MS); materials science and engineering (MS, PhD); mechanical engineering (MS, MSME, MSMP, MSNE, PhD); medical physics (MS, MSMP); nuclear and radiological engineering (PhD); nuclear and radiological engineering and medical physics (MS, MSMP, MSNE, PhD); nuclear engineering (MSNE); operations research (MS, PhD). Electronic applications accepted.

College of Sciences *Program availability:* Part-time. Offers applied physiology (PhD); biology (MS, PhD); chemistry and biochemistry (MS, PhD); earth and atmospheric sciences (MS, PhD); mathematics (MS, PhD); physics (MS, PhD); prosthetics and orthotics (MS); psychology (MS, PhD); sciences (MS, PhD). Electronic applications accepted.

Ivan Allen College of Liberal Arts *Program availability:* Part-time. Offers digital media (MS, PhD); economics (MS, PhD); history and sociology of technology and science (MS, PhD); international affairs (MS); liberal arts (MS, PhD); public policy (MS, PhD). Electronic applications accepted.

Scheller College of Business *Program availability:* Part-time, evening/weekend. Offers business (MBA, MS, PhD); business administration (MBA); global business (MBA); management (MS, PhD); management of technology (MBA). Electronic applications accepted.

GEORGIAN COURT UNIVERSITY, Lakewood, NJ 08701-2697

General Information Independent-religious, coed, comprehensive institution. *Enrollment:* 149 full-time matriculated graduate/professional students (122 women), 521 part-time matriculated graduate/professional students (408 women). *Enrollment by degree level:* 670 master's. *Graduate faculty:* 30 full-time (16 women), 45 part-time/adjunct (29 women). *Tuition:* Full-time $856; part-time $856 per credit hour. *Required fees:* $968; $496 per unit. $248 per semester. Tuition and fees vary according to campus/location and program. *Graduate housing:* Room and/or apartments available on a first-come, first-served basis to single students; on-campus housing not available to married students. Housing application deadline: 5/1. *Student services:* Campus employment opportunities, campus safety program, career counseling, exercise/wellness program, free psychological counseling, low-cost health insurance, services for students with disabilities, teacher training. *Library facilities:* The Sister Mary Joseph Cunningham Library. *Collection:* Books: 129,447 (physical), 117,590 (digital/electronic); Serial titles: 2,898 (physical), 33,651 (digital/electronic); Databases: 115. Weekly public service hours: 85; students can reserve study rooms.

Computer facilities: 221 computers available on campus for general student use. A campuswide network can be accessed from student residence rooms and from off campus. Online class registration is available.
Website: http://www.georgian.edu/

General Application Contact: Patrick Givens, Director of Graduate and Professional Studies Admissions, 732-987-2736, Fax: 732-987-2000, E-mail: gps@georgian.edu.

GRADUATE UNITS

School of Arts and Sciences Students: 90 full-time (84 women), 99 part-time (67 women); includes 28 minority (9 Black or African American, non-Hispanic/Latino; 1 Asian, non-Hispanic/Latino; 14 Hispanic/Latino; 4 Two or more races, non-Hispanic/Latino), 2 international. Average age 34. 138 applicants, 59% accepted, 60 enrolled. *Faculty:* 15 full-time (9 women), 11 part-time/adjunct (9 women). Expenses: Contact institution. *Financial support:* Scholarships/grants, health care benefits, and unspecified assistantships available. Financial award application deadline: 4/15; financial award applicants required to submit FAFSA. In 2018, 68 master's, 19 other advanced degrees awarded. *Program availability:* Part-time, evening/weekend. Offers applied behavior analysis (MA); autism spectrum disorders (Certificate); clinical mental health counseling (MA); criminal justice and human rights (MS); holistic health studies (MA, Certificate); homeland security (Certificate); instructional technology (CPC); mercy spirituality (Certificate); parish business management (Certificate); professional counselor (Certificate); school psychology (MA, Certificate); theology (MA, Certificate). *Application deadline:* For fall admission, 8/15 for domestic students, 5/1 for international students; for spring admission, 1/15 for domestic students, 10/1 for international students. Applications are processed on a rolling basis. *Application fee:* $40. Electronic applications accepted. *Application Contact:* Patrick Givens, Director of Graduate and Professional Studies Admissions, 732-987-2736, Fax: 732-987-2000, E-mail: gps@georgian.edu. *Dean,* Dr. Mary Chinery, 732-987-2493, Fax: 732-987-2007, E-mail: mchinery@georgian.edu.

School of Business and Digital Media Students: 27 full-time (13 women), 26 part-time (17 women); includes 15 minority (5 Black or African American, non-Hispanic/Latino; 4 Asian, non-Hispanic/Latino; 5 Hispanic/Latino; 1 Two or more races, non-Hispanic/Latino), 3 international. Average age 30. 59 applicants, 59% accepted, 19 enrolled. *Faculty:* 5 full-time (1 woman), 6 part-time/adjunct (3 women). Expenses: Contact institution. *Financial support:* Scholarships/grants, health care benefits, and unspecified assistantships available. Financial award application deadline: 4/15; financial award applicants required to submit FAFSA. In 2018, 23 master's, 3 other advanced degrees awarded. *Program availability:* Part-time, evening/weekend. Offers business (MBA); business essentials (Certificate); nonprofit management (Certificate). *Application deadline:* For fall admission, 8/15 for domestic students, 5/1 for international students; for spring admission, 1/15 for domestic students, 10/1 for international students. Applications are processed on a rolling basis. *Application fee:* $40. Electronic applications accepted. *Application Contact:* Patrick Givens, Director of Graduate and Professional Studies Admissions, 732-987-2736, Fax: 732-987-2000, E-mail: gps@georgian.edu. *Dean School of Business and Digital Media,* Dr. Jennifer Edmonds, 732-987-2662, Fax: 732-987-2024, E-mail: jedmonds@georgian.edu.

School of Education Students: 32 full-time (25 women), 396 part-time (324 women); includes 84 minority (35 Black or African American, non-Hispanic/Latino; 10 Asian, non-Hispanic/Latino; 36 Hispanic/Latino; 3 Two or more races, non-Hispanic/Latino). Average age 34. 323 applicants, 67% accepted, 148 enrolled. *Faculty:* 10 full-time (6 women), 28 part-time/adjunct (17 women). Expenses: Contact institution. *Financial support:* Scholarships/grants, health care benefits, and unspecified assistantships available. Financial award application deadline: 4/15; financial award applicants required to submit FAFSA. In 2018, 152 master's, 4 other advanced degrees awarded. *Program availability:* Part-time, evening/weekend. Offers administration and leadership (MA); autism spectrum disorders (Certificate); education (M Ed, MAT); instructional technology (M Mat SE, MA, Certificate). *Application deadline:* For fall admission, 8/15 priority date for domestic students, 5/1 for international students; for spring admission, 1/15 priority date for domestic students, 10/1 for international students. Applications are processed on a rolling basis. *Application fee:* $40. Electronic applications accepted. *Application Contact:* Patrick Givens, Director of Graduate and Professional Studies Admissions, 732-987-2736, Fax: 732-987-2000, E-mail: gps@georgian.edu. *Dean of School of Education,* Dr. Christopher Campisano, 732-987-2729, E-mail: ccampisano@georgian.edu.

GEORGIA SOUTHERN UNIVERSITY, Statesboro, GA 30458

General Information State-supported, coed, university. CGS member. *Enrollment:* 26,408 graduate, professional, and undergraduate students; 1,336 full-time matriculated graduate/professional students (888 women), 1,925 part-time matriculated graduate/professional students (1,365 women). *Enrollment by degree level:* 2,346 master's, 600 doctoral, 315 other advanced degrees. *Graduate faculty:* 731 full-time (310 women), 42 part-time/adjunct (20 women). *Tuition, area resident:* Part-time $3324 per semester. Tuition, state resident: full-time $5814; part-time $3324 per semester. Tuition, nonresident: full-time $23,204; part-time $13,260 per semester. *Required fees:* $2092; $2092. Tuition and fees vary according to course load, degree level, campus/location and program. *Graduate housing:* Room and/or apartments available on a first-come, first-served basis to single students; on-campus housing not available to married students. Typical cost: $5900 per year ($9650 including board). Room and board charges vary according to board plan, campus/location and housing facility selected. Housing application deadline: 5/1. *Student services:* Campus employment opportunities, campus safety program, exercise/wellness program, free psychological counseling, grant writing training, international student services, low-cost health insurance, multicultural affairs office, services for students with disabilities, teacher training, writing training. *Library facilities:* Henderson Library. *Collection:* Books: 649,104 (physical), 656,518 (digital/electronic); Serial titles: 15,006 (physical), 104,711 (digital/electronic); Databases: 325. Weekly public service hours: 143; study areas open 24 hours, 5–7 days a week; students can reserve study rooms.

Computer facilities: Computer purchase and lease plans are available. 3,743 computers available on campus for general student use. A campuswide network can be accessed from student residence rooms and from off campus. Online class registration, online degree audit, online career services, and online healthcare are available.
Website: http://www.georgiasouthern.edu/

General Application Contact: Naronda C. Wright, Office of Graduate Admissions, 912-478-5384, Fax: 912-478-0740, E-mail: gradadmissions@georgiasouthern.edu.

GRADUATE UNITS

Jack N. Averitt College of Graduate Studies *Program availability:* Part-time, evening/weekend, 100% online, blended/hybrid learning. Electronic applications accepted.

Allen E. Paulson College of Engineering and Computing *Program availability:* Part-time, blended/hybrid learning. Offers civil engineering and construction management (MSAE); computer science (MS); electrical and electronic systems (MSAE); engineering and computing (MS, MSAE, Graduate Certificate); engineering and information technology (MSAE); engineering and manufacturing management (Graduate Certificate); engineering/energy science (MSAE); engineering/engineering management (MSAE); engineering/mechatronics (MSAE); information technology (MSAE); occupational safety and environmental compliance (Graduate Certificate). Electronic applications accepted.

College of Arts and Humanities *Program availability:* Part-time. Offers arts and humanities (MA, MFA, MM, MPA, MS, Psy D, Certificate, Graduate Certificate); composition (MM); conducting (MM); English (MA); fine arts (MFA); history (MA); music education (MM); music technology (MM); performance (MM); professional communication and leadership (MA, Certificate); public history (Graduate Certificate); Spanish (MA). Electronic applications accepted.

College of Behavioral and Social Sciences Offers behavioral and social sciences (MA, MPA, MS, Psy D, Certificate, Graduate Certificate); clinical psychology (Psy D); criminal justice (MS); cyber crime (Certificate); psychology (MS); public administration (MPA, Graduate Certificate); public and nonprofit management (MPA, Graduate Certificate); social science (MA).

College of Education *Program availability:* Part-time, evening/weekend, 100% online, blended/hybrid learning. Offers counselor education (M Ed); curriculum and instruction - accomplished teaching (M Ed); curriculum studies (Ed D); education (M Ed, MAT, Ed D, Ed S); educational leadership (M Ed, Ed D, Ed S); elementary education (M Ed, MAT, Ed S); evaluation, assessment, research, and learning (M Ed); higher education (M Ed, Ed D); higher education administration (M Ed); higher education leadership (Ed D); instructional technology (M Ed, Ed S); mental health counseling (M Ed); middle grades education (M Ed, MAT, Ed S); P-12 leadership (M Ed, Ed D, Ed S); reading education (M Ed, Ed S); school counseling (M Ed); school library media (M Ed, Ed S); school psychology (Ed S); secondary education (M Ed, MAT, Ed S); Spanish P-12 education (MAT); special education (M Ed, MAT, Ed S); special education transition specialist (Certificate). Electronic applications accepted.

College of Science and Mathematics *Program availability:* Part-time. Offers applied mathematics (MS); applied physical science (MS); biology (MS); science and mathematics (MS, Certificate). Electronic applications accepted.

Jiann-Ping Hsu College of Public Health Students: 148 full-time (103 women), 95 part-time (69 women); includes 135 minority (107 Black or African American, non-Hispanic/Latino; 11 Asian, non-Hispanic/Latino; 5 Hispanic/Latino; 12 Two or more races, non-Hispanic/Latino), 47 international. Average age 32. 223 applicants, 84% accepted, 64 enrolled. *Faculty:* 39 full-time (18 women), 1 (woman) part-time/adjunct. Expenses: Contact institution. *Financial support:* In 2018–19, 113 students received support, including 53 fellowships with full tuition reimbursements available (averaging $7,750 per year), 3 research assistantships with full tuition reimbursements available (averaging $7,750 per year), 1 teaching assistantship with full tuition reimbursement available (averaging $7,750 per year); scholarships/grants, tuition waivers (full), and unspecified assistantships also available. Support available to part-time students. Financial award application deadline: 6/30; financial award applicants required to submit FAFSA. In 2018, 49 master's, 12 doctorates awarded. *Program availability:* Part-time. Offers applied public health, biostatistics, community health education, environmental health sciences, epidemiology, health policy & management (MPH); biostatistics (MPH, Dr PH); community health behavior and education (Dr PH); community health education (MPH); environmental health sciences (MPH); epidemiology (MPH); epidemiology, biostatistics, public health leadership, community health behavior and education (Dr PH); health policy and management (MPH, Dr PH). *Application deadline:* For fall admission, 2/1 priority date for domestic and international students. Applications are processed on a rolling basis. *Application fee:* $135. Electronic applications accepted. *Application Contact:* Monica H Brister, Academic Services Coordinator, 912-478-2674, Fax: 912-4782479, E-mail: mbrister@georgiasouthern.edu. *Interim dean,* Dr. Stuart H Tedders, 912-478-2674, Fax: 912-478-5811, E-mail: stedders@georgiasouthern.edu.

Parker College of Business *Program availability:* Part-time, evening/weekend, 100% online. Offers applied economics (MS); business (M Acc, MBA, MS, PhD, Graduate Certificate); business administration (MBA); enterprise resources planning (Graduate Certificate); forensic accounting (M Acc); information systems (Graduate Certificate); logistics and supply chain management (PhD). Electronic applications accepted.

Waters College of Health Professions *Program availability:* Part-time, evening/weekend, 100% online, blended/hybrid learning. Offers communication sciences and disorders (MS); dietetics (Certificate); family nurse practitioner (MSN); health administration (MHA); health professions (MHA, MS, MSN, MSSM, DNP, DPT, Certificate); kinesiology (MS); nurse educator (Certificate); nurse practitioner (MSN); nursing science (DNP); physical therapy (DPT); psychiatric mental health nurse practitioner (MSN); sport management (MS); sports medicine (MSSM, Certificate); strength and conditioning (MSSM, Certificate). Electronic applications accepted.

GEORGIA SOUTHWESTERN STATE UNIVERSITY, Americus, GA 31709-4693

General Information State-supported, coed, comprehensive institution. *Graduate housing:* Room and/or apartments available on a first-come, first-served basis to single students; on-campus housing not available to married students.

GRADUATE UNITS

College of Nursing and Health Sciences *Program availability:* Part-time, online only, all theory courses are offered online. Offers family nurse practitioner (MSN); health informatics (Postbaccalaureate Certificate); nurse educator (Post Master's Certificate); nursing educator (MSN); nursing informatics (MSN); nursing leadership (MSN). MSN program offered by the Georgia Intercollegiate Consortium for Graduate Nursing Education, a partnership with Columbus State University. Electronic applications accepted.

School of Business Administration *Program availability:* Part-time, online only, 100% online. Offers business administration (MBA). Electronic applications accepted.

School of Computing and Mathematics *Program availability:* Part-time, 100% online, blended/hybrid learning. Offers computer information systems (Graduate Certificate); computer science (MS). Electronic applications accepted.

School of Education Offers early childhood education (M Ed, Ed S); middle grades education (Ed S); middle grades language arts (M Ed); middle grades mathematics (M Ed); special education (M Ed). Electronic applications accepted.

GEORGIA STATE UNIVERSITY, Atlanta, GA 30302-3083

General Information State-supported, coed, university. CGS member. *Enrollment:* 34,274 graduate, professional, and undergraduate students; 4,930 full-time matriculated graduate/professional students (2,977 women), 1,956 part-time matriculated graduate/professional students (1,274 women). *Enrollment by degree level:* 4,227 master's, 2,502 doctoral, 112 other advanced degrees. *Graduate faculty:* 845 full-time (378 women), 132 part-time/adjunct (65 women). *International tuition:* $30,024 full-time. *Tuition, area resident:* Full-time $9360; part-time $390 per credit hour. *Tuition, state resident:* full-time $9360; part-time $390 per credit hour. Tuition, nonresident: full-time $30,024; part-time $1251 per credit hour. *Required fees:* $2128. *Graduate housing:* Rooms and/or apartments available on a first-come, first-served basis to single and married students. Housing application deadline: 2/5. *Student services:* Campus safety program, career counseling, child daycare facilities, exercise/wellness program, international student services, services for students with disabilities. *Library facilities:* University Library plus 6 others. *Collection:* Books: 1.9 million (physical), 686,132 (digital/electronic); Serial titles: 21,654 (digital/electronic). Students can reserve study rooms.

Computer facilities: 2,040 computers available on campus for general student use. A campuswide network can be accessed from student residence rooms and from off campus. Online class registration is available.
Website: http://www.gsu.edu/

GRADUATE UNITS

Andrew Young School of Policy Studies Students: 385 full-time (254 women), 144 part-time (103 women); includes 254 minority (183 Black or African American, non-Hispanic/Latino; 18 Asian, non-Hispanic/Latino; 29 Hispanic/Latino; 24 Two or more races, non-Hispanic/Latino), 99 international. Average age 30. 785 applicants, 51% accepted, 195 enrolled. *Faculty:* 54 full-time (20 women), 3 part-time/adjunct (0 women). Expenses: Contact institution. *Financial support:* Unspecified assistantships available. Financial award application deadline: 2/15; financial award applicants required to submit FAFSA. In 2018, 150 master's, 24 doctorates, 8 other advanced degrees awarded. *Program availability:* Part-time, evening/weekend. Offers criminal justice (MPA, MS); criminal justice and criminology (PhD); disaster management (Certificate); disaster policy (MPA); economics (MA); environmental economics (PhD); environmental policy (PhD); experimental economics (PhD); health policy (PhD); labor economics (PhD); management and finance (MPA); nonprofit management (MPA, Certificate); nonprofit policy (MPA); planning and economic development (MPP, Certificate); policy (MA); policy analysis and evaluation (MPA); policy studies (MA, MPA, MPP, MS, MSW, PhD, Certificate); public and nonprofit management (PhD); public finance (PhD); public finance and budgeting (PhD); public finance policy (MPA); public health (MPA); urban and regional economics (PhD). *Application deadline:* For fall admission, 1/15 for domestic and international students. *Application fee:* $50. Electronic applications accepted. *Application Contact:* Dr. Sally Wallace, Dean, 404-413-0000, Fax: 404-413-0004. *Dean,* Dr. Sally Wallace, 404-413-0000, Fax: 404-413-0004.

School of Social Work Students: 108 full-time (101 women), 19 part-time (18 women); includes 84 minority (68 Black or African American, non-Hispanic/Latino; 2 Asian, non-Hispanic/Latino; 7 Hispanic/Latino; 7 Two or more races, non-Hispanic/Latino). Average age 31. 168 applicants, 50% accepted, 44 enrolled. *Faculty:* 13 full-time (9 women), 1 part-time/adjunct (0 women). Expenses: Contact institution. *Financial support:* In 2018–19, research assistantships with tuition reimbursements (averaging $4,000 per year), teaching assistantships with tuition reimbursements (averaging $4,000 per year) were awarded; career-related internships or fieldwork, institutionally sponsored loans, scholarships/grants, tuition waivers, and unspecified assistantships also available. Financial award application deadline: 2/1; financial award applicants required to submit FAFSA. In 2018, 61 master's awarded. *Program availability:* Part-time. Offers child welfare leadership (Certificate); community partnerships (MSW); forensic social work (Certificate). *Application deadline:* For fall admission, 2/1 priority date for domestic and international students. *Application fee:* $50. Electronic applications accepted. *Application Contact:* Brian Bride, Director of School of Social Work, 404-413-1052, Fax: 404-413-1075, E-mail: bbride@gsu.edu. *Director of School of Social Work,* Brian Bride, 404-413-1052, Fax: 404-413-1075, E-mail: bbride@gsu.edu.

Byrdine F. Lewis School of Nursing Students: 368 full-time (288 women), 221 part-time (196 women); includes 240 minority (145 Black or African American, non-Hispanic/Latino; 50 Asian, non-Hispanic/Latino; 28 Hispanic/Latino; 17 Two or more races, non-Hispanic/Latino), 15 international. Average age 27. 533 applicants, 48% accepted, 167 enrolled. *Faculty:* 57 full-time (40 women), 7 part-time/adjunct (5 women). Expenses: Contact institution. *Financial support:* In 2018–19, research assistantships with tuition reimbursements (averaging $1,666 per year), teaching assistantships with tuition reimbursements (averaging $1,920 per year) were awarded; scholarships/grants, tuition waivers (full and partial), and unspecified assistantships also available. Support available to part-time students. Financial award application deadline: 8/1; financial award applicants required to submit FAFSA. In 2018, 113 master's, 46 doctorates, 19 other advanced degrees awarded. *Program availability:* Part-time, blended/hybrid learning. Offers adult health clinical nurse specialist/nurse practitioner (MS, Certificate); child health clinical nurse specialist/pediatric nurse practitioner (MS, Certificate); family nurse practitioner (MS, Certificate); family psychiatric mental health nurse practitioner (MS, Certificate); nursing (PhD); nursing leadership in healthcare innovations (MS); nutrition (MS); occupational therapy (MOT); perinatal clinical nurse specialist/women's health nurse practitioner (MS, Certificate); physical therapy (DPT); respiratory therapy (MS). *Application deadline:* For fall admission, 2/1 priority date for domestic and international students; for spring admission, 9/15 for domestic and international students. Applications are processed on a rolling basis. *Application fee:* $50. Electronic applications accepted. *Application Contact:* Nancy Kropf, Dean of Nursing, 404-413-1101, Fax: 404-413-1090, E-mail: nkropf@gsu.edu. *Dean of Nursing,* Nancy Kropf, 404-413-1101, Fax: 404-413-1090, E-mail: nkropf@gsu.edu.

Division of Nutrition Students: 45 full-time (41 women), 3 part-time (2 women); includes 12 minority (4 Black or African American, non-Hispanic/Latino; 3 Asian, non-Hispanic/Latino; 5 Hispanic/Latino). Average age 29. 54 applicants, 57% accepted, 24 enrolled. *Faculty:* 8 full-time (6 women), 1 (woman) part-time/adjunct. Expenses: Contact institution. *Financial support:* In 2018–19, research assistantships with tuition reimbursements (averaging $1,647 per year), teaching assistantships with full tuition reimbursements (averaging $2,666 per year) were awarded. Financial award application deadline: 4/1. In 2018, 18 master's awarded. *Program availability:* Part-time. Offers nutrition (MS). *Application deadline:* For fall admission, 5/15 for domestic and international students; for spring admission, 10/1 for domestic and international students. *Application fee:* $50. Electronic applications accepted. *Application Contact:* Dr. Anita Nucci, Associate Professor and Graduate Program Director, 404-413-1234, Fax: 404-413-1228, E-mail: anucci@gsu.edu. *Associate Professor and Graduate Program Director,* Dr. Anita Nucci, 404-413-1234, Fax: 404-413-1228, E-mail: anucci@gsu.edu.

Division of Physical Therapy Students: 125 full-time (79 women), 2 part-time (1 woman); includes 37 minority (9 Black or African American, non-Hispanic/Latino; 15 Asian, non-Hispanic/Latino; 6 Hispanic/Latino; 7 Two or more races, non-Hispanic/Latino). Average age 26. *Faculty:* 11 full-time (5 women), 1 (woman) part-time/adjunct. Expenses: Contact institution. *Financial support:* In 2018–19, research assistantships with full tuition reimbursements (averaging $2,000 per year), teaching assistantships with full tuition reimbursements (averaging $2,000 per year) were awarded; scholarships/grants, tuition waivers (partial), and unspecified assistantships also available. Financial award application deadline: 4/1; financial award applicants required to submit FAFSA. In 2018, 35 doctorates awarded. Offers physical therapy (DPT). *Application deadline:* For fall admission, 11/15 for domestic and international students. *Application fee:* $50. Electronic applications accepted. *Application Contact:* Dr. Sujay Galen, Chair, 404-413-1243, Fax: 404-413-1230, E-mail: sgalen@gsu.edu. *Chair,* Dr. Sujay Galen, 404-413-1243, Fax: 404-413-1230, E-mail: sgalen@gsu.edu.

Division of Respiratory Therapy Students: 38 full-time (23 women), 5 part-time (3 women); includes 15 minority (5 Black or African American, non-Hispanic/Latino; 5 Asian, non-Hispanic/Latino; 5 Hispanic/Latino), 14 international. Average age 30. 47 applicants, 62% accepted, 19 enrolled. *Faculty:* 7 full-time (2 women). Expenses: Contact institution. *Financial support:* In 2018–19, research assistantships with full tuition reimbursements (averaging $2,000 per year), teaching assistantships with full tuition reimbursements (averaging $2,000 per year) were awarded; scholarships/grants and unspecified assistantships also available. Financial award application deadline: 6/1; financial award applicants required to submit FAFSA. In 2018, 26 master's awarded. Offers respiratory therapy (MS). *Application deadline:* For fall admission, 5/1 for domestic and international students; for spring admission, 9/15 for domestic and international students. *Application fee:* $50. Electronic applications accepted. *Application Contact:* Dr. Douglas Gardenhire, Department Head, 404-413-1270, Fax: 404-413-1230, E-mail: dgardenhire@gsu.edu. *Department Head,* Dr. Douglas Gardenhire, 404-413-1270, Fax: 404-413-1230, E-mail: dgardenhire@gsu.edu.

College of Arts

College of Arts and Sciences Students: 1,471 full-time (811 women), 374 part-time (215 women); includes 581 minority (312 Black or African American, non-Hispanic/Latino; 2 American Indian or Alaska Native, non-Hispanic/Latino; 109 Asian, non-Hispanic/Latino; 96 Hispanic/Latino; 1 Native Hawaiian or other Pacific Islander, non-Hispanic/Latino; 61 Two or more races, non-Hispanic/Latino), 519 international. Average age 32. 2,269 applicants, 38% accepted, 471 enrolled. *Faculty:* 365 full-time (147 women), 19 part-time/adjunct (9 women). Expenses: Contact institution. *Financial support:* Fellowships with tuition reimbursements, research assistantships with tuition reimbursements, teaching assistantships with tuition reimbursements, career-related internships or fieldwork, scholarships/grants, health care benefits, tuition waivers (partial), and unspecified assistantships available. Support available to part-time students. Financial award application deadline: 4/15; financial award applicants required to submit FAFSA. In 2018, 448 master's, 140 doctorates, 26 other advanced degrees awarded. *Program availability:* Part-time, evening/weekend. Offers African-American studies (MA); analytical chemistry (MS, PhD); anthropology (MA); applied and environmental microbiology (MS, PhD); applied linguistics (MA, PhD); applied linguistics and pedagogy (MA Ed); arts and sciences (MA, MA Ed, MFA, MHP, MM, MS, PhD, Certificate, Graduate Certificate); astronomy (PhD); biochemistry (MS, PhD); bioinformatics (MS, PhD); biophysical chemistry (PhD); biostatistics (MS, PhD); cellular and molecular biology and physiology (MS, PhD); clinical psychology (PhD); cognitive sciences (PhD); community psychology (PhD); computational chemistry (MS, PhD); computer science (MS, PhD); creative writing (MA, MFA, PhD); developmental psychology (PhD); discrete mathematics (MS); English (MA, PhD); fiction (MA, MFA); film, video, and digital imaging (MA); French (MA); French studies (MA); geochemistry (PhD); geographic information systems (Certificate); geography (MS); geology (MS); heritage preservation (MHP); historic preservation (MA); history (MA, PhD); human communication and social influence (MA); interpretation (Certificate); Latin American studies (Certificate); literary studies (MA, PhD); literature and culture (MA); mass communication (MA); mathematics (MS, PhD); media and society (PhD); molecular genetics and biochemistry (MS, PhD); moving image studies (PhD); neurobiology and behavior (MS, PhD); neuropsychology and behavioral neuroscience (PhD); organic/medicinal chemistry (MS, PhD); philosophy (MA); physical chemistry (MS); physics (MS, PhD); poetry (MA, MFA); political science (MA, PhD); public communication (PhD); public history (MA); religious studies (MA); rhetoric and composition (MA, PhD); rhetoric and politics (PhD); scientific computing (MS); sociology (MA, PhD); Spanish (MA); statistics (MS); translation (Certificate); translation and interpretation (Certificate); world history (MA). *Application deadline:* For fall admission, 7/1 for domestic and international students; for spring admission, 11/15 for domestic and international students. *Application fee:* $50. Electronic applications accepted. *Application Contact:* Amber Amari, Assistant Dean for Graduate Programs, 404-413-5037, E-mail: aamari@gsu.edu. *Dean,* Dr. Sara Rosen, 404-413-5114, Fax: 404-413-5117, E-mail: rosen@gsu.edu.

Gerontology Institute Students: 20 full-time (17 women), 13 part-time (10 women); includes 21 minority (14 Black or African American, non-Hispanic/Latino; 4 Asian, non-Hispanic/Latino; 2 Hispanic/Latino; 1 Two or more races, non-Hispanic/Latino), 6 international. Average age 44. 20 applicants, 95% accepted, 15 enrolled. *Faculty:* 4 full-time (all women), 1 (woman) part-time/adjunct. Expenses: Contact institution. *Financial support:* In 2018–19, research assistantships with full tuition reimbursements (averaging $6,000 per year) were awarded; career-related internships or fieldwork, scholarships/grants, and unspecified assistantships also available. Financial award application deadline: 4/15; financial award applicants required to submit FAFSA. In 2018, 8 master's, 7 other advanced degrees awarded. *Program availability:* Part-time. Offers gerontology (MA, Certificate). *Application deadline:* For fall admission, 4/15 for domestic and international students; for spring admission, 10/15 for domestic and international students. Applications are processed on a rolling basis. *Application fee:* $50. Electronic applications accepted. *Application Contact:* Dr. Candace L. Kemp, Director of Graduate Studies, 404-413-5210, Fax: 404-413-5219, E-mail: ckemp@gsu.edu. *Director,* Dr. Elizabeth O. Burgess, 404-413-5210, Fax: 404-413-5219, E-mail: eburgess@gsu.edu.

Institute for Women's, Gender, and Sexuality Studies Students: 13 full-time (all women), 3 part-time (all women); includes 8 minority (5 Black or African American, non-Hispanic/Latino; 1 Hispanic/Latino; 2 Two or more races, non-Hispanic/Latino), 3 international. Average age 36. 22 applicants, 73% accepted, 7 enrolled. *Faculty:* 4 full-time (all women). Expenses: Contact institution. *Financial support:* In 2018–19, research assistantships with full tuition reimbursements (averaging $7,000 per year), teaching assistantships with full tuition reimbursements (averaging $7,500 per year) were awarded; career-related internships or fieldwork, health care benefits, and unspecified assistantships also available. Financial award application deadline: 2/15. In 2018, 5 master's, 4 other advanced degrees awarded. *Program availability:* Part-time. Offers women's, gender, and sexuality studies (MA, Graduate Certificate). *Application deadline:* For fall admission, 2/15 for domestic and international students. *Application fee:* $50. Electronic applications accepted. *Application Contact:* Dr. Megan Sinnott, Director of Graduate Studies, Fax: 404-413-6585, E-mail: megansinnott@gsu.edu.

Neuroscience Institute Students: 59 full-time (30 women), 1 part-time (0 women); includes 21 minority (1 Black or African American, non-Hispanic/Latino; 9 Asian, non-Hispanic/Latino; 8 Hispanic/Latino; 3 Two or more races, non-Hispanic/Latino), 8 international. Average age 28. 61 applicants, 43% accepted, 13 enrolled. *Faculty:* 20 full-time (8 women). Expenses: Contact institution. *Financial support:* In 2018–19, fellowships (averaging $22,000 per year), research assistantships (averaging $22,000

per year) were awarded. Financial award applicants required to submit FAFSA. In 2018, 7 doctorates awarded. Offers neuroscience (PhD). *Application deadline:* For fall admission, 12/10 for domestic and international students. *Application fee:* $50. Electronic applications accepted. *Application Contact:* Dr. Laura L. Carruth, Director of Graduate Studies, 404-413-5340, E-mail: lcarruth@gsu.edu. *Director,* Prof. Walter Wilczynski, 404-413-6307, E-mail: wwilczynski@gsu.edu.

Ernest G. Welch School of Art and Design Students: 60 full-time (37 women), 9 part-time (6 women); includes 21 minority (10 Black or African American, non-Hispanic/Latino; 1 Asian, non-Hispanic/Latino; 5 Hispanic/Latino; 5 Two or more races, non-Hispanic/Latino), 7 international. Average age 33. 156 applicants, 27% accepted, 28 enrolled. *Faculty:* 71 full-time (28 women), 9 part-time/adjunct (2 women). Expenses: Contact institution. *Financial support:* In 2018–19, fellowships with full tuition reimbursements (averaging $11,000 per year), research assistantships with full tuition reimbursements (averaging $6,000 per year), teaching assistantships with full tuition reimbursements (averaging $7,000 per year) were awarded; scholarships/grants and unspecified assistantships also available. Financial award application deadline: 4/15; financial award applicants required to submit FAFSA. In 2018, 23 master's awarded. Offers art and design (MA, MA Ed, MFA); art education (MA Ed); art history (MA); ceramics (MFA); drawing and painting (MFA); graphic design (MFA); interior design (MFA); photography (MFA); printmaking (MFA); sculpture (MFA); textiles (MFA). *Application deadline:* For fall admission, 1/6 for domestic and international students; for spring admission, 1/15 priority date for domestic and international students. *Application fee:* $50. Electronic applications accepted. *Application Contact:* Michael White, Director, Welch School of Art and Design, 404-413-5228, E-mail: mwhite@gsu.edu. *Director, Welch School of Art and Design,* Michael White, 404-413-5228, E-mail: mwhite@gsu.edu.

College of Education and Human Development Students: 908 full-time (676 women), 553 part-time (388 women); includes 805 minority (568 Black or African American, non-Hispanic/Latino; 64 Asian, non-Hispanic/Latino; 109 Hispanic/Latino; 1 Native Hawaiian or other Pacific Islander, non-Hispanic/Latino; 63 Two or more races, non-Hispanic/Latino), 39 international. Average age 32. 1,209 applicants, 44% accepted, 399 enrolled. *Faculty:* 121 full-time (80 women), 52 part-time/adjunct (38 women). Expenses: Contact institution. *Financial support:* In 2018–19, fellowships with full tuition reimbursements (averaging $25,000 per year), research assistantships with tuition reimbursements (averaging $4,867 per year), teaching assistantships with tuition reimbursements (averaging $4,683 per year) were awarded; career-related internships or fieldwork, Federal Work-Study, scholarships/grants, tuition waivers (partial), and unspecified assistantships also available. Support available to part-time students. Financial award applicants required to submit FAFSA. In 2018, 404 master's, 66 doctorates, 18 other advanced degrees awarded. *Program availability:* Part-time, evening/weekend, online learning. Offers autism spectrum disorders (PhD); behavior and learning disabilities (M Ed); behavior disorders (PhD); communication disorders (M Ed, PhD); counseling psychology (PhD); counselor education and practice (PhD); curriculum and instruction (Ed D); early childhood and elementary education (PhD); early childhood education (M Ed, Ed S); early childhood special education (PhD); education and human development (M Ed, MAT, MS, Ed D, PhD, Ed S); education of students with exceptionalities (PhD); educational leadership (M Ed, Ed D, Ed S); educational psychology (MS, PhD); educational research (MS, PhD); English education (MAT); exercise science (MS); health and physical education (M Ed); kinesiology (PhD); learning disabilities (PhD); mathematics education (M Ed, MAT); mental health counseling (MS, Ed S); mental retardation (PhD); middle level education (MAT); multiple and severe disabilities (M Ed); orthopedic impairments (PhD); reading, language and literacy education (M Ed, MAT); rehabilitation counseling (MS); school counseling (M Ed, Ed S); school psychology (M Ed, PhD, Ed S); science education (M Ed, MAT); sensory impairments (PhD); social foundations of education (MS, PhD); social studies education (M Ed, MAT); sports administration (MS); sports medicine (MS); teaching and learning (PhD); urban education (M Ed); urban teacher leadership (M Ed). *Application fee:* $50. Electronic applications accepted. *Application Contact:* Nancy Keita, Assistant Dean for Student Services, 404-413-8001, E-mail: nkeita@gsu.edu. *Dean,* Dr. Paul A. Alberto, 404-413-8100, Fax: 404-413-8103, E-mail: palberto@gsu.edu.

Learning Technologies Division *Faculty:* 7 full-time (3 women). Expenses: Contact institution. *Financial support:* Federal Work-Study and institutionally sponsored loans available. In 2018, 6 master's, 3 doctorates awarded. *Program availability:* Part-time, evening/weekend. Offers instructional design and technology (MS); instructional technology (PhD). *Application deadline:* For fall admission, 1/15 for domestic and international students; for summer admission, 1/15 for domestic and international students. *Application fee:* $50. Electronic applications accepted. *Application Contact:* Nancy Keita, Director, Office of Academic Assistance and Graduate Admissions, 404-413-8001, E-mail: nkeita@gsu.edu.

College of Law Students: 480 full-time (239 women), 159 part-time (85 women); includes 202 minority (88 Black or African American, non-Hispanic/Latino; 2 American Indian or Alaska Native, non-Hispanic/Latino; 42 Asian, non-Hispanic/Latino; 54 Hispanic/Latino; 16 Two or more races, non-Hispanic/Latino), 15 international. Average age 28. 1,478 applicants, 41% accepted, 214 enrolled. *Faculty:* 52 full-time (29 women), 10 part-time/adjunct (3 women). Expenses: Contact institution. *Financial support:* In 2018–19, research assistantships with tuition reimbursements (averaging $2,500 per year), teaching assistantships (averaging $2,500 per year) were awarded; scholarships/grants, tuition waivers, and unspecified assistantships also available. Financial award application deadline: 4/1; financial award applicants required to submit FAFSA. In 2018, 179 doctorates awarded. *Program availability:* Part-time, evening/weekend. Offers law (JD). *Application deadline:* For fall admission, 3/15 for domestic students, 3/15 priority date for international students. Applications are processed on a rolling basis. *Application fee:* $50. Electronic applications accepted. *Application Contact:* Dr. Monique McCarthy, Senior Director of Admissions, 404-413-9004, Fax: 404-413-9203, E-mail: mmccarthy18@gsu.edu. *Interim Dean, College of Law,* Dr. Leslie E. Wolf, 404-413-9035, Fax: 404-413-9227, E-mail: lwolf@gsu.edu.

J. Mack Robinson College of Business Students: 893 full-time (430 women), 328 part-time (158 women); includes 481 minority (234 Black or African American, non-Hispanic/Latino; 4 American Indian or Alaska Native, non-Hispanic/Latino; 149 Asian, non-Hispanic/Latino; 61 Hispanic/Latino; 33 Two or more races, non-Hispanic/Latino), 361 international. Average age 32. 1,926 applicants, 59% accepted, 629 enrolled. *Faculty:* 81 full-time (16 women), 21 part-time/adjunct (3 women). Expenses: Contact institution. *Financial support:* Research assistantships, teaching assistantships, scholarships/grants, tuition waivers, and unspecified assistantships available. Financial award applicants required to submit FAFSA. In 2018, 697 master's, 33 doctorates, 26 other advanced degrees awarded. *Program availability:* Part-time, evening/weekend. Offers actuarial science (MAS); business (EMBA, Exec MS, GMBA, M Tax, MAS, MBA, MIB, MPA, MPA, MS, MSCIS, MSHA, MSIS, MSRE, PMBA, EDB, PhD, Certificate); business administration (MBA); business analysis (MBA, MS); computer information systems (PhD); enterprise risk management (MBA, Certificate); entrepreneurship

(MBA); executive business administration (EMBA); finance (MBA, MS, PhD); financial risk management (MBA); global business administration (GMBA); health informatics (MBA, MS); hotel real estate (MBA); human resources management (MBA, MS); information systems (MSIS, Certificate); information systems development and project management (MBA); information systems management (MBA); managing information technology (Exec MS); marketing (MBA, MS, PhD); mathematical risk management (MS); operations management (MBA, MS); organization behavior/human resource management (PhD); organization management (MBA); organizational change (MS); professional business administration (PMBA); real estate (MBA, MS, PhD, Certificate); risk and insurance (MS); risk management and insurance (MBA, MS, PhD, Certificate); strategic management (PhD); the wireless organization (MBA). *Application deadline:* For fall admission, 5/1 priority date for domestic students, 2/1 priority date for international students; for spring admission, 9/15 priority date for domestic students, 4/1 priority date for international students. Applications are processed on a rolling basis. *Application fee:* $50. Electronic applications accepted. *Application Contact:* Toby McChesney, Assistant Dean for Graduate Recruiting and Student Services, 404-413-7167, Fax: 404-413-7162, E-mail: rcbgradadmissions@gsu.edu. *Dean of the J. Mack Robinson College of Business,* Dr. Richard D. Phillips, 404-413-7000, Fax: 404-413-7035, E-mail: rphillips@gsu.edu.

Institute of Health Administration Students: 42 full-time (21 women), 14 part-time (6 women); includes 19 minority (8 Black or African American, non-Hispanic/Latino; 9 Asian, non-Hispanic/Latino; 1 Hispanic/Latino; 1 Two or more races, non-Hispanic/Latino), 7 international. Average age 31. 75 applicants, 39% accepted, 24 enrolled. *Faculty:* 4 full-time (1 woman). Expenses: Contact institution. *Financial support:* Research assistantships, teaching assistantships, scholarships/grants, tuition waivers, and unspecified assistantships available. In 2018, 49 master's awarded. *Program availability:* Part-time, evening/weekend. Offers health administration (MBA, MSHA); health informatics (MBA, MSCIS). *Application deadline:* For fall admission, 5/1 priority date for domestic students, 2/1 priority date for international students; for spring admission, 9/15 priority date for domestic students, 4/1 priority date for international students. Applications are processed on a rolling basis. *Application fee:* $50. Electronic applications accepted. *Application Contact:* Toby McChesney, Assistant Dean for Graduate Recruiting and Student Services, 404-413-7167, Fax: 404-413-7162, E-mail: rcbgradadmissions@gsu.edu. *Chair in Health Administration/Director of the Institute of Health,* Dr. Andrew T. Sumner, 404-413-7630, Fax: 404-413-7631.

Institute of International Business Students: 18 full-time (8 women); includes 6 minority (3 Black or African American, non-Hispanic/Latino; 1 Asian, non-Hispanic/Latino; 1 Hispanic/Latino; 1 Two or more races, non-Hispanic/Latino), 8 international. Average age 29. 48 applicants, 73% accepted, 22 enrolled. *Faculty:* 5 full-time (3 women). Expenses: Contact institution. *Financial support:* Research assistantships, teaching assistantships, scholarships/grants, tuition waivers (partial), and unspecified assistantships available. Financial award application deadline: 5/1. In 2018, 40 master's awarded. *Program availability:* Part-time, evening/weekend. Offers international business (GMBA, MBA, MIB); international business and information technology (MBA); international entrepreneurship (MBA). *Application deadline:* For fall admission, 5/1 priority date for domestic students, 2/1 priority date for international students; for spring admission, 9/15 priority date for domestic students, 5/1 priority date for international students. Applications are processed on a rolling basis. *Application fee:* $50. Electronic applications accepted. *Application Contact:* Toby McChesney, Assistant Dean for Graduate Recruiting and Student Services, 404-413-7167, Fax: 404-413-7162, E-mail: rcbgradadmissions@gsu.edu. *Professor/Director of the Institute of International Business,* Dr. Daniel Bello, 404-413-7275, Fax: 404-413-7276.

School of Accountancy Students: 131 full-time (83 women), 121 part-time (79 women); includes 134 minority (57 Black or African American, non-Hispanic/Latino; 50 Asian, non-Hispanic/Latino; 20 Hispanic/Latino; 7 Two or more races, non-Hispanic/Latino), 37 international. Average age 30. 200 applicants, 70% accepted, 104 enrolled. *Faculty:* 9 full-time (3 women), 8 part-time/adjunct (0 women). Expenses: Contact institution. *Financial support:* Research assistantships, teaching assistantships, scholarships/grants, tuition waivers, and unspecified assistantships available. Financial award applicants required to submit FAFSA. In 2018, 146 master's awarded. *Program availability:* Part-time, evening/weekend. Offers accounting (MBA, PhD); information systems audit and control (MS); professional accountancy (MPA); taxation (M Tax). *Application deadline:* For fall admission, 5/1 priority date for domestic students, 2/1 priority date for international students; for spring admission, 9/15 priority date for domestic students, 4/1 priority date for international students. Applications are processed on a rolling basis. *Application fee:* $50. Electronic applications accepted. *Application Contact:* Toby McChesney, Assistant Dean for Graduate Recruiting and Student Services, 404-413-7167, Fax: 404-413-7162, E-mail: rcbgradadmissions@gsu.edu. *Director of the School of Accountancy,* Dr. Douglas E. Stevens, 404-413-7212, Fax: 404-413-7203, E-mail: dstevens11@gsu.edu.

School of Public Health Students: 225 full-time (175 women), 96 part-time (75 women); includes 186 minority (131 Black or African American, non-Hispanic/Latino; 32 Asian, non-Hispanic/Latino; 15 Hispanic/Latino; 8 Two or more races, non-Hispanic/Latino), 39 international. Average age 30. 526 applicants, 51% accepted, 108 enrolled. *Faculty:* 32 full-time (17 women). Expenses: Contact institution. *Financial support:* In 2018–19, fellowships (averaging $2,500 per year), research assistantships with full tuition reimbursements (averaging $22,000 per year), teaching assistantships with full tuition reimbursements (averaging $22,000 per year) were awarded; career-related internships or fieldwork, scholarships/grants, health care benefits, unspecified assistantships, and out-of-state tuition waivers also available. In 2018, 140 master's, 7 doctorates, 6 other advanced degrees awarded. *Program availability:* Part-time. Offers public health (MPH, Dr PH, PhD, Certificate). *Application deadline:* For fall admission, 2/1 for domestic and international students; for spring admission, 10/1 for domestic and international students. *Application fee:* $50. Electronic applications accepted. *Application Contact:* Dr. Rodney Lyn, Interim Dean, Associate Professor, Senior Associate Dean for Academic and Strategic Initiatives, 404-413-1133, Fax: 404-413-1140, E-mail: rlyn1@gsu.edu. *Interim Dean, Associate Professor, Senior Associate Dean for Academic and Strategic Initiatives,* Dr. Rodney Lyn, 404-413-1133, Fax: 404-413-1140, E-mail: rlyn1@gsu.edu.

GERSTNER SLOAN KETTERING GRADUATE SCHOOL OF BIOMEDICAL SCIENCES, New York, NY 10021

General Information Independent, coed, graduate-only institution. *Enrollment by degree level:* 74 doctoral. *Graduate faculty:* 128 full-time (28 women). *Graduate housing:* Rooms and/or apartments guaranteed to single and married students. Typical cost: $10,728 per year for single students; $16,248 per year for married students. Room charges vary according to housing facility selected. Housing application deadline: 5/5.

Student services: Campus employment opportunities, campus safety program, career counseling, child daycare facilities, free psychological counseling, grant writing training, international student services, low-cost health insurance, multicultural affairs office, services for students with disabilities, writing training. *Library facilities:* Memorial Sloan Kettering Cancer Center Library. *Collection:* Books: 4,210 (physical), 20,871 (digital/electronic); Serial titles: 5,153 (digital/electronic). Weekly public service hours: 53; students can reserve study rooms.

Computer facilities: 74 computers available on campus for general student use. A campuswide network can be accessed from student residence rooms and from off campus. Online class registration is available.
Website: https://www.sloankettering.edu/gerstner

General Application Contact: Julie Masen, Main Office, 646-888-6639, Fax: 646-422-2351, E-mail: gradstudies@sloankettering.edu.

GRADUATE UNITS

Program in Cancer Biology Students: 74 full-time (34 women); includes 12 minority (1 Black or African American, non-Hispanic/Latino; 5 Asian, non-Hispanic/Latino; 6 Hispanic/Latino), 29 international. *Faculty:* 130 full-time (30 women). Expenses: Contact institution. *Financial support:* In 2018–19, 74 students received support. Teaching assistantships and fellowship package including stipend ($38,655), full-tuition scholarship, first-year allowance, and comprehensive medical and dental insurance available. In 2018, 14 doctorates awarded. Offers cancer biology (PhD). *Application deadline:* For fall admission, 12/1 for domestic and international students. Electronic applications accepted. *Application Contact:* Julie Masen, Admissions Coordinator, 646-888-6639, Fax: 646-422-2351, E-mail: gradstudies@sloankettering.edu. *Associate Dean,* Linda Burnley, 646-888-6639, E-mail: burnleyl@sloankettering.edu.

GLION INSTITUTE OF HIGHER EDUCATION, CH-1823 Glion-sur-Montreux, Switzerland

General Information Proprietary, coed, comprehensive institution.

GRADUATE UNITS

Graduate Programs *Program availability:* Evening/weekend.

GLOBAL UNIVERSITY, Springfield, MO 65804

General Information Independent-religious, coed, comprehensive institution. *Graduate housing:* On-campus housing not available.

GRADUATE UNITS

Graduate School of Theology *Program availability:* Part-time, evening/weekend, online learning. Offers bible and theology (D Min); biblical language (M Div); biblical studies (MA); Christian ministry (M Div, D Min); ministerial studies (MA). Electronic applications accepted.

GODDARD COLLEGE, Plainfield, VT 05667-9432

General Information Independent, coed, comprehensive institution. *Graduate housing:* On-campus housing not available.

GRADUATE UNITS

Graduate Division *Program availability:* Part-time, online learning. Offers clinical mental health counseling (MA); community education (MA); consciousness studies (MA); creative writing (MFA); embodiment studies (MA); expressive arts therapy (MA); health arts and sciences (MA); interdisciplinary arts (MFA); psychology (MA); sexual orientation (MA); social innovation and sustainability (MA); teacher licensure (MA); transformative language arts (MA). Electronic applications accepted.

GOLDEN GATE UNIVERSITY, San Francisco, CA 94105-2968

General Information Independent, coed, university. *Graduate housing:* On-campus housing not available.

GRADUATE UNITS

Ageno School of Business *Program availability:* Part-time, evening/weekend. Offers accounting (MBA); adaptive leadership (MBA); advanced financial planning (MS); business administration (EMBA, MBA, DBA); business analytics (MBA, MS); entrepreneurship (MBA); finance (MBA, MS, Certificate); financial life planning (Certificate); financial planning (MS, Certificate); global supply chain management (MBA, Certificate); human resource management (MBA, MS, Certificate); information technology management (MBA, MS, Certificate); international business (MBA); marketing (MBA, MS, Certificate); project management (MBA, MS, Certificate); psychology (MA, Certificate); public administration (EMPA, MBA); public administration leadership (Certificate). Electronic applications accepted.

School of Accounting *Program availability:* Part-time, evening/weekend. Offers financial accounting and reporting (M Ac, MSA, Graduate Certificate); forensic accounting (M Ac, MSA, Graduate Certificate); internal auditing (M Ac, MSA, Certificate); management accounting (M Ac, MSA); taxation (M Ac, MSA). Electronic applications accepted.

School of Law *Program availability:* Part-time, evening/weekend. Offers environmental law (LL M); estate planning (LL M); intellectual property law (LL M); international legal studies (LL M, SJD); law (JD); taxation law (LL M); U.S. legal studies (LL M). Electronic applications accepted.

School of Taxation *Program availability:* Part-time, evening/weekend. Offers advanced studies in taxation (Certificate); estate planning (Certificate); financial planning and taxation (MS); international taxation (Certificate); state and local taxation (Certificate); taxation (MS, Certificate). Electronic applications accepted.

GOLDEY-BEACOM COLLEGE, Wilmington, DE 19808-1999

General Information Independent, coed, comprehensive institution. *Graduate housing:* Room and/or apartments available on a first-come, first-served basis to single students; on-campus housing not available to married students.

GRADUATE UNITS

Graduate Program *Program availability:* Part-time, evening/weekend. Offers business administration (MBA); finance (MS); financial management (MBA); health care management (MBA); human resource management (MBA); information technology (MBA); international business management (MBA); major finance (MBA); major taxation (MBA); management (MM); marketing management (MBA); taxation (MBA, MS). Electronic applications accepted.

GOLDFARB SCHOOL OF NURSING AT BARNES-JEWISH COLLEGE, St. Louis, MO 63110

General Information Independent, coed, primarily women, comprehensive institution. *Graduate housing:* On-campus housing not available.

GRADUATE UNITS

Graduate Programs *Program availability:* Part-time, online learning. Offers adult-gerontology (MSN); adult-gerontology (MSN); health systems and population health leadership (MSN); nurse anesthesia (MSN).

GONZAGA UNIVERSITY, Spokane, WA 99258

General Information Independent-religious, coed, university. *Graduate housing:* Rooms and/or apartments available on a first-come, first-served basis to single and married students. Housing application deadline: 5/1.

GRADUATE UNITS

College of Arts and Sciences *Program availability:* Part-time, blended/hybrid learning. Offers philosophy (MA); theology and leadership (MA). Electronic applications accepted.

English Language Center *Program availability:* Part-time. Offers teaching English as a second language (MA). Electronic applications accepted.

School of Business Administration *Program availability:* Part-time, evening/weekend. Offers accountancy (M Acc); American Indian entrepreneurship (MBA); business administration (MBA); taxation (MS). Electronic applications accepted.

School of Education *Program availability:* Part-time, evening/weekend, 100% online, blended/hybrid learning. Offers clinical mental health counseling (MA); educational leadership (M Ed, Ed D); elementary education (MIT); marriage and family counseling (MA); school counseling (MA); secondary education (MIT); special education (M Ed, MIT); sport and athletic administration (MA). Electronic applications accepted.

School of Engineering and Applied Science *Program availability:* Part-time-only, evening/weekend, online only, 100% online. Offers transmission and distribution engineering (M Eng, Certificate). Electronic applications accepted.

School of Law *Program availability:* Part-time. Offers law (JD). Electronic applications accepted.

School of Leadership Studies *Program availability:* Part-time, evening/weekend, 100% online, blended/hybrid learning, immersion weekends. Offers communication and leadership (MA); leadership studies (PhD); organizational leadership (MA). Electronic applications accepted.

School of Nursing and Human Physiology *Program availability:* Part-time, evening/weekend, 100% online, immersion weekends. Offers nursing and human physiology (MSN, DNP, DNP-A). Electronic applications accepted.

GORDON COLLEGE, Wenham, MA 01984-1899

General Information Independent-religious, coed, comprehensive institution. *Graduate housing:* Room and/or apartments available on a first-come, first-served basis to single students; on-campus housing not available to married students. Housing application deadline: 6/15. *Research affiliation:* National Association for Music Education (music education), Feierabend Association for Music Education (early childhood music education), American Choral Directors Association (choral music education), Embracing the New Music Educators Association (mentoring for new music teaching professionals).

GRADUATE UNITS

Graduate Education Program *Program availability:* Part-time, evening/weekend. Offers early childhood (M Ed); educational leadership (M Ed, Ed S); elementary education (M Ed); English as a second language (M Ed, Ed S); math specialist (M Ed); mathematics specialist (Ed S); middle school education (M Ed); moderate disabilities (M Ed); Montessori education (M Ed); reading (M Ed, Ed S); secondary education (M Ed).

Graduate Financial Analysis Program *Program availability:* Part-time, evening/weekend. Offers financial analysis (MS). Electronic applications accepted.

Graduate Leadership Program Offers leadership (MA, Ed S).

Graduate Music Education Program *Program availability:* Part-time. Offers music education (MM Ed).

GORDON-CONWELL THEOLOGICAL SEMINARY, South Hamilton, MA 01982-2395

General Information Independent-religious, coed, graduate-only institution. *Graduate housing:* Rooms and/or apartments available to single and married students. Housing application deadline: 4/1.

GRADUATE UNITS

Graduate and Professional Programs *Program availability:* Part-time, evening/weekend. Offers Biblical languages (MABL); church history (MACH); counseling (MACO); ministry (D Min); missions/evangelism (MAME); New Testament (MANT); Old Testament (MAOT); religion (MAR); theology (M Div, MATH, Th M, Th D).

GOSHEN COLLEGE, Goshen, IN 46526-4794

General Information Independent-religious, coed, comprehensive institution. *Graduate housing:* On-campus housing not available.

GRADUATE UNITS

Merry Lea Environmental Learning Center Offers environmental education (MA). Electronic applications accepted.

Program in Nursing *Program availability:* Part-time, evening/weekend. Offers family nurse practitioner (MSN). Electronic applications accepted.

GOUCHER COLLEGE, Baltimore, MD 21204-2794

General Information Independent, coed, comprehensive institution. *Graduate housing:* On-campus housing not available. *Research affiliation:* Sheppard-Pratt Hospital (education).

GRADUATE UNITS

Graduate Programs in Education *Program availability:* Part-time, evening/weekend. Offers at-risk and diverse learners (M Ed, Certificate); athletic program leadership and administration (M Ed, Certificate); elementary education (MAT); literacy strategies for content learning (M Ed); middle school (M Ed, Certificate); Montessori studies (M Ed); reading instruction (M Ed, Certificate); reducing student, classroom, and school disruption (M Ed); school improvement leadership (M Ed); secondary education (MAT); special education (MAT); special education for certified elementary and secondary teachers (M Ed); teacher as leader in technology (M Ed). Electronic applications accepted.

MA and MFA Programs *Program availability:* Part-time, evening/weekend, blended/hybrid learning. Offers art and technology (MFA); arts administration (MA); cultural sustainability (MA); digital arts (MA); historic preservation (MA); nonfiction (MFA). Electronic applications accepted.

Post-Baccalaureate Premedical Program Offers premedical studies (Certificate). Electronic applications accepted.

GOVERNORS STATE UNIVERSITY, University Park, IL 60484

General Information State-supported, coed, university. CGS member. *Enrollment by degree level:* 1,533 master's, 196 doctoral. *Graduate housing:* Rooms and/or apartments available on a first-come, first-served basis to single and married students. Housing application deadline: 6/1. *Student services:* Campus employment opportunities, career counseling, child daycare facilities, exercise/wellness program, free psychological counseling, international student services, multicultural affairs office, services for students with disabilities, writing training. *Library facilities:* University Library. *Collection:* Books: 284,377 (physical), 339,176 (digital/electronic); Serial titles: 2,438 (physical), 11,484 (digital/electronic); Databases: 176. Weekly public service hours: 75; students can reserve study rooms.

Computer facilities: A campuswide network can be accessed from student residence rooms. Online class registration, student portal are available. Website: http://www.govst.edu/

General Application Contact: Paul McGuinness, Executive Director, Enrollment Management/Director, Admissions, 708-534-5000 Ext. 7308, E-mail: pmcguinness@govst.edu.

GRADUATE UNITS

College of Arts and Sciences Students: 1,067 full-time (541 women), 811 part-time (432 women); includes 1,125 minority (782 Black or African American, non-Hispanic/Latino; 1 American Indian or Alaska Native, non-Hispanic/Latino; 37 Asian, non-Hispanic/Latino; 238 Hispanic/Latino; 67 Two or more races, non-Hispanic/Latino), 66 international. Average age 29. 269 applicants, 70% accepted, 76 enrolled. *Faculty:* 97 full-time (48 women), 118 part-time/adjunct (55 women). Expenses: Contact institution. *Financial support:* Federal Work-Study and unspecified assistantships available. Financial award application deadline: 5/1; financial award applicants required to submit FAFSA. In 2018, 203 master's awarded. *Program availability:* Part-time. Offers actuarial science (MS); analytical chemistry (MS); art (MA); arts and sciences (MA, MFA, MPA, MS); communication studies (MS); computer science (MS); criminal justice (MA); English (MA); environmental biology (MS); independent film and digital imaging (MFA); political and justice studies (MA); public administration (MPA). *Application deadline:* For fall admission, 4/1 for domestic students. Applications are processed on a rolling basis. *Application fee:* $50. Electronic applications accepted. *Application Contact:* Paul McGuinness, Assistant Vice President, Enrollment Management/Director, Admissions, 708-534-5000 Ext. 7308, E-mail: pmcguinness@govst.edu. *Dean, College of Arts and Sciences/Dean, Graduate Studies,* Andrae Marak, 708-534-5000 Ext. 4589, E-mail: amarak@govst.edu.

College of Business Students: 35 full-time (19 women), 103 part-time (58 women); includes 78 minority (55 Black or African American, non-Hispanic/Latino; 7 Asian, non-Hispanic/Latino; 11 Hispanic/Latino; 5 Two or more races, non-Hispanic/Latino), 3 international. Average age 36. 108 applicants, 46% accepted, 38 enrolled. *Faculty:* 25 full-time (8 women), 34 part-time/adjunct (11 women). Expenses: Contact institution. *Financial support:* Federal Work-Study and unspecified assistantships available. Financial award application deadline: 5/1; financial award applicants required to submit FAFSA. In 2018, 54 master's awarded. *Program availability:* Part-time. Offers accounting (MS); business (MBA, MS); business administration (MBA); management information systems (MS). *Application deadline:* For fall admission, 4/1 for domestic students. Applications are processed on a rolling basis. *Application fee:* $50. Electronic applications accepted. *Application Contact:* Paul McGuinness, Assistant Vice President, Enrollment Management/Director, Admissions, 708-534-5000 Ext. 7308, E-mail: pmcguinness@govst.edu. *Dean, College of Business,* Jun Zhao, 708-534-5000 Ext. 4953, E-mail: jzhao@govst.edu.

College of Education Students: 154 full-time (133 women), 249 part-time (191 women); includes 217 minority (164 Black or African American, non-Hispanic/Latino; 4 Asian, non-Hispanic/Latino; 40 Hispanic/Latino; 9 Two or more races, non-Hispanic/Latino), 3 international. Average age 37. 197 applicants, 52% accepted, 87 enrolled. *Faculty:* 46 full-time (32 women), 53 part-time/adjunct (37 women). Expenses: Contact institution. *Financial support:* Federal Work-Study and unspecified assistantships available. Financial award application deadline: 5/1; financial award applicants required to submit FAFSA. In 2018, 99 master's, 17 doctorates awarded. *Program availability:* Part-time. Offers counseling (MA); early childhood education (MA); education (MA, Ed D); educational administration and supervision (MA); higher education administration (Ed D); multi-categorical special education (MA); psychology (MA); reading (MA). *Application deadline:* For fall admission, 4/1 for domestic students. Applications are processed on a rolling basis. *Application fee:* $50. Electronic applications accepted. *Application Contact:* Paul McGuinness, Assistant Vice President, Enrollment Management/Director, Admissions, 708-534-5000 Ext. 7308, E-mail: pmcguinness@govst.edu. *Dean, College of Education,* Shannon Dermer, 708-534-5000 Ext. 8396, E-mail: sdermer@govst.edu.

College of Health and Human Services Students: 344 full-time (263 women), 351 part-time (303 women); includes 348 minority (237 Black or African American, non-Hispanic/Latino; 25 Asian, non-Hispanic/Latino; 74 Hispanic/Latino; 12 Two or more races, non-Hispanic/Latino), 11 international. Average age 34. 516 applicants, 28% accepted, 105 enrolled. *Faculty:* 56 full-time (48 women), 85 part-time/adjunct (61 women). Expenses: Contact institution. *Financial support:* Federal Work-Study and unspecified assistantships available. Financial award application deadline: 5/1; financial award applicants required to submit FAFSA. In 2018, 203 master's, 38 doctorates awarded. *Program availability:* Part-time. Offers addiction studies and behavioral health (MHS); communication disorders (MHS); health administration (MHA); health and human services (MHA, MHS, MOT, MSN, MSW, DPT); nursing (MSN); occupational therapy (MOT); physical therapy (DPT); social work (MSW). *Application deadline:* For fall admission, 4/1 for domestic students. Applications are processed on a rolling basis. *Application fee:* $50. Electronic applications accepted. *Application Contact:* Paul McGuinness, Assistant Vice President, Enrollment Management/Director, Admission, 708-534-5000 Ext. 7308, E-mail: pmcguinness@govst.edu. *Dean, College of Health and Human Services,* Catherine Balthazar, 708-534-5000 Ext. 4592, E-mail: cbalthazar@govst.edu.

GRACE COLLEGE, Winona Lake, IN 46590-1294

General Information Independent-religious, coed, comprehensive institution. *Graduate housing:* On-campus housing not available.

GRADUATE UNITS

Department of Graduate Counseling *Program availability:* Part-time. Offers clinical mental health counseling (MA). Electronic applications accepted.

GRACE COLLEGE OF DIVINITY, Fayetteville, NC 28314

General Information Independent-religious, coed, comprehensive institution.

GRADUATE UNITS

Graduate Program Offers theology (MCL).

GRACELAND UNIVERSITY, Lamoni, IA 50140

General Information Independent-religious, coed, comprehensive institution. *Enrollment:* 1,992 graduate, professional, and undergraduate students; 449 full-time matriculated graduate/professional students (385 women), 363 part-time matriculated graduate/professional students (321 women). *Enrollment by degree level:* 734 master's, 20 doctoral, 58 other advanced degrees. *Tuition:* Part-time $800 per credit hour. *Graduate housing:* On-campus housing not available. *Student services:* Campus safety program, career counseling, free psychological counseling, services for students with disabilities, teacher training, writing training. *Library facilities:* F. M. Smith Library. *Collection:* Books: 80,000 (physical), 350,000 (digital/electronic); Serial titles: 130 (physical), 60 (digital/electronic); Databases: 50. Weekly public service hours: 80; students can reserve study rooms.

Computer facilities: 178 computers available on campus for general student use. A campuswide network can be accessed from student residence rooms and from off campus. Online class registration is available.
Website: http://www.graceland.edu/

General Application Contact: Lisa Libich, Director of Retention Operations for College of Graduate and Continuing Studies, 816-423-4730, Fax: 816-833-2990, E-mail: libich@graceland.edu.

GRADUATE UNITS

Community of Christ Seminary Students: 11 full-time (6 women), 15 part-time (8 women); includes 1 minority (American Indian or Alaska Native, non-Hispanic/Latino), 3 international. Average age 44. 12 applicants, 100% accepted, 9 enrolled. *Faculty:* 1 full-time (0 women), 1 part-time/adjunct (0 women). *Expenses:* Contact institution. *Financial support:* In 2018–19, 2 students received support. Scholarships/grants available. Financial award application deadline: 5/31; financial award applicants required to submit FAFSA. *Program availability:* Evening/weekend. Offers theology (MAR). *Application deadline:* For fall admission, 5/31 for domestic and international students. Applications are processed on a rolling basis. *Application fee:* $50. Electronic applications accepted. *Application Contact:* Sharon Ward, Administrative Assistant, 816-423-4676, Fax: 816-423-4753, E-mail: ward@graceland.edu. *Director,* Zac Harmon-McLaughlin, 816-423-4693, E-mail: zmclaugh@graceland.edu.

Gleazer School of Education Students: 70 full-time (58 women), 36 part-time (34 women); includes 4 minority (1 Black or African American, non-Hispanic/Latino; 1 Asian, non-Hispanic/Latino; 1 Hispanic/Latino; 1 Two or more races, non-Hispanic/Latino). Average age 34. 29 applicants, 21% accepted, 1 enrolled. *Expenses:* Contact institution. *Financial support:* Tuition waivers (partial) available. Financial award applicants required to submit FAFSA. In 2018, 76 master's awarded. *Program availability:* Part-time, 100% online. Offers curriculum and instruction: collaborative learning and teaching (M Ed); differentiated instruction (M Ed); instructional leadership (M Ed); literacy instruction (M Ed); management in a quality classroom (M Ed); special education (M Ed); technology integration (M Ed). *Application deadline:* For winter admission, 11/1 for domestic students; for spring admission, 2/1 priority date for domestic students; for summer admission, 7/1 for domestic students. Applications are processed on a rolling basis. *Application fee:* $50. Electronic applications accepted. *Application Contact:* Susan Freeze, Admissions Representative, 816-423-4676, Fax: 816-833-2990, E-mail: sfreeze1@graceland.edu. *Dean,* Dr. Michele Dickey-Kotz, 641-784-5202, E-mail: dickey@graceland.edu.

School of Nursing Students: 368 full-time (321 women), 312 part-time (279 women); includes 110 minority (38 Black or African American, non-Hispanic/Latino; 6 American Indian or Alaska Native, non-Hispanic/Latino; 18 Asian, non-Hispanic/Latino; 29 Hispanic/Latino; 19 Two or more races, non-Hispanic/Latino), 2 international. Average age 36. 236 applicants, 68% accepted, 121 enrolled. *Expenses:* Contact institution. *Financial support:* Institutionally sponsored loans available. Support available to part-time students. Financial award application deadline: 6/1; financial award applicants required to submit FAFSA. In 2018, 152 master's, 5 doctorates awarded. *Program availability:* Part-time, online only, 100% online. Offers adult and gerontology acute care (MSN, PMC); family nurse practitioner (MSN, PMC); nurse educator (MSN, PMC); organizational leadership (DNP). *Application deadline:* For fall admission, 7/1 priority date for domestic students; for winter admission, 11/1 priority date for domestic students; for spring admission, 11/1 priority date for domestic students; for summer admission, 3/1 priority date for domestic students. Applications are processed on a rolling basis. *Application fee:* $50. Electronic applications accepted. *Application Contact:* Barbie Bell, Admissions Representative, 816-423-4717, Fax: 816-833-2990, E-mail: distancelearning@graceland.edu. *Dean of School of Nursing & Professor of Nursing,* Dr. Sharon Little-Stoetzel, 816-423-4670, E-mail: stoetzel@graceland.edu.

GRACE MISSION UNIVERSITY, Fullerton, CA 92833

General Information Independent, coed, comprehensive institution.

GRADUATE UNITS

Graduate School Offers missions (M Div, MACE, MAICS, D Miss).

GRACE SCHOOL OF THEOLOGY, Conroe, TX 77384-4894

General Information Independent, coed, comprehensive institution.

GRADUATE UNITS

Graduate Programs Offers theology (M Div, MABS, MM, Th M).

GRACE THEOLOGICAL SEMINARY, Winona Lake, IN 46590-9907

General Information Independent-religious, coed, primarily men, graduate-only institution. *Graduate housing:* On-campus housing not available.

GRADUATE UNITS

Graduate and Professional Programs *Program availability:* Part-time, online learning. Offers biblical studies (Certificate); chaplaincy (M Div); exegetical studies (M Div); intercultural studies (M Div, MA, D Min); local church ministry (MA); pastoral counseling (M Div); pastoral studies (M Div, D Min); theology (Diploma). Electronic applications accepted.

THE GRADUATE CENTER, CITY UNIVERSITY OF NEW YORK, New York, NY 10016-4039

General Information State and locally supported, coed, graduate-only institution. CGS member. *Graduate housing:* Rooms and/or apartments available to single and married students. Housing application deadline: 5/1. *Research affiliation:* American Museum of Natural History (anthropology), Roche Institute of Molecular Biology (biological sciences), New York Botanical Gardens (biological sciences).

GRADUATE UNITS

Graduate Studies Offers accounting (PhD); anthropological linguistics (PhD); archaeology (PhD); architecture (PhD); audiology (Au D); basic applied neurocognition (PhD); behavioral science (PhD); biochemistry (PhD); biology (PhD); biopsychology (PhD); chemistry (PhD); classics (MA, PhD); clinical psychology (PhD); cognitive neuroscience (MS); comparative literature (MA, PhD); computer science (PhD); criminal justice (PhD); cultural anthropology (PhD); data analysis (MS); data science (MS); data studies (MS); data visualization (MS); data visualization and mapping (MA); developmental psychology (PhD); digital pedagogy (MA); earth and environmental sciences (PhD); economics (PhD); educational psychology (PhD); English (PhD); environmental psychology (PhD); experimental psychology (PhD); finance (PhD); French (PhD); graphic arts (PhD); history (PhD); industrial psychology (PhD); Latin American, Iberian and Latino cultures (PhD); learning processes (PhD); liberal studies (MA); linguistics (MA, PhD); management planning systems (PhD); mathematics (PhD); music (DMA, PhD); neuropsychology (PhD); nursing (PhD); painting (PhD); philosophy (MA, PhD); photography (PhD); physical anthropology (PhD); physics (PhD); political science (MA, PhD); psychology (PhD); quantitative methods in the social sciences (MS); sculpture (PhD); social personality (PhD); social welfare (DSW, PhD); sociology (PhD); speech-language-hearing sciences (PhD); textual analysis (MA); theatre (PhD); urban education (PhD). Electronic applications accepted.

GRADUATE THEOLOGICAL UNION, Berkeley, CA 94709-1212

General Information Independent-religious, coed, graduate-only institution. *Graduate housing:* Rooms and/or apartments available on a first-come, first-served basis to single and married students. Housing application deadline: 6/1.

GRADUATE UNITS

Graduate Programs Offers art and religion (MA, PhD, Th D); biblical languages (MA); biblical studies (MA); Biblical studies (PhD, Th D); Buddhist studies (MA); Christian spirituality (MA, PhD, Th D); cultural and historical studies of religions (MA, PhD, Th D); ethics and social theory (PhD, Th D); history (MA, PhD, Th D); homiletics (MA, PhD, Th D); interdisciplinary studies (PhD, Th D); Jewish studies (MA, PhD, Th D, Certificate); liturgical studies (MA, PhD, Th D); Near Eastern religions (PhD, Th D); Orthodox Christian studies (MA); religion and psychology (MA, PhD, Th D); religion and society/ethics and social theory (MA); systematic and philosophical theology (MA, PhD, Th D). PhD programs in Jewish studies and Near Eastern religions offered jointly with University of California, Berkeley. Electronic applications accepted.

GRAMBLING STATE UNIVERSITY, Grambling, LA 71245

General Information State-supported, coed, university. CGS member. *Graduate housing:* On-campus housing not available. *Research affiliation:* U.S. Department of Defense (cyberspace technology, materials and manufacturing), National Institutes of Justice (technology and equipment in forensic science), U.S. Department of Housing and Urban Development (HUD) (housing preservation in low-income areas), National Science Foundation (science and engineering), NASA (aeronautics research), National Institutes of Health (biomedical sciences).

GRADUATE UNITS

School of Graduate Studies and Research *Program availability:* Part-time, evening/weekend. Electronic applications accepted.

College of Arts and Sciences *Program availability:* Part-time. Offers arts and sciences (MA, MPA); health services administration (MPA); human resource management (MPA); public management (MPA); social sciences (MA); state and local government (MPA). Electronic applications accepted.

College of Education *Program availability:* Part-time, evening/weekend. Offers curriculum and instruction (MS); developmental education (MS, Ed D, PMC); education (M Ed, MAT, MS, Ed D, PMC); educational leadership (M Ed); special education (M Ed); sports administration (MS). Electronic applications accepted.

College of Professional Studies *Program availability:* Part-time. Offers criminal justice (MS); family nurse practitioner (PMC); mass communication (MA); nursing (MSN); social work (MSW). Electronic applications accepted.

GRAND CANYON UNIVERSITY, Phoenix, AZ 85017-1097

General Information Independent-religious, coed, comprehensive institution. *Graduate housing:* Rooms and/or apartments available on a first-come, first-served basis to single and married students.

GRADUATE UNITS

Colangelo College of Business *Program availability:* Part-time, evening/weekend, online learning. Offers accounting (MBA, MS); business analytics (MS); disaster preparedness and executive fire service leadership (MS); finance (MBA); general management (MBA); health systems management (MBA); information technology management (MS); leadership (MBA, MS); marketing (MBA); organizational leadership and entrepreneurship (MS); project management (MBA); sports business (MBA); strategic human resource management (MBA). Electronic applications accepted.

College of Doctoral Studies Offers data analytics (DBA); general psychology (PhD); management (DBA); marketing (DBA); organizational leadership (Ed D).

College of Education *Program availability:* Part-time, evening/weekend, online learning. Offers autism spectrum disorders (MA); curriculum and instruction (MA); early childhood education (M Ed); educational administration (M Ed); educational leadership (M Ed); elementary education (M Ed); gifted education (MA); instructional technology (MS); K-12 leadership (Ed S); reading (MA); secondary education (M Ed); secondary humanities education (M Ed); secondary STEM education (M Ed); special education (M Ed); teaching and learning (Ed D); teaching English to speakers of other languages (MA). Electronic applications accepted.

College of Nursing and Health Care Professions *Program availability:* Part-time, evening/weekend, online learning. Offers acute care nurse practitioner (MSN, PMC); family nurse practitioner (MSN, PMC); health care administration (MS); health care informatics (MS, MSN); leadership in health care systems (MSN); nursing (DNP); nursing education (MSN, PMC); public health (MPH, MSN).

GRAND RAPIDS THEOLOGICAL SEMINARY OF CORNERSTONE UNIVERSITY, Grand Rapids, MI 49525-5897

General Information Independent-religious, coed, graduate-only institution. *Graduate housing:* Rooms and/or apartments available on a first-come, first-served basis to single and married students. Housing application deadline: 6/1.

GRADUATE UNITS

Graduate Programs *Program availability:* Part-time, evening/weekend, 100% online, blended/hybrid learning. Offers academic (M Div); chaplaincy ministries (M Div); Christian formation (MA); counseling (MA); formation and soul care ministries (M Div); intercultural ministries (M Div); interdisciplinary studies (MA); New Testament (Th M); Old Testament (Th M); pastoral ministries (M Div); small group and discipleship ministries (M Div); student and family ministries (M Div). Electronic applications accepted.

GRAND VALLEY STATE UNIVERSITY, Allendale, MI 49401-9403

General Information State-supported, coed, comprehensive institution. CGS member. *Enrollment:* 24,677 graduate, professional, and undergraduate students; 1,412 full-time matriculated graduate/professional students (1,039 women), 1,449 part-time matriculated graduate/professional students (991 women). *Enrollment by degree level:* 2,560 master's, 286 doctoral, 15 other advanced degrees. *Graduate faculty:* 299 full-time (148 women), 91 part-time/adjunct (60 women). Tuition and fees vary according to degree level and program. *Graduate housing:* Rooms and/or apartments available on a first-come, first-served basis to single and married students. Housing application deadline: 2/1. *Student services:* Campus employment opportunities, campus safety program, career counseling, child daycare facilities, exercise/wellness program, free psychological counseling, grant writing training, international student services, low-cost health insurance, multicultural affairs office, services for students with disabilities, teacher training, writing training. *Library facilities:* Mary Idema Pew Library Learning and Information Commons plus 5 others. *Collection:* Books: 567,197 (physical), 1 million (digital/electronic). Students can reserve study rooms.

Computer facilities: 2,600 computers available on campus for general student use. A campuswide network can be accessed from student residence rooms and from off campus. Online class registration, transcript, degree audit, credit card payments are available.
Website: http://www.gvsu.edu/

General Application Contact: Tracey James-Heer, Associate Director of Admissions, 616-331-2025, Fax: 616-331-2000, E-mail: james-ht@gvsu.edu.

GRADUATE UNITS

College of Community and Public Service Students: 273 full-time (231 women), 245 part-time (193 women); includes 100 minority (41 Black or African American, non-Hispanic/Latino; 7 American Indian or Alaska Native, non-Hispanic/Latino; 11 Asian, non-Hispanic/Latino; 28 Hispanic/Latino; 13 Two or more races, non-Hispanic/Latino), 13 international. Average age 29. 334 applicants, 92% accepted, 150 enrolled. *Faculty:* 29 full-time (13 women), 22 part-time/adjunct (13 women). Expenses: Contact institution. *Financial support:* In 2018–19, 91 students received support, including 51 fellowships, 52 research assistantships with full and partial tuition reimbursements available (averaging $8,000 per year); teaching assistantships, career-related internships or fieldwork, Federal Work-Study, institutionally sponsored loans, and unspecified assistantships also available. Financial award application deadline: 5/1. In 2018, 220 master's awarded. *Program availability:* Part-time, evening/weekend. Offers community and public service (MHA, MPA, MPNL, MS, MSW). *Application deadline:* For fall admission, 5/1 priority date for domestic students; for winter admission, 11/1 priority date for domestic students; for spring admission, 4/10 priority date for domestic students. Applications are processed on a rolling basis. *Application fee:* $30. Electronic applications accepted. *Application Contact:* Tracey James-Heer, Associate Director of Admissions, 616-331-2025, Fax: 616-331-2000, E-mail: james-ht@gvsu.edu. *Dean,* George Grant, 616-331-6850.

School of Criminal Justice Students: 11 full-time (8 women), 8 part-time (5 women); includes 5 minority (2 Black or African American, non-Hispanic/Latino; 3 Hispanic/Latino), 1 international. Average age 28. 22 applicants, 95% accepted, 7 enrolled. *Faculty:* 5 full-time (1 woman). Expenses: Contact institution. *Financial support:* In 2018–19, 6 students received support, including 6 research assistantships with full and partial tuition reimbursements available (averaging $4,000 per year); fellowships, career-related internships or fieldwork, Federal Work-Study, scholarships/grants, and unspecified assistantships also available. Financial award application deadline: 5/1. In 2018, 3 master's awarded. *Program availability:* Part-time, evening/weekend. Offers criminal justice (MS). *Application deadline:* For fall admission, 5/1 priority date for domestic students; for winter admission, 11/1 priority date for domestic students; for spring admission, 4/1 priority date for domestic students. Applications are processed on a rolling basis. *Application fee:* $30. Electronic applications accepted. *Application Contact:* Tonisha Jones, Graduate Program Director/Recruiting Contact, 616-331-7187, Fax: 616-331-7155, E-mail: jontonis@gvsu.edu. *Director,* Dr. Patrick Gerkin, 616-331-7130, Fax: 616-331-7155, E-mail: gerkinp@gvsu.edu.

School of Public, Nonprofit and Health Administration Students: 31 full-time (20 women), 79 part-time (52 women); includes 18 minority (6 Black or African American, non-Hispanic/Latino; 3 American Indian or Alaska Native, non-Hispanic/Latino; 2 Asian, non-Hispanic/Latino; 4 Hispanic/Latino; 3 Two or more races, non-Hispanic/Latino), 4 international. Average age 30. 76 applicants, 91% accepted, 23 enrolled. *Faculty:* 12 full-time (5 women), 4 part-time/adjunct (2 women). Expenses: Contact institution. *Financial support:* In 2018–19, 27 students received support, including 18 fellowships, 15 research assistantships with full and partial tuition reimbursements available (averaging $4,000 per year); career-related internships or fieldwork, Federal Work-Study, scholarships/grants, and unspecified assistantships also available. Financial award application deadline: 5/1. In 2018, 40 master's awarded. *Program availability:* Part-time, evening/weekend. Offers health administration (MHA); philanthropy and nonprofit leadership (MPNL); public, nonprofit and health administration (MHA, MPA, MPNL). *Application deadline:* For fall admission, 5/1 priority date for domestic students; for winter admission, 11/1 priority date for domestic students. Applications are processed on a rolling basis. *Application fee:* $30. Electronic applications accepted. *Application Contact:* Davia Downey, Graduate Program Director/Recruiting Contact, 616-331-6681, Fax: 616-331-7120, E-mail: downeyd@gvsu.edu. *Director,* Dr. Richard Jelier, 616-331-6575, Fax: 616-331-7120, E-mail: jelierr@gvsu.edu.

School of Social Work Students: 196 full-time (177 women), 110 part-time (97 women); includes 62 minority (29 Black or African American, non-Hispanic/Latino; 4 American Indian or Alaska Native, non-Hispanic/Latino; 4 Asian, non-Hispanic/Latino; 19 Hispanic/Latino; 6 Two or more races, non-Hispanic/Latino), 1 international. Average age 28. 191 applicants, 93% accepted, 101 enrolled. *Faculty:* 12 full-time (7 women), 18 part-time/adjunct (11 women). Expenses: Contact institution. *Financial support:* In 2018–19, 45 students received support, including 27 fellowships, 23 research assistantships with full and partial tuition reimbursements available (averaging $4,000 per year); career-related internships or fieldwork, Federal Work-Study, institutionally sponsored loans, and unspecified assistantships also available. In 2018, 151 master's awarded. *Program availability:* Part-time. Offers social work (MSW). *Application deadline:* For fall admission, 5/1 priority date for domestic students; for winter admission, 10/1 priority date for domestic students; for spring admission, 3/15 priority date for domestic students. Applications are processed on a rolling basis. *Application fee:* $30. Electronic applications accepted. *Application Contact:* Dr. Cray Mulder, Graduate Program Director/Recruiting Contact, 616-331-6596, Fax: 616-331-6570, E-mail: muldercra@gvsu.edu. *Chair,* Dr. Scott Berlin, 616-331-6556, Fax: 616-331-6570, E-mail: berlins@gvsu.edu.

College of Education Students: 124 full-time (77 women), 655 part-time (524 women); includes 92 minority (43 Black or African American, non-Hispanic/Latino; 6 American Indian or Alaska Native, non-Hispanic/Latino; 8 Asian, non-Hispanic/Latino; 27 Hispanic/Latino; 8 Two or more races, non-Hispanic/Latino), 13 international. Average age 33. 312 applicants, 93% accepted, 110 enrolled. *Faculty:* 42 full-time (26 women), 12 part-time/adjunct (9 women). Expenses: Contact institution. *Financial support:* In 2018–19, 236 students received support, including 178 fellowships, 50 research assistantships with full and partial tuition reimbursements available (averaging $8,000 per year); career-related internships or fieldwork, Federal Work-Study, scholarships/grants, and unspecified assistantships also available. In 2018, 271 master's, 9 Ed Ss awarded. *Program availability:* Part-time, evening/weekend, 100% online. Offers adult and higher education (M Ed); cognitive impairment (M Ed); college student affairs leadership (M Ed); early childhood developmental delay (M Ed); early childhood education (M Ed); education (M Ed, Ed S); educational differentiation (M Ed); educational leadership (M Ed); educational technology (M Ed); educational technology integration (M Ed); elementary education (M Ed); emotional impairment (M Ed); higher education (M Ed); instruction and curriculum (M Ed); leadership (Ed S); learning disabilities (M Ed); literacy studies (M Ed); middle level education (M Ed); reading and language arts (M Ed); school counseling (M Ed); school library media services (M Ed); secondary level education (M Ed); special education (M Ed); teaching English to speakers of other languages (M Ed). *Application deadline:* Applications are processed on a rolling basis. *Application fee:* $30. Electronic applications accepted. *Application Contact:* Annukka Thelen, Director, Student Information and Services Center, 616-331-6650, Fax: 616-331-6217, E-mail: thelenant@gvsu.edu. *Interim Dean,* Dr. Sherril Soman, 616-331-2987, Fax: 616-331-6515, E-mail: somans@gvsu.edu.

College of Health Professions Students: 652 full-time (527 women), 38 part-time (32 women); includes 65 minority (15 Black or African American, non-Hispanic/Latino; 1 American Indian or Alaska Native, non-Hispanic/Latino; 17 Asian, non-Hispanic/Latino; 20 Hispanic/Latino; 12 Two or more races, non-Hispanic/Latino), 5 international. Average age 25. 1,271 applicants, 31% accepted, 292 enrolled. *Faculty:* 58 full-time (45 women), 22 part-time/adjunct (20 women). Expenses: Contact institution. *Financial support:* In 2018–19, 98 students received support, including 69 fellowships, 40 research assistantships with full and partial tuition reimbursements available (averaging $8,000 per year); career-related internships or fieldwork, Federal Work-Study, institutionally sponsored loans, and scholarships/grants also available. Financial award application deadline: 2/15. In 2018, 221 master's, 60 doctorates awarded. Offers clinical dietetics (MS); health professions (MPAS, MPH, MS, DPT); medical dosimetry (MS); occupational therapy (MS); physical therapy (DPT); physician assistant studies (MPAS); public health (MPH); speech-language pathology (MS). *Application deadline:* For winter admission, 1/15 priority date for domestic and international students. Applications are processed on a rolling basis. Electronic applications accepted. *Application Contact:* Darlene Zwart, Student Services Coordinator, 616-331-3958, E-mail: zwartda@gvsu.edu. *Dean,* Dr. Roy Olsson, 616-331-3356, Fax: 616-331-3350, E-mail: olssonr@gvsu.edu.

College of Liberal Arts and Sciences Students: 142 full-time (83 women), 128 part-time (85 women); includes 42 minority (16 Black or African American, non-Hispanic/Latino; 1 American Indian or Alaska Native, non-Hispanic/Latino; 4 Asian, non-Hispanic/Latino; 8 Hispanic/Latino; 13 Two or more races, non-Hispanic/Latino), 24 international. Average age 28. 212 applicants, 79% accepted, 91 enrolled. *Faculty:* 93 full-time (37 women), 5 part-time/adjunct (1 woman). Expenses: Contact institution. *Financial support:* In 2018–19, 101 students received support, including 18 fellowships, 86 research assistantships; career-related internships or fieldwork, Federal Work-Study, institutionally sponsored loans, scholarships/grants, and unspecified assistantships also available. In 2018, 97 master's, 12 other advanced degrees awarded. *Program availability:* Part-time, evening/weekend. Offers applied linguistics (MA); biology (MS); biomedical sciences (MHS); biostatistics (MS); cell and molecular biology (MS); English (MA); liberal arts and sciences (MA, MHS, MS, Psy S); school psychology (MS, Psy S). *Application deadline:* Applications are processed on a rolling basis. *Application fee:* $30. Electronic applications accepted. *Application Contact:* Betty Schaner, Assistant Dean of Advising and Student Services, 616-331-2495, Fax: 616-331-3675, E-mail: schanerb@gvsu.edu. *Dean,* Dr. Frederick Antczak, 616-331-2495, Fax: 616-331-3675, E-mail: antczakf@gvsu.edu.

School of Communications Students: 21 full-time (11 women), 30 part-time (16 women); includes 18 minority (7 Black or African American, non-Hispanic/Latino; 2 Asian, non-Hispanic/Latino; 5 Hispanic/Latino; 4 Two or more races, non-Hispanic/Latino), 5 international. Average age 30. 46 applicants, 98% accepted, 15 enrolled. *Faculty:* 2 full-time (0 women), 1 part-time/adjunct (0 women). Expenses: Contact institution. *Financial support:* In 2018–19, 13 students received support, including 9 fellowships, 4 research assistantships with full and partial tuition reimbursements available (averaging $8,000 per year); career-related internships or fieldwork, Federal Work-Study, and institutionally sponsored loans also available. Support available to part-time students. Financial award application deadline: 4/15. In 2018, 22 master's awarded. *Program availability:* Part-time, evening/weekend. Offers communications (MS). *Application deadline:* For fall admission, 8/15 priority date for domestic students; for winter admission, 12/15 priority date for domestic students; for spring admission, 4/15 priority date for domestic students. Applications are processed on a rolling basis. *Application fee:* $30. Electronic applications accepted. *Application Contact:* Dr. Alex Nesterenko, Graduate Program Director, 616-331-3667, Fax: 616-331-2700, E-mail: nesterea@gvsu.edu. *Department Director,* Dr. Jonathan Hodge, 616-331-3668, Fax: 616-895-2700, E-mail: hodgejo@gvsu.edu.

Kirkhof College of Nursing Students: 63 full-time (58 women), 55 part-time (48 women); includes 17 minority (9 Black or African American, non-Hispanic/Latino; 4 Asian, non-Hispanic/Latino; 3 Hispanic/Latino; 1 Two or more races, non-Hispanic/Latino), 4 international. Average age 33. 39 applicants, 97% accepted, 24 enrolled. *Faculty:* 17 full-time (16 women), 6 part-time/adjunct (5 women). Expenses: Contact institution. *Financial support:* In 2018–19, 39 students received support, including 14 fellowships, 29 research assistantships with partial tuition reimbursements available (averaging $4,000 per year); career-related internships or fieldwork, Federal Work-Study, institutionally sponsored loans, and traineeships also available. Financial award application deadline: 2/15. In 2018, 7 master's, 49 doctorates awarded. *Program availability:* Part-time. Offers advanced practice (MSN); case management (MSN); nursing administration (MSN); nursing education (MSN); nursing practice (DNP). *Application deadline:* For fall admission, 3/15 priority date for domestic students. Applications are processed on a rolling basis. *Application fee:* $30. Electronic applications accepted. *Application Contact:* Dr. Katherine Moran, Graduate Program Director, 616-331-5458, Fax: 616-331-2510, E-mail: morakath@gvsu.edu. *Dean,* Dr. Cynthia McCurren, 616-331-3558, Fax: 616-331-2510, E-mail: mccurrec@gvsu.edu.

Padnos College of Engineering and Computing Students: 82 full-time (30 women), 131 part-time (27 women); includes 24 minority (5 Black or African American, non-Hispanic/Latino; 11 Asian, non-Hispanic/Latino; 4 Hispanic/Latino; 4 Two or more races, non-Hispanic/Latino), 78 international. Average age 27. 185 applicants, 72% accepted, 57 enrolled. *Faculty:* 31 full-time (5 women). Expenses: Contact institution. *Financial support:* In 2018–19, 69 students received support, including 18 fellowships, 56 research assistantships with full and partial tuition reimbursements available (averaging $8,000 per year); unspecified assistantships also available. In 2018, 71 master's awarded. *Program availability:* Part-time. Offers engineering and computing (MS, MSE); medical and bioinformatics (MS). *Application deadline:* For fall admission, 2/1 for domestic students. Applications are processed on a rolling basis. *Application fee:* $30. Electronic applications accepted. *Application Contact:* Sara Wheeler, Director, Advising Center, 616-331-6025, Fax: 616-331-6770, E-mail: wheelesa@gvsu.edu. *Dean,* Dr. Paul Plotkowski, 616-331-6260, Fax: 616-331-6770, E-mail: plotkowp@gvsu.edu.

School of Computing and Information Systems Students: 26 full-time (10 women), 53 part-time (7 women); includes 10 minority (2 Black or African American, non-Hispanic/Latino; 6 Asian, non-Hispanic/Latino; 1 Hispanic/Latino; 1 Two or more races, non-Hispanic/Latino), 21 international. Average age 29. 56 applicants, 70% accepted, 15 enrolled. *Faculty:* 10 full-time (0 women). Expenses: Contact institution. *Financial support:* In 2018–19, 13 students received support, including 6 fellowships, 5 research assistantships with full and partial tuition reimbursements available (averaging $8,000 per year). In 2018, 23 master's awarded. *Program availability:* Part-time, evening/weekend. Offers computer information systems (MS). *Application deadline:* For fall admission, 6/1 for international students; for winter admission, 9/1 for international students. Applications are processed on a rolling basis. *Application fee:* $30. Electronic applications accepted. *Application Contact:* Dr. D. Robert Adams, Graduate Program Director, 616-331-3885, Fax: 616-331-2144, E-mail: adamsr@gvsu.edu. *Director,* Dr. Paul Leidig, 616-331-2060, Fax: 616-331-2144, E-mail: leidigp@gvsu.edu.

School of Engineering Students: 26 full-time (5 women), 50 part-time (7 women); includes 6 minority (1 Black or African American, non-Hispanic/Latino; 2 Asian, non-Hispanic/Latino; 1 Hispanic/Latino; 2 Two or more races, non-Hispanic/Latino), 39 international. Average age 26. 52 applicants, 62% accepted, 13 enrolled. *Faculty:* 19 full-time (5 women). Expenses: Contact institution. *Financial support:* In 2018–19, 40 students received support, including 8 fellowships, 34 research assistantships with full and partial tuition reimbursements available (averaging $4,000 per year); career-related internships or fieldwork, Federal Work-Study, institutionally sponsored loans, scholarships/grants, and unspecified assistantships also available. In 2018, 32 master's awarded. *Program availability:* Part-time, evening/weekend. Offers electrical and computer engineering (MSE); manufacturing operations (MSE); mechanical engineering (MSE); product design and manufacturing engineering (MSE). *Application deadline:* Applications are processed on a rolling basis. *Application fee:* $30. Electronic applications accepted. *Application Contact:* Dr. Shabbir Choudhuri, Graduate Program Director, 616-331-6845, Fax: 616-331-7215, E-mail: choudhus@gvsu.edu. *Director,* Dr. Wael Mokhtar, 616-331-6015, Fax: 616-331-7215, E-mail: mokhtarw@gvsu.edu.

Seidman College of Business Students: 76 full-time (33 women), 197 part-time (82 women); includes 38 minority (4 Black or African American, non-Hispanic/Latino; 1 American Indian or Alaska Native, non-Hispanic/Latino; 11 Asian, non-Hispanic/Latino; 14 Hispanic/Latino; 8 Two or more races, non-Hispanic/Latino), 13 international. Average age 30. 130 applicants, 95% accepted, 42 enrolled. *Faculty:* 24 full-time (4 women), 9 part-time/adjunct (2 women). Expenses: Contact institution. *Financial support:* In 2018–19, 50 students received support, including 36 fellowships, 19 research assistantships; Federal Work-Study, institutionally sponsored loans, and unspecified assistantships also available. Support available to part-time students. Financial award application deadline: 2/15; financial award applicants required to submit FAFSA. In 2018, 111 master's awarded. *Program availability:* Part-time, evening/weekend. Offers accounting (MSA); business (MBA, MSA, MST); business administration (MBA); taxation (MST). *Application deadline:* For fall admission, 8/1 priority date for domestic students, 5/1 priority date for international students; for winter admission, 12/1 priority date for domestic students, 11/1 priority date for international students; for spring admission, 4/1 priority date for domestic students, 3/1 priority date for international students. Applications are processed on a rolling basis. *Application fee:* $30. Electronic applications accepted. *Application Contact:* Koleta Moore, Assistant Dean of Student Engagement, Graduate Program Operations, 616-331-7400, Fax: 616-331-7389, E-mail: moorekol@gvsu.edu. *Dean,* Dr. Diana Lawson, 616-331-7385, Fax: 616-331-7380, E-mail: lawsond1@gvsu.edu.

GRAND VIEW UNIVERSITY, Des Moines, IA 50316-1599

General Information Independent-religious, coed, comprehensive institution.

GRADUATE UNITS

Graduate Studies *Program availability:* Part-time, evening/weekend. Offers athletic training (MS); clinical nurse leader (MSN, Post Master's Certificate); nursing education (MSN, Post Master's Certificate); organizational leadership (MS); sport management (MS); teacher leadership (M Ed); urban education (M Ed). Electronic applications accepted.

GRANITE STATE COLLEGE, Concord, NH 03301

General Information State and locally supported, coed, comprehensive institution. *Graduate housing:* On-campus housing not available.

GRADUATE UNITS

MS in Instruction and Leadership Program *Program availability:* Part-time, evening/weekend. Offers instruction and leadership (MS). Electronic applications accepted.

MS in Leadership Program *Program availability:* Part-time, evening/weekend, 100% online, blended/hybrid learning. Offers leadership (MS). Electronic applications accepted.

MS in Management Program *Program availability:* Part-time, 100% online, blended/hybrid learning. Offers management (MS). Electronic applications accepted.

MS in Project Management Program *Program availability:* Part-time, 100% online, blended/hybrid learning. Offers project management (MS). Electronic applications accepted.

GRANTHAM UNIVERSITY, Lenexa, KS 66219

General Information Proprietary, coed, comprehensive institution. *Enrollment:* 891 full-time matriculated graduate/professional students (410 women), 461 part-time matriculated graduate/professional students (209 women). *Enrollment by degree level:* 1,327 master's, 25 other advanced degrees. *Tuition:* Full-time $4200; part-time $350 per credit hour. *Required fees:* $50; $50 per credit hour. *Student services:* Career counseling, services for students with disabilities, writing training. *Library facilities:* Grantham Online Library.

Computer facilities: Online class registration is available. Website: http://www.grantham.edu/

General Application Contact: Lauren Cook, Director of Admissions, 800-955-2527 Ext. 803, Fax: 877-3044467, E-mail: admissions@grantham.edu.

GRADUATE UNITS

College of Engineering and Computer Science Students: 168 full-time (40 women), 65 part-time (19 women); includes 102 minority (73 Black or African American, non-Hispanic/Latino; 1 American Indian or Alaska Native, non-Hispanic/Latino; 10 Asian, non-Hispanic/Latino; 10 Hispanic/Latino; 8 Two or more races, non-Hispanic/Latino). Average age 40. 52 applicants, 96% accepted, 44 enrolled. Expenses: Contact institution. *Financial support:* Scholarships/grants available. Financial award applicants required to submit FAFSA. In 2018, 84 master's awarded. *Program availability:* Part-time, evening/weekend, online only, 100% online. Offers information management (MS); information management technology (MS); information technology (MS). *Application deadline:* Applications are processed on a rolling basis. *Application fee:* $0. Electronic applications accepted. *Application Contact:* Lauren Cook, Director of Admissions, 800-955-2527 Ext. 803, Fax: 877-304-4467, E-mail: admissions@grantham.edu. *Dean of the College of Engineering and Computer Science,* Dr. Nancy Miller, 913-309-4738, Fax: 855-681-5201, E-mail: nmiller@grantham.edu.

College of Nursing and Allied Health Students: 182 full-time (138 women), 95 part-time (68 women); includes 114 minority (77 Black or African American, non-Hispanic/Latino; 2 American Indian or Alaska Native, non-Hispanic/Latino; 20 Asian, non-Hispanic/Latino; 8 Hispanic/Latino; 2 Native Hawaiian or other Pacific Islander, non-Hispanic/Latino; 5 Two or more races, non-Hispanic/Latino). Average age 41. 90 applicants, 92% accepted, 65 enrolled. Expenses: Contact institution. *Financial support:* Scholarships/grants available. Financial award applicants required to submit FAFSA. In 2018, 87 master's awarded. *Program availability:* Part-time, evening/weekend, online only, 100% online. Offers case management (MSN); health systems management (MS); healthcare administration (MHA); nursing education (MSN); nursing informatics (MSN); nursing management and organizational leadership (MSN). *Application deadline:* Applications are processed on a rolling basis. *Application fee:* $0. Electronic applications accepted. *Application Contact:* Lauren Cook, Director of Admissions, 800-955-2527 Ext. 803, Fax: 877-304-4467, E-mail: admissions@grantham.edu. *Dean of the College of Nursing and Allied Health,* Dr. Cheryl Rules, 913-309-4783, Fax: 844-897-6490, E-mail: crules@grantham.edu.

Mark Skousen School of Business Students: 556 full-time (238 women), 301 part-time (122 women); includes 369 minority (268 Black or African American, non-Hispanic/Latino; 5 American Indian or Alaska Native, non-Hispanic/Latino; 16 Asian, non-Hispanic/Latino; 50 Hispanic/Latino; 4 Native Hawaiian or other Pacific Islander, non-Hispanic/Latino; 26 Two or more races, non-Hispanic/Latino), 1 international. Average age 40. 206 applicants, 90% accepted, 159 enrolled. Expenses: Contact institution. *Financial support:* Scholarships/grants available. Financial award applicants required to submit FAFSA. In 2018, 284 master's, 16 other advanced degrees awarded. *Program availability:* Part-time, evening/weekend, online only, 100% online. Offers business administration (MBA); business intelligence (MS); human resources (Certificate); information management (MBA); performance improvement (MS); project management (MBA, Certificate). *Application deadline:* Applications are processed on a rolling basis. *Application fee:* $0. Electronic applications accepted. *Application Contact:* Lauren Cook, Director of Admissions, 800-955-2527 Ext. 803, Fax: 877-304-4467, E-mail: admissions@grantham.edu. *Dean of the Mark Skousen School of Business,* Dr. David Marker, 913-309-4747, Fax: 844-260-6287, E-mail: dmarker@grantham.edu.

GRATZ COLLEGE, Melrose Park, PA 19027

General Information Independent-religious, coed, graduate-only institution. *Graduate housing:* On-campus housing not available.

GRADUATE UNITS

Graduate Programs *Program availability:* Part-time, evening/weekend, online learning. Offers education (MA); education leadership (Ed D); Holocaust and genocide studies (MA, PhD); Jewish Christian studies (Graduate Certificate); Jewish communal service (MA, Certificate); Jewish instructional education (MA); Jewish studies (MA); nonprofit management (MS).

GREENSBORO COLLEGE, Greensboro, NC 27401-1875

General Information Independent-religious, coed, comprehensive institution. *Graduate housing:* Rooms and/or apartments guaranteed to single students and available on a first-come, first-served basis to married students. Housing application deadline: 6/1.

GRADUATE UNITS

Program in Education *Program availability:* Part-time, evening/weekend. Offers elementary education (M Ed); special education (M Ed). Electronic applications accepted.

Program in Teaching English to Speakers of Other Languages *Program availability:* Part-time, evening/weekend. Offers teaching English to speakers of other languages (MA). Electronic applications accepted.

Program in Theology, Ethics and Culture Offers theology, ethics and culture (MA).

GREENVILLE UNIVERSITY, Greenville, IL 62246-0159

General Information Independent-religious, coed, comprehensive institution. *Graduate housing:* On-campus housing not available.

GRADUATE UNITS

Program in Education Offers education (MAT); elementary education (MAE); secondary education (MAE). Electronic applications accepted.

Program in Leadership and Ministry *Program availability:* Part-time. Offers leadership and ministry (MA). Electronic applications accepted.

GUILFORD COLLEGE, Greensboro, NC 27410-4173

General Information Independent-religious, coed, comprehensive institution.

GRADUATE UNITS

Master in Criminal Justice Students: 4 full-time (2 women), 2 part-time (1 woman); includes 2 minority (both Black or African American, non-Hispanic/Latino). Average age 36. 6 applicants, 100% accepted, 6 enrolled. *Faculty:* 2 full-time (1 woman), 1 (1 woman) part-time/adjunct. Expenses: Contact institution. *Financial support:* Applicants required to submit FAFSA. *Program availability:* Part-time, evening/weekend. Offers criminal justice (MS). *Application deadline:* Applications are processed on a rolling basis. *Application fee:* $75. Electronic applications accepted. *Application Contact:* Will Pizio, Coordinator, 336-316-2418, E-mail: wpizio@guilford.edu. *Coordinator,* Will Pizio, 336-316-2418, E-mail: wpizio@guilford.edu.

GWYNEDD MERCY UNIVERSITY, Gwynedd Valley, PA 19437-0901

General Information Independent-religious, coed, comprehensive institution. *Graduate housing:* On-campus housing not available.

GRADUATE UNITS

Frances M. Maguire School of Nursing and Health Professions *Program availability:* Part-time, blended/hybrid learning. Offers clinical nurse specialist (MSN); nurse educator (MSN); nurse practitioner (MSN); nursing (DNP). Electronic applications accepted.

School of Education *Program availability:* Part-time, evening/weekend, 100% online. Offers education (Ed D); educational administration (MS); master teacher (MS); school counseling (MS); special education (MS).

School of Graduate and Professional Studies *Program availability:* Part-time, evening/weekend. Offers health care administration (MBA); management (MSM); strategic management and leadership (MBA).

HALLMARK UNIVERSITY, San Antonio, TX 78230

General Information Independent, coed, comprehensive institution. *Graduate housing:* On-campus housing not available.

GRADUATE UNITS

School of Business Offers global management (MBA).

HAMLINE UNIVERSITY, St. Paul, MN 55104-1284

General Information Independent-religious, coed, comprehensive institution. *Graduate housing:* Rooms and/or apartments available on a first-come, first-served basis to single and married students. *Research affiliation:* Minnesota Women Elected Officials.

GRADUATE UNITS

College of Liberal Arts *Program availability:* Part-time, evening/weekend. Offers creative writing (MFA); creative writing for children and young adults (MFA); law (MSL). Electronic applications accepted.

School of Business *Program availability:* Part-time, evening/weekend, blended/hybrid learning. Offers business administration (MBA); nonprofit management (MNM); public administration (MPA, DPA). Electronic applications accepted.

School of Education *Program availability:* Part-time, evening/weekend, 100% online, blended/hybrid learning. Offers education (MA Ed, Ed D); English as a second language (MA); literacy education (MA); natural science and environmental education (MA Ed); teaching (MAT); teaching English to speakers of other languages (MA). Electronic applications accepted.

HAMPTON UNIVERSITY, Hampton, VA 23668

General Information Independent, coed, comprehensive institution. CGS member. *Enrollment by degree level:* 284 master's, 217 doctoral. *Graduate housing:* Rooms and/or apartments available on a first-come, first-served basis to single and married students. Housing application deadline: 6/1. *Student services:* Campus employment opportunities, campus safety program, career counseling, child daycare facilities, exercise/wellness program, free psychological counseling, international student services, services for students with disabilities, teacher training, writing training. *Library facilities:* William R. and Norma B. Harvey Library plus 4 others. *Collection:* Books: 307,143 (physical), 91,991 (digital/electronic); Serial titles: 8,240 (physical); Databases: 115. Study areas open 24 hours, 5–7 days a week; students can reserve study rooms. *Research affiliation:* NASA (Atmospheric and Planetary Sciences), NASA (Atmospheric and Planetary Sciences, Engineering), National Oceanic and Atmospheric Administration (NOAA) (Atmospheric, Planetary, Marine & Environmental Sciences), Thomas Jefferson National Accelerator Lab (Physics, Medical Physics), L'Oreal (Dermatology, Cancer Research), The Cancer Action Coalition of Virginia (Biology, Nursing, Pharmacy, Medical Physics, Biochemistry & Chemistry).

Computer facilities: Computer purchase and lease plans are available. 1,500 computers available on campus for general student use. A campuswide network can be accessed from student residence rooms and from off campus. Online class registration, learning management system are available.
Website: http://www.hamptonu.edu/

General Application Contact: Dr. Michelle Penn-Marshall, Dean, Graduate College, 757-727-5454, E-mail: hugrad@hamptonu.edu.

GRADUATE UNITS

Program in Business Administration Students: 24 full-time (12 women), 12 part-time (4 women); includes 32 minority (31 Black or African American, non-Hispanic/Latino; 1 Hispanic/Latino), 2 international. Average age 28. 24 applicants, 42% accepted, 8 enrolled. Expenses: Contact institution. *Financial support:* Research assistantships, teaching assistantships, career-related internships or fieldwork, Federal Work-Study, institutionally sponsored loans, scholarships/grants, health care benefits, tuition waivers, unspecified assistantships, and stipends available. Support available to part-time students. Financial award application deadline: 6/30; financial award applicants required to submit FAFSA. In 2018, 21 master's, 3 doctorates awarded. *Program availability:* Part-time, online learning. Offers business administration (MBA, PhD). *Application deadline:* For fall admission, 6/1 priority date for domestic students, 4/1 priority date for international students; for spring admission, 11/1 priority date for domestic students, 9/1 priority date for international students; for summer admission, 4/1 priority date for domestic students, 2/1 priority date for international students. Applications are processed on a rolling basis. *Application fee:* $35. Electronic applications accepted. *Application Contact:* Dr. Ziette Hayes, Dean, School of Business, 757-727-5361. *Dean,* School of Business, Dr. Ziette Hayes, 757-727-5361.

School of Liberal Arts and Education Students: 107 full-time (74 women), 39 part-time (30 women); includes 136 minority (135 Black or African American, non-Hispanic/Latino; 1 Asian, non-Hispanic/Latino). Average age 34. 71 applicants, 62% accepted, 33 enrolled. Expenses: Contact institution. *Financial support:* Fellowships, research assistantships, teaching assistantships, career-related internships or fieldwork, Federal Work-Study, institutionally sponsored loans, and scholarships/grants available. Support available to part-time students. Financial award application deadline: 5/1; financial award applicants required to submit FAFSA. In 2018, 31 master's, 4 doctorates, 5 other advanced degrees awarded. *Program availability:* Part-time, evening/weekend. Offers college student development (MA); community agency counseling (MA); counseling (Ed S); counselor education and supervision (PhD); educational leadership (MA); educational management (PhD); English education 6-12 (MT); intercollegiate athletics (MS); international sports (MS); liberal arts and education (MA, MS, MT, PhD, Ed S); marriage and family studies (MS); mathematics education 6-12 (MT); organizational behavior and sport business leadership (MS); pastoral counseling (MA); psychology (MS); school counseling (MA). *Application deadline:* For fall admission, 6/1 priority date for domestic students, 4/1 priority date for international students; for winter admission, 9/1 priority date for international students; for spring admission, 11/1 priority date for domestic students; for summer admission, 4/15 for domestic students, 2/1 priority date for international students. Applications are processed on a rolling basis. *Application fee:* $35. Electronic applications accepted. *Application Contact:* Dr. Michelle Penn-Marshall, Dean, Graduate College, 757-727-5454, E-mail: hugrad@hamptonu.edu. *Dean,* Dr. Linda Malone-Colon, 757-727-5400.

School of Nursing Students: 4 full-time (all women), 23 part-time (21 women); includes 25 minority (24 Black or African American, non-Hispanic/Latino; 1 Hispanic/Latino). Average age 49. 5 applicants, 0% accepted, 0 enrolled. Expenses: Contact institution. *Financial support:* In 2018–19, 2 students received support. Fellowships, research assistantships, teaching assistantships, career-related internships or fieldwork, Federal Work-Study, institutionally sponsored loans, and scholarships/grants available. Support available to part-time students. Financial award application deadline: 6/30; financial award applicants required to submit FAFSA. In 2018, 3 master's, 6 doctorates awarded. *Program availability:* Part-time, online learning. Offers community health nursing (MS); family nurse practitioner (MS); family research (PhD); nursing administration (MS); nursing education (MS). *Application deadline:* For fall admission, 6/1 priority date for domestic students, 4/1 priority date for international students; for spring admission, 11/1 priority date for domestic students, 9/1 priority date for international students; for summer admission, 4/1 priority date for domestic students, 2/1 priority date for international students. Applications are processed on a rolling basis. *Application fee:* $35. Electronic applications accepted. *Application Contact:* Dr. Shevellanie Lott, Dean, 757-727-5654, E-mail: shevellanie.lott@hamptonu.edu. *Dean,* Dr. Shevellanie Lott, 757-727-5654, E-mail: shevellanie.lott@hamptonu.edu.

School of Science Students: 236 full-time (164 women), 28 part-time (20 women); includes 185 minority (157 Black or African American, non-Hispanic/Latino; 3 American Indian or Alaska Native, non-Hispanic/Latino; 15 Asian, non-Hispanic/Latino; 10 Hispanic/Latino), 11 international. Average age 26. 823 applicants, 12% accepted, 49 enrolled. Expenses: Contact institution. *Financial support:* Fellowships, research assistantships, teaching assistantships, career-related internships or fieldwork, Federal Work-Study, institutionally sponsored loans, scholarships/grants, and stipends available. Support available to part-time students. Financial award application deadline: 6/30; financial award applicants required to submit FAFSA. In 2018, 50 master's, 23 doctorates awarded. *Program availability:* Part-time, evening/weekend, online learning. Offers atmospheric science (MS, PhD); biology (MS); chemistry (MS); communicative sciences and disorders (MA); computational mathematics (MS); computer science (MS); environmental science (MS); information assurance (MS); medical physics (PhD); medical science (MS); nonlinear science (MS); nuclear physics (MS, PhD); optical physics (MS, PhD); physical therapy (DPT); planetary science (MS, PhD); science (MA, MS, DPT, PhD); statistics and probability (MS). *Application deadline:* For fall admission, 6/1 for domestic students, 4/1 for international students; for winter admission, 11/1 for domestic students, 9/1 for international students; for spring admission, 11/1 for domestic students; for summer admission, 4/1 for domestic students, 2/1 for international students. Applications are processed on a rolling basis. *Application fee:* $35. Electronic applications accepted. *Application Contact:* Dr. Calvin Lowe, Dean, 757-722-5239. *Dean,* Dr. Calvin Lowe, 757-722-5239.

HANNIBAL-LAGRANGE UNIVERSITY, Hannibal, MO 63401-1999

General Information Independent-religious, coed, comprehensive institution.

GRADUATE UNITS

Program in Education *Program availability:* Part-time, evening/weekend. Offers literacy (MS Ed); teaching and learning (MS Ed).

HARDING SCHOOL OF THEOLOGY, Memphis, TN 38117-5499

General Information Independent-religious, coed, primarily men, graduate-only institution. *Graduate housing:* Rooms and/or apartments available on a first-come, first-served basis to single and married students.

GRADUATE UNITS

Graduate Programs *Program availability:* Part-time, online learning. Offers Christian ministry (MA); historical theology (MA); ministry (M Div); New Testament (MA); Old Testament (MA); systematic theology (MA); transforming leadership (D Min). Electronic applications accepted.

HARDING UNIVERSITY, Searcy, AR 72149-0001

General Information Independent-religious, coed, university. *Graduate housing:* Rooms and/or apartments available on a first-come, first-served basis to single and married students.

GRADUATE UNITS

Cannon-Clary College of Education *Program availability:* Part-time, evening/weekend. Offers advanced studies in teaching and learning (M Ed); art (MSE); behavioral science (MSE); counseling (MS, Ed S); early childhood special education (M Ed, MSE); education (MSE); educational leadership (M Ed, Ed S); elementary education (M Ed); English (MSE); French (MSE); history/social science (MSE); kinesiology (MSE); math (MSE); reading (M Ed); secondary education (M Ed); Spanish (MSE); teaching (MAT); teaching English as a second language (MSE).

College of Allied Health Offers allied health (MS, DPT); communication sciences and disorders (MS); physical therapy (DPT); physician assistant (MS).

College of Bible and Ministry *Program availability:* Part-time, online learning. Offers Bible and ministry (M Min).

College of Pharmacy Offers pharmacy (Pharm D). Electronic applications accepted.

Paul R. Carter College of Business Administration *Program availability:* Part-time, evening/weekend, 100% online. Offers international business (MBA); leadership and organizational management (MBA).

HARDIN-SIMMONS UNIVERSITY, Abilene, TX 79698-0001

General Information Independent-religious, coed, comprehensive institution. *Enrollment:* 2,343 graduate, professional, and undergraduate students; 276 full-time matriculated graduate/professional students (148 women), 297 part-time matriculated graduate/professional students (152 women). *Enrollment by degree level:* 425 master's, 147 doctoral, 1 other advanced degree. *Graduate faculty:* 90 full-time (39 women), 16 part-time/adjunct (2 women). *Tuition:* Full-time $750; part-time $750 per credit hour. *Required fees:* $1300; $880 per credit. Tuition and fees vary according to degree level and program. *Graduate housing:* Rooms and/or apartments available on a first-come, first-served basis to single and married students. Typical cost: $6000 per year for single students; $5280 per year for married students. Room charges vary according to board plan and housing facility selected. *Student services:* Campus employment opportunities, career counseling, exercise/wellness program, free psychological counseling, international student services, services for students with disabilities. *Library facilities:* Richardson Library plus 1 other. *Collection:* Books: 201,169 (physical), 41,773 (digital/electronic); Serial titles: 183 (physical), 67,899 (digital/electronic); Databases: 142. Weekly public service hours: 89.

Computer facilities: 115 computers available on campus for general student use. A campuswide network can be accessed from student residence rooms and from off campus. Online class registration is available.
Website: http://www.hsutx.edu/

General Application Contact: Joel Templeton, Graduate Admissions Counselor, 325-670-1682, Fax: 325-671-2115, E-mail: gradoff@hsutx.edu.

GRADUATE UNITS

Graduate School Students: 276 full-time (148 women), 297 part-time (152 women); includes 202 minority (49 Black or African American, non-Hispanic/Latino; 10 Asian, non-Hispanic/Latino; 86 Hispanic/Latino; 57 Two or more races, non-Hispanic/Latino), 14 international. Average age 32. 1,689 applicants, 16% accepted, 175 enrolled. *Faculty:* 90 full-time (39 women), 16 part-time/adjunct (2 women). Expenses: Contact institution. *Financial support:* Fellowships, career-related internships or fieldwork, scholarships/grants, and recreation assistantships, coaching assistantships available. Support available to part-time students. Financial award application deadline: 6/30; financial award applicants required to submit FAFSA. In 2018, 88 master's, 33 doctorates awarded. *Program availability:* Part-time. *Application deadline:* For fall admission, 8/15 priority date for domestic students, 4/1 for international students; for spring admission, 1/5 priority date for domestic students, 9/1 for international students. Applications are processed on a rolling basis. *Application fee:* $50. Electronic applications accepted. *Application Contact:* Joel Templeton, Graduate Admissions Counselor, 325-670-1682, E-mail: gradoff@hsutx.edu. *Dean of Graduate Studies,* Dr. Nancy Kucinski, 325-670-1298, Fax: 325-670-1564, E-mail: gradoff@hsutx.edu.

College of Fine Arts Students: 1 (woman) full-time, 5 part-time (2 women); includes 4 minority (1 Black or African American, non-Hispanic/Latino; 1 Hispanic/Latino; 2 Two or more races, non-Hispanic/Latino). Average age 31. 7 applicants, 71% accepted, 1 enrolled. *Faculty:* 12 full-time (4 women), 2 part-time/adjunct (0 women). Expenses: Contact institution. *Financial support:* Fellowships, career-related internships or fieldwork, and scholarships/grants available. Support available to part-time students. Financial award application deadline: 6/30; financial award applicants required to submit FAFSA. In 2018, 1 master's awarded. *Program availability:* Part-time. Offers church music (MM); music education (MM); music performance (MM); theory and composition (MM). *Application deadline:* For fall admission, 8/15 priority date for domestic students, 4/1 for international students; for spring admission, 1/5 priority date for domestic students, 9/1 for international students. Applications are processed on a rolling basis. *Application fee:* $50. Electronic applications accepted. *Application Contact:* Dr. Nancy Kucinski, Dean of Graduate Studies, 325-670-1298, Fax: 325-670-1564, E-mail: gradoff@hsutx.edu. *Dean, College of Fine Arts,* Dr. Robert Tucker, 325-670-1498, E-mail: robert.l.tucker@hsutx.edu.

College of Human Sciences and Educational Studies Students: 12 full-time (7 women), 114 part-time (80 women); includes 33 minority (13 Black or African American, non-Hispanic/Latino; 1 Asian, non-Hispanic/Latino; 16 Hispanic/Latino; 3 Two or more races, non-Hispanic/Latino), 2 international. Average age 33. 51 applicants, 90% accepted, 38 enrolled. *Faculty:* 14 full-time (8 women), 2 part-time/adjunct (both women). Expenses: Contact institution. *Financial support:* Fellowships, career-related internships or fieldwork, scholarships/grants, and coaching assistantships available. Support available to part-time students. Financial award application deadline: 6/30; financial award applicants required to submit FAFSA. In 2018, 33 master's, 5 doctorates awarded. *Program availability:* Part-time. Offers counseling and human development (M Ed); educational leadership in superintendence (Ed D); gifted education (M Ed); higher education leadership (Ed D); human sciences and educational studies (M Ed, Ed D); kinesiology, sport, and recreation (M Ed); reading education (M Ed); reading specialist education (M Ed). *Application deadline:* For fall admission, 8/15 priority date for domestic students, 4/1 for international students; for spring admission, 1/5 priority date for domestic students, 9/1 for international students. Applications are processed on a rolling basis. *Application fee:* $50. Electronic applications accepted. *Application Contact:* Dr. Nancy Kucinski, Dean of Graduate Studies, 325-670-1298, Fax: 325-670-1564, E-mail: gradoff@hsutx.edu. *Dean,* Dr. Perry Kay Brown, 325-670-1021, Fax: 325-670-5859, E-mail: pkbrown@hsutx.edu.

Cynthia Ann Parker College of Liberal Arts Students: 20 full-time (14 women), 14 part-time (12 women); includes 8 minority (2 Black or African American, non-Hispanic/Latino; 5 Hispanic/Latino; 1 Two or more races, non-Hispanic/Latino), 1 international. Average age 30. 16 applicants, 94% accepted, 10 enrolled. *Faculty:* 15 full-time (7 women). Expenses: Contact institution. *Financial support:* Fellowships and scholarships/grants available. Support available to part-time students. Financial award application deadline: 6/30; financial award applicants required to submit FAFSA. In 2018, 12 master's awarded. *Program availability:* Part-time. Offers clinical counseling and marriage and family therapy (MA); liberal arts (MA). *Application deadline:* For fall admission, 8/15 priority date for domestic students, 4/1 for international students; for spring admission, 1/5 priority date for domestic students, 9/1 for international students. Applications are processed on a rolling basis. *Application fee:* $50. Electronic applications accepted. *Application Contact:* Dr. Nancy Kucinski, Dean of Graduate Studies, 325-670-1298, Fax: 325-670-1564, E-mail: gradoff@hsutx.edu. *Dean, Cynthia Ann Parker College of Liberal Arts,* Dr. Stephen Cook, 325-670-1487, E-mail: stephen.cook@hsutx.edu.

Holland School of Sciences and Mathematics Students: 148 full-time (101 women), 4 part-time (3 women); includes 37 minority (8 Black or African American, non-Hispanic/Latino; 5 Asian, non-Hispanic/Latino; 23 Hispanic/Latino; 1 Two or more races, non-Hispanic/Latino), 1 international. Average age 25. 1,498 applicants, 6% accepted, 61 enrolled. *Faculty:* 19 full-time (10 women), 2 part-time/adjunct. Expenses: Contact institution. *Financial support:* Fellowships, career-related internships or fieldwork, and scholarships/grants available. Support available to part-time students. Financial award application deadline: 6/30; financial award applicants required to submit FAFSA. In 2018, 10 master's, 26 doctorates awarded. *Program availability:* Part-time. Offers physical therapy (DPT); physician assistant studies (MPAS). *Application deadline:* For fall admission, 8/15 priority date for domestic students, 4/1 for international students; for spring admission, 1/5 priority date for domestic students, 9/1 for international students. Applications are processed on a rolling basis. *Application fee:* $50. Electronic applications accepted. *Application Contact:* Dr. Nancy Kucinski, Dean of Graduate Studies, 325-670-1298, Fax: 325-670-1564, E-mail: gradoff@hsutx.edu. *Dean, Holland School of Sciences and Mathematics,* Dr. Andrea Jensen, 325-670-1382, E-mail: ajensen@hsutx.edu.

Kelley College of Business Students: 32 full-time (6 women), 55 part-time (23 women); includes 16 minority (5 Black or African American, non-Hispanic/Latino; 11 Hispanic/Latino), 2 international. Average age 29. 48 applicants, 96% accepted, 41 enrolled. *Faculty:* 10 full-time (3 women). Expenses: Contact institution. *Financial support:* Fellowships and scholarships/grants available. Support available to part-time students. Financial award application deadline: 6/30; financial award applicants required to submit FAFSA. In 2018, 27 master's awarded. *Program availability:* Part-time. Offers business administration (MBA); information science (MS); sports management (MBA). *Application deadline:* For fall admission, 8/15 priority date for domestic students, 4/1 for international students; for spring admission, 1/5 priority date for domestic students, 9/1 for international students. Applications are processed

on a rolling basis. *Application fee:* $50. Electronic applications accepted. *Application Contact:* Dr. Nancy Kucinski, Dean of Graduate Studies, 325-670-1298, Fax: 325-670-1564, E-mail: gradoff@hsutx.edu. *Program Director,* Dr. Jennifer Plantier, 325-671-2166, Fax: 325-670-1523, E-mail: jplantier@hsutx.edu.

Logsdon Seminary Students: 63 full-time (19 women), 91 part-time (24 women); includes 52 minority (20 Black or African American, non-Hispanic/Latino; 4 Asian, non-Hispanic/Latino; 28 Hispanic/Latino), 7 international. Average age 40. 25 applicants, 88% accepted, 18 enrolled. *Faculty:* 16 full-time (3 women), 10 part-time/adjunct. Expenses: Contact institution. *Financial support:* Fellowships and scholarships/grants available. Support available to part-time students. Financial award application deadline: 6/30; financial award applicants required to submit FAFSA. In 2018, 4 master's, 2 doctorates awarded. *Program availability:* Part-time, evening/weekend. Offers family ministry (MA); ministry (D Min); religion (MA); theology (M Div, MA, D Min). *Application deadline:* For fall admission, 8/15 priority date for domestic students, 4/1 for international students; for spring admission, 1/5 priority date for domestic students, 9/1 for international students. Applications are processed on a rolling basis. *Application fee:* $50. Electronic applications accepted. *Application Contact:* Dr. Nancy Kucinski, Dean of Graduate Studies, 325-670-1298, Fax: 325-670-1564, E-mail: gradoff@hsutx.edu. *Dean,* Dr. Robert Ellis, 325-670-5841, Fax: 325-671-2157, E-mail: rellis@hsutx.edu.

Patty Hanks Shelton School of Nursing Students: 14 part-time (8 women); includes 2 minority (both Hispanic/Latino), 1 international. Average age 34. 6 applicants, 100% accepted, 6 enrolled. *Faculty:* 4 full-time (all women). Expenses: Contact institution. *Financial support:* Career-related internships or fieldwork and scholarships/grants available. Support available to part-time students. Financial award application deadline: 6/30; financial award applicants required to submit FAFSA. In 2018, 6 master's awarded. *Program availability:* Part-time. Offers education (MSN); family nurse practitioner (MSN). Programs offered jointly with McMurry University. *Application deadline:* For fall admission, 8/15 priority date for domestic students, 4/1 for international students; for spring admission, 1/5 priority date for domestic students, 9/1 for international students. Applications are processed on a rolling basis. *Application fee:* $50. Electronic applications accepted. *Application Contact:* Dr. Nancy Kucinski, Dean of Graduate Studies, 325-670-1298, Fax: 325-670-1564, E-mail: gradoff@hsutx.edu. *Dean,* Dr. Donalyn Alexander, 325-670-1198, E-mail: donalyn.alexander@phssn.edu.

HARRISBURG UNIVERSITY OF SCIENCE AND TECHNOLOGY, Harrisburg, PA 17101

General Information Independent, coed, comprehensive institution. *Graduate housing:* On-campus housing not available. *Research affiliation:* MistIQ Technologies (data analytics), WildFig Data Company (data analytics).

GRADUATE UNITS

Learning Technologies and Media Systems Program *Program availability:* Part-time, evening/weekend. Offers games and simulations (MS); instructional design (MS); instructional development (MS); instructional technology (MS); integration and leadership (MS). Electronic applications accepted.

Program in Human-Centered Interaction Design Offers human-centered interaction design (MS).

Program in Information Systems Engineering and Management *Program availability:* Part-time, evening/weekend. Offers analytics (MS); digital government (MS); digital health (MS); entrepreneurship (MS); information security (MS); software engineering and systems development (MS). Electronic applications accepted.

Program in Project Management *Program availability:* Part-time, evening/weekend. Offers information technology (MS). Electronic applications accepted.

Program in Techpreneurship Offers techpreneurship (MS).

HARRISON MIDDLETON UNIVERSITY, Tempe, AZ 85282

General Information Independent, coed, graduate-only institution.

GRADUATE UNITS

Graduate Program *Program availability:* Part-time, evening/weekend, online learning. Offers education (MA, Ed D); humanities (MA); imaginative literature (MA); interdisciplinary studies (DA); jurisprudence (MA); natural science (MA); philosophy and religion (MA); social science (MA). Electronic applications accepted.

HARTFORD SEMINARY, Hartford, CT 06105-2279

General Information Independent-religious, coed, graduate-only institution. *Graduate housing:* Rooms and/or apartments available on a first-come, first-served basis to single and married students. Housing application deadline: 7/15.

GRADUATE UNITS

Graduate Programs *Program availability:* Part-time, evening/weekend, online learning. Offers Islamic studies (MA); ministry (D Min); religious studies (MA); spirituality (Certificate).

HARVARD UNIVERSITY, Cambridge, MA 02138

General Information Independent, coed, university. CGS member. *Graduate housing:* Rooms and/or apartments available on a first-come, first-served basis to single and married students. *Research affiliation:* Woods Hole Oceanographic Institution (biology).

GRADUATE UNITS

Cyprus International Institute for the Environment and Public Health in Association with Harvard School of Public Health Offers environmental health (MS); environmental/public health (PhD); epidemiology and biostatistics (MS). Electronic applications accepted.

Extension School *Program availability:* Part-time, evening/weekend. Offers applied sciences (CAS); biotechnology (ALM); educational technologies (ALM); educational technology (CET); English for graduate and professional studies (DGP); environmental management (ALM, CEM); information technology (ALM); journalism (ALM); liberal arts (ALM); management (ALM, CM); mathematics for teaching (ALM); museum studies (ALM); premedical studies (Diploma); publication and communication (CPC).

Graduate School of Arts and Sciences Offers African and African American studies (PhD); African history (PhD); Akkadian and Sumerian (AM, PhD); American history (PhD); ancient art (PhD); ancient Near Eastern art (PhD); ancient, medieval, early modern, and modern Europe (PhD); anthropology and Middle Eastern studies (PhD); Arabic (AM, PhD); archaeology (PhD); architecture (PhD); Armenian (AM, PhD); arts and sciences (AM, MDE, ME, MFS, SM, PhD); astronomy (PhD); astrophysics (PhD); Baroque art (PhD); biblical history (AM); biochemical chemistry (PhD); biological anthropology (PhD); biological sciences in dental medicine (PhD); biology (PhD); biophysics (PhD); biostatistics (PhD); business economics (PhD); Byzantine art (PhD); Byzantine Greek (PhD); chemical biology (PhD); chemical physics (PhD); Chinese (PhD); Chinese studies (AM); classical archaeology (PhD); classical art (PhD); classical philology (PhD); classical philosophy (PhD); comparative literature (PhD); composition (AM, PhD); critical theory (PhD); descriptive linguistics (PhD); diplomatic history (PhD); earth and planetary sciences (AM, PhD); East Asian history (PhD); economic and social history (PhD); economics (PhD); economics and Middle Eastern studies (PhD); eighteenth-century literature (PhD); experimental physics (PhD); fine arts and Middle Eastern studies (PhD); forest science (MFS); French (AM, PhD); German (PhD); health policy (PhD); Hebrew (AM, PhD); historical linguistics (PhD); history and Middle Eastern studies (PhD); history of American civilization (PhD); history of science (AM, PhD); Indian art (PhD); Indian philosophy (AM, PhD); Indo-Muslim culture (AM, PhD); information, technology and management (PhD); Inner Asian and Altaic studies (PhD); inorganic chemistry (PhD); intellectual history (PhD); Iranian (AM, PhD); Irish (PhD); Islamic art (PhD); Italian (AM, PhD); Japanese (PhD); Japanese and Chinese art (PhD); Japanese studies (AM); Jewish history and literature (AM, PhD); Korean (PhD); Korean studies (AM); landscape architecture (PhD); Latin American history (PhD); legal anthropology (AM); literature: nineteenth-century to the present (PhD); mathematics (PhD); medical anthropology (AM); medical engineering/medical physics (PhD); medieval art (PhD); medieval Latin (PhD); medieval literature and language (PhD); modern art (PhD); modern British and American literature (PhD); molecular and cellular biology (PhD); Mongolian (PhD); Mongolian studies (AM); musicology (AM); musicology and ethnomusicology (PhD); Near Eastern history (PhD); neurobiology (PhD); oceanic history (PhD); oral literature (PhD); organic chemistry (PhD); organizational behavior (PhD); Pali (AM, PhD); Persian (AM, PhD); philosophy (PhD); physical chemistry (PhD); Polish (PhD); political economy and government (PhD); political science (PhD); Portuguese (AM, PhD); psychology (PhD); public policy (PhD); regional studies–Middle East (AM); regional studies-Russia, Eastern Europe, and Central Asia (AM); Renaissance and modern architecture (PhD); Renaissance art (PhD); Renaissance literature (PhD); Russian (PhD); Sanskrit (AM, PhD); Scandinavian (PhD); Semitic philology (AM, PhD); Serbo-Croatian (PhD); Slavic philology (PhD); social anthropology (AM, PhD); social change and development (AM); social policy (PhD); social psychology (PhD); sociology (PhD); Spanish (AM, PhD); statistics (AM, PhD); study of religion (PhD); Syro-Palestinian archaeology (AM, PhD); systems biology (PhD); theoretical linguistics (PhD); theoretical physics (PhD); theory (AM, PhD); Tibetan (AM, PhD); Turkish (AM, PhD); Ukrainian (PhD); urban planning (PhD); Urdu (AM, PhD); Vietnamese (PhD); Vietnamese studies (AM); Welsh (PhD). Electronic applications accepted.

Division of Medical Sciences Offers biological chemistry and molecular pharmacology (PhD); cell biology (PhD); genetics (PhD); microbiology and molecular genetics (PhD); pathology (PhD).

Harvard John A. Paulson School of Engineering and Applied Sciences Program availability: Part-time. Offers applied mathematics (PhD); applied physics (PhD); computational science and engineering (ME, SM); computer science (PhD); data science (SM); design engineering (MDE); engineering science (ME); engineering sciences (SM, PhD). MDE offered in collaboration with Graduate School of Design. Electronic applications accepted.

Graduate School of Design Offers architecture (M Arch); design (M Arch, M Des S, MAUD, MLA, MLAUD, MUP, Dr DES); design studies (M Des S); landscape architecture (MLA); urban planning (MUP); urban planning and design (MAUD, MLAUD). Electronic applications accepted.

Harvard Business School Offers accounting and management (DBA); business (MBA, DBA, PhD); business administration (MBA); business economics (PhD); health policy management (PhD); management (DBA); marketing (DBA); organizational behavior (PhD); science, technology and management (PhD); strategy (DBA); technology and operations management (DBA).

Harvard Divinity School Offers divinity (M Div, MTS, Th M). Electronic applications accepted.

Harvard Graduate School of Education Program availability: Part-time. Offers arts in education (Ed M); education (Ed M, Ed L D, PhD); education leadership (Ed L D); education policy and management (Ed M); higher education (Ed M); human development and psychology (Ed M); international education policy (Ed M); language and literacy (Ed M); learning and teaching (Ed M); mind, brain, and education (Ed M); prevention science and practice (Ed M); school leadership (Ed M); special studies (Ed M); teacher education (Ed M); technology, innovation, and education (Ed M). Electronic applications accepted.

Harvard Medical School Offers medicine (M Eng, SM, MD, PhD, Sc D). Electronic applications accepted.

Harvard T.H. Chan School of Public Health Students: 1,290 full-time (859 women), 331 part-time (165 women); includes 419 minority (78 Black or African American, non-Hispanic/Latino; 1 American Indian or Alaska Native, non-Hispanic/Latino; 197 Asian, non-Hispanic/Latino; 89 Hispanic/Latino; 54 Two or more races, non-Hispanic/Latino), 626 international. Average age 29. Faculty: 376 full-time (146 women), 128 part-time/adjunct (45 women). Expenses: Contact institution. Financial support: Fellowships, research assistantships, teaching assistantships, career-related internships or fieldwork, Federal Work-Study, scholarships/grants, traineeships, and unspecified assistantships available. Support available to part-time students. Financial award application deadline: 2/15; financial award applicants required to submit FAFSA. In 2018, 518 master's, 128 doctorates awarded. Program availability: Part-time. Offers biological sciences in public health (PhD); biostatistics (SM, PhD); cancer epidemiology (SM); cardiovascular epidemiology (SM); clinical effectiveness (MPH); clinical epidemiology (SM); computational biology and quantitative genetics (SM); environmental and occupational epidemiology (SM); environmental epidemiology (SM); environmental exposure assessment (SM); environmental health (PhD); epidemiologic methods (SM); epidemiology (PhD); epidemiology of aging (SM); ergonomics and safety (SM); genetic epidemiology and statistical genetics (SM); global health (MPH); global health and population (SM, PhD); health and social behavior (PhD); health data science (SM); health management (MPH); health policy (MPH); health policy and management (MHCM, SM, PhD); infectious disease epidemiology (SM); neuro-psychiatric epidemiology (SM); nutrition (PhD); nutritional epidemiology (SM); occupational and environmental health (MPH); occupational health (SM); occupational hygiene (SM); pharmacoepidemiology (SM); population health sciences (PhD); public health (MHCM, MPH, SM, Dr PH, PhD); quantitative methods (MPH); reproductive epidemiology (SM); risk and decision science (SM); social and behavioral sciences (PhD). SM program offered jointly with Simmons College. Application deadline: For fall admission, 12/1 for domestic and international students. Application fee: $135. Electronic applications accepted. Application Contact: Vincent W. James, Director of Admissions, 617-432-1031, Fax: 617-432-7080, E-mail: admissions@hsph.harvard.edu. Dean of the Faculty, Dr. Michelle Williams, 617-432-1025, Fax: 617-277-5320, E-mail: deansoff@hsph.harvard.edu.

John F. Kennedy School of Government Offers government (MPA, MPAID, MPP, PhD); political economy and government (PhD); public administration (MPA); public administration in international development (MPAID); public policy (MPP). Electronic applications accepted.

Law School Offers international and comparative law (JD); law (LL M, JD, SJD); law and business (JD); law and government (JD); law and social change (JD); law, science and technology (JD).

School of Dental Medicine Offers advanced general dentistry (Certificate); dental medicine (M Med Sc, D Med Sc, DMD, Certificate); dental public health (Certificate); endodontics (Certificate); general practice residency (Certificate); oral biology (M Med Sc, D Med Sc); oral implantology (Certificate); oral medicine (Certificate); oral pathology (Certificate); oral surgery (Certificate); orthodontics (Certificate); pediatric dentistry (Certificate); periodontics (Certificate); prosthodontics (Certificate). Electronic applications accepted.

HASTINGS COLLEGE, Hastings, NE 68901
General Information Independent-religious, coed, comprehensive institution. Graduate housing: On-campus housing not available.
GRADUATE UNITS
Department of Teacher Education Program availability: Part-time. Offers teacher education (MAT). Electronic applications accepted.

HAWAI'I PACIFIC UNIVERSITY, Honolulu, HI 96813
General Information Independent, coed, comprehensive institution. Graduate housing: Rooms and/or apartments available on a first-come, first-served basis to single and married students. Research affiliation: Oceanic Institute (marine science).
GRADUATE UNITS
College of Business Program availability: Part-time, evening/weekend, 100% online, blended/hybrid learning. Offers business (MA, MBA, MSIS); finance (MBA); human resource management (MBA); information systems (MSIS); international business (MBA); management (MBA); marketing (MBA); organizational change (MA); organizational change and development (MBA). Electronic applications accepted.
College of Health and Society Program availability: Part-time, evening/weekend, 100% online, blended/hybrid learning. Offers health and society (MPH, MSN, MSW, DNP); nursing (MSN, DNP); public health (MPH); social work (MSW). Electronic applications accepted.
College of Liberal Arts Program availability: Part-time, evening/weekend. Offers clinical mental health counseling (MA); communication (MA); diplomacy and military studies (MA); global leadership and sustainable development (MA); liberal arts (MA); teaching English to speakers of other languages (MA). Electronic applications accepted.
College of Natural and Computational Sciences Program availability: Part-time. Offers marine science (MS); natural and computational sciences (MS). Electronic applications accepted.
College of Professional Studies Program availability: Part-time, evening/weekend, 100% online, blended/hybrid learning. Offers educational leadership (M Ed); elementary education (M Ed); public administration (MPA); secondary education (M Ed). Electronic applications accepted.

HAZELDEN BETTY FORD GRADUATE SCHOOL OF ADDICTION STUDIES, Center City, MN 55012
General Information Independent, coed, graduate-only institution. CGS member. Graduate housing: On-campus housing not available.
GRADUATE UNITS
Graduate Programs Program availability: Part-time. Offers addiction counseling (MA, Certificate).

HEBREW COLLEGE, Newton Centre, MA 02459
General Information Independent-religious, coed, graduate-only institution. Graduate housing: On-campus housing not available.
GRADUATE UNITS
Cantor Educator Program Offers cantor educator (MJ Ed).
Program in Jewish Studies Program availability: Part-time, evening/weekend, online learning. Offers Jewish liturgical music (Certificate); Jewish music education (Certificate); Jewish studies (MA).
Rabbinical School Offers rabbinics (MA).
Shoolman Graduate School of Jewish Education Program availability: Part-time, evening/weekend, online learning. Offers early childhood Jewish education (Certificate); Jewish day school education (Certificate); Jewish education (MJ Ed); Jewish family education (Certificate); Jewish special education (Certificate); Jewish youth education, informal education and camping (Certificate).

HEBREW UNION COLLEGE–JEWISH INSTITUTE OF RELIGION, New York, NY 10012-1186
General Information Independent-religious, coed, graduate-only institution. Graduate housing: On-campus housing not available.
GRADUATE UNITS
Rabbinical School Offers rabbinical studies (MAHL).
School of Education Program availability: Part-time. Offers education (MARE).
School of Graduate Studies Program availability: Part-time. Offers Hebrew letters (DHL); Judaic studies (MAJS); pastoral counseling (D Min).
School of Jewish Nonprofit Management Offers Jewish nonprofit management (MA).
School of Sacred Music Offers sacred music (MSM).

HEC MONTREAL, Montréal, QC H3T 2A7, Canada
General Information Province-supported, coed, comprehensive institution. Enrollment: 1,836 full-time matriculated graduate/professional students (917 women), 1,417 part-time matriculated graduate/professional students (790 women). Enrollment by degree level: 1,776 master's, 130 doctoral, 1,347 other advanced degrees. Graduate faculty: 305 full-time (107 women), 490 part-time/adjunct (172 women). International tuition: $20,905.20 Canadian dollars full-time. Tuition, area resident: Full-time $3052.80 Canadian dollars; part-time $84.80 Canadian dollars per credit. Tuition, province resident: full-time $3816 Canadian dollars; part-time $264.67 Canadian dollars per credit. Tuition, Canadian resident: full-time $11,910 Canadian dollars. Required fees: $1805.34 Canadian dollars; part-time $43.62 Canadian dollars per credit. $71.78 Canadian dollars per term. Tuition and fees vary according to degree level and program. Graduate housing: Rooms and/or apartments available on a first-come, first-served basis to single students and guaranteed to married students. Typical cost: $3960 Canadian dollars per year for single students; $6450 Canadian dollars per year for married students. Student services: Campus employment opportunities, campus safety program, career counseling, child daycare facilities, exercise/wellness program, free psychological

counseling, grant writing training, international student services, low-cost health insurance, multicultural affairs office, services for students with disabilities. *Library facilities:* HEC Montreal Library plus 1 other. *Collection:* Books: 116,690 (physical), 206,337 (digital/electronic); Serial titles: 952 (physical), 111,941 (digital/electronic); Databases: 161. Weekly public service hours: 100; students can reserve study rooms.

Computer facilities: 159 computers available on campus for general student use. A campuswide network can be accessed from student residence rooms. Online class registration, learning management system, corporate calendar and Web sites for resources available for classes are available.
Website: http://www.hec.ca/

General Application Contact: Virginie Lefebvre, Registrar, 514-340-6000, Fax: 514-340-6411, E-mail: aide@hec.ca.

GRADUATE UNITS

School of Business Administration Students: 1,836 full-time (917 women), 1,417 part-time (790 women). 2,610 applicants, 64% accepted, 1136 enrolled. *Faculty:* 305 full-time (107 women), 490 part-time/adjunct (172 women). Expenses: Contact institution. *Financial support:* In 2018–19, 858 students received support. Research assistantships, teaching assistantships, and scholarships/grants available. Financial award application deadline: 9/2. In 2018, 656 master's, 19 doctorates, 611 other advanced degrees awarded. Offers accounting (PhD); accounting, management, control, and audit (M Sc); applied economics (M Sc, PhD); applied financial economics (M Sc); business administration (LL M, M Sc, MBA, MM, PhD, Graduate Certificate); business administration and management (MBA); business analysis - information technology (Graduate Diploma); business analysis and information technologies (M Sc); business analytics (M Sc); business intelligence (M Sc); data science (PhD); e-business (Graduate Diploma); electronic commerce (M Sc); entrepreneurship (Graduate Diploma); entrepreneurship-intrapreneurship-innovation (M Sc); finance (M Sc, PhD); financial engineering (M Sc, PhD); financial professions (Graduate Diploma); global supply chain management (M Sc); human resources (Graduate Diploma); human resources management (M Sc); information technology (PhD); international business (M Sc, PhD); international logistics (M Sc); logistics and operations management (PhD); management (M Sc, Graduate Diploma); management and social innovations (M Sc); management and sustainable development (Graduate Diploma); management control (M Sc); management in cultural enterprises (MM); management of cultural organizations (Graduate Diploma); management science (PhD); management, strategy and organizations (PhD); marketing (M Sc); marketing communication (Graduate Diploma); operations management (M Sc); organizational behaviour and human resources (PhD); organizational development (M Sc); professional accounting (Graduate Diploma); strategy (M Sc); supply chain management (Graduate Diploma); taxation (Graduate Diploma); user experience in business context (M Sc). Most courses are given in French. *Application fee:* $91 Canadian dollars ($191 Canadian dollars for international students). Electronic applications accepted. *Application Contact:* Virginie Lefebvre, Registrar, 514-340-6000, Fax: 514-340-6411, E-mail: aide@hec.ca. *Director,* Dr. Federico Pasin, 514-340-6411, Fax: 514-340-6411, E-mail: federico.pasin@hec.ca.

HEIDELBERG UNIVERSITY, Tiffin, OH 44883-2462

General Information Independent-religious, coed, comprehensive institution. *Enrollment:* 75 full-time matriculated graduate/professional students (41 women), 55 part-time matriculated graduate/professional students (36 women). *Enrollment by degree level:* 130 master's. *Graduate faculty:* 12 full-time (9 women), 15 part-time/adjunct (8 women). *Tuition:* Part-time $575 per semester hour. *Graduate housing:* On-campus housing not available. *Student services:* Campus employment opportunities, campus safety program, career counseling, exercise/wellness program, free psychological counseling, international student services, multicultural affairs office, services for students with disabilities, teacher training, writing training. *Library facilities:* Beeghly Library plus 1 other. *Collection:* Books: 86,891 (physical), 279,499 (digital/electronic); Serial titles: 1,293 (physical), 61,058 (digital/electronic); Databases: 198. Weekly public service hours: 83.

Computer facilities: 125 computers available on campus for general student use. A campuswide network can be accessed from student residence rooms and from off campus. Online class registration is available.
Website: http://www.heidelberg.edu/

General Application Contact: Katie Zeyen, Graduate Admissions Coordinator, 419-448-2602, Fax: 419-448-2565, E-mail: kzeyen@heidelberg.edu.

GRADUATE UNITS

Master of Arts in Counseling Program Students: 31 full-time (26 women), 30 part-time (23 women). 71 applicants, 90% accepted, 37 enrolled. Expenses: Contact institution. *Financial support:* In 2018–19, 16 students received support. Scholarships/grants and unspecified assistantships available. Financial award applicants required to submit FAFSA. In 2018, 12 master's awarded. *Program availability:* Part-time, evening/weekend. Offers school counseling (MA). *Application deadline:* For fall admission, 8/15 for domestic students, 6/1 for international students; for spring admission, 12/3 for domestic students, 11/1 for international students; for summer admission, 5/1 for domestic students, 4/1 for international students. Applications are processed on a rolling basis. *Application fee:* $0. Electronic applications accepted. *Application Contact:* Katie Zeyen, Graduate Admissions Coordinator, 419-448-2602, Fax: 419-448-2565, E-mail: kzeyen@heidelberg.edu. *Director of Graduate Studies in Counseling,* Dr. Marjorie Shavers, 419-448-2308, E-mail: mshavers@heidelberg.edu.

Master of Arts in Education Program Students: 6 full-time (1 woman), 10 part-time (5 women). 10 applicants, 80% accepted, 6 enrolled. Expenses: Contact institution. *Financial support:* Unspecified assistantships available. Financial award applicants required to submit FAFSA. In 2018, 14 master's awarded. *Program availability:* Part-time, evening/weekend. Offers education (MAE). *Application deadline:* For fall admission, 8/15 for domestic students; for spring admission, 12/3 for domestic students; for summer admission, 5/1 for domestic students. Applications are processed on a rolling basis. *Application fee:* $0. Electronic applications accepted. *Application Contact:* Katie Zeyen, Graduate Admissions Coordinator, 419-448-2602, Fax: 419-448-2565, E-mail: kzeyen@heidelberg.edu. *Director of the School of Education,* Dr. Karen Jones, 419-448-2130, E-mail: kjones9@heidelberg.edu.

Master of Business Administration Program Students: 38 full-time (14 women), 15 part-time (8 women). 75 applicants, 84% accepted, 37 enrolled. Expenses: Contact institution. *Financial support:* In 2018–19, 53 students received support. Scholarships/grants and unspecified assistantships available. Financial award applicants required to submit FAFSA. In 2018, 32 master's awarded. *Program availability:* Part-time, evening/weekend. Offers business administration (MBA). *Application deadline:* For fall admission, 6/1 for domestic and international students; for spring admission, 12/3 for domestic students, 12/1 for international students; for summer admission, 5/15 for domestic students, 4/1 for international students. Applications are processed on a rolling basis. *Application fee:* $0. Electronic applications accepted.

Application Contact: Katie Zeyen, Graduate Admissions Coordinator, 419-448-2602, Fax: 419-448-2565, E-mail: kzeyen@heidelberg.edu. *Dean of Business and Technology,* Dr. Scott Johnson, 419-448-2284, E-mail: sjohnson@heidelberg.edu.

Master of Music Education Program Expenses: Contact institution. *Financial support:* Unspecified assistantships available. Financial award applicants required to submit FAFSA. In 2018, 1 master's awarded. *Program availability:* Part-time. Offers music education (MME). Program offered in summer only. *Application deadline:* For fall admission, 6/1 for domestic students. Applications are processed on a rolling basis. *Application fee:* $0. Electronic applications accepted. *Application Contact:* Katie Zeyen, Graduate Studies Coordinator, 419-448-2602, Fax: 419-448-2565, E-mail: kzeyen@heidelberg.edu. *Director,* Dr. Carol Dusdieker, 419-448-2080, E-mail: cdusdiek@heidelberg.edu.

HENDERSON STATE UNIVERSITY, Arkadelphia, AR 71999-0001

General Information State-supported, coed, comprehensive institution. CGS member. *Graduate housing:* Room and/or apartments available on a first-come, first-served basis to single students; on-campus housing not available to married students. Housing application deadline: 8/1.

GRADUATE UNITS

Graduate Studies *Program availability:* Part-time, 100% online.
Ellis College of Arts and Sciences *Program availability:* Part-time. Offers arts and sciences (MLA).
School of Business *Program availability:* Part-time, 100% online. Offers business (MBA).
Teachers College *Program availability:* Part-time, 100% online. Offers clinical mental health counseling (MS); curriculum leadership (Ed S); developmental therapy (MS, MSE, Graduate Certificate); dyslexia therapy (Graduate Certificate); education (MAT); educational leadership (MSE, Ed S, Graduate Certificate); educational technology leadership (Graduate Certificate); English as a second language (MSE, Graduate Certificate); instructional facilitator (MSE, Graduate Certificate); middle level education (MAT); secondary school counseling (MSE); special education (K-12) (MAT, MSE); special education/early childhood (MAT); sports administration (MS).

HENDRIX COLLEGE, Conway, AR 72032

General Information Independent-religious, coed, comprehensive institution. *Graduate housing:* Room and/or apartments available on a first-come, first-served basis to single students. Housing application deadline: 6/1.

GRADUATE UNITS

Program in Accounting *Program availability:* Part-time. Offers accounting (MA).

HENLEY-PUTNAM SCHOOL OF STRATEGIC SECURITY, Rapid City, SD 57701

General Information Proprietary, coed, comprehensive institution.

GRADUATE UNITS

Doctorate Program in Strategic Security *Program availability:* Part-time, online learning. Offers strategic security (DSS).
Master of Science Program in Intelligence Management *Program availability:* Part-time, online learning. Offers intelligence management (MS).
Master of Science Program in Strategic Security and Protection Management *Program availability:* Part-time, online learning. Offers extremist organizations (MS).
Master of Science Program in Terrorism and Counterterrorism Studies *Program availability:* Part-time, online learning. Offers intelligence operations (MS); protective intelligence (MS).

HERITAGE CHRISTIAN UNIVERSITY, Florence, AL 35630

General Information Independent-religious, coed, primarily men, comprehensive institution.

GRADUATE UNITS

Graduate Programs Offers counseling (MM); Greek (MA); ministry (MM); New Testament (MA).

HERITAGE COLLEGE AND SEMINARY, Cambridge, ON N3C 3T2, Canada

General Information Independent-religious, coed, comprehensive institution. *Graduate housing:* Room and/or apartments available on a first-come, first-served basis to single students; on-campus housing not available to married students. Housing application deadline: 5/31.

GRADUATE UNITS

Graduate and Professional Programs Offers general (M Div); intercultural studies (M Div); pastoral (M Div); research (M Div); theological studies (MTS, CTS).

HERITAGE UNIVERSITY, Toppenish, WA 98948-9599

General Information Independent, coed, comprehensive institution. *Graduate housing:* On-campus housing not available.

GRADUATE UNITS

Graduate Programs in Education *Program availability:* Part-time, evening/weekend. Offers bilingual education/ESL (M Ed); biology (M Ed); counseling (M Ed); educational administration (M Ed); English and literature (M Ed); professional studies (M Ed); reading/literacy (M Ed); special education (M Ed); teaching (MIT).

HERZING UNIVERSITY ONLINE, Menomonee Falls, WI 53051

General Information Independent, coed, comprehensive institution. CGS member.

GRADUATE UNITS

Program in Business Administration *Program availability:* Online learning. Offers accounting (MBA); business administration (MBA); business management (MBA); healthcare management (MBA); human resources (MBA); marketing (MBA); project management (MBA); technology management (MBA).
Program in Nursing *Program availability:* Online learning. Offers nursing (MSN); nursing education (MSN); nursing management (MSN).

HIGH POINT UNIVERSITY, High Point, NC 27268

General Information Independent-religious, coed, university. *Graduate housing:* On-campus housing not available.

GRADUATE UNITS

Norcross Graduate School *Program availability:* Part-time, evening/weekend. Offers athletic training (MSAT); business administration (MBA); educational leadership (M Ed, Ed D); elementary education (M Ed, MAT); pharmacy (Pharm D); physical therapy (DPT); physician assistant studies (MPAS); secondary mathematics (M Ed, MAT); special education (M Ed); strategic communication (MA). Electronic applications accepted.

HIGH TECH HIGH GRADUATE SCHOOL OF EDUCATION, San Diego, CA 92106

General Information Private, coed, graduate-only institution.

GRADUATE UNITS

Program in Educational Leadership *Program availability:* Part-time. Offers educational leadership (M Ed).

HILBERT COLLEGE, Hamburg, NY 14075-1597

General Information Independent-religious, coed, comprehensive institution. *Graduate housing:* On-campus housing not available.

GRADUATE UNITS

Program in Criminal Justice Administration *Program availability:* Evening/weekend. Offers criminal justice administration (MS). Electronic applications accepted.

Program in Public Administration *Program availability:* Evening/weekend. Offers health administration (MPA); public administration (MPA). Electronic applications accepted.

HILLSDALE COLLEGE, Hillsdale, MI 49242-1298

General Information Independent, coed, comprehensive institution.

GRADUATE UNITS

Van Andel Graduate School of Statesmanship Students: 59 full-time. Average age 27. *Faculty:* 11 full-time, 1 part-time/adjunct. Expenses: Contact institution. *Financial support:* In 2018–19, 59 students received support, including 23 fellowships with full tuition reimbursements available (averaging $20,000 per year), 28 research assistantships with full tuition reimbursements available (averaging $4,000 per year); institutionally sponsored loans, scholarships/grants, and unspecified assistantships also available. Financial award application deadline: 12/15. In 2018, 10 master's, 2 doctorates awarded. Offers politics (MA, PhD). *Application deadline:* For fall admission, 12/15 priority date for domestic and international students; for spring admission, 10/15 for domestic and international students. *Application fee:* $25. Electronic applications accepted. *Application Contact:* Mariel Stauff, Graduate Program Coordinator, 517-607-2483, E-mail: gradschool@hillsdale.edu. *Dean*, Dr. Ronald J. Pestritto, 517-607-2483, E-mail: gradschool@hillsdale.edu.

HIRAM COLLEGE, Hiram, OH 44234

General Information Independent, coed, comprehensive institution.

GRADUATE UNITS

Graduate Studies *Program availability:* Part-time, evening/weekend. Offers interdisciplinary studies (MAIS).

HODGES UNIVERSITY, Naples, FL 34119

General Information Independent, coed, comprehensive institution. *Graduate housing:* On-campus housing not available.

GRADUATE UNITS

Graduate Programs *Program availability:* Part-time, evening/weekend, 100% online, blended/hybrid learning. Offers accounting (M Acc); business administration (MBA); clinical mental health counseling (MS); health services administration (MS); information systems management (MIS); legal studies (MS); management (MSM). Electronic applications accepted.

HOFSTRA UNIVERSITY, Hempstead, NY 11549

General Information Independent, coed, university. CGS member. *Enrollment:* 10,871 graduate, professional, and undergraduate students. *Enrollment by degree level:* 2,678 master's, 1,433 doctoral, 59 other advanced degrees. *Graduate housing:* Room and/or apartments available on a first-come, first-served basis to single students; on-campus housing not available to married students. Housing application deadline: 5/1. *Student services:* Campus employment opportunities, campus safety program, career counseling, child daycare facilities, exercise/wellness program, free psychological counseling, grant writing training, international student services, multicultural affairs office, services for students with disabilities, teacher training, writing training. *Library facilities:* Axinn Library plus 3 others. *Collection:* Books: 859,300 (physical), 214,032 (digital/electronic); Serial titles: 1,761 (physical), 17,415 (digital/electronic); Databases: 241. Weekly public service hours: 110; study areas open 24 hours, 5–7 days a week; students can reserve study rooms.

Computer facilities: Computer purchase and lease plans are available. 1,536 computers available on campus for general student use. A campuswide network can be accessed from student residence rooms and from off campus. Online class registration, Emergency alert system, online course management system, online card services balance update, online e-portfolio, software tutoring, support for specific tech-enhanced assignments, repair and rebuilding-after-virus services, and printing services are available.

Website: http://www.hofstra.edu/

General Application Contact: Sunil Samuel, Assistant Vice President of Admissions, 516-463-4723, Fax: 516-463-4664, E-mail: graduateadmission@hofstra.edu.

GRADUATE UNITS

College of Liberal Arts and Sciences Students: 273 full-time (190 women), 47 part-time (29 women); includes 76 minority (15 Black or African American, non-Hispanic/Latino; 2 American Indian or Alaska Native, non-Hispanic/Latino; 17 Asian, non-Hispanic/Latino; 40 Hispanic/Latino; 2 Two or more races, non-Hispanic/Latino), 28 international. Average age 27. 456 applicants, 57% accepted, 118 enrolled. *Faculty:* 68 full-time (26 women), 45 part-time/adjunct (21 women). Expenses: Contact institution. *Financial support:* In 2018–19, 221 students received support, including 171 fellowships with full and partial tuition reimbursements available (averaging $7,395 per year), 6 research assistantships with full and partial tuition reimbursements available (averaging $6,773 per year); career-related internships or fieldwork, Federal Work-Study, institutionally sponsored loans, scholarships/grants, traineeships, tuition waivers (full and partial), unspecified assistantships, and scholarships and endowed scholarships also available. Support available to part-time students. Financial award applicants required to submit FAFSA. In 2018, 95 master's, 33 doctorates awarded. *Program availability:* Part-time, evening/weekend, online learning. Offers applied linguistics (TESOL) (MA); applied organizational psychology (PhD); biology (MA, MS); clinical psychology (PhD); creative writing (MFA); industrial/organizational psychology (MA); liberal arts and sciences (MA, MFA, MS, PhD, Psy D); linguistics (MA); medical physics (MS); school-community psychology (Psy D); sustainability studies (MA); urban ecology (MA, MS). *Application deadline:* Applications are processed on a rolling basis. *Application fee:* $75. Electronic applications accepted. *Application Contact:* Sunil Samuel, Assistant Vice President of Admissions, 516-463-4723, Fax: 516-463-4664,

E-mail: graduateadmission@hofstra.edu. *Dean*, Dr. Benjamin Rifkin, 516-463-5411, Fax: 516-463-4861, E-mail: benjamin.rifkin@hofstra.edu.

Donald and Barbara Zucker School of Medicine at Hofstra/Northwell Students: 419 full-time (196 women); includes 186 minority (24 Black or African American, non-Hispanic/Latino; 98 Asian, non-Hispanic/Latino; 50 Hispanic/Latino; 4 Native Hawaiian or other Pacific Islander, non-Hispanic/Latino; 10 Two or more races, non-Hispanic/Latino), 1 international. Average age 25. 5,358 applicants, 7% accepted, 102 enrolled. *Faculty:* 19 full-time (13 women), 14 part-time/adjunct (8 women). Expenses: Contact institution. *Financial support:* In 2018–19, 325 students received support, including 315 fellowships with full and partial tuition reimbursements available (averaging $25,722 per year); research assistantships with full and partial tuition reimbursements available, career-related internships or fieldwork, Federal Work-Study, institutionally sponsored loans, scholarships/grants, tuition waivers (full and partial), unspecified assistantships, and scholarships and endowed scholarships also available. Support available to part-time students. Financial award applicants required to submit FAFSA. In 2018, 91 doctorates awarded. Offers medicine (MD); molecular basis of medicine (PhD). *Application deadline:* For fall admission, 12/1 priority date for domestic students. Applications are processed on a rolling basis. *Application fee:* $100. Electronic applications accepted. *Application Contact:* Sunil Samuel, Assistant Vice President of Admissions, 516-463-4723, Fax: 516-463-4664. *Dean*, Dr. Lawrence Smith, 516-463-7517, Fax: 516-463-7543, E-mail: lawrence.smith@hofstra.edu.

Frank G. Zarb School of Business Students: 533 full-time (227 women), 260 part-time (118 women); includes 192 minority (37 Black or African American, non-Hispanic/Latino; 2 American Indian or Alaska Native, non-Hispanic/Latino; 77 Asian, non-Hispanic/Latino; 67 Hispanic/Latino; 9 Two or more races, non-Hispanic/Latino), 306 international. Average age 28. 1,222 applicants, 74% accepted, 294 enrolled. *Faculty:* 46 full-time (14 women), 30 part-time/adjunct (8 women). Expenses: Contact institution. *Financial support:* In 2018–19, 262 students received support, including 229 fellowships with full and partial tuition reimbursements available (averaging $4,875 per year), 4 research assistantships with full and partial tuition reimbursements available (averaging $5,652 per year); career-related internships or fieldwork, Federal Work-Study, institutionally sponsored loans, scholarships/grants, tuition waivers (full and partial), unspecified assistantships, and scholarships and endowed scholarships also available. Support available to part-time students. Financial award applicants required to submit FAFSA. In 2018, 457 master's awarded. *Program availability:* Part-time, evening/weekend, blended/hybrid learning. Offers accounting (MS, Advanced Certificate); business (EMBA, MBA, MS, Advanced Certificate); business administration (MBA); business analytics (MS); corporate finance (Advanced Certificate); executive program in management (EMBA); finance (MS); general management (Advanced Certificate); human resource management (MS, Advanced Certificate); information systems (MS, Advanced Certificate); international business (Advanced Certificate); investment management (Advanced Certificate); marketing (MS, Advanced Certificate); marketing research (MS); quantitative finance (MS); taxation (MS, Advanced Certificate). *Application deadline:* Applications are processed on a rolling basis. *Application fee:* $75. Electronic applications accepted. *Application Contact:* Sunil Samuel, Assistant Vice President of Admissions, 516-463-4723, Fax: 516-463-4664, E-mail: graduateadmission@hofstra.edu. *Dean*, Dr. Janet Lenaghan, 516-463-6574, Fax: 516-463-5268, E-mail: janet.a.lenaghan@hofstra.edu.

Fred DeMatteis School of Engineering and Applied Sciences Students: 30 full-time (9 women), 13 part-time (1 woman); includes 11 minority (1 Black or African American, non-Hispanic/Latino; 5 Asian, non-Hispanic/Latino; 5 Hispanic/Latino), 15 international. Average age 27. 82 applicants, 66% accepted, 19 enrolled. *Faculty:* 10 full-time (4 women), 5 part-time/adjunct. Expenses: Contact institution. *Financial support:* In 2018–19, 24 students received support, including 11 fellowships with full and partial tuition reimbursements available (averaging $4,482 per year); research assistantships with full and partial tuition reimbursements available, career-related internships or fieldwork, Federal Work-Study, institutionally sponsored loans, scholarships/grants, tuition waivers (full and partial), unspecified assistantships, and scholarships and endowed scholarships also available. Support available to part-time students. Financial award applicants required to submit FAFSA. In 2018, 18 master's awarded. *Program availability:* Part-time, evening/weekend, blended/hybrid learning. Offers computer science (MS). *Application deadline:* Applications are processed on a rolling basis. *Application fee:* $75. Electronic applications accepted. *Application Contact:* Sunil Samuel, Assistant Vice President of Admissions, 516-463-4723, Fax: 516-463-4664, E-mail: graduateadmission@hofstra.edu. *Dean*, Dr. Sina Rabbany, 516-463-6672, E-mail: sina.y.rabbany@hofstra.edu.

Hofstra Northwell School of Graduate Nursing and Physician Assistant Studies Students: 178 full-time (130 women), 130 part-time (112 women); includes 106 minority (19 Black or African American, non-Hispanic/Latino; 3 American Indian or Alaska Native, non-Hispanic/Latino; 39 Asian, non-Hispanic/Latino; 43 Hispanic/Latino; 2 Native Hawaiian or other Pacific Islander, non-Hispanic/Latino), 2 international. Average age 29. 2,139 applicants, 9% accepted, 131 enrolled. *Faculty:* 13 full-time (11 women), 17 part-time/adjunct (14 women). Expenses: Contact institution. *Financial support:* In 2018–19, 13 students received support, including 11 fellowships with full and partial tuition reimbursements available (averaging $12,268 per year), 2 research assistantships with full and partial tuition reimbursements available (averaging $6,490 per year); career-related internships or fieldwork, Federal Work-Study, institutionally sponsored loans, scholarships/grants, traineeships, tuition waivers (full and partial), unspecified assistantships, and scholarships and endowed scholarships also available. Support available to part-time students. Financial award applicants required to submit FAFSA. In 2018, 72 master's awarded. Offers adult-gerontology acute care nurse practitioner (MS); family nurse practitioner (MS); nursing and physician assistant studies (MS); physician assistant studies (MS); psychiatric-mental health np (MS). *Application deadline:* For fall admission, 11/1 for domestic students. *Application fee:* $75. Electronic applications accepted. *Application Contact:* Sunil Samuel, Assistant Vice President of Admissions, 516-463-4723, Fax: 516-463-4664, E-mail: graduateadmission@hofstra.edu. *Dean*, Kathleen Gallo, 516-463-7475, Fax: 516-463-7495, E-mail: kathleen.gallo@hofstra.edu.

Lawrence Herbert School of Communication Students: 47 full-time (24 women), 18 part-time (14 women); includes 34 minority (21 Black or African American, non-Hispanic/Latino; 2 Asian, non-Hispanic/Latino; 10 Hispanic/Latino; 1 Native Hawaiian or other Pacific Islander, non-Hispanic/Latino), 3 international. Average age 27. 76 applicants, 79% accepted, 30 enrolled. *Faculty:* 9 full-time (5 women), 7 part-time/adjunct (4 women). Expenses: Contact institution. *Financial support:* In 2018–19, 34 students received support, including 33 fellowships with full and partial tuition reimbursements available (averaging $3,487 per year), 1 research assistantship with full and partial tuition reimbursement available (averaging $6,180 per year); career-related internships or fieldwork, Federal Work-Study, institutionally sponsored loans, scholarships/grants, tuition waivers (full and partial), unspecified assistantships, and scholarships and endowed scholarships also available. Support available to part-time students. Financial award applicants required to submit FAFSA. In 2018, 29 master's awarded. *Program availability:* Part-time, evening/weekend. Offers communication (MA); journalism (MA); public relations (MA). *Application deadline:* Applications are processed on a rolling basis. *Application fee:* $75. Electronic applications accepted. *Application Contact:* Sunil Samuel, Assistant Vice President of Admissions, 516-463-4723, Fax: 516-463-4664, E-mail: graduateadmission@hofstra.edu. *Dean,* Mark Lukasiewicz, 516-463-5213, E-mail: Mark.Lukasiewicz@hofstra.edu.

Maurice A. Deane School of Law Students: 712 full-time (374 women), 137 part-time (88 women); includes 181 minority (53 Black or African American, non-Hispanic/Latino; 2 American Indian or Alaska Native, non-Hispanic/Latino; 34 Asian, non-Hispanic/Latino; 82 Hispanic/Latino; 7 Native Hawaiian or other Pacific Islander, non-Hispanic/Latino; 3 Two or more races, non-Hispanic/Latino), 13 international. Average age 27. 3,104 applicants, 50% accepted, 301 enrolled. *Faculty:* 41 full-time (21 women), 78 part-time/adjunct (24 women). Expenses: Contact institution. *Financial support:* In 2018–19, 578 students received support, including 565 fellowships with full and partial tuition reimbursements available (averaging $32,425 per year); research assistantships with full and partial tuition reimbursements available, career-related internships or fieldwork, Federal Work-Study, institutionally sponsored loans, scholarships/grants, tuition waivers (full and partial), unspecified assistantships, and scholarships and endowed scholarships also available. Support available to part-time students. Financial award applicants required to submit FAFSA. In 2018, 37 master's, 234 doctorates awarded. *Program availability:* Part-time, 100% online. Offers alternative dispute resolution (JD); American legal studies (LL M); business law honors (JD); clinical bioethics (Certificate); corporate compliance (JD); criminal law and procedure (JD); family law (LL M, JD); health law (JD); health law and policy (LL M, MA); intellectual property law honors (JD); international law honors (JD). *Application deadline:* For fall admission, 4/15 priority date for domestic and international students. Applications are processed on a rolling basis. *Application fee:* $0. Electronic applications accepted. *Application Contact:* Sunil Samuel, Assistant Vice President of Admissions, 516-463-4723, Fax: 516-463-4664. *Dean,* Gail Prudenti, 516-463-4068, E-mail: gail.prudenti@hofstra.edu.

School of Education *Program availability:* Part-time, evening/weekend, blended/hybrid learning. Offers applied behavior analysis (Advanced Certificate); bilingual education (MA); bilingual extension (Advanced Certificate); business education (MS Ed); childhood special education (MS Ed); curriculum studies (MS Ed); early childhood and childhood education (MS Ed); early childhood education (MA, MS Ed); early childhood special education (MS Ed, Advanced Certificate); education (MA, MS, MS Ed, Ed D, Advanced Certificate); educational and policy leadership (Ed D); educational leadership (Advanced Certificate); educational leadership and policy studies (MS Ed); educational technology (Advanced Certificate); elementary education (MA, MS Ed); elementary special education (MS Ed); English education (MS Ed); family and consumer science (MS Ed); fine arts and music education (Advanced Certificate); fine arts education (MS Ed); foreign language and TESOL (MS Ed); foreign language education (MA, MS Ed); gifted education (Advanced Certificate); health education (MS); health professions pedagogy and leadership (MS); higher education leadership and policy studies (MS Ed); inclusive early childhood special education (MS Ed); inclusive elementary special education (MS Ed); inclusive secondary special education (MS Ed); languages other than English and teaching English as a second language (MA); learning and teaching (Ed D); literacy studies (MA, MS Ed, Ed D, Advanced Certificate); mathematics education (MA, MS Ed); middle childhood extension (Advanced Certificate); music education (MA, MS Ed); pedagogy for health professions (Advanced Certificate); physical education (MS); school district business leader (Advanced Certificate); science education (MA); secondary education (Advanced Certificate); secondary education generalist - students with disabilities 7-12 (MS Ed); secondary special education generalist - secondary education (MS Ed); social studies education (MA, MS Ed); special education (MS Ed, Advanced Certificate); special education assessment and diagnosis (Advanced Certificate); special education early childhood intervention (MS Ed); special education: international perspectives (MS Ed); teaching languages other than English and TESOL (MS Ed); teaching students with severe or multiple disabilities (Advanced Certificate); technology for learning (MA); TESOL (MS Ed, Advanced Certificate); TESOL with specialization in STEM (MA); work based learning extension (Advanced Certificate). Electronic applications accepted.

School of Health Professions and Human Services Students: 517 full-time (427 women), 170 part-time (132 women); includes 276 minority (99 Black or African American, non-Hispanic/Latino; 1 American Indian or Alaska Native, non-Hispanic/Latino; 81 Asian, non-Hispanic/Latino; 79 Hispanic/Latino; 11 Native Hawaiian or other Pacific Islander, non-Hispanic/Latino; 5 Two or more races, non-Hispanic/Latino), 24 international. Average age 28. 1,384 applicants, 46% accepted, 256 enrolled. *Faculty:* 32 full-time (18 women), 68 part-time/adjunct (39 women). Expenses: Contact institution. *Financial support:* In 2018–19, 257 students received support, including 184 fellowships with full and partial tuition reimbursements available (averaging $3,508 per year), 11 research assistantships with full and partial tuition reimbursements available (averaging $5,695 per year); career-related internships or fieldwork, Federal Work-Study, institutionally sponsored loans, scholarships/grants, traineeships, tuition waivers (full and partial), unspecified assistantships, and scholarships and endowed scholarships also available. Support available to part-time students. Financial award applicants required to submit FAFSA. In 2018, 230 master's, 6 doctorates, 10 other advanced degrees awarded. *Program availability:* Part-time, evening/weekend. Offers audiology (Au D); counseling (MS Ed, PD); creative arts therapy (MA); foundations of public health (Advanced Certificate); health administration (MHA); health informatics (MS); health professions and human services (MA, MHA, MPH, MS, MS Ed, Au D, Advanced Certificate, PD); interdisciplinary transition specialist (Advanced Certificate); marriage and family therapy (MA); mental health counseling (MA, Advanced Certificate); occupational therapy (MS); public health (MPH); rehabilitation administration (PD); rehabilitation counseling (MS Ed, Advanced Certificate); rehabilitation counseling in mental health (MS Ed, Advanced Certificate); security and privacy in health information systems (Advanced Certificate); speech-language pathology (MA); sports science (MS); teacher of students with speech-language disabilities (Advanced Certificate). *Application deadline:* Applications are processed on a rolling basis. *Application fee:* $75. Electronic applications accepted. *Application Contact:* Sunil Samuel, Assistant Vice President of Admissions, 516-463-4723, Fax: 516-463-4664, E-mail: graduateadmission@hofstra.edu. *Dean,* Dr. Holly Seirup, 516-463-5301, Fax: 516-463-5317, E-mail: holly.j.seirup@hofstra.edu.

HOLLINS UNIVERSITY, Roanoke, VA 24020

General Information Independent, Undergraduate: women only; graduate: coed, comprehensive institution. *Enrollment:* 804 graduate, professional, and undergraduate students; 50 full-time matriculated graduate/professional students (39 women), 77 part-time matriculated graduate/professional students (67 women). *Enrollment by degree level:* 127 master's, 2 other advanced degrees. *Graduate faculty:* 15 full-time (8 women), 11 part-time/adjunct (6 women). *Required fees:* $675; $81.25. Tuition and fees vary

according to program. *Graduate housing:* On-campus housing not available. *Student services:* Campus safety program, career counseling, services for students with disabilities, teacher training, writing training. *Library facilities:* Wyndham Robertson Library plus 1 other. *Collection:* Books: 246,065 (physical), 122,121 (digital/electronic); Serial titles: 1,160 (physical), 51,262 (digital/electronic); Databases: 130. Weekly public service hours: 94.

Computer facilities: Computer purchase and lease plans are available. 102 computers available on campus for general student use. A campuswide network can be accessed from student residence rooms. Online class registration is available. Website: http://www.hollins.edu/

General Application Contact: Cathy S. Koon, Manager of Graduate Services, 540-362-6326, Fax: 540-362-6288, E-mail: ckoon@hollins.edu.

GRADUATE UNITS

Graduate Programs 158 applicants, 27% accepted, 29 enrolled. Expenses: Contact institution. *Financial support:* Fellowships, teaching assistantships, Federal Work-Study, and scholarships/grants available. Financial award application deadline: 7/15; financial award applicants required to submit FAFSA. In 2018, 79 master's awarded. *Program availability:* 100% online, blended/hybrid learning. Offers children's book illustration (Certificate); children's book writing and illustrating (MFA); children's literature (MA, MFA); creative writing (MFA); dance (MFA); humanities (MALS); interdisciplinary studies (MALS); leadership (MALS); new play directing (Certificate); new play performance (Certificate); playwriting (MFA); screenwriting (MFA); screenwriting and film studies (MA); social sciences (MALS); teaching (MAT); teaching and learning (MA); visual and performing arts (MALS). *Application deadline:* For fall admission, 1/6 priority date for domestic and international students. Applications are processed on a rolling basis. *Application fee:* $40. Electronic applications accepted. *Application Contact:* Dawn Barnett, Graduate Studies Assistant, 540-362-6575, Fax: 540-362-6288, E-mail: hugrad@hollins.edu. *Vice President for Academic Affairs,* Dr. Patricia Hammer, 540-3626326, Fax: 540-362-6288, E-mail: hugrad@hollins.edu.

HOLMES INSTITUTE, Golden, CO 80401

General Information Independent-religious, coed, graduate-only institution. *Graduate housing:* On-campus housing not available.

GRADUATE UNITS

Graduate Program *Program availability:* Online learning. Offers consciousness studies (MS).

HOLY APOSTLES COLLEGE AND SEMINARY, Cromwell, CT 06416-2005

General Information Independent-religious, coed, comprehensive institution. *Graduate housing:* On-campus housing not available.

GRADUATE UNITS

Department of Theology *Program availability:* Part-time, evening/weekend, online learning. Offers bioethics (MA, Certificate, Post Master's Certificate); church history (MA, Certificate, Post Master's Certificate); dogmatic theology (MA, Certificate, Post Master's Certificate); liturgical music (MA, Certificate, Post Master's Certificate); liturgy (MA, Certificate, Post Master's Certificate); moral theology (MA, Certificate, Post Master's Certificate); philosophical theology (MA, Certificate, Post Master's Certificate); religious education (MA, Certificate, Post Master's Certificate); sacred scripture (MA, Post Master's Certificate); sacred scriptures (Certificate); theology (M Div). Electronic applications accepted.

HOLY CROSS GREEK ORTHODOX SCHOOL OF THEOLOGY, Brookline, MA 02445-7496

General Information Independent-religious, coed, primarily men, graduate-only institution. *Graduate housing:* Rooms and/or apartments available on a first-come, first-served basis to single and married students.

GRADUATE UNITS

Theological Programs *Program availability:* Part-time. Offers theology (M Div, MTS, Th M).

HOLY FAMILY UNIVERSITY, Philadelphia, PA 19114

General Information Independent-religious, coed, comprehensive institution. *Graduate housing:* On-campus housing not available.

GRADUATE UNITS

Graduate and Professional Programs *Program availability:* Part-time, evening/weekend. Electronic applications accepted.

School of Arts and Sciences *Program availability:* Part-time, evening/weekend. Offers counseling psychology (MS); criminal justice (MA). Electronic applications accepted.

School of Business Administration *Program availability:* Part-time, evening/weekend. Offers accountancy (MS); finance (MBA); health care administration (MBA); human resource management (MBA); information systems management (MBA). Electronic applications accepted.

School of Education *Program availability:* Part-time, evening/weekend. Offers early elementary education (PreK-Grade 4) (M Ed); education (M Ed, Ed D); education leadership (M Ed); educational leadership and professional studies (Ed D); general education (M Ed); reading specialist (M Ed); special education (M Ed); TESOL and literacy (M Ed). Electronic applications accepted.

School of Nursing and Allied Health Professions *Program availability:* Part-time, evening/weekend. Offers nursing administration (MSN); nursing education (MSN). Electronic applications accepted.

HOLY NAMES UNIVERSITY, Oakland, CA 94619-1699

General Information Independent-religious, coed, comprehensive institution. *Enrollment:* 130 full-time matriculated graduate/professional students (97 women), 198 part-time matriculated graduate/professional students (161 women). *Enrollment by degree level:* 292 master's, 36 other advanced degrees. *Required fees:* $1003. *Graduate housing:* Room and/or apartments available on a first-come, first-served basis to single students; on-campus housing not available to married students. Housing application deadline: 8/15. *Student services:* Campus employment opportunities, campus safety program, career counseling, exercise/wellness program, free psychological counseling, international student services, low-cost health insurance, services for students with disabilities, writing training. *Library facilities:* Cushing Library. *Collection:* Books: 41,811 (physical), 137,046 (digital/electronic); Databases: 49. Students can reserve study rooms.

Computer facilities: 92 computers available on campus for general student use. A campuswide network can be accessed from student residence rooms. Online class registration is available. Website: http://www.hnu.edu/

General Application Contact: Graduate Admissions Office, 510-436-1351, Fax: 510-436-1325, E-mail: graduateadmissions@hnu.edu.

GRADUATE UNITS

Graduate Division Students: 130 full-time (97 women), 198 part-time (161 women); includes 207 minority (86 Black or African American, non-Hispanic/Latino; 2 American Indian or Alaska Native, non-Hispanic/Latino; 46 Asian, non-Hispanic/Latino; 70 Hispanic/Latino; 3 Two or more races, non-Hispanic/Latino), 13 international. Average age 35. 268 applicants, 64% accepted, 118 enrolled. Expenses: Contact institution. *Financial support:* Career-related internships or fieldwork, scholarships/grants, and unspecified assistantships available. Support available to part-time students. Financial award application deadline: 3/2; financial award applicants required to submit FAFSA. In 2018, 292 master's, 36 other advanced degrees awarded. *Program availability:* Part-time, evening/weekend. Offers administration/management (MSN, PMC); care transition management (MSN); counseling and forensic counseling (MA); counseling psychology (MA); creative writing (MA); educational therapy (Certificate); family nurse practitioner (MSN, PMC); finance (MBA); forensic psychology (MA); informatics (MSN); Kodaly (Certificate); management and leadership (MBA); marketing (MBA); mild/moderate disabilities (Ed S); multiple subject teaching (Credential); music education with Kodaly emphasis (MM); nurse educator (PMC); piano pedagogy (MM); single subject teaching (Credential); urban education: educational therapy (M Ed); urban education: K-12 education (M Ed); urban education: special education (M Ed); vocal pedagogy (MM). *Application deadline:* For fall admission, 8/1 priority date for domestic students, 7/15 for international students; for spring admission, 12/1 priority date for domestic students, 12/1 for international students; for summer admission, 5/1 priority date for domestic students, 5/1 for international students. Applications are processed on a rolling basis. *Application fee:* $65. Electronic applications accepted. *Application Contact:* Graduate Admissions Office. *Director of Admissions,* Chris Rascon, 510-436-1351, Fax: 510-436-1325, E-mail: graduateadmissions@hnu.edu.

HOOD COLLEGE, Frederick, MD 21701-8575

General Information Independent, coed, comprehensive institution. CGS member. *Enrollment:* 2,052 graduate, professional, and undergraduate students; 161 full-time matriculated graduate/professional students (81 women), 756 part-time matriculated graduate/professional students (517 women). *Enrollment by degree level:* 742 master's, 53 doctoral, 122 other advanced degrees. *Graduate faculty:* 37 full-time (21 women), 60 part-time/adjunct (35 women). *Tuition:* Full-time $17,640; part-time $4410 per semester. *Required fees:* $125 per semester. Tuition and fees vary according to degree level and program. *Graduate housing:* On-campus housing not available. *Student services:* Campus employment opportunities, campus safety program, career counseling, international student services, multicultural affairs office, services for students with disabilities, teacher training. *Library facilities:* Beneficial-Hodson Library and Information Technology Center plus 1 other. *Collection:* Books: 113,587 (physical), 367,563 (digital/electronic); Serial titles: 1,546 (physical), 2,440 (digital/electronic); Databases: 148. Students can reserve study rooms.

Computer facilities: Computer purchase and lease plans are available. 470 computers available on campus for general student use. A campuswide network can be accessed from student residence rooms and from off campus. Online class registration, Virtual Computer Lab (VCL), wireless printing are available.
Website: http://www.hood.edu/

General Application Contact: Dr. April Boulton, Dean of Graduate School, 301-696-3600, Fax: 301-696-3597, E-mail: gofurther@hood.edu.

GRADUATE UNITS

Graduate School Students: 161 full-time (81 women), 756 part-time (517 women); includes 176 minority (77 Black or African American, non-Hispanic/Latino; 1 American Indian or Alaska Native, non-Hispanic/Latino; 25 Asian, non-Hispanic/Latino; 50 Hispanic/Latino; 2 Native Hawaiian or other Pacific Islander, non-Hispanic/Latino; 21 Two or more races, non-Hispanic/Latino), 119 international. Average age 33. 323 applicants, 94% accepted, 200 enrolled. *Faculty:* 37 full-time (21 women), 60 part-time/adjunct (35 women). Expenses: Contact institution. *Financial support:* Research assistantships with full tuition reimbursements, tuition waivers (full and partial), and unspecified assistantships available. Financial award applicants required to submit FAFSA. In 2018, 231 master's, 89 other advanced degrees awarded. *Program availability:* Part-time, evening/weekend. Offers accounting (MBA); bioinformatics (MS, Certificate); biotechnology/molecular biology (MS); ceramic arts (Certificate); ceramics (MA, MFA); clinical mental health counseling (MS); computer science (MS); curriculum and instruction (MS); cybersecurity (MS, Certificate); education, multidisciplinary studies (MS); educational leadership (MS, Certificate); environmental biology (MS); geographic information systems (Certificate); high school (MS); humanities (MA); information systems (MBA); information technology (MS); interdisciplinary studies in human behavior (MA); management information systems (MS); middle school (MS); organizational leadership (DBA, DOL); organizational management (Certificate); reading specialization (MS); school counseling (MS); secondary mathematics education (Certificate); STEM education (Certificate); thanatology (Certificate). *Application deadline:* For fall admission, 8/15 priority date for domestic students, 8/5 for international students; for spring admission, 12/1 priority date for domestic students, 12/1 for international students; for summer admission, 5/1 priority date for domestic students, 4/15 for international students. Applications are processed on a rolling basis. *Application fee:* $50 ($100 for international students). Electronic applications accepted. *Application Contact:* Christian DiGregorio, Director of Graduate Admissions, 301-696 Ext. 3604, E-mail: gofurther@hood.edu. *Dean of the Graduate School,* Dr. April M Boulton, 301-696-3600, E-mail: gofurther@hood.edu.

HOOD THEOLOGICAL SEMINARY, Salisbury, NC 28144

General Information Independent-religious, coed, graduate-only institution. *Graduate housing:* Rooms and/or apartments guaranteed to single students and available on a first-come, first-served basis to married students. Housing application deadline: 8/15.

GRADUATE UNITS

Graduate and Professional Programs *Program availability:* Part-time, evening/weekend, online learning. Offers theology (M Div, MTS, D Min).

HOPE INTERNATIONAL UNIVERSITY, Fullerton, CA 92831-3138

General Information Independent-religious, coed, comprehensive institution. *Graduate housing:* Room and/or apartments available on a first-come, first-served basis to single students; on-campus housing not available to married students. Housing application deadline: 7/1.

GRADUATE UNITS

School of Graduate and Professional Studies *Program availability:* Part-time, evening/weekend, online learning. Offers Christian leadership (MCM); church music (MA); church music (Korean track) (MCM); church planting (MCM); education

administration (MA); elementary education (ME); general management (MBA, MSM); intercultural studies (MCM); international development (MBA, MSM); marketing management (MBA, MSM); marriage and family therapy (MA, MFT); non-profit management (MBA, MSM); secondary education (ME); worship (MCM). Electronic applications accepted.

HOUGHTON COLLEGE, Houghton, NY 14744

General Information Independent-religious, coed, comprehensive institution. *Graduate housing:* On-campus housing not available.

GRADUATE UNITS

Greatbatch School of Music Offers collaborative performance (MMus); composition (MMus); conducting (MMus); music (MA); performance (MMus); world music with theology and intercultural studies (MA). Electronic applications accepted.

HOUSTON BAPTIST UNIVERSITY, Houston, TX 77074-3298

General Information Independent-religious, coed, comprehensive institution. *Graduate housing:* Rooms and/or apartments available on a first-come, first-served basis to single and married students. Housing application deadline: 4/1.

GRADUATE UNITS

Archie W. Dunham College of Business *Program availability:* Part-time, evening/weekend, 100% online. Offers business (MBA, MIB, MSHRM); business administration (MBA); human resources management (MSHRM); international business (MIB). Electronic applications accepted.

College of Education and Behavioral Sciences *Program availability:* Part-time, evening/weekend, 100% online. Offers bilingual education (M Ed); Christian counseling (MACC); counseling (MAC); counselor education (M Ed); curriculum and instruction (M Ed); curriculum and instruction (EC-6 bilingual) (M Ed); curriculum and instruction in all-level art, Spanish, music, or physical education (M Ed); curriculum and instruction in EC-6 and special education (EC-12) (M Ed); curriculum and instruction in instructional technology (M Ed); curriculum and instruction in mathematics, science, or social studies (4-8) (M Ed); curriculum and instruction with EC-6 generalist (M Ed); curriculum and instruction with English language arts and reading (4-8) (M Ed); education and behavioral sciences (M Ed, MA, MAC, MACC, MAP, Ed D); educational administration (M Ed); educational diagnostician (M Ed); executive educational leadership (Ed D); higher education in business management (M Ed); higher education in Christian studies (M Ed); higher education in counseling (M Ed); higher education in educational technology (M Ed); marriage and family therapy (MA); pastoral counseling (MA); reading (M Ed); school psychology (MAP); special educational leadership (Ed D). Electronic applications accepted.

School of Christian Thought *Program availability:* Part-time, evening/weekend. Offers Biblical languages (M Div); Christian leadership (MA); Christian thought (M Div, MA); cultural apologetics (MA); English languages (M Div); philosophical apologetics (MA); theological studies (MA). Electronic applications accepted.

School of Fine Arts *Program availability:* Part-time, evening/weekend. Offers studio art (MFA). Electronic applications accepted.

School of Humanities *Program availability:* Part-time, evening/weekend. Offers education (EC-12 art, music, physical education, or Spanish) (MLA); education (EC-6 generalist) (MLA); general liberal arts (MLA); humanities (MA, MLA); philosophy (MLA); specialization in education (4-8 or 7-12) (MLA). Electronic applications accepted.

School of Nursing and Allied Health *Program availability:* Part-time, evening/weekend, online only, 100% online. Offers family nurse practitioner (MSN); nursing and allied health (MSK, MSN); pediatric nurse practitioner in primary care (MSN); sport management (MSK). Electronic applications accepted.

HOUSTON GRADUATE SCHOOL OF THEOLOGY, Houston, TX 77092

General Information Independent-religious, coed, graduate-only institution. *Graduate housing:* On-campus housing not available.

GRADUATE UNITS

Graduate Programs *Program availability:* Part-time, evening/weekend. Offers counseling (MA); pastoral ministry (M Div, D Min); theology (MA).

HOWARD PAYNE UNIVERSITY, Brownwood, TX 76801-2715

General Information Independent-religious, coed, comprehensive institution. *Graduate housing:* Room and/or apartments available on a first-come, first-served basis to single students; on-campus housing not available to married students.

GRADUATE UNITS

Program in Business Administration *Program availability:* Part-time, evening/weekend. Offers business administration (MBA). Electronic applications accepted.

Program in Criminal Justice *Program availability:* Part-time, evening/weekend, online only, 100% online. Offers criminal justice (MS). Electronic applications accepted.

Program in Instructional Leadership *Program availability:* Part-time, evening/weekend, online only. Offers instructional leadership (M Ed). Electronic applications accepted.

Program in Sport and Wellness Leadership *Program availability:* Part-time. Offers sport and wellness leadership (M Ed). Electronic applications accepted.

Program in Theology and Ministry *Program availability:* Part-time. Offers theology and ministry (MA). Electronic applications accepted.

Program in Youth Ministry *Program availability:* Part-time. Offers youth ministry (MA). Electronic applications accepted.

HOWARD UNIVERSITY, Washington, DC 20059-0002

General Information Independent, coed, university. CGS member. *Graduate housing:* Rooms and/or apartments available on a first-come, first-served basis to single and married students. Housing application deadline: 4/1. *Research affiliation:* Ewing Marion Kauffman Foundation (science education), The Tokyo Foundation (women's studies, international affairs), National Oceanic and Atmospheric Administration (NOAA) (atmospheric science and nanotechnology), National Institute of Mental Health (NIMH) (genomics), Akilu Lamma Institute of Pathobiology (HIV/AIDS infection, water resources development, population movement), Labor Research Laboratories and Medical Center in Benin City, Nigeria (infectious diseases).

GRADUATE UNITS

Cathy Hughes School of Communications *Program availability:* Part-time, evening/weekend. Offers communication sciences (PhD); communications (MA, MFA, MS, PhD); film (MFA); intercultural communication (MA, PhD); organizational communication (MA, PhD); speech pathology (MS). Electronic applications accepted.

Department of Communication, Culture and Media Studies *Program availability:* Part-time, evening/weekend. Offers mass communication (MA, PhD); media studies (MA, PhD). Electronic applications accepted.

College of Dentistry Offers advanced education in general dentistry (Certificate); dentistry (DDS); general dentistry practice (Certificate); oral and maxillofacial surgery (Certificate); orthodontics (Certificate); pediatric dentistry (Certificate).

College of Engineering, Architecture, and Computer Sciences *Program availability:* Part-time. Offers engineering, architecture, and computer sciences (M Eng, MCS, MS, PhD). Electronic applications accepted.

School of Engineering and Computer Science *Program availability:* Part-time. Offers chemical engineering (MS); civil engineering (M Eng); electrical engineering (M Eng, PhD); engineering and computer science (M Eng, MCS, MS, PhD); mechanical engineering (M Eng, PhD); systems and computer science (MCS). Electronic applications accepted.

College of Medicine Offers biochemistry and molecular biology (PhD); biotechnology (MS); medicine (MPH, MS, MD, PhD); microbiology (PhD); pharmacology (MS, PhD); public health (MPH).

College of Nursing and Allied Health Sciences *Program availability:* Part-time. Offers nursing and allied health sciences (MPA, MSN, MSOT, DPT, Certificate). Electronic applications accepted.

Division of Allied Health Sciences Offers occupational therapy (MSOT); physical therapy (DPT); physician assistant (MPA).

Division of Nursing *Program availability:* Part-time. Offers family nurse practitioner (MSN); nurse educator (MSN).

College of Pharmacy *Program availability:* Online learning. Offers pharmacy (Pharm D). Electronic applications accepted.

Graduate School *Program availability:* Part-time, evening/weekend. Offers African diaspora (MA, PhD); African history (MA, PhD); African studies (MA, PhD); analytical chemistry (MS, PhD); anatomy (MS, PhD); applied mathematics (MS, PhD); atmospheric (MS, PhD); atmospheric sciences (MS, PhD); biochemistry (MS, PhD); biology (MS, PhD); biophysics (PhD); clinical psychology (PhD); developmental psychology (PhD); economics (MA, PhD); English (MA, PhD); environmental (MS, PhD); exercise physiology (MS); experimental psychology (PhD); French (MA); health education (MS); inorganic chemistry (MS, PhD); Latin America and the Caribbean (MA, PhD); mathematics (MS, PhD); neuropsychology (PhD); nutrition (MS, PhD); organic chemistry (MS, PhD); personality psychology (PhD); philosophy (MA); physical chemistry (MS, PhD); physics (MS, PhD); physiology (PhD); political science (MA, MAPA, PhD); psychology (MS); public administration (MAPA); public history (MA); social psychology (PhD); sociology (MA, PhD); Spanish (MA); sports studies (MS); United States history (MA, PhD); urban recreation (MS). Electronic applications accepted.

Division of Fine Arts *Program availability:* Part-time. Offers 3D reality (sculpture and ceramics) (MFA); applied music (MM); art history (MA); design (MFA); electronic studio (MFA); fine arts (MFA); history of art and visual culture (MA); instrument (MM Ed); jazz studies (MM); organ (MM Ed); painting (MFA); photography (MFA); piano (MM Ed); voice (MM Ed).

School of Business *Program availability:* Part-time, evening/weekend, online learning. Offers accounting (MBA); business (MBA); entrepreneurship (MBA); finance (MBA); general management (MBA); human resources management (MBA); information systems (MBA); international business (MBA); marketing (MBA); supply chain management (MBA).

School of Divinity *Program availability:* Part-time, evening/weekend. Offers theology (M Div, MARS, D Min). Electronic applications accepted.

School of Education Students: 128 full-time (91 women), 48 part-time (32 women); includes 151 minority (150 Black or African American, non-Hispanic/Latino; 1 Hispanic/Latino), 23 international. Average age 31. 181 applicants, 39% accepted, 57 enrolled. *Faculty:* 38 full-time (26 women), 9 part-time/adjunct (4 women). Expenses: Contact institution. *Financial support:* In 2018–19, 69 students received support, including 5 fellowships (averaging $49,000 per year), 17 research assistantships (averaging $24,500 per year); career-related internships or fieldwork, Federal Work-Study, institutionally sponsored loans, scholarships/grants, tuition waivers (full and partial), and unspecified assistantships also available. Financial award application deadline: 2/15; financial award applicants required to submit FAFSA. In 2018, 17 master's, 23 doctorates awarded. Offers counseling psychology (PhD); education (M Ed, Ed D, PhD, CAGS); educational administration (Ed D); educational administration and supervision (M Ed, CAGS); educational psychology (PhD); elementary education (M Ed); school psychology (PhD); school psychology and counseling services (M Ed); secondary education (M Ed); special education (M Ed). *Application deadline:* For fall admission, 1/15 for domestic and international students. *Application fee:* $75. Electronic applications accepted. *Application Contact:* Dr. Scott J. Dantley, Associate Dean for Academic Affairs, 202-806-7340, Fax: 202-806-7018, E-mail: scott.dantley@howard.edu. *Dean, School of Education,* Dr. Dawn G. Williams, 202-806-7340, Fax: 202-806-7018, E-mail: dgwilliams@howard.edu.

School of Law Offers law (LL M, JD). Electronic applications accepted.

School of Social Work *Program availability:* Part-time. Offers social work (MSW, PhD). Electronic applications accepted.

HULT INTERNATIONAL BUSINESS SCHOOL, Cambridge, MA 02141

General Information Independent, coed, comprehensive institution. *Graduate housing:* On-campus housing not available.

GRADUATE UNITS

Graduate Programs Offers business administration (EMBA); business analytics (MBA, MIB); business statistics (MBS); disruptive innovation (MDI); entrepreneurship (MBA, MIB); family business (MBA, MIB); finance (MBA, MF, MIB); international marketing (MIM); marketing (MBA, MIB); project management (MBA, MIB). MDI and MBS offered in San Francisco; MBA also offered in Boston, San Francisco, Dubai, Shanghai, and New York. Electronic applications accepted.

HUMBOLDT STATE UNIVERSITY, Arcata, CA 95521-8299

General Information State-supported, coed, comprehensive institution. *Enrollment:* 7,774 graduate, professional, and undergraduate students; 311 full-time matriculated graduate/professional students (207 women), 260 part-time matriculated graduate/professional students (164 women). *Enrollment by degree level:* 571 master's. *Graduate faculty:* 157 full-time (72 women), 210 part-time/adjunct (130 women). *Tuition:* Part-time $4649 per semester. *Required fees:* $2121; $1673. Tuition and fees vary according to program. *Graduate housing:* Room and/or apartments available on a first-come, first-served basis to single students; on-campus housing not available to married students. Typical cost: $6216 per year ($13,562 including board). Room and board

charges vary according to board plan and housing facility selected. Housing application deadline: 3/1. *Student services:* Campus employment opportunities, campus safety program, career counseling, child daycare facilities, exercise/wellness program, free psychological counseling, international student services, low-cost health insurance, multicultural affairs office, services for students with disabilities, teacher training. *Library facilities:* Humbolt State University Library. *Collection:* Books: 487,338 (physical), 165,816 (digital/electronic); Serial titles: 34,235 (physical), 190 (digital/electronic); Databases: 89. Weekly public service hours: 100; students can reserve study rooms.

Computer facilities: Computer purchase and lease plans are available. 1,098 computers available on campus for general student use. A campuswide network can be accessed from student residence rooms and from off campus. Online class registration is available.
Website: http://www.humboldt.edu/

General Application Contact: Cynthia Werner, Admissions Coordinator, 707-826-6250, E-mail: apply@humboldt.edu.

GRADUATE UNITS

Academic Programs Students: 311 full-time (207 women), 260 part-time (164 women); includes 187 minority (7 Black or African American, non-Hispanic/Latino; 17 American Indian or Alaska Native, non-Hispanic/Latino; 15 Asian, non-Hispanic/Latino; 117 Hispanic/Latino; 31 Two or more races, non-Hispanic/Latino), 9 international. Average age 31. 482 applicants, 53% accepted, 193 enrolled. *Faculty:* 157 full-time (72 women), 210 part-time/adjunct (130 women). Expenses: Contact institution. *Financial support:* Fellowships, research assistantships, teaching assistantships, career-related internships or fieldwork, Federal Work-Study, and institutionally sponsored loans available. Support available to part-time students. Financial award application deadline: 3/1; financial award applicants required to submit FAFSA. In 2018, 230 master's awarded. *Program availability:* Part-time, evening/weekend. *Application deadline:* Applications are processed on a rolling basis. *Application fee:* $55. Electronic applications accepted. *Application Contact:* Terri Fisher, Graduate Coordinator, 707-826-5194, E-mail: terri.fisher@humboldt.edu. Vice Provost, Dr. Mary Oling-Sisay, 707-826-3722.

College of Arts, Humanities, and Social Sciences Students: 49 full-time (36 women), 56 part-time (37 women); includes 34 minority (1 Black or African American, non-Hispanic/Latino; 6 American Indian or Alaska Native, non-Hispanic/Latino; 3 Asian, non-Hispanic/Latino; 21 Hispanic/Latino; 3 Two or more races, non-Hispanic/Latino). Average age 31. 35 applicants, 77% accepted, 16 enrolled. *Faculty:* 30 full-time (20 women), 53 part-time/adjunct (36 women). Expenses: Contact institution. *Financial support:* Fellowships, teaching assistantships, career-related internships or fieldwork, Federal Work-Study, and institutionally sponsored loans available. Support available to part-time students. Financial award application deadline: 3/1; financial award applicants required to submit FAFSA. In 2018, 9 master's awarded. *Program availability:* Part-time. Offers applied anthropology (MA); arts, humanities, and social sciences (MA); English (MA); environment and community (MA); sociology (MA). *Application deadline:* Applications are processed on a rolling basis. *Application fee:* $55. Electronic applications accepted. *Application Contact:* Cynthia Werner, Graduate Admissions Office Coordinator, 707-826 Ext. 6250, E-mail: cw7001@humboldt.edu. *Dean,* Dr. Lisa Bond-Maupin, 707-826-4491, Fax: 707-826-4498, E-mail: ljb20@humboldt.edu.

College of Natural Resources and Sciences Students: 74 full-time (40 women), 84 part-time (37 women); includes 38 minority (2 Black or African American, non-Hispanic/Latino; 2 American Indian or Alaska Native, non-Hispanic/Latino; 5 Asian, non-Hispanic/Latino; 23 Hispanic/Latino; 6 Two or more races, non-Hispanic/Latino), 5 international. Average age 29. 134 applicants, 40% accepted, 35 enrolled. *Faculty:* 78 full-time (24 women), 71 part-time/adjunct (35 women). Expenses: Contact institution. *Financial support:* Fellowships, career-related internships or fieldwork, and Federal Work-Study available. Support available to part-time students. Financial award application deadline: 3/1; financial award applicants required to submit FAFSA. In 2018, 45 master's awarded. *Program availability:* Part-time. Offers biological sciences (MS); environmental systems (MS); natural resources (MS); natural resources and sciences (MA, MS, Certificate). *Application deadline:* Applications are processed on a rolling basis. *Application fee:* $55. *Application Contact:* Dr. Dale Oliver, Dean, 707-826-3256, E-mail: dale.oliver@humboldt.edu. *Dean,* Dr. Dale Oliver, 707-826-3256, E-mail: dale.oliver@humboldt.edu.

College of Professional Studies Students: 188 full-time (131 women), 120 part-time (90 women); includes 115 minority (4 Black or African American, non-Hispanic/Latino; 9 American Indian or Alaska Native, non-Hispanic/Latino; 7 Asian, non-Hispanic/Latino; 73 Hispanic/Latino; 22 Two or more races, non-Hispanic/Latino), 4 international. Average age 32. 257 applicants, 52% accepted, 114 enrolled. *Faculty:* 49 full-time (28 women), 86 part-time/adjunct (59 women). Expenses: Contact institution. *Financial support:* Fellowships, teaching assistantships, career-related internships or fieldwork, Federal Work-Study, and institutionally sponsored loans available. Support available to part-time students. Financial award application deadline: 3/1; financial award applicants required to submit FAFSA. In 2018, 149 master's awarded. *Program availability:* Part-time, evening/weekend. Offers business (MBA); education (MA); kinesiology (MS); psychology (MA); social work (MSW). *Application deadline:* Applications are processed on a rolling basis. *Application fee:* $55. *Application Contact:* Dr. Shawna Young, Dean, 707-826-3961, Fax: 707-826-3963, E-mail: shy4@humboldt.edu. *Dean,* Dr. Shawna Young, 707-826-3961, Fax: 707-826-3963, E-mail: shy4@humboldt.edu.

HUMPHREYS UNIVERSITY, Stockton, CA 95207-3896

General Information Independent, coed, comprehensive institution. *Graduate housing:* On-campus housing not available.

GRADUATE UNITS

Drivon School of Law *Program availability:* Part-time, evening/weekend. Offers law (JD). Electronic applications accepted.

HUNTER COLLEGE OF THE CITY UNIVERSITY OF NEW YORK, New York, NY 10065-5085

General Information State and locally supported, coed, comprehensive institution. *Graduate housing:* Room and/or apartments available on a first-come, first-served basis to single students; on-campus housing not available to married students. *Research affiliation:* Mount Sinai Medical Center, Bellevue Hospital Center, Cornell University Medical Center, New York Hospital.

GRADUATE UNITS

Graduate School *Program availability:* Part-time, evening/weekend.

Hunter-Bellevue School of Nursing *Program availability:* Part-time. Offers adult-gerontology clinical nurse specialist (MS); adult-gerontology nurse practitioner (DNP); community/public health nursing (MS); family nurse practitioner (DNP); gerontological/adult nurse practitioner (MS); nursing (MS, DNP, AC); psychiatric-mental health nurse practitioner (MS, AC).

School of Arts and Sciences *Program availability:* Part-time, evening/weekend. Offers accounting (MS); adolescent mathematics education (MA); animal behavior and conservation (MA, Certificate); anthropology (MA); applied mathematics (MA); applied social research (MS); art history (MA); arts and sciences (MA, MFA, MS, MUP, PhD, Certificate); biochemistry (MA, PhD); bioinformatics (MA); biological sciences (MA, PhD); chemistry (MA, PhD); composition (MA); creative writing (MFA); economics (MA); ethnomusicology (MA); fiction (MFA); French (MA); general psychology (MA); geographic information science (Certificate); geography (MA); geoinformatics (MS); history (MA); integrated media arts (MFA); Italian (MA); literature, language, and theory (MA); memoir (MFA); music history (MA); music theory (MA); performance (MA); physics and astronomy (MA, PhD); playwriting (MFA); poetry (MFA); pure mathematics (MA); Spanish (MA); statistics (MA); studio art (MFA); teaching Chinese (MA); teaching Latin (MA); theatre (MA, MFA); urban affairs (MS); urban planning (MUP); urban policy and leadership (MS).

School of Education *Program availability:* Part-time, evening/weekend. Offers administration and supervision (AC); bilingual education (MS); biology education (MA); blind and visually impaired (MS Ed); chemistry education (MA); early childhood education (MS); earth science (MA); education (MA, MS, MS Ed, Ed D, AC); educational supervision and administration (Ed D, AC); English education (MA); French education (MA); instructional leadership (Ed D); Italian education (MA); mathematics education (MA); music education (MA); physics education (MA); rehabilitation counseling (MS Ed); school counseling (MS Ed); severe/multiple disabilities (MS Ed); social studies education (MA); Spanish education (MA); teaching English as a second language (MA). Electronic applications accepted.

School of Health Professions *Program availability:* Part-time, evening/weekend. Offers health professions (MS, DPT, AC); physical therapy (DPT); speech-language pathology (MS).

School of Urban Public Health *Program availability:* Part-time. Offers nutrition (MS).

Silberman School of Social Work Offers social work (MSW).

HUNTINGTON UNIVERSITY, Huntington, IN 46750-1299

General Information Independent-religious, coed, comprehensive institution. *Graduate housing:* On-campus housing not available. *Research affiliation:* Link Institute (youth ministry).

GRADUATE UNITS

Graduate School *Program availability:* Part-time, online learning. Offers adolescent and young adult education (M Ed); business administration (MBA); counseling (MA); early adolescent education (M Ed); elementary education (M Ed); global youth ministry (MA); occupational therapy (OTD); organizational leadership (MA); pastoral leadership (MA); TESOL education (M Ed). Electronic applications accepted.

HUNTINGTON UNIVERSITY OF HEALTH SCIENCES, Knoxville, TN 37918

General Information Proprietary, coed, comprehensive institution.

GRADUATE UNITS

Program in Nutrition *Program availability:* Part-time, evening/weekend, online learning. Offers clinical nutrition (DHS); nutrition (MS); personalized option (DHS). Electronic applications accepted.

HUNTSVILLE BIBLE COLLEGE, Huntsville, AL 35811-1632

General Information Independent, coed, comprehensive institution.

GRADUATE UNITS

Program in Ministry Offers biblical leadership (MM); pastoral studies (MM).

HUSSON UNIVERSITY, Bangor, ME 04401-2999

General Information Independent, coed, comprehensive institution. *Graduate housing:* Room and/or apartments available on a first-come, first-served basis to single students; on-campus housing not available to married students. Housing application deadline: 6/1.

GRADUATE UNITS

Doctorate in Physical Therapy Program Offers physical therapy (DPT). Electronic applications accepted.

Graduate Nursing Program *Program availability:* Part-time, evening/weekend. Offers educational leadership (MSN); family and community nurse practitioner (MSN, PMC); psychiatric mental health nurse practitioner (MSN, PMC). Electronic applications accepted.

Graduate Programs in Counseling and Human Relations *Program availability:* Part-time, evening/weekend. Offers clinical mental health counseling (MS); human relations (MS); school counseling (MS). Electronic applications accepted.

Master of Business Administration Program *Program availability:* Part-time, evening/weekend, 100% online, blended/hybrid learning. Offers athletic administration (MBA); biotechnology and innovation (MBA); general business administration (MBA); healthcare management (MBA); hospitality and tourism management (MBA); organizational management (MBA); risk management (MBA). Electronic applications accepted.

Master of Science in Criminal Justice Administration Program *Program availability:* Part-time, evening/weekend. Offers criminal justice administration (MS). Electronic applications accepted.

School of Pharmacy Offers pharmacology (MS); pharmacy (Pharm D). Electronic applications accepted.

HUSTON-TILLOTSON UNIVERSITY, Austin, TX 78702-2795

General Information Independent-religious, coed, comprehensive institution.

GRADUATE UNITS

Graduate Programs Offers educational leadership (M Ed).

ICAHN SCHOOL OF MEDICINE AT MOUNT SINAI, New York, NY 10029-6504

General Information Independent, coed, graduate-only institution. *Graduate housing:* Rooms and/or apartments guaranteed to single and married students. Housing application deadline: 6/1.

GRADUATE UNITS

The Bioethics Program Offers bioethics (MS). Program offered jointly with Union Graduate College.

Department of Medical Education Offers medical education (MD). Electronic applications accepted.

Graduate School of Biomedical Sciences Offers biomedical sciences (MS, PhD); clinical research education (MS, PhD); community medicine (MPH); genetic counseling (MS); neurosciences (PhD). Electronic applications accepted.

IDAHO STATE UNIVERSITY, Pocatello, ID 83209

General Information State-supported, coed, university. CGS member. *Graduate housing:* Rooms and/or apartments available on a first-come, first-served basis to single and married students. Housing application deadline: 5/1. *Research affiliation:* S.M. Stoller Corporation (ecology, waste management), ON Semiconductor (computer sciences, environmental management), Inland Northwest Research Alliance (INRA) (science), J.R. Simplot Company (plant sciences, environmental studies), Bechtel BWXT Idaho, LLC (environmental management, nuclear sciences), Environmental Science and Research Foundation (waste management, ecology).

GRADUATE UNITS

Graduate School *Program availability:* Part-time. Electronic applications accepted.

College of Arts and Letters *Program availability:* Part-time. Offers anthropology (MA, MS); art (MFA); arts and letters (MA, MFA, MNS, MPA, MS, DA, PhD, Post-Master's Certificate, Postbaccalaureate Certificate); clinical psychology (PhD); communication (MA); English (MA); English and the teaching of English (PhD); experimental psychology (PhD); historical resources management (MA); political science (MA, DA); public administration (MPA); sociology (MA); TESOL (Post-Master's Certificate); theatre (MA). Electronic applications accepted.

College of Business *Program availability:* Part-time. Offers business administration (MBA, Postbaccalaureate Certificate); computer information systems (MS, Postbaccalaureate Certificate). Electronic applications accepted.

College of Education *Program availability:* Part-time. Offers athletic administration (MPE); athletic training (MSAT); deaf education (M Ed); education (M Ed, MPE, Ed D, PhD, 5th Year Certificate, 6th Year Certificate, Ed S); educational administration (M Ed, 6th Year Certificate, Ed S); educational leadership (Ed D); elementary education (M Ed); human exceptionality (M Ed); human resource development (MS); instructional design (PhD); instructional technology (M Ed); literacy (M Ed); music education (M Ed); school psychology (M Ed, Ed S); secondary education (M Ed). Electronic applications accepted.

College of Health Professions *Program availability:* Part-time. Offers advanced general dentistry (Post-Doctoral Certificate); counseling (M Coun, Ed S); counselor education and counseling (PhD); dental hygiene (MS); family medicine (Post-Master's Certificate); health education (MHE); health professions (M Coun, MHE, MPH, MS, PhD, Ed S); physician assistant studies (MPAS); public health (MPH). Electronic applications accepted.

College of Nursing *Program availability:* Part-time. Offers nursing (MS, DNP, PhD). Electronic applications accepted.

College of Pharmacy *Program availability:* Part-time. Offers biopharmaceutical analysis (PhD); drug delivery (PhD); medicinal chemistry (PhD); pharmaceutical sciences (MS); pharmacology (PhD); pharmacy (MS, PhD, Pharm D); pharmacy administration (MS, PhD). Electronic applications accepted.

College of Rehabilitation and Communication Sciences Offers audiology (Au D); occupational therapy (MOT); physical therapy (DPT); rehabilitation and communication sciences (MOT, MS, Au D, DPT); speech language pathology (MS).

College of Science and Engineering *Program availability:* Part-time. Offers applied physics (PhD); biology (MNS, MS, DA, PhD); chemistry (MNS, MS); civil engineering (MS); clinical laboratory science (MS); environmental engineering (MS); environmental science and management (MS); geographic information science (MS); geology (MNS, MS); geology with emphasis in environmental geoscience (MS); geophysics/hydrology/geology (MS); geotechnology (Postbaccalaureate Certificate); health physics (MS); mathematics (MS, DA); mathematics for secondary teachers (MA); measurement and control engineering (MS); mechanical engineering (MS); microbiology (MS); nuclear science and engineering (MS, PhD); physics (MNS); science and engineering (MA, MNS, MS, DA, PhD, Postbaccalaureate Certificate). Electronic applications accepted.

IGLOBAL UNIVERSITY, Vienna, VA 22182

General Information Proprietary, coed, comprehensive institution.

GRADUATE UNITS

Graduate Programs

ILIFF SCHOOL OF THEOLOGY, Denver, CO 80210-4798

General Information Independent-religious, coed, graduate-only institution. *Graduate housing:* Rooms and/or apartments available on a first-come, first-served basis to single and married students.

GRADUATE UNITS

Graduate and Professional Programs *Program availability:* Part-time, evening/weekend. Offers biblical studies (MA); church history (MA); religion (MA); religion and social change (MA); specialized ministry (MASM); theology (M Div, MTS, D Min, PhD); theology/ethics (MA). PhD offered jointly with University of Denver. Electronic applications accepted.

ILLINOIS COLLEGE, Jacksonville, IL 62650-2299

General Information Independent-religious, coed, comprehensive institution. *Graduate housing:* On-campus housing not available.

GRADUATE UNITS

Program in Education *Program availability:* Part-time-only, evening/weekend. Offers education (MA Ed). Electronic applications accepted.

ILLINOIS COLLEGE OF OPTOMETRY, Chicago, IL 60616-3878

General Information Independent, coed, graduate-only institution. *Graduate housing:* Rooms and/or apartments available on a first-come, first-served basis to single and married students. Housing application deadline: 6/1. *Research affiliation:* Rush University (cataract development), University of Chicago (vision science), University of Illinois at Chicago (neuropharmacology), Vision Service Plan (pediatric optometry), Ciba Vision (contact lenses).

GRADUATE UNITS

Professional Program Offers optometry (OD). Electronic applications accepted.

ILLINOIS INSTITUTE OF TECHNOLOGY, Chicago, IL 60616

General Information Independent, coed, university. CGS member. *Graduate housing:* Rooms and/or apartments available on a first-come, first-served basis to single and married students. Housing application deadline: 6/1.

GRADUATE UNITS

Chicago-Kent College of Law *Program availability:* Part-time, evening/weekend. Offers family law (LL M); financial services law (LL M); international intellectual property law (LL M); law (JD); legal studies (JSD); taxation (LL M); U.S., international, and transnational law (LL M). Electronic applications accepted.

Graduate College *Program availability:* Part-time, evening/weekend, online learning. Electronic applications accepted.

Armour College of Engineering *Program availability:* Part-time, evening/weekend, online learning. Offers architectural engineering (M Arch E); biological engineering (MAS); biomedical engineering (MAS, MS, PhD); biomedical imaging and signals (MAS); chemical engineering (MAS, MS, PhD); civil engineering (MS, PhD); computer engineering (MS, PhD); construction engineering and management (MCEM); electrical engineering (MS, PhD); electricity markets (MAS); engineering (M Arch E, M Env E, M Geoenv E, M Trans E, MAS, MCEM, MGE, MPW, MS, MSE, PhD); environmental engineering (M Env E, MS, PhD); geoenvironmental engineering (M Geoenv E); geotechnical engineering (MGE); infrastructure engineering and management (MPW); manufacturing engineering (MAS, MS); materials science and engineering (MAS, MS, PhD); mechanical and aerospace engineering (MAS, MS, PhD); network engineering (MAS); power engineering (MAS); structural engineering (MSE); telecommunications and software engineering (MAS); transportation engineering (M Trans E); VLSI and microelectronics (MAS). Electronic applications accepted.

College of Architecture *Program availability:* Part-time. Offers architecture (M Arch, MLA, MS Arch, PhD). Electronic applications accepted.

College of Science *Program availability:* Part-time, evening/weekend, online learning. Offers analytical chemistry (MAS); applied life sciences (MAS); applied mathematics (MS, PhD); applied physics (MS); biochemistry (MS); biology (MS, PhD); business (MCS); cell and molecular biology (MS); chemistry (MAS, MS, PhD); computational intelligence (MCS); computer science (MCS, MS, PhD); cyber-physical systems (MCS); data analytics (MCS); data science (MAS); database systems (MCS); distributed and cloud computing (MCS); education (MCS); finance (MCS); health physics (MAS); information security and assurance (MCS); materials chemistry (MAS); mathematical finance (MAS); mathematics education (MAS, PhD); microbiology (MS); molecular biochemistry and biophysics (MS, PhD); networking and communications (MCS); physics (MS); science (MAS, MCS, MS, PhD); science education (MAS, PhD); software engineering (MCS); telecommunications and software engineering (MAS). Electronic applications accepted.

Institute of Design *Program availability:* Part-time. Offers design (M Des, MDM, PhD). Electronic applications accepted.

Lewis College of Human Sciences Offers clinical psychology (PhD); human sciences (MS, PhD); industrial and organizational psychology (PhD); information architecture (MS); personnel and human resource development (MS); rehabilitation and mental health counseling (MS); rehabilitation counseling education (PhD); technical communication (PhD); technical communication and information design (MS).

School of Applied Technology *Program availability:* Part-time, evening/weekend, online learning. Offers applied technology (MAS, MFPE, MFST, MS); cyber forensics and security (MAS); food process engineering (MFPE, MS); food safety and technology (MFST, MS); industrial technology and management (MAS); information technology and management (MAS). Electronic applications accepted.

Stuart School of Business *Program availability:* Part-time, evening/weekend. Offers business (MBA, MMF, MPA, MS, PhD); environmental management and sustainability (MS); finance (MS); management science (PhD); marketing analytics and communication (MS); mathematical finance (MMF); public administration (MPA); sustainability (MBA); technological entrepreneurship (MTE). Electronic applications accepted.

ILLINOIS STATE UNIVERSITY, Normal, IL 61790

General Information State-supported, coed, university. CGS member. *Enrollment:* 1,277 full-time matriculated graduate/professional students (797 women), 1,087 part-time matriculated graduate/professional students (769 women). *Enrollment by degree level:* 1,832 master's, 428 doctoral, 104 other advanced degrees. *Graduate faculty:* 892 full-time (458 women), 434 part-time/adjunct (276 women). *International tuition:* $15,089.40 full-time. *Tuition, area resident:* Full-time $7264.62. *Tuition, state resident:* full-time $9466. *Tuition, nonresident:* full-time $17,290. *Required fees:* $1481.04. *Graduate housing:* Rooms and/or apartments available on a first-come, first-served basis to single and married students. Typical cost: $7094 per year ($9352 including board) for single students; $5738 per year for married students. Room and board charges vary according to board plan and housing facility selected. Housing application deadline: 5/1. *Student services:* Campus employment opportunities, campus safety program, career counseling, child daycare facilities, exercise/wellness program, free psychological counseling, international student services, low-cost health insurance, multicultural affairs office, services for students with disabilities, teacher training, writing training. *Library facilities:* Milner Library. *Collection:* Books: 1.4 million (physical), 190,817 (digital/electronic); Serial titles: 97,570 (digital/electronic); Databases: 251. Students can reserve study rooms.

Computer facilities: Computer purchase and lease plans are available. 2,500 computers available on campus for general student use. A campuswide network can be accessed from student residence rooms and from off campus. Online class registration is available.
Website: http://www.illinoisstate.edu/

General Application Contact: Dr. Noelle Selkow, Interim Director of Graduate Studies, 309-438-2583, Fax: 309-438-7912, E-mail: gradinfo@ilstu.edu.

GRADUATE UNITS

Graduate School Students: 1,277 full-time (797 women), 1,087 part-time (769 women); includes 359 minority (138 Black or African American, non-Hispanic/Latino; 3 American Indian or Alaska Native, non-Hispanic/Latino; 40 Asian, non-Hispanic/Latino; 127 Hispanic/Latino; 1 Native Hawaiian or other Pacific Islander, non-Hispanic/Latino; 50 Two or more races, non-Hispanic/Latino), 343 international. Average age 30. 1,742 applicants, 70% accepted, 699 enrolled. *Faculty:* 892 full-time (458 women) 434 part-time/adjunct (276 women). Expenses: Contact institution. *Financial support:* In 2018–19, 362 research assistantships, 445 teaching assistantships were awarded; fellowships, career-related internships or fieldwork, Federal Work-Study, institutionally sponsored loans, tuition waivers (full and partial), and unspecified assistantships also available. Support available to part-time students. Financial award application deadline: 4/1. In 2018, 677 master's, 50 doctorates, 143 other advanced degrees awarded. *Program availability:* Part-time. *Application deadline:* Applications are processed on a rolling basis. *Application fee:* $40. Electronic applications accepted. *Application Contact:* Dr. Noelle Selkow, Interim Director of Graduate Studies, 309-438-2583, Fax: 309-438-7912, E-mail: gradinfo@ilstu.edu. *Interim Director of Graduate Studies,* Dr. Noelle Selkow, 309-438-2583, Fax: 309-438-7912, E-mail: gradinfo@ilstu.edu.

College of Applied Science and Technology Students: 255 full-time (141 women), 115 part-time (52 women); includes 52 minority (15 Black or African American, non-Hispanic/Latino; 1 American Indian or Alaska Native, non-Hispanic/Latino; 7 Asian, non-Hispanic/Latino; 19 Hispanic/Latino; 10 Two or more races, non-Hispanic/Latino), 85 international. Average age 27. 362 applicants, 64% accepted, 135 enrolled. *Faculty:* 148 full-time (74 women), 87 part-time/adjunct (37 women). Expenses: Contact institution. *Financial support:* Fellowships, research assistantships, teaching assistantships, career-related internships or fieldwork, Federal Work-Study, institutionally sponsored loans, tuition waivers (full and partial), and unspecified assistantships available. Support available to part-time students. Financial award application deadline: 4/1. In 2018, 169 master's, 67 other advanced degrees awarded. *Program availability:* Part-time. Offers agribusiness (MS); applied science and technology (MA, MS, Certificate, Graduate Certificate); criminal justice sciences (MA, MS); family and consumer sciences (MA, MS); health education (MS); information technology (MS); technology (MS). *Application deadline:* Applications are processed on a rolling basis. *Application fee:* $40. *Application Contact:* Dr. Todd McLoda, Dean, 309-438-7602, E-mail: tamclod@IllinoisState.edu. *Dean,* Dr. Todd McLoda, 309-438-7602, E-mail: tamclod@IllinoisState.edu.

College of Arts and Sciences Students: 633 full-time (445 women), 235 part-time (154 women); includes 133 minority (39 Black or African American, non-Hispanic/Latino; 1 American Indian or Alaska Native, non-Hispanic/Latino; 19 Asian, non-Hispanic/Latino; 54 Hispanic/Latino; 20 Two or more races, non-Hispanic/Latino), 148 international. Average age 28. 750 applicants, 65% accepted, 254 enrolled. *Faculty:* 381 full-time (179 women), 115 part-time/adjunct (64 women). Expenses: Contact institution. *Financial support:* In 2018–19, 98 research assistantships, 329 teaching assistantships were awarded; career-related internships or fieldwork, Federal Work-Study, institutionally sponsored loans, tuition waivers (full and partial), and unspecified assistantships also available. Support available to part-time students. Financial award application deadline: 4/1. In 2018, 213 master's, 27 doctorates, 21 other advanced degrees awarded. *Program availability:* Part-time. Offers animal behavior (MS); arts and sciences (MA, MS, MSW, MM, SSP); bacteriology (MS); biochemistry (MS); biological sciences (MS); biology (PhD); biophysics (MS); biotechnology (MS); botany (MS, PhD); cell biology (MS); chemistry (MCE, MS, MSCE); communication (MA, MS); communication sciences and disorders (MA, MS); conservation biology (MS); developmental biology (MS); ecology (MS, PhD); economics (MA, MS); English (MA, MS, PhD); entomology (MS); evolutionary biology (MS); French (MA); French and German (MA); French and Spanish (MA); genetics (MS, PhD); geography-geology (Graduate Certificate); German (MA); German and Spanish (MA); historical archaeology (MA, MS); history (MA, MS); immunology (MS); mathematics (MA, MS); mathematics education (MA, PhD); microbiology (MS, PhD); molecular biology (MS); molecular genetics (MS); neurobiology (MS); neuroscience (MS); parasitology (MS); physiology (MS, PhD); plant biology (MS); plant molecular biology (MS); plant sciences (MS); politics and government (MA, MS); psychology (MA, MS); school psychology (PhD, SSP); social work (MSW); sociology (MA, MS); Spanish (MS); structural biology (MS); writing (MA, MS); zoology (MS, PhD). *Application deadline:* Applications are processed on a rolling basis. *Application fee:* $40. *Application Contact:* Dr. Noelle Selkow, Interim Director of Graduate Studies, 309-438-2583, Fax: 309-438-7912, E-mail: gradinfo@ilstu.edu. *Interim Dean,* Dr. Diane Zosky, 309-438-5669, E-mail: dlzosky@IllinoisState.edu.

College of Business Students: 185 full-time (81 women), 48 part-time (24 women); includes 16 minority (2 Black or African American, non-Hispanic/Latino; 5 Asian, non-Hispanic/Latino; 2 Hispanic/Latino; 7 Two or more races, non-Hispanic/Latino), 53 international. Average age 27. 137 applicants, 91% accepted, 84 enrolled. *Faculty:* 108 full-time (41 women), 24 part-time/adjunct (8 women). Expenses: Contact institution. *Financial support:* In 2018–19, 56 research assistantships were awarded; career-related internships or fieldwork, Federal Work-Study, institutionally sponsored loans, and tuition waivers (full and partial) also available. Support available to part-time students. Financial award application deadline: 4/1. In 2018, 99 master's awarded. *Program availability:* Part-time. Offers accounting (MPA, MS); business (MBA, MPA, MS); business administration (MBA). *Application deadline:* Applications are processed on a rolling basis. *Application fee:* $40. *Application Contact:* Dr. Noelle Selkow, Interim Director of Graduate Studies, 309-438-2583, Fax: 309-438-7912, E-mail: gradinfo@ilstu.edu. *Dean of the College of Business,* Dr. Ajay Samant, 309-438-2251, E-mail: asamant@IllinoisState.edu.

College of Education Students: 65 full-time (46 women), 550 part-time (418 women); includes 115 minority (72 Black or African American, non-Hispanic/Latino; 1 American Indian or Alaska Native, non-Hispanic/Latino; 1 Asian, non-Hispanic/Latino; 34 Hispanic/Latino; 7 Two or more races, non-Hispanic/Latino), 13 international. Average age 35. 195 applicants, 79% accepted, 98 enrolled. *Faculty:* 102 full-time (76 women), 132 part-time/adjunct (107 women). Expenses: Contact institution. *Financial support:* In 2018–19, 37 research assistantships were awarded; career-related internships or fieldwork, Federal Work-Study, institutionally sponsored loans, tuition waivers (full and partial), and unspecified assistantships also available. Support available to part-time students. Financial award application deadline: 4/1. In 2018, 93 master's, 18 doctorates, 54 other advanced degrees awarded. *Program availability:* Part-time. Offers college student personnel administration (MS); curriculum and instruction (MS, MS Ed, Ed D); education (MS, MS Ed, Ed D, PhD, Certificate); educational administration (MS, MS Ed, Ed D, PhD); educational policies (Ed D); postsecondary education (Ed D); reading (MS Ed); special education (MS, MS Ed, Ed D, Certificate); supervision (Ed D). *Application deadline:* Applications are processed on a rolling basis. *Application fee:* $40. *Application Contact:* Dr. Noelle Selkow, Interim Director of Graduate Studies, 309-438-2583, Fax: 309-438-7912, E-mail: gradinfo@ilstu.edu. *Dean of College of Education,* Kevin Laudner, 309-438-2453, E-mail: klaudne@ilstu.edu.

College of Fine Arts Students: 112 full-time (68 women), 27 part-time (24 women); includes 22 minority (3 Black or African American, non-Hispanic/Latino; 4 Asian, non-Hispanic/Latino; 12 Hispanic/Latino; 3 Two or more races, non-Hispanic/Latino), 28 international. Average age 28. 105 applicants, 60% accepted, 34 enrolled. *Faculty:* 112 full-time (49 women), 30 part-time/adjunct (18 women). Expenses: Contact institution. *Financial support:* In 2018–19, 77 teaching assistantships were awarded; career-related internships or fieldwork, Federal Work-Study, institutionally sponsored loans, tuition waivers (full and partial), and unspecified assistantships also available. Support available to part-time students. Financial award application deadline: 4/1. In 2018, 44 master's awarded. *Program availability:* Part-time. Offers art history (MA, MS); arts technology (MS); ceramics (MFA, MS); drawing (MFA, MS); fibers (MFA, MS); fine arts (MA, MFA, MM, MM Ed, MS); glass (MFA, MS); graphic design (MFA, MS); metals (MFA, MS); music (MM, MM Ed); painting (MFA, MS); photography (MFA, MS); printmaking (MFA, MS); sculpture (MFA, MS); theatre (MA, MFA, MS). *Application deadline:* Applications are processed on a rolling basis. *Application fee:* $40. *Application Contact:* Dr. Noelle Selkow, Interim Director of Graduate Studies, 309-438-2583, Fax: 309-438-7912, E-mail: gradinfo@ilstu.edu. *Dean of the College of Fine Arts,* Dr. Jean M.K. Miller, 309-438-8321, E-mail: jmmill5@ilstu.edu.

Mennonite College of Nursing Students: 11 full-time (8 women), 112 part-time (97 women); includes 21 minority (7 Black or African American, non-Hispanic/Latino; 4

Asian, non-Hispanic/Latino; 6 Hispanic/Latino; 1 Native Hawaiian or other Pacific Islander, non-Hispanic/Latino; 3 Two or more races, non-Hispanic/Latino). Average age 37. 44 applicants, 27% accepted, 10 enrolled. *Faculty:* 40 full-time (38 women), 46 part-time/adjunct (42 women). Expenses: Contact institution. *Financial support:* In 2018–19, 5 teaching assistantships were awarded. In 2018, 30 master's, 5 doctorates, 1 other advanced degree awarded. Offers family nurse practitioner (PMC); nursing (MSN, PhD). *Application fee:* $40. *Application Contact:* Dr. Noelle Selkow, Interim Director of Graduate Studies, 309-438-2583, Fax: 309-438-7912, E-mail: gradinfor@ilstu.edu. *Dean of Mennonite College of Nursing,* Dr. Judy Neubrander, 309-438-2174, E-mail: jlneubr@IllinoisState.edu.

IMMACULATA UNIVERSITY, Immaculata, PA 19345

General Information Independent-religious, coed, university. CGS member. *Graduate housing:* Rooms and/or apartments available on a first-come, first-served basis to single and married students.

GRADUATE UNITS

College of Graduate Studies *Program availability:* Part-time, evening/weekend. Offers bilingual studies (MA); clinical mental health counseling (MA); clinical psychology (Psy D); educational leadership (MA, Ed D); forensic psychology (Graduate Certificate); integrative psychotherapy (Graduate Certificate); music therapy (MA); neuropsychology (Graduate Certificate); nutrition education for the registered dietitian (MA); nutrition education with dietetic internship (MA); nutrition education with wellness promotion (MA); organization leadership (MA); principal (Certificate); psychodynamic psychotherapy (Graduate Certificate); psychological testing (Graduate Certificate); school counseling (MA, Graduate Certificate); school psychology (MA); secondary education (Certificate); supervisor of special education (Certificate); TESOL (MA). Electronic applications accepted.

Division of Nursing *Program availability:* Part-time, evening/weekend. Offers nursing administration (MSN); nursing education (MSN).

INDEPENDENCE UNIVERSITY, Salt Lake City, UT 84107

General Information Proprietary, coed, comprehensive institution. *Graduate housing:* On-campus housing not available.

GRADUATE UNITS

Program in Business Administration Offers business administration (MBA).

Program in Business Administration in Health Care *Program availability:* Part-time, evening/weekend, online learning. Offers health care administration (MBA).

Program in Health Care Administration *Program availability:* Part-time, evening/weekend, online learning. Offers health care administration (MSHCA).

Program in Health Services *Program availability:* Part-time, evening/weekend, online learning. Offers community health (MSHS); wellness promotion (MSHS).

Program in Nursing Offers community health (MSN); gerontology (MSN); nursing administration (MSN); wellness promotion (MSN).

Program in Public Health *Program availability:* Part-time, evening/weekend, online learning. Offers public health (MPH).

INDIANA STATE UNIVERSITY, Terre Haute, IN 47809

General Information State-supported, coed, university. CGS member. *Graduate housing:* Rooms and/or apartments available on a first-come, first-served basis to single and married students. Housing application deadline: 4/18. *Research affiliation:* Indiana Space Grant (remote sensing), Indiana University School of Medicine (cancer and Lupus research), Cranberry Lake Biological Station (psychosocial impacts of cancer), Boston Museum of Science (remote sensing, biology), Great Lakes Northern Forest Cooperative Ecosystem Study Unit (biology, life sciences).

GRADUATE UNITS

College of Graduate and Professional Studies *Program availability:* Part-time, evening/weekend, online learning. Offers technology management (PhD). Electronic applications accepted.

Bayh College of Education *Program availability:* Part-time, evening/weekend. Offers clinical mental health counseling (MS); communication disorders (MS); curriculum and instruction (M Ed, PhD); education (M Ed, MS, PhD, Ed S); educational administration (PhD); educational technology (MS); higher education leadership (PhD); K-12 district leadership (PhD); school administration (Ed S); school administration and supervision (M Ed); school counseling (M Ed); school psychology (PhD, Ed S); student affairs and higher education (MS). Electronic applications accepted.

College of Arts and Sciences *Program availability:* Part-time, evening/weekend. Offers applied linguistics/teaching English as a second language (MA); arts and sciences (MA, MFA, MM, MPA, MS, PhD, Psy D, CAS); British and American literature (MA); cellular and molecular biology (PhD); ceramics (MA, MFA); clinical psychology (Psy D); communication studies (MA); computer science (MS); conducting (MM); criminology and criminal justice (MA, MS); drawing (MA, MFA); ecology, systematics and evolution (PhD); English (MA); general psychology (MA, MS); graphic design (MA, MFA); history (MA, MS); language education (PhD); life sciences (MS); mathematics (MA, MS); music education (MM); music performance (MM); painting (MA, MFA); photography (MA, MFA); physiology (PhD); printmaking (MA, MFA); public administration (MPA); radio, television and film (MA); science education (MS); sculpture (MA, MFA); Spanish/teaching English as a second language (MA); TESL/TEFL (CAS); writing (MA). Electronic applications accepted.

College of Health and Human Services Offers advanced practice nursing (DNP); applied health sciences (MS, DHS); athletic training (MS, DAT); family nurse practitioner (MS); health and human services (MA, MS, MSW, DAT, DNP, DPT, PhD); nursing administration (MS); nursing education (MS); occupational therapy (MS); physical education (MS); physical therapy (DPT); physician assistant (MS); recreation and sport management (MS); social work (MSW); sport management (PhD). Electronic applications accepted.

College of Technology Offers career and technical education (MS); electronics and computer technology (MS); human resource development (MS); occupational safety management (MS); technology (MS); technology management (MS). Electronic applications accepted.

Scott College of Business *Program availability:* Part-time, evening/weekend. Offers business (MBA). Electronic applications accepted.

INDIANA TECH, Fort Wayne, IN 46803-1297

General Information Independent, coed, comprehensive institution. *Graduate housing:* Room and/or apartments available on a first-come, first-served basis to single students; on-campus housing not available to married students. Housing application deadline: 8/15.

GRADUATE UNITS

Program in Business Administration *Program availability:* Part-time, evening/weekend, online learning. Offers accounting (MBA); health care management (MBA); human resources (MBA); management (MBA); marketing (MBA). Electronic applications accepted.

Program in Engineering Management *Program availability:* Part-time, evening/weekend, online only, 100% online. Offers engineering management (MSE). Electronic applications accepted.

Program in Global Leadership *Program availability:* Part-time, evening/weekend, online only, 100% online. Offers global leadership (PhD). Electronic applications accepted.

Program in Management *Program availability:* Part-time, evening/weekend, 100% online. Offers management (MSM). Electronic applications accepted.

Program in Organizational Leadership *Program availability:* Part-time, evening/weekend, online only, 100% online. Offers organizational leadership (MS). Electronic applications accepted.

Program in Psychology Offers psychology (MS).

INDIANA UNIVERSITY BLOOMINGTON, Bloomington, IN 47405-7000

General Information State-supported, coed, university. CGS member. *Graduate housing:* Rooms and/or apartments available to single and married students. Housing application deadline: 5/11.

GRADUATE UNITS

Jacobs School of Music Offers music (MA, MM, MME, MS, DM, DME, PhD, Artist Diploma, Performance Diploma, Spec). Electronic applications accepted.

Kelley School of Business Offers business (MBA, MPA, MS, DBA, PhD). PhD offered through University Graduate School. Electronic applications accepted.

Maurer School of Law Offers comparative law (MCL); juridical science (SJD); law (LL M, JD); law and social sciences (PhD); legal studies (Certificate). PhD offered through University Graduate School. Electronic applications accepted.

School of Education *Program availability:* Part-time, 100% online, blended/hybrid learning. Offers art education (MS, Ed D, PhD); counseling (MS, Ed D, Ed S); counselor education (MS, Ed S); curriculum studies (Ed D, PhD); education (MS, Ed D, PhD, Ed S, Graduate Certificate); educational leadership (MS, Ed D, Ed S); educational psychology (MS, PhD); elementary education (MS, Ed D, PhD, Ed S); higher education (Ed D, PhD); higher education and student affairs (MS); history and philosophy of education (MS); history, philosophy, and policy in education (PhD); inquiry methodology (PhD); instructional systems technology (MS, PhD); international and comparative education (MS); learning and developmental sciences (MS, PhD); literacy, culture, and language education (MS, Ed D, PhD, Ed S); mathematics education (MS, Ed D, PhD); school psychology (PhD, Ed S); science education (MS, Ed D, PhD); secondary education (MS, Ed D, PhD); social studies education (MS, PhD); special education (PhD, Ed S). Electronic applications accepted.

School of Informatics, Computing, and Engineering *Program availability:* Part-time, online learning. Offers bioinformatics (MS); computer science (MS, PhD); cybersecurity risk management (MS); data science (MS, Graduate Certificate); informatics (MS, PhD); informatics, computing, and engineering (MIS, MLS, MS, PhD, Graduate Certificate, Sp LIS); information architecture (Graduate Certificate); information science (MIS, PhD); intelligent systems engineering (PhD); library and information science (Sp LIS); library science (MLS); secure computing (MS, Graduate Certificate); visual heritage (PhD). PhD offered through University Graduate School. Electronic applications accepted.

School of Optometry Offers optometry (MS, OD, PhD). Electronic applications accepted.

School of Public and Environmental Affairs *Program availability:* Part-time, 100% online, blended/hybrid learning. Offers applied ecology (MSES); arts administration (MAAA); economic development (MPA); energy (MPA, MSES); environmental chemistry, toxicology, and risk assessment (MSES); environmental policy (PhD); environmental policy and natural resource management (MPA); environmental science (PhD); hazardous materials management (Certificate); information systems (MPA); international development (MPA); local government management (MPA); nonprofit management (MPA, Certificate); policy analysis (MPA); public and environmental affairs (MAAA, MES, MPA, MSES, PhD, Certificate); public budgeting and financial management (Certificate); public finance (PhD); public financial administration (MPA); public management (MPA, PhD, Certificate); public policy analysis (PhD); social entrepreneurship (Certificate); specialized environmental science (MSES); specialized public affairs (MPA); sustainability and sustainable development (MPA); water resources (MSES). Electronic applications accepted.

School of Public Health *Program availability:* Part-time, online learning. Offers applied sport science (MS); athletic administration/sport management (MS); athletic training (MS); behavioral, social, and community health (MPH); biomechanics (MS); biostatistics (MPH); environmental health (MPH, PhD); epidemiology (MPH, PhD); ergonomics (MS); exercise physiology (MS); family health (MPH); health behavior (PhD); human performance (PhD); leisure behavior (PhD); motor learning/control (MS); nutrition science (MS); outdoor recreation (MS); park and public lands management (MS); physical activity (MPH); physical activity, fitness and wellness (MS); professional health education (MPH); public health (MPH, MS, PhD); public health administration (MPH); recreation administration (MS); recreational sports administration (MS); recreational therapy (MS); safety management (MS); school and college health education (MS); tourism management (MS). Electronic applications accepted.

University Graduate School *Program availability:* Part-time. Electronic applications accepted.

College of Arts and Sciences *Program availability:* Part-time. Offers acting (MFA); African American and African diaspora studies (MA, PhD); African languages and linguistics (PhD); African studies (MA); analytical chemistry (PhD); anthropology (MA, PhD); apparel merchandising (MS); applied mathematics (MA); applied statistics (MS); architecture (M Arch); arts and sciences (MA, MAT, MFA, MS, Au D, PhD, Certificate); astronomy (MA, PhD); astrophysics (PhD); audiology (Au D); auditory sciences (Au D, PhD); biochemistry (PhD); biogeochemistry (MS, PhD); biology teaching (MAT); biotechnology (MA); Central Eurasian studies (MA, PhD); chemical biology (PhD); chemistry (MAT); Chinese (MA, PhD); Chinese language pedagogy (MA); classical studies (MA, MAT, PhD); clinical science (PhD); cognitive neuroscience (PhD); cognitive psychology (PhD); cognitive science (PhD); comparative literature (MA, MAT, PhD); computational linguistics (MA, MS, PhD); creative writing (MA, MFA); crime and youth development (MA, PhD); crime, law and psychology (MA, PhD); criminal justice (MA, PhD); criminal justice institutions and practices (MA, PhD); criminology (MA, PhD); design and technology (MFA); developmental criminology (MA, PhD); developmental psychology (PhD); directing

(MFA); East Asian studies (MA); economic geology (MS, PhD); economics (MS, PhD); ethnomusicology (MA, PhD); European studies (MA); evolution, ecology, and behavior (MA, PhD); French (MA, PhD); gender studies (PhD); genetics (PhD); geobiology (MS, PhD); geography (PhD); geophysics, structural geology and tectonics (MS, PhD); German philology and linguistics (PhD); German studies (MA, PhD); global and international studies (MA, MS, PhD, Certificate); history (MA, MAT, PhD); history and philosophy of science and medicine (MA, PhD); hydrogeology (MS, PhD); inorganic chemistry (PhD); interdisciplinary studies in crime and punishment (PhD); interdisciplinary studies of crime and punishment (MA); international studies (MA, MS); Italian (MA, PhD); Japanese (MA, PhD); Japanese language pedagogy (MA); Jewish studies (MA); Jewish studies and history (MA); language sciences (PhD); Latin American and Caribbean studies (MA); linguistics (MA, PhD); literature (PhD); materials chemistry (PhD); mathematical physics (PhD); mathematics education (MAT); media (MS); media arts and sciences (MA, PhD); medical physics (MS); medieval German studies (PhD); methods of behavior (MA); microbiology (MA, PhD); mineralogy (MS, PhD); molecular systems neuroscience (MA); molecular, cellular, and developmental biology (PhD); Near Eastern languages and cultures (MA, PhD); neuroscience (PhD); organic chemistry (PhD); philosophy (MA, PhD); physical chemistry (PhD); physics (MAT, MS, PhD); plant sciences (MA, PhD); playwriting (MFA); political science (PhD); Portuguese (MA, PhD); pure mathematics (MA, PhD); religious studies (MA, PhD); rhetoric (PhD); Russian and East European studies (MA, Certificate); second language studies (MA, PhD); Slavic and East European languages and cultures (MA, MAT, PhD); social psychology (PhD); sociology (MA, PhD); Spanish (MA, PhD); speech and hearing sciences (MA, Au D, PhD); speech and voice sciences (PhD); speech-language pathology (MA); statistical science (MS, PhD); stratigraphy and sedimentology (MS, PhD); studies in science literacy and responsible research (MA); studio art (MFA); teaching German (MAT); TESOL and applied linguistics (MA); the relationship between crime and gender, race and ethnicity (MA, PhD); theatre history, theory, and literature (MA, PhD); theoretical analyses of criminology (MA, PhD); zoology (MA, PhD). Electronic applications accepted.

INDIANA UNIVERSITY EAST, Richmond, IN 47374-1289
General Information State-supported, coed, comprehensive institution.
GRADUATE UNITS
School of Education Offers education (MS Ed).
School of Nursing Offers nursing (MSN).
School of Social Work Offers social work (MSW).

INDIANA UNIVERSITY KOKOMO, Kokomo, IN 46902-9003
General Information State-supported, coed, comprehensive institution. *Graduate housing:* On-campus housing not available.
GRADUATE UNITS
Department of Public Administration and Health Management *Program availability:* Part-time, evening/weekend. Offers health management (MPM, Graduate Certificate); public management (Graduate Certificate); public management and policy (MPM). Electronic applications accepted.

School of Business *Program availability:* Part-time, evening/weekend. Offers accounting (Postbaccalaureate Certificate); business administration (MBA); business fundamentals (Postbaccalaureate Certificate). Electronic applications accepted.

School of Nursing Offers family nurse practitioner (MSN); nurse administrator (MSN); nurse educator (MSN). Electronic applications accepted.

INDIANA UNIVERSITY NORTHWEST, Gary, IN 46408-1197
General Information State-supported, coed, comprehensive institution. *Graduate housing:* On-campus housing not available.
GRADUATE UNITS
College of Arts and Sciences *Program availability:* Part-time, evening/weekend. Offers clinical counseling (MS); community development/urban studies (Graduate Certificate); computer information systems (Graduate Certificate); liberal studies (MLS); race-ethnic studies (Graduate Certificate); women's and gender studies (Graduate Certificate). Electronic applications accepted.

School of Business and Economics *Program availability:* Part-time, evening/weekend. Offers accounting (Graduate Certificate); management (Certificate); management and administrative studies (MBA). Electronic applications accepted.

School of Education *Program availability:* Part-time, evening/weekend. Offers educational leadership (MS Ed); elementary education (MS Ed); K-12 online teaching (Graduate Certificate); secondary education (MS Ed). Electronic applications accepted.

School of Public and Environmental Affairs *Program availability:* Part-time. Offers criminal justice (MPA); environmental affairs (Graduate Certificate); health services (MPA); nonprofit management (Certificate); public management (MPA, Graduate Certificate). Electronic applications accepted.

School of Social Work *Program availability:* Part-time, evening/weekend. Offers health (MSW); mental health and addictions (MSW). Electronic applications accepted.

INDIANA UNIVERSITY OF PENNSYLVANIA, Indiana, PA 15705
General Information State-supported, coed, university. CGS member. *Enrollment:* 11,325 graduate, professional, and undergraduate students; 794 full-time matriculated graduate/professional students (485 women), 1,316 part-time matriculated graduate/professional students (826 women). *Enrollment by degree level:* 1,212 master's, 811 doctoral, 87 other advanced degrees. *Graduate faculty:* 234 full-time (105 women), 16 part-time/adjunct (9 women). *Tuition, state resident:* full-time $12,384; part-time $516 per credit hour. *Tuition, nonresident:* full-time $18,576; part-time $774 per credit hour. *Required fees:* $4454; $186 per credit hour. $65 per semester. Tuition and fees vary according to program and reciprocity agreements. *Graduate housing:* Room and/or apartments available on a first-come, first-served basis to single students; on-campus housing not available to married students. Housing application deadline: 4/15. *Student services:* Campus employment opportunities, campus safety program, career counseling, free psychological counseling, international student services, low-cost health insurance, multicultural affairs office, services for students with disabilities. *Library facilities:* Stapleton Library plus 1 other. *Collection:* Books: 514,631 (physical), 100,229 (digital/electronic); Serial titles: 4,858 (physical). Weekly public service hours: 101; study areas open 24 hours, 5–7 days a week; students can reserve study rooms.

Computer facilities: Computer purchase and lease plans are available. 2,363 computers available on campus for general student use. A campuswide network can be accessed from student residence rooms and from off campus. Online class registration is available.
Website: http://www.iup.edu/

General Application Contact: Paula Stossel, Assistant Dean for Administration, 724-357-2222, Fax: 724-357-4862, E-mail: graduate-admissions@iup.edu.
GRADUATE UNITS

School of Graduate Studies and Research Students: 794 full-time (485 women), 1,316 part-time (826 women); includes 265 minority (129 Black or African American, non-Hispanic/Latino; 4 American Indian or Alaska Native, non-Hispanic/Latino; 36 Asian, non-Hispanic/Latino; 54 Hispanic/Latino; 1 Native Hawaiian or other Pacific Islander, non-Hispanic/Latino; 41 Two or more races, non-Hispanic/Latino), 361 international. Average age 36. 2,110 applicants, 62% accepted, 794 enrolled. *Faculty:* 234 full-time (105 women), 16 part-time/adjunct (9 women). Expenses: Contact institution. *Financial support:* In 2018–19, 29 fellowships with full tuition reimbursements (averaging $971 per year), 430 research assistantships with tuition reimbursements (averaging $3,300 per year), 26 teaching assistantships with partial tuition reimbursements (averaging $17,551 per year) were awarded; career-related internships or fieldwork, Federal Work-Study, scholarships/grants, tuition waivers (full and partial), and unspecified assistantships also available. Support available to part-time students. Financial award application deadline: 3/15; financial award applicants required to submit FAFSA. In 2018, 290 master's, 150 doctorates, 7 other advanced degrees awarded. *Program availability:* Part-time, evening/weekend, blended/hybrid learning. *Application deadline:* Applications are processed on a rolling basis. *Application fee:* $50. Electronic applications accepted. *Application Contact:* Paula Stossel, Vice President for Graduate Enrollment, 724-357-4511, Fax: 724-357-4862, E-mail: paula.stossel@iup.edu. *Director of Graduate Marketing,* Simon Stuchlik, 724-357-2127, Fax: 724-357-4862, E-mail: stuchlik@iup.edu.

College of Education and Communications Students: 266 full-time (202 women), 405 part-time (277 women); includes 100 minority (54 Black or African American, non-Hispanic/Latino; 6 Asian, non-Hispanic/Latino; 18 Hispanic/Latino; 1 Native Hawaiian or other Pacific Islander, non-Hispanic/Latino; 21 Two or more races, non-Hispanic/Latino), 17 international. Average age 33. 690 applicants, 60% accepted, 258 enrolled. *Faculty:* 50 full-time (33 women), 11 part-time/adjunct (7 women). Expenses: Contact institution. *Financial support:* In 2018–19, 21 fellowships (averaging $842 per year), 132 research assistantships with tuition reimbursements (averaging $4,244 per year), 9 teaching assistantships with tuition reimbursements (averaging $21,032 per year) were awarded; career-related internships or fieldwork, Federal Work-Study, scholarships/grants, and unspecified assistantships also available. Support available to part-time students. Financial award application deadline: 4/15; financial award applicants required to submit FAFSA. In 2018, 161 master's, 36 doctorates, 24 other advanced degrees awarded. *Program availability:* Part-time, evening/weekend. Offers administration and leadership studies (D Ed); adult and community education (MA); adult and community education/communications technology (MA); business/administrative (M Ed); business/business specialist (M Ed); business/workforce development (M Ed); clinical mental health counseling (MA); communication disorders, special education, and disability services (M Ed, MS, Certificate); communications media and instructional technology (PhD); community counseling (MA); curriculum and instruction (D Ed); education (M Ed); education and communications (M Ed, MA, MS, D Ed, PhD, Certificate); educational and school psychology (M Ed, D Ed, Certificate); educational psychology (M Ed, Certificate); literacy (M Ed, Certificate); principal (Certificate); reading (Certificate); school counseling (M Ed); school psychology (D Ed, Certificate); special education (M Ed); speech-language pathology (MS); student affairs in higher education (MA). *Application deadline:* Applications are processed on a rolling basis. *Application fee:* $50. Electronic applications accepted. *Application Contact:* Paula Stossel, Assistant Dean for Administration, 724-357-4511, Fax: 724-357-4862, E-mail: graduate-admissions@iup.edu. *Dean,* Dr. Lara Luetkehans, 724-357-2480, Fax: 724-357-5595.

College of Fine Arts Students: 23 full-time (10 women), 26 part-time (16 women); includes 5 minority (2 Asian, non-Hispanic/Latino; 3 Hispanic/Latino), 2 international. Average age 28. 30 applicants, 90% accepted, 19 enrolled. *Faculty:* 20 full-time (6 women), 1 (woman) part-time/adjunct. Expenses: Contact institution. *Financial support:* In 2018–19, 25 research assistantships with tuition reimbursements (averaging $4,262 per year) were awarded; fellowships with full tuition reimbursements, career-related internships or fieldwork, Federal Work-Study, scholarships/grants, and unspecified assistantships also available. Support available to part-time students. Financial award application deadline: 4/15; financial award applicants required to submit FAFSA. In 2018, 15 master's awarded. *Program availability:* Part-time. Offers art (MA, MFA); fine arts (MA, MFA); music education (MA); music performance (MA). *Application deadline:* Applications are processed on a rolling basis. *Application fee:* $50. Electronic applications accepted. *Application Contact:* Dr. Susan Palmisano, Graduate Coordinator, 724-357-2536, E-mail: palmisan@iup.edu. *Dean,* Curtis A. Scheib, 724-357-2397, Fax: 724-357-7778, E-mail: Curtis.Scheib@iup.edu.

College of Health and Human Services Students: 189 full-time (113 women), 307 part-time (215 women); includes 60 minority (36 Black or African American, non-Hispanic/Latino; 2 American Indian or Alaska Native, non-Hispanic/Latino; 6 Asian, non-Hispanic/Latino; 9 Hispanic/Latino; 7 Two or more races, non-Hispanic/Latino), 23 international. Average age 32. 408 applicants, 79% accepted, 196 enrolled. *Faculty:* 41 full-time (21 women), 1 (woman) part-time/adjunct. Expenses: Contact institution. *Financial support:* In 2018–19, 10 fellowships with full tuition reimbursements (averaging $562 per year), 91 research assistantships with tuition reimbursements (averaging $3,346 per year), 4 teaching assistantships with partial tuition reimbursements (averaging $21,371 per year) were awarded; career-related internships or fieldwork, Federal Work-Study, scholarships/grants, and unspecified assistantships also available. Support available to part-time students. Financial award application deadline: 4/15; financial award applicants required to submit FAFSA. In 2018, 205 master's, 15 doctorates awarded. *Program availability:* Part-time, evening/weekend, online learning. Offers criminology (MA, PhD); employment and labor relations (MA, MS); food and nutrition (MS); health and human services (M Ed, MA, MS, PhD, Certificate); health and physical education (M Ed); health services administration (MS); nursing (PhD); nursing administration (MS); nursing and allied health (MS, PhD); nursing education (MS); safety sciences (MS, PhD); sport science/exercise science (MS); sport science/sport management (MS); sport science/sport studies (MS). *Application deadline:* Applications are processed on a rolling basis. *Application fee:* $50. Electronic applications accepted. *Application Contact:* Paula Stossel, Assistant Dean, 724-357-4511, Fax: 724-357-4862, E-mail: graduate-admissions@iup.edu. *Acting Dean,* Dr. Mary Williams, 724-357-2560, Fax: 724-357-6205, E-mail: mary.e.williams@iup.edu.

College of Humanities and Social Sciences Students: 123 full-time (68 women), 303 part-time (183 women); includes 57 minority (25 Black or African American, non-Hispanic/Latino; 2 American Indian or Alaska Native, non-Hispanic/Latino; 10 Asian, non-Hispanic/Latino; 12 Hispanic/Latino; 8 Two or more races, non-Hispanic/Latino),

85 international. Average age 36. 345 applicants, 74% accepted, 92 enrolled. *Faculty:* 52 full-time (25 women), 2 part-time/adjunct (0 women). Expenses: Contact institution. *Financial support:* In 2018–19, 18 fellowships with full tuition reimbursements (averaging $1,102 per year), 82 research assistantships with tuition reimbursements (averaging $4,070 per year), 10 teaching assistantships with partial tuition reimbursements (averaging $20,150 per year) were awarded; career-related internships or fieldwork, Federal Work-Study, scholarships/grants, and unspecified assistantships also available. Support available to part-time students. Financial award application deadline: 4/15; financial award applicants required to submit FAFSA. In 2018, 51 master's, 39 doctorates awarded. *Program availability:* Part-time, evening/weekend. Offers administration and leadership studies (PhD); applied archaeology (MA); composition and literature (MA); composition and teaching English to speakers of other languages (PhD); English: generalist (MA); English: literature (MA); English: TESOL (MA); environmental planning (MS); geographic information science and geospatial techniques (Certificate); geographic information science/cartography (MS); geography (MA); history (MA); humanities and social sciences (MA, MS, PhD, Certificate); literature and criticism (PhD); political science (MA); public affairs (MA); public history (MA); regional planning (MS); sociology (MA, PhD); teaching English (MA). *Application deadline:* Applications are processed on a rolling basis. *Application fee:* $50. Electronic applications accepted. *Application Contact:* Paula Stossel, Assistant Dean, 724-357-4511, E-mail: graduate-admissions@iup.edu. *Dean,* Dr. Yaw Asamoah, 724-357-5764, E-mail: osebo@iup.edu.

College of Natural Sciences and Mathematics Students: 82 full-time (48 women), 45 part-time (32 women); includes 18 minority (3 Black or African American, non-Hispanic/Latino; 6 Asian, non-Hispanic/Latino; 7 Hispanic/Latino; 2 Two or more races, non-Hispanic/Latino), 14 international. Average age 27. 270 applicants, 34% accepted, 34 enrolled. *Faculty:* 43 full-time (16 women). Expenses: Contact institution. *Financial support:* In 2018–19, 61 research assistantships with tuition reimbursements (averaging $3,064 per year), 10 teaching assistantships (averaging $24,425 per year) were awarded; fellowships with full tuition reimbursements, career-related internships or fieldwork, Federal Work-Study, scholarships/grants, and unspecified assistantships also available. Support available to part-time students. Financial award application deadline: 4/15; financial award applicants required to submit FAFSA. In 2018, 36 master's, 11 doctorates awarded. *Program availability:* Part-time. Offers applied and industrial chemistry (PSM); applied mathematics (MS); biology (MS); chemistry (PSM); clinical psychology (Psy D); elementary and middle school mathematics education (M Ed); nanoscience/industrial materials (PSM); natural sciences and mathematics (M Ed, MA, MS, PSM, Psy D); physics (MA, PSM); psychology (MA); secondary mathematics education (M Ed). *Application deadline:* Applications are processed on a rolling basis. *Application fee:* $50. Electronic applications accepted. *Application Contact:* Paula Stossel, Assistant Dean of Administration, 724-357-4511, Fax: 724-357-4862, E-mail: graduate-admissions@iup.edu. *Dean,* Dr. Deanne Snavely, 724-357-2609, Fax: 724-357-5700, E-mail: snavely@iup.edu.

Eberly College of Business and Information Technology Students: 110 full-time (44 women), 221 part-time (98 women); includes 25 minority (11 Black or African American, non-Hispanic/Latino; 6 Asian, non-Hispanic/Latino; 5 Hispanic/Latino; 3 Two or more races, non-Hispanic/Latino), 215 international. Average age 28. 291 applicants, 82% accepted, 201 enrolled. *Faculty:* 28 full-time (4 women), 1 part-time/adjunct (0 women). Expenses: Contact institution. *Financial support:* Fellowships, research assistantships, career-related internships or fieldwork, Federal Work-Study, scholarships/grants, and unspecified assistantships available. Support available to part-time students. Financial award application deadline: 4/15; financial award applicants required to submit FAFSA. In 2018, 188 master's awarded. *Program availability:* Part-time, evening/weekend. Offers business administration (MBA); business and information technology (M Ed, MBA). *Application deadline:* Applications are processed on a rolling basis. *Application fee:* $50. Electronic applications accepted. *Application Contact:* Paula Stossel, Assistant Dean, 724-357-4511, Fax: 724-357-4862, E-mail: graduate-admissions@iup.edu. *Dean,* Dr. Robert Camp, 724-357-7889, E-mail: bobcamp@iup.edu.

INDIANA UNIVERSITY–PURDUE UNIVERSITY INDIANAPOLIS, Indianapolis, IN 46202

General Information State-supported, coed, university. *Graduate housing:* Rooms and/or apartments available on a first-come, first-served basis to single and married students. Housing application deadline: 3/15.

GRADUATE UNITS

Herron School of Art and Design Offers art therapy (MA); visual art (MFA); visual communication design (MFA). Electronic applications accepted.

Indiana University School of Medicine Offers anatomy and cell biology (MS, PhD); biochemistry and molecular biology (MS, PhD); genetic counseling (MS); medical and molecular genetics (MS, PhD); medicine (MS, MD, PhD); microbiology and immunology (MS, PhD); pathology and laboratory medicine (MS, PhD); pharmacology (MS, PhD); toxicology (MS, PhD).

Stark Neurosciences Research Institute Offers medical neuroscience (PhD).

Kelley School of Business Offers accounting (MBA); business (MBA, MSA); business of medicine (MBA); entrepreneurship (MBA); finance (MBA); general administration (MBA); marketing (MBA); supply chain management (MBA).

Lilly Family School of Philanthropy Offers philanthropy (MA, XMA, PhD).

Richard M. Fairbanks School of Public Health Offers biostatistics (MS, PhD); environmental health (MPH); epidemiology (MPH, PhD); global health leadership (Dr PH); health administration (MHA); health policy (Graduate Certificate); health policy and management (MPH, PhD); health systems management (Graduate Certificate); product stewardship (MS); public health (Graduate Certificate); social and behavioral sciences (MPH).

Robert H. McKinney School of Law *Program availability:* Part-time. Offers advocacy skills (Certificate); American law for foreign lawyers (LL M); civil and human rights (Certificate); corporate and commercial law (LL M, Certificate); criminal law (Certificate); environmental and natural resources (Certificate); health law (Certificate); health law, policy and bioethics (LL M); intellectual property law (LL M, Certificate); international and comparative law (LL M, Certificate); international human rights law (LL M); law (MJ, JD, SJD). Electronic applications accepted.

School of Dentistry Offers cariology and operative dentistry (MSD); dental materials (MS, MSD); dental sciences (PhD); dentistry (DDS, Certificate); endodontics (MSD); oral and maxillofacial surgery (MSD); orthodontics (MSD); pediatric dentistry (MSD); periodontics (MSD); prosthodontics (MSD). Electronic applications accepted.

School of Education *Program availability:* Part-time, evening/weekend. Offers curriculum and instruction (MS); early childhood (MS); educational leadership (MS,

Certificate); English as a second language (Certificate); kindergarten (Certificate); language education (MS); reading (Certificate); school counseling (MS); special education (MS, Certificate). Electronic applications accepted.

School of Engineering and Technology *Program availability:* Part-time, evening/weekend. Offers applied data management and analytics (MS); biomedical engineering (MS, PhD); electrical and computer engineering (MS, PhD); engineering (MSE); engineering and technology (MS, MS Bm E, MSE, MSME, PhD); facilities management (MS); information security and assurance (MS); mechanical engineering (MSME, PhD); motorsports (MS); music technology (MS, PhD); music therapy (MS); organizational leadership (MS); technical communication (MS). Electronic applications accepted.

School of Health and Rehabilitation Sciences *Program availability:* Part-time, evening/weekend. Offers health and rehabilitation sciences (PhD); health sciences (MS); nutrition and dietetics (MS); occupational therapy (OTD); physical therapy (DPT); physician assistant (MPAS). Electronic applications accepted.

School of Informatics and Computing *Program availability:* Part-time, evening/weekend. Offers bioinformatics (MS, PhD); health informatics (MS, PhD); human-computer interaction (MS, PhD); informatics (MS); informatics and computing (MLS, MS, PhD, Certificate); library and information science (MLS); media arts and science (MS). Electronic applications accepted.

School of Liberal Arts Offers American philosophy (Certificate); American studies (PhD); applied communication (MA); bioethics (Certificate); economics (MA); English (MA); European history (MA); general sociology (MA); geographic information systems (MS, Certificate); health communication (PhD); liberal arts (MA, MS, PhD, Certificate); medical sociology (MA); museum studies (MA, Certificate); philosophy (MA); philosophy/bioethics (MA); political science (MA); public history (MA); teaching English to speakers of other languages (TESOL) (MA, Certificate); teaching literature (Certificate); teaching writing (Certificate); United States history (MA).

School of Nursing *Program availability:* Part-time, blended/hybrid learning. Offers adult/gerontology acute care nurse practitioner (MSN); adult/gerontology clinical nurse specialist (MSN); adult/gerontology primary care nurse practitioner (MSN); clinical nursing science (PhD); executive leadership (DNP); family nurse practitioner (MSN); health systems (PhD); nursing (MSN, DNP, PhD); nursing education (MSN); nursing leadership in health systems (MSN); pediatric clinical nurse specialist (MSN); pediatric nurse practitioner (MSN). Electronic applications accepted.

School of Physical Education and Tourism Management Offers event tourism (MS); kinesiology (MS); public health (Graduate Certificate). Electronic applications accepted.

School of Public and Environmental Affairs *Program availability:* Part-time, evening/weekend, online learning. Offers criminal justice and public safety (MS); homeland security and emergency management (Graduate Certificate); library management (Graduate Certificate); nonprofit management (Graduate Certificate); public affairs (MPA); public management (Graduate Certificate); social entrepreneurship: nonprofit and public benefit organizations (Graduate Certificate). Electronic applications accepted.

School of Science *Program availability:* Part-time, evening/weekend. Offers addiction neuroscience (PhD); applied earth sciences (PhD); applied social and organizational psychology (PhD); biocomputing (Graduate Certificate); biology (MS, PhD); biometrics (Graduate Certificate); chemistry and chemical biology (MS, PhD); clinical psychology (PhD); computer science (MS, PhD); computer security (Graduate Certificate); databases and data mining (Graduate Certificate); forensic and investigative sciences (MS); geology (MS); industrial/organizational psychology (MS); mathematics (MS, PhD); physics (MS, PhD); science (MS, PhD, Graduate Certificate); software engineering (Graduate Certificate). Electronic applications accepted.

School of Social Work *Program availability:* Part-time, evening/weekend. Offers social work (MSW, PhD, Certificate).

INDIANA UNIVERSITY SOUTH BEND, South Bend, IN 46615

General Information State-supported, coed, comprehensive institution. *Graduate housing:* On-campus housing not available.

GRADUATE UNITS

College of Liberal Arts and Sciences *Program availability:* Part-time, evening/weekend. Offers advanced computer programming (Graduate Certificate); applied informatics (Graduate Certificate); applied mathematics and computer science (MS); behavior modification (Graduate Certificate); computer applications (Graduate Certificate); computer programming (Graduate Certificate); correctional management and supervision (Graduate Certificate); English (MA); health systems management (Graduate Certificate); international studies (Graduate Certificate); liberal studies (MLS); nonprofit management (Graduate Certificate); paralegal studies (Graduate Certificate); professional writing (Graduate Certificate); public affairs (MPA); public management (Graduate Certificate); social and cultural diversity (Graduate Certificate); strategic sustainability leadership (Graduate Certificate); technology for administration (Graduate Certificate).

Ernestine M. Raclin School of the Arts *Program availability:* Part-time. Offers communication studies (MA); music (MM); music performance (AD). Electronic applications accepted.

Judd Leighton School of Business and Economics *Program availability:* Part-time, evening/weekend. Offers accounting (MSA); business (Graduate Certificate); business administration (MBA). Electronic applications accepted.

School of Education *Program availability:* Part-time, evening/weekend. Offers addiction counseling (MS Ed); alcohol and drug counseling (Graduate Certificate); clinical mental health counseling (MS Ed); educational leadership (MS Ed); elementary education (MS Ed); marriage, couple, and family counseling (MS Ed); school counseling (MS Ed); secondary education (MS Ed); special education (MAT, MS Ed). Electronic applications accepted.

School of Social Work *Program availability:* Part-time, evening/weekend. Offers social work (MSW).

Vera Z. Dwyer College of Health Sciences Offers health sciences (MSN).

School of Nursing *Program availability:* Part-time, evening/weekend. Offers family nurse practitioner (MSN).

INDIANA UNIVERSITY SOUTHEAST, New Albany, IN 47150-6405

General Information State-supported, coed, comprehensive institution. *Graduate housing:* On-campus housing not available.

GRADUATE UNITS

Master of Interdisciplinary Studies Program *Program availability:* Part-time. Offers interdisciplinary studies (MIS, Graduate Certificate). Electronic applications accepted.

School of Business *Program availability:* Part-time. Offers business administration (MBA); strategic finance (MS). Electronic applications accepted.

School of Education *Program availability:* Part-time, evening/weekend. Offers counselor education (MS Ed); elementary education (MS Ed); secondary education (MS Ed). Electronic applications accepted.

INDIANA WESLEYAN UNIVERSITY, Marion, IN 46953-4974
General Information Independent-religious, coed, comprehensive institution. *Graduate housing:* On-campus housing not available. *Research affiliation:* Eli Lilly and Company.
GRADUATE UNITS
College of Adult and Professional Studies *Program availability:* Part-time, evening/weekend, online learning. Offers accounting (MBA, Graduate Certificate); applied management (MBA); business administration (MBA); health care (MBA, Graduate Certificate); human resources (MBA, Graduate Certificate); management (MS); organizational leadership (Ed D). Electronic applications accepted.
School of Educational Leadership *Program availability:* Part-time, evening/weekend, online learning. Offers educational leadership (M Ed, Ed S). Electronic applications accepted.
Graduate School *Program availability:* Part-time, evening/weekend, online learning. Electronic applications accepted.
College of Arts and Sciences *Program availability:* Part-time. Offers addictions counseling (MS); clinical mental health counseling (MS); community counseling (MS); marriage and family therapy (MS); school counseling (MS); student development counseling and administration (MS). Electronic applications accepted.
School of Health Sciences Offers athletic training (MS); occupational therapy (OTD); public health (MPH).
School of Nursing *Program availability:* Part-time, online learning. Offers nursing administration (MS); nursing education (MS); primary care nursing (MS).
Wesley Seminary Offers children, youth and family ministry (MA); divinity (M Div); ministerial leadership (MA); ministry (MA).

INSTITUTE FOR CHRISTIAN STUDIES, Toronto, ON M5S 2E6, Canada
General Information Independent-religious, coed, graduate-only institution. *Graduate housing:* On-campus housing not available.
GRADUATE UNITS
Graduate Programs *Program availability:* Part-time, online learning. Offers education (M Phil F, PhD); history of philosophy (M Phil F, PhD); philosophical aesthetics (M Phil F, PhD); philosophy of religion (M Phil F, PhD); political theory (M Phil F, PhD); systematic philosophy (M Phil F, PhD); theology (M Phil F, PhD); worldview studies (MWS).

INSTITUTE FOR CLINICAL SOCIAL WORK, Chicago, IL 60601
General Information Independent, coed, primarily women, graduate-only institution. *Graduate housing:* On-campus housing not available.
GRADUATE UNITS
Graduate Programs *Program availability:* Part-time. Offers clinical social work (PhD).

INSTITUTE FOR DOCTORAL STUDIES IN THE VISUAL ARTS, Portland, ME 04102
General Information Independent, coed, graduate-only institution. *Enrollment by degree level:* 60 doctoral. *Graduate faculty:* 3 full-time, 7 part-time/adjunct. Website: https://www.idsva.edu/
General Application Contact: Molly Davis, Director of Administration/Director of Admissions, 207-771-8887, E-mail: info@idsva.edu.
GRADUATE UNITS
PhD Program in Visual Art: Philosophy, Aesthetics, and Art Theory Students: 60 full-time. Average age 43. *Faculty:* 3 full-time, 7 part-time/adjunct. Expenses: Contact institution. *Financial support:* Fellowships, teaching assistantships, and scholarships/grants available. Financial award applicants required to submit FAFSA. In 2018, 4 doctorates awarded. *Program availability:* Blended/hybrid learning. Offers art theory (PhD); art theory, philosophy and aesthetics (PhD); philosophy (PhD). *Application deadline:* Applications are processed on a rolling basis. *Application fee:* $60. Electronic applications accepted. *Application Contact:* Molly Davis, Director of Administration/Director of Admissions, 207-771-8887, E-mail: info@idsva.edu. *Director of Administration/ Director of Admissions,* Molly Davis, 207-7718887, E-mail: mdavis@idsva.edu.

INSTITUTE OF AMERICAN INDIAN ARTS, Santa Fe, NM 87508
General Information Federally supported, coed, comprehensive institution. *Graduate housing:* On-campus housing not available.
GRADUATE UNITS
Low Residency MFA in Creative Writing Program *Program availability:* Low-residency. Offers creative writing (MFA). Electronic applications accepted.

INSTITUTE OF CLINICAL ACUPUNCTURE AND ORIENTAL MEDICINE, Honolulu, HI 96817
General Information Proprietary, coed, graduate-only institution.
GRADUATE UNITS
Program in Oriental Medicine Offers Oriental medicine (MSOM).

INSTITUTE OF PUBLIC ADMINISTRATION, Dublin 4, Ireland
General Information Proprietary, coed, comprehensive institution.
GRADUATE UNITS
Programs in Public Administration Offers healthcare management (MA); local government management (MA); public management (MA, Diploma).

INSTITUTE OF TAOIST EDUCATION AND ACUPUNCTURE, Louisville, CO 80027
General Information Independent, coed, graduate-only institution.
GRADUATE UNITS
Graduate Program Offers classical five-element acupuncture (M Ac).

THE INSTITUTE OF WORLD POLITICS, Washington, DC 20036
General Information Independent, coed, graduate-only institution. *Graduate housing:* On-campus housing not available.
GRADUATE UNITS
Graduate Programs in National Security, Intelligence, and International Affairs *Program availability:* Part-time, evening/weekend. Offers American foreign policy (Certificate); comparative political culture (Certificate); conflict prevention (Certificate); counterintelligence (Certificate); counterterrorism (Certificate); cyber statecraft (Certificate); economic statecraft (Certificate); homeland security (Certificate); intelligence (Certificate); international politics (Certificate); national security affairs (Executive MA, Certificate); nonviolent conflict (Certificate); peace building, stabilization, and humanitarian affairs (Certificate); public diplomacy and strategic influence (Certificate); statecraft and international affairs (MA); statecraft and national security (MA, DSNS); strategic communication (Certificate); strategic intelligence studies (MA, Professional MA); strategic soft power (Certificate). Electronic applications accepted.

INSTITUT FRANCO-EUROPÉEN DE CHIROPRAXIE, 94200, France
General Information Independent, coed, graduate-only institution.
GRADUATE UNITS
Professional Program Offers chiropractic (DC).

INSTITUTO CENTROAMERICANO DE ADMINISTRACIÓN DE EMPRESAS, La Garita, Alajuela, Costa Rica
General Information Independent, coed, graduate-only institution. *Graduate housing:* Rooms and/or apartments guaranteed to single students and available to married students. *Research affiliation:* Tropical Agricultural Research and Higher Education Center (agribusiness), Harvard Institute for International Development (macroeconomics and environment), Earth University (agribusiness), Inter-American Institute for Cooperation on Agriculture (agribusiness), David Rockefeller Center for Latin American Studies (competitiveness), Zamarano (agribusiness).
GRADUATE UNITS
Graduate Programs Offers agribusiness management (MIAM); business administration (EMBA); finance (MBA); real estate management (MGREM); sustainable development (MBA); technology (MBA). Electronic applications accepted.

INSTITUTO TECNOLÓGICO Y DE ESTUDIOS SUPERIORES DE MONTERREY, CAMPUS CENTRAL DE VERACRUZ, 94500 Córdoba, Veracruz, Mexico
General Information Independent, coed, comprehensive institution.
GRADUATE UNITS
Graduate Programs *Program availability:* Part-time, evening/weekend, online learning. Electronic applications accepted.

INSTITUTO TECNOLÓGICO Y DE ESTUDIOS SUPERIORES DE MONTERREY, CAMPUS CHIAPAS, 29000 Tuxtla Gutiérrez, Chiapas, Mexico
General Information Independent, coed, comprehensive institution.

INSTITUTO TECNOLÓGICO Y DE ESTUDIOS SUPERIORES DE MONTERREY, CAMPUS CHIHUAHUA, 31300 Chihuahua, Chihuahua, Mexico
General Information Independent, coed, comprehensive institution.
GRADUATE UNITS
Graduate Programs Offers computer systems engineering (Ingeniero); electrical engineering (Ingeniero); electromechanical engineering (Ingeniero); electronic engineering (Ingeniero); engineering administration (MEA); industrial engineering (MIE, Ingeniero); international trade (MIT); mechanical engineering (Ingeniero).

INSTITUTO TECNOLÓGICO Y DE ESTUDIOS SUPERIORES DE MONTERREY, CAMPUS CIUDAD DE MÉXICO, 14380 Ciudad de Mexico, DF, Mexico
General Information Independent, coed, comprehensive institution. *Graduate housing:* On-campus housing not available. *Research affiliation:* McGill University (management), Concordia University (business and management), Eli Lilly S. A. de C. U. (technological development), Ford Motor Company (industrial organizations), German Research Center on Artificial Intelligence (informatics), Brent University (telecommunications).
GRADUATE UNITS
School of Business Administration *Program availability:* Part-time, evening/weekend, online learning. Offers business administration (EMBA, MBA, PhD); economy (MBA); finance (MBA). EMBA program offered jointly with The University of Texas at Austin.
School of Design, Engineering and Architecture *Program availability:* Part-time, evening/weekend, online learning. Offers management (MA); telecommunications (MA).
School of Humanities and Social Sciences *Program availability:* Part-time, evening/weekend. Offers humanities and social sciences (LL B).
Virtual University Division *Program availability:* Part-time, evening/weekend, online learning.

INSTITUTO TECNOLÓGICO Y DE ESTUDIOS SUPERIORES DE MONTERREY, CAMPUS CIUDAD JUÁREZ, 32320 Ciudad Juárez, Chihuahua, Mexico
General Information Independent, coed, comprehensive institution.
GRADUATE UNITS
Program in Administration of Information Technology Offers administration of information technology (MAIT).
Program in Applied Public Management Offers applied public management (MPM).
Program in Business Administration *Program availability:* Part-time, online learning. Offers business administration (MBA).
Program in Education Offers education (M Ed).
Program in Educational Administration Offers educational administration (MEA).
Program in Educational Innovation Offers educational innovation (DE).
Program in Educational Technology Offers educational technology (MTE).
Program in Electronic Commerce Offers electronic commerce (MEC).
Program in Humanistic Studies Offers humanistic studies (MEH).
Program in Quality Management Offers quality management (MQM).

INSTITUTO TECNOLÓGICO Y DE ESTUDIOS SUPERIORES DE MONTERREY, CAMPUS CIUDAD OBREGÓN, 85000 Ciudad Obregón, Sonora, Mexico
General Information Independent, coed, comprehensive institution.
GRADUATE UNITS
Program in Administration Offers administration (MA).

Program in Administration of Information Technology Offers administration of information technology (MATI).

Program in Administration of Telecommunications Offers administration of telecommunications (MAT).

Program in Engineering Offers engineering (ME).

Program in Finance Offers finance (MF).

Program in International Relations Offers international relations (MIR).

Program in Marketing Technology Offers marketing technology (MMT).

Programs in Education Offers cognitive development (ME); communications (ME); mathematics (ME).

INSTITUTO TECNOLÓGICO Y DE ESTUDIOS SUPERIORES DE MONTERREY, CAMPUS COLIMA, 28010 Colima, Colima, Mexico

General Information Independent, coed, comprehensive institution.

INSTITUTO TECNOLÓGICO Y DE ESTUDIOS SUPERIORES DE MONTERREY, CAMPUS CUERNAVACA, 62000 Temixco, Morelos, Mexico

General Information Independent, coed, comprehensive institution.

GRADUATE UNITS

Programs in Business Administration Offers finance (MA); human resources management (MA); international business (MA); marketing (MA).

Programs in Information Science Offers administration of information technology (MATI); computer science (MCC, DCC); information technology (MTI).

INSTITUTO TECNOLÓGICO Y DE ESTUDIOS SUPERIORES DE MONTERREY, CAMPUS ESTADO DE MÉXICO, Estado de Mexico 52926, Mexico

General Information Independent, coed, comprehensive institution. *Graduate housing:* On-campus housing not available. *Research affiliation:* Transportadora San Marcos, S. A. de C. V. (quality control), Microsoft Visual Studio (computer science), Sony Electronics (new products), Kaltex (quality control), Texas Instruments (semiconductors).

GRADUATE UNITS

Professional and Graduate Division *Program availability:* Part-time, online learning. Offers administration of information technologies (MITA); architecture (M Arch); business administration (GMBA, MBA); computer sciences (MCS, PhD); education (M Ed); educational institution administration (MAD); educational technology and innovation (PhD); electronic commerce (MEC); environmental systems (MS); finance (MAF); humanistic studies (MHS); information sciences and knowledge management (MISKM); information systems (MS); manufacturing systems (MS); marketing (MEM); quality systems and productivity (MS); science and materials engineering (PhD); telecommunications management (MTM).

INSTITUTO TECNOLÓGICO Y DE ESTUDIOS SUPERIORES DE MONTERREY, CAMPUS GUADALAJARA, 45140 Zapopan, Jalisco, Mexico

General Information Independent, coed, comprehensive institution. *Graduate housing:* Rooms and/or apartments available to single and married students. Housing application deadline: 8/30.

GRADUATE UNITS

Program in Business Administration *Program availability:* Part-time, evening/weekend, online learning. Offers business administration (IEMBA, M Ad).

Program in Finance Offers finance (MF).

INSTITUTO TECNOLÓGICO Y DE ESTUDIOS SUPERIORES DE MONTERREY, CAMPUS HIDALGO, 42090 Pachuca, Hidalgo, Mexico

General Information Independent, coed, comprehensive institution.

INSTITUTO TECNOLÓGICO Y DE ESTUDIOS SUPERIORES DE MONTERREY, CAMPUS IRAPUATO, 36660 Irapuato, Guanajuato, Mexico

General Information Independent, coed, comprehensive institution.

GRADUATE UNITS

Graduate Programs Offers administration (MBA); administration of information technology (MAIT); administration of telecommunications (MAT); architecture (M Arch); computer science (MCS); education (M Ed); educational administration (MEA); educational innovation and technology (DEIT); educational technology (MET); electronic commerce (MBA); environmental administration and planning (MEAP); environmental systems (MES); finances (MBA); humanistic studies (MHS); international management for Latin American executives (MIMLAE); library and information science (MLIS); manufacturing quality management (MMQM); marketing research (MBA).

INSTITUTO TECNOLÓGICO Y DE ESTUDIOS SUPERIORES DE MONTERREY, CAMPUS LAGUNA, 27250 Torreón, Coahuila, Mexico

General Information Independent, coed, comprehensive institution. *Graduate housing:* On-campus housing not available.

GRADUATE UNITS

Graduate School *Program availability:* Part-time. Offers business administration (MBA); industrial engineering (MIE); management information systems (MS).

INSTITUTO TECNOLÓGICO Y DE ESTUDIOS SUPERIORES DE MONTERREY, CAMPUS LEÓN, 37120 León, Guanajuato, Mexico

General Information Independent, coed, comprehensive institution.

GRADUATE UNITS

Program in Business Administration *Program availability:* Part-time. Offers business administration (MBA).

INSTITUTO TECNOLÓGICO Y DE ESTUDIOS SUPERIORES DE MONTERREY, CAMPUS MONTERREY, 64849 Monterrey, Nuevo León, Mexico

General Information Independent, coed, comprehensive institution. *Graduate housing:* Room and/or apartments available to single students; on-campus housing not available to married students. *Research affiliation:* IBM de Mexico (computer science), Southwest Research Institute (environment), Hylsa (steel), Vitro (glass products), Cydsa (petrochemicals), Cemex (cement).

GRADUATE UNITS

Graduate and Research Division *Program availability:* Part-time, evening/weekend. Offers agricultural parasitology (PhD); agricultural sciences (MS); applied statistics (M Eng); artificial intelligence (PhD); automation engineering (M Eng); biotechnology (MS); chemical engineering (M Eng); chemistry (MS, PhD); civil engineering (M Eng); communications (MS); computer science (MS); education (MA); electrical engineering (MS); electronic engineering (M Eng); environmental engineering (M Eng); farming productivity (MS); food processing engineering (MS); industrial engineering (M Eng, PhD); informatics (PhD); information systems (MS); information technology (MS); manufacturing engineering (M Eng); mechanical engineering (M Eng); phytopathology (MS); systems and quality engineering (M Eng).

Graduate School of Business Administration and Leadership *Program availability:* Part-time. Offers business administration (MA, MBA); finance (M Sc); international business (M Sc); management (PhD); management and leadership (M Sc, MA, MBA, PhD); marketing (M Sc).

INSTITUTO TECNOLÓGICO Y DE ESTUDIOS SUPERIORES DE MONTERREY, CAMPUS QUERÉTARO, 76130 Querétaro, Querétaro, Mexico

General Information Independent, coed, comprehensive institution. *Graduate housing:* Room and/or apartments guaranteed to single students; on-campus housing not available to married students. Housing application deadline: 6/15. *Research affiliation:* Transmisiones y Equipos Mecanicos (manufacturing design).

GRADUATE UNITS

School of Business Offers business (MBA).

INSTITUTO TECNOLÓGICO Y DE ESTUDIOS SUPERIORES DE MONTERREY, CAMPUS SALTILLO, 25270 Saltillo, Coahuila, Mexico

General Information Independent, coed, comprehensive institution.

INSTITUTO TECNOLÓGICO Y DE ESTUDIOS SUPERIORES DE MONTERREY, CAMPUS SAN LUIS POTOSÍ, 78140 San Luis Potosí, SLP, Mexico

General Information Independent, coed, comprehensive institution.

INSTITUTO TECNOLÓGICO Y DE ESTUDIOS SUPERIORES DE MONTERREY, CAMPUS SINALOA, 80800 Culiacán, Sinaloa, Mexico

General Information Independent, coed, comprehensive institution.

INSTITUTO TECNOLÓGICO Y DE ESTUDIOS SUPERIORES DE MONTERREY, CAMPUS SONORA NORTE, 83000 Hermosillo, Sonora, Mexico

General Information Independent, coed, comprehensive institution. *Graduate housing:* On-campus housing not available. *Research affiliation:* National Council for Science and Technology (engineering).

GRADUATE UNITS

Program in Business Offers business (MA).

Program in Education Offers education (MA).

Program in Technological Information Management Offers technological information management (MA).

INSTITUTO TECNOLÓGICO Y DE ESTUDIOS SUPERIORES DE MONTERREY, CAMPUS TAMPICO, 89120 Altimira, Tamaulipas, Mexico

General Information Independent, coed, comprehensive institution.

INSTITUTO TECNOLÓGICO Y DE ESTUDIOS SUPERIORES DE MONTERREY, CAMPUS TOLUCA, 50252 Toluca, Estado de Mexico, Mexico

General Information Independent, coed, comprehensive institution.

GRADUATE UNITS

Graduate Programs *Program availability:* Part-time, evening/weekend.

INSTITUTO TECNOLÓGICO Y DE ESTUDIOS SUPERIORES DE MONTERREY, CAMPUS ZACATECAS, 98000 Zacatecas, Zacatecas, Mexico

General Information Independent, coed, comprehensive institution.

INTER AMERICAN UNIVERSITY OF PUERTO RICO, AGUADILLA CAMPUS, Aguadilla, PR 00605

General Information Independent, coed, comprehensive institution.

GRADUATE UNITS

Graduate School *Program availability:* Part-time, evening/weekend. Electronic applications accepted.

INTER AMERICAN UNIVERSITY OF PUERTO RICO, ARECIBO CAMPUS, Arecibo, PR 00614-4050

General Information Independent, coed, comprehensive institution.

GRADUATE UNITS

Program in Anesthesia Offers anesthesia (MS).

Program in Business Administration Offers accounting (MBA); finance (MBA); human resources (MBA).

Program in Nursing Offers critical care nursing (MSN); surgical nursing (MSN).

Programs in Education Offers administration and educational supervision (MA Ed); counseling and guidance (MA Ed); curriculum and teaching (MA Ed); elementary education (MA Ed).

INTER AMERICAN UNIVERSITY OF PUERTO RICO, BARRANQUITAS CAMPUS, Barranquitas, PR 00794

General Information Independent, coed, comprehensive institution. *Graduate housing:* On-campus housing not available.

GRADUATE UNITS

Business Administration Program *Program availability:* Part-time, evening/weekend. Offers accounting (MBA); human resources (MBA); managerial information systems (MBA). Electronic applications accepted.

Program in Biotechnology *Program availability:* Part-time, evening/weekend. Offers general biotechnology (MSB); plants biotechnology (MSB). Electronic applications accepted.

Program in Criminal Justice *Program availability:* Evening/weekend. Offers criminal justice (MA). Electronic applications accepted.

Program in Education *Program availability:* Part-time, evening/weekend. Offers curriculum and teaching (M Ed); educational leadership and management (MA); elementary education (M Ed); information and library service technology (M Ed); special education (MA). Electronic applications accepted.

Program in Nursing *Program availability:* Part-time, evening/weekend. Offers critical care nursing (MSN); medical surgical nursing (MSN). Electronic applications accepted.

INTER AMERICAN UNIVERSITY OF PUERTO RICO, BAYAMÓN CAMPUS, Bayamón, PR 00957

General Information Independent, coed, comprehensive institution. *Enrollment:* 4,293 graduate, professional, and undergraduate students; 4 full-time matriculated graduate/professional students (all women), 100 part-time matriculated graduate/professional students (66 women). *Enrollment by degree level:* 104 master's. *Graduate faculty:* 9 full-time (2 women), 3 part-time/adjunct (2 women). *Tuition:* Full-time $3816; part-time $1908 per trimester. *Required fees:* $735; $642. *Graduate housing:* Room and/or apartments available on a first-come, first-served basis to single students; on-campus housing not available to married students. Typical cost: $4000 per year ($7993 including board). *Student services:* Career counseling, free psychological counseling, international student services, services for students with disabilities. *Library facilities:* Centro de Acceso a la Informacion plus 1 other. *Collection:* Books: 28,998 (physical), 248,232 (digital/electronic); Serial titles: 123 (physical); Databases: 88. Weekly public service hours: 75; students can reserve study rooms.

Computer facilities: 730 computers available on campus for general student use. A campuswide network can be accessed from student residence rooms. Online class registration is available.
Website: http://bayamon.inter.edu/

General Application Contact: Aurelis Baez, Director of Students Services, 787-279-1912 Ext. 2017, Fax: 787-279-2205, E-mail: abaez@bayamon.inter.edu.

GRADUATE UNITS

Graduate School *Program availability:* Part-time, evening/weekend. Offers biology (MS); electrical engineering (ME); human resources (MBA); mechanical engineering (ME, MS).

INTER AMERICAN UNIVERSITY OF PUERTO RICO, FAJARDO CAMPUS, Fajardo, PR 00738-7003

General Information Independent, coed, comprehensive institution. *Graduate housing:* On-campus housing not available.

GRADUATE UNITS

Graduate Programs *Program availability:* Online learning. Offers computer science (MS); educational management and leadership (MA Ed); general business (MBA); human resources (MBA); management information systems (MBA); marketing (MBA); special education (MA Ed).

INTER AMERICAN UNIVERSITY OF PUERTO RICO, GUAYAMA CAMPUS, Guayama, PR 00785

General Information Independent, coed, comprehensive institution.

GRADUATE UNITS

Department of Business Administration Offers marketing (MBA).

Department of Education and Social Sciences *Program availability:* Part-time. Offers early childhood education (0-4 years) (M Ed); elementary education (M Ed). Electronic applications accepted.

Department of Natural and Applied Sciences Offers computer security and networks (MS); networking and security (MCS).

INTER AMERICAN UNIVERSITY OF PUERTO RICO, METROPOLITAN CAMPUS, San Juan, PR 00919-1293

General Information Independent, coed, comprehensive institution. CGS member. *Graduate housing:* On-campus housing not available. *Research affiliation:* Innovation Technology (electronics).

GRADUATE UNITS

Graduate Programs *Program availability:* Part-time, evening/weekend. Offers accounting (MBA); administration of clinical laboratories (MS); advanced clinical services (MSW); advanced social work administration (MSW); American history (PhD); Christian education (PhD); clinical services (MSW); commercial education (MA); counseling psychology (MA, PhD); criminal justice (MA); curriculum and instruction (Ed D); educational administration (Ed D); educational computing (MA); elementary education (MA); English (MA); environmental evaluation and protection (MS); finance (MBA); general business (MBA); guidance and counseling (MA, Ed D); higher education administration (MA); history (MA, PhD); history education (MA); human resources (MBA); industrial management (MBA); industrial/organizational psychology (MA, PhD); international business (MIB); interregional and international business (PhD); labor relations (MA); management information systems (MBA); marketing (MBA); molecular microbiology (MS); music education (MM); occupational education (MA); open information systems (MS); pastoral theology (PhD); school psychology (MA, PhD); social work administration (MSW); Spanish (MA); Spanish education (MA); special education (MA); special education administration (Ed D); teaching English as a second language (MA); teaching of math (MA); teaching of physical education (MA); teaching of science (MA); theological studies (PhD); training and sport performance (MA); women's and gender studies (MA). Electronic applications accepted.

INTER AMERICAN UNIVERSITY OF PUERTO RICO, PONCE CAMPUS, Mercedita, PR 00715-1602

General Information Independent, coed, comprehensive institution.

GRADUATE UNITS

Graduate School

INTER AMERICAN UNIVERSITY OF PUERTO RICO, SAN GERMÁN CAMPUS, San Germán, PR 00683-5008

General Information Independent, coed, university. *Enrollment:* 4,450 graduate, professional, and undergraduate students; 459 full-time matriculated graduate/professional students (291 women), 204 part-time matriculated graduate/professional students (137 women). *Enrollment by degree level:* 355 master's, 275 doctoral, 33 other advanced degrees. *Graduate faculty:* 96 full-time (56 women), 180 part-time/adjunct (113 women). *Tuition:* Full-time $212; part-time $212 per credit. *Required fees:* $366 per semester. One-time fee: $31. Tuition and fees vary according to degree level and program. *Graduate housing:* Rooms and/or apartments available on a first-come, first-served basis to single and married students. Typical cost: $1200 per year ($3900 including board) for single students; $6000 per year for married students. Room and board charges vary according to housing facility selected. Housing application deadline: 6/15. *Student services:* Campus employment opportunities, campus safety program, career counseling, child daycare facilities, exercise/wellness program, free psychological counseling, international student services, low-cost health insurance, services for students with disabilities, teacher training. *Library facilities:* Juan Cancio Ortiz Library. *Collection:* Books: 125,059 (physical), 3,850 (digital/electronic); Serial titles: 240 (physical), 594,924 (digital/electronic); Databases: 96. Weekly public service hours: 69.

Computer facilities: 950 computers available on campus for general student use. A campuswide network can be accessed from student residence rooms and from off campus. Online class registration is available.
Website: http://www.sg.inter.edu/

General Application Contact: Dr. Zulma Quiñones, Director of School for Graduate Studies and Research, 787-264-1912 Ext. 7357, Fax: 787-892-6350, E-mail: zulma_quinones@intersg.edu.

GRADUATE UNITS

Graduate Studies Center *Program availability:* Part-time, evening/weekend. Offers accounting (MBA); applied mathematics (MA); business education (MA); counseling psychology (MA, PhD); curriculum and instruction (Ed D); drawing (MFA); education: counseling (MA, PhD); elementary education (MA); environmental sciences (MS); finance (MBA); general business administration (MBA); graphic design (MFA); health and physical education (MA); human resources (MBA, PhD); industrial relations (MBA); information systems (MBA); international and interregional business (PhD); library sciences (MLS); management (MBA); marketing (MBA); music (MA); music teacher education (MA); painting (MFA); photography (MFA); printmaking (MFA); school psychology (MA, PhD); science education (MA); sculpture (MFA); special education (MA); teaching English as a second language (MA).

INTER AMERICAN UNIVERSITY OF PUERTO RICO SCHOOL OF LAW, San Juan, PR 00936-8351

General Information Independent, coed, graduate-only institution.

GRADUATE UNITS

Professional Program *Program availability:* Part-time, evening/weekend. Offers law (JD).

INTER AMERICAN UNIVERSITY OF PUERTO RICO SCHOOL OF OPTOMETRY, Bayamón, PR 00957

General Information Independent, coed, graduate-only institution. *Graduate housing:* Room and/or apartments available on a first-come, first-served basis to single students; on-campus housing not available to married students.

GRADUATE UNITS

Professional Program Offers optometry (OD). Electronic applications accepted.

INTERDENOMINATIONAL THEOLOGICAL CENTER, Atlanta, GA 30314-4112

General Information Independent-religious, coed, graduate-only institution. *Graduate housing:* Room and/or apartments available on a first-come, first-served basis to single students; on-campus housing not available to married students. Housing application deadline: 8/1. *Research affiliation:* Atlanta University Center, Inc., Columbia Theological Seminary Library, Candler School of Theology Library, Emory University Library.

GRADUATE UNITS

Graduate and Professional Programs *Program availability:* Part-time, evening/weekend, blended/hybrid learning. Offers Christian education (MACE); ministry (D Min); pastoral counseling (Th D); theology (M Div). D Min and Th D programs offered in collaboration with the Atlanta Theological Association. Electronic applications accepted.

INTERIOR DESIGNERS INSTITUTE, Newport Beach, CA 92660

General Information Proprietary, coed, comprehensive institution.

GRADUATE UNITS

Graduate Program Offers interior design (MA).

INTERNATIONAL BAPTIST COLLEGE AND SEMINARY, Chandler, AZ 85286

General Information Independent-religious, coed, comprehensive institution. *Graduate housing:* Room and/or apartments available on a first-come, first-served basis to single students; on-campus housing not available to married students.

GRADUATE UNITS

Program in Biblical Studies Offers Biblical studies (MA).

Program in Education Offers education (M Ed).

Program in Ministry Offers ministry (M Min, D Min).

INTERNATIONAL INSTITUTE FOR RESTORATIVE PRACTICES, Bethlehem, PA 18018

General Information Independent, coed, graduate-only institution. CGS member. *Enrollment by degree level:* 67 master's. *Graduate faculty:* 5 full-time (4 women). *Tuition:* Full-time $1761; part-time $1761 per course.

Computer facilities: Online class registration is available.
Website: http://www.iirp.edu/

General Application Contact: Jamie Kaintz, Director of Student Services, 610-807-9221, Fax: 610-807-0423, E-mail: registrar@iirp.edu.

GRADUATE UNITS

Graduate Programs Students: 1 (woman) full-time, 66 part-time (49 women). *Faculty:* 5 full-time (4 women), 5 part-time/adjunct (2 women). Expenses: Contact institution.

Financial support: Institutionally sponsored loans and scholarships/grants available. *Program availability:* Online learning. Offers restorative practices (MS, Certificate). *Application Contact:* Jamie Kaintz, Registrar, 610-807-9221, E-mail: registrar@iirp.edu.

INTERNATIONAL TECHNOLOGICAL UNIVERSITY, San Jose, CA 95134

General Information Independent, coed, graduate-only institution. CGS member. *Research affiliation:* Linux Works, Inc. (software), @Channel (software), New Trends Technology, Inc. (hardware), Pico Turbo, Inc. (hardware).

GRADUATE UNITS

Program in Business Administration *Program availability:* Part-time, evening/weekend. Offers business administration (MBA, DBA). Electronic applications accepted.

Program in Computer Engineering *Program availability:* Part-time, evening/weekend. Offers computer engineering (MSCE). Electronic applications accepted.

Program in Digital Arts *Program availability:* Part-time. Offers digital arts (MA). Electronic applications accepted.

Program in Electrical Engineering *Program availability:* Part-time, evening/weekend. Offers electrical engineering (MSEE, PhD). Electronic applications accepted.

Program in Engineering Management *Program availability:* Part-time, evening/weekend. Offers engineering management (MSEM). Electronic applications accepted.

Program in Software Engineering *Program availability:* Part-time, evening/weekend. Offers software engineering (MSSE). Electronic applications accepted.

INTERNATIONAL UNIVERSITY IN GENEVA, CH-1215 Geneva 15, Switzerland

General Information Private, coed, comprehensive institution. *Graduate housing:* Room and/or apartments available on a first-come, first-served basis to single students; on-campus housing not available to married students. Housing application deadline: 7/31.

GRADUATE UNITS

Business Programs *Program availability:* Part-time, evening/weekend. Offers business administration (MBA, DBA); entrepreneurship (MBA); international business (MIB); international trade (MIT); sales and marketing (MBA). Electronic applications accepted.

Leadership Programs Offers international relations and diplomacy (MIRD); media and communication (MA); public administration (DPA). Electronic applications accepted.

THE INTERNATIONAL UNIVERSITY OF MONACO, MC-98000 Principality of Monaco, Monaco

General Information Independent, coed, comprehensive institution. *Graduate housing:* Rooms and/or apartments guaranteed to single and married students. *Research affiliation:* Alpstar (hedge funds).

GRADUATE UNITS

Graduate Programs *Program availability:* Part-time. Offers entrepreneurship (EMBA, MBA); financial engineering (M Sc); hedge fund and private equity (M Sc); international marketing (EMBA, MBA); international wealth management (M Sc); luxury goods and services (EMBA, M Sc, MBA); wealth and asset management (EMBA, MBA). Electronic applications accepted.

IONA COLLEGE, New Rochelle, NY 10801-1890

General Information Independent-religious, coed, comprehensive institution. *Enrollment:* 3,926 graduate, professional, and undergraduate students; 345 full-time matriculated graduate/professional students (235 women), 294 part-time matriculated graduate/professional students (171 women). *Enrollment by degree level:* 639 master's. *Graduate faculty:* 83 full-time (30 women), 42 part-time/adjunct (16 women). *Tuition:* Full-time $14,064; part-time $7032 per credit. *Required fees:* $245 per semester. *One-time fee:* $250. Tuition and fees vary according to program. *Graduate housing:* On-campus housing not available. *Student services:* Campus employment opportunities, campus safety program, career counseling, exercise/wellness program, free psychological counseling, international student services, multicultural affairs office, services for students with disabilities, writing training. *Library facilities:* Ryan Library plus 1 other. *Collection:* Books: 268,290 (physical), 330,337 (digital/electronic); Serial titles: 112 (physical), 369 (digital/electronic); Databases: 160. Weekly public service hours: 101; students can reserve study rooms.

Computer facilities: Computer purchase and lease plans are available. A campuswide network can be accessed from student residence rooms and from off campus. Online class registration, bill payment are available. Website: http://www.iona.edu/

General Application Contact: Katelyn Brunck, Associate Director of Graduate Admissions, 914-633-2451, Fax: 914-633-2277, E-mail: kbrunck@iona.edu.

GRADUATE UNITS

School of Arts and Science Students: 216 full-time (175 women), 100 part-time (73 women); includes 131 minority (48 Black or African American, non-Hispanic/Latino; 9 Asian, non-Hispanic/Latino; 69 Hispanic/Latino; 1 Native Hawaiian or other Pacific Islander, non-Hispanic/Latino; 4 Two or more races, non-Hispanic/Latino), 10 international. Average age 25. 377 applicants, 84% accepted, 114 enrolled. *Faculty:* 50 full-time (24 women), 24 part-time/adjunct (10 women). Expenses: Contact institution. *Financial support:* In 2018–19, 10 students received support. Tuition waivers (partial) and unspecified assistantships available. Support available to part-time students. Financial award application deadline: 4/15; financial award applicants required to submit FAFSA. In 2018, 134 master's, 11 other advanced degrees awarded. *Program availability:* Part-time, evening/weekend. Offers adolescence education: biology (MS Ed, MST); adolescence education: English (MS Ed); adolescence education: mathematics (MST); adolescence education: social studies (MS Ed, MST); adolescence education: Spanish (MS Ed); adolescence special education 5-12 (MST); arts and science (MA, MS, MS Ed, MST, AC, Certificate); childhood and special education (MST); communication sciences and disorders (MA); computer science (MS); criminal justice (MS); cyber security (MS); cybercrime and security (AC); early childhood and childhood (MST); educational leadership (MS Ed); English (MA); forensic criminology and criminal justice systems (Certificate); game development (MS); general-experimental psychology (MA); history (MA); human resources (Certificate); industrial-organizational psychology (MA); marriage and family therapy (MS); mental health counseling (MA); organizational behavior (Certificate); psychology (MA); public relations (MA); school psychology (MA); sports communication and media (MA). *Application deadline:* For fall admission, 8/1 priority date for domestic students, 5/1 priority date for international students; for winter admission, 12/1 priority date for domestic students, 8/1 priority date for international students; for spring admission, 1/1 priority date for domestic students, 9/1 priority date

for international students; for summer admission, 5/1 priority date for domestic students, 1/1 priority date for international students. Applications are processed on a rolling basis. Electronic applications accepted. *Application Contact:* Dr. Katherine Zaromatidis, Director of Graduate Studies, School of Arts and Science, 914-633-2375, E-mail: kzaromatidis@iona.edu. *Dean, School of Arts and Science,* Joseph Stabile, PhD, 914-633-2253, Fax: 914-633-2023, E-mail: jstabile@iona.edu.

School of Business Students: 127 full-time (59 women), 190 part-time (96 women); includes 118 minority (36 Black or African American, non-Hispanic/Latino; 2 American Indian or Alaska Native, non-Hispanic/Latino; 16 Asian, non-Hispanic/Latino; 63 Hispanic/Latino; 1 Native Hawaiian or other Pacific Islander, non-Hispanic/Latino), 17 international. Average age 28. 189 applicants, 93% accepted, 89 enrolled. *Faculty:* 26 full-time (4 women), 6 part-time/adjunct (4 women). Expenses: Contact institution. *Financial support:* In 2018–19, 173 students received support. Scholarships/grants, tuition waivers (partial), and unspecified assistantships available. Support available to part-time students. Financial award application deadline: 4/15; financial award applicants required to submit FAFSA. In 2018, 191 master's, 144 other advanced degrees awarded. *Program availability:* Part-time, evening/weekend, 100% online, blended/hybrid learning. Offers accounting and information systems (MS); business (MBA, MS, AC, PMC); business continuity and risk management (AC); finance (MS); financial management (MBA, PMC); financial services (MS); general accounting (MBA, AC); health care analytics (AC); human resource management (PMC); information systems (MBA, MS, PMC); international business (AC, PMC); international finance (MS); management (MBA, PMC); marketing (MBA); project management (MS); public accounting (MBA, MS, AC); sports and entertainment management (AC). *Application deadline:* For fall admission, 8/15 priority date for domestic students, 8/1 priority date for international students; for winter admission, 11/15 priority date for domestic students, 11/1 priority date for international students; for spring admission, 2/15 priority date for domestic students, 2/1 priority date for international students; for summer admission, 5/15 priority date for domestic students, 5/1 priority date for international students. Applications are processed on a rolling basis. *Application fee:* $0. Electronic applications accepted. *Application Contact:* Kimberly Kelly, Director of Graduate Business Admissions, 914-633-2271, Fax: 914-633-2012, E-mail: kkelly@iona.edu. *Interim Dean of the School of Business,* Richard Highfield, PhD, 914-633-2789, Fax: 914-633-2708, E-mail: rhighfield@iona.edu.

IOWA STATE UNIVERSITY OF SCIENCE AND TECHNOLOGY, Ames, IA 50011

General Information State-supported, coed, university. CGS member. *Graduate housing:* Rooms and/or apartments available on a first-come, first-served basis to single and married students. Housing application deadline: 6/15. *Research affiliation:* National Veterinary Services Laboratories, National Animal Disease Center, National Soil Tilth Laboratory, North Central Regional Center for Rural Development, U.S. Department of Energy-Ames Laboratory.

GRADUATE UNITS

Bioinformatics and Computational Biology Program Offers bioinformatics and computational biology (MS, PhD). Electronic applications accepted.

Department of Accounting Offers accounting (M Acc). Electronic applications accepted.

Department of Aerospace Engineering and Engineering Mechanics Offers aerospace engineering (M Eng, MS, PhD); engineering mechanics (M Eng, MS, PhD). Electronic applications accepted.

Department of Agricultural Education and Studies Offers agricultural education and studies (MS, PhD). Electronic applications accepted.

Department of Agronomy Offers agricultural meteorology (MS, PhD); agronomy (MS); crop production and physiology (MS, PhD); plant breeding (MS, PhD); soil science (MS, PhD). Electronic applications accepted.

Department of Animal Science Offers animal breeding and genetics (MS, PhD); animal physiology (MS); animal psychology (PhD); animal science (MS, PhD); meat science (MS, PhD). Electronic applications accepted.

Department of Anthropology Offers anthropology (MA). Electronic applications accepted.

Department of Apparel, Events, and Hospitality Management *Program availability:* Online learning. Offers apparel, merchandising, and design (MS, PhD); hospitality management (MS, PhD). Electronic applications accepted.

Department of Architecture Offers architectural studies (MSAS); architecture (M Arch, MS). Electronic applications accepted.

Department of Biomedical Sciences Offers biomedical sciences (MS, PhD). Electronic applications accepted.

Department of Chemical and Biological Engineering Offers chemical and biological engineering (M Eng, MS, PhD). Electronic applications accepted.

Department of Chemistry Offers chemistry (MS, PhD). Electronic applications accepted.

Department of Civil and Construction Engineering Offers civil engineering (MS, PhD). Electronic applications accepted.

Department of Community and Regional Planning Offers community and regional planning (MCRP); transportation (MS). Electronic applications accepted.

Department of Computer Science Offers computer science (MS, PhD). Electronic applications accepted.

Department of Economics Offers agricultural economics (MS, PhD); economics (MS, PhD). JD/MS and JD/PhD offered jointly with Drake University and The University of Iowa. Electronic applications accepted.

Department of Education Offers curriculum and instructional technology (M Ed, MS, PhD); elementary education (M Ed, MS); historical, philosophical, and comparative studies in education (M Ed, MS); special education (M Ed, MS, PhD). Electronic applications accepted.

Department of Educational Leadership and Policy Studies Offers counselor education (M Ed, MS); educational administration (M Ed, MS); educational leadership (PhD); higher education (M Ed, MS); organizational learning and human resource development (M Ed, MS); research and evaluation (MS); student affairs (MS). Electronic applications accepted.

Department of Electrical and Computer Engineering Offers computer engineering (M Eng, MS, PhD); electrical engineering (M Eng, MS, PhD). Electronic applications accepted.

Department of English Offers creative writing (MFA); English (MA); rhetoric and professional communication (PhD). Electronic applications accepted.

Department of Entomology Offers entomology (MS, PhD). Electronic applications accepted.

Department of Food Science and Human Nutrition Offers food science and technology (MS, PhD); nutrition (MS, PhD). Electronic applications accepted.

Department of Geological and Atmospheric Sciences Offers earth science (MS, PhD); environmental science (MS, PhD); geology (MS, PhD); meteorology (MS, PhD). Electronic applications accepted.

Department of History Offers history (MA); rural, agricultural, technological, and environmental history (PhD). Electronic applications accepted.

Department of Horticulture Offers horticulture (MS, PhD). Electronic applications accepted.

Department of Human Development and Family Studies Offers human development and family studies (MFCS, MS, PhD). Electronic applications accepted.

Department of Industrial and Manufacturing Systems Engineering Offers industrial engineering (M Eng, MS, PhD); operations research (MS); systems engineering (M Eng). Electronic applications accepted.

Department of Kinesiology Offers kinesiology (MS, PhD). Electronic applications accepted.

Department of Landscape Architecture *Program availability:* Part-time. Offers landscape architecture (MLA, MS). Electronic applications accepted.

Department of Materials Science and Engineering Offers materials science and engineering (M Eng, MS, PhD). Electronic applications accepted.

Department of Mathematics Offers applied mathematics (MS, PhD); mathematics (MS, PhD); school mathematics (MSM). Electronic applications accepted.

Department of Mechanical Engineering Offers mechanical engineering (M Eng, MS, PhD); systems engineering (M Eng). Electronic applications accepted.

Department of Natural Resource Ecology and Management Offers forestry (MS, PhD); wildlife ecology (MS, PhD). Electronic applications accepted.

Department of Physics and Astronomy Offers applied physics (MS, PhD); astrophysics (MS, PhD); condensed matter physics (MS, PhD); high energy physics (MS, PhD); nuclear physics (MS, PhD); physics (MS, PhD). Electronic applications accepted.

Department of Plant Pathology Offers plant pathology (MS, PhD). Electronic applications accepted.

Department of Political Science Offers political science (MA); public administration (MPA). JD/MA offered jointly with Drake University. Electronic applications accepted.

Department of Psychology Offers cognitive psychology (PhD); counseling psychology (PhD); psychology (MS, PhD); social psychology (PhD). Electronic applications accepted.

Department of Sociology Offers rural sociology (MS, PhD); sociology (MS, PhD). Electronic applications accepted.

Department of Statistics Offers statistics (MS, PhD). Electronic applications accepted.

Department of Veterinary Clinical Sciences Offers veterinary clinical sciences (MS). Electronic applications accepted.

Department of Veterinary Diagnostic and Production Animal Medicine Offers veterinary preventative medicine (MS). Electronic applications accepted.

Department of Veterinary Microbiology and Preventive Medicine Offers veterinary microbiology (MS, PhD). Electronic applications accepted.

Department of Veterinary Pathology Offers veterinary pathology (MS, PhD). Electronic applications accepted.

Greenlee School of Journalism and Communication Offers journalism and mass communication (MS). Electronic applications accepted.

Program in Agricultural and Biosystems Engineering Offers agricultural and biosystems engineering (M En, MS, PhD). Electronic applications accepted.

Program in Agricultural Economics Offers agricultural economics (MS, PhD). Electronic applications accepted.

Program in Agricultural Meteorology Offers agricultural meteorology (MS, PhD). Electronic applications accepted.

Program in Analytical Chemistry Offers analytical chemistry (MS, PhD). Electronic applications accepted.

Program in Animal Breeding and Genetics Offers animal breeding and genetics (MS); immunogenetics (PhD); molecular genetics (PhD); quantitative genetics (PhD). Electronic applications accepted.

Program in Animal Physiology Offers animal physiology (MS, PhD). Electronic applications accepted.

Program in Apparel, Merchandising, and Design Offers apparel, merchandising, and design (MS, PhD). Electronic applications accepted.

Program in Applied Linguistics and Technology Offers applied linguistics and technology (PhD). Electronic applications accepted.

Program in Applied Mathematics Offers applied mathematics (MS, PhD). Electronic applications accepted.

Program in Applied Physics Offers applied physics (MS, PhD). Electronic applications accepted.

Program in Astrophysics Offers astrophysics (MS, PhD).

Program in Biophysics Offers biophysics (MS, PhD). Electronic applications accepted.

Program in Biorenewable Resources and Technology Offers biorenewable resources and technology (MS, PhD). Electronic applications accepted.

Program in Business Administration Offers business administration (MBA). Electronic applications accepted.

Program in Business Analytics *Program availability:* Online learning. Offers business analytics (MS).

Program in Business and Technology Offers business and technology (PhD). Electronic applications accepted.

Program in Computer Engineering Offers computer engineering (M Eng, MS, PhD). Electronic applications accepted.

Program in Condensed Matter Physics Offers condensed matter physics (MS, PhD). Electronic applications accepted.

Program in Creative Writing and Environment Offers creative writing and environment (MFA). Electronic applications accepted.

Program in Crop Production and Physiology Offers crop production and physiology (MS, PhD). Electronic applications accepted.

Program in Diet and Exercise Offers diet and exercise (MS). Electronic applications accepted.

Program in Earth Science Offers earth science (MS, PhD). Electronic applications accepted.

Program in Ecology and Evolutionary Biology Offers ecology and evolutionary biology (MS, PhD). Electronic applications accepted.

Program in Engineering Mechanics Offers engineering mechanics (M Eng, MS, PhD). Electronic applications accepted.

Program in Environmental Sciences Offers environmental sciences (MS, PhD). Electronic applications accepted.

Program in Family and Consumer Sciences Offers family and consumer sciences (MFCS). Electronic applications accepted.

Program in Finance Offers finance (M Fin).

Program in Fisheries Biology Offers fisheries biology (MS, PhD). Electronic applications accepted.

Program in Forestry Offers forestry (MS, PhD). Electronic applications accepted.

Program in Genetics Offers genetics (MS, PhD). Electronic applications accepted.

Program in Graphic Design Offers graphic design (MA, MFA). Electronic applications accepted.

Program in High Energy Physics Offers high energy physics (MS, PhD). Electronic applications accepted.

Program in Human-Computer Interaction Offers human-computer interaction (MS, PhD). Electronic applications accepted.

Program in Immunobiology Offers immunobiology (MS, PhD). Electronic applications accepted.

Program in Industrial Agriculture and Technology Offers industrial agriculture and technology (MS, PhD). Electronic applications accepted.

Program in Industrial Design Offers industrial design (MID). Electronic applications accepted.

Program in Information Assurance Offers information assurance (M Eng, MS). Electronic applications accepted.

Program in Information Systems Offers information systems (MS). Electronic applications accepted.

Program in Inorganic Chemistry Offers inorganic chemistry (MS, PhD). Electronic applications accepted.

Program in Integrated Visual Arts Offers integrated visual arts (MFA).

Program in Interdisciplinary Graduate Studies Offers interdisciplinary graduate studies (MA, MS). Electronic applications accepted.

Program in Interior Design Offers interior design (MA, MFA). Electronic applications accepted.

Program in Meat Science Offers meat science (MS, PhD). Electronic applications accepted.

Program in Meteorology Offers meteorology (MS, PhD). Electronic applications accepted.

Program in Microbiology Offers microbiology (MS, PhD). Electronic applications accepted.

Program in Molecular, Cellular, and Developmental Biology Offers molecular, cellular, and developmental biology (MS, PhD). Electronic applications accepted.

Program in Neuroscience Offers neuroscience (MS, PhD). Electronic applications accepted.

Program in Nuclear Physics Offers nuclear physics (MS, PhD). Electronic applications accepted.

Program in Nutritional Sciences Offers nutritional sciences (MS, PhD). Electronic applications accepted.

Program in Organic Chemistry Offers organic chemistry (MS, PhD). Electronic applications accepted.

Program in Physical Chemistry Offers physical chemistry (MS, PhD). Electronic applications accepted.

Program in Plant Biology Offers plant biology (MS, PhD). Electronic applications accepted.

Program in Plant Breeding Offers plant breeding (MS, PhD). Electronic applications accepted.

Program in Rhetoric and Professional Communication Offers rhetoric and professional communication (PhD). Electronic applications accepted.

Program in Rhetoric, Composition, and Professional Communication Offers rhetoric, composition, and professional communication (MA). Electronic applications accepted.

Program in Rural Sociology Offers rural sociology (MS, PhD). Electronic applications accepted.

Program in School Mathematics Offers school mathematics (MSM). Electronic applications accepted.

Program in Science Education Offers science education (MAT). Electronic applications accepted.

Program in Seed Technology and Business Offers seed technology and business (MS). Electronic applications accepted.

Program in Soil Science Offers soil science (MS, PhD). Electronic applications accepted.

Program in Sustainable Agriculture Offers sustainable agriculture (MS, PhD). Electronic applications accepted.

Program in Systems Engineering Offers systems engineering (M Eng). Electronic applications accepted.

Program in Teaching English as a Second Language/Applied Linguistics Offers teaching English as a second language/applied linguistics (MA). Electronic applications accepted.

Program in Toxicology Offers toxicology (MS, PhD). Electronic applications accepted.

Program in Transportation Offers transportation (MS). Electronic applications accepted.

Rural, Agricultural, Technological, and Environmental History Program Offers rural, agricultural, technological, and environmental history (PhD). Electronic applications accepted.

IOWA WESLEYAN UNIVERSITY, Mount Pleasant, IA 52641-1398

General Information Independent-religious, coed, comprehensive institution.

GRADUATE UNITS

Program in Curriculum and Instruction Offers effective teaching and instruction (M Ed).

IRELL & MANELLA GRADUATE SCHOOL OF BIOLOGICAL SCIENCES, Duarte, CA 91010

General Information Independent, coed, graduate-only institution. *Graduate housing:* Room and/or apartments available on a first-come, first-served basis to single students; on-campus housing not available to married students. Housing application deadline: 7/31.

GRADUATE UNITS

Graduate Program Offers brain metastatic cancer (PhD); cancer and stem cell metabolism (PhD); cancer biology (PhD); cancer biology and developmental therapeutics (PhD); cell biology (PhD); chemical biology (PhD); chromosomal break repair (PhD); diabetes and pancreatic progenitor cell biology (PhD); DNA repair and cancer biology (PhD); germline epigenetic remodeling and endocrine disruptors (PhD); hematology and hematopoietic cell transplantation (PhD); hematology and immunology (PhD); inflammation and cancer (PhD); micrornas and gene regulation in cardiovascular disease (PhD); mixed chimerism for reversal of autoimmunity (PhD); molecular and cellular biology (PhD); molecular biology and genetics (PhD); nanoparticle mediated twist1 silencing in metastatic cancer (PhD); neuro-oncology and stem cell biology (PhD); neuroscience (PhD); RNA directed therapies for HIV-1 (PhD); small RNA-induced transcriptional gene activation (PhD); stem cell regulation by the microenvironment (PhD); translational oncology and pharmaceutical sciences (PhD); tumor biology (PhD). Electronic applications accepted.

ITHACA COLLEGE, Ithaca, NY 14850

General Information Independent, coed, comprehensive institution. *Enrollment:* 6,517 graduate, professional, and undergraduate students; 354 full-time matriculated graduate/professional students (266 women), 60 part-time matriculated graduate/professional students (35 women). *Enrollment by degree level:* 242 master's, 172 doctoral. *Graduate faculty:* 149 full-time (70 women), 3 part-time/adjunct (all women). *Graduate housing:* On-campus housing not available. *Student services:* Campus employment opportunities, campus safety program, career counseling, exercise/wellness program, free psychological counseling, international student services, low-cost health insurance, multicultural affairs office, services for students with disabilities, teacher training, writing training. *Library facilities:* Ithaca College Library. *Collection:* Books: 315,000 (physical), 165,000 (digital/electronic); Serial titles: 640 (physical), 68,858 (digital/electronic); Databases: 155. Weekly public service hours: 148; study areas open 24 hours, 5–7 days a week.

Computer facilities: 640 computers available on campus for general student use. A campuswide network can be accessed. Online class registration is available. Website: http://www.ithaca.edu/

General Application Contact: Nicole Eversley Bradwell, Director, Office of Admission, 800-429-4274, Fax: 607-274-1263, E-mail: admission@ithaca.edu.

GRADUATE UNITS

Roy H. Park School of Communications Students: 12 part-time (8 women); includes 6 minority (1 Black or African American, non-Hispanic/Latino; 3 Hispanic/Latino; 2 Two or more races, non-Hispanic/Latino), 2 international. Average age 29. 18 applicants, 67% accepted, 6 enrolled. *Faculty:* 7 full-time (2 women). Expenses: Contact institution. *Financial support:* In 2018–19, 12 students received support, including 12 fellowships (averaging $5,596 per year); career-related internships or fieldwork, Federal Work-Study, and scholarships/grants also available. Support available to part-time students. Financial award application deadline: 2/1; financial award applicants required to submit FAFSA. In 2018, 4 master's awarded. *Program availability:* Part-time. Offers communications (MFA, MS); communications innovation (MS); image text (MFA). *Application deadline:* For fall admission, 2/1 for domestic and international students. Applications are processed on a rolling basis. *Application fee:* $40. Electronic applications accepted. *Application Contact:* Nicole Eversley Bradwell, Director, Office of Admission, 800-429-4274, Fax: 607-274-1263, E-mail: admission@ithaca.edu. *Dean,* Dr. Diane Gayeski, 607-274-3895, E-mail: gayeski@ithaca.edu.

School of Business Students: 36 full-time (10 women), 2 part-time (1 woman); includes 3 minority (1 Asian, non-Hispanic/Latino; 2 Hispanic/Latino), 1 international. Average age 22. 50 applicants, 78% accepted, 36 enrolled. Expenses: Contact institution. *Financial support:* In 2018–19, 30 students received support, including 28 fellowships (averaging $7,750 per year); career-related internships or fieldwork, Federal Work-Study, and scholarships/grants also available. Support available to part-time students. Financial award application deadline: 3/1; financial award applicants required to submit FAFSA. In 2018, 42 master's awarded. *Program availability:* Part-time. Offers accounting (MS); business (MBA, MS); sport management (MBA). *Application deadline:* For fall admission, 5/15 for domestic and international students; for spring admission, 11/1 for domestic and international students. Applications are processed on a rolling basis. *Application fee:* $40. Electronic applications accepted. *Application Contact:* Nicole Eversley Bradwell, Director, Office of Admission, 607-274-3341, Fax: 607-274-1263, E-mail: admission@ithaca.edu. *Dean,* Dr. Sean Reid, 607-274-3341, E-mail: sreid@ithaca.edu.

School of Health Sciences and Human Performance Students: 290 full-time (232 women), 20 part-time (13 women); includes 44 minority (7 Black or African American, non-Hispanic/Latino; 15 Asian, non-Hispanic/Latino; 10 Hispanic/Latino; 12 Two or more races, non-Hispanic/Latino), 1 international. Average age 23. 301 applicants, 56% accepted, 165 enrolled. *Faculty:* 54 full-time (36 women). Expenses: Contact institution. *Financial support:* In 2018–19, 213 students received support, including 62 research assistantships (averaging $13,552 per year); career-related internships or fieldwork, Federal Work-Study, and scholarships/grants also available. Support available to part-time students. Financial award applicants required to submit FAFSA. In 2018, 109 master's, 85 doctorates awarded. *Program availability:* Part-time. Offers exercise and sport sciences (MS); health education (MS); health sciences and human performance (MS, DPT); occupational therapy (MS); physical education (MS); physical therapy (DPT); speech-language pathology and audiology (MS). *Application deadline:* Applications are processed on a rolling basis. *Application fee:* $40. Electronic applications accepted. *Application Contact:* Nicole Eversley Bradwell, Director, Office of Admission, 607-800-429-4274, Fax: 607-274-1263, E-mail: admission@ithaca.edu. *Dean,* Dr. Linda Petrosino, 607-274-3237, Fax: 607-274-1263, E-mail: lpetrosino@ithaca.edu.

School of Humanities and Sciences Students: 20 full-time (13 women); includes 2 minority (1 Asian, non-Hispanic/Latino; 1 Hispanic/Latino). Average age 30. 31 applicants, 87% accepted, 19 enrolled. *Faculty:* 14 full-time (7 women). Expenses: Contact institution. *Financial support:* In 2018–19, 19 students received support, including 19 research assistantships (averaging $11,475 per year); career-related internships or fieldwork, Federal Work-Study, and scholarships/grants also available. Financial award application deadline: 3/1; financial award applicants required to submit FAFSA. In 2018, 14 master's awarded. Offers agriculture education (MAT); childhood education (MS); English (MAT); humanities and sciences (MAT, MS). *Application deadline:* For fall admission, 3/19 for domestic and international students. Applications

are processed on a rolling basis. *Application fee:* $40. Electronic applications accepted. *Application Contact:* Nicole Eversley Bradwell, Director, Office of Admission, 800-429-4274/274-3124, Fax: 607-274-1263, E-mail: admission@ithaca.edu. *Dean, School of Humanities and Sciences,* Dr. Melanie Stein, 274-3102, E-mail: mstein2@ithaca.edu.

School of Music Students: 20 full-time (9 women), 23 part-time (11 women); includes 11 minority (2 Black or African American, non-Hispanic/Latino; 6 Asian, non-Hispanic/Latino; 3 Hispanic/Latino), 6 international. Average age 24. 99 applicants, 53% accepted, 19 enrolled. *Faculty:* 62 full-time (20 women), 3 part-time/adjunct (all women). Expenses: Contact institution. *Financial support:* In 2018–19, 42 students received support, including 41 teaching assistantships (averaging $10,447 per year); career-related internships or fieldwork, Federal Work-Study, and scholarships/grants also available. Support available to part-time students. Financial award application deadline: 12/1; financial award applicants required to submit FAFSA. In 2018, 27 master's awarded. *Program availability:* Part-time. Offers composition (MM); music (MM, MS); music education (MS); performance (MM). *Application deadline:* For fall admission, 12/1 for domestic and international students. Applications are processed on a rolling basis. *Application fee:* $40. Electronic applications accepted. *Application Contact:* Nicole Eversley Bradwell, Director, Office of Admission, 800-429-4274, Fax: 607-274-1263, E-mail: admission@ithaca.edu. *Dean, School of Music,* Dr. Karl Paulnack, 607-274-3343, E-mail: kpaulnack@ithaca.edu.

JACKSON STATE UNIVERSITY, Jackson, MS 39217

General Information State-supported, coed, university. CGS member. *Graduate housing:* Room and/or apartments available on a first-come, first-served basis to single students; on-campus housing not available to married students. Housing application deadline: 7/15. *Research affiliation:* Lawrence A. Berkeley Laboratories (biology, chemistry), U.S. Department of Energy (biology), National Science Foundation (biology, chemistry), Environmental Protection Agency, Oak Ridge Associated Universities (science), Raytheon Systems Company (computer science).

GRADUATE UNITS

Graduate School *Program availability:* Part-time, evening/weekend, online only, 100% online, blended/hybrid learning. Electronic applications accepted.

College of Business *Program availability:* Part-time, evening/weekend. Offers accounting (MPA); business (MBA, MPA, PhD); business administration (MBA, PhD). Electronic applications accepted.

College of Education and Human Development *Program availability:* Part-time, evening/weekend, 100% online, blended/hybrid learning. Offers clinical mental health (MS); early childhood education (MS Ed, Ed D); education administration and supervision (Ed S); education and human development (MS, MS Ed, Ed D, PhD, Ed S); educational administration and supervision (MS Ed, PhD); elementary education (MS Ed, Ed S); higher education (Ed S); physical education (MS Ed); reading education (MS Ed); rehabilitation counseling (MS); school counseling (MS Ed); special education (MS Ed, Ed S); sport science (MS). Electronic applications accepted.

College of Liberal Arts *Program availability:* Part-time, evening/weekend. Offers clinical psychology (PhD); criminology and justice services (MA); English (MA); history (MA); liberal arts (MA, MAT, MM Ed, PhD); music education (MM Ed); political science (MA); sociology (MA); teaching English (MAT). Electronic applications accepted.

College of Public Service Offers public administration (PhD); public policy and administration (MPPA); public service (MA, MPPA, MSW, PhD); social work (MSW, PhD); urban and regional planning (MA, PhD).

College of Science, Engineering and Technology *Program availability:* Part-time, evening/weekend. Offers applied mathematics (MS); biology (MS); chemistry and biochemistry (MS, PhD); civil engineering (MS, PhD); coastal engineering (MS, PhD); computer science (MS); environmental engineering (MS, PhD); environmental science (MS); hazardous materials management (MS); mathematics education (MST); physical science (MS, PhD); pure mathematics (MS); science education (MST); science, engineering and technology (MS, MS Ed, MST, PhD); technology education (MS Ed).

School of Public Health Offers communicative disorders (MS); public health (MPH, MS, Dr PH).

JACKSONVILLE STATE UNIVERSITY, Jacksonville, AL 36265-1602

General Information State-supported, coed, comprehensive institution. *Graduate housing:* Rooms and/or apartments available on a first-come, first-served basis to single and married students.

GRADUATE UNITS

Graduate Studies *Program availability:* Part-time, evening/weekend, 100% online, blended/hybrid learning. Offers nursing (MSN). Electronic applications accepted.

School of Arts and Humanities Offers arts and humanities (MA); English (MA); history (MA); liberal studies (MA); music (MA).

School of Business and Industry *Program availability:* Part-time, evening/weekend, 100% online, blended/hybrid learning. Offers business and industry (MBA). Electronic applications accepted.

School of Education *Program availability:* Part-time, evening/weekend, 100% online, blended/hybrid learning. Offers early childhood education (MS Ed); education (MS, MS Ed, Ed S); elementary education (MS Ed); guidance and counseling (MS Ed); instructional leadership (MS Ed, Ed S); library media (MS Ed); physical education (MS Ed, Ed S); reading specialist (MS Ed); secondary education (MS Ed); special education (MS Ed). Electronic applications accepted.

School of Human Services and Social Sciences Offers criminal justice (MS); emergency management (MS, D Sc); human services and social sciences (MPA, MS, MSW, D Sc); psychology (MS); public administration (MPA); social work (MSW).

School of Science *Program availability:* Part-time, evening/weekend, 100% online, blended/hybrid learning. Offers biology (MS); computer systems and software design (MS); mathematics (MS); science (MS).

JACKSONVILLE UNIVERSITY, Jacksonville, FL 32211

General Information Independent, coed, comprehensive institution. *Graduate housing:* Room and/or apartments available on a first-come, first-served basis to single students; on-campus housing not available to married students. Housing application deadline: 8/1.

GRADUATE UNITS

Brooks Rehabilitation College of Healthcare Sciences *Program availability:* Part-time, 100% online, blended/hybrid learning. Offers healthcare sciences (MS, MSN, DNP, OTD, Certificate). Electronic applications accepted.

Keigwin School of Nursing *Program availability:* Part-time, 100% online, blended/hybrid learning. Offers adult gerontology acute care nurse practitioner (MSN);

adult-gerontology acute care nurse practitioner (Certificate); clinical nurse educator (MSN, Certificate); emergency nurse practitioner (Certificate); family nurse practitioner (MSN, Certificate); family nurse practitioner/emergency nurse practitioner (MSN, Certificate); leadership in healthcare systems (Certificate); leadership in the healthcare system (MSN); nursing informatics (MSN); nursing practice (DNP); psychiatric mental health nurse practitioner (Certificate); psychiatric nurse practitioner (MSN). Electronic applications accepted.

School of Applied Health Sciences *Program availability:* Part-time, 100% online, blended/hybrid learning. Offers clinical mental health counseling (MS); health informatics (MS); kinesiological sciences (MS); occupational therapy (OTD); speech-language pathology (MS); sport management (MS). Electronic applications accepted.

School of Orthodontics Offers dentistry (MS); orthodontics (Certificate). Electronic applications accepted.

College of Arts and Sciences *Program availability:* Evening/weekend. Offers arts and sciences (MA, MS); leadership and learning (MS); mathematics (MA). Electronic applications accepted.

Marine Science Research Institute *Program availability:* Part-time. Offers marine science (MA, MS). MPP/MS offered jointly with JU's Public Policy Institute. Electronic applications accepted.

College of Fine Arts *Program availability:* Blended/hybrid learning. Offers choreography (MFA); fine arts (MFA); visual arts (MFA). Electronic applications accepted.

Davis College of Business *Program availability:* Part-time, evening/weekend, 100% online. Offers accounting and finance (MBA); business (MBA, MS, DBA); business administration (MBA, DBA); business management (MBA); consumer goods and services marketing (MBA); leadership development (MBA); management (MBA); management accounting (MBA); organizational leadership (MS). MBA/JD offered jointly with Florida School of Law; MSN/MBA offered jointly with JU's Keigwin School of Nursing; MBA/MPP offered jointly with JU's Public Policy Institute. Electronic applications accepted.

Public Policy Institute *Program availability:* Part-time, evening/weekend. Offers public policy (MPP). MPP/JD offered in partnership with Florida Coastal School of Law; MPP/MBA with JU's Davis College of Business; MPP/MS with JU's Marine Science Research Institute. Electronic applications accepted.

JAMES MADISON UNIVERSITY, Harrisonburg, VA 22807

General Information State-supported, coed, comprehensive institution. CGS member. *Enrollment:* 1,033 full-time matriculated graduate/professional students (744 women), 641 part-time matriculated graduate/professional students (414 women). *Enrollment by degree level:* 1,405 master's, 195 doctoral, 74 other advanced degrees. *Graduate faculty:* 769. Tuition, state resident: full-time $10,848. Tuition, nonresident: full-time $27,888. *Required fees:* $1128. *Graduate housing:* On-campus housing not available. *Student services:* Campus employment opportunities, campus safety program, career counseling, exercise/wellness program, free psychological counseling, international student services, multicultural affairs office, services for students with disabilities, teacher training, writing training. *Library facilities:* Carrier Library plus 2 others. *Collection:* Students can reserve study rooms.

Computer facilities: Computer purchase and lease plans are available. A campuswide network can be accessed from student residence rooms and from off campus. Online class registration is available.
Website: http://www.jmu.edu/

General Application Contact: John Burgess, Interim Dean, The Graduate School, 540-568-4213, Fax: 540-568-7860, E-mail: grad@jmu.edu.

GRADUATE UNITS

The Graduate School Students: 1,033 full-time (744 women), 641 part-time (414 women); includes 260 minority (94 Black or African American, non-Hispanic/Latino; 1 American Indian or Alaska Native, non-Hispanic/Latino; 48 Asian, non-Hispanic/Latino; 73 Hispanic/Latino; 44 Two or more races, non-Hispanic/Latino; 47 international. Average age 30. 2,268 applicants, 48% accepted, 732 enrolled. *Faculty:* 769. Expenses: Contact institution. *Financial support:* In 2018–19, 393 students received support, including 273 fellowships with full tuition reimbursements available (averaging $7,911 per year), 40 teaching assistantships with full tuition reimbursements available (averaging $9,284 per year); research assistantships, career-related internships or fieldwork, Federal Work-Study, tuition waivers, unspecified assistantships, and athletic assistantships (averaging $9284), doctoral assistantships (stipend varies) also available. Financial award application deadline: 3/1; financial award applicants required to submit FAFSA. In 2018, 778 master's, 37 doctorates, 28 other advanced degrees awarded. *Program availability:* Part-time, evening/weekend, 100% online, blended/hybrid learning. *Application fee:* $60. Electronic applications accepted. *Application Contact:* Lynette D. Michael, Director of Graduate Admissions, 540-568-6131 Ext. 6395, Fax: 540-568-7860, E-mail: michaeld@jmu.edu. *Interim Dean, The Graduate School,* John Burgess, 540-568-4213, Fax: 540-568-7860, E-mail: grad@jmu.edu.

College of Arts and Letters Students: 100 full-time (62 women), 32 part-time (20 women); includes 23 minority (10 Black or African American, non-Hispanic/Latino; 4 Asian, non-Hispanic/Latino; 5 Hispanic/Latino; 4 Two or more races, non-Hispanic/Latino; 4 international. Average age 30. *Faculty:* 130. Expenses: Contact institution. *Financial support:* In 2018–19, 83 students received support, including 18 teaching assistantships with full tuition reimbursements available (averaging $9,284 per year); fellowships and Federal Work-Study also available. Financial award application deadline: 3/1; financial award applicants required to submit FAFSA. In 2018, 54 master's awarded. *Program availability:* Part-time. Offers arts and letters (MA, MPA, MA); English (MA); environmental communication (MA); health communication (MA); individualized (MPA); political science (MA); public history (MA); public management (MPA); strategic communication (MA); U.S. history (MA); world history (MA); writing, rhetoric, and technical communication (MA, MS). *Application fee:* $55. Electronic applications accepted. *Application Contact:* Lynette D. Michael, Director of Graduate Admissions, 540-568-6131 Ext. 6395, Fax: 540-568-7860, E-mail: michaeld@jmu.edu. *Dean,* Dr. David K. Jeffrey, 540-568-7044.

College of Business Students: 114 full-time (41 women), 115 part-time (47 women); includes 44 minority (11 Black or African American, non-Hispanic/Latino; 10 Asian, non-Hispanic/Latino; 18 Hispanic/Latino; 5 Two or more races, non-Hispanic/Latino; 12 international. Average age 30. *Faculty:* 69. Expenses: Contact institution. *Financial support:* In 2018–19, 39 students received support. Fellowships, career-related internships or fieldwork, Federal Work-Study, and assistantships (averaging $7911), 6 doctoral assistantships, 1 service assistantship available. Financial award application deadline: 3/1; financial award applicants required to submit FAFSA. In 2018, 152 master's, 7 doctorates awarded. *Program availability:* Part-time, evening/weekend, blended/hybrid learning. Offers accounting information systems (MS); business (MBA, MS, PhD); postsecondary analysis and leadership (PhD); taxation (MS). *Application fee:* $60. Electronic applications accepted. *Application Contact:* Lynette D. Michael,

Director of Graduate Admissions, 540-568-6395, Fax: 540-568-7860, E-mail: michaeld@jmu.edu. *Dean,* Dr. Mary A. Gowan, 540-568-3254, E-mail: gowanma@jmu.edu.

College of Education Students: 293 full-time (254 women), 220 part-time (153 women); includes 71 minority (21 Black or African American, non-Hispanic/Latino; 1 American Indian or Alaska Native, non-Hispanic/Latino; 8 Asian, non-Hispanic/Latino; 24 Hispanic/Latino; 17 Two or more races, non-Hispanic/Latino), 2 international. Average age 30. *Faculty:* 126. Expenses: Contact institution. *Financial support:* In 2018–19, 36 students received support. Teaching assistantships, career-related internships or fieldwork, Federal Work-Study, and assistantships (averaging $7911) available. Financial award application deadline: 3/1; financial award applicants required to submit FAFSA. In 2018, 330 master's awarded. *Program availability:* Part-time, evening/weekend, 100% online, blended/hybrid learning. Offers adapted curriculum (MAT); autism (M Ed); behavior specialist (M Ed); early childhood education (MAT); early childhood education (preK-3) (MAT); early childhood special education (MAT); education (M Ed, MAT, MS Ed); educational leadership (M Ed); educational technology (M Ed); elementary education (MAT); equity and cultural diversity (M Ed); general curriculum K-12 special education (MAT); gifted education (M Ed); higher education (MS Ed); human resource management (MS Ed); inclusive early childhood education (MAT); inclusive early childhood special education (MAT); individualized (MS Ed); instructional design (MS Ed); instructional specialist (M Ed); K-12 special education (MAT); K-8 math specialist (M Ed); K-8 mathematics specialist (M Ed); leadership and facilitation (MS Ed); mathematics (MAT); middle education (MAT); program evaluation and measurement (MS Ed); reading education (M Ed); secondary education (MAT); Spanish language and culture for educators (M Ed); TESOL (MAT); visual impairments (MAT). *Application fee:* $60. Electronic applications accepted. *Application Contact:* Lynette D. Michael, Director of Graduate Admissions, 540-568-6131 Ext. 6395, Fax: 540-568-7860, E-mail: michaeld@jmu.edu. *Dean,* Dr. Phillip M. Wishon, 540-568-6572, E-mail: wishonpm@jmu.edu.

College of Health and Behavioral Studies Students: 424 full-time (334 women), 124 part-time (110 women); includes 84 minority (32 Black or African American, non-Hispanic/Latino; 18 Asian, non-Hispanic/Latino; 20 Hispanic/Latino; 14 Two or more races, non-Hispanic/Latino), 7 international. Average age 30. *Faculty:* 212. Expenses: Contact institution. *Financial support:* In 2018–19, 189 students received support, including 16 teaching assistantships with full tuition reimbursements available (averaging $9,284 per year); career-related internships or fieldwork, Federal Work-Study, unspecified assistantships, and athletic assistantships (averaging $8837); service assistantships (averaging $7530), doctoral assistantships also available. Financial award application deadline: 3/1; financial award applicants required to submit FAFSA. In 2018, 189 master's, 19 doctorates, 17 other advanced degrees awarded. *Program availability:* Part-time, evening/weekend, 100% online, blended/hybrid learning. Offers adult/gerontology primary care nurse practitioner (MSN); applied research (MA); assessment and measurement (PhD); audiology (Au D); behavior analysis (MA); clinical and school psychology (Psy D); clinical exercise physiology (MS); clinical mental health counseling/clinical nurse leader (MSN); communication sciences and disorders (PhD); counseling and supervision (PhD); exercise physiology (MS); experimental psychology (MA); family nurse practitioner (MSN); health and behavioral studies (M Ed, MA, MAT, MOT, MPAS, MS, MSN, Au D, DNP, PhD, Psy D, Ed S); kinesiology (MAT, MS); nurse administrator (MSN); nurse midwifery (MSN); nursing (MSN, DNP); nutrition and exercise (MS); nutrition and physical activity (MS); occupational therapy (MOT); physical and health education (MAT); physician assistant studies (MPAS); psychiatric mental health nurse practitioner (MSN); quantitative psychology (MA); school psychology (MA, Ed S); speech-language pathology (MS); sport and recreation leadership (MS). *Application fee:* $55. Electronic applications accepted. *Application Contact:* Lynette D. Michael, Director of Graduate Admissions, 540-568-6131 Ext. 6395, Fax: 540-568-7860, E-mail: michaeld@jmu.edu. *Dean,* Dr. Sharon E. Lovell, 540-568-2705, Fax: 540-568-2747, E-mail: lovellse@jmu.edu.

College of Integrated Science and Engineering Students: 3 full-time (0 women), 51 part-time (11 women); includes 13 minority (7 Black or African American, non-Hispanic/Latino; 3 Asian, non-Hispanic/Latino; 2 Hispanic/Latino; 1 Two or more races, non-Hispanic/Latino), 2 international. Average age 30. *Faculty:* 75. Expenses: Contact institution. *Financial support:* In 2018–19, 2 students received support. Career-related internships or fieldwork, Federal Work-Study, and 4 assistantships (averaging $7911) available. Financial award application deadline: 3/1; financial award applicants required to submit FAFSA. In 2018, 20 master's awarded. *Program availability:* Part-time, evening/weekend, 100% online, blended/hybrid learning, study abroad. Offers digital forensics (MS); environmental management and sustainability (MS); information security (MS); integrated science and engineering (MS). *Application fee:* $60. Electronic applications accepted. *Application Contact:* Lynette D. Michael, Director of Graduate Admissions, 540-568-6395, Fax: 540-568-7860, E-mail: michaeld@jmu.edu. *Dean,* Dr. Robert A. Kolvoord, 540-568-2752, E-mail: kolvoora@jmu.edu.

College of Science and Mathematics Students: 20 full-time (13 women), 25 part-time (17 women); includes 3 minority (1 Black or African American, non-Hispanic/Latino; 1 Asian, non-Hispanic/Latino; 1 Hispanic/Latino). Average age 30. *Faculty:* 69. Expenses: Contact institution. *Financial support:* In 2018–19, 15 students received support. Fellowships, Federal Work-Study, and assistantships (averaging $7911) available. Financial award application deadline: 3/1; financial award applicants required to submit FAFSA. In 2018, 8 master's awarded. *Program availability:* Part-time. Offers biology (MS); mathematics (M Ed); science and mathematics (M Ed, MS). *Application fee:* $60. Electronic applications accepted. *Application Contact:* Lynette D. Michael, Director of Graduate Admissions, 540-568-6131 Ext. 6395, Fax: 540-568-7860, E-mail: michaeld@jmu.edu. *Dean,* Dr. David F. Brakke, 540-568-3508, E-mail: brakkedf@jmu.edu.

College of Visual and Performing Arts Students: 50 full-time (25 women), 18 part-time (11 women); includes 9 minority (4 Black or African American, non-Hispanic/Latino; 1 Asian, non-Hispanic/Latino; 3 Hispanic/Latino; 1 Two or more races, non-Hispanic/Latino), 17 international. Average age 30. *Faculty:* 88. Expenses: Contact institution. *Financial support:* In 2018–19, 39 students received support, including 2 teaching assistantships with full tuition reimbursements available (averaging $9,284 per year); fellowships, Federal Work-Study, and assistantships (averaging $7911), 17 doctoral assistantships (stipend varies) also available. Financial award application deadline: 3/1; financial award applicants required to submit FAFSA. In 2018, 9 master's, 3 doctorates awarded. *Program availability:* Part-time. Offers art education (MA); composition (MM); conducting (MM, DMA); music education (MM); performance (MM, DMA); studio art (MA, MFA); visual and performing arts (MA, MFA, MM, DMA). *Application fee:* $60. Electronic applications accepted. *Application Contact:* Lynette D. Michael, Director of Graduate Admissions and Student Records, 540-568-6131 Ext. 6395, Fax: 540-568-7860, E-mail: michaeld@jmu.edu. *Dean,* Dr. George Sparks, 540-568-6247, E-mail: sparksge@jmu.edu.

JEFFERSON COLLEGE OF HEALTH SCIENCES, Roanoke, VA 24013

General Information Independent, coed, comprehensive institution. *Graduate housing:* Room and/or apartments available on a first-come, first-served basis to single students; on-campus housing not available to married students. *Research affiliation:* Carilion Clinic (hospital and medical services), Virginia Polytechnic Institute and State University/Carilion Medical School (medicine).

GRADUATE UNITS

Program in Nursing *Program availability:* Part-time. Offers nursing education (MSN); nursing management (MSN). Electronic applications accepted.

Program in Occupational Therapy *Program availability:* Part-time. Offers occupational therapy (MS). Electronic applications accepted.

Program in Physician Assistant Offers physician assistant (MS). Electronic applications accepted.

THE JEWISH THEOLOGICAL SEMINARY, New York, NY 10027-4649

General Information Independent-religious, coed, university. *Graduate housing:* Rooms and/or apartments available on a first-come, first-served basis to single and married students. Housing application deadline: 5/15.

GRADUATE UNITS

The Graduate School *Program availability:* Part-time. Offers ancient Judaism (MA, DHL, PhD); Bible and ancient Semitic languages (MA, DHL, PhD); interdepartmental studies (MA); Jewish art and visual culture (MA); Jewish gender and women's studies (MA); Jewish history (MA, DHL, PhD); Jewish literature (MA, DHL, PhD); Jewish philosophy (DHL); Jewish thought (MA, DHL, PhD); liturgy (MA, DHL, PhD); medieval Jewish studies (MA, DHL, PhD); Midrash (DHL); Midrash and scriptural interpretation (MA, PhD); modern Jewish studies (MA, DHL, PhD); Talmud and rabbinics (MA, DHL, PhD). MA/MSW offered jointly with Columbia University.

H. L. Miller Cantorial School and College of Jewish Music Offers Jewish music (MSM).

The Rabbinical School Offers theology (MA, Rabbi).

William Davidson Graduate School of Jewish Education *Program availability:* Part-time, online learning. Offers Jewish education (MA, Ed D). Offered in conjunction with The Rabbinical School; H. L. Miller Cantorial School and College of Jewish Music; Teacher's College, Columbia University; and Union Theological Seminary.

JOHN BROWN UNIVERSITY, Siloam Springs, AR 72761-2121

General Information Independent-religious, coed, comprehensive institution. *Graduate housing:* Rooms and/or apartments available on a first-come, first-served basis to single and married students.

GRADUATE UNITS

Graduate Counseling Programs *Program availability:* Part-time, evening/weekend. Offers clinical mental health counseling (MS); marriage and family therapy (MS); play therapy (Graduate Certificate); school counseling (MS). Electronic applications accepted.

Graduate Education Programs *Program availability:* Part-time, evening/weekend. Offers curriculum and instruction (M Ed); secondary education (MAT). Electronic applications accepted.

Soderquist College of Business *Program availability:* Part-time, evening/weekend, online only, 100% online, blended/hybrid learning. Offers international business (MBA); leadership and ethics (MBA, MS). Electronic applications accepted.

JOHN CABOT UNIVERSITY, Rome 00165, Italy

General Information Independent, coed, comprehensive institution. *Enrollment:* 1,512 graduate, professional, and undergraduate students; 15 full-time matriculated graduate/professional students. *Enrollment by degree level:* 15 master's. *Graduate faculty:* 10 full-time. One-time fee: $21,000 full-time. *Graduate housing:* On-campus housing not available. *Student services:* Campus safety program, career counseling, exercise/wellness program, free psychological counseling, international student services, services for students with disabilities. *Library facilities:* Frohring Library. *Collection:* Books: 34,218 (physical); Databases: 39. Weekly public service hours: 86; students can reserve study rooms.

Computer facilities: 153 computers available on campus for general student use. A campuswide network can be accessed from student residence rooms and from off campus. Online class registration is available. Website: http://www.johncabot.edu/

General Application Contact: Stefania Corrado, Associate Coordinator of DS Admissions, 39-0668191 Ext. 271, E-mail: scorrado@johncabot.edu.

GRADUATE UNITS

John Cabot University - Graduate School Students: 15 full-time. Average age 34. 39 applicants, 46% accepted, 9 enrolled. *Faculty:* 10 full-time. Expenses: Contact institution. *Financial support:* Scholarships/grants and G.I. Bill available. Financial award application deadline: 2/1; financial award applicants required to submit FAFSA. In 2018, 7 master's awarded. Offers art history (MA). *Application deadline:* For fall admission, 7/31 for domestic students, 2/1 for international students. *Application fee:* $50. Electronic applications accepted. *Application Contact:* Lauren Rice, Associate Coordinator for Graduate Admissions, E-mail: lrice@johncabot.edu.

JOHN CARROLL UNIVERSITY, University Heights, OH 44118

General Information Independent-religious, coed, comprehensive institution. CGS member. *Enrollment:* 234 full-time matriculated graduate/professional students (156 women), 241 part-time matriculated graduate/professional students (132 women). *Enrollment by degree level:* 449 master's, 26 other advanced degrees. *Graduate faculty:* 40 full-time (20 women), 26 part-time/adjunct (12 women). *Tuition:* Full-time $13,140; part-time $730 per credit hour. Tuition and fees vary according to program. *Graduate housing:* On-campus housing not available. *Student services:* Campus employment opportunities, campus safety program, career counseling, exercise/wellness program, free psychological counseling, international student services, multicultural affairs office, services for students with disabilities, teacher training, writing training. *Library facilities:* Grasselli Library. *Collection:* Books: 456,260 (physical), 91,554 (digital/electronic); Serial titles: 459,633 (physical), 115,548 (digital/electronic); Databases: 279. Weekly public service hours: 111; students can reserve study rooms.

Computer facilities: Computer purchase and lease plans are available. 396 computers available on campus for general student use. A campuswide network can be accessed from student residence rooms and from off campus. Online class registration, campus student online registration, billing, advising system, JCU mobile app, course

---

management site (BlackBoard), online financial aid and billing; online course sites; online housing selection are available. Website: http://www.jcu.edu/

General Application Contact: Dr. Rebecca E. Drenovsky, Associate Dean for Graduate and Professional Programs, 216-397-4284, E-mail: rdrenovsky@jcu.edu.

GRADUATE UNITS

Graduate Studies Students: 234 full-time (156 women), 241 part-time (132 women); includes 73 minority (38 Black or African American, non-Hispanic/Latino; 11 Asian, non-Hispanic/Latino; 13 Hispanic/Latino; 11 Two or more races, non-Hispanic/Latino), 24 international. 262 applicants, 57% accepted, 67 enrolled. *Faculty:* 40 full-time (20 women), 26 part-time/adjunct (12 women). Expenses: Contact institution. *Financial support:* In 2018–19, 404 students received support. Research assistantships, teaching assistantships, scholarships/grants, and unspecified assistantships available. Support available to part-time students. Financial award applicants required to submit FAFSA. In 2018, 192 master's, 13 other advanced degrees awarded. *Program availability:* Part-time, evening/weekend. Offers biology (MA, MS); clinical counseling (MA); community counseling (MA); educational psychology (M Ed, Ed S); English (MA); humanities (MA); mathematics (MA); nonprofit administration (MA); professional teacher education (M Ed, MA); school counseling (M Ed); school psychology (Ed S); theology and religious studies (MA). *Application deadline:* Applications are processed on a rolling basis. *Application fee:* $0. Electronic applications accepted. *Application Contact:* Colleen K. Sommerfeld, Assistant Dean for Graduate Admission & Retention, 216-397-4902, Fax: 216-397-1835, E-mail: csommerfeld@jcu.edu. *Associate Dean for Graduate & Professional Programs*, Dr. Rebecca E. Drenovsky, 216-397-4451, Fax: 216-397-1835, E-mail: rdrenovsky@jcu.edu.

John M. and Mary Jo Boler College of Business Expenses: Contact institution. *Financial support:* Fellowships, scholarships/grants, and unspecified assistantships available. Financial award applicants required to submit FAFSA. *Program availability:* Part-time, evening/weekend. Offers accountancy (MS); business (MBA); laboratory administration (MS). *Application deadline:* For fall admission, 8/1 priority date for domestic and international students; for spring admission, 12/1 priority date for domestic and international students; for summer admission, 4/1 priority date for domestic and international students. Applications are processed on a rolling basis. Electronic applications accepted. *Application Contact:* Kristopher Tibbs, Assistant Dean, Graduate Business Programs, 216-397-1970, Fax: 216-397-1833, E-mail: gradbusiness@jcu.edu. *Dean, Boler College of Business,* Dr. Alan R. Miciak, 216-397-4391, Fax: 216-397-1833.

JOHN F. KENNEDY UNIVERSITY, Pleasant Hill, CA 94523-4817

General Information Independent, coed, primarily women, upper-level institution. *Graduate housing:* On-campus housing not available.

GRADUATE UNITS

College of Business and Professional Studies *Program availability:* Part-time, evening/weekend, online learning. Offers business administration (MBA); business and professional studies (MA, MBA, Certificate); finance (MBA); health care (MBA); holistic health education (MA); human resources (MBA); information technology (MBA); management (MBA); museum studies (Certificate); sales management (MBA); strategic management (MBA).

College of Law *Program availability:* Part-time, evening/weekend, blended/hybrid learning. Offers law (JD). Program also offered on San Jose campus.

College of Psychology *Program availability:* Part-time, evening/weekend. Offers consciousness and transformative studies (MA); counseling psychology (MA); depth and transpersonal psychotherapy (MA); expressive arts (MA); holistic studies (MA); psychology (MA, Psy D, Certificate, Graduate Certificate); somatic psychology (MA); sport psychology (MA, Graduate Certificate).

JOHN JAY COLLEGE OF CRIMINAL JUSTICE OF THE CITY UNIVERSITY OF NEW YORK, New York, NY 10019

General Information State and locally supported, coed, comprehensive institution. CGS member. *Graduate housing:* On-campus housing not available. *Research affiliation:* Criminal Justice Center, Criminal Justice Research and Evaluation Center, Center on Violence and Human Survival, Center for Dispute Resolution, The Fire Science Institute, The Institute For Criminal Justice Ethics.

GRADUATE UNITS

Graduate Studies *Program availability:* Part-time, evening/weekend. Offers criminal justice (MA, PhD); criminology and deviance (PhD); forensic psychology (PhD); forensic science (PhD); international crime and justice (MA); law and philosophy (PhD); organizational behavior (PhD); protection management (MS); public administration (MPA); public policy (PhD).

THE JOHN MARSHALL LAW SCHOOL, Chicago, IL 60604-3968

General Information Independent, coed, graduate-only institution. *Graduate housing:* On-campus housing not available.

GRADUATE UNITS

Graduate and Professional Programs *Program availability:* Part-time, evening/weekend, 100% online, blended/hybrid learning. Offers law (LL M, MJ, JD). Electronic applications accepted.

JOHN PAUL THE GREAT CATHOLIC UNIVERSITY, Escondido, CA 92025

General Information Independent-religious, coed, comprehensive institution.

GRADUATE UNITS

School of Theology Offers biblical theology (MA).

JOHNS HOPKINS UNIVERSITY, Baltimore, MD 21218

General Information Independent, coed, university. CGS member. *Enrollment:* 8,155 full-time matriculated graduate/professional students (4,310 women), 9,213 part-time matriculated graduate/professional students (4,836 women). *Enrollment by degree level:* 13,068 master's, 3,778 doctoral, 522 other advanced degrees. *Graduate faculty:* 4,542 full-time (1,969 women), 226 part-time/adjunct (105 women). *Graduate housing:* On-campus housing not available. *Student services:* Campus employment opportunities, campus safety program, career counseling, exercise/wellness program, free psychological counseling, grant writing training, international student services, low-cost health insurance, multicultural affairs office, services for students with disabilities, teacher training, writing training. *Library facilities:* The Sheridan Libraries plus 2 others. *Collection:* Books: 2.4 million (physical), 1.8 million (digital/electronic); Serial titles: 51,824 (physical), 154,044 (digital/electronic); Databases: 836. Study areas open 24 hours, 5–7 days a week; students can reserve study rooms.

Computer facilities: Computer purchase and lease plans are available. 200 computers available on campus for general student use. A campuswide network can be accessed from student residence rooms and from off campus. Online class registration is available.

Website: http://www.jhu.edu/

GRADUATE UNITS

Advanced Academic Programs Students: 585 full-time (328 women), 3,055 part-time (1,831 women). 1,751 applicants, 74% accepted, 680 enrolled. Expenses: Contact institution. *Financial support:* In 2018–19, 275 students received support. Institutionally sponsored loans available. Financial award applicants required to submit FAFSA. In 2018, 1,217 master's, 83 other advanced degrees awarded. *Program availability:* Part-time, evening/weekend, online learning. Offers applied economics (MA); bioinformatics (MS); biotechnology (MS); biotechnology enterprise and entrepreneurship (MBEE); communication (MA); digital curation (Certificate); energy policy and climate (MS); environmental sciences (MS); film and media (MA); geographic information systems (MS, Certificate); global security studies (MA); government (MA); liberal arts (MA, Certificate); museum studies (MA); national securities study (Certificate); nonprofit management (Certificate); public management (MA); regulatory science (MS); research administration (MS); science writing (MA, Certificate); writing (MA). *Application deadline:* For fall admission, 5/31 priority date for domestic students, 4/30 priority date for international students; for spring admission, 10/31 priority date for domestic students, 10/15 priority date for international students. Applications are processed on a rolling basis. *Application fee:* $75. Electronic applications accepted. *Application Contact:* Melissa Edwards, Admissions Manager, 202-452-1941, Fax: 202-452-1970, E-mail: aapadmissions@jhu.edu. *Senior Associate Dean,* Dr. Kathleen Burke, 800-847-3330, Fax: 202-452-1970, E-mail: aapadmissions@jhu.edu.

Bloomberg School of Public Health Students: 1,466 full-time, 1,184 part-time. Average age 32. 5,156 applicants, 45% accepted, 1146 enrolled. *Faculty:* 729 full-time, 847 part-time/adjunct. Expenses: Contact institution. *Financial support:* In 2018–19, 1,857 students received support. Fellowships, research assistantships, teaching assistantships, career-related internships or fieldwork, Federal Work-Study, scholarships/grants, traineeships, health care benefits, and unspecified assistantships available. Support available to part-time students. Financial award application deadline: 3/15; financial award applicants required to submit FAFSA. In 2018, 831 master's, 121 doctorates awarded. *Program availability:* Part-time, 100% online, blended/hybrid learning. Offers biochemistry and molecular biology (MHS, Sc M, PhD); bioethics and policy (PhD); biostatistics (MHS, Sc M, PhD); cancer epidemiology (MHS, Sc M, PhD, Sc D); cardiovascular disease and clinical epidemiology (MHS, Sc M, PhD, Sc D); children's mental health services (PhD); clinical investigation (MHS, PhD); clinical trials (PhD, Sc D); clinical trials and evidence synthesis (MHS, Sc M, PhD, Sc D); demography (MHS); environmental epidemiology (MHS, Sc M, PhD, Sc D); environmental health (MHS, Sc M, Dr PH, PhD); epidemiology of aging (MHS, Sc M, PhD, Sc D); general epidemiology and methodology (MHS, Sc M); genetic counseling (Sc M); genetic epidemiology (MHS, Sc M, PhD, Sc D); global disease epidemiology and control (MSPH, PhD); global health economics (MHS); health administration (MHA); health and public policy (PhD); health economics (MHS); health economics and policy (PhD); health education and health communication (MSPH); health finance and management (MHS); health policy (MSPH); health policy and management (Dr PH); health services research and policy (PhD); health systems (MSPH, PhD); human nutrition (MSPH, PhD); infectious disease epidemiology (MHS, Sc M, PhD, Sc D); mental health (MHS); molecular microbiology and immunology (MHS, Sc M, PhD); occupational and environmental hygiene (MSPH); population, family and reproductive health (MHS, MSPH, PhD); public health (MBE, MHA, MHS, MHS, MPH, MPP, MSPH, Sc M, Dr PH, PhD, Sc D); public policy (MPP); social and behavioral interventions (MSPH, PhD); social and behavioral sciences (PhD); social factors in health (MHS); toxicity testing and human health risk assessment of environmental agents (MSPH). *Application fee:* $135. Electronic applications accepted. *Application Contact:* Office of Admissions, 410-955-3543, Fax: 410-955-0464, E-mail: jhsph.admiss@jhu.edu. *Dean,* Dr. Ellen J. MacKenzie, 410-955-3540, Fax: 410-955-0121, E-mail: jhsph.deansoffice@jhu.edu.

Master of Bioethics Program Students: 5 full-time, 6 part-time. 21 applicants, 71% accepted, 9 enrolled. *Faculty:* 15 full-time (9 women). Expenses: Contact institution. *Financial support:* Application deadline: 3/15. In 2018, 4 master's awarded. *Program availability:* Part-time. Offers bioethics (MBE). *Application deadline:* Applications are processed on a rolling basis. *Application fee:* $135. Electronic applications accepted. *Application Contact:* Office of Admissions, 410-955-3543, Fax: 410-955-0464, E-mail: jhsph.admiss@jhu.edu. *Director of the Johns Hopkins Berman Institute of Bioethics,* Dr. Jeffrey Kahn, 410-614-5679, E-mail: jeffkahn@jhu.edu.

Carey Business School Students: 1,077 full-time (611 women), 1,129 part-time (480 women). 3,933 applicants, 69% accepted, 1131 enrolled. *Faculty:* 98 full-time (33 women). Expenses: Contact institution. *Financial support:* In 2018–19, 674 students received support. Scholarships/grants available. Support available to part-time students. Financial award application deadline: 4/15; financial award applicants required to submit FAFSA. In 2018, 1,208 master's, 18 other advanced degrees awarded. *Program availability:* Part-time, evening/weekend, online only, blended/hybrid learning, on-site residency requirement. Offers business (MBA, MS, Certificate); business administration (MBA); business analytics and risk management (MS); finance (MS); financial management (Certificate); health care management (MS); information systems (MS); investments (Certificate); marketing (MS); real estate and infrastructure (MS). *Application deadline:* For fall admission, 5/1 for domestic and international students. Applications are processed on a rolling basis. *Application fee:* $100. Electronic applications accepted. *Application Contact:* Office of Admissions, 410-234-9220, Fax: 443-529-1554, E-mail: carey.admissions@jhu.edu. *Dean,* Dr. Bernard T. Ferrari, 410-234-9210, E-mail: bferrari@jhu.edu.

Engineering Program for Professionals Students: 2,455 part-time (630 women). 1,379 applicants, 46% accepted, 406 enrolled. *Faculty:* 13 full-time (4 women), 305 part-time/adjunct (48 women). Expenses: Contact institution. In 2018, 770 master's, 14 other advanced degrees awarded. *Program availability:* Part-time, evening/weekend, 100% online, blended/hybrid learning. Offers applied and computational mathematics (MS, Post-Master's Certificate); applied biomedical engineering (MS, Post-Master's Certificate); applied physics (MS, Post-Master's Certificate); chemical and biomolecular engineering (M Ch E); civil engineering (MCE, Graduate Certificate); communications and networking (MS); computer science (Post-Master's Certificate); cybersecurity (MS, Post-Master's Certificate); electrical and computer engineering (Graduate Certificate, Post-Master's Certificate); engineering (M Ch E, M Mat SE, MCE, MEE, MEM, MME, MS, MSE, D Eng, Graduate Certificate, Post Master's Certificate, Post-Master's Certificate); engineering management (MEM); environmental engineering (MS, Graduate Certificate, Post-Master's Certificate); environmental engineering and science (MEE, MS, Graduate Certificate, Post-Master's Certificate); environmental planning and management (MS, Graduate Certificate, Post-Master's Certificate); financial mathematics (MS); financial risk management (Graduate Certificate); information

systems engineering (MS, Graduate Certificate, Post-Master's Certificate); mechanical engineering (MME, Post Master's Certificate); nanotechnology (M Mat SE); nanotechnology (MS); quantitative portfolio management (Graduate Certificate); securitization (Graduate Certificate); space systems engineering (MS); systems engineering (MS, MSE, Graduate Certificate, Post-Master's Certificate); technical management (MS, Graduate Certificate, Post-Master's Certificate). *Application deadline:* Applications are processed on a rolling basis. *Application fee:* $0. Electronic applications accepted. *Application Contact:* Doug Schiller, Director of Admissions & Student Services, 410-516-2300, Fax: 410-579-8049, E-mail: schiller@jhu.edu. *Associate Dean,* Dr. Daniel Horn, 410-516-2300, Fax: 410-579-8049, E-mail: dhorn@jhu.edu.

G. W. C. Whiting School of Engineering Students: 1,697 full-time (548 women), 143 part-time (55 women). 5,304 applicants, 34% accepted, 734 enrolled. *Faculty:* 269 full-time (57 women). Expenses: Contact institution. *Financial support:* In 2018–19, 953 students received support, including 165 fellowships with full and partial tuition reimbursements available, 695 research assistantships with full and partial tuition reimbursements available, 93 teaching assistantships with full and partial tuition reimbursements available; Federal Work-Study, institutionally sponsored loans, scholarships/grants, health care benefits, tuition waivers (full and partial), and unspecified assistantships also available. Support available to part-time students. Financial award applicants required to submit FAFSA. In 2018, 622 master's, 105 doctorates, 1 other advanced degree awarded. Offers bioengineering innovation and design (MSE); biomaterials (MSEM); biomedical engineering (MSE, PhD); chemical and biomolecular engineering (MSE, PhD); civil engineering (MSE, PhD); communications science (MSEM); computational medicine (PhD); computer science (MSEM); discrete mathematics (MA, MSE, PhD); electrical and computer engineering (MSE, PhD); engineering (M Ch E, M Mat SE, MA, MEE, MME, MS, MSE, MSEM, MSSI, D Eng, PhD, Certificate, Post-Master's Certificate); environmental health and engineering (MA, MS, MSE, PhD); environmental systems analysis, economics and public policy (MSEM); financial mathematics (MSE); fluid mechanics (MSEM); materials science and engineering (MSEM); mechanical engineering (MSEM); mechanics and materials (MSEM); nano-biotechnology (MSEM); nanomaterials and nanotechnology (MSEM); operations research (MSEM); operations research/optimization (MA, MSE, PhD); probability and statistics (MSEM); robotics (MSE); security informatics (MSSI); smart product and device design (MSEM); statistics/probability (MA, MSE, PhD). *Application fee:* $75. Electronic applications accepted. *Application Contact:* Lauren McGhee, Director of Engineering Graduate Admissions, 410-516-0505, Fax: 410-516-0780, E-mail: lauren.mcghee@jhu.edu. *Dean,* Dr. T. E. Schlesinger, 410-516-8350 Ext. 3, Fax: 410-516-8627.

National Institutes of Health Sponsored Programs Students: 126 full-time (72 women); includes 36 minority (3 Black or African American, non-Hispanic/Latino; 1 American Indian or Alaska Native, non-Hispanic/Latino; 21 Asian, non-Hispanic/Latino; 11 Hispanic/Latino), 19 international. 282 applicants, 26% accepted, 36 enrolled. *Faculty:* 25 full-time (4 women). Expenses: Contact institution. *Financial support:* In 2018–19, 24 fellowships (averaging $23,000 per year), 93 research assistantships (averaging $23,000 per year), 22 teaching assistantships (averaging $23,000 per year) were awarded; Federal Work-Study, institutionally sponsored loans, scholarships/grants, traineeships, health care benefits, tuition waivers (partial), and unspecified assistantships also available. Financial award application deadline: 4/15; financial award applicants required to submit FAFSA. In 2018, 15 doctorates awarded. Offers biology (PhD); cell, molecular, and developmental biology and biophysics (PhD). Applicants must apply to NIH Graduate Partnerships Program. *Application deadline:* For fall admission, 12/1 priority date for domestic students. *Application fee:* $60. Electronic applications accepted. *Application Contact:* Joan Miller, Academic Affairs Administrator, 410-516-5502, Fax: 410-516-5213, E-mail: joan@jhu.edu. *Chair,* Dr. Vincent Hilser, 410-516-4693, Fax: 410-516-5213, E-mail: vhilser@jhu.edu.

Peabody Conservatory Students: 315 full-time (166 women), 7 part-time (5 women). 733 applicants, 48% accepted, 151 enrolled. *Faculty:* 110 full-time (48 women). Expenses: Contact institution. *Financial support:* In 2018–19, 271 students received support, including 65 teaching assistantships (averaging $25,240 per year); fellowships, Federal Work-Study, institutionally sponsored loans, scholarships/grants, and unspecified assistantships also available. Financial award application deadline: 2/1; financial award applicants required to submit CSS PROFILE or FAFSA. In 2018, 127 master's, 13 doctorates, 26 other advanced degrees awarded. Offers music (MA, MM, DMA, AD, GPD). *Application deadline:* For fall admission, 12/1 priority date for domestic and international students. *Application fee:* $120. Electronic applications accepted. *Application Contact:* John Huling, Director of Admissions, 800-368-2521, E-mail: admissions@peabody.jhu.edu. *Dean,* Dr. Fred Bronstein, 667-208-6500.

Program in Molecular Biophysics Offers molecular biophysics (PhD).

School of Advanced International Studies Students: 857 full-time (435 women), 32 part-time (17 women). 1,302 applicants, 89% accepted, 471 enrolled. *Faculty:* 103 full-time (37 women). Expenses: Contact institution. *Financial support:* In 2018–19, 431 students received support, including 431 fellowships (averaging $20,358 per year); research assistantships, teaching assistantships, Federal Work-Study, institutionally sponsored loans, and scholarships/grants also available. Support available to part-time students. Financial award application deadline: 2/15; financial award applicants required to submit FAFSA. In 2018, 592 master's, 6 doctorates, 38 other advanced degrees awarded. *Program availability:* Evening/weekend. Offers global risk (MA); international development (MA, Certificate); international economics (Certificate); international economics and finance (MA); international public policy (MIPP); international relations (PhD); international studies (Certificate); Japan studies (MA); Korea studies (MA); South Asia studies (MA); Southeast Asia studies (MA). Dual-degree with Nanjing University (MAIS); other dual degree programs offered with Johns Hopkins, University of Pennsylvania; INSEAD, and others. *Application deadline:* For fall admission, 1/7 for domestic and international students; for spring admission, 10/15 for domestic and international students. *Application fee:* $85. Electronic applications accepted. *Application Contact:* Karen Ohen, Director of Admissions, 202-663-5700, Fax: 202-663-7788, E-mail: sais.dc.admissions@jhu.edu. *Dean,* Eliot Cohen, 202-663-5781, E-mail: ecohen1@jhu.edu.

School of Education Students: 593 full-time (454 women), 1,807 part-time (1,356 women). 1,541 applicants, 53% accepted, 625 enrolled. *Faculty:* 118 full-time (86 women). Expenses: Contact institution. *Financial support:* In 2018–19, 206 students received support, including 23 fellowships (averaging $25,500 per year); research assistantships, teaching assistantships, Federal Work-Study, and scholarships/grants also available. Support available to part-time students. Financial award application deadline: 4/1; financial award applicants required to submit FAFSA. In 2018, 937 master's, 61 doctorates, 183 other advanced degrees awarded. *Program availability:* Part-time, evening/weekend, 100% online, blended/hybrid learning. Offers education (M Ed, MAT, MS, Ed D, PhD, Advanced Certificate, Graduate Certificate, Post-Master's Certificate). *Application deadline:* For fall admission, 4/1 priority date for domestic students, 4/1 for international students; for spring admission, 10/1 priority date for domestic students, 10/1 for international students; for summer admission, 2/1 priority date for domestic students, 2/1 for international students. Applications are processed on a rolling basis. *Application fee:* $80. Electronic applications accepted. *Application Contact:* Elisabeth Woodward, Director of Admissions, 410-516-9797, E-mail: admissions@jhu.edu. *Dean*, Dr. Christopher C. Morphew, 410-516-7820, E-mail: soe.dean@jhu.edu.

School of Medicine Students: 1,274 full-time (667 women), 31 part-time (15 women). *Faculty:* 2,811 full-time (1,190 women). Expenses: Contact institution. *Financial support:* Fellowships, research assistantships, teaching assistantships, career-related internships or fieldwork, Federal Work-Study, institutionally sponsored loans, and tuition waivers (full) available. In 2018, 29 master's, 233 doctorates, 2 other advanced degrees awarded. Offers medicine (MA, MS, MD, PhD, Certificate). *Application deadline:* Applications are processed on a rolling basis. *Application fee:* $85. Electronic applications accepted. *Application Contact:* Dr. Paul B. Rothman, Dean of Medical Faculty/Chief Executive Officer, 410-955-3180. *Dean of Medical Faculty/Chief Executive Officer*, Dr. Paul B. Rothman, 410-955-3180.

Graduate Programs in Medicine 1,967 applicants, 16% accepted, 160 enrolled. Expenses: Contact institution. *Financial support:* Fellowships, research assistantships, teaching assistantships, career-related internships or fieldwork, Federal Work-Study, institutionally sponsored loans, and tuition waivers (full) available. Financial award applicants required to submit FAFSA. Offers applied health sciences informatics (MS); biochemistry, cellular and molecular biology (PhD); biological chemistry (PhD); cellular and molecular medicine (PhD); cellular and molecular physiology (PhD); clinical informatics (Certificate); functional anatomy and evolution (PhD); health sciences informatics (PhD); health sciences informatics research (MS); immunology (PhD); medical and biological illustration (MA); medicine (MA, PhD); molecular biophysics (MS, PhD); neuroscience (PhD); pathobiology (PhD); pharmacology and molecular sciences (PhD); physiology (PhD). *Application deadline:* For fall admission, 1/10 for domestic students, 1/10 priority date for international students. *Application fee:* $85. Electronic applications accepted. *Application Contact:* Catherine L. Will, Program/Projects Manager, Office of Graduate Student Affairs, 410-634-3385, E-mail: grad_study@jhmi.edu. *Program/Projects Manager, Office of Graduate Student Affairs*, Catherine L. Will, 410-634-3385, E-mail: grad_study@jhmi.edu.

School of Nursing Students: 513 full-time (458 women), 229 part-time (216 women); includes 287 minority (95 Black or African American, non-Hispanic/Latino; 95 Asian, non-Hispanic/Latino; 67 Hispanic/Latino; 1 Native Hawaiian or other Pacific Islander, non-Hispanic/Latino; 29 Two or more races, non-Hispanic/Latino), 16 international. 1,042 applicants, 54% accepted, 333 enrolled. *Faculty:* 73 full-time (65 women), 7 part-time/adjunct (all women). Expenses: Contact institution. *Financial support:* In 2018–19, 554 students received support, including 42 fellowships with full and partial tuition reimbursements available (averaging $5,000 per year), 15 research assistantships with full tuition reimbursements available (averaging $8,000 per year), 9 teaching assistantships (averaging $3,000 per year); Federal Work-Study, scholarships/grants, and tuition waivers (full and partial) also available. Support available to part-time students. Financial award application deadline: 3/1; financial award applicants required to submit FAFSA. In 2018, 242 master's, 38 doctorates, 32 other advanced degrees awarded. *Program availability:* Part-time, 100% online, blended/hybrid learning. Offers nursing (MSN, DNP, PhD, Certificate). *Application deadline:* For fall admission, 11/1 priority date for domestic and international students; for spring admission, 7/1 priority date for domestic and international students; for summer admission, 11/1 priority date for domestic and international students. *Application fee:* $70. Electronic applications accepted. *Application Contact:* Cathy Wilson, Director of Admissions, 410-955-7548, Fax: 410-614-7086, E-mail: jhuson@jhu.edu. *Dean*, Dr. Patricia M. Davidson, 410-955-7544, Fax: 410-955-4890, E-mail: sondeansoffice@jhu.edu.

Zanvyl Krieger School of Arts and Sciences Students: 936 full-time (395 women). 2,825 applicants, 15% accepted, 203 enrolled. *Faculty:* 510 full-time (202 women). Expenses: Contact institution. *Financial support:* Fellowships with full and partial tuition reimbursements, research assistantships with full and partial tuition reimbursements, teaching assistantships with full and partial tuition reimbursements, career-related internships or fieldwork, Federal Work-Study, institutionally sponsored loans, scholarships/grants, health care benefits, tuition waivers (full and partial), and unspecified assistantships available. Support available to part-time students. Financial award applicants required to submit FAFSA. In 2018, 157 master's, 125 doctorates, 28 other advanced degrees awarded. Offers anthropology (PhD); archaeology (PhD); arts and sciences (MA, MBEE, MFA, MS, PhD, Certificate); Assyriology (PhD); astronomy (PhD); biophysics (PhD); cell, molecular, developmental biology, and biophysics (PhD); chemical biology (MS, PhD); chemistry (MA, PhD); classics (PhD); cognitive science (MA, PhD); comparative literature (PhD); earth and planetary sciences (MA, PhD); economics (PhD); Egyptology (PhD); English and American literature (PhD); fiction writing (MFA); German (MA, PhD); Hebrew Bible/Northwest Semitics (PhD); history (PhD); history of art (MA, PhD); history of science and technology (MA, PhD); intellectual history (PhD); mathematics (PhD); philosophy (MA, PhD); physics (PhD); poetry (MFA); political science (MA, PhD); psychological and brain sciences (PhD); romance languages (PhD); sociology (PhD). *Application fee:* $75. Electronic applications accepted. *Application Contact:* Richard Helman, Director, Graduate Admissions and Enrollment, 410-516-7125, E-mail: graduateadmissions@jhu.edu. *Dean*, Dr. Beverly Wendland, 410-516-8220, E-mail: kriegerschooldean@jhu.edu.

JOHNSON & WALES UNIVERSITY, Providence, RI 02903-3703

General Information Independent, coed, comprehensive institution. *Graduate housing:* On-campus housing not available. *Research affiliation:* Consortium of Rhode Island Academic and Research Libraries, Association of Institutional Research.

GRADUATE UNITS

Graduate Studies *Program availability:* Part-time, evening/weekend. Offers accounting (MBA); addiction counseling (MS); business administration (MBA); business education and secondary special education (MAT); clinical mental health counseling (MS); criminal justice (MS); culinary arts education (MAT); data analytics (MS); educational leadership (Ed D); elementary education and elementary special education (MAT); finance (MBA); global fashion merchandising and management (MBA); global tourism and sustainable economic development (MS); hospitality (MBA); human resource management (MS); information security/assurance (MS); information technology (MBA); nonprofit management (MBA); occupational therapy (OTD); operations and supply chain management (MBA); organizational leadership (MBA); organizational psychology (MBA); physician assistant studies (MS); sport leadership (MBA); teaching and learning (M Ed).

JOHNSON C. SMITH UNIVERSITY, Charlotte, NC 28216-5398

General Information Independent, coed, comprehensive institution. *Enrollment:* 1,565 graduate, professional, and undergraduate students; 72 full-time matriculated graduate/professional students (66 women), 13 part-time matriculated graduate/professional students (12 women). *Enrollment by degree level:* 85 master's. *Graduate faculty:* 6 full-time (2 women), 4 part-time/adjunct (all women). Full-time $8640. *Graduate housing:* Room and/or apartments available on a first-come, first-served basis to single students; on-campus housing not available to married students. Typical cost: $6000 per year. Room charges vary according to board plan and housing facility selected. *Student services:* Exercise/wellness program, free psychological counseling, services for students with disabilities. *Library facilities:* James B. Duke Library. *Collection:* Books: 105,422 (physical), 203,337 (digital/electronic); Serial titles: 107 (physical), 23,465 (digital/electronic); Databases: 99. Weekly public service hours: 79; study areas open 24 hours, 5–7 days a week; students can reserve study rooms. **Computer facilities:** Computer purchase and lease plans are available. 125 computers available on campus for general student use. A campuswide network can be accessed from student residence rooms and from off campus. Online class registration is available. Website: http://www.jcsu.edu/

General Application Contact: Vory L Billups, Director of Admissions, 704-378-1081.

GRADUATE UNITS

Program in Social Work Students: 72 full-time (66 women), 13 part-time (12 women); includes 79 minority (78 Black or African American, non-Hispanic/Latino; 1 American Indian or Alaska Native, non-Hispanic/Latino). Average age 32. *Faculty:* 6 full-time (2 women), 4 part-time/adjunct (all women). Expenses: Contact institution. *Financial support:* Federal Work-Study, scholarships/grants, and unspecified assistantships available. Financial award applicants required to submit FAFSA. In 2018, 37 master's awarded. *Program availability:* Part-time, evening/weekend. Offers social work (MSW). *Application deadline:* Applications are processed on a rolling basis. *Application fee:* $40. Electronic applications accepted. *Application Contact:* Vory Billups, Director of Admissions, 704-3781081, E-mail: vbillups@jcsu.edu. *Director of MSW Program*, Dr. Melvin Herring, 704-371-6754, E-mail: mherring@jcsu.edu.

JOHNSON UNIVERSITY, Knoxville, TN 37998-1001

General Information Independent-religious, coed, comprehensive institution. *Graduate housing:* Rooms and/or apartments available on a first-come, first-served basis to single and married students. Housing application deadline: 8/1.

GRADUATE UNITS

Graduate and Professional Programs *Program availability:* Part-time, evening/weekend, 100% online, blended/hybrid learning. Offers biblical interpretation (Graduate Certificate); business administration (MBA); Christian ministries (Graduate Certificate); clinical mental health counseling (MA); educational technology (MA); intercultural studies (MA); leadership (MBA); leadership studies (PhD); New Testament (MA); nonprofit management (MBA); school counseling (MA); spiritual formation and leadership (Graduate Certificate); strategic ministry (MA); teacher education (MA). Electronic applications accepted.

JOHNSON UNIVERSITY FLORIDA, Kissimmee, FL 34744-5301

General Information Independent-religious, coed, comprehensive institution.

GRADUATE UNITS

Program in Strategic Ministry *Program availability:* Online learning. Offers children and family (MSM); church administration (MSM); church planting (MSM); intercultural studies (MSM); pastoral ministry (MSM); special needs (MSM); sports ministry (MSM); worship (MSM); youth ministry (MSM).

JOSE MARIA VARGAS UNIVERSITY, Pembroke Pines, FL 33026

General Information Proprietary, coed, comprehensive institution.

GRADUATE UNITS

Program in Preschool Education Offers preschool education (MS).

THE JUDGE ADVOCATE GENERAL'S SCHOOL, U.S. ARMY, Charlottesville, VA 22903-1781

General Information Federally supported, coed, primarily men, graduate-only institution. *Graduate housing:* On-campus housing not available.

GRADUATE UNITS

Graduate Programs Offers military law (LL M). Program available only to active duty military lawyers.

JUDSON UNIVERSITY, Elgin, IL 60123-1498

General Information Independent-religious, coed, comprehensive institution. *Enrollment:* 1,256 graduate, professional, and undergraduate students; 125 full-time matriculated graduate/professional students (83 women), 88 part-time matriculated graduate/professional students (65 women). *Enrollment by degree level:* 132 master's, 22 doctoral, 1 other advanced degree. *Graduate faculty:* 25 full-time (13 women), 48 part-time/adjunct (22 women). *Required fees:* $250. One-time fee: $125 full-time. Tuition and fees vary according to program. *Graduate housing:* Rooms and/or apartments available on a first-come, first-served basis to single and married students. Typical cost: $9988 (including board) for single students. Housing application deadline: 8/1. *Student services:* Campus employment opportunities, campus safety program, career counseling, exercise/wellness program, free psychological counseling, international student services, low-cost health insurance, multicultural affairs office, services for students with disabilities, writing training. *Library facilities:* Benjamin P. Browne Library. *Collection:* Books: 120,765 (physical), 6,280 (digital/electronic); Serial titles: 158 (physical), 48,401 (digital/electronic); Databases: 53. Weekly public service hours: 76; students can reserve study rooms. **Computer facilities:** 140 computers available on campus for general student use. A campuswide network can be accessed from student residence rooms and from off campus. Online class registration is available. Website: http://www.judsonu.edu/

General Application Contact: Maria Aguirre, Student Academic Advisor, 847-628-1160, E-mail: maguirre@judsonu.edu.

GRADUATE UNITS

Doctor of Education in Literacy Program Students: 13 full-time (all women), 19 part-time (17 women); includes 1 minority (Hispanic/Latino). Average age 43. 15 applicants, 93% accepted, 14 enrolled. *Faculty:* 5 full-time (3 women), 10 part-time/adjunct (all women). Expenses: Contact institution. *Financial support:* Teaching assistantships available. Financial award application deadline: 11/15; financial award applicants required to submit FAFSA. In 2018, 9 doctorates awarded. Offers literacy (Ed D). *Application deadline:* For fall admission, 11/15 for domestic and international students. *Application fee:* $200. *Application Contact:* Brenda Buckley-Hughes, Co-Director, 847-628-1060, E-mail: bbuckley-hughes@judsonu.edu. *Co-Director*, Dr. Brenda Buckley-Hughes, 847-628-1060, E-mail: bbuckley-hughes@judsonu.edu.

Master of Architecture Program Students: 18 full-time (6 women); includes 10 minority (all Hispanic/Latino). Average age 24. *Faculty:* 3 full-time (0 women), 2 part-time/adjunct (0 women). Expenses: Contact institution. *Financial support:* In 2018–19, 9 students received support. Fellowships, research assistantships, teaching assistantships, scholarships/grants, and 8 assistantships available. Financial award application deadline: 5/1; financial award applicants required to submit FAFSA. In 2018, 9 master's awarded. *Program availability:* Part-time. Offers architecture (M Arch); sustainable design (M Arch); traditional architecture and urbanism (M Arch). *Application deadline:* For fall admission, 2/15 priority date for domestic and international students; for winter admission, 11/15 for domestic students; for spring admission, 11/15 for domestic and international students. Applications are processed on a rolling basis. *Application fee:* $100. Electronic applications accepted. *Application Contact:* Annelise Pollard, Admissions Representative, 847-628-2519, E-mail: annelise.pollard@judsonu.edu. *Interim Chair,* Dr. Curtis Sartor, 847-628-1017, E-mail: csartor@judsonu.edu.

Master of Arts in Clinical Mental Health Counseling Program Students: 27 full-time (24 women), 13 part-time (12 women); includes 10 minority (8 Black or African American, non-Hispanic/Latino; 2 Hispanic/Latino). Average age 38. 15 applicants, 100% accepted, 11 enrolled. *Faculty:* 3 full-time (2 women), 5 part-time/adjunct (4 women). Expenses: Contact institution. *Financial support:* Unspecified assistantships available. *Program availability:* Evening/weekend. Offers clinical mental health counseling (MA). *Application deadline:* Applications are processed on a rolling basis. *Application fee:* $35. Electronic applications accepted. *Application Contact:* Kim Surin, Enrollment Manager, 847-628-5033, E-mail: kim.surin@info.judsonu.edu. *Program Director,* Dr. Amber Randolph, 847-628-1544, E-mail: amber.randolph@judsonu.edu.

Master of Arts in Human Services Administration Students: 11 full-time (8 women), 3 part-time (all women); includes 3 minority (2 Black or African American, non-Hispanic/Latino; 1 Hispanic/Latino). Average age 39. 9 applicants, 67% accepted, 4 enrolled. *Faculty:* 7 full-time (6 women). Expenses: Contact institution. *Financial support:* Unspecified assistantships available. In 2018, 18 master's awarded. *Program availability:* Evening/weekend. Offers human services administration (MA). *Application deadline:* Applications are processed on a rolling basis. *Application fee:* $35. Electronic applications accepted. *Application Contact:* Kim Surin, Enrollment Manager, 847-628-5033, E-mail: kim.surin@info.judsonu.edu.

Master of Arts in Organizational Leadership Students: 16 full-time (11 women), 4 part-time (3 women); includes 6 minority (4 Black or African American, non-Hispanic/Latino; 2 Hispanic/Latino). Average age 36. 15 applicants, 73% accepted, 9 enrolled. *Faculty:* 7 full-time (4 women), 31 part-time/adjunct (9 women). Expenses: Contact institution. *Financial support:* Institutionally sponsored loans and unspecified assistantships available. Financial award applicants required to submit FAFSA. In 2018, 16 master's awarded. *Program availability:* Part-time, evening/weekend, 100% online, blended/hybrid learning. Offers organizational leadership (MA). *Application deadline:* Applications are processed on a rolling basis. *Application fee:* $35. Electronic applications accepted. *Application Contact:* Kim Surin, Enrollment Manager, 847-628-5033, E-mail: kim.surin@info.judsonu.edu. *Chair,* Karen Love, 847-628-1524, E-mail: klove@judsonu.edu.

Master of Business Administration Program Students: 40 full-time (21 women), 20 part-time (7 women); includes 25 minority (13 Black or African American, non-Hispanic/Latino; 1 Asian, non-Hispanic/Latino; 11 Hispanic/Latino), 3 international. Average age 36. 23 applicants, 100% accepted, 23 enrolled. *Faculty:* 7 full-time (5 women), 100 part-time/adjunct (50 women). Expenses: Contact institution. *Financial support:* In 2018–19, 6 teaching assistantships were awarded; tuition waivers (partial) also available. Financial award applicants required to submit FAFSA. In 2018, 20 master's awarded. *Program availability:* Evening/weekend, 100% online. Offers business administration (MBA). *Application deadline:* Applications are processed on a rolling basis. *Application fee:* $35. Electronic applications accepted. *Application Contact:* Kim Surin, Enrollment Manager, 847-628-5033, E-mail: kim.surin@info.judsonu.edu. *Chair,* John C. Boggs, 847-628-1041, E-mail: john.boggs@judsonu.edu.

Master of Education in Literacy Program Students: 19 full-time (all women); includes 2 minority (both Hispanic/Latino). Average age 31. 19 applicants, 100% accepted, 19 enrolled. *Faculty:* 4 full-time (2 women), 8 part-time/adjunct (7 women). Expenses: Contact institution. *Financial support:* Tuition discounts available. Financial award application deadline: 4/15; financial award applicants required to submit FAFSA. Offers literacy (M Ed). *Application deadline:* For fall admission, 4/15 for domestic and international students. Applications are processed on a rolling basis. *Application fee:* $55. *Application Contact:* Dr. Kristy Piebenga, Director, 847-628-1086, E-mail: kristy.piebenga@judsonu.edu. *Director,* Dr. Kristy Piebenga, 847-628-1086, E-mail: kristy.piebenga@judsonu.edu.

Master of Leadership in Ministry Program Students: 10 part-time (4 women); includes 5 minority (3 Black or African American, non-Hispanic/Latino; 2 Hispanic/Latino). Average age 39. 9 applicants, 100% accepted, 9 enrolled. *Faculty:* 4 full-time (2 women), 6 part-time/adjunct (2 women). Expenses: Contact institution. *Financial support:* In 2018–19, 5 students received support. Scholarships/grants and tuition waivers available. Financial award application deadline: 8/15; financial award applicants required to submit FAFSA. *Program availability:* Evening/weekend, online only, blended/hybrid learning. Offers leadership in ministry (MLM). *Application deadline:* Applications are processed on a rolling basis. *Application fee:* $35. Electronic applications accepted. *Application Contact:* Dr. David Sanders, Director, 847-628-1052, E-mail: dsanders@judsonu.edu. *Director,* Dr. David Sanders, 847-628-1052, E-mail: dsanders@judsonu.edu.

THE JUILLIARD SCHOOL, New York, NY 10023-6588

General Information Independent, coed, comprehensive institution. *Graduate housing:* Room and/or apartments available on a first-come, first-served basis to single students; on-campus housing not available to married students. Housing application deadline: 5/15.

GRADUATE UNITS

Graduate Programs Offers acting (MFA); jazz studies (Artist Diploma); music (MM, DMA, Diploma); music performance (Artist Diploma); opera studies (Artist Diploma); string quartet (Artist Diploma). Electronic applications accepted.

JUNIATA COLLEGE, Huntingdon, PA 16652-2119

General Information Independent-religious, coed, comprehensive institution. *Graduate housing:* On-campus housing not available.

GRADUATE UNITS

Department of Accounting, Business, and Economics Offers accounting (M Acc); business administration (MBA); organizational leadership (MOL).

KANSAS CITY UNIVERSITY OF MEDICINE AND BIOSCIENCES, Kansas City, MO 64106-1453

General Information Independent, coed, graduate-only institution. CGS member. *Graduate housing:* On-campus housing not available. *Research affiliation:* Boehringer

Ingelheim (HIV/AIDS), Mylanta-Bertek (hypertension), Covance (hypertension), Novartis Pharmaceuticals (Chronic Obstructive Pulmonary Disease (COPD)).

GRADUATE UNITS

College of Biosciences *Program availability:* Part-time. Offers bioethics (MA); biomedical sciences (MS).

College of Osteopathic Medicine Offers osteopathic medicine (DO).

KANSAS STATE UNIVERSITY, Manhattan, KS 66506

General Information State-supported, coed, university. CGS member. *Graduate housing:* Rooms and/or apartments available on a first-come, first-served basis to single and married students. Housing application deadline: 2/1. *Research affiliation:* Visteon Corporation, Midwest Research Institute, NASA-Research Center, U.S. Grain Marketing Research Laboratory.

GRADUATE UNITS

Graduate School *Program availability:* Part-time, evening/weekend, online learning. Electronic applications accepted.

College of Agriculture *Program availability:* Part-time, online learning. Offers agricultural economics (MAB, MS, PhD); agricultural education and communication (MS); agriculture (MAB, MS, PhD, Certificate); crop science (MS, PhD); entomology (MS, PhD); food science (MS, PhD); genetics (MS, PhD); grain science and industry (MS, PhD); grassland management (Certificate); horticulture and natural resources (MS, PhD); meat science (MS, PhD); monogastric nutrition (MS, PhD); physiology (MS, PhD); plant breeding and genetics (MS, PhD); plant pathology (MS, PhD); range and forage science (MS, PhD); ruminant nutrition (MS, PhD); soil and environmental science (MS, PhD); weed science (MS, PhD). Electronic applications accepted.

College of Architecture, Planning and Design *Program availability:* Part-time. Offers architecture (M Arch, MS Arch); architecture, planning and design (M Arch, MIAPD, MLA, MRCP, MS, MS Arch, PhD); community development (MS); environmental design and planning (PhD); interior architecture and product design (MIAPD); landscape architecture (MLA); regional and community planning (MRCP). Electronic applications accepted.

College of Arts and Sciences *Program availability:* Part-time, online learning. Offers advertising (MS); art (MFA); arts and sciences (MA, MFA, MM, MPA, MS, PhD, Graduate Certificate); biochemistry and molecular biophysics (MS, PhD); biology (MS); chemistry (MS, PhD); communication studies (MA); community journalism (MS); economics (MA, PhD); English (MA); gender, women and sexuality studies (Graduate Certificate); geographic information science (Graduate Certificate); geography (MA, PhD); geology (MS); global communication (MS); health communication (MS); history (MA, PhD); literature (MA); mathematics (MS, PhD, Graduate Certificate); media management (MS); music, theatre and dance (MA, MM); physics (MS, PhD); political science (MA); psychological sciences (PhD); public administration (MPA); public relations (MS); second language acquisition (MA); security studies (MA, PhD); sociology (MA, PhD); statistics (MS, PhD, Graduate Certificate); technical writing and professional communication (Graduate Certificate). Electronic applications accepted.

College of Business *Program availability:* Part-time. Offers accounting (M Acc); business (M Acc, MBA, Certificate); data analytics (MBA); finance (MBA); management (MBA); marketing (MBA); technology entrepreneurship (MBA). Electronic applications accepted.

College of Education *Program availability:* Part-time, evening/weekend, online learning. Offers academic advising (MS, Certificate); adult learning (Certificate); counseling and student development (MS); curriculum and instruction (Ed D, PhD); digital teaching and learning (MS); education (MS, Ed D, PhD, Certificate); educational computing, design and online learning (MS); educational leadership (MS, Ed D, PhD); elementary/middle level curriculum and instruction (MS); leadership dynamics for adult learners (Certificate); online learning (Certificate); qualitative research (Certificate); reading specialist endorsement (MS); reading/language arts (MS); social justice education (Certificate); special education (MS, Ed D); special education, counseling, and student affairs (PhD); teacher leader/school improvement (MS); teaching and learning (Certificate); teaching English as a second language for adult learners (Certificate). Electronic applications accepted.

College of Engineering *Program availability:* Part-time, online learning. Offers architectural engineering and construction science (MS); biological and agricultural engineering (MS, PhD); chemical engineering (MS, PhD, Graduate Certificate); civil engineering (MS, PhD); computer science (MS, MSE, PhD); electrical engineering (MS); engineering (MEM, MS, MSE, PhD, Graduate Certificate); engineering management (MEM); environmental engineering (MS, PhD); geotechnical engineering (MS, PhD); industrial engineering (MS); mechanical engineering (MS, PhD); nuclear engineering (PhD); operations research (MS); structural engineering (MS, PhD); transportation engineering (MS, PhD); water resources engineering (MS, PhD). Electronic applications accepted.

College of Human Ecology *Program availability:* Part-time, online learning. Offers apparel and textiles (MS, PhD); applied family sciences (MS, PhD); communication sciences and disorders (MS); conflict resolution (Graduate Certificate); couple and family therapy (MS, PhD); dietetics (MS); early childhood education (MS); family and community service (MS); gerontology (MS, Graduate Certificate); hospitality administration (PhD); hospitality and dietetics administration (MS); human ecology (MS, PhD, Graduate Certificate); human nutrition (PhD); kinesiology (MS, PhD); life-span human development (MS, PhD); nutrition, dietetics and sensory sciences (MS); nutritional sciences (PhD); personal financial planning (MS, PhD, Graduate Certificate); public health nutrition (PhD); public health physical activity (PhD); sensory analysis and consumer behavior (PhD); youth development (MS, Graduate Certificate). Electronic applications accepted.

College of Technology and Aviation *Program availability:* Part-time, evening/weekend, 100% online. Offers technology and aviation (MT). Electronic applications accepted.

College of Veterinary Medicine Offers biomedical science (MS); clinical sciences (MPH, Graduate Certificate); diagnostic medicine/pathobiology (PhD); physiology (PhD); veterinary medicine (MPH, MS, DVM, PhD, Graduate Certificate). Electronic applications accepted.

School of Applied and Interdisciplinary Studies *Program availability:* Part-time, 100% online, blended/hybrid learning. Offers applied science and technology (PSM); professional interdisciplinary sciences (Graduate Certificate); professional skills for STEM practitioners (Graduate Certificate). Electronic applications accepted.

KANSAS WESLEYAN UNIVERSITY, Salina, KS 67401-6196

General Information Independent-religious, coed, comprehensive institution. *Graduate housing:* Rooms and/or apartments available to single and married students.

GRADUATE UNITS

Program in Business Administration *Program availability:* Part-time, evening/weekend. Offers business administration (MBA); sports management (MBA).

KEAN UNIVERSITY, Union, NJ 07083

General Information State-supported, coed, university. *Enrollment:* 14,056 graduate, professional, and undergraduate students; 1,030 full-time matriculated graduate/professional students (798 women), 770 part-time matriculated graduate/professional students (581 women). *Enrollment by degree level:* 1,574 master's, 188 doctoral, 38 other advanced degrees. *Graduate faculty:* 267 full-time (146 women). Tuition, state resident: full-time $15,025; part-time $733.50 per credit. Tuition, nonresident: full-time $19,890; part-time $884.50 per credit. *Required fees:* $2107.50; $89.50 per credit. Tuition and fees vary according to course level, course load, degree level and program. *Graduate housing:* Room and/or apartments available on a first-come, first-served basis to single students; on-campus housing not available to married students. Housing application deadline: 5/1. *Student services:* Campus employment opportunities, campus safety program, career counseling, child daycare facilities, exercise/wellness program, free psychological counseling, grant writing training, international student services, low-cost health insurance, multicultural affairs office, services for students with disabilities, teacher training, writing training. *Library facilities:* Nancy Thompson Library. *Collection:* Books: 177,961 (physical), 12,121 (digital/electronic); Serial titles: 59,728 (digital/electronic); Databases: 244. Weekly public service hours: 102.

Computer facilities: 1,700 computers available on campus for general student use. A campuswide network can be accessed from student residence rooms and from off campus. Online class registration is available.
Website: http://www.kean.edu/

General Application Contact: Helen Ramirez, Associate Director, 908-737-7137, E-mail: hramirez@kean.edu.

GRADUATE UNITS

College of Business and Public Management Students: 136 full-time (84 women), 102 part-time (63 women); includes 159 minority (67 Black or African American, non-Hispanic/Latino; 19 Asian, non-Hispanic/Latino; 67 Hispanic/Latino; 2 Native Hawaiian or other Pacific Islander, non-Hispanic/Latino; 4 Two or more races, non-Hispanic/Latino), 21 international. Average age 31. 119 applicants, 95% accepted, 72 enrolled. *Faculty:* 28 full-time (6 women). Expenses: Contact institution. *Financial support:* Federal Work-Study, scholarships/grants, and unspecified assistantships available. Financial award applicants required to submit FAFSA. In 2018, 94 master's awarded. *Program availability:* Part-time. Offers accounting (MS); business and public management (MA, MBA, MPA, MS); criminal justice (MA); executive management (MBA); global management (MBA); health services administration (MPA); non-profit management (MPA); public administration (MPA). *Application deadline:* For fall admission, 6/30 for domestic and international students; for spring admission, 12/1 for domestic and international students. Applications are processed on a rolling basis. *Application fee:* $75. Electronic applications accepted. *Application Contact:* Pedro Lopes, Admissions Counselor, 908-737-7100, E-mail: gradadmissions@kean.edu. *Dean,* Dr. Jin Wang, 908-737-4700, Fax: 908-737-4755, E-mail: cbpm@kean.edu.
College of Education Students: 35 full-time (27 women), 126 part-time (89 women); includes 64 minority (20 Black or African American, non-Hispanic/Latino; 12 Asian, non-Hispanic/Latino; 30 Hispanic/Latino; 1 Native Hawaiian or other Pacific Islander, non-Hispanic/Latino; 1 Two or more races, non-Hispanic/Latino), 2 international. Average age 33. 73 applicants, 100% accepted, 58 enrolled. *Faculty:* 52 full-time (33 women). Expenses: Contact institution. *Financial support:* Scholarships/grants and unspecified assistantships available. Financial award applicants required to submit FAFSA. In 2018, 85 master's awarded. *Program availability:* Part-time. Offers bilingual/bicultural education (MA); early childhood education (MA); education (MA, MS); exercise science (MS); Hindi and Urdu language pedagogy (MA); special education (MA); teaching English as a second language (MA). *Application deadline:* For fall admission, 6/30 for domestic and international students; for spring admission, 12/1 for domestic and international students. Applications are processed on a rolling basis. *Application fee:* $75. Electronic applications accepted. *Application Contact:* Brittany Gerstenhaber, Admissions Counselor, 908-737-7100, E-mail: gradadmissions@kean.edu.
College of Liberal Arts Students: 159 full-time (131 women), 110 part-time (87 women); includes 153 minority (72 Black or African American, non-Hispanic/Latino; 15 Asian, non-Hispanic/Latino; 60 Hispanic/Latino; 6 Two or more races, non-Hispanic/Latino), 4 international. Average age 29. 160 applicants, 88% accepted, 94 enrolled. *Faculty:* 95 full-time (55 women). Expenses: Contact institution. *Financial support:* Scholarships/grants and unspecified assistantships available. Financial award applicants required to submit FAFSA. In 2018, 78 master's awarded. *Program availability:* Part-time. Offers communication studies (MA); English writing studies (MA); fine arts education (MA); forensic psychology (MA); Holocaust and genocide studies (MA); human behavior and organizational psychology (MA); liberal arts (MA); marriage and family therapy (MA); psychological services (MA). *Application deadline:* For fall admission, 6/30 for domestic and international students; for spring admission, 12/1 for domestic and international students. Applications are processed on a rolling basis. *Application fee:* $75. Electronic applications accepted. *Application Contact:* Amy Clark, Program Assistant, 908-737-7100, E-mail: gradadmissions@kean.edu. *Acting Dean,* Dr. Jonathan Mercantini, 908-737-0430, Fax: 908-737-0435, E-mail: jmercant@kean.edu.
College of Natural, Applied and Health Sciences Students: 14 full-time (6 women), 30 part-time (25 women); includes 21 minority (11 Black or African American, non-Hispanic/Latino; 6 Asian, non-Hispanic/Latino; 2 Hispanic/Latino; 2 Two or more races, non-Hispanic/Latino), 10 international. Average age 37. 26 applicants, 88% accepted, 12 enrolled. *Faculty:* 31 full-time (16 women). Expenses: Contact institution. *Financial support:* Scholarships/grants and unspecified assistantships available. Financial award applicants required to submit FAFSA. In 2018, 57 master's awarded. *Program availability:* Part-time. Offers clinical management (MSN); community health nursing (MSN); computer information systems (MS); natural, applied and health sciences (MS, MSN, PhD). *Application deadline:* For fall admission, 6/30 for domestic and international students; for spring admission, 12/1 for domestic and international students. Applications are processed on a rolling basis. *Application fee:* $75. Electronic applications accepted. *Application Contact:* Pedro Lopes, Admissions Counselor, 908-737-7100, E-mail: gradadmissions@kean.edu. *Dean,* Dr. George Chang, 908-737-3600, Fax: 908-737-3606, E-mail: gchang@kean.edu.
Nathan Weiss Graduate College Students: 648 full-time (527 women), 394 part-time (311 women); includes 465 minority (213 Black or African American, non-Hispanic/Latino; 1 American Indian or Alaska Native, non-Hispanic/Latino; 32 Asian, non-Hispanic/Latino; 197 Hispanic/Latino; 22 Two or more races, non-Hispanic/Latino), 4 international. Average age 31. 1,521 applicants, 36% accepted, 347 enrolled. *Faculty:* 51 full-time (34 women). Expenses: Contact institution. *Financial support:* Scholarships/grants and unspecified assistantships available. Financial award

applicants required to submit FAFSA. In 2018, 270 master's, 20 doctorates, 14 other advanced degrees awarded. *Program availability:* Part-time. Offers alcohol and drug abuse counseling (MA); clinical mental health counseling (MA); combined school and clinical psychology (Psy D); educational leadership (Ed D); occupational therapy (MS); physical therapy (DPT); school business administrator (MA); school counseling (MA); school psychology (Diploma); social work (MSW); speech-language pathology (MA, SLPD); supervisor and principal (MA); supervisors, principals, and school business administrators (MA). *Application deadline:* For fall admission, 6/1 for domestic and international students; for spring admission, 12/1 for domestic and international students. Applications are processed on a rolling basis. *Application fee:* $75. Electronic applications accepted. *Application Contact:* Ann-Marie Kay, Associate Director, Graduate Admissions, 908-737-7100, E-mail: grad-adm@kean.edu. *Dean,* Dr. Jeffrey Beck, 908-737-5902, Fax: 908-737-5905, E-mail: jbeck@kean.edu.
New Jersey Center for Science, Technology and Mathematics Students: 38 full-time (23 women), 8 part-time (6 women); includes 23 minority (6 Black or African American, non-Hispanic/Latino; 4 Asian, non-Hispanic/Latino; 13 Hispanic/Latino), 4 international. Average age 26. 15 applicants, 87% accepted, 6 enrolled. *Faculty:* 7 full-time (1 woman). Expenses: Contact institution. *Financial support:* Scholarships/grants and unspecified assistantships available. Financial award applicants required to submit FAFSA. In 2018, 23 master's awarded. Offers biotechnology science (MS); instruction and curriculum (MA). *Application deadline:* For fall admission, 6/30 for domestic and international students; for spring admission, 12/1 for domestic and international students. Applications are processed on a rolling basis. *Application fee:* $75. Electronic applications accepted. *Application Contact:* Pedro Lopes, Admissions Counselor, 908-737-7100, E-mail: gradcoordinatorcdd@kean.edu. *Dean,* Dr. Keith Bostian, 908-737-7200, E-mail: kbostian@kean.edu.

KECK GRADUATE INSTITUTE, Claremont, CA 91711

General Information Independent, coed, graduate-only institution. CGS member.

GRADUATE UNITS

Henry E. Riggs School of Applied Life Sciences Offers applied life sciences (PhD); bioscience (MBS); bioscience management (Certificate). Electronic applications accepted.
Minerva Schools at KGI
School of Pharmacy and Health Sciences Offers pharmacy and health sciences (Pharm D).

KEENE STATE COLLEGE, Keene, NH 03435

General Information State-supported, coed, comprehensive institution. *Enrollment:* 9 full-time matriculated graduate/professional students (8 women), 37 part-time matriculated graduate/professional students (20 women). *Enrollment by degree level:* 36 master's, 10 other advanced degrees. *Graduate faculty:* 6 full-time (3 women), 6 part-time/adjunct (3 women). Tuition, state resident: full-time $9540; part-time $530 per credit. Tuition, nonresident: full-time $10,440; part-time $580 per credit. *Required fees:* $1998; $111 per credit. Tuition and fees vary according to course load. *Graduate housing:* Room and/or apartments available on a first-come, first-served basis to single students; on-campus housing not available to married students. Typical cost: $7358 per year ($11,026 including board). Room and board charges vary according to board plan and housing facility selected. Housing application deadline: 5/1. *Student services:* Campus employment opportunities, campus safety program, career counseling, exercise/wellness program, free psychological counseling, grant writing training, international student services, multicultural affairs office, services for students with disabilities, teacher training, writing training. *Library facilities:* Mason Library. *Collection:* Books: 247,720 (physical), 319,081 (digital/electronic); Serial titles: 142 (physical), 73,114 (digital/electronic); Databases: 92. Weekly public service hours: 102; students can reserve study rooms.

Computer facilities: Computer purchase and lease plans are available. 600 computers available on campus for general student use. A campuswide network can be accessed from student residence rooms and from off campus. Online class registration is available.
Website: http://www.keene.edu/

General Application Contact: Robert Baker, Director of Continuing Education, 603-358-2338, E-mail: kscgraduatestudies@keene.edu.

GRADUATE UNITS

The School of Arts, Education, and Culture
The School of Sciences, Sustainability, and Health

KEHILATH YAKOV RABBINICAL SEMINARY, Ossining, NY 10562

General Information Independent-religious, men only, comprehensive institution.

GRADUATE UNITS
Graduate Programs

KEISER UNIVERSITY, Fort Lauderdale, FL 33309

General Information Independent, coed, university.

GRADUATE UNITS

Doctor of Business Administration Program Offers global business (DBA); global management (DBA); marketing (DBA).
Ed S in Educational Leadership Program Offers educational leadership (Ed S).
Ed S in Instructional Design and Technology Program Offers instructional design and technology (Ed S).
Joint MS Ed/MBA Program
MA in Criminal Justice Program *Program availability:* Part-time, online learning. Offers criminal justice (MA).
MA in Homeland Security Program Offers homeland security (MA).
Master of Accountancy Program Offers forensic accounting (M Acc).
Master of Business Administration Program *Program availability:* Part-time, online learning. Offers accounting (MBA); health services administration (MBA); international business (MBA); management (MBA); marketing (MBA); technology management (MBA). All concentrations except technology management also offered in Mandarin.
Master of Science in Education Program *Program availability:* Part-time, online learning. Offers allied health teaching and leadership (MS Ed); career college administration (MS Ed); leadership (MS Ed); online teaching and learning (MS Ed); teaching and learning (MS Ed).
Master of Science in Nursing Program Offers family nurse practitioner (MSN); nursing (MSN).
MS in Information Security Program Offers information security (MS).

MS in Information Technology Leadership Program Offers information technology leadership (MS).

MS in Occupational Therapy Program Offers occupational therapy (MS).

MS in Organizational Leadership Program Offers organizational leadership (MSOL).

MS in Organizational Psychology Program Offers organizational psychology (MS).

MS in Physician Assistant Program Offers physician assistant (MS).

MS in Psychology Program Offers psychology (MS).

Nurse Anesthesia Programs Offers nurse anesthesia (MSNA, DNAP).

PhD in Educational Leadership Program Offers educational leadership (PhD).

PhD in Industrial and Organizational Psychology Program Offers industrial and organizational psychology (PhD).

PhD in Instructional Design and Technology Program Offers instructional design and technology (PhD).

PhD in Psychology Program Offers psychology (PhD).

KENNESAW STATE UNIVERSITY, Kennesaw, GA 30144

General Information State-supported, coed, comprehensive institution. CGS member. *Enrollment:* 35,420 graduate, professional, and undergraduate students; 978 full-time matriculated graduate/professional students (601 women), 2,171 part-time matriculated graduate/professional students (1,303 women). *Enrollment by degree level:* 2,275 master's, 238 doctoral, 636 other advanced degrees. *International tuition:* $25,080 full-time. *Tuition, area resident:* Full-time $6960; part-time $290 per credit hour. Tuition, state resident: full-time $6960; part-time $290 per credit hour. Tuition, nonresident: full-time $25,080; part-time $1045 per credit hour. *Required fees:* $2006; $1706 per semester. $853 per semester. *Graduate housing:* Room and/or apartments available on a first-come, first-served basis to single students; on-campus housing not available to married students. *Student services:* Campus employment opportunities, campus safety program, career counseling, exercise/wellness program, free psychological counseling, international student services, low-cost health insurance, multicultural affairs office, services for students with disabilities, teacher training, writing training. *Library facilities:* Kennesaw State University Library System plus 2 others. *Collection:* Books: 378,276 (physical), 656,005 (digital/electronic); Serial titles: 1,273 (physical), 115,672 (digital/electronic); Databases: 476. Students can reserve study rooms.

Computer facilities: Computer purchase and lease plans are available. 4,500 computers available on campus for general student use. A campuswide network can be accessed from student residence rooms and from off campus. Online class registration is available.

Website: http://www.kennesaw.edu/

General Application Contact: Admissions Counselor, 470-578-4377, Fax: 470-578-9172, E-mail: ksugrad@kennesaw.edu.

GRADUATE UNITS

Analytics and Data Science Institute Students: 20 full-time (9 women), 1 part-time (0 women); includes 1 minority (Black or African American, non-Hispanic/Latino), 13 international. Average age 33. 52 applicants, 10% accepted, 5 enrolled. Expenses: Contact institution. *Financial support:* In 2018–19, 5 research assistantships with full and partial tuition reimbursements (averaging $36,000 per year) were awarded. Offers analytics and data science (PhD). *Application deadline:* For fall admission, 2/1 for domestic and international students. *Application fee:* $60. Electronic applications accepted. *Application Contact:* Admissions Counselor, 470-578-4377, Fax: 470-578-9172, E-mail: ksugrad@kennesaw.edu. *Program Director,* Sherrill Hayes, 470-578-6499, E-mail: shayes32@kennesaw.edu.

Bagwell College of Education Students: 186 full-time (161 women), 909 part-time (701 women); includes 316 minority (236 Black or African American, non-Hispanic/Latino; 1 American Indian or Alaska Native, non-Hispanic/Latino; 22 Asian, non-Hispanic/Latino; 44 Hispanic/Latino; 2 Native Hawaiian or other Pacific Islander, non-Hispanic/Latino; 11 Two or more races, non-Hispanic/Latino), 1 international. Average age 36. 456 applicants, 72% accepted, 272 enrolled. Expenses: Contact institution. *Financial support:* Research assistantships with tuition reimbursements, Federal Work-Study, and unspecified assistantships available. Support available to part-time students. Financial award application deadline: 4/1; financial award applicants required to submit FAFSA. In 2018, 197 master's, 27 doctorates, 191 other advanced degrees awarded. *Program availability:* Part-time, 100% online, blended/hybrid learning. Offers art education (MAT); curriculum and instruction (Ed S); early childhood education (M Ed); education (M Ed, MAT, Ed D, Ed S); educational leadership (M Ed); instructional technology (M Ed, Ed D, Ed S); middle grades and secondary education (Ed D, Ed S); reading (M Ed); secondary English (MAT); secondary mathematics (MAT); secondary science (MAT); special education (M Ed, Ed D, Ed S); teacher leadership (M Ed, Ed D, Ed S); teaching English to speakers of other languages (MAT). *Application deadline:* For fall admission, 7/1 for domestic and international students; for spring admission, 11/1 for domestic and international students; for summer admission, 4/1 for domestic and international students. Applications are processed on a rolling basis. *Application fee:* $60. Electronic applications accepted. *Application Contact:* Admission Counselor, 470-578-4377, Fax: 470-578-9172, E-mail: ksugrad@kennesaw.edu. *Dean,* Cynthia Reed, 470-578-6117, Fax: 470-578-6567.

Coles College of Business Students: 146 full-time (67 women), 428 part-time (218 women); includes 249 minority (155 Black or African American, non-Hispanic/Latino; 2 American Indian or Alaska Native, non-Hispanic/Latino; 38 Asian, non-Hispanic/Latino; 39 Hispanic/Latino; 15 Two or more races, non-Hispanic/Latino), 27 international. Average age 35. 441 applicants, 56% accepted, 190 enrolled. Expenses: Contact institution. *Financial support:* Research assistantships with tuition reimbursements, Federal Work-Study, and unspecified assistantships available. Support available to part-time students. Financial award application deadline: 4/1; financial award applicants required to submit FAFSA. In 2018, 283 master's, 12 doctorates awarded. *Program availability:* Part-time, evening/weekend, 100% online. Offers accounting (M Acc); business (EMBA, M Acc, MBA, MS, MSIS, DBA); business administration (EMBA, MBA, DBA); health management and informatics (MS); information systems (MSIS). *Application deadline:* For fall admission, 7/1 for domestic and international students; for spring admission, 11/1 for domestic and international students; for summer admission, 4/1 for domestic and international students. Applications are processed on a rolling basis. *Application fee:* $60. Electronic applications accepted. *Application Contact:* Admissions Counselor, 470-578-4377, Fax: 470-578-9172, E-mail: ksugrad@kennesaw.edu. *Interim Dean,* Dr. Robin Cheramie, 470-578-6425, E-mail: rcheram1@kennesaw.edu.

College of Architecture and Construction Management Students: 4 full-time (1 woman), 10 part-time (3 women); includes 5 minority (3 Black or African American, non-Hispanic/Latino; 1 Asian, non-Hispanic/Latino; 1 Hispanic/Latino), 5 international. Average age 40. 10 applicants, 30% accepted, 3 enrolled. Expenses: Contact institution. *Financial support:* Research assistantships with tuition reimbursements, career-related internships or fieldwork, scholarships/grants, and unspecified assistantships available. Support available to part-time students. Financial award applicants required to submit FAFSA. In 2018, 9 master's awarded. *Program availability:* Part-time, evening/weekend. Offers architecture and construction management (MS, MS Arch); construction management (MS). *Application deadline:* For fall admission, 7/1 priority date for domestic students, 5/1 priority date for international students; for spring admission, 11/1 priority date for domestic students, 9/1 priority date for international students. Applications are processed on a rolling basis. *Application fee:* $60. Electronic applications accepted. *Application Contact:* Admission Counselor, 470-578-4377, Fax: 470-578-9172, E-mail: ksugrad@kennesaw.edu.

College of Computing and Software Engineering Students: 211 full-time (84 women), 354 part-time (114 women); includes 249 minority (129 Black or African American, non-Hispanic/Latino; 77 Asian, non-Hispanic/Latino; 29 Hispanic/Latino; 1 Native Hawaiian or other Pacific Islander, non-Hispanic/Latino; 13 Two or more races, non-Hispanic/Latino), 98 international. Average age 32. 301 applicants, 76% accepted, 164 enrolled. Expenses: Contact institution. *Financial support:* Research assistantships with full and partial tuition reimbursements, teaching assistantships with full tuition reimbursements, career-related internships or fieldwork, scholarships/grants, and unspecified assistantships available. Support available to part-time students. Financial award applicants required to submit FAFSA. In 2018, 115 master's awarded. *Program availability:* Part-time, evening/weekend, blended/hybrid learning. Offers computer science (MS); computing and software engineering (MS, MSIT, MSSWE, Graduate Certificate, Postbaccalaureate Certificate); data management and analytics (Graduate Certificate); health information technology (Postbaccalaureate Certificate); information technology (MSIT); information technology foundations (Postbaccalaureate Certificate); information technology security (Graduate Certificate); software engineering (MSSWE, Graduate Certificate); software engineering foundations (Graduate Certificate). *Application deadline:* For fall admission, 7/1 priority date for domestic students, 5/1 priority date for international students; for spring admission, 11/1 priority date for domestic students, 9/1 priority date for international students; for summer admission, 4/1 priority date for domestic students, 3/1 priority date for international students. Applications are processed on a rolling basis. *Application fee:* $60. Electronic applications accepted. *Application Contact:* Admission Counselor, 470-578-4377, Fax: 470-578-9172, E-mail: ksugrad@kennesaw.edu. *Dean,* Dr. Jon Preston, 470-578-5572, E-mail: jprest20@kennesaw.edu.

College of Humanities and Social Sciences Students: 141 full-time (98 women), 200 part-time (140 women); includes 144 minority (105 Black or African American, non-Hispanic/Latino; 10 Asian, non-Hispanic/Latino; 19 Hispanic/Latino; 10 Two or more races, non-Hispanic/Latino), 19 international. Average age 34. 237 applicants, 72% accepted, 136 enrolled. Expenses: Contact institution. *Financial support:* Research assistantships with full tuition reimbursements, teaching assistantships with full tuition reimbursements, Federal Work-Study, and unspecified assistantships available. Support available to part-time students. Financial award applicants required to submit FAFSA. In 2018, 70 master's, 7 doctorates awarded. *Program availability:* Part-time, evening/weekend, 100% online. Offers American studies (MA); conflict management (MSCM); criminal justice (MS); humanities and social sciences (MA, MAPW, MPA, MS, MSCM, PhD); integrated global communication (MA); international conflict management (PhD); international policy management (MS); professional writing (MAPW); public administration (MPA). *Application deadline:* For fall admission, 6/1 priority date for domestic and international students; for spring admission, 10/1 priority date for domestic and international students. Applications are processed on a rolling basis. *Application fee:* $60. Electronic applications accepted. *Application Contact:* Admissions Counselor, 470-578-4377, Fax: 470-578-9172, E-mail: ksugrad@kennesaw.edu.

College of Science and Mathematics Students: 61 full-time (28 women), 33 part-time (16 women); includes 29 minority (14 Black or African American, non-Hispanic/Latino; 6 Asian, non-Hispanic/Latino; 6 Hispanic/Latino; 1 Native Hawaiian or other Pacific Islander, non-Hispanic/Latino; 2 Two or more races, non-Hispanic/Latino), 4 international. Average age 31. 178 applicants, 44% accepted, 53 enrolled. Expenses: Contact institution. *Financial support:* Research assistantships with full tuition reimbursements, Federal Work-Study, and unspecified assistantships available. Support available to part-time students. Financial award applicants required to submit FAFSA. In 2018, 39 master's awarded. *Program availability:* Part-time, 100% online, blended/hybrid learning. Offers applied statistics (MSAS); biochemistry (MS); chemistry (MS); integrative biology (MS); science and mathematics (MS, MSAS). *Application deadline:* For fall admission, 6/1 for domestic and international students; for spring admission, 10/1 for domestic and international students. Applications are processed on a rolling basis. *Application fee:* $60. Electronic applications accepted. *Application Contact:* Admissions Counselor, 470-578-4377, Fax: 470-578-9172, E-mail: ksugrad@kennesaw.edu. *Interim Dean,* Dr. Don McGarey.

Southern Polytechnic College of Engineering and Engineering Technology Students: 31 full-time (9 women), 158 part-time (46 women); includes 80 minority (39 Black or African American, non-Hispanic/Latino; 17 Asian, non-Hispanic/Latino; 16 Hispanic/Latino; 8 Two or more races, non-Hispanic/Latino), 8 international. Average age 35. 178 applicants, 44% accepted, 53 enrolled. Expenses: Contact institution. *Financial support:* Research assistantships with tuition reimbursements, teaching assistantships with partial tuition reimbursements, career-related internships or fieldwork, scholarships/grants, and unspecified assistantships available. Support available to part-time students. Financial award applicants required to submit FAFSA. In 2018, 47 master's awarded. *Program availability:* Part-time, evening/weekend, online learning. Offers electrical engineering (MS); engineering and engineering technology (MS); engineering management (MS); environmental engineering (MS); geotechnical engineering (MS); mechanical engineering (MS); quality assurance (MS); structural engineering (MS); systems engineering (MS); transportation and pavement engineering (MS); water resources engineering (MS). *Application deadline:* For fall admission, 7/1 priority date for domestic students, 5/1 priority date for international students; for spring admission, 11/1 priority date for domestic students, 9/1 priority date for international students. Applications are processed on a rolling basis. *Application fee:* $60. Electronic applications accepted. *Application Contact:* Admissions Counselor, 470-578-4377, E-mail: ksugrad@kennesaw.edu.

University College Students: 3 full-time (all women), 7 part-time (4 women); includes 4 minority (3 Black or African American, non-Hispanic/Latino; 1 American Indian or Alaska Native, non-Hispanic/Latino). Average age 39. Expenses: Contact institution. *Financial support:* Applicants required to submit FAFSA. In 2018, 6 master's awarded. Offers first-year studies (MS). *Application fee:* $60. *Application Contact:* Admissions Counselor, 770-420-4377, Fax: 770-423-6885, E-mail: ksugrad@kennesaw.edu.

WellStar College of Health and Human Services Students: 175 full-time (141 women), 60 part-time (53 women); includes 86 minority (55 Black or African American, non-Hispanic/Latino; 9 Asian, non-Hispanic/Latino; 13 Hispanic/Latino; 9 Two or more races, non-Hispanic/Latino), 4 international. Average age 31. 228 applicants, 74% accepted, 121 enrolled. Expenses: Contact institution. *Financial support:* Research assistantships with full tuition reimbursements and Federal Work-Study available. Support available to part-time students. Financial award applicants required to submit FAFSA. In 2018, 78 master's, 2 doctorates awarded. *Program availability:* Part-time, evening/weekend, online learning. Offers exercise physiology (MS); health and human services (MS, MSN, MSW, DNS); nursing administration (MSN); nursing education (MSN); nursing science (DNS); primary care nurse practitioner (MSN); social work (MSW); sport management (MS). *Application deadline:* For fall admission, 6/1 for domestic and international students. *Application fee:* $60. Electronic applications accepted. *Application Contact:* Admissions Counselor, 470-578-4377, Fax: 470-578-9172, E-mail: ksugrad@kennesaw.edu. *Dean,* Dr. Mark Tillman, 470-578-6565, E-mail: mtillm13@kennesaw.edu.

KENRICK-GLENNON SEMINARY, St. Louis, MO 63119-4330

General Information Independent-religious, men only, graduate-only institution. *Graduate housing:* Room and/or apartments available to single students; on-campus housing not available to married students.

GRADUATE UNITS

Graduate and Professional Programs Offers theology (M Div, MA).

KENT STATE UNIVERSITY, Kent, OH 44242-0001

General Information State-supported, coed, university. CGS member. *Enrollment:* 3,040 full-time matriculated graduate/professional students (1,841 women), 2,287 part-time matriculated graduate/professional students (1,669 women). *Enrollment by degree level:* 3,542 master's, 1,633 doctoral, 152 other advanced degrees. *Graduate faculty:* 667. *International tuition:* $21,952 full-time. Tuition, state resident: full-time $11,766; part-time $536 per credit. Tuition, nonresident: full-time $21,952; part-time $999 per credit. Tuition and fees vary according to course load. *Graduate housing:* Room and/or apartments available on a first-come, first-served basis to single students; on-campus housing not available to married students. *Student services:* Campus employment opportunities, campus safety program, career counseling, child daycare facilities, exercise/wellness program, free psychological counseling, grant writing training, international student services, low-cost health insurance, multicultural affairs office, services for students with disabilities, teacher training, writing training. *Library facilities:* Kent State University Main Library plus 4 others. *Collection:* Books: 3 million (physical), 1.2 million (digital/electronic); Serial titles: 35,857 (physical), 14,996 (digital/electronic); Databases: 355. Weekly public service hours: 146; study areas open 24 hours, 5–7 days a week; students can reserve study rooms.

Computer facilities: Computer purchase and lease plans are available. A campuswide network can be accessed from student residence rooms and from off campus. Online class registration is available.
Website: http://www.kent.edu/

General Application Contact: Lana Whitehead, Director of Graduate Admissions, 330-672-6336, E-mail: lwhiteh2@kent.edu.

GRADUATE UNITS

College of Aeronautics and Engineering Students: 27 full-time (5 women), 21 part-time (3 women); includes 2 minority (both Hispanic/Latino), 27 international. Average age 27. 49 applicants, 82% accepted, 14 enrolled. *Faculty:* 11 full-time (0 women), 2 part-time/adjunct (1 woman). Expenses: Contact institution. *Financial support:* Research assistantships, teaching assistantships, career-related internships or fieldwork, Federal Work-Study, scholarships/grants, and unspecified assistantships available. Financial award application deadline: 2/1; financial award applicants required to submit FAFSA. In 2018, 63 master's awarded. *Program availability:* Part-time, 100% online. Offers technology (MTC). *Application deadline:* For fall admission, 7/23 for domestic and international students; for spring admission, 12/14 for domestic and international students; for summer admission, 4/30 for domestic and international students. Applications are processed on a rolling basis. *Application fee:* $45 ($70 for international students). Electronic applications accepted. *Application Contact:* Richard Mangrum, Coordinator, Graduate Program, 330-672-1933, E-mail: rmangum@kent.edu. *Dean,* Christina Bloebaum, 330-672-9780, E-mail: cbloebau@kent.edu.

College of Architecture and Environmental Design Students: 75 full-time (39 women), 6 part-time (2 women); includes 7 minority (2 Black or African American, non-Hispanic/Latino; 1 Asian, non-Hispanic/Latino; 3 Hispanic/Latino; 1 Two or more races, non-Hispanic/Latino), 12 international. Average age 26. 110 applicants, 85% accepted, 64 enrolled. *Faculty:* 15 full-time (4 women), 8 part-time/adjunct (2 women). Expenses: Contact institution. *Financial support:* Research assistantships with full tuition reimbursements, teaching assistantships with full tuition reimbursements, Federal Work-Study, scholarships/grants, and unspecified assistantships available. Financial award application deadline: 2/1; financial award applicants required to submit FAFSA. In 2018, 43 master's awarded. *Program availability:* Part-time. Offers architecture (M Arch); architecture and environmental design (MS); health care design (MHCD); landscape architecture (MLA); urban design (MUD). *Application deadline:* For fall admission, 1/15 for domestic students; for winter admission, 6/1 for domestic students; for spring admission, 6/1 for domestic students. Applications are processed on a rolling basis. *Application fee:* $45 ($70 for international students). Electronic applications accepted. *Application Contact:* Johnathan Fleming, Assistant Professor and Director, Master of Architecture, 330-672-0934, E-mail: jpflemi1@kent.edu. *Dean,* Mark Mistur, 330-672-2917, E-mail: mmistur1@kent.edu.

College of Arts and Sciences Students: 894 full-time (455 women), 296 part-time (182 women); includes 124 minority (54 Black or African American, non-Hispanic/Latino; 1 American Indian or Alaska Native, non-Hispanic/Latino; 25 Asian, non-Hispanic/Latino; 25 Hispanic/Latino; 19 Two or more races, non-Hispanic/Latino), 383 international. Average age 31. 1,349 applicants, 47% accepted, 291 enrolled. *Faculty:* 285 full-time (101 women), 16 part-time/adjunct (5 women). Expenses: Contact institution. *Financial support:* Fellowships with full tuition reimbursements, research assistantships with full tuition reimbursements, teaching assistantships with full tuition reimbursements, career-related internships or fieldwork, Federal Work-Study, scholarships/grants, and unspecified assistantships available. Financial award application deadline: 2/1; financial award applicants required to submit FAFSA. In 2018, 234 master's, 86 doctorates awarded. *Program availability:* Part-time, 100% online. Offers anthropology (MA); applied geology (PhD); applied mathematics (MA, MS, PhD); arts and sciences (MA, MFA, MGIS, MLS, MPA, MS, PhD); biological sciences (MA, MS, PhD); chemical physics (MS, PhD); chemistry (MA, MS, PhD); clinical psychology (MA, PhD); computer science (MA, MS, PhD); creative writing (MFA); criminology and criminal justice (MA); English (MA, PhD); English for teachers (MA); experimental psychology (MA, PhD); French (MA); geographic information science (MGIS); geography (MA, PhD); geology (MS); German (MA); history (MA, PhD); Latin (MA); literature and writing (MA); mathematics for secondary teachers (MA); philosophy (MA); physics (MA, MS, PhD); political science (MA, PhD); public administration (MPA); pure mathematics (MA, MS, PhD); rhetoric and composition (PhD); sociology (MA, PhD); Spanish (MA); teaching English as a second language (MA); translation (MA); translation studies (PhD). *Application deadline:*

Applications are processed on a rolling basis. *Application fee:* $45 ($70 for international students). Electronic applications accepted. *Application Contact:* Dr. Manfred Van Dulman, Associate Dean, Graduate Studies, 330-672-8973, E-mail: mvandul@kent.edu. *Dean,* Dr. James L. Blank, 330-672-2650, E-mail: jblank@kent.edu.

Center for Comparative and Integrative Programs Students: 4 full-time (2 women), 5 part-time (3 women); includes 2 minority (1 Black or African American, non-Hispanic/Latino; 1 Hispanic/Latino). Average age 30. 8 applicants, 100% accepted, 5 enrolled. *Faculty:* 1 full-time. Expenses: Contact institution. *Financial support:* Career-related internships or fieldwork and Federal Work-Study available. Financial award application deadline: 2/1; financial award applicants required to submit FAFSA. In 2018, 1 master's awarded. *Program availability:* Part-time, 100% online. Offers comparative and integrative programs (MLS). *Application deadline:* For fall admission, 6/15 for domestic and international students; for spring admission, 11/29 for domestic and international students. Applications are processed on a rolling basis. *Application fee:* $45 ($70 for international students). Electronic applications accepted. *Application Contact:* Dr. David W. Odell-Scott, Director of Center for Comparative and Integrative Programs, 330-672-0271, E-mail: dodellsc@kent.edu. *Director of Center for Comparative and Integrative Programs,* Dr. David W. Odell-Scott, 330-672-0271, E-mail: dodellsc@kent.edu.

School of Biomedical Sciences Students: 75 full-time (47 women); includes 11 minority (2 Black or African American, non-Hispanic/Latino; 3 Asian, non-Hispanic/Latino; 3 Hispanic/Latino; 3 Two or more races, non-Hispanic/Latino), 23 international. Average age 28. 64 applicants, 28% accepted, 12 enrolled. *Faculty:* 22 full-time (9 women). Expenses: Contact institution. *Financial support:* Research assistantships with full tuition reimbursements, teaching assistantships, and unspecified assistantships available. Financial award application deadline: 1/1. In 2018, 1 master's, 12 doctorates awarded. Offers biological anthropology (PhD); biomedical mathematics (MS, PhD); cellular and molecular biology (MS, PhD); neurosciences (MS, PhD); pharmacology (MS, PhD); physiology (MS, PhD). *Application deadline:* For fall admission, 1/1 for domestic students, 12/15 for international students. Applications are processed on a rolling basis. *Application fee:* $45 ($70 for international students). Electronic applications accepted. *Application Contact:* Dr. Ernest J. Freeman, Director, School of Biomedical Sciences, 330-672-2363, E-mail: efreema2@kent.edu. *Director, School of Biomedical Sciences,* Dr. Ernest J. Freeman, 330-672-2363, E-mail: efreema2@kent.edu.

College of Business Administration Students: 169 full-time (72 women), 62 part-time (33 women); includes 17 minority (8 Black or African American, non-Hispanic/Latino; 1 Asian, non-Hispanic/Latino; 1 Hispanic/Latino; 7 Two or more races, non-Hispanic/Latino), 78 international. Average age 30. 325 applicants, 68% accepted, 130 enrolled. *Faculty:* 53 full-time (18 women). Expenses: Contact institution. *Financial support:* In 2018–19, 13 research assistantships with full tuition reimbursements (averaging $5,200 per year), 35 teaching assistantships with full tuition reimbursements (averaging $23,000 per year) were awarded; fellowships with full tuition reimbursements, career-related internships or fieldwork, Federal Work-Study, and unspecified assistantships also available. Financial award applicants required to submit FAFSA. In 2018, 98 master's, 8 doctorates awarded. *Program availability:* Part-time, evening/weekend. Offers accounting (MS, PhD); business administration (MA, MBA, MS, MSBA, PhD); business analytics (MS); economics (MA); finance (PhD); management systems (PhD); marketing (PhD). *Application fee:* $45 ($70 for international students). Electronic applications accepted. *Application Contact:* Louise M. Ditchey, Administrative Director, 330-672-2282, Fax: 330-672-7303, E-mail: gradbus@kent.edu. *Associate Dean for Graduate Programs,* Dr. Cathy L.Z. Dubois, 330-672-1103, E-mail: cdubois@kent.edu.

College of Communication and Information Students: 245 full-time (183 women), 586 part-time (412 women); includes 100 minority (48 Black or African American, non-Hispanic/Latino; 1 American Indian or Alaska Native, non-Hispanic/Latino; 12 Asian, non-Hispanic/Latino; 25 Hispanic/Latino; 1 Native Hawaiian or other Pacific Islander, non-Hispanic/Latino; 13 Two or more races, non-Hispanic/Latino), 52 international. Average age 33. 347 applicants, 91% accepted, 196 enrolled. *Faculty:* 53 full-time (34 women), 23 part-time/adjunct (10 women). Expenses: Contact institution. *Financial support:* Fellowships with full tuition reimbursements, research assistantships with full tuition reimbursements, teaching assistantships with full tuition reimbursements, career-related internships or fieldwork, Federal Work-Study, scholarships/grants, and unspecified assistantships available. Financial award application deadline: 1/15; financial award applicants required to submit FAFSA. In 2018, 496 master's awarded. *Program availability:* Part-time, online learning. Offers communication and information (MA, MDS, MFA, MLIS, MS). *Application deadline:* For fall admission, 1/15 for domestic students, 12/15 for international students; for spring admission, 11/25 for domestic students, 10/25 for international students. Applications are processed on a rolling basis. *Application fee:* $45 ($70 for international students). Electronic applications accepted. *Application Contact:* Nzinga Hart, Graduate Academic Program Coordinator, 330-672-2502, E-mail: nbodden@kent.edu. *Professor and Dean,* Amy Reynolds, 330-672-2950, E-mail: areyno24@kent.edu.

School of Communication Studies Students: 14 full-time (9 women), 5 part-time (all women); includes 1 minority (Hispanic/Latino), 4 international. Average age 27. 273 applicants, 58% accepted, 37 enrolled. *Faculty:* 18 full-time (2 women), 3 part-time/adjunct (0 women). Expenses: Contact institution. *Financial support:* Research assistantships with full tuition reimbursements, teaching assistantships with full tuition reimbursements, career-related internships or fieldwork, and unspecified assistantships available. Financial award application deadline: 1/15. In 2018, 16 master's awarded. *Program availability:* Part-time. Offers communication studies (MA). *Application deadline:* For fall admission, 1/15 for domestic students, 12/25 for international students; for spring admission, 11/15 for domestic students, 10/25 for international students. Applications are processed on a rolling basis. *Application fee:* $45 ($70 for international students). Electronic applications accepted. *Application Contact:* Dr. Suzy D'Enbeau, Associate Professor and Graduate Coordinator, 330-672-3802, E-mail: sdenbeau@kent.edu. *Director,* Dr. Elizabeth E. Graham, 330-672-3087, E-mail: egraha18@kent.edu.

School of Digital Sciences Students: 21 full-time (10 women), 28 part-time (12 women); includes 2 minority (both Black or African American, non-Hispanic/Latino), 28 international. Average age 32. 47 applicants, 72% accepted, 12 enrolled. *Faculty:* 2 full-time (1 woman), 5 part-time/adjunct (2 women). Expenses: Contact institution. *Financial support:* Career-related internships or fieldwork and scholarships/grants available. In 2018, 121 master's awarded. *Program availability:* Part-time. Offers digital sciences (MDS); digital systems management (MDS); digital systems software development (MDS); digital systems telecommunication network (MDS); digital systems training technology (MDS); enterprise architecture (MDS). *Application deadline:* For fall admission, 7/1 for domestic students, 5/15 for international students; for spring admission, 11/15 for domestic students, 10/1 for international students; for summer admission, 4/15 for domestic students, 3/15 for international students.

Applications are processed on a rolling basis. *Application fee:* $45 ($70 for international students). Electronic applications accepted. *Application Contact:* Amy Copus, Academic Advisor II for Graduate Students, 330-672-9105, E-mail: acopus@kent.edu. *Interim Director,* Jeff Fruit, 330-672-9105, E-mail: jfruit@kent.edu.

School of Information Students: 114 full-time (91 women), 235 part-time (162 women); includes 52 minority (24 Black or African American, non-Hispanic/Latino; 8 Asian, non-Hispanic/Latino; 15 Hispanic/Latino; 5 Two or more races, non-Hispanic/Latino; 4 international. Average age 32. 212 applicants, 99% accepted, 147 enrolled. *Faculty:* 16 full-time (13 women), 10 part-time/adjunct (6 women). Expenses: Contact institution. *Financial support:* Fellowships with full tuition reimbursements, research assistantships with full tuition reimbursements, teaching assistantships with full tuition reimbursements, scholarships/grants, and unspecified assistantships available. Financial award application deadline: 3/1. In 2018, 308 master's awarded. *Program availability:* Part-time, 100% online. Offers health informatics (MS); library and information science (MLIS). *Application deadline:* For fall admission, 3/15 priority date for domestic students, 3/15 for international students; for spring admission, 9/15 priority date for domestic students, 9/15 for international students; for summer admission, 1/15 priority date for domestic students, 1/15 for international students. Applications are processed on a rolling basis. *Application fee:* $45 ($70 for international students). Electronic applications accepted. *Application Contact:* Dr. Karen Gracy, Graduate Co-Coordinator/Associate Professor, 330-672-2782, E-mail: kgracy@kent.edu. *Director and Professor,* Dr. Kendra Albright, 330-672-8535, E-mail: kalbrig7@kent.edu.

School of Journalism and Mass Communication Students: 12 full-time (8 women), 44 part-time (29 women); includes 7 minority (5 Black or African American, non-Hispanic/Latino; 1 Hispanic/Latino; 1 Two or more races, non-Hispanic/Latino), 3 international. Average age 36. 23 applicants, 78% accepted, 12 enrolled. *Faculty:* 14 full-time (9 women), 4 part-time/adjunct (2 women). Expenses: Contact institution. *Financial support:* Research assistantships with full tuition reimbursements, teaching assistantships with full tuition reimbursements, scholarships/grants, and unspecified assistantships available. Financial award application deadline: 3/1. In 2018, 41 master's awarded. *Program availability:* Part-time, 100% online. Offers journalism and mass communication (MA). *Application deadline:* For fall admission, 7/1 for domestic and international students. Applications are processed on a rolling basis. *Application fee:* $45 ($70 for international students). Electronic applications accepted. *Application Contact:* Mark Goodman, Graduate Coordinator/Professor, 330-672-6239, E-mail: mgoodm10@kent.edu. *Interim Director and Professor,* Jeff Fruit, 330-672-2572, E-mail: jmc@kent.edu.

School of Visual Communication Design Students: 18 full-time (14 women), 10 part-time (4 women); includes 5 minority (3 Black or African American, non-Hispanic/Latino; 1 Asian, non-Hispanic/Latino; 1 Two or more races, non-Hispanic/Latino), 7 international. Average age 30. 13 applicants, 85% accepted, 6 enrolled. *Faculty:* 8 full-time (5 women), 4 part-time/adjunct. Expenses: Contact institution. *Financial support:* Scholarships/grants and unspecified assistantships available. Financial award application deadline: 3/5; financial award applicants required to submit FAFSA. In 2018, 10 master's awarded. *Program availability:* Part-time. Offers visual communication design (MA, MFA). *Application deadline:* For fall admission, 3/1 for domestic and international students; for spring admission, 10/1 for domestic and international students. Applications are processed on a rolling basis. *Application fee:* $45 ($70 for international students). Electronic applications accepted. *Application Contact:* Ken Visocky O'Grady, Graduate Coordinator and Professor, 330-672-1353, E-mail: kogrady@kent.edu. *Interim Director,* Dr. David Robins, 330-672-2782, E-mail: drobins@kent.edu.

College of Education, Health and Human Services Students: 865 full-time (619 women), 559 part-time (425 women); includes 199 minority (103 Black or African American, non-Hispanic/Latino; 9 American Indian or Alaska Native, non-Hispanic/Latino; 42 Asian, non-Hispanic/Latino; 15 Hispanic/Latino; 27 Native Hawaiian or other Pacific Islander, non-Hispanic/Latino; 3 Two or more races, non-Hispanic/Latino), 91 international. *Faculty:* 188 full-time (116 women), 130 part-time/adjunct (87 women). Expenses: Contact institution. *Financial support:* In 2018–19, 112 research assistantships with full tuition reimbursements (averaging $10,564 per year), 28 teaching assistantships (averaging $11,938 per year) were awarded; scholarships/grants, health care benefits, unspecified assistantships, and 30 administrative assistantships (averaging $10,406 per year) also available. Financial award application deadline: 4/1; financial award applicants required to submit FAFSA. In 2018, 401 master's, 27 doctorates, 62 other advanced degrees awarded. *Program availability:* Part-time, evening/weekend, online learning. Offers education, health and human services (M Ed, MA, MAT, MS, Au D, PhD, Ed S). *Application deadline:* Applications are processed on a rolling basis. *Application fee:* $45 ($60 for international students). Electronic applications accepted. *Application Contact:* Cheryl Slusarczyk, Academic Program Director, Office of Graduate Student Services, 330-672-2576, Fax: 330-672-9162, E-mail: cslusarc@kent.edu. *Dean,* Dr. James Hannon, 330-672-0566, Fax: 330-672-3407, E-mail: jhannon5@kent.edu.

School of Foundations, Leadership and Administration Students: 229 full-time (125 women), 148 part-time (102 women); includes 81 minority (43 Black or African American, non-Hispanic/Latino; 3 American Indian or Alaska Native, non-Hispanic/Latino; 15 Asian, non-Hispanic/Latino; 5 Hispanic/Latino; 14 Native Hawaiian or other Pacific Islander, non-Hispanic/Latino; 1 Two or more races, non-Hispanic/Latino), 38 international. 405 applicants, 40% accepted. *Faculty:* 32 full-time (21 women), 36 part-time/adjunct (15 women). Expenses: Contact institution. *Financial support:* In 2018–19, 31 research assistantships with full tuition reimbursements (averaging $9,855 per year), 5 teaching assistantships with full tuition reimbursements (averaging $12,000 per year) were awarded; Federal Work-Study, scholarships/grants, tuition waivers (full), unspecified assistantships, and 10 administrative assistantships (averaging $9,550 per year) also available. Financial award application deadline: 3/15. In 2018, 94 master's, 4 doctorates, 17 other advanced degrees awarded. Offers cultural foundations (M Ed, MA, PhD); evaluation and measurement (M Ed, PhD); higher education (PhD, Ed S); higher education and student personnel (M Ed); hospitality and tourism management (MS); K-12 leadership (M Ed, PhD, Ed S); sport and recreation management (MA); sports recreation and management (MA); sports studies (MA). *Application deadline:* Applications are processed on a rolling basis. *Application fee:* $45 ($60 for international students). Electronic applications accepted. *Application Contact:* Cheryl Slusarczyk, Academic Program Director, 330-672-2576, Fax: 330-672-9162, E-mail: ogs@kent.edu. *Director,* Dr. Kim Schimmel, 330-672-0232, Fax: 330-672-3063, E-mail: kschimme@kent.edu.

School of Health Sciences Students: 179 full-time (134 women), 63 part-time (47 women); includes 29 minority (14 Black or African American, non-Hispanic/Latino; 9 Asian, non-Hispanic/Latino; 1 Hispanic/Latino; 4 Native Hawaiian or other Pacific Islander, non-Hispanic/Latino; 1 Two or more races, non-Hispanic/Latino), 20

international. 504 applicants, 33% accepted. *Faculty:* 42 full-time (33 women), 7 part-time/adjunct (5 women). Expenses: Contact institution. *Financial support:* In 2018–19, 25 research assistantships with full tuition reimbursements (averaging $9,760 per year), 12 teaching assistantships with full tuition reimbursements (averaging $10,250 per year) were awarded; Federal Work-Study, scholarships/grants, unspecified assistantships, and 1 administrative assistantship (averaging $12,000 per year) also available. Financial award application deadline: 4/1; financial award applicants required to submit FAFSA. In 2018, 74 master's, 7 doctorates awarded. *Program availability:* Part-time, evening/weekend. Offers athletic training (MS); audiology (Au D, PhD); exercise physiology (MS, PhD); health education and promotion (M Ed, PhD); nutrition (MS); speech language pathology (MA, PhD). *Application deadline:* Applications are processed on a rolling basis. *Application fee:* $45 ($60 for international students). Electronic applications accepted. *Application Contact:* Cheryl Slusarczyk, Academic Program Director, Office of Graduate Student Services, 330-672-2576, Fax: 330-672-9162, E-mail: ogs@kent.edu. *Director,* Dr. Ellen Glickman, 330-672-0575, E-mail: eglickma@kent.edu.

School of Lifespan Development and Educational Sciences Students: 341 full-time (272 women), 238 part-time (193 women); includes 66 minority (40 Black or African American, non-Hispanic/Latino; 5 American Indian or Alaska Native, non-Hispanic/Latino; 5 Asian, non-Hispanic/Latino; 8 Hispanic/Latino; 7 Native Hawaiian or other Pacific Islander, non-Hispanic/Latino; 1 Two or more races, non-Hispanic/Latino), 16 international. 461 applicants, 35% accepted. *Faculty:* 71 full-time (37 women), 80 part-time/adjunct (61 women). Expenses: Contact institution. *Financial support:* In 2018–19, 35 research assistantships with full tuition reimbursements (averaging $10,000 per year), 8 teaching assistantships with full tuition reimbursements (averaging $12,000 per year) were awarded; Federal Work-Study, scholarships/grants, unspecified assistantships, and 16 administrative assistantships (averaging $9,594 per year) also available. Financial award application deadline: 4/1. In 2018, 162 master's, 21 doctorates, 14 other advanced degrees awarded. *Program availability:* Part-time, evening/weekend. Offers clinical mental health counseling (M Ed); counseling (Ed S); counseling and human development services (PhD); deaf education (M Ed); early childhood education (M Ed); educational interpreter K-12 (M Ed); educational psychology (M Ed, MA); general special education (M Ed); human development and family studies (MA); instructional technology (M Ed, PhD); mild/moderate intervention (M Ed); rehabilitation counseling (M Ed); school counseling (M Ed); school psychology (PhD, Ed S); special education (M Ed, PhD, Ed S); transition to work (M Ed). *Application deadline:* Applications are processed on a rolling basis. *Application fee:* $45 ($60 for international students). Electronic applications accepted. *Application Contact:* Cheryl Slusarczyk, Academic Program Director, Office of Graduate Student Services, 330-672-2576, Fax: 330-672-9162, E-mail: ogs@kent.edu. *Director,* Dr. Mary Dellmann-Jenkins, 330-672-6958, E-mail: mdellman@kent.edu.

School of Teaching, Learning and Curriculum Studies Students: 116 full-time (88 women), 110 part-time (83 women); includes 23 minority (6 Black or African American, non-Hispanic/Latino; 1 American Indian or Alaska Native, non-Hispanic/Latino; 13 Asian, non-Hispanic/Latino; 1 Hispanic/Latino; 2 Native Hawaiian or other Pacific Islander, non-Hispanic/Latino), 17 international. 202 applicants, 35% accepted. *Faculty:* 43 full-time (25 women), 7 part-time/adjunct (6 women). Expenses: Contact institution. *Financial support:* In 2018–19, 21 research assistantships with full tuition reimbursements (averaging $12,642 per year), 3 teaching assistantships with full tuition reimbursements (averaging $13,500 per year) were awarded; Federal Work-Study, scholarships/grants, unspecified assistantships, and 3 administrative assistantships (averaging $10,500 per year) also available. Financial award application deadline: 4/1. In 2018, 71 master's, 13 doctorates, 2 other advanced degrees awarded. *Program availability:* Part-time, evening/weekend. Offers career technical teacher education (M Ed); curriculum and instruction (M Ed, PhD, Ed S); early childhood education (M Ed, MA, MAT); junior high/middle school (M Ed, MA); math specialization (M Ed, MA); reading specialization (M Ed, MA); secondary education (MAT). *Application deadline:* Applications are processed on a rolling basis. *Application fee:* $45 ($60 for international students). Electronic applications accepted. *Application Contact:* Cheryl Slusarczyk, Academic Program Director, Office of Graduate Student Services, 330-672-2576, Fax: 330-672-9162, E-mail: ogs@kent.edu. *Director,* Dr. Alexa Sandmann, 330-672-0652, E-mail: asandman@kent.edu.

College of Nursing Students: 168 full-time (147 women), 484 part-time (422 women); includes 65 minority (30 Black or African American, non-Hispanic/Latino; 12 Asian, non-Hispanic/Latino; 12 Hispanic/Latino; 1 Native Hawaiian or other Pacific Islander, non-Hispanic/Latino; 10 Two or more races, non-Hispanic/Latino), 7 international. Average age 34. 360 applicants, 71% accepted, 194 enrolled. *Faculty:* 28 full-time (27 women), 11 part-time/adjunct (9 women). Expenses: Contact institution. *Financial support:* Federal Work-Study and scholarships/grants available. Financial award application deadline: 2/1. In 2018, 130 master's, 14 doctorates awarded. *Program availability:* Part-time, online learning. Offers advanced nursing practice (DNP); nursing (MSN, PhD). *Application deadline:* For fall admission, 3/1 for domestic and international students; for spring admission, 10/1 for domestic and international students. Applications are processed on a rolling basis. *Application fee:* $45 ($70 for international students). Electronic applications accepted. *Application Contact:* Dr. Wendy A. Umberger, Associate Dean for Graduate Programs/Professor, 330-672-8813, E-mail: wlewando@kent.edu. *Dean,* Dr. Barbara Broome, 330-672-3777, E-mail: bbroome1@kent.edu.

College of Podiatric Medicine Students: 417 full-time (166 women); includes 118 minority (34 Black or African American, non-Hispanic/Latino; 1 American Indian or Alaska Native, non-Hispanic/Latino; 75 Asian, non-Hispanic/Latino; 7 Hispanic/Latino; 1 Native Hawaiian or other Pacific Islander, non-Hispanic/Latino), 13 international. Average age 27. 572 applicants, 40% accepted, 109 enrolled. *Faculty:* 18 full-time (7 women), 6 part-time/adjunct (3 women). Expenses: Contact institution. *Financial support:* Career-related internships or fieldwork, Federal Work-Study, institutionally sponsored loans, and scholarships/grants available. Financial award applicants required to submit FAFSA. In 2018, 105 doctorates awarded. Offers podiatric medicine (DPM). *Application deadline:* For fall admission, 7/31 priority date for domestic students, 7/31 for international students. Applications are processed on a rolling basis. *Application fee:* $180. Electronic applications accepted. *Application Contact:* Carla Ronnenbaum, Director, Enrollment Management, 216-9167488, E-mail: cronneba@kent.edu. *Dean,* Dr. Allan Boike, 216-231-3300, E-mail: aboike1@kent.edu.

College of Public Health Students: 136 full-time (95 women), 178 part-time (140 women); includes 71 minority (47 Black or African American, non-Hispanic/Latino; 10 Asian, non-Hispanic/Latino; 6 Hispanic/Latino; 8 Two or more races, non-Hispanic/Latino), 45 international. Average age 32. 197 applicants, 85% accepted, 112 enrolled. *Faculty:* 20 full-time (10 women), 1 part-time/adjunct (0 women). Expenses: Contact institution. *Financial support:* Career-related internships or fieldwork, Federal Work-Study, scholarships/grants, and unspecified assistantships available. In 2018, 77 master's, 6 doctorates awarded. *Program availability:* Part-time, 100% online. Offers public health (MPH, PhD). *Application deadline:* For fall admission, 6/15 for domestic and international students; for spring admission, 10/15 for domestic and international students; for summer admission, 3/15 for domestic and international students. Applications are processed on a rolling basis. *Application fee:* $45 ($70 for international students). Electronic applications accepted. *Application Contact:* Dr. Jeffrey S. Hallam, Professor/Associate Dean for Research and Graduate Studies, 330-672-0679, E-mail: jhallam1@kent.edu. *Dean and Professor of Health Policy and Management,* Dr. Sonia Alemagno, 330-672-6500, E-mail: salemagn@kent.edu.

College of the Arts Students: 129 full-time (74 women), 188 part-time (128 women); includes 29 minority (13 Black or African American, non-Hispanic/Latino; 3 Asian, non-Hispanic/Latino; 5 Hispanic/Latino; 1 Native Hawaiian or other Pacific Islander, non-Hispanic/Latino; 7 Two or more races, non-Hispanic/Latino), 37 international. Average age 31. 174 applicants, 83% accepted, 98 enrolled. *Faculty:* 60 full-time (27 women), 26 part-time/adjunct (17 women). Expenses: Contact institution. *Financial support:* Research assistantships with full tuition reimbursements, teaching assistantships with full tuition reimbursements, scholarships/grants, and unspecified assistantships available. Financial award application deadline: 2/2. In 2018, 112 master's, 2 doctorates awarded. *Program availability:* Part-time, 100% online. Offers arts (MA, MFA, MM, PhD). *Application deadline:* For fall admission, 2/2 for domestic and international students; for spring admission, 10/15 for domestic and international students. Applications are processed on a rolling basis. *Application fee:* $45 ($70 for international students). Electronic applications accepted. *Application Contact:* Yuko Kurahashi, Graduate Coordinator, 330-672-9483, E-mail: ykurahashi@kent.edu. *Dean and Professor,* Dr. John R. Crawford-Spinelli, 330-672-2760, E-mail: jcrawfo1@kent.edu.

Hugh A. Glauser School of Music Students: 70 full-time (35 women), 160 part-time (104 women); includes 22 minority (11 Black or African American, non-Hispanic/Latino; 2 Asian, non-Hispanic/Latino; 3 Hispanic/Latino; 1 Native Hawaiian or other Pacific Islander, non-Hispanic/Latino; 5 Two or more races, non-Hispanic/Latino), 30 international. Average age 31. 91 applicants, 85% accepted, 57 enrolled. *Faculty:* 29 full-time (8 women), 24 part-time/adjunct (16 women). Expenses: Contact institution. *Financial support:* Teaching assistantships with full and partial tuition reimbursements, scholarships/grants, and unspecified assistantships available. Financial award application deadline: 4/1. In 2018, 82 master's, 2 doctorates awarded. *Program availability:* Part-time, 100% online. Offers conducting (MM); ethnomusicology (MA); music composition (MA); music education (MM, PhD); music theory (MA); music theory-composition (PhD); performance (MM). *Application deadline:* For fall admission, 2/9 priority date for domestic and international students. Applications are processed on a rolling basis. *Application fee:* $45 ($70 for international students). Electronic applications accepted. *Application Contact:* Michael Chunn, Graduate Coordinator/Trumpet Professor, 330-672-9234, Fax: 330-672-7837, E-mail: mchunn@kent.edu. *Interim Director and Voice-Professor,* Jane Dressler, 330-672-9239, E-mail: jdressle@kent.edu.

School of Art Students: 34 full-time (23 women), 27 part-time (24 women); includes 1 minority (Black or African American, non-Hispanic/Latino), 1 international. Average age 31. 41 applicants, 73% accepted, 16 enrolled. *Faculty:* 17 full-time (10 women), 1 (woman) part-time/adjunct. Expenses: Contact institution. *Financial support:* Career-related internships or fieldwork, scholarships/grants, and unspecified assistantships available. Financial award application deadline: 3/16. In 2018, 22 master's awarded. *Program availability:* Part-time, 100% online, blended/hybrid learning. Offers art education (MA); art history (MA); crafts (MA); fine arts (MA); studio art (MFA). *Application deadline:* For fall admission, 2/2 priority date for domestic students, 2/2 for international students; for spring admission, 10/15 for domestic and international students. Applications are processed on a rolling basis. *Application fee:* $45 ($70 for international students). Electronic applications accepted. *Application Contact:* Peter Christian Johnson, Graduate Coordinator and Associate Professor Ceramics, 330-672-3360, E-mail: pjohns35@kent.edu. *Director,* Marie Bukowski, 330-672-2192, E-mail: mbukows1@kent.edu.

School of Theatre and Dance Students: 17 full-time (8 women), 1 part-time (0 women); includes 3 minority (1 Black or African American, non-Hispanic/Latino; 1 Asian, non-Hispanic/Latino; 1 Two or more races, non-Hispanic/Latino), 3 international. Average age 37. 19 applicants, 84% accepted, 10 enrolled. *Faculty:* 10 full-time (5 women), 1 part-time/adjunct (0 women). Expenses: Contact institution. *Financial support:* Teaching assistantships with full tuition reimbursements, career-related internships or fieldwork, Federal Work-Study, scholarships/grants, and unspecified assistantships available. Financial award application deadline: 5/1. In 2018, 8 master's awarded. *Program availability:* Part-time. Offers theatre studies (MFA). *Application deadline:* Applications are processed on a rolling basis. *Application fee:* $45 ($70 for international students). Electronic applications accepted. *Application Contact:* Yuko Kurahashi, Graduate Coordinator and Associate Professor of Theatre, 330-672-9483, E-mail: ykurahas@kent.edu. *Director and Associate Professor,* Eric van Baars, 330-672-0102, E-mail: fvanbaar@kent.edu.

KENT STATE UNIVERSITY AT STARK, Canton, OH 44720-7599

General Information State-supported, coed, comprehensive institution.

GRADUATE UNITS

Graduate School of Education, Health and Human Services Offers curriculum and instruction studies (M Ed, MA).

Professional MBA Program Offers business administration (MBA).

KENTUCKY CHRISTIAN UNIVERSITY, Grayson, KY 41143-2205

General Information Independent-religious, coed, comprehensive institution. *Graduate housing:* Rooms and/or apartments available on a first-come, first-served basis to single and married students.

GRADUATE UNITS

Graduate School *Program availability:* Part-time. Offers Biblical studies (MA); Christian leadership (MA). Electronic applications accepted.

KENTUCKY STATE UNIVERSITY, Frankfort, KY 40601

General Information State-related, coed, comprehensive institution. *Enrollment:* 60 full-time matriculated graduate/professional students (27 women), 54 part-time matriculated graduate/professional students (33 women). *Enrollment by degree level:* 109 master's, 5 doctoral. *Graduate faculty:* 39 full-time (12 women), 1 (woman) part-time/adjunct. *International tuition:* $11,550 full-time. *Tuition, area resident:* Full-time $7560; part-time $420 per credit hour. *Tuition, state resident:* full-time $7560; part-time $420 per credit hour. *Tuition, nonresident:* full-time $11,550; part-time $630 per credit hour. Tuition and fees vary according to course load. *Graduate housing:* Room and/or apartments available on a first-come, first-served basis to single students; on-campus housing not available to married students. Typical cost: $3340 per year ($6690 including board). Room and board charges vary according to board plan and housing facility selected.

Housing application deadline: 6/1. *Student services:* Campus safety program, career counseling, exercise/wellness program, international student services, services for students with disabilities. *Library facilities:* Paul G. Blazer Library. *Collection:* Books: 170,726 (physical), 23,417 (digital/electronic); Serial titles: 1,894 (physical), 38,647 (digital/electronic); Databases: 56. Weekly public service hours: 101; study areas open 24 hours, 5–7 days a week. *Research affiliation:* National Science Foundation (Brain Neuron simulation; Promoting STEM minority), Verison (Innovative learning program), NASA (Signal processing simulation), Alltech (Aquaculture).

Computer facilities: 142 computers available on campus for general student use. A campuswide network can be accessed from student residence rooms and from off campus. Online class registration, student bill-pay, address verification, ability to accept financial aid awards are available.
Website: http://www.kysu.edu/

General Application Contact: Dr. Ken Andries, Interim Director of Graduate Programs, 502-597-5094, E-mail: kenneth.andries@kysu.edu.

GRADUATE UNITS

Program in Aquaculture Students: 9 full-time (2 women), 8 part-time (6 women); includes 2 minority (both Black or African American, non-Hispanic/Latino), 3 international. Average age 29. 5 applicants, 80% accepted, 3 enrolled. *Faculty:* 7 full-time (0 women). Expenses: Contact institution. *Financial support:* In 2018–19, 11 students received support, including 8 research assistantships (averaging $23,375 per year); scholarships/grants and unspecified assistantships also available. Financial award application deadline: 6/30; financial award applicants required to submit FAFSA. *Program availability:* Evening/weekend. *Application deadline:* For fall admission, 7/1 for domestic and international students; for spring admission, 11/15 for domestic and international students; for summer admission, 5/1 for domestic and international students. Applications are processed on a rolling basis. *Application fee:* $30 ($100 for international students). Electronic applications accepted. *Application Contact:* Dr. James H Tidwell, Chair, 502-597-8104, Fax: 502-597-8118, E-mail: james.tidwell@kysu.edu. *Chair,* Dr. James H Tidwell, 502-597-8104, Fax: 502-597-8118, E-mail: james.tidwell@kysu.edu.

Program in Business Administration Students: 5 full-time (3 women), 9 part-time (3 women); includes 7 minority (all Black or African American, non-Hispanic/Latino), 1 international. Average age 31. 5 applicants, 60% accepted, 2 enrolled. *Faculty:* 7 full-time. Expenses: Contact institution. *Financial support:* In 2018–19, 13 students received support, including 1 research assistantship (averaging $23,833 per year); scholarships/grants and unspecified assistantships also available. Financial award application deadline: 6/30; financial award applicants required to submit FAFSA. *Program availability:* Part-time, evening/weekend. *Application deadline:* For fall admission, 7/1 for domestic and international students; for spring admission, 11/15 for domestic and international students; for summer admission, 5/1 for domestic and international students. Applications are processed on a rolling basis. *Application fee:* $30 ($100 for international students). Electronic applications accepted. *Application Contact:* Dr. James Obielodan, Interim Chair, 502-597-6915, E-mail: james.obielodan@kysu.edu. *Interim Chair,* Dr. James Obielodan, 502-597-6915, E-mail: james.obielodan@kysu.edu.

Program in Computer Science Technology Students: 2 full-time (both women), 5 part-time (2 women); includes 4 minority (2 Black or African American, non-Hispanic/Latino; 2 Asian, non-Hispanic/Latino), 1 international. Average age 34. 6 applicants, 50% accepted, 1 enrolled. *Faculty:* 4 full-time (1 woman). Expenses: Contact institution. *Financial support:* In 2018–19, 4 students received support, including 1 research assistantship (averaging $13,519 per year); scholarships/grants and unspecified assistantships also available. Financial award application deadline: 6/30; financial award applicants required to submit FAFSA. *Program availability:* Evening/weekend. *Application deadline:* For fall admission, 7/1 for domestic and international students; for spring admission, 11/15 for domestic and international students; for summer admission, 5/1 for domestic and international students. Applications are processed on a rolling basis. *Application fee:* $30 ($100 for international students). Electronic applications accepted. *Application Contact:* Dr. Mike Unuakhalu, Coordinator, 502-597-6382, Fax: 502-597-6179, E-mail: mike.unuakhalu@kysu.edu. *Chair,* Dr. Chi Shen, 502-597-6083, Fax: 502-597-6179, E-mail: chi.shen@kysu.edu.

Program in Environmental Studies Students: 18 full-time (4 women), 10 part-time (8 women); includes 4 minority (3 Black or African American, non-Hispanic/Latino; 1 Hispanic/Latino), 9 international. Average age 32. 10 applicants, 70% accepted, 4 enrolled. *Faculty:* 5 full-time (1 woman). Expenses: Contact institution. *Financial support:* In 2018–19, 22 students received support, including 7 research assistantships (averaging $23,310 per year); scholarships/grants and unspecified assistantships also available. Financial award application deadline: 6/30; financial award applicants required to submit FAFSA. *Program availability:* Evening/weekend. *Application deadline:* For fall admission, 7/1 for domestic and international students; for spring admission, 11/15 for domestic and international students; for summer admission, 5/1 for domestic and international students. Applications are processed on a rolling basis. *Application fee:* $30 ($100 for international students). Electronic applications accepted. *Application Contact:* Dr. John Sedlacek, Chair, 502-597-6582. *Chair,* Dr. John Sedlacek, 502-597-6582.

Program in Interdisciplinary Behavioral Science Students: 7 full-time (3 women), 2 part-time (1 woman); includes 6 minority (all Black or African American, non-Hispanic/Latino). Average age 30. 3 applicants, 33% accepted, 1 enrolled. *Faculty:* 5 full-time (4 women). Expenses: Contact institution. *Financial support:* In 2018–19, 8 students received support. Scholarships/grants and unspecified assistantships available. Financial award application deadline: 6/30; financial award applicants required to submit FAFSA. *Program availability:* Part-time, evening/weekend. *Application deadline:* For fall admission, 7/1 for domestic and international students; for spring admission, 11/15 for domestic and international students; for summer admission, 5/1 for domestic and international students. Applications are processed on a rolling basis. *Application fee:* $30 ($100 for international students). Electronic applications accepted. *Application Contact:* Dr. Mara Lee Merlino, 502-597-5053, Fax: 502-597-6714, E-mail: mara.merlino@kysu.edu. *Chair,* Dr. Tierra Freeman Taylor, 502-597-5932, Fax: 502-597-6714, E-mail: tierra.freeman@kysu.edu.

Program in Nursing Practice Students: 5 full-time (4 women); includes 1 minority (Black or African American, non-Hispanic/Latino). Average age 39. 3 applicants, 100% accepted, 1 enrolled. *Faculty:* 4 full-time (all women), 1 (woman) part-time/adjunct. Expenses: Contact institution. *Financial support:* In 2018–19, 3 students received support. Scholarships/grants available. Financial award application deadline: 6/30; financial award applicants required to submit FAFSA. *Application deadline:* For fall admission, 3/15 for domestic and international students. *Application fee:* $30 ($100 for international students). Electronic applications accepted. *Application Contact:* Dr. Wanda Gonsalves, Interim Dean, 502-597-6129, E-mail: wanda.gonsalves@kysu.edu. *Interim Dean,* Dr. Wanda Gonsalves, 502-597-6129, E-mail: wanda.gonsalves@kysu.edu.

Program in Public Administration Students: 10 full-time (6 women), 17 part-time (10 women); includes 22 minority (21 Black or African American, non-Hispanic/Latino; 1 Two or more races, non-Hispanic/Latino), 1 international. Average age 33. 9 applicants, 100% accepted, 9 enrolled. *Faculty:* 4 full-time (1 woman). Expenses: Contact institution. *Financial support:* In 2018–19, 26 students received support. Scholarships/grants and unspecified assistantships available. Financial award application deadline: 6/30; financial award applicants required to submit FAFSA. *Program availability:* Evening/weekend. *Application deadline:* For fall admission, 7/1 for domestic and international students; for spring admission, 11/15 for domestic and international students; for summer admission, 5/1 for domestic and international students. Applications are processed on a rolling basis. *Application fee:* $30 ($100 for international students). Electronic applications accepted. *Application Contact:* Dr. Elgie McFayden, Chair, 502-597-5899, Fax: 502-597-6715, E-mail: elgie.mcfayden@kysu.edu. *Chair,* Dr. Elgie McFayden, 502-597-5899, Fax: 502-597-6715, E-mail: elgie.mcfayden@kysu.edu.

Program in Special Education Students: 4 full-time (3 women), 3 part-time (all women); includes 3 minority (all Black or African American, non-Hispanic/Latino). Average age 28. 4 applicants, 50% accepted, 2 enrolled. *Faculty:* 3 full-time (1 woman). Expenses: Contact institution. *Financial support:* In 2018–19, 6 students received support. Scholarships/grants available. Financial award application deadline: 6/30; financial award applicants required to submit FAFSA. *Program availability:* Evening/weekend, online only, blended/hybrid learning. *Application deadline:* For fall admission, 7/1 for domestic and international students; for spring admission, 11/15 for domestic and international students; for summer admission, 5/1 for domestic and international students. Applications are processed on a rolling basis. *Application fee:* $30 ($100 for international students). Electronic applications accepted. *Application Contact:* Dr. Kevin Jones, Interim Chair, 502-597-5919, E-mail: kevin.m.jones@kysu.edu. *Interim Chair,* Dr. Kevin Jones, 502-597-5919, E-mail: kevin.m.jones@kysu.edu.

KETTERING COLLEGE, Kettering, OH 45429-1299

General Information Independent-religious, coed, primarily women, comprehensive institution.

GRADUATE UNITS

Program in Occupational Therapy Offers occupational therapy (OTD).

Program in Physician Assistant Studies Offers physician assistant studies (MPAS).

KETTERING UNIVERSITY, Flint, MI 48504

General Information Independent, coed, comprehensive institution. CGS member. *Graduate housing:* Rooms and/or apartments available on a first-come, first-served basis to single students and available to married students. Housing application deadline: 7/15. *Research affiliation:* McLaren Foundation (orthopedic surgery biomechanics), Shin-Estu Chemical Company (atmospheric plasma technology), Broad-Ocean Technologies (electric vehicle battery systems), Landaal Packaging Systems (space utilization and process flow of operations), Mahindra Tractor Assembly, dba Mahindra GenZe (electric power and control boards), TRW (crash safety).

GRADUATE UNITS

Graduate School *Program availability:* Part-time, evening/weekend, online learning. Offers business (MBA, MS); engineering (MS). Electronic applications accepted.

KEUKA COLLEGE, Keuka Park, NY 14478

General Information Independent-religious, coed, comprehensive institution. *Graduate housing:* Room and/or apartments available on a first-come, first-served basis to single students; on-campus housing not available to married students. Housing application deadline: 5/1.

GRADUATE UNITS

Program in Childhood Education/Literacy Offers literacy 5-12 (MS); literacy B-6 (MS). Electronic applications accepted.

Program in Criminal Justice Administration *Program availability:* Part-time, evening/weekend. Offers criminal justice administration (MS). Electronic applications accepted.

Program in Management *Program availability:* Part-time, evening/weekend, 100% online, blended/hybrid learning. Offers management (MS).

Program in Nursing Offers adult gerontology (MS); nursing education (MS). Electronic applications accepted.

Program in Occupational Therapy Offers occupational therapy (MS). Electronic applications accepted.

Program in Social Work Offers social work (MSW). Electronic applications accepted.

KEYSTONE COLLEGE, La Plume, PA 18440

General Information Independent, coed, comprehensive institution. *Enrollment:* 1,423 graduate, professional, and undergraduate students; 47 full-time matriculated graduate/professional students (42 women), 37 part-time matriculated graduate/professional students (29 women). *Enrollment by degree level:* 84 master's. *Graduate faculty:* 4 full-time (3 women), 5 part-time/adjunct (all women). *Tuition:* Part-time $575 per credit. One-time fee: $100. Tuition and fees vary according to program. *Graduate housing:* On-campus housing not available. *Student services:* Campus employment opportunities, campus safety program, career counseling, exercise/wellness program, free psychological counseling, grant writing training, international student services, multicultural affairs office, services for students with disabilities, writing training. *Library facilities:* Miller Library.

Computer facilities: 100 computers available on campus for general student use. A campuswide network can be accessed from student residence rooms and from off campus. Online class registration is available.
Website: http://www.keystone.edu/

General Application Contact: Jennifer Sekol, Director of Admissions, 570-945-8117, Fax: 570-945-7916, E-mail: jennifer.sekol@keystone.edu.

GRADUATE UNITS

Master's in Business Administration Students: 22. Expenses: Contact institution. *Financial support:* Unspecified assistantships available. Financial award applicants required to submit FAFSA. *Program availability:* Part-time, online only, 100% online. Offers business administration (MBA). *Application deadline:* For fall admission, 8/1 for domestic students; for spring admission, 3/1 for domestic students; for summer admission, 7/1 for domestic students. Applications are processed on a rolling basis. *Application fee:* $0. Electronic applications accepted. *Application Contact:* Sarah Louzon, Admissions Counselor, 570-945-8126, Fax: 570-945-7916, E-mail: sarah.louzon@keystone.edu. *Associate Professor/Coordinator of MBA Program,* Dr. Dana Harris, 570-945-8421, E-mail: dana.harris@keystone.edu.

Master's in Early Childhood Education Leadership Students: 48. 22 applicants, 100% accepted, 18 enrolled. *Faculty:* 1 (woman) full-time, 4 part-time/adjunct (all women). Expenses: Contact institution. *Financial support:* Unspecified assistantships available. Financial award application deadline: 5/1; financial award applicants required to submit FAFSA. In 2018, 20 master's awarded. *Program availability:* Part-time, blended/hybrid learning. Offers early childhood education leadership (M Ed). *Application deadline:* For fall admission, 8/1 for domestic students; for spring admission, 1/1 for domestic students; for summer admission, 5/1 for domestic students. Applications are processed on a rolling basis. *Application fee:* $0. Electronic applications accepted. *Application Contact:* Jennifer Sekol, Director of Admissions, 570-945-8117, Fax: 570-945-7916, E-mail: jennifer.sekol@keystone.edu. *Professor,* Heather Shanks-McElroy, PhD, 570-945-8475, E-mail: heather.mcelroy@keystone.edu.

MS Program in Criminal Justice

KING'S COLLEGE, Wilkes-Barre, PA 18711-0801

General Information Independent-religious, coed, comprehensive institution. *Graduate housing:* On-campus housing not available.

GRADUATE UNITS

Program in Education *Program availability:* Part-time, evening/weekend. Offers education (M Ed).

Program in Physician Assistant Studies Offers physician assistant studies (MSPAS). Electronic applications accepted.

William G. McGowan School of Business *Program availability:* Part-time. Offers health care administration (MS).

THE KING'S UNIVERSITY, Southlake, TX 76092

General Information Independent-religious, coed, comprehensive institution.

GRADUATE UNITS

Graduate and Professional Programs Offers Biblical studies (Graduate Certificate); Christian ministry (Graduate Certificate); ministry (M Div, MPT, D Min).

KINGSWOOD UNIVERSITY, Sussex, NB E4E 5L2, Canada

General Information Independent-religious, coed, comprehensive institution. *Enrollment:* 6 full-time matriculated graduate/professional students (1 woman), 1 part-time matriculated graduate/professional student. *Enrollment by degree level:* 7 master's. *Graduate faculty:* 1 full-time (0 women), 1 part-time/adjunct (0 women). *Tuition:* Part-time $360 Canadian dollars per credit hour. One-time fee: $150 Canadian dollars part-time. *Graduate housing:* On-campus housing not available. *Library facilities:* The Earle and Marion Trouten Library.

Computer facilities: 8 computers available on campus for general student use. A campuswide network can be accessed from student residence rooms and from off campus.
Website: http://www.kingswood.edu/

General Application Contact: Enrolment Office, 506-432-4422, Fax: 506-432-4442, E-mail: enrolment@kingswood.edu.

GRADUATE UNITS

Program in Pastoral Theology Offers pastoral theology (MA).

KING UNIVERSITY, Bristol, TN 37620-2699

General Information Independent-religious, coed, comprehensive institution. *Enrollment:* 1,948 graduate, professional, and undergraduate students; 332 full-time matriculated graduate/professional students (228 women), 37 part-time matriculated graduate/professional students (33 women). *Enrollment by degree level:* 348 master's, 12 doctoral, 9 other advanced degrees. *Graduate faculty:* 26 full-time (16 women), 26 part-time/adjunct (16 women). *Tuition:* Full-time $13,365; part-time $495 per semester hour. *Required fees:* $900; $100 per course. One-time fee: $175. Tuition and fees vary according to class time, degree level and program. *Graduate housing:* Room and/or apartments available on a first-come, first-served basis to single students; on-campus housing not available to married students. Typical cost: $4532 per year ($9024 including board). Housing application deadline: 8/18. *Student services:* Campus employment opportunities, campus safety program, career counseling, exercise/wellness program, free psychological counseling, international student services, services for students with disabilities, writing training. *Library facilities:* E. W. King Library plus 3 others. *Collection:* Books: 75,745 (physical), 191,050 (digital/electronic); Serial titles: 150 (physical); Databases: 99. Weekly public service hours: 85.

Computer facilities: 90 computers available on campus for general student use. A campuswide network can be accessed from student residence rooms and from off campus. Online class registration, Student Portal are available.
Website: http://www.king.edu/

General Application Contact: Ashley Hartless, Interim Director of Enrollment Management Adult, Graduate & Professional Studies/Tri Cities, 276-964-7471, Fax: 423-652-4727, E-mail: ajhartless@king.edu.

GRADUATE UNITS

School of Business, Economics, and Technology Students: 182 full-time (107 women), 8 part-time (6 women); includes 18 minority (7 Black or African American, non-Hispanic/Latino; 4 Hispanic/Latino; 1 Native Hawaiian or other Pacific Islander, non-Hispanic/Latino; 6 Two or more races, non-Hispanic/Latino), 2 international. Average age 32. 143 applicants, 98% accepted, 68 enrolled. *Faculty:* 11 full-time (9 women), 10 part-time/adjunct (7 women). Expenses: Contact institution. *Financial support:* Unspecified assistantships available. Financial award applicants required to submit FAFSA. In 2018, 125 master's awarded. *Program availability:* Part-time, evening/weekend, 100% online, blended/hybrid learning. Offers accounting (MBA); finance (MBA); healthcare management (MBA); human resources management (MBA); leadership (MBA); management (MBA); marketing (MBA); project management (MBA). *Application deadline:* Applications are processed on a rolling basis. *Application fee:* $0 ($50 for international students). Electronic applications accepted. *Application Contact:* Nancy Beverly, Territory Manager/Enrollment Counselor, 423-341-9495, Fax: 423-652-4727, E-mail: nmbeverly@king.edu. *Dean, School of Business, Economics and Technology,* Dr. Mark Pate, 423-652-4814, E-mail: mjpate@king.edu.

School of Education Students: 33 full-time (17 women), 3 part-time (all women); includes 2 minority (both Black or African American, non-Hispanic/Latino), 1 international. Average age 29. 43 applicants, 56% accepted, 21 enrolled. *Faculty:* 4 full-time (2 women), 6 part-time/adjunct (all women). Expenses: Contact institution. *Financial support:* Unspecified assistantships available. Financial award applicants required to submit FAFSA. *Program availability:* Part-time, evening/weekend, 100% online, blended/hybrid learning. *Application deadline:* Applications are processed on a rolling basis. *Application fee:* $50 for international students. Electronic applications accepted. *Application Contact:* Ashley Hartless, Interim Director of Enrollment

Management Adult, Graduate & Professional Studies/Tri Cities, 276-964-7471, Fax: 423-652-4727, E-mail: ajhartless@king.edu. *Dean, School of Education*, Dr. Donna Watson, 423-652-4843, E-mail: dhwatson@king.edu.

School of Nursing Students: 117 full-time (104 women), 26 part-time (24 women); includes 13 minority (7 Black or African American, non-Hispanic/Latino; 3 Asian, non-Hispanic/Latino; 1 Hispanic/Latino; 2 Two or more races, non-Hispanic/Latino). Average age 37. 145 applicants, 92% accepted, 63 enrolled. *Faculty*: 11 full-time (all women), 5 part-time/adjunct (3 women). Expenses: Contact institution. *Financial support*: Unspecified assistantships available. Financial award applicants required to submit FAFSA. In 2018, 89 master's, 1 doctorate, 6 other advanced degrees awarded. *Program availability*: Part-time, evening/weekend, 100% online, blended/hybrid learning. Offers family nurse practitioner (MSN, Post-Master's Certificate); nurse educator (MSN, Post-Master's Certificate); nursing (DNP); nursing administration (MSN); pediatric nurse practitioner (MSN). *Application deadline*: Applications are processed on a rolling basis. *Application fee*: $0 ($50 for international students). Electronic applications accepted. *Application Contact*: Natalie Blankenship, Territory Manager/Enrollment Counselor, 652-652-4159, Fax: 652-652-4727, E-mail: nblankenship@king.edu. *Dean, School of Nursing*, Dr. Tracy Slemp, 423-652-6335, E-mail: tjslemp@king.edu.

KNOX COLLEGE, Toronto, ON M5S 2E6, Canada
General Information Independent-religious, coed, graduate-only institution. *Graduate housing*: Room and/or apartments available on a first-come, first-served basis to single students; on-campus housing not available to married students. Housing application deadline: 5/31.

GRADUATE UNITS

College of Theology *Program availability*: Part-time. Offers theology (M Div, MRE, MTS, Th M, D Min, Th D). Applicants for D Min, Th M, and Th D must apply to Toronto School of Theology; MRE, M Div, MTS, and Th M programs offered jointly with University of Toronto.

KNOX THEOLOGICAL SEMINARY, Fort Lauderdale, FL 33308
General Information Independent-religious, coed, primarily men, graduate-only institution. *Graduate housing*: On-campus housing not available.

GRADUATE UNITS

Graduate Programs *Program availability*: Part-time, blended/hybrid learning. Offers Biblical and theological studies (MA); Christian and classical studies (MA); divinity (M Div); ministry (D Min).

KUTZTOWN UNIVERSITY OF PENNSYLVANIA, Kutztown, PA 19530-0730
General Information State-supported, coed, comprehensive institution. CGS member. *Enrollment*: 294 full-time matriculated graduate/professional students (220 women), 604 part-time matriculated graduate/professional students (466 women). *Enrollment by degree level*: 777 master's, 40 doctoral, 81 other advanced degrees. *Graduate faculty*: 96 full-time (60 women), 10 part-time/adjunct (5 women). Tuition, state resident: part-time $516 per credit. Tuition, nonresident: part-time $774 per credit. *Required fees*: $119 per credit. One-time fee: $50 part-time. Tuition and fees vary according to degree level. *Graduate housing*: Rooms and/or apartments available on a first-come, first-served basis to single and married students. Housing application deadline: 5/1. *Student services*: Campus employment opportunities, campus safety program, career counseling, exercise/wellness program, free psychological counseling, international student services, low-cost health insurance, multicultural affairs office, services for students with disabilities. *Library facilities*: Rohrbach Library. *Collection*: Books: 317,044 (physical), 299,170 (digital/electronic); Serial titles: 88,613 (digital/electronic); Databases: 134. Weekly public service hours: 92; students can reserve study rooms.

Computer facilities: Computer purchase and lease plans are available. 1,075 computers available on campus for general student use. A campuswide network can be accessed from student residence rooms. Online class registration is available. Website: http://www.kutztown.edu/

General Application Contact: Kelly Hish, Admissions Clerk, 610-683-4190, Fax: 610-683-1375, E-mail: graduate@kutztown.edu.

GRADUATE UNITS

College of Business Students: 12 full-time (4 women), 19 part-time (7 women); includes 1 minority (Hispanic/Latino), 3 international. Average age 30. 37 applicants, 86% accepted, 14 enrolled. *Faculty*: 7 full-time (5 women). Expenses: Contact institution. *Financial support*: Career-related internships or fieldwork, Federal Work-Study, and unspecified assistantships available. Financial award application deadline: 3/1; financial award applicants required to submit FAFSA. In 2018, 12 master's awarded. *Program availability*: Part-time, evening/weekend, 100% online, blended/hybrid learning. Offers business (MBA); business administration (MBA). *Application deadline*: For fall admission, 8/1 priority date for domestic and international students; for spring admission, 12/1 priority date for domestic and international students. Applications are processed on a rolling basis. *Application fee*: $35. Electronic applications accepted. *Application Contact*: Dr. Anne Carroll, Dean, 610-683-4575, Fax: 610-683-4573, E-mail: acarroll@kutztown.edu. *Dean*, Dr. Anne Carroll, 610-683-4575, Fax: 610-683-4573, E-mail: acarroll@kutztown.edu.

College of Education Students: 188 full-time (151 women), 413 part-time (323 women); includes 91 minority (27 Black or African American, non-Hispanic/Latino; 6 Asian, non-Hispanic/Latino; 43 Hispanic/Latino; 15 Two or more races, non-Hispanic/Latino), 3 international. Average age 30. 416 applicants, 83% accepted, 206 enrolled. *Faculty*: 34 full-time (26 women), 5 part-time/adjunct (1 woman). Expenses: Contact institution. *Financial support*: Career-related internships or fieldwork, Federal Work-Study, and unspecified assistantships available. Financial award application deadline: 3/1; financial award applicants required to submit FAFSA. In 2018, 177 master's awarded. *Program availability*: Part-time, evening/weekend, 100% online, blended/hybrid learning. Offers biology (M Ed); counseling psychology (MA); curriculum and instruction (M Ed); education (M Ed, MA, MLS, MS, Ed D); elementary education (M Ed); English (M Ed); instructional technology (M Ed); library science (MLS); mathematics (M Ed); middle level (M Ed); reading (M Ed); school counseling (MS); social studies (M Ed); student affairs in higher education (M Ed); teaching (M Ed); transformational teaching and learning (Ed D). *Application deadline*: For fall admission, 8/1 for domestic and international students; for spring admission, 12/1 for domestic and international students. *Application fee*: $35. Electronic applications accepted. *Application Contact*: Dr. Kenneth Teitelbaum, Dean, 610-683-4253, Fax: 610-683-4255, E-mail: teitelba@kutztown.edu. *Dean*, Dr. Kenneth Teitelbaum, 610-683-4253, Fax: 610-683-4255, E-mail: teitelba@kutztown.edu.

College of Liberal Arts and Sciences Students: 69 full-time (47 women), 90 part-time (68 women); includes 38 minority (18 Black or African American, non-Hispanic/Latino; 1 American Indian or Alaska Native, non-Hispanic/Latino; 2 Asian, non-Hispanic/Latino; 11 Hispanic/Latino; 1 Native Hawaiian or other Pacific Islander, non-Hispanic/Latino; 5 Two or more races, non-Hispanic/Latino), 1 international. Average age 31. 148 applicants, 86% accepted, 72 enrolled. *Faculty*: 41 full-time (21 women). Expenses: Contact institution. *Financial support*: Career-related internships or fieldwork, Federal Work-Study, and unspecified assistantships available. Financial award application deadline: 3/1; financial award applicants required to submit FAFSA. In 2018, 68 master's, 6 doctorates awarded. *Program availability*: Part-time, evening/weekend. Offers computer science (MS); English (MA); liberal arts and sciences (MA, MPA, MS, MSW, DSW); public administration (MPA); social work (MSW, DSW). *Application deadline*: For fall admission, 8/1 for domestic and international students; for spring admission, 12/1 for domestic and international students. *Application fee*: $35. Electronic applications accepted. *Application Contact*: Dr. David Beougher, Dean, 610-683-4305, Fax: 610-683-4633, E-mail: clas@kutztown.edu. *Dean*, Dr. David Beougher, 610-683-4305, Fax: 610-683-4633, E-mail: clas@kutztown.edu.

College of Visual and Performing Arts Students: 25 full-time (18 women), 82 part-time (68 women); includes 8 minority (2 Black or African American, non-Hispanic/Latino; 1 Asian, non-Hispanic/Latino; 1 Hispanic/Latino; 4 Two or more races, non-Hispanic/Latino). Average age 31. 66 applicants, 95% accepted, 33 enrolled. *Faculty*: 14 full-time (8 women), 5 part-time/adjunct (4 women). Expenses: Contact institution. *Financial support*: Career-related internships or fieldwork, Federal Work-Study, institutionally sponsored loans, and unspecified assistantships available. Financial award application deadline: 3/1; financial award applicants required to submit FAFSA. In 2018, 18 master's awarded. *Program availability*: Part-time. Offers art education (M Ed); arts administration (MA); communication design (MFA); music education (M Ed); visual and performing arts (M Ed, MA, MFA). *Application deadline*: For fall admission, 8/1 for domestic and international students; for spring admission, 12/1 for domestic and international students. *Application fee*: $35. Electronic applications accepted. *Application Contact*: Dr. Michelle Kiec, Dean, 610-683-4500, Fax: 610-683-4547, E-mail: kiec@kutztown.edu. *Dean*, Dr. Michelle Kiec, 610-683-4500, Fax: 610-683-4547, E-mail: kiec@kutztown.edu.

LAGRANGE COLLEGE, LaGrange, GA 30240-2999
General Information Independent-religious, coed, comprehensive institution. *Graduate housing*: Room and/or apartments available on a first-come, first-served basis to single students; on-campus housing not available to married students. Housing application deadline: 5/1.

GRADUATE UNITS

Graduate Programs *Program availability*: Part-time, evening/weekend. Offers clinical mental health counseling (MS); curriculum and instruction (M Ed, Ed S); middle grades (MAT); organizational leadership (MA); secondary education (MAT). Electronic applications accepted.

Program in Strength and Conditioning

LAGUNA COLLEGE OF ART & DESIGN, Laguna Beach, CA 92651-1136
General Information Independent, coed, comprehensive institution.

GRADUATE UNITS

Graduate Program Electronic applications accepted.

LAKE ERIE COLLEGE, Painesville, OH 44077-3389
General Information Independent, coed, comprehensive institution. *Graduate housing*: On-campus housing not available.

GRADUATE UNITS

School of Business *Program availability*: Part-time, evening/weekend. Offers general management (MBA); health care administration (MBA); information technology management (MBA). Electronic applications accepted.

School of Education and Professional Studies *Program availability*: Part-time, evening/weekend. Offers education and professional studies (M Ed). Electronic applications accepted.

LAKE ERIE COLLEGE OF OSTEOPATHIC MEDICINE, Erie, PA 16509-1025
General Information Independent, coed, graduate-only institution. *Graduate housing*: On-campus housing not available. *Research affiliation*: West Virginia University (neurology), Neuro Structural Research Laboratories (neurology), Cornelli Consulting (CORCON) (neurology), University of Maryland (neurology), Duke University (neurology).

GRADUATE UNITS

Professional Programs Offers biomedical sciences (Postbaccalaureate Certificate); medical education (MS); osteopathic medicine (DO); pharmacy (Pharm D). Electronic applications accepted.

LAKE FOREST COLLEGE, Lake Forest, IL 60045
General Information Independent, coed, comprehensive institution. *Graduate housing*: On-campus housing not available. *Research affiliation*: Argonne National Laboratory (physics), Merck & Company, Inc., Chicago History Museum (Chicago history), Lake Forest Hospital (genomes), The Art Institute of Chicago (Asian art), Newberry Library (medieval and Renaissance history, American West).

GRADUATE UNITS

Graduate Program in Liberal Studies *Program availability*: Part-time, evening/weekend. Offers American studies (MLS); cinema in East Asia (MLS); environmental studies (MLS); history (MLS); Medieval and Renaissance art (MLS); philosophy (MLS); Spanish (MLS); writing (MLS). Electronic applications accepted.

Master of Arts in Teaching Program Offers elementary education (MAT); K-12 French (MAT); K-12 music (MAT); K-12 Spanish (MAT); K-12 visual art (MAT); secondary biology (MAT); secondary chemistry (MAT); secondary English (MAT); secondary history (MAT); secondary mathematics (MAT).

LAKE FOREST GRADUATE SCHOOL OF MANAGEMENT, Lake Forest, IL 60045
General Information Independent, coed, graduate-only institution. *Graduate housing*: On-campus housing not available.

GRADUATE UNITS

The Immersion MBA Program (iMBA) *Program availability*: Online learning. Offers global business (MBA).

The Leadership MBA Program *Program availability*: Part-time, evening/weekend. Offers finance (MBA); global business (MBA); healthcare management (MBA); management (MBA); marketing (MBA); organizational behavior (MBA). Electronic applications accepted.

LAKEHEAD UNIVERSITY, Thunder Bay, ON P7B 5E1, Canada

General Information Province-supported, coed, comprehensive institution. *Graduate housing:* Rooms and/or apartments available to single students and available on a first-come, first-served basis to married students. Housing application deadline: 3/10. *Research affiliation:* Falcon Bridge (biology), Placer Dome (biology), Centre for Northern Forest Ecosystem Research (biology, forestry, tourism), Thunder Bay Regional Cancer Centre (psychosocial oncology), Bowater Inc. (chemistry, engineering).

GRADUATE UNITS

Graduate Studies *Program availability:* Part-time, evening/weekend. Offers biology (M Sc); chemistry (M Sc); clinical psychology (PhD); economics (MA); experimental psychology (MA); geology (M Sc); gerontology (M Ed, M Sc, MA, MSW); physics (M Sc); women's studies (M Ed, MA, MSW).

Faculty of Education *Program availability:* Part-time, evening/weekend. Offers educational studies (PhD); gerontology (M Ed); women's studies (M Ed).

Faculty of Engineering *Program availability:* Part-time. Offers control engineering (M Sc Engr); electrical/computer engineering (M Sc Engr); environmental engineering (M Sc Engr).

Faculty of Natural Resources Management *Program availability:* Part-time. Offers forest sciences (PhD); forestry (M Sc F).

Faculty of Social Sciences and Humanities *Program availability:* Part-time, evening/weekend. Offers English (MA); gerontology (MA); health services and policy research (MA); history (MA); social sciences and humanities (MA); sociology (MA); women's studies (MA).

School of Kinesiology *Program availability:* Part-time. Offers kinesiology (M Sc); kinesiology and gerontology (M Sc).

School of Mathematical Sciences *Program availability:* Part-time, evening/weekend. Offers computer science (M Sc); mathematical science (MA).

School of Social Work *Program availability:* Part-time. Offers gerontology (MSW); social work (MSW); women's studies (MSW).

LAKELAND UNIVERSITY, Plymouth, WI 53073

General Information Independent-religious, coed, comprehensive institution. *Graduate housing:* On-campus housing not available.

GRADUATE UNITS

Graduate Studies Division *Program availability:* Part-time, evening/weekend. Offers accounting (MBA); counseling (MA); education (M Ed); finance (MBA); healthcare management (MBA); project management (MBA); theology (MAT).

LAMAR UNIVERSITY, Beaumont, TX 77710

General Information State-supported, coed, university. CGS member. *Enrollment:* 14,783 graduate, professional, and undergraduate students; 722 full-time matriculated graduate/professional students (450 women), 5,157 part-time matriculated graduate/professional students (3,817 women). *Enrollment by degree level:* 4,448 master's, 335 doctoral, 1,095 other advanced degrees. *Graduate faculty:* 483 full-time (222 women), 131 part-time/adjunct (80 women). *International tuition:* $6852 full-time. Tuition, state resident: full-time $6234; part-time $346 per credit hour. Tuition, nonresident: full-time $6852; part-time $761 per credit hour. *Required fees:* $1940; $327 per credit hour. Tuition and fees vary according to course load, campus/location, program and reciprocity agreements. *Graduate housing:* Rooms and/or apartments available on a first-come, first-served basis to single and married students. Typical cost: $5670 per year ($9170 including board) for single students. Room and board charges vary according to board plan. *Student services:* Campus employment opportunities, campus safety program, career counseling, exercise/wellness program, free psychological counseling, grant writing training, international student services, low-cost health insurance, multicultural affairs office, services for students with disabilities, teacher training, writing training. *Library facilities:* Mary and John Gray Library plus 1 other. *Collection:* Books: 496,121 (physical), 91,469 (digital/electronic); Serial titles: 42,694 (physical), 47,629 (digital/electronic); Databases: 142. Weekly public service hours: 87; students can reserve study rooms.

Computer facilities: 1,104 computers available on campus for general student use. A campuswide network can be accessed from student residence rooms and from off campus. Online class registration is available.
Website: http://www.lamar.edu/

General Application Contact: Celeste Contreras, Director, Admissions and Recruitment, 409-880-7870, Fax: 409-880-8180, E-mail: gradadmissions@lamar.edu.

GRADUATE UNITS

College of Graduate Studies Students: 722 full-time (450 women), 5,157 part-time (3,817 women); includes 2,532 minority (1,271 Black or African American, non-Hispanic/Latino; 24 American Indian or Alaska Native, non-Hispanic/Latino; 109 Asian, non-Hispanic/Latino; 1,075 Hispanic/Latino; 4 Native Hawaiian or other Pacific Islander, non-Hispanic/Latino; 49 Two or more races, non-Hispanic/Latino), 368 international. Average age 36. 5,062 applicants, 84% accepted, 1375 enrolled. *Faculty:* 483 full-time (222 women), 131 part-time/adjunct (80 women). Expenses: Contact institution. *Financial support:* In 2018–19, 258 students received support. Fellowships with partial tuition reimbursements available, research assistantships, teaching assistantships, career-related internships or fieldwork, Federal Work-Study, institutionally sponsored loans, scholarships/grants, and tuition waivers (partial) available. Support available to part-time students. Financial award applicants required to submit FAFSA. In 2018, 2,197 master's, 101 doctorates, 755 other advanced degrees awarded. *Program availability:* Part-time, evening/weekend. *Application deadline:* Applications are processed on a rolling basis. *Application fee:* $25 ($50 for international students). Electronic applications accepted. *Application Contact:* Celeste Contreras, Director, Admissions, 409-880-8888, Fax: 409-880-7419, E-mail: gradmissions@lamar.edu. *Dean,* Dr. William E. Harn, 409-880-8229, Fax: 409-880-1723, E-mail: lugradstudies@lamar.edu.

College of Arts and Sciences Students: 116 full-time (51 women), 313 part-time (202 women); includes 185 minority (101 Black or African American, non-Hispanic/Latino; 1 American Indian or Alaska Native, non-Hispanic/Latino; 12 Asian, non-Hispanic/Latino; 62 Hispanic/Latino; 9 Two or more races, non-Hispanic/Latino), 97 international. Average age 32. 431 applicants, 83% accepted, 123 enrolled. *Faculty:* 215 full-time (106 women), 54 part-time/adjunct (32 women). Expenses: Contact institution. *Financial support:* In 2018–19, 33 students received support. Fellowships, research assistantships, teaching assistantships with tuition reimbursements available, career-related internships or fieldwork, Federal Work-Study, institutionally sponsored loans, scholarships/grants, and tuition waivers (partial) available. Support available to part-time students. Financial award applicants required to submit FAFSA. In 2018, 207 master's awarded. *Program availability:* Part-time, evening/weekend. Offers arts and sciences (MA, MPA, MS, MSN); biology (MS); chemistry and biochemistry (MS); computer science (MS); English (MA); history (MA); mathematics

(MS); nursing administration (MSN); nursing education (MSN); political science (MPA); psychology (MS); sociology, social work, and criminal justice (MS); teaching Spanish (MA). *Application deadline:* Applications are processed on a rolling basis. *Application fee:* $25 ($50 for international students). Electronic applications accepted. *Application Contact:* Celeste Contreras, Director, Admissions, 409-880-8888, E-mail: gradmissions@lamar.edu. *Dean,* Dr. Lynn Maurer, 409-880-8508, Fax: 409-880-8007.

College of Business Students: 38 full-time (18 women), 242 part-time (141 women); includes 113 minority (60 Black or African American, non-Hispanic/Latino; 13 Asian, non-Hispanic/Latino; 34 Hispanic/Latino; 6 Two or more races, non-Hispanic/Latino), 25 international. Average age 33. 184 applicants, 97% accepted, 48 enrolled. *Faculty:* 48 full-time (14 women), 8 part-time/adjunct (3 women). Expenses: Contact institution. *Financial support:* In 2018–19, 33 students received support. Fellowships with tuition reimbursements available, research assistantships with partial tuition reimbursements, career-related internships or fieldwork, Federal Work-Study, institutionally sponsored loans, scholarships/grants, and tuition waivers (partial) available. Support available to part-time students. Financial award applicants required to submit FAFSA. In 2018, 90 master's awarded. *Program availability:* Part-time, evening/weekend. Offers accounting (MBA). *Application deadline:* Applications are processed on a rolling basis. *Application fee:* $25 ($50 for international students). Electronic applications accepted. *Application Contact:* Celeste Contreras, Director, Admissions and Academic Services, 409-880-8888, Fax: 409-880-7419, E-mail: gradmissions@lamar.edu. *Dean,* Dr. Dan French, 409-880-8603, Fax: 409-880-8088, E-mail: dan.french@lamar.edu.

College of Education and Human Development Students: 302 full-time (263 women), 4,473 part-time (3,437 women); includes 2,172 minority (1,038 Black or African American, non-Hispanic/Latino; 22 American Indian or Alaska Native, non-Hispanic/Latino; 70 Asian, non-Hispanic/Latino; 949 Hispanic/Latino; 4 Native Hawaiian or other Pacific Islander, non-Hispanic/Latino; 89 Two or more races, non-Hispanic/Latino), 17 international. Average age 37. 3,981 applicants, 85% accepted, 1092 enrolled. *Faculty:* 82 full-time (58 women), 48 part-time/adjunct (36 women). Expenses: Contact institution. *Financial support:* In 2018–19, 135 students received support. Fellowships, research assistantships, teaching assistantships, career-related internships or fieldwork, Federal Work-Study, institutionally sponsored loans, and scholarships/grants available. Support available to part-time students. Financial award applicants required to submit FAFSA. In 2018, 1,673 master's, 73 doctorates, 755 other advanced degrees awarded. *Program availability:* Part-time, evening/weekend, online learning. Offers clinical mental health counseling (M Ed); digital learning and leading (M Ed); education administration (M Ed); education and human development (M Ed, MS, Ed D, Certificate); educational leadership (Ed D); educational technology (M Ed); family and consumer sciences (MS); health and kinesiology (MS); school counseling (M Ed); special education (MS); teacher education (M Ed). *Application deadline:* Applications are processed on a rolling basis. *Application fee:* $25 ($50 for international students). Electronic applications accepted. *Application Contact:* Celeste Contreras, Director, Admissions and Academic Services, 409-880-8888, Fax: 409-880-7419, E-mail: gradmissions@lamar.edu. *Dean,* Dr. Robert Spina, 409-880-8661.

College of Engineering Students: 152 full-time (19 women), 100 part-time (18 women); includes 13 minority (1 Black or African American, non-Hispanic/Latino; 1 American Indian or Alaska Native, non-Hispanic/Latino; 8 Asian, non-Hispanic/Latino; 2 Hispanic/Latino; 1 Two or more races, non-Hispanic/Latino), 220 international. Average age 28. 359 applicants, 74% accepted, 56 enrolled. *Faculty:* 53 full-time (6 women), 2 part-time/adjunct (0 women). Expenses: Contact institution. *Financial support:* In 2018–19, 15 students received support. Fellowships with partial tuition reimbursements available, research assistantships with partial tuition reimbursements available, teaching assistantships with partial tuition reimbursements available, career-related internships or fieldwork, Federal Work-Study, institutionally sponsored loans, scholarships/grants, tuition waivers (full and partial), and laboratory assistantships available. Support available to part-time students. Financial award applicants required to submit FAFSA. In 2018, 185 master's, 15 doctorates awarded. *Program availability:* Part-time, evening/weekend. Offers chemical engineering (ME, PhD); civil and environmental engineering (ME, MES, MS, DE); electrical engineering (ME, MES, DE); engineering (ME, MEM, MES, MS, DE, PhD); industrial engineering (ME, MEM, MES, DE); mechanical engineering (ME, MES, DE). *Application deadline:* Applications are processed on a rolling basis. *Application fee:* $25 ($50 for international students). Electronic applications accepted. *Application Contact:* Celeste Contreras, Director, Admissions and Academic Services, 409-880-8888, Fax: 409-880-7419, E-mail: gradmissions@lamar.edu. *Dean,* Dr. Brian Craig, 409-880-8784, Fax: 409-880-2197.

College of Fine Arts and Communication Students: 114 full-time (99 women), 29 part-time (19 women); includes 49 minority (12 Black or African American, non-Hispanic/Latino; 6 Asian, non-Hispanic/Latino; 28 Hispanic/Latino; 3 Two or more races, non-Hispanic/Latino), 9 international. Average age 27. 107 applicants, 75% accepted, 56 enrolled. *Faculty:* 82 full-time (36 women), 19 part-time/adjunct (9 women). Expenses: Contact institution. *Financial support:* In 2018–19, 42 students received support. Fellowships, research assistantships, teaching assistantships, career-related internships or fieldwork, Federal Work-Study, institutionally sponsored loans, and tuition waivers (partial) available. Support available to part-time students. Financial award applicants required to submit FAFSA. In 2018, 42 master's, 13 doctorates awarded. *Program availability:* Part-time, evening/weekend. Offers audiology (Au D); deaf studies and deaf education (MS, Ed D); fine arts and communication (MM, MS, Au D, Ed D); music (MM); speech language pathology (MS). *Application deadline:* Applications are processed on a rolling basis. *Application fee:* $25 ($50 for international students). Electronic applications accepted. *Application Contact:* Celeste Contreras, Director, Admissions and Academic Services, 409-880-8888, Fax: 409-880-7419, E-mail: gradmissions@lamar.edu. *Dean,* Dr. Derina Holtzhausen, 409-880-8137, Fax: 409-880-2286.

LANCASTER BIBLE COLLEGE, Lancaster, PA 17601

General Information Independent-religious, coed, comprehensive institution. *Enrollment:* 2,122 graduate, professional, and undergraduate students; 94 full-time matriculated graduate/professional students (47 women), 89 part-time matriculated graduate/professional students (45 women). *Enrollment by degree level:* 183 master's. *Graduate faculty:* 8 full-time (1 woman), 5 part-time/adjunct (1 woman). *Graduate housing:* On-campus housing not available. *Student services:* Campus employment opportunities, career counseling, international student services. *Library facilities:* Lancaster Bible College Library.

Computer facilities: 50 computers available on campus for general student use. A campuswide network can be accessed from student residence rooms.
Website: http://www.lbc.edu/

General Application Contact: Dr. Gary Bredfeldt, Associate Vice President/Dean of iLead Center, 717-560-8297, Fax: 717-560-8236, E-mail: gbredfeldt@lbc.edu.

GRADUATE UNITS

Capital Bible Seminary Students: 98 full-time (32 women), 276 part-time (114 women); includes 215 minority (169 Black or African American, non-Hispanic/Latino; 39 Asian, non-Hispanic/Latino; 7 Hispanic/Latino); 12 international. Average age 41. 105 applicants, 95% accepted, 84 enrolled. *Faculty:* 11 full-time (0 women), 12 part-time/adjunct (0 women). Expenses: Contact institution. *Financial support:* In 2018–19, 181 students received support. Career-related internships or fieldwork available. In 2018, 36 master's, 3 other advanced degrees awarded. *Program availability:* Part-time, evening/weekend. Offers biblical studies (MA, Certificate); Christian counseling and discipleship (MA, Certificate); ministry (MA); theology (M Div). *Application deadline:* For fall admission, 7/30 priority date for domestic students; for spring admission, 12/1 priority date for domestic students. Applications are processed on a rolling basis. *Application fee:* $30.

Graduate School Students: 94 full-time (47 women), 89 part-time (45 women); includes 21 minority (15 Black or African American, non-Hispanic/Latino; 5 Asian, non-Hispanic/Latino; 1 Hispanic/Latino). Average age 36. *Faculty:* 8 full-time (1 woman), 5 part-time/adjunct (1 woman). Expenses: Contact institution. *Financial support:* In 2018–19, 31 students received support. Teaching assistantships, scholarships/grants, and unspecified assistantships available. Support available to part-time students. Financial award application deadline: 6/1; financial award applicants required to submit FAFSA. *Program availability:* Part-time, evening/weekend. Offers adult ministries (MA); Bible (MA); children and family ministry (MA); church planting (MA); consulting resource teacher (M Ed); elementary school counseling (M Ed); leadership (PhD); leadership studies (MA); marriage and family counseling (MA); mental health counseling (MA); pastoral studies (MA); secondary school counseling (M Ed); sports ministry (MA); student ministry (MA); town and country ministry (MA). *Application deadline:* Applications are processed on a rolling basis. *Application fee:* $25. *Application Contact:* Mark Wilson, Admissions Counselor, 717-560-8229, E-mail: mwilson@lbc.edu. *Associate Vice President/Dean of iLead Center*, Dr. Gary Bredfeldt, 717-560-8297, Fax: 717-560-8236.

LANCASTER THEOLOGICAL SEMINARY, Lancaster, PA 17603-2812

General Information Independent-religious, coed, graduate-only institution. *Graduate housing:* Rooms and/or apartments available on a first-come, first-served basis to single and married students. Housing application deadline: 8/1.

GRADUATE UNITS

Graduate and Professional Programs Offers biblical studies (MAR); Christian education (MAR); Christianity and the arts (MAR); church history (MAR); congregational life (MAR); lay leadership (Certificate); theological studies (M Div); theology (D Min); theology and ethics (MAR).

LANDER UNIVERSITY, Greenwood, SC 29649-2099

General Information State-supported, coed, comprehensive institution. *Graduate housing:* Room and/or apartments available on a first-come, first-served basis to single students; on-campus housing not available to married students.

GRADUATE UNITS

Graduate Studies *Program availability:* Part-time, online learning. Offers clinical nurse leader (MSN); emergency management (MS); Montessori education (M Ed); teaching and learning (M Ed). Electronic applications accepted.

LANGSTON UNIVERSITY, Langston, OK 73050

General Information State-supported, coed, comprehensive institution. CGS member. *Graduate housing:* Rooms and/or apartments available on a first-come, first-served basis to single and married students.

GRADUATE UNITS

School of Education and Behavioral Sciences *Program availability:* Part-time. Offers bilingual/multicultural (M Ed); elementary education (M Ed); English as a second language (M Ed); rehabilitation counseling (M Sc); urban education (M Ed).

School of Physical Therapy Offers physical therapy (DPT).

LA ROCHE UNIVERSITY, Pittsburgh, PA 15237-5898

General Information Independent-religious, coed, comprehensive institution. *Enrollment:* 69 full-time matriculated graduate/professional students (50 women), 45 part-time matriculated graduate/professional students (50 women). *Enrollment by degree level:* 147 master's, 2 doctoral, 5 other advanced degrees. *Graduate faculty:* 12 full-time (11 women), 17 part-time/adjunct (8 women). *Tuition:* Part-time $735 per unit. *Required fees:* $80; $80 per unit. *Graduate housing:* On-campus housing not available. *Student services:* Campus employment opportunities, career counseling, free psychological counseling, international student services, low-cost health insurance, multicultural affairs office, services for students with disabilities. *Library facilities:* John J. Wright Library plus 1 other. *Collection:* Books: 75,803 (physical), 221,000 (digital/electronic); Databases: 1,248.

Computer facilities: Computer purchase and lease plans are available. A campuswide network can be accessed. Online class registration is available.
Website: http://www.laroche.edu/

General Application Contact: Erin Pottgen, Assistant Director, Graduate Admissions, 412-847-2509, Fax: 412-536-1283, E-mail: erin.pottgen@laroche.edu.

GRADUATE UNITS

Doctoral Program of Nurse Anesthesia Practice

Program in Education

Program in Information Systems

School of Graduate Studies and Adult Education Students: 69 full-time (50 women), 85 part-time (50 women); includes 7 minority (3 Black or African American, non-Hispanic/Latino; 3 Hispanic/Latino; 1 Two or more races, non-Hispanic/Latino), 25 international. Average age 32. 213 applicants, 77% accepted, 52 enrolled. *Faculty:* 12 full-time (11 women), 17 part-time/adjunct (8 women). Expenses: Contact institution. *Financial support:* Unspecified assistantships available. Financial award application deadline: 3/31; financial award applicants required to submit FAFSA. In 2018, 55 master's, 2 doctorates awarded. *Program availability:* Part-time, evening/weekend, 100% online. Offers accounting (MS); clinical nurse leader (MSN); human resources management (MS, Certificate); nurse anesthesia (MSN); nursing education (MSN); nursing management (MSN). *Application deadline:* For fall admission, 8/15 for domestic and international students; for spring admission, 12/15 for domestic and international students. Applications are processed on a rolling basis. *Application fee:* $50. Electronic applications accepted. *Application Contact:* Erin Pottgen, Assistant Director, Graduate Admissions, 412-847-2509, Fax: 412-536-1283, E-mail:

erin.pottgen@laroche.edu. *Dean,* Dr. Rosemary McCarthy, 412-536-1193, Fax: 412-536-1763, E-mail: rosemary.mccarthy@laroche.edu.

LA SALLE UNIVERSITY, Philadelphia, PA 19141-1199

General Information Independent-religious, coed, comprehensive institution. CGS member. *Graduate housing:* Room and/or apartments available on a first-come, first-served basis to single students; on-campus housing not available to married students.

GRADUATE UNITS

School of Arts and Sciences *Program availability:* Part-time, evening/weekend, 100% online, blended/hybrid learning. Offers American history (Certificate); application development (Certificate); arts and sciences (MA, MS, Psy D, Certificate); autism spectrum disorders (MA, Certificate); bilingual/bicultural studies (MA); child clinical psychology (Psy D); classroom management (MA); clinical health psychology (Psy D); clinical psychology (MA); communication consulting and development (MA); communication management (MA); computer information science (MS); corporate fraud (MS); dual early childhood and special education (MA); dual middle-level science and math and special education (MA); education (MA); English (MA); English as a second language (Certificate); European history (Certificate); fraud and forensic accounting (Certificate); general practice psychology (Psy D); general professional communication (MA); history (MA); history for educators (MA); industrial/organizational psychology (MA); information technology leadership (MS); instructional coach (Certificate); instructional leadership (MA); instructional technology management (MS, Certificate); marriage and family therapy (MA); network security (MS); professional and business communication (Certificate); professional clinical counseling (MA); public history (MA); public relations (MA); reading specialist (MA, Certificate); secondary education (MA); social and new media (Certificate); software project leadership (Certificate); special education (MA, Certificate); teaching advanced placement history (Certificate); world history (Certificate). Electronic applications accepted.

Hispanic Institute *Program availability:* Part-time, evening/weekend. Offers bilingual/bicultural studies (MA); ESL program specialist (Certificate); interpretation: English/Spanish-Spanish/English (Certificate); teaching English to speakers of other languages (MA); translation and interpretation (MA); translation: English/Spanish-Spanish/English (Certificate). Electronic applications accepted.

School of Business *Program availability:* Part-time, evening/weekend, 100% online, blended/hybrid learning. Offers accounting (MBA, Post-MBA Certificate); business administration (MBA, Post-MBA Certificate); business systems and analytics (MBA, Post-MBA Certificate); finance (MBA, Post-MBA Certificate); general business administration (MBA, Post-MBA Certificate); human capital development (MS, Certificate); human resource management (MBA, Post-MBA Certificate); international business (Post-MBA Certificate); management (MBA, Post-MBA Certificate); marketing (Post-MBA Certificate); nonprofit leadership (MS). Electronic applications accepted.

School of Nursing and Health Sciences *Program availability:* Part-time, evening/weekend. Offers adult gerontology primary care nurse practitioner (MSN, Certificate); adult health and illness clinical nurse specialist (MSN); adult-gerontology clinical nurse specialist (MSN, Certificate); clinical nurse leader (MSN); family primary care nurse practitioner (MSN, Certificate); gerontology (Certificate); nurse anesthetist (MSN, Certificate); nursing (MSN, Certificate); nursing administration (MSN, Certificate); nursing and health sciences (MPH, MS, MSN, DNP, Certificate); nursing education (Certificate); nursing practice (DNP); nursing service administration (MSN); public health (MPH); public health nursing (MSN, Certificate); school nursing (Certificate); speech-language pathology (MS). Electronic applications accepted.

LASELL COLLEGE, Newton, MA 02466-2709

General Information Independent, coed, comprehensive institution. *Enrollment:* 2,116 graduate, professional, and undergraduate students; 140 full-time matriculated graduate/professional students (90 women), 302 part-time matriculated graduate/professional students (181 women). *Enrollment by degree level:* 430 master's, 12 other advanced degrees. *Graduate faculty:* 22 full-time (13 women), 39 part-time/adjunct (25 women). *Tuition:* Part-time $600 per credit. *Required fees:* $40 per course. *Graduate housing:* On-campus housing not available. *Student services:* Campus employment opportunities, career counseling, exercise/wellness program, international student services, multicultural affairs office, services for students with disabilities. *Library facilities:* Brennan Library. *Collection:* Books: 35,093 (physical), 59,782 (digital/electronic); Serial titles: 63 (physical), 113,658 (digital/electronic); Databases: 88. Weekly public service hours: 83; students can reserve study rooms.

Computer facilities: Computer purchase and lease plans are available. 219 computers available on campus for general student use. A campuswide network can be accessed from student residence rooms and from off campus. Online class registration, online tutoring are available.
Website: http://www.lasell.edu/

General Application Contact: Adrienne Franciosi, Assistant Vice President of Graduate and Professional Studies, 617-243-2400, Fax: 617-243-2450, E-mail: gradinfo@lasell.edu.

GRADUATE UNITS

Graduate and Professional Studies in Communication Students: 27 full-time (18 women), 28 part-time (18 women); includes 12 minority (5 Black or African American, non-Hispanic/Latino; 6 Hispanic/Latino; 1 Two or more races, non-Hispanic/Latino), 17 international. Average age 30. 55 applicants, 44% accepted, 21 enrolled. *Faculty:* 5 full-time (4 women), 8 part-time/adjunct (4 women). Expenses: Contact institution. *Financial support:* Federal Work-Study, scholarships/grants, and tuition discounts available. Support available to part-time students. Financial award application deadline: 8/31; financial award applicants required to submit FAFSA. In 2018, 34 master's, 2 other advanced degrees awarded. *Program availability:* Part-time, evening/weekend, 100% online, blended/hybrid learning. Offers health communication (MSC, Graduate Certificate); integrated marketing communication (MSC, Graduate Certificate); public relations (MSC, Graduate Certificate). *Application deadline:* For fall admission, 8/31 priority date for domestic students, 6/30 priority date for international students; for spring admission, 12/31 priority date for domestic students, 10/31 priority date for international students. Applications are processed on a rolling basis. Electronic applications accepted. *Application Contact:* Adrienne Franciosi, Assistant Vice President of Graduate and Professional Studies, 617-243-2214, Fax: 617-243-2450, E-mail: gradinfo@lasell.edu. *Vice President of Graduate and Professional Studies,* Eric Turner, 617-243-2071, Fax: 617-243-2450, E-mail: gradinfo@lasell.edu.

Graduate and Professional Studies in Criminal Justice Students: 36 full-time (18 women), 63 part-time (21 women); includes 24 minority (7 Black or African American, non-Hispanic/Latino; 2 Asian, non-Hispanic/Latino; 12 Hispanic/Latino; 3 Two or more races, non-Hispanic/Latino). Average age 31. 37 applicants, 73% accepted, 23 enrolled. *Faculty:* 2 full-time (1 woman), 4 part-time/adjunct (2 women). Expenses: Contact institution. *Financial support:* Federal Work-Study, scholarships/grants, and tuition discounts available. Support available to part-time students. Financial award application deadline: 8/31; financial award applicants required to submit FAFSA. In 2018, 33 master's awarded. *Program availability:* Part-time, evening/weekend, online only, 100% online. Offers emergency and crisis management (MS, Certificate); homeland security and global justice (MS, Certificate); violence prevention and advocacy (MS, Certificate). *Application deadline:* For fall admission, 8/31 priority date for domestic students, 6/30 priority date for international students; for spring admission, 12/31 priority date for domestic students, 10/31 priority date for international students. Applications are processed on a rolling basis. Electronic applications accepted. *Application Contact:* Adrienne Franciosi, Assistant Vice President of Graduate and Professional Studies, 617-243-2214, Fax: 617-243-2450, E-mail: gradinfo@lasell.edu. *Vice President of Graduate and Professional Studies,* Eric Turner, 617-243-2071, Fax: 617-243-2450, E-mail: gradinfo@lasell.edu.

Graduate and Professional Studies in Education Students: 4 full-time (3 women), 45 part-time (37 women); includes 4 minority (3 Asian, non-Hispanic/Latino; 1 Hispanic/Latino). Average age 28. 23 applicants, 70% accepted, 10 enrolled. *Faculty:* 1 (woman) full-time, 5 part-time/adjunct (4 women). Expenses: Contact institution. *Financial support:* Federal Work-Study, scholarships/grants, and tuition discounts available. Support available to part-time students. Financial award application deadline: 8/31; financial award applicants required to submit FAFSA. In 2018, 22 master's awarded. *Program availability:* Part-time-only, evening/weekend, blended/hybrid learning. Offers curriculum, leadership, and inclusion (M Ed); elementary education (M Ed); special education (M Ed); teaching bilingual/English learners with disabilities (Graduate Certificate). *Application deadline:* For fall admission, 8/31 priority date for domestic students, 6/30 priority date for international students; for spring admission, 12/31 priority date for domestic students, 10/31 priority date for international students. Applications are processed on a rolling basis. Electronic applications accepted. *Application Contact:* Adrienne Franciosi, Director of Graduate Enrollment, 617-243-2214, Fax: 617-243-2450, E-mail: gradinfo@lasell.edu. *Vice President of Graduate and Professional Studies,* Eric Turner, 617-243-2071, Fax: 617-243-2450, E-mail: gradinfo@lasell.edu.

Graduate and Professional Studies in Management Students: 37 full-time (28 women), 76 part-time (48 women); includes 22 minority (12 Black or African American, non-Hispanic/Latino; 1 Asian, non-Hispanic/Latino; 9 Hispanic/Latino), 20 international. Average age 32. 68 applicants, 54% accepted, 20 enrolled. *Faculty:* 7 full-time (4 women), 14 part-time/adjunct (9 women). Expenses: Contact institution. *Financial support:* Federal Work-Study, scholarships/grants, and tuition discounts available. Support available to part-time students. Financial award application deadline: 8/31; financial award applicants required to submit FAFSA. In 2018, 62 master's, 1 other advanced degree awarded. *Program availability:* Part-time, evening/weekend, 100% online, blended/hybrid learning. Offers business administration (MBA); elder care management (MSM); hospitality and event management (MSM); human resources management (MSM, Graduate Certificate); management (MSM, Graduate Certificate); marketing (MS, Graduate Certificate); project management (MSM, Graduate Certificate). *Application deadline:* For fall admission, 8/31 priority date for domestic students, 6/30 priority date for international students; for spring admission, 12/31 priority date for domestic students, 10/31 priority date for international students. Applications are processed on a rolling basis. Electronic applications accepted. *Application Contact:* Adrienne Franciosi, Assistant Vice President of Graduate and Professional Studies, 617-243-2214, Fax: 617-243-2450, E-mail: gradinfo@lasell.edu. *Vice President of Graduate and Professional Studies,* Eric Turner, 617-243-2071, Fax: 617-243-2450, E-mail: gradinfo@lasell.edu.

Graduate and Professional Studies in Rehabilitation Science Students: 2 full-time (both women), 19 part-time (16 women); includes 3 minority (2 Black or African American, non-Hispanic/Latino; 1 Hispanic/Latino). Average age 26. 21 applicants, 43% accepted, 8 enrolled. *Faculty:* 1 full-time (0 women), 2 part-time/adjunct (both women). Expenses: Contact institution. *Financial support:* Federal Work-Study, scholarships/grants, and tuition discounts available. Support available to part-time students. Financial award application deadline: 8/31; financial award applicants required to submit FAFSA. In 2018, 6 master's awarded. *Program availability:* Part-time, evening/weekend, online only, 100% online. Offers rehabilitation science (MS). *Application deadline:* For fall admission, 8/31 priority date for domestic students, 6/30 priority date for international students; for spring admission, 12/31 priority date for domestic students, 10/31 priority date for international students. Applications are processed on a rolling basis. Electronic applications accepted. *Application Contact:* Adrienne Franciosi, Assistant Vice President of Graduate and Professional Studies, 617-243-2214, Fax: 617-243-2450, E-mail: gradinfo@lasell.edu. *Dean of Graduate and Professional Studies,* Eric Turner, 617-243-2071, Fax: 617-243-2450, E-mail: gradinfo@lasell.edu.

Graduate and Professional Studies in Sport Management Students: 15 full-time (7 women), 32 part-time (11 women); includes 17 minority (12 Black or African American, non-Hispanic/Latino; 4 Hispanic/Latino; 1 Two or more races, non-Hispanic/Latino). Average age 29. 36 applicants, 39% accepted, 11 enrolled. *Faculty:* 4 full-time (1 woman), 4 part-time/adjunct (2 women). Expenses: Contact institution. *Financial support:* Federal Work-Study, scholarships/grants, and tuition discounts available. Support available to part-time students. Financial award application deadline: 8/31; financial award applicants required to submit FAFSA. In 2018, 20 master's awarded. *Program availability:* Part-time, evening/weekend, online only, 100% online. Offers athletic administration (MS); parks and recreation (MS); sport leadership (MS, Graduate Certificate); sport tourism and hospitality (MS). *Application deadline:* For fall admission, 8/31 priority date for domestic students, 6/30 priority date for international students; for spring admission, 12/31 priority date for domestic students, 10/31 priority date for international students. Applications are processed on a rolling basis. Electronic applications accepted. *Application Contact:* Adrienne Franciosi, Assistant Vice President of Graduate and Professional Studies, 617-243-2214, Fax: 617-243-2450, E-mail: gradinfo@lasell.edu. *Vice President of Graduate and Professional Studies,* Eric Turner, 617-243-2071, Fax: 617-243-2450, E-mail: gradinfo@lasell.edu.

LA SIERRA UNIVERSITY, Riverside, CA 92505

General Information Independent-religious, coed, comprehensive institution. CGS member. *Graduate housing:* Rooms and/or apartments available on a first-come, first-served basis to single students and available to married students.

GRADUATE UNITS

College of Arts and Sciences *Program availability:* Part-time. Offers arts and sciences (MA); communication (MA); English (MA).

School of Business and Management Offers accounting (MBA); finance (MBA); general management (MBA); human resources management (MBA); leadership, values, and ethics for business and management (Certificate); marketing (MBA).

School of Education *Program availability:* Part-time, evening/weekend. Offers administration and leadership (MA, Ed D, Ed S); counseling (MA); curriculum and

instruction (MA, Ed D, Ed S); education (MA, MAT, Ed D, Ed S); educational psychology (Ed S); school psychology (Ed S); teaching (MAT).

School of Religion *Program availability:* Part-time. Offers pastoral ministry (M Div); religion (MA); religious education (MA); religious studies (MA).

LAURENTIAN UNIVERSITY, Sudbury, ON P3E 2C6, Canada

General Information Province-supported, coed, comprehensive institution. *Graduate housing:* Rooms and/or apartments available on a first-come, first-served basis to single and married students.

GRADUATE UNITS

School of Graduate Studies and Research *Program availability:* Part-time, evening/weekend. Offers analytical chemistry (M Sc); applied psychology (MA); applied social research (MA); biochemistry (M Sc); biology (M Sc); boreal ecology (PhD); environmental chemistry (M Sc); European history (MA); experimental psychology (MA); geology (M Sc); history of Northern Ontario (MA); human development (M Sc, MA); humanities: interpretation and values (MA); mineral deposits and precambrian geology (PhD); mineral exploration (M Sc); North American history (MA); nursing (M Sc N); organic chemistry (M Sc); physical/theoretical chemistry (M Sc); physics (M Sc); rural and Northern health (PhD); science communication (G Dip).

School of Commerce and Administration *Program availability:* Part-time, evening/weekend. Offers commerce and administration (MBA).

School of Engineering *Program availability:* Part-time. Offers mineral resources engineering (M Eng, MA Sc); natural resources engineering (PhD).

School of Social Work *Program availability:* Part-time. Offers social work (MSW). Open only to French-speaking students.

LAWRENCE TECHNOLOGICAL UNIVERSITY, Southfield, MI 48075-1058

General Information Independent, coed, university. *Graduate housing:* Rooms and/or apartments available on a first-come, first-served basis to single and married students. Housing application deadline: 5/1. *Research affiliation:* Ford Motor Company (engineering), Clinton River Watershed Council (storm water analysis), Detroit Economic Growth Association (Great Lakes Shoreline Cities Green Infrastructure Project), Hyundai-KIA America Technical Center, Inc. (improvement of built-in hands-free cell phone performance), Johnson Controls Battery Group, Inc. (vehicle system power management testing), Meijer Foundation (engineering).

GRADUATE UNITS

College of Architecture and Design *Program availability:* Part-time, evening/weekend. Offers architecture (M Arch, MA); build information modeling (Graduate Certificate); interior design (MID); social practice (MFA); transportation design (Graduate Certificate); urban design (MUD). Electronic applications accepted.

College of Arts and Sciences *Program availability:* Part-time, evening/weekend. Offers bioinformatics (Graduate Certificate); computer science (MS); educational technology (MA); instructional design, communication, and presentation (Graduate Certificate); integrated science (MA); science education (MA); technical and professional communication (MS, Graduate Certificate); writing for the digital age (Graduate Certificate). Electronic applications accepted.

College of Engineering *Program availability:* Part-time, evening/weekend. Offers architectural engineering (MS); automotive engineering (MS); biomedical engineering (MS); civil engineering (MA, MS, PhD); construction engineering management (MS); electrical and computer engineering (MS); engineering management (MEM); engineering technology (MS); fire engineering (MS); industrial engineering (MS); manufacturing systems (ME); mechanical engineering (MS, DE, PhD); mechatronic systems engineering (MS). Electronic applications accepted.

College of Management *Program availability:* Part-time, evening/weekend, 100% online. Offers business administration (MBA, DBA); cybersecurity (Graduate Certificate); health IT management (Graduate Certificate); information assurance management (Graduate Certificate); information systems (MS); information technology (MS, DM); management (PhD); nonprofit management and leadership (Graduate Certificate); operations management (MS); project management (Graduate Certificate). Electronic applications accepted.

LEBANESE AMERICAN UNIVERSITY, Beirut, Lebanon

General Information Private, coed, comprehensive institution.

GRADUATE UNITS

School of Arts and Sciences Offers computer science (MS); international affairs (MA).

School of Business Offers business (MBA).

School of Pharmacy Offers pharmacy (Pharm D).

LEBANON VALLEY COLLEGE, Annville, PA 17003-1400

General Information Independent-religious, coed, comprehensive institution. *Graduate housing:* Room and/or apartments available on a first-come, first-served basis to single students; on-campus housing not available to married students. Housing application deadline: 3/3.

GRADUATE UNITS

Program in Athletic Training Offers athletic training (MAT). Electronic applications accepted.

Program in Business Administration *Program availability:* Part-time, evening/weekend. Offers business administration (MBA); healthcare management (MBA); human resources (MBA); leadership and ethics (MBA); project management (MBA). Electronic applications accepted.

Program in Music Education *Program availability:* Part-time-only, evening/weekend. Offers music education (MME). Electronic applications accepted.

Program in Physical Therapy Offers physical therapy (DPT). Electronic applications accepted.

Program in Science Education *Program availability:* Part-time-only, evening/weekend, 100% online, blended/hybrid learning. Offers integrative STEM education (Certificate); STEM education (MSE). Electronic applications accepted.

Program in Speech-Language Pathology Offers speech-language pathology (MSLP).

LEE UNIVERSITY, Cleveland, TN 37320-3450

General Information Independent-religious, coed, comprehensive institution. *Enrollment:* 5,386 graduate, professional, and undergraduate students. *Enrollment by degree level:* 482 master's, 5 other advanced degrees. *Graduate housing:* Rooms and/or apartments available on a first-come, first-served basis to single and married students. Housing application deadline: 9/1. *Student services:* Campus employment opportunities, campus safety program, career counseling, exercise/wellness program, free psychological counseling, international student services, services for students with disabilities, teacher training, writing training. *Library facilities:* William G. Squires Library plus 2 others. *Collection:* Books: 158,156 (physical), 303,576 (digital/electronic); Serial titles: 244 (physical), 97,212 (digital/electronic); Databases: 137. Weekly public service hours: 93; students can reserve study rooms.

Computer facilities: 460 computers available on campus for general student use. A campuswide network can be accessed from student residence rooms and from off campus. Online class registration is available. Website: http://www.leeuniversity.edu/

General Application Contact: Jeffery McGirt, Director of Graduate Enrollment, 423-614-8691, Fax: 423-614-8317, E-mail: jmcgirt@leeuniversity.edu.

GRADUATE UNITS

Graduate Studies in Counseling Students: 89 full-time (71 women), 29 part-time (19 women); includes 26 minority (8 Black or African American, non-Hispanic/Latino; 17 Hispanic/Latino; 1 Two or more races, non-Hispanic/Latino). Average age 30. 50 applicants, 76% accepted, 31 enrolled. *Faculty:* 8 full-time (4 women), 2 part-time/adjunct (0 women). Expenses: Contact institution. *Financial support:* In 2018–19, 46 students received support. Career-related internships or fieldwork, Federal Work-Study, institutionally sponsored loans, scholarships/grants, and unspecified assistantships available. Financial award application deadline: 3/1; financial award applicants required to submit FAFSA. In 2018, 46 master's awarded. *Program availability:* Part-time, 100% online. Offers holistic child development (MS); marriage and family studies (MS); marriage and family therapy (MS); school counseling (MS). *Application deadline:* For fall admission, 4/1 priority date for domestic and international students; for spring admission, 11/1 priority date for domestic and international students. Applications are processed on a rolling basis. *Application fee:* $25. Electronic applications accepted. *Application Contact:* Jeffery McGirt, Director of Graduate Enrollment, 423-614-8691, Fax: 423-614-8317, E-mail: jmcgirt@leeuniversity.edu. *Director,* Dr. Trevor Milliron, 423-614-8126, Fax: 423-614-8124, E-mail: tmilliron@leeuniversity.edu.

MBA Program Students: 13 full-time (7 women), 54 part-time (26 women); includes 7 minority (4 Black or African American, non-Hispanic/Latino; 1 Asian, non-Hispanic/Latino; 1 Hispanic/Latino; 1 Two or more races, non-Hispanic/Latino), 11 international. Average age 29. 30 applicants, 80% accepted, 23 enrolled. *Faculty:* 5 full-time (1 woman). Expenses: Contact institution. *Financial support:* In 2018–19, 36 students received support. Scholarships/grants available. Financial award application deadline: 3/1; financial award applicants required to submit FAFSA. In 2018, 27 master's awarded. *Program availability:* Part-time, evening/weekend, 100% online. Offers business administration (MBA). *Application deadline:* For fall admission, 4/1 priority date for domestic and international students; for spring admission, 10/1 priority date for domestic and international students. Applications are processed on a rolling basis. *Application fee:* $25. Electronic applications accepted. *Application Contact:* Jeffery McGirt, Director of Graduate Enrollment, 423-614-8691, Fax: 423-614-8317, E-mail: jmcgirt@leeuniversity.edu. *Director,* Dr. Shane Griffith, 423-614-8694, E-mail: mba@leeuniversity.edu.

Program in Education Students: 32 full-time (26 women), 73 part-time (49 women); includes 13 minority (10 Black or African American, non-Hispanic/Latino; 3 Two or more races, non-Hispanic/Latino), 3 international. Average age 30. 56 applicants, 73% accepted, 34 enrolled. *Faculty:* 13 full-time (5 women), 13 part-time/adjunct (7 women). Expenses: Contact institution. *Financial support:* In 2018–19, 43 students received support. Career-related internships or fieldwork, Federal Work-Study, institutionally sponsored loans, scholarships/grants, and unspecified assistantships available. Financial award application deadline: 3/1; financial award applicants required to submit FAFSA. In 2018, 60 master's, 3 other advanced degrees awarded. *Program availability:* Part-time. Offers art (MAT); curriculum and instruction (M Ed, Ed S); early childhood (MAT); educational leadership (M Ed, Ed S); elementary education (MAT); English and math (MAT); English and science (MAT); English and social studies (MAT); higher education administration (MS); history (MAT); history and economics (MAT); math and science (MAT); math and social studies (MAT); middle grades (MAT); science and social studies (MASW); secondary education (MAT); Spanish (MAT); special education (M Ed, MAT); TESOL (MAT). *Application deadline:* For fall admission, 6/1 priority date for domestic and international students; for spring admission, 11/1 priority date for domestic and international students; for summer admission, 4/1 priority date for domestic and international students. Applications are processed on a rolling basis. *Application fee:* $25. Electronic applications accepted. *Application Contact:* Jeffery McGirt, Director of Graduate Enrollment, 423-614-8691, Fax: 423-614-8317, E-mail: jmcgirt@leeuniversity.edu. *Director,* Dr. William Kamm, 423-614-8544, E-mail: wkamm@leeuniversity.edu.

Program in Music Students: 18 full-time (8 women), 6 part-time (4 women); includes 3 minority (all Asian, non-Hispanic/Latino), 5 international. Average age 26. 15 applicants, 93% accepted, 10 enrolled. *Faculty:* 24 full-time (6 women), 6 part-time/adjunct (4 women). Expenses: Contact institution. *Financial support:* In 2018–19, 26 students received support. Career-related internships or fieldwork, Federal Work-Study, institutionally sponsored loans, scholarships/grants, and unspecified assistantships available. Financial award application deadline: 3/1; financial award applicants required to submit FAFSA. In 2018, 12 master's awarded. *Program availability:* Part-time, online only, 100% online. Offers conducting (MM); music education (MM); music performance (MM); religious studies (MCM); sacred music (MCM). *Application deadline:* For fall admission, 4/1 priority date for domestic and international students; for spring admission, 10/1 priority date for domestic and international students. Applications are processed on a rolling basis. *Application fee:* $25. Electronic applications accepted. *Application Contact:* Jeffery McGirt, Director of Graduate Enrollment, 423-614-8691, Fax: 423-614-8317, E-mail: jmcgirt@leeuniversity.edu. *Director,* Dr. Brad J. Moffett, 423-614-8240, Fax: 423-614-8245, E-mail: gradmusic@leeuniversity.edu.

Programs in Religion Students: 35 full-time (7 women), 112 part-time (34 women); includes 70 minority (11 Black or African American, non-Hispanic/Latino; 55 Hispanic/Latino; 4 Two or more races, non-Hispanic/Latino), 3 international. Average age 37. 14 applicants, 93% accepted, 10 enrolled. *Faculty:* 14 full-time (3 women), 7 part-time/adjunct (0 women). Expenses: Contact institution. *Financial support:* In 2018–19, 58 students received support, including 14 teaching assistantships (averaging $1,593 per year); career-related internships or fieldwork, Federal Work-Study, institutionally sponsored loans, scholarships/grants, and unspecified assistantships also available. Financial award application deadline: 3/1; financial award applicants required to submit FAFSA. In 2018, 15 master's awarded. *Program availability:* Part-time, 100% online. Offers biblical studies (MA); ministry studies/leadership (MA); ministry studies/worship (MA); ministry studies/youth and family (MA); theological studies (MA). *Application deadline:* For fall admission, 4/1 priority date for domestic and international students; for spring admission, 10/1 priority date for domestic and international students. Applications are processed on a rolling basis. *Application fee:* $25. Electronic applications accepted. *Application Contact:* Jeffery McGirt, Director of Graduate

Enrollment, 423-614-8691, Fax: 423-614-8317, E-mail: jmcgirt@leeuniversity.edu. *Director,* Dr. Lisa Long, 423-303-5100, E-mail: llong@leeuniversity.edu.

LEHIGH UNIVERSITY, Bethlehem, PA 18015

General Information Independent, coed, university. CGS member. *Enrollment:* 1,110 full-time matriculated graduate/professional students (452 women), 614 part-time matriculated graduate/professional students (300 women). *Enrollment by degree level:* 1,026 master's, 691 doctoral, 7 other advanced degrees. *Graduate faculty:* 365 full-time (115 women), 56 part-time/adjunct (29 women). Tuition and fees vary according to program. *Graduate housing:* Rooms and/or apartments available on a first-come, first-served basis to single and married students. *Student services:* Campus employment opportunities, campus safety program, career counseling, child daycare facilities, exercise/wellness program, free psychological counseling, international student services, low-cost health insurance, multicultural affairs office, services for students with disabilities, teacher training, writing training. *Library facilities:* E. W. Fairchild-Martindale Library plus 1 other. *Collection:* Books: 798,207 (physical), 402,504 (digital/electronic); Serial titles: 2,050 (physical), 61,205 (digital/electronic); Databases: 191. Weekly public service hours: 83; students can reserve study rooms.

Computer facilities: Computer purchase and lease plans are available. 597 computers available on campus for general student use. A campuswide network can be accessed from student residence rooms and from off campus. Online class registration is available. Website: http://www.lehigh.edu/

GRADUATE UNITS

College of Arts and Sciences Students: 265 full-time (129 women), 66 part-time (39 women); includes 37 minority (8 Black or African American, non-Hispanic/Latino; 1 American Indian or Alaska Native, non-Hispanic/Latino; 9 Asian, non-Hispanic/Latino; 15 Hispanic/Latino; 4 Two or more races, non-Hispanic/Latino), 74 international. Average age 28. 524 applicants, 39% accepted, 91 enrolled. *Faculty:* 166 full-time (66 women), 7 part-time/adjunct (2 women). Expenses: Contact institution. *Financial support:* Application deadline: 1/1. In 2018, 59 master's, 29 doctorates awarded. *Program availability:* Part-time, online learning. Offers Africana studies (Graduate Certificate); American studies (MA); applied mathematics (MS, PhD); arts and sciences (MA, MS, PhD, Graduate Certificate); Atlantic world (PhD); biochemistry (PhD); British history (PhD); cell and molecular biology (PhD); chemistry (MS, PhD); documentary film (Graduate Certificate); earth and environmental sciences (MS, PhD); English (MA, PhD); environmental health (Graduate Certificate); environmental justice (Graduate Certificate); environmental policy and law (Graduate Certificate); environmental policy design (MA); history (MA); industrial and modern America (PhD); integrative biology (PhD); mathematics (MS, PhD); molecular biology (MS); photonics (MS); physics (MS, PhD); politics and policy (MA); psychology (MS, PhD); public history (MA); sociology (MA); statistics (MS); sustainable development (Graduate Certificate); urban environmental policy (Graduate Certificate). *Application deadline:* For fall admission, 7/1 for domestic students, 7/15 for international students; for spring admission, 12/1 for domestic and international students. *Application fee:* $75. Electronic applications accepted. *Application Contact:* Tyler Frey, Administrative Clerk, 610-758-4281, Fax: 610-758-6232, E-mail: trf218@lehigh.edu. *Associate Dean of Graduate Studies,* Dr. Dominic Packer, 610-758-4282, Fax: 610-758-6232, E-mail: dlp208@lehigh.edu.

College of Business Students: 138 full-time (73 women), 176 part-time (47 women); includes 34 minority (4 Black or African American, non-Hispanic/Latino; 18 Asian, non-Hispanic/Latino; 8 Hispanic/Latino; 1 Native Hawaiian or other Pacific Islander, non-Hispanic/Latino; 3 Two or more races, non-Hispanic/Latino), 106 international. Average age 30. 457 applicants, 59% accepted, 115 enrolled. *Faculty:* 31 full-time (4 women), 10 part-time/adjunct (4 women). Expenses: Contact institution. *Financial support:* In 2018–19, 10 fellowships with partial tuition reimbursements, 1 research assistantship with full tuition reimbursement (averaging $19,700 per year), 15 teaching assistantships with full tuition reimbursements (averaging $19,700 per year) were awarded; scholarships/grants and unspecified assistantships also available. Support available to part-time students. Financial award application deadline: 1/15. In 2018, 158 master's, 1 doctorate awarded. *Program availability:* Part-time, evening/weekend, synchronous with live classroom. Offers accounting and information analysis (MS); analytical finance (MS); business administration (MBA); business and economics (MBA, MS, PhD); economics (MS, PhD); project management (MBA). *Application deadline:* For fall admission, 7/15 for domestic students, 5/1 for international students; for spring admission, 12/1 for domestic and international students. *Application fee:* $75. *Application Contact:* Mary Theresa Taglang, Director of Recruitment and Admissions, 610-758-4386, Fax: 610-758-5283, E-mail: mtt4@lehigh.edu. *Dean,* Georgette Chapman-Phillips, 610-758-6725, Fax: 610-758-4499, E-mail: gcp214@lehigh.edu.

College of Education Students: 145 full-time (125 women), 251 part-time (168 women); includes 68 minority (17 Black or African American, non-Hispanic/Latino; 12 Asian, non-Hispanic/Latino; 36 Hispanic/Latino; 1 Native Hawaiian or other Pacific Islander, non-Hispanic/Latino; 2 Two or more races, non-Hispanic/Latino), 51 international. Average age 31. 322 applicants, 48% accepted, 70 enrolled. *Faculty:* 32 full-time (22 women), 34 part-time/adjunct (22 women). Expenses: Contact institution. *Financial support:* In 2018–19, 127 students received support, including 3 fellowships with tuition reimbursements available (averaging $2,500 per year), 45 research assistantships with full and partial tuition reimbursements available (averaging $13,778 per year); career-related internships or fieldwork, scholarships/grants, and unspecified assistantships also available. Financial award application deadline: 3/1. In 2018, 147 master's, 23 doctorates awarded. *Program availability:* Part-time, evening/weekend, blended/hybrid learning. Offers counseling and human services (M Ed); counseling psychology (PhD); curriculum and instruction (Certificate); education (M Ed, MA, MS, Ed D, PhD, Certificate, Ed S, Graduate Certificate); educational leadership (M Ed, Ed D); elementary education (M Ed); instructional technology (MS); international counseling (M Ed, Certificate); K-12 principal (Certificate); school counseling (M Ed); school psychology (PhD, Ed S); special education (M Ed, PhD); superintendent letter (Certificate); teaching, learning and technology (PhD). *Application deadline:* For fall admission, 1/1 for domestic and international students; for spring admission, 12/15 for domestic and international students; for summer admission, 4/15 for domestic and international students. Applications are processed on a rolling basis. *Application fee:* $65. Electronic applications accepted. *Application Contact:* Donna M. Johnson, Manager of Admissions and Recruitment, 610-758-3231, Fax: 610-758-6223, E-mail: dmj4@lehigh.edu. *Dean,* Dr. William Gaudelli, 610-758-3221, Fax: 610-758-6223, E-mail: wig318@lehigh.edu.

P.C. Rossin College of Engineering and Applied Science Students: 562 full-time (125 women), 121 part-time (46 women); includes 58 minority (13 Black or African American, non-Hispanic/Latino; 18 Asian, non-Hispanic/Latino; 19 Hispanic/Latino; 2 Native Hawaiian or other Pacific Islander, non-Hispanic/Latino; 6 Two or more races, non-Hispanic/Latino), 425 international. Average age 29. 1,598 applicants, 37% accepted, 188 enrolled. *Faculty:* 145 full-time (26 women), 9 part-time/adjunct (1 woman). Expenses: Contact institution. *Financial support:* In 2018–19, 257 students received support, including 42 fellowships with tuition reimbursements available (averaging $22,050 per year), 160 research assistantships with tuition reimbursements available (averaging $29,400 per year), 55 teaching assistantships with tuition reimbursements available (averaging $22,050 per year); scholarships/grants, tuition waivers (full and partial), and unspecified assistantships also available. Financial award application deadline: 1/15. In 2018, 284 master's, 60 doctorates awarded. *Program availability:* Part-time, 100% online, blended/hybrid learning. Offers analytical finance (MS); bioengineering (MS, PhD); biological chemical engineering (M Eng); chemical energy engineering (M Eng); chemical engineering (M Eng, MS, PhD); civil and environmental engineering (M Eng, MS, PhD); computer engineering (M Eng, MS, PhD); computer science (M Eng, MS, PhD); electrical engineering (M Eng, MS, PhD); energy systems engineering (M Eng); engineering and applied science (M Eng, MS, PhD, Certificate); healthcare systems engineering (M Eng, Certificate); industrial and systems engineering (M Eng, MS, PhD); management science and engineering (M Eng, MS); materials science and engineering (M Eng, MS, PhD); mechanical engineering (M Eng, MS, PhD); photonics (MS); polymer science/engineering (M Eng, MS, PhD); technical entrepreneurship (M Eng). MBA & E - Rossin College of Engineering & Applied Science/College of Business; MS Fin engineering (Formerly AFIN) - RCEAS/College of Bus/Coll of Arts & Sc. *Application deadline:* For fall admission, 7/15 for domestic students, 6/15 for international students; for spring admission, 12/1 for domestic and international students. *Application fee:* $75. Electronic applications accepted. *Application Contact:* Brianne Lisk, Manager of Graduate Programs, 610-758-6310, Fax: 610-758-5623, E-mail: brie.lisk@lehigh.edu. *Dean,* Dr. Stephen P. DeWeerth, 610-758-5308, Fax: 610-758-5623, E-mail: steve.deweerth@lehigh.edu.

Center for Polymer Science and Engineering Students: 10 full-time (5 women), 35 part-time (14 women); includes 13 minority (3 Black or African American, non-Hispanic/Latino; 6 Asian, non-Hispanic/Latino; 3 Hispanic/Latino; 1 Native Hawaiian or other Pacific Islander, non-Hispanic/Latino), 5 international. Average age 31. 47 applicants, 36% accepted, 14 enrolled. Expenses: Contact institution. *Financial support:* In 2018–19, 1 research assistantship with full tuition reimbursement (averaging $11,025 per year), 1 teaching assistantship with full tuition reimbursement (averaging $11,025 per year) were awarded; health care benefits also available. Financial award application deadline: 1/15. In 2018, 6 master's awarded. *Program availability:* Part-time, evening/weekend, 100% online, blended/hybrid learning. Offers polymer science and engineering (M Eng, MS, PhD). *Application deadline:* For fall admission, 7/15 for domestic students, 1/15 for international students; for spring admission, 12/1 for domestic and international students; for summer admission, 4/30 for domestic and international students. Applications are processed on a rolling basis. *Application fee:* $75. Electronic applications accepted. *Application Contact:* James E. Roberts, Chair, Polymer Education Committee, 610-758-4841, Fax: 610-758-6536, E-mail: jer1@lehigh.edu. *Director,* Dr. Raymond A. Pearson, 610-758-3857, Fax: 610-758-3526, E-mail: rp02@lehigh.edu.

LEHMAN COLLEGE OF THE CITY UNIVERSITY OF NEW YORK, Bronx, NY 10468-1589

General Information State and locally supported, coed, comprehensive institution. *Graduate housing:* On-campus housing not available. *Research affiliation:* New York Botanical Gardens, Montefiore Hospital and Medical Center.

GRADUATE UNITS

School of Arts and Humanities *Program availability:* Part-time, evening/weekend. Offers applied music and music teaching (MAT); art education (MA); art studio (MA, MFA); arts and humanities (MA, MAT, MFA); English (MA); history (MA); Spanish (MA).

School of Education *Program availability:* Part-time, evening/weekend. Offers bilingual special education (MS Ed); childhood education (MS Ed); counselor education/school counseling (MS Ed); early childhood education (MS Ed); early childhood special education (MS Ed); education (MA, MS Ed); English education (MS Ed); literacy studies (MS Ed); mathematics education (MA); science education (MS Ed); social studies education (MA); special education (MS Ed); teaching English to speakers of other languages (MS Ed).

School of Health Sciences, Human Services and Nursing Offers adult health nursing (MS); clinical nutrition (MS); community nutrition (MS); dietetic internship (MS); health education and promotion (MA); health N–12 teacher (MS Ed); health sciences, human services and nursing (MA, MS, MS Ed, MSN, MSW); nursing of older adults (MS); nutrition (MS); parent-child nursing (MS); pediatric nurse practitioner (MS); recreation education (MS Ed); social work (MSW); speech-language pathology (MA).

School of Natural and Social Sciences *Program availability:* Part-time, evening/weekend. Offers accounting (MS); biology (MA); business (MS); computer science (MS); mathematics (MS); natural and social sciences (MA, MS, MS Ed, PhD).

LE MOYNE COLLEGE, Syracuse, NY 13214

General Information Independent-religious, coed, comprehensive institution. *Enrollment:* 320 full-time matriculated graduate/professional students (239 women), 251 part-time matriculated graduate/professional students (178 women). *Enrollment by degree level:* 521 master's, 50 other advanced degrees. *Graduate faculty:* 38 full-time (20 women), 47 part-time/adjunct (33 women). *Tuition:* Full-time $14,465; part-time $803 per credit hour. *Required fees:* $50; $50 per unit. $25 per semester. One-time fee: $50 part-time. Tuition and fees vary according to degree level and program. *Graduate housing:* On-campus housing not available. *Student services:* Campus employment opportunities, campus safety program, career counseling, exercise/wellness program, free psychological counseling, international student services, low-cost health insurance, multicultural affairs office, services for students with disabilities, teacher training, writing training. *Library facilities:* Noreen Reale Falcone Library. *Collection:* Books: 261,183 (physical), 206,330 (digital/electronic); Serial titles: 1,391 (physical), 508 (digital/electronic); Databases: 270. Weekly public service hours: 109; study areas open 24 hours, 5–7 days a week; students can reserve study rooms.

Computer facilities: 330 computers available on campus for general student use. A campuswide network can be accessed from student residence rooms and from off campus. Online class registration, ECHO (campus-wide portal), some virtual access from off campus are available.
Website: http://www.lemoyne.edu/

General Application Contact: Dr. Timothy M. Lee, Vice President for Enrollment Management, 315-445-5444, Fax: 315-445-6092, E-mail: trapaskp@lemoyne.edu.

GRADUATE UNITS

Department of Education Students: 35 full-time (28 women), 119 part-time (84 women); includes 14 minority (5 Black or African American, non-Hispanic/Latino; 1 Asian, non-Hispanic/Latino; 7 Hispanic/Latino; 1 Two or more races, non-Hispanic/Latino), 1 international. Average age 30. 123 applicants, 89% accepted, 96 enrolled. *Faculty:* 7 full-time (5 women), 16 part-time/adjunct (11 women). Expenses: Contact institution. *Financial support:* In 2018–19, 44 students received support.

Career-related internships or fieldwork, scholarships/grants, and health care benefits available. Support available to part-time students. Financial award applicants required to submit FAFSA. In 2018, 66 master's, 48 CASs awarded. *Program availability:* Part-time, evening/weekend. Offers adolescent education (MS Ed, MST); adolescent education/special education (MS Ed, MST); adolescent English (MST); adolescent English/special education (MST); adolescent foreign language (MST); adolescent history (MST); childhood education (MS Ed); childhood education/special education (MS Ed); elementary education (MS Ed); general education (MS Ed); inclusive childhood education (MST); literacy education (MS Ed); school building leader (MS Ed); school building leadership (CAS); school district business leader (MS Ed, CAS); school district leader (MS Ed); school district leadership (CAS); secondary education (MS Ed); special education (MS Ed); teaching English to speakers of other languages (MS Ed); urban studies (MS Ed). *Application deadline:* For fall admission, 4/1 priority date for domestic and international students; for spring admission, 10/1 priority date for domestic and international students; for summer admission, 3/1 priority date for domestic and international students. Applications are processed on a rolling basis. Electronic applications accepted. *Application Contact:* Jody F Manning, Assistant Director for Graduate Admission, 315-445-5444, Fax: 315-445-6092, E-mail: manninjf@lemoyne.edu. *Chair, Department of Education,* Dr. Stephen C. Fleury, 315-445-4376, Fax: 315-445-4744, E-mail: fleurysc@lemoyne.edu.

Department of Nursing Students: 27 full-time (22 women), 54 part-time (50 women); includes 14 minority (6 Black or African American, non-Hispanic/Latino; 6 Hispanic/Latino; 2 Two or more races, non-Hispanic/Latino). Average age 33. 39 applicants, 95% accepted, 32 enrolled. *Faculty:* 3 full-time (all women), 5 part-time/adjunct (all women). Expenses: Contact institution. *Financial support:* In 2018–19, 15 students received support. Career-related internships or fieldwork, scholarships/grants, health care benefits, and unspecified assistantships available. Support available to part-time students. Financial award applicants required to submit FAFSA. In 2018, 32 master's, 3 other advanced degrees awarded. *Program availability:* Part-time, evening/weekend. Offers family nurse practitioner (MS, CAS); informatics (MS, CAS); nursing administration (MS, CAS); nursing education (MS, CAS). *Application deadline:* For fall admission, 8/1 priority date for domestic students, 8/1 for international students; for spring admission, 11/15 priority date for domestic students, 11/15 for international students; for summer admission, 5/1 priority date for domestic students, 5/1 for international students. Applications are processed on a rolling basis. *Application fee:* $50. Electronic applications accepted. *Application Contact:* Timothy M. Lee, Vice President for Enrollment Management, 315-445-5444, Fax: 315-445-6092. *Professor/Chair of Nursing,* Dr. Margaret M. Wells, 315-445-5435, Fax: 315-445-6024, E-mail: wellsmm@lemoyne.edu.

Department of Occupational Therapy Students: 75 full-time (69 women), 4 part-time (3 women); includes 15 minority (2 Black or African American, non-Hispanic/Latino; 10 Asian, non-Hispanic/Latino; 2 Hispanic/Latino; 1 Native Hawaiian or other Pacific Islander, non-Hispanic/Latino). Average age 25. 99 applicants, 85% accepted, 45 enrolled. *Faculty:* 3 full-time (all women), 6 part-time/adjunct (4 women). Expenses: Contact institution. *Financial support:* Career-related internships or fieldwork, scholarships/grants, and health care benefits available. Financial award applicants required to submit FAFSA. In 2018, 39 master's awarded. Offers occupational therapy (MS). *Application deadline:* For fall admission, 3/30 for domestic and international students. Applications are processed on a rolling basis. *Application fee:* $125. Electronic applications accepted. *Application Contact:* Timothy M. Lee, Vice President for Enrollment Management, 315-445-5444, Fax: 315-445-6092. *Interim Chair,* Dr. Deborah Marr, 315-445-5432, E-mail: occupationaltherapy@lemoyne.edu.

Department of Physician Assistant Studies Students: 131 full-time (97 women), 2 part-time (both women); includes 9 minority (4 Black or African American, non-Hispanic/Latino; 3 Asian, non-Hispanic/Latino; 1 Hispanic/Latino; 1 Two or more races, non-Hispanic/Latino), 1 international. Average age 26. 1,284 applicants, 7% accepted, 64 enrolled. *Faculty:* 6 full-time (4 women), 13 part-time/adjunct (10 women). Expenses: Contact institution. *Financial support:* In 2018–19, 14 students received support. Career-related internships or fieldwork, scholarships/grants, and health care benefits available. Financial award applicants required to submit FAFSA. In 2018, 67 master's awarded. Offers physician assistant (MS). *Application deadline:* For fall admission, 10/1 priority date for domestic and international students. *Application fee:* $175. Electronic applications accepted. *Application Contact:* Elizabeth W. Mercer, Interim Director, Department of Physician Assistant Studies, 315-445-4745, Fax: 315-445-6092, E-mail: mercerew@lemoyne.edu. *Interim Director, Department of Physician Assistant Studies,* Elizabeth W. Mercer, 315-445-4745, Fax: 315-445-4602, E-mail: mercerew@lemoyne.edu.

Madden School of Business Students: 48 full-time (21 women), 63 part-time (30 women); includes 11 minority (3 Black or African American, non-Hispanic/Latino; 1 American Indian or Alaska Native, non-Hispanic/Latino; 3 Asian, non-Hispanic/Latino; 4 Hispanic/Latino), 4 international. Average age 27. 69 applicants, 94% accepted, 61 enrolled. *Faculty:* 18 full-time (5 women), 5 part-time/adjunct (1 woman). Expenses: Contact institution. *Financial support:* In 2018–19, 35 students received support. Career-related internships or fieldwork, scholarships/grants, health care benefits, and unspecified assistantships available. Support available to part-time students. Financial award applicants required to submit FAFSA. In 2018, 60 master's awarded. *Program availability:* Part-time, evening/weekend. Offers business administration (MBA); information systems (MS). *Application deadline:* For fall admission, 7/1 priority date for domestic and international students; for spring admission, 11/1 priority date for domestic and international students; for summer admission, 4/1 priority date for domestic and international students. Applications are processed on a rolling basis. *Application fee:* $0. Electronic applications accepted. *Application Contact:* Teresa M. Renn, Senior Assistant Director for Graduate Admission, 315-445-5444, Fax: 315-445-6092, E-mail: renntm@lemoyne.edu. *Dean of Madden School of Business,* James Joseph, 315-445-4280, Fax: 315-445-4787, E-mail: josepjae@lemoyne.edu.

Program in Arts Administration Students: 4 full-time (2 women), 9 part-time (all women); includes 3 minority (2 Black or African American, non-Hispanic/Latino; 1 Two or more races, non-Hispanic/Latino). Average age 30. 15 applicants, 80% accepted, 10 enrolled. *Faculty:* 1 full-time (0 women), 2 part-time/adjunct (both women). Expenses: Contact institution. *Financial support:* In 2018–19, 5 students received support. Career-related internships or fieldwork, scholarships/grants, and health care benefits available. Support available to part-time students. Financial award applicants required to submit FAFSA. In 2018, 7 master's awarded. *Program availability:* Part-time, evening/weekend. Offers arts administration (MS). *Application deadline:* For fall admission, 7/1 priority date for domestic and international students; for spring admission, 11/1 priority date for domestic and international students; for summer admission, 4/1 priority date for domestic and international students. Applications are processed on a rolling basis. *Application fee:* $50. Electronic applications accepted. *Application Contact:* Teresa M. Renn, Senior Assistant Director for Graduate Admission, 315-445-5444, Fax: 315-445-6092, E-mail: renntm@lemoyne.edu. *Assistant Professor and Director of Arts Administration,* Travis Newton, 315-445-4201, E-mail: newtontm@lemoyne.edu.

LENOIR-RHYNE UNIVERSITY, Hickory, NC 28601

General Information Independent-religious, coed, comprehensive institution. *Graduate housing:* Room and/or apartments available on a first-come, first-served basis to single students; on-campus housing not available to married students. Housing application deadline: 5/1.

GRADUATE UNITS

Graduate Programs *Program availability:* Part-time, evening/weekend, online learning. Electronic applications accepted.

Charles M. Snipes School of Business *Program availability:* Part-time, evening/weekend, online learning. Offers accounting (MBA); business analytics and information technology (MBA); entrepreneurship (MBA); global business (MBA); healthcare administration (MBA); innovation and change management (MBA); leadership development (MBA). Electronic applications accepted.

Lutheran Theological Southern Seminary *Program availability:* Part-time. Offers theology (M Div, MACM, MAR, STM).

School of Arts and Letters Offers arts and letters (MA); writing (MA). Electronic applications accepted.

School of Counseling and Human Services *Program availability:* Part-time, evening/weekend. Offers clinical mental health counseling (MA); counseling and human services (MA); school counseling (MA). Electronic applications accepted.

School of Education *Program availability:* Part-time, evening/weekend, online learning. Offers community and nonprofit leadership (MA); community college administration (MA); education (MA, MAT, MS); general management (MA); higher education leadership (MA); management (MA); online teaching and instructional design (MS); second language community services (MA); secondary education (MAT); substance abuse (MA); vocational strategies (MA). Electronic applications accepted.

School of Health, Exercise and Sport Science *Program availability:* Part-time. Offers athletic training (MS); public health (MPH).

School of Natural Sciences *Program availability:* Part-time, evening/weekend, online learning. Offers natural sciences (MS); sustainability studies (MS). Electronic applications accepted.

School of Nursing *Program availability:* Online only. Offers nursing (MSN); nursing administration (MSN); nursing education (MSN). Electronic applications accepted.

School of Occupational Therapy Offers occupational therapy (MS).

School of Physician Assistant Studies Offers physician assistant studies (MS).

LESLEY UNIVERSITY, Cambridge, MA 02138-2790

General Information Independent, coed, primarily women, comprehensive institution. *Graduate housing:* Room and/or apartments available to single students; on-campus housing not available to married students. *Research affiliation:* TERC (education research and development).

GRADUATE UNITS

College of Art and Design *Program availability:* Part-time. Offers photography (MFA); visual arts (MFA). Electronic applications accepted.

Graduate School of Arts and Social Sciences *Program availability:* Part-time, online learning. Offers clinical mental health counseling (MA); counseling psychology (MA, CAGS); creative writing (MFA); expressive therapies (MA, PhD, CAGS); independent studies (CAGS); independent study (MA); intercultural relations (MA, CAGS); interdisciplinary studies (MA); urban environmental leadership (MA). Electronic applications accepted.

Graduate School of Education *Program availability:* Part-time, evening/weekend, online learning. Offers arts, community, and education (M Ed); autism studies (Certificate); curriculum and instruction (M Ed, CAGS); early childhood education (M Ed); ecological teaching and learning (MS); educational studies (PhD); elementary education (M Ed); emergent technologies for educators (Certificate); ESLArts: language learning through the arts (M Ed); high school education (M Ed); individually designed (M Ed); integrated teaching through the arts (M Ed); literacy for K-8 classroom teachers (M Ed); mathematics education (M Ed); middle school education (M Ed); moderate disabilities (M Ed); online learning (Certificate); reading (CAGS); science in education (M Ed); severe disabilities (CAGS); special needs (CAGS); specialist teacher of reading (M Ed); teacher of visual art (M Ed); technology in education (M Ed, CAGS). Electronic applications accepted.

LES ROCHES INTERNATIONAL SCHOOL OF HOTEL MANAGEMENT, CH-3975 Bluche, Switzerland

General Information Private, coed, comprehensive institution.

GRADUATE UNITS

Program in Hospitality Management Offers hospitality management (MBA). Available only at Switzerland campus.

LETOURNEAU UNIVERSITY, Longview, TX 75607-7001

General Information Independent-religious, coed, comprehensive institution. *Enrollment:* 3,175 graduate, professional, and undergraduate students; 61 full-time matriculated graduate/professional students (47 women), 311 part-time matriculated graduate/professional students (248 women). *Enrollment by degree level:* 372 master's. *Graduate housing:* Rooms and/or apartments available on a first-come, first-served basis to single and married students. *Student services:* Campus employment opportunities, campus safety program, career counseling, exercise/wellness program, free psychological counseling, international student services, low-cost health insurance, multicultural affairs office, services for students with disabilities, writing training. *Library facilities:* Margaret Estes Library plus 1 other. *Collection:* Books: 36,096 (physical), 233,126 (digital/electronic); Serial titles: 29,406 (digital/electronic); Databases: 95. Weekly public service hours: 87.

Computer facilities: Computer purchase and lease plans are available. A campuswide network can be accessed from student residence rooms and from off campus. Online class registration is available. Website: http://www.letu.edu/

GRADUATE UNITS

Graduate Programs Students: 61 full-time (47 women), 311 part-time (248 women); includes 184 minority (117 Black or African American, non-Hispanic/Latino; 3 American Indian or Alaska Native, non-Hispanic/Latino; 1 Asian, non-Hispanic/Latino; 35 Hispanic/Latino; 28 Two or more races, non-Hispanic/Latino), 2 international. Average age 37. Expenses: Contact institution. *Financial support:* Research assistantships, teaching assistantships, unspecified assistantships, and employee tuition waivers and institutionally sponsored loans available. Financial award applicants required to submit FAFSA. In 2018, 97 master's awarded. *Program availability:* Part-time, 100% online, blended/hybrid learning. Offers business administration (MBA); counseling (MA);

curriculum and instruction (M Ed); educational administration (M Ed); engineering (ME, MS); engineering management (MEM); health care administration (MS); marriage and family therapy (MA); psychology (MA); strategic leadership (MSL); teacher leadership (M Ed); teaching and learning (M Ed). *Application deadline:* Applications are processed on a rolling basis. Electronic applications accepted.

LEWIS & CLARK COLLEGE, Portland, OR 97219-7899

General Information Independent, coed, comprehensive institution. *Graduate housing:* On-campus housing not available.

GRADUATE UNITS

Graduate School of Education and Counseling *Program availability:* Part-time, evening/weekend. Offers curriculum and instruction (M Ed); education and counseling (M Ed, MA, MAT, MS, Ed D, Ed S); educational administration (M Ed, Ed S); educational leadership (M Ed, MA, Ed D, Ed S); elementary education (MAT); marriage, couple, and family therapy (MA, MS); professional mental health counseling (MA, MS); professional mental health counseling - addictions (MA, MS); school counseling (M Ed); school psychology (Ed S); secondary education (MAT); special education (M Ed); student affairs administration (MA). Electronic applications accepted.

Lewis & Clark Law School *Program availability:* Part-time, evening/weekend. Offers animal law (LL M); environmental, natural resources, and energy law (LL M, MSL); law (JD). Electronic applications accepted.

LEWIS UNIVERSITY, Romeoville, IL 60446

General Information Independent-religious, coed, comprehensive institution. CGS member. *Enrollment:* 486 full-time matriculated graduate/professional students (319 women), 1,462 part-time matriculated graduate/professional students (981 women). *Enrollment by degree level:* 1,872 master's, 76 doctoral. *Graduate housing:* Room and/or apartments available on a first-come, first-served basis to single students; on-campus housing not available to married students. Housing application deadline: 7/1. *Student services:* Campus employment opportunities, campus safety program, career counseling, exercise/wellness program, free psychological counseling, international student services, low-cost health insurance, multicultural affairs office, services for students with disabilities, teacher training, writing training. *Library facilities:* Lewis University Library. *Collection:* Books: 120,468 (physical), 527,534 (digital/electronic); Serial titles: 1,622 (physical), 151,185 (digital/electronic); Databases: 115. Weekly public service hours: 102; students can reserve study rooms.

Computer facilities: 350 computers available on campus for general student use. A campuswide network can be accessed from student residence rooms and from off campus. Online class registration, online help desk, online billing, online financial aid, online payments, online admission application, online housing application, online application for graduation, online Blackboard course management system, online tutoring are available.
Website: http://www.lewisu.edu/

General Application Contact: Dr. Leslie Jacobson, Director, Graduate Admission, 815-836-5610, E-mail: grad@lewisu.edu.

GRADUATE UNITS

College of Arts and Sciences Students: 218 full-time (138 women), 456 part-time (198 women); includes 194 minority (53 Black or African American, non-Hispanic/Latino; 1 American Indian or Alaska Native, non-Hispanic/Latino; 39 Asian, non-Hispanic/Latino; 82 Hispanic/Latino; 3 Native Hawaiian or other Pacific Islander, non-Hispanic/Latino; 16 Two or more races, non-Hispanic/Latino), 23 international. Average age 31. Expenses: Contact institution. *Financial support:* Federal Work-Study, scholarships/grants, tuition waivers (partial), and unspecified assistantships available. Financial award application deadline: 5/1; financial award applicants required to submit FAFSA. *Program availability:* Part-time, evening/weekend, 100% online, blended/hybrid learning. Offers adult mental health counseling (MA); arts and sciences (MA, MS, MSW); aviation and transportation (MS); chemical physics (MS); chemistry (MS); computational biology and bioinformatics (MS); computer science (MS); criminal justice (MS); cyber security (MS); higher education/student services (MA); intelligent systems (MS); organizational and leadership coaching (MA); physics (MS); public safety administration (MS); school counseling (MA); social work (MSW); software engineering (MS); technical (MS); training and development (MA). *Application deadline:* For fall admission, 5/1 priority date for international students; for spring admission, 11/15 priority date for international students. Applications are processed on a rolling basis. *Application fee:* $40. Electronic applications accepted. *Application Contact:* Linda Campbell, Graduate Admission Counselor, 815-836-5610, E-mail: grad@lewisu.edu. *Dean,* Dr. Bonnie Bondavalli.

College of Business Students: 160 full-time (96 women), 375 part-time (247 women); includes 165 minority (65 Black or African American, non-Hispanic/Latino; 2 American Indian or Alaska Native, non-Hispanic/Latino; 18 Asian, non-Hispanic/Latino; 69 Hispanic/Latino; 11 Two or more races, non-Hispanic/Latino), 35 international. Average age 34. Expenses: Contact institution. *Financial support:* Career-related internships or fieldwork, Federal Work-Study, scholarships/grants, and unspecified assistantships available. Financial award application deadline: 5/1; financial award applicants required to submit FAFSA. *Program availability:* Part-time, evening/weekend, 100% online, blended/hybrid learning. Offers accounting (MBA); business (MBA, MS); custom elective option (MBA); e-business (MBA); finance (MBA); financial analytics (MS); healthcare analytics (MS); healthcare management (MBA); human resources management (MBA); information security - management (MS); international business (MBA); management information systems (MBA); marketing (MBA); marketing analytics (MS); operations analytics (MS); project management (MBA); technology and operations management (MBA). *Application deadline:* For fall admission, 5/1 priority date for international students; for spring admission, 11/15 priority date for international students. Applications are processed on a rolling basis. *Application fee:* $40. Electronic applications accepted. *Application Contact:* Office of Graduate Admission, 815-836-5610, E-mail: grad@lewisu.edu. *Dean,* Dr. Ryan Butt.

College of Education Students: 76 full-time (56 women), 192 part-time (134 women); includes 74 minority (22 Black or African American, non-Hispanic/Latino; 7 Asian, non-Hispanic/Latino; 40 Hispanic/Latino; 5 Two or more races, non-Hispanic/Latino), 8 international. Average age 33. Expenses: Contact institution. *Financial support:* Career-related internships or fieldwork, Federal Work-Study, scholarships/grants, and unspecified assistantships available. Financial award application deadline: 5/1; financial award applicants required to submit FAFSA. *Program availability:* Part-time, evening/weekend. Offers chemistry (MA); curriculum and instruction: literacy and English language learning (M Ed); curriculum and instruction: technology learning and design (M Ed); early childhood special education (M Ed); education (M Ed, MA, Ed D); educational leadership for teaching and learning (Ed D); educational leadership with principal preparation endorsement (M Ed, MA); educational leadership with teacher leader endorsement (M Ed); elementary education (MA); English (MA); English as a second language (M Ed); foreign language instruction (MA); history (MA); middle level education (MA); physics (MA); psychology and social science (MA); reading and literacy

(M Ed, MA); special education (MA). *Application deadline:* For fall admission, 5/1 priority date for international students; for spring admission, 11/15 priority date for international students. Applications are processed on a rolling basis. *Application fee:* $40. Electronic applications accepted. *Application Contact:* Kathy Lisak, Graduate Admission Counselor, 815-836-5610, E-mail: grad@lewisu.edu. *Dean,* Dr. Bonnie Bondavalli.

College of Nursing and Health Professions Students: 32 full-time (29 women), 439 part-time (402 women); includes 123 minority (30 Black or African American, non-Hispanic/Latino; 36 Asian, non-Hispanic/Latino; 50 Hispanic/Latino; 7 Two or more races, non-Hispanic/Latino), 2 international. Average age 36. Expenses: Contact institution. *Financial support:* Federal Work-Study, scholarships/grants, and unspecified assistantships available. Financial award application deadline: 5/1; financial award applicants required to submit FAFSA. *Program availability:* Part-time, evening/weekend, 100% online, blended/hybrid learning. Offers adult gerontology clinical nurse specialist (MSN); adult gerontology primary care nurse practitioner (MSN); family nurse practitioner (MSN); healthcare systems leadership (MSN); nursing and health professions (MSN, DNP); nursing education (MSN); school nurse (MSN). *Application deadline:* For fall admission, 5/1 priority date for international students; for spring admission, 11/15 priority date for international students. Applications are processed on a rolling basis. *Application fee:* $40. Electronic applications accepted. *Application Contact:* Nancy Wiksten, Graduate Admission Counselor, 815-836-5610, E-mail: grad@lewisu.edu. *Dean,* Dr. Peggy Rice.

LEXINGTON THEOLOGICAL SEMINARY, Lexington, KY 40508-3218

General Information Independent-religious, coed, graduate-only institution. *Graduate housing:* Rooms and/or apartments available on a first-come, first-served basis to single and married students. Housing application deadline: 6/15.

GRADUATE UNITS

Graduate and Professional Programs *Program availability:* Part-time, evening/weekend. Offers theology (M Div, MA, MAPS, D Min). M Div/MSW offered jointly with University of Kentucky.

LIBERTY UNIVERSITY, Lynchburg, VA 24515

General Information Independent-religious, coed, comprehensive institution. *Enrollment:* 14,379 full-time matriculated graduate/professional students (8,780 women), 18,582 part-time matriculated graduate/professional students (11,056 women). *Enrollment by degree level:* 25,567 master's, 6,287 doctoral, 1,107 other advanced degrees. *Tuition:* Full-time $10,851; part-time $562 per credit hour. *Graduate housing:* Room and/or apartments available on a first-come, first-served basis to single students; on-campus housing not available to married students. *Student services:* Campus employment opportunities, career counseling, exercise/wellness program, free psychological counseling, international student services, multicultural affairs office, services for students with disabilities, writing training. *Library facilities:* Jerry Falwell Library plus 1 other. *Collection:* Books: 313,657 (physical), 377,967 (digital/electronic); Serial titles: 4,323 (physical), 118,877 (digital/electronic); Databases: 512. Students can reserve study rooms.

Computer facilities: 1,640 computers available on campus for general student use. A campuswide network can be accessed from student residence rooms and from off campus. Online class registration is available.
Website: http://www.liberty.edu/

General Application Contact: Dr. Nina Shenkle, Dean of Admissions, 877-298-9617, Fax: 434-522-0430, E-mail: residentgraduate@liberty.edu.

GRADUATE UNITS

College of Arts and Sciences Students: 231 full-time (139 women), 404 part-time (225 women); includes 144 minority (90 Black or African American, non-Hispanic/Latino; 3 American Indian or Alaska Native, non-Hispanic/Latino; 1 Asian, non-Hispanic/Latino; 23 Hispanic/Latino; 27 Two or more races, non-Hispanic/Latino), 8 international. Average age 38. 748 applicants, 39% accepted, 165 enrolled. Expenses: Contact institution. *Financial support:* In 2018–19, 659 students received support. Teaching assistantships with tuition reimbursements available and Federal Work-Study available. In 2018, 152 master's awarded. *Program availability:* Part-time, online learning. Offers English (MA); history (MA); professional writing (MA). *Application deadline:* For fall admission, 6/1 for domestic students; for spring admission, 11/1 for domestic students. Applications are processed on a rolling basis. *Application fee:* $50. Electronic applications accepted. *Application Contact:* Dr. Terry Elam, Director of Graduate Admissions, 434-592-3966, Fax: 434-522-0430, E-mail: gradadmissions@liberty.edu. *Dean,* Dr. Roger Schultz, 434-592-4031, Fax: 434-522-0430, E-mail: rschultz@liberty.edu.

College of Osteopathic Medicine Students: 611 full-time (282 women), 5 part-time (2 women); includes 100 minority (13 Black or African American, non-Hispanic/Latino; 1 American Indian or Alaska Native, non-Hispanic/Latino; 60 Asian, non-Hispanic/Latino; 16 Hispanic/Latino; 10 Two or more races, non-Hispanic/Latino), 28 international. Average age 27. 2,069 applicants, 8% accepted, 160 enrolled. Expenses: Contact institution. *Financial support:* In 2018–19, 167 students received support. Teaching assistantships and Federal Work-Study available. In 2018, 126 doctorates awarded. Offers osteopathic medicine (DO). *Application deadline:* Applications are processed on a rolling basis. Electronic applications accepted. *Application Contact:* Jay Bridge, Director of Admissions, 800-424-9595, Fax: 800-628-7977, E-mail: gradadmissions@liberty.edu. *Dean,* Dr. Peter A. Bell, 434-592-6515.

Helms School of Government Students: 615 full-time (329 women), 975 part-time (408 women); includes 476 minority (330 Black or African American, non-Hispanic/Latino; 6 American Indian or Alaska Native, non-Hispanic/Latino; 15 Asian, non-Hispanic/Latino; 69 Hispanic/Latino; 1 Native Hawaiian or other Pacific Islander, non-Hispanic/Latino; 55 Two or more races, non-Hispanic/Latino), 26 international. Average age 35. 2,345 applicants, 46% accepted, 563 enrolled. Expenses: Contact institution. *Financial support:* In 2018–19, 808 students received support. Teaching assistantships and Federal Work-Study available. In 2018, 291 master's awarded. *Program availability:* Part-time, online learning. Offers criminal justice (MS); international relations (MS); political science (MS); public administration (MPA); public policy (MA). *Application deadline:* Applications are processed on a rolling basis. *Application fee:* $50. Electronic applications accepted. *Application Contact:* Jay Bridge, Director of Admissions, 800-424-9595, Fax: 800-628-7977, E-mail: gradadmissions@liberty.edu. *Dean,* Ron Miller, 434-592-4986, E-mail: govtdean@liberty.edu.

School of Behavioral Sciences Students: 3,163 full-time (2,537 women), 4,813 part-time (3,790 women); includes 2,399 minority (1,847 Black or African American, non-Hispanic/Latino; 39 American Indian or Alaska Native, non-Hispanic/Latino; 77 Asian, non-Hispanic/Latino; 244 Hispanic/Latino; 13 Native Hawaiian or other Pacific Islander, non-Hispanic/Latino; 179 Two or more races, non-Hispanic/Latino), 129 international. Average age 39. 8,226 applicants, 38% accepted, 1752 enrolled. Expenses: Contact institution. *Financial support:* In 2018–19, 1,003 students received support. Teaching assistantships and Federal Work-Study available. Financial award applicants required to submit FAFSA. In 2018, 2,420 master's, 21 doctorates, 79 other advanced degrees awarded. *Program availability:* Part-time, online learning. Offers applied psychology (MA); clinical mental health counseling (MA); community care and counseling (Ed D); counselor education and supervision (PhD); human services counseling (MA); marriage and family counseling (MA); marriage and family therapy (MA); military resilience (Certificate); pastoral counseling (MA); professional counseling (MA); psychology (MS); school counseling (M Ed). *Application deadline:* Applications are processed on a rolling basis. *Application fee:* $50. Electronic applications accepted. *Application Contact:* Jay Bridge, Director of Admissions, 800-424-9595, Fax: 800-628-7977, E-mail: gradadmissions@liberty.edu. *Founding Dean, School of Behavioral Sciences,* Dr. Ronald Hawkins, E-mail: provost@liberty.edu.

School of Business Students: 2,871 full-time (1,496 women), 4,437 part-time (1,969 women); includes 2,069 minority (1,424 Black or African American, non-Hispanic/Latino; 44 American Indian or Alaska Native, non-Hispanic/Latino; 133 Asian, non-Hispanic/Latino; 282 Hispanic/Latino; 16 Native Hawaiian or other Pacific Islander, non-Hispanic/Latino; 170 Two or more races, non-Hispanic/Latino), 154 international. Average age 36. 8,980 applicants, 45% accepted, 2009 enrolled. Expenses: Contact institution. *Financial support:* In 2018–19, 990 students received support. Teaching assistantships and Federal Work-Study available. Financial award applicants required to submit FAFSA. In 2018, 1,988 master's, 25 doctorates awarded. *Program availability:* Part-time, online learning. Offers accounting (MBA, MS); cyber security (MS); executive leadership (MA); international business (DBA); leadership (DBA); marketing (MBA, MS, DBA); project management (MBA, DBA); public relations (MBA). *Application deadline:* Applications are processed on a rolling basis. *Application fee:* $50. Electronic applications accepted. *Application Contact:* Jay Bridge, Director of Graduate Admissions, 800-424-9595, Fax: 800-628-7977, E-mail: gradadmissions@liberty.edu. *Dean,* Dr. Dave Bratt, 434-592-7321, E-mail: dabrat@liberty.edu.

School of Communication and Digital Content Students: 185 full-time (133 women), 204 part-time (141 women); includes 107 minority (70 Black or African American, non-Hispanic/Latino; 1 American Indian or Alaska Native, non-Hispanic/Latino; 5 Asian, non-Hispanic/Latino; 21 Hispanic/Latino; 1 Native Hawaiian or other Pacific Islander, non-Hispanic/Latino; 9 Two or more races, non-Hispanic/Latino), 12 international. Average age 32. 709 applicants, 36% accepted, 136 enrolled. Expenses: Contact institution. *Financial support:* In 2018–19, 882 students received support. Federal Work-Study and unspecified assistantships available. Financial award applicants required to submit FAFSA. In 2018, 75 master's awarded. *Program availability:* Part-time. Offers communication (MA); promotion and video content (MA); social media management (MS); strategic communication (MA). *Application deadline:* For fall admission, 6/1 for domestic students; for spring admission, 11/1 for domestic students. Applications are processed on a rolling basis. *Application fee:* $50. Electronic applications accepted. *Application Contact:* Dr. Terry Elam, Director of Graduate Admissions, 434-582-2111, Fax: 434-582-7836, E-mail: gradadmissions@liberty.edu. *Dean,* Dr. Ronald Hawkins, E-mail: provost@liberty.edu.

School of Divinity Students: 2,414 full-time (700 women), 2,600 part-time (757 women); includes 1,336 minority (965 Black or African American, non-Hispanic/Latino; 29 American Indian or Alaska Native, non-Hispanic/Latino; 88 Asian, non-Hispanic/Latino; 164 Hispanic/Latino; 10 Native Hawaiian or other Pacific Islander, non-Hispanic/Latino; 80 Two or more races, non-Hispanic/Latino), 115 international. Average age 42. 4,358 applicants, 35% accepted, 957 enrolled. Expenses: Contact institution. *Financial support:* Teaching assistantships with tuition reimbursements, career-related internships or fieldwork, and Federal Work-Study available. Financial award applicants required to submit FAFSA. In 2018, 1,331 master's, 82 doctorates awarded. *Program availability:* Part-time, online learning. Offers Biblical exposition (MA); Biblical languages (M Div); Biblical studies (M Div, MA, MAR, Th M, D Min); chaplaincy (M Div, D Min); Christian apologetics (M Div, MA, MAR, Th M); Christian leadership and church ministries (M Div); Christian ministries (M Div); Christian ministry (MA); Christian thought (M Div); church history (M Div, MAR, Th M); community chaplaincy (M Div, MAR); discipleship (D Min); discipleship and church ministry (M Div, MAR, MCM); evangelism and church planting (MAR, MCM, D Min); expository preaching (D Min); global ministry (MA); global studies (M Div, MAR, MCM, MGS, Th M); healthcare chaplaincy (M Div); homiletics (M Div, MAR, Th M); leadership (M Div, MAR); marketplace chaplaincy (M Div, MCM); ministry leadership (Ed D); pastoral counseling (M Div, MA, MAR, D Min); pastoral leadership (D Min); pastoral ministries (M Div, M Serv Soc, MCM); religious education (MRE); sports chaplaincy (MA); theology (M Div, MAR, MTS, Th M); theology and apologetics (D Min, PhD); worship (M Div, MA, MCM, D Min); youth and family ministries (M Div). *Application deadline:* For fall admission, 6/1 for domestic students; for spring admission, 11/1 for domestic students. Applications are processed on a rolling basis. *Application fee:* $50. Electronic applications accepted. *Application Contact:* Jay Bridge, Director of Graduate Admissions, 800-424-9595, Fax: 800-628-7977, E-mail: gradadmissions@liberty.edu. *Dean,* Dr. Ed Hindson, 434-582-2569, E-mail: divinity@liberty.edu.

School of Education Students: 2,922 full-time (2,241 women), 3,559 part-time (2,621 women); includes 1,770 minority (1,342 Black or African American, non-Hispanic/Latino; 38 American Indian or Alaska Native, non-Hispanic/Latino; 68 Asian, non-Hispanic/Latino; 177 Hispanic/Latino; 18 Native Hawaiian or other Pacific Islander, non-Hispanic/Latino; 127 Two or more races, non-Hispanic/Latino), 71 international. Average age 38. 9,077 applicants, 37% accepted, 1886 enrolled. Expenses: Contact institution. *Financial support:* In 2018–19, 265 students received support. Federal Work-Study and tuition waivers (partial) available. In 2018, 1,020 master's, 173 doctorates, 402 other advanced degrees awarded. *Program availability:* Part-time, online learning. Offers reading specialist (M Ed). *Application deadline:* For fall admission, 6/1 for domestic students; for spring admission, 11/1 for domestic students. Applications are processed on a rolling basis. *Application fee:* $50. Electronic applications accepted. *Application Contact:* Jay Bridge, Director of Graduate Admissions, 800-424-9595, Fax: 800-628-7977, E-mail: gradadmissions@liberty.edu. *Dean,* Dr. Deanna Keith, 434-582-2417, E-mail: dkeith@liberty.edu.

School of Health Sciences Students: 729 full-time (530 women), 760 part-time (555 women); includes 505 minority (327 Black or African American, non-Hispanic/Latino; 9 American Indian or Alaska Native, non-Hispanic/Latino; 38 Asian, non-Hispanic/Latino; 80 Hispanic/Latino; 4 Native Hawaiian or other Pacific Islander, non-Hispanic/Latino; 47 Two or more races, non-Hispanic/Latino), 71 international. Average age 31. 3,363 applicants, 32% accepted, 522 enrolled. Expenses: Contact institution. *Financial support:* In 2018–19, 918 students received support. Federal Work-Study available. Financial award applicants required to submit FAFSA. In 2018, 373 master's awarded. *Program availability:* Part-time, online learning. Offers anatomy and cell biology (PhD); biomedical sciences (MS); epidemiology (MPH); exercise science (MS); global health (MPH); health promotion (MPH); medical sciences (MA); nutrition (MPH). *Application* *fee:* $50. *Application Contact:* Jay Bridge, Director of Admissions, 800-424-9595, Fax: 800-628-7977, E-mail: gradadmissions@liberty.edu. *Dean,* Dr. Ralph Linstra.

School of Law Students: 258 full-time (131 women), 138 part-time (63 women); includes 97 minority (45 Black or African American, non-Hispanic/Latino; 2 American Indian or Alaska Native, non-Hispanic/Latino; 10 Asian, non-Hispanic/Latino; 20 Hispanic/Latino; 1 Native Hawaiian or other Pacific Islander, non-Hispanic/Latino; 19 Two or more races, non-Hispanic/Latino), 7 international. Average age 33. 387 applicants, 50% accepted, 142 enrolled. Expenses: Contact institution. *Financial support:* In 2018–19, 208 students received support. Federal Work-Study available. Financial award applicants required to submit FAFSA. *Program availability:* Online learning. Offers American legal studies (JM); international legal studies (JM, LL M). *Application deadline:* For fall admission, 6/1 for domestic students. *Application Contact:* Joleen Thaxton, Assistant Director of Admissions, 434-592-5300, Fax: 434-592-5400, E-mail: lawadmissions@liberty.edu. *Dean,* B. Keith Faulkner, 434-592-5300, Fax: 434-592-5400, E-mail: law@liberty.edu.

School of Music Students: 118 full-time (48 women), 187 part-time (92 women); includes 73 minority (49 Black or African American, non-Hispanic/Latino; 6 Asian, non-Hispanic/Latino; 15 Hispanic/Latino; 3 Two or more races, non-Hispanic/Latino), 16 international. Average age 37. 429 applicants, 29% accepted, 56 enrolled. Expenses: Contact institution. *Financial support:* In 2018–19, 619 students received support. Federal Work-Study available. Financial award applicants required to submit FAFSA. In 2018, 48 master's, 6 doctorates awarded. *Program availability:* Part-time, online learning. Offers ethnomusicology (MA); music and worship (MA); music education (MA); worship studies (MA, DWS). *Application deadline:* Applications are processed on a rolling basis. *Application fee:* $50. Electronic applications accepted. *Application Contact:* Jay Bridge, Director of Admissions, 800-424-9595, Fax: 800-628-7977, E-mail: gradadmissions@liberty.edu. *Dean,* Dr. Vernon Whaley, 434-592-3463, E-mail: vwhaley@liberty.edu.

School of Nursing Students: 202 full-time (177 women), 449 part-time (402 women); includes 121 minority (66 Black or African American, non-Hispanic/Latino; 1 American Indian or Alaska Native, non-Hispanic/Latino; 16 Asian, non-Hispanic/Latino; 22 Hispanic/Latino; 1 Native Hawaiian or other Pacific Islander, non-Hispanic/Latino; 15 Two or more races, non-Hispanic/Latino), 8 international. Average age 39. 849 applicants, 27% accepted, 143 enrolled. Expenses: Contact institution. *Financial support:* In 2018–19, 128 students received support. Federal Work-Study available. Financial award applicants required to submit FAFSA. In 2018, 147 master's, 13 doctorates awarded. *Program availability:* Part-time, online learning. Offers family nurse practitioner (DNP); nurse educator (MSN); nursing administration (MSN); nursing informatics (MSN). *Application deadline:* Applications are processed on a rolling basis. *Application fee:* $50. Electronic applications accepted. *Application Contact:* Jay Bridge, Director of Admissions, 800-424-9595, Fax: 800-628-7977, E-mail: gradadmissions@liberty.edu. *Dean,* Dr. Shanna Akers, 434-592-3618, E-mail: lusondean@liberty.edu.

School of Visual and Performing Arts Students: 60 full-time (37 women), 51 part-time (31 women); includes 19 minority (7 Black or African American, non-Hispanic/Latino; 5 Asian, non-Hispanic/Latino; 2 Hispanic/Latino; 5 Two or more races, non-Hispanic/Latino), 2 international. Average age 33. 253 applicants, 24% accepted, 35 enrolled. Expenses: Contact institution. *Financial support:* In 2018–19, 614 students received support. Federal Work-Study available. In 2018, 9 master's awarded. Offers graphic design (MFA); studio art (MFA); visual communication design (MA). *Application fee:* $50. Electronic applications accepted. *Application Contact:* Jay Bridge, Director of Admissions, 800-424-9595, Fax: 800-628-7977, E-mail: gradadmissions@liberty.edu. *Dean,* Scott Hayes, 434-592-6744, E-mail: smhayes@liberty.edu.

LIFE CHIROPRACTIC COLLEGE WEST, Hayward, CA 94545

General Information Independent, coed, graduate-only institution. *Graduate housing:* On-campus housing not available. *Research affiliation:* National Center for Complimentary Medicine, National Center for Complementary and Alternative Medicine/University Cancer Research Fund, Advanced Orthogonality, San Jose State University, University of Calgary.

GRADUATE UNITS

Professional Program Offers chiropractic (DC). Electronic applications accepted.

LIFE UNIVERSITY, Marietta, GA 30060-2903

General Information Independent, coed, comprehensive institution. *Graduate housing:* Rooms and/or apartments available on a first-come, first-served basis to single and married students.

GRADUATE UNITS

College of Chiropractic Offers chiropractic (DC). Electronic applications accepted.

College of Graduate and Undergraduate Studies *Program availability:* Part-time, 100% online, blended/hybrid learning. Offers athletic training (MAT); chiropractic sport science (MS); nutrition and sport science (MS); positive psychology (MS); sport coaching (MS); sport injury management (MS); sports health science (MS). Electronic applications accepted.

LIM COLLEGE, New York, NY 10022-5268

General Information Proprietary, coed, primarily women, comprehensive institution. *Enrollment:* 1,781 graduate, professional, and undergraduate students; 153 full-time matriculated graduate/professional students (136 women), 125 part-time matriculated graduate/professional students (118 women). *Enrollment by degree level:* 278 master's. *Graduate faculty:* 2 full-time, 21 part-time/adjunct. *Tuition:* Full-time $28,500; part-time $950 per credit hour. *Required fees:* $500; $100 per semester. *Graduate housing:* Room and/or apartments available on a first-come, first-served basis to single students; on-campus housing not available to married students. *Typical cost:* $16,840 per year ($20,840 including board). *Student services:* Campus employment opportunities, career counseling, exercise/wellness program, free psychological counseling, international student services, low-cost health insurance, services for students with disabilities, writing training. *Library facilities:* Adrian G. Marcuse Library. *Collection:* Books: 15,000 (physical), 700 (digital/electronic); Serial titles: 172 (physical); Databases: 55. Students can reserve study rooms.

Computer facilities: Computer purchase and lease plans are available. 352 computers available on campus for general student use. A campuswide network can be accessed from student residence rooms and from off campus. Online class registration is available.
Website: http://www.limcollege.edu/

General Application Contact: George Toledo, Assistant Director of Graduate Admissions, 212-310-0634, E-mail: graduateadmissions@limcollege.edu.

GRADUATE UNITS

MPS Program Students: 125 full-time (109 women), 45 part-time (44 women); includes 64 minority (31 Black or African American, non-Hispanic/Latino; 15 Asian, non-

Hispanic/Latino; 18 Hispanic/Latino), 67 international. Average age 25. 292 applicants, 67% accepted, 125 enrolled. *Faculty:* 2 full-time, 21 part-time/adjunct. Expenses: Contact institution. In 2018, 146 master's awarded. *Program availability:* Part-time, 100% online. Offers business of fashion (MPS); fashion marketing (MPS); fashion merchandising and retail management (MPS); global fashion supply chain management (MPS). *Application deadline:* Applications are processed on a rolling basis. *Application fee:* $40. Electronic applications accepted. *Application Contact:* George Toledo, Assistant Director of Graduate Admissions, 212-310-0634, E-mail: graduateadmissions@limcollege.edu. *Chair of Graduate Studies,* John Keane, E-mail: graduatestudies@limcollege.edu.

LIMESTONE COLLEGE, Gaffney, SC 29340-3799

General Information Independent, coed, comprehensive institution. *Enrollment:* 2,346 graduate, professional, and undergraduate students; 43 full-time matriculated graduate/professional students (22 women), 28 part-time matriculated graduate/professional students (14 women). *Enrollment by degree level:* 71 master's. *Graduate faculty:* 10 full-time (3 women). *Tuition:* Full-time $11,700; part-time $7800 per credit hour. *Required fees:* $300; $150 per credit hour. $75 per term. *Graduate housing:* On-campus housing not available. *Student services:* Career counseling, free psychological counseling, services for students with disabilities. *Library facilities:* A. J. Eastwood Library plus 1 other. *Collection:* Books: 67,000 (physical), 239,537 (digital/electronic); Serial titles: 111 (physical), 482,082 (digital/electronic); Databases: 156. Weekly public service hours: 70.

Computer facilities: 137 computers available on campus for general student use. A campuswide network can be accessed from student residence rooms and from off campus. Online class registration is available.
Website: http://www.limestone.edu/

General Application Contact: Adair Haynes, Director of Graduate Studies in Enrollment and Admissions, 800-795-7151 Ext. 4370, Fax: 864-487-8706, E-mail: ahaynes@limestone.edu.

GRADUATE UNITS

MBA Program Students: 43 full-time (22 women), 28 part-time (14 women); includes 30 minority (28 Black or African American, non-Hispanic/Latino; 1 Asian, non-Hispanic/Latino; 1 Two or more races, non-Hispanic/Latino), 3 international. Average age 36. 69 applicants, 39% accepted, 9 enrolled. *Faculty:* 10 full-time (3 women). Expenses: Contact institution. *Financial support:* Scholarships/grants available. Financial award application deadline: 6/15; financial award applicants required to submit FAFSA. In 2018, 30 master's awarded. *Program availability:* Part-time, evening/weekend, 100% online, but there are three 1-hour group dynamics classes offered during weekends between semesters. Offers business administration (MBA). *Application deadline:* For fall admission, 8/1 priority date for domestic and international students; for winter admission, 12/12 priority date for domestic and international students; for spring admission, 4/1 priority date for domestic and international students. Applications are processed on a rolling basis. *Application fee:* $25. Electronic applications accepted. *Application Contact:* Adair Hudson, Director of Graduate Studies in Enrollment and Admissions, 800-795-7151 Ext. 4370, Fax: 864-467-8706, E-mail: ahaynes@limestone.edu. *Director of Graduate Studies in Enrollment and Admissions,* Adair Hudson, 864-488-4370, Fax: 864-487-8706, E-mail: ahudson@limestone.edu.

LINCOLN CHRISTIAN SEMINARY, Lincoln, IL 62656-2167

General Information Independent-religious, coed, graduate-only institution. *Graduate housing:* Rooms and/or apartments available on a first-come, first-served basis to single and married students.

GRADUATE UNITS

Graduate and Professional Programs *Program availability:* Part-time. Offers Bible and theology (MA); Christian ministries (MA); counseling (MA); divinity (M Div); leadership ministry (D Min); religious education (MRE). Electronic applications accepted.

LINCOLN CHRISTIAN UNIVERSITY, Lincoln, IL 62656-2167

General Information Independent-religious, coed, comprehensive institution. *Enrollment:* 732 graduate, professional, and undergraduate students; 92 full-time matriculated graduate/professional students (38 women), 225 part-time matriculated graduate/professional students (76 women). *Enrollment by degree level:* 301 master's, 16 doctoral. *Graduate faculty:* 10 full-time (1 woman), 51 part-time/adjunct (13 women). *Tuition:* Full-time $7920; part-time $5280 per credit hour. *Required fees:* $150; $150 per credit hour. Tuition and fees vary according to program. *Graduate housing:* Rooms and/or apartments available on a first-come, first-served basis to single and married students. *Typical cost:* $3600 per year ($7920 including board) for single students; $3600 per year ($7920 including board) for married students. Housing application deadline: 8/15. *Student services:* Campus employment opportunities, campus safety program, free psychological counseling, international student services, services for students with disabilities, writing training. *Library facilities:* Jessie Eury Library. *Collection:* Books: 92,813 (physical), 55,082 (digital/electronic); Serial titles: 719 (physical), 15,442 (digital/electronic); Databases: 52. Weekly public service hours: 82; students can reserve study rooms.

Computer facilities: 51 computers available on campus for general student use. A campuswide network can be accessed from student residence rooms and from off campus. Online class registration is available.
Website: http://www.lincolnchristian.edu/

General Application Contact: Lindsey Clark, Associate Director of Graduate Enrollment, 217-732-3168 Ext. 2398, E-mail: lclark@lincolnchristian.edu.

GRADUATE UNITS

Graduate Programs *Program availability:* Online learning. Offers Bible and theology (MA); Biblical studies (MA); church history/historical theology (MA); counseling (MA); formative worship (MA); intercultural studies (MA); ministry (MA); organizational leadership (MA); philosophy and apologetics (MA); spiritual formation (MA); theology (MA). MA in spiritual formation offered in Normal, IL.

LINCOLN MEMORIAL UNIVERSITY, Harrogate, TN 37752-1901

General Information Independent, coed, university. *Graduate housing:* Rooms and/or apartments available on a first-come, first-served basis to single and married students.

GRADUATE UNITS

Carter and Moyers School of Education *Program availability:* Part-time, evening/weekend, online learning. Offers administration and supervision (M Ed, Ed S); counseling and guidance (M Ed); curriculum and instruction (M Ed, Ed D, Ed S); English (M Ed); executive leadership (Ed D); higher education administration (Ed D); human resource development (Ed D); leadership and administration (Ed D).

Caylor School of Nursing *Program availability:* Part-time. Offers family nurse practitioner (MSN); nurse anesthesia (MSN); psychiatric mental health nurse practitioner (MSN).

College of Veterinary Medicine Offers veterinary medicine (DVM).

DeBusk College of Osteopathic Medicine Offers osteopathic medicine (DO).

Duncan School of Law *Program availability:* Part-time. Offers law (JD). Electronic applications accepted.

School of Business *Program availability:* Part-time, evening/weekend. Offers business (MBA).

LINCOLN UNIVERSITY, Oakland, CA 94612

General Information Independent, coed, comprehensive institution.

GRADUATE UNITS

Graduate Studies *Program availability:* Part-time. Offers finance and investments (DBA); finance management (MS); finance management and investments (MBA); general business (MBA); human resource management (MBA, DBA); international business (MBA, MS); management information systems (MBA). Electronic applications accepted.

LINCOLN UNIVERSITY, Jefferson City, MO 65101

General Information State-supported, coed, comprehensive institution. *Enrollment:* 37 full-time matriculated graduate/professional students (23 women), 52 part-time matriculated graduate/professional students (25 women). *Enrollment by degree level:* 82 master's, 7 advanced degrees. *International tuition:* $12,996 full-time. *Tuition, area resident:* Full-time $6984; part-time $291 per credit. *Tuition, state resident:* full-time $6984; part-time $291 per credit. *Tuition, nonresident:* full-time $12,996; part-time $541.50 per credit. *Required fees:* $1242.20. *Graduate housing:* Room and/or apartments available on a first-come, first-served basis to single students; on-campus housing not available to married students. *Housing application deadline:* 7/1. *Student services:* Campus employment opportunities, career counseling, international student services, services for students with disabilities. *Library facilities:* Inman E. Page Library. *Collection:* Books: 99,126 (physical), 197,476 (digital/electronic); Serial titles: 1,194 (physical), 19,000 (digital/electronic); Databases: 39. Weekly public service hours: 88.

Computer facilities: Computer purchase and lease plans are available. 365 computers available on campus for general student use. A campuswide network can be accessed from student residence rooms and from off campus. Online class registration is available.
Website: http://www.lincolnu.edu/

General Application Contact: Dr. Benjamin Arnold, Assistant Vice President of Academic Affairs, 573-681-5247, Fax: 573-681-5106, E-mail: gradschool@lincolnu.edu.

GRADUATE UNITS

Graduate Studies Students: 37 full-time (23 women), 52 part-time (25 women); includes 26 minority (24 Black or African American, non-Hispanic/Latino; 1 Asian, non-Hispanic/Latino; 1 Two or more races, non-Hispanic/Latino), 11 international. Average age 34. 67 applicants, 52% accepted, 29 enrolled. Expenses: Contact institution. *Financial support:* In 2018–19, 9 research assistantships with tuition reimbursements (averaging $4,050 per year) were awarded; fellowships with tuition reimbursements, Federal Work-Study, scholarships/grants, and unspecified assistantships also available. Support available to part-time students. Financial award application deadline: 3/1; financial award applicants required to submit FAFSA. In 2018, 48 master's awarded. *Program availability:* Part-time, evening/weekend, 100% online, blended/hybrid learning. Offers business administration (MBA); counseling (M Ed); environmental science (MS); higher education (MA); history (MA); natural sciences (MS); school teaching middle school with certification (M Ed); school teaching-elementary (M Ed); school teaching-secondary (M Ed); sociology (MA); sociology/criminal justice (MA); sustainable agriculture (MS). *Application deadline:* For fall admission, 7/1 priority date for domestic students, 5/1 priority date for international students; for spring admission, 11/1 priority date for domestic students, 10/1 priority date for international students; for summer admission, 6/1 priority date for domestic students. Applications are processed on a rolling basis. *Application fee:* $30. Electronic applications accepted. *Application Contact:* Sarah Robinett, Administrative Assistant, 573-681-5247, Fax: 573-681-5106, E-mail: gradschool@lincolnu.edu. *Assistant Vice President of Academic Affairs,* Dr. Benjamin Arnold, 573-681-5247, Fax: 573-681-5106, E-mail: gradschool@lincolnu.edu.

LINCOLN UNIVERSITY, Lincoln University, PA 19352

General Information State-related, coed, comprehensive institution. *Enrollment by degree level:* 264 master's. *Graduate housing:* On-campus housing not available. *Student services:* Campus employment opportunities, campus safety program, career counseling, free psychological counseling, international student services, low-cost health insurance, services for students with disabilities, teacher training, writing training. *Library facilities:* Langston Hughes Memorial Library. *Collection:* Weekly public service hours: 80; study areas open 24 hours, 5–7 days a week; students can reserve study rooms.

Computer facilities: 280 computers available on campus for general student use. A campuswide network can be accessed from student residence rooms and from off campus. Online class registration is available.
Website: http://www.lincoln.edu/

General Application Contact: Jernice Lea, Director, University City Student Services and Admissions, 215-590-8231, Fax: 215-387-3859, E-mail: jlea@lincoln.edu.

GRADUATE UNITS

The School of Adult & Continuing Education Students: 192 full-time (154 women), 62 part-time (40 women); includes 230 minority (218 Black or African American, non-Hispanic/Latino; 9 Hispanic/Latino; 3 Two or more races, non-Hispanic/Latino), 3 international. Average age 33. 278 applicants, 58% accepted, 94 enrolled. *Faculty:* 8 full-time (3 women), 22 part-time/adjunct (12 women). Expenses: Contact institution. *Financial support:* Scholarships/grants available. Financial award application deadline: 4/1; financial award applicants required to submit FAFSA. In 2018, 105 master's awarded. *Program availability:* Part-time, evening/weekend. Offers counseling (MSC); early childhood education (M Ed); early childhood education and special education (M Ed); educational leadership (M Ed); finance (MBA); human resources management (MBA); human services delivery (MAHS). *Application deadline:* For fall admission, 8/19 for domestic and international students; for spring admission, 12/30 for domestic and international students. Applications are processed on a rolling basis. *Application fee:* $50. Electronic applications accepted. *Application Contact:* Jernice Lea, Director, Student Services and Admissions, 215-590-8231, Fax: 215-387-3859, E-mail: jlea@lincoln.edu. *Dean of Faculty,* Dr. Patricia Joseph, 484-365-7659, E-mail: joseph@lincoln.edu.

LINDENWOOD UNIVERSITY, St. Charles, MO 63301-1695

General Information Independent-religious, coed, comprehensive institution. *Enrollment:* 9,468 graduate, professional, and undergraduate students; 1,401 full-time matriculated graduate/professional students (904 women), 1,461 part-time matriculated graduate/professional students (1,091 women). *Enrollment by degree level:* 2,464 master's, 266 doctoral, 132 other advanced degrees. *Graduate faculty:* 94 full-time (48 women), 244 part-time/adjunct (130 women). *Tuition:* Full-time $16,900; part-time $480 per credit hour. *Required fees:* $700; $350 per unit. Tuition and fees vary according to degree level. *Graduate housing:* Rooms and/or apartments available on a first-come, first-served basis to single and married students. Typical cost: $8700 (including board) for single students. Housing application deadline: 8/26. *Student services:* Campus employment opportunities, campus safety program, career counseling, exercise/wellness program, free psychological counseling, international student services, services for students with disabilities, teacher training, writing training. *Library facilities:* Library and Academic Resource Center plus 1 other. *Collection:* Books: 74,836 (physical), 278,834 (digital/electronic); Serial titles: 193 (physical), 97 (digital/electronic); Databases: 141. Students can reserve study rooms.

Computer facilities: 231 computers available on campus for general student use. A campuswide network can be accessed from student residence rooms and from off campus. Online class registration is available.
Website: http://www.lindenwood.edu/

General Application Contact: Kara Schilli, Assistant Vice President University Admissions, 636-949-4349, Fax: 636-949-4109, E-mail: adultadmissions@lindenwood.edu.

GRADUATE UNITS

Graduate Programs Students: 1,401 full-time (904 women), 1,461 part-time (1,091 women); includes 763 minority (585 Black or African American, non-Hispanic/Latino; 10 American Indian or Alaska Native, non-Hispanic/Latino; 19 Asian, non-Hispanic/Latino; 87 Hispanic/Latino; 2 Native Hawaiian or other Pacific Islander, non-Hispanic/Latino; 60 Two or more races, non-Hispanic/Latino), 162 international. Average age 35. 1,242 applicants, 58% accepted, 570 enrolled. *Faculty:* 94 full-time (48 women), 244 part-time/adjunct (130 women). Expenses: Contact institution. *Financial support:* In 2018–19, 1,051 students received support. Career-related internships or fieldwork, Federal Work-Study, institutionally sponsored loans, scholarships/grants, tuition waivers (full), and unspecified assistantships available. Financial award application deadline: 6/30; financial award applicants required to submit FAFSA. In 2018, 1,123 master's, 64 doctorates, 66 other advanced degrees awarded. *Program availability:* Part-time, evening/weekend, 100% online. *Application deadline:* For fall admission, 8/9 priority date for domestic students, 6/1 priority date for international students; for spring admission, 12/20 priority date for domestic students, 11/1 priority date for international students; for summer admission, 5/15 priority date for domestic students, 3/27 priority date for international students. Applications are processed on a rolling basis. *Application fee:* $0 ($100 for international students). Electronic applications accepted. *Application Contact:* Kara Schilli, Assistant Vice President, University Admissions, 636-949-4349, Fax: 636-949-4109, E-mail: KSchilli@lindenwood.edu. *Provost and Vice President of Academic Affairs,* Dr. Marilyn Abbott, 636-949-4846, Fax: 636-949-4912, E-mail: mabbott@lindenwood.edu.

Plaster School of Business and Entrepreneurship Students: 234 full-time (133 women), 221 part-time (139 women); includes 121 minority (95 Black or African American, non-Hispanic/Latino; 1 American Indian or Alaska Native, non-Hispanic/Latino; 3 Asian, non-Hispanic/Latino; 12 Hispanic/Latino; 10 Two or more races, non-Hispanic/Latino), 53 international. Average age 32. 251 applicants, 38% accepted, 95 enrolled. *Faculty:* 14 full-time (4 women), 26 part-time/adjunct (9 women). Expenses: Contact institution. *Financial support:* In 2018–19, 283 students received support. Career-related internships or fieldwork, Federal Work-Study, institutionally sponsored loans, scholarships/grants, tuition waivers (partial), and unspecified assistantships available. Financial award application deadline: 6/30; financial award applicants required to submit FAFSA. In 2018, 210 master's awarded. *Program availability:* Part-time, evening/weekend, 100% online. Offers business and entrepreneurship (M Acc, MA, MBA, MS). *Application deadline:* For fall admission, 8/9 priority date for domestic students, 6/1 priority date for international students; for winter admission, 12/20 priority date for domestic students, 11/1 priority date for international students; for spring admission, 2/28 priority date for domestic students, 1/3 priority date for international students; for summer admission, 5/15 priority date for domestic students, 3/27 priority date for international students. Applications are processed on a rolling basis. *Application fee:* $0 ($100 for international students). Electronic applications accepted. *Application Contact:* Kara Schilli, Assistant Vice President, University Admissions, 636-949-4349, Fax: 636-949-4109, E-mail: adultadmissions@lindenwood.edu. *Dean, School of Business and Entrepreneurship,* Roger Ellis, 636-949-4839, E-mail: rellis@lindenwood.edu.

School of Accelerated Degree Programs Students: 652 full-time (398 women), 66 part-time (45 women); includes 241 minority (182 Black or African American, non-Hispanic/Latino; 1 American Indian or Alaska Native, non-Hispanic/Latino; 8 Asian, non-Hispanic/Latino; 25 Hispanic/Latino; 1 Native Hawaiian or other Pacific Islander, non-Hispanic/Latino; 24 Two or more races, non-Hispanic/Latino), 81 international. Average age 36. 359 applicants, 54% accepted, 170 enrolled. *Faculty:* 15 full-time (8 women), 62 part-time/adjunct (22 women). Expenses: Contact institution. *Financial support:* In 2018–19, 372 students received support. Career-related internships or fieldwork, institutionally sponsored loans, scholarships/grants, tuition waivers (partial), and unspecified assistantships available. Financial award application deadline: 6/30; financial award applicants required to submit FAFSA. In 2018, 416 master's, 2 other advanced degrees awarded. *Program availability:* Part-time, evening/weekend, 100% online. Offers administration (MSA); business administration (MBA); communications (MA); criminal justice and administration (MS); healthcare administration (MS); human resource management (MS); information technology (Certificate); managing information security (MS); managing information technology (MS); managing virtualization and cloud computing (MS); writing (MFA). *Application deadline:* For fall admission, 9/30 priority date for domestic and international students; for winter admission, 1/6 priority date for domestic and international students; for spring admission, 4/6 priority date for domestic and international students; for summer admission, 7/8 priority date for domestic and international students. Applications are processed on a rolling basis. *Application fee:* $0 ($100 for international students). Electronic applications accepted. *Application Contact:* Kara Schilli, Assistant Vice President, University Admissions, 636-949-4349, Fax: 636-949-4109, E-mail: adultadmissions@lindenwood.edu. *Dean, Accelerated Degree Programs,* Dr. Gina Ganahl, 636-949-4501, Fax: 636-949-4505, E-mail: gganahl@lindenwood.edu.

School of Arts, Media, and Communications Students: 40 full-time (23 women), 26 part-time (21 women); includes 18 minority (7 Black or African American, non-Hispanic/Latino; 1 American Indian or Alaska Native, non-Hispanic/Latino; 8

Hispanic/Latino; 2 Two or more races, non-Hispanic/Latino), 7 international. Average age 33. 98 applicants, 65% accepted, 23 enrolled. *Faculty:* 15 full-time (2 women), 7 part-time/adjunct (6 women). Expenses: Contact institution. *Financial support:* In 2018–19, 29 students received support. Career-related internships or fieldwork, institutionally sponsored loans, scholarships/grants, tuition waivers (partial), and unspecified assistantships available. Financial award application deadline: 6/30; financial award applicants required to submit FAFSA. In 2018, 12 master's awarded. *Program availability:* Part-time, 100% online. Offers advertising (MA); art history (MA); cinema and media arts (MFA); communications (MA); digital and Web design (MA); fashion and business design (MS); journalism (MA); mass communications (MA); social media and digital content (MS). *Application deadline:* For fall admission, 8/9 priority date for domestic students, 6/1 priority date for international students; for spring admission, 12/20 for domestic students, 11/1 priority date for international students; for summer admission, 5/15 priority date for domestic students, 3/27 priority date for international students. Applications are processed on a rolling basis. *Application fee:* $0 ($100 for international students). Electronic applications accepted. *Application Contact:* Kara Schilli, Assistant Vice President, University Admissions, 636-949-4349, Fax: 636-949-4109, E-mail: adultadmissions@lindenwood.edu. *Dean, School of Arts, Media, and Communications,* Dr. Jason Lively, 636-949-4164, Fax: 636-949-4910, E-mail: JLively@lindenwood.edu.

School of Education Students: 456 full-time (341 women), 1,107 part-time (851 women); includes 374 minority (296 Black or African American, non-Hispanic/Latino; 7 American Indian or Alaska Native, non-Hispanic/Latino; 8 Asian, non-Hispanic/Latino; 38 Hispanic/Latino; 1 Native Hawaiian or other Pacific Islander, non-Hispanic/Latino; 24 Two or more races, non-Hispanic/Latino), 17 international. Average age 36. 496 applicants, 72% accepted, 275 enrolled. *Faculty:* 38 full-time (28 women), 111 part-time/adjunct (66 women). Expenses: Contact institution. *Financial support:* In 2018–19, 316 students received support. Career-related internships or fieldwork, Federal Work-Study, institutionally sponsored loans, scholarships/grants, tuition waivers (partial), and unspecified assistantships available. Financial award application deadline: 6/30; financial award applicants required to submit FAFSA. In 2018, 454 master's, 64 doctorates, 66 other advanced degrees awarded. *Program availability:* Part-time, evening/weekend, 100% online, blended/hybrid learning. Offers behavioral analysis (MA); education (MA); educational administration (MA, Ed D, Ed S); English to speakers of other languages (MA); instructional leadership (Ed D, Ed S); library media (MA); professional counseling (MA); school administration (MA, Ed S); school counseling (MA); teaching (MA). *Application deadline:* For fall admission, 8/9 priority date for domestic students, 6/1 priority date for international students; for spring admission, 12/20 priority date for domestic students, 11/1 priority date for international students; for summer admission, 5/15 priority date for domestic students, 3/27 priority date for international students. Applications are processed on a rolling basis. *Application fee:* $0 ($100 for international students). Electronic applications accepted. *Application Contact:* Kara Schilli, Assistant Vice President, University Admissions, 636-949-4349, Fax: 636-949-4109, E-mail: adultadmissions@lindenwood.edu. *Dean, School of Education,* Dr. Anthony Scheffler, 636-949-4618, Fax: 636-949-4197, E-mail: ascheffler@lindenwood.edu.

School of Health Sciences Students: 19 full-time (9 women), 41 part-time (35 women); includes 9 minority (5 Black or African American, non-Hispanic/Latino; 4 Hispanic/Latino), 4 international. Average age 33. 65 applicants, 49% accepted, 22 enrolled. *Faculty:* 9 full-time (4 women), 4 part-time/adjunct (3 women). Expenses: Contact institution. *Financial support:* In 2018–19, 46 students received support. Career-related internships or fieldwork, Federal Work-Study, institutionally sponsored loans, scholarships/grants, tuition waivers (partial), and unspecified assistantships available. Financial award application deadline: 6/30; financial award applicants required to submit FAFSA. In 2018, 27 master's awarded. *Program availability:* Part-time, blended/hybrid learning. Offers human performance (MS); nursing (MS). *Application deadline:* For fall admission, 8/9 priority date for domestic students, 6/1 priority date for international students; for spring admission, 12/20 priority date for domestic students, 11/1 priority date for international students; for summer admission, 5/15 priority date for domestic students, 3/27 priority date for international students. Applications are processed on a rolling basis. *Application fee:* $0 ($100 for international students). Electronic applications accepted. *Application Contact:* Kara Schilli, Assistant Vice President, University Admissions, 636-949-4349, Fax: 636-949-4109, E-mail: adultadmissions@lindenwood.edu. *Dean, School of Health Sciences,* Dr. Cynthia Schroeder, 636-949-4318, E-mail: cschroeder@lindenwood.edu.

LINDENWOOD UNIVERSITY–BELLEVILLE, Belleville, IL 62226

General Information Independent-religious, coed, comprehensive institution.

GRADUATE UNITS
Graduate Programs

LINDSEY WILSON COLLEGE, Columbia, KY 42728

General Information Independent-religious, coed, comprehensive institution. *Graduate housing:* Rooms and/or apartments available on a first-come, first-served basis to single and married students.

GRADUATE UNITS
Division of Education *Program availability:* Online learning. Offers teacher as leader (M Ed).

Louisville Center for Design *Program availability:* Online learning. Offers interactive design (MA).

School of Professional Counseling *Program availability:* Part-time, evening/weekend, online learning. Offers counseling and human development (M Ed); counselor education and supervision (PhD).

LIPSCOMB UNIVERSITY, Nashville, TN 37204-3951

General Information Independent-religious, coed, university. CGS member. *Graduate housing:* Room and/or apartments available on a first-come, first-served basis to single students; on-campus housing not available to married students. Housing application deadline: 7/15.

GRADUATE UNITS
College of Business *Program availability:* Part-time, evening/weekend. Offers accounting and finance (MBA); audit/accounting (M Acc); business (Certificate); business administration (MM); healthcare management (MBA); leadership (MBA); tax (M Acc). Electronic applications accepted.

College of Computing and Technology *Program availability:* Part-time, evening/weekend. Offers data science (MS, Certificate); information technology (MS, Certificate); software engineering (MS, Certificate). Electronic applications accepted.

College of Education *Program availability:* Part-time, evening/weekend, 100% online. Offers applied behavior analysis (MS, Certificate); coaching for learning (M Ed, Certificate,

Ed S); educational leadership (M Ed, Ed S); English language learning (M Ed, Ed S); instructional coaching (M Ed, Certificate, Ed S); instructional practice (M Ed); learning organizations and strategic change (Ed D); literacy coaching (Certificate, Ed S); reading specialty (M Ed, Ed S); school counseling (M Ed, Ed S); special education (M Ed); teaching, learning, and leading (M Ed); technology integration (M Ed, Ed S); technology integration specialist (Certificate). Electronic applications accepted.

College of Pharmacy Offers healthcare informatics (MS); pharmacy (Pharm D). Electronic applications accepted.

Department of Psychology, Counseling, and Family Science *Program availability:* Part-time, evening/weekend. Offers clinical mental health counseling (MS); counseling psychology (Certificate); marriage and family therapy (MMFT); psychology (MS). Electronic applications accepted.

Hazelip School of Theology *Program availability:* Part-time, evening/weekend, online learning. Offers missional and spiritual formation (D Min); theology (M Div). Electronic applications accepted.

Institute for Conflict Management *Program availability:* Part-time, evening/weekend. Offers conflict management (MA, Certificate). Electronic applications accepted.

Institute for Sustainable Practice *Program availability:* Part-time, evening/weekend, online learning. Offers sustainable practice (MS, Certificate). Electronic applications accepted.

Nelson and Sue Andrews Institute for Civic Leadership *Program availability:* Part-time, evening/weekend. Offers civic leadership (MA, Graduate Certificate); cross sector collaboration (MA); non-profit leadership (MA). Electronic applications accepted.

Program in Biomolecular Science *Program availability:* Part-time, evening/weekend. Offers human disease (MS); laboratory research (MS). Electronic applications accepted.

Program in Exercise and Nutrition Science *Program availability:* Part-time, evening/weekend. Offers exercise and nutrition science (MS). Electronic applications accepted.

Program in Film and Creative Media *Program availability:* Part-time, evening/weekend. Offers writer/director (MFA). Electronic applications accepted.

Program in Organizational Leadership *Program availability:* Part-time, online only, blended/hybrid learning. Offers aging services leadership (Certificate); global leadership (Certificate); organizational leadership (MPS); performance coaching (Certificate); strategic leadership (Certificate). Electronic applications accepted.

School of Public Policy Offers leadership and public service (MA). Electronic applications accepted.

LOCK HAVEN UNIVERSITY OF PENNSYLVANIA, Lock Haven, PA 17745-2390

General Information State-supported, coed, comprehensive institution. *Graduate housing:* Room and/or apartments available on a first-come, first-served basis to single students; on-campus housing not available to married students. Housing application deadline: 6/1.

GRADUATE UNITS
College of Liberal Arts and Education *Program availability:* Part-time, evening/weekend, online learning. Offers alternative education (M Ed); educational leadership (M Ed); teaching and learning (M Ed). Electronic applications accepted.

College of Natural, Behavioral and Health Sciences Offers actuarial science (PSM); athletic training (MS); health promotion/education (MHS); healthcare management (MHS); physician assistant (MHS). Program also offered at the Clearfield, Coudersport, and Harrisburg campuses. Electronic applications accepted.

The Stephen Poorman College of Business, Information Systems, and Human Services *Program availability:* Online learning. Offers clinical mental health counseling (MS); sport science (MS). Electronic applications accepted.

LOGAN UNIVERSITY, Chesterfield, MO 63017

General Information Independent, coed, upper-level institution. *Graduate housing:* On-campus housing not available. *Research affiliation:* BTE-Multi-Cervical Unit (cervical spine analysis), Cadwell (electrophysiological diagnosis), Standard Process (nutrition and lipid management), Biofreeze (topical analgesics), Foot Levelers, Inc. (orthotics).

GRADUATE UNITS
College of Chiropractic Offers chiropractic (DC). Electronic applications accepted.

College of Health Sciences *Program availability:* Part-time, online only, 100% online. Offers health informatics (MS); health professions education (DHPE); nutrition and human performance (MS); sports science and rehabilitation (MS). Electronic applications accepted.

LOGOS EVANGELICAL SEMINARY, El Monte, CA 91731

General Information Independent-religious, coed, graduate-only institution. *Graduate housing:* Rooms and/or apartments available on a first-come, first-served basis to single and married students. Housing application deadline: 7/15.

GRADUATE UNITS
Graduate Programs *Program availability:* Part-time, 100% online, blended/hybrid learning. Offers theology (M Div, MA, MAFM, MAICS, Th M, D Min, PhD, Diploma). Electronic applications accepted.

LOMA LINDA UNIVERSITY, Loma Linda, CA 92350

General Information Independent-religious, coed, university. CGS member. *Graduate housing:* Room and/or apartments available on a first-come, first-served basis to single students; on-campus housing not available to married students. *Research affiliation:* City of Hope Hospital (cancer research), Children's Hospital Los Angeles (cancer research), Children's Hospital Orange County (cancer research).

GRADUATE UNITS
School of Allied Health Professions Offers allied health professions (MOT, MPA, MS, DPT, OTD, PhD, SLPD); occupational therapy (MOT, OTD); physical therapy (DPT, PhD); physician assistant sciences (MPA); rehabilitation (MS); speech-language pathology (MS, SLPD). Electronic applications accepted.

School of Behavioral Health Offers behavioral health (MS, MSW, DMFT, PhD, Psy D, Certificate); child life specialist (MS); clinical mediation (Certificate); clinical psychology (PhD, Psy D); counseling (MS); criminal justice (MS); drug and alcohol counseling (Certificate); family life education (Certificate); gerontology (MS); marital and family therapy (DMFT); school counseling (Certificate); social policy and social research (PhD); social work (MSW). Electronic applications accepted.

School of Dentistry Offers dentistry (MS, DDS, Certificate); endodontics (MS, Certificate); implant dentistry (MS, Certificate); oral and maxillofacial surgery (MS, Certificate); orthodontics and dentofacial orthopedics (MS, Certificate); periodontics (MS).

School of Medicine Offers biochemistry (MS, PhD); human anatomy (PhD); medicine (MS, MD, PhD); microbiology (PhD); pathology (PhD); pharmacology (PhD); physiology (PhD).

School of Nursing *Program availability:* Part-time. Offers adult/gerontology (MS); nursing (MS, DNP, PhD); nursing administration (MS); obstetrics-pediatrics (MS). Electronic applications accepted.

School of Pharmacy Offers pharmacy (Pharm D).

School of Public Health *Program availability:* Part-time. Offers biostatistics (MPH); environmental and occupational health (MPH); epidemiology (MPH, Dr PH, PhD); global health (MPH); health education (MPH, Dr PH); healthcare administration (MBA); public health (MBA, MPH, MS, Dr PH, PhD); public health nutrition (MPH, Dr PH). Electronic applications accepted.

School of Religion Offers bioethics (MA, Certificate); chaplaincy (MS); religion (MA, MS, Certificate); religion and society (MA). Electronic applications accepted.

LONDON METROPOLITAN UNIVERSITY, London N7 8DB, United Kingdom
General Information Private, coed, university.
GRADUATE UNITS
Graduate Programs

LONG ISLAND UNIVERSITY–BRENTWOOD CAMPUS, Brentwood, NY 11717
General Information Independent, coed, upper-level institution. *Graduate housing:* On-campus housing not available.
GRADUATE UNITS
Graduate Programs *Program availability:* Part-time. Offers childhood education (MS); childhood education/literacy B-6 (MS); childhood education/special education (grades 1-6) (MS); clinical mental health counseling (MS, Advanced Certificate); criminal justice (MS); early childhood education (MS); educational leadership (MS Ed); family nurse practitioner (MS, Advanced Certificate); health administration (MPA); library and information science (MS); literacy (B-6) (MS Ed); school counselor (MS, Advanced Certificate); social work (MSW); special education (MS Ed); students with disabilities generalist (grades 7-12) (Advanced Certificate). Electronic applications accepted.

LONG ISLAND UNIVERSITY–HUDSON, Purchase, NY 10577
General Information Independent, coed, graduate-only institution. *Graduate housing:* On-campus housing not available.
GRADUATE UNITS
Graduate School *Program availability:* Part-time, evening/weekend. Offers autism (Advanced Certificate); bilingual education (Advanced Certificate); childhood education (MS Ed); crisis management (Advanced Certificate); early childhood education (MS Ed); educational leadership (MS Ed); health administration (MPA); literacy (MS Ed); marriage and family therapy (MS); mental health counseling (MS, Advanced Certificate); middle childhood and adolescence education (MS Ed); pharmaceutics (MS); public administration (MPA); school counseling (MS Ed, Advanced Certificate); school psychology (MS Ed); special education (MS Ed); TESOL (MS Ed); TESOL (all grades) (Advanced Certificate). Electronic applications accepted.

LONG ISLAND UNIVERSITY–LIU BROOKLYN, Brooklyn, NY 11201-8423
General Information Independent, coed, university. *Graduate housing:* Room and/or apartments available on a first-come, first-served basis to single students; on-campus housing not available to married students. Housing application deadline: 5/1. *Research affiliation:* California Table Grape Commission (pharmacy), Latitude Pharmaceuticals, Inc. (pharmacy), National Institute for Pharmaceutical Technology and Education (pharmacy), Natoli Engineering Company (pharmacy), Onconova Therapeutics, Inc. (pharmacy), Simcyp Limited (pharmacy).
GRADUATE UNITS
Arnold and Marie Schwartz College of Pharmacy and Health Sciences *Program availability:* Part-time. Offers drug regulatory affairs (MS); pharmaceutics (MS, PhD); pharmacology and toxicology (MS); pharmacy (Pharm D). Electronic applications accepted.

Harriet Rothkopf Heilbrunn School of Nursing *Program availability:* Part-time, evening/weekend, blended/hybrid learning. Offers adult nurse practitioner (MS, Advanced Certificate); family nurse practitioner (MS, Advanced Certificate); nurse educator (MS). Electronic applications accepted.

Richard L. Conolly College of Liberal Arts and Sciences *Program availability:* Part-time. Offers biology (MS); chemistry (MS); clinical psychology (PhD); creative writing (MFA); English (MA); media arts (MA, MFA); political science (MA); psychology (MA); social science (MS); United Nations (Advanced Certificate); urban studies (MA); writing and production for television (MFA). Electronic applications accepted.

School of Business, Public Administration and Information Sciences *Program availability:* Part-time, evening/weekend. Offers accounting (MBA); accounting (MS); business administration (MBA); computer science (MS); gerontology (Advanced Certificate); health administration (MPA); human resources management (MS); not-for-profit management (Advanced Certificate); public administration (MPA); taxation (MS). Electronic applications accepted.

School of Education *Program availability:* Part-time, evening/weekend, 100% online. Offers adolescence urban education (MS Ed); applied behavior analysis (Advanced Certificate); bilingual education (Advanced Certificate); bilingual education in urban setting (MS Ed); bilingual school counselor (MS Ed, Advanced Certificate); childhood urban education (MS Ed); childhood/early childhood education (MS Ed); childhood/early childhood urban education (MS Ed); early childhood urban education (MS Ed, Advanced Certificate); educational leadership (MS, Advanced Certificate); marriage and family therapy (MS, Advanced Certificate); mental health counseling (MS, Advanced Certificate); school building district leader (Advanced Certificate); school counselor (MS Ed, Advanced Certificate); school psychologist (MS Ed); teaching students with disabilities (MS Ed); teaching urban children with disabilities (MS Ed); TESOL (MS Ed, Advanced Certificate). Electronic applications accepted.

School of Health Professions Offers athletic training and sport sciences (MS); community health (MS Ed); exercise science (MS); forensic social work (Advanced Certificate); occupational therapy (MS); physical therapy (DPT); physician assistant (MS); public health (MPH); social work (MSW); speech-language pathology (MS). Electronic applications accepted.

LONG ISLAND UNIVERSITY–LIU POST, Brookville, NY 11548-1300
General Information Independent, coed, university. *Graduate housing:* Room and/or apartments available on a first-come, first-served basis to single students; on-campus housing not available to married students. Housing application deadline: 5/1. *Research affiliation:* Structure-ase Inc. (biology).
GRADUATE UNITS
College of Arts, Communications and Design Offers art (MA); clinical art therapy (MA); clinical art therapy and counseling (MA); digital game design and development (MA); fine arts and design (MFA); interactive multimedia arts (MA); museum studies (MA); music (MA); theatre (MFA). Electronic applications accepted.

College of Education, Information and Technology *Program availability:* Part-time, 100% online, blended/hybrid learning. Offers adolescence education (MS); adolescence education 7-12 (MS); archives and records management (AC); art education (MS); childhood education (MS); childhood education/literacy B-6 (MS); childhood education/special education (MS); clinical mental health counseling (MS, AC); early childhood education (MS); early childhood education/childhood education (MS); educational leadership (AC); educational technology (MS); information studies (PhD); interdisciplinary educational studies (Ed D); middle childhood education (MS); music education (MS); public library administration (AC); school counselor (MS); special education (MS Ed); speech-language pathology (MA); students with disabilities, 7-12 generalist (AC); TESOL (MA). Electronic applications accepted.

College of Liberal Arts and Sciences *Program availability:* Part-time, evening/weekend, blended/hybrid learning. Offers applied mathematics (MA); behavior analysis (MA); biology (MS); criminal justice (MS); earth science (MS); English (MA); environmental sustainability (MS); genetic counseling (MS); history (MA); interdisciplinary studies (MA, MS); political science (MA); psychology (MA). Electronic applications accepted.

College of Management *Program availability:* Part-time, evening/weekend, blended/hybrid learning. Offers accountancy (MS); finance (MBA); information systems (MS); international business (MBA); management (MBA); management engineering (MS); marketing (MBA); taxation (MS); technical project management (MS). Electronic applications accepted.

School of Health Professions and Nursing *Program availability:* Part-time, blended/hybrid learning. Offers biomedical science (MS); cardiovascular perfusion (MS); clinical lab sciences (MS); clinical laboratory management (MS); dietetic internship (Advanced Certificate); family nurse practitioner (MS, Advanced Certificate); forensic social work (Advanced Certificate); gerontology (Advanced Certificate); health administration (MPA); non-profit management (Advanced Certificate); nursing education (MS); nutrition (MS); public administration (MPA); social work (MSW). Electronic applications accepted.

LONG ISLAND UNIVERSITY–RIVERHEAD, Riverhead, NY 11901
General Information Independent, coed, graduate-only institution. *Graduate housing:* On-campus housing not available.
GRADUATE UNITS
Graduate Programs *Program availability:* Part-time. Offers applied behavior analysis (Advanced Certificate); childhood education (MS); cybersecurity policy (Advanced Certificate); homeland security management (MS, Advanced Certificate); literacy education (MS); literacy education B-6 (MS); teaching students with disabilities (MS); TESOL (Advanced Certificate). Electronic applications accepted.

LONGWOOD UNIVERSITY, Farmville, VA 23909
General Information State-supported, coed, comprehensive institution. CGS member. *Graduate housing:* On-campus housing not available.
GRADUATE UNITS
College of Graduate and Professional Studies *Program availability:* Part-time, evening/weekend. Electronic applications accepted.

College of Business and Economics *Program availability:* Part-time, online only, 100% online. Offers general business (MBA); real estate (MBA); retail management (MBA). Electronic applications accepted.

College of Education and Human Services *Program availability:* Part-time, evening/weekend. Offers communication sciences and disorders (MS); education (MS); reading, literacy and learning (M Ed); school librarianship (M Ed); social work and communication sciences and disorders (MS). Electronic applications accepted.

LORAS COLLEGE, Dubuque, IA 52004-0178
General Information Independent-religious, coed, comprehensive institution. *Graduate housing:* On-campus housing not available.
GRADUATE UNITS
Graduate Division *Program availability:* Part-time, evening/weekend. Offers applied psychology (MA); educational leadership (MA); instructional strategist I K-6 and 7-12 (MA); ministry (MA); theology (MA).

LOUISIANA COLLEGE, Pineville, LA 71359-0001
General Information Independent-religious, coed, comprehensive institution.
GRADUATE UNITS
Graduate Programs

LOUISIANA STATE UNIVERSITY AND AGRICULTURAL & MECHANICAL COLLEGE, Baton Rouge, LA 70803
General Information State-supported, coed, university. CGS member. *Graduate housing:* Rooms and/or apartments available on a first-come, first-served basis to single and married students. Housing application deadline: 3/15. *Research affiliation:* Arctic Research Consortium of the U.S., Organization for Tropical Studies, Coalition for Academic Scientific Computing, Albert Einstein Institute, Inter-University Consortium for Political and Social Research, Laser Interferometer Gravitational Wave Observatory.
GRADUATE UNITS
Graduate School *Program availability:* Part-time, evening/weekend. Electronic applications accepted.

College of Agriculture Offers agricultural economics and agribusiness (MS, PhD); agriculture (M App St, MS, PhD); agronomy (MS, PhD); animal sciences (MS, PhD); applied statistics (M App St); entomology (MS, PhD); fisheries (MS); forestry (MS, PhD); horticulture (MS, PhD); human ecology (MS, PhD); nutrition and food sciences (MS, PhD); plant health (MS, PhD); soil science (MS, PhD); wildlife (MS); wildlife and fisheries science (PhD).

College of Art and Design Offers architecture (M Arch); art and design (M Arch, MA, MFA, MLA); art history (MA); ceramics (MFA); graphic design (MFA); landscape architecture (MLA); painting and drawing (MFA); photography (MFA); printmaking (MFA); sculpture (MFA); studio art (MFA).

Louisiana State University and Agricultural & Mechanical College

College of Engineering Offers biological and agricultural engineering (MSBAE); chemical engineering (MS Ch E, PhD); computer science (MSSS, PhD); construction management (MS, PhD); digital media arts and engineering (M Sc); electrical and computer engineering (MSEE, PhD); engineering (M Sc, MS, MS Ch E, MS Pet E, MSBAE, MSCE, MSEE, MSES, MSME, MSSS, PhD); engineering science (MS, PhD); environmental engineering (MSCE, PhD); geotechnical engineering (MSCE, PhD); mechanical and industrial engineering (MSME, PhD); petroleum engineering (MS Pet E, PhD); structural engineering and mechanics (MSCE, PhD); systems science (MSSS); transportation engineering (MSCE, PhD); water resources (MSCE, PhD).

College of Humanities and Social Sciences Offers biological psychology (MA, PhD); clinical psychology (MA, PhD); cognitive psychology (MA, PhD); communication sciences and disorders (MA, PhD); communication studies (MA, PhD); comparative literature (MA, PhD); creative writing (MFA); developmental psychology (MA, PhD); English (MA, PhD); French literature and linguistics (MA, PhD); geography (MA, MS); geography and anthropology (PhD); Hispanic studies (MA); history (MA, PhD); humanities and social sciences (MA, MALA, MFA, MS, PhD); liberal arts (MALA); philosophy (MA); political science (MA, PhD); school psychology (MA, PhD); sociology (MA, PhD).

College of Human Sciences and Education Offers agriculture and extension education and youth development (MS, PhD); career and technical education (MS, PhD); comprehensive vocational education (MS, PhD); counseling (M Ed, MA, Ed S); educational administration (M Ed, MA, PhD, Ed S); educational technology (MA); elementary education (M Ed, MAT); extension and international education (MS, PhD); higher education (PhD); human resource and leadership development (MS, PhD); human sciences and education (M Ed, MA, MAT, MLIS, MS, MSW, PhD, Ed S); industrial education (MS); kinesiology (MS, PhD); library and information science (MLIS); research methodology (PhD); secondary education (M Ed, MAT); social work (MSW, PhD); vocational agriculture education (MS, PhD); vocational business education (MS); vocational home economics education (MS).

College of Music and Dramatic Arts Offers acting (MFA); directing (MFA); music (MM, DMA, PhD); music and dramatic arts (MFA, MM, DMA, PhD); music education (PhD); theatre (PhD); theatre design/technology (MFA).

College of Science Offers astronomy (MS, PhD); astrophysics (PhD); biochemistry (MS, PhD); biological science (MS, PhD); chemistry (MS, PhD); geology and geophysics (MS, PhD); mathematics (MS, PhD); medical physics (MS); natural sciences (MNS); physics (MS, PhD); science (MNS).

E. J. Ourso College of Business Offers accounting (MS, PhD); business (EMBA, MBA, MPA, MS, PMBA, PhD); business administration (PhD); economics (MS, PhD); finance (MS); information systems and decision sciences (MS, PhD); public administration (MPA).

Manship School of Mass Communication Offers mass communication (MMC, PhD).

School of the Coast and Environment Offers environmental planning and management (MS); environmental science (PhD); environmental toxicology (MS); oceanography and coastal sciences (MS, PhD); the coast and environment (MS, PhD).

Paul M. Hebert Law Center Students: 569 full-time (262 women); includes 114 minority (44 Black or African American, non-Hispanic/Latino; 2 American Indian or Alaska Native, non-Hispanic/Latino; 13 Asian, non-Hispanic/Latino; 42 Hispanic/Latino; 13 Two or more races, non-Hispanic/Latino), 8 international. Average age 26. 899 applicants, 62% accepted, 205 enrolled. *Faculty:* 39 full-time (17 women), 19 part-time/adjunct (1 woman). Expenses: Contact institution. *Financial support:* In 2018–19, 528 students received support. Scholarships/grants and tuition waivers (full and partial) available. Financial award application deadline: 7/1; financial award applicants required to submit FAFSA. In 2018, 8 master's awarded. Offers law (LL M, JD). *Application deadline:* For fall admission, 3/1 priority date for domestic and international students. Applications are processed on a rolling basis. *Application fee:* $50. Electronic applications accepted. *Application Contact:* Jake T. Henry, III, Director of Admissions, 225-578-8646, Fax: 225-578-8647, E-mail: jakeh@lsu.edu. *Dean,* Thomas Galligan, 225-578-8491, Fax: 225-578-8202, E-mail: tgalligan@lsu.edu.

School of Veterinary Medicine Offers comparative biomedical sciences (MS, PhD); pathobiological sciences (MS, PhD); veterinary clinical sciences (MS, PhD); veterinary medicine (MS, DVM, PhD).

LOUISIANA STATE UNIVERSITY HEALTH SCIENCES CENTER, New Orleans, LA 70112-2223

General Information State-supported, coed, university. CGS member. *Graduate housing:* Rooms and/or apartments available on a first-come, first-served basis to single and married students. Housing application deadline: 5/1.

GRADUATE UNITS

School of Allied Health Professions Students: 389 full-time (320 women); includes 56 minority (22 Black or African American, non-Hispanic/Latino; 18 Asian, non-Hispanic/Latino; 5 Hispanic/Latino; 1 Native Hawaiian or other Pacific Islander, non-Hispanic/Latino; 10 Two or more races, non-Hispanic/Latino), 2 international. Average age 25. 1,032 applicants, 14% accepted, 141 enrolled. *Faculty:* 29 full-time (23 women), 4 part-time/adjunct (all women). Expenses: Contact institution. *Financial support:* Work assistantships available. Financial award application deadline: 4/15; financial award applicants required to submit FAFSA. In 2018, 104 master's, 44 doctorates awarded. Offers allied health professions (MCD, MHS, MOT, MPAS, Au D, DPT); audiology (Au D); clinical rehabilitation and counseling (MHS); occupational therapy (MOT); physical therapy (DPT); physician assistant studies (MPAS); speech pathology (MCD). *Application deadline:* For fall admission, 4/15 priority date for domestic students; for spring admission, 1/15 priority date for domestic students. *Application fee:* $150. Electronic applications accepted. *Application Contact:* Yudialys Delgado Cazanas, Student Affairs Director, 504-568-4253, Fax: 504-568-3185, E-mail: ydelga@lsuhsc.edu. *Dean,* Dr. Jimmy M. Cairo, 504-556-3400, Fax: 504-568-4249, E-mail: jcairo@lsuhsc.edu.

School of Dentistry Offers dentistry (DDS).

School of Graduate Studies in New Orleans Offers cell biology and anatomy (PhD); human genetics (PhD); medicine (PhD); microbiology and immunology (PhD); neuroscience (PhD); pharmacology and experimental therapeutics (PhD); physiology (PhD).

School of Medicine in New Orleans Offers medicine (MPH, MD). Open only to Louisiana residents. Electronic applications accepted.

School of Nursing *Program availability:* Part-time. Offers adult gerontology acute care nurse practitioner (DNP, Post-Master's Certificate); adult gerontology clinical nurse specialist (DNP, Post-Master's Certificate); adult gerontology primary care nurse practitioner (DNP, Post-Master's Certificate); clinical nurse leader (MSN); executive nurse leader (DNP, Post-Master's Certificate); neonatal nurse practitioner (DNP, Post-Master's Certificate); nurse anesthesia (DNP, Post-Master's Certificate); nurse educator (MSN); nursing (DNS); primary care family nurse practitioner (DNP, Post-Master's Certificate); public/community health nursing (DNP, Post-Master's Certificate). Electronic applications accepted.

School of Public Health *Program availability:* Part-time. Offers behavioral and community health sciences (MPH); biostatistics (MPH, MS, PhD); community health sciences (PhD); environmental and occupational health sciences (MPH); epidemiology (MPH, PhD); health policy and systems management (MPH). Electronic applications accepted.

LOUISIANA STATE UNIVERSITY HEALTH SCIENCES CENTER AT SHREVEPORT, Shreveport, LA 71130-3932

General Information State-supported, coed, university. *Research affiliation:* Pennington Biomedical Research Center (metabolic disorders/obesity).

GRADUATE UNITS

Department of Biochemistry and Molecular Biology Offers biochemistry and molecular biology (MS, PhD). Electronic applications accepted.

Department of Cellular Biology and Anatomy Offers cellular biology and anatomy (MS, PhD).

Department of Microbiology and Immunology Offers microbiology and immunology (MS, PhD). Electronic applications accepted.

Department of Molecular and Cellular Physiology Offers physiology (MS, PhD).

Department of Pharmacology, Toxicology and Neuroscience Offers pharmacology (PhD).

Master of Science in Biomedical Sciences Program Offers biomedical sciences (MS).

School of Medicine Offers medicine (MD).

LOUISIANA STATE UNIVERSITY IN SHREVEPORT, Shreveport, LA 71115-2399

General Information State-supported, coed, comprehensive institution. *Research affiliation:* Micromanufacturing Institute (manufacturing technology), U.S. Department of Agriculture (USDA) (crop science), Louisiana Manufacturing Science Center (robotics), Biomedical Research Institute, Cotton, Incorporated (plant physiology).

GRADUATE UNITS

College of Arts and Sciences *Program availability:* Part-time, evening/weekend, 100% online. Offers arts and sciences (MA, MS); biological sciences (MS); computer systems technology (MS); liberal arts (MA); nonprofit administration (MS). Electronic applications accepted.

College of Business, Education, and Human Development *Program availability:* Part-time. Offers business administration (MBA); business, education, and human development (M Ed, MBA, MHA, MPH, MS, Ed D, SSP); counseling (MS); curriculum and instruction (M Ed); health administration (MHA); leadership (M Ed); leadership studies (Ed D); public health (MPH); school psychology (SSP). Electronic applications accepted.

LOUISIANA TECH UNIVERSITY, Ruston, LA 71272

General Information State-supported, coed, university. *Graduate housing:* Rooms and/or apartments available on a first-come, first-served basis to single and married students. Housing application deadline: 1/15.

GRADUATE UNITS

Graduate School *Program availability:* Part-time, evening/weekend. Electronic applications accepted.

College of Applied and Natural Sciences *Program availability:* Part-time. Offers biology (MS); dietetics (Graduate Certificate); health informatics (MHI); molecular science and nanotechnology (MS, PhD). Electronic applications accepted.

College of Business *Program availability:* Part-time, evening/weekend, 100% online, blended/hybrid learning. Offers accounting (M Acc, DBA); computer information systems (DBA); finance (MBA, DBA); information assurance (MBA); innovation (MBA); management (DBA); marketing (MBA, DBA). Electronic applications accepted.

College of Education *Program availability:* Part-time. Offers counseling and guidance (MA); counseling psychology (PhD); curriculum and instruction (M Ed); cyber education (Graduate Certificate); dynamics of domestic and family violence (Graduate Certificate); early childhood education - PreK-3 (MAT); educational leadership (M Ed, Ed D); elementary education and special education mild/moderate grades 1-5 (MAT); higher education administration (Graduate Certificate); industrial/organizational psychology (MA, PhD); kinesiology (MS); middle school education (MAT); orientation and mobility (Graduate Certificate); rehabilitation teaching for the blind (Graduate Certificate); secondary education (MAT); special education: visually impaired (MAT); teacher leader education (Graduate Certificate); visual impairments - blind education (Graduate Certificate). Electronic applications accepted.

College of Engineering and Science *Program availability:* Part-time-only. Offers applied physics (MS); biomedical engineering (PhD); computer science (MS); engineering (MS, PhD); engineering and technology management (MS); mathematics (MS); molecular science and nanotechnology (MS, PhD). Electronic applications accepted.

College of Liberal Arts *Program availability:* Part-time. Offers architecture (M Arch); art (MFA); audiology (Au D); communication (MA); English (MA); history (MA); speech pathology (MA); technical writing and communication (Graduate Certificate). Electronic applications accepted.

LOUISVILLE PRESBYTERIAN THEOLOGICAL SEMINARY, Louisville, KY 40205-1798

General Information Independent-religious, coed, graduate-only institution. *Enrollment by degree level:* 93 master's, 50 doctoral. *Graduate faculty:* 18 full-time (7 women), 8 part-time/adjunct (6 women). *Tuition:* Full-time $11,502; part-time $6390 per semester. *Required fees:* $286; $286. *Graduate housing:* Rooms and/or apartments available on a first-come, first-served basis to single and married students. Housing application deadline: 4/15. *Student services:* Campus employment opportunities, career counseling, international student services, services for students with disabilities, writing training. *Library facilities:* E.M. White Library. *Collection:* Books: 165,449 (physical), 11,301 (digital/electronic); Serial titles: 1,276 (physical), 2,618 (digital/electronic); Databases: 45. Students can reserve study rooms.

Computer facilities: 22 computers available on campus for general student use. Website: http://www.lpts.edu/

General Application Contact: Rev. Sandra Moon, Director of Admissions, 502-895-3411 Ext. 371, Fax: 502-895-1096, E-mail: smoon@lpts.edu.

GRADUATE UNITS

Graduate and Professional Programs Students: 96 full-time (63 women), 47 part-time (29 women); includes 46 minority (38 Black or African American, non-Hispanic/Latino; 3 Asian, non-Hispanic/Latino; 4 Hispanic/Latino; 1 Native Hawaiian or other Pacific Islander, non-Hispanic/Latino), 1 international. Average age 41. *Faculty:* 18 full-time (7 women), 8 part-time/adjunct (6 women). Expenses: Contact institution. *Financial support:* Career-related internships or fieldwork, Federal Work-Study, institutionally sponsored loans, and scholarships/grants available. Financial award application deadline: 2/1. In 2018, 25 master's, 10 doctorates awarded. *Program availability:* Part-time. Offers Bible (MAR); divinity (M Div); ministry (D Min); religious thought (MAR). JD/M Div, M Div/MBA, and M Div/MSSW offered jointly with University of Louisville. *Application deadline:* For fall admission, 6/15 priority date for domestic students, 2/1 priority date for international students. Applications are processed on a rolling basis. *Application fee:* $50. Electronic applications accepted. *Application Contact:* Rev. Sandra Moon, Director of Admissions, 502-895-3411, Fax: 502-895-1096, E-mail: smoon@lpts.edu. *Acting Dean,* Dr. Steve Cook, 502-895-3411, Fax: 502-895-1096, E-mail: scook@lpts.edu.

LOURDES UNIVERSITY, Sylvania, OH 43560-2898

General Information Independent-religious, coed, comprehensive institution. *Graduate housing:* Rooms and/or apartments available to single and married students. Housing application deadline: 5/1.

GRADUATE UNITS

Graduate School *Program availability:* Evening/weekend. Offers business (MBA); leadership (M Ed); nurse anesthesia (MSN); nurse educator (MSN); nurse leader (MSN); organizational leadership (MOL); reading (M Ed); teaching and curriculum (M Ed); theology (MA).

LOYOLA MARYMOUNT UNIVERSITY, Los Angeles, CA 90045

General Information Independent-religious, coed, comprehensive institution. CGS member. *Enrollment:* 9,838 graduate, professional, and undergraduate students; 2,258 full-time matriculated graduate/professional students (1,391 women), 393 part-time matriculated graduate/professional students (219 women). *Enrollment by degree level:* 1,553 master's, 1,098 doctoral. *Graduate faculty:* 232 full-time (101 women), 250 part-time/adjunct (127 women). *Graduate housing:* Room and/or apartments available on a first-come, first-served basis to single students; on-campus housing not available to married students. *Student services:* Campus employment opportunities, career counseling, child daycare facilities, exercise/wellness program, free psychological counseling, international student services, low-cost health insurance, multicultural affairs office, services for students with disabilities, teacher training. *Library facilities:* William H. Hannon Library. *Collection:* Study areas open 24 hours, 5–7 days a week; students can reserve study rooms.

Computer facilities: Computer purchase and lease plans are available. 820 computers available on campus for general student use. A campuswide network can be accessed from student residence rooms and from off campus. Online class registration is available.
Website: http://www.lmu.edu/

General Application Contact: Ammar Dalal, Assistant Vice Provost for Graduate Enrollment, 310-338-2721, Fax: 310-338-6086, E-mail: graduateinfo@lmu.edu.

GRADUATE UNITS

Bellarmine College of Liberal Arts Students: 143 full-time (75 women), 18 part-time (10 women); includes 69 minority (7 Black or African American, non-Hispanic/Latino; 12 Asian, non-Hispanic/Latino; 40 Hispanic/Latino; 2 Native Hawaiian or other Pacific Islander, non-Hispanic/Latino; 8 Two or more races, non-Hispanic/Latino), 24 international. Average age 39. 135 applicants, 81% accepted, 62 enrolled. *Faculty:* 38 full-time (13 women), 6 part-time/adjunct (2 women). Expenses: Contact institution. *Financial support:* Research assistantships, teaching assistantships, Federal Work-Study, scholarships/grants, and unspecified assistantships available. Support available to part-time students. Financial award application deadline: 5/1; financial award applicants required to submit FAFSA. In 2018, 53 master's awarded. *Program availability:* Part-time, evening/weekend. Offers bioethics (MA); English (MA); liberal arts (MA); pastoral theology (MA); philosophy (MA); theology (MA); yoga studies (MA). *Application fee:* $50. Electronic applications accepted. *Application Contact:* Ammar Dalal, Assistant Vice Provost for Graduate Enrollment, 310-338-2721, Fax: 310-338-6086, E-mail: graduateinfo@lmu.edu. *Dean, Bellarmine College of Liberal Arts,* Dr. Robbin D. Crabtree, 310-338-2716, E-mail: robbin.crabtree@lmu.edu.

College of Business Administration Students: 111 full-time (50 women), 4 part-time (0 women); includes 50 minority (12 Black or African American, non-Hispanic/Latino; 1 American Indian or Alaska Native, non-Hispanic/Latino; 11 Asian, non-Hispanic/Latino; 23 Hispanic/Latino; 1 Native Hawaiian or other Pacific Islander, non-Hispanic/Latino; 2 Two or more races, non-Hispanic/Latino), 24 international. Average age 31. 185 applicants, 52% accepted, 50 enrolled. *Faculty:* 33 full-time (7 women), 12 part-time/adjunct (2 women). Expenses: Contact institution. *Financial support:* Research assistantships, career-related internships or fieldwork, institutionally sponsored loans, scholarships/grants, and unspecified assistantships available. Support available to part-time students. Financial award application deadline: 5/1; financial award applicants required to submit FAFSA. In 2018, 92 master's awarded. *Program availability:* Part-time. Offers accounting (MS); business administration (MBA, MS); executive business administration (MBA). *Application fee:* $50. Electronic applications accepted. *Application Contact:* Ammar Dalal, Assistant Vice Provost for Graduate Enrollment, 310-338-2721, Fax: 310-338-6086, E-mail: graduateinfo@lmu.edu. *Dean, College of Business Administration,* Dr. Dayle Smith, 310-338-7504, E-mail: dayle.smith@lmu.edu.

College of Communication and Fine Arts Students: 49 full-time (47 women); includes 25 minority (1 Black or African American, non-Hispanic/Latino; 9 Asian, non-Hispanic/Latino; 14 Hispanic/Latino; 1 Two or more races, non-Hispanic/Latino). Average age 31. 35 applicants, 86% accepted, 22 enrolled. *Faculty:* 5 full-time (4 women), 13 part-time/adjunct (11 women). Expenses: Contact institution. *Financial support:* Research assistantships, career-related internships or fieldwork, institutionally sponsored loans, scholarships/grants, and unspecified assistantships available. Financial award application deadline: 5/1; financial award applicants required to submit FAFSA. In 2018, 24 master's awarded. Offers communication and fine arts (MA); marital and family therapy (MA). *Application fee:* $50. Electronic applications accepted. *Application Contact:* Ammar Dalal, Assistant Vice Provost for Graduate Enrollment, 310-338-2721, Fax: 310-338-6086, E-mail: graduateinfo@lmu.edu. *Dean, College of Communication and Fine Arts,* Dr. Bryant Keith Alexander, 310-338-7430, E-mail: bryantkeithalexander@lmu.edu.

Frank R. Seaver College of Science and Engineering Students: 93 full-time (34 women), 30 part-time (9 women); includes 69 minority (11 Black or African American, non-Hispanic/Latino; 18 Asian, non-Hispanic/Latino; 30 Hispanic/Latino; 1 Native Hawaiian or other Pacific Islander, non-Hispanic/Latino; 9 Two or more races, non-Hispanic/Latino), 27 international. Average age 29. 99 applicants, 81% accepted, 36 enrolled. *Faculty:* 19 full-time (4 women), 15 part-time/adjunct (4 women). Expenses: Contact institution. *Financial support:* Research assistantships, Federal Work-Study, scholarships/grants, unspecified assistantships, and laboratory assistantships available. Support available to part-time students. Financial award application deadline: 5/1; financial award applicants required to submit FAFSA. In 2018, 48 master's awarded. *Program availability:* Part-time. Offers civil engineering (MSE); electrical engineering (MS); environmental science (MS); healthcare systems engineering (MS); mechanical engineering (MSE); science and engineering (MAT, MS, MSE); systems engineering (MS); systems engineering leadership teaching management (MAT). *Application fee:* $50. Electronic applications accepted. *Application Contact:* Ammar Dalal, Assistant Vice Provost for Graduate Enrollment, 310-338-2721, Fax: 310-338-6086, E-mail: graduateinfo@lmu.edu. *Dean, Frank R. Seaver College of Science and Engineering,* Dr. Tina Choe, 310-338-2834, E-mail: tina.choe@lmu.edu.

Loyola Law School Los Angeles Students: 913 full-time (510 women), 194 part-time (95 women); includes 445 minority (48 Black or African American, non-Hispanic/Latino; 2 American Indian or Alaska Native, non-Hispanic/Latino; 117 Asian, non-Hispanic/Latino; 225 Hispanic/Latino; 1 Native Hawaiian or other Pacific Islander, non-Hispanic/Latino; 52 Two or more races, non-Hispanic/Latino), 80 international. Average age 27. 4,012 applicants, 36% accepted, 309 enrolled. *Faculty:* 65 full-time (33 women), 120 part-time/adjunct (47 women). Expenses: Contact institution. *Financial support:* In 2018–19, 645 students received support, including 40 research assistantships (averaging $1,823 per year); career-related internships or fieldwork, Federal Work-Study, scholarships/grants, and tuition waivers (partial) also available. Support available to part-time students. Financial award application deadline: 3/15; financial award applicants required to submit FAFSA. In 2018, 62 master's, 281 doctorates awarded. *Program availability:* Part-time, evening/weekend. Offers law (LL M, MLS, JD, JSD); law/business (LL M, LL M in Tax, MLS, MT, JD, JSD); law/tax law (LL M, LL M in Tax, MLS, MT, JD, JSD); tax law (LL M in Tax, MT). *Application deadline:* For fall admission, 2/1 priority date for domestic students, 2/1 for international students. Applications are processed on a rolling basis. *Application fee:* $0. Electronic applications accepted. *Application Contact:* Jannell Lundy Roberts, Senior Assistant Dean, Admissions and Enrollment Services, 213-736-1074, Fax: 213-736-6523, E-mail: admissions@lls.edu. *Dean,* Michael Waterstone, 213-736-2243, Fax: 213-487-6736, E-mail: michael.waterstone@lls.edu.

School of Education Students: 774 full-time (594 women), 136 part-time (97 women); includes 551 minority (65 Black or African American, non-Hispanic/Latino; 74 Asian, non-Hispanic/Latino; 387 Hispanic/Latino; 2 Native Hawaiian or other Pacific Islander, non-Hispanic/Latino; 23 Two or more races, non-Hispanic/Latino), 60 international. Average age 29. 544 applicants, 67% accepted, 276 enrolled. *Faculty:* 38 full-time (25 women), 114 part-time/adjunct (79 women). Expenses: Contact institution. *Financial support:* Research assistantships, teaching assistantships, institutionally sponsored loans, scholarships/grants, and unspecified assistantships available. Support available to part-time students. Financial award application deadline: 5/1; financial award applicants required to submit FAFSA. In 2018, 466 master's, 17 doctorates awarded. *Program availability:* Part-time, evening/weekend. Offers bilingual elementary education (MA); bilingual secondary education (MA); counseling (MA); education (MA, Ed D); educational leadership for social justice (Ed D); educational studies (MA); elementary education (MA); guidance and counseling (MA); higher education administration (MA); literacy education (MA); literacy instruction for urban environments (MA); literacy/language arts (MA); reading instruction (MA); school administration (MA); school counseling (MA); school psychology (MA); secondary education (MA); special education (MA); urban education (MA). *Application fee:* $50. Electronic applications accepted. *Application Contact:* Ammar Dalal, Assistant Vice Provost for Graduate Enrollment, 310-338-2721, Fax: 310-338-6086, E-mail: graduateinfo@lmu.edu. *Interim Dean, School of Education,* Dr. Mary McCullough, 310-338-7312, E-mail: Mary.McCullough@lmu.edu.

School of Film and Television Students: 187 full-time (89 women), 2 part-time (0 women); includes 74 minority (31 Black or African American, non-Hispanic/Latino; 9 Asian, non-Hispanic/Latino; 24 Hispanic/Latino; 10 Two or more races, non-Hispanic/Latino), 47 international. Average age 26. 316 applicants, 58% accepted, 77 enrolled. *Faculty:* 30 full-time (13 women), 29 part-time/adjunct (9 women). Expenses: Contact institution. *Financial support:* Research assistantships, teaching assistantships, career-related internships or fieldwork, and scholarships/grants available. Support available to part-time students. Financial award application deadline: 5/1; financial award applicants required to submit FAFSA. In 2018, 60 master's awarded. Offers film and television (MFA); film and television production (MFA); writing and producing for television (MFA); writing for the screen (MFA). *Application fee:* $50. Electronic applications accepted. *Application Contact:* Ammar Dalal, Assistant Vice Provost for Graduate Enrollment, 310-338-2721, Fax: 310-338-6086, E-mail: graduateinfo@lmu.edu. *Dean, School of Film and Television,* Peggy M. Rajski, 310-338-5800, E-mail: Peggy.Rajski@lmu.edu.

LOYOLA UNIVERSITY CHICAGO, Chicago, IL 60660

General Information Independent-religious, coed, university. CGS member. *Enrollment:* 17,007 graduate, professional, and undergraduate students; 3,915 full-time matriculated graduate/professional students (2,460 women), 1,300 part-time matriculated graduate/professional students (943 women). *Enrollment by degree level:* 3,045 master's, 2,022 doctoral, 148 other advanced degrees. *Graduate faculty:* 924 full-time (436 women), 750 part-time/adjunct (402 women). *Tuition:* Full-time $1033; part-time $788 per credit hour. *Required fees:* $700; $400 per credit hour. *One-time fee:* $400. One-time fee: $100. Tuition and fees vary according to course level, course load, degree level, program and student level. *Graduate housing:* Rooms and/or apartments available on a first-come, first-served basis to single and married students. Typical cost: $10,526 (including board) for single students. Room and board charges vary according to board plan, campus/location and housing facility selected. Housing application deadline: 5/1. *Student services:* Campus employment opportunities, campus safety program, career counseling, exercise/wellness program, free psychological counseling, international student services, low-cost health insurance, multicultural affairs office, services for students with disabilities, teacher training, writing training. *Library facilities:* Cudahy Library plus 7 others. *Collection:* Books: 1.9 million (physical), 568,720 (digital/electronic); Serial titles: 2,245 (physical), 58,389 (digital/electronic); Databases: 545. Weekly public service hours: 144; study areas open 24 hours, 5–7 days a week; students can reserve study rooms.

Computer facilities: Computer purchase and lease plans are available. 1,300 computers available on campus for general student use. A campuswide network can be accessed from student residence rooms and from off campus. Online class registration is available.
Website: http://www.luc.edu/

GRADUATE UNITS

General Application Contact: Jill Schur, Director, Graduate Enrollment Management, 312-915-8902, E-mail: gradinfo@luc.edu.

GRADUATE UNITS

Graduate School Students: 950 full-time (570 women), 272 part-time (155 women); includes 369 minority (101 Black or African American, non-Hispanic/Latino; 2 American Indian or Alaska Native, non-Hispanic/Latino; 112 Asian, non-Hispanic/Latino; 119 Hispanic/Latino; 10 Native Hawaiian or other Pacific Islander, non-Hispanic/Latino; 25 Two or more races, non-Hispanic/Latino), 112 international. Average age 31. 1,433 applicants, 39% accepted, 267 enrolled. Expenses: Contact institution. *Financial support:* Fellowships with full tuition reimbursements, research assistantships with full tuition reimbursements, teaching assistantships with tuition reimbursements, career-related internships or fieldwork, Federal Work-Study, institutionally sponsored loans, scholarships/grants, and unspecified assistantships available. Support available to part-time students. Financial award application deadline: 2/1; financial award applicants required to submit FAFSA. In 2018, 1,218 master's, 121 doctorates, 147 other advanced degrees awarded. *Program availability:* Part-time, evening/weekend, 100% online, blended/hybrid learning. Offers 19th century studies (PhD); applied philosophy and philosophy (MA); applied statistics (MS); biochemistry and molecular biology (MS, PhD); biology (MA); cell and molecular physiology (MS, PhD); cellular & molecular oncology (MS); chemistry (PhD); chemistry/biochemistry (MS); clinical psychology (MA, PhD); clinical research methods (MS); computer science (MS); criminal justice (MA); developmental psychology (MA, PhD); digital humanities (MA); English (MA); epidemiology (MPH); global politics (PhD); history (MA, PhD); infectious disease and immunology (MS); information technology (MS); integrative cell biology (MS, PhD); mathematics (MS); Medieval and Renaissance literature (PhD); microbiology and immunology (MS, PhD); modern literature and culture (PhD); molecular pharmacology and therapeutics (MS, PhD); neuroscience (MS, PhD); philosophy (PhD); political science (MA); public history (MA); public policy (MPP); sociology (MA, PhD); software engineering (MS); Spanish (MA); textual studies and digital humanities (PhD); theology (PhD); thesis (MA); urban affairs (MA); women's studies and gender studies (MA). *Application deadline:* Applications are processed on a rolling basis. *Application fee:* $50. Electronic applications accepted. *Application Contact:* Jill Schur, Director of Graduate Enrollment Management, 312-915-8902, E-mail: gradinfo@luc.edu. *Dean,* Dr. Thomas Regan, 773-508-3505, Fax: 773-508-3514, E-mail: tregan1@luc.edu.

Marcella Niehoff School of Nursing Students: 177 full-time (164 women), 241 part-time (223 women); includes 110 minority (24 Black or African American, non-Hispanic/Latino; 40 Asian, non-Hispanic/Latino; 38 Hispanic/Latino; 1 Native Hawaiian or other Pacific Islander, non-Hispanic/Latino; 7 Two or more races, non-Hispanic/Latino), 5 international. Average age 35. 193 applicants, 64% accepted, 103 enrolled. *Faculty:* 24 full-time (22 women), 21 part-time/adjunct (19 women). Expenses: Contact institution. *Financial support:* In 2018–19, 10 students received support, including 3 research assistantships with full tuition reimbursements available (averaging $18,000 per year), 1 teaching assistantship with full tuition reimbursement available (averaging $18,000 per year); scholarships/grants, unspecified assistantships, and nurse faculty loan program also available. Financial award application deadline: 5/1; financial award applicants required to submit FAFSA. In 2018, 106 master's, 13 doctorates, 21 other advanced degrees awarded. *Program availability:* Part-time, blended/hybrid learning. Offers adult clinical nurse specialist (MSN, Certificate); adult nurse practitioner (Certificate); dietetics (MS); family nurse practitioner (Certificate); family, adult, and women's health nurse practitioner (MSN); health systems leadership (MSN); healthcare quality using education in safety and technology (DNP); infection prevention (MSN, DNP); nursing science (PhD); women's health clinical nurse specialist (Certificate). *Application deadline:* For fall admission, 6/1 priority date for domestic and international students; for spring admission, 11/15 priority date for domestic and international students; for summer admission, 3/15 priority date for domestic and international students. Applications are processed on a rolling basis. *Application fee:* $50. Electronic applications accepted. *Application Contact:* Toni Topalova, Enrollment Advisor, 708-216-3751, Fax: 708-216-9555, E-mail: atopalova@luc.edu. *Dean,* Dr. Vickie Keough, 708-216-5448, Fax: 708-216-9555, E-mail: vkeough@luc.edu.

Neiswanger Institute for Bioethics Students: 35 full-time (24 women), 98 part-time (57 women); includes 30 minority (12 Black or African American, non-Hispanic/Latino; 2 American Indian or Alaska Native, non-Hispanic/Latino; 7 Asian, non-Hispanic/Latino; 7 Hispanic/Latino; 2 Two or more races, non-Hispanic/Latino). Average age 47. 38 applicants, 76% accepted, 26 enrolled. *Faculty:* 7 full-time (4 women), 6 part-time/adjunct (2 women). Expenses: Contact institution. *Financial support:* In 2018–19, 93 students received support. Institutionally sponsored loans and scholarships/grants available. Financial award applicants required to submit FAFSA. In 2018, 24 master's, 15 doctorates, 10 other advanced degrees awarded. *Program availability:* Part-time, online only, 100% online, blended/hybrid learning. Offers clinical bioethics, bioethics and health policy, catholic health care ethics (Certificate); clinical bioethics, catholic bioethics, organizational ethics, research ethics, public health ethics (D Be). *Application deadline:* For fall admission, 8/1 for domestic and international students; for spring admission, 1/5 for domestic and international students; for summer admission, 5/1 for domestic and international students. *Application Contact:* Robbin Hiller, Coordinator, Bioethics Education, 708-321-9219, Fax: 708-327-9209, E-mail: rhiller@luc.edu. *Coordinator, Bioethics Education,* Robbin Hiller, 708-327-9212, Fax: 708-327-9209, E-mail: rhiller@luc.edu.

School of Communication Students: 50 full-time (34 women), 13 part-time (11 women); includes 18 minority (9 Black or African American, non-Hispanic/Latino; 2 Asian, non-Hispanic/Latino; 6 Hispanic/Latino; 1 Two or more races, non-Hispanic/Latino), 18 international. Average age 29. 100 applicants, 56% accepted, 29 enrolled. Expenses: Contact institution. *Financial support:* Applicants required to submit FAFSA. In 2018, 17 master's awarded. Offers digital storytelling (MC); global strategic communication (MS). *Application Contact:* Ron Martin, Associate Director of Enrollment Management, 312-915-8950, Fax: 312-915-8905, E-mail: gradapp@luc.edu. *Dean,* Dr. Don Heider, 312-915-6548, E-mail: dheider@luc.edu.

Institute of Pastoral Studies Students: 80 full-time (51 women), 150 part-time (107 women); includes 58 minority (24 Black or African American, non-Hispanic/Latino; 7 Asian, non-Hispanic/Latino; 27 Hispanic/Latino), 28 international. Average age 45. 128 applicants, 79% accepted, 72 enrolled. *Faculty:* 9 full-time (3 women), 20 part-time/adjunct (7 women). Expenses: Contact institution. *Financial support:* In 2018–19, 111 students received support. Career-related internships or fieldwork, Federal Work-Study, scholarships/grants, and unspecified assistantships available. Support available to part-time students. Financial award application deadline: 3/15. In 2018, 53 master's, 5 other advanced degrees awarded. *Program availability:* Part-time, evening/weekend, 100% online, blended/hybrid learning. Offers Christian spirituality (MA); church management (Certificate); counseling for ministry (MA); divinity (M Div); health care ministry leadership (Certificate); health care mission leadership (MA); pastoral counseling (MA, Certificate); pastoral studies (MA); religious education (Certificate);

social justice (MA, Certificate); spiritual direction (Certificate). MSW/MA offered with School of Social Work. *Application deadline:* Applications are processed on a rolling basis. *Application fee:* $50. Electronic applications accepted. *Application Contact:* Dr. Peter L Jones, Interim Dean, 312-915-7400, Fax: 312-915-7504, E-mail: pjones5@luc.edu. *Interim Dean,* Dr. Peter L Jones, 312-915-7400, Fax: 312-915-7504, E-mail: pjones5@luc.edu.

Quinlan School of Business *Program availability:* Part-time, evening/weekend. Offers accountancy (MSA); accounting (MBA); asset management (MSF); business (MBA, MS, MSA, MSF, MSHR, MSSCM, Certificate); business data analytics (MS, Certificate); business ethics (MBA); data warehousing (Certificate); derivative markets (MBA); economics (MBA); entrepreneurship (MBA); finance (MBA); healthcare management (MBA); human resources (MSHR); human resources management (MBA); information systems (MS, Certificate); information systems management (MBA); integrated marketing communications (MS); international business (MBA); management (MBA); marketing (MBA); risk management (MBA); supply chain management (MBA, MSSCM, Certificate). Electronic applications accepted.

School of Education Students: 308 full-time (237 women), 182 part-time (135 women); includes 188 minority (71 Black or African American, non-Hispanic/Latino; 29 Asian, non-Hispanic/Latino; 73 Hispanic/Latino; 1 Native Hawaiian or other Pacific Islander, non-Hispanic/Latino; 14 Two or more races, non-Hispanic/Latino), 20 international. Average age 31. 608 applicants, 63% accepted, 146 enrolled. *Faculty:* 49 full-time (32 women), 69 part-time/adjunct (50 women). Expenses: Contact institution. *Financial support:* In 2018–19, 293 students received support, including 120 fellowships with partial tuition reimbursements available, 80 research assistantships with full tuition reimbursements available (averaging $14,000 per year), 93 teaching assistantships (averaging $4,000 per year); career-related internships or fieldwork, Federal Work-Study, institutionally sponsored loans, scholarships/grants, traineeships, health care benefits, and unspecified assistantships also available. Support available to part-time students. Financial award application deadline: 2/1; financial award applicants required to submit FAFSA. In 2018, 174 master's, 45 doctorates, 19 other advanced degrees awarded. *Program availability:* Part-time, evening/weekend. Offers administration and supervision (M Ed, Ed D, Certificate); clinical mental health counseling (Ed S); community counseling (M Ed, MA); counseling psychology (PhD); cultural and educational policy studies (M Ed, MA, PhD); curriculum and instruction (M Ed, Ed D); education (M Ed, MA, Ed D, PhD, Certificate, Ed S); elementary education (M Ed); English language teaching and learning (M Ed); higher education (M Ed, PhD); international higher education (M Ed); measurement $ quantitative methods (Certificate); research methodology (PhD); school counseling (M Ed, Certificate); school psychology (Ed D, PhD, Ed S); secondary education (M Ed); special education (M Ed). *Application fee:* $50. Electronic applications accepted. *Application Contact:* Dr. Siobhan Cafferty, Program Chair, 312-915-7002, E-mail: scaffer@luc.edu. *Dean,* Dr. Malik Henfield, 312-915-7002, E-mail: mhenfield@luc.edu.

School of Law Students: 870 full-time (530 women), 239 part-time (185 women); includes 380 minority (134 Black or African American, non-Hispanic/Latino; 64 Asian, non-Hispanic/Latino; 142 Hispanic/Latino; 40 Two or more races, non-Hispanic/Latino), 34 international. Average age 31. 2,711 applicants, 46% accepted, 387 enrolled. *Faculty:* 69 full-time (36 women), 306 part-time/adjunct (148 women). Expenses: Contact institution. *Financial support:* In 2018–19, 598 students received support, including 67 fellowships; research assistantships, Federal Work-Study, scholarships/grants, and health care benefits also available. Financial award application deadline: 3/1; financial award applicants required to submit FAFSA. In 2018, 151 master's, 193 doctorates, 152 Certificates awarded. *Program availability:* Part-time, evening/weekend, 100% online, blended/hybrid learning. Offers advocacy (LL M); business and compliance (MJ); business law (LL M); child and family (LL M); child and family law (MJ, Certificate); global competition (LL M, MJ); health law (LL M, MJ, Certificate); international law (LL M); law (JD); public interest law (Certificate); rule of law for development (LL M, MJ); tax (LL M); tax law (Certificate); transactional law (Certificate); trial advocacy (Certificate). *Application deadline:* For fall admission, 4/1 for domestic and international students. Applications are processed on a rolling basis. *Application fee:* $0. Electronic applications accepted. *Application Contact:* Jill Schur, Director, Graduate Enrollment Management, 312-915-8902, E-mail: gradinfo@luc.edu. *Associate Dean for Administration, Law School,* Dr. James Faught, JD, 312-915-7131, Fax: 312-915-6911, E-mail: law-admissions@luc.edu.

School of Social Work *Program availability:* Part-time. Offers social work (MSW, PhD, PGC).

LOYOLA UNIVERSITY MARYLAND, Baltimore, MD 21210-2699

General Information Independent-religious, coed, university. CGS member. *Graduate housing:* On-campus housing not available.

GRADUATE UNITS

Graduate Programs *Program availability:* Part-time, evening/weekend. Electronic applications accepted.

Loyola College of Arts and Sciences *Program availability:* Part-time, evening/weekend. Offers arts and sciences (MA, MS, MTS, PhD, Psy D, CAS, Certificate); clinical psychology (MS, Psy D, CAS); counseling psychology (MS, CAS); emerging media (MA); speech-language pathology (MS); theology (MTS). Electronic applications accepted.

School of Education *Program availability:* Part-time, evening/weekend. Offers curriculum and instruction (MA); education (M Ed, MA, MAT, CAS); educational leadership (M Ed, CAS); educational technology (M Ed, MA); elementary education (M Ed, MAT); Kodaly music education (M Ed); literacy teacher (M Ed); Montessori education (CAS); reading specialist (M Ed); school counseling (M Ed, MA, CAS); secondary education (MAT). Electronic applications accepted.

Sellinger School of Business *Program availability:* Part-time, evening/weekend. Offers business (M Acc, MBA); business administration (MBA); finance (MBA); information systems (MBA); investments and applied portfolio management (MBA); management (MBA); marketing (MBA). Electronic applications accepted.

LOYOLA UNIVERSITY NEW ORLEANS, New Orleans, LA 70118-6195

General Information Independent-religious, coed, comprehensive institution. *Enrollment:* 4,261 graduate, professional, and undergraduate students; 607 full-time matriculated graduate/professional students (368 women), 628 part-time matriculated graduate/professional students (507 women). *Enrollment by degree level:* 635 master's, 598 doctoral, 2 other advanced degrees. *Graduate faculty:* 98 full-time (56 women), 61 part-time/adjunct (27 women). *Tuition:* Full-time $818; part-time $818 per credit hour. *Required fees:* $1516; $760 per unit. $380 per semester. One-time fee: $300. Tuition and fees vary according to degree level and program. *Graduate housing:* Room and/or apartments available on a first-come, first-served basis to single students; on-campus housing not available to married students. Typical cost: $12,876 (including board). Room and board charges vary according to housing facility selected. Housing application deadline: 8/1. *Student services:* Campus employment opportunities, campus safety program, career counseling, child daycare facilities, exercise/wellness program, free psychological counseling, international student services, low-cost health insurance, multicultural affairs office, services for students with disabilities. *Library facilities:* Monroe Library plus 1 other. *Collection:* Books: 353,685 (physical), 42,981 (digital/electronic); Serial titles: 1,385 (physical), 250,962 (digital/electronic); Databases: 129. Weekly public service hours: 114; students can reserve study rooms.

Computer facilities: Computer purchase and lease plans are available. 525 computers available on campus for general student use. A campuswide network can be accessed from student residence rooms and from off campus. Online class registration is available.
Website: http://www.loyno.edu/

General Application Contact: Tharren Poplion, Assistant Director, Admissions, 504-865-3240, E-mail: poplion@loyno.edu.

GRADUATE UNITS

College of Arts and Sciences Students: 30 full-time (24 women), 24 part-time (17 women); includes 24 minority (18 Black or African American, non-Hispanic/Latino; 2 American Indian or Alaska Native, non-Hispanic/Latino; 1 Asian, non-Hispanic/Latino; 2 Hispanic/Latino; 1 Two or more races, non-Hispanic/Latino). Average age 33. 58 applicants, 81% accepted, 35 enrolled. *Faculty:* 6 full-time (4 women), 2 part-time/adjunct (1 woman). Expenses: Contact institution. *Financial support:* Research assistantships, teaching assistantships, career-related internships or fieldwork, Federal Work-Study, scholarships/grants, and tuition waivers (partial) available. Support available to part-time students. Financial award application deadline: 5/1; financial award applicants required to submit FAFSA. In 2018, 5 master's awarded. *Program availability:* Part-time, evening/weekend. Offers arts and sciences (MAT, MCJ); criminology and justice (MCJ); teaching (MAT). Application fee: $20. Electronic applications accepted. *Application Contact:* Tharren Poplion, Assistant Director, Admissions, 504-865-3240, E-mail: poplion@loyno.edu. *Interim Dean,* Uriel Quesada, 504-865-3049, Fax: 504-865-2059, E-mail: uquesada@loyno.edu.

College of Law Students: 429 full-time (242 women), 80 part-time (37 women); includes 185 minority (85 Black or African American, non-Hispanic/Latino; 12 American Indian or Alaska Native, non-Hispanic/Latino; 16 Asian, non-Hispanic/Latino; 66 Hispanic/Latino; 6 Two or more races, non-Hispanic/Latino; 6 international. Average age 27. 795 applicants, 61% accepted, 170 enrolled. *Faculty:* 42 full-time (21 women), 26 part-time/adjunct (11 women). Expenses: Contact institution. *Financial support:* Fellowships, research assistantships, teaching assistantships, career-related internships or fieldwork, institutionally sponsored loans, scholarships/grants, traineeships, health care benefits, tuition waivers, and unspecified assistantships available. Support available to part-time students. Financial award applicants required to submit FAFSA. In 2018, 4 master's, 144 doctorates awarded. *Program availability:* Part-time, online learning. Offers law (LL M, JD). *Application deadline:* For fall admission, 8/1 priority date for domestic and international students. Applications are processed on a rolling basis. *Application fee:* $0. Electronic applications accepted. *Application Contact:* Kimberly Jones, Director of Law Admissions, 504-861-5575, Fax: 504-861-5772, E-mail: ladmit@loyno.edu. *Dean,* Madeleine Landrieu, 504-861-5847, Fax: 504-861-5677, E-mail: lmoore@loyno.edu.

College of Music and Media Students: 10 full-time (6 women), 37 part-time (26 women); includes 21 minority (10 Black or African American, non-Hispanic/Latino; 1 Asian, non-Hispanic/Latino; 6 Hispanic/Latino; 4 Two or more races, non-Hispanic/Latino), 2 international. Average age 29. 35 applicants, 91% accepted, 16 enrolled. *Faculty:* 13 full-time (7 women), 13 part-time/adjunct (4 women). Expenses: Contact institution. *Financial support:* Career-related internships or fieldwork, Federal Work-Study, institutionally sponsored loans, scholarships/grants, unspecified assistantships, and talent-based music scholarships available. Support available to part-time students. Financial award application deadline: 5/1; financial award applicants required to submit FAFSA. In 2018, 10 master's awarded. *Program availability:* Part-time. Offers music therapy (MMT); performance (MM). *Application deadline:* For fall admission, 8/15 priority date for domestic and international students; for spring admission, 1/1 priority date for domestic and international students. Applications are processed on a rolling basis. *Application fee:* $20. Electronic applications accepted. *Application Contact:* Dr. Kern Maass, Dean, 504-865-3039, Fax: 504-865-2852, E-mail: kdmaass@loyno.edu. *Dean,* Dr. Kern Maass, 504-865-3039, Fax: 504-865-2852, E-mail: kdmaass@loyno.edu.

College of Nursing and Health Students: 90 full-time (71 women), 439 part-time (394 women); includes 166 minority (108 Black or African American, non-Hispanic/Latino; 5 American Indian or Alaska Native, non-Hispanic/Latino; 18 Asian, non-Hispanic/Latino; 31 Hispanic/Latino; 3 Native Hawaiian or other Pacific Islander, non-Hispanic/Latino; 1 Two or more races, non-Hispanic/Latino), 4 international. Average age 40. 245 applicants, 80% accepted, 144 enrolled. *Faculty:* 23 full-time (18 women), 14 part-time/adjunct (10 women). Expenses: Contact institution. In 2018, 118 master's, 19 doctorates awarded. *Program availability:* Part-time. Offers counseling (MS); nursing and health (MPS, MRE, MS, MSN, DNP, Certificate). *Application deadline:* Applications are processed on a rolling basis. *Application fee:* $0. Electronic applications accepted. *Application Contact:* Tharren Poplion, Assistant Director, Admissions, 504-865-3240, E-mail: poplion@loyno.edu. *Dean,* Dr. Laurie Ann Ferguson, 504-865-2880, E-mail: ferguson@loyno.edu.

Loyola Institute for Ministry Students: 31 full-time (18 women), 68 part-time (52 women); includes 21 minority (8 Black or African American, non-Hispanic/Latino; 2 American Indian or Alaska Native, non-Hispanic/Latino; 3 Asian, non-Hispanic/Latino; 8 Hispanic/Latino), 2 international. Average age 47. 35 applicants, 100% accepted, 26 enrolled. *Faculty:* 2 full-time (1 woman), 6 part-time/adjunct (3 women). Expenses: Contact institution. *Financial support:* Career-related internships or fieldwork, scholarships/grants, health care benefits, and tuition waivers (partial) available. Support available to part-time students. Financial award application deadline: 5/1; financial award applicants required to submit FAFSA. In 2018, 21 master's awarded. *Program availability:* Part-time, evening/weekend, online learning. Offers pastoral studies (MPS); religious education (MRE); theology and ministry (Certificate). *Application deadline:* For fall admission, 8/15 for domestic and international students; for spring admission, 1/1 for domestic and international students. Applications are processed on a rolling basis. *Application fee:* $20. Electronic applications accepted. *Application Contact:* Diane Blair, Manager of Admissions, 504-865-3728, Fax: 504-865-2066, E-mail: lim@loyno.edu. *Director,* Dr. Tom Ryan, 504-865-2069, Fax: 504-865-2066, E-mail: tfryan@loyno.edu.

School of Nursing Students: 35 full-time (all women), 316 part-time (291 women); includes 128 minority (90 Black or African American, non-Hispanic/Latino; 3 American Indian or Alaska Native, non-Hispanic/Latino; 15 Asian, non-Hispanic/Latino; 16 Hispanic/Latino; 3 Native Hawaiian or other Pacific Islander, non-Hispanic/Latino; 1 Two or more races, non-Hispanic/Latino). Average age 39. 160 applicants, 72%

accepted, 85 enrolled. *Faculty:* 17 full-time (15 women), 5 part-time/adjunct (4 women). Expenses: Contact institution. *Financial support:* Traineeships and Incumbent Workers Training Program grants available. Financial award application deadline: 5/1; financial award applicants required to submit FAFSA. In 2018, 81 master's, 19 doctorates awarded. *Program availability:* Part-time, online learning. Offers family nurse practitioner (DNP); nursing (MSN). *Application deadline:* For fall admission, 8/1 priority date for domestic and international students; for winter admission, 12/15 priority date for domestic and international students; for spring admission, 5/15 priority date for domestic and international students. Applications are processed on a rolling basis. *Application fee:* $40. Electronic applications accepted. *Application Contact:* Elizabeth Wadsworth, Executive Assistant to the Director, 504-865-2307, Fax: 504-865-3254, E-mail: edwadswo@loyno.edu. *Interim Director,* Dr. Laurie Ann Ferguson, 504-865-2880, Fax: 504-865-3254, E-mail: nursing@loyno.edu.

Joseph A. Butt, S.J., College of Business Students: 48 full-time (25 women), 48 part-time (33 women); includes 34 minority (20 Black or African American, non-Hispanic/Latino; 1 Asian, non-Hispanic/Latino; 11 Hispanic/Latino; 2 Two or more races, non-Hispanic/Latino), 6 international. Average age 31. 79 applicants, 92% accepted, 43 enrolled. *Faculty:* 14 full-time (6 women), 6 part-time/adjunct (1 woman). Expenses: Contact institution. *Financial support:* Research assistantships, scholarships/grants, tuition waivers (partial), and unspecified assistantships available. Financial award application deadline: 5/1; financial award applicants required to submit FAFSA. In 2018, 22 master's awarded. *Program availability:* Part-time, evening/weekend, online learning. Offers business (MBA); organizational performance excellence (MBA). *Application deadline:* For fall admission, 6/15 priority date for domestic students, 5/15 priority date for international students; for spring admission, 11/15 priority date for domestic students, 10/15 priority date for international students. Applications are processed on a rolling basis. *Application fee:* $50. Electronic applications accepted. *Application Contact:* Ashley Francis, Director of Graduate Programs, 504-864-7979, Fax: 504-864-7970, E-mail: mba@loyno.edu. *Interim Dean,* Dr. J. Patrick O'Brien, 504-864-7990, Fax: 504-864-7970, E-mail: mba@loyno.edu.

LUBBOCK CHRISTIAN UNIVERSITY, Lubbock, TX 79407-2099

General Information Independent-religious, coed, comprehensive institution. *Graduate housing:* Rooms and/or apartments available to single and married students. Housing application deadline: 8/15.

GRADUATE UNITS

Graduate Biblical Studies *Program availability:* Part-time. Offers Bible and ministry (MS); biblical interpretation (MA).

LUTHERAN SCHOOL OF THEOLOGY AT CHICAGO, Chicago, IL 60615-5199

General Information Independent-religious, coed, graduate-only institution. *Graduate housing:* Rooms and/or apartments available on a first-come, first-served basis to single and married students. Housing application deadline: 5/15. *Research affiliation:* Chicago Center for Public Ministry, Zygon Center for Religion and Science.

GRADUATE UNITS

Graduate and Professional Programs *Program availability:* Part-time. Offers ministry (MAM, D Min); theological studies (MATS, PhD); theology (M Div).

LUTHERAN THEOLOGICAL SEMINARY SASKATOON, Saskatoon, SK S7N 0X3, Canada

General Information Independent-religious, coed, graduate-only institution. *Graduate housing:* Room and/or apartments available to single students; on-campus housing not available to married students. Housing application deadline: 4/30.

GRADUATE UNITS

Graduate and Professional Programs *Program availability:* Part-time. Offers Biblical studies (MTS); church history (MTS); ethics/church and society (MTS); history of Christianity (STM); New Testament (STM); Old Testament (STM); pastoral studies (STM); pastoral theology (MTS); systematic theology (MTS); systematic theology and philosophy of religion (STM); theology (M Div, D Div). STM programs offered jointly with College of Emmanuel and St. Chad and St. Andrew's College.

LUTHER RICE COLLEGE & SEMINARY, Lithonia, GA 30038-2454

General Information Independent-religious, coed, comprehensive institution. *Graduate housing:* On-campus housing not available.

GRADUATE UNITS

Graduate Programs *Program availability:* Part-time, evening/weekend, online learning. Offers apologetics (MA); Bible languages (M Div); Biblical counseling (MA); Christian ministry (M Div, D Min); Christian studies (MA); leadership (MA). Electronic applications accepted.

LUTHER SEMINARY, St. Paul, MN 55108-1445

General Information Independent-religious, coed, graduate-only institution. *Graduate housing:* Rooms and/or apartments available on a first-come, first-served basis to single and married students.

GRADUATE UNITS

Graduate and Professional Programs *Program availability:* Part-time, online learning. Offers aging and health (MA); Biblical preaching (D Min); children, youth and family (M Div, MA); congregational mission and leadership (M Th, MA, D Min); history of Christianity (M Th, MA); missions and world religions (M Th); New Testament (M Th, MA); Old Testament (M Th, MA); pastoral care: clinical pastoral theology (M Th); pastoral theology and ministry (M Th); systematic theology (M Th, MA). Electronic applications accepted.

LYNN UNIVERSITY, Boca Raton, FL 33431-5598

General Information Independent, coed, comprehensive institution. *Enrollment:* 467 full-time matriculated graduate/professional students (270 women), 393 part-time matriculated graduate/professional students (214 women). *Enrollment by degree level:* 754 master's, 70 doctoral, 36 other advanced degrees. *Graduate faculty:* 137 full-time (58 women), 82 part-time/adjunct (44 women). *Tuition:* Full-time $17,760; part-time $740 per course. One-time fee: $100. Tuition and fees vary according to class time, course load and degree level. *Graduate housing:* On-campus housing not available. *Student services:* Campus employment opportunities, campus safety program, career counseling, exercise/wellness program, free psychological counseling, international student services, low-cost health insurance, multicultural affairs office, services for students with disabilities. *Library facilities:* Eugene M. and Christine E. Lynn Library. *Collection:* Books: 58,952 (physical), 239,257 (digital/electronic); Serial titles: 401 (physical), 43,029 (digital/electronic); Databases: 118. Weekly public service hours: 96.

Computer facilities: Computer purchase and lease plans are available. 150 computers available on campus for general student use. A campuswide network can be accessed from student residence rooms and from off campus. Online registration with advisor approval for juniors, seniors and MBA students available.
Website: http://www.lynn.edu/

General Application Contact: Steven Pruitt, Assistant Director of Graduate Admissions, 561-237-7834, Fax: 561-237-7100, E-mail: admission@lynn.edu.

GRADUATE UNITS

College of Arts and Sciences Students: 73 full-time (59 women), 43 part-time (25 women); includes 52 minority (25 Black or African American, non-Hispanic/Latino; 1 Asian, non-Hispanic/Latino; 25 Hispanic/Latino; 1 Two or more races, non-Hispanic/Latino), 6 international. Average age 32. 110 applicants, 65% accepted, 53 enrolled. *Faculty:* 54 full-time (25 women), 33 part-time/adjunct (24 women). Expenses: Contact institution. *Financial support:* In 2018–19, 24 students received support. Career-related internships or fieldwork, Federal Work-Study, scholarships/grants, tuition waivers (full and partial), and unspecified assistantships available. Support available to part-time students. Financial award application deadline: 3/1; financial award applicants required to submit FAFSA. In 2018, 39 master's awarded. *Program availability:* Part-time, evening/weekend, 100% online, blended/hybrid learning. Offers criminal justice (MS); mental health counseling (MS); psychology (MS). *Application deadline:* For fall admission, 8/18 for domestic students, 8/4 for international students; for spring admission, 12/15 for domestic students, 12/1 for international students; for summer admission, 4/17 for domestic students, 4/3 for international students. Applications are processed on a rolling basis. *Application fee:* $45. Electronic applications accepted. *Application Contact:* Steven Pruitt, Director of Graduate and Online Admission, 561-237-7834, Fax: 561-237-7100, E-mail: admissionpm@lynn.edu. *Dean, College of Arts and Sciences,* Dr. Gary Villa, 561-237-7025, E-mail: gvilla@lynn.edu.

College of Business and Management Students: 283 full-time (149 women), 211 part-time (101 women); includes 132 minority (61 Black or African American, non-Hispanic/Latino; 17 Asian, non-Hispanic/Latino; 45 Hispanic/Latino; 9 Two or more races, non-Hispanic/Latino), 136 international. Average age 30. 331 applicants, 83% accepted, 205 enrolled. *Faculty:* 34 full-time (14 women), 22 part-time/adjunct (9 women). Expenses: Contact institution. *Financial support:* In 2018–19, 137 students received support. Career-related internships or fieldwork, Federal Work-Study, scholarships/grants, tuition waivers (full and partial), and unspecified assistantships available. Support available to part-time students. Financial award application deadline: 3/1; financial award applicants required to submit FAFSA. In 2018, 259 master's awarded. *Program availability:* Part-time, evening/weekend, 100% online, blended/hybrid learning. Offers business administration (MBA). *Application deadline:* For fall admission, 8/18 for domestic students, 8/4 for international students; for spring admission, 12/15 for domestic students, 12/1 for international students; for summer admission, 4/17 for domestic students, 4/3 for international students. Applications are processed on a rolling basis. *Application fee:* $45. Electronic applications accepted. *Application Contact:* Steven Pruitt, Director of Graduate and Undergraduate Evening Admission, 561-237-7834, Fax: 561-237-7100, E-mail: spruitt@lynn.edu. *Dean of the College of Business and Management,* Dr. RT Good, 561-237-7458, E-mail: rgood@lynn.edu.

Conservatory of Music Students: 33 full-time (11 women), 30 part-time (12 women); includes 6 minority (5 Hispanic/Latino; 1 Two or more races, non-Hispanic/Latino), 31 international. Average age 26. 112 applicants, 43% accepted, 29 enrolled. *Faculty:* 12 full-time (3 women), 10 part-time/adjunct (2 women). Expenses: Contact institution. *Financial support:* In 2018–19, 63 students received support. Federal Work-Study, scholarships/grants, and unspecified assistantships available. Support available to part-time students. Financial award application deadline: 3/1; financial award applicants required to submit FAFSA. In 2018, 16 master's, 1 Certificate awarded. *Program availability:* Part-time, evening/weekend. Offers composition (MM); instrumental collaborative piano (MM); performance (MM); professional performance (Certificate). *Application deadline:* For fall admission, 8/18 for domestic students, 8/4 for international students; for spring admission, 12/15 for domestic students, 12/1 for international students; for summer admission, 4/17 for domestic students, 4/3 for international students. Applications are processed on a rolling basis. *Application fee:* $50. Electronic applications accepted. *Application Contact:* Steven Pruitt, Director of Graduate Admissions, 561-237-7834, Fax: 561-237-7100, E-mail: admission@lynn.edu. *Dean,* Dr. Jon Robertson, 561-237-7702, Fax: 561-237-9002, E-mail: jrobertson@lynn.edu.

Donald E. and Helen L. Ross College of Education Students: 38 full-time (30 women), 85 part-time (63 women); includes 50 minority (33 Black or African American, non-Hispanic/Latino; 1 Asian, non-Hispanic/Latino; 15 Hispanic/Latino; 1 Two or more races, non-Hispanic/Latino), 5 international. Average age 38. 78 applicants, 65% accepted, 41 enrolled. *Faculty:* 6 full-time (4 women), 8 part-time/adjunct (7 women). Expenses: Contact institution. *Financial support:* In 2018–19, 85 students received support. Career-related internships or fieldwork, Federal Work-Study, scholarships/grants, tuition waivers (partial), and unspecified assistantships available. Support available to part-time students. Financial award application deadline: 3/1; financial award applicants required to submit FAFSA. In 2018, 13 master's, 14 doctorates awarded. *Program availability:* Part-time, evening/weekend, online learning. Offers educational leadership (M Ed, Ed D); exceptional student education (M Ed). *Application deadline:* For fall admission, 8/18 for domestic students, 8/4 for international students; for spring admission, 12/15 for domestic students, 12/1 for international students; for summer admission, 4/17 for domestic students, 4/3 for international students. Applications are processed on a rolling basis. *Application fee:* $45. Electronic applications accepted. *Application Contact:* Steven Pruitt, Director of Graduate and Undergraduate Evening Admission, 561-237-7834, Fax: 561-237-7100, E-mail: spruitt@lynn.edu. *Dean, College of Education,* Dr. Kathleen Weigel, 561-237-7441, E-mail: kweigel@lynn.edu.

Eugene M. and Christine E. Lynn College of Communication and Design Students: 28 full-time (10 women), 5 part-time (2 women); includes 22 minority (11 Black or African American, non-Hispanic/Latino; 1 Asian, non-Hispanic/Latino; 9 Hispanic/Latino; 1 Two or more races, non-Hispanic/Latino), 11 international. Average age 28. 58 applicants, 84% accepted, 28 enrolled. *Faculty:* 14 full-time (9 women), 7 part-time/adjunct (1 woman). Expenses: Contact institution. *Financial support:* In 2018–19, 18 students received support. Career-related internships or fieldwork, Federal Work-Study, institutionally sponsored loans, scholarships/grants, tuition waivers (partial), and unspecified assistantships available. Support available to part-time students. Financial award application deadline: 8/1; financial award applicants required to submit FAFSA. In 2018, 30 master's awarded. *Program availability:* Part-time, evening/weekend. Offers communication and media (MS); digital media (Certificate); graphic and Web design (MFA); visual effects animation (MFA). *Application deadline:* For fall admission, 8/18 for domestic students, 8/4 for international students; for spring admission, 12/15 for domestic students, 12/1 for international students; for summer admission, 4/17 for domestic students, 4/3 for international students. Applications are processed on a rolling basis. *Application fee:* $45. Electronic applications accepted. *Application Contact:*

Steven Pruitt, Director of Graduate Admission, 561-237-7834, Fax: 561-237-7100, E-mail: admission@lynn.edu. *Dean,* Dr. David L. Jaffe, 561-237-7099, Fax: 561-237-7097, E-mail: djaffe@lynn.edu.

MAASTRICHT SCHOOL OF MANAGEMENT, 6201 BE Maastricht, Netherlands
General Information Private, coed, graduate-only institution.

GRADUATE UNITS

Graduate Programs Offers business administration (MBA, DBA, PhD); facility management (Exec MBA); management (M Sc); sustainability (Exec MBA).

MACHZIKEI HADATH RABBINICAL COLLEGE, Brooklyn, NY 11204-1805
General Information Independent-religious, men only, comprehensive institution. *Graduate housing:* Room and/or apartments available to single students; on-campus housing not available to married students.

GRADUATE UNITS
Graduate Programs

MADONNA UNIVERSITY, Livonia, MI 48150-1173
General Information Independent-religious, coed, comprehensive institution. *Enrollment:* 3,044 graduate, professional, and undergraduate students; 112 full-time matriculated graduate/professional students (90 women), 472 part-time matriculated graduate/professional students (351 women). *Enrollment by degree level:* 530 master's, 25 doctoral, 29 other advanced degrees. *Graduate faculty:* 45 full-time (30 women), 44 part-time/adjunct (28 women). *Tuition:* Full-time $15,030; part-time $835 per credit hour. Tuition and fees vary according to degree level and program. *Graduate housing:* Room and/or apartments available on a first-come, first-served basis to single students; on-campus housing not available to married students. Typical cost: $5000 per year ($9950 including board). Room and board charges vary according to board plan and housing facility selected. Housing application deadline: 3/31. *Student services:* Campus employment opportunities, campus safety program, free psychological counseling, international student services, low-cost health insurance, services for students with disabilities, writing training. *Library facilities:* Madonna University Library. *Collection:* Books: 71,562 (physical), 181,927 (digital/electronic); Serial titles: 190 (physical), 70,781 (digital/electronic); Databases: 130. Weekly public service hours: 100; students can reserve study rooms.

Computer facilities: Computer purchase and lease plans are available. 205 computers available on campus for general student use. A campuswide network can be accessed from student residence rooms and from off campus. Online class registration, online payments, online statements, online unofficial transcripts are available.
Website: http://www.madonna.edu/

General Application Contact: Trish Everett, Director of Graduate and Online Admissions, 734-432-5388, Fax: 734-432-5862, E-mail: peverett@madonna.edu.

GRADUATE UNITS

Department of Psychology *Program availability:* Part-time, evening/weekend. Offers clinical psychology (MSCP). Electronic applications accepted.

Program in Health Services *Program availability:* Part-time. Offers health services (MSHS). Electronic applications accepted.

Program in Hospice *Program availability:* Part-time, evening/weekend. Offers hospice (MSH). Electronic applications accepted.

Program in Liberal Studies Offers liberal studies (MALS).

Program in Nursing *Program availability:* Part-time. Offers adult health: chronic health conditions (MSN); adult nurse practitioner (MSN); nursing administration (MSN). Electronic applications accepted.

Program in Religious Studies Offers pastoral ministry (MA).

Program in Social Work Offers social work (MSW).

Program in Teaching English to Speakers of Other Languages *Program availability:* Part-time, evening/weekend. Offers teaching English to speakers of other languages (MATESOL). Electronic applications accepted.

Programs in Education *Program availability:* Part-time, evening/weekend. Offers Catholic school leadership (MSA); educational leadership (MSA); learning disabilities (MAT); literacy education (MAT); teaching and learning (MAT). Electronic applications accepted.

School of Business *Program availability:* Part-time, evening/weekend, online learning. Offers business administration (MBA); international business (MSBA); leadership studies (MSBA); leadership studies in criminal justice (MSBA); quality and operations management (MSBA). Electronic applications accepted.

MAHARISHI UNIVERSITY OF MANAGEMENT, Fairfield, IA 52557
General Information Independent, coed, university. *Enrollment:* 1,599 graduate, professional, and undergraduate students; 747 full-time matriculated graduate/professional students (161 women), 528 part-time matriculated graduate/professional students (156 women). *Enrollment by degree level:* 1,205 master's, 51 doctoral. *Graduate faculty:* 118 full-time (33 women), 49 part-time/adjunct (12 women). *Tuition:* Full-time $29,000; part-time $4800 per credit hour. *Required fees:* $530. *Graduate housing:* Room and/or apartments guaranteed to single students; on-campus housing not available to married students. Typical cost: $7400 (including board). Housing application deadline: 8/1. *Student services:* Campus employment opportunities, campus safety program, career counseling, child daycare facilities, exercise/wellness program, free psychological counseling, international student services, teacher training, writing training. *Library facilities:* Maharishi University of Management Library. *Collection:* Weekly public service hours: 55.

Computer facilities: A campuswide network can be accessed.
Website: http://www.mum.edu/

General Application Contact: Gwen Stowe, Director of Admissions, 641-472-1110, Fax: 641-472-1179, E-mail: admissions@mum.edu.

GRADUATE UNITS

Graduate Studies *Program availability:* Evening/weekend, online learning. Offers accounting (MBA); computer science (MS); Maharishi Vedic science (MA, PhD); management (PhD); physiology (PhD); screenwriting (MFA); sustainability (MBA). Electronic applications accepted.

MAINE COLLEGE OF ART, Portland, ME 04101
General Information Independent, coed, comprehensive institution.
GRADUATE UNITS
Program in Studio Art Offers studio art (MA, MFA). Electronic applications accepted.

MAINE MARITIME ACADEMY, Castine, ME 04420

General Information State-supported, coed, primarily men, comprehensive institution. *Graduate housing:* Rooms and/or apartments available on a first-come, first-served basis to single and married students. Housing application deadline: 4/15.

GRADUATE UNITS

Loeb-Sullivan School of International Business and Logistics *Program availability:* Part-time, 100% online. Offers global logistics and maritime management (MS); international logistics management (MS). Electronic applications accepted.

MALONE UNIVERSITY, Canton, OH 44709

General Information Independent-religious, coed, comprehensive institution. *Enrollment:* 75 full-time matriculated graduate/professional students (43 women), 366 part-time matriculated graduate/professional students (252 women). *Enrollment by degree level:* 441 master's. *Graduate faculty:* 39 full-time (24 women), 41 part-time/adjunct (28 women). *Graduate housing:* On-campus housing not available. *Student services:* Exercise/wellness program, multicultural affairs office, services for students with disabilities. *Library facilities:* Everett L. Cattell Library plus 1 other. *Collection:* Books: 169,479 (physical), 312,753 (digital/electronic); Serial titles: 2,035 (physical), 39,854 (digital/electronic); Databases: 176. Weekly public service hours: 88.

Computer facilities: Computer purchase and lease plans are available. 254 computers available on campus for general student use. A campuswide network can be accessed from student residence rooms and from off campus. Online class registration, online advising, online financial aid information, and online credit card payments are available. Website: http://www.malone.edu/

General Application Contact: Graduate and Professional Studies, E-mail: gps@malone.edu.

GRADUATE UNITS

Graduate Program in Business *Program availability:* Part-time, evening/weekend, online learning. Offers business (MBA).

Graduate Program in Counseling and Human Development *Program availability:* Part-time, evening/weekend. Offers clinical counseling (MA); school counseling (MA).

Graduate Program in Education *Program availability:* Part-time, evening/weekend. Offers curriculum and instruction (MA); curriculum, instruction, and professional development (MA); educational leadership (principal license) (MA); intervention specialist (MA).

Graduate Program in Nursing *Program availability:* Part-time, evening/weekend. Offers family nurse practitioner (MSN).

Graduate Program in Organizational Leadership *Program availability:* Part-time, evening/weekend. Offers organizational leadership (MAOL).

MANCHESTER UNIVERSITY, North Manchester, IN 46962-1225

General Information Independent-religious, coed, comprehensive institution. *Enrollment:* 1,530 graduate, professional, and undergraduate students; 290 full-time matriculated graduate/professional students (168 women), 53 part-time matriculated graduate/professional students (41 women). *Enrollment by degree level:* 67 master's, 276 doctoral. *Graduate faculty:* 43 full-time (23 women), 7 part-time/adjunct (3 women). *Graduate housing:* On-campus housing not available. *Student services:* Campus safety program, career counseling, multicultural affairs office. *Library facilities:* Funderburg Library. *Collection:* Study areas open 24 hours, 5–7 days a week.

Computer facilities: Computer purchase and lease plans are available. 226 computers available on campus for general student use. A campuswide network can be accessed from student residence rooms and from off campus. Online class registration is available. Website: http://www.manchester.edu/

General Application Contact: Dr. Mark Huntington, Graduate Program Director, 260-982-5033, E-mail: mwhuntington@manchester.edu.

GRADUATE UNITS

Doctor of Pharmacy Program Students: 280 full-time (160 women), 8 part-time (4 women); includes 88 minority (36 Black or African American, non-Hispanic/Latino; 39 Asian, non-Hispanic/Latino; 10 Hispanic/Latino; 1 Native Hawaiian or other Pacific Islander, non-Hispanic/Latino; 2 Two or more races, non-Hispanic/Latino), 3 international. Average age 25. 449 applicants, 28% accepted, 73 enrolled. *Faculty:* 32 full-time (17 women), 1 (woman) part-time/adjunct. Expenses: Contact institution. Offers pharmacy (Pharm D). *Application deadline:* For fall admission, 3/1 for domestic students. *Application fee:* $175. Electronic applications accepted. *Application Contact:* Greg Hetrick, Director of Admissions and Enrollment Management, 260-470-2656, E-mail: gbhetrick@manchester.edu. *Dean of Pharmacy Programs/Professor of Pharmaceutical Sciences*, W. Thomas Smith, 260-470-2668, E-mail: wtsmith@manchester.edu.

Master of Athletic Training Program Students: 3 full-time (2 women); includes 1 minority (Hispanic/Latino). Average age 24. 18 applicants, 72% accepted, 2 enrolled. *Faculty:* 3 full-time, 3 part-time/adjunct (2 women). Expenses: Contact institution. *Financial support:* Fellowships and fellowships are in form of tuition discounts available. Financial award application deadline: 5/1; financial award applicants required to submit FAFSA. In 2018, 12 master's awarded. Offers athletic training (MAT). *Application deadline:* For fall admission, 1/1 priority date for domestic students. Applications are processed on a rolling basis. *Application fee:* $60. Electronic applications accepted. *Application Contact:* Mark Huntington, Program Director, Graduate Athletic Training Education, 260-982-5033, E-mail: mwhuntington@manchester.edu. *Program Director, Graduate Athletic Training Education*, Mark Huntington, 260-982-5033, E-mail: mwhuntington@manchester.edu.

Master of Science in Pharmacogenomics Program Students: 47 part-time (33 women). 82 applicants, 84% accepted, 49 enrolled. *Faculty:* 8 full-time (6 women), 3 part-time/adjunct (0 women). Expenses: Contact institution. *Program availability:* Part-time, 100% online, blended/hybrid learning. Offers pharmacogenomics (MS). *Application deadline:* Applications are processed on a rolling basis. *Application fee:* $50. Electronic applications accepted. *Application Contact:* Greg Hetrick, Director of Admissions and Enrollment Management, 260-470-2656, E-mail: gbhetrick@manchester.edu. *Director of Pharmacogenomics Education*, Dr. Dave F. Kisor, 260-470-2747, E-mail: dfkisor@manchester.edu.

MANHATTAN COLLEGE, Riverdale, NY 10471

General Information Independent-religious, coed, comprehensive institution. *Graduate housing:* Rooms and/or apartments available on a first-come, first-served basis to single and married students.

GRADUATE UNITS

Graduate Programs *Program availability:* Part-time, evening/weekend.

School of Business *Program availability:* Part-time, 100% online, blended/hybrid learning. Offers business (MBA). Electronic applications accepted.

School of Continuing and Professional Studies Students: 64 full-time (34 women), 22 part-time (13 women); includes 41 minority (17 Black or African American, non-Hispanic/Latino; 4 Asian, non-Hispanic/Latino; 18 Hispanic/Latino; 2 Two or more races, non-Hispanic/Latino). Average age 33. 36 applicants, 94% accepted, 30 enrolled. *Faculty:* 14 part-time/adjunct (10 women). Expenses: Contact institution. *Financial support:* Fellowships, research assistantships, teaching assistantships, and tuition waivers available. Financial award application deadline: 2/15; financial award applicants required to submit FAFSA. In 2018, 28 master's awarded. *Program availability:* Part-time, evening/weekend, 100% online, blended/hybrid learning. Offers organizational leadership (MS). *Application deadline:* For fall admission, 8/1. for domestic students; for spring admission, 11/15 for domestic students. Applications are processed on a rolling basis. *Application fee:* $75. Electronic applications accepted. *Application Contact:* William Bisset, Vice President for Enrollment Management, 718-862-7199, Fax: 718-862-8019, E-mail: william.bisset@manhattan.edu. *Dean*, Cheryl Harrison, 718-862-7862, E-mail: cheryl.harrison@manhattan.edu.

School of Education and Health *Program availability:* Part-time, evening/weekend, online learning. Offers adolescence education students with disabilities generalist extension in English or math or social studies - grades 7-12 (MS Ed); advanced leadership studies (MS Ed, Advanced Certificate); bilingual education (Advanced Certificate); bilingual pupil personnel services (Professional Diploma); dual childhood/students with disabilities - grades 1-6 (MS Ed); education and health (MA, MS, MS Ed, Advanced Certificate, Certificate, Professional Diploma); instructional design and delivery (MS); marriage and family therapy (MS); mental health counseling (MS, Advanced Certificate); school building leadership (MS Ed, Advanced Certificate); school counseling (MA, Professional Diploma); students with disabilities - grades 1-6 (MS Ed).

School of Engineering *Program availability:* Part-time, evening/weekend. Offers chemical engineering (MS); civil engineering (MS); computer engineering (MS); construction management (MS); electrical engineering (MS); environmental engineering (ME, MS); mechanical engineering (MS).

School of Science Offers applied mathematics - data analytics (MS); mathematics (MS).

MANHATTAN SCHOOL OF MUSIC, New York, NY 10027-4698

General Information Independent, coed, comprehensive institution. *Enrollment:* 449 full-time matriculated graduate/professional students (256 women), 51 part-time matriculated graduate/professional students (28 women). *Graduate faculty:* 272 full-time (84 women), 27 part-time/adjunct (12 women). *Tuition:* Full-time $48,280. *Required fees:* $850. *Graduate housing:* Room and/or apartments available on a first-come, first-served basis to single students; on-campus housing not available to married students. Typical cost: $14,720 per year ($17,425 including board). Room and board charges vary according to board plan and housing facility selected. Housing application deadline: 5/1. *Student services:* Campus employment opportunities, campus safety program, career counseling, exercise/wellness program, free psychological counseling, grant writing training, international student services, low-cost health insurance, services for students with disabilities. *Library facilities:* Peter J. Sharp Library plus 1 other.

Computer facilities: 20 computers available on campus for general student use. A campuswide network can be accessed from student residence rooms and from off campus. Online class registration is available. Website: http://www.msmnyc.edu/

General Application Contact: Christina Quental, Director of Admission, 917-493-4436, E-mail: cquental@msmnyc.edu.

GRADUATE UNITS

Graduate Programs Offers composition (MM, DMA); jazz (MM, DMA); music performance (MM, DMA); orchestral performance (MM). Electronic applications accepted.

Professional Studies Certificate Program Offers instrumental music (CPS); vocal music (CPS). Electronic applications accepted.

MANHATTANVILLE COLLEGE, Purchase, NY 10577-2132

General Information Independent, coed, comprehensive institution. *Enrollment:* 2,492 graduate, professional, and undergraduate students; 321 full-time matriculated graduate/professional students (194 women), 485 part-time matriculated graduate/professional students (356 women). *Enrollment by degree level:* 642 master's, 111 doctoral, 53 other advanced degrees. *Graduate faculty:* 28 full-time (17 women), 141 part-time/adjunct (87 women). *Tuition:* Full-time $16,830; part-time $935 per credit. *Required fees:* $210; $105 per semester. $105 per semester. Tuition and fees vary according to course load, degree level and program. *Graduate housing:* Rooms and/or apartments available on a first-come, first-served basis to single and married students. Typical cost: $10,850 per year ($16,690 including board) for single students; $10,850 per year ($16,690 including board) for married students. Room and board charges vary according to board plan. *Student services:* Campus employment opportunities, campus safety program, career counseling, exercise/wellness program, free psychological counseling, grant writing training, international student services, low-cost health insurance, multicultural affairs office, services for students with disabilities, teacher training, writing training. *Library facilities:* Manhattanville College Library. *Collection:* Books: 189,313 (physical), 177,686 (digital/electronic); Serial titles: 926 (physical), 60,205 (digital/electronic); Databases: 122. Weekly public service hours: 109; study areas open 24 hours, 5–7 days a week.

Computer facilities: 125 computers available on campus for general student use. A campuswide network can be accessed from student residence rooms and from off campus. Online class registration, Mobile Apps are available. Website: http://www.mville.edu/

General Application Contact: Brian Sondey, Director of Graduate Admissions, 914-323-1490, Fax: 914-694-1732, E-mail: Brian.Sondey@mville.edu.

GRADUATE UNITS

Master of Fine Arts in Creative Writing Program Students: 4 full-time (3 women), 13 part-time (9 women); includes 1 minority (Hispanic/Latino). Average age 44. 21 applicants, 81% accepted, 12 enrolled. *Faculty:* 5 part-time/adjunct (3 women). Expenses: Contact institution. *Financial support:* In 2018–19, 5 students received support. Fellowships, Federal Work-Study, scholarships/grants, tuition waivers (partial), and unspecified assistantships available. Financial award application deadline: 3/15; financial award applicants required to submit FAFSA. In 2018, 3 master's awarded. *Program availability:* Part-time, evening/weekend. Offers creative writing (MFA). *Application deadline:* Applications are processed on a rolling basis. *Application fee:* $75. Electronic applications accepted. *Application Contact:* Brian Sondey, Director of

Graduate Admissions, 914-323-1490, Fax: 914-694-1732, E-mail: Brian.Sondey@mville.edu. *Program Director*, Lori Soderlind, 914-323-5239, E-mail: Lori.Soderlind@mville.edu.

School of Education Students: 235 full-time (148 women), 448 part-time (335 women); includes 119 minority (46 Black or African American, non-Hispanic/Latino; 1 American Indian or Alaska Native, non-Hispanic/Latino; 12 Asian, non-Hispanic/Latino; 53 Hispanic/Latino; 4 Native Hawaiian or other Pacific Islander, non-Hispanic/Latino; 3 Two or more races, non-Hispanic/Latino), 3 international. Average age 32. 304 applicants, 64% accepted, 153 enrolled. *Faculty:* 28 full-time (17 women), 110 part-time/adjunct (75 women). Expenses: Contact institution. *Financial support:* In 2018–19, 86 students received support. Teaching assistantships, career-related internships or fieldwork, Federal Work-Study, institutionally sponsored loans, scholarships/grants, and unspecified assistantships available. Financial award application deadline: 3/15; financial award applicants required to submit FAFSA. In 2018, 220 master's, 12 doctorates, 35 other advanced degrees awarded. *Program availability:* Part-time, evening/weekend. Offers adolescence education (grades 7-12) foreign language(French, Spanish, Italian and Latin) (MAT, Advanced Certificate); adult and international settings (MPS); bilingual education (childhood/Spanish) (Advanced Certificate); biology and special education (MPS); chemistry and special education (MPS); childhood education (grades 1-6) (MAT); childhood education (grades 1-6) and special education: childhood (grades 1-6) (MPS); childhood education and special education (grades 1-6) (MPS); early childhood (birth-grade 2) & childhood ed (grades 1-6) (MAT); early childhood (birth-grade 2) and special education: early childhood (birth-grade 2) (MPS); early childhood education (birth-grade 2) (MAT); education (Advanced Certificate); education entrepreneurship (M Ed); education for sustainability (Advanced Certificate); education leadership (Ed D); educational leadership (MPS); educational leadership - school building leader (PD); educational leadership - school building leader and school district leader (PD); educational studies (M Ed); English (5-9 and 7-12); special ed generalist (7-12); se English (7-12) (MPS); English and special education (MPS); English and special education (grades 5-12) (MPS); health and wellness specialist (Advanced Certificate); higher education leadership (Ed D); literacy (birth-grade 6) and special education childhood (grades 1-6) (MPS); literacy 5-12; special education generalist 7-12; special ed specialist 7-12 (MPS); literacy and special education (MPS); literacy specialist (MPS); literacy specialist (birth-grade 6) (MPS); literacy specialist (grades 5-12) (MPS); math (5-9 and 7-12); special ed generalist (7-12); se math (7-12) (MPS); math and special education (MPS); mathematics (Advanced Certificate); mathematics and special education (grades 5-12) (MPS); middle childhood/adolescence ed science (biology or chemistry grades 5-12) or (physics grades 7-12) (MAT); middle childhood/adolescence education (grades 5-12) English (MAT, Advanced Certificate); middle childhood/adolescence education (grades 5-12) mathematics (MAT, Advanced Certificate); middle childhood/adolescence education (grades 5-12) science (biology chemistry, physics, earth science) (Advanced Certificate); middle childhood/adolescence education (grades 5-12) social studies (MAT, Advanced Certificate); music education (all grades) (MAT); physical education and sport pedagogy (MAT); physics (MAT, Advanced Certificate); school district leader (Advanced Certificate); science and special education (grades 5-12) (MPS); science of reading: multisensory instruction – the rose institute for learning and literacy (Advanced Certificate); science: biology or chemistry (5-9 and 7-12); special ed generalist (7-12); se science (7-12) (MPS); social studies (MAT); social studies (5-9 and 7-12); special generalist (7-12); se soc.st. (7-12) (MPS); social studies and special education (MPS); social studies and special education (grades 5-12) (MPS); Spanish (grades 7-12) (MAT); special ed early childhood and childhood (birth-grade 6) (MPS); special education childhood (grades 1-6) (MPS); special education generalist (MPS); special education: childhood (grades 1-6) (Certificate); special education: early childhood (birth-grade 2) (MPS, Certificate); special education: early childhood (birth-grade 2) and childhood (grades 1-6) (Certificate); special education: grades 7-12 generalist (MPS, Certificate); teaching English as a second language (all grades) (MPS, Certificate); tesol - teaching English as a second language (all grades) (MPS); visual arts education(all grades) (MAT, Certificate). *Application deadline:* For summer admission, 1/1 for domestic students. Applications are processed on a rolling basis. *Application fee:* $75. Electronic applications accepted. *Application Contact:* Alissa Wilson, Director, SOE Graduate Enrollment Management, 914-323-3153, E-mail: edschool@mville.edu. *Dean*, Dr. Shelley Wepner, 914-323-3153, Fax: 914-323-5493, E-mail: Shelly.Wepner@mville.edu.

School of Professional Studies Students: 82 full-time (43 women), 24 part-time (12 women); includes 39 minority (9 Black or African American, non-Hispanic/Latino; 1 American Indian or Alaska Native, non-Hispanic/Latino; 2 Asian, non-Hispanic/Latino; 25 Hispanic/Latino; 2 Two or more races, non-Hispanic/Latino), 11 international. Average age 30. 120 applicants, 40% accepted, 30 enrolled. *Faculty:* 27 part-time/adjunct (10 women). Expenses: Contact institution. *Financial support:* Federal Work-Study, institutionally sponsored loans, scholarships/grants, and unspecified assistantships available. Financial award application deadline: 3/15; financial award applicants required to submit FAFSA. In 2018, 60 master's awarded. *Program availability:* Part-time, evening/weekend. Offers business leadership (Advanced Certificate); finance (MS, Advanced Certificate); human resource management (MS, Advanced Certificate); international management (MS, Advanced Certificate); marketing communication management (MS); sport business and entertainment management (MS, Advanced Certificate). *Application deadline:* Applications are processed on a rolling basis. *Application fee:* $75. Electronic applications accepted. *Application Contact:* Monika Pottgen, Assistant Director of Recruitment and Admissions, 914-323-5150, E-mail: sps@mville.edu. *Associate Dean*, Laura Persky, 914-323-5188, E-mail: Laura.Persky@mville.edu.

MANSFIELD UNIVERSITY OF PENNSYLVANIA, Mansfield, PA 16933

General Information State-supported, coed, comprehensive institution. *Graduate housing:* Room and/or apartments available on a first-come, first-served basis to single students; on-campus housing not available to married students.

GRADUATE UNITS

Graduate Studies *Program availability:* Part-time, evening/weekend, online learning. Offers art education (M Ed); band conducting (MA); choral conducting (MA); elementary education (M Ed); library science (M Ed); nursing (MSN); organizational leadership (MA); performance (MA); secondary education (MS); special education (M Ed). Electronic applications accepted.

MAPLE SPRINGS BAPTIST BIBLE COLLEGE AND SEMINARY, Capitol Heights, MD 20743

General Information Independent-religious, coed, comprehensive institution. *Graduate housing:* On-campus housing not available.

GRADUATE UNITS

Graduate and Professional Programs Offers biblical studies (MA, Certificate); Christian counseling (MA); church administration (MA); divinity (M Div); ministry (D Min); religious education (MRE).

MARANATHA BAPTIST UNIVERSITY, Watertown, WI 53094

General Information Independent-religious, coed, comprehensive institution. *Graduate housing:* Room and/or apartments available to single students; on-campus housing not available to married students.

GRADUATE UNITS

Chaplaincy Program Offers chaplaincy (M Div).

Doctor of Ministry Program Offers ministry (D Min).

Master of Arts in English Bible Program *Program availability:* Part-time, 100% online. Offers English Bible (MA).

Master of Arts in Intercultural Studies Program *Program availability:* Part-time. Offers intercultural studies (MA).

Master of Divinity Program *Program availability:* Part-time. Offers divinity (M Div).

Program in Biblical Counseling *Program availability:* Part-time. Offers Biblical counseling (MA).

Program in Biblical Studies *Program availability:* Part-time. Offers Biblical studies (MA).

Program in Organizational Leadership Offers organizational leadership (MOL).

Program in Teaching and Learning *Program availability:* Part-time, evening/weekend, 100% online. Offers teaching and learning (M Ed).

MARCONI INTERNATIONAL UNIVERSITY, Miami, FL 33132

General Information Proprietary, coed, comprehensive institution.

GRADUATE UNITS

Graduate Programs

MARIAN UNIVERSITY, Indianapolis, IN 46222-1997

General Information Independent-religious, coed, comprehensive institution. *Enrollment:* 3,592 graduate, professional, and undergraduate students; 854 full-time matriculated graduate/professional students (450 women), 310 part-time matriculated graduate/professional students (224 women). *Enrollment by degree level:* 407 master's, 707 doctoral. *Graduate faculty:* 38 full-time (19 women), 48 part-time/adjunct (34 women). *Tuition:* Full-time $8910; part-time $8910 per semester. One-time fee: $40 full-time. Tuition and fees vary according to program. *Graduate housing:* On-campus housing not available. *Student services:* Campus safety program, career counseling, exercise/wellness program, free psychological counseling, international student services, low-cost health insurance, multicultural affairs office, services for students with disabilities, teacher training, writing training. *Library facilities:* Mother Theresa Hackelmeier Memorial Library. *Collection:* Books: 80,118 (physical); Serial titles: 150 (physical), 44,749 (digital/electronic). Weekly public service hours: 95.

Computer facilities: Computer purchase and lease plans are available. 201 computers available on campus for general student use. A campuswide network can be accessed from student residence rooms. Online class registration is available. Website: http://www.marian.edu/

General Application Contact: College of Graduate and Online Programs, 317-9556128, E-mail: GRadmissions@marian.edu.

GRADUATE UNITS

College of Osteopathic Medicine Offers osteopathic medicine (MS, DO). Electronic applications accepted.

Educators College *Program availability:* Part-time, evening/weekend, 100% online. Offers education (MA, MAT). Electronic applications accepted.

Leighton School of Nursing *Program availability:* Part-time. Offers family nurse practitioner (DNP); nurse anesthesia (DNP); nursing education (MSN). Electronic applications accepted.

Master of Science in Counseling Program *Program availability:* Part-time. Offers clinical mental health counseling (MS); school counseling (MS). Electronic applications accepted.

MARIAN UNIVERSITY, Fond du Lac, WI 54935-4699

General Information Independent-religious, coed, comprehensive institution. *Graduate housing:* On-campus housing not available.

GRADUATE UNITS

School of Business and Public Safety *Program availability:* Part-time, evening/weekend. Offers organizational leadership (MS). Electronic applications accepted.

School of Education *Program availability:* Part-time, evening/weekend, online learning. Offers curriculum and instruction leadership (PhD); educational administration (PhD); educational leadership (MAE); educational technology (MAE); leadership studies (PhD); special education (MAE); teacher education (MAE).

School of Nursing and Health Professions *Program availability:* Part-time, evening/weekend. Offers adult nurse practitioner (MSN); nurse educator (MSN); thanatology (MS). Electronic applications accepted.

MARIETTA COLLEGE, Marietta, OH 45750-4000

General Information Independent, coed, comprehensive institution. *Graduate housing:* On-campus housing not available.

GRADUATE UNITS

Program in Physician Assistant Studies Offers physician assistant studies (MS). Electronic applications accepted.

Program in Psychology *Program availability:* Part-time. Offers psychology (MAP).

MARIST COLLEGE, Poughkeepsie, NY 12601-1387

General Information Independent, coed, comprehensive institution. *Graduate housing:* On-campus housing not available. *Research affiliation:* Center for Advanced Brain Imaging Psychology (psychology), New York State Office of Technology and Academic Research (NYSTAR) (technology), Hudson Valley Technology Development Corporation (HVTDC) (technology), Hudson River Psychiatric Center (psychology), St. Francis Hospital, Dutchess County Community Mental Health Center (mental health).

GRADUATE UNITS

Graduate Programs *Program availability:* Part-time, evening/weekend, online learning. Electronic applications accepted.

School of Communication and the Arts *Program availability:* Part-time, online learning. Offers communication (MA); integrated marketing communication (MA); museum studies (MA). Electronic applications accepted.

School of Computer Science and Mathematics *Program availability:* Part-time, evening/weekend, online learning. Offers business analytics (Adv C); computer science/software development (MS); information systems (MS, Adv C). Electronic applications accepted.

School of Management *Program availability:* Part-time, evening/weekend, online learning. Offers business administration (MBA, Adv C); executive leadership (Adv C); professional accountancy (MS); public administration (MPA). Electronic applications accepted.

School of Science Offers physical therapy (DPT).

School of Social and Behavioral Sciences *Program availability:* Part-time, evening/weekend. Offers education (M Ed, MA); mental health counseling (MA); school psychology (MA, Adv C). Electronic applications accepted.

MARLBORO COLLEGE, Marlboro, VT 05344

General Information Independent, coed, comprehensive institution. *Graduate housing:* On-campus housing not available.

GRADUATE UNITS

Graduate and Professional Studies *Program availability:* Part-time, evening/weekend, blended/hybrid learning. Offers educational technology (Certificate); mission-driven organizations (MBA, MS); project management (MBA, MS); social innovation (MBA, MS); teaching English to speakers of other languages (MAT); teaching for social justice (MAT); teaching with technology (MAT). Electronic applications accepted.

MARQUETTE UNIVERSITY, Milwaukee, WI 53201-1881

General Information Independent-religious, coed, university. CGS member. *Graduate housing:* Rooms and/or apartments available on a first-come, first-served basis to single and married students. *Research affiliation:* Shriners Hospital for Children in Chicago, Rehabilitation Institute of Chicago, Froedtert Memorial Lutheran Hospital, Children's Hospital of Wisconsin, Blood Center of Wisconsin, Department of Orthopedic Surgery, Medical College of Wisconsin.

GRADUATE UNITS

Graduate School *Program availability:* Part-time, evening/weekend, online learning. Offers interdisciplinary studies (PhD); transfusion medicine (MSTM). Electronic applications accepted.

College of Arts and Sciences *Program availability:* Part-time. Offers American literature (PhD); analytical chemistry (MS, PhD); ancient philosophy (PhD); arts and sciences (MA, MACD, MS, PhD); bioanalytical chemistry (MS, PhD); bioinformatics (MS); biophysical chemistry (MS, PhD); British and American literature (MA); British empiricism and analytic philosophy (PhD); British literature (PhD); cell biology (MS, PhD); chemical physics (MS, PhD); Christian philosophy (PhD); computational sciences (MS, PhD); computing (MS); developmental biology (MS, PhD); early modern European philosophy (PhD); ecology (MS, PhD); epithelial physiology (MS, PhD); ethics (PhD); European history (MA, PhD); genetics (MS, PhD); German philosophy (PhD); global studies (MA); history of philosophy (MA); inorganic chemistry (MS, PhD); international affairs (MA); mathematics education (MS); medieval philosophy (PhD); microbiology (MS, PhD); molecular biology (MS, PhD); muscle and exercise physiology (MS, PhD); neuroscience (PhD); organic chemistry (MS, PhD); phenomenology and existentialism (PhD); philosophy of religion (PhD); physical chemistry (MS, PhD); political science (MA); psychology (PhD); public service (MA); social and applied philosophy (MA); Spanish (MA); theology (MA, PhD); United States history (MA, PhD). Electronic applications accepted.

College of Communication *Program availability:* Part-time, evening/weekend. Offers advertising and public relations (MA); communication studies (MA); digital storytelling (Certificate); journalism (MA); mass communication (MA); science, health and environmental communication (MA). Electronic applications accepted.

College of Education *Program availability:* Part-time. Offers clinical mental health counseling (MS); college student personnel administration (M Ed); community counseling (MA); counseling psychology (PhD); curriculum and instruction (MA); education (M Ed, MA, MS, PhD, Certificate); educational administration (M Ed); educational policy and foundations (MA); elementary education (Certificate); literacy (MA); principal (Certificate); reading specialist (Certificate); reading teacher (Certificate); school counseling (MA); secondary education (Certificate); superintendent (Certificate).

College of Engineering *Program availability:* Part-time, evening/weekend. Offers biocomputing (ME); bioimaging (ME); bioinstrumentation (ME); bioinstrumentation/computers (MS, PhD); biomechanics (ME); biomechanics/biomaterials (MS, PhD); biorehabilitation (ME); construction engineering and management (MS, PhD, Certificate); digital signal processing (Certificate); electric machines, drives, and controls (Certificate); electrical and computer engineering (MS, PhD); engineering (ME, MS, MSEM, PhD, Certificate); engineering innovation (Certificate); engineering management (MSEM); environmental engineering (MS, PhD); functional imaging (PhD); healthcare technologies management (MS); mechanical engineering (MS, PhD); microwaves and antennas (Certificate); new product and process development (Certificate); rehabilitation bioengineering (PhD); sensors and smart systems (Certificate); structural design (Certificate); structural engineering and structural mechanics (MS, PhD); systems physiology (MS, PhD); transportation (Certificate); transportation engineering and materials (MS, PhD); waste and wastewater treatment processes (Certificate); water resources engineering (Certificate). Electronic applications accepted.

College of Health Sciences Offers bilingual English/Spanish (Certificate); clinical and translational rehabilitation science (MS, PhD); health sciences (MPAS, MS, DPT, PhD, Certificate); physical therapy (DPT); physician assistant studies (MPAS); speech-language pathology (MS). Electronic applications accepted.

College of Nursing Offers acute care nurse practitioner (Certificate); adult clinical nurse specialist (Certificate); adult nurse practitioner (Certificate); advanced practice nursing (MSN, DNP); family nurse practitioner (Certificate); nurse-midwifery (Certificate); nursing (PhD); pediatric acute care (Certificate); pediatric primary care (Certificate); systems leadership and healthcare quality (Certificate). Electronic applications accepted.

Graduate School of Management *Program availability:* Part-time, evening/weekend. Offers accounting (MSA); business administration (MBA); business economics (MSAE); economics (MBA); entrepreneurship (Certificate); finance (MBA); financial economics (MSAE); human resources (MBA); international business (MBA); international economics (MSAE); management (MBA, MSA, MSAE, MSHR, Certificate); management information systems (MBA); marketing (MBA); marketing research

(MSAE); operations and supply chain management (MBA); real estate economics (MSAE); sports business (MBA). Electronic applications accepted.

Law School *Program availability:* Part-time, evening/weekend. Offers law (JD). Electronic applications accepted.

School of Dentistry Offers advanced training in general dentistry (MS, Certificate); dental biomaterials (MS); dentistry (MS, DDS, Certificate); endodontics (MS, Certificate); orthodontics (MS, Certificate); periodontics (MS, Certificate); prosthodontics (MS, Certificate).

MARSHALL B. KETCHUM UNIVERSITY, Fullerton, CA 92831-1615

General Information Independent, coed, graduate-only institution. *Graduate housing:* On-campus housing not available. *Research affiliation:* Alcon Laboratories (ophthalmic products), Essilor (spectacle lenses), Allergan (ophthalmic products).

GRADUATE UNITS

Graduate and Professional Programs Offers optometry (OD); pharmacy (Pharm D); vision science (MS). Electronic applications accepted.

MARSHALL UNIVERSITY, Huntington, WV 25755

General Information State-supported, coed, university. *Graduate housing:* Rooms and/or apartments available on a first-come, first-served basis to single and married students. *Research affiliation:* Bayer Corporation, Kanawha Valley Local Port District, Greenbrier County Commission, Dominion Power, Wyeth-Ayerst (clinical pharmaceutical study).

GRADUATE UNITS

Academic Affairs Division *Program availability:* Part-time, evening/weekend.

College of Arts and Media *Program availability:* Evening/weekend. Offers arts and media (MA, MAJ, Certificate); journalism (MAJ, Certificate); music (MA).

College of Business *Program availability:* Part-time, evening/weekend. Offers accountancy (MS); business (MBA, MS, DMPNA, Certificate, Graduate Certificate); business administration (MBA); health care administration (MS); human resource management (MS); management foundations (Certificate); nurse anesthesia (DMPNA).

College of Education and Professional Development *Program availability:* Part-time, evening/weekend. Offers adult and continuing education (MS); counseling (MA); education (MA, MS, Ed D, Certificate, Ed S); education and professional development (MA, MAT, MS, Ed D, Certificate, Ed S); leadership studies (MA); literacy education (MA); school psychology (Ed S); special education (MA); teaching (MAT). Electronic applications accepted.

College of Health Professions Offers athletic training (MS); biomechanics (MS); communication disorders (MS); dietetics (MS, Certificate); exercise science (MS); health informatics (MS); health professions (MPH, MS, MSN, MSW, DPT, Certificate); kinesiology (MS); nursing (MSN, Certificate); physical therapy (DPT); public health (MPH); social work (MSW); sport administration (MS).

College of Information Technology and Engineering *Program availability:* Part-time, evening/weekend. Offers computer science (MS); electrical and computer engineering (MSEE); engineering management (MSE); environmental engineering (MSE); environmental science (MS); information systems (MS); information technology and engineering (MS, MSE, MSEE, MSME, Certificate); mechanical engineering (MSME); safety (MS); technology management (MS, Certificate); transportation and infrastructure engineering (MSE).

College of Liberal Arts *Program availability:* Evening/weekend. Offers clinical psychology (Certificate); communication studies (MA); English (MA, Graduate Certificate); geography (MA, MS, Certificate); history (MA, Certificate); humanities (MA, Certificate); liberal arts (MA, MPA, MS, Psy D, Certificate, Graduate Certificate); political science (MA, MPA); psychology (MA, Psy D); sociology (MA).

College of Science Offers biological science (MA, MS); chemistry (MS); criminal justice (MS); mathematics (MA); physical and applied science (MA, MS); science (MA, MS).

Forensic Science Center Offers forensic science (MS, Graduate Certificate).

School of Pharmacy Offers pharmacy (Pharm D).

Joan C. Edwards School of Medicine Offers biomedical sciences (MS, PhD); medicine (MS, MD, PhD). Electronic applications accepted.

MARS HILL UNIVERSITY, Mars Hill, NC 28754

General Information Independent-religious, coed, comprehensive institution.

GRADUATE UNITS

Adult and Graduate Studies

MARTIN LUTHER COLLEGE, New Ulm, MN 56073

General Information Independent-religious, coed, comprehensive institution. *Enrollment:* 972 graduate, professional, and undergraduate students; 1 full-time matriculated graduate/professional student, 86 part-time matriculated graduate/professional students (26 women). *Enrollment by degree level:* 87 master's. *Graduate faculty:* 13 full-time (2 women), 31 part-time/adjunct (10 women). *Graduate housing:* On-campus housing not available. *Library facilities:* Martin Luther College Library.

Computer facilities: A campuswide network can be accessed from student residence rooms.
Website: http://www.mlc-wels.edu/

General Application Contact: John E. Meyer, Director of Graduate Studies, 507-354-8221 Ext. 398, Fax: 507-354-8225, E-mail: meyerjd@mlc-wels.edu.

GRADUATE UNITS

Graduate Studies Students: 1 full-time (0 women), 86 part-time (26 women); includes 1 minority (Two or more races, non-Hispanic/Latino), 1 international. Average age 38. 35 applicants, 100% accepted, 35 enrolled. *Faculty:* 13 full-time (2 women), 31 part-time/adjunct (10 women). Expenses: Contact institution. *Financial support:* In 2018–19, 1 student received support. Scholarships/grants available. Financial award application deadline: 9/1. In 2018, 26 master's awarded. *Program availability:* Part-time, evening/weekend, online only, 100% online. Offers early childhood director (MS Ed Admin); educational technology (MS Ed); instruction (MS Ed); leadership (MS Ed); principal (MS Ed Admin); special education (MS Ed). *Application deadline:* Applications are processed on a rolling basis. *Application fee:* $35. Electronic applications accepted. *Application Contact:* John E. Meyer, Director of Graduate Studies, 507-354-8221 Ext. 398, E-mail: meyerjd@mlc-wels.edu. *Director of Graduate Studies,* John E. Meyer, 507-354-8221 Ext. 398, E-mail: meyerjd@mlc-wels.edu.

MARTIN UNIVERSITY, Indianapolis, IN 46218-3867

General Information Independent, coed, comprehensive institution. *Graduate housing:* On-campus housing not available.

GRADUATE UNITS

Division of Psychology *Program availability:* Part-time, evening/weekend. Offers community psychology (MS).

Graduate School of Urban Ministry *Program availability:* Part-time, evening/weekend. Offers urban ministry studies (MA).

MARY BALDWIN UNIVERSITY, Staunton, VA 24401-3610

General Information Independent, coed, primarily women, comprehensive institution. *Graduate housing:* On-campus housing not available.

GRADUATE UNITS

Graduate Studies *Program availability:* Part-time, evening/weekend, online learning. Offers acting (M Litt); applied behavior analysis (MS); autism spectrum disorders (M Ed); directing (M Litt); dramaturgy (M Litt); elementary education (M Ed, MAT); English as a second language (M Ed); environment-based learning (M Ed); gifted education (M Ed); higher education (MS); leadership (M Ed); middle grades education (MAT); occupational therapy (OTD); patient safety and healthcare quality (MSN); physical therapy (DPT); physician assistant (MSPA); reading education (M Ed); Shakespeare and performance (MFA); special education (M Ed); teaching (M Litt).

MARYGROVE COLLEGE, Detroit, MI 48221-2599

General Information Independent-religious, coed, primarily women, graduate-only institution. *Graduate housing:* On-campus housing not available.

GRADUATE UNITS

Graduate Studies *Program availability:* Part-time, evening/weekend, 100% online, blended/hybrid learning. Offers autism spectrum disorders (M Ed, Certificate); curriculum instruction and assessment (MAT); educational leadership (MA); educational technology (M Ed); effective teaching in the 21st century-classroom focus (MAT); effective teaching in the 21st century-technology focus (MAT); human resource management (MA, Certificate); mathematics 6-8 (MAT); mathematics K-5 (MAT); reading and literacy K-6 (MAT); reading specialist (M Ed); school administrator (Certificate); social justice (MA); special education (MAT); special education - learning disabilities (M Ed); teaching - pre-elementary education (M Ed); teaching - pre-secondary education (M Ed). Electronic applications accepted.

MARYLAND INSTITUTE COLLEGE OF ART, Baltimore, MD 21217

General Information Independent, coed, comprehensive institution. *Graduate housing:* Room and/or apartments available on a first-come, first-served basis to single students; on-campus housing not available to married students. Housing application deadline: 5/15.

GRADUATE UNITS

Graduate Studies *Program availability:* Part-time, online learning. Offers art education (MA); business of art and design (MPS); community arts (MFA); curatorial practice (MFA); filmmaking (MFA); fine arts (Postbaccalaureate Certificate); graphic design (MA, MFA); illustration practice (MFA); information visualization (MPS); photographic and electronic media (MFA); social design (MA); studio art (MFA); teaching (MAT). Electronic applications accepted.

LeRoy E. Hoffberger School of Painting Offers painting (MFA). Electronic applications accepted.

Mount Royal School of Art Offers painting (MFA). Electronic applications accepted.

Rinehart School of Sculpture Offers sculpture (MFA). Electronic applications accepted.

MARYLAND UNIVERSITY OF INTEGRATIVE HEALTH, Laurel, MD 20723

General Information Independent, coed, primarily women, graduate-only institution. *Graduate housing:* On-campus housing not available. *Research affiliation:* Food as Medicine, Georgetown University School of Complementary and Alternative Medicine, Natural Gourmet Institute, Institute for Integrative Nutrition.

GRADUATE UNITS

Program in Herbal Medicine Offers clinical herbalism (Certificate); herbal studies (Certificate); therapeutic herbalism (MS).

Program in Naturopathic Medicine Offers naturopathic medicine (ND).

Programs in Acupuncture and Oriental Medicine Offers acupuncture (M Ac, D Ac); Chinese herbs (Certificate); Oriental medicine (MOM, DOM).

Programs in Health and Wellness Coaching Offers health and wellness coaching (MA, Postbaccalaureate Certificate).

Programs in Health Promotion and Yoga Therapy Offers health promotion (MS); yoga therapy (MS).

Programs in Nutrition Offers clinical nutrition (DCN); nutrition and integrative health (MS, Post Master's Certificate).

MARYMOUNT CALIFORNIA UNIVERSITY, Rancho Palos Verdes, CA 90275-6299

General Information Independent-religious, coed, comprehensive institution.

GRADUATE UNITS

Program in Business Administration Offers business administration (MBA).

Program in Community Psychology Offers community psychology (MS).

Program in Leadership and Global Development Offers leadership and global development (MS).

MARYMOUNT UNIVERSITY, Arlington, VA 22207-4299

General Information Independent-religious, coed, comprehensive institution. *Enrollment:* 3,418 graduate, professional, and undergraduate students; 616 full-time matriculated graduate/professional students (465 women), 501 part-time matriculated graduate/professional students (350 women). *Enrollment by degree level:* 935 master's, 162 doctoral, 20 other advanced degrees. *Graduate faculty:* 63 full-time (50 women), 65 part-time/adjunct (42 women). *Tuition:* Full-time $18,900; part-time $1050 per credit. *Required fees:* $396; $22 per credit hour. One-time fee: $270. Tuition and fees vary according to program. *Graduate housing:* Rooms and/or apartments available on a first-come, first-served basis to single and married students. Typical cost: $16,912 (including board) for single students; $16,912 (including board) for married students. Room and board charges vary according to housing facility selected. Housing application deadline: 5/1. *Student services:* Campus employment opportunities, campus safety program, career counseling, free psychological counseling, international student services, low-cost health insurance, services for students with disabilities, teacher training. *Library facilities:* Emerson C. Reinsch Library plus 1 other. *Collection:* Weekly public service hours: 104; students can reserve study rooms.

Computer facilities: 270 computers available on campus for general student use. A campuswide network can be accessed from student residence rooms and from off campus. Online class registration, Online drive space are available. Website: http://www.marymount.edu/

General Application Contact: Rebecca Esposito, Senior Associate Director, Graduate Admissions, 703-284-5901, Fax: 703-527-3815, E-mail: grad.admissions@marymount.edu.

GRADUATE UNITS

Malek School of Health Professions Students: 146 full-time (96 women), 57 part-time (52 women); includes 60 minority (24 Black or African American, non-Hispanic/Latino; 17 Asian, non-Hispanic/Latino; 11 Hispanic/Latino; 8 Two or more races, non-Hispanic/Latino), 11 international. Average age 30. 402 applicants, 46% accepted, 71 enrolled. *Faculty:* 18 full-time (15 women), 20 part-time/adjunct (14 women). Expenses: Contact institution. *Financial support:* In 2018–19, 16 students received support. Research assistantships, teaching assistantships, career-related internships or fieldwork, scholarships/grants, and unspecified assistantships available. Support available to part-time students. Financial award application deadline: 3/1; financial award applicants required to submit FAFSA. In 2018, 20 master's, 45 doctorates, 1 other advanced degree awarded. *Program availability:* Part-time, evening/weekend. Offers family nurse practitioner (MSN, Certificate); health education and promotion (MS); health professions (MS, MSN, DNP, DPT, Certificate); nursing (DNP); physical therapy (DPT). *Application deadline:* For fall admission, 3/1 priority date for domestic and international students; for spring admission, 11/1 priority date for domestic and international students. Applications are processed on a rolling basis. *Application fee:* $40. Electronic applications accepted. *Application Contact:* Rebecca Esposito, Senior Associate Director, Graduate Admissions, 703-284-5901, Fax: 703-527-3815, E-mail: grad.admissions@marymount.edu. *Dean,* Dr. Jeanne Matthews, 703-284-1580, Fax: 703-284-3819, E-mail: jeanne.matthews@marymount.edu.

School of Business and Technology Students: 123 full-time (67 women), 225 part-time (114 women); includes 170 minority (71 Black or African American, non-Hispanic/Latino; 1 American Indian or Alaska Native, non-Hispanic/Latino; 44 Asian, non-Hispanic/Latino; 41 Hispanic/Latino; 2 Native Hawaiian or other Pacific Islander, non-Hispanic/Latino; 11 Two or more races, non-Hispanic/Latino), 65 international. Average age 32. 281 applicants, 98% accepted, 138 enrolled. *Faculty:* 17 full-time (11 women), 14 part-time/adjunct (3 women). Expenses: Contact institution. *Financial support:* In 2018–19, 14 students received support. Research assistantships, teaching assistantships, career-related internships or fieldwork, scholarships/grants, and unspecified assistantships available. Support available to part-time students. Financial award application deadline: 3/1; financial award applicants required to submit FAFSA. In 2018, 144 master's, 14 other advanced degrees awarded. *Program availability:* Part-time, evening/weekend. Offers association and nonprofit management (Certificate); business administration (MBA); business administration with health care management (MBA); business administration with human resource management (MBA); business and technology (MBA, MS, D Sc, Certificate); cybersecurity (MS); cybersecurity with information technology (MS, D Sc, Certificate); health care informatics (Certificate); health care management (MS); health care management with business administration (MS); health care management with information technology (MS); human resource management (Certificate); human resource management with business administration (Certificate); information technology (MS, Certificate); information technology project management and technology leadership (Certificate); information technology with business administration (MS, Certificate); information technology with health care management (MS, Certificate); leadership and management (MS); management studies (Certificate); organization development (Certificate). *Application deadline:* For fall admission, 7/16 priority date for domestic and international students; for spring admission, 11/16 priority date for domestic and international students; for summer admission, 4/16 for domestic and international students. Applications are processed on a rolling basis. *Application fee:* $40. Electronic applications accepted. *Application Contact:* Rebecca Esposito, Senior Associate Director, Graduate Admissions, 703-284-5901, Fax: 703-527-3815, E-mail: grad.admissions@marymount.edu. *Interim Dean,* Jonathan Aberman, 703-284-5910, Fax: 703-527-3830, E-mail: jonathan.aberman@marymount.edu.

School of Design, Arts, and Humanities Students: 56 full-time (53 women), 39 part-time (34 women); includes 26 minority (12 Black or African American, non-Hispanic/Latino; 5 Asian, non-Hispanic/Latino; 6 Hispanic/Latino; 1 Native Hawaiian or other Pacific Islander, non-Hispanic/Latino; 2 Two or more races, non-Hispanic/Latino), 14 international. Average age 36. 59 applicants, 97% accepted, 27 enrolled. *Faculty:* 6 full-time (5 women), 10 part-time/adjunct (8 women). Expenses: Contact institution. *Financial support:* In 2018–19, 7 students received support. Research assistantships, teaching assistantships, career-related internships or fieldwork, scholarships/grants, and unspecified assistantships available. Support available to part-time students. Financial award application deadline: 3/1; financial award applicants required to submit FAFSA. In 2018, 17 master's awarded. *Program availability:* Part-time, evening/weekend. Offers arts and sciences (MA, Certificate); English and humanities (MA); interior design (MA); teaching English at the community college (Certificate). *Application deadline:* For fall admission, 7/15 priority date for domestic and international students; for spring admission, 11/1 priority date for domestic and international students; for summer admission, 4/15 for domestic and international students. Applications are processed on a rolling basis. *Application fee:* $40. Electronic applications accepted. *Application Contact:* Rebecca Esposito, Senior Associate Director, Graduate Admissions, 703-284-5901, Fax: 703-527-3815, E-mail: grad.admissions@marymount.edu. *Dean,* Dr. Christina Clark, 703-284-1560, Fax: 703-284-3859, E-mail: christina.clark@marymount.edu.

School of Sciences, Mathematics, and Education Students: 291 full-time (249 women), 180 part-time (150 women); includes 121 minority (41 Black or African American, non-Hispanic/Latino; 1 American Indian or Alaska Native, non-Hispanic/Latino; 21 Asian, non-Hispanic/Latino; 47 Hispanic/Latino; 1 Native Hawaiian or other Pacific Islander, non-Hispanic/Latino; 10 Two or more races, non-Hispanic/Latino), 16 international. Average age 29. 340 applicants, 89% accepted, 180 enrolled. *Faculty:* 22 full-time (19 women), 21 part-time/adjunct (17 women). Expenses: Contact institution. *Financial support:* In 2018–19, 24 students received support. Research assistantships, teaching assistantships, career-related internships or fieldwork, scholarships/grants, and unspecified assistantships available. Support available to part-time students. Financial award application deadline: 3/1; financial award applicants required to submit FAFSA. In 2018, 180 master's awarded. *Program availability:* Part-time, evening/weekend. Offers clinical mental health counseling (MA); counseling with forensic and legal studies (MA); curriculum and instruction (M Ed); education and human services (M Ed, MA); elementary education (M Ed); forensic and legal psychology (MA); forensic and legal psychology with counseling (MA); pastoral counseling (MA); professional studies (M Ed); school counseling (MA); secondary education (M Ed); special education: general curriculum (M Ed). *Application deadline:*

For fall admission, 1/15 priority date for domestic and international students; for spring admission, 10/5 for domestic and international students. Applications are processed on a rolling basis. *Application fee:* $40. Electronic applications accepted. *Application Contact:* Rebecca Esposito, Senior Associate Director, Graduate Admissions, 703-284-5901, Fax: 703-527-3815, E-mail: grad.admissions@marymount.edu. *Dean,* Dr. Catherine Wehlburg, 703-284-1620, Fax: 703-284-1631, E-mail: catherine.wehlburg@marymount.edu.

MARYVILLE UNIVERSITY OF SAINT LOUIS, St. Louis, MO 63141-7299

General Information Independent, coed, university. *Enrollment:* 9,139 graduate, professional, and undergraduate students; 714 full-time matriculated graduate/professional students (469 women), 4,747 part-time matriculated graduate/professional students (3,812 women). *Enrollment by degree level:* 4,210 master's, 631 doctoral, 620 other advanced degrees. *Graduate faculty:* 83 full-time (59 women), 289 part-time/adjunct (189 women). *Tuition:* Full-time $13,035; part-time $714 per credit hour. One-time fee: $350. Tuition and fees vary according to course load, degree level and program. *Graduate housing:* Room and/or apartments available on a first-come, first-served basis to single students; on-campus housing not available to married students. Typical cost: $7800 per year ($10,088 including board). Room and board charges vary according to board plan and housing facility selected. Housing application deadline: 5/1. *Student services:* Campus employment opportunities, campus safety program, career counseling, exercise/wellness program, free psychological counseling, international student services, low-cost health insurance, multicultural affairs office, services for students with disabilities, teacher training, writing training. *Library facilities:* University Library. *Collection:* Books: 57,027 (physical), 252,154 (digital/electronic); Serial titles: 78,331 (digital/electronic); Databases: 138. Weekly public service hours: 103; study areas open 24 hours a day, 5–7 days a week.

Computer facilities: 563 computers available on campus for general student use. A campuswide network can be accessed from student residence rooms and from off campus. Online class registration, specialized software, university catalog are available. Website: http://www.maryville.edu/

General Application Contact: Jeannie DeLuca, Director of Admissions and Advising for Online Programs, 314-529-9355, Fax: 314-529-9927, E-mail: jdeluca@maryville.edu.

GRADUATE UNITS

College of Arts and Sciences Students: 62 full-time (33 women), 37 part-time (28 women); includes 11 minority (5 Black or African American, non-Hispanic/Latino; 3 Asian, non-Hispanic/Latino; 1 Hispanic/Latino; 2 Two or more races, non-Hispanic/Latino), 52 international. Average age 28. *Faculty:* 7 full-time (5 women), 11 part-time/adjunct (5 women). Expenses: Contact institution. *Financial support:* Application deadline: 4/1; applicants required to submit FAFSA. In 2018, 32 master's awarded. *Program availability:* Part-time. Offers actuarial science (MS); data science (MS); strategic communication and leadership (MA). *Application deadline:* Applications are processed on a rolling basis. Electronic applications accepted. *Application Contact:* Shani Lenore-Jenkins, Associate Vice President of Enrollment, 314-529-9359, E-mail: slenore@maryville.edu. *Interim Dean,* Jennifer Yukna, 314-529-6858, Fax: 314-529-9965, E-mail: jyukna@maryville.edu.

The John E. Simon School of Business Students: 338 full-time (166 women), 739 part-time (356 women); includes 310 minority (161 Black or African American, non-Hispanic/Latino; 6 American Indian or Alaska Native, non-Hispanic/Latino; 59 Asian, non-Hispanic/Latino; 57 Hispanic/Latino; 27 Two or more races, non-Hispanic/Latino), 30 international. Average age 33. *Faculty:* 5 full-time (1 woman), 77 part-time/adjunct (19 women). Expenses: Contact institution. *Financial support:* Career-related internships or fieldwork, Federal Work-Study, tuition waivers (partial), and campus employment available. Financial award application deadline: 4/1; financial award applicants required to submit FAFSA. In 2018, 143 master's awarded. *Program availability:* Part-time, 100% online, blended/hybrid learning. Offers accounting (MBA, MS, Certificate); business studies (Certificate); cybersecurity (MBA, MS, Certificate); financial services (MBA, Certificate); health administration (MBA); healthcare administration (Certificate); human resource management (MBA); human resources management (Certificate); information technology (MBA); information technology management (Certificate); management (MBA, Certificate); management and leadership (MA); marketing (MBA, Certificate); project management (MBA, Certificate); sport business management (MBA); supply chain management (Certificate); supply chain management/logistics (MBA). *Application deadline:* Applications are processed on a rolling basis. Electronic applications accepted. *Application Contact:* Chris Gourdine, Assistant Dean Business Administration, 314-529-6861, Fax: 314-529-9975, E-mail: cgourdine@maryville.edu. *Interim Dean,* Tammy Gocial, 314-529-9401, Fax: 314-529-9975, E-mail: tgocial@maryville.edu.

Myrtle E. and Earl E. Walker College of Health Professions Students: 302 full-time (258 women), 3,652 part-time (3,189 women); includes 1,011 minority (489 Black or African American, non-Hispanic/Latino; 53 American Indian or Alaska Native, non-Hispanic/Latino; 175 Asian, non-Hispanic/Latino; 212 Hispanic/Latino; 82 Two or more races, non-Hispanic/Latino), 12 international. Average age 35. *Faculty:* 49 full-time (40 women), 148 part-time/adjunct (127 women). Expenses: Contact institution. *Financial support:* Career-related internships or fieldwork, Federal Work-Study, and campus employment available. Financial award application deadline: 4/1; financial award applicants required to submit FAFSA. In 2018, 958 master's, 79 doctorates awarded. *Program availability:* Part-time, 100% online, blended/hybrid learning. Offers health professions (MARC, MMT, MOT, MS, MSN, DNP, DPT, Post-MSN Certificate); marriage and family therapy (MARC); music therapy (MARC); occupational therapy (MOT); physical therapy (DPT); speech-language pathology (MS); substance abuse (MARC). *Application deadline:* Applications are processed on a rolling basis. Electronic applications accepted. *Application Contact:* Jeannie DeLuca, Director of Admissions and Advising, 314-529-9355, Fax: 314-529-9927, E-mail: jdeluca@maryville.edu. *Dean,* Michelle Jenkins-Unterberg, 314-529-9590, Fax: 314-529-9495, E-mail: munterberg@maryville.edu.

The Catherine McAuley School of Nursing Students: 74 full-time (68 women), 3,448 part-time (3,021 women); includes 953 minority (459 Black or African American, non-Hispanic/Latino; 53 American Indian or Alaska Native, non-Hispanic/Latino; 161 Asian, non-Hispanic/Latino; 199 Hispanic/Latino; 81 Two or more races, non-Hispanic/Latino), 11 international. Average age 37. *Faculty:* 14 full-time (all women), 134 part-time/adjunct (114 women). Expenses: Contact institution. *Financial support:* Federal Work-Study and campus employment available. Support available to part-time students. Financial award application deadline: 4/1; financial award applicants required to submit FAFSA. In 2018, 887 master's, 42 doctorates awarded. *Program availability:* 100% online, blended/hybrid learning. Offers acute care nurse practitioner (MSN); adult gerontology nurse practitioner (MSN); advanced practice nursing (DNP); family nurse practitioner (MSN); pediatric nurse practitioner (MSN). *Application deadline:* Applications are processed on a rolling basis. Electronic applications accepted. *Application Contact:* Jeannie DeLuca, Director of Admissions and Advising, 314-929-9355, Fax: 314-529-9927, E-mail: jdeluca@maryville.edu. *Assistant Dean/Director of Online Nursing,* Dr. Elizabeth Buck, 314-529-9453, Fax: 314-529-9139, E-mail: ebuck@maryville.edu.

School of Education Students: 12 full-time (all women), 311 part-time (234 women); includes 99 minority (84 Black or African American, non-Hispanic/Latino; 2 Asian, non-Hispanic/Latino; 9 Hispanic/Latino; 4 Two or more races, non-Hispanic/Latino), 2 international. Average age 38. *Faculty:* 16 full-time (8 women), 18 part-time/adjunct (11 women). Expenses: Contact institution. *Financial support:* Career-related internships or fieldwork, Federal Work-Study, tuition waivers (partial), and professional educator discounts available. Financial award application deadline: 4/1; financial award applicants required to submit FAFSA. In 2018, 25 master's, 100 doctorates awarded. *Program availability:* Part-time, 100% online, blended/hybrid learning. Offers early childhood education (MA Ed); educational leadership (Ed D); educational leadership w/principal certification (MA Ed); elementary education (MA Ed); gifted (MA Ed); higher education leadership (Ed D); middle grades education (MA Ed); reading/literacy specialist (MA Ed); teacher as leader (Ed D). *Application deadline:* Applications are processed on a rolling basis. Electronic applications accepted. *Application Contact:* Stacey Ruffin, Director of Clinical Experiences & Partnerships, 314-529-9542, Fax: 314-529-9921, E-mail: sruffin@maryville.edu. *Dean,* Dr. Maschael Schappe, 314-529-9670, Fax: 314-529-9921, E-mail: mschappe@maryville.edu.

MARYWOOD UNIVERSITY, Scranton, PA 18509-1598

General Information Independent-religious, coed, comprehensive institution. *Graduate housing:* Room and/or apartments available on a first-come, first-served basis to single students; on-campus housing not available to married students.

GRADUATE UNITS

Academic Affairs *Program availability:* Part-time, evening/weekend, online learning. Electronic applications accepted.

Center for Interdisciplinary Studies *Program availability:* Part-time. Offers human development (PhD). Electronic applications accepted.

College of Health and Human Services *Program availability:* Part-time, online learning. Offers dietetic internship (Certificate); gerontology (MS); health and human services (MHSA, MPA, MS, MSW, Certificate); health services administration (MHSA); nutrition (MS); physician assistant studies (MS); public administration (MPA); social work (MHSA, MPA, MS, MSW); sports nutrition and exercise science (MS). Electronic applications accepted.

Insalaco College of Creative and Performing Arts *Program availability:* Part-time. Offers art (Graduate Certificate); art education (MA); art therapy (MA, Graduate Certificate); clay (MA, MFA); communication arts (MA); creative and performing arts (MA, MFA, MMT, Graduate Certificate); graphic design (MFA); illustration (MFA); music education (MA); painting (MA, MFA); photography (MA, MFA); printmaking (MA, MFA); sculpture (MA, MFA); studio art (MA); visual arts (MFA). Electronic applications accepted.

Munley College of Liberal Arts and Sciences *Program availability:* Part-time, online learning. Offers biotechnology (MS); criminal justice (MS); finance/investment (MBA); general management (MBA); information security (MS); liberal arts and sciences (MBA, MS); management information systems (MBA, MS). Electronic applications accepted.

Reap College of Education and Human Development *Program availability:* Part-time. Offers clinical psychology (Psy D); clinical services (MA); counselor education (MS); early childhood intervention (MS); education and human development (M Ed, MA, MAT, MS, Psy D, Certificate, Post-Master's Certificate); general theoretical psychology (MA); higher education administration (MS); instructional leadership (M Ed); mental health counseling (MA); PK-4 education (MAT); psychology (MA); reading education (MS); school leadership (MS); secondary/K-12 education (MAT); special education (MS); special education administration and supervision (MS); speech-language pathology (MS).

School of Architecture *Program availability:* Part-time. Offers architecture (M Arch, MA); interior architecture/design (MA). Electronic applications accepted.

MASSACHUSETTS COLLEGE OF ART AND DESIGN, Boston, MA 02115-5882

General Information State-supported, coed, comprehensive institution. *Graduate housing:* Room and/or apartments available on a first-come, first-served basis to single students; on-campus housing not available to married students. Housing application deadline: 5/1.

GRADUATE UNITS

Graduate Programs Offers 2D fine arts (MFA); 3D fine arts (MFA); architecture (M Arch); art education (M Ed, MAT); art teacher preparation (Postbaccalaureate Certificate); design (MFA, Postbaccalaureate Certificate); design innovation (M Des); fine arts (MFA); media arts (MFA, Postbaccalaureate Certificate). Electronic applications accepted.

MASSACHUSETTS COLLEGE OF LIBERAL ARTS, North Adams, MA 01247-4100

General Information State-supported, coed, comprehensive institution. *Graduate housing:* On-campus housing not available.

GRADUATE UNITS

Graduate Programs *Program availability:* Part-time, evening/weekend. Offers business (MBA); educational administration (M Ed); educational leadership (CAGS); instruction and curriculum (M Ed); instructional technology (M Ed); physical education and health (M Ed); reading (M Ed); special education (M Ed).

MASSACHUSETTS INSTITUTE OF TECHNOLOGY, Cambridge, MA 02139-4307

General Information Independent, coed, university. CGS member. *Enrollment:* 11,574 graduate, professional, and undergraduate students; 6,817 full-time matriculated graduate/professional students (2,416 women), 12 part-time matriculated graduate/professional students (3 women). *Enrollment by degree level:* 2,859 master's, 3,970 doctoral. *Graduate faculty:* 1,042 full-time (246 women), 14 part-time/adjunct (5 women). *Tuition:* Full-time $51,520; part-time $800 per credit hour. *Required fees:* $312. *Graduate housing:* Rooms and/or apartments available to single and married students. Housing application deadline: 5/15. *Student services:* Campus employment opportunities, campus safety program, career counseling, child daycare facilities, exercise/wellness program, free psychological counseling, grant writing training, international student services, low-cost health insurance, services for students with disabilities, teacher training, writing training. *Library facilities:* MIT Libraries plus 5 others. *Collection:* Books: 1.3 million (physical), 758,981 (digital/electronic); Serial titles: 50,139 (physical), 58,996 (digital/electronic); Databases: 336. Weekly public service hours: 95;

study areas open 24 hours, 5–7 days a week; students can reserve study rooms. *Research affiliation:* Woods Hole Oceanographic Institute (applied ocean science and engineering), Broad Institute (genomics and biomedical research), Whitehead Institute for Biomedical Research (developmental biology).

Computer facilities: Computer purchase and lease plans are available. 1,050 computers available on campus for general student use. A campuswide network can be accessed from student residence rooms and from off campus. Online class registration is available.
Website: http://www.mit.edu/

General Application Contact: Graduate Admissions, 617-324-6730, E-mail: gradadmissions@mit.edu.

GRADUATE UNITS

MIT Sloan School of Management Expenses: Contact institution. *Financial support:* Fellowships with tuition reimbursements, research assistantships with tuition reimbursements, teaching assistantships with tuition reimbursements, Federal Work-Study, institutionally sponsored loans, scholarships/grants, health care benefits, and unspecified assistantships available. Support available to part-time students. Offers management (M Fin, MBA, MS, SM, PhD). Electronic applications accepted. *Application Contact:* Rod Garcia, Director of Admissions, 617-253-5434, Fax: 617-253-6405, E-mail: mbaadmissions@sloan.mit.edu. *Dean,* David C. Schmittlein, 617-253-2804, Fax: 617-258-6617, E-mail: dschmitt@mit.edu.

Operations Research Center Offers operations research (SM, PhD). Electronic applications accepted.

School of Architecture and Planning Offers architecture (M Arch, PhD); architecture and planning (M Arch, MCP, MSRED, SM, SM Arch S, SMACT, SMBT, PhD); architecture studies (SM Arch S); art, culture and technology (SMACT); building technology (SMBT); city planning (MCP); media arts and sciences (SM, PhD); media technology (SM); urban and regional planning (PhD); urban and regional studies (PhD); urban studies and planning (SM). Electronic applications accepted.

Center for Real Estate Offers real estate development (MSRED). Electronic applications accepted.

School of Engineering Offers aeronautics and astronautics (SM, PhD, Sc D, EAA); aerospace computational engineering (PhD, Sc D); air transportation systems (PhD, Sc D); air-breathing propulsion (PhD, Sc D); aircraft systems engineering (PhD, Sc D); applied biosciences (PhD, Sc D); archaeological materials (PhD, Sc D); autonomous systems (PhD, Sc D); bioengineering (PhD, Sc D); biological engineering (PhD, Sc D); biological oceanography (PhD, Sc D); biomedical engineering (M Eng); chemical engineering (PhD, Sc D); chemical engineering practice (SM, PhD); chemical oceanography (PhD, Sc D); civil and environmental engineering (M Eng, SM, PhD, Sc D); civil and environmental systems (PhD, Sc D); civil engineering (PhD, Sc D, CE); civil engineering and computation (PhD); coastal engineering (PhD, Sc D); communications and networks (PhD, Sc D); computation for design and optimization (SM); computational and systems biology (PhD); computer science (PhD, Sc D, ECS); computer science and engineering (PhD, Sc D); computer science and molecular biology (M Eng); construction engineering and management (PhD, Sc D); controls (PhD, Sc D); electrical engineering (PhD, Sc D, EE); electrical engineering and computer science (M Eng, SM, PhD, Sc D); engineering (M Eng, SM, PhD, Sc D, CE, EAA, ECS, EE, Mat E, Mech E, NE, Naval E); engineering and management (SM); environmental biology (PhD, Sc D); environmental chemistry (PhD, Sc D); environmental engineering (PhD, Sc D); environmental engineering and computation (PhD); environmental fluid mechanics (PhD, Sc D); geotechnical and geoenvironmental engineering (PhD, Sc D); health sciences and technology (SM, PhD, Sc D); humans in aerospace (PhD, Sc D); hydrology (PhD, Sc D); information technology (PhD, Sc D); logistics (M Eng); manufacturing (M Eng); materials and structures (PhD, Sc D); materials engineering (Mat E); materials science and engineering (SM, PhD, Sc D); mechanical engineering (SM, PhD, Sc D, Mech E); naval architecture and marine engineering (SM, PhD, Sc D); naval engineering (Naval E); nuclear science and engineering (SM, PhD, Sc D, NE); ocean engineering (SM, PhD, Sc D); oceanographic engineering (SM, PhD, Sc D); space propulsion (PhD, Sc D); space systems (PhD, Sc D); structures and materials (PhD, Sc D); toxicology (SM); transportation (PhD, Sc D). Electronic applications accepted.

Institute for Data, Systems, and Society Offers social and engineering systems (PhD); technology and policy (SM). Electronic applications accepted.

School of Humanities, Arts, and Social Sciences Offers comparative media studies (SM); economics (SM, PhD); history, anthropology, and science, technology and society (PhD); humanities, arts, and social sciences (SM, PhD); linguistics (PhD); philosophy (PhD); political science (SM, PhD); science writing (SM). Electronic applications accepted.

School of Science Offers atmospheric chemistry (PhD, Sc D); atmospheric science (SM, PhD, Sc D); biochemistry (PhD); biological chemistry (PhD); biological oceanography (PhD); biology (PhD); biophysical chemistry and molecular structure (PhD); cell biology (PhD); chemical oceanography (SM, PhD, Sc D); climate physics and chemistry (SM, PhD, Sc D); cognitive science (PhD); computational systems biology (PhD); developmental biology (PhD); earth and planetary sciences (SM); genetics (PhD); geochemistry (PhD, Sc D); geology (PhD, Sc D); geophysics (PhD, Sc D); immunology (PhD); inorganic chemistry (PhD); marine geology and geophysics (SM, PhD, Sc D); mathematics (PhD); microbiology (PhD); molecular biology (PhD); neurobiology (PhD); neuroscience (PhD); organic chemistry (PhD); physical chemistry (PhD); physical oceanography (SM, PhD, Sc D); physics (SM, PhD); planetary sciences (PhD, Sc D); science (SM, PhD, Sc D). Electronic applications accepted.

MASSACHUSETTS MARITIME ACADEMY, Buzzards Bay, MA 02532-1803

General Information State-supported, coed, comprehensive institution. *Enrollment:* 1,802 graduate, professional, and undergraduate students; 93 full-time matriculated graduate/professional students (24 women). *Enrollment by degree level:* 93 master's. *Graduate housing:* On-campus housing not available. *Student services:* Career counseling. *Library facilities:* American Bureau of Shipping Information Commons plus 1 other. *Collection:* Databases: 124.

Computer facilities: 130 computers available on campus for general student use. A campuswide network can be accessed from student residence rooms and from off campus. Online class registration, course-supported e-learning are available.
Website: http://www.maritime.edu/

General Application Contact: Anna Woringer, Staff Assistant, 508-830-5019, E-mail: dce@maritime.edu.

GRADUATE UNITS
Master's in Maritime Business Management Program

Program in Emergency Management Students: 42 full-time (15 women). Expenses: Contact institution. In 2018, 17 master's awarded. *Program availability:* Evening/weekend. Offers emergency management (MS). *Application deadline:* Applications are processed on a rolling basis. Electronic applications accepted. *Application Contact:* Anna Woringer, Staff Assistant, 508-830-5019, E-mail: dce@maritime.edu. *Dean, Graduate and Continuing Education,* James McDonald, 508-830-5096, E-mail: dce@maritime.edu.

Program in Facilities Management Students: 36 full-time (2 women). Expenses: Contact institution. In 2018, 20 master's awarded. *Program availability:* Evening/weekend. Offers facilities management (MS). *Application deadline:* Applications are processed on a rolling basis. Electronic applications accepted. *Application Contact:* Anna Woringer, Staff Assistant, 508-830-5019, E-mail: dce@maritime.edu. *Dean, Graduate and Continuing Education,* James McDonald, 508-830-5096, E-mail: dce@maritime.edu.

MASSACHUSETTS SCHOOL OF LAW AT ANDOVER, Andover, MA 01810

General Information Independent, coed, graduate-only institution. *Graduate housing:* On-campus housing not available.

GRADUATE UNITS

Professional Program *Program availability:* Part-time, evening/weekend. Offers law (JD). Electronic applications accepted.

THE MASTER'S UNIVERSITY, Santa Clarita, CA 91321-1200

General Information Independent-religious, coed, comprehensive institution. *Graduate housing:* On-campus housing not available.

GRADUATE UNITS

The Master's Seminary *Program availability:* Part-time. Offers biblical counseling (MABC); New Testament (Th D); Old Testament (Th D); preaching (D Min); theology (M Div, M Th, Th D).

MAYO CLINIC ALIX SCHOOL OF MEDICINE, Rochester, MN 55905

General Information Independent, coed, graduate-only institution. *Graduate housing:* On-campus housing not available.

GRADUATE UNITS

Professional Program Offers medicine (MD). MD offered through the Mayo Foundation's Division of Education; MD/PhD, MD/Certificate with Mayo Graduate School. Electronic applications accepted.

MAYO CLINIC GRADUATE SCHOOL OF BIOMEDICAL SCIENCES, Rochester, MN 55905

General Information Independent, coed, graduate-only institution. *Enrollment by degree level:* 181 doctoral. *Graduate faculty:* 341 full-time (78 women). *Graduate housing:* On-campus housing not available. *Student services:* Campus safety program, career counseling, exercise/wellness program, free psychological counseling, grant writing training, international student services, low-cost health insurance, multicultural affairs office, services for students with disabilities, writing training. *Library facilities:* Mayo Clinic Libraries plus 11 others. *Collection:* Books: 400,000 (digital/electronic); Databases: 4,300. Study areas open 24 hours, 5–7 days a week; students can reserve study rooms.

Computer facilities: Online class registration is available.
Website: https://college.mayo.edu/academics/biomedical-research-training/

General Application Contact: Sarah E. Giese, PhD Admissions Coordinator, 507-538-1160, Fax: 507-293-0838, E-mail: phd.training@mayo.edu.

GRADUATE UNITS

Program in Biochemistry and Molecular Biology Students: 40 full-time (20 women); includes 18 minority (1 Black or African American, non-Hispanic/Latino; 1 American Indian or Alaska Native, non-Hispanic/Latino; 10 Asian, non-Hispanic/Latino; 6 Hispanic/Latino). 52 applicants, 25% accepted, 7 enrolled. *Faculty:* 104 full-time (16 women). Expenses: Contact institution. *Financial support:* Fellowships with full tuition reimbursements available. Offers biochemistry and molecular biology (MS, PhD). *Application deadline:* For fall admission, 12/1 for domestic and international students. *Application fee:* $50. Electronic applications accepted. *Application Contact:* Sarah E Giese, Admissions Coordinator, 507-538-1160, E-mail: phd.training@mayo.edu. *Director,* Dr. David J. Katzmann, 507-284-3320, E-mail: katzmann.david@mayo.edu.

Program in Biomedical Engineering and Physiology Students: 26 full-time (12 women); includes 2 minority (1 American Indian or Alaska Native, non-Hispanic/Latino; 1 Asian, non-Hispanic/Latino). 42 applicants, 36% accepted, 5 enrolled. *Faculty:* 77 full-time (10 women). Expenses: Contact institution. *Financial support:* Fellowships with full tuition reimbursements available. Offers biomedical engineering and physiology (MS, PhD). *Application deadline:* For fall admission, 12/1 for domestic and international students. *Application fee:* $50. Electronic applications accepted. *Application Contact:* Sarah E. Giese, Admissions Coordinator, 507-538-1160, E-mail: phd.training@mayo.edu. *Director,* Dr. Carlos B. Mantilla, 507-255-8544, E-mail: mantilla.carlos@mayo.edu.

Program in Clinical and Translational Science Students: 22 full-time (15 women); includes 12 minority (2 Black or African American, non-Hispanic/Latino; 5 Asian, non-Hispanic/Latino; 4 Hispanic/Latino; 1 Native Hawaiian or other Pacific Islander, non-Hispanic/Latino). 12 applicants, 50% accepted, 3 enrolled. *Faculty:* 69 full-time (16 women). Expenses: Contact institution. *Financial support:* Fellowships with full tuition reimbursements available. Offers clinical and translational science (MS); laboratory-based translational science (PhD); patient-based translational science (PhD); population-based translational science (PhD). *Application deadline:* For fall admission, 12/1 for domestic and international students. *Application fee:* $50. Electronic applications accepted. *Application Contact:* Sarah E. Giese, PhD Admissions Coordinator, 507-538-1160, E-mail: phd.training@mayo.edu. *Director,* Anthony J. Windebank, MD, 507-293-7602, E-mail: windebank.anthony@mayo.edu.

Program in Immunology Students: 29 full-time (15 women); includes 9 minority (1 Black or African American, non-Hispanic/Latino; 1 American Indian or Alaska Native, non-Hispanic/Latino; 5 Asian, non-Hispanic/Latino; 2 Hispanic/Latino). 39 applicants, 51% accepted, 8 enrolled. *Faculty:* 27 full-time (7 women). Expenses: Contact institution. *Financial support:* Fellowships with full tuition reimbursements available. Offers immunology (PhD). *Application deadline:* For fall admission, 12/1 for domestic and international students. *Application fee:* $50. Electronic applications accepted. *Application Contact:* Sarah E Giese, Admissions Coordinator, 507-538-1160, E-mail: phd.training@mayo.edu. *Director,* Dr. Karen Hedin, 507-284-2713, E-mail: hedin.karen@mayo.edu.

Program in Molecular Pharmacology and Experimental Therapeutics Students: 26 full-time (18 women); includes 10 minority (2 Black or African American, non-Hispanic/Latino; 1 American Indian or Alaska Native, non-Hispanic/Latino; 7 Asian, non-Hispanic/Latino). 26 applicants, 19% accepted, 4 enrolled. *Faculty:* 19 full-time (1 woman). Expenses: Contact institution. *Financial support:* Fellowships with full tuition reimbursements available. Offers molecular pharmacology and experimental therapeutics (MS, PhD). *Application deadline:* For fall admission, 12/1 for domestic and international students. *Application fee:* $50. Electronic applications accepted. *Application Contact:* Sarah E Giese, Admissions Coordinator, 507-538-1160, E-mail: phd.training@mayo.edu. *Director*, Dr. Richard Weinshilboum, 507-284-4308, E-mail: weinshilboum.richard@mayo.edu.

Program in Neuroscience Students: 18 full-time (14 women); includes 5 minority (all Asian, non-Hispanic/Latino). 21 applicants, 33% accepted, 4 enrolled. *Faculty:* 32 full-time (7 women). Expenses: Contact institution. *Financial support:* Fellowships with full tuition reimbursements available. Offers neuroscience (MS, PhD). *Application deadline:* For fall admission, 12/1 priority date for domestic students, 12/1 for international students. *Application fee:* $50. Electronic applications accepted. *Application Contact:* Sarah E. Giese, Admissions Coordinator, 507-538-1160, E-mail: phd.training@mayo.edu. *Director*, Pamela J. McLean, 904-953-6692, E-mail: mclean.pamela@mayo.edu.

Program in Virology and Gene Therapy Students: 17 full-time (6 women); includes 4 minority (3 Asian, non-Hispanic/Latino; 1 Hispanic/Latino). 19 applicants, 53% accepted, 3 enrolled. *Faculty:* 12 full-time (4 women). Expenses: Contact institution. *Financial support:* Fellowships available. Offers virology and gene therapy (PhD). *Application deadline:* For fall admission, 12/1 for domestic and international students. *Application fee:* $50. Electronic applications accepted. *Application Contact:* Sarah E. Giese, Admissions Coordinator, 507-538-1160, E-mail: phd.training@mayo.edu. *Director*, Dr. Michael Barry, 507-538-1188, E-mail: barry.michael@mayo.edu.

MAYO CLINIC SCHOOL OF HEALTH SCIENCES, Rochester, MN 55905

General Information Independent, coed, graduate-only institution. *Enrollment:* 207 full-time matriculated graduate/professional students (136 women). *Enrollment by degree level:* 207 doctoral. *Graduate faculty:* 20 full-time (11 women). *Student services:* Campus employment opportunities, campus safety program, career counseling, exercise/wellness program, free psychological counseling, international student services, multicultural affairs office, services for students with disabilities, teacher training, writing training. *Library facilities:* Venables Health Sciences Library plus 3 others. *Collection:* Study areas open 24 hours, 5–7 days a week; students can reserve study rooms.

Computer facilities: A campuswide network can be accessed from student residence rooms and from off campus. Online class registration is available. Website: http://www.mayo.edu/mayo-clinic-school-of-health-sciences

General Application Contact: Kammi Englund, Education Coordinator, 507-284-3678, Fax: 507-284-0656, E-mail: englund.kammi@mayo.edu.

GRADUATE UNITS

Doctor of Nurse Anesthesia Practice Program Offers nurse anesthesia practice (DNAP). Electronic applications accepted.

Program in Physical Therapy Offers physical therapy (DPT). Electronic applications accepted.

MCCORMICK THEOLOGICAL SEMINARY, Chicago, IL 60615

General Information Independent-religious, coed, graduate-only institution. *Graduate housing:* Rooms and/or apartments available on a first-come, first-served basis to single and married students. Housing application deadline: 7/1.

GRADUATE UNITS

Graduate and Professional Programs *Program availability:* Part-time, evening/weekend. Offers ministry (D Min); theological studies (MATS, Certificate); theology (M Div). M Div/MSW offered jointly with Loyola University Chicago, University of Chicago, and University of Illinois at Chicago.

MCDANIEL COLLEGE, Westminster, MD 21157-4390

General Information Independent, coed, comprehensive institution. *Graduate housing:* On-campus housing not available.

GRADUATE UNITS

Graduate and Professional Studies *Program availability:* Part-time, evening/weekend, 100% online, blended/hybrid learning. Offers counseling (MS); curriculum and instruction (MS); deaf education (MS); educational leadership (MS); elementary education (MS); elementary STEM instructional leader (Postbaccalaureate Certificate); equity and excellence in education (Postbaccalaureate Certificate); gerontology (MS, Postbaccalaureate Certificate); human resources development (MS); human services management (MS); kinesiology (MS); learning technology specialist (Postbaccalaureate Certificate; liberal arts (MLA); reading specialists: literacy leadership (MS); school librarianship (MS); secondary education (MS); special education (MS); teaching of English to speakers of other languages (MS); writing for children and young adults (Postbaccalaureate Certificate). Electronic applications accepted.

MCGILL UNIVERSITY, Montréal, QC H3A 2T5, Canada

General Information Province-supported, coed, university. CGS member. *Graduate housing:* Room and/or apartments available to married students; on-campus housing not available to single students.

GRADUATE UNITS

Faculty of Graduate and Postdoctoral Studies

Desautels Faculty of Management Offers administration (PhD); entrepreneurial studies (MBA); finance (MBA); general management (Post Master's Certificate); global manufacturing and supply chain management (MMM); information systems (MBA); international business (MBA); international practicing management (MM); management (MBA); management for development (MBA); marketing (MBA); operations management (MBA); public accountancy (Diploma); strategic management (MMM). MMM offered jointly with Faculty of Engineering; PhD with Concordia University, HEC Montreal, Université de Montréal, Université du Québec à Montréal.

Faculty of Agricultural and Environmental Sciences Offers agricultural and environmental sciences (M Sc, M Sc A, PhD, Certificate, Graduate Diploma); agricultural economics (M Sc); animal science (M Sc, M Sc A, PhD); biotechnology (M Sc A, Certificate); computer applications (M Sc, M Sc A, PhD); dietetics (M Sc A, Graduate Diploma); entomology (M Sc, PhD); environmental assessment (M Sc); food engineering (M Sc, M Sc A, PhD); food science and agricultural chemistry (M Sc, PhD); forest science (M Sc, PhD); grain drying (M Sc, M Sc A, PhD); human nutrition (M Sc, M Sc A, PhD); irrigation and drainage (M Sc, M Sc A, PhD); machinery (M Sc, M Sc A, PhD); microbiology (M Sc, PhD); micrometeorology (M Sc, PhD); neotropical environment (M Sc, PhD); parasitology (M Sc, PhD); plant science (M Sc, M Sc A, PhD, Certificate); pollution control (M Sc, M Sc A, PhD); post-harvest technology (M Sc, M Sc A, PhD); soil dynamics (M Sc, M Sc A, PhD); soil science (M Sc, PhD); structure and environment (M Sc, M Sc A, PhD); vegetable and fruit storage (M Sc, M Sc A, PhD); wildlife biology (M Sc, PhD).

Faculty of Arts Offers anthropology (MA, PhD); art history and communication studies (MA, PhD); arts (MA, MSW, PhD, Diploma); bioethics (MA); East Asian studies (MA, PhD); economics (MA, PhD); English (MA, PhD); French language and literature (MA, PhD); German studies (MA, PhD); Hispanic studies (MA, PhD); history (MA, PhD); history of medicine (MA, PhD, Diploma); Islamic studies (MA, PhD, Diploma); Italian studies (MA, PhD); Jewish studies (MA); language acquisition (D); linguistics (MA, PhD); medical anthropology (MA); medical sociology (MA); neo-tropical environment (MA); philosophy (PhD); political science (MA, PhD); Russian literature (MA, PhD); social statistics (MA); social work (MSW, PhD, Diploma); sociology (MA, PhD, Diploma).

Faculty of Dentistry Offers forensic dentistry (Certificate); oral and maxillofacial surgery (M Sc, PhD).

Faculty of Education Offers counseling psychology (MA, PhD); culture and values in education (MA, PhD); curriculum studies (MA); education (M Ed, M Sc, MA, MLIS, PhD, Certificate, Diploma); educational leadership (MA, Certificate); educational psychology (M Ed, MA, PhD); educational studies (PhD); information studies (MLIS, PhD, Certificate, Diploma); integrated studies in education (M Ed); kinesiology and physical education (M Sc, MA, PhD, Certificate, Diploma); school/applied child psychology and applied developmental psychology (M Ed, MA, PhD, Diploma); second language education (MA, PhD).

Faculty of Engineering Offers aerospace (M Eng); affordable homes (M Arch II, Diploma); architectural history and theory (M Arch II); architecture (PhD); chemical engineering (M Eng, PhD); domestic environment (M Arch II); domestic environments (Diploma); electrical and computer engineering (M Eng, PhD); engineering (M Arch I, M Arch II, M Eng, M Sc, MMM, MUP, PhD, Diploma); environmental engineering (M Eng, M Sc, PhD); environmental planning (MUP); fluid mechanics (M Sc); fluid mechanics and hydraulic engineering (M Eng, PhD); housing (MUP); manufacturing management (MMM); materials engineering (M Eng, PhD); mechanical engineering (M Eng, M Sc, PhD); minimum cost housing in developing countries (M Arch II, Diploma); mining engineering (M Eng, M Sc, PhD, Diploma); professional architecture (M Arch I); rehabilitation of urban infrastructure (M Eng, PhD); soil behavior (M Eng, PhD); soil mechanics and foundations (M Eng, PhD); structures and structural mechanics (M Eng, PhD); transportation (MUP); urban design (MUP); urban planning, policy and design (PhD); water resources (M Sc); water resources engineering (M Eng, PhD).

Faculty of Law Offers air and space law (LL M, DCL, Graduate Certificate); bioethics (LL M); comparative law (LL M, DCL, Graduate Certificate); law (LL M, DCL). Applications for LL M with specialization in bioethics are made initially through the Biomedical Ethics Unit in the Faculty of Medicine.

Faculty of Medicine Offers anatomy and cell biology (M Sc, PhD); assessing driving capability (PGC); biochemistry (M Sc, PhD); biomedical engineering (M Eng, PhD); biostatistics (M Sc, PhD); communication science and disorders (M Sc); communication sciences and disorders (PhD); epidemiology (M Sc, PhD); experimental medicine (M Sc, PhD); genetic counseling (M Sc); human genetics (M Sc, PhD); medical anthropology (MA, PhD); medical history (MA, PhD); medical physics (M Sc, PhD); medical sociology (MA, PhD); medicine (M Eng, M Sc, M Sc A, MA, PhD, Diploma, Graduate Diploma, PGC); microbiology and immunology (M Sc, M Sc A, PhD); neurology and neurosurgery (M Sc, PhD); nurse practitioner (Graduate Diploma); nursing (M Sc A, PhD); occupational health (M Sc A); otolaryngology (M Sc); pathology (M Sc, PhD); pharmacology and therapeutics (M Sc, PhD); physiology (M Sc, PhD); psychiatry (M Sc); public health (MSPH); rehabilitation science (M Sc, PhD); speech-language pathology (M Sc A); surgery (M Sc, PhD).

Faculty of Religious Studies Offers religious studies (MA, STM, PhD).

Faculty of Science Offers atmospheric science (M Sc); bioinformatics (M Sc, PhD); chemical biology (M Sc, PhD); chemistry (M Sc, PhD); clinical psychology (PhD); computational science and engineering (M Sc); computer science (M Sc, PhD); earth and planetary sciences (M Sc, PhD); environment (M Sc, PhD); experimental psychology (M Sc, MA, PhD); geography (M Sc, MA, PhD); mathematics and statistics (M Sc, MA, PhD); neo-tropical environment (M Sc, MA, PhD); physical oceanography (M Sc, PhD); physics (M Sc, PhD); science (M Sc, MA, PhD); social statistics (MA).

Schulich School of Music Offers composition (M Mus, D Mus, PhD); music education (MA, PhD); music technology (MA, PhD); musicology (MA, PhD); performance (M Mus); performance studies (D Mus); sound recording (M Mus, PhD); theory (MA, PhD).

Professional Program in Dentistry Offers dentistry (DMD). Electronic applications accepted.

Professional Program in Medicine Offers medicine.

MCKENDREE UNIVERSITY, Lebanon, IL 62254-1299

General Information Independent-religious, coed, university. *Graduate housing:* On-campus housing not available.

GRADUATE UNITS

Graduate Programs *Program availability:* Part-time, evening/weekend. Offers business administration (MBA); clinical mental health counseling (MA); curriculum design and instruction (Ed D, Ed S); educational administration and leadership (MA Ed); educational studies (MA Ed); higher education administrative services (MA Ed); human resource management (MBA); international business (MBA); music education (MA Ed); nursing education (MSN); nursing management/administration (MSN); reading (MA Ed); special education (MA Ed); teacher leadership (MA Ed); teaching certification (MA Ed). Electronic applications accepted.

MCMASTER UNIVERSITY, Hamilton, ON L8S 4M2, Canada

General Information Province-supported, coed, university. CGS member. *Graduate housing:* Room and/or apartments available to single students; on-campus housing not available to married students. Housing application deadline: 6/30. *Research affiliation:* Commonwealth Development (telecommunications), Canadian Centre for Inland Waters (chemical and civil engineering).

GRADUATE UNITS

Faculty of Health Sciences *Program availability:* Part-time, online learning. Offers biochemistry and biomedical sciences (M Sc, PhD); blood and vascular (M Sc, PhD); genetics and cancer (M Sc, PhD); health research methodology (M Sc, PhD); health sciences (M Sc, PhD); immunity and infection (M Sc, PhD); metabolism and nutrition

(M Sc, PhD); neurosciences and behavioral sciences (M Sc, PhD); nursing (M Sc, PhD); occupational therapy (M Sc); physiology/pharmacology (M Sc, PhD); physiotherapy (M Sc); rehabilitation science (M Sc, PhD); rehabilitation science (course-based) (M Sc).

McMaster Divinity College *Program availability:* Part-time. Offers Biblical studies (MA, MTS, Diploma); biblical studies (M Div); Christian interpretation/history (M Div, MA, MTS, Diploma); Christian ministry (M Div, MA, MTS, Diploma); Christian Studies (Certificate); Christian theology (PhD). Affiliated with the Toronto School of Theology.

School of Graduate Studies *Program availability:* Part-time.

DeGroote School of Business *Program availability:* Part-time. Offers business (MBA, PhD); human resources and management (MBA, PhD); information systems (PhD).

Faculty of Engineering *Program availability:* Part-time. Offers chemical engineering (M Eng, MA Sc, PhD); civil engineering (M Eng, MA Sc, PhD); computer science (M Sc, PhD); electrical engineering (M Eng, MA Sc, PhD); engineering (M Eng, M Sc, MA Sc, PhD); engineering physics (M Eng, MA Sc, PhD); materials engineering (M Eng, MA Sc, PhD); materials science (M Eng, PhD); mechanical engineering (M Eng, MA Sc, PhD); nuclear engineering (PhD); software engineering (M Eng, MA Sc, PhD).

Faculty of Humanities *Program availability:* Part-time, evening/weekend. Offers classics (MA, PhD); cultural studies and critical theory (MA); English (MA, PhD); French (MA); history (MA, PhD); humanities (MA, PhD); philosophy (MA, PhD).

Faculty of Science *Program availability:* Part-time, evening/weekend. Offers analytical chemistry (M Sc, PhD); applied statistics (M Sc); astrophysics (PhD); biology (M Sc, PhD); chemical physics (M Sc, PhD); chemistry (M Sc, PhD); geochemistry (PhD); geology (M Sc, PhD); health and radiation physics (M Sc); human geography (MA, PhD); inorganic chemistry (M Sc, PhD); mathematics (M Sc, PhD); medical physics (M Sc, PhD); medical statistics (M Sc); organic chemistry (M Sc, PhD); physical chemistry (M Sc, PhD); physical geography (M Sc, PhD); physics (PhD); polymer chemistry (M Sc, PhD); psychology (M Sc, PhD); science (M Sc, MA, PhD); statistical theory (M Sc); statistics (M Sc).

Faculty of Social Sciences *Program availability:* Part-time, evening/weekend. Offers analysis of social welfare policy (MSW); analysis of social work practice (MSW); anthropology (MA, PhD); economics (MA, PhD); globalization studies (MA); human biodynamics (M Sc, PhD); international relations (PhD); political science (MA); public and the global economy (MA); public policy (PhD); public policy and administration (MA); religious studies (MA, PhD); social sciences (M Sc, MA, MSW, PhD); sociology (MA, PhD); work and society (MA).

MCMURRY UNIVERSITY, Abilene, TX 79697

General Information Independent-religious, coed, comprehensive institution.

GRADUATE UNITS
Graduate Studies

MCNEESE STATE UNIVERSITY, Lake Charles, LA 70609

General Information State-supported, coed, comprehensive institution. *Graduate housing:* Room and/or apartments available on a first-come, first-served basis to single students. Housing application deadline: 8/15.

GRADUATE UNITS
Doré School of Graduate Studies *Program availability:* Part-time, evening/weekend.

Burton College of Education *Program availability:* Part-time, evening/weekend. Offers academically gifted education (M Ed); applied behavior analysis (MA, Graduate Certificate); counseling psychology (MA); curriculum and instruction (M Ed); early childhood education grades PK-3 (Postbaccalaureate Certificate); education (M Ed, MA, MAT, MS, Ed S, Graduate Certificate, Postbaccalaureate Certificate); educational leadership (M Ed, Ed S); educational technology (Ed S); educational technology leadership (M Ed); elementary education (MAT); elementary education grades 1-5 (Postbaccalaureate Certificate); exercise physiology (MS); general/experimental psychology (MA); health promotion (MS); instructional technology (MS); middle school education grades 4-8 (Postbaccalaureate Certificate); multiple levels grades K-12 (Postbaccalaureate Certificate); nutrition and wellness (MS); reading (M Ed); school counseling (M Ed); school librarian (Postbaccalaureate Certificate); secondary education (MAT); secondary education grades 6-12 (Postbaccalaureate Certificate); special education (M Ed); special education - mild/moderate grades 1-12 (MAT); special education, mild/moderate for elementary education grades 1-5 (Postbaccalaureate Certificate).

College of Business *Program availability:* Part-time, evening/weekend. Offers business (MBA); business administration (MBA).

College of Engineering and Computer Science *Program availability:* Part-time, evening/weekend. Offers chemical engineering (M Eng); civil engineering (M Eng); electrical engineering (M Eng); engineering management (M Eng); mechanical engineering (M Eng).

College of Liberal Arts *Program availability:* Part-time, evening/weekend. Offers creative writing (MFA); criminal justice (MS); liberal arts (MA, MFA, MS, Postbaccalaureate Certificate); literature (MA).

College of Nursing and Health Professions Offers family nurse practitioner (MSN); nurse educator (MSN); nursing and health professions (MSN, PMC); psychiatric/mental health nurse practitioner (MSN).

College of Science and Agriculture *Program availability:* Part-time, evening/weekend. Offers agricultural sciences (MS); computer science (MS); environmental and chemical sciences (MS); environmental science (MS); mathematics (MS); science and agriculture (MS); statistics (MS).

MCPHERSON COLLEGE, McPherson, KS 67460-1402

General Information Independent-religious, coed, comprehensive institution. *Graduate housing:* On-campus housing not available.

GRADUATE UNITS
Program in Education Offers education (M Ed).

MCPHS UNIVERSITY, Boston, MA 02115-5896

General Information Independent, coed, university. *Graduate housing:* Room and/or apartments available on a first-come, first-served basis to single students; on-campus housing not available to married students. Housing application deadline: 5/1. *Research affiliation:* Cephrim Biosciences, Inc. (pharmaceutics), Center for Analytical Science (analytical medicinal chemistry).

GRADUATE UNITS
Graduate Studies *Program availability:* Part-time. Offers drug regulatory affairs and health policy (MS); medicinal chemistry (MS, PhD); nursing (MS);

pharmaceutics/industrial pharmacy (MS, PhD); pharmacology (MS, PhD); pharmacy (Pharm D); pharmacy and health sciences (MPAS, MPH, MS, PhD, Pharm D); physician assistant studies (MPAS); public health (MPH).

New England School of Acupuncture *Program availability:* Part-time. Offers acupuncture (M Ac); acupuncture and Oriental medicine (MAOM).

School of Optometry Offers optometry (OD).

School of Pharmacy–Worcester/Manchester Offers pharmacy (Pharm D).

School of Physical Therapy Offers physical therapy (DPT).

MEADVILLE LOMBARD THEOLOGICAL SCHOOL, Chicago, IL 60637-1602

General Information Independent-religious, coed, graduate-only institution. *Graduate housing:* Rooms and/or apartments available on a first-come, first-served basis to single and married students. Housing application deadline: 3/15.

GRADUATE UNITS

Graduate and Professional Programs *Program availability:* Part-time, online learning. Offers divinity (M Div); ministry (D Min); religion (MA). M Div/MSW offered jointly with University of Chicago.

MEDAILLE COLLEGE, Buffalo, NY 14214-2695

General Information Independent, coed, comprehensive institution. *Graduate housing:* Rooms and/or apartments available on a first-come, first-served basis to single and married students. Housing application deadline: 8/15.

GRADUATE UNITS

Program in Business Administration - Amherst *Program availability:* Evening/weekend. Offers business administration (MBA); organizational leadership (MA). Electronic applications accepted.

Program in Business Administration - Rochester *Program availability:* Evening/weekend. Offers business administration (MBA); organizational leadership (MA).

Program in Education *Program availability:* Part-time, evening/weekend. Offers adolescent education (MS Ed); curriculum and instruction (MS Ed); education preparation (MS Ed); literacy (MS Ed); special education (MS). Electronic applications accepted.

Programs in Psychology *Program availability:* Part-time, evening/weekend. Offers clinical psychology (Psy D); marriage and family therapy (MA); mental health counseling (MA); psychology (MA). Electronic applications accepted.

MEDICAL COLLEGE OF WISCONSIN, Milwaukee, WI 53226-0509

General Information Independent, coed, graduate-only institution. CGS member. *Graduate housing:* On-campus housing not available. *Research affiliation:* General Electric Medical Systems (biophysics, radiology).

GRADUATE UNITS

Graduate School *Program availability:* Part-time, evening/weekend, online learning. Offers biochemistry (PhD); biomedical sciences (MA, MPH, MS, PhD, Graduate Certificate); biostatistics (PhD); clinical and translational science (MS); neuroscience (PhD); pharmacology and toxicology (PhD); physiology (PhD); public and community health (PhD); public health (MPH, Graduate Certificate). Electronic applications accepted.

Center for Bioethics and Medical Humanities *Program availability:* Part-time. Offers bioethics (MA); clinical bioethics (Graduate Certificate); research ethics (Graduate Certificate).

Medical Scientist Training Program

Interdisciplinary Program in Biomedical Sciences Offers biomedical sciences (PhD).

Medical School *Program availability:* Part-time, online learning. Offers anesthesiology (MSA); medicine (MSA, MD).

Pharmacy School Offers pharmacy (Pharm D).

MEDICAL UNIVERSITY OF SOUTH CAROLINA, Charleston, SC 29425

General Information State-supported, coed, upper-level institution. CGS member. *Research affiliation:* Novartis Pharmaceuticals (cancer), Boston Scientific Corporation (cardiovascular diseases), Genentech (Alzheimer's disease), AstraZeneca (cancer/cardiovascular diseases), Merck & Company, Inc. (neuroscience), Eli Lilly and Company (substance abuse).

GRADUATE UNITS

College of Dental Medicine Offers dental medicine (DMD). Electronic applications accepted.

College of Graduate Studies Offers biochemistry and molecular biology (MS, PhD); cancer biology (PhD); cardiovascular biology (PhD); cardiovascular imaging (PhD); cell and molecular pharmacology and experimental therapeutics (MS, PhD); cell injury and repair (PhD); cell regulation (PhD); craniofacial biology (PhD); drug discovery (PhD); genetics and development (PhD); marine biomedicine (PhD); medicinal chemistry (PhD); microbiology and immunology (MS, PhD); neurosciences (MS, PhD); pathology and laboratory medicine (MS, PhD); toxicology (PhD). Electronic applications accepted.

Division of Biostatistics and Epidemiology Offers biostatistics (MS, PhD); epidemiology (MS, PhD). Electronic applications accepted.

South Carolina Clinical and Translational Research Institute *Program availability:* Online learning. Offers clinical and translational research (MS). Electronic applications accepted.

College of Health Professions *Program availability:* Part-time. Offers anesthesia for nurses (MSNA); health administration (DHA); health administration-executive (MHA); health administration-global (MHA); health administration-residential (MHA); health and rehabilitation science (PhD); health professions (MHA, MS, MSNA, MSOT, DHA, DPT, PhD); occupational therapy (MSOT); physical therapy (DPT); physician assistant studies (MS). Electronic applications accepted.

College of Medicine Offers medicine (MD). Electronic applications accepted.

College of Nursing *Program availability:* Part-time, online learning. Offers adult-gerontology health nurse practitioner (MSN, DNP); advanced practice nursing (DNP); family nurse practitioner (MSN, DNP); nurse administrator (MSN); nurse educator (MSN); nursing (MSN, DNP, PhD); pediatric nurse practitioner (MSN, DNP). Electronic applications accepted.

South Carolina College of Pharmacy Offers pharmacy (Pharm D). Electronic applications accepted.

MEHARRY MEDICAL COLLEGE, Nashville, TN 37208-9989

General Information Independent-religious, coed, graduate-only institution. CGS member. *Graduate housing:* Rooms and/or apartments available on a first-come, first-served basis to single and married students.

GRADUATE UNITS

School of Dentistry Offers dentistry (DDS, PhD).

School of Graduate Studies *Program availability:* Online learning. Offers biochemistry and cancer biology (PhD); microbiology and immunology (PhD); neuroscience (PhD); pharmacology (PhD). Electronic applications accepted.

Division of Public Health Practice *Program availability:* Part-time, evening/weekend. Offers occupational medicine (MSPH); public health administration (MSPH).

School of Medicine Offers medicine (MD). Electronic applications accepted.

MELBOURNE BUSINESS SCHOOL, Carlton, Victoria 3053, Australia

General Information Independent, coed, graduate-only institution.

GRADUATE UNITS

Graduate Programs Offers business administration (Exec MBA, MBA); management (PhD); management science (PhD); marketing (PhD); social impact (Graduate Certificate).

MEMORIAL UNIVERSITY OF NEWFOUNDLAND, St. John's, NL A1C 5S7, Canada

General Information Province-supported, coed, university. CGS member. *Graduate housing:* Rooms and/or apartments available on a first-come, first-served basis to single and married students. *Research affiliation:* Eastern Regional Health Authority (health research).

GRADUATE UNITS

Faculty of Medicine *Program availability:* Part-time, online learning. Offers medicine (M Sc, PhD, Diploma). Electronic applications accepted.

Graduate Programs in Medicine *Program availability:* Part-time. Offers applied health services research (M Sc); cancer (M Sc, PhD); cardiovascular (M Sc, PhD); clinical epidemiology (M Sc, PhD, Diploma); community health (M Sc, PhD, Diploma); human genetics (M Sc, PhD); immunology (M Sc, PhD); medicine (M Sc, PhD, Diploma); neuroscience (M Sc, PhD). Electronic applications accepted.

School of Graduate Studies *Program availability:* Part-time, evening/weekend, 100% online, blended/hybrid learning. Offers applied psychological sciences (MAPS); aquaculture (M Sc); archaeology and physical anthropology (MA, PhD); atomic and molecular physics (PhD); biochemistry (M Sc, PhD); biology (M Sc, PhD); chemistry (M Sc, PhD); classics (MA); clinical psychology (Psy D); cognitive and behavioral ecology (M Sc, PhD); computer engineering (MA Sc); computer science (M Sc, PhD); condensed matter physics (PhD); economics (MA); employment relations (MER); English (MA, PhD); environmental science (M Env Sc, M Sc, PhD); environmental systems engineering and management (MA Sc); ethnomusicology (MA, PhD); experimental psychology (M Sc, PhD); fisheries resource management (MMS, Graduate Diploma); folklore (MA, PhD); food science (M Sc, PhD); French studies (MA); gender (PhD); gender studies (MGS); geography (M Sc, MA, PhD); geology (M Sc, PhD); geophysics (M Sc, PhD); German language and literature (M Phil, MA); history (MA, PhD); humanities (M Phil); instrumental analysis (M Sc); linguistics (MA, PhD); marine spatial planning and management (MMS); maritime sociology (PhD); mathematics (M Sc, PhD); philosophy (MA, PhD); physical oceanography (M Sc, PhD); physics (M Sc); political science (MA); religious studies (MA); scientific computing (M Sc); social and cultural anthropology (MA, PhD); sociology (M Phil, MA); statistics (M Sc, MAS, PhD); work and development (PhD). Electronic applications accepted.

Faculty of Business Administration *Program availability:* Part-time. Offers business administration (MBA). Electronic applications accepted.

Faculty of Education *Program availability:* Part-time. Offers counseling psychology (M Ed); curriculum, teaching, and learning studies (M Ed); education (PhD); educational leadership studies (M Ed, Graduate Diploma); information technology (M Ed); post-secondary studies (M Ed, Diploma). Electronic applications accepted.

Faculty of Engineering and Applied Science *Program availability:* Part-time. Offers civil engineering (M Eng, PhD); electrical and computer engineering (M Eng, PhD); mechanical engineering (M Eng, PhD); ocean and naval architecture engineering (M Eng, PhD). Electronic applications accepted.

School of Human Kinetics and Recreation *Program availability:* Part-time. Offers administration, curriculum and supervision (MPE); biomechanics/ergonomics (MS Kin); exercise and work physiology (MS Kin); psychology of sport, exercise and recreation (MS Kin); socio-cultural studies of physical activity and health (MS Kin). Electronic applications accepted.

School of Music Offers conducting (MMus); performance pedagogy (MMus); performing (MMus). Electronic applications accepted.

School of Nursing *Program availability:* Part-time. Offers nursing (MN, PhD). Electronic applications accepted.

School of Pharmacy *Program availability:* Part-time. Offers pharmacy (MSCPharm, PhD). Electronic applications accepted.

School of Social Work Offers social work (MSW, PhD). Electronic applications accepted.

MEMPHIS THEOLOGICAL SEMINARY, Memphis, TN 38104-4395

General Information Independent-religious, coed, graduate-only institution. *Graduate housing:* Rooms and/or apartments available on a first-come, first-served basis to single and married students. Housing application deadline: 7/15. *Research affiliation:* Lilly Foundation (technology, religion), Wabash Center for Teaching and Learning (theology, religion).

GRADUATE UNITS

Graduate and Professional Programs *Program availability:* Part-time. Offers theology (M Div, MAR, D Min).

MERCER UNIVERSITY, Macon, GA 31207

General Information Independent-religious, coed, university. *Enrollment:* 7,315 graduate, professional, and undergraduate students; 2,814 full-time matriculated graduate/professional students (1,762 women), 1,089 part-time matriculated graduate/professional students (783 women). *Enrollment by degree level:* 1,968 master's, 1,890 doctoral, 45 other advanced degrees. *Graduate faculty:* 224 full-time (103 women), 122 part-time/adjunct (72 women). *Graduate housing:* On-campus housing not available. *Student services:* Campus employment opportunities, campus safety program, career counseling, exercise/wellness program, free psychological counseling, international student services, low-cost health insurance, services for students with disabilities. *Library facilities:* Jack Tarver Library plus 3 others. *Collection:* Study areas open 24 hours, 5–7 days a week; students can reserve study rooms.

Computer facilities: A campuswide network can be accessed from student residence rooms and from off campus. Online class registration is available. Website: http://www.mercer.edu.

General Application Contact: Tracey M. Wofford, Director of Graduate Admissions, 678-547-6422, Fax: 678-547-6422, E-mail: wofford_tm@mercer.edu.

GRADUATE UNITS

Graduate Studies, Cecil B. Day Campus Students: 1,672 full-time (1,182 women), 908 part-time (664 women); includes 1,397 minority (957 Black or African American, non-Hispanic/Latino; 4 American Indian or Alaska Native, non-Hispanic/Latino; 289 Asian, non-Hispanic/Latino; 119 Hispanic/Latino; 28 Two or more races, non-Hispanic/Latino), 127 international. Average age 31. *Faculty:* 130 full-time (71 women), 89 part-time/adjunct (65 women). Expenses: Contact institution. *Financial support:* Teaching assistantships, career-related internships or fieldwork, Federal Work-Study, and scholarships/grants available. Support available to part-time students. Financial award applicants required to submit FAFSA. In 2018, 722 master's, 234 doctorates, 14 other advanced degrees awarded. *Program availability:* Part-time, evening/weekend, 100% online, blended/hybrid learning. *Application Contact:* Tracey M. Wofford, Director of Admissions, 678-547-6422, E-mail: wofford_tm@mercer.edu. Provost, Dr. Scott Davis, 478-301-2110, E-mail: davis_ds@mercer.edu.

College of Health Professions Students: 369 full-time (280 women), 67 part-time (56 women); includes 173 minority (110 Black or African American, non-Hispanic/Latino; 35 Asian, non-Hispanic/Latino; 26 Hispanic/Latino; 2 Two or more races, non-Hispanic/Latino), 6 international. Average age 26. *Faculty:* 26 full-time (16 women), 12 part-time/adjunct (7 women). Expenses: Contact institution. *Financial support:* Federal Work-Study, traineeships, and unspecified assistantships available. In 2018, 141 master's, 51 doctorates awarded. Offers athletic training (MAT); clinical medical psychology (Psy D); physical therapy (DPT); physician assistant studies (MM Sc); public health (MPH). *Application Contact:* Laura Ellison, Director of Admissions and Student Affairs, 678-547-6391, E-mail: ellison_la@mercer.edu. Dean/Clinical Professor, Dr. Lisa Lundquist, 678-547-6308, E-mail: lundquist_lm@mercer.edu.

College of Pharmacy Offers pharmaceutical sciences (PhD); pharmacy (Pharm D). PharmD/MBA offered jointly with Eugene W. Stetson School of Business and Economics; PharmD/MPH with College of Health Professions; PharmD/MSHI with Penfield College. Electronic applications accepted.

Eugene W. Stetson School of Business and Economics (Atlanta) *Program availability:* Part-time, evening/weekend, 100% online, blended/hybrid learning. Offers accounting (M Acc); innovation (PMBA); international business (MBA). Electronic applications accepted.

Georgia Baptist College of Nursing Students: 55 full-time (50 women), 36 part-time (30 women); includes 46 minority (32 Black or African American, non-Hispanic/Latino; 1 American Indian or Alaska Native, non-Hispanic/Latino; 9 Asian, non-Hispanic/Latino; 3 Hispanic/Latino; 1 Two or more races, non-Hispanic/Latino), 1 international. Average age 36. 95 applicants, 55% accepted, 38 enrolled. *Faculty:* 16 full-time (14 women), 5 part-time/adjunct (4 women). Expenses: Contact institution. *Financial support:* In 2018–19, 19 students received support, including 1 research assistantship with partial tuition reimbursement available (averaging $10,500 per year), 1 teaching assistantship with partial tuition reimbursement available (averaging $7,000 per year); scholarships/grants also available. Financial award application deadline: 6/30; financial award applicants required to submit FAFSA. In 2018, 29 master's, 9 doctorates awarded. *Program availability:* Part-time, blended/hybrid learning. Offers adult gerontology acute care nurse practitioner (MSN, Certificate); family nurse practitioner (MSN, Certificate); nursing (PhD); nursing practice (DNP). *Application deadline:* For fall admission, 7/1 for domestic students; for spring admission, 12/1 for domestic students; for summer admission, 4/15 for domestic students. Applications are processed on a rolling basis. *Application fee:* $50. Electronic applications accepted. *Application Contact:* Janda Anderson, Director of Admissions, 678-547-6700, Fax: 678-547-6794, E-mail: anderson_j@mercer.edu. Dean/Professor, Dr. Linda Streit, 678-547-6793, Fax: 678-547-6796, E-mail: streit_la@mercer.edu.

James and Carolyn McAfee School of Theology Students: 71 full-time (46 women), 68 part-time (28 women); includes 80 minority (73 Black or African American, non-Hispanic/Latino; 1 Asian, non-Hispanic/Latino; 5 Hispanic/Latino; 1 Two or more races, non-Hispanic/Latino), 2 international. Average age 38. 101 applicants, 43% accepted, 33 enrolled. *Faculty:* 10 full-time (4 women), 4 part-time/adjunct (2 women). Expenses: Contact institution. *Financial support:* In 2018–19, 50 students received support, including 2 fellowships with full tuition reimbursements available (averaging $3,000 per year); career-related internships or fieldwork, Federal Work-Study, scholarships/grants, and stipends also available. Support available to part-time students. Financial award application deadline: 1/15; financial award applicants required to submit FAFSA. In 2018, 39 master's, 3 doctorates awarded. *Program availability:* Part-time, 100% online. Offers Christian ministry (MACM); Christian spirituality (D Min); divinity (M Div); preaching (D Min). *Application deadline:* For fall admission, 5/31 priority date for domestic and international students; for spring admission, 11/15 priority date for domestic and international students. Applications are processed on a rolling basis. *Application fee:* $50. Electronic applications accepted. *Application Contact:* Nathan Cost, Director of Admissions, 678-547-6451, E-mail: cost_na@mercer.edu. Interim Dean, Dr. C. Gregory DeLoach, 678-547-6620, E-mail: deloach_cg@mercer.edu.

Penfield College *Program availability:* Part-time, evening/weekend, 100% online, blended/hybrid learning. Offers certified rehabilitation counseling (MS); clinical mental health (MS); counselor education and supervision (PhD); criminal justice and public safety leadership (MS); health informatics (MS); human services (MS); organizational leadership (MS); school counseling (MS). Electronic applications accepted.

Tift College of Education (Atlanta) *Program availability:* Part-time, evening/weekend. Offers curriculum and instruction (PhD); early childhood education (M Ed, MAT, Ed S); educational leadership (PhD); educational leadership P-12 (M Ed, Ed S); higher education leadership (M Ed); independent and charter school leadership (M Ed); middle grades education (M Ed, MAT); secondary education (M Ed, MAT); teacher leadership (Ed S). Electronic applications accepted.

Graduate Studies, Macon Campus Students: 170 full-time (75 women), 167 part-time (108 women); includes 132 minority (92 Black or African American, non-Hispanic/Latino; 2 American Indian or Alaska Native, non-Hispanic/Latino; 20 Asian, non-Hispanic/Latino; 16 Hispanic/Latino; 2 Two or more races, non-Hispanic/Latino), 14 international. Average age 29. *Faculty:* 94 full-time (35 women), 18 part-time/adjunct (4 women). Expenses: Contact institution. *Financial support:* Career-related internships or fieldwork, Federal Work-Study, and institutionally sponsored loans available. In 2018,

151 master's, 4 doctorates awarded. *Program availability:* Part-time, evening/weekend. *Application Contact:* Tracey M. Wofford, Director of Graduate Admissions, 678-547-6422, E-mail: wofford_trn@mercer.edu. *Interim Dean of Graduate Studies/Professor of Mathematics,* Keith Howard, 478-301-5983, E-mail: howard_ke@mercer.edu.

Eugene W. Stetson School of Business and Economics (Macon) *Program availability:* Part-time, evening/weekend. Offers business and economics (MBA); health care (MBA); innovation (MBA). Electronic applications accepted.

School of Engineering *Program availability:* Part-time-only, evening/weekend, online learning. Offers biomedical engineering (MSE); computer engineering (MSE); electrical engineering (MSE); engineering management (MSE); environmental engineering (MSE); environmental systems (MS); mechanical engineering (MSE); software engineering (MSE); software systems (MS); technical communications management (MS); technical management (MS).

Tift College of Education (Macon) *Program availability:* Part-time, evening/weekend, 100% online, blended/hybrid learning. Offers curriculum and instruction (PhD); early childhood education (M Ed, Ed S); educational leadership (M Ed, PhD, Ed S); higher education leadership (M Ed); independent and charter school leadership (M Ed); secondary education (MAT); teacher leadership (Ed S). Electronic applications accepted.

Townsend School of Music Offers choral conducting (MM); church music (MM); collaborative piano (MM); instrumental conducting (MM); performance (MM).

Mercer University School of Law Offers law (JD). JD/MBA offered jointly with Eugene W. Stetson School of Business and Economics. Electronic applications accepted.

School of Medicine Offers medicine (MFT, MPH, MSA, MD).

MERCY COLLEGE, Dobbs Ferry, NY 10522-1189

General Information Independent-religious, coed, comprehensive institution. CGS member. *Enrollment:* 9,031 graduate, professional, and undergraduate students; 1,165 full-time matriculated graduate/professional students (842 women), 1,018 part-time matriculated graduate/professional students (858 women). *Enrollment by degree level:* 2,021 master's, 119 doctoral, 43 other advanced degrees. *Graduate faculty:* 80 full-time (56 women), 143 part-time/adjunct (72 women). *Tuition:* Full-time $15,696; part-time $872 per credit. *Required fees:* $642; $161 per term. Tuition and fees vary according to course load, degree level and program. *Graduate housing:* Room and/or apartments available on a first-come, first-served basis to single students; on-campus housing not available to married students. Typical cost: $9750 per year ($14,400 including board). Room and board charges vary according to board plan, campus/location and housing facility selected. Housing application deadline: 7/1. *Student services:* Campus employment opportunities, campus safety program, career counseling, exercise/wellness program, free psychological counseling, international student services, services for students with disabilities, teacher training, writing training. *Library facilities:* Mercy College Library plus 3 others. *Collection:* Books: 78,894 (physical), 72,328 (digital/electronic); Serial titles: 26 (physical), 61,974 (digital/electronic); Databases: 43. Students can reserve study rooms.

Computer facilities: Computer purchase and lease plans are available. 1,000 computers available on campus for general student use. A campuswide network can be accessed from student residence rooms and from off campus. Online class registration is available.

Website: http://www.mercy.edu/

General Application Contact: Allison Gurdineer, Executive Director of Admissions, 877-637-2946, Fax: 914-674-7382, E-mail: admissions@mercy.edu.

GRADUATE UNITS

School of Business Students: 379 full-time (232 women), 132 part-time (93 women); includes 358 minority (160 Black or African American, non-Hispanic/Latino; 2 American Indian or Alaska Native, non-Hispanic/Latino; 33 Asian, non-Hispanic/Latino; 153 Hispanic/Latino; 1 Native Hawaiian or other Pacific Islander, non-Hispanic/Latino; 9 Two or more races, non-Hispanic/Latino), 26 international. Average age 32. 376 applicants, 71% accepted, 174 enrolled. Expenses: Contact institution. *Financial support:* Career-related internships or fieldwork, Federal Work-Study, scholarships/grants, and unspecified assistantships available. Support available to part-time students. Financial award applicants required to submit FAFSA. In 2018, 271 master's awarded. *Program availability:* Part-time, evening/weekend, 100% online, blended/hybrid learning. Offers accounting (MS); business (MBA, MS); business administration (MBA); human resource management (MS); organizational leadership (MS). *Application deadline:* Applications are processed on a rolling basis. *Application fee:* $40. Electronic applications accepted. *Application Contact:* Allison Gurdineer, Executive Director of Admissions, 877-637-2946, E-mail: admissions@mercy.edu. *Dean, School of Business,* Dr. Lloyd Gibson, 914-674-7159, Fax: 914-674-7493, E-mail: lgibson@mercy.edu.

School of Education Students: 176 full-time (143 women), 351 part-time (307 women); includes 267 minority (85 Black or African American, non-Hispanic/Latino; 1 American Indian or Alaska Native, non-Hispanic/Latino; 17 Asian, non-Hispanic/Latino; 154 Hispanic/Latino; 2 Native Hawaiian or other Pacific Islander, non-Hispanic/Latino; 8 Two or more races, non-Hispanic/Latino). Average age 33. 466 applicants, 53% accepted, 163 enrolled. Expenses: Contact institution. *Financial support:* Career-related internships or fieldwork, Federal Work-Study, scholarships/grants, and unspecified assistantships available. Support available to part-time students. Financial award applicants required to submit FAFSA. In 2018, 185 master's, 26 other advanced degrees awarded. *Program availability:* Part-time, evening/weekend, 100% online, blended/hybrid learning. Offers adolescence education (MS); childhood education (MS); early childhood education (MS); education (MS, Advanced Certificate); educational leadership (Advanced Certificate); teaching English to speakers of other languages (TESOL) (MS, Advanced Certificate); teaching literacy (Advanced Certificate); teaching literacy, birth-6 (MS); teaching literacy, grades 5-12 (MS). *Application deadline:* Applications are processed on a rolling basis. *Application fee:* $40. Electronic applications accepted. *Application Contact:* Allison Gurdineer, Executive Director of Admissions, 877-637-2946, Fax: 914-674-7382, E-mail: admissions@mercy.edu. *Interim Dean for the School of Education,* Dr. Eric Martone, 914-674-7618, Fax: 914-674-7352, E-mail: emartone@mercy.edu.

School of Health and Natural Sciences Students: 374 full-time (283 women), 179 part-time (165 women); includes 262 minority (72 Black or African American, non-Hispanic/Latino; 69 Asian, non-Hispanic/Latino; 99 Hispanic/Latino; 4 Native Hawaiian or other Pacific Islander, non-Hispanic/Latino; 18 Two or more races, non-Hispanic/Latino), 1 international. Average age 31. 1,391 applicants, 25% accepted, 187 enrolled. Expenses: Contact institution. *Financial support:* Career-related internships or fieldwork, Federal Work-Study, scholarships/grants, and unspecified assistantships available. Support available to part-time students. Financial award applicants required to submit FAFSA. In 2018, 178 master's, 24 doctorates awarded. *Program availability:* Part-time, evening/weekend, blended/hybrid learning. Offers communication disorders (MS); nursing (MS); nursing administration (MS); nursing education (MS); occupational

therapy (MS); physical therapy (DPT); physician assistant studies (MS). *Application deadline:* Applications are processed on a rolling basis. *Application fee:* $40. Electronic applications accepted. *Application Contact:* Allison Gurdineer, Executive Director of Admissions, 877-637-2946, Fax: 914-674-7382, E-mail: admissions@mercy.edu. *Dean, School of Health and Natural Sciences,* Dr. Joan Toglia, 914-674-7746, Fax: 914-674-7250, E-mail: jtoglia@mercy.edu.

School of Liberal Arts Students: 26 full-time (5 women), 71 part-time (45 women); includes 32 minority (14 Black or African American, non-Hispanic/Latino; 4 Asian, non-Hispanic/Latino; 13 Hispanic/Latino; 1 Two or more races, non-Hispanic/Latino), 5 international. Average age 35. 66 applicants, 68% accepted, 31 enrolled. Expenses: Contact institution. *Financial support:* Career-related internships or fieldwork, Federal Work-Study, scholarships/grants, and unspecified assistantships available. Support available to part-time students. Financial award applicants required to submit FAFSA. In 2018, 44 master's awarded. *Program availability:* Part-time, evening/weekend, 100% online, blended/hybrid learning. Offers cybersecurity (MS); English literature (MA). *Application deadline:* Applications are processed on a rolling basis. *Application fee:* $40. Electronic applications accepted. *Application Contact:* Allison Gurdineer, Executive Director of Admissions, 877-637-2946, Fax: 914-674-7382, E-mail: admissions@mercy.edu. *Interim Dean, School of Liberal Arts,* Stephen Ward, 914-674-7432, Fax: 914-674-7518, E-mail: sward@mercy.edu.

School of Social and Behavioral Sciences Students: 210 full-time (179 women), 285 part-time (248 women); includes 361 minority (162 Black or African American, non-Hispanic/Latino; 11 Asian, non-Hispanic/Latino; 182 Hispanic/Latino; 1 Native Hawaiian or other Pacific Islander, non-Hispanic/Latino; 5 Two or more races, non-Hispanic/Latino), 5 international. Average age 32. 401 applicants, 40% accepted, 112 enrolled. Expenses: Contact institution. *Financial support:* Career-related internships or fieldwork, Federal Work-Study, scholarships/grants, and unspecified assistantships available. Support available to part-time students. Financial award applicants required to submit FAFSA. In 2018, 157 master's awarded. *Program availability:* Part-time, evening/weekend, 100% online, blended/hybrid learning. Offers counseling (MS, Certificate); family counseling (Certificate); health services management (MPA, MS); marriage and family therapy (MS); mental health counseling (MS); psychology (MS); school counseling (Certificate); school psychology (MS). *Application deadline:* Applications are processed on a rolling basis. *Application fee:* $40. Electronic applications accepted. *Application Contact:* Allison Gurdineer, Executive Director of Admissions, 877-637-2946, Fax: 914-674-7382, E-mail: admissions@mercy.edu. *Dean, School of Social and Behavioral Sciences,* Dr. Karol Dean, 914-674-7517, Fax: 914-674-7413, E-mail: kdean@mercy.edu.

MERCY COLLEGE OF OHIO, Toledo, OH 43604

General Information Independent-religious, coed, primarily women, comprehensive institution. *Enrollment:* 1,511 graduate, professional, and undergraduate students; 48 part-time matriculated graduate/professional students (40 women). *Enrollment by degree level:* 48 master's. *Tuition:* Part-time $624 per credit hour. *Required fees:* $450. One-time fee: $250 part-time. *Graduate housing:* On-campus housing not available. *Student services:* Career counseling, free psychological counseling, low-cost health insurance, multicultural affairs office, services for students with disabilities, writing training. *Library facilities:* Mercy College of Ohio Library. *Collection:* Books: 7,081 (physical), 98,167 (digital/electronic); Serial titles: 334 (physical), 82,313 (digital/electronic); Databases: 15. Weekly public service hours: 57; students can reserve study rooms.

Computer facilities: 121 computers available on campus for general student use. A campuswide network can be accessed. Online class registration is available.

Website: http://www.mercycollege.edu/

GRADUATE UNITS

Program in Health Administration Students: 28 part-time (22 women); includes 4 minority (2 Black or African American, non-Hispanic/Latino; 1 Native Hawaiian or other Pacific Islander, non-Hispanic/Latino; 1 Two or more races, non-Hispanic/Latino). Average age 40. *Faculty:* 1 (woman) full-time, 9 part-time/adjunct (all women). Expenses: Contact institution. *Financial support:* Applicants required to submit FAFSA. *Program availability:* Part-time-only, online only, 100% online. Offers health administration (MHA). *Application fee:* $0. Electronic applications accepted. *Application Contact:* Amy Mergen, Director of Enrollment Management, 888-806-3729, E-mail: admissions@mercycollege.edu. *Dean Health Sciences; Program Director: Master of Health Administration,* Dr. Kimberly Watson, 419-251-1852, E-mail: kim.watson@mercycollege.edu.

Program in Nursing Students: 28 part-time (22 women). Average age 39. *Faculty:* 1 (woman) full-time, 7 part-time/adjunct (6 women). Expenses: Contact institution. *Financial support:* Applicants required to submit FAFSA. In 2018, 10 master's awarded. *Program availability:* Part-time-only, online only, 100% online, Practicum Experiences: 140 hours total. Offers nursing (MSN). *Application fee:* $0. Electronic applications accepted. *Application Contact:* Amy Mergen, Director of Enrollment Management, 888-806-3729, E-mail: admissions@mercycollege.edu. *MSN Program Director,* Dr. Deborah Karns, 419-251-1718, E-mail: deborah.karns@mercycollege.edu.

MERCYHURST UNIVERSITY, Erie, PA 16546

General Information Independent-religious, coed, comprehensive institution. *Graduate housing:* On-campus housing not available.

GRADUATE UNITS

Graduate Studies *Program availability:* Part-time, evening/weekend. Offers accounting (MS); administration of justice (MS); applied behavior analysis (MS); applied intelligence (MS, Certificate); archaeology and geological archaeology (MS); autism (MS); data science (MS); forensic and biological anthropology (MS); generalist (MS); higher education administration (MS); higher education leadership and disabilities (MS); human resources (MS); organizational leadership (MS, Certificate); physician assistant studies (MS); secondary education: pedagogy and practice (MS); sports leadership (MS); strategy and innovation (MS). Electronic applications accepted.

MEREDITH COLLEGE, Raleigh, NC 27607-5298

General Information Independent, Undergraduate: women only; graduate: coed, comprehensive institution. *Enrollment:* 134 full-time matriculated graduate/professional students (118 women), 165 part-time matriculated graduate/professional students (143 women). *Enrollment by degree level:* 213 master's, 86 other advanced degrees. *Graduate housing:* On-campus housing not available. *Student services:* Campus safety program, career counseling, free psychological counseling, international student services, services for students with disabilities. *Library facilities:* Carlyle Campbell Library.

Computer facilities: A campuswide network can be accessed from student residence rooms. Online class registration is available.

Website: http://www.meredith.edu/

General Application Contact: Cindy Bell, Admissions Coordinator, 919-760-8787, E-mail: bellcyn@meredith.edu.

GRADUATE UNITS

School of Business Students: 1 (woman) full-time, 88 part-time (69 women); includes 37 minority (28 Black or African American, non-Hispanic/Latino; 2 Asian, non-Hispanic/Latino; 6 Hispanic/Latino; 1 Two or more races, non-Hispanic/Latino), 5 international. Average age 35. Expenses: Contact institution. *Financial support:* Career-related internships or fieldwork, institutionally sponsored loans, scholarships/grants, and tuition waivers (partial) available. Support available to part-time students. Financial award application deadline: 2/15; financial award applicants required to submit FAFSA. In 2018, 29 master's awarded. *Program availability:* Part-time, evening/weekend. Offers business (MBA). *Application deadline:* For fall admission, 7/1 priority date for domestic and international students; for spring admission, 11/1 priority date for domestic and international students. Applications are processed on a rolling basis. *Application fee:* $50. Electronic applications accepted. *Application Contact:* Kristie Ogilvie, Dean, 919-760-8432, Fax: 919-760-8470. *Dean,* Kristie Ogilvie, 919-760-8432, Fax: 919-760-8470.

School of Education, Health and Human Sciences Students: 97 full-time (89 women), 76 part-time (73 women); includes 39 minority (17 Black or African American, non-Hispanic/Latino; 1 American Indian or Alaska Native, non-Hispanic/Latino; 9 Asian, non-Hispanic/Latino; 10 Hispanic/Latino; 2 Two or more races, non-Hispanic/Latino). Average age 28. Expenses: Contact institution. *Financial support:* Career-related internships or fieldwork, institutionally sponsored loans, and tuition waivers (partial) available. Support available to part-time students. Financial award application deadline: 2/15; financial award applicants required to submit FAFSA. In 2018, 56 master's, 36 other advanced degrees awarded. *Program availability:* Part-time, evening/weekend. Offers academically and intellectually gifted (M Ed); dietetic internship (Postbaccalaureate Certificate); elementary education (M Ed, MAT); English as a second language (M Ed, MAT); health and physical education (MAT); industrial/organizational psychology (MA); nutrition (MS); nutrition, health and human performance (MS, Postbaccalaureate Certificate); psychology (MA); reading (M Ed); special education (MAT); special education (general curriculum) (M Ed). *Application deadline:* For fall admission, 7/1 priority date for domestic students; for spring admission, 11/1 priority date for domestic students. Applications are processed on a rolling basis. *Application fee:* $50. Electronic applications accepted. *Application Contact:* Dr. Monica McKinney, Graduate Program Manager, 919-760-8056, Fax: 919-760-2303, E-mail: mckinneym@meredith.edu. *Graduate Program Manager,* Dr. Monica McKinney, 919-760-8056, Fax: 919-760-2303, E-mail: mckinneym@meredith.edu.

MERRIMACK COLLEGE, North Andover, MA 01845-5800

General Information Independent-religious, coed, comprehensive institution. CGS member. *Enrollment:* 4,516 graduate, professional, and undergraduate students; 586 full-time matriculated graduate/professional students (416 women), 192 part-time matriculated graduate/professional students (145 women). *Enrollment by degree level:* 772 master's, 6 other advanced degrees. *Graduate faculty:* 44 full-time (23 women), 64 part-time/adjunct (40 women). *Tuition:* Full-time $23,840; part-time $745 per credit hour. *Required fees:* $100; $100. Tuition and fees vary according to course load and program. *Graduate housing:* On-campus housing not available. *Student services:* Campus employment opportunities, campus safety program, career counseling, exercise/wellness program, free psychological counseling, international student services, low-cost health insurance, multicultural affairs office, services for students with disabilities, teacher training, writing training. *Library facilities:* McQuade Library. *Collection:* Books: 90,940 (physical), 179,938 (digital/electronic); Serial titles: 56 (physical), 155,880 (digital/electronic); Databases: 231.

Computer facilities: Computer purchase and lease plans are available. A campuswide network can be accessed from student residence rooms and from off campus. Online class registration is available.
Website: http://www.merrimack.edu/

General Application Contact: Megan Goddard, Office of Graduate Studies, 978-837-3563, E-mail: graduate@merrimack.edu.

GRADUATE UNITS

Girard School of Business Students: 81 full-time (33 women), 32 part-time (17 women); includes 11 minority (6 Black or African American, non-Hispanic/Latino; 3 Asian, non-Hispanic/Latino; 2 Two or more races, non-Hispanic/Latino), 11 international. Average age 30. 200 applicants, 75% accepted, 79 enrolled. *Faculty:* 5 full-time (1 woman), 3 part-time/adjunct (1 woman). Expenses: Contact institution. *Financial support:* Career-related internships or fieldwork, scholarships/grants, health care benefits, and unspecified assistantships available. Support available to part-time students. Financial award application deadline: 5/1; financial award applicants required to submit FAFSA. In 2018, 78 master's awarded. *Program availability:* Part-time, evening/weekend, 100% online. Offers accounting (MS); business analytics (MS); management (MS). *Application deadline:* For fall admission, 8/24 for domestic students, 7/30 for international students; for spring admission, 1/10 for domestic and international students; for summer admission, 5/10 for domestic students, 4/10 for international students. Applications are processed on a rolling basis. *Application fee:* $0. Electronic applications accepted. *Application Contact:* Jennifer Greenwood, Graduate Admission Counselor, 978-837-3563, E-mail: graduate@merrimack.edu. *Dean,* Dr. Catherine Usoff, 978-837-5044, E-mail: usoffc@merrimack.edu.

School of Education and Social Policy Students: 324 full-time (274 women), 120 part-time (108 women); includes 48 minority (11 Black or African American, non-Hispanic/Latino; 2 Asian, non-Hispanic/Latino; 22 Hispanic/Latino; 1 Native Hawaiian or other Pacific Islander, non-Hispanic/Latino; 12 Two or more races, non-Hispanic/Latino), 3 international. Average age 27. 511 applicants, 85% accepted, 291 enrolled. *Faculty:* 11 full-time (7 women), 53 part-time/adjunct (39 women). Expenses: Contact institution. *Financial support:* Fellowships with full tuition reimbursements, career-related internships or fieldwork, scholarships/grants, and health care benefits available. Support available to part-time students. Financial award application deadline: 5/1; financial award applicants required to submit FAFSA. In 2018, 177 master's awarded. *Program availability:* Part-time, evening/weekend, 100% online courses with immersion events and in-classroom practicum close to home. Offers criminology and criminal justice (MS); educational leadership (CAGS); English as a second language (prek-6) (M Ed). *Application deadline:* For fall admission, 8/24 for domestic students, 7/30 for international students; for spring admission, 1/10 for domestic students, 12/10 for international students; for summer admission, 5/10 for domestic students, 4/10 for international students. Applications are processed on a rolling basis. *Application fee:* $0. Electronic applications accepted. *Application Contact:* Alyssa Orlando, Graduate Admissions Counselor, 978-837-5338, E-mail: orlandoaf@merrimack.edu. *Dean,* Dr. Isabelle Cherney, 978-837-5338, E-mail: cherneyi@merrimack.edu.

School of Health Sciences Students: 93 full-time (62 women), 12 part-time (10 women); includes 3 minority (all Black or African American, non-Hispanic/Latino), 4 international. Average age 26. 163 applicants, 92% accepted, 82 enrolled. *Faculty:* 11 full-time (10 women), 2 part-time/adjunct (both women). Expenses: Contact institution. *Financial support:* Fellowships with partial tuition reimbursements, career-related internships or fieldwork, scholarships/grants, and health care benefits available. Support available to part-time students. Financial award application deadline: 5/1; financial award applicants required to submit FAFSA. In 2018, 71 master's awarded. *Program availability:* Part-time, evening/weekend. Offers athletic training (MS); community health education (MS); exercise and sport science (MS); health and wellness management (MS). *Application deadline:* For fall admission, 8/24 for domestic students, 7/30 for international students; for summer admission, 5/10 for domestic students, 4/10 for international students. Applications are processed on a rolling basis. *Application fee:* $0. Electronic applications accepted. *Application Contact:* Allison Pena, Office of Graduate Studies, 978-837-3563, E-mail: graduate@merrimack.edu. *Dean,* Dr. Janet Blum, 978-837-5396, E-mail: blumj@merrimack.edu.

School of Liberal Arts Students: 35 full-time (29 women), 11 part-time (5 women); includes 3 minority (1 Black or African American, non-Hispanic/Latino; 1 Asian, non-Hispanic/Latino; 1 Hispanic/Latino), 3 international. Average age 33. 66 applicants, 79% accepted, 31 enrolled. *Faculty:* 6 full-time (2 women), 1 part-time/adjunct (0 women). Expenses: Contact institution. *Financial support:* Career-related internships or fieldwork, scholarships/grants, and health care benefits available. Support available to part-time students. Financial award application deadline: 5/1; financial award applicants required to submit FAFSA. In 2018, 11 master's awarded. *Program availability:* Part-time, evening/weekend. Offers clinical mental health counseling (MS); interfaith spirituality (Certificate); public affairs (MPA); spiritual direction (MA, Certificate); spirituality (MA). *Application deadline:* For fall admission, 8/24 for domestic students, 7/30 for international students; for spring admission, 1/10 for domestic students, 12/10 for international students; for summer admission, 5/10 for domestic students, 4/10 for international students. Applications are processed on a rolling basis. *Application fee:* $0. Electronic applications accepted. *Application Contact:* Jennifer Greenwood, Graduate Admissions Counselor, 978-837-3563, E-mail: greenwoodjl@merrimack.edu. *Dean,* Dr. Karen Ryan, 978-837-5880, E-mail: ryankl@merrimack.edu.

School of Science and Engineering Students: 53 full-time (18 women), 17 part-time (5 women); includes 14 minority (6 Black or African American, non-Hispanic/Latino; 6 Asian, non-Hispanic/Latino; 2 Two or more races, non-Hispanic/Latino), 9 international. Average age 34. 183 applicants, 61% accepted, 40 enrolled. *Faculty:* 10 full-time (2 women), 6 part-time/adjunct (1 woman). Expenses: Contact institution. *Financial support:* Career-related internships or fieldwork, scholarships/grants, health care benefits, and unspecified assistantships available. Support available to part-time students. Financial award application deadline: 5/1; financial award applicants required to submit FAFSA. In 2018, 27 master's awarded. *Program availability:* Part-time, evening/weekend, 100% online. Offers civil engineering (MS); computer science (MS); data science (MS); engineering management (MS); mechanical engineering (MS). *Application deadline:* For fall admission, 8/24 for domestic students, 7/30 for international students; for spring admission, 1/10 for domestic students, 12/10 for international students; for summer admission, 5/10 for domestic students, 4/10 for international students. Applications are processed on a rolling basis. *Application fee:* $0. Electronic applications accepted. *Application Contact:* Allison Pena, Graduate Admissions Counselor, 978-837-3563, E-mail: penaa@merrimack.edu. *Dean,* Dr. Naira Campbell-Kyureghyan, 978-837-5265, E-mail: campbellnk@merrimack.edu.

MESIVTA OF EASTERN PARKWAY–YESHIVA ZICHRON MEILECH, Brooklyn, NY 11218-5559

General Information Independent-religious, men only, comprehensive institution.

GRADUATE UNITS

Graduate Programs

MESIVTA TORAH VODAATH RABBINICAL SEMINARY, Brooklyn, NY 11218-5299

General Information Independent-religious, men only, comprehensive institution.

GRADUATE UNITS

Graduate Programs Offers rabbinical studies (Certificate); theological and ministerial studies (Certificate).

MESIVTHA TIFERETH JERUSALEM OF AMERICA, New York, NY 10002-6301

General Information Independent-religious, men only, comprehensive institution.

GRADUATE UNITS

Graduate Programs

MESSIAH COLLEGE, Mechanicsburg, PA 17055

General Information Independent-religious, coed, comprehensive institution.

GRADUATE UNITS

Program in Business and Leadership *Program availability:* Online learning. Offers leadership (MBA, Certificate); management (Certificate); strategic leadership (MA).

Program in Conducting *Program availability:* Part-time, online learning. Offers choral conducting (MM); orchestral conducting (MM); wind conducting (MM). Electronic applications accepted.

Program in Counseling *Program availability:* Part-time, online learning. Offers clinical mental health counseling (MAC); counseling (CAGS); marriage, couple, and family counseling (MAC); school counseling (MAC). Electronic applications accepted.

Program in Education *Program availability:* Part-time, online learning. Offers curriculum and instruction (M Ed); special education (M Ed); teaching English to speakers of other languages (M Ed). Electronic applications accepted.

Program in Higher Education *Program availability:* Part-time. Offers college athletics management (MA); self-designed concentration (MA); student affairs (MA). Electronic applications accepted.

Program in Nursing Offers nurse educator (MSN).

METHODIST THEOLOGICAL SCHOOL IN OHIO, Delaware, OH 43015-8004

General Information Independent-religious, coed, graduate-only institution. *Graduate housing:* Rooms and/or apartments available on a first-come, first-served basis to single students and available to married students. Housing application deadline: 8/15.

GRADUATE UNITS

Graduate and Professional Programs *Program availability:* Part-time. Offers theology (M Div, MACE, MACM, MTS, D Min).

METHODIST UNIVERSITY, Fayetteville, NC 28311-1498

General Information Independent-religious, coed, comprehensive institution. *Graduate housing:* Room and/or apartments available on a first-come, first-served basis to single students; on-campus housing not available to married students. Housing application deadline: 6/1.

GRADUATE UNITS

School of Graduate Studies *Program availability:* Part-time, evening/weekend. Offers business administration (MBA); justice administration (MJA); physician assistant studies (MMS). Electronic applications accepted.

METROPOLITAN COLLEGE OF NEW YORK, New York, NY 10006

General Information Independent, coed, comprehensive institution. *Graduate housing:* On-campus housing not available. *Research affiliation:* U.S. Department of Homeland Security (homeland security), U.S. Federal Emergency Management Administration (higher education).

GRADUATE UNITS

Program in Business Administration *Program availability:* Evening/weekend. Offers financial services (MBA); general management (MBA); healthcare systems and risk management (MBA); media management (MBA). Electronic applications accepted.

Program in Childhood/Special Education Offers dual childhood 1-6 special education (MS). Electronic applications accepted.

Program in Public Administration *Program availability:* Evening/weekend. Offers emergency and disaster management (MPA); public affairs and administration (MPA). Electronic applications accepted.

METROPOLITAN STATE UNIVERSITY, St. Paul, MN 55106-5000

General Information State-supported, coed, comprehensive institution. *Graduate housing:* On-campus housing not available.

GRADUATE UNITS

College of Community Studies and Public Affairs Offers alcohol and drug counseling (MS); co-occurring disorders recovery counseling (MS); public administration (MPA); public and nonprofit administration (MPNA).

College of Liberal Arts *Program availability:* Part-time, evening/weekend. Offers liberal studies (MA); technical communication (MS). Electronic applications accepted.

College of Management *Program availability:* Part-time, evening/weekend. Offers business administration (MBA, DBA); business analytics (Graduate Certificate); database administration (Graduate Certificate); global supply chain management (Graduate Certificate); information assurance security (Graduate Certificate); management information systems (MMIS); MIS generalist (Graduate Certificate); MIS systems analysis and design (Graduate Certificate); project management (Graduate Certificate). Electronic applications accepted.

College of Nursing and Health Sciences *Program availability:* Part-time. Offers advanced dental therapy (MS); leadership and management (MSN); nurse educator (MSN); nursing (DNP).

College of Sciences Offers computer science (MS, PSM).

School of Law Enforcement and Criminal Justice *Program availability:* Part-time, evening/weekend. Offers criminal justice (MS). Electronic applications accepted.

School of Urban Education Offers curriculum, pedagogy and schooling (MS); English as a second language (MS); secondary education (MS); special education (MS).

METROPOLITAN STATE UNIVERSITY OF DENVER, Denver, CO 80204

General Information State-supported, coed, comprehensive institution. CGS member.

GRADUATE UNITS

College of Letters, Arts and Sciences Offers individual and families (MSW); macro practice (MSW); social work (MSW).

School of Business Offers accounting (MP Acc); fraud exam and forensic auditing (MP Acc); internal audit (MP Acc); public accounting (MP Acc); taxation (MP Acc).

School of Education Offers elementary education (MAT); special education (MAT).

MGH INSTITUTE OF HEALTH PROFESSIONS, Boston, MA 02129

General Information Independent, coed, primarily women, graduate-only institution. *Graduate housing:* On-campus housing not available. *Research affiliation:* Health and Disability Research Institute, Boston University (efficacy of a post-rehabilitation exercise intervention in patients after hip fracture), Eunice Kennedy Shriver National Institute of Child and Health Development (dyadic intervention for women at risk for postpartum depression and their infants), National Institutes of Health (postnatal parental depression, family dynamics in early parenting), Robert Wood Johnson Foundation (mother-infant intervention for the prevention of postpartum depression and associated mother-infant relationship dysfunction), U.S. Department of Defense (robotic nursing assistant to H-star technology), The American Academy of Nursing/John W. Hartford Foundation (building academic geriatric nursing capacity).

GRADUATE UNITS

School of Health and Rehabilitation Sciences *Program availability:* Part-time. Offers health and rehabilitation sciences (MPAS, MS, DPT, OTD, Certificate); occupational therapy (OTD); physical therapy (MS, DPT, Certificate); physician assistant studies (MPAS); reading (Certificate); speech-language pathology (MS). Electronic applications accepted.

School of Nursing Offers advanced practice nursing (MSN); gerontological nursing (MSN); nursing (DNP); pediatric nursing (MSN); psychiatric nursing (MSN); teaching and learning for health care education (Certificate); women's health nursing (MSN). Electronic applications accepted.

MIAMI INTERNATIONAL UNIVERSITY OF ART & DESIGN, Miami, FL 33132-1418

General Information Proprietary, coed, comprehensive institution.

GRADUATE UNITS

Program in Design and Media Management Offers design and media management (MA).

Program in Film *Program availability:* Online learning. Offers film (MFA).

MIAMI REGIONAL UNIVERSITY, Miami Springs, FL 33166

General Information Proprietary, coed, comprehensive institution.

GRADUATE UNITS

School of Nursing and Health Sciences Offers nursing (MSN); nursing education (MSN); nursing leadership (MSN).

MIAMI UNIVERSITY, Oxford, OH 45056

General Information State-related, coed, university. CGS member. *Enrollment:* 19,934 graduate, professional, and undergraduate students; 991 full-time matriculated graduate/professional students (585 women), 1,362 part-time matriculated graduate/professional students (1,022 women). *Enrollment by degree level:* 1,997 master's, 356 doctoral. *Graduate faculty:* 624 full-time (254 women). *Graduate housing:* Room and/or apartments available on a first-come, first-served basis to single students; on-campus housing not available to married students. *Student services:* Campus employment opportunities, campus safety program, career counseling, child daycare facilities, exercise/wellness program, free psychological counseling, grant writing training, international student services, low-cost health insurance, multicultural affairs office, services for students with disabilities, teacher training, writing training. *Library facilities:* King Library plus 3 others. *Collection:* Books: 1.3 million (physical), 773,916 (digital/electronic); Serial titles: 41,080 (physical), 287,002 (digital/electronic); Databases: 778. Weekly public service hours: 168; study areas open 24 hours, 5–7 days a week; students can reserve study rooms.

Computer facilities: Computer purchase and lease plans are available. 652 computers available on campus for general student use. A campuswide network can be accessed from student residence rooms and from off campus. Online class registration is available.

Website: http://miamioh.edu/

General Application Contact: Graduate Admission Coordinator, 513-529-3734, E-mail: applygrad@miamioh.edu.

GRADUATE UNITS

College of Arts and Science Students: 566 full-time (328 women), 902 part-time (734 women); includes 194 minority (22 Black or African American, non-Hispanic/Latino; 5 American Indian or Alaska Native, non-Hispanic/Latino; 31 Asian, non-Hispanic/Latino; 84 Hispanic/Latino; 2 Native Hawaiian or other Pacific Islander, non-Hispanic/Latino; 50 Two or more races, non-Hispanic/Latino), 170 international. Average age 31. *Faculty:* 296 full-time (132 women). Expenses: Contact institution. In 2018, 435 master's, 37 doctorates awarded. *Program availability:* Part-time. Offers arts and science (M Env, MA, MAT, MGS, MPSG, MS, MS Stat, PhD); biology (MA, MAT, MS, PhD); chemistry and biochemistry (MS, PhD); English (MA, MAT, PhD); French (MA); geography (MA); geology (MA, MS, PhD); gerontology (MGS); history (MA); mathematics (MA, MAT, MS); microbiology (MS, PhD); philosophy (MA); physics (MS); political science (MA); population and social gerontology (MPSG); psychology (MA, PhD); social gerontology (PhD); speech pathology and audiology (MA, MS); statistics (MS Stat). *Application Contact:* Admission Coordinator, 513-529-3734, E-mail: applygrad@miamioh.edu. *Dean,* Dr. Chris Makaroff, 513-529-1234, E-mail: cas@miamioh.edu.

College of Creative Arts Students: 71 full-time (44 women); includes 10 minority (3 Black or African American, non-Hispanic/Latino; 4 Asian, non-Hispanic/Latino; 3 Hispanic/Latino), 22 international. Average age 28. *Faculty:* 70 full-time (30 women). Expenses: Contact institution. In 2018, 23 master's awarded. Offers architecture and interior design (M Arch); art education (MA); creative arts (A Arch, MA, MFA, MM); music education (MM); music performance (MM); studio art (MFA); theatre (MA). *Application Contact:* Graduate Admission Coordinator, 513-529-3734, E-mail: applygrad@miamioh.edu. *Dean,* Dr. Liz Mullenix, 513-529-6010, E-mail: cca@miamioh.edu.

College of Education, Health and Society Students: 267 full-time (187 women), 346 part-time (260 women); includes 102 minority (52 Black or African American, non-Hispanic/Latino; 11 Asian, non-Hispanic/Latino; 22 Hispanic/Latino; 17 Two or more races, non-Hispanic/Latino), 42 international. Average age 32. *Faculty:* 90 full-time (50 women). Expenses: Contact institution. In 2018, 252 master's, 26 doctorates awarded. Offers education, health and society (M Ed, MA, MAT, MS, Ed D, PhD, Ed S); educational leadership (Ed D, PhD); educational psychology (M Ed, MA, MS, Ed S); family studies and social work (MA); kinesiology and health (MS); school leadership (M Ed); student affairs in higher education (MS, PhD); teacher education (M Ed, MAT); transformative education (M Ed). *Application Contact:* Graduate Admission Coordinator, 513-529-3734, E-mail: applygrad@miamioh.edu. *Dean,* Dr. Michael Dantley, 513-529-6317, E-mail: ehs@miamioh.edu.

College of Engineering and Computing Students: 57 full-time (15 women), 7 part-time (1 woman); includes 4 minority (1 Black or African American, non-Hispanic/Latino; 1 Asian, non-Hispanic/Latino; 2 Hispanic/Latino), 34 international. Average age 25. *Faculty:* 60 full-time (10 women). Expenses: Contact institution. In 2018, 34 master's awarded. Offers chemical, paper and biomedical engineering (MS); computer science (MCS); electrical and computer engineering (MS); engineering and computing (MCS, MS); mechanical and manufacturing engineering (MS). *Application Contact:* Graduate Admission Coordinator, 513-529-3734, E-mail: applygrad@miamioh.edu. *Dean,* Dr. Marek Dollar, 513-529-0700, E-mail: cec@miamioh.edu.

Farmer School of Business Students: 30 full-time (11 women), 107 part-time (27 women); includes 22 minority (4 Black or African American, non-Hispanic/Latino; 7 Asian, non-Hispanic/Latino; 6 Hispanic/Latino; 5 Two or more races, non-Hispanic/Latino), 9 international. Average age 32. *Faculty:* 108 full-time (32 women). Expenses: Contact institution. In 2018, 131 master's awarded. Offers accountancy (M Acc); business (M Acc, MA, MBA); business administration (MBA); economics (MA). *Application Contact:* Admission Coordinator, 513-529-3734, E-mail: applygrad@miamioh.edu. *Dean/Chair in Business Leadership,* Dr. Marc Rubin, 513-529-3381, E-mail: deanofbusiness@miamioh.edu.

Institute for the Environment and Sustainability Students: 22 full-time (14 women), 19 part-time (8 women); includes 4 minority (1 Black or African American, non-Hispanic/Latino; 1 American Indian or Alaska Native, non-Hispanic/Latino; 1 Hispanic/Latino; 1 Two or more races, non-Hispanic/Latino), 7 international. Average age 26. *Faculty:* 1 (woman) full-time. Expenses: Contact institution. In 2018, 17 master's awarded. Offers environment and sustainability (M Env). Electronic applications accepted. *Application Contact:* Dr. Jonathan Levy, Director/Associate Professor of Geology and Environmental Earth Science, 513-529-1947, E-mail: levyj@miamioh.edu. *Director/Associate Professor of Geology and Environmental Earth Science,* Dr. Jonathan Levy, 513-529-1947, E-mail: levyj@miamioh.edu.

MICHIGAN SCHOOL OF PSYCHOLOGY, Farmington Hills, MI 48334

General Information Independent, coed, graduate-only institution. *Graduate housing:* On-campus housing not available.

GRADUATE UNITS

MA and Psy D Programs in Clinical Psychology *Program availability:* Part-time, evening/weekend. Offers clinical psychology (MA, Psy D). Electronic applications accepted.

MICHIGAN STATE UNIVERSITY, East Lansing, MI 48824

General Information State-supported, coed, university. CGS member. *Graduate housing:* Rooms and/or apartments available on a first-come, first-served basis to single and married students. *Research affiliation:* Argonne National Laboratory (high-energy physics and structural biology), Association of Sea Grant Programs (fresh water ecosystems), Fraunhofer Center (manufacturing), Michigan Economic Development Corporation (life sciences, homeland security, automotive technologies), Oak Ridge Associated Universities (scientific research and education), Southern Astrophysical Research (SOAR) Telescope (astronomy).

GRADUATE UNITS

College of Human Medicine Offers biochemistry and molecular biology (MS, PhD); epidemiology (MS, PhD); human medicine (MD); human medicine/medical scientist training program (MD); microbiology (MS); microbiology and molecular genetics (PhD); pharmacology and toxicology (MS, PhD); physiology (MS, PhD); public health (MPH).

College of Osteopathic Medicine Offers biochemistry and molecular biology (MS, PhD); integrative pharmacology (MS); microbiology (MS); microbiology and molecular genetics (PhD); osteopathic medicine (MS, DO, PhD); pharmacology and toxicology (MS, PhD); pharmacology and toxicology-environmental toxicology (PhD); physiology (MS, PhD).

College of Veterinary Medicine Offers animal science–environmental toxicology (PhD); biochemistry and molecular biology–environmental toxicology (PhD); chemistry–environmental toxicology (PhD); comparative medicine and integrative biology (MS, PhD); comparative medicine and integrative biology–environmental toxicology (PhD); crop and soil sciences–environmental toxicology (PhD); environmental engineering–environmental toxicology (PhD); environmental geosciences–environmental toxicology (PhD); fisheries and wildlife–environmental toxicology (PhD); food safety (MS); food safety and toxicology (MS); food science–environmental toxicology (PhD); forestry–environmental toxicology (PhD); genetics–environmental toxicology (PhD); human nutrition–environmental toxicology (PhD); integrative toxicology (PhD); large animal clinical sciences (MS, PhD); microbiology and molecular genetics (MS, PhD); microbiology–environmental toxicology (PhD); pathobiology and diagnostic investigation (MS, PhD); pathology (MS, PhD); pathology–environmental toxicology (PhD); pharmacology and toxicology (MS, PhD); pharmacology and toxicology–environmental toxicology (PhD); physiology (MS, PhD); small animal clinical sciences (MS); veterinary medicine (MS, DVM, PhD); veterinary medicine/medical scientist training program (DVM); zoology–environmental toxicology (PhD).

The Graduate School *Program availability:* Part-time, evening/weekend, online learning. Electronic applications accepted.

College of Agriculture and Natural Resources Offers agricultural economics (MS, PhD); agricultural, food, and resource economics (MS, PhD); agriculture and natural resources (MA, MIPS, MS, MURP, PhD); animal science (MS, PhD); animal science-environmental toxicology (PhD); biosystems engineering (MS, PhD); community sustainability (MS, PhD); construction management (MS, PhD); crop and soil sciences (MS, PhD); crop and soil sciences-environmental toxicology (PhD); entomology (MS, PhD); environmental design (MA); fisheries and wildlife (MS, PhD); fisheries and wildlife - environmental toxicology (PhD); food science (MS, PhD); food science - environmental toxicology (PhD); forestry (MS, PhD); forestry-environmental toxicology (PhD); horticulture (MS, PhD); human nutrition (MS, PhD); human nutrition-environmental toxicology (PhD); integrated pest management (MS); interior design and facilities management (MA); international planning studies (MIPS); packaging (MS, PhD); plant breeding and genetics (MS, PhD); plant breeding and genetics-crop and soil sciences (MS); plant breeding, genetics and biotechnology-crop and soil sciences (PhD); plant breeding, genetics and biotechnology-forestry (MS, PhD); plant breeding, genetics and biotechnology-horticulture (MS, PhD); plant pathology (MS, PhD); urban and regional planning (MURP).

College of Arts and Letters Offers African American and African studies (MA, PhD); American studies (MA, PhD); arts and letters (MA, MFA, PhD); critical studies in literacy and pedagogy (MA); digital rhetoric and professional writing (MA); English (PhD); French (MA); French language and literature (PhD); German studies (MA, PhD); Hispanic cultural studies (PhD); Hispanic literatures (MA); linguistics (MA, PhD); literature in English (MA); philosophy (MA, PhD); rhetoric and writing (PhD); second language studies (PhD); Spanish as a second or bilingual language (MA); studio art (MFA); teaching English to speakers of other languages (MA); theatre (MA, MFA). Electronic applications accepted.

College of Communication Arts and Sciences Offers advertising (MA); communication (MA, PhD); communication arts and sciences (MA, MS, PhD); communication arts and sciences–information and media (PhD); communicative sciences and disorders (MA, PhD); health communication (MA); journalism (MA); media and information management (MA); public relations (MA); serious game design (MA).

College of Education Offers counseling (MA); curriculum, instruction and teacher education (PhD, Ed S); education (MA, MS, PhD, Ed S); educational policy (PhD); educational psychology and educational technology (PhD); educational technology (MA); higher, adult and lifelong education (MA, PhD); K–12 educational administration (MA, PhD, Ed S); kinesiology (MS, PhD); literacy instruction (MA); measurement and quantitative methods (PhD); rehabilitation counseling (MA); rehabilitation counselor education (PhD); school psychology (MA, PhD, Ed S); special education (MA, PhD); student affairs administration (MA); teaching and curriculum (MA). Electronic applications accepted.

College of Engineering *Program availability:* Part-time. Offers chemical engineering (MS, PhD); civil engineering (MS, PhD); computer science (MS, PhD); electrical engineering (MS, PhD); engineering (MS, PhD); engineering mechanics (MS, PhD); environmental engineering (MS, PhD); environmental engineering-environmental toxicology (PhD); materials science and engineering (MS, PhD); mechanical engineering (MS, PhD). Electronic applications accepted.

College of Music Offers collaborative piano (M Mus); jazz studies (M Mus); music (PhD); music composition (M Mus, DMA); music conducting (M Mus, DMA); music education (M Mus); music performance (M Mus, DMA); music theory (M Mus); music therapy (M Mus); musicology (MA); piano pedagogy (M Mus). Electronic applications accepted.

College of Natural Science Offers applied mathematics (MS, PhD); applied statistics (MS); astrophysics and astronomy (MS, PhD); biochemistry and molecular biology (MS, PhD); biochemistry and molecular biology/environmental toxicology (PhD); biomedical laboratory operations (MS); cell and molecular biology (MS, PhD); cell and molecular biology/environmental toxicology (PhD); cellular and molecular biology (PhD); chemical physics (PhD); chemistry (MS, PhD); chemistry-environmental toxicology (PhD); clinical laboratory sciences (MS); computational chemistry (MS); crop and soil sciences (PhD); ecology, evolutionary biology and behavior (MS, PhD); environmental geosciences (MS, PhD); environmental geosciences-environmental

toxicology (PhD); genetics (MS, PhD); genetics–environmental toxicology (PhD); geological sciences (MS, PhD); industrial mathematics (MS); industrial microbiology (MS, PhD); integrative biology (MS, PhD); mathematics (MAT, MS, PhD); mathematics education (MS); microbiology (MS, PhD); microbiology and molecular genetics (MS, PhD); microbiology–environmental toxicology (PhD); natural science (MAT, MS, PhD); neuroscience (MS, PhD); physics (MS, PhD); physiology (MS, PhD); plant biology (MS, PhD); plant breeding, genetics and biotechnology - plant biology (MS, PhD); plant physiology (PhD); quantitative biology (PhD); statistics (MS, PhD). Electronic applications accepted.

College of Nursing *Program availability:* Part-time, online learning. Offers nursing (MSN, PhD). Electronic applications accepted.

College of Social Science Offers anthropology (MA, PhD); Chicano/Latino studies (PhD); child development (MS); clinical social work (MSW); criminal justice (MS, PhD); economics (MA, PhD); family and community services (MA); forensic science (MS); geography (MA, PhD); history (MA, PhD); history-secondary school teaching (MA); human development and family studies (MS, PhD); human resources and labor relations (MLRHR, PhD); law enforcement intelligence and analysis (MS); organizational and community practice (MSW); political science (MA, PhD); professional applications in anthropology (MA); psychology (MA, PhD); public policy (MPP); social science (MA, MIPS, MLRHR, MPP, MS, MSW, MURP, PhD); social work (PhD); sociology (MA, PhD); youth development (MA). Electronic applications accepted.

Eli Broad College of Business *Program availability:* Evening/weekend. Offers accounting (MS, PhD); business (MBA, MS, PhD); business analytics (MS); business information systems (PhD); finance (MS, PhD); foodservice business management (MS); hospitality business management (MS); human resource management (MBA); integrative management (MBA); logistics (PhD); management (PhD); management, strategy, and leadership (MS); marketing (MBA, PhD); marketing research (MS); operations and sourcing management (PhD); supply chain management (MBA, MS). Electronic applications accepted.

National Superconducting Cyclotron Laboratory Offers chemistry (PhD); physics (PhD).

MICHIGAN STATE UNIVERSITY COLLEGE OF LAW, East Lansing, MI 48824-1300

General Information Independent, coed, graduate-only institution. *Enrollment by degree level:* 69 master's, 708 doctoral. *Graduate faculty:* 54 full-time (24 women), 68 part-time/adjunct (24 women). *Tuition:* Full-time $44,200. *Required fees:* $37. *Graduate housing:* Rooms and/or apartments available on a first-come, first-served basis to single and married students. Typical cost: $7780 (including board) for single students; $10,350 per year ($13,365 including board) for married students. Room and board charges vary according to board plan. Housing application deadline: 5/1. *Student services:* Campus employment opportunities, campus safety program, career counseling, exercise/wellness program, international student services, low-cost health insurance, multicultural affairs office, services for students with disabilities, writing training. *Library facilities:* John F. Schaefer Law Library plus 2 others. *Collection:* Books: 111,715 (physical), 42,605 (digital/electronic); Serial titles: 3,356 (physical), 5,374 (digital/electronic); Databases: 31. Weekly public service hours: 71; students can reserve study rooms.

Computer facilities: 100 computers available on campus for general student use. A campuswide network can be accessed from student residence rooms. Online class registration is available.
Website: http://www.law.msu.edu/

General Application Contact: Ian McInnis, Director of Admissions, 517-432-6949, Fax: 517-432-6801, E-mail: ian.mcinnis@law.msu.edu.

GRADUATE UNITS

Graduate and Professional Programs *Program availability:* Part-time. Offers American legal system (LL M, MJ); global food law (LL M, MJ); intellectual property law (LL M, MJ); law (JD); legal studies (MLS). Electronic applications accepted.

MICHIGAN TECHNOLOGICAL UNIVERSITY, Houghton, MI 49931

General Information State-supported, coed, university. CGS member. *Enrollment:* 1,059 full-time matriculated graduate/professional students (309 women), 280 part-time matriculated graduate/professional students (92 women). *Enrollment by degree level:* 781 master's, 546 doctoral, 12 other advanced degrees. *Graduate faculty:* 462 full-time (125 women), 164 part-time/adjunct (33 women). *International tuition:* $18,126 full-time. *Tuition, area resident:* Full-time $18,126; part-time $1007 per credit. Tuition, state resident: full-time $18,126; part-time $1007 per credit. Tuition, nonresident: full-time $18,126; part-time $1007 per credit. *Required fees:* $248; $124 per semester. Tuition and fees vary according to course load and program. *Graduate housing:* Rooms and/or apartments available on a first-come, first-served basis to single and married students. Typical cost: $4530 per year ($9304 including board) for single students. Room and board charges vary according to board plan and housing facility selected. *Student services:* Campus employment opportunities, campus safety program, career counseling, child daycare facilities, exercise/wellness program, free psychological counseling, grant writing training, international student services, low-cost health insurance, multicultural affairs office, services for students with disabilities, teacher training, writing training. *Library facilities:* J. R. Van Pelt and John and Ruanne Opie Library. *Collection:* Books: 362,342 (physical), 142,603 (digital/electronic); Serial titles: 14,050 (physical), 124,764 (digital/electronic); Databases: 347. Weekly public service hours: 105; study areas open 24 hours, 5–7 days a week; students can reserve study rooms. *Research affiliation:* Ariens Company (Materials testing), E3 Sparkplugs (Automotive technology design), Faurecia Emissions Control Technologies (Emissions Testing), Osmose Inc (Materials Testing), Nostrum Energy LLC (Control system design).

Computer facilities: 1,079 computers available on campus for general student use. A campuswide network can be accessed from student residence rooms and from off campus. Online class registration is available.
Website: http://www.mtu.edu/

General Application Contact: Carol T. Wingerson, Administrative Aide, 906-487-2328, Fax: 906-487-2284, E-mail: gradadms@mtu.edu.

GRADUATE UNITS

Graduate School Students: 1,059 full-time (309 women), 280 part-time (92 women); includes 63 minority (17 Black or African American, non-Hispanic/Latino; 2 American Indian or Alaska Native, non-Hispanic/Latino; 7 Asian, non-Hispanic/Latino; 12 Hispanic/Latino; 25 Two or more races, non-Hispanic/Latino), 786 international. Average age 28. 4,252 applicants, 35% accepted, 400 enrolled. *Faculty:* 462 full-time (125 women), 164 part-time/adjunct (33 women). Expenses: Contact institution. *Financial support:* In 2018–19, 938 students received support, including 107 fellowships with tuition reimbursements available (averaging $16,590 per year), 218 research assistantships with tuition reimbursements available (averaging $16,590 per year), 229 teaching assistantships with tuition reimbursements available (averaging $16,590 per year); career-related internships or fieldwork, Federal Work-Study, scholarships/grants, traineeships, health care benefits, unspecified assistantships, and cooperative program also available. Financial award applicants required to submit FAFSA. In 2018, 419 master's, 85 doctorates, 63 other advanced degrees awarded. *Program availability:* Part-time, 100% online, blended/hybrid learning. Offers automotive systems and controls (Graduate Certificate); biochemistry and molecular biology (PhD); computational science and engineering (PhD); data science (Graduate Certificate); sustainability (Graduate Certificate). *Application deadline:* Applications are processed on a rolling basis. Electronic applications accepted. *Application Contact:* Carol T. Wingerson, Administrative Aide, 906-487-2328, Fax: 906-487-2284, E-mail: gradadms@mtu.edu. *Dean of the Graduate School/Associate Provost for Graduate Education*, Dr. Pushpalatha Murthy, 906-487-2326, Fax: 906-487-2284, E-mail: ppmurthy@mtu.edu.

College of Computing Students: 50 full-time (17 women), 14 part-time (7 women); includes 5 minority (1 Black or African American, non-Hispanic/Latino; 1 Asian, non-Hispanic/Latino; 3 Two or more races, non-Hispanic/Latino). Average age 28. 500 applicants, 28% accepted, 22 enrolled. *Faculty:* 30 full-time (6 women), 4 part-time/adjunct. Expenses: Contact institution. *Financial support:* In 2018–19, 43 students received support, including 1 fellowship with tuition reimbursement available (averaging $16,590 per year), 10 research assistantships with tuition reimbursements available (averaging $16,590 per year), 16 teaching assistantships with tuition reimbursements available (averaging $16,590 per year); career-related internships or fieldwork, Federal Work-Study, scholarships/grants, and health care benefits also available. Financial award applicants required to submit FAFSA. *Program availability:* Part-time, 100% online, blended/hybrid learning. *Application deadline:* Applications are processed on a rolling basis. Electronic applications accepted. *Application Contact:* Cheryl Simpkins, Office Assistant, 906-487-2209, Fax: 906-487-2283, E-mail: cisimpki@mtu.edu. *Dean*, Dr. Adrienne R. Minerick, 906-487-2209, Fax: 906-487-2283, E-mail: minerick@mtu.edu.

College of Engineering Students: 634 full-time (123 women), 144 part-time (32 women); includes 30 minority (8 Black or African American, non-Hispanic/Latino; 6 Asian, non-Hispanic/Latino; 10 Hispanic/Latino; 6 Two or more races, non-Hispanic/Latino), 537 international. Average age 27. 2,309 applicants, 39% accepted, 228 enrolled. *Faculty:* 261 full-time (48 women), 99 part-time/adjunct (16 women). Expenses: Contact institution. *Financial support:* In 2018–19, 546 students received support, including 54 fellowships with tuition reimbursements available (averaging $16,590 per year), 140 research assistantships with tuition reimbursements available (averaging $16,590 per year), 77 teaching assistantships with tuition reimbursements available (averaging $16,590 per year); career-related internships or fieldwork, Federal Work-Study, scholarships/grants, health care benefits, unspecified assistantships, and cooperative program also available. Financial award applicants required to submit FAFSA. In 2018, 304 master's, 42 doctorates, 61 other advanced degrees awarded. *Program availability:* Part-time, 100% online, blended/hybrid learning. Offers advanced electric power engineering (Graduate Certificate); biomedical engineering (MS, PhD); chemical engineering (MS, PhD); civil engineering (MS, PhD); electrical engineering (PhD); engineering (MS, PhD, Graduate Certificate); engineering mechanics (MS); environmental engineering (MS, PhD); environmental engineering science (MS); geology (MS); geophysics (PhD); hybrid electric drive vehicle engineering (Graduate Certificate); materials science and engineering (MS, PhD); mechanical engineering-engineering mechanics (PhD); mining engineering (PhD). *Application deadline:* Applications are processed on a rolling basis. Electronic applications accepted. *Application Contact:* Carol T. Wingerson, Administrative Aide, 906-487-2328, Fax: 906-487-2284, E-mail: gradadms@mtu.edu. *Dean*, Dr. Janet Callahan, 906-487-2005, E-mail: callahan@mtu.edu.

College of Sciences and Arts Students: 221 full-time (103 women), 54 part-time (27 women); includes 16 minority (5 Black or African American, non-Hispanic/Latino; 1 American Indian or Alaska Native, non-Hispanic/Latino; 1 Hispanic/Latino; 9 Two or more races, non-Hispanic/Latino), 128 international. Average age 30. 688 applicants, 35% accepted, 82 enrolled. *Faculty:* 223 full-time (85 women), 50 part-time/adjunct (12 women). Expenses: Contact institution. *Financial support:* In 2018–19, 219 students received support, including 35 fellowships with tuition reimbursements available (averaging $16,590 per year), 36 research assistantships with tuition reimbursements available (averaging $16,590 per year), 115 teaching assistantships with tuition reimbursements available (averaging $16,590 per year); career-related internships or fieldwork, Federal Work-Study, scholarships/grants, traineeships, health care benefits, unspecified assistantships, and cooperative program also available. Financial award applicants required to submit FAFSA. In 2018, 49 master's, 33 doctorates, 2 other advanced degrees awarded. *Program availability:* Part-time, blended/hybrid learning. Offers applied cognitive science and human factors (MS, PhD); applied physics (MS, PhD); applied science education (MS); biological sciences (MS, PhD); chemistry (MS, PhD); environmental and energy policy (MS); integrative physiology (PhD); kinesiology (MS); mathematical sciences (MS, PhD); physics (MS, PhD); post-secondary STEM education (Graduate Certificate); rhetoric, theory and culture (MS); sciences and arts (MS, PhD, Graduate Certificate). *Application deadline:* For fall admission, 4/1 for domestic and international students; for spring admission, 9/1 for domestic and international students. Applications are processed on a rolling basis. Electronic applications accepted. *Application Contact:* Carol T. Wingerson, Administrative Aide, 906-487-2328, Fax: 906-487-2284, E-mail: gradadms@mtu.edu. *Dean*, Dr. David Hemmer, 906-487-2156, Fax: 906-487-3347, E-mail: djhemmer@mtu.edu.

School of Business and Economics Students: 37 full-time (17 women), 28 part-time (16 women); includes 3 minority (1 Hispanic/Latino; 2 Two or more races, non-Hispanic/Latino), 17 international. Average age 28. 166 applicants, 25% accepted, 29 enrolled. *Faculty:* 24 full-time (9 women), 1 part-time/adjunct. Expenses: Contact institution. *Financial support:* In 2018–19, 25 students received support. Health care benefits and unspecified assistantships available. Financial award application deadline: 4/1; financial award applicants required to submit FAFSA. In 2018, 26 master's awarded. *Program availability:* Part-time, evening/weekend. Offers applied natural resource economics (MS); business administration (MBA). *Application deadline:* For fall admission, 7/1 for domestic and international students; for spring admission, 12/1 for domestic and international students. Applications are processed on a rolling basis. Electronic applications accepted. *Application Contact:* Carol T. Wingerson, Administrative Aide, 906-487-2328, Fax: 906-487-2284, E-mail: gradadms@mtu.edu. *Dean*, Dr. Dean Johnson, 906-487-2668, Fax: 906-487-1863, E-mail: dean@mtu.edu.

School of Forest Resources and Environmental Science Students: 50 full-time (21 women), 16 part-time (7 women); includes 4 minority (1 Black or African American, non-Hispanic/Latino; 3 Two or more races, non-Hispanic/Latino), 13 international. Average age 30. 110 applicants, 30% accepted, 22 enrolled. *Faculty:* 38 full-time (11 women), 24 part-time/adjunct (7 women). Expenses: Contact institution. *Financial support:* In 2018–19, 41 students received support, including 2 fellowships with tuition reimbursements available (averaging $16,590 per year), 18 research assistantships with tuition reimbursements available (averaging $16,590 per year), 8 teaching assistantships with tuition reimbursements available (averaging $16,590 per year); career-related internships or fieldwork, Federal Work-Study, scholarships/grants, health care benefits, unspecified assistantships, and cooperative program also available. Financial award applicants required to submit FAFSA. In 2018, 20 master's, 6 doctorates awarded. *Program availability:* Part-time. Offers forest resources and environmental science (MGIS). *Application deadline:* Applications are processed on a rolling basis. Electronic applications accepted. *Application Contact:* Dr. Audrey L. Mayer, Graduate Director/Professor, 906-487-3448, Fax: 906-487-2915, E-mail: almayer@mtu.edu. *Dean*, Dr. Andrew J. Storer, 906-487-3470, Fax: 906-487-2915, E-mail: storer@mtu.edu.

MID-AMERICA BAPTIST THEOLOGICAL SEMINARY, Cordova, TN 38016

General Information Independent-religious, men only, comprehensive institution. *Graduate housing:* Rooms and/or apartments available on a first-come, first-served basis to single and married students. Housing application deadline: 7/31.

GRADUATE UNITS

Graduate and Professional Programs Offers biblical counseling (M Div); Christian education (M Div, MACE); ministry (D Min); missiology and intercultural studies (M Div); pastoral ministry (M Div); theology (MA, PhD); worship (MA). Electronic applications accepted.

MID-AMERICA BAPTIST THEOLOGICAL SEMINARY NORTHEAST BRANCH, Schenectady, NY 12303-3463

General Information Independent-religious, coed, primarily men, graduate-only institution. *Graduate housing:* Rooms and/or apartments available on a first-come, first-served basis to single and married students.

GRADUATE UNITS

Program in Theology *Program availability:* Part-time, evening/weekend. Offers theology (M Div). Electronic applications accepted.

MID-AMERICA CHRISTIAN UNIVERSITY, Oklahoma City, OK 73170-4504

General Information Independent-religious, coed, comprehensive institution.

GRADUATE UNITS

Program in Business Administration Offers business administration (MBA).

Program in Counseling Offers marital and family therapy (MS); pastoral/spiritual direction (MS); professional counselor (MS).

Program in Leadership Offers leadership (MA).

Program in Public Administration Offers public administration (MA).

MIDAMERICA NAZARENE UNIVERSITY, Olathe, KS 66062-1899

General Information Independent-religious, coed, comprehensive institution. *Graduate housing:* On-campus housing not available.

GRADUATE UNITS

Professional and Graduate Studies in Education *Program availability:* Part-time, evening/weekend, online only, 100% online. Offers ESOL (M Ed); reading specialist (M Ed); technology enhanced teaching (M Ed). Electronic applications accepted.

School of Behavioral Sciences and Counseling *Program availability:* Evening/weekend. Offers counseling (MA). Electronic applications accepted.

School of Business *Program availability:* Part-time, evening/weekend, 100% online, blended/hybrid learning. Offers management (MBA, MSM). Electronic applications accepted.

School of Nursing and Health Science *Program availability:* Part-time, evening/weekend, 100% online, blended/hybrid learning. Offers healthcare administration (MSN); healthcare quality management (MSN); nursing education (MSN); public health (MSN). Electronic applications accepted.

MID-AMERICA REFORMED SEMINARY, Dyer, IN 46311

General Information Independent-religious, men only, graduate-only institution.

GRADUATE UNITS

Graduate Programs Offers theology (M Div, MTS).

MIDDLEBURY COLLEGE, Middlebury, VT 05753-6002

General Information Independent, coed, comprehensive institution. *Enrollment:* 2,626 graduate, professional, and undergraduate students; 47 part-time matriculated graduate/professional students (39 women). *Enrollment by degree level:* 47 master's. *Graduate housing:* Room and/or apartments guaranteed to single students; on-campus housing not available to married students. *Student services:* Campus safety program, career counseling, free psychological counseling, international student services, services for students with disabilities, teacher training. *Library facilities:* Davis Family Library plus 2 others. *Collection:* Books: 764,667 (physical), 644,056 (digital/electronic); Databases: 695. Weekly public service hours: 112; students can reserve study rooms.

Computer facilities: Computer purchase and lease plans are available. A campuswide network can be accessed from student residence rooms and from off campus. Online class registration, personal Web pages, file servers are available. Website: http://www.middlebury.edu/

General Application Contact: Admissions Office, 802-443-3000, Fax: 802-443-2056, E-mail: admissions@middlebury.edu.

GRADUATE UNITS

Language Schools Expenses: Contact institution. *Financial support:* Fellowships and scholarships/grants available. Financial award applicants required to submit FAFSA. Offers language (MA, DML). *Application deadline:* For summer admission, 5/1 for domestic and international students. Applications are processed on a rolling basis. *Application fee:* $75. Electronic applications accepted. *Application Contact:* Kara Gennarelli, Technical and Lead Coordinator, Language Schools Office, 802-443-5727, Fax: 802-443-2075, E-mail: languages@middlebury.edu. *Dean*, Dr. Stephen B. Snyder, 802-443-5979, Fax: 802-443-2075, E-mail: ssnyder@middlebury.edu.

Arabic School Expenses: Contact institution. *Financial support:* Fellowships and scholarships/grants available. Financial award application deadline: 3/14; financial award applicants required to submit FAFSA. Offers Arabic (MA). *Application deadline:* For summer admission, 5/1 for domestic and international students. Applications are processed on a rolling basis. *Application fee:* $75. Electronic applications accepted. *Application Contact:* Barbara Walter, Coordinator, 802-443-5230, Fax: 802-443-2075, E-mail: bwalter@middlebury.edu. *Director,* Dr. Mahmoud Abdalla, 802-443-5230, Fax: 802-443-2075, E-mail: mabdalla@miis.edu.

Chinese School Expenses: Contact institution. *Financial support:* Fellowships and scholarships/grants available. Financial award application deadline: 3/15; financial award applicants required to submit FAFSA. Offers Chinese (MA). *Application deadline:* Applications are processed on a rolling basis. *Application fee:* $75. Electronic applications accepted. *Application Contact:* Mimi Clark, Coordinator, 802-443-5520, Fax: 802-443-2075, E-mail: chineseschool@middlebury.edu. *Director,* Cecilia Chang, 802-443-5520, Fax: 802-443-3510, E-mail: cchang@middlebury.edu.

French School Expenses: Contact institution. *Financial support:* Fellowships and scholarships/grants available. Financial award application deadline: 3/10; financial award applicants required to submit FAFSA. Offers French (MA, DML). *Application deadline:* Applications are processed on a rolling basis. *Application fee:* $75. Electronic applications accepted. *Application Contact:* Sheila Schwaneflugel, Coordinator, 802-443-5526, Fax: 802-443-2075, E-mail: sschwaneflugel@middlebury.edu. *Director,* Armelle Crouzieres-Ingenthron, 802-443-2427, Fax: 802-443-2075, E-mail: crouzier@middlebury.edu.

German School Expenses: Contact institution. *Financial support:* Fellowships and scholarships/grants available. Financial award application deadline: 3/9; financial award applicants required to submit FAFSA. Offers German (MA, DML). *Application deadline:* Applications are processed on a rolling basis. *Application fee:* $75. Electronic applications accepted. *Application Contact:* Christina Ellison, Coordinator, 802-443-5203, Fax: 802-443-2075, E-mail: germanschool@middlebury.edu. *Director,* Dr. Bettina Matthias, 802-443-3527, Fax: 802-443-2075, E-mail: bmatthia@middlebury.edu.

Hebrew School Expenses: Contact institution. *Financial support:* Fellowships and scholarships/grants available. Financial award application deadline: 3/28; financial award applicants required to submit FAFSA. *Program availability:* Blended/hybrid learning. Offers Hebrew (MA). *Application deadline:* Applications are processed on a rolling basis. *Application fee:* $75. Electronic applications accepted. *Application Contact:* Vardit Ringvald, Director, 802-443-3574, E-mail: vringval@middlebury.edu. *Director,* Vardit Ringvald, 802-443-3574, E-mail: vringval@middlebury.edu.

Italian School Expenses: Contact institution. *Financial support:* Fellowships and scholarships/grants available. Financial award application deadline: 3/10; financial award applicants required to submit FAFSA. Offers Italian (MA, DML). *Application deadline:* Applications are processed on a rolling basis. *Application fee:* $75. Electronic applications accepted. *Application Contact:* Joseph Tamagni, Coordinator, 802-443-5727, Fax: 802-443-2075, E-mail: italianschool@middlebury.edu. *Director,* Dr. Antonio Vitti, 802-443-5727, Fax: 802-443-2075, E-mail: acvitti@middlebury.edu.

Russian School Expenses: Contact institution. *Financial support:* Fellowships and scholarships/grants available. Financial award application deadline: 3/14; financial award applicants required to submit FAFSA. Offers Russian (MA, DML). *Application deadline:* Applications are processed on a rolling basis. *Application fee:* $75. Electronic applications accepted. *Application Contact:* Oliver Carling, Coordinator, 802-443-2006, Fax: 802-443-2075, E-mail: ocarling@middlebury.edu. *Director,* Dr. Jason Merrill, 802-443-5230, Fax: 802-443-2075, E-mail: jmerrill@middlebury.edu.

Spanish School Expenses: Contact institution. *Financial support:* Fellowships and scholarships/grants available. Financial award application deadline: 3/8; financial award applicants required to submit FAFSA. Offers Spanish (MA, DML). *Application deadline:* Applications are processed on a rolling basis. *Application fee:* $75. Electronic applications accepted. *Application Contact:* Audrey LaRock, Coordinator, 802-443-5539, Fax: 802-443-2075, E-mail: larock@middlebury.edu. *Director,* Dr. Jacobo Sefami, 802-443-5539, Fax: 802-443-2075, E-mail: jsefami@midtlelbury.edu.

Middlebury Bread Loaf School of English *Program availability:* Part-time. Offers English (M Litt, MA). Offered during summer only. Electronic applications accepted.

MIDDLEBURY INSTITUTE OF INTERNATIONAL STUDIES AT MONTEREY, Monterey, CA 93940-2691

General Information Independent, coed, graduate-only institution. *Graduate housing:* On-campus housing not available.

GRADUATE UNITS

Graduate School of International Policy and Management Offers international education management (MA); international environmental policy (MA); international policy and development (MA); international policy and management (MA, MPA); international trade and economic diplomacy (MA); nonproliferation and terrorism studies (MA); public administration (MPA). Electronic applications accepted.

Graduate School of Translation, Interpretation and Language Education Offers conference interpretation (MA); teaching English to speakers of other languages (MATESOL); teaching foreign language (MATFL); translation (MA); translation and interpretation (MA); translation and localization management (MA); translation, interpretation and language education (MA, MATESOL, MATFL). Electronic applications accepted.

MIDDLE GEORGIA STATE UNIVERSITY, Macon, GA 31206

General Information State-supported, coed, comprehensive institution.

GRADUATE UNITS

Office of Graduate Studies Offers adult/gerontology acute care nurse practitioner (MSN); information technology (MS).

MIDDLE TENNESSEE SCHOOL OF ANESTHESIA, Madison, TN 37116

General Information Independent-religious, coed, graduate-only institution. *Graduate housing:* On-campus housing not available.

GRADUATE UNITS

Graduate Programs Offers anesthesia (MS, DNAP).

MIDDLE TENNESSEE STATE UNIVERSITY, Murfreesboro, TN 37132

General Information State-supported, coed, university. CGS member. *Graduate housing:* Rooms and/or apartments available on a first-come, first-served basis to single and married students.

GRADUATE UNITS

College of Graduate Studies *Program availability:* Part-time, evening/weekend, online learning. Offers mathematics and science education (PhD). Electronic applications accepted.

College of Basic and Applied Sciences *Program availability:* Part-time, evening/weekend, online learning. Offers actuarial sciences (MS); aerospace education (M Ed); aviation administration (MS); basic and applied sciences (M Ed, MS, MSN, MST, PhD, Graduate Certificate); biology (MS); biostatistics (MS); biotechnology (MS); chemistry (MS); computational science (PhD); computer science (MS); engineering management (MS); engineering technology (MS); health care informatics (MS); horse science (MS); mathematics (MS, MST); molecular biosciences (PhD). Electronic applications accepted.

College of Behavioral and Health Sciences Offers behavioral and health sciences (MA, MCJ, MS, MSN, MSW, PhD, Ed S, Graduate Certificate); clinical psychology (MA); criminal justice administration (MCJ); exercise science (MS); experimental psychology (MA); family nurse practitioner (MSN, Graduate Certificate); health and human performance (MS); health, physical education and recreation (MS); human performance (PhD); industrial/organizational psychology (MA); leisure and sport management (MS); nursing (MSN, Graduate Certificate); psychology (MA, Ed S); quantitative psychology (MA); school psychology (MA); social work (MSW). Electronic applications accepted.

College of Education *Program availability:* Part-time, evening/weekend, online learning. Offers administration and supervision (M Ed, Ed S); curriculum and instruction (M Ed, Ed S); early childhood education (M Ed); education (M Ed, PhD, Ed S); elementary education (M Ed, Ed S); English as a second language (M Ed, Ed S); literacy studies (PhD); mental health counseling (M Ed); middle school education (M Ed); professional counseling (M Ed); reading (M Ed); school counseling (M Ed); secondary education (M Ed); special education (M Ed); technology and curriculum design (Ed S). Electronic applications accepted.

College of Liberal Arts *Program availability:* Part-time, evening/weekend, online learning. Offers archival management (Graduate Certificate); English (MA, PhD); foreign languages (MAT); geosciences (Graduate Certificate); gerontology (Graduate Certificate); history (MA); international affairs (MA); liberal arts (MA, MAT, MSW, PhD, Graduate Certificate); music (MA); public history (PhD); sociology (MA); women's and gender studies (Graduate Certificate). Electronic applications accepted.

College of Mass Communication *Program availability:* Part-time, evening/weekend, online learning. Offers mass communication (MFA, MS); recording arts and technologies (MFA). Electronic applications accepted.

Jennings A. Jones College of Business *Program availability:* Part-time, evening/weekend, online learning. Offers accounting (M Acc); business (M Acc, MA, MBA, MBE, MS, PhD); business administration (MBA); business education (MBE); computer information systems (MS); economics (MA, PhD); management (MS). Electronic applications accepted.

University College *Program availability:* Part-time, evening/weekend, online learning. Offers advanced studies in teaching and learning (M Ed); human resources leadership (MPS); nursing administration (MSN); nursing education (MSN); strategic leadership (MPS); training and development (MPS).

MIDWAY UNIVERSITY, Midway, KY 40347-1120

General Information Independent-religious, coed, comprehensive institution. *Graduate housing:* On-campus housing not available.

GRADUATE UNITS

Graduate Programs Offers education (MAT); leadership (MBA).

MIDWEST COLLEGE OF ORIENTAL MEDICINE, Racine, WI 53403-9747

General Information Proprietary, coed, graduate-only institution. *Graduate housing:* On-campus housing not available. *Research affiliation:* Guangzhou University of Traditional Chinese Medicine (pharmacology).

GRADUATE UNITS

Graduate Programs *Program availability:* Part-time, evening/weekend. Offers acupuncture (Certificate); Oriental medicine (MSOM).

Graduate Programs-Chicago *Program availability:* Part-time, evening/weekend.

MIDWESTERN BAPTIST THEOLOGICAL SEMINARY, Kansas City, MO 64118-4697

General Information Independent-religious, coed, graduate-only institution. *Graduate housing:* Rooms and/or apartments guaranteed to single and married students.

GRADUATE UNITS

Graduate and Professional Programs *Program availability:* Part-time, online learning. Offers Christian education (MACE); Christian foundations (Graduate Certificate); church music (MCM); counseling (MA); ministry (D Ed Min, D Min); Old or New Testament studies (PhD); theology (M Div). Electronic applications accepted.

MIDWESTERN STATE UNIVERSITY, Wichita Falls, TX 76308

General Information State-supported, coed, comprehensive institution. CGS member. *Graduate housing:* Rooms and/or apartments available on a first-come, first-served basis to single and married students.

GRADUATE UNITS

Billie Doris McAda Graduate School *Program availability:* Part-time, evening/weekend. Electronic applications accepted.

College of Science and Mathematics *Program availability:* Part-time, evening/weekend. Offers biology (MS); computer science (MS); science and mathematics (MS). Electronic applications accepted.

Dillard College of Business Administration *Program availability:* Part-time, evening/weekend. Offers business administration (MBA). Electronic applications accepted.

Prothro-Yeager College of Humanities and Social Sciences *Program availability:* Part-time, evening/weekend. Offers clinical/counseling psychology (MA); English (MA); history (MA); humanities and social sciences (MA, PhD); philosophy (PhD); political science (MA). Electronic applications accepted.

Robert D. and Carol Gunn College of Health Sciences and Human Services *Program availability:* Part-time, evening/weekend. Offers criminal justice (MA); exercise physiology (MS); family nurse practitioner (MSN); family psychiatric mental health nurse practitioner (MSN); health information management (MHA); health sciences and human services (MA, MHA, MS, MSN, Graduate Certificate); health services administration (Graduate Certificate); medical practice management (MHA); nurse educator (MSN); public and community sector health care management (MHA); radiologic sciences (MS); rural and urban hospital management (MHA). Electronic applications accepted.

West College of Education *Program availability:* Part-time, evening/weekend. Offers counseling (MA); curriculum and instruction (M Ed); education (M Ed, MA);

educational leadership (M Ed); educational technology (M Ed); human resource development (MA); reading (M Ed); school counseling (M Ed); special education (M Ed); sport administration (M Ed); training and development (MA). Electronic applications accepted.

MIDWESTERN UNIVERSITY, DOWNERS GROVE CAMPUS, Downers Grove, IL 60515-1235

General Information Independent, coed, graduate-only institution. *Graduate housing:* Rooms and/or apartments available on a first-come, first-served basis to single and married students.

GRADUATE UNITS

Chicago College of Optometry Offers optometry (OD).

Chicago College of Osteopathic Medicine Offers osteopathic medicine (DO).

Chicago College of Pharmacy *Program availability:* Part-time, online learning. Offers pharmacy (Pharm D).

College of Dental Medicine-Illinois Offers dental medicine (DMD).

College of Graduate Studies Offers biomedical sciences (MA, MBS).

College of Health Sciences, Illinois Campus Offers clinical psychology (Psy D); health sciences (MA, MBS, MMS, MOT, MS, DPT, Psy D); occupational therapy (MOT); physical therapy (DPT); physician assistant studies (MMS); speech-language pathology (MS).

MIDWESTERN UNIVERSITY, GLENDALE CAMPUS, Glendale, AZ 85308

General Information Independent, coed, graduate-only institution. *Graduate housing:* Rooms and/or apartments available on a first-come, first-served basis to single and married students.

GRADUATE UNITS

Arizona College of Optometry Offers optometry (OD).

Arizona College of Osteopathic Medicine Offers osteopathic medicine (DO). Electronic applications accepted.

College of Dental Medicine Offers dental medicine (DMD).

College of Health Sciences, Arizona Campus *Program availability:* Part-time. Offers biomedical sciences (MA, MBS); cardiovascular science (MCVS); clinical psychology (Psy D); health sciences (MA, MBS, MCVS, MMS, MOT, MS, DPM, DPT, Psy D); nurse anesthesia (MS); occupational therapy (MOT); physical therapy (DPT); physician assistant studies (MMS); podiatric medicine (DPM); speech-language pathology (MS).

College of Pharmacy-Glendale Offers pharmacy (Pharm D).

College of Veterinary Medicine Offers veterinary medicine (DVM).

MIDWEST UNIVERSITY, Wentzville, MO 63385

General Information Independent-religious, coed, university. *Graduate housing:* Rooms and/or apartments available on a first-come, first-served basis to single and married students. Housing application deadline: 1/21.

GRADUATE UNITS

Graduate Programs *Program availability:* Part-time, online learning. Offers asset management/investment/real estate (MBA); Christian counseling (D Min); Christian education (D Min); counseling (MA); divinity (M Div); educational (MA); global business management (MBA); global leadership (MBA); leadership (PhD); mission studies (D Min); music (MM, DMA); pastoral theology (D Min); public policy/administration (MBA); teaching English to speakers of other languages (MA).

MIDWIVES COLLEGE OF UTAH, Salt Lake City, UT 84106

General Information Independent, women only, comprehensive institution. *Graduate housing:* On-campus housing not available.

GRADUATE UNITS

Graduate Program *Program availability:* Part-time. Offers midwifery (MS). Electronic applications accepted.

MILLENNIA ATLANTIC UNIVERSITY, Doral, FL 33178

General Information Proprietary, coed, comprehensive institution.

GRADUATE UNITS

Graduate Programs *Program availability:* Online learning.

MILLERSVILLE UNIVERSITY OF PENNSYLVANIA, Millersville, PA 17551-0302

General Information State-supported, coed, university. CGS member. *Enrollment:* 7,781 graduate, professional, and undergraduate students; 181 full-time matriculated graduate/professional students (131 women), 617 part-time matriculated graduate/professional students (451 women). *Enrollment by degree level:* 752 master's, 46 doctoral. *Graduate faculty:* 82 full-time (50 women), 50 part-time/adjunct (35 women). *International tuition:* $13,932 full-time. *Tuition, area resident:* Full-time $9288; part-time $516 per credit. *Tuition, state resident:* full-time $9288; part-time $516 per credit. *Tuition, nonresident:* full-time $13,932; part-time $774 per credit. *Required fees:* $2623.50; $145.75 per credit. Tuition and fees vary according to course load, degree level and program. *Graduate housing:* Room and/or apartments available on a first-come, first-served basis to single students; on-campus housing not available to married students. Typical cost: $8608 per year ($12,688 including board). Room and board charges vary according to board plan and housing facility selected. *Student services:* Campus employment opportunities, campus safety program, career counseling, exercise/wellness program, free psychological counseling, grant writing training, international student services, multicultural affairs office, services for students with disabilities, teacher training, writing training. *Library facilities:* The Francine G. McNairy Library and Learning Forum at Ganser Hall. *Collection:* Books: 316,579 (physical), 54,885 (digital/electronic); Serial titles: 4,191 (physical), 399,958 (digital/electronic); Databases: 179. Weekly public service hours: 94; students can reserve study rooms. *Research affiliation:* Chincoteague Bay Field Station for the Marine Science Consortium (Biology).

Computer facilities: 430 computers available on campus for general student use. A campuswide network can be accessed from student residence rooms and from off campus. Online class registration is available. Website: http://www.millersville.edu.

General Application Contact: Dr. James A. Delle, Acting Dean of College of Graduate Studies and Adult Learning/Associate Provost, Academic Administration, 717-871-7462, E-mail: james.delle@millersville.edu.

GRADUATE UNITS

College of Graduate Studies and Adult Learning Students: 181 full-time (131 women), 617 part-time (451 women); includes 121 minority (45 Black or African American, non-Hispanic/Latino; 2 American Indian or Alaska Native, non-Hispanic/Latino; 11 Asian, non-Hispanic/Latino; 52 Hispanic/Latino; 11 Two or more races, non-Hispanic/Latino), 6 international. Average age 32. 447 applicants, 87% accepted, 266 enrolled. *Faculty:* 82 full-time (50 women), 50 part-time/adjunct (35 women). Expenses: Contact institution. *Financial support:* In 2018–19, 102 students received support. Unspecified assistantships available. Financial award application deadline: 3/15; financial award applicants required to submit FAFSA. In 2018, 258 master's, 9 doctorates awarded. *Program availability:* Part-time, evening/weekend, 100% online, blended/hybrid learning. Doctor of Educational Leadership: Collaborative program with Shippensburg University; Doctor of Social Work: Collaborative program with Kutztown University; Master of Social Work: Collaborative program with Shippensburg University; Language and Culture Studies (French, German, & Spanish): Collaborative program with West Chester University. *Application fee:* $40. Electronic applications accepted. *Application Contact:* Chad E. Baker, Director of Graduate Admissions and Recruitment, 717-871-7644, E-mail: chad.baker@millersville.edu. *Acting Dean of College of Graduate Studies and Adult Learning/Associate Provost, Academic Administration,* Dr. James A. Delle, 717-871-7462, E-mail: James.Delle@millersville.edu.

College of Arts, Humanities and Social Sciences Students: 8 full-time (7 women), 52 part-time (31 women); includes 9 minority (2 Black or African American, non-Hispanic/Latino; 7 Hispanic/Latino), 1 international. Average age 34. 22 applicants, 100% accepted, 16 enrolled. *Faculty:* 18 full-time (13 women), 3 part-time/adjunct (2 women). Expenses: Contact institution. *Financial support:* In 2018–19, 9 students received support. Unspecified assistantships available. Financial award application deadline: 3/15; financial award applicants required to submit FAFSA. In 2018, 17 master's awarded. *Program availability:* Part-time. Offers art education (M Ed); English (M Ed, MA); english (MA); history (MA); language and cultures (MA); languages and cultures (MA); writing (Postbaccalaureate Certificate). Language and Culture Studies (French, German, Spanish): Collaborative program with West Chester University. *Application deadline:* Applications are processed on a rolling basis. *Application fee:* $40. Electronic applications accepted. *Application Contact:* Dr. James A. Delle, Acting Dean of College of Graduate Studies and Adult Learning/Associate Provost, Academic Administration, 717-871-7462, E-mail: James.Delle@millersville.edu. *Interim Dean,* Dr. Orlando J. Perez, 717-871-5631, Fax: 717-871-7947, E-mail: orlando.perez@millersville.edu.

College of Education and Human Services Students: 147 full-time (115 women), 390 part-time (311 women); includes 81 minority (33 Black or African American, non-Hispanic/Latino; 1 American Indian or Alaska Native, non-Hispanic/Latino; 6 Asian, non-Hispanic/Latino; 34 Hispanic/Latino; 7 Two or more races, non-Hispanic/Latino), 2 international. Average age 31. 304 applicants, 88% accepted, 179 enrolled. *Faculty:* 44 full-time (31 women), 30 part-time/adjunct (20 women). Expenses: Contact institution. *Financial support:* In 2018–19, 78 students received support. Unspecified assistantships available. Financial award application deadline: 3/15; financial award applicants required to submit FAFSA. In 2018, 170 master's, 9 doctorates awarded. *Program availability:* Part-time, evening/weekend, 100% online, blended/hybrid learning. The DSW coursework is 100% online and students attend weekend residency at start of each semester. Offers assessment, curriculum and teaching - online teaching (M Ed); assessment, curriculum and teaching - stem education (M Ed); assessment, curriculum, and teaching (M Ed); coaching education (Post-Master's Certificate); early childhood education (M Ed); educational leadership (Ed D); gifted education (M Ed); language and literacy (M Ed); language and literacy education (M Ed); leadership for teaching and learning (M Ed); psychology (MS); school counseling (M Ed); social work (MSW, DSW); special education (M Ed); special education: 7-12 (M Ed); special education: PreK-8 (M Ed); sport management (M Ed); sport management: athletic coaching (Post-Master's Certificate). Doctor of Educational Leadership: Collaborative program with Shippensburg University; Doctor of Social Work: Collaborative program with Kutztown University; Master of Social Work: Collaborative program with Shippensburg University. *Application fee:* $40. Electronic applications accepted. *Application Contact:* Dr. James A. Delle, Acting Dean of College of Graduate Studies and Adult Learning/Associate Provost, Academic Administration, 717-871-7462, E-mail: James.Delle@millersville.edu. *Dean,* Dr. George Drake, 717-871-7333, E-mail: george.drake@millersville.edu.

College of Science and Technology Students: 26 full-time (9 women), 175 part-time (109 women); includes 31 minority (10 Black or African American, non-Hispanic/Latino; 1 American Indian or Alaska Native, non-Hispanic/Latino; 5 Asian, non-Hispanic/Latino; 11 Hispanic/Latino; 4 Two or more races, non-Hispanic/Latino), 3 international. Average age 36. 121 applicants, 82% accepted, 71 enrolled. *Faculty:* 20 full-time (6 women), 17 part-time/adjunct (13 women). Expenses: Contact institution. *Financial support:* In 2018–19, 15 students received support. Unspecified assistantships available. Financial award application deadline: 3/15; financial award applicants required to submit FAFSA. In 2018, 62 master's awarded. *Program availability:* Part-time, 100% online. Offers emergency management (MS); family nurse practitioner (MSN, Post-Master's Certificate); integrated scientific applications (MS); mathematics (M Ed); nursing education (MSN, Post-Master's Certificate); nursing practice (DNP); technology and innovation (M Ed, MS). *Application deadline:* Applications are processed on a rolling basis. *Application fee:* $40. Electronic applications accepted. *Application Contact:* Dr. James A. Delle, Acting Dean of Graduate Studies and Adult Learning/Associate Provost, Academic Administration, 717-871-7462, E-mail: James.Delle@millersville.edu. *Dean, College of Science and Technology,* Dr. Michael Jackson, 717-871-4292, E-mail: michael.jackson@millersville.edu.

MILLIGAN COLLEGE, Milligan College, TN 37682

General Information Independent-religious, coed, comprehensive institution. *Enrollment:* 1,225 graduate, professional, and undergraduate students; 311 full-time matriculated graduate/professional students (194 women), 79 part-time matriculated graduate/professional students (36 women). *Enrollment by degree level:* 360 master's, 28 doctoral, 2 other advanced degrees. *Graduate faculty:* 40 full-time (17 women), 34 part-time/adjunct (16 women). *Graduate housing:* Rooms and/or apartments available on a first-come, first-served basis to single and married students. Typical cost: $600 per year for single students; $450 per year for married students. Room charges vary according to housing facility selected. Housing application deadline: 4/1. *Student services:* Campus employment opportunities, campus safety program, career counseling, exercise/wellness program, free psychological counseling, international student services, multicultural affairs office, services for students with disabilities, teacher training, writing training. *Library facilities:* P. H. Welshimer Memorial Library plus 1 other. *Collection:* Books: 173,242 (physical), 281,617 (digital/electronic); Serial titles: 932 (physical), 44,498 (digital/electronic); Databases: 95. Weekly public service hours: 89; students can reserve study rooms.

Computer facilities: 102 computers available on campus for general student use. A campuswide network can be accessed from student residence rooms and from off campus. Online class registration is available.
Website: http://www.milligan.edu/

General Application Contact: Pam Smith, Operations Assistant, 423-461-8482, Fax: 423-461-8789, E-mail: pbsmith@milligan.edu.

GRADUATE UNITS

Area of Business Administration Students: 50 full-time (17 women), 1 part-time (0 women); includes 3 minority (1 Black or African American, non-Hispanic/Latino; 1 Asian, non-Hispanic/Latino; 1 Two or more races, non-Hispanic/Latino), 2 international. Average age 36. 42 applicants, 93% accepted, 35 enrolled. *Faculty:* 3 full-time (0 women), 5 part-time/adjunct (1 woman). Expenses: Contact institution. *Financial support:* Scholarships/grants available. Financial award application deadline: 12/1; financial award applicants required to submit FAFSA. In 2018, 29 master's awarded. *Program availability:* Blended/hybrid learning. Offers health sector management (MBA, Graduate Certificate); leadership (MBA, Graduate Certificate); operations management (MBA, Graduate Certificate). *Application deadline:* For fall admission, 8/1 for domestic students, 6/1 for international students; for spring admission, 1/15 for domestic students, 12/1 for international students. Applications are processed on a rolling basis. *Application fee:* $30. Electronic applications accepted. *Application Contact:* Rebecca Banton, Graduate Admissions Recruiter, Business Area, 423-461-8662, Fax: 423-461-8789, E-mail: rbbanton@milligan.edu. *Area Chair of Business,* Dr. David Campbell, 423-461-8674, Fax: 423-461-8677, E-mail: dacampbell@milligan.edu.

Area of Computer Science

Area of Counselor Education Programs Students: 21 full-time (15 women), 3 part-time (all women); includes 2 minority (1 Black or African American, non-Hispanic/Latino; 1 Two or more races, non-Hispanic/Latino). Average age 31. 24 applicants, 88% accepted, 13 enrolled. *Faculty:* 3 full-time (all women), 2 part-time/adjunct (1 woman). Expenses: Contact institution. *Financial support:* Scholarships/grants available. Financial award application deadline: 12/1; financial award applicants required to submit FAFSA. In 2018, 15 master's awarded. *Program availability:* Part-time. Offers clinical mental health counseling (MSC); counseling ministry (Graduate Certificate); school counseling (MSC). *Application deadline:* For fall admission, 8/1 for domestic students, 6/1 for international students. Applications are processed on a rolling basis. *Application fee:* $30. Electronic applications accepted. *Application Contact:* Stacy Shankle, Graduate Admissions Recruiter, Healthcare Programs, 423-461-8424, Fax: 423-461-8789, E-mail: srshankle@milligan.edu. *Director of Master of Science in Counseling Program,* Dr. Rebecca Sapp, 423-461-3071, E-mail: rlsapp@milligan.edu.

Area of Education Students: 38 full-time (31 women), 8 part-time (4 women); includes 2 minority (1 Hispanic/Latino; 1 Two or more races, non-Hispanic/Latino), 1 international. Average age 35. 36 applicants, 97% accepted, 32 enrolled. *Faculty:* 5 full-time (3 women), 6 part-time/adjunct (3 women). Expenses: Contact institution. *Financial support:* Scholarships/grants available. Financial award application deadline: 12/1; financial award applicants required to submit FAFSA. In 2018, 18 master's awarded. *Program availability:* Part-time, 100% online, blended/hybrid learning. Offers combined preK-3/K-5 education (M Ed); educational leadership (Ed D); educational specialist (Ed S); K-5 education (M Ed); middle grades education (M Ed); preK-3 education (M Ed); preK-3 special education (M Ed); secondary education (M Ed). *Application deadline:* For fall admission, 8/1 priority date for domestic students, 6/1 for international students; for spring admission, 11/15 priority date for domestic students, 12/1 for international students; for summer admission, 4/1 for domestic students. Applications are processed on a rolling basis. *Application fee:* $30. Electronic applications accepted. *Application Contact:* Melissa Dillow, Graduate Admissions Recruiter, Education, 423-461-8306, Fax: 423-461-8982, E-mail: msdillow@milligan.edu. *Area Chair of Education,* Dr. Angela Hilton-Prillhart, 423-461-8769, Fax: 423-461-3103, E-mail: anhilton-prillhart@milligan.edu.

Area of Humane Learning

Area of Physician Assistant Studies Students: 24 full-time (13 women); includes 3 minority (1 Black or African American, non-Hispanic/Latino; 1 Asian, non-Hispanic/Latino; 1 Two or more races, non-Hispanic/Latino). Average age 30. 280 applicants, 15% accepted, 23 enrolled. *Faculty:* 3 full-time (2 women), 4 part-time/adjunct (2 women). Expenses: Contact institution. *Financial support:* Scholarships/grants available. Financial award application deadline: 12/1; financial award applicants required to submit FAFSA. Offers physician assistant studies (MSPAS). *Application deadline:* For spring admission, 9/1 for domestic students. *Application fee:* $120. Electronic applications accepted. *Application Contact:* Rebekah Bess, Program Secretary, 423-461-1557, Fax: 423-461-1518, E-mail: rbess@milligan.edu. *Area Chair and Director,* Andrew Hull, 423-461-1558, Fax: 423-461-1518, E-mail: awhull@milligan.edu.

Emmanuel Christian Seminary at Milligan College Students: 70 full-time (29 women), 67 part-time (29 women); includes 15 minority (7 Black or African American, non-Hispanic/Latino; 1 American Indian or Alaska Native, non-Hispanic/Latino; 1 Asian, non-Hispanic/Latino; 5 Hispanic/Latino; 1 Two or more races, non-Hispanic/Latino), 9 international. Average age 37. 61 applicants, 98% accepted, 49 enrolled. *Faculty:* 12 full-time (1 woman), 10 part-time/adjunct (1 woman). Expenses: Contact institution. *Financial support:* Scholarships/grants and unspecified assistantships available. Financial award application deadline: 12/1; financial award applicants required to submit FAFSA. In 2018, 13 master's, 2 doctorates awarded. *Program availability:* Part-time, blended/hybrid learning. Offers Christian care and counseling (M Div); Christian education (M Div); Christian ministries (MACM, Graduate Certificate); Christian ministry (M Div); Christian theology (M Div, MAR); church history (MAR); church history/historical theology (M Div); general studies (M Div); ministry (D Min); New Testament (M Div, MAR); Old Testament (M Div, MAR); urban ministry (M Div); world missions (M Div). *Application deadline:* For fall admission, 8/1 for domestic students, 6/1 for international students; for spring admission, 12/15 for domestic students, 8/1 for international students. Applications are processed on a rolling basis. *Application fee:* $30 ($0 for international students). Electronic applications accepted. *Application Contact:* Lauren Gullett, Director of Admissions and Recruitment for Emmanuel Christian Seminary, 423-461-1535, Fax: 423-926-6198, E-mail: lwgullett@milligan.edu. *Academic Dean, Emmanuel Christian Seminary,* Dr. Rollin Ramsaran, 423-461-1524, Fax: 423-926-6198, E-mail: raramsaran@milligan.edu.

Program in Occupational Therapy Students: 96 full-time (84 women); includes 5 minority (3 Hispanic/Latino; 2 Two or more races, non-Hispanic/Latino). Average age 25. 231 applicants, 33% accepted, 32 enrolled. *Faculty:* 6 full-time (4 women), 10 part-time/adjunct (9 women). Expenses: Contact institution. *Financial support:* Career-related internships or fieldwork and institutionally sponsored loans available. Financial award application deadline: 4/15; financial award applicants required to submit FAFSA. In 2018, 28 master's awarded. Offers occupational therapy (MSOT). *Application deadline:* For spring admission, 11/15 for domestic and international students. Application fee: $120. Electronic applications accepted. *Application Contact:* Kristia Brown, Office Manager and Admissions Representative, 423-975-8010, Fax: 423-975-8019, E-mail: lkbrown@milligan.edu. *Program Director and Area Chair of Occupational Therapy;,* Dr. Christy Isbell, 423-461-1548, Fax: 423-975-8019, E-mail: cisbell@milligan.edu.

MILLIKIN UNIVERSITY, Decatur, IL 62522-2084

General Information Independent-religious, coed, comprehensive institution. *Enrollment:* 2,068 graduate, professional, and undergraduate students; 82 full-time matriculated graduate/professional students (49 women), 25 part-time matriculated graduate/professional students (17 women). *Enrollment by degree level:* 67 master's, 40 doctoral. *Graduate faculty:* 24 full-time (18 women), 12 part-time/adjunct (4 women). Tuition and fees vary according to course load, degree level and program. *Student services:* Campus employment opportunities, career counseling, exercise/wellness program, grant writing training, international student services, multicultural affairs office, services for students with disabilities, writing training. *Library facilities:* Staley Library. *Collection:* Books: 122,725 (physical), 23,745 (digital/electronic); Serial titles: 543 (physical), 49 (digital/electronic); Databases: 49. Weekly public service hours: 113; students can reserve study rooms.

Computer facilities: 135 computers available on campus for general student use. A campuswide network can be accessed from student residence rooms. Online class registration, online degree audit, online financials (view and pay bills, financial aid) are available.
Website: http://www.millikin.edu/

General Application Contact: Marianne Taylor, Director of Graduate Admission, 217-420-6771, Fax: 217-425-4669, E-mail: mgtaylor@millikin.edu.

GRADUATE UNITS

School of Nursing Students: 49 full-time (35 women), 21 part-time (16 women); includes 14 minority (7 Black or African American, non-Hispanic/Latino; 4 Asian, non-Hispanic/Latino; 3 Hispanic/Latino). Average age 30. 135 applicants, 38% accepted, 28 enrolled. *Faculty:* 18 full-time (16 women), 1 part-time/adjunct (3 women). Expenses: Contact institution. *Financial support:* In 2018–19, 1 student received support. Traineeships and unspecified assistantships available. Financial award applicants required to submit FAFSA. In 2018, 4 master's, 11 doctorates awarded. *Program availability:* Part-time. Offers completion program (DNP); entry into nursing practice (MSN). *Application deadline:* For spring admission, 7/1 priority date for domestic and international students; for summer admission, 11/1 priority date for domestic and international students. Applications are processed on a rolling basis. *Application fee:* $0. Electronic applications accepted. *Application Contact:* Marianne Taylor, Director, Graduate Admission, 217-420-6771, Fax: 217-425-4669, E-mail: mgtaylor@millikin.edu. *Interim Director,* Dr. Elizabeth Gephart, 217-424-6397, Fax: 217-420-6731, E-mail: egephart@millikin.edu.

Tabor School of Business Students: 33 full-time (14 women), 4 part-time (1 woman); includes 10 minority (7 Black or African American, non-Hispanic/Latino; 1 Hispanic/Latino; 2 Two or more races, non-Hispanic/Latino), 1 international. Average age 29. 69 applicants, 65% accepted, 32 enrolled. *Faculty:* 6 full-time (2 women), 7 part-time/adjunct (1 woman). Expenses: Contact institution. *Financial support:* In 2018–19, 19 students received support, including 1 research assistantship with partial tuition reimbursement available (averaging $6,000 per year), 3 teaching assistantships with partial tuition reimbursements available (averaging $6,000 per year); tuition waivers (full) also available. Financial award applicants required to submit FAFSA. In 2018, 25 master's awarded. *Program availability:* Evening/weekend. Offers business (MBA). *Application deadline:* For fall admission, 6/1 priority date for domestic students, 5/1 priority date for international students; for spring admission, 11/1 priority date for domestic students, 8/1 priority date for international students. Applications are processed on a rolling basis. *Application fee:* $0. Electronic applications accepted. *Application Contact:* Marianne Taylor, Director, Graduate Admission, 217-420-6771, Fax: 217-424-6286, E-mail: mgtaylor@millikin.edu. *Dean,* Dr. Najiba Benabess, 217-420-6762, E-mail: nbenabess@millikin.edu.

MILLSAPS COLLEGE, Jackson, MS 39210

General Information Independent-religious, coed, comprehensive institution. *Graduate housing:* Room and/or apartments available to single students; on-campus housing not available to married students. Housing application deadline: 6/1. *Research affiliation:* Downtown Jackson Partners Group (real estate development), Oxbow Ventures (commercialization of renewable energy), Midtown Partners (economic development).

GRADUATE UNITS

Else School of Management *Program availability:* Part-time. Offers accounting (M Acc); business administration (MBA). Electronic applications accepted.

MILLS COLLEGE, Oakland, CA 94613-1000

General Information Independent, Undergraduate: women only; graduate: coed, comprehensive institution. *Graduate housing:* Rooms and/or apartments available on a first-come, first-served basis to single and married students. Housing application deadline: 6/15.

GRADUATE UNITS

Graduate Studies *Program availability:* Part-time, evening/weekend. Offers art (MFA); book art and creative writing (MFA); ceramics (MFA); composition (MA); computer science (Certificate); dance (MA, MFA); electronic music and recording media (MFA); infant mental health (MA); interdisciplinary computer science (MA); intermedia (MFA); literature (MA); music performance and literature (MFA); painting (MFA); photography (MFA); poetry (MFA); pre-medical studies (Certificate); prose (MFA); public policy (MPP); sculpture (MFA); Spanish creative writing (Certificate); translation (MFA). Electronic applications accepted.

Lorry I. Lokey Graduate School of Business *Program availability:* Part-time. Offers applied economics (MA); management (MBA, MM).

School of Education *Program availability:* Part-time, evening/weekend. Offers education (MA, Ed D, Certificate). Electronic applications accepted.

MILWAUKEE SCHOOL OF ENGINEERING, Milwaukee, WI 53202-3109

General Information Independent, coed, primarily men, comprehensive institution. *Graduate housing:* Rooms and/or apartments available on a first-come, first-served basis to single and married students. Housing application deadline: 7/1. *Research affiliation:* Keen Foundation (entrepreneurship and engineering education), National Fluid Power Association (hydraulics and pneumatics), 3dMD (biomolecular modeling), National Additive Manufacturing Innovation Institute (rapid prototyping), Caterpillar, Inc. (electrohydraulics), Clinical Translational Science Institute (medical and healthcare innovation and transfer).

GRADUATE UNITS

MBA in STEM Leadership Program *Program availability:* Part-time, evening/weekend. Offers STEM leadership (MBA). Electronic applications accepted.

MBA Program in Education Leadership *Program availability:* Part-time, evening/weekend. Offers education leadership (MBA). Electronic applications accepted.

MS Program in Architectural Engineering *Program availability:* Part-time, evening/weekend. Offers architectural engineering (MS). Electronic applications accepted.

MS Program in Civil Engineering *Program availability:* Part-time, evening/weekend. Offers civil engineering (MS). Electronic applications accepted.

MS Program in Engineering *Program availability:* Part-time, evening/weekend. Offers engineering (MS). Electronic applications accepted.

MS Program in Engineering Management *Program availability:* Part-time, evening/weekend. Offers engineering management (MS). Electronic applications accepted.

MS Program in Marketing and Export Management *Program availability:* Part-time, evening/weekend. Offers marketing and export management (MS). Electronic applications accepted.

MS Program in New Product Management *Program availability:* Part-time, evening/weekend. Offers new product management (MS). Electronic applications accepted.

MS Program in Nursing - Leadership and Management *Program availability:* Part-time, evening/weekend, 100% online, blended/hybrid learning. Offers nursing - leadership and management (MSN). Electronic applications accepted.

MS Program in Perfusion Offers perfusion (MS). Electronic applications accepted.

Program in Business Administration *Program availability:* Part-time, evening/weekend, 100% online, blended/hybrid learning. Offers business administration (MBA). Electronic applications accepted.

MINNEAPOLIS COLLEGE OF ART AND DESIGN, Minneapolis, MN 55404-4347

General Information Independent, coed, comprehensive institution. *Graduate housing:* On-campus housing not available.

GRADUATE UNITS

Certificate Programs *Program availability:* Part-time, 100% online, blended/hybrid learning. Offers graphic design (Certificate); media (Certificate); sustainable design (Certificate). Electronic applications accepted.

Program in Graphic and Web Design Offers graphic and Web design (MA).

Program in Sustainable Design Offers sustainable design (MA).

Program in Visual Studies *Program availability:* Part-time. Offers animation (MFA); comic art (MFA); drawing (MFA); filmmaking (MFA); fine arts (MFA); furniture design (MFA); graphic design (MFA); illustration (MFA); interactive media (MFA); painting (MFA); photography (MFA); printmaking (MFA); sculpture (MFA). Electronic applications accepted.

MINNESOTA STATE UNIVERSITY MANKATO, Mankato, MN 56001

General Information State-supported, coed, university. CGS member. *Graduate housing:* Room and/or apartments available on a first-come, first-served basis to single students; on-campus housing not available to married students.

GRADUATE UNITS

College of Graduate Studies and Research *Program availability:* Part-time, online learning. Offers cross-disciplinary studies (MS). Electronic applications accepted.

College of Allied Health and Nursing *Program availability:* Part-time. Offers allied health and nursing (MA, MS, MSN, DNP, Postbaccalaureate Certificate); communication disorders (MS); community health education (MS); family nurse practitioner (MSN); nurse educator (MSN); nursing (DNP); physical education (MA, MS); public health education (Postbaccalaureate Certificate); rehabilitation counseling (MS); school health education (MS, Postbaccalaureate Certificate). Electronic applications accepted.

College of Arts and Humanities *Program availability:* Part-time, evening/weekend. Offers art (MA); art education (MAT); arts and humanities (MA, MAT, MFA, MM, MS, Certificate); choral conducting (MM); communication and composition (MA); communication education (Certificate); communication studies (MA, MS); creative writing (MFA); English studies (MA); forensics (MFA); French (MS); French education (MS); music education (MAT); piano performance (MM); professional communication (Certificate); Spanish (MS); Spanish education (MS); Spanish for the professions (MS); teaching English as a second language (MA, Certificate); technical communication (MA, Certificate); theatre arts (MA, MFA); wind band conducting (MM).

College of Business Offers accounting (MSA); business (MBA). Electronic applications accepted.

College of Education *Program availability:* Part-time, evening/weekend. Offers college student affairs (MS); counselor education and supervision (Ed D); education (MAT, MS, Ed D, Certificate); educational leadership (MS, Ed D); emotional and behavioral disorders (MS, Certificate); experiential education (MS); learning disabilities (MS, Certificate); mental health counseling (MS); professional school counseling (K-12) (MS). Electronic applications accepted.

College of Science, Engineering and Technology *Program availability:* Part-time. Offers applied statistics (MS); biology (MS); biology education (MS); environmental sciences (MS); information technology (MS); manufacturing engineering technology (MS); mathematics (MA, MS); mathematics education (MS); physics (MS); physics education (MS); science, engineering and technology (MA, MAT, MS, Certificate); statistics (MS). Electronic applications accepted.

College of Social and Behavioral Sciences *Program availability:* Part-time. Offers aging studies (MS); applied anthropology (MS); clinical psychology (MA); ethnic studies (MS); gender and women's studies (MS); geography (MS); history (MA, MS); industrial/organizational psychology (MA); local government management (Certificate); non-profit leadership (Certificate); public administration (MPA); school psychology (Psy D); social and behavioral sciences (MA, MAT, MPA, MS, MSW, Psy D, Certificate); social studies (MAT); social work (MSW); sociology (MA); sociology: college teaching (MA); sociology: corrections (MS); sociology: human services planning and administration (MS); urban and regional studies (MA); urban planning (MA, Certificate). Electronic applications accepted.

MINNESOTA STATE UNIVERSITY MOORHEAD, Moorhead, MN 56563

General Information State-supported, coed, comprehensive institution. CGS member. *Enrollment:* 5,860 graduate, professional, and undergraduate students; 176 full-time matriculated graduate/professional students (135 women), 585 part-time matriculated graduate/professional students (422 women). *Enrollment by degree level:* 629 master's, 38 doctoral, 96 other advanced degrees. Tuition and fees vary according to course load, degree level, program and reciprocity agreements. *Graduate housing:* Room and/or apartments available on a first-come, first-served basis to single students; on-campus housing not available to married students. Typical cost: $6312 per year ($9560 including board). Room and board charges vary according to board plan and housing facility selected. Housing application deadline: 3/1. *Student services:* Campus employment opportunities, campus safety program, career counseling, child daycare facilities, exercise/wellness program, free psychological counseling, grant writing training, international student services, low-cost health insurance, multicultural affairs office, services for students with disabilities, teacher training. *Library facilities:* Livingston Lord Library plus 1 other. *Collection:* Books: 326,187 (physical), 20,401 (digital/electronic); Serial titles: 1,634 (physical), 18,041 (digital/electronic); Databases: 84. Weekly public service hours: 79.

Computer facilities: Computer purchase and lease plans are available. 1,500 computers available on campus for general student use. A campuswide network can be accessed from student residence rooms and from off campus. Online class registration is available.

Website: http://www.mnstate.edu/

General Application Contact: Karla Wenger, Office Manager, 218-477-2344, Fax: 218-477-2344, E-mail: wengerk@mnstate.edu.

GRADUATE UNITS

Graduate and Extended Learning Students: 176 full-time (135 women), 585 part-time (422 women); includes 47 minority (14 Black or African American, non-Hispanic/Latino; 5 American Indian or Alaska Native, non-Hispanic/Latino; 10 Asian, non-Hispanic/Latino; 7 Hispanic/Latino; 11 Two or more races, non-Hispanic/Latino), 10 international. Average age 32. 298 applicants, 64% accepted. *Faculty:* 78. Expenses: Contact institution. *Financial support:* Federal Work-Study and unspecified assistantships available. Financial award application deadline: 10/1; financial award applicants required to submit FAFSA. In 2018, 263 master's, 29 other advanced degrees awarded. *Program availability:* Part-time, evening/weekend, 100% online, blended/hybrid learning. *Application deadline:* Applications are processed on a rolling basis. *Application fee:* $35. Electronic applications accepted. *Application Contact:* Karla Wenger, Office Manager, 218-236-2344, Fax: 218-236-2482, E-mail: wengerk@mnstate.edu. *Interim Dean of Graduate and Extended Learning*, Dr. Lisa Karch, 218-477-2699, Fax: 218-236-2482, E-mail: lisa.karch@mnstate.edu.

College of Business and Innovation Students: 19 full-time (8 women), 32 part-time (15 women); includes 1 minority (Asian, non-Hispanic/Latino), 8 international. Average age 28. 39 applicants, 44% accepted. *Faculty:* 13. Expenses: Contact institution. *Financial support:* Federal Work-Study and unspecified assistantships available. Financial award application deadline: 10/1; financial award applicants required to submit FAFSA. In 2018, 26 master's awarded. *Program availability:* Part-time, evening/weekend, 100% online, blended/hybrid learning. Offers accounting and finance (MS); business administration (MBA). *Application deadline:* For fall admission, 4/15 for domestic students; for spring admission, 11/15 for domestic students; for summer admission, 4/15 for domestic students. Applications are processed on a rolling basis. *Application fee:* $35. Electronic applications accepted. *Application Contact:* Karla Wenger, Office Manager, 218-477-2344, E-mail: wengerk@mnstate.edu. *Interim Dean*, Joshua Behl, 218-477-2667, E-mail: joshua.behl@mnstate.edu.

College of Education and Human Services Students: 129 full-time (105 women), 425 part-time (300 women); includes 32 minority (8 Black or African American, non-Hispanic/Latino; 4 American Indian or Alaska Native, non-Hispanic/Latino; 6 Asian, non-Hispanic/Latino; 7 Hispanic/Latino; 7 Two or more races, non-Hispanic/Latino), 1 international. Average age 33. 154 applicants, 77% accepted. Expenses: Contact institution. *Financial support:* Federal Work-Study and unspecified assistantships available. Financial award application deadline: 10/1; financial award applicants required to submit FAFSA. In 2018, 198 master's, 29 other advanced degrees awarded. *Program availability:* Part-time, evening/weekend, 100% online, blended/hybrid learning. Offers counseling and student affairs (MS); educational leadership (MS, Ed D, Ed S). *Application deadline:* For fall admission, 7/1 priority date for domestic students; for spring admission, 11/15 priority date for domestic students. Applications are processed on a rolling basis. *Application fee:* $35. Electronic applications accepted. *Application Contact:* Karla Wenger, Office Manager, 218-477-2344, Fax: 218-477-2482, E-mail: wengerk@mnstate.edu. *Dean*, Dr. Ok-Hee Lee, 218-477-2095, E-mail: okheelee@mnstate.edu.

College of Humanities and Social Sciences Students: 10 part-time (9 women). Average age 35. 3 applicants, 33% accepted. Expenses: Contact institution. *Financial support:* Federal Work-Study and unspecified assistantships available. Financial award application deadline: 10/1; financial award applicants required to submit FAFSA. In 2018, 7 master's awarded. *Program availability:* Part-time, evening/weekend. Offers teaching English as a second language (MA). *Application deadline:* For fall admission, 4/15 for domestic students; for spring admission, 11/15 for domestic students; for summer admission, 4/15 for domestic students. Applications are processed on a rolling basis. *Application fee:* $35. Electronic applications accepted. *Application Contact:* Karla Wenger, Office Manager, 218-477-2344, Fax: 218-477-2482, E-mail: wengerk@mnstate.edu. *Interim Dean*, Dr. Annette Morrow, 218-477-2813, E-mail: morrowan@mnstate.edu.

College of Science, Health and the Environment Students: 28 full-time (22 women), 119 part-time (98 women). Average age 32. 102 applicants, 53% accepted. Expenses: Contact institution. *Financial support:* Federal Work-Study and unspecified assistantships available. Financial award application deadline: 10/1; financial award applicants required to submit FAFSA. In 2018, 40 master's, 11 other advanced degrees awarded. *Program availability:* Part-time, evening/weekend, 100% online, blended/hybrid learning. Offers healthcare administration (MHA); nursing (MS); school psychology (MS, Psy S). *Application deadline:* Applications are processed on a rolling basis. *Application fee:* $35. Electronic applications accepted. *Application Contact:* Karla Wenger, Office Manager, 218-477-2344, Fax: 218-477-2482, E-mail: wengerk@mnstate.edu. *Interim Dean*, Dr. Elizabeth Nawrot, 218-477-5892, E-mail: nawrot@mnstate.edu.

MINOT STATE UNIVERSITY, Minot, ND 58707-0002

General Information State-supported, coed, comprehensive institution. *Graduate housing:* Rooms and/or apartments available on a first-come, first-served basis to single and married students. Housing application deadline: 6/30. *Research affiliation:* Rural Crime and Justice Center (criminal justice research), North Dakota Center for Persons with Disabilities (NDCPD).

GRADUATE UNITS

Graduate School *Program availability:* Part-time, 100% online, blended/hybrid learning. Offers deaf/hard of hearing education (MS); elementary education (M Ed); information systems (MSIS); management (MSM); mathematics (MAT); school psychology (Ed Sp); science (MAT); specific learning disabilities (MS); speech-language pathology (MS). Electronic applications accepted.

MIRRER YESHIVA CENTRAL INSTITUTE, Brooklyn, NY 11223-2010

General Information Independent-religious, men only, comprehensive institution.

GRADUATE UNITS
Graduate Programs

MISERICORDIA UNIVERSITY, Dallas, PA 18612-1098

General Information Independent-religious, coed, comprehensive institution. *Graduate housing:* On-campus housing not available.

GRADUATE UNITS

College of Business *Program availability:* Part-time, evening/weekend. Offers accounting (MBA); business (MBA, MS); healthcare management (MBA, MS); human resource management (MBA, MS); management (MBA, MS); sport management (MBA). Electronic applications accepted.

College of Health Sciences and Education *Program availability:* Part-time, evening/weekend. Offers health sciences and education (MS, MSN, MSOT, MSSLP, DNP, DPT, OTD); instructional technology (MS); nursing (MSN, DNP); occupational therapy (MSOT, OTD); physical therapy (DPT); reading specialist (MS); special education (MS); speech-language pathology (MSSLP). Electronic applications accepted.

MISSIO SEMINARY, Hatfield, PA 19440-2499

General Information Independent-religious, coed, graduate-only institution. *Enrollment by degree level:* 172 master's, 22 doctoral, 10 other advanced degrees. *Graduate faculty:* 9 full-time (1 woman), 20 part-time/adjunct (5 women). *Tuition:* Full-time $14,420. *Required fees:* $100; $100 per credit. *Graduate housing:* On-campus housing not available. *Student services:* Campus employment opportunities, career counseling, international student services. *Library facilities:* Missio Seminary Library plus 1 other. *Collection:* Books: 30,304 (physical), 140,000 (digital/electronic); Serial titles: 13,572 (physical), 220 (digital/electronic); Databases: 10. Weekly public service hours: 36.

Computer facilities: 15 computers available on campus for general student use. Website: http://www.missio.edu/

General Application Contact: Rev. Michael Heath, Admissions Counselor and Recruiter, 215-368-5000 Ext. 152, Fax: 215-368-7002, E-mail: mheath@missio.edu.

GRADUATE UNITS

Graduate and Professional Programs Students: 117 full-time (33 women), 87 part-time (32 women); includes 69 minority (43 Black or African American, non-Hispanic/Latino; 23 Asian, non-Hispanic/Latino; 2 Hispanic/Latino; 1 Two or more races, non-Hispanic/Latino), 74 international. Average age 39. 83 applicants, 64% accepted, 49 enrolled. *Faculty:* 9 full-time (1 woman), 20 part-time/adjunct (5 women). Expenses: Contact institution. *Financial support:* In 2018–19, 155 students received support. Career-related internships or fieldwork, institutionally sponsored loans, and scholarships/grants available. Support available to part-time students. Financial award application deadline: 8/30; financial award applicants required to submit FAFSA. In 2018, 50 master's, 10 doctorates awarded. *Program availability:* Part-time, evening/weekend. Offers advanced missional leadership (D Min); advanced pastoral studies (Certificate); biblical counseling (Certificate); biblical studies (MA, Certificate); counseling (MA); ministry (M Div, MA); missional theology (MA). *Application deadline:* Applications are processed on a rolling basis. *Application fee:* $30. Electronic applications accepted. *Application Contact:* Rev. Michael Heath, Student Advancement Counselor, 215-368-5000 Ext. 152, Fax: 215-368-7002, E-mail: mheath@missio.edu. *Dean of the Faculty,* Dr. Dave Lamb, 215-368-5000 Ext. 135, E-mail: dlamb@missio.edu.

MISSISSIPPI COLLEGE, Clinton, MS 39058

General Information Independent-religious, coed, comprehensive institution. *Graduate housing:* Room and/or apartments available on a first-come, first-served basis to single students; on-campus housing not available to married students. Housing application deadline: 8/15. *Research affiliation:* Gulf Coast Research Laboratory (marine biology).

GRADUATE UNITS

Graduate School *Program availability:* Part-time, evening/weekend, online learning. Offers health services administration (MHSA); liberal studies (MLS). Electronic applications accepted.

College of Arts and Sciences *Program availability:* Part-time, evening/weekend. Offers administration of justice (MSS); applied communication (MSC); applied music performance (MM); art (M Ed, MA, MFA); arts and sciences (M Ed, MA, MCS, MFA, MM, MS, MSC, MSS, Certificate); biological science (M Ed); biology (MCS); biology-biological sciences (MS); biology-medical sciences (MS); chemistry and biochemistry (MCS, MS); Christian studies and the arts (M Ed, MA, MFA, MM, MSC); computer science (M Ed, MS); conducting (MM); cybersecurity and information assurance (MS); English (M Ed, MA); history (M Ed, MA, MSS); humanities and social sciences (M Ed, MA, MS, MSS, Certificate); mathematics (M Ed, MCS, MS); music education (MM); music performance: organ (MM); paralegal studies (Certificate); political science (MSS); public relations and corporate communication (MSC); science and mathematics (M Ed, MCS, MS); social sciences (M Ed, MSS); teaching English to speakers of other languages (MA, MS); vocal pedagogy (MM). Electronic applications accepted.

School of Business *Program availability:* Part-time, evening/weekend. Offers accounting (Certificate); business administration (MBA); business education (M Ed); finance (MBA, Certificate). Electronic applications accepted.

School of Education *Program availability:* Part-time, evening/weekend, online learning. Offers art (M Ed); athletic administration (MS); biological science (M Ed); business education (M Ed); computer science (M Ed); counseling (Ed S); dyslexia therapy (M Ed); education (M Ed, MS, Ed D, Ed S); educational leadership (M Ed, Ed D, Ed S); elementary education (M Ed, Ed S); English (M Ed); higher education administration (MS); marriage and family counseling (MS); mathematics (M Ed); mental health counseling (MS); school counseling (M Ed); secondary education (M Ed); social studies (history) (M Ed); teaching arts (M Ed). Electronic applications accepted.

School of Law Offers civil law studies (Certificate); law (JD). Electronic applications accepted.

MISSISSIPPI STATE UNIVERSITY, Mississippi State, MS 39762

General Information State-supported, coed, university. CGS member. *Enrollment:* 1,862 full-time matriculated graduate/professional students (1,019 women), 1,515 part-time matriculated graduate/professional students (704 women). *Enrollment by degree level:* 1,826 master's, 1,511 doctoral, 40 other advanced degrees. *Graduate faculty:* 811 full-time (260 women), 19 part-time/adjunct (6 women). Tuition, state resident: full-time $8450; part-time $360.59 per credit hour. Tuition, nonresident: full-time $23,140; part-time $969.09 per credit hour. *Required fees:* $110. One-time fee: $55 full-time. Part-time tuition and fees vary according to course load, degree level, campus/location and reciprocity agreements. *Graduate housing:* Room and/or apartments available on a first-come, first-served basis to single students; on-campus housing not available to married students. Typical cost: $5983 per year ($9764 including board). Room and board charges vary according to board plan and housing facility selected. Housing application deadline: 4/1. *Student services:* Campus employment opportunities, campus safety program, career counseling, child daycare facilities, exercise/wellness program, free psychological counseling, grant writing training, international student services, low-cost health insurance, multicultural affairs office, services for students with disabilities, teacher training, writing training. *Library facilities:* Mitchell Memorial Library plus 2 others. *Collection:* Books: 257,296 (physical), 56,456 (digital/electronic); Serial titles: 1,646 (physical), 231,031 (digital/electronic); Databases: 185. Weekly public service hours: 110; students can reserve study rooms.

Computer facilities: 1,000 computers available on campus for general student use. A campuswide network can be accessed from student residence rooms and from off campus. Online class registration is available. Website: http://www.msstate.edu/

General Application Contact: Forest Sparks, Admissions Manager, 662-325-7400, Fax: 662-325-1967, E-mail: grad@grad.msstate.edu.

GRADUATE UNITS

Bagley College of Engineering Students: 346 full-time (102 women), 335 part-time (77 women); includes 102 minority (46 Black or African American, non-Hispanic/Latino; 25 Asian, non-Hispanic/Latino; 28 Hispanic/Latino; 1 Native Hawaiian or other Pacific Islander, non-Hispanic/Latino; 2 Two or more races, non-Hispanic/Latino), 213 international. Average age 31. 492 applicants, 46% accepted, 131 enrolled. *Faculty:* 100 full-time (15 women), 6 part-time/adjunct (2 women). Expenses: Contact institution. *Financial support:* In 2018–19, 178 research assistantships with full tuition reimbursements (averaging $16,993 per year), 69 teaching assistantships with full tuition reimbursements (averaging $15,123 per year) were awarded; Federal Work-Study, institutionally sponsored loans, scholarships/grants, and unspecified assistantships also available. Financial award application deadline: 4/1; financial award applicants required to submit FAFSA. In 2018, 131 master's, 47 doctorates awarded. *Program availability:* Part-time, 100% online. Offers aerospace engineering (MS); civil and environmental engineering (MS, PhD); computer science and engineering (MS, PhD); electrical and computer engineering (MS, PhD); engineering (M Eng, MS, PhD); human factors and ergonomics (MS); industrial and systems engineering (PhD); industrial systems (MS); management systems (MS); manufacturing systems (MS); mechanical engineering (MS); operations research (MS). *Application deadline:* For fall admission, 7/1 for domestic students, 5/1 for international students; for spring admission, 11/1 for domestic students, 9/1 for international students. Applications are processed on a rolling basis. *Application fee:* $60 ($80 for international students). Electronic applications accepted. *Application Contact:* Angie Campbell, Admissions and Enrollment Assistant, 662-325-9514, E-mail: acampbell@grad.msstate.edu. *Dean,* Dr. Jason Keith, 662-325-7183, Fax: 662-325-8573, E-mail: keith@bagley.msstate.edu.

Dave C. Swalm School of Chemical Engineering Students: 16 full-time (7 women), 4 part-time (1 woman); includes 2 minority (both Asian, non-Hispanic/Latino), 15 international. Average age 29. 21 applicants, 29% accepted, 5 enrolled. *Faculty:* 10 full-time (2 women). Expenses: Contact institution. *Financial support:* In 2018–19, 13 research assistantships with full tuition reimbursements (averaging $17,669 per year), 1 teaching assistantship with full tuition reimbursement (averaging $17,669 per year) were awarded; Federal Work-Study, institutionally sponsored loans, and unspecified assistantships also available. Financial award application deadline: 4/1; financial award applicants required to submit FAFSA. In 2018, 1 master's, 3 doctorates awarded. Offers chemical engineering (MS, PhD). *Application deadline:* For fall admission, 4/1 priority date for domestic students, 5/1 for international students; for spring admission, 8/1 priority date for domestic students, 9/1 for international students. Applications are processed on a rolling basis. *Application fee:* $60 ($80 for international students). Electronic applications accepted. *Application Contact:* Angie Campbell, Admissions and Enrollment Assistant, 662-325-9514, E-mail: acampbell@grad.msstate.edu. *Director/Earnest W. Deavenport Jr. Chair,* Dr. Bill Elmore, 662-325-2480, Fax: 662-325-2482, E-mail: elmore@che.msstate.edu.

College of Agriculture and Life Sciences Students: 231 full-time (136 women), 144 part-time (83 women); includes 45 minority (32 Black or African American, non-Hispanic/Latino; 1 American Indian or Alaska Native, non-Hispanic/Latino; 3 Asian, non-Hispanic/Latino; 6 Hispanic/Latino; 3 Two or more races, non-Hispanic/Latino), 80 international. Average age 30. 185 applicants, 52% accepted, 78 enrolled. *Faculty:* 183 full-time (51 women). Expenses: Contact institution. *Financial support:* In 2018–19, 161 research assistantships with full tuition reimbursements (averaging $15,255 per year), 14 teaching assistantships with full tuition reimbursements (averaging $13,356 per year) were awarded; career-related internships or fieldwork, Federal Work-Study, institutionally sponsored loans, scholarships/grants, tuition waivers (partial), and unspecified assistantships also available. Financial award application deadline: 4/1; financial award applicants required to submit FAFSA. In 2018, 81 master's, 39 doctorates awarded. *Program availability:* Blended/hybrid learning. Offers agricultural economics (MS); agricultural life sciences (MS); agricultural science (PhD); agricultural sciences (MS, PhD); agriculture (MS); agriculture and life sciences (MABM, MLA, MS, PhD); biochemistry (MS, PhD); biological engineering (MS, PhD); biomedical engineering (MS, PhD); entomology (MS, PhD); food science and technology (MS, PhD); health promotion (MS); landscape architecture (MLA); life sciences (PhD); nutrition (MS, PhD); plant pathology (MS, PhD); weed science (MS, PhD). *Application deadline:* For fall admission, 7/1 for domestic students, 5/1 for international students; for spring admission, 11/1 for domestic students, 9/1 for international students. Applications are processed on a rolling basis. *Application fee:* $60 ($80 for international students). Electronic applications accepted. *Application Contact:* Ryan King, Admissions and Enrollment Assistant, 662-325-8951, Fax: 662-325-1967, E-mail: rjk101@grad.msstate.edu. *Dean of Agriculture and Life Sciences/Director of Mississippi Agricultural and Forestry Experiment Station,* Dr. George Hopper, 662-325-2953, Fax: 662-325-8580, E-mail: dean@cfr.msstate.edu.

School of Human Sciences Students: 30 full-time (28 women), 51 part-time (35 women); includes 17 minority (13 Black or African American, non-Hispanic/Latino; 1 Hispanic/Latino; 3 Two or more races, non-Hispanic/Latino; 4 international. Average age 34. 26 applicants, 62% accepted, 16 enrolled. *Faculty:* 21 full-time (12 women). Expenses: Contact institution. *Financial support:* In 2018–19, 14 research assistantships (averaging $12,575 per year) were awarded; Federal Work-Study, institutionally sponsored loans, and unspecified assistantships also available. Financial award application deadline: 4/1; financial award applicants required to submit FAFSA. In 2018, 8 master's, 12 doctorates awarded. *Program availability:* Part-time. Offers agriculture and extension education (MS); agriculture science (PhD); fashion design and merchandising (MS); human development and family studies (MS, PhD). *Application deadline:* For fall admission, 7/1 for domestic students, 5/1 for international students; for spring admission, 11/1 for domestic students, 9/1 for international students. Applications are processed on a rolling basis. *Application fee:* $60 ($80 for international students). Electronic applications accepted. *Application Contact:* Ryan King, Admissions and Enrollment Assistant, 662-325-8951, E-mail: rjk101@grad.msstate.edu. *Professor and Director,* Dr. Michael Newman, 662-325-2950, E-mail: mnewman@humansci.msstate.edu.

College of Arts and Sciences Students: 422 full-time (193 women), 325 part-time (160 women); includes 119 minority (58 Black or African American, non-Hispanic/Latino; 3 American Indian or Alaska Native, non-Hispanic/Latino; 11 Asian, non-Hispanic/Latino; 38 Hispanic/Latino; 1 Native Hawaiian or other Pacific Islander, non-Hispanic/Latino; 8 Two or more races, non-Hispanic/Latino), 145 international. Average age 30. 578 applicants, 62% accepted, 212 enrolled. *Faculty:* 230 full-time (89 women), 3 part-time/adjunct (0 women). Expenses: Contact institution. *Financial support:* In 2018–19, 153 research assistantships with full tuition reimbursements (averaging $15,750 per year), 310 teaching assistantships with full tuition reimbursements (averaging $14,654 per year) were awarded; Federal Work-Study, institutionally sponsored loans, scholarships/grants, tuition waivers (partial), and unspecified assistantships also available. Financial award application deadline: 4/1; financial award applicants required to submit FAFSA. In 2018, 173 master's, 32 doctorates awarded. *Program availability:* Part-time, evening/weekend. Offers Africa (MA, PhD); anthropology and Middle Eastern cultures (MA); applied meteorology (MS); applied psychology (PhD); arts and sciences (MA, MPPA, MS, PhD); Asia (MA, PhD); biological sciences (MS, PhD); broadcast meteorology (MS); chemistry (MA, MS, PhD); earth and atmospheric science (PhD); English (MA); environmental geosciences (MS); Europe (MA, PhD); French (MA); general biology (MS); geography (MS); geology (MS); geospatial sciences (MS); Latin America (MA, PhD); mathematical sciences (MS); mathematics (MS); physics (MS, PhD); political science (MA); professional meteorology/climatology (MS); psychology (MS); public policy and administration (MPPA, PhD); sociology (MS, PhD); statistics (MS); teachers in geosciences (MS); United States (MA, PhD); world history (MA, PhD). *Application deadline:* For fall admission, 7/1 for domestic students, 5/1 for international students; for spring admission, 11/1 for domestic students, 9/1 for international students. Applications are processed on a rolling basis. *Application fee:* $60 ($80 for international students). Electronic applications accepted. *Application Contact:* Robbie Salters, Admissions and Enrollment Assistant, 662-325-7400, E-mail: rsk139@msstate.edu. *Dean and Professor,* Dr. Rick Travis, 662-325-2646, Fax: 662-325-8740, E-mail: rtravis@deanas.msstate.edu.

College of Business Students: 138 full-time (69 women), 224 part-time (69 women); includes 42 minority (23 Black or African American, non-Hispanic/Latino; 2 American Indian or Alaska Native, non-Hispanic/Latino; 5 Asian, non-Hispanic/Latino; 11 Hispanic/Latino; 1 Two or more races, non-Hispanic/Latino), 27 international. Average age 30. 182 applicants, 59% accepted, 80 enrolled. *Faculty:* 56 full-time (11 women), 2 part-time/adjunct (0 women). Expenses: Contact institution. *Financial support:* In 2018–19, 2 research assistantships (averaging $10,908 per year), 41 teaching assistantships (averaging $13,407 per year) were awarded; career-related internships or fieldwork, Federal Work-Study, institutionally sponsored loans, scholarships/grants, and unspecified assistantships also available. Financial award application deadline: 4/1; financial award applicants required to submit FAFSA. In 2018, 164 master's, 9 doctorates awarded. *Program availability:* Part-time, evening/weekend, blended/hybrid learning. Offers applied economics (PhD); business (MA, MBA, MPA, MSIS, PhD); business administration (MBA, PhD); economics (MA); information systems (MSIS, PhD); management (PhD); project management (MBA). *Application deadline:* For fall admission, 3/1 priority date for domestic students, 5/1 for international students; for spring admission, 11/1 for domestic students, 9/1 for international students. Applications are processed on a rolling basis. *Application fee:* $60 ($80 for international students). Electronic applications accepted. *Application Contact:* Robbie Salters, Admissions and Enrollment Assistant, 662-325-7400, E-mail: rsalters@grad.msstate.edu. *Dean and Professor,* Dr. Sharon Oswald, 662-325-2580, Fax: 662-325-2410, E-mail: slo49@msstate.edu.

Adkerson School of Accountancy Students: 63 full-time (43 women), 1 part-time (0 women); includes 2 minority (1 Asian, non-Hispanic/Latino; 1 Hispanic/Latino), 1 international. Average age 24. 32 applicants, 78% accepted, 20 enrolled. *Faculty:* 10 full-time (0 women). Expenses: Contact institution. *Financial support:* Career-related internships or fieldwork, Federal Work-Study, institutionally sponsored loans, scholarships/grants, and unspecified assistantships available. Support available to part-time students. Financial award application deadline: 4/1; financial award applicants required to submit FAFSA. In 2018, 59 master's awarded. Offers accountancy (MPA); systems (MPA). *Application deadline:* For fall admission, 7/1 for domestic students, 5/1 for international students; for spring admission, 11/1 for domestic students, 9/1 for international students. Applications are processed on a rolling basis. *Application fee:* $60 ($80 for international students). Electronic applications accepted. *Application Contact:* Robbie Salters, Admissions and Enrollment Assistant, 662-325-7400, E-mail: rsalters@grad.msstate.edu. *Professor and Director,* Dr. Shawn Mauldin, 662-325-3710, Fax: 662-325-1646, E-mail: smauldin@business.msstate.edu.

College of Education Students: 252 full-time (170 women), 413 part-time (281 women); includes 226 minority (188 Black or African American, non-Hispanic/Latino; 5 American Indian or Alaska Native, non-Hispanic/Latino; 4 Asian, non-Hispanic/Latino; 18 Hispanic/Latino; 11 Two or more races, non-Hispanic/Latino), 19 international. Average age 32. 317 applicants, 67% accepted, 164 enrolled. *Faculty:* 89 full-time (46 women), 3 part-time/adjunct (all women). Expenses: Contact institution. *Financial support:* In 2018–19, 13 research assistantships (averaging $10,862 per year), 22 teaching assistantships (averaging $9,923 per year) were awarded; career-related internships or fieldwork, Federal Work-Study, institutionally sponsored loans, scholarships/grants, and unspecified assistantships also available. Financial award application deadline: 4/1; financial award applicants required to submit FAFSA. In 2018, 168 master's, 29 doctorates, 22 other advanced degrees awarded. *Program availability:* Part-time, evening/weekend, blended/hybrid learning. Offers clinical mental health (MS); college counseling (MS); community college education (MAT); community college leadership (PhD); counseling/mental health (PhD); counseling/school psychology (PhD);

counselor education (Ed S); disability studies (MS); early childhood education (PhD); education (MAT, MS, MSIT, MST, PhD, Ed S); educational psychology/general educational psychology (PhD); educational psychology/school psychology (PhD); elementary education (MS, PhD, Ed S); exercise physiology (MS); exercise science (PhD); general curriculum and instruction (PhD); general educational psychology (MS); higher education leadership (PhD); instructional systems and workforce development (MSIT, PhD); P-12 school leadership (PhD); psychometry (MS); reading education (PhD); rehabilitation counseling (MS); school administration (MS, Ed S); school counseling (MS); school psychology (Ed S); secondary education (MAT, MS, PhD, Ed S); special education (MAT, MS, PhD, Ed S); sport administration (MS); sport pedagogy (MS); sport studies (PhD); student affairs (MS); student affairs and higher education (MS); technology (MST, Ed S); workforce education leadership (MS). *Application deadline:* For fall admission, 7/1 for domestic students, 5/1 for international students; for spring admission, 11/1 for domestic students, 9/1 for international students. Applications are processed on a rolling basis. *Application fee:* $60 ($80 for international students). Electronic applications accepted. *Application Contact:* Ryan King, Admissions and Enrollment Assistant, 662-325-8951, E-mail: rjk101@grad.msstate.edu. *Dean,* Dr. Richard Blackbourn, 662-325-3717, Fax: 662-325-8784, E-mail: rlb277@msstate.edu.

College of Forest Resources Students: 92 full-time (38 women), 30 part-time (6 women); includes 8 minority (3 Black or African American, non-Hispanic/Latino; 1 American Indian or Alaska Native, non-Hispanic/Latino; 1 Asian, non-Hispanic/Latino; 2 Hispanic/Latino; 1 Two or more races, non-Hispanic/Latino), 35 international. Average age 29. 56 applicants, 54% accepted, 26 enrolled. *Faculty:* 61 full-time (9 women), 1 part-time/adjunct (0 women). Expenses: Contact institution. *Financial support:* In 2018–19, 92 research assistantships with full tuition reimbursements (averaging $15,602 per year) were awarded; career-related internships or fieldwork, Federal Work-Study, institutionally sponsored loans, and unspecified assistantships also available. Financial award application deadline: 4/1; financial award applicants required to submit FAFSA. In 2018, 35 master's, 14 doctorates awarded. *Program availability:* Part-time. Offers forest resources (PhD); forestry (MS); sustainable bioproducts (MS); wildlife, fisheries and aquaculture (MS, PhD). *Application deadline:* For fall admission, 7/1 for domestic students, 5/1 for international students; for spring admission, 11/1 for domestic students, 9/1 for international students. Applications are processed on a rolling basis. *Application fee:* $60 ($80 for international students). Electronic applications accepted. *Application Contact:* Nathan Drake, Admissions and Enrollment Assistant, 662-325-3804, E-mail: ndrake@grad.msstate.edu. *Dean,* Dr. George Hopper, 662-325-2953, Fax: 662-325-8726, E-mail: ghopper@cfr.msstate.edu.

College of Veterinary Medicine Students: 381 full-time (311 women), 44 part-time (28 women); includes 36 minority (7 Black or African American, non-Hispanic/Latino; 2 American Indian or Alaska Native, non-Hispanic/Latino; 5 Asian, non-Hispanic/Latino; 16 Hispanic/Latino; 6 Two or more races, non-Hispanic/Latino), 19 international. Average age 26. 1,125 applicants, 9% accepted, 103 enrolled. *Faculty:* 67 full-time (31 women), 3 part-time/adjunct (1 woman). Expenses: Contact institution. *Financial support:* In 2018–19, 235 students received support, including 25 research assistantships with full tuition reimbursements available (averaging $16,988 per year); fellowships also available. Financial award application deadline: 6/30; financial award applicants required to submit CSS PROFILE or FAFSA. In 2018, 7 master's, 13 doctorates awarded. Offers veterinary medical science (MS, PhD); veterinary medicine (MS, DVM, PhD). *Application deadline:* For fall admission, 9/15 for domestic and international students. *Application fee:* $60 ($80 for international students). Electronic applications accepted. *Application Contact:* Jennifer Burns, Academic Affairs Manager, 662-325-1078, Fax: 663-325-1027, E-mail: jenny.burns@msstate.edu. *Dean,* Dr. Kent H. Hoblet, 662-325-1131, Fax: 662-325-1498, E-mail: hoblet@cvm.msstate.edu.

MISSISSIPPI UNIVERSITY FOR WOMEN, Columbus, MS 39701-9998

General Information State-supported, coed, comprehensive institution. *Graduate housing:* Rooms and/or apartments available on a first-come, first-served basis to single and married students.

GRADUATE UNITS

Graduate School *Program availability:* Part-time.

College of Education and Human Sciences *Program availability:* Part-time. Offers differentiated instruction (M Ed); educational leadership (M Ed); gifted studies (M Ed); reading/literacy (M Ed); teaching (MAT).

College of Nursing and Health Sciences *Program availability:* Part-time. Offers nursing (MSN, DNP, PMC); public health education (MPH); speech-language pathology (MS).

MISSISSIPPI VALLEY STATE UNIVERSITY, Itta Bena, MS 38941-1400

General Information State-supported, coed, comprehensive institution. *Graduate housing:* On-campus housing not available.

GRADUATE UNITS

College of Education Students: 4 full-time (1 woman), 63 part-time (46 women); includes 65 minority (64 Black or African American, non-Hispanic/Latino; 1 Asian, non-Hispanic/Latino). Average age 35. *Faculty:* 6 full-time (5 women), 2 part-time/adjunct (both women). Expenses: Contact institution. *Financial support:* Institutionally sponsored loans available. Financial award application deadline: 8/1; financial award applicants required to submit FAFSA. In 2018, 12 master's awarded. *Program availability:* Part-time, evening/weekend. Offers education (MAT, MS). *Application deadline:* Applications are processed on a rolling basis. *Application fee:* $0. *Application Contact:* Dr. Danisha Williams, Director of Admissions, 601-254-3344, Fax: 662-254-3759, E-mail: danisha.williams@mvsu.edu. *Interim Chair,* Dr. Kalanya Moore, 662-254-3619, Fax: 662-254-3623, E-mail: kalanya.moore@mvsu.edu.

Department of Criminal Justice Students: 3 full-time (1 woman), 40 part-time (28 women); all minorities (all Black or African American, non-Hispanic/Latino). Average age 33. 13 applicants, 100% accepted, 12 enrolled. *Faculty:* 5 full-time (3 women), 5 part-time/adjunct (all women). Expenses: Contact institution. *Financial support:* In 2018–19, 22 students received support, including research assistantships with full tuition reimbursements available (averaging $3,640 per year); Federal Work-Study and scholarships/grants also available. Support available to part-time students. Financial award application deadline: 4/15; financial award applicants required to submit FAFSA. In 2018, 10 master's awarded. *Program availability:* Part-time, evening/weekend, 100% online. Offers criminal justice (MS). *Application deadline:* For fall admission, 4/1 priority date for domestic students; for spring admission, 12/15 priority date for domestic students. Applications are processed on a rolling basis. *Application fee:* $0. Electronic applications accepted. *Application Contact:* Dr. Danisha Willliams, Director of Admissions, 662-254-3344, Fax: 662-254-3759, E-mail: danisha.williams@mvsu.edu. *Chair,* Dr. Emmanuel Amadi, 601-254-3363, Fax: 601-254-3646, E-mail: amadi@mvsu.edu.

Department of Natural Sciences and Environmental Health Students: 12 full-time (8 women), 7 part-time (5 women); includes 18 minority (17 Black or African American, non-Hispanic/Latino; 1 Asian, non-Hispanic/Latino). Average age 26. *Faculty:* 4 full-time (2 women), 1 part-time/adjunct (0 women). Expenses: Contact institution. *Financial support:* Research assistantships, teaching assistantships, career-related internships or fieldwork, Federal Work-Study, scholarships/grants, and unspecified assistantships available. Financial award application deadline: 4/1; financial award applicants required to submit FAFSA. In 2018, 6 master's awarded. *Program availability:* Part-time, evening/weekend. Offers environmental health (MS). *Application deadline:* For fall admission, 4/1 for domestic students; for spring admission, 12/15 for domestic students. Applications are processed on a rolling basis. *Application fee:* $0. *Application Contact:* Dr. Danisha Williams, Office of Admissions, 601-254-3344, Fax: 662-254-3759, E-mail: danisha.williams@mvsu.edu. *Chair,* Dr. Manju Pande, 662-254-3377, Fax: 662-254-3668, E-mail: mpande@mvsu.edu.

MISSOURI BAPTIST UNIVERSITY, St. Louis, MO 63141-8660
General Information Independent-religious, coed, comprehensive institution.
GRADUATE UNITS
Graduate Programs

MISSOURI SOUTHERN STATE UNIVERSITY, Joplin, MO 64801-1595
General Information State-supported, coed, comprehensive institution.
GRADUATE UNITS
Program in Business Administration *Program availability:* Online learning. Offers business administration (MBA). Program offered jointly with Northwest Missouri State University.
Program in Criminal Justice Administration *Program availability:* Online learning. Offers criminal justice administration (MS). Program offered jointly with Southeast Missouri State University.
Program in Dental Hygiene *Program availability:* Part-time. Offers dental hygiene (MS). Program offered jointly with University of Missouri–Kansas City. Electronic applications accepted.
Program in Early Childhood Education Offers early childhood education (MS Ed). Program offered jointly with Northwest Missouri State University.
Program in Instructional Technology Offers instructional technology (MS Ed). Program offered jointly with Northwest Missouri State University.
Program in Nursing *Program availability:* Part-time. Offers nursing (MSN). Program offered jointly with University of Missouri–Kansas City. Electronic applications accepted.
Program in Teaching Offers teaching (MAT). Program offered jointly with Missouri State University.

MISSOURI STATE UNIVERSITY, Springfield, MO 65897
General Information State-supported, coed, comprehensive institution. CGS member. *Enrollment:* 1,521 full-time matriculated graduate/professional students (964 women), 1,691 part-time matriculated graduate/professional students (1,015 women). *Enrollment by degree level:* 2,687 master's, 373 doctoral, 152 other advanced degrees. *Graduate faculty:* 743 full-time (364 women), 392 part-time/adjunct (210 women). Tuition and fees vary according to class time, course level, course load, degree level, campus/location, program and student level. *Graduate housing:* Rooms and/or apartments available on a first-come, first-served basis to single and married students. *Student services:* Campus employment opportunities, campus safety program, career counseling, child daycare facilities, exercise/wellness program, free psychological counseling, grant writing training, international student services, low-cost health insurance, multicultural affairs office, services for students with disabilities, teacher training, writing training. *Library facilities:* Meyer Library.
Computer facilities: A campuswide network can be accessed from student residence rooms and from off campus. Online class registration is available.
Website: http://www.missouristate.edu/
General Application Contact: Lakan Drinker, Director, Graduate Enrollment Management, 417-836-5330, Fax: 417-836-6200, E-mail: graduateadmissions@missouristate.edu.
GRADUATE UNITS
Graduate College Students: 1,521 full-time (964 women), 1,691 part-time (1,015 women); includes 330 minority (97 Black or African American, non-Hispanic/Latino; 15 American Indian or Alaska Native, non-Hispanic/Latino; 50 Asian, non-Hispanic/Latino; 103 Hispanic/Latino; 4 Native Hawaiian or other Pacific Islander, non-Hispanic/Latino; 61 Two or more races, non-Hispanic/Latino), 389 international. Average age 25. 3,205 applicants, 43% accepted, 1150 enrolled. *Faculty:* 743 full-time (364 women), 392 part-time/adjunct (210 women). Expenses: Contact institution. *Financial support:* In 2018–19, 585 students received support, including 53 research assistantships with full tuition reimbursements available (averaging $8,772 per year), 104 teaching assistantships with full tuition reimbursements available (averaging $8,772 per year); Federal Work-Study, institutionally sponsored loans, scholarships/grants, health care benefits, and unspecified assistantships also available. Financial award application deadline: 1/31; financial award applicants required to submit FAFSA. In 2018, 1,000 master's, 115 doctorates, 10 other advanced degrees awarded. *Program availability:* Part-time, 100% online, blended/hybrid learning. Offers administrative studies (Certificate); applied communication (MS); criminal justice (MS); environmental management (MS); homeland security (MS); individualized (MS); professional studies (MS); screenwriting and producing (MS); sports management (MS). *Application deadline:* For fall admission, 7/20 priority date for domestic students, 5/1 for international students; for spring admission, 12/20 priority date for domestic students, 9/1 for international students. Applications are processed on a rolling basis. *Application fee:* $55 ($60 for international students). Electronic applications accepted. *Application Contact:* Lakan Drinker, Director, Graduate Enrollment Management, 417-836-5330, Fax: 417-836-6200, E-mail: lakandrinker@missouristate.edu. *Associate Provost/Dean,* Dr. Julie Masterson, 417-836-5335, Fax: 417-836-6200, E-mail: juliemasterson@missouristate.edu.
College of Arts and Letters Students: 109 full-time (78 women), 136 part-time (107 women); includes 24 minority (8 Black or African American, non-Hispanic/Latino; 2 Asian, non-Hispanic/Latino; 9 Hispanic/Latino; 1 Native Hawaiian or other Pacific Islander, non-Hispanic/Latino; 4 Two or more races, non-Hispanic/Latino), 28 international. Average age 25. 156 applicants, 65% accepted, 93 enrolled. *Faculty:* 74 full-time (32 women), 7 part-time/adjunct (5 women). Expenses: Contact institution. *Financial support:* In 2018–19, 61 teaching assistantships with full tuition reimbursements (averaging $8,772 per year) were awarded; Federal Work-Study, institutionally sponsored loans, scholarships/grants, health care benefits, and unspecified assistantships also available. Financial award application deadline: 1/31;

financial award applicants required to submit FAFSA. In 2018, 67 master's awarded. *Program availability:* Part-time, evening/weekend, 100% online, blended/hybrid learning. Offers applied second language acquisition (MASLA); arts and letters (MA, MASLA, MFA, MM, MS Ed, Certificate); communication (MA); English (MA); English education (MS Ed); music (MM, MS Ed); teaching English to speakers of other languages (Certificate); visual studies (MFA); writing (MA). *Application deadline:* For fall admission, 7/20 priority date for domestic students, 5/1 for international students; for spring admission, 12/20 priority date for domestic students, 9/1 for international students; for summer admission, 5/20 priority date for domestic students. Applications are processed on a rolling basis. *Application fee:* $55 ($60 for international students). Electronic applications accepted. *Application Contact:* Lakan Drinker, Director, Graduate Enrollment Management, 417-836-5330, Fax: 417-836-6200, E-mail: lakandrinker@missouristate.edu. *Dean,* Dr. Shawn Wahl, 417-836-4366, Fax: 417-836-6940, E-mail: shawnwahl@missouristate.edu.
College of Business Students: 354 full-time (188 women), 513 part-time (200 women); includes 91 minority (27 Black or African American, non-Hispanic/Latino; 3 American Indian or Alaska Native, non-Hispanic/Latino; 22 Asian, non-Hispanic/Latino; 27 Hispanic/Latino; 1 Native Hawaiian or other Pacific Islander, non-Hispanic/Latino; 11 Two or more races, non-Hispanic/Latino), 201 international. Average age 24. 504 applicants, 62% accepted. *Faculty:* 50 full-time (13 women), 8 part-time/adjunct (1 woman). Expenses: Contact institution. *Financial support:* In 2018–19, 4 teaching assistantships with full tuition reimbursements (averaging $10,672 per year) were awarded; Federal Work-Study, institutionally sponsored loans, scholarships/grants, and unspecified assistantships also available. Financial award application deadline: 1/31; financial award applicants required to submit FAFSA. In 2018, 346 master's awarded. *Program availability:* Part-time, evening/weekend, 100% online, blended/hybrid learning. Offers accountancy (M Acc); business (M Acc, MBA, MHA, MS, MS Ed); business administration (MBA); project management (MS). *Application deadline:* For fall admission, 7/20 priority date for domestic students, 5/1 for international students; for spring admission, 12/20 priority date for domestic students, 9/1 for international students; for summer admission, 5/20 priority date for domestic students. Applications are processed on a rolling basis. *Application fee:* $55 ($60 for international students). Electronic applications accepted. *Application Contact:* Lakan Drinker, Director, Graduate Enrollment Management, 417-836-5330, Fax: 417-836-6200, E-mail: lakandrinker@missouristate.edu. *Dean,* Dr. David Meinert, 417-836-4408, Fax: 417-836-4407, E-mail: coba@missouristate.edu.
College of Education Students: 147 full-time (115 women), 492 part-time (399 women); includes 59 minority (16 Black or African American, non-Hispanic/Latino; 1 American Indian or Alaska Native, non-Hispanic/Latino; 3 Asian, non-Hispanic/Latino; 23 Hispanic/Latino; 16 Two or more races, non-Hispanic/Latino), 11 international. Average age 24. 381 applicants, 71% accepted. *Faculty:* 43 full-time (26 women), 11 part-time/adjunct (6 women). Expenses: Contact institution. *Financial support:* Teaching assistantships, Federal Work-Study, institutionally sponsored loans, scholarships/grants, and unspecified assistantships available. Financial award application deadline: 1/31; financial award applicants required to submit FAFSA. In 2018, 182 master's, 10 other advanced degrees awarded. *Program availability:* Part-time. Offers counseling (MS); counseling and assessment (Ed S); early childhood and family development (MS); education (MAT, MS, MS Ed, Ed S); educational administration (MS Ed, Ed S); educational technology (MS Ed); elementary education (MS Ed); elementary principal (MS Ed, Ed S); literacy (MS Ed, Graduate Certificate); mental health counseling (MS); secondary principal (MS Ed, Ed S); special education (MS Ed); student affairs in higher education (MS); superintendent (Ed S); teacher leadership (Certificate, Ed S); teaching (MAT); teaching and learning (MA, Certificate). *Application deadline:* For fall admission, 7/20 for domestic students, 5/1 for international students; for spring admission, 12/20 for domestic students, 9/1 for international students; for summer admission, 5/20 for domestic students. Applications are processed on a rolling basis. *Application fee:* $55 ($60 for international students). Electronic applications accepted. *Application Contact:* Lakan Drinker, Director, Graduate Enrollment Management, 417-836-5330, Fax: 417-836-6200, E-mail: lakandrinker@missouristate.edu. *Dean,* Dr. David Hough, 417-836-5254, Fax: 417-836-4884, E-mail: collegeofeducation@missouristate.edu.
College of Health and Human Services Students: 614 full-time (445 women), 205 part-time (155 women); includes 100 minority (32 Black or African American, non-Hispanic/Latino; 7 American Indian or Alaska Native, non-Hispanic/Latino; 16 Asian, non-Hispanic/Latino; 24 Hispanic/Latino; 2 Native Hawaiian or other Pacific Islander, non-Hispanic/Latino; 19 Two or more races, non-Hispanic/Latino), 29 international. Average age 23. 367 applicants, 35% accepted. *Faculty:* 89 full-time (58 women), 33 part-time/adjunct (21 women). Expenses: Contact institution. *Financial support:* In 2018–19, 9 research assistantships with full tuition reimbursements (averaging $8,772 per year), 33 teaching assistantships with full tuition reimbursements (averaging $8,772 per year) were awarded; Federal Work-Study, institutionally sponsored loans, scholarships/grants, and unspecified assistantships also available. Financial award application deadline: 1/31; financial award applicants required to submit FAFSA. In 2018, 180 master's, 115 doctorates awarded. *Program availability:* Part-time. Offers applied behavior analysis (MS); athletic training (MS); cell and molecular biology (MS); clinical psychology (MS); communication sciences and disorders (Au D); dietetic internship (Certificate); experimental psychology (MS); forensic child psychology (Certificate); health and human services (MOT, MPH, MS, MS Ed, MSN, MSW, Au D, DNAP, DNP, DPT, Certificate); health promotion and wellness management (MS); industrial/organizational psychology (MS); nurse anesthesia (DNAP); nursing (MSN); nursing practice (DNP); occupational therapy (MOT); physical therapy (DPT); physician assistant studies (MS); public health (MPH); secondary education (MS Ed); social work (MSW); speech language pathology (MS). *Application fee:* $55 ($60 for international students). Electronic applications accepted. *Application Contact:* Lakan Drinker, Director, Graduate Enrollment Management, 417-836-5330, Fax: 417-836-6200, E-mail: lakandrinker@missouristate.edu. *Interim Dean,* Dr. Letitia White-Minnis, 417-836-4176, Fax: 417-836-6905, E-mail: chhs@missouristate.edu.
College of Humanities and Public Affairs Students: 84 full-time (35 women), 163 part-time (56 women); includes 24 minority (6 Black or African American, non-Hispanic/Latino; 1 American Indian or Alaska Native, non-Hispanic/Latino; 5 Asian, non-Hispanic/Latino; 10 Hispanic/Latino; 2 Two or more races, non-Hispanic/Latino), 9 international. Average age 24. 137 applicants, 62% accepted. *Faculty:* 66 full-time (20 women), 21 part-time/adjunct (5 women). Expenses: Contact institution. *Financial support:* In 2018–19, 3 teaching assistantships with partial tuition reimbursements (averaging $2,150 per year) were awarded; Federal Work-Study, institutionally sponsored loans, scholarships/grants, and unspecified assistantships also available. Financial award application deadline: 1/31; financial award applicants required to submit FAFSA. In 2018, 86 master's awarded. *Program availability:* Part-time. Offers community corrections (Certificate); criminology and criminal justice (MS); defense

and strategic studies (Certificate); general weapons of mass destruction (MS); global studies (MGS); history (MA); history education (MS Ed); history for teachers (Certificate); homeland security and defense (Certificate); humanities and public affairs (MA, MGS, MIAA, MPA, MS, MS Ed, Certificate); public administration (MPA); public management (Certificate); religious studies (MA, Certificate). *Application deadline:* For fall admission, 7/20 priority date for domestic students, 5/1 for international students; for spring admission, 12/20 priority date for domestic students, 9/1 for international students; for summer admission, 5/20 priority date for domestic students. Applications are processed on a rolling basis. *Application fee:* $55 ($60 for international students). Electronic applications accepted. *Application Contact:* Lakan Drinker, Director, Graduate Enrollment Management, 417-836-5330, Fax: 417-836-6200, E-mail: lakandrinker@missouristate.edu. *Dean,* Dr. Victor Matthews, 417-836-5529, Fax: 417-836-8472, E-mail: victormatthews@missouristate.edu.

College of Natural and Applied Sciences Students: 97 full-time (33 women), 69 part-time (37 women); includes 12 minority (1 Black or African American, non-Hispanic/Latino; 1 American Indian or Alaska Native, non-Hispanic/Latino; 1 Asian, non-Hispanic/Latino; 5 Hispanic/Latino; 4 Two or more races, non-Hispanic/Latino), 49 international. Average age 24. 120 applicants, 58% accepted. *Faculty:* 87 full-time (14 women), 8 part-time/adjunct (2 women). Expenses: Contact institution. *Financial support:* In 2018–19, 11 research assistantships with full tuition reimbursements (averaging $10,672 per year), 81 teaching assistantships with full tuition reimbursements (averaging $9,483 per year) were awarded; Federal Work-Study, institutionally sponsored loans, scholarships/grants, and unspecified assistantships also available. Financial award application deadline: 1/31; financial award applicants required to submit FAFSA. In 2018, 56 master's awarded. *Program availability:* Part-time, evening/weekend. Offers biology (MS); chemistry (MS); geography, geology, and planning (Certificate); materials science (MS); mathematics (MS); natural and applied science (MNAS); natural and applied sciences (MNAS, MS, MS Ed, Certificate); secondary education (MS Ed). *Application deadline:* For fall admission, 7/20 priority date for domestic students, 5/1 for international students; for spring admission, 12/20 priority date for domestic students, 9/1 for international students; for summer admission, 5/20 priority date for domestic students. Applications are processed on a rolling basis. *Application fee:* $55 ($60 for international students). Electronic applications accepted. *Application Contact:* Lakan Drinker, Director, Graduate Enrollment Management, 417-836-5330, Fax: 417-836-6200, E-mail: lakandrinker@missouristate.edu. *Dean,* Dr. Tamera Jahnke, 417-836-5249, Fax: 417-836-6934, E-mail: tamerajahnke@missouristate.edu.

Darr College of Agriculture Students: 22 full-time (9 women), 32 part-time (17 women); includes 3 minority (1 American Indian or Alaska Native, non-Hispanic/Latino; 2 Two or more races, non-Hispanic/Latino). Average age 23. 24 applicants, 42% accepted. *Faculty:* 16 full-time (5 women), 1 part-time/adjunct (0 women). Expenses: Contact institution. *Financial support:* In 2018–19, 7 research assistantships with full tuition reimbursements (averaging $9,365 per year), 6 teaching assistantships with full tuition reimbursements (averaging $8,450 per year) were awarded; Federal Work-Study, institutionally sponsored loans, scholarships/grants, and unspecified assistantships also available. Financial award application deadline: 1/31; financial award applicants required to submit FAFSA. In 2018, 21 master's awarded. *Program availability:* Part-time. Offers plant science (MS); secondary education (MS Ed). *Application deadline:* For fall admission, 7/20 priority date for domestic students, 5/1 for international students; for spring admission, 12/20 priority date for domestic students, 9/1 for international students; for summer admission, 5/20 priority date for domestic students. Applications are processed on a rolling basis. *Application fee:* $55 ($60 for international students). Electronic applications accepted. *Application Contact:* Lakan Drinker, Director, Graduate Enrollment Management, 417-836-5330, Fax: 417-836-6200, E-mail: lakandrinker@missouristate.edu. *Dean,* Dr. Ronald Del Vecchio, 417-836-5050, E-mail: darr@missouristate.edu.

MISSOURI UNIVERSITY OF SCIENCE AND TECHNOLOGY, Rolla, MO 65409

General Information State-supported, coed, university. CGS member. *Enrollment:* 1,052 full-time matriculated graduate/professional students (223 women), 707 part-time matriculated graduate/professional students (164 women). *Enrollment by degree level:* 734 master's, 713 doctoral, 196 other advanced degrees. *Graduate faculty:* 326 full-time (70 women), 36 part-time/adjunct (7 women). *International tuition:* $23,518.80 full-time. Tuition, state resident: full-time $7545.60; part-time $419.20 per credit hour. Tuition, nonresident: full-time $22,169; part-time $1231.60 per credit hour. *Required fees:* $4523.05. Full-time tuition and fees vary according to course load, campus/location, program and reciprocity agreements. *Graduate housing:* Rooms and/or apartments available on a first-come, first-served basis to single and married students. *Student services:* Campus employment opportunities, campus safety program, career counseling, exercise/wellness program, free psychological counseling, grant writing training, international student services, low-cost health insurance, multicultural affairs office, services for students with disabilities, teacher training, writing training. *Library facilities:* Curtis Laws Wilson Library. *Collection:* Books: 305,834 (physical), 447,868 (digital/electronic); Serial titles: 14,178 (physical), 79,586 (digital/electronic); Databases: 180. Weekly public service hours: 112; students can reserve study rooms.

Computer facilities: Computer purchase and lease plans are available. 980 computers available on campus for general student use. A campuswide network can be accessed from student residence rooms and from off campus. Online class registration is available.
Website: http://www.mst.edu/

General Application Contact: Adrienne Neckermann, Manager, Office of Graduate Studies, 573-341-7712, E-mail: neckermanna@mst.edu.

GRADUATE UNITS

Department of Biological Sciences Offers applied and environmental biology (MS).

Department of Business and Information Technology Offers business administration (MBA); information science and technology (MS). Electronic applications accepted.

Department of Chemical and Biochemical Engineering Offers chemical engineering (MS, PhD). Electronic applications accepted.

Department of Chemistry Offers chemistry (MS, MST, PhD). Electronic applications accepted.

Department of Civil, Architectural, and Environmental Engineering *Program availability:* Part-time, evening/weekend. Offers civil engineering (MS, DE, PhD); environmental engineering (MS). Electronic applications accepted.

Department of Computer Science *Program availability:* Part-time. Offers computer science (MS, PhD). Electronic applications accepted.

Department of Electrical and Computer Engineering *Program availability:* Part-time, evening/weekend. Offers computer engineering (MS, DE, PhD); electrical engineering (MS, DE, PhD). Electronic applications accepted.

Department of Engineering Management and Systems Engineering Offers engineering management (MS, PhD); systems engineering (MS, PhD). Electronic applications accepted.

Department of English and Technical Communication Offers technical communication (MS).

Department of Geosciences and Geological and Petroleum Engineering *Program availability:* Part-time. Offers geological engineering (MS, DE, PhD); geology and geophysics (MS, PhD); petroleum engineering (MS, DE, PhD). Electronic applications accepted.

Department of Materials Science and Engineering Offers ceramic engineering (MS, PhD); materials science and engineering (MS, PhD); metallurgical engineering (MS, PhD). Electronic applications accepted.

Department of Mathematics and Statistics Offers applied mathematics (MS); mathematics (MST, PhD). Electronic applications accepted.

Department of Mechanical and Aerospace Engineering *Program availability:* Part-time, evening/weekend. Offers aerospace engineering (MS, PhD); manufacturing engineering (M Eng, MS); mechanical engineering (MS, PhD). Electronic applications accepted.

Department of Mining and Nuclear Engineering Offers explosives engineering (MS, PhD); mining engineering (MS, DE, PhD); nuclear engineering (MS, DE, PhD). Electronic applications accepted.

Department of Physics Offers physics (MS, MST, PhD). Electronic applications accepted.

Department of Psychological Science Offers industrial-organizational psychology (MS).

Program in Geotechnics Offers geotechnics (ME).

MISSOURI VALLEY COLLEGE, Marshall, MO 65340-3197

General Information Independent-religious, coed, comprehensive institution.

GRADUATE UNITS

Graduate Studies

MISSOURI WESTERN STATE UNIVERSITY, St. Joseph, MO 64507-2294

General Information State-supported, coed, comprehensive institution. CGS member. *Enrollment:* 81 full-time matriculated graduate/professional students (32 women), 145 part-time matriculated graduate/professional students (100 women). *Enrollment by degree level:* 217 master's, 9 other advanced degrees. *Graduate faculty:* 42 full-time (15 women), 7 part-time/adjunct (5 women). *Tuition, area resident:* Part-time $359.39 per credit hour. Tuition, state resident: part-time $359.39 per credit hour. Tuition, nonresident: part-time $643.39 per credit hour. Tuition and fees vary according to program. *Graduate housing:* Room and/or apartments available on a first-come, first-served basis to single students; on-campus housing not available to married students. *Student services:* Campus employment opportunities, campus safety program, career counseling, child daycare facilities, exercise/wellness program, free psychological counseling, international student services, low-cost health insurance, multicultural affairs office, services for students with disabilities. *Library facilities:* Missouri Western State University Library. *Collection:* Books: 166,649 (physical), 215,083 (digital/electronic); Serial titles: 1,585 (physical), 57,298 (digital/electronic); Databases: 65.

Computer facilities: Computer purchase and lease plans are available. A campuswide network can be accessed from student residence rooms and from off campus. Online class registration, personal online storage are available.
Website: http://www.missouriwestern.edu/

General Application Contact: Dr. Susan Bashinski, Dean of the Graduate School, 816-271-4394, Fax: 816-271-4525, E-mail: graduate@missouriwestern.edu.

GRADUATE UNITS

CyberSecurity Students: 9 full-time (2 women), 2 part-time (0 women); includes 1 minority (Asian, non-Hispanic/Latino), 7 international. Average age 27. 30 applicants, 63% accepted, 6 enrolled. Expenses: Contact institution. *Financial support:* Scholarships/grants and unspecified assistantships available. Support available to part-time students. In 2018, 6 master's awarded. *Program availability:* Part-time. Offers information technology assurance administration (MS). *Application deadline:* For fall admission, 7/15 for domestic and international students; for spring admission, 11/1 for domestic and international students; for summer admission, 4/29 for domestic and international students. Applications are processed on a rolling basis. *Application fee:* $45 ($50 for international students). Electronic applications accepted. *Application Contact:* Dr. Susan Bashinski, Dean of the Graduate School, 816-271-4394, Fax: 816-271-4525, E-mail: graduate@missouriwestern.edu. *Assistant Professor,* Dr. Yipkei Kwok, 816-271-4523, E-mail: ykwok@missouriwestern.edu.

Program in Applied Science Students: 35 full-time (11 women), 14 part-time (5 women); includes 4 minority (1 Black or African American, non-Hispanic/Latino; 1 Asian, non-Hispanic/Latino; 1 Hispanic/Latino; 1 Two or more races, non-Hispanic/Latino), 10 international. Average age 25. 31 applicants, 94% accepted, 20 enrolled. Expenses: Contact institution. *Financial support:* Scholarships/grants and unspecified assistantships available. Support available to part-time students. In 2018, 18 master's awarded. *Program availability:* Part-time. Offers chemistry (MAS); engineering technology management (MAS); industrial life science (MAS); sport and fitness management (MAS). *Application deadline:* For fall admission, 7/15 for domestic and international students; for spring admission, 11/1 for domestic and international students; for summer admission, 4/29 for domestic and international students. Applications are processed on a rolling basis. *Application fee:* $45 ($50 for international students). Electronic applications accepted. *Application Contact:* Dr. Susan Bashinski, Dean of the Graduate School, 816-271-4394, Fax: 816-271-4525, E-mail: graduate@missouriwestern.edu. *Dean of the Graduate School,* Dr. Susan Bashinski, 816-271-4394, Fax: 816-271-4525, E-mail: graduate@missouriwestern.edu.

Program in Assessment Students: 1 (woman) full-time, 33 part-time (32 women); includes 3 minority (2 American Indian or Alaska Native, non-Hispanic/Latino; 1 Asian, non-Hispanic/Latino). Average age 40. 16 applicants, 100% accepted, 8 enrolled. Expenses: Contact institution. *Financial support:* Scholarships/grants and unspecified assistantships available. Support available to part-time students. In 2018, 4 other advanced degrees awarded. *Program availability:* Part-time. Offers K-12 cross-categorical special education (MAS); TESOL (Graduate Certificate). *Application deadline:* For fall admission, 7/15 for domestic and international students; for spring admission, 11/1 for domestic and international students; for summer admission, 4/29 for domestic and international students. Applications are processed on a rolling basis. *Application fee:* $45 ($50 for international students). Electronic applications accepted. *Application Contact:* Dr. Susan Bashinski, Dean of Graduate Programs, 816-271-4394, Fax: 816-271-4525, E-mail: graduate@missouriwestern.edu. *Dean of Graduate Programs,* Dr. Susan Bashinski, 816-271-4394, E-mail: graduate@missouriwestern.edu.

Program in Business Administration Students: 25 full-time (12 women), 41 part-time (17 women); includes 8 minority (3 Black or African American, non-Hispanic/Latino; 2 American Indian or Alaska Native, non-Hispanic/Latino; 2 Asian, non-Hispanic/Latino; 1 Two or more races, non-Hispanic/Latino), 1 international. Average age 32. 45 applicants, 93% accepted, 25 enrolled. Expenses: Contact institution. *Financial support:* Scholarships/grants and unspecified assistantships available. Support available to part-time students. In 2018, 19 master's awarded. *Program availability:* Part-time, 100% online. Offers animal and life sciences (MBA); enterprise resource planning (MBA); forensic accounting (MBA); general business (MBA). *Application deadline:* For fall admission, 7/15 for domestic and international students; for spring admission, 11/1 for domestic and international students; for summer admission, 4/29 for domestic and international students. Applications are processed on a rolling basis. *Application fee:* $45 ($50 for international students). Electronic applications accepted. *Application Contact:* Dr. Susan Bashinski, Dean of the Graduate School, 816-271-4394, Fax: 816-271-4525, E-mail: graduate@missouriwestern.edu. *Dean of Craig School of Business,* Dr. Logan Jones, 816-271-4338, E-mail: jones@missouriwestern.edu.

Program in Forensic Investigations Students: 4 full-time (3 women), 12 part-time (10 women); includes 4 minority (2 Black or African American, non-Hispanic/Latino; 1 Asian, non-Hispanic/Latino; 1 Two or more races, non-Hispanic/Latino). Average age 26. 5 applicants, 100% accepted, 5 enrolled. Expenses: Contact institution. *Financial support:* Scholarships/grants and unspecified assistantships available. Support available to part-time students. In 2018, 8 master's awarded. *Program availability:* Part-time. Offers forensic investigations (MAS, Graduate Certificate). *Application deadline:* For fall admission, 7/15 for domestic and international students; for spring admission, 11/1 for domestic and international students; for summer admission, 4/29 for domestic and international students. Applications are processed on a rolling basis. *Application fee:* $45 ($50 for international students). Electronic applications accepted. *Application Contact:* Dr. Susan Bashinski, Dean of the Graduate School, 816-271-4394, Fax: 816-271-4525, E-mail: graduate@missouriwestern.edu. *Forensics Graduate Program Director,* Dr. Monty Smith, 816-271-4434, E-mail: msmith84@missouriwestern.edu.

Program in Nursing Students: 3 full-time (all women), 32 part-time (31 women); includes 3 minority (1 Black or African American, non-Hispanic/Latino; 1 Asian, non-Hispanic/Latino; 1 Hispanic/Latino), 2 international. Average age 37. 6 applicants, 100% accepted, 5 enrolled. Expenses: Contact institution. *Financial support:* Scholarships/grants and unspecified assistantships available. Support available to part-time students. In 2018, 12 master's, 1 other advanced degree awarded. *Program availability:* Part-time. Offers health care leadership (MSN); nurse educator (MSN, Graduate Certificate). *Application deadline:* For fall admission, 7/15 for domestic and international students; for spring admission, 11/1 for domestic and international students; for summer admission, 4/29 for domestic and international students. Applications are processed on a rolling basis. *Application fee:* $45 ($50 for international students). Electronic applications accepted. *Application Contact:* Dr. Susan Bashinski, Dean of the Graduate School, 816-271-4394, Fax: 816-271-4525, E-mail: graduate@missouriwestern.edu. *MSN Program Director and Assistant Professor,* Dr. Jacklyn Gentry, 816-271-4415, E-mail: jgentry8@missouriwestern.edu.

Technical Communication Students: 1 full-time (0 women), 3 part-time (all women); includes 1 minority (Two or more races, non-Hispanic/Latino), 1 international. Average age 47. 2 applicants, 100% accepted, 1 enrolled. Expenses: Contact institution. *Financial support:* Scholarships/grants and unspecified assistantships available. Support available to part-time students. In 2018, 7 master's, 2 other advanced degrees awarded. *Program availability:* Part-time. Offers teaching of writing (Graduate Certificate); technical communication (MAA); writing studies (MAA). *Application deadline:* For fall admission, 7/15 for domestic and international students; for spring admission, 11/1 for domestic and international students; for summer admission, 4/29 for domestic and international students. Applications are processed on a rolling basis. *Application fee:* $45 ($50 for international students). Electronic applications accepted. *Application Contact:* Dr. Susan Bashinski, Dean of the Graduate School, 816-271-4394, Fax: 816-271-4525, E-mail: graduate@missouriwestern.edu. *Associate Professor,* Dr. Michael Charlton, 816-271-4310, E-mail: mcharlton@missouriwestern.edu.

MITCHELL HAMLINE SCHOOL OF LAW, Saint Paul, MN 55105-3076

General Information Independent, coed, graduate-only institution.

GRADUATE UNITS

Graduate and Professional Programs *Program availability:* Part-time, evening/weekend, blended/hybrid learning. Offers law (LL M, JD). Electronic applications accepted.

MOLLOY COLLEGE, Rockville Centre, NY 11571-5002

General Information Independent, coed, comprehensive institution. *Enrollment:* 4,929 graduate, professional, and undergraduate students; 322 full-time matriculated graduate/professional students (252 women), 997 part-time matriculated graduate/professional students (803 women). *Enrollment by degree level:* 1,171 master's, 100 doctoral, 48 other advanced degrees. *Graduate faculty:* 83 full-time (69 women), 76 part-time/adjunct (44 women). *Tuition:* Full-time $20,790; part-time $1155 per credit. *Required fees:* $1060; $900. Tuition and fees vary according to course load and degree level. *Graduate housing:* On-campus housing not available. *Student services:* Campus employment opportunities, campus safety program, career counseling, free psychological counseling, international student services, low-cost health insurance, services for students with disabilities, teacher training, writing training. *Library facilities:* James Edward Tobin Library plus 1 other. *Collection:* Books: 33,809 (physical), 295,138 (digital/electronic); Serial titles: 48 (physical), 62,642 (digital/electronic); Databases: 198.

Computer facilities: 750 computers available on campus for general student use. A campuswide network can be accessed from student residence rooms and from off campus. Online class registration is available.
Website: http://www.molloy.edu/

General Application Contact: Faye Hood, Assistant Director for Admissions, 516-323-4009, E-mail: fhood@molloy.edu.

GRADUATE UNITS

The Barbara H. Hagan School of Nursing Students: 22 full-time (20 women), 570 part-time (514 women); includes 356 minority (186 Black or African American, non-Hispanic/Latino; 2 American Indian or Alaska Native, non-Hispanic/Latino; 113 Asian, non-Hispanic/Latino; 41 Hispanic/Latino; 2 Native Hawaiian or other Pacific Islander, non-Hispanic/Latino; 12 Two or more races, non-Hispanic/Latino), 4 international. Average age 44. 263 applicants, 62% accepted, 121 enrolled. *Faculty:* 33 full-time (32 women), 14 part-time/adjunct (6 women). Expenses: Contact institution. *Financial support:* Research assistantships with partial tuition reimbursements, teaching

assistantships with partial tuition reimbursements, institutionally sponsored loans, scholarships/grants, and unspecified assistantships available. Support available to part-time students. Financial award application deadline: 3/1; financial award applicants required to submit FAFSA. In 2018, 103 master's, 14 doctorates, 11 other advanced degrees awarded. *Program availability:* Part-time, evening/weekend. Offers adult-gerontology clinical nurse specialist (DNP); adult-gerontology nurse practitioner (MS, DNP); clinical nurse specialist: adult-gerontology (MS); family nurse practitioner (MS, DNP); family psychiatric/mental health nurse practitioner (MS, DNP); nursing (PhD, Advanced Certificate); nursing administration with informatics (MS); nursing education (MS); pediatric nurse practitioner (MS, DNP). *Application deadline:* For fall admission, 9/2 priority date for domestic students; for spring admission, 1/20 priority date for domestic students. Applications are processed on a rolling basis. *Application fee:* $60. Electronic applications accepted. *Application Contact:* Faye Hood, Assistant Director for Admissions, 516-323-4009, E-mail: fhood@molloy.edu. *Dean, The Barbara H. Hagan School of Nursing,* Dr. Marcia R. Gardner, 516-323-3651, E-mail: mgardner@molloy.edu.

Criminal Justice Program Students: 12 full-time (7 women), 14 part-time (9 women); includes 9 minority (4 Black or African American, non-Hispanic/Latino; 4 Hispanic/Latino; 1 Native Hawaiian or other Pacific Islander, non-Hispanic/Latino). Average age 36. 22 applicants, 68% accepted, 9 enrolled. *Faculty:* 4 full-time (2 women), 5 part-time/adjunct (1 woman). Expenses: Contact institution. *Financial support:* Application deadline: 3/1; applicants required to submit FAFSA. In 2018, 13 master's awarded. *Program availability:* Part-time, evening/weekend. Offers criminal justice (MS). *Application deadline:* Applications are processed on a rolling basis. *Application fee:* $60. Electronic applications accepted. *Application Contact:* Faye Hood, Assistant Director for Admissions, 516-323-4009, E-mail: fhood@molloy.edu. *Associate Dean/Graduate Program Director,* Dr. John Eterno, 516-323-3804, E-mail: jeterno@molloy.edu.

Graduate Business Program Students: 75 full-time (45 women), 164 part-time (88 women); includes 100 minority (45 Black or African American, non-Hispanic/Latino; 21 Asian, non-Hispanic/Latino; 30 Hispanic/Latino; 1 Native Hawaiian or other Pacific Islander, non-Hispanic/Latino; 3 Two or more races, non-Hispanic/Latino), 3 international. Average age 40. 97 applicants, 78% accepted, 65 enrolled. *Faculty:* 9 full-time (2 women), 20 part-time/adjunct (8 women). Expenses: Contact institution. *Financial support:* Application deadline: 3/1; applicants required to submit FAFSA. In 2018, 91 master's, 1 other advanced degree awarded. *Program availability:* Part-time, evening/weekend. Offers accounting (MBA); finance (MBA, Post-Master's Certificate, Postbaccalaureate Certificate); healthcare (MBA, Post-Master's Certificate, Postbaccalaureate Certificate); management (MBA); marketing (MBA, Post-Master's Certificate, Postbaccalaureate Certificate); personal financial planning (MBA). *Application deadline:* Applications are processed on a rolling basis. *Application fee:* $60. Electronic applications accepted. *Application Contact:* Faye Hood, Assistant Director for Admissions, 516-323-4009, E-mail: fhood@molloy.edu. *Dean, Division of Business/Director of Graduate Programs,* Dr. Maureen Mackenzie, 516-323-3080, E-mail: mmackenzie@molloy.edu.

Graduate Education Program Students: 106 full-time (78 women), 203 part-time (154 women); includes 65 minority (14 Black or African American, non-Hispanic/Latino; 5 Asian, non-Hispanic/Latino; 41 Hispanic/Latino; 5 Two or more races, non-Hispanic/Latino). Average age 41. 147 applicants, 63% accepted, 79 enrolled. *Faculty:* 24 full-time (22 women), 26 part-time/adjunct (19 women). Expenses: Contact institution. *Financial support:* Application deadline: 3/1; applicants required to submit FAFSA. In 2018, 120 master's, 1 other advanced degree awarded. *Program availability:* Part-time, evening/weekend. Offers adolescent education in biology (MS); adolescent special education (Advanced Certificate); bilingual extension (Advanced Certificate); childhood education (MS); childhood special education (Advanced Certificate); early childhood education (MS); educational technology (MS); English (MS); mathematics (MS); social studies (MS); Spanish (MS); special education on both childhood and adolescent levels (MS); teaching English to speakers of other languages (TESOL) in grades pre-K to 12 (MS); TESOL (Advanced Certificate). *Application deadline:* Applications are processed on a rolling basis. *Application fee:* $60. Electronic applications accepted. *Application Contact:* Faye Hood, Assistant Director for Admissions, 516-323-4009, E-mail: fhood@molloy.edu. *Dean,* Joanne O'Brien, 516-323-3116, E-mail: jobrien@molloy.edu.

Graduate Music Therapy Program Students: 12 full-time (9 women), 19 part-time (13 women); includes 8 minority (1 Black or African American, non-Hispanic/Latino; 1 Asian, non-Hispanic/Latino; 5 Hispanic/Latino; 1 Two or more races, non-Hispanic/Latino), 5 international. Average age 31. 27 applicants, 52% accepted, 8 enrolled. *Faculty:* 4 full-time (3 women), 5 part-time/adjunct (4 women). Expenses: Contact institution. *Financial support:* Application deadline: 3/1; applicants required to submit FAFSA. In 2018, 11 master's awarded. *Program availability:* Part-time, evening/weekend. Offers music therapy (MS). *Application deadline:* Applications are processed on a rolling basis. *Application fee:* $60. Electronic applications accepted. *Application Contact:* Faye Hood, Assistant Director for Admissions, 516-323-4009, E-mail: fhood@molloy.edu. *Associate Dean/Director of Graduate Music Therapy,* Suzanne Sorel, 516-323-3322, E-mail: ssorel@molloy.edu.

Program in Clinical Mental Health Counseling Students: 7 full-time (all women), 27 part-time (25 women); includes 10 minority (5 Black or African American, non-Hispanic/Latino; 1 Asian, non-Hispanic/Latino; 3 Hispanic/Latino; 1 Two or more races, non-Hispanic/Latino). Average age 37. 28 applicants, 46% accepted, 10 enrolled. *Faculty:* 5 full-time (4 women), 1 (woman) part-time/adjunct. Expenses: Contact institution. *Financial support:* Application deadline: 3/1; applicants required to submit FAFSA. *Program availability:* Part-time-only, evening/weekend. Offers clinical mental health counseling (MS). *Application deadline:* Applications are processed on a rolling basis. *Application fee:* $60. Electronic applications accepted. *Application Contact:* Faye Hood, Assistant Director for Admissions, 516-323-4009, E-mail: fhood@molloy.edu. *Associate Dean and Director for Department of Clinical Mental Health Counseling,* Dr. Laura B. Kestemberg, 516-323-3842, E-mail: lkestemberg@molloy.edu.

Program in Speech-Language Pathology Students: 88 full-time (86 women); includes 22 minority (3 Black or African American, non-Hispanic/Latino; 1 Asian, non-Hispanic/Latino; 16 Hispanic/Latino; 2 Two or more races, non-Hispanic/Latino). Average age 26. 271 applicants, 43% accepted, 45 enrolled. *Faculty:* 4 full-time (all women), 5 part-time/adjunct (all women). Expenses: Contact institution. *Financial support:* Application deadline: 3/1; applicants required to submit FAFSA. In 2018, 38 master's awarded. *Program availability:* Part-time, evening/weekend. Offers speech-language pathology (MS). *Application deadline:* For fall admission, 2/1 for domestic and international students. *Application fee:* $60. Electronic applications accepted. *Application Contact:* Faye Hood, Assistant Director for Admissions, 516-323-4009, E-mail: fhood@molloy.edu. *Associate Dean,* Susan Alimonti, 516-323-3517, E-mail: salimonti@molloy.edu.

MONMOUTH UNIVERSITY, West Long Branch, NJ 07764-1898

General Information Independent, coed, comprehensive institution. CGS member. *Enrollment:* 658 full-time matriculated graduate/professional students (498 women), 879 part-time matriculated graduate/professional students (679 women). *Enrollment by degree level:* 1,369 master's, 81 doctoral, 87 other advanced degrees. *Graduate faculty:* 128 full-time (75 women), 88 part-time/adjunct (51 women). *Tuition:* Part-time $1233 per credit. *Required fees:* $178 per term. *Graduate housing:* Room and/or apartments available on a first-come, first-served basis to single students; on-campus housing not available to married students. *Student services:* Campus employment opportunities, campus safety program, career counseling, exercise/wellness program, free psychological counseling, international student services, low-cost health insurance, multicultural affairs office, services for students with disabilities, teacher training, writing training. *Library facilities:* Monmouth University Library. *Collection:* Books: 275,000 (physical), 40,416 (digital/electronic); Serial titles: 1,622 (physical), 73,909 (digital/electronic); Databases: 189. Weekly public service hours: 111; students can reserve study rooms.

Computer facilities: Computer purchase and lease plans are available. 1,000 computers available on campus for general student use. A campuswide network can be accessed from student residence rooms and from off campus. Online class registration is available.

Website: http://www.monmouth.edu/

General Application Contact: Lauren Vento-Cifelli, Associate Vice President of Undergraduate and Graduate Admission, 732-571-3562, Fax: 732-263-5123, E-mail: gradadm@monmouth.edu.

GRADUATE UNITS

Graduate Studies Students: 658 full-time (498 women), 874 part-time (675 women); includes 340 minority (111 Black or African American, non-Hispanic/Latino; 2 American Indian or Alaska Native, non-Hispanic/Latino; 64 Asian, non-Hispanic/Latino; 137 Hispanic/Latino; 1 Native Hawaiian or other Pacific Islander, non-Hispanic/Latino; 25 Two or more races, non-Hispanic/Latino), 54 international. Average age 31. *Faculty:* 128 full-time (75 women), 88 part-time/adjunct (51 women). Expenses: Contact institution. *Financial support:* In 2018–19, 1,059 students received support. Career-related internships or fieldwork, institutionally sponsored loans, scholarships/grants, and unspecified assistantships available. Support available to part-time students. Financial award applicants required to submit FAFSA. In 2018, 556 master's, 14 other advanced degrees awarded. *Program availability:* Part-time, evening/weekend, 100% online, blended/hybrid learning. Offers addiction studies (MA); anthropology (MA); clinical mental health counseling (MS); computer science (MS); creative writing (MA); criminal justice (MA); criminal justice administration (Certificate); European history (MA); literature (MA); professional counseling (PMC); public service communication specialist (Certificate); rhetoric and writing (MA); software engineering (MS, Certificate); strategic public relations and new media (Certificate); United States history (MA). *Application deadline:* For fall admission, 7/15 priority date for domestic students, 6/1 for international students; for spring admission, 12/1 priority date for domestic students, 11/1 for international students; for summer admission, 5/1 for domestic students. Applications are processed on a rolling basis. *Application fee:* $50. Electronic applications accepted. *Application Contact:* Laurie Kuhn, Associate Director of Graduate Admission, 732-571-3452, Fax: 732-263-5123, E-mail: gradadm@monmouth.edu. *Vice Provost for Graduate Studies,* Dr. Michael A. Palladino, 732-571-7550, Fax: 732-263-5142.

Leon Hess Business School Students: 91 full-time (47 women), 81 part-time (35 women); includes 17 minority (2 Black or African American, non-Hispanic/Latino; 6 Asian, non-Hispanic/Latino; 7 Hispanic/Latino; 2 Two or more races, non-Hispanic/Latino), 12 international. Average age 29. *Faculty:* 22 full-time (5 women), 8 part-time/adjunct (1 woman). Expenses: Contact institution. *Financial support:* In 2018–19, 131 students received support. Institutionally sponsored loans, scholarships/grants, and unspecified assistantships available. Support available to part-time students. Financial award applicants required to submit FAFSA. In 2018, 79 master's, 1 other advanced degree awarded. *Program availability:* Part-time, evening/weekend. Offers accounting (MBA, Certificate); business administration (MBA); finance (MBA); management (MBA); marketing (MBA); real estate (MBA). *Application deadline:* For fall admission, 7/15 priority date for domestic students, 6/1 for international students; for spring admission, 12/1 priority date for domestic students, 11/1 for international students; for summer admission, 5/1 for domestic students. Applications are processed on a rolling basis. *Application fee:* $50. Electronic applications accepted. *Application Contact:* Laurie Kuhn, Associate Director of Graduate Admission, 732-571-3452, Fax: 732-263-5123, E-mail: gradadm@monmouth.edu. *MBA Program Director,* Dr. Susan Gupta, 732-571-3639, Fax: 732-571-5517, E-mail: sgupta@monmouth.edu.

Marjorie K. Unterberg School of Nursing and Health Studies Students: 92 full-time (68 women), 271 part-time (253 women); includes 124 minority (41 Black or African American, non-Hispanic/Latino; 42 Asian, non-Hispanic/Latino; 37 Hispanic/Latino; 1 Native Hawaiian or other Pacific Islander, non-Hispanic/Latino; 3 Two or more races, non-Hispanic/Latino), 1 international. Average age 37. *Faculty:* 14 full-time (all women), 17 part-time/adjunct (10 women). Expenses: Contact institution. *Financial support:* In 2018–19, 234 students received support. Institutionally sponsored loans, scholarships/grants, and unspecified assistantships available. Support available to part-time students. Financial award applicants required to submit FAFSA. In 2018, 100 master's, 14 doctorates, 10 other advanced degrees awarded. *Program availability:* Part-time, evening/weekend, 100% online, blended/hybrid learning. Offers adult-gerontological primary care nurse practitioner (Post-Master's Certificate); forensic nursing (MSN). *Application deadline:* For fall admission, 7/15 priority date for domestic students, 6/1 for international students; for spring admission, 12/1 priority date for domestic students, 11/1 for international students; for summer admission, 5/1 for domestic students. Applications are processed on a rolling basis. *Application fee:* $50. Electronic applications accepted. *Application Contact:* Lucia Fedele, Graduate Admission Counselor, 732-571-3452, Fax: 732-263-5123, E-mail: gradadm@monmouth.edu. *Dean,* Dr. Janet Mahoney, 732-571-3443, Fax: 732-263-5131, E-mail: jmahoney@monmouth.edu.

School of Education Students: 214 full-time (187 women), 148 part-time (127 women); includes 60 minority (13 Black or African American, non-Hispanic/Latino; 2 Asian, non-Hispanic/Latino; 40 Hispanic/Latino; 5 Two or more races, non-Hispanic/Latino). Average age 27. *Faculty:* 29 full-time (23 women), 32 part-time/adjunct (24 women). Expenses: Contact institution. *Financial support:* In 2018–19, 290 students received support. Institutionally sponsored loans, scholarships/grants, and unspecified assistantships available. Support available to part-time students. Financial award applicants required to submit FAFSA. In 2018, 108 master's, 9 other advanced degrees awarded. *Program availability:* Part-time, evening/weekend, 100% online, blended/hybrid learning. Offers applied behavior analysis (Certificate); autism (Certificate); director of school counseling services (Post-Master's Certificate); early childhood (M Ed); educational leadership (Ed D); elementary education (MAT); English as a second language (M Ed); learning disabilities teacher-consultant (Post-Master's Certificate); literacy (MS Ed); school counseling (MS Ed); special education (MS Ed); speech-language pathology (MS Ed); student affairs and college counseling (MS Ed); supervisor (Post-Master's Certificate); teaching English to speakers of other languages (Certificate). *Application deadline:* For fall admission, 7/15 priority date for domestic students, 7/1 for international students; for spring admission, 12/1 priority date for domestic students, 11/1 for international students; for summer admission, 5/1 for domestic students. Applications are processed on a rolling basis. *Application fee:* $50. Electronic applications accepted. *Application Contact:* Kirsten Sneeringer, Graduate Admission Counselor, 732-571-3452, Fax: 732-263-5123, E-mail: gradadm@monmouth.edu. *Dean,* Dr. John E. Henning, 732-263-5513, Fax: 732-263-5277, E-mail: kodonnel@monmouth.edu.

School of Social Work Students: 102 full-time (97 women), 100 part-time (77 women); includes 73 minority (34 Black or African American, non-Hispanic/Latino; 1 American Indian or Alaska Native, non-Hispanic/Latino; 3 Asian, non-Hispanic/Latino; 28 Hispanic/Latino; 7 Two or more races, non-Hispanic/Latino). Average age 30. *Faculty:* 12 full-time (7 women), 14 part-time/adjunct (12 women). Expenses: Contact institution. *Financial support:* In 2018–19, 122 students received support. Institutionally sponsored loans, scholarships/grants, and unspecified assistantships available. Support available to part-time students. Financial award applicants required to submit FAFSA. In 2018, 91 master's, 2 other advanced degrees awarded. *Program availability:* Part-time, evening/weekend. Offers clinical practice with families and children (MSW); international and community development (MSW); play therapy (Certificate). *Application deadline:* For fall admission, 3/15 for domestic and international students. Applications are processed on a rolling basis. *Application fee:* $50. Electronic applications accepted. *Application Contact:* Lucia Fedele, Graduate Admission Counselor, 732-571-3452, Fax: 732-263-5123, E-mail: gradm@monmouth.edu. *Program Director,* Dr. Carolyn Bradley, 732-263-5477, Fax: 732-263-5217, E-mail: cbradley@monmouth.edu.

Monmouth University (International Student Information)

MONROE COLLEGE, Bronx, NY 10468

General Information Proprietary, coed, comprehensive institution. *Graduate housing:* Rooms and/or apartments available on a first-come, first-served basis to single and married students. Housing application deadline: 5/1.

GRADUATE UNITS

King Graduate School *Program availability:* Online learning. Offers accounting (MS); business administration (MBA); computer science (MS); criminal justice (MS); hospitality management (MS); public health (MPH).

MONTANA STATE UNIVERSITY, Bozeman, MT 59717

General Information State-supported, coed, university. CGS member. *Graduate housing:* Rooms and/or apartments available on a first-come, first-served basis to single and married students. *Research affiliation:* Phillips Environmental (microbial technology), Microvision (information transmission systems), LigoCyte Pharmaceuticals, Inc. (pharmaceuticals), Eli Lilly and Company (antifungal technology), S2 Corporation (instrumentation), ILX Lightwave (laser diodes, electro-optical test equipment).

GRADUATE UNITS

The Graduate School *Program availability:* Part-time, online learning. Electronic applications accepted.

College of Agriculture *Program availability:* Part-time, online learning. Offers agricultural education (MS); agriculture (MS, PhD); animal and range sciences (MS, PhD); immunology and infectious diseases (MS, PhD); land rehabilitation (interdisciplinary) (MS); land resources and environmental sciences (MS); plant pathology (MS); plant sciences (MS, PhD). Electronic applications accepted.

College of Arts and Architecture *Program availability:* Part-time. Offers architecture (M Arch); art (MFA); art history (MA); arts and architecture (M Arch, MA, MFA); science and natural history filmmaking (MFA). Electronic applications accepted.

College of Business *Program availability:* Part-time. Offers professional accountancy (MP Ac). Electronic applications accepted.

College of Education, Health, and Human Development *Program availability:* Part-time, online learning. Offers adult and higher education (Ed D); curriculum and instruction (M Ed, Ed D); education (M Ed); education, health, and human development (M Ed, MS, Ed D, Ed S); educational leadership (Ed D, Ed S); family and consumer sciences (MS). Electronic applications accepted.

College of Engineering *Program availability:* Part-time. Offers chemical engineering (MS); civil engineering (MS); computer science (MS, PhD); construction engineering management (MCEM); electrical engineering (MS); engineering (PhD); environmental engineering (MS); industrial and management engineering (MS); mechanical engineering (MS). Electronic applications accepted.

College of Letters and Science *Program availability:* Part-time, online learning. Offers biochemistry (MS, PhD); biological sciences (PhD); chemistry (MS, PhD); earth sciences (MS, PhD); ecological and environmental statistics (MS); ecology and environmental sciences (PhD); English (MA); fish and wildlife biology (PhD); fish and wildlife management (MS); history (MA, PhD); letters and science (MA, MPA, MS, PhD); mathematics (MS, PhD); microbiology (MS, PhD); Native American studies (MA); neuroscience (MS, PhD); physics (MS, PhD); psychology (MS); public administration (MPA); statistics (MS, PhD). Electronic applications accepted.

College of Nursing *Program availability:* Part-time, online learning. Offers clinical nurse leader (MN); family and individual nurse practitioner (DNP); family nurse practitioner (MN, Post-Master's Certificate); nursing education (Certificate, Post-Master's Certificate); psychiatric mental health nurse practitioner (MN); psychiatric/mental health nurse practitioner (DNP). Electronic applications accepted.

MONTANA STATE UNIVERSITY BILLINGS, Billings, MT 59101

General Information State-supported, coed, comprehensive institution. *Graduate housing:* Rooms and/or apartments available on a first-come, first-served basis to single and married students. Housing application deadline: 5/1.

GRADUATE UNITS

College of Allied Health Professions *Program availability:* Part-time, evening/weekend, 100% online, blended/hybrid learning. Offers allied health professions (MHA, MS); athletic training (MS); clinical rehabilitation and mental health counseling (MS); health administration (MHA). Electronic applications accepted.

College of Arts and Sciences *Program availability:* Part-time, 100% online, blended/hybrid learning. Offers arts and sciences (MS); psychology (MS); public relations (MS). Electronic applications accepted.

College of Education *Program availability:* Part-time, 100% online, blended/hybrid learning. Offers advanced studies (MS Sp Ed); applied behavior analysis (MS Sp Ed);

curriculum and instruction (M Ed); education (M Ed, MS Sp Ed, Certificate); generalist (MS Sp Ed); interdisciplinary studies (M Ed); K-8 elementary education (M Ed); online instructional technologies (M Ed); reading (M Ed); school counseling (M Ed); secondary education (M Ed); special education (MS Sp Ed); teaching (Certificate). Electronic applications accepted.

MONTANA STATE UNIVERSITY–NORTHERN, Havre, MT 59501-7751

General Information State-supported, coed, comprehensive institution. *Graduate housing:* Rooms and/or apartments available on a first-served basis to single students and available to married students. Housing application deadline: 8/22.

GRADUATE UNITS

Graduate Programs *Program availability:* Part-time, evening/weekend, online learning. Offers counselor education (M Ed); education (M Ed, MS Ed); instruction and learning (MS Ed). Electronic applications accepted.

MONTANA TECH OF THE UNIVERSITY OF MONTANA, Butte, MT 59701-8997

General Information State-supported, coed, comprehensive institution. CGS member. *Graduate housing:* Rooms and/or apartments available on a first-come, first-served basis to single and married students. Housing application deadline: 7/1. *Research affiliation:* Newmont Mining (mining and mineral processing), Stillwater Mining (mineral production and training), NorthWestern Energy (electric efficiency), Edison Welding Institute (fuel cell design), Montana Resources, Inc. (mine reclamation and revegetation), QualTech, Inc. (battery monitor technology).

GRADUATE UNITS

Department of Environmental Engineering *Program availability:* Part-time. Offers environmental engineering (MS). Electronic applications accepted.

Department of General Engineering *Program availability:* Part-time. Offers general engineering (MS). Electronic applications accepted.

Department of Industrial Hygiene *Program availability:* Part-time, online learning. Offers industrial hygiene (MS). Electronic applications accepted.

Department of Metallurgical/Mineral Processing Engineering *Program availability:* Part-time. Offers metallurgical/mineral processing engineering (MS). Electronic applications accepted.

Department of Petroleum Engineering *Program availability:* Part-time, evening/weekend. Offers petroleum engineering (MS). Electronic applications accepted.

Department of Technical Communication *Program availability:* Part-time. Offers technical communication (MS). Electronic applications accepted.

Electrical Engineering Program *Program availability:* Part-time. Offers electrical engineering (MS). Electronic applications accepted.

Geosciences Programs *Program availability:* Part-time. Offers geochemistry (MS); geological engineering (MS); geology (MS); geophysical engineering (MS); hydrogeological engineering (MS); hydrogeology (MS). Electronic applications accepted.

Health Care Informatics Program *Program availability:* Part-time, evening/weekend, online learning. Offers health care informatics (Certificate). Electronic applications accepted.

Interdisciplinary Program *Program availability:* Part-time. Offers interdisciplinary studies (MS).

Mining Engineering Program *Program availability:* Part-time. Offers mining engineering (MS). Electronic applications accepted.

Program in Materials Science Offers materials science (PhD).

Project Engineering and Management Program *Program availability:* Part-time, evening/weekend, online learning. Offers project engineering and management (MPEM). Electronic applications accepted.

MONTCLAIR STATE UNIVERSITY, Montclair, NJ 07043-1624

General Information State-supported, coed, university. CGS member. *Graduate housing:* Room and/or apartments available on a first-come, first-served basis to single students; on-campus housing not available to married students. Housing application deadline: 3/1. *Research affiliation:* Spencer Foundation (education improvement), The International Society for Optical Engineering (optics and photonics), Deafness Research Foundation (heating science).

GRADUATE UNITS

The Graduate School *Program availability:* Part-time, evening/weekend. Electronic applications accepted.

College of Education and Human Services *Program availability:* Part-time, evening/weekend. Offers art (MAT); biology (MAT); certified alcohol and drug counselor (Certificate); chemistry (MAT); counseling (MA); counselor education (PhD); developmental models of autism intervention (Certificate); dietetics (Postbaccalaureate Certificate); earth science (MAT); education and human services (M Ed, MA, MAT, MPH, MS, Ed D, PhD, Certificate, Post Master's Certificate, Postbaccalaureate Certificate); educational leadership (MA); English (MAT); exercise science (MA); family and child studies (MA); family studies (PhD); French (MAT); health and physical education (MAT); health education (MAT); inclusive early childhood education (M Ed); infant and early childhood mental health (Certificate); learning disabilities (M Ed); mathematics (MAT); music (MAT); nutrition and exercise science (Certificate); nutrition and food science (MS); physical education (MAT); physical science (MAT); program evaluation (Certificate); public health (MPH); reading (MA); social studies (MAT); Spanish (MAT); sports administration and coaching (MA); teacher education and teacher development (PhD); teacher of English as a second language (MAT); teaching and supervision in physical education (MA). Electronic applications accepted.

College of Humanities and Social Sciences *Program availability:* Part-time, evening/weekend. Offers adolescent advocacy (Certificate); applied linguistics (MA); audiology (Sc D); child advocacy and policy (MA, Certificate); clinical psychology (MA); communication sciences and disorders (MA); computational linguistics (Certificate); conflict management and peace studies (MA); conflict management in the workplace (Certificate); data collection and management (Certificate); English (MA); family/civil forensic psychology (Certificate); forensic psychology (Certificate); French literature (MA); French studies (MA); governance, compliance and regulation (MA); humanities and social sciences (MA, Sc D, Certificate); industrial and organizational psychology (MA); intellectual property (MA); law and governance (MA); legal management (MA); paralegal studies (Certificate); psychology (MA); Spanish (MA); teaching English to speakers of other languages (Certificate); teaching writing (Certificate); translation and interpreting in Spanish (Certificate). Electronic applications accepted.

College of Science and Mathematics *Program availability:* Part-time, evening/weekend. Offers biological science/education (MS); biology (MS); chemistry (MS); computer networking (Certificate); computer science (MS); earth and environmental science (MS); ecology and evolution (MS); environmental education (MA); environmental forensics (Certificate); environmental management (MA); environmental science (MA); geographic information science (Certificate); geoscience (MS); information technology (MS); marine biology and coastal sciences (MS); mathematics education (Ed D); molecular biology (MS, Certificate); pharmaceutical biochemistry (MS); physiology (MS); pure and applied mathematics (MS); science and mathematics (MA, MAT, MS, Ed D, PhD, Certificate); statistics (MS); sustainability science (MS); teaching middle grades mathematics (MA, Certificate); teaching physical education (MAT); water resource management (Certificate). Electronic applications accepted.

College of the Arts *Program availability:* Part-time, evening/weekend. Offers arts (MA, MFA, AD, Performer's Certificate, Postbaccalaureate Certificate); arts management (MA); museum management (MA); music (MA, AD, Performer's Certificate); music education (MA); music therapy (MA, Postbaccalaureate Certificate); performance (MA); production/stage management (MA); public and organizational relations (MA); studio (MA); studio art (MFA); theatre studies (MA); theory/composition (MA). Electronic applications accepted.

Feliciano School of Business *Program availability:* Part-time, evening/weekend. Offers accounting (MS, Post Master's Certificate); business (MBA, MS, Graduate Certificate, Post Master's Certificate); business analytics (MBA); digital marketing (MBA); finance (MBA); forensic accounting (Graduate Certificate); general business administration (MBA); human resources management (MBA); management (MBA); management of information and technology (MBA); marketing (MBA); project management (MBA). Electronic applications accepted.

MONTREAT COLLEGE, Montreat, NC 28757-1267

General Information Independent-religious, coed, comprehensive institution. *Graduate housing:* On-campus housing not available.

GRADUATE UNITS

School of Professional and Adult Studies *Program availability:* Part-time, evening/weekend, online learning. Electronic applications accepted.

MOODY BIBLE INSTITUTE, Chicago, IL 60610-3284

General Information Independent-religious, coed, comprehensive institution. *Graduate housing:* Rooms and/or apartments guaranteed to single students and available on a first-come, first-served basis to married students. Housing application deadline: 6/1.

GRADUATE UNITS

Graduate School *Program availability:* Part-time. Offers biblical studies (MABS, Graduate Certificate); intercultural studies (MAIS, Graduate Certificate); ministry (M Div, M Min); spiritual formation and discipleship (MASF, Graduate Certificate); urban studies (MA, Graduate Certificate).

MOODY THEOLOGICAL SEMINARY–MICHIGAN, Plymouth, MI 48170

General Information Independent-religious, coed, graduate-only institution. *Graduate housing:* On-campus housing not available.

GRADUATE UNITS

Graduate Programs *Program availability:* Part-time, evening/weekend. Offers Bible (Graduate Certificate); Christian education (MA); counseling psychology (MA); divinity (M Div); theological studies (MA).

MOORE COLLEGE OF ART & DESIGN, Philadelphia, PA 19103

General Information Independent, Undergraduate: women only; graduate: coed, comprehensive institution.

GRADUATE UNITS

Program in Art Education *Program availability:* Part-time. Offers art education (MA).

Program in Community Practice Offers community practice (MFA).

Program in Interior Design *Program availability:* Evening/weekend. Offers interior design (MFA).

Program in Social Engagement *Program availability:* Part-time. Offers social engagement (MA).

Program in Studio Art Offers studio art (MFA).

MORAVIAN COLLEGE, Bethlehem, PA 18018-6650

General Information Independent-religious, coed, comprehensive institution. *Enrollment:* 62 full-time matriculated graduate/professional students (42 women), 240 part-time matriculated graduate/professional students (181 women). *Enrollment by degree level:* 291 master's, 11 doctoral. *Graduate faculty:* 11 full-time (5 women), 29 part-time/adjunct (13 women). *Graduate housing:* On-campus housing not available. *Student services:* Campus employment opportunities, campus safety program, career counseling, exercise/wellness program, international student services, multicultural affairs office, services for students with disabilities, teacher training, writing training. *Library facilities:* Reeves Library. *Collection:* Books: 198,012 (physical), 168,981 (digital/electronic); Serial titles: 2,490 (physical), 183 (digital/electronic); Databases: 67. Weekly public service hours: 86.

Computer facilities: Computer purchase and lease plans are available. 230 computers available on campus for general student use. A campuswide network can be accessed from student residence rooms and from off campus. Online class registration is available.
Website: http://www.moravian.edu/

General Application Contact: Scott Dams, Dean of Graduate & Adult Enrollment, 610-861-1400, E-mail: graduate@moravian.edu.

GRADUATE UNITS

Graduate and Continuing Studies Students: 62 full-time (42 women), 240 part-time (181 women); includes 35 minority (9 Black or African American, non-Hispanic/Latino; 5 Asian, non-Hispanic/Latino; 21 Hispanic/Latino), 2 international. Average age 32. 475 applicants, 69% accepted, 249 enrolled. *Faculty:* 11 full-time (5 women), 29 part-time/adjunct (13 women). Expenses: Contact institution. *Financial support:* Applicants required to submit FAFSA. In 2018, 83 master's awarded. *Program availability:* Part-time, evening/weekend, 100% online. Offers accounting (MBA); athletic training (MS, DAT); business management (MBA); curriculum and instruction (M Ed); education (MAT); health administration (MHA); HR leadership (MSHRM); speech-language pathology (MS); supply chain management (MBA). *Application deadline:* For fall admission, 8/1 priority date for domestic and international students; for spring admission, 1/1 priority date for domestic and international students; for summer admission, 5/1 priority date for domestic and international students. Applications are processed on a rolling basis. Electronic applications accepted. *Application Contact:* Kristina Sullivan, Director of Student Recruitment Operations, 610-861-1400, Fax: 610-861-1466, E-mail: graduate@moravian.edu. *Dean of Graduate and Adult Enrollment,* Scott Dams, 610-861-1400, Fax: 610-861-1466, E-mail: graduate@moravian.edu.

Helen S. Breidegam School of Nursing Students: 6 full-time (5 women), 82 part-time (77 women); includes 13 minority (4 Black or African American, non-Hispanic/Latino; 4 Asian, non-Hispanic/Latino; 5 Hispanic/Latino), 1 international. Average age 37. 78 applicants, 67% accepted, 54 enrolled. *Faculty:* 2 full-time (1 woman), 7 part-time/adjunct (5 women). Expenses: Contact institution. *Financial support:* Applicants required to submit FAFSA. In 2018, 22 master's awarded. *Program availability:* Part-time, evening/weekend. Offers clinical nurse leader (MS); nurse administrator (MS); nurse educator (MS); nurse practitioner - acute care (MS); nurse practitioner - primary care (MS). *Application deadline:* For fall admission, 8/1 priority date for domestic and international students; for spring admission, 1/1 priority date for domestic and international students; for summer admission, 5/1 priority date for domestic and international students. Applications are processed on a rolling basis. Electronic applications accepted. *Application Contact:* Caroline Bechtel, Student Experience Mentor, 610-861-1400, Fax: 610-861-1466, E-mail: graduate@moravian.edu.

MORAVIAN THEOLOGICAL SEMINARY, Bethlehem, PA 18018-6614

General Information Independent-religious, coed, graduate-only institution. *Enrollment by degree level:* 61 master's, 12 other advanced degrees. *Graduate faculty:* 9 full-time (4 women), 1 (woman) part-time/adjunct. *Tuition:* Part-time $650 per credit hour. *Required fees:* $215. *Graduate housing:* Rooms and/or apartments available on a first-come, first-served basis to single and married students. Typical cost: $833 per year for single students; $833 per year for married students. Room charges vary according to housing facility selected. Housing application deadline: 7/31. *Student services:* Campus employment opportunities, campus safety program, exercise/wellness program, international student services, low-cost health insurance, multicultural affairs office, services for students with disabilities, writing training. *Library facilities:* Reeves Library. *Collection:* Books: 192,017 (physical), 137,800 (digital/electronic); Serial titles: 6,082 (physical), 2,168 (digital/electronic); Databases: 62. Weekly public service hours: 100; students can reserve study rooms.

Computer facilities: 227 computers available on campus for general student use. A campuswide network can be accessed from student residence rooms and from off campus. Online class registration is available.
Website: http://www.moravianseminary.edu/

General Application Contact: Rev. Randy D'Angelo, Director of Seminary Enrollment, 610-861-1512, Fax: 610-861-1569, E-mail: dangelor@moravian.edu.

GRADUATE UNITS

Graduate and Certificate Programs Students: 20 full-time (16 women), 53 part-time (38 women); includes 15 minority (4 Black or African American, non-Hispanic/Latino; 10 Hispanic/Latino; 1 Two or more races, non-Hispanic/Latino), 1 international. Average age 43. 37 applicants, 65% accepted, 22 enrolled. *Faculty:* 9 full-time (4 women), 1 (woman) part-time/adjunct. Expenses: Contact institution. *Financial support:* In 2018–19, 52 students received support. Career-related internships or fieldwork, Federal Work-Study, and scholarships/grants available. Support available to part-time students. Financial award application deadline: 7/15; financial award applicants required to submit FAFSA. In 2018, 20 master's, 6 other advanced degrees awarded. *Program availability:* Part-time. Offers Biblical studies (Graduate Certificate); formative spirituality (M Div, Graduate Certificate); spiritual direction (MATS, Graduate Certificate). Marywood University. *Application deadline:* For fall admission, 7/15 for domestic students, 4/1 priority date for international students; for spring admission, 11/15 for domestic students, 9/1 priority date for international students. Applications are processed on a rolling basis. *Application fee:* $50. Electronic applications accepted. *Application Contact:* Randy D'Angelo, Director of Seminary Enrollment, 610-861-1512, Fax: 610-861-1569, E-mail: dangelor@moravian.edu. *Dean and Vice President,* Rev. Dr. Frank L. Crouch, 610-861-1516, E-mail: crouchf@moravian.edu.

MOREHEAD STATE UNIVERSITY, Morehead, KY 40351

General Information State-supported, coed, comprehensive institution. *Graduate housing:* Room and/or apartments available on a first-come, first-served basis to single students; on-campus housing not available to married students. Housing application deadline: 3/12.

GRADUATE UNITS

Graduate School *Program availability:* Part-time, evening/weekend, online learning. Electronic applications accepted.

Caudill College of Arts, Humanities and Social Sciences *Program availability:* Part-time, evening/weekend, online learning. Offers art education (MA); arts, humanities and social sciences (MA, MM); communication (MA); criminology (MA); English (MA); general sociology (MA); gerontology (MA); graphic design (MA); music education (MM); music performance (MM); sociology regional analysis (MA); sociology/chemical dependency (MA); studio art (MA). Electronic applications accepted.

College of Education *Program availability:* Part-time, evening/weekend. Offers adult and higher education (MA, Ed S); business and marketing education (MAT); certified professional counselor (Ed S); counseling P-12 (MA); curriculum and instruction (Ed S); education (MA, MA Ed, MAT, Ed S); educational technology (MA Ed); English/language arts 5-9 (MAT); French (MAT); health P-12 (MAT); instructional leadership (Ed S); learning and behavioral disorders P-12 (MAT); mathematics 5-9 (MAT); moderate and severe disabilities P-12 (MAT); physical education P-12 (MAT); school administration (MA); school counseling (Ed S); science 5-9 (MAT); secondary biology (MAT); secondary chemistry (MAT); secondary earth science (MAT); secondary English (MAT); secondary math (MAT); secondary physics (MAT); secondary social studies (MAT); social studies 5-9 (MAT); Spanish (MAT); teacher leader business and marketing content (MA Ed); teacher leader business and marketing technology (MA Ed); teacher leader educational technology (MA Ed); teacher leader English (MA Ed); teacher leader gifted education (MA Ed); teacher leader IECE certification (MA Ed); teacher leader interdisciplinary education P-5 (MA Ed); teacher leader middle grades (MA Ed); teacher leader non IECE certification (MA Ed); teacher leader reading/writing - non-certification (MA Ed); teacher leader reading/writing certification (MA Ed); teacher leader school communication - certification (MA Ed); teacher leader school communication - non-certification (MA Ed); teacher leader social studies (MA Ed); teacher leader special education (MA Ed). Electronic applications accepted.

College of Science *Program availability:* Part-time, evening/weekend. Offers biology (MS); biology regional analysis (MS); career and technical agricultural education

(MS); clinical/counseling psychology (MS); general/experimental psychology (MS); science (MA, MS); wellness promotion (MA). Electronic applications accepted.

Elmer R. Smith College of Business and Technology *Program availability:* Part-time, evening/weekend, online learning. Offers business administration (MBA); business and technology (MA, MBA, MPA, MSIS); career and technical education (MS); computer information systems and analytics (MS); engineering and technology (MS). Electronic applications accepted.

Institute for Regional Analysis and Public Policy Offers public administration (MPA). Electronic applications accepted.

MOREHOUSE SCHOOL OF MEDICINE, Atlanta, GA 30310-1495

General Information Independent, coed, graduate-only institution. CGS member. *Graduate housing:* On-campus housing not available. *Research affiliation:* Merck & Company, Inc. (hypotension), CareStat (renal insufficiency), Wyeth (helicobacter pylori study), Bristol-Myers Squibb (pharmacokinetics), Parke-Davis (cardiovascular risk factors), NitroMel, Inc. (heart failure).

GRADUATE UNITS

Graduate Programs in Biomedical Sciences Offers biomedical research (MS); biomedical sciences (PhD); biomedical technology (MS); medical sciences (MS). Electronic applications accepted.

Master of Public Health Program *Program availability:* Part-time. Offers public health (MPH). Electronic applications accepted.

Master of Science in Clinical Research Program *Program availability:* Part-time. Offers clinical research (MS). Electronic applications accepted.

Professional Program Offers medicine (MD). Electronic applications accepted.

MORGAN STATE UNIVERSITY, Baltimore, MD 21251

General Information State-supported, coed, university. CGS member. *Graduate housing:* Rooms and/or apartments available on a first-come, first-served basis to single and married students.

GRADUATE UNITS

School of Graduate Studies *Program availability:* Part-time, evening/weekend.

Clarence M. Mitchell, Jr. School of Engineering *Program availability:* Part-time, evening/weekend. Offers civil engineering (M Eng, D Eng); electrical and computer engineering (M Eng, MS, D Eng); industrial and systems engineering (M Eng, D Eng); transportation (MS, PhD, Postbaccalaureate Certificate); transportation and urban infrastructure studies (MS, PhD, Postbaccalaureate Certificate).

College of Liberal Arts *Program availability:* Part-time. Offers African-American studies (MA); economics (MA); English (MA, PhD); history (MA, PhD); international studies (MA); liberal arts (MA, MS, PhD); museum studies and historic preservation (MA); music (MA); psychometrics (MS, PhD); sociology (MA, MS).

Earl G. Graves School of Business and Management *Program availability:* Part-time, evening/weekend. Offers accounting (MS); business administration (MBA, PhD); business and management (MBA, PhD); hospitality management (MS); project management (MS).

School of Architecture and Planning Offers architecture (M Arch); city and regional planning (MCRP); landscape architecture (MLA).

School of Community Health and Policy Offers nursing (MS, PhD); public health (MPH, Dr PH).

School of Computer, Mathematical, and Natural Sciences Offers bioenvironmental science (PhD); bioinformatics (MS); biology (MS); chemistry (MS); computer science (MS); computer, mathematical, and natural sciences (MA, MS, PhD); industrial and computational mathematics (PhD); mathematics (MA); physics (MS).

School of Education and Urban Studies *Program availability:* Part-time. Offers community college leadership (Ed D); education and urban studies (MA, MAT, MS, Ed D, PhD); elementary education (MAT); higher education (PhD); higher education administration (MA, PhD); higher education and student affairs administration (MA); mathematics education (MS, Ed D); science education (MS, Ed D); urban educational leadership (Ed D).

School of Global Journalism and Communication Offers journalism (MA).

School of Social Work Offers social work (MSW).

MORNINGSIDE COLLEGE, Sioux City, IA 51106

General Information Independent-religious, coed, comprehensive institution. *Graduate housing:* On-campus housing not available. *Research affiliation:* Iowa Public Service Company (biology, chemistry, physics).

GRADUATE UNITS

Graduate Programs *Program availability:* Part-time, evening/weekend, online only, 100% online. Electronic applications accepted.

Nylen School of Nursing *Program availability:* Part-time, online only, 100% online. Offers adult gerontology primary care nurse practitioner (MSN); clinical nurse leader (MSN); family primary care nurse practitioner (MSN). Electronic applications accepted.

Sharon Walker School of Education *Program availability:* Part-time, online only, 100% online. Offers professional educator (MAT); special education (MAT). Electronic applications accepted.

MOUNT ALLISON UNIVERSITY, Sackville, NB E4L 1E4, Canada

General Information Province-supported, coed, comprehensive institution. *Graduate housing:* Room and/or apartments guaranteed to single students; on-campus housing not available to married students. Housing application deadline: 8/31. *Research affiliation:* Atlantic Cancer Institute (medical research), Moncton Hospital (medical research), Huntsman Marine Science Centre (marine biology).

GRADUATE UNITS

Department of Biology Offers biology (M Sc).

Department of Chemistry and Biochemistry Offers chemistry (M Sc).

MOUNT ALOYSIUS COLLEGE, Cresson, PA 16630-1999

General Information Independent-religious, coed, comprehensive institution. *Graduate housing:* On-campus housing not available. *Student services:* Campus employment opportunities, campus safety program, career counseling, child daycare facilities, exercise/wellness program, free psychological counseling, international student services, services for students with disabilities, writing training. *Library facilities:* Mount Aloysius College Library.

Computer facilities: Computer purchase and lease plans are available. A campuswide network can be accessed from student residence rooms and from off campus. Online class registration is available.
Website: http://www.mtaloy.edu/

General Application Contact: Matthew P. Bodenschatz, Director of Graduate and Continuing Education Admissions, 814-886-6556, Fax: 814-886-6441, E-mail: mbodenschatz@mtaloy.edu.

GRADUATE UNITS

Program in Business Administration Expenses: Contact institution. *Financial support:* Unspecified assistantships available. Financial award applicants required to submit FAFSA. *Program availability:* Part-time, evening/weekend. Offers accounting (MBA); health and human services administration (MBA); non-profit management (MBA); project management (MBA). *Application deadline:* For fall admission, 8/1 for domestic students; for spring admission, 12/1 for domestic students. Applications are processed on a rolling basis. *Application fee:* $30. Electronic applications accepted. *Application Contact:* Matthew P. Bodenschatz, Director of Graduate and Continuing Education Admissions, 814-886-6556, Fax: 814-886-6441, E-mail: mbodenschatz@mtaloy.edu.

Program in Community Counseling Expenses: Contact institution. *Financial support:* Unspecified assistantships available. Financial award applicants required to submit FAFSA. *Program availability:* Evening/weekend. Offers community counseling (MS). *Application deadline:* For fall admission, 8/1 for domestic students; for spring admission, 12/1 for domestic students. Applications are processed on a rolling basis. *Application fee:* $30. Electronic applications accepted. *Application Contact:* Matthew P. Bodenschatz, Director of Graduate and Continuing Education Admissions, 814-886-6556, Fax: 814-886-6441, E-mail: mbodenschatz@mtaloy.edu.

MOUNT ANGEL SEMINARY, Saint Benedict, OR 97373

General Information Independent-religious, Undergraduate: men only; graduate: coed, comprehensive institution. *Graduate housing:* Room and/or apartments guaranteed to single students; on-campus housing not available to married students.

GRADUATE UNITS

Program in Theology *Program availability:* Part-time. Offers theology (M Div, MA).

MOUNT CARMEL COLLEGE OF NURSING, Columbus, OH 43222

General Information Independent, coed, primarily women, comprehensive institution. *Enrollment:* 1,090 graduate, professional, and undergraduate students; 97 full-time matriculated graduate/professional students (81 women), 107 part-time matriculated graduate/professional students (94 women). *Enrollment by degree level:* 204 master's, 4 doctoral, 2 other advanced degrees. *Graduate faculty:* 8 full-time (all women), 7 part-time/adjunct (6 women). *Tuition:* Full-time $11,403; part-time $543 per credit hour. *Required fees:* $85; $85 per unit. *Graduate housing:* Rooms and/or apartments available on a first-come, first-served basis to single and married students. Typical cost: $5000 per year for married students. Housing application deadline: 7/1. *Student services:* Free psychological counseling, multicultural affairs office, services for students with disabilities, teacher training, writing training. *Library facilities:* The Mount Carmel Health Sciences Library plus 1 other. *Collection:* Books: 8,163 (physical), 297,441 (digital/electronic); Serial titles: 683 (physical), 48,768 (digital/electronic); Databases: 178. Weekly public service hours: 61; study areas open 24 hours, 5–7 days a week; students can reserve study rooms.

Computer facilities: 25 computers available on campus for general student use. A campuswide network can be accessed from student residence rooms. Online class registration is available.

Website: http://www.mccn.edu/

General Application Contact: Dr. Kim Campbell, Director of Recruitment and Admissions, 614-234-5144, Fax: 614-234-5427, E-mail: kcampbell@mccn.edu.

GRADUATE UNITS

Nursing Program Students: 106 full-time (89 women), 111 part-time (96 women); includes 49 minority (30 Black or African American, non-Hispanic/Latino; 7 Asian, non-Hispanic/Latino; 5 Hispanic/Latino; 7 Two or more races, non-Hispanic/Latino). Average age 35. 135 applicants, 77% accepted, 68 enrolled. *Faculty:* 8 full-time (all women), 7 part-time/adjunct (6 women). Expenses: Contact institution. *Financial support:* In 2018–19, 11 students received support. Institutionally sponsored loans and scholarships/grants available. Financial award application deadline: 3/1; financial award applicants required to submit FAFSA. In 2018, 57 master's awarded. *Program availability:* Part-time. Offers adult gerontology acute care nurse practitioner (MS); adult health clinical nurse specialist (MS); family nurse practitioner (MS); nursing (DNP); nursing administration (MS); nursing education (MS). *Application deadline:* For fall admission, 2/1 priority date for domestic students; for spring admission, 11/1 priority date for domestic students. Applications are processed on a rolling basis. *Application fee:* $30. Electronic applications accepted. *Application Contact:* Dr. Kim Campbell, Director of Recruitment and Admissions, 614-234-5144, Fax: 614-234-5427, E-mail: kcampbell@mccn.edu. *Interim Associate Dean Graduate Studies,* Dr. Jami Nininger, 614-234-1777, Fax: 614-234-2875, E-mail: jnininger@mccn.edu.

MOUNT HOLYOKE COLLEGE, South Hadley, MA 01075

General Information Independent, women only, comprehensive institution. *Enrollment:* 16 full-time matriculated graduate/professional students (15 women), 111 part-time matriculated graduate/professional students (91 women). *Enrollment by degree level:* 127 master's. *Graduate faculty:* 48 part-time/adjunct (38 women). *Tuition:* Full-time $27,900; part-time $775 per credit hour. One-time fee: $150. Tuition and fees vary according to course level, course load, program and student level. *Graduate housing:* On-campus housing not available. *Student services:* Campus employment opportunities, campus safety program, career counseling, exercise/wellness program, free psychological counseling, international student services, multicultural affairs office, services for students with disabilities, teacher training, writing training. *Library facilities:* Williston Memorial Library plus 2 others. *Collection:* Books: 662,010 (physical), 853,290 (digital/electronic); Serial titles: 603 (physical), 8,098 (digital/electronic); Databases: 227. Weekly public service hours: 115; students can reserve study rooms.

Computer facilities: Computer purchase and lease plans are available. 392 computers available on campus for general student use. A campuswide network can be accessed from student residence rooms and from off campus. Online class registration, personal Web pages are available.

Website: http://www.mtholyoke.edu/

General Application Contact: Dr. Tiffany Espinosa, Executive Director of Professional and Graduate Education, 413-538-3478, Fax: 413-538-3098, E-mail: tespinos@mtholyoke.edu.

GRADUATE UNITS

Professional and Graduate Education (PaGE) Students: 16 full-time (15 women), 111 part-time (91 women); includes 23 minority (5 Black or African American, non-Hispanic/Latino; 2 Asian, non-Hispanic/Latino; 10 Hispanic/Latino; 6 Two or more races, non-Hispanic/Latino), 7 international. Average age 36. 86 applicants, 91% accepted, 50 enrolled. *Faculty:* 48 part-time/adjunct (38 women). Expenses: Contact institution. *Financial support:* In 2018–19, 134 students received support, including 5 fellowships with partial tuition reimbursements available (averaging $3,390 per year); scholarships/grants and unspecified assistantships also available. Financial award applicants required to submit FAFSA. In 2018, 32 master's awarded. *Program availability:* Part-time, evening/weekend, blended/hybrid learning. Offers initial teacher licensure (MAT); mathematics teaching (MAMT); teacher leadership (MATL). *Application deadline:* For fall admission, 8/1 for domestic and international students; for winter admission, 12/1 for domestic and international students; for spring admission, 1/15 for domestic and international students; for summer admission, 5/15 for domestic and international students. Applications are processed on a rolling basis. *Application fee:* $50. Electronic applications accepted. *Application Contact:* Dr. Tiffany Espinosa, Executive Director of Professional and Graduate Education, 413-538-3478, Fax: 413-538-3098, E-mail: tespinos@mtholyoke.edu. *Executive Director of Professional and Graduate Education,* Dr. Tiffany Espinosa, 413-538-3478, Fax: 413-538-3098, E-mail: tespinos@mtholyoke.edu.

MOUNT MARTY COLLEGE, Yankton, SD 57078-3724

General Information Independent-religious, coed, comprehensive institution. *Graduate housing:* On-campus housing not available.

GRADUATE UNITS

Graduate Studies Division Offers business administration (MBA); nurse anesthesia (MS); nursing (MSN); pastoral ministries (MPM). Electronic applications accepted.

MOUNT MARY UNIVERSITY, Milwaukee, WI 53222-4597

General Information Independent-religious, Undergraduate: women only; graduate: coed, comprehensive institution. CGS member. *Graduate housing:* Room and/or apartments available on a first-come, first-served basis to single students; on-campus housing not available to married students.

GRADUATE UNITS

Graduate Programs *Program availability:* Part-time, evening/weekend, 100% online, blended/hybrid learning. Offers art therapy (MS, DAT); clinical mental health counseling (MS, Certificate); clinical rehabilitation counseling (MS, Certificate); creative writing (MA); dietetics (MS); dietetics internship (MS); general management (MBA); health systems leadership (MBA); occupational therapy (MS, OTD); professional and new media writing (MA); professional development (MA); school counseling (MS, Certificate); vocational rehabilitation counseling (MS, Certificate). Electronic applications accepted.

MOUNT MERCY UNIVERSITY, Cedar Rapids, IA 52402-4797

General Information Independent-religious, coed, comprehensive institution.

GRADUATE UNITS

Program in Business Administration *Program availability:* Evening/weekend. Offers human resource (MBA); quality management (MBA). Electronic applications accepted.

Program in Criminal Justice *Program availability:* Evening/weekend, online learning. Offers criminal justice (MA).

Program in Education Offers reading (MA Ed); special education (MA Ed); teacher leadership (MA Ed). Electronic applications accepted.

Program in Marriage and Family Therapy *Program availability:* Evening/weekend. Offers marriage and family therapy (MA).

Program in Nursing *Program availability:* Evening/weekend. Offers health advocacy (MSN); nurse administration (MSN); nurse education (MSN).

Program in Strategic Leadership *Program availability:* Evening/weekend. Offers strategic leadership (MSL).

MOUNT ST. JOSEPH UNIVERSITY, Cincinnati, OH 45233-1670

General Information Independent-religious, coed, comprehensive institution. CGS member. *Graduate housing:* Room and/or apartments available on a first-come, first-served basis to single students; on-campus housing not available to married students. Housing application deadline: 4/1.

GRADUATE UNITS

Doctor of Nursing Practice Program *Program availability:* Part-time-only. Offers health systems leadership (DNP). Electronic applications accepted.

Graduate Education Program *Program availability:* Part-time, evening/weekend, 100% online, blended/hybrid learning. Offers adolescent to young adult education (MA); dyslexia (Certificate); inclusive early childhood education (MA); middle childhood education (MA); multicultural special education (MA); reading science (MA). Electronic applications accepted.

Graduate Program in Religious Studies *Program availability:* Part-time, evening/weekend. Offers religious studies (MA); spirituality and wellness (Certificate). Electronic applications accepted.

Master of Business Administration Program *Program availability:* Part-time, evening/weekend. Offers business administration (MBA). Electronic applications accepted.

Master of Science in Nursing Program *Program availability:* Part-time. Offers administration (MSN); clinical nurse leader (MSN); education (MSN). Electronic applications accepted.

Master of Science in Organizational Leadership Program *Program availability:* Part-time, evening/weekend. Offers organizational leadership (MS). Electronic applications accepted.

Master's Graduate Entry-Level into Nursing (MAGELIN) Program Offers nursing (MSN). Electronic applications accepted.

Physical Therapy Program Offers physical therapy (DPT). Electronic applications accepted.

MOUNT SAINT MARY COLLEGE, Newburgh, NY 12550-3494

General Information Independent, coed, comprehensive institution. *Enrollment:* 2,352 graduate, professional, and undergraduate students; 61 full-time matriculated graduate/professional students (33 women), 277 part-time matriculated graduate/professional students (244 women). *Enrollment by degree level:* 327 master's, 11 other advanced degrees. *Graduate faculty:* 19 full-time (15 women), 16 part-time/adjunct (13 women). *Tuition:* Full-time $14,454; part-time $803 per credit. *Required fees:* $172; $86 per semester. *Graduate housing:* Room and/or apartments guaranteed to single students; on-campus housing not available to married students. Typical cost: $9776 per year ($16,132 including board). Housing application deadline: 5/1. *Student services:* Campus employment opportunities, campus safety program, career counseling, free psychological counseling, international student services, services for students with disabilities. *Library facilities:* Kaplan Family Library and Learning Center. *Collection:* Books: 84,909 (physical), 11,569 (digital/electronic); Serial titles: 195 (physical), 59,481 (digital/electronic); Databases: 93. Students can reserve study rooms.

Computer facilities: Computer purchase and lease plans are available. 470 computers available on campus for general student use. A campuswide network can be accessed from student residence rooms and from off campus. Online class registration is available.
Website: http://www.msmc.edu/

General Application Contact: Eileen Bardney, Director of Admissions, 845-569-3254, Fax: 845-569-3438, E-mail: Eileen.Bardney@msmc.edu.

GRADUATE UNITS

Division of Education Students: 19 full-time (14 women), 78 part-time (64 women); includes 7 minority (5 Hispanic/Latino; 1 Native Hawaiian or other Pacific Islander, non-Hispanic/Latino; 1 Two or more races, non-Hispanic/Latino). Average age 28. 31 applicants, 61% accepted, 17 enrolled. *Faculty:* 7 full-time (6 women), 7 part-time/adjunct (all women). Expenses: Contact institution. *Financial support:* In 2018–19, 17 students received support. Institutionally sponsored loans, scholarships/grants, and unspecified assistantships available. Financial award application deadline: 4/15; financial award applicants required to submit FAFSA. In 2018, 28 master's awarded. *Program availability:* Part-time, evening/weekend. Offers adolescence and special education (MS Ed); childhood education (MS Ed); literacy education (MS Ed); middle school (7-9) (MS Ed). *Application deadline:* Applications are processed on a rolling basis. *Application fee:* $45. Electronic applications accepted. *Application Contact:* Eileen Bardney, Director of Admissions, 845-569-3254, Fax: 845-569-3438, E-mail: Eileen.Bardney@msmc.edu. *Graduate Coordinator,* Dr. Vicki Caruana, 845-569-3530, Fax: 845-569-3551, E-mail: Victoria.caruana@msmc.edu.

School of Business Students: 37 full-time (14 women), 30 part-time (19 women); includes 14 minority (3 Black or African American, non-Hispanic/Latino; 1 Asian, non-Hispanic/Latino; 10 Hispanic/Latino). Average age 30. 16 applicants, 81% accepted, 10 enrolled. *Faculty:* 6 full-time (3 women), 3 part-time/adjunct (0 women). Expenses: Contact institution. *Financial support:* In 2018–19, 13 students received support. Scholarships/grants and unspecified assistantships available. Financial award application deadline: 4/15; financial award applicants required to submit FAFSA. In 2018, 48 master's awarded. *Program availability:* Part-time, evening/weekend. Offers business (MBA); financial planning (MBA); health care management (MBA). *Application deadline:* Applications are processed on a rolling basis. *Application fee:* $45. Electronic applications accepted. *Application Contact:* Eileen Bardney, Director of Admissions, 845-569-3254, Fax: 845-569-3438, E-mail: Eileen.Bardney@msmc.edu. *Graduate Coordinator,* Dr. Veronica McMillian, 845-569-3119, Fax: 845-569-3885, E-mail: veronica.mcmillan@msmc.edu.

School of Nursing Students: 5 full-time (all women), 169 part-time (161 women); includes 41 minority (20 Black or African American, non-Hispanic/Latino; 1 American Indian or Alaska Native, non-Hispanic/Latino; 7 Asian, non-Hispanic/Latino; 10 Hispanic/Latino; 1 Native Hawaiian or other Pacific Islander, non-Hispanic/Latino; 2 Two or more races, non-Hispanic/Latino). Average age 37. 36 applicants, 81% accepted, 24 enrolled. *Faculty:* 6 full-time (all women), 6 part-time/adjunct (all women). Expenses: Contact institution. *Financial support:* In 2018–19, 10 students received support. Scholarships/grants and unspecified assistantships available. Financial award application deadline: 4/15; financial award applicants required to submit FAFSA. In 2018, 32 master's, 5 other advanced degrees awarded. *Program availability:* Part-time, evening/weekend, blended/hybrid learning. Offers adult nurse practitioner (MS, Advanced Certificate); family nurse practitioner (Advanced Certificate); nursing education (Advanced Certificate). *Application deadline:* For fall admission, 6/3 priority date for domestic students; for spring admission, 10/31 priority date for domestic students. Applications are processed on a rolling basis. *Application fee:* $45. Electronic applications accepted. *Application Contact:* Eileen Bardney, Director of Admissions, 845-569-3254, Fax: 845-569-3438, E-mail: Eileen.Bardney@msmc.edu. *Graduate Coordinator,* Christine Berte, 845-569-3141, Fax: 845-562-6762, E-mail: christine.berte@msmc.edu.

MOUNT SAINT MARY'S UNIVERSITY, Los Angeles, CA 90049

General Information Independent-religious, coed, primarily women, comprehensive institution. CGS member. *Enrollment:* 689 full-time matriculated graduate/professional students (569 women), 178 part-time matriculated graduate/professional students (143 women). *Enrollment by degree level:* 515 master's, 92 doctoral, 260 other advanced degrees. *Graduate faculty:* 41 full-time (33 women), 159 part-time/adjunct (118 women). *Tuition:* Full-time $45,260. *Required fees:* $170. Full-time tuition and fees vary according to course load and program. *Graduate housing:* Room and/or apartments available on a first-come, first-served basis to single students; on-campus housing not available to married students. *Student services:* Campus employment opportunities, career counseling, exercise/wellness program, free psychological counseling, low-cost health insurance, services for students with disabilities, writing training. *Library facilities:* Charles Willard Coe Library plus 1 other. *Collection:* Books: 88,758 (physical), 396,855 (digital/electronic); Serial titles: 168 (physical), 39,316 (digital/electronic); Databases: 215. Weekly public service hours: 91; study areas open 24 hours, 5–7 days a week.

Computer facilities: 170 computers available on campus for general student use. A campuswide network can be accessed from student residence rooms and from off campus. Online class registration is available.
Website: http://www.msmu.edu/

General Application Contact: Albert Ramos, Director of Graduate Admissions, 213-477-2800, Fax: 213-477-2797, E-mail: gradprograms@msmu.edu.

GRADUATE UNITS

Graduate Division *Program availability:* Part-time, evening/weekend. Offers business administration (MBA); counseling psychology (MS); creative writing (MFA); education (MS, Certificate); film and television (MFA); health policy and management (MS); humanities (MA); nursing (MSN, Certificate); physical therapy (DPT); religious studies (MA). Electronic applications accepted.

MOUNT ST. MARY'S UNIVERSITY, Emmitsburg, MD 21727-7799

General Information Independent-religious, coed, comprehensive institution. *Enrollment:* 184 full-time matriculated graduate/professional students (36 women), 268 part-time matriculated graduate/professional students (155 women). *Enrollment by degree level:* 440 master's, 12 other advanced degrees. *Graduate faculty:* 34 full-time (12 women), 27 part-time/adjunct (13 women). *Graduate housing:* Room and/or apartments available on a first-come, first-served basis to single students; on-campus housing not available to married students. *Student services:* Campus employment opportunities, campus safety program, career counseling, exercise/wellness program, free psychological counseling, international student services, low-cost health insurance, multicultural affairs office, services for students with disabilities, teacher training, writing training. *Library facilities:* Phillips Library. *Collection:* Books: 149,657 (physical), 280,598 (digital/electronic); Serial titles: 1,207 (physical), 26,497 (digital/electronic); Databases: 157.

Computer facilities: 80 computers available on campus for general student use. A campuswide network can be accessed from student residence rooms. Online class registration, tuition payment, course management system are available.
Website: http://www.msmary.edu/

GRADUATE UNITS

Graduate Seminary Offers theology (M Div, MA).

Program in Biotechnology and Management *Program availability:* Part-time-only, evening/weekend. Offers biotechnology and management (MS). Electronic applications accepted.

Program in Business Administration *Program availability:* Part-time, evening/weekend. Offers business administration (MBA). Electronic applications accepted.

Program in Education Offers education (M Ed, MAT). Electronic applications accepted.

Program in Health Administration *Program availability:* Part-time, evening/weekend. Offers health administration (MHA). Electronic applications accepted.

Program in Philosophical Studies *Program availability:* Part-time. Offers philosophical studies (MA).

Program in Sport Management *Program availability:* Part-time, evening/weekend. Offers sport management (MS). Electronic applications accepted.

MOUNT SAINT VINCENT UNIVERSITY, Halifax, NS B3M 2J6, Canada

General Information Province-supported, coed, primarily women, comprehensive institution. *Graduate housing:* Room and/or apartments available on a first-come, first-served basis to single students; on-campus housing not available to married students. Housing application deadline: 5/15.

GRADUATE UNITS

Graduate Programs *Program availability:* Part-time, evening/weekend, online learning. Offers applied human nutrition (M Sc AHN, MAHN); child and youth study (MA); communication (MA); family studies and gerontology (MA); public relations (MPR); women's studies (MA). Electronic applications accepted.

Faculty of Education *Program availability:* Part-time, evening/weekend, online learning. Offers education (M Ed, MA, MA Ed, MA-R); education of the blind or visually impaired (M Ed); education of the deaf or hard of hearing (M Ed); educational foundations (M Ed, MA Ed, MA-R); educational psychology (MA-R); elementary and middle school education (M Ed, MA Ed, MA-R); evaluation (M Ed); general curriculum studies (M Ed, MA Ed, MA-R); human relations (M Ed); lifelong learning (M Ed, MA Ed, MA-R); literacy education (M Ed, MA Ed, MA-R); school psychology (MA); teaching English to speakers of other languages (M Ed, MA Ed, MA-R). Electronic applications accepted.

MOUNT VERNON NAZARENE UNIVERSITY, Mount Vernon, OH 43050-9500

General Information Independent-religious, coed, comprehensive institution. *Graduate housing:* On-campus housing not available.

GRADUATE UNITS

Department of Education *Program availability:* Part-time, evening/weekend. Offers education (MA Ed); professional educator's license (MA Ed).

Program in Management *Program availability:* Part-time, evening/weekend. Offers management (MSM).

Program in Ministry *Program availability:* Part-time, evening/weekend. Offers ministry (M Min).

MULTNOMAH UNIVERSITY, Portland, OR 97220-5898

General Information Independent-religious, coed, comprehensive institution. *Enrollment:* 166 full-time matriculated graduate/professional students (87 women), 122 part-time matriculated graduate/professional students (42 women). *Enrollment by degree level:* 261 master's, 21 doctoral, 6 other advanced degrees. *Graduate faculty:* 10 full-time (6 women), 23 part-time/adjunct (9 women). *Tuition:* Full-time $13,440; part-time $6720 per semester hour. *Required fees:* $390; $250 per unit. Tuition and fees vary according to course load. *Graduate housing:* Room and/or apartments available on a first-come, first-served basis to single students; on-campus housing not available to married students. Typical cost: $10,000 (including board). Room and board charges vary according to housing facility selected. Housing application deadline: 7/15. *Student services:* Campus employment opportunities, career counseling, free psychological counseling, low-cost health insurance, multicultural affairs office, writing training. *Library facilities:* John Mitchell Library. *Collection:* Books: 120,106 (physical), 152,698 (digital/electronic); Serial titles: 548 (physical), 20,000 (digital/electronic); Databases: 45. Weekly public service hours: 82; students can reserve study rooms.

Computer facilities: 36 computers available on campus for general student use. A campuswide network can be accessed from student residence rooms and from off campus. Online class registration is available.
Website: http://www.multnomah.edu/

General Application Contact: Mindy Kate Hasenkamp, Director of Admissions, 503-251-6483, Fax: 503-254-1268, E-mail: admiss@multnomah.edu.

GRADUATE UNITS

Graduate Programs *Program availability:* Part-time, evening/weekend. Offers counseling (MA); global development and justice (MA); teaching (MA); TESOL (MA). Electronic applications accepted.

Multnomah Biblical Seminary *Program availability:* Part-time. Offers theology (M Div, MABS, MACL, MATS, Th M, D Min).

MURRAY STATE UNIVERSITY, Murray, KY 42071

General Information State-supported, coed, university. *Graduate housing:* Rooms and/or apartments available on a first-come, first-served basis to single and married students.

GRADUATE UNITS

Arthur J. Bauernfeind College of Business *Program availability:* Part-time, evening/weekend, 100% online, blended/hybrid learning. Offers accounting (MBA); business (MA, MBA, MS, MSIS, Certificate); computer science and information systems (MSIS); economic development (MS); economics (MS); finance (MBA); global communications (MBA); human resource management (MBA); marketing (MBA); mass communications (MA, MS); nursing education (MA). MS in telecommunications systems management is an interdisciplinary program with the Jesse D. Jones College of Science, Engineering and Technology. Electronic applications accepted.

College of Education and Human Services *Program availability:* Part-time, evening/weekend, 100% online, blended/hybrid learning. Offers career and technical education (MS); college advising (Certificate); education administration (MA Ed); education and human services (MA Ed, MS, Ed D, Certificate, Ed S); elementary teacher leader (MA Ed); human development and leadership (MS, Certificate); interdisciplinary early childhood education (MA Ed); library media (MA Ed); middle school teacher leader (MA Ed); nonprofit leadership studies (MS, Certificate); P-20 and community leadership (Ed D); postsecondary education administration (MA Ed); school counseling (MA Ed); school guidance and counseling (Ed S); secondary teacher leader (MA Ed); special education (MA Ed); teacher education and professional development (Ed S). PhD, EdD offered jointly with University of Kentucky. Electronic applications accepted.

Center for Communication Disorders *Program availability:* Part-time. Offers interdisciplinary brain injury studies (Certificate); speech-language pathology (MS). Electronic applications accepted.

College of Humanities and Fine Arts *Program availability:* Part-time, evening/weekend, 100% online, blended/hybrid learning. Offers clinical psychology (MA, MS); creative writing (MFA); English (MA); English pedagogy and technology (DA); gender studies (Certificate); general experimental psychology (MA, MS); history (MA); humanities and fine arts (MA, MFA, MME, MPA, MS, DA, Certificate); music education (MME); political science and sociology (MPA); research design and analysis (Certificate); teaching English to speakers of other languages (TESOL) (MA). Electronic applications accepted.

Hutson School of Agriculture *Program availability:* Part-time, 100% online, blended/hybrid learning. Offers agriculture (MS); veterinary hospital management (Certificate). Electronic applications accepted.

Jesse D. Jones College of Science, Engineering and Technology *Program availability:* Part-time, evening/weekend, 100% online, blended/hybrid learning. Offers biology (MS); chemistry (MS); environmental science (MS); geosciences (MS); geospatial data science (Certificate); mathematics (MA, MS); mathematics teacher leader (MAT); science, engineering and technology (MA, MAT, MS, Certificate). Electronic applications accepted.

Institute of Engineering *Program availability:* Part-time. Offers applied engineering and technology management (MS); telecommunications systems management (MS). Electronic applications accepted.

School of Nursing and Health Professions *Program availability:* Part-time, evening/weekend, 100% online, blended/hybrid learning. Offers family nurse practitioner (DNP); nurse anesthetist (DNP); nursing and health professions (MS, DNP, Certificate); nutrition (MS); registered dietitian (Certificate). Electronic applications accepted.

MUSKINGUM UNIVERSITY, New Concord, OH 43762

General Information Independent-religious, coed, comprehensive institution. *Graduate housing:* On-campus housing not available.

GRADUATE UNITS

Graduate Programs in Education *Program availability:* Part-time. Offers education (MAE, MAT).

NAROPA UNIVERSITY, Boulder, CO 80302-6697

General Information Independent, coed, comprehensive institution. *Graduate housing:* Room and/or apartments available on a first-come, first-served basis to single students; on-campus housing not available to married students. Housing application deadline: 7/1.

GRADUATE UNITS

Graduate Programs *Program availability:* Part-time, blended/hybrid learning. Offers contemplative psychotherapy and Buddhist psychology (MA); creative writing (MFA); creative writing and poetics (MFA); divinity (M Div); ecopsychology (MA); mindfulness-based transpersonal counseling (MA); religious studies (MA); religious studies with language (MA); resilient leadership (MA); somatic counseling: body psychotherapy (MA); somatic counseling: dance/movement therapy (MA); theater: contemporary performance (MFA); transpersonal art therapy (MA); transpersonal wilderness therapy (MA). Electronic applications accepted.

NASHOTAH HOUSE THEOLOGICAL SEMINARY, Nashotah, WI 53058-9793

General Information Independent-religious, coed, primarily men, graduate-only institution. *Graduate housing:* Rooms and/or apartments available on a first-come, first-served basis to single and married students. Housing application deadline: 5/1.

GRADUATE UNITS

Graduate Programs *Program availability:* Part-time. Offers Anglican studies (Certificate); Biblical studies (STM); Christian spirituality (STM); church history (STM); liturgy (STM); ministry (M Div, MM); pastoral ministry (MPM); theological studies (MTS); theology (STM, D Min). Electronic applications accepted.

NATIONAL AMERICAN UNIVERSITY, Austin, TX 78731

General Information Proprietary, coed, graduate-only institution.

GRADUATE UNITS

Roueche Graduate Center *Program availability:* Part-time, evening/weekend, online learning. Offers accounting (MBA); aviation management (MBA, MM); care coordination (MSN); community college leadership (Ed D); criminal justice (MM); e-marketing (MBA, MM); health care administration (MBA, MM); higher education (MM); human resources management (MBA, MM); information technology management (MBA, MM); international business (MBA); leadership (EMBA); management (MBA); nursing administration (MSN); nursing education (MSN); nursing informatics (MSN); operations and configuration management (MBA, MM); project and process management (MBA, MM). Master's programs offered online through the Harold D. Buckingham Graduate School. Electronic applications accepted.

NATIONAL COLLEGE OF MIDWIFERY, Taos, NM 87571

General Information Independent, women only, comprehensive institution.

GRADUATE UNITS

Graduate Programs *Program availability:* Part-time, evening/weekend, online learning. Offers midwifery (MS, PhD). Electronic applications accepted.

NATIONAL DEFENSE UNIVERSITY, Washington, DC 20319-5066

General Information Federally supported, coed, graduate-only institution. *Graduate housing:* On-campus housing not available.

GRADUATE UNITS

College of International Security Affairs *Program availability:* Part-time, evening/weekend. Offers strategic security studies (MA).

The Dwight D. Eisenhower School for National Security and Resource Strategy Offers national resource strategy (MS). Open only to Department of Defense employees and specific federal agencies.

Joint Advanced Warfighting School Offers joint campaign planning and strategy (MS). Open only to Department of Defense employees and specific federal agencies.

National War College Offers national security strategy (MS). Open only to Department of Defense employees and specific federal agencies.

NATIONAL INTELLIGENCE UNIVERSITY, Washington, DC 20340-5100

General Information Federally supported, coed, upper-level institution. *Graduate housing:* On-campus housing not available.

GRADUATE UNITS

Graduate Program *Program availability:* Part-time, evening/weekend. Offers strategic intelligence (MSSI). Open only to federal government employees.

NATIONAL LOUIS UNIVERSITY, Chicago, IL 60603

General Information Independent, coed, university.

GRADUATE UNITS

College of Arts and Sciences *Program availability:* Part-time, evening/weekend, online learning. Offers adult education (Ed D); counseling and human services (MS); language and academic development (M Ed, Certificate); psychology (MA, PhD, Certificate); public policy (MA); written communication (MS, Certificate). Electronic applications accepted.

College of Management and Business *Program availability:* Part-time, evening/weekend. Offers business administration (MBA); human resource management and development (MS); management (MS).

National College of Education *Program availability:* Part-time, evening/weekend. Offers administration and supervision (M Ed, Ed D, CAS, Ed S); curriculum and instruction (M Ed, MS Ed, CAS); early childhood administration (M Ed, CAS); early childhood education (M Ed, MAT, MS Ed, CAS); education (Ed D); educational psychology/human learning and development M Ed, MS Ed, CAS, Ed S); elementary education (MAT); interdisciplinary curriculum and instruction (M Ed); mathematics education (M Ed, MS Ed, CAS); middle grades education (MAT); reading and language (M Ed, MS Ed, CAS); school psychology (M Ed, Ed S); science education (M Ed, MS Ed, CAS); secondary education (MAT); special education (M Ed, MAT, CAS); technology in education (M Ed, CAS).

NATIONAL PARALEGAL COLLEGE, Phoenix, AZ 85014

General Information Proprietary, coed, comprehensive institution.

GRADUATE UNITS

Graduate Programs *Program availability:* Part-time. Offers compliance law (MS); legal studies (MS); taxation (MS). Electronic applications accepted.

NATIONAL TEST PILOT SCHOOL, Mojave, CA 93502-0658

General Information Independent, coed, graduate-only institution.

GRADUATE UNITS

National Flight Institute Offers flight test and evaluation (MS); flight test engineering (MS).

NATIONAL UNIVERSITY, La Jolla, CA 92037-1011

General Information Independent, coed, comprehensive institution. CGS member. *Enrollment:* 16,930 graduate, professional, and undergraduate students; 6,531 full-time matriculated graduate/professional students (4,439 women), 1,451 part-time matriculated graduate/professional students (933 women). *Enrollment by degree level:* 7,925 master's, 103 other advanced degrees. *Graduate faculty:* 141 full-time (73 women), 500 part-time/adjunct (257 women). *Tuition:* Full-time $10,320; part-time $430 per unit. Tuition and fees vary according to degree level. *Graduate housing:* On-campus housing not available. *Student services:* Campus employment opportunities, campus safety program, career counseling, international student services, services for students with disabilities, teacher training, writing training. *Library facilities:* National University Library. *Collection:* Books: 201,123 (physical), 368,486 (digital/electronic); Serial titles: 3,050 (physical), 95,256 (digital/electronic); Databases: 190. Weekly public service hours: 72; students can reserve study rooms.

Computer facilities: 2,800 computers available on campus for general student use. A campuswide network can be accessed from off campus. Online class registration is available.
Website: http://www.nu.edu/

General Application Contact: Brandon Jouganatos, Vice President for Enrollment Services, 800-628-8648, E-mail: advisor@nu.edu.

GRADUATE UNITS

College of Letters and Sciences *Program availability:* Part-time, evening/weekend, 100% online, blended/hybrid learning. Offers biology (MS); counseling psychology (MA); creative writing (MFA); English (MA); film studies (MA); forensic and crime scene investigations (Certificate); forensic sciences (MFS); human behavior (MA); mathematics for educators (MS); performance psychology (MA); strategic communications (MA). Electronic applications accepted.

Sanford College of Education *Program availability:* Part-time, evening/weekend, 100% online, blended/hybrid learning. Offers advanced teaching practices (MS); applied behavior analysis (MS); applied school leadership (MS); e-teaching and learning (Certificate); education (MA); educational administration (MS); educational and instructional technology (MS); educational counseling (MS); higher education administration (MS); inspired teaching and learning (M Ed); school psychology (MS); special education (MA, MS). Electronic applications accepted.

School of Business and Management *Program availability:* Part-time, evening/weekend, 100% online, blended/hybrid learning. Offers accountancy (M Acc, Certificate); business administration (GMBA, MBA); business analytics (MS); cause leadership (MA); global management (MGM); human resource management (MA); management information systems (MS); marketing (MS); organizational leadership (MS). GMBA offered in Spanish. Electronic applications accepted.

School of Engineering and Computing *Program availability:* Part-time, evening/weekend, 100% online, blended/hybrid learning. Offers computer science (MS); cyber security and information assurance (MS); data analytics (MS); electrical engineering (MS); engineering management (MS); information technology management (MS); management information systems (MS); sustainability management (MS). Electronic applications accepted.

School of Health and Human Services *Program availability:* Part-time, evening/weekend, 100% online, blended/hybrid learning. Offers clinical affairs (MS);

clinical regulatory affairs (MS); complementary and integrative healthcare (MS); family nurse practitioner (MSN); health and life science analytics (MS); health informatics (MS, Certificate); healthcare administration (MHA); nurse anesthesia (MSNA); nursing administration (MSN); nursing informatics (MSN); psychiatric-mental health nurse practitioner (MSN); public health (MPH). Electronic applications accepted.

School of Professional Studies *Program availability:* Part-time, evening/weekend, 100% online, blended/hybrid learning. Offers criminal justice (MCJ); digital cinema production (MFA); digital journalism (MA); homeland security and emergency management (MS); juvenile justice (MS); professional screenwriting (MFA); public administration (MPA). Electronic applications accepted.

NATIONAL UNIVERSITY COLLEGE, Bayamón, PR 00960

General Information Proprietary, coed, comprehensive institution.

GRADUATE UNITS

Graduate Programs

NATIONAL UNIVERSITY OF HEALTH SCIENCES, Lombard, IL 60148-4583

General Information Independent, coed, graduate-only institution. *Graduate housing:* Rooms and/or apartments available on a first-come, first-served basis to single and married students. *Research affiliation:* University of Illinois at Chicago (public health), Canadian Memorial Chiropractic College (mechanisms of CAM), Cox Technic F/D Enterprise LLC (mechanisms of CAM), Logan Chiropractic College (behavior research), Foot Levelers, Inc. (orthotics/biomechanics), Auburn University (mechanisms of CAM).

GRADUATE UNITS

Graduate Programs Offers acupuncture (MSAC); chiropractic (DC); diagnostic imaging (MS); naturopathic medicine (ND); Oriental medicine (MSOM).

NATIONAL UNIVERSITY OF NATURAL MEDICINE, Portland, OR 97201

General Information Independent, coed, primarily women, graduate-only institution. *Graduate housing:* On-campus housing not available. *Research affiliation:* Metagenics, Inc. (effects of methylation diet, nutrition supplements), Divinia Water (product safety and tolerability, case reports, water).

GRADUATE UNITS

College of Classical Chinese Medicine Offers classical Chinese medicine (M Ac, MSOM, DOM). Electronic applications accepted.

College of Naturopathic Medicine Offers integrative medicine research (MS); naturopathic medicine (ND). Electronic applications accepted.

School of Graduate Studies Offers Ayurveda (MS); global health (MS); integrative medicine research (MS); integrative mental health (MS); nutrition (MS). Electronic applications accepted.

NAVAJO TECHNICAL UNIVERSITY, Crownpoint, NM 87313

General Information Independent, coed, comprehensive institution.

GRADUATE UNITS

Program in Dine Studies Offers dine studies (MA).

NAVAL POSTGRADUATE SCHOOL, Monterey, CA 93943

General Information Federally supported, coed, graduate-only institution. *Graduate housing:* Rooms and/or apartments available to single and married students. *Research affiliation:* U.S. Department of Homeland Security, National Reconnaissance Office, National Oceanic and Atmospheric Administration (NOAA), National Security Agency, Federal Law Enforcement Training.

GRADUATE UNITS

Departments and Academic Groups *Program availability:* Part-time, online learning. Offers applied mathematics (MS, PhD); applied physics (MS, PhD); applied science (MS); astronautical engineer (AstE); astronautical engineering (MS); combat systems technology (MS); command and control (MS); communications (MS); computer engineering (MS); computer science (MS, PhD); cost estimating analysis (MS); defense analysis (MS); electrical engineer (EE); electrical engineering (MS, PhD); electronic warfare systems engineering (MS); engineering acoustics (MS, PhD); engineering science (MS); engineering systems (MS); financial management (MS); human systems integration (MS); identity management and cyber security (MA); information operations (MS); information sciences (PhD); information systems and operations (MS); information technology management (MS); information warfare systems engineering (MS); irregular warfare (MS); knowledge superiority (Certificate); mechanical and aerospace engineering (PhD); mechanical engineer (ME); mechanical engineering (MS, MSME); meteorology (MS, PhD); meteorology and physical oceanography (MS); modeling of virtual environments and simulations (MS, PhD); national security affairs (MS); operations analysis (MS); operations research (MS, PhD); physical oceanography (MS, PhD); physics (MS, PhD); product development (MS); remote sensing intelligence (MS); security studies (MA, PhD); software engineering (MS, PhD); space systems (Engr); space systems operations (MS); special operations (MA, MS); system technology (command, control and communications) (MS); systems analysis (MS); systems engineering (MS, PhD, Certificate); systems engineering analysis (MS, PhD); systems engineering management (MS, PhD); tactile missiles (MS); terrorist operations and financing (MS). Programs only open to commissioned officers of the United States and friendly nations and selected United States federal civilian employees.

Graduate School of Business and Public Policy *Program availability:* Part-time, online learning. Offers acquisition and contract management (MBA); business administration (EMBA, MBA); contract management (MS); defense business management (MBA); defense systems analysis (MS); defense systems management (international) (MBA); financial management (MBA); information management (MBA); manpower systems analysis (MS); material logistics support management (MBA); program management (MS); resource planning and management for international defense (MBA); supply chain management (MBA); systems acquisition management (MBA); transportation management (MBA). Program only open to commissioned officers of the United States and friendly nations and selected United States federal civilian employees.

NAVAL WAR COLLEGE, Newport, RI 02841-1207

General Information Federally supported, coed, primarily men, graduate-only institution.

GRADUATE UNITS

Program in National Security and Strategic Studies Offers national security and strategic studies (MA). Program open only to full-time military personnel.

NAZARENE THEOLOGICAL SEMINARY, Kansas City, MO 64131-1263

General Information Independent-religious, coed, graduate-only institution. *Graduate housing:* Rooms and/or apartments available on a first-come, first-served basis to single and married students. *Research affiliation:* University of Missouri-Kansas City (religious studies).

GRADUATE UNITS

Graduate and Professional Programs *Program availability:* Part-time. Offers Christian formation and discipleship (MA); intercultural studies (MA); pastoral theology (Graduate Certificate); theological studies (MA); theology (M Div, D Min). Electronic applications accepted.

NAZARETH COLLEGE OF ROCHESTER, Rochester, NY 14618

General Information Independent, coed, comprehensive institution. CGS member. *Graduate housing:* Room and/or apartments available on a first-come, first-served basis to single students; on-campus housing not available to married students. Housing application deadline: 5/15.

GRADUATE UNITS

Graduate Studies *Program availability:* Part-time, evening/weekend. Offers art education (MS Ed); art therapy (MS); communication sciences and disorders (MS); educational technology (MS Ed); human resource management (MS); inclusive adolescence education (MS Ed); inclusive childhood education (MS Ed); inclusive early childhood education (MS Ed); literacy education (MS Ed); management (MS); music education (MS Ed); music performance and pedagogy (MM); music therapy (MS); physical therapy (DPT); social work (MSW); teaching English to speakers of other languages (MS Ed).

NEBRASKA CHRISTIAN COLLEGE OF HOPE INTERNATIONAL UNIVERSITY, Papillion, NE 68046

General Information Independent-religious, coed, comprehensive institution.

GRADUATE UNITS

Graduate Programs

NEBRASKA METHODIST COLLEGE, Omaha, NE 68114

General Information Independent-religious, coed, comprehensive institution. *Graduate housing:* Rooms and/or apartments available on a first-come, first-served basis to single students and available to married students. Housing application deadline: 4/1.

GRADUATE UNITS

Program in Healthcare Operations Management *Program availability:* Part-time, evening/weekend, online learning. Offers healthcare operations management (MS).

Program in Health Promotion Management *Program availability:* Part-time, evening/weekend, online learning. Offers health promotion management (MS).

Program in Nursing *Program availability:* Evening/weekend, online learning. Offers nurse educator (MSN); nurse executive (MSN).

Program in Occupational Therapy Offers occupational therapy (MOT).

NEBRASKA WESLEYAN UNIVERSITY, Lincoln, NE 68504-2796

General Information Independent-religious, coed, comprehensive institution. *Enrollment:* 38 full-time matriculated graduate/professional students (27 women), 206 part-time matriculated graduate/professional students (146 women). *Enrollment by degree level:* 244 master's. *Graduate faculty:* 18 full-time (12 women), 21 part-time/adjunct (11 women). *Tuition:* Full-time $5388; part-time $449 per credit hour. One-time fee: $100. Tuition and fees vary according to program. *Student services:* Career counseling, multicultural affairs office, services for students with disabilities. *Library facilities:* Cochrane Woods Library. *Collection:* Books: 316,222 (physical), 185,022 (digital/electronic); Serial titles: 1,711 (physical), 16,353 (digital/electronic); Databases: 69. Weekly public service hours: 91; students can reserve study rooms.

Computer facilities: 360 computers available on campus for general student use. A campuswide network can be accessed from student residence rooms and from off campus. Online class registration is available.
Website: http://www.nebrwesleyan.edu/

General Application Contact: Graduate, Adult and Transfer Admissions Office, 402-465-2329, Fax: 402-465-2179, E-mail: adultadmissions@nebrwesleyan.edu.

GRADUATE UNITS

Graduate Programs Students: 38 full-time (27 women), 206 part-time (146 women); includes 20 minority (6 Black or African American, non-Hispanic/Latino; 1 American Indian or Alaska Native, non-Hispanic/Latino; 3 Asian, non-Hispanic/Latino; 3 Hispanic/Latino; 7 Two or more races, non-Hispanic/Latino), 3 international. Average age 35. 112 applicants, 55% accepted, 40 enrolled. *Faculty:* 18 full-time (12 women), 21 part-time/adjunct (11 women). Expenses: Contact institution. In 2018, 74 master's awarded. *Program availability:* Part-time. Offers nursing (MSN). *Application fee:* $0. Electronic applications accepted. *Application Contact:* Graduate, Adult and Transfer Admissions, 402-465-2329, Fax: 402-465-2179, E-mail: adultadmissions@nebrwesleyan.edu. *Dean of Graduate Programs,* Dr. Jennifer Ziegler, 402-465-2110, E-mail: jziegle2@nebrwesleyan.edu.

Program in Business Administration

Program in Education

NER ISRAEL RABBINICAL COLLEGE, Baltimore, MD 21208

General Information Independent-religious, men only, comprehensive institution. *Graduate housing:* Rooms and/or apartments guaranteed to single students and available on a first-come, first-served basis to married students.

GRADUATE UNITS

Graduate Programs Offers rabbinics (MTL, DTL, Professional Certificate).

NER ISRAEL YESHIVA COLLEGE OF TORONTO, Thornhill, ON L4J 8A7, Canada

General Information Independent-religious, men only, comprehensive institution.

GRADUATE UNITS

Graduate Programs

NEUMANN UNIVERSITY, Aston, PA 19014-1298

General Information Independent-religious, coed, comprehensive institution. *Graduate housing:* On-campus housing not available.

GRADUATE UNITS

Graduate Program in Education *Program availability:* Part-time, evening/weekend, 100% online, blended/hybrid learning. Offers education (MS). Electronic applications accepted.

Graduate Program in Nursing *Program availability:* Part-time, evening/weekend. Offers adult-gerontology nurse practitioner (MS, Certificate). Electronic applications accepted.

Graduate Programs in Business and Information Management *Program availability:* Part-time, evening/weekend. Offers accounting (MS); sport business (MS). Electronic applications accepted.

Program in Educational Leadership *Program availability:* Part-time, evening/weekend. Offers educational leadership (Ed D). Electronic applications accepted.

Program in Organizational and Strategic Leadership *Program availability:* Part-time, evening/weekend, 100% online, blended/hybrid learning. Offers organizational and strategic leadership (MS). Electronic applications accepted.

Program in Pastoral Clinical Mental Health Counseling *Program availability:* Part-time, evening/weekend. Offers pastoral care specialist (Certificate); pastoral clinical mental health counseling (MS); pastoral clinical mental health counseling certificate of advanced study (Certificate); pastoral counseling (PhD); spiritual formation and direction (CSD); spiritual formation and direction supervision certificate of advanced study (Certificate). Electronic applications accepted.

Program in Physical Therapy *Program availability:* Evening/weekend. Offers physical therapy (DPT). Electronic applications accepted.

NEW BRUNSWICK THEOLOGICAL SEMINARY, New Brunswick, NJ 08901-1196

General Information Independent-religious, coed, graduate-only institution. *Graduate housing:* Rooms and/or apartments available on a first-come, first-served basis to single and married students. Housing application deadline: 6/30.

GRADUATE UNITS

Graduate and Professional Programs *Program availability:* Part-time, evening/weekend. Offers pastoral care and counseling (D Min). Electronic applications accepted.

NEW CHARTER UNIVERSITY, Salt Lake City, UT 84101

General Information Proprietary, coed, comprehensive institution. *Enrollment:* 13 part-time matriculated graduate/professional students (9 women). *Enrollment by degree level:* 13 master's. *Graduate faculty:* 12 part-time/adjunct (7 women). *Tuition:* Full-time $4491; part-time $1497 per term. *Required fees:* $50 per term. *Graduate housing:* On-campus housing not available.

Computer facilities: A campuswide network can be accessed from off campus. Website: http://www.new.edu/

General Application Contact: Stephen Mann, Admissions Advisor, 801-515-3085, Fax: 801-855-5922, E-mail: smann@new.edu.

GRADUATE UNITS

College of Business Students: 16 part-time. Average age 40. 1 applicant, 100% accepted, 1 enrolled. *Faculty:* 13 part-time/adjunct (1 woman). Expenses: Contact institution. *Financial support:* In 2018–19, 1 student received support. Scholarships/grants available. In 2018, 10 master's awarded. *Program availability:* Part-time, evening/weekend, online only, 100% online. Offers finance (MBA); health care management (MBA); management (MBA). *Application deadline:* Applications are processed on a rolling basis. *Application fee:* $50. Electronic applications accepted. *Application Contact:* Stephen Mann, Admissions Advisor, 801-515-3085, E-mail: smann@new.edu. *Academic Dean,* Timothy Harrington, 801-8838336, E-mail: tharrington@new.edu.

NEW COLLEGE OF FLORIDA, Sarasota, FL 34243

General Information State-supported, coed, comprehensive institution.

GRADUATE UNITS

Program in Data Science Offers data science (MDS).

NEW ENGLAND COLLEGE, Henniker, NH 03242-3293

General Information Independent, coed, comprehensive institution. *Graduate housing:* Room and/or apartments available on a first-come, first-served basis to single students; on-campus housing not available to married students. Housing application deadline: 5/1.

GRADUATE UNITS

Program in Community Mental Health Counseling *Program availability:* Part-time, evening/weekend. Offers human services (MS); mental health counseling (MS).

Program in Education *Program availability:* Part-time, evening/weekend. Offers higher education administration (MS, Ed D); K-12 leadership (Ed D); literacy and language arts (M Ed); meeting the needs of all learners/special education (M Ed); teacher leadership/school reform (M Ed).

Program in Management *Program availability:* Part-time, evening/weekend. Offers accounting (MSA); healthcare administration (MS); international relations (MA); marketing management (MS); nonprofit leadership (MS); project management (MS); strategic leadership (MS). Electronic applications accepted.

Program in Public Policy *Program availability:* Part-time, evening/weekend, online learning. Offers public policy (MA). Electronic applications accepted.

Program in Sports and Recreation Management: Coaching Offers sports and recreation management: coaching (MS).

Programs in Writing *Program availability:* Part-time, evening/weekend. Offers poetry (MFA); professional writing (MA). Electronic applications accepted.

NEW ENGLAND COLLEGE OF BUSINESS AND FINANCE, Boston, MA 02111-2645

General Information Independent, coed, primarily women, comprehensive institution.

GRADUATE UNITS

Program in Business Ethics and Compliance *Program availability:* Online learning. Offers business ethics and compliance (MS).

Program in Finance *Program availability:* Online learning. Offers finance (MSF).

Program in Quality Systems Management Offers quality systems management (MS).

NEW ENGLAND COLLEGE OF OPTOMETRY, Boston, MA 02115-1100

General Information Independent, coed, graduate-only institution. *Graduate housing:* On-campus housing not available. *Research affiliation:* Vistakon-Johnson & Johnson (contact lenses), Boston University School of Medicine (vision science).

GRADUATE UNITS

Graduate and Professional Programs Offers optometry (OD); vision science (MS). Electronic applications accepted.

NEW ENGLAND CONSERVATORY OF MUSIC, Boston, MA 02115-5000

General Information Independent, coed, comprehensive institution. *Graduate housing:* Room and/or apartments available on a first-come, first-served basis to single students; on-campus housing not available to married students. Housing application deadline: 6/15.

GRADUATE UNITS

Graduate Program in Music Offers music (MM, DMA, Diploma). Electronic applications accepted.

NEW ENGLAND INSTITUTE OF TECHNOLOGY, East Greenwich, RI 02818

General Information Independent, coed, comprehensive institution. *Graduate housing:* On-campus housing not available.

GRADUATE UNITS

Program in Construction Management Students: 14 full-time (6 women), 4 part-time (2 women), 5 international. Average age 32. Expenses: Contact institution. *Program availability:* Part-time, evening/weekend, online only, 100% online, blended/hybrid learning. Offers construction management (MS). *Application deadline:* Applications are processed on a rolling basis. *Application fee:* $25. Electronic applications accepted. *Application Contact:* Lynn M Fawthrop, Vice President of Enrollment Management and Marketing, 401-739-5000 Ext. 3315, Fax: 401-886-0859, E-mail: lmfawthrop@neit.edu. *Senior Vice President and Provost,* Dr. Douglas H. Sherman, 401-739-5000 Ext. 3481, Fax: 401-886-0859, E-mail: dsherman@neit.edu.

Program in Engineering Management Students: 16 full-time (0 women), 1 (woman) part-time; includes 5 minority (3 Black or African American, non-Hispanic/Latino; 2 Hispanic/Latino), 1 international. Average age 29. Expenses: Contact institution. *Program availability:* Part-time, evening/weekend, 100% online, blended/hybrid learning. Offers engineering management (MSEM). *Application deadline:* Applications are processed on a rolling basis. *Application fee:* $25. Electronic applications accepted. *Application Contact:* Lynn M Fawthrop, Vice President of Enrollment Management and Marketing, 401-739-5000 Ext. 3315, Fax: 401-886-0859, E-mail: lmfawthrop@neit.edu. *Senior Vice President and Provost,* Dr. Douglas H. Sherman, 401-739-5000 Ext. 3481, Fax: 401-886-0859, E-mail: dsherman@neit.edu.

Program in Information Technology Students: 14 full-time (6 women), 7 part-time (1 woman), 7 international. Average age 31. Expenses: Contact institution. *Program availability:* Part-time, evening/weekend, 100% online, blended/hybrid learning. Offers information technology (MS). *Application deadline:* Applications are processed on a rolling basis. *Application fee:* $25. Electronic applications accepted. *Application Contact:* Lynn M Fawthrop, Vice President of Enrollment Management and Marketing, 401-739-5000 Ext. 3315, Fax: 401-886-0859, E-mail: lmfawthrop@neit.edu. *Senior Vice President and Provost,* Dr. Douglas H. Sherman, 401-739-5000 Ext. 3481, Fax: 401-886-0859, E-mail: dsherman@neit.edu.

Program in Occupational Therapy Students: 96 full-time (84 women), 8 part-time (7 women); includes 17 minority (3 Black or African American, non-Hispanic/Latino; 4 Asian, non-Hispanic/Latino; 10 Hispanic/Latino). Average age 31. Expenses: Contact institution. *Program availability:* Part-time, evening/weekend, 100% online, blended/hybrid learning. Offers occupational therapy (MS, OTD). *Application deadline:* Applications are processed on a rolling basis. *Application fee:* $25. Electronic applications accepted. *Application Contact:* Lynn M Fawthrop, Vice President of Enrollment Management and Marketing, 800-736-7744 Ext. 3315, Fax: 401-886-0859, E-mail: lmfawthrop@neit.edu. *Senior Vice President and Provost,* Douglas H. Sherman, 401-739-5000 Ext. 3481, Fax: 401-886-0859, E-mail: dsherman@neit.edu.

Program in Public Health Students: 15 full-time (11 women), 2 part-time (1 woman); includes 2 minority (1 Black or African American, non-Hispanic/Latino; 1 Hispanic/Latino). Average age 32. Expenses: Contact institution. *Program availability:* Part-time, evening/weekend, online only, 100% online, blended/hybrid learning. Offers public health (MPH). *Application deadline:* Applications are processed on a rolling basis. *Application fee:* $25. Electronic applications accepted. *Application Contact:* Lynn M Fawthrop, Vice President of Enrollment Management and Marketing, 401-739-5000 Ext. 3315, Fax: 401-886-0859, E-mail: lmfawthrop@neit.edu. *Senior Vice President and Provost,* Douglas H. Sherman, 401-739-5000 Ext. 3481, Fax: 401-886-0859, E-mail: dsherman@neit.edu.

NEW ENGLAND LAW—BOSTON, Boston, MA 02116-5687

General Information Independent, coed, graduate-only institution. *Graduate housing:* On-campus housing not available.

GRADUATE UNITS

Graduate Programs *Program availability:* Part-time, evening/weekend. Offers American law (LL M); law (JD). Electronic applications accepted.

NEW HAMPSHIRE INSTITUTE OF ART, Manchester, NH 03104

General Information Independent, coed, comprehensive institution. *Graduate housing:* Room and/or apartments available on a first-come, first-served basis to single students; on-campus housing not available to married students. Housing application deadline: 6/15.

GRADUATE UNITS

Graduate Studies Offers art education (MA); creative writing (MFA); photography (MFA); teaching visual arts (MAT); visual arts (MFA). Electronic applications accepted.

NEW JERSEY CITY UNIVERSITY, Jersey City, NJ 07305-1597

General Information State-supported, coed, comprehensive institution. *Graduate housing:* On-campus housing not available.

GRADUATE UNITS

College of Professional Studies *Program availability:* Part-time, evening/weekend. Offers civil security leadership (D Sc); community health education (MS); criminal justice (MS); health administration (MS); national security studies (MS, Certificate); school health education (MS).

Debra Cannon Partridge Wolfe College of Education *Program availability:* Part-time, evening/weekend. Offers bilingual/bicultural education (MA); counselor education (MA); early childhood education (MAT); education (MA, MAT, Ed D); educational administration and supervision (MA); educational technology (MA); educational technology leadership (Ed D); elementary education (MAT); English as a second language (MA); secondary education (MAT); special education (MA); urban education (MA); urban education world language (MA).

New Jersey City University

Graduate Studies and Continuing Education *Program availability:* Part-time, evening/weekend, online learning.

School of Business *Program availability:* Part-time, evening/weekend. Offers accounting (MS, Graduate Certificate); business (MBA, MS, Graduate Certificate); finance (MBA, MS, Graduate Certificate); marketing (MBA); organizational management and leadership (MBA).

William J. Maxwell College of Arts and Sciences *Program availability:* Part-time, evening/weekend. Offers art (MFA); art education (MA); arts and sciences (MA, MFA, MM); mathematics education (MA); music education (MA); performance (MM); studio art (MFA).

NEW JERSEY INSTITUTE OF TECHNOLOGY, Newark, NJ 07102
General Information State-supported, coed, university. CGS member. *Enrollment:* 11,423 graduate, professional, and undergraduate students; 1,745 full-time matriculated graduate/professional students (546 women), 1,146 part-time matriculated graduate/professional students (317 women). *Enrollment by degree level:* 2,345 master's, 482 doctoral, 64 other advanced degrees. *Graduate faculty:* 439 full-time (101 women), 357 part-time/adjunct (90 women). *International tuition:* $29,960 full-time. *Tuition, area resident:* Full-time $20,232; part-time $1101 per credit hour. Tuition, state resident: full-time $20,232; part-time $1101 per credit hour. Tuition, nonresident: full-time $29,960; part-time $1583 per credit hour. *Required fees:* $3142; $185 per credit hour. $1110 per semester. *Graduate housing:* Room and/or apartments available on a first-come, first-served basis to single students; on-campus housing not available to married students. Typical cost: $4734 per year ($6355 including board). Room and board charges vary according to board plan, campus/location and housing facility selected. Housing application deadline: 3/31. *Student services:* Campus employment opportunities, campus safety program, career counseling, exercise/wellness program, free psychological counseling, grant writing training, international student services, low-cost health insurance, multicultural affairs office, services for students with disabilities, teacher training, writing training. *Library facilities:* Van Houten Library plus 1 other. *Collection:* Books: 138,456 (physical), 185,262 (digital/electronic); Serial titles: 50 (physical), 185,301 (digital/electronic); Databases: 35. Weekly public service hours: 111; students can reserve study rooms.

Computer facilities: Computer purchase and lease plans are available. 1,938 computers available on campus for general student use. A campuswide network can be accessed from student residence rooms and from off campus. Online class registration is available.
Website: http://www.njit.edu/

General Application Contact: Stephen Eck, Director of Admissions, 973-596-3300, Fax: 973-596-3461, E-mail: admissions@njit.edu.

GRADUATE UNITS
College of Science and Liberal Arts Students: 200 full-time (79 women), 63 part-time (29 women); includes 61 minority (17 Black or African American, non-Hispanic/Latino; 29 Asian, non-Hispanic/Latino; 11 Hispanic/Latino; 4 Two or more races, non-Hispanic/Latino), 136 international. Average age 28. 429 applicants, 49% accepted, 89 enrolled. *Faculty:* 150 full-time (43 women), 115 part-time/adjunct (47 women). Expenses: Contact institution. *Financial support:* In 2018–19, 134 students received support, including 17 fellowships with full tuition reimbursements available (averaging $22,000 per year), 74 research assistantships with full tuition reimbursements available (averaging $22,000 per year), 71 teaching assistantships with full tuition reimbursements available (averaging $22,000 per year); scholarships/grants, traineeships, health care benefits, and unspecified assistantships also available. Financial award application deadline: 1/15. In 2018, 43 master's, 16 doctorates, 2 other advanced degrees awarded. *Program availability:* Part-time, evening/weekend. Offers applied mathematics (MS); applied physics (MS, PhD); applied statistics (MS, Certificate); biology (MS, PhD); biostatistics (MS); chemistry (MS, PhD); environmental and sustainability policy (MS); environmental science (MS, PhD); history (MA, MAT); materials science and engineering (MS, PhD); mathematical and computational finance (MS); mathematical sciences (PhD); pharmaceutical chemistry (MS); professional and technical communications (MS); technical communication essentials (Certificate). *Application deadline:* For fall admission, 6/1 priority date for domestic students, 5/1 priority date for international students; for spring admission, 11/15 priority date for domestic and international students. Applications are processed on a rolling basis. *Application fee:* $75. Electronic applications accepted. *Application Contact:* Stephen Eck, Director of Admissions, 973-596-3300, Fax: 973-596-3461, E-mail: admissions@njit.edu. *Dean,* Dr. Kevin Belfield, 973-596-3676, Fax: 973-565-0586, E-mail: kevin.d.belfield@njit.edu.

J. Robert and Barbara A. Hillier College of Architecture and Design Students: 55 full-time (39 women), 2 part-time (1 woman); includes 13 minority (2 Black or African American, non-Hispanic/Latino; 2 Asian, non-Hispanic/Latino; 9 Hispanic/Latino), 25 international. Average age 28. 106 applicants, 38% accepted, 24 enrolled. *Faculty:* 25 full-time (9 women), 33 part-time/adjunct (13 women). Expenses: Contact institution. *Financial support:* In 2018–19, 40 students received support, including 3 fellowships with full tuition reimbursements available (averaging $22,000 per year), 1 research assistantship with full tuition reimbursement available (averaging $22,000 per year), 8 teaching assistantships with full tuition reimbursements available (averaging $22,000 per year); career-related internships or fieldwork, Federal Work-Study, scholarships/grants, traineeships, unspecified assistantships, and studio assistantships (1 averaging $10,000) also available. Financial award application deadline: 1/15. In 2018, 16 master's awarded. *Program availability:* Part-time, evening/weekend. Offers architecture (M Arch); infrastructure planning (MIP); urban systems (PhD). *Application deadline:* For fall admission, 6/1 priority date for domestic students, 5/1 priority date for international students; for spring admission, 11/15 priority date for domestic and international students. Applications are processed on a rolling basis. *Application fee:* $75. Electronic applications accepted. *Application Contact:* Stephen Eck, Director of Admissions, 973-596-3300, Fax: 973-596-3461, E-mail: admissions@njit.edu. *Dean,* Dr. Branko Kolarevic, 973-596-3080, E-mail: branko.r.kolarevic@njit.edu.

Martin Tuchman School of Management Students: 132 full-time (30 women), 128 part-time (67 women); includes 141 minority (39 Black or African American, non-Hispanic/Latino; 1 American Indian or Alaska Native, non-Hispanic/Latino; 51 Asian, non-Hispanic/Latino; 44 Hispanic/Latino; 6 Two or more races, non-Hispanic/Latino), 37 international. Average age 30. 339 applicants, 57% accepted, 88 enrolled. *Faculty:* 32 full-time (8 women), 22 part-time/adjunct (6 women). Expenses: Contact institution. *Financial support:* In 2018–19, 37 students received support, including 6 fellowships with full tuition reimbursements available (averaging $22,000 per year), 9 research assistantships with full tuition reimbursements available (averaging $22,000 per year), 10 teaching assistantships (averaging $22,000 per year); career-related internships or fieldwork, Federal Work-Study, scholarships/grants, and unspecified assistantships also available. Financial award application deadline: 1/15. In 2018, 82 master's, 11 other advanced degrees awarded. *Program availability:* Part-time, evening/weekend. Offers business data science (PhD); management (MS); management of technology (MBA,

Certificate). *Application deadline:* For fall admission, 6/1 priority date for domestic students, 5/1 priority date for international students; for spring admission, 11/15 priority date for domestic and international students. Applications are processed on a rolling basis. *Application fee:* $75. Electronic applications accepted. *Application Contact:* Stephen Eck, Director of Admissions, 973-596-3300, Fax: 973-596-3461, E-mail: admissions@njit.edu. *Dean,* Dr. Oya Tukel, 973-596-3248, Fax: 973-596-3074, E-mail: oya.i.tukel@njit.edu.

Newark College of Engineering Students: 690 full-time (163 women), 594 part-time (130 women); includes 427 minority (79 Black or African American, non-Hispanic/Latino; 181 Asian, non-Hispanic/Latino; 140 Hispanic/Latino; 27 Two or more races, non-Hispanic/Latino), 553 international. Average age 27. 2,334 applicants, 57% accepted, 452 enrolled. *Faculty:* 147 full-time (26 women), 133 part-time/adjunct (16 women). Expenses: Contact institution. *Financial support:* In 2018–19, 396 students received support, including 52 fellowships with full tuition reimbursements available (averaging $22,000 per year), 113 research assistantships with full tuition reimbursements available (averaging $22,000 per year), 101 teaching assistantships with full tuition reimbursements available (averaging $22,000 per year); career-related internships or fieldwork, Federal Work-Study, scholarships/grants, and unspecified assistantships also available. Financial award application deadline: 1/15. In 2018, 418 master's, 31 doctorates awarded. *Program availability:* Part-time, evening/weekend. Offers biomedical engineering (MS, PhD); biopharmaceutical engineering (MS); chemical engineering (MS, PhD); civil engineering (MS, PhD); computer engineering (MS); critical infrastructure systems (MS); electrical engineering (MS, PhD); engineering management (MS); engineering science (MS); environmental engineering (MS, PhD); healthcare systems management (MS); industrial engineering (MS, PhD); internet engineering (MS); manufacturing systems engineering (MS); materials science & engineering (PhD); materials science and engineering (MS); mechanical engineering (MS, PhD); occupational safety and health engineering (MS). *Application deadline:* For fall admission, 6/1 priority date for domestic students, 5/1 priority date for international students; for spring admission, 11/15 priority date for domestic and international students. Applications are processed on a rolling basis. *Application fee:* $75. Electronic applications accepted. *Application Contact:* Stephen Eck, Director of Admissions, 973-596-3300, Fax: 973-596-3461, E-mail: admissions@njit.edu. *Dean,* Dr. Moshe Kam, 973-596-5534, Fax: 973-596-2316, E-mail: moshe.kam@njit.edu.

Ying Wu College of Computing Students: 699 full-time (229 women), 269 part-time (67 women); includes 260 minority (44 Black or African American, non-Hispanic/Latino; 145 Asian, non-Hispanic/Latino; 59 Hispanic/Latino; 12 Two or more races, non-Hispanic/Latino), 614 international. Average age 26. 2,216 applicants, 55% accepted, 366 enrolled. *Faculty:* 69 full-time (13 women), 38 part-time/adjunct (4 women). Expenses: Contact institution. *Financial support:* In 2018–19, 366 students received support, including 10 fellowships with full tuition reimbursements available (averaging $22,000 per year), 47 research assistantships with full tuition reimbursements available (averaging $22,000 per year), 28 teaching assistantships with full tuition reimbursements available (averaging $22,000 per year); career-related internships or fieldwork, Federal Work-Study, scholarships/grants, and unspecified assistantships also available. Financial award application deadline: 1/15. In 2018, 418 master's, 5 doctorates, 13 other advanced degrees awarded. *Program availability:* Part-time, evening/weekend. Offers big data management and mining (Certificate); business and information systems (Certificate); computer science (PhD); computing and business (MS); data mining (Certificate); data science (MS); information security (Certificate); information systems (PhD); information technology administration and security (MS); IT administration (Certificate); network security and information assurance (Certificate); software engineering (MS); software engineering analysis/design (Certificate); Web systems development (Certificate). *Application deadline:* For fall admission, 6/1 priority date for domestic students, 5/1 priority date for international students; for spring admission, 11/15 priority date for domestic and international students. Applications are processed on a rolling basis. *Application fee:* $75. Electronic applications accepted. *Application Contact:* Stephen Eck, Director of Admissions, 973-596-3300, Fax: 973-596-3461, E-mail: admissions@njit.edu. *Dean,* Dr. Craig Gotsman, 973-596-3366, Fax: 973-596-5777, E-mail: craig.gotsman@njit.edu.

NEWMAN THEOLOGICAL COLLEGE, Edmonton, AB T6V 1H3, Canada
General Information Independent-religious, coed, graduate-only institution. *Enrollment:* 30 full-time matriculated graduate/professional students (4 women), 88 part-time matriculated graduate/professional students (72 women). *Enrollment by degree level:* 115 master's, 3 other advanced degrees. *Graduate faculty:* 14 full-time (3 women), 8 part-time/adjunct (2 women). *Tuition:* Full-time $6630 Canadian dollars; part-time $663 Canadian dollars per course. *Required fees:* $230 Canadian dollars; $85 Canadian dollars per semester. $85 Canadian dollars per semester. One-time fee: $45 Canadian dollars. Tuition and fees vary according to course load and campus/location. *Graduate housing:* On-campus housing not available. *Student services:* Campus employment opportunities, career counseling, free psychological counseling, services for students with disabilities. *Library facilities:* Sopchyshyn Family Library. *Collection:* Books: 72,000 (physical); Serial titles: 181 (physical); Databases: 13. Weekly public service hours: 45; students can reserve study rooms.

Computer facilities: 5 computers available on campus for general student use.
Website: http://www.newman.edu.

General Application Contact: Maria Saulnier, Registrar, 780-392-2451, Fax: 780-462-4013, E-mail: registrar@newman.edu.

GRADUATE UNITS
Religious Education Programs Students: 1 (woman) full-time, 80 part-time (66 women). Average age 40. 20 applicants, 100% accepted, 20 enrolled. *Faculty:* 2 full-time (1 woman), 4 part-time/adjunct (1 woman). Expenses: Contact institution. *Financial support:* In 2018–19, 9 students received support. Tuition bursaries available. Support available to part-time students. Financial award application deadline: 5/31. In 2018, 15 master's awarded. *Program availability:* Part-time, blended/hybrid learning. Offers religious education (MRE, Graduate Certificate). *Application deadline:* For fall admission, 8/19 priority date for domestic students, 2/19 priority date for international students; for winter admission, 11/20 priority date for domestic students; for spring admission, 2/19 priority date for domestic students. Applications are processed on a rolling basis. *Application fee:* $45 ($250 for international students). *Application Contact:* Maria Saulnier, Registrar, 780-392-2451, Fax: 780-462-4013, E-mail: registrar@newman.edu. *Director,* Sandra Talarico, 780-392-2450 Ext. 2214, Fax: 780-462-4013, E-mail: sandra.talarico@newman.edu.

Theology Programs Students: 29 full-time (3 women), 8 part-time (6 women). Average age 30. 15 applicants, 100% accepted, 14 enrolled. *Faculty:* 14 full-time (3 women), 5 part-time/adjunct (1 woman). Expenses: Contact institution. *Financial support:* In 2018–19, 6 students received support. Tuition bursaries available. Support available to part-time students. Financial award application deadline: 5/31. In 2018, 12 master's awarded.

Program availability: Part-time, 100% online. Offers theology (M Div, M Th, MTS). *Application deadline:* For fall admission, 8/19 priority date for domestic students, 2/19 priority date for international students; for winter admission, 11/20 priority date for domestic students; for spring admission, 2/19 priority date for domestic students. Applications are processed on a rolling basis. *Application fee:* $45 ($250 for international students). *Application Contact:* Maria Saulnier, Registrar, 780-392-2451, Fax: 780-462-4013, E-mail: registrar@newman.edu. *Academic Dean/Vice President,* Dr. Ryan Topping, 780-392-2450 Ext. 2444, Fax: 780-462-4013, E-mail: ryan.topping@newman.edu.

NEWMAN UNIVERSITY, Wichita, KS 67213-2097

General Information Independent-religious, coed, comprehensive institution. *Graduate housing:* Rooms and/or apartments available on a first-come, first-served basis to single and married students. Housing application deadline: 8/1.

GRADUATE UNITS

Graduate Theology Program *Program availability:* Part-time, online learning. Offers theological studies (MTS); theology (MA).

Master of Science in Education Program *Program availability:* Part-time, evening/weekend, online learning. Offers building leadership (MS Ed); curriculum and instruction (MS Ed); organizational leadership (MS Ed). Electronic applications accepted.

MBA Program *Program availability:* Part-time. Offers finance (MBA); international business (MBA); leadership (MBA); management (MBA); management information technology (MBA). Electronic applications accepted.

School of Nursing and Allied Health Offers nurse anesthesia (MS). Electronic applications accepted.

School of Social Work *Program availability:* Online learning. Offers social work (MSW).

NEW MEXICO HIGHLANDS UNIVERSITY, Las Vegas, NM 87701

General Information State-supported, coed, comprehensive institution. CGS member. *Graduate housing:* Rooms and/or apartments guaranteed to single and married students. *Research affiliation:* Spectra Gases, Inc. (chemistry), Los Alamos National Laboratory (chemistry), Sigma Aldrich (chemistry).

GRADUATE UNITS

Graduate Studies *Program availability:* Part-time.

College of Arts and Sciences *Program availability:* Part-time. Offers arts and sciences (MA, MS); chemistry (MS); English (MA); human performance and sport (MA); media arts and computer science (MS); natural science (MS); psychology (MS); public affairs (MA); Southwest studies (MA). Electronic applications accepted.

Facundo Valdez School of Social Work *Program availability:* Part-time. Offers bilingual/bicultural clinical practice (MSW); clinical practice (MSW).

School of Business, Media and Technology Offers business administration (MBA); media arts and computer science (MA); media arts and technology (MA).

School of Education *Program availability:* Part-time. Offers curriculum and instruction (MA); educational leadership (MA); professional counseling (MA); special education (MA).

NEW MEXICO INSTITUTE OF MINING AND TECHNOLOGY, Socorro, NM 87801

General Information State-supported, coed, university. CGS member. *Graduate housing:* Rooms and/or apartments available on a first-come, first-served basis to single and married students. Housing application deadline: 6/1. *Research affiliation:* Gas Technology Institute (natural gas recovery), Optical Surface Technologies LLC (custom optical components), National Center for Atmospheric Research (atmosphere research), National Radio Astronomy Observatory (astronomy), Joint Center for Materials Research (materials engineering, metallurgy).

GRADUATE UNITS

Center for Graduate Studies Offers applied and industrial mathematics (PhD); astrophysics (PhD); atmospheric physics (PhD); biology (MS); chemistry (MS, PhD); computer science (MS, PhD); electrical engineering (MS); environmental engineering (MS); explosives engineering (MS); fluid and thermal sciences (MS); geobiology (PhD); geochemistry (MS, PhD); geology (MS, PhD); geophysics (MS, PhD); geotechnical engineering (MS); hydrology (MS, PhD); industrial mathematics (MS); instrumentation (MS); materials engineering (MS, PhD); mathematical physics (PhD); mathematics (MS); mechatronics systems engineering (MS); mining engineering (MS); operations research and statistics (MS); petroleum engineering (MS, PhD); physics (MS); science teaching (MST); solid mechanics (MS); STEM education (MEM). Electronic applications accepted.

NEW MEXICO STATE UNIVERSITY, Las Cruces, NM 88003-8001

General Information State-supported, coed, university. CGS member. *Enrollment:* 1,405 full-time matriculated graduate/professional students (779 women), 1,095 part-time matriculated graduate/professional students (659 women). *Enrollment by degree level:* 1,748 master's, 722 doctoral, 30 other advanced degrees. *Graduate faculty:* 501 full-time (208 women), 47 part-time/adjunct (27 women). *International tuition:* $12,769.30 full-time. *Tuition, area resident:* Full-time $4216.70; part-time $252.70 per credit hour. *Tuition, state resident:* Full-time $4216.70; part-time $252.70 per credit hour. *Tuition, nonresident:* full-time $12,769; part-time $881.10 per credit hour. *Required fees:* $878.40; $48.80 per credit hour. Full-time tuition and fees vary according to course load and reciprocity agreements. *Graduate housing:* Rooms and/or apartments available on a first-come, first-served basis to single and married students. Typical cost: $5350 per year ($9252 including board) for single students; $8025 per year ($13,878 including board) for married students. Room and board charges vary according to board plan, campus/location and housing facility selected. Housing application deadline: 7/1. *Student services:* Campus employment opportunities, campus safety program, career counseling, child daycare facilities, exercise/wellness program, free psychological counseling, grant writing training, international student services, low-cost health insurance, multicultural affairs office, services for students with disabilities, teacher training, writing training. *Library facilities:* New Mexico State University Library - Zuhl plus 1 other. *Collection:* Books: 1.2 million (physical), 160,068 (digital/electronic); Serial titles: 23,730 (physical), 135,113 (digital/electronic); Databases: 410. Weekly public service hours: 112; students can reserve study rooms.

Computer facilities: Computer purchase and lease plans are available. 708 computers available on campus for general student use. A campuswide network can be accessed from student residence rooms and from off campus. Online class registration, antivirus software; student portal online with file share/storage space, student employee clock-in, payments system, hardware rentals, short-term tablet checkout, software discounts are available.
Website: http://www.nmsu.edu/

General Application Contact: Dr. Luis Cifuentes, Dean, 575-646-5746, Fax: 575-646-7758, E-mail: gradinfo@nmsu.edu.

GRADUATE UNITS

College of Agricultural, Consumer and Environmental Sciences Students: 153 full-time (93 women), 51 part-time (30 women); includes 72 minority (2 Black or African American, non-Hispanic/Latino; 2 American Indian or Alaska Native, non-Hispanic/Latino; 65 Hispanic/Latino; 3 Two or more races, non-Hispanic/Latino), 41 international. Average age 29. 114 applicants, 59% accepted, 56 enrolled. *Faculty:* 74 full-time (28 women), 4 part-time/adjunct (1 woman). Expenses: Contact institution. *Financial support:* In 2018–19, 157 students received support, including 4 fellowships (averaging $4,548 per year), 81 research assistantships (averaging $17,800 per year), 50 teaching assistantships (averaging $13,130 per year); career-related internships or fieldwork, Federal Work-Study, scholarships/grants, traineeships, health care benefits, and unspecified assistantships also available. Support available to part-time students. Financial award application deadline: 3/1. In 2018, 62 master's, 4 doctorates awarded. *Program availability:* Part-time. Offers agribusiness (MBA); agricultural and extension education (MA); agriculture (M Ag); animal science (MS, PhD); clothing, textiles, and merchandising (MS); economic development (DED); entomology, plant pathology and weed science (MS); family and child science (MS); family and consumer science education (MS); family and consumer sciences (MS); fish, wildlife and conservation ecology (MS); food science and technology (MS); horticulture (MS); hotel, restaurant, and tourism management (MS); human nutrition and dietetic sciences (MS); plant and environmental sciences (MS, PhD); range science (MS, PhD); water science management (MS). *Application deadline:* For fall admission, 8/15 for domestic and international students; for spring admission, 12/15 for domestic and international students; for summer admission, 5/15 for domestic and international students. Applications are processed on a rolling basis. *Application fee:* $40 ($50 for international students). Electronic applications accepted. *Application Contact:* Dr. Donald Conner, Associate Dean, 575-646-1109, Fax: 575-646-5975, E-mail: deconner@nmsu.edu. *Dean,* Dr. Rolando A. Flores, 575-646-3748, Fax: 575-646-5975, E-mail: agdean@nmsu.edu.

College of Arts and Sciences Students: 478 full-time (238 women), 232 part-time (133 women); includes 249 minority (19 Black or African American, non-Hispanic/Latino; 7 American Indian or Alaska Native, non-Hispanic/Latino; 15 Asian, non-Hispanic/Latino; 184 Hispanic/Latino; 1 Native Hawaiian or other Pacific Islander, non-Hispanic/Latino; 23 Two or more races, non-Hispanic/Latino), 179 international. Average age 32. 689 applicants, 45% accepted, 152 enrolled. *Faculty:* 210 full-time (80 women), 9 part-time/adjunct (2 women). Expenses: Contact institution. *Financial support:* In 2018–19, 463 students received support, including 25 fellowships (averaging $4,066 per year), 64 research assistantships (averaging $18,823 per year), 301 teaching assistantships (averaging $16,209 per year); career-related internships or fieldwork, Federal Work-Study, scholarships/grants, traineeships, health care benefits, and unspecified assistantships also available. Support available to part-time students. Financial award application deadline: 3/1. In 2018, 177 master's, 40 doctorates, 21 other advanced degrees awarded. *Program availability:* Part-time, online learning. Offers anthropology (MA); applied geography (MAG); art history (MA); astronomy (MS, PhD); behavioral, ecological & evolutionary biology (PhD); bioinformatics (MS); biology (MS); biotechnology (MS); chemistry (MS, PhD); communication studies (MA); computer science (MS, PhD); conducting (MM); creative writing (MFA); criminal justice (MCJ); cultural resource management (Graduate Certificate); English (MA); experimental psychology (MA, PhD); fine arts (MFA); geography (MAG); geological sciences (MS); government (MA); history (MA); mathematical sciences (MS, PhD); museum studies (Graduate Certificate); music (MM); music education (MM); performance (MM); public administration (MPA); public history (MA); rhetoric and professional communication (PhD); sociology (MA); space physics (MS); Spanish (MA); studio art (MFA). *Application fee:* $40 ($50 for international students). Electronic applications accepted. *Application Contact:* Dr. James Murphy, Associate Dean, 575-646-3500, Fax: 575-646-6799, E-mail: murphy@nmsu.edu. *Dean,* Dr. Enrico Pontelli, 575-646-3500, Fax: 575-646-6799, E-mail: epontell@nmsu.edu.

College of Business Students: 127 full-time (61 women), 157 part-time (92 women); includes 151 minority (10 Black or African American, non-Hispanic/Latino; 4 American Indian or Alaska Native, non-Hispanic/Latino; 8 Asian, non-Hispanic/Latino; 123 Hispanic/Latino; 6 Two or more races, non-Hispanic/Latino), 43 international. Average age 32. 229 applicants, 77% accepted, 48 enrolled. *Faculty:* 48 full-time (12 women). Expenses: Contact institution. *Financial support:* In 2018–19, 122 students received support, including 8 fellowships (averaging $4,548 per year), 12 research assistantships (averaging $11,672 per year), 42 teaching assistantships (averaging $15,128 per year); career-related internships or fieldwork, Federal Work-Study, scholarships/grants, traineeships, health care benefits, and unspecified assistantships also available. Support available to part-time students. Financial award application deadline: 3/1. In 2018, 100 master's, 15 doctorates, 15 other advanced degrees awarded. *Program availability:* Part-time, 100% online. Offers accountancy (MACCT); agribusiness (MBA); applied statistics (MS); business administration (PhD); economic development (DED); economics (MA); finance (MBA, Graduate Certificate); information systems (MBA); management (PhD); public utility regulation and economics (Graduate Certificate). *Application deadline:* For fall admission, 7/1 priority date for domestic students; for spring admission, 11/1 for domestic students. Applications are processed on a rolling basis. *Application fee:* $40 ($50 for international students). Electronic applications accepted. *Application Contact:* Graduate Admissions, 575-646-3121, E-mail: admissions@nmsu.edu. *Dean,* Dr. James Hoffman, 575-646-2821, Fax: 575-646-6155, E-mail: jhoffman@nmsu.edu.

College of Education Students: 257 full-time (190 women), 405 part-time (294 women); includes 367 minority (20 Black or African American, non-Hispanic/Latino; 14 American Indian or Alaska Native, non-Hispanic/Latino; 15 Asian, non-Hispanic/Latino; 302 Hispanic/Latino; 1 Native Hawaiian or other Pacific Islander, non-Hispanic/Latino; 15 Two or more races, non-Hispanic/Latino), 46 international. Average age 36. 404 applicants, 45% accepted, 128 enrolled. *Faculty:* 66 full-time (47 women), 12 part-time/adjunct (9 women). Expenses: Contact institution. *Financial support:* In 2018–19, 256 students received support, including 14 fellowships (averaging $4,548 per year), 26 research assistantships (averaging $11,172 per year), 48 teaching assistantships (averaging $12,418 per year); career-related internships or fieldwork, Federal Work-Study, scholarships/grants, traineeships, health care benefits, and unspecified assistantships also available. Support available to part-time students. Financial award application deadline: 3/1. In 2018, 156 master's, 29 doctorates, 26 other advanced degrees awarded. *Program availability:* Part-time-only, evening/weekend, blended/hybrid learning. Offers bilingual education (MA); communication disorders (MA); counseling psychology (PhD); curriculum and instruction (Ed D, PhD, Ed S); early childhood education (MA); education (MA); education specialist (Ed S); educational administration (MA); educational diagnostics (MA, Ed S); educational leadership (Ed D, PhD); kinesiology (PhD); language, literacy and culture (MA); learning design and technologies

(MA); online teaching and learning (Graduate Certificate); school psychology (Ed S); special education (Ed D, PhD); teaching (MAT); teaching English to speakers of other languages (MA). *Application deadline:* For fall admission, 3/15 for international students; for spring admission, 10/15 for international students. Applications are processed on a rolling basis. *Application fee:* $40 ($50 for international students). Electronic applications accepted. *Application Contact:* Dr. David Rutledge, Graduate Education Advising, 575-646-5411, Fax: 575-646-6032, E-mail: rutledge@nmsu.edu. *Interim Dean,* Dr. Susan Brown, 575-646-5858, Fax: 575-646-6032, E-mail: susanbro@nmsu.edu.

College of Engineering Students: 218 full-time (56 women), 162 part-time (39 women); includes 132 minority (9 Black or African American, non-Hispanic/Latino; 3 American Indian or Alaska Native, non-Hispanic/Latino; 12 Asian, non-Hispanic/Latino; 100 Hispanic/Latino; 8 Two or more races, non-Hispanic/Latino), 137 international. Average age 31. 292 applicants, 56% accepted, 79 enrolled. *Faculty:* 63 full-time (12 women), 2 part-time/adjunct (0 women). Expenses: Contact institution. *Financial support:* In 2018–19, 237 students received support, including 18 fellowships (averaging $3,125 per year), 82 research assistantships (averaging $14,613 per year), 70 teaching assistantships (averaging $13,034 per year); career-related internships or fieldwork, Federal Work-Study, scholarships/grants, traineeships, health care benefits, and unspecified assistantships also available. Support available to part-time students. Financial award application deadline: 3/1. In 2018, 111 master's, 21 doctorates, 6 other advanced degrees awarded. *Program availability:* Part-time, online learning. Offers aerospace engineering (MSAE); chemical engineering (MS Ch E, PhD); civil and geological engineering (PhD); civil engineering (MSCE); electrical & computer engineering (MSEE); environmental engineering (MS Env E); industrial engineering (MSIE, PhD); master of science (MS Env E, MSAE, MSCE, MSIE, MSME); mechanical engineering (MSME, PhD); systems engineering (Graduate Certificate). *Application deadline:* For fall admission, 7/1 priority date for domestic students; for spring admission, 11/1 for domestic students. Applications are processed on a rolling basis. *Application fee:* $40 ($50 for international students). Electronic applications accepted. *Application Contact:* Graduate Admissions, 575-646-3121, E-mail: admissions@nmsu.edu. *Dean,* Dr. Lakshmi Reddi, 575-646-7234, Fax: 575-646-3549, E-mail: engrdean@nmsu.edu.

Klipsch School of Electrical and Computer Engineering Students: 58 full-time (15 women), 51 part-time (12 women); includes 39 minority (1 Black or African American, non-Hispanic/Latino; 5 Asian, non-Hispanic/Latino; 31 Hispanic/Latino; 2 Two or more races, non-Hispanic/Latino), 41 international. Average age 31. 75 applicants, 67% accepted, 18 enrolled. *Faculty:* 18 full-time (1 woman), 1 part-time/adjunct (0 women). Expenses: Contact institution. *Financial support:* In 2018–19, 67 students received support, including 1 fellowship (averaging $4,548 per year), 24 research assistantships (averaging $14,776 per year), 17 teaching assistantships (averaging $10,680 per year); career-related internships or fieldwork, Federal Work-Study, scholarships/grants, traineeships, health care benefits, and unspecified assistantships also available. Support available to part-time students. Financial award application deadline: 3/1. In 2018, 25 master's, 7 doctorates, 5 other advanced degrees awarded. *Program availability:* Part-time, evening/weekend, 100% online. Offers electrical and computer engineering (PhD); master of science (MSEE). *Application deadline:* For fall admission, 3/1 priority date for domestic and international students; for spring admission, 8/1 priority date for domestic and international students. Applications are processed on a rolling basis. *Application fee:* $40 ($50 for international students). Electronic applications accepted. *Application Contact:* Dr. Steven Stochaj, Interim Department Head, 575-646-3115, Fax: 575-646-1435, E-mail: sstochaj@nmsu.edu. *Interim Department Head,* Dr. Steven Stochaj, 575-646-3115, Fax: 575-646-1435, E-mail: sstochaj@nmsu.edu.

College of Health and Social Services Students: 178 full-time (148 women), 87 part-time (70 women); includes 158 minority (17 Black or African American, non-Hispanic/Latino; 4 American Indian or Alaska Native, non-Hispanic/Latino; 6 Asian, non-Hispanic/Latino; 127 Hispanic/Latino; 4 Two or more races, non-Hispanic/Latino), 4 international. Average age 35. 208 applicants, 76% accepted, 112 enrolled. *Faculty:* 35 full-time (28 women), 20 part-time/adjunct (15 women). Expenses: Contact institution. *Financial support:* In 2018–19, 116 students received support, including 20 research assistantships (averaging $10,267 per year), 10 teaching assistantships (averaging $8,992 per year); career-related internships or fieldwork, Federal Work-Study, scholarships/grants, traineeships, health care benefits, and unspecified assistantships also available. Support available to part-time students. Financial award application deadline: 3/1. In 2018, 74 master's, 20 doctorates, 9 other advanced degrees awarded. *Program availability:* Part-time, evening/weekend, online learning. Offers nursing (MSN); nursing practice (DNP); public health (MPH, Graduate Certificate); social work (MSW). *Application deadline:* For fall admission, 7/1 priority date for domestic students. Applications are processed on a rolling basis. *Application fee:* $40 ($50 for international students). Electronic applications accepted. *Application Contact:* Graduate Admissions, 575-646-3121, E-mail: admissions@nmsu.edu. *Dean,* Dr. Sonya Cooper, 575-646-3526, Fax: 575-646-6166, E-mail: socooper@nmsu.edu.

School of Nursing Students: 41 full-time (35 women), 35 part-time (29 women); includes 40 minority (6 Black or African American, non-Hispanic/Latino; 3 Asian, non-Hispanic/Latino; 31 Hispanic/Latino). Average age 41. 40 applicants, 90% accepted, 23 enrolled. *Faculty:* 13 full-time (all women). Expenses: Contact institution. *Financial support:* In 2018–19, 29 students received support, including 5 teaching assistantships (averaging $11,952 per year); career-related internships or fieldwork, Federal Work-Study, scholarships/grants, traineeships, health care benefits, and unspecified assistantships also available. Support available to part-time students. Financial award application deadline: 3/1. In 2018, 4 master's, 21 doctorates, 5 other advanced degrees awarded. *Program availability:* Part-time, blended/hybrid learning. Offers family nurse practitioner (Graduate Certificate); nursing (MSN); nursing practice (DNP); nursing science (PhD); psychiatric/mental health nurse practitioner (Graduate Certificate). *Application deadline:* For fall admission, 2/1 priority date for domestic students, 2/1 for international students. *Application fee:* $40 ($50 for international students). Electronic applications accepted. *Application Contact:* Alyce Kolenovsky, Academic Advisor, 575-646-3812, Fax: 575-646-2167, E-mail: nursing@nmsu.edu. *Director,* Dr. Alexa Doig, 575-646-3812, Fax: 575-646-2167, E-mail: adoig@nmsu.edu.

School of Social Work Students: 117 full-time (100 women), 6 part-time (5 women); includes 87 minority (8 Black or African American, non-Hispanic/Latino; 2 American Indian or Alaska Native, non-Hispanic/Latino; 2 Asian, non-Hispanic/Latino; 72 Hispanic/Latino; 3 Two or more races, non-Hispanic/Latino), 1 international. Average age 32. 122 applicants, 76% accepted, 68 enrolled. *Faculty:* 11 full-time (9 women), 16 part-time/adjunct (12 women). Expenses: Contact institution. *Financial support:* In 2018–19, 62 students received support, including 11 research assistantships (averaging $8,384 per year); career-related internships or fieldwork, Federal Work-Study, scholarships/grants, traineeships, health care benefits, and unspecified assistantships also available. Support available to part-time students. Financial award

application deadline: 3/1. In 2018, 47 master's awarded. *Program availability:* Part-time, blended/hybrid learning. Offers social work (MSW). *Application deadline:* For fall admission, 1/16 priority date for domestic students, 2/16 priority date for international students. Applications are processed on a rolling basis. *Application fee:* $40 ($50 for international students). Electronic applications accepted. *Application Contact:* MSW Program Coordinator, 575-646-2143, Fax: 575-646-4116, E-mail: socwork@nmsu.edu. *Interim Department Head,* Dr. Loui Reyes, 575-646-4820, Fax: 575-646-4116, E-mail: louireye@nmsu.edu.

Graduate School Students: 38 full-time (21 women), 21 part-time (7 women); includes 13 minority (1 American Indian or Alaska Native, non-Hispanic/Latino; 12 Hispanic/Latino), 23 international. Average age 36. 34 applicants, 56% accepted, 9 enrolled. *Faculty:* 5 full-time (1 woman). Expenses: Contact institution. *Financial support:* In 2018–19, 45 students received support, including 5 fellowships (averaging $4,548 per year), 9 research assistantships (averaging $18,448 per year), 3 teaching assistantships (averaging $17,099 per year); career-related internships or fieldwork, Federal Work-Study, scholarships/grants, traineeships, health care benefits, and unspecified assistantships also available. Support available to part-time students. Financial award application deadline: 3/1. In 2018, 4 master's, 5 doctorates awarded. *Program availability:* Part-time, evening/weekend, online learning. Offers interdisciplinary studies (MA, MS, PhD); molecular biology (MS, PhD); water science management (MS, PhD). *Application fee:* $40 ($50 for international students). Electronic applications accepted. *Application Contact:* Graduate Admissions, 575-646-3121, E-mail: admissions@nmsu.edu. *Dean,* Dr. Luis Cifuentes, 575-646-5746, Fax: 575-646-7758, E-mail: gradinfo@nmsu.edu.

NEW ORLEANS BAPTIST THEOLOGICAL SEMINARY, New Orleans, LA 70126-4858

General Information Independent-religious, coed, primarily men, comprehensive institution. *Graduate housing:* Rooms and/or apartments available to single and married students.

GRADUATE UNITS

Graduate and Professional Programs *Program availability:* Evening/weekend. Offers theology (M Div, MA, MACE, MAMFC, MMCM, D Min, DEM, DMA, PhD).

Division of Biblical Studies Offers biblical studies (M Div, MA, PhD).

Division of Christian Education Ministries Program availability: Evening/weekend, online learning. Offers Christian education (M Div, MACE, D Min, DEM, PhD).

Division of Church Music Ministries Program availability: Online learning. Offers church music ministries (M Div, MMCM, DMA).

Division of Pastoral Ministries Program availability: Online learning. Offers pastoral ministries (M Div, MAMFC, D Min, PhD).

Division of Theological and Historical Studies Program availability: Online learning. Offers theological and historical studies (M Div, MA, D Min, PhD).

NEW SAINT ANDREWS COLLEGE, Moscow, ID 83843

General Information Independent-religious, coed, comprehensive institution. *Enrollment:* 29 full-time matriculated graduate/professional students (13 women), 2 part-time matriculated graduate/professional students (both women). *Enrollment by degree level:* 31 master's. *Graduate faculty:* 13 part-time/adjunct (0 women). *Tuition:* Part-time $475 per credit. *Graduate housing:* On-campus housing not available. *Student services:* Campus employment opportunities, career counseling, international student services. *Library facilities:* Tyndale Library plus 1 other. *Collection:* Students can reserve study rooms.

Computer facilities: 4 computers available on campus for general student use. A campuswide network can be accessed from off campus. Online class registration is available.

Website: http://www.nsa.edu/

General Application Contact: Brenda Schlect, Director of Admissions, 208-882-1566 Ext. 113, Fax: 208-882-4293, E-mail: admissions@nsa.edu.

GRADUATE UNITS

Graduate School *Program availability:* Part-time, blended/hybrid learning. Offers classical Christian studies (Graduate Certificate); creative writing (MFA); theology and letters (MA). Electronic applications accepted.

THE NEW SCHOOL, New York, NY 10011

General Information Independent, coed, university. *Graduate housing:* Room and/or apartments available on a first-come, first-served basis to single students; on-campus housing not available to married students. Housing application deadline: 6/15. *Research affiliation:* The Goldman Sachs Group, Inc., Siemens, Raytheon Corporation, National Geospatial-Intelligence Agency, Environmental Systems Research Institute, Dow Jones & Company, Inc.

GRADUATE UNITS

College of Performing Arts *Program availability:* Part-time. Offers performing arts (MFA, MM, Advanced Diploma). Electronic applications accepted.

Mannes School of Music Program availability: Part-time. Offers composition (MM, Advanced Diploma); guitar (MM, Advanced Diploma); harpsichord (MM, Advanced Diploma); music theory (MM); orchestral conducting (MM, Advanced Diploma); orchestral instruments (MM, Advanced Diploma); piano (MM, Advanced Diploma); piano and collaborative piano (MM, Advanced Diploma); theory (Advanced Diploma); voice (MM, Advanced Diploma). Electronic applications accepted.

School of Drama Program availability: Part-time. Offers acting (MFA); directing (MFA); playwriting (MFA). Electronic applications accepted.

The New School for Social Research Program availability: Part-time. Offers anthropology (MA, PhD); clinical psychology (PhD); cognitive, social, and developmental psychology (PhD); economics (MA, MS, PhD); global political economy and finance (MA); historical studies (MA, PhD); liberal studies (MA); philosophy (MA); politics (M Phil, MA, PhD); psychoanalysis (PhD); psychology (MA); social research (M Phil, MA, MS, PhD); sociology (M Phil, MA, PhD). Electronic applications accepted.

Parsons Paris Program availability: Part-time. Offers art and design (MA); fashion studies (MA); history of design and curatorial studies (MA). Electronic applications accepted.

Parsons School of Design Program availability: Part-time. Offers architecture (M Arch); business of design (Advanced Certificate); communication design (MPS); data visualization (MS); design (M Arch, MA, MFA, MPS, MS, Advanced Certificate); design and technology (MFA); design and urban ecologies (MS); design studies (MA); fashion design and society (MFA); fashion studies (MA); fine arts (MFA); history of design and curatorial studies (MA); industrial design (MFA); interior design (MFA); lighting design (MFA); photography (MFA); strategic design and management (MS); theories of urban practice (MA); transdisciplinary design (MFA). Electronic applications accepted.

Schools of Public Engagement *Program availability:* Part-time, 100% online. Offers cities and social justice (MA); conflict and security (MA); creative writing (MFA); development (MA); documentary media studies (Graduate Certificate); environmental policy and sustainability management (MS); governance and rights (MA); international affairs (MS); leadership and change (Graduate Certificate); media and culture (MA); media management (MS, Graduate Certificate); media studies (MA); nonprofit management (MS); organizational change management (MS); organizational development (Graduate Certificate); public and urban policy (PhD); public engagement (MA, MFA, MS, PhD, Graduate Certificate); teaching English to speakers of other languages (MA). Electronic applications accepted.

NEWSCHOOL OF ARCHITECTURE AND DESIGN, San Diego, CA 92101-6634

General Information Proprietary, coed, primarily men, comprehensive institution. *Research affiliation:* Academy of Neuroscience for Architecture (neuroscience and architecture).

GRADUATE UNITS

Program in Architecture *Program availability:* Part-time, online learning. Offers architecture (M Arch, MS).

Program in Construction Management *Program availability:* Part-time, online learning. Offers construction management (MCM). Electronic applications accepted.

NEW YORK ACADEMY OF ART, New York, NY 10013-2911

General Information Independent, coed, graduate-only institution. *Graduate housing:* On-campus housing not available.

GRADUATE UNITS

Master of Fine Arts Program Offers anatomy (MFA); drawing (MFA); fine arts (MFA); painting (MFA); printmaking (MFA); sculpture (MFA). Electronic applications accepted.

NEW YORK CHIROPRACTIC COLLEGE, Seneca Falls, NY 13148-0800

General Information Independent, coed, graduate-only institution. *Graduate housing:* Rooms and/or apartments available on a first-come, first-served basis to single and married students. *Research affiliation:* Foot Levelers, Inc. (orthotics research), Atrium Innovations (nutrition), Nimmo Education Foundation (muscle physiology).

GRADUATE UNITS

Doctor of Chiropractic Program Offers chiropractic (DC). Electronic applications accepted.

Finger Lakes School of Acupuncture and Oriental Medicine Offers acupuncture (MS); acupuncture and Oriental medicine (MS). Electronic applications accepted.

Program in Applied Clinical Nutrition *Program availability:* Part-time, evening/weekend. Offers applied clinical nutrition (MS). Electronic applications accepted.

Program in Clinical Anatomy Offers clinical anatomy (MS). Electronic applications accepted.

Program in Human Anatomy and Physiology Instruction *Program availability:* Online learning. Offers human anatomy and physiology (MS).

NEW YORK COLLEGE OF HEALTH PROFESSIONS, Syosset, NY 11791-4413

General Information Independent, coed, comprehensive institution. *Graduate housing:* On-campus housing not available. *Research affiliation:* North Shore Hospital (acupuncture).

GRADUATE UNITS

Graduate School of Oriental Medicine *Program availability:* Part-time. Offers acupuncture (MS); Oriental medicine (MS).

NEW YORK COLLEGE OF PODIATRIC MEDICINE, New York, NY 10035

General Information Independent, coed, graduate-only institution. *Graduate housing:* Rooms and/or apartments available on a first-come, first-served basis to single and married students. Housing application deadline: 8/15. *Research affiliation:* Cyberlogics (ultrasound use), Novartis Pharmaceuticals (fungal diseases of nail), Prescription Dispensing Laboratories (topical verapamil), Anodyne Corporation (light energy applications).

GRADUATE UNITS

Professional Program Offers podiatric medicine (DPM).

NEW YORK COLLEGE OF TRADITIONAL CHINESE MEDICINE, Mineola, NY 11501

General Information Independent, coed, graduate-only institution.

GRADUATE UNITS

Graduate Programs Offers Oriental medicine (MAOM).

NEW YORK FILM ACADEMY, Burbank, CA 91505

General Information Independent, coed, comprehensive institution.

GRADUATE UNITS

Program in Filmmaking–Los Angeles Offers acting for film (MFA); cinematography (MFA); documentary film (MFA); film and media production (MA); filmmaking (MFA); game design (MFA); photography (MFA); producing (MA, MFA); screenwriting (MA, MFA).

Program in Filmmaking–South Beach, Florida Offers acting for film (MFA); cinematography (MFA); documentary film (MFA); film and media production (MA); filmmaking (MFA); game design (MFA); photography (MFA); producing (MA, MFA); screenwriting (MA, MFA).

NEW YORK INSTITUTE OF TECHNOLOGY, Old Westbury, NY 11568-8000

General Information Independent, coed, comprehensive institution. *Enrollment:* 2,862 full-time matriculated graduate/professional students (1,418 women), 602 part-time matriculated graduate/professional students (331 women). *Enrollment by degree level:* 1,679 master's, 1,730 doctoral, 55 other advanced degrees. *Tuition:* Full-time $1285; part-time $1285 per credit. *Required fees:* $215; $175 per unit. Tuition and fees vary according to course load, degree level and campus/location. *Graduate housing:* Room and/or apartments available on a first-come, first-served basis to single students; on-campus housing not available to married students. Typical cost: $9320 per year ($14,290 including board). Room and board charges vary according to campus/location. *Student*

services: Campus employment opportunities, campus safety program, career counseling, exercise/wellness program, free psychological counseling, international student services, low-cost health insurance, services for students with disabilities, writing training. *Library facilities:* George and Gertrude Wisser Memorial Library plus 3 others. *Collection:* Books: 89,426 (physical), 70,248 (digital/electronic); Serial titles: 2,279 (physical), 23,926 (digital/electronic). Weekly public service hours: 78; students can reserve study rooms.

Computer facilities: 1,250 computers available on campus for general student use. A campuswide network can be accessed from student residence rooms and from off campus. Online class registration is available.
Website: http://www.nyit.edu/

General Application Contact: Alice Dolitsky, Director, Graduate Admissions, 516-686-7520, Fax: 516-686-1116, E-mail: admissions@nyit.edu.

GRADUATE UNITS

College of Arts and Sciences Students: 130 full-time (82 women), 20 part-time (14 women); includes 23 minority (6 Black or African American, non-Hispanic/Latino; 4 Asian, non-Hispanic/Latino; 9 Hispanic/Latino; 4 Two or more races, non-Hispanic/Latino), 103 international. Average age 26. 377 applicants, 65% accepted, 147 enrolled. Expenses: Contact institution. *Financial support:* Career-related internships or fieldwork, Federal Work-Study, scholarships/grants, tuition waivers (full and partial), and unspecified assistantships available. Support available to part-time students. Financial award application deadline: 2/15; financial award applicants required to submit FAFSA. In 2018, 92 master's awarded. *Program availability:* Part-time, evening/weekend, 100% online, blended/hybrid learning. Offers arts and sciences (MA, MFA); communication arts (MA); computer graphics (MFA). *Application deadline:* For fall admission, 7/1 for international students. Applications are processed on a rolling basis. *Application fee:* $50. Electronic applications accepted. *Application Contact:* Alice Dolitsky, Director, Graduate Admissions, 516-686-1316, Fax: 516-686-1116, E-mail: admissions@nyit.edu. *Dean,* Dr. Daniel Quigley, 516-686-7756, E-mail: dquigley@nyit.edu.

College of Engineering and Computing Sciences Students: 350 full-time (97 women), 209 part-time (60 women); includes 120 minority (29 Black or African American, non-Hispanic/Latino; 55 Asian, non-Hispanic/Latino; 30 Hispanic/Latino; 1 Native Hawaiian or other Pacific Islander, non-Hispanic/Latino; 5 Two or more races, non-Hispanic/Latino), 353 international. Average age 27. 1,673 applicants, 59% accepted, 159 enrolled. Expenses: Contact institution. *Financial support:* Fellowships with partial tuition reimbursements, teaching assistantships with partial tuition reimbursements, career-related internships or fieldwork, Federal Work-Study, scholarships/grants, tuition waivers (full and partial), and unspecified assistantships available. Support available to part-time students. Financial award application deadline: 2/15; financial award applicants required to submit FAFSA. In 2018, 400 master's awarded. *Program availability:* Part-time, evening/weekend, 100% online, blended/hybrid learning. Offers bioengineering (MS); computer science (MS); electrical and computer engineering (MS); energy technology (Advanced Certificate); engineering and computing sciences (MS, Advanced Certificate); environmental management (Advanced Certificate); environmental technology and sustainability (MS); facilities management (Advanced Certificate); information, network, and computer security (MS); infrastructure security management (Advanced Certificate); mechanical engineering (MS). *Application deadline:* For fall admission, 7/1 for international students; for spring admission, 12/15 for international students. Applications are processed on a rolling basis. *Application fee:* $50. Electronic applications accepted. *Application Contact:* Alice Dolitsky, Director, Graduate Admissions, 516-686-7520, Fax: 516-686-1116, E-mail: admissions@nyit.edu. *Dean,* Dr. Babek Beheshti, 516-686-7437, E-mail: deanofengineering@nyit.edu.

College of Osteopathic Medicine Students: 1,612 full-time (767 women); includes 738 minority (65 Black or African American, non-Hispanic/Latino; 584 Asian, non-Hispanic/Latino; 63 Hispanic/Latino; 26 Two or more races, non-Hispanic/Latino). Average age 27. 7,036 applicants, 13% accepted, 436 enrolled. *Faculty:* 94 full-time (44 women), 36 part-time/adjunct (16 women). Expenses: Contact institution. *Financial support:* Federal Work-Study and scholarships/grants available. Financial award application deadline: 2/15; financial award applicants required to submit FAFSA. Offers global health (Certificate). *Application deadline:* For fall admission, 3/1 for domestic students. *Application fee:* $80. Electronic applications accepted. *Application Contact:* Gina Moses, Director, Admissions Recruitment, 516-686-1227, E-mail: gmoses@nyit.edu. *Dean,* Dr. Jerry Balentine, 516-686-3999, Fax: 516-686-3830, E-mail: Jerry.Balentine@nyit.edu.

School of Architecture and Design Students: 24 full-time (15 women); includes 3 minority (1 Asian, non-Hispanic/Latino; 2 Hispanic/Latino), 18 international. Average age 29. 74 applicants, 38% accepted, 17 enrolled. *Faculty:* 3 full-time (1 woman), 3 part-time/adjunct (0 women). Expenses: Contact institution. *Financial support:* Career-related internships or fieldwork, Federal Work-Study, institutionally sponsored loans, scholarships/grants, tuition waivers (full and partial), and unspecified assistantships available. Support available to part-time students. Financial award application deadline: 2/15; financial award applicants required to submit FAFSA. In 2018, 6 master's awarded. *Program availability:* Part-time. Offers architecture (M Arch); architecture, urban and regional design (MS). *Application deadline:* For fall admission, 3/1 for domestic and international students. Applications are processed on a rolling basis. *Application fee:* $50. Electronic applications accepted. *Application Contact:* Alice Dolitsky, Director, Graduate Admissions, 516-686-1116, E-mail: admissions@nyit.edu. *Chair,* Robert Cody, 516-686-7401, E-mail: rcody@nyit.edu.

School of Health Professions Students: 366 full-time (258 women), 41 part-time (35 women); includes 105 minority (13 Black or African American, non-Hispanic/Latino; 48 Asian, non-Hispanic/Latino; 36 Hispanic/Latino; 8 Two or more races, non-Hispanic/Latino), 1 international. Average age 25. 2,569 applicants, 11% accepted, 138 enrolled. Expenses: Contact institution. *Financial support:* Career-related internships or fieldwork, Federal Work-Study, scholarships/grants, tuition waivers (full and partial), and unspecified assistantships available. Support available to part-time students. Financial award application deadline: 2/15; financial award applicants required to submit FAFSA. In 2018, 88 master's, 42 doctorates awarded. *Program availability:* Part-time, evening/weekend, 100% online. Offers clinical nutrition (MS); health professions (MS, DPT); occupational therapy (MS); physical therapy (DPT); physician assistant studies (MS). *Application fee:* $50. Electronic applications accepted. *Application Contact:* Alice Dolitsky, Director, Graduate Admissions, 516-686-7520, Fax: 516-686-1116, E-mail: admissions@nyit.edu. *Dean,* Dr. Gordon Schmidt, 516-686-3939, E-mail: shp@nyit.edu.

School of Management Students: 310 full-time (134 women), 116 part-time (69 women); includes 59 minority (12 Black or African American, non-Hispanic/Latino; 1 American Indian or Alaska Native, non-Hispanic/Latino; 21 Asian, non-Hispanic/Latino; 19 Hispanic/Latino; 1 Native Hawaiian or other Pacific Islander, non-Hispanic/Latino; 5 Two or more races, non-Hispanic/Latino), 307 international. Average age 27. 604 applicants, 68% accepted, 128 enrolled. Expenses: Contact institution. *Financial support:* Career-related internships or fieldwork, Federal Work-Study, scholarships/grants, tuition waivers (full and partial), and unspecified assistantships available. Support available to part-time students. Financial award application deadline: 2/15; financial award applicants required to submit FAFSA. In 2018, 317 master's, 1 other advanced degree awarded. *Program availability:* Part-time. Offers executive management (MBA); human resource management (Advanced Certificate); human resource management and labor relations (MS); management (MBA, MS, Advanced Certificate). *Application deadline:* Applications are processed on a rolling basis. *Application fee:* $50. Electronic applications accepted. *Application Contact:* Alice Dolitsky, Director, Graduate Admissions, 516-686-7520, Fax: 516-686-1116, E-mail: admissions@nyit.edu. *Dean,* Dr. Jess Boronico, 516-686-7838, Fax: 516-686-7430, E-mail: jboronic@nyit.edu.

NEW YORK LAW SCHOOL, New York, NY 10013

General Information Independent, coed, graduate-only institution. *Enrollment by degree level:* 26 master's, 1,016 doctoral. *Graduate faculty:* 56 full-time (27 women), 83 part-time/adjunct (26 women). *Tuition:* Full-time $50,008; part-time $38,536 per year. *Required fees:* $1724; $1224 per unit. Tuition and fees vary according to course load and degree level. *Graduate housing:* Room and/or apartments available on a first-come, first-served basis to single students; on-campus housing not available to married students. Typical cost: $22,872 per year. Room charges vary according to housing facility selected. Housing application deadline: 7/1. *Student services:* Campus employment opportunities, campus safety program, career counseling, exercise/wellness program, free psychological counseling, international student services, low-cost health insurance, multicultural affairs office, services for students with disabilities, writing training. *Library facilities:* The Mendik Library. *Collection:* Books: 274,045 (physical), 246,875 (digital/electronic); Serial titles: 5,525 (physical), 256,670 (digital/electronic); Databases: 139. Weekly public service hours: 93.

Computer facilities: 70 computers available on campus for general student use. A campuswide network can be accessed from off campus. Online class registration is available.
Website: http://www.nyls.edu/

General Application Contact: Ella Mae Estrada, Associate Dean for Enrollment Management, Financial Aid and Diversity Initiatives, 212-431-2888, Fax: 212-966-1522, E-mail: admissions@nyls.edu.

GRADUATE UNITS

Graduate Programs Students: 791 full-time (467 women), 251 part-time (136 women); includes 334 minority (61 Black or African American, non-Hispanic/Latino; 74 Asian, non-Hispanic/Latino; 170 Hispanic/Latino; 1 Native Hawaiian or other Pacific Islander, non-Hispanic/Latino; 28 Two or more races, non-Hispanic/Latino), 26 international. Average age 27. 2,837 applicants, 52% accepted, 385 enrolled. *Faculty:* 56 full-time (27 women), 83 part-time/adjunct (26 women). Expenses: Contact institution. *Financial support:* In 2018–19, 698 students received support, including 107 fellowships (averaging $4,110 per year), 22 research assistants (averaging $4,663 per year), 19 teaching assistantships (averaging $4,661 per year); career-related internships or fieldwork, Federal Work-Study, and scholarships/grants also available. Support available to part-time students. Financial award application deadline: 7/1; financial award applicants required to submit FAFSA. In 2018, 13 master's, 272 doctorates awarded. *Program availability:* Part-time, evening/weekend. Offers law (LL M, JD). JD/MBA offered jointly with Baruch College of the City University of New York; JD/MA in forensic psychology offered jointly with John Jay College of Criminal Justice of the City University of New York. *Application deadline:* For fall admission, 7/1 priority date for domestic and international students. Applications are processed on a rolling basis. *Application fee:* $0. Electronic applications accepted. *Application Contact:* Ella Mae Estrada, Associate Dean for Enrollment Management, Financial Aid and Diversity Initiatives, 212-431-2888, Fax: 212-966-1522, E-mail: admissions@nyls.edu. *Dean and President,* Anthony W. Crowell, 212-431-2840, Fax: 212-219-3752, E-mail: anthony.crowell@nyls.edu.

NEW YORK MEDICAL COLLEGE, Valhalla, NY 10595

General Information Independent, coed, graduate-only institution. CGS member. *Enrollment by degree level:* 418 master's, 1,037 doctoral, 5 other advanced degrees. *Graduate faculty:* 1,103 full-time (459 women), 1,487 part-time/adjunct (575 women). *Tuition:* Full-time $54,040; part-time $1165 per credit. *Required fees:* $500; $500 per credit. Tuition and fees vary according to course load. *Graduate housing:* Rooms and/or apartments available on a first-come, first-served basis to single and married students. Typical cost: $10,500 per year for single students; $17,220 per year for married students. Room charges vary according to housing facility selected. *Student services:* Campus employment opportunities, campus safety program, career counseling, exercise/wellness program, free psychological counseling, international student services, low-cost health insurance, multicultural affairs office, services for students with disabilities, writing training. *Library facilities:* Health Sciences Library plus 2 others. *Collection:* Books: 30,759 (physical), 12,923 (digital/electronic); Serial titles: 1,731 (physical), 17,194 (digital/electronic); Databases: 115. Weekly public service hours: 83; study areas open 24 hours, 5–7 days a week; students can reserve study rooms. *Research affiliation:* Touro College & University System (biomedical research), Westchester Medical Center (biomedical research), Metropolitan Hospital (biomedical research), Westchester Institute for Human Development (biomedical research), Columbia University College of Physicians and Surgeons (neurosciences), Seattle Children's Hospital (pediatric pulmonary disease).

Computer facilities: 60 computers available on campus for general student use. A campuswide network can be accessed. Online class registration is available.
Website: http://www.nymc.edu/

General Application Contact: Robin Baum, Director of Admissions, 914-594-4882, Fax: 914-594-4613, E-mail: mdadmit@nymc.edu.

GRADUATE UNITS

Graduate School of Basic Medical Sciences Students: 119 full-time (71 women), 16 part-time (8 women); includes 59 minority (14 Black or African American, non-Hispanic/Latino; 1 American Indian or Alaska Native, non-Hispanic/Latino; 19 Asian, non-Hispanic/Latino; 19 Hispanic/Latino; 1 Native Hawaiian or other Pacific Islander, non-Hispanic/Latino; 5 Two or more races, non-Hispanic/Latino), 22 international. Average age 29. 261 applicants, 57% accepted, 69 enrolled. *Faculty:* 86 full-time (21 women). Expenses: Contact institution. *Financial support:* Federal Work-Study, scholarships/grants, unspecified assistantships, and Student Federal Loans available. Financial award application deadline: 4/30; financial award applicants required to submit FAFSA. In 2018, 28 master's, 5 doctorates awarded. *Program availability:* Part-time, evening/weekend. Offers biochemistry and molecular biology (MS, PhD); cell biology (MS, PhD); microbiology and immunology (MS, PhD); pathology (MS, PhD); pharmacology (MS, PhD); physiology (MS, PhD). *Application deadline:* For fall admission, 7/1 priority date for domestic students, 5/1 priority date for international students; for spring admission, 12/1 priority date for domestic students, 9/15 priority date

for international students. Applications are processed on a rolling basis. *Application fee:* $75 ($100 for international students). Electronic applications accepted. *Application Contact:* Valerie Romeo-Messana, Director of Admissions, 914-594-4110, Fax: 914-594-4944, E-mail: v_romeomessana@nymc.edu. *Dean,* Dr. Marina K Holz, 914-594-4110, Fax: 914-594-4944, E-mail: mholz@nymc.edu.

School of Health Sciences and Practice Students: 245 full-time (181 women), 233 part-time (167 women); includes 208 minority (79 Black or African American, non-Hispanic/Latino; 2 American Indian or Alaska Native, non-Hispanic/Latino; 59 Asian, non-Hispanic/Latino; 57 Hispanic/Latino; 1 Native Hawaiian or other Pacific Islander, non-Hispanic/Latino; 10 Two or more races, non-Hispanic/Latino), 13 international. Average age 27. 484 applicants, 68% accepted, 88 enrolled. *Faculty:* 47 full-time (34 women), 239 part-time/adjunct (141 women). Expenses: Contact institution. *Financial support:* In 2018–19, 4 students received support. Federal Work-Study, scholarships/grants, unspecified assistantships, and Federal student loans available. Financial award application deadline: 4/30; financial award applicants required to submit FAFSA. In 2018, 113 master's, 47 doctorates awarded. *Program availability:* Part-time, evening/weekend, 100% online, blended/hybrid learning. Offers behavioral sciences and health promotion (MPH); biostatistics (MS); children with special health care (Graduate Certificate); emergency preparedness (Graduate Certificate); environmental health science (MPH); epidemiology (MPH, MS); global health (Graduate Certificate); health education (Graduate Certificate); health policy and management (MPH, Dr PH); industrial hygiene (Graduate Certificate); pediatric dysphagia (Post-Graduate Certificate); physical therapy (DPT); public health (Graduate Certificate); speech-language pathology (MS). *Application deadline:* For fall admission, 8/1 for domestic students, 4/15 for international students; for spring admission, 12/1 for domestic students; for summer admission, 5/1 for domestic students, 4/15 for international students. Applications are processed on a rolling basis. *Application fee:* $128 ($120 for international students). Electronic applications accepted. *Application Contact:* Irene Bundziak, Assistant to Director of Admissions, 914-594-4905, E-mail: irene_bundziak@nymc.edu. *Vice Dean,* Ben Johnson, PhD, 914-594-4531, E-mail: bjohnson23@nymc.edu.

School of Medicine Students: 849 full-time (460 women); includes 384 minority (69 Black or African American, non-Hispanic/Latino; 1 American Indian or Alaska Native, non-Hispanic/Latino; 219 Asian, non-Hispanic/Latino; 73 Hispanic/Latino; 22 Two or more races, non-Hispanic/Latino), 7 international. Average age 26. 11,789 applicants, 5% accepted, 210 enrolled. *Faculty:* 1,056 full-time (425 women), 1,248 part-time/adjunct (434 women). Expenses: Contact institution. *Financial support:* In 2018–19, 396 students received support. Federal Work-Study, institutionally sponsored loans, scholarships/grants, unspecified assistantships, and Federal Student Loans available. Financial award application deadline: 4/30; financial award applicants required to submit FAFSA. In 2018, 200 doctorates awarded. Offers medicine (MD). *Application deadline:* For fall admission, 1/31 for domestic and international students. Applications are processed on a rolling basis. *Application fee:* $130. Electronic applications accepted. *Application Contact:* Robin Baum, Assistant Dean of Admissions, 914-594-4882, Fax: 914-594-4613, E-mail: mdadmit@nymc.edu. *Senior Associate Dean for Medical Education,* Jennifer Koestler, MD, 914-594-4500, E-mail: jennifer_koestler@nymc.edu.

NEW YORK SCHOOL OF INTERIOR DESIGN, New York, NY 10021-5110

General Information Independent, coed, primarily women, comprehensive institution. *Graduate housing:* Room and/or apartments available on a first-come, first-served basis to single students; on-campus housing not available to married students. Housing application deadline: 5/1. *Research affiliation:* Metropolitan New York Library Council-Research Consortium.

GRADUATE UNITS

Program in Healthcare Interior Design Offers healthcare interior design (MPS). Electronic applications accepted.

Program in Interior Design (Post-Professional Level) Offers interior design (MFA). Electronic applications accepted.

Program in Interior Design (Professional-Level) Offers interior design (MFA). Electronic applications accepted.

Program in Interior Lighting Design Offers interior lighting design (MPS). Electronic applications accepted.

Program in Sustainable Interior Environments Offers sustainable interior environments (MPS). Electronic applications accepted.

NEW YORK STUDIO SCHOOL OF DRAWING, PAINTING AND SCULPTURE, New York, NY 10011

General Information Independent, coed, comprehensive institution.

GRADUATE UNITS

Certificate Program Offers studio art (Certificate).

MFA Program Offers painting (MFA); sculpture (MFA).

NEW YORK THEOLOGICAL SEMINARY, New York, NY 10115

General Information Independent-religious, coed, graduate-only institution. *Graduate housing:* On-campus housing not available. *Research affiliation:* Bellevue Hospital Center, Goldwater Memorial Hospital, Institutes of Religion and Health, Lutheran Medical Center, Postgraduate Center for Mental Health.

GRADUATE UNITS

Graduate and Professional Programs *Program availability:* Part-time. Offers theology (M Div, MPS, MSW, D Min). MSW offered jointly with Fordham University.

NEW YORK UNIVERSITY, New York, NY 10012-1019

General Information Independent, coed, university. CGS member. *Graduate housing:* Room and/or apartments available on a first-come, first-served basis to single students; on-campus housing not available to married students. Housing application deadline: 5/1. *Research affiliation:* Center for the Study of Complex Malaria in India, National Institutes of Health (biology), Training in Systems and Integrative Neuroscience, National Institutes of Health (neural science), Research Network on Opening Governance, MacArthur Foundation (technology management and innovation), Data Science Environments Program, Gordon and Betty Moore Foundation (data science).

GRADUATE UNITS

College of Dentistry Offers biomaterials science (MS); clinical research (MS); dentistry (MS, DDS, Advanced Certificate); endodontics (Advanced Certificate); oral and maxillofacial surgery (Advanced Certificate); orthodontics (Advanced Certificate); pediatric dentistry (Advanced Certificate); periodontics (Advanced Certificate); prosthodontics (Advanced Certificate). Electronic applications accepted.

College of Global Public Health *Program availability:* Part-time, online learning. Offers biological basis of public health (PhD); community and international health (MPH); global health leadership (MPH); health systems and health services research (PhD); population and community health (PhD); public health nutrition (MPH); social and behavioral sciences (MPH); socio-behavioral health (PhD). Electronic applications accepted.

Gallatin School of Individualized Study Students: 75 full-time (54 women), 72 part-time (49 women); includes 46 minority (19 Black or African American, non-Hispanic/Latino; 8 Asian, non-Hispanic/Latino; 13 Hispanic/Latino; 1 Native Hawaiian or other Pacific Islander, non-Hispanic/Latino; 5 Two or more races, non-Hispanic/Latino), 28 international. Average age 32. 184 applicants, 65% accepted, 58 enrolled. *Faculty:* 52 full-time (30 women), 49 part-time/adjunct (28 women). Expenses: Contact institution. *Financial support:* In 2018–19, 52 students received support, including 5 fellowships (averaging $5,000 per year); research assistantships, Federal Work-Study, institutionally sponsored loans, scholarships/grants, health care benefits, tuition waivers (full and partial), and unspecified assistantships also available. Support available to part-time students. Financial award application deadline: 1/15; financial award applicants required to submit FAFSA. In 2018, 49 master's awarded. *Program availability:* Part-time, evening/weekend. Offers individualized study (MA). *Application deadline:* For fall admission, 1/15 priority date for domestic and international students; for spring admission, 10/1 for domestic and international students. Applications are processed on a rolling basis. *Application fee:* $50. Electronic applications accepted. *Application Contact:* Frances R. Levin, Director of Enrollment, 212-998-7349, E-mail: gallatin.gradadmissions@nyu.edu. *Dean,* Dr. Susanne L. Wofford, 212-998-7370.

Graduate School of Arts and Science Students: 3,555 full-time (1,847 women), 869 part-time (476 women); includes 769 minority (126 Black or African American, non-Hispanic/Latino; 5 American Indian or Alaska Native, non-Hispanic/Latino; 260 Asian, non-Hispanic/Latino; 280 Hispanic/Latino; 98 Two or more races, non-Hispanic/Latino), 1,998 international. Average age 27. 15,197 applicants, 27% accepted, 1390 enrolled. *Faculty:* 597 full-time (159 women). Expenses: Contact institution. *Financial support:* Fellowships with tuition reimbursements, research assistantships with tuition reimbursements, teaching assistantships with tuition reimbursements, career-related internships or fieldwork, Federal Work-Study, institutionally sponsored loans, scholarships/grants, health care benefits, tuition waivers (partial), unspecified assistantships, and instructorships available. Financial award applicants required to submit FAFSA. In 2018, 1,128 master's, 222 doctorates, 18 other advanced degrees awarded. *Program availability:* Part-time, evening/weekend. Offers African diaspora (PhD); African history (PhD); Africana studies (MA); American studies (MA, PhD); anthropology (MA, PhD); anthropology and French studies (PhD); applied economic analysis (Advanced Certificate); archival management (Advanced Certificate); arts and science (MA, MFA, MS, PhD, Advanced Certificate); Atlantic history (PhD); biology (PhD); biomedical journalism (MS); cancer and molecular biology (PhD); chemistry (MS, PhD); classics (MA, PhD); cognition and perception (PhD); comparative literature (MA, PhD); composition and theory (MA, PhD); computational biology (PhD); computers in biological research (MS); creative writing (MA, MFA); data science (MS); developmental genetics (PhD); early music performance (Advanced Certificate); East Asian studies (MA, PhD); economics (MA, PhD); English and American literature (MA, PhD); environmental medicine (MS, PhD); ethnomusicology (MA, PhD); French studies/history (PhD); general biology (MS); general psychology (MA); German studies and critical thought (MA, PhD); Hebrew and Judaic studies (MA, PhD); Hebrew and Judaic studies/history (PhD); Hebrew and Judaic studies/museum studies (MA); historical and sustainable architecture (MA); history (MA, PhD); humanities and social thought (MA); immunology and microbiology (PhD); industrial/organizational psychology (MA); Irish and Irish American studies (MA); Italian studies (MA, PhD); linguistics (MA, PhD); Middle Eastern history (MA); Middle Eastern studies/history (PhD); molecular genetics (PhD); museum studies (Advanced Certificate); neurobiology (PhD); oral biology (MS); philosophy (MA, PhD); physics (MS, PhD); plant biology (PhD); poetics and theory (Advanced Certificate); political campaign management (MA); politics (MA, PhD); Portuguese (MA, PhD); psychotherapy and psychoanalysis (Advanced Certificate); public history (Advanced Certificate); recombinant DNA technology (MS); religion (Advanced Certificate); religious studies (MA); Slavic literature (MA); social psychology (PhD); social theory (Advanced Certificate); sociology (MA, PhD); Spanish (PhD); Spanish and Latin American literatures and cultures (MA); Spanish language and translation (MA); world history (MA). *Application fee:* $110. Electronic applications accepted. *Application Contact:* Roberta Popik, Associate Dean for Graduate Enrollment Services, 212-998-8050, Fax: 212-995-4557, E-mail: gsas.admissions@nyu.edu. *Dean,* Dr. Phillip Brian Harper, 212-998-8040.

Arthur L. Carter Journalism Institute Students: 166 full-time (122 women), 32 part-time (22 women); includes 45 minority (14 Black or African American, non-Hispanic/Latino; 1 American Indian or Alaska Native, non-Hispanic/Latino; 5 Asian, non-Hispanic/Latino; 18 Hispanic/Latino; 7 Two or more races, non-Hispanic/Latino), 61 international. Average age 26. 350 applicants, 56% accepted, 100 enrolled. Expenses: Contact institution. *Financial support:* Fellowships, teaching assistantships, Federal Work-Study, institutionally sponsored loans, scholarships/grants, and tuition waivers (partial) available. Financial award application deadline: 1/4; financial award applicants required to submit FAFSA. In 2018, 111 master's, 25 other advanced degrees awarded. *Program availability:* Part-time. Offers biomedical journalism (MS); cultural reporting and criticism (MA); French studies/journalism (MA); journalism (MA); Latin American and Caribbean studies/journalism (MA); Near Eastern studies/journalism (MA); science and environmental reporting (Advanced Certificate). *Application deadline:* For fall admission, 1/4 priority date for domestic students, 1/4 for international students. *Application fee:* $110. *Application Contact:* Charles Seife, Director of Graduate Studies, 212-998-7980, Fax: 212-995-4148, E-mail: graduate.journalism@nyu.edu. *Chair,* Perri Klass, 212-998-7980, Fax: 212-995-4148, E-mail: graduate.journalism@nyu.edu.

Center for European Studies Students: 14 full-time (9 women), 1 (woman) part-time; includes 1 minority (Hispanic/Latino), 2 international. Average age 27. 33 applicants, 100% accepted, 10 enrolled. *Faculty:* 4 full-time (0 women). Expenses: Contact institution. *Financial support:* Fellowships with tuition reimbursements, teaching assistantships, career-related internships or fieldwork, Federal Work-Study, institutionally sponsored loans, and scholarships/grants available. Financial award application deadline: 2/1; financial award applicants required to submit FAFSA. In 2018, 9 master's awarded. Offers European studies (MA). *Application deadline:* For fall admission, 2/1 priority date for domestic students, 2/1 for international students. *Application fee:* $110. Electronic applications accepted. *Application Contact:* Mikhala Stein, Administrator, 212-998-3838, Fax: 212-995-4188, E-mail: european.studies@nyu.edu. *Director,* Larry Wolff, 212-998-3838, Fax: 212-995-4188, E-mail: european.studies@nyu.edu.

Center for French Civilization and Culture Students: 70 full-time (50 women), 1 part-time (0 women); includes 9 minority (3 Black or African American, non-Hispanic/Latino; 2 Asian, non-Hispanic/Latino; 4 Hispanic/Latino), 14 international. Average age 27. 103 applicants, 52% accepted, 30 enrolled. Expenses: Contact institution. *Financial support:* Fellowships, research assistantships, teaching assistantships, Federal Work-Study, institutionally sponsored loans, scholarships/grants, traineeships, unspecified assistantships, and instructorships available. Financial award application deadline: 1/4; financial award applicants required to submit FAFSA. In 2018, 17 master's, 8 doctorates awarded. *Program availability:* Part-time, evening/weekend. Offers French (PhD); French civilization (PhD); French civilization and culture (MA, PhD, Advanced Certificate); French language and civilization (MA); French studies (MA, PhD, Advanced Certificate); French studies and anthropology (PhD); French studies and history (PhD); French studies and journalism (MA); French studies and sociology (PhD); Romance languages and literatures (MA). *Application deadline:* For fall admission, 1/4 for domestic and international students. *Application fee:* $110. *Application Contact:* Erin Brau, Graduate Department Administrator, 212-998-8700, Fax: 212-995-4187, E-mail: french.grad@nyu.edu. *Director of Graduate Studies,* Lucien Nouis, 212-998-8700, Fax: 212-995-4187, E-mail: french.grad@nyu.edu.

Center for Latin American and Caribbean Studies Students: 16 full-time (13 women), 6 part-time (4 women); includes 12 minority (1 Black or African American, non-Hispanic/Latino; 10 Hispanic/Latino; 1 Two or more races, non-Hispanic/Latino), 2 international. Average age 27. 21 applicants, 100% accepted, 10 enrolled. Expenses: Contact institution. *Financial support:* Fellowships with tuition reimbursements, teaching assistantships with tuition reimbursements, Federal Work-Study, institutionally sponsored loans, scholarships/grants, health care benefits, and unspecified assistantships available. Financial award application deadline: 2/1; financial award applicants required to submit FAFSA. In 2018, 14 master's awarded. *Program availability:* Part-time. Offers Latin American and Caribbean studies (MA). *Application deadline:* For fall admission, 2/1 priority date for domestic students, 2/1 for international students. *Application fee:* $110. *Application Contact:* Amalia Cordova, Program Administrator, 212-998-8686, Fax: 212-995-4163, E-mail: clacs.info@nyu.edu. *Director,* Jill Lane, 212-998-8686, Fax: 212-995-4163, E-mail: clacs.info@nyu.edu.

Center for Neural Science Students: 62 full-time (26 women), 1 (woman) part-time; includes 16 minority (5 Asian, non-Hispanic/Latino; 8 Hispanic/Latino; 3 Two or more races, non-Hispanic/Latino), 23 international. Average age 27. 479 applicants, 4% accepted, 7 enrolled. *Faculty:* 15 full-time (3 women). Expenses: Contact institution. *Financial support:* Fellowships with tuition reimbursements, research assistantships with tuition reimbursements, career-related internships or fieldwork, Federal Work-Study, institutionally sponsored loans, scholarships/grants, health care benefits, and unspecified assistantships available. Financial award application deadline: 12/1; financial award applicants required to submit FAFSA. In 2018, 10 doctorates awarded. Offers neural science (PhD). *Application deadline:* For fall admission, 12/1 for domestic and international students. *Application fee:* $110. *Application Contact:* Michael Hawken, Director of Graduate Studies, 212-998-7780, Fax: 212-995-4011, E-mail: admissions@cns.nyu.edu. *Chair,* J. Anthony Movshon, 212-998-7780, Fax: 212-995-4011, E-mail: admissions@cns.nyu.edu.

Courant Institute of Mathematical Sciences Students: 678 full-time (216 women), 134 part-time (30 women); includes 94 minority (4 Black or African American, non-Hispanic/Latino; 1 American Indian or Alaska Native, non-Hispanic/Latino; 66 Asian, non-Hispanic/Latino; 15 Hispanic/Latino; 8 Two or more races, non-Hispanic/Latino), 584 international. Average age 25. 3,703 applicants, 26% accepted, 305 enrolled. Expenses: Contact institution. *Financial support:* Fellowships, research assistantships, teaching assistantships, career-related internships or fieldwork, Federal Work-Study, institutionally sponsored loans, scholarships/grants, health care benefits, tuition waivers (full and partial), and unspecified assistantships available. Financial award application deadline: 12/18; financial award applicants required to submit FAFSA. In 2018, 284 master's, 19 doctorates awarded. *Program availability:* Part-time, evening/weekend. Offers computer science (MS, PhD); information systems (MS); mathematics (MS, PhD); mathematics and statistics/operations research (MS); mathematics in finance (MS); scientific computing (MS). *Application deadline:* For fall admission, 12/18 for domestic and international students. *Application fee:* $110. *Application Contact:* Tamar Arnon, Graduate Administrator, 212-998-3238, Fax: 212-995-4121, E-mail: admissions@math.nyu.edu. *Director of Graduate Studies,* Fedor Bogomolov, 212-998-3238, Fax: 212-995-4121, E-mail: admissions@math.nyu.edu.

Hagop Kevorkian Center for Near Eastern Studies Students: 62 full-time (33 women), 12 part-time (8 women); includes 4 minority (1 Black or African American, non-Hispanic/Latino; 2 Asian, non-Hispanic/Latino; 1 Hispanic/Latino), 19 international. Average age 28. 173 applicants, 29% accepted, 19 enrolled. Expenses: Contact institution. *Financial support:* Fellowships, teaching assistantships, Federal Work-Study, and institutionally sponsored loans available. Financial award application deadline: 12/18; financial award applicants required to submit FAFSA. In 2018, 16 master's, 5 doctorates awarded. *Program availability:* Part-time, evening/weekend. Offers Middle Eastern and Islamic studies (MA, PhD); Middle Eastern and Islamic studies/history (PhD); Near Eastern studies (MA, PhD); Near Eastern studies/museum studies (MA). *Application deadline:* For fall admission, 12/18 for domestic and international students. *Application fee:* $110. *Application Contact:* Everett Rowson, Acting Director of Graduate Studies, 212-998-8880, E-mail: kevorkian.center@nyu.edu. *Chair,* Zvi Ben-Dor Benite, 212-998-8880, Fax: 212-995-4689, E-mail: kevorkian.center@nyu.edu.

Institute for Law and Society Expenses: Contact institution. *Financial support:* Fellowships, teaching assistantships, career-related internships or fieldwork, Federal Work-Study, institutionally sponsored loans, scholarships/grants, health care benefits, and unspecified assistantships available. Financial award applicants required to submit FAFSA. In 2018, 1 doctorate awarded. Offers law and society (MA, PhD). *Application Contact:* Carly Vignogna, Graduate Administrator, 212-998-8040, Fax: 212-995-4557, E-mail: gsas.admissions@nyu.edu. *Director of Graduate Studies,* Jo Dixon, 212-998-8040, Fax: 212-995-4557, E-mail: gsas.admissions@nyu.edu.

Institute for the Study of the Ancient World Students: 24 full-time (15 women), 1 (woman) part-time; includes 2 minority (1 Asian, non-Hispanic/Latino; 1 Two or more races, non-Hispanic/Latino), 15 international. Average age 29. 36 applicants, 19% accepted, 5 enrolled. Expenses: Contact institution. *Financial support:* Fellowships and stipends available. Financial award application deadline: 1/4; financial award applicants required to submit FAFSA. In 2018, 4 doctorates awarded. Offers study of the ancient world (PhD). *Application deadline:* For fall admission, 1/4 for domestic and international students. *Application fee:* $110. Electronic applications accepted. *Application Contact:* Marc Leblanc, Graduate Department Administrator, 212-992-7843, Fax: 212-992-7809, E-mail: isaw@nyu.edu. *Director,* Dr. Roger Bagnall, 212-992-7843, Fax: 212-992-7809, E-mail: isaw@nyu.edu.

Institute of Fine Arts Students: 184 full-time (151 women), 4 part-time (all women); includes 27 minority (1 Black or African American, non-Hispanic/Latino; 9 Asian, non-Hispanic/Latino; 10 Hispanic/Latino; 7 Two or more races, non-Hispanic/Latino), 50 international. Average age 29. 355 applicants, 42% accepted, 53 enrolled. Expenses: Contact institution. *Financial support:* Fellowships, research assistantships, teaching assistantships, career-related internships or fieldwork, Federal Work-Study, institutionally sponsored loans, and tuition waivers (partial) available. Financial award application deadline: 12/18; financial award applicants required to submit FAFSA. In 2018, 53 master's, 9 doctorates awarded. *Program availability:* Part-time. Offers architectural studies (PhD); art history and archaeology (MA, PhD); classical art and archaeology (PhD); curatorial studies (PhD); East and South Asian art (PhD); Near Eastern art and archaeology (PhD). *Application deadline:* For fall admission, 12/18 for domestic and international students. *Application fee:* $110. *Application Contact:* Alexander Nagel, Director of Graduate Studies, 212-992-5800, Fax: 212-992-5807, E-mail: ifa.program@nyu.edu. *Chair,* Patricia Rubin, 212-992-5800, Fax: 212-992-5807, E-mail: ifa.program@nyu.edu.

Leonard N. Stern School of Business *Program availability:* Part-time, evening/weekend. Offers accounting (MBA, PhD); business (MBA, PhD); economics (MBA, PhD); entertainment, media and technology (MBA); finance (MBA, PhD); general marketing (MBA); information systems (MBA, PhD); management organizations (MBA); marketing (PhD); operations management (MBA, PhD); organization theory (PhD); organizational behavior (PhD); product management (MBA); statistics (MBA, PhD); strategy (PhD). Electronic applications accepted.

Rory Meyers College of Nursing *Program availability:* Part-time, evening/weekend. Offers adult-gerontology acute care nurse practitioner (MS, Advanced Certificate); adult-gerontology primary care nurse practitioner (MS, Advanced Certificate); family nurse practitioner (MS, Advanced Certificate); gerontology nurse practitioner (Advanced Certificate); nurse-midwifery (MS, Advanced Certificate); nursing (MS, DNP, PhD, Advanced Certificate); nursing administration (MS, Advanced Certificate); nursing education (MS, Advanced Certificate); nursing informatics (MS, Advanced Certificate); nursing research and theory development (PhD); pediatrics nurse practitioner (MS, Advanced Certificate); psychiatric-mental health nurse practitioner (MS, Advanced Certificate). Electronic applications accepted.

School of Law *Program availability:* Part-time, blended/hybrid learning. Offers law (LL M, JD, JSD); law and business (Advanced Certificate); taxation (MSL, Advanced Certificate). Electronic applications accepted.

School of Medicine Offers medicine (MS, MD, PhD). Electronic applications accepted.

Sackler Institute of Graduate Biomedical Sciences Students: 275 full-time (167 women), 2 part-time (1 woman); includes 111 minority (15 Black or African American, non-Hispanic/Latino; 1 American Indian or Alaska Native, non-Hispanic/Latino; 65 Asian, non-Hispanic/Latino; 30 Hispanic/Latino), 85 international. Average age 27. 847 applicants, 15% accepted, 49 enrolled. *Faculty:* 267 full-time (71 women). Expenses: Contact institution. *Financial support:* Institutionally sponsored loans, health care benefits, tuition waivers (full), and unspecified assistantships available. In 2018, 56 doctorates awarded. Offers biomedical sciences (PhD). *Application deadline:* For fall admission, 12/2 for domestic and international students. Applications are processed on a rolling basis. *Application fee:* $100. Electronic applications accepted. *Application Contact:* Jessica Dong, Program Manager, 212-263-5648, E-mail: sackler-info@nyulangone.org. *Associate Dean for Biomedical Sciences/Director, Sackler Institute,* Dr. Naoko Tanese, 212-263-8945, E-mail: naoko.tanese@nyulangone.org.

Center for Applied Liberal Arts *Program availability:* Part-time, evening/weekend. Offers applied liberal arts (MS); professional writing (MS); translation (MS). Electronic applications accepted.

Center for Global Affairs *Program availability:* Part-time, evening/weekend. Offers global affairs (MS). Electronic applications accepted.

Center for Publishing *Program availability:* Part-time, evening/weekend. Offers publishing: digital and print media (MS). Electronic applications accepted.

Division of Programs in Business *Program availability:* Part-time, evening/weekend, 100% online, blended/hybrid learning. Offers human resource management and development (MS); integrated marketing (MS); leadership and human capital management (MS); management and systems (MS); marketing and public relations (MS); project management (MS); public relations and corporate communication (MS). Electronic applications accepted.

Jonathan M. Tisch Center of Hospitality *Program availability:* Part-time, evening/weekend. Offers hospitality industry studies (MS); tourism management (MS). Electronic applications accepted.

Preston Robert Tisch Institute for Global Sport *Program availability:* Part-time, evening/weekend. Offers sports business (MS). Electronic applications accepted.

Schack Institute of Real Estate *Program availability:* Part-time, evening/weekend. Offers construction management (MS); real estate (MS); real estate development (MS). Electronic applications accepted.

Silver School of Social Work Students: 780 full-time (682 women), 324 part-time (283 women); includes 415 minority (117 Black or African American, non-Hispanic/Latino; 1 American Indian or Alaska Native, non-Hispanic/Latino; 44 Asian, non-Hispanic/Latino; 195 Hispanic/Latino; 58 Two or more races, non-Hispanic/Latino), 76 international. Average age 29. 1,550 applicants, 82% accepted, 554 enrolled. *Faculty:* 34 full-time (26 women), 133 part-time/adjunct (99 women). Expenses: Contact institution. *Financial support:* In 2018–19, 1,004 students received support, including 6 fellowships (averaging $22,000 per year), 3 teaching assistantships with full and partial tuition reimbursements available (averaging $28,145 per year); career-related internships or fieldwork, Federal Work-Study, scholarships/grants, health care benefits, tuition waivers (full and partial), and unspecified assistantships also available. Support available to part-time students. Financial award application deadline: 2/15; financial award applicants required to submit FAFSA. In 2018, 557 master's, 28 doctorates awarded. *Program availability:* Part-time, evening/weekend. Offers social work (MSW, PhD). Sarah Lawrence College offers the MA in Child Development. All other dual degrees are offered within graduate professional schools at New York University. *Application deadline:* For fall admission, 1/10 priority date for domestic and international students; for spring admission, 10/4 priority date for domestic and international students; for summer admission, 3/20 priority date for domestic students. Applications are processed on a rolling basis. *Application fee:* $60. Electronic applications accepted. *Application Contact:* Robert W. Sommo, Jr., Assistant Dean for Enrollment Services, 212-998-5910, Fax: 212-995-4171, E-mail: silver.admissions@nyu.edu. *Dean and Paulette Goddard Professor of Social Work,* Dr. Neil B. Guterman, 212-998-5959, Fax: 212-995-4172.

Steinhardt School of Culture, Education, and Human Development *Program availability:* Part-time. Offers advanced occupational therapy (MA); applied statistics for social science research (MS); art education (MA); art therapy (MA); art, education, and community practice (MA); bilingual education (MA, PhD, Advanced Certificate); business and workplace education (MA, Advanced Certificate); business education (MA, Advanced Certificate); childhood (MA); childhood education (MA); clinical nutrition (MS); clinically rich integrated science (MA); clinically-based English education, grades 7-12 (MA); communication sciences and disorders (MS, PhD); costume studies (MA); counseling (MA, PhD, Advanced Certificate); counseling and guidance (MA, Advanced Certificate); counseling for mental health and wellness (MA); counseling psychology (PhD); culture, education, and human development (MA, MFA, MM, MPH, MS, DPS, DPT, Ed D, PhD, Advanced Certificate, Post Master's Certificate, Postbaccalaureate Certificate); dance education (MA, Advanced Certificate); developmental psychology (PhD); digital media design for learning (MA, Advanced Certificate); drama therapy (MA); early childhood (MA); early childhood and childhood education (MA); early childhood education (MA); early childhood education/early childhood special education (MA); education and Jewish studies (MA, PhD); education policy (MA); educational and developmental psychology (MA, PhD); educational communication and technology (MA, MS, PhD, Advanced Certificate); educational leadership (MA, Ed D, PhD, Advanced Certificate); educational leadership, politics and advocacy (MA); educational theatre (MA, Ed D, MA); educational theatre and English 7-12 (MA); educational theatre and social studies 7-12 (MA); educational theatre in colleges and communities (MA, Ed D, PhD); educational theatre, all grades (MA); English education (MA, PhD, Advanced Certificate); English education, grades 7-12 (MA); environmental conservation education (MA); food studies (MA, PhD); foreign language education (MA); games for learning (MS); higher and postsecondary education (PhD); higher education (MA, Ed D, PhD); higher education administration (Ed D); higher education and student affairs (MA); history of education (MA, PhD); human development and social intervention (MA); instrumental performance (MM); international education (MA, PhD, Advanced Certificate); LGBT health, education, and social services (Advanced Certificate); literacy education (MA); mathematics education (MA); media, culture and communication (MA, PhD); multilingual/multicultural studies (MA, PhD, Advanced Certificate); music business (MA); music education (MA); music performance and composition (MM, PhD, Advanced Certificate); music technology (MA, MM, PhD); music theatre (MM); music theory and composition (MM); music therapy (MA); nutrition and dietetics (MS, PhD); occupational therapy (MS, DPS); orthopedic physical therapy (Advanced Certificate); performing arts administration (MA); physical therapy (MA, DPT, PhD); piano performance (MM); psychology and social intervention (PhD); rehabilitation sciences (PhD); research in occupational therapy (Advanced Certificate); school building leader (MA); school district leader (Advanced Certificate); social and cultural studies of education (MA); social studies education (MA); sociology of education (MA, PhD); special education (MA); studio art (MA, MFA, Advanced Certificate); teachers of art, all grades (MA); teaching and learning (Ed D, PhD); teaching art/social studies 7-12 (MA); teaching dance in the professions (MA); teaching dance, all grades (MA, Advanced Certificate); teaching English to speakers of other languages (MA, PhD); teaching foreign languages, 7-12 (MA); teaching French as a foreign language (MA); teaching social studies 7-12 (MA); teaching Spanish as a foreign language (MA); visual arts administration (MA); visual culture (MA); vocal pedagogy (Advanced Certificate); vocal performance (MM); workplace learning (Advanced Certificate). Electronic applications accepted.

Tandon School of Engineering Students: 2,157 full-time (707 women), 523 part-time (148 women); includes 334 minority (41 Black or African American, non-Hispanic/Latino; 180 Asian, non-Hispanic/Latino; 90 Hispanic/Latino; 23 Two or more races, non-Hispanic/Latino), 1,987 international. Average age 25. 9,976 applicants, 38% accepted, 1241 enrolled. *Faculty:* 179 full-time (41 women), 232 part-time/adjunct (32 women). Expenses: Contact institution. *Financial support:* Application deadline: 2/15. In 2018, 1,316 master's, 40 doctorates, 6 other advanced degrees awarded. *Program availability:* Part-time, 100% online, blended/hybrid learning. Offers applied physics (MS, Advanced Certificate); bioinformatics (MS, Advanced Certificate); biomedical engineering (MS); biotechnology (MS, PhD); biotechnology and entrepreneurship (MS); chemical engineering (MS); chemistry (MS); civil engineering (MS, PhD); computer engineering (MS); computer science (MS, PhD); construction management (MS); cyber security (MS); cybersecurity risk and strategy (MS); electrical engineering (MS, PhD); environmental engineering (MS); environmental science (MS); financial engineering (MS); industrial engineering (MS); integrated digital media (MS); management (MS); management of technology (MS); manufacturing engineering (MS); materials chemistry (PhD); mathematics (MS); mechanical engineering (MS, PhD); mechatronics and robotics (MS); organizational behavior, systems and analytics (MS); software engineering (Graduate Certificate); technology management (PhD); transportation management (MS); transportation planning and engineering (MS, PhD); urban systems engineering and management (MS). *Application deadline:* For fall admission, 2/15 for domestic and international students; for spring admission, 11/1 for domestic and international students. Applications are processed on a rolling basis. *Application fee:* $75. Electronic applications accepted. *Application Contact:* Elizabeth Ensweiler, Senior Director of Graduate Enrollment and Graduate Admissions, 646-997-3182, E-mail: elizabeth.ensweiler@nyu.edu. *Dean of NYU Tandon School of Engineering,* Dr. Jelena Kovacevic, 646-997-3503, E-mail: jk184@nyu.edu.

Tisch School of the Arts Offers acting (MFA); arts (MA, MFA, MPS, PhD); arts politics (MA); cinema studies (MA, PhD); dance (MFA); design for stage and film (MFA); dramatic writing (MFA); interactive telecommunications (MPS); moving image archiving and preservation (MA); musical theatre writing (MFA); performance studies (MA, PhD). Electronic applications accepted.

Game Center Students: 68 full-time (37 women); includes 51 minority (2 Black or African American, non-Hispanic/Latino; 1 American Indian or Alaska Native, non-Hispanic/Latino; 45 Asian, non-Hispanic/Latino; 3 Hispanic/Latino). Average age 26. 226 applicants, 25% accepted, 33 enrolled. *Faculty:* 11 full-time (4 women), 33 part-time/adjunct (8 women). Expenses: Contact institution. *Financial support:* In 2018–19, 52 students received support, including 20 teaching assistantships (averaging $3,600 per year); career-related internships or fieldwork and scholarships/grants also available. Financial award application deadline: 1/1. In 2018, 33 master's awarded. Offers game design (MFA). *Application deadline:* For fall admission, 1/1 for domestic students. *Application fee:* $65. Electronic applications accepted. *Application Contact:* Jessica Lam, Department Administrator, 646-9970708, E-mail: gamecenter@nyu.edu. *Director,* Frank Lantz, 646-997-0746, E-mail: frank.lantz@nyu.edu.

Kanbar Institute of Film and Television Students: 115 full-time (55 women); includes 31 minority (12 Black or African American, non-Hispanic/Latino; 9 Asian, non-Hispanic/Latino; 6 Hispanic/Latino; 4 Two or more races, non-Hispanic/Latino), 52 international. 747 applicants, 7% accepted, 38 enrolled. *Faculty:* 19 full-time (9 women), 26 part-time/adjunct (14 women). Expenses: Contact institution. *Financial support:* Fellowships, teaching assistantships, Federal Work-Study, institutionally sponsored loans, scholarships/grants, health care benefits, tuition waivers (full and partial), and unspecified assistantships available. Financial award application deadline: 2/15; financial award applicants required to submit FAFSA. In 2018, 68 master's awarded. Offers film and television (MFA). *Application deadline:* For fall admission, 12/1 for domestic and international students. *Application fee:* $60.

Electronic applications accepted. *Application Contact:* Dan Sandford, Director of Graduate Admissions, 212-998-1918, Fax: 212-995-4060, E-mail: tisch.gradadmissions@nyu.edu. *Chair,* John Tintori, 212-998-1780, E-mail: jt42@nyu.edu.

Wagner Graduate School of Public Service *Program availability:* Part-time. Offers global public policy and management (EMPA); health finance (MPA); health policy analysis (MPA); health services management (MPA); international health (MPA); public administration (PhD); public and nonprofit management and policy (MPA, Advanced Certificate); public service (EMPA, MPA, MUP, PhD, Advanced Certificate); urban planning (MUP). Electronic applications accepted.

NIAGARA UNIVERSITY, Niagara University, NY 14109

General Information Independent-religious, coed, comprehensive institution. *Enrollment:* 509 full-time matriculated graduate/professional students (319 women), 404 part-time matriculated graduate/professional students (286 women). *Enrollment by degree level:* 774 master's, 59 doctoral, 80 other advanced degrees. Tuition and fees vary according to program. *Graduate housing:* Room and/or apartments available to single students; on-campus housing not available to married students. Typical cost: $11,700 (including board). Room and board charges vary according to housing facility selected. Housing application deadline: 8/1. *Student services:* Campus employment opportunities, campus safety program, career counseling, exercise/wellness program, free psychological counseling, international student services, multicultural affairs office, services for students with disabilities, teacher training, writing training. *Library facilities:* Our Lady of Angels Library. *Collection:* Books: 122,720 (physical), 348,406 (digital/electronic); Serial titles: 32,000 (digital/electronic); Databases: 111. Weekly public service hours: 107; study areas open 24 hours, 5–7 days a week; students can reserve study rooms.

Computer facilities: 81 computers available on campus for general student use. A campuswide network can be accessed from student residence rooms. Online class registration is available.
Website: http://www.niagara.edu/

General Application Contact: Evan Pierce, Associate Director of Graduate Studies, 716-286-8327, Fax: 716-286-8710, E-mail: epierce@niagara.edu.

GRADUATE UNITS

Graduate Division of Arts and Sciences Students: 34 full-time (18 women), 22 part-time (9 women); includes 10 minority (3 Black or African American, non-Hispanic/Latino; 2 American Indian or Alaska Native, non-Hispanic/Latino; 2 Asian, non-Hispanic/Latino; 2 Hispanic/Latino; 1 Two or more races, non-Hispanic/Latino), 9 international. Average age 29. Expenses: Contact institution. *Financial support:* Research assistantships with tuition reimbursements, teaching assistantships with tuition reimbursements, career-related internships or fieldwork, Federal Work-Study, scholarships/grants, and unspecified assistantships available. Support available to part-time students. Financial award application deadline: 4/15; financial award applicants required to submit FAFSA. In 2018, 22 master's awarded. *Program availability:* Part-time. Offers criminal justice (MS); criminal justice administration (MS); information security and digital forensics (MS); interdisciplinary studies (MA). *Application deadline:* For fall admission, 8/1 for domestic students. Applications are processed on a rolling basis. Electronic applications accepted. *Application Contact:* Evan Pierce, Associate Director, Graduate Studies, 716-286-8327, Fax: 716-286-8710, E-mail: epierce@niagara.edu. *Dean,* Dr. Peter Butera, 716-286-8060, Fax: 716-286-8061, E-mail: pbutera@niagara.edu.

Graduate Division of Business Administration Students: 224 full-time (116 women), 56 part-time (22 women); includes 36 minority (9 Black or African American, non-Hispanic/Latino; 2 American Indian or Alaska Native, non-Hispanic/Latino; 6 Asian, non-Hispanic/Latino; 12 Hispanic/Latino; 7 Two or more races, non-Hispanic/Latino), 82 international. Average age 26. Expenses: Contact institution. *Financial support:* Research assistantships, teaching assistantships, career-related internships or fieldwork, Federal Work-Study, scholarships/grants, and unspecified assistantships available. Support available to part-time students. Financial award application deadline: 4/15; financial award applicants required to submit FAFSA. In 2018, 134 master's awarded. *Program availability:* Part-time, evening/weekend, 100% online, blended/hybrid learning. Offers accounting (MBA); business administration (MBA); finance (MBA, MS); financial planning (MBA); healthcare administration (MBA, MHA); human resources (MBA); international business (MBA); marketing (MBA); professional accountancy (MBA); strategic management (MBA); supply chain management (MBA). *Application deadline:* For fall admission, 8/1 for domestic students; for spring admission, 11/1 for domestic students. Applications are processed on a rolling basis. Electronic applications accepted. *Application Contact:* Evan Pierce, Associate Director for Graduate Recruitment, 716-286-8327, Fax: 716-286-8710, E-mail: epierce@niagara.edu. *MBA Director/Chair of the Marketing Department,* Dr. Paul Richardson, 716-286-8169, Fax: 716-286-8206, E-mail: mba@niagara.edu.

Graduate Division of Education Students: 241 full-time (181 women), 319 part-time (250 women); includes 73 minority (36 Black or African American, non-Hispanic/Latino; 3 American Indian or Alaska Native, non-Hispanic/Latino; 6 Asian, non-Hispanic/Latino; 19 Hispanic/Latino; 9 Two or more races, non-Hispanic/Latino), 110 international. Average age 31. Expenses: Contact institution. *Financial support:* Research assistantships with tuition reimbursements, teaching assistantships with tuition reimbursements, career-related internships or fieldwork, Federal Work-Study, scholarships/grants, and unspecified assistantships available. Support available to part-time students. Financial award application deadline: 4/15; financial award applicants required to submit FAFSA. In 2018, 164 master's, 15 doctorates, 44 other advanced degrees awarded. *Program availability:* Part-time, evening/weekend, 100% online, blended/hybrid learning. Offers applied behavior analysis (Certificate); early childhood and childhood education (MS Ed, Certificate); early childhood special education (MS); educational leadership (MS Ed, PhD, Certificate); leadership and policy (PhD); literacy instruction (MS Ed); mental health counseling (MS, Certificate); middle and adolescence education (MS Ed); school building leader (MS Ed); school counseling (MS Ed, Certificate); school district business leader (Certificate); school district leader (MS Ed, Certificate); school psychology (MS); special education (MS Ed); special education (grades 1-12) (Certificate); teacher education (MS, MS Ed, Certificate); teaching English to speakers of other languages (MS Ed, Certificate). *Application deadline:* For fall admission, 8/1 for domestic students. Applications are processed on a rolling basis. Electronic applications accepted. *Application Contact:* Evan Pierce, Associate Director for Graduate Recruitment, 716-286-8327, Fax: 716-286-8710, E-mail: epierce@niagara.edu. *Dean, College of Education,* Dr. Chandra Foote, 716-286-8549, Fax: 716-286-8561, E-mail: cjf@niagara.edu.

NICHOLLS STATE UNIVERSITY, Thibodaux, LA 70310

General Information State-supported, coed, comprehensive institution. *Graduate housing:* Rooms and/or apartments available on a first-come, first-served basis to single and married students. Housing application deadline: 4/15.

GRADUATE UNITS

Graduate Studies *Program availability:* Part-time, evening/weekend, online learning.

College of Arts and Sciences *Program availability:* Part-time, evening/weekend. Offers arts and sciences (MS); marine and environmental biology (MS). Electronic applications accepted.

College of Business Administration *Program availability:* Part-time, evening/weekend. Offers business administration (MBA). Electronic applications accepted.

College of Education *Program availability:* Part-time, evening/weekend. Offers clinical mental health counseling (MA); curriculum and instruction (M Ed); education (M Ed, MA, MAT, SSP); educational leadership (M Ed); elementary education (MAT); human performance education (MAT); middle school education (MAT); school counseling (M Ed); school psychology (SSP); secondary education (MAT). Electronic applications accepted.

College of Nursing and Allied Health Offers family nurse practitioner (MSN); nurse executive (MSN); nursing education (MSN); psychiatric/mental health nurse practitioner (MSN).

NICHOLS COLLEGE, Dudley, MA 01571-5000

General Information Independent, coed, comprehensive institution. *Graduate housing:* On-campus housing not available.

GRADUATE UNITS

Graduate and Professional Studies *Program availability:* Part-time, evening/weekend, online learning. Offers business administration (MBA); counterterrorism (MS); organizational leadership (MSOL). Electronic applications accepted.

NIPISSING UNIVERSITY, North Bay, ON P1B 8L7, Canada

General Information Province-supported, coed, comprehensive institution. *Graduate housing:* Room and/or apartments available to single students; on-campus housing not available to married students. Housing application deadline: 6/13. *Research affiliation:* Canada Space Agency (CSA) and MacDonald, Dettwiler and Associates Ltd. (MDA–RADARSAT-2) (remote sensing), Education Quality and Accountability Office (EQAO) (assessing educational quality), Ontario Association of Deans of Education (OADE) (assessing pre-service practicum processes), Tembec (forestry restoration), Metals in the Human Environment Research Network (MITHE-RN) (assessing environmental pollutants on aquatic ecosystems).

GRADUATE UNITS

Faculty of Education *Program availability:* Part-time, evening/weekend. Offers education (M Ed, Certificate).

NORFOLK STATE UNIVERSITY, Norfolk, VA 23504

General Information State-supported, coed, comprehensive institution. CGS member. *Graduate housing:* Room and/or apartments available to single students; on-campus housing not available to married students. Housing application deadline: 3/1. *Research affiliation:* U.S. Department of Energy/NASA (fundamental and applied research studies), NASA Langley Research Center (aerospace applications, lidar application), National Science Foundation (fundamental and applied research studies), U.S. Department of Education (DOE) (Title III projects, No Child Left Behind initiative), University of Virginia's Integrative Graduate Education and Research Traineeship (IGERT) (science and engineering interactions with matter), Applied Research Center (technology transfer).

GRADUATE UNITS

School of Graduate Studies *Program availability:* Part-time. Electronic applications accepted.

Ethelyn R. Strong School of Social Work *Program availability:* Part-time. Offers social work (MSW, PhD).

School of Education *Program availability:* Part-time. Offers early childhood education (MAT); education (MA, MAT); pre-elementary education (MA); principal preparation (MA); secondary education (MAT); severe disabilities (MA); teaching (MA); urban education/administration (MA).

School of Liberal Arts *Program availability:* Part-time. Offers community/clinical psychology (MA); criminal justice (MA); liberal arts (MA, MFA, MM, Psy D); media and communication (MA); music (MM); music education (MM); performance (MM); psychology (Psy D); theory and composition (MM); urban affairs (MA); visual studies (MA, MFA).

School of Science and Technology Offers computer science (MS); electronics engineering (MS); materials science (MS); optical engineering (MS); science and technology (MS).

NORTH AMERICAN UNIVERSITY, Stafford, TX 77477

General Information Independent, coed, comprehensive institution.

GRADUATE UNITS

Program in Educational Leadership Offers educational leadership (M Ed).

NORTH CAROLINA AGRICULTURAL AND TECHNICAL STATE UNIVERSITY, Greensboro, NC 27411

General Information State-supported, coed, university. CGS member. *Graduate housing:* Room and/or apartments available on a first-come, first-served basis to single students; on-campus housing not available to married students. Housing application deadline: 5/8. *Research affiliation:* North Carolina Biotechnology Research Center (biotechnology), Boeing (aerospace engineering), Northrop Grumman Corporation (high performance computing), Research Triangle Institute (environmental protection, advanced technology), Rockwell, Inc. (avionics technology, communications technology), Honeywell (industrial automation control).

GRADUATE UNITS

The Graduate College *Program availability:* Part-time, evening/weekend. Electronic applications accepted.

College of Agriculture and Environmental Sciences *Program availability:* Part-time, evening/weekend. Offers agribusiness and food industry management (MS); agricultural education (MS); agriculture and environmental sciences (MAT, MS); child development, early education and family studies (MAT); family and consumer sciences education (MAT); food and nutritional sciences (MS); integrated animal health systems (MS); plant, soil and environmental science (MS).

College of Arts, Humanities, and Social Sciences *Program availability:* Part-time, evening/weekend. Offers arts, humanities, and social sciences (MA, MAT); English and African-American literature (MA); English education (MAT).

College of Business and Economics Offers accounting (MBA); business education (MAT); human resources management (MBA); supply chain systems (MBA).

College of Education *Program availability:* Part-time, evening/weekend. Offers adult education (MS); education (MA Ed, MAT, MS, MSA, PhD); elementary education (MA Ed); instructional technology (MS); interdisciplinary leadership studies (PhD); mental health counseling (MS); reading education (MA Ed); rehabilitation counseling and rehabilitation counselor education (PhD); school administration (MSA); school counseling (MS).

College of Engineering *Program availability:* Part-time. Offers bioengineering (MS); biological engineering (MS); chemical engineering (MS); civil engineering (MSCE); computer science (MSCS, PhD); electrical engineering (MSEE, PhD); engineering (MS, MSCE, MSCS, MSE, MSEE, MSIE, MSME, PhD); industrial and systems engineering (PhD); industrial engineering (MSIE); mechanical engineering (MSME, PhD).

College of Health and Human Sciences Offers health and human sciences (MSW); social work (MSW).

College of Science and Technology *Program availability:* Part-time, evening/weekend. Offers applied mathematics (MS); biology (MS); biology education (MAT); chemistry (MAT, MS); computational sciences (MS); mathematics (MAT); physics (MS); science and technology (MAT, MS, MSIT, MSTM).

NORTH CAROLINA CENTRAL UNIVERSITY, Durham, NC 27707-3129

General Information State-supported, coed, comprehensive institution. CGS member. *Graduate housing:* Room and/or apartments available on a first-come, first-served basis to single students; on-campus housing not available to married students. Housing application deadline: 7/1.

GRADUATE UNITS

College of Arts and Sciences Offers arts and sciences (MA, MM, MS); biological and biomedical sciences (MS); chemistry (MS); earth sciences (MS); English (MA); environmental and geographic sciences (MS); history (MA); jazz studies (MM); mathematics (MS); physics (MS).

College of Behavioral and Social Sciences Offers behavioral and social sciences (MA, MPA, MS, MSW); clinical psychology (MA); criminal justice (MS); general physical education (MS); general psychology (MA); public administration (MPA); recreation administration (MS); social work (MSW).

School of Business *Program availability:* Part-time, evening/weekend. Offers business (MBA).

School of Education *Program availability:* Part-time, evening/weekend. Offers career counseling (MA); clinical mental health counseling (MA); communication disorders (MS); education (M Ed, MA, MAT, MS, MSA); educational technology (MA); emotional disabilities (M Ed, MAT); learning disabilities (M Ed, MAT); school administration (MSA); school counseling (MA); visual impairment (M Ed, MAT).

School of Law *Program availability:* Part-time, evening/weekend. Offers law (JD).

School of Library and Information Sciences *Program availability:* Part-time, evening/weekend. Offers library and information sciences (MIS, MLS).

NORTH CAROLINA STATE UNIVERSITY, Raleigh, NC 27695

General Information State-supported, coed, university. CGS member. *Graduate housing:* Rooms and/or apartments available on a first-come, first-served basis to single and married students. *Research affiliation:* Triangle Universities Nuclear Laboratory, Research Triangle Institute, Highlands Biological Station, National Humanities Center, Microelectronics Center of North Carolina, North Carolina-Japan Center.

GRADUATE UNITS

College of Veterinary Medicine *Program availability:* Part-time. Offers cell biology (MS, PhD); infectious disease (MS, PhD); pathology (MS, PhD); pharmacology (MS, PhD); population medicine (MS, PhD); veterinary medicine (MS, PhD). Electronic applications accepted.

Graduate School *Program availability:* Part-time, evening/weekend, online learning. Electronic applications accepted.

College of Agriculture and Life Sciences *Program availability:* Part-time. Offers agricultural and resource economics (MS, PhD); agriculture and life sciences (MBAE, MFG, MFM, MFS, MMB, MN, MP, MS, PhD, Certificate); animal and poultry science (PhD); animal science (MS); biological and agricultural engineering (MBAE, MS, PhD, Certificate); entomology (MS, PhD); financial mathematics (MFM); food, bioprocessing and nutrition sciences (MFS, MS, PhD); functional genomics (MFG, MS, PhD); horticultural science (MS, PhD, Certificate); microbiology (MS, PhD); molecular and structural biochemistry (PhD); plant biology (MS, PhD); poultry science (MS); soil science (MS, PhD). Electronic applications accepted.

College of Design *Program availability:* Part-time. Offers architecture (M Arch); art and design (MAD); design (M Arch, MAD, MGD, MID, MLA, PhD); graphic design (MGD); industrial design (MID); landscape architecture (MLA). Electronic applications accepted.

College of Education *Program availability:* Part-time. Offers adult and community college education (M Ed, MS, Ed D); agency counseling (M Ed, MS); business and marketing education (M Ed, MS); counselor education (M Ed, MS, PhD); curriculum and instruction (M Ed, MS, PhD); education (M Ed, MS, MSA, Ed D, PhD, Certificate); educational administration and supervision (Ed D); educational research and policy analysis (PhD); elementary education (M Ed); human resource development (MS); mathematics education (M Ed, MS, PhD); middle grades education (M Ed, MS); school administration (MSA); science education (M Ed, MS, PhD); special education (M Ed, MS); technology education (M Ed, MS, Ed D); training and development (M Ed, Ed D, Certificate). Electronic applications accepted.

College of Engineering *Program availability:* Part-time. Offers aerospace engineering (MS, PhD); chemical engineering (M Ch E, MS, PhD); civil engineering (MCE, MS, PhD); computer engineering (MS, PhD); computer networking (MS); computer science (MC Sc, MS, PhD); electrical engineering (MS, PhD); engineering (M Ch E, M Eng, MC Sc, MCE, MIE, MIMS, MMSE, MNAE, MNE, MOR, MS, PhD); environmental engineering (MS); industrial engineering (MIE, MS, PhD); integrated manufacturing systems engineering (MIMS); materials science and engineering (MMSE, MNAE, MS, PhD); mechanical engineering (MS, PhD); nuclear engineering (MNE, MS, PhD); operations research (MOR, MS, PhD). Electronic applications accepted.

College of Humanities and Social Sciences *Program availability:* Part-time, evening/weekend. Offers anthropology (MA); applied social and community psychology (PhD); communication (MS); communication, rhetoric, and digital media (MS, PhD); creative writing (MFA); English (MA, MFA); French language and literature (MA); history (MA); human factors and applied cognition (PhD); humanities and social sciences (M Soc, MA, MFA, MIS, MPA, MS, MSW, PhD, Certificate); industrial/organizational psychology (PhD); international studies (MIS); lifespan developmental psychology (PhD); nonprofit management (Certificate); public administration (MPA, PhD); public history (MA); school psychology (PhD); social work (MSW); sociology (PhD); Spanish language and literature (MA). Electronic applications accepted.

College of Natural Resources *Program availability:* Part-time. Offers forestry and environmental resources (MF, MS, PhD); natural resource management (MPRTM, MS); natural resources (MF, MPRTM, MS, PhD); park and recreation management (MPRTM, MS); parks, recreation and tourism management (PhD); recreational sport management (MPRTM, MS); spatial information science (MPRTM, MS); tourism policy and development (MPRTM, MS). Electronic applications accepted.

College of Sciences *Program availability:* Part-time. Offers chemistry (MS, PhD); marine, earth, and atmospheric sciences (MS, PhD); mathematics (MS, PhD); meteorology (MS, PhD); oceanography (MS, PhD); physics (MS, PhD); sciences (M Stat, MS, PhD); statistics (M Stat, MS, PhD). Electronic applications accepted.

Poole College of Management *Program availability:* Part-time. Offers accounting (MAC); biosciences management (MBA); economics (M Econ, MA, PhD); entrepreneurship and technology commercialization (MBA); financial management (MBA); innovation management (MBA); management (M Econ, MA, MAC, MBA, MS, PhD); marketing management (MBA); services management (MBA); supply chain management (MBA). Electronic applications accepted.

Wilson College of Textiles *Program availability:* Part-time, evening/weekend, online learning. Offers fiber and polymer science (PhD); textile and apparel technology and management (MS, MT); textile chemistry (MS); textile engineering (MS); textile technology management (PhD); textiles (MS, MT, PhD). Electronic applications accepted.

NORTH CENTRAL COLLEGE, Naperville, IL 60566-7063

General Information Independent-religious, coed, comprehensive institution. CGS member. *Graduate housing:* Room and/or apartments available on a first-come, first-served basis to single students; on-campus housing not available to married students. Housing application deadline: 4/15.

GRADUATE UNITS

School of Graduate and Professional Studies *Program availability:* Part-time, evening/weekend. Offers change management (MBA); computer science (MS); culture and society (MALS); education (MA Ed); finance (MBA); human resource management (MBA); leadership studies (MLD); management (MBA). Electronic applications accepted.

NORTHCENTRAL UNIVERSITY, San Diego, CA 92106

General Information Proprietary, coed, upper-level institution. CGS member. *Enrollment:* 4,759 full-time matriculated graduate/professional students (2,997 women), 5,939 part-time matriculated graduate/professional students (3,987 women). *Enrollment by degree level:* 4,009 master's, 6,206 doctoral, 454 other advanced degrees. *Graduate faculty:* 119 full-time (77 women), 379 part-time/adjunct (195 women). *Tuition:* Full-time $893. *Required fees:* $95. Tuition and fees vary according to degree level and program. *Graduate housing:* On-campus housing not available. *Student services:* Services for students with disabilities, writing training. *Library facilities:* Northcentral University Library (Virtual). *Collection:* Databases: 123. Weekly public service hours: 79.

Computer facilities: Online class registration is available. Website: http://www.ncu.edu/

General Application Contact: Enrollment Advisor, 866-776-0331, Fax: 928-541-7817, E-mail: admissions@ncu.edu.

GRADUATE UNITS

Graduate Studies Students: 5,036 full-time (3,291 women), 5,747 part-time (3,977 women); includes 3,777 minority (2,550 Black or African American, non-Hispanic/Latino; 76 American Indian or Alaska Native, non-Hispanic/Latino; 192 Asian, non-Hispanic/Latino; 603 Hispanic/Latino; 39 Native Hawaiian or other Pacific Islander, non-Hispanic/Latino; 317 Two or more races, non-Hispanic/Latino). Average age 45. *Faculty:* 98 full-time (63 women), 385 part-time/adjunct (203 women). Expenses: Contact institution. *Financial support:* Scholarships/grants available. In 2018, 929 master's, 782 doctorates, 278 other advanced degrees awarded. *Program availability:* Part-time, evening/weekend, online only, 100% online. Offers business (MBA, DBA, PhD, Postbaccalaureate Certificate); education (M Ed, Ed D, PhD, Ed S, Post-Master's Certificate, Postbaccalaureate Certificate); marriage and family therapy (MA, DMFT, PhD, Post-Master's Certificate, Postbaccalaureate Certificate); psychology (MA, PhD, Post-Master's Certificate, Postbaccalaureate Certificate); technology (MS, PhD). *Application deadline:* Applications are processed on a rolling basis. *Application fee:* $0. Electronic applications accepted. *Application Contact:* Ken Boutelle, Vice President, Enrollment Services, 888-628-4979, E-mail: enrollmentservices@ncu.edu. *Acting Provost,* Dr. David Harpool, 888-327-2877 Ext. 8181, E-mail: provost@ncu.edu.

NORTH DAKOTA STATE UNIVERSITY, Fargo, ND 58102

General Information State-supported, coed, university. CGS member. *Graduate housing:* Rooms and/or apartments available on a first-come, first-served basis to single and married students. *Research affiliation:* U.S. Department of Agriculture (USDA), Metabolism and Radiation Laboratory.

GRADUATE UNITS

College of Graduate and Interdisciplinary Studies *Program availability:* Part-time, evening/weekend, 100% online, blended/hybrid learning. Offers cellular and molecular biology (PhD); college teaching (Certificate); environmental and conservation sciences (MS, PhD); food safety (MS, PhD); genomics and bioinformatics (MS, PhD); managerial logistics (MML); materials and nanotechnology (MS, PhD); STEM education (PhD); transportation and logistics (PhD); transportation and urban systems (MS). Electronic applications accepted.

College of Agriculture, Food Systems, and Natural Resources *Program availability:* Part-time. Offers agribusiness and applied economics (MS); agriculture, food systems, and natural resources (MS, PhD); animal sciences (MS, PhD); cereal science (MS, PhD); entomology (MS, PhD); horticulture (MS); international agribusiness (MS); microbiology (MS); molecular pathogenesis (PhD); natural resources management (MS); plant pathology (MS, PhD); plant sciences (MS, PhD); soil sciences (MS, PhD). Electronic applications accepted.

College of Arts, Humanities and Social Sciences *Program availability:* Part-time, evening/weekend. Offers anthropology (MA, MS); architecture (M Arch); arts, humanities and social sciences (M Arch, M Ed, MA, MLA, MM, MS, DMA, PhD); communication (PhD); community development (MA, MS); composition (MA); conducting (MM, DMA); criminal justice (PhD); criminal justice administration (MS); history (MA, MS, PhD); landscape architecture (MLA); mass communication (MA); music education (MM); performance (MM, DMA); rhetoric, writing and culture (PhD); sociology (MS); speech communication (MS). Electronic applications accepted.

College of Business Program availability: Part-time, evening/weekend. Offers accountancy (M Acc); business administration (MBA). Electronic applications accepted.

College of Engineering Program availability: Part-time. Offers agricultural and biosystems engineering (MS, PhD); civil engineering (MS, PhD); construction management (MCM, MS, Graduate Certificate); electrical and computer engineering (M Eng, MS, PhD); engineering (M Eng, MCM, MS, PhD, Graduate Certificate); environmental and conservation science (PhD); environmental engineering (MS); industrial and manufacturing engineering (MS, PhD); manufacturing engineering (MS); materials and nanotechnology (PhD); mechanical engineering (MS, PhD); natural resource management (PhD); STEM education (PhD); transportation and logistics (PhD). Electronic applications accepted.

College of Health Professions Program availability: Part-time. Offers American Indian public health (MPH); community health sciences (MPH); health professions (MPH, MS, DNP, PhD, Pharm D); management of infectious diseases (MPH); nursing (DNP); pharmacy (MS, PhD, Pharm D). Electronic applications accepted.

College of Human Development and Education Program availability: Part-time, evening/weekend, online learning. Offers advanced athletic training (MS); agricultural education (M Ed, MS); athletic training (MAT); clinical mental health counseling (M Ed, MS); counselor education (M Ed, MS); counselor education and supervision (PhD); developmental science (PhD); dietetics (MS); educational leadership (M Ed, MS, Ed S); exercise science and nutrition (PhD); family and consumer sciences education (M Ed, MS); family financial planning (MS, Certificate); gerontology (PhD, Certificate); health, nutrition and exercise science (MS); human development and education (M Ed, MAT, MPH, MS, Ed D, PhD, Certificate, Ed S); school counseling (M Ed, MS); youth development (MS). Electronic applications accepted.

College of Science and Mathematics Program availability: Part-time. Offers applied mathematics (MS, PhD); biochemistry (MS, PhD); biology (MS); botany (MS, PhD); chemistry (MS, PhD); clinical psychology (MS); coatings and polymeric materials (MS, PhD); computer science (MS, PhD); health and social psychology (PhD); mathematics (MS, PhD); physics (MS, PhD); psychological clinical science (PhD); psychology (MS); science and mathematics (MS, MSE, PhD, Certificate); software engineering (MS, MSE, PhD, Certificate); sports statistics (MS); statistics (MS); visual and cognitive neuroscience (PhD); zoology (MS, PhD). Electronic applications accepted.

NORTHEASTERN ILLINOIS UNIVERSITY, Chicago, IL 60625-4699

General Information State-supported, coed, comprehensive institution. *Graduate housing:* Room and/or apartments available to single students; on-campus housing not available to married students. *Research affiliation:* Advocate Health Care Network (health care cost containment), Lutheran General Hospital (clinical cardiology), Advocate Medical Group (health care outcomes research).

GRADUATE UNITS

College of Graduate Studies and Research Program availability: Part-time, evening/weekend. Electronic applications accepted.

College of Arts and Sciences Program availability: Part-time, evening/weekend. Offers arts and sciences (MA, MS, MSW, Graduate Certificate); biology (MS); chemistry (MS); communication, media and theatre (MA); computer science (MS); English (MA); geographic information science (Graduate Certificate); geography and environmental studies (MA); gerontology (MA); history (MA); Latin American literatures and cultures (MA); linguistics (MA); mathematics (MS); music (MA); political science (MA); secondary education mathematics (MS); social work (MSW); teaching English to speakers of other languages (MA). Electronic applications accepted.

College of Business and Management Program availability: Part-time, evening/weekend. Offers accounting (MSA); business administration (MBA). Electronic applications accepted.

Daniel L. Goodwin College of Education Program availability: Part-time, evening/weekend. Offers clinical mental health counseling (MA); early childhood education (MAT); education (MA, MAT, MS, MSI); educational administration and supervision (MA); elementary education (MAT); English language arts (MAT); exercise science (MS); family counseling (MA); gifted education (MA); human resource development (MA); inner city studies (MA); language arts - secondary education (MSI); learning behavior specialist (MA, MS); literacy education (MA); mathematics (MAT); middle level education (MAT); rehabilitation counseling (MA); school counseling (MA); science (MAT); social science (MAT). Electronic applications accepted.

NORTHEASTERN SEMINARY AT ROBERTS WESLEYAN COLLEGE, Rochester, NY 14624

General Information Independent-religious, coed, graduate-only institution. *Enrollment by degree level:* 103 master's, 15 doctoral, 20 other advanced degrees. *Graduate faculty:* 7 full-time (3 women), 18 part-time/adjunct (6 women). *Tuition:* Full-time $9612; part-time $534 per credit hour. *Required fees:* $500. *Graduate housing:* On-campus housing not available. *Student services:* Campus safety program, career counseling, exercise/wellness program, international student services, services for students with disabilities, writing training. *Library facilities:* B. Thomas Golisano Library plus 1 other. *Collection:* Books: 129,401 (physical), 151,162 (digital/electronic); Serial titles: 172 (physical), 49,225 (digital/electronic); Databases: 151. Weekly public service hours: 80; study areas open 24 hours, 5–7 days a week; students can reserve study rooms.

Computer facilities: A campuswide network can be accessed. Online class registration is available.
Website: http://www.nes.edu/

General Application Contact: JP Anderson, Associate Vice President for Enrollment, 585-594-6832, Fax: 585-594-6801, E-mail: anderson_jp@roberts.edu.

GRADUATE UNITS

Graduate and Professional Programs Students: 63 full-time (24 women), 75 part-time (44 women); includes 55 minority (44 Black or African American, non-Hispanic/Latino; 1 Asian, non-Hispanic/Latino; 9 Hispanic/Latino; 1 Two or more races, non-Hispanic/Latino). Average age 45. 51 applicants, 76% accepted, 34 enrolled. *Faculty:* 8 full-time (3 women), 18 part-time/adjunct (6 women). Expenses: Contact institution. *Financial support:* Teaching assistantships with partial tuition reimbursements, career-related internships or fieldwork, institutionally sponsored loans, scholarships/grants, and tuition waivers (partial) available. Financial award applicants required to submit FAFSA. In 2018, 17 master's, 5 doctorates awarded. *Program availability:* Part-time, evening/weekend, 100% online, blended/hybrid learning. Offers ministry (D Min); theological studies (MA); theology (M Div); theology and social justice (MA); transformational leadership (MA). MDiv/MSW offered jointly with Roberts Wesleyan College. *Application deadline:* For fall admission, 4/1 priority date for domestic and international students; for spring admission, 11/1 priority date for domestic and

international students; for summer admission, 4/1 priority date for domestic and international students. Applications are processed on a rolling basis. *Application fee:* $0. Electronic applications accepted. *Application Contact:* Monica Ross, Admissions Liaison, 585-594-6802, Fax: 585-594-6801, E-mail: ross_monica@roberts.edu. *Vice President and Dean*, Dr. Douglas R. Cullum, 585-594-6331, Fax: 585-594-6801, E-mail: cullumd@roberts.edu.

NORTHEASTERN STATE UNIVERSITY, Tahlequah, OK 74464-2399

General Information State-supported, coed, comprehensive institution. *Enrollment:* 7,899 graduate, professional, and undergraduate students; 527 full-time matriculated graduate/professional students (385 women), 640 part-time matriculated graduate/professional students (481 women). *Enrollment by degree level:* 1,055 master's, 112 doctoral. *Graduate faculty:* 120 full-time (58 women), 23 part-time/adjunct (12 women). *International tuition:* $9999 full-time. *Tuition, area resident:* Full-time $4500; part-time $250 per credit hour. *Tuition, state resident:* full-time $4500; part-time $250 per credit hour. *Tuition, nonresident:* full-time $9999; part-time $555.50 per credit hour. *Required fees:* $601.20; $33.40 per credit hour. *Graduate housing:* Rooms and/or apartments available on a first-come, first-served basis to single and married students. Housing application deadline: 6/1. *Student services:* Campus employment opportunities, campus safety program, career counseling, exercise/wellness program, free psychological counseling, international student services, low-cost health insurance, multicultural affairs office, services for students with disabilities, teacher training, writing training. *Library facilities:* John Vaughn Library. *Collection:* Books: 415,253 (physical), 64,575 (digital/electronic); Serial titles: 30,893 (physical), 92,125 (digital/electronic); Databases: 143. Weekly public service hours: 114.

Computer facilities: Computer purchase and lease plans are available. 1,160 computers available on campus for general student use. A campuswide network can be accessed from student residence rooms and from off campus. Online class registration is available.
Website: http://www.nsuok.edu/

General Application Contact: Josh McCollum, Graduate Coordinator, Advising and Admissions, 918-444-2093, E-mail: mccolluj@nsuok.edu.

GRADUATE UNITS

College of Business and Technology Students: 44 full-time (19 women), 115 part-time (68 women); includes 77 minority (13 Black or African American, non-Hispanic/Latino; 18 American Indian or Alaska Native, non-Hispanic/Latino; 7 Asian, non-Hispanic/Latino; 10 Hispanic/Latino; 29 Two or more races, non-Hispanic/Latino), 3 international. Average age 33. *Faculty:* 14 full-time (2 women), 2 part-time/adjunct (0 women). Expenses: Contact institution. *Financial support:* Teaching assistantships and Federal Work-Study available. Financial award application deadline: 3/1. In 2018, 34 master's awarded. *Program availability:* Part-time, evening/weekend. Offers accounting and financial analysis (MS); business administration (MBA, PMBA); business and technology (MBA, MS, PMBA). *Application deadline:* For fall admission, 6/1 priority date for domestic students. Applications are processed on a rolling basis. *Application fee:* $0 ($25 for international students). Electronic applications accepted. *Application Contact:* Josh McCollum, Graduate Coordinator, 918-444-2093, E-mail: mccolluj@nsuok.edu. *Dean*, Dr. Roger Collier, 918-444-2900, E-mail: colliere@nsuok.edu.

College of Education Students: 162 full-time (126 women), 299 part-time (239 women); includes 187 minority (19 Black or African American, non-Hispanic/Latino; 70 American Indian or Alaska Native, non-Hispanic/Latino; 5 Asian, non-Hispanic/Latino; 16 Hispanic/Latino; 77 Two or more races, non-Hispanic/Latino), 8 international. Average age 34. *Faculty:* 31 full-time (21 women), 9 part-time/adjunct (5 women). Expenses: Contact institution. *Financial support:* Teaching assistantships, career-related internships or fieldwork, and Federal Work-Study available. Financial award application deadline: 3/1. In 2018, 170 master's awarded. *Program availability:* Part-time, evening/weekend. Offers counseling (MS); early childhood education (M Ed); education (M Ed, MS); health and kinesiology (MS); higher education leadership (MS); instructional leadership (M Ed); library media and information technology (MS); reading (M Ed); school administration (M Ed); special education-autism spectrum disorders (M Ed). *Application deadline:* For fall admission, 6/1 priority date for domestic students. Applications are processed on a rolling basis. *Application fee:* $25. Electronic applications accepted. *Application Contact:* Josh McCollum, Graduate Coordinator, 918-444-2093, E-mail: mccolluj@nsuok.edu. *Interim Dean of the College of Education*, Dr. Vanessa Anton, 918-444-3700, Fax: 918-458-2351, E-mail: anton@nsuok.edu.

College of Liberal Arts Students: 58 full-time (39 women), 66 part-time (39 women); includes 60 minority (15 Black or African American, non-Hispanic/Latino; 19 American Indian or Alaska Native, non-Hispanic/Latino; 5 Hispanic/Latino; 1 Native Hawaiian or other Pacific Islander, non-Hispanic/Latino; 20 Two or more races, non-Hispanic/Latino), 1 international. Average age 34. *Faculty:* 25 full-time (7 women), 4 part-time/adjunct (1 woman). Expenses: Contact institution. *Financial support:* Teaching assistantships and Federal Work-Study available. Financial award application deadline: 3/1. In 2018, 17 master's awarded. *Program availability:* Part-time, evening/weekend. Offers American studies (MA); communication arts (MA); criminal justice (MS); English (MA); liberal arts (MA, MS). *Application deadline:* For fall admission, 6/1 priority date for domestic students. Applications are processed on a rolling basis. *Application fee:* $25. Electronic applications accepted. *Application Contact:* Josh McCollum, Graduate Coordinator, 918-444-2093, E-mail: mccolluj@nsuok.edu. *Interim Dean of Liberal Arts*, Dr. Robyn Pursley, 918-444-3600, Fax: 918-458-2348, E-mail: cola@nsuok.edu.

College of Science and Health Professions Students: 147 full-time (137 women), 69 part-time (60 women); includes 78 minority (4 Black or African American, non-Hispanic/Latino; 27 American Indian or Alaska Native, non-Hispanic/Latino; 8 Asian, non-Hispanic/Latino; 11 Hispanic/Latino; 28 Two or more races, non-Hispanic/Latino), 1 international. Average age 30. *Faculty:* 26 full-time (14 women), 8 part-time/adjunct (6 women). Expenses: Contact institution. In 2018, 68 master's awarded. Offers mathematics education (M Ed); natural sciences (MS); nursing (MSN); nursing education (MSN); occupational therapy (MS); science and health professions (M Ed, MS, MSN); science education (M Ed); speech-language pathology (MS). *Application deadline:* Applications are processed on a rolling basis. *Application fee:* $25. Electronic applications accepted. *Application Contact:* Josh McCollum, Graduate Coordinator, 918-444-2093, E-mail: mccolluj@nsuok.edu. *Dean*, Dr. Pamela Hathorn, 918-444-3800, E-mail: hathorn@nsuok.edu.

Oklahoma College of Optometry Students: 112 full-time (61 women); includes 29 minority (2 Black or African American, non-Hispanic/Latino; 7 American Indian or Alaska Native, non-Hispanic/Latino; 8 Asian, non-Hispanic/Latino; 4 Hispanic/Latino; 8 Two or more races, non-Hispanic/Latino). Average age 25. *Faculty:* 15 full-time (5 women). Expenses: Contact institution. *Financial support:* Federal Work-Study, institutionally sponsored loans, scholarships/grants, tuition waivers (partial), and residencies available. Financial award application deadline: 5/1; financial award applicants required to submit FAFSA. In 2018, 27 doctorates awarded. Offers optometry (OD). *Application deadline:* For fall admission, 2/1 for domestic students. Applications are processed on a rolling basis. *Application fee:* $45. Electronic applications accepted. *Application Contact:* Sandy Medearis, Optometric Student and Alumni Services Director, 918-444-4006, Fax: 918-458-2104, E-mail: medearis@nsuok.edu. *Dean of Oklahoma College of Optometry,* Dr. Douglas Penisten, 918-444-4025, E-mail: penisten@nsuok.edu.

NORTHEASTERN UNIVERSITY, Boston, MA 02115-5096

General Information Independent, coed, university. CGS member. *Research affiliation:* Jobs for America's Graduates (labor studies), Cytyc Corporation (medical technology), BBN Technologies (information technology), Analog Devices, Inc. (electronics), General Electric Company (GE) (engineering).

GRADUATE UNITS

Bouvé College of Health Sciences *Program availability:* Part-time, evening/weekend, online learning. Offers applied behavior analysis (MS); audiology (Au D); counseling psychology (MS, PhD, CAGS); exercise science (MS); nursing (MS, PhD, CAGS); nursing practice (DNP); pharmaceutical sciences (MS, PhD); pharmacology (MS); pharmacy (Pharm D); school psychology (PhD); speech-language pathology (MS); urban health (MPH). Electronic applications accepted.

College of Arts, Media and Design Offers architecture (M Arch); arts administration and cultural entrepreneurship (MS); experience design (MFA, MS); game science and design (MS); information design and visualization (MFA); interdisciplinary arts (MFA); journalism (MA); media advocacy (MS); music industry leadership (MS); sustainable building systems (MS); sustainable urban environments (M Des). Electronic applications accepted.

College of Computer and Information Science *Program availability:* Part-time, evening/weekend. Offers computer science (MS, PhD); data science (MS); game science and design (MS); health informatics (MS); information assurance (MS); network science (PhD); personal health informatics (PhD). Electronic applications accepted.

College of Engineering *Program availability:* Part-time, online learning. Offers bioengineering (MS, PhD); chemical engineering (MS, PhD); civil engineering (MS, PhD); computer engineering (PhD); computer systems engineering (MS); electrical and computer engineering (MS); electrical and computer engineering leadership (MS); electrical engineering (PhD); energy systems (MS); engineering and public policy (MS); engineering management (MS, Certificate); environmental engineering (MS); industrial engineering (MS, PhD); information assurance (PhD); information systems (MS); interdisciplinary engineering (PhD); mechanical engineering (PhD); operations research (MS); telecommunication systems management (MS). Electronic applications accepted.

College of Professional Studies *Program availability:* Part-time, evening/weekend, 100% online, blended/hybrid learning. Offers applied nutrition (MS); college athletics administration (MSL); commerce and economic development (MS); corporate and organizational communication (MS); criminal justice (MS); digital media (MPS); elearning and instructional design (M Ed); elementary education (MAT); geographic information technology (MPS); global studies and international relations (MS); higher education administration (M Ed); homeland security (MA); human services (MS); informatics (MPS); leadership (MS); learning analytics (M Ed); learning and instruction (M Ed); nonprofit management (MS); professional sports administration (MSL); project management (MS); regulatory affairs for drugs, biologics, and medical devices (MS); respiratory care leadership (MS); special education (M Ed); technical communication (MS). Electronic applications accepted.

College of Science *Program availability:* Part-time. Offers applied mathematics (MS); bioinformatics (MS); biology (PhD); biotechnology (MS); chemistry and chemical biology (MS, PhD); environmental science and policy (MS); marine and environmental sciences (PhD); marine biology (MS); mathematics (MS, PhD); operations research (MSOR); physics (MS, PhD); psychology (PhD). Electronic applications accepted.

College of Social Sciences and Humanities *Program availability:* Online learning. Offers criminology and criminal justice (MSCJ); criminology and justice policy (PhD); economics (MA, PhD); English (MA, PhD); international affairs (MA); law and public policy (PhD); political science (MA, PhD); public administration (MPA); public policy (MPP); security and resilience studies (MS); sociology (MA, PhD); urban and regional policy (MS); urban informatics (MS); world history (MA, PhD). Electronic applications accepted.

D'Amore-McKim School of Business *Program availability:* Part-time, evening/weekend, online learning. Offers accounting (MS); business administration (EMBA, MBA); finance (MS); innovation (MS); international business (MS); international management (MS); taxation (MS); technological entrepreneurship (MS). Electronic applications accepted.

School of Law *Program availability:* Online learning. Offers law (LL M, MLS, JD). JD/MPH offered jointly with Tufts University; JD/MSA/MBA with Graduate School of Professional Accounting; JD/MS with Program in Law and Public Policy; JD/MELP with Vermont Law School; and JD/MA with Brandeis University. Electronic applications accepted.

NORTHEAST OHIO MEDICAL UNIVERSITY, Rootstown, OH 44272-0095

General Information State-supported, coed, graduate-only institution. *Graduate housing:* On-campus housing not available. *Research affiliation:* American Heart Association (physiology, biochemistry), National Science Foundation (anatomy), National Institutes of Health (anatomy, biochemistry, immunology, neurobiology, microbiology), Summa Health Systems (orthopedics, anatomy), Margaret Clark Morgan Foundation (schizophrenia, mental illness), Austen BioInnovation Institute in Akron (pharmacology, drug delivery, biotechnology, community health).

GRADUATE UNITS

College of Graduate Studies *Program availability:* Part-time, evening/weekend. Offers bioethics (Certificate); health-system pharmacy administration (MS); integrated pharmaceutical medicine (MS, PhD); medical ethics and humanities (MS); public health (MPH). MPH offered as part of consortium with The University of Akron, Youngstown State University, Ohio University, and Cleveland State University. Electronic applications accepted.

College of Medicine Offers medicine (MD). Electronic applications accepted.

College of Pharmacy Offers pharmacy (Pharm D). Electronic applications accepted.

NORTHERN ARIZONA UNIVERSITY, Flagstaff, AZ 86011

General Information State-supported, coed, university. CGS member. *Graduate housing:* Rooms and/or apartments available on a first-come, first-served basis to single and married students. Housing application deadline: 5/1. *Research affiliation:* W.L. Gore and Associates, Inc. (biomedical engineering), Museum of Northern Arizona (anthropology), Lowell Observatory (physics and astronomy), Rocky Mountain Forest and Range Experiment Station (forestry), U.S. Naval Observatory (physics and astronomy), U.S. Geological Survey (USGS) (geology).

GRADUATE UNITS

College of Arts and Letters *Program availability:* Part-time, 100% online, blended/hybrid learning. Offers applied linguistics (PhD); arts and letters (MA, MAT, MFA, MM, PhD, Graduate Certificate); creative writing (MFA); English (MA); history (MA); professional writing (Graduate Certificate); rhetoric, writing and digital media studies (Graduate Certificate); Spanish (MAT); Spanish education (MAT); teaching English as a second language (MA, Graduate Certificate). Electronic applications accepted.

School of Music *Program availability:* Part-time. Offers music (MM); music performance (Graduate Certificate). Electronic applications accepted.

College of Education *Program availability:* Part-time, 100% online, blended/hybrid learning. Offers autism spectrum disorders (Certificate); bilingual/multicultural education (M Ed); career and technical education (M Ed, Certificate); clinical mental health counseling (MA); combined counseling/school psychology (PhD); community college teaching and learning (Graduate Certificate); counseling (M Ed); curriculum and instruction (Ed D); early childhood education (M Ed); education (M Ed, MA, Ed D, PhD, Certificate, Ed S, Graduate Certificate); educational leadership (M Ed, Ed D); educational technology (M Ed, Certificate); elementary education (M Ed); English as a second language (Certificate); human relations (M Ed); positive behavior support (Certificate); principal (Graduate Certificate); psychology of human development and learning (Graduate Certificate); school psychology (Ed S); secondary education (M Ed); special education (M Ed); superintendent (Graduate Certificate). Electronic applications accepted.

College of Engineering, Informatics, and Applied Sciences Offers bioengineering (PhD); engineering (M Eng); informatics and computing (PhD).

Engineering Division *Program availability:* Part-time. Offers engineering (MS). Electronic applications accepted.

College of Environment, Forestry, and Natural Sciences *Program availability:* Part-time, 100% online, blended/hybrid learning. Offers applied physics (MS); applied statistics (Graduate Certificate); astronomy and planetary science (PhD); biology (MS, PhD); chemistry (MS); engineering, forestry, and natural sciences (M Eng, MA, MAT, MF, MS, MSF, PhD, Graduate Certificate); mathematics (MS); mathematics education (MS); statistics (MS); teaching introductory community college mathematics (Graduate Certificate). Electronic applications accepted.

Center for Science Teaching and Learning *Program availability:* Part-time, 100% online, blended/hybrid learning. Offers science teaching (MA); science with certification (MAT). Electronic applications accepted.

School of Earth Sciences and Environmental Sustainability *Program availability:* Part-time. Offers climate science and solutions (MS); conservation ecology (Graduate Certificate); earth sciences and environmental sustainability (PhD); environmental sciences and policy (MS); geology (MS). Electronic applications accepted.

School of Forestry *Program availability:* Part-time. Offers forest science (PhD); forestry (MF, MSF). Electronic applications accepted.

College of Health and Human Services *Program availability:* Part-time, 100% online, blended/hybrid learning. Offers clinical speech-language pathology (MS); exercise science (MS); health and human services (MPAS, MS, DNP, DPT, OTD, Certificate); occupational therapy (OTD); physical education (MS); physical therapy (DPT); physician assistant studies (MPAS). Electronic applications accepted.

School of Nursing *Program availability:* Part-time, 100% online, blended/hybrid learning. Offers family nurse practitioner (Certificate); nursing (MS); nursing practice (DNP). Electronic applications accepted.

College of Social and Behavioral Sciences *Program availability:* Part-time, 100% online, blended/hybrid learning. Offers anthropology (MA); applied criminology (MS); applied geospatial sciences (MS); applied sociology (MA); community planning (Certificate); ethnic studies (Graduate Certificate); geographic information systems (Certificate); indigenous and tribal nation-building (Graduate Certificate); interdisciplinary health (PhD); parks and recreation management (MS); political science (MA, PhD, Graduate Certificate); psychological sciences (MA); public administration (MPA); public management (Graduate Certificate); social and behavioral sciences (MA, MPA, MS, PhD, Certificate, Graduate Certificate); sustainable communities (MA); women's and gender studies (Graduate Certificate). Electronic applications accepted.

Institute for Human Development *Program availability:* Part-time. Offers assistive technology (Graduate Certificate). Electronic applications accepted.

School of Communication *Program availability:* Part-time, 100% online, blended/hybrid learning. Offers communication (MA); communication studies (Graduate Certificate); science communication (Graduate Certificate). Electronic applications accepted.

Office of the Provost *Program availability:* Part-time, blended/hybrid learning. Offers global business administration (MGBA). Electronic applications accepted.

Online, Statewide and Education Innovation

The W. A. Franke College of Business *Program availability:* Part-time, 100% online, blended/hybrid learning. Offers business administration (MBA); business foundations (Graduate Certificate). Electronic applications accepted.

NORTHERN ILLINOIS UNIVERSITY, De Kalb, IL 60115-2854

General Information State-supported, coed, university. CGS member. *Enrollment:* 17,169 graduate, professional, and undergraduate students; 1,994 full-time matriculated graduate/professional students (1,040 women), 2,387 part-time matriculated graduate/professional students (1,400 women). *Enrollment by degree level:* 3,388 master's, 930 doctoral, 63 other advanced degrees. *Graduate faculty:* 672 full-time (248 women), 66 part-time/adjunct (17 women). *Graduate housing:* Rooms and/or apartments available on a first-come, first-served basis to single and married students. *Student services:* Campus employment opportunities, campus safety program, career counseling, child daycare facilities, exercise/wellness program, free psychological counseling, grant writing training, international student services, low-cost health insurance, services for students with disabilities, teacher training, writing training. *Library facilities:* Founders Memorial Library plus 4 others. *Collection:* Books: 1.8 million (physical), 595,551 (digital/electronic); Serial titles: 1,206 (physical), 82,960 (digital/electronic); Databases: 311. Weekly public service hours: 100; students can reserve study rooms.

Computer facilities: 1,500 computers available on campus for general student use. A campuswide network can be accessed from student residence rooms and from off campus. Online class registration is available. Website: http://www.niu.edu/

General Application Contact: Dr. Bradley G. Bond, Dean, Graduate School, 815-753-0395, Fax: 815-753-6366, E-mail: gradsch@niu.edu.

GRADUATE UNITS

College of Law Students: 221 full-time (105 women), 39 part-time (15 women); includes 61 minority (27 Black or African American, non-Hispanic/Latino; 8 Asian, non-

Hispanic/Latino; 18 Hispanic/Latino; 2 Native Hawaiian or other Pacific Islander, non-Hispanic/Latino; 6 Two or more races, non-Hispanic/Latino), 3 international. Average age 27. 611 applicants, 51% accepted, 92 enrolled. *Faculty:* 22 full-time (11 women). Expenses: Contact institution. *Financial support:* In 2018–19, 8 teaching assistantships were awarded; research assistantships, career-related internships or fieldwork, Federal Work-Study, tuition waivers (full and partial), and unspecified assistantships also available. Support available to part-time students. Financial award application deadline: 3/1; financial award applicants required to submit FAFSA. In 2018, 77 doctorates awarded. *Program availability:* Part-time. Offers law (JD). *Application deadline:* For fall admission, 4/1 priority date for domestic and international students. Applications are processed on a rolling basis. Electronic applications accepted. *Application Contact:* Amanda Noascono, Director of Admissions and Financial Aid, 815-753-8595, Fax: 815-753-5680, E-mail: law-admit@niu.edu. *Interim Dean,* Laurel Rigertas, 815-753-5300, Fax: 815-753-8552, E-mail: lrigertas@niu.edu.

Graduate School Students: 1,773 full-time (935 women), 2,348 part-time (1,385 women); includes 936 minority (278 Black or African American, non-Hispanic/Latino; 6 American Indian or Alaska Native, non-Hispanic/Latino; 191 Asian, non-Hispanic/Latino; 362 Hispanic/Latino; 99 Two or more races, non-Hispanic/Latino), 701 international. Average age 32. 3,152 applicants, 60% accepted, 851 enrolled. *Faculty:* 672 full-time (248 women), 66 part-time/adjunct (17 women). Expenses: Contact institution. *Financial support:* In 2018–19, 411 research assistantships with full tuition reimbursements, 896 teaching assistantships with full tuition reimbursements were awarded; fellowships with full tuition reimbursements, career-related internships or fieldwork, Federal Work-Study, scholarships/grants, tuition waivers (full), and staff assistantships also available. Support available to part-time students. Financial award applicants required to submit FAFSA. In 2018, 1,399 master's, 159 doctorates, 7 other advanced degrees awarded. *Program availability:* Part-time, evening/weekend, online learning. *Application deadline:* For fall admission, 8/1 for domestic students, 5/1 for international students; for spring admission, 12/1 for domestic students, 10/1 for international students. Applications are processed on a rolling basis. *Application fee:* $40. Electronic applications accepted. *Application Contact:* Graduate School Information, 815-753-0395, E-mail: gradsch@niu.edu. *Dean,* Dr. Bradley G. Bond, 815-753-9403, Fax: 815-753-6366, E-mail: bbond@niu.edu.

College of Business Students: 350 full-time (144 women), 387 part-time (138 women); includes 221 minority (46 Black or African American, non-Hispanic/Latino; 1 American Indian or Alaska Native, non-Hispanic/Latino; 77 Asian, non-Hispanic/Latino; 81 Hispanic/Latino; 16 Two or more races, non-Hispanic/Latino), 163 international. Average age 30. 479 applicants, 77% accepted, 178 enrolled. *Faculty:* 53 full-time (17 women), 3 part-time/adjunct (0 women). Expenses: Contact institution. *Financial support:* In 2018–19, 5 research assistantships with full tuition reimbursements, 3 teaching assistantships with full tuition reimbursements were awarded; fellowships with full tuition reimbursements, career-related internships or fieldwork, Federal Work-Study, scholarships/grants, tuition waivers (full), and unspecified assistantships also available. Support available to part-time students. Financial award applicants required to submit FAFSA. In 2018, 496 master's awarded. *Program availability:* Part-time, evening/weekend. Offers accountancy (MAC, MAS, MST); business (MAC, MAS, MBA, MS, MST); management information systems (MS). *Application deadline:* For fall admission, 6/1 for domestic students, 5/1 for international students; for spring admission, 11/1 for domestic students, 10/1 for international students. Applications are processed on a rolling basis. *Application fee:* $40. Electronic applications accepted. *Application Contact:* Office of Graduate Studies in Business, 815-753-6301. *Dean,* Balaji Rajagopalan, 815-753-6225, Fax: 815-753-5305, E-mail: brajagopalan@niu.edu.

College of Education Students: 333 full-time (205 women), 888 part-time (629 women); includes 315 minority (125 Black or African American, non-Hispanic/Latino; 2 American Indian or Alaska Native, non-Hispanic/Latino; 36 Asian, non-Hispanic/Latino; 111 Hispanic/Latino; 41 Two or more races, non-Hispanic/Latino), 74 international. Average age 36. 479 applicants, 77% accepted, 178 enrolled. *Faculty:* 110 full-time (66 women), 5 part-time/adjunct (3 women). Expenses: Contact institution. *Financial support:* In 2018–19, 1 research assistantship with full tuition reimbursement was awarded; fellowships with full tuition reimbursements, teaching assistantships with full tuition reimbursements, career-related internships or fieldwork, Federal Work-Study, scholarships/grants, tuition waivers (full), and staff assistantships also available. Support available to part-time students. Financial award applicants required to submit FAFSA. In 2018, 308 master's, 61 doctorates, 2 other advanced degrees awarded. *Program availability:* Part-time, evening/weekend, online learning. Offers adult and higher education (MS Ed, Ed D); counseling (MS Ed, Ed D); curriculum and instruction (MS Ed, Ed D); early childhood education (MS Ed); education (MS, MS Ed, Ed D, Ed S); educational administration (MS Ed, Ed D, Ed S); educational psychology (MS Ed, Ed D); educational research and evaluation (MS); elementary education (MS Ed); foundations of education (MS Ed); instructional technology (MS Ed, Ed D); kinesiology and physical education (MS, MS Ed); literacy education (MS Ed); school business management (MS Ed); special education (MS Ed). *Application deadline:* For fall admission, 6/1 for domestic students, 5/1 for international students; for spring admission, 11/1 for domestic students, 10/1 for international students. Applications are processed on a rolling basis. *Application fee:* $40. Electronic applications accepted. *Application Contact:* Graduate School Office, 815-753-0395, E-mail: gradsch@niu.edu. *Dean,* Laurie Elish-Piper, 815-753-1949, Fax: 851-753-2100.

College of Engineering and Engineering Technology Students: 125 full-time (29 women), 125 part-time (18 women); includes 34 minority (11 Black or African American, non-Hispanic/Latino; 12 Asian, non-Hispanic/Latino; 8 Hispanic/Latino; 3 Native Hawaiian or other Pacific Islander, non-Hispanic/Latino), 147 international. Average age 28. 329 applicants, 62% accepted, 65 enrolled. *Faculty:* 36 full-time (2 women), 2 part-time/adjunct (0 women). Expenses: Contact institution. *Financial support:* In 2018–19, 1 research assistantship with full tuition reimbursement was awarded; fellowships with full tuition reimbursements, teaching assistantships with full tuition reimbursements, career-related internships or fieldwork, Federal Work-Study, scholarships/grants, tuition waivers (full), and unspecified assistantships also available. Support available to part-time students. Financial award applicants required to submit FAFSA. In 2018, 125 master's awarded. *Program availability:* Part-time, evening/weekend. Offers electrical engineering (MS); engineering and engineering technology (MS); industrial engineering (MS); industrial management (MS); mechanical engineering (MS). *Application deadline:* For fall admission, 6/1 for domestic students, 5/1 for international students; for spring admission, 11/1 for domestic students, 10/1 for international students. Applications are processed on a rolling basis. *Application fee:* $40. Electronic applications accepted. *Application Contact:* Graduate School Office, 815-753-0395, E-mail: gradsch@niu.edu. *Dean,* Dr. Donald R Peterson, 815-753-1281, Fax: 815-753-1310, E-mail: drpeterson@niu.edu.

College of Health and Human Sciences Students: 290 full-time (233 women), 219 part-time (188 women); includes 136 minority (42 Black or African American, non-Hispanic/Latino; 2 American Indian or Alaska Native, non-Hispanic/Latino; 27 Asian, non-Hispanic/Latino; 55 Hispanic/Latino; 10 Two or more races, non-Hispanic/Latino), 7 international. Average age 30. 560 applicants, 47% accepted, 117 enrolled. *Faculty:* 46 full-time (37 women), 5 part-time/adjunct (3 women). Expenses: Contact institution. *Financial support:* In 2018–19, 5 research assistantships with full tuition reimbursements were awarded; fellowships with full tuition reimbursements, teaching assistantships with full tuition reimbursements, career-related internships or fieldwork, Federal Work-Study, scholarships/grants, tuition waivers (full) and staff assistantships also available. Support available to part-time students. Financial award applicants required to submit FAFSA. In 2018, 130 master's, 43 doctorates awarded. *Program availability:* Part-time, evening/weekend. Offers applied human development and family sciences (MS); audiology (Au D); communicative disorders (MA, Au D); health and human sciences (MA, MPH, MS, Au D, DNP, DPT); nursing (MS, DNP); nutrition and dietetics (MS); physical therapy (DPT); public health (MPH); speech-language pathology (MA). *Application deadline:* For fall admission, 6/1 for domestic students, 5/1 for international students; for spring admission, 11/1 for domestic students, 10/1 for international students. Applications are processed on a rolling basis. *Application fee:* $40. Electronic applications accepted. *Application Contact:* Graduate School Office, 815-753-0395, E-mail: gradsch@niu.edu. *Dean,* Dr. Derryl Block, 815-753-6157.

College of Liberal Arts and Sciences Students: 544 full-time (256 women), 340 part-time (158 women); includes 124 minority (27 Black or African American, non-Hispanic/Latino; 26 Asian, non-Hispanic/Latino; 54 Hispanic/Latino; 17 Two or more races, non-Hispanic/Latino), 268 international. Average age 30. 1,135 applicants, 49% accepted, 202 enrolled. *Faculty:* 342 full-time (99 women), 36 part-time/adjunct (7 women). Expenses: Contact institution. *Financial support:* In 2018–19, 2 research assistantships with full tuition reimbursements were awarded; fellowships with full tuition reimbursements, teaching assistantships with full tuition reimbursements, career-related internships or fieldwork, Federal Work-Study, scholarships/grants, tuition waivers (full), and unspecified assistantships also available. Support available to part-time students. Financial award applicants required to submit FAFSA. In 2018, 292 master's, 51 doctorates awarded. *Program availability:* Part-time, evening/weekend. Offers anthropology (MA); biological sciences (MS, PhD); chemistry and biochemistry (MS, PhD); communication studies (MA); computer science (MS); economics (MA, PhD); English (MA, PhD); French (MA); geography (MS, PhD); geology and environmental geosciences (MS, PhD); history (MA, PhD); liberal arts and sciences (MA, MPA, MS, PhD); mathematical sciences (PhD); mathematics (MS); philosophy (MA); physics (MS, PhD); political science (MA, PhD); psychology (MA, PhD); public administration (MPA); sociology (MA); Spanish (MA); statistics (MS). *Application deadline:* For fall admission, 6/1 for domestic students, 5/1 for international students; for spring admission, 11/1 for domestic students, 10/1 for international students. Applications are processed on a rolling basis. *Application fee:* $40. Electronic applications accepted. *Application Contact:* Graduate School Office, 815-753-0395, E-mail: gradsch@niu.edu. *Acting Dean,* Dr. Judy K Ledgerwood, 815-753-1061, Fax: 815-753-7950, E-mail: mccord@niu.edu.

College of Visual and Performing Arts Students: 103 full-time (47 women), 57 part-time (35 women); includes 25 minority (3 Black or African American, non-Hispanic/Latino; 5 Asian, non-Hispanic/Latino; 11 Hispanic/Latino; 6 Two or more races, non-Hispanic/Latino), 31 international. Average age 30. 135 applicants, 68% accepted, 43 enrolled. *Faculty:* 85 full-time (27 women), 15 part-time/adjunct (4 women). Expenses: Contact institution. *Financial support:* Fellowships with full tuition reimbursements, research assistantships with full tuition reimbursements, teaching assistantships with full tuition reimbursements, career-related internships or fieldwork, Federal Work-Study, scholarships/grants, tuition waivers (full), and staff assistantships available. Support available to part-time students. Financial award applicants required to submit FAFSA. In 2018, 48 master's, 5 other advanced degrees awarded. *Program availability:* Part-time, evening/weekend. Offers art (MA, MFA, MS); music (MM, Performer's Certificate); theatre and dance (MFA); visual and performing arts (MA, MFA, MM, MS, Performer's Certificate). *Application deadline:* For fall admission, 5/1 for international students; for spring admission, 10/1 for international students. Applications are processed on a rolling basis. *Application fee:* $40. Electronic applications accepted. *Application Contact:* Graduate School Office, 815-753-0395, E-mail: gradsch@niu.edu. *Dean,* Dr. Paul Kassel, 815-753-1138, Fax: 815-753-8372, E-mail: pkassel@niu.edu.

NORTHERN KENTUCKY UNIVERSITY, Highland Heights, KY 41099

General Information State-supported, coed, comprehensive institution. CGS member. *Graduate housing:* Room and/or apartments available on a first-come, first-served basis to single students; on-campus housing not available to married students. Housing application deadline: 5/1.

GRADUATE UNITS

Chase College of Law Students: 283 full-time (147 women), 154 part-time (84 women); includes 48 minority (30 Black or African American, non-Hispanic/Latino; 6 Asian, non-Hispanic/Latino; 12 Hispanic/Latino). Average age 27. 542 applicants, 68% accepted, 140 enrolled. *Faculty:* 25 full-time (8 women), 37 part-time/adjunct (9 women). Expenses: Contact institution. *Financial support:* Fellowships, research assistantships, career-related internships or fieldwork, Federal Work-Study, scholarships/grants, and unspecified assistantships available. Support available to part-time students. Financial award application deadline: 3/1; financial award applicants required to submit FAFSA. In 2018, 93 doctorates awarded. *Program availability:* Part-time, evening/weekend. Offers law (JD). *Application deadline:* For fall admission, 4/1 priority date for domestic and international students; for summer admission, 3/15 priority date for domestic students, 3/15 for international students. Applications are processed on a rolling basis. *Application fee:* $40. Electronic applications accepted. *Application Contact:* Ashley Siemer, Director of Student Affairs and Enrollment Management, 859-572-5841, E-mail: graya4@nku.edu. *Dean,* Judith Daar.

Office of Graduate Programs *Program availability:* Part-time, evening/weekend, online learning. Electronic applications accepted.

College of Arts and Sciences *Program availability:* Part-time, evening/weekend, online learning. Offers arts and sciences (MA, MPA, MS, Certificate); composition and rhetoric (Certificate); creative writing (Certificate); cultural studies and discourses (Certificate); English (MA); industrial psychology (Certificate); industrial-organizational psychology (MS); integrative studies (MA); non-profit management (Certificate); occupational health psychology (Certificate); organizational psychology (Certificate); professional writing (Certificate); public administration (MPA); public history (MA). Electronic applications accepted.

College of Business *Program availability:* Part-time, evening/weekend. Offers accountancy (M Acc); advanced taxation (Certificate); business (M Acc, MBA, MS, Certificate); business administration (MBA, Certificate); executive leadership and organizational change (MS). Electronic applications accepted.

College of Education and Human Services Program availability: Part-time, evening/weekend. Offers clinical mental health counseling (MS); education (MA, Certificate); education and human services (MA, MAT, MS, MSW, Ed D, Certificate, Ed S); educational leadership (Ed D, Ed S); school counseling (MA); social work (MSW); special education (Certificate); teaching (MAT). Electronic applications accepted.

College of Informatics Program availability: Part-time, evening/weekend. Offers business informatics (MS, Certificate); communication (MA); communication teaching (Certificate); computer information technology (MSCIT); computer science (MSCS); corporate information security (Certificate); documentary studies (Certificate); enterprise resource planning (Certificate); geographic information systems (Certificate); health informatics (MS, Certificate); informatics (MA, MS, MSCIT, MSCS, Certificate); public relations (Certificate); relationships (Certificate); secure software engineering (Certificate). Electronic applications accepted.

School of Nursing and Health Professions Program availability: Part-time, evening/weekend, online learning. Offers health science (MS); nursing (MSHS, MSN, DNP, Certificate, Post-Master's Certificate); nursing and health professions (MS, MSHS, MSN, DNP, Certificate, Post-Master's Certificate). Electronic applications accepted.

NORTHERN MICHIGAN UNIVERSITY, Marquette, MI 49855-5301

General Information State-supported, coed, comprehensive institution. CGS member. *Graduate housing:* Rooms and/or apartments available on a first-come, first-served basis to single and married students. Housing application deadline: 7/15.

GRADUATE UNITS

Office of Graduate Education and Research Program availability: Part-time, evening/weekend, online learning. Electronic applications accepted.

College of Arts and Sciences Program availability: Part-time, online learning. Offers applied behavior analysis (MS); arts and sciences (MA, MFA, MS, Graduate Certificate); biology (MS); creative writing (MFA); integrated biosciences (MS); literature (MA); pedagogy (MA); psychological science (MS); teaching English to speakers of other languages (Graduate Certificate); theater (MA); writing (MA). Electronic applications accepted.

College of Business Program availability: Part-time. Offers business (MBA). Electronic applications accepted.

College of Health Sciences and Professional Studies Program availability: Part-time. Offers administration and supervision (MAE); clinical molecular genetics (MS); exercise science (MS); health sciences and professional studies (MA, MA Ed, MAE, MS, DNP); instruction (MAE); learning disabilities (MAE); nursing (DNP); postsecondary biology education (MS); reading education (MAE).

NORTHERN SEMINARY, Lombard, IL 60148-5698

General Information Independent-religious, coed, primarily men, graduate-only institution. *Graduate housing:* On-campus housing not available.

GRADUATE UNITS

Graduate and Professional Programs Program availability: Part-time, evening/weekend. Offers Biblical studies (M Div); Christian community development (MA, D Min); Christian ministry (MACM); contextual theology (D Min); missional church ministry (M Div); New Testament (M Div, MANT); New Testament context (D Min); Old Testament (M Div); preaching (D Min); theology (M Div); theology and mission (MA); urban leadership (MA); worship (M Div, MAW). Electronic applications accepted.

NORTHERN STATE UNIVERSITY, Aberdeen, SD 57401-7198

General Information State-supported, coed, comprehensive institution. *Graduate housing:* Room and/or apartments available on a first-come, first-served basis to single students; on-campus housing not available to married students. Housing application deadline: 8/1. *Research affiliation:* AASCU–Grants Resource Center.

GRADUATE UNITS

MME Program in Music Education Program availability: Part-time, online learning. Offers music education (MME). Electronic applications accepted.

MS Ed Program in Counseling Program availability: Part-time, online learning. Offers clinical mental health counseling (MS Ed); school counseling (MS Ed). Electronic applications accepted.

MS Ed Program in Educational Studies Program availability: Part-time, online learning. Offers educational studies (MS Ed). Electronic applications accepted.

MS Ed Program in Instructional Design in E-learning Program availability: Part-time, online learning. Offers instructional design in e-learning (MS Ed). Electronic applications accepted.

MS Ed Program in Leadership and Administration Program availability: Part-time, evening/weekend, online learning. Offers leadership and administration (MS Ed). Electronic applications accepted.

MS Ed Program in Sport Performance and Leadership Program availability: Part-time. Offers sport performance and leadership (MS Ed). Electronic applications accepted.

MS Ed Program in Teaching and Learning Program availability: Part-time, evening/weekend, online learning. Offers teaching and learning (MS Ed). Electronic applications accepted.

MS Program in Banking and Financial Services Program availability: Part-time, online learning. Offers banking and financial services (MS). Electronic applications accepted.

MS Program in Training and Development in E-learning Program availability: Part-time, online learning. Offers training and development in e-learning (MS). Electronic applications accepted.

NORTHERN VERMONT UNIVERSITY–JOHNSON, Johnson, VT 05656

General Information State-supported, coed, comprehensive institution. *Graduate housing:* Rooms and/or apartments available on a first-come, first-served basis to single and married students. Housing application deadline: 3/15.

GRADUATE UNITS

Program in Counseling Program availability: Part-time. Offers addictions counseling (MA); clinical mental health counseling (MA); general counseling (MA); school counseling (MA). Electronic applications accepted.

Program in Education Program availability: Part-time. Offers applied behavior analysis (MA Ed); curriculum and instruction (MA Ed); foundations of education (MA Ed); special education (MA Ed). Electronic applications accepted.

Program in Studio Arts Program availability: Part-time, online learning. Offers ceramics (MFA); digital media (MFA); drawing (MFA); painting (MFA); photography (MFA); printmaking (MFA); sculpture (MFA). Electronic applications accepted.

NORTHERN VERMONT UNIVERSITY–LYNDON, Lyndonville, VT 05851

General Information State-supported, coed, comprehensive institution. *Graduate housing:* On-campus housing not available.

GRADUATE UNITS

Graduate Programs in Education Program availability: Part-time, evening/weekend. Offers curriculum and instruction (M Ed); education (M Ed); natural sciences (MST); reading specialist (M Ed); science education (MST); special education (M Ed); teaching and counseling (M Ed).

NORTH GREENVILLE UNIVERSITY, Tigerville, SC 29688-1892

General Information Independent-religious, coed, comprehensive institution. *Graduate housing:* Room and/or apartments available on a first-come, first-served basis to single students; on-campus housing not available to married students. Housing application deadline: 8/1.

GRADUATE UNITS

T. Walter Brashier Graduate School Program availability: Part-time, evening/weekend, online learning. Offers Christian ministry (MCM, D Min); education (M Ed, MAT); financial planning (MBA); human resources (MBA). Electronic applications accepted.

NORTH PARK THEOLOGICAL SEMINARY, Chicago, IL 60625-4895

General Information Independent-religious, coed, graduate-only institution. *Enrollment by degree level:* 225 master's, 40 doctoral, 60 other advanced degrees. *Graduate faculty:* 17 full-time (4 women), 13 part-time/adjunct (3 women). *Graduate housing:* Rooms and/or apartments available on a first-come, first-served basis to single and married students. Housing application deadline: 9/1. *Student services:* Campus employment opportunities, campus safety program, career counseling, free psychological counseling, international student services, low-cost health insurance, multicultural affairs office, writing training. *Library facilities:* Brandel Library. Website: http://www.northpark.edu/sem/

General Application Contact: Baily Warman Manwatkar, Admission Counselor, 773-244-6229, E-mail: semadmissions@northpark.edu.

GRADUATE UNITS

Graduate and Professional Programs Program availability: Part-time. Offers adult ministry (Certificate); camping and retreat ministry (Certificate); children and family ministry (Certificate); Christian formation (MA); Christian ministry (MACM); faith and health (Certificate); intercultural studies (Certificate); justice ministry (Certificate); leadership and administration (Certificate); preaching (D Min); spiritual direction (Certificate); theological studies (MATS); theology (M Div); youth ministry (Certificate).

NORTH PARK UNIVERSITY, Chicago, IL 60625-4895

General Information Independent-religious, coed, comprehensive institution. *Graduate housing:* Rooms and/or apartments available to single and married students.

GRADUATE UNITS

School of Business and Nonprofit Management Program availability: Part-time, evening/weekend, online learning. Offers business and nonprofit management (MBA, MHEA, MHRM, MM, MNA).

School of Education Offers education (MA).

School of Music Offers vocal performance (MM).

School of Nursing and Health Sciences Program availability: Part-time, evening/weekend. Offers advanced practice nursing (MS); leadership and management (MS).

NORTHWEST CHRISTIAN UNIVERSITY, Eugene, OR 97401-3745

General Information Independent-religious, coed, comprehensive institution. *Graduate housing:* On-campus housing not available.

GRADUATE UNITS

School of Business and Management Program availability: Part-time, evening/weekend, online only, 100% online. Offers accounting (MBA); management (MBA). Electronic applications accepted.

School of Education and Counseling Program availability: Part-time, evening/weekend, online learning. Offers clinical mental health counseling (MA); elementary teaching (MAT); English for speakers of other languages (MAT); physical education (MAT); school counseling (MA); secondary teaching (MAT); special education (MAT). Electronic applications accepted.

NORTHWESTERN COLLEGE, Orange City, IA 51041-1996

General Information Independent-religious, coed, comprehensive institution.

GRADUATE UNITS

Program in Education Program availability: Online learning. Offers early childhood (M Ed); master teacher (M Ed); teacher leadership (M Ed, Graduate Certificate).

NORTHWESTERN HEALTH SCIENCES UNIVERSITY, Bloomington, MN 55431-1599

General Information Independent, coed, graduate-only institution. *Graduate housing:* On-campus housing not available. *Research affiliation:* University of Minnesota, Center for Spirituality and Healing (education research), University of Western States (clinical research), University of Pittsburgh (education research).

GRADUATE UNITS

College of Chiropractic Offers chiropractic (DC). Electronic applications accepted.

College of Health and Wellness Offers acupuncture (M Ac); applied clinical nutrition (MHS); Oriental medicine (MOM). Electronic applications accepted.

NORTHWESTERN OKLAHOMA STATE UNIVERSITY, Alva, OK 73717-2799

General Information State-supported, coed, comprehensive institution. *Graduate housing:* Room and/or apartments available to single students; on-campus housing not available to married students.

GRADUATE UNITS

Program in American Studies Program availability: Part-time. Offers American studies (MA).

School of Professional Studies Program availability: Part-time. Offers adult education management and administration (M Ed); counseling psychology (MCP); curriculum and instruction (M Ed); educational leadership (M Ed); elementary education (M Ed); reading specialist (M Ed); school counseling (M Ed); secondary education (M Ed).

NORTHWESTERN POLYTECHNIC UNIVERSITY, Fremont, CA 94539-7482

General Information Independent, coed, comprehensive institution. *Graduate housing:* Room and/or apartments available on a first-come, first-served basis to single students; on-campus housing not available to married students. Housing application deadline: 7/15.

GRADUATE UNITS

School of Business and Information Technology *Program availability:* Part-time, evening/weekend. Offers business and information technology (MBA, DBA).

School of Engineering *Program availability:* Part-time, evening/weekend. Offers computer engineering (DCE); computer science (MS); computer systems engineering (MS); electrical engineering (MS).

NORTHWESTERN STATE UNIVERSITY OF LOUISIANA, Natchitoches, LA 71497

General Information State-supported, coed, comprehensive institution. CGS member. *Graduate housing:* Room and/or apartments available on a first-come, first-served basis to single students; on-campus housing not available to married students. Housing application deadline: 3/1. *Research affiliation:* NASA (Strategic Defense Initiative), Central State Hospital, Federal Records and Archives Services.

GRADUATE UNITS

Graduate Studies and Research *Program availability:* Part-time, evening/weekend, online learning. Offers clinical psychology (MS); English (MA); health and human performance (MS); homeland security (MS). Electronic applications accepted.

College of Education and Human Development Offers adult and continuing education (MA); counseling (Ed S); curriculum and instruction (M Ed); early childhood education and teaching (M Ed, MAT); education and human development (M Ed, MA, MAT, Ed S); educational leadership (M Ed, Ed S); educational technology (Ed S); educational technology leadership (M Ed); elementary education (MAT); elementary teaching (Ed S); middle school education (MAT); reading (Ed S); school counseling (MA); secondary education (MAT); secondary teaching (Ed S); special education (Ed S); student affairs in higher education (MA). Electronic applications accepted.

College of Nursing and School of Allied Health *Program availability:* Part-time. Offers nursing and allied health (MS, MSN); radiologic sciences (MS). Electronic applications accepted.

School of Creative and Performing Arts Offers art (MA); fine and graphic arts (MA); music (MM). Electronic applications accepted.

NORTHWESTERN UNIVERSITY, Evanston, IL 60208

General Information Independent, coed, university. CGS member. *Graduate housing:* Rooms and/or apartments available on a first-come, first-served basis to single students and available to married students. Housing application deadline: 9/1. *Research affiliation:* Dow Chemical Company (materials science and engineering), E.I. du Pont de Nemours and Company (physics), Exxon Chemical Company (chemical engineering), Ford Motor Company (mechanical engineering), Medtronics, Inc. (cardiology), Amoco Oil Company (materials science and engineering).

GRADUATE UNITS

Feinberg School of Medicine Offers biostatistics (PhD); clinical investigation (MSCI); clinical psychology (PhD); epidemiology (PhD); health and biomedical informatics (PhD); health services and outcomes research (PhD); healthcare quality and patient safety (PhD); medicine (MS, MSCI, DPT, MD, PhD); neuroscience (PhD); physical therapy (DPT); public health (MPH); translational outcomes in science (PhD). Electronic applications accepted.

The Graduate School *Program availability:* Part-time, evening/weekend. Offers biochemistry (PhD); bioengineering and biotechnology (PhD); biotechnology (PhD); cell and molecular biology (PhD); clinical investigation (MSCI, Certificate); developmental and systems biology (PhD); gender and sexuality studies (Graduate Certificate); genetic counseling (MS); marital and family therapy (MS); nanotechnology (PhD); neurobiology (PhD); neuroscience (PhD); structural biology and biophysics (PhD). Electronic applications accepted.

Center for International and Comparative Studies Offers international and comparative studies (Certificate).

Judd A. and Marjorie Weinberg College of Arts and Sciences *Program availability:* Part-time, evening/weekend. Offers African American studies (PhD); African studies (Graduate Certificate); ancient philosophy (PhD); anthropology (PhD); applied physics (PhD); art history (PhD); arts and sciences (MA, MFA, MS, PhD, Graduate Certificate); brain, behavior and cognition (PhD); chemistry (PhD); clinical psychology (PhD); cognitive psychology (PhD); comparative literary studies (PhD); earth and planetary sciences (PhD); economics (PhD); English (MA, PhD); French/Francophone studies (PhD); German literature and critical thought (PhD); history (PhD); Italian studies (Graduate Certificate); linguistics (PhD); mathematics (PhD); neurobiology and physiology (MS); personality psychology (PhD); philosophy (PhD); physics and astronomy (PhD); plant biology and conservation (MA, PhD); political science (PhD); religious studies (PhD); Slavic languages and literature (PhD); social psychology (PhD); sociology (PhD); Spanish and Portuguese (PhD); statistics (MS, PhD); visual arts (MFA).

Kellogg School of Management *Program availability:* Part-time, evening/weekend. Offers accounting information and management (MBA, PhD); analytical finance (MBA); business administration (MBA); decision sciences (MBA); entrepreneurship and innovation (MBA); finance (PhD); health enterprise management (MBA); human resources management (MBA); international business (MBA); management (MBA, MS, PhD); management and organizations (MBA, PhD); management and organizations and sociology (PhD); management and strategy (PhD); management studies (MS); managerial analytics (MBA); managerial economics (MBA); managerial economics and decision sciences (PhD); managerial economics and strategy (PhD); marketing (MBA, PhD); marketing management (MBA); media management (MBA); operations management (MBA, PhD); real estate (MBA); social enterprise at Kellogg (MBA). PhD admissions and degree offered through The Graduate School. Electronic applications accepted.

School of Communication *Program availability:* Part-time. Offers audiology (Au D); communication (MA, MFA, MS, MSC, Au D, PhD); communication sciences and disorders (PhD); communication studies (PhD); directing (MFA); documentary media (MFA); leadership for creative enterprises (MS); managerial communication (MSC); media, technology and society (PhD); performance studies (MA, PhD); screen cultures (MA, PhD); speech, language, and learning (MS); stage design (MFA); technology and social behavior (PhD); theatre and drama (PhD); writing for the screen and stage (MFA). MA, MFA, and PhD admissions and degrees offered through The

Graduate School; MSC admissions and degrees offered through the School of Communication.

School of Education and Social Policy *Program availability:* Part-time, evening/weekend. Offers education (MS); elementary teaching (MS); human development and social policy (PhD); learning and organizational change (MS); learning sciences (MA, PhD); secondary teaching (MS); teacher leadership (MS). MA and PhD admissions and degrees offered through The Graduate School. Electronic applications accepted.

Henry and Leigh Bienen School of Music Offers brass performance (MM, DMA); composition (DMA); conducting (MM, DMA); jazz studies (MM); music education (MME, PhD); music theory (MM); music theory and cognition (PhD); musicology (MM, PhD); percussion performance (MM, DMA); performance (MM); piano pedagogy (MME); piano performance (MM, DMA); piano performance and collaborative arts (MM, DMA); piano performance and pedagogy (MM, DMA); string performance (MM, DMA); theory (MM); voice and opera performance (MM, DMA); woodwind performance (MM, DMA). PhD admissions and degree offered through The Graduate School. Electronic applications accepted.

McCormick School of Engineering and Applied Science *Program availability:* Part-time, evening/weekend. Offers analytics (MS); biomedical engineering (MS, PhD); biotechnology (MS); chemical engineering (MS, PhD); computer engineering (MS, PhD); computer science (MS, PhD); design innovation (MBA, MS); electrical engineering (MS, PhD); engineering and applied science (MBA, MEM, MIT, MME, MMM, MPD, MS, PhD, Certificate); engineering management (MEM); engineering sciences and applied mathematics (MS, PhD); environmental engineering and science (MS, PhD); geotechnical engineering (MS, PhD); industrial engineering and management science (MS, PhD); information technology (MS); integrated computational materials engineering (Certificate); materials science and engineering (MS, PhD); mechanical engineering (MS, PhD); mechanics of materials and solids (MS, PhD); product design and development management (MS); project management (MS); robotics (MS); structural engineering and materials (MS, PhD); theoretical and applied mechanics (MS, PhD); transportation systems analysis and planning (MS, PhD). MS and PhD admissions and degrees offered through The Graduate School. Electronic applications accepted.

Segal Design Institute Offers engineering design and innovation (MS).

Medill School of Journalism, Media, and Integrated Marketing Communications Offers brand strategy (MSIMC); content marketing (MSIMC); direct and interactive marketing (MSIMC); integrated marketing communications (MSIMC); interactive publishing (MSJ); magazine writing/editing (MSJ); marketing analytics (MSIMC); reporting (MSJ); strategic communications (MSIMC); video/broadcast (MSJ). Electronic applications accepted.

Pritzker School of Law *Program availability:* Part-time, online learning. Offers international human rights (LL M); law (MSL, JD); tax (LL M in Tax). Executive LL M programs offered in Madrid (Spain), Seoul (South Korea), and Tel Aviv (Israel). Electronic applications accepted.

School of Professional Studies Offers American literature (MA); American studies (MA); analytics and business intelligence (MS); British literature (MA); clinical research (MS); comparative and world literature (MA); computer-based data mining (MS); creative writing (MA, MFA); database and Internet technologies (MS); global health (MS); global policy (MA); health informatics (MS); health services policy (MA); healthcare compliance (MS); history (MA); information design and strategy (MS); information systems (MS); information systems management (MS); information systems security (MS); marketing analytics (MS); medical informatics (MS); predictive modeling (MS); public administration (MA); public policy (MA); quality systems (MS); religious and ethical studies (MA); risk analytics (MS); software project management and development (MS); sports administration (MA); Web analytics (MS).

NORTHWEST MISSOURI STATE UNIVERSITY, Maryville, MO 64468-6001

General Information State-supported, coed, comprehensive institution. *Enrollment:* 6,857 graduate, professional, and undergraduate students; 452 full-time matriculated graduate/professional students (251 women), 751 part-time matriculated graduate/professional students (469 women). *Enrollment by degree level:* 1,159 master's, 16 doctoral, 28 other advanced degrees. *Graduate faculty:* 150 full-time (52 women). *International tuition:* $9103 full-time. *Tuition, area resident:* Full-time $4551; part-time $252.86 per credit hour. *Tuition, state resident:* full-time $4551; part-time $252.86 per credit hour. *Tuition, nonresident:* full-time $9103; part-time $505.72 per credit hour. *Required fees:* $2668; $148.20 per credit hour. Tuition and fees vary according to program. *Graduate housing:* Rooms and/or apartments available on a first-come, first-served basis to single and married students. Typical cost: $6356 per year ($10,016 including board) for single students. Room and board charges vary according to board plan and housing facility selected. Housing application deadline: 6/1. *Student services:* Campus employment opportunities, campus safety program, career counseling, exercise/wellness program, free psychological counseling, international student services, low-cost health insurance, multicultural affairs office, services for students with disabilities, teacher training, writing training. *Library facilities:* Owens Library. *Collection:* Books: 165,794 (physical), 213,591 (digital/electronic). Weekly public service hours: 95; students can reserve study rooms.

Computer facilities: Computer purchase and lease plans are available. 260 computers available on campus for general student use. A campuswide network can be accessed from student residence rooms and from off campus. Online class registration, online courses with library and databases are available. Website: http://www.nwmissouri.edu/

General Application Contact: Dr. Gregory Haddock, Dean of Graduate School, 660-562-1145, Fax: 660-562-1096, E-mail: gradsch@nwmissouri.edu.

GRADUATE UNITS

Graduate School Students: 452 full-time (251 women), 751 part-time (469 women); includes 95 minority (43 Black or African American, non-Hispanic/Latino; 3 American Indian or Alaska Native, non-Hispanic/Latino; 9 Asian, non-Hispanic/Latino; 25 Hispanic/Latino; 1 Native Hawaiian or other Pacific Islander, non-Hispanic/Latino; 14 Two or more races, non-Hispanic/Latino), 261 international. Average age 31. 907 applicants, 76% accepted, 409 enrolled. *Faculty:* 150 full-time (52 women). Expenses: Contact institution. *Financial support:* Research assistantships with full tuition reimbursements, teaching assistantships with full tuition reimbursements, career-related internships or fieldwork, Federal Work-Study, institutionally sponsored loans, scholarships/grants, unspecified assistantships, and administrative assistantships, tutorial assistantships available. Financial award application deadline: 4/1; financial award applicants required to submit FAFSA. In 2018, 389 master's, 11 other advanced degrees awarded. *Program availability:* Part-time, evening/weekend. *Application deadline:* For fall admission, 7/1 for domestic and international students; for spring admission, 11/15 for domestic and international students. Applications are processed on a rolling basis. *Application fee:* $0 ($75 for international students). Electronic applications accepted. *Application Contact:* Cynthia Williams, Executive Secretary, 660-562-1144, Fax: 660-562-1096, E-mail: gradsch@nwmissouri.edu. *Dean,* Dr. Gregory Haddock, 660-562-1145, Fax: 660-562-1096, E-mail: gradsch@nwmissouri.edu.

College of Arts and Sciences Students: 15 full-time (9 women), 66 part-time (30 women); includes 6 minority (2 Black or African American, non-Hispanic/Latino; 1 American Indian or Alaska Native, non-Hispanic/Latino; 1 Hispanic/Latino; 2 Two or more races, non-Hispanic/Latino), 2 international. Average age 34. 32 applicants, 66% accepted, 19 enrolled. *Faculty:* 20 full-time (9 women). Expenses: Contact institution. *Financial support:* Research assistantships with full tuition reimbursements, teaching assistantships with full tuition reimbursements, and administrative assistantships, tutorial assistantships available. Financial award application deadline: 4/1; financial award applicants required to submit FAFSA. In 2018, 17 master's awarded. *Program availability:* Part-time. Offers biology (MS); elementary mathematics specialist (MS Ed); English (MA); English education (MS Ed); English pedagogy (MA); geographic information science (MS, Certificate); history (MS Ed); mathematics (MS); mathematics education (MS Ed); teaching: science (MS Ed). *Application deadline:* For fall admission, 7/1 for domestic and international students; for spring admission, 11/15 for domestic and international students. Applications are processed on a rolling basis. *Application fee:* $0 ($75 for international students). Electronic applications accepted. *Application Contact:* Dr. Michael Steiner, Dean, 660-562-1197. *Dean,* Dr. Michael Steiner, 660-562-1197.

Melvin and Valorie Booth College of Business and Professional Studies Students: 56 full-time (31 women), 220 part-time (126 women); includes 47 minority (23 Black or African American, non-Hispanic/Latino; 6 Asian, non-Hispanic/Latino; 10 Hispanic/Latino; 8 Two or more races, non-Hispanic/Latino), 15 international. Average age 32. 154 applicants, 75% accepted, 104 enrolled. *Faculty:* 24 full-time (12 women). Expenses: Contact institution. *Financial support:* Research assistantships with full tuition reimbursements, teaching assistantships with full tuition reimbursements, career-related internships or fieldwork, unspecified assistantships, and administrative assistantships, tutorial assistantships available. Financial award application deadline: 4/1; financial award applicants required to submit FAFSA. In 2018, 53 master's awarded. *Program availability:* Part-time. Offers agricultural economics (MBA); business decision and analytics (MBA); general management (MBA); human resource management (MBA); marketing (MBA). *Application deadline:* For fall admission, 7/1 for domestic and international students; for spring admission, 11/15 for domestic and international students; for summer admission, 4/1 for domestic and international students. Applications are processed on a rolling basis. *Application fee:* $0 ($50 for international students). Electronic applications accepted. *Application Contact:* Dr. Steve Ludwig, Director of the Melvin And Valorie Booth School of Business, 660-562-1749, Fax: 660-562-1096, E-mail: sludwig@nwmissouri.edu. *Director of the Melvin And Valorie Booth School of Business,* Dr. Steve Ludwig, 660-562-1749, Fax: 660-562-1096, E-mail: sludwig@nwmissouri.edu.

School of Agricultural Sciences Students: 9 full-time (7 women), 4 international. Average age 23. 8 applicants, 63% accepted, 4 enrolled. *Faculty:* 6 full-time (1 woman). Expenses: Contact institution. *Financial support:* Research assistantships with full tuition reimbursements, teaching assistantships with full tuition reimbursements, and unspecified assistantships available. Financial award application deadline: 4/1; financial award applicants required to submit FAFSA. In 2018, 1 master's awarded. *Program availability:* Part-time. Offers agricultural economics (MBA); agricultural education (MS Ed); agriculture (MS); teaching: agriculture (MS Ed). *Application deadline:* For fall admission, 7/1 for domestic and international students; for spring admission, 11/15 for domestic and international students. Applications are processed on a rolling basis. *Application fee:* $0 ($75 for international students). Electronic applications accepted. *Application Contact:* Rodney Barr, Director, 660-562-1620. *Director,* Rodney Barr, 660-562-1620.

School of Computer Science and Information Systems Students: 205 full-time (82 women), 36 part-time (14 women); includes 1 minority (Two or more races, non-Hispanic/Latino), 233 international. Average age 24. 459 applicants, 79% accepted, 116 enrolled. *Faculty:* 13 full-time (5 women). Expenses: Contact institution. *Financial support:* Research assistantships, teaching assistantships with full tuition reimbursements, and unspecified assistantships available. Financial award application deadline: 4/1; financial award applicants required to submit FAFSA. In 2018, 185 master's awarded. *Program availability:* Part-time. Offers applied computer science (MS); information systems (MS); instructional technology (MS). *Application deadline:* Applications are processed on a rolling basis. *Application fee:* $0 ($75 for international students). *Application Contact:* Dr. Gregory Haddock, Dean of Graduate School, 660-562-1145, Fax: 660-562-1096, E-mail: gradsch@nwmissouri.edu. *Director of School of Computer Science and Information Systems,* Dr. Douglas Hawley, 660-562-1200, Fax: 660-562-1963, E-mail: hawley@nwmissouri.edu.

School of Education Students: 109 full-time (87 women), 385 part-time (270 women); includes 30 minority (10 Black or African American, non-Hispanic/Latino; 2 American Indian or Alaska Native, non-Hispanic/Latino; 3 Asian, non-Hispanic/Latino; 12 Hispanic/Latino; 1 Native Hawaiian or other Pacific Islander, non-Hispanic/Latino; 2 Two or more races, non-Hispanic/Latino), 1 international. Average age 33. 210 applicants, 72% accepted, 142 enrolled. *Faculty:* 26 full-time (16 women). Expenses: Contact institution. *Financial support:* Research assistantships with full tuition reimbursements, teaching assistantships with full tuition reimbursements, and unspecified assistantships available. Financial award application deadline: 4/1; financial award applicants required to submit FAFSA. In 2018, 71 master's, 11 other advanced degrees awarded. *Program availability:* Part-time. Offers early childhood education (MS Ed); education leadership (MS Ed); educational leadership (Ed S); educational leadership and policy analysis (Ed D); elementary education (MS Ed); elementary mathematics (MS Ed); higher education leadership (MS); middle school education (MS Ed); reading (MS Ed); special education (MS Ed); teacher leadership (MS Ed); teaching English language learners (MS Ed). *Application deadline:* For fall admission, 7/1 for domestic and international students; for spring admission, 11/15 for domestic and international students. Applications are processed on a rolling basis. *Application fee:* $0 ($75 for international students). Electronic applications accepted. *Application Contact:* Dr. Tim Wall, Director, 660-562-1179, E-mail: timwall@nwmissouri.edu. *Director,* Dr. Tim Wall, 660-562-1179, E-mail: timwall@nwmissouri.edu.

School of Health Science and Wellness Students: 58 full-time (35 women), 27 part-time (17 women); includes 9 minority (7 Black or African American, non-Hispanic/Latino; 1 Hispanic/Latino; 1 Two or more races, non-Hispanic/Latino), 6 international. Average age 26. 50 applicants, 74% accepted, 23 enrolled. *Faculty:* 15 full-time (7 women). Expenses: Contact institution. *Financial support:* Teaching assistantships with full tuition reimbursements and unspecified assistantships available. Financial award application deadline: 4/1; financial award applicants required to submit FAFSA. In 2018, 54 master's awarded. *Program availability:* Part-

time. Offers applied health and sport sciences (MS); guidance and counseling (MS Ed); health and physical education (MS Ed); recreation (MS); sport and exercise psychology (MS). *Application deadline:* For fall admission, 7/1 for domestic and international students; for spring admission, 11/15 for domestic and international students. Applications are processed on a rolling basis. *Application fee:* $0 ($75 for international students). *Application Contact:* Gina Smith, Office Manager, 660-562-1297, Fax: 660-562-1963, E-mail: smigina@nwmissouri.edu. *Director, School of Health Science and Wellness,* Dr. Terry Long, 660-562-1706, Fax: 660-562-1483, E-mail: tlong@nwmissouri.edu.

NORTHWEST NAZARENE UNIVERSITY, Nampa, ID 83686-5897

General Information Independent-religious, coed, comprehensive institution. *Enrollment:* 541 full-time matriculated graduate/professional students (354 women), 187 part-time matriculated graduate/professional students (97 women). *Enrollment by degree level:* 690 master's, 36 doctoral. *Graduate faculty:* 20 full-time (13 women), 117 part-time/adjunct (57 women). *Tuition:* Full-time $6744; part-time $3372 per credit. *Required fees:* $190; $190 per unit. $95 per semester. Tuition and fees vary according to course load, degree level and program. *Graduate housing:* On-campus housing not available. *Student services:* Career counseling, free psychological counseling, multicultural affairs office, services for students with disabilities, teacher training, writing training. *Library facilities:* John E. Riley Library.

Computer facilities: Computer purchase and lease plans are available. A campuswide network can be accessed from student residence rooms. Online class registration is available.
Website: http://www.nnu.edu/

General Application Contact: Dr. Paula Kellerer, Dean, College of Adult and Graduate Studies, 208-467-8729, Fax: 208-467-8252, E-mail: pkellerer@nnu.edu.

GRADUATE UNITS

Graduate Business Programs Students: 45 full-time (24 women), 26 part-time (15 women). Average age 34. 26 applicants, 62% accepted, 11 enrolled. *Faculty:* 7 full-time (2 women), 8 part-time/adjunct (3 women). Expenses: Contact institution. *Financial support:* In 2018–19, 129,205 students received support. Scholarships/grants available. Financial award applicants required to submit FAFSA. In 2018, 32 master's awarded. *Program availability:* Part-time, evening/weekend, 100% online, blended/hybrid learning, 100% Face-to-face. Offers business administration (MBA). *Application deadline:* Applications are processed on a rolling basis. *Application fee:* $50. Electronic applications accepted. *Application Contact:* Melinda Siems, Program Coordinator, 208-467-8100, Fax: 208-467-8440, E-mail: mba@nnu.edu. *Director of Graduate Studies,* Dr. Joshua Jensen, 208-467-8852, Fax: 208-467-8440, E-mail: mba@nnu.edu.

Graduate Education Program Students: 128 full-time (83 women), 59 part-time (37 women); includes 22 minority (3 Black or African American, non-Hispanic/Latino; 1 Asian, non-Hispanic/Latino; 3 Hispanic/Latino; 15 Two or more races, non-Hispanic/Latino), 1 international. Average age 44. 124 applicants, 84% accepted, 87 enrolled. *Faculty:* 4 full-time (3 women), 18 part-time/adjunct (7 women). Expenses: Contact institution. *Financial support:* Application deadline: 1/15; applicants required to submit FAFSA. In 2018, 37 master's, 18 doctorates, 28 other advanced degrees awarded. *Program availability:* Part-time, online only, 100% online, 2-week face-to-face residency (for doctoral programs). Offers curriculum and instruction (M Ed); educational leadership (M Ed, Ed D, PhD, Ed S). *Application deadline:* Applications are processed on a rolling basis. *Application fee:* $50. Electronic applications accepted. *Application Contact:* Charlene Brown, Admissions Counselor, 208-467-8492, Fax: 208-467-8384, E-mail: gradeducationinfo@nnu.edu. *Chair,* Dr. Heidi Curtis, 208-467-8250, E-mail: hlcurtis@nnu.edu.

NNU Graduate School of Theology Students: 82 full-time (38 women); includes 12 minority (6 Black or African American, non-Hispanic/Latino; 1 American Indian or Alaska Native, non-Hispanic/Latino; 3 Hispanic/Latino; 2 Native Hawaiian or other Pacific Islander, non-Hispanic/Latino). Average age 40. 43 applicants, 74% accepted, 23 enrolled. *Faculty:* 10 full-time (3 women), 16 part-time/adjunct. Expenses: Contact institution. *Financial support:* In 2018–19, 67 students received support. Scholarships/grants available. Financial award applicants required to submit FAFSA. In 2018, 22 master's awarded. *Program availability:* Part-time, online only, 100% online. Offers leadership and formation (MA); missional leadership (M Div); pastoral ministry (MA); spiritual formation (M Div); youth, children, and family ministry (M Div). *Application deadline:* For fall admission, 7/31 for domestic students, 7/1 for international students; for spring admission, 2/1 for domestic students, 1/5 for international students. Applications are processed on a rolling basis. *Application fee:* $50. Electronic applications accepted. *Application Contact:* Vicki Funk, Program Coordinator, 208-467-8432, Fax: 208-467-8252, E-mail: vlfunk@nnu.edu. *Director, Graduate Studies,* Dr. Jay Akkerman, 208-467-8437, Fax: 208-467-8252.

Program in Counselor Education Average age 35. 47 applicants, 66% accepted, 25 enrolled. *Faculty:* 5 full-time (3 women), 28 part-time/adjunct (15 women). Expenses: Contact institution. *Financial support:* Applicants required to submit FAFSA. In 2018, 49 master's awarded. *Program availability:* Part-time, evening/weekend. Offers clinical counseling (MS); marriage and family counseling (MS); school counseling (MS). *Application deadline:* For fall admission, 2/15 for domestic and international students; for spring admission, 9/15 for domestic and international students. *Application fee:* $50. Electronic applications accepted. *Application Contact:* Christy Gilliam, Graduate Admissions Counselor, 208-467-8853, E-mail: cgilliam@nnu.edu. *Chair,* Dr. Lori Fairgrieve, 208-467-8343.

Program in Nursing Students: 38 full-time (32 women); includes 4 minority (1 Black or African American, non-Hispanic/Latino; 3 Two or more races, non-Hispanic/Latino). Average age 38. 124 applicants, 40% accepted, 42 enrolled. *Faculty:* 2 full-time (both women), 11 part-time/adjunct (10 women). Expenses: Contact institution. *Financial support:* Health care benefits available. Financial award application deadline: 2/1; financial award applicants required to submit FAFSA. In 2018, 26 master's awarded. *Program availability:* Part-time, evening/weekend, online only, 100% online, And Residential LABS for FNP. Offers leadership/education (MSN). *Application deadline:* For fall admission, 5/15 for domestic and international students; for spring admission, 9/1 for domestic and international students. *Application fee:* $0. Electronic applications accepted. *Application Contact:* Sandy Blom, Graduate Nursing Coordinator, 208-467-8642, Fax: 208-467-8651, E-mail: sblom@nnu.edu. *Director,* Dr. Leonie Sutherland, 208-467-8679, E-mail: lsutherland@nnu.edu.

Program in Social Work *Program availability:* Part-time-only, evening/weekend. Offers clinical mental health and addictions practice (MSW). Electronic applications accepted.

NORTHWEST UNIVERSITY, Kirkland, WA 98033

General Information Independent-religious, coed, comprehensive institution. *Graduate housing:* Rooms and/or apartments available on a first-come, first-served basis to single and married students.

GRADUATE UNITS

College of Business *Program availability:* Part-time, evening/weekend. Offers business administration (MBA); international business (MBA); project management (MBA); social entrepreneurship (MBA). Electronic applications accepted.

College of Ministry *Program availability:* Part-time, evening/weekend, online learning. Offers ministry (MIM); missional leadership (MA); theology and culture (MA). Electronic applications accepted.

College of Social and Behavioral Sciences *Program availability:* Evening/weekend. Offers counseling psychology (MA, Psy D); international community development (MA).

School of Education *Program availability:* Part-time, evening/weekend. Offers education (M Ed); teaching (MIT). Electronic applications accepted.

NORTHWOOD UNIVERSITY, MICHIGAN CAMPUS, Midland, MI 48640-2398

General Information Independent, coed, comprehensive institution. *Enrollment:* 1,594 graduate, professional, and undergraduate students; 41 full-time matriculated graduate/professional students (19 women), 314 part-time matriculated graduate/professional students (164 women). *Enrollment by degree level:* 355 master's. *Graduate faculty:* 3 full-time (0 women), 43 part-time/adjunct (12 women). *Tuition:* Full-time $37,080; part-time $18,540 per year. Tuition and fees vary according to course load and program. *Graduate housing:* Rooms and/or apartments guaranteed to single and married students. Typical cost: $5460 per year ($8810 including board) for single students; $10,920 per year ($17,620 including board) for married students. Room and board charges vary according to board plan and housing facility selected. Housing application deadline: 8/20. *Student services:* Campus employment opportunities, campus safety program, career counseling, exercise/wellness program, free psychological counseling, international student services, low-cost health insurance, multicultural affairs office, services for students with disabilities. *Library facilities:* Strosacker Library. *Collection:* Books: 30,504 (physical); Databases: 26. Weekly public service hours: 89; students can reserve study rooms.

Computer facilities: 215 computers available on campus for general student use. A campuswide network can be accessed from student residence rooms and from off campus. Online class registration is available. Website: http://www.northwood.edu/

General Application Contact: Lucille Pagan, Director of Admissions, Devos, 989-837-4893, Fax: 989-837-4800, E-mail: DeVos@northwood.edu.

GRADUATE UNITS

DeVos Graduate School Students: 44 full-time (21 women), 267 part-time (98 women); includes 34 minority (22 Black or African American, non-Hispanic/Latino; 1 American Indian or Alaska Native, non-Hispanic/Latino; 7 Asian, non-Hispanic/Latino; 4 Hispanic/Latino), 53 international. Average age 32. 127 applicants, 71% accepted, 84 enrolled. *Faculty:* 6 full-time (1 woman), 8 part-time/adjunct (2 women). *Expenses:* Contact institution. *Financial support:* In 2018–19, 130 students received support. Federal Work-Study and scholarships/grants available. Support available to part-time students. Financial award application deadline: 6/30; financial award applicants required to submit FAFSA. In 2018, 127 master's awarded. *Program availability:* Part-time, evening/weekend, online learning. Offers management (MBA, MSOL). MBA also offered on Florida and Texas campuses; MSOL offered online only. *Application deadline:* For fall admission, 7/1 priority date for domestic and international students; for winter admission, 12/1 priority date for domestic students. Applications are processed on a rolling basis. *Application fee:* $50. Electronic applications accepted. *Application Contact:* Matt Bennett, Director of Enrollment, 989-837-4178, Fax: 989-837-4800, E-mail: mba@northwood.edu. *Dean and Chief Operating Officer,* Dr. William T Busby, 989-837-4488, Fax: 989-837-4800, E-mail: busby@northwood.edu.

NORWICH UNIVERSITY, Northfield, VT 05663

General Information Independent, coed, comprehensive institution.

GRADUATE UNITS

College of Graduate and Continuing Studies *Program availability:* Evening/weekend, online only, mostly all online with a week-long residency requirement. Offers construction management (MBA, MCE); criminal justice (MS); criminal justice and public safety (MPA); diplomacy (MA); energy management (MBA); environmental (MCE); executive leadership (MS); finance (MBA); fiscal management (MPA); geotechnical (MCE); history (MA); information security and assurance (MS); international development and influence (MPA); international relations (MA); leadership (MS); logistics (MBA); military history (MA); municipal governance (MPA); nonprofit management (MPA); nursing administration (MSN); nursing education (MSN); organizational leadership (MBA); policy analysis and analytics (MPA); project management (MBA); public administration leadership and crisis management (MPA); public works and sustainability (MPA); structural (MCE); supply chain management (MBA). Electronic applications accepted.

NOTRE DAME COLLEGE, South Euclid, OH 44121-4293

General Information Independent-religious, coed, comprehensive institution. *Graduate housing:* On-campus housing not available.

GRADUATE UNITS

Graduate Programs *Program availability:* Part-time, evening/weekend. Offers mild/moderate needs (M Ed); reading (M Ed); security policy studies (MA, Graduate Certificate); technology (M Ed).

NOTRE DAME DE NAMUR UNIVERSITY, Belmont, CA 94002-1908

General Information Independent-religious, coed, comprehensive institution. *Enrollment:* 146 full-time matriculated graduate/professional students (121 women), 298 part-time matriculated graduate/professional students (218 women). *Enrollment by degree level:* 18 doctoral. *Graduate faculty:* 26 full-time (16 women), 48 part-time/adjunct (34 women). *Tuition:* Full-time $16,596; part-time $11,064 per semester. *Required fees:* $130; $130 per unit. $65 per semester. Tuition and fees vary according to program. *Graduate housing:* On-campus housing not available. *Student services:* Campus employment opportunities, campus safety program, career counseling, free psychological counseling, international student services, low-cost health insurance, multicultural affairs office, services for students with disabilities, teacher training, writing training. *Library facilities:* The Carl Gellert and Celia Berta Gellert Library plus 1 other. *Collection:* Books: 88,990 (physical), 194,534 (digital/electronic); Databases: 50.

Computer facilities: 100 computers available on campus for general student use. A campuswide network can be accessed from student residence rooms and from off campus. Online class registration is available. Website: http://www.ndnu.edu/

General Application Contact: Kenia Salgado Villareal, Assistant Director of Admissions Operations, 650-508-3600, Fax: 650-508-3426, E-mail: ksalgadovillarreal@ndnu.edu.

GRADUATE UNITS

Division of Academic Affairs *Program availability:* Part-time, evening/weekend, online learning. Electronic applications accepted.

School of Business and Management *Program availability:* Part-time, online learning. Offers business and management (MBA, MPA); finance (MBA); public administration (MPA). Electronic applications accepted.

School of Education and Psychology *Program availability:* Part-time, evening/weekend. Offers art therapy (MA); art therapy psychology (PhD); clinical psychology (MS); clinical psychology: marital and family therapy (MS); curriculum and instruction (MA); disciplinary studies (MA); education and psychology (MA, MS, PhD); school administration (MA); special education (MA). Electronic applications accepted.

NOTRE DAME OF MARYLAND UNIVERSITY, Baltimore, MD 21210-2476

General Information Independent-religious, coed, primarily women, comprehensive institution. *Graduate housing:* On-campus housing not available.

GRADUATE UNITS

Graduate Studies *Program availability:* Part-time, evening/weekend. Offers contemporary communication (MA); instructional leadership for changing populations (PhD); leadership in teaching (MA); liberal studies (MA); management (MA); nonprofit management (MA); pharmacy (Pharm D); teaching (MA); teaching English to speakers of other languages (MA). Electronic applications accepted.

NOTRE DAME SEMINARY, New Orleans, LA 70118-4391

General Information Independent-religious, coed, primarily men, graduate-only institution. *Graduate housing:* Room and/or apartments guaranteed to single students; on-campus housing not available to married students. Housing application deadline: 7/31.

GRADUATE UNITS

Graduate School of Theology *Program availability:* Part-time. Offers theology (M Div, MA).

NOVA SOUTHEASTERN UNIVERSITY, Fort Lauderdale, FL 33314-7796

General Information Independent, coed, university. *Graduate housing:* Rooms and/or apartments available on a first-come, first-served basis to single and married students.

GRADUATE UNITS

Abraham S. Fischler College of Education *Program availability:* Part-time, evening/weekend, 100% online, blended/hybrid learning. Offers education (MS, Ed D, PhD, Ed S); instructional technology and distance education (MS); teaching and learning (MA). Electronic applications accepted.

College of Arts, Humanities, and Social Sciences *Program availability:* Part-time, evening/weekend, 100% online, blended/hybrid learning. Offers advanced conflict resolution practice (Graduate Certificate); child protection (MHS); college student affairs (MS); conflict analysis and resolution (MS, PhD); criminal justice (MS, PhD); cross-disciplinary studies (MA); developmental disabilities (MS); family studies (Graduate Certificate); family systems health care (Graduate Certificate); family therapy (MS, PhD); marriage and family therapy (DMFT); peace studies (Graduate Certificate); qualitative research (Graduate Certificate); solution focused coaching (Graduate Certificate). Electronic applications accepted.

College of Dental Medicine Offers dental medicine (DMD); dentistry (MS). Electronic applications accepted.

College of Engineering and Computing *Program availability:* Part-time, evening/weekend, blended/hybrid learning. Offers computer science (MS, PhD); information assurance (PhD); information assurance and cybersecurity (MS); information systems (PhD); information technology (MS); management information systems (MS). Electronic applications accepted.

College of Medical Sciences Offers biomedical sciences (MBS).

College of Optometry *Program availability:* Online learning. Offers optometry (MS, OD). Electronic applications accepted.

College of Pharmacy Offers pharmaceutical affairs (MS); pharmaceutical sciences (MS, PhD); pharmacy (Pharm D). Electronic applications accepted.

College of Psychology *Program availability:* 100% online, blended/hybrid learning. Offers clinical mental health counseling (MS); clinical psychology (PhD, Psy D); counseling (MS); experimental psychology (MS); forensic psychology (MS); general psychology (MS); school counseling (MS); school psychology (Psy D, Psy S); substance abuse counseling (MS); substance abuse counseling and education (MS). Electronic applications accepted.

Dr. Kiran C. Patel College of Allopathic Medicine Offers allopathic medicine (MD).

Dr. Kiran C. Patel College of Osteopathic Medicine Offers biomedical informatics (MS, Graduate Certificate); disaster and emergency management (MS); medical education (MS); nutrition (MS, Graduate Certificate); osteopathic medicine (DO); public health (MPH, Graduate Certificate); social medicine (Graduate Certificate). Electronic applications accepted.

Dr. Pallavi Patel College of Health Care Sciences Offers anesthesiologist assistant (MSA); audiology (Au D); health science (MH Sc, DHSc, PhD); occupational therapy (MOT, Dr OT, PhD); physical therapy (DPT, TDPT); physician assistant (MMS); speech-language pathology (MS). Electronic applications accepted.

Halmos College of Natural Sciences and Oceanography *Program availability:* Part-time, evening/weekend, blended/hybrid learning. Offers biological sciences (MS); marine biology and oceanography (PhD). Electronic applications accepted.

H. Wayne Huizenga College of Business and Entrepreneurship *Program availability:* Part-time, evening/weekend, 100% online, blended/hybrid learning. Offers accounting (M Acc); business (MBA); business intelligence/analytics (MBA); complex health systems (MBA); enterprise informatics (MBA); entrepreneurship (MBA); finance (MBA); human resource management (MBA); international business (MBA); management (MBA); marketing (MBA); process improvement (MBA); public administration (MPA); real estate development (MS); sport revenue generation (MBA); supply chain management (MBA). Electronic applications accepted.

Ron and Kathy Assaf College of Nursing *Program availability:* Part-time, evening/weekend, 100% online, blended/hybrid learning, annual one-week summer institute delivered face-to-face on main campus. Offers advanced practice registered nurse (MSN); executive nurse leadership (MSN); nursing (PhD); nursing education (MSN); nursing informatics (MSN); nursing practice (DNP). Electronic applications accepted.

Shepard Broad College of Law *Program availability:* Part-time, evening/weekend, 100% online, blended/hybrid learning. Offers education law (MS); employment law (MS); health law (MS, JD); international law (JD); law and policy (MS). Electronic applications accepted.

NSCAD UNIVERSITY, Halifax, NS B3J 3J6, Canada

General Information Province-supported, coed, comprehensive institution. *Graduate housing:* On-campus housing not available.

GRADUATE UNITS

Program in Fine Arts Offers craft (MFA); design (M Des); fine and media arts (MFA).

NYACK COLLEGE, Nyack, NY 10960

General Information Independent-religious, coed, comprehensive institution. *Enrollment:* 433 full-time matriculated graduate/professional students (247 women), 575 part-time matriculated graduate/professional students (331 women). *Enrollment by degree level:* 933 master's, 75 doctoral. *Graduate faculty:* 23 full-time (11 women), 46 part-time/adjunct (16 women). *Graduate housing:* Rooms and/or apartments available on a first-come, first-served basis to single and married students. Housing application deadline: 9/1. *Student services:* Campus employment opportunities, career counseling, free psychological counseling, international student services, services for students with disabilities, writing training. *Library facilities:* Bailey Library plus 3 others.

Computer facilities: A campuswide network can be accessed. Online class registration is available.
Website: http://www.nyack.edu/

GRADUATE UNITS

Alliance Graduate School of Counseling Students: 74 full-time (60 women), 134 part-time (107 women); includes 172 minority (68 Black or African American, non-Hispanic/Latino; 1 American Indian or Alaska Native, non-Hispanic/Latino; 46 Asian, non-Hispanic/Latino; 50 Hispanic/Latino; 7 Two or more races, non-Hispanic/Latino), 7 international. Average age 37. Expenses: Contact institution. *Financial support:* Career-related internships or fieldwork and scholarships/grants available. Financial award applicants required to submit FAFSA. In 2018, 62 master's awarded. *Program availability:* Part-time, evening/weekend, 100% online. Offers marriage and family therapy (MA); mental health counseling (MA). *Application deadline:* For fall admission, 8/1 for domestic students, 2/15 for international students; for spring admission, 12/15 for domestic students, 7/15 for international students. Applications are processed on a rolling basis. *Application fee:* $30. Electronic applications accepted. *Application Contact:* Chastity Crespo, Admissions Associate, 646-378-6199, E-mail: admissions.grad@nyack.edu. *Director,* Dr. Antoinette Gines-Rivera, 646-378-6160.

Alliance Theological Seminary Students: 250 full-time (103 women), 366 part-time (168 women); includes 468 minority (153 Black or African American, non-Hispanic/Latino; 2 American Indian or Alaska Native, non-Hispanic/Latino; 106 Asian, non-Hispanic/Latino; 194 Hispanic/Latino; 2 Native Hawaiian or other Pacific Islander, non-Hispanic/Latino; 11 Two or more races, non-Hispanic/Latino), 44 international. Average age 43. Expenses: Contact institution. *Financial support:* Career-related internships or fieldwork, Federal Work-Study, and scholarships/grants available. Financial award applicants required to submit FAFSA. In 2018, 107 master's, 21 doctorates awarded. *Program availability:* Part-time, evening/weekend, 100% online, blended/hybrid learning. Offers Biblical literature (MA); Biblical studies (MA); Christian ministry (MPS); intercultural studies (MA); ministry (D Min); theology and missions (M Div); urban ministry (MPS). *Application deadline:* Applications are processed on a rolling basis. *Application fee:* $30. Electronic applications accepted. *Application Contact:* Jennifer Reimer, Associate Director of Admissions, 845-770-5709, E-mail: admissions.grad@nyack.edu. *Dean,* Dr. Ronald Walborn, 845-770-5715, Fax: 845-358-1663.

College of Bible and Christian Ministry Students: 5 part-time (1 woman); includes 2 minority (both Black or African American, non-Hispanic/Latino). Average age 47. Expenses: Contact institution. *Financial support:* Applicants required to submit FAFSA. In 2018, 1 master's awarded. *Program availability:* Part-time, evening/weekend, 100% online, blended/hybrid learning. Offers ancient Judaism and Christian origins (MA). *Application deadline:* Applications are processed on a rolling basis. *Application fee:* $30. Electronic applications accepted. *Application Contact:* Dr. Steven Notley, Director, 646-378-6148, E-mail: steven.notley@nyack.edu. *Director,* Dr. Steven Notley, 646-378-6148, E-mail: steven.notley@nyack.edu.

School of Business and Leadership Students: 31 full-time (18 women), 10 part-time (6 women); includes 32 minority (20 Black or African American, non-Hispanic/Latino; 1 Asian, non-Hispanic/Latino; 10 Hispanic/Latino; 1 Two or more races, non-Hispanic/Latino), 4 international. Average age 37. Expenses: Contact institution. *Financial support:* Scholarships/grants available. Financial award applicants required to submit FAFSA. In 2018, 26 master's awarded. *Program availability:* Part-time, evening/weekend, 100% online, blended/hybrid learning. Offers business administration (MBA); organizational leadership (MS). *Application deadline:* Applications are processed on a rolling basis. *Application fee:* $50. Electronic applications accepted. *Application Contact:* Dr. Anita Underwood, Dean, 845-675-4511. *Dean,* Dr. Anita Underwood, 845-675-4511.

School of Education Students: 28 full-time (24 women), 22 part-time (19 women); includes 21 minority (10 Black or African American, non-Hispanic/Latino; 1 American Indian or Alaska Native, non-Hispanic/Latino; 3 Asian, non-Hispanic/Latino; 6 Hispanic/Latino; 1 Two or more races, non-Hispanic/Latino), 4 international. Average age 32. Expenses: Contact institution. *Financial support:* Scholarships/grants available. Financial award applicants required to submit FAFSA. In 2018, 17 master's awarded. *Program availability:* Part-time, evening/weekend, 100% online, blended/hybrid learning. Offers childhood education (MS); childhood special education (MS); TESOL (MAT, MS). *Application deadline:* Applications are processed on a rolling basis. *Application fee:* $30. Electronic applications accepted. *Application Contact:* Dr. JoAnn Looney, Dean, 845-675-4538. *Dean,* Dr. JoAnn Looney, 845-675-4538.

School of Social Work Students: 50 full-time (42 women), 38 part-time (30 women); includes 78 minority (48 Black or African American, non-Hispanic/Latino; 5 Asian, non-Hispanic/Latino; 25 Hispanic/Latino), 2 international. Average age 35. Expenses: Contact institution. *Financial support:* Scholarships/grants available. Financial award applicants required to submit FAFSA. In 2018, 26 master's awarded. *Program availability:* Part-time, evening/weekend. Offers clinical social work practice (MSW); leadership in organizations and communities (MSW). *Application deadline:* Applications are processed on a rolling basis. *Application fee:* $45. Electronic applications accepted. *Application Contact:* Dr. Janet Furness, Director of MSW Program, 646-378-6169. *Director of MSW Program,* Dr. Janet Furness, 646-378-6169.

OAKLAND CITY UNIVERSITY, Oakland City, IN 47660-1099

General Information Independent-religious, coed, comprehensive institution. *Graduate housing:* Rooms and/or apartments guaranteed to single students and available on a first-come, first-served basis to married students. Housing application deadline: 7/1.

GRADUATE UNITS

Chapman Seminary *Program availability:* Part-time. Offers ministry (M Div); pastoral care (M Div); theology (D Min).

School of Business *Program availability:* Part-time, evening/weekend. Offers business administration (MBA); strategic management (MS).

School of Education Offers building level administration (MS Ed); curriculum and instruction (MS Ed, Ed D); education (MS Ed); elementary education (MAT); organizational management (Ed D); secondary education (MAT); superintendency (Ed D).

OAKLAND UNIVERSITY, Rochester, MI 48309-4401

General Information State-supported, coed, university. CGS member. *Graduate housing:* Rooms and/or apartments available on a first-come, first-served basis to single and married students. Housing application deadline: 9/1. *Research affiliation:* Beaumont Hospital Corporation (eye research, nursing), Henry Ford Health Systems (medical physics, health sciences).

GRADUATE UNITS

Graduate Study and Lifelong Learning *Program availability:* Part-time. Electronic applications accepted.

College of Arts and Sciences *Program availability:* Part-time, evening/weekend. Offers applied mathematical sciences (PhD); applied statistics (MS); arts and sciences (MA, MM, MPA, MS, PhD, Certificate, Graduate Certificate, PMC); biological and biomedical sciences (PhD); biology (MA, MS); biomedical sciences (PhD, Graduate Certificate); chemistry (MS); English (MA); history (MA); industrial applied mathematics (MS); liberal studies (MA); linguistics (MA); local government management (Graduate Certificate); mathematical statistics (MS); mathematics (MA); medical physics (PhD); non-profit and organizational management (PMC); physics (MS); public administration (MPA); statistical methods (Certificate); teaching English as a second language (Certificate). Electronic applications accepted.

School of Business Administration *Program availability:* Part-time, evening/weekend. Offers accounting (M Acc, Certificate); business administration (EMBA, M Acc, MBA, MS, Certificate); economics (MBA, Certificate); entrepreneurship (Certificate); finance (Certificate); general management (Certificate); human resource management (Certificate); information technology management (MS); international business (Certificate); management and marketing (EMBA); management information systems (Certificate); marketing (Certificate); production and operations management (Certificate). Electronic applications accepted.

School of Education and Human Services *Program availability:* Part-time, evening/weekend. Offers advanced microcomputer applications (Graduate Certificate); applied behavior analysis (Graduate Certificate); autism spectrum disorder (Graduate Certificate); counseling (MA, PhD, Certificate); digital literacies and learning (Graduate Certificate); early childhood education (M Ed, PhD, Ed S); early education and intervention (Ed S); education and human services (M Ed, MA, MAT, PhD, Certificate, Ed S, Graduate Certificate, PMC); educational leadership (M Ed, PhD); educational studies (M Ed); elementary education (MAT); emotional impairment (Graduate Certificate); higher education (PhD); microcomputer applications (Graduate Certificate); reading and language arts (MAT); reading education (PhD); reading, language arts and literature (PMC); school administration (Ed S); secondary education (MAT); special education (M Ed, Graduate Certificate); specific learning disabilities (Graduate Certificate); teaching and learning (Graduate Certificate). Electronic applications accepted.

School of Engineering and Computer Science *Program availability:* Part-time, evening/weekend. Offers computer science (MS); computer science and informatics (PhD); electrical and computer engineering (MS, PhD); embedded systems (MS); engineering and computer science (MS, PhD, Graduate Certificate); engineering management (MS); industrial and systems engineering (MS); mechanical engineering (MS, PhD); mechatronics (MS); productivity improvement (Graduate Certificate); software engineering and information technology (MS); systems engineering (PhD). Electronic applications accepted.

School of Health Sciences Offers clinical exercise science (Dr Sc PT); complementary medicine and wellness (Dr Sc PT); corporate worksite wellness (Dr Sc PT); exercise science (Dr Sc PT); health sciences (MS, DPT, Dr Sc PT, TDPT, Graduate Certificate); neurological rehabilitation (Dr Sc PT, TDPT); orthopedic manual physical therapy (Dr Sc PT, TDPT, Graduate Certificate); orthopedic physical therapy (Graduate Certificate); orthopedics (Dr Sc PT, TDPT); pediatric rehabilitation (Dr Sc PT, TDPT); physical therapy (DPT); public health (MPH); safety management (MS); teaching and learning for rehabilitation professionals (Dr Sc PT, TDPT). Electronic applications accepted.

School of Nursing *Program availability:* Part-time, evening/weekend. Offers adult gerontological nurse practitioner (MSN, PMC); family nurse practitioner (MSN, PMC); nurse anesthesia (MSN, PMC); nursing (MSN, DNP, PMC); nursing practice (DNP). Electronic applications accepted.

School of Music, Theatre and Dance Offers music (MM); music education (PhD). Electronic applications accepted.

OAKWOOD UNIVERSITY, Huntsville, AL 35896

General Information Independent-religious, coed, comprehensive institution. *Graduate housing:* On-campus housing not available.

GRADUATE UNITS

Program in Pastoral Studies Offers pastoral studies (MA).

OBERLIN COLLEGE, Oberlin, OH 44074

General Information Independent, coed, comprehensive institution. *Graduate housing:* Rooms and/or apartments available on a first-come, first-served basis to single students and available to married students. Housing application deadline: 6/15.

GRADUATE UNITS

Conservatory of Music Offers conducting (MM); contemporary chamber music (MM); historical performance (MM); performance (AD); piano technology (AD). Electronic applications accepted.

OBLATE SCHOOL OF THEOLOGY, San Antonio, TX 78216-6693

General Information Independent-religious, coed, graduate-only institution. *Graduate housing:* On-campus housing not available.

GRADUATE UNITS

Graduate and Professional Programs *Program availability:* Part-time, 100% online, blended/hybrid learning. Offers African-American pastoral leadership (D Min); divinity (M Div); pastoral leadership (D Min); pastoral ministry (MAP Min); pastoral studies (Certificate); spiritual formation in the local community (D Min); spirituality (MA Sp, PhD); spirituality and ministry (D Min); theology (MA Th); U.S. Hispanic/Latino ministry (D Min). Electronic applications accepted.

OCCIDENTAL COLLEGE, Los Angeles, CA 90041-3314

General Information Independent, coed, comprehensive institution. *Graduate housing:* On-campus housing not available.

GRADUATE UNITS

Department of Biology *Program availability:* Part-time. Offers biology (MA).

OGLALA LAKOTA COLLEGE, Kyle, SD 57752-0490

General Information State and locally supported, coed, comprehensive institution. *Graduate housing:* On-campus housing not available.

GRADUATE UNITS

Graduate Studies *Program availability:* Part-time, evening/weekend. Offers educational administration (MA); Lakota leadership and management (MA).

OHIO CHRISTIAN UNIVERSITY, Circleville, OH 43113

General Information Independent-religious, coed, comprehensive institution.

GRADUATE UNITS

Graduate Programs

OHIO DOMINICAN UNIVERSITY, Columbus, OH 43219-2099

General Information Independent-religious, coed, comprehensive institution. *Enrollment:* 1,716 graduate, professional, and undergraduate students; 162 full-time matriculated graduate/professional students (105 women), 366 part-time matriculated graduate/professional students (242 women). *Enrollment by degree level:* 528 master's. *Graduate faculty:* 28 full-time (12 women), 26 part-time/adjunct (6 women). *Tuition:* Full-time $10,800; part-time $600 per credit hour. *Required fees:* $450; $225 per semester. Tuition and fees vary according to program. *Graduate housing:* Room and/or apartments available on a first-come, first-served basis to single students; on-campus housing not available to married students. Typical cost: $11,000 per year. Room charges vary according to board plan. Housing application deadline: 8/20. *Student services:* Campus employment opportunities, campus safety program, career counseling, exercise/wellness program, free psychological counseling, international student services, multicultural affairs office, services for students with disabilities, teacher training, writing training. *Library facilities:* Ohio Dominican Library. *Collection:* Books: 76,976 (physical), 149,521 (digital/electronic); Serial titles: 5,327 (physical), 29,439 (digital/electronic); Databases: 216. Students can reserve study rooms.

Computer facilities: 350 computers available on campus for general student use. A campuswide network can be accessed from student residence rooms and from off campus. Online class registration is available. Website: http://www.ohiodominican.edu/

General Application Contact: John W. Naughton, Vice President of Enrollment and Student Success, 614-251-4721, Fax: 614-251-6654, E-mail: grad@ohiodominican.edu.

GRADUATE UNITS

Division of Arts and Letters Students: 1 (woman) full-time, 58 part-time (38 women); includes 3 minority (2 Black or African American, non-Hispanic/Latino; 1 Hispanic/Latino). Average age 40. 32 applicants, 47% accepted, 11 enrolled. *Faculty:* 6 full-time (2 women), 2 part-time/adjunct (1 woman). Expenses: Contact institution. In 2018, 13 master's awarded. *Program availability:* Part-time, evening/weekend, 100% online. Offers English (MA); theology (MA). *Application deadline:* For fall admission, 8/20 for domestic students, 7/15 for international students; for spring admission, 1/3 for domestic students, 12/15 for international students; for summer admission, 6/3 for domestic students, 5/15 for international students. Applications are processed on a rolling basis. *Application fee:* $25. Electronic applications accepted. *Application Contact:* John W. Naughton, Vice President for Enrollment and Student Success, 614-251-4721, Fax: 614-251-6654, E-mail: grad@ohiodominican.edu. Chair, Dr. Bruce Gartner, 614-251-4604, Fax: 614-253-3656, E-mail: gartnerb@ohiodominican.edu.

Division of Business Students: 60 full-time (24 women), 100 part-time (48 women); includes 38 minority (24 Black or African American, non-Hispanic/Latino; 1 American Indian or Alaska Native, non-Hispanic/Latino; 4 Asian, non-Hispanic/Latino; 5 Hispanic/Latino; 4 Two or more races, non-Hispanic/Latino), 22 international. Average age 30. 141 applicants, 43% accepted, 38 enrolled. *Faculty:* 13 full-time (4 women), 17 part-time/adjunct (3 women). Expenses: Contact institution. *Financial support:* Applicants required to submit FAFSA. In 2018, 70 master's awarded. *Program availability:* Part-time, evening/weekend, 100% online, blended/hybrid learning. Offers accounting (MBA); business administration (MBA); data analytics (MBA); finance (MBA); healthcare administration (MS); leadership (MBA); risk management (MBA); sport management (MBA, MS). *Application deadline:* For fall admission, 8/15 for domestic students, 6/10 for international students; for spring admission, 1/4 for domestic students, 11/2 for international students. Applications are processed on a rolling basis. *Application fee:* $25. Electronic applications accepted. *Application Contact:* John W. Naughton, Vice President for Enrollment & Student Success, 614-251-4721, Fax: 614-251-6654, E-mail: grad@ohiodominican.edu. Chair, Dr. Kenneth C. Fah, 614-251-4566, E-mail: fahk@ohiodominican.edu.

Division of Education Students: 6 full-time (5 women), 111 part-time (82 women); includes 12 minority (5 Black or African American, non-Hispanic/Latino; 3 Hispanic/Latino; 4 Two or more races, non-Hispanic/Latino), 8 international. Average age 34. 49 applicants, 53% accepted, 23 enrolled. *Faculty:* 7 full-time (4 women), 7 part-time/adjunct (4 women). Expenses: Contact institution. *Financial support:* Tuition waivers and tuition discounts (for diocesan teachers) available. Financial award applicants required to submit FAFSA. In 2018, 64 master's awarded. *Program availability:* Part-time, evening/weekend, 100% online, blended/hybrid learning. Offers curriculum and instruction (M Ed); educational leadership (M Ed); teaching English to speakers of other languages (MA). *Application deadline:* For fall admission, 8/15 for domestic students, 6/10 for international students; for spring admission, 1/4 for domestic students, 11/2 for international students. Applications are processed on a rolling basis. *Application fee:* $25. Electronic applications accepted. *Application Contact:* John W. Naughton, Vice President for Enrollment and Student Success, 614-251-4721, Fax: 614-251-6654, E-mail: grad@ohiodominican.edu. Chair, Division of Education, Dr. Marlissa Stauffer, 614-251-4621, E-mail: stauffem@ohiodominican.edu.

Division of Physician Assistant Studies Students: 99 full-time (75 women), 51 part-time (34 women); includes 11 minority (1 Black or African American, non-Hispanic/Latino; 1 American Indian or Alaska Native, non-Hispanic/Latino; 4 Asian, non-Hispanic/Latino; 2 Hispanic/Latino; 3 Two or more races, non-Hispanic/Latino). Average age 25. 500 applicants, 17% accepted, 48 enrolled. *Faculty:* 7 full-time (4 women), 2 part-time/adjunct (0 women). Expenses: Contact institution. *Financial support:* Applicants required to submit FAFSA. In 2018, 51 master's awarded. Offers physician assistant studies (MS). *Application deadline:* For fall admission, 10/1 for domestic and international students. Applications are processed on a rolling basis. Electronic applications accepted. *Application Contact:* John W. Naughton, Vice President for Enrollment and Student Success, 614-251-4721, Fax: 614-251-6654, E-mail: grad@ohiodominican.edu. *Program Director*, Prof. Shonna Riedlinger, 614-251-8988, E-mail: riedlins@ohiodominican.edu.

OHIO NORTHERN UNIVERSITY, Ada, OH 45810-1599

General Information Independent-religious, coed, comprehensive institution. *Graduate housing:* Room and/or apartments available on a first-come, first-served basis to single students; on-campus housing not available to married students.

GRADUATE UNITS

Claude W. Pettit College of Law Offers law (LL M, JD). Electronic applications accepted.

College of Business Offers business (MSA).

Raabe College of Pharmacy Offers pharmacy (Pharm D). Students enter the program as undergraduates.

THE OHIO STATE UNIVERSITY, Columbus, OH 43210

General Information State-supported, coed, university. CGS member. *Enrollment:* 61,170 graduate, professional, and undergraduate students; 11,956 full-time matriculated graduate/professional students (6,492 women), 1,877 part-time matriculated graduate/professional students (1,164 women). *Enrollment by degree level:* 5,439 master's, 8,280 doctoral, 114 other advanced degrees. *Graduate housing:* Rooms and/or apartments available on a first-come, first-served basis to single and married students. *Student services:* Campus employment opportunities, campus safety program, career counseling, child daycare facilities, exercise/wellness program, free psychological counseling, grant writing training, international student services, low-cost health insurance, multicultural affairs office, services for students with disabilities, teacher training, writing training. *Library facilities:* William Oxley Thompson Library plus 10 others. *Collection:* Books: 5 million (physical), 1.3 million (digital/electronic); Serial titles: 664,616 (physical), 55,339 (digital/electronic); Databases: 2,046. Study areas open 24 hours, 5–7 days a week; students can reserve study rooms.

Computer facilities: A campuswide network can be accessed. Online class registration, admission applications, fee payment are available. Website: http://www.osu.edu/

General Application Contact: Graduate and Professional Admissions, 614-292-9444, Fax: 614-292-3895, E-mail: gpadmissions@osu.edu.

GRADUATE UNITS

College of Dentistry Students: 530 full-time (245 women), 9 part-time (3 women). Average age 26. *Faculty:* 93. Expenses: Contact institution. *Financial support:* Fellowships with tuition reimbursements, research assistantships with tuition reimbursements, teaching assistantships with tuition reimbursements, Federal Work-Study, institutionally sponsored loans, and health care benefits available. Financial award application deadline: 2/15. In 2018, 24 master's, 108 doctorates awarded. Offers dental anesthesiology (MS); dental hygiene (MDH); dentistry (DDS); endodontics (MS); oral and maxillofacial pathology (MS); oral and maxillofacial surgery (MS); oral biology (PhD); orthodontics (MS); pediatric dentistry (MS); periodontology (MS); prosthodontics (MS). *Application deadline:* For fall admission, 10/1 for domestic and international students; for summer admission, 4/11 for domestic students, 3/10 for international students. Applications are processed on a rolling basis. Electronic applications accepted. *Application Contact:* Graduate and Professional Admissions, 614-292-9444, Fax: 614-292-3895, E-mail: gpadmissions@osu.edu. *Dean*, Dr. Patrick M. Lloyd, 614-292-9755, E-mail: lloyd.256@osu.edu.

College of Medicine Students: 1,333 full-time (815 women), 125 part-time (87 women). Average age 26. *Faculty:* 1,858. Expenses: Contact institution. *Financial support:* Fellowships with tuition reimbursements, research assistantships with tuition reimbursements, teaching assistantships with tuition reimbursements, Federal Work-Study, institutionally sponsored loans, and scholarships/grants available. Support available to part-time students. Financial award application deadline: 2/15; financial award applicants required to submit FAFSA. In 2018, 90 master's, 280 doctorates awarded. Offers biomedical sciences (PhD); medicine (MOT, MS, DPT, MD, PhD). *Application deadline:* Applications are processed on a rolling basis. Electronic applications accepted. *Application Contact:* Graduate and Professional Admissions, 614-292-9444, Fax: 614-292-3895, E-mail: gpadmissions@osu.edu. *Dean and Vice President of Health Sciences*, Dr. K. Craig Kent, MD, 614-292-2600, Fax: 614-292-1301.

School of Health and Rehabilitation Sciences Students: 382 full-time (309 women), 20 part-time (16 women); includes 57 minority (6 Black or African American, non-Hispanic/Latino; 19 Asian, non-Hispanic/Latino; 20 Hispanic/Latino; 12 Two or more races, non-Hispanic/Latino). Average age 25. *Faculty:* 44. Expenses: Contact institution. *Financial support:* Fellowships with tuition reimbursements, research assistantships with full tuition reimbursements, teaching assistantships with full tuition reimbursements, traineeships, unspecified assistantships, and administrative assistantships available. Financial award application deadline: 3/1. In 2018, 57 master's, 64 doctorates awarded. *Program availability:* Part-time. Offers allied health (MS); anatomy (MS, PhD); health and rehabilitation sciences (MOT, MS, DPT, PhD); occupational therapy (MOT); physical therapy (DPT). *Application deadline:* Applications are processed on a rolling basis. *Application fee:* $60 ($70 for international students). Electronic applications accepted. *Application Contact:* Graduate and Professional Admissions, 614-292-9444, Fax: 614-292-3895, E-mail: gpadmissions@osu.edu. *Associate Dean and Director*, Dr. Deborah S. Larsen, 614-292-5645, Fax: 614-292-0210, E-mail: larsen.64@osu.edu.

College of Optometry Students: 275 (185 women); includes 52 minority (14 Black or African American, non-Hispanic/Latino; 21 Asian, non-Hispanic/Latino; 7 Hispanic/Latino; 10 Two or more races, non-Hispanic/Latino). Average age 24. *Faculty:* 34. Expenses: Contact institution. *Financial support:* Research assistantships with full tuition reimbursements, teaching assistantships with full tuition reimbursements, institutionally sponsored loans, and scholarships/grants available. Financial award application deadline: 2/15; financial award applicants required to submit FAFSA. In 2018, 14 master's, 67 doctorates awarded. Offers optometry (OD); vision science (MS, PhD). *Application deadline:* For fall admission, 3/31 for domestic and international students; for spring admission, 12/1 for domestic students, 11/1 for international students. Applications are processed on a rolling basis. *Application fee:* $60 ($70 for international students). Electronic applications accepted. *Application Contact:* Office of Student Affairs, College of Optometry, 614-292-2647, Fax: 614-292-7493, E-mail: admissions@optometry.osu.edu. *Dean*, Dr. Karla Zadnik, 614-292-6603, E-mail: zadnik.4@osu.edu.

College of Pharmacy Students: 606 (345 women); includes 178 minority (44 Black or African American, non-Hispanic/Latino; 96 Asian, non-Hispanic/Latino; 22 Hispanic/Latino; 16 Two or more races, non-Hispanic/Latino), 61 international. Average age 25. *Faculty:* 49. Expenses: Contact institution. *Financial support:* Fellowships with full tuition reimbursements, research assistantships with full tuition reimbursements, teaching assistantships with full tuition reimbursements, career-related internships or fieldwork, Federal Work-Study, institutionally sponsored loans, scholarships/grants, and traineeships available. In 2018, 17 master's, 135 doctorates awarded. Offers pharmacy (MS, PhD, Pharm D). *Application deadline:* For fall admission, 12/15 for domestic and international students. *Application fee:* $60 ($70 for international students). Electronic applications accepted. *Application Contact:* Dr. Henry J. Mann, Dean and Professor, 614-292-5711, Fax: 614-292-2588, E-mail: mann.414@osu.edu. *Dean and Professor*, Dr. Henry J. Mann, 614-292-5711, Fax: 614-292-2588, E-mail: mann.414@osu.edu.

College of Public Health Students: 272 full-time (195 women), 65 part-time (50 women); includes 86 minority (28 Black or African American, non-Hispanic/Latino; 28 Asian, non-Hispanic/Latino; 20 Hispanic/Latino; 10 Two or more races, non-Hispanic/Latino), 24 international. Average age 27. *Faculty:* 54. Expenses: Contact institution. *Financial support:* Fellowships with tuition reimbursements and research assistantships with tuition reimbursements available. In 2018, 108 master's, 4 doctorates awarded. *Program availability:* Part-time. Offers public health (MHA, MPH, MS, PhD). *Application deadline:* For fall admission, 12/1 priority date for domestic students, 11/1 priority date for international students. Applications are processed on a rolling basis. *Application fee:* $60 ($70 for international students). Electronic applications accepted. *Application Contact:* Dr. Amy L. Fairchild, Dean and Professor, 614-292-8350, E-mail: fairchild.139@osu.edu. *Dean and Professor*, Dr. Amy L. Fairchild, 614-292-8350, E-mail: fairchild.139@osu.edu.

College of Veterinary Medicine Students: 687 full-time (526 women), 53 part-time (39 women). Average age 26. *Faculty:* 107. Expenses: Contact institution. In 2018, 17 master's, 162 doctorates awarded. Offers comparative and veterinary medicine (MS, PhD); veterinary medicine (MS, DVM, PhD). *Application deadline:* For fall admission, 9/15 for domestic and international students. Applications are processed on a rolling basis. *Application fee:* $60 ($70 for international students). Electronic applications accepted. *Application Contact:* Graduate and Professional Admissions, 614-292-9444, Fax: 614-292-3895, E-mail: gpadmissions@osu.edu. *Dean/Chair/Professor*, Dr. Rustin M. Moore, 614-688-8749, Fax: 614-292-3544, E-mail: moore.66@osu.edu.

Graduate School Students: 8,260 full-time (4,185 women), 1,618 part-time (981 women); includes 1,511 minority (465 Black or African American, non-Hispanic/Latino; 10 American Indian or Alaska Native, non-Hispanic/Latino; 354 Asian, non-Hispanic/Latino; 431 Hispanic/Latino; 3 Native Hawaiian or other Pacific Islander, non-Hispanic/Latino; 248 Two or more races, non-Hispanic/Latino), 2,526 international. Average age 28. Expenses: Contact institution. *Financial support:* Fellowships with tuition reimbursements, research assistantships with tuition reimbursements, teaching assistantships with tuition reimbursements, career-related internships or fieldwork, Federal Work-Study, institutionally sponsored loans, and unspecified assistantships available. Support available to part-time students. In 2018, 2,478 master's, 906 doctorates, 17 other advanced degrees awarded. *Program availability:* Part-time, evening/weekend. Offers biostatistics (PhD). *Application deadline:* For fall admission, 8/12 for domestic students, 7/1 for international students; for spring admission, 3/1 for domestic students, 2/1 for international students. Applications are processed on a rolling basis. *Application fee:* $60 ($70 for international students). Electronic applications accepted. *Application Contact:* Graduate and Professional Admissions, 614-292-9444, Fax: 614-292-3895, E-mail: gpadmissions@osu.edu. *Vice Provost and Dean*, Dr. Alicia L. Bertone, 614-292-6031, E-mail: bertone.1@osu.edu.

Center for Applied Plant Sciences Students: 9 full-time (5 women). Average age 27. Expenses: Contact institution. *Financial support:* Fellowships with tuition reimbursements and research assistantships with tuition reimbursements available. In 2018, 3 doctorates awarded. Offers applied plant sciences (PhD). *Application deadline:* For fall admission, 11/15 priority date for domestic and international students. Applications are processed on a rolling basis. *Application fee:* $60 ($70 for international students). Electronic applications accepted. *Application Contact:* Graduate and Professional Admissions, 614-292-9444, Fax: 614-292-3895, E-mail: gpadmissions@osu.edu. *Graduate Studies Committee Chair*, Dr. Thomas Mitchell, 614-292-1728, E-mail: mitchell.815@osu.edu.

Center for Latin American Studies Students: 4. Expenses: Contact institution. *Financial support:* Fellowships with tuition reimbursements available. In 2018, 1 master's awarded. Offers Latin American studies (MA). *Application deadline:* For fall admission, 12/13 priority date for domestic students, 11/30 priority date for international students; for spring admission, 12/12 for domestic students, 11/10 for international students; for summer admission, 4/10 for domestic students, 3/13 for international students. Applications are processed on a rolling basis. *Application fee:* $60 ($70 for international students). Electronic applications accepted. *Application Contact:* Graduate and Professional Admissions, 614-292-9444, Fax: 614-292-3895, E-mail: gpadmissions@osu.edu. *Director*, Dr. Terrell Morgan, 614-292-9555, E-mail: morgan.3@osu.edu.

Center for Slavic and East European Studies Students: 9 full-time (3 women). Expenses: Contact institution. *Financial support:* Fellowships, Federal Work-Study, and institutionally sponsored loans available. Support available to part-time students. In 2018, 7 master's awarded. Offers Slavic and East European studies (MA). *Application deadline:* For fall admission, 12/13 priority date for domestic students, 11/30 priority date for international students; for spring admission, 11/10 for domestic and international students; for summer admission, 3/13 for domestic and international students. Applications are processed on a rolling basis. *Application fee:* $60 ($70 for international students). Electronic applications accepted. *Application Contact:* Graduate and Professional Admissions, 614-292-9444, Fax: 614-292-3895, E-mail: gpadmissions@osu.edu. *Director*, Dr. Yana Hashamova, E-mail: hashamova.1@osu.edu.

College of Arts and Sciences Students: 2,638 full-time (1,292 women), 69 part-time (55 women). Average age 28. *Faculty:* 932. Expenses: Contact institution. *Financial support:* Fellowships, research assistantships, teaching assistantships, career-related internships or fieldwork, Federal Work-Study, institutionally sponsored loans, and unspecified assistantships available. Support available to part-time students. In 2018, 379 master's, 377 doctorates awarded. *Program availability:* Part-time. Offers acting (MFA); actuarial and quantitative risk management (MAQRM); African-American and African studies (MA, PhD); ancient Greek and Latin (MA, PhD); anthropology (MA, PhD); art (MFA); art education (MA); arts administration, education and policy (PhD); arts and humanities (MA, MFA, MM, DMA, PhD); arts and sciences (M Mus, MA, MAQRM, MFA, MMS, MS, DMA, PhD); arts policy and administration (MA); astronomy (MS, PhD); atmospheric sciences (MS, PhD); audiology (Au D); behavioral neuroscience (PhD); biochemistry (PhD); biophysics (MS, PhD); biostatistics (PhD); cell and developmental biology (MS, PhD); chemical physics (MS,

PhD); chemistry (MS, PhD); Chinese (MA, PhD); choreography (MFA); clinical psychology (PhD); cognitive psychology (PhD); communication (MA, PhD); comparative studies (MA, PhD); computational sciences (MMS); dance (MFA, PhD); dance and technology (MFA); dance studies (PhD); design (MA, MFA); design research and development (MFA); developmental psychology (PhD); digital animation and interactive media (MFA); earth sciences (MS, PhD); economics (MA, PhD); English (MA, MFA, PhD); evolution, ecology, and organismal biology (MS, PhD); French (MA, PhD); genetics (MS, PhD); geodetic science (MS, PhD); geography (MA, PhD); geological sciences (MS, PhD); Germanic languages and literatures (MA, PhD); Greek studies (MA); hearing science (PhD); history (MA, PhD); history of art (MA, PhD); history, theory and literature (MFA); intellectual and developmental disabilities psychology (PhD); Italian (MA); Italian studies (PhD); Japanese (MA, PhD); Latin studies (MA, PhD); lighting and production (MFA); linguistics (MA, PhD); mathematical biosciences (MMS); mathematics (PhD); mathematics for educators (MMS); microbiology (MS, PhD); modern Greek (MA, PhD); molecular biology (MS, PhD); molecular, cellular and developmental biology (MS, PhD); movement analysis, Laban studies, notation and dance documentation (MFA); music (MA, MM, DMA, PhD); natural and mathematical sciences (M Appl Stat, MAQRM, MMS, MS, PhD); Near Eastern languages and cultures (MA, PhD); neuroscience (PhD); performance (MFA); philosophy (MA, PhD); physics (MS, PhD); political science (PhD); quantitative psychology (PhD); Slavic linguistics (MA, PhD); Slavic literature, film, and cultural studies (MA, PhD); social and behavioral sciences (MA, MS, Au D, PhD); social psychology (PhD); sociology (PhD); Spanish and Portuguese (MA, PhD); speech-language pathology (MA); speech-language science (PhD); statistics (M Appl Stat, MS, PhD); theatre (PhD); theatre studies (MA); women's, gender and sexuality studies (MA, PhD). *Application deadline:* For fall admission, 8/1 for domestic students, 7/1 for international students; for spring admission, 3/1 for domestic students, 2/1 for international students. Applications are processed on a rolling basis. *Application fee:* $60 ($70 for international students). Electronic applications accepted. *Application Contact:* Graduate and Professional Admissions, 614-292-9444, Fax: 614-292-3895, E-mail: gpadmissions@osu.edu. *Executive Dean and Vice Provost*, Dr. Gretchen Ritter, 614-292-3236, E-mail: ritter.1596@osu.edu.

College of Education and Human Ecology Students: 770 full-time (519 women), 294 part-time (203 women). Average age 31. *Faculty:* 160. Expenses: Contact institution. *Financial support:* Fellowships with tuition reimbursements, research assistantships with tuition reimbursements, teaching assistantships with tuition reimbursements, career-related internships or fieldwork, Federal Work-Study, institutionally sponsored loans, scholarships/grants, traineeships, health care benefits, and unspecified assistantships available. Support available to part-time students. In 2018, 319 master's, 96 doctorates, 13 other advanced degrees awarded. Offers consumer sciences (MS, PhD); education and human ecology (M Ed, MA, MS, Ed D, PhD, Ed S); educational studies (M Ed, MA, PhD, Ed S); human development and family science (PhD); human nutrition (MS, PhD); kinesiology (MA, Ed D, PhD); teaching and learning (M Ed, MA, PhD, Ed S). *Application deadline:* Applications are processed on a rolling basis. *Application fee:* $60 ($70 for international students). Electronic applications accepted. *Application Contact:* Graduate and Professional Admissions, 614-292-9444, Fax: 614-292-3895, E-mail: gpadmissions@osu.edu. *Dean*, Dr. Donald B. Pope-Davis, E-mail: pope-davis.1@osu.edu.

College of Engineering Students: 1,749 full-time (406 women), 156 part-time (32 women). Average age 26. *Faculty:* 364. Expenses: Contact institution. *Financial support:* Fellowships with tuition reimbursements, research assistantships with tuition reimbursements, teaching assistantships with tuition reimbursements, career-related internships or fieldwork, Federal Work-Study, institutionally sponsored loans, and unspecified assistantships available. Support available to part-time students. In 2018, 496 master's, 159 doctorates awarded. *Program availability:* Part-time, evening/weekend. Offers aerospace engineering (MS, PhD); architecture (M Arch); biomedical engineering (MS, PhD); chemical engineering (MS, PhD); city and regional planning (MCRP, PhD); civil engineering (MS, PhD); computer science and engineering (MS, PhD); electrical and computer engineering (MS, PhD); electrical engineering (MS, PhD); engineering (M Arch, M Land Arch, MCRP, MS, PhD); industrial and systems engineering (MS, PhD); landscape architecture (M Land Arch); materials science and engineering (MS, PhD); mechanical engineering (MS, PhD); nuclear engineering (MS, PhD); welding engineering (MS, PhD). *Application deadline:* For fall admission, 11/30 priority date for domestic and international students. Applications are processed on a rolling basis. *Application fee:* $60 ($70 for international students). Electronic applications accepted. *Application Contact:* Graduate and Professional Admissions, 614-292-9444, Fax: 614-292-3895, E-mail: gpadmissions@osu.edu. *Dean*, Dr. David B. Williams, 614-292-2836, Fax: 614-292-9615, E-mail: williams.4219@osu.edu.

College of Food, Agricultural, and Environmental Sciences Students: 478 full-time (273 women), 58 part-time (32 women); includes 73 minority (18 Black or African American, non-Hispanic/Latino; 17 Asian, non-Hispanic/Latino; 26 Hispanic/Latino; 12 Two or more races, non-Hispanic/Latino), 166 international. Average age 28. *Faculty:* 327. Expenses: Contact institution. *Financial support:* Fellowships with tuition reimbursements, research assistantships with tuition reimbursements, teaching assistantships with tuition reimbursements, career-related internships or fieldwork, Federal Work-Study, institutionally sponsored loans, and unspecified assistantships available. Support available to part-time students. In 2018, 112 master's, 59 doctorates awarded. *Program availability:* Part-time. Offers agricultural and extension education (M Ed, MS, PhD); agricultural, environmental, and development economics (MS, PhD); animal sciences (MAS, MS, PhD); ecological restoration (MS, PhD); ecosystem science (MS, PhD); entomology (MPHM, MS, PhD); environment and natural resources (MENR); environmental science (MS, PhD); environmental social sciences (MS, PhD); fisheries and wildlife science (MS, PhD); food science and technology (MS, PhD); food, agricultural, and biological engineering (MS, PhD); food, agricultural, and environmental sciences (M Ed, MAS, MENR, MPHM, MS, PhD); forest science (MS, PhD); horticulture and crop science (MS, PhD); plant pathology (MPHM, MS, PhD); rural sociology (MS, PhD); soil science (MS, PhD). *Application deadline:* Applications are processed on a rolling basis. *Application fee:* $60 ($70 for international students). Electronic applications accepted. *Application Contact:* Graduate and Professional Admissions, 614-292-9444, Fax: 614-292-3895, E-mail: gpadmissions@osu.edu. *Vice President and Dean*, Dr. Cathann A. Kress, 614-292-6164, E-mail: kress.98@osu.edu.

College of Nursing Students: 597 full-time (491 women), 400 part-time (343 women). Average age 33. *Faculty:* 64. Expenses: Contact institution. *Financial support:* Fellowships, research assistantships, teaching assistantships, Federal Work-Study, institutionally sponsored loans, and unspecified assistantships available. Support available to part-time students. In 2018, 230 master's, 18 doctorates awarded. *Program availability:* Part-time. Offers nursing (MHI, MS, DNP). *Application deadline:* For fall admission, 12/13 priority date for domestic students, 11/30 priority date for international students; for summer admission, 10/12 for domestic and international students. Applications are processed on a rolling basis. *Application fee:* $60 ($70 for international students). Electronic applications accepted. *Application Contact:* Graduate and Professional Admissions, 614-292-9444, Fax: 614-292-3895, E-mail: gpadmissions@osu.edu. *Dean,* Dr. Bernadette M. Melnyk, 614-292-4844, Fax: 614-292-4535, E-mail: melnyk.15@osu.edu.

College of Social Work Students: 595 full-time (507 women), 110 part-time (88 women). Average age 29. *Faculty:* 31. Expenses: Contact institution. *Financial support:* Fellowships, research assistantships, teaching assistantships, Federal Work-Study, institutionally sponsored loans, and unspecified assistantships available. Support available to part-time students. In 2018, 266 master's, 8 doctorates awarded. *Program availability:* Part-time. Offers social work (MSW, PhD). *Application deadline:* For fall admission, 12/13 priority date for domestic students, 11/30 priority date for international students; for summer admission, 4/1 for domestic students, 3/1 for international students. Applications are processed on a rolling basis. *Application fee:* $60 ($70 for international students). Electronic applications accepted. *Application Contact:* Graduate and Professional Admissions, 614-292-6031, Fax: 614-292-3656, E-mail: gpadmissions@osu.edu. *Dean,* Dr. Tom Gregoire, 614-292-9426, E-mail: gregoire.5@osu.edu.

East Asian Studies Center Average age 25. Expenses: Contact institution. In 2018, 7 master's awarded. Offers East Asian studies (MA). *Application deadline:* For fall admission, 12/13 priority date for domestic students, 11/30 priority date for international students; for spring admission, 12/1 for domestic students, 11/1 for international students; for summer admission, 4/10 for domestic students, 3/13 for international students. Applications are processed on a rolling basis. *Application fee:* $60 ($70 for international students). Electronic applications accepted. *Application Contact:* Graduate and Professional Admissions, 614-292-9444, Fax: 614-292-3895, E-mail: gpadmissions@osu.edu. *Associate Professor,* Dr. Etsuyo Yuasa, 614-292-5816, E-mail: yuasa.1@osu.edu.

John Glenn College of Public Affairs Students: 141 full-time (80 women), 45 part-time (25 women). Average age 29. *Faculty:* 21. Expenses: Contact institution. *Financial support:* Fellowships, research assistantships, teaching assistantships, Federal Work-Study, institutionally sponsored loans, and unspecified assistantships available. Support available to part-time students. In 2018, 78 master's, 6 doctorates awarded. *Program availability:* Part-time. Offers public administration (MA, MPA); public policy and management (PhD). *Application deadline:* For fall admission, 12/1 priority date for domestic students, 11/30 priority date for international students; for spring admission, 11/15 for domestic and international students; for summer admission, 4/1 for domestic and international students. Applications are processed on a rolling basis. *Application fee:* $60 ($70 for international students). Electronic applications accepted. *Application Contact:* Graduate and Professional Admissions, 614-292-6031, Fax: 614-292-3656, E-mail: gpadmissions@osu.edu. *Dean,* Dr. Trevor Brown, 614-292-4533, Fax: 614-292-4868, E-mail: brown.2296@osu.edu.

Max M. Fisher College of Business Students: 623 full-time (284 women), 420 part-time (159 women). Average age 30. *Faculty:* 105. Expenses: Contact institution. *Financial support:* Fellowships, research assistantships, teaching assistantships, career-related internships or fieldwork, Federal Work-Study, institutionally sponsored loans, and unspecified assistantships available. Support available to part-time students. In 2018, 500 master's, 10 doctorates awarded. *Program availability:* Part-time, evening/weekend. Offers accounting (M Acc); business (M Acc, MA, MBA, MBLE, MBOE, MF, MHRM, PhD); business administration (MA, MBA, PhD); business logistics engineering (MBLE); business operational excellence (MBOE); finance (MF); human resource management (MHRM, PhD); labor and human resources (PhD); management information systems (PhD). *Application deadline:* Applications are processed on a rolling basis. *Application fee:* $60 ($70 for international students). Electronic applications accepted. *Application Contact:* Graduate and Professional Admissions, 614-292-9444, Fax: 614-292-3656, E-mail: gpadmissions@osu.edu. *Dean/Chair,* Dr. Anil K. Makhija, 614-292-2666, E-mail: makhija.1@osu.edu.

Moritz College of Law Offers law (LL M, MSL, JD). Electronic applications accepted.

THE OHIO STATE UNIVERSITY AT LIMA, Lima, OH 45804

General Information State-supported, coed, comprehensive institution. *Graduate housing:* On-campus housing not available.

GRADUATE UNITS

Graduate Programs *Program availability:* Part-time. Offers social work (MSW). Electronic applications accepted.

THE OHIO STATE UNIVERSITY AT MANSFIELD, Mansfield, OH 44906-1599

General Information State-supported, coed, comprehensive institution. *Enrollment:* 1,099 graduate, professional, and undergraduate students; 2 matriculated graduate/professional students. *Graduate housing:* On-campus housing not available. *Student services:* Campus employment opportunities, campus safety program, career counseling, child daycare facilities, exercise/wellness program, free psychological counseling, grant writing training, international student services, low-cost health insurance, multicultural affairs office, services for students with disabilities, teacher training, writing training. *Library facilities:* Bromfield Library & Information Commons. *Collection:* Books: 43,903 (physical), 1.4 million (digital/electronic); Serial titles: 126 (physical), 54,781 (digital/electronic); Databases: 2,075. Weekly public service hours: 63; students can reserve study rooms.

Computer facilities: A campuswide network can be accessed. Online class registration is available.
Website: http://www.mansfield.osu.edu/

General Application Contact: Graduate and Professional Admissions, 614-292-9444, Fax: 614-292-3895, E-mail: gpadmissions@osu.edu.

GRADUATE UNITS

Graduate Programs Students: 2. Expenses: Contact institution. *Financial support:* Teaching assistantships with full tuition reimbursements, Federal Work-Study, and scholarships/grants available. Support available to part-time students. Financial award application deadline: 2/15; financial award applicants required to submit FAFSA. *Program availability:* Part-time. Offers education (MA); social work (MSW). *Application deadline:* For fall admission, 4/1 for domestic students, 3/1 for international students; for spring admission, 10/15 for domestic and international students. Applications are processed on a rolling basis. *Application fee:* $60 ($70 for international students). Electronic applications accepted. *Application Contact:* Graduate and Professional Admissions, 614-292-9444, Fax: 614-292-3895, E-mail: gpadmissions@osu.edu. *Dean and Director,* Dr. Norman W. Jones, 419-755-4222, E-mail: jones.2376@osu.edu.

THE OHIO STATE UNIVERSITY AT MARION, Marion, OH 43302-5695

General Information State-supported, coed, comprehensive institution. *Graduate housing:* On-campus housing not available. *Student services:* Campus employment opportunities, campus safety program, career counseling, child daycare facilities, exercise/wellness program, free psychological counseling, grant writing training, international student services, low-cost health insurance, multicultural affairs office, services for students with disabilities, teacher training, writing training. *Library facilities:* Marion Campus Library. *Collection:* Books: 46,290 (physical), 1.4 million (digital/electronic); Serial titles: 54,781 (digital/electronic); Databases: 2,056. Weekly public service hours: 57; students can reserve study rooms.

Computer facilities: A campuswide network can be accessed. Online class registration is available.
Website: http://osumarion.osu.edu/

General Application Contact: Graduate and Professional Admissions, 614-292-9444, Fax: 614-292-3985, E-mail: gpadmissions@osu.edu.

GRADUATE UNITS

Graduate Programs Expenses: Contact institution. *Financial support:* Application deadline: 2/15; applicants required to submit FAFSA. *Program availability:* Part-time. Offers education (MA). *Application deadline:* Applications are processed on a rolling basis. *Application fee:* $60 ($70 for international students). Electronic applications accepted. *Application Contact:* Graduate and Professional Admissions, 614-292-9444, Fax: 614-292-3895, E-mail: gpadmissions@osu.edu. *Dean/Director,* Dr. Gregory S. Rose, 740-725-6218, E-mail: rose.9@osu.edu.

THE OHIO STATE UNIVERSITY AT NEWARK, Newark, OH 43055-1797

General Information State-supported, coed, comprehensive institution. *Enrollment:* 2,882 graduate, professional, and undergraduate students; 8 matriculated graduate/professional students (5 women). *Graduate housing:* Rooms and/or apartments available on a first-come, first-served basis to single and married students. *Student services:* Campus safety program, career counseling, child daycare facilities, exercise/wellness program, free psychological counseling, grant writing training, international student services, low-cost health insurance, multicultural affairs office, services for students with disabilities, teacher training, writing training. *Library facilities:* John L. and Christine Warner Library. *Collection:* Books: 52,380 (physical), 1.4 million (digital/electronic); Serial titles: 491 (physical), 54,576 (digital/electronic); Databases: 2,056. Weekly public service hours: 69; students can reserve study rooms.

Computer facilities: A campuswide network can be accessed. Online class registration is available.
Website: http://www.newark.osu.edu/

General Application Contact: Graduate and Professional Admissions, 614-292-9444, Fax: 614-292-3985, E-mail: gpadmissions@osu.edu.

GRADUATE UNITS

Graduate Programs Students: 8 (5 women). Average age 37. *Faculty:* 49. Expenses: Contact institution. *Financial support:* Application deadline: 2/15. *Program availability:* Part-time. Offers education - teaching and learning (MA); social work (MSW). *Application deadline:* For fall admission, 3/1 for domestic and international students. Applications are processed on a rolling basis. *Application fee:* $60 ($70 for international students). Electronic applications accepted. *Application Contact:* Graduate and Professional Admissions, 614-292-9444, Fax: 614-292-3985, E-mail: gpadmissions@osu.edu. *Dean and Director,* Dr. William L. MacDonald, 740-366-9333 Ext. 330, E-mail: macdonald.24@osu.edu.

OHIO UNIVERSITY, Athens, OH 45701-2979

General Information State-supported, coed, university. CGS member. *Graduate housing:* Rooms and/or apartments available on a first-come, first-served basis to single and married students. Housing application deadline: 5/1.

GRADUATE UNITS

Graduate College *Program availability:* Part-time, evening/weekend, online learning. Electronic applications accepted.

Center for International Studies *Program availability:* Part-time. Offers African studies (MA); Asian studies (MA); communications and development studies (MA); international development studies (MA); international studies (MA); Latin American studies (MA). Electronic applications accepted.

College of Arts and Sciences *Program availability:* Part-time, evening/weekend. Offers applied economics (MA); applied linguistics (MA); arts and sciences (MA, MFE, MS, MSS, PhD); astronomy (MS, PhD); biological sciences (MS, PhD); cell biology and physiology (MS, PhD); chemistry and biochemistry (MS, PhD); clinical psychology (PhD); ecology and evolutionary biology (MS, PhD); English language and literature (MA, PhD); environmental and plant biology (MS, PhD); environmental geochemistry (MS); exercise physiology and muscle biology (MS, PhD); experimental psychology (PhD); financial economics (MFE); French (MA); geography (MA, MS); history (MA, PhD); mathematics (MS, PhD); microbiology (MS, PhD); molecular and cellular biology (PhD); neuroscience (MS, PhD); organizational psychology (PhD); philosophy (MA); physics (MS, PhD); political science (MA); social sciences (MSS); sociology (MA); Spanish (MA). Electronic applications accepted.

College of Business *Program availability:* Part-time, evening/weekend, online learning. Offers athletic administration (MS); business (MBA, MS); executive management (MBA). Electronic applications accepted.

College of Fine Arts *Program availability:* Part-time, evening/weekend, online learning. Offers accompanying (MM); art history (MA); ceramics (MFA); composition (MM); conducting (MM); film (MFA); film studies (MA); fine arts (MA, MFA, MM, PhD, Certificate); graphic design (MFA); history/literature (MM); interdisciplinary arts (PhD); music education (MM); music therapy (MM); painting (MFA); performance (MM, Certificate); performance/pedagogy (MM); photography (MFA); printmaking (MFA); sculpture (MFA); theater (MA, MFA); theory (MM). Electronic applications accepted.

College of Health Sciences and Professions *Program availability:* Part-time, evening/weekend, online learning. Offers advanced clinical practice (DNP); athletic training (MS); clinical audiology (Au D); communication sciences and disorders (MA, Au D, PhD); early child development and family life (MS); executive practice (DNP); family nurse practitioner (MSN); family studies (MS); food and nutrition (MS); health administration (MHA); health sciences and professions (MA, MHA, MPH, MS, MSN, MSW, Au D, DNP, DPT, PhD); hearing science (PhD); human and consumer sciences (MS); nurse educator (MSN); physical therapy (DPT); physiology of exercise (MS); public health (MPH); social work (MSW); speech language pathology (MA); speech language science (PhD). Electronic applications accepted.

Gladys W. and David H. Patton College of Education and Human Services *Program availability:* Part-time, evening/weekend. Offers adolescent to young adult education (M Ed); coaching education (MS); college student personnel (M Ed); community/agency counseling (M Ed); computer education and technology (M Ed); counselor education (PhD); curriculum and instruction (M Ed, PhD); early childhood/special education (M Ed); education and human services (M Ed, MS, MSA, Ed D, PhD); educational administration (M Ed, Ed D); educational research and evaluation (M Ed, PhD); higher education (PhD); instructional technology (PhD); intervention specialist/mild-moderate needs (M Ed); intervention specialist/moderate-intensive needs (M Ed); middle childhood education (M Ed); reading education (M Ed); recreation studies (MS); rehabilitation counseling (M Ed); school counseling (M Ed). Electronic applications accepted.

Russ College of Engineering and Technology *Program availability:* Part-time. Offers biomedical engineering (MS); chemical engineering (MS, PhD); civil engineering (PhD); construction engineering and management (MS); electrical engineering (MS); electrical engineering and computer science (PhD); engineering and technology (M Eng Mgt, MS, PhD); environmental (MS); geoenvironmental (MS); geotechnical (MS); industrial and systems engineering (MS); mechanical and systems engineering (PhD); mechanical engineering (MS); mechanics (MS); structures (MS); transportation (MS); water resources (MS). Electronic applications accepted.

Scripps College of Communication *Program availability:* Part-time. Offers communication (MA, MCTP, MFA, MS, PhD); communication media arts (MFA); health communication (PhD); information and telecommunication systems (MCTP); journalism (MS); mass communication (PhD); media arts and studies (MA); organizational communication (MA); relating and organizing (PhD); rhetoric and public culture (PhD); visual communication (MA). Electronic applications accepted.

Voinovich School of Leadership and Public Affairs Offers environmental studies (MS, Certificate); public administration (MPA). Electronic applications accepted.

Heritage College of Osteopathic Medicine Offers osteopathic medicine (DO). Applicants must be U.S. residents to apply. Electronic applications accepted.

OHIO VALLEY UNIVERSITY, Vienna, WV 26105-8000
General Information Independent-religious, coed, comprehensive institution.
GRADUATE UNITS
School of Graduate Education *Program availability:* Online learning. Offers curriculum and instruction (M Ed).

OHR HAMEIR THEOLOGICAL SEMINARY, Cortlandt Manor, NY 10567
General Information Independent-religious, men only, comprehensive institution.
GRADUATE UNITS
Graduate Programs

OKLAHOMA BAPTIST UNIVERSITY, Shawnee, OK 74804
General Information Independent-religious, coed, comprehensive institution. *Enrollment:* 2,085 graduate, professional, and undergraduate students; 49 full-time matriculated graduate/professional students (34 women), 76 part-time matriculated graduate/professional students (41 women). *Enrollment by degree level:* 125 master's. *Graduate faculty:* 1 (woman) full-time, 27 part-time/adjunct (5 women). *Tuition:* Full-time $9900; part-time $6600 per credit hour. *Graduate housing:* Rooms and/or apartments available on a first-come, first-served basis to single and married students. *Typical cost:* $4300 per year ($5850 including board) for single students; $8520 per year ($10,070 including board) for married students. Room and board charges vary according to board plan. Housing application deadline: 7/31. *Student services:* Campus employment opportunities, campus safety program, career counseling, exercise/wellness program, free psychological counseling, international student services, low-cost health insurance, services for students with disabilities. *Library facilities:* Mabee Learning Center. *Collection:* Books: 162,334 (physical), 188,606 (digital/electronic); Serial titles: 1,140 (physical); Databases: 60. Weekly public service hours: 91; students can reserve study rooms.

Computer facilities: 175 computers available on campus for general student use. A campuswide network can be accessed from student residence rooms. Online class registration, campus portal, online course work are available.
Website: http://www.okbu.edu/

General Application Contact: Will Brantley, Director of Recruitment for Graduate College, 405-585-4607, Fax: 405-585-4646, E-mail: will.brantley@okbu.edu.

GRADUATE UNITS
Master of Business Administration in Transformational Leadership Students: 18 full-time (8 women), 33 part-time (15 women); includes 14 minority (1 Black or African American, non-Hispanic/Latino; 11 American Indian or Alaska Native, non-Hispanic/Latino; 1 Hispanic/Latino; 1 Two or more races, non-Hispanic/Latino), 5 international. Average age 32. Expenses: Contact institution. *Financial support:* Applicants required to submit FAFSA. *Program availability:* Part-time, evening/weekend, 100% online, blended/hybrid learning. Offers energy management (MBA); transformational leadership (MBA). *Application deadline:* Applications are processed on a rolling basis. *Application fee:* $0. Electronic applications accepted. *Application Contact:* Will Brantley, Director of Recruitment, 405-5854607, Fax: 405-5854646, E-mail: will.brantley@okbu.edu. *Director of Recruitment,* Will Brantley, 405-5854607, Fax: 405-5854646, E-mail: will.brantley@okbu.edu.

Program in Marriage and Family Therapy *Program availability:* Part-time, evening/weekend. Offers marriage and family therapy (MS). Electronic applications accepted.

Program in Nursing Offers global nursing (MSN); nursing education (MSN).

OKLAHOMA CHRISTIAN UNIVERSITY, Oklahoma City, OK 73136-1100
General Information Independent-religious, coed, comprehensive institution. *Enrollment:* 2,248 graduate, professional, and undergraduate students; 263 full-time matriculated graduate/professional students (89 women), 221 part-time matriculated graduate/professional students (66 women). *Enrollment by degree level:* 484 master's. *Graduate faculty:* 23 full-time (5 women), 27 part-time/adjunct (2 women). *Tuition:* Full-time $5400; part-time $600 per credit hour. Tuition and fees vary according to program. *Graduate housing:* Rooms and/or apartments available on a first-come, first-served basis to single and married students. Housing application deadline: 8/31. *Student services:* Campus employment opportunities, campus safety program, exercise/wellness program, free psychological counseling, international student services, writing training. *Library facilities:* Tom and Ada Beam Library. *Collection:* Books: 108,575 (physical), 66,843 (digital/electronic); Serial titles: 1,241 (physical), 42,377 (digital/electronic); Databases: 76. Weekly public service hours: 82; students can reserve study rooms.

Computer facilities: 101 computers available on campus for general student use. A campuswide network can be accessed from student residence rooms and from off campus. Online class registration is available.
Website: http://www.oc.edu/

General Application Contact: Angie Ricketts, Admissions Counselor, 405-425-5587, E-mail: angie.ricketts@oc.edu.

GRADUATE UNITS
Graduate School of Business *Program availability:* Part-time, 100% online. Offers accounting (M Acc, MBA); financial services (MBA); general business (MBA); health services management (MBA); human resources (MBA); international business (MBA); leadership and organizational development (MBA); marketing (MBA); nonprofit management (MBA); project management (MBA). Electronic applications accepted.

Graduate School of Engineering and Computer Science *Program availability:* Part-time. Offers electrical and computer engineering (MSE); engineering management (MSE); mechanical engineering (MSE); software engineering (MSCS, MSE). Electronic applications accepted.

Graduate School of Theology Students: 12 full-time (0 women), 30 part-time (4 women). Average age 32. 12 applicants, 100% accepted, 10 enrolled. *Faculty:* 8 full-time (0 women). Expenses: Contact institution. *Financial support:* In 2018–19, 38 students received support. Federal Work-Study and scholarships/grants available. Financial award application deadline: 8/15; financial award applicants required to submit FAFSA. In 2018, 8 master's awarded. *Program availability:* Part-time, 100% online, blended/hybrid learning. Offers ministry (MACM); scripture (MTS); theology (M Div, MTS). *Application deadline:* For fall admission, 8/15 priority date for domestic and international students; for spring admission, 1/3 priority date for domestic and international students. Applications are processed on a rolling basis. *Application fee:* $25. Electronic applications accepted. *Application Contact:* Josh Bailey, Program Director, 405-425-5389, Fax: 405-425-5076, E-mail: josh.bailey@oc.edu. *Dean,* Dr. Charles Rix, 405-425-5379, E-mail: charles.rix@oc.edu.

OKLAHOMA CITY UNIVERSITY, Oklahoma City, OK 73106-1402
General Information Independent-religious, coed, comprehensive institution. *Graduate housing:* Rooms and/or apartments available on a first-come, first-served basis to single and married students. Housing application deadline: 6/15.
GRADUATE UNITS
Kramer School of Nursing *Program availability:* Part-time, evening/weekend, online learning. Offers clinical nurse leader (MSN); nursing (DNP, PhD); nursing education (MSN). Electronic applications accepted.

Meinders School of Business *Program availability:* Part-time, evening/weekend, 100% online. Offers business (MBA, MSA); computer science (MS); energy legal studies (MS); energy management (MS). Electronic applications accepted.

Petree College of Arts and Sciences *Program availability:* Part-time, evening/weekend. Offers applied behavioral studies (M Ed); applied sociology: nonprofit leadership (MA); creative writing (MFA); criminology (MS); early childhood education (M Ed); elementary education (M Ed); general studies (MLA); leadership/management (MLA); moving image arts (MFA); professional counseling (M Ed); teaching (MA); teaching English to speakers of other languages (MA). Electronic applications accepted.

School of Law *Program availability:* Part-time, evening/weekend. Offers law (LL M, JD). Electronic applications accepted.

Wanda L. Bass School of Music *Program availability:* Part-time. Offers composition (MM); conducting (MM); musical theatre (MM); opera performance (MM); performance (MM); vocal coaching (MM). Electronic applications accepted.

OKLAHOMA STATE UNIVERSITY, Stillwater, OK 74078
General Information State-supported, coed, university. CGS member. *Enrollment:* 24,649 graduate, professional, and undergraduate students; 1,634 full-time matriculated graduate/professional students (973 women), 2,441 part-time matriculated graduate/professional students (1,104 women). *Enrollment by degree level:* 2,160 master's, 1,772 doctoral, 143 other advanced degrees. *Graduate faculty:* 1,235 full-time (484 women), 178 part-time/adjunct (100 women). *International tuition:* $10,517 full-time. *Tuition, area resident:* Full-time $4148. Tuition, state resident: full-time $4148. Tuition, nonresident: full-time $10,517. *Required fees:* $4394; $2929 per credit hour. Tuition and fees vary according to course load and program. *Graduate housing:* Rooms and/or apartments available on a first-come, first-served basis to single and married students. Typical cost: $8996 (including board) for single students; $14,436 (including board) for married students. Room and board charges vary according to board plan and housing facility selected. *Student services:* Campus employment opportunities, campus safety program, career counseling, exercise/wellness program, free psychological counseling, grant writing training, international student services, low-cost health insurance, multicultural affairs office, services for students with disabilities, teacher training, writing training. *Library facilities:* Edmon Low Library plus 3 others. *Collection:* Weekly public service hours: 146; study areas open 24 hours, 5–7 days a week; students can reserve study rooms. *Research affiliation:* Allens, Inc. (horticulture and landscape architecture), General Motors (industrial engineering and management), Simons Foundation (mathematics), Howard Hughes Medical Institute (educational studies), Narramore Christian Foundation (Human Development and Family Science.), LiteCure, LLC (veterinary clinical sciences).

Computer facilities: Computer purchase and lease plans are available. A campuswide network can be accessed from student residence rooms and from off campus. Online class registration, Computer labs are available.
Website: http://www.okstate.edu/

General Application Contact: Dr. Sheryl Tucker, Dean, 405-744-6368, Fax: 405-744-0355, E-mail: gradi@okstate.edu.

GRADUATE UNITS
Center for Veterinary Health Sciences *Program availability:* Online learning. Offers veterinary biomedical sciences (MS, PhD); veterinary health sciences (MS, DVM, PhD); veterinary medicine (DVM).

College of Agricultural Science and Natural Resources Students: 117 full-time (68 women), 271 part-time (138 women); includes 51 minority (15 Black or African American, non-Hispanic/Latino; 7 American Indian or Alaska Native, non-Hispanic/Latino; 4 Asian, non-Hispanic/Latino; 13 Hispanic/Latino; 12 Two or more races, non-Hispanic/Latino), 103 international. Average age 28. 209 applicants, 55% accepted, 100 enrolled. *Faculty:* 213 full-time (55 women), 5 part-time/adjunct (2 women). Expenses: Contact institution. *Financial support:* In 2018–19, 220 research assistantships (averaging $3,640 per year), 53 teaching assistantships (averaging $3,144 per year) were awarded; fellowships, career-related internships or fieldwork, Federal Work-Study, scholarships/grants, health care benefits, tuition waivers (partial), and unspecified assistantships also available. Support available to part-time students.

Financial award application deadline: 3/1; financial award applicants required to submit FAFSA. In 2018, 128 master's, 35 doctorates awarded. *Program availability:* Online learning. Offers agricultural economics (M Ag, MS, PhD); agricultural education, communications and leadership (M Ag, MS, PhD); agricultural science and natural resources (M Ag, MS, PhD); animal sciences (M Ag, MS); biochemistry and molecular biology (MS, PhD); biosystems engineering (MS, PhD); crop science (PhD); entomology (PhD); entomology and plant pathology (MS); environmental and natural resources (MS, PhD); food science (PhD); horticulture (M Ag, MS, PhD); natural resource ecology and management (M Ag, MS, PhD); plant and soil sciences (MS); soil science (M Ag). *Application deadline:* For fall admission, 3/1 priority date for domestic and international students; for spring admission, 8/1 priority date for domestic and international students. Applications are processed on a rolling basis. *Application fee:* $40 ($75 for international students). Electronic applications accepted. *Application Contact:* Dr. Sheryl Tucker, Vice Prov/Dean/Prof, 405-744-6368, Fax: 405-744-0355, E-mail: gradi@okstate.edu. *Vice President/Dean,* Dr. Thomas Coon, 405-744-2474, E-mail: thomas.coon@okstate.edu.

College of Arts and Sciences Offers applied mathematics (MS, PhD); art history (MA); arts and sciences (MA, MFA, MM, MS, PhD); botany (MS); chemistry (MS, PhD); clinical psychology (PhD); communication sciences and disorders (MS); computer science (MS, PhD); creative writing (MFA); English (MA, PhD); environmental science (PhD); fire and emergency management administration (MS, PhD); general psychology (MS); geography (MS, PhD); graphic design (MA); history (MA, PhD); integrative biology (MS, PhD); microbiology and molecular genetics (MS, PhD); philosophy (MS, PhD); photonics (MS, PhD); political science (MA); sociology (MS, PhD); statistics (MS, PhD); theatre (MA). Electronic applications accepted.

Boone Pickens School of Geology Students: 28 full-time (8 women), 51 part-time (14 women); includes 8 minority (2 Black or African American, non-Hispanic/Latino; 1 American Indian or Alaska Native, non-Hispanic/Latino; 3 Hispanic/Latino; 2 Two or more races, non-Hispanic/Latino), 20 international. Average age 30. 85 applicants, 20% accepted, 14 enrolled. *Faculty:* 15 full-time (3 women), 1 (woman) part-time/adjunct. Expenses: Contact institution. *Financial support:* Research assistantships, teaching assistantships, career-related internships or fieldwork, Federal Work-Study, scholarships/grants, health care benefits, tuition waivers (partial), and unspecified assistantships available. Support available to part-time students. Financial award application deadline: 3/1; financial award applicants required to submit FAFSA. In 2018, 23 master's, 2 doctorates awarded. Offers geology (MS, PhD). *Application deadline:* For fall admission, 3/1 priority date for international students; for spring admission, 8/1 priority date for international students. Applications are processed on a rolling basis. *Application fee:* $40 ($75 for international students). Electronic applications accepted. *Application Contact:* Dr. Sheryl Tucker, Dean, 405-744-6368, Fax: 405-744-0355, E-mail: gradi@okstate.edu. *Department Head,* Dr. Camelia Knapp, 405-744-6358, Fax: 405-744-7841, E-mail: camelia.knapp@okstate.edu.

Michael and Anne Greenwood School of Music Students: 21 full-time (9 women), 6 part-time (2 women); includes 2 minority (1 Black or African American, non-Hispanic/Latino; 1 Asian, non-Hispanic/Latino), 4 international. Average age 26. 37 applicants, 49% accepted, 13 enrolled. *Faculty:* 33 full-time (14 women), 9 part-time/adjunct (2 women). Expenses: Contact institution. *Financial support:* Teaching assistantships, career-related internships or fieldwork, Federal Work-Study, scholarships/grants, health care benefits, tuition waivers (partial), and unspecified assistantships available. Support available to part-time students. Financial award application deadline: 3/1; financial award applicants required to submit FAFSA. In 2018, 7 master's awarded. Offers pedagogy and performance (MM). *Application deadline:* For fall admission, 3/1 priority date for international students; for spring admission, 8/1 priority date for international students. Applications are processed on a rolling basis. *Application fee:* $40 ($75 for international students). Electronic applications accepted. *Application Contact:* Dr. Sheryl Tucker, Dean, 405-744-6368, Fax: 405-744-0355, E-mail: gradi@okstate.edu. *Department Head,* Dr. Howard Potter, 405-744-8997, Fax: 405-744-9324, E-mail: osumusic@okstate.edu.

School of Media and Strategic Communications Students: 10 full-time (5 women), 14 part-time (10 women); includes 5 minority (1 Black or African American, non-Hispanic/Latino; 1 American Indian or Alaska Native, non-Hispanic/Latino; 1 Hispanic/Latino; 2 Two or more races, non-Hispanic/Latino), 2 international. Average age 27. 12 applicants, 83% accepted, 9 enrolled. *Faculty:* 17 full-time (6 women), 5 part-time/adjunct (1 woman). Expenses: Contact institution. *Financial support:* Research assistantships, teaching assistantships, career-related internships or fieldwork, Federal Work-Study, scholarships/grants, health care benefits, tuition waivers (partial), and unspecified assistantships available. Support available to part-time students. Financial award application deadline: 3/1; financial award applicants required to submit FAFSA. In 2018, 17 master's awarded. Offers mass communication (MS). *Application deadline:* For fall admission, 3/1 priority date for international students; for spring admission, 8/1 priority date for international students. Applications are processed on a rolling basis. *Application fee:* $40 ($75 for international students). Electronic applications accepted. *Application Contact:* Dr. Sheryl Tucker, Dean, 405-744-6368, Fax: 405-744-0355, E-mail: gradi@okstate.edu. *Director,* Dr. Max Andrews, 405-744-4207, Fax: 405-744-7104, E-mail: max.andrews@okstate.edu.

College of Education, Health and Aviation *Program availability:* Part-time, online learning. Offers education, health and aviation (MS, Ed D, PhD, Ed S). Electronic applications accepted.

School of Applied Health and Educational Psychology *Program availability:* Part-time. Offers applied behavioral studies (Ed D); applied health and educational psychology (MS, PhD, Ed S). Electronic applications accepted.

School of Educational Studies *Program availability:* Part-time. Offers higher education (Ed D). Electronic applications accepted.

School of Teaching and Curriculum Leadership *Program availability:* Part-time. Offers teaching and curriculum leadership (MS, PhD). Electronic applications accepted.

College of Engineering, Architecture and Technology *Program availability:* Online learning. Offers engineering, architecture and technology (MS, PhD). Electronic applications accepted.

School of Chemical Engineering Students: 13 full-time (2 women), 29 part-time (6 women); includes 3 minority (1 Asian, non-Hispanic/Latino; 2 Two or more races, non-Hispanic/Latino), 26 international. Average age 29. 64 applicants, 20% accepted, 13 enrolled. *Faculty:* 12 full-time (2 women), 1 part-time/adjunct (0 women). Expenses: Contact institution. *Financial support:* Research assistantships, teaching assistantships, career-related internships or fieldwork, Federal Work-Study, scholarships/grants, health care benefits, tuition waivers (partial), and unspecified assistantships available. Support available to part-time students. Financial award application deadline: 3/1; financial award applicants required to submit FAFSA. In 2018, 8 master's, 2 doctorates awarded. Offers chemical engineering (MS, PhD). *Application deadline:* For fall admission, 3/1 priority date for international students; for spring admission, 8/1 priority date for international students. Applications are processed on a rolling basis. *Application fee:* $40 ($75 for international students). Electronic applications accepted. *Application Contact:* Dr. Sheryl Tucker, Dean, 405-744-6368, Fax: 405-744-0355, E-mail: gradi@okstate.edu. *Head,* Dr. Gier Hareland, 405-744-5280, Fax: 405-744-6338.

School of Civil and Environmental Engineering Students: 20 full-time (5 women), 41 part-time (12 women); includes 6 minority (3 American Indian or Alaska Native, non-Hispanic/Latino; 1 Hispanic/Latino; 2 Two or more races, non-Hispanic/Latino), 31 international. Average age 29. 74 applicants, 26% accepted, 11 enrolled. *Faculty:* 21 full-time (2 women), 2 part-time/adjunct (0 women). Expenses: Contact institution. *Financial support:* Research assistantships, teaching assistantships, career-related internships or fieldwork, Federal Work-Study, scholarships/grants, health care benefits, tuition waivers (partial), and unspecified assistantships available. Support available to part-time students. Financial award application deadline: 3/1; financial award applicants required to submit FAFSA. In 2018, 17 master's, 4 doctorates awarded. Offers civil engineering (MS, PhD). *Application deadline:* For fall admission, 3/1 priority date for international students; for spring admission, 8/1 priority date for international students. Applications are processed on a rolling basis. *Application fee:* $40 ($75 for international students). Electronic applications accepted. *Application Contact:* Dr. Sheryl Tucker, Dean, 405-744-6368, Fax: 405-744-0355, E-mail: gradi@okstate.edu. *Department Head,* Dr. Norb Delatte, 405-744-5190, Fax: 405-744-7554, E-mail: norb.delatte@okstate.edu.

School of Electrical and Computer Engineering Students: 25 full-time (7 women), 38 part-time (6 women); includes 7 minority (2 Black or African American, non-Hispanic/Latino; 1 Asian, non-Hispanic/Latino; 2 Hispanic/Latino; 2 Two or more races, non-Hispanic/Latino), 50 international. Average age 29. 159 applicants, 23% accepted, 18 enrolled. *Faculty:* 20 full-time (2 women), 1 part-time/adjunct (0 women). Expenses: Contact institution. *Financial support:* Research assistantships, teaching assistantships, career-related internships or fieldwork, Federal Work-Study, scholarships/grants, health care benefits, tuition waivers (partial), and unspecified assistantships available. Support available to part-time students. Financial award application deadline: 3/1; financial award applicants required to submit FAFSA. In 2018, 31 master's, 3 doctorates awarded. *Program availability:* Online learning. Offers electrical and computer engineering (MS, PhD). *Application deadline:* For fall admission, 3/1 priority date for international students; for spring admission, 8/1 priority date for international students. Applications are processed on a rolling basis. *Application fee:* $40 ($75 for international students). Electronic applications accepted. *Application Contact:* Dr. R. G. Ramakumar, Graduate Coordinator, 405-744-5157, Fax: 405-744-9198, E-mail: ramakum@okstate.edu. *Department Head,* Dr. Jeffrey Young, 405-744-5151, Fax: 405-744-9198, E-mail: jl.young@okstate.edu.

School of Industrial Engineering and Management Students: 22 full-time (5 women), 107 part-time (17 women); includes 23 minority (5 Black or African American, non-Hispanic/Latino; 1 American Indian or Alaska Native, non-Hispanic/Latino; 5 Asian, non-Hispanic/Latino; 6 Hispanic/Latino; 1 Native Hawaiian or other Pacific Islander, non-Hispanic/Latino; 5 Two or more races, non-Hispanic/Latino), 34 international. Average age 30. 247 applicants, 21% accepted, 44 enrolled. *Faculty:* 13 full-time (4 women), 1 part-time/adjunct (0 women). Expenses: Contact institution. *Financial support:* Research assistantships, teaching assistantships, career-related internships or fieldwork, Federal Work-Study, scholarships/grants, health care benefits, tuition waivers (partial), and unspecified assistantships available. Support available to part-time students. Financial award application deadline: 3/1; financial award applicants required to submit FAFSA. In 2018, 101 master's, 6 doctorates awarded. *Program availability:* Online learning. Offers industrial engineering and management (MS, PhD). *Application deadline:* For fall admission, 3/1 priority date for international students; for spring admission, 8/1 priority date for international students. Applications are processed on a rolling basis. *Application fee:* $40 ($75 for international students). Electronic applications accepted. *Application Contact:* Dr. Baski Balasundaram, Director of Graduate Program, 405-744-6055, Fax: 405-744-4654, E-mail: baski@okstate.edu. *Head,* Dr. Sunderesh Heragu, 405-744-6055, Fax: 405-744-4654, E-mail: sunderesh.heragu@okstate.edu.

School of Materials Science and Engineering Students: 2 full-time (0 women), 16 part-time (4 women); includes 4 minority (2 American Indian or Alaska Native, non-Hispanic/Latino; 1 Asian, non-Hispanic/Latino; 1 Two or more races, non-Hispanic/Latino), 7 international. Average age 29. 14 applicants, 29% accepted, 4 enrolled. *Faculty:* 7 full-time (0 women), 2 part-time/adjunct (0 women). Expenses: Contact institution. *Financial support:* Research assistantships and teaching assistantships available. In 2018, 3 master's, 1 doctorate awarded. Offers materials science and engineering (MS, PhD). *Application deadline:* For fall admission, 3/1 for domestic students; for spring admission, 8/1 for domestic students. *Application fee:* $40 ($75 for international students). Electronic applications accepted. *Application Contact:* Dr. Sheryl Tucker, Dean, 405-744-6368, Fax: 405-744-0355, E-mail: gradi@okstate.edu. *Head,* Dr. Raman P Singh, 918-594-8155, E-mail: raman.singh@okstate.edu.

School of Mechanical and Aerospace Engineering Students: 25 full-time (1 woman), 92 part-time (14 women); includes 14 minority (3 American Indian or Alaska Native, non-Hispanic/Latino; 4 Asian, non-Hispanic/Latino; 2 Hispanic/Latino; 5 Two or more races, non-Hispanic/Latino), 50 international. Average age 26. 181 applicants, 22% accepted, 37 enrolled. *Faculty:* 31 full-time (1 woman), 3 part-time/adjunct (1 woman). Expenses: Contact institution. *Financial support:* Research assistantships, teaching assistantships, career-related internships or fieldwork, Federal Work-Study, scholarships/grants, health care benefits, tuition waivers (partial), and unspecified assistantships available. Support available to part-time students. Financial award application deadline: 3/1; financial award applicants required to submit FAFSA. In 2018, 25 master's, 4 doctorates awarded. *Program availability:* Online learning. Offers mechanical and aerospace engineering (MS, PhD). *Application deadline:* For fall admission, 3/1 priority date for international students; for spring admission, 8/1 priority date for international students. Applications are processed on a rolling basis. *Application fee:* $40 ($75 for international students). Electronic applications accepted. *Application Contact:* Dr. Charlotte Fore, Manager of Graduate Studies and Research Development, 405-744-5900, Fax: 405-744-7873, E-mail: charlotte.fore@okstate.edu. *Department Head,* Dr. Daniel E. Fisher, 405-744-5900, Fax: 405-744-7873, E-mail: maehead@okstate.edu.

College of Human Sciences *Program availability:* Online learning. Offers design, housing and merchandising (MS, PhD); human development and family science (MS, PhD); human sciences (MS, PhD); nutritional sciences (MS, PhD). Electronic applications accepted.

School of Hospitality and Tourism Management Students: 18 full-time (11 women), 19 part-time (10 women); includes 3 minority (all Asian, non-Hispanic/Latino), 30 international. Average age 28. 17 applicants, 65% accepted, 8 enrolled. *Faculty:* 16 full-time (9 women), 7 part-time/adjunct (1 woman). Expenses: Contact institution.

Financial support: Research assistantships, teaching assistantships, career-related internships or fieldwork, Federal Work-Study, scholarships/grants, health care benefits, tuition waivers (partial), and unspecified assistantships available. Support available to part-time students. Financial award application deadline: 3/1; financial award applicants required to submit FAFSA. In 2018, 9 master's awarded. Offers hospitality and tourism management (MS, PhD). *Application deadline:* For fall admission, 3/1 priority date for international students; for spring admission, 8/1 priority date for international students. Applications are processed on a rolling basis. *Application fee:* $40 ($75 for international students). Electronic applications accepted. *Application Contact:* Dr. Li Miao, Graduate Coordinator, 405-744-1277, Fax: 405-744-6299, E-mail: lm@okstate.edu. *Interim Director,* Dr. Li Miao, 405-744-6713, Fax: 405-744-6299, E-mail: htm@okstate.edu.

Graduate College Offers aerospace security (Graduate Certificate); bioenergy and sustainable technology (Graduate Certificate); business data mining (Graduate Certificate); business sustainability (Graduate Certificate); environmental science (MS); international studies (MS); non-profit management (Graduate Certificate); teaching English to speakers of other languages (Graduate Certificate); telecommunications management (MS). Programs are interdisciplinary. Electronic applications accepted.

Spears School of Business *Program availability:* Part-time, online learning. Offers business (MBA, MS, PhD); economics and legal studies in business (MS, PhD); entrepreneurship (MBA, MS, PhD); finance (MS, PhD); management (MBA, MS, PhD); management information systems (MS); management science and information systems (PhD); telecommunications management (MS). Electronic applications accepted.

School of Accounting Students: 43 full-time (27 women), 18 part-time (13 women); includes 16 minority (2 Black or African American, non-Hispanic/Latino; 2 American Indian or Alaska Native, non-Hispanic/Latino; 4 Asian, non-Hispanic/Latino; 1 Hispanic/Latino; 7 Two or more races, non-Hispanic/Latino), 5 international. Average age 23. 34 applicants, 50% accepted, 12 enrolled. *Faculty:* 16 full-time (8 women), 4 part-time/adjunct (3 women). Expenses: Contact institution. *Financial support:* Research assistantships, teaching assistantships, career-related internships or fieldwork, Federal Work-Study, scholarships/grants, health care benefits, tuition waivers (partial), and unspecified assistantships available. Support available to part-time students. Financial award application deadline: 3/1; financial award applicants required to submit FAFSA. In 2018, 38 master's awarded. *Program availability:* Part-time. Offers accounting (MS, PhD). *Application deadline:* For fall admission, 3/1 priority date for international students; for spring admission, 8/1 priority date for international students. Applications are processed on a rolling basis. *Application fee:* $40 ($75 for international students). Electronic applications accepted. *Application Contact:* Dr. Alyssa Vowell, Graduate Coordinator, 405-744-6635, Fax: 405-744-1680, E-mail: alyssa.vowell@okstate.edu. *Department Head,* Dr. Audrey Gramling, 405-744-1245, Fax: 405-744-1680, E-mail: audrey.gramling@okstate.edu.

School of Marketing and International Business Students: 71 full-time (22 women), 34 part-time (17 women); includes 8 minority (1 Black or African American, non-Hispanic/Latino; 3 Asian, non-Hispanic/Latino; 4 Hispanic/Latino), 74 international. Average age 27. 234 applicants, 20% accepted, 42 enrolled. *Faculty:* 21 full-time (5 women), 5 part-time/adjunct (2 women). Expenses: Contact institution. *Financial support:* Research assistantships, teaching assistantships, career-related internships or fieldwork, Federal Work-Study, scholarships/grants, health care benefits, tuition waivers (partial), and unspecified assistantships available. Support available to part-time students. Financial award application deadline: 3/1; financial award applicants required to submit FAFSA. In 2018, 39 master's awarded. *Program availability:* Part-time. Offers business administration (MS); marketing (MBA). *Application deadline:* For fall admission, 3/1 priority date for international students; for spring admission, 8/1 priority date for international students. Applications are processed on a rolling basis. *Application fee:* $40 ($75 for international students). Electronic applications accepted. *Application Contact:* Dr. Kevin Voss, PhD Coordinator, 405-744-5106, Fax: 405-744-5180, E-mail: kevin.voss@okstate.edu. *Department Head,* Dr. Tom Brown, 405-744-5113, Fax: 405-744-5180, E-mail: tom.brown@okstate.edu.

OKLAHOMA STATE UNIVERSITY CENTER FOR HEALTH SCIENCES, Tulsa, OK 74107-1898

General Information State-supported, coed, graduate-only institution. *Graduate housing:* On-campus housing not available. *Research affiliation:* Viropharma, Inc. (pharmaceutical sciences), Ingenex (pharmaceutical sciences), The Procter & Gamble Company (pharmaceutical sciences), Glaxo-Smith Kline (pharmaceutical sciences), Sun River, Inc. (cognitive rehabilitation), Merck & Company, Inc. (pharmaceutical sciences).

GRADUATE UNITS

College of Osteopathic Medicine Offers osteopathic medicine (DO). Electronic applications accepted.

Graduate Program in Forensic Sciences *Program availability:* Part-time, evening/weekend, 100% online, blended/hybrid learning. Offers forensic sciences (MS). Electronic applications accepted.

Program in Biomedical Sciences Offers biomedical sciences (MS, PhD). Electronic applications accepted.

Program in Health Care Administration *Program availability:* Part-time, evening/weekend, 100% online. Offers health care administration (MS).

OKLAHOMA WESLEYAN UNIVERSITY, Bartlesville, OK 74006-6299

General Information Independent-religious, coed, comprehensive institution.

GRADUATE UNITS

Professional Studies Division

OLD DOMINION UNIVERSITY, Norfolk, VA 23529

General Information State-supported, coed, university. CGS member. *Graduate housing:* Room and/or apartments available on a first-come, first-served basis to single students; on-campus housing not available to married students. Housing application deadline: 5/1. *Research affiliation:* Commonwealth Center for Advanced Manufacturing (CCAM) (advanced engineering and manufacturing), Huntington Ingalls Industries (Newport News Shipbuilding) (digital shipbuilding), Thomas Jefferson National Accelerator Facility (high energy physics and laser processing), NASA Langley Research Center (aeronautics and data analytics), Eastern Virginia Medical School (medicine), Virginia Institute of Marine Science (marine science and coastal resilience).

GRADUATE UNITS

College of Arts and Letters *Program availability:* Part-time, evening/weekend, 100% online. Offers applied studies or conducting (MME); arts and entrepreneurship (Certificate); arts and letters (MA, MFA, MME, PhD, Certificate); conflict and cooperation (MA, PhD); creative writing (MFA); criminal justice (MA); criminology and criminal justice (PhD); cultural and human geography (MA); cultural studies (MA); English (MA, PhD); gender and sexuality studies (MA); general sociology (MA); health, communication and culture (Certificate); history (MA); interdependence and transnationalism (MA, PhD); international cultural studies (MA, PhD); international political economy and development (MA, PhD); lifespan and digital communication (MA); literature (MA); media and popular culture studies (MA); modeling and simulation (MA, PhD); pedagogy (MME); philosophy and religious studies (MA); professional writing (MA); research (MME); rhetoric and composition (MA); social justice and entrepreneurship (Certificate); sociolinguistics (MA); TESOL (MA); U.S. foreign policy and international relations (MA, PhD); visual studies (MA); women's studies (MA); world cultures (MA). Electronic applications accepted.

College of Health Sciences *Program availability:* Part-time, evening/weekend, 100% online, blended/hybrid learning. Offers health sciences (MS, MSAT, MSN, DNP, DPT, PhD); health services research (PhD). Electronic applications accepted.

School of Community and Environmental Health Offers general environmental health (MS); industrial hygiene (MS). Electronic applications accepted.

School of Dental Hygiene *Program availability:* Part-time, evening/weekend, blended/hybrid learning. Offers dental hygiene (MS). Electronic applications accepted.

School of Nursing *Program availability:* Part-time, 100% online, blended/hybrid learning. Offers adult gerontology clinical nurse specialist/administrator (MSN); adult gerontology clinical nurse specialist/educator (MSN); advanced practice (DNP); family nurse practitioner (MSN); neonatal clinical nurse specialist (MSN); neonatal nurse practitioner (MSN); nurse administrator (MSN); nurse anesthesia (DNP); nurse executive (DNP); nursing (MSN, DNP); pediatric clinical nurse specialist (MSN); pediatric nurse practitioner (MSN). MSN in nurse midwifery, MSN in psychiatric mental health offered in cooperation with Shenandoah University. Electronic applications accepted.

School of Physical Therapy and Athletic Training Offers athletic training (MSAT); kinesiology and rehabilitation (PhD); physical therapy (DPT). Electronic applications accepted.

College of Sciences *Program availability:* Part-time, evening/weekend, 100% online. Offers analytical chemistry (MS, PhD); applied mathematics (MS, PhD); applied psychological sciences (PhD); biochemistry (MS, PhD); biology (MS); biomedical sciences (PhD); biostatistics (MS); clinical psychology (PhD); computer information systems (MS); computer science (MS, PhD); ecological sciences (PhD); environmental chemistry (MS, PhD); human factors psychology (PhD); industrial/organizational psychology (PhD); inorganic chemistry (MS, PhD); microbiology and immunology (MS); ocean and earth sciences (MS); oceanography (PhD); organic chemistry (MS, PhD); physical chemistry (MS, PhD); physics (MS, PhD); psychology (MS, PhD); sciences (MS, PhD); statistics (MS); statistics/biostatistics (PhD). Electronic applications accepted.

Darden College of Education *Program availability:* Part-time, evening/weekend, 100% online, blended/hybrid learning. Offers adapted curriculum K-12 (MS Ed); adapted physical education (MS Ed); chemistry (MS Ed); clinical mental health counseling (MS Ed); coaching education (MS Ed); college counseling (MS Ed); community college leadership (PhD); community college teaching (MS Ed); counseling (Ed S); counselor education (PhD); curriculum and instruction (MS Ed, PhD); early childhood education (MS Ed, PhD); early childhood special education (MS Ed); education (PhD); educational leadership (MS Ed, PhD, Ed S); elementary education (Postbaccalaureate Certificate); English (MS Ed); exercise science and wellness (MS Ed); general curriculum K-12 (MS Ed); higher education (MS Ed, PhD, Ed S); human movement science (PhD); human movement sciences (PhD); human resources training (PhD); instructional design and technology (PhD); instructional technology (MS Ed); library science (MS Ed); literacy leadership (PhD); park, recreation and tourism (MS); physical education (MS Ed); reading specialist (MS Ed); school counseling (MS Ed); secondary education (MS Ed); special education (PhD); speech-language pathology (MS); sport management (MS); technology education (PhD). Electronic applications accepted.

Frank Batten College of Engineering and Technology *Program availability:* Part-time, evening/weekend, 100% online, blended/hybrid learning. Offers aerospace engineering (ME, MS, D Eng, PhD); biomedical engineering (ME, MS, PhD); civil and environmental engineering (D Eng, PhD); civil engineering (ME, MS); electrical and computer engineering (ME, MS, D Eng, PhD); engineering and technology (ME, MS, D Eng, PhD); engineering management (MEM, MS); engineering management and systems engineering (D Eng, PhD); environmental engineering (ME, MS); mechanical engineering (ME, MS, D Eng, PhD); modeling and simulation (ME, MS, D Eng, PhD); systems engineering (ME). Electronic applications accepted.

Strome College of Business *Program availability:* Part-time, evening/weekend, online learning. Offers accounting (MS); business (MA, MBA, MPA, MS, PhD); business administration (MBA, PhD); economics (MA); maritime trade and supply chain management (MS); multi-sector public service (MPA); public administration (MPA); public administration and policy (PhD). Electronic applications accepted.

OLIVET COLLEGE, Olivet, MI 49076-9701

General Information Independent-religious, coed, comprehensive institution.

GRADUATE UNITS

Master of Business Administration in Insurance Program *Program availability:* Part-time, online only, 100% online, blended/hybrid learning. Offers insurance (MBA). Electronic applications accepted.

OLIVET NAZARENE UNIVERSITY, Bourbonnais, IL 60914

General Information Independent-religious, coed, comprehensive institution. *Graduate housing:* Room and/or apartments available to single students; on-campus housing not available to married students. Housing application deadline: 8/15.

GRADUATE UNITS

Graduate School *Program availability:* Part-time, evening/weekend. Offers business administration (MBA); family nurse practitioner (MSN); nursing (MSN); practical ministries (MPM).

Division of Education *Program availability:* Evening/weekend. Offers curriculum and instruction (MAE); elementary education (MAT); library information specialist (MAE); reading specialist (MAE); school leadership (MAE); secondary education (MAT).

Division of Religion *Program availability:* Part-time. Offers biblical literature (MA); religion (MA); theology (MA).

Program in Organizational Leadership Offers organizational leadership (MOL).

OMEGA GRADUATE SCHOOL, Dayton, TN 37321-6736

General Information Independent-religious, coed, graduate-only institution. *Graduate housing:* Rooms and/or apartments guaranteed to single students and available on a first-come, first-served basis to married students.

GRADUATE UNITS

Graduate Programs Offers family life education (M Litt); integration of religion and society (D Phil); organizational leadership (M Litt).

OPEN UNIVERSITY, Milton Keynes MK7 6AA, United Kingdom

General Information Public, coed, comprehensive institution.

GRADUATE UNITS

Graduate Programs

ORAL ROBERTS UNIVERSITY, Tulsa, OK 74171

General Information Independent-religious, coed, comprehensive institution. *Graduate housing:* Room and/or apartments available on a first-come, first-served basis to single students; on-campus housing not available to married students.

GRADUATE UNITS

School of Business *Program availability:* Part-time, online learning. Offers accounting (MBA); entrepreneurship (MBA); finance (MBA); international business (MBA); management (MBA); marketing (MBA); not for profit management (MNM). Electronic applications accepted.

School of Education *Program availability:* Part-time, online learning. Offers Christian school administration (K-12) (MA Ed, Ed D); college and higher education administration (Ed D); curriculum and instruction (MA Ed); initial teaching with alternative licensure (MAT); initial teaching with licensure (MAT); public school administration (K-12) (MA Ed, Ed D). Electronic applications accepted.

School of Theology and Missions *Program availability:* Part-time, online learning. Offers biblical literature (MA); church ministries and leadership (D Min); clinical pastoral education (M Div); missions (MA); pastoral care and chaplaincy (M Div, D Min); practical theology (MA); professional counseling (MA); theological/historical studies (MA). Electronic applications accepted.

OREGON COLLEGE OF ORIENTAL MEDICINE, Portland, OR 97216

General Information Independent, coed, graduate-only institution. *Graduate housing:* On-campus housing not available.

GRADUATE UNITS

Graduate Program in Acupuncture and Oriental Medicine *Program availability:* Part-time. Offers acupuncture and Oriental medicine (M Ac OM, MAcOM, DAOM).

OREGON HEALTH & SCIENCE UNIVERSITY, Portland, OR 97239-3098

General Information State-related, coed, upper-level institution. CGS member. *Graduate housing:* On-campus housing not available. *Research affiliation:* Oregon Regional Primate Research Center.

GRADUATE UNITS

School of Dentistry Offers biomaterials and biomechanics (MS); dentistry (MS, DMD, Certificate); endodontics (Certificate); oral and maxillofacial surgery (Certificate); oral molecular biology (MS); orthodontics (MS, Certificate); pediatric dentistry (Certificate); periodontology (MS, Certificate); restorative dentistry (MS). Electronic applications accepted.

School of Medicine Students: 938 full-time (533 women), 299 part-time (154 women); includes 306 minority (19 Black or African American, non-Hispanic/Latino; 3 American Indian or Alaska Native, non-Hispanic/Latino; 160 Asian, non-Hispanic/Latino; 64 Hispanic/Latino; 1 Native Hawaiian or other Pacific Islander, non-Hispanic/Latino; 59 Two or more races, non-Hispanic/Latino), 77 international. Average age 29. Expenses: Contact institution. *Financial support:* Fellowships, research assistantships, teaching assistantships, career-related internships or fieldwork, Federal Work-Study, institutionally sponsored loans, scholarships/grants, health care benefits, and full-tuition and stipends (for PhD students) available. Support available to part-time students. Financial award application deadline: 3/1; financial award applicants required to submit FAFSA. In 2018, 173 master's, 191 doctorates, 78 other advanced degrees awarded. *Program availability:* Part-time. Offers medicine (MBA, MBI, MBST, MCR, MPAS, MS, MSCNU, MD, PhD, Certificate, Graduate Certificate). *Application deadline:* Applications are processed on a rolling basis. Electronic applications accepted. *Application Contact:* Registrar's Office, 503-494-7800. *Dean of the School of Medicine,* Dr. Sharon Anderson, 503-494-8220, Fax: 503-494-3400.

Graduate Programs in Medicine Students: 404 full-time (230 women), 347 part-time (183 women); includes 178 minority (11 Black or African American, non-Hispanic/Latino; 3 American Indian or Alaska Native, non-Hispanic/Latino; 88 Asian, non-Hispanic/Latino; 47 Hispanic/Latino; 29 Two or more races, non-Hispanic/Latino), 78 international. Average age 32. 816 applicants, 32% accepted, 177 enrolled. *Faculty:* 883. Expenses: Contact institution. *Financial support:* Fellowships, research assistantships, teaching assistantships, scholarships/grants, health care benefits, and full-tuition and stipends (for PhD students) available. Financial award application deadline: 3/1; financial award applicants required to submit FAFSA. In 2018, 173 master's, 44 doctorates, 74 other advanced degrees awarded. *Program availability:* Part-time. Offers behavioral neuroscience (PhD); biochemistry and molecular biology (PhD); bioinformatics and computational biology (MS, PhD); biomedical engineering (MBI, MS, PhD); cancer biology (PhD); cell and developmental biology (PhD); clinical informatics (MBI, MS, PhD, Certificate); computer science and engineering (MS, PhD); dietetics (Certificate); electrical engineering (MS, PhD); environmental science and engineering (MS, PhD); health information management (Certificate); healthcare management (MBA, MS, Certificate); human investigations (MCR, Certificate); human nutrition (MS); medicine (MBA, MBI, MCR, MPAS, MS, MSCNU, PhD, Certificate); molecular and cellular biosciences (PhD); molecular and medical genetics (PhD); molecular microbiology and immunology (PhD); neuroscience (PhD); physician assistant studies (MPAS); physiology and pharmacology (PhD). *Application fee:* $70. Electronic applications accepted. *Application Contact:* Lorie Gookin, Admissions Coordinator, 503-494-6222, E-mail: somgrad@ohsu.edu. *Associate Dean for Graduate Studies,* Dr. Allison Fryer, 503-494-6222, E-mail: somgrad@ohsu.edu.

School of Nursing *Program availability:* Part-time, 100% online, blended/hybrid learning. Offers adult gerontology acute care nurse practitioner (MN); family nurse practitioner (MN); health systems and organizational leadership (MN); nurse anesthesia (MN); nurse midwifery (MN); nursing (MN, DNP, PhD, Post Master's Certificate); nursing education (MN, Post Master's Certificate); pediatric nurse practitioner (MN); psychiatric mental health nurse practitioner (MN). Electronic applications accepted.

OREGON INSTITUTE OF TECHNOLOGY, Klamath Falls, OR 97601-8801

General Information State-supported, coed, comprehensive institution. *Graduate housing:* Room and/or apartments available on a first-come, first-served basis to single students; on-campus housing not available to married students. Housing application deadline: 3/1.

GRADUATE UNITS

Program in Manufacturing Engineering Technology *Program availability:* Part-time, online learning. Offers manufacturing engineering technology (MS). Electronic applications accepted.

OREGON STATE UNIVERSITY, Corvallis, OR 97331

General Information State-supported, coed, university. CGS member. *Graduate housing:* Rooms and/or apartments guaranteed to single students and available on a first-come, first-served basis to married students. Housing application deadline: 5/1. *Research affiliation:* W.M. Keck Foundation (science, engineering), David and Lucille Packard Foundation (science, environmental science), William and Flora Hewlett Foundation (science, engineering), George and Betty Moore Foundation (medical research, science education), Comer Science and Educational Foundation (science).

GRADUATE UNITS

College of Agricultural Sciences *Program availability:* Part-time, online learning. Offers agricultural sciences (MA, MS, PSM, PhD); agroforestry (MS, PhD); animal science (MS); animal-habitat relationships (MS, PhD); applied systematics (MS); aquaculture (MS); breeding, genetics, and biotechnology (MS, PhD); brewing (MS, PhD); community and landscape horticultural systems (MS, PhD); conservation biology (MS, PhD); crop science (MS, PhD); ecology (MS, PhD); enology (MS, PhD); environmental chemistry and ecotoxicology (MS, PhD); environmental soil science (MS, PhD); fish genetics (MS, PhD); fisheries and wildlife administration (PSM); flavor chemistry (MS, PhD); food and seafood processing (MS, PhD); food chemistry/biochemistry (MS, PhD); food engineering (MS, PhD); food microbiology/biotechnology (MS, PhD); genetics (MS, PhD); genomics and computational biology (MS, PhD); ichthyology (MS, PhD); leadership and communication in agriculture (MS); limnology (MS, PhD); mechanistic toxicology (MS, PhD); molecular and cellular biology (MS, PhD); molecular and cellular toxicology (MS, PhD); mycology (MS, PhD); neurotoxicology (MS, PhD); parasites and diseases (MS, PhD); physiology and ecology of marine and freshwater fishes (MS, PhD); plant pathology (MS, PhD); plant physiology (MS, PhD); poultry science (MS, PhD); public health economics (MA, MS, PhD); sensory evaluation (MS, PhD); stream ecology (MS, PhD); sustainable crop production (MS, PhD); toxicology (MS, PhD); water pollution biology (MS, PhD).

College of Business *Program availability:* Part-time, blended/hybrid learning. Offers business (MBA, PhD); business administration (PhD); corporate finance (MBA).

College of Earth, Ocean, and Atmospheric Sciences Offers atmospheric sciences (MA, MS, PhD); earth, ocean, and atmospheric sciences (MA, MS, PhD); geochemistry (MA, MS, PhD); geographic information science (MA, MS, PhD); geomorphology (MA, MS, PhD); geophysics (MA, MS, PhD); glacial geology (MA, MS, PhD); hydrology and hydrogeology (MA, MS, PhD); igneous petrology (MA, MS, PhD); marine resource management (MS); neotonics (MA, MS, PhD); oceanography (MA, MS, PhD); paleoclimatology (MA); physical geography (MA, MS, PhD); resource geography (MA, MS, PhD); structural geology (MA, MS, PhD).

College of Education *Program availability:* Part-time, 100% online, blended/hybrid learning. Offers adult and higher education (Ed M, Ed D, PhD); agricultural education (PhD); clinical mental health counseling (M Coun); clinically based elementary education (MAT); counseling (Ed M, M Coun, MAT, MS, Ed D, PhD); elementary education (MAT); language arts (MAT); language equity and education policy (PhD); mathematics (MAT); mathematics education (MS); music education (MAT); school counseling (M Coun); science (MAT); science education (MS); science/mathematics education (PhD); social studies (MAT).

College of Engineering *Program availability:* Part-time, 100% online. Offers advanced manufacturing (M Eng, MS, PhD); algorithms and cryptography (M Eng, MS, PhD); application of nuclear techniques (M Eng, MHP, MS, PhD); bio-based products and fuels (M Eng, MS, PhD); biological systems analysis (M Eng, MS, PhD); biomaterials (M Eng, MS, PhD); biomedical devices and instrumentation (M Eng, MS, PhD); bioprocessing (M Eng, MS, PhD); bioremediation (M Eng, MS, PhD); chemical engineering (MS, PhD); chemistry (MS, PhD); civil engineering (M Eng, MS, PhD); coastal and ocean engineering (M Eng, MS, PhD); construction engineering management (M Eng, MS, PhD); ecosystems analysis and modeling (M Eng, MS, PhD); electrical and computer engineering (M Eng, MS, PhD); engineering (M Eng, MHP, MMP, MS, PhD); engineering education (M Eng, MS, PhD); engineering management (M Eng); forest products (MS, PhD); geomatics (M Eng, MS, PhD); geotechnical engineering (M Eng, MS, PhD); human performance engineering (M Eng, MS, PhD); human systems engineering (M Eng, MS, PhD); information systems engineering (M Eng, MS, PhD); infrastructure materials (M Eng, MS, PhD); manufacturing systems engineering (M Eng, MS, PhD); mathematics (MS, PhD); mechanical engineering (MS, PhD); medical health physics (MMP, MS); medical imaging (M Eng, MS, PhD); nuclear engineering (MS, PhD); physics (MS, PhD); robotics (M Eng, MS, PhD); structural engineering (M Eng, MS, PhD); systems and computational biology (M Eng, MS, PhD); therapeutic radiologic physics (PhD); transportation engineering (M Eng); water quality (M Eng, MS, PhD); water resources (M Eng, MS, PhD).

College of Forestry *Program availability:* Part-time, 100% online. Offers biodeterioration and materials protection (MS, PhD); engineering for sustainable forestry (MF, MS, PhD); fisheries management (MNR); forest biology (MF); forest, wildlife and landscape ecology (MS, PhD); forestry (MF, MNR, MS, PhD); forests and climate change (MNR); genetics and physiology (MS, PhD); geographic information science (MNR); integrated social and ecological systems (MS, PhD); science of conservation, restoration and sustainable management (MS, PhD); silviculture (MF); social science, policy, and natural resources (MS, PhD); soil-plant-atmosphere continuum (MS, PhD); sustainable natural resources (MNR); sustainable recreation and tourism (MS); urban forestry (MNR); water conflict management and transformation (MNR); wildlife management (MNR).

College of Liberal Arts *Program availability:* Part-time. Offers applied anthropology (MA); applied cognition (MS, PhD); biomedical ethics (MA); college student services administration (Ed M, MS); contemporary Hispanic studies (MA); development of the physical, biological, and environmental sciences (MA, MS, PhD); energy policy (MPP, PhD); engineering psychology (MS, PhD); environmental action (MA); environmental policy (MPP, PhD); feminist leadership (PhD); fiction (MFA); film and visual studies (MA); health psychology (MS, PhD); international policy (MPP, PhD); law, crime and policy (MPP, PhD); liberal arts (Ed M, MA, MFA, MPP, MS, PhD); literature and culture (MA); rhetoric, writing and composition (MA); rural policy (MPP, PhD); science and technology policy (MPP, PhD); social policy (MPP, PhD).

College of Pharmacy Offers biopharmaceutics (MS, PhD); pharmacy (MS, PhD, Pharm D).

College of Public Health and Human Sciences Offers athletic training (MATRN); biophysical kinesiology (MS, PhD); biostatistics (MPH); environmental and occupational health (MPH, PhD); epidemiology (MPH, PhD); global health (MPH, PhD); human development and family studies (MS, PhD); nutrition (MS, PhD); psychosocial kinesiology (MS, PhD); public health and human sciences (MATRN, MPH, MS, PhD). Electronic applications accepted.

College of Science *Program availability:* Part-time. Offers analytical chemistry (MA, MS, PhD); atomic physics (MA, MS, PhD); behavioral ecology (PhD); biochemistry and biophysics (MA, MS, PhD); computational physics (MA, MS, PhD); data analytics (MS); differential geometry (MA, MS, PhD); environmental microbiology (MA, MS, PhD); experimental physics (MA, MS, PhD); financial and actuarial mathematics (MA, MS, PhD); food microbiology (MA, MS, PhD); genomics (MA, MS, PhD); immunology (MA, MS, PhD); mathematical biology (MA, MS, PhD); mathematics education (MS, PhD); microbial ecology (MA, MS, PhD); microbial evolution (MA, MS, PhD); nuclear and particle physics (MA, MS, PhD); number theory (MA, MS, PhD); numerical analysis (MA, MS, PhD); optical physics (MA, MS, PhD); parasitology (MA, MS, PhD); pathogenic microbiology (MA, MS, PhD); probability (MA); science (MA, MS, PhD); solid state physics (MA, MS, PhD); statistics (MA, MS, PhD); virology (MA).

College of Veterinary Medicine Offers veterinary medicine (DVM). DVM admissions open only to residents of Oregon and other states participating in the Western Interstate Commission for Higher Education.

Interdisciplinary/Institutional Programs *Program availability:* Part-time. Offers biogeochemistry (MA, MS, PSM, PhD); bioinformatics (PhD); biomedical sciences (MS, PhD); biotechnology (PhD); ecology (MA, MS, PSM, PhD); environmental education (MA, MS, PhD); genome biology (PhD); interdisciplinary studies (MAIS); molecular virology (PhD); plant molecular biology (PhD); quantitative analysis (PSM); social science (MA, MS, PSM, PhD); water resources (MA, MS, PhD); water resources engineering (MS, PhD); water resources policy and management (MS); water resources science (MS, PhD).

OREGON STATE UNIVERSITY–CASCADES, Bend, OR 97701

General Information State-supported, coed, comprehensive institution.

GRADUATE UNITS

Program in Counseling Offers community counseling (MS); school counseling (MS).
Program in Education Offers education (MAT).

OTIS COLLEGE OF ART AND DESIGN, Los Angeles, CA 90045-9785

General Information Independent, coed, comprehensive institution. *Graduate housing:* On-campus housing not available.

GRADUATE UNITS

Program in Fine Arts Offers new genres (MFA); painting (MFA); photography (MFA); sculpture (MFA). Electronic applications accepted.
Program in Graphic Design Offers graphic design (MFA). Electronic applications accepted.
Program in Public Practice Offers public practice (MFA). Electronic applications accepted.
Program in Writing Offers writing (MFA). Electronic applications accepted.

OTTAWA UNIVERSITY, Ottawa, KS 66067-3399

General Information Independent-religious, coed, comprehensive institution. *Graduate housing:* On-campus housing not available.

GRADUATE UNITS

Graduate Studies-Arizona *Program availability:* Part-time, evening/weekend, online learning. Offers business administration (MBA); Christian counseling (MA); community college counseling (MA); curriculum and instruction (MA); early childhood (MA); education intervention (MA); education leadership (MA); education technology (MA); expressive arts therapy (MA); finance (MBA); human resources (MA, MBA); leadership (MBA); marketing (MBA); marriage and family therapy (MA); Montessori early childhood education (MA); Montessori elementary education (MA); professional development (MA); school guidance counseling (MA); special education - cross categorical (MA); treatment of trauma, abuse and deprivation (MA). Electronic applications accepted.
Graduate Studies-International *Program availability:* Online learning. Offers business administration (MBA). Electronic applications accepted.
Graduate Studies-Kansas City *Program availability:* Part-time, evening/weekend, online learning. Offers business administration (MBA); human resources (MA). Electronic applications accepted.
Graduate Studies-Wisconsin *Program availability:* Part-time, evening/weekend, online learning. Offers business administration (MBA). Electronic applications accepted.

OTTERBEIN UNIVERSITY, Westerville, OH 43081

General Information Independent-religious, coed, comprehensive institution. CGS member. *Graduate housing:* On-campus housing not available.

GRADUATE UNITS

Department of Business, Accounting and Economics *Program availability:* Part-time, evening/weekend. Offers business, accounting and economics (MBA).
Department of Education Offers education (MAE, MAT).
Department of Nursing *Program availability:* Part-time, evening/weekend, online learning. Offers advanced practice nurse educator (Certificate); clinical nurse leader (MSN); family nurse practitioner (MSN, Certificate); nurse anesthesia (MSN, Certificate); nursing (DNP); nursing service administration (MSN).

OUR LADY OF THE LAKE UNIVERSITY, San Antonio, TX 78207-4689

General Information Independent-religious, coed, comprehensive institution. *Enrollment:* 1,527 full-time matriculated graduate/professional students (1,244 women), 202 part-time matriculated graduate/professional students (162 women). *Enrollment by degree level:* 1,419 master's, 310 doctoral. *Graduate faculty:* 71 full-time (55 women), 99 part-time/adjunct (65 women). *Tuition:* Full-time $16,326; part-time $907 per credit. *Graduate housing:* Room and/or apartments available on a first-come, first-served basis to single students; on-campus housing not available to married students. Housing application deadline: 7/15. *Student services:* Campus employment opportunities, campus safety program, career counseling, exercise/wellness program, free psychological counseling, international student services, low-cost health insurance, services for students with disabilities, teacher training. *Library facilities:* The Sueltenfuss Library. *Collection:* Books: 82,924 (physical), 51,160 (digital/electronic); Serial titles: 16,651 (physical), 167,665 (digital/electronic); Databases: 96. Weekly public service hours: 95; study areas open 24 hours, 5–7 days a week.

Computer facilities: 236 computers available on campus for general student use. A campuswide network can be accessed from student residence rooms and from off campus. Online class registration is available. Website: http://www.ollusa.edu/

General Application Contact: Graduate Admissions Office, 210-431-3995, Fax: 210-431-3945, E-mail: gradadm@ollusa.edu.

GRADUATE UNITS

College of Arts and Sciences Students: 12 full-time (9 women), 5 part-time (3 women); includes 12 minority (1 Black or African American, non-Hispanic/Latino; 10 Hispanic/Latino; 1 Two or more races, non-Hispanic/Latino). Average age 32. 10 applicants, 70% accepted, 4 enrolled. *Faculty:* 3 full-time (2 women). Expenses: Contact institution. *Financial support:* In 2018–19, 7 students received support. Federal Work-Study, scholarships/grants, unspecified assistantships, and tuition discounts available. Support available to part-time students. Financial award application deadline: 5/1; financial award applicants required to submit FAFSA. In 2018, 7 master's awarded. *Program availability:* Part-time, evening/weekend. Offers arts and sciences (MA); literature, creative writing, and social justice (MA). *Application deadline:* For fall admission, 7/15 for domestic and international students; for spring admission, 11/15 for domestic and international students; for summer admission, 2/15 for domestic and international students. *Application fee:* $40 ($50 for international students). Electronic applications accepted. *Application Contact:* Graduate Admission, 210-431-3995, Fax: 210-431-3945, E-mail: gradadm@lake.ollusa.edu. *Interim Dean for the College of Arts and Science,* Dr. Rosa Rivera-Hainaj, 210-431-6564, E-mail: rhainaj@lake.ollusa.edu.

College of Professional Studies Students: 1,022 full-time (935 women), 151 part-time (130 women); includes 764 minority (269 Black or African American, non-Hispanic/Latino; 7 American Indian or Alaska Native, non-Hispanic/Latino; 10 Asian, non-Hispanic/Latino; 452 Hispanic/Latino; 2 Native Hawaiian or other Pacific Islander, non-Hispanic/Latino; 24 Two or more races, non-Hispanic/Latino). Average age 33. 417 applicants, 61% accepted, 188 enrolled. *Faculty:* 5 full-time (all women), 3 part-time/adjunct (2 women). Expenses: Contact institution. *Financial support:* In 2018–19, 111 students received support. Research assistantships, teaching assistantships, Federal Work-Study, scholarships/grants, unspecified assistantships, and tuition discounts available. Support available to part-time students. Financial award application deadline: 5/1; financial award applicants required to submit FAFSA. In 2018, 418 master's, 5 doctorates awarded. *Program availability:* Part-time, evening/weekend, 100% online, blended/hybrid learning. Offers communication and learning disorders (MA); counseling psychology (Psy D); integrated science teaching (M Ed); marriage and family therapy (MS); school counseling (M Ed); school psychology (MS); sociology (MA). *Application fee:* $40 ($50 for international students). Electronic applications accepted. *Application Contact:* Graduate Admissions, 210-431-3995 Ext. 2314, Fax: 210-431-3945, E-mail: gradadm@lake.ollusa.edu. *Dean,* Dr. Mo Cuevas, 210-431-6516, E-mail: mccuevas@ollusa.edu.

School of Business and Leadership Students: 493 full-time (300 women), 46 part-time (29 women); includes 405 minority (53 Black or African American, non-Hispanic/Latino; 7 Asian, non-Hispanic/Latino; 341 Hispanic/Latino; 2 Native Hawaiian or other Pacific Islander, non-Hispanic/Latino; 2 Two or more races, non-Hispanic/Latino), 1 international. Average age 40. 150 applicants, 90% accepted, 100 enrolled. *Faculty:* 15 full-time (all women), 42 part-time/adjunct (10 women). Expenses: Contact institution. *Financial support:* Teaching assistantships, Federal Work-Study, unspecified assistantships, and tuition discounts available. Support available to part-time students. Financial award application deadline: 5/1; financial award applicants required to submit FAFSA. In 2018, 123 master's, 23 doctorates awarded. *Program availability:* Part-time, evening/weekend, 100% online, blended/hybrid learning. Offers accounting (MS); finance (MBA); healthcare management (MBA); information systems and security (MS); leadership studies (PhD); management (MBA); nonprofit management (MS); organizational leadership (MS). *Application fee:* $40 ($50 for international students). Electronic applications accepted. *Associate Dean,* Kathryn Winney, 210-434-6711 Ext. 7051, E-mail: kmwinney@ollusa.edu.

Worden School of Social Service Students: 787 full-time (724 women), 100 part-time (88 women); includes 567 minority (241 Black or African American, non-Hispanic/Latino; 7 American Indian or Alaska Native, non-Hispanic/Latino; 6 Asian, non-Hispanic/Latino; 291 Hispanic/Latino; 2 Native Hawaiian or other Pacific Islander, non-Hispanic/Latino; 20 Two or more races, non-Hispanic/Latino). Average age 35. 190 applicants, 90% accepted, 124 enrolled. *Faculty:* 11 full-time (8 women), 63 part-time/adjunct (49 women). Expenses: Contact institution. *Financial support:* In 2018–19, 29 students received support, including 1 research assistantship (averaging $15,300 per year); teaching assistantships, Federal Work-Study, scholarships/grants, unspecified assistantships, and tuition discounts also available. Support available to part-time students. Financial award application deadline: 5/1; financial award applicants required to submit FAFSA. In 2018, 335 master's awarded. *Program availability:* Part-time, evening/weekend, 100% online, blended/hybrid learning. Offers social work (MSW, PhD). *Application deadline:* For fall admission, 6/15 for domestic and international students; for spring admission, 11/15 for domestic and international students; for summer admission, 4/15 for domestic and international students. Applications are processed on a rolling basis. *Application fee:* $40 ($50 for international students). Electronic applications accepted. *Application Contact:* Office of Graduate Admissions, 210-431-3995, Fax: 210-431-3945, E-mail: gradadm@lake.ollusa.edu. *Program Director,* Rebecca Gomez, 210-434-6711 Ext. 5578, E-mail: rjgomez@ollusa.edu.

PACE UNIVERSITY, New York, NY 10038

General Information Independent, coed, university. *Enrollment:* 13,609 graduate, professional, and undergraduate students; 2,335 full-time matriculated graduate/professional students (1,383 women), 2,209 part-time matriculated graduate/professional students (1,453 women). *Enrollment by degree level:* 3,545 master's, 950 doctoral, 49 other advanced degrees. *Graduate housing:* Room and/or apartments available on a first-come, first-served basis to single students; on-campus housing not available to married students. *Student services:* Campus employment opportunities, career counseling, free psychological counseling, grant writing training, international student services, low-cost health insurance, multicultural affairs office, services for students with disabilities, teacher training, writing training. *Library facilities:* Henry Birnbaum Library. *Collection:* Books: 382,858 (physical), 224,418 (digital/electronic); Serial titles: 73 (physical), 576,860 (digital/electronic); Databases: 172. Weekly public service hours: 93; students can reserve study rooms.

Computer facilities: 209 computers available on campus for general student use. A campuswide network can be accessed. Online class registration, administrative functions (tuition, student records, financial aid, health insurance waiver) are available. Website: http://www.pace.edu/nyc

General Application Contact: Susan Ford-Goldschein, Director of Graduate Admissions, 212-346-1531, Fax: 212-346-1585, E-mail: graduateadmission@pace.edu.

GRADUATE UNITS

College of Health Professions Average age 32. 1,817 applicants, 22% accepted, 245 enrolled. Expenses: Contact institution. *Financial support:* Research assistantships, teaching assistantships, career-related internships or fieldwork, institutionally sponsored loans, scholarships/grants, and unspecified assistantships available. Financial award application deadline: 2/15; financial award applicants required to submit FAFSA. In 2018, 847 master's, 45 doctorates, 27 other advanced degrees awarded. *Program availability:* Part-time. Offers communication sciences and disorders (MS); health professions (MS, DNP, PhD, CAGS); physician assistant studies (MS). *Application deadline:* For fall admission, 3/1 for domestic students; for spring admission, 9/1 for domestic students. Applications are processed on a rolling basis. *Application fee:* $70. Electronic applications accepted. *Application Contact:* Susan Ford-Goldschein, Dean of Graduate Admissions, 212-346-1531, Fax: 212-346-1585, E-mail: graduateadmission@pace.edu. *Dean, College of Health Professions,* Dr. Harriet R. Feldman, 914-773-3341, Fax: 914-773-3341, E-mail: hfeldman@pace.edu.

Lienhard School of Nursing Average age 35. 289 applicants, 74% accepted, 138 enrolled. Expenses: Contact institution. *Financial support:* Research assistantships, teaching assistantships, career-related internships or fieldwork, Federal Work-Study, institutionally sponsored loans, tuition waivers (partial), and unspecified assistantships available. Support available to part-time students. Financial award application deadline: 2/15; financial award applicants required to submit FAFSA. In 2018, 483 master's, 45 doctorates, 27 other advanced degrees awarded. *Program availability:* Part-time. Offers adult acute care nurse practitioner (MS, CAGS); family nurse practitioner (MS, CAGS); nursing (DNP, PhD); professional nursing leadership (MS, CAGS). *Application deadline:* For fall admission, 3/1 for domestic and international students. Applications are processed on a rolling basis. *Application fee:* $70. Electronic applications accepted. *Application Contact:* Susan Ford-Goldschein, Director of Graduate Admissions, 212-346-1531, Fax: 212-346-1585, E-mail: graduateadmission@pace.edu. *Dean, College of Health Professions,* Dr. Harriet R. Feldman, 914-773-3341, E-mail: hfeldman@pace.edu.

Dyson College of Arts and Sciences Students: 439 full-time (313 women), 606 part-time (400 women); includes 319 minority (113 Black or African American, non-Hispanic/Latino; 1 American Indian or Alaska Native, non-Hispanic/Latino; 47 Asian, non-Hispanic/Latino; 117 Hispanic/Latino; 1 Native Hawaiian or other Pacific Islander, non-Hispanic/Latino; 40 Two or more races, non-Hispanic/Latino), 67 international. Average age 32. 1,126 applicants, 78% accepted, 570 enrolled. Expenses: Contact institution. *Financial support:* Research assistantships with partial tuition reimbursements, teaching assistantships, career-related internships or fieldwork, Federal Work-Study, scholarships/grants, and tuition waivers (partial) available. Support available to part-time students. Financial award application deadline: 2/15; financial award applicants required to submit FAFSA. In 2018, 241 master's, 19 doctorates, 4 other advanced degrees awarded. *Program availability:* Part-time, evening/weekend, 100% online, blended/hybrid learning. Offers acting (MFA); arts and sciences (MA, MFA, MPA, MS, MS Ed, PhD, Psy D, Certificate); biochemistry and molecular biology (MS); book publishing (Certificate); business side of publishing (Certificate); digital publishing (Certificate); directing (MFA); environmental science (MS); forensic science (MS); government management (MPA); grief and loss (MS); health care administration (MPA); magazine publishing (Certificate); management for public safety and homeland security professionals (MA); media and communication arts (MA); mental health counseling (MS, PhD); not-for-profit management (MPA); playwriting (MFA); psychology (MA); publishing (MS); school psychology (MS Ed); school-clinical child psychology (MS Ed, Psy D); substance abuse (MS). *Application deadline:* For fall admission, 8/1 for domestic students, 6/1 for international students; for spring admission, 12/1 for domestic students, 10/1 for international students. Applications are processed on a rolling basis. *Application fee:* $70. Electronic applications accepted. *Application Contact:* Susan Ford-Goldschein, Director of Admissions, 212-346-1531, Fax: 212-346-1585, E-mail: graduateadmission@pace.edu. *Dean,* Dr. Nira Herrmann, 212-346-1517, Fax: 212-346-1725, E-mail: nherrmann@pace.edu.

Elisabeth Haub School of Law *Program availability:* Part-time. Offers comparative legal studies (LL M); environmental law (LL M, SJD); law (JD). JD/MA offered jointly with Sarah Lawrence College; JD/MEM offered jointly with Yale University School of Forestry and Environmental Studies. Electronic applications accepted.

Lubin School of Business Students: 397 full-time (229 women), 330 part-time (182 women); includes 185 minority (56 Black or African American, non-Hispanic/Latino; 70 Asian, non-Hispanic/Latino; 46 Hispanic/Latino; 1 Native Hawaiian or other Pacific Islander, non-Hispanic/Latino; 12 Two or more races, non-Hispanic/Latino), 311 international. Average age 30. 765 applicants, 74% accepted, 246 enrolled. Expenses: Contact institution. *Financial support:* Research assistantships, career-related internships or fieldwork, Federal Work-Study, tuition waivers (full and partial), and unspecified assistantships available. Support available to part-time students. Financial award application deadline: 2/15; financial award applicants required to submit FAFSA. In 2018, 366 master's, 8 doctorates awarded. *Program availability:* Part-time, evening/weekend, blended/hybrid learning. Offers business (MBA, MS, DPS, APC); business economics (APC); customer intelligence & analytics (MS); e-business (APC); entrepreneurial studies (MBA); entrepreneurship (MS); finance (DPS); financial management (MBA, MS, APC); financial risk management (MS); human resource management (MBA, MS); information systems (MS); international business (MBA); international economics (APC); international finance (MBA); investment management (MBA, MS, APC); management (DPS); marketing (DPS, APC); marketing management (MBA); public accounting (MBA, MS, APC); social media and mobile marketing (MS); strategic management (MBA, MS); taxation (MBA, MS). *Application deadline:* For fall admission, 8/1 priority date for domestic students, 6/1 for international students; for spring admission, 12/1 priority date for domestic students, 10/1 for international students; for summer admission, 5/1 priority date for domestic students, 3/1 for international students. Applications are processed on a rolling basis. *Application fee:* $70. Electronic applications accepted. *Application Contact:* Susan Ford-Goldschein, Director of Graduate Admissions, 212-346-1531, Fax: 212-346-1585, E-mail: graduateadmission@pace.edu. *Dean, Lubin School of Business,* Neil S. Braun, 212-618-6600, Fax: 212-618-6603, E-mail: nbraun@pace.edu.

School of Education Students: 98 full-time (82 women), 542 part-time (391 women); includes 256 minority (116 Black or African American, non-Hispanic/Latino; 2 American Indian or Alaska Native, non-Hispanic/Latino; 45 Asian, non-Hispanic/Latino; 83 Hispanic/Latino; 10 Two or more races, non-Hispanic/Latino), 4 international. Average age 30. 223 applicants, 89% accepted, 130 enrolled. Faculty: 19 full-time (13 women), 86 part-time/adjunct (49 women). Expenses: Contact institution. *Financial support:* In 2018–19, 17 students received support, including 17 research assistantships with partial tuition reimbursements available (averaging $6,020 per year); career-related internships or fieldwork, Federal Work-Study, scholarships/grants, and unspecified assistantships also available. Financial award application deadline: 9/1; financial award applicants

required to submit FAFSA. In 2018, 269 master's, 12 other advanced degrees awarded. *Program availability:* Part-time, evening/weekend, 100% online, blended/hybrid learning. Offers adolescent education (MST); childhood education (MST); early childhood development, learning and intervention (MST); educational technology studies (MS); inclusive adolescent education (MST); integrated instruction for educational technology (Certificate); integrated instruction for literacy and technology (Certificate); literacy (MS Ed); special education (MS Ed). *Application deadline:* For fall admission, 8/1 priority date for domestic students, 6/1 for international students; for spring admission, 12/1 priority date for domestic students, 10/1 for international students. Applications are processed on a rolling basis. *Application fee:* $70. Electronic applications accepted. *Application Contact:* Susan Ford-Goldschein, Director of Graduate Admissions, 212-346-1531, Fax: 212-346-1585, E-mail: graduateadmission@pace.edu. *Dean, School of Education,* Dr. Harriet Feldman, 914-773-3829, E-mail: hfeldman@pace.edu.

Seidenberg School of Computer Science and Information Systems Students: 515 full-time (172 women), 288 part-time (90 women); includes 183 minority (67 Black or African American, non-Hispanic/Latino; 3 American Indian or Alaska Native, non-Hispanic/Latino; 50 Asian, non-Hispanic/Latino; 52 Hispanic/Latino; 1 Native Hawaiian or other Pacific Islander, non-Hispanic/Latino; 10 Two or more races, non-Hispanic/Latino), 497 international. Average age 30. 817 applicants, 93% accepted, 235 enrolled. Faculty: 26 full-time (7 women), 7 part-time/adjunct (2 women). Expenses: Contact institution. *Financial support:* In 2018–19, 45 students received support. Research assistantships, career-related internships or fieldwork, scholarships/grants, and unspecified assistantships available. Support available to part-time students. Financial award application deadline: 2/15; financial award applicants required to submit FAFSA. In 2018, 383 master's, 15 doctorates, 1 other advanced degree awarded. *Program availability:* Part-time, evening/weekend, online only, 100% online, blended/hybrid learning. Offers chief information security officer (APC); computer science (MS, PhD); enterprise analytics (MS); information and communication technology strategy and innovation (APC); information systems (MS, APC); information technology (MS); professional studies in computing (DPS); secure software and information engineering (APC); security and information assurance (Certificate); software development and engineering (MS, Certificate); telecommunications systems and networks (MS, Certificate). *Application deadline:* For fall admission, 8/1 priority date for domestic students, 6/1 for international students; for spring admission, 12/1 for domestic students, 10/1 for international students. Applications are processed on a rolling basis. *Application fee:* $70. Electronic applications accepted. *Application Contact:* Susan Ford-Goldschein, Director of Graduate Admissions, 914-422-4283, Fax: 212-346-1585, E-mail: graduateadmission@pace.edu. *Dean, Seidenberg School of Computer Science and Information Systems,* Dr. Jonathan Hill, 212-346-1864, E-mail: jhill@pace.edu.

PACIFICA GRADUATE INSTITUTE, Carpinteria, CA 93013

General Information Proprietary, coed, graduate-only institution. *Graduate housing:* Rooms and/or apartments guaranteed to single and married students. Housing application deadline: 8/15. *Research affiliation:* Elton B. Stevens Company (EBSCO) (journal management), American Psychological Association (psychology), North California Consortium of Psychology Libraries (psychology).

GRADUATE UNITS

Graduate Programs Offers clinical psychology (PhD); counseling psychology (MA); depth psychology (MA, PhD); mythological studies (MA, PhD).

PACIFIC COLLEGE OF ORIENTAL MEDICINE, San Diego, CA 92108

General Information Proprietary, coed, graduate-only institution. *Graduate housing:* On-campus housing not available. *Research affiliation:* National Institutes of Health (complimentary and alternative medicine).

GRADUATE UNITS

Graduate Program *Program availability:* Part-time, evening/weekend. Offers Oriental medicine (MSTOM, DAOM).

PACIFIC COLLEGE OF ORIENTAL MEDICINE–CHICAGO, Chicago, IL 60601

General Information Proprietary, coed, graduate-only institution. *Graduate housing:* On-campus housing not available. *Research affiliation:* Children's Memorial Hospital of Chicago (pediatric research).

GRADUATE UNITS

Graduate Program *Program availability:* Part-time, evening/weekend. Offers oriental medicine (MTOM).

PACIFIC COLLEGE OF ORIENTAL MEDICINE-NEW YORK, New York, NY 10010

General Information Proprietary, coed, graduate-only institution. *Graduate housing:* On-campus housing not available.

GRADUATE UNITS

Graduate Program *Program availability:* Part-time, evening/weekend. Offers Oriental medicine (MSTOM).

PACIFIC LUTHERAN UNIVERSITY, Tacoma, WA 98447

General Information Independent-religious, coed, comprehensive institution. *Graduate housing:* Rooms and/or apartments available on a first-come, first-served basis to single and married students. Housing application deadline: 5/1.

GRADUATE UNITS

Division of Humanities *Program availability:* Part-time, blended/hybrid learning. Offers creative writing (MFA). Electronic applications accepted.

Division of Social Sciences Offers marriage and family therapy (MA). Electronic applications accepted.

School of Business *Program availability:* Part-time, evening/weekend. Offers accounting (MSA); business (MBA, MS, MSA, MSF); business administration (MBA); finance (MSF); market research (MS). Electronic applications accepted.

School of Education and Kinesiology *Program availability:* Part-time, evening/weekend. Offers education and kinesiology (MAE); initial teaching certification (MAE). Electronic applications accepted.

School of Nursing Offers entry level nursing (MSN); nursing (MSN, DNP). Electronic applications accepted.

PACIFIC NORTHWEST COLLEGE OF ART, Portland, OR 97209

General Information Independent, coed, comprehensive institution.

GRADUATE UNITS

Program in Applied Craft and Design Offers applied craft and design (MFA). Program offered in collaboration with Oregon College of Art & Craft.

Program in Collaborative Design Offers collaborative design (MFA).

Program in Critical Studies Offers critical studies (MA).

Program in Print Media Offers print media (MFA).

Program in Visual Studies Offers visual studies (MFA).

PACIFIC NORTHWEST UNIVERSITY OF HEALTH SCIENCES, Yakima, WA 98901

General Information Independent, coed, graduate-only institution. *Graduate housing:* On-campus housing not available. *Research affiliation:* Yakima Valley Community Foundation (health care), Arnold P. Gold Foundation (health care), Health Resources and Services Administration (health care).

GRADUATE UNITS

College of Osteopathic Medicine Offers osteopathic medicine (DO). Electronic applications accepted.

PACIFIC OAKS COLLEGE, Pasadena, CA 91103

General Information Independent, coed, primarily women, upper-level institution. *Graduate housing:* Room and/or apartments available to single students; on-campus housing not available to married students.

GRADUATE UNITS

Graduate School *Program availability:* Part-time, evening/weekend, online learning. Offers early childhood education (MA); human development (MA); marriage, family and child counseling (MA); preliminary education specialist (MA); preliminary multiple subject (MA).

PACIFIC RIM CHRISTIAN UNIVERSITY, Honolulu, HI 96819

General Information Independent-religious, coed, comprehensive institution.

GRADUATE UNITS

Program in Christian Ministry Offers Christian ministry (MA).

PACIFIC SCHOOL OF RELIGION, Berkeley, CA 94709-1323

General Information Independent, coed, graduate-only institution. *Graduate housing:* Rooms and/or apartments guaranteed to single and married students. Housing application deadline: 4/1. *Research affiliation:* Center for Women and Religion (women's studies), Center for Ethics and Social Policy (business ethics), Disciples Seminary Foundation (theology), Swedenborgian House of Studies (theology), Bay Area Faith and Health Consortium (public health).

GRADUATE UNITS

Graduate and Professional Programs *Program availability:* Part-time. Offers religion (M Div, MA, MTS, D Min, PhD, Th D, CAPS, CMS, CSS, CTS). MA, PhD, Th D offered jointly with Graduate Theological Union; D Min with Church Divinity School of the Pacific. Electronic applications accepted.

PACIFIC STATES UNIVERSITY, Los Angeles, CA 90010

General Information Independent, coed, comprehensive institution. *Graduate housing:* Room and/or apartments available on a first-come, first-served basis to single students; on-campus housing not available to married students.

GRADUATE UNITS

College of Business *Program availability:* Part-time, evening/weekend, online learning. Offers accounting (MBA, Certificate); beauty management (MBA); finance (MBA); international business (MBA); management of information technology (MBA); project management (Certificate); real estate management (MBA).

College of Computer Science and Information Systems *Program availability:* Part-time, evening/weekend. Offers computer science (MS); information systems (MS).

PACIFIC UNION COLLEGE, Angwin, CA 94508-9707

General Information Independent-religious, coed, comprehensive institution. *Graduate housing:* Room and/or apartments available on a first-come, first-served basis to married students; on-campus housing not available to single students.

GRADUATE UNITS

Education Department Students: 3 full-time (2 women). Average age 20. 4 applicants, 100% accepted, 4 enrolled. *Faculty:* 3 full-time (1 woman), 1 (woman) part-time/adjunct. Expenses: Contact institution. *Financial support:* Scholarships/grants available. Support available to part-time students. Financial award application deadline: 9/25. In 2018, 1 master's awarded. *Program availability:* Part-time. Offers education (M Ed); elementary teaching (MAT); secondary teaching (MAT). *Application deadline:* For fall admission, 8/30 for domestic and international students; for summer admission, 6/1 for domestic and international students. Applications are processed on a rolling basis. *Application fee:* $0. *Application Contact:* Sarah Gitter, Credential Analyst, 707-965-6643, Fax: 707-965-6645, E-mail: teachingcredentials@puc.edu. *Department Chair,* Dr. Jean Buller, 707-965-7266, Fax: 707-965-6645, E-mail: jbuller@puc.edu.

PACIFIC UNIVERSITY, Forest Grove, OR 97116-1797

General Information Independent, coed, comprehensive institution. *Graduate housing:* On-campus housing not available. *Research affiliation:* NEI/PEDIG–JAEB Center of Health Research (amblyopia treatment), BSK, CIBA Vision (contact lenses), Cooper Vision (contact lenses), The Ohio State University/Vistakon-Johnson & Johnson (adolescent and child vision care).

GRADUATE UNITS

College of Business Offers business administration (MBA); finance (MSF).

College of Education *Program availability:* Part-time, evening/weekend. Offers early childhood education (MAT); education (MAE); elementary education (MAT); ESOL (MAT); high school education (MAT); middle school education (MAT); special education (MAT); speech-language pathology (MS); STEM education (MAT); talented and gifted (M Ed); visual function in learning (M Ed). Electronic applications accepted.

College of Optometry Offers optometry (OD); vision science (MS, PhD). Electronic applications accepted.

Healthcare Administration Program Offers healthcare administration (MHA).

Program in Social Work Offers social work (MSW).

Program in Writing *Program availability:* Part-time. Offers writing (MFA).

School of Audiology Offers audiology (Au D).

School of Occupational Therapy Offers occupational therapy (OTD). Electronic applications accepted.

School of Pharmacy Offers pharmacy (Pharm D). Electronic applications accepted.

School of Physical Therapy Offers athletic training (MSAT); physical therapy (DPT). Electronic applications accepted.

School of Physician Assistant Studies Offers physician assistant studies (MS).

School of Professional Psychology *Program availability:* Part-time. Offers applied psychological science (MA, MS); clinical psychology (PhD, Psy D). Electronic applications accepted.

PALM BEACH ATLANTIC UNIVERSITY, West Palm Beach, FL 33416-4708

General Information Independent-religious, coed, comprehensive institution. *Enrollment:* 3,705 graduate, professional, and undergraduate students; 570 full-time matriculated graduate/professional students (406 women), 280 part-time matriculated graduate/professional students (192 women). *Enrollment by degree level:* 472 master's, 378 doctoral. *Graduate faculty:* 36 full-time (17 women), 32 part-time/adjunct (21 women). *Tuition:* Part-time $767 per credit. Tuition and fees vary according to program. *Graduate housing:* On-campus housing not available. *Student services:* Campus employment opportunities, campus safety program, career counseling, exercise/wellness program, multicultural affairs office, services for students with disabilities, writing training. *Library facilities:* Warren Library plus 1 other. *Collection:* Books: 143,334 (physical), 126,921 (digital/electronic); Serial titles: 114 (physical), 121,795 (digital/electronic); Databases: 143. Weekly public service hours: 100; students can reserve study rooms.

Computer facilities: 350 computers available on campus for general student use. A campuswide network can be accessed. Online class registration is available. Website: http://www.pba.edu/

General Application Contact: Joseph Bryan, Assistant Vice President for Admissions, 888-468-6722, E-mail: grad@pba.edu.

GRADUATE UNITS

Gregory School of Pharmacy Students: 247 full-time (163 women), 23 part-time (15 women); includes 148 minority (29 Black or African American, non-Hispanic/Latino; 35 Asian, non-Hispanic/Latino; 72 Hispanic/Latino; 12 Two or more races, non-Hispanic/Latino), 14 international. Average age 27. 321 applicants, 40% accepted, 69 enrolled. *Faculty:* 24 full-time (12 women), 5 part-time/adjunct (3 women). Expenses: Contact institution. *Financial support:* In 2018–19, 63 students received support. Scholarships/grants and employee education grants available. Financial award application deadline: 5/1; financial award applicants required to submit FAFSA. In 2018, 67 doctorates awarded. Offers pharmacy (Pharm D). *Application deadline:* For fall admission, 3/1 priority date for domestic and international students. Applications are processed on a rolling basis. *Application fee:* $0. Electronic applications accepted. *Application Contact:* Lucas Whittaker, Director of Pharmacy Admissions, 561-803-2751, E-mail: lucas_whittaker@pba.edu. *Dean,* Dr. Jeff Lewis, 561-803-2701, E-mail: jeff_lewis@pba.edu.

MacArthur School of Leadership Students: 1 full-time (0 women), 81 part-time (58 women); includes 37 minority (21 Black or African American, non-Hispanic/Latino; 11 Hispanic/Latino; 5 Two or more races, non-Hispanic/Latino), 5 international. Average age 39. *Faculty:* 8 full-time (3 women), 1 part-time/adjunct (0 women). Expenses: Contact institution. *Financial support:* In 2018–19, 44 students received support. Scholarships/grants and employee education grants available. Financial award application deadline: 5/1; financial award applicants required to submit FAFSA. In 2018, 17 master's awarded. *Program availability:* Part-time, evening/weekend, 100% online, blended/hybrid learning. Offers leadership (MS). *Application deadline:* Applications are processed on a rolling basis. *Application fee:* $50. Electronic applications accepted. *Application Contact:* Graduate Admissions, 888-468-6722, E-mail: grad@pba.edu. *Dean,* Dr. Craig Domeck, 561-803-2318, E-mail: craig_domeck@pba.edu.

Rinker School of Business Students: 36 full-time (19 women), 40 part-time (20 women); includes 26 minority (8 Black or African American, non-Hispanic/Latino; 2 Asian, non-Hispanic/Latino; 16 Hispanic/Latino), 20 international. Average age 31. *Faculty:* 2 full-time (1 woman), 3 part-time/adjunct (1 woman). Expenses: Contact institution. *Financial support:* In 2018–19, 46 students received support. Scholarships/grants and employee education grants available. Financial award application deadline: 5/1; financial award applicants required to submit FAFSA. In 2018, 17 master's awarded. *Program availability:* Part-time, evening/weekend. Offers business (MACC, MBA). *Application deadline:* Applications are processed on a rolling basis. *Application fee:* $50. Electronic applications accepted. *Application Contact:* Graduate Admissions, 888-468-6722, Fax: 561-803-2115, E-mail: grad@pba.edu. *MBA Program Director,* Dr. David Smith, 561-803-2473, E-mail: david_smith@pba.edu.

School of Education and Behavioral Studies Students: 182 full-time (149 women), 69 part-time (56 women); includes 130 minority (53 Black or African American, non-Hispanic/Latino; 3 Asian, non-Hispanic/Latino; 60 Hispanic/Latino; 14 Two or more races, non-Hispanic/Latino), 5 international. Average age 35. *Faculty:* 9 full-time (2 women), 12 part-time/adjunct (9 women). Expenses: Contact institution. *Financial support:* In 2018–19, 63 students received support. Career-related internships or fieldwork, scholarships/grants, and employee education grants available. Financial award application deadline: 5/1; financial award applicants required to submit FAFSA. In 2018, 101 master's awarded. *Program availability:* Part-time, evening/weekend. Offers counseling psychology (MS). *Application deadline:* Applications are processed on a rolling basis. *Application fee:* $50. Electronic applications accepted. *Application Contact:* Graduate Admissions, 888-468-6722, E-mail: grad@pba.edu. *Dean,* Dr. Chelly Templeton, 561-803-2353.

School of Ministry Students: 22 full-time (6 women), 28 part-time (9 women); includes 16 minority (8 Black or African American, non-Hispanic/Latino; 7 Hispanic/Latino; 1 Two or more races, non-Hispanic/Latino), 2 international. Average age 28. *Faculty:* 5 full-time (3 women), 2 part-time/adjunct (1 woman). Expenses: Contact institution. *Financial support:* In 2018–19, 17 students received support. Scholarships/grants, unspecified assistantships, and employee education grants available. Financial award application deadline: 5/1; financial award applicants required to submit FAFSA. In 2018, 8 master's awarded. *Program availability:* Part-time. Offers Christian studies (MA); ministry (M Div). *Application deadline:* Applications are processed on a rolling basis. *Application fee:* $50. Electronic applications accepted. *Application Contact:* Graduate Admissions, 888-468-6722, E-mail: grad@pba.edu. *Director of the M Div Program,* Dr. Justin Hardin, 561-803-2377.

School of Nursing Students: 69 full-time (61 women), 39 part-time (31 women); includes 54 minority (34 Black or African American, non-Hispanic/Latino; 2 Asian, non-Hispanic/Latino; 15 Hispanic/Latino; 3 Two or more races, non-Hispanic/Latino), 1 international. Average age 32. *Faculty:* 3 full-time (all women), 5 part-time/adjunct (all women). Expenses: Contact institution. *Financial support:* In 2018–19, 24 students received support. Scholarships/grants and employee education grants available. Financial award application deadline: 5/1; financial award applicants required to submit FAFSA. In 2018, 39 master's, 19 doctorates awarded. *Program availability:* Part-time.

Offers family nurse practitioner (DNP); health systems leadership (MSN). *Application deadline:* Applications are processed on a rolling basis. *Application fee:* $50. Electronic applications accepted. *Application Contact:* Graduate Admissions, 888-468-6722, E-mail: grad@pba.edu. *Dean,* Phyllis King, 561-803-2827.

PALMER COLLEGE OF CHIROPRACTIC, Davenport, IA 52803-5287

General Information Independent, coed, comprehensive institution.

GRADUATE UNITS

Division of Graduate Studies *Program availability:* Part-time. Offers clinical research (MS). Electronic applications accepted.

Professional Program *Program availability:* Part-time. Offers chiropractic (DC). Electronic applications accepted.

Professional Program–Florida Campus *Program availability:* Part-time. Offers chiropractic (DC).

Professional Program–West Campus *Program availability:* Part-time. Offers chiropractic (DC). Electronic applications accepted.

PALO ALTO UNIVERSITY, Palo Alto, CA 94304

General Information Independent, coed, upper-level institution. *Graduate housing:* On-campus housing not available.

GRADUATE UNITS

MA in Counseling Program *Program availability:* Part-time, 100% online, blended/hybrid learning. Offers clinical mental health (MA); marriage, family and child (MA). Electronic applications accepted.

MS in Psychology (PhD Prep) Program *Program availability:* Part-time, online only, online program with 1-week on-campus intensive. Offers psychology (MS). Electronic applications accepted.

PGSP-Stanford Psy D Consortium Program Offers psychology (Psy D). Program offered jointly with Stanford University. Electronic applications accepted.

PhD in Clinical Psychology Program Offers clinical psychology (PhD). Electronic applications accepted.

PARIS COLLEGE OF ART, 75010 Paris, France

General Information Independent, coed, comprehensive institution.

GRADUATE UNITS

Graduate Programs Offers accessories design (MA); fashion design: new materials and technologies (MA); fashion film and photography (MA); interior design (MA); transdisciplinary new media (MA, MFA).

PARKER UNIVERSITY, Dallas, TX 75229-5668

General Information Independent, coed, graduate-only institution. *Graduate housing:* On-campus housing not available.

GRADUATE UNITS

Doctor of Chiropractic Program *Program availability:* Part-time. Offers chiropractic (DC). Electronic applications accepted.

PARK UNIVERSITY, Parkville, MO 64152-3795

General Information Independent, coed, comprehensive institution. CGS member.

GRADUATE UNITS

School of Graduate and Professional Studies *Program availability:* Part-time, evening/weekend, online learning. Offers adult education (M Ed); business and government leadership (Graduate Certificate); business, government, and global society (MPA); communication and leadership (MA); creative and life writing (Graduate Certificate); disaster and emergency management (MPA, Graduate Certificate); educational leadership (M Ed); finance (MBA, Graduate Certificate); general business (MBA); global business (Graduate Certificate); healthcare administration (MHA); healthcare services management and leadership (Graduate Certificate); international business (MBA); language and literacy (M Ed); leadership of international healthcare organizations (Graduate Certificate); management information systems (MBA, Graduate Certificate); music performance (ADP, Graduate Certificate); nonprofit and community services management (MPA); nonprofit leadership (Graduate Certificate); performance (MM); public management (MPA); social work (MSW); teacher leadership (M Ed). Electronic applications accepted.

PAYNE THEOLOGICAL SEMINARY, Wilberforce, OH 45384-3474

General Information Independent-religious, coed, graduate-only institution. *Graduate housing:* Rooms and/or apartments available on a first-come, first-served basis to single and married students. Housing application deadline: 8/15.

GRADUATE UNITS

Program in Theology *Program availability:* Part-time, evening/weekend, online learning. Offers theology (M Div).

PEIRCE COLLEGE, Philadelphia, PA 19102-4699

General Information Independent, coed, primarily women, comprehensive institution.

GRADUATE UNITS

Program in Organizational Leadership and Management Offers organizational leadership and management (MS).

PENN STATE ERIE, THE BEHREND COLLEGE, Erie, PA 16563

General Information State-related, coed, comprehensive institution. *Graduate housing:* Room and/or apartments available on a first-come, first-served basis to single students; on-campus housing not available to married students.

GRADUATE UNITS

Graduate School *Program availability:* Part-time. Offers accounting (MPAC); applied clinical psychology (MA); business administration (MBA); quality and manufacturing management (MMM). Electronic applications accepted.

PENN STATE GREAT VALLEY, Malvern, PA 19355-1488

General Information State-related, coed, graduate-only institution. *Graduate housing:* On-campus housing not available.

GRADUATE UNITS

Graduate Studies *Program availability:* Part-time, evening/weekend. Electronic applications accepted.

Engineering Division Offers engineering management (MEM); software engineering (MSE); systems engineering (M Eng, Certificate).

Management Division Offers business administration (MBA); cyber security (Certificate); data analytics (MPS, MS, Certificate); distributed energy and grid modernization (Certificate); finance (M Fin); health sector management (Certificate); human resource management (Certificate); information science (MSIS); leadership development (MLD); new ventures and entrepreneurship (Certificate); sustainable management practices (Certificate).

PENN STATE HARRISBURG, Middletown, PA 17057

General Information State-related, coed, comprehensive institution. *Graduate housing:* Room and/or apartments available on a first-served basis to single students; on-campus housing not available to married students.

GRADUATE UNITS

Graduate School *Program availability:* Part-time, evening/weekend. Electronic applications accepted.

School of Behavioral Sciences and Education *Program availability:* Part-time, evening/weekend. Offers adult education in the health and medical professions (Certificate); applied behavior analysis (MA); applied clinical psychology (MA); applied psychological research (MA); community psychology and social change (MA); English as a second language (ESL) program specialist and leadership (Certificate); health education (M Ed); lifelong learning and adult education (M Ed, D Ed); literacy education (M Ed); literacy leadership (Certificate); psychology: applications in clinical psychology (Certificate); psychology: health psychology (Certificate); teaching and curriculum (M Ed); training and development (M Ed, Certificate).

School of Business Administration *Program availability:* Part-time, evening/weekend. Offers accounting (MPAC, Certificate); business administration (MBA); information systems (MS); operations and supply chain management (Certificate).

School of Humanities *Program availability:* Part-time, evening/weekend. Offers American studies (MA, PhD); communications (MA); folklore and ethnography (Certificate); heritage and museum practice (Certificate); humanities (MA).

School of Public Affairs Offers criminal justice (MA); health administration (MHA); health administration: long term care (Certificate); homeland security (MPS, Certificate); public administration (MPA, PhD); public administration: non-profit administration (Certificate); public budgeting and financial management (Certificate); public sector human resource management (Certificate).

School of Science, Engineering and Technology *Program availability:* Part-time, evening/weekend. Offers civil engineering (MS); computer science (MS); electrical engineering (M Eng, MS); engineering management (MPS); engineering science (M Eng); environmental engineering (M Eng); environmental pollution control (MEPC, MS); mechanical engineering (MS); structural engineering (Certificate).

PENN STATE HERSHEY MEDICAL CENTER, Hershey, PA 17033-2360

General Information State-related, coed, graduate-only institution. *Graduate housing:* Rooms and/or apartments available on a first-come, first-served basis to single and married students.

GRADUATE UNITS

College of Medicine Offers medicine (MPAS, MPH, MS, Dr PH, MD, PhD). Electronic applications accepted.

Graduate School Programs in the Biomedical Sciences Offers anatomy (MS, PhD); biochemistry and molecular genetics (MS, PhD); biomedical sciences (MS, PhD); biostatistics (PhD); cell and developmental biology (PhD); cellular and integrative physiology (MS, PhD); laboratory animal medicine (MS); life sciences (MS, PhD); molecular medicine (PhD); molecular toxicology (PhD); neurobiology (PhD); neuroscience (MS, PhD); public health (MPH, Dr PH); public health sciences (MS); translational therapeutics (MS, PhD); virology and immunology (MS, PhD). Electronic applications accepted.

PENN STATE UNIVERSITY–DICKINSON LAW, Carlisle, PA 17013

General Information State-related, coed, graduate-only institution. *Graduate housing:* On-campus housing not available.

GRADUATE UNITS

Graduate and Professional Programs Offers law (LL M, JD). Electronic applications accepted.

PENN STATE UNIVERSITY PARK, University Park, PA 16802

General Information State-related, coed, university. CGS member. *Graduate housing:* Rooms and/or apartments available on a first-come, first-served basis to single and married students.

GRADUATE UNITS

Graduate School *Program availability:* Part-time, evening/weekend, online learning. Electronic applications accepted.

College of Agricultural Sciences *Program availability:* Part-time. Offers agricultural and biological engineering (MS, PhD); agricultural and extension education (M Ed, MS, PhD, Certificate); agricultural sciences (M Ed, MPS, MS, PhD, Certificate); agronomy (MS, PhD); animal science (MPS, MS, PhD); applied youth, family and community education (M Ed); biorenewable systems (MS, PhD); energy, environmental, and food economics (MS, PhD); entomology (MS, PhD); food science (MS, PhD); forest resources (MS, PhD); horticulture (MS, PhD); pathobiology (MS, PhD); plant pathology (MS, PhD); rural sociology (MS, PhD); soil science (MS, PhD); wildlife and fisheries science (MS, PhD). Electronic applications accepted.

College of Arts and Architecture *Program availability:* Part-time, evening/weekend. Offers architecture (M Arch, MS, PhD); art (MFA); art education (MS, PhD, Certificate); art history (MA, PhD); arts and architecture (M Arch, M Mus, MA, MFA, MLA, MME, MS, DMA, PhD, Certificate); composition-theory (M Mus); conducting (M Mus); landscape architecture (MLA, MS); music (MA); music education (MME, PhD, Certificate); pedagogy and performance (M Mus); performance (M Mus); piano performance (DMA); theatre (MFA). Electronic applications accepted.

College of Earth and Mineral Sciences Offers earth and mineral sciences (MS, PhD); energy and mineral engineering (MS, PhD); geography (MS, PhD); geosciences (MS, PhD); meteorology (MS, PhD). Electronic applications accepted.

College of Education *Program availability:* Part-time, evening/weekend. Offers counselor education (M Ed, D Ed, PhD, Certificate); curriculum and instruction (M Ed, MS, PhD, Certificate); education (M Ed, MA, MS, D Ed, PhD, Certificate); educational leadership (M Ed, D Ed, PhD, Certificate); educational psychology (MS, PhD, Certificate); educational theory and policy (MA, PhD); higher education (M Ed, D Ed, PhD); learning, design, and technology (M Ed, MS, PhD, Certificate); lifelong learning and adult education (M Ed, D Ed, PhD, Certificate); school psychology (M Ed, MS, PhD, Certificate); special education (M Ed, MS, PhD); workforce education and development (M Ed, MS, PhD). Electronic applications accepted.

College of Engineering *Program availability:* Part-time, evening/weekend. Offers additive manufacturing and design (MS); aerospace engineering (M Eng, MS, PhD); architectural engineering (M Eng, MAE, MS, PhD); chemical engineering (MS, PhD); civil engineering (M Eng, MS, PhD); computer science and engineering (M Eng, MS, PhD); electrical engineering (MS, PhD); engineering (M Eng, MAE, MFR, MS, PhD); engineering at the nano-scale (MS); engineering design (M Eng, MS); engineering leadership and innovation management (M Eng); engineering mechanics (M Eng); engineering science and mechanics (MS, PhD); environmental engineering (M Eng, MS, PhD); facilities engineering and management (M Eng); industrial engineering (MS, PhD); mechanical engineering (MS, PhD); nuclear engineering (M Eng, MS, PhD). Electronic applications accepted.

College of Health and Human Development *Program availability:* Part-time, evening/weekend. Offers biobehavioral health (MS, PhD); communication sciences and disorders (MS, PhD, Certificate); health and human development (MHA, MS, PhD, Certificate); health policy and administration (MHA, MS, PhD); hospitality management (MS, PhD); human development and family studies (MS, PhD); kinesiology (MS, PhD, Certificate); nutritional sciences (MS, PhD); recreation, park and tourism management (MS, PhD). Electronic applications accepted.

College of Information Sciences and Technology *Program availability:* Part-time, evening/weekend. Offers information sciences (MPS); information sciences and technology (MS, PhD). Electronic applications accepted.

College of Nursing *Program availability:* Part-time, evening/weekend. Offers nursing (MSN). Electronic applications accepted.

College of the Liberal Arts *Program availability:* Part-time, evening/weekend. Offers anthropology (MA, PhD); applied linguistics (PhD); communication arts and sciences (MA, PhD); comparative literature (MA, PhD); criminology (MA, PhD); economics (MA, PhD); English (MA, MFA, PhD); French (MA, PhD); German (MA, PhD); history (MA, PhD); human resources and employment relations (MS); labor and global workers' rights (MPS); liberal arts (MA, MFA, MPS, MS, PhD); philosophy (MA, PhD); political science (MA, PhD); psychology (MS, PhD); Russian and comparative literature (MA); sociology (MA, PhD); Spanish (MA, PhD); teaching English as a second language (MA). Electronic applications accepted.

Donald P. Bellisario College of Communications *Program availability:* Part-time, evening/weekend. Offers communications (MA, PhD); mass communications (PhD); media studies (MA). Electronic applications accepted.

Eberly College of Science *Program availability:* Part-time, evening/weekend. Offers applied statistics (MAS); astronomy and astrophysics (MS, PhD); biochemistry, microbiology, and molecular biology (MS, PhD); biology (MS, PhD); biotechnology (MBIOT); chemistry (MS, PhD); forensic science (MPS); mathematics (M Ed, MA, D Ed, PhD); physics (M Ed, MS, PhD); science (M Ed, MA, MAS, MBIOT, MPS, MS, D Ed, PhD); statistics (MA, MS, PhD). Electronic applications accepted.

Intercollege Graduate Programs *Program availability:* Part-time, evening/weekend. Offers acoustics (PhD); bioengineering (MS, PhD); ecology (MS, PhD); environmental pollution control (MEPC, MS); integrative and biomedical physiology (MS, PhD); materials science and engineering (MS, PhD); molecular, cellular, and integrative biosciences (MS, PhD); plant biology (MS, PhD); renewable energy and sustainability systems (MPS). Electronic applications accepted.

School of International Affairs *Program availability:* Part-time, evening/weekend. Offers international affairs (MIA). Electronic applications accepted.

Smeal College of Business *Program availability:* Part-time, evening/weekend. Offers accounting (M Acc); business administration (MBA, MS, PhD); management and organizational leadership (MPS). Electronic applications accepted.

Penn State Law Offers law (LL M, JD, SJD). Electronic applications accepted.

PENN STATE YORK, York, PA 17403

General Information State-related, coed, comprehensive institution.

GRADUATE UNITS

Graduate School Offers ESL specialist (Certificate); teaching and curriculum (M Ed).

PENNSYLVANIA ACADEMY OF THE FINE ARTS, Philadelphia, PA 19102

General Information Independent, coed, comprehensive institution. *Enrollment:* 74 graduate, professional, and undergraduate students; 74 full-time matriculated graduate/professional students (49 women). *Enrollment by degree level:* 68 master's, 6 other advanced degrees. *Graduate faculty:* 6 full-time (2 women), 18 part-time/adjunct (11 women). *Tuition:* Full-time $39,906. *Required fees:* $1450. *Graduate housing:* On-campus housing not available. *Student services:* Campus employment opportunities, campus safety program, career counseling, free psychological counseling, international student services, low-cost health insurance, writing training. *Library facilities:* Arcadia Fine Arts Library.

Computer facilities: 75 computers available on campus for general student use. Website: http://www.pafa.edu/

General Application Contact: Sam Schetina, Graduate Admissions Counselor, 215-391-4398, Fax: 215-569-0153, E-mail: sschetina@pafa.edu.

GRADUATE UNITS

Division of Graduate Studies Students: 74 full-time (49 women); includes 13 minority (5 Black or African American, non-Hispanic/Latino; 2 Asian, non-Hispanic/Latino; 3 Hispanic/Latino; 3 Two or more races, non-Hispanic/Latino), 9 international. *Faculty:* 6 full-time (2 women), 18 part-time/adjunct (11 women). Expenses: Contact institution. *Financial support:* In 2018–19, 74 students received support. Teaching assistantships, Federal Work-Study, institutionally sponsored loans, scholarships/grants, and unspecified assistantships available. Financial award application deadline: 3/1; financial award applicants required to submit FAFSA. Offers painting (MFA, Postbaccalaureate Certificate); printmaking (MFA, Postbaccalaureate Certificate); sculpture (MFA, Postbaccalaureate Certificate); studio art (MFA, Postbaccalaureate Certificate). MFA program also available in a low-residency format. *Application deadline:* For fall admission, 1/15 for domestic and international students. Applications are processed on a rolling basis. *Application fee:* $60. Electronic applications accepted. *Application Contact:* Sam Schetina, Graduate Admissions Counselor, 215-391-4398, Fax: 215-569-0153, E-mail: sschetina@pafa.edu. *Interim Chair of Graduate Programs,* Dr. Kevin Richards, Fax: 215-569-0153, E-mail: richards@pobox.pafa.edu.

PENNSYLVANIA COLLEGE OF HEALTH SCIENCES, Lancaster, PA 17601

General Information Independent, coed, comprehensive institution.

GRADUATE UNITS

Graduate Programs Offers administration (MSN); education (MSHS, MSN); healthcare administration (MHA).

PENSACOLA CHRISTIAN COLLEGE, Pensacola, FL 32503-2267

General Information Independent-religious, coed, comprehensive institution.

GRADUATE UNITS

Graduate Studies

PENTECOSTAL THEOLOGICAL SEMINARY, Cleveland, TN 37320-3330

General Information Independent-religious, coed, graduate-only institution. *Graduate housing:* Rooms and/or apartments available to single and married students.

GRADUATE UNITS

Graduate and Professional Programs *Program availability:* Part-time. Offers biblical studies (MTS); church ministries (MA); counseling (MA); discipleship and Christian formation (MA); ministry (D Min); Pentecostal theology (MTS); theology (M Div).

PEPPERDINE UNIVERSITY, Malibu, CA 90263

General Information Independent-religious, coed, university. *Enrollment:* 7,961 graduate, professional, and undergraduate students; 2,281 full-time matriculated graduate/professional students (1,378 women), 2,019 part-time matriculated graduate/professional students (1,385 women). *Enrollment by degree level:* 3,207 master's, 1,072 doctoral, 21 other advanced degrees. *Graduate housing:* Rooms and/or apartments available on a first-come, first-served basis to single and married students. *Student services:* Campus employment opportunities, campus safety program, career counseling, exercise/wellness program, free psychological counseling, international student services, low-cost health insurance, multicultural affairs office, services for students with disabilities, teacher training. *Library facilities:* Payson Library plus 5 others. *Collection:* Books: 311,392 (physical), 356,075 (digital/electronic); Serial titles: 312 (physical), 66,464 (digital/electronic); Databases: 128. Weekly public service hours: 112; students can reserve study rooms.

Computer facilities: Computer purchase and lease plans are available. 240 computers available on campus for general student use. A campuswide network can be accessed from student residence rooms and from off campus. Online class registration is available.

Website: http://www.pepperdine.edu/

General Application Contact: Kristy Paredes Collins, Dean of Enrollment Management, 310-506-4392, Fax: 310-506-4861, E-mail: admission-seaver@pepperdine.edu.

GRADUATE UNITS

Graduate School of Education and Psychology Students: 790 full-time (627 women), 1,041 part-time (811 women); includes 855 minority (229 Black or African American, non-Hispanic/Latino; 5 American Indian or Alaska Native, non-Hispanic/Latino; 158 Asian, non-Hispanic/Latino; 372 Hispanic/Latino; 13 Native Hawaiian or other Pacific Islander, non-Hispanic/Latino; 78 Two or more races, non-Hispanic/Latino), 129 international. Average age 34. 1,519 applicants, 84% accepted, 655 enrolled. *Faculty:* 46 full-time (25 women), 153 part-time/adjunct (104 women). Expenses: Contact institution. *Financial support:* Research assistantships, teaching assistantships, career-related internships or fieldwork, Federal Work-Study, institutionally sponsored loans, scholarships/grants, and unspecified assistantships available. Support available to part-time students. Financial award applicants required to submit FAFSA. In 2018, 421 master's, 119 doctorates awarded. *Program availability:* Part-time, evening/weekend, 100% online, blended/hybrid learning. Offers education and psychology (MA, MS, Ed D, PhD, Psy D). *Application fee:* $65. Electronic applications accepted. *Application Contact:* Chris Costa, Director of Enrollment, 310-568-2850, E-mail: chris.costa@pepperdine.edu. *Dean,* Dr. Helen Easterling Williams, 310-568-5620, E-mail: Helen.Williams@pepperdine.edu.

Pepperdine Graziadio Business School Students: 852 full-time (404 women), 685 part-time (368 women); includes 389 minority (129 Black or African American, non-Hispanic/Latino; 6 American Indian or Alaska Native, non-Hispanic/Latino; 193 Asian, non-Hispanic/Latino; 60 Hispanic/Latino; 1 Two or more races, non-Hispanic/Latino), 388 international. Average age 32. 3,371 applicants, 58% accepted, 468 enrolled. *Faculty:* 93 full-time (26 women), 17 part-time/adjunct (5 women). Expenses: Contact institution. *Financial support:* Institutionally sponsored loans and scholarships/grants available. Financial award applicants required to submit FAFSA. In 2018, 927 master's awarded. *Program availability:* Part-time, evening/weekend, 100% online. Offers business (MBA, MS). 5 Year BS/MBA, JD/MBA, MBA/MPP, BS/MBA. *Application deadline:* For fall admission, 5/15 for domestic students, 4/1 for international students; for spring admission, 11/15 for domestic students, 10/15 for international students; for summer admission, 4/1 for domestic and international students. Applications are processed on a rolling basis. *Application fee:* $150. Electronic applications accepted. *Application Contact:* Amanda Karr, Executive Director, Enrollment Management, 310-5685663, E-mail: amanda.karr@pepperdine.edu. *Dean,* Graziadio Business School, Deryck J. van Rensburg, 310-568-5500, E-mail: deryck.rensburg@pepperdine.edu.

School of Law Students: 580 full-time (320 women), 219 part-time (160 women); includes 280 minority (85 Black or African American, non-Hispanic/Latino; 2 American Indian or Alaska Native, non-Hispanic/Latino; 41 Asian, non-Hispanic/Latino; 108 Hispanic/Latino; 4 Native Hawaiian or other Pacific Islander, non-Hispanic/Latino; 40 Two or more races, non-Hispanic/Latino), 59 international. Average age 31. *Faculty:* 29 full-time (9 women), 37 part-time/adjunct (11 women). Expenses: Contact institution. *Financial support:* Fellowships, research assistantships, teaching assistantships, career-related internships or fieldwork, Federal Work-Study, institutionally sponsored loans, and scholarships/grants available. Support available to part-time students. Financial award application deadline: 4/1; financial award applicants required to submit FAFSA. In 2018, 76 master's, 168 doctorates awarded. Offers law (LL M, MDR, JD). *Application deadline:* For fall admission, 3/1 for domestic and international students. Applications are processed on a rolling basis. *Application fee:* $65. Electronic applications accepted. *Application Contact:* Shannon Phillips, Dean of Admissions and Student Services and Executive Staff Director, 310-506-4631, Fax: 310-506-4266, E-mail: shannon.phillips@pepperdine.edu. *Dean,* Dr. Paul Caron, 310-506-4621, E-mail: paul.caron@pepperdine.edu.

School of Public Policy Students: 53 full-time (26 women), 4 part-time (all women); includes 14 minority (4 Black or African American, non-Hispanic/Latino; 5 Asian, non-Hispanic/Latino; 4 Hispanic/Latino; 1 Native Hawaiian or other Pacific Islander, non-Hispanic/Latino), 11 international. Average age 25. 125 applicants, 59% accepted, 33 enrolled. *Faculty:* 4 full-time (2 women), 5 part-time/adjunct. Expenses: Contact institution. *Financial support:* In 2018–19, 67 students received support. Research assistantships, Federal Work-Study, institutionally sponsored loans, scholarships/grants, and unspecified assistantships available. Support available to part-time students. Financial award application deadline: 7/17; financial award applicants required to submit FAFSA. In 2018, 22 master's awarded. Offers American politics (MPP); economics (MPP); international relations (MPP); state and local policy (MPP). *Application deadline:*

For fall admission, 7/17 for domestic students, 6/19 for international students. Applications are processed on a rolling basis. *Application fee:* $0. Electronic applications accepted. *Application Contact:* Carson Bruno, Assistant Dean for Program Relations Admission and Program Relations, 310-506-7493, E-mail: carson.bruno@pepperdine.edu. *Dean, School of Public Policy,* Pete Peterson, 310-506-7490, Fax: 310-506-7494, E-mail: pete.n.peterson@pepperdine.edu.

Seaver College Students: 6 full-time (1 woman), 70 part-time (42 women); includes 19 minority (6 Black or African American, non-Hispanic/Latino; 1 American Indian or Alaska Native, non-Hispanic/Latino; 2 Asian, non-Hispanic/Latino; 5 Hispanic/Latino; 1 Native Hawaiian or other Pacific Islander, non-Hispanic/Latino; 4 Two or more races, non-Hispanic/Latino), 11 international. Average age 30. 54 applicants, 65% accepted, 29 enrolled. Expenses: Contact institution. *Financial support:* Fellowships, research assistantships, teaching assistantships, career-related internships or fieldwork, Federal Work-Study, institutionally sponsored loans, scholarships/grants, and tuition waivers (partial) available. Support available to part-time students. Financial award application deadline: 2/15; financial award applicants required to submit FAFSA. In 2018, 27 master's awarded. Offers business (MS); communication (MFA); humanities (MA, MFA); religion (M Div, MA, MS). *Application deadline:* For fall admission, 2/1 priority date for domestic students. Applications are processed on a rolling basis. *Application fee:* $65. *Application Contact:* Joy Brown, Admission Counselor, 310-506-4392, E-mail: joy.brown@pepperdine.edu. *Assistant Dean, Special Academic and Graduate Programs for Seaver College,* Dr. Dana Dudley, 310-506-6047, Fax: 310-506-4816, E-mail: dana.dudley@pepperdine.edu.

PERU STATE COLLEGE, Peru, NE 68421
General Information State-supported, coed, comprehensive institution. *Graduate housing:* Rooms and/or apartments available to single and married students.

GRADUATE UNITS

Graduate Programs *Program availability:* Part-time, online learning. Offers curriculum and instruction (MS Ed); organizational management (MS).

PFEIFFER UNIVERSITY, Misenheimer, NC 28109-0960
General Information Independent-religious, coed, comprehensive institution. *Graduate housing:* On-campus housing not available.

GRADUATE UNITS

Program in Business Administration *Program availability:* Part-time, evening/weekend, online learning. Offers business administration (MBA).
Program in Elementary Education Offers elementary education (MAT, MS).
Program in Health Administration Offers health administration (MHA).
Program in Leadership and Organizational Change Offers leadership and organizational change (MS).
Program in Practical Theology *Program availability:* Part-time, evening/weekend. Offers practical theology (MA).

PHILADELPHIA COLLEGE OF OSTEOPATHIC MEDICINE, Philadelphia, PA 19131-1694
General Information Independent, coed, graduate-only institution. *Enrollment by degree level:* 449 master's, 1,253 doctoral, 33 other advanced degrees. *Graduate faculty:* 152 full-time (67 women), 1,639 part-time/adjunct (435 women). Tuition and fees vary according to course load, degree level and program. *Graduate housing:* On-campus housing not available. *Student services:* Campus employment opportunities, campus safety program, career counseling, exercise/wellness program, free psychological counseling, low-cost health insurance, multicultural affairs office, services for students with disabilities, writing training. *Library facilities:* PCOM Library plus 1 other. *Collection:* Study areas open 24 hours, 5–7 days a week; students can reserve study rooms.
Computer facilities: 142 computers available on campus for general student use. Online class registration is available.
Website: http://www.pcom.edu/
General Application Contact: Kari A. Shotwell, Director of Admissions, 215-871-6700, Fax: 215-871-6719, E-mail: karis@pcom.edu.

PHILLIPS GRADUATE UNIVERSITY, Chatsworth, CA 91311
General Information Independent, coed, graduate-only institution. *Graduate housing:* On-campus housing not available.

GRADUATE UNITS

Doctoral Program in Organizational Management and Consulting *Program availability:* Evening/weekend. Offers organizational management and consulting (Psy D). Electronic applications accepted.
Master's Program in Psychology *Program availability:* Evening/weekend. Offers art therapy (MA); marriage and family therapy (MA); school counseling (MA); school psychology (MA). Electronic applications accepted.

PHILLIPS THEOLOGICAL SEMINARY, Tulsa, OK 74116
General Information Independent-religious, coed, graduate-only institution. *Graduate housing:* On-campus housing not available.

GRADUATE UNITS

Programs in Theology *Program availability:* Part-time, online learning. Offers administration of church agencies (M Div); campus ministry (M Div); church-related social work (M Div); college and seminary teaching (M Div); global mission work (M Div); institutional chaplaincy (M Div); ministerial vocations in Christian education (M Div); ministry (D Min); ministry and culture (MAMC); ministry of music (M Div); parish ministry (D Min); pastoral care and counseling (M Div); pastoral counseling (D Min); pastoral ministry (D Min); practices of ministry (D Min); theological studies (MTS).

PHOENIX INSTITUTE OF HERBAL MEDICINE & ACUPUNCTURE, Phoenix, AZ 85018
General Information Proprietary, coed, graduate-only institution.

GRADUATE UNITS

Graduate Programs Offers acupuncture (MSAC); Oriental medicine (MSOM).

PHOENIX SEMINARY, Phoenix, AZ 85018
General Information Independent-religious, coed, graduate-only institution.

GRADUATE UNITS

Graduate Programs *Program availability:* Part-time, evening/weekend. Offers Biblical and theological studies (Graduate Diploma); Biblical communication (M Div); Biblical leadership (MA); Christian counseling (Graduate Diploma); counseling and family (M Div); leadership development (M Div); ministry (D Min); professional counseling (MA).

PIEDMONT COLLEGE, Demorest, GA 30535
General Information Independent-religious, coed, comprehensive institution. *Enrollment:* 2,490 graduate, professional, and undergraduate students; 523 full-time matriculated graduate/professional students (427 women), 663 part-time matriculated graduate/professional students (567 women). *Enrollment by degree level:* 442 master's, 81 doctoral, 663 other advanced degrees. *Tuition:* Full-time $9738; part-time $541 per credit. *Required fees:* $200 per semester. *Graduate housing:* Room and/or apartments available on a first-come, first-served basis to single students; on-campus housing not available to married students. *Student services:* Campus employment opportunities, campus safety program, career counseling, exercise/wellness program, services for students with disabilities, teacher training, writing training. *Library facilities:* Arrendale Library plus 2 others. *Collection:* Books: 85,631 (physical), 766,654 (digital/electronic); Serial titles: 76 (physical); Databases: 197. Students can reserve study rooms.
Computer facilities: 225 computers available on campus for general student use. A campuswide network can be accessed from student residence rooms and from off campus. Online class registration is available.
Website: http://www.piedmont.edu/
General Application Contact: Kathleen Carter, Director of Graduate Enrollment Management, 706-778-8500 Ext. 1181, Fax: 706-776-0150, E-mail: kanderson@piedmont.edu.

GRADUATE UNITS

School of Business Students: 27 full-time (11 women), 13 part-time (7 women); includes 13 minority (6 Black or African American, non-Hispanic/Latino; 1 Asian, non-Hispanic/Latino; 4 Hispanic/Latino; 2 Native Hawaiian or other Pacific Islander, non-Hispanic/Latino). Average age 29. 10 applicants, 70% accepted, 7 enrolled. Expenses: Contact institution. *Financial support:* Federal Work-Study and unspecified assistantships available. Financial award applicants required to submit FAFSA. In 2018, 23 master's awarded. *Program availability:* Part-time, evening/weekend. Offers business (MBA). *Application deadline:* For fall admission, 7/15 for domestic students; for spring admission, 12/1 for domestic students. Applications are processed on a rolling basis. Electronic applications accepted. *Application Contact:* Kathleen Carter, Director of Graduate Enrollment Management, 706-778-3000, E-mail: kcarter@piedmont.edu. *Dean,* Dr. Edward Taylor, 706-778-3000, E-mail: etaylor@piedmont.edu.
School of Education Students: 496 full-time (416 women), 650 part-time (560 women); includes 185 minority (137 Black or African American, non-Hispanic/Latino; 2 American Indian or Alaska Native, non-Hispanic/Latino; 13 Asian, non-Hispanic/Latino; 31 Hispanic/Latino; 1 Native Hawaiian or other Pacific Islander, non-Hispanic/Latino; 1 Two or more races, non-Hispanic/Latino). Average age 37. 483 applicants, 89% accepted, 372 enrolled. Expenses: Contact institution. *Financial support:* Career-related internships or fieldwork, Federal Work-Study, and unspecified assistantships available. Support available to part-time students. Financial award applicants required to submit FAFSA. In 2018, 275 master's, 10 doctorates, 229 other advanced degrees awarded. *Program availability:* Part-time, evening/weekend. Offers art education (MAT); curriculum and instruction (Ed D, Ed S); early childhood education (MA, MAT); middle grades education (MA, MAT); music education (MAT); secondary education (MA, MAT); special education (MA, MAT). *Application deadline:* For fall admission, 7/15 for domestic students; for spring admission, 12/1 for domestic students. Applications are processed on a rolling basis. Electronic applications accepted. *Application Contact:* Kathleen Carter, Director of Graduate Enrollment Management, 706-778-8500 Ext. 1181, Fax: 706-778-0150, E-mail: kanderson@piedmont.edu. *Dean,* Dr. R.D. Nordgren, 706-778-3000 Ext. 1201, Fax: 706-776-9608, E-mail: rdnordgren@piedmont.edu.

PIEDMONT INTERNATIONAL UNIVERSITY, Winston-Salem, NC 27101-5197
General Information Independent-religious, coed, university. *Graduate housing:* Rooms and/or apartments available on a first-come, first-served basis to single and married students. Housing application deadline: 5/1.

GRADUATE UNITS

Graduate School *Program availability:* Part-time, online learning. Offers Biblical studies (PhD); curriculum and instruction (M Ed); divinity (M Div); educational leadership (M Ed); leadership (MA, PhD); ministry (MA Min, D Min); non-language track (MABS); PhD preparation track (MABS). Electronic applications accepted.
Temple Baptist Seminary *Program availability:* Part-time, evening/weekend, online learning. Offers theology (M Div, D Min).

PILLAR COLLEGE, Newark, NJ 07102
General Information Independent-religious, coed, comprehensive institution.

GRADUATE UNITS

Program in Counseling Offers counseling (MA).

PITTSBURGH THEOLOGICAL SEMINARY, Pittsburgh, PA 15206-2596
General Information Independent-religious, coed, graduate-only institution. *Graduate housing:* Rooms and/or apartments available on a first-come, first-served basis to single and married students. Housing application deadline: 6/1.

GRADUATE UNITS

Graduate and Professional Programs *Program availability:* Part-time, evening/weekend. Offers divinity (M Div); theological studies (MA); theology (Th M); theology and ministry (MA, D Min). M Div/MSW offered jointly with University of Pittsburgh; JD/M Div with Duquesne University; M Div/MSPPM with Carnegie Mellon University. Electronic applications accepted.

PITTSBURG STATE UNIVERSITY, Pittsburg, KS 66762
General Information State-supported, coed, comprehensive institution. *Graduate housing:* Rooms and/or apartments available on a first-come, first-served basis to single and married students. Housing application deadline: 8/15. *Research affiliation:* Cargill, Inc. (vegetable oil).

GRADUATE UNITS

Graduate School *Program availability:* Part-time, evening/weekend, 100% online, blended/hybrid learning. Electronic applications accepted.
College of Arts and Sciences *Program availability:* Part-time, 100% online, blended/hybrid learning. Offers arts and sciences (MA, MM, MS, MSN, DNP); biology (MS); chemistry (MS); communication (MA); conducting (MM); education (MM); English (MA); history (MA); mathematics (MS); nursing (DNP); nursing education (MSN); performance (MM); physics (MS); polymer chemistry (MS). Electronic applications accepted.
College of Education *Program availability:* Part-time, 100% online, blended/hybrid learning. Offers advanced studies in leadership (Ed S); autism spectrum disorder

(Certificate); counselor education (MS); district level (Certificate); education (MS); educational leadership (MS); educational technology (MS); general school administration (Ed S); health, human performance, and recreation (MS); psychology (MS); school counseling (MS); school psychology (Ed S); secondary education (MAT); special education (MAT, MS); teaching (MS); TESOL (Certificate). Electronic applications accepted.

College of Technology *Program availability:* Part-time, 100% online, blended/hybrid learning. Offers career and technical education (MS); construction engineering technology (MET); construction management (MS); electrical engineering technology (MET); general engineering technology (MET); human resource development (MS); manufacturing engineering technology (MET); mechanical engineering technology (MET); plastics engineering technology (MET); technology (MS); workforce development and education (Ed S). Electronic applications accepted.

Kelce College of Business Offers accounting (MBA); business (MBA); general administration (MBA); international business (MBA). Electronic applications accepted.

PLYMOUTH STATE UNIVERSITY, Plymouth, NH 03264-1595

General Information State-supported, coed, comprehensive institution. *Graduate housing:* Rooms and/or apartments available on a first-come, first-served basis to single students and guaranteed to married students. Housing application deadline: 5/1. *Research affiliation:* Hubbard Brook Experimental Forest (science), New Hampshire Department of Environmental Services (science), White Mountain National Forest (science), National Oceanic and Atmospheric Administration (NOAA) (science).

GRADUATE UNITS

College of Graduate Studies *Program availability:* Part-time, evening/weekend, online learning.

Graduate Studies in Business *Program availability:* Part-time, evening/weekend, online learning. Offers accounting (MS); general management (MBA).

Graduate Studies in Education *Program availability:* Part-time, evening/weekend, online learning. Offers addictions treatment (MS); administrative leadership (Ed D); art education (MAT); athletic training (MS); clinical mental health counseling (CAGS); couples and family therapy (MS); curriculum and instruction (Ed D); eating disorders (M Ed); education (M Ed, MAT, MS, Ed D, CAGS); educational leadership (CAGS); English education (M Ed); health education (M Ed); health promotion (MS); heritage studies (M Ed); higher education (CAGS); integrated arts (M Ed); learning, leadership and community (Ed D); mathematics education (M Ed); music education (M Ed); play therapy (MS); school psychology (CAGS).

Program in Historic Preservation Offers historic preservation (MA, Graduate Certificate).

Program in Personal and Organizational Wellness Offers personal and organizational wellness (MA, Graduate Certificate).

POINT LOMA NAZARENE UNIVERSITY, San Diego, CA 92106-2899

General Information Independent-religious, coed, comprehensive institution. *Graduate housing:* On-campus housing not available.

GRADUATE UNITS

College of Extended Learning Offers marriage and family therapy (MA); organizational leadership (MA); professional clinical counselor (MA).

Department of Biology *Program availability:* Part-time. Offers biology (MS). Electronic applications accepted.

Department of Kinesiology *Program availability:* Part-time, online learning. Offers exercise science (MS); sport performance (MS).

Fermanian School of Business *Program availability:* Part-time, evening/weekend. Offers general business (MBA); healthcare management (MBA); innovation and entrepreneurship (MBA); organizational leadership (MBA); project management (MBA). Electronic applications accepted.

School of Education *Program availability:* Part-time, evening/weekend. Offers counseling and guidance (MA); education (MA, MAT); educational administration (MA); leadership in learning (MA); special education (MA); teaching (MAT). Electronic applications accepted.

School of Nursing *Program availability:* Part-time. Offers adult/gerontology (MSN); clinical nurse specialist (Post-MSN Certificate); family/individual health (MSN); nursing (MSN, DNP, Post-MSN Certificate); pediatrics (MSN).

School of Theology and Christian Ministry *Program availability:* Part-time, online only, nine-week quads with eight weeks of online coursework and a one-week intensive. Offers theology and Christian ministry (M Min). Electronic applications accepted.

POINT PARK UNIVERSITY, Pittsburgh, PA 15222-1984

General Information Independent, coed, university. CGS member. *Graduate housing:* Room and/or apartments available on a first-come, first-served basis to single students; on-campus housing not available to married students. Housing application deadline: 7/31.

GRADUATE UNITS

Center for Innovative Learning Offers community engagement (PhD).

Conservatory of Performing Arts *Program availability:* Blended/hybrid learning. Offers screenwriting and playwriting (MFA). Electronic applications accepted.

Rowland School of Business *Program availability:* Part-time, evening/weekend, 100% online. Offers business (MA, MBA, MS); business analytics (MBA); global management and administration (MBA); health care administration and management (MS); health systems management (MBA); international business (MBA); leadership (MA); management (MBA); management information systems (MBA); sports, arts and entertainment management (MBA). Electronic applications accepted.

School of Arts and Sciences *Program availability:* Part-time, evening/weekend, online learning. Offers adult learning and training (MA); arts and sciences (M Ed, MA, MS, Ed D, Psy D); athletic coaching (M Ed); clinical-community psychology (MA, Psy D); criminal justice administration (MS); curriculum and instruction (MA); educational administration (MA); engineering management (MS); environmental studies (MS); intelligence and global security (MA); leadership and administration (Ed D); secondary education (M Ed); special education grades 7-12 (M Ed); special education PreK-grade 8 (M Ed). Electronic applications accepted.

School of Communication *Program availability:* Part-time, evening/weekend. Offers communication technology (MA); media communication (MA). Electronic applications accepted.

POINT UNIVERSITY, West Point, GA 31833

General Information Independent-religious, coed, comprehensive institution. *Enrollment:* 2,248 graduate, professional, and undergraduate students; 8 full-time matriculated graduate/professional students (1 woman), 27 part-time matriculated graduate/professional students (19 women). *Enrollment by degree level:* 35 master's. *Graduate faculty:* 2 full-time (both women), 8 part-time/adjunct (3 women). *Tuition:* Full-time $515; part-time $515 per credit hour. *Required fees:* $250 per term. Tuition and fees vary according to program. *Library facilities:* Point University Library plus 1 other.

Computer facilities: 115 computers available on campus for general student use. A campuswide network can be accessed from student residence rooms. Online class registration is available.
Website: http://point.edu/

General Application Contact: Rusty Hassell, Executive Director of Enrollment, 706-385-1503, E-mail: rusty.hassell@point.edu.

GRADUATE UNITS

Graduate Programs Students: 8 full-time (1 woman), 27 part-time (19 women); includes 19 minority (15 Black or African American, non-Hispanic/Latino; 2 Hispanic/Latino; 2 Two or more races, non-Hispanic/Latino), 1 international. Average age 40. *Faculty:* 2 full-time (both women), 8 part-time/adjunct (3 women). Expenses: Contact institution. *Program availability:* Part-time, online only, 100% online. Offers business transformation (MBA); transformative ministry (MTM). *Application deadline:* Applications are processed on a rolling basis. *Application fee:* $0. Electronic applications accepted. *Application Contact:* Rusty Hassell, Executive Director of Enrollment, 706-385-1503, E-mail: rhassell@point.edu.

POLYTECHNIC UNIVERSITY OF PUERTO RICO, Hato Rey, PR 00918

General Information Independent, coed, comprehensive institution. CGS member. *Graduate housing:* On-campus housing not available. *Research affiliation:* University of Missouri (engineering, mathematics and science), University of Puerto Rico, Mayaguez Campus (electrical engineering), Virginia Polytechnic Institute and State University (mechanical and electrical engineering), Naval Research Laboratories (mechanical and electrical engineering), U.S. Department of Energy Laboratories (electrical engineering).

GRADUATE UNITS

Graduate School *Program availability:* Part-time, evening/weekend.

POLYTECHNIC UNIVERSITY OF PUERTO RICO, MIAMI CAMPUS, Miami, FL 33166

General Information Independent, coed, comprehensive institution.

GRADUATE UNITS

Graduate School *Program availability:* Part-time, evening/weekend, online learning. Electronic applications accepted.

POLYTECHNIC UNIVERSITY OF PUERTO RICO, ORLANDO CAMPUS, Orlando, FL 32825

General Information Independent, coed, comprehensive institution. *Graduate housing:* On-campus housing not available.

GRADUATE UNITS

Graduate School *Program availability:* Part-time, evening/weekend, online learning. Electronic applications accepted.

PONCE HEALTH SCIENCES UNIVERSITY, Ponce, PR 00732-7004

General Information Independent, coed, graduate-only institution. *Research affiliation:* The University of Texas at San Antonio (health disparities, proteomics, bioinformatics), H.L. Moffitt Cancer Center (cancer biology, oncology), Oregon Health & Science University (neurosciences, cancer, inflammation), University of Puerto Rico, Mayaguez Campus (cancer biology, molecular genetics), University of Puerto Rico, Medical Sciences Campus (translational research), University of Maryland–Institute of Human Virology (HIV/AIDS research).

GRADUATE UNITS

DrPH Program in Epidemiology

Masters Program in Public Health Offers epidemiology (Dr PH); public health (MPH).

MD Program

MPH Program in Environmental Health

MPH Program in Epidemiology

MS Program in Medical Sciences

MS Program in School Psychology

PhD Program in Biomedical Sciences Offers biomedical sciences (PhD).

PhD Program in Clinical Psychology Offers clinical psychology (PhD, Psy D).

Post Graduate Certificate Program in Neuroscience of Learning

Professional Certificate Program in Family and Couples Therapy

PsyD Program in Clinical Psychology

PONTIFICAL CATHOLIC UNIVERSITY OF PUERTO RICO, Ponce, PR 00717-0777

General Information Independent-religious, coed, university. *Graduate housing:* Room and/or apartments available to single students; on-campus housing not available to married students. Housing application deadline: 7/15.

GRADUATE UNITS

College of Arts and Humanities *Program availability:* Part-time, evening/weekend. Offers arts and humanities (MA, Professional Certificate); grammar and writing (Professional Certificate); Hispanic studies (MA); history (MA); painting and drawing (MA); theology and philosophy (M Div).

College of Business Administration *Program availability:* Part-time, evening/weekend. Offers accounting (MBA); business administration (MBA, DBA, PhD, Professional Certificate); finance (MBA); general business (MBA, Professional Certificate); human resources (MBA, Professional Certificate); international business (MBA); management (MBA); management and accounting (Professional Certificate); management information systems (MBA, Professional Certificate); maritime logistics and transportation (Professional Certificate); marketing (MBA); office administration (MBA, MS).

College of Education *Program availability:* Part-time, evening/weekend. Offers business teacher education (M Ed, PhD); counselor education (M Ed); curriculum and instruction (M Ed, PhD); education (M Ed, MA Ed, MRE, PhD); education-general (M Ed, MA Ed); educational leadership and administration (PhD); educational psychology (M Ed); English as a second language (M Ed).

College of Graduate Studies in Behavioral Science and Community Affairs *Program availability:* Part-time, evening/weekend. Offers clinical psychology (PhD, Psy D); clinical social work (MSW); criminology (MA); industrial psychology (PhD); psychology (PhD); public administration (MSS); rehabilitation counseling (MA).

College of Sciences *Program availability:* Part-time, evening/weekend. Offers chemistry (MS); environmental sciences (MS); medical-surgical nursing (MSN); mental health and psychiatric nursing (MSN); sciences (MS, Certificate).

School of Medical Technology Offers medical technology (Certificate).

School of Law *Program availability:* Part-time, evening/weekend. Offers law (JD).

PONTIFICAL COLLEGE JOSEPHINUM, Columbus, OH 43235

General Information Independent-religious, men only, comprehensive institution. *Graduate housing:* Room and/or apartments guaranteed to single students; on-campus housing not available to married students. Housing application deadline: 8/15.

GRADUATE UNITS

School of Theology *Program availability:* Part-time. Offers theology (M Div, MA). All students are sponsored/selected by their diocese.

PONTIFICAL JOHN PAUL II INSTITUTE FOR STUDIES ON MARRIAGE AND FAMILY, Washington, DC 20064

General Information Independent-religious, coed, graduate-only institution.

GRADUATE UNITS

Graduate Programs Offers biotechnology and ethics (MTS); marriage and family (MTS, STD, STL); theology (PhD).

POPE ST. JOHN XXIII NATIONAL SEMINARY, Weston, MA 02493-2618

General Information Independent-religious, men only, graduate-only institution. *Graduate housing:* Room and/or apartments available to single students; on-campus housing not available to married students. Housing application deadline: 8/1.

GRADUATE UNITS

Graduate Program Offers theology (M Div).

PORTLAND STATE UNIVERSITY, Portland, OR 97207-0751

General Information State-supported, coed, university. CGS member. *Graduate housing:* Rooms and/or apartments available on a first-come, first-served basis to single and married students. Housing application deadline: 5/1. *Research affiliation:* DesignMedix Inc (chemistry, drug development for infectious diseases), Metron Inc. (computer engineering, advanced mathematical methods), Portland General Electric (electrical engineering), Semiconductor Research Corporation (computer science), Oregon Nanoscience and Microtechnologies Institute (electrical and computer engineering), Tektronix (electrical engineering).

GRADUATE UNITS

Graduate Studies *Program availability:* Part-time, evening/weekend, online learning.

College of Liberal Arts and Sciences *Program availability:* Part-time, evening/weekend. Offers anthropology (MA, MS); applied physics (PhD); applied statistics (Certificate); biology (MA, MS, PhD); chemistry (MA, MS, PhD); computational intelligence (Certificate); computer modeling and simulation (Certificate); conflict resolution (MA, MS); creative writing (MFA); English (MA); environmental management (MEM); environmental science and management (PSM); environmental sciences and resources (PhD); environmental sciences/biology (PhD); environmental sciences/chemistry (PhD); environmental sciences/civil engineering (PhD); environmental sciences/geography (PhD); environmental sciences/geology (PhD); environmental sciences/physics (PhD); environmental studies (MS); French (MA); general arts and letters education (MAT, MST); general science education (MAT, MST); general social science education (MAT, MST); general speech communication (MA, MS, Certificate); geography (MA, MAT, MS, MST, PhD); geology (MA, MS, Certificate); German (MA); history (MA); hydrology (Certificate); Japanese (MA); liberal arts and sciences (PhD); mathematical sciences (PhD); mathematics education (PhD); mathematics for middle school (Certificate); mathematics for teachers (MS); physics (MA, MS); psychology (MA, MS, PhD); science/geology (MAT, MST); sociology (MA, MS, PhD); Spanish (MA); speech-language pathology (MA, MS); statistics (MS); systems science (MS); systems science/anthropology (PhD); systems science/business administration (PhD); systems science/civil engineering (PhD); systems science/economics (PhD); systems science/engineering management (PhD); systems science/general (PhD); systems science/mathematical sciences (PhD); systems science/mechanical engineering (PhD); systems science/psychology (PhD); systems science/sociology (PhD); teaching English as a second language (Certificate); teaching English to speakers of other languages (MA); world literature and language (MA).

College of the Arts *Program availability:* Part-time. Offers architecture (M Arch); conducting (Mus M); contemporary art practice: art and social practice (MFA); contemporary art practice: studio practice (MFA); jazz studies (Mus M); music (Mus M); performance (Mus M); the arts (M Arch, MFA, Mus M).

College of Urban and Public Affairs *Program availability:* Part-time, evening/weekend. Offers applied social demography (Certificate); collaborative governance (Certificate); criminology and criminal justice (MS); economics (MA, MS); energy policy and management (Certificate); environmental and resource economics (Certificate); global management and leadership (MPA); government (EMPA, MA, MPA, MS, PhD, Certificate); health administration (MPA); human resource management (MPA); local government (MPA); natural resource policy and administration (MPA); nonprofit and public management (Certificate); nonprofit management (MPA); political science (MA); public administration (EMPA); public affairs and policy (PhD); real estate development (Certificate); sustainable food systems (Certificate); transportation (Certificate); urban and public affairs (EMPA, MA, MPA, MRED, MS, MURP, MUS, PhD, Certificate); urban design (Certificate); urban studies (PhD); urban studies and planning (MRED, MURP, MUS); urban studies: regional science (PhD).

Maseeh College of Engineering and Computer Science *Program availability:* Part-time, evening/weekend. Offers civil and environmental engineering (M Eng, MS, PhD); computer science (MS, PhD); computer security (Certificate); electrical and computer engineering (MS, PhD); engineering and computer science (M Eng, MS, MSME, MSMSE, PhD, Certificate); engineering and technology management (MS); mechanical engineering (PhD); technology management (PhD).

OHSU-PSU School of Public Health *Program availability:* Part-time. Offers community health (PhD); health management and policy (MPH); health promotion (MPH); health studies (MA); health systems and policy (PhD); public health (MA, MPH, PhD).

The School of Business *Program availability:* Part-time, evening/weekend. Offers business (MBA, MIM, MRED, MS, MSF, MSFA, PhD); business administration (MBA); financial analysis (MSF); global supply chain management (MS); international management (MIM); real estate development (MRED). Electronic applications accepted.

School of Education *Program availability:* Part-time, evening/weekend. Offers education (M Ed, MA, MAT, MS, MST, Ed D). Electronic applications accepted.

School of Social Work *Program availability:* Part-time. Offers social work (MSW); social work and social research (PhD).

POST UNIVERSITY, Waterbury, CT 06723-2540

General Information Independent, coed, comprehensive institution. *Enrollment:* 349 full-time matriculated graduate/professional students (177 women), 47 part-time matriculated graduate/professional students (27 women). *Enrollment by degree level:* 396 master's. *Graduate faculty:* 10 full-time, 69 part-time/adjunct. *Tuition:* Full-time $8300; part-time $570 per credit. *Required fees:* $140 per term. Tuition and fees vary according to course level, campus/location and program. *Student services:* Campus employment opportunities, campus safety program, career counseling, international student services, multicultural affairs office, services for students with disabilities, writing training. *Library facilities:* Trauriq Library and Resource Center. *Collection:* Books: 10,320 (physical), 160,000 (digital/electronic); Serial titles: 250 (physical), 36,199 (digital/electronic); Databases: 43. Weekly public service hours: 75; students can reserve study rooms.

Computer facilities: Computer purchase and lease plans are available. 150 computers available on campus for general student use. A campuswide network can be accessed. Online class registration, software applications are available. Website: http://www.post.edu/

General Application Contact: Jeanna Sinn, Vice President, Admissions, 203-591-5238, E-mail: jsinn@post.edu.

GRADUATE UNITS

Program in Business Administration *Program availability:* Online learning. Offers accounting (MSA); business administration (MBA); corporate finance (MBA); corporate innovation (MBA); healthcare systems leadership (MBA); leadership (MBA); marketing (MBA); project management (MBA, MS).

Program in Counseling and Human Services *Program availability:* Part-time, evening/weekend, online learning. Offers counseling and human services (MS); counseling and human services/alcohol and drug counseling (MS); counseling and human services/clinical mental health counseling (MS); counseling and human services/forensic mental health counseling (MS); counseling and human services/non-profit management (MS).

Program in Education *Program availability:* Online learning. Offers curriculum and instruction (M Ed); education (M Ed); educational technology (M Ed); higher education administration (MS); learning design and technology (M Ed); online teaching (M Ed); teaching English to speakers of other languages (TESOL) (M Ed).

Program in Public Administration *Program availability:* Online learning. Offers emergency management and homeland security (MPA).

PRAIRIE VIEW A&M UNIVERSITY, Prairie View, TX 77446

General Information State-supported, coed, university. *Enrollment:* 9,516 graduate, professional, and undergraduate students; 474 full-time matriculated graduate/professional students (277 women), 518 part-time matriculated graduate/professional students (357 women). *Enrollment by degree level:* 853 master's, 132 doctoral, 7 other advanced degrees. *Graduate faculty:* 112 full-time (45 women), 14 part-time/adjunct (9 women). *Tuition, area resident:* Full-time $3172; part-time $317 per credit. Tuition, state resident: full-time $3172; part-time $317 per credit. Tuition, nonresident: full-time $7965; part-time $796 per credit. *Required fees:* $4847; $485 per credit. *Graduate housing:* Room and/or apartments available on a first-come, first-served basis to single students; on-campus housing not available to married students. Typical cost: $5774 per year ($8743 including board). Room and board charges vary according to board plan, campus/location and housing facility selected. Housing application deadline: 4/16. *Student services:* Campus employment opportunities, campus safety program, career counseling, exercise/wellness program, free psychological counseling, grant writing training, international student services, low-cost health insurance, multicultural affairs office, services for students with disabilities, teacher training, writing training. *Library facilities:* John B. Coleman Library plus 3 others. *Collection:* Books: 232,516 (physical), 344,581 (digital/electronic); Serial titles: 199 (physical); Databases: 23. Weekly public service hours: 97; students can reserve study rooms.

Computer facilities: 3,500 computers available on campus for general student use. A campuswide network can be accessed from student residence rooms and from off campus. Online class registration is available. Website: http://www.pvamu.edu/

General Application Contact: Pauline Walker, Office of Graduate Admissions, 936-261-3521, Fax: 936-261-3529, E-mail: gradadmissions@pvamu.edu.

GRADUATE UNITS

College of Agriculture and Human Sciences Average age 31. 57 applicants, 88% accepted, 36 enrolled. Expenses: Contact institution. *Financial support:* Research assistantships, career-related internships or fieldwork, Federal Work-Study, institutionally sponsored loans, scholarships/grants, tuition waivers (full and partial), and unspecified assistantships available. Support available to part-time students. Financial award application deadline: 4/1; financial award applicants required to submit FAFSA. In 2018, 24 master's awarded. *Program availability:* Part-time, evening/weekend. Offers agriculture and human sciences (MS). *Application deadline:* For fall admission, 5/1 priority date for domestic and international students; for spring admission, 10/11 priority date for domestic students, 9/1 priority date for international students; for summer admission, 3/1 priority date for domestic students, 2/1 priority date for international students. Applications are processed on a rolling basis. *Application fee:* $50. Electronic applications accepted. *Application Contact:* Pauline Walker, Administrative Assistant II, 936-261-3521, Fax: 936-261-3529, E-mail: gradadmissions@pvamu.edu. Interim Dean and Director of Land-Grant Programs, Dr. Ali Fares, 936-261-5019, E-mail: alfares@pvamu.edu.

College of Arts and Sciences Students: 32 full-time (23 women), 9 part-time (8 women); includes 35 minority (all Black or African American, non-Hispanic/Latino), 4 international. Average age 31. 27 applicants, 89% accepted, 21 enrolled. *Faculty:* 9 full-time (2 women), 1 (woman) part-time/adjunct. Expenses: Contact institution. *Financial support:* Research assistantships, teaching assistantships, career-related internships or fieldwork, Federal Work-Study, institutionally sponsored loans, and tuition waivers (full and partial) available. Support available to part-time students. Financial award application deadline: 4/1; financial award applicants required to submit FAFSA. *Program availability:* Part-time, evening/weekend. Offers arts and sciences (MA, MS); chemistry (MS). *Application deadline:* For fall admission, 5/1 priority date for domestic and international students; for spring admission, 10/11 priority date for domestic students, 9/1 priority date for international students; for summer admission, 3/1 priority date for domestic students, 2/1 priority date for international students. Applications are processed on a rolling basis. *Application fee:* $50. Electronic applications accepted. *Application Contact:* Pauline Walker, Administrative Assistant II, Research and Graduate Studies, 936-261-3521, Fax: 936-261-3529, E-mail: gradadmissions@pvamu.edu. *Dean,* Dr. Danny R. Kelley, 936-261-3180, Fax: 936-261-3188, E-mail: drkelley@pvamu.edu.

Division of Social Work, Behavioral and Political Sciences Students: 23 full-time (20 women), 5 part-time (4 women); includes 27 minority (all Black or African American, non-Hispanic/Latino). Average age 32. 13 applicants, 85% accepted, 10 enrolled. *Faculty:* 4 full-time (2 women), 1 (woman) part-time/adjunct. Expenses: Contact institution. *Financial support:* In 2018–19, 1 research assistantship (averaging $5,000 per year) was awarded; Federal Work-Study, institutionally sponsored loans, scholarships/grants, and tuition waivers also available. Support available to part-time students. Financial award application deadline: 4/1; financial award applicants required to submit FAFSA. In 2018, 2 master's awarded. *Program availability:* Part-time, evening/weekend. Offers sociology (MA). *Application deadline:* For fall admission, 5/1 priority date for domestic and international students; for spring admission, 10/1 priority date for domestic students, 9/1 priority date for international students; for summer admission, 3/1 priority date for domestic students, 2/1 priority date for international students. Applications are processed on a rolling basis. *Application fee:* $50. Electronic applications accepted. *Application Contact:* Pauline Walker, Administrative Assistant II, Research and Graduate Studies, 936-261-3521, Fax: 936-261-3529, E-mail: gradadmissions@pvamu.edu. *Division Head,* Dr. Walle Engedayehu, 936-261-3202, Fax: 936-261-3229, E-mail: waengedayehu@pvamu.edu.

College of Business Students: 57 full-time (33 women), 132 part-time (85 women); includes 174 minority (148 Black or African American, non-Hispanic/Latino; 1 American Indian or Alaska Native, non-Hispanic/Latino; 13 Asian, non-Hispanic/Latino; 10 Hispanic/Latino; 1 Native Hawaiian or other Pacific Islander, non-Hispanic/Latino; 1 Two or more races, non-Hispanic/Latino), 9 international. Average age 29. 90 applicants, 86% accepted, 59 enrolled. *Faculty:* 18 full-time (2 women), 1 part-time/adjunct (0 women). Expenses: Contact institution. *Financial support:* In 2018–19, 3 research assistantships (averaging $1,600 per year) were awarded; scholarships/grants and unspecified assistantships also available. Financial award application deadline: 4/1; financial award applicants required to submit FAFSA. In 2018, 98 master's awarded. *Program availability:* Part-time, evening/weekend. Offers accounting (MS); business administration (MBA). *Application deadline:* For fall admission, 5/1 for domestic students, 5/1 priority date for international students; for spring admission, 10/1 for domestic students, 9/1 priority date for international students; for summer admission, 3/1 for domestic students, 2/1 for international students. Applications are processed on a rolling basis. *Application fee:* $50. Electronic applications accepted. *Application Contact:* Gabriel Crosby, Director, Graduate Programs in Business, 936-261-9217, Fax: 936-261-9232, E-mail: mba@pvamu.edu. *Dean,* Dr. Munir Quddus, 936-261-9200, Fax: 936-261-9241, E-mail: cob@pvamu.edu.

College of Education Students: 84 full-time (59 women), 185 part-time (141 women); includes 257 minority (242 Black or African American, non-Hispanic/Latino; 14 Hispanic/Latino; 1 Two or more races, non-Hispanic/Latino), 6 international. Average age 35. 86 applicants, 86% accepted, 58 enrolled. *Faculty:* 22 full-time (13 women), 3 part-time/adjunct (2 women). Expenses: Contact institution. *Financial support:* Career-related internships or fieldwork, institutionally sponsored loans, scholarships/grants, and unspecified assistantships available. Support available to part-time students. Financial award application deadline: 4/1; financial award applicants required to submit FAFSA. In 2018, 121 master's, 4 doctorates awarded. *Program availability:* Part-time, evening/weekend, blended/hybrid learning. Offers curriculum and instruction (M Ed, MA Ed, MS Ed); education (M Ed, MA, MA Ed, MS, MS Ed, PhD); educational leadership and counseling (M Ed, MA, MS Ed, PhD); health and kinesiology (M Ed, MS). *Application deadline:* For fall admission, 5/1 priority date for domestic and international students; for spring admission, 10/1 priority date for domestic students, 9/1 priority date for international students; for summer admission, 3/1 priority date for domestic students, 2/1 priority date for international students. Applications are processed on a rolling basis. *Application fee:* $50. Electronic applications accepted. *Application Contact:* Pauline Walker, Administrative Assistant II, Research and Graduate Studies, 936-261-3521, Fax: 936-261-3529, E-mail: gradadmissions@pvamu.edu. *Interim Dean,* Dr. Michael L McFrazier, 936-261-3600 Ext. 2102, Fax: 936-261-3621, E-mail: mlmcFrazier@pvamu.edu.

College of Engineering Students: 134 full-time (34 women), 67 part-time (24 women); includes 84 minority (67 Black or African American, non-Hispanic/Latino; 12 Asian, non-Hispanic/Latino; 5 Hispanic/Latino), 102 international. Average age 31. 130 applicants, 80% accepted, 52 enrolled. *Faculty:* 29 full-time (8 women), 1 part-time/adjunct (0 women). Expenses: Contact institution. *Financial support:* Fellowships, research assistantships, teaching assistantships, career-related internships or fieldwork, institutionally sponsored loans, scholarships/grants, health care benefits, tuition waivers (full), and unspecified assistantships available. Financial award application deadline: 4/1; financial award applicants required to submit FAFSA. In 2018, 67 master's, 3 doctorates awarded. *Program availability:* Part-time, evening/weekend. Offers computer information systems (MSCIS); computer science (MSCS); electrical engineering (MSEE, PhDEE); general engineering (MS Engr). *Application deadline:* For fall admission, 5/1 priority date for domestic and international students; for spring admission, 10/1 priority date for domestic students, 9/1 priority date for international students; for summer admission, 3/1 priority date for domestic students, 2/1 priority date for international students. Applications are processed on a rolling basis. *Application fee:* $50. Electronic applications accepted. *Application Contact:* Pauline Walker, Administrative Assistant II, Research and Graduate Studies, 936-261-3521, Fax: 936-261-3529, E-mail: gradadmissions@pvamu.edu. *Dean,* Dr. Pamela H Obiomon, 936-261-9890, Fax: 936-261-9868, E-mail: phobiomon@pvamu.edu.

College of Juvenile Justice and Psychology Students: 19 full-time (13 women), 20 part-time (17 women); includes 35 minority (29 Black or African American, non-Hispanic/Latino; 5 Hispanic/Latino; 1 Two or more races, non-Hispanic/Latino), 3 international. Average age 32. 28 applicants, 32% accepted, 7 enrolled. *Faculty:* 8 full-time (4 women). Expenses: Contact institution. *Financial support:* In 2018–19, 21 research assistantships with full tuition reimbursements (averaging $22,000 per year), 6 teaching assistantships with full tuition reimbursements (averaging $18,000 per year) were awarded; career-related internships or fieldwork, institutionally sponsored loans, scholarships/grants, health care benefits, tuition waivers (full), and unspecified assistantships also available. Support available to part-time students. Financial award application deadline: 4/1; financial award applicants required to submit FAFSA. In 2018, 14 master's, 1 doctorate awarded. *Program availability:* Part-time, evening/weekend, online only, 100% online, Master's in Juvenile Justice. Offers clinical adolescent psychology (PhD); juvenile forensic psychology (MSJFP); juvenile justice (MSJJ, PhD). *Application deadline:* For fall admission, 5/1 priority date for domestic and international students; for spring admission, 10/1 priority date for domestic students, 9/1 priority date for international students; for summer admission, 3/1 priority date for domestic students, 2/1 priority date for international students. Applications are processed on a rolling basis.

Application fee: $50. Electronic applications accepted. *Application Contact:* Pauline Walker, Executive Secretary, Graduate Program, 936-261-3521, Fax: 936-261-3529, E-mail: gradadmissions@pvamu.edu. *Interim Dean,* Dr. Camille Gibson, 936-261-5265 Ext. 5265, Fax: 936-261-5253, E-mail: cbgibson@pvamu.edu.

College of Nursing Students: 59 full-time (51 women), 64 part-time (51 women); includes 118 minority (89 Black or African American, non-Hispanic/Latino; 22 Asian, non-Hispanic/Latino; 7 Hispanic/Latino), 1 international. Average age 36. 45 applicants, 89% accepted, 33 enrolled. *Faculty:* 11 full-time (10 women), 5 part-time/adjunct (4 women). Expenses: Contact institution. *Financial support:* In 2018–19, 1 teaching assistantship (averaging $16,000 per year) was awarded; career-related internships or fieldwork, Federal Work-Study, institutionally sponsored loans, scholarships/grants, and traineeships also available. Support available to part-time students. Financial award application deadline: 4/1; financial award applicants required to submit FAFSA. In 2018, 24 master's, 3 doctorates awarded. *Program availability:* Part-time, evening/weekend. Offers nursing (MSN, DNP). *Application deadline:* For fall admission, 5/1 priority date for domestic and international students; for spring admission, 10/1 priority date for domestic students, 9/1 priority date for international students; for summer admission, 3/1 priority date for domestic students, 2/1 priority date for international students. Applications are processed on a rolling basis. *Application fee:* $50. Electronic applications accepted. *Application Contact:* Dr. Forest Smith, Director of Student Services and Admissions, 713-797-7031, Fax: 713-797-7012, E-mail: fdsmith@pvamu.edu. *Dean,* Dr. Betty N. Adams, 713-797-7009, Fax: 713-797-7013, E-mail: bnadams@pvamu.edu.

School of Architecture Students: 36 full-time (15 women), 12 part-time (6 women); includes 42 minority (34 Black or African American, non-Hispanic/Latino; 1 Asian, non-Hispanic/Latino; 7 Hispanic/Latino), 2 international. Average age 29. 27 applicants, 81% accepted, 18 enrolled. *Faculty:* 4 full-time (0 women), 3 part-time/adjunct (2 women). Expenses: Contact institution. *Financial support:* Career-related internships or fieldwork, Federal Work-Study, institutionally sponsored loans, scholarships/grants, tuition waivers (full and partial), and unspecified assistantships available. Support available to part-time students. Financial award application deadline: 4/1; financial award applicants required to submit FAFSA. In 2018, 30 master's awarded. *Program availability:* Part-time, evening/weekend. Offers architecture (M Arch, MCD). *Application deadline:* For fall admission, 5/1 priority date for domestic and international students; for spring admission, 10/1 priority date for domestic students, 9/1 priority date for international students; for summer admission, 3/1 priority date for domestic students, 2/1 priority date for international students. Applications are processed on a rolling basis. *Application fee:* $50. Electronic applications accepted. *Application Contact:* Pauline Walker, Administrative Assistant II, Research and Graduate Studies, 936-261-3521, Fax: 936-261-3529, E-mail: pmwalker@pvamu.edu. *Dean,* Dr. Ikhlas Sabouni, 936-261-9800, Fax: 936-261-2350, E-mail: isabouni@pvamu.edu.

PRATT INSTITUTE, Brooklyn, NY 11205-3899

General Information Independent, coed, comprehensive institution. *Enrollment:* 1,186 full-time matriculated graduate/professional students (859 women), 177 part-time matriculated graduate/professional students (140 women). *Enrollment by degree level:* 1,359 master's, 4 other advanced degrees. *Graduate faculty:* 86 full-time (50 women), 543 part-time (280 women). *Tuition:* Full-time $33,246; part-time $1847 per credit. *Required fees:* $1980. *Graduate housing:* Room and/or apartments available on a first-come, first-served basis to single students; on-campus housing not available to married students. Typical cost: $22,150 per year ($26,022 including board). Housing application deadline: 5/1. *Student services:* Campus employment opportunities, campus safety program, career counseling, exercise/wellness program, free psychological counseling, grant writing training, international student services, low-cost health insurance, multicultural affairs office, services for students with disabilities, teacher training, writing training. *Library facilities:* Pratt Institute Library.

Computer facilities: A campuswide network can be accessed from student residence rooms and from off campus. Online class registration is available. Website: http://www.pratt.edu.

General Application Contact: Natalie Capannelli, Director of Graduate Admissions, 718-636-3551, Fax: 718-636-3670, E-mail: ncapanne@pratt.edu.

GRADUATE UNITS

School of Architecture Students: 318 full-time (190 women), 50 part-time (26 women); includes 83 minority (19 Black or African American, non-Hispanic/Latino; 1 American Indian or Alaska Native, non-Hispanic/Latino; 21 Asian, non-Hispanic/Latino; 36 Hispanic/Latino; 6 Two or more races, non-Hispanic/Latino), 180 international. Average age 27. 730 applicants, 83% accepted, 118 enrolled. Expenses: Contact institution. *Financial support:* Career-related internships or fieldwork, Federal Work-Study, institutionally sponsored loans, scholarships/grants, health care benefits, and unspecified assistantships available. Support available to part-time students. Financial award application deadline: 2/1; financial award applicants required to submit FAFSA. In 2018, 149 master's awarded. Offers architecture (M Arch, MS, MS Arch, MSCRP); architecture (first-professional) (M Arch); architecture (post-professional) (MS Arch); architecture and urban design (MS); city and regional planning (MSCRP); facilities management (MS); historic preservation (MS); real estate practice (MS); sustainable environmental systems (MS); urban placemaking and management (MS). *Application deadline:* For fall admission, 1/5 for domestic and international students; for spring admission, 10/1 for domestic and international students. *Application fee:* $50 ($90 for international students). Electronic applications accepted. *Application Contact:* Natalie Capannelli, Director of Graduate Admissions, 718-636-3551, Fax: 718-399-4242, E-mail: ncapanne@pratt.edu. *Dean,* Thomas Hanrahan, 718-399-4308, Fax: 718-399-4315, E-mail: hanrahan@pratt.edu.

School of Art Students: 258 full-time (192 women), 96 part-time (82 women); includes 92 minority (30 Black or African American, non-Hispanic/Latino; 18 Asian, non-Hispanic/Latino; 35 Hispanic/Latino; 9 Two or more races, non-Hispanic/Latino), 129 international. Average age 29. 955 applicants, 48% accepted, 155 enrolled. *Faculty:* 27 full-time (15 women), 11 part-time/adjunct (5 women). Expenses: Contact institution. *Financial support:* Career-related internships or fieldwork, Federal Work-Study, institutionally sponsored loans, scholarships/grants, health care benefits, and unspecified assistantships available. Support available to part-time students. Financial award application deadline: 2/1; financial award applicants required to submit FAFSA. In 2018, 124 master's awarded. *Program availability:* Part-time. Offers art (MA, MFA, MPS, MS, Adv C); art and design education (MA, MS, Adv C); art therapy and creativity development (MPS); arts and cultural management (MPS); dance/movement therapy (MS); design management (MPS); digital arts (MFA); fine arts (MFA). *Application deadline:* For fall admission, 1/5 for domestic and international students; for spring admission, 10/1 for domestic and international students. *Application fee:* $50 ($90 for international students). Electronic applications accepted. *Application Contact:* Natalie Capannelli, Director of Graduate Admissions, 718-636-3551, Fax: 718-399-4242, E-mail: ncapanne@pratt.edu. *Acting Dean,* Jorge Oliver, 718-636-3671, E-mail: joliver6@pratt.edu.

School of Design Students: 390 full-time (296 women), 7 part-time (5 women); includes 36 minority (5 Black or African American, non-Hispanic/Latino; 20 Asian, non-Hispanic/Latino; 7 Hispanic/Latino; 1 Native Hawaiian or other Pacific Islander, non-Hispanic/Latino; 3 Two or more races, non-Hispanic/Latino), 313 international. Average age 25. 966 applicants, 49% accepted, 176 enrolled. *Faculty:* 17 full-time (8 women), 248 part-time/adjunct (111 women). Expenses: Contact institution. *Financial support:* Career-related internships or fieldwork, Federal Work-Study, institutionally sponsored loans, scholarships/grants, health care benefits, and unspecified assistantships available. Support available to part-time students. Financial award application deadline: 2/1; financial award applicants required to submit FAFSA. In 2018, 139 master's awarded. *Program availability:* Part-time. Offers communications design (MFA); design (MFA, MID, MS); industrial design (MID); interior design (MFA); package design (MS). *Application deadline:* For fall admission, 1/5 for domestic and international students; for spring admission, 10/1 for domestic and international students. *Application fee:* $50 ($90 for international students). Electronic applications accepted. *Application Contact:* Natalie Capannelli, Director of Graduate Admissions, 718-636-3551, Fax: 718-636-3670, E-mail: ncapanne@pratt.edu. *Dean, School of Design,* Anita Cooney, 718-687-5744, Fax: 718-636-3410, E-mail: acooney@pratt.edu.

School of Information Average age 30. 303 applicants, 75% accepted, 67 enrolled. *Faculty:* 10 full-time (8 women), 21 part-time/adjunct (11 women). Expenses: Contact institution. *Financial support:* Career-related internships or fieldwork, Federal Work-Study, institutionally sponsored loans, scholarships/grants, health care benefits, and unspecified assistantships available. Support available to part-time students. Financial award application deadline: 2/1; financial award applicants required to submit FAFSA. In 2018, 59 master's, 1 other advanced degree awarded. *Program availability:* Part-time. Offers information (MS, Adv C). *Application deadline:* For fall admission, 1/5 for domestic and international students; for spring admission, 10/1 for domestic and international students. Applications are processed on a rolling basis. *Application fee:* $50 ($90 for international students). Electronic applications accepted. *Application Contact:* Natalie Capannelli, Director of Graduate Admissions, 718-636-3551, Fax: 718-399-4242, E-mail: ncapanne@pratt.edu. *Interim Dean,* Anthony Cocciolo, 212-647-7702, Fax: 212-367-2442, E-mail: acocciol@pratt.edu.

School of Liberal Arts and Sciences Students: 68 full-time (54 women), 9 part-time (6 women); includes 24 minority (11 Black or African American, non-Hispanic/Latino; 1 American Indian or Alaska Native, non-Hispanic/Latino; 4 Asian, non-Hispanic/Latino; 6 Hispanic/Latino; 2 Two or more races, non-Hispanic/Latino), 16 international. Average age 28. 196 applicants, 57% accepted, 28 enrolled. *Faculty:* 22 full-time (15 women), 188 part-time/adjunct (102 women). Expenses: Contact institution. *Financial support:* Career-related internships or fieldwork, Federal Work-Study, institutionally sponsored loans, scholarships/grants, health care benefits, and unspecified assistantships available. Support available to part-time students. Financial award application deadline: 2/1; financial award applicants required to submit FAFSA. In 2018, 32 master's awarded. Offers liberal arts and sciences (MA, MFA); media studies (MA); performance and performance studies (MFA); writing (MFA). *Application deadline:* For fall admission, 1/5 for domestic and international students; for spring admission, 10/1 for domestic and international students. *Application fee:* $50 ($90 for international students). Electronic applications accepted. *Application Contact:* Natalie Capannelli, Director of Graduate Admissions, 718-636-3551, Fax: 718-399-4242, E-mail: ncapanne@pratt.edu. *Interim Dean,* Dr. Helio Takai, 718-636-3570, Fax: 718-399-4586, E-mail: htakai@pratt.edu.

PRESBYTERIAN COLLEGE, Clinton, SC 29325

General Information Independent-religious, coed, comprehensive institution. *Enrollment:* 246 full-time matriculated graduate/professional students (184 women), 4 part-time matriculated graduate/professional students (2 women). *Enrollment by degree level:* 250 doctoral. *Graduate faculty:* 7 full-time (0 women), 17 part-time/adjunct (0 women). *Tuition:* Full-time $35,300. *Required fees:* $1600. Full-time tuition and fees vary according to degree level. *Graduate housing:* On-campus housing not available. *Student services:* Campus employment opportunities, campus safety program, career counseling, exercise/wellness program, free psychological counseling, international student services, multicultural affairs office, services for students with disabilities, writing training. *Library facilities:* James H. Thomason Library. *Collection:* Books: 108,925 (physical), 227,396 (digital/electronic); Serial titles: 702 (physical), 16,342 (digital/electronic); Databases: 71. Study areas open 24 hours, 5–7 days a week; students can reserve study rooms.

Computer facilities: 100 computers available on campus for general student use. A campuswide network can be accessed from student residence rooms and from off campus. Online class registration is available. Website: http://www.presby.edu/

General Application Contact: Deanie Kane, Director of Admissions, 864-938-3913, E-mail: kjkane@presby.edu.

GRADUATE UNITS

Presbyterian College School of Pharmacy (PCSP) Students: 246 full-time (184 women), 4 part-time (2 women); includes 70 minority (38 Black or African American, non-Hispanic/Latino; 2 American Indian or Alaska Native, non-Hispanic/Latino; 18 Asian, non-Hispanic/Latino; 5 Hispanic/Latino; 7 Two or more races, non-Hispanic/Latino), 1 international. Average age 25. 164 applicants, 49% accepted, 61 enrolled. *Faculty:* 7 full-time (0 women), 17 part-time/adjunct (0 women). Expenses: Contact institution. *Financial support:* In 2018–19, 13 students received support, including 6 research assistantships (averaging $3,000 per year); Federal Work-Study and health care benefits also available. Financial award application deadline: 4/1; financial award applicants required to submit FAFSA. In 2018, 69 doctorates awarded. Offers pharmacy (Pharm D). *Application deadline:* For fall admission, 4/1 for domestic and international students. Applications are processed on a rolling basis. *Application fee:* $175. Electronic applications accepted. *Application Contact:* Deanie Kane, Director of Admissions, 864-938-3913, E-mail: kjkane@presby.edu. *Dean,* Dr. Richard E. Stull.

PRESCOTT COLLEGE, Prescott, AZ 86301

General Information Independent, coed, comprehensive institution. *Graduate housing:* Room and/or apartments available on a first-come, first-served basis to single students; on-campus housing not available to married students. Housing application deadline: 5/1. *Research affiliation:* Marshall Foundation (youth and wilderness), U.S. Department of Agriculture (USDA) (agro-ecology), National Park Service (forest health), Packard Foundation (Kino Bay research).

GRADUATE UNITS

Graduate Programs *Program availability:* Part-time, online learning. Offers adventure education (MA); adventure-based environmental education (MA); adventure-based psychotherapy (MA); counseling psychology (MA); early childhood education (MA); early childhood special education (MA); ecopsychology (MA); ecotherapy (MA); education (MA); elementary education (MA); environmental education leadership and administration (MA); environmental studies (MA); equine-assisted learning (MA);

equine-assisted mental health (MA); expressive arts therapy (MA); humanities (MA); school guidance counseling (MA); secondary education (MA); social justice and human rights (MA); somatic psychology (MA); special education: learning disabilities (MA); special education: mental retardation (MA); special education: serious emotional disabilities (MA); student-directed concentration (MA); student-directed independent study (MA); sustainability education (PhD). Electronic applications accepted.

PRESIDIO GRADUATE SCHOOL, San Francisco, CA 94129

General Information Independent, coed, graduate-only institution.

GRADUATE UNITS

Graduate Programs - San Francisco Offers sustainable energy management (Certificate); sustainable management (MBA, MPA, Certificate). MBA/JD offered in conjunction with the University of California, Hastings College of the Law.

MBA Programs - Seattle *Program availability:* Part-time, evening/weekend, blended/hybrid learning. Offers cooperative management (Certificate); sustainable business (MBA); sustainable systems (MBA). Electronic applications accepted.

PRINCETON THEOLOGICAL SEMINARY, Princeton, NJ 08542-0803

General Information Independent-religious, coed, graduate-only institution. *Graduate housing:* Rooms and/or apartments available on a first-come, first-served basis to single and married students. *Research affiliation:* Center of Theological Inquiry.

GRADUATE UNITS

Graduate and Professional Programs *Program availability:* Part-time. Offers theology (M Div, MA, Th M, D Min, PhD). Electronic applications accepted.

PRINCETON UNIVERSITY, Princeton, NJ 08544-1019

General Information Independent, coed, university. CGS member. *Graduate housing:* Rooms and/or apartments available to single and married students. Housing application deadline: 4/15. *Research affiliation:* Institute for Advanced Study (physics and mathematics), Brookhaven National Laboratory (experimental physics), Textile Research Institute (polymer research), National Oceanic and Atmospheric Administration (NOAA)–GFD Laboratory (weather prediction).

GRADUATE UNITS

Graduate School Offers anthropology (PhD); applied and computational mathematics (PhD); astronomy (PhD); atmospheric and oceanic sciences (PhD); chemistry (PhD); classical and Hellenic studies (PhD); classical art and archaeology (PhD); classical philosophy (PhD); comparative literature (PhD); composition (PhD); demography (PhD, Certificate); East Asian art and archaeology (PhD); East Asian studies (PhD); ecology and evolutionary biology (PhD); economics (PhD); economics and demography (PhD); English (PhD); French language and literature (PhD); geosciences (PhD); German (PhD); history (PhD); history (the ancient world) (PhD); history of science (PhD); industrial chemistry (MS); literature and philology (PhD); mathematics (PhD); molecular biology (PhD); musicology (PhD); Near Eastern studies (MA, PhD); neuroscience (PhD); ocean sciences and marine biology (PhD); philosophy (PhD); philosophy of science (PhD); physics (PhD); plasma physics (PhD); political philosophy (PhD); politics (PhD); psychology (PhD); public affairs and demography (PhD); religion (PhD); Russian and Slavic linguistics (PhD); Russian literature (PhD); sociology (PhD); sociology and demography (PhD); Spanish and Portuguese (PhD). Electronic applications accepted.

Bendheim Center for Finance Students: 49 full-time (23 women); includes 3 minority (2 Asian, non-Hispanic/Latino; 1 Two or more races, non-Hispanic/Latino), 43 international. Average age 23. 565 applicants, 7% accepted, 29 enrolled. *Faculty:* 9 full-time (1 woman), 7 part-time/adjunct. Expenses: Contact institution. *Financial support:* In 2018–19, 9 students received support, including 10 teaching assistantships (averaging $10,000 per year); scholarships/grants also available. In 2018, 27 master's awarded. Offers finance (M Fin). *Application deadline:* For fall admission, 12/31 for domestic and international students. *Application fee:* $0. Electronic applications accepted. *Application Contact:* Graduate Admissions Office, 609-258-3034, Fax: 609-258-7262, E-mail: gsadmit@princeton.edu. *Director of Graduate Studies,* Rene Carmona, 609-258-2310, Fax: 609-258-3791, E-mail: rcarmona@princeton.edu.

School of Architecture Offers architecture (M Arch, PhD). Electronic applications accepted.

School of Engineering and Applied Science Offers chemical and biological engineering (M Eng, MSE, PhD); civil and environmental engineering (M Eng, MSE, PhD); computer science (MSE, PhD); electrical engineering (M Eng, PhD); engineering and applied science (M Eng, MSE, PhD); mechanical and aerospace engineering (M Eng, MSE, PhD); operations research and financial engineering (M Eng, MSE, PhD). Electronic applications accepted.

Woodrow Wilson School of Public and International Affairs Offers public affairs (MPA, PhD); public policy (MPP). JD/MPA offered jointly with Columbia University, New York University, Stanford University. Electronic applications accepted.

Princeton Institute for the Science and Technology of Materials (PRISM) Offers materials (PhD).

Princeton Neuroscience Institute Offers neuroscience (PhD). Electronic applications accepted.

PROVIDENCE COLLEGE, Providence, RI 02918

General Information Independent-religious, coed, comprehensive institution. *Graduate housing:* On-campus housing not available.

GRADUATE UNITS

Department of History *Program availability:* Part-time, evening/weekend. Offers American history (MA); modern European history (MA).

Department of Theology *Program availability:* Part-time, evening/weekend. Offers Biblical studies (MA); theology (MA, MTS).

Program in Counseling *Program availability:* Part-time, evening/weekend. Offers counseling (M Ed).

Program in Literacy *Program availability:* Part-time, evening/weekend. Offers literacy (M Ed).

Program in Special Education *Program availability:* Part-time, evening/weekend. Offers special education (M Ed).

Program in Teaching Mathematics *Program availability:* Part-time, evening/weekend. Offers teaching mathematics (MA).

Program in Urban Teaching *Program availability:* Part-time, evening/weekend. Offers urban teaching (M Ed).

Programs in Administration *Program availability:* Part-time, evening/weekend. Offers elementary administration (M Ed); secondary administration (M Ed).

Providence Alliance for Catholic Teachers (PACT) Program Offers secondary education (M Ed).

School of Business *Program availability:* Part-time, evening/weekend. Offers accounting (MBA); finance (MBA); international business (MBA); management (MBA); marketing (MBA).

PROVIDENCE UNIVERSITY COLLEGE & THEOLOGICAL SEMINARY, Otterburne, MB R0A 1G0, Canada

General Information Independent-religious, coed, comprehensive institution. *Graduate housing:* Rooms and/or apartments guaranteed to single students and available on a first-come, first-served basis to married students. Housing application deadline: 8/15.

GRADUATE UNITS

Theological Seminary *Program availability:* Part-time. Offers children's ministry (Certificate); Christian studies (MA, Certificate); counseling (MA); cross-cultural discipleship (Certificate); divinity (M Div); educational studies (MA); global studies (MA); lay counseling (Diploma); ministry (D Min); teaching English to speakers of other languages (Certificate); theological studies (MA); training teacher of English to speakers of other languages (Certificate); youth ministry (Certificate).

PURCHASE COLLEGE, STATE UNIVERSITY OF NEW YORK, Purchase, NY 10577-1400

General Information State-supported, coed, comprehensive institution. *Enrollment:* 4,263 graduate, professional, and undergraduate students; 91 full-time matriculated graduate/professional students (47 women), 9 part-time matriculated graduate/professional students (4 women). *Enrollment by degree level:* 100 master's. *Tuition, area resident:* Full-time $11,090; part-time $462 per credit hour. Tuition, state resident: full-time $11,310. Tuition, nonresident: full-time $23,100; part-time $944 per credit hour. *Required fees:* $1883; $75.57 per credit hour. One-time fee: $210 full-time. *Graduate housing:* Room and/or apartments available on a first-come, first-served basis to single students; on-campus housing not available to married students. Typical cost: $10,488 per year ($13,914 including board). Room and board charges vary according to board plan and housing facility selected. Housing application deadline: 6/21. *Student services:* Campus employment opportunities, campus safety program, career counseling, child daycare facilities, exercise/wellness program, free psychological counseling, international student services, low-cost health insurance, multicultural affairs office, services for students with disabilities. *Library facilities:* Purchase College Library plus 1 other. *Collection:* Books: 237,710 (physical), 11,422 (digital/electronic); Serial titles: 107 (physical), 65,714 (digital/electronic); Databases: 176.

Computer facilities: 600 computers available on campus for general student use. A campuswide network can be accessed from student residence rooms and from off campus. Online class registration; CNC-routers; 3D printers; Laser cutters; Vinyl Printers; a Virtual Reality Lab; a fabrication lab; Non-liner edit labs for film; Music Digital Audio Workstations, 24 and 48" plotters for high-quality photographic output; a digital embroidery machine are available.
Website: http://www.purchase.edu/

General Application Contact: Bea Martin-Ruiz, Admissions Counselor, 914-250-6704, Fax: 914-251-6314, E-mail: admissn@purchase.edu.

GRADUATE UNITS

Conservatory of Music Offers classical composition (MM); instrumental performance (MM); jazz studies (MM); studio composition (MM); voice and opera studies (MM). Electronic applications accepted.

School of Art and Design Offers art history/visual arts (MA); visual arts (MFA). Electronic applications accepted.

School of Film and Media Studies Offers media arts and culture (MFA).

School of Humanities Offers art history (MA). Electronic applications accepted.

School of the Arts *Program availability:* Part-time. Offers entrepreneurship in the arts (MA).

PURDUE UNIVERSITY, West Lafayette, IN 47907

General Information State-supported, coed, university. CGS member. *Enrollment:* 43,411 graduate, professional, and undergraduate students; 6,017 full-time matriculated graduate/professional students (2,374 women), 3,507 part-time matriculated graduate/professional students (1,585 women). *Enrollment by degree level:* 4,555 master's, 4,828 doctoral, 141 other advanced degrees. *Graduate faculty:* 2,086 full-time (691 women), 96 part-time/adjunct (35 women). *Graduate housing:* Rooms and/or apartments available on a first-come, first-served basis to single and married students. Housing application deadline: 3/1. *Student services:* Campus employment opportunities, campus safety program, career counseling, child daycare facilities, exercise/wellness program, free psychological counseling, grant writing training, international student services, low-cost health insurance, multicultural affairs office, services for students with disabilities, teacher training, writing training. *Library facilities:* Purdue University Libraries plus 9 others. *Collection:* Books: 946,376 (physical), 2.5 million (digital/electronic); Serial titles: 44,788 (physical), 136,167 (digital/electronic); Databases: 580. Weekly public service hours: 168; study areas open 24 hours, 5–7 days a week; students can reserve study rooms.

Computer facilities: Computer purchase and lease plans are available. 5,237 computers available on campus for general student use. A campuswide network can be accessed from student residence rooms and from off campus. Online class registration is available.
Website: http://www.purdue.edu/

General Application Contact: Marcia Fritzlen, Graduate School Admissions, 765-494-2600, Fax: 765-494-0136, E-mail: gradinfo@purdue.edu.

GRADUATE UNITS

College of Engineering *Program availability:* Part-time, 100% online, blended/hybrid learning. Offers biomedical engineering (MSBME, PhD); engineering (MS, MSABE, MSBME, MSCE, MSChE, MSE, MSECE, MSIE, MSME, MSMSE, MSNE, PhD, Certificate); interdisciplinary engineering (MS, MSE). Electronic applications accepted.

Davidson School of Chemical Engineering Offers chemical engineering (MSChE, PhD). Electronic applications accepted.

Division of Environmental and Ecological Engineering Offers environmental and ecological engineering (MS, PhD).

Lyles School of Civil Engineering *Program availability:* Part-time. Offers civil engineering (MS, MSCE, MSE, PhD). Electronic applications accepted.

School of Aeronautics and Astronautics *Program availability:* Part-time, 100% online. Offers aeronautics and astronautics (MS, PhD). Electronic applications accepted.

School of Agricultural and Biological Engineering *Program availability:* Part-time. Offers agricultural and biological engineering (MS, MSABE, MSE, PhD). Electronic applications accepted.

School of Electrical and Computer Engineering *Program availability:* Part-time, online learning. Offers electrical and computer engineering (MSECE, PhD). MS and PhD degree programs in biomedical engineering offered jointly with School of Mechanical Engineering and School of Chemical Engineering. Electronic applications accepted.

School of Engineering Education Offers engineering education (PhD). Electronic applications accepted.

School of Industrial Engineering *Program availability:* Part-time, online learning. Offers industrial engineering (MS, MSIE, PhD). Electronic applications accepted.

School of Materials Engineering Offers materials engineering (MSMSE, PhD). Electronic applications accepted.

School of Mechanical Engineering *Program availability:* Part-time, online learning. Offers mechanical engineering (MS, MSE, MSME, PhD, Certificate). MS and PhD degree programs in biomedical engineering offered jointly with School of Electrical and Computer Engineering and School of Chemical Engineering. Electronic applications accepted.

School of Nuclear Engineering *Program availability:* Part-time. Offers nuclear engineering (MS, MSNE, PhD). Electronic applications accepted.

College of Pharmacy Students: 724 full-time (475 women), 12 part-time (7 women); includes 169 minority (25 Black or African American, non-Hispanic/Latino; 3 American Indian or Alaska Native, non-Hispanic/Latino; 97 Asian, non-Hispanic/Latino; 28 Hispanic/Latino; 16 Two or more races, non-Hispanic/Latino), 95 international. Average age 23. 658 applicants, 33% accepted, 179 enrolled. *Faculty:* 67 full-time (31 women), 8 part-time/adjunct (4 women). Expenses: Contact institution. *Financial support:* Fellowships, research assistantships, teaching assistantships, career-related internships or fieldwork, Federal Work-Study, scholarships/grants, and traineeships available. Support available to part-time students. Financial award applicants required to submit FAFSA. In 2018, 1 master's, 18 doctorates, 145 other advanced degrees awarded. *Program availability:* Part-time. Offers biophysical and computational chemistry (PhD); cancer research (PhD); clinical pharmacy (PhD); immunology and infectious disease (PhD); industrial and physical pharmacy (PhD, Certificate); medicinal biochemistry and molecular biology (PhD); medicinal chemistry and chemical biology (PhD); molecular pharmacology (PhD); neuropharmacology, neurodegeneration, and neurotoxicity (PhD); pharmaceutics (PhD); pharmacy (MS, MS, PharmD, Certificate); pharmacy administration (MS, PhD); pharmacy and pharmacal sciences (MS, PhD, PharmD, Certificate); pharmacy practice (MS); regulatory quality compliance (MS, Certificate); systems biology and functional genomics (PhD). *Application deadline:* Applications are processed on a rolling basis. *Application fee:* $60 ($75 for international students). Electronic applications accepted. *Application Contact:* Danzhou Yang, Associate Dean for Research and Graduate Programs, 765-494-1362, E-mail: yangdz@purdue.edu. *Dean:* Eric L. Barker, 765-494-1368, E-mail: barkerel@purdue.edu.

Graduate School Students: 5,895 full-time (2,314 women), 3,499 part-time (1,580 women); includes 1,266 minority (290 Black or African American, non-Hispanic/Latino; 16 American Indian or Alaska Native, non-Hispanic/Latino; 425 Asian, non-Hispanic/Latino; 382 Hispanic/Latino; 5 Native Hawaiian or other Pacific Islander, non-Hispanic/Latino; 148 Two or more races, non-Hispanic/Latino), 4,138 international. Average age 29. 15,871 applicants, 33% accepted, 2365 enrolled. *Faculty:* 2,086 full-time (691 women), 96 part-time/adjunct (35 women). Expenses: Contact institution. *Financial support:* Fellowships with tuition reimbursements, research assistantships with tuition reimbursements, teaching assistantships with tuition reimbursements, career-related internships or fieldwork, scholarships/grants, tuition waivers (full and partial), and instructorships available. Support available to part-time students. Financial award applicants required to submit FAFSA. In 2018, 2,264 master's, 740 doctorates, 313 other advanced degrees awarded. *Program availability:* Part-time, evening/weekend, online learning. Offers biomedical sciences (PhD); biomolecular structure and biophysics (PhD); biotechnology (PhD); chemical biology (PhD); chromatin and regulation of gene expression (PhD); ecological sciences and engineering (MS, PhD); information security (PhD); integrative neuroscience (PhD); integrative plant sciences (PhD); membrane biology (PhD); microbiology (PhD); molecular evolutionary and cancer biology (PhD); molecular evolutionary genetics (PhD); molecular virology (PhD); philosophy and literature (PhD). MD/PhD offered jointly with Indiana University–Purdue University Indianapolis. *Application deadline:* Applications are processed on a rolling basis. *Application fee:* $60 ($75 for international students). Electronic applications accepted. *Application Contact:* Graduate School Admissions, 765-494-2600, Fax: 765-494-0136, E-mail: gradinfo@purdue.edu. *Dean:* Dr. Linda J. Mason, 765-494-0245, E-mail: lmason@purdue.edu.

College of Agriculture Students: 550 full-time (255 women), 119 part-time (51 women); includes 77 minority (14 Black or African American, non-Hispanic/Latino; 5 American Indian or Alaska Native, non-Hispanic/Latino; 18 Asian, non-Hispanic/Latino; 25 Hispanic/Latino; 1 Native Hawaiian or other Pacific Islander, non-Hispanic/Latino; 14 Two or more races, non-Hispanic/Latino), 284 international. Average age 28. 620 applicants, 32% accepted, 141 enrolled. *Faculty:* 285 full-time (75 women), 12 part-time/adjunct (4 women). Expenses: Contact institution. *Financial support:* Fellowships with tuition reimbursements, research assistantships with tuition reimbursements, teaching assistantships with tuition reimbursements, career-related internships or fieldwork, and tuition waivers (partial) available. Support available to part-time students. Financial award applicants required to submit FAFSA. In 2018, 127 master's, 88 doctorates awarded. *Program availability:* Part-time. Offers agricultural economics (EMBA, MS, PhD); agriculture (EMBA, M Agr, MA, MS, MSF, PhD); agronomy (MS, PhD); animal sciences (MS, PhD); biochemistry (MS, PhD); botany and plant pathology (MS, PhD); entomology (MS, PhD); fisheries and aquatic sciences (MS, MSF, PhD); food science (MS, PhD); forest biology (MS, MSF, PhD); horticulture (M Agr, MS, PhD); natural resource social science (MS, PhD); natural resources social science (MSF); quantitative ecology (MS, MSF, PhD); wildlife science (MS, MSF, PhD); wood products and wood products manufacturing (MS, MSF, PhD); youth development and agricultural education (MA, PhD). *Application deadline:* Applications are processed on a rolling basis. *Application fee:* $60 ($75 for international students). Electronic applications accepted. *Application Contact:* Graduate School Admissions, 765-494-2600, Fax: 765-494-0136, E-mail: gradinfo@purdue.edu. *Dean:* Karen Plaut, 765-494-7420, E-mail: kplaut@purdue.edu.

College of Education Students: 147 full-time (107 women), 606 part-time (466 women); includes 132 minority (42 Black or African American, non-Hispanic/Latino; 1 American Indian or Alaska Native, non-Hispanic/Latino; 26 Asian, non-Hispanic/Latino; 45 Hispanic/Latino; 1 Native Hawaiian or other Pacific Islander, non-Hispanic/Latino; 17 Two or more races, non-Hispanic/Latino), 90 international. Average age 35. 402 applicants, 65% accepted, 139 enrolled. *Faculty:* 64 full-time (45 women), 5 part-time/adjunct (1 woman). Expenses: Contact institution. *Financial* *support:* Fellowships with full tuition reimbursements, research assistantships with full tuition reimbursements, teaching assistantships with full tuition reimbursements, career-related internships or fieldwork, and tuition waivers (full) available. Support available to part-time students. Financial award application deadline: 3/1; financial award applicants required to submit FAFSA. In 2018, 227 master's, 30 doctorates, 41 other advanced degrees awarded. *Program availability:* Part-time, evening/weekend. Offers administration (MS Ed, Ed S); agricultural and extension education (MS, MS Ed, PhD, Ed S); art education (PhD); career and technical education (MS Ed, PhD, Ed S); curriculum studies (MS Ed, PhD, Ed S); educational technology (MS Ed, PhD, Ed S); elementary education (MS Ed); family and consumer sciences education (MS Ed, PhD, Ed S); foreign language education (MS Ed, PhD, Ed S); foundations of education (MS Ed); higher education administration (PhD); industrial technology (PhD, Ed S); language arts (MS Ed, Ed S); literacy (MS Ed, PhD, Ed S); mathematics education (MS, MS Ed, PhD, Ed S); science education (MS, MS Ed, PhD, Ed S); social studies education (MS Ed, PhD, Ed S). *Application deadline:* For fall admission, 12/15 for domestic students, 3/1 for international students; for spring admission, 9/15 for domestic students, 8/1 for international students. *Application fee:* $60 ($75 for international students). Electronic applications accepted. *Application Contact:* Graduate School Admissions, 765-494-2600, Fax: 765-494-0136, E-mail: gradinfo@purdue.edu. *Dean,* Dr. Nancy Marchand-Martella, 765-494-2336, E-mail: nmarchand-martella@purdue.edu.

College of Health and Human Sciences Students: 441 full-time (352 women), 155 part-time (115 women); includes 107 minority (30 Black or African American, non-Hispanic/Latino; 34 Asian, non-Hispanic/Latino; 23 Hispanic/Latino; 20 Two or more races, non-Hispanic/Latino), 111 international. Average age 29. 1,027 applicants, 36% accepted, 209 enrolled. *Faculty:* 219 full-time (134 women), 12 part-time/adjunct (10 women). Expenses: Contact institution. *Financial support:* Fellowships, research assistantships, teaching assistantships, and career-related internships or fieldwork available. Support available to part-time students. Financial award applicants required to submit FAFSA. In 2018, 117 master's, 57 doctorates, 6 other advanced degrees awarded. *Program availability:* Part-time. Offers adult gerontology primary care nurse practitioner (MS, Post Master's Certificate); animal health (MS, PhD); athletic training education administration (MS, PhD); audiology clinic (MS, Au D, PhD); behavioral neuroscience (PhD); biochemical and molecular nutrition (MS, PhD); biomechanics (MS, PhD); clinical psychology (PhD); cognitive psychology (PhD); consumer sciences and retailing (MS, PhD); developmental studies (MS, PhD); exercise physiology (MS, PhD); family studies (MS, PhD); growth and development (MS, PhD); health and human sciences (MS, Au D, DNP, PhD, Post Master's Certificate); health education (MS, PhD); health physics (MS, PhD); history/philosophy of sport (MS, PhD); hospitality and tourism management (MS, PhD); human and clinical nutrition (MS, PhD); industrial/organizational psychology (PhD); linguistics (MS, PhD); marriage and family therapy (MS, PhD); mathematical and computational cognitive science (PhD); medical physics (MS, PhD); motor control and development (MS, PhD); nursing (DNP); occupational and environmental health science (MS, PhD); physical education pedagogy (PhD); physical education teacher education (MS); primary care family nurse practitioner (MS, Post Master's Certificate); primary care pediatric nurse practitioner (MS, Post Master's Certificate); public health and education (MS, PhD); radiological health (PhD); recreation and sport management (MS, PhD); speech and hearing science (MS, PhD); speech-language pathology (MS, PhD); sport and exercise psychology (MS, PhD); toxicology (PhD). *Application deadline:* Applications are processed on a rolling basis. *Application fee:* $60 ($75 for international students). Electronic applications accepted. *Application Contact:* Graduate School Admissions, 765-494-2600, Fax: 765-494-0136, E-mail: gradinfo@purdue.edu. *Dean,* Dr. Marion K. Underwood, 765-494-8210.

College of Liberal Arts Students: 442 full-time (260 women), 575 part-time (420 women); includes 199 minority (74 Black or African American, non-Hispanic/Latino; 1 American Indian or Alaska Native, non-Hispanic/Latino; 27 Asian, non-Hispanic/Latino; 78 Hispanic/Latino; 19 Two or more races, non-Hispanic/Latino), 161 international. Average age 33. 985 applicants, 36% accepted, 235 enrolled. *Faculty:* 261 full-time (125 women), 13 part-time/adjunct (6 women). Expenses: Contact institution. *Financial support:* Fellowships, research assistantships, teaching assistantships, career-related internships or fieldwork, scholarships/grants, and tuition waivers (full) available. Support available to part-time students. Financial award applicants required to submit FAFSA. In 2018, 314 master's, 85 doctorates awarded. *Program availability:* Part-time, evening/weekend. Offers American studies (MA, PhD); anthropology (MS, PhD); art education (MA, PhD); communication (MA, MS, PhD); comparative literature (MA, PhD); creative writing (MFA); French (MA, MAT, PhD); German (MA, MAT, PhD); history (MA, PhD); industrial design (MFA); interior design (MFA); Japanese pedagogy (MA); liberal arts (MA, MAT, MFA, MS, Au D, PhD); linguistics (MS, PhD); literature (MA, PhD); philosophy (MA, PhD); political science (MA, PhD); sociology (MS, PhD); Spanish (MA, MAT, PhD); theatre (MFA); visual communications design (MFA). *Application deadline:* Applications are processed on a rolling basis. *Application fee:* $60 ($75 for international students). Electronic applications accepted. *Application Contact:* Graduate School Admissions, 765-494-2600, Fax: 765-494-0136, E-mail: gradinfo@purdue.edu. *Dean,* David A. Reingold, 765-494-3661, E-mail: reingold@purdue.edu.

College of Science Students: 1,119 full-time (360 women), 170 part-time (48 women); includes 146 minority (27 Black or African American, non-Hispanic/Latino; 3 American Indian or Alaska Native, non-Hispanic/Latino; 50 Asian, non-Hispanic/Latino; 52 Hispanic/Latino; 1 Native Hawaiian or other Pacific Islander, non-Hispanic/Latino; 13 Two or more races, non-Hispanic/Latino), 767 international. Average age 26. 3,751 applicants, 20% accepted, 276 enrolled. *Faculty:* 341 full-time (66 women), 4 part-time/adjunct. Expenses: Contact institution. *Financial support:* Fellowships with tuition reimbursements, research assistantships with tuition reimbursements, teaching assistantships with tuition reimbursements, career-related internships or fieldwork, and tuition waivers (partial) available. Support available to part-time students. Financial award applicants required to submit FAFSA. In 2018, 135 master's, 170 doctorates, 15 other advanced degrees awarded. *Program availability:* Part-time. Offers analytical chemistry (PhD); applied statistics, mathematical statistics and probability, joint statistics and computer science, computational finance (MS); biochemistry (MS, PhD); cell and developmental biology (PhD); chemical education (MS, PhD); computer sciences (MS, PhD); earth and atmospheric sciences (MS, PhD); genetics (MS); inorganic chemistry (PhD); mathematics (MS, PhD); microbiology (MS, PhD); neurobiology (MS, PhD); organic chemistry (MS, PhD); physical chemistry (PhD); physics (MS, PhD); science (MS, PhD, Certificate). *Application fee:* $60 ($75 for international students). Electronic applications accepted. *Application Contact:* Graduate School Admissions, 765-494-2600, Fax: 765-494-0136, E-mail: gradinfo@purdue.edu. *Dean,* Patrick Wolfe, 765-494-1730, E-mail: patrick@purdue.edu.

Krannert School of Management Offers business administration (MBA); economics (PhD); finance (MSF); global executive business administration (MBA); human resource management (MSHRM); management (MBA, MSF, MSHRM, MSIA, PhD); organizational behavior and human resource management (PhD). Electronic applications accepted.

Purdue Polytechnic Institute Students: 312 full-time (119 women), 419 part-time (143 women); includes 96 minority (26 Black or African American, non-Hispanic/Latino; 1 American Indian or Alaska Native, non-Hispanic/Latino; 32 Asian, non-Hispanic/Latino; 28 Hispanic/Latino; 1 Native Hawaiian or other Pacific Islander, non-Hispanic/Latino; 8 Two or more races, non-Hispanic/Latino), 296 international. Average age 31. 726 applicants, 53% accepted, 222 enrolled. *Faculty:* 182 full-time (44 women), 9 part-time/adjunct (2 women). Expenses: Contact institution. *Financial support:* In 2018–19, 37 teaching assistantships were awarded; fellowships also available. Support available to part-time students. Financial award applicants required to submit FAFSA. In 2018, 217 master's, 17 doctorates awarded. *Program availability:* Online learning. Offers aviation and aerospace management (MS); building construction management (MS); computer and information technology (MS); computer graphics technology (MS, PhD); leadership (MS, PhD); organizational leadership (MS); technology (MS, PhD); technology innovation (MS). *Application deadline:* Applications are processed on a rolling basis. *Application fee:* $60 ($75 for international students). Electronic applications accepted. *Application Contact:* Graduate School Admissions, 765-494-2600, Fax: 765-494-0136, E-mail: gradinfo@purdue.edu. *Dean,* Dr. Gary R. Bertoline, 765-494-2552, E-mail: bertoline@purdue.edu.

School of Veterinary Medicine *Program availability:* Part-time, evening/weekend. Offers anatomy (MS, PhD); basic medical sciences (MS, PhD); comparative epidemiology and public health (MS); comparative epidemiology and public heath (PhD); comparative microbiology and immunology (MS, PhD); comparative pathobiology (MS, PhD); interdisciplinary studies (MS); lab animal medicine (MS); pharmacology (MS, PhD); physiology (MS, PhD); veterinary anatomic pathology (MS); veterinary clinical pathology (MS); veterinary clinical sciences (MS, PhD); veterinary medicine (MS, DVM, PhD).

PURDUE UNIVERSITY FORT WAYNE, Fort Wayne, IN 46805-1499

General Information State-supported, coed, comprehensive institution. *Graduate housing:* Room and/or apartments available on a first-come, first-served basis to single students; on-campus housing not available to married students. *Research affiliation:* Regenstrief Institute, Inc. (nursing), Earthwatch (biology), PHD, Inc. (engineering), Bendix Commercial Vehicle Systems, LLC (engineering, technology, and computer science), Northeast Indiana Fund (education and public policy), Fort Wayne Metals (geosciences).

GRADUATE UNITS

College of Arts and Sciences *Program availability:* Part-time, evening/weekend. Offers applied mathematics (MS); applied statistics (Certificate); arts and sciences (MA, MAT, MS, Certificate); biology (MS); English (MA, MAT); mathematics (MS); operations research (MS); professional communication (MA, MS); teaching (MAT); TENL (teaching English as a new language) (Certificate).

College of Engineering, Technology, and Computer Science *Program availability:* Part-time. Offers applied computer science (MS); civil engineering (MSE); computer engineering (MSE); electrical engineering (MSE); engineering, technology, and computer science (MS, MSE, Certificate); facilities/construction management (MS); human resources (MS); industrial technology/manufacturing (MS); information technology/advanced computer applications (MS); leadership (MS); mechanical engineering (MSE); organizational leadership and supervision (Certificate); systems engineering (MSE). Electronic applications accepted.

College of Health and Human Services *Program availability:* Part-time. Offers adult-gerontology primary care nurse practitioner (MS); family nurse practitioner (MS); health and human services (MS, DNP, Certificate); nurse executive (MS); nursing administration (Certificate); nursing education (MS). Electronic applications accepted.

College of Professional Studies *Program availability:* Part-time. Offers public management (MPM, Certificate).

School of Education *Program availability:* Part-time. Offers couple and family counseling (MS Ed); educational leadership (MS Ed); elementary education (MS Ed); school counseling (MS Ed); secondary education (MS Ed); special education (MS Ed, Certificate).

Doermer School of Business *Program availability:* Part-time. Offers business (MBA).

PURDUE UNIVERSITY GLOBAL, Davenport, IA 52807

General Information Independent, coed, comprehensive institution.

GRADUATE UNITS

School of Business *Program availability:* Part-time, evening/weekend, online learning. Offers business administration (MBA); change leadership (MS); entrepreneurship (MBA); finance (MBA); health care management (MBA, MS); human resource (MBA); international business (MBA); management (MS); marketing (MBA); project management (MBA, MS); supply chain management and logistics (MBA, MS). Electronic applications accepted.

School of Criminal Justice *Program availability:* Part-time, evening/weekend, online learning. Offers corrections (MSCJ); global issues in criminal justice (MSCJ); law (MSCJ); leadership and executive management (MSCJ); policing (MSCJ). Electronic applications accepted.

School of Higher Education Studies *Program availability:* Part-time, evening/weekend, online learning. Offers college administration and leadership (MS); college teaching and learning (MS); student services (MS).

School of Information Technology *Program availability:* Part-time, evening/weekend, online learning. Offers decision support systems (MS); information security and assurance (MS).

School of Legal Studies *Program availability:* Part-time, evening/weekend, online learning. Offers health care delivery (MS); pathway to paralegal (Postbaccalaureate Certificate); state and local government (MS).

School of Nursing *Program availability:* Part-time, evening/weekend, online learning. Offers nurse administrator (MS); nurse educator (MS).

School of Teacher Education *Program availability:* Part-time, evening/weekend, online learning. Offers education (M Ed); secondary education (M Ed); teaching and learning (MA); teaching literacy and language: grades 6-12 (MA); teaching literacy and language: grades K-6 (MA); teaching mathematics: grades 6-8 (MA); teaching mathematics: grades 9-12 (MA); teaching mathematics: grades K-5 (MA); teaching science: grades 6-12 (MA); teaching science: grades K-6 (MA); teaching students with special needs (MA); teaching with technology (MA).

PURDUE UNIVERSITY NORTHWEST, Hammond, IN 46323-2094

General Information State-supported, coed, comprehensive institution. *Graduate housing:* Room and/or apartments available on a first-come, first-served basis to single students; on-campus housing not available to married students.

GRADUATE UNITS

Graduate Studies Office *Program availability:* Part-time, evening/weekend, online learning. Electronic applications accepted.

School of Education Offers counseling (MS Ed); educational administration (MS Ed); human services (MS Ed); instructional technology (MS Ed); mental health counseling (MS Ed); school counseling (MS Ed); special education (MS Ed).

School of Engineering, Mathematics, and Science *Program availability:* Part-time, evening/weekend, online learning. Offers biology (MS); biology teaching (MS); biotechnology (MS); computer engineering (MSE); computer science (MS); electrical engineering (MSE); engineering (MS); engineering, mathematics, and science (MAT, MS, MSE); mathematics (MAT, MS); mechanical engineering (MSE). Electronic applications accepted.

School of Liberal Arts and Social Sciences *Program availability:* Part-time. Offers child development and family studies (MS); communication (MA); English (MA); history (MA); liberal arts and social sciences (MA, MS); marriage and family therapy (MS).

School of Management *Program availability:* Part-time, evening/weekend. Offers accountancy (M Acc); business administration (MBA); business administration for executives (EMBA). Electronic applications accepted.

School of Nursing *Program availability:* Part-time, online learning. Offers adult health clinical nurse specialist (MS); critical care clinical nurse specialist (MS); family nurse practitioner (MS); nurse executive (MS). Electronic applications accepted.

School of Technology Offers technology (MS).

QUEENS COLLEGE OF THE CITY UNIVERSITY OF NEW YORK, Queens, NY 11367-1597

General Information State and locally supported, coed, comprehensive institution. *Enrollment:* 19,746 graduate, professional, and undergraduate students. *Enrollment by degree level:* 2,693 master's, 352 other advanced degrees. *Graduate housing:* Room and/or apartments available on a first-come, first-served basis to single students; on-campus housing not available to married students. *Student services:* Campus employment opportunities, career counseling, child daycare facilities, free psychological counseling, international student services, low-cost health insurance, services for students with disabilities, teacher training, writing training. *Library facilities:* The Benjamin S. Rosenthal Library plus 1 other. *Collection:* Books: 842,531 (physical), 405,360 (digital/electronic); Serial titles: 198 (physical), 226,727 (digital/electronic); Databases: 291. Weekly library service hours: 94; students can reserve study rooms.

Computer facilities: 2,477 computers available on campus for general student use. A campuswide network can be accessed from student residence rooms and from off campus. Online class registration is available.
Website: http://www.qc.cuny.edu/

General Application Contact: Richard Alvarez, Vice President for Enrollment and Student Retention, 718-997-5929, Fax: 718-997-5193, E-mail: graduate_admissions@qc.cuny.edu.

GRADUATE UNITS

Arts and Humanities Division Students: 82 full-time (55 women), 384 part-time (258 women); includes 190 minority (29 Black or African American, non-Hispanic/Latino; 1 American Indian or Alaska Native, non-Hispanic/Latino; 65 Asian, non-Hispanic/Latino; 82 Hispanic/Latino; 13 Two or more races, non-Hispanic/Latino), 44 international. Average age 30. 795 applicants, 40% accepted, 203 enrolled. *Faculty:* 198 full-time (101 women), 340 part-time/adjunct (187 women). Expenses: Contact institution. *Financial support:* Fellowships, research assistantships, career-related internships or fieldwork, and scholarships/grants available. Financial award application deadline: 4/1; financial award applicants required to submit FAFSA. In 2018, 157 master's, 16 other advanced degrees awarded. *Program availability:* Part-time. Offers applied linguistics (MA); art history (MA); arts and humanities (MA, MFA, MM, MS Ed, AC, Advanced Certificate, Advanced Diploma, Post-Master's Certificate); creative writing and literary translation (MFA); English (MA); French (MA); Italian (MA); media studies (MA); Spanish (MA); speech-language pathology (MA); studio art (MFA); TESOL (MS Ed, Post-Master's Certificate); TESOL and bilingual education (Post-Master's Certificate). *Application deadline:* For fall admission, 4/1 for domestic students; for spring admission, 11/1 for domestic students. Applications are processed on a rolling basis. *Application fee:* $125. Electronic applications accepted. *Application Contact:* Elizabeth D'Amico-Ramirez, Assistant Director of Graduate Admissions, 718-997-5203, E-mail: elizabeth.damicoramirez@qc.cuny.edu. *Dean,* Dr. William McClure, 718-997-5790, E-mail: william.mcclure@qc.cuny.edu.

Aaron Copland School of Music Students: 21 full-time (6 women), 153 part-time (75 women); includes 60 minority (8 Black or African American, non-Hispanic/Latino; 1 American Indian or Alaska Native, non-Hispanic/Latino; 22 Asian, non-Hispanic/Latino; 22 Hispanic/Latino; 7 Two or more races, non-Hispanic/Latino), 33 international. Average age 30. 72 applicants, 63% accepted, 19 enrolled. *Faculty:* 25 full-time (7 women), 74 part-time/adjunct (28 women). Expenses: Contact institution. *Financial support:* In 2018–19, 20 students received support. Career-related internships or fieldwork, Federal Work-Study, institutionally sponsored loans, and scholarships/grants available. Financial award application deadline: 4/1; financial award applicants required to submit FAFSA. In 2018, 50 master's, 5 other advanced degrees awarded. *Program availability:* Part-time. Offers classical performance (MM, Advanced Diploma); jazz studies (MM); music (MA); music education (MS Ed, Advanced Certificate). *Application deadline:* For fall admission, 4/1 for domestic students; for spring admission, 11/1 for domestic students. Applications are processed on a rolling basis. *Application fee:* $125. Electronic applications accepted. *Application Contact:* Elizabeth D'Amico-Ramirez, Assistant Director of Graduate Admissions, 718-997-5203, E-mail: elizabeth.damicoramirez@qc.cuny.edu. *Chair,* Michael Lipsey, 718-997-3800, E-mail: Michael.Lipsey@qc.cuny.edu.

Division of Education Students: 240 full-time (204 women), 1,114 part-time (888 women); includes 2,763 minority (84 Black or African American, non-Hispanic/Latino; 1 American Indian or Alaska Native, non-Hispanic/Latino; 190 Asian, non-Hispanic/Latino; 359 Hispanic/Latino; 5 Native Hawaiian or other Pacific Islander, non-Hispanic/Latino; 2,124 Two or more races, non-Hispanic/Latino), 34 international. Average age 29. 1,255 applicants, 66% accepted, 643 enrolled. *Faculty:* 67 full-time (47 women), 157 part-time/adjunct (115 women). Expenses: Contact institution. *Financial support:* Fellowships, career-related internships or fieldwork, and scholarships/grants available. Financial award application deadline: 4/1; financial award applicants required to submit FAFSA. In 2018, 385 master's, 235 other advanced degrees awarded. *Program*

availability: Part-time, evening/weekend. Offers adolescent biology (MAT); art (MS Ed); bilingual education (MAT, MS Ed, AC); bilingual pupil personnel (AC); biology (MS Ed, AC); chemistry (MS Ed, AC); childhood education (MAT, MS Ed); counselor education (MS Ed); early childhood education birth-2 (MAT, MS Ed, AC); earth sciences (MS Ed, AC); education (MA, MAT, MS Ed, AC); English (MS Ed, AC); French (MS Ed); Italian (MS Ed, AC); literacy education (MS Ed); literacy education birth-grade 6 (MS Ed, AC); mathematics (MS Ed, AC); mental health counseling (MS); music (MS Ed, AC); physics (MS Ed, AC); school building leader (AC); school district leader (AC); school psychologist (MS Ed); social studies (MS Ed, AC); Spanish (MS Ed, AC); special education-childhood education (AC); special education-early childhood (MS Ed); teacher of special education 1-6 (MS Ed); teacher of special education birth-2 (MS Ed); teaching students with disabilities, grades 7-12 (MS Ed, AC). *Application deadline:* For fall admission, 4/1 for domestic students; for spring admission, 11/1 for domestic students. Applications are processed on a rolling basis. *Application fee:* $125. Electronic applications accepted. *Application Contact:* Elizabeth D'Amico-Ramirez, Assistant Director of Graduate Admissions, 718-997-5203, E-mail: elizabeth.damicoramirez@qc.cuny.edu. *Dean,* Dr. Craig Michaels, 718-997-5220, E-mail: craig.michaels@qc.cuny.edu.

Division of Social Sciences Students: 62 full-time (40 women), 695 part-time (457 women); includes 393 minority (89 Black or African American, non-Hispanic/Latino; 1 American Indian or Alaska Native, non-Hispanic/Latino; 141 Asian, non-Hispanic/Latino; 140 Hispanic/Latino; 2 Native Hawaiian or other Pacific Islander, non-Hispanic/Latino; 20 Two or more races, non-Hispanic/Latino), 42 international. Average age 32. *Faculty:* 177 full-time (73 women), 226 part-time/adjunct (85 women). Expenses: Contact institution. *Financial support:* Career-related internships or fieldwork available. Financial award application deadline: 4/1; financial award applicants required to submit FAFSA. In 2018, 254 master's, 1 other advanced degree awarded. *Program availability:* Part-time, evening/weekend. Offers accounting (MS); data analytics and applied social research (MA); history (MA); liberal studies (MA); risk management: accounting (MS); risk management: dynamic financial analysis (MS); risk management: finance (MS); social sciences (MA, MLS, MS, AC); urban affairs (MA). *Application deadline:* For fall admission, 4/1 for domestic students; for spring admission, 11/1 for domestic students. Applications are processed on a rolling basis. *Application fee:* $125. Electronic applications accepted. *Application Contact:* Elizabeth D'Amico-Ramirez, Assistant Director of Graduate Admissions, 718-997-5203, E-mail: elizabeth.damicoramirez@qc.cuny.edu. *Dean,* Dr. Michael Wolfe, 718-997-5210, E-mail: michael.wolfe@qc.cuny.edu.

Graduate School of Library and Information Studies Students: 26 full-time (17 women), 309 part-time (231 women); includes 123 minority (39 Black or African American, non-Hispanic/Latino; 1 American Indian or Alaska Native, non-Hispanic/Latino; 17 Asian, non-Hispanic/Latino; 56 Hispanic/Latino; 1 Native Hawaiian or other Pacific Islander, non-Hispanic/Latino; 9 Two or more races, non-Hispanic/Latino), 4 international. Average age 32. *Faculty:* 9 full-time (5 women), 13 part-time/adjunct (9 women). Expenses: Contact institution. *Financial support:* Career-related internships or fieldwork and unspecified assistantships available. Financial award application deadline: 4/1; financial award applicants required to submit FAFSA. In 2018, 88 master's, 1 other advanced degree awarded. *Program availability:* Part-time, evening/weekend. Offers archives and preservation of cultural materials (AC); children's and young adult services in the public library (AC); librarianship (AC); library science (MLS); school library media specialist (MLS). *Application deadline:* For fall admission, 4/1 for domestic students; for spring admission, 11/1 for domestic students. Applications are processed on a rolling basis. *Application fee:* $125. Electronic applications accepted. *Application Contact:* Elizabeth D'Amico-Ramirez, Assistant Director of Graduate Admissions, 718-997-5203, E-mail: elizabeth.damicoramirez@qc.cuny.edu. *Director/Chair,* Kwong Bor Ng, 718-997-3790, E-mail: kwongbor.ng@qc.cuny.edu.

Mathematics and Natural Sciences Division Students: 44 full-time (17 women), 365 part-time (208 women); includes 204 minority (42 Black or African American, non-Hispanic/Latino; 69 Asian, non-Hispanic/Latino; 78 Hispanic/Latino; 1 Native Hawaiian or other Pacific Islander, non-Hispanic/Latino; 14 Two or more races, non-Hispanic/Latino), 43 international. Average age 29. *Faculty:* 165 full-time (62 women), 316 part-time/adjunct (151 women). Expenses: Contact institution. *Financial support:* Research assistantships, career-related internships or fieldwork, and scholarships/grants available. Financial award application deadline: 4/1; financial award applicants required to submit FAFSA. In 2018, 126 master's, 21 other advanced degrees awarded. *Program availability:* Part-time. Offers applied behavior analysis (MA); applied mathematics (MA); behavioral neuroscience (MA); biology (MA); chemistry (MA); computer science (MA); exercise science specialist (MS); family and consumer science (K-12) (AC); family and consumer science/teaching curriculum (K-12) (MS Ed); general psychology (MA); mathematics and natural sciences (MA, MAT, MS, MS Ed, AC); nutrition and exercise science (MS); nutrition specialist (MS); photonics (MS); physical education (K-12) (AC); physical education/teaching curriculum (pre K-12) (MS Ed); physics (MA); pure mathematics (MA). *Application deadline:* For fall admission, 4/1 for domestic students; for spring admission, 11/1 for domestic students. Applications are processed on a rolling basis. *Application fee:* $125. Electronic applications accepted. *Application Contact:* Elizabeth D'Amico-Ramirez, Assistant Director of Graduate Admissions, 718-997-5203, E-mail: elizabeth.damicoramirez@qc.cuny.edu. *Interim Dean,* Dr. Susan A. Rotenberg, 718-997-4105, E-mail: susan.rotenberg@qc.cuny.edu.

School of Earth and Environmental Sciences Students: 1 (woman) full-time, 14 part-time (5 women); includes 3 minority (2 Black or African American, non-Hispanic/Latino; 1 Asian, non-Hispanic/Latino), 1 international. Average age 28. 11 applicants, 73% accepted, 6 enrolled. *Faculty:* 17 full-time (5 women), 16 part-time/adjunct (8 women). Expenses: Contact institution. *Financial support:* In 2018–19, 10 teaching assistantships (averaging $11,968 per year) were awarded; career-related internships or fieldwork and unspecified assistantships also available. Financial award application deadline: 4/1; financial award applicants required to submit FAFSA. In 2018, 11 master's awarded. *Program availability:* Part-time, evening/weekend. Offers applied environmental geosciences (MS); geological and environmental sciences (MA). *Application deadline:* For fall admission, 4/1 for domestic students; for spring admission, 11/1 for domestic students. Applications are processed on a rolling basis. *Application fee:* $125. Electronic applications accepted. *Application Contact:* Gregory O'Mullan, Graduate Advisor, 718-997-3452, E-mail: gomullan@qc.cuny.edu. *Chair,* Jeffrey Bird, 718-997-3300, E-mail: jeffrey.bird@qc.cuny.edu.

QUEEN'S UNIVERSITY AT KINGSTON, Kingston, ON K7L 3N6, Canada

General Information Province-supported, coed, university. CGS member. *Graduate housing:* Rooms and/or apartments available to single students and available on a first-come, first-served basis to married students. Housing application deadline: 6/15.

GRADUATE UNITS

Faculty of Law *Program availability:* Part-time. Offers law (LL M, JD).

School of Graduate Studies *Program availability:* Part-time. Offers industrial relations (MIR).

Faculty of Arts and Science *Program availability:* Part-time. Offers arts and science (M Phil, M Pl, M Sc, M Sc Eng, MA, MIR, PhD); biology (M Sc, PhD); brain behavior and cognitive science (MA, PhD); Canadian politics (MA, PhD); chemistry (M Sc, PhD); classics (MA); clinical psychology (MA, PhD); communication and information technology (MA, PhD); comparative politics (MA, PhD); computing (M Sc, PhD); developmental psychology (MA, PhD); English language and literature (M Phil, MA, PhD); feminist sociology (MA, PhD); French studies (MA, PhD); gender and politics (MA, PhD); geography (M Sc, MA, PhD); geological sciences and geological engineering (M Sc, PhD); international relations (MA, PhD); mathematics (M Sc, PhD); philosophy (MA, PhD); physics, engineering physics and astronomy (M Sc, M Sc Eng, PhD); political theory (MA, PhD); religion (MA); social personality psychology (MA, PhD); socio-legal studies (MA, PhD); sociological theory (MA, PhD); statistics (M Sc, PhD); urban and regional planning (M Pl). Electronic applications accepted.

Faculty of Education *Program availability:* Part-time. Offers education (M Ed, PhD).

Faculty of Engineering and Applied Science *Program availability:* Part-time. Offers chemical engineering (M Sc, PhD); civil engineering (M Eng, M Sc Eng, PhD); electrical and computer engineering (M Eng, M Sc, M Sc Eng, PhD); engineering and applied science (M Eng, M Sc, M Sc Eng, PhD); mechanical and materials engineering (M Eng, M Sc, M Sc Eng, PhD); mining engineering (M Eng, M Sc, M Sc Eng, PhD). Electronic applications accepted.

Faculty of Health Sciences *Program availability:* Part-time. Offers epidemiology (M Sc, PhD); health and chronic illness (M Sc); health sciences (M Sc, M Sc OT, M Sc PT, MPH, MD, PhD, Certificate); nurse scientist (PhD); occupational therapy (M Sc OT); pathology and molecular medicine (M Sc, PhD); physical therapy (M Sc PT); policy research and clinical epidemiology (M Sc); primary health care nurse practitioner (Certificate); public health (MPH); rehabilitation science (M Sc, PhD); women's and children's health (M Sc). Electronic applications accepted.

School of Kinesiology and Health Studies *Program availability:* Part-time. Offers biomechanics and ergonomics (M Sc, PhD); exercise physiology (M Sc, PhD); health promotion (M Sc, PhD); physical activity epidemiology (M Sc, PhD); sociocultural studies of sport, health and the body (MA, PhD); sport psychology (M Sc, PhD). Electronic applications accepted.

School of Policy Studies *Program availability:* Part-time. Offers policy studies (MPA).

School of Medicine Offers medicine (MD). Electronic applications accepted.

Smith School of Business Offers analytics (M Sc, PhD); artificial intelligence (MM); business (M Sc, MBA, MIB, MM, PhD); business economics (M Sc, PhD); consulting and project management (MBA); finance (M Sc, MBA, PhD); innovation and entrepreneurship (MBA); international business (MIB); management information systems (M Sc, MBA, PhD); marketing (M Sc, MBA, PhD); organizational behavior (M Sc, PhD); strategy (M Sc, PhD).

QUEENS UNIVERSITY OF CHARLOTTE, Charlotte, NC 28274-0002
General Information Independent-religious, coed, comprehensive institution. *Graduate housing:* On-campus housing not available.

GRADUATE UNITS

College of Arts and Sciences *Program availability:* Part-time, online learning. Offers creative writing (MFA); interior design (MA). Electronic applications accepted.

Knight School of Communication *Program availability:* Part-time, evening/weekend, online learning. Offers organizational and strategic communication (MA).

McColl School of Business *Program availability:* Part-time, evening/weekend, online learning. Offers business administration (EMBA, MBA, PMBA); organization development (MSOD). Electronic applications accepted.

Presbyterian School of Nursing Offers clinical nurse leader (MSN); nurse educator (MSN); nursing administrator (MSN). Electronic applications accepted.

Wayland H. Cato, Jr. School of Education *Program availability:* Part-time, evening/weekend, online learning. Offers educational leadership (MA); K-6 (MAT); literacy K-12 (M Ed).

QUINCY UNIVERSITY, Quincy, IL 62301-2699
General Information Independent-religious, coed, comprehensive institution. *Graduate housing:* Room and/or apartments available to single students; on-campus housing not available to married students.

GRADUATE UNITS

Master of Science in Education Counseling Program *Program availability:* Part-time, evening/weekend. Offers clinical mental health counseling (MS Ed); college student personnel (MS Ed); school counseling (MS Ed). Electronic applications accepted.

Master of Science in Education Programs *Program availability:* Part-time, evening/weekend, online learning. Offers curriculum and instruction (MS Ed); education studies (MS Ed); leadership (MS Ed); reading education (MS Ed); teacher leader (MS Ed). Electronic applications accepted.

MBA Program *Program availability:* Part-time, evening/weekend, online learning. Offers business administration (MBA). Electronic applications accepted.

QUINNIPIAC UNIVERSITY, Hamden, CT 06518-1940
General Information Independent, coed, comprehensive institution. *Graduate housing:* Room and/or apartments available on a first-come, first-served basis to married students; on-campus housing not available to single students.

GRADUATE UNITS

College of Arts and Sciences *Program availability:* Part-time, evening/weekend. Offers arts and sciences (MS); molecular and cell biology (MS). Electronic applications accepted.

Frank H. Netter MD School of Medicine Offers anesthesiologist assistant (MMS); medicine (MMS, MD). Electronic applications accepted.

School of Business *Program availability:* Part-time, evening/weekend, 100% online, blended/hybrid learning. Offers accounting (MS); business (MBA, MS); finance (MBA); health care management (MBA); organizational leadership (MS); supply chain management (MBA). Electronic applications accepted.

School of Communications *Program availability:* Part-time, evening/weekend, online learning. Offers communications (MS); interactive media (MS); journalism (MS); media design (MS); public relations (MS); social media (MS); sports journalism (MS); UX design (MS). Electronic applications accepted.

School of Education Offers biology (MAT); education (MAT, MS, Diploma); educational leadership (Diploma); elementary education (MAT); English (MAT); history (MAT); instructional design (MS); mathematics (MAT); Spanish (MAT); teacher leadership (MS). Electronic applications accepted.

School of Engineering Offers cybersecurity (MS).

School of Health Sciences Offers biomedical sciences (MHS); cardiovascular perfusion (MHS); health sciences (MHS, MSW); pathologists' assistant (MHS); physician assistant (MHS); radiologist assistant (MHS); social work (MSW). Electronic applications accepted.

School of Law *Program availability:* Part-time, evening/weekend. Offers law (LL M, JD). Electronic applications accepted.

School of Nursing Offers adult nurse practitioner (DNP); care of populations (DNP); family nurse practitioner (DNP); nurse anesthesia (DNP); nursing (DNP); nursing leadership (DNP). Electronic applications accepted.

RABBINICAL ACADEMY MESIVTA RABBI CHAIM BERLIN, Brooklyn, NY 11230-4715
General Information Independent-religious, men only, comprehensive institution. *Graduate housing:* Room and/or apartments available to single students; on-campus housing not available to married students. Housing application deadline: 9/30.

GRADUATE UNITS

Graduate Program Offers Talmudic law and rabbinics (Advanced Talmudic Degree, Second Talmudic Degree).

RABBINICAL COLLEGE BETH SHRAGA, Monsey, NY 10952-3035
General Information Independent-religious, men only, comprehensive institution.

GRADUATE UNITS

Graduate Programs Offers theology.

RABBINICAL COLLEGE BOBOVER YESHIVA B'NEI ZION, Brooklyn, NY 11219
General Information Independent-religious, men only, comprehensive institution. *Graduate housing:* Room and/or apartments available to single students; on-campus housing not available to married students.

GRADUATE UNITS

Graduate Programs Offers theology (First Talmudic Degree, Rabbi).

RABBINICAL COLLEGE OF LONG ISLAND, Long Beach, NY 11561-3305
General Information Independent-religious, men only, comprehensive institution.

GRADUATE UNITS

Graduate Programs Offers theology.

RABBINICAL SEMINARY OF AMERICA, Flushing, NY 11367
General Information Independent-religious, men only, comprehensive institution. *Graduate housing:* Room and/or apartments available to single students; on-campus housing not available to married students. Housing application deadline: 6/15.

GRADUATE UNITS

Graduate Programs School offers a master's and first professional degree.

RADFORD UNIVERSITY, Radford, VA 24142
General Information State-supported, coed, university. CGS member. *Enrollment:* 9,335 graduate, professional, and undergraduate students; 530 full-time matriculated graduate/professional students (414 women), 376 part-time matriculated graduate/professional students (283 women). *Enrollment by degree level:* 716 master's, 140 doctoral, 50 other advanced degrees. *Graduate faculty:* 151 full-time (96 women), 41 part-time/adjunct (30 women). *Tuition, area resident:* Full-time $8915; part-time $371 per credit hour. Tuition, state resident: full-time $8915; part-time $371 per credit hour. Tuition, nonresident: full-time $17,441. *Required fees:* $3288; $138 per credit hour. *Graduate housing:* On-campus housing not available. *Student services:* Campus employment opportunities, campus safety program, career counseling, exercise/wellness program, free psychological counseling, international student services, multicultural affairs office, services for students with disabilities, teacher training, writing training. *Library facilities:* McConnell Library. *Collection:* Books: 271,383 (physical), 332,165 (digital/electronic); Serial titles: 558 (physical), 28,298 (digital/electronic); Databases: 535. Students can reserve study rooms.

Computer facilities: Computer purchase and lease plans are available. 900 computers available on campus for general student use. A campuswide network can be accessed from student residence rooms and from off campus. Online class registration, online financial aid status and student accounts payable are available. Website: http://www.radford.edu/

General Application Contact: Rebecca Conner, Director of Graduate Enrollment, 540-831-5431, Fax: 540-831-6061, E-mail: gradcollege@radford.edu.

GRADUATE UNITS

College of Graduate Studies and Research Students: 530 full-time (414 women), 376 part-time (283 women); includes 136 minority (79 Black or African American, non-Hispanic/Latino; 2 American Indian or Alaska Native, non-Hispanic/Latino; 13 Asian, non-Hispanic/Latino; 19 Hispanic/Latino; 23 Two or more races, non-Hispanic/Latino), 16 international. Average age 29. 1,149 applicants, 59% accepted, 413 enrolled. *Faculty:* 151 full-time (96 women), 41 part-time/adjunct (30 women). Expenses: Contact institution. *Financial support:* In 2018-19, 185 students received support, including 10 research assistantships (averaging $6,250 per year), 70 teaching assistantships (averaging $10,043 per year); career-related internships or fieldwork, scholarships/grants, and unspecified assistantships also available. Support available to part-time students. Financial award application deadline: 3/1; financial award applicants required to submit FAFSA. In 2018, 307 master's, 40 doctorates, 23 other advanced degrees awarded. *Program availability:* Part-time, evening/weekend, 100% online, blended/hybrid learning. Offers art (MFA); business administration (MBA); clinical-counseling psychology (MA, MS); communication sciences and disorders (MA, MS); counseling psychology (Psy D); counselor education (MS); criminal justice (MA, MS, Certificate); early childhood education (MS); educational leadership (MS); English (MA, MS); experimental psychology (MA); industrial-organizational psychology (MA, MS); literacy education (MS); mathematics education (MS); music (MA, MS); nursing practice (DNP); occupational therapy (MOT); physical therapy (DPT); school psychology (Ed S); social work (MSW); special education (MS, Certificate); strategic communication (MS). *Application deadline:* Applications are processed on a rolling basis. *Application fee:* $50. Electronic applications accepted. *Application Contact:* Rebecca Conner, Director, Graduate Enrollment, 540-831-5431, Fax: 540-831-6061, E-mail: gradcollege@radford.edu. *Dean,* Dr. Benjamin Caldwell, 540-831-5723, Fax: 540-831-6061, E-mail: gradcollege@radford.edu.

Program in Data and Information Management Students: 4 full-time (1 woman), 3 part-time (0 women); includes 1 minority (Asian, non-Hispanic/Latino), 3 international. Average age 30. 4 applicants, 50% accepted, 1 enrolled. *Faculty:* 4 full-time (0 women). Expenses: Contact institution. *Financial support:* In 2018–19, 3 students received support, including 3 teaching assistantships (averaging $10,000 per year); scholarships/grants and unspecified assistantships also available. Support available to part-time students. Financial award application deadline: 3/1; financial award applicants required to submit FAFSA. In 2018, 5 master's awarded. *Program availability:* Part-time. Offers data and information management (MS). *Application deadline:* Applications are processed on a rolling basis. *Application fee:* $50. Electronic applications accepted. *Application Contact:* Dr. Jeff Pittges, Graduate Coordinator and Director, 540-831-5381, E-mail: jpittges@radford.edu. *Graduate Coordinator and Director*, Dr. Jeff Pittges, 540-831-5381, E-mail: jpittges@radford.edu.

RADIOLOGICAL TECHNOLOGIES UNIVERSITY VT, South Bend, IN 46601

General Information Proprietary, coed, comprehensive institution.

GRADUATE UNITS
Graduate Programs

RAMAPO COLLEGE OF NEW JERSEY, Mahwah, NJ 07430-1680

General Information State-supported, coed, comprehensive institution. *Enrollment:* 146 full-time matriculated graduate/professional students (111 women), 404 part-time matriculated graduate/professional students (306 women). *Enrollment by degree level:* 550 master's. *Graduate faculty:* 15 full-time (10 women), 36 part-time/adjunct (21 women). Tuition, state resident: part-time $706.15 per credit. Tuition, nonresident: part-time $706.15 per credit. *Required fees:* $57.50 per credit. *Graduate housing:* Room and/or apartments available on a first-come, first-served basis to single students; on-campus housing not available to married students. Typical cost: $9000 per year. Housing application deadline: 7/1. *Student services:* Career counseling, services for students with disabilities. *Library facilities:* George T. Potter Library.

Computer facilities: A campuswide network can be accessed from student residence rooms and from off campus. Online class registration is available.
Website: http://www.ramapo.edu/

General Application Contact: Anthony Dovi, Associate Director of Admissions, Adult Learners and Graduate Programs, 201-684-7305, Fax: 201-684-7964, E-mail: adovi@ramapo.edu.

GRADUATE UNITS

Master of Arts in Educational Leadership Program Students: 31 full-time (23 women), 30 part-time (18 women); includes 5 minority (2 Black or African American, non-Hispanic/Latino; 1 Asian, non-Hispanic/Latino; 2 Hispanic/Latino). Average age 33. 57 applicants, 93% accepted, 38 enrolled. *Faculty:* 1 full-time (0 women), 11 part-time/adjunct (1 woman). Expenses: Contact institution. *Financial support:* Career-related internships or fieldwork available. Financial award application deadline: 3/1; financial award applicants required to submit FAFSA. In 2018, 37 master's awarded. *Program availability:* Part-time. Offers educational leadership (MA). *Application deadline:* For fall admission, 5/1 for domestic and international students; for spring admission, 12/1 for domestic and international students; for summer admission, 5/1 for domestic and international students. Applications are processed on a rolling basis. *Application fee:* $65. Electronic applications accepted. *Application Contact:* Karen Viviani, Graduate Program Assistant, 201-684-7638, Fax: 201-684-7983, E-mail: kdroubi@ramapo.edu. *Assistant Dean, Teacher Education*, Dr. Brian P. Chinni, 201-684-7613, E-mail: bchinni@ramapo.edu.

Master of Arts in Special Education Program Students: 50 part-time (45 women); includes 6 minority (1 Asian, non-Hispanic/Latino; 4 Hispanic/Latino; 1 Two or more races, non-Hispanic/Latino). Average age 29. 41 applicants, 90% accepted, 25 enrolled. *Faculty:* 1 (woman) full-time, 2 part-time/adjunct (both women). Expenses: Contact institution. *Financial support:* Career-related internships or fieldwork available. Financial award application deadline: 3/1; financial award applicants required to submit FAFSA. In 2018, 19 master's awarded. *Program availability:* Part-time, evening/weekend. Offers special education (MA). *Application deadline:* For fall admission, 5/1 for domestic and international students. Applications are processed on a rolling basis. *Application fee:* $65. Electronic applications accepted. *Application Contact:* Karen Viviani, Graduate Program Assistant, 201-684-7638, Fax: 201-684-7983, E-mail: kdroubi@ramapo.edu. *Director*, Dr. Julie Norflus-Good, 201-684-7246, E-mail: jgood@ramapo.edu.

Master of Business Administration Program Students: 66 part-time (35 women); includes 18 minority (1 Black or African American, non-Hispanic/Latino; 4 Asian, non-Hispanic/Latino; 13 Hispanic/Latino). Average age 31. 90 applicants, 53% accepted, 34 enrolled. *Faculty:* 3 full-time (all women). Expenses: Contact institution. *Financial support:* In 2018–19, 5 students received support. Career-related internships or fieldwork and scholarships/grants available. Financial award application deadline: 3/1; financial award applicants required to submit FAFSA. In 2018, 30 master's awarded. *Program availability:* Part-time-only, evening/weekend. Offers leadership (MBA). *Application deadline:* For fall admission, 5/1 for domestic and international students. Applications are processed on a rolling basis. *Application fee:* $65. Electronic applications accepted. *Application Contact:* Timothy Landers, Assistant Dean/Director of the MBA Program, 201-684-7771, E-mail: tlanders@ramapo.edu. *Dean of the Anisfield School of Business*, Dr. Edward Petkus, 201-684-7377, E-mail: epetkus@ramapo.edu.

Master of Science in Accounting Program Students: 24 full-time (9 women), 17 part-time (12 women); includes 8 minority (4 Asian, non-Hispanic/Latino; 4 Hispanic/Latino), 1 international. Average age 28. 52 applicants, 77% accepted, 28 enrolled. *Faculty:* 3 full-time (1 woman). Expenses: Contact institution. *Financial support:* Career-related internships or fieldwork available. Financial award application deadline: 3/1; financial award applicants required to submit FAFSA. In 2018, 8 master's awarded. *Program availability:* Part-time. Offers accounting (MS). *Application deadline:* For fall admission, 5/1 for domestic and international students; for spring admission, 12/1 for domestic and international students; for summer admission, 5/1 for domestic and international students. Applications are processed on a rolling basis. *Application fee:* $65. Electronic applications accepted. *Application Contact:* Dr. Constance Crawford, Director of the Master of Science in Accounting Program, 201-684-7396, E-mail: ccrawfor@ramapo.edu. *Dean of the Anisfield School of Business*, Dr. Edward Petkus, 201-684-7377, E-mail: epetkus@ramapo.edu.

Master of Science in Educational Technology Program Students: 5 full-time (all women), 104 part-time (76 women); includes 14 minority (6 Black or African American, non-Hispanic/Latino; 2 Asian, non-Hispanic/Latino; 6 Hispanic/Latino), 1 international. Average age 35. 73 applicants, 95% accepted, 59 enrolled. *Faculty:* 8 part-time/adjunct (3 women). Expenses: Contact institution. *Financial support:* Career-related internships or fieldwork available. Financial award application deadline: 3/1; financial award

applicants required to submit FAFSA. In 2018, 75 master's awarded. *Program availability:* Part-time, evening/weekend. Offers educational technology (MS). *Application deadline:* For fall admission, 5/1 for domestic and international students; for spring admission, 12/1 for domestic and international students. Applications are processed on a rolling basis. *Application fee:* $65. Electronic applications accepted. *Application Contact:* Karen Viviani, Graduate Program Assistant, 201-684-7638, Fax: 201-684-7983, E-mail: kdroubi@ramapo.edu. *Director of the Master in Educational Technology Program*, Dr. Richard Russo, 201-684-7899, Fax: 201-684-6699, E-mail: rrusso@ramapo.edu.

Master of Science in Nursing Program Students: 113 part-time (100 women); includes 48 minority (10 Black or African American, non-Hispanic/Latino; 27 Asian, non-Hispanic/Latino; 10 Hispanic/Latino; 1 Two or more races, non-Hispanic/Latino). Average age 33. 84 applicants, 71% accepted, 41 enrolled. *Faculty:* 3 full-time (all women), 5 part-time/adjunct (4 women). Expenses: Contact institution. *Financial support:* Career-related internships or fieldwork available. Financial award application deadline: 3/1; financial award applicants required to submit FAFSA. In 2018, 4 master's awarded. *Program availability:* Part-time. Offers family nurse practitioner (MSN); nursing administrator (MSN); nursing education (MSN). *Application deadline:* For fall admission, 5/1 for domestic and international students; for spring admission, 12/1 for domestic and international students. Applications are processed on a rolling basis. *Application fee:* $65. Electronic applications accepted. *Application Contact:* Anthony Dovi, Associate Director of Admissions, Adult Learners and Graduate Programs, 201-684-7305, Fax: 201-684-7964, E-mail: adovi@ramapo.edu. *Assistant Dean of Nursing Programs/Professor*, Dr. Kathleen M. Burke, 201-684-7737, Fax: 201-684-7954, E-mail: kmburke@ramapo.edu.

Master of Social Work Program Students: 86 full-time (74 women), 24 part-time (20 women); includes 34 minority (12 Black or African American, non-Hispanic/Latino; 4 Asian, non-Hispanic/Latino; 18 Hispanic/Latino). Average age 30. 224 applicants, 61% accepted, 74 enrolled. *Faculty:* 4 full-time (2 women), 11 part-time/adjunct (all women). Expenses: Contact institution. *Financial support:* In 2018–19, 4 students received support. Scholarships/grants available. Financial award application deadline: 3/1; financial award applicants required to submit FAFSA. In 2018, 56 master's awarded. *Program availability:* Part-time. Offers social work (MSW). *Application deadline:* For fall admission, 3/1 for domestic and international students. Applications are processed on a rolling basis. *Application fee:* $65. Electronic applications accepted. *Application Contact:* Joyce Wilson, Master of Social Work Coordinator, 201-684-7721, Fax: 201-684-7257, E-mail: jwilson@ramapo.edu. *Director of the Master of Social Work program*, Dr. Kathleen Ray, 201-684-7814, Fax: 201-684-7257, E-mail: kray1@ramapo.edu.

RANDALL UNIVERSITY, Moore, OK 73160-1208

General Information Independent-religious, coed, comprehensive institution. *Graduate housing:* Room and/or apartments available on a first-come, first-served basis to single students.

GRADUATE UNITS
Department of Bible Studies *Program availability:* Part-time, evening/weekend. Offers ministry (MA).

RANDOLPH COLLEGE, Lynchburg, VA 24503

General Information Independent-religious, coed, comprehensive institution.

GRADUATE UNITS
Program in Creative Writing Offers creative writing (MFA).

Programs in Education Offers curriculum and instruction (MAT); special education-learning disabilities (M Ed, MAT).

RECONSTRUCTIONIST RABBINICAL COLLEGE, Wyncote, PA 19095-1898

General Information Independent-religious, coed, graduate-only institution. *Graduate housing:* On-campus housing not available.

GRADUATE UNITS
Graduate Programs *Program availability:* Part-time. Offers Jewish studies (MAJS); rabbinics (MAHL, DHL); women's studies (Certificate). Certificate offered jointly with Temple University.

REED COLLEGE, Portland, OR 97202-8199

General Information Independent, coed, comprehensive institution. *Graduate housing:* On-campus housing not available.

GRADUATE UNITS
Graduate Program in Liberal Studies Students: 30 part-time (17 women); includes 3 minority (1 Black or African American, non-Hispanic/Latino; 1 Asian, non-Hispanic/Latino; 1 Hispanic/Latino). Average age 44. 6 applicants, 67% accepted, 4 enrolled. *Faculty:* 9 part-time/adjunct (2 women). Expenses: Contact institution. *Financial support:* In 2018–19, 8 students received support. Scholarships/grants and health care benefits available. Support available to part-time students. Financial award application deadline: 5/1; financial award applicants required to submit CSS PROFILE or FAFSA. In 2018, 5 master's awarded. *Program availability:* Part-time-only, evening/weekend. Offers liberal studies (MALS). *Application deadline:* For fall admission, 7/1 priority date for domestic students, 5/1 for international students; for spring admission, 12/1 priority date for domestic students, 9/1 for international students; for summer admission, 4/1 for domestic students, 2/1 for international students. Applications are processed on a rolling basis. *Application fee:* $75. Electronic applications accepted. *Application Contact:* Barbara A. Amen, Graduate Studies, 503-777-7259, Fax: 503-517-7345, E-mail: bamen@reed.edu. *Director, Graduate Studies*, Barbara A. Amen, 503-777-7259, Fax: 503-517-7345, E-mail: bamen@reed.edu.

REFORMED EPISCOPAL SEMINARY, Blue Bell, PA 19422

General Information Independent-religious, coed, graduate-only institution. *Graduate housing:* Room and/or apartments available on a first-come, first-served basis to single students; on-campus housing not available to married students.

GRADUATE UNITS
Graduate Program Offers theology (M Div).

REFORMED PRESBYTERIAN THEOLOGICAL SEMINARY, Pittsburgh, PA 15208-2594

General Information Independent-religious, coed, primarily men, graduate-only institution. *Graduate housing:* Rooms and/or apartments available on a first-come, first-served basis to single and married students.

GRADUATE UNITS

Graduate and Professional Programs *Program availability:* Part-time, evening/weekend. Offers theology (M Div, MTS, D Min). Electronic applications accepted.

REFORMED THEOLOGICAL SEMINARY–ATLANTA CAMPUS, Marietta, GA 30067

General Information Independent-religious, coed, primarily men, graduate-only institution.

GRADUATE UNITS

Graduate Programs Offers theology (M Div, MABS, MAR, D Min, Certificate).

REFORMED THEOLOGICAL SEMINARY–CHARLOTTE CAMPUS, Charlotte, NC 28226-6318

General Information Independent-religious, coed, primarily men, graduate-only institution. *Graduate housing:* On-campus housing not available.

GRADUATE UNITS

Graduate and Professional Programs *Program availability:* Part-time. Offers biblical studies (MA); ministry (D Min); pastoral ministry (M Div); theological studies (MA). Electronic applications accepted.

REFORMED THEOLOGICAL SEMINARY–DALLAS CAMPUS, Dallas, TX 75207

General Information Independent-religious, coed, graduate-only institution.

GRADUATE UNITS

Graduate and Professional Programs Offers theological studies (MA); theology (M Div).

REFORMED THEOLOGICAL SEMINARY–HOUSTON CAMPUS, Houston, TX 77024

General Information Independent-religious, coed, primarily men, graduate-only institution. *Graduate housing:* On-campus housing not available.

GRADUATE UNITS

Graduate Program Offers Biblical studies (MA). Electronic applications accepted.

REFORMED THEOLOGICAL SEMINARY–JACKSON CAMPUS, Jackson, MS 39209-3004

General Information Independent-religious, coed, primarily men, graduate-only institution. *Graduate housing:* Rooms and/or apartments available on a first-come, first-served basis to single and married students.

GRADUATE UNITS

Graduate and Professional Programs Offers Bible, theology, and missions (Certificate); Biblical exegesis (M Div); biblical studies (MA); Christian education (MA); counseling (M Div); marriage and family therapy (MA); ministry (D Min); missions (M Div, MA, D Min); theological studies (MA).

REFORMED THEOLOGICAL SEMINARY–ORLANDO CAMPUS, Oviedo, FL 32765

General Information Independent-religious, coed, primarily men, graduate-only institution. *Graduate housing:* Rooms and/or apartments available on a first-come, first-served basis to single and married students.

GRADUATE UNITS

Graduate Programs *Program availability:* Part-time, online learning. Offers Bible (Certificate); biblical studies (MA); counseling (MA); missions (Certificate); reformed expository preaching (D Min); reformed theology and ministry (D Min); theological studies (MA); theology (M Div, Certificate). Electronic applications accepted.

REFORMED THEOLOGICAL SEMINARY–WASHINGTON D.C., McLean, VA 22102

General Information Independent-religious, coed, primarily men, graduate-only institution. *Graduate housing:* On-campus housing not available.

GRADUATE UNITS

Graduate and Professional Programs *Program availability:* Part-time, evening/weekend. Offers Bible (M Div); biblical studies (MA); practical theology (M Div); religion (MA); theology (M Div). Electronic applications accepted.

REFORMED UNIVERSITY, Lawrenceville, GA 30043

General Information Independent-religious, coed, comprehensive institution.

GRADUATE UNITS

Graduate Programs

REGENT COLLEGE, Vancouver, BC V6T 2E4, Canada

General Information Independent-religious, coed, graduate-only institution. *Enrollment by degree level:* 455 master's. *Graduate faculty:* 16 full-time (2 women), 26 part-time/adjunct (7 women). *Graduate housing:* On-campus housing not available. *Student services:* Campus employment opportunities, campus safety program, career counseling, international student services, low-cost health insurance, services for students with disabilities, writing training. *Library facilities:* The John Richard Allison Library plus 15 others. *Collection:* Books: 200,000 (physical); Databases: 12. Students can reserve study rooms.

Computer facilities: 8 computers available on campus for general student use. Online class registration is available.
Website: http://www.regent-college.edu/

General Application Contact: Admissions, 604-224-3245, Fax: 604-224-3097, E-mail: admissions@regent-college.edu.

GRADUATE UNITS

Program in Theology *Program availability:* Part-time. Offers Christian history and theology (M Div, MATS); Christian studies (MATS, G Dip); Christianity, church and culture (M Div, MATS); scripture (M Div, MATS); theology (Th M). Electronic applications accepted.

REGENT'S UNIVERSITY LONDON, London NW1 4NS, United Kingdom

General Information Independent, coed, comprehensive institution.

GRADUATE UNITS

Webster Graduate School *Program availability:* Part-time. Offers business (MBA); finance (MS); human resources (MA); information technology management (MA); international business (MA); international non-governmental organizations (MA); international relations (MA); management and leadership (MA); marketing (MA).

REGENT UNIVERSITY, Virginia Beach, VA 23464-9800

General Information Independent-religious, coed, comprehensive institution. *Graduate housing:* Rooms and/or apartments available on a first-come, first-served basis to single and married students. Housing application deadline: 5/1.

GRADUATE UNITS

Graduate School *Program availability:* Part-time, evening/weekend, 100% online, blended/hybrid learning. Electronic applications accepted.

Robertson School of Government *Program availability:* Part-time, evening/weekend, 100% online, blended/hybrid learning. Offers government (MA); national security studies (MA); public administration (MPA). Electronic applications accepted.

School of Business and Leadership *Program availability:* Part-time, evening/weekend, 100% online, blended/hybrid learning. Offers business administration (MBA); business analytics (MS); business and design management (MA); church leadership (MA); leadership (Certificate); organizational leadership (MA, PhD); strategic leadership (DSL). Electronic applications accepted.

School of Communication and the Arts *Program availability:* Part-time, evening/weekend, 100% online, blended/hybrid learning. Offers acting (MFA); communication (MA, PhD); film and TV (MA); film-television (MFA); journalism (MA); theatre (MA). Electronic applications accepted.

School of Divinity *Program availability:* Part-time, evening/weekend, 100% online, blended/hybrid learning. Offers Christian spirituality and formation (MA); divinity (M Div); leadership and renewal (D Min); practical theology (MA); renewal theology (PhD); theological studies (MTS); theology (Th M). Electronic applications accepted.

School of Education *Program availability:* Part-time, evening/weekend, 100% online, blended/hybrid learning. Offers education (M Ed, Ed D, PhD); educational specialist (Ed S). Electronic applications accepted.

School of Law *Program availability:* Part-time, 100% online, blended/hybrid learning. Offers American legal studies (LL M); human rights (LL M); law (MA, JD). Electronic applications accepted.

School of Psychology and Counseling *Program availability:* Part-time, evening/weekend, 100% online, blended/hybrid learning. Offers clinical mental health counseling (MA); clinical psychology (Psy D); counseling and psychological studies - clinical (PhD); counseling and psychological studies - research (PhD); counseling studies (CAGS); counselor education and supervision (PhD); general psychology (MS); human services (MA); marriage, couple, and family counseling (MA); pastoral counseling (MA); school counseling (MA). Electronic applications accepted.

REGIS COLLEGE, Toronto, ON M5S 2Z5, Canada

General Information Independent-religious, coed, graduate-only institution. *Graduate housing:* Room and/or apartments available on a first-come, first-served basis to single students; on-campus housing not available to married students. *Research affiliation:* Lonergan Research Institute (theology/philosophy), Lupina Foundation (research and innovation related to health/society issues).

GRADUATE UNITS

Graduate and Professional Programs Offers eastern Christian studies (Certificate); Ignatian spirituality (Diploma); ministry (D Min); ministry and spirituality (MAMS); philosophical studies (Diploma); retreat direction (Certificate); sacred theology (STM, STD, STB, STL); spiritual direction (Diploma); theological studies (MTS, Diploma); theology (M Div, MA, Th M, PhD, Th D).

REGIS COLLEGE, Weston, MA 02493

General Information Independent-religious, coed, comprehensive institution. *Enrollment:* 200 full-time matriculated graduate/professional students, 1,900 part-time matriculated graduate/professional students. *Graduate housing:* Room and/or apartments available on a first-come, first-served basis to single students; on-campus housing not available to married students. *Student services:* Campus employment opportunities, campus safety program, career counseling, exercise/wellness program, international student services, low-cost health insurance, multicultural affairs office, services for students with disabilities, teacher training, writing training. *Library facilities:* Regis College Library. *Collection:* Books: 108,313 (physical), 421,975 (digital/electronic); Serial titles: 126 (physical), 153 (digital/electronic); Databases: 58. Weekly public service hours: 108.

Computer facilities: 196 computers available on campus for general student use. A campuswide network can be accessed from student residence rooms and from off campus. Online class registration, online bills, financial aid award letters and check-in requirements are available.
Website: http://www.regiscollege.edu/

General Application Contact: Shelagh Tomaino, Dean of Graduate Admission, 781-768-7330, Fax: 781-768-8218, E-mail: graduatedepartment@regiscollege.edu.

GRADUATE UNITS

Department of Education Expenses: Contact institution. *Financial support:* Federal Work-Study, scholarships/grants, and unspecified assistantships available. Financial award applicants required to submit FAFSA. *Program availability:* Part-time, evening/weekend. Offers elementary teacher (M Ed); higher education leadership (Ed D); special education (M Ed). *Application deadline:* Applications are processed on a rolling basis. *Application fee:* $65. Electronic applications accepted. *Application Contact:* Dr. Priscilla Boerger, Department Chair/Graduate Program Director, 781-768-7422, E-mail: priscilla.boerger@regiscollege.edu. Department Chair/Graduate Program Director, Dr. Priscilla Boerger, 781-768-7422, E-mail: priscilla.boerger@regiscollege.edu.

Nursing and Health Sciences School Expenses: Contact institution. *Financial support:* Federal Work-Study, scholarships/grants, and unspecified assistantships available. Support available to part-time students. Financial award applicants required to submit FAFSA. *Program availability:* Part-time, evening/weekend, 100% online, blended/hybrid learning. Offers applied behavior analysis (MS); counseling psychology (MA); health administration (MS); nurse practitioner (Certificate); nursing (MS, DNP); nursing education (Certificate); occupational therapy (MS). *Application deadline:* Applications are processed on a rolling basis. *Application fee:* $75. Electronic applications accepted. *Application Contact:* Hillary Lyons, Graduate Admission Counselor, 781-768-7746, E-mail: hillary.lyons@regiscollege.edu.

Strategic Communication Program Expenses: Contact institution. *Financial support:* Federal Work-Study and unspecified assistantships available. Financial award applicants required to submit FAFSA. *Program availability:* Part-time, evening/weekend. Offers strategic communication (MA). *Application deadline:* Applications are processed on a rolling basis. *Application fee:* $65. Electronic applications accepted. *Application Contact:* Dr. Colleen Malachowski, Director, 781-768-7373, E-mail: colleen.malachowski@regiscollege.edu. *Director,* Dr. Colleen Malachowski, 781-768-7373, E-mail: colleen.malachowski@regiscollege.edu.

REGIS UNIVERSITY, Denver, CO 80221-1099

General Information Independent-religious, coed, comprehensive institution. *Graduate housing:* Room and/or apartments available on a first-come, first-served basis to single students; on-campus housing not available to married students. Housing application deadline: 5/1. *Research affiliation:* Commission for Accelerated Programs, Learning Anytime Anywhere Partnership (Internet-based technology), Transparency by Design (online programs, best practices).

GRADUATE UNITS

College of Business and Economics *Program availability:* Part-time, evening/weekend, 100% online, blended/hybrid learning. Offers accounting (MS); executive leadership (Certificate); finance (MS); finance and accounting (MBA); health industry leadership (MBA); human resource management and leadership (MSOL); management (MBA); marketing (MBA); nonprofit leadership (Post-Graduate Certificate); nonprofit management (MNM); nonprofit organizational capacity building (Certificate); operations management (MBA); organizational leadership and management (MSOL); project leadership and management (MS, MSOL); strategic business management (Certificate); strategic human resource integration (Certificate); strategic management (MBA). Programs offered at Colorado Springs Campus, Northwest Denver Campus, Southeast Denver Campus, Fort Collins Campus, Broomfield Campus, Henderson (Nevada) Campus, and Summerlin (Nevada) Campus. Electronic applications accepted.

College of Computer and Information Sciences *Program availability:* Part-time, evening/weekend, 100% online, blended/hybrid learning. Offers agile technologies (Certificate); cybersecurity (Certificate); data science (M Sc); database administration with Oracle (Certificate); database development (Certificate); database technologies (M Sc); enterprise Java software development (Certificate); enterprise resource planning (Certificate); executive information technology (Certificate); health care informatics (Certificate); health care informatics and information management (M Sc); information assurance (M Sc); information assurance policy management (Certificate); information technology management (M Sc); mobile software development (Certificate); software engineering (M Sc, Certificate); software engineering and database technology (M Sc); storage area networks (Certificate); systems engineering (M Sc, Certificate). Electronic applications accepted.

College of Contemporary Liberal Studies *Program availability:* Part-time, evening/weekend, 100% online, blended/hybrid learning. Offers creative writing (MFA); criminology (M Sc); curriculum, instruction and assessment (M Ed); education - teacher leadership (M Ed); educational leadership (M Ed); elementary education (M Ed); literacy (Certificate); reading (M Ed); secondary education (M Ed); special education (M Ed); teacher academic leadership (Certificate); teacher leadership (MA); teacher/educational leadership (M Ed); teaching the linguistically diverse (M Ed). Electronic applications accepted.

Regis College *Program availability:* Part-time. Offers biomedical sciences (MS); developmental practice (MDP); education (MA); environmental biology (MS). Electronic applications accepted.

Rueckert-Hartman College for Health Professions *Program availability:* Part-time, evening/weekend, 100% online, blended/hybrid learning. Offers advanced practice nurse (DNP); counseling (MA); counseling children and adolescents (Post-Graduate Certificate); counseling military families (Post-Graduate Certificate); depth psychotherapy (Post-Graduate Certificate); fellowship in orthopedic manual physical therapy (Certificate); health care business management (Certificate); health care quality and patient safety (Certificate); health industry leadership (MBA); health services administration (MS); marriage and family therapy (MA, Post-Graduate Certificate); neonatal nurse practitioner (MSN); nursing education (MSN); nursing leadership (MSN); occupational therapy (OTD); pharmacy (Pharm D); physical therapy (DPT). Electronic applications accepted.

REINHARDT UNIVERSITY, Waleska, GA 30183-2981

General Information Independent-religious, coed, comprehensive institution. *Enrollment:* 1,566 graduate, professional, and undergraduate students; 42 full-time matriculated graduate/professional students (24 women), 51 part-time matriculated graduate/professional students (15 women). *Enrollment by degree level:* 93 master's. *Graduate faculty:* 9 full-time (4 women), 13 part-time/adjunct (8 women). *Tuition:* Full-time $8732; part-time $495 per credit. *Required fees:* $200. Tuition and fees vary according to course load and program. *Graduate housing:* Room and/or apartments available on a first-come, first-served basis to single students; on-campus housing not available to married students. *Typical cost:* $8600 (including board). Room and board charges vary according to board plan and housing facility selected. *Student services:* Campus safety program, career counseling, exercise/wellness program, free psychological counseling, international student services, services for students with disabilities. *Library facilities:* Hill Freeman Library/Spruill Learning Center plus 1 other. *Collection:* Books: 61,496 (physical), 183,453 (digital/electronic); Serial titles: 52 (physical), 27,855 (digital/electronic); Databases: 167.

Computer facilities: A campuswide network can be accessed from student residence rooms and from off campus. Online class registration is available.
Website: http://www.reinhardt.edu/

GRADUATE UNITS

McCamish School of Business & Sport Studies Students: 7 full-time (1 woman), 37 part-time (12 women); includes 13 minority (10 Black or African American, non-Hispanic/Latino; 2 Hispanic/Latino; 1 Two or more races, non-Hispanic/Latino), 2 international. Average age 44. *Faculty:* 5 full-time (3 women). Expenses: Contact institution. *Financial support:* Application deadline: 7/1; applicants required to submit FAFSA. In 2018, 12 master's awarded. *Program availability:* Part-time, evening/weekend, 100% online. Offers business (MBA). *Application deadline:* Applications are processed on a rolling basis. *Application fee:* $50. Electronic applications accepted. *Application Contact:* Dr. Dana L. Hall, Program Coordinator, 770-720-5756, Fax: 770-720-9236, E-mail: dlh@reinhardt.edu. *Interim Dean,* Jacob Harney, 770-720-9102, E-mail: jph@reinhardt.edu.

Price School of Education Students: 17 full-time (14 women); includes 4 minority (3 Black or African American, non-Hispanic/Latino; 1 Hispanic/Latino). Average age 33. *Faculty:* 2 full-time (both women), 3 part-time/adjunct (all women). Expenses: Contact institution. *Financial support:* Application deadline: 7/1; applicants required to submit FAFSA. In 2018, 54 master's awarded. *Program availability:* Part-time. Offers education (M Ed, MAT). *Application deadline:* Applications are processed on a rolling basis. *Application fee:* $50. Electronic applications accepted. *Application Contact:* Graduate

Admissions, 770-720-5760, E-mail: gradadmissions@reinhardt.edu. *Dean,* Dr. Nancy Marsh, 770-720-5657, Fax: 770-720-9173, E-mail: njm@reinhardt.edu.

School of Arts & Humanities Students: 18 full-time (9 women), 1 (woman) part-time; includes 3 minority (2 Black or African American, non-Hispanic/Latino; 1 Two or more races, non-Hispanic/Latino). Average age 33. *Faculty:* 1 full-time (0 women), 10 part-time/adjunct (5 women). Expenses: Contact institution. *Financial support:* Application deadline: 5/7; applicants required to submit FAFSA. *Program availability:* Blended/hybrid learning. Offers creative writing (MFA). *Application deadline:* Applications are processed on a rolling basis. *Application fee:* $50. *Application Contact:* Graduate Admissions, 770-720-9191, E-mail: gradadmissions@reinhardt.edu. *Dean,* Dr. Wayne Glowka, 770-720-5628, E-mail: awg@reinhardt.edu.

School of Professional Studies Students: 13 part-time (2 women); includes 1 minority (Black or African American, non-Hispanic/Latino). Average age 42. *Faculty:* 1 full-time (0 women). Expenses: Contact institution. *Financial support:* Application deadline: 7/7; applicants required to submit FAFSA. In 2018, 4 master's awarded. *Program availability:* Part-time-only, blended/hybrid learning. Offers public administration (MPA). *Application deadline:* Applications are processed on a rolling basis. Electronic applications accepted. *Application Contact:* Graduate Admissions, 770-720-5760, Fax: 770-720-5739, E-mail: gradadmissions@reinhardt.edu. *Interim Dean,* Lester W. Drawdy, 770-720-5927, E-mail: lwd@reinhardt.edu.

RELAY GRADUATE SCHOOL OF EDUCATION, New York, NY 10011

General Information Independent, coed, graduate-only institution.

GRADUATE UNITS

Graduate Programs *Program availability:* Online learning. Offers education (MAT). Program also offered at Chicago, Delaware, Houston, Memphis, New Orleans, and Newark campuses.

RENSSELAER AT HARTFORD, Hartford, CT 06120-2991

General Information Independent, coed, graduate-only institution. *Graduate housing:* On-campus housing not available.

GRADUATE UNITS

Department of Computer and Information Science *Program availability:* Part-time, evening/weekend. Offers computer science (MS); information technology (MS). Electronic applications accepted.

Department of Engineering *Program availability:* Part-time, evening/weekend. Offers computer and systems engineering (ME); electrical engineering (ME, MS); engineering (ME, MS); engineering science (MS); mechanical engineering (ME, MS). Electronic applications accepted.

Lally School of Management and Technology *Program availability:* Part-time, evening/weekend, online learning. Offers management and technology (MBA, MS). Electronic applications accepted.

RENSSELAER POLYTECHNIC INSTITUTE, Troy, NY 12180-3590

General Information Independent, coed, university. CGS member. *Enrollment:* 1,120 full-time matriculated graduate/professional students (341 women), 93 part-time matriculated graduate/professional students (40 women). *Enrollment by degree level:* 388 master's, 825 doctoral. *Graduate faculty:* 477 full-time (120 women), 50 part-time/adjunct (10 women). *Graduate housing:* Rooms and/or apartments available on a first-come, first-served basis to single and married students. *Student services:* Campus employment opportunities, campus safety program, career counseling, exercise/wellness program, free psychological counseling, grant writing training, international student services, low-cost health insurance, multicultural affairs office, services for students with disabilities, teacher training, writing training. *Library facilities:* Folsom Library plus 2 others. *Collection:* Students can reserve study rooms.

Computer facilities: Computer purchase and lease plans are available. A campuswide network can be accessed from student residence rooms and from off campus. Online class registration, billing, downloadable software, webpages are available.
Website: http://www.rpi.edu/

General Application Contact: Jarron Decker, Director of Graduate Admissions, 518-276-6216, Fax: 518-276-4072, E-mail: gradadmissions@rpi.edu.

GRADUATE UNITS

Graduate School Students: 1,188 full-time (394 women), 141 part-time (29 women); includes 168 minority (27 Black or African American, non-Hispanic/Latino; 1 American Indian or Alaska Native, non-Hispanic/Latino; 59 Asian, non-Hispanic/Latino; 40 Hispanic/Latino; 41 Two or more races, non-Hispanic/Latino), 620 international. Average age 26. 3,675 applicants, 32% accepted, 301 enrolled. *Faculty:* 477 full-time (120 women), 50 part-time/adjunct (10 women). Expenses: Contact institution. *Financial support:* In 2018–19, 968 students received support, including research assistantships with full tuition reimbursements available (averaging $23,000 per year), teaching assistantships with full tuition reimbursements available (averaging $23,000 per year); fellowships with full tuition reimbursements available, scholarships/grants, health care benefits, and tuition waivers (full) also available. Financial award application deadline: 1/1. In 2018, 352 master's, 162 doctorates awarded. *Program availability:* Part-time-only, evening/weekend. *Application deadline:* For fall admission, 1/1 priority date for domestic and international students; for spring admission, 8/15 priority date for domestic and international students. Applications are processed on a rolling basis. *Application fee:* $75. Electronic applications accepted. *Application Contact:* Jarron Decker, Director of Graduate Admissions, 518-276-6216, Fax: 518-276-4072, E-mail: gradadmissions@rpi.edu.

Lally School of Management Students: 201 full-time (97 women), 32 part-time (11 women); includes 27 minority (5 Black or African American, non-Hispanic/Latino; 8 Asian, non-Hispanic/Latino; 9 Hispanic/Latino; 5 Two or more races, non-Hispanic/Latino), 158 international. Average age 24. 1,198 applicants, 40% accepted, 142 enrolled. *Faculty:* 36 full-time (9 women), 5 part-time/adjunct (0 women). Expenses: Contact institution. *Financial support:* In 2018–19, 64 students received support. Scholarships/grants available. Financial award application deadline: 1/1; financial award applicants required to submit FAFSA. In 2018, 124 master's, 6 doctorates awarded. *Program availability:* Part-time. Offers business analytics (MS); management (MBA, MS, PhD); quantitative finance and risk analytics (MS); supply chain management (MS); technology commercialization and entrepreneurship (MS). *Application deadline:* For fall admission, 1/1 priority date for domestic and international students. Applications are processed on a rolling basis. *Application fee:* $75. Electronic applications accepted. *Application Contact:* Jarron Decker, Director of Graduate Admissions, 518-276-6216, Fax: 518-276-4072, E-mail: gradadmissions@rpi.edu. *Associate Dean, Lally School of Management,* Dr. Chanaka Edirisinghe, 518-276-3336, E-mail: edirin@rpi.edu.

School of Architecture Students: 52 full-time (22 women), 3 part-time (1 woman); includes 7 minority (1 Black or African American, non-Hispanic/Latino; 3 Asian, non-Hispanic/Latino; 1 Hispanic/Latino; 2 Two or more races, non-Hispanic/Latino), 19 international. Average age 28. 122 applicants, 79% accepted, 34 enrolled. *Faculty:* 33 full-time (8 women), 13 part-time/adjunct (1 woman). Expenses: Contact institution. *Financial support:* In 2018–19, research assistantships (averaging $23,000 per year), teaching assistantships (averaging $23,000 per year) were awarded; fellowships and scholarships/grants also available. Financial award application deadline: 1/1. In 2018, 25 master's, 5 doctorates awarded. Offers architectural acoustics (PhD); architecture (M Arch, MS, PhD); built ecologies (PhD); lighting (PhD). *Application deadline:* For fall admission, 1/1 priority date for domestic and international students; for spring admission, 8/15 for domestic and international students; for summer admission, 1/1 for domestic and international students. Applications are processed on a rolling basis. *Application fee:* $75. Electronic applications accepted. *Application Contact:* Jarron Decker, Director of Graduate Admissions, 518-276-6216, Fax: 518-276-4072, E-mail: gradadmissions@rpi.edu. *Dean, School of Architecture,* Evan Douglis, 518-276-6460, E-mail: douglis@rpi.edu.

School of Engineering Students: 533 full-time (137 women), 84 part-time (11 women); includes 76 minority (12 Black or African American, non-Hispanic/Latino; 1 American Indian or Alaska Native, non-Hispanic/Latino; 29 Asian, non-Hispanic/Latino; 13 Hispanic/Latino; 21 Two or more races, non-Hispanic/Latino), 298 international. Average age 26. 1,413 applicants, 36% accepted, 162 enrolled. *Faculty:* 179 full-time (28 women), 8 part-time/adjunct (0 women). Expenses: Contact institution. *Financial support:* In 2018–19, 462 students received support, including research assistantships (averaging $23,000 per year), teaching assistantships (averaging $23,000 per year); fellowships also available. Financial award application deadline: 1/1. In 2018, 127 master's, 89 doctorates awarded. *Program availability:* Part-time. Offers aeronautical engineering (M Eng, MS, PhD); biomedical engineering (M Eng, MS, D Eng, PhD); chemical engineering (M Eng, MS, PhD); civil engineering (M Eng, MS, PhD); computer and systems engineering (M Eng, MS, PhD); decision sciences and engineering systems (PhD); electrical engineering (M Eng, MS, PhD); engineering (M Eng, MS, D Eng, PhD); engineering physics (MS, PhD); environmental engineering (M Eng, MS, PhD); industrial and management engineering (M Eng, MS); materials engineering (M Eng, MS, D Eng, PhD); mechanical engineering (M Eng, MS, D Eng, PhD); nuclear engineering and science (M Eng, MS, D Eng, PhD); systems engineering and technology management (M Eng); transportation engineering (M Eng, MS, PhD). *Application deadline:* For fall admission, 1/1 priority date for domestic and international students; for spring admission, 8/15 priority date for domestic and international students. Applications are processed on a rolling basis. *Application fee:* $75. Electronic applications accepted. *Application Contact:* Jarron Decker, Director of Graduate Admissions, 518-276-6216, Fax: 518-276-4072, E-mail: gradadmissions@rpi.edu. *Dean,* Shekhar Garde, 518-276-6298, E-mail: gardes@rpi.edu.

School of Humanities, Arts, and Social Sciences Students: 63 full-time (33 women), 9 part-time (4 women); includes 10 minority (3 Asian, non-Hispanic/Latino; 5 Hispanic/Latino; 2 Two or more races, non-Hispanic/Latino), 11 international. Average age 32. 73 applicants, 37% accepted, 13 enrolled. *Faculty:* 92 full-time (36 women), 12 part-time/adjunct (5 women). Expenses: Contact institution. *Financial support:* In 2018–19, research assistantships (averaging $23,000 per year), teaching assistantships (averaging $23,000 per year) were awarded; fellowships and scholarships/grants also available. Financial award application deadline: 1/1. *Program availability:* Part-time, evening/weekend, online learning. Offers cognitive science (PhD); communication and rhetoric (MS, PhD); electronic arts (PhD); humanities, arts, and social sciences (MS); science and technology studies (MS, PhD). *Application deadline:* For fall admission, 1/1 priority date for domestic students, 1/15 priority date for international students; for spring admission, 8/15 priority date for domestic and international students. Applications are processed on a rolling basis. *Application fee:* $75. Electronic applications accepted. *Application Contact:* Jarron Decker, Director of Graduate Admissions, 518-276-6216, Fax: 518-276-4072, E-mail: gradadmissions@rpi.edu. *Associate Dean for Research and Graduate Studies,* Dr. Curtis Bahn, 518-276-6065, E-mail: crb@rpi.edu.

School of Science Students: 332 full-time (102 women), 17 part-time (4 women); includes 50 minority (9 Black or African American, non-Hispanic/Latino; 16 Asian, non-Hispanic/Latino; 14 Hispanic/Latino; 11 Two or more races, non-Hispanic/Latino), 128 international. Average age 26. 1,070 applicants, 28% accepted, 80 enrolled. *Faculty:* 127 full-time (33 women), 9 part-time/adjunct (4 women). Expenses: Contact institution. *Financial support:* In 2018–19, research assistantships (averaging $23,000 per year), teaching assistantships (averaging $23,000 per year) were awarded; fellowships also available. Financial award application deadline: 1/1. In 2018, 71 master's, 47 doctorates awarded. Offers applied mathematics (MS); astronomy (MS); biochemistry and biophysics (MS, PhD); biology (MS, PhD); chemistry (MS, PhD); computer science (MS, PhD); geology (MS, PhD); information technology (MS); mathematics (MS, PhD); multi-disciplinary science (MS, PhD); physics (MS, PhD); science (MS, PhD). *Application deadline:* For fall admission, 1/1 priority date for domestic and international students; for spring admission, 8/15 priority date for domestic and international students. Applications are processed on a rolling basis. *Application fee:* $75. Electronic applications accepted. *Application Contact:* Jarron Decker, Director of Graduate Admissions, 518-276-6216, Fax: 518-276-4072, E-mail: gradadmissions@rpi.edu. *Associate Dean, School of Science,* Dr. Christian Wetzel, 518-276-3755, E-mail: wetzel@rpi.edu.

RESEARCH COLLEGE OF NURSING, Kansas City, MO 64132

General Information Independent, coed, primarily women, comprehensive institution. *Enrollment:* 1 full-time matriculated graduate/professional student, 130 part-time matriculated graduate/professional students (108 women). *Enrollment by degree level:* 131 master's. *Graduate faculty:* 9 full-time (all women), 4 part-time/adjunct (2 women). *Tuition:* Part-time $550 per credit hour. *Required fees:* $25 per credit hour. Part-time tuition and fees vary according to student level. *Graduate housing:* Rooms and/or apartments available on a first-come, first-served basis to single and married students. Typical cost: $5400 per year for single students; $10,800 per year for married students. Housing application deadline: 1/15. *Student services:* Campus safety program, child daycare facilities. *Library facilities:* Greenlease Library.

Computer facilities: 125 computers available on campus for general student use. A campuswide network can be accessed from student residence rooms and from off campus. Online class registration is available.
Website: http://www.researchcollege.edu/

General Application Contact: Leslie Burry, Director of Admission, 816-995-2820, Fax: 816-995-2813, E-mail: leslie.burry@researchcollege.edu.

GRADUATE UNITS

Nursing Program *Program availability:* Part-time-only, 100% online. Offers adult-gerontological nurse practitioner (MSN); executive practice and healthcare leadership (MSN); family nurse practitioner (MSN). Electronic applications accepted.

RESURRECTION UNIVERSITY, Chicago, IL 60622

General Information Independent, coed, upper-level institution.

GRADUATE UNITS

Nursing Program Offers nursing (MSN).

RHODE ISLAND COLLEGE, Providence, RI 02908-1991

General Information State-supported, coed, comprehensive institution. *Enrollment:* 7,771 graduate, professional, and undergraduate students; 250 full-time matriculated graduate/professional students (205 women), 516 part-time matriculated graduate/professional students (404 women). *Enrollment by degree level:* 673 master's, 63 doctoral, 31 other advanced degrees. *Graduate faculty:* 106 full-time (70 women), 87 part-time/adjunct (66 women). *Tuition, area resident:* Part-time $407 per credit. Tuition, nonresident: part-time $792 per credit. *Required fees:* $29 per credit. $100 per semester. *Graduate housing:* Room and/or apartments guaranteed to single students; on-campus housing not available to married students. Typical cost: $7106 per year. Room charges vary according to board plan and housing facility selected. Housing application deadline: 5/15. *Student services:* Campus employment opportunities, career counseling, free psychological counseling, grant writing training, international student services, low-cost health insurance, multicultural affairs office, services for students with disabilities. *Library facilities:* Adams Library. *Collection:* Books: 306,080 (physical), 302,387 (digital/electronic); Serial titles: 3,081 (physical), 52,652 (digital/electronic); Databases: 123. Weekly public service hours: 80.

Computer facilities: Computer purchase and lease plans are available. 250 computers available on campus for general student use. A campuswide network can be accessed. Online class registration is available.
Website: http://www.ric.edu/

General Application Contact: Dr. Leslie Schuster, Interim Dean of Graduate Studies, 401-456-9723, E-mail: graduatestudies@ric.edu.

GRADUATE UNITS

School of Graduate Studies Students: 250 full-time (205 women), 516 part-time (404 women); includes 168 minority (51 Black or African American, non-Hispanic/Latino; 3 American Indian or Alaska Native, non-Hispanic/Latino; 21 Asian, non-Hispanic/Latino; 87 Hispanic/Latino; 1 Native Hawaiian or other Pacific Islander, non-Hispanic/Latino; 5 Two or more races, non-Hispanic/Latino). Average age 32. *Faculty:* 106 full-time (70 women), 87 part-time/adjunct (66 women). Expenses: Contact institution. *Financial support:* Research assistantships, teaching assistantships, career-related internships or fieldwork, Federal Work-Study, traineeships, health care benefits, tuition waivers (full and partial), and unspecified assistantships available. Support available to part-time students. Financial award application deadline: 5/15; financial award applicants required to submit FAFSA. In 2018, 269 master's, 9 doctorates, 36 other advanced degrees awarded. *Program availability:* Part-time, evening/weekend. Joint PhD program in Education with University of Rhode Island. *Application deadline:* For fall admission, 3/1 priority date for domestic students; for spring admission, 11/1 for domestic students. Applications are processed on a rolling basis. *Application fee:* $50. Electronic applications accepted. *Application Contact:* Graduate Studies, 401-456-8700. *Interim Dean of Graduate Studies,* Dr. Leslie Schuster, 401-456-9723, E-mail: graduatestudies@ric.edu.

Faculty of Arts and Sciences Students: 9 full-time (5 women), 39 part-time (21 women); includes 7 minority (3 Black or African American, non-Hispanic/Latino; 1 American Indian or Alaska Native, non-Hispanic/Latino; 1 Asian, non-Hispanic/Latino; 2 Hispanic/Latino). Average age 31. *Faculty:* 39 full-time (18 women), 5 part-time/adjunct (2 women). Expenses: Contact institution. *Financial support:* Research assistantships with tuition reimbursements, teaching assistantships, career-related internships or fieldwork, Federal Work-Study, scholarships/grants, health care benefits, and unspecified assistantships available. Support available to part-time students. Financial award application deadline: 5/15; financial award applicants required to submit FAFSA. In 2018, 19 master's, 2 other advanced degrees awarded. *Program availability:* Part-time, evening/weekend. Offers art education (MA, MAT); arts and sciences (MA, MAT, MM Ed, MPA, CGS); biology (MA); creative writing (MA, CGS); English (MA); health psychology (CGS); history (MA); justice studies (MA); literature (CGS); mathematics (MA); mathematics content specialist (CGS); media studies (MA); modern biological sciences (CGS); music education (MAT, MM Ed); psychology (MA). *Application deadline:* For fall admission, 3/1 for domestic students; for spring admission, 11/1 for domestic students. Applications are processed on a rolling basis. *Application fee:* $50. Electronic applications accepted. *Application Contact:* Graduate Studies, 401-456-8700, E-mail: graduatestudies@ric.edu. *Dean,* Dr. Earl Simson, 401-456-8106, E-mail: esimson@ric.edu.

Feinstein School of Education and Human Development Students: 87 full-time (74 women), 237 part-time (193 women); includes 49 minority (11 Black or African American, non-Hispanic/Latino; 1 American Indian or Alaska Native, non-Hispanic/Latino; 12 Asian, non-Hispanic/Latino; 23 Hispanic/Latino; 2 Two or more races, non-Hispanic/Latino). Average age 32. *Faculty:* 38 full-time (30 women), 35 part-time/adjunct (26 women). Expenses: Contact institution. *Financial support:* Teaching assistantships, career-related internships or fieldwork, Federal Work-Study, scholarships/grants, health care benefits, and unspecified assistantships available. Support available to part-time students. Financial award application deadline: 5/15; financial award applicants required to submit FAFSA. In 2018, 115 master's, 5 doctorates, 31 other advanced degrees awarded. *Program availability:* Part-time, evening/weekend. Offers advanced counseling (CGS); advanced studies in teaching and learning (M Ed); agency counseling (MA); autism education (CGS); clinical mental health counseling (MS); co-occurring disorders (MA, CGS); early childhood education (M Ed); education (PhD); education and human development (M Ed, MA, MAT, MS, PhD, CAGS, CGS); educational leadership (M Ed); elementary education (M Ed, MAT); English (MAT); French (MAT); health education (M Ed); history (MAT); math (MAT); mental health counseling (CAGS); physical education (CGS); reading (M Ed); school counseling (MA); school psychology (CAGS); secondary education (MAT); severe intellectual disabilities (CGS); Spanish (MAT); special education (M Ed); teacher leadership (CGS); teaching English as a second language (M Ed). *Application deadline:* For fall admission, 3/1 for domestic students; for spring admission, 11/1 for domestic students. Applications are processed on a rolling basis. *Application fee:* $50. Electronic applications accepted. *Application Contact:* Dr. Jeannine Dingus-Eason, Dean, 401-456-8110, E-mail: jdinguseason@ric.edu. *Dean,* Dr. Jeannine Dingus-Eason, 401-456-8110, E-mail: jdinguseason@ric.edu.

School of Business Students: 9 full-time (8 women), 24 part-time (15 women); includes 16 minority (7 Black or African American, non-Hispanic/Latino; 9 Hispanic/Latino). Average age 27. *Faculty:* 4 full-time (3 women), 9 part-time/adjunct (3 women). Expenses: Contact institution. *Financial support:* Research assistantships, teaching assistantships, Federal Work-Study, scholarships/grants, health care benefits, and unspecified assistantships available. Support available to part-time students. Financial award application deadline: 5/15; financial award applicants required to submit FAFSA. In 2018, 8 master's awarded. *Program availability:* Part-time, evening/weekend. Offers accounting (MP Ac); business (MP Ac, MS, CGS); financial planning (CGS); health care administration (MS). *Application deadline:* For fall admission, 3/1 for domestic students. Applications are processed on a rolling basis. *Application fee:* $50. Electronic applications accepted. *Application Contact:* Dr. Jeffrey Mello, Dean, 401-456-8009, E-mail: jmello@ric.edu. *Dean,* Dr. Jeffrey Mello, 401-456-8009, E-mail: jmello@ric.edu.

School of Nursing Students: 19 full-time (13 women), 81 part-time (67 women); includes 11 minority (2 Black or African American, non-Hispanic/Latino; 4 Asian, non-Hispanic/Latino; 3 Hispanic/Latino; 1 Native Hawaiian or other Pacific Islander, non-Hispanic/Latino; 1 Two or more races, non-Hispanic/Latino). Average age 36. *Faculty:* 10 full-time (all women), 16 part-time/adjunct (14 women). Expenses: Contact institution. *Financial support:* Teaching assistantships, Federal Work-Study, scholarships/grants, health care benefits, and unspecified assistantships available. Support available to part-time students. Financial award application deadline: 5/15; financial award applicants required to submit FAFSA. In 2018, 30 master's, 4 doctorates awarded. *Program availability:* Part-time. Offers nursing (MSN, DNP). *Application deadline:* For fall admission, 2/15 for domestic students. Applications are processed on a rolling basis. *Application fee:* $50. Electronic applications accepted. *Application Contact:* Dr. Debra Servello, Interim Dean, 401-456-8014, E-mail: dservello@ric.edu. *Interim Dean,* Dr. Debra Servello, 401-456-8014, E-mail: dservello@ric.edu.

School of Social Work Students: 126 full-time (105 women), 135 part-time (108 women); includes 85 minority (28 Black or African American, non-Hispanic/Latino; 1 American Indian or Alaska Native, non-Hispanic/Latino; 4 Asian, non-Hispanic/Latino; 50 Hispanic/Latino; 2 Two or more races, non-Hispanic/Latino). Average age 31. *Faculty:* 15 full-time (9 women), 22 part-time/adjunct (21 women). Expenses: Contact institution. *Financial support:* Career-related internships or fieldwork, Federal Work-Study, scholarships/grants, health care benefits, and unspecified assistantships available. Support available to part-time students. Financial award application deadline: 5/15; financial award applicants required to submit FAFSA. In 2018, 97 master's awarded. *Program availability:* Part-time. Offers social work (MSW). *Application deadline:* For fall admission, 2/1 for domestic students. Applications are processed on a rolling basis. *Application fee:* $50. Electronic applications accepted. *Application Contact:* Dr. Jayashree Nimmagadda, Interim Dean, 401-456-8042, E-mail: jnimmagadda@ric.edu. *Interim Dean,* Dr. Jayashree Nimmagadda, 401-456-8042, E-mail: jnimmagadda@ric.edu.

RHODE ISLAND SCHOOL OF DESIGN, Providence, RI 02903-2784

General Information Independent, coed, comprehensive institution. Enrollment: 2,468 graduate, professional, and undergraduate students; 474 full-time matriculated graduate/professional students (301 women). Enrollment by degree level: 474 master's. *Graduate faculty:* 78 full-time (35 women), 100 part-time/adjunct (37 women). *Tuition:* Full-time $49,900. *Required fees:* $1060. *Graduate housing:* Rooms and/or apartments available on a first-come, first-served basis to single and married students. Typical cost: $12,850 per year ($17,230 including board) for single students. Room and board charges vary according to board plan and housing facility selected. Housing application deadline: 5/15. *Student services:* Campus employment opportunities, campus safety program, career counseling, exercise/wellness program, free psychological counseling, grant writing training, international student services, low-cost health insurance, multicultural affairs office, services for students with disabilities, teacher training, writing training. *Library facilities:* Fleet Library. *Collection:* Books: 131,412 (physical), 178,450 (digital/electronic); Serial titles: 1,662 (physical), 800 (digital/electronic); Databases: 48. Weekly public service hours: 89; students can reserve study rooms.

Computer facilities: Computer purchase and lease plans are available. 65 computers available on campus for general student use. A campuswide network can be accessed from student residence rooms and from off campus. Online class registration is available.
Website: http://www.risd.edu/

General Application Contact: Molly Pettengill, Associate Director for Graduate Recruitment, 401-454-6312, Fax: 401-454-6309, E-mail: admissions@risd.edu.

GRADUATE UNITS

Department of Architecture Students: 88 full-time (48 women); includes 12 minority (3 Black or African American, non-Hispanic/Latino; 2 Asian, non-Hispanic/Latino; 7 Hispanic/Latino), 46 international. Average age 25. 314 applicants, 47% accepted, 37 enrolled. Expenses: Contact institution. *Financial support:* Fellowships, research assistantships, teaching assistantships, Federal Work-Study, and unspecified assistantships available. Financial award application deadline: 2/15; financial award applicants required to submit FAFSA. In 2018, 29 master's awarded. Offers architecture (M Arch). *Application deadline:* For fall admission, 1/10 for domestic and international students. *Application fee:* $60. Electronic applications accepted. *Application Contact:* Molly Pettengill, Assistant Director for Graduate Recruitment, 401-454-6312, Fax: 401-454-6309, E-mail: mpetteng@risd.edu. *Department Head,* Amy Kulper, 401-454-6281, Fax: 401-454-6299, E-mail: archgrad@risd.edu.

Department of Ceramics Students: 10 full-time (8 women); includes 1 minority (Asian, non-Hispanic/Latino), 4 international. Average age 28. 21 applicants, 38% accepted, 4 enrolled. Expenses: Contact institution. *Financial support:* Fellowships, research assistantships, teaching assistantships, Federal Work-Study, scholarships/grants, and unspecified assistantships available. Financial award application deadline: 2/1; financial award applicants required to submit FAFSA. In 2018, 4 master's awarded. Offers ceramics (MFA). *Application deadline:* For fall admission, 1/10 for domestic and international students. *Application fee:* $60. Electronic applications accepted. *Application Contact:* Molly Pettengill, Associate Director for Graduate Recruitment, 401-454-6312, Fax: 401-454-6309, E-mail: ceramics@risd.edu. *Department Head and Graduate Coordinator,* Katy Schimert, 401-454-6190, Fax: 401-454-6191, E-mail: ceramics@risd.edu.

Department of Digital and Media Students: 21 full-time (13 women); includes 3 minority (1 Asian, non-Hispanic/Latino; 1 Hispanic/Latino; 1 Two or more races, non-Hispanic/Latino), 14 international. Average age 28. 137 applicants, 26% accepted, 9 enrolled. Expenses: Contact institution. *Financial support:* Fellowships, research assistantships, teaching assistantships, Federal Work-Study, scholarships/grants, and unspecified assistantships available. Financial award application deadline: 2/1; financial award applicants required to submit FAFSA. In 2018, 8 master's awarded. Offers digital and media (MFA). *Application deadline:* For fall admission, 1/10 for domestic and international students. *Application fee:* $60. Electronic applications accepted. *Application Contact:* Molly Pettengill, Associate Director for Graduate Recruitment, 401-454-6312, Fax: 401-454-6309, E-mail: mpetteng@risd.edu. *Department Head and Graduate Program Director,* Shona Kitchen, 401-454-6139, Fax: 401-277-4966, E-mail: digital@risd.edu.

Department of Furniture Design Students: 20 full-time (8 women); includes 4 minority (2 Asian, non-Hispanic/Latino; 2 Two or more races, non-Hispanic/Latino), 9 international. Average age 27. 24 applicants, 50% accepted, 6 enrolled. Expenses: Contact institution. *Financial support:* Fellowships, research assistantships, teaching assistantships, Federal Work-Study, scholarships/grants, and unspecified assistantships available. Financial award application deadline: 2/1; financial award applicants required to submit FAFSA. In 2018, 7 master's awarded. Offers furniture design (MFA). *Application deadline:* For fall admission, 1/10 for domestic and international students. *Application fee:* $60. Electronic applications accepted. *Application Contact:* Molly Pettengill, Associate Director for Graduate Recruitment, 401-454-6312, Fax: 401-454-6309, E-mail: mpetteng@risd.edu. *Department Head,* Lothar Windels, 401-454-6102, E-mail: furniture@risd.edu.

Department of Glass Students: 7 full-time (6 women); includes 1 minority (Asian, non-Hispanic/Latino), 4 international. Average age 28. 14 applicants, 36% accepted, 2 enrolled. Expenses: Contact institution. *Financial support:* Fellowships, research assistantships, teaching assistantships, Federal Work-Study, scholarships/grants, and unspecified assistantships available. Financial award application deadline: 2/1; financial award applicants required to submit FAFSA. In 2018, 2 master's awarded. Offers glass (MFA). *Application deadline:* For fall admission, 1/10 for domestic and international students. *Application fee:* $60. Electronic applications accepted. *Application Contact:* Molly Pettengill, Associate Director for Graduate Recruitment, 401-454-6312, Fax: 401-454-6309, E-mail: mpetteng@risd.edu. *Department Head and Graduate Program Director,* Jocelyne Prince, 401-454-6190, Fax: 401-454-6680, E-mail: jprince@risd.edu.

Department of Graphic Design Students: 37 full-time (20 women); includes 7 minority (4 Asian, non-Hispanic/Latino; 2 Hispanic/Latino; 1 Two or more races, non-Hispanic/Latino), 11 international. Average age 29. 284 applicants, 7% accepted, 13 enrolled. Expenses: Contact institution. *Financial support:* Fellowships, research assistantships, teaching assistantships, Federal Work-Study, scholarships/grants, and unspecified assistantships available. Financial award application deadline: 2/1; financial award applicants required to submit FAFSA. In 2018, 13 master's awarded. Offers graphic design (MFA). *Application deadline:* For fall admission, 1/10 for domestic and international students. *Application fee:* $60. Electronic applications accepted. *Application Contact:* Molly Pettengill, Associate Director for Graduate Recruitment, 401-454-6312, Fax: 401-454-6309, E-mail: mpetteng@risd.edu. *Department Head,* Lucy Hitchcock, 401-454-6171, Fax: 401-454-6117, E-mail: gd@risd.edu.

Department of Industrial Design Students: 40 full-time (17 women); includes 7 minority (4 Asian, non-Hispanic/Latino; 2 Hispanic/Latino; 1 Two or more races, non-Hispanic/Latino), 23 international. Average age 26. 218 applicants, 26% accepted, 16 enrolled. Expenses: Contact institution. *Financial support:* Fellowships, research assistantships, teaching assistantships, Federal Work-Study, scholarships/grants, and unspecified assistantships available. Financial award application deadline: 2/1; financial award applicants required to submit FAFSA. In 2018, 19 master's awarded. Offers industrial design (MID). *Application deadline:* For fall admission, 1/10 for domestic and international students. *Application fee:* $60. Electronic applications accepted. *Application Contact:* Molly Pettengill, Associate Director for Graduate Recruitment, 401-454-6312, Fax: 401-454-6309, E-mail: mpetteng@risd.edu. *Department Head,* Peter Yeadon, 401-454-6160, Fax: 401-454-6157, E-mail: idgradprogram@risd.edu.

Department of Interior Architecture Students: 80 full-time (62 women); includes 3 minority (2 Asian, non-Hispanic/Latino; 1 Two or more races, non-Hispanic/Latino), 64 international. Average age 25. 198 applicants, 41% accepted, 45 enrolled. Expenses: Contact institution. *Financial support:* Fellowships, research assistantships, teaching assistantships, Federal Work-Study, scholarships/grants, and unspecified assistantships available. Financial award application deadline: 2/1; financial award applicants required to submit FAFSA. In 2018, 39 master's awarded. Offers exhibition and narrative environments (M Des); interior studies/adaptive reuse (M Des, MA). *Application deadline:* For fall admission, 1/10 for domestic and international students. *Application fee:* $60. Electronic applications accepted. *Application Contact:* Molly Pettengill, Associate Director for Graduate Recruitment, 401-454-6312, Fax: 401-454-6309, E-mail: mpetteng@risd.edu. *Department Head,* Liliane Wong, 401-454-6272, Fax: 401-277-4962, E-mail: lwong@risd.edu.

Department of Jewelry and Metalsmithing Students: 9 full-time (8 women), 5 international. Average age 24. 54 applicants, 15% accepted, 5 enrolled. Expenses: Contact institution. *Financial support:* Fellowships, research assistantships, teaching assistantships, Federal Work-Study, scholarships/grants, and unspecified assistantships available. Financial award application deadline: 2/1; financial award applicants required to submit FAFSA. In 2018, 4 master's awarded. Offers jewelry and metalsmithing (MFA). *Application deadline:* For fall admission, 1/10 for domestic and international students. *Application fee:* $60. Electronic applications accepted. *Application Contact:* Molly Pettengill, Associate Director for Graduate Recruitment, 401-454-6312, Fax: 401-454-6309, E-mail: mpetteng@risd.edu. *Department Head,* Tim Veske-McMahon, 401-454-6190, Fax: 401-454-6191, E-mail: jewelry@risd.edu.

Department of Landscape Architecture Students: 74 full-time (52 women); includes 2 minority (both Asian, non-Hispanic/Latino), 61 international. Average age 24. 129 applicants, 84% accepted, 32 enrolled. Expenses: Contact institution. *Financial support:* Fellowships, research assistantships, teaching assistantships, Federal Work-Study, scholarships/grants, and unspecified assistantships available. Financial award application deadline: 2/1; financial award applicants required to submit FAFSA. In 2018, 26 master's awarded. Offers landscape architecture (MLA). *Application deadline:* For fall admission, 1/10 for domestic and international students. *Application fee:* $60. Electronic applications accepted. *Application Contact:* Molly Pettengill, Associate Director for Graduate Recruitment, 401-454-6312, Fax: 401-454-6309, E-mail: mpetteng@risd.edu. *Department Head,* Johanna Barthmeier-Payne, 401-454-6282, Fax: 401-454-6299, E-mail: ldardept@risd.edu.

Department of Painting Students: 19 full-time (8 women); includes 2 minority (1 Black or African American, non-Hispanic/Latino; 1 Hispanic/Latino), 3 international. Average age 27. 258 applicants, 7% accepted, 10 enrolled. Expenses: Contact institution. *Financial support:* Fellowships, research assistantships, teaching assistantships, Federal Work-Study, scholarships/grants, and unspecified assistantships available. Financial award application deadline: 2/1; financial award applicants required to submit FAFSA. In 2018, 10 master's awarded. Offers painting (MFA). *Application deadline:* For fall admission, 1/10 for domestic and international students. *Application fee:* $60. Electronic applications accepted. *Application Contact:* Molly Pettengill, Associate Director for Graduate Recruitment, 401-454-6312, Fax: 401-454-6309, E-mail: mpetteng@risd.edu. *Department Head,* Kevin Zucker, 401-454-6158, Fax: 401-454-6681, E-mail: painting@risd.edu.

Department of Photography Students: 15 full-time (8 women); includes 3 minority (1 Black or African American, non-Hispanic/Latino; 2 Hispanic/Latino), 5 international. Average age 26. 125 applicants, 18% accepted, 6 enrolled. Expenses: Contact institution. *Financial support:* Fellowships, research assistantships, teaching assistantships, Federal Work-Study, scholarships/grants, and unspecified assistantships available. Financial award application deadline: 2/1; financial award applicants required to submit FAFSA. In 2018, 7 master's awarded. Offers photography (MFA). *Application deadline:* For fall admission, 1/10 for domestic and international students. *Application fee:* $60. Electronic applications accepted. *Application Contact:* Molly Pettengill, Associate Director for Graduate Recruitment, 401-454-6312, Fax: 401-454-6309, E-mail: mpetteng@risd.edu. *Department Head,* Brian Ulrich, 401-454-6122, Fax: 401-454-6385, E-mail: photo@risd.edu.

Department of Printmaking Students: 13 full-time (9 women); includes 3 minority (1 Asian, non-Hispanic/Latino; 1 Hispanic/Latino; 1 Two or more races, non-Hispanic/Latino), 4 international. Average age 26. 44 applicants, 34% accepted, 8 enrolled. Expenses: Contact institution. *Financial support:* Fellowships, research assistantships, teaching assistantships, Federal Work-Study, scholarships/grants, and unspecified assistantships available. Financial award application deadline: 2/1; financial award applicants required to submit FAFSA. In 2018, 8 master's awarded. Offers printmaking (MFA). *Application deadline:* For fall admission, 1/10 for domestic and international students. *Application fee:* $60. Electronic applications accepted. *Application Contact:* Molly Pettengill, Associate Director for Graduate Recruitment, 401-454-6312, Fax: 401-454-6309, E-mail: mpetteng@risd.edu. *Department Head,* Cornelia McSheehy, 401-454-6224, Fax: 401-454-6707, E-mail: printmaking@risd.edu.

Department of Sculpture Students: 14 full-time (10 women); includes 4 minority (1 Asian, non-Hispanic/Latino; 2 Hispanic/Latino; 1 Two or more races, non-Hispanic/Latino), 7 international. Average age 28. 70 applicants, 17% accepted, 5 enrolled. Expenses: Contact institution. *Financial support:* Fellowships, research assistantships, teaching assistantships, Federal Work-Study, scholarships/grants, and unspecified assistantships available. Financial award application deadline: 2/1; financial award applicants required to submit FAFSA. In 2018, 4 master's awarded. Offers sculpture (MFA). *Application deadline:* For fall admission, 1/10 for domestic and international students. *Application fee:* $60. Electronic applications accepted. *Application Contact:* Molly Pettengill, Associate Director for Graduate Recruitment, 401-454-6312, Fax: 401-454-6309, E-mail: mpetteng@risd.edu. *Department Head,* Lisi Raskin, 401-454-6190, Fax: 401-454-6191, E-mail: sculpture@risd.edu.

Department of Teaching and Learning in Art and Design Students: 11 full-time (all women); includes 3 minority (2 Asian, non-Hispanic/Latino; 1 Hispanic/Latino), 4 international. Average age 25. 26 applicants, 69% accepted, 11 enrolled. Expenses: Contact institution. *Financial support:* Fellowships, research assistantships, teaching assistantships, Federal Work-Study, scholarships/grants, and unspecified assistantships available. Financial award application deadline: 2/1; financial award applicants required to submit FAFSA. In 2018, 21 master's awarded. Offers art education (MAT). *Application deadline:* For fall admission, 1/10 for domestic and international students. *Application fee:* $60. Electronic applications accepted. *Application Contact:* Molly Pettengill, Associate Director for Graduate Recruitment, 401-454-6312, Fax: 401-454-6309, E-mail: mpetteng@risd.edu. *Department Head and Graduate Program Director,* Paul Sproll, 401-454-6695, Fax: 401-454-6694, E-mail: teachlearn@risd.edu.

Department of Textiles Students: 10 full-time (8 women); includes 2 minority (1 Black or African American, non-Hispanic/Latino; 1 Two or more races, non-Hispanic/Latino), 5 international. Average age 28. 49 applicants, 16% accepted, 5 enrolled. Expenses: Contact institution. *Financial support:* Fellowships, research assistantships, teaching assistantships, Federal Work-Study, scholarships/grants, and unspecified assistantships available. Financial award application deadline: 2/1; financial award applicants required to submit FAFSA. In 2018, 6 master's awarded. Offers textiles (MFA). *Application deadline:* For fall admission, 1/10 for domestic and international students. *Application fee:* $60. Electronic applications accepted. *Application Contact:* Molly Pettengill, Associate Director for Graduate Recruitment, 401-454-6312, Fax: 401-454-6309, E-mail: mpetteng@risd.edu. *Department Head,* Anaïs Missakian, 401-427-6967, Fax: 401-277-4883, E-mail: textiles@risd.edu.

RHODES COLLEGE, Memphis, TN 38112-1690

General Information Independent, coed, comprehensive institution. *Enrollment:* 2,035 graduate, professional, and undergraduate students; 25 full-time matriculated graduate/professional students (10 women), 3 part-time matriculated graduate/professional students (2 women). *Enrollment by degree level:* 22 master's, 6 other advanced degrees. *Graduate faculty:* 7 full-time (all women), 2 part-time/adjunct (0 women). *Tuition:* Full-time $47,580. *Required fees:* $310. *Graduate housing:* Room and/or apartments available on a first-come, first-served basis to single students; on-campus housing not available to married students. Typical cost: $11,403 (including board). Housing application deadline: 3/1. *Student services:* Campus employment opportunities, campus safety program, career counseling, exercise/wellness program, free psychological counseling, international student services, low-cost health insurance, multicultural affairs office, services for students with disabilities, writing training. *Library facilities:* Paul Barret, Jr. Library. *Collection:* Books: 246,054 (physical); Serial titles: 94,665 (digital/electronic); Databases: 151. Weekly public service hours: 113.

Computer facilities: 1,000 computers available on campus for general student use. A campuswide network can be accessed from student residence rooms and from off campus. Online class registration is available.
Website: http://www.rhodes.edu/

General Application Contact: Dr. Pamela H. Church, Program Director, 901-843-3863, Fax: 901-843-3736, E-mail: church@rhodes.edu.

GRADUATE UNITS

Department of Business Students: 18 full-time (4 women); includes 2 minority (1 American Indian or Alaska Native, non-Hispanic/Latino; 1 Two or more races, non-Hispanic/Latino). Average age 22. *Faculty:* 2 full-time (both women), 2 part-time/adjunct (0 women). Expenses: Contact institution. *Financial support:* Career-related internships or fieldwork and scholarships/grants available. Financial award application deadline: 3/1; financial award applicants required to submit FAFSA. In 2018, 21 master's awarded. *Program availability:* Part-time. Offers accounting (MS). *Application deadline:* For fall admission, 3/1 for domestic students. Electronic applications accepted. *Application Contact:* Dr. Pamela H. Church, Program Director, 901-843-3863, Fax: 901-843-3798, E-mail: church@rhodes.edu.

RICE UNIVERSITY, Houston, TX 77251-1892

General Information Independent, coed, university. CGS member. *Graduate housing:* Rooms and/or apartments available on a first-come, first-served basis to single and married students. Housing application deadline: 7/15. *Research affiliation:* Fermi National Accelerator Laboratory, Los Alamos National Laboratory, Brookhaven National Laboratory, Arecibo Observatory, Houston Area Research Center.

GRADUATE UNITS

Graduate Programs *Program availability:* Part-time. Offers education (MAT). Electronic applications accepted.

George R. Brown School of Engineering *Program availability:* Part-time. Offers bioengineering (MS, PhD); bioinformatics (PhD); biostatistics (PhD); chemical and biomolecular engineering (MS, PhD); chemical engineering (M Ch E); circuits, controls, and communication systems (MS, PhD); civil engineering (MCE, MS, PhD); computational and applied mathematics (MA, MCAM, PhD); computational finance (PhD); computational science and engineering (PhD); computer science (MCS, MS, PhD); computer science and engineering (MS, PhD); electrical engineering (MEE); engineering (M Ch E, M Stat, MA, MBE, MCAM, MCE, MCS, MEE, MEE, MES, MME, MMS, MS, PhD); environmental engineering (MEE, MES, MS, PhD); environmental science (MEE, MES, MS, PhD); general statistics (PhD); lasers, microwaves, and solid-state electronics (MS, PhD); materials science (MMS, MS, PhD); mechanical engineering (MME, MS, PhD); statistics (M Stat, MA). MD/PhD offered jointly with Baylor College of Medicine, The University of Texas Health Science Center at Houston. Electronic applications accepted.

Jesse H. Jones Graduate School of Business *Program availability:* Evening/weekend. Offers business administration (EMBA, MBA, PMBA). Electronic applications accepted.

School of Architecture Offers architecture (M Arch, D Arch); urban design (M Arch). Electronic applications accepted.

School of Humanities Offers African religions (PhD); African-American religions (PhD); art history (PhD); contemplative studies (PhD); English (MA, PhD); ghosticism, esotericism, mysticism (PhD); history (MA, PhD); humanities (MA, PhD); Islam (PhD); Jewish thought and philosophy (PhD); linguistics (MA, PhD); modern Christianity in thought and popular culture (PhD); philosophy (MA, PhD); psychology of religion (PhD); the Bible and beyond (PhD).

School of Social Sciences Offers archaeology (MA, PhD); cognitive sciences (MA, PhD); economics (PhD); energy economics (MEECON); industrial-organizational/social psychology (MA, PhD); political science (PhD); psychology (MA, PhD); social sciences (MA, MEECON, PhD); social-cultural anthropology (MA, PhD); sociology (PhD).

Shepherd School of Music Offers composition (MM, DMA); conducting (MM); musicology (MM); performance (MM, DMA); theory (MM).

Susanne M. Glasscock School of Continuing Studies *Program availability:* Part-time, evening/weekend. Offers liberal studies (MLS).

Wiess School of Natural Sciences *Program availability:* Part-time. Offers biochemistry and cell biology (MA, PhD); chemistry (MA); earth science (MS, PhD); ecology and evolutionary biology (MA, MS, PhD); inorganic chemistry (PhD); mathematics (PhD); nanoscale physics (MS); natural sciences (MA, MS, MST, PhD); organic chemistry (PhD); physical chemistry (PhD); physics and astronomy (PhD); science teaching (MST). Electronic applications accepted.

Wiess School–Professional Science Master's Programs Offers bioscience research and health policy (MS); environmental analysis and decision making (MS); geophysics (MS); nanoscale physics (MS); professional science (MS).

Rice Quantum Institute Offers quantum physics (MS, PhD). Electronic applications accepted.

RICHMOND, THE AMERICAN INTERNATIONAL UNIVERSITY IN LONDON, Richmond, Surrey TW10 6JP, United Kingdom

General Information Independent, coed, comprehensive institution. *Graduate housing:* Room and/or apartments available on a first-come, first-served basis to single students; on-campus housing not available to married students. Housing application deadline: 8/1.

GRADUATE UNITS

MA in Art History Program *Program availability:* Part-time. Offers art history (MA). Electronic applications accepted.

MA in International Relations Program *Program availability:* Part-time. Offers international relations (MA). Electronic applications accepted.

RICHMONT GRADUATE UNIVERSITY, Atlanta, GA 30339

General Information Independent-religious, coed, graduate-only institution.

GRADUATE UNITS

School of Counseling *Program availability:* Part-time, evening/weekend. Offers clinical mental health counseling (MA); marriage and family therapy (MA). Electronic applications accepted.

School of Ministry *Program availability:* Part-time, evening/weekend, 100% online, blended/hybrid learning. Offers ministry (MA); spiritual direction (Graduate Certificate); spiritual formation and direction (MA). Electronic applications accepted.

RIDER UNIVERSITY, Lawrenceville, NJ 08648-3001

General Information Independent, coed, comprehensive institution. *Enrollment:* 4,825 graduate, professional, and undergraduate students; 305 full-time matriculated graduate/professional students (199 women), 622 part-time matriculated graduate/professional students (411 women). *Enrollment by degree level:* 797 master's, 33 doctoral, 91 other advanced degrees. *Tuition:* Full-time $850; part-time $850 per credit hour. *Required fees:* $50; $50 per course. Tuition and fees vary according to program. *Graduate housing:* Room and/or apartments available on a first-come, first-served basis to single students; on-campus housing not available to married students. Typical cost: $6540 per year ($9300 including board). Room and board charges vary according to board plan, campus/location and housing facility selected. *Student services:* Campus employment opportunities, campus safety program, career counseling, exercise/wellness program, free psychological counseling, international student services, multicultural affairs office, services for students with disabilities. *Library facilities:* Franklin F. Moore Library plus 1 other. *Collection:* Books: 311,713 (physical), 174,115 (digital/electronic); Serial titles: 723 (physical), 54,382 (digital/electronic); Databases: 171. Study areas open 24 hours, 5–7 days a week; students can reserve study rooms.

Computer facilities: Computer purchase and lease plans are available. 300 computers available on campus for general student use. A campuswide network can be accessed. Online class registration is available.
Website: http://www.rider.edu/

General Application Contact: Jamie L. Mitchell, Director of Graduate and Continuing Studies Admission, 609-896-5036, Fax: 609-895-5680, E-mail: jmitchell@rider.edu.

GRADUATE UNITS

College of Business Administration Students: 72 full-time (33 women), 178 part-time (80 women); includes 56 minority (21 Black or African American, non-Hispanic/Latino; 1 American Indian or Alaska Native, non-Hispanic/Latino; 15 Asian, non-Hispanic/Latino;

14 Hispanic/Latino; 5 Two or more races, non-Hispanic/Latino), 28 international. Average age 31. 153 applicants, 76% accepted, 63 enrolled. Expenses: Contact institution. *Financial support:* Applicants required to submit FAFSA. In 2018, 84 master's, 6 other advanced degrees awarded. *Program availability:* Part-time, evening/weekend. Offers accountancy (M Acc, Certificate); business administration (EMBA, M Acc, MBA, MS, Certificate); corporate finance (MS). *Application deadline:* For fall admission, 8/1 priority date for domestic students, 3/15 priority date for international students; for spring admission, 12/1 priority date for domestic students, 11/1 priority date for international students. Applications are processed on a rolling basis. *Application fee:* $50. Electronic applications accepted. *Application Contact:* Jamie L. Mitchell, Director of Graduate Admissions, 609-896-5036, Fax: 609-895-5680, E-mail: jmitchell@rider.edu. *Dean,* Dr. Eugene Kutcher, 609-895-5152, E-mail: ekutcher@rider.edu.

College of Continuing Studies

College of Education and Human Services Students: 137 full-time (112 women), 292 part-time (226 women); includes 103 minority (49 Black or African American, non-Hispanic/Latino; 2 American Indian or Alaska Native, non-Hispanic/Latino; 11 Asian, non-Hispanic/Latino; 38 Hispanic/Latino; 3 Two or more races, non-Hispanic/Latino). Average age 33. 279 applicants, 67% accepted, 117 enrolled. Expenses: Contact institution. *Financial support:* In 2018–19, 316 students received support. Applicants required to submit FAFSA. In 2018, 144 master's, 137 other advanced degrees awarded. *Program availability:* Part-time, evening/weekend. Offers bilingual education (MAT); clinical mental health counseling (MA); developing people and organizations (MA); director of counseling services (Ed S); early childhood education (MAT); education and human services (MA, MAT, Certificate, Ed S); elementary education (MAT); English as a second language (MAT); life and career coaching (MA); school counseling (MA, Certificate, Ed S); school psychology (Certificate, Ed S); secondary education (MAT); special education (MA); teacher of students with disabilities (Certificate); world language (MAT). *Application deadline:* For fall admission, 5/1 priority date for domestic students, 3/15 priority date for international students; for spring admission, 10/1 priority date for domestic students, 11/1 priority date for international students. Applications are processed on a rolling basis. *Application fee:* $50. Electronic applications accepted. *Application Contact:* Jamie L. Mitchell, Director of Graduate Admissions, 609-896-5036, Fax: 609-895-5680, E-mail: jmitchell@rider.edu. *Dean,* Dr. Sharon J. Sherman, 609-895-5048, E-mail: ssherman@rider.edu.

College of Liberal Arts and Sciences Students: 24 full-time (15 women), 117 part-time (87 women); includes 39 minority (15 Black or African American, non-Hispanic/Latino; 6 Asian, non-Hispanic/Latino; 14 Hispanic/Latino; 4 Two or more races, non-Hispanic/Latino), 6 international. Average age 30. 98 applicants, 69% accepted, 58 enrolled. Expenses: Contact institution. *Financial support:* Applicants required to submit FAFSA. In 2018, 65 master's awarded. *Program availability:* Part-time, evening/weekend. Offers business communication studies (MA); domestic security (MA); global security (MA); health communication (MA); liberal arts and sciences (MA). *Application deadline:* For fall admission, 8/1 priority date for domestic students; for spring admission, 12/1 priority date for domestic students. Applications are processed on a rolling basis. *Application fee:* $50. Electronic applications accepted. *Application Contact:* Jamie L. Mitchell, Director of Graduate Admissions, 609-896-5036, Fax: 609-895-5680, E-mail: jmitchell@rider.edu. *Dean,* Kelly Bidle, 609-895-5418, E-mail: kbidle@rider.edu.

School of Fine and Performing Arts Expenses: Contact institution. Offers arts management and executive leadership (MA). *Application Contact:* Jamie L. Mitchell, Director of Graduate and Continuing Studies Admission, 609-896-5036, Fax: 609-895-5680, E-mail: jmitchell@rider.edu. *Interim Program Director,* Todd Dellinger, 609-896-5246, E-mail: tdellinger@rider.edu.

Westminster Choir College Students: 59 full-time (35 women), 14 part-time (10 women); includes 10 minority (1 Black or African American, non-Hispanic/Latino; 3 Asian, non-Hispanic/Latino; 1 Hispanic/Latino; 1 Native Hawaiian or other Pacific Islander, non-Hispanic/Latino; 4 Two or more races, non-Hispanic/Latino), 9 international. Average age 29. 82 applicants, 60% accepted, 20 enrolled. Expenses: Contact institution. In 2018, 60 master's awarded. Offers American and public musicology (MM); choral conducting (MM); composition (MM); music (MM, MME, MVP); music education (MME); organ performance (MM); piano accompanying and coaching (MM); piano pedagogy and performance (MM); piano performance (MM); sacred music (MM); voice pedagogy and performance (MM, MVP). *Application deadline:* For fall admission, 5/1 priority date for domestic students, 3/15 priority date for international students; for spring admission, 11/1 priority date for domestic and international students. Applications are processed on a rolling basis. *Application fee:* $50. Electronic applications accepted. *Application Contact:* Kimberly Apadula, Assistant Director, WCC Admissions, 609-921-7100, Fax: 609-921-2538, E-mail: wccadmission@rider.edu. *Dean,* Dr. Marshall Onofrio, 609-921-7100 Ext. 8206, E-mail: monofrio@rider.edu.

RIVIER UNIVERSITY, Nashua, NH 03060

General Information Independent-religious, coed, comprehensive institution. *Graduate housing:* On-campus housing not available.

GRADUATE UNITS

School of Graduate Studies *Program availability:* Part-time. Offers business administration (MBA); clinical psychology (MS); computer information systems (MS); computer science (MS); curriculum and instruction (M Ed); early childhood education (M Ed); educational administration (M Ed); educational studies (M Ed); elementary education (M Ed); elementary education and general special education (M Ed); emotional and behavioral disorders (M Ed); English (MAT); experimental psychology (MS); general social education (M Ed); leadership and learning (Ed D, CAGS); learning disabilities (M Ed); learning disabilities and reading (M Ed); mathematics (MAT); mental health counseling (MA); reading (M Ed); school counseling (M Ed); social studies education (MAT); Spanish (MAT); writing and literature (MA). Electronic applications accepted.

Division of Nursing and Health Professions *Program availability:* Part-time, evening/weekend. Offers family nurse practitioner (MS); leadership in health systems management (MS); nursing education (MS); nursing practice (DNP); psychiatric/mental health nurse practitioner (MS); public health (MPH). Electronic applications accepted.

THE ROBERT E. WEBBER INSTITUTE FOR WORSHIP STUDIES, Jacksonville, FL 32207

General Information Independent-religious, coed, graduate-only institution.

GRADUATE UNITS

Doctor of Worship Studies Program Offers worship studies (DWS).

Master of Worship Studies Program Offers worship studies (MWS).

ROBERT MORRIS UNIVERSITY, Moon Township, PA 15108-1189

General Information Independent, coed, university. *Enrollment:* 890 part-time matriculated graduate/professional students (482 women). *Enrollment by degree level:* 617 master's, 273 doctoral, 42 other advanced degrees. *Graduate faculty:* 70 full-time (31 women), 16 part-time/adjunct (4 women). *Tuition:* Part-time $925 per credit hour. *Required fees:* $80 per credit hour. Tuition and fees vary according to degree level. *Graduate housing:* On-campus housing not available. *Student services:* Campus employment opportunities, campus safety program, career counseling, exercise/wellness program, international student services, multicultural affairs office, services for students with disabilities, teacher training. *Library facilities:* Robert Morris University Library. *Collection:* Books: 97,693 (physical), 172,931 (digital/electronic); Serial titles: 244 (physical), 47,791 (digital/electronic); Databases: 104. Weekly public service hours: 101; study areas open 24 hours, 5–7 days a week; students can reserve study rooms.

Computer facilities: Computer purchase and lease plans are available. 375 computers available on campus for general student use. A campuswide network can be accessed from student residence rooms and from off campus. Online class registration, online payment are available.

Website: http://www.rmu.edu/

General Application Contact: Kellie L. Laurenzi, Associate Vice President, 412-397-5200, Fax: 412-397-2425, E-mail: graduateadmissions@rmu.edu.

GRADUATE UNITS

School of Business Students: 214 part-time (84 women); includes 12 minority (6 Black or African American, non-Hispanic/Latino; 5 Asian, non-Hispanic/Latino; 1 Two or more races, non-Hispanic/Latino), 7 international. Average age 30. 77 applicants, 97% accepted, 71 enrolled. *Faculty:* 18 full-time (7 women), 1 (woman) part-time/adjunct. Expenses: Contact institution. *Financial support:* Institutionally sponsored loans available. Support available to part-time students. Financial award application deadline: 5/1; financial award applicants required to submit FAFSA. In 2018, 83 master's awarded. *Program availability:* Part-time-only, evening/weekend, 100% online. Offers business administration (MBA); human resource management (MS); taxation (MS). *Application deadline:* For fall admission, 7/1 priority date for domestic and international students; for spring admission, 11/1 priority date for domestic and international students. Applications are processed on a rolling basis. *Application fee:* $35. Electronic applications accepted. *Application Contact:* Dr. Jodi Potter, Director, MBA Program, 412-397-6387, E-mail: potterj@rmu.edu. *Dean,* Dr. Michelle L. Patrick, 412-397-5445, Fax: 412-397-2585, E-mail: patrick@rmu.edu.

School of Engineering, Mathematics and Science Students: 20 part-time (4 women); includes 1 minority (Black or African American, non-Hispanic/Latino), 9 international. Average age 28. 34 applicants, 18% accepted, 6 enrolled. *Faculty:* 7 full-time (1 woman), 1 part-time/adjunct (0 women). Expenses: Contact institution. *Financial support:* Federal Work-Study, institutionally sponsored loans, and unspecified assistantships available. Financial award application deadline: 5/1; financial award applicants required to submit FAFSA. In 2018, 33 master's awarded. *Program availability:* Part-time-only, evening/weekend, 100% online. Offers engineering management (MS). *Application deadline:* For fall admission, 7/1 priority date for domestic and international students; for spring admission, 11/1 priority date for domestic and international students. Applications are processed on a rolling basis. *Application fee:* $35. Electronic applications accepted. *Application Contact:* Dr. Maria V. Kalevitch, Dean, 412-397-4020, E-mail: kalevitch@rmu.edu. *Dean,* Dr. Maria V. Kalevitch, 412-397-4020, E-mail: kalevitch@rmu.edu.

School of Informatics, Humanities and Social Sciences Students: 262 part-time (94 women); includes 57 minority (31 Black or African American, non-Hispanic/Latino; 13 Asian, non-Hispanic/Latino; 8 Hispanic/Latino; 5 Two or more races, non-Hispanic/Latino), 43 international. Average age 35. 150 applicants, 92% accepted, 79 enrolled. *Faculty:* 22 full-time (7 women), 10 part-time/adjunct (0 women). Expenses: Contact institution. *Financial support:* Institutionally sponsored loans available. Support available to part-time students. Financial award application deadline: 5/1; financial award applicants required to submit FAFSA. In 2018, 133 master's, 11 doctorates awarded. *Program availability:* Part-time-only, evening/weekend, 100% online. Offers communication and information systems (MS); cyber security (MS); data analytics (MS); information security and assurance (MS); information systems and communications (D Sc); information systems management (MS); information technology project management (MS); Internet information systems (MS); organizational leadership (MS). *Application deadline:* For fall admission, 7/1 priority date for domestic and international students; for spring admission, 11/1 priority date for domestic and international students. Applications are processed on a rolling basis. *Application fee:* $35. Electronic applications accepted. *Application Contact:* Jon A. Radermacher, Interim Dean, School of Informatics, Humanities and Social Sciences, 412-397-4088, E-mail: radermacher@rmu.edu. *Interim Dean, School of Informatics, Humanities and Social Sciences,* Jon A. Radermacher, 412-397-4088, E-mail: radermacher@rmu.edu.

School of Nursing, Education and Human Studies Students: 393 part-time (300 women); includes 47 minority (27 Black or African American, non-Hispanic/Latino; 7 Asian, non-Hispanic/Latino; 5 Hispanic/Latino; 8 Two or more races, non-Hispanic/Latino), 5 international. Average age 35. 130 applicants, 86% accepted, 86 enrolled. *Faculty:* 23 full-time (16 women), 4 part-time/adjunct (3 women). Expenses: Contact institution. *Financial support:* Federal Work-Study, institutionally sponsored loans, and unspecified assistantships available. Financial award application deadline: 5/1; financial award applicants required to submit FAFSA. In 2018, 53 master's, 43 doctorates awarded. *Program availability:* Part-time-only, evening/weekend, 100% online. Offers nursing and health sciences (MSN, DNP). *Application deadline:* For fall admission, 7/1 priority date for domestic and international students; for spring admission, 11/1 priority date for domestic and international students. Applications are processed on a rolling basis. *Application fee:* $35. Electronic applications accepted. *Application Contact:* Dr. George W. Semich, Interim Dean, School of Nursing, Education and Human Studies, 412-397-6032, E-mail: semich@rmu.edu. *Interim Dean, School of Nursing, Education and Human Studies,* Dr. George W. Semich, 412-397-6032, E-mail: semich@rmu.edu.

See Display on the next page and Close-Up on page 741.

ROBERT MORRIS UNIVERSITY ILLINOIS, Chicago, IL 60605

General Information Independent, coed, comprehensive institution. *Graduate housing:* Room and/or apartments available to single students.

GRADUATE UNITS

Morris Graduate School of Management *Program availability:* Part-time, evening/weekend. Offers accounting (MBA); accounting/finance (MBA); business analytics (MIS); health care administration (MM); higher education administration (MM); human performance (MS); human resource management (MBA); information security (MIS); information systems management (MIS); law enforcement administration (MM); management (MBA); management/finance (MBA); management/human resource management (MBA); sports administration (MM). Electronic applications accepted.

ROBERTS WESLEYAN COLLEGE, Rochester, NY 14624-1997

General Information Independent-religious, coed, comprehensive institution. *Graduate housing:* Rooms and/or apartments available on a first-come, first-served basis to single and married students.

GRADUATE UNITS

Department of Nursing *Program availability:* Evening/weekend, online learning. Offers nursing education (MSN); nursing informatics (MSN); nursing leadership and administration (MSN). Electronic applications accepted.

Department of Social Work Offers child and family practice (MSW); mental health practice (MSW).

Graduate Business Programs *Program availability:* Evening/weekend. Offers strategic leadership (MS); strategic marketing (MS).

Graduate Psychology Programs *Program availability:* Part-time, evening/weekend. Offers clinical/school psychology (Psy D); school counseling (MS); school psychology (MS). Electronic applications accepted.

Graduate Teacher Education Programs *Program availability:* Part-time, evening/weekend. Offers adolescence and special education (M Ed); childhood and special education (M Ed); literacy education (M Ed); special education (M Ed). Electronic applications accepted.

Health Administration Programs *Program availability:* Evening/weekend, online learning. Offers health administration (MS); healthcare informatics administration (MS).

ROCHESTER COLLEGE, Rochester Hills, MI 48307-2764

General Information Independent-religious, coed, comprehensive institution.

GRADUATE UNITS

Center for Missional Leadership Offers missional leadership (MRE).

ROCHESTER INSTITUTE OF TECHNOLOGY, Rochester, NY 14623-5603

General Information Independent, coed, university. CGS member. *Enrollment:* 16,463 graduate, professional, and undergraduate students; 2,247 full-time matriculated graduate/professional students (862 women), 869 part-time matriculated graduate/professional students (358 women). *Enrollment by degree level:* 2,814 master's, 277 doctoral, 25 other advanced degrees. *Graduate housing:* Rooms and/or apartments available on a first-come, first-served basis to single and married students. *Student services:* Campus employment opportunities, campus safety program, career counseling, child daycare facilities, exercise/wellness program, free psychological counseling, grant writing training, international student services, low-cost health insurance, multicultural affairs office, services for students with disabilities, teacher training, writing training. *Library facilities:* Wallace Memorial Library. *Collection:* Books: 429,176 (physical), 240,712 (digital/electronic); Serial titles: 58,293 (digital/electronic); Databases: 113. Weekly public service hours: 147; study areas open 24 hours, 5–7 days a week; students can reserve study rooms.

Computer facilities: Computer purchase and lease plans are available. 3,500 computers available on campus for general student use. A campuswide network can be accessed from student residence rooms and from off campus. Online class registration, student account information are available.
Website: http://www.rit.edu/

General Application Contact: Diane Ellison, Senior Associate Vice President, Graduate Enrollment Services, 585-475-2229, Fax: 585-475-7164, E-mail: gradinfo@rit.edu.

GRADUATE UNITS

Graduate Enrollment Services Students: 2,259 full-time (823 women), 903 part-time (326 women); includes 215 minority (46 Black or African American, non-Hispanic/Latino; 2 American Indian or Alaska Native, non-Hispanic/Latino; 76 Asian, non-Hispanic/Latino; 57 Hispanic/Latino; 34 Two or more races, non-Hispanic/Latino), 1,790 international. Average age 27. 4,415 applicants, 58% accepted, 904 enrolled. Expenses: Contact institution. *Financial support:* In 2018–19, 2,338 students received support. Research assistantships, teaching assistantships, career-related internships or fieldwork, scholarships/grants, health care benefits, and unspecified assistantships available. Support available to part-time students. Financial award applicants required to submit FAFSA. In 2018, 944 master's, 9 doctorates, 86 other advanced degrees awarded. *Program availability:* Part-time, evening/weekend, 100% online, blended/hybrid learning. *Application deadline:* Applications are processed on a rolling basis. *Application fee:* $65. Electronic applications accepted. *Application Contact:* Dr. Diane Ellison, Senior Associate Vice President, Graduate Enrollment Services, 585-475-2229, Fax: 585-475-7164, E-mail: gradinfo@rit.edu. *Senior Associate Vice President, Graduate Enrollment Services,* Dr. Diane Ellison, 585-475-2229, Fax: 585-475-7164, E-mail: gradinfo@rit.edu.

College of Applied Science and Technology Students: 160 full-time (47 women), 60 part-time (16 women); includes 20 minority (6 Black or African American, non-Hispanic/Latino; 5 Asian, non-Hispanic/Latino; 6 Hispanic/Latino; 3 Two or more races, non-Hispanic/Latino), 161 international. Average age 26. 253 applicants, 79% accepted, 67 enrolled. Expenses: Contact institution. *Financial support:* In 2018–19, 184 students received support. Teaching assistantships with partial tuition reimbursements available, career-related internships or fieldwork, scholarships/grants, and unspecified assistantships available. Support available to part-time students. Financial award applicants required to submit FAFSA. In 2018, 100 master's awarded. *Program availability:* Part-time, evening/weekend, 100% online, blended/hybrid learning. Offers applied science and technology (MS, Advanced Certificate); engineering technology (MS); environmental, health and safety management (MS); hospitality and tourism management (MS); human resources development (MS); international hospitality and service innovation (MS, Advanced Certificate); manufacturing and mechanical systems integration (MS); organizational learning (Advanced Certificate); packaging science (MS); service leadership and innovation (MS); telecommunications engineering technology (MS); workplace learning and instruction (Advanced Certificate). *Application deadline:* Applications are processed on a rolling basis. *Application fee:* $65. Electronic applications accepted. *Application Contact:* Diane Ellison, Senior Associate Vice President, Graduate Enrollment Services, 585-475-2229, Fax: 585-475-7164, E-mail: gradinfo@rit.edu. *Interim Dean,* Dr. S. Manian Ramkumar, 585-475-5955, E-mail: smrmet@rit.edu.

College of Health Sciences and Technology Students: 18 full-time (15 women), 18 part-time (13 women); includes 11 minority (3 Black or African American, non-Hispanic/Latino; 4 Asian, non-Hispanic/Latino; 4 Hispanic/Latino), 4 international. Average age 30. 17 applicants, 94% accepted, 12 enrolled. Expenses: Contact institution. *Financial support:* In 2018–19, 16 students received support. Research assistantships with partial tuition reimbursements available, teaching assistantships with partial tuition reimbursements available, career-related internships or fieldwork,

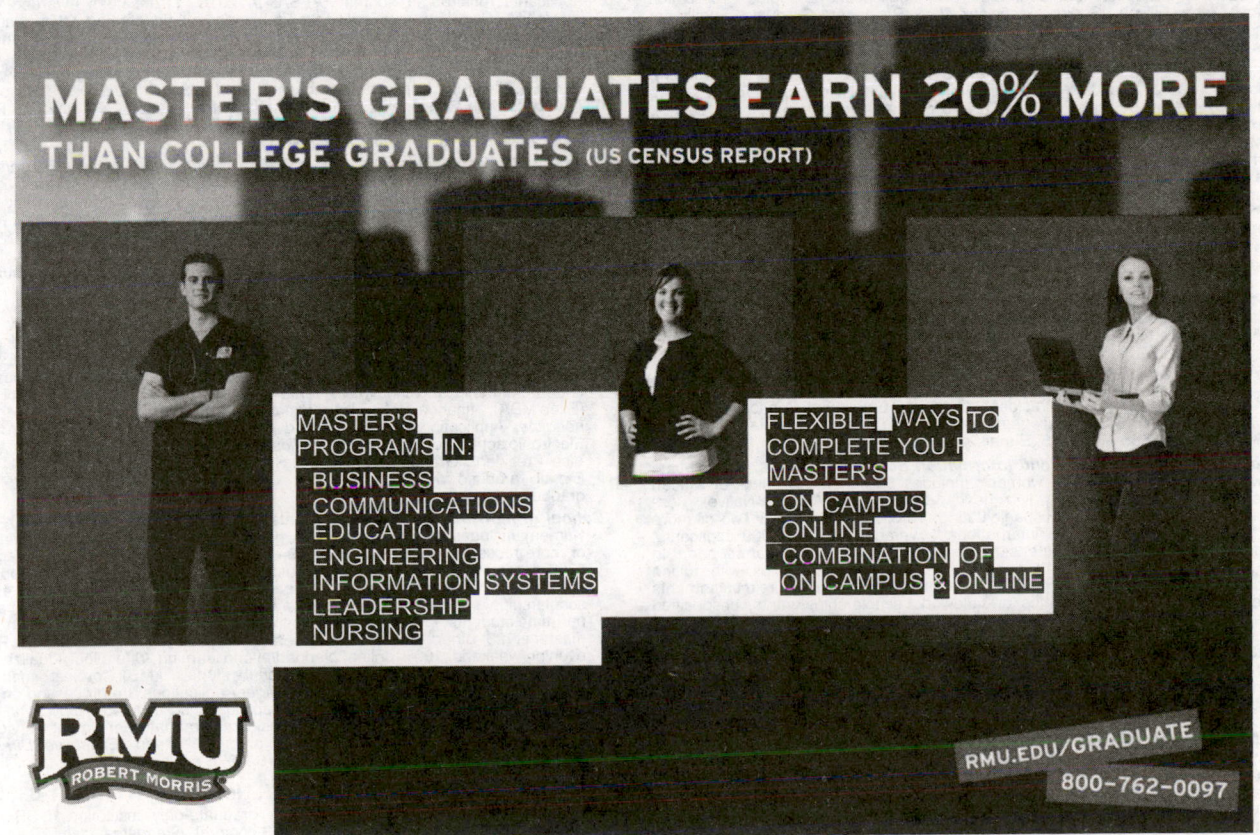

scholarships/grants, and unspecified assistantships available. Support available to part-time students. Financial award applicants required to submit FAFSA. In 2018, 10 master's, 4 other advanced degrees awarded. *Program availability:* Part-time, evening/weekend, 100% online. Offers health care finance (Advanced Certificate); health sciences and technology (MFA, MS, Advanced Certificate); health systems administration (MS); medical illustration (MFA). *Application deadline:* Applications are processed on a rolling basis. *Application fee:* $65. Electronic applications accepted. *Application Contact:* Diane Ellison, Senior Associate Vice President, Graduate Enrollment Services, 585-475-2229, Fax: 585-475-7164, E-mail: gradinfo@rit.edu. *Vice President and Dean, Institute and College of Health Sciences and Technology,* Dr. Daniel Ornt, 585-475-4017, Fax: 585-475-4330, E-mail: daniel.ornt@rit.edu.

College of Imaging Arts and Sciences Students: 207 full-time (140 women), 61 part-time (37 women); includes 23 minority (2 Black or African American, non-Hispanic/Latino; 7 Asian, non-Hispanic/Latino; 7 Hispanic/Latino; 7 Two or more races, non-Hispanic/Latino), 182 international. Average age 26. 586 applicants, 52% accepted, 101 enrolled. Expenses: Contact institution. *Financial support:* In 2018–19, 181 students received support. Teaching assistantships with partial tuition reimbursements available, career-related internships or fieldwork, scholarships/grants, and unspecified assistantships available. Support available to part-time students. Financial award applicants required to submit FAFSA. In 2018, 78 master's, 4 other advanced degrees awarded. *Program availability:* Part-time, 100% online. Offers American crafts (MFA); ceramics (MFA); design (MFA, Advanced Certificate); film and animation (MFA); fine arts studio (MFA); furniture design (MFA); glass (MFA); imaging arts and sciences (MFA, MS, MST, Advanced Certificate); industrial design (MFA); media arts and technology (MS); media sciences (MS); metals and jewelry design (MFA); photographic arts and sciences (MFA); photography and related media (MFA); print media (MS); user experience design and development (Advanced Certificate); visual arts-all grades (MST); visual communication design (MFA). *Application deadline:* For fall admission, 2/15 priority date for domestic and international students. Applications are processed on a rolling basis. *Application fee:* $65. Electronic applications accepted. *Application Contact:* Diane Ellison, Senior Associate Vice President, Graduate Enrollment Services, 585-475-2229, Fax: 585-475-7164, E-mail: gradinfo@rit.edu. *Interim Dean,* Dr. Robin Cass, 585-475-2683, E-mail: robin.cass@rit.edu.

College of Liberal Arts Students: 56 full-time (40 women), 23 part-time (16 women); includes 17 minority (6 Black or African American, non-Hispanic/Latino; 2 Asian, non-Hispanic/Latino; 2 Two or more races, non-Hispanic/Latino), 14 international. Average age 26. 113 applicants, 52% accepted, 34 enrolled. Expenses: Contact institution. *Financial support:* In 2018–19, 42 students received support. Research assistantships with partial tuition reimbursements available, teaching assistantships with partial tuition reimbursements available, career-related internships or fieldwork, scholarships/grants, and unspecified assistantships available. Support available to part-time students. Financial award applicants required to submit FAFSA. In 2018, 23 master's, 9 other advanced degrees awarded. *Program availability:* Part-time, 100% online. Offers communication and digital media (Advanced Certificate); communication and media technologies (MS); criminal justice (MS); engineering psychology (Advanced Certificate); experimental psychology (MS); liberal arts (MS, Advanced Certificate); school psychology (MS, Advanced Certificate); science, technology and public policy (MS). *Application deadline:* For fall admission, 2/15 priority date for domestic and international students; for spring admission, 12/15 priority date for domestic and international students. Applications are processed on a rolling basis. *Application fee:* $65. Electronic applications accepted. *Application Contact:* Diane Ellison, Senior Associate Vice President, Graduate Enrollment Services, 585-475-2229, Fax: 585-475-7164, E-mail: gradinfo@rit.edu. *Dean,* Dr. James Winebrake, 585-475-2929, Fax: 585-475-7120, E-mail: libarts@rit.edu.

College of Science Students: 221 full-time (95 women), 110 part-time (37 women); includes 29 minority (2 Black or African American, non-Hispanic/Latino; 12 Asian, non-Hispanic/Latino; 8 Hispanic/Latino; 7 Two or more races, non-Hispanic/Latino), 129 international. Average age 27. 497 applicants, 41% accepted, 87 enrolled. Expenses: Contact institution. *Financial support:* In 2018–19, 251 students received support. Research assistantships, teaching assistantships, career-related internships or fieldwork, institutionally sponsored loans, scholarships/grants, unspecified assistantships, and health care benefits (for PhD program only) available. Support available to part-time students. Financial award applicants required to submit FAFSA. In 2018, 47 master's, 3 doctorates awarded. *Program availability:* Part-time, evening/weekend, 100% online. Offers applied and computational mathematics (MS); applied statistics (MS, Advanced Certificate); astrophysical science and technology (MS, PhD); bioinformatics (MS); chemistry (MS); color science (MS, PhD); environmental science (MS); imaging science (MS, PhD); life sciences (MS); materials science and engineering (MS); mathematical modeling (PhD); science (MS, PhD, Advanced Certificate). *Application deadline:* For fall admission, 2/15 priority date for domestic and international students; for spring admission, 12/15 priority date for domestic and international students. Applications are processed on a rolling basis. *Application fee:* $65. Electronic applications accepted. *Application Contact:* Diane Ellison, Senior Associate Vice President, Graduate Enrollment Services, 585-475-2229, Fax: 585-475-7164, E-mail: gradinfo@rit.edu. *Dean,* Dr. Sophia Maggelakis, 585-475-5221, Fax: 585-475-2398, E-mail: science@rit.edu.

Golisano College of Computing and Information Sciences Students: 709 full-time (198 women), 192 part-time (62 women); includes 53 minority (7 Black or African American, non-Hispanic/Latino; 1 American Indian or Alaska Native, non-Hispanic/Latino; 24 Asian, non-Hispanic/Latino; 13 Hispanic/Latino; 8 Two or more races, non-Hispanic/Latino), 733 international. Average age 26. 2,369 applicants, 42% accepted, 262 enrolled. Expenses: Contact institution. *Financial support:* In 2018–19, 833 students received support. Research assistantships with tuition reimbursements available, teaching assistantships with tuition reimbursements available, career-related internships or fieldwork, scholarships/grants, unspecified assistantships, and health care benefits (for PhD program only) available. Support available to part-time students. Financial award applicants required to submit FAFSA. In 2018, 234 master's, 1 doctorate, 62 other advanced degrees awarded. *Program availability:* Part-time, evening/weekend, 100% online. Offers big data analytics (Advanced Certificate); computer science (MS, Advanced Certificate); computing and information sciences (PhD); computing security (MS); cybersecurity (Advanced Certificate); game design and development (MS); health informatics (MS); human computer interaction (MS); information sciences and technologies (MS); networking and systems administration (MS); networking, planning and design (Advanced Certificate); software engineering (MS); Web development (Advanced Certificate). *Application deadline:* For fall admission, 2/15 priority date for domestic and international students; for spring admission, 12/15 priority date for domestic and international students. Applications are processed on a rolling basis. *Application fee:* $65. Electronic applications accepted. *Application Contact:* Diane Ellison, Senior

Associate Vice President, Graduate Enrollment Services, 585-475-2229, Fax: 585-475-7164, E-mail: gradinfo@rit.edu. *Dean,* Dr. Anne Haake, 585-475-7203, Fax: 585-475-4775, E-mail: gccis-email@rit.edu.

Golisano Institute for Sustainability Students: 62 full-time (33 women), 21 part-time (10 women); includes 5 minority (1 Asian, non-Hispanic/Latino; 3 Hispanic/Latino; 1 Two or more races, non-Hispanic/Latino), 51 international. Average age 29. 164 applicants, 55% accepted, 22 enrolled. Expenses: Contact institution. *Financial support:* In 2018–19, 73 students received support. Research assistantships with tuition reimbursements available, teaching assistantships with tuition reimbursements available, career-related internships or fieldwork, scholarships/grants, unspecified assistantships, and health care benefits (for PhD program only) available. Support available to part-time students. Financial award applicants required to submit FAFSA. In 2018, 9 master's, 1 doctorate awarded. *Program availability:* Part-time. Offers architecture (M Arch); sustainability (PhD); sustainable systems (MS). *Application deadline:* For fall admission, 2/15 priority date for domestic and international students; for spring admission, 12/15 priority date for domestic and international students. Applications are processed on a rolling basis. *Application fee:* $65. Electronic applications accepted. *Application Contact:* Diane Ellison, Senior Associate Vice President, Graduate Enrollment Services, 585-475-2229, Fax: 585-475-7164, E-mail: gradinfo@rit.edu. *Associate Provost and Director,* Dr. Nabil Nasr, 585-475-5101, E-mail: info@sustainability.rit.edu.

Kate Gleason College of Engineering Students: 409 full-time (82 women), 182 part-time (29 women); includes 29 minority (4 Black or African American, non-Hispanic/Latino; 12 Asian, non-Hispanic/Latino; 12 Hispanic/Latino; 1 Two or more races, non-Hispanic/Latino), 315 international. Average age 26. 1,355 applicants, 39% accepted, 166 enrolled. Expenses: Contact institution. *Financial support:* In 2018–19, 489 students received support. Fellowships, research assistantships, teaching assistantships, career-related internships or fieldwork, scholarships/grants, tuition waivers (full and partial), unspecified assistantships, and health care benefits (for PhD program only) available. Support available to part-time students. Financial award applicants required to submit FAFSA. In 2018, 200 master's, 5 doctorates, 10 other advanced degrees awarded. *Program availability:* Part-time, evening/weekend, 100% online. Offers computer engineering (MS); electrical engineering (MS); engineering (ME, MS, PhD, Advanced Certificate); engineering management (ME); industrial and systems engineering (ME, MS); Lean Six Sigma (Advanced Certificate); manufacturing leadership (MS); mechanical engineering (ME, MS); microelectronic engineering (MS); microelectronic manufacturing engineering (ME); microsystems engineering (PhD); product development (MS); sustainable engineering (ME, MS). *Application deadline:* For fall admission, 2/15 priority date for domestic and international students. Applications are processed on a rolling basis. *Application fee:* $65. Electronic applications accepted. *Application Contact:* Diane Ellison, Senior Associate Vice President, Graduate Enrollment Services, 585-475-2229, Fax: 585-475-7164, E-mail: gradinfo@rit.edu. *Dean,* Dr. Doreen Edwards, 585-475-2145, Fax: 585-475-6879, E-mail: coe@rit.edu.

National Technical Institute for the Deaf Students: 17 full-time (12 women), 12 part-time (11 women); includes 4 minority (1 Asian, non-Hispanic/Latino; 3 Hispanic/Latino), 5 international. Average age 32. 24 applicants, 33% accepted, 5 enrolled. Expenses: Contact institution. *Financial support:* Fellowships with partial tuition reimbursements, research assistantships with partial tuition reimbursements, career-related internships or fieldwork, scholarships/grants, and unspecified assistantships available. Support available to part-time students. Financial award applicants required to submit FAFSA. In 2018, 11 master's awarded. *Program availability:* Part-time, evening/weekend, blended/hybrid learning. Offers deaf studies (MS); health care interpretation (MS); secondary education for the deaf and hard of hearing (MS). *Application deadline:* For fall admission, 2/15 priority date for domestic and international students. Applications are processed on a rolling basis. *Application fee:* $65. Electronic applications accepted. *Application Contact:* Diane Ellison, Senior Associate Vice President, Graduate Enrollment Services, 585-475-2229, Fax: 585-475-7164, E-mail: gradinfo@rit.edu. *President,* Dr. Gerard J. Buckley, 585-475-6317, Fax: 585-475-5978, E-mail: gbuckley@ntid.rit.edu.

Saunders College of Business Students: 221 full-time (102 women), 150 part-time (73 women); includes 38 minority (11 Black or African American, non-Hispanic/Latino; 13 Asian, non-Hispanic/Latino; 8 Hispanic/Latino; 6 Two or more races, non-Hispanic/Latino), 101 international. Average age 30. 588 applicants, 49% accepted, 138 enrolled. Expenses: Contact institution. *Financial support:* In 2018–19, 221 students received support. Research assistantships with partial tuition reimbursements available, teaching assistantships with partial tuition reimbursements available, career-related internships or fieldwork, Federal Work-Study, scholarships/grants, and unspecified assistantships available. Support available to part-time students. Financial award applicants required to submit FAFSA. In 2018, 145 master's awarded. *Program availability:* Part-time, evening/weekend, 100% online, blended/hybrid learning. Offers accounting (MBA, MS); business (Exec MBA, MBA, MS); business administration (MBA); computational finance (MS); entrepreneurship and innovative ventures (MS); executive business administration (Exec MBA); finance (MS); management (MS); marketing (MBA). *Application deadline:* Applications are processed on a rolling basis. *Application fee:* $65. Electronic applications accepted. *Application Contact:* Diane Ellison, Senior Associate Vice President, Graduate Enrollment Services, 585-475-2229, Fax: 585-475-7164, E-mail: gradinfo@rit.edu. *Dean,* Dr. Jacqueline Mozrall, 585-475-6025, E-mail: gradbus@saunders.rit.edu.

School of Individualized Study Students: 23 full-time (11 women), 70 part-time (40 women); includes 11 minority (5 Asian, non-Hispanic/Latino; 5 Hispanic/Latino; 1 Two or more races, non-Hispanic/Latino), 9 international. Average age 33. 60 applicants, 57% accepted, 15 enrolled. Expenses: Contact institution. *Financial support:* In 2018–19, 10 students received support. Career-related internships or fieldwork, scholarships/grants, and unspecified assistantships available. Support available to part-time students. Financial award applicants required to submit FAFSA. In 2018, 18 master's, 23 other advanced degrees awarded. *Program availability:* Part-time, evening/weekend, 100% online, blended/hybrid learning. Offers individualized studies (MS, Advanced Certificate); professional studies (MS); project management (Advanced Certificate). *Application deadline:* Applications are processed on a rolling basis. *Application fee:* $65. Electronic applications accepted. *Application Contact:* Diane Ellison, Senior Associate Vice President, Graduate Enrollment Services, 585-475-2229, Fax: 585-475-7164, E-mail: gradinfo@rit.edu. *Executive Director,* Dr. James Hall, 585-475-2295, Fax: 585-475-6292, E-mail: sois@rit.edu.

THE ROCKEFELLER UNIVERSITY, New York, NY 10021-6399

General Information Independent, coed, graduate-only institution. CGS member. *Enrollment by degree level:* 19 master's, 213 doctoral. *Graduate faculty:* 79 full-time (12 women). *Graduate housing:* Rooms and/or apartments guaranteed to single and married students. Housing application deadline: 6/1. *Student services:* Campus safety program, career counseling, child daycare facilities, exercise/wellness program, free psychological counseling, grant writing training, low-cost health insurance, teacher training. *Library facilities:* Rita and Frits Markus Library. *Collection:* Books: 44,511 (physical), 199,577 (digital/electronic); Serial titles: 7,202 (digital/electronic); Databases: 9. Weekly public service hours: 40; study areas open 24 hours, 5–7 days a week; students can reserve study rooms.

Computer facilities: 32 computers available on campus for general student use. A campuswide network can be accessed from student residence rooms and from off campus. Online class registration is available.
Website: http://www.rockefeller.edu/

General Application Contact: Kristen Cullen, Graduate Admissions Administrator/Registrar, 212-327-8086, Fax: 212-327-8505, E-mail: phd@rockefeller.edu.

GRADUATE UNITS

The David Rockefeller Graduate Program in Bioscience Students: 239 full-time (104 women); includes 55 minority (9 Black or African American, non-Hispanic/Latino; 24 Asian, non-Hispanic/Latino; 21 Hispanic/Latino; 1 Native Hawaiian or other Pacific Islander, non-Hispanic/Latino), 76 international. Average age 25. 1,017 applicants, 8% accepted, 32 enrolled. *Faculty:* 79 full-time (12 women). Expenses: Contact institution. *Financial support:* In 2018–19, 239 students received support, including 239 fellowships with full tuition reimbursements available; institutionally sponsored loans, scholarships/grants, traineeships, and health care benefits also available. In 2018, 6 master's, 30 doctorates awarded. Offers bioscience (MS, PhD). *Application deadline:* For fall and winter admission, 12/1 for domestic and international students. *Application fee:* $50. Electronic applications accepted. *Application Contact:* Kristen Cullen, Graduate Admissions Administrator/Registrar, 212-327-8086, Fax: 212-327-8505, E-mail: phd@rockefeller.edu. *Dean of Graduate and Postdoctoral Studies/Vice President,* Dr. Sidney Strickland, 212-327-8086, Fax: 212-327-8505, E-mail: phd@rockefeller.edu.

ROCKFORD UNIVERSITY, Rockford, IL 61108-2393

General Information Independent, coed, comprehensive institution. *Graduate housing:* Room and/or apartments available on a first-come, first-served basis to single students; on-campus housing not available to married students.

GRADUATE UNITS

Graduate Studies *Program availability:* Part-time, evening/weekend. Offers business administration (MBA); early childhood education (MAT); elementary education (MAT); instructional strategies (MAT); reading (MAT); secondary education (MAT); special education (MAT). Electronic applications accepted.

ROCKHURST UNIVERSITY, Kansas City, MO 64110-2561

General Information Independent-religious, coed, comprehensive institution. *Graduate housing:* Room and/or apartments available on a first-come, first-served basis to single students; on-campus housing not available to married students.

GRADUATE UNITS

College of Health and Human Services *Program availability:* Part-time, evening/weekend. Offers communication sciences and disorders (MS); education (M Ed); health and human services (M Ed, MOT, MS, DPT); occupational therapy (MOT); physical therapy (DPT).

Helzberg School of Management *Program availability:* Part-time, evening/weekend. Offers accounting (MBA); business intelligence (MBA, Certificate); business intelligence and analytics (MS); data science (MBA, Certificate); entrepreneurship (MBA); finance (MBA); fundraising leadership (MBA, Certificate); healthcare management (MBA, Certificate); human capital (Certificate); international business (Certificate); management (MA, MBA, Certificate); nonprofit administration (Certificate); organizational development (Certificate); science leadership (Certificate). Electronic applications accepted.

ROCKY MOUNTAIN COLLEGE, Billings, MT 59102-1796

General Information Independent-religious, coed, comprehensive institution. *Enrollment:* 997 graduate, professional, and undergraduate students; 89 full-time matriculated graduate/professional students (50 women), 3 part-time matriculated graduate/professional students (1 woman). *Enrollment by degree level:* 92 master's. *Graduate faculty:* 12 full-time (7 women), 2 part-time/adjunct (1 woman). *Tuition:* Full-time $28,962. *Required fees:* $590; $590. Tuition and fees vary according to degree level and program. *Graduate housing:* Rooms and/or apartments available on a first-come, first-served basis to single and married students. Typical cost: $7290 per year for single students; $7290 per year for married students. Room charges vary according to board plan and housing facility selected. *Student services:* Campus employment opportunities, campus safety program, career counseling, free psychological counseling, international student services, services for students with disabilities, teacher training, writing training. *Library facilities:* Paul M. Adams Memorial Library. *Collection:* Books: 46,877 (physical), 172,956 (digital/electronic); Serial titles: 379 (physical), 92,127 (digital/electronic); Databases: 119. Weekly public service hours: 89.

Computer facilities: 113 computers available on campus for general student use. A campuswide network can be accessed from student residence rooms and from off campus. Online class registration is available.
Website: http://www.rocky.edu/

General Application Contact: Austin Mapston, Dean of Enrollment Services, 406-657-1026, Fax: 406-657-1189, E-mail: admissions@rocky.edu.

GRADUATE UNITS

Program in Accountancy Students: 2 part-time (0 women); includes 1 minority (American Indian or Alaska Native, non-Hispanic/Latino). Average age 34. *Faculty:* 2 full-time (0 women). Expenses: Contact institution. *Financial support:* In 2018–19, 1 student received support. Campus work-study available. Financial award applicants required to submit FAFSA. In 2018, 6 master's awarded. *Program availability:* Part-time-only. Offers accountancy (M Acc). *Application deadline:* Applications are processed on a rolling basis. *Application fee:* $35 ($40 for international students). Electronic applications accepted. *Application Contact:* Austin Mapston, Dean of Enrollment Services, 406-657-1026, Fax: 406-657-1189, E-mail: admissions@rocky.edu. *Professor of Business Administration and Economics,* Anthony Piltz, 406-657-1069, E-mail: piltza@rocky.edu.

Program in Educational Leadership Students: 17 full-time (9 women), 1 (woman) part-time; includes 1 minority (Hispanic/Latino). Average age 33. *Faculty:* 2 full-time (both women). Expenses: Contact institution. *Financial support:* In 2018–19, 17 students received support. Scholarships/grants available. Financial award applicants required to submit FAFSA. In 2018, 18 master's awarded. Offers educational leadership (M Ed). *Application deadline:* Applications are processed on a rolling basis. *Application fee:* $35 ($40 for international students). Electronic applications accepted. *Application Contact:*

Austin Mapston, Dean of Enrollment Services, 406-657-1026, Fax: 406-657-1189, E-mail: admissions@rocky.edu. *Director of Educational Leadership and Distance Education,* Dr. Stevie Schmitz, 406-657-1134, E-mail: schmitzs@rocky.edu.

Program in Occupational Therapy *Faculty:* 2 full-time (both women). Expenses: Contact institution. *Financial support:* Unspecified assistantships and campus work-study available. Financial award applicants required to submit FAFSA. Offers occupational therapy (OTD). *Application deadline:* Applications are processed on a rolling basis. *Application fee:* $190. Electronic applications accepted. *Application Contact:* Cody Halverson, Coordinator of Admissions for Health Professions, 406-657-1198, E-mail: halversonc@rocky.edu. *Director,* Dr. Twylla M. Kirchen, 406-657-1165, E-mail: twylla.kirchen@rocky.edu.

Program in Physician Assistant Studies Students: 72 full-time (41 women); includes 7 minority (3 Asian, non-Hispanic/Latino; 2 Hispanic/Latino; 2 Two or more races, non-Hispanic/Latino). Average age 27. *Faculty:* 6 full-time (3 women), 2 part-time/adjunct (1 woman). Expenses: Contact institution. *Financial support:* Applicants required to submit FAFSA. In 2018, 36 master's awarded. Offers physician assistant studies (MPAS). *Application deadline:* Applications are processed on a rolling basis. *Application fee:* $45. Electronic applications accepted. *Application Contact:* Cody Halverson, Coordinator of Admissions for Health Professions, 406-657-1198, E-mail: halversonc@rocky.edu. *Program Director,* Heather Heggem, 406-657-1190, E-mail: heather.heggem@rocky.edu.

ROCKY MOUNTAIN COLLEGE OF ART + DESIGN, Lakewood, CO 80214

General Information Proprietary, coed, comprehensive institution.

GRADUATE UNITS

Program in Education, Leadership + Emerging Technologies *Program availability:* Online learning. Offers education, leadership and emerging technologies (MA).

ROCKY MOUNTAIN UNIVERSITY OF HEALTH PROFESSIONS, Provo, UT 84606

General Information Proprietary, coed, graduate-only institution. *Research affiliation:* Aegis Corporation.

GRADUATE UNITS

Doctor of Nursing Practice Program Offers nursing practice (DNP).

Doctor of Science Program in Clinical Electrophysiology *Program availability:* Online learning. Offers clinical electrophysiology (D Sc).

Program in Occupational Therapy *Program availability:* Online learning. Offers occupational therapy (OTD). Electronic applications accepted.

Program in Physician Assistant Studies Offers physician assistant studies (MPAS).

Program in Speech-Language Pathology Offers speech-language pathology (Clin Sc D).

Programs in Physical Therapy Offers physical therapy (DPT, TDPT).

ROCKY VISTA UNIVERSITY, Parker, CO 80134

General Information Proprietary, coed, graduate-only institution.

GRADUATE UNITS

College of Osteopathic Medicine Offers osteopathic medicine (DO).

Program in Biomedical Sciences Offers biomedical sciences (MS).

Program in Physician Assistant Studies Offers physician assistant studies (MPAS).

ROGERS STATE UNIVERSITY, Claremore, OK 74017-3252

General Information State-supported, coed, comprehensive institution.

GRADUATE UNITS

Program in Business Administration Offers business administration (MBA).

ROGER WILLIAMS UNIVERSITY, Bristol, RI 02809

General Information Independent, coed, comprehensive institution. *Enrollment:* 182 full-time matriculated graduate/professional students (106 women), 140 part-time matriculated graduate/professional students (75 women). *Enrollment by degree level:* 313 master's, 9 other advanced degrees. *Graduate faculty:* 49 full-time (19 women), 29 part-time/adjunct (8 women). *Graduate housing:* On-campus housing not available. *Student services:* Campus employment opportunities, campus safety program, career counseling, exercise/wellness program, free psychological counseling, international student services, low-cost health insurance, services for students with disabilities, teacher training. *Library facilities:* Roger Williams University Library plus 1 other. *Collection:* Books: 219,429 (physical), 448,637 (digital/electronic); Serial titles: 493 (physical), 52,585 (digital/electronic); Databases: 189. Weekly public service hours: 111; students can reserve study rooms.

Computer facilities: 100 computers available on campus for general student use. A campuswide network can be accessed from student residence rooms and from off campus. Online class registration is available.
Website: http://www.rwu.edu/

General Application Contact: Marcus Hanscom, Director of Graduate Admission, 401-254-3345, Fax: 401-254-3557, E-mail: mhanscom@rwu.edu.

GRADUATE UNITS

Feinstein School of Humanities, Arts and Education Students: 7 part-time (all women). Average age 36. 1 applicant, 100% accepted, 1 enrolled. *Faculty:* 5 full-time (4 women), 5 part-time/adjunct (2 women). Expenses: Contact institution. *Financial support:* Application deadline: 3/15; applicants required to submit FAFSA. In 2018, 6 master's awarded. *Program availability:* Part-time-only, evening/weekend. Offers literacy education (MA); middle school certification (Certificate). *Application deadline:* Applications are processed on a rolling basis. *Application fee:* $50. Electronic applications accepted. *Application Contact:* Marcus Hanscom, Director of Graduate Admissions, 401-254-3345, Fax: 401-254-3557, E-mail: gradadmit@rwu.edu. *Dean,* Dr. Cynthia Scheinberg, 401-254-3828, E-mail: cscheinberg@rwu.edu.

Feinstein School of Social and Natural Sciences Students: 41 full-time (34 women), 1 (woman) part-time; includes 10 minority (1 Black or African American, non-Hispanic/Latino; 2 Asian, non-Hispanic/Latino; 5 Hispanic/Latino; 1 Native Hawaiian or other Pacific Islander, non-Hispanic/Latino; 1 Two or more races, non-Hispanic/Latino). Average age 24. 99 applicants, 48% accepted, 20 enrolled. *Faculty:* 9 full-time (4 women), 2 part-time/adjunct (1 woman). Expenses: Contact institution. *Financial support:* In 2018–19, 18 students received support. Scholarships/grants and unspecified assistantships available. Financial award application deadline: 3/16; financial award applicants required to submit FAFSA. In 2018, 19 master's awarded. Offers clinical psychology (MA); forensic psychology (MA). *Application deadline:* For fall admission, 2/15 for domestic students. *Application fee:* $50. Electronic applications accepted. *Application Contact:* Marcus Hanscom, Director of Graduate Admissions, 401-254-3345, Fax: 401-254-3557, E-mail: gradadmit@rwu.edu. *Dean*, Benjamin Greenstein, 401-254-3337, E-mail: bgreenstein@rwu.edu.

Mario J. Gabelli School of Business Students: 19 full-time (10 women); includes 3 minority (2 Hispanic/Latino; 1 Two or more races, non-Hispanic/Latino). Average age 24. 39 applicants, 72% accepted, 19 enrolled. *Faculty:* 5 full-time (2 women), 1 part-time/adjunct. Expenses: Contact institution. *Financial support:* In 2018–19, 9 students received support. Scholarships/grants available. Financial award application deadline: 3/15; financial award applicants required to submit FAFSA. In 2018, 6 master's awarded. Offers business (MBA). *Application deadline:* For fall admission, 4/1 priority date for domestic students. *Application fee:* $50. Electronic applications accepted. *Application Contact:* Marcus Hanscom, Director of Graduate Admissions, 401-254-3345, Fax: 401-254-3557, E-mail: mhanscom@rwu.edu. *Dean*, Dr. Susan McTiernan, 401-254-3444, E-mail: smctiernan@rwu.edu.

School of Architecture, Art and Historic Preservation Students: 106 full-time (53 women), 8 part-time (4 women); includes 9 minority (1 Black or African American, non-Hispanic/Latino; 2 Asian, non-Hispanic/Latino; 5 Hispanic/Latino; 1 Two or more races, non-Hispanic/Latino), 8 international. Average age 24. 86 applicants, 87% accepted, 49 enrolled. *Faculty:* 17 full-time (4 women), 10 part-time/adjunct (2 women). Expenses: Contact institution. *Financial support:* In 2018–19, 104 students received support. Scholarships/grants and unspecified assistantships available. Financial award application deadline: 3/15; financial award applicants required to submit FAFSA. In 2018, 57 master's awarded. Offers architecture (M Arch); art and architectural history (MA); historical preservation (MS, Certificate); urban and regional planning (Certificate). *Application deadline:* For fall admission, 4/1 for domestic students; for spring admission, 11/15 for domestic students. *Application fee:* $50. Electronic applications accepted. *Application Contact:* Marcus Hanscom, Director of Graduate Admission, 401-254-3345, Fax: 401-254-3557, E-mail: gradadmit@rwu.edu. *Dean*, Stephen White, 401-254-3607, E-mail: swhite@rwu.edu.

School of Engineering

School of Justice Studies Students: 13 full-time (8 women), 109 part-time (51 women); includes 30 minority (10 Black or African American, non-Hispanic/Latino; 1 Asian, non-Hispanic/Latino; 18 Hispanic/Latino; 1 Two or more races, non-Hispanic/Latino), 2 international. Average age 35. 90 applicants, 71% accepted, 35 enrolled. *Faculty:* 10 full-time (5 women), 3 part-time/adjunct (all women). Expenses: Contact institution. *Financial support:* In 2018–19, 2 students received support. Scholarships/grants and unspecified assistantships available. Financial award application deadline: 3/15; financial award applicants required to submit FAFSA. In 2018, 39 master's awarded. *Program availability:* Part-time, evening/weekend, 100% online, blended/hybrid learning. Offers criminal justice (MS); cybersecurity (MS); leadership (MS); public administration (MPA). *Application deadline:* For fall admission, 8/1 for domestic students; for spring admission, 1/1 for domestic students. Applications are processed on a rolling basis. *Application fee:* $50. Electronic applications accepted. *Application Contact:* Marcus Hanscom, Director of Graduate Admission, 401-254-3345, Fax: 401-254-3557, E-mail: gradadmit@rwu.edu. *Dean*, Dr. Eric Bronson, 401-254-3336, E-mail: ebronson@rwu.edu.

School of Law Students: 461 full-time (244 women); includes 125 minority (35 Black or African American, non-Hispanic/Latino; 1 American Indian or Alaska Native, non-Hispanic/Latino; 16 Asian, non-Hispanic/Latino; 54 Hispanic/Latino; 19 Two or more races, non-Hispanic/Latino), 6 international. Average age 27. 849 applicants, 71% accepted, 161 enrolled. *Faculty:* 27 full-time (16 women), 31 part-time/adjunct (14 women). Expenses: Contact institution. *Financial support:* In 2018–19, 255 students received support, including 9 fellowships (averaging $1,739 per year), 51 research assistantships (averaging $931 per year); Federal Work-Study also available. Financial award application deadline: 3/15; financial award applicants required to submit FAFSA. In 2018, 4 master's, 129 doctorates awarded. *Program availability:* Part-time. Offers law (MSL, JD). JD/MMA and JD/MLRHR offered jointly with University of Rhode Island. *Application deadline:* For fall admission, 4/1 priority date for domestic and international students. Applications are processed on a rolling basis. *Application fee:* $60. Electronic applications accepted. *Application Contact:* Michael W. Donnelly-Boylen, Assistant Dean of Admissions, 401-254-4555, Fax: 401-254-4516, E-mail: mdonnelly-boylen@rwu.edu. *Dean*, Michael Yelnosky, 401-254-4500, Fax: 401-254-3525, E-mail: myelnosky@rwu.edu.

University College

ROLLINS COLLEGE, Winter Park, FL 32789-4499

General Information Independent, coed, comprehensive institution. *Graduate housing:* Room and/or apartments available on a first-come, first-served basis to single students; on-campus housing not available to married students.

GRADUATE UNITS

Crummer Graduate School of Business *Program availability:* Part-time, evening/weekend, online learning. Offers entrepreneurship (MBA); finance (MBA); international business (MBA); management (MBA). Electronic applications accepted.

Hamilton Holt School *Program availability:* Part-time, evening/weekend. Offers applied behavior analysis and clinical science (MA); clinical mental health counseling (MA); elementary education (M Ed, MAT); human resources (MHR); liberal studies (MLS); public health (MPH).

ROOSEVELT UNIVERSITY, Chicago, IL 60605

General Information Independent, coed, comprehensive institution. *Graduate housing:* Room and/or apartments available on a first-come, first-served basis to single students; on-campus housing not available to married students. Housing application deadline: 7/1.

GRADUATE UNITS

Graduate Division *Program availability:* Part-time, evening/weekend. Electronic applications accepted.

Chicago College of Performing Arts Offers brass (Diploma); brass performance (MM); classical guitar (MM, Diploma); music (MM); music composition (MM); opera (Diploma); orchestral studies (MM, Diploma); percussion (MM, Diploma); performing arts (MA, MM, Diploma); performing arts administration (MA); piano (Diploma); piano performance (MM); strings (MM, Diploma); theatre directing (MA); voice (MM); woodwinds (MM, Diploma). Electronic applications accepted.

College of Arts and Sciences *Program availability:* Part-time, evening/weekend. Offers actuarial science (MS); arts and sciences (MA, MFA, MPA, MS, MSIMC, PhD, Psy D); biology (MS); biomedical sciences (MS); biotechnology and chemical science (MS); clinical psychology (MA, Psy D); clinical psychology - counseling practice (MA); community development and action (MA); computer science (MS); creative writing (MFA); economics (MA); history (MA); industrial/organizational psychology (MA, PhD); integrated marketing communications (MSIMC); mathematics (MS); public administration (MPA). Electronic applications accepted.

College of Education *Program availability:* Part-time, evening/weekend. Offers clinical mental health counseling (MA); early childhood education (MA); education (MA); elementary education (MA); instructional leadership (MA); reading teacher education (MA); school counseling (MA); secondary education (MA); special education (MA); training and development (MA). Electronic applications accepted.

College of Pharmacy Offers pharmacy (Pharm D). Electronic applications accepted.

Walter E. Heller College of Business *Program availability:* Part-time, evening/weekend. Offers accounting (MSA); accounting forensics (MSAF); business (MA, MBA, MS, MSA, MSAF, MSHRM); business administration (MBA); hospitality and tourism management (MS); human resource management (MSHRM); organization development (MA); real estate (MS). Electronic applications accepted.

ROSALIND FRANKLIN UNIVERSITY OF MEDICINE AND SCIENCE, North Chicago, IL 60064-3095

General Information Independent, coed, graduate-only institution. CGS member. *Graduate housing:* Rooms and/or apartments available on a first-come, first-served basis to single and married students. Housing application deadline: 3/13. *Research affiliation:* Argonne National Laboratory (medical physics), Veterans Administration Hospital (pulmonary medicine).

GRADUATE UNITS

Chicago Medical School Offers medicine (MD).

College of Health Professions *Program availability:* Part-time, online learning. Offers biomedical sciences (MS); clinical nutrition (MS); clinical psychology (MS, PhD); health professions (MS, D Sc, DNAP, DPT, PhD, TDPT, Certificate); health professions education (MS); health promotion and wellness (MS); healthcare administration and management (MS, Certificate); interprofessional studies (D Sc, PhD); nurse anesthesia (DNAP); nutrition education (MS); pathologists' assistant (MS); physical therapy (MS, DPT, TDPT); physician assistant (MS).

College of Pharmacy Offers pharmacy (Pharm D).

Dr. William M. Scholl College of Podiatric Medicine Offers podiatric medicine (DPM).

School of Graduate and Postdoctoral Studies - Interdisciplinary Graduate Program in Biomedical Sciences Offers biochemistry and molecular biology (PhD); cell biology and anatomy (PhD); cellular and molecular pharmacology (MS, PhD); microbiology and immunology (PhD); neuroscience (PhD); physiology and biophysics (MS, PhD). Electronic applications accepted.

ROSE-HULMAN INSTITUTE OF TECHNOLOGY, Terre Haute, IN 47803-3999

General Information Independent, coed, primarily men, comprehensive institution. *Enrollment:* 30 full-time matriculated graduate/professional students (6 women), 27 part-time matriculated graduate/professional students (5 women). *Enrollment by degree level:* 57 master's. *Graduate faculty:* 110 full-time (28 women), 5 part-time/adjunct (1 woman). *Tuition:* Full-time $46,641. *Graduate housing:* Room and/or apartments available on a first-come, first-served basis to single students; on-campus housing not available to married students. Typical cost: $8988 per year ($14,766 including board). *Student services:* Campus employment opportunities, career counseling, exercise/wellness program, free psychological counseling, international student services, low-cost health insurance, multicultural affairs office, services for students with disabilities. *Library facilities:* John A. Logan Library. *Collection:* Books: 29,406 (physical), 301,291 (digital/electronic); Serial titles: 42 (physical), 41,278 (digital/electronic); Databases: 33. Weekly public service hours: 101; students can reserve study rooms.

Computer facilities: Computer purchase and lease plans are available. 48 computers available on campus for general student use. A campuswide network can be accessed from student residence rooms and from off campus. Online class registration is available. Website: http://www.rose-hulman.edu/

General Application Contact: Dr. Craig Downing, Associate Dean of Lifelong Learning, 812-877-8822, E-mail: downing@rose-hulman.edu.

GRADUATE UNITS

Graduate Studies Students: 30 full-time (6 women), 27 part-time (5 women); includes 8 minority (4 Asian, non-Hispanic/Latino; 3 Hispanic/Latino; 1 Two or more races, non-Hispanic/Latino), 21 international. Average age 25. 57 applicants, 60% accepted, 21 enrolled. *Faculty:* 110 full-time (28 women), 5 part-time/adjunct (1 woman). Expenses: Contact institution. *Financial support:* In 2018–19, 49 students received support. Fellowships with tuition reimbursements available, research assistantships with tuition reimbursements available, institutionally sponsored loans, scholarships/grants, and tuition waivers (full and partial) available. Financial award application deadline: 2/1; financial award applicants required to submit FAFSA. In 2018, 33 master's awarded. *Program availability:* Part-time. Offers biology and biomedical engineering (MS); chemical engineering (M Eng, MS); civil engineering (MS); electrical and computer engineering (M Eng); electrical engineering (MS); engineering and applied sciences (M Eng, MS); engineering management (M Eng, MS); environmental engineering (MS); mechanical engineering (M Eng, MS); optical engineering (MS); systems engineering and management (MS). *Application deadline:* For fall admission, 2/1 priority date for domestic and international students; for winter admission, 10/1 for domestic students, 8/1 for international students; for spring admission, 1/15 for domestic students, 11/1 for international students. Applications are processed on a rolling basis. *Application fee:* $0. Electronic applications accepted. *Application Contact:* Dr. Craig Downing, Associate Dean of Lifelong Learning, 812-877-8822, E-mail: downing@rose-hulman.edu. *Associate Dean of Lifelong Learning*, Dr. Craig Downing, 812-877-8822, E-mail: downing@rose-hulman.edu.

ROSEMAN UNIVERSITY OF HEALTH SCIENCES, Henderson, NV 89014

General Information Private, coed, graduate-only institution. *Graduate housing:* On-campus housing not available.

GRADUATE UNITS

College of Dental Medicine - Henderson Campus Offers business administration (MBA); dental medicine (Post-Doctoral Certificate).

College of Dental Medicine - South Jordan, Utah Campus Offers dental medicine (DMD). Electronic applications accepted.

College of Pharmacy Offers pharmacy (Pharm D). Electronic applications accepted.

MBA Program *Program availability:* Part-time, evening/weekend. Offers business administration (MBA).

ROSEMONT COLLEGE, Rosemont, PA 19010-1699

General Information Independent-religious, coed, comprehensive institution. *Graduate housing:* Room and/or apartments available on a first-come, first-served basis to single students; on-campus housing not available to married students. Housing application deadline: 8/1.

GRADUATE UNITS

Schools of Graduate and Professional Studies *Program availability:* Part-time, evening/weekend, online learning. Offers business administration (MBA); creative writing (MFA); elementary certification (MA); human services (MA); leadership (MS); management (MS); PreK-4 (MA); publishing (MA); school counseling (MA). Electronic applications accepted.

ROWAN UNIVERSITY, Glassboro, NJ 08028-1701

General Information State-supported, coed, comprehensive institution. CGS member. *Graduate housing:* Room and/or apartments available on a first-come, first-served basis to single students; on-campus housing not available to married students. Housing application deadline: 5/1.

GRADUATE UNITS

Cooper Medical School Offers medicine (MD).

Graduate School *Program availability:* Part-time, evening/weekend. Electronic applications accepted.

College of Communication and Creative Arts *Program availability:* Part-time, evening/weekend. Offers communication and creative arts (MA); editing and publishing (CGS); integrated marketing communication and new media (CGS); public relations/advertising (MA); writing (MA); writing, composition, and rhetoric (CGS). Electronic applications accepted.

College of Education *Program availability:* Part-time, evening/weekend. Offers autism spectrum disorders (CGS); counseling in educational settings (MA); education (M Ed, MA, MST, Ed D, CAGS, CGS, Ed S, Postbaccalaureate Certificate); educational leadership (Ed D, CAGS); educational technology (CGS); ESL education (CGS); higher education administration (MA); learning disabilities (MA, CGS); principal preparation (CAGS); reading education (MA, CGS); reading/writing literacy (CGS); school administration (MA); school and public librarianship (MA); school nursing (Postbaccalaureate Certificate); school psychology (MA, Ed S); special education (MA, CGS); STEM education (MA); subject matter education (MST); supervisor (CAGS); teacher leadership (M Ed); teacher of reading (Postbaccalaureate Certificate); teacher of students with disabilities (Postbaccalaureate Certificate); teaching and learning (CGS); theatre education (MST). Electronic applications accepted.

College of Engineering *Program availability:* Part-time, evening/weekend. Offers chemical engineering (MS); civil engineering (MEM, MS); electrical engineering (MS); engineering (MEM, MS, MSE); mechanical engineering (MS). Electronic applications accepted.

College of Humanities and Social Sciences Offers criminal justice (MA); history (MA, CGS); humanities and social sciences (MA, CGS).

College of Performing Arts *Program availability:* Part-time, evening/weekend. Offers performance (MM); performing arts (MA, MM, MST); theatre arts administration (MA). Electronic applications accepted.

College of Science and Mathematics *Program availability:* Part-time, evening/weekend. Offers applied behavioral analysis (MA, CAGS); bioinformatics (MS); biological science (MS); clinical mental health counseling (MA, CAGS); computer science (MS); mathematics (MA); middle grades math education (CGS); networks (CGS); nursing (MS); pharmaceutical sciences (MS); psychology (MA, CAGS); science and mathematics (MA, MS, CAGS, CGS). Electronic applications accepted.

Rohrer College of Business *Program availability:* Part-time, evening/weekend. Offers business (MBA, CAGS, CGS); business administration (MBA). Electronic applications accepted.

School of Biomedical Science and Health Professions *Program availability:* Part-time, evening/weekend, online learning. Offers health and exercise science (MA); wellness and lifestyle management (MA). Electronic applications accepted.

School of Osteopathic Medicine Offers osteopathic medicine (DO). Electronic applications accepted.

ROYAL MILITARY COLLEGE OF CANADA, Kingston, ON K7K 7B4, Canada

General Information Federally supported, coed, university.

GRADUATE UNITS

Division of Graduate Studies *Program availability:* Part-time, online learning. Electronic applications accepted.

Continuing Studies Offers business administration (MBA); defense management and policy (MA); history (PhD); war studies (MA). Electronic applications accepted.

Faculty of Engineering Offers civil engineering (M Eng, MA Sc, PhD); computer engineering (M Eng, PhD); electrical engineering (M Eng, PhD); engineering (M Eng, M Sc, MA Sc, PhD); mechanical engineering (M Eng, MA Sc, PhD); software engineering (M Eng, PhD). Electronic applications accepted.

Faculty of Science Offers chemical engineering (M Eng, MA Sc, PhD); chemistry (M Sc, PhD); computer science (M Sc); mathematics (M Sc); physics (M Sc); science (M Eng, M Sc, MA Sc, PhD). Electronic applications accepted.

ROYAL ROADS UNIVERSITY, Victoria, BC V9B 5Y2, Canada

General Information Province-supported, coed, upper-level institution. *Enrollment:* 3,452 full-time matriculated graduate/professional students (2,103 women). *Enrollment by degree level:* 2,854 master's, 104 doctoral, 494 other advanced degrees. *Graduate faculty:* 49 full-time, 315 part-time/adjunct. *Tuition, area resident:* Full-time $27,000 Canadian dollars. Tuition, province resident: full-time $27,000 Canadian dollars. Tuition, Canadian resident: full-time $33,000 Canadian dollars. *Required fees:* $662 Canadian dollars. *Graduate housing:* Room and/or apartments available on a first-come, first-served basis to single students; on-campus housing not available to married students. *Student services:* Campus safety program, career counseling, child daycare facilities, exercise/wellness program, free psychological counseling, international student services, multicultural affairs office, services for students with disabilities, writing training. *Library facilities:* Coronel Memorial Library.

Computer facilities: A campuswide network can be accessed. Online class registration, free file storage are available.
Website: http://www.royalroads.ca/

General Application Contact: Director of Admissions/Registrar, 250-391-2511, Fax: 250-391-2522, E-mail: rruregistrar@royalroads.ca.

GRADUATE UNITS

Graduate Studies *Program availability:* Blended/hybrid learning. Offers conflict analysis (G Dip); conflict analysis and management (MA); disaster and emergency management (MA, G Dip); environment and management (M Sc, MA); environment and sustainability (MAIS); environmental education and communication (MA, G Dip, Graduate Certificate); human security and peacebuilding (MA, G Dip); justice studies (G Dip); peace and conflict studies (MAIS); tourism management (MA, Graduate Certificate). Electronic applications accepted.

RUSH UNIVERSITY, Chicago, IL 60612-3832

General Information Independent, coed, upper-level institution. CGS member. *Graduate housing:* Rooms and/or apartments available on a first-come, first-served basis to single and married students.

GRADUATE UNITS

College of Health Sciences Expenses: Contact institution. *Financial support:* Career-related internships or fieldwork, Federal Work-Study, institutionally sponsored loans, and scholarships/grants available. Support available to part-time students. Financial award application deadline: 4/1; financial award applicants required to submit FAFSA. *Program availability:* Part-time. Offers audiology (Au D); clinical laboratory management (MS); clinical nutrition (MS); health sciences (MS, Au D, OTD, PhD); health systems management (MS, PhD); medical laboratory science (MS); occupational therapy (OTD); perfusion technology (MS); physician assistant studies (MS); respiratory care (MS); speech-language pathology (MS). Electronic applications accepted.

College of Nursing *Program availability:* 100% online, blended/hybrid learning. Offers adult gerontology acute care clinical nurse specialist (DNP); adult gerontology acute care nurse practitioner (DNP, Post-Graduate Certificate); adult gerontology primary care nurse practitioner (DNP); advanced public health nursing (DNP); clinical nurse leader (MSN); family nurse practitioner (DNP); neonatal clinical nurse specialist (DNP); neonatal nurse practitioner (DNP, Post-Graduate Certificate); nurse anesthesia (DNP); nursing (MSN, DNP, PhD, Post-Graduate Certificate); nursing science (PhD); pediatric acute care nurse practitioner (DNP, Post-Graduate Certificate); pediatric clinical nurse specialist (DNP); pediatric primary care nurse practitioner (DNP); psychiatric mental health nurse practitioner (DNP); transformative leadership: population health (DNP); transformative leadership: systems (DNP). Electronic applications accepted.

Graduate College *Program availability:* Part-time. Offers physiology (PhD). Electronic applications accepted.

Division of Anatomy and Cell Biology Offers anatomy and cell biology (MS, PhD). Electronic applications accepted.

Division of Biochemistry Offers biochemistry (MS, PhD). Electronic applications accepted.

Division of Immunology and Microbiology Offers immunology (MS, PhD); microbiology (PhD); virology (MS, PhD).

Division of Medical Physics Offers medical physics (MS, PhD). Electronic applications accepted.

Division of Neuroscience Offers neuroscience (MS, PhD). Electronic applications accepted.

Division of Pharmacology Offers clinical research (MS); pharmacology (MS, PhD).

Rush Medical College Offers medicine (MD). Electronic applications accepted.

RUTGERS UNIVERSITY–CAMDEN, Camden, NJ 08102-1401

General Information State-supported, coed, university. *Graduate housing:* Rooms and/or apartments available to single and married students.

GRADUATE UNITS

Graduate School of Arts and Sciences *Program availability:* Part-time, evening/weekend. Offers American and public history (MA); biology (MS); chemistry (MS); childhood studies (MA, PhD); computational and integrative biology (MS, PhD); computer science (MS); creative writing (MFA); criminal justice (MA); education policy and leadership (MPA); English (MA); industrial mathematics (MBS); industrial/applied mathematics (MS); international public service and development (MPA); liberal studies (MALS); mathematical computer science (MS); physical therapy (DPT); psychology (MA); public management (MPA); pure mathematics (MS); teaching in mathematical sciences (MS). Electronic applications accepted.

School of Business *Program availability:* Part-time, evening/weekend. Offers business (MBA). Electronic applications accepted.

School of Law *Program availability:* Part-time, evening/weekend. Offers law (JD). JD/MCRP, JD/MA, JD/MPA, JD/MSW, JD/MS offered jointly with Rutgers, The State University of New Jersey, New Brunswick; JD/MPA, JD/MD, JD/DO with University of Medicine and Dentistry of New Jersey. Electronic applications accepted.

School of Nursing–Camden Offers adult gerontology primary care nurse practitioner (DNP); family nurse practitioner (DNP).

School of Public Health *Program availability:* Part-time, evening/weekend. Offers general public health (Certificate); health systems and policy (MPH). Electronic applications accepted.

RUTGERS UNIVERSITY–NEWARK, Newark, NJ 07102

General Information State-supported, coed, university. CGS member. *Graduate housing:* Room and/or apartments available to single students; on-campus housing not available to married students. Housing application deadline: 5/15.

GRADUATE UNITS

Graduate School *Program availability:* Part-time, evening/weekend. Offers accounting (PhD); accounting information systems (PhD); American political system (MA); American studies (MA, PhD); analytical chemistry (MS, PhD); applied physics (MS, PhD); biochemistry (MS, PhD); biology (PhD); cognitive neuroscience (PhD); cognitive science (PhD); computational biology (MS); computer information systems (PhD); creative writing (MFA); economics (MA); English (MA); environmental geology (MS); environmental science (MS, PhD); finance (PhD); health care administration (MPA); history (MA, MAT); human resources administration (MPA); information technology (PhD); inorganic chemistry (MS, PhD); international business (PhD); international relations (MA); jazz history and research (MA); management science (PhD); marketing (PhD); mathematical sciences (PhD); organic chemistry (MS, PhD); organization management (PhD); perception (PhD); physical chemistry (MS, PhD); psychobiology (PhD); public administration (PhD); public management (MPA); public policy analysis (MPA); social cognition (PhD); urban systems (PhD); urban systems and issues (MPA). Electronic applications accepted.

Division of Global Affairs *Program availability:* Part-time, evening/weekend. Offers global affairs (MS, PhD). Electronic applications accepted.

Graduate School of Biomedical Sciences *Program availability:* Part-time, evening/weekend. Offers biochemistry and molecular biology (MS, PhD); biomedical engineering (Certificate); biomedical sciences (PhD, Certificate); biomedical sciences (interdisciplinary) (PhD); cell biology and molecular medicine (PhD); integrative neuroscience (PhD); microbiology and molecular genetics (PhD); molecular pathology and immunology (PhD); pharmacology and physiology (PhD). PhD in biomedical engineering offered jointly with New Jersey Institute of Technology. Electronic applications accepted.

School of Criminal Justice Offers criminal justice (MA, PhD). Electronic applications accepted.

New Jersey Medical School Offers medicine (MD). Electronic applications accepted.

Rutgers Business School–Newark and New Brunswick *Program availability:* Part-time, evening/weekend. Offers accountancy (M Accy); accounting (PhD); accounting information systems (PhD); business (MBA, MFA, MHSM, MIT, MRE); business administration (MBA); business of fashion (MBA); economics (PhD); finance (PhD); financial analysis (MFA); healthcare services management (MHSM); individualized study (PhD); information technology (PhD); international business (PhD); management science (PhD); marketing science (PhD); organizational management (PhD); pharmaceutical management (MBA); professional accounting (MBA); quantitative finance (MQF); real estate and logistics (MRE); science, technology and management (PhD); supply chain management (PhD). Electronic applications accepted.

Rutgers School of Dental Medicine Offers dental science (MS); dentistry (DMD); endodontics (Certificate); oral medicine (Certificate); orthodontics (Certificate); pediatric dentistry (Certificate); periodontics (Certificate); prosthodontics (Certificate). DMD/MPH offered jointly with New Jersey Institute of Technology, Rutgers, The State University of New Jersey, Camden. Electronic applications accepted.

Rutgers School of Nursing *Program availability:* Part-time. Offers adult health (MSN); adult occupational health (MSN); advanced practice nursing (MSN, Post Master's Certificate); family nurse practitioner (MSN); nurse anesthesia (MSN); nursing (MSN); nursing informatics (MSN); urban health (PhD); women's health practitioner (MSN). Electronic applications accepted.

School of Health Related Professions *Program availability:* Part-time. Offers biomedical informatics (MS, PhD); clinical laboratory sciences (MS); clinical nutrition (MS, DCN); community counseling (MS); dietetic internship (Certificate); health care informatics (Certificate); health care management (MS); health related professions (MS, DCN, DPT, PhD, Certificate); health sciences (MS, PhD); nutrition (PhD); physical therapy (DPT); physician assistant (MS); psychiatric rehabilitation (MS, PhD); radiologist assistant (MS); rehabilitation counseling (MS). Electronic applications accepted.

School of Law *Program availability:* Part-time, evening/weekend. Offers law (JD). JD/MCRP, JD/PhD offered jointly with Rutgers, The State University of New Jersey, New Brunswick.

School of Public Health *Program availability:* Part-time, evening/weekend. Offers clinical epidemiology (Certificate); dental public health (MPH); general public health (Certificate); public policy and oral health services administration (Certificate); quantitative methods (MPH); urban health (MPH). Electronic applications accepted.

RUTGERS UNIVERSITY–NEW BRUNSWICK, Piscataway, NJ 08854-8097

General Information State-supported, coed, university. CGS member. *Graduate housing:* Rooms and/or apartments available to single and married students.

GRADUATE UNITS

Edward J. Bloustein School of Planning and Public Policy *Program availability:* Part-time, evening/weekend, online learning. Offers planning and public policy (MCRP, MCRS, MPAP, MPI, MPP, PhD); public informatics (MPI); public policy (MPAP, MPP); urban planning and policy development (MCRP, MCRS). Electronic applications accepted.

Ernest Mario School of Pharmacy Offers medicinal chemistry (MS, PhD); pharmaceutical science (MS, PhD); pharmacy (Pharm D). Electronic applications accepted.

Graduate School–New Brunswick *Program availability:* Part-time, evening/weekend, online learning. Offers African-American history (PhD); air pollution and resources (MS, PhD); American politics (PhD); anthropology (MA, PhD); applied mathematics (MS, PhD); applied statistics (MS); aquatic biology (MS, PhD); aquatic chemistry (MS, PhD); art history (MA, PhD); astronomy (MS, PhD); atmospheric science (MS, PhD); behavioral neuroscience (PhD); bilingualism and second language acquisition (MA, PhD); biochemistry (PhD); biological chemistry (MS, PhD); biophysics (PhD); biostatistics (MS); cell and developmental biology (MS, PhD); chemical and biochemical engineering (MS, PhD); chemistry and physics of aerosol and hydrosol systems (MS, PhD); civil and environmental engineering (MS, PhD); classics (MA, MAT, PhD); clinical psychology (PhD); cognitive psychology (PhD); communications and solid-state electronics (MS, PhD); comparative literature (MA, PhD); comparative politics (PhD); computational biology and molecular biophysics (PhD); computer engineering (MS, PhD); computer science (MS, PhD); condensed matter physics (MS, PhD); control systems (MS, PhD); cultural heritage and preservation studies (MA); curatorial studies (Certificate); data mining (MS); design and control (MS, PhD); digital signal processing (MS, PhD); early American history (PhD); early modern European history (PhD); east Asian history (PhD); East Asian languages and cultures (MA); ecology and evolution (MS, PhD); economics (MA, PhD); elementary particle physics (MS, PhD); endocrinology and animal biosciences (MS, PhD); entomology (MS, PhD); environmental chemistry (MS, PhD); environmental microbiology (MS, PhD); environmental toxicology (MS, PhD); exposure assessment (MS, PhD); fate and effects of pollutants (MS, PhD); fluid mechanics (MS, PhD); food and business economics (MS); food science (M Phil, MS, PhD); French (MA, PhD); French studies (MAT); geography (MA, MS, PhD); geological sciences (PhD); German (MAT, PhD); German literature (MA, PhD); global and comparative history (PhD); historic preservation (Certificate); history (PhD); history of diplomacy and foreign relations (PhD); history of technology, environment and health (PhD); history of the Atlantic cultures and African diaspora (PhD); horticulture and plant technology (MS, PhD); industrial and systems engineering (MS, PhD); industrial-occupational toxicology (MS, PhD); information technology (MS); inorganic chemistry (MS, PhD); interdisciplinary classical studies and ancient history (MA, PhD); interdisciplinary health psychology (PhD); intermediate energy nuclear physics (MS); international relations (PhD); Italian (MA, PhD); Italian literature and literary criticism (MA); Jewish studies (MA, Certificate); landscape architecture (MLA); language, literature and culture (MAT); Latin American history (PhD); linguistics (PhD); literatures in English (PhD); manufacturing systems engineering (MS); materials science and engineering (MS, PhD); mathematics (MS, PhD); mechanics (MS, PhD); medieval history (PhD); microbiology and molecular genetics (MS, PhD); modern European history (PhD); molecular and cellular biology (MS, PhD); nineteenth and twentieth century American history (PhD); nuclear physics (MS, PhD); nutritional sciences (MS, PhD); nutritional toxicology (MS, PhD); oceanography (MS, PhD); operations research (PhD); organic chemistry (MS, PhD); organismal and population biology (MS, PhD); pharmaceutical toxicology (MS, PhD); philosophy (PhD); physical chemistry (MS, PhD); physics (MST); plant pathology (MS, PhD); political theory (PhD); pollution prevention and control (MS, PhD); public law (PhD); quality and productivity management (MS); quality and reliability engineering (MS); religious studies (MA, Graduate Certificate); social psychology (PhD); sociology (MA, PhD); solid mechanics (MS, PhD); Spanish (MA, MAT, PhD); Spanish literature (MA, PhD); statistics (MS, PhD); surface science

(PhD); theoretical physics (MS, PhD); thermal sciences (MS, PhD); translation (MA); United Nations and global policy studies (MA); water and wastewater treatment (MS, PhD); water resources (MS, PhD); women and politics (PhD); women's and gender history (PhD); women's and gender studies (MA, PhD).

Graduate School of Applied and Professional Psychology Offers applied and professional psychology (Psy M, Psy D); clinical psychology (Psy M, Psy D); school psychology (Psy M, Psy D). Electronic applications accepted.

Graduate School of Biomedical Sciences Offers biochemistry (MS, PhD); biochemistry and molecular biology (MS, PhD); biomedical engineering (MS, PhD); biomedical science (MS); biomedical sciences (MBS, MS, PhD); cellular and molecular pharmacology (MS, PhD); clinical and translational science (MS); environmental sciences/exposure assessment (PhD); exposure science and assessment (PhD); microbiology and molecular genetics (MS, PhD); molecular genetics, microbiology and immunology (MS, PhD); neuroscience (MS, PhD); physiology and integrative biology (MS, PhD); toxicology (PhD). Electronic applications accepted.

Graduate School of Education *Program availability:* Part-time, evening/weekend. Offers college student affairs (Ed M); early childhood/elementary education (Ed M, Ed D); education (Ed M, Ed D, PhD); educational administration and supervision (Ed M, Ed D); educational policy (PhD); educational psychology (PhD); educational statistics, measurement and evaluation (Ed M); English as a second language education (Ed M); English education (Ed M); language education (Ed M, Ed D); learning, cognition and development (Ed M); literacy education (Ed M, Ed D, PhD); mathematics education (Ed M, Ed D); reading education (Ed M); school counseling and counseling psychology (Ed M); science education (Ed M, Ed D); social and philosophical foundations of education (Ed M); social studies education (Ed M, Ed D); special education (Ed M, Ed D). Electronic applications accepted.

Mason Gross School of the Arts *Program availability:* Part-time. Offers acting (MFA); arts (MFA, MM, DMA, AD); collaborative piano (MM, DMA); conducting: choral (MM, DMA); conducting: instrumental (MM, DMA); conducting: orchestral (MM, DMA); design (MFA); drawing (MFA); jazz studies (MM); music (DMA, AD); music education (MM, DMA); music performance (MM); painting (MFA); playwriting (MFA); sculpture (MFA); stage management (MFA); technical direction (MFA); visual arts (MFA).

Robert Wood Johnson Medical School Offers medicine (MD). Electronic applications accepted.

School of Communication and Information *Program availability:* Part-time, online learning. Offers communication and information (MCIS, MI, MLS, PhD); communication and information studies (MCIS); communication, information and library studies (PhD); information (MI). Electronic applications accepted.

School of Management and Labor Relations *Program availability:* Part-time, evening/weekend. Offers human resource management (MHRM); industrial relations and human resources (PhD); labor and employment relations (MLER). Electronic applications accepted.

School of Public Health *Program availability:* Part-time, evening/weekend. Offers biostatistics (MPH, MS, Dr PH, PhD); clinical epidemiology (Certificate); environmental and occupational health (MPH, Dr PH, PhD, Certificate); epidemiology (MPH, Dr PH, PhD); general public health (Certificate); health education and behavioral science (MPH, Dr PH, PhD); health systems and policy (MPH, PhD); public health (MPH, Dr PH, PhD); public health preparedness (Certificate). Electronic applications accepted.

School of Social Work *Program availability:* Part-time. Offers social work (MSW, PhD). Electronic applications accepted.

RYERSON UNIVERSITY, Toronto, ON M5B 2K3, Canada

General Information Province-supported, coed, comprehensive institution. CGS member.

GRADUATE UNITS

School of Graduate Studies Offers photographic preservation and collections management (MA).

Ted Rogers School of Management Offers global business administration (MBA); management (MSM); management of technology and innovation (MBA).

SACRED HEART MAJOR SEMINARY, Detroit, MI 48206-1799

General Information Independent-religious, coed, comprehensive institution. *Graduate housing:* Room and/or apartments guaranteed to single students; on-campus housing not available to married students. Housing application deadline: 8/1.

GRADUATE UNITS

School of Theology *Program availability:* Part-time, evening/weekend. Offers pastoral studies (MAPS); theology (M Div, MA).

SACRED HEART SEMINARY AND SCHOOL OF THEOLOGY, Hales Corners, WI 53130-0429

General Information Independent-religious, coed, primarily men, graduate-only institution. *Graduate housing:* Room and/or apartments guaranteed to single students; on-campus housing not available to married students.

GRADUATE UNITS

Graduate and Professional Programs *Program availability:* Part-time. Offers priestly formation (Certificate); theology (M Div, MA).

SACRED HEART UNIVERSITY, Fairfield, CT 06825

General Information Independent-religious, coed, comprehensive institution. CGS member. *Graduate housing:* On-campus housing not available.

GRADUATE UNITS

Graduate Programs *Program availability:* Part-time, evening/weekend, online learning. Electronic applications accepted.

College of Arts and Sciences Offers applied psychology (MS); arts and sciences (MA, MA Comm, MPA, MS, MSW); bioinformatics (MS); chemistry (MS); computer science (MS); computer science gaming (MS); corporate communications and public relations (MA Comm); criminal justice (MA); cybersecurity (MS); digital multimedia journalism (MA Comm); digital multimedia production (MA Comm); film and television production (MA); information technology (MS); media literacy and digital culture (MA); molecular biology (MS); public administration (MPA); social work (MSW); sports communication and media (MA). Electronic applications accepted.

College of Health Professions *Program availability:* Part-time, evening/weekend, 100% online, blended/hybrid learning. Offers exercise science and nutrition (MS); health professions (MPAS, MPH, MS, MSOT, DPT); healthcare informatics (MS); occupational therapy (MSOT); physical therapy (DPT); physician assistant studies (MPAS); public health (MPH); speech-language pathology (MS). Electronic applications accepted.

College of Nursing Program availability: Part-time, evening/weekend, 100% online, blended/hybrid learning. Offers clinical (DNP); clinical nurse leader (MSN); family nurse practitioner (MSN, Post-Master's Certificate); leadership (DNP); nursing education (MSN); nursing management and executive leadership (MSN). Electronic applications accepted.

Isabelle Farrington College of Education Program availability: Part-time, evening/weekend. Offers advanced studies in administration (Professional Certificate); advanced studies in literacy (Professional Certificate); education (M Ed, MAT, Professional Certificate); teaching: education (MAT). Electronic applications accepted.

Jack Welch College of Business Program availability: Part-time, evening/weekend. Offers accounting (MBA, MS, Graduate Certificate); administration (MBA, DBA); business (MBA, MS, DBA, Graduate Certificate); digital marketing (MS); finance (MBA, Graduate Certificate); finance and investment management (MS); human resource management (MS, Graduate Certificate); management (Graduate Certificate); marketing (MBA, Graduate Certificate). Electronic applications accepted.

SAGE GRADUATE SCHOOL, Troy, NY 12180-4115

General Information Independent, coed, graduate-only institution. Enrollment by degree level: 871 master's, 229 doctoral, 94 other advanced degrees. Graduate faculty: 58 full-time (49 women), 55 part-time/adjunct (41 women). Graduate housing: Room and/or apartments available on a first-come, first-served basis to single students; on-campus housing not available to married students. Housing application deadline: 5/1. Student services: Career counseling. Library facilities: James Wheelock Clark Library plus 1 other. Collection: Books: 194,209 (physical), 160,067 (digital/electronic); Serial titles: 245 (physical), 63,276 (digital/electronic); Databases: 105. Weekly public service hours: 65; students can reserve study rooms.

Computer facilities: 441 computers available on campus for general student use. Online class registration is available.
Website: http://www.sage.edu/

General Application Contact: Wendy D. Diefendorf, Director of Graduate and Adult Admission, 518-244-2443, Fax: 518-244-6880, E-mail: sgsadm@sage.edu.

GRADUATE UNITS

Esteves School of Education Students: 79 full-time (62 women), 332 part-time (255 women); includes 120 minority (54 Black or African American, non-Hispanic/Latino; 1 American Indian or Alaska Native, non-Hispanic/Latino; 16 Asian, non-Hispanic/Latino; 40 Hispanic/Latino; 1 Native Hawaiian or other Pacific Islander, non-Hispanic/Latino; 8 Two or more races, non-Hispanic/Latino). Average age 33. 482 applicants, 47% accepted, 138 enrolled. Faculty: 16 full-time (12 women), 24 part-time/adjunct (16 women). Expenses: Contact institution. Financial support: Fellowships, research assistantships, scholarships/grants, and unspecified assistantships available. Financial award application deadline: 3/1; financial award applicants required to submit FAFSA. In 2018, 126 master's, 33 doctorates, 16 other advanced degrees awarded. Program availability: Part-time, evening/weekend. Offers applied behavior analysis and autism (MS, Post Master's Certificate); childhood education/literacy (MS); childhood special education (MS Ed); education (MS, MS Ed, Ed D, Post Master's Certificate); educational leadership (Ed D); literacy (MS Ed); literacy/childhood special education (MS Ed); school counseling (MS, Post Master's Certificate); school health education (MS); special education (MS Ed). Application deadline: Applications are processed on a rolling basis. Application fee: $30. Electronic applications accepted. Application Contact: Michael Jones, SR Associate Director of Graduate Enrollment Management, 518-292-8615, Fax: 518-292-1912, E-mail: jonesm4@sage.edu. Dean, Esteves School of Education, Dr. John Pelizza, 518-244-2051, Fax: 518-244-2334, E-mail: pelizj@sage.edu.

School of Health Sciences Students: 322 full-time (261 women), 304 part-time (267 women); includes 102 minority (35 Black or African American, non-Hispanic/Latino; 2 American Indian or Alaska Native, non-Hispanic/Latino; 29 Asian, non-Hispanic/Latino; 22 Hispanic/Latino; 14 Two or more races, non-Hispanic/Latino). Average age 30. 773 applicants, 34% accepted, 159 enrolled. Faculty: 37 full-time (33 women), 27 part-time/adjunct (26 women). Expenses: Contact institution. Financial support: Fellowships, research assistantships, scholarships/grants, and unspecified assistantships available. Financial award application deadline: 3/1; financial award applicants required to submit FAFSA. In 2018, 135 master's, 33 doctorates, 54 other advanced degrees awarded. Program availability: Part-time, evening/weekend. Offers adult gerontology nurse practitioner (MS, Certificate); applied nutrition (MS); community psychology (MA); counseling and community psychology (MA); dietetic internship (Certificate); education and leadership (DNS); family nurse practitioner (MS); forensic mental health (MS, Certificate); health sciences (MA, MS, DNS, DPT, Certificate, Post Master's Certificate, Postbaccalaureate Certificate); nursing (MS, DNS, Certificate, Post Master's Certificate); nutrition (Certificate); occupational therapy (MS); physical therapy (DPT); psychiatric mental health nurse practitioner (MS, Post Master's Certificate); psychology (MA, Certificate). Application deadline: Applications are processed on a rolling basis. Application fee: $30. Electronic applications accepted. Application Contact: Michael Jones, SR Associate Director of Graduate Enrollment Management, 518-292-8615, Fax: 518-292-1912, E-mail: jonesm4@sage.edu. Dean, School of Health Sciences, Dr. Kathleen Kelly, 518-244-2030, E-mail: kellyk5@sage.edu.

School of Management Students: 25 full-time (12 women), 82 part-time (64 women); includes 24 minority (11 Black or African American, non-Hispanic/Latino; 2 American Indian or Alaska Native, non-Hispanic/Latino; 2 Asian, non-Hispanic/Latino; 8 Hispanic/Latino; 1 Two or more races, non-Hispanic/Latino), 1 international. Average age 32. 100 applicants, 45% accepted, 23 enrolled. Faculty: 5 full-time (3 women), 4 part-time/adjunct (1 woman). Expenses: Contact institution. Financial support: Fellowships, research assistantships, and unspecified assistantships available. Financial award application deadline: 3/1; financial award applicants required to submit FAFSA. In 2018, 36 master's awarded. Program availability: Part-time, evening/weekend, 100% online, blended/hybrid learning. Offers business administration (MBA); gerontology (MS); management (MBA, MS); organization management (MS). Application deadline: Applications are processed on a rolling basis. Application fee: $30. Electronic applications accepted. Application Contact: Michael Jones, SR Associate Director of Graduate Enrollment Management, 518-292-8615, Fax: 518-292-1912, E-mail: jonesm4@sage.edu. Dean, School of Management, Dr. Kimberly Fredericks, 518-292-1782, Fax: 518-292-1964, E-mail: fredek1@sage.edu.

SAGINAW VALLEY STATE UNIVERSITY, University Center, MI 48710

General Information State-supported, coed, comprehensive institution. Enrollment: 8,535 graduate, professional, and undergraduate students; 271 full-time matriculated graduate/professional students (214 women), 519 part-time matriculated graduate/professional students (395 women). Enrollment by degree level: 738 master's, 32 doctoral, 20 other advanced degrees. Graduate faculty: 63 full-time (39 women), 29 part-time/adjunct (18 women). International tuition: $14,215 full-time. Tuition, area

resident: Full-time $6225; part-time $623 per credit hour. Tuition, state resident: full-time $6225; part-time $623 per credit hour. Tuition, nonresident: full-time $14,215; part-time $1185 per credit hour. Required fees: $263; $14.60 per credit hour. Tuition and fees vary according to degree level. Graduate housing: Room and/or apartments available on a first-come, first-served basis to single students; on-campus housing not available to married students. Typical cost: $4430 per year ($10,440 including board). Room and board charges vary according to board plan and housing facility selected. Housing application deadline: 5/1. Student services: Campus employment opportunities, career counseling, exercise/wellness program, free psychological counseling, international student services, multicultural affairs office, services for students with disabilities, writing training. Library facilities: Zahnow Library. Collection: Books: 217,900 (physical), 107,479 (digital/electronic); Serial titles: 127 (physical), 50,164 (digital/electronic); Databases: 63. Weekly public service hours: 92.

Computer facilities: Computer purchase and lease plans are available. 424 computers available on campus for general student use. A campuswide network can be accessed from student residence rooms and from off campus. Online class registration is available.
Website: http://www.svsu.edu/

General Application Contact: Jenna Briggs, Director, Graduate and International Admissions, 989-964-6096, Fax: 989-964-2788, E-mail: gradadm@svsu.edu.

GRADUATE UNITS

College of Arts and Behavioral Sciences Students: 25 full-time (14 women), 23 part-time (14 women); includes 7 minority (3 Black or African American, non-Hispanic/Latino; 1 Asian, non-Hispanic/Latino; 2 Hispanic/Latino; 1 Two or more races, non-Hispanic/Latino), 14 international. Average age 29. 30 applicants, 73% accepted, 9 enrolled. Faculty: 9 full-time (3 women), 3 part-time/adjunct (0 women). Expenses: Contact institution. Financial support: Federal Work-Study and scholarships/grants available. Support available to part-time students. Financial award applicants required to submit FAFSA. In 2018, 11 master's awarded. Program availability: Part-time, evening/weekend. Offers arts and behavioral sciences (MA); communication and media administration (MA); public administration (MA). Application deadline: For fall admission, 7/15 for international students; for winter admission, 11/15 for international students; for spring admission, 4/15 for international students. Applications are processed on a rolling basis. Application fee: $30 ($90 for international students). Electronic applications accepted. Application Contact: Jenna Briggs, Director, Graduate and International Admissions, 989-964-6096, Fax: 989-964-2788, E-mail: gradadm@svsu.edu. Dean, Dr. Marc Peretz, 989-964-4062, Fax: 989-964-7232, E-mail: mhp@svsu.edu.

College of Business and Management Students: 16 full-time (7 women), 44 part-time (16 women); includes 12 minority (3 Black or African American, non-Hispanic/Latino; 2 Asian, non-Hispanic/Latino; 4 Hispanic/Latino; 3 Two or more races, non-Hispanic/Latino), 14 international. Average age 30. 58 applicants, 62% accepted, 21 enrolled. Faculty: 9 full-time (2 women), 1 part-time/adjunct (0 women). Expenses: Contact institution. Financial support: Federal Work-Study and scholarships/grants available. Support available to part-time students. Financial award application deadline: 4/1; financial award applicants required to submit FAFSA. In 2018, 10 master's awarded. Program availability: Part-time, evening/weekend, online only, 100% online, blended/hybrid learning. Offers business administration (MBA); business and management (MBA). Application deadline: For fall admission, 7/15 for international students; for winter admission, 11/15 for international students; for spring admission, 4/15 for international students. Applications are processed on a rolling basis. Application fee: $30 ($90 for international students). Electronic applications accepted. Application Contact: Jenna Briggs, Director, Graduate and International Admissions, 989-964-6096, Fax: 989-964-2788, E-mail: gradadm@svsu.edu. MBA Program Coordinator, Dr. Mark McCartney, 989-964-4064.

College of Education Students: 22 full-time (15 women), 192 part-time (155 women); includes 19 minority (6 Black or African American, non-Hispanic/Latino; 1 Asian, non-Hispanic/Latino; 6 Hispanic/Latino; 6 Two or more races, non-Hispanic/Latino), 12 international. Average age 35. 53 applicants, 94% accepted, 47 enrolled. Faculty: 14 full-time (12 women), 14 part-time/adjunct (9 women). Expenses: Contact institution. Financial support: Federal Work-Study and scholarships/grants available. Support available to part-time students. Financial award applicants required to submit FAFSA. In 2018, 20 master's, 28 other advanced degrees awarded. Program availability: Part-time, evening/weekend, online learning. Offers early childhood education (MAT); education (M Ed, MA, MAT, Ed S); educational leadership (M Ed, Ed S); instructional technology (MA); K-12 literacy specialist (MAT); reading education (MAT); special education (MAT); teaching Chinese as a foreign language (MAT). Application deadline: For fall admission, 7/15 for international students; for winter admission, 11/15 for international students; for spring admission, 4/15 for international students. Applications are processed on a rolling basis. Application fee: $30 ($90 for international students). Electronic applications accepted. Application Contact: Jenna Briggs, Director, Graduate and International Admissions, 989-964-6096, Fax: 989-964-2788, E-mail: gradadm@svsu.edu. Dean, Dr. Craig Douglas, 989-964-4057, Fax: 989-964-4563, E-mail: coeconnect@svsu.edu.

College of Health and Human Services Students: 198 full-time (177 women), 248 part-time (207 women); includes 58 minority (26 Black or African American, non-Hispanic/Latino; 8 Asian, non-Hispanic/Latino; 9 Hispanic/Latino; 15 Two or more races, non-Hispanic/Latino), 7 international. Average age 29. 126 applicants, 94% accepted, 99 enrolled. Faculty: 28 full-time (24 women), 10 part-time/adjunct (9 women). Expenses: Contact institution. Financial support: Federal Work-Study and scholarships/grants available. Support available to part-time students. Financial award application deadline: 4/1; financial award applicants required to submit FAFSA. In 2018, 70 master's awarded. Program availability: Part-time, evening/weekend. Offers clinical nurse specialist (MSN); health and human services (MS, MSN, MSOT, MSW, DNP); health leadership (MS); nurse practitioner (MSN, DNP); nursing (MSN); occupational therapy (MSOT); social work (MSW). Application deadline: For fall admission, 7/15 for international students; for winter admission, 11/15 for international students; for spring admission, 4/15 for international students. Applications are processed on a rolling basis. Application fee: $30 ($90 for international students). Electronic applications accepted. Application Contact: Jenna Briggs, Director, Graduate and International Admissions, 989-964-6096, Fax: 989-964-2788, E-mail: gradadm@svsu.edu. Dean, Dr. Judith Ruland, 989-964-4145, Fax: 989-964-4024, E-mail: jruland@svsu.edu.

College of Science, Engineering, and Technology Students: 10 full-time (1 woman), 12 part-time (3 women); includes 1 minority (Asian, non-Hispanic/Latino), 8 international. Average age 32. 35 applicants, 80% accepted, 8 enrolled. Faculty: 5 full-time (0 women), 1 part-time/adjunct (0 women). Expenses: Contact institution. Financial support: Federal Work-Study and scholarships/grants available. Support available to part-time students. Financial award application deadline: 4/1; financial award applicants required to submit FAFSA. Program availability: Part-time, evening/weekend. Offers computer science and information systems (MS); energy and materials (MS). Application deadline: For fall admission, 7/15 for international students; for winter admission, 11/15 for international students; for spring admission, 4/15 for international students. Applications are processed on a rolling basis. *Application fee:* $30 ($90 for international students). Electronic applications accepted. *Application Contact:* Jenna Briggs, Director, Graduate and International Admissions, 989-964-6096, Fax: 989-964-2788, E-mail: gradadm@svsu.edu. *Program Coordinator*, Dr. Robert Tuttle, 989-964-4144, Fax: 989-964-2717.

ST. AMBROSE UNIVERSITY, Davenport, IA 52803-2898

General Information Independent-religious, coed, comprehensive institution. CGS member. *Graduate housing:* Room and/or apartments available on a first-come, first-served basis to single students; on-campus housing not available to married students. Housing application deadline: 3/1.

GRADUATE UNITS

College of Arts and Sciences *Program availability:* Part-time, evening/weekend. Offers arts and sciences (MCJ, MP Th, MSITM); criminal justice (MCJ); information technology management (MSITM); juvenile justice education (MCJ); pastoral theology (MP Th). Electronic applications accepted.

College of Business *Program availability:* Part-time, evening/weekend. Offers accounting (MAC); business (MAC, MBA, MOL, DBA); business administration (DBA); health care (MBA); human resources (MBA); organizational leadership (MOL). Electronic applications accepted.

College of Health and Human Services *Program availability:* Part-time, evening/weekend, online learning. Offers exercise physiology (MS); health and human services (MPAS, MPH, MS, MSLP, MSW, DPT, OTD); occupational therapy (OTD); physical therapy (DPT); physician assistant studies (MPAS); public health (MPH); social work (MSW); speech-language pathology (MSLP). Electronic applications accepted.

School of Education *Program availability:* Part-time, evening/weekend, online learning. Offers early childhood education (M Ed); educational administration (M Ed). Electronic applications accepted.

ST. ANDREW'S COLLEGE, Saskatoon, SK S7N 0W3, Canada

General Information Independent-religious, coed, graduate-only institution.

GRADUATE UNITS

Graduate Programs in Theology Offers theology (M Div, MTS, STM, D Min, Diploma).

ST. ANDREW'S COLLEGE IN WINNIPEG, Winnipeg, MB R3T 2M7, Canada

General Information Independent-religious, coed, primarily men, graduate-only institution. *Graduate housing:* Rooms and/or apartments available to single and married students. Housing application deadline: 7/31.

GRADUATE UNITS

Graduate Programs Offers theology (M Div).

SAINT ANTHONY COLLEGE OF NURSING, Rockford, IL 61114

General Information Independent-religious, coed, primarily women, upper-level institution.

GRADUATE UNITS

Graduate Program *Program availability:* Part-time. Offers nursing (MSN).

ST. AUGUSTINE'S SEMINARY OF TORONTO, Scarborough, ON M1M 1M3, Canada

General Information Independent-religious, coed, primarily men, graduate-only institution. *Graduate housing:* On-campus housing not available.

GRADUATE UNITS

Graduate and Professional Programs *Program availability:* Part-time, evening/weekend. Offers divinity (M Div); lay ministry (Diploma); religious education (MRE); theological studies (MTS, Diploma).

ST. BERNARD'S SCHOOL OF THEOLOGY AND MINISTRY, Rochester, NY 14618

General Information Independent-religious, coed, graduate-only institution. *Graduate housing:* On-campus housing not available. *Research affiliation:* Colgate Rochester Crozer Divinity School.

GRADUATE UNITS

Graduate and Professional Programs *Program availability:* Part-time, evening/weekend. Offers pastoral studies (MA, Certificate); theological studies (MA); theology (M Div).

ST. BONAVENTURE UNIVERSITY, St. Bonaventure, NY 14778-2284

General Information Independent-religious, coed, comprehensive institution. CGS member. *Enrollment by degree level:* 409 master's, 43 other advanced degrees. *Graduate housing:* Room and/or apartments available on a first-come, first-served basis to single students; on-campus housing not available to married students. Housing application deadline: 3/19. *Student services:* Career counseling, international student services, low-cost health insurance, multicultural affairs office. *Library facilities:* Friedsam Memorial Library. *Collection:* Books: 371,691 (physical), 1.6 million (digital/electronic); Serial titles: 253 (physical), 269,989 (digital/electronic); Databases: 64. Weekly public service hours: 109; students can reserve study rooms.

Computer facilities: 320 computers available on campus for general student use. A campuswide network can be accessed from student residence rooms and from off campus. Online class registration is available. Website: http://www.sbu.edu/

General Application Contact: Bruce Campbell, Director of Graduate Admissions, 716-375-2429, Fax: 716-375-4015, E-mail: gradsch@sbu.edu.

GRADUATE UNITS

School of Graduate School Students: 149 full-time (88 women), 405 part-time (263 women); includes 84 minority (35 Black or African American, non-Hispanic/Latino; 5 American Indian or Alaska Native, non-Hispanic/Latino; 3 Asian, non-Hispanic/Latino; 29 Hispanic/Latino; 12 Two or more races, non-Hispanic/Latino), 9 international. Average age 31. 279 applicants, 99% accepted, 181 enrolled. *Faculty:* 34 full-time (18 women), 34 part-time/adjunct (20 women). Expenses: Contact institution. *Financial support:* In 2018–19, 26 students received support. Scholarships/grants and unspecified assistantships available. Financial award application deadline: 4/15; financial award applicants required to submit FAFSA. In 2018, 221 master's, 33 other advanced degrees awarded. *Program availability:* Part-time, evening/weekend, 100% online, blended/hybrid learning. *Application deadline:* For fall admission, 3/15 priority

date for domestic students, 2/1 priority date for international students; for spring admission, 10/15 priority date for domestic students, 7/1 priority date for international students. Applications are processed on a rolling basis. *Application fee:* $0. Electronic applications accepted. *Application Contact:* Matthew Retchless, Director of Graduate Admissions, 716-375-2021, Fax: 716-375-4015, E-mail: gradsch@sbu.edu. *Dean*, Dr. Lisa Buenaventura, 716-375-2394, Fax: 716-375-2360, E-mail: lbuenave@sbu.edu.

Jandoli School of Communication Students: 19 full-time (10 women), 76 part-time (43 women); includes 22 minority (12 Black or African American, non-Hispanic/Latino; 1 American Indian or Alaska Native, non-Hispanic/Latino; 8 Hispanic/Latino; 1 Two or more races, non-Hispanic/Latino), 1 international. Average age 33. 35 applicants, 100% accepted, 22 enrolled. *Faculty:* 6 full-time (4 women), 4 part-time/adjunct (2 women). Expenses: Contact institution. *Financial support:* In 2018–19, 8 students received support. Scholarships/grants, health care benefits, and unspecified assistantships available. Support available to part-time students. Financial award application deadline: 4/15; financial award applicants required to submit FAFSA. In 2018, 46 master's awarded. *Program availability:* Part-time, evening/weekend, online only, 100% online. Offers communication (MA); integrated marketing communications (MA); strategic leadership (MA). *Application deadline:* For fall admission, 3/15 priority date for domestic students, 2/1 priority date for international students; for spring admission, 10/15 priority date for domestic students, 7/1 priority date for international students. Applications are processed on a rolling basis. *Application fee:* $0. Electronic applications accepted. *Application Contact:* Matthew Retchless, Director of Graduate Admissions, 716-375-2021, Fax: 716-375-4015, E-mail: gradsch@sbu.edu. *Dean*, Aaron Chimbel, 716-375-2040, Fax: 716-375-2588, E-mail: achimbel@sbu.edu.

School of Business Students: 86 full-time (44 women), 108 part-time (52 women); includes 16 minority (7 Black or African American, non-Hispanic/Latino; 1 Asian, non-Hispanic/Latino; 5 Hispanic/Latino; 3 Two or more races, non-Hispanic/Latino), 8 international. Average age 28. 88 applicants, 98% accepted, 71 enrolled. *Faculty:* 15 full-time (4 women), 6 part-time/adjunct (3 women). Expenses: Contact institution. *Financial support:* In 2018–19, 9 students received support. Career-related internships or fieldwork, scholarships/grants, health care benefits, and unspecified assistantships available. Financial award application deadline: 4/15; financial award applicants required to submit FAFSA. In 2018, 125 master's awarded. *Program availability:* Part-time, evening/weekend, 100% online. Offers general business (MBA); professional accountancy (MBA). *Application deadline:* For fall admission, 3/15 priority date for domestic students, 2/1 priority date for international students; for spring admission, 10/15 priority date for domestic students, 7/1 priority date for international students. Applications are processed on a rolling basis. *Application fee:* $0. Electronic applications accepted. *Application Contact:* Matthew Retchless, Director of Graduate Admissions, 716-375-2021, Fax: 716-375-4015, E-mail: gradsch@sbu.edu. *Dean*, Dr. Matrecia James, 716-375-2200, Fax: 716-372-2191, E-mail: mjames@sbu.edu.

School of Education Students: 44 full-time (34 women), 219 part-time (166 women); includes 43 minority (16 Black or African American, non-Hispanic/Latino; 1 American Indian or Alaska Native, non-Hispanic/Latino; 2 Asian, non-Hispanic/Latino; 16 Hispanic/Latino; 8 Two or more races, non-Hispanic/Latino). Average age 32. 156 applicants, 99% accepted, 88 enrolled. *Faculty:* 11 full-time (9 women), 22 part-time/adjunct (14 women). Expenses: Contact institution. *Financial support:* In 2018–19, 12 students received support. Career-related internships or fieldwork, scholarships/grants, health care benefits, and unspecified assistantships available. Financial award application deadline: 4/15; financial award applicants required to submit FAFSA. In 2018, 48 master's, 33 Adv Cs awarded. *Program availability:* Part-time, evening/weekend, 100% online, blended/hybrid learning. Offers adolescence education (MS Ed); adolescent literacy 5-12 (MS Ed); childhood literacy B-6 (MS Ed); community mental health counseling (MS Ed); education (MS Ed, Adv C); educational leadership (MS Ed); gifted education (MS Ed, Adv C); gifted education and students with disabilities (MS Ed); rehabilitation counseling (MS Ed); school building leader (Adv C); school counseling (MS Ed); school counselor (Adv C); school district leader (Adv C). *Application deadline:* For fall admission, 3/15 priority date for domestic students, 2/1 priority date for international students; for spring admission, 10/15 priority date for domestic students, 7/1 priority date for international students. Applications are processed on a rolling basis. *Application fee:* $0. Electronic applications accepted. *Application Contact:* Matthew Retchless, Director of Graduate Admissions, 716-375-2021, Fax: 716-375-4015, E-mail: gradsch@sbu.edu. *Dean*, Dr. Lisa Buenaventura, 716-375-2394, Fax: 716-375-2360, E-mail: lbuenave@sbu.edu.

ST. CATHERINE UNIVERSITY, St. Paul, MN 55105

General Information Independent-religious, Undergraduate: women only; graduate: coed, comprehensive institution. CGS member. *Graduate housing:* Rooms and/or apartments available on a first-come, first-served basis to single and married students. Housing application deadline: 5/1.

GRADUATE UNITS

Graduate Programs *Program availability:* Part-time, evening/weekend, online learning. Offers adult-gerontological nurse practitioner (MS); education - initial licensure (MA, Certificate); education - Montessori education (MA); education–curriculum and instruction (MA); global health (MPH); health informatics (MHI); healthcare (MBA); holistic health studies (MA); integrated marketing communications (MBA); library and information science (MLIS); management (MBA); nurse educator (MS); nursing (DNP); nursing: entry-level (MS); occupational therapy (MA, OTD); organizational leadership (MA); pastoral ministry (Certificate); pediatric nurse practitioner (MS); physical therapy (DPT); physician assistant studies (MPAS); social work (MSW, DSW); spiritual direction (Certificate); theology (MA).

SAINT CHARLES BORROMEO SEMINARY, OVERBROOK, Wynnewood, PA 19096

General Information Independent-religious, coed, primarily men, comprehensive institution. *Graduate housing:* Room and/or apartments guaranteed to single students; on-campus housing not available to married students. Housing application deadline: 7/15.

GRADUATE UNITS

School of Theological Studies *Program availability:* Part-time, evening/weekend. Offers philosophical studies (MA); theological studies (MA); theology (MA).

ST. CLOUD STATE UNIVERSITY, St. Cloud, MN 56301-4498

General Information State-supported, coed, comprehensive institution. CGS member. *Graduate housing:* Room and/or apartments available on a first-come, first-served basis to single students; on-campus housing not available to married students. Housing application deadline: 4/15.

GRADUATE UNITS

School of Graduate Studies *Program availability:* Part-time, evening/weekend, online learning. Electronic applications accepted.

College of Liberal Arts Offers English (MS); English studies (MA); history (MA, MS); industrial-organizational psychology (MS); liberal arts (MA, MS); mass communications (MS); rhetoric and writing (MA).

College of Science and Engineering Offers biology (MA, MS); computer science (MS); electrical engineering (MS); information assurance (MS); instructional technology (Graduate Certificate); regulatory affairs and services (MS, Graduate Certificate); science and engineering (MA, MS, Graduate Certificate). Electronic applications accepted.

College of Social Sciences *Program availability:* Part-time. Offers applied economics (MS); criminal justice (MS); criminal justice administration (MS); cultural resource management archeology (MS, Graduate Certificate); geography and planning (MS, Graduate Certificate); public safety executive leadership (MS); social sciences (MA, MS, Graduate Certificate). Electronic applications accepted.

Herberger Business School *Program availability:* Part-time, evening/weekend. Offers business administration (MBA); information assurance (MS). Electronic applications accepted.

School of Education *Program availability:* Part-time, evening/weekend, online learning. Offers child and family studies (MS); college counseling and student development (MS); developmental and cognitive disabilities (MS, Ed D, Graduate Certificate); higher education administration (Ed D); information media (MS, Graduate Certificate); social responsibility (MS).

School of Health and Human Services Offers applied behavior analysis (MS); communication sciences and disorders (MS); educational administration and leadership (MS); educational leadership and community psychology (Spt); gerontology (MS, Graduate Certificate); health and human services (MS, MSW, Graduate Certificate, Spt); marriage and family therapy (MS); social work (MSW).

ST. EDWARD'S UNIVERSITY, Austin, TX 78704

General Information Independent-religious, coed, comprehensive institution. *Graduate housing:* On-campus housing not available.

GRADUATE UNITS

Bill Munday School of Business *Program availability:* Part-time, evening/weekend. Offers accounting (MBA); business (M Ac, MBA, MS); digital management (MBA); leadership and change (MS). Electronic applications accepted.

School of Behavioral and Social Sciences Offers environmental management and sustainability (PSM). Electronic applications accepted.

School of Education *Program availability:* Part-time, evening/weekend. Offers college student development (MA); counseling (MA); education (Certificate); humanities (MLA); liberal arts (MLA, Certificate). Electronic applications accepted.

ST. FRANCIS COLLEGE, Brooklyn Heights, NY 11201-4398

General Information Independent-religious, coed, comprehensive institution.

GRADUATE UNITS

Program in Professional Accountancy Offers professional accountancy (MS).

SAINT FRANCIS MEDICAL CENTER COLLEGE OF NURSING, Peoria, IL 61603-3783

General Information Independent-religious, coed, primarily women, upper-level institution. *Graduate housing:* Room and/or apartments available on a first-come, first-served basis to single students; on-campus housing not available to married students. Housing application deadline: 3/15.

GRADUATE UNITS

Graduate Programs Students: 2 full-time (both women), 217 part-time (184 women); includes 23 minority (10 Black or African American, non-Hispanic/Latino; 4 Asian, non-Hispanic/Latino; 6 Hispanic/Latino; 3 Two or more races, non-Hispanic/Latino). Average age 37. *Faculty:* 12 full-time (all women), 5 part-time/adjunct (all women). *Expenses:* Contact institution. *Financial support:* In 2018–19, 13 students received support. Scholarships/grants and tuition waivers (partial) available. Support available to part-time students. Financial award application deadline: 6/15; financial award applicants required to submit FAFSA. In 2018, 51 master's, 11 doctorates awarded. *Program availability:* Part-time, online only, 100% online, blended/hybrid learning. Offers adult gerontology (MSN); clinical nurse leader (MSN); family nurse practitioner (MSN, Post-Graduate Certificate); family psychiatric mental health nurse practitioner (MSN); neonatal nurse practitioner (MSN); nurse clinician (Post-Graduate Certificate); nurse educator (MSN, Post-Graduate Certificate); nursing (DNP); nursing management leadership (MSN). *Application deadline:* For fall admission, 6/1 priority date for domestic and international students; for spring admission, 11/15 priority date for domestic and international students. Applications are processed on a rolling basis. *Application fee:* $50. *Application Contact:* Dr. Kim A. Mitchell, Dean, Graduate Program, 309-655-2201, Fax: 309-624-8973, E-mail: kim.a.mitchell@osfhealthcare.org. *President of OSF Colleges of Health Sciences,* Dr. Sandie S Soldwisch, 815-282-7909, Fax: 309-624-8973, E-mail: Sandie.S.Soldwisch@osfhealthcare.org.

SAINT FRANCIS UNIVERSITY, Loretto, PA 15940-0600

General Information Independent-religious, coed, comprehensive institution. *Graduate housing:* On-campus housing not available.

GRADUATE UNITS

Cancer Care Program Offers cancer care (MS). Electronic applications accepted.

Department of Occupational Therapy Offers occupational therapy (MOT). Electronic applications accepted.

Department of Physical Therapy Offers physical therapy (DPT). Electronic applications accepted.

Department of Physician Assistant Sciences Offers physician assistant sciences (MPAS). Electronic applications accepted.

Graduate Education Program *Program availability:* Part-time, 100% online, blended/hybrid learning. Offers education (M Ed); leadership (M Ed); reading (M Ed). Electronic applications accepted.

Health Science Program *Program availability:* Part-time, evening/weekend, 100% online. Offers health science (MHS). Electronic applications accepted.

Medical Science Program *Program availability:* Part-time, evening/weekend, online learning. Offers medical science (MMS). Electronic applications accepted.

Nursing Program *Program availability:* Part-time, online only, blended/hybrid learning. Offers leadership/education (MSN). Electronic applications accepted.

School of Business *Program availability:* Part-time, evening/weekend. Offers business administration (MBA); human resource management (MHRM). Electronic applications accepted.

ST. FRANCIS XAVIER UNIVERSITY, Antigonish, NS B2G 2W5, Canada

General Information Independent-religious, coed, comprehensive institution. *Enrollment:* 48 full-time matriculated graduate/professional students (27 women), 426 part-time matriculated graduate/professional students (314 women). *Enrollment by degree level:* 405 master's, 11 doctoral, 58 other advanced degrees. *International tuition:* $932.49 Canadian dollars full-time. *Tuition, area resident:* Full-time $7547 Canadian dollars. Tuition, province resident: Full-time $7547 Canadian dollars; part-time $804.19 Canadian dollars per course. Tuition, Canadian resident: full-time $8839 Canadian dollars; part-time $932.49 Canadian dollars per course. *Required fees:* $90.20 Canadian dollars; $90.20 Canadian dollars per course. One-time fee: $6 Canadian dollars. Tuition and fees vary according to course load, degree level and program. *Graduate housing:* Room and/or apartments available on a first-come, first-served basis to single students; on-campus housing not available to married students. *Student services:* Campus employment opportunities, campus safety program, career counseling, child daycare facilities, exercise/wellness program, free psychological counseling, international student services, low-cost health insurance, multicultural affairs office, services for students with disabilities, teacher training, writing training. *Library facilities:* Angus L. Macdonald Library plus 1 other.

Computer facilities: 500 computers available on campus for general student use. A campuswide network can be accessed from student residence rooms and from off campus. Online class registration, online financial account, personal network storage, personal Web publishing, WirelessSynch iPods, Smartphones are available. Website: http://www.stfx.ca/

GRADUATE UNITS

Graduate Studies *Program availability:* Part-time, online learning. Offers adult education (M Ad Ed); biology (M Sc); Celtic studies (MA); chemistry (M Sc); community development (M Ad Ed); computer science (M Sc); curriculum and instruction (M Ed); earth sciences (M Sc); educational administration and leadership (M Ed).

ST. JOHN FISHER COLLEGE, Rochester, NY 14618-3597

General Information Independent-religious, coed, comprehensive institution. *Enrollment:* 3,719 graduate, professional, and undergraduate students; 545 full-time matriculated graduate/professional students (361 women), 422 part-time matriculated graduate/professional students (318 women). *Enrollment by degree level:* 527 master's, 440 doctoral. *Graduate faculty:* 72 full-time (45 women), 21 part-time/adjunct (13 women). *Tuition:* Full-time $950; part-time $950 per credit hour. *Required fees:* $15; $15 per semester. *Graduate housing:* On-campus housing not available. *Student services:* Campus employment opportunities, campus safety program, career counseling, child daycare facilities, exercise/wellness program, free psychological counseling, international student services, low-cost health insurance, multicultural affairs office, services for students with disabilities, teacher training, writing training. *Library facilities:* Charles J. Lavery Library plus 1 other. *Collection:* Books: 138,569 (physical), 297,511 (digital/electronic); Databases: 156. Students can reserve study rooms.

Computer facilities: 550 computers available on campus for general student use. A campuswide network can be accessed from student residence rooms and from off campus. Online class registration is available. Website: http://www.sjfc.edu/

General Application Contact: Michelle Gosier, Director of Transfer and Graduate Admissions, 585-385-8064, Fax: 585-385-8344, E-mail: mgosier@sjfc.edu.

GRADUATE UNITS

Ralph C. Wilson Jr. School of Education Students: 133 full-time (87 women), 70 part-time (55 women); includes 78 minority (64 Black or African American, non-Hispanic/Latino; 12 Hispanic/Latino; 2 Two or more races, non-Hispanic/Latino). Average age 40. 76 applicants, 72% accepted, 22 enrolled. *Faculty:* 21 full-time (15 women), 7 part-time/adjunct (6 women). *Expenses:* Contact institution. *Financial support:* Scholarships/grants available. Financial award applicants required to submit FAFSA. In 2018, 69 master's, 60 doctorates awarded. *Program availability:* Part-time, evening/weekend. Offers adolescence education: biology with special education (MS Ed); adolescence education: chemistry with special education (MS Ed); adolescence education: English with special education (MS Ed); adolescence education: French with special education (MS Ed); adolescence education: math with special education (MS Ed); adolescence education: physics with special education (MS Ed); adolescence education: social studies with special education (MS Ed); adolescence education: Spanish with special education (MS Ed); childhood education (MS); childhood education/special education (Certificate); education (MS, MS Ed, Ed D, Certificate); educational leadership (MS Ed); executive leadership (Ed D); library media (MS); literacy birth to grade 6 (MS); literacy grades 5 to 12 (MS). *Application deadline:* Applications are processed on a rolling basis. *Application fee:* $30. Electronic applications accepted. *Application Contact:* Michelle Gosier, Director of Transfer and Graduate Admissions, 585-385-8064, E-mail: mgosier@sjfc.edu. *Dean,* Dr. Michael Wischnowski, 585-385-7361, E-mail: mwischnowski@sjfc.edu.

School of Arts and Sciences Students: 13 part-time (6 women); includes 4 minority (2 Black or African American, non-Hispanic/Latino; 2 Asian, non-Hispanic/Latino). Average age 28. 26 applicants, 100% accepted, 13 enrolled. *Faculty:* 2 full-time (0 women). *Expenses:* Contact institution. *Financial support:* Scholarships/grants available. Financial award applicants required to submit FAFSA. *Program availability:* Part-time, evening/weekend. Offers arts and sciences (MS); math, science, and technology education (MS). *Application deadline:* Applications are processed on a rolling basis. *Application fee:* $30. Electronic applications accepted. *Application Contact:* Michelle Gosier, Director of Transfer and Graduate Admissions, 585-385-8064, E-mail: mgosier@sjfc.edu. *Dean,* Ann Marie Fallon, 585-385-8477, E-mail: afallon@sjfc.edu.

School of Business Students: 53 full-time (29 women), 70 part-time (28 women); includes 18 minority (5 Black or African American, non-Hispanic/Latino; 7 Asian, non-Hispanic/Latino; 5 Hispanic/Latino; 1 Two or more races, non-Hispanic/Latino), 2 international. Average age 27. 97 applicants, 89% accepted, 52 enrolled. *Faculty:* 6 full-time (0 women), 7 part-time/adjunct (2 women). *Expenses:* Contact institution. *Financial support:* Scholarships/grants available. Financial award applicants required to submit FAFSA. In 2018, 67 master's awarded. *Program availability:* Part-time, evening/weekend. Offers business (MBA, MS); business administration (MBA). *Application deadline:* Applications are processed on a rolling basis. *Application fee:* $30. Electronic applications accepted. *Application Contact:* Michelle Gosier, Director of Transfer and Graduate Admissions, 585-385-8064, E-mail: mgosier@sjfc.edu. *Dean, School of Business,* Rama Yelkur, 585-385-8446, E-mail: ryelkur@sjfc.edu.

Wegmans School of Nursing Students: 61 full-time (52 women), 263 part-time (226 women); includes 56 minority (27 Black or African American, non-Hispanic/Latino; 1 American Indian or Alaska Native, non-Hispanic/Latino; 11 Asian, non-Hispanic/Latino; 14 Hispanic/Latino; 3 Two or more races, non-Hispanic/Latino). Average age 31. 208 applicants, 60% accepted, 97 enrolled. *Faculty:* 22 full-time (18 women), 7 part-time/adjunct (5 women). Expenses: Contact institution. *Financial support:* Scholarships/grants available. Financial award applicants required to submit FAFSA. In 2018, 82 master's, 5 doctorates awarded. *Program availability:* Part-time, evening/weekend. Offers advanced practice nursing (MS, Certificate); mental health counseling (MS); nursing (MS, DNP, Certificate); nursing practice (DNP). *Application deadline:* Applications are processed on a rolling basis. Electronic applications accepted. *Application Contact:* Michelle Gosier, Director of Transfer and Graduate Admissions, 585-385-8064, E-mail: mgosier@sjfc.edu. *Dean,* Dr. Diane Cooney-Miner, 585-385-8241, Fax: 585-385-8466, E-mail: dcooney-miner@sjfc.edu.

Wegmans School of Pharmacy Students: 298 full-time (193 women), 6 part-time (3 women); includes 59 minority (10 Black or African American, non-Hispanic/Latino; 35 Asian, non-Hispanic/Latino; 6 Hispanic/Latino; 8 Two or more races, non-Hispanic/Latino), 3 international. Average age 24. 337 applicants, 31% accepted, 56 enrolled. *Faculty:* 18 full-time (11 women). Expenses: Contact institution. *Financial support:* Scholarships/grants available. Financial award applicants required to submit FAFSA. In 2018, 82 doctorates awarded. Offers pharmacy (Pharm D). *Application deadline:* For fall admission, 3/1 for domestic students. Applications are processed on a rolling basis. *Application fee:* $30. Electronic applications accepted. *Application Contact:* Michelle Gosier, Director of Transfer and Graduate Admissions, 585-385-8064, E-mail: mgosier@sjfc.edu. *Dean,* Dr. Christine Birnie, 585-385-7202, E-mail: cbirnie@sjfc.edu.

ST. JOHN'S COLLEGE, Annapolis, MD 21401

General Information Independent, coed, comprehensive institution. *Graduate housing:* On-campus housing not available.

GRADUATE UNITS

Graduate Institute *Program availability:* Evening/weekend. Offers liberal arts (MALA). Electronic applications accepted.

ST. JOHN'S COLLEGE, Santa Fe, NM 87505

General Information Independent, coed, comprehensive institution. *Graduate housing:* Rooms and/or apartments available on a first-come, first-served basis to single and married students. Housing application deadline: 4/1.

GRADUATE UNITS

Graduate Institute in Liberal Education *Program availability:* Evening/weekend. Offers Eastern classics (MA); liberal arts (MA); liberal education (MA).

ST. JOHN'S SEMINARY, Camarillo, CA 93012-2598

General Information Independent-religious, coed, primarily men, graduate-only institution. *Graduate housing:* Room and/or apartments guaranteed to single students; on-campus housing not available to married students.

GRADUATE UNITS

Graduate and Professional Programs *Program availability:* Part-time. Offers divinity (M Div); pastoral ministry (MAPM); theology (MA). Electronic applications accepted.

SAINT JOHN'S SEMINARY, Brighton, MA 02135

General Information Independent-religious, coed, graduate-only institution. *Graduate housing:* Room and/or apartments available to single students; on-campus housing not available to married students. Housing application deadline: 8/1.

GRADUATE UNITS

Graduate Programs Offers theology (M Div, MA Th, MAM).

SAINT JOHN'S UNIVERSITY, Collegeville, MN 56321

General Information Independent-religious, Undergraduate: men only; graduate: coed, comprehensive institution. *Graduate housing:* Rooms and/or apartments available on a first-come, first-served basis to single and married students. *Research affiliation:* Hill Monastic Manuscript Library (monastic studies, liturgy, spirituality), Center for Ecumenical and Cultural Research, Arca Artium (visual and book arts).

GRADUATE UNITS

Saint John's School of Theology and Seminary *Program availability:* Part-time, online learning. Offers divinity (M Div); liturgical music (MA); liturgical studies (MA); pastoral ministry (MA); theology (MA). Electronic applications accepted.

ST. JOHN'S UNIVERSITY, Queens, NY 11439

General Information Independent-religious, coed, university. CGS member. *Graduate housing:* Room and/or apartments available on a first-come, first-served basis to single students; on-campus housing not available to married students. Housing application deadline: 5/1. *Research affiliation:* Raybiotech (biotechnology), Amneal Pharmaceuticals (pharmaceutical research), RAND Corporation, Jewish Board of Family and Children's Services (mental health and social services), Merck & Company, Inc. (pharmaceutical research), ABITEC (specialty chemicals).

GRADUATE UNITS

College of Pharmacy and Health Sciences *Program availability:* Part-time, evening/weekend. Offers pharmaceutical sciences (MPH, MS, PhD); pharmacy administration (MS); pharmacy and health sciences (MPH, MS, PhD); public health (MPH); toxicology (MS). Electronic applications accepted.

College of Professional Studies Offers data mining and predictive analytics (MS); homeland security and criminal justice leadership (MPS); international communications (MS); sport management (MPS). Electronic applications accepted.

Institute for Biotechnology Offers biological and pharmaceutical biotechnology (MS). Electronic applications accepted.

The Peter J. Tobin College of Business Offers accounting (MS); business (MBA, MS); business administration (MBA); business analytics and information systems (MBA); finance (MBA, MS); taxation (MBA, MS). Electronic applications accepted.

School of Risk Management, Insurance and Actuarial Science Offers actuarial science (MS); business administration (MBA); enterprise risk management (MBA, MS); risk management and insurance (MS). Electronic applications accepted.

St. John's College of Liberal Arts and Sciences *Program availability:* Part-time, evening/weekend, 100% online, blended/hybrid learning. Offers applied and computational mathematics (MA); audiology (Au D); biological sciences (MS, PhD); chemistry (MS); clinical psychology (MA, PhD); clinical psychology-child (PhD); clinical psychology-general (PhD); criminology and justice (MA); English (MA, PhD); global development and social justice (MA); government and politics (MA, Adv C); history (MA, PhD); international law and diplomacy (Adv C); liberal arts and sciences (MA, MS, Au D,

PhD, Psy D, Adv C); liberal studies (MA); museum administration (MA); psychology (MA, MS, PhD, Psy D); public administration (Adv C); public history (MA); school psychology (MS, Psy D); sociology (MA); Spanish (MA); speech language pathology (MA); theology (MA). Electronic applications accepted.

Division of Library and Information Science *Program availability:* Part-time, online only, 100% online. Offers library science (MS); management for information professionals (Adv C). Electronic applications accepted.

Institute of Asian Studies *Program availability:* Part-time, evening/weekend. Offers Chinese studies (MA); East Asian studies (MA). Electronic applications accepted.

The School of Education Offers administration and supervision (Ed D); adolescent education (MS Ed); bilingual education (Adv C); childhood and childhood special education (MS Ed); childhood education (MS Ed); childhood education and teaching English to speakers of other languages (MS Ed); clinical mental health counseling (MS Ed, Adv C); curriculum and instruction (PhD); early childhood (PhD); early childhood education (MS Ed); education (MS Ed, Ed D, PhD, Adv C); gifted education (Adv C); global education (PhD); instructional leadership (Ed D, Adv C); literacy (MS Ed, PhD, Adv C); literacy leadership (Adv C); school building leadership (MS Ed, Adv C); school building leadership/school district leadership (Adv C); school counseling (MS Ed, Adv C); school district leadership (Adv C); special education (MS Ed, Adv C); STEM education (PhD); teaching children with disabilities in adolescent education (Adv C); teaching children with disabilities in adolescent education (7-12) (MS Ed); teaching children with disabilities in childhood education (Adv C); teaching children with disabilities in childhood education (1-6) (MS Ed); teaching English to speakers of other languages (MS Ed, Adv C); teaching English to speakers of other languages and bilingual education (MS Ed, Adv C); teaching literacy (MS Ed, Adv C); teaching literacy (5-12) and TESOL (K-12) (MS Ed); teaching literacy (B-6) and teaching children with disabilities in childhood education (MS Ed); teaching literacy (B-6) and TESOL (K-12) (MS Ed); teaching students with disabilities and early childhood education (B-2) (MS Ed); teaching, learning, and knowing (PhD). Electronic applications accepted.

School of Law *Program availability:* Part-time, evening/weekend. Offers bankruptcy (LL M); law (LL M, JD); transnational legal practice (LL M); U.S. legal studies (LL M). Electronic applications accepted.

ST. JOSEPH'S COLLEGE, LONG ISLAND CAMPUS, Patchogue, NY 11772-2399

General Information Independent, coed, comprehensive institution. *Enrollment:* 4,115 graduate, professional, and undergraduate students; 133 full-time matriculated graduate/professional students (91 women), 714 part-time matriculated graduate/professional students (543 women). *Enrollment by degree level:* 847 master's, 104 other advanced degrees. *Graduate faculty:* 34 full-time (22 women), 55 part-time/adjunct (26 women). *Tuition:* Full-time $18,450; part-time $1025 per credit. *Required fees:* $414. *Graduate housing:* On-campus housing not available. *Student services:* Campus employment opportunities, campus safety program, career counseling, exercise/wellness program, free psychological counseling, low-cost health insurance, multicultural affairs office, services for students with disabilities, teacher training, writing training. *Library facilities:* Callahan Library plus 1 other. *Collection:* Books: 113,712 (physical), 161,062 (digital/electronic); Serial titles: 224 (physical), 59,853 (digital/electronic); Databases: 129. Weekly public service hours: 80; students can reserve study rooms.

Computer facilities: 267 computers available on campus for general student use. A campuswide network can be accessed from off campus. Online class registration, library databases, learning management system, course evaluations, print management, virtual application labs, office 365, student suggestion box are available. Website: http://www.sjcny.edu/

General Application Contact: Christina Seifert, Director of Graduate and Professional Studies Admissions, 631-687-4525, E-mail: cseifert@sjcny.edu.

GRADUATE UNITS

Program in Forensic Computing Students: 6 full-time (3 women), 14 part-time (4 women); includes 8 minority (4 Black or African American, non-Hispanic/Latino; 4 Hispanic/Latino). Average age 28. 13 applicants, 77% accepted, 7 enrolled. *Faculty:* 1 full-time (0 women), 2 part-time/adjunct (0 women). Expenses: Contact institution. *Financial support:* In 2018–19, 3 students received support. *Program availability:* Part-time, evening/weekend. Offers forensic computing (MS). *Application deadline:* Applications are processed on a rolling basis. *Application fee:* $25. Electronic applications accepted. *Application Contact:* Victoria Hong, Director of M.S. in Forensic Computing, Chairperson, Assistant Professor, 631-687-2646, E-mail: vhong@sjcny.edu. *Director of M.S. in Forensic Computing, Chairperson, Assistant Professor,* Victoria Hong, 631-687-2646, E-mail: vhong@sjcny.edu.

Program in Nursing Students: 1 (woman) full-time, 52 part-time (47 women); includes 17 minority (9 Black or African American, non-Hispanic/Latino; 4 Asian, non-Hispanic/Latino; 4 Hispanic/Latino). Average age 41. 43 applicants, 67% accepted, 21 enrolled. *Faculty:* 3 full-time (all women), 1 (woman) part-time/adjunct. Expenses: Contact institution. *Financial support:* In 2018–19, 37 students received support. In 2018, 3 master's awarded. *Program availability:* Part-time, evening/weekend. Offers adult-gerontology clinical nurse specialist (MS); adult-gerontology primary care nurse practitioner (MS); nursing education (MS). *Application deadline:* Applications are processed on a rolling basis. *Application fee:* $25. Electronic applications accepted. *Application Contact:* Dr. Maria Fletcher, RN, Director, Associate Professor, 631-687-5180, E-mail: mfletcher@sjcny.edu. *Director, Associate Professor,* Dr. Maria Fletcher, RN, 631-687-5180, E-mail: mfletcher@sjcny.edu.

Programs in Business Management and Administration Students: 52 full-time (28 women), 144 part-time (72 women); includes 48 minority (12 Black or African American, non-Hispanic/Latino; 9 Asian, non-Hispanic/Latino; 25 Hispanic/Latino; 1 Native Hawaiian or other Pacific Islander, non-Hispanic/Latino; 1 Two or more races, non-Hispanic/Latino). Average age 32. 134 applicants, 66% accepted, 57 enrolled. *Faculty:* 13 full-time (5 women), 23 part-time/adjunct (8 women). Expenses: Contact institution. *Financial support:* In 2018–19, 46 students received support. Federal Work-Study available. In 2018, 47 master's awarded. *Program availability:* Part-time, evening/weekend, 100% online, blended/hybrid learning. Offers accounting (MBA); business administration (MBA); business management and administration (EMBA, MBA). *Application deadline:* Applications are processed on a rolling basis. *Application fee:* $25. Electronic applications accepted. *Application Contact:* Mary A. Chance, Assistant Professor, Interim Director of Graduate Management Studies, 631-687-1297, E-mail: mchance@sjcny.edu. *Assistant Professor, Interim Director of Graduate Management Studies,* Mary A. Chance, 631-687-1297, E-mail: mchance@sjcny.edu.

Field of Executive Business Administration Students: 25 full-time (15 women), 94 part-time (50 women); includes 33 minority (10 Black or African American, non-Hispanic/Latino; 4 Asian, non-Hispanic/Latino; 17 Hispanic/Latino; 1 Native Hawaiian or other Pacific Islander, non-Hispanic/Latino; 1 Two or more races, non-

Hispanic/Latino). Average age 34. 85 applicants, 62% accepted, 33 enrolled. *Faculty:* 13 full-time (5 women), 23 part-time/adjunct (8 women). Expenses: Contact institution. *Financial support:* In 2018–19, 23 students received support. In 2018, 23 master's awarded. *Program availability:* Part-time, evening/weekend, 100% online, blended/hybrid learning. Offers executive business administration (EMBA). *Application deadline:* Applications are processed on a rolling basis. *Application fee:* $25. Electronic applications accepted. *Application Contact:* Mary A. Chance, Assistant Professor/Interim Director of Graduate Management Studies, 631-687-1297, E-mail: mchance@sjcny.edu. *Assistant Professor/Interim Director of Graduate Management Studies*, Mary A. Chance, 631-687-1297, E-mail: mchance@sjcny.edu.

Programs in Education Students: 33 full-time (26 women), 335 part-time (293 women); includes 45 minority (5 Black or African American, non-Hispanic/Latino; 2 American Indian or Alaska Native, non-Hispanic/Latino; 3 Asian, non-Hispanic/Latino; 30 Hispanic/Latino; 1 Native Hawaiian or other Pacific Islander, non-Hispanic/Latino; 4 Two or more races, non-Hispanic/Latino). Average age 26. 250 applicants, 82% accepted, 134 enrolled. *Faculty:* 14 full-time (11 women), 23 part-time/adjunct (14 women). Expenses: Contact institution. *Financial support:* In 2018–19, 127 students received support. Federal Work-Study available. In 2018, 180 master's awarded. *Program availability:* Part-time, evening/weekend. Offers educational leadership (MA); mathematics education (MA); special education (MA). *Application deadline:* Applications are processed on a rolling basis. *Application fee:* $25. Electronic applications accepted. *Application Contact:* Nancy Gilchriest, Associate Professor and Department Chair, 631-687-1472, E-mail: ngilchriest@sjcny.edu. *Associate Professor and Department Chair,* Nancy Gilchriest, 631-687-1472, E-mail: ngilchriest@sjcny.edu.

Field in Special Education Students: 14 full-time (12 women), 94 part-time (74 women); includes 10 minority (1 Asian, non-Hispanic/Latino; 8 Hispanic/Latino; 1 Two or more races, non-Hispanic/Latino). Average age 25. 79 applicants, 82% accepted, 44 enrolled. *Faculty:* 9 full-time (7 women), 10 part-time/adjunct (4 women). Expenses: Contact institution. *Financial support:* In 2018–19, 42 students received support. Federal Work-Study available. In 2018, 69 master's awarded. *Program availability:* Part-time, evening/weekend. Offers special education (MA). *Application deadline:* Applications are processed on a rolling basis. *Application fee:* $25. Electronic applications accepted. *Application Contact:* Joan Silver, Associate Professor/Director of MA in Childhood and Adolescence Education with an annotation in Severe and Multiple Disabilities, 631-687-1219, E-mail: jsilver@sjcny.edu. *Associate Professor/Director of MA in Childhood and Adolescence Education with an annotation in Severe and Multiple Disabilities,* Joan Silver, 631-687-1219, E-mail: jsilver@sjcny.edu.

Field of Infant/Toddler Early Childhood Special Education Students: 12 full-time (9 women), 128 part-time (118 women); includes 18 minority (3 Black or African American, non-Hispanic/Latino; 1 American Indian or Alaska Native, non-Hispanic/Latino; 1 Asian, non-Hispanic/Latino; 13 Hispanic/Latino). Average age 28. 98 applicants, 80% accepted, 48 enrolled. *Faculty:* 4 full-time (all women), 7 part-time/adjunct (all women). Expenses: Contact institution. *Financial support:* In 2018–19, 32 students received support. In 2018, 37 master's awarded. *Program availability:* Part-time, evening/weekend. Offers infant/toddler early childhood special education (MA). *Application deadline:* Applications are processed on a rolling basis. *Application fee:* $25. Electronic applications accepted. *Application Contact:* Katherine Granelli, Director of MA in Infant/Toddler Early Childhood Special Education, 631-687-1217, E-mail: kgranelli@sjcny.edu. *Director of MA in Infant/Toddler Early Childhood Special Education,* Katherine Granelli, 631-687-1217, E-mail: kgranelli@sjcny.edu.

Field of Literacy and Cognition Students: 6 full-time (5 women), 91 part-time (86 women); includes 13 minority (1 Black or African American, non-Hispanic/Latino; 1 American Indian or Alaska Native, non-Hispanic/Latino; 1 Asian, non-Hispanic/Latino; 7 Hispanic/Latino; 3 Two or more races, non-Hispanic/Latino). Average age 25. 64 applicants, 88% accepted, 38 enrolled. *Faculty:* 2 part-time/adjunct (both women). Expenses: Contact institution. *Financial support:* In 2018–19, 43 students received support. In 2018, 63 master's awarded. *Program availability:* Part-time, evening/weekend. Offers literacy 5-12 (MA); literacy and cognition birth-6 (MA); literacy birth-12 (MA); literacy/cognition and special education (MA). *Application deadline:* Applications are processed on a rolling basis. *Application fee:* $25. Electronic applications accepted. *Application Contact:* Karen Megay-Nespoli, Associate Professor/Director of MA in Literacy and Cognition, 631-687-1212, E-mail: kmegay-nespoli@sjcny.edu. *Associate Professor/Director of MA in Literacy and Cognition,* Karen Megay-Nespoli, 631-687-1212, E-mail: kmegay-nespoli@sjcny.edu.

Programs in Health Care Administration Students: 6 full-time (4 women), 18 part-time (11 women); includes 6 minority (2 Black or African American, non-Hispanic/Latino; 1 Asian, non-Hispanic/Latino; 3 Hispanic/Latino). Average age 37. 10 applicants, 50% accepted, 2 enrolled. *Faculty:* 13 full-time (5 women), 23 part-time/adjunct (8 women). Expenses: Contact institution. *Financial support:* In 2018–19, 13 students received support. In 2018, 13 master's awarded. *Program availability:* Part-time, evening/weekend, 100% online, blended/hybrid learning. Offers health care administration (MBA); health care management (MBA); health care management - health information systems (MBA). *Application deadline:* Applications are processed on a rolling basis. *Application fee:* $25. Electronic applications accepted. *Application Contact:* Mary A. Chance, Assistant Professor/Interim Director of Graduate Management Studies, 631-687-1297, E-mail: mchance@sjcny.edu. *Assistant Professor/Interim Director of Graduate Management Studies,* Mary A. Chance, 631-687-1297, E-mail: mchance@sjcny.edu.

Programs in Management Students: 35 full-time (29 women), 151 part-time (116 women); includes 64 minority (30 Black or African American, non-Hispanic/Latino; 3 Asian, non-Hispanic/Latino; 26 Hispanic/Latino; 5 Two or more races, non-Hispanic/Latino). Average age 35. 165 applicants, 62% accepted, 77 enrolled. *Faculty:* 13 full-time (5 women), 23 part-time/adjunct (8 women). Expenses: Contact institution. *Financial support:* In 2018–19, 31 students received support. In 2018, 38 master's awarded. *Program availability:* Part-time, evening/weekend, 100% online, blended/hybrid learning. Offers health care management (MS); human resources management (MS); human services leadership (MS); organizational management (MS). *Application deadline:* Applications are processed on a rolling basis. *Application fee:* $25. Electronic applications accepted. *Application Contact:* Mary A. Chance, Assistant Professor/Interim Director of Graduate Management Studies, 631-687-1297, E-mail: mchance@sjcny.edu. *Assistant Professor/Interim Director of Graduate Management Studies,* Mary A. Chance, 631-687-1297, E-mail: mchance@sjcny.edu.

ST. JOSEPH'S COLLEGE, NEW YORK, Brooklyn, NY 11205-3688

General Information Independent, coed, comprehensive institution. *Enrollment:* 1,179 graduate, professional, and undergraduate students; 41 full-time matriculated graduate/professional students (29 women), 188 full-time matriculated graduate/professional students (146 women). *Enrollment by degree level:* 229 master's, 2 other advanced degrees. *Graduate faculty:* 11 full-time (10 women), 18 part-

time/adjunct (12 women). *Tuition:* Full-time $18,450; part-time $1025 per credit. *Required fees:* $414. *Graduate housing:* On-campus housing not available. *Student services:* Campus employment opportunities, campus safety program, career counseling, exercise/wellness program, free psychological counseling, low-cost health insurance, multicultural affairs office, services for students with disabilities, teacher training, writing training. *Library facilities:* McEntegart Hall Library plus 1 other. *Collection:* Books: 91,695 (physical), 161,062 (digital/electronic); Serial titles: 36 (physical), 59,853 (digital/electronic); Databases: 129. Weekly public service hours: 83; students can reserve study rooms.

Computer facilities: 207 computers available on campus for general student use. A campuswide network can be accessed from off campus. Online class registration, library databases, learning management system, course evaluations, print management, virtual application labs, office software, student suggestion box are available. Website: http://www.sjcny.edu/

General Application Contact: Roberto Figueroa, Director of Transfer, Adult, and Graduate Admissions, 718-940-5828, E-mail: rfigueroa@sjcny.edu.

GRADUATE UNITS

Program in Creative Writing Students: 8 full-time (6 women); includes 4 minority (1 Black or African American, non-Hispanic/Latino; 1 Asian, non-Hispanic/Latino; 2 Hispanic/Latino). Average age 34. 18 applicants, 72% accepted, 5 enrolled. *Faculty:* 1 (woman) full-time, 3 part-time/adjunct (1 woman). Expenses: Contact institution. *Financial support:* In 2018–19, 7 students received support. In 2018, 12 master's awarded. *Program availability:* Part-time, evening/weekend. Offers creative writing (MFA). *Application deadline:* Applications are processed on a rolling basis. *Application fee:* $25. Electronic applications accepted. *Application Contact:* Grace Bonner, E-mail: gbonner@sjcny.edu.

Program in Forensic Computing Students: 3 full-time (1 woman), 7 part-time (2 women); includes 8 minority (4 Black or African American, non-Hispanic/Latino; 4 Hispanic/Latino). Average age 31. 11 applicants, 91% accepted, 4 enrolled. *Faculty:* 1 full-time (0 women), 2 part-time/adjunct (0 women). Expenses: Contact institution. *Financial support:* In 2018–19, 2 students received support. In 2018, 1 master's awarded. *Program availability:* Part-time, evening/weekend. Offers forensic computing (MS). *Application deadline:* Applications are processed on a rolling basis. *Application fee:* $25. Electronic applications accepted. *Application Contact:* Roberto Figueroa, Director of Transfer, Adult and Graduate Admissions, 718-940-5828, E-mail: rfigueroa@sjcny.edu. *Associate Professor,* Dr. Joseph Pascarella, 718-940-5775, E-mail: jpascarella2@sjcny.edu.

Program in Nursing Students: 51 part-time (49 women); includes 41 minority (36 Black or African American, non-Hispanic/Latino; 2 Asian, non-Hispanic/Latino; 1 Hispanic/Latino; 2 Two or more races, non-Hispanic/Latino). Average age 43. 45 applicants, 60% accepted, 13 enrolled. *Faculty:* 3 full-time (all women), 4 part-time/adjunct (all women). Expenses: Contact institution. *Financial support:* In 2018–19, 9 students received support. In 2018, 7 master's awarded. *Program availability:* Part-time, evening/weekend. Offers adult-gerontology clinical nurse specialist (MS); adult-gerontology primary care nurse practitioner (MS); nursing education (MS). *Application deadline:* Applications are processed on a rolling basis. *Application fee:* $25. Electronic applications accepted. *Application Contact:* Maria Fletcher, Director, Associate Professor, 718-940-5891, E-mail: mfletcher@sjcny.edu. *Director, Associate Professor,* Maria Fletcher, 718-940-5891, E-mail: mfletcher@sjcny.edu.

Programs in Business Management and Administration Students: 11 full-time (5 women), 33 part-time (20 women); includes 33 minority (23 Black or African American, non-Hispanic/Latino; 2 Asian, non-Hispanic/Latino; 6 Hispanic/Latino; 2 Two or more races, non-Hispanic/Latino). Average age 37. 25 applicants, 72% accepted, 13 enrolled. *Faculty:* 5 part-time/adjunct (4 women). Expenses: Contact institution. *Financial support:* In 2018–19, 11 students received support. In 2018, 17 master's awarded. *Program availability:* Part-time, evening/weekend, 100% online, blended/hybrid learning. Offers accounting (MBA); business administration (MBA); management (MS). *Application deadline:* Applications are processed on a rolling basis. *Application fee:* $25. Electronic applications accepted. *Application Contact:* Mary A. Chance, Interim Director and Assistant Professor, 631-687-1297, E-mail: mchance@sjcny.edu. *Interim Director and Assistant Professor,* Mary A. Chance, 631-687-1297, E-mail: mchance@sjcny.edu.

Field of Executive Business Administration Students: 10 full-time (5 women), 25 part-time (16 women); includes 26 minority (17 Black or African American, non-Hispanic/Latino; 2 Asian, non-Hispanic/Latino; 5 Hispanic/Latino; 2 Two or more races, non-Hispanic/Latino). Average age 39. 17 applicants, 76% accepted, 11 enrolled. *Faculty:* 5 part-time/adjunct (4 women). Expenses: Contact institution. *Financial support:* In 2018–19, 10 students received support. In 2018, 15 master's awarded. *Program availability:* Part-time, evening/weekend, 100% online, blended/hybrid learning. Offers executive business administration (EMBA). *Application deadline:* Applications are processed on a rolling basis. *Application fee:* $25. Electronic applications accepted. *Application Contact:* Dr. Sharon Didier, Co-Director of Graduate Management Studies/Assistant Professor, 718-940-5790, E-mail: sdidier@sjcny.edu. *Co-Director of Graduate Management Studies/Assistant Professor,* Dr. Sharon Didier, 718-940-5790, E-mail: sdidier@sjcny.edu.

Programs in Education Students: 34 part-time (28 women); includes 11 minority (2 Black or African American, non-Hispanic/Latino; 9 Hispanic/Latino). Average age 24. 26 applicants, 77% accepted, 16 enrolled. *Faculty:* 5 full-time (all women), 2 part-time/adjunct (both women). Expenses: Contact institution. *Financial support:* In 2018–19, 22 students received support. In 2018, 16 master's awarded. *Program availability:* Part-time, evening/weekend. Offers educational leadership (MA); literacy and cognition (MA); special education (MA). *Application deadline:* Applications are processed on a rolling basis. *Application fee:* $25. Electronic applications accepted. *Application Contact:* Nancy Gilchriest, Associate Professor, Department Chair, 631-687-1472, E-mail: ngilchriest@sjcny.edu. *Associate Professor, Department Chair,* Nancy Gilchriest, 631-687-1472, E-mail: ngilchriest@sjcny.edu.

Field of Literacy and Cognition Students: 13 part-time (12 women); includes 6 minority (all Hispanic/Latino). Average age 23. 11 applicants, 82% accepted, 7 enrolled. *Faculty:* 2 full-time (both women), 2 part-time/adjunct (both women). Expenses: Contact institution. *Financial support:* In 2018–19, 8 students received support. In 2018, 8 master's awarded. *Program availability:* Part-time, evening/weekend. Offers literacy and cognition (MA). *Application deadline:* Applications are processed on a rolling basis. *Application fee:* $25. Electronic applications accepted. *Application Contact:* Esther Berkowitz, Associate Professor/Director of the Literacy and Cognition Program, 718-940-5692, E-mail: eberkowitz@sjcny.edu. *Associate Professor/Director of the Literacy and Cognition Program,* Esther Berkowitz, 718-940-5692, E-mail: eberkowitz@sjcny.edu.

Field of Special Education Students: 14 part-time (12 women); includes 2 minority (both Hispanic/Latino). Average age 23. 12 applicants, 67% accepted, 7 enrolled. *Faculty:* 3 full-time (all women). Expenses: Contact institution. *Financial support:* In

2018–19, 10 students received support. In 2018, 8 master's awarded. *Program availability:* Part-time, evening/weekend. Offers severe and multiple disabilities (MA). *Application deadline:* Applications are processed on a rolling basis. *Application fee:* $25. Electronic applications accepted. *Application Contact:* Susan Straut-Collard, Professor/Associate Chair/Director of the MA in Childhood and Adolescence Special Education, 718-940-5689, E-mail: sstrautcollard@sjcny.edu. *Professor/Associate Chair/Director of the MA in Childhood and Adolescence Special Education*, Susan Straut-Collard, 718-940-5689, E-mail: sstrautcollard@sjcny.edu.

Programs in Health Care Administration Students: 2 full-time (both women), 12 part-time (9 women); includes 10 minority (6 Black or African American, non-Hispanic/Latino; 2 Asian, non-Hispanic/Latino; 2 Hispanic/Latino). Average age 37. *Faculty:* 5 part-time/adjunct (4 women). Expenses: Contact institution. *Financial support:* In 2018–19, 6 students received support. In 2018, 7 master's awarded. *Program availability:* Part-time, evening/weekend, 100% online, blended/hybrid learning. Offers health care administration (MBA); health care management (MBA). *Application deadline:* Applications are processed on a rolling basis. *Application fee:* $25. Electronic applications accepted. *Application Contact:* Lauren Pete, Associate Professor and Chair, 718-940-5890, E-mail: lpete@sjcny.edu. *Associate Professor and Chair*, Lauren Pete, 718-940-5890, E-mail: lpete@sjcny.edu.

Field in Health Care Management - Health Information Systems Students: 9 part-time (7 women); includes 6 minority (4 Black or African American, non-Hispanic/Latino; 2 Asian, non-Hispanic/Latino). Average age 36. *Faculty:* 5 part-time/adjunct (4 women). Expenses: Contact institution. *Financial support:* In 2018–19, 4 students received support. In 2018, 6 master's awarded. *Program availability:* Part-time, evening/weekend, 100% online, blended/hybrid learning. Offers health care management - health information systems (MBA). *Application deadline:* Applications are processed on a rolling basis. *Application fee:* $25. Electronic applications accepted. *Application Contact:* Lauren Pete, Chair, 718-940-5890, E-mail: lpete@sjcny.edu. *Chair*, Lauren Pete, 718-940-5890, E-mail: lpete@sjcny.edu.

Programs in Management Students: 17 full-time (15 women), 51 part-time (38 women); includes 52 minority (27 Black or African American, non-Hispanic/Latino; 6 Asian, non-Hispanic/Latino; 17 Hispanic/Latino; 2 Two or more races, non-Hispanic/Latino). Average age 38. 46 applicants, 65% accepted, 17 enrolled. *Faculty:* 5 part-time/adjunct (4 women). Expenses: Contact institution. *Financial support:* In 2018–19, 13 students received support. In 2018, 26 master's awarded. *Program availability:* Part-time, evening/weekend, 100% online, blended/hybrid learning. Offers human resources management (MS); management (MBA, MS); organizational management (MS). *Application deadline:* Applications are processed on a rolling basis. *Application fee:* $25. Electronic applications accepted. *Application Contact:* Sharon Didier, Assistant Chair/Co-Director of Graduate Management Studies/Associate Professor, 718-940-5790, E-mail: sdidier@sjcny.edu. *Assistant Chair/Co-Director of Graduate Management Studies/Associate Professor*, Sharon Didier, 718-940-5790, E-mail: sdidier@sjcny.edu.

Field in Health Care Management Students: 9 full-time (all women), 20 part-time (14 women); includes 22 minority (10 Black or African American, non-Hispanic/Latino; 1 Asian, non-Hispanic/Latino; 9 Hispanic/Latino; 1 Two or more races, non-Hispanic/Latino). Average age 35. 19 applicants, 42% accepted, 7 enrolled. *Faculty:* 5 part-time/adjunct (4 women). Expenses: Contact institution. *Financial support:* In 2018–19, 5 students received support. In 2018, 9 master's awarded. *Program availability:* Part-time, evening/weekend, 100% online, blended/hybrid learning. Offers health care management (MBA). *Application deadline:* Applications are processed on a rolling basis. *Application fee:* $25. Electronic applications accepted. *Application Contact:* Lauren Pete, Associate Professor/Chair, 718-940-5890, E-mail: lpete@sjcny.edu. *Associate Professor/Chair*, Lauren Pete, 718-940-5890, E-mail: lpete@sjcny.edu.

Field in Human Services Management and Leadership Students: 2 full-time (both women), 13 part-time (10 women); includes 11 minority (6 Black or African American, non-Hispanic/Latino; 2 Asian, non-Hispanic/Latino; 3 Hispanic/Latino). Average age 42. 11 applicants, 82% accepted, 5 enrolled. *Faculty:* 5 part-time/adjunct (4 women). Expenses: Contact institution. *Financial support:* In 2018–19, 5 students received support. In 2018, 5 master's awarded. *Program availability:* Part-time, evening/weekend, 100% online, blended/hybrid learning. Offers human services management and leadership (MS). *Application deadline:* Applications are processed on a rolling basis. *Application fee:* $25. Electronic applications accepted. *Application Contact:* Sharon Didier, Assistant Chair/Co-Director of Graduate Management Studies/Associate Professor, 718-940-5790, E-mail: sdidier@sjcny.edu. *Assistant Chair/Co-Director of Graduate Management Studies/Associate Professor*, Sharon Didier, 718-940-5790, E-mail: sdidier@sjcny.edu.

SAINT JOSEPH'S COLLEGE OF MAINE, Standish, ME 04084

General Information Independent-religious, coed, comprehensive institution. *Graduate housing:* On-campus housing not available.

GRADUATE UNITS

Master of Accountancy Program *Program availability:* Part-time, online learning. Offers accountancy (M Acc). Electronic applications accepted.

Master of Arts in Pastoral Theology Program *Program availability:* Part-time, online learning. Offers pastoral theology (MA).

Master of Business Administration in Leadership Program *Program availability:* Part-time, online learning. Offers leadership (MBA).

Master of Health Administration Program *Program availability:* Part-time, online learning. Offers health administration (MHA). Degree program is external; available only by correspondence and online. Electronic applications accepted.

Master of Science in Education Program *Program availability:* Part-time, online learning. Offers adult education and training (MS Ed); Catholic school leadership (MS Ed); health care educator (MS Ed); school educator (MS Ed). Program available by correspondence. Electronic applications accepted.

Master of Science in Nursing Program *Program availability:* Part-time, online learning. Offers administration (MSN); education (MSN); family nurse practitioner (MSN); nursing administration and leadership (Certificate); nursing and health care education (Certificate). Electronic applications accepted.

ST. JOSEPH'S SEMINARY, Yonkers, NY 10704

General Information Independent-religious, coed, graduate-only institution. *Graduate housing:* Room and/or apartments guaranteed to single students; on-campus housing not available to married students.

GRADUATE UNITS

Graduate and Professional Programs Offers Catholic philosophical studies (MA); divinity (M Div); pastoral studies (MAPS); theology (MA).

SAINT JOSEPH'S UNIVERSITY, Philadelphia, PA 19131-1395

General Information Independent-religious, coed, comprehensive institution. *Graduate housing:* On-campus housing not available.

GRADUATE UNITS

College of Arts and Sciences *Program availability:* Part-time, evening/weekend, 100% online, blended/hybrid learning. Offers arts and sciences (MA, MS, Ed D, Certificate, Post-Master's Certificate); behavior analysis (MS, Post-Master's Certificate); behavior management (MS); biology (MA, MS); computer science (MS); criminal justice (MS); curriculum supervisor (Certificate); educational leadership (MS, Ed D); elementary education (MS, Certificate); elementary/middle school education (Certificate); federal law enforcement (MS); health administration (MS); health informatics (MS); intelligence and crime analysis (MS); mathematics and computer science (Post-Master's Certificate); organizational development and leadership (MS); organizations development and leadership (MS); principal (Certificate); professional education (MS); psychology (MS); reading specialist (MS, Certificate); reading supervisor (Certificate); secondary education (MS, Certificate); special education (MS); special education 7-12 (Certificate); special education PK-8 (Certificate); superintendent's letter of eligibility (Certificate); supervisor of special education (Certificate); teacher of the deaf and hard of hearing (Certificate); writing studies (MA). Electronic applications accepted.

Erivan K. Haub School of Business *Program availability:* Part-time-only, evening/weekend, 100% online. Offers accounting (MBA); business (MBA, MS, Post Master's Certificate, Postbaccalaureate Certificate); business intelligence analytics (MBA); business intelligence and analytics (MS); customer analytics and insights (MS); executive business administration (MBA); finance (MBA); financial analysis reporting (Postbaccalaureate Certificate); financial services (MS); food marketing (MBA, MS); general business (MBA); health and medical services administration (MBA); international business (MBA); international marketing (MBA, MS); leading (MBA); marketing (MBA); pharmaceutical and healthcare marketing (MBA, Post Master's Certificate); strategic human resources management (MS). Electronic applications accepted.

SAINT LEO UNIVERSITY, Saint Leo, FL 33574-6665

General Information Independent-religious, coed, comprehensive institution. *Enrollment:* 5,232 graduate, professional, and undergraduate students; 88 full-time matriculated graduate/professional students (69 women), 4,118 part-time matriculated graduate/professional students (2,577 women). *Enrollment by degree level:* 3,971 master's, 230 doctoral, 5 other advanced degrees. *Graduate faculty:* 97 full-time (41 women), 134 part-time/adjunct (64 women). *Tuition:* Full-time $12,960; part-time $720 per credit hour. Tuition and fees vary according to degree level, campus/location and program. *Graduate housing:* Room and/or apartments available on a first-come, first-served basis to single students; on-campus housing not available to married students. *Student services:* Campus employment opportunities, campus safety program, career counseling, exercise/wellness program, free psychological counseling, international student services, low-cost health insurance, multicultural affairs office, services for students with disabilities, teacher training, writing training. *Library facilities:* Cannon Memorial Library plus 1 other. *Collection:* Books: 86,985 (physical), 363,788 (digital/electronic); Serial titles: 1,430 (physical), 100,630 (digital/electronic); Databases: 121. Weekly public service hours: 112.

Computer facilities: Computer purchase and lease plans are available. 150 computers available on campus for general student use. A campuswide network can be accessed from student residence rooms and from off campus. Online class registration is available.
Website: http://www.saintleo.edu/

General Application Contact: Mark Russum, Assistant Vice President, Enrollment, 800-707-8846, Fax: 352-588-7873, E-mail: grad.admissions@saintleo.edu.

GRADUATE UNITS

Graduate Studies in Business Students: 8 full-time (3 women), 2,209 part-time (1,288 women); includes 1,046 minority (691 Black or African American, non-Hispanic/Latino; 10 American Indian or Alaska Native, non-Hispanic/Latino; 47 Asian, non-Hispanic/Latino; 249 Hispanic/Latino; 5 Native Hawaiian or other Pacific Islander, non-Hispanic/Latino; 44 Two or more races, non-Hispanic/Latino; 71 international. Average age 37. 760 applicants, 83% accepted, 498 enrolled. *Faculty:* 51 full-time (16 women), 54 part-time/adjunct (22 women). Expenses: Contact institution. *Financial support:* In 2018–19, 213 students received support. Scholarships/grants, unspecified assistantships, and tuition remission for Saint Leo employees and their dependents available. Financial award application deadline: 3/1; financial award applicants required to submit FAFSA. In 2018, 763 master's, 14 doctorates awarded. *Program availability:* Part-time, evening/weekend, 100% online, blended/hybrid learning. Offers accounting (M Acc); cybersecurity management (MBA); health care management (MBA); human resource management (MBA); marketing (MBA); marketing research and social media analytics (MBA); software engineering (MS). *Application deadline:* For fall admission, 7/1 priority date for domestic and international students; for spring admission, 11/12 priority date for domestic students, 11/1 for international students. Applications are processed on a rolling basis. *Application fee:* $80. Electronic applications accepted. *Application Contact:* Mark Russum, Assistant Vice President, Enrollment, 800-707-8846, Fax: 352-588-7873, E-mail: grad.admissions@saintleo.edu. *Dean, School of Business*, Dr. Robyn Parker, 352-588-8599, Fax: 352-588-8912, E-mail: mbaslu@saintleo.edu.

Graduate Studies in Creative Writing Students: 34 part-time (24 women); includes 11 minority (6 Black or African American, non-Hispanic/Latino; 4 Hispanic/Latino; 1 Two or more races, non-Hispanic/Latino). Average age 41. 15 applicants, 87% accepted, 4 enrolled. *Faculty:* 4 full-time (2 women), 2 part-time/adjunct (1 woman). Expenses: Contact institution. *Financial support:* In 2018–19, 6 students received support. Tuition remission for Saint Leo employees and their dependents available. Financial award application deadline: 3/1; financial award applicants required to submit FAFSA. In 2018, 14 master's awarded. *Program availability:* Part-time. Offers creative writing (MA); war literature and writing for veterans (MA). *Application deadline:* For fall admission, 7/1 priority date for domestic and international students; for spring admission, 11/1 priority date for domestic and international students. Applications are processed on a rolling basis. *Application fee:* $80. Electronic applications accepted. *Application Contact:* Mark Russum, Assistant Vice President, Enrollment, 800-707-8846, Fax: 352-588-7873, E-mail: grad.admissions@saintleo.edu. *Director*, Dr. Steve Kistulentz, 352-588-7218, Fax: 352-588-8300, E-mail: steven.kistulentz@saintleo.edu.

Graduate Studies in Education Average age 37. 214 applicants, 69% accepted, 125 enrolled. Expenses: Contact institution. *Financial support:* In 2018–19, 17 students received support. Career-related internships or fieldwork, scholarships/grants, health care benefits, and tuition remission for Saint Leo employees and their dependents available. Financial award application deadline: 3/1; financial award applicants required to submit FAFSA. In 2018, 139 master's, 9 other advanced degrees awarded. *Program availability:* Part-time, evening/weekend, online only, 100% online. Offers school leadership (Ed D). *Application deadline:* For fall admission, 7/1 priority date for domestic students, 7/1 for international students; for winter admission, 7/1 for international students; for spring admission, 11/1 priority date for domestic students. Applications are processed on a rolling basis. *Application fee:* $80. Electronic applications accepted. *Application Contact:* Mark Russum, Assistant Vice President, Enrollment, 800-707-8846, Fax: 352-588-7873, E-mail: grad.admissions@saintleo.edu. *Director of Graduate Studies in Education*, Dr. Fern Aefsky, 352-588-8309, Fax: 352-588-8861, E-mail: kara.winkler@saintleo.edu.

Graduate Studies in Human Services Average age 40. 77 applicants, 65% accepted, 47 enrolled. Expenses: Contact institution. *Financial support:* In 2018–19, 4 students received support. Career-related internships or fieldwork, scholarships/grants, health care benefits, and tuition remission for Saint Leo employees and their dependents available. Financial award application deadline: 3/1; financial award applicants required to submit FAFSA. In 2018, 44 master's awarded. *Program availability:* Part-time, evening/weekend, 100% online. Offers human services (MS). *Application deadline:* For fall admission, 7/1 for domestic and international students; for spring admission, 11/1 for domestic and international students. Applications are processed on a rolling basis. *Application fee:* $80. Electronic applications accepted. *Application Contact:* Mary Martinez-Drovie, Graduate Enrollment Counselor, 352-588-5802, Fax: 352-588-8289, E-mail: mary.martinez-drovie@saintleo.edu. *Dean, School of Education and Social Services*, Dr. Susan Kinsella, 352-588-8272, Fax: 352-588-8289, E-mail: susan.kinsella@saintleo.edu.

Graduate Studies in Psychology Students: 59 part-time (47 women); includes 30 minority (20 Black or African American, non-Hispanic/Latino; 1 American Indian or Alaska Native, non-Hispanic/Latino; 1 Asian, non-Hispanic/Latino; 6 Hispanic/Latino; 2 Two or more races, non-Hispanic/Latino). Average age 35. 62 applicants, 65% accepted, 32 enrolled. *Faculty:* 4 full-time (3 women), 3 part-time/adjunct (1 woman). Expenses: Contact institution. *Financial support:* In 2018–19, 3 students received support. Scholarships/grants and tuition remission for Saint Leo employees and their dependents available. Financial award application deadline: 3/1; financial award applicants required to submit FAFSA. In 2018, 5 master's awarded. *Program availability:* Part-time-only, evening/weekend, online only, 100% online. Offers psychology (MS). *Application deadline:* For fall admission, 7/1 priority date for domestic students, 7/1 for international students; for spring admission, 11/1 priority date for domestic students, 11/1 for international students. Applications are processed on a rolling basis. *Application fee:* $80. Electronic applications accepted. *Application Contact:* Mark Russum, Assistant Vice President, Enrollment, 800-707-8846, Fax: 352-588-7873, E-mail: grad.admissions@saintleo.edu. *Director, Graduate Studies in Psychology*, Dr. Cathleen Dunn, 352-588-8294, Fax: 352-588-8300.

Graduate Studies in Public Safety Administration Students: 3 full-time (1 woman), 800 part-time (492 women); includes 400 minority (281 Black or African American, non-Hispanic/Latino; 3 American Indian or Alaska Native, non-Hispanic/Latino; 8 Asian, non-Hispanic/Latino; 90 Hispanic/Latino; 1 Native Hawaiian or other Pacific Islander, non-Hispanic/Latino; 17 Two or more races, non-Hispanic/Latino; 1 international. Average age 37. 300 applicants, 86% accepted, 195 enrolled. *Faculty:* 8 full-time (3 women), 29 part-time/adjunct (7 women). Expenses: Contact institution. *Financial support:* In 2018–19, 21 students received support. Scholarships/grants and tuition remission for Saint Leo employees and their dependents available. Financial award application deadline: 3/1; financial award applicants required to submit FAFSA. In 2018, 235 master's awarded. *Program availability:* Part-time, evening/weekend, 100% online, blended/hybrid learning. Offers criminal justice (MS, DCJ); emergency and disaster management (MS). *Application deadline:* For fall admission, 7/1 priority date for domestic and international students; for spring admission, 11/1 priority date for domestic and international students. Applications are processed on a rolling basis. *Application fee:* $80. Electronic applications accepted. *Application Contact:* Mark Russum, Assistant Vice President, Enrollment, 800-707-8846, Fax: 352-588-7873, E-mail: grad.admissions@saintleo.edu. *Director of Graduate Studies in Public Safety Administration*, Dr. Robert Diemer, 352-588-8974, Fax: 352-588-8660, E-mail: graduatepublicsafety@saintleo.edu.

Graduate Studies in Social Work Students: 71 full-time (63 women), 205 part-time (174 women); includes 126 minority (91 Black or African American, non-Hispanic/Latino; 33 Hispanic/Latino; 2 Two or more races, non-Hispanic/Latino). Average age 36. 201 applicants, 64% accepted, 100 enrolled. *Faculty:* 9 full-time (7 women), 14 part-time/adjunct (13 women). Expenses: Contact institution. *Financial support:* In 2018–19, 4 students received support. Scholarships/grants, unspecified assistantships, and tuition remission for Saint Leo employees and their dependents available. Financial award application deadline: 3/1. In 2018, 77 master's awarded. *Program availability:* Online only, blended/hybrid learning. Offers advanced clinical practice (MSW). *Application deadline:* For fall admission, 6/1 for domestic and international students. *Application fee:* $80. Electronic applications accepted. *Application Contact:* Mark Russum, Assistant Vice President, Enrollment, 800-707-8846, Fax: 352-588-7873, E-mail: grad.admissions@saintleo.edu. *Director of Graduate Studies in Social Work*, Dr. Courtney Wiest, 352-588-8015, Fax: 352-588-8289.

Graduate Studies in Theology Students: 5 full-time (2 women), 239 part-time (86 women); includes 41 minority (24 Black or African American, non-Hispanic/Latino; 1 Asian, non-Hispanic/Latino; 14 Hispanic/Latino; 1 Native Hawaiian or other Pacific Islander, non-Hispanic/Latino; 1 Two or more races, non-Hispanic/Latino), 1 international. Average age 50. 86 applicants, 87% accepted, 51 enrolled. *Faculty:* 11 full-time (0 women), 7 part-time/adjunct (3 women). Expenses: Contact institution. *Financial support:* In 2018–19, 4 students received support. Fellowships, scholarships/grants, and tuition remission for Saint Leo employees and their dependents available. Financial award application deadline: 3/1; financial award applicants required to submit FAFSA. In 2018, 46 master's awarded. *Program availability:* Part-time, evening/weekend, 100% online, blended/hybrid learning. Offers theology (MA, Certificate). *Application deadline:* For fall admission, 7/1 priority date for domestic and international students; for spring admission, 11/1 priority date for domestic and international students. Applications are processed on a rolling basis. *Application fee:* $80. Electronic applications accepted. *Application Contact:* Mark Russum, Assistant Vice President, Enrollment, 800-707-8846, Fax: 352-588-7873, E-mail: grad.admissions@saintleo.edu. *Director, Graduate Theology*, Dr. Randall Woodard, 352-588-8239, Fax: 352-588-8404, E-mail: randall.woodard@saintleo.edu.

ST. LOUIS COLLEGE OF PHARMACY, St. Louis, MO 63110-1088

General Information Independent, coed, comprehensive institution. *Enrollment:* 786 full-time matriculated graduate/professional students (476 women), 25 part-time matriculated graduate/professional students (15 women). *Enrollment by degree level:* 811 doctoral. *Graduate faculty:* 52 full-time (31 women), 44 part-time/adjunct (30 women). *Tuition:* Full-time $35,756; part-time $1117 per credit hour. *Required fees:* $1641; $1641 per unit. *Graduate housing:* Room and/or apartments available on a first-come, first-served basis to single students; on-campus housing not available to married students. Typical cost: $6498 per year ($11,919 including board). Room and board

charges vary according to board plan and housing facility selected. Housing application deadline: 6/1. *Student services:* Campus employment opportunities, campus safety program, career counseling, exercise/wellness program, free psychological counseling, international student services, low-cost health insurance, multicultural affairs office, services for students with disabilities, writing training. *Library facilities:* O. J. Cloughly Alumni Library. *Collection:* Books: 14,941 (physical), 180,979 (digital/electronic); Serial titles: 445 (physical), 43,334 (digital/electronic); Databases: 62. Weekly public service hours: 101; study areas open 24 hours, 5–7 days a week; students can reserve study rooms.

Computer facilities: Computer purchase and lease plans are available. 1,390 computers available on campus for general student use. A campuswide network can be accessed from student residence rooms and from off campus. Online class registration is available.
Website: http://www.stlcop.edu/

General Application Contact: Jill Gebke, Director of Admissions, 314-446-8140, Fax: 314-446-8309, E-mail: jill.gebke@stlcop.edu.

GRADUATE UNITS

School of Pharmacy Students: 786 full-time (476 women), 25 part-time (15 women); includes 288 minority (72 Black or African American, non-Hispanic/Latino; 2 American Indian or Alaska Native, non-Hispanic/Latino; 191 Asian, non-Hispanic/Latino; 11 Hispanic/Latino; 12 Two or more races, non-Hispanic/Latino), 27 international. Average age 24. 295 applicants, 71% accepted, 192 enrolled. *Faculty:* 52 full-time (31 women), 44 part-time/adjunct (30 women). Expenses: Contact institution. *Financial support:* In 2018–19, 393 students received support. Federal Work-Study and scholarships/grants available. Financial award application deadline: 3/15; financial award applicants required to submit FAFSA. In 2018, 241 doctorates awarded. Offers pharmacy (Pharm D). *Application deadline:* For fall admission, 3/1 for domestic and international students. Applications are processed on a rolling basis. *Application fee:* $55. Electronic applications accepted. *Application Contact:* Jill Gebke, Director of Admissions, 314-446-8140, Fax: 314-446-8309, E-mail: jill.gebke@stlcop.edu. *Dean of Pharmacy*, Dr. Bruce Canaday, 314-446-8184.

SAINT LOUIS UNIVERSITY, St. Louis, MO 63103

General Information Independent-religious, coed, university. CGS member. *Graduate housing:* Rooms and/or apartments available to single and married students. Housing application deadline: 5/1. *Research affiliation:* AT&T Foundation (communication), National Center for Atmospheric Research (earth and atmospheric sciences), Argonne National Laboratory (energy, physics, chemistry, mathematics and computer science), Small Business Administration (business, administration and entrepreneurship), Monsanto Chemical Corporation (chemistry), Missouri Botanical Garden (biology, plant science).

GRADUATE UNITS

Graduate Programs *Program availability:* Part-time, evening/weekend, online learning. Electronic applications accepted.

Center for Advanced Dental Education Offers endodontics (MSD); orthodontics (MSD); periodontics (MSD). Electronic applications accepted.

Center for Health Care Ethics Offers clinical health care ethics (Certificate); health care ethics (PhD). Electronic applications accepted.

College for Public Health and Social Justice *Program availability:* Part-time. Offers administration of justice (MA); applied behavior analysis (MS); community health (MPH, MS, MSPH); emergency management (MA); health administration (MHA); health policy (MPH); public health and social justice (MA, MHA, MPH, MS, MSPH, MSW, PhD, Certificate); public health studies (PhD); social work (MSW, PhD); treatment and rehabilitation (MA); urban planning and development (MS).

College of Arts and Sciences *Program availability:* Part-time, evening/weekend. Offers American studies (MA, MA-R, PhD); arts and sciences (M Pr Met, MA, MA-R, MS, MS-R, PhD); bioinformatics and computational biology (MS); biology (MS, MS-R, PhD); chemistry (MS, MS-R, PhD); clinical psychology (MS-R, PhD); communication (MA, MA-R); computer science (MS); English (MA, MA-R, PhD); experimental psychology (MS-R, PhD); French (MA); geophysics (PhD); geoscience (MS); historical theology (MA, PhD); history (MA, MA-R, PhD); industrial-organizational psychology (PhD); mathematics (MA, PhD); meteorology (M Pr Met, MS-R, PhD); philosophy (MA, MA-R, PhD); political science (MA); psychology (PhD); software engineering (MS); Spanish (MA); theology (MA). Electronic applications accepted.

Doisy College of Health Sciences *Program availability:* Part-time. Offers athletic training (MAT); communication sciences and disorders (MA); health sciences (MAT, MMS, MOT, MS, DPT, PhD, Certificate); medical dietetics (MS); nutrition and physical performance (MS); occupational science and occupational therapy (MOT); physical therapy (DPT); physician assistant education (MMS).

John Cook School of Business *Program availability:* Part-time, evening/weekend. Offers accounting (M Acct, MBA); business (EMIB, M Acct, MBA, MSF, PhD); business administration (MBA); executive international business (EMIB); finance (MBA, MSF); international business (MBA). Electronic applications accepted.

Parks College of Engineering, Aviation, and Technology *Program availability:* Part-time, online learning. Offers biomedical engineering (MS, MS-R, PhD); engineering, aviation, and technology (MS, MS-R, PhD).

School of Education *Program availability:* Part-time. Offers Catholic school leadership (MA); curriculum and instruction (MA, Ed D, PhD); education (MA, MA-R, MAT, Ed D, PhD, Certificate, Ed S); educational administration (MA, Ed D, PhD, Ed S); educational foundations (MA, Ed D, PhD); higher education (MA, Ed D, PhD); special education (MA); student personnel administration (MA); teaching (MAT). Electronic applications accepted.

School of Medicine Offers anatomy (MS-R, PhD); biochemistry and molecular biology (PhD); biomedical sciences (MS-R, PhD); medicine (MS-R, MD, PhD); molecular microbiology and immunology (PhD); pathology (PhD); pharmacological and physiological science (PhD). Electronic applications accepted.

School of Nursing *Program availability:* Part-time, online learning. Offers nursing (MSN, DNP, PhD, Certificate). Electronic applications accepted.

School of Law *Program availability:* Part-time, evening/weekend. Offers law (LL M, JD). Electronic applications accepted.

SAINT LOUIS UNIVERSITY–MADRID CAMPUS, 28003 Madrid, Spain

General Information Independent-religious, coed, comprehensive institution. *Graduate housing:* Room and/or apartments guaranteed to single students. *Research affiliation:* Universidad Autónoma de Madrid (English philology), Pontificia Universidade Catolica do Rio de Janeiro, Sogang University, Korea.

GRADUATE UNITS

Graduate Programs *Program availability:* Part-time. Offers English (MA); Spanish (MA).

SAINT MARTIN'S UNIVERSITY, Lacey, WA 98503

General Information Independent-religious, coed, comprehensive institution. *Enrollment:* 1,609 graduate, professional, and undergraduate students; 68 full-time matriculated graduate/professional students (36 women), 180 part-time matriculated graduate/professional students (120 women). *Enrollment by degree level:* 233 master's, 15 other advanced degrees. *Graduate faculty:* 23 full-time (11 women), 27 part-time/adjunct (13 women). *Tuition:* Full-time $22,950; part-time $1275 per credit. Tuition and fees vary according to course load, campus/location and program. *Graduate housing:* Room and/or apartments available on a first-come, first-served basis to single students; on-campus housing not available to married students. Housing application deadline: 3/15. *Student services:* Campus employment opportunities, campus safety program, career counseling, exercise/wellness program, free psychological counseling, international student services, low-cost health insurance, multicultural affairs office, services for students with disabilities, writing training. *Library facilities:* O'Grady Library. *Collection:* Books: 88,291 (physical), 233,172 (digital/electronic); Serial titles: 98 (physical), 54,407 (digital/electronic); Databases: 114. Weekly public service hours: 88; students can reserve study rooms.

Computer facilities: 80 computers available on campus for general student use. A campuswide network can be accessed from student residence rooms. Online class registration is available.
Website: http://www.stmartin.edu/
General Application Contact: Casey Caronna, Administrative Assistant III, 360-412-6128, E-mail: ccaronna@stmartin.edu.

GRADUATE UNITS

Office of Graduate Studies Students: 66 full-time (36 women), 199 part-time (132 women); includes 80 minority (24 Black or African American, non-Hispanic/Latino; 4 American Indian or Alaska Native, non-Hispanic/Latino; 19 Asian, non-Hispanic/Latino; 23 Hispanic/Latino; 10 Two or more races, non-Hispanic/Latino), 13 international. Average age 36. 149 applicants, 61% accepted, 65 enrolled. *Faculty:* 21 full-time (11 women), 28 part-time/adjunct (11 women). Expenses: Contact institution. *Financial support:* Career-related internships or fieldwork, institutionally sponsored loans, and scholarships/grants available. Support available to part-time students. Financial award application deadline: 3/1; financial award applicants required to submit FAFSA. In 2018, 112 master's awarded. *Program availability:* Part-time, evening/weekend. Offers civil engineering (MCE); counseling psychology (MAC); engineering management (M Eng Mgt); mechanical engineering (MME). *Application deadline:* For fall admission, 4/1 priority date for domestic and international students; for spring admission, 11/1 for domestic students, 11/1 priority date for international students. Applications are processed on a rolling basis. *Application fee:* $50. Electronic applications accepted. *Application Contact:* Chantelle Petron Marker, Senior Recruiter, 360-412-6128, E-mail: cmarker@stmartin.edu. *Associate Dean of Graduate and Professional Programs,* Christopher Maund, 360-410-6142, E-mail: cmaund@stmartin.edu.

College of Education Students: 34 full-time (18 women), 40 part-time (31 women); includes 16 minority (3 Black or African American, non-Hispanic/Latino; 5 Asian, non-Hispanic/Latino; 5 Hispanic/Latino; 3 Two or more races, non-Hispanic/Latino), 1 international. Average age 37. 28 applicants, 46% accepted, 11 enrolled. *Faculty:* 9 full-time (6 women), 10 part-time/adjunct (6 women). Expenses: Contact institution. *Financial support:* Career-related internships or fieldwork, Federal Work-Study, institutionally sponsored loans, and unspecified assistantships available. Support available to part-time students. Financial award application deadline: 3/1; financial award applicants required to submit FAFSA. In 2018, 16 master's awarded. *Program availability:* Part-time, evening/weekend. Offers education (M Ed, MIT). *Application deadline:* For fall admission, 4/1 priority date for domestic and international students; for spring admission, 11/1 priority date for domestic and international students. Applications are processed on a rolling basis. *Application fee:* $50. Electronic applications accepted. *Application Contact:* Chantelle Petron Marker, Senior Recruiter, 360-412-6128, E-mail: cmarker@stmartin.edu. *College of Education and Counseling,* Dr. Fumie Hashimoto, 360-438-4333, Fax: 360-438-4486, E-mail: fhashimoto@stmartin.edu.

School of Business Students: 36 full-time (15 women), 25 part-time (9 women); includes 28 minority (8 Black or African American, non-Hispanic/Latino; 9 Asian, non-Hispanic/Latino; 8 Hispanic/Latino; 3 Two or more races, non-Hispanic/Latino), 8 international. Average age 33. 64 applicants, 61% accepted, 29 enrolled. *Faculty:* 5 full-time (3 women), 12 part-time/adjunct (2 women). Expenses: Contact institution. *Financial support:* Career-related internships or fieldwork and scholarships/grants available. Support available to part-time students. Financial award application deadline: 3/1; financial award applicants required to submit FAFSA. In 2018, 32 master's awarded. *Program availability:* Part-time, evening/weekend. Offers business (MBA). *Application deadline:* For fall admission, 7/1 priority date for domestic and international students; for spring admission, 12/1 for domestic students, 12/1 priority date for international students. Applications are processed on a rolling basis. *Application fee:* $50. Electronic applications accepted. *Application Contact:* Chantelle Petron Marker, Senior Recruiter, 360-412-6128, E-mail: cmarker@stmartin.edu. *Interim Dean, School of Business,* Dr. Jeff Crane, 360-438-4564, E-mail: jcrane@stmartin.edu.

SAINT MARY-OF-THE-WOODS COLLEGE, Saint Mary of the Woods, IN 47876

General Information Independent-religious, coed, primarily women, comprehensive institution. *Graduate housing:* On-campus housing not available.

GRADUATE UNITS

Master of Arts in Art Therapy Program *Program availability:* Part-time. Offers art therapy (MA, Post-Master's Certificate). Electronic applications accepted.
Master of Arts in Music Therapy Program *Program availability:* Part-time, blended/hybrid learning. Offers music therapy (MA). Electronic applications accepted.
Master of Healthcare Administration Program Offers healthcare administration (MHA).
Master of Leadership Development Program *Program availability:* Part-time. Offers not-for-profit leadership (MLD); organizational leadership (MLD). Electronic applications accepted.
Master of Science in Nursing Program Offers nursing (MSN).

SAINT MARY'S COLLEGE, Notre Dame, IN 46556

General Information Independent-religious, women only, comprehensive institution. *Enrollment:* 67 full-time matriculated graduate/professional students (65 women), 59 part-time matriculated graduate/professional students (54 women). *Enrollment by degree level:* 67 master's, 59 doctoral. *Graduate faculty:* 14 full-time (13 women), 4 part-time/adjunct (3 women). *Tuition:* Full-time $56,415. Tuition and fees vary according to course load and program. *Graduate housing:* Room and/or apartments available on a first-come, first-served basis to single students; on-campus housing not available to married students. Typical cost: $12,580 (including board). Room and board charges vary according to board plan and housing facility selected. Housing application deadline: 5/1. *Student services:* Campus employment opportunities, campus safety program, career counseling, child daycare facilities, exercise/wellness program, free psychological counseling, international student services, multicultural affairs office, services for students with disabilities, writing training. *Library facilities:* Cushwa-Leighton Library. *Collection:* Books: 260,077 (physical), 140,170 (digital/electronic); Serial titles: 4,136 (physical), 205,506 (digital/electronic); Databases: 74. Weekly public service hours: 54; study areas open 24 hours, 5–7 days a week; students can reserve study rooms.

Computer facilities: Computer purchase and lease plans are available. 291 computers available on campus for general student use. A campuswide network can be accessed from student residence rooms and from off campus. Online class registration is available.
Website: http://www.saintmarys.edu/
General Application Contact: Melissa Fruscione, Associate Director of Admission, Graduate Programs, 574-284-5098, E-mail: mfruscione@saintmarys.edu.

GRADUATE UNITS

Graduate Programs Students: 67 full-time (65 women), 59 part-time (54 women); includes 33 minority (11 Black or African American, non-Hispanic/Latino; 1 American Indian or Alaska Native, non-Hispanic/Latino; 7 Asian, non-Hispanic/Latino; 6 Hispanic/Latino; 8 Two or more races, non-Hispanic/Latino). Average age 29. *Faculty:* 14 full-time (13 women), 4 part-time/adjunct (3 women). Expenses: Contact institution. *Financial support:* Application deadline: 3/1; applicants required to submit FAFSA. *Program availability:* Online learning. Offers adult - gerontology acute care (DNP); adult - gerontology primary care (DNP); data science (MS); family nurse practitioner (DNP); speech language pathology (MS). *Application Contact:* Melissa Fruscione, Director of Graduate Admissions, 574-284-5098, E-mail: graduateadmission@saintmarys.edu.

SAINT MARY'S COLLEGE OF CALIFORNIA, Moraga, CA 94575

General Information Independent-religious, coed, upper-level institution. CGS member. *Graduate housing:* Room and/or apartments available on a first-come, first-served basis to single students; on-campus housing not available to married students. Housing application deadline: 6/1.

GRADUATE UNITS

Kalmanovitz School of Education *Program availability:* Part-time, evening/weekend. Offers career counseling (MA); coaching and facilitation (MA); college student services (Credential); education (M Ed, MA, MA Ed, Ed D, Credential); educational administration (MA); educational leadership (Ed D); general counseling (MA); marriage and family therapy (MA); Montessori education (MA); organizational leadership and change (MA); peacebuilding and conflict transformation (MA); preliminary administrative services (Credential); pupil personnel services (Credential); school counseling (MA); school psychology (MA); social justice (MA); special education (M Ed); supervision and leadership (MA); teaching (MA Ed); teaching leadership (MA).

School of Economics and Business Administration *Program availability:* Part-time, evening/weekend. Offers accounting (MS); business analytics (MS); executive business administration (MBA); financial analysis and investment management (MS); management (MS); professional business administration (MBA).

School of Liberal Arts *Program availability:* Part-time. Offers creative writing (MFA); dance: creative practice (MFA); dance: design and production (MFA); fitness management (MA); liberal arts (MA, MFA); sport management (MA); sport studies (MA).

ST. MARY'S COLLEGE OF MARYLAND, St. Mary's City, MD 20686-3001

General Information State-supported, coed, comprehensive institution. *Graduate housing:* Room and/or apartments available on a first-come, first-served basis to single students; on-campus housing not available to married students. Housing application deadline: 5/1.

GRADUATE UNITS

Department of Educational Studies Offers educational studies (MAT). Electronic applications accepted.

SAINT MARY SEMINARY AND GRADUATE SCHOOL OF THEOLOGY, Wickliffe, OH 44092-2527

General Information Independent-religious, coed, primarily men, graduate-only institution. *Graduate housing:* Room and/or apartments available to single students; on-campus housing not available to married students.

GRADUATE UNITS

Graduate and Professional Programs *Program availability:* Part-time. Offers theology (M Div, MA, D Min).

ST. MARY'S SEMINARY AND UNIVERSITY, Baltimore, MD 21210-1994

General Information Independent-religious, coed, primarily men, graduate-only institution. *Graduate housing:* Room and/or apartments guaranteed to single students; on-campus housing not available to married students. Housing application deadline: 8/15.

GRADUATE UNITS

Ecumenical Institute of Theology *Program availability:* Part-time, evening/weekend. Offers church ministries (MA); theology (MA Th, Certificate).
School of Theology *Program availability:* Part-time. Offers theology (M Div, MA Th, STD, STB, STL).

SAINT MARY'S UNIVERSITY, Halifax, NS B3H 3C3, Canada

General Information Province-supported, coed, comprehensive institution. *Graduate housing:* Rooms and/or apartments available on a first-come, first-served basis to single students and available to married students.

GRADUATE UNITS

Faculty of Arts *Program availability:* Part-time, evening/weekend. Offers arts (MA, Certificate, Graduate Diploma); Atlantic Canada studies (MA, Certificate); criminology (MA); history (MA); international development studies (MA, Graduate Diploma); philosophy (MA); theology and religious studies (MA); women and gender studies (MA).
Faculty of Science *Program availability:* Part-time. Offers applied psychology (M Sc, PhD); applied science (M Sc); astronomy (M Sc, PhD); science (M Sc, PhD).

Sobey School of Business *Program availability:* Part-time, evening/weekend. Offers business (MBA, MF, PhD).

ST. MARY'S UNIVERSITY, San Antonio, TX 78228

General Information Independent-religious, coed, comprehensive institution. CGS member. *Enrollment:* 3,648 graduate, professional, and undergraduate students; 885 full-time matriculated graduate/professional students (452 women), 390 part-time matriculated graduate/professional students (230 women). *Enrollment by degree level:* 465 master's, 127 doctoral, 13 other advanced degrees. *Graduate faculty:* 10 full-time (5 women), 28 part-time/adjunct (8 women). *Tuition:* Full-time $16,830; part-time $935 per credit hour. *Required fees:* $1055. Tuition and fees vary according to program. *Graduate housing:* Room and/or apartments available on a first-come, first-served basis to single students; on-campus housing not available to married students. Typical cost: $8856 per year ($12,596 including board). Housing application deadline: 5/1. *Student services:* Campus employment opportunities, career counseling, exercise/wellness program, free psychological counseling, international student services, low-cost health insurance, services for students with disabilities. *Library facilities:* Louis J. Blume Library plus 1 other. *Collection:* Books: 207,131 (physical), 479,714 (digital/electronic); Serial titles: 429 (physical), 99,503 (digital/electronic); Databases: 134. Weekly public service hours: 100.

Computer facilities: Computer purchase and lease plans are available. 200 computers available on campus for general student use. A campuswide network can be accessed from student residence rooms and from off campus. Online class registration is available.
Website: http://www.stmarytx.edu/

General Application Contact: Kim Thornton, Director of Graduate Admission, 210-436-3126, E-mail: kthornton@stmarytx.edu.

GRADUATE UNITS

Graduate Studies Students: 885 full-time (452 women), 390 part-time (230 women); includes 701 minority (75 Black or African American, non-Hispanic/Latino; 8 American Indian or Alaska Native, non-Hispanic/Latino; 36 Asian, non-Hispanic/Latino; 571 Hispanic/Latino; 2 Native Hawaiian or other Pacific Islander, non-Hispanic/Latino; 9 Two or more races, non-Hispanic/Latino), 90 international. Average age 30. 446 applicants, 71% accepted, 128 enrolled. *Faculty:* 62 full-time (27 women), 57 part-time/adjunct (13 women). *Expenses:* Contact institution. *Financial support:* Fellowships, research assistantships, career-related internships or fieldwork, Federal Work-Study, institutionally sponsored loans, scholarships/grants, health care benefits, tuition waivers, and unspecified assistantships available. Financial award application deadline: 3/31; financial award applicants required to submit FAFSA. In 2018, 216 master's, 218 doctorates, 5 other advanced degrees awarded. *Program availability:* Part-time, evening/weekend, 100% online. Offers Catholic school leadership (MA); clinical mental health counseling (MA); communication studies (MA); conflict transformation (Certificate); counselor education and supervision (PhD); education (MA); educational leadership (MA); English literature and language (MA); industrial/organizational psychology (MA, MS); international conflict resolution (MA); international development (MA); international relations (MA); public administration (MPA); public communication, public policy and public leadership (Certificate); security policy (MA); theology (MA). *Application deadline:* For fall admission, 7/1 for domestic students; for spring admission, 11/15 for domestic students; for summer admission, 4/1 for domestic students. Applications are processed on a rolling basis. Electronic applications accepted. *Application Contact:* Kim Thornton, Director of Graduate Admission, 210-436-3101, E-mail: kthornton@stmarytx.edu. *Interim Dean of Graduate Studies,* Dr. Leona Pallansch, 210-436-3204, E-mail: lpallansch@stmarytx.edu.

Greehey School of Business Students: 34 full-time (18 women), 52 part-time (25 women); includes 44 minority (7 Black or African American, non-Hispanic/Latino; 1 Asian, non-Hispanic/Latino; 34 Hispanic/Latino; 1 Native Hawaiian or other Pacific Islander, non-Hispanic/Latino; 1 Two or more races, non-Hispanic/Latino), 13 international. Average age 33. 84 applicants, 55% accepted, 29 enrolled. *Expenses:* Contact institution. *Financial support:* Research assistantships, institutionally sponsored loans, scholarships/grants, and unspecified assistantships available. Financial award application deadline: 3/31; financial award applicants required to submit FAFSA. In 2018, 67 master's awarded. *Program availability:* Part-time, evening/weekend. Offers business administration (MBA). *Application deadline:* For fall admission, 7/1 for domestic students; for spring admission, 11/15 for domestic students; for summer admission, 4/1 for domestic students. *Application fee:* $0. Electronic applications accepted. *Application Contact:* Jeremy Grace, Director, Master of Business Administration Programs, 210-431-2027, E-mail: jmgrace@stmarytx.edu. *Director, Master of Business Administration Programs,* Jeremy Grace, 210-431-2027, E-mail: jmgrace@stmarytx.edu.

School of Law Students: 687 full-time (339 women), 100 part-time (61 women); includes 451 minority (40 Black or African American, non-Hispanic/Latino; 7 American Indian or Alaska Native, non-Hispanic/Latino; 21 Asian, non-Hispanic/Latino; 382 Hispanic/Latino; 1 Native Hawaiian or other Pacific Islander, non-Hispanic/Latino), 8 international. Average age 29. *Faculty:* 52 full-time (22 women), 29 part-time/adjunct (5 women). *Expenses:* Contact institution. *Financial support:* Application deadline: 2/15; applicants required to submit FAFSA. In 2018, 18 master's, 212 doctorates awarded. *Program availability:* Part-time. Offers American legal studies (LL M); business and entrepreneurship law (MJ); commercial law (MJ); compliance, business law and risk (MJ); criminal justice (MJ); education law (MJ); environmental law (MJ); health law (MJ); healthcare compliance (MJ); international and comparative law (LL M); international comparative law (MJ); international criminal law (LL M); law (LL M, MJ, JD); military and national security law (MJ); natural resource law (MJ); tax law (MJ). *Application deadline:* For fall admission, 3/1 for domestic students. *Application fee:* $0. *Application Contact:* Kim Thornton, Director of Graduate Admission, 210-436-3101, E-mail: kthornton@stmarytx.edu. *Dean,* Stephen Sheppard, 210-436-3530, E-mail: sheppard@stmarytx.edu.

School of Science, Engineering and Technology Students: 37 full-time (7 women), 43 part-time (15 women); includes 30 minority (3 Black or African American, non-Hispanic/Latino; 2 Asian, non-Hispanic/Latino; 25 Hispanic/Latino), 37 international. Average age 29. 80 applicants, 60% accepted, 7 enrolled. *Expenses:* Contact institution. *Financial support:* Application deadline: 3/31; applicants required to submit FAFSA. In 2018, 45 master's, 2 other advanced degrees awarded. *Program availability:* Part-time, evening/weekend, blended/hybrid learning. Offers computer engineering (MS); computer information systems (MS); cybersecurity (MS, Certificate); electrical engineering (MS); engineering systems management (MS); industrial engineering (MS); science, engineering and technology (MS, Certificate); software engineering (MS, Certificate). *Application deadline:* For fall admission, 7/1 for domestic students; for spring admission, 11/15 for domestic students; for summer admission, 4/1 for domestic students. Applications are processed on a rolling basis. *Application fee:* $0. Electronic applications accepted. *Application Contact:* Dr. Winston F. Erevelles, Dean, 210-436-3996, E-mail: werevelles@stmarytx.edu. *Dean,* Dr. Winston F. Erevelles, 210-436-3996, E-mail: werevelles@stmarytx.edu.

SAINT MARY'S UNIVERSITY OF MINNESOTA, Winona, MN 55987-1399

General Information Independent-religious, coed, comprehensive institution. *Enrollment:* 5,560 graduate, professional, and undergraduate students. *Enrollment by degree level:* 3,493 master's, 354 doctoral, 176 other advanced degrees. *Student services:* Campus safety program, services for students with disabilities, teacher training, writing training. *Library facilities:* Fitzgerald Library plus 1 other. *Collection:* Books: 210,639 (physical), 10,144 (digital/electronic); Serial titles: 169 (physical), 82,154 (digital/electronic); Databases: 77. Weekly public service hours: 97; students can reserve study rooms.

Computer facilities: 200 computers available on campus for general student use. A campuswide network can be accessed from student residence rooms and from off campus. Online class registration is available.
Website: http://www.smumn.edu/

General Application Contact: James Callinan, Director of Admission for Graduate and Professional Programs, 612-728-5158, Fax: 612-728-5121, E-mail: jcallina@smumn.edu.

GRADUATE UNITS

Schools of Graduate and Professional Programs Students: 2,655 full-time (1,817 women), 1,234 part-time (835 women); includes 685 minority (360 Black or African American, non-Hispanic/Latino; 15 American Indian or Alaska Native, non-Hispanic/Latino; 160 Asian, non-Hispanic/Latino; 141 Hispanic/Latino; 3 Native Hawaiian or other Pacific Islander, non-Hispanic/Latino; 6 Two or more races, non-Hispanic/Latino), 101 international. Average age 35. *Faculty:* 56 full-time (36 women), 292 part-time/adjunct (169 women). *Expenses:* Contact institution. *Financial support:* Applicants required to submit FAFSA. In 2018, 1,297 master's, 36 doctorates, 124 other advanced degrees awarded. *Program availability:* Part-time, evening/weekend, 100% online, blended/hybrid learning. *Application deadline:* Applications are processed on a rolling basis. Electronic applications accepted. *Application Contact:* Laura Roy, Director of Admission of Schools of Graduate and Professional Programs, 507-457-8606, Fax: 612-728-5121, E-mail: lroy@smumn.edu. *Provost and Dean of Faculties,* Brian Schmisek, 507-457-1756, E-mail: bschmise@smumn.edu.

Graduate School of Business and Technology Students: 965 full-time (578 women), 324 part-time (180 women); includes 326 minority (182 Black or African American, non-Hispanic/Latino; 7 American Indian or Alaska Native, non-Hispanic/Latino; 69 Asian, non-Hispanic/Latino; 65 Hispanic/Latino; 1 Native Hawaiian or other Pacific Islander, non-Hispanic/Latino; 2 Two or more races, non-Hispanic/Latino), 75 international. Average age 36. *Expenses:* Contact institution. *Program availability:* Part-time, evening/weekend, 100% online, blended/hybrid learning. Offers accountancy (MS); business administration (MBA, DBA); business and technology (MA, MBA, MS, DBA, Certificate); business intelligence and data analytics (MS); cybersecurity (MS); geographic information science (MS, Certificate); human development (MA); human resource management (MA); international development (MA); management (MA); organizational leadership (MA); philanthropy and development (MA); project management (MS, Certificate); public administration (MA). *Application deadline:* Applications are processed on a rolling basis. Electronic applications accepted. *Application Contact:* Laurie Roy, Director of Admission of Schools of Graduate and Professional Programs, 507-457-8606, E-mail: lroy@smumn.edu. *Dean,* Dr. Michelle Wieser, 507-457-1451, E-mail: mwieser@smumn.edu.

Graduate School of Education Students: 943 full-time (692 women), 689 part-time (471 women); includes 176 minority (77 Black or African American, non-Hispanic/Latino; 5 American Indian or Alaska Native, non-Hispanic/Latino; 47 Asian, non-Hispanic/Latino; 45 Hispanic/Latino; 1 Native Hawaiian or other Pacific Islander, non-Hispanic/Latino; 1 Two or more races, non-Hispanic/Latino), 14 international. Average age 35. *Expenses:* Contact institution. *Program availability:* Part-time, evening/weekend, 100% online, blended/hybrid learning. Offers behavioral disorders (Certificate); education (M Ed, MA, Ed D, Certificate, Ed S); educational administration (Certificate, Ed S); educational leadership (MA, Ed D); instruction (MA); K-12 reading teacher (Certificate); LaSallian leadership (MA); LaSallian studies (MA); learning design and technology (M Ed); learning disabilities (Certificate); literacy education (MA); special education (MA); teaching and learning (M Ed). *Application deadline:* Applications are processed on a rolling basis. Electronic applications accepted. *Application Contact:* Laurie Roy, Director of Admission of Schools of Graduate and Professional Programs, 507-457-8606, Fax: 612-728-5121, E-mail: lroy@smumn.edu. *Dean,* Dr. Rebecca Hopkins, 507-457-6620, E-mail: rhopkins@smumn.edu.

Graduate School of Health and Human Services Students: 747 full-time (547 women), 221 part-time (184 women); includes 183 minority (101 Black or African American, non-Hispanic/Latino; 3 American Indian or Alaska Native, non-Hispanic/Latino; 44 Asian, non-Hispanic/Latino; 31 Hispanic/Latino; 1 Native Hawaiian or other Pacific Islander, non-Hispanic/Latino; 3 Two or more races, non-Hispanic/Latino), 12 international. Average age 33. *Expenses:* Contact institution. *Program availability:* Part-time, evening/weekend, 100% online, blended/hybrid learning. Offers counseling and psychological services (MA, Certificate); counseling psychology (Psy D); health and human services (MA, MS, Psy D, Certificate); health and human services administration (MA); marriage and family therapy (MA); nurse anesthesia (MS). *Application deadline:* Applications are processed on a rolling basis. Electronic applications accepted. *Application Contact:* Laurie Roy, Director of Admission of Schools of Graduate and Professional Programs, 507-313-5564, Fax: 612-728-5121, E-mail: lroy@smumn.edu. *Dean,* Dr. Todd Reinhart, 507-457-1758, E-mail: treinhar@smumn.edu.

SAINT MEINRAD SCHOOL OF THEOLOGY, Saint Meinrad, IN 47577

General Information Independent-religious, coed, primarily men, graduate-only institution. *Enrollment by degree level:* 166 master's. *Graduate faculty:* 19 full-time (2 women), 5 part-time/adjunct (1 woman). *Tuition:* Full-time $27,714; part-time $520 per credit. *Required fees:* $3100; $34 per course. Tuition and fees vary according to program. *Graduate housing:* On-campus housing not available. *Student services:* Campus employment opportunities, campus safety program, exercise/wellness program, free psychological counseling, writing training. *Library facilities:* Archabbey Library. *Collection:* Students can reserve study rooms.

Computer facilities: 30 computers available on campus for general student use. A campuswide network can be accessed from student residence rooms and from off campus.
Website: http://www.saintmeinrad.edu/

General Application Contact: Dr. John Schlachter, Director of Admissions, 812-357-6142, Fax: 812-357-6816, E-mail: apply@saintmeinrad.edu.

GRADUATE UNITS

Master of Arts (Catholic Philosophical Studies) Program Students: 32 full-time (0 women); includes 1 minority (Black or African American, non-Hispanic/Latino), 3 international. Average age 28. *Faculty:* 6 full-time (1 woman), 4 part-time/adjunct (1 woman). Expenses: Contact institution. *Financial support:* Federal Work-Study and scholarships/grants available. Financial award applicants required to submit FAFSA. In 2018, 11 master's awarded. Offers Catholic philosophical studies (MA). *Application deadline:* For fall admission, 7/1 priority date for domestic and international students; for winter admission, 11/15 for domestic and international students. Applications are processed on a rolling basis. *Application fee:* $30. *Application Contact:* Dr. John Schlachter, Director of Admissions, 812-357-6142, Fax: 812-357-6816, E-mail: jschlachter@saintmeinrad.edu. *Academic Dean*, Dr. Robert Alvis, 812-357-6543, Fax: 812-357-6816, E-mail: ralvis@saintmeinrad.edu.

Master of Arts (Theology) Program Students: 6 full-time (4 women), 39 part-time (17 women); includes 6 minority (2 Black or African American, non-Hispanic/Latino; 4 Hispanic/Latino), 3 international. Average age 46. *Faculty:* 20 full-time (2 women), 6 part-time/adjunct (1 woman). Expenses: Contact institution. *Financial support:* Federal Work-Study, institutionally sponsored loans, and scholarships/grants available. Support available to part-time students. Financial award application deadline: 7/1; financial award applicants required to submit FAFSA. In 2018, 20 master's awarded. *Program availability:* Part-time, evening/weekend. Offers theology (MA). *Application deadline:* For fall admission, 7/1 for domestic and international students; for winter admission, 11/15 for domestic and international students. Applications are processed on a rolling basis. *Application fee:* $30. Electronic applications accepted. *Application Contact:* Dr. John Schlachter, Director of Admissions, 812-357-6142, Fax: 812-357-6816, E-mail: apply@saintmeinrad.edu. *Director of Graduate Theology Programs*, Sr. Jeana Visel, OSB, 812-357-6721, Fax: 812-357-6816.

Master of Divinity Program Students: 79 full-time (0 women); includes 6 minority (1 Black or African American, non-Hispanic/Latino; 1 Asian, non-Hispanic/Latino; 4 Hispanic/Latino), 24 international. Average age 31. *Faculty:* 21 full-time (2 women), 6 part-time/adjunct (1 woman). Expenses: Contact institution. *Financial support:* Federal Work-Study, institutionally sponsored loans, and scholarships/grants available. Financial award application deadline: 7/31; financial award applicants required to submit FAFSA. In 2018, 18 master's awarded. Offers divinity (M Div). *Application deadline:* For fall admission, 7/1 priority date for domestic students, 7/1 for international students; for winter admission, 11/15 for domestic and international students. Applications are processed on a rolling basis. *Application fee:* $0. *Application Contact:* Dr. John Schlachter, Director of Admissions, 812-357-6142, Fax: 812-357-6816, E-mail: apply@saintmeinrad.edu. *Academic Dean*, Dr. Robert Alvis, 812-357-6543, Fax: 812-357-6816, E-mail: ralvis@saintmeinrad.edu.

SAINT MICHAEL'S COLLEGE, Colchester, VT 05439

General Information Independent-religious, coed, comprehensive institution. *Enrollment:* 56 full-time matriculated graduate/professional students (38 women), 83 part-time matriculated graduate/professional students (69 women). *Enrollment by degree level:* 139 master's. *Tuition:* Part-time $590 per credit. *Graduate housing:* On-campus housing not available. *Student services:* Campus employment opportunities, campus safety program, career counseling, international student services, multicultural affairs office, services for students with disabilities. *Library facilities:* Durick Library. *Collection:* Books: 231,418 (physical), 231,171 (digital/electronic); Serial titles: 1,653 (physical), 128,515 (digital/electronic); Databases: 142. Weekly public service hours: 102.

Computer facilities: Computer purchase and lease plans are available. 97 computers available on campus for general student use. A campuswide network can be accessed from student residence rooms and from off campus. Online class registration is available.
Website: http://www.smcvt.edu/

General Application Contact: Alex Bertoni, Marketing Director, 802-654-2536.

GRADUATE UNITS

Graduate Programs *Program availability:* Part-time, evening/weekend. Offers arts in education (CAGS); clinical psychology (MA); literacy (M Ed); school leadership (CAGS); special education (M Ed); teaching English to speakers of other languages (MATESOL, Certificate). Electronic applications accepted.

ST. NORBERT COLLEGE, De Pere, WI 54115-2099

General Information Independent-religious, coed, comprehensive institution. *Enrollment:* 2,228 graduate, professional, and undergraduate students; 112 part-time matriculated graduate/professional students (67 women). *Enrollment by degree level:* 112 master's. *Graduate faculty:* 10 full-time (3 women), 18 part-time/adjunct (6 women). *Tuition:* Part-time $750 per credit. *Required fees:* $37.50 per course. Tuition and fees vary according to course load and program. *Graduate housing:* On-campus housing not available. *Student services:* Campus safety program, career counseling, child daycare facilities, exercise/wellness program, free psychological counseling, international student services, multicultural affairs office, services for students with disabilities, writing training. *Library facilities:* Miriam B. and James J. Mulva Library plus 1 other. *Collection:* Books: 252,444 (physical), 207,312 (digital/electronic); Serial titles: 103,421 (physical), 103,236 (digital/electronic). Weekly public service hours: 116; students can reserve study rooms.

Computer facilities: Computer purchase and lease plans are available. 167 computers available on campus for general student use. A campuswide network can be accessed from student residence rooms and from off campus. Online class registration is available.
Website: http://www.snc.edu/

General Application Contact: Brenda Busch, Associate Director of Graduate Recruitment, 920-403-3942, Fax: 920-403-4072, E-mail: brenda.busch@snc.edu.

GRADUATE UNITS

Master of Arts in Liberal Studies Program Students: 8 part-time (6 women); includes 1 minority (Hispanic/Latino). Average age 37. *Faculty:* 2 part-time/adjunct (0 women). Expenses: Contact institution. *Financial support:* Applicants required to submit FAFSA. *Program availability:* Part-time-only, evening/weekend. Offers liberal studies (MA). *Application deadline:* Applications are processed on a rolling basis. *Application fee:* $50. Electronic applications accepted. *Application Contact:* Danielle Wahlen, Program Coordinator, 920-403-3957, E-mail: danielle.wahlen@snc.edu. *Director*, Dr. Howard Ebert, 920-403-3956, E-mail: howard.ebert@snc.edu.

Master of Business Administration Program Students: 66 part-time (38 women); includes 6 minority (1 American Indian or Alaska Native, non-Hispanic/Latino; 2 Asian, non-Hispanic/Latino; 2 Hispanic/Latino; 1 Two or more races, non-Hispanic/Latino).

Average age 33. 15 applicants, 100% accepted, 14 enrolled. *Faculty:* 11 full-time (3 women), 10 part-time/adjunct (3 women). Expenses: Contact institution. *Financial support:* Federal Work-Study available. Financial award application deadline: 1/1; financial award applicants required to submit FAFSA. In 2018, 31 master's awarded. *Program availability:* Part-time-only, evening/weekend. Offers business (MBA); health care (MBA); supply chain and manufacturing (MBA). *Application deadline:* For fall admission, 8/4 for domestic students; for winter admission, 12/15 for domestic students; for spring admission, 3/2 for domestic students; for summer admission, 4/20 for domestic students. Applications are processed on a rolling basis. *Application fee:* $50. Electronic applications accepted. *Application Contact:* Brenda Busch, Associate Director of Graduate Recruitment, 920-403-3942, Fax: 920-403-4072, E-mail: brenda.busch@snc.edu. *Coordinator of MBA Program*, Lisa Gray, 920-403-3449, E-mail: lisa.gray@snc.edu.

Master of Theological Studies Program Students: 38 part-time (23 women); includes 14 minority (13 Hispanic/Latino; 1 Two or more races, non-Hispanic/Latino). Average age 60. 1 applicant, 100% accepted, 0 enrolled. *Faculty:* 8 part-time/adjunct (4 women). Expenses: Contact institution. *Financial support:* In 2018–19, 18 students received support. Scholarships/grants available. Support available to part-time students. Financial award application deadline: 8/26. In 2018, 2 master's awarded. *Program availability:* Part-time-only, evening/weekend, students from New Mexico site video conference in to a live class in DePere. Offers theological studies (MTS). *Application deadline:* Applications are processed on a rolling basis. *Application fee:* $50. Electronic applications accepted. *Application Contact:* Danielle Wahlen, Program Coordinator, 920-403-3957, E-mail: danielle.wahlen@snc.edu. *Director*, Dr. Howard Ebert, 920-403-3956, E-mail: howard.ebert@snc.edu.

ST. PATRICK'S SEMINARY & UNIVERSITY, Menlo Park, CA 94025-3596

General Information Independent-religious, coed, primarily men, graduate-only institution. *Graduate housing:* Room and/or apartments guaranteed to single students; on-campus housing not available to married students. Housing application deadline: 8/15.

GRADUATE UNITS

School of Theology *Program availability:* Part-time. Offers theology (M Div, MA, STB). STB offered jointly with St. Mary's Seminary and University.

SAINT PAUL SCHOOL OF THEOLOGY, Overland Park, KS 66211

General Information Independent-religious, coed, graduate-only institution. *Graduate housing:* Rooms and/or apartments available to single and married students. Housing application deadline: 5/31.

GRADUATE UNITS

Graduate and Professional Programs *Program availability:* Part-time. Offers theology (M Div, MA, MTS, D Min).

SAINT PAUL UNIVERSITY, Ottawa, ON K1S 1C4, Canada

General Information Province-supported, coed, university. *Graduate housing:* Room and/or apartments available to single students; on-campus housing not available to married students.

GRADUATE UNITS

Faculty of Canon Law *Program availability:* Part-time. Offers canon law (MCL, JCD, PhD, Graduate Certificate, JCL); canonical practice (Graduate Certificate); ecclesiastical administration (Graduate Certificate).

Faculty of Human Sciences Offers conflict studies (MA); counseling and spirituality (MA); individual and/or marital/couple counseling (MA Past St); individual or marital/couple counseling (MA); mission and interreligious studies (MA); pastoral care in health care services (MA Past St); spiritual care (MA). Programs offered in French and English.

Faculty of Theology Offers theology (MA Th, MP Th, MRE, D Min, D Th, PhD, L Th).

ST. PETER'S SEMINARY, London, ON N6A 3Y1, Canada

General Information Independent-religious, coed, primarily men, graduate-only institution.

GRADUATE UNITS

Department of Theology Offers theology (M Div, MTS).

SAINT PETER'S UNIVERSITY, Jersey City, NJ 07306-5997

General Information Independent-religious, coed, comprehensive institution. *Graduate housing:* On-campus housing not available.

GRADUATE UNITS

Graduate Business Programs *Program availability:* Part-time, evening/weekend. Offers accountancy (MS); business (MBA, MS); business analytics (MS); finance (MBA); health care administration (MBA); human resource management (MBA); international business (MBA); management (MBA); management information systems (MS); marketing (MBA); mobile intelligence (MS); risk management (MBA). Electronic applications accepted.

Graduate Programs in Education *Program availability:* Part-time, evening/weekend. Offers 6-8 middle school education (MA Ed, Certificate); director of school counseling services (Certificate); educational leadership (MA Ed, Ed D); general administration (MHE); higher education (MHE, Ed D); K-12 secondary education (MA Ed, Certificate); K-5 elementary education (MA Ed, Certificate); literacy (MA Ed); middle school mathematics (Certificate); professional/associate counselor (Certificate); reading (MA Ed); school business administrator (Certificate); school counseling (MA, Certificate); special education (MA Ed, Certificate); teaching (MA Ed, Certificate). Electronic applications accepted.

Program in Criminal Justice Administration *Program availability:* Part-time, evening/weekend. Offers federal law enforcement administration (MA); police administration (MA). Electronic applications accepted.

Program in Public Administration Offers public administration (MPA).

School of Nursing *Program availability:* Part-time, evening/weekend. Offers adult nurse practitioner (MSN, Certificate); advanced practice (DNP); case management (MSN, DNP); nursing (MSN, DNP, Certificate). Electronic applications accepted.

SAINTS CYRIL AND METHODIUS SEMINARY, Orchard Lake, MI 48324

General Information Independent-religious, coed, graduate-only institution. *Graduate housing:* Room and/or apartments guaranteed to single students; on-campus housing not available to married students. Housing application deadline: 7/1.

GRADUATE UNITS

Graduate and Professional Programs *Program availability:* Part-time. Offers pastoral ministry (MAPM); religious education (MARE); theology (M Div, MA).

ST. STEPHEN'S COLLEGE, Edmonton, AB T6G 2J6, Canada

General Information Independent-religious, coed, graduate-only institution. *Enrollment by degree level:* 85 master's, 27 doctoral, 11 other advanced degrees. *Graduate faculty:* 1 full-time (0 women), 38 part-time/adjunct (23 women). *Tuition:* Part-time $30,695 Canadian dollars per degree program. *Graduate housing:* On-campus housing not available. *Library facilities:* University of Alberta Library.

Computer facilities: 2 computers available on campus for general student use. Website: http://ststephenscollege.ca/

General Application Contact: Shelley Westermann, Registrar, 780-439-7311, Fax: 780-433-8875, E-mail: westerma@ualberta.ca.

GRADUATE UNITS

Programs in Theology *Program availability:* Part-time, evening/weekend, online learning. Offers ministry (D Min); pastoral counseling (MA); social transformation ministry (MA); spirituality and liturgy (MA); theological studies (MTS); theology (M Th). Electronic applications accepted.

ST. THOMAS AQUINAS COLLEGE, Sparkill, NY 10976

General Information Independent, coed, comprehensive institution. *Graduate housing:* On-campus housing not available. *Research affiliation:* Lederle Laboratories (science education), Lamont Doherty Laboratories (science education).

GRADUATE UNITS

Division of Business Administration *Program availability:* Part-time, evening/weekend. Offers business administration (MBA); finance (MBA); management (MBA); marketing (MBA). Electronic applications accepted.

Division of Teacher Education *Program availability:* Part-time, evening/weekend. Offers adolescence education (MST); childhood and special education (MST); childhood education (MST); educational leadership (MS Ed); reading (MS Ed, PMC); special education (MS Ed, PMC); teaching (MS Ed). Electronic applications accepted.

ST. THOMAS UNIVERSITY, Miami Gardens, FL 33054-6459

General Information Independent-religious, coed, university. *Graduate housing:* Room and/or apartments available on a first-come, first-served basis to single students; on-campus housing not available to married students. Housing application deadline: 7/1.

GRADUATE UNITS

Biscayne College Offers guidance and counseling (MS, Post-Master's Certificate); marriage and family therapy (MS, Post-Master's Certificate); mental health counseling (MS).

School of Business Offers accounting (MBA); business (M Acc, MBA, MIB, MS, MSM, Certificate); business administration (M Acc, MBA, Certificate); general management (MSM, Certificate); health management (MBA, MSM, Certificate); human resource management (MBA, MSM, Certificate); international business (MBA, MIB, MSM, Certificate); justice administration (MSM, Certificate); management accounting (MSM, Certificate); public management (MSM, Certificate); sports administration (MS).

School of Law *Program availability:* Online learning. Offers international human rights (LL M); international taxation (LL M); law (JD). Electronic applications accepted.

School of Leadership Studies *Program availability:* Part-time, evening/weekend. Offers art management (MA); electronic media (MA); executive management (MPS); Hispanic media (MA, Certificate); leadership studies (MA, MPS, MS, Ed D, Certificate).

Institute for Education *Program availability:* Part-time, evening/weekend. Offers earth/space science (Certificate); educational administration (MS, Certificate); educational leadership (Ed D); elementary education (MS); ESOL (Certificate); gifted education (Certificate); instructional technology (MS, Certificate); professional studies (Certificate); reading (MS, Certificate); special education (MS). Electronic applications accepted.

School of Theology and Ministry Offers theology and ministry (MA, PhD, Certificate).

Institute for Pastoral Ministries *Program availability:* Part-time, evening/weekend. Offers pastoral ministries (MA, Certificate); practical theology (PhD). Electronic applications accepted.

ST. TIKHON'S ORTHODOX THEOLOGICAL SEMINARY, South Canaan, PA 18459

General Information Independent-religious, men only, graduate-only institution. *Graduate housing:* Room and/or apartments guaranteed to single students; on-campus housing not available to married students.

GRADUATE UNITS

Divinity Program *Program availability:* Part-time. Offers divinity (M Div).

SAINT VINCENT COLLEGE, Latrobe, PA 15650-2690

General Information Independent-religious, coed, comprehensive institution. *Graduate housing:* Room and/or apartments available on a first-come, first-served basis to single students; on-campus housing not available to married students.

GRADUATE UNITS

Program in Business Offers business (MS).

Program in Education *Program availability:* Part-time, evening/weekend. Offers curriculum and instruction (MS); instructional design and technology (MS); school administration and supervision (MS); special education (MS).

Program in Health Science Offers nurse anesthesia (MS).

ST. VINCENT DE PAUL REGIONAL SEMINARY, Boynton Beach, FL 33436-4899

General Information Independent-religious, coed, primarily men, graduate-only institution. *Graduate housing:* Room and/or apartments guaranteed to single students; on-campus housing not available to married students.

GRADUATE UNITS

Graduate and Professional Programs *Program availability:* Part-time. Offers theology (M Div, MA Th).

SAINT VINCENT SEMINARY, Latrobe, PA 15650-2690

General Information Independent-religious, coed, primarily men, graduate-only institution. *Enrollment by degree level:* 51 master's. *Graduate faculty:* 6 full-time (1 woman), 12 part-time/adjunct (2 women). *Tuition:* Full-time $29,018; part-time $964 per credit. *Graduate housing:* Room and/or apartments guaranteed to single students; on-campus housing not available to married students. Typical cost: $7148 per year ($14,070

including board). Housing application deadline: 8/15. *Student services:* Campus safety program, exercise/wellness program, free psychological counseling, international student services, services for students with disabilities, writing training. *Library facilities:* Latimer Family Library - currently under construction. *Collection:* Weekly public service hours: 84.

Computer facilities: 150 computers available on campus for general student use. A campuswide network can be accessed from student residence rooms. Online class registration is available.

Website: http://www.saintvincentseminary.edu/

General Application Contact: Rev. Patrick T. Cronauer, OSB, Academic Dean, 724-805-2324, Fax: 724-805-2880, E-mail: patrick.cronauer@stvincent.edu.

GRADUATE UNITS

School of Theology Students: 43 full-time (0 women), 8 part-time (0 women); includes 4 minority (2 Asian, non-Hispanic/Latino; 1 Hispanic/Latino; 1 Two or more races, non-Hispanic/Latino), 12 international. Average age 27. 11 applicants, 100% accepted, 11 enrolled. *Faculty:* 7 full-time (2 women), 12 part-time/adjunct (2 women). *Expenses:* Contact institution. *Financial support:* In 2018–19, 51 students received support. Scholarships/grants available. Support available to part-time students. In 2018, 9 master's awarded. *Program availability:* Part-time, evening/weekend. Offers Catholic philosophical studies (MA); ecclesial ministry (MA); ministry (M Div); monastic studies (MA); sacred scripture (MA); systematic theology (MA). Saint Vincent College provides philosophy courses for the MA in Catholic Philosophical Studies degree program only. *Application deadline:* For fall admission, 8/15 for domestic and international students. Applications are processed on a rolling basis. *Application fee:* $34. *Application Contact:* Rev. Patrick T. Cronauer, OSB, Academic Dean, 724-805-2324, Fax: 724-805-2880, E-mail: patrick.cronauer@stvincent.edu. *President/Rector,* Very Rev. Edward M. Mazich, OSB, 724-805-2845, Fax: 724-532-5052, E-mail: edward.mazich@stvincent.edu.

ST. VLADIMIR'S ORTHODOX THEOLOGICAL SEMINARY, Crestwood, NY 10707-1699

General Information Independent-religious, coed, primarily men, graduate-only institution. *Graduate housing:* Rooms and/or apartments available on a first-come, first-served basis to single and married students. Housing application deadline: 5/1.

GRADUATE UNITS

Graduate School of Theology *Program availability:* Part-time. Offers general theological studies (MA); theology (M Div, M Th, D Min). MA and M Div offered jointly with St. Nersess Armenian Seminary. Electronic applications accepted.

SAINT XAVIER UNIVERSITY, Chicago, IL 60655-3105

General Information Independent-religious, coed, comprehensive institution. CGS member. *Graduate housing:* Room and/or apartments available on a first-come, first-served basis to single students; on-campus housing not available to married students. Housing application deadline: 8/15. *Research affiliation:* Alexian Brothers Hospital, Holy Cross Hospital, Little Company of Mary Hospital, Mercy Center for Health Care Services.

GRADUATE UNITS

Graduate Studies *Program availability:* Part-time, evening/weekend. Electronic applications accepted.

College of Arts and Sciences *Program availability:* Part-time, evening/weekend. Offers arts and sciences (MA, MACS, MS); computer science (MACS); speech-language pathology (MS).

Graham School of Management *Program availability:* Part-time, evening/weekend. Offers employee health benefits (Certificate); finance (MBA); financial fraud examination and management (MBA, Certificate); financial planning (MBA, Certificate); generalist/individualized (MBA); health administration (MBA); managed care (Certificate); management (MBA); marketing (MBA); project management (MBA, Certificate). Electronic applications accepted.

School of Education *Program availability:* Part-time, evening/weekend. Offers counseling (MA); curriculum and instruction (MA); early childhood education (MA); educational administration (MA); elementary education (MA); individualized studies (MA); music education (MA); reading (MA); secondary education (MA); Spanish education (MA); special education (MA); teaching and leadership (MA).

School of Nursing *Program availability:* Part-time, evening/weekend. Offers nursing (MSN, Certificate).

SALEM COLLEGE, Winston-Salem, NC 27101

General Information Independent-religious, coed, primarily women, comprehensive institution. *Graduate housing:* On-campus housing not available.

GRADUATE UNITS

Graduate Studies *Program availability:* Part-time, evening/weekend, online learning. Offers art education (MAT); elementary education (M Ed, MAT); language and literacy (M Ed); middle school education (MAT); organ (MM); piano (MM); school counseling (M Ed); second language studies (MAT); secondary education (MAT); special education (M Ed, MAT). Electronic applications accepted.

SALEM INTERNATIONAL UNIVERSITY, Salem, WV 26426-0500

General Information Independent, coed, comprehensive institution. *Graduate housing:* Rooms and/or apartments available on a first-come, first-served basis to single students and available to married students.

GRADUATE UNITS

School of Business *Program availability:* Part-time, online learning. Offers information security (MBA); international business (MBA). Electronic applications accepted.

School of Education *Program availability:* Part-time, evening/weekend, online learning. Offers curriculum and instruction (M Ed); educational leadership (M Ed). Electronic applications accepted.

SALEM STATE UNIVERSITY, Salem, MA 01970-5353

General Information State-supported, coed, comprehensive institution. CGS member. *Graduate housing:* On-campus housing not available.

GRADUATE UNITS

School of Graduate Studies *Program availability:* Part-time, evening/weekend. Offers adult-gerontology primary care nursing (MSN); advanced professional studies in counseling (Graduate Certificate); art (MAT); business administration (MBA); chemistry (MAT); counseling and psychological services (MS, Graduate Certificate); criminal justice (MS); early childhood education (M Ed); education (CAGS); elementary education (M Ed); English (MA, MAT); geo-information science (MS); higher education in student affairs (M Ed); history (MA, MAT); humanities (M Ed); library media studies (M Ed); math/science (MAT); mathematics (MAT, MS); middle school general science

Salisbury University

(MAT); middle school math (MAT); nursing administration (MSN); nursing education (MSN); occupational therapy (MS); physical education (M Ed); reading (M Ed); school counseling (M Ed); secondary education (M Ed); social work (MSW); Spanish (MAT); special education (M Ed); teaching English as a second language (MAT).

SALISBURY UNIVERSITY, Salisbury, MD 21801-6837

General Information State-supported, coed, comprehensive institution. CGS member. *Enrollment:* 8,567 graduate, professional, and undergraduate students; 510 full-time matriculated graduate/professional students (406 women), 324 part-time matriculated graduate/professional students (245 women). *Enrollment by degree level:* 743 master's, 80 doctoral, 11 other advanced degrees. *Graduate faculty:* 111 full-time (63 women), 51 part-time/adjunct (41 women). *Graduate housing:* On-campus housing not available. *Student services:* Campus employment opportunities, campus safety program, career counseling, exercise/wellness program, free psychological counseling, international student services, multicultural affairs office, services for students with disabilities, teacher training, writing training. *Library facilities:* Guerrieri Academic Commons plus 2 others. *Collection:* Books: 269,531 (physical), 347 (digital/electronic); Serial titles: 694 (physical), 150 (digital/electronic); Databases: 106. Weekly public service hours: 112; study areas open 24 hours, 5–7 days a week; students can reserve study rooms.

Computer facilities: 1,000 computers available on campus for general student use. A campuswide network can be accessed from student residence rooms and from off campus. Online class registration, university accounts, student web hosting are available.
Website: http://www.salisbury.edu/

General Application Contact: Lacie Doyle, Graduate Enrollment Management Specialist, 410-548-3546, Fax: 410-677-0052, E-mail: lhdoyle@salisbury.edu.

GRADUATE UNITS

Department of Conflict Analysis and Dispute Resolution Students: 29 full-time (15 women), 3 part-time (all women); includes 10 minority (8 Black or African American, non-Hispanic/Latino; 2 Two or more races, non-Hispanic/Latino), 1 international. Average age 29. 18 applicants, 89% accepted, 12 enrolled. *Faculty:* 5 full-time (0 women). Expenses: Contact institution. *Financial support:* In 2018–19, 14 students received support, including 3 research assistantships with full tuition reimbursements available (averaging $8,667 per year), 6 teaching assistantships with full tuition reimbursements available (averaging $8,000 per year); career-related internships or fieldwork and scholarships/grants also available. Support available to part-time students. Financial award application deadline: 3/1; financial award applicants required to submit FAFSA. In 2018, 19 master's awarded. *Program availability:* Part-time, evening/weekend. Offers conflict analysis and dispute resolution (MA). *Application deadline:* For fall admission, 5/1 priority date for domestic and international students. Applications are processed on a rolling basis. *Application fee:* $65. Electronic applications accepted. *Application Contact:* Dr. Ignaciyas Soosaipillai, Graduate Program Director, 410-543-6435, E-mail: iksoosaipillai@salisbury.edu. *Graduate Program Director,* Dr. Ignaciyas Soosaipillai, 410-543-6435, E-mail: iksoosaipillai@salisbury.edu.

Department of English Students: 12 full-time (10 women), 9 part-time (8 women); includes 1 minority (Hispanic/Latino), 3 international. Average age 35. 16 applicants, 88% accepted, 4 enrolled. *Faculty:* 10 full-time (5 women). Expenses: Contact institution. *Financial support:* In 2018–19, 2 students received support, including 8 teaching assistantships with full tuition reimbursements available (averaging $11,050 per year); career-related internships or fieldwork and scholarships/grants also available. Support available to part-time students. Financial award application deadline: 3/1; financial award applicants required to submit FAFSA. In 2018, 14 master's awarded. *Program availability:* Part-time, evening/weekend. Offers English (MA). *Application deadline:* For fall admission, 8/1 for domestic and international students; for spring admission, 1/1 for domestic and international students. *Application fee:* $65. Electronic applications accepted. *Application Contact:* Dr. John Nieves, Graduate Program Director, 410-677-6511, E-mail: janieves@salisbury.edu. *Graduate Program Director,* Dr. John Nieves, 410-677-6511, E-mail: janieves@salisbury.edu.

Department of History Students: 5 full-time (1 woman), 6 part-time (1 woman); includes 1 minority (Two or more races, non-Hispanic/Latino). Average age 37. 5 applicants, 80% accepted, 4 enrolled. *Faculty:* 5 full-time (0 women). Expenses: Contact institution. *Financial support:* In 2018–19, 3 students received support, including 5 research assistantships with full tuition reimbursements available (averaging $8,000 per year); career-related internships or fieldwork and scholarships/grants also available. Support available to part-time students. Financial award application deadline: 3/1; financial award applicants required to submit FAFSA. In 2018, 5 master's awarded. *Program availability:* Part-time, evening/weekend. Offers history (MA). *Application deadline:* For fall admission, 4/15 priority date for domestic and international students; for spring admission, 10/15 priority date for domestic and international students. Applications are processed on a rolling basis. *Application fee:* $65. Electronic applications accepted. *Application Contact:* Dr. Celine Carayon, Graduate Program Director, 410-677-4601, E-mail: cxcarayon@salisbury.edu. *Graduate Program Director,* Dr. Celine Carayon, 410-677-4601, E-mail: cxcarayon@salisbury.edu.

Department of Social Work Students: 309 full-time (280 women), 61 part-time (56 women); includes 95 minority (70 Black or African American, non-Hispanic/Latino; 1 American Indian or Alaska Native, non-Hispanic/Latino; 2 Asian, non-Hispanic/Latino; 9 Hispanic/Latino; 2 Native Hawaiian or other Pacific Islander, non-Hispanic/Latino; 11 Two or more races, non-Hispanic/Latino), 1 international. Average age 32. 337 applicants, 71% accepted, 169 enrolled. *Faculty:* 24 full-time (20 women), 42 part-time/adjunct (33 women). Expenses: Contact institution. *Financial support:* In 2018–19, 22 students received support, including 2 research assistantships with full tuition reimbursements available (averaging $2,000 per year), 2 teaching assistantships with full tuition reimbursements available (averaging $8,000 per year); career-related internships or fieldwork and scholarships/grants also available. Support available to part-time students. Financial award application deadline: 3/1; financial award applicants required to submit FAFSA. In 2018, 169 master's awarded. *Program availability:* Part-time, evening/weekend, 100% online, blended/hybrid learning. Offers social work (MSW). *Application deadline:* For fall admission, 1/15 priority date for domestic and international students; for summer admission, 1/15 priority date for domestic and international students. Applications are processed on a rolling basis. *Application fee:* $65. Electronic applications accepted. *Application Contact:* Lindsey Shockley, Admissions Program Specialist, 410-677-5363, E-mail: lrshockley@salisbury.edu. *Graduate Program Director,* Dr. Mary Hylton, 410-677-5346, E-mail: mehylton@salisbury.edu.

DNP Program Students: 34 full-time (31 women), 3 part-time (all women); includes 8 minority (5 Black or African American, non-Hispanic/Latino; 1 Asian, non-Hispanic/Latino; 1 Hispanic/Latino; 1 Two or more races, non-Hispanic/Latino). Average age 33. 16 applicants, 75% accepted, 10 enrolled. *Faculty:* 15 full-time (14 women), 4 part-time/adjunct (all women). Expenses: Contact institution. *Financial support:* In 2018–19, 1 student received support. Career-related internships or fieldwork and scholarships/grants available. Support available to part-time students. Financial award application deadline: 3/1; financial award applicants required to submit FAFSA. In 2018, 7 doctorates awarded. *Program availability:* Part-time, evening/weekend, 100% online, blended/hybrid learning. Offers family nurse practitioner (DNP); nursing leadership (DNP). *Application deadline:* For fall admission, 3/1 priority date for domestic and international students. Applications are processed on a rolling basis. *Application fee:* $65. Electronic applications accepted. *Application Contact:* Carmel Boger, Administrative Assistant I, 410-543-6420, E-mail: ciboger@salisbury.edu. *Graduate Program Director,* Dr. Dorothea Winter, 410-548-5562, E-mail: dmwinter@salisbury.edu.

MS in Nursing Program Students: 2 part-time (both women); includes 1 minority (Hispanic/Latino). Average age 23. 3 applicants, 33% accepted, 1 enrolled. *Faculty:* 15 full-time (14 women), 4 part-time/adjunct (all women). Expenses: Contact institution. *Financial support:* In 2018–19, 1 student received support, including 1 research assistantship with full tuition reimbursement available (averaging $8,000 per year); career-related internships or fieldwork and scholarships/grants also available. Support available to part-time students. Financial award application deadline: 3/1; financial award applicants required to submit FAFSA. *Program availability:* Part-time, evening/weekend, 100% online, blended/hybrid learning. Offers nursing (MS). *Application deadline:* For fall admission, 3/1 priority date for domestic and international students. *Application fee:* $65. Electronic applications accepted. *Application Contact:* Carmel Boger, Administrative Assistant I, 410-543-6420, E-mail: ciboger@salisbury.edu. *Graduate Program Director,* Dr. Dorothea Winter, 410-548-5562, E-mail: dmwinter@salisbury.edu.

Perdue School of Business Students: 39 full-time (23 women), 30 part-time (14 women); includes 14 minority (9 Black or African American, non-Hispanic/Latino; 1 Asian, non-Hispanic/Latino; 4 Two or more races, non-Hispanic/Latino), 1 international. Average age 29. 77 applicants, 75% accepted, 45 enrolled. *Faculty:* 6 full-time (1 woman). Expenses: Contact institution. *Financial support:* In 2018–19, 18 students received support, including 10 research assistantships with full tuition reimbursements available (averaging $8,000 per year), 8 teaching assistantships with full tuition reimbursements available (averaging $8,500 per year); career-related internships or fieldwork and scholarships/grants also available. Support available to part-time students. Financial award application deadline: 3/1; financial award applicants required to submit FAFSA. In 2018, 38 master's awarded. *Program availability:* Part-time, evening/weekend, 100% online, blended/hybrid learning. Offers business administration (MBA). *Application deadline:* For fall admission, 3/1 priority date for domestic and international students. Applications are processed on a rolling basis. *Application fee:* $65. Electronic applications accepted. *Application Contact:* Yvonne Hanley, Graduate Program Director, 410-548-3983, E-mail: yxdownie@salisbury.edu. *Graduate Program Director,* Yvonne Hanley, 410-548-3983, E-mail: yxdownie@salisbury.edu.

Program in Applied Biology Students: 8 full-time (4 women), 3 part-time (2 women); includes 2 minority (1 Asian, non-Hispanic/Latino; 1 Native Hawaiian or other Pacific Islander, non-Hispanic/Latino). Average age 24. 9 applicants, 56% accepted, 5 enrolled. *Faculty:* 14 full-time (7 women). Expenses: Contact institution. *Financial support:* In 2018–19, 5 students received support, including 9 teaching assistantships with full tuition reimbursements available (averaging $13,000 per year); career-related internships or fieldwork and scholarships/grants also available. Support available to part-time students. Financial award application deadline: 3/1; financial award applicants required to submit FAFSA. In 2018, 2 master's awarded. Offers applied biology (MS). *Application deadline:* For fall admission, 3/1 for domestic and international students; for spring admission, 10/1 for domestic and international students. *Application fee:* $65. Electronic applications accepted. *Application Contact:* Dr. Dana Price, Graduate Program Director, 410-543-6498, E-mail: dlprice@salisbury.edu. *Graduate Program Director,* Dr. Dana Price, 410-543-6498, E-mail: dlprice@salisbury.edu.

Program in Applied Health Physiology Students: 22 full-time (10 women), 5 part-time (2 women); includes 5 minority (2 Black or African American, non-Hispanic/Latino; 1 American Indian or Alaska Native, non-Hispanic/Latino; 1 Hispanic/Latino; 1 Two or more races, non-Hispanic/Latino). Average age 24. 17 applicants, 82% accepted, 9 enrolled. *Faculty:* 5 full-time (1 woman). Expenses: Contact institution. *Financial support:* In 2018–19, 10 students received support, including 1 research assistantship with full tuition reimbursement available (averaging $8,000 per year), 9 teaching assistantships with full tuition reimbursements available (averaging $8,111 per year); career-related internships or fieldwork and scholarships/grants also available. Support available to part-time students. Financial award application deadline: 3/1; financial award applicants required to submit FAFSA. In 2018, 16 master's awarded. *Program availability:* Part-time, evening/weekend. Offers applied health physiology (MS). *Application deadline:* For fall admission, 8/1 for domestic and international students; for spring admission, 12/1 for domestic and international students. *Application fee:* $65. Electronic applications accepted. *Application Contact:* Dr. Thomas Pellinger, Graduate Program Director, 410-677-0144, E-mail: tkpellinger@salisbury.edu. *Graduate Program Director,* Dr. Thomas Pellinger, 410-677-0144, E-mail: tkpellinger@salisbury.edu.

Program in Athletic Training Students: 10 full-time (7 women), 3 part-time (1 woman); includes 3 minority (2 Black or African American, non-Hispanic/Latino; 1 Two or more races, non-Hispanic/Latino). Average age 24. 17 applicants, 82% accepted, 10 enrolled. *Faculty:* 2 full-time (both women). Expenses: Contact institution. *Financial support:* In 2018–19, 1 student received support. Career-related internships or fieldwork and scholarships/grants available. Support available to part-time students. Financial award application deadline: 3/1; financial award applicants required to submit FAFSA. In 2018, 3 master's awarded. Offers athletic training (MSAT). *Application deadline:* For summer admission, 1/15 priority date for domestic and international students. Applications are processed on a rolling basis. *Application fee:* $65. Electronic applications accepted. *Application Contact:* Dr. Laura Marinaro, Graduate Program Director, 410-548-3529, E-mail: lmmarinaro@salisbury.edu. *Graduate Program Director,* Dr. Laura Marinaro, 410-548-3529, E-mail: lmmarinaro@salisbury.edu.

Program in Contemporary Curriculum Theory and Instruction: Literacy Students: 18 full-time (14 women), 25 part-time (20 women); includes 3 minority (2 Black or African American, non-Hispanic/Latino; 1 Two or more races, non-Hispanic/Latino), 2 international. Average age 40. 19 applicants, 89% accepted, 15 enrolled. *Faculty:* 6 full-time (4 women). Expenses: Contact institution. *Financial support:* In 2018–19, 4 students received support, including 3 teaching assistantships with full tuition reimbursements available (averaging $8,000 per year); career-related internships or fieldwork and scholarships/grants also available. Support available to part-time students. Financial award application deadline: 3/1; financial award applicants required to submit FAFSA. *Program availability:* Part-time, evening/weekend, 100% online, blended/hybrid learning. Offers literacy (Ed D). *Application deadline:* For fall admission, 3/31 priority date for domestic and international students. Applications are processed on a rolling basis. *Application fee:* $65. Electronic applications accepted. *Application Contact:* Dr. Judith Franzak, Graduate Program Director, 410-677-0238, E-mail: jkfranzak@salisbury.edu. *Graduate Program Director,* Dr. Judith Franzak, 410-677-0238, E-mail: jkfranzak@salisbury.edu.

Program in Curriculum and Instruction Students: 11 full-time (2 women), 83 part-time (67 women); includes 14 minority (7 Black or African American, non-Hispanic/Latino; 1 Asian, non-Hispanic/Latino; 2 Hispanic/Latino; 4 Two or more races, non-Hispanic/Latino). Average age 29. 35 applicants, 80% accepted, 27 enrolled. *Faculty:* 10 full-time (7 women), 4 part-time/adjunct (3 women). Expenses: Contact institution. *Financial support:* In 2018–19, 8 students received support, including 11 teaching assistantships with full tuition reimbursements available (averaging $8,364 per year); career-related internships or fieldwork and scholarships/grants also available. Support available to part-time students. Financial award application deadline: 3/1; financial award applicants required to submit FAFSA. In 2018, 27 master's awarded. *Program availability:* Part-time, evening/weekend. Offers curriculum and instruction (M Ed). *Application deadline:* For fall admission, 4/1 priority date for domestic and international students; for spring admission, 10/1 priority date for domestic and international students; for summer admission, 4/1 priority date for domestic and international students. Applications are processed on a rolling basis. *Application fee:* $65. Electronic applications accepted. *Application Contact:* Dr. Douglas DeWitt, Graduate Program Director, 410-543-6286, E-mail: dmdewitt@salisbury.edu. *Graduate Program Director*, Dr. Douglas DeWitt, 410-543-6286, E-mail: dmdewitt@salisbury.edu.

Program in Educational Leadership Students: 2 full-time (both women), 46 part-time (29 women); includes 8 minority (7 Black or African American, non-Hispanic/Latino; 1 Two or more races, non-Hispanic/Latino). Average age 31. 22 applicants, 86% accepted, 15 enrolled. *Faculty:* 3 full-time (0 women), 1 (woman) part-time/adjunct. Expenses: Contact institution. *Financial support:* Career-related internships or fieldwork and scholarships/grants available. Support available to part-time students. Financial award application deadline: 3/1; financial award applicants required to submit FAFSA. In 2018, 8 master's awarded. *Program availability:* Part-time, evening/weekend. Offers educational leadership (M Ed). *Application deadline:* For fall admission, 4/1 priority date for domestic and international students; for spring admission, 10/1 priority date for domestic and international students; for summer admission, 4/1 priority date for domestic and international students. Applications are processed on a rolling basis. *Application fee:* $65. Electronic applications accepted. *Application Contact:* Dr. Douglas DeWitt, Graduate Program Director, 410-543-6286, E-mail: dmdewitt@salisbury.edu. *Graduate Program Director*, Dr. Douglas DeWitt, 410-543-6286, E-mail: dmdewitt@salisbury.edu.

Program in Geographic Information Systems Management Students: 5 full-time (2 women), 7 part-time (2 women); includes 1 minority (Two or more races, non-Hispanic/Latino). Average age 29. 10 applicants, 80% accepted, 7 enrolled. *Faculty:* 2 full-time. Expenses: Contact institution. *Financial support:* In 2018–19, 5 research assistantships with full tuition reimbursements available (averaging $8,000 per year) were awarded; career-related internships or fieldwork and scholarships/grants also available. Support available to part-time students. Financial award application deadline: 3/1; financial award applicants required to submit FAFSA. In 2018, 12 master's awarded. *Program availability:* Part-time, evening/weekend, online only, 100% online. Offers geographic information systems management (MS). *Application deadline:* For fall admission, 8/1 for domestic and international students; for spring admission, 1/3 for domestic and international students; for summer admission, 5/1 for domestic and international students. Applications are processed on a rolling basis. *Application fee:* $65. Electronic applications accepted. *Application Contact:* Dr. Stuart Hamilton, Graduate Program Director, 410-543-6459, E-mail: sehamilton@salisbury.edu. *Graduate Program Director*, Dr. Stuart Hamilton, 410-543-6459, E-mail: sehamilton@salisbury.edu.

Program in Mathematics Education Students: 1 (woman) full-time, 11 part-time (10 women). Average age 26. 7 applicants, 100% accepted, 6 enrolled. *Faculty:* 2 full-time (1 woman). Expenses: Contact institution. *Financial support:* In 2018–19, 1 teaching assistantship with full tuition reimbursement (averaging $8,000 per year) was awarded; career-related internships or fieldwork and scholarships/grants also available. Support available to part-time students. Financial award application deadline: 3/1; financial award applicants required to submit FAFSA. In 2018, 1 master's awarded. *Program availability:* Part-time. Offers mathematics (MSME). *Application deadline:* For fall admission, 8/15 priority date for domestic and international students; for spring admission, 10/1 priority date for domestic and international students. Applications are processed on a rolling basis. *Application fee:* $65. Electronic applications accepted. *Application Contact:* Dr. Jennifer Bergner, Graduate Program Director, 410-677-5429, E-mail: jabergner@salisbury.edu. *Graduate Program Director*, Dr. Jennifer Bergner, 410-677-5429, E-mail: jabergner@salisbury.edu.

Program in Reading Specialist Students: 23 part-time (22 women); includes 2 minority (both Asian, non-Hispanic/Latino). Average age 28. 10 applicants, 80% accepted, 8 enrolled. *Faculty:* 1 full-time (1 woman). Expenses: Contact institution. *Financial support:* In 2018–19, 4 students received support. Career-related internships or fieldwork and scholarships/grants available. Support available to part-time students. Financial award application deadline: 3/1; financial award applicants required to submit FAFSA. In 2018, 4 master's awarded. *Program availability:* Part-time, evening/weekend. Offers reading specialist (M Ed). *Application deadline:* For fall admission, 3/1 priority date for domestic and international students; for spring admission, 10/1 priority date for domestic and international students; for summer admission, 3/1 priority date for domestic and international students. Applications are processed on a rolling basis. *Application fee:* $65. Electronic applications accepted. *Application Contact:* Dr. Joyce Wiencek, Graduate Program Director, 410-543-6288, E-mail: bjwiencek@salisbury.edu. *Graduate Program Director*, Dr. Joyce Wiencek, 410-543-6288, E-mail: bjwiencek@salisbury.edu.

Program in Teaching Students: 5 full-time (4 women), 3 part-time (all women). Average age 30. 2 applicants, 100% accepted, 2 enrolled. *Faculty:* 5 full-time (3 women). Expenses: Contact institution. *Financial support:* In 2018–19, 4 students received support, including 2 teaching assistantships with full tuition reimbursements available (averaging $8,000 per year); career-related internships or fieldwork and scholarships/grants also available. Support available to part-time students. Financial award application deadline: 3/1; financial award applicants required to submit FAFSA. In 2018, 5 master's awarded. *Program availability:* Part-time, evening/weekend. Offers secondary education (MAT). *Application deadline:* For winter admission, 10/1 priority date for domestic and international students. *Application fee:* $65. Electronic applications accepted. *Application Contact:* Claire Williams, Program Management Specialist, 410-677-0001, E-mail: clwilliams@salisbury.edu. *Graduate Program Director*, Dr. Alexander Pope, IV, 410-543-6391, E-mail: axpope@salisbury.edu.

See Display below and Close-Up on page 743.

SALUS UNIVERSITY, Elkins Park, PA 19027-1598
General Information Independent, coed, graduate-only institution. *Graduate housing:* On-campus housing not available. *Research affiliation:* Dynamis Pharmaceuticals (diabetes research), DakDak (photobiology).

GRADUATE UNITS

College of Education and Rehabilitation *Program availability:* Part-time, online learning. Offers education of children and youth with visual and multiple impairments

(M Ed, Certificate); low vision rehabilitation (MS, Certificate); occupational therapy (MS); orientation and mobility therapy (MS, Certificate); speech-language pathology (MS); vision rehabilitation therapy (MS, Certificate).

College of Health Sciences Offers physician assistant (MMS); public health (MPH). Electronic applications accepted.

Osborne College of Audiology Offers audiology (Au D). Electronic applications accepted.

Pennsylvania College of Optometry Offers optometry (OD). Electronic applications accepted.

SALVE REGINA UNIVERSITY, Newport, RI 02840-4192

General Information Independent-religious, coed, comprehensive institution. *Enrollment:* 2,647 graduate, professional, and undergraduate students; 227 full-time matriculated graduate/professional students (148 women), 367 part-time matriculated graduate/professional students (233 women). *Enrollment by degree level:* 444 master's, 104 doctoral, 46 other advanced degrees. *Graduate faculty:* 27 full-time (14 women), 46 part-time/adjunct (19 women). *Tuition:* Full-time $10,530; part-time $585 per credit. *Required fees:* $60 per term. Tuition and fees vary according to course level, course load, degree level and program. *Graduate housing:* On-campus housing not available. *Student services:* Campus employment opportunities, campus safety program, career counseling, international student services, multicultural affairs office, services for students with disabilities. *Library facilities:* McKillop Library. *Collection:* Books: 147,721 (physical), 347,549 (digital/electronic); Serial titles: 195 (physical), 75,064 (digital/electronic); Databases: 82. Weekly public service hours: 58; students can reserve study rooms.

Computer facilities: Computer purchase and lease plans are available. 215 computers available on campus for general student use. A campuswide network can be accessed from student residence rooms and from off campus. Online class registration is available.

Website: http://www.salve.edu/

General Application Contact: Laurie Reilly, Graduate Admissions Manager, 401-341-2153, Fax: 401-341-2973, E-mail: laurie.reilly@salve.edu.

GRADUATE UNITS

The Newport MFA in Creative Writing Program Offers creative writing (MFA).

Program in Administration of Justice and Homeland Security *Program availability:* Part-time, evening/weekend, online learning. Offers administration of justice and homeland security (MS); cybersecurity and intelligence (CGS); digital forensics (CGS); leadership in justice (CGS). Electronic applications accepted.

Program in Applied Behavior Analysis Offers applied behavior analysis (MA, CAGS).

Program in Business Administration *Program availability:* Part-time, evening/weekend, online learning. Offers cybersecurity issues in business (MBA); entrepreneurial enterprise (MBA); health care administration and management (MBA); nonprofit management (MBA); social ventures (MBA). Electronic applications accepted.

Program in Healthcare Administration and Management *Program availability:* Part-time, evening/weekend, online learning. Offers healthcare administration and management (MS). Electronic applications accepted.

Program in Humanities *Program availability:* Part-time, evening/weekend, online learning. Offers humanitarian assistance (MA); humanities (PhD); public humanities (MA); religion, peace and justice (MA). Electronic applications accepted.

Program in International Relations *Program availability:* Part-time, evening/weekend, online learning. Offers international relations (MA, PhD, CGS). Electronic applications accepted.

Program in Management *Program availability:* Part-time, evening/weekend, online learning. Offers business studies (CGS); human resource management (CGS); innovation and strategic management (MS); management (CGS); nonprofit management (CGS); social entrepreneurship (CGS). Electronic applications accepted.

Program in Nursing *Program availability:* Part-time, evening/weekend. Offers nursing (DNP). Electronic applications accepted.

Program in Rehabilitation Counseling *Program availability:* Part-time, evening/weekend. Offers clinical rehabilitation and mental health counseling (MA); mental health (CAGS); rehabilitation (CAGS); rehabilitation counseling (MA); substance abuse and treatment (CAGS). Electronic applications accepted.

SAMFORD UNIVERSITY, Birmingham, AL 35229

General Information Independent-religious, coed, university. *Enrollment:* 5,589 graduate, professional, and undergraduate students; 1,824 full-time matriculated graduate/professional students (1,159 women), 223 part-time matriculated graduate/professional students (157 women). *Enrollment by degree level:* 622 master's, 1,396 doctoral, 29 other advanced degrees. *Graduate faculty:* 164 full-time (90 women), 55 part-time/adjunct (24 women). *Tuition:* Full-time $17,255; part-time $837 per credit. *Required fees:* $610; $305 per term. Tuition and fees vary according to course load, degree level, program and student level. *Graduate housing:* On-campus housing not available. *Student services:* Campus employment opportunities, campus safety program, career counseling, exercise/wellness program, free psychological counseling, grant writing training, international student services, low-cost health insurance, multicultural affairs office, services for students with disabilities, teacher training, writing training. *Library facilities:* University Library plus 2 others. *Collection:* Books: 574,434 (physical), 299,458 (digital/electronic); Serial titles: 6,045 (physical), 117,199 (digital/electronic); Databases: 296. Weekly public service hours: 99; students can reserve study rooms.

Computer facilities: 330 computers available on campus for general student use. A campuswide network can be accessed from student residence rooms and from off campus. Online class registration, free online storage and tech support are available. Website: http://www.samford.edu/

General Application Contact: Brian L. Kennedy, Director of Recruitment, 205-726-4176, Fax: 205-726-2171, E-mail: blkenned@samford.edu.

GRADUATE UNITS

Beeson School of Divinity Students: 131 full-time (26 women), 18 part-time (9 women); includes 20 minority (all Black or African American, non-Hispanic/Latino), 7 international. Average age 31. 54 applicants, 98% accepted, 27 enrolled. *Faculty:* 14 full-time (2 women), 3 part-time/adjunct (1 woman). Expenses: Contact institution. *Financial support:* In 2018–19, 129 students received support, including 6 teaching assistantships (averaging $1,200 per year); Federal Work-Study and scholarships/grants also available. Financial award application deadline: 2/15; financial award applicants required to submit FAFSA. In 2018, 31 master's, 3 doctorates awarded. *Program availability:* Part-time. Offers divinity (M Div, MATS, D Min). Samford Universtiy. *Application deadline:* For fall admission, 2/15 for domestic and international students; for spring admission, 10/1 for domestic and international students. *Application fee:* $35. Electronic applications

accepted. *Application Contact:* Sherri S. Brown, Director of Admission, 205-726-2066, E-mail: sbrown5@samford.edu. *Dean, Professor of Divinity,* Dr. Douglas A Sweeney, 205-726-2632, E-mail: dsweeney@samford.edu.

Brock School of Business Students: 76 full-time (30 women), 20 part-time (11 women); includes 8 minority (4 Black or African American, non-Hispanic/Latino; 1 Asian, non-Hispanic/Latino; 1 Hispanic/Latino; 2 Two or more races, non-Hispanic/Latino), 7 international. Average age 28. 41 applicants, 88% accepted, 26 enrolled. *Faculty:* 7 full-time (1 woman), 4 part-time/adjunct (0 women). Expenses: Contact institution. *Financial support:* In 2018–19, 46 students received support. Scholarships/grants available. Financial award application deadline: 2/15; financial award applicants required to submit FAFSA. In 2018, 74 master's awarded. *Program availability:* Part-time, 100% online, blended/hybrid learning. Offers accountancy (M Acc); entrepreneurship (MBA); finance (MBA); marketing (MBA). Programs offered jointly with Cumberland School of Law, Beeson School of Divinity, Howard College of Arts and Sciences, and McWhorter School of Pharmacy. *Application deadline:* For fall admission, 8/1 for domestic and international students; for spring admission, 1/1 for domestic and international students. Applications are processed on a rolling basis. *Application fee:* $35. Electronic applications accepted. *Application Contact:* Elizabeth Gambrell, Associate Director, 205-726-2040, Fax: 205-726-2540, E-mail: eagambre@samford.edu. *Assistant Dean,* Dr. Barbara Cartledge, 205-726-2935, Fax: 205-726-2540, E-mail: bhcartle@samford.edu.

Cumberland School of Law Students: 453 full-time (231 women), 11 part-time (4 women); includes 87 minority (55 Black or African American, non-Hispanic/Latino; 5 American Indian or Alaska Native, non-Hispanic/Latino; 6 Asian, non-Hispanic/Latino; 17 Hispanic/Latino; 1 Native Hawaiian or other Pacific Islander, non-Hispanic/Latino; 3 Two or more races, non-Hispanic/Latino), 1 international. Average age 27. 607 applicants, 74% accepted, 170 enrolled. *Faculty:* 17 full-time (7 women), 21 part-time/adjunct (8 women). Expenses: Contact institution. *Financial support:* In 2018–19, 374 students received support. Scholarships/grants available. Financial award application deadline: 3/1; financial award applicants required to submit FAFSA. In 2018, 13 master's, 142 doctorates awarded. *Program availability:* Part-time, 100% online. Offers law (LL M, MCL, MSL, JD). Samford University, University of Alabama Birmingham. *Application deadline:* For fall admission, 6/1 for domestic students, 6/1 priority date for international students. Electronic applications accepted. *Application Contact:* Whitney Dachelet, Interim Director of Admissions and Student Recruiting, 205-726-2702, Fax: 205-726-2057, E-mail: wdachele@samford.edu. *Dean and* Ethel P. *Malugen Professor of Law,* Henry C. Strickland, 205-726-2704, Fax: 205-726-4457, E-mail: hcstrick@samford.edu.

Howard College of Arts and Sciences Students: 7 full-time (3 women); includes 4 minority (3 Black or African American, non-Hispanic/Latino; 1 Asian, non-Hispanic/Latino). Average age 28. 18 applicants, 28% accepted, 4 enrolled. *Faculty:* 8 full-time (2 women), 1 part-time/adjunct (0 women). Expenses: Contact institution. *Financial support:* Application deadline: 2/15; applicants required to submit FAFSA. In 2018, 4 master's awarded. *Program availability:* Part-time, online only, 100% online. Offers energy (MSEM); environmental management (MSEM); public health (MSEM). *Application fee:* $40. *Application Contact:* David Frings, Assistant Graduate Director, 205-726-4537, E-mail: dmfrings@samford.edu. *Professor and Chair,* Dr. Anthony Scott Overton, 205-726-4537, E-mail: aoverton@samford.edu.

Ida Moffett School of Nursing Students: 287 full-time (245 women), 52 part-time (45 women); includes 71 minority (42 Black or African American, non-Hispanic/Latino; 1 American Indian or Alaska Native, non-Hispanic/Latino; 9 Asian, non-Hispanic/Latino; 8 Hispanic/Latino; 1 Native Hawaiian or other Pacific Islander, non-Hispanic/Latino; 10 Two or more races, non-Hispanic/Latino). Average age 36. 81 applicants, 74% accepted, 48 enrolled. *Faculty:* 18 full-time (17 women), 3 part-time/adjunct (0 women). Expenses: Contact institution. *Financial support:* In 2018–19, 59 students received support. Application deadline: 2/15; applicants required to submit FAFSA. In 2018, 132 master's, 52 doctorates awarded. *Program availability:* Part-time, evening/weekend, blended/hybrid learning. Offers administration (DNP); advanced practice (DNP); dual nurse practitioner (family/emergency) (DNP); family nurse practitioner (MSN, DNP); nurse anesthesia (MSN, DNP); nursing administration (DNP). *Application deadline:* For fall admission, 4/1 for domestic and international students; for spring admission, 8/1 for domestic and international students; for summer admission, 1/1 for domestic and international students. *Application fee:* $50. Electronic applications accepted. *Application Contact:* Allyson Maddox, Director of Graduate Student Services, 205-726-2047, E-mail: amaddox@samford.edu. *Vice Provost, College of Health Sciences/Ida Moffett School of Nursing Dean/Professor,* Dr. Nena F. Sanders, 205-726-2612, E-mail: nfsander@samford.edu.

McWhorter School of Pharmacy Students: 464 full-time (306 women), 11 part-time (6 women); includes 95 minority (48 Black or African American, non-Hispanic/Latino; 4 American Indian or Alaska Native, non-Hispanic/Latino; 29 Asian, non-Hispanic/Latino; 7 Hispanic/Latino; 7 Two or more races, non-Hispanic/Latino), 5 international. Average age 24. 314 applicants, 39% accepted, 119 enrolled. *Faculty:* 36 full-time (23 women), 1 part-time/adjunct (0 women). Expenses: Contact institution. *Financial support:* In 2018–19, 217 students received support. Institutionally sponsored loans and scholarships/grants available. Financial award application deadline: 2/15; financial award applicants required to submit FAFSA. In 2018, 110 doctorates awarded. Offers pharmacy (Pharm D). *Application deadline:* For fall admission, 5/1 priority date for domestic and international students. Applications are processed on a rolling basis. Electronic applications accepted. *Application Contact:* Jonathan Parker, Director of Pharmacy Admissions, 205-726-4242, Fax: 205-726-4141, E-mail: jmparker@samford.edu. *Dean/Professor,* Dr. Michael Crouch, 205-726-4475, E-mail: mcrouch@samford.edu.

Orlean Beeson School of Education Students: 156 full-time (111 women), 101 part-time (73 women); includes 106 minority (100 Black or African American, non-Hispanic/Latino; 1 American Indian or Alaska Native, non-Hispanic/Latino; 5 Two or more races, non-Hispanic/Latino), 1 international. Average age 37. 107 applicants, 94% accepted, 65 enrolled. *Faculty:* 12 full-time (10 women), 16 part-time/adjunct (11 women). Expenses: Contact institution. *Financial support:* In 2018–19, 173 students received support. Scholarships/grants available. Financial award application deadline: 2/15; financial award applicants required to submit FAFSA. In 2018, 94 master's, 40 doctorates, 11 other advanced degrees awarded. *Program availability:* Part-time, evening/weekend, 100% online, blended/hybrid learning. Offers educational leadership (MSE, Ed D); elementary education (MS Ed, MSE); gifted (MSE); instructional design and technology (MSE); instructional leadership (MSE, Ed S); secondary education (MSE); special education (MSE). *Application deadline:* For fall admission, 7/15 for domestic and international students; for winter admission, 11/15 for domestic and international students; for spring admission, 11/15 for domestic and international students; for summer admission, 4/15 for domestic and international students. Applications are processed on a rolling basis. *Application fee:* $35. Electronic applications accepted. *Application Contact:* Brooke Karr, Graduate Admissions Office Coordinator, 205-729-2783, E-mail: kbgilrea@samford.edu. *Interim Dean,* Dr. Howard Finch, 205-726-2745, E-mail: hfinch@samford.edu.

School of Health Professions Students: 152 full-time (120 women); includes 16 minority (5 Black or African American, non-Hispanic/Latino; 1 American Indian or Alaska Native, non-Hispanic/Latino; 4 Hispanic/Latino; 6 Two or more races, non-Hispanic/Latino). Average age 24. 645 applicants, 32% accepted, 9 enrolled. *Faculty:* 24 full-time (13 women), 1 (woman) part-time/adjunct. Expenses: Contact institution. *Financial support:* In 2018–19, 5 students received support. Scholarships/grants available. Financial award application deadline: 5/1; financial award applicants required to submit FAFSA. In 2018, 50 master's awarded. Offers athletic training (MAT); physical therapy (DPT); respiratory care (MS); speech language pathology (MS). *Application deadline:* For fall admission, 8/1 for domestic students; for spring admission, 12/1 for domestic students; for summer admission, 1/1 for domestic students. *Application fee:* $120. Electronic applications accepted. *Application Contact:* Dr. Marian Carter, Ed.D., Assistant Dean of Enrollment Management and Student Services, 205-726-2611, E-mail: mwcarter@samford.edu. *Dean of the School of Health Professions*, Dr. Alan Jung, Ph.D., 205-726-2716, E-mail: apjung@samford.edu.

School of Public Health Students: 86 full-time (79 women), 6 part-time (all women); includes 18 minority (15 Black or African American, non-Hispanic/Latino; 1 Hispanic/Latino; 2 Two or more races, non-Hispanic/Latino). Average age 28. 93 applicants, 73% accepted, 30 enrolled. *Faculty:* 18 full-time (11 women), 1 (woman) part-time/adjunct. Expenses: Contact institution. *Financial support:* In 2018–19, 39 students received support. Scholarships/grants available. Financial award application deadline: 5/1; financial award applicants required to submit FAFSA. In 2018, 59 master's awarded. *Program availability:* Part-time, online only, 100% online. Offers health informatics (MSHI); healthcare administration (MHA); nutrition (MS); public health (MPH); social work (MSW). *Application deadline:* For fall admission, 10/1 for domestic students; for winter admission, 12/1 for domestic students; for spring admission, 5/1 for domestic students. Applications are processed on a rolling basis. *Application fee:* $75. Electronic applications accepted. *Application Contact:* Dr. Marian Carter, Ed.D, Assistant Dean of Enrollment Management and Student Services, 205-726-2611, E-mail: mwcarter@samford.edu. *Dean, School of Public Health*, Dr. Keith Elder, Ph.D., 205-726-4655, E-mail: kelder@samford.edu.

School of the Arts Students: 12 full-time (8 women), 4 part-time (3 women); includes 2 minority (both Black or African American, non-Hispanic/Latino), 2 international. Average age 26. 9 applicants, 89% accepted, 3 enrolled. *Faculty:* 10 full-time (4 women), 4 part-time/adjunct (2 women). Expenses: Contact institution. *Financial support:* In 2018–19, 13 students received support. Scholarships/grants available. Financial award application deadline: 2/15; financial award applicants required to submit FAFSA. In 2018, 4 master's awarded. *Program availability:* Part-time. Offers church music (MM); instrumental performance (MM); piano performance and pedagogy (MM); vocal performance (MM); vocal/choral or instrumental music (MME). *Application deadline:* For fall admission, 1/17 for domestic and international students; for spring admission, 10/18 for domestic and international students. Applications are processed on a rolling basis. *Application fee:* $35. Electronic applications accepted. *Application Contact:* Dr. Mark Lackey, Assistant Professor, 205-726-4623, Fax: 205-726-2615, E-mail: mlckey@samford.edu. *Dean of the School of the Arts/Professor*, Dr. Joseph Hopkin, 205-726-2778, E-mail: jhopkins@samford.edu.

SAM HOUSTON STATE UNIVERSITY, Huntsville, TX 77341

General Information State-supported, coed, university. CGS member. *Graduate housing:* Room and/or apartments available on a first-come, first-served basis to single students; on-campus housing not available to married students. Housing application deadline: 8/20. *Research affiliation:* Texas Criminal Justice Division, Texas Department of Corrections, Research Division.

GRADUATE UNITS

College of Business Administration *Program availability:* Part-time, evening/weekend, online learning. Offers accounting (MS); banking and financial institutions (EMBA); business administration (EMBA, MBA, MS); project management (MS). Electronic applications accepted.

College of Criminal Justice *Program availability:* Part-time, evening/weekend, online learning. Offers criminal justice (MS, PhD); criminal justice and criminology (MA); criminal justice leadership and management (MS); forensic science (MS); homeland security studies (MS); victim services management (MS). Electronic applications accepted.

College of Education *Program availability:* Part-time, evening/weekend, online learning. Offers administration (M Ed); counseling (M Ed, MA, PhD); curriculum and instruction (M Ed); developmental education administration (Ed D); education (M Ed, MA, MLS, Ed D, PhD); educational leadership (Ed D); higher education administration (MA); higher education leadership (Ed D); instructional leadership (M Ed, MA); international literacy (M Ed); library science (MLS); reading (M Ed); special education (M Ed, MA). Electronic applications accepted.

College of Fine Arts and Mass Communication *Program availability:* Part-time. Offers dance (MFA); digital media (MA); fine arts and mass communication (MA, MFA, MM). Electronic applications accepted.

School of Music *Program availability:* Part-time. Offers music (MM). Electronic applications accepted.

College of Health Sciences *Program availability:* Part-time. Offers dietetics (MS); family and consumer sciences (MS); health (MA); health sciences (MA, MS); sport and human performance (MA); sport management (MA). Electronic applications accepted.

College of Humanities and Social Sciences *Program availability:* Part-time, online learning. Offers communication studies (MA); creative writing, editing, and publishing (MFA); English (MA); history (MA); humanities and social sciences (MA, MFA, MPA, PhD, SSP); political science (MA); psychology (MA, PhD, SSP); public administration (MPA); sociology (MA); Spanish (MA). Electronic applications accepted.

College of Sciences *Program availability:* Part-time, evening/weekend. Offers agriculture (MS); applied geographic information science (MS); biological sciences (MA, MS); chemistry (MS); computing and information science (MS); digital forensics (MS); geographic information science (Certificate); information assurance and security (MS); mathematics (MA, MS); sciences (MA, MS, PhD, Certificate); statistics (MS). Electronic applications accepted.

SAMUEL MERRITT UNIVERSITY, Oakland, CA 94609-3108

General Information Independent, coed, primarily women, upper-level institution. *Graduate housing:* On-campus housing not available. *Research affiliation:* Summit Medical Center (nursing).

GRADUATE UNITS

California School of Podiatric Medicine Offers podiatric medicine (DPM). Electronic applications accepted.

Department of Occupational Therapy Offers occupational therapy (OTD). Electronic applications accepted.

Department of Physical Therapy Offers physical therapy (DPT). Electronic applications accepted.

Department of Physician Assistant Studies Offers physician assistant studies (MPA). Electronic applications accepted.

School of Nursing *Program availability:* Part-time, evening/weekend, 100% online, blended/hybrid learning. Offers case management (MSN); family nurse practitioner (MSN, DNP, Certificate); nurse anesthetist (MSN, Certificate); nursing (DNP). Electronic applications accepted.

SAN DIEGO CHRISTIAN COLLEGE, Santee, CA 92071

General Information Independent-religious, coed, comprehensive institution.

GRADUATE UNITS

Graduate Programs

SAN DIEGO STATE UNIVERSITY, San Diego, CA 92182

General Information State-supported, coed, university. CGS member. *Graduate housing:* Room and/or apartments available on a first-come, first-served basis to single students; on-campus housing not available to married students. Housing application deadline: 5/1. *Research affiliation:* Robert Wood Johnson Foundation (public health), General Atomics (technical student services), William and Flora Hewlett Foundation (teacher education), American Heart Association (biology), Children's Hospital and Research Center (children's health), Qualcomm (wireless and telecommunications).

GRADUATE UNITS

Graduate and Research Affairs *Program availability:* Part-time, evening/weekend. Offers interdisciplinary studies (MA, MS). Electronic applications accepted.

College of Arts and Letters *Program availability:* Part-time, evening/weekend. Offers anthropology (MA); applied linguistics and English as a second language (CAL); arts and letters (MA, MFA, PhD, CAL); Asian studies (MA); computational linguistics (MA); creative writing (MFA); economics (MA); English (MA); English as a second language/applied linguistics (MA); European studies (MA); general linguistics (MA); geography (MA, PhD); history (MA); Latin American studies (MA); lesbian, gay, bisexual and transgender studies (Graduate Certificate); liberal arts and sciences (MA); philosophy (MA); political science (MA); rhetoric and writing studies (MA); sociology (MA); Spanish (MA); women's studies (MA). Electronic applications accepted.

College of Education *Program availability:* Part-time, evening/weekend. Offers child development (MS); counseling and school psychology (MS); education (MA, MS, Ed D, PhD); educational leadership (MA); educational leadership in post-secondary education (MA); educational technology (MA); educational technology and teaching and learning (Ed D); elementary curriculum and instruction (MA); multi-cultural emphasis (PhD); policy studies in language and cross cultural education (MA); reading education (MA); rehabilitation counseling (MS); secondary curriculum and instruction (MA); special education (MA). Electronic applications accepted.

College of Engineering *Program availability:* Part-time, evening/weekend. Offers aerospace engineering (MS); civil engineering (MS); electrical engineering (MS); engineering (MS, PhD); engineering mechanics (MS); engineering sciences and applied mechanics (PhD); flight dynamics (MS); fluid dynamics (MS); manufacture and design (MS); mechanical engineering (MS). Electronic applications accepted.

College of Health and Human Services *Program availability:* Part-time, evening/weekend. Offers audiology (Au D); biometry (MPH); communicative disorders (MA); environmental health (MPH); epidemiology (MPH, PhD); exercise physiology (MS); gerontology (MS); global emergency preparedness and response (MS); global health (PhD); health and human services (MA, MPH, MS, MSW, Au D, DPT, PhD); health behavior (PhD); health promotion (MPH); health services administration (MPH); kinesiology (MA); language and communicative disorders (PhD); nursing (MS); nutritional sciences (MS); physical therapy (DPT); social work (MSW); toxicology (MS). Electronic applications accepted.

College of Professional Studies and Fine Arts *Program availability:* Part-time. Offers advertising and public relations (MA); city planning (MCP); composition (acoustic and electronic) (MM); conducting (MM); criminal justice administration (MPA); criminal justice and criminology (MS); critical-cultural studies (MA); design and technology (MFA); ethnomusicology (MA); film and television production (MFA); hospitality and tourism (MA); interaction studies (MA); intercultural and international studies (MA); jazz studies (MM); meeting and event management (MA); musical theatre (MFA); musicology (MA); new media studies (MA); news and information studies (MA); performance (MM); piano pedagogy (MA); professional studies and fine arts (MA, MCP, MFA, MM, MPA, MS); public administration (MPA); studio arts (MA, MFA); telecommunications and media management (MA); theatre arts (MA); theory (MA).

College of Sciences *Program availability:* Part-time. Offers applied mathematics (MS); astronomy (MS); biology (MA, MS); cell and molecular biology (PhD); chemistry and biochemistry (MA, MS, PhD); clinical psychology (MS, PhD); computational science (MS, PhD); computer science (MS); ecology (MS); geological sciences (MS); industrial and organizational psychology (MS); mathematics (MA); mathematics and science education (PhD); microbiology (MS); molecular biology (MA, MS); physics (MA, MS); program evaluation (MS); psychology (MS); radiological physics (MS); regulatory affairs (MS); sciences (MA, MS, PhD); statistics (MS). Electronic applications accepted.

Fowler College of Business *Program availability:* Part-time, evening/weekend. Offers accountancy (MS); business (MBA, MS); business administration (MBA); entrepreneurship (MS); finance (MS); human resources management (MS); information systems (MS); management science (MS); marketing (MS); sports business management (MBA). Electronic applications accepted.

SANFORD BURNHAM PREBYS MEDICAL DISCOVERY INSTITUTE, La Jolla, CA 92037

General Information Independent, coed, graduate-only institution.

GRADUATE UNITS

Graduate School of Biomedical Sciences Offers biomedical sciences (PhD).

SAN FRANCISCO ART INSTITUTE, San Francisco, CA 94133

General Information Independent, coed, comprehensive institution. *Graduate housing:* Room and/or apartments available on a first-come, first-served basis to single students; on-campus housing not available to married students. Housing application deadline: 6/1. *Research affiliation:* San Francisco Museum of Modern Art (art history, museum studies, contemporary art), Yerba Buena Center for the Arts (art exhibits), Headlands Center for the Arts (multidisciplinary art exhibition), Kadist Art Foundation (contemporary art exhibition), Tremaine Foundation (education; art, environment, and learning disabilities), Prelinger Library (library).

GRADUATE UNITS

Master of Arts Programs Offers exhibition and museum studies (MA); history and theory of contemporary art (MA). Electronic applications accepted.

Master of Fine Arts Programs Offers studio art (MFA, Certificate). Electronic applications accepted.

SAN FRANCISCO CONSERVATORY OF MUSIC, San Francisco, CA 94102

General Information Independent, coed, comprehensive institution. *Graduate housing:* Rooms and/or apartments available on a first-come, first-served basis to single and married students. Housing application deadline: 5/31.

GRADUATE UNITS

Graduate Division Offers brass (MM); chamber music (MM, Artist Certificate); composition (MM); conducting (MM); guitar (MM); harp (MM); historical performance (MM); percussion (MM); piano (MM, MM, Artist Diploma); strings (MM, Artist Diploma); voice (MM, Postgraduate Diploma); woodwinds (MM). Electronic applications accepted.

SAN FRANCISCO STATE UNIVERSITY, San Francisco, CA 94132-1722

General Information State-supported, coed, university. *Graduate housing:* Room and/or apartments available on a first-come, first-served basis to single students; on-campus housing not available to married students.

GRADUATE UNITS

Division of Graduate Studies *Program availability:* Part-time, evening/weekend.

College of Business Offers accounting (MSA); business (EMBA, MA, MBA, MSA); decision sciences/operations research (MBA); economics (MA); ethics and compliance (MBA); finance (MBA); global business and innovation (MBA); healthcare administration (MBA); hospitality and tourism management (MBA); information systems (MBA); leadership (MBA); marketing (MBA); nonprofit and social enterprise leadership (MBA); sustainable business (MBA).

College of Education Offers adult education (MA); augmentative and alternative communication (AC); autism spectrum (AC); communicative disorders (MS); early childhood education (MA); early childhood practices (AC); education (MA, MS, Ed D, PhD, AC, Certificate, Credential); education specialist (Credential); educational administration (MA, Credential); educational leadership (Ed D); elementary education (MA); equity and social justice (MA); instructional technologies (MA); language and literacy education (MA, Certificate, Credential); mathematics education (MA); orientation and mobility (Credential); reading (Certificate); reading and literacy leadership (Credential); secondary education (MA, Credential); special education (MA, PhD); special interest (MA).

College of Ethnic Studies Expenses: Contact institution. *Program availability:* Part-time. Offers Asian American studies (MA); ethnic studies (MA). *Application Contact:* Dr. Catriona Esquibel, Associate Dean, 415-338-1693, Fax: 415-338-1739, E-mail: ktrion@sfsu.edu. *Dean,* Dr. Amy H. Sueyoshi, 415-338-1693, Fax: 415-338-1739, E-mail: ethnicst@sfsu.edu.

College of Health and Social Sciences *Program availability:* Part-time. Offers adult acute care (MS); clinical mental health counseling (MS); clinical nurse specialist (MS); community health education (MPH); community/public health nursing (MS); criminal justice administration (MPA); environmental administration and policy (MPA); family and consumer sciences (MA); family nurse practitioner (Certificate); gerontology (MA); health and social sciences (MA, MPA, MPH, MS, MSW, DPT, Certificate); kinesiology (MS); marriage, family and child counseling (MS); nonprofit administration (MPA); nursing administration (MS); pediatrics (MS); physical therapy (DPT); public management (MPA); public policy (MPA); recreation, parks, and tourism (MS); sexuality studies (MA); social work (MSW); urban administration (MPA); women's health (MS).

College of Liberal and Creative Arts Expenses: Contact institution. *Financial support:* Teaching assistantships, career-related internships or fieldwork, and Federal Work-Study available. *Program availability:* Part-time, evening/weekend. Offers archaeology (MA); art (MFA); biological anthropology (MA); broadcast and electronic communication arts (MA); chamber music (MM); Chinese (MA); cinema (MA, MFA); classical performance (MM); classics (MA); communication studies (MA); comparative literature (MA); composition (MA, Certificate); conducting (MM); creative writing (MA, MFA); cultural anthropology (MA); French (MA); German (MA); history (MA); humanities and liberal studies (MA); immigrant literacies (Certificate); industrial arts (MA); international relations (MA); Italian (MA); Japanese (MA); liberal and creative arts (MA, MFA, MM, Certificate); linguistics (MA); literature (MA); museum studies (MA); music education (MA); music history (MA); philosophy (MA); political science (MA); Spanish (MA); teaching composition (Certificate); teaching English to speakers of other languages (MA); teaching post-secondary reading (Certificate); theatre arts (MA, MFA); visual anthropology (MA); women and gender studies (MA). *Application Contact:* Michelle Rashleger, Chief of Staff, 415-405-4281, Fax: 415-338-6159, E-mail: mrash@sfsu.edu. *Dean,* Dr. Andrew Harris, 415-338-1471, Fax: 415-338-6159, E-mail: a1harris@sfsu.edu.

College of Science and Engineering Expenses: Contact institution. *Program availability:* Part-time. Offers astronomy (MS); biochemistry (MS); biotechnology (PSM); cell and molecular biology (MS); chemistry (MS); clinical psychology (MS); computer science (MS); developmental psychology (MS); ecology, evolution, and conservation biology (MS); embedded electrical and computer systems (MS); energy systems (MS); geographic information science (MS); geography (MA); geosciences (MS); industrial/organizational psychology (MS); interdisciplinary marine and estuarine science (MS); marine biology (MS); mathematics (MS); microbiology (MS); mind, brain, and behavior (MA); physics (MS); physiology and behavioral biology (MS); resource management and environmental planning (MA); school psychology (MS, Credential); science (PSM); science and engineering (MA, MS, PSM, Credential); social, personality, and affective science psychology (MA); stem cell science (PSM); structural/earthquake engineering (MS). *Application deadline:* Applications are processed on a rolling basis. Electronic applications accepted. *Application Contact:* Nadia Chan, Executive Assistant to the Dean, 415-338-1571, Fax: 415-338-6136, E-mail: nadiach@sfsu.edu. *Dean,* Dr. Carmen Domingo, 415-338-1571, Fax: 415-338-6136, E-mail: cdomingo@sfsu.edu.

SAN FRANCISCO THEOLOGICAL SEMINARY, San Anselmo, CA 94960

General Information Independent-religious, coed, graduate-only institution. *Graduate housing:* Rooms and/or apartments available on a first-come, first-served basis to single and married students. Housing application deadline: 5/1.

GRADUATE UNITS

Graduate and Professional Programs *Program availability:* Part-time. Offers theology (M Div, MA, MATS, D Min, PhD, Th D). MA, Th D, PhD, M Div/MA offered jointly with Graduate Theological Union.

SAN IGNACIO UNIVERSITY, Doral, FL 33178

General Information Proprietary, coed, comprehensive institution.

GRADUATE UNITS

Graduate Programs

SAN JOAQUIN COLLEGE OF LAW, Clovis, CA 93612-1312

General Information Independent, coed, graduate-only institution. *Graduate housing:* On-campus housing not available.

GRADUATE UNITS

Law Program *Program availability:* Part-time, evening/weekend. Offers law (JD).

SAN JOSE STATE UNIVERSITY, San Jose, CA 95192-0001

General Information State-supported, coed, comprehensive institution. *Graduate housing:* Room and/or apartments available on a first-come, first-served basis to single students; on-campus housing not available to married students. Housing application deadline: 5/1. *Research affiliation:* Moss Landing Marine Laboratories (oceanography/marine science).

GRADUATE UNITS

EdD Leadership Program

Moss Landing Marine Laboratories Offers marine science (MS). Electronic applications accepted.

Program in Anthropology Offers applied anthropology (MA).

Program in Applied Data Science

Program in Art and Art History

Program in Audiology

Program in Aviation and Technology Offers quality assurance (MS). Electronic applications accepted.

Program in Biological Sciences *Program availability:* Part-time. Offers biological sciences (MA, MS); molecular biology and microbiology (MS); organismal biology, conservation and ecology (MS); physiology (MS). Electronic applications accepted.

Program in Biomedical Engineering

Program in Business Graduate Programs

Program in Chemical & Materials Engineering *Program availability:* Part-time. Offers chemical engineering (MS); materials engineering (MS). Electronic applications accepted.

Program in Chemistry *Program availability:* Part-time, evening/weekend. Offers chemistry (MA, MS). Electronic applications accepted.

Program in Chicana and Chicano Studies

Program in Child & Adolescent Development Offers child and adolescent development (MA). Electronic applications accepted.

Program in Civil & Environmental Engineering Offers civil engineering (MS). Electronic applications accepted.

Program in Communication Studies Offers communication studies (MA). Electronic applications accepted.

Program in Communicative Disorders and Sciences *Program availability:* Evening/weekend. Offers speech-language pathology (MA). Electronic applications accepted.

Program in Computer Engineering Offers computer engineering (MS); software engineering (MS). Electronic applications accepted.

Program in Computer Science

Program in Counselor Education *Program availability:* Evening/weekend. Offers counselor education (MA). Electronic applications accepted.

Program in Economics *Program availability:* Part-time. Offers applied economics (MA); economics (MA). Electronic applications accepted.

Program in Educational Leadership Offers educational administration (K-12) (MA); educational leadership (Ed D); higher education administration (MA). Electronic applications accepted.

Program in Electrical Engineering Offers electrical engineering (MS). Electronic applications accepted.

Program in Elementary Education Offers curriculum and instruction (MA); reading (Certificate). Electronic applications accepted.

Program in English and Comparative Literature

Program in Environmental Studies *Program availability:* Part-time. Offers environmental studies (MS). Electronic applications accepted.

Program in Film and Theatre Offers theatre arts (MA). Electronic applications accepted.

Program in General Engineering

Program in Geography Offers geographic information science (Certificate); geography (MA). Electronic applications accepted.

Program in Geology Offers geology (MS). Electronic applications accepted.

Program in Health Science and Recreation

Program in History Offers history (MA); history education (MA). Electronic applications accepted.

Program in Industrial and Systems Engineering *Program availability:* Part-time. Offers industrial and systems engineering (MS). Electronic applications accepted.

Program in Journalism and Mass Communication *Program availability:* Part-time. Offers mass communications (MS). Electronic applications accepted.

Program in Justice Studies *Program availability:* Part-time. Offers justice studies (MS). Electronic applications accepted.

Program in Kinesiology Offers kinesiology (MA). Electronic applications accepted.

Program in Linguistics and Language Development Offers computational linguistics (Certificate); linguistics (MA); teaching English to speakers of other languages (MA, Certificate). Electronic applications accepted.

Program in Mathematics and Statistics

Program in Mechanical and Aerospace Engineering *Program availability:* Part-time. Offers aerospace engineering (MS); mechanical engineering (MS). Electronic applications accepted.

Program in Meteorology and Climate Science Offers meteorology (MS). Electronic applications accepted.

Program in Music and Dance

Program in Nursing *Program availability:* Part-time, evening/weekend. Offers gerontology nurse practitioner (MS); nursing (Certificate); nursing administration (MS); nursing education (MS). Electronic applications accepted.

Program in Nutrition, Food Science, and Packaging Offers nutritional science (MS). Electronic applications accepted.

Program in Occupational Therapy Offers occupational therapy (MS). Electronic applications accepted.

Program in Philosophy Offers philosophy (MA). Electronic applications accepted.

Program in Physics and Astronomy *Program availability:* Part-time, evening/weekend. Offers computational physics (MS); physics (MS). Electronic applications accepted.

Program in Political Science *Program availability:* Part-time, evening/weekend. Offers public administration (MPA). Electronic applications accepted.

Program in Psychology Offers clinical psychology (MS); experimental psychology (MA); industrial/organizational psychology (MS); psychology (MA). Electronic applications accepted.

Program in Secondary Education

Program in Social Work *Program availability:* Part-time. Offers social work (MA, MSW, MUP, Certificate). Electronic applications accepted.

Program in Sociology *Program availability:* Part-time, evening/weekend. Offers sociology (MA). Electronic applications accepted.

Program in Special Education *Program availability:* Evening/weekend. Offers special education (MA). Electronic applications accepted.

Program in Technology

Program in Urban and Regional Planning

Program in World Languages and Literature

Program Recreation and Leisure Studies

School of Information

SAN JUAN BAUTISTA SCHOOL OF MEDICINE, Caguas, PR 00726-4968

General Information Independent, coed, graduate-only institution. *Graduate housing:* On-campus housing not available. *Research affiliation:* Universidad Central del Caribe (molecular biology), Fundación de Investigacion de Puerto Rico (clinical and translational research), University of Puerto Rico, Medical Sciences Campus (molecular biology, microbiology, neurosciences, pediatrics, public health), Ponce School of Medicine and Health Sciences (virology, immunology), Veteran Affairs (clinical research).

GRADUATE UNITS

Graduate and Professional Programs

THE SANS TECHNOLOGY INSTITUTE, Bethesda, MD 20814

General Information Proprietary, coed, graduate-only institution.

GRADUATE UNITS

Programs in Information Security Offers information security engineering (MS); information security management (MS).

THE SANTA BARBARA AND VENTURA COLLEGES OF LAW–SANTA BARBARA, Santa Barbara, CA 93101

General Information Independent, coed, graduate-only institution.

GRADUATE UNITS

Graduate and Professional Programs Offers law (MLS, JD).

THE SANTA BARBARA AND VENTURA COLLEGES OF LAW–VENTURA, Ventura, CA 93003

General Information Independent, coed, graduate-only institution.

GRADUATE UNITS

Graduate and Professional Programs Offers law (MLS, JD).

SANTA CLARA UNIVERSITY, Santa Clara, CA 95053

General Information Independent-religious, coed, university. *Enrollment:* 2,118 full-time matriculated graduate/professional students (1,135 women), 975 part-time matriculated graduate/professional students (518 women). *Enrollment by degree level:* 2,249 master's, 756 doctoral, 88 other advanced degrees. *Graduate faculty:* 271 full-time (104 women), 197 part-time/adjunct (84 women). *Graduate housing:* Rooms and/or apartments available on a first-come, first-served basis to single and married students. Housing application deadline: 3/28. *Student services:* Campus employment opportunities, campus safety program, career counseling, exercise/wellness program, free psychological counseling, international student services, low-cost health insurance, multicultural affairs office, services for students with disabilities. *Library facilities:* University Library plus 1 other. *Collection:* Books: 606,483 (physical), 658,072 (digital/electronic); Serial titles: 14,096 (physical), 84,245 (digital/electronic); Databases: 356. Weekly public service hours: 121; students can reserve study rooms.

Computer facilities: Computer purchase and lease plans are available. A campuswide network can be accessed from student residence rooms and from off campus. Online class registration is available. Website: http://www.scu.edu/

GRADUATE UNITS

College of Arts and Sciences Students: 7 full-time (6 women), 40 part-time (26 women); includes 29 minority (3 Black or African American, non-Hispanic/Latino; 6 Asian, non-Hispanic/Latino; 18 Hispanic/Latino; 1 Native Hawaiian or other Pacific Islander, non-Hispanic/Latino; 1 Two or more races, non-Hispanic/Latino). Average age 49. 9 applicants, 100% accepted, 8 enrolled. *Faculty:* 3 full-time (0 women), 5 part-time/adjunct (4 women). Expenses: Contact institution. *Financial support:* Fellowships, Federal Work-Study, and scholarships/grants available. Support available to part-time students. Financial award applicants required to submit FAFSA. In 2018, 24 master's awarded. *Program availability:* Part-time, online learning. Offers pastoral ministries (MA). *Application deadline:* For fall admission, 8/15 for domestic students; for winter admission, 10/5 for domestic students; for spring admission, 3/4 for domestic students; for summer admission, 5/4 for domestic students. Applications are processed on a rolling basis. *Application fee:* $50. Electronic applications accepted. *Application Contact:* Joseph A Morris, Director, Graduate Program in Pastoral Ministries, 408-554-2357, Fax: 408-554-7830, E-mail: jamorris@scu.edu. *Director, Graduate Program in Pastoral Ministries,* Joseph A Morris, 408-554-2357, Fax: 408-554-7830, E-mail: jamorris@scu.edu.

Jesuit School of Theology Students: 97 full-time (16 women), 13 part-time (8 women); includes 23 minority (1 Black or African American, non-Hispanic/Latino; 1 American Indian or Alaska Native, non-Hispanic/Latino; 7 Asian, non-Hispanic/Latino; 9 Hispanic/Latino; 1 Native Hawaiian or other Pacific Islander, non-Hispanic/Latino; 4 Two or more races, non-Hispanic/Latino), 52 international. Average age 37. 117 applicants, 72% accepted, 52 enrolled. *Faculty:* 17 full-time (6 women), 6 part-time/adjunct (4 women). Expenses: Contact institution. *Financial support:* Fellowships, Federal Work-Study, and scholarships/grants available. Support available to part-time students. Financial award applicants required to submit FAFSA. In 2018, 40 master's, 24 doctorates awarded. *Program availability:* Part-time, online learning. Offers Biblical studies (MTS); Christian spirituality (MTS); church history (MTS); cultural and historical studies of Catholicism (MTS); divinity (M Div); ethics and social theory/religion and society (MTS); history of art and religion (MTS); liturgical studies (MTS); sacred theology (STD, STB, STL); systematic and philosophical theology (MTS); theology (Th M). *Application deadline:* For fall admission, 3/1 for domestic students; for spring admission, 9/1 for domestic students. *Application fee:* $50. Electronic applications accepted. *Application Contact:* Alison Benders, J.D., Ph.D., Interim Dean, 510-549-5055, E-mail: ambenders@scu.edu. *Interim Dean,* Alison Benders, J.D., Ph.D., 510-549-5055, E-mail: ambenders@scu.edu.

Leavey School of Business Students: 487 full-time (278 women), 326 part-time (139 women); includes 295 minority (14 Black or African American, non-Hispanic/Latino; 207 Asian, non-Hispanic/Latino; 39 Hispanic/Latino; 35 Two or more races, non-Hispanic/Latino), 294 international. Average age 31. 694 applicants, 65% accepted, 281 enrolled. *Faculty:* 101 full-time (32 women), 47 part-time/adjunct (15 women). Expenses: Contact institution. *Financial support:* In 2018–19, 192 students received support. Fellowships, Federal Work-Study, and scholarships/grants available. Support available to part-time students. Financial award applicants required to submit FAFSA. In 2018, 195 master's awarded. *Program availability:* Part-time, online learning. Offers business administration (MBA); business analytics (MS); finance (MS); information systems (MS); supply chain management and analytics (MS). *Application fee:* $100 ($150 for international students). Electronic applications accepted. *Application Contact:* Caryn Beck-Dudley, Dean, 408-554-4523, E-mail: cbeckdudley@scu.edu. *Dean,* Caryn Beck-Dudley, 408-554-4523, E-mail: cbeckdudley@scu.edu.

School of Education and Counseling Psychology Students: 291 full-time (235 women), 298 part-time (238 women); includes 301 minority (15 Black or African American, non-Hispanic/Latino; 1 American Indian or Alaska Native, non-Hispanic/Latino; 87 Asian, non-Hispanic/Latino; 146 Hispanic/Latino; 52 Two or more races, non-Hispanic/Latino), 44 international. Average age 31. 319 applicants, 79% accepted, 143 enrolled. *Faculty:* 31 full-time (19 women), 35 part-time/adjunct (24 women). Expenses: Contact institution. *Financial support:* Fellowships, Federal Work-Study, and scholarships/grants available. Support available to part-time students. Financial award applicants required to submit FAFSA. In 2018, 223 master's awarded. *Program availability:* Part-time, online learning. Offers alternative and correctional education (Certificate); counseling (MA); counseling psychology (MA); educational leadership (MA); interdisciplinary education (MA); teaching + clear teaching certificate for catholic school teachers (MAT); teaching + teaching credential (mattc) - multiple subjects (MAT); teaching + teaching credential (mattc) - single subjects (MAT). *Application deadline:* For fall admission, 9/23 for domestic students; for winter admission, 1/6 for domestic students. Applications are processed on a rolling basis. *Application fee:* $50. Electronic applications accepted. *Application Contact:* Victoria Rodriguez, Graduate Admissions Advisor, 408-554-4723, Fax: 408-554-4367, E-mail: vlrodriguez@scu.edu. *Dean,* Dr. Sabrina Zirkel, 408-551-3074, Fax: 408-554-4367, E-mail: szirkel@scu.edu.

School of Engineering Students: 555 full-time (211 women), 269 part-time (91 women); includes 208 minority (8 Black or African American, non-Hispanic/Latino; 1 American Indian or Alaska Native, non-Hispanic/Latino; 145 Asian, non-Hispanic/Latino; 28 Hispanic/Latino; 26 Two or more races, non-Hispanic/Latino), 472 international. Average age 27. 1,309 applicants, 36% accepted, 269 enrolled. *Faculty:* 72 full-time (24 women), 52 part-time/adjunct (9 women). Expenses: Contact institution. *Financial support:* Fellowships, Federal Work-Study, and scholarships/grants available. Support available to part-time students. Financial award applicants required to submit FAFSA. In 2018, 320 master's, 7 doctorates awarded. *Program availability:* Part-time. Offers applied mathematics (MS); bioengineering (MS); civil, environmental, and sustainable engineering (MS); computer science and engineering (MS, PhD, Engineer); electrical engineering (MS, PhD, Engineer); engineering management and leadership (MS); mechanical engineering (MS, PhD, Engineer); power systems and sustainable energy (MS); software engineering (MS). *Application deadline:* For fall admission, 6/1 for domestic students; for winter admission, 9/6 for domestic students; for spring admission, 1/10 for domestic students; for summer admission, 3/6 for domestic students. *Application fee:* $60. Electronic applications accepted. *Application Contact:* Stacey Tinker, Director of Admissions and Marketing, 408-554-4748, Fax: 408-554-4323, E-mail: stinker@scu.edu. *Dean,* Dr. Elaine Scott, 408-554-3512, E-mail: epscott@scu.edu.

School of Law Students: 681 full-time (389 women), 29 part-time (16 women); includes 310 minority (22 Black or African American, non-Hispanic/Latino; 128 Asian, non-Hispanic/Latino; 152 Hispanic/Latino; 4 Native Hawaiian or other Pacific Islander, non-Hispanic/Latino; 4 Two or more races, non-Hispanic/Latino), 38 international. Average age 27. 2,126 applicants, 57% accepted, 246 enrolled. *Faculty:* 47 full-time (23 women), 52 part-time/adjunct (28 women). Expenses: Contact institution. *Financial support:* Fellowships, Federal Work-Study, and scholarships/grants available. Support available to part-time students. Financial award applicants required to submit FAFSA. In 2018, 54 master's, 217 doctorates awarded. *Program availability:* Part-time, online learning. Offers high tech law (Certificate); intellectual property (LL M); international and comparative law (LL M); international law (Certificate); law (JD); public interest and social justice law (Certificate); United States law (LL M). *Application fee:* $75 ($0 for international students). Electronic applications accepted. *Application Contact:* Anna Han, Interim Dean, 408-554-4362, Fax: 408-554-5095, E-mail: lkloppenberg@scu.edu. *Interim Dean,* Anna Han, 408-554-4362, Fax: 408-554-5095, E-mail: lkloppenberg@scu.edu.

SARAH LAWRENCE COLLEGE, Bronxville, NY 10708-5999

General Information Independent, coed, comprehensive institution. CGS member. *Graduate housing:* On-campus housing not available. *Research affiliation:* Westchester Medical Center/New York Medical College, New York Hospital–Cornell Medical Center, Albert Einstein College of Medicine, New York University Medical Center, Columbia University Medical Center.

GRADUATE UNITS

Graduate Studies *Program availability:* Part-time. Offers art of teaching (MS Ed); child development (MA); creative non-fiction (MFA); dance (MFA); dance/movement therapy (MS); fiction (MFA); health advocacy (MS); human genetics (MS); poetry (MFA); theater (MFA); women's history (MA). Electronic applications accepted.

SAVANNAH COLLEGE OF ART AND DESIGN, Savannah, GA 31402-3146

General Information Independent, coed, comprehensive institution. CGS member. *Enrollment:* 14,832 graduate, professional, and undergraduate students; 1,920 full-time matriculated graduate/professional students (1,239 women), 690 part-time matriculated graduate/professional students (457 women). *Enrollment by degree level:* 2,610 master's. *Graduate faculty:* 578 full-time (237 women), 148 part-time/adjunct (83 women). *Tuition:* Full-time $37,530; part-time $4170 per course. One-time fee: $500. *Graduate housing:* Room and/or apartments available on a first-come, first-served basis to single students; on-campus housing not available to married students. Housing application deadline: 4/1. *Student services:* Campus employment opportunities, campus safety program, career counseling, exercise/wellness program, free psychological counseling, international student services, multicultural affairs office, services for students with disabilities, writing training. *Library facilities:* Jen Library plus 4 others. *Collection:* Books: 264,695 (physical), 215,544 (digital/electronic); Serial titles: 901 (physical), 50,630 (digital/electronic); Databases: 81. Weekly public service hours: 106; students can reserve study rooms.

Computer facilities: 3,464 computers available on campus for general student use. A campuswide network can be accessed from student residence rooms and from off campus. Online class registration is available. Website: http://www.scad.edu/

General Application Contact: Jenny Jaquillard, Executive Director of Admission Recruitment, 912-525-5100, E-mail: admission@scad.edu.

GRADUATE UNITS

Creative Business Leadership Students: 17 full-time (12 women), 52 part-time (46 women); includes 12 minority (10 Black or African American, non-Hispanic/Latino; 1 Asian, non-Hispanic/Latino; 1 Hispanic/Latino), 11 international. Average age 29. 93 applicants, 25% accepted, 14 enrolled. *Faculty:* 2 full-time (0 women), 2 part-time/adjunct (1 woman). Expenses: Contact institution. *Financial support:* Career-related internships or fieldwork, Federal Work-Study, and scholarships/grants available. Financial award application deadline: 4/1; financial award applicants required to submit FAFSA. In 2018, 44 master's awarded. *Program availability:* Part-time, 100% online. Offers business design and arts leadership (MA). *Application deadline:* For fall admission, 4/1 for domestic and international students. Applications are processed on a rolling basis. *Application fee:* $40. Electronic applications accepted. *Application Contact:* Jenny Jaquillard, Executive Director of Admission Recruitment, 912-525-5100, E-mail: admission@scad.edu. *Dean, school of design,* Victor Ermoli.

Program in Accessory Design Students: 9 full-time (8 women), 5 part-time (all women); includes 4 minority (2 Black or African American, non-Hispanic/Latino; 1 Asian, non-Hispanic/Latino; 1 Hispanic/Latino), 8 international. Average age 27. 14 applicants, 50% accepted, 5 enrolled. *Faculty:* 4 full-time (all women). Expenses: Contact institution. *Financial support:* Career-related internships or fieldwork, Federal Work-Study, and scholarships/grants available. Financial award application deadline: 4/1; financial award applicants required to submit FAFSA. In 2018, 14 master's awarded. *Program availability:* Part-time. Offers accessory design (MA, MFA). *Application deadline:* For fall admission, 4/1 for domestic and international students. Applications are processed on a rolling basis. *Application fee:* $40. Electronic applications accepted. *Application Contact:* Jenny Jaquillard, Executive Director of Admission Recruitment, 912-525-5100, E-mail: admission@scad.edu. *Associate Chair, accessory design,* Sophia Susassi.

Program in Advertising Students: 26 full-time (19 women), 5 part-time (3 women); includes 9 minority (6 Black or African American, non-Hispanic/Latino; 1 American Indian or Alaska Native, non-Hispanic/Latino; 1 Asian, non-Hispanic/Latino; 1 Hispanic/Latino), 17 international. Average age 27. 69 applicants, 25% accepted, 10 enrolled. *Faculty:* 9 full-time (4 women), 6 part-time/adjunct (2 women). Expenses: Contact institution. *Financial support:* Career-related internships or fieldwork, Federal Work-Study, and scholarships/grants available. Financial award application deadline: 4/1; financial award applicants required to submit FAFSA. In 2018, 14 master's awarded. *Program availability:* Part-time. Offers advertising (MA, MFA). *Application deadline:* For fall admission, 4/1 for domestic and international students. Applications are processed on a rolling basis. *Application fee:* $40. Electronic applications accepted. *Application Contact:* Jenny Jaquillard, Executive Director of Admission Recruitment, 912-525-5100, Fax: 912-525-5985, E-mail: admission@scad.edu. *Chair of Advertising Design,* Duke Greenhill.

Program in Animation Students: 219 full-time (121 women), 60 part-time (28 women); includes 57 minority (29 Black or African American, non-Hispanic/Latino; 1 American Indian or Alaska Native, non-Hispanic/Latino; 13 Asian, non-Hispanic/Latino; 14 Hispanic/Latino), 129 international. Average age 26. 220 applicants, 52% accepted, 68 enrolled. *Faculty:* 33 full-time (6 women), 8 part-time/adjunct (4 women). Expenses: Contact institution. *Financial support:* Career-related internships or fieldwork, Federal Work-Study, and scholarships/grants available. Financial award application deadline: 4/1; financial award applicants required to submit FAFSA. In 2018, 82 master's awarded. *Program availability:* Part-time, 100% online. Offers animation (MA, MFA). *Application deadline:* For fall admission, 4/1 for domestic and international students. Applications are processed on a rolling basis. *Application fee:* $40. Electronic applications accepted. *Application Contact:* Jenny Jaquillard, Executive Director of Admission Recruitment, 912-525-5100, E-mail: admission@scad.edu. *Chair, animation,* Chris Gallagher, 912-525-5100.

Program in Architectural History Students: 5 full-time (all women). Average age 29. 7 applicants, 57% accepted, 1 enrolled. *Faculty:* 9 full-time (1 woman). Expenses: Contact institution. *Financial support:* Career-related internships or fieldwork, Federal Work-Study, and scholarships/grants available. Financial award application deadline: 4/1; financial award applicants required to submit FAFSA. In 2018, 1 master's awarded. *Program availability:* Part-time. Offers architectural history (MFA). *Application deadline:* For fall admission, 4/1 for domestic and international students. Applications are processed on a rolling basis. *Application fee:* $40. Electronic applications accepted. *Application Contact:* Jenny Jaquillard, Executive Director of Admission Recruitment, 912-525-5100, E-mail: admission@scad.edu. *Chair, architectural history,* Dr. Robin Williams.

Program in Architecture Students: 59 full-time (30 women), 23 part-time (7 women); includes 17 minority (5 Black or African American, non-Hispanic/Latino; 1 Asian, non-Hispanic/Latino; 11 Hispanic/Latino), 47 international. Average age 26. 155 applicants, 58% accepted, 21 enrolled. *Faculty:* 18 full-time (7 women), 5 part-time/adjunct (0 women). Expenses: Contact institution. *Financial support:* Career-related internships or fieldwork, Federal Work-Study, and scholarships/grants available. Financial award application deadline: 4/1; financial award applicants required to submit FAFSA. In 2018, 36 master's awarded. *Program availability:* Part-time. Offers architecture (M Arch). *Application deadline:* For fall admission, 4/1 for domestic and international students. Applications are processed on a rolling basis. *Application fee:* $40. Electronic applications accepted. *Application Contact:* Jenny Jaquillard, Executive Director of

Admission Recruitment, 912-525-5100, E-mail: admission@scad.edu. *Dean, school of building arts,* Geoffrey Taylor.

Program in Art History Students: 8 full-time (7 women), 4 part-time (all women); includes 1 minority (Hispanic/Latino), 2 international. Average age 28. 28 applicants, 46% accepted, 5 enrolled. *Faculty:* 39 full-time (29 women), 5 part-time/adjunct (3 women). Expenses: Contact institution. *Financial support:* Career-related internships or fieldwork, Federal Work-Study, and scholarships/grants available. Financial award application deadline: 4/1; financial award applicants required to submit FAFSA. In 2018, 3 master's awarded. *Program availability:* Part-time. Offers art history (MA). *Application deadline:* For fall admission, 4/1 for domestic and international students. Applications are processed on a rolling basis. *Application fee:* $40. Electronic applications accepted. *Application Contact:* Jenny Jaquillard, Executive Director of Admission Recruitment, 912-525-5100, E-mail: admission@scad.edu. *Chair, art history,* Art DiFuria.

Program in Cinema Studies Students: 4 full-time (2 women), 3 part-time (all women); includes 2 minority (both Black or African American, non-Hispanic/Latino). Average age 26. 12 applicants, 50% accepted, 3 enrolled. *Faculty:* 2 full-time (1 woman), 1 (woman) part-time/adjunct. Expenses: Contact institution. *Financial support:* Career-related internships or fieldwork, Federal Work-Study, and scholarships/grants available. Financial award application deadline: 4/1; financial award applicants required to submit FAFSA. In 2018, 3 master's awarded. *Program availability:* Part-time. Offers cinema studies (MA). *Application deadline:* For fall admission, 4/1 for domestic and international students. Applications are processed on a rolling basis. *Application fee:* $40. Electronic applications accepted. *Application Contact:* Jenny Jaquillard, Executive Director of Admission Recruitment, 912-525-5100, E-mail: admission@scad.edu. *Chair, art history,* Art Difuria.

Program in Design for Sustainability Students: 13 full-time (10 women), 2 part-time (both women), 11 international. Average age 27. 16 applicants, 38% accepted, 3 enrolled. Expenses: Contact institution. *Financial support:* Career-related internships or fieldwork, Federal Work-Study, and scholarships/grants available. Financial award application deadline: 4/1; financial award applicants required to submit FAFSA. In 2018, 13 master's awarded. *Program availability:* Part-time. Offers built environment (MFA); management (MFA); packaging and print media (MFA); products (MFA). *Application deadline:* For fall admission, 4/1 for domestic and international students. Applications are processed on a rolling basis. *Application fee:* $40. Electronic applications accepted. *Application Contact:* Jenny Jaquillard, Executive Director of Admission Recruitment, 912-525-5100, E-mail: admission@scad.edu. *Dean, school of design,* Victor Ermoli.

Program in Design Management Students: 46 full-time (31 women), 65 part-time (48 women); includes 21 minority (7 Black or African American, non-Hispanic/Latino; 6 Asian, non-Hispanic/Latino; 8 Hispanic/Latino), 44 international. Average age 30. 90 applicants, 40% accepted, 14 enrolled. *Faculty:* 4 full-time (1 woman), 5 part-time/adjunct (2 women). Expenses: Contact institution. *Financial support:* Career-related internships or fieldwork, Federal Work-Study, and scholarships/grants available. Financial award application deadline: 4/1; financial award applicants required to submit FAFSA. In 2018, 55 master's awarded. *Program availability:* Part-time, 100% online. Offers design management (MA, MFA). *Application deadline:* For fall admission, 4/1 for domestic and international students. Applications are processed on a rolling basis. *Application fee:* $40. Electronic applications accepted. *Application Contact:* Jenny Jaquillard, Executive Director of Admission Recruitment, 912-525-5100, E-mail: admission@scad.edu. *Dean, school of design,* Victor Ermoli.

Program in Dramatic Writing Students: 24 full-time (13 women), 1 part-time (0 women); includes 8 minority (6 Black or African American, non-Hispanic/Latino; 1 Hispanic/Latino; 1 Native Hawaiian or other Pacific Islander, non-Hispanic/Latino), 5 international. Average age 25. 27 applicants, 52% accepted, 9 enrolled. *Faculty:* 5 full-time (2 women), 1 (woman) part-time/adjunct. Expenses: Contact institution. *Financial support:* Career-related internships or fieldwork, Federal Work-Study, and scholarships/grants available. Financial award application deadline: 4/1; financial award applicants required to submit FAFSA. In 2018, 9 master's awarded. *Program availability:* Part-time. Offers dramatic writing (MFA). *Application deadline:* For fall admission, 4/1 for domestic and international students. Applications are processed on a rolling basis. *Application fee:* $40. Electronic applications accepted. *Application Contact:* Jenny Jaquillard, Executive Director of Admission Recruitment, 912-525-5100, E-mail: admission@scad.edu. *Chair, dramatic writing,* Averie Storck.

Program in Fashion Students: 59 full-time (52 women), 24 part-time (22 women); includes 19 minority (14 Black or African American, non-Hispanic/Latino; 4 Asian, non-Hispanic/Latino; 1 Hispanic/Latino), 55 international. Average age 27. 119 applicants, 38% accepted, 18 enrolled. *Faculty:* 26 full-time (14 women), 3 part-time/adjunct (all women). Expenses: Contact institution. *Financial support:* Career-related internships or fieldwork, Federal Work-Study, and scholarships/grants available. Financial award application deadline: 4/1; financial award applicants required to submit FAFSA. In 2018, 27 master's awarded. *Program availability:* Part-time, 100% online. Offers fashion (MA, MFA). *Application deadline:* For fall admission, 4/1 for domestic and international students. Applications are processed on a rolling basis. *Application fee:* $40. Electronic applications accepted. *Application Contact:* Jenny Jaquillard, Executive Director of Admission Recruitment, 912-525-5100, E-mail: admission@scad.edu. *Chair, fashion,* Jens Kaeumle.

Program in Fibers Students: 22 full-time (20 women), 3 part-time (all women); includes 4 minority (1 Black or African American, non-Hispanic/Latino; 3 Hispanic/Latino), 12 international. Average age 25. 31 applicants, 58% accepted, 8 enrolled. *Faculty:* 8 full-time (7 women), 2 part-time/adjunct (both women). Expenses: Contact institution. *Financial support:* Career-related internships or fieldwork, Federal Work-Study, and scholarships/grants available. Financial award application deadline: 4/1; financial award applicants required to submit FAFSA. In 2018, 13 master's awarded. *Program availability:* Part-time. Offers fibers (MA, MFA). *Application deadline:* For fall admission, 4/1 for domestic and international students. Applications are processed on a rolling basis. *Application fee:* $40. Electronic applications accepted. *Application Contact:* Jenny Jaquillard, Executive Director of Admission Recruitment, 912-525-5100, E-mail: admission@scad.edu. *Chair, fibers,* Cayewah Easley.

Program in Film and Television Students: 208 full-time (103 women), 25 part-time (12 women); includes 81 minority (68 Black or African American, non-Hispanic/Latino; 1 American Indian or Alaska Native, non-Hispanic/Latino; 4 Asian, non-Hispanic/Latino; 8 Hispanic/Latino), 111 international. Average age 26. 283 applicants, 51% accepted, 73 enrolled. *Faculty:* 22 full-time (2 women), 2 part-time/adjunct (1 woman). Expenses: Contact institution. *Financial support:* Career-related internships or fieldwork, Federal Work-Study, and scholarships/grants available. Financial award application deadline: 4/1; financial award applicants required to submit FAFSA. In 2018, 57 master's awarded. *Program availability:* Part-time. Offers film and television (MA, MFA). *Application deadline:* For fall admission, 4/1 for domestic and international students. Applications are processed on a rolling basis. *Application fee:* $40. Electronic applications accepted. *Application Contact:* Jenny Jaquillard, Executive Director of Admission Recruitment, 912-525-5100, E-mail: admission@scad.edu. *Chair, film and television,* Donald Moffett.

Program in Furniture Design Students: 23 full-time (14 women); includes 3 minority (1 Black or African American, non-Hispanic/Latino; 2 Hispanic/Latino), 12 international. Average age 27. 27 applicants, 48% accepted, 7 enrolled. *Faculty:* 4 full-time (1 woman). Expenses: Contact institution. *Financial support:* Career-related internships or fieldwork, Federal Work-Study, and scholarships/grants available. Financial award application deadline: 4/1; financial award applicants required to submit FAFSA. In 2018, 12 master's awarded. *Program availability:* Part-time. Offers furniture design (MA, MFA). *Application deadline:* For fall admission, 4/1 for domestic and international students. Applications are processed on a rolling basis. *Application fee:* $40. Electronic applications accepted. *Application Contact:* Jenny Jaquillard, Executive Director of Admission Recruitment, 912-525-5100, E-mail: admission@scad.edu. *Associate Chair, furniture,* Fred Spector.

Program in Graphic Design and Visual Experience Students: 100 full-time (68 women), 43 part-time (27 women); includes 12 minority (4 Black or African American, non-Hispanic/Latino; 4 Asian, non-Hispanic/Latino; 4 Hispanic/Latino), 100 international. Average age 28. 334 applicants, 20% accepted, 32 enrolled. *Faculty:* 17 full-time (8 women), 7 part-time/adjunct (2 women). Expenses: Contact institution. *Financial support:* Career-related internships or fieldwork, Federal Work-Study, and scholarships/grants available. Financial award application deadline: 4/1; financial award applicants required to submit FAFSA. In 2018, 40 master's awarded. *Program availability:* Part-time, 100% online. Offers graphic design and visual experience (MA, MFA). *Application deadline:* For fall admission, 4/1 for domestic and international students. Applications are processed on a rolling basis. *Application fee:* $40. Electronic applications accepted. *Application Contact:* Jenny Jaquillard, Executive Director of Admission Recruitment, 912-525-5100, E-mail: admission@scad.edu. *Chair, graphic design,* Duke Greenhill.

Program in Illustration Students: 143 full-time (111 women), 49 part-time (33 women); includes 22 minority (6 Black or African American, non-Hispanic/Latino; 2 American Indian or Alaska Native, non-Hispanic/Latino; 8 Asian, non-Hispanic/Latino; 5 Hispanic/Latino; 1 Two or more races, non-Hispanic/Latino), 102 international. Average age 28. 189 applicants, 59% accepted, 68 enrolled. *Faculty:* 18 full-time (3 women), 5 part-time/adjunct (2 women). Expenses: Contact institution. *Financial support:* Career-related internships or fieldwork, Federal Work-Study, and scholarships/grants available. Financial award application deadline: 4/1; financial award applicants required to submit FAFSA. In 2018, 48 master's awarded. *Program availability:* Part-time, 100% online. Offers illustration (MA, MFA). *Application deadline:* For fall admission, 4/1 for domestic and international students. Applications are processed on a rolling basis. *Application fee:* $40. Electronic applications accepted. *Application Contact:* Jenny Jaquillard, Executive Director of Admission Recruitment, 912-525-5100, E-mail: admission@scad.edu. *Chair, illustration,* George Spears.

Program in Industrial Design Students: 125 full-time (52 women), 20 part-time (8 women); includes 5 minority (1 Black or African American, non-Hispanic/Latino; 2 Hispanic/Latino), 127 international. Average age 25. 162 applicants, 70% accepted, 46 enrolled. *Faculty:* 16 full-time (1 woman), 2 part-time/adjunct (1 woman). Expenses: Contact institution. *Financial support:* Career-related internships or fieldwork, Federal Work-Study, and scholarships/grants available. Financial award application deadline: 4/1; financial award applicants required to submit FAFSA. In 2018, 58 master's awarded. *Program availability:* Part-time. Offers industrial design (MA, MFA). *Application deadline:* For fall admission, 4/1 for domestic and international students. Applications are processed on a rolling basis. *Application fee:* $40. Electronic applications accepted. *Application Contact:* Jenny Jaquillard, Executive Director of Admission Recruitment, 912-525-5100, E-mail: admission@scad.edu. *Chair, industrial design,* Cesar Pieri Ferreira Jorge.

Program in Interactive Design and Game Development Students: 83 full-time (33 women), 27 part-time (8 women); includes 18 minority (6 Black or African American, non-Hispanic/Latino; 5 Asian, non-Hispanic/Latino; 7 Hispanic/Latino), 67 international. Average age 27. 196 applicants, 43% accepted, 29 enrolled. *Faculty:* 16 full-time (4 women), 4 part-time/adjunct (1 woman). Expenses: Contact institution. *Financial support:* Career-related internships or fieldwork, Federal Work-Study, and scholarships/grants available. Financial award application deadline: 4/1; financial award applicants required to submit FAFSA. In 2018, 33 master's awarded. *Program availability:* Part-time, 100% online. Offers interactive design and game development (MA, MFA). *Application deadline:* For fall admission, 4/1 for domestic and international students. Applications are processed on a rolling basis. *Application fee:* $40. Electronic applications accepted. *Application Contact:* Jenny Jaquillard, Executive Director of Admission Recruitment, 912-525-5100, E-mail: admission@scad.edu. *Chair, interactive design and game development,* SuAnne Fu.

Program in Interior Design Students: 129 full-time (101 women), 19 part-time (16 women); includes 8 minority (3 Black or African American, non-Hispanic/Latino; 1 Asian, non-Hispanic/Latino; 4 Hispanic/Latino), 121 international. Average age 26. 265 applicants, 40% accepted, 54 enrolled. *Faculty:* 17 full-time (9 women), 12 part-time/adjunct (8 women). Expenses: Contact institution. *Financial support:* Career-related internships or fieldwork, Federal Work-Study, and scholarships/grants available. Financial award application deadline: 4/1; financial award applicants required to submit FAFSA. In 2018, 42 master's awarded. *Program availability:* Part-time, 100% online. Offers interior design (MA, MFA). *Application deadline:* For fall admission, 4/1 for domestic and international students. Applications are processed on a rolling basis. *Application fee:* $40. Electronic applications accepted. *Application Contact:* Jenny Jaquillard, Executive Director of Admission Recruitment, 912-525-5100, E-mail: admission@scad.edu. *Chair, interior design,* Ryan Hansen.

Program in Jewelry Students: 22 full-time (all women), 4 part-time (3 women); includes 1 minority (Black or African American, non-Hispanic/Latino), 22 international. Average age 26. 27 applicants, 59% accepted, 5 enrolled. *Faculty:* 4 full-time (2 women). Expenses: Contact institution. *Financial support:* Career-related internships or fieldwork, Federal Work-Study, and scholarships/grants available. Financial award application deadline: 4/1; financial award applicants required to submit FAFSA. In 2018, 8 master's awarded. *Program availability:* Part-time. Offers jewelry (MA, MFA). *Application deadline:* For fall admission, 4/1 for domestic and international students. Applications are processed on a rolling basis. *Application fee:* $40. Electronic applications accepted. *Application Contact:* Jenny Jaquillard, Executive Director of Admission Recruitment, 912-525-5100, E-mail: admission@scad.edu. *Chair, jewelry,* Jay Song.

Program in Luxury and Fashion Management Students: 121 full-time (102 women), 50 part-time (45 women); includes 40 minority (27 Black or African American, non-Hispanic/Latino; 5 Asian, non-Hispanic/Latino; 8 Hispanic/Latino), 93 international. Average age 26. 200 applicants, 44% accepted, 51 enrolled. *Faculty:* 15 full-time (7 women), 1 (woman) part-time/adjunct. Expenses: Contact institution. *Financial support:* Career-related internships or fieldwork, Federal Work-Study, and scholarships/grants available. Financial award application deadline: 4/1; financial award applicants required to submit FAFSA. In 2018, 84 master's awarded. *Program availability:* Part-time, 100%

online. Offers luxury and fashion management (MA, MFA). *Application deadline:* For fall admission, 4/1 for domestic and international students. Applications are processed on a rolling basis. *Application fee:* $40. Electronic applications accepted. *Application Contact:* Jenny Jaquillard, Executive Director of Admission, 912-525-5100, E-mail: admission@scad.edu. *Associate Chair, luxury and fashion management,* Alessandro Cannata.

Program in Motion Media Design Students: 48 full-time (32 women), 34 part-time (19 women); includes 16 minority (5 Black or African American, non-Hispanic/Latino; 4 Asian, non-Hispanic/Latino; 7 Hispanic/Latino), 36 international. Average age 30. 49 applicants, 47% accepted, 17 enrolled. *Faculty:* 12 full-time (3 women), 3 part-time/adjunct (all women). Expenses: Contact institution. *Financial support:* Career-related internships or fieldwork, Federal Work-Study, and scholarships/grants available. Financial award application deadline: 4/1; financial award applicants required to submit FAFSA. In 2018, 25 master's awarded. *Program availability:* Part-time, 100% online. Offers motion media design (MA, MFA). *Application deadline:* For fall admission, 4/1 for domestic and international students. Applications are processed on a rolling basis. *Application fee:* $40. Electronic applications accepted. *Application Contact:* Jenny Jaquillard, Executive Director of Admission Recruitment, 912-525-5100, E-mail: admission@scad.edu. *Chair, motion media design,* Kelly Carlton.

Program in Painting Students: 58 full-time (45 women), 38 part-time (25 women); includes 12 minority (5 Black or African American, non-Hispanic/Latino; 2 Asian, non-Hispanic/Latino; 5 Hispanic/Latino), 24 international. Average age 36. 91 applicants, 42% accepted, 15 enrolled. *Faculty:* 10 full-time (2 women), 1 (woman) part-time/adjunct. Expenses: Contact institution. *Financial support:* Career-related internships or fieldwork, Federal Work-Study, and scholarships/grants available. Financial award application deadline: 4/1; financial award applicants required to submit FAFSA. In 2018, 27 master's awarded. *Program availability:* Part-time, 100% online. Offers painting (MA, MFA). *Application deadline:* For fall admission, 4/1 for domestic and international students. Applications are processed on a rolling basis. *Application fee:* $40. Electronic applications accepted. *Application Contact:* Jenny Jaquillard, Executive Director of Admission Recruitment, 912-525-5100, E-mail: admission@scad.edu. *Chair, fine arts,* Christopher Williams.

Program in Performing Arts Students: 36 full-time (23 women), 6 part-time (3 women); includes 21 minority (16 Black or African American, non-Hispanic/Latino; 1 Asian, non-Hispanic/Latino; 4 Hispanic/Latino), 2 international. Average age 26. 70 applicants, 43% accepted, 12 enrolled. *Faculty:* 13 full-time (5 women), 5 part-time/adjunct (4 women). Expenses: Contact institution. *Financial support:* Career-related internships or fieldwork, Federal Work-Study, and scholarships/grants available. Financial award application deadline: 4/1; financial award applicants required to submit FAFSA. In 2018, 25 master's awarded. *Program availability:* Part-time. Offers performing arts (MFA). *Application deadline:* For fall admission, 4/1 for domestic and international students. Applications are processed on a rolling basis. *Application fee:* $40. Electronic applications accepted. *Application Contact:* Jenny Jaquillard, Executive Director of Admission Recruitment, 912-525-5100, E-mail: admission@scad.edu. *Chair, performing arts,* Mark Tymchyshyn.

Program in Photography Students: 57 full-time (34 women), 31 part-time (19 women); includes 16 minority (7 Black or African American, non-Hispanic/Latino; 1 American Indian or Alaska Native, non-Hispanic/Latino; 3 Asian, non-Hispanic/Latino; 5 Hispanic/Latino), 32 international. Average age 33. 129 applicants, 39% accepted, 24 enrolled. *Faculty:* 21 full-time (8 women), 3 part-time/adjunct (0 women). Expenses: Contact institution. *Financial support:* Career-related internships or fieldwork, Federal Work-Study, and scholarships/grants available. Financial award application deadline: 4/1; financial award applicants required to submit FAFSA. In 2018, 31 master's awarded. *Program availability:* Part-time, 100% online. Offers photography (MA, MFA). *Application deadline:* For fall admission, 4/1 for domestic and international students. Applications are processed on a rolling basis. *Application fee:* $40. Electronic applications accepted. *Application Contact:* Jenny Jaquillard, Executive Director of Admission Recruitment, 912-525-5100, E-mail: admission@scad.edu. *Chair, photography,* Rick English.

Program in Preservation Design Students: 13 full-time (10 women), 27 part-time (25 women); includes 1 minority (Hispanic/Latino), 1 international. Average age 33. 47 applicants, 45% accepted, 14 enrolled. *Faculty:* 2 full-time (both women). Expenses: Contact institution. *Financial support:* Career-related internships or fieldwork, Federal Work-Study, and scholarships/grants available. Financial award application deadline: 4/1; financial award applicants required to submit FAFSA. In 2018, 20 master's awarded. *Program availability:* Part-time, 100% online. Offers preservation design (MA, MFA). *Application deadline:* For fall admission, 4/1 for domestic and international students. Applications are processed on a rolling basis. *Application fee:* $40. Electronic applications accepted. *Application Contact:* Jenny Jaquillard, Executive Director of Admission Recruitment, 912-525-5100, E-mail: admission@scad.edu. *Dean, school of building arts,* Geoffrey Taylor.

Program in Production Design Students: 17 full-time (15 women), 1 (woman) part-time; includes 5 minority (3 Black or African American, non-Hispanic/Latino; 1 Asian, non-Hispanic/Latino; 1 Hispanic/Latino), 8 international. Average age 28. 31 applicants, 52% accepted, 9 enrolled. *Faculty:* 5 full-time (all women), 1 (woman) part-time/adjunct. Expenses: Contact institution. *Financial support:* Career-related internships or fieldwork, Federal Work-Study, and scholarships/grants available. Financial award application deadline: 4/1; financial award applicants required to submit FAFSA. In 2018, 15 master's awarded. *Program availability:* Part-time. Offers production design (MA, MFA). *Application deadline:* For fall admission, 4/1 for domestic and international students. Applications are processed on a rolling basis. *Application fee:* $40. Electronic applications accepted. *Application Contact:* Jenny Jaquillard, Executive Director of Admission Recruitment, 912-525-5100, E-mail: admission@scad.edu. *Dean, school of entertainment arts,* Andra Reeve-Raab.

Program in Sculpture Students: 9 full-time (6 women), 1 part-time (0 women), 6 international. Average age 33. 7 applicants, 71% accepted, 1 enrolled. *Faculty:* 1 full-time (0 women), 1 part-time/adjunct (0 women). Expenses: Contact institution. *Financial support:* Career-related internships or fieldwork, Federal Work-Study, and scholarships/grants available. Financial award application deadline: 4/1; financial award applicants required to submit FAFSA. In 2018, 4 master's awarded. *Program availability:* Part-time. Offers sculpture (MA, MFA). *Application deadline:* For fall admission, 4/1 for domestic and international students. Applications are processed on a rolling basis. *Application fee:* $40. Electronic applications accepted. *Application Contact:* Jenny Jaquillard, Executive Director of Admission Recruitment, 912-525-5100, E-mail: admission@scad.edu. *Chair, sculpture,* Christopher Williams.

Program in Sequential Art Students: 47 full-time (35 women), 11 part-time (7 women); includes 13 minority (4 Black or African American, non-Hispanic/Latino; 4 Asian, non-Hispanic/Latino; 5 Hispanic/Latino), 24 international. Average age 27. 45 applicants, 58% accepted, 15 enrolled. *Faculty:* 13 full-time (5 women), 5 part-time/adjunct (2 women). Expenses: Contact institution. *Financial support:* Career-related internships or fieldwork, Federal Work-Study, and scholarships/grants available. Financial award application deadline: 4/1; financial award applicants required to submit FAFSA. In 2018, 8 master's awarded. *Program availability:* Part-time. Offers sequential art (MA, MFA). *Application deadline:* For fall admission, 4/1 for domestic and international students. Applications are processed on a rolling basis. *Application fee:* $40. Electronic applications accepted. *Application Contact:* Jenny Jaquillard, Executive Director of Admission Recruitment, 912-525-5100, E-mail: admission@scad.edu. *Chair, sequential art,* George Spears.

Program in Service Design Students: 22 full-time (15 women), 7 part-time (4 women); includes 4 minority (1 Black or African American, non-Hispanic/Latino; 1 Asian, non-Hispanic/Latino; 2 Hispanic/Latino), 18 international. Average age 27. 60 applicants, 60% accepted, 8 enrolled. *Faculty:* 2 full-time (1 woman). Expenses: Contact institution. *Financial support:* Career-related internships or fieldwork, Federal Work-Study, and scholarships/grants available. Financial award application deadline: 4/1; financial award applicants required to submit FAFSA. In 2018, 4 master's awarded. *Program availability:* Part-time. Offers service design (MFA). *Application deadline:* For fall admission, 4/1 for domestic and international students. Applications are processed on a rolling basis. *Application fee:* $40. Electronic applications accepted. *Application Contact:* Jenny Jaquillard, Executive Director of Admission Recruitment, 912-525-5100, E-mail: admission@scad.edu. *Associate Chair, service design,* Xenia Viladas.

Program in Sound Design Students: 28 full-time (11 women), 5 part-time (0 women); includes 7 minority (4 Black or African American, non-Hispanic/Latino; 2 Asian, non-Hispanic/Latino; 1 Hispanic/Latino), 15 international. Average age 26. 36 applicants, 58% accepted, 11 enrolled. *Faculty:* 6 full-time (0 women), 1 part-time/adjunct (0 women). Expenses: Contact institution. *Financial support:* Career-related internships or fieldwork, Federal Work-Study, and scholarships/grants available. Financial award application deadline: 4/1; financial award applicants required to submit FAFSA. In 2018, 13 master's awarded. *Program availability:* Part-time. Offers sound design (MA, MFA). *Application deadline:* For fall admission, 4/1 for domestic and international students. Applications are processed on a rolling basis. *Application fee:* $40. Electronic applications accepted. *Application Contact:* Jenny Jaquillard, Executive Director of Admission Recruitment, 912-525-5100, E-mail: admission@scad.edu. *Chair, sound design,* Mitchell Gettleman.

Program in Themed Entertainment Design Students: 36 full-time (27 women), 5 part-time (2 women); includes 6 minority (1 Asian, non-Hispanic/Latino; 5 Hispanic/Latino), 10 international. Average age 26. 33 applicants, 64% accepted, 14 enrolled. *Faculty:* 1 full-time (0 women). Expenses: Contact institution. *Financial support:* Career-related internships or fieldwork, Federal Work-Study, and scholarships/grants available. Financial award application deadline: 4/1; financial award applicants required to submit FAFSA. In 2018, 8 master's awarded. *Program availability:* Part-time. Offers themed entertainment design (MFA). *Application deadline:* For fall admission, 4/1 for domestic and international students. Applications are processed on a rolling basis. *Application fee:* $40. Electronic applications accepted. *Application Contact:* Jenny Jaquillard, Executive Director of Admission Recruitment, 912-525-5100, E-mail: admission@scad.edu. *Dean, school of entertainment arts,* Andra Reeve-Raab.

Program in Urban Design Students: 8 full-time (4 women), 1 part-time (0 women), 8 international. Average age 27. 22 applicants, 64% accepted, 1 enrolled. *Faculty:* 1 full-time (0 women). Expenses: Contact institution. *Financial support:* Career-related internships or fieldwork, Federal Work-Study, and scholarships/grants available. Financial award application deadline: 4/1; financial award applicants required to submit FAFSA. In 2018, 3 master's awarded. *Program availability:* Part-time. Offers urban design (MUD). *Application deadline:* For fall admission, 4/1 for domestic and international students. Applications are processed on a rolling basis. *Application fee:* $40. Electronic applications accepted. *Application Contact:* Jenny Jaquillard, Executive Director of Admission Recruitment, 912-525-5100, E-mail: admission@scad.edu. *Dean, school of building arts,* Geoffrey Taylor.

Program in Visual Effects Students: 39 full-time (17 women), 12 part-time (5 women); includes 7 minority (3 Asian, non-Hispanic/Latino; 4 Hispanic/Latino), 30 international. Average age 27. 37 applicants, 35% accepted, 9 enrolled. *Faculty:* 15 full-time (3 women). Expenses: Contact institution. *Financial support:* Career-related internships or fieldwork, Federal Work-Study, and scholarships/grants available. Financial award application deadline: 4/1; financial award applicants required to submit FAFSA. In 2018, 26 master's awarded. *Program availability:* Part-time. Offers visual effects (MA, MFA). *Application deadline:* For fall admission, 4/1 for domestic and international students. Applications are processed on a rolling basis. *Application fee:* $40. Electronic applications accepted. *Application Contact:* Jenny Jaquillard, Executive Director of Admission Recruitment, 912-525-5100, E-mail: admission@scad.edu. *Dean, school of digital media,* Max Almy.

Program in Writing Students: 32 full-time (24 women), 26 part-time (23 women); includes 19 minority (15 Black or African American, non-Hispanic/Latino; 1 Asian, non-Hispanic/Latino; 3 Hispanic/Latino), 5 international. Average age 31. 51 applicants, 31% accepted, 8 enrolled. *Faculty:* 7 full-time (3 women), 2 part-time/adjunct (1 woman). Expenses: Contact institution. *Financial support:* Career-related internships or fieldwork, Federal Work-Study, and scholarships/grants available. Financial award application deadline: 4/1; financial award applicants required to submit FAFSA. In 2018, 11 master's awarded. *Program availability:* Part-time, 100% online. Offers writing (MFA). *Application deadline:* For fall admission, 4/1 for domestic and international students. Applications are processed on a rolling basis. *Application fee:* $40. Electronic applications accepted. *Application Contact:* Jenny Jaquillard, Executive Director of Admission Recruitment, 912-525-5100, E-mail: admission@scad.edu. *Chair, writing,* Christopher Millis.

SAVANNAH STATE UNIVERSITY, Savannah, GA 31404

General Information State-supported, coed, comprehensive institution. CGS member. *Graduate housing:* Room and/or apartments available on a first-come, first-served basis to single students; on-campus housing not available to married students. Housing application deadline: 5/1. *Research affiliation:* Office of Naval Research (ONR) (marine science), Living Marine Resources Cooperative Science Center (LMRCSC) (marine science), National Institute of Mental Health (NIMH) (social work), U.S. Department of Homeland Security (urban studies and planning), Skidaway Institute of Oceanography (marine science), University of Georgia Marine Education Center & Aquarium (marine science).

GRADUATE UNITS

Master of Business Administration Program *Program availability:* Part-time, evening/weekend. Offers business administration (MBA). Electronic applications accepted.

Master of Public Administration Program *Program availability:* Part-time. Offers city management (MPA); human resources (MPA). Electronic applications accepted.

Master of Science in Marine Sciences Program *Program availability:* Part-time. Offers applied marine science (MSMS); marine science research (MSMS); professional advancement (MSMS). Electronic applications accepted.

Master of Science in Urban Studies and Planning Program *Program availability:* Part-time. Offers urban studies and planning (MSUS). Electronic applications accepted.
Master of Social Work Program Offers social work (MSW).

SAYBROOK UNIVERSITY, San Francisco, CA 94612

General Information Independent, coed, graduate-only institution. *Research affiliation:* Rollo May Center for Humanistic Studies.

GRADUATE UNITS

LIOS MA Residential Programs Offers leadership and organization development (MA); psychology counseling (MA).
School of Clinical Psychology Offers clinical psychology (MA). Program offered jointly with Bastyr University.
School of Mind-Body Medicine Offers mind-body medicine (MS, PhD, Certificate). Electronic applications accepted.
School of Organizational Leadership and Transformation Offers organizational leadership and transformation (MA). Program offered jointly with Bastyr University.
School of Psychology and Interdisciplinary Inquiry *Program availability:* Online learning. Offers human science (MA, PhD); organizational systems (MA, PhD); psychology (MA, PhD). Electronic applications accepted.

SCHILLER INTERNATIONAL UNIVERSITY, 69115 Heidelberg, Germany

General Information Independent, coed, comprehensive institution. *Graduate housing:* Room and/or apartments available on a first-come, first-served basis to single students; on-campus housing not available to married students.

GRADUATE UNITS

MBA Programs, Heidelberg, Germany *Program availability:* Part-time, evening/weekend. Offers international business (MBA, MIM); management of information technology (MBA).

SCHILLER INTERNATIONAL UNIVERSITY, F-75015 Paris, France

General Information Independent, coed, comprehensive institution. *Graduate housing:* On-campus housing not available.

GRADUATE UNITS

MBA Program Paris, France *Program availability:* Part-time, evening/weekend, online learning. Offers international business (MBA). Bilingual French/English MBA available for native French speakers.
Program in International Relations and Diplomacy *Program availability:* Part-time, evening/weekend. Offers international relations and diplomacy (MA).

SCHILLER INTERNATIONAL UNIVERSITY, 28002 Madrid, Spain

General Information Independent, coed, comprehensive institution. *Graduate housing:* On-campus housing not available.

GRADUATE UNITS

MBA Program, Madrid, Spain *Program availability:* Part-time. Offers international business (MBA).

SCHILLER INTERNATIONAL UNIVERSITY, Largo, FL 33771

General Information Independent, coed, comprehensive institution. *Graduate housing:* Room and/or apartments available on a first-come, first-served basis to single students; on-campus housing not available to married students. Housing application deadline: 8/1.

GRADUATE UNITS

MBA Programs, Florida *Program availability:* Part-time, evening/weekend, online learning. Offers financial planning (MBA); information technology (MBA); international business (MBA); international hotel and tourism management (MBA).

SCHOOL OF ADVANCED AIR AND SPACE STUDIES, Maxwell AFB, AL 36112-6424

General Information Federally supported, coed, primarily men, graduate-only institution.

GRADUATE UNITS

Program in Airpower Art and Science Offers airpower art and science (MA). Available to active duty military officers only.

SCHOOL OF ARCHITECTURE AT TALIESIN, Scottsdale, AZ 85261-4430

General Information Independent, coed, graduate-only institution. *Graduate housing:* Rooms and/or apartments guaranteed to single students and available on a first-come, first-served basis to married students. Housing application deadline: 3/20.

GRADUATE UNITS

Graduate Program Offers architecture (M Arch). Summer session held in Spring Green, WI. Electronic applications accepted.

SCHOOL OF THE ART INSTITUTE OF CHICAGO, Chicago, IL 60603-3103

General Information Independent, coed, comprehensive institution. *Enrollment:* 686 full-time matriculated graduate/professional students (489 women), 60 part-time matriculated graduate/professional students (45 women). *Enrollment by degree level:* 717 master's, 29 other advanced degrees. *Tuition:* Full-time $39,960; part-time $1665 per credit hour. *Required fees:* $920; $305 per semester. $305 per semester. Tuition and fees vary according to course load, program and student level. *Graduate housing:* Room and/or apartments available on a first-come, first-served basis to single students; on-campus housing not available to married students. Typical cost: $12,300 per year ($14,770 including board). Room and board charges vary according to campus/location and housing facility selected. Housing application deadline: 8/27. *Student services:* Campus employment opportunities, career counseling, free psychological counseling, international student services, low-cost health insurance, multicultural affairs office, services for students with disabilities. *Library facilities:* The John M. Flaxman Library plus 1 other. *Collection:* Books: 110,287 (physical), 203,725 (digital/electronic); Serial titles: 19,541 (physical), 204,634 (digital/electronic); Databases: 177.

Computer facilities: Computer purchase and lease plans are available. 300 computers available on campus for general student use. A campuswide network can be accessed from student residence rooms and from off campus. Online class registration is available.
Website: http://www.saic.edu/

General Application Contact: Associate Director of Graduate Admissions, 312-899-5219, Fax: 312-899-1840, E-mail: admiss@artic.edu.

SCHOOL OF VISUAL ARTS, New York, NY 10010-3994

General Information Proprietary, coed, comprehensive institution. CGS member. *Graduate housing:* Room and/or apartments available on a first-come, first-served basis to single students; on-campus housing not available to married students.

GRADUATE UNITS

Graduate Programs Offers art education (MAT); art practice (MFA); art therapy (MPS); art writing (MFA); branding (MPS); computer art (MFA); critical theory and the arts (MA); curatorial practice (MA); design (MFA); design for social innovation (MFA); design research, writing and criticism (MA); digital photography (MPS); directing (MPS); fashion photography (MPS); fine arts (MFA); illustration as visual essay (MFA); interaction design (MFA); photography, video and related media (MFA); products of design (MFA); social documentary film (MFA); visual narrative (MFA). Electronic applications accepted.

SCHREINER UNIVERSITY, Kerrville, TX 78028-5697

General Information Independent-religious, coed, comprehensive institution. *Graduate housing:* Room and/or apartments available on a first-come, first-served basis to single students; on-campus housing not available to married students.

GRADUATE UNITS

Department of Education *Program availability:* Part-time, evening/weekend, online learning. Offers education (M Ed); principal (Certificate). Electronic applications accepted.

MBA Program *Program availability:* Part-time, online learning. Offers ethical leadership (MBA). Electronic applications accepted.

THE SCRIPPS RESEARCH INSTITUTE, La Jolla, CA 92037

General Information Independent, coed, graduate-only institution. *Graduate housing:* On-campus housing not available.

GRADUATE UNITS

Kellogg School of Science and Technology Offers chemical and biological sciences (PhD). Electronic applications accepted.

SEATTLE INSTITUTE OF EAST ASIAN MEDICINE, Seattle, WA 98115

General Information Proprietary, coed, primarily women, graduate-only institution. *Graduate housing:* On-campus housing not available.

GRADUATE UNITS

Graduate Program Offers Oriental medicine (M Ac OM).

SEATTLE PACIFIC UNIVERSITY, Seattle, WA 98119-1997

General Information Independent-religious, coed, comprehensive institution. *Enrollment:* 327 full-time matriculated graduate/professional students (240 women), 451 part-time matriculated graduate/professional students (320 women). *Enrollment by degree level:* 534 master's, 184 doctoral, 60 other advanced degrees. *Graduate housing:* Rooms and/or apartments available on a first-come, first-served basis to single and married students. Housing application deadline: 8/1. *Student services:* Campus employment opportunities, campus safety program, career counseling, exercise/wellness program, free psychological counseling, international student services, low-cost health insurance, multicultural affairs office, services for students with disabilities, teacher training, writing training. *Library facilities:* University Library.

Computer facilities: 150 computers available on campus for general student use. A campuswide network can be accessed from student residence rooms and from off campus. Online class registration is available. Website: http://www.spu.edu/

GRADUATE UNITS

Doctoral Program in Education Students: 11 part-time (7 women); includes 2 minority (1 Black or African American, non-Hispanic/Latino; 1 American Indian or Alaska Native, non-Hispanic/Latino), 2 international. Average age 50. 8 applicants, 50% accepted, 4 enrolled. Expenses: Contact institution. *Financial support:* Career-related internships or fieldwork available. Financial award applicants required to submit FAFSA. In 2018, 14 doctorates awarded. Offers education (Ed D, PhD). *Application deadline:* For fall admission, 8/15 for domestic students; for winter admission, 11/15 for domestic students; for spring admission, 2/15 for domestic students; for summer admission, 5/15 for domestic students. Applications are processed on a rolling basis. *Application fee:* $50. *Application Contact:* Nyaradzo Mvududu, Director of Doctoral Programs, 206-281-2551, E-mail: nyaradzo@spu.edu. *Director of Doctoral Programs,* Nyaradzo Mvududu, 206-281-2551, E-mail: nyaradzo@spu.edu.

Educational Leadership Programs Students: 2 full-time (1 woman), 55 part-time (33 women); includes 8 minority (3 Black or African American, non-Hispanic/Latino; 1 Asian, non-Hispanic/Latino; 3 Hispanic/Latino; 1 Two or more races, non-Hispanic/Latino). Average age 41. 20 applicants, 90% accepted, 18 enrolled. Expenses: Contact institution. *Financial support:* Career-related internships or fieldwork available. Financial award applicants required to submit FAFSA. In 2018, 15 master's awarded. *Program availability:* Part-time, evening/weekend. Offers educational leadership (M Ed, Ed D); principal (Certificate); program administrator (Certificate); superintendent (Certificate). *Application deadline:* For fall admission, 8/15 priority date for domestic students; for winter admission, 11/15 for domestic students; for spring admission, 2/15 priority date for domestic students; for summer admission, 5/15 for domestic students. Applications are processed on a rolling basis. *Application fee:* $50. Electronic applications accepted. *Application Contact:* The Graduate Center, 206-281-2091. *Chair,* Dr. William Prenevost, 206-281-2370, Fax: 206-281-2756, E-mail: prenew@spu.edu.

Industrial-Organizational Psychology Program Students: 53 full-time (38 women), 28 part-time (20 women); includes 21 minority (2 Black or African American, non-Hispanic/Latino; 1 American Indian or Alaska Native, non-Hispanic/Latino; 12 Asian, non-Hispanic/Latino; 5 Hispanic/Latino; 1 Two or more races, non-Hispanic/Latino), 2 international. Average age 28. 62 applicants, 52% accepted, 25 enrolled. Expenses: Contact institution. *Financial support:* Applicants required to submit FAFSA. In 2018, 30 master's, 8 doctorates awarded. Offers industrial-organizational psychology (MA, PhD). *Application deadline:* For fall admission, 12/15 for domestic and international students. *Application fee:* $50. Electronic applications accepted. *Application Contact:* The Graduate Center, 206-281-2091. *Chair,* Dr. Robert B. McKenna, 206-281-2629, E-mail: rmckenna@spu.edu.

MA in Teaching English to Speakers of Other Languages Program Students: 1 full-time (0 women), 1 (woman) part-time. Average age 43. Expenses: Contact institution. In 2018, 12 master's awarded. *Program availability:* Part-time. Offers K-12 (MA). *Application Contact:* Dr. Kathryn Bartholomew, Program Director, 206-281-3533, Fax: 206-281-2500, E-mail: kbarthol@spu.edu. *Program Director,* Dr. Kathryn Bartholomew, 206-281-3533, Fax: 206-281-2500, E-mail: kbarthol@spu.edu.

Master of Arts in Management Program Students: 12 part-time (9 women); includes 3 minority (2 Black or African American, non-Hispanic/Latino; 1 Asian, non-Hispanic/Latino), 4 international. Average age 31. 11 applicants, 45% accepted, 2 enrolled. Expenses: Contact institution. Offers business intelligence and data analytics (MA); cybersecurity (MA); faith and business (MA); human resources (MA); social and sustainable management (MA). *Application deadline:* For fall admission, 8/1 for domestic students, 6/1 for international students; for winter admission, 11/1 for domestic students, 9/1 for international students; for spring admission, 2/1 for domestic students, 12/1 for international students; for summer admission, 5/1 for domestic students. *Application fee:* $50.

Master of Arts in Teaching Program Students: 56 full-time (35 women), 59 part-time (43 women); includes 20 minority (1 American Indian or Alaska Native, non-Hispanic/Latino; 9 Asian, non-Hispanic/Latino; 6 Hispanic/Latino; 4 Two or more races, non-Hispanic/Latino). Average age 33. 54 applicants, 74% accepted, 28 enrolled. Expenses: Contact institution. *Financial support:* Scholarships/grants available. Financial award applicants required to submit FAFSA. In 2018, 78 master's awarded. *Program availability:* Part-time, evening/weekend. Offers teaching (MAT). *Application deadline:* For fall admission, 3/15 for domestic students. *Application fee:* $50. Electronic applications accepted. *Application Contact:* Graduate Admission, 206-281-2091.

Master of Arts in Theology Program Students: 21 full-time (12 women), 29 part-time (13 women); includes 22 minority (9 Black or African American, non-Hispanic/Latino; 8 Asian, non-Hispanic/Latino; 3 Hispanic/Latino; 2 Two or more races, non-Hispanic/Latino), 3 international. Average age 34. 9 applicants, 78% accepted, 1 enrolled. Expenses: Contact institution. *Financial support:* Application deadline: 4/1; applicants required to submit FAFSA. In 2018, 22 master's awarded. Offers Asian American ministry (MA); business and applied theology (MA); Christian leadership (MA); Christian scripture (MA); Christian studies (Graduate Certificate); reconciliation and intercultural studies (MA); theology (MA). *Application deadline:* For fall admission, 7/31 for domestic students, 6/15 for international students; for winter admission, 11/15 for domestic students; for spring admission, 2/15 for domestic students; for summer admission, 5/1 for domestic students. Applications are processed on a rolling basis. *Application fee:* $50. Electronic applications accepted. *Application Contact:* Dr. Doug Strong, Dean, 206-281-2473, E-mail: dstrong@spu.edu. *Dean,* Dr. Doug Strong, 206-281-2473, E-mail: dstrong@spu.edu.

Master of Business Administration Program Students: 2 full-time (1 woman), 40 part-time (25 women); includes 13 minority (4 Black or African American, non-Hispanic/Latino; 5 Asian, non-Hispanic/Latino; 2 Hispanic/Latino; 2 Two or more races, non-Hispanic/Latino), 9 international. Average age 32. 36 applicants, 53% accepted, 7 enrolled. Expenses: Contact institution. *Financial support:* Scholarships/grants available. Financial award applicants required to submit FAFSA. In 2018, 14 master's awarded. *Program availability:* Part-time. Offers business administration (MBA); social and sustainable enterprise (MBA). *Application deadline:* For fall admission, 8/1 for domestic and international students; for winter admission, 11/1 for domestic and international students; for spring admission, 2/1 for domestic and international students. Applications are processed on a rolling basis. *Application fee:* $50. Electronic applications accepted. *Application Contact:* Gary Karns, Associate Dean for Graduate Studies, 206-281-2948, Fax: 206-281-2733. *Associate Dean for Graduate Studies,* Gary Karns, 206-281-2948, Fax: 206-281-2733.

Master of Divinity Program Students: 3 full-time (1 woman), 1 part-time (0 women). Average age 32. 22 applicants, 95% accepted, 15 enrolled. Expenses: Contact institution. *Financial support:* Scholarships/grants available. Financial award applicants required to submit FAFSA. Offers divinity (M Div). *Application deadline:* For fall admission, 7/31 for domestic students; for winter admission, 11/15 for domestic students; for spring admission, 2/15 for domestic students; for summer admission, 5/1 for domestic students. *Application fee:* $50. *Application Contact:* Dr. Doug Strong, Dean, 206-281-2473, E-mail: dstrong@spu.edu. *Dean,* Dr. Doug Strong, 206-281-2473, E-mail: dstrong@spu.edu.

Master of Education in Literacy Program Students: 13 part-time (all women); includes 1 minority (Asian, non-Hispanic/Latino). Average age 30. 2 applicants, 100% accepted, 2 enrolled. Expenses: Contact institution. *Financial support:* Scholarships/grants available. Financial award applicants required to submit FAFSA. In 2018, 6 master's awarded. *Program availability:* Part-time. Offers literacy (M Ed). *Application deadline:* For fall admission, 8/15 for domestic students; for winter admission, 11/15 for domestic students; for spring admission, 2/15 for domestic students; for summer admission, 5/15 for domestic students. Applications are processed on a rolling basis. *Application fee:* $50. Electronic applications accepted. *Application Contact:* The Graduate Center, 206-281-2091. *Chair,* Dr. Scott F. Beers, 206-281-2707, E-mail: sbeers@spu.edu.

Master of Education in School Counseling Program Students: 53 full-time (46 women), 34 part-time (27 women); includes 23 minority (2 Black or African American, non-Hispanic/Latino; 1 American Indian or Alaska Native, non-Hispanic/Latino; 12 Asian, non-Hispanic/Latino; 4 Hispanic/Latino; 1 Native Hawaiian or other Pacific Islander, non-Hispanic/Latino; 3 Two or more races, non-Hispanic/Latino), 4 international. Average age 29. 65 applicants, 71% accepted, 24 enrolled. Expenses: Contact institution. *Financial support:* Scholarships/grants available. Financial award applicants required to submit FAFSA. In 2018, 19 master's awarded. *Program availability:* Part-time. Offers school counseling (M Ed, Certificate). *Application deadline:* For fall admission, 4/1 priority date for domestic students. *Application fee:* $50. Electronic applications accepted. *Application Contact:* Dr. June Hyun, Chair, 206-281-2671, Fax: 206-281-2756, E-mail: jhyun@spu.edu. *Chair,* Dr. June Hyun, 206-281-2671, Fax: 206-281-2756, E-mail: jhyun@spu.edu.

Master of Education in Teacher Leadership Program Students: 1 (woman) full-time, 35 part-time (27 women); includes 5 minority (2 Black or African American, non-Hispanic/Latino; 2 Asian, non-Hispanic/Latino; 1 Hispanic/Latino), 1 international. Average age 36. 14 applicants, 93% accepted, 11 enrolled. Expenses: Contact institution. *Financial support:* Applicants required to submit FAFSA. In 2018, 21 master's awarded. *Program availability:* Part-time, evening/weekend. Offers teacher leadership (M Ed). *Application deadline:* For fall admission, 8/15 priority date for domestic students, 7/1 for international students; for winter admission, 11/15 for domestic students; for spring admission, 2/15 for domestic students, 3/1 for international students; for summer admission, 5/15 for domestic students. Applications are processed on a rolling basis. *Application fee:* $50. Electronic applications accepted. *Application Contact:* The Graduate Center, 206-281-2091. *Chair,* Robin Henrikson, 206-281-2186, E-mail: henrir@spu.edu.

Master of Fine Arts in Creative Writing Program Students: 37 part-time (27 women); includes 3 minority (1 Asian, non-Hispanic/Latino; 1 Hispanic/Latino; 1 Two or more races, non-Hispanic/Latino), 1 international. Average age 33. 16 applicants, 113% accepted, 15 enrolled. Expenses: Contact institution. *Financial support:* Applicants required to submit FAFSA. In 2018, 11 master's awarded. *Program availability:* Part-time. Offers creative writing (MFA). *Application deadline:* For winter admission, 11/1 for domestic students; for summer admission, 5/1 for domestic students. *Application fee:* $50. Electronic applications accepted. *Application Contact:* The Graduate Center, 206-281-2091. *Director,* Dr. Scott Cairns, 206-281-2109, E-mail: gwolfe@spu.edu.

Master of Science in Information Systems Management Program Students: 2 full-time (both women), 20 part-time (11 women); includes 7 minority (4 Black or African American, non-Hispanic/Latino; 2 Asian, non-Hispanic/Latino; 1 Hispanic/Latino), 10 international. Average age 32. 18 applicants, 61% accepted, 9 enrolled. Expenses: Contact institution. *Financial support:* Applicants required to submit FAFSA. In 2018, 10 master's awarded. *Program availability:* Part-time. Offers information systems management (MS). *Application deadline:* For fall admission, 8/1 for domestic students, 6/1 for international students; for winter admission, 11/1 for domestic and international students; for spring admission, 2/1 for domestic students, 12/1 for international students; for summer admission, 5/1 for domestic students. Applications are processed on a rolling basis. *Application fee:* $50. Electronic applications accepted. *Application Contact:* Gary Karns, Associate Dean for Graduate Studies, 206-281-2948, Fax: 206-281-2733. *Associate Dean for Graduate Studies,* Gary Karns, 206-281-2948, Fax: 206-281-2733.

MS in Marriage and Family Therapy Program Students: 44 full-time (35 women), 18 part-time (12 women); includes 13 minority (3 Black or African American, non-Hispanic/Latino; 6 Asian, non-Hispanic/Latino; 2 Hispanic/Latino; 2 Two or more races, non-Hispanic/Latino). Average age 30. 57 applicants, 79% accepted, 29 enrolled. Expenses: Contact institution. *Financial support:* Fellowships and Federal Work-Study available. Financial award applicants required to submit FAFSA. In 2018, 21 master's awarded. *Program availability:* Part-time. Offers marriage and family therapy (MS); medical family therapy (Certificate). *Application deadline:* For fall admission, 1/23 for domestic students, 2/1 for international students. Applications are processed on a rolling basis. *Application fee:* $50. Electronic applications accepted. *Application Contact:* Dr. Scott Edwards, Chair, 206-281-2681, E-mail: sedwards@spu.edu. *Chair,* Dr. Scott Edwards, 206-281-2681, E-mail: sedwards@spu.edu.

MS in Nursing Program Students: 26 full-time (23 women), 26 part-time (23 women); includes 25 minority (6 Black or African American, non-Hispanic/Latino; 14 Asian, non-Hispanic/Latino; 4 Hispanic/Latino; 1 Two or more races, non-Hispanic/Latino). Average age 34. 45 applicants, 89% accepted, 23 enrolled. Expenses: Contact institution. *Financial support:* Fellowships and scholarships/grants available. Financial award applicants required to submit FAFSA. In 2018, 25 master's awarded. *Program availability:* Part-time. Offers administration (MSN); adult/gerontology nurse practitioner (MSN); clinical nurse specialist (MSN); family nurse practitioner (MSN, Certificate); informatics (MSN); nurse educator (MSN). *Application deadline:* For fall admission, 1/15 priority date for domestic students; for spring admission, 1/15 for domestic students. Applications are processed on a rolling basis. *Application fee:* $50. Electronic applications accepted. *Application Contact:* Dr. Christine Hoyle, Associate Dean, 206-281-2649, E-mail: hoylec@spu.edu. *Associate Dean,* Dr. Christine Hoyle, 206-281-2649, E-mail: hoylec@spu.edu.

PhD in Clinical Psychology Program Students: 51 full-time (40 women), 21 part-time (19 women); includes 18 minority (3 Black or African American, non-Hispanic/Latino; 6 Asian, non-Hispanic/Latino; 7 Hispanic/Latino; 2 Two or more races, non-Hispanic/Latino), 4 international. Average age 28. 90 applicants, 31% accepted, 12 enrolled. Expenses: Contact institution. *Financial support:* Fellowships and scholarships/grants available. Financial award applicants required to submit FAFSA. In 2018, 16 doctorates awarded. Offers clinical psychology (PhD). *Application deadline:* For fall admission, 12/15 for domestic and international students. Electronic applications accepted. *Application Contact:* Dr. Amy Mezulis, Chair of Clinical Psychology, 206-281-2820, E-mail: mezulis@spu.edu. *Chair of Clinical Psychology,* Dr. Amy Mezulis, 206-281-2820, E-mail: mezulis@spu.edu.

PhD in Counselor Education Program Students: 7 part-time (5 women); includes 3 minority (2 Asian, non-Hispanic/Latino; 1 Two or more races, non-Hispanic/Latino). Average age 35. 1 applicant, 100% accepted, 1 enrolled. Expenses: Contact institution. In 2018, 1 doctorate awarded. Offers counselor education (PhD). *Application deadline:* For fall admission, 8/15 for domestic students; for winter admission, 11/15 for domestic students; for spring admission, 2/15 for domestic students; for summer admission, 5/15 for domestic students. *Application fee:* $50. *Application Contact:* Munyi Shea, Chair, 206-281-2369, E-mail: mshea@spu.edu. *Chair,* Munyi Shea, 206-281-2369, E-mail: mshea@spu.edu.

Program in Digital Education Leadership Students: 1 (woman) full-time, 14 part-time (12 women); includes 3 minority (1 American Indian or Alaska Native, non-Hispanic/Latino; 1 Asian, non-Hispanic/Latino; 1 Hispanic/Latino). Average age 36. 11 applicants, 91% accepted, 8 enrolled. Expenses: Contact institution. In 2018, 9 master's awarded. Offers digital education leadership (M Ed). *Application deadline:* For fall admission, 9/8 for domestic students. *Application Contact:* Graduate Center, 206-281-2091. *Dean,* Rick Eigenbrood, 206-281-2710, E-mail: eigend@spu.edu.

Program in Teaching Mathematics and Science Students: 11 full-time (4 women), 2 part-time (both women); includes 2 minority (1 Asian, non-Hispanic/Latino; 1 Two or more races, non-Hispanic/Latino). Average age 33. 38 applicants, 55% accepted, 13 enrolled. Expenses: Contact institution. In 2018, 15 master's awarded. Offers teaching mathematics and science (MTMS). *Application deadline:* For fall admission, 8/15 for domestic students; for winter admission, 11/15 for domestic students; for spring admission, 2/15 for domestic students; for summer admission, 5/15 for domestic students. *Application Contact:* David W. Dento, Graduate Teacher Education Chair, 206-281-2504, E-mail: dentod@spu.edu. *Graduate Teacher Education Chair,* David W. Dento, 206-281-2504, E-mail: dentod@spu.edu.

THE SEATTLE SCHOOL OF THEOLOGY AND PSYCHOLOGY, Seattle, WA 98121

General Information Independent-religious, coed, graduate-only institution.

GRADUATE UNITS

Graduate Programs *Program availability:* Part-time.

SEATTLE UNIVERSITY, Seattle, WA 98122-1090

General Information Independent-religious, coed, comprehensive institution. *Enrollment:* 7,291 graduate, professional, and undergraduate students; 879 full-time matriculated graduate/professional students (620 women), 990 part-time matriculated graduate/professional students (606 women). *Enrollment by degree level:* 1,549 master's, 416 doctoral, 657 other advanced degrees. *Graduate faculty:* 509 full-time (264 women), 217 part-time/adjunct (118 women). *Graduate housing:* Room and/or apartments available on a first-come, first-served basis to single students; on-campus housing not available to married students. *Student services:* Campus employment opportunities, campus safety program, career counseling, exercise/wellness program, free psychological counseling, international student services, low-cost health insurance, multicultural affairs office, services for students with disabilities, teacher training, writing training. *Library facilities:* Lemieux Library & McGoldrick Learning Commons plus 1 other. *Collection:* Books: 472,572 (physical), 257,641 (digital/electronic); Serial titles: 118,353 (physical), 8,597 (digital/electronic); Databases: 235. Students can reserve study rooms.

Computer facilities: Computer purchase and lease plans are available. 467 computers available on campus for general student use. A campuswide network can be accessed from student residence rooms and from off campus. Online class registration is available.
Website: http://www.seattleu.edu/

General Application Contact: Janet Shandley, Director of Graduate Admissions, 206-296-5900, Fax: 206-298-5656, E-mail: grad_admissions@seattleu.edu.

GRADUATE UNITS

Albers School of Business and Economics Students: 246 full-time (138 women), 305 part-time (137 women); includes 123 minority (11 Black or African American, non-Hispanic/Latino; 2 American Indian or Alaska Native, non-Hispanic/Latino; 64 Asian, non-Hispanic/Latino; 33 Hispanic/Latino; 1 Native Hawaiian or other Pacific Islander, non-Hispanic/Latino; 12 Two or more races, non-Hispanic/Latino), 143 international. Average age 30. 454 applicants, 63% accepted, 162 enrolled. *Faculty:* 67 full-time (24 women), 17 part-time/adjunct (8 women). Expenses: Contact institution. *Financial support:* In 2018–19, 174 students received support. Fellowships with partial tuition reimbursements available, research assistantships, career-related internships or fieldwork, Federal Work-Study, scholarships/grants, and unspecified assistantships available. Support available to part-time students. Financial award application deadline: 6/1; financial award applicants required to submit FAFSA. In 2018, 254 master's, 66 other advanced degrees awarded. *Program availability:* Part-time, evening/weekend. Offers business administration (MBA, Certificate); business analytics (MSBA, Certificate); business and economics (EMBA, MBA, MPAC, MSBA, MSF, Certificate); finance (MSF, Certificate); professional accounting (MPAC). *Application deadline:* For fall admission, 8/20 priority date for domestic students, 4/1 priority date for international students; for winter admission, 11/20 priority date for domestic students, 9/1 priority date for international students; for spring admission, 2/20 priority date for domestic students, 12/1 priority date for international students; for summer admission, 5/20 priority date for domestic students, 1/1 priority date for international students. Applications are processed on a rolling basis. *Application fee:* $55. Electronic applications accepted. *Application Contact:* Jeff Millard, Assistant Dean of Graduate Programs, 206-296-5700, E-mail: albersgrad@seattleu.edu. *Dean,* Dr. Joseph M. Phillips, Jr., 206-296-5700, Fax: 206-296-5795, E-mail: phillipsj@seattleu.edu.

Center for Leadership Formation Students: 52 full-time (31 women), 1 (woman) part-time; includes 6 minority (3 Black or African American, non-Hispanic/Latino; 1 Asian, non-Hispanic/Latino; 1 Hispanic/Latino; 1 Two or more races, non-Hispanic/Latino). Average age 42. 40 applicants, 98% accepted, 31 enrolled. *Faculty:* 2 part-time/adjunct (both women). Expenses: Contact institution. *Financial support:* In 2018–19, 17 students received support. Scholarships/grants available. Financial award applicants required to submit FAFSA. In 2018, 25 master's, 16 other advanced degrees awarded. *Program availability:* Evening/weekend. Offers leadership (EMBA, Certificate). *Application deadline:* Applications are processed on a rolling basis. *Application fee:* $55. Electronic applications accepted. *Application Contact:* Sommer Harrison, Manager, Graduate Programs Outreach, 206-296-2529, E-mail: emba@seattleu.edu. *Associate Dean of Executive Education,* Dr. Marilyn Gist, 206-296-5413, E-mail: gistm@seattleu.edu.

College of Arts and Sciences Students: 113 full-time (81 women), 254 part-time (183 women); includes 112 minority (24 Black or African American, non-Hispanic/Latino; 3 American Indian or Alaska Native, non-Hispanic/Latino; 26 Asian, non-Hispanic/Latino; 42 Hispanic/Latino; 17 Two or more races, non-Hispanic/Latino), 12 international. Average age 30. 306 applicants, 71% accepted, 135 enrolled. *Faculty:* 197 full-time (104 women), 91 part-time/adjunct (45 women). Expenses: Contact institution. *Financial support:* In 2018–19, 161 students received support. Career-related internships or fieldwork, Federal Work-Study, scholarships/grants, and unspecified assistantships available. Support available to part-time students. Financial award application deadline: 3/15; financial award applicants required to submit FAFSA. In 2018, 169 master's, 10 other advanced degrees awarded. *Program availability:* Part-time, evening/weekend. Offers arts and sciences (MA Psych, MACJ, MFA, MNPL, MPA, MSAL, MSW, Certificate); arts leadership (MFA); crime analysis (Certificate); criminal justice (MACJ); existential and phenomenological therapeutic psychology (MA Psych); social work (MSW). *Application deadline:* For fall admission, 1/15 for domestic and international students; for winter admission, 10/15 for domestic and international students; for spring admission, 2/15 for domestic and international students. Applications are processed on a rolling basis. *Application fee:* $55. Electronic applications accepted. *Application Contact:* Janet Shandley, Director of Graduate Admissions, 206-296-5900, Fax: 206-298-5656, E-mail: grad_admissions@seattleu.edu. *Dean,* Dr. David Powers, 206-296-5300, E-mail: powersda@seattleu.edu.

Center for the Study of Sport and Exercise Students: 8 full-time (2 women), 31 part-time (11 women); includes 6 minority (1 Black or African American, non-Hispanic/Latino; 5 Asian, non-Hispanic/Latino), 5 international. Average age 26. 1 applicant, 100% accepted, 1 enrolled. *Faculty:* 3 full-time (1 woman). Expenses: Contact institution. *Financial support:* In 2018–19, 20 students received support. Research assistantships and scholarships/grants available. Financial award applicants required to submit FAFSA. In 2018, 22 master's awarded. *Program availability:* Part-time, evening/weekend. Offers sport and exercise (MSAL). *Application deadline:* For fall admission, 2/15 for domestic and international students. *Application fee:* $55. Electronic applications accepted. *Application Contact:* Janet Shandley, Associate Dean of Graduate Admissions, 206-296-5900, Fax: 206-298-5656, E-mail: grad_admissions@seattleu.edu. *Director,* Dr. Dan Tripps, 206-398-4605, E-mail: trippsd@seattleu.edu.

Institute of Public Service Students: 10 full-time (5 women), 126 part-time (81 women); includes 49 minority (12 Black or African American, non-Hispanic/Latino; 1 American Indian or Alaska Native, non-Hispanic/Latino; 9 Asian, non-Hispanic/Latino; 24 Hispanic/Latino; 3 Two or more races, non-Hispanic/Latino), 2 international. Average age 31. 53 applicants, 91% accepted, 35 enrolled. *Faculty:* 7 full-time (4 women), 3 part-time/adjunct (2 women). Expenses: Contact institution. *Financial support:* In 2018–19, 23 students received support. Career-related internships or fieldwork, Federal Work-Study, and unspecified assistantships available. Support available to part-time students. Financial award applicants required to submit FAFSA. In 2018, 50 master's awarded. *Program availability:* Part-time, evening/weekend. Offers public service (MNPL, MPA). *Application deadline:* For fall admission, 7/20 priority date for domestic students, 7/20 for international students; for winter admission, 10/20 priority date for domestic students, 10/20 for international students; for spring admission, 2/20 priority date for domestic students, 2/20 for international students. Applications are processed on a rolling basis. *Application fee:* $55. Electronic applications accepted. *Application Contact:* Janet Shandley, Associate Dean of Graduate Admissions, 206-296-5900, Fax: 206-298-5656, E-mail: grad_admissions@seattleu.edu. *Interim Director, Institute of Public Service,* Dr. John Collins, 206-296-5442, Fax: 206-296-5997, E-mail: collinsj@seattleu.edu.

College of Education Students: 255 full-time (208 women), 205 part-time (152 women); includes 163 minority (24 Black or African American, non-Hispanic/Latino; 3 American Indian or Alaska Native, non-Hispanic/Latino; 52 Asian, non-Hispanic/Latino; 61 Hispanic/Latino; 2 Native Hawaiian or other Pacific Islander, non-Hispanic/Latino; 21 Two or more races, non-Hispanic/Latino), 14 international. Average age 30. 465 applicants, 53% accepted, 148 enrolled. *Faculty:* 30 full-time (17 women), 19 part-time/adjunct (12 women). Expenses: Contact institution. *Financial support:* In 2018–19, 134 students received support. Career-related internships or fieldwork, Federal Work-Study, scholarships/grants, and unspecified assistantships available. Support available to part-time students. Financial award applicants required to submit FAFSA. In 2018, 177 master's, 21 doctorates, 27 other advanced degrees awarded. *Program availability:* Part-time, evening/weekend. Offers adult education and training (M Ed, MA, Certificate); counseling and school psychology (MA, Certificate, Ed S); education (M Ed, MA, MIT, Ed D, Certificate, Ed S, Post-Master's Certificate); educational administration (M Ed, MA, Certificate, Ed S); educational leadership (Ed D); special education (M Ed, MA, Certificate); student development administration (M Ed, MA); teacher education (MIT); teaching English to speakers of other languages (M Ed, MA, Certificate). *Application deadline:* Applications are processed on a rolling basis. *Application fee:* $55. Electronic applications accepted. *Application Contact:* Janet Shandley, Director of Graduate Admissions, 206-296-5900, Fax: 206-298-5656, E-mail: grad_admissions@seattleu.edu. *Dean,* Dr. Deanna Sands, 206-296-5758, E-mail: sandsd@seattleu.edu.

College of Nursing Students: 167 full-time (140 women), 44 part-time (35 women); includes 73 minority (20 Black or African American, non-Hispanic/Latino; 1 American Indian or Alaska Native, non-Hispanic/Latino; 22 Asian, non-Hispanic/Latino; 23 Hispanic/Latino; 7 Two or more races, non-Hispanic/Latino), 1 international. Average age 32. 16 applicants, 88% accepted, 9 enrolled. *Faculty:* 92 full-time (86 women), 56 part-time/adjunct (52 women). Expenses: Contact institution. *Financial support:* In 2018–19, 95 students received support. Fellowships, research assistantships, career-related internships or fieldwork, Federal Work-Study, and scholarships/grants available. Support available to part-time students. Financial award applicants required to submit FAFSA. In 2018, 9 doctorates awarded. *Program availability:* Part-time, evening/weekend. Offers nursing (DNP). *Application deadline:* For fall admission, 7/1 for domestic students. *Application fee:* $55. *Application Contact:* Janet Shandley, Director of Graduate Admissions, 206-296-5900, Fax: 206-298-5656, E-mail: grad_admissions@seattleu.edu. *Dean,* Dr. Kristen Swanson, 206-296-5676.

College of Science and Engineering Students: 75 full-time (30 women), 80 part-time (26 women); includes 37 minority (1 Black or African American, non-Hispanic/Latino; 19 Asian, non-Hispanic/Latino; 12 Hispanic/Latino; 5 Two or more races, non-Hispanic/Latino), 51 international. Average age 28. 136 applicants, 57% accepted, 56 enrolled. *Faculty:* 104 full-time (42 women), 15 part-time/adjunct (7 women). Expenses: Contact institution. *Financial support:* In 2018–19, 17 students received support. Career-related internships or fieldwork and Federal Work-Study available. Support available to part-time students. Financial award applicants required to submit FAFSA. In 2018, 32 master's awarded. *Program availability:* Part-time, evening/weekend. Offers computer science (MSCS); science and engineering (MSCS). *Application deadline:* For fall admission, 7/1 for domestic students. *Application fee:* $55. *Application Contact:* Janet Shandley, Director of Graduate Admissions, 206-296-5900, Fax: 206-298-5656, E-mail: grad_admissions@seattleu.edu. *Dean,* Dr. Michael Quinn, 206-296-5500, Fax: 206-296-2071.

School of Law *Program availability:* Part-time, evening/weekend. Offers American legal studies (LL M); business development (MLS); elder law (LL M); health law (LL M); innovation and technology (LL M, MLS); tribal law and governance (LL M, MLS). Electronic applications accepted.

School of Theology and Ministry Students: 29 full-time (26 women), 105 part-time (74 women); includes 38 minority (14 Black or African American, non-Hispanic/Latino; 11 Asian, non-Hispanic/Latino; 10 Hispanic/Latino; 1 Native Hawaiian or other Pacific Islander, non-Hispanic/Latino; 2 Two or more races, non-Hispanic/Latino), 3 international. Average age 42. 38 applicants, 89% accepted, 20 enrolled. *Faculty:* 22 full-time (12 women), 22 part-time/adjunct (14 women). Expenses: Contact institution. *Financial support:* In 2018–19, 92 students received support. Career-related internships or fieldwork, Federal Work-Study, and scholarships/grants available. Support available to part-time students. Financial award application deadline: 6/1; financial award applicants required to submit FAFSA. In 2018, 32 master's, 5 doctorates, 5 other advanced degrees awarded. *Program availability:* Part-time, online learning. Offers couples and family therapy (MA); divinity (M Div, D Min); pastoral studies (MAPS); theology and ministry (M Div, MA, MAPS, MATL, MATS, D Min, Certificate); transformational leadership (MATL); transforming spirituality (MATS, Certificate). *Application deadline:* For fall admission, 6/1 priority date for domestic students, 4/1 for international students. *Application fee:* $55. Electronic applications accepted. *Application Contact:* Colette Meda Casavant, Admissions Coordinator, 206-296-5333, Fax: 206-296-5329, E-mail: casavant@seattleu.edu. *Dean,* Dr. Mark Markuly, 206-296-5330, Fax: 206-296-5329, E-mail: stm@seattleu.edu.

SELMA UNIVERSITY, Selma, AL 36701-5299

General Information Independent-religious, coed, comprehensive institution.

GRADUATE UNITS

Graduate Programs Offers Bible and Christian education (MA); Bible and pastoral ministry (MA).

SEMINARY OF THE SOUTHWEST, Austin, TX 78768-2247

General Information Independent-religious, coed, graduate-only institution. *Enrollment by degree level:* 121 master's, 2 other advanced degrees. *Graduate faculty:* 12 full-time (6 women), 15 part-time/adjunct (9 women). *Tuition:* Full-time $15,576; part-time $7788 per year. *Required fees:* $778; $506. One-time fee: $99 full-time; $52 part-time. Tuition and fees vary according to class time and course load. *Graduate housing:* Rooms and/or apartments available on a first-come, first-served basis to single and married students. Typical cost: $5868 per year for single students; $8496 per year for married students. Room charges vary according to housing facility selected. Housing application deadline: 8/1. *Student services:* Campus safety program, exercise/wellness program, writing training. *Library facilities:* Booher Library. *Collection:* Books: 119,122 (physical), 178,977 (digital/electronic); Serial titles: 405 (physical), 27,622 (digital/electronic); Databases: 75. Weekly public service hours: 86; students can reserve study rooms.

Computer facilities: 8 computers available on campus for general student use. Online class registration is available.
Website: http://www.ssw.edu/

General Application Contact: Beth Jordan, Enrollment Manager, 512-472-4133 Ext. 357, Fax: 512-472-3098, E-mail: beth.jordan@ssw.edu.

SETON HALL UNIVERSITY, South Orange, NJ 07079-2697

General Information Independent-religious, coed, university. CGS member. *Graduate housing:* On-campus housing not available.

GRADUATE UNITS

College of Arts and Sciences *Program availability:* Part-time, evening/weekend, online learning. Offers analytical chemistry (MS, PhD); arts and sciences (MA, MPA, MS, PhD, Graduate Certificate); Asian studies (MA); biochemistry (MS, PhD); biology (MS); biology/business administration (MS); chemistry (MS); experimental psychology (MS); history (MA); inorganic chemistry (MS, PhD); Jewish-Christian studies (MA); literature (MA); microbiology (MS); molecular bioscience (PhD); molecular bioscience/neuroscience (PhD); nonprofit organization management (Graduate Certificate); organic chemistry (MS, PhD); physical chemistry (MS, PhD); public administration (MPA); social work (MSW). Electronic applications accepted.

College of Communication and the Arts *Program availability:* Part-time, evening/weekend, online learning. Offers exhibition development (MA); museum management (MA); museum professions (MA); museum registration (MA); public relations (MA); strategic communication (MA). Electronic applications accepted.

College of Education and Human Services *Program availability:* Part-time, evening/weekend, 100% online, blended/hybrid learning. Offers college student personnel administration (MA); counseling psychology (MA, PhD); education and human services (MA, MS, Ed D, Exec Ed D, PhD, Ed S); education research, assessment and program evaluation (PhD); higher education administration (Ed D, PhD); human resource training and development (MA); individualized (MA); instructional design and technology (MA); K–12 administration and supervision (Ed D, Exec Ed D, Ed S); K–12 leadership, management and policy (Ed D, Exec Ed D, Ed S); marriage and family therapy (MA); psychological studies (MA); school counseling (MA); school psychology (MA); special education (MA); sport and exercise psychology (MA). Electronic applications accepted.

College of Nursing *Program availability:* Part-time, online learning. Offers advanced practice in primary health care (MSN, DNP); entry into practice (MSN); health systems administration (MSN, DNP); nursing (PhD); nursing case management (MSN); nursing education (MA); school nurse (MSN). Electronic applications accepted.

Immaculate Conception Seminary School of Theology *Program availability:* Part-time, evening/weekend. Offers Christian spirituality (Certificate); great spiritual books (Certificate); pastoral ministry (M Div, MA, Certificate); scripture studies (Certificate); Seminary's Theological Education for Parish Services (STEPS) (Certificate); theology (MA). Electronic applications accepted.

School of Diplomacy and International Relations *Program availability:* Part-time, evening/weekend, 100% online, blended/hybrid learning. Offers diplomacy and international relations (MA); global health management (Graduate Certificate); post-conflict state reconstruction and sustainability (Graduate Certificate); United Nations studies (Graduate Certificate). Electronic applications accepted.

School of Health and Medical Sciences *Program availability:* Part-time, evening/weekend. Offers athletic training (MS); health and medical sciences (MHA, MS, DPT, PhD); health sciences (PhD); healthcare administration (MHA); occupational therapy (MS); physician assistant (MS); professional physical therapy (DPT); speech-language pathology (MS). Electronic applications accepted.

School of Law *Program availability:* Part-time, evening/weekend. Offers health law (LL M, JD); intellectual property (LL M, JD); law (MSJ). MD/JD, MD/MSJ offered jointly with University of Medicine and Dentistry of New Jersey. Electronic applications accepted.

School of Medicine Offers medicine (MD).

Stillman School of Business Students: 87 full-time (39 women), 491 part-time (198 women); includes 81 minority (30 Black or African American, non-Hispanic/Latino; 14 Asian, non-Hispanic/Latino; 28 Hispanic/Latino; 9 Two or more races, non-Hispanic/Latino), 294 international. Average age 33. 449 applicants, 86% accepted, 230 enrolled. *Faculty:* 27 full-time (5 women), 18 part-time/adjunct (2 women). Expenses: Contact institution. *Financial support:* Research assistantships with full tuition reimbursements, career-related internships or fieldwork, scholarships/grants, and unspecified assistantships available. Financial award application deadline: 6/30; financial award applicants required to submit FAFSA. In 2018, 135 master's awarded. *Program availability:* Part-time, evening/weekend. Offers accounting (MBA, MS, Certificate); entrepreneurial studies (Certificate); finance (MBA); financial decision making (Certificate); information technology management (MBA); international business (MBA); management (MBA); marketing (MBA); professional accounting (MS); sport management (MBA); supply chain management (MBA, Certificate); taxation (Certificate). *Application deadline:* For fall admission, 5/31 priority date for domestic students, 3/31 priority date for international students; for spring admission, 10/31 priority date for domestic students, 9/30 priority date for international students; for summer admission, 4/30 priority date for domestic students, 3/31 priority date for international students. Applications are processed on a rolling basis. *Application fee:* $75. Electronic applications accepted. *Application Contact:* Alfred Ayoub, Director of Graduate Admissions, 973-761-9262, Fax: 973-761-9208, E-mail: alfred.ayoub@shu.edu. *Dean,* Dr. Joyce Strawser, 973-761-9013, Fax: 973-275-2465, E-mail: joyce.strawser@shu.edu.

SETON HILL UNIVERSITY, Greensburg, PA 15601

General Information Independent-religious, coed, comprehensive institution. *Enrollment:* 2,080 graduate, professional, and undergraduate students; 250 full-time matriculated graduate/professional students (173 women), 120 part-time matriculated graduate/professional students (92 women). *Enrollment by degree level:* 370 master's, 3 other advanced degrees. *Graduate faculty:* 14 full-time, 15 part-time/adjunct. *Graduate housing:* Room and/or apartments available on a first-come, first-served basis to single students; on-campus housing not available to married students. Housing application deadline: 7/1. *Student services:* Campus employment opportunities, campus safety program, career counseling, exercise/wellness program, free psychological counseling, international student services, multicultural affairs office, services for students with disabilities, teacher training, writing training. *Library facilities:* Reeves Memorial Library. *Collection:* Books: 72,274 (physical), 127,160 (digital/electronic); Serial titles: 2,919 (physical); Databases: 37. Students can reserve study rooms.

Computer facilities: Computer purchase and lease plans are available. 66 computers available on campus for general student use. A campuswide network can be accessed from student residence rooms and from off campus. Online class registration is available.
Website: http://www.setonhill.edu/

General Application Contact: Director of Graduate and Adult Studies, 724-838-4208, Fax: 724-830-1891, E-mail: gadmit@setonhill.edu.

GRADUATE UNITS

MA Program in Art Therapy Expenses: Contact institution. *Financial support:* Federal Work-Study, scholarships/grants, and tuition discounts available. Financial award application deadline: 8/15; financial award applicants required to submit FAFSA. *Program availability:* Part-time. Offers art therapy (MA). *Application deadline:* For fall admission, 7/1 for domestic and international students; for spring admission, 11/30 for domestic and international students. Applications are processed on a rolling basis. *Application fee:* $0. Electronic applications accepted.

Master of Arts Program in Elementary/Middle Level Education Expenses: Contact institution. *Financial support:* Federal Work-Study, scholarships/grants, and tuition discounts available. Financial award application deadline: 8/15; financial award applicants required to submit FAFSA. *Program availability:* Part-time, evening/weekend, blended/hybrid learning. Offers elementary/middle level education (MA). *Application deadline:* Applications are processed on a rolling basis. *Application fee:* $0. Electronic applications accepted.

Master of Arts Program in Special Education Expenses: Contact institution. *Financial support:* Scholarships/grants and tuition discounts available. Financial award application deadline: 8/15; financial award applicants required to submit FAFSA. *Program availability:* Part-time, evening/weekend, blended/hybrid learning. Offers special education (MA). *Application deadline:* Applications are processed on a rolling basis. *Application fee:* $0. Electronic applications accepted.

Master of Science Program in Physician Assistant Expenses: Contact institution. *Financial support:* Application deadline: 8/15; applicants required to submit FAFSA. Offers physician assistant (MS). *Application deadline:* Applications are processed on a rolling basis. Electronic applications accepted.

Master's and Certificate Program in Orthodontics Expenses: Contact institution. *Financial support:* Application deadline: 5/15; applicants required to submit FAFSA. Offers orthodontics (MS, Certificate). *Application deadline:* Applications are processed on a rolling basis. Electronic applications accepted.

MBA Program Expenses: Contact institution. *Financial support:* Federal Work-Study, scholarships/grants, and tuition discounts available. Financial award application deadline: 8/15; financial award applicants required to submit FAFSA. *Program availability:* Part-time, evening/weekend. Offers entrepreneurship (MBA); forensic accounting and fraud examination (MBA); healthcare administration (MBA); management (MBA). *Application deadline:* Applications are processed on a rolling basis. *Application fee:* $0. Electronic applications accepted. *Application Contact:* Dr. Douglas Nelson, Associate Professor, Business/MBA Program Director, E-mail: dnelson@setonhill.edu. *Associate Professor, Business/MBA Program Director,* Dr. Douglas Nelson, E-mail: dnelson@setonhill.edu.

MFA Program in Writing Popular Fiction Expenses: Contact institution. *Financial support:* Scholarships/grants and tuition discounts available. Financial award application deadline: 8/15; financial award applicants required to submit FAFSA. *Program availability:* Part-time. Offers writing popular fiction (MFA). *Application deadline:* For fall admission, 10/1 priority date for domestic students; for spring admission, 3/1 priority date for domestic students. Applications are processed on a rolling basis. Electronic applications accepted. *Application Contact:* Dr. Nicole Peeler, Associate Professor, English/Program Director, Writing Popular Fiction, E-mail: peeler@setonhill.edu. *Associate Professor, English/Program Director, Writing Popular Fiction,* Dr. Nicole Peeler, E-mail: peeler@setonhill.edu.

Program in Innovative Instruction Average age 34. 21 applicants, 48% accepted, 9 enrolled. Expenses: Contact institution. *Financial support:* In 2018–19, 7 students received support. Scholarships/grants, tuition waivers (partial), and unspecified assistantships available. Support available to part-time students. Financial award application deadline: 8/15; financial award applicants required to submit FAFSA. In 2018, 5 master's awarded. *Program availability:* Part-time, evening/weekend. Offers innovative instruction (M Ed). *Application deadline:* Applications are processed on a rolling basis. *Application fee:* $35. Electronic applications accepted.

SHASTA BIBLE COLLEGE, Redding, CA 96002

General Information Independent-religious, coed, comprehensive institution. *Graduate housing:* Rooms and/or apartments available on a first-come, first-served basis to single and married students.

GRADUATE UNITS

Program in Biblical Counseling *Program availability:* Part-time. Offers biblical counseling and Christian family life education (MA).

Program in Christian Ministry *Program availability:* Part-time, online learning. Offers Christian ministry (MA).

Program in School and Church Administration *Program availability:* Part-time, evening/weekend. Offers school and church administration (MS).

SHAWNEE STATE UNIVERSITY, Portsmouth, OH 45662

General Information State-supported, coed, comprehensive institution.

GRADUATE UNITS

Program in Curriculum and Instruction Offers curriculum and instruction (M Ed).

Program in Occupational Therapy Offers occupational therapy (MOT).

SHAW UNIVERSITY, Raleigh, NC 27601-2399

General Information Independent-religious, coed, comprehensive institution. *Enrollment:* 63 full-time matriculated graduate/professional students (31 women), 43 part-time matriculated graduate/professional students (25 women). *Enrollment by degree level:* 106 master's. *Graduate faculty:* 6 full-time (4 women), 8 part-time/adjunct (3 women). *Tuition:* Full-time $10,404; part-time $578 per credit hour. *Required fees:* $2784; $408 per credit hour. $1023 per semester. *Graduate housing:* Room and/or apartments available on a first-come, first-served basis to single students; on-campus housing not available to married students. Typical cost: $3842 per year ($8514 including board). *Student services:* Campus employment opportunities, campus safety program, career counseling, child daycare facilities, free psychological counseling, international student services, low-cost health insurance, services for students with disabilities, teacher training, writing training. *Library facilities:* James E. Cheek Learning Resources Center.

Computer facilities: A campuswide network can be accessed from student residence rooms and from off campus. Online class registration is available.
Website: http://www.shawu.edu/

General Application Contact: Anthony Brooks, Chief Enrollment Management Officer, 919-719-1983, Fax: 919-546-8271, E-mail: anthony.brooks@shawu.edu.

GRADUATE UNITS

Department of Education & Child Development Students: 1 (woman) full-time, 8 part-time (6 women); includes 5 minority (4 Black or African American, non-Hispanic/Latino; 1 Hispanic/Latino), 1 international. Average age 33. 4 applicants, 100% accepted, 4 enrolled. *Faculty:* 1 (woman) full-time, 2 part-time/adjunct (both women). Expenses: Contact institution. *Financial support:* In 2018–19, 14 students received support. Career-related internships or fieldwork, Federal Work-Study, scholarships/grants, and tuition waivers (full) available. Support available to part-time students. Financial award applicants required to submit FAFSA. In 2018, 9 master's awarded. *Program availability:* Part-time, evening/weekend. Offers early childhood education (MS). *Application deadline:* For fall admission, 4/1 priority date for domestic students, 1/30 priority date for international students; for spring admission, 10/31 priority date for domestic students, 8/30 priority date for international students. Applications are processed on a rolling basis. *Application fee:* $50. Electronic applications accepted. *Application Contact:* Dr. Paula Moten-Tolson, Program Coordinator/Asst. Professor, 919-546-8544, Fax: 919-546-8531, E-mail: pmoten@shawu.edu. *Department Head,* Dr. Lucy Wilson, 919-546-8322, Fax: 919-546-8531, E-mail: lwilson@shawu.edu.

Divinity School Students: 62 full-time (30 women), 35 part-time (19 women); includes 73 minority (70 Black or African American, non-Hispanic/Latino; 1 Asian, non-Hispanic/Latino; 1 Hispanic/Latino; 1 Two or more races, non-Hispanic/Latino), 1 international. Average age 46. 25 applicants, 100% accepted, 19 enrolled. *Faculty:* 6 full-time (3 women), 7 part-time/adjunct (1 woman). Expenses: Contact institution. *Financial support:* In 2018–19, 14 students received support. Federal Work-Study, scholarships/grants, and tuition waivers (full) available. Support available to part-time students. Financial award applicants required to submit FAFSA. In 2018, 19 master's awarded. *Program availability:* Part-time, evening/weekend. Offers divinity (M Div, MACE). *Application deadline:* For fall admission, 7/30 priority date for domestic students, 1/30 priority date for international students; for spring admission, 11/30 priority date for domestic students, 8/30 priority date for international students. Applications are processed on a rolling basis. *Application fee:* $50. Electronic applications accepted. *Application Contact:* Dr. Johnny Bernard Hill, Dean, 919-546-8612, Fax: 919-546-8571, E-mail: jhill@shawu.edu. *Dean,* Dr. Johnny Bernard Hill, 919-546-8612, Fax: 919-546-8571, E-mail: jhill@shawu.edu.

SHENANDOAH UNIVERSITY, Winchester, VA 22601-5195

General Information Independent-religious, coed, university. *Enrollment:* 942 full-time matriculated graduate/professional students (683 women), 723 part-time matriculated graduate/professional students (551 women). *Enrollment by degree level:* 703 master's, 863 doctoral, 99 other advanced degrees. *Graduate faculty:* 147 full-time (94 women), 116 part-time/adjunct (81 women). *Tuition:* Full-time $15,750. *Required fees:* $1230; $615. Tuition and fees vary according to course load and program. *Graduate housing:* Rooms and/or apartments available on a first-come, first-served basis to single and married students. Typical cost: $10,370 (including board) for single students; $9216 per year for married students. Room and board charges vary according to board plan and housing facility selected. Housing application deadline: 3/2. *Student services:* Campus employment opportunities, campus safety program, career counseling, child daycare facilities, exercise/wellness program, free psychological counseling, international student services, low-cost health insurance, multicultural affairs office, services for students with disabilities, teacher training, writing training. *Library facilities:* Alson H. Smith, Jr. Library plus 1 other. *Collection:* Books: 122,422 (physical), 217,000 (digital/electronic); Serial titles: 700 (physical), 86,500 (digital/electronic); Databases: 135. Weekly public service hours: 96; students can reserve study rooms.

Computer facilities: 32 computers available on campus for general student use. A campuswide network can be accessed from student residence rooms and from off campus. Online class registration, online student account information are available. Website: http://www.su.edu/

General Application Contact: Andrew Woodall, Executive Dean of Admissions, 540-665-4581, Fax: 540-665-4627, E-mail: admit@su.edu.

GRADUATE UNITS

Bernard J. Dunn School of Pharmacy Students: 312 full-time (219 women), 187 part-time (120 women); includes 134 minority (60 Black or African American, non-Hispanic/Latino; 60 Asian, non-Hispanic/Latino; 9 Hispanic/Latino; 1 Native Hawaiian or other Pacific Islander, non-Hispanic/Latino; 4 Two or more races, non-Hispanic/Latino), 18 international. Average age 33. 397 applicants, 68% accepted, 163 enrolled. *Faculty:* 40 full-time (25 women), 7 part-time/adjunct (4 women). Expenses: Contact institution. *Financial support:* In 2018–19, 42 students received support. Scholarships/grants and unspecified assistantships available. Financial award application deadline: 1/15; financial award applicants required to submit FAFSA. In 2018, 120 doctorates awarded. *Program availability:* Part-time, evening/weekend, 100% online. Offers pharmacy (Pharm D). *Application deadline:* For fall admission, 6/1 for domestic and international students. *Application fee:* $30. Electronic applications accepted. *Application Contact:* Andrew Woodall, Assistant Vice President of Recruitment and Admissions, 540-665-4581, Fax: 540-665-4627, E-mail: admit@su.edu. *Dean of Pharmacy,* Robert DiCenzo, PhD, 540-542-6529, Fax: 540-665-1283, E-mail: rdicenzo@su.edu.

College of Arts and Sciences Students: 18 full-time (15 women), 5 part-time (all women); includes 6 minority (3 Black or African American, non-Hispanic/Latino; 1 Asian, non-Hispanic/Latino; 2 Hispanic/Latino). Average age 29. 17 applicants, 88% accepted, 11 enrolled. *Faculty:* 1 (woman) full-time, 4 part-time/adjunct (3 women). Expenses: Contact institution. *Financial support:* Scholarships/grants and unspecified assistantships available. Financial award application deadline: 1/15; financial award applicants required to submit FAFSA. In 2018, 11 master's awarded. *Program availability:* Part-time, evening/weekend. Offers applied behavior analysis (MS). *Application deadline:* For fall admission, 7/15 for domestic and international students. *Application fee:* $30. Electronic applications accepted. *Application Contact:* Andrew Woodall, Assistant Vice President of Recruitment and Admissions, 540-665-4581, Fax: 540-665-4627, E-mail: admit@su.edu. *Dean of the College of Arts and Sciences,* Jeff W. Coker, PhD, 540-665-4587, Fax: 540-665-4644, E-mail: jcoker2@su.edu.

Eleanor Wade Custer School of Nursing Average age 37. 52 applicants, 88% accepted, 34 enrolled. Expenses: Contact institution. *Financial support:* In 2018–19, 32 students received support. Scholarships/grants and unspecified assistantships available. Financial award applicants required to submit FAFSA. In 2018, 18 master's, 1 doctorate, 28 other advanced degrees awarded. Offers adult gerontology primary care nurse practitioner (Graduate Certificate); adult-gerontology primary care nurse practitioner (MSN); family nurse practitioner (MSN, DNP, Graduate Certificate); general (MSN); health systems leadership (DNP); health systems management (MSN, Graduate Certificate); nurse midwifery (MSN); nurse-midwifery (Graduate Certificate); nursing education (Graduate Certificate); nursing practice (DNP); psychiatric mental health nurse practitioner (MSN, DNP, Graduate Certificate). *Application deadline:* For fall admission, 4/15 priority date for domestic and international students; for spring admission, 11/1 for domestic and international students; for summer admission, 3/1 for domestic and international students. *Application fee:* $30. Electronic applications accepted. *Application Contact:* Andrew Woodall, Executive Director of Recruitment and Admissions, 540-665-4581, Fax: 540-665-4627, E-mail: admit@su.edu. *Dean,* Dr. Kathleen LaSala, RN, 540-678-4381, Fax: 540-665-5519, E-mail: klasala@su.edu.

Harry F. Byrd, Jr. School of Business Students: 45 full-time (12 women), 34 part-time (18 women); includes 11 minority (3 Black or African American, non-Hispanic/Latino; 1 American Indian or Alaska Native, non-Hispanic/Latino; 2 Asian, non-Hispanic/Latino; 4 Hispanic/Latino; 1 Two or more races, non-Hispanic/Latino), 22 international. Average age 29. 73 applicants, 93% accepted, 44 enrolled. *Faculty:* 9 full-time (3 women), 4 part-time/adjunct (0 women). Expenses: Contact institution. *Financial support:* In 2018–19, 27 students received support. Scholarships/grants and unspecified assistantships available. Financial award application deadline: 1/15; financial award applicants required to submit FAFSA. In 2018, 47 master's, 12 other advanced degrees awarded. *Program availability:* Part-time, evening/weekend. Offers business (MBA, Certificate). *Application deadline:* For fall admission, 6/15 for domestic students, 5/15 for international students; for spring admission, 11/15 for domestic students, 10/15 for international students; for summer admission, 3/1 for domestic and international students. *Application fee:* $30. Electronic applications accepted. *Application Contact:* Andrew Woodall, Assistant Vice President for Admissions and Recruitment, 540-665-4581, Fax: 540-665-4627, E-mail: admit@su.edu. *Dean of Harry F. Byrd, Jr. School of Business,* Astrid Sheil, PhD, 540-545-7253, Fax: 540-665-5437, E-mail: asheil@su.edu.

School of Education and Leadership Students: 11 full-time (8 women), 211 part-time (163 women); includes 27 minority (14 Black or African American, non-Hispanic/Latino; 1 American Indian or Alaska Native, non-Hispanic/Latino; 4 Asian, non-Hispanic/Latino; 3 Hispanic/Latino; 1 Native Hawaiian or other Pacific Islander, non-Hispanic/Latino; 4 Two or more races, non-Hispanic/Latino), 2 international. Average age 38. 82 applicants, 96% accepted, 54 enrolled. *Faculty:* 8 full-time (6 women), 26 part-time/adjunct (19 women). Expenses: Contact institution. *Financial support:* In 2018–19, 3 students received support. Scholarships/grants and unspecified assistantships available. Financial award application deadline: 1/15; financial award applicants required to submit FAFSA. In 2018, 62 master's, 11 doctorates, 34 other advanced degrees awarded. *Program availability:* Part-time, evening/weekend. Offers early childhood literacy (MS); reading licensure (MS); writing (MS). *Application deadline:* For fall admission, 3/15 for domestic students, 3/17 for international students. Applications are processed on a rolling basis. *Application fee:* $30. Electronic applications accepted. *Application Contact:* Andrew Woodall, Assistant Vice President for Admissions & Recruitment, 540-665-4581, Fax: 540-665-4627, E-mail: admit@su.edu. *Director, School of Education and Leadership,* Jill Lindsey, PhD, 540-545-7324, Fax: 540-665-4726, E-mail: jlindsey@su.edu.

School of Health Professions Students: 471 full-time (371 women), 149 part-time (128 women); includes 61 minority (9 Black or African American, non-Hispanic/Latino; 2 American Indian or Alaska Native, non-Hispanic/Latino; 17 Asian, non-Hispanic/Latino; 20 Hispanic/Latino; 13 Two or more races, non-Hispanic/Latino), 23 international. Average age 28. 1,124 applicants, 33% accepted, 226 enrolled. *Faculty:* 39 full-time (31 women), 24 part-time/adjunct (14 women). Expenses: Contact institution. *Financial support:* In 2018–19, 21 students received support. Scholarships/grants and unspecified assistantships available. Financial award application deadline: 1/15; financial award applicants required to submit FAFSA. In 2018, 104 master's, 88 doctorates, 6 other advanced degrees awarded. *Program availability:* Part-time, all online except for two on-site weekend sessions (for DPT). Offers athletic training (MSAT); occupational therapy (MS); performing arts medicine (Certificate); physical therapy (DPT); physician assistant studies (MS); public health (MPH, Certificate). *Application deadline:* For fall admission, 10/1 for domestic and international students; for spring admission, 12/1 for domestic and international students; for summer admission, 10/1 for domestic and international students. *Application fee:* $30. Electronic applications accepted. *Application Contact:* Katie Olivo, Associate Director of Graduate and International Admissions, 540-665-4581, Fax: 540-665-4627, E-mail: kolivo@su.edu. *Dean of Health Professions,* Karen Elizabeth Abraham-Justice, Ph.D., 540-542-6209, Fax: 540-665-5530, E-mail: kabraham@su.edu.

Shenandoah Conservatory Students: 67 full-time (41 women), 65 part-time (46 women); includes 18 minority (7 Black or African American, non-Hispanic/Latino; 1 Asian, non-Hispanic/Latino; 8 Hispanic/Latino; 2 Two or more races, non-Hispanic/Latino), 22 international. Average age 30. 74 applicants, 76% accepted, 34 enrolled. *Faculty:* 61 full-time (21 women), 58 part-time/adjunct (31 women). Expenses: Contact institution. *Financial support:* In 2018–19, 44 students received support. Scholarships/grants and unspecified assistantships available. Financial award application deadline: 1/15; financial award applicants required to submit FAFSA. In 2018, 30 master's, 9 doctorates, 8 other advanced degrees awarded. *Program availability:* Part-time. Offers music (Artist Diploma). *Application deadline:* For fall admission, 1/15 for domestic and international students; for summer admission, 4/15 for domestic and international students. *Application fee:* $30. Electronic applications accepted. *Application Contact:* Andrew Woodall, Executive Director of Recruitment and Advancement, 540-665-4581, Fax: 540-665-4627, E-mail: admit@su.edu. *Dean,* Dr. Michael J. Stepniak, 540-542-6201, Fax: 540-665-5402, E-mail: mstepnia@su.edu.

SHEPHERDS THEOLOGICAL SEMINARY, Cary, NC 27518
General Information Independent-religious, coed, graduate-only institution. *Graduate housing:* On-campus housing not available.

GRADUATE UNITS

Graduate Programs Offers Biblical literature and languages (MA); church ministry (MA); ministry (MTS); New Testament (M Div); Old Testament (M Div); theology (M Div).

SHEPHERD UNIVERSITY, Shepherdstown, WV 25443
General Information State-supported, coed, comprehensive institution.

GRADUATE UNITS

Program in Curriculum and Instruction Offers curriculum and instruction (MA).

SHERMAN COLLEGE OF CHIROPRACTIC, Spartanburg, SC 29304-1452
General Information Independent, coed, graduate-only institution. *Graduate housing:* Room and/or apartments available to single students. *Research affiliation:* American Public Health Service (chiropractic research), Upper Cervical Research Foundation (chiropractic).

GRADUATE UNITS

Professional Program Offers chiropractic (DC). Electronic applications accepted.

SHILOH UNIVERSITY, Kalona, IA 52247
General Information Independent, coed, comprehensive institution. *Graduate housing:* On-campus housing not available.

GRADUATE UNITS

Graduate Programs *Program availability:* Part-time, evening/weekend, online only, 100% online. Offers Christian ministries (M Div); leadership of church and spiritual formation (D Min); theological studies (MA). Electronic applications accepted.

SHIPPENSBURG UNIVERSITY OF PENNSYLVANIA, Shippensburg, PA 17257-2299
General Information State-supported, coed, comprehensive institution. CGS member. *Enrollment:* 251 full-time matriculated graduate/professional students (174 women), 518 part-time matriculated graduate/professional students (305 women). *Enrollment by degree level:* 718 master's, 44 doctoral, 7 other advanced degrees. *Graduate faculty:* 127 full-time (53 women), 21 part-time/adjunct (13 women). Tuition, state resident: part-time $516 per credit. Tuition, nonresident: part-time $750 per credit. *Required fees:* $149 per credit. *Graduate housing:* On-campus housing not available. *Student services:* Campus employment opportunities, campus safety program, career counseling, child daycare facilities, exercise/wellness program, free psychological counseling, grant writing training, international student services, low-cost health insurance, multicultural affairs office, services for students with disabilities, teacher training, writing training. *Library facilities:* Ezra Lehman Memorial Library plus 1 other. *Collection:* Books: 359,138 (physical), 189,092 (digital/electronic); Serial titles: 50 (physical), 255 (digital/electronic); Databases: 106. Weekly public service hours: 97.

Computer facilities: 1,100 computers available on campus for general student use. A campuswide network can be accessed from student residence rooms and from off campus. Online class registration, personal Web pages are available. Website: http://www.ship.edu/

General Application Contact: Maya T. Mapp, Director of Admissions, 717-477-1231, Fax: 717-477-4016, E-mail: mtmapp@ship.edu.

GRADUATE UNITS

School of Graduate Studies Students: 251 full-time (174 women), 518 part-time (305 women); includes 121 minority (61 Black or African American, non-Hispanic/Latino; 11 Asian, non-Hispanic/Latino; 33 Hispanic/Latino; 16 Two or more races, non-Hispanic/Latino), 37 international. Average age 31. 706 applicants, 64% accepted, 283 enrolled. *Faculty:* 127 full-time (53 women), 21 part-time/adjunct (13 women). Expenses: Contact institution. *Financial support:* In 2018–19, 158 students received support. Career-related internships or fieldwork, scholarships/grants, unspecified assistantships, and resident hall director and student payroll positions available. Support available to part-time students. Financial award application deadline: 3/1; financial award applicants required to submit FAFSA. In 2018, 364 master's, 2 doctorates, 8 other advanced degrees awarded. *Program availability:* Part-time, evening/weekend, 100% online, blended/hybrid learning. *Application deadline:* For fall admission, 4/30 for international students; for spring admission, 9/30 for international students. Applications are processed on a rolling basis. *Application fee:* $45. Electronic applications accepted. *Application Contact:* Maya T. Mapp, Director of Admissions, 717-477-1231, Fax: 717-477-4016, E-mail: mtmapp@ship.edu. *Associate Provost and Dean of Graduate Studies,* Dr. Tracy A. Schoolcraft, 717-477-1148, Fax: 717-477-4038, E-mail: tascho@ship.edu.

College of Arts and Sciences Students: 70 full-time (37 women), 85 part-time (48 women); includes 26 minority (14 Black or African American, non-Hispanic/Latino; 1 Asian, non-Hispanic/Latino; 7 Hispanic/Latino; 4 Two or more races, non-Hispanic/Latino), 15 international. Average age 29. 181 applicants, 76% accepted, 67 enrolled. *Faculty:* 67 full-time (27 women), 2 part-time/adjunct (1 woman). Expenses: Contact institution. *Financial support:* In 2018–19, 69 students received support. Career-related internships or fieldwork, scholarships/grants, unspecified assistantships, and resident hall director and student payroll positions available. Support available to part-time students. Financial award application deadline: 3/1; financial award applicants required to submit FAFSA. In 2018, 95 master's awarded. *Program availability:* Part-time, evening/weekend. Offers agile software engineering (Certificate); applied history (MA); arts and sciences (MA, MPA, MS, Certificate); biology (MS); communication studies (MS); computer science (MS); geoenvironmental studies (MS); IT leadership (Certificate); organizational development and leadership (MS); psychological science (MS); public administration (MPA). *Application deadline:* For fall admission, 4/30 for international students; for spring admission, 9/30 for international students. Applications are processed on a rolling basis. *Application fee:* $45. Electronic applications accepted. *Application Contact:* Maya T. Mapp, Director of Admissions, 717-477-1231, Fax: 717-477-4016, E-mail: mtmapp@ship.edu. *Dean,* Dr. James H. Mike, 717-477-1151, Fax: 717-477-4026, E-mail: jhmike@ship.edu.

College of Education and Human Services Students: 150 full-time (123 women), 259 part-time (190 women); includes 62 minority (30 Black or African American, non-Hispanic/Latino; 4 Asian, non-Hispanic/Latino; 19 Hispanic/Latino; 9 Two or more races, non-Hispanic/Latino), 9 international. Average age 31. 376 applicants, 60% accepted, 156 enrolled. *Faculty:* 40 full-time (22 women), 17 part-time/adjunct (12 women). Expenses: Contact institution. *Financial support:* In 2018–19, 74 students received support. Career-related internships or fieldwork, scholarships/grants, unspecified assistantships, and resident hall director and student payroll positions available. Support available to part-time students. Financial award application deadline: 3/1; financial award applicants required to submit FAFSA. In 2018, 165 master's, 2 doctorates awarded. *Program availability:* Part-time, evening/weekend, 100% online, blended/hybrid learning. Offers college counseling (MS); college student personnel (MS); counselor education and supervision (Ed D); criminal justice (MS); curriculum and instruction (M Ed); education and human services (M Ed, MAT, MS, MSW, Ed D); educational leadership (M Ed, Ed D); mental health counseling (MS); reading (M Ed); school counseling (M Ed); social work (MSW); special education (M Ed); STEM education (MAT). *Application deadline:* For fall admission, 4/30 for international students; for spring admission, 9/30 for international students. Applications are processed on a rolling basis. *Application fee:* $45. Electronic applications accepted. *Application Contact:* Maya T. Mapp, Director of Admissions, 717-477-1231, Fax: 717-477-4016, E-mail: mtmapp@ship.edu. *Dean of the College of Education and Human Services,* Dr. Nicole R. Hill, 717-477-1373, Fax: 717-477-4012, E-mail: nrhill@ship.edu.

John L. Grove College of Business Students: 31 full-time (14 women), 174 part-time (67 women); includes 33 minority (17 Black or African American, non-Hispanic/Latino; 6 Asian, non-Hispanic/Latino; 7 Hispanic/Latino; 3 Two or more races, non-Hispanic/Latino), 13 international. Average age 33. 149 applicants, 61% accepted, 60 enrolled. *Faculty:* 20 full-time (4 women), 2 part-time/adjunct (0 women). Expenses: Contact institution. *Financial support:* In 2018–19, 15 students received support. Career-related internships or fieldwork, scholarships/grants, unspecified assistantships, and resident hall director and student payroll positions available. Support available to part-time students. Financial award application deadline: 3/1; financial award applicants required to submit FAFSA. In 2018, 104 master's, 1 other advanced degree awarded. *Program availability:* Part-time, evening/weekend, 100% online, blended/hybrid learning. Offers advanced studies in business (Certificate); advanced supply chain and logistics management (Certificate); business administration (MBA, DBA); finance (Certificate); health care management

(Certificate); management information systems (Certificate). *Application deadline:* For fall admission, 4/30 for international students; for spring admission, 9/30 for international students. Applications are processed on a rolling basis. *Application fee:* $45. Electronic applications accepted. *Application Contact:* Maya T. Mapp, Director of Admissions, 717-477-1231, Fax: 717-477-4016, E-mail: mtmapp@ship.edu. *Dean of the College of Business,* Dr. John G. Kooti, 717-477-1435, Fax: 717-477-4003, E-mail: jgkooti@ship.edu.

SHORTER UNIVERSITY, Rome, GA 30165
General Information Independent-religious, coed, comprehensive institution. *Graduate housing:* Room and/or apartments available on a first-come, first-served basis to single students; on-campus housing not available to married students. Housing application deadline: 3/30.

GRADUATE UNITS

Professional Studies *Program availability:* Evening/weekend. Offers accountancy (MAC); business administration (MBA); management (MM). Electronic applications accepted.

SH'OR YOSHUV RABBINICAL COLLEGE, Lawrence, NY 11559-1714
General Information Independent-religious, men only, comprehensive institution.

GRADUATE UNITS
Graduate Programs

SIENA COLLEGE, Loudonville, NY 12211-1462
General Information Independent-religious, coed, comprehensive institution. *Graduate housing:* On-campus housing not available.

GRADUATE UNITS

School of Business *Program availability:* Evening/weekend. Offers accounting (MS).

SIENA HEIGHTS UNIVERSITY, Adrian, MI 49221-1796
General Information Independent-religious, coed, comprehensive institution. *Enrollment:* 34 full-time matriculated graduate/professional students (20 women), 183 part-time matriculated graduate/professional students (126 women). *Enrollment by degree level:* 217 master's. *Graduate faculty:* 10 full-time (6 women), 16 part-time/adjunct (10 women). *Tuition:* Full-time $11,340; part-time $7560 per year. *Required fees:* $454; $454 per unit. $227 per semester. One-time fee: $100. Tuition and fees vary according to program. *Graduate housing:* Room and/or apartments available on a first-come, first-served basis to single and married students. Typical cost: $10,620 (including board) for single students; $10,620 (including board) for married students. Room and board charges vary according to housing facility selected. Housing application deadline: 5/1. *Student services:* Campus employment opportunities, campus safety program, career counseling, free psychological counseling, international student services, low-cost health insurance, multicultural affairs office, services for students with disabilities, teacher training, writing training. *Library facilities:* Siena Heights University Library plus 1 other.
Computer facilities: 180 computers available on campus for general student use. A campuswide network can be accessed from student residence rooms and from off campus. Online class registration is available.
Website: http://www.sienaheights.edu/
General Application Contact: Elizabeth Brooks, Assistant Director, 517-264-7662, Fax: 517-264-7165, E-mail: ebrooks@sienaheights.edu.

GRADUATE UNITS

Graduate College Students: 34 full-time (20 women), 183 part-time (126 women); includes 64 minority (38 Black or African American, non-Hispanic/Latino; 2 American Indian or Alaska Native, non-Hispanic/Latino; 4 Asian, non-Hispanic/Latino; 14 Hispanic/Latino; 6 Two or more races, non-Hispanic/Latino). Average age 36. 97 applicants, 41% accepted, 30 enrolled. *Faculty:* 10 full-time (6 women), 16 part-time/adjunct (6 women). Expenses: Contact institution. *Financial support:* In 2018–19, 55 students received support. Scholarships/grants, tuition waivers (full and partial), unspecified assistantships, and State of Michigan Scholarships/Grants available. Support available to part-time students. Financial award application deadline: 9/1; financial award applicants required to submit FAFSA. In 2018, 72 master's awarded. *Program availability:* Part-time, evening/weekend. Offers clinical mental health counseling (MA); educational leadership (Specialist); leadership (MA); teacher education (MA). *Application deadline:* Applications are processed on a rolling basis. *Application fee:* $50. Electronic applications accepted. *Application Contact:* Elizabeth Brooks, Assistant Director, 517-264-7662, Fax: 517-264-7714, E-mail: ebrooks@sienaheights.edu. *Dean, College for Professional Studies and Graduate College,* Dr. Cheryl Betz, 517-264-7234, Fax: 517-264-7714, E-mail: cbetz@sienaheights.edu.

SIERRA NEVADA COLLEGE, Incline Village, NV 89451
General Information Independent, coed, comprehensive institution. *Graduate housing:* On-campus housing not available.

GRADUATE UNITS

Teacher Education Program *Program availability:* Part-time, evening/weekend, online learning. Offers advanced teaching and leadership (M Ed); elementary education (MAT); secondary education (MAT). Electronic applications accepted.

SILVER LAKE COLLEGE OF THE HOLY FAMILY, Manitowoc, WI 54220-9319
General Information Independent-religious, coed, comprehensive institution. *Graduate housing:* Room and/or apartments guaranteed to single students; on-campus housing not available to married students. Housing application deadline: 6/1.

GRADUATE UNITS

Graduate School *Program availability:* Part-time. Offers administrative leadership (MA Ed); leadership and organizational development (MS); music education-Kodaly emphasis (MM); teacher leadership (MA Ed). Electronic applications accepted.

SIMMONS UNIVERSITY, Boston, MA 02115
General Information Independent, Undergraduate: women only; graduate: coed, university. *Enrollment:* 1,488 full-time matriculated graduate/professional students (1,275 women), 2,785 part-time matriculated graduate/professional students (2,462 women). *Enrollment by degree level:* 3,987 master's, 204 doctoral, 82 other advanced degrees. *Graduate faculty:* 137 full-time (106 women), 599 part-time/adjunct (536 women). *Tuition:* Full-time $21,726; part-time $1207 per credit hour. *Required fees:* $168; $168 per unit. *Graduate housing:* Room and/or apartments available on a first-come, first-served basis to single students; on-campus housing not available to married students. Housing application deadline: 3/31. *Student services:* Campus employment opportunities, campus safety program, career counseling, exercise/wellness program, free psychological counseling, grant writing training, international student services, low-cost health insurance, multicultural affairs office, services for students with disabilities, writing training. *Library facilities:* Beatley Library. *Collection:* Books: 154,852 (physical), 37,362 (digital/electronic); Serial titles: 13 (physical), 278,000 (digital/electronic); Databases: 137. Weekly public service hours: 105; students can reserve study rooms.
Computer facilities: Computer purchase and lease plans are available. 570 computers available on campus for general student use. A campuswide network can be accessed from student residence rooms and from off campus. Online class registration is available.
Website: http://www.simmons.edu/
General Application Contact: Kristen Haack, Associate Vice President, Enrollment Management, 617-521-2917, Fax: 617-521-3058, E-mail: kristen.haack@simmons.edu.

GRADUATE UNITS

College of Natural, Behavioral, and Health Sciences Students: 363 full-time (318 women), 1,578 part-time (1,428 women); includes 385 minority (140 Black or African American, non-Hispanic/Latino; 4 American Indian or Alaska Native, non-Hispanic/Latino; 95 Asian, non-Hispanic/Latino; 107 Hispanic/Latino; 4 Native Hawaiian or other Pacific Islander, non-Hispanic/Latino; 35 Two or more races, non-Hispanic/Latino; 20 international. Average age 32. 1,304 applicants, 64% accepted, 512 enrolled. *Faculty:* 39 full-time (31 women), 311 part-time/adjunct (285 women). Expenses: Contact institution. *Financial support:* In 2018–19, 24 students received support, including 21 fellowships (averaging $4,650 per year), 3 teaching assistantships (averaging $2,000 per year); scholarships/grants also available. Financial award applicants required to submit FAFSA. In 2018, 423 master's, 39 doctorates awarded. *Program availability:* Part-time, 100% online, blended/hybrid learning. Offers nursing (MS, MSN); nursing practice (DNP). *Application deadline:* For fall admission, 6/1 for international students. *Application fee:* $50. Electronic applications accepted. *Application Contact:* Brett DiMarzo, Director of Graduate Admission, 617-521-2651, Fax: 617-521-3137, E-mail: brett.dimarzo@simmons.edu. *Dean,* Dr. Lepaine Sharp-McHenry.

College of Organizational, Computational, and Information Sciences Students: 315 full-time (263 women), 473 part-time (406 women); includes 102 minority (12 Black or African American, non-Hispanic/Latino; 20 Asian, non-Hispanic/Latino; 42 Hispanic/Latino; 28 Two or more races, non-Hispanic/Latino), 12 international. Average age 31. 493 applicants, 87% accepted, 240 enrolled. *Faculty:* 32 full-time (22 women), 38 part-time/adjunct (30 women). Expenses: Contact institution. *Financial support:* In 2018–19, 16 students received support, including 5 fellowships (averaging $22,000 per year), 11 teaching assistantships (averaging $19,500 per year); scholarships/grants also available. Financial award applicants required to submit FAFSA. In 2018, 740 master's awarded. *Program availability:* Part-time, 100% online, blended/hybrid learning. Offers business administration (MBA); health care (MBA). *Application deadline:* For fall admission, 7/18 priority date for domestic students; for summer admission, 4/24 priority date for domestic students. Applications are processed on a rolling basis. *Application fee:* $75. Electronic applications accepted. *Application Contact:* Kate Benson, Director, Library Science Admission Office, 617-5212801, E-mail: kate.benson@simmons.edu. *Dean,* Dr. Marie desJardins, E-mail: marie.desjardins@simmons.edu.

College of Social Sciences, Policy, and Practice Students: 805 full-time (689 women), 663 part-time (566 women); includes 412 minority (205 Black or African American, non-Hispanic/Latino; 1 American Indian or Alaska Native, non-Hispanic/Latino; 40 Asian, non-Hispanic/Latino; 125 Hispanic/Latino; 2 Native Hawaiian or other Pacific Islander, non-Hispanic/Latino; 39 Two or more races, non-Hispanic/Latino), 6 international. Average age 31. 1,382 applicants, 71% accepted, 457 enrolled. *Faculty:* 50 full-time (40 women), 246 part-time/adjunct (218 women). Expenses: Contact institution. *Financial support:* In 2018–19, 14 students received support, including 12 fellowships (averaging $2,400 per year), 2 teaching assistantships (averaging $2,000 per year); scholarships/grants also available. Support available to part-time students. Financial award applicants required to submit FAFSA. In 2018, 597 master's, 4 doctorates awarded. *Program availability:* Part-time, 100% online, blended/hybrid learning. Offers social work (MSW, PhD). *Application deadline:* For fall admission, 8/1 for domestic students; for spring admission, 12/15 for domestic students; for summer admission, 5/1 for domestic students. Applications are processed on a rolling basis. *Application fee:* $35. Electronic applications accepted. *Application Contact:* Carlos D. Frontado, Director of Admissions, 617-521-3920, Fax: 617-521-3980, E-mail: ssw@simmons.edu. *Dean,* Dr. Stephanie Berzin, 617-521-2759, E-mail: stephanie.berzin@simmons.edu.

Gwen Ifill College of Media, Arts, and Humanities Students: 5 full-time (all women), 70 part-time (61 women); includes 12 minority (2 Black or African American, non-Hispanic/Latino; 4 Asian, non-Hispanic/Latino; 4 Hispanic/Latino; 2 Two or more races, non-Hispanic/Latino). Average age 29. 84 applicants, 79% accepted, 32 enrolled. *Faculty:* 16 full-time (13 women), 4 part-time/adjunct (3 women). Expenses: Contact institution. *Financial support:* In 2018–19, 14 students received support, including 1 fellowship (averaging $15,360 per year), 13 teaching assistantships (averaging $2,000 per year); scholarships/grants also available. Financial award applicants required to submit FAFSA. In 2018, 24 master's awarded. *Program availability:* Part-time. Offers behavior analysis (MS, PhD, Ed S); children's literature (MA); dietetics (Certificate); elementary education (MAT); English (MA); gender/cultural studies (MA); history (MA); nutrition and health promotion (MS); physical therapy (DPT); public health (MPH); public policy (MPP); special education: moderate and severe disabilities (MS Ed); sports nutrition (Certificate); writing for children (MFA). *Application deadline:* For fall admission, 8/1 for domestic and international students; for spring admission, 12/15 for domestic and international students; for summer admission, 5/1 for domestic and international students. Applications are processed on a rolling basis. *Application fee:* $35. Electronic applications accepted. *Application Contact:* Patricia Flaherty, Director, Graduate Studies Admission, 617-521-3902, Fax: 617-521-3058, E-mail: gsa@simmons.edu. *Dean,* Dr. Brian Norman, 617-521-2472, E-mail: brian.norman@simmons.edu.

SIMON FRASER UNIVERSITY, Burnaby, BC V5A 1S6, Canada
General Information Province-supported, coed, university. *Graduate housing:* Room and/or apartments available on a first-come, first-served basis to single students; on-campus housing not available to married students. Housing application deadline: 12/1. *Research affiliation:* BC Cancer Agency (health sciences, biomedical sciences, physiology, kinesiology), TRIUMF (physics), Ballard Power Systems (mechatronics), Bamfield Marine Research Station (marine biology, ecology, archaeology).

GRADUATE UNITS

Office of Graduate Studies and Postdoctoral Fellows *Program availability:* Part-time, evening/weekend, online learning. Electronic applications accepted.

Faculty of Applied Sciences Offers applied sciences (M Eng, M Sc, MA Sc, PhD, Graduate Certificate); computing science (M Sc, PhD); engineering science (M Eng, MA Sc, PhD); mechatronic systems engineering (MA Sc, PhD). Electronic applications accepted.

Faculty of Arts and Social Sciences *Program availability:* Part-time, evening/weekend. Offers anthropology (MA, PhD); applied legal studies (MA); arts and social sciences (M Pub, M Sc, M Urb, MA, MALS, MPP, PhD, Graduate Certificate, Graduate Diploma); criminology (MA, PhD); economics (MA, PhD); English (MA, PhD); French (MA); gender, sexuality and women's studies (MA, PhD); gerontology (MA, PhD); history (MA, PhD); humanities (MA); international studies (MA); Latin American studies (MA, Graduate Certificate); liberal studies (MALS); linguistics (MA, PhD); philosophy (MA, PhD); political science (MA, PhD); psychology (MA, PhD); public policy (MPP); sociology (MA, PhD); teachers of English (MA); urban studies (M Urb, Graduate Diploma). Electronic applications accepted.

Faculty of Business Administration *Program availability:* Online learning. Offers business administration (EMBA, PhD, Graduate Diploma); finance (M Sc); management of technology (MBA); management of technology/biotechnology (MBA).

Faculty of Communication, Art and Technology Offers communication (MA, PhD); communication, art and technology (M Pub, M Sc, MA, MFA, PhD); contemporary arts (MA, MFA); interactive arts and technology (M Sc, MA, PhD); publishing (M Pub).

Faculty of Education Offers arts education (M Ed, MA, Ed D, PhD); counseling psychology (M Ed, MA); curriculum and instruction (M Ed); curriculum and instruction foundations (M Ed, MA); curriculum theory and implementation (PhD); education (M Ed, M Sc, MA, Ed D, PhD, Graduate Diploma); educational leadership (M Ed, MA, Ed D); educational practice (M Ed); educational psychology (M Ed, MA, PhD); educational technology and learning design (M Ed, MA, PhD); languages, cultures, and literacies (PhD); mathematics education (PhD); philosophy of education (PhD); secondary mathematics education (M Ed, M Sc); teaching English as a second/foreign language (M Ed). Electronic applications accepted.

Faculty of Environment Offers archaeology (MA, PhD); environment (M Sc, MA, MRM, PhD, Graduate Diploma); geography (M Sc, MA, PhD); quantitative methods in fisheries management (Graduate Diploma); resource and environmental management (MRM, PhD); resource and environmental planning (MRM).

Faculty of Health Sciences Offers global health (Graduate Diploma); health sciences (M Sc, PhD); public health (MPH). Electronic applications accepted.

Faculty of Science Offers actuarial science (M Sc); applied and computational mathematics (M Sc, PhD); bioinformatics (Graduate Diploma); biological sciences (M Sc, PhD); biomedical physiology and kinesiology (M Sc, PhD); chemistry (M Sc, PhD); earth sciences (M Sc, PhD); environmental toxicology (MET); mathematics (M Sc, PhD); molecular biology and biochemistry (M Sc, PhD); operations research (M Sc, PhD); pest management (MPM); physics (M Sc, PhD); science (M Sc, MET, MPM, PhD, Graduate Diploma); statistics (M Sc, PhD). Electronic applications accepted.

SIMPSON COLLEGE, Indianola, IA 50125-1297

General Information Independent-religious, coed, comprehensive institution.

GRADUATE UNITS

Department of Education Offers secondary education (MAT).

Department of Social Sciences *Program availability:* Evening/weekend. Offers criminal justice (MACJ).

SIMPSON UNIVERSITY, Redding, CA 96003-8606

General Information Independent-religious, coed, comprehensive institution. *Graduate housing:* On-campus housing not available.

GRADUATE UNITS

A.W. Tozer Theological Seminary *Program availability:* Part-time, evening/weekend, 100% online, blended/hybrid learning. Offers ministry leadership (MA). Electronic applications accepted.

School of Education *Program availability:* Part-time, evening/weekend. Offers education (MA); education and preliminary administrative services credential (MA); education and preliminary teaching credential (MA); teaching (MA). Electronic applications accepted.

School of Graduate Studies *Program availability:* Evening/weekend, 100% online, blended/hybrid learning. Offers counseling psychology (MA); organizational leadership (MA). Electronic applications accepted.

SINTE GLESKA UNIVERSITY, Mission, SD 57555

General Information Independent, coed, comprehensive institution. *Graduate housing:* Rooms and/or apartments available on a first-come, first-served basis to single and married students.

GRADUATE UNITS

Graduate Education Program *Program availability:* Part-time, evening/weekend. Offers elementary education (M Ed).

SIOUX FALLS SEMINARY, Sioux Falls, SD 57105-1599

General Information Independent-religious, coed, graduate-only institution. *Graduate housing:* On-campus housing not available.

GRADUATE UNITS

Graduate and Professional Programs *Program availability:* Part-time. Offers Bible and theology (MA); Christian leadership (MA); counseling (MA); marriage and family therapy (M Div); ministry (D Min); pastoral care and counseling (M Div); theological studies (Certificate).

SIT GRADUATE INSTITUTE, Brattleboro, VT 05302-0676

General Information Independent, coed, graduate-only institution. *Graduate housing:* Rooms and/or apartments available on a first-come, first-served basis to single and married students. Housing application deadline: 7/1.

GRADUATE UNITS

Graduate Programs *Program availability:* Part-time, online learning. Offers climate change and global sustainability (MA); global leadership and social innovation (MA); global youth development and leadership (M Ed); intercultural service, leadership, and management (self-designed) (MA); international education (MA); peace and justice leadership (MA); sustainable development (MA); teaching English as a second language (MAT). Electronic applications accepted.

SITTING BULL COLLEGE, Fort Yates, ND 58538-9701

General Information Independent, coed, comprehensive institution. *Graduate housing:* Rooms and/or apartments available on a first-come, first-served basis to single and married students. Housing application deadline: 4/30.

GRADUATE UNITS

Graduate Programs Offers curriculum and instruction (M Ed); environmental science (MS).

SLIPPERY ROCK UNIVERSITY OF PENNSYLVANIA, Slippery Rock, PA 16057-1383

General Information State-supported, coed, university. *Enrollment:* 553 full-time matriculated graduate/professional students (390 women), 621 part-time matriculated graduate/professional students (469 women). *Enrollment by degree level:* 957 master's, 217 doctoral. *Graduate faculty:* 84 full-time (54 women), 7 part-time/adjunct (5 women). *International tuition:* $9468 full-time. *Tuition, area resident:* Full-time $9288; part-time $6192 per credit hour. Tuition, state resident: full-time $9288; part-time $6192 per credit hour. Tuition, nonresident: full-time $9468; part-time $6312 per credit hour. *Required fees:* $105.40; $105.40 per credit hour. $1264.80 per semester. Tuition and fees vary according to course load, degree level and program. *Graduate housing:* Room and/or apartments available on a first-come, first-served basis to single students; on-campus housing not available to married students. Typical cost: $6880 per year ($10,530 including board). Room and board charges vary according to board plan and housing facility selected. Housing application deadline: 6/1. *Student services:* Campus employment opportunities, campus safety program, career counseling, child daycare facilities, exercise/wellness program, free psychological counseling, international student services, multicultural affairs office, services for students with disabilities, writing training. *Library facilities:* Bailey Library. *Collection:* Books: 282,009 (physical), 286,118 (digital/electronic); Serial titles: 248 (physical), 49,191 (digital/electronic); Databases: 134. Weekly public service hours: 98; students can reserve study rooms.

Computer facilities: Computer purchase and lease plans are available. 1,654 computers available on campus for general student use. A campuswide network can be accessed from student residence rooms and from off campus. Online class registration is available.
Website: http://www.sru.edu/

General Application Contact: Brandi Weber-Mortimer, Director of Graduate Admissions, 724-738-2051, Fax: 724-738-2146, E-mail: graduate.admissions@sru.edu.

GRADUATE UNITS

Graduate Studies (Recruitment) Students: 553 full-time (390 women), 621 part-time (469 women); includes 84 minority (33 Black or African American, non-Hispanic/Latino; 2 American Indian or Alaska Native, non-Hispanic/Latino; 15 Asian, non-Hispanic/Latino; 20 Hispanic/Latino; 14 Two or more races, non-Hispanic/Latino), 5 international. Average age 29. 1,752 applicants, 51% accepted, 490 enrolled. *Faculty:* 101 full-time (55 women), 16 part-time/adjunct (12 women). Expenses: Contact institution. *Financial support:* In 2018–19, 169 students received support. Career-related internships or fieldwork, Federal Work-Study, institutionally sponsored loans, scholarships/grants, tuition waivers (partial), and unspecified assistantships available. Support available to part-time students. Financial award application deadline: 5/1; financial award applicants required to submit FAFSA. In 2018, 435 master's, 66 doctorates awarded. *Program availability:* Part-time, evening/weekend, 100% online, blended/hybrid learning. *Application deadline:* For fall admission, 1/15 priority date for domestic and international students; for spring admission, 10/1 priority date for domestic students, 9/1 priority date for international students. Applications are processed on a rolling basis. *Application fee:* $25 ($30 for international students). Electronic applications accepted. *Application Contact:* Brandi Weber-Mortimer, Director of Graduate Admissions, 724-738-4340, Fax: 724-738-2146, E-mail: graduate.admissions@sru.edu. *Director of Graduate Admissions,* Brandi Weber-Mortimer, 724-738-4340, Fax: 724-738-2146, E-mail: graduate.admissions@sru.edu.

College of Business Students: 21 full-time (8 women), 22 part-time (15 women); includes 3 minority (1 Black or African American, non-Hispanic/Latino; 1 Asian, non-Hispanic/Latino; 1 Hispanic/Latino). Average age 29. 53 applicants, 62% accepted, 23 enrolled. *Faculty:* 12 full-time (7 women), 1 part-time/adjunct (0 women). Expenses: Contact institution. *Financial support:* In 2018–19, 9 students received support. Career-related internships or fieldwork, Federal Work-Study, institutionally sponsored loans, scholarships/grants, tuition waivers (partial), and unspecified assistantships available. Support available to part-time students. Financial award application deadline: 5/1; financial award applicants required to submit FAFSA. In 2018, 23 master's awarded. *Program availability:* Part-time, evening/weekend. Offers accounting/finance (MBA); business (MBA); general (MBA); marketing/management (MBA). *Application deadline:* For fall admission, 3/1 priority date for domestic students, 5/1 priority date for international students; for spring admission, 10/1 priority date for domestic students, 9/1 priority date for international students. Applications are processed on a rolling basis. *Application fee:* $25 ($30 for international students). Electronic applications accepted. *Application Contact:* Brandi Weber-Mortimer, Director of Graduate Admissions, 724-738-2051, Fax: 724-738-2146, E-mail: graduate.admissions@sru.edu. *Dean,* Dr. Lawrence Shao, 724-738-2687, Fax: 724-738-4767, E-mail: lawrence.shao@sru.edu.

College of Education Students: 186 full-time (141 women), 397 part-time (328 women); includes 31 minority (12 Black or African American, non-Hispanic/Latino; 1 American Indian or Alaska Native, non-Hispanic/Latino; 3 Asian, non-Hispanic/Latino; 9 Hispanic/Latino; 6 Two or more races, non-Hispanic/Latino), 3 international. Average age 30. 510 applicants, 76% accepted, 223 enrolled. *Faculty:* 101 full-time (55 women), 16 part-time/adjunct (12 women). Expenses: Contact institution. *Financial support:* In 2018–19, 91 students received support. Career-related internships or fieldwork, Federal Work-Study, institutionally sponsored loans, scholarships/grants, tuition waivers (partial), and unspecified assistantships available. Support available to part-time students. Financial award application deadline: 5/1; financial award applicants required to submit FAFSA. In 2018, 231 master's, 12 doctorates awarded. *Program availability:* Part-time, evening/weekend, 100% online. Offers adapted physical activity (MS); autism (M Ed); clinical mental health (MA); education (M Ed, MA, MS, Ed D); instructional coach (M Ed); K-12 reading (M Ed); K-12 science and math (M Ed); master teacher (M Ed); reading specialist (M Ed); school counseling (M Ed); secondary education (M Ed); special education (Ed D); student affairs in higher education (MA); student affairs in higher education with college counseling (MA); supervision (M Ed); technology for online instruction (M Ed). *Application deadline:* For fall admission, 3/1 priority date for domestic students, 5/1 priority date for international students; for spring admission, 10/1 priority date for domestic students, 9/1 priority date for international students. Applications are processed on a rolling basis. *Application fee:* $25 ($30 for international students). Electronic applications accepted. *Application Contact:* Brandi Weber-Mortimer, Director of Graduate Admissions, 724-738-2051, Fax: 724-738-2146, E-mail: graduate.admissions@sru.edu. *Dean,* Dr. A. Keith Dils, 724-738-2007, Fax: 724-738-2880, E-mail: keith.dils@sru.edu.

College of Health, Environment, and Science Students: 313 full-time (222 women), 113 part-time (68 women); includes 38 minority (14 Black or African American, non-Hispanic/Latino; 10 Asian, non-Hispanic/Latino; 7 Hispanic/Latino; 7 Two or more races, non-Hispanic/Latino), 2 international. Average age 27. 1,027 applicants, 37% accepted, 186 enrolled. *Faculty:* 101 full-time (55 women), 16 part-time/adjunct (12 women). Expenses: Contact institution. *Financial support:* In 2018–19, 57 students received support. Career-related internships or fieldwork, Federal Work-Study, institutionally sponsored loans, scholarships/grants, tuition waivers (partial), and unspecified assistantships available. Support available to part-time students. Financial award application deadline: 5/1; financial award applicants required to submit FAFSA. In 2018, 112 master's, 54 doctorates awarded. *Program availability:* Part-time, evening/weekend, 100% online. Offers data analytics (MS); environmental education (M Ed); health informatics (MS); health, environment, and science (M Ed, MPH, MS, DPT); park and resource management (MS); physical therapy (DPT); physician assistant studies (MS); public health (MPH). *Application deadline:* For fall admission, 3/1 priority date for domestic students, 5/1 priority date for international students; for spring admission, 10/1 priority date for domestic students, 9/1 priority date for international students. Applications are processed on a rolling basis. *Application fee:* $25 ($30 for international students). Electronic applications accepted. *Application Contact:* Brandi Weber-Mortimer, Director of Graduate Admissions, 724-738-2051, Fax: 724-738-2146, E-mail: graduate.admissions@sru.edu. *Interim Dean,* Dr. Jerry Chmielewski, 724-738-2489, Fax: 724-738-2881, E-mail: jerry.chmielewski@sru.edu.

College of Liberal Arts Students: 33 full-time (19 women), 89 part-time (58 women); includes 12 minority (6 Black or African American, non-Hispanic/Latino; 1 American Indian or Alaska Native, non-Hispanic/Latino; 1 Asian, non-Hispanic/Latino; 3 Hispanic/Latino; 1 Two or more races, non-Hispanic/Latino). Average age 33. 140 applicants, 62% accepted, 58 enrolled. *Faculty:* 16 full-time (12 women), 101 part-time/adjunct (55 women). Expenses: Contact institution. *Financial support:* In 2018–19, 10 students received support. Career-related internships or fieldwork, Federal Work-Study, institutionally sponsored loans, scholarships/grants, tuition waivers (partial), and unspecified assistantships available. Support available to part-time students. Financial award application deadline: 5/1; financial award applicants required to submit FAFSA. In 2018, 42 master's awarded. *Program availability:* Part-time, evening/weekend, online only, 100% online. Offers criminal justice (MA); English (MA); history (MA); liberal arts (MA, MMT); music therapy (MMT); teaching English to speakers of other languages (MA). *Application deadline:* For fall admission, 3/1 priority date for domestic students, 5/1 priority date for international students; for spring admission, 10/1 priority date for domestic students, 9/1 priority date for international students. Applications are processed on a rolling basis. *Application fee:* $25 ($30 for international students). Electronic applications accepted. *Application Contact:* Brandi Weber-Mortimer, Director of Graduate Admissions, 724-738-2051, Fax: 724-738-2146, E-mail: graduate.admissions@sru.edu. *Dean,* Dr. Dan Bauer, 724-738-4262, Fax: 724-738-2188, E-mail: dan.bauer@sru.edu.

SMITH COLLEGE, Northampton, MA 01063

General Information Independent, Undergraduate: women only; graduate: coed, comprehensive institution. *Enrollment:* 378 full-time matriculated graduate/professional students (325 women), 23 part-time matriculated graduate/professional students (19 women). *Enrollment by degree level:* 336 master's, 61 doctoral, 4 other advanced degrees. *Graduate faculty:* 290 full-time (165 women), 20 part-time/adjunct (13 women). *Tuition:* Full-time $39,120; part-time $1630 per credit. Tuition and fees vary according to course load and program. *Graduate housing:* Room and/or apartments available on a first-come, first-served basis to single students; on-campus housing not available to married students. Typical cost: $8800 per year ($17,520 including board). Housing application deadline: 5/1. *Student services:* Campus safety program, career counseling, child daycare facilities, exercise/wellness program, international student services, low-cost health insurance, multicultural affairs office, services for students with disabilities, teacher training, writing training. *Library facilities:* Neilson Library.

Computer facilities: Computer purchase and lease plans are available. A campuswide network can be accessed. Online class registration is available. Website: http://www.smith.edu/

General Application Contact: Patricia DiBartolo, Dean of the Faculty/Dean for Academic Development, 413-585-3000, Fax: 413-585-3054, E-mail: pdibarto@smith.edu.

GRADUATE UNITS

Graduate and Special Programs Students: 61 full-time (48 women), 16 part-time (13 women); includes 16 minority (6 Black or African American, non-Hispanic/Latino; 5 Asian, non-Hispanic/Latino; 5 Hispanic/Latino), 3 international. Average age 26. 154 applicants, 47% accepted, 44 enrolled. *Faculty:* 276 full-time (155 women), 12 part-time/adjunct (7 women). Expenses: Contact institution. *Financial support:* In 2018–19, 73 students received support, including 6 fellowships with full tuition reimbursements available, 5 research assistantships with full tuition reimbursements available (averaging $13,850 per year), 7 teaching assistantships with full tuition reimbursements available (averaging $13,850 per year); scholarships/grants, tuition waivers (full and partial), and human resources employee benefit also available. Support available to part-time students. Financial award application deadline: 1/15; financial award applicants required to submit CSS PROFILE or FAFSA. In 2018, 43 master's, 8 other advanced degrees awarded. *Program availability:* Part-time. Offers biological sciences (MAT, MS); dance (MFA); elementary education (MAT); exercise and sport studies (MS); middle school education (MAT); secondary education (MAT); theatre (MFA); women in mathematics (Postbaccalaureate Certificate). *Application deadline:* For fall admission, 1/15 for domestic and international students; for spring admission, 12/1 for domestic students. *Application fee:* $60. *Application Contact:* Ruth Morgan, Program Coordinator, 413-585-3050, Fax: 413-585-3054, E-mail: gradstdy@smith.edu. *Director,* Patricia DiBartolo, 413-585-3050, Fax: 413-585-3054, E-mail: pdibarto@smith.edu.

School for Social Work Students: 273 full-time (245 women), 50 part-time (41 women); includes 97 minority (31 Black or African American, non-Hispanic/Latino; 2 American Indian or Alaska Native, non-Hispanic/Latino; 22 Asian, non-Hispanic/Latino; 27 Hispanic/Latino; 15 Two or more races, non-Hispanic/Latino), 8 international. Average age 33. 398 applicants, 53% accepted, 114 enrolled. *Faculty:* 15 full-time (11 women), 94 part-time/adjunct (68 women). Expenses: Contact institution. *Financial support:* In 2018–19, 265 students received support. Research assistantships, career-related internships or fieldwork, and scholarships/grants available. Financial award application deadline: 3/1; financial award applicants required to submit FAFSA. In 2018, 132 master's, 6 doctorates awarded. Offers clinical social work (MSW, PhD). *Application deadline:* For fall admission, 2/21 for domestic students, 2/15 for international students. Applications are processed on a rolling basis. *Application fee:* $60. Electronic applications accepted. *Application Contact:* Irene Rodriguez Martin, Associate Dean, Graduate Enrollment and Student Services, 413-585-7960, Fax: 413-585-7994, E-mail: imartin@smith.edu. *Dean/Professor,* Dr. Marianne Yoshioka, 413-585-7977, E-mail: myoshioka@smith.edu.

SOFIA UNIVERSITY, Palo Alto, CA 94303

General Information Independent, coed, graduate-only institution. *Graduate housing:* On-campus housing not available.

GRADUATE UNITS

Hybrid: Face-to-Face/Online Programs *Program availability:* Online learning. Offers transpersonal psychology (MA, PhD). Electronic applications accepted.

Residential Programs *Program availability:* Part-time, evening/weekend. Offers clinical psychology (Psy D); computer science (MS); counseling psychology (MA); transpersonal psychology (MA, PhD). Electronic applications accepted.

SOKA UNIVERSITY OF AMERICA, Aliso Viejo, CA 92656

General Information Independent, coed, comprehensive institution. *Graduate housing:* Room and/or apartments available to single students; on-campus housing not available to married students.

GRADUATE UNITS

Graduate School *Program availability:* Evening/weekend. Offers educational leadership and societal change (MA).

SONOMA STATE UNIVERSITY, Rohnert Park, CA 94928-3609

General Information State-supported, coed, comprehensive institution. *Enrollment:* 9,201 graduate, professional, and undergraduate students; 380 full-time matriculated graduate/professional students (296 women), 256 part-time matriculated graduate/professional students (182 women). *Graduate faculty:* 56 full-time (26 women), 27 part-time/adjunct (23 women). *Graduate housing:* Room and/or apartments available on a first-come, first-served basis to single students; on-campus housing not available to married students. Housing application deadline: 1/1. *Student services:* Campus employment opportunities, career counseling, child daycare facilities, exercise/wellness program, free psychological counseling, international student services, multicultural affairs office, services for students with disabilities. *Library facilities:* Jean and Charles Schultz Information Center plus 1 other. *Collection:* Students can reserve study rooms.

Computer facilities: A campuswide network can be accessed from student residence rooms and from off campus. Online class registration is available. Website: http://www.sonoma.edu/

General Application Contact: Gillian King-Bailey, Analyst, Academic Programs, 707-664-4286, Fax: 707-664-4060, E-mail: kingbail@sonoma.edu.

GRADUATE UNITS

Department of English *Program availability:* Part-time, evening/weekend. Offers American literature (MA); creative writing (MA); English literature (MA); world literature (MA).

School of Business and Economics *Program availability:* Part-time, evening/weekend. Offers wine business (Exec MBA, MBA).

School of Education *Program availability:* Part-time, evening/weekend. Offers administrative services (Credential); curriculum, teaching, and learning (MA); early childhood education (MA); education specialist (Credential); educational leadership (MA); multiple subject (Credential); reading and literacy (MA, Credential); single subject (Credential); special education (MA).

School of Science and Technology *Program availability:* Part-time. Offers biochemistry (MA); exercise science/pre-physical therapy (MA); family nurse practitioner (MSN); interdisciplinary (MA); interdisciplinary pre-occupational therapy (MA); lifetime physical activity (MA); science and technology (MA, MS, MSN).

School of Social Sciences *Program availability:* Part-time, evening/weekend. Offers clinical mental health counseling (MA); cultural resources management (MA); history (MA); public administration (MPA); school counseling (MA); social sciences (MA, MPA, Certificate).

SOTHEBY'S INSTITUTE OF ART–LONDON, WC1B 3EE London, United Kingdom

General Information Private, coed, graduate-only institution. *Graduate housing:* On-campus housing not available. *Research affiliation:* University of Manchester.

GRADUATE UNITS

Graduate Programs Offers art business (MA); contemporary art (MA); fine and decorative art and design (MA); modern and contemporary Asian art (MA). Electronic applications accepted.

SOTHEBY'S INSTITUTE OF ART–NEW YORK, New York, NY 10021

General Information Proprietary, coed, graduate-only institution. *Graduate housing:* On-campus housing not available.

GRADUATE UNITS

Graduate Programs Offers art business (MA); contemporary art (MA); fine and decorative art and design (MA). Electronic applications accepted.

SOUTH BAYLO UNIVERSITY, Anaheim, CA 92801-1701

General Information Independent, coed, graduate-only institution. *Graduate housing:* On-campus housing not available. *Research affiliation:* University of Illinois at Chicago (testing of herbal formulations), University of California Irvine College of Medicine (complimentary and alternative medicine), National Nutritional Foods Association (herbs and nutritional supplements), Henan College of Traditional Chinese Medicine (herbology and acupuncture), Kaiser Permanente (patient care: acupuncture and Oriental medicine).

GRADUATE UNITS

Program in Oriental Medicine and Acupuncture *Program availability:* Evening/weekend. Offers Oriental medicine and acupuncture (MS). Electronic applications accepted.

SOUTH CAROLINA STATE UNIVERSITY, Orangeburg, SC 29117-0001

General Information State-supported, coed, comprehensive institution. *Enrollment:* 250 full-time matriculated graduate/professional students (190 women), 135 part-time matriculated graduate/professional students (97 women). *Enrollment by degree level:* 290 master's, 62 doctoral, 33 other advanced degrees. *Graduate faculty:* 44 full-time (23 women), 25 part-time/adjunct (14 women). *Tuition, area resident:* Full-time $9928; part-time $552 per credit hour. Tuition, state resident: full-time $9928. Tuition, nonresident: full-time $21,038; part-time $1169 per credit hour. *Required fees:* $1532; $85 per credit hour. *Graduate housing:* Room and/or apartments available on a first-come, first-served basis to single students; on-campus housing not available to married students. Typical cost: $8000 per year. Room charges vary according to board plan and housing facility selected. Housing application deadline: 7/31. *Student services:* Campus employment opportunities, career counseling, exercise/wellness program, free psychological counseling, international student services, low-cost health insurance, multicultural affairs office, services for students with disabilities, teacher training, writing training. *Library facilities:* Miller F. Whittaker Library. *Collection:* Books: 317,233 (physical), 195,578 (digital/electronic); Serial titles: 18,334 (digital/electronic); Databases: 114. Weekly public service hours: 74; students can reserve study rooms.

Computer facilities: 600 computers available on campus for general student use. A campuswide network can be accessed from student residence rooms. Online class registration is available.
Website: http://www.scsu.edu/

General Application Contact: Dr. Frederick Evans, Dean, College of Graduate and Professional Studies, 803-536-7097, Fax: 803-536-8812, E-mail: fevans6@scsu.edu.

GRADUATE UNITS

College of Graduate and Professional Studies Students: 250 full-time (190 women), 135 part-time (97 women); includes 334 minority (331 Black or African American, non-Hispanic/Latino; 3 Asian, non-Hispanic/Latino); 3 international. Average age 33. 270 applicants, 94% accepted, 124 enrolled. *Faculty:* 44 full-time (23 women), 25 part-time/adjunct (14 women). Expenses: Contact institution. *Financial support:* Fellowships, career-related internships or fieldwork, Federal Work-Study, scholarships/grants, and unspecified assistantships available. Financial award application deadline: 6/1. In 2018, 83 master's, 11 doctorates, 11 other advanced degrees awarded. *Program availability:* Part-time, evening/weekend. Offers counselor education (M Ed); early childhood education (MAT); education (M Ed); elementary education (M Ed, MAT); English (MAT); general science/biology (MAT); individual and family development (MS); mathematics (MAT); nutritional sciences (MS); rehabilitation counseling (MA); secondary education (M Ed); special education (M Ed); speech pathology and audiology (MA); transportation (MS). *Application deadline:* For fall admission, 6/15 for domestic and international students; for spring admission, 11/1 for domestic and international students. *Application fee:* $25. Electronic applications accepted. *Application Contact:* Curtis Foskey, Coordinator of Graduate Admission, 803-536-8419, Fax: 803-536-8812, E-mail: cfoskey@scsu.edu. *Dean, College of Graduate and Professional Studies,* Dr. Frederick Evans, 803-536-7097, Fax: 803-536-8812, E-mail: fevans6@scsu.edu.

Department of Business Administration Students: 20 full-time (9 women), 6 part-time (2 women); all minorities (all Black or African American, non-Hispanic/Latino). Average age 28. 12 applicants, 92% accepted, 9 enrolled. *Faculty:* 7 full-time (2 women). Expenses: Contact institution. *Financial support:* Fellowships, research assistantships, career-related internships or fieldwork, Federal Work-Study, scholarships/grants, and unspecified assistantships available. Financial award application deadline: 6/1. In 2018, 14 master's awarded. *Program availability:* Part-time, evening/weekend. Offers agribusiness (MBA); entrepreneurship (MBA); general business administration (MBA); healthcare management (MBA). *Application deadline:* For fall admission, 6/15 for domestic and international students; for spring admission, 11/1 for domestic and international students. *Application fee:* $25. Electronic applications accepted. *Application Contact:* Ellen R. Ricoma, MBA Program Director, 803-533-3777, Fax: 803-516-4651, E-mail: ericoma1@scsu.edu. *Interim Chair,* Dr. David Jamison, 803-536-8443, Fax: 803-536-8078, E-mail: djamison@scsu.edu.

SOUTH COLLEGE, Knoxville, TN 37917

General Information Proprietary, coed, primarily women, comprehensive institution.

GRADUATE UNITS

Program in Pharmacy Offers pharmacy (Pharm D).

Program in Physician Assistant Studies Offers physician assistant studies (MHS).

SOUTH DAKOTA SCHOOL OF MINES AND TECHNOLOGY, Rapid City, SD 57701-3995

General Information State-supported, coed, university. CGS member. *Graduate housing:* Room and/or apartments available on a first-come, first-served basis to single students; on-campus housing not available to married students. *Research affiliation:* Raven Industries (composite and thin films), Black Hills Power (NDA-Lightning (experimental and data collection)), CalxAqua (filtration media), RESPEC, Inc. (mining and waste storage), HF Webster (cold spray applications), Nanofiber Sperations (cutting edge separation media composed of functionalized nanofibers).

GRADUATE UNITS

Graduate Division *Program availability:* Part-time. Offers atmospheric and environmental sciences (MS, PhD); biomedical engineering (MS, PhD); chemical and biological engineering (PhD); chemical engineering (MS); civil and environmental engineering (MS, PhD); computational sciences and robotics (MS); construction engineering management (MS); electrical engineering (MS); engineering management (MS); geology and geological engineering (MS, PhD); materials engineering and science (MS, PhD); mechanical engineering (MS, PhD); mining engineering (MS); nanoscience and nanoengineering (PhD); paleontology (MS); physics (MS, PhD). Electronic applications accepted.

College of Engineering *Program availability:* Part-time, online learning. Offers engineering (MS, PhD). Electronic applications accepted.

College of Science and Letters *Program availability:* Part-time. Offers science and letters (MS, PhD).

SOUTH DAKOTA STATE UNIVERSITY, Brookings, SD 57007

General Information State-supported, coed, university. CGS member. *Graduate housing:* Rooms and/or apartments available to single and married students.

GRADUATE UNITS

Graduate School *Program availability:* Part-time, evening/weekend, online learning. Offers geospatial science and engineering (PhD).

College of Agriculture, Food and Environmental Sciences *Program availability:* Part-time. Offers agricultural and biosystems engineering (MS, PhD); agriculture, food and environmental sciences (MS, PhD); animal science (MS, PhD); biological sciences (MS, PhD); dairy science (MS, PhD); economics (MS); food science (MS, PhD); plant science (MS, PhD); wildlife and fisheries sciences (MS, PhD).

College of Arts, Humanities and Social Sciences *Program availability:* Part-time. Offers arts, humanities and social sciences (MA, MS, PhD); communication studies and journalism (MS); English (MA); industrial/organizational psychology (MS); sociology (MS, PhD).

College of Education and Human Sciences Offers agricultural education (MS); athletic training (MS); counseling and human resource development (M Ed, MS); curriculum and instruction (M Ed); dietetics (MS); education and human sciences (M Ed, MFCS, MS, PhD); educational administration (M Ed); family financial planning (MS); human sciences (MS); merchandising (MS); nutrition and exercise sciences (MS, PhD); sport and recreation studies (MS).

College of Natural Sciences Offers biochemistry (PhD); biological sciences (MS, PhD); chemistry (MS, PhD); engineering (MS); geography (MS); natural sciences (MS, PhD).

College of Nursing *Program availability:* Part-time, evening/weekend, online learning. Offers nursing (MS, PhD).

College of Pharmacy and Allied Health Professions Offers biological science (MS); pharmaceutical sciences (PhD); pharmacy (Pharm D); pharmacy and allied health professions (MS, PhD, Pharm D).

Jerome J. Lohr College of Engineering *Program availability:* Part-time. Offers agricultural, biosystems and mechanical engineering (PhD); biological sciences (MS, PhD); computational science and statistics (PhD); electrical engineering (PhD); engineering (MS); mathematics (MS); mechanical engineering (MS); operations management (MS); statistics (MS).

SOUTHEASTERN BAPTIST THEOLOGICAL SEMINARY, Wake Forest, NC 27587

General Information Independent-religious, coed, comprehensive institution. *Graduate housing:* Rooms and/or apartments available on a first-come, first-served basis to single and married students.

GRADUATE UNITS

Graduate and Professional Programs Offers advanced biblical studies (M Div); Christian education (M Div, MACE); Christian ethics (PhD); Christian ministry (M Div); Christian planting (M Div); church music (MACM); counseling (MACO); evangelism (PhD); language (M Div); ministry (D Min); New Testament (PhD); Old Testament (PhD); philosophy (PhD); theology (Th M, PhD); women's studies (M Div).

SOUTHEASTERN LOUISIANA UNIVERSITY, Hammond, LA 70402

General Information State-supported, coed, comprehensive institution. *Enrollment:* 14,327 graduate, professional, and undergraduate students; 369 full-time matriculated graduate/professional students (249 women), 598 part-time matriculated graduate/professional students (474 women). *Enrollment by degree level:* 763 master's, 110 doctoral, 94 other advanced degrees. *Graduate faculty:* 154 full-time (83 women), 1 (woman) part-time/adjunct. *Tuition, area resident:* Full-time $6684. Tuition, state resident: full-time $6684. Tuition, nonresident: full-time $19,162. *Required fees:* $2097. *Graduate housing:* Room and/or apartments available on a first-come, first-served basis to single students; on-campus housing not available to married students. Typical cost: $4940 per year ($8420 including board). Room and board charges vary according to board plan and housing facility selected. Housing application deadline: 6/15. *Student services:* Campus employment opportunities, campus safety program, career counseling, exercise/wellness program, free psychological counseling, international student services, low-cost health insurance, multicultural affairs office, services for students with disabilities, teacher training, writing training. *Library facilities:* Linus A. Sims Memorial Library plus 1 other. *Collection:* Books: 1.3 million (physical), 428,672 (digital/electronic); Serial titles: 338 (physical), 561 (digital/electronic). Students can reserve study rooms.

Computer facilities: 1,031 computers available on campus for general student use. A campuswide network can be accessed from student residence rooms and from off campus. Online class registration, campus Webmail, student newspaper, transcripts, bookstore are available.
Website: http://www.southeastern.edu/

General Application Contact: John Boulahanis, Director of Graduate Studies, 985-549-2610, Fax: 985-549-5882, E-mail: graduatestudies@southeastern.edu.

GRADUATE UNITS

College of Arts, Humanities and Social Sciences Students: 62 full-time (33 women), 83 part-time (50 women); includes 38 minority (13 Black or African American, non-Hispanic/Latino; 1 Asian, non-Hispanic/Latino; 11 Hispanic/Latino; 1 Native Hawaiian or other Pacific Islander, non-Hispanic/Latino; 12 Two or more races, non-Hispanic/Latino), 6 international. Average age 27. 105 applicants, 66% accepted, 41 enrolled. *Faculty:* 57 full-time (25 women). Expenses: Contact institution. *Financial support:* In 2018–19, 104 students received support, including 1 fellowship with tuition reimbursement available (averaging $3,500 per year), 30 research assistantships with tuition reimbursements available (averaging $8,791 per year), 18 teaching assistantships with tuition reimbursements available (averaging $11,294 per year); career-related internships or fieldwork, institutionally sponsored loans, scholarships/grants, tuition waivers (full), and unspecified assistantships also available. Support available to part-time students. Financial award application deadline: 5/1; financial award applicants required to submit FAFSA. In 2018, 54 master's awarded. *Program availability:* Part-time, evening/weekend. Offers arts, humanities and social sciences (M Mus, MA, MS); choral conducting (M Mus); creative writing (MA); criminal justice (MS); globalization and sustainability (MS); health communications (MA); history (MA); instrumental conducting (M Mus); journalism (MA); language and literacy (MA); marketing (MA); music performance (M Mus); music theory (M Mus); professional writing (MA); psychology (MA); public relations (MA); publishing studies (MA); sociology (MA). *Application deadline:* For fall admission, 7/15 priority date for domestic students, 6/1 priority date for international students; for spring admission, 12/1 priority date for domestic students, 10/1 priority date for international students. Applications are processed on a rolling basis. *Application fee:* $20 ($30 for international students). Electronic applications accepted. *Application Contact:* Office of Admissions, 985-549-5637, Fax: 985-549-5822, E-mail: admissions@southeastern.edu. *Dean,* Dr. Karen Fontenot, 985-549-2101, Fax: 985-549-5014, E-mail: ahss@southeastern.edu.

College of Business Students: 89 full-time (39 women), 18 part-time (12 women); includes 14 minority (5 Black or African American, non-Hispanic/Latino; 7 Hispanic/Latino; 2 Two or more races, non-Hispanic/Latino), 13 international. Average age 27. 72 applicants, 44% accepted, 24 enrolled. *Faculty:* 17 full-time (3 women). Expenses: Contact institution. *Financial support:* In 2018–19, 62 students received support, including 1 fellowship with tuition reimbursement available (averaging $3,500 per year); career-related internships or fieldwork, Federal Work-Study, institutionally sponsored loans, scholarships/grants, and unspecified assistantships also available. Support available to part-time students. Financial award application deadline: 5/1; financial award applicants required to submit FAFSA. In 2018, 60 master's awarded. *Program availability:* Part-time. Offers business (MBA). *Application deadline:* For fall admission, 7/15 priority date for domestic students, 6/1 priority date for international students; for spring admission, 12/1 priority date for domestic students, 10/1 priority date for international students. Applications are processed on a rolling basis. *Application fee:* $20 ($30 for international students). Electronic applications accepted. *Application Contact:* Dr. Antoinette Phillips, Dean, 985-549-2258, Fax: 985-549-5038, E-mail: business@southeastern.edu. *Dean,* Dr. Antoinette Phillips, 985-549-2258, Fax: 985-549-5038, E-mail: business@southeastern.edu.

College of Education Students: 34 full-time (29 women), 295 part-time (246 women); includes 95 minority (74 Black or African American, non-Hispanic/Latino; 9 Hispanic/Latino; 12 Two or more races, non-Hispanic/Latino), 1 international. Average age 38. 126 applicants, 73% accepted, 70 enrolled. *Faculty:* 19 full-time (13 women). Expenses: Contact institution. *Financial support:* In 2018–19, 8 students received support, including 1 fellowship with tuition reimbursement available (averaging $3,500 per year); career-related internships or fieldwork, Federal Work-Study, institutionally sponsored loans, scholarships/grants, and unspecified assistantships also available. Support available to part-time students. Financial award application deadline: 5/1; financial award applicants required to submit FAFSA. In 2018, 33 master's, 14 doctorates awarded. *Program availability:* Part-time, evening/weekend. Offers curriculum and instruction (M Ed); education (M Ed, MAT, Ed D); educational leadership (M Ed, Ed D); elementary education (MAT); special education (M Ed); special education: early interventionist (MAT). *Application deadline:* For fall admission, 7/15 priority date for domestic students, 6/1 priority date for international students; for spring admission, 12/1 priority date for domestic students, 10/1 priority date for international students. Applications are processed on a rolling basis. *Application fee:* $20 ($30 for international students). Electronic applications accepted. *Application Contact:* Dr. Paula Calderon, Dean, 985-549-2217, Fax: 985-549-2070, E-mail: collegeofeducation@southeastern.edu. *Dean,* Dr. Paula Calderon, 985-549-2217, Fax: 985-549-2070, E-mail: collegeofeducation@southeastern.edu.

College of Nursing and Health Sciences Students: 151 full-time (132 women), 186 part-time (159 women); includes 89 minority (43 Black or African American, non-Hispanic/Latino; 2 American Indian or Alaska Native, non-Hispanic/Latino; 3 Asian, non-Hispanic/Latino; 24 Hispanic/Latino; 2 Native Hawaiian or other Pacific Islander, non-Hispanic/Latino; 15 Two or more races, non-Hispanic/Latino), 3 international. Average age 31. 271 applicants, 52% accepted, 65 enrolled. *Faculty:* 42 full-time (34 women), 1 (woman) part-time/adjunct. Expenses: Contact institution. *Financial support:* In 2018–19, 111 students received support, including 1 fellowship with tuition reimbursement available (averaging $3,500 per year), 9 research assistantships with tuition reimbursements available (averaging $10,067 per year), 4 teaching assistantships with tuition reimbursements available (averaging $21,249 per year); career-related internships or fieldwork, Federal Work-Study, institutionally sponsored loans, scholarships/grants, and unspecified assistantships also available. Support available to part-time students. Financial award application deadline: 5/1; financial award applicants required to submit FAFSA. In 2018, 110 master's, 5 doctorates awarded. *Program availability:* Part-time, evening/weekend. Offers communication sciences and disorders (MS); counseling (MS); health and kinesiology (MS); nursing and health sciences (MS, MSN, DNP). *Application deadline:* For fall admission, 7/15 priority date for domestic students, 6/1 priority date for international students; for spring admission, 12/1 priority date for domestic students, 10/1 priority date for international students. Applications are processed on a rolling basis. *Application fee:* $20 ($30 for international students). Electronic applications accepted. *Application Contact:* Office of Admissions, 985-549-5637, Fax: 985-549-5632, E-mail: admissions@southeastern.edu. *Dean,* Dr. Ann Carruth, 985-549-3772, Fax: 985-549-5179, E-mail: cnhs@southeastern.edu.

School of Nursing Students: 27 full-time (24 women), 113 part-time (97 women); includes 26 minority (16 Black or African American, non-Hispanic/Latino; 2 Asian, non-Hispanic/Latino; 6 Hispanic/Latino; 2 Two or more races, non-Hispanic/Latino). Average age 35. 57 applicants, 51% accepted, 23 enrolled. *Faculty:* 17 full-time (16 women), 1 (woman) part-time/adjunct. Expenses: Contact institution. *Financial support:* In 2018–19, 1 student received support. Federal Work-Study, institutionally sponsored loans, scholarships/grants, traineeships, tuition waivers (full), and unspecified assistantships available. Support available to part-time students. Financial award application deadline: 5/1; financial award applicants required to submit FAFSA. In 2018, 46 master's, 5 doctorates awarded. *Program availability:* Part-time. Offers nurse practitioner (DNP); nursing (MSN). *Application deadline:* For fall admission, 4/1 for domestic and international students; for spring admission, 10/1 for domestic and international students. *Application fee:* $20 ($30 for international students). Electronic applications accepted. *Application Contact:* Office of Admissions, 985-549-5637, Fax: 985-549-5632, E-mail: admissions@southeastern.edu. *Department Head, School of Nursing,* Dr. Ken Tillman, 985-549-2156, Fax: 985-549-2869, E-mail: nursing@selu.edu.

College of Science and Technology Students: 33 full-time (16 women), 7 part-time (1 woman); includes 7 minority (1 Black or African American, non-Hispanic/Latino; 5 Hispanic/Latino; 1 Two or more races, non-Hispanic/Latino). Average age 26. 32 applicants, 56% accepted, 12 enrolled. *Faculty:* 19 full-time (8 women). Expenses: Contact institution. *Financial support:* In 2018–19, 35 students received support, including 1 fellowship with tuition reimbursement available (averaging $3,500 per year), 7 research assistantships with tuition reimbursements available (averaging $18,576 per year), 9 teaching assistantships with tuition reimbursements available (averaging $16,765 per year); career-related internships or fieldwork, Federal Work-Study, institutionally sponsored loans, and unspecified assistantships also available. Support available to part-time students. Financial award application deadline: 5/1; financial award applicants required to submit FAFSA. In 2018, 14 master's awarded. *Program availability:* Part-time, evening/weekend. Offers biological sciences (MS); integrated science and technology (MS); science and technology (MS). *Application deadline:* For fall admission, 7/15 priority date for domestic students, 6/1 priority date for international students; for spring admission, 12/1 priority date for domestic students, 10/1 priority date for international students. Applications are processed on a rolling basis. *Application fee:* $20 ($30 for international students). Electronic applications accepted. *Application Contact:* Office of Admissions, 985-549-5637, Fax: 985-549-5632, E-mail: admissions@southeastern.edu. *Dean,* Dr. Daniel McCarthy, 985-549-2055, Fax: 985-549-3396, E-mail: dmccarthy@southeastern.edu.

SOUTHEASTERN OKLAHOMA STATE UNIVERSITY, Durant, OK 74701-0609

General Information State-supported, coed, comprehensive institution. *Graduate housing:* Rooms and/or apartments available on a first-come, first-served basis to single and married students. Housing application deadline: 6/15. *Research affiliation:* U.S. Department of the Interior (biological sciences), U.S. Department of Agriculture (USDA) (biological sciences), National Science Foundation (chemistry, computer science, physical sciences), U.S. Fish and Wildlife Service (biological sciences), National Institutes of Health (biological sciences, chemistry, computer science, physical sciences).

GRADUATE UNITS

Department of Aviation Science *Program availability:* Part-time, evening/weekend. Offers aerospace administration and logistics (MS). Electronic applications accepted.

John Massey School of Business *Program availability:* Part-time, evening/weekend. Offers business (MBA). Electronic applications accepted.

School of Arts and Sciences *Program availability:* Part-time, evening/weekend. Offers biology (MT); computer information systems (MT); occupational safety and health (MT). Electronic applications accepted.

School of Behavioral Sciences *Program availability:* Part-time, evening/weekend. Offers clinical mental health counseling (MS). Electronic applications accepted.

School of Education *Program availability:* Part-time, evening/weekend. Offers math specialist (M Ed); reading specialist (M Ed); school administration (M Ed); school counseling (M Ed). Electronic applications accepted.

SOUTHEASTERN UNIVERSITY, Lakeland, FL 33801-6099

General Information Independent-religious, coed, comprehensive institution. *Graduate housing:* On-campus housing not available.

GRADUATE UNITS

Barnett College of Ministry and Theology *Program availability:* Evening/weekend, online learning. Offers family ministry (MA); ministerial leadership (MA, D Min); theological studies (MA); theology (M Div). Electronic applications accepted.

College of Behavioral and Social Sciences *Program availability:* Evening/weekend. Offers human services (MA); international community development (MA); marriage and family counseling (MS); professional counseling (MS); school counseling (MS); social work (MSW). Electronic applications accepted.

College of Education Offers curriculum and instruction (Ed D); educational leadership (M Ed); elementary education (M Ed); exceptional student education (M Ed); exceptional student education/educational therapy (M Ed); kinesiology (M Ed); organizational leadership (Ed D); reading education (M Ed); teaching English to speakers of other languages (M Ed). Electronic applications accepted.

Jannetides College of Business and Entrepreneurial Leadership *Program availability:* Evening/weekend, online learning. Offers executive leadership (MBA); global business administration (MBA); healthcare administration (MBA); missional leadership (MBA); organizational leadership (PhD); sport management (MBA); strategic leadership (DSL). Electronic applications accepted.

SOUTHEAST MISSOURI STATE UNIVERSITY, Cape Girardeau, MO 63701-4799

General Information State-supported, coed, comprehensive institution. CGS member. *Enrollment:* 11,071 graduate, professional, and undergraduate students; 381 full-time matriculated graduate/professional students (236 women), 640 part-time matriculated graduate/professional students (443 women). Enrollment by degree level: 921 master's, 12 doctoral, 88 other advanced degrees. *Graduate faculty:* 196 full-time (104 women), 16 part-time/adjunct (8 women). *International tuition:* $516 full-time. *Tuition, area resident:* Full-time $277; part-time $277 per credit hour. Tuition, state resident: full-time $277; part-time $277 per credit hour. Tuition, nonresident: full-time $516; part-time $516 per credit hour. *Required fees:* $39; $39 per credit hour. One-time fee: $100. Tuition and fees vary according to degree level and program. *Graduate housing:* Room and/or apartments available on a first-come, first-served basis to single students; on-campus housing not available to married students. Typical cost: $5084 per year ($6934 including board). Room and board charges vary according to board plan, campus/location and housing facility selected. Housing application deadline: 12/1. *Student services:* Campus employment opportunities, campus safety program, career counseling, child daycare facilities, exercise/wellness program, free psychological counseling, international student services, multicultural affairs office, services for students with disabilities, teacher training, writing training. *Library facilities:* Kent Library. *Collection:* Books: 380,006 (physical), 263,780 (digital/electronic); Serial titles: 4,163 (physical), 58,594 (digital/electronic); Databases: 159. Weekly public service hours: 92.

Computer facilities: 1,550 computers available on campus for general student use. A campuswide network can be accessed from student residence rooms. Online class registration is available.
Website: http://www.semo.edu/

GRADUATE UNITS

School of Graduate Studies Students: 382 full-time (237 women), 665 part-time (466 women); includes 88 minority (53 Black or African American, non-Hispanic/Latino; 4 American Indian or Alaska Native, non-Hispanic/Latino; 12 Asian, non-Hispanic/Latino; 14 Hispanic/Latino; 1 Native Hawaiian or other Pacific Islander, non-Hispanic/Latino; 4 Two or more races, non-Hispanic/Latino), 174 international. Average age 31. 694 applicants, 80% accepted, 448 enrolled. *Faculty:* 196 full-time (104 women), 16 part-time/adjunct (8 women). Expenses: Contact institution. *Financial support:* In 2018–19, 316 students received support, including 84 teaching assistantships with full tuition reimbursements available; career-related internships or fieldwork, Federal Work-Study, scholarships/grants, traineeships, tuition waivers (full), and unspecified assistantships also available. Financial award application deadline: 6/30; financial award applicants required to submit FAFSA. In 2018, 409 master's, 68 other advanced degrees awarded. *Program availability:* Part-time, evening/weekend, 100% online, blended/hybrid learning. Offers biology (MNS); career counseling (MA); chemistry (MNS); communication disorders (MA); counseling (MA, Ed S); criminal justice (MS); educational administration (MA, Ed D, Ed S); educational leadership (Ed D); elementary education (MA); environmental science (MS); exceptional child education (MA); health, human performance and recreation (MS); heritage interpretation (Certificate); higher education administration (MA); historic preservation (Certificate); history (MA); human environmental studies (MA); mathematics (MNS); mental health counseling (MA); middle and secondary education (MA); nursing (MSN); political science, philosophy and religion (MPA); polytechnic studies (MS); public history (MA); school counseling (MA); secondary administration (MA); teacher leadership (MA, Ed S); teaching English to speakers of other languages (MA). *Application deadline:* For fall admission, 8/1 for domestic students, 6/1 for international students; for spring admission, 11/1 for domestic students, 10/1 for international students; for summer admission, 5/15 for domestic students. Applications are processed on a rolling basis. *Application fee:* $30 ($40 for international students). Electronic applications accepted. *Application Contact:* Alisa Aleen McFerron, Assistant Director of Admissions for Operations, 573-651-5937, E-mail: amcferron@semo.edu. *Coordinator of Academic Operations,* Brian Hopkins, 573-651-2062, Fax: 573-651-2001, E-mail: graduateschool@semo.edu.

Harrison College of Business and Computing Students: 94 full-time (50 women), 88 part-time (39 women); includes 18 minority (9 Black or African American, non-Hispanic/Latino; 4 Asian, non-Hispanic/Latino; 5 Hispanic/Latino), 79 international. Average age 29. 80 applicants, 100% accepted, 80 enrolled. *Faculty:* 27 full-time (7 women), 1 (woman) part-time/adjunct. Expenses: Contact institution. *Financial support:* In 2018–19, 16 students received support. Career-related internships or fieldwork, Federal Work-Study, scholarships/grants, traineeships, tuition waivers (full), and unspecified assistantships available. Financial award application deadline: 6/30; financial award applicants required to submit FAFSA. In 2018, 62 master's awarded. *Program availability:* Part-time, evening/weekend, 100% online. Offers accounting

(MBA); entrepreneurship (MBA); financial management (MBA); sport management (MBA). *Application deadline:* For fall admission, 8/1 for domestic students, 6/1 for international students; for spring admission, 11/21 for domestic students, 10/1 for international students; for summer admission, 5/15 for domestic students. Applications are processed on a rolling basis. *Application fee:* $30 ($40 for international students). Electronic applications accepted. *Application Contact:* Dr. Alberto Davila, Dean, 573-651-2112, E-mail: adavila@semo.edu. *Dean,* Dr. Alberto Davila, 573-651-2112, E-mail: adavila@semo.edu.

SOUTHERN ADVENTIST UNIVERSITY, Collegedale, TN 37315-0370

General Information Independent-religious, coed, comprehensive institution. *Enrollment:* 390 matriculated graduate/professional students (312 women). *Enrollment by degree level:* 334 master's, 48 doctoral, 11 other advanced degrees. *Graduate housing:* Rooms and/or apartments available on a first-come, first-served basis to single and married students. Housing application deadline: 7/1. *Student services:* Campus employment opportunities, campus safety program, career counseling, exercise/wellness program, free psychological counseling, international student services, low-cost health insurance, multicultural affairs office, services for students with disabilities, teacher training, writing training. *Library facilities:* McKee Library plus 7 others. *Collection:* Books: 173,284 (physical), 107,663 (digital/electronic); Serial titles: 510 (physical), 170 (digital/electronic); Databases: 160. Weekly public service hours: 82; students can reserve study rooms.

Computer facilities: 300 computers available on campus for general student use. A campuswide network can be accessed from student residence rooms and from off campus. Online class registration is available.
Website: http://www.southern.edu/

General Application Contact: Laurie Gauthier, Director of Graduate Marketing and Enrollment Management, 423-236-2585, Fax: 423-236-1694, E-mail: graduatestudies@southern.edu.

GRADUATE UNITS

School of Business 23 applicants, 48% accepted, 8 enrolled. *Faculty:* 7 full-time (2 women). Expenses: Contact institution. *Financial support:* Scholarships/grants and unspecified assistantships available. Financial award application deadline: 9/1; financial award applicants required to submit FAFSA. In 2018, 8 master's awarded. *Program availability:* Part-time, evening/weekend, 100% online. Offers accounting (MBA); computer information systems (MBA); finance (MBA); healthcare administration (MBA); management (MBA). *Application deadline:* For fall admission, 7/1 for domestic students, 5/1 for international students; for winter admission, 11/1 for domestic students, 9/1 for international students; for summer admission, 4/1 for domestic students, 2/1 for international students. Applications are processed on a rolling basis. *Application fee:* $40. Electronic applications accepted. *Application Contact:* Teshia Price, Graduate Studies Coordinator, 423-236-2751, Fax: 423-236-1527, E-mail: tprice@southern.edu. *Dean,* Dr. Stephanie Sheehan, 423-236-2659, Fax: 423-236-1527, E-mail: ssheehan@southern.edu.

School of Computing Students: 17 full-time (0 women), 3 part-time (0 women); includes 5 minority (all Hispanic/Latino), 6 international. Average age 27. 5 applicants, 20% accepted, 1 enrolled. *Faculty:* 4 full-time (0 women). Expenses: Contact institution. *Financial support:* Career-related internships or fieldwork, tuition waivers (full and partial), and unspecified assistantships available. Financial award application deadline: 8/1; financial award applicants required to submit FAFSA. In 2018, 4 master's awarded. *Program availability:* Part-time. Offers computer science (MS). *Application deadline:* For fall admission, 3/1 priority date for domestic students, 3/1 for international students; for winter admission, 10/1 priority date for domestic students, 10/1 for international students. Applications are processed on a rolling basis. *Application fee:* $25. Electronic applications accepted. *Application Contact:* Tyson Hall, Program Coordinator, 423-236-2916, E-mail: tyson@southern.edu. *Dean,* Rick Halterman, 423-236-2871, E-mail: halterman@southern.edu.

School of Education and Psychology Students: 42 full-time (32 women), 40 part-time (29 women). 13 applicants, 38% accepted, 4 enrolled. *Faculty:* 11 full-time (8 women), 11 part-time/adjunct (5 women). Expenses: Contact institution. *Financial support:* Scholarships/grants and unspecified assistantships available. Support available to part-time students. Financial award application deadline: 4/1; financial award applicants required to submit FAFSA. *Program availability:* Part-time, evening/weekend, 100% online, blended/hybrid learning. Offers clinical mental health counseling (MS); instructional leadership (MS Ed); literacy education (MS Ed); outdoor education (MS Ed); professional school counseling (MS). *Application deadline:* For fall admission, 7/1 priority date for domestic students, 6/1 priority date for international students; for winter admission, 11/1 priority date for domestic students, 10/1 priority date for international students; for spring admission, 4/1 priority date for domestic students, 3/1 priority date for international students. Applications are processed on a rolling basis. *Application fee:* $40. Electronic applications accepted. *Application Contact:* Mikhaile Spence, Graduate Program Manager, 423-236-2496, Fax: 423-236-1765, E-mail: maspence@southern.edu. *Dean,* Dr. Tammy Overstreet, 423-236-2444, Fax: 423-236-1765, E-mail: toverstreet@southern.edu.

School of Nursing 74 applicants, 64% accepted, 37 enrolled. *Faculty:* 16 full-time (15 women), 7 part-time/adjunct (4 women). Expenses: Contact institution. *Financial support:* Teaching assistantships with full and partial tuition reimbursements available. Financial award application deadline: 8/1; financial award applicants required to submit FAFSA. *Program availability:* Part-time, 100% online. Offers acute care-adult/gerontology nurse practitioner (MSN, DNP); healthcare administration (MSN, DNP); lifestyle medicine (DNP); nurse educator (MSN, DNP); primary care-adult/gerontology nurse practitioner (MSN); primary care-family nurse practitioner (MSN, DNP); primary care-psychiatric mental health nurse practitioner (MSN, DNP). *Application deadline:* For fall admission, 7/1 for domestic and international students; for winter admission, 12/1 for domestic and international students. Applications are processed on a rolling basis. *Application fee:* $40. Electronic applications accepted. *Application Contact:* Frances Johnson, DNP, Associate Dean and Graduate Program Coordinator, 423-236-2941, Fax: 423-236-1957, E-mail: francesj@southern.edu. *Dean,* Dr. Holly Gadd, 423-236-2942, Fax: 423-236-1940, E-mail: hgadd@southern.edu.

School of Religion *Faculty:* 11 full-time, 5 part-time/adjunct. Expenses: Contact institution. *Financial support:* Tuition waivers (full) and Employee Sponsored available. Support available to part-time students. Financial award application deadline: 8/1; financial award applicants required to submit FAFSA. *Program availability:* Part-time. Offers evangelism and ministry (M Min); old Testament studies (MA); religious studies (MA). *Application deadline:* For spring admission, 5/1 priority date for domestic students, 4/30 for international students. Applications are processed on a rolling basis. *Application fee:* $40. *Application Contact:* Dr. Alan Parker, Program Coordinator, 423-236-2683, Fax: 423-236-1976, E-mail: parker@southern.edu. *Dean,* Dr. Greg A. King, 423-236-2975, Fax: 423-236-1976, E-mail: gking@southern.edu.

School of Social Work Students: 53 full-time (46 women), 23 part-time (18 women); includes 34 minority (21 Black or African American, non-Hispanic/Latino; 1 Asian, non-Hispanic/Latino; 11 Hispanic/Latino; 1 Two or more races, non-Hispanic/Latino). Average age 37. 60 applicants, 60% accepted, 31 enrolled. *Faculty:* 8 full-time (7 women). Expenses: Contact institution. *Financial support:* Unspecified assistantships and Employee Sponsored available. Financial award application deadline: 8/1; financial award applicants required to submit FAFSA. In 2018, 34 master's awarded. *Program availability:* Part-time, evening/weekend. Offers mental health practice in social work (MSW). *Application deadline:* For fall admission, 7/1 for domestic students, 5/1 for international students; for winter admission, 11/1 for domestic students, 9/1 for international students. Applications are processed on a rolling basis. *Application fee:* $40. Electronic applications accepted. *Application Contact:* Tricia Foster, Program Manager, 423-236-2629, Fax: 423-236-1768, E-mail: gradstudies@southern.edu. *Dean,* Kristie Wilder, JD, 423-236-2206, E-mail: kwilder@southern.edu.

SOUTHERN ARKANSAS UNIVERSITY–MAGNOLIA, Magnolia, AR 71753

General Information State-supported, coed, comprehensive institution. *Enrollment:* 4,468 graduate, professional, and undergraduate students; 164 full-time matriculated graduate/professional students (77 women), 762 part-time matriculated graduate/professional students (510 women). *Enrollment by degree level:* 926 master's. *Graduate faculty:* 36 full-time (21 women), 32 part-time/adjunct (15 women). *International tuition:* $7866 full-time. *Tuition, area resident:* Full-time $5130; part-time $3420 per year. Tuition, state resident: full-time $5130; part-time $3420 per year. Tuition, nonresident: full-time $7866; part-time $5244 per year. *Required fees:* $1052; $710 per unit. Tuition and fees vary according to course load. *Graduate housing:* Rooms and/or apartments available on a first-come, first-served basis to single and married students. Typical cost: $3105 per year ($3580 including board) for single students; $4228 per year ($4703 including board) for married students. Room and board charges vary according to board plan, campus/location and housing facility selected. Housing application deadline: 8/1. *Student services:* Campus employment opportunities, campus safety program, career counseling, exercise/wellness program, free psychological counseling, international student services, low-cost health insurance, multicultural affairs office, services for students with disabilities, writing training. *Library facilities:* Magale Library. *Collection:* Books: 138,050 (physical), 10,973 (digital/electronic); Serial titles: 130 (physical), 86 (digital/electronic); Databases: 187. Weekly public service hours: 87.

Computer facilities: 199 computers available on campus for general student use. A campuswide network can be accessed from student residence rooms and from off campus. Online class registration is available.
Website: http://www.saumag.edu/

General Application Contact: Talia Jett, Admissions Coordinator, School of Graduate Studies, 870-235-5450, Fax: 870-235-5227, E-mail: taliajett@saumag.edu.

GRADUATE UNITS

School of Graduate Studies Students: 164 full-time (77 women), 762 part-time (510 women); includes 192 minority (163 Black or African American, non-Hispanic/Latino; 7 American Indian or Alaska Native, non-Hispanic/Latino; 13 Asian, non-Hispanic/Latino; 1 Hispanic/Latino; 8 Two or more races, non-Hispanic/Latino), 213 international. Average age 28. 363 applicants, 100% accepted, 237 enrolled. *Faculty:* 36 full-time (21 women), 32 part-time/adjunct (15 women). Expenses: Contact institution. *Financial support:* Career-related internships or fieldwork, Federal Work-Study, scholarships/grants, tuition waivers (full), and unspecified assistantships available. Financial award applicants required to submit FAFSA. In 2018, 716 master's awarded. *Program availability:* Part-time, 100% online, blended/hybrid learning. Offers agriculture (MS); business administration (MBA); clinical and mental health counseling (MS); computer and information sciences (MS); gifted and talented (M Ed); higher, adult and lifelong education (M Ed); kinesiology (M Ed); library media and information specialist (M Ed); public administration (MPA); school counseling K-12 (M Ed); student affairs and college counseling (MS); teaching (MAT). *Application deadline:* For fall admission, 8/1 for domestic and international students; for spring admission, 12/1 for domestic students, 11/15 for international students; for summer admission, 4/1 for domestic students, 5/10 for international students. Applications are processed on a rolling basis. *Application fee:* $25 ($90 for international students). Electronic applications accepted. *Application Contact:* Talia Jett, Admissions Coordinator, 870-2355450, Fax: 870-235-5227, E-mail: taliajett@saumag.edu. *Dean, School of Graduate Studies,* Dr. Kim Bloss, 870-235-4150, Fax: 870-235-5227, E-mail: kkbloss@saumag.edu.

THE SOUTHERN BAPTIST THEOLOGICAL SEMINARY, Louisville, KY 40280-0004

General Information Independent-religious, coed, comprehensive institution. *Graduate housing:* Rooms and/or apartments available on a first-come, first-served basis to single and married students.

GRADUATE UNITS

Billy Graham School of Missions, Evangelism and Ministry *Program availability:* Part-time, evening/weekend, online learning. Offers ministry (D Min); missiology (MA, D Miss); missions and evangelism (M Div, Th M, PhD); theological studies (MA).

School of Theology *Program availability:* Part-time, evening/weekend, online learning. Offers applied theology (D Min); biblical and theological studies (M Div); biblical counseling (M Div, MA, D Min); biblical spirituality (D Min); Christian ministry (M Div); expository preaching (D Min); pastoral studies (M Div); theological studies (MA); theology (Th M, PhD); worldview and apologetics (M Div).

SOUTHERN CALIFORNIA INSTITUTE OF ARCHITECTURE, Los Angeles, CA 90013

General Information Independent, coed, comprehensive institution. *Graduate housing:* On-campus housing not available.

GRADUATE UNITS

Center for Advanced Studies
Graduate Program in Architecture Offers architecture (M Arch). Electronic applications accepted.

SOUTHERN CALIFORNIA SEMINARY, El Cajon, CA 92019

General Information Independent-religious, coed, comprehensive institution. *Graduate housing:* Rooms and/or apartments available on a first-come, first-served basis to single and married students.

GRADUATE UNITS

Graduate and Professional Programs *Program availability:* Part-time, evening/weekend, online learning. Offers Biblical studies (MABS); counseling psychology (MACP); marriage and family therapy (MAMFT); psychology (Psy D); religious studies (MRS); theology (M Div). Electronic applications accepted.

SOUTHERN CALIFORNIA UNIVERSITY OF HEALTH SCIENCES, Whittier, CA 90609-1166

General Information Independent, coed, graduate-only institution. *Graduate housing:* On-campus housing not available. *Research affiliation:* Samueli Institute (alternative health care), Anton B. Burg Foundation (alternative health care).

GRADUATE UNITS

College of Eastern Medicine *Program availability:* Part-time, evening/weekend. Offers Eastern medicine (MAOM, DAOM). Electronic applications accepted.

Los Angeles College of Chiropractic Offers chiropractic (DC). Electronic applications accepted.

SOUTHERN COLLEGE OF OPTOMETRY, Memphis, TN 38104-2222

General Information Independent, coed, graduate-only institution. *Graduate housing:* On-campus housing not available.

GRADUATE UNITS

Professional Program Offers optometry (OD).

SOUTHERN CONNECTICUT STATE UNIVERSITY, New Haven, CT 06515-1355

General Information State-supported, coed, comprehensive institution. CGS member. *Graduate housing:* Room and/or apartments available on a first-come, first-served basis to single students; on-campus housing not available to married students.

GRADUATE UNITS

School of Graduate Studies *Program availability:* Part-time, evening/weekend, online learning. Electronic applications accepted.

School of Arts and Sciences Offers art education (MS); arts and sciences (MA, MFA, MS, Diploma); biology (MS); chemistry (MS); computer science (MS); English (MA, MS); environmental education (MS); history (MA, MS); mathematics (MS); multicultural-bilingual education/teaching English to speakers of other languages (MS); political science (MS); psychology (MA); romance languages (MA); science education (MS, Diploma); sociology (MS); women's studies (MA). Electronic applications accepted.

School of Business *Program availability:* Part-time, evening/weekend. Offers business (MBA); business administration (MBA). Electronic applications accepted.

School of Education *Program availability:* Part-time. Offers classroom teacher specialist (Diploma); community counseling (MS); counseling (Diploma); education (MLS, MS, MS Ed, Ed D, Diploma); educational coach (Diploma); educational leadership (Ed D, Diploma); elementary education (MS); information studies (Diploma); library science (MLS); reading (MS, Diploma); research, statistics, and measurement (MS); school counseling (MS); school psychology (MS, Diploma); special education (MS Ed). Electronic applications accepted.

School of Health and Human Services *Program availability:* Part-time, evening/weekend. Offers family nurse practitioner (MSN); health and human services (MPH, MS, MSN, MSW, Ed D); human performance (MS); nursing (Ed D); nursing education (MSN); physical education (MS); public health (MPH); recreation and leisure studies (MS); school health education (MS); social work (MSW); speech pathology (MS). Electronic applications accepted.

SOUTHERN EVANGELICAL SEMINARY, Matthews, NC 28105

General Information Independent-religious, coed, primarily men, graduate-only institution. *Enrollment by degree level:* 112 master's, 36 doctoral. *Graduate faculty:* 8 full-time (0 women), 11 part-time/adjunct (0 women). *Graduate housing:* On-campus housing not available. *Student services:* Campus employment opportunities, career counseling, international student services, writing training. *Library facilities:* Jamison Library. *Collection:* Books: 80,000 (physical); Databases: 6. Weekly public service hours: 40.

Computer facilities: 10 computers available on campus for general student use. A campuswide network can be accessed. Online class registration is available. Website: http://www.ses.edu/

General Application Contact: Adam Tucker, Director of Recruitment, 704-847-5600 Ext. 211, E-mail: dpotter@ses.edu.

GRADUATE UNITS

Graduate Programs *Program availability:* Part-time, evening/weekend, online learning. Offers apologetics (MA, D Min, Certificate); Christian education (MA); church ministry (MA, Certificate); divinity (Certificate); Islamic studies (MA, Certificate); Jewish studies (MA); philosophy (MA); philosophy of religion (PhD); religion (MA); theology (M Div); youth ministry (MA).

SOUTHERN ILLINOIS UNIVERSITY CARBONDALE, Carbondale, IL 62901-4701

General Information State-supported, coed, university. CGS member. *Graduate housing:* Rooms and/or apartments available on a first-come, first-served basis to single and married students. *Research affiliation:* NASA-Ames Research Center, Argonne National Laboratory.

GRADUATE UNITS

Graduate School *Program availability:* Part-time. Offers molecular, cellular and systemic physiology (MS, PhD); molecular, cellular, and systemic physiology (PhD); pharmacology (MS, PhD); physician assistant studies (MSPA).

College of Agriculture *Program availability:* Part-time. Offers agribusiness economics (MS); agriculture (MS); animal science (MS); food and nutrition (MS); forestry (MS); plant, soil, and general agriculture (MS).

College of Applied Science Offers applied science (M Arch, MS); architecture (M Arch); fire service and homeland security (MS); medical dosimetry (MS). Electronic applications accepted.

College of Business and Administration *Program availability:* Part-time. Offers accountancy (M Acc, PhD); business administration (MBA, PhD); business and administration (M Acc, MBA, PhD). Electronic applications accepted.

College of Education and Human Services *Program availability:* Part-time. Offers behavior analysis and therapy (MS); communication disorders and sciences (MS); community health education (MPH); curriculum and instruction (MS Ed, PhD); education (MS Ed); education and human services (MPH, MS, MS Ed, MSW, PhD); educational administration (MS Ed, PhD); educational psychology (MS Ed, PhD); health education (MS Ed, PhD); higher education (MS Ed); kinesiology (MS Ed); recreation (MS Ed); social work (MSW); special education (MS Ed, PhD); workforce education and development (MS Ed, PhD). Electronic applications accepted.

College of Engineering Offers biomedical engineering (ME, MS); civil and environmental engineering (ME); civil engineering (MS); electrical and computer engineering (MS, PhD); engineering (ME, MS, PhD); engineering science (PhD); engineering sciences (PhD); mechanical engineering (MS); mining engineering (MS); quality engineering and management (MS).

College of Liberal Arts *Program availability:* Part-time. Offers anthropology (MA, PhD); clinical psychology (PhD); communication studies (MA, MS, PhD); composition (MA, PhD); counseling psychology (PhD); creative writing (MFA); criminology and criminal justice (MA, PhD); drawing (MFA); economics (MA, MS, PhD); experimental psychology (MA, MS); fiber/weaving (MFA); foreign languages and literatures (MA); geography (MS, PhD); glass (MFA); history (MA, PhD); liberal arts (MA, MFA, MM, MPA, MS, PhD); linguistics (MA); metalsmithing/blacksmithing (MFA); music (MM); painting (MFA); philosophy (MA, PhD); political science (MA, PhD); public administration (MPA); sociology (MA, PhD); speech/theater (PhD); teaching English to speakers of other languages (MA); theater (MFA).

College of Mass Communication and Media Arts *Program availability:* Part-time. Offers mass communication and media arts (MA, MFA, MS, PhD); media theory and research (MA); professional media and media management studies (MS).

College of Science *Program availability:* Part-time. Offers biological sciences (MS); chemistry and biochemistry (MS, PhD); computer science (MS, PhD); environmental resources and policy (PhD); geology (MS); geosciences (PhD); mathematics (MA, MS, PhD); molecular biology, microbiology, and biochemistry (MS, PhD); physics (MS, PhD); plant biology (MS, PhD); science (MA, MS, PhD); zoology (MS, PhD).

School of Law *Program availability:* Part-time. Offers general law (LL M, MLS); health law and policy (LL M, MLS); law (JD); legal studies (MLS). Electronic applications accepted.

SOUTHERN ILLINOIS UNIVERSITY EDWARDSVILLE, Edwardsville, IL 62026

General Information State-supported, coed, university. CGS member. *Graduate housing:* Rooms and/or apartments available on a first-come, first-served basis to single and married students. Housing application deadline: 5/1. *Research affiliation:* Long Island Veterinary Clinic (electrical engineering), SSM DePaul Health Center (nursing), Nurturenergy (mechanical engineering), Tulsa Dental Products (dental medicine), Mallinckrodt (pharmacy), Schlumberger (mechanical engineering).

GRADUATE UNITS

Graduate School *Program availability:* Part-time, evening/weekend, blended/hybrid learning. Offers cultural heritage and resources management (MA, MS); diversity training (MA, MS); healthcare informatics (MS); organizational design thinking (MS); sustainability (MS). Electronic applications accepted.

College of Arts and Sciences *Program availability:* Part-time, evening/weekend, online learning. Offers art studio (MFA); art therapy counseling (MA); arts and sciences (MA, MFA, MM, MPA, MS, MSW, PSM, Postbaccalaureate Certificate); biology (MA, MS); chemistry (MS); computational and applied mathematics (MS); corporate and organizational communication (MA); creative writing (MA); environmental science management (PSM); environmental sciences (MS); geography (MS); health communication (MA); history (MS); interpersonal communication (MA); literature (MA, Postbaccalaureate Certificate); mass communications (MS); media literacy (Postbaccalaureate Certificate); museum studies (Postbaccalaureate Certificate); music (MM); music education (MM); music performance (MM); piano pedagogy (Postbaccalaureate Certificate); postsecondary mathematics education (MS); public administration (MPA); public relations (MS); pure mathematics (MS); school social work (MSW); social work (MSW); sociology (MA); statistics and operations research (MS); teaching English as a second language (MA, Postbaccalaureate Certificate); teaching of writing (MA, Postbaccalaureate Certificate); vocal pedagogy (Postbaccalaureate Certificate). Electronic applications accepted.

School of Business *Program availability:* Part-time, evening/weekend. Offers accountancy (MSA); business (MA, MBA, MMR, MS, MSA); business analytics (MBA); computer management and information systems (MS); economics and finance (MA, MS); management information systems (MBA); marketing research (MMR); project management (MBA); taxation (MSA). Electronic applications accepted.

School of Education, Health, and Human Behavior *Program availability:* Part-time, evening/weekend. Offers clinical child and school psychology (MS); clinical psychology (MA); college student personnel administration (MS Ed); curriculum and instruction (MS Ed); education, health, and human behavior (MA, MS, MS Ed, Ed D, Ed S, Post-Master's Certificate, Postbaccalaureate Certificate, SD); educational administration (MS Ed, Ed S); educational leadership (MS Ed, Ed D, Ed S, Postbaccalaureate Certificate); exercise and sport psychology (MS); exercise physiology (MS); industrial-organizational psychology (MA); instructional technology (MS Ed); learning, culture, and society (MS Ed); literacy education (MS Ed); literacy specialist (Post-Master's Certificate); physical education and coaching pedagogy (MS Ed); school psychology (SD); special education (MS Ed, Post-Master's Certificate); speech-language pathology (MS); Web-based learning (Postbaccalaureate Certificate). Electronic applications accepted.

School of Engineering *Program availability:* Part-time, evening/weekend. Offers computer science (MS); electrical engineering (MS); engineering (MS); environmental engineering (MS); geotechnical engineering (MS); industrial engineering (MS); mechanical engineering (MS); structural engineering (MS); transportation engineering (MS). Electronic applications accepted.

School of Nursing *Program availability:* Part-time, evening/weekend. Offers family nurse practitioner (MS, Post-Master's Certificate); health care and nursing administration (MS, Post-Master's Certificate); nurse anesthesia (DNP); nurse educator (MS, Post-Master's Certificate); nursing (MS, DNP, Post-Master's Certificate). Electronic applications accepted.

School of Dental Medicine Offers dental medicine (DMD). Electronic applications accepted.

School of Pharmacy Offers pharmacy education (Pharm D); pharmacy pediatrics (Pharm D). Electronic applications accepted.

SOUTHERN METHODIST UNIVERSITY, Dallas, TX 75275

General Information Independent-religious, coed, university. CGS member. *Graduate housing:* Rooms and/or apartments available on a first-come, first-served basis to single and married students. Housing application deadline: 6/1.

GRADUATE UNITS

Cox School of Business *Program availability:* Part-time, evening/weekend. Offers accounting (MSA); business (EMBA, MBA, MS, MSA, MSF, MSM); business analytics (MS); finance (MS); information technology and operations management (MBA, PMBA); management (MBA, PMBA); marketing (MBA, PMBA); real estate (MBA, PMBA); strategy and entrepreneurship (MBA, PMBA). Electronic applications accepted.

Dedman College of Humanities and Sciences *Program availability:* Part-time, evening/weekend. Offers American history (MA, PhD); applied economics (MA); applied economics and predictive analytics (MS); applied geophysics (MS); applied medical anthropology (MA); applied statistics and data analytics (MS); archaeology (PhD); biostatistics (PhD); chemistry (MS); clinical psychology (PhD); computational and applied mathematics (MS, PhD); cultural anthropology (PhD); earth sciences (MS, PhD); economics (PhD); English (MA, PhD); experimental chemistry (PhD); global history (MA); Hebrew Bible/Old Testament (PhD); humanities and sciences (MA, MS, PhD); law and economics (MA); medical anthropology (PhD); medieval studies (MA); molecular and cellular biology (MA, MS, PhD); physics (MS, PhD); religious studies (MA); statistical science (PhD); theoretical and computational chemistry (PhD). Electronic applications accepted.

Dedman School of Law *Program availability:* Part-time, evening/weekend. Offers general law (LL M); international and comparative law (LL M); law (JD, SJD); taxation (LL M). Electronic applications accepted.

Lyle School of Engineering *Program availability:* Part-time, evening/weekend, online learning. Offers civil and environmental engineering (PhD); civil engineering (MS); computer engineering (MS, PhD); computer science (MS, PhD); data science (MS); datacenter systems engineering (MS); design and innovation (MA); electrical engineering (MS, PhD); engineering (MA, MS, MSIEM, DE, PhD); engineering entrepreneurship (MS); engineering management (MS, DE); environmental engineering (MS); information engineering and management (MSIEM); manufacturing systems management (MS); mechanical engineering (MS, PhD); operations research (MS, PhD); security engineering (MS); software engineering (MS, DE); sustainability and development (MA); systems engineering (MS); telecommunications and network engineering (MS).

Meadows School of the Arts *Program availability:* Evening/weekend. Offers arts (MA, MFA, MM, MM, MSM, PhD, Diploma). Electronic applications accepted.

Division of Art Offers studio art (MFA).

Division of Art History *Program availability:* Part-time, evening/weekend. Offers art history (MA); rhetorics of art, space and culture (PhD).

Division of Arts Management and Arts Entrepreneurship Offers international arts management (MM). MM offered jointly with Bocconi University Graduate School of Management in Milan and HEC Montreal. Electronic applications accepted.

Division of Music *Program availability:* Part-time. Offers composition (MM); conducting (MM); music education (MM); musicology (MM); performance (MM); theory pedagogy (MM). Electronic applications accepted.

Division of Theatre Offers acting (MFA); design (MFA). Electronic applications accepted.

Temerlin Advertising Institute Offers advertising (MA). Electronic applications accepted.

Perkins School of Theology *Program availability:* Part-time. Offers ministry (M Div, D Min); sacred music (MSM); theological studies (MTS).

Simmons School of Education and Human Development *Program availability:* Part-time, evening/weekend. Offers applied physiology (PhD); bilingual education (MBE); counseling (MS); dispute resolution (MA, Graduate Certificate); education (M Ed, PhD); education and human development (M Ed, MA, MBE, MLS, MS, DLS, PhD, Graduate Certificate); English as a second language (M Ed); gifted and talented (M Ed); health promotion management (MS); healthcare collaboration and conflict engagement (Graduate Certificate); higher education (M Ed, Ed D); liberal studies (MLS, DLS); literacy studies (M Ed); PK-12 school leadership (M Ed, Ed D); special education (M Ed); sport management (MS).

SOUTHERN NAZARENE UNIVERSITY, Bethany, OK 73008
General Information Independent-religious, coed, comprehensive institution. *Graduate housing:* Rooms and/or apartments available on a first-come, first-served basis to single and married students. Housing application deadline: 8/1.

GRADUATE UNITS

College of Professional and Graduate Studies *Program availability:* Part-time, evening/weekend. Offers counseling psychology (MA, MSCP); marital and family therapy (MA). Electronic applications accepted.

School of Business *Program availability:* Part-time, evening/weekend, online learning. Offers business administration (MBA); health care management (MBA); management (MS Mgt). Electronic applications accepted.

School of Kinesiology Offers sports management and administration (MA).

School of Nursing *Program availability:* Part-time, evening/weekend. Offers nursing education (MS); nursing leadership (MS).

SOUTHERN NEW HAMPSHIRE UNIVERSITY, Manchester, NH 03106-1045
General Information Independent, coed, university. *Graduate housing:* Room and/or apartments available on a first-come, first-served basis to single students; on-campus housing not available to married students.

GRADUATE UNITS

Program in Nursing *Program availability:* Online only, 100% online. Offers clinical nurse leader (MSN); nurse educator (MSN); nursing (MSN); patient safety and quality (MSN, Post Master's Certificate). Electronic applications accepted.

School of Arts and Sciences *Program availability:* Part-time, evening/weekend. Offers clinical mental health counseling (MS); creative writing (MA); criminal justice (MS); cyber security (MS); English (MS); fiction and nonfiction (MFA); history (MA); political science (MS); psychology (MS). Electronic applications accepted.

School of Business *Program availability:* Part-time, evening/weekend, online learning. Offers accounting (MBA, Graduate Certificate); accounting finance (MS); accounting/auditing (MS); accounting/forensic accounting (MS); accounting/management accounting (MS); accounting/taxation (MS); applied economics (MS); athletic administration (MBA, Graduate Certificate); business administration (IMBA, Certificate); business analytics (MBA); business intelligence (MBA); communication (MA); community economic development (MBA); criminal justice (MBA); data analytics (MS); economics (MBA); engineering management (MBA); entrepreneurship (MBA); finance (MBA, MS, Graduate Certificate); finance/corporate finance (MS); finance/investments (MS); forensic accounting (MBA); forensic accounting and fraud examination (Graduate Certificate); healthcare informatics (MBA); healthcare management (MBA); human resource management (MS); human resources (MS); information technology (MS); information technology management (MBA); international business (PhD); Internet marketing (MBA); leadership (MBA); leadership of nonprofit organizations (Graduate Certificate); management (MS); marketing (MBA, MS, Graduate Certificate); music business (MBA); operations and project management (MS); operations and supply chain management (MBA, Graduate Certificate); organizational

leadership (MS); project management (MBA, Graduate Certificate); public administration (MBA, Graduate Certificate); quantitative analysis (MBA); Six Sigma (Graduate Certificate); Six Sigma quality (MBA); social media marketing (MBA, Graduate Certificate); sport management (MBA, MS, Graduate Certificate); sustainability and environmental compliance (MBA). Electronic applications accepted.

School of Education *Program availability:* Part-time, evening/weekend, online learning. Offers curriculum and instruction (M Ed); dyslexia studies and language-based learning disabilities (Certificate); early childhood and special education (M Ed); educational leadership (M Ed, Ed D); educational studies (M Ed); elementary and special education (M Ed); field based education (M Ed); higher education administration (MS); teaching English as a foreign language (MS). Electronic applications accepted.

SOUTHERN OREGON UNIVERSITY, Ashland, OR 97520
General Information State-supported, coed, comprehensive institution. *Graduate housing:* Rooms and/or apartments available on a first-come, first-served basis to single and married students. Housing application deadline: 8/1. *Research affiliation:* U.S. Forest Service (biology, ecology studies), U.S. Fish and Wildlife Service (forensics), Oregon Shakespeare Festival (theatre arts), Crater Lake National Park (scientific studies), Bureau of Land Management (ecological studies), Bear Creek Corporation (environmental studies).

GRADUATE UNITS

Graduate Studies *Program availability:* Part-time, evening/weekend, online learning. Offers applied computer science (PSM); environmental education (MS); French language teaching (MA); interdisciplinary studies (MS); performance (MM); psychology (MHC); Spanish language teaching (MA). Electronic applications accepted.

Ashland Center for Theatre Studies *Program availability:* Part-time. Offers theatre studies (MTS). Electronic applications accepted.

School of Business *Program availability:* Part-time, evening/weekend, online learning. Offers accounting (Postbaccalaureate Certificate); business administration (MBA); international management (MIM). Electronic applications accepted.

School of Education *Program availability:* Online learning. Offers elementary education (MA Ed, MS Ed); secondary education (MA Ed, MS Ed); teaching (MAT). Electronic applications accepted.

SOUTHERN STATES UNIVERSITY, San Diego, CA 92110
General Information Proprietary, coed, comprehensive institution.

GRADUATE UNITS

Graduate Programs

SOUTHERN UNIVERSITY AND AGRICULTURAL AND MECHANICAL COLLEGE, Baton Rouge, LA 70813
General Information State-supported, coed, university. CGS member. *Graduate housing:* Room and/or apartments available on a first-come, first-served basis to single students; on-campus housing not available to married students. Housing application deadline: 6/30. *Research affiliation:* Michigan State University (language screening of African-Americans), University of Georgia (substance abuse prevention), The University of Alabama (diabetes), NASA (drinking water remote sensing, mechanical engineering), Livingston Observatory (gravitational waves, cosmic gravity waves, black waves).

GRADUATE UNITS

College of Business Offers business (MBA).

College of Nursing and Allied Health Offers nursing and allied health (MS, MSN, DNP, PhD); speech-language pathology and audiology (MS); therapeutic recreation (MS).

School of Nursing *Program availability:* Part-time. Offers educator/administrator (PhD); family health nursing (MSN); family nurse practitioner (Post Master's Certificate); geriatric nurse practitioner/gerontology (PhD); nursing (DNP).

Graduate School *Program availability:* Part-time.

College of Agricultural, Family and Consumer Sciences Offers urban forestry (MS); urban forestry and natural resources (MS).

College of Humanities and Interdisciplinary Studies Offers administration and supervision (M Ed); counselor education (MA); education (M Ed, MA, MS, PhD); educational leadership (M Ed); elementary education (M Ed); humanities and interdisciplinary studies (MA); mass communication (MA); media (M Ed); mental health counseling (MA); secondary education (M Ed).

College of Sciences and Engineering *Program availability:* Part-time. Offers analytical chemistry (MS); biochemistry (MS); biology (MS); environmental sciences (MS); information systems (MS); inorganic chemistry (MS); mathematics (MS); micro/minicomputer architecture (MS); operating systems (MS); organic chemistry (MS); physical chemistry (MS); physics (MS); science/mathematics education (PhD); sciences and engineering (MA, ME, MS).

Nelson Mandela College of Government and Social Sciences Offers criminal justice (MS); government and social sciences (MA, MPA, MS, PhD); public administration (MPA); public policy (PhD); rehabilitation counseling (MS); social sciences (MA).

Southern University Law Center *Program availability:* Part-time, evening/weekend. Offers law (JD). Electronic applications accepted.

SOUTHERN UNIVERSITY AT NEW ORLEANS, New Orleans, LA 70126-1009
General Information State-supported, coed, primarily women, comprehensive institution. *Graduate housing:* Room and/or apartments available on a first-come, first-served basis to single students; on-campus housing not available to married students.

GRADUATE UNITS

School of Graduate Studies *Program availability:* Part-time, evening/weekend. Offers criminal justice (MA); management information systems (MS); museum studies (MA); social work (MSW).

SOUTHERN UTAH UNIVERSITY, Cedar City, UT 84720-2498
General Information State-supported, coed, comprehensive institution. *Enrollment:* 225 full-time matriculated graduate/professional students (99 women), 675 part-time matriculated graduate/professional students (380 women). *Enrollment by degree level:* 840 master's, 60 other advanced degrees. *Graduate faculty:* 58 full-time (18 women), 35 part-time/adjunct (6 women). *Tuition, area resident:* Full-time $7574; part-time $339 per credit hour. *Tuition, state resident:* full-time $7574; part-time $339 per credit hour. *Tuition, nonresident:* full-time $23,784; part-time $1069 per credit hour. *Required fees:* $764. Tuition and fees vary according to course load and program. *Graduate housing:* Room and/or apartments available on a first-come, first-served basis to single students; on-campus housing not available to married students. Typical cost: $3350 per year ($7250 including board). Room and board charges vary according to board plan and housing facility selected. *Student services:* Campus employment opportunities, campus

safety program, exercise/wellness program, free psychological counseling, international student services, low-cost health insurance, multicultural affairs office, services for students with disabilities, teacher training. *Library facilities:* Gerald R Sherratt Library. *Collection:* Books: 241,434 (physical), 441,219 (digital/electronic); Serial titles: 676 (physical), 22,603 (digital/electronic); Databases: 218. Students can reserve study rooms.

Computer facilities: A campuswide network can be accessed from student residence rooms and from off campus. Online class registration is available. Website: http://www.suu.edu/

General Application Contact: https://www.suu.edu/graduatestudies/, 435-8658665.

GRADUATE UNITS

Master of Accountancy/MBA Dual Degree Program Students: 1. 9 applicants, 100% accepted, 0 enrolled. Expenses: Contact institution. *Financial support:* Unspecified assistantships available. *Program availability:* Part-time, online only, 100% online. *Application deadline:* For fall admission, 7/15 for domestic and international students; for spring admission, 12/1 for domestic and international students; for summer admission, 5/1 for domestic and international students. Applications are processed on a rolling basis. *Application fee:* $60 ($65 for international students). Electronic applications accepted.

Program in Accounting Students: 43 full-time (12 women), 48 part-time (16 women); includes 11 minority (2 Black or African American, non-Hispanic/Latino; 2 American Indian or Alaska Native, non-Hispanic/Latino; 1 Asian, non-Hispanic/Latino; 6 Hispanic/Latino), 2 international. Average age 29. 40 applicants, 95% accepted, 31 enrolled. *Faculty:* 7 full-time (0 women), 1 part-time/adjunct (0 women). Expenses: Contact institution. *Financial support:* Unspecified assistantships available. In 2018, 62 master's awarded. *Program availability:* Part-time, 100% online. Offers accounting (M Acc). *Application deadline:* For fall admission, 7/15 for domestic and international students; for spring admission, 12/1 for domestic and international students; for summer admission, 5/1 for domestic and international students. Applications are processed on a rolling basis. *Application fee:* $60 ($65 for international students). Electronic applications accepted. *Application Contact:* Dr. Robin Boneck, Department Chair, 435-586-7773, Fax: 435-586-5493, E-mail: boneck@suu.edu. *Department Chair,* Dr. Robin Boneck, 435-586-7773, Fax: 435-586-5493, E-mail: boneck@suu.edu.

Program in Arts Administration Students: 15 full-time (10 women), 22 part-time (15 women); includes 4 minority (2 Black or African American, non-Hispanic/Latino; 2 Hispanic/Latino). Average age 31. 31 applicants, 77% accepted, 19 enrolled. *Faculty:* 3 full-time (2 women), 4 part-time/adjunct (1 woman). Expenses: Contact institution. *Financial support:* Tuition waivers and unspecified assistantships available. In 2018, 13 master's awarded. *Program availability:* Part-time, 100% online. Offers arts administration (MA, MFA). *Application deadline:* For fall admission, 2/15 for domestic and international students. Applications are processed on a rolling basis. *Application fee:* $60 ($65 for international students). Electronic applications accepted. *Application Contact:* Rachel Parker, Program Director/Assistant Professor, 435-586-7873, Fax: 435-865-8657, E-mail: rachelparker@suu.edu. *Program Director/Assistant Professor,* Rachel Parker, 435-586-7873, Fax: 435-865-8657, E-mail: rachelparker@suu.edu.

Program in Business Administration Students: 35 full-time (12 women), 49 part-time (16 women); includes 10 minority (2 Black or African American, non-Hispanic/Latino; 2 American Indian or Alaska Native, non-Hispanic/Latino; 2 Asian, non-Hispanic/Latino; 4 Hispanic/Latino), 8 international. Average age 31. 56 applicants, 52% accepted, 29 enrolled. *Faculty:* 7 full-time (0 women), 2 part-time/adjunct (0 women). Expenses: Contact institution. *Financial support:* Scholarships/grants available. In 2018, 31 master's awarded. *Program availability:* Part-time, 100% online. Offers business administration (MBA). *Application deadline:* For fall admission, 7/15 for domestic and international students; for spring admission, 12/1 for domestic and international students; for summer admission, 5/1 for domestic and international students. Applications are processed on a rolling basis. *Application fee:* $60 ($65 for international students). Electronic applications accepted. *Application Contact:* Kenneth Hall, MBA Program Director, 435-865-8541, Fax: 435-586-5493, E-mail: kennethhall2@suu.edu. *MBA Program Director,* Kenneth Hall, 435-865-8541, Fax: 435-586-5493, E-mail: kennethhall2@suu.edu.

Program in Communication Students: 15 full-time (12 women), 33 part-time (18 women); includes 2 minority (both Black or African American, non-Hispanic/Latino), 1 international. Average age 31. 22 applicants, 77% accepted, 16 enrolled. *Faculty:* 6 full-time (0 women), 1 part-time/adjunct (0 women). Expenses: Contact institution. *Financial support:* Teaching assistantships with tuition reimbursements and unspecified assistantships available. Financial award application deadline: 3/15. In 2018, 23 master's awarded. *Program availability:* Part-time, 100% online. Offers communication (MA). *Application deadline:* For fall admission, 6/15 for domestic and international students; for spring admission, 10/15 for domestic and international students; for summer admission, 4/15 for domestic and international students. Applications are processed on a rolling basis. *Application fee:* $60 ($65 for international students). Electronic applications accepted. *Application Contact:* Dr. Kevin Stein, Program Director, 435-586-7874, E-mail: stein@suu.edu. *Department Chair,* Dr. Matt Barton, 435-586-7970, E-mail: bartonm@suu.edu.

Program in Cyber Security and Information Assurance Students: 5 full-time (1 woman), 26 part-time (3 women); includes 6 minority (1 Black or African American, non-Hispanic/Latino; 1 Asian, non-Hispanic/Latino; 3 Hispanic/Latino; 1 Native Hawaiian or other Pacific Islander, non-Hispanic/Latino). Average age 36. 13 applicants, 54% accepted, 14 enrolled. *Faculty:* 2 full-time (1 woman), 3 part-time/adjunct (0 women). Expenses: Contact institution. In 2018, 5 master's awarded. *Program availability:* Part-time, online only, 100% online. Offers cyber and web security (MS). *Application fee:* $60 ($65 for international students). Electronic applications accepted. *Application Contact:* Mary Gillins, Administrative Assistant, 435-586-5405, Fax: 435-865-8444, E-mail: marygillins@suu.edu. *Department Chair/Interim Graduate Program Director,* Dr. Nathan Barker, 435-586-5414, Fax: 435-865-8444, E-mail: barkern@suu.edu.

Program in Education Students: 7 full-time (all women), 346 part-time (240 women); includes 21 minority (3 Black or African American, non-Hispanic/Latino; 1 American Indian or Alaska Native, non-Hispanic/Latino; 5 Asian, non-Hispanic/Latino; 10 Hispanic/Latino; 2 Native Hawaiian or other Pacific Islander, non-Hispanic/Latino), 3 international. Average age 38. 78 applicants, 96% accepted, 55 enrolled. *Faculty:* 13 full-time (6 women), 10 part-time/adjunct (4 women). Expenses: Contact institution. In 2018, 198 master's awarded. *Program availability:* Part-time, 100% online. Offers administrative licensure (Certificate); music education (MMus). *Application deadline:* For fall admission, 7/15 for domestic and international students; for spring admission, 11/15 for domestic and international students; for summer admission, 4/15 for domestic and international students. Applications are processed on a rolling basis. *Application fee:* $60 ($65 for international students). Electronic applications accepted. *Application Contact:* Tamara Lovell, Program Specialist, 435-865-8759, Fax: 435-865-8485, E-mail:

tamaralovell@suu.edu. *Department Chair,* Dr. Shawn Christiansen, 435-865-8171, Fax: 435-865-8485, E-mail: reynolds@suu.edu.

Program in Interdisciplinary Studies Students: 17 full-time (8 women), 13 part-time (9 women); includes 4 minority (1 Asian, non-Hispanic/Latino; 3 Hispanic/Latino; 2 international. Average age 37. 17 applicants, 82% accepted, 10 enrolled. *Faculty:* 2 full-time (1 woman), 4 part-time/adjunct (0 women). Expenses: Contact institution. *Program availability:* 100% online. Offers interdisciplinary studies (MIS). *Application fee:* $60 ($65 for international students). *Application Contact:* Dr. Cynthia Kimball Davis, Department Chair, 435-586-7850, E-mail: cynthiakimballdavis@suu.edu. *Department Chair,* Dr. Cynthia Kimball Davis, 435-586-7850, E-mail: cynthiakimballdavis@suu.edu.

Program in Music Students: 19 full-time (2 women), 6 part-time (1 woman); includes 1 minority (Hispanic/Latino). Average age 34. 29 applicants, 90% accepted, 20 enrolled. *Faculty:* 1 full-time (0 women), 4 part-time/adjunct (0 women). Expenses: Contact institution. In 2018, 11 master's awarded. *Program availability:* Part-time, 100% online. Offers performance technology (MMus). *Application fee:* $60 ($65 for international students). *Application Contact:* Dr. Lawrence Johnson, Department Chair, 435-865-7150, E-mail: johsonl@suu.edu. *Department Chair,* Dr. Lawrence Johnson, 435-865-7150, E-mail: johsonl@suu.edu.

Program in Public Administration Students: 56 full-time (30 women), 76 part-time (41 women); includes 22 minority (2 Black or African American, non-Hispanic/Latino; 2 American Indian or Alaska Native, non-Hispanic/Latino; 5 Asian, non-Hispanic/Latino; 9 Hispanic/Latino; 3 Native Hawaiian or other Pacific Islander, non-Hispanic/Latino; 1 Two or more races, non-Hispanic/Latino), 5 international. Average age 32. 53 applicants, 79% accepted, 33 enrolled. *Faculty:* 5 full-time (2 women), 6 part-time/adjunct (1 woman). Expenses: Contact institution. *Financial support:* Tuition waivers (full and partial) and unspecified assistantships available. Financial award application deadline: 6/15. In 2018, 48 master's awarded. *Program availability:* Part-time, evening/weekend, 100% online. Offers public administration (MPA). *Application deadline:* For fall admission, 7/15 for domestic and international students; for spring admission, 11/15 for domestic and international students; for summer admission, 4/15 for domestic and international students. Applications are processed on a rolling basis. *Application fee:* $60 ($65 for international students). Electronic applications accepted. *Application Contact:* Dr. Angela Pool-Funai, MPA Program Director, 435-865-8153, Fax: 435-586-1925, E-mail: angelapoolfunai@suu.edu. *MPA Program Director,* Dr. Angela Pool-Funai, 435-865-8153, Fax: 435-586-1925, E-mail: angelapoolfunai@suu.edu.

Program in Sports Conditioning and Performance Students: 13 full-time (5 women), 56 part-time (21 women); includes 10 minority (1 Black or African American, non-Hispanic/Latino; 1 American Indian or Alaska Native, non-Hispanic/Latino; 3 Asian, non-Hispanic/Latino; 3 Hispanic/Latino; 2 Native Hawaiian or other Pacific Islander, non-Hispanic/Latino). Average age 29. 19 applicants, 89% accepted, 9 enrolled. *Faculty:* 8 full-time (4 women). Expenses: Contact institution. *Financial support:* Available to part-time students. In 2018, 7 master's awarded. *Program availability:* Part-time, online only, three intensive summer courses/clinical workshops on campus for 1-2 weeks. Offers sports conditioning and performance (MS). *Application deadline:* For fall admission, 7/15 for domestic and international students; for spring admission, 10/15 for domestic and international students; for summer admission, 2/15 for domestic and international students. Applications are processed on a rolling basis. *Application fee:* $60 ($65 for international students). Electronic applications accepted. *Application Contact:* Joan Anderson, Administrative Assistant, 435-586-7816, Fax: 435-865-8057, E-mail: anderson_j@suu.edu. *Department Chair,* Dr. Camille Thomas, 435-586-7815, Fax: 435-865-8057, E-mail: camillethomas1@suu.edu.

SOUTHERN WESLEYAN UNIVERSITY, Central, SC 29630-1020

General Information Independent-religious, coed, comprehensive institution. *Graduate housing:* On-campus housing not available.

GRADUATE UNITS

Program in Business Administration *Program availability:* Evening/weekend. Offers business administration (MBA).

Program in Christian Ministries *Program availability:* Part-time, evening/weekend. Offers Christian ministries (M Min).

Program in Education *Program availability:* Evening/weekend. Offers education (M Ed). Program also offered at Greenville, S. C. site.

Program in Management *Program availability:* Evening/weekend. Offers management (MSM).

SOUTH FLORIDA BIBLE COLLEGE AND THEOLOGICAL SEMINARY, Deerfield Beach, FL 33442

General Information Proprietary, coed, comprehensive institution.

GRADUATE UNITS

Graduate Programs Offers biblical studies (MA); theology (M Div).

SOUTH TEXAS COLLEGE OF LAW HOUSTON, Houston, TX 77002-7000

General Information Independent, coed, graduate-only institution.

GRADUATE UNITS

Professional Program *Program availability:* Part-time, evening/weekend. Offers law (JD). Electronic applications accepted.

SOUTH UNIVERSITY, Montgomery, AL 36116-1120

General Information Independent, coed, comprehensive institution.

GRADUATE UNITS

Program in Business Administration Offers business administration (MBA).

Program in Clinical Mental Health Counseling Offers clinical mental health counseling (MA).

Program in Criminal Justice Offers criminal justice (MS).

Program in Healthcare Administration Offers healthcare administration (MBA).

Program in Information Systems and Technology Offers information systems and technology (MS).

Program in Nursing Offers nursing (MSN).

Program in Public Administration Offers public administration (MPA).

SOUTH UNIVERSITY, Royal Palm Beach, FL 33411

General Information Independent, coed, comprehensive institution.

GRADUATE UNITS

Program in Business Administration Offers business administration (MBA); healthcare administration (MBA).

Program in Clinical Mental Health Counseling Offers clinical mental health counseling (MA).
Program in Criminal Justice Offers criminal justice (MS).
Program in Information Systems and Technology Offers information systems and technology (MS).
Program in Nursing Offers family nurse practitioner (MS).
Program in Occupational Therapy Offers occupational therapy (OTD).
Program in Public Administration Offers public administration (MPA).

SOUTH UNIVERSITY, Tampa, FL 33614
General Information Independent, coed, comprehensive institution.
GRADUATE UNITS
Program in Business Administration Offers business administration (MBA).
Program in Criminal Justice Offers criminal justice (MS).
Program in Healthcare Administration Offers healthcare administration (MBA).
Program in Information Systems and Technology Offers information systems and technology (MS).
Program in Nursing Offers adult health nurse practitioner (MS); family nurse practitioner (MS); nurse educator (MS).
Program in Physician Assistant Studies Offers physician assistant studies (MS).

SOUTH UNIVERSITY, Savannah, GA 31406
General Information Independent, coed, comprehensive institution.
GRADUATE UNITS
Graduate Programs
College of Arts and Sciences Offers arts and sciences (MA, MS); clinical mental health counseling (MA); criminal justice (MS).
College of Business Offers corrections (MBA); entrepreneurship and small business (MBA); healthcare administration (MBA); hospitality management (MBA); leadership (MS); public administration (MPA); sustainability (MBA).
College of Health Professions Offers anesthesiologist assistant (MM Sc); health professions (MM Sc, MS); physician assistant studies (MS).
College of Nursing Offers nurse educator (MS).
Doctor of Ministry Program Offers ministry (D Min).
School of Pharmacy

SOUTH UNIVERSITY, Columbia, SC 29203
General Information Independent, coed, comprehensive institution.
GRADUATE UNITS
Program in Business Administration Offers business administration (MBA).
Program in Clinical Mental Health Counseling Offers clinical mental health counseling (MA).
Program in Criminal Justice Offers criminal justice (MS).
Program in Healthcare Administration Offers healthcare administration (MBA).
Program in Leadership Offers leadership (MS).
Program in Nursing Offers nursing (MSN).
Program in Pharmacy Offers pharmacy (Pharm D).

SOUTH UNIVERSITY, Round Rock, TX 78681
General Information Independent, coed, comprehensive institution.
GRADUATE UNITS
Program in Business Administration Offers business administration (MBA).
Program in Clinical Mental Health Counseling Offers clinical mental health counseling (MA).
Program in Information Systems and Technology Offers information systems and technology (MS).

SOUTH UNIVERSITY, Glen Allen, VA 23060
General Information Independent, coed, comprehensive institution.
GRADUATE UNITS
Program in Business Administration Offers business administration (MBA).
Program in Clinical Mental Health Counseling Offers clinical mental health counseling (MA).
Program in Nursing Offers nursing (MSN).

SOUTH UNIVERSITY, Virginia Beach, VA 23452
General Information Independent, coed, comprehensive institution.
GRADUATE UNITS
Program in Business Administration Offers business administration (MBA).
Program in Clinical Mental Health Counseling Offers clinical mental health counseling (MA).
Program in Information Systems and Technology Offers information systems and technology (MS).
Program in Leadership Offers leadership (MS).
Program in Nursing Offers family nurse practitioner (MSN).

SOUTHWEST ACUPUNCTURE COLLEGE, Santa Fe, NM 87505
General Information Private, coed, primarily women, graduate-only institution. *Graduate housing:* On-campus housing not available.
GRADUATE UNITS
Program in Oriental Medicine, Boulder Campus *Program availability:* Part-time. Offers Oriental medicine (MS).
Program in Oriental Medicine, Santa Fe Campus *Program availability:* Part-time. Offers Oriental medicine (MS). Electronic applications accepted.

SOUTHWEST BAPTIST UNIVERSITY, Bolivar, MO 65613-2597
General Information Independent-religious, coed, comprehensive institution. *Graduate housing:* Room and/or apartments available on a first-come, first-served basis to single students; on-campus housing not available to married students.
GRADUATE UNITS
Program in Business *Program availability:* Part-time, online learning. Offers business administration (MBA); health administration (MBA).
Program in Education *Program availability:* Part-time. Offers education (MS); educational administration (MS, Ed S).

Program in Physical Therapy Offers physical therapy (DPT).

SOUTHWEST COLLEGE OF NATUROPATHIC MEDICINE AND HEALTH SCIENCES, Tempe, AZ 85282
General Information Independent, coed, graduate-only institution. *Graduate housing:* On-campus housing not available. *Research affiliation:* Gaia Herbs, Arizona State University, Biodesign Institute (immune modulation, virology, genomics, herbal medicine), Emory University, Aviratek, LLC (antimicrobial botanicals).
GRADUATE UNITS
Doctor of Naturopathic Medicine Program Offers naturopathic medicine (ND). Electronic applications accepted.

SOUTHWESTERN ADVENTIST UNIVERSITY, Keene, TX 76059
General Information Independent-religious, coed, comprehensive institution. *Graduate housing:* Rooms and/or apartments available on a first-come, first-served basis to single and married students. Housing application deadline: 8/31.
GRADUATE UNITS
Business Administration Department *Program availability:* Part-time, evening/weekend. Offers accounting (MBA); finance (MBA); management/leadership (MBA).
Education Department *Program availability:* Part-time, evening/weekend. Offers curriculum and instruction with reading emphasis (M Ed); educational leadership (M Ed).

SOUTHWESTERN ASSEMBLIES OF GOD UNIVERSITY, Waxahachie, TX 75165-5735
General Information Independent-religious, coed, comprehensive institution. *Graduate housing:* Room and/or apartments guaranteed to single students.
GRADUATE UNITS
Thomas F. Harrison School of Graduate Studies *Program availability:* Part-time, evening/weekend, online learning. Offers Bible and theology (MS); Biblical studies (M Div); Christian school administration (MS); counseling (M Div); counseling psychology (clinical) (MCP); cross cultural missions (M Div); curriculum development (MS); early education administration (M Ed); history (MA); human services counseling (MS); middle and secondary education (M Ed); practical theology (M Div); theological studies (M Div). Electronic applications accepted.

SOUTHWESTERN BAPTIST THEOLOGICAL SEMINARY, Fort Worth, TX 76122-0000
General Information Independent-religious, coed, primarily men, graduate-only institution. *Graduate housing:* Rooms and/or apartments available on a first-come, first-served basis to single and married students. *Research affiliation:* Campus Crusade for Christ/Jesus Film Project (evangelical missions), DAWN: Discipling A Whole Nation (evangelical missions).
GRADUATE UNITS
Jack D. Terry School of Church and Family Ministries *Program availability:* Part-time, evening/weekend. Offers church and family ministries (MA, MACE, MACSE, DEM, PhD). Electronic applications accepted.
Roy Fish School of Evangelism and Missions Offers cross-cultural missions (MTS); evangelism (M Div); evangelism and missions (D Min); international church planting (M Div); Islamic studies (M Div, MA Islamic); missiology (MA Miss); missions (M Div); North American church planting (M Div); North American evangelism and international missions (D Min); theology (Th M); world Christian studies (PhD).
School of Church Music *Program availability:* Part-time. Offers church music (MACM, MAWSHP, MM, DMA, PhD). Electronic applications accepted.
School of Preaching Offers preaching (Th M, D Min, PhD, Certificate).
School of Theology *Program availability:* Part-time, evening/weekend. Offers ministry (D Min); theology (PhD). Electronic applications accepted.

SOUTHWESTERN CHRISTIAN UNIVERSITY, Bethany, OK 73008-0340
General Information Independent-religious, coed, comprehensive institution.
GRADUATE UNITS
Program in Ministry *Program availability:* Part-time. Offers church planting (M Min); church revitalization and renewal (M Min); intercultural studies (M Min); leadership (M Min); life coaching (M Min); pastoral ministries (M Min); work place ministries (M Min). Electronic applications accepted.

SOUTHWESTERN COLLEGE, Winfield, KS 67156-2499
General Information Independent-religious, coed, comprehensive institution. *Enrollment:* 44 full-time matriculated graduate/professional students (15 women), 124 part-time matriculated graduate/professional students (74 women). *Enrollment by degree level:* 126 master's, 40 doctoral, 2 other advanced degrees. *Graduate faculty:* 12 full-time (7 women), 33 part-time/adjunct (16 women). *Tuition:* Full-time $11,502; part-time $639 per credit hour. *Required fees:* $60. Tuition and fees vary according to degree level, campus/location and program. *Graduate housing:* Rooms and/or apartments available on a first-come, first-served basis to single and married students. Typical cost: $7760 (including board) for single students. Room and board charges vary according to board plan and housing facility selected. *Student services:* Campus employment opportunities, campus safety program, career counseling, free psychological counseling, international student services, services for students with disabilities, teacher training, writing training. *Library facilities:* Harold and Mary Ellen Deets Library. *Collection:* Books: 49,349 (physical), 479,970 (digital/electronic); Serial titles: 10 (physical), 21,560 (digital/electronic); Databases: 84. Weekly public service hours: 91; students can reserve study rooms.
Computer facilities: Computer purchase and lease plans are available. 45 computers available on campus for general student use. A campuswide network can be accessed from student residence rooms and from off campus. Online class registration, everything in Self-Service and BlackBoard are available.
Website: http://www.sckans.edu/
General Application Contact: Adam Jenkins, Vice President for Enrollment Management, 620-229-6091, Fax: 620-229-6384, E-mail: adam.jenkins@sckans.edu.
GRADUATE UNITS
Education Programs Students: 6 full-time (5 women), 79 part-time (54 women); includes 11 minority (4 Black or African American, non-Hispanic/Latino; 2 American Indian or Alaska Native, non-Hispanic/Latino; 1 Asian, non-Hispanic/Latino; 3 Hispanic/Latino; 1 Two or more races, non-Hispanic/Latino), 4 international. Average age 38. 31 applicants, 74% accepted, 18 enrolled. *Faculty:* 7 full-time (5 women), 14

part-time/adjunct (12 women). Expenses: Contact institution. *Financial support:* In 2018–19, 13 students received support. Unspecified assistantships and employee tuition waivers available. Financial award applicants required to submit FAFSA. In 2018, 24 master's, 8 doctorates awarded. *Program availability:* Part-time, evening/weekend, 100% online, blended/hybrid learning. Offers curriculum and instruction (M Ed); early childhood education (M Ed); educational leadership (Ed D); special education (M Ed); teaching (MA). *Application deadline:* Applications are processed on a rolling basis. *Application fee:* $40. Electronic applications accepted. *Application Contact:* Jen Caughron, Director of Enrollment Services & Marketing, 888-684-5335 Ext. 3312, Fax: 888-684-5218, E-mail: jennifer.caughron@sckans.edu. *Education Division Chair,* J.K. Campbell, 620-229-6115, E-mail: JK.Campbell@sckans.edu.

Fifth-Year Graduate Programs Students: 18 full-time (5 women), 2 part-time (both women); includes 7 minority (6 Black or African American, non-Hispanic/Latino; 1 Hispanic/Latino), 5 international. Average age 25. 25 applicants, 52% accepted, 10 enrolled. *Faculty:* 5 full-time (2 women). Expenses: Contact institution. *Financial support:* In 2018–19, 14 students received support. Fellowships, unspecified assistantships, and employee tuition waivers available. Financial award applicants required to submit FAFSA. In 2018, 9 master's awarded. *Program availability:* Part-time. Offers management (MBA). *Application deadline:* For fall admission, 8/26 for domestic students; for spring admission, 1/21 for domestic students. Applications are processed on a rolling basis. *Application fee:* $25. Electronic applications accepted. *Application Contact:* Adam Jenkins, Vice President for Enrollment Management, 620-229-6091, E-mail: adam.jenkins@sckans.edu. *Professor/Division Chair,* Dr. Kurt Keiser, 620-229-6361, E-mail: kurt.keiser@sckans.edu.

Professional Studies Programs Students: 20 full-time (5 women), 43 part-time (18 women); includes 16 minority (8 Black or African American, non-Hispanic/Latino; 1 Asian, non-Hispanic/Latino; 5 Hispanic/Latino; 2 Two or more races, non-Hispanic/Latino). Average age 37. 24 applicants, 100% accepted, 17 enrolled. *Faculty:* 19 part-time/adjunct (4 women). Expenses: Contact institution. *Financial support:* In 2018–19, 11 students received support. Unspecified assistantships and employee tuition waivers available. Financial award applicants required to submit FAFSA. In 2018, 37 master's awarded. *Program availability:* Part-time, evening/weekend, online only, 100% online. Offers business administration (MBA); leadership (MS); management (MS); security administration (MS); specialized ministries (MA). *Application deadline:* Applications are processed on a rolling basis. *Application fee:* $40. Electronic applications accepted. *Application Contact:* Jen Caughron, Director of Enrollment Services & Marketing, 888-684-5335 Ext. 3312, Fax: 316-688-5218, E-mail: jennifer.caughron@sckans.edu. *Director of Enrollment Services & Marketing,* Jen Caughron, 888-684-5335 Ext. 3312, Fax: 316-688-5218, E-mail: jennifer.caughron@sckans.edu.

SOUTHWESTERN COLLEGE, Santa Fe, NM 87502-4788

General Information Independent, coed, primarily women, graduate-only institution. *Graduate housing:* On-campus housing not available.

GRADUATE UNITS

Program in Art Therapy/Counseling *Program availability:* Part-time, evening/weekend. Offers art therapy/counseling (MA).

Program in Counseling *Program availability:* Part-time, evening/weekend. Offers counseling (MA).

Program in Grief, Loss and Trauma Counseling *Program availability:* Part-time, evening/weekend, online learning. Offers grief, loss and trauma counseling (MA, Certificate).

Program in Integral Somatic Psychology Offers integral somatic psychology (Certificate).

Program in Psychodrama and Action Methods Offers psychodrama and action methods (Certificate).

Program in Transformational Ecopsychology Offers transformational ecopsychology (Certificate).

SOUTHWESTERN LAW SCHOOL, Los Angeles, CA 90010

General Information Independent, coed, graduate-only institution. *Enrollment by degree level:* 718 doctoral. *Graduate faculty:* 60 full-time (30 women), 83 part-time/adjunct (37 women). *Tuition:* Full-time $53,966; part-time $35,994 per year. *Required fees:* $200; $200 per unit. Tuition and fees vary according to program. *Graduate housing:* Rooms and/or apartments available on a first-come, first-served basis to single and married students. Typical cost: $20,520 (including board) for single students; $20,520 (including board) for married students. Room and board charges vary according to housing facility selected. *Student services:* Campus employment opportunities, campus safety program, career counseling, exercise/wellness program, free psychological counseling, international student services, low-cost health insurance, multicultural affairs office, services for students with disabilities, writing training. *Library facilities:* Leigh H. Taylor Law Library. *Collection:* Books: 84,135 (physical), 242,870 (digital/electronic); Serial titles: 9,537 (physical), 5,610 (digital/electronic); Databases: 117. Weekly public service hours: 102; students can reserve study rooms.

Computer facilities: 102 computers available on campus for general student use. A campuswide network can be accessed from student residence rooms. Online class registration is available.
Website: http://www.swlaw.edu/

General Application Contact: Lisa Gear, Assistant Dean of Admissions, 213-738-6834, Fax: 213-738-6899, E-mail: admissions@swlaw.edu.

GRADUATE UNITS

Graduate and Professional Programs Students: 517 full-time (270 women), 200 part-time (129 women); includes 338 minority (43 Black or African American, non-Hispanic/Latino; 58 Asian, non-Hispanic/Latino; 195 Hispanic/Latino; 3 Native Hawaiian or other Pacific Islander, non-Hispanic/Latino; 39 Two or more races, non-Hispanic/Latino), 14 international. Average age 27. 1,752 applicants, 46% accepted, 271 enrolled. *Faculty:* 60 full-time (30 women), 83 part-time/adjunct (37 women). Expenses: Contact institution. *Financial support:* In 2018–19, 369 students received support. Federal Work-Study, institutionally sponsored loans, and scholarships/grants available. Support available to part-time students. Financial award application deadline: 6/1; financial award applicants required to submit FAFSA. In 2018, 7 master's, 182 doctorates awarded. *Program availability:* Part-time, evening/weekend. Offers entertainment and media law (LL M); individualized studies (LL M); law (JD). *Application deadline:* For fall admission, 4/1 priority date for domestic and international students. Applications are processed on a rolling basis. *Application fee:* $60. Electronic applications accepted. *Application Contact:* Lisa Gear, Assistant Dean of Admissions, 213-738-6834, Fax: 213-738-6899, E-mail: admissions@swlaw.edu. *Dean,* Susan Westerberg Prager, 213-738-6710, Fax: 213-383-1688.

SOUTHWESTERN OKLAHOMA STATE UNIVERSITY, Weatherford, OK 73096-3098

General Information State-supported, coed, comprehensive institution. *Graduate housing:* Rooms and/or apartments available on a first-come, first-served basis to single and married students. Housing application deadline: 8/19. *Research affiliation:* Gulf Coast Research Laboratory.

GRADUATE UNITS

College of Arts and Sciences *Program availability:* Part-time. Offers art education (M Ed); arts and sciences (M Ed, MM); music education (MM); music performance (MM); music therapy (MM).

College of Pharmacy Offers pharmacy (Pharm D); pharmacy leadership (Pharm D).

College of Professional and Graduate Studies *Program availability:* Part-time, evening/weekend, online learning.

Everett Dobson School of Business and Technology *Program availability:* Part-time, evening/weekend, online learning. Offers business and technology (MBA, MSM). MBA distance learning degree program offered to Oklahoma residents only.

School of Behavioral Sciences and Education *Program availability:* Part-time, evening/weekend, online learning. Offers biomedical science and microbiology (M Ed); community counseling (MS); early childhood education (M Ed); education administration (M Ed); elementary education (M Ed); health and physical education (M Ed); kinesiology (M Ed); mathematics (M Ed); natural sciences (M Ed); parks and recreation management (M Ed); school counseling (M Ed); school psychology (Ed S); school psychometry (M Ed); social sciences (M Ed); special education (M Ed); sports management (M Ed).

SOUTHWEST MINNESOTA STATE UNIVERSITY, Marshall, MN 56258

General Information State-supported, coed, comprehensive institution. *Graduate housing:* Room and/or apartments available to single students; on-campus housing not available to married students.

GRADUATE UNITS

Department of Business and Public Affairs *Program availability:* Part-time, evening/weekend, online learning. Offers leadership (MBA); management (MBA); marketing (MBA). Electronic applications accepted.

Department of Education *Program availability:* Part-time, evening/weekend, online learning. Offers ESL (MS); math (MS); reading (MS); special education (MS); teaching, learning and leadership (MS).

SOUTHWEST UNIVERSITY, Kenner, LA 70062

General Information Proprietary, coed, comprehensive institution.

GRADUATE UNITS

MBA Program Offers business administration (MBA); management (MBA); organizational management (MBA).

Program in Criminal Justice Offers criminal justice (MS).

Program in Management Offers management (MA).

Program in Organizational Management Offers organizational management (MA).

SOUTHWEST UNIVERSITY OF VISUAL ARTS, Tucson, AZ 85716-2505

General Information Proprietary, coed, comprehensive institution.

GRADUATE UNITS

MFA Programs Offers motion arts (MFA); painting and drawing (MFA); photography (MFA).

SPALDING UNIVERSITY, Louisville, KY 40203-2188

General Information Independent, coed, comprehensive institution. CGS member. *Graduate housing:* Room and/or apartments available on a first-come, first-served basis to single students; on-campus housing not available to married students.

GRADUATE UNITS

Graduate Studies *Program availability:* Part-time, evening/weekend.

College of Education *Program availability:* Part-time, evening/weekend. Offers art teacher education (MAT); business teacher education (MAT); education (M Ed, MA, MAT, Ed D); elementary school education (MAT); executive (Ed D); foreign language (MAT); high school education (MAT); middle school education (MAT); scholar-practitioner (Ed D); secondary education (MAT); special education (learning and behavioral disorders) (MAT); student guidance counselor (MA); teacher leader (M Ed). Electronic applications accepted.

College of Social Sciences and Humanities *Program availability:* Part-time, evening/weekend, online learning. Offers business and communication (MS); social sciences and humanities (MFA, MS); writing (MFA).

Kosair College of Health and Natural Sciences *Program availability:* Part-time, evening/weekend. Offers adult nurse practitioner (MSN); athletic training (MS); clinical psychology (MA, Psy D); family nurse practitioner (MSN); health and natural sciences (MA, MS, MSN, MSW, DNP, Psy D, Post-Master's Certificate); leadership in nursing and healthcare (MSN); nurse educator (Post-Master's Certificate); nurse practitioner (Post-Master's Certificate); occupational therapy (MS); pediatric nurse practitioner (MSN); social work (MSW).

SPERTUS INSTITUTE FOR JEWISH LEARNING AND LEADERSHIP, Chicago, IL 60605-1901

General Information Independent, coed, graduate-only institution. *Graduate housing:* On-campus housing not available.

GRADUATE UNITS

Program in Jewish Studies *Program availability:* Part-time, evening/weekend, online learning. Offers Jewish studies (MAJPS, MAJS, DJS, DSJS).

SPRING ARBOR UNIVERSITY, Spring Arbor, MI 49283-9799

General Information Independent-religious, coed, comprehensive institution. *Graduate housing:* Rooms and/or apartments available on a first-come, first-served basis to single and married students. Housing application deadline: 5/1.

GRADUATE UNITS

Gainey School of Business *Program availability:* Part-time, evening/weekend, online learning. Offers business (MBA).

School of Arts and Sciences *Program availability:* Part-time, online learning. Offers communication (MA); spiritual formation and leadership (MA).

School of Education *Program availability:* Part-time, evening/weekend, online learning. Offers education (MAE); reading (MAR); special education (MSE). Electronic applications accepted.

School of Human Services *Program availability:* Part-time, evening/weekend, online learning. Offers counseling (MAC); family studies (MAFS); nursing (MSN); social work (MSW). Electronic applications accepted.

SPRINGFIELD COLLEGE, Springfield, MA 01109-3797

General Information Independent, coed, comprehensive institution. CGS member. *Graduate housing:* Rooms and/or apartments available on a first-come, first-served basis to single and married students.

GRADUATE UNITS

Graduate Programs *Program availability:* Part-time, evening/weekend. Offers adapted physical education (MS); advanced-level coaching (M Ed); art therapy (M Ed, MS, CAGS); athletic administration (MS); athletic counseling (MS, CAGS); athletic training (MS); business administration (MBA); clinical exercise physiology (MS); clinical mental health counseling (M Ed, CAGS); counseling psychology (Psy D); early childhood education (M Ed); educational studies (M Ed); elementary education (M Ed); exercise physiology (MS, PhD); general counseling (M Ed); health promotion and disease prevention (MS); industrial/organizational psychology (M Ed, CAGS); mental health counseling (MS); occupational therapy (MS); organizational management and leadership (MS); physical education initial licensure (CAGS); physical therapy (DPT); physician assistant (MS); recreation management (M Ed, MS); rehabilitation counseling (M Ed, MS); school counseling (M Ed, CAGS); secondary education (M Ed); special education (M Ed, CAGS); sport and exercise psychology (MS, PhD); sport management (M Ed, MS); strength and conditioning (MS); student personnel administration in higher education (M Ed, CAGS); teaching and administration (PhD); therapeutic recreation management (M Ed, MS). Electronic applications accepted.

School of Social Work *Program availability:* Part-time, evening/weekend. Offers advanced practice with children and adolescents (Post-Master's Certificate); social work (MSW). Electronic applications accepted.

SPRING HILL COLLEGE, Mobile, AL 36608-1791

General Information Independent-religious, coed, comprehensive institution. *Enrollment:* 1,395 graduate, professional, and undergraduate students; 8 full-time matriculated graduate/professional students (6 women), 117 part-time matriculated graduate/professional students (41 women). *Enrollment by degree level:* 99 master's, 26 other advanced degrees. *Graduate faculty:* 15 full-time (4 women), 8 part-time/adjunct (6 women). *Tuition:* Full-time $9270; part-time $515 per credit hour. Tuition and fees vary according to program. *Graduate housing:* On-campus housing not available. *Student services:* Campus safety program, career counseling, exercise/wellness program, writing training. *Library facilities:* Marnie and John Burke Memorial Library plus 1 other.

Computer facilities: A campuswide network can be accessed from student residence rooms and from off campus. Online class registration is available. Website: http://www.shc.edu/

General Application Contact: Gary Bracken, Vice President of Enrollment Management, 251-380-3038, Fax: 251-460-2186, E-mail: gbracken@shc.edu.

GRADUATE UNITS

Graduate Programs Students: 8 full-time (6 women), 117 part-time (41 women); includes 21 minority (10 Black or African American, non-Hispanic/Latino; 1 American Indian or Alaska Native, non-Hispanic/Latino; 3 Asian, non-Hispanic/Latino; 4 Hispanic/Latino; 3 Two or more races, non-Hispanic/Latino), 6 international. Average age 36. *Faculty:* 15 full-time (4 women), 8 part-time/adjunct (6 women). Expenses: Contact institution. *Financial support:* Fellowships, research assistantships, teaching assistantships, and tuition waivers available. Financial award applicants required to submit FAFSA. In 2018, 36 master's, 4 other advanced degrees awarded. *Program availability:* Part-time, online learning. Offers business administration (MBA); early childhood education (MAT, MS Ed); educational theory (MS Ed); elementary education (MAT, MS Ed); fine arts (MLA); leadership and ethics (MLA, Postbaccalaureate Certificate); literature (MLA); nursing (MSN, Post-Master's Certificate); secondary education (MAT, MA, MPS, MTS, Postbaccalaureate Certificate); theology (MA, MPS, MTS, Postbaccalaureate Certificate). *Application deadline:* For fall admission, 8/1 priority date for domestic and international students; for spring admission, 12/1 priority date for domestic and international students. Applications are processed on a rolling basis. *Application fee:* $25 ($35 for international students). Electronic applications accepted. *Application Contact:* Gary Bracken, Vice President of Enrollment Management, 251-380-3038, Fax: 251-460-2186, E-mail: gbracken@shc.edu. *Vice President of Enrollment Management,* Gary Bracken, 251-380-3038, Fax: 251-460-2186, E-mail: gbracken@shc.edu.

STANBRIDGE UNIVERSITY, Irvine, CA 92612

General Information Proprietary, coed, comprehensive institution.

GRADUATE UNITS

Program in Nursing *Program availability:* Online learning. Offers nursing (MSN).

Program in Occupational Therapy Offers occupational therapy (MS).

STANFORD UNIVERSITY, Stanford, CA 94305-2004

General Information Independent, coed, university. CGS member. *Enrollment:* 9,157 full-time matriculated graduate/professional students (3,860 women), 280 part-time matriculated graduate/professional students (89 women). *Enrollment by degree level:* 3,481 master's, 5,956 doctoral. *Graduate faculty:* 2,208 full-time (650 women), 32 part-time/adjunct (11 women). *Tuition:* Full-time $50,703; part-time $32,970 per year. *Required fees:* $651. *Graduate housing:* Rooms and/or apartments guaranteed to single and married students. Typical cost: $11,643 per year for single students; $20,547 per year for married students. Room charges vary according to housing facility selected. Housing application deadline: 5/9. *Student services:* Campus employment opportunities, campus safety program, career counseling, child daycare facilities, exercise/wellness program, free psychological counseling, grant writing training, international student services, low-cost health insurance, multicultural affairs office, services for students with disabilities, teacher training, writing training. *Library facilities:* Green Library plus 20 others. *Collection:* Books: 9.5 million (physical), 1.5 million (digital/electronic); Serial titles: 77,000 (physical). Study areas open 24 hours, 5–7 days a week; students can reserve study rooms.

Computer facilities: Computer purchase and lease plans are available. 1,000 computers available on campus for general student use. A campuswide network can be accessed from student residence rooms and from off campus. Online class registration is available.

Website: http://www.stanford.edu/

General Application Contact: Graduate Admissions, 866-432-7472, Fax: 650-723-8371, E-mail: gradadmissions@stanford.edu.

GRADUATE UNITS

Graduate School of Business Expenses: Contact institution. Offers business (MBA, PhD).

Graduate School of Education Expenses: Contact institution. Offers curriculum and teacher education (MA); education (MA, MAE, PhD); elementary education (MAE); international comparative education (MA, PhD); learning, design, and technology (MA); policy, organization, and leadership studies (MA); secondary education (MAE).

Law School Expenses: Contact institution. Offers corporate governance and practice (LL M); environmental law and policy (LL M); international economic law, business and policy (LL M); international legal studies (JSM); law (JD, JSD); law, science and technology (LL M); legal studies (MLS). *Application Contact:* Graduate Admissions, 866-432-7472, Fax: 650-723-8371, E-mail: gradadmissions@stanford.edu. *Dean,* M. Elizabeth Magill, 650-723-4455, Fax: 650-725-0253, E-mail: emagill@law.stanford.edu.

School of Earth, Energy and Environmental Sciences Expenses: Contact institution. Offers earth system science (MS, PhD); earth, energy and environmental sciences (MS, PhD, Eng); energy resources engineering (MS, PhD, Eng); geological sciences (MS, PhD, Eng); geophysics (MS, PhD); petroleum engineering (MS, PhD).

School of Engineering Expenses: Contact institution. Offers aeronautics and astronautics (MS, PhD, Eng); atmosphere and energy (MS, PhD); biomechanical engineering (MSE); chemical engineering (MS, PhD); computer science (MS, PhD); construction (MS); design impact (MSE); electrical engineering (MS, PhD); engineering (MS, MSE, PhD, Engr); environmental engineering and science (MS, PhD, Eng); environmental fluid mechanics and hydrology (PhD); geomechanics (MS); management science and engineering (MS, PhD); materials science and engineering (MS, PhD, Engr); mechanical engineering (MS, PhD, Engr); product design (MS); structural engineering (MS).

Institute for Computational and Mathematical Engineering Expenses: Contact institution. Offers computational and mathematical engineering (MS, PhD).

School of Humanities and Sciences Expenses: Contact institution. Offers anthropology (MA); applied and engineering physics (MS); applied physics (PhD); archaeology (PhD); art history (PhD); art practice (MFA); biology (MS, PhD); biophysics (PhD); chemistry (PhD); Chinese (MA, PhD); classics (MA, PhD); communication (MA, PhD); comparative literature (PhD); composition (DMA); computer-based music theory and acoustics (PhD); culture and society (PhD); data science (MS); design (MFA); documentary film and video (MFA); ecology and environment (PhD); economics (PhD); English (MA, PhD); financial mathematics (MS); French (MA, PhD); French and Italian (PhD); German studies (MA, PhD); history (MA, PhD); humanities and sciences (MA, MFA, MS, DMA, PhD); Italian (MA, PhD); Japanese (MA, PhD); linguistics (MA, PhD); mathematics (PhD); modern thought and literature (PhD); music, science, and technology (MA); musicology (PhD); philosophy (MA, PhD); physics (PhD); political science (MA, PhD); psychology (PhD); religious studies (PhD); Slavic languages and literatures (PhD); sociology (PhD); Spanish (MA, PhD); statistics (PhD); theater and performance studies (PhD).

Center for East Asian Studies Expenses: Contact institution. Offers East Asian studies (MA).

Center for Russian, East European and Eurasian Studies Expenses: Contact institution. Offers Russian, East European and Eurasian studies (MA).

School of Medicine Expenses: Contact institution. Offers bioengineering (MS, PhD); medicine (MS, MD, PhD).

Graduate Programs in Medicine Expenses: Contact institution. Offers biochemistry (PhD); biostatistics (PhD); chemical and systems biology (PhD); developmental biology (MS, PhD); epidemiology and clinical research (MS, PhD); genetics (PhD); health policy (MS, PhD); medicine (MS, PhD); microbiology and immunology (PhD); molecular and cellular physiology (PhD); structural biology (PhD).

Stanford Center for Biomedical Informatics Research Expenses: Contact institution. Offers biomedical informatics research (MS, PhD).

STARR KING SCHOOL FOR THE MINISTRY, Berkeley, CA 94709-1209

General Information Independent-religious, coed, graduate-only institution. *Graduate housing:* On-campus housing not available.

GRADUATE UNITS

Professional Program Offers theology (M Div).

STATE UNIVERSITY OF NEW YORK AT FREDONIA, Fredonia, NY 14063-1136

General Information State-supported, coed, comprehensive institution. *Enrollment:* 4,656 graduate, professional, and undergraduate students; 151 full-time matriculated graduate/professional students (122 women), 73 part-time matriculated graduate/professional students (59 women). *Enrollment by degree level:* 218 master's, 6 other advanced degrees. *Graduate faculty:* 97 full-time (55 women), 64 part-time/adjunct (37 women). *International tuition:* $16,650 full-time. Tuition, state resident: full-time $6870; part-time $462 per credit hour. Tuition, nonresident: full-time $16,650; part-time $944 per credit hour. *Required fees:* $25; $2 per credit hour. $1 per semester. *Graduate housing:* Room and/or apartments available on a first-come, first-served basis to single students; on-campus housing not available to married students. Typical cost: $7500 per year ($12,630 including board). Housing application deadline: 8/24. *Student services:* Campus employment opportunities, campus safety program, career counseling, child daycare facilities, exercise/wellness program, free psychological counseling, grant writing training, international student services, low-cost health insurance, multicultural affairs office, services for students with disabilities, teacher training, writing training. *Library facilities:* Daniel A. Reed Library. *Collection:* Books: 18 million (physical); Serial titles: 48,000 (physical). Weekly public service hours: 68; students can reserve study rooms.

Computer facilities: Computer purchase and lease plans are available. 500 computers available on campus for general student use. A campuswide network can be accessed. Online class registration is available.

Website: http://www.fredonia.edu/

General Application Contact: Wendy S. Dunst, Graduate Admissions Coordinator (Graduate Recruit/Admissions Associate), 716-673-4971, Fax: 716-673-3712, E-mail: wendy.dunst@fredonia.edu.

GRADUATE UNITS

College of Education Students: 39 full-time (33 women), 44 part-time (36 women); includes 5 minority (1 Asian, non-Hispanic/Latino; 3 Hispanic/Latino; 1 Two or more races, non-Hispanic/Latino), 4 international. Average age 27. 44 applicants, 89% accepted, 34 enrolled. *Faculty:* 16 full-time (14 women), 13 part-time/adjunct (11 women). Expenses: Contact institution. *Financial support:* In 2018–19, 13 students received support. Unspecified assistantships available. Financial award application deadline: 3/15; financial award applicants required to submit FAFSA. In 2018, 25 master's awarded. *Program availability:* Part-time. Offers curriculum and instruction (MS Ed); literacy education (MS Ed); music education (M Mus); TESOL (MS Ed). *Application deadline:* For fall admission, 4/1 priority date for domestic and international students; for spring admission, 11/1 priority date for domestic students, 11/1 for international students. Applications are processed on a rolling basis. *Application fee:* $75. Electronic applications accepted. *Application Contact:* Wendy S. Dunst, Interim Graduate Recruitment and Admissions Associate, 716-673-3808, Fax: 716-673-3712, E-mail: wendy.dunst@fredonia.edu. *Dean,* Dr. Christine Givner, 716-673-3311, E-mail: christine.givner@fredonia.edu.

College of Liberal Arts and Sciences Students: 67 full-time (60 women), 6 part-time (5 women); includes 9 minority (2 Black or African American, non-Hispanic/Latino; 5 Asian, non-Hispanic/Latino; 1 Hispanic/Latino; 1 Two or more races, non-Hispanic/Latino), 9 international. Average age 23. 131 applicants, 77% accepted, 36 enrolled. *Faculty:* 23 full-time (12 women), 3 part-time/adjunct (1 woman). Expenses: Contact institution. *Financial support:* In 2018–19, 17 students received support, including 14 teaching assistantships with full and partial tuition reimbursements available (averaging $5,957 per year); tuition waivers (full and partial) and unspecified assistantships also available. In 2018, 37 master's, 1 other advanced degree awarded. *Program availability:* Part-time, evening/weekend. Offers biology (MS); English (MA); English education 7-12 (MA); interdisciplinary studies (MA, MS); math education (MS Ed); professional writing (CAS); speech pathology (MS). *Application deadline:* For fall admission, 4/1 for domestic and international students; for spring admission, 11/1 for domestic and international students. Applications are processed on a rolling basis. *Application fee:* $75. Electronic applications accepted. *Application Contact:* Wendy S. Dunst, Interim Graduate Recruitment and Admissions Associate, 716-673-3808, Fax: 716-673-3712, E-mail: wendy.dunst@fredonia.edu. *Dean,* Dr. Andy Karafa, 716-673-3173, Fax: 716-673-3338, E-mail: andy.karafa@gmail.com.

School of Music Students: 44 full-time (28 women), 18 part-time (13 women); includes 5 minority (2 Black or African American, non-Hispanic/Latino; 1 Asian, non-Hispanic/Latino; 1 Hispanic/Latino; 1 Two or more races, non-Hispanic/Latino), 16 international. Average age 25. 63 applicants, 59% accepted, 24 enrolled. *Faculty:* 40 full-time (17 women), 15 part-time/adjunct (9 women). Expenses: Contact institution. *Financial support:* In 2018–19, 14 students received support. Unspecified assistantships available. Financial award application deadline: 3/15; financial award applicants required to submit FAFSA. In 2018, 87 master's awarded. *Program availability:* Part-time. Offers music education (MM); music performance (MM); music theory/composition (MM); music therapy (MM). *Application deadline:* For fall admission, 4/1 priority date for domestic and international students; for spring admission, 11/1 priority date for domestic students, 11/1 for international students. Applications are processed on a rolling basis. *Application fee:* $75. Electronic applications accepted. *Application Contact:* Dr. Barry Kilpatrick, Admissions Coordinator, School of Music, 716-673-4635, E-mail: barry.kilpatrick@fredonia.edu. *Director, School of Music,* Dr. Melvin Unger, 716-673-3151, E-mail: melvin.unger@fredonia.edu.

STATE UNIVERSITY OF NEW YORK AT NEW PALTZ, New Paltz, NY 12561

General Information State-supported, coed, comprehensive institution. *Enrollment:* 449 full-time matriculated graduate/professional students (320 women), 467 part-time matriculated graduate/professional students (347 women). *Enrollment by degree level:* 916 master's. *Graduate faculty:* 116 full-time (60 women), 55 part-time/adjunct (38 women). *Graduate housing:* On-campus housing not available. *Student services:* Campus employment opportunities, campus safety program, career counseling, child daycare facilities, free psychological counseling, international student services, low-cost health insurance, services for students with disabilities, teacher training, writing training. *Library facilities:* Sojourner Truth Library. *Collection:* Books: 455,728 (physical), 149,851 (digital/electronic); Serial titles: 234 (physical), 85,306 (digital/electronic); Databases: 98. Weekly public service hours: 103; students can reserve study rooms.

Computer facilities: 800 computers available on campus for general student use. A campuswide network can be accessed from student residence rooms and from off campus. Online class registration is available.
Website: http://www.newpaltz.edu/

General Application Contact: Vika Shock, Director of Graduate Admissions, 845-257-3285, Fax: 845-257-3284, E-mail: gradstudies@newpaltz.edu.

GRADUATE UNITS

Graduate and Extended Learning School Students: 455 full-time (324 women), 474 part-time (353 women); includes 157 minority (26 Black or African American, non-Hispanic/Latino; 17 Asian, non-Hispanic/Latino; 101 Hispanic/Latino; 1 Native Hawaiian or other Pacific Islander, non-Hispanic/Latino; 12 Two or more races, non-Hispanic/Latino), 65 international. 714 applicants, 64% accepted, 288 enrolled. *Faculty:* 116 full-time (60 women), 55 part-time/adjunct (38 women). Expenses: Contact institution. *Financial support:* In 2018–19, 15 fellowships with partial tuition reimbursements (averaging $1,360 per year), 30 research assistantships with partial tuition reimbursements (averaging $5,000 per year), 40 teaching assistantships with partial tuition reimbursements (averaging $5,000 per year) were awarded; career-related internships or fieldwork, scholarships/grants, traineeships, health care benefits, and unspecified assistantships also available. Financial award application deadline: 8/1; financial award applicants required to submit FAFSA. In 2018, 372 master's, 45 other advanced degrees awarded. *Program availability:* Part-time, evening/weekend. *Application fee:* $50. Electronic applications accepted. *Application Contact:* Vika Shock, Director of Graduate Admissions, 845-257-3285, Fax: 845-257-3284, E-mail: shockv@newpaltz.edu. *Assistant Vice President,* Dr. Shala Mills, 845-257-3947, Fax: 845-257-3284, E-mail: millss@newpaltz.edu.

School of Business Students: 61 full-time (33 women), 48 part-time (24 women); includes 24 minority (6 Black or African American, non-Hispanic/Latino; 6 Asian, non-Hispanic/Latino; 11 Hispanic/Latino; 1 Two or more races, non-Hispanic/Latino), 8 international. 49 applicants, 96% accepted, 38 enrolled. *Faculty:* 14 full-time (2 women), 4 part-time/adjunct (1 woman). Expenses: Contact institution. *Financial support:* In 2018–19, 6 research assistantships with partial tuition reimbursements (averaging $5,000 per year), 1 teaching assistantship with partial tuition reimbursement (averaging $5,000 per year) were awarded; scholarships/grants, traineeships, and unspecified assistantships also available. Financial award application deadline: 8/1. In 2018, 42 master's awarded. *Program availability:* Part-time, evening/weekend. Offers business administration (MBA); public accountancy (MBA). *Application deadline:* Applications are processed on a rolling basis. *Application fee:* $50. Electronic applications accepted. *Application Contact:* Aaron Hines, Director of MBA Program, 845-257-2968, E-mail: mba@newpaltz.edu. *Dean,* Dr. Kristin Backhaus, 845-257-2930, E-mail: mba@newpaltz.edu.

School of Education Students: 147 full-time (104 women), 296 part-time (241 women); includes 72 minority (11 Black or African American, non-Hispanic/Latino; 2 Asian, non-Hispanic/Latino; 54 Hispanic/Latino; 5 Two or more races, non-Hispanic/Latino). 180 applicants, 83% accepted, 122 enrolled. *Faculty:* 26 full-time (19 women), 24 part-time/adjunct (19 women). Expenses: Contact institution. *Financial support:* Scholarships/grants available. Financial award application deadline: 8/1. In 2018, 169 master's, 45 other advanced degrees awarded. *Program availability:* Part-time, evening/weekend. Offers adolescence education: biology (MAT, MS Ed); adolescence education: chemistry (MAT, MS Ed); adolescence education: earth science (MAT, MS Ed); adolescence education: English (MAT, MS Ed); adolescence education: French (MAT, MS Ed); adolescence education: social studies (MAT, MS Ed); adolescence education: Spanish (MAT, MS Ed); adolescence special education (7-12) (MS Ed); adolescence special education and literacy (MS Ed); childhood education (MS Ed); childhood education 1-6 (MST); childhood special education (1-6) (MS Ed); childhood special education and literacy (MS Ed); early childhood special education (B-2) (MS Ed); education (MAT, MPS, MS Ed, MST, AC, CAS); humanistic/multicultural education (MPS, AC); multicultural education (AC); school building leader (CAS); school district leader alternate route: transition d (CAS); school leadership (MS Ed, CAS); second language education (MS Ed, AC); second language education (tesol) (MS Ed); special education (MS Ed); teaching English to speakers of other languages: cr-iti (AC). *Application deadline:* For fall admission, 3/1 for domestic and international students; for spring admission, 10/1 for domestic and international students. *Application fee:* $50. Electronic applications accepted. *Application Contact:* Vika Shock, Director of Graduate Admissions, 845-257-3285, Fax: 845-257-3286, E-mail: gradstudies@newpaltz.edu. *Dean,* Dr. Michael Rosenberg, 845-257-2800, E-mail: schoolofed@newpaltz.edu.

School of Fine and Performing Arts Students: 54 full-time (39 women), 16 part-time (all women); includes 11 minority (3 Asian, non-Hispanic/Latino; 8 Hispanic/Latino), 11 international. 84 applicants, 58% accepted, 26 enrolled. *Faculty:* 20 full-time (11 women), 14 part-time/adjunct (10 women). Expenses: Contact institution. *Financial support:* In 2018–19, 8 research assistantships with partial tuition reimbursements (averaging $5,000 per year), 7 teaching assistantships with partial tuition reimbursements (averaging $5,000 per year) were awarded; scholarships/grants also available. Financial award application deadline: 8/1. In 2018, 47 master's awarded. *Program availability:* Part-time, evening/weekend. Offers ceramic, metal, painting-drawing, printmaking or sculpture (MFA); ceramics (MFA); metal (MFA); music therapy (MS); painting-drawing (MFA); printmaking (MFA); sculpture (MFA); visual arts education (MS Ed). *Application deadline:* For fall admission, 2/15 priority date for domestic students, 2/15 for international students. Applications are processed on a rolling basis. *Application fee:* $50. Electronic applications accepted. *Application Contact:* Vika Shock, Director of Graduate Admissions, 845-257-3286, Fax: 845-257-3284, E-mail: gradstudies@newpaltz.edu. *Dean,* Prof. Jeni Mokren, 845-257-3860, E-mail: mokrenj@newpaltz.edu.

School of Liberal Arts and Sciences Students: 139 full-time (120 women), 52 part-time (32 women); includes 37 minority (5 Black or African American, non-Hispanic/Latino; 2 Asian, non-Hispanic/Latino; 23 Hispanic/Latino; 1 Native Hawaiian or other Pacific Islander, non-Hispanic/Latino; 6 Two or more races, non-Hispanic/Latino), 1 international. 254 applicants, 53% accepted, 80 enrolled. *Faculty:* 39 full-time (24 women), 9 part-time/adjunct (7 women). Expenses: Contact institution. *Financial support:* In 2018–19, 1 research assistantship with partial tuition reimbursement (averaging $5,000 per year), 28 teaching assistantships with partial tuition reimbursements (averaging $5,000 per year) were awarded. Financial award application deadline: 8/1. In 2018, 72 master's, 5 other advanced degrees awarded. *Program availability:* Part-time, evening/weekend. Offers clinical mental health counseling (MS); communication disorders (MS); English (MA); mental health counseling (AC); psychological science (MS); school counseling (MS); speech-language disabilities (MS); trauma and disaster mental health (AC). *Application deadline:* For fall admission, 2/1 for domestic and international students; for spring admission, 11/15 for domestic and international students. Applications are processed on a rolling basis. *Application fee:* $50. Electronic applications accepted. *Application Contact:* Vika Shock, Director of Graduate Admissions, 845-257-3286, E-mail: gradstudies@newpaltz.edu. *Dean,* Dr. Laura Barrett, 845-257-3520, E-mail: barrett@newpaltz.edu.

School of Science and Engineering Students: 51 full-time (25 women), 16 part-time (6 women); includes 7 minority (3 Black or African American, non-Hispanic/Latino; 3 Asian, non-Hispanic/Latino; 1 Hispanic/Latino), 44 international. 122 applicants, 64% accepted, 21 enrolled. *Faculty:* 17 full-time (4 women), 4 part-time/adjunct (1 woman). Expenses: Contact institution. *Financial support:* In 2018–19, 15 fellowships with partial tuition reimbursements (averaging $1,360 per year), 4 teaching assistantships with partial tuition reimbursements (averaging $5,000 per year) were awarded. Financial award application deadline: 8/1. In 2018, 29 master's awarded. *Program availability:* Part-time, evening/weekend. Offers computer science (MS); electrical engineering (MS). *Application deadline:* For fall admission, 5/15 for domestic and international students; for spring admission, 11/15 for domestic and international students. Applications are processed on a rolling basis. *Application fee:* $50. Electronic applications accepted. *Application Contact:* Vika Shock, Director of Graduate Admission, 845-257-3286, E-mail: gradstudies@newpaltz.edu. *Dean,* Dr. Daniel Freedman, 845-257-3728, E-mail: freedmad@newpaltz.edu.

STATE UNIVERSITY OF NEW YORK AT OSWEGO, Oswego, NY 13126

General Information State-supported, coed, comprehensive institution. CGS member. *Graduate housing:* Room and/or apartments available on a first-come, first-served basis to single students; on-campus housing not available to married students. Housing application deadline: 4/1. *Research affiliation:* Intel Corporation (research and education), IBM (research and education), Alcan (research and education), MACTEC (research and education), Entergy (research and education).

GRADUATE UNITS

Graduate Studies *Program availability:* Part-time. Offers art (MA); graphic design and digital media (MA); health informatics professional (MS); health informatics: intelligent health systems (MS); health information management: health data science (MS).

College of Liberal Arts and Sciences *Program availability:* Part-time. Offers chemistry (MS); English (MA); history (MA); human computer interaction (MA); liberal arts and sciences (MA, MS).

School of Business *Program availability:* Part-time, evening/weekend. Offers business (MBA).

School of Communication, Media and the Arts Offers strategic communication (MA).

School of Education *Program availability:* Part-time. Offers adolescence education (MST); agriculture (MS Ed); art education (MAT); business and marketing (MS Ed); childhood education (MST); curriculum and instruction (MS Ed); education (MAT, MS,

MS Ed, MST, CAS); educational administration (CAS); family and consumer sciences (MS Ed); health careers (MS Ed); literacy education (MS Ed); mental health counseling (MS); school building leadership (CAS); special education (MS Ed); technical education (MS Ed); technology (MS Ed); trade education (MS Ed).

STATE UNIVERSITY OF NEW YORK AT PLATTSBURGH, Plattsburgh, NY 12901-2681

General Information State-supported, coed, comprehensive institution. *Graduate housing:* Room and/or apartments available on a first-come, first-served basis to single students; on-campus housing not available to married students. Housing application deadline: 5/1. *Research affiliation:* New York State Sea Grant (environmental science), Miner Agricultural Research Institute (environmental science).

GRADUATE UNITS

School of Arts and Sciences *Program availability:* Part-time. Offers arts and sciences (MA, MS, PSM, CAS); natural science (MS, PSM); school psychology (MA, CAS).

School of Education, Health, and Human Services *Program availability:* Part-time. Offers adolescence education (MST); biology 7-12 (MST); birth to grade 2 (MS Ed); birth to grade 6 (MS Ed); birth-grade 6 (MS Ed); chemistry 7-12 (MST); childhood education (grades 1-6) (MST); clinical mental health counseling (MS, Advanced Certificate); early childhood birth-grade 6 (Advanced Certificate); earth science 7-12 (MST); education, health, and human services (MA, MS, MS Ed, MST, Advanced Certificate, CAS); educational leadership (CAS); English 7-12 (MST); French 7-12 (MST); grades 1 to 6 (MS Ed); grades 5-12 (MS Ed); grades 7 to 12 (MS Ed); mathematics 7-12 (MST); physics 7-12 (MST); school counselor (MS Ed, CAS); social studies 7-12 (MST); Spanish 7-12 (MST); speech-language pathology (MA); student affairs counseling (MS); teacher education: teaching and learning (MS Ed).

STATE UNIVERSITY OF NEW YORK COLLEGE AT CORTLAND, Cortland, NY 13045

General Information State-supported, coed, comprehensive institution. *Graduate housing:* Room and/or apartments available on a first-come, first-served basis to single students; on-campus housing not available to married students.

GRADUATE UNITS

Graduate Studies *Program availability:* Part-time, evening/weekend. Electronic applications accepted.

School of Arts and Sciences *Program availability:* Part-time, evening/weekend. Offers arts and sciences (MA, MAT, MS Ed); biology (MAT); chemistry (MAT); English (MA); history (MA); mathematics (MAT); mathematics and physics (MS Ed); physics (MAT, MS Ed); second language education (MS Ed).

School of Education *Program availability:* Part-time, evening/weekend. Offers childhood education (MST); education (MS Ed, MST, CAS); literacy education (MS Ed); school building leader (CAS); school building leader and school district leader (CAS); school district business leader (CAS); school district leader (CAS); teaching students with disabilities (MS Ed).

School of Professional Studies *Program availability:* Part-time, evening/weekend. Offers adapted physical education (MS Ed); coaching pedagogy (MS Ed); communication sciences and disorders (MS); community health (MS); health education (MST); international sport management (MS); outdoor education (MS, MS Ed); physical education leadership (MS Ed); recreation management (MS, MS Ed); sport management (MS); therapeutic recreation (MS, MS Ed).

STATE UNIVERSITY OF NEW YORK COLLEGE AT GENESEO, Geneseo, NY 14454-1401

General Information State-supported, coed, comprehensive institution. *Graduate housing:* Room and/or apartments available on a first-come, first-served basis to single students; on-campus housing not available to married students. Housing application deadline: 5/1. *Research affiliation:* Rochester City School District/School #19 (education), Avon School District (education), The Community Place of Greater Rochester (reading literacy), Central Library of Rochester (education), The Genesee Valley Educational Partnership (education), Greater Rochester Summer Learning Association (education).

GRADUATE UNITS

Graduate Studies *Program availability:* Part-time. Electronic applications accepted.

School of Business Offers accounting (MS). Electronic applications accepted.

School of Education *Program availability:* Part-time. Offers childhood multicultural education (MS Ed); education (MS Ed); English 7-12 (MS Ed); French 7-12 (MS Ed); reading and literacy B-12 (MS Ed); social studies 7-12 (MS Ed); Spanish 7-12 (MS Ed). Electronic applications accepted.

STATE UNIVERSITY OF NEW YORK COLLEGE AT OLD WESTBURY, Old Westbury, NY 11568-0210

General Information State-supported, coed, comprehensive institution. *Enrollment:* 233 full-time matriculated graduate/professional students (123 women), 163 part-time matriculated graduate/professional students (70 women). *Enrollment by degree level:* 187 master's, 5 other advanced degrees. *Graduate faculty:* 15 full-time (4 women), 3 part-time/adjunct (2 women). *Graduate housing:* Room and/or apartments available on a first-come, first-served basis to single students; on-campus housing not available to married students. *Student services:* Campus safety program, career counseling, child daycare facilities, exercise/wellness program, free psychological counseling, international student services, services for students with disabilities, teacher training, writing training. *Library facilities:* SUNY College at Old Westbury Library plus 1 other. *Collection:* Books: 156,872 (physical), 144,263 (digital/electronic); Databases: 138. Weekly public service hours: 99.

Computer facilities: 480 computers available on campus for general student use. A campuswide network can be accessed from student residence rooms and from off campus. Online class registration, financial aid, billing information are available. Website: http://www.oldwestbury.edu/

General Application Contact: Philip D'Angelo, Graduate Programs Admissions Counselor, 516-876-3077, E-mail: enroll@oldwestbury.edu.

GRADUATE UNITS

Program in Liberal Studies Students: 5 full-time (1 woman), 4 part-time (3 women); includes 4 minority (1 Black or African American, non-Hispanic/Latino; 1 Asian, non-Hispanic/Latino; 2 Hispanic/Latino). Average age 38. 10 applicants, 80% accepted, 5 enrolled. *Faculty:* 2 full-time (both women). Expenses: Contact institution. *Financial support:* Applicants required to submit FAFSA. In 2018, 1 master's awarded. *Program availability:* Part-time, evening/weekend. Offers liberal studies (MA). *Application deadline:* Applications are processed on a rolling basis. *Application fee:* $50. Electronic applications accepted. *Application Contact:* Philip D'Angelo, Graduate Admissions

Office, 516-876-3073, E-mail: enroll@oldwestbury.edu. *Associate Professor, American Studies,* Dr. Amanda Frisken, 516-876-4853, E-mail: friskena@oldwestbury.edu.
Program in Mental Health Counseling Offers mental health counseling (MS).
School of Business *Program availability:* Part-time, evening/weekend. Offers accounting (MS); taxation (MS). Electronic applications accepted.
School of Education *Program availability:* Part-time, evening/weekend. Offers biology (MAT, MS); chemistry (MAT, MS); English language arts (MAT, MS); math (MAT, MS); social studies (MAT, MS); Spanish (MAT, MS).

STATE UNIVERSITY OF NEW YORK COLLEGE AT ONEONTA, Oneonta, NY 13820-4015

General Information State-supported, coed, comprehensive institution. *Graduate housing:* Room and/or apartments available on a first-come, first-served basis to single students; on-campus housing not available to married students. Housing application deadline: 5/1. *Research affiliation:* New York State Historical Association (museum studies (history and science)).

GRADUATE UNITS

Graduate Programs *Program availability:* Part-time, evening/weekend, online learning. Offers biology (MS); history museum studies (MA); lake management (MS); nutrition and dietetics (MS); science museum studies (MA).

Division of Education *Program availability:* Part-time, evening/weekend. Offers childhood education (MS Ed); educational psychology, counseling and special education (MS Ed, CAS); elementary education and reading (MS Ed); literacy education (MS Ed); school counselor K-12 (MS Ed, CAS); special education (MS Ed).

STATE UNIVERSITY OF NEW YORK COLLEGE AT POTSDAM, Potsdam, NY 13676

General Information State-supported, coed, comprehensive institution. *Graduate housing:* Room and/or apartments available on a first-come, first-served basis to single students; on-campus housing not available to married students.

GRADUATE UNITS

Crane School of Music *Program availability:* Part-time. Offers music education (MM); music performance (MM). Electronic applications accepted.

School of Arts and Sciences *Program availability:* Part-time. Offers arts and sciences (MA); mathematics (MA). Electronic applications accepted.

School of Education and Professional Studies *Program availability:* Online learning. Offers adolescence (grades 7-12) (MS Ed); childhood (grades 1-6) (MS Ed); childhood education (MST); community health (MS); curriculum and instruction (MS Ed); early childhood (birth-grade 2) (MS Ed); education and professional studies (MS, MS Ed, MST); educational technology specialist (MS Ed); English education (MST); literacy educator (MS Ed); literacy specialist (MS Ed); mathematics education (MST); organizational performance and technology (MS); science education (MST); social studies education (MST). Electronic applications accepted.

STATE UNIVERSITY OF NEW YORK COLLEGE OF ENVIRONMENTAL SCIENCE AND FORESTRY, Syracuse, NY 13210-2779

General Information State-supported, coed, university. CGS member. *Enrollment:* 2,256 graduate, professional, and undergraduate students; 325 full-time matriculated graduate/professional students (166 women), 65 part-time matriculated graduate/professional students (26 women). *Enrollment by degree level:* 221 master's, 162 doctoral, 7 other advanced degrees. *Graduate faculty:* 128 full-time (43 women), 48 part-time/adjunct (18 women). *International tuition:* $22,650 full-time. Tuition, *area resident:* Full-time $11,090; part-time $462 per credit hour. Tuition, state resident: full-time $11,090; part-time $462 per credit hour. Tuition, nonresident: full-time $22,650; part-time $944 per credit hour. Required fees: $1733; $178.58 per credit hour. *Graduate housing:* On-campus housing not available. *Student services:* Campus employment opportunities, campus safety program, career counseling, exercise/wellness program, free psychological counseling, grant writing training, international student services, low-cost health insurance, multicultural affairs office, writing training. *Library facilities:* F. Franklin Moon Library plus 1 other. *Collection:* Books: 57,565 (physical), 444,963 (digital/electronic); Serial titles: 1,568 (physical), 163,166 (digital/electronic); Databases: 181. Weekly public service hours: 97.

Computer facilities: Computer purchase and lease plans are available. 350 computers available on campus for general student use. A campuswide network can be accessed from student residence rooms and from off campus. Online class registration is available.
Website: http://www.esf.edu/

General Application Contact: Scott Shannon, Dean, Instruction and Graduate Studies, 315-470-6599, Fax: 315-470-6978, E-mail: esfgrad@esf.edu.

GRADUATE UNITS

Department of Chemistry Students: 37 full-time (14 women), 3 part-time (2 women); includes 1 minority (Asian, non-Hispanic/Latino), 13 international. Average age 28. 51 applicants, 53% accepted, 13 enrolled. *Faculty:* 14 full-time (1 woman), 1 part-time/adjunct (0 women). Expenses: Contact institution. *Financial support:* In 2018–19, 13 students received support. Unspecified assistantships available. Financial award application deadline: 6/30; financial award applicants required to submit FAFSA. In 2018, 4 master's, 5 doctorates awarded. *Program availability:* Part-time. Offers biochemistry (MPS, MS, PhD); environmental chemistry (MPS, MS, PhD); organic chemistry of natural products (MPS, MS, PhD); polymer chemistry (MPS, MS, PhD). *Application deadline:* For fall admission, 2/1 priority date for domestic and international students; for spring admission, 11/1 priority date for domestic and international students. Applications are processed on a rolling basis. *Application fee:* $60. Electronic applications accepted. *Application Contact:* Scott Shannon, Associate Provost for Instruction/Dean of the Graduate School, 315-470-6599, Fax: 315-470-6978, E-mail: sshannon@esf.edu. *Chair,* Dr. Avik Chatterrjee, 315-470-4747, Fax: 315-470-6855, E-mail: achatter@esf.edu.

Department of Environmental and Forest Biology Students: 107 full-time (57 women), 21 part-time (8 women); includes 9 minority (6 American Indian or Alaska Native, non-Hispanic/Latino; 2 Asian, non-Hispanic/Latino; 1 Hispanic/Latino), 18 international. Average age 30. 79 applicants, 49% accepted, 24 enrolled. *Faculty:* 35 full-time (10 women), 4 part-time/adjunct (3 women). Expenses: Contact institution. *Financial support:* In 2018–19, 46 students received support. Unspecified assistantships available. Financial award application deadline: 6/30; financial award applicants required to submit FAFSA. In 2018, 30 master's, 3 doctorates awarded. *Program availability:* Part-time. Offers applied ecology (MPS); chemical ecology (MPS, MS, PhD); conservation biology (MPS, MS, PhD); ecology (MPS, MS, PhD); entomology (MPS, MS, PhD); environmental interpretation (MPS, MS, PhD); environmental physiology (MPS, MS, PhD); fish and wildlife biology and management (MPS, MS, PhD); forest pathology and mycology (MPS, MS, PhD); plant biotechnology (MPS); plant science and biotechnology (MPS, MS, PhD). *Application deadline:* For fall admission, 2/1 priority date for domestic and international students; for spring admission, 11/1 priority date for domestic and international students. Applications are processed on a rolling basis. *Application fee:* $60. Electronic applications accepted. *Application Contact:* Scott Shannon, Associate Provost for Instruction/Dean of the Graduate School, 315-470-6599, E-mail: esfgrad@esf.edu. Chair, Dr. Melissa K. Fierke, 315-470-6809, Fax: 315-470-6743, E-mail: mkfierke@esf.edu.

Department of Environmental Resources Engineering Students: 32 full-time (12 women), 8 part-time (0 women); includes 2 minority (1 Black or African American, non-Hispanic/Latino; 1 Asian, non-Hispanic/Latino), 19 international. Average age 41. 31 applicants, 58% accepted, 7 enrolled. *Faculty:* 9 full-time (1 woman), 3 part-time/adjunct (0 women). Expenses: Contact institution. *Financial support:* In 2018–19, 9 students received support. Unspecified assistantships available. Financial award application deadline: 6/30; financial award applicants required to submit FAFSA. In 2018, 11 master's, 1 doctorate awarded. *Program availability:* Part-time. Offers ecological engineering (MPS, MS, PhD); environmental management (MPS); environmental resources engineering (MPS, MS, PhD); geospatial information science and engineering (MPS, MS, PhD); water resources engineering (MPS, MS, PhD). *Application deadline:* For fall admission, 1/15 priority date for domestic and international students; for spring admission, 11/1 priority date for domestic and international students. Applications are processed on a rolling basis. *Application fee:* $60. Electronic applications accepted. *Application Contact:* Scott Shannon, Associate Provost for Instruction/Dean of the Graduate School, 315-470-6599, Fax: 315-470-6978, E-mail: esfgrad@esf.edu. Chair, Dr. Lindi Quackenbush, 315-470-4727, Fax: 315-470-4710, E-mail: ljquackc@esf.edu.

Department of Environmental Studies Students: 8 full-time (6 women), 2 part-time (both women), 1 international. Average age 26. 9 applicants, 78% accepted, 5 enrolled. *Faculty:* 10 full-time (7 women), 3 part-time/adjunct (2 women). Expenses: Contact institution. *Financial support:* In 2018–19, 2 students received support. Unspecified assistantships available. Financial award application deadline: 6/30; financial award applicants required to submit FAFSA. In 2018, 3 master's awarded. *Program availability:* Part-time. Offers environmental communication (MPS, MS); environmental policy (MPS, MS). *Application deadline:* Applications are processed on a rolling basis. *Application fee:* $60. Electronic applications accepted. *Application Contact:* Scott Shannon, Associate Provost for Instruction/Dean of the Graduate School, 315-470-6599, Fax: 315-470-6978, E-mail: esfgrad@esf.edu. Chair, Dr. Bennette Whitmore, 315-470-6636, E-mail: bwhitmor@esf.edu.

Department of Forest and Natural Resources Management Students: 42 full-time (19 women), 5 part-time (2 women); includes 5 minority (1 Black or African American, non-Hispanic/Latino; 1 American Indian or Alaska Native, non-Hispanic/Latino; 2 Asian, non-Hispanic/Latino; 1 Hispanic/Latino), 13 international. Average age 30. 26 applicants, 81% accepted, 4 enrolled. *Faculty:* 33 full-time (8 women), 7 part-time/adjunct (0 women). Expenses: Contact institution. *Financial support:* In 2018–19, 13 students received support. Unspecified assistantships available. Financial award application deadline: 6/30; financial award applicants required to submit FAFSA. In 2018, 14 master's awarded. *Program availability:* Part-time. Offers ecology and ecosystems (MPS, MS, PhD); economics, governance and human dimensions (MPS, MS, PhD); forest and natural resources management (MPS, MS, PhD); forest resources management (MF); monitoring, analysis and modeling (MPS, MS, PhD). *Application deadline:* For fall admission, 2/1 priority date for domestic and international students; for spring admission, 11/1 priority date for domestic and international students. Applications are processed on a rolling basis. *Application fee:* $60. *Application Contact:* Scott Shannon, Associate Provost for Instruction/Dean of the Graduate School, 315-470-6599, Fax: 315-470-6978, E-mail: esfgrad@esf.edu. Chair, Dr. Christopher Nowak, 315-470-6575, Fax: 315-470-6536, E-mail: canowak@esf.edu.

Department of Landscape Architecture Students: 25 full-time (16 women), 2 part-time (1 woman); includes 2 minority (both Black or African American, non-Hispanic/Latino), 6 international. Average age 25. 40 applicants, 70% accepted, 8 enrolled. *Faculty:* 10 full-time (4 women), 7 part-time/adjunct (5 women). Expenses: Contact institution. *Financial support:* In 2018–19, 11 students received support. Unspecified assistantships available. Financial award application deadline: 6/30; financial award applicants required to submit FAFSA. In 2018, 7 master's awarded. *Program availability:* Part-time. Offers community design and planning (MLA, MS); cultural landscape studies and conservation (MLA, MS); landscape and urban ecology (MLA, MS). *Application deadline:* For fall admission, 2/1 priority date for domestic and international students; for spring admission, 11/1 priority date for domestic and international students. Applications are processed on a rolling basis. *Application fee:* $60. Electronic applications accepted. *Application Contact:* Scott Shannon, Associate Provost for Instruction/Dean of the Graduate School, 315-470-6599, Fax: 315-470-6978, E-mail: esfgrad@esf.edu. Chair, Dr. Douglas Johnston, 315-470-6544, Fax: 315-470-6540, E-mail: dmjohnst@esf.edu.

Department of Paper and Bioprocess Engineering Students: 20 full-time (11 women), 1 part-time (0 women); includes 29 minority (28 American Indian or Alaska Native, non-Hispanic/Latino; 1 Hispanic/Latino), 14 international. Average age 28. 18 applicants, 100% accepted, 11 enrolled. *Faculty:* 13 full-time (2 women), 1 part-time/adjunct (0 women). Expenses: Contact institution. *Financial support:* In 2018–19, 17 students received support. Unspecified assistantships available. Financial award application deadline: 6/30; financial award applicants required to submit FAFSA. In 2018, 2 master's awarded. *Program availability:* Part-time. Offers biomaterials engineering (MS, PhD); bioprocess engineering (MPS, MS, PhD); bioprocessing (Advanced Certificate); paper science and engineering (MPS, MS, PhD); sustainable engineering management (MPS). *Application deadline:* For fall admission, 2/1 priority date for domestic and international students; for spring admission, 11/1 priority date for domestic and international students. Applications are processed on a rolling basis. *Application fee:* $60. Electronic applications accepted. *Application Contact:* Scott Shannon, Associate Provost and Dean, Instruction and Graduate Studies, 315-470-6599, Fax: 315-470-6978, E-mail: esfgrad@esf.edu. Interim Chair, Dr. Bandaru Ramarao, 315-470-6502, Fax: 315-470-6945, E-mail: bvramara@esf.edu.

Program in Environmental Science Students: 52 full-time (30 women), 13 part-time (9 women); includes 3 minority (1 Asian, non-Hispanic/Latino; 2 Hispanic/Latino), 26 international. Average age 32. 51 applicants, 73% accepted, 17 enrolled. *Faculty:* 1 full-time (0 women), 1 (woman) part-time/adjunct. Expenses: Contact institution. *Financial support:* In 2018–19, 24 students received support. Unspecified assistantships available. Financial award application deadline: 6/30; financial award applicants required to submit FAFSA. In 2018, 14 master's, 8 doctorates awarded. *Program availability:* Part-time. Offers biophysical and ecological economics (MPS); coupled natural and human systems (MPS); ecosystem restoration (MPS); environmental and community land planning (MPS, MS); environmental and natural resources policy (PhD); environmental communication and participatory processes (PhD); environmental monitoring and modeling (MPS); water and wetland resource studies (MPS, MS). *Application deadline:*

For fall admission, 2/1 priority date for domestic and international students; for spring admission, 11/1 priority date for domestic and international students. Applications are processed on a rolling basis. *Application fee:* $60. Electronic applications accepted. *Application Contact:* Scott Shannon, Associate Provost for Instruction/Dean of the Graduate School, 315-470-6599, Fax: 315-470-6978, E-mail: esfgrad@esf.edu. *Director of the Division of Environmental Science,* Dr. Russell Briggs, 315-470-6989, Fax: 315-470-6700, E-mail: rdbriggs@esf.edu.

STATE UNIVERSITY OF NEW YORK COLLEGE OF OPTOMETRY, New York, NY 10036
General Information State-supported, coed, graduate-only institution. *Graduate housing:* On-campus housing not available. *Research affiliation:* Schnurmacher Institute for Vision Research (vision science).

GRADUATE UNITS

Graduate Programs *Program availability:* Part-time. Offers vision science (PhD).
Professional Program Offers optometry (OD). Electronic applications accepted.

STATE UNIVERSITY OF NEW YORK COLLEGE OF TECHNOLOGY AT DELHI, Delhi, NY 13753
General Information State-supported, coed, comprehensive institution. *Graduate housing:* On-campus housing not available.

GRADUATE UNITS

Program in Nursing *Program availability:* Online only, 100% online. Offers nursing administration (MS); nursing education (MS).

STATE UNIVERSITY OF NEW YORK DOWNSTATE MEDICAL CENTER, Brooklyn, NY 11203-2098
General Information State-supported, coed, upper-level institution. *Graduate housing:* Rooms and/or apartments available on a first-come, first-served basis to single and married students. Housing application deadline: 5/29. *Research affiliation:* Brooklyn Veterans Administration Medical Center, Polytechnic Institute of New York University (biomedical engineering).

GRADUATE UNITS

College of Medicine Offers medicine (MPH, MD); urban and immigrant health (MPH).
College of Nursing *Program availability:* Part-time, evening/weekend. Offers clinical nurse specialist (MS, Post Master's Certificate); nurse anesthesia (MS); nurse midwifery (MS, Post Master's Certificate); nurse practitioner (MS, Post Master's Certificate); nursing (MS, Post Master's Certificate).
School of Graduate Studies Offers bioimaging and neuroengineering (PhD); biomedical engineering (MS); molecular and cellular biology (PhD); neural and behavioral science (PhD); occupational therapy (MS).

STATE UNIVERSITY OF NEW YORK EMPIRE STATE COLLEGE, Saratoga Springs, NY 12866-4391
General Information State-supported, coed, comprehensive institution. *Graduate housing:* On-campus housing not available.

GRADUATE UNITS

School for Graduate Studies *Program availability:* Part-time, evening/weekend, online learning. Offers adult learning (MA); community and economic development (MA); global leadership (MBA); labor and policy studies (MA); learning and emerging technologies (MA); liberal studies (MA); management (MBA); nursing education (MSN); social policy (MA); teaching (MAT); teaching and learning (M Ed). Electronic applications accepted.

STATE UNIVERSITY OF NEW YORK MARITIME COLLEGE, Throggs Neck, NY 10465-4198
General Information State-supported, coed, comprehensive institution. *Graduate housing:* Room and/or apartments available to single students; on-campus housing not available to married students. *Research affiliation:* Port Authority of New York and New Jersey (transportation), Transportation Infrastructure Research Consortium, Transportation Research Board (maritime transportation).

GRADUATE UNITS

Program in International Transportation Management *Program availability:* Part-time, evening/weekend. Offers international transportation management (MS).

STATE UNIVERSITY OF NEW YORK POLYTECHNIC INSTITUTE, Utica, NY 13502
General Information State-supported, coed, comprehensive institution. *Enrollment:* 250 full-time matriculated graduate/professional students (123 women), 499 part-time matriculated graduate/professional students (311 women). *Enrollment by degree level:* 694 master's, 46 doctoral, 9 other advanced degrees. *Graduate faculty:* 56 full-time (14 women), 37 part-time/adjunct (23 women). *International tuition:* $16,992 full-time. *Tuition, area resident:* Full-time $8316; part-time $462 per credit hour. Tuition, nonresident: full-time $16,992; part-time $944 per credit hour. *Required fees:* $1023; $56.87 per credit hour. Tuition and fees vary according to course load, campus/location and program. *Graduate housing:* Room and/or apartments available to single students; on-campus housing not available to married students. *Student services:* Campus employment opportunities, campus safety program, career counseling, exercise/wellness program, free psychological counseling, international student services, multicultural affairs office, services for students with disabilities, writing training. *Library facilities:* Peter J. Cayan Library. *Collection:* Books: 139,500 (physical), 108,500 (digital/electronic); Serial titles: 2,175 (physical), 49,045 (digital/electronic); Databases: 50. Weekly public service hours: 87; students can reserve study rooms. *Research affiliation:* Griffiss Institute (Innovation and Entrepreneurship).

Computer facilities: 380 computers available on campus for general student use. A campuswide network can be accessed from student residence rooms and from off campus. Online class registration is available.
Website: http://www.sunypoly.edu/

General Application Contact: Alicia Foster, Director of Graduate Admissions, 315-792-7347, E-mail: alicia.foster@sunypoly.edu.

GRADUATE UNITS

College of Nanoscale Science and Engineering Students: 34 full-time (10 women), 36 part-time (14 women); includes 27 minority (17 Asian, non-Hispanic/Latino; 4 Hispanic/Latino; 6 Two or more races, non-Hispanic/Latino), 13 international. Average age 28. 65 applicants, 31% accepted, 10 enrolled. Expenses: Contact institution. *Financial support:* Fellowships, research assistantships, teaching assistantships, and tuition waivers available. Financial award application deadline: 6/1; financial award applicants required to submit FAFSA. In 2018, 8 master's, 5 doctorates awarded. Offers nanoscale engineering (PhD); nanoscale science (MS). *Application deadline:* For fall admission, 7/1 for domestic and international students; for spring admission, 12/1 for domestic students, 11/1 for international students. Applications are processed on a rolling basis. *Application fee:* $60. Electronic applications accepted. *Application Contact:* Krista Thompson, Assistant Dean of Graduate Studies, 518-956-7011, E-mail: kthompson@sunypoly.edu.

MBA Program in Technology Management Students: 29 full-time (13 women), 85 part-time (41 women); includes 18 minority (4 Black or African American, non-Hispanic/Latino; 8 Asian, non-Hispanic/Latino; 6 Hispanic/Latino). Average age 32. 54 applicants, 54% accepted, 26 enrolled. Expenses: Contact institution. *Financial support:* Fellowships, research assistantships, and unspecified assistantships available. Financial award application deadline: 6/1; financial award applicants required to submit FAFSA. In 2018, 29 master's awarded. *Program availability:* Part-time, 100% online. Offers accounting and finance (MBA); business management (MBA); health informatics (MBA); human resource management (MBA); marketing management (MBA). *Application deadline:* For fall admission, 7/1 priority date for domestic students, 7/1 for international students; for spring admission, 12/1 for domestic students, 11/1 for international students. Applications are processed on a rolling basis. *Application fee:* $60. Electronic applications accepted. *Application Contact:* Alicia Foster, Director of Graduate Admissions, 315-792-7347, E-mail: fostera3@sunypoly.edu. *Coordinator,* Dr. Rafael Romero, 315-792-7207, E-mail: rafael.romero@sunypoly.edu.

Program in Advanced Technology Students: 2 full-time (0 women), 4 part-time (0 women); includes 4 minority (1 Black or African American, non-Hispanic/Latino; 3 Asian, non-Hispanic/Latino). Average age 31. 10 applicants, 70% accepted, 6 enrolled. Expenses: Contact institution. *Financial support:* Fellowships, research assistantships, and unspecified assistantships available. Financial award application deadline: 6/1; financial award applicants required to submit FAFSA. Offers advanced technology (MS). *Application deadline:* For fall admission, 7/1 for domestic and international students; for spring admission, 11/1 for domestic and international students. Applications are processed on a rolling basis. *Application fee:* $60. Electronic applications accepted. *Application Contact:* Alicia Foster, Director of Graduate Admissions, 315-792-7345, E-mail: fostera3@sunypoly.edu. *Interim Dean of Engineering,* Dr. Michael Carpenter.

Program in Computer and Information Science Students: 78 full-time (18 women), 25 part-time (4 women); includes 7 minority (5 Asian, non-Hispanic/Latino; 2 Hispanic/Latino), 76 international. Average age 24. 153 applicants, 64% accepted, 39 enrolled. Expenses: Contact institution. *Financial support:* Research assistantships, scholarships/grants, and unspecified assistantships available. Financial award application deadline: 6/1; financial award applicants required to submit FAFSA. In 2018, 36 master's awarded. *Program availability:* Part-time. Offers computer and information science (MS). *Application deadline:* For fall admission, 7/1 for domestic and international students; for spring admission, 12/1 for domestic students, 11/1 for international students. Applications are processed on a rolling basis. *Application fee:* $60. Electronic applications accepted. *Application Contact:* Alicia Foster, Director of Graduate Admissions, 315-792-7347, E-mail: fostera3@sunypoly.edu. *Program Coordinator,* Dr. Roger Cavallo, 315-792-7231, E-mail: roger.cavallo@sunypoly.edu.

Program in Family Nurse Practitioner Students: 40 full-time (36 women), 143 part-time (132 women); includes 26 minority (7 Black or African American, non-Hispanic/Latino; 8 Asian, non-Hispanic/Latino; 7 Hispanic/Latino; 4 Two or more races, non-Hispanic/Latino). Average age 36. 150 applicants, 56% accepted, 62 enrolled. Expenses: Contact institution. *Financial support:* Fellowships and scholarships/grants available. Financial award application deadline: 6/1; financial award applicants required to submit FAFSA. In 2018, 49 master's awarded. *Program availability:* Part-time. Offers family nurse practitioner (MS, CAS). *Application deadline:* For fall admission, 2/1 for domestic and international students. *Application fee:* $60. *Application Contact:* Alicia Foster, Director of Graduate Admissions, 315-792-7347, E-mail: fostera3@sunypoly.edu. *Assistant Professor,* Dr. Lynne Longtin, 315-792-7555, E-mail: lynne.longtin@sunypoly.edu.

Program in Information Design and Technology Students: 10 full-time (5 women), 55 part-time (27 women); includes 18 minority (4 Black or African American, non-Hispanic/Latino; 4 Asian, non-Hispanic/Latino; 7 Hispanic/Latino; 3 Two or more races, non-Hispanic/Latino). Average age 36. 26 applicants, 50% accepted, 16 enrolled. Expenses: Contact institution. *Financial support:* Applicants required to submit FAFSA. In 2018, 21 master's awarded. *Program availability:* Part-time. Offers information design and technology (MS). *Application deadline:* For fall admission, 7/1 for domestic and international students; for spring admission, 12/1 for domestic students, 11/1 for international students. Applications are processed on a rolling basis. *Application fee:* $60. Electronic applications accepted. *Application Contact:* Alicia Foster, Director of Graduate Admissions, 315-792-7347, E-mail: fostera3@sunypoly.edu. *Professor,* Dr. Kathryn Stam, 315-792-7241, E-mail: Kathryn.Stam@sunypoly.edu.

Program in Network and Computer Security Students: 15 full-time (1 woman), 13 part-time (3 women); includes 2 minority (1 Asian, non-Hispanic/Latino; 1 Hispanic/Latino), 11 international. Average age 30. 42 applicants, 52% accepted, 14 enrolled. Faculty: 3 full-time (0 women), 3 part-time/adjunct (0 women). Expenses: Contact institution. *Financial support:* Research assistantships and unspecified assistantships available. Financial award applicants required to submit FAFSA. In 2018, 12 master's awarded. *Program availability:* Part-time. Offers network and computer security (MS). *Application deadline:* For fall admission, 7/1 for domestic and international students; for spring admission, 12/1 for domestic students, 11/1 for international students. Applications are processed on a rolling basis. *Application fee:* $60. Electronic applications accepted. *Application Contact:* Alicia Foster, Director of Graduate Admissions, 315-792-7347, E-mail: alicia.foster@sunyit.edu. *Chair, NCS Department,* Dr. John Marsh, 315-792-7125, E-mail: john.marsh@sunypoly.edu.

Program in Nursing Education Students: 1 (woman) full-time, 39 part-time (36 women); includes 6 minority (3 Black or African American, non-Hispanic/Latino; 2 Asian, non-Hispanic/Latino; 1 Hispanic/Latino). Average age 41. 17 applicants, 41% accepted, 6 enrolled. Expenses: Contact institution. *Financial support:* Scholarships/grants available. Financial award applicants required to submit FAFSA. In 2018, 17 master's awarded. *Program availability:* Part-time, 100% online. Offers nursing education (MS, CAS). *Application deadline:* For fall admission, 7/1 for domestic and international students; for spring admission, 12/1 for domestic students, 11/1 for international students. Applications are processed on a rolling basis. *Application fee:* $60. Electronic applications accepted. *Application Contact:* Alicia Foster, Director of Graduate Admissions, 315-792-7347, E-mail: fostera3@sunypoly.edu. *Program Coordinator,* Dr. Darlene DelPrato, 315-792-7283, E-mail: delprad@sunypoly.edu.

State University of New York Polytechnic Institute Students: 24 full-time (15 women), 77 part-time (40 women); includes 32 minority (5 Black or African American, non-Hispanic/Latino; 1 American Indian or Alaska Native, non-Hispanic/Latino; 10 Asian, non-Hispanic/Latino; 12 Hispanic/Latino; 1 Native Hawaiian or other Pacific Islander, non-Hispanic/Latino; 3 Two or more races, non-Hispanic/Latino). Average age 31. 76 applicants, 53% accepted, 28 enrolled. Expenses: Contact institution. *Financial support:*

Fellowships, research assistantships, and unspecified assistantships available. Financial award application deadline: 6/1; financial award applicants required to submit FAFSA. In 2018, 19 master's awarded. *Program availability:* Part-time, 100% online. Offers accountancy (MS). *Application deadline:* For fall admission, 7/1 for domestic and international students; for spring admission, 11/1 for domestic and international students. Applications are processed on a rolling basis. *Application fee:* $60. Electronic applications accepted. *Application Contact:* Alicia Foster, Director of Graduate Admissions, 315-792-7347, E-mail: fostera3@sunypoly.edu. *Program Coordinator,* Peter Karl, 315-792-7120, E-mail: pak3rd@sunypoly.edu.

STATE UNIVERSITY OF NEW YORK UPSTATE MEDICAL UNIVERSITY, Syracuse, NY 13210

General Information State-supported, coed, upper-level institution. CGS member. *Graduate housing:* Rooms and/or apartments available on a first-come, first-served basis to single and married students. Housing application deadline: 8/1.

GRADUATE UNITS

College of Graduate Studies Offers anatomy (MS, PhD); biochemistry (MS); biochemistry and molecular biology (PhD); microbiology (MS); microbiology and immunology (PhD); neuroscience (PhD); pharmacology (PhD); physiology (MS, PhD); public health (MPH). Electronic applications accepted.

College of Medicine Offers medicine (MD). Electronic applications accepted.

College of Nursing *Program availability:* Part-time, online learning. Offers nurse practitioner (Post Master's Certificate); nursing (MS). Electronic applications accepted.

Department of Physical Therapy *Program availability:* Part-time, evening/weekend, online learning. Offers physical therapy (DPT). Electronic applications accepted.

Program in Medical Technology Offers medical technology (MS).

STEPHEN F. AUSTIN STATE UNIVERSITY, Nacogdoches, TX 75962

General Information State-supported, coed, comprehensive institution. *Graduate housing:* Rooms and/or apartments available on a first-come, first-served basis to single students and available to married students. Housing application deadline: 6/1. *Research affiliation:* University Health Center at Tyler (biotechnology, environmental science).

GRADUATE UNITS

Graduate School *Program availability:* Part-time, evening/weekend, online learning. Electronic applications accepted.

Arthur Temple College of Forestry and Agriculture Offers agriculture (MS); forestry (MF, MS, PhD); forestry and agriculture (MF, MS, PhD).

College of Fine Arts *Program availability:* Part-time. Offers art (MA); art education (MAAE); design (MFA); drawing (MFA); filmmaking (MFA); fine arts (MA, MAAE, MFA, MM); music (MA, MM); painting (MFA); sculpture (MFA).

College of Liberal and Applied Arts *Program availability:* Part-time, evening/weekend. Offers communication (MA); cultural heritage (MIS); English (MA); Hispanic studies (MA); history (MA); interdisciplinary studies (MIS); liberal and applied arts (MA, MIS, MPA, MSW); mass communication (MA); psychology (MA); public administration (MPA); publishing (MA); social work (MSW).

College of Sciences and Mathematics *Program availability:* Part-time. Offers biology (MS); biotechnology (MS); chemistry (MS); cyber security (MS); environmental science (MS); family nurse practitioner (MSN); geology (MS, MSNS); mathematics (MS); mathematics education (MS); physics (MS, PhD); sciences and mathematics (MS, MSNS, PhD); statistics (MS).

James I. Perkins College of Education *Program availability:* Part-time, evening/weekend. Offers athletic training (MS); counseling (MA); early childhood education (M Ed); education (M Ed, MA, MAT, MS, Ed D); educational leadership (Ed D); elementary education (M Ed); human sciences (MS); kinesiology (MS); school psychology (MA); secondary education (M Ed); secondary education leadership (MAT); special education (M Ed); speech-language pathology (MS).

Nelson Rusche College of Business *Program availability:* Part-time, evening/weekend. Offers business (MBA, MPA); management and marketing (MBA); professional accountancy (MPA).

STEPHENS COLLEGE, Columbia, MO 65215-0002

General Information Independent, Undergraduate: women only; graduate: coed, comprehensive institution. *Graduate housing:* On-campus housing not available.

GRADUATE UNITS

Division of Graduate and Continuing Studies *Program availability:* Part-time, evening/weekend, online learning. Offers counseling (M Ed); health information administration (Postbaccalaureate Certificate); physician assistant studies (MPAS); TV and screenwriting (MFA). Electronic applications accepted.

STETSON UNIVERSITY, DeLand, FL 32723

General Information Independent, coed, comprehensive institution. *Enrollment:* 4,341 graduate, professional, and undergraduate students; 1,023 full-time matriculated graduate/professional students (602 women), 162 part-time matriculated graduate/professional students (87 women). *Enrollment by degree level:* 361 master's, 824 doctoral. *Graduate faculty:* 69 full-time (34 women), 66 part-time/adjunct (30 women). *Graduate housing:* Rooms and/or apartments available to single and married students. *Student services:* Campus employment opportunities, campus safety program, career counseling, free psychological counseling, international student services, multicultural affairs office, services for students with disabilities, teacher training. *Library facilities:* DuPont-Ball Library plus 1 other. *Collection:* Books: 230,712 (physical), 194,199 (digital/electronic); Serial titles: 227 (physical), 159,553 (digital/electronic); Databases: 134. Weekly public service hours: 104; students can reserve study rooms.

Computer facilities: 600 computers available on campus for general student use. A campuswide network can be accessed from student residence rooms and from off campus. Online class registration is available.
Website: http://www.stetson.edu/

General Application Contact: Jamie Vanderlip, Director of Admissions for Graduate, Transfer and Adult Populations, 386-822-7100, Fax: 386-822-7112, E-mail: gradadmissions@stetson.edu.

GRADUATE UNITS

College of Arts and Sciences Students: 157 full-time (127 women), 7 part-time (6 women); includes 55 minority (16 Black or African American, non-Hispanic/Latino; 3 American Indian or Alaska Native, non-Hispanic/Latino; 21 Hispanic/Latino; 15 Two or more races, non-Hispanic/Latino), 8 international. Average age 33. 114 applicants, 63% accepted, 58 enrolled. Faculty: 13 full-time (9 women), 9 part-time/adjunct (5 women). Expenses: Contact institution. *Financial support:* In 2018–19, 53 students received support. Career-related internships or fieldwork, Federal Work-Study, scholarships/grants, unspecified assistantships, and tuition waivers (for staff and dependents) available. Support available to part-time students. Financial award applicants required to submit FAFSA. In 2018, 83 master's awarded. *Program availability:* Part-time, evening/weekend. Offers English (MFA). *Application deadline:* For fall admission, 8/1 priority date for domestic students; for spring admission, 1/1 priority date for domestic students; for summer admission, 5/1 priority date for domestic students. Applications are processed on a rolling basis. *Application fee:* $50. Electronic applications accepted. *Application Contact:* Jamie Vanderlip, Director of Admissions for Graduate, Transfer and Adult Programs, 386-822-7100, Fax: 386-822-7112, E-mail: jlvander@stetson.edu. *Dean,* Dr. Elizabeth Skomp, 386-822-7515.

Division of Education Students: 141 full-time (113 women), 7 part-time (6 women); includes 50 minority (16 Black or African American, non-Hispanic/Latino; 3 American Indian or Alaska Native, non-Hispanic/Latino; 20 Hispanic/Latino; 11 Two or more races, non-Hispanic/Latino), 7 international. Average age 32. 103 applicants, 62% accepted, 52 enrolled. *Faculty:* 12 full-time (8 women), 4 part-time/adjunct (3 women). Expenses: Contact institution. *Financial support:* In 2018–19, 53 students received support. Career-related internships or fieldwork, Federal Work-Study, institutionally sponsored loans, scholarships/grants, unspecified assistantships, and tuition waivers (for staff and dependents) available. Support available to part-time students. Financial award applicants required to submit FAFSA. In 2018, 72 master's awarded. *Program availability:* Part-time, evening/weekend. Offers counselor education (MS); educational leadership (M Ed); teacher education (M Ed). *Application deadline:* For fall admission, 8/1 priority date for domestic students; for spring admission, 1/1 priority date for domestic students; for summer admission, 5/1 priority date for domestic students. Applications are processed on a rolling basis. *Application fee:* $50. Electronic applications accepted. *Application Contact:* Jamie Vanderlip, Director of Admissions for Graduate, Transfer and Adult Programs, 386-822-7100, Fax: 386-822-7112, E-mail: jlvander@stetson.edu. *Dean of the College of Arts and Sciences,* Dr. Elizabeth Skomp, 386-822-7515.

College of Law Students: 764 full-time (415 women), 130 part-time (67 women); includes 245 minority (67 Black or African American, non-Hispanic/Latino; 3 American Indian or Alaska Native, non-Hispanic/Latino; 19 Asian, non-Hispanic/Latino; 124 Hispanic/Latino; 32 Two or more races, non-Hispanic/Latino), 15 international. Average age 27. 2,029 applicants, 47% accepted, 316 enrolled. *Faculty:* 42 full-time (22 women), 56 part-time/adjunct (24 women). Expenses: Contact institution. *Financial support:* In 2018–19, 669 students received support, including 50 research assistantships (averaging $1,370 per year), 53 teaching assistantships (averaging $949 per year); career-related internships or fieldwork, Federal Work-Study, scholarships/grants, unspecified assistantships, and tuition waivers (for staff and dependents) also available. Support available to part-time students. Financial award application deadline: 8/15; financial award applicants required to submit FAFSA. In 2018, 27 master's, 247 doctorates awarded. *Program availability:* Part-time, evening/weekend, 100% online. Offers law (LL M, M Jur, JD). *Application deadline:* For fall admission, 5/15 for domestic and international students. Applications are processed on a rolling basis. *Application fee:* $55. Electronic applications accepted. *Application Contact:* Darren Kettles, Director of Admissions, 727-562-7802, Fax: 727-562-7670, E-mail: lawadmit@law.stetson.edu. *Dean/Professor of Law,* Michèle Alexandre, 727-562-7809, Fax: 727-562-7800, E-mail: malexandre@law.stetson.edu.

School of Business Administration Students: 102 full-time (60 women), 25 part-time (14 women); includes 43 minority (11 Black or African American, non-Hispanic/Latino; 5 Asian, non-Hispanic/Latino; 17 Hispanic/Latino; 10 Two or more races, non-Hispanic/Latino), 8 international. Average age 31. 96 applicants, 69% accepted, 57 enrolled. *Faculty:* 14 full-time (3 women), 1 (woman) part-time/adjunct. Expenses: Contact institution. *Financial support:* In 2018–19, 30 students received support. Career-related internships or fieldwork, Federal Work-Study, institutionally sponsored loans, scholarships/grants, unspecified assistantships, and tuition waivers (for staff and dependents) available. Support available to part-time students. Financial award applicants required to submit FAFSA. In 2018, 77 master's awarded. *Program availability:* Part-time, evening/weekend. Offers accounting (M Acc); business administration (EMBA, M Acc, MBA). *Application deadline:* For fall admission, 8/1 for domestic students; for spring admission, 1/1 for domestic students; for summer admission, 5/1 for domestic students. Applications are processed on a rolling basis. *Application fee:* $50. Electronic applications accepted. *Application Contact:* Jamie Vanderlip, Director of Admissions for Graduate, Transfer and Adult Programs, 386-822-7100, Fax: 386-822-7112, E-mail: jlvander@stetson.edu. *Dean, School of Business Administration,* Dr. Neal P. Mero, 386-822-7405.

STEVENS-HENAGER COLLEGE, Salt Lake City, UT 84123
General Information Independent, coed, comprehensive institution.

STEVENS INSTITUTE OF TECHNOLOGY, Hoboken, NJ 07030
General Information Independent, coed, university. CGS member. *Enrollment:* 6,929 graduate, professional, and undergraduate students; 2,292 full-time matriculated graduate/professional students (627 women), 1,105 part-time matriculated graduate/professional students (356 women). *Enrollment by degree level:* 2,925 master's, 375 doctoral, 97 other advanced degrees. *Graduate faculty:* 307 full-time (77 women), 128 part-time/adjunct (25 women). *Tuition:* Full-time $35,960; part-time $1620 per credit. *Required fees:* $1290; $600 per semester. Tuition and fees vary according to course load. *Graduate housing:* Room and/or apartments available on a first-come, first-served basis to single students; on-campus housing not available to married students. Typical cost: $16,930 (including board). Room and board charges vary according to board plan and housing facility selected. Housing application deadline: 1/31. *Student services:* Campus employment opportunities, campus safety program, career counseling, exercise/wellness program, free psychological counseling, grant writing training, international student services, low-cost health insurance, multicultural affairs office, services for students with disabilities, teacher training, writing training. *Library facilities:* Samuel C. Williams Library. *Collection:* Books: 66,492 (physical), 210,243 (digital/electronic); Serial titles: 898 (physical), 35,353 (digital/electronic); Databases: 71. Students can reserve study rooms.

Computer facilities: 11 computers available on campus for general student use. A campuswide network can be accessed. Online class registration, online account information, debit dining program, laundry status are available. Website: http://www.stevens.edu/

GRADUATE UNITS

Charles V. Schaefer Jr. School of Engineering and Science Students: 1,258 full-time (286 women), 271 part-time (65 women); includes 133 minority (29 Black or African American, non-Hispanic/Latino; 3 American Indian or Alaska Native, non-Hispanic/Latino; 96 Asian, non-Hispanic/Latino; 5 Hispanic/Latino), 1,069 international. Average age 26. *Faculty:* 179 full-time (40 women), 72 part-time/adjunct (8 women). Expenses: Contact institution. *Financial support:* Fellowships, research

assistantships, teaching assistantships, career-related internships or fieldwork, Federal Work-Study, scholarships/grants, and unspecified assistantships available. Financial award application deadline: 2/15; financial award applicants required to submit FAFSA. In 2018, 783 master's, 36 doctorates, 124 other advanced degrees awarded. *Program availability:* Part-time, evening/weekend, 100% online, blended/hybrid learning. Offers applied mathematics (MS); armament engineering (M Eng); autonomous robotics (Certificate); biomedical engineering (M Eng, PhD, Certificate); chemical biology (MS, PhD, Certificate); chemical engineering (M Eng, PhD, Engr); chemistry (MS, PhD, Certificate); civil engineering (PhD, Certificate); computer and electrical engineering (M Eng); computer engineering (PhD, Certificate); computer science (MS, PhD, Certificate); computer systems (M Eng); construction management (MS, Certificate); data communications and networks (M Eng); digital systems design (M Eng); electrical engineering (M Eng, PhD, Certificate); engineered software systems (M Eng); engineering and science (M Eng, MS, PhD, Certificate, Engr); environmental engineering (PhD, Certificate); environmental processes (M Eng); geotechnical/geoenvironmental engineering (M Eng, Engr); hydrologic modeling (M Eng); image processing and multimedia (M Eng); information system security (M Eng); information systems (M Eng); inland and coastal environmental hydrodynamics (M Eng); manufacturing technologies (M Eng); materials science and engineering (M Eng, PhD); mathematics (MS, PhD); mechanical engineering (M Eng, PhD, Eng); media and broadcast engineering (MS); modeling of environmental systems (M Eng); networked information systems (MS, Certificate); ocean engineering (M Eng, PhD); pharmaceutical manufacturing (M Eng, MS, Certificate); product architecture and engineering (M Eng); soil and groundwater pollution control (M Eng); stochastic systems (MS, Certificate); stormwater management (M Eng); structural engineering (M Eng, Engr); systems reliability and design (M Eng); transportation engineering (M Eng); water resources engineering (M Eng). *Application deadline:* For fall admission, 4/15 for domestic and international students; for spring admission, 11/1 for domestic and international students; for summer admission, 5/1 for domestic students. Applications are processed on a rolling basis. *Application fee:* $60. Electronic applications accepted. *Application Contact:* Graduate Admissions, 888-783-8367, Fax: 888-555-1306, E-mail: graduate@stevens.edu. *Dean,* Dr. Jean Zu, 201-216-2833, E-mail: jean.zu@stevens.edu.

College of Arts and Letters Students: 1 full-time (0 women), 2 part-time (both women). Average age 29. *Faculty:* 40 full-time (20 women), 30 part-time/adjunct (12 women). Expenses: Contact institution. *Financial support:* Fellowships, research assistantships, teaching assistantships, career-related internships or fieldwork, Federal Work-Study, scholarships/grants, and unspecified assistantships available. Financial award application deadline: 2/15; financial award applicants required to submit FAFSA. *Program availability:* Part-time, evening/weekend. Offers arts and letters (MA, Graduate Certificate); policy and innovation (MA, Graduate Certificate). *Application deadline:* For fall admission, 4/15 for domestic and international students; for spring admission, 11/1 for domestic and international students; for summer admission, 5/1 for domestic students. Applications are processed on a rolling basis. *Application fee:* $60. Electronic applications accepted. *Application Contact:* Graduate Admission, 888-783-8367, Fax: 888-511-1306, E-mail: graduate@stevens.edu. *Dean of CAL,* Dr. Kelland Thomas, 201-216-3728, Fax: 201-216-8245, E-mail: Kelland.Thomas@stevens.edu.

School of Business Students: 837 full-time (297 women), 549 part-time (214 women); includes 188 minority (42 Black or African American, non-Hispanic/Latino; 4 American Indian or Alaska Native, non-Hispanic/Latino; 137 Asian, non-Hispanic/Latino; 5 Hispanic/Latino), 824 international. Average age 30. *Faculty:* 58 full-time (8 women), 18 part-time/adjunct (3 women). Expenses: Contact institution. *Financial support:* Fellowships, research assistantships, teaching assistantships, career-related internships or fieldwork, Federal Work-Study, scholarships/grants, and unspecified assistantships available. Financial award application deadline: 2/15; financial award applicants required to submit FAFSA. In 2018, 651 master's, 11 doctorates, 175 other advanced degrees awarded. *Program availability:* Part-time, evening/weekend, 100% online, blended/hybrid learning. Offers business (MS); business administration (EMBA); business intelligence and analytics (MBA); computer science (MS); e-commerce (MS); engineering management (MBA); enterprise systems (MS); entrepreneurial information technology (MS); finance (MS); financial engineering (MS, PhD, Certificate); general management (MS); global innovation management (MS); human resource management (MS); information architecture (MS); information management (MS, PhD, Certificate); information security (MS); information systems (MBA); information technology in financial services industry (MS); information technology in the pharmaceutical industry (MS); information technology outsourcing management (MS); innovation and entrepreneurship (MS); management of wireless networks (MS); marketing (MBA); network and communication management and services (MS); online security, technology and business (MS); pharmaceutical management (MBA); project management (MBA, MS, Certificate); software engineering (MS); technical management (MS); technology commercialization (MS); technology management (EMBA, MBA, MS, PhD); telecommunications (MS); telecommunications management (MBA, PhD, Certificate). *Application deadline:* For fall admission, 4/1 for domestic and international students; for spring admission, 11/1 for domestic and international students; for summer admission, 5/1 for domestic students. Applications are processed on a rolling basis. *Application fee:* $60. Electronic applications accepted. *Application Contact:* Graduate Admissions, 888-793-8367, Fax: 888-511-1306, E-mail: graduate@stevens.edu. *Dean of SB,* Dr. Gregory Prastacos, 201-216-8366, E-mail: gprastac@stevens.edu.

School of Systems and Enterprises Students: 196 full-time (43 women), 283 part-time (75 women); includes 52 minority (17 Black or African American, non-Hispanic/Latino; 2 American Indian or Alaska Native, non-Hispanic/Latino; 31 Asian, non-Hispanic/Latino; 2 Hispanic/Latino), 152 international. Average age 30. *Faculty:* 28 full-time (8 women), 5 part-time/adjunct (1 woman). Expenses: Contact institution. *Financial support:* Fellowships, research assistantships, teaching assistantships, career-related internships or fieldwork, Federal Work-Study, scholarships/grants, and unspecified assistantships available. Financial award application deadline: 2/15; financial award applicants required to submit FAFSA. In 2018, 232 master's, 5 doctorates, 233 other advanced degrees awarded. *Program availability:* Part-time, evening/weekend, 100% online, blended/hybrid learning. Offers engineering management (M Eng, PhD, Certificate); socio-technical systems (MS, PhD); software engineering (MS, Certificate); space systems engineering (M Eng, Certificate); systems and enterprises (M Eng, MS, PhD, Certificate); systems and supportability engineering (Certificate); systems engineering (M Eng, PhD); systems engineering and architecting (Certificate); systems engineering management (Certificate); systems engineering of embedded/cyber-physical systems (Certificate); systems engineering security (Certificate). *Application deadline:* For fall admission, 4/15 for domestic and international students; for spring admission, 11/1 for domestic and international students; for summer admission, 5/1 for domestic students. Applications are processed on a rolling basis. *Application fee:* $60. Electronic applications accepted. *Application Contact:* Graduate Admissions, 888-783-8367, Fax: 888-511-1306, E-mail: graduate@stevens.edu. *Dean of SSE,* Dr. Yehia Massoud, 201-216.8025, E-mail: yehia.massoud@stevens.edu.

STEVENSON UNIVERSITY, Stevenson, MD 21153

General Information Independent, coed, comprehensive institution. *Enrollment:* 93 full-time matriculated graduate/professional students (63 women), 508 part-time matriculated graduate/professional students (403 women). *Enrollment by degree level:* 601 master's. *Graduate faculty:* 7 full-time (6 women), 57 part-time/adjunct (31 women). *Tuition:* Part-time $695 per credit. Tuition and fees vary according to program. *Graduate housing:* On-campus housing not available. *Student services:* Campus employment opportunities, campus safety program, career counseling, exercise/wellness program, multicultural affairs office, services for students with disabilities, writing training. *Library facilities:* Stevenson University Learning Resource Center-Greenspring Campus plus 2 others. *Collection:* Books: 67,987 (physical), 342,648 (digital/electronic); Serial titles: 476 (physical), 72,885 (digital/electronic); Databases: 88. Weekly public service hours: 136; students can reserve study rooms.

Computer facilities: Computer purchase and lease plans are available. 515 computers available on campus for general student use. A campuswide network can be accessed from student residence rooms and from off campus. Online class registration is available.
Website: http://www.stevenson.edu/

General Application Contact: Amanda Millar, Director, SUO Admissions, 443-352-4243, Fax: 443-352-4440, E-mail: amillar@stevenson.edu.

GRADUATE UNITS

Master of Arts in Teaching Program Students: 13 part-time (9 women); includes 5 minority (1 Black or African American, non-Hispanic/Latino; 2 Asian, non-Hispanic/Latino; 2 Hispanic/Latino). Average age 31. 8 applicants, 75% accepted, 6 enrolled. *Faculty:* 5 part-time/adjunct (all women). Expenses: Contact institution. *Financial support:* Unspecified assistantships available. Financial award applicants required to submit FAFSA. *Program availability:* Part-time, blended/hybrid learning. Offers secondary biology (MAT); secondary chemistry (MAT); secondary mathematics (MAT). *Application deadline:* Applications are processed on a rolling basis. Electronic applications accepted. *Application Contact:* Amanda Millar, Director, Admissions, 443-352-4243, Fax: 443-352-4440, E-mail: amillar@stevenson.edu. *Dean, Stevenson University Online,* Dr. Anne P. Davis.

Master of Forensic Science Students: 29 full-time (26 women), 37 part-time (34 women); includes 39 minority (33 Black or African American, non-Hispanic/Latino; 1 American Indian or Alaska Native, non-Hispanic/Latino; 3 Asian, non-Hispanic/Latino; 2 Hispanic/Latino). Average age 27. 45 applicants, 67% accepted, 19 enrolled. *Faculty:* 1 full-time (0 women), 7 part-time/adjunct (3 women). Expenses: Contact institution. *Financial support:* Unspecified assistantships available. Financial award applicants required to submit FAFSA. In 2018, 15 master's awarded. *Program availability:* Part-time. Offers biology (MS); chemistry (MS); crime scene investigation (MS). Program offered in partnership with Maryland State Police Forensic Sciences Division. *Application deadline:* Applications are processed on a rolling basis. *Application fee:* $0. Electronic applications accepted. *Application Contact:* Amanda Millar, Director, Admissions, 443-333-3334, Fax: 443-394-0538, E-mail: amillar@stevenson.edu. *Program Coordinator,* Carolyn Johnson, E-mail: CHJOHNSON@stevenson.edu.

Program in Business and Technology Management Students: 26 full-time (7 women), 82 part-time (45 women); includes 42 minority (32 Black or African American, non-Hispanic/Latino; 3 American Indian or Alaska Native, non-Hispanic/Latino; 3 Asian, non-Hispanic/Latino; 4 Hispanic/Latino). Average age 29. 37 applicants, 49% accepted, 16 enrolled. *Faculty:* 1 full-time (0 women), 9 part-time/adjunct (2 women). Expenses: Contact institution. *Financial support:* Unspecified assistantships available. Financial award applicants required to submit FAFSA. In 2018, 66 master's awarded. *Program availability:* Part-time, online only, 100% online. Offers emerging technology (MS); innovative leadership (MS). *Application deadline:* Applications are processed on a rolling basis. *Application fee:* $0. Electronic applications accepted. *Application Contact:* Amanda Millar, Director, Admissions, 443-352-4058, Fax: 443-394-0538, E-mail: amillar@stevenson.edu. *Coordinator,* Steven Engorn, 443-352-4220, Fax: 443-394-0538, E-mail: sengorn@stevenson.edu.

Program in Communication Studies Students: 5 full-time (3 women), 18 part-time (14 women); includes 13 minority (9 Black or African American, non-Hispanic/Latino; 1 American Indian or Alaska Native, non-Hispanic/Latino; 2 Asian, non-Hispanic/Latino; 1 Hispanic/Latino). Average age 27. 29 applicants, 69% accepted, 6 enrolled. *Faculty:* 5 part-time/adjunct (3 women). Expenses: Contact institution. *Financial support:* Unspecified assistantships available. Financial award applicants required to submit FAFSA. In 2018, 11 master's awarded. *Program availability:* Part-time, online only, 100% online, blended/hybrid learning. Offers communication studies (MS). *Application deadline:* Applications are processed on a rolling basis. Electronic applications accepted. *Application Contact:* Amanda Millar, Director, Admissions, 443-352-4243, Fax: 443-352-4440, E-mail: amillar@stevenson.edu. *Associate Dean, Communications Studies,* Dr. Nadene Vevea, 443-394-9498, E-mail: nvevea@stevenson.edu.

Program in Community-Based Education and Leadership Students: 6 full-time (5 women), 27 part-time (23 women); includes 14 minority (11 Black or African American, non-Hispanic/Latino; 1 Asian, non-Hispanic/Latino; 1 Hispanic/Latino; 1 Two or more races, non-Hispanic/Latino). Average age 32. 25 applicants, 68% accepted, 13 enrolled. *Faculty:* 1 (woman) full-time, 2 part-time/adjunct (both women). Expenses: Contact institution. *Financial support:* Unspecified assistantships available. Financial award applicants required to submit FAFSA. In 2018, 10 master's awarded. *Program availability:* Part-time, evening/weekend. Offers community-based education and leadership (MS). *Application deadline:* Applications are processed on a rolling basis. Electronic applications accepted. *Application Contact:* Amanda Millar, Director, Admissions, 443-334-3334, Fax: 443-394-0538, E-mail: amillar@stevenson.edu. *Program Coordinator,* Lisa Moyer.

Program in Crime Scene Investigation Students: 15 full-time (14 women), 35 part-time (24 women); includes 32 minority (24 Black or African American, non-Hispanic/Latino; 1 American Indian or Alaska Native, non-Hispanic/Latino; 2 Asian, non-Hispanic/Latino; 5 Hispanic/Latino). Average age 27. 45 applicants, 69% accepted, 23 enrolled. *Faculty:* 1 full-time (0 women), 7 part-time/adjunct (3 women). Expenses: Contact institution. *Financial support:* Teaching assistantships and unspecified assistantships available. *Program availability:* Part-time. *Application deadline:* Applications are processed on a rolling basis. *Application Contact:* Amanda Millar, Director, SUO Admissions, 443-352-4243, Fax: 443-352-4440, E-mail: amillar@stevenson.edu.

Program in Cyber Forensics Students: 16 part-time (5 women); includes 6 minority (4 Black or African American, non-Hispanic/Latino; 1 American Indian or Alaska Native, non-Hispanic/Latino; 1 Asian, non-Hispanic/Latino). Average age 32. 12 applicants, 92%

accepted, 7 enrolled. *Faculty:* 6 part-time/adjunct (1 woman). Expenses: Contact institution. *Financial support:* Unspecified assistantships available. Financial award applicants required to submit FAFSA. In 2018, 9 master's awarded. *Program availability:* Part-time, 100% online. Offers cyber forensics (MS). *Application deadline:* Applications are processed on a rolling basis. Electronic applications accepted. *Application Contact:* Amanda Millar, Director, Admissions, 443-334-3334, Fax: 443-394-0538, E-mail: amillar@stevenson.edu. *Program Coordinator,* Carolyn Johnson, E-mail: CHJOHNSON@stevenson.edu.

Program in Forensic Accounting Students: 2 full-time (both women), 29 part-time (18 women); includes 13 minority (10 Black or African American, non-Hispanic/Latino; 1 American Indian or Alaska Native, non-Hispanic/Latino; 1 Asian, non-Hispanic/Latino; 1 Hispanic/Latino). Average age 36. 18 applicants, 67% accepted, 9 enrolled. *Faculty:* 3 part-time/adjunct (0 women). Expenses: Contact institution. *Financial support:* Unspecified assistantships available. *Program availability:* Part-time. *Application deadline:* Applications are processed on a rolling basis. Electronic applications accepted. *Application Contact:* Amanda Millar, Director, SUO Admissions, 443-352-4243, Fax: 443-352-4440, E-mail: amillar@stevenson.edu.

Program in Forensic Investigations Students: 2 full-time (both women), 34 part-time (31 women); includes 22 minority (19 Black or African American, non-Hispanic/Latino; 1 American Indian or Alaska Native, non-Hispanic/Latino; 1 Asian, non-Hispanic/Latino; 1 Hispanic/Latino). Average age 28. 25 applicants, 84% accepted, 12 enrolled. *Faculty:* 2 part-time/adjunct (0 women). Expenses: Contact institution. *Financial support:* Unspecified assistantships available. *Program availability:* Part-time. *Application deadline:* Applications are processed on a rolling basis. Electronic applications accepted. *Application Contact:* Amanda Millar, Director, SUO Admissions, 443-352-4243, Fax: 443-352-4440, E-mail: amillar@stevenson.edu. *Program Coordinator,* Carolyn Johnson, Esq..

Program in Forensic Studies Students: 1 (woman) full-time, 26 part-time (21 women); includes 16 minority (12 Black or African American, non-Hispanic/Latino; 2 Asian, non-Hispanic/Latino; 2 Hispanic/Latino). Average age 30. 17 applicants, 65% accepted, 5 enrolled. *Faculty:* 2 full-time (both women), 8 part-time/adjunct (1 woman). Expenses: Contact institution. *Financial support:* Unspecified assistantships available. Financial award applicants required to submit FAFSA. In 2018, 8 master's awarded. *Program availability:* Part-time, blended/hybrid learning. Offers computer forensics (MS); criminalistics (MS); forensic accounting (MS); forensic legal professional (MS); interdisciplinary track (MS); investigations (MS). *Application deadline:* Applications are processed on a rolling basis. *Application fee:* $0. Electronic applications accepted. *Application Contact:* Amanda Millar, Director, Admissions, 443-334-3334, Fax: 443-394-0538, E-mail: amillar@stevenson.edu. *Program Coordinator,* Carolyn Johnson, JD, E-mail: CHJOHNSON@stevenson.edu.

Program in Healthcare Management Students: 4 full-time (1 woman), 36 part-time (30 women); includes 17 minority (11 Black or African American, non-Hispanic/Latino; 2 Asian, non-Hispanic/Latino; 1 Hispanic/Latino; 3 Two or more races, non-Hispanic/Latino). Average age 32. 32 applicants, 41% accepted, 9 enrolled. *Faculty:* 1 (woman) full-time, 7 part-time/adjunct (6 women). Expenses: Contact institution. *Financial support:* Unspecified assistantships available. Financial award applicants required to submit FAFSA. In 2018, 18 master's awarded. *Program availability:* Part-time, online only, 100% online. Offers project management (MS); quality management and patient safety (MS). *Application deadline:* Applications are processed on a rolling basis. Electronic applications accepted. *Application Contact:* Amanda Millar, Director, Admissions, 443-352-4243, Fax: 443-394-0538, E-mail: amillar@stevenson.edu. *Coordinator,* Sharon Buchbinder, PhD, 443-394-9290, Fax: 443-394-0538, E-mail: sbuchbinder@stevenson.edu.

Program in Nursing Students: 150 part-time (145 women); includes 36 minority (29 Black or African American, non-Hispanic/Latino; 1 American Indian or Alaska Native, non-Hispanic/Latino; 3 Asian, non-Hispanic/Latino; 3 Hispanic/Latino). Average age 39. 48 applicants, 85% accepted, 27 enrolled. *Faculty:* 2 full-time (both women), 13 part-time/adjunct (all women). Expenses: Contact institution. *Financial support:* Unspecified assistantships available. Financial award applicants required to submit FAFSA. In 2018, 50 master's awarded. *Program availability:* Part-time, blended/hybrid learning. Offers nursing education (MS); nursing leadership/management (MS); population-based care coordination (MS). *Application deadline:* Applications are processed on a rolling basis. *Application fee:* $0. Electronic applications accepted. *Application Contact:* Amanda Millar, Director, Admissions, 443-352-4243, Fax: 443-394-0538, E-mail: amillar@stevenson.edu. *Associate Dean,* Judith Feustle, PhD, 443-352-4292, Fax: 443-394-0538, E-mail: jfeustle@stevenson.edu.

STOCKTON UNIVERSITY, Galloway, NJ 08205-9441

General Information State-supported, coed, comprehensive institution. CGS member. *Enrollment:* 9,621 graduate, professional, and undergraduate students; 590 full-time matriculated graduate/professional students (430 women), 396 part-time matriculated graduate/professional students (297 women). *Enrollment by degree level:* 801 master's, 185 doctoral. *Graduate faculty:* 117 full-time (65 women), 37 part-time/adjunct (28 women). *International tuition:* $17,282 full-time. *Tuition, area resident:* Full-time $11,226; part-time $623.69 per credit hour. Tuition, state resident: Full-time $11,226; part-time $623.69 per credit hour. Tuition, nonresident: full-time $17,282; part-time $960.10 per credit hour. *Required fees:* $3376; $187.56 per credit hour. *Graduate housing:* Room and/or apartments available on a first-come, first-served basis to single students; on-campus housing not available to married students. Housing application deadline: 6/1. *Student services:* Campus employment opportunities, campus safety program, career counseling, child daycare facilities, exercise/wellness program, free psychological counseling, grant writing training, international student services, low-cost health insurance, services for students with disabilities, teacher training, writing training. *Library facilities:* Richard E. Bjork Library. *Collection:* Books: 215,712 (physical), 165,452 (digital/electronic); Serial titles: 85 (physical), 133,008 (digital/electronic); Databases: 184. Weekly public service hours: 91.

Computer facilities: 1,224 computers available on campus for general student use. A campuswide network can be accessed from student residence rooms and from off campus. Online class registration is available.
Website: http://www.stockton.edu/

General Application Contact: Tara Williams, Assistant Director of Graduate Enrollment Management, 609-626-3640, E-mail: gradschool@stockton.edu.

GRADUATE UNITS

Office of Graduate Studies Students: 590 full-time (430 women), 396 part-time (297 women); includes 240 minority (82 Black or African American, non-Hispanic/Latino; 2 American Indian or Alaska Native, non-Hispanic/Latino; 43 Asian, non-Hispanic/Latino; 83 Hispanic/Latino; 2 Native Hawaiian or other Pacific Islander, non-Hispanic/Latino; 28 Two or more races, non-Hispanic/Latino), 3 international. Average age 32. 1,431 applicants, 41% accepted, 328 enrolled. *Faculty:* 117 full-time (65 women), 37 part-time/adjunct (28 women). Expenses: Contact institution. *Financial support:* Fellowships, research assistantships, career-related internships or fieldwork, Federal Work-Study, scholarships/grants, and unspecified assistantships available. Support available to part-time students. Financial award application deadline: 3/1; financial award applicants required to submit FAFSA. In 2018, 259 master's, 30 doctorates awarded. *Program availability:* Part-time, evening/weekend, 100% online, blended/hybrid learning. Offers American studies (MA, Certificate); business administration (MBA); communication disorders (MS); criminal justice (MA); data science and strategic analytics (MS); education (MA); environmental science (PSM); Holocaust and genocide studies (MA); instructional technology (MA); nursing (MSN); occupational therapy (MSOT); organizational leadership (Ed D); physical therapy (DPT); social work (MSW). *Application deadline:* For fall admission, 7/1 for domestic and international students. Applications are processed on a rolling basis. *Application fee:* $50. Electronic applications accepted. *Application Contact:* Tara Williams, Assistant Director of Graduate Enrollment, 609-626-3640, Fax: 609-626-6050, E-mail: gradschool@stockton.edu. *Director of Graduate Enrollment Management,* AmyBeth Glass, 609-652-4298, E-mail: graduatestudies@stockton.edu.

STONEHILL COLLEGE, Easton, MA 02357

General Information Independent-religious, coed, comprehensive institution. *Graduate housing:* On-campus housing not available.

GRADUATE UNITS

Program in Integrated Marketing Communications Expenses: Contact institution. Offers integrated marketing communications (MA). *Application Contact:* Melissa Ratliff, Dean of Graduate Admission, 508-565-1877, Fax: 508-565-1601, E-mail: mratliff@stonehill.edu. *Director,* Lee McGinnis, 508-565-1971, E-mail: lmcginnis@stonehill.edu.

Program in Special Education Expenses: Contact institution. *Financial support:* Applicants required to submit FAFSA. *Program availability:* Part-time, evening/weekend. Offers special education (MA). *Application deadline:* Applications are processed on a rolling basis. Electronic applications accepted. *Application Contact:* Melissa Ratliff, Dean of Graduate Admission, 508-5651877, Fax: 508-565-1601, E-mail: mratliff@stonehill.edu.

STONY BROOK UNIVERSITY, STATE UNIVERSITY OF NEW YORK, Stony Brook, NY 11794

General Information State-supported, coed, university. CGS member. *Enrollment:* 5,332 full-time matriculated graduate/professional students (2,636 women), 3,042 part-time matriculated graduate/professional students (2,195 women). *Enrollment by degree level:* 5,095 master's, 2,658 doctoral, 621 other advanced degrees. *Graduate faculty:* 1,908 full-time (793 women), 699 part-time/adjunct (355 women). *International tuition:* $22,650 full-time. *Tuition, area resident:* Full-time $11,090; part-time $462 per credit hour. *Tuition, state resident:* Full-time $11,090; part-time $462 per credit hour. Tuition, nonresident: full-time $22,650; part-time $944 per credit hour. *Required fees:* $1917. *Graduate housing:* Rooms and/or apartments available to single and married students. Housing application deadline: 5/1. *Student services:* Campus employment opportunities, campus safety program, career counseling, child daycare facilities, exercise/wellness program, free psychological counseling, grant writing training, international student services, multicultural affairs office, services for students with disabilities, teacher training, writing training. *Library facilities:* Frank Melville, Jr. Memorial Library plus 7 others. *Collection:* Books: 1.9 million (physical), 348,868 (digital/electronic); Serial titles: 1,225 (physical), 190,674 (digital/electronic); Databases: 679. Weekly public service hours: 131; study areas open 24 hours, 5–7 days a week; students can reserve study rooms.

Computer facilities: Computer purchase and lease plans are available. 1,590 computers available on campus for general student use. A campuswide network can be accessed from student residence rooms and from off campus. Online class registration is available.
Website: http://www.stonybrook.edu/

General Application Contact: Melissa Jordan, Senior Assistant Dean for Records and Admission, 631-632-9712, Fax: 631-632-7243, E-mail: gradadmissions@stonybrook.edu.

GRADUATE UNITS

Graduate School Students: 3,263 full-time (1,299 women), 787 part-time (364 women); includes 648 minority (103 Black or African American, non-Hispanic/Latino; 2 American Indian or Alaska Native, non-Hispanic/Latino; 277 Asian, non-Hispanic/Latino; 215 Hispanic/Latino; 51 Two or more races, non-Hispanic/Latino), 1,948 international. Average age 28. 7,304 applicants, 41% accepted, 1139 enrolled. *Faculty:* 913 full-time (314 women), 290 part-time/adjunct (130 women). Expenses: Contact institution. *Financial support:* In 2018–19, 131 fellowships, 568 research assistantships, 864 teaching assistantships were awarded; career-related internships or fieldwork, Federal Work-Study, institutionally sponsored loans, scholarships/grants, traineeships, health care benefits, tuition waivers (full), and unspecified assistantships also available. In 2018, 959 master's, 307 doctorates, 77 other advanced degrees awarded. *Program availability:* Part-time, evening/weekend. *Application deadline:* For fall admission, 1/15 for domestic and international students; for spring admission, 10/1 for domestic and international students. *Application fee:* $100. Electronic applications accepted. *Application Contact:* Melissa Jordan, Assistant Dean for Records and Admission, 631-632-9712, Fax: 631-632-7243, E-mail: gradadmissions@stonybrook.edu. *Vice Provost for Graduate and Professional Education Dean of the Graduate School,* Dr. Eic Wertheimer, 631-632-7035, Fax: 631-632-7112, E-mail: Eric.Wertheimer@stonybrook.edu.

College of Arts and Sciences Students: 1,519 full-time (710 women), 148 part-time (93 women); includes 291 minority (46 Black or African American, non-Hispanic/Latino; 2 American Indian or Alaska Native, non-Hispanic/Latino; 103 Asian, non-Hispanic/Latino; 112 Hispanic/Latino; 28 Two or more races, non-Hispanic/Latino), 644 international. Average age 29. 3,090 applicants, 30% accepted, 375 enrolled. *Faculty:* 526 full-time (207 women), 113 part-time/adjunct (43 women). Expenses: Contact institution. *Financial support:* In 2018–19, 67 fellowships, 232 research assistantships, 590 teaching assistantships were awarded; career-related internships or fieldwork, Federal Work-Study, scholarships/grants, traineeships, health care benefits, and unspecified assistantships also available. Financial award applicants required to submit FAFSA. In 2018, 224 master's, 194 doctorates, 32 other advanced degrees awarded. *Program availability:* Part-time, evening/weekend. Offers Africana studies (MA, Certificate); anthropological sciences (PhD); anthropology (MA, PhD); applied ecology (MA); art history and criticism (MA, PhD); arts and sciences (MA, MAPP, MAT, MFA, MM, MS, DMA, PhD, Advanced Certificate, Certificate, Graduate Certificate); astronomy (PhD); biochemistry and cell biology (MA, MS, PhD); biochemistry and structural biology (PhD); chemistry (MS, PhD); clinical psychology (PhD); cognitive psychology (PhD); comparative literature (MA, PhD);

contemporary Asian and Asian American studies (MA); cultural studies (PhD, Certificate); dramaturgy (MFA); ecology and evolution (PhD); economics (MA, PhD); English (MA, MAT, PhD); French (MA); genetics (PhD); geosciences (MAT, MS, PhD); Hispanic languages and literature (MA, PhD); history (MA, PhD); integrative neuroscience (PhD); Italian (MA); linguistics (MA, PhD); mathematics (MA, MAT, PhD); molecular and cellular biology (MA, PhD); music history/theory (MA, PhD); music performance (MM, DMA); neuroscience (MS, PhD); philosophy (MA, PhD, Advanced Certificate); physics (MA, MAT, MS, PhD); political science (MA, PhD); psychology (MA); public policy (MAPP); public policy and urban development (MA); social and health psychology (PhD); sociology (MA, PhD); STEM education (MA); studio art (MFA); teaching English to speakers of other languages (MA); teaching writing (Graduate Certificate); theatre arts (MA, MFA); women's, gender, and sexuality studies (Certificate). *Application deadline:* For fall admission, 1/15 for domestic students; for spring admission, 10/1 for domestic students. *Application fee:* $100. Electronic applications accepted. *Application Contact:* Melissa Jordan, Assistant Dean for Records and Admission, 631-632-9712, Fax: 631-632-7243, E-mail: melissa.jordan@stonybrook.edu. *Interim Dean,* Dr. Nicole S Sampson, 631-632-6976, Fax: 631-632-6900, E-mail: Nicole.Sampson@stonybrook.edu.

College of Business Students: 182 full-time (85 women), 163 part-time (86 women); includes 85 minority (17 Black or African American, non-Hispanic/Latino; 35 Asian, non-Hispanic/Latino; 29 Hispanic/Latino; 4 Two or more races, non-Hispanic/Latino), 48 international. Average age 28. 361 applicants, 66% accepted, 130 enrolled. *Faculty:* 38 full-time (13 women), 8 part-time/adjunct (3 women). Expenses: Contact institution. *Financial support:* Research assistantships and teaching assistantships available. In 2018, 215 master's, 2 other advanced degrees awarded. Offers accounting (MS); business (MBA, MS, AGC, Certificate); business administration (MBA); finance (MS, AGC); health care management (MBA); human resources (MBA); innovation (MBA); management (MBA); marketing (MBA); operations management (MBA). *Application deadline:* For fall admission, 12/1 for domestic students, 10/15 priority date for international students; for spring admission, 11/15 for domestic students. *Application fee:* $100. *Application Contact:* Joyce Gibson, Graduate Coordinator, 631-632-7171, Fax: 631-632-8181, E-mail: Joyce.Gibson@stonybrook.edu. *Dean,* Dr. Manuel London, 631-632-7159, E-mail: manuel.london@stonybrook.edu.

College of Engineering and Applied Sciences Students: 1,225 full-time (313 women), 367 part-time (108 women); includes 173 minority (18 Black or African American, non-Hispanic/Latino; 104 Asian, non-Hispanic/Latino; 40 Hispanic/Latino; 11 Two or more races, non-Hispanic/Latino), 1,194 international. Average age 26. 3,381 applicants, 46% accepted, 485 enrolled. *Faculty:* 171 full-time (28 women), 38 part-time/adjunct (11 women). Expenses: Contact institution. *Financial support:* In 2018–19, 9 fellowships, 255 research assistantships, 226 teaching assistantships were awarded; career-related internships or fieldwork also available. In 2018, 396 master's, 87 doctorates, 4 other advanced degrees awarded. *Program availability:* Part-time, evening/weekend. Offers applied mathematics and statistics (MS, PhD, Advanced Certificate); biomedical engineering (MS, PhD, Certificate); biomedical informatics (MS, PhD, AGC); civil engineering (MS, PhD, Graduate Certificate); computer engineering (MS, PhD); computer science (MS, PhD, Certificate); educational technology (MS); electrical engineering (MS, PhD); energy technology and policy (MS); engineering and applied sciences (MS, PhD, AGC, Advanced Certificate, Certificate, Graduate Certificate); global technology management (MS); information systems engineering (MS); materials science and engineering (MS, PhD); mechanical engineering (MS, PhD); medical physics (MS, PhD); networking and wireless communications (Certificate); technology, policy, and innovation (PhD). *Application deadline:* For fall admission, 1/15 for domestic students; for spring admission, 10/1 for domestic students. *Application fee:* $100. *Application Contact:* Melissa Jordan, Assistant Dean for Records and Admission, 631-632-9712, Fax: 631-632-7243, E-mail: gradadmissions@stonybrook.edu. *Dean,* Dr. Fotis Sotiropoulos, 631-632-8380, Fax: 631-632-8205, E-mail: fotis.sotiropoulos@stonybrook.edu.

School of Marine and Atmospheric Sciences Students: 117 full-time (58 women), 14 part-time (6 women); includes 17 minority (6 Asian, non-Hispanic/Latino; 7 Hispanic/Latino; 4 Two or more races, non-Hispanic/Latino), 26 international. Average age 28. 126 applicants, 42% accepted, 29 enrolled. *Faculty:* 52 full-time (15 women), 10 part-time/adjunct (3 women). Expenses: Contact institution. *Financial support:* In 2018–19, 13 fellowships, 42 research assistantships, 26 teaching assistantships were awarded; career-related internships or fieldwork and tuition waivers (full) also available. In 2018, 28 master's, 8 doctorates, 7 other advanced degrees awarded. Offers atmospheric sciences (MS, PhD); geospatial sciences (Graduate Certificate); marine and atmospheric sciences (MA, MS, PhD, Graduate Certificate); marine conservation and policy (MA); marine sciences (MS, PhD). *Application deadline:* For fall admission, 1/15 for domestic students; for spring admission, 10/1 for domestic students. *Application fee:* $100. *Application Contact:* Ginny Clancy, Educational Programs Coordinator, 631-632-8681, Fax: 631-632-8200. *Dean,* Dr. Paul Shepson, 631-632-8700, Fax: 631-632-8820, E-mail: Paul.Shepson@stonybrook.edu.

School of Journalism Students: 2 part-time (both women). Average age 31. 3 applicants, 0% accepted, 0 enrolled. *Faculty:* 9 full-time (3 women), 20 part-time/adjunct (7 women). Expenses: Contact institution. *Financial support:* Teaching assistantships available. Offers health communication (Certificate); journalism (MS). *Application deadline:* For fall admission, 1/15 for domestic students; for spring admission, 10/1 for domestic students. *Application fee:* $100. *Application Contact:* Maureen Robinson, Coordinator, 631-632-7403, Fax: 631-632-7550, E-mail: maureen.robinson@stonybrook.edu. *Interim Dean,* Dr. Laura Lindenfeld, 631-632-7403, E-mail: laura.lindenfeld@stonybrook.edu.

School of Professional Development Students: 214 full-time (138 women), 1,100 part-time (813 women); includes 313 minority (117 Black or African American, non-Hispanic/Latino; 2 American Indian or Alaska Native, non-Hispanic/Latino; 32 Asian, non-Hispanic/Latino; 140 Hispanic/Latino; 3 Native Hawaiian or other Pacific Islander, non-Hispanic/Latino; 19 Two or more races, non-Hispanic/Latino), 7 international. Average age 33. 483 applicants, 89% accepted, 337 enrolled. *Faculty:* 3 full-time (2 women), 94 part-time/adjunct (40 women). Expenses: Contact institution. *Financial support:* Fellowships, research assistantships, teaching assistantships, and career-related internships or fieldwork available. Support available to part-time students. In 2018, 315 master's, 178 other advanced degrees awarded. *Program availability:* Part-time, evening/weekend, online learning. Offers coaching (Graduate Certificate); environmental management (MPS); German (MAT); higher education administration (MA, Certificate); human resource management (MS, Graduate Certificate); Italian (MAT); liberal studies (MA); mathematics (MAT); school district business leadership (Advanced Certificate); social studies (MAT); Spanish (MAT). *Application deadline:* For fall admission, 1/15 for domestic students, 6/1 for international students; for spring admission, 10/1 for domestic and international students. Applications are processed on a rolling basis. *Application fee:* $100. *Application Contact:* Melissa Jordan, Assistant

Dean, 631-632-7751, E-mail: melissa.jordan@stonybrook.edu. *Associate Vice President for Professional Education and Assistant Provost for Engaged Learning*, Patricia Malone, 631-632-7512, Fax: 631-632-9046, E-mail: patricia.malone@stonybrook.edu.

Stony Brook Medicine Students: 2,024 full-time (1,297 women), 1,190 part-time (1,043 women); includes 1,185 minority (278 Black or African American, non-Hispanic/Latino; 7 American Indian or Alaska Native, non-Hispanic/Latino; 486 Asian, non-Hispanic/Latino; 350 Hispanic/Latino; 5 Native Hawaiian or other Pacific Islander, non-Hispanic/Latino; 59 Two or more races, non-Hispanic/Latino), 73 international. 10,047 applicants, 19% accepted, 1142 enrolled. Expenses: Contact institution. *Financial support:* In 2018–19, 36 fellowships, 29 research assistantships were awarded; teaching assistantships also available. In 2018, 750 master's, 295 doctorates, 50 other advanced degrees awarded. Offers medicine (MHA, MPH, MS, MSW, DDS, DNP, DPT, MD, PhD, Advanced Certificate, Certificate). *Application deadline:* For fall admission, 1/15 for domestic students; for spring admission, 10/1 for domestic students. *Application fee:* $100. Electronic applications accepted. *Application Contact:* Melissa Jordan, Assistant Dean for Records and Admission, 631-632-9712, Fax: 631-632-7243, E-mail: gradadmissions@stonybrook.edu. *Dean*, Dr. Kenneth Kaushansky, 631-444-8234, E-mail: kenneth.kaushansky@stonybrook.edu.

School of Dental Medicine Students: 204 full-time (107 women), 4 part-time (all women); includes 69 minority (2 Black or African American, non-Hispanic/Latino; 54 Asian, non-Hispanic/Latino; 9 Hispanic/Latino; 4 Two or more races, non-Hispanic/Latino), 6 international. Average age 26. 1,185 applicants, 9% accepted, 54 enrolled. *Faculty:* 35 full-time (15 women), 80 part-time/adjunct (21 women). Expenses: Contact institution. *Financial support:* Fellowships, research assistantships, teaching assistantships, and Federal Work-Study available. In 2018, 43 doctorates awarded. Offers dental medicine (DDS); endodontics (Certificate); oral biology and pathology (MS, PhD); orthodontics (Certificate); periodontics (Certificate). *Application deadline:* For fall admission, 1/15 for domestic students; for spring admission, 10/1 for domestic students. *Application fee:* $100. *Application Contact:* Marcia Simon, Coordinator, 631-632-8922, Fax: 631-632-7130, E-mail: Marcia.Simon@stonybrook.edu. *Dean*, Dr. Mary R. Truhlar, 631-632-6985, Fax: 631-632-6621, E-mail: mary.truhlar@stonybrookmedicine.edu.

School of Health Technology and Management Students: 595 full-time (407 women), 67 part-time (51 women); includes 202 minority (29 Black or African American, non-Hispanic/Latino; 97 Asian, non-Hispanic/Latino; 62 Hispanic/Latino; 1 Native Hawaiian or other Pacific Islander, non-Hispanic/Latino; 13 Two or more races, non-Hispanic/Latino), 13 international. Average age 26. 2,386 applicants, 17% accepted, 256 enrolled. *Faculty:* 61 full-time (41 women), 56 part-time/adjunct (36 women). Expenses: Contact institution. *Financial support:* In 2018–19, 1 research assistantship was awarded; fellowships, teaching assistantships, career-related internships or fieldwork, Federal Work-Study, and institutionally sponsored loans also available. Financial award application deadline: 3/15. In 2018, 158 master's, 89 doctorates, 27 other advanced degrees awarded. Offers applied health informatics (MS); disability studies (Certificate); health administration (MHA); health and rehabilitation sciences (PhD); health care management (Advanced Certificate); health care policy and management (MS); occupational therapy (MS); physical therapy (DPT); physician assistant (MS). *Application deadline:* For fall admission, 1/15 for domestic students; for spring admission, 10/1 for domestic students. *Application fee:* $100. *Application Contact:* Frances Shaw, Department Secretary, 631-444-3240, Fax: 631-444-7621, E-mail: frances.shaw@stonybrook.edu. *Interim Dean*, Lisa M Johnson, 631-444-3181, Fax: 631-444-7621, E-mail: lisa.johnson@stonybrook.edu.

School of Medicine Students: 745 full-time (379 women), 100 part-time (80 women); includes 348 minority (42 Black or African American, non-Hispanic/Latino; 2 American Indian or Alaska Native, non-Hispanic/Latino; 221 Asian, non-Hispanic/Latino; 69 Hispanic/Latino; 14 Two or more races, non-Hispanic/Latino), 52 international. Average age 26. 4,991 applicants, 11% accepted, 212 enrolled. *Faculty:* 891 full-time (406 women), 125 part-time/adjunct (85 women). Expenses: Contact institution. *Financial support:* In 2018–19, 36 fellowships, 25 research assistantships were awarded; teaching assistantships, career-related internships or fieldwork, Federal Work-Study, and tuition waivers (full) also available. In 2018, 88 master's, 139 doctorates awarded. Offers anatomical sciences (PhD); community health (MPH); evaluation sciences (MPH); family violence (MPH); health communication (Certificate); health economics (MPH); health education and promotion (Certificate); medicine (MPH, MS, MD, PhD, Pharm D, Advanced Certificate, Certificate); molecular and cellular pharmacology (MS, PhD); molecular genetics and microbiology (PhD); nutrition (MS, Advanced Certificate); pharmacological sciences (MS, PhD); physiology and biophysics (PhD); population health (MPH); population health and clinical outcomes research (PhD); substance abuse (MPH). *Application deadline:* For fall admission, 1/15 for domestic students; for spring admission, 10/1 for domestic students. *Application fee:* $100. *Application Contact:* Dr. Jack Fuhrer, Associate Dean of Admissions, 631-444-2113, Fax: 631-444-6032, E-mail: somadmissions@stonybrook.edu. *Dean*, Dr. Kenneth Kaushansky, 631-444-2121, Fax: 631-632-6621, E-mail: kenneth.kaushansky@stonybrook.edu.

School of Nursing Students: 34 full-time (31 women), 944 part-time (846 women); includes 358 minority (128 Black or African American, non-Hispanic/Latino; 5 American Indian or Alaska Native, non-Hispanic/Latino; 98 Asian, non-Hispanic/Latino; 104 Hispanic/Latino; 3 Native Hawaiian or other Pacific Islander, non-Hispanic/Latino; 20 Two or more races, non-Hispanic/Latino). Average age 36. 803 applicants, 53% accepted, 353 enrolled. *Faculty:* 36 full-time (33 women), 40 part-time/adjunct (37 women). Expenses: Contact institution. *Financial support:* Fellowships, research assistantships, teaching assistantships, career-related internships or fieldwork, Federal Work-Study, institutionally sponsored loans, and traineeships available. Financial award application deadline: 3/15. In 2018, 266 master's, 20 doctorates, 19 other advanced degrees awarded. *Program availability:* Blended/hybrid learning. Offers adult health nurse practitioner (Certificate); adult health/primary care nursing (MS, DNP); child health nurse practitioner (Certificate); child health nursing (MS, DNP); family nurse practitioner (MS, DNP, Certificate); neonatal nurse practitioner (Certificate); neonatal nursing (MS, DNP); nurse midwifery (MS, DNP, Certificate); nursing (MS, DNP, PhD, Certificate); nursing education (MS, Certificate); nursing leadership (MS, Certificate); nursing practice (DNP); perinatal women's health nursing (MS, DNP, Certificate); psychiatric-mental health nurse practitioner (MS, DNP, Certificate). *Application deadline:* For fall admission, 2/27 for domestic students. *Application fee:* $100. Electronic applications accepted. *Application Contact:* Karen Allard, Admissions Coordinator, 631-444-6628, Fax: 631-444-3136, E-mail: karen.allard@stonybrook.edu. *Dean*, Dr. Annette B Wysocki, 631-444-3200, Fax: 631-444-3136, E-mail: annette.wysocki@stonybrook.edu.

School of Social Welfare Students: 446 full-time (373 women), 75 part-time (62 women); includes 208 minority (77 Black or African American, non-Hispanic/Latino; 16 Asian, non-Hispanic/Latino; 106 Hispanic/Latino; 1 Native Hawaiian or other Pacific Islander, non-Hispanic/Latino; 8 Two or more races, non-Hispanic/Latino), 2 international. Average age 30. 420 applicants, 92% accepted, 267 enrolled. *Faculty:* 17 full-time (11 women), 45 part-time/adjunct (33 women). Expenses: Contact institution. *Financial support:* Fellowships, research assistantships, teaching assistantships, career-related internships or fieldwork, Federal Work-Study, and institutionally sponsored loans available. Financial award applicants required to submit FAFSA. In 2018, 238 master's, 4 doctorates awarded. *Program availability:* Part-time. Offers social welfare (PhD); social work (MSW). *Application deadline:* For fall admission, 1/15 for domestic students; for spring admission, 10/1 for domestic students. *Application fee:* $100. *Application Contact:* Jamie Weissbach, Coordinator, 631-444-3146, Fax: 631-444-7565, E-mail: jamie.weissbach@stonybrook.edu. *Dean and Assistant Vice President for Social Determinants of Health*, Dr. Jacqueline B. Mondros, 631-444-2139, E-mail: jacqueline.mondros@stonybrook.edu.

Stony Brook Southampton Students: 51 full-time (35 women), 58 part-time (44 women); includes 18 minority (5 Black or African American, non-Hispanic/Latino; 5 Asian, non-Hispanic/Latino; 7 Hispanic/Latino; 1 Two or more races, non-Hispanic/Latino), 3 international. Average age 37. 99 applicants, 71% accepted, 30 enrolled. *Faculty:* 9 full-time (4 women), 40 part-time/adjunct (20 women). Expenses: Contact institution. *Financial support:* In 2018–19, 4 teaching assistantships were awarded. In 2018, 34 master's, 18 other advanced degrees awarded. Offers fiction (MFA); film (MFA); poetry (MFA); scientific writing (MFA); scriptwriting (MFA). *Application deadline:* For fall admission, 1/15 for domestic students; for spring admission, 10/1 for domestic students. Applications are processed on a rolling basis. *Application fee:* $100. *Application Contact:* Margaret S Grigonis, Administrative Coordinator, 631-632-5028, Fax: 631-982-7318, E-mail: margaret.grigonis@stonybrook.edu. *Associate Provost*, Dr. Robert Reeves, 631-632-5030, Fax: 631-982-7318, E-mail: robert.reeves@stonybrook.edu.

STRATFORD UNIVERSITY, Baltimore, MD 21202

General Information Proprietary, coed, comprehensive institution.

GRADUATE UNITS

Program in International Hospitality Management *Program availability:* Part-time, evening/weekend, online learning. Offers international hospitality management (MS).

STRATFORD UNIVERSITY, Falls Church, VA 22043

General Information Proprietary, coed, comprehensive institution. *Enrollment:* 391 full-time matriculated graduate/professional students (173 women), 289 part-time matriculated graduate/professional students (125 women). *Enrollment by degree level:* 668 master's, 3 doctoral, 9 other advanced degrees. *Tuition:* Full-time $22,275; part-time $11,137 per year. One-time fee: $385. *Graduate housing:* On-campus housing not available. *Student services:* Campus employment opportunities, career counseling, exercise/wellness program, international student services, multicultural affairs office, services for students with disabilities, writing training. *Library facilities:* Learning Resource Center.

Computer facilities: A campuswide network can be accessed from off campus. Online class registration is available.
Website: http://www.stratford.edu/

General Application Contact: Lori Smith, Admissions, 214-649-7113, E-mail: lasmith@stratford.edu.

GRADUATE UNITS

School of Graduate Studies *Program availability:* Part-time, evening/weekend, 100% online, blended/hybrid learning. Offers accounting (MS); business administration (MBA, DBA); cyber security (MS); cyber security leadership and policy (MS); digital forensics (MS); healthcare administration (MS); information systems (MS); information technology (DIT); networking and telecommunications (MS); software engineering (MS). Electronic applications accepted.

STRAYER UNIVERSITY, Washington, DC 20005-2603

General Information Proprietary, coed, comprehensive institution. *Graduate housing:* On-campus housing not available.

GRADUATE UNITS

Graduate Studies *Program availability:* Part-time, evening/weekend, online learning. Offers accounting (MS); acquisition (MBA); business administration (MBA); communications technology (MS); educational management (M Ed); finance (MBA); health services administration (MHSA); hospitality and tourism management (MBA); human resource management (MBA); information systems (MS); management (MBA); management information systems (MS); marketing (MBA); professional accounting (MS); public administration (MPA); supply chain management (MBA); technology in education (M Ed). Programs also offered at campus locations in Birmingham, AL; Chamblee, GA; Cobb County, GA; Morrow, GA; White Marsh, MD; Charleston, SC; Columbia, SC; Greensboro, NC; Greenville, SC; Lexington, KY; Louisville, KY; Nashville, TN; North Raleigh, NC; Washington, DC. Electronic applications accepted.

SUFFOLK UNIVERSITY, Boston, MA 02108-2770

General Information Independent, coed, comprehensive institution. *Enrollment:* 1,071 full-time matriculated graduate/professional students (635 women), 883 part-time matriculated graduate/professional students (509 women). *Enrollment by degree level:* 822 master's, 1,129 doctoral, 3 other advanced degrees. *Graduate faculty:* 104 full-time (51 women), 53 part-time/adjunct (23 women). *Graduate housing:* On-campus housing not available. *Student services:* Campus employment opportunities, campus safety program, career counseling, exercise/wellness program, free psychological counseling, grant writing training, international student services, low-cost health insurance, multicultural affairs office, services for students with disabilities, writing training. *Library facilities:* Mildred Sawyer Library plus 3 others. *Collection:* Books: 128,945 (physical), 249,567 (digital/electronic); Serial titles: 307 (physical), 65,782 (digital/electronic); Databases: 174. Weekly public service hours: 103; students can reserve study rooms.

Computer facilities: Computer purchase and lease plans are available. 675 computers available on campus for general student use. A campuswide network can be accessed from student residence rooms and from off campus. Online class registration is available.
Website: http://www.suffolk.edu/

General Application Contact: Heather O'Leary, Director of Graduate Admissions, 617-573-8302, Fax: 617-305-1733, E-mail: grad.admission@suffolk.edu.

GRADUATE UNITS

College of Arts and Sciences Students: 126 full-time (108 women), 94 part-time (75 women); includes 45 minority (17 Black or African American, non-Hispanic/Latino; 9 Asian, non-Hispanic/Latino; 14 Hispanic/Latino; 5 Two or more races, non-Hispanic/Latino), 28 international. Average age 28. 529 applicants, 50% accepted, 87 enrolled. *Faculty:* 46 full-time (25 women), 20 part-time/adjunct (11 women). Expenses:

Contact institution. *Financial support:* In 2018–19, 150 students received support, including 98 fellowships (averaging $2,855 per year); career-related internships or fieldwork, Federal Work-Study, institutionally sponsored loans, scholarships/grants, and unspecified assistantships also available. Support available to part-time students. Financial award application deadline: 4/1; financial award applicants required to submit FAFSA. In 2018, 131 master's, 6 doctorates, 3 other advanced degrees awarded. *Program availability:* Part-time, evening/weekend. Offers administration of higher education (M Ed, CAGS); arts and sciences (M Ed, MA, MAC, MS, MSCJS, MSPS, PhD, CAGS, Certificate, Graduate Certificate); clinical psychology (PhD); college admission counseling (Certificate); communication studies (MAC); disability services (Certificate); ethics and public policy (MS); integrated marketing communication (MAC); international relations (MSPS); mental health counseling (MS); political science (MSPS); professional politics (MSPS, CAGS); public relations and advertising (MAC); school counseling (MS); sociology (MSCJS). *Application deadline:* For fall admission, 3/15 priority date for domestic and international students; for spring admission, 10/15 priority date for domestic students, 10/1 priority date for international students. Applications are processed on a rolling basis. *Application fee:* $50. Electronic applications accepted. *Application Contact:* Mara Marzocchi, Associate Director of Graduate Admissions, 617-573-8302, Fax: 617-305-1733, E-mail: grad.admission@suffolk.edu. *Dean,* Maria Toyoda, 617-573-8265, Fax: 617-573-8513, E-mail: mtoyada@suffolk.edu.

Law School Students: 730 full-time (341 women), 363 part-time (192 women); includes 198 minority (42 Black or African American, non-Hispanic/Latino; 48 Asian, non-Hispanic/Latino; 85 Hispanic/Latino; 2 Native Hawaiian or other Pacific Islander, non-Hispanic/Latino; 21 Two or more races, non-Hispanic/Latino), 50 international. Average age 27. 1,971 applicants, 65% accepted, 374 enrolled. *Faculty:* 64 full-time (31 women), 51 part-time/adjunct (19 women). Expenses: Contact institution. *Financial support:* In 2018–19, 778 students received support, including 1 fellowship (averaging $31,390 per year); career-related internships or fieldwork, Federal Work-Study, institutionally sponsored loans, and scholarships/grants also available. Support available to part-time students. Financial award application deadline: 3/1; financial award applicants required to submit FAFSA. In 2018, 18 master's, 290 doctorates awarded. *Program availability:* Part-time, evening/weekend. Offers business law and financial services (JD); civil litigation (JD); global law and technology (LL M); health and biomedical law (JD); intellectual property law (JD); international law (JD). *Application deadline:* For fall admission, 4/1 for domestic and international students. Applications are processed on a rolling basis. *Application fee:* $60. Electronic applications accepted. *Application Contact:* Matthew Gavin, Assistant Dean for Admissions and Financial Aid, 617-573-8144, Fax: 617-994-6838, E-mail: lawadm@suffolk.edu. *Dean,* Andrew Perlman, 617-573-8144, Fax: 617-994-6838, E-mail: lawadmin@suffolk.edu.

New England School of Art and Design Students: 26 full-time (25 women), 10 part-time (9 women); includes 4 minority (2 Asian, non-Hispanic/Latino; 2 Hispanic/Latino), 10 international. Average age 28. 61 applicants, 69% accepted, 12 enrolled. *Faculty:* 7 full-time (4 women), 4 part-time/adjunct (2 women). Expenses: Contact institution. *Financial support:* In 2018–19, 33 students received support, including 6 fellowships (averaging $2,700 per year); career-related internships or fieldwork, Federal Work-Study, institutionally sponsored loans, scholarships/grants, and unspecified assistantships also available. Financial award application deadline: 4/1; financial award applicants required to submit FAFSA. In 2018, 31 master's awarded. *Program availability:* Part-time, evening/weekend. Offers graphic design (MA); interior architecture (MA). *Application deadline:* For fall admission, 3/15 priority date for domestic and international students; for spring admission, 10/15 priority date for domestic and international students. Applications are processed on a rolling basis. *Application fee:* $50. Electronic applications accepted. *Application Contact:* Mara Marzocchi, Associate Director of Graduate Admissions, 617-573-8302, Fax: 617-305-1733, E-mail: grad.admission@suffolk.edu. *Department Chair,* Audrey Goldstein, 617-997-4290, E-mail: agoldstein@suffolk.edu.

Sawyer Business School Students: 215 full-time (138 women), 426 part-time (263 women); includes 192 minority (68 Black or African American, non-Hispanic/Latino; 53 Asian, non-Hispanic/Latino; 60 Hispanic/Latino; 11 Two or more races, non-Hispanic/Latino), 116 international. Average age 30. 1,204 applicants, 71% accepted, 332 enrolled. *Faculty:* 59 full-time (26 women), 32 part-time/adjunct (11 women). Expenses: Contact institution. *Financial support:* In 2018–19, 423 students received support, including 19 fellowships (averaging $3,189 per year); career-related internships or fieldwork, Federal Work-Study, institutionally sponsored loans, scholarships/grants, and unspecified assistantships also available. Support available to part-time students. Financial award application deadline: 4/1; financial award applicants required to submit FAFSA. In 2018, 433 master's awarded. *Program availability:* Part-time, evening/weekend, 100% online, blended/hybrid learning. Offers accounting (MBA, MSA, Graduate Certificate); business (EMBA, GMBA, MBA, MBAH, MHA, MPA, MS, MSA, MSBA, MSF, MSFSB, MST, Graduate Certificate); business analytics (MS, MSBA); community health (MPA); entrepreneurship (MBA); executive business administration (EMBA); finance (MSF, MSFSB); global business administration (GMBA); global marketing (MS); health (MBAH); health administration (MBA); healthcare administration (MHA); information systems, performance management, and big data analytics (MPA); international business (MBA); market research and customer insights (MS); marketing (MBA); nonprofit management (MBA, MPA); organizational behavior (MBA); product management (MS); state and local government (MPA); strategic management (MBA); supply chain management (MBA); taxation (MBA, MST). *Application deadline:* For fall admission, 3/15 priority date for domestic and international students; for spring admission, 10/15 for domestic students, 3/15 for international students. Applications are processed on a rolling basis. *Application fee:* $50. Electronic applications accepted. *Application Contact:* Mara Marzocchi, Associate Director of Graduate Admissions, 617-573-8302, Fax: 617-305-1733, E-mail: grad.admission@suffolk.edu. *Dean,* William J. O'Neill, JD, 617-573-2665, Fax: 617-573-8704, E-mail: woneill@suffolk.edu.

SULLIVAN UNIVERSITY, Louisville, KY 40205

General Information Proprietary, coed, comprehensive institution. *Graduate housing:* On-campus housing not available.

GRADUATE UNITS

College of Pharmacy Offers pharmacy (Pharm D).

School of Business *Program availability:* Part-time, online learning. Offers business (EMBA, MBA, MPM, MSCM, MSCS, MSHRL, MSM, MSMIT, PhD, Pharm D).

SUL ROSS STATE UNIVERSITY, Alpine, TX 79832

General Information State-supported, coed, comprehensive institution. *Graduate housing:* Rooms and/or apartments available on a first-come, first-served basis to single and married students. *Research affiliation:* Chihuahuan Desert Research Institute (biology, geology), Big Bend National Park (biology, geology).

GRADUATE UNITS

College of Arts and Sciences *Program availability:* Part-time, evening/weekend. Offers art history (MA); arts and sciences (MA); biology (MS); English (MA); geology (MS); history (MA); political science (MA); psychology (MA); studio art (MA).

College of Professional Studies *Program availability:* Part-time, evening/weekend. Offers business administration (EMBA, MBA); counseling (M Ed); criminal justice (MS); educational diagnostics (M Ed, Certificate); homeland security (MS); master reading teacher (Certificate); physical education (M Ed); reading specialist (M Ed, Certificate); school administration (M Ed); Texas reading specialist (M Ed). Two-year Executive MBA program in cooperation with La Universidad de Chihuahua, Mexico (UACH).

Division of Agricultural and Natural Resource Science *Program availability:* Part-time. Offers agricultural and natural resource science (M Ag, MS); animal science (M Ag, MS); range and wildlife management (M Ag, MS).

Rio Grande College of Sul Ross State University *Program availability:* Part-time, evening/weekend, online learning. Offers business administration (MBA); teacher education (M Ed).

SUM BIBLE COLLEGE & THEOLOGICAL SEMINARY, Oakland, CA 94603

General Information Independent-religious, coed, comprehensive institution.

GRADUATE UNITS

Graduate Programs Offers biblical studies (MA); Christian leadership (MA); theology (M Div).

SWEDISH INSTITUTE, COLLEGE OF HEALTH SCIENCES, New York, NY 10001-6700

General Information Proprietary, coed, comprehensive institution. *Graduate housing:* On-campus housing not available.

GRADUATE UNITS

Graduate Program *Program availability:* Part-time, evening/weekend.

SWEET BRIAR COLLEGE, Sweet Briar, VA 24595

General Information Independent, women only, comprehensive institution. *Graduate housing:* Room and/or apartments available on a first-come, first-served basis to single students; on-campus housing not available to married students.

GRADUATE UNITS

Department of Education *Program availability:* Part-time. Offers education (M Ed, MAT). Electronic applications accepted.

SYRACUSE UNIVERSITY, Syracuse, NY 13244

General Information Independent, coed, university. CGS member. *Enrollment:* 22,803 graduate, professional, and undergraduate students; 4,517 full-time matriculated graduate/professional students (2,293 women), 2,891 part-time matriculated graduate/professional students (1,289 women). *Enrollment by degree level:* 5,432 master's, 1,851 doctoral, 125 other advanced degrees. *Graduate faculty:* 1,148 full-time (497 women), 611 part-time/adjunct (273 women). *Graduate housing:* On-campus housing not available. *Student services:* Campus employment opportunities, campus safety program, career counseling, child daycare facilities, exercise/wellness program, free psychological counseling, grant writing training, international student services, low-cost health insurance, multicultural affairs office, services for students with disabilities, teacher training, writing training. *Library facilities:* E. S. Bird Library plus 4 others. *Collection:* Books: 2.6 million (physical), 545,994 (digital/electronic); Serial titles: 33,881 (physical), 125,294 (digital/electronic); Databases: 586. Weekly public service hours: 146; study areas open 24 hours, 5–7 days a week; students can reserve study rooms.

Computer facilities: Computer purchase and lease plans are available. 3,500 computers available on campus for general student use. A campuswide network can be accessed from student residence rooms and from off campus. Online class registration, Library; web conferencing; learning management system (Blackboard); blogging service; personal websites; "View My Advising Report," digital asset management system (Collage);Microsoft Office 365;Lynda.com online video training are available. Website: http://www.syracuse.edu/

GRADUATE UNITS

College of Arts and Sciences Students: 751 full-time (452 women), 40 part-time (20 women); includes 152 minority (37 Black or African American, non-Hispanic/Latino; 3 American Indian or Alaska Native, non-Hispanic/Latino; 31 Asian, non-Hispanic/Latino; 59 Hispanic/Latino; 1 Native Hawaiian or other Pacific Islander, non-Hispanic/Latino; 21 Two or more races, non-Hispanic/Latino), 200 international. Average age 27. 2,374 applicants, 25% accepted, 266 enrolled. *Faculty:* 370 full-time (162 women), 135 part-time/adjunct (79 women). Expenses: Contact institution. *Financial support:* Fellowships with full tuition reimbursements, research assistantships with tuition reimbursements, teaching assistantships with tuition reimbursements, career-related internships or fieldwork, Federal Work-Study, scholarships/grants, health care benefits, tuition waivers, and unspecified assistantships available. Support available to part-time students. Financial award application deadline: 1/1. In 2018, 192 master's, 58 doctorates, 49 other advanced degrees awarded. *Program availability:* Part-time. Offers advanced forensic science (MS); applied statistics (MS); art history (MA); arts and sciences (MA, MFA, MS, Au D, PhD, CAS); audiology (Au D, PhD); biology (MS, PhD); biomedical forensic science (MS); chemistry (MS, PhD); clinical psychology (PhD); cognition, brain, and behavior (PhD); college science teaching (PhD); composition and cultural rhetoric (PhD); computational linguistics (MS); creative writing (MFA); earth sciences (MS, PhD); English (MA, PhD); firearm and tool mark examination (CAS); French and Francophone studies (MA); general forensic science (MS); language teaching: TESOL/TLOTE (CAS); linguistic studies (MA); math education (PhD); mathematics (MS, PhD); mathematics education (MS); medicolegal death investigation (MS, CAS); neuroscience (PhD); nuclear forensics (MS); Pan-African studies (MA); philosophy (MA, PhD); physics (MS, PhD); religion (MA, PhD); school psychology (PhD); social psychology (PhD); Spanish literature and culture (MA); speech-language pathology (MS). *Application fee:* $75. *Application Contact:* Christopher N. Anderson, Director of Undergraduate and Graduate Recruiting, 315-443-4322, E-mail: asadmissions@syr.edu. *Dean,* Dr. Karin Ruhlandt, 315-443-1306, E-mail: kruhland@syr.edu.

College of Engineering and Computer Science Students: 927 full-time (242 women), 362 part-time (63 women); includes 126 minority (37 Black or African American, non-Hispanic/Latino; 62 Asian, non-Hispanic/Latino; 15 Hispanic/Latino; 12 Two or more races, non-Hispanic/Latino), 914 international. Average age 27. 2,999 applicants, 40% accepted, 450 enrolled. *Faculty:* 88 full-time (24 women), 21 part-time/adjunct (2 women). Expenses: Contact institution. *Financial support:* Fellowships with full tuition reimbursements, research assistantships with tuition reimbursements, teaching assistantships with tuition reimbursements, scholarships/grants, and tuition waivers (partial) available. Financial award application deadline: 1/1; financial award applicants required to submit FAFSA. In 2018, 365 master's, 35 doctorates, 2 other advanced degrees awarded. *Program availability:* Part-time, evening/weekend. Offers bioengineering (MS, PhD); chemical engineering (MS, PhD); civil engineering (MS, PhD); computer and information science and engineering (PhD); computer engineering (MS); computer science (MS); cybersecurity (MS, CAS); electrical and computer engineering (PhD); electrical engineering (MS); engineering and computer science (MS, PhD, CAS); engineering management (MS); environmental engineering (MS); environmental engineering science (MS); environmental health (CAS); mechanical and aerospace engineering (MS, PhD); sustainable enterprise (CAS). *Application deadline:* For fall admission, 7/1 priority date for domestic students, 6/1 priority date for international students; for spring admission, 11/15 priority date for domestic students, 10/15 priority date for international students. Applications are processed on a rolling basis. *Application fee:* $75. Electronic applications accepted. *Application Contact:* Kathleen Joyce, Assistant Dean, 314-443-2219, E-mail: topgrads@syr.edu. *Dean, College of Engineering and Computer Science,* Dr. Teresa Dahlberg, 315-443-2545, E-mail: dahlberg@syr.edu.

College of Law Students: 580 full-time (316 women), 8 part-time (5 women); includes 136 minority (43 Black or African American, non-Hispanic/Latino; 30 Asian, non-Hispanic/Latino; 52 Hispanic/Latino; 1 Native Hawaiian or other Pacific Islander, non-Hispanic/Latino; 10 Two or more races, non-Hispanic/Latino), 57 international. Average age 26. 1,822 applicants, 52% accepted, 297 enrolled. *Faculty:* 45 full-time (19 women), 17 part-time/adjunct (5 women). Expenses: Contact institution. *Financial support:* In 2018–19, 487 students received support. Fellowships, research assistantships, career-related internships or fieldwork, Federal Work-Study, institutionally sponsored loans, scholarships/grants, and tuition waivers (partial) available. Support available to part-time students. Financial award application deadline: 2/15. In 2018, 31 master's, 175 doctorates awarded. *Program availability:* Part-time. Offers American law (LL M); law (LL M, JD). *Application deadline:* For fall admission, 4/1 priority date for domestic and international students. Applications are processed on a rolling basis. *Application fee:* $70. Electronic applications accepted. *Application Contact:* Steve Budgar, Director of Admissions, 315-443-1962, Fax: 315-443-9568, E-mail: admissions@law.syr.edu. *Dean and Professor of Law,* Craig M. Boise, 315-443-9580, E-mail: cmboise@law.syr.edu.

College of Visual and Performing Arts Students: 199 full-time (117 women), 12 part-time (4 women); includes 26 minority (7 Black or African American, non-Hispanic/Latino; 3 Asian, non-Hispanic/Latino; 7 Hispanic/Latino; 9 Two or more races, non-Hispanic/Latino), 84 international. Average age 27. 517 applicants, 42% accepted, 98 enrolled. *Faculty:* 133 full-time (63 women), 113 part-time/adjunct (51 women). Expenses: Contact institution. *Financial support:* Fellowships with full tuition reimbursements, teaching assistantships, institutionally sponsored loans, and unspecified assistantships available. Financial award application deadline: 1/1; financial award applicants required to submit FAFSA. In 2018, 83 master's awarded. Offers art photography (MFA); art video (MFA); audio arts (MA); communication and rhetorical studies (MA); composition (MM); computer art (MFA); conducting (MM); film (MFA); illustration (MFA); museum studies (MA); music and performance (MM); studio arts (MFA); visual and performing arts (M Mus, M Mus, MA, MFA, MM, MS); voice pedagogy (MM). *Application deadline:* For fall admission, 2/1 priority date for domestic and international students; for spring admission, 3/1 priority date for domestic and international students; for summer admission, 2/1 priority date for domestic and international students. *Application fee:* $75. Electronic applications accepted. *Application Contact:* Caitlin Jarvis, Graduate Recruitment Specialist, 315-443-2769, E-mail: admissg@syr.edu. *Dean, College of Visual and Performing Arts,* Dr. Michael S. Tick, 315-443-8070, E-mail: mtick1@syr.edu.

David B. Falk College of Sport and Human Dynamics Students: 200 full-time (172 women), 102 part-time (86 women); includes 66 minority (30 Black or African American, non-Hispanic/Latino; 2 American Indian or Alaska Native, non-Hispanic/Latino; 7 Asian, non-Hispanic/Latino; 20 Hispanic/Latino; 7 Two or more races, non-Hispanic/Latino), 25 international. Average age 29. 366 applicants, 76% accepted, 139 enrolled. *Faculty:* 74 full-time (43 women), 22 part-time/adjunct (13 women). Expenses: Contact institution. *Financial support:* Fellowships with full tuition reimbursements, research assistantships, teaching assistantships, and tuition waivers available. Financial award application deadline: 1/1; financial award applicants required to submit FAFSA. In 2018, 124 master's, 5 doctorates, 38 other advanced degrees awarded. *Program availability:* Part-time, evening/weekend. Offers addiction studies (MA, CAS); food studies (MS, CAS); global health (MS); human development and family science (MA, MS, PhD); marriage and family therapy (MA, PhD); nutrition science (MA, MS, PhD); social work (MSW); sport and human dynamics (MA, MS, MSW, PhD, CAS); sport venue and event management (MS); trauma-informed practice (CAS). *Application deadline:* For fall admission, 2/15 priority date for domestic and international students; for spring admission, 11/15 priority date for domestic students, 11/15 for international students; for summer admission, 3/15 priority date for domestic students, 3/15 for international students. Applications are processed on a rolling basis. *Application fee:* $75. Electronic applications accepted. *Application Contact:* Felicia Otero, Director of College Admissions, 315-443-5555, Fax: 315-443-2562, E-mail: falk@syr.edu. *Dean,* Dr. Diane Lyden Murphy, 315-443-5582, Fax: 315-443-2562.

Martin J. Whitman School of Management Students: 336 full-time (159 women), 1,113 part-time (360 women); includes 461 minority (171 Black or African American, non-Hispanic/Latino; 3 American Indian or Alaska Native, non-Hispanic/Latino; 102 Asian, non-Hispanic/Latino; 136 Hispanic/Latino; 6 Native Hawaiian or other Pacific Islander, non-Hispanic/Latino; 43 Two or more races, non-Hispanic/Latino), 220 international. Average age 33. 1,327 applicants, 66% accepted, 326 enrolled. *Faculty:* 73 full-time (28 women), 66 part-time/adjunct (15 women). Expenses: Contact institution. *Financial support:* In 2018–19, 45 students received support. Fellowships with full tuition reimbursements available, research assistantships, teaching assistantships, career-related internships or fieldwork, and scholarships/grants available. Financial award application deadline: 2/15. In 2018, 475 master's, 4 doctorates awarded. *Program availability:* Part-time, 100% online. Offers accounting (MBA); business analytics (MS); entrepreneurship (MBA); finance (PhD); management (MBA, MS, PhD); management information systems (PhD); marketing management (MBA); professional accounting (MS); real estate (MBA); supply chain management (MS). *Application deadline:* For fall admission, 11/30 for domestic and international students; for winter admission, 1/1 for domestic and international students; for spring admission, 2/15 for domestic and international students; for summer admission, 4/19 for domestic students. *Application fee:* $75. Electronic applications accepted. *Application Contact:* Shri Ramakrishnan, Assistant Director, Graduate Recruitment, 315-443-3497, Fax: 315-443-9517, E-mail: sramak01@syr.edu. *Dean,* Eugene Anderson, 315-443-9494, Fax: 315-443-9517, E-mail: genea@syr.edu.

Maxwell School of Citizenship and Public Affairs Students: 470 full-time (250 women), 156 part-time (73 women); includes 98 minority (33 Black or African American, non-Hispanic/Latino; 1 American Indian or Alaska Native, non-Hispanic/Latino; 25 Asian, non-Hispanic/Latino; 29 Hispanic/Latino; 1 Native Hawaiian or other Pacific Islander, non-Hispanic/Latino; 9 Two or more races, non-Hispanic/Latino), 184 international. Average age 32. 1,213 applicants, 46% accepted, 245 enrolled. *Faculty:* 155 full-time (60 women), 34 part-time/adjunct (9 women). Expenses: Contact institution. *Financial support:* Fellowships with full tuition reimbursements, research assistantships, and teaching assistantships available. Financial award application deadline: 1/1. In 2018, 265 master's, 35 doctorates, 131 other advanced degrees awarded. *Program availability:* Part-time, online learning. Offers anthropology (MA, PhD); citizenship and public affairs (EMIR, EMPA, MA, MPA, MPH, MS Sc, PhD, CAS); conflict resolution (CAS); economics (MA, PhD); geography (MA, PhD); health services management and policy (CAS); history (MA, PhD); international relations (EMIR, MA); leadership of international and non-governmental organizations (CAS); political science (MA, PhD); public administration (EMPA, MPA, PhD); public diplomacypublic infrastructure management and leadership (CAS); social sciences (MA, PhD); sociology (MA, PhD). *Application deadline:* For fall admission, 2/1 priority date for domestic and international students. Applications are processed on a rolling basis. *Application fee:* $75. Electronic applications accepted. *Application Contact:* Megan Begert, Enrollment Manager, 315-443-4000, E-mail: msbegert@syr.edu. *Dean,* Dr. David Van Slyke, 315-443-3461, E-mail: vanslyke@maxwell.syr.edu.

School of Architecture Students: 109 full-time (56 women), 1 part-time (0 women); includes 6 minority (1 Black or African American, non-Hispanic/Latino; 1 Asian, non-Hispanic/Latino; 4 Hispanic/Latino), 83 international. Average age 26. 273 applicants, 59% accepted, 35 enrolled. *Faculty:* 40 full-time (14 women), 14 part-time/adjunct (5 women). Expenses: Contact institution. *Financial support:* Fellowships with full tuition reimbursements, research assistantships, and teaching assistantships available. Financial award application deadline: 1/1. In 2018, 40 master's awarded. Offers architecture (M Arch, MS). *Application deadline:* For fall admission, 2/1 priority date for domestic and international students. *Application fee:* $75. Electronic applications accepted. *Application Contact:* Vittoria Buccina, Director, Graduate and Undergraduate Recruitment, 315-443-5074, E-mail: vabuccin@syr.edu. *Dean, School of Architecture,* Michael Speaks, 315-443-0790, E-mail: maspeaks@syr.edu.

School of Education Students: 246 full-time (173 women), 216 part-time (152 women); includes 103 minority (47 Black or African American, non-Hispanic/Latino; 4 American Indian or Alaska Native, non-Hispanic/Latino; 4 Asian, non-Hispanic/Latino; 32 Hispanic/Latino; 16 Two or more races, non-Hispanic/Latino), 77 international. Average age 34. 480 applicants, 55% accepted, 114 enrolled. *Faculty:* 54 full-time (32 women), 51 part-time/adjunct (33 women). Expenses: Contact institution. *Financial support:* Fellowships with full tuition reimbursements, research assistantships, teaching assistantships, career-related internships or fieldwork, institutionally sponsored loans, scholarships/grants, health care benefits, tuition waivers (partial), and unspecified assistantships available. Financial award application deadline: 1/15; financial award applicants required to submit FAFSA. In 2018, 148 master's, 17 doctorates, 32 other advanced degrees awarded. *Program availability:* Part-time. Offers art education (MS); biology (MS); chemistry (MS, PhD); clinical mental health counseling (MS); counseling and counselor education (PhD); cultural foundations of education (MS, PhD, CAS); disability studies (CAS); early childhood special education (MS); education (M Mus, MM, MS, Ed D, PhD, CAS); educational leadership (MS, Ed D, CAS); educational technology (CAS); English education preparation (grades 7-12) (MS); exercise science (MS); higher education (MS, PhD); inclusive special education (grades 1-6) (MS); inclusive special education (grades 7-12) (MS); inclusive special education: severe/multiple disabilities (MS); instructional design foundations (CAS); instructional design, development, and evaluation (MS, PhD, CAS); instructional technology (MS); literacy education (PhD); literacy education (birth - grade 12) (MS); mathematics education (MS, PhD); music education (MM, MS); school counseling (MS, CAS); school district business leadership (CAS); social studies education preparation (grades 7-12) (MS); special education (PhD); student affairs counseling (MS); teaching and curriculum (MS, PhD); teaching English language learners (Pre-K-12) (MS). *Application deadline:* Applications are processed on a rolling basis. *Application fee:* $75. Electronic applications accepted. *Application Contact:* Speranza Migliore, Graduate Recruiter, School of Education, 315-443-2505, E-mail: gradrcrt@syr.edu. *Dean,* Dr. Joanna Masingila, 315-443-4751, E-mail: jomasing@syr.edu.

School of Information Studies Students: 475 full-time (209 women), 641 part-time (334 women); includes 248 minority (80 Black or African American, non-Hispanic/Latino; 4 American Indian or Alaska Native, non-Hispanic/Latino; 72 Asian, non-Hispanic/Latino; 60 Hispanic/Latino; 2 Native Hawaiian or other Pacific Islander, non-Hispanic/Latino; 30 Two or more races, non-Hispanic/Latino), 376 international. Average age 31. 1,580 applicants, 50% accepted, 395 enrolled. *Faculty:* 34 full-time (16 women), 65 part-time/adjunct (29 women). Expenses: Contact institution. *Financial support:* Fellowships with full tuition reimbursements, research assistantships, teaching assistantships, and scholarships/grants available. Financial award application deadline: 1/1. In 2018, 256 master's, 6 doctorates, 237 other advanced degrees awarded. *Program availability:* Part-time, evening/weekend, online learning. Offers applied data science (MS); data science (CAS); e-government management and leadership (CAS); enterprise data systems (CAS); information management (MS); information science and technology (PhD); information security management (CAS); information studies (MS, PhD, CAS); library and information science (MS); library and information science: school media (MS); school media (CAS). *Application deadline:* For fall admission, 1/1 priority date for domestic students, 2/1 priority date for international students; for spring admission, 10/15 priority date for domestic and international students. Applications are processed on a rolling basis. *Application fee:* $75. Electronic applications accepted. *Application Contact:* Susan Corieri, Director of Enrollment Management, 315-443-2575, E-mail: ist@syr.edu. *Dean/Professor,* Dr. Elizabeth D. Liddy, 315-443-2736, E-mail: liddy@syr.edu.

S. I. Newhouse School of Public Communications Students: 224 full-time (147 women), 240 part-time (192 women); includes 179 minority (93 Black or African American, non-Hispanic/Latino; 4 American Indian or Alaska Native, non-Hispanic/Latino; 15 Asian, non-Hispanic/Latino; 45 Hispanic/Latino; 2 Native Hawaiian or other Pacific Islander, non-Hispanic/Latino; 20 Two or more races, non-Hispanic/Latino), 81 international. Average age 28. 802 applicants, 65% accepted, 245 enrolled. *Faculty:* 80 full-time (36 women), 64 part-time/adjunct (27 women). Expenses: Contact institution. *Financial support:* Fellowships with full tuition reimbursements, research assistantships with partial tuition reimbursements, scholarships/grants, and instructional associate positions with partial tuition reimbursements available. Financial award application deadline: 2/1. In 2018, 321 master's, 2 doctorates awarded. *Program availability:* Online learning. Offers advertising (MS); arts journalism (MA); broadcast and digital journalism (MS); communications management (MS); magazine, newspaper and online journalism (MA); mass communications (PhD); media studies (MA); new media management (MS); photography (MS); public communications (MA, MS, PhD); public diplomacypublic relations (MS); television, radio, and film (MA). *Application deadline:* For fall admission, 1/15 priority date for domestic and international students; for summer admission, 1/15 priority date for domestic and international students.

Application fee: $45. Electronic applications accepted. *Application Contact:* Martha Coria, Graduate Records Office, 315-443-4039, Fax: 315-443-1834, E-mail: pcgrad@syr.edu. *Dean,* Lorraine Branham, 315-443-3372, E-mail: lbranham@syr.edu.

TABOR COLLEGE, Hillsboro, KS 67063

General Information Independent-religious, coed, comprehensive institution.

GRADUATE UNITS

Graduate Program Offers accounting (MBA). Program offered at the Wichita campus only.

TAFT UNIVERSITY SYSTEM, Denver, CO 80246

General Information Proprietary, coed, graduate-only institution.

GRADUATE UNITS

The Boyer Graduate School of Education Offers education (M Ed).

Taft Law School Offers American jurisprudence (LL M); law (JD); taxation (LL M).

W. Edwards Deming School of Business Offers taxation (MS).

TALMUDICAL ACADEMY OF NEW JERSEY, Adelphia, NJ 07710

General Information Independent-religious, men only, comprehensive institution.

GRADUATE UNITS

Graduate Program

TALMUDIC UNIVERSITY, Miami Beach, FL 33140

General Information Independent-religious, men only, comprehensive institution. *Graduate housing:* Rooms and/or apartments available on a first-come, first-served basis to single and married students.

GRADUATE UNITS

Program in Talmudic Law Offers Talmudic law (MRE).

TARLETON STATE UNIVERSITY, Stephenville, TX 76402

General Information State-supported, coed, comprehensive institution. *Enrollment:* 400 full-time matriculated graduate/professional students (260 women), 1,331 part-time matriculated graduate/professional students (837 women). *Enrollment by degree level:* 1,608 master's, 123 doctoral. *Graduate faculty:* 162 full-time (77 women), 53 part-time/adjunct (27 women). *International tuition:* $11,750 full-time. Tuition, state resident: full-time $4200; part-time $652 per credit hour. Tuition, nonresident: full-time $11,750; part-time $652 per credit hour. *Required fees:* $1540. Tuition and fees vary according to degree level and program. *Graduate housing:* Rooms and/or apartments available on a first-come, first-served basis to single and married students. Typical cost: $6750 per year ($10,700 including board) for single students. Room and board charges vary according to board plan and housing facility selected. Housing application deadline: 8/1. *Student services:* Campus employment opportunities, campus safety program, career counseling, child daycare facilities, exercise/wellness program, free psychological counseling, grant writing training, international student services, low-cost health insurance, multicultural affairs office, services for students with disabilities, teacher training, writing training. *Library facilities:* Dick Smith Library plus 1 other. *Collection:* Students can reserve study rooms.

Computer facilities: 1,200 computers available on campus for general student use. A campuswide network can be accessed from student residence rooms and from off campus. Online class registration is available. Website: http://www.tarleton.edu/

General Application Contact: Wendy Weiss, Graduate Admissions Coordinator, 254-968-9104, Fax: 254-968-9670, E-mail: weiss@tarleton.edu.

GRADUATE UNITS

College of Graduate Studies Students: 422 full-time (292 women), 1,377 part-time (891 women); includes 514 minority (202 Black or African American, non-Hispanic/Latino; 7 American Indian or Alaska Native, non-Hispanic/Latino; 26 Asian, non-Hispanic/Latino; 229 Hispanic/Latino; 50 Two or more races, non-Hispanic/Latino), 33 international. Average age 36. 922 applicants, 68% accepted, 478 enrolled. *Faculty:* 145 full-time (72 women), 52 part-time/adjunct (25 women). Expenses: Contact institution. *Financial support:* Research assistantships, teaching assistantships, career-related internships or fieldwork, Federal Work-Study, institutionally sponsored loans, scholarships/grants, and tuition waivers (partial) available. Support available to part-time students. Financial award application deadline: 5/1; financial award applicants required to submit FAFSA. In 2018, 471 master's, 14 doctorates awarded. *Program availability:* Part-time, evening/weekend, 100% online, blended/hybrid learning. *Application deadline:* For fall admission, 8/15 priority date for domestic students; for spring admission, 1/7 for domestic students. *Application fee:* $50 ($130 for international students). Electronic applications accepted. *Application Contact:* Wendy Weiss, Graduate Admissions Coordinator, 254-968-9104, Fax: 254-968-9670, E-mail: weiss@tarleton.edu. *Dean,* Dr. Barry Lambert, 254-968-9463, Fax: 254-968-9670, E-mail: blambert@tarleton.edu.

College of Agricultural and Environmental Sciences Students: 69 full-time (44 women), 37 part-time (23 women); includes 20 minority (5 Black or African American, non-Hispanic/Latino; 1 American Indian or Alaska Native, non-Hispanic/Latino; 1 Asian, non-Hispanic/Latino; 9 Hispanic/Latino; 4 Two or more races, non-Hispanic/Latino), 2 international. Average age 25. 55 applicants, 91% accepted, 40 enrolled. *Faculty:* 18 full-time (6 women), 8 part-time/adjunct (3 women). Expenses: Contact institution. *Financial support:* Research assistantships, teaching assistantships, career-related internships or fieldwork, Federal Work-Study, and institutionally sponsored loans available. Support available to part-time students. Financial award application deadline: 5/1; financial award applicants required to submit FAFSA. In 2018, 35 master's awarded. *Program availability:* Part-time, evening/weekend, 100% online, blended/hybrid learning. Offers agricultural and consumer resources (MS); agricultural and environmental sciences (MS); agricultural and natural resource sciences (MS). *Application deadline:* For fall admission, 8/15 priority date for domestic students; for spring admission, 1/7 for domestic students. Applications are processed on a rolling basis. *Application fee:* $50 ($130 for international students). Electronic applications accepted. *Application Contact:* Wendy Weiss, Information Contact, 254-968-9104, Fax: 254-968-9670, E-mail: gradoffice@tarleton.edu. *Dean,* Dr. Steve Damron, 254-968-9227, Fax: 254-968-9655, E-mail: sdamron@tarleton.edu.

College of Business Administration Students: 66 full-time (43 women), 471 part-time (282 women); includes 141 minority (45 Black or African American, non-Hispanic/Latino; 2 American Indian or Alaska Native, non-Hispanic/Latino; 13 Asian, non-Hispanic/Latino; 63 Hispanic/Latino; 18 Two or more races, non-Hispanic/Latino), 14 international. Average age 33. 250 applicants, 87% accepted, 176 enrolled. *Faculty:* 30 full-time (5 women), 6 part-time/adjunct (2 women). Expenses: Contact institution. *Financial support:* Research assistantships, teaching assistantships,

career-related internships or fieldwork, Federal Work-Study, and institutionally sponsored loans available. Support available to part-time students. Financial award application deadline: 5/1; financial award applicants required to submit FAFSA. In 2018, 167 master's awarded. *Program availability:* Part-time, evening/weekend, 100% online, blended/hybrid learning. Offers accounting (M Acc); business administration (M Acc, MBA, MS); human resources management (MS); information systems (MS). *Application deadline:* For fall admission, 8/15 priority date for domestic students; for spring admission, 1/7 for domestic students. Applications are processed on a rolling basis. *Application fee:* $50 ($130 for international students). Electronic applications accepted. *Application Contact:* Jodie Dearing, Graduate Program Manager, 254-968-9055, E-mail: jdearing@tarleton.edu. *Dean,* Dr. Chris Shao, 254-968-9350, E-mail: shao@tarleton.edu.

College of Education Students: 74 full-time (54 women), 372 part-time (288 women); includes 134 minority (64 Black or African American, non-Hispanic/Latino; 3 American Indian or Alaska Native, non-Hispanic/Latino; 1 Asian, non-Hispanic/Latino; 57 Hispanic/Latino; 9 Two or more races, non-Hispanic/Latino), 3 international. Average age 38. 168 applicants, 84% accepted, 114 enrolled. *Faculty:* 32 full-time (19 women), 12 part-time/adjunct (8 women). Expenses: Contact institution. *Financial support:* Research assistantships, teaching assistantships with partial tuition reimbursements, career-related internships or fieldwork, Federal Work-Study, institutionally sponsored loans, and tuition waivers (partial) available. Support available to part-time students. Financial award application deadline: 5/1; financial award applicants required to submit FAFSA. In 2018, 172 master's, 28 doctorates awarded. *Program availability:* Part-time, evening/weekend, 100% online, blended/hybrid learning. Offers applied psychology (MS); athletic training (MS); curriculum and instruction (MS); education (M Ed, MS, Ed D, Certificate); educational administration (M Ed); educational diagnostician (M Ed); educational leadership (Ed D, Certificate); elementary education (M Ed); instructional design and technology (M Ed); instructional leadership (M Ed); kinesiology (MS); secondary education (M Ed); special education (M Ed); technology applications (M Ed); technology director (M Ed). *Application deadline:* For fall admission, 8/15 priority date for domestic students; for spring admission, 1/7 for domestic students. Applications are processed on a rolling basis. *Application fee:* $50 ($130 for international students). Electronic applications accepted. *Application Contact:* Wendy Weiss, Information Contact, 254-968-9104, Fax: 254-968-9670, E-mail: weiss@tarleton.edu. *Dean,* Dr. Jordan Barkley, 254-968-9088, Fax: 254-968-9525, E-mail: jbarkley@tarleton.edu.

College of Health Sciences and Human Services Students: 92 full-time (83 women), 163 part-time (134 women); includes 89 minority (38 Black or African American, non-Hispanic/Latino; 1 American Indian or Alaska Native, non-Hispanic/Latino; 1 Asian, non-Hispanic/Latino; 46 Hispanic/Latino; 3 Two or more races, non-Hispanic/Latino), 6 international. Average age 32. 218 applicants, 87% accepted, 128 enrolled. *Faculty:* 20 full-time (18 women), 7 part-time/adjunct (6 women). Expenses: Contact institution. *Financial support:* Research assistantships, teaching assistantships, career-related internships or fieldwork, Federal Work-Study, scholarships/grants, and unspecified assistantships available. Financial award application deadline: 2/15; financial award applicants required to submit FAFSA. In 2018, 21 master's awarded. *Program availability:* Part-time. Offers health sciences and human services (MS, MSN, MSW, Certificate); medical laboratory sciences (MS); nursing administration (MSN); nursing education (MSN); social work (MSW). *Application deadline:* For fall admission, 8/15 for domestic students, 6/15 for international students; for spring admission, 1/5 for domestic students, 11/15 for international students; for summer admission, 5/1 for domestic students, 4/15 for international students. Applications are processed on a rolling basis. *Application fee:* $50 ($130 for international students). Electronic applications accepted. *Application Contact:* Wendy Weiss, Graduate Admissions Coordinator, 254-968-9104, Fax: 254-968-9670, E-mail: weiss@tarleton.edu. *Associate Dean,* Sally Lewis, 254-968-1692.

College of Liberal and Fine Arts Students: 30 full-time (15 women), 261 part-time (137 women); includes 106 minority (45 Black or African American, non-Hispanic/Latino; 7 Asian, non-Hispanic/Latino; 43 Hispanic/Latino; 11 Two or more races, non-Hispanic/Latino), 3 international. Average age 35. 112 applicants, 86% accepted, 81 enrolled. *Faculty:* 24 full-time (13 women), 12 part-time/adjunct (5 women). Expenses: Contact institution. *Financial support:* Research assistantships, teaching assistantships, Federal Work-Study, scholarships/grants, and unspecified assistantships available. Financial award application deadline: 5/1; financial award applicants required to submit FAFSA. In 2018, 67 master's awarded. *Program availability:* Part-time, evening/weekend, 100% online, blended/hybrid learning. Offers communication studies (MA); criminal justice (MCJ); English (MA); history (MA); liberal and fine arts (MA, MCJ, MM, MPA); music education (MM). *Application deadline:* For fall admission, 8/15 priority date for domestic students; for spring admission, 1/7 for domestic students. Applications are processed on a rolling basis. *Application fee:* $50 ($130 for international students). Electronic applications accepted. *Application Contact:* Wendy Weiss, Information Contact, 254-968-9104, Fax: 254-968-9670, E-mail: weiss@tarleton.edu. *Interim Dean,* Dr. Eric Morrow, 254-968-9141, Fax: 254-968-9784, E-mail: morrow@tarleton.edu.

College of Science and Technology Students: 22 full-time (7 women), 65 part-time (20 women); includes 23 minority (4 Black or African American, non-Hispanic/Latino; 3 Asian, non-Hispanic/Latino; 11 Hispanic/Latino; 5 Two or more races, non-Hispanic/Latino), 5 international. Average age 32. 38 applicants, 89% accepted, 26 enrolled. *Faculty:* 16 full-time (8 women), 5 part-time/adjunct (1 woman). Expenses: Contact institution. *Financial support:* Research assistantships, teaching assistantships, career-related internships or fieldwork, Federal Work-Study, and tuition waivers (partial) available. Support available to part-time students. Financial award application deadline: 5/1; financial award applicants required to submit FAFSA. In 2018, 38 master's awarded. *Program availability:* Part-time, evening/weekend, 100% online, blended/hybrid learning. Offers biology (MS); environmental science (MS); mathematics (MS); quality and engineering management (MS); science and technology (MS). *Application deadline:* For fall admission, 8/15 priority date for domestic students; for spring admission, 1/7 for domestic students. Applications are processed on a rolling basis. *Application fee:* $50 ($130 for international students). Electronic applications accepted. *Application Contact:* Wendy Weiss, Information Contact, 254-968-9104, Fax: 254-968-9670, E-mail: weiss@tarleton.edu. *Dean,* Dr. James Pierce, 254-968-9781, Fax: 254-968-0549, E-mail: jrpierce@tarleton.edu.

TAYLOR COLLEGE AND SEMINARY, Edmonton, AB T6J 4T3, Canada

General Information Independent-religious, coed, comprehensive institution. *Graduate housing:* Room and/or apartments available on a first-come, first-served basis to single students; on-campus housing not available to married students. Housing application deadline: 8/1.

GRADUATE UNITS

Graduate and Professional Programs *Program availability:* Part-time, online learning. Offers Christian studies (Diploma); intercultural studies (MA, Diploma); theology (M Div, MTS).

TAYLOR UNIVERSITY, Upland, IN 46989-1001

General Information Independent-religious, coed, comprehensive institution. *Graduate housing:* On-campus housing not available.

GRADUATE UNITS

Master of Arts in Higher Education Program *Program availability:* Part-time. Offers higher education (MA).

TEACHERS COLLEGE, COLUMBIA UNIVERSITY, New York, NY 10027-6696

General Information Independent, coed, graduate-only institution. *Enrollment by degree level:* 3,307 master's, 1,290 doctoral, 37 other advanced degrees. *Graduate faculty:* 237 full-time. *Graduate housing:* Rooms and/or apartments available on a first-come, first-served basis to single and married students. Housing application deadline: 12/1. *Student services:* Campus employment opportunities, campus safety program, career counseling, exercise/wellness program, free psychological counseling, grant writing training, international student services, low-cost health insurance, multicultural affairs office, services for students with disabilities, teacher training, writing training. *Library facilities:* The Gottesman Libraries. *Collection:* Students can reserve study rooms.

Computer facilities: Online class registration is available. Website: http://www.tc.columbia.edu/

General Application Contact: Kelly Sutton-Skinner, Director of Admissions & New Student Enrollment, E-mail: kms2237@tc.columbia.edu.

GRADUATE UNITS

Department of Arts and Humanities Students: 267 full-time (216 women), 569 part-time (400 women); includes 235 minority (62 Black or African American, non-Hispanic/Latino; 2 American Indian or Alaska Native, non-Hispanic/Latino; 88 Asian, non-Hispanic/Latino; 69 Hispanic/Latino; 14 Two or more races, non-Hispanic/Latino), 229 international. Average age 31. 1,075 applicants, 56% accepted, 342 enrolled. Expenses: Contact institution. *Financial support:* Fellowships, research assistantships, teaching assistantships, career-related internships or fieldwork, Federal Work-Study, institutionally sponsored loans, tuition waivers (full and partial), and unspecified assistantships available. Support available to part-time students. *Program availability:* Part-time, evening/weekend. Offers applied linguistics (MA, Ed D); art and art education (Ed M, MA, Ed D, Ed DCT); arts administration (MA); bilingual and bicultural education (MA); global competence (Certificate); history and education (Ed D, PhD); music and music education (Ed DCT); philosophy and education (MA, Ed D, PhD); social studies education (Ed M, PhD); teaching English to speakers of other languages (Ed M); teaching of English and English education (Ed M, MA, Ed D, PhD); teaching of social studies (MA); TESOL (MA, Ed D). *Application Contact:* Kelly Sutton-Skinner, Director of Admissions & New Student Enrollment, E-mail: kms2237@tc.columbia.edu. *Department Chair,* Prof. ZhaoHong Han, E-mail: zhh2@tc.columbia.edu.

Department of Biobehavioral Sciences Students: 126 full-time (111 women), 203 part-time (162 women); includes 137 minority (24 Black or African American, non-Hispanic/Latino; 42 Asian, non-Hispanic/Latino; 62 Hispanic/Latino; 9 Two or more races, non-Hispanic/Latino), 36 international. Average age 28. 643 applicants, 51% accepted, 150 enrolled. Expenses: Contact institution. *Program availability:* Part-time, evening/weekend. Offers applied exercise physiology (Ed M, MA, Ed D); communication sciences and disorders (MS, Ed D, PhD); kinesiology (PhD); motor learning and control (Ed M, MA); motor learning/movement science (Ed D); neuroscience and education (MS); physical education (MA, Ed D). *Application Contact:* Kelly Sutton-Skinner, Director of Admission & New Student Enrollment, 212-678-3305, E-mail: kms2237@tc.columbia.edu. *Chair,* Prof. Carol Garber, 212-678-3891, E-mail: garber@tc.columbia.edu.

Department of Counseling and Clinical Psychology Students: 298 full-time (260 women), 376 part-time (314 women); includes 235 minority (52 Black or African American, non-Hispanic/Latino; 75 Asian, non-Hispanic/Latino; 89 Hispanic/Latino; 19 Two or more races, non-Hispanic/Latino), 140 international. Average age 28. 1,586 applicants, 37% accepted, 295 enrolled. Expenses: Contact institution. *Program availability:* Part-time. Offers clinical psychology (PhD); counseling psychology (Ed M, Ed D, PhD); mental health counseling (ME); psychological counseling (ME, ND); psychology in education (MA, ND); school counselor (ME). *Application Contact:* Kelly Sutton-Skinner, Director of Admission & New Student Enrollment, E-mail: kms2237@tc.columbia.edu. *Chair,* Prof. George Bonanno, 212-678-3468, E-mail: gab38@tc.columbia.edu.

Department of Curriculum and Teaching Students: 88 full-time (77 women), 264 part-time (239 women); includes 129 minority (45 Black or African American, non-Hispanic/Latino; 1 American Indian or Alaska Native, non-Hispanic/Latino; 41 Asian, non-Hispanic/Latino; 28 Hispanic/Latino; 14 Two or more races, non-Hispanic/Latino), 48 international. Average age 30. 460 applicants, 73% accepted, 149 enrolled. Expenses: Contact institution. *Program availability:* Part-time, evening/weekend. Offers curriculum and teaching (Ed M, MA, Ed D); curriculum and teaching: elementary education (MA); curriculum and teaching: secondary education (MA); early childhood education (MA, Ed D); early childhood education: special education (MA); elementary education-gifted extension (MA); elementary inclusive education (MA); gifted education (MA); literacy specialist (MA); secondary inclusive education (MA); special inclusive elementary education (MA). *Application Contact:* Kelly Sutton-Skinner, Director of Admission & New Student Enrollment, E-mail: kms2237@tc.columbia.edu. *Chair,* Prof. Daniel Friedrich, 212-678-3263, E-mail: friedrich@exchange.tc.columbia.edu.

Department of Education Policy and Social Analysis Students: 82 full-time (67 women), 181 part-time (140 women); includes 91 minority (39 Black or African American, non-Hispanic/Latino; 1 American Indian or Alaska Native, non-Hispanic/Latino; 19 Asian, non-Hispanic/Latino; 27 Hispanic/Latino; 5 Two or more races, non-Hispanic/Latino), 79 international. Average age 28. 497 applicants, 54% accepted, 110 enrolled. Expenses: Contact institution. Offers economics and education (Ed M, MA, PhD); education policy (Ed M, MA, Ed D, PhD); politics and education (Ed M, MA, Ed D, PhD); sociology and education (Ed M, MA, Ed D, PhD). *Application Contact:* Kelly Sutton-Skinner, Director of Admissions & New Student Enrollment, E-mail: kms2237@tc.columbia.edu. *Chair,* Dr. Aaron Pallas, 212-678-8119, E-mail: amp155@tc.columbia.edu.

Department of Health and Behavior Studies Students: 157 full-time (145 women), 344 part-time (310 women); includes 169 minority (46 Black or African American, non-Hispanic/Latino; 2 American Indian or Alaska Native, non-Hispanic/Latino; 55 Asian, non-Hispanic/Latino; 57 Hispanic/Latino; 9 Two or more races, non-Hispanic/Latino), 64 international. Average age 31. 495 applicants, 64% accepted, 171 enrolled. Expenses: Contact institution. *Program availability:* Part-time, evening/weekend. Offers applied behavior analysis (MA, PhD); applied educational psychology: school psychology (Ed M, PhD); behavioral nutrition (PhD); community health education (MS); community nutrition education (Ed M); education of deaf and hard of hearing (MA, Ed D); health education (MA, Ed D); hearing impairment (Ed D); intellectual disability/autism (MA, Ed D, PhD); nursing education (Ed D, Advanced Certificate); nutrition and education (MS); nutrition and exercise physiology (MS); nutrition and public health (MS); nutrition education (Ed D); physical disabilities (Ed D); reading specialist (MA); severe or multiple disabilities (MA); special education (Ed M, MA, Ed D); teaching of sign language (MA). *Application Contact:* Kelly Sutton-Skinner, Director of Admission & New Student Enrollment, E-mail: kms2237@tc.columbia.edu. *Chair,* Prof. Dolores Perin, 212-678-3091, E-mail: dp111@tc.columbia.edu.

Department of Human Development Students: 114 full-time (89 women), 168 part-time (119 women); includes 75 minority (19 Black or African American, non-Hispanic/Latino; 36 Asian, non-Hispanic/Latino; 18 Hispanic/Latino; 2 Two or more races, non-Hispanic/Latino), 132 international. Average age 29. 401 applicants, 56% accepted, 109 enrolled. Expenses: Contact institution. *Program availability:* Part-time. Offers applied statistics (MS); cognitive studies in education (MA, Ed D, PhD); developmental psychology (MA, Ed D, PhD); educational psychology-human cognition and learning (Ed M, MA, Ed D, PhD); learning analytics (MS); measurement and evaluation (ME, Ed D, PhD); measurement, evaluation, and statistics (MA, MS, Ed D, PhD). *Application Contact:* Kelly Sutton-Skinner, Director of Admission & New Student Enrollment, E-mail: kms2237@tc.columbia.edu. *Chair,* Jim Corter, 212-678-3843, E-mail: jec34@tc.columbia.edu.

Department of International and Transcultural Studies Students: 94 full-time (79 women), 166 part-time (141 women); includes 90 minority (17 Black or African American, non-Hispanic/Latino; 32 Asian, non-Hispanic/Latino; 9 Two or more races, non-Hispanic/Latino), 99 international. Average age 29. 389 applicants, 56% accepted, 99 enrolled. Expenses: Contact institution. *Program availability:* Part-time. Offers anthropology and education (MA, Ed D, PhD); applied anthropology (PhD); comparative and international education (MA, Ed D, PhD); international educational development (Ed M, MA, Ed D, PhD). *Application Contact:* Kelly Sutton Skinner, Director of Admission & New Student Enrollment, E-mail: kms2237@tc.columbia.edu. *Chair,* Prof. Herve Varenne, 212-678-3190, E-mail: varenne@tc.columbia.edu.

Department of Mathematics, Science and Technology Students: 155 full-time (114 women), 254 part-time (162 women); includes 136 minority (44 Black or African American, non-Hispanic/Latino; 1 American Indian or Alaska Native, non-Hispanic/Latino; 59 Asian, non-Hispanic/Latino; 23 Hispanic/Latino; 9 Two or more races, non-Hispanic/Latino), 140 international. Average age 31. 484 applicants, 60% accepted, 138 enrolled. Expenses: Contact institution. *Program availability:* Part-time, evening/weekend, online learning. Offers biology 7-12 (MA); chemistry 7-12 (MA); communication and education (MA, Ed D); computing in education (MA); earth science 7-12 (MA); instructional technology and media (Ed M, MA, Ed D); mathematics education (Ed M, MA, Ed D, Ed DCT, PhD); physics 7-12 (MA); science and dental education (MA); science education (Ed M, MS, Ed DCT, PhD); supervisor/teacher of science education (MA); technology specialist (MA). *Application Contact:* Kelly Sutton Skinner, Director of Admission & New Student Enrollment, E-mail: kms2237@tc.columbia.edu. *Chair,* Prof. Erica Walker, 212-678-8246, E-mail: ewalker@tc.columbia.edu.

Department of Organization and Leadership Students: 249 full-time (165 women), 427 part-time (299 women); includes 275 minority (99 Black or African American, non-Hispanic/Latino; 75 Asian, non-Hispanic/Latino; 82 Hispanic/Latino; 1 Native Hawaiian or other Pacific Islander, non-Hispanic/Latino; 18 Two or more races, non-Hispanic/Latino), 84 international. Average age 34. 770 applicants, 59% accepted, 267 enrolled. Expenses: Contact institution. *Program availability:* Part-time, evening/weekend. Offers adult education guided intensive study (Ed D); adult learning and leadership (Ed M, MA, Ed D); educational leadership (Ed D); higher and postsecondary education (MA, Ed D); leadership, policy and politics (Ed D); nurse executive (MA, Ed D); private school leadership (Ed M, MA); public school building leadership (Ed M, MA); social and organizational psychology (MA); urban education leaders (Ed D). *Application Contact:* Kelly Sutton-Skinner, Director of Admission & New Student Enrollment, E-mail: kms2237@tc.columbia.edu. *Chair,* Prof. Bill Baldwin, 212-678-3043, E-mail: wjb12@tc.columbia.edu.

Interdisciplinary Programs Students: 10 full-time (6 women), 30 part-time (19 women); includes 12 minority (4 Black or African American, non-Hispanic/Latino; 4 Asian, non-Hispanic/Latino; 2 Hispanic/Latino; 1 Native Hawaiian or other Pacific Islander, non-Hispanic/Latino; 1 Two or more races, non-Hispanic/Latino), 8 international. Average age 41. 4 applicants, 50% accepted, 2 enrolled. Expenses: Contact institution. *Program availability:* Part-time. Offers interdisciplinary studies (Ed M, MA, ME, Ed D). *Application Contact:* Kelly Sutton-Skinner, Director of Admissions & New Student Enrollment, E-mail: kms2237@tc.columbia.edu.

TEACHERS COLLEGE OF SAN JOAQUIN, Stockton, CA 95206

General Information Public, coed, graduate-only institution. *Enrollment by degree level:* 301 master's, 630 other advanced degrees. *Graduate faculty:* 7 full-time (all women), 32 part-time/adjunct (23 women). *Tuition:* Full-time $5520. Tuition and fees vary according to course load and program. *Graduate housing:* On-campus housing not available. *Student services:* Campus employment opportunities, career counseling, services for students with disabilities, teacher training, writing training. *Collection:* Books: 1,250 (physical), 2,800 (digital/electronic).

Computer facilities: 65 computers available on campus for general student use. A campuswide network can be accessed from off campus. Online class registration is available. Website: http://www.sjcoe.org/tcsj/

General Application Contact: Katie Turner, Community and College Liaison, 209-4689164, E-mail: kturner@sjcoe.net.

GRADUATE UNITS

Master's Program in Education Offers early education (M Ed); educational inquiry (M Ed); educational leadership and school development (M Ed); science, technology, engineering, and mathematics (M Ed); special education (M Ed).

TÉLÉ-UNIVERSITÉ, Québec, QC G1K 9H5, Canada

General Information Province-supported, coed, comprehensive institution. *Graduate housing:* On-campus housing not available.

GRADUATE UNITS

Graduate Programs *Program availability:* Part-time. Offers computer science (PhD); corporate finance (MS); distance learning (MS).

TELSHE YESHIVA–CHICAGO, Chicago, IL 60625-5598

General Information Independent-religious, men only, comprehensive institution.

GRADUATE UNITS

Graduate Program

TEMPLE UNIVERSITY, Philadelphia, PA 19122-6096

General Information State-related, coed, university. CGS member. *Enrollment:* 39,755 graduate, professional, and undergraduate students; 4,455 full-time matriculated graduate/professional students (2,651 women), 1,233 part-time matriculated graduate/professional students (848 women). *Enrollment by degree level:* 2,573 master's, 3,037 doctoral, 78 other advanced degrees. *Graduate faculty:* 959 full-time (452 women), 578 part-time/adjunct (283 women). *Graduate housing:* Rooms and/or apartments available on a first-come, first-served basis to single and married students. Housing application deadline: 5/1. *Student services:* Campus employment opportunities, campus safety program, career counseling, exercise/wellness program, free psychological counseling, grant writing training, international student services, low-cost health insurance, multicultural affairs office, services for students with disabilities, teacher training, writing training. *Library facilities:* Paley Library plus 6 others. *Collection:* Books: 3.4 million (physical), 1.6 million (digital/electronic); Serial titles: 61,478 (physical), 189,776 (digital/electronic); Databases: 773. Students can reserve study rooms.

Computer facilities: Computer purchase and lease plans are available. 15,100 computers available on campus for general student use. A campuswide network can be accessed from student residence rooms and from off campus. Online class registration, student accounts, Web hosting are available. Website: http://www.temple.edu/

General Application Contact: Temple University Graduate School, 215-204-1380, E-mail: grad@temple.edu.

GRADUATE UNITS

Beasley School of Law *Program availability:* Part-time, evening/weekend. Offers Asian law (LL M); business law (Certificate); employee benefits (Certificate); estate planning (Certificate); law (LL M, JD, SJD, Certificate); legal education (SJD); taxation (LL M); transnational law (LL M); trial advocacy (LL M); trial advocacy and litigation (Certificate). Electronic applications accepted.

Center for the Performing and Cinematic Arts Students: 290 full-time (167 women), 51 part-time (32 women); includes 57 minority (28 Black or African American, non-Hispanic/Latino; 4 Asian, non-Hispanic/Latino; 13 Hispanic/Latino; 12 Two or more races, non-Hispanic/Latino), 96 international. 593 applicants, 41% accepted, 113 enrolled. *Faculty:* 81 full-time (41 women), 103 part-time/adjunct (42 women). Expenses: Contact institution. *Financial support:* Fellowships, research assistantships, teaching assistantships, Federal Work-Study, scholarships/grants, health care benefits, and unspecified assistantships available. Financial award applicants required to submit FAFSA. In 2018, 104 master's, 12 doctorates awarded. *Program availability:* Part-time, evening/weekend, online learning. Offers performing and cinematic arts (Ed M, MA, MFA, MM, MMT, DMA, PhD). *Application fee:* $60. Electronic applications accepted. *Application Contact:* James Short, Assistant Dean, Undergraduate & Graduate Admissions/CPCA, 215-204-8598, E-mail: james.short@temple.edu. *Dean/Vice Provost for the Arts,* Dr. Robert Stroker, 215-204-5004, E-mail: robert.stroker@temple.edu.

Boyer College of Music and Dance Students: 235 full-time (140 women), 45 part-time (27 women); includes 40 minority (19 Black or African American, non-Hispanic/Latino; 3 Asian, non-Hispanic/Latino; 10 Hispanic/Latino; 8 Two or more races, non-Hispanic/Latino), 86 international. 442 applicants, 46% accepted, 88 enrolled. *Faculty:* 50 full-time (26 women), 60 part-time/adjunct (26 women). Expenses: Contact institution. *Financial support:* Fellowships with tuition reimbursements, research assistantships with tuition reimbursements, teaching assistantships with tuition reimbursements, career-related internships or fieldwork, Federal Work-Study, scholarships/grants, health care benefits, and unspecified assistantships available. Financial award application deadline: 3/1; financial award applicants required to submit FAFSA. In 2018, 77 master's, 12 doctorates awarded. *Program availability:* Part-time, evening/weekend, online learning. Offers choral conducting (MM); collaborative piano/chamber music (MM); collaborative piano/opera coaching (MM); composition (MM, PhD); dance (MA, MFA, PhD); instrumental conducting (MM); music and dance (MA, MFA, MM, MMT, DMA, PhD); music education (MM, PhD); music history (MM); music performance (MM, DMA); music studies (PhD); music theory (MM, PhD); music therapy (MMT, PhD); musicology (MM, PhD); opera (MM); piano pedagogy (MM); string pedagogy (MM). *Application fee:* $60. Electronic applications accepted. *Application Contact:* James Short, Director of Undergraduate and Graduate Admissions, 215-204-8598, Fax: 215-204-4957, E-mail: james.short@temple.edu. *Dean,* Dr. Robert Stroker, 215-204-5004, Fax: 215-204-4957, E-mail: rstroker@temple.edu.

School of Theater, Film and Media Arts Students: 55 full-time (27 women), 6 part-time (5 women); includes 17 minority (9 Black or African American, non-Hispanic/Latino; 1 Asian, non-Hispanic/Latino; 3 Hispanic/Latino; 4 Two or more races, non-Hispanic/Latino), 10 international. 151 applicants, 26% accepted, 25 enrolled. *Faculty:* 31 full-time (15 women), 43 part-time/adjunct (16 women). Expenses: Contact institution. *Financial support:* Fellowships, teaching assistantships, Federal Work-Study, and health care benefits available. Financial award application deadline: 3/1; financial award applicants required to submit FAFSA. In 2018, 27 master's awarded. Offers acting (MFA); design (MFA); directing (MFA); film and media arts (MA, MFA); musical theater collaboration (MFA); musical theater studies (MA); playwriting (MFA); theater, film and media arts (MA, MFA). *Application fee:* $60. Electronic applications accepted. *Application Contact:* Paury Flowers, Recruitment Coordinator, 215-777-9135, E-mail: pflowers@temple.edu. *Dean/Vice Provost for the Arts,* Dr. Robert Stroker, 215-204-8598, E-mail: robert.stroker@temple.edu.

College of Education Students: 453 full-time (321 women), 373 part-time (259 women); includes 253 minority (145 Black or African American, non-Hispanic/Latino; 3 American Indian or Alaska Native, non-Hispanic/Latino; 37 Asian, non-Hispanic/Latino; 48 Hispanic/Latino; 1 Native Hawaiian or other Pacific Islander, non-Hispanic/Latino; 19 Two or more races, non-Hispanic/Latino), 33 international. 881 applicants, 53% accepted, 260 enrolled. *Faculty:* 54 full-time (34 women), 93 part-time/adjunct (62 women). Expenses: Contact institution. *Financial support:* Fellowships, Federal Work-Study, scholarships/grants, health care benefits, and unspecified assistantships available. Financial award applicants required to submit FAFSA. In 2018, 291 master's, 59 doctorates, 70 other advanced degrees awarded. *Program availability:* Part-time, evening/weekend. Offers applied behavior analysis (MS Ed); career and technical education (Ed M); counseling psychology (Ed M); education (Ed M, MS Ed, Ed D, PhD, Ed S); educational leadership (Ed M, Ed D); educational psychology (Ed M); middle grades education (Ed M); school psychology (PhD, Ed S); secondary education (Ed M); teaching English to speakers of other languages (MS Ed); urban education (Ed M).

Application fee: $60. Electronic applications accepted. *Application Contact:* Joseph Paris, Assistant Dean of Marketing & Enrollment Management, 215-204-2810, E-mail: educate@temple.edu. *Dean,* Dr. Gregory Anderson, 215-204-8017, Fax: 215-204-5622, E-mail: gregory.anderson@temple.edu.

College of Engineering *Program availability:* Part-time, 100% online, blended/hybrid learning. Offers bioengineering (PhD); civil engineering (MSCE, PhD); electrical and computer engineering (PhD); electrical engineering (MSEE, PhD); engineering (MS, MS Env E, MSCE, MSEE, MSME, PhD, Certificate, Graduate Certificate); engineering management (MS, Certificate); environmental engineering (MS Env E, PhD); mechanical engineering (MSME); storm water management (Graduate Certificate). Electronic applications accepted.

College of Liberal Arts Students: 576 full-time (338 women), 106 part-time (60 women); includes 184 minority (82 Black or African American, non-Hispanic/Latino; 2 American Indian or Alaska Native, non-Hispanic/Latino; 25 Asian, non-Hispanic/Latino; 49 Hispanic/Latino; 26 Two or more races, non-Hispanic/Latino), 80 international. 1,187 applicants, 29% accepted, 145 enrolled. *Faculty:* 298 full-time (137 women), 105 part-time/adjunct (46 women). Expenses: Contact institution. *Financial support:* Fellowships, research assistantships, teaching assistantships, Federal Work-Study, and health care benefits available. Financial award applicants required to submit FAFSA. In 2018, 107 master's, 68 doctorates, 11 other advanced degrees awarded. *Program availability:* Part-time. Offers African American studies (MA, PhD); anthropology (PhD); creative writing (MFA); criminal justice (MA, PhD); economics (MA, PhD); English (MA, PhD); geographic information systems (PSM, Graduate Certificate); geography and urban studies (MA, PhD); history (MA, PhD); liberal arts (MA, MFA, MS, PSM, PhD, Graduate Certificate); philosophy (MA, PhD); political science (MA, PhD); psychology (MA, MS, PhD); religion (MA, PhD); sociology (MA, PhD); Spanish (MA, PhD). *Application fee:* $60. Electronic applications accepted. *Application Contact:* Amy Defibaugh, Director, Graduate Affairs, 215-204-8504, E-mail: amy.defibaugh@temple.edu. *Dean,* Richard Deeg, 215-204-7747, Fax: 215-204-5022, E-mail: rdeeg@temple.edu.

College of Public Health Students: 739 full-time (572 women), 321 part-time (257 women); includes 330 minority (161 Black or African American, non-Hispanic/Latino; 3 American Indian or Alaska Native, non-Hispanic/Latino; 55 Asian, non-Hispanic/Latino; 70 Hispanic/Latino; 41 Two or more races, non-Hispanic/Latino), 35 international. 1,175 applicants, 53% accepted, 250 enrolled. *Faculty:* 132 full-time (89 women), 31 part-time/adjunct (21 women). Expenses: Contact institution. *Financial support:* Fellowships, research assistantships, teaching assistantships, Federal Work-Study, scholarships/grants, health care benefits, and unspecified assistantships available. Support available to part-time students. Financial award applicants required to submit FAFSA. In 2018, 300 master's, 84 doctorates awarded. *Program availability:* Part-time, evening/weekend, online learning. Offers adult-gerontology primary care (DNP); applied biostatistics (MPH); athletic training (MSAT, DAT); communication sciences and disorders (PhD); environmental health (MPH); epidemiology (MPH, MS, PhD); family-individual across the lifespan (DNP); health informatics (MS); health policy (PhD); health policy and management (MPH); kinesiology (MS, PhD); neuromotor science (MS, PhD); nursing (DNP); occupational therapy (MOT, DOT); public health (MA, MOT, MPH, MS, MSAT, MSW, DAT, DNP, DOT, DPT, PhD, TDPT); recreational therapy (MS); social and behavioral sciences (MPH, PhD); speech-language-hearing (MA). *Application fee:* $60. *Application Contact:* Michael Usino, Assistant Dean of Admissions, 215-204-5717, E-mail: michael.usino@temple.edu. *Dean,* Laura Siminoff, 215-707-8624, E-mail: laura.siminoff@temple.edu.

School of Social Work Students: 224 full-time (197 women), 89 part-time (80 women); includes 136 minority (90 Black or African American, non-Hispanic/Latino; 2 American Indian or Alaska Native, non-Hispanic/Latino; 6 Asian, non-Hispanic/Latino; 26 Hispanic/Latino; 12 Two or more races, non-Hispanic/Latino), 239 applicants, 80% accepted, 82 enrolled. *Faculty:* 21 full-time (12 women), 11 part-time/adjunct (8 women). Expenses: Contact institution. *Financial support:* Career-related internships or fieldwork, Federal Work-Study, and scholarships/grants available. Financial award application deadline: 1/15; financial award applicants required to submit FAFSA. In 2018, 154 master's awarded. *Program availability:* Part-time, evening/weekend, online learning. Offers social work (MSW). *Application deadline:* For fall admission, 1/15 priority date for domestic students; for spring admission, 11/1 for domestic students; for summer admission, 1/15 priority date for domestic students. Applications are processed on a rolling basis. *Application fee:* $60. Electronic applications accepted. *Application Contact:* Tre Grue, Assistant Director of Admissions, 215-204-5806, E-mail: tre@temple.edu. *Director of the School of Social Work,* Philip McCallion, 215-204-8137, E-mail: philip.mccallion@temple.edu.

College of Science and Technology Students: 411 full-time (140 women), 49 part-time (20 women); includes 64 minority (16 Black or African American, non-Hispanic/Latino; 33 Asian, non-Hispanic/Latino; 11 Hispanic/Latino; 4 Two or more races, non-Hispanic/Latino), 225 international. 522 applicants, 46% accepted, 109 enrolled. *Faculty:* 175 full-time (44 women), 15 part-time/adjunct (3 women). Expenses: Contact institution. *Financial support:* Fellowships, research assistantships, teaching assistantships, career-related internships or fieldwork, Federal Work-Study, scholarships/grants, health care benefits, and unspecified assistantships available. Support available to part-time students. Financial award applicants required to submit FAFSA. In 2018, 73 master's, 27 doctorates awarded. *Program availability:* Part-time, evening/weekend. Offers applied and computational mathematics (MS); biology (MS, PSM, PhD); biotechnology (MS); chemistry (MA, PhD); computational data science (MS); computer and information sciences (PhD); computer science (MS); cyber defense and information assurance (PSM); geology (MS); geoscience (PhD); information science and technology (MS); mathematics (MS, PhD); physics (MS, PhD); science and technology (MA, MS, PSM, PhD). *Application fee:* $60. Electronic applications accepted. *Application Contact:* Caitlyn Moynahan, Graduate Admissions Coordinator, 215-204-5295, E-mail: cst.gradinfo@temple.edu. *Dean,* Michael Klein, 215-204-1927, E-mail: cst.dean@temple.edu.

Fox School of Business *Program availability:* Part-time, evening/weekend, online learning. Offers accountancy (MS); accounting (MBA, PhD); actuarial science (MS); business (EMBA, IMBA, MBA, MHM, MS, PhD); business management (MBA); entrepreneurship (PhD); finance (MS, PhD); financial engineering (MS); financial management (MBA); healthcare and life sciences innovation (MBA); human resource management (MBA, MS); innovation management and entrepreneurship (MS); international business (IMBA, PhD); IT management (MBA); management information systems (PhD); marketing (MS, PhD); marketing management (MBA); pharmaceutical management (MBA); risk management and insurance (PhD); statistics (MS, PhD); strategic management (EMBA, MBA, PhD); tourism and sport (PhD). Electronic applications accepted.

Klein College of Media and Communication Students: 87 full-time (59 women), 27 part-time (14 women); includes 29 minority (17 Black or African American, non-Hispanic/Latino; 2 Asian, non-Hispanic/Latino; 7 Hispanic/Latino; 3 Two or more races, non-Hispanic/Latino), 30 international. 159 applicants, 59% accepted, 47 enrolled.

Faculty: 71 full-time (39 women), 63 part-time/adjunct (31 women). Expenses: Contact institution. *Financial support:* Fellowships, teaching assistantships, Federal Work-Study, scholarships/grants, health care benefits, unspecified assistantships, and travel award available. Financial award applicants required to submit FAFSA. In 2018, 37 master's, 3 doctorates awarded. *Program availability:* Part-time, evening/weekend, online learning. Offers communication management (MS); globalization and development communication (MS); journalism (MJ); media and communication (MA, MJ, MS, PhD); media studies and production (MA). *Application fee:* $60. Electronic applications accepted. *Application Contact:* Nicole McKenna, Graduate Office Director, 215-204-1497, E-mail: nmckenna@temple.edu. *Dean,* David Boardman, 215-204-8422, Fax: 215-204-4811, E-mail: dboardman@temple.edu.

Kornberg School of Dentistry Offers advanced education in general dentistry (Certificate); dentistry (MS, DMD, Certificate); endodontology (Certificate); oral biology (MS); orthodontics (Certificate); periodontology (Certificate). Electronic applications accepted.

Lewis Katz School of Medicine Students: 990 full-time (535 women), 18 part-time (14 women); includes 402 minority (81 Black or African American, non-Hispanic/Latino; 187 Asian, non-Hispanic/Latino; 105 Hispanic/Latino; 1 Native Hawaiian or other Pacific Islander, non-Hispanic/Latino; 28 Two or more races, non-Hispanic/Latino; 26 international. 7,509 applicants, 7% accepted, 230 enrolled. *Faculty:* 20 full-time (8 women). Expenses: Contact institution. *Financial support:* Fellowships, research assistantships, Federal Work-Study, institutionally sponsored loans, scholarships/grants, and health care benefits available. Financial award applicants required to submit FAFSA. In 2018, 22 master's, 250 doctorates awarded. Offers biomedical sciences (MS); medicine (MS, MD, PhD). *Application fee:* $60. Electronic applications accepted. *Application Contact:* Jacob Ufberg, Associate Dean of Admissions, 215-707-5308, E-mail: medadmissions@temple.edu. *Dean,* Larry R. Kaiser, 215-707-8773, E-mail: sks@temple.edu.

School of Pharmacy Students: 578 full-time (321 women), 206 part-time (151 women); includes 358 minority (55 Black or African American, non-Hispanic/Latino; 132 Asian, non-Hispanic/Latino; 24 Hispanic/Latino; 147 Two or more races, non-Hispanic/Latino; 42 international. 569 applicants, 44% accepted, 156 enrolled. *Faculty:* 33 full-time (17 women), 37 part-time/adjunct (13 women). Expenses: Contact institution. *Financial support:* Fellowships, research assistantships, teaching assistantships, Federal Work-Study, and unspecified assistantships available. Financial award application deadline: 3/1; financial award applicants required to submit FAFSA. In 2018, 92 master's, 140 doctorates awarded. *Program availability:* Part-time, evening/weekend, online learning. Offers medicinal chemistry (MS, PhD); pharmaceutics (MS, PhD); pharmacodynamics (MS, PhD); pharmacy (MS, PhD, Pharm D); regulatory affairs and quality assurance (MS). *Application fee:* $60. Electronic applications accepted. *Application Contact:* Joan Hankins, Director of Admissions, 215-707-4900, E-mail: joan.hankins@temple.edu. *Interim Dean,* Michael Borenstein, 215-707-2976, E-mail: michael.borenstein@temple.edu.

School of Podiatric Medicine Offers podiatric medicine (DPM). DPM/PhD offered jointly with Drexel University, University of Pennsylvania.

School of Sport, Tourism and Hospitality Management Students: 153 full-time (70 women), 56 part-time (25 women); includes 48 minority (28 Black or African American, non-Hispanic/Latino; 5 Asian, non-Hispanic/Latino; 10 Hispanic/Latino; 5 Two or more races, non-Hispanic/Latino, 33 international. 215 applicants, 76% accepted, 107 enrolled. *Faculty:* 24 full-time (9 women), 11 part-time/adjunct (4 women). Expenses: Contact institution. *Financial support:* Scholarships/grants, health care benefits, and unspecified assistantships available. Financial award application deadline: 3/1; financial award applicants required to submit FAFSA. In 2018, 71 master's awarded. *Program availability:* Part-time, evening/weekend, online learning. Offers sport business (MS); tourism and hospitality management (MTHM); tourism and sport (PhD); travel and tourism (MS). *Application deadline:* For fall admission, 12/15 priority date for domestic students, 3/1 for international students; for spring admission, 11/1 for domestic students, 8/1 for international students. Applications are processed on a rolling basis. *Application fee:* $60. Electronic applications accepted. *Application Contact:* Michelle Rosar, Assistant Director of Graduate Enrollment, 215-204-3315, E-mail: michelle.rosar@temple.edu. *Dean,* Ronald C. Anderson, 215-204-8701, E-mail: sthm@temple.edu.

Tyler School of Art and Architecture Students: 178 full-time (128 women), 26 part-time (16 women); includes 34 minority (10 Black or African American, non-Hispanic/Latino; 6 Asian, non-Hispanic/Latino; 11 Hispanic/Latino; 7 Two or more races, non-Hispanic/Latino), 27 international. 467 applicants, 34% accepted, 77 enrolled. *Faculty:* 71 full-time (34 women), 120 part-time/adjunct (61 women). Expenses: Contact institution. *Financial support:* Fellowships with full tuition reimbursements, research assistantships with full tuition reimbursements, teaching assistantships with full tuition reimbursements, Federal Work-Study, institutionally sponsored loans, scholarships/grants, health care benefits, and travel scholarships/grants available. Financial award application deadline: 1/6; financial award applicants required to submit FAFSA. In 2018, 73 master's, 7 doctorates awarded. *Program availability:* Part-time, evening/weekend. Offers architecture (M Arch); art (Ed M, M Arch, MA, MFA, ML Arch, MS, PhD, Graduate Certificate); art education (Ed M); art history (MA, PhD); ceramics/glass (MFA); fibers and material studies (MFA); glass (MFA); graphic and interactive design (MFA); metals/jewelry/CAD-CAM (MFA); photography (MFA); printmaking (MFA). *Application fee:* $60. Electronic applications accepted. *Application Contact:* Lauren O'Neill, Director of Admissions, 215-777-9159, E-mail: tyleradmissions@temple.edu. *Dean,* Susan E. Cahan, 215-777-9000, E-mail: tyler@temple.edu.

TENNESSEE STATE UNIVERSITY, Nashville, TN 37209-1561

General Information State-supported, coed, comprehensive institution. CGS member. *Graduate housing:* Rooms and/or apartments available on a first-come, first-served basis to single and married students. Housing application deadline: 8/1.

GRADUATE UNITS

The School of Graduate Studies and Research

College of Agriculture, Human and Natural Sciences Program availability: Part-time, evening/weekend. Offers agricultural sciences (MS); biological sciences (MS, PhD); biotechnology (PhD); chemistry (MS).

College of Business Program availability: Part-time, evening/weekend, online learning. Offers business (MBA). Electronic applications accepted.

College of Education Program availability: Part-time, evening/weekend. Offers counseling psychology (MS); curriculum and instruction (M Ed, Ed D); education (M Ed, MA Ed, MS, Ed D, PhD, Ed S); elementary education (M Ed); special education (M Ed).

College of Engineering Program availability: Part-time, evening/weekend. Offers biomedical engineering (ME); civil engineering (ME); computer and information systems engineering (MS, PhD); electrical engineering (ME); environmental engineering (ME); manufacturing engineering (ME); mathematical sciences (MS); mechanical engineering (ME).

College of Health Sciences Program availability: Part-time, evening/weekend. Offers exercise science (MA Ed); family nurse practitioner (MSN, Certificate); health sciences (MA Ed, MOT, MPH, MS, MSN, DPT, Certificate); holistic nurse practitioner (MSN); holistic nursing (Certificate); nursing education (MSN, Certificate); occupational therapy (MOT); physical therapy (DPT); public health (MPH); speech and hearing science (MS); sports administration (MA Ed). Electronic applications accepted.

College of Liberal Arts Program availability: Part-time, evening/weekend. Offers criminal justice (MCJ); liberal arts (MCJ). Electronic applications accepted.

College of Public Service Program availability: Part-time, evening/weekend. Offers human resource management (MPS); public administration (MPA, PhD); social work (MSW); strategic leadership (MPS); training and development (MPS).

TENNESSEE TECHNOLOGICAL UNIVERSITY, Cookeville, TN 38505

General Information State-supported, coed, university. CGS member. *Enrollment:* 308 full-time matriculated graduate/professional students (167 women), 853 part-time matriculated graduate/professional students (477 women). *Enrollment by degree level:* 904 master's, 174 doctoral, 83 other advanced degrees. *Graduate faculty:* 341 full-time (62 women). *Graduate housing:* Rooms and/or apartments available on a first-come, first-served basis to single and married students. Housing application deadline: 6/1. *Student services:* Campus employment opportunities, campus safety program, career counseling, child daycare facilities, exercise/wellness program, free psychological counseling, international student services, low-cost health insurance, multicultural affairs office, services for students with disabilities, teacher training. *Library facilities:* Angelo and Jennette Volpe Library and Media Center. *Collection:* Books: 235,249 (physical), 267,168 (digital/electronic); Serial titles: 120,118 (physical); Databases: 193.

Computer facilities: 227 computers available on campus for general student use. A campuswide network can be accessed. Online class registration, 590 additional computers are available for student use in individual departmental labs are available. Website: http://www.tntech.edu/

General Application Contact: Shelia K. Kendrick, Coordinator of Graduate Studies, 931-372-3808, Fax: 931-372-3497, E-mail: skendrick@tntech.edu.

GRADUATE UNITS

College of Graduate Studies Students: 308 full-time (167 women), 853 part-time (477 women); includes 88 minority (42 Black or African American, non-Hispanic/Latino; 9 Asian, non-Hispanic/Latino; 17 Hispanic/Latino; 20 Two or more races, non-Hispanic/Latino), 123 international. 861 applicants, 65% accepted, 343 enrolled. *Faculty:* 341 full-time (62 women). Expenses: Contact institution. *Financial support:* In 2018–19, 354 students received support, including 50 fellowships (averaging $8,000 per year), 143 research assistantships (averaging $6,973 per year), 156 teaching assistantships (averaging $6,213 per year); career-related internships or fieldwork and Federal Work-Study also available. Support available to part-time students. Financial award application deadline: 4/1; financial award applicants required to submit FAFSA. In 2018, 333 master's, 19 doctorates, 34 other advanced degrees awarded. *Program availability:* Part-time, evening/weekend, 100% online, blended/hybrid learning. *Application deadline:* For fall admission, 7/1 for domestic students, 5/1 for international students; for spring admission, 12/1 for domestic students, 10/1 for international students; for summer admission, 5/1 for domestic students, 2/1 for international students. Applications are processed on a rolling basis. *Application fee:* $35 ($40 for international students). Electronic applications accepted. *Application Contact:* Shelia K. Kendrick, Coordinator of Graduate Studies, 931-372-3808, Fax: 931-372-3497, E-mail: skendrick@tntech.edu. *Senior Associate Provost and Dean of Graduate Studies,* Dr. Mark A. Stephens, 931-372-3233, Fax: 931-372-3497, E-mail: mstephens@tntech.edu.

College of Arts and Sciences Students: 25 full-time (15 women), 28 part-time (13 women); includes 1 minority (Two or more races, non-Hispanic/Latino), 5 international. 47 applicants, 53% accepted, 17 enrolled. *Faculty:* 78 full-time (15 women). Expenses: Contact institution. *Financial support:* In 2018–19, 8 research assistantships (averaging $7,600 per year), 45 teaching assistantships (averaging $6,630 per year) were awarded; fellowships and career-related internships or fieldwork also available. Support available to part-time students. Financial award application deadline: 4/1. In 2018, 20 master's awarded. *Program availability:* Part-time. Offers arts and sciences (MA, MS); chemistry (MS); English (MA); fish, game, and wildlife management (MS); mathematics (MS). *Application deadline:* For fall admission, 8/1 for domestic students, 5/1 for international students; for spring admission, 12/1 for domestic students, 10/1 for international students; for summer admission, 5/1 for domestic students, 2/1 for international students. Applications are processed on a rolling basis. *Application fee:* $35 ($40 for international students). Electronic applications accepted. *Application Contact:* Shelia K. Kendrick, Coordinator of Graduate Studies, 931-372-3808, Fax: 931-372-3497, E-mail: skendrick@tntech.edu. *Dean,* Dr. Paul Semmes, 931-372-3118, Fax: 931-372-6142, E-mail: psemmes@tntech.edu.

College of Business Students: 39 full-time (14 women), 179 part-time (83 women); includes 18 minority (7 Black or African American, non-Hispanic/Latino; 2 Asian, non-Hispanic/Latino; 6 Hispanic/Latino; 3 Two or more races, non-Hispanic/Latino), 5 international. 161 applicants, 67% accepted, 78 enrolled. *Faculty:* 28 full-time (5 women). Expenses: Contact institution. *Financial support:* In 2018–19, 2 research assistantships (averaging $4,400 per year), 4 teaching assistantships (averaging $4,400 per year) were awarded; fellowships also available. Support available to part-time students. Financial award application deadline: 4/1. In 2018, 88 master's awarded. *Program availability:* Part-time, evening/weekend, online learning. Offers accountancy (M Acc); business (M Acc, MBA); finance (MBA); human resource management (MBA); international business (MBA); management information systems (MBA). *Application deadline:* For fall admission, 8/1 for domestic students, 5/1 for international students; for spring admission, 12/1 for domestic students, 10/1 for international students; for summer admission, 5/1 for domestic students, 2/1 for international students. Applications are processed on a rolling basis. *Application fee:* $35 ($40 for international students). Electronic applications accepted. *Application Contact:* Shelia K. Kendrick, Coordinator of Graduate Studies, 931-372-3808, Fax: 931-372-3497, E-mail: skendrick@tntech.edu. *Director,* Kate Nicewicz, 931-372-3600, Fax: 931-372-6249, E-mail: knicewicz@tntech.edu.

College of Education Students: 123 full-time (96 women), 288 part-time (215 women); includes 32 minority (17 Black or African American, non-Hispanic/Latino; 3 Asian, non-Hispanic/Latino; 5 Hispanic/Latino; 7 Two or more races, non-Hispanic/Latino), 8 international. 221 applicants, 76% accepted, 120 enrolled. *Faculty:* 58 full-time (16 women). Expenses: Contact institution. *Financial support:* Fellowships, research assistantships, teaching assistantships, and career-related internships or fieldwork available. Support available to part-time students. Financial award application deadline: 4/1. In 2018, 105 master's, 8 doctorates, 33 other advanced degrees awarded. *Program availability:* Part-time, evening/weekend. Offers adapted physical education (MA); applied behavior analysis (PhD); counseling and psychology (MA, Ed S); curriculum (MA, Ed S); early childhood education (MA, Ed S); education (MA, PhD, Ed S); educational technology (MA, Ed S); elementary education (MA, Ed S); elementary/middle school physical education (MA); exceptional learning (PhD); instructional leadership (MA, Ed S); library science (MA, Ed S); lifetime wellness (MA); literacy (MA, PhD, Ed S); music (MA); program planning and evaluation (PhD); reading (MA, Ed S); secondary education (MA, Ed S); special education (Ed S); sport management (MA); STEM education (MA, PhD, Ed S). *Application deadline:* For fall admission, 8/1 for domestic students, 5/1 for international students; for spring admission, 12/1 for domestic students, 10/1 for international students; for summer admission, 5/1 for domestic students, 2/1 for international students. Applications are processed on a rolling basis. *Application fee:* $35 ($40 for international students). Electronic applications accepted. *Application Contact:* Shelia K. Kendrick, Coordinator of Graduate Studies, 931-372-3808, Fax: 931-372-3497, E-mail: skendrick@tntech.edu. *Dean,* Dr. Lisa Zagumny, 931-372-3124, Fax: 931-372-6319, E-mail: lzagumny@tntech.edu.

College of Engineering Students: 68 full-time (11 women), 156 part-time (24 women); includes 9 minority (3 Black or African American, non-Hispanic/Latino; 3 Asian, non-Hispanic/Latino; 2 Hispanic/Latino; 1 Two or more races, non-Hispanic/Latino), 99 international. 273 applicants, 58% accepted, 52 enrolled. *Faculty:* 76 full-time (2 women). Expenses: Contact institution. *Financial support:* Fellowships, research assistantships, teaching assistantships, and career-related internships or fieldwork available. Support available to part-time students. Financial award application deadline: 4/1. In 2018, 50 master's, 8 doctorates awarded. *Program availability:* Part-time. Offers chemical engineering (MS); civil and environmental engineering (MS); computer science (MS, PhD); electrical and computer engineering (MS); engineering (MS, PhD); mechanical engineering (MS). *Application deadline:* For fall admission, 8/1 for domestic students, 5/1 for international students; for spring admission, 12/1 for domestic students, 10/1 for international students. Applications are processed on a rolling basis. *Application fee:* $35 ($40 for international students). Electronic applications accepted. *Application Contact:* Shelia K. Kendrick, Coordinator of Graduate Studies, 931-372-3808, Fax: 931-372-3497, E-mail: skendrick@tntech.edu. *Interim Dean,* Dr. Darrell Hoy, 931-372-3172, Fax: 931-372-6172, E-mail: dhoy@tntech.edu.

College of Interdisciplinary Studies Students: 34 full-time (15 women), 104 part-time (55 women); includes 22 minority (14 Black or African American, non-Hispanic/Latino; 3 Hispanic/Latino; 5 Two or more races, non-Hispanic/Latino), 6 international. 69 applicants, 65% accepted, 37 enrolled. Expenses: Contact institution. *Financial support:* Research assistantships and teaching assistantships available. In 2018, 35 master's, 3 doctorates awarded. *Program availability:* Part-time. Offers agriculture (PhD); biology (PhD); chemistry (PhD); environmental informatics (PSM); environmental studies (PSM, PhD); geosciences (PhD); health care administration (MPS); human resources leadership (MPS); integrated research (PhD); interdisciplinary studies (MPS, PSM, PhD); manufacturing sustainability (PSM); public safety (MPS); strategic leadership (MPS); teaching English to speakers of other languages (MPS); training and development (MPS). *Application deadline:* For fall admission, 7/1 for domestic students, 5/1 for international students; for spring admission, 11/1 for domestic students, 10/1 for international students; for summer admission, 5/1 for domestic students, 2/1 for international students. Applications are processed on a rolling basis. *Application fee:* $35 ($40 for international students). Electronic applications accepted. *Application Contact:* Shelia K. Kendrick, Coordinator of Graduate Studies, 931-372-3808, Fax: 931-372-3497, E-mail: skendrick@tntech.edu. *Dean,* Dr. Mike Gotcher, 931-372-6238, E-mail: mgotcher@tntech.edu.

Whitson-Hester School of Nursing Students: 19 full-time (16 women), 98 part-time (87 women); includes 6 minority (1 Black or African American, non-Hispanic/Latino; 1 Asian, non-Hispanic/Latino; 1 Hispanic/Latino; 3 Two or more races, non-Hispanic/Latino). 90 applicants, 57% accepted, 36 enrolled. Expenses: Contact institution. *Financial support:* Teaching assistantships available. Financial award application deadline: 4/1. In 2018, 35 master's awarded. *Program availability:* Part-time, evening/weekend, online learning. Offers adult-gerontology acute care nurse practitioner (DNP); executive leadership in nursing (DNP); family nurse practitioner (MSN, DNP); nursing (MSN, DNP); nursing administration (MSN); nursing education (MSN); pediatric nurse practitioner–primary care (DNP); psychiatric/mental health nurse practitioner (DNP); women's health care nurse practitioner (DNP). *Application deadline:* For fall admission, 7/1 for domestic students, 5/1 for international students; for spring admission, 11/1 for domestic students, 10/1 for international students; for summer admission, 5/1 for domestic students, 2/1 for international students. Applications are processed on a rolling basis. *Application fee:* $35 ($40 for international students). Electronic applications accepted. *Application Contact:* Shelia K. Kendrick, Coordinator of Graduate Studies, 931-372-3808, Fax: 931-372-3497, E-mail: skendrick@tntech.edu. *Dean,* Dr. Kim Hanna, 931-372-3547, Fax: 931-372-6244, E-mail: khanna@tntech.edu.

TENNESSEE WESLEYAN UNIVERSITY, Athens, TN 37303

General Information Independent-religious, coed, comprehensive institution. *Enrollment:* 12 full-time matriculated graduate/professional students (8 women), 19 part-time matriculated graduate/professional students (13 women). *Enrollment by degree level:* 31 master's. *Graduate faculty:* 4 full-time (1 woman), 1 (woman) part-time/adjunct. *Tuition:* Full-time $9000; part-time $500 per credit hour. *Graduate housing:* On-campus housing not available. *Student services:* Career counseling, international student services, multicultural affairs office, services for students with disabilities. *Library facilities:* Merner-Pfeiffer Library plus 1 other. *Collection:* Books: 52,465 (physical), 356,697 (digital/electronic); Serial titles: 82 (physical); Databases: 76. Weekly public service hours: 69.

Computer facilities: 205 computers available on campus for general student use. A campuswide network can be accessed from student residence rooms. Online class registration is available. Website: http://www.tnwesleyan.edu/

General Application Contact: Makhaila Woodlief, Adult and Graduate Admissions Counselor, 423-746-5285, Fax: 423-745-9335, E-mail: mbucco@tnwesleyan.edu.

GRADUATE UNITS

Graduate Programs Students: 12 full-time (8 women), 19 part-time (13 women). Average age 28. 29 applicants, 83% accepted, 16 enrolled. *Faculty:* 4 full-time (1 woman), 2 part-time/adjunct (1 woman). Expenses: Contact institution. *Financial support:* Application deadline: 4/30; applicants required to submit FAFSA. In 2018, 9 master's awarded. *Program availability:* Part-time. Offers accounting (MBA); management (MBA). *Application deadline:* For fall admission, 8/19 for domestic students; for spring admission, 1/14 for domestic students; for summer admission, 5/6

for domestic students. Electronic applications accepted. *Application Contact:* Makhaila Woodlief, Adult and Graduate Admissions Counselor, 423-746-5285, Fax: 423-745-9335, E-mail: mwoodlief@tnwesleyan.edu.

TEXAS A&M INTERNATIONAL UNIVERSITY, Laredo, TX 78041

General Information State-supported, coed, comprehensive institution. CGS member. *Graduate housing:* Rooms and/or apartments available on a first-come, first-served basis to single and married students.

GRADUATE UNITS

Office of Graduate Studies and Research *Program availability:* Part-time.

A.R. Sanchez, Jr. School of Business *Program availability:* Part-time, evening/weekend. Offers accounting (MP Acc); business (MBA, MP Acc, MSIS, PhD); information systems (MSIS); international banking and finance (MBA); international business management (MBA, PhD).

College of Arts and Sciences *Program availability:* Part-time, online learning. Offers arts and sciences (MA, MACP, MPA, MS, PhD); biology (MS); counseling psychology (MACP); criminal justice (MS); English (MA); history and political thought (MA); language, literature and translation (MA); mathematics (MS); psychology (MS); public administration (MPA); sociology (MA).

College of Education *Program availability:* Part-time, evening/weekend. Offers curriculum and pedagogy (MS); education (MS, MS Ed); educational administration (MS Ed); generic special education (MS Ed); school counseling (MS).

College of Nursing and Health Sciences Offers family nurse practitioner (MSN).

TEXAS A&M UNIVERSITY, College Station, TX 77843

General Information State-supported, coed, university. CGS member. *Enrollment:* 13,118 full-time matriculated graduate/professional students (5,768 women), 3,078 part-time matriculated graduate/professional students (1,480 women). *Enrollment by degree level:* 6,987 master's, 7,708 doctoral, 95 other advanced degrees. *Graduate faculty:* 1,931. *Graduate housing:* Rooms and/or apartments available on a first-come, first-served basis to single and married students. *Student services:* Campus employment opportunities, campus safety program, career counseling, child daycare facilities, exercise/wellness program, free psychological counseling, grant writing training, international student services, low-cost health insurance, multicultural affairs office, services for students with disabilities, teacher training, writing training. *Library facilities:* Sterling C. Evans Library plus 9 others. *Collection:* Books: 4.3 million (physical), 1.9 million (digital/electronic); Serial titles: 10,083 (physical), 199,378 (digital/electronic); Databases: 1,162. Weekly public service hours: 144; study areas open 24 hours, 5–7 days a week; students can reserve study rooms.

Computer facilities: 2,776 computers available on campus for general student use. A campuswide network can be accessed from student residence rooms and from off campus. Online class registration is available.
Website: http://www.tamu.edu/

GRADUATE UNITS

Bush School of Government and Public Service Students: 327 full-time (161 women), 77 part-time (23 women); includes 96 minority (17 Black or African American, non-Hispanic/Latino; 1 American Indian or Alaska Native, non-Hispanic/Latino; 13 Asian, non-Hispanic/Latino; 53 Hispanic/Latino; 12 Two or more races, non-Hispanic/Latino), 36 international. Average age 29. 273 applicants, 99% accepted, 178 enrolled. *Faculty:* 66. Expenses: Contact institution. *Financial support:* In 2018–19, 393 students received support, including 22 fellowships with tuition reimbursements available (averaging $12,348 per year), 79 research assistantships with tuition reimbursements available (averaging $11,067 per year), 2 teaching assistantships with tuition reimbursements available (averaging $10,375 per year); career-related internships or fieldwork, institutionally sponsored loans, scholarships/grants, traineeships, health care benefits, tuition waivers (full and partial), and unspecified assistantships also available. Support available to part-time students. Financial award application deadline: 3/15; financial award applicants required to submit FAFSA. In 2018, 187 master's awarded. Offers international affairs (MIA). *Application deadline:* For fall admission, 1/15 for domestic and international students. *Application fee:* $50 ($90 for international students). Electronic applications accepted. *Application Contact:* Kathryn Meyer, Director of Recruitment and Admissions, 979-458-4767, Fax: 979-845-4155, E-mail: bushschooladmissions@tamu.edu. *Dean,* Dr. Mark Welsh, 979-862-8007, E-mail: mwelsh@tamu.edu.

College of Agriculture and Life Sciences Students: 978 full-time (512 women), 279 part-time (141 women); includes 204 minority (36 Black or African American, non-Hispanic/Latino; 3 American Indian or Alaska Native, non-Hispanic/Latino; 27 Asian, non-Hispanic/Latino; 121 Hispanic/Latino; 1 Native Hawaiian or other Pacific Islander, non-Hispanic/Latino; 16 Two or more races, non-Hispanic/Latino), 416 international. Average age 30. 515 applicants, 61% accepted, 238 enrolled. *Faculty:* 349. Expenses: Contact institution. *Financial support:* In 2018–19, 1,013 students received support, including 159 fellowships with tuition reimbursements available (averaging $13,554 per year), 575 research assistantships with tuition reimbursements available (averaging $14,017 per year), 337 teaching assistantships with tuition reimbursements available (averaging $13,020 per year); career-related internships or fieldwork, institutionally sponsored loans, scholarships/grants, traineeships, health care benefits, tuition waivers (full and partial), and unspecified assistantships also available. Support available to part-time students. Financial award application deadline: 3/15; financial award applicants required to submit FAFSA. In 2018, 224 master's, 102 doctorates awarded. *Program availability:* Part-time, blended/hybrid learning. Offers agricultural development (M Agr); agricultural economics (M Agr, MS, PhD); agricultural education (Ed D); agricultural leadership, education and communication (M Ed, MS); agricultural systems management (M Agr, MS); agriculture and life sciences (M Agr, M Ed, M Engr, MEIM, MNRD, MRRD, MS, MWSc, Ed D, PhD); animal breeding, animal science (MS); animal science (M Agr); biochemistry (MS, PhD); biological and agricultural engineering (MS, PhD); ecosystem science and management (M Agr, MNRD, MS, PhD); entomology (MS); equine industry management (MEIM); food science and technology (M Agr, MS); horticulture (M Agr); nutrition (MS, PhD); physiology of reproduction (PhD); plant pathology (MS); poultry science (PhD); recreation and resources development (MRRD); recreation, park, and tourism science (PhD); soil science (MS, PhD); wildlife and fisheries sciences (MS); wildlife science (MWSc). *Application deadline:* For fall admission, 7/21 priority date for domestic students, 6/1 priority date for international students; for spring admission, 12/1 priority date for domestic students, 10/1 priority date for international students. Applications are processed on a rolling basis. *Application fee:* $50 ($90 for international students). Electronic applications accepted. *Application Contact:* Graduate Admissions, 979-845-1044, E-mail: graduate-admissions@tamu.edu. *Vice Chancellor and Dean for Agriculture and Life Sciences,* Dr. Mark A. Hussey, 979-845-4747, Fax: 979-845-9938, E-mail: mhussey@tamu.edu.

College of Architecture Students: 395 full-time (204 women), 53 part-time (26 women); includes 80 minority (13 Black or African American, non-Hispanic/Latino; 17 Asian, non-Hispanic/Latino; 48 Hispanic/Latino; 2 Two or more races, non-Hispanic/Latino; 207 international. Average age 28. 370 applicants, 80% accepted, 132 enrolled. *Faculty:* 117. Expenses: Contact institution. *Financial support:* In 2018–19, 360 students received support, including 11 fellowships with tuition reimbursements available (averaging $7,732 per year), 119 research assistantships with tuition reimbursements available (averaging $9,294 per year), 125 teaching assistantships with tuition reimbursements available (averaging $8,627 per year); career-related internships or fieldwork, institutionally sponsored loans, scholarships/grants, traineeships, health care benefits, tuition waivers (full and partial), and unspecified assistantships also available. Support available to part-time students. Financial award application deadline: 3/15; financial award applicants required to submit FAFSA. In 2018, 155 master's, 17 doctorates awarded. Offers architecture (M Arch, MS); construction management (MS); land and property development (MLPD); landscape architecture (MLA); urban and regional planning (MUP); urban and regional science (PhD); visualization (MS). *Application deadline:* For fall admission, 1/15 priority date for domestic and international students. Applications are processed on a rolling basis. *Application fee:* $50 ($90 for international students). Electronic applications accepted. *Application Contact:* Graduate Admissions, 979-458-0427, E-mail: admissions@tamu.edu. *Dean,* Dr. Jorge Vanegas, 979-845-1223, Fax: 979-845-4491, E-mail: jvanegas@arch.tamu.edu.

College of Dentistry Students: 503 full-time (265 women), 26 part-time (10 women); includes 288 minority (52 Black or African American, non-Hispanic/Latino; 1 American Indian or Alaska Native, non-Hispanic/Latino; 113 Asian, non-Hispanic/Latino; 112 Hispanic/Latino; 10 Two or more races, non-Hispanic/Latino; 26 international. Average age 27. 13 applicants, 62% accepted, 3 enrolled. *Faculty:* 45. Expenses: Contact institution. *Financial support:* In 2018–19, 276 students received support, including 24 research assistantships with tuition reimbursements available (averaging $12,742 per year), 45 teaching assistantships with tuition reimbursements available (averaging $20,772 per year); career-related internships or fieldwork, institutionally sponsored loans, scholarships/grants, traineeships, health care benefits, tuition waivers (full and partial), and unspecified assistantships also available. Support available to part-time students. Financial award applicants required to submit FAFSA. In 2018, 13 master's, 2 doctorates, 109 other advanced degrees awarded. Offers maxillofacial surgery (Certificate); pediatric dentistry (Certificate). *Application fee:* $35. Electronic applications accepted. *Application Contact:* Ernestine S. Lacy, Associate Dean for Student Affairs and Student Diversity, 214-828-8374, Fax: 214-874-4572, E-mail: eslacy@tamhsc.edu. *Dean,* Dr. Lawrence E. Wolinsky, 214-828-8300, E-mail: wolinsky@tamhsc.edu.

College of Education and Human Development Students: 721 full-time (531 women), 863 part-time (632 women); includes 560 minority (148 Black or African American, non-Hispanic/Latino; 6 American Indian or Alaska Native, non-Hispanic/Latino; 50 Asian, non-Hispanic/Latino; 328 Hispanic/Latino; 2 Native Hawaiian or other Pacific Islander, non-Hispanic/Latino; 26 Two or more races, non-Hispanic/Latino), 154 international. Average age 33. 589 applicants, 62% accepted, 283 enrolled. *Faculty:* 183. Expenses: Contact institution. *Financial support:* In 2018–19, 802 students received support, including 13 fellowships with tuition reimbursements available (averaging $22,861 per year), 221 research assistantships with tuition reimbursements available (averaging $10,462 per year), 132 teaching assistantships with tuition reimbursements available (averaging $9,872 per year); career-related internships or fieldwork, institutionally sponsored loans, scholarships/grants, traineeships, health care benefits, tuition waivers (full and partial), and unspecified assistantships also available. Support available to part-time students. Financial award application deadline: 3/15; financial award applicants required to submit FAFSA. In 2018, 531 master's, 108 doctorates awarded. *Program availability:* Part-time, evening/weekend, blended/hybrid learning. Offers athletic training (MS); bilingual education (M Ed, MS); counseling psychology (PhD); curriculum and instruction (M Ed, MS, Ed D, PhD); education and human development (M Ed, MS, Ed D, PhD); educational administration (M Ed, MS, Ed D); educational human resource development (PhD); educational psychology (M Ed, MS, PhD); educational technology (M Ed); health education (MS, PhD); kinesiology (MS, PhD); school psychology (PhD); special education (M Ed, MS); sports management (MS). *Application deadline:* Applications are processed on a rolling basis. *Application fee:* $50 ($90 for international students). Electronic applications accepted. *Application Contact:* Dr. Beverly Irby, Professor and Associate Dean for Academic Affairs, 979-845-5311, E-mail: beverly.irby@tamu.edu. *Professor and Dean,* Dr. Joyce Alexander, 979-862-6649, E-mail: joycemalexander@tamu.edu.

College of Engineering Students: 3,525 full-time (800 women), 691 part-time (138 women); includes 491 minority (57 Black or African American, non-Hispanic/Latino; 175 Asian, non-Hispanic/Latino; 215 Hispanic/Latino; 2 Native Hawaiian or other Pacific Islander, non-Hispanic/Latino; 42 Two or more races, non-Hispanic/Latino), 2,814 international. Average age 28. 8,711 applicants, 33% accepted, 1191 enrolled. *Faculty:* 525. Expenses: Contact institution. *Financial support:* In 2018–19, 2,779 students received support, including 355 fellowships with tuition reimbursements available (averaging $10,340 per year), 1,572 research assistantships with tuition reimbursements available (averaging $15,351 per year), 573 teaching assistantships with tuition reimbursements available (averaging $12,719 per year); career-related internships or fieldwork, institutionally sponsored loans, scholarships/grants, traineeships, health care benefits, tuition waivers (full and partial), and unspecified assistantships also available. Support available to part-time students. Financial award applicants required to submit FAFSA. In 2018, 987 master's, 262 doctorates awarded. *Program availability:* Part-time, online learning. Offers aerospace engineering (M Eng); biomedical engineering (PhD); chemical engineering (MS); civil engineering (M Eng, MS, PhD); computer engineering (M Eng, MS, PhD); computer science (MCS, MS, PhD); electrical engineering (M Eng); engineering (M Eng, MCS, METM, MID, MS, PhD); engineering systems management (MS); industrial distribution (MID); industrial engineering (M Eng, MS, PhD); materials science and engineering (M Eng); mechanical engineering (PhD); nuclear engineering (M Eng, PhD); petroleum engineering (M Eng); technical management (METM). *Application fee:* $50 ($90 for international students). Electronic applications accepted. *Application Contact:* Dr. John C. Criscione, Assistant Dean for Graduate Programs, 979-845-5428, E-mail: jccriscione@tamu.edu. *Dean and Vice Chancellor,* Dr. M. Katherine Banks, 979-845-1306, E-mail: k-banks@tamu.edu.

College of Geosciences Students: 261 full-time (98 women), 97 part-time (43 women); includes 64 minority (6 Black or African American, non-Hispanic/Latino; 1 American Indian or Alaska Native, non-Hispanic/Latino; 12 Asian, non-Hispanic/Latino; 37 Hispanic/Latino; 8 Two or more races, non-Hispanic/Latino), 119 international. Average age 30. 372 applicants, 36% accepted, 77 enrolled. *Faculty:* 101. Expenses: Contact institution. *Financial support:* In 2018–19, 244 students received support, including 62 fellowships with tuition reimbursements available (averaging $7,874 per year), 126 research assistantships with tuition reimbursements available (averaging $14,591 per year), 75 teaching assistantships with tuition reimbursements available (averaging $13,353 per year); career-related internships or fieldwork, institutionally sponsored

loans, traineeships, health care benefits, tuition waivers (full and partial), and unspecified assistantships also available. Support available to part-time students. Financial award application deadline: 3/15; financial award applicants required to submit FAFSA. In 2018, 52 master's, 23 doctorates awarded. *Program availability:* Part-time. Offers atmospheric science (MS); geography (MS); geology (MS, PhD); geophysics (PhD); geosciences (MS, PhD); oceanography (PhD). *Application deadline:* For fall admission, 1/1 priority date for domestic students; for spring admission, 8/15 for domestic students. Applications are processed on a rolling basis. *Application fee:* $50 ($90 for international students). Electronic applications accepted. *Application Contact:* Dr. Eric A. Riggs, Associate Professor/Associate Dean, 979-845-3651, E-mail: emriggs@geos.tamu.edu. *Dean,* Dr. Kate C. Miller, 979-845-3651, E-mail: dean@geosciences.tamu.edu.

College of Liberal Arts Students: 695 full-time (353 women), 148 part-time (79 women); includes 178 minority (31 Black or African American, non-Hispanic/Latino; 27 Asian, non-Hispanic/Latino; 110 Hispanic/Latino; 10 Two or more races, non-Hispanic/Latino), 328 international. Average age 30. 1,075 applicants, 41% accepted, 225 enrolled. *Faculty:* 331. Expenses: Contact institution. *Financial support:* In 2018–19, 630 students received support, including 58 fellowships with tuition reimbursements available (averaging $16,962 per year), 182 research assistantships with tuition reimbursements available (averaging $13,844 per year), 365 teaching assistantships with tuition reimbursements available (averaging $11,270 per year); career-related internships or fieldwork, institutionally sponsored loans, scholarships/grants, traineeships, health care benefits, tuition waivers (full and partial), unspecified assistantships, and assistant lecturer positions also available. Support available to part-time students. Financial award application deadline: 3/15; financial award applicants required to submit FAFSA. In 2018, 120 master's, 87 doctorates awarded. *Program availability:* Part-time. Offers anthropology (MA, PhD); clinical psychology (PhD); communication (PhD); economics (MS); English (PhD); Hispanic studies (PhD); history (PhD); liberal arts (MA, MS, PhD); maritime archaeology and conservation (MS); performance studies (MA); philosophy (MA); political science (PhD); psychology (MS); sociology (MS, PhD). *Application fee:* $50 ($90 for international students). Electronic applications accepted. *Application Contact:* Dr. Patricia A. Hurley, Associate Dean for Faculty and Graduate Programs, 979-845-8541, Fax: 979-845-5164, E-mail: pat-hurley@tamu.edu. *Dean,* Dr. Pamela R. Matthews, 979-862-6797, Fax: 979-845-5164, E-mail: p-matthews@tamu.edu.

College of Medicine Students: 1,530 full-time (742 women), 48 part-time (32 women); includes 776 minority (48 Black or African American, non-Hispanic/Latino; 2 American Indian or Alaska Native, non-Hispanic/Latino; 508 Asian, non-Hispanic/Latino; 172 Hispanic/Latino; 46 Two or more races, non-Hispanic/Latino), 102 international. Average age 27. 140 applicants, 31% accepted, 38 enrolled. *Faculty:* 72. Expenses: Contact institution. *Financial support:* In 2018–19, 322 students received support, including 2 fellowships with tuition reimbursements available (averaging $4,125 per year), 112 research assistantships with tuition reimbursements available (averaging $22,494 per year); career-related internships or fieldwork, institutionally sponsored loans, scholarships/grants, traineeships, health care benefits, tuition waivers (full and partial), and unspecified assistantships also available. Support available to part-time students. Financial award applicants required to submit FAFSA. In 2018, 10 master's, 44 doctorates awarded. Offers medical sciences (PhD); medicine (MD). *Application deadline:* For fall admission, 9/30 for domestic students. *Application fee:* $200. Electronic applications accepted. *Application Contact:* Filomeno G. Maldonado, Associate Dean of Admissions, 979-436-0231, Fax: 979-436-0097, E-mail: fgmaldonado@medicine.tamhsc.edu. *Interim Senior Vice President and Chief Operating Officer,* Dr. Paul E. Ogden, MD, 979-436-0202, Fax: 979-436-0092, E-mail: ogden@medicine.tamhsc.edu.

College of Nursing Students: 5 full-time (all women), 71 part-time (62 women); includes 20 minority (2 Black or African American, non-Hispanic/Latino; 1 American Indian or Alaska Native, non-Hispanic/Latino; 2 Asian, non-Hispanic/Latino; 14 Hispanic/Latino; 1 Two or more races, non-Hispanic/Latino). Average age 35. 90 applicants, 37% accepted, 24 enrolled. *Faculty:* 19. Expenses: Contact institution. *Financial support:* In 2018–19, 14 students received support, including 3 fellowships (averaging $1,400 per year), 1 research assistantship (averaging $1,043 per year); career-related internships or fieldwork, institutionally sponsored loans, scholarships/grants, traineeships, health care benefits, tuition waivers (full and partial), and unspecified assistantships also available. Support available to part-time students. Financial award applicants required to submit FAFSA. In 2018, 23 master's awarded. Offers family nurse practitioner (MSN); forensic nursing (MSN); nursing education (MSN). *Application Contact:* Jennifer Frank, Program Coordinator for Recruitment and Admission, 979-436-0110, E-mail: conadmissions@tamhsc.edu. *Founding Dean,* Dr. Sharon A. Wilkerson, 979-436-0111, Fax: 979-436-0098, E-mail: wilkerson@tamhsc.edu.

College of Science Students: 886 full-time (250 women), 423 part-time (148 women); includes 242 minority (24 Black or African American, non-Hispanic/Latino; 2 American Indian or Alaska Native, non-Hispanic/Latino; 107 Asian, non-Hispanic/Latino; 82 Hispanic/Latino; 27 Two or more races, non-Hispanic/Latino), 487 international. Average age 30. 1,109 applicants, 51% accepted, 314 enrolled. *Faculty:* 247. Expenses: Contact institution. *Financial support:* In 2018–19, 778 students received support, including 128 fellowships with tuition reimbursements available (averaging $10,667 per year), 287 research assistantships with tuition reimbursements available (averaging $15,719 per year), 448 teaching assistantships with tuition reimbursements available (averaging $18,576 per year); career-related internships or fieldwork, institutionally sponsored loans, scholarships/grants, traineeships, health care benefits, tuition waivers (full and partial), and unspecified assistantships also available. Support available to part-time students. Financial award applicants required to submit FAFSA. In 2018, 176 master's, 137 doctorates awarded. *Program availability:* Part-time. Offers analytics (MS); applied physics (PhD); astronomy (MS); biology (PhD); chemistry (MS); mathematics (MS, PhD); microbiology (MS, PhD); physics (PhD); quantitative finance (MS); science (MS, PhD); statistics (MS, PhD). *Application fee:* $50 ($90 for international students). *Application Contact:* Mark Zoran, Associate Dean for Graduate Studies, 979-458-8001, Fax: 979-845-6077, E-mail: zoran@science.tamu.edu. *Dean,* Dr. Meigan Aronson, 979-845-8817, Fax: 979-845-6077, E-mail: maronson@science.tamu.edu.

College of Veterinary Medicine and Biomedical Sciences Students: 762 full-time (582 women), 42 part-time (36 women); includes 196 minority (22 Black or African American, non-Hispanic/Latino; 45 Asian, non-Hispanic/Latino; 110 Hispanic/Latino; 19 Two or more races, non-Hispanic/Latino), 44 international. Average age 26. 274 applicants, 80% accepted, 198 enrolled. *Faculty:* 130. Expenses: Contact institution. *Financial support:* In 2018–19, 752 students received support, including 23 fellowships with tuition reimbursements available (averaging $18,131 per year), 113 research assistantships with tuition reimbursements available (averaging $17,994 per year), 31 teaching assistantships with tuition reimbursements available (averaging $15,356 per year); career-related internships or fieldwork, institutionally sponsored loans, scholarships/grants, traineeships, health care benefits, tuition waivers (full and partial), unspecified assistantships, and clinical associateships also available. Support available to part-time students. Financial award application deadline: 3/15; financial award applicants required to submit FAFSA. In 2018, 88 master's, 21 doctorates awarded. *Program availability:* Part-time. Offers veterinary medicine and biomedical sciences (MS, DVM, PhD). *Application deadline:* For fall admission, 6/1 for domestic students, 3/1 for international students; for spring admission, 11/1 for domestic students, 8/1 for international students; for summer admission, 3/1 for domestic students, 12/1 for international students. *Application fee:* $50 ($90 for international students). *Application Contact:* Graduate Admissions, 979-845-1044, E-mail: admissions@tamu.edu. *Dean,* Dr. Eleanor M. Green, 979-845-5053, Fax: 979-845-5088, E-mail: emgreen@tamu.edu.

Galveston Campus Students: 175 full-time (76 women), 45 part-time (9 women); includes 43 minority (5 Black or African American, non-Hispanic/Latino; 15 Asian, non-Hispanic/Latino; 15 Hispanic/Latino; 8 Two or more races, non-Hispanic/Latino), 9 international. Average age 28. 64 applicants, 95% accepted, 48 enrolled. *Faculty:* 56. Expenses: Contact institution. *Financial support:* In 2018–19, 106 students received support, including 1 fellowship with tuition reimbursement available (averaging $34,000 per year), 53 research assistantships with tuition reimbursements available (averaging $9,421 per year), 60 teaching assistantships with tuition reimbursements available (averaging $14,587 per year). In 2018, 96 master's, 3 doctorates awarded. Offers marine biology (MS); marine resources management (MMRM); maritime administration and logistics (MMAL). *Application Contact:* Nicole Kinslow, Director of Graduate Studies, 409-740-4937, Fax: 409-740-4754, E-mail: kinslown@tamug.edu.

Irma Lerma Rangel College of Pharmacy Students: 278 full-time (184 women), 80 part-time (53 women); includes 148 minority (44 Black or African American, non-Hispanic/Latino; 31 Asian, non-Hispanic/Latino; 66 Hispanic/Latino; 1 Native Hawaiian or other Pacific Islander, non-Hispanic/Latino; 6 Two or more races, non-Hispanic/Latino), 80 international. Average age 29. 169 applicants, 100% accepted, 135 enrolled. *Faculty:* 59. Expenses: Contact institution. *Financial support:* In 2018–19, 163 students received support, including 1 teaching assistantship (averaging $13,500 per year); career-related internships or fieldwork, institutionally sponsored loans, scholarships/grants, traineeships, health care benefits, tuition waivers (full and partial), and unspecified assistantships also available. Support available to part-time students. Financial award applicants required to submit FAFSA. In 2018, 9 doctorates awarded. Offers pharmacy (Pharm D). *Application deadline:* For fall admission, 11/1 for domestic students. *Application fee:* $100. Electronic applications accepted. *Application Contact:* Maria de Leon, Director of Admission, 361-221-0642, E-mail: mdeleon@tamhsc.edu. *Dean,* Dr. Indra K. Reddy, 361-593-4273, Fax: 361-593-4929, E-mail: ireddy@pharmacy.tamhsc.edu.

Mays Business School Students: 1,170 full-time (498 women), 21 part-time (8 women); includes 219 minority (28 Black or African American, non-Hispanic/Latino; 2 American Indian or Alaska Native, non-Hispanic/Latino; 68 Asian, non-Hispanic/Latino; 114 Hispanic/Latino; 7 Two or more races, non-Hispanic/Latino), 274 international. Average age 27. 1,617 applicants, 45% accepted, 415 enrolled. *Faculty:* 116. Expenses: Contact institution. *Financial support:* In 2018–19, 823 students received support, including 77 fellowships with tuition reimbursements available (averaging $4,347 per year), 134 research assistantships with tuition reimbursements available (averaging $12,080 per year), 112 teaching assistantships with tuition reimbursements available (averaging $6,604 per year); career-related internships or fieldwork, institutionally sponsored loans, scholarships/grants, traineeships, health care benefits, tuition waivers, and unspecified assistantships also available. Support available to part-time students. Financial award application deadline: 3/15; financial award applicants required to submit FAFSA. In 2018, 754 master's awarded. Offers accounting (MS); business (MBA, MFM, MRE, MS); entrepreneurial leadership (MS); finance (MS); financial management (MFM); human resource management (MS); land economics and real estate (MRE); management information systems (MS); marketing (MS). *Application deadline:* Applications are processed on a rolling basis. *Application fee:* $50 ($90 for international students). Electronic applications accepted. *Application Contact:* Director, MBA Program, 979-845-4714, Fax: 979-862-2393, E-mail: msprogram@mays.tamu.edu. *Dean,* Dr. Eli Jones, 979-845-4711, Fax: 979-845-6639, E-mail: elijones@tamu.edu.

School of Law Students: 465 full-time (251 women), 112 part-time (39 women); includes 174 minority (38 Black or African American, non-Hispanic/Latino; 5 American Indian or Alaska Native, non-Hispanic/Latino; 14 Asian, non-Hispanic/Latino; 112 Hispanic/Latino; 5 Two or more races, non-Hispanic/Latino), 5 international. Average age 30. 463 applicants, 100% accepted, 233 enrolled. *Faculty:* 82. Expenses: Contact institution. *Financial support:* In 2018–19, 447 students received support, including 4 fellowships with tuition reimbursements available (averaging $20,207 per year); career-related internships or fieldwork, institutionally sponsored loans, scholarships/grants, traineeships, health care benefits, and tuition waivers (full and partial) also available. Support available to part-time students. Financial award applicants required to submit FAFSA. In 2018, 1 master's awarded. Offers intellectual property (M Jur); jurisprudence (M Jur); law (JD). *Application deadline:* For fall admission, 7/1 for domestic students. Applications are processed on a rolling basis. *Application fee:* $55. *Application Contact:* Law School Admissions, 817-212-4040, E-mail: law-admissions@law.tamu.edu. *Dean,* Dr. Andrew P. Morriss, 817-212-4139, Fax: 817-212-4139, E-mail: amorriss@law.tamu.edu.

School of Public Health Students: 278 full-time (184 women), 80 part-time (53 women); includes 147 minority (44 Black or African American, non-Hispanic/Latino; 31 Asian, non-Hispanic/Latino; 66 Hispanic/Latino; 6 Two or more races, non-Hispanic/Latino), 80 international. Average age 29. 169 applicants, 100% accepted, 135 enrolled. *Faculty:* 59. Expenses: Contact institution. *Financial support:* In 2018–19, 199 students received support, including 6 fellowships with tuition reimbursements available (averaging $18,326 per year), 53 research assistantships with tuition reimbursements available (averaging $13,190 per year), 28 teaching assistantships with tuition reimbursements available (averaging $17,245 per year); career-related internships or fieldwork, institutionally sponsored loans, scholarships/grants, traineeships, health care benefits, tuition waivers (full and partial), and unspecified assistantships also available. Support available to part-time students. Financial award applicants required to submit FAFSA. In 2018, 142 master's, 9 doctorates awarded. *Program availability:* Part-time, blended/hybrid learning. Offers biostatistics (MPH, MSPH); environmental health (MPH, MSPH); epidemiology (MPH, MSPH); health administration (MHA); health policy and management (MPH); health services research (PhD); occupational safety and health (MPH). *Application fee:* $120. Electronic applications accepted. *Application Contact:* Erin E. Schneider, Associate Director of Admissions and Recruitment, 979-436-9380, E-mail: eschneider@sph.tamhsc.edu. *Dean,* Dr. Jay Maddock, 979-436-9322, Fax: 979-458-1878, E-mail: maddock@tamhsc.edu.

TEXAS A&M UNIVERSITY–CENTRAL TEXAS, Killeen, TX 76549

General Information State-supported, coed, upper-level institution. CGS member.

GRADUATE UNITS

Graduate Studies and Research

TEXAS A&M UNIVERSITY–COMMERCE, Commerce, TX 75429

General Information State-supported, coed, university. CGS member. *Enrollment:* 1,071 full-time matriculated graduate/professional students (668 women), 2,868 part-time matriculated graduate/professional students (1,909 women). *Enrollment by degree level:* 3,311 master's, 525 doctoral, 103 other advanced degrees. *Graduate faculty:* 247 full-time (108 women), 50 part-time/adjunct (26 women). *International tuition:* $11,100 full-time. *Tuition, area resident:* Full-time $3630. Tuition, state resident: full-time $3630. Tuition, nonresident: full-time $11,100. *Required fees:* $2794. Tuition and fees vary according to course load, degree level and program. *Graduate housing:* Rooms and/or apartments available on a first-come, first-served basis to single and married students. Typical cost: $5158 per year ($7950 including board) for single students; $5254 per year ($8154 including board) for married students. Room and board charges vary according to board plan and housing facility selected. *Student services:* Campus employment opportunities, campus safety program, career counseling, child daycare facilities, exercise/wellness program, free psychological counseling, international student services, multicultural affairs office, services for students with disabilities, teacher training, writing training. *Library facilities:* Gee Library.

Computer facilities: A campuswide network can be accessed from student residence rooms and from off campus. Online class registration is available. Website: http://www.tamuc.edu/

General Application Contact: Kimberly Stringer, Graduate Liaison, 903-468-3066, E-mail: kimberly.stringer@tamuc.edu.

GRADUATE UNITS

College of Agricultural Sciences and Natural Resources Students: 21 full-time (14 women), 31 part-time (24 women); includes 15 minority (1 Black or African American, non-Hispanic/Latino; 1 American Indian or Alaska Native, non-Hispanic/Latino; 1 Asian, non-Hispanic/Latino; 7 Hispanic/Latino; 5 Two or more races, non-Hispanic/Latino), 3 international. Average age 27. 27 applicants, 59% accepted, 13 enrolled. *Faculty:* 9 full-time (1 woman), 1 (woman) part-time/adjunct. Expenses: Contact institution. *Financial support:* In 2018–19, 17 students received support, including 45 research assistantships with partial tuition reimbursements available (averaging $2,736 per year), 1 teaching assistantship with partial tuition reimbursement available (averaging $4,725 per year); career-related internships or fieldwork, Federal Work-Study, institutionally sponsored loans, scholarships/grants, health care benefits, and unspecified assistantships also available. Financial award application deadline: 5/1; financial award applicants required to submit FAFSA. In 2018, 21 master's awarded. *Program availability:* Part-time, evening/weekend, 100% online, blended/hybrid learning. Offers agricultural sciences (MS). *Application deadline:* For fall admission, 6/1 priority date for international students; for spring admission, 10/15 priority date for international students; for summer admission, 10/15 priority date for international students. Applications are processed on a rolling basis. *Application fee:* $50 ($75 for international students). Electronic applications accepted. *Application Contact:* Vicky Turner, Doctoral Degree and Special Programs Coordinator, 903-886-5167, E-mail: vicky.turner@tamuc.edu. *Dean,* Dr. Randy Harp, 903-886-5351, Fax: 903-886-5990, E-mail: randy.harp@tamuc.edu.

College of Business Students: 391 full-time (209 women), 948 part-time (511 women); includes 583 minority (249 Black or African American, non-Hispanic/Latino; 4 American Indian or Alaska Native, non-Hispanic/Latino; 89 Asian, non-Hispanic/Latino; 205 Hispanic/Latino; 1 Native Hawaiian or other Pacific Islander, non-Hispanic/Latino; 35 Two or more races, non-Hispanic/Latino), 156 international. Average age 33. 930 applicants, 58% accepted, 355 enrolled. *Faculty:* 48 full-time (15 women), 2 part-time/adjunct (1 woman). Expenses: Contact institution. *Financial support:* In 2018–19, 61 students received support, including 57 research assistantships with partial tuition reimbursements available (averaging $3,286 per year); Federal Work-Study, institutionally sponsored loans, scholarships/grants, health care benefits, and unspecified assistantships also available. Financial award application deadline: 5/1; financial award applicants required to submit FAFSA. In 2018, 628 master's awarded. *Program availability:* Part-time, evening/weekend, 100% online, blended/hybrid learning. Offers accounting (MSA); business administration (MBA); business analytics (MS); finance (MSF); management (MS); marketing (MS). *Application deadline:* For fall admission, 6/1 priority date for international students; for spring admission, 10/15 priority date for international students; for summer admission, 3/15 priority date for international students. Applications are processed on a rolling basis. *Application fee:* $50 ($75 for international students). Electronic applications accepted. *Application Contact:* Shanna Hoskison, Director, Graduate Advising, 903-886-5190, E-mail: shanna.hoskison@tamuc.edu. *Dean of College of Business,* Dr. Shanan Gwaltney Gibson, 903-886-5191, Fax: 903-886-5650, E-mail: shanan.gibson@tamuc.edu.

College of Education and Human Services Students: 356 full-time (295 women), 1,262 part-time (992 women); includes 683 minority (349 Black or African American, non-Hispanic/Latino; 9 American Indian or Alaska Native, non-Hispanic/Latino; 30 Asian, non-Hispanic/Latino; 238 Hispanic/Latino; 57 Two or more races, non-Hispanic/Latino), 9 international. Average age 37. 951 applicants, 42% accepted, 304 enrolled. *Faculty:* 95 full-time (59 women), 29 part-time/adjunct (22 women). Expenses: Contact institution. *Financial support:* In 2018–19, 116 students received support, including 94 research assistantships with partial tuition reimbursements available (averaging $3,863 per year), 38 teaching assistantships with partial tuition reimbursements available (averaging $4,728 per year); career-related internships or fieldwork, Federal Work-Study, institutionally sponsored loans, scholarships/grants, health care benefits, and unspecified assistantships also available. Financial award application deadline: 5/1; financial award applicants required to submit FAFSA. In 2018, 532 master's, 51 doctorates awarded. *Program availability:* Part-time, evening/weekend, 100% online, blended/hybrid learning. Offers counseling (M Ed, MS, PhD); early childhood education (M Ed, MS); educational administration (M Ed, MS, Ed D); educational psychology (PhD); educational technology leadership (M Ed, MS); educational technology library science (M Ed, MS); elementary education (M Ed); health, kinesiology and sports studies (MS); higher education (MS, Ed D); psychology (MS); reading (M Ed, MS); school psychology (SSP); secondary education (M Ed, MS); social work (MSW); special education (M Ed, MS); supervision, curriculum and instruction-elementary education (Ed D); training and development (MS). *Application deadline:* For fall admission, 6/1 priority date for international students; for spring admission, 10/15 priority date for international students; for summer admission, 3/15 priority date for international students. Applications are processed on a rolling basis. *Application fee:* $50 ($75 for international students). Electronic applications accepted. *Application Contact:* Vicky Turner, Doctoral Degree and Special Programs Coordinator, 903-886-5167, E-mail: vicky.turner@tamuc.edu. *Interim Dean,* Dr. Madeline Justice, 903-886-5181, Fax: 903-886-5905, E-mail: madeline.justice@tamuc.edu.

College of Humanities, Social Sciences and Arts Students: 125 full-time (83 women), 393 part-time (278 women); includes 197 minority (75 Black or African American, non-Hispanic/Latino; 2 American Indian or Alaska Native, non-Hispanic/Latino; 13 Asian, non-Hispanic/Latino; 92 Hispanic/Latino; 1 Native Hawaiian or other Pacific Islander, non-Hispanic/Latino; 14 Two or more races, non-Hispanic/Latino, 16 international. Average age 37. 261 applicants, 46% accepted, 106 enrolled. *Faculty:* 50 full-time (26 women), 11 part-time/adjunct (2 women). Expenses: Contact institution. *Financial support:* In 2018–19, 39 students received support, including 18 research assistantships with partial tuition reimbursements available (averaging $3,231 per year), 136 teaching assistantships with partial tuition reimbursements available (averaging $4,053 per year); Federal Work-Study, institutionally sponsored loans, scholarships/grants, health care benefits, and unspecified assistantships also available. Financial award application deadline: 5/1; financial award applicants required to submit FAFSA. In 2018, 124 master's, 8 doctorates awarded. *Program availability:* Part-time. Offers applied criminology (MS); applied linguistics (MA, MS); art (MA, MFA); computational linguistics (Graduate Certificate); creative writing (Graduate Certificate); criminal justice management (Graduate Certificate); criminal justice studies (Graduate Certificate); English (MA, MS, PhD); film studies (Graduate Certificate); history (MA, MS); history of Christianity (Graduate Certificate); Holocaust studies (Graduate Certificate); homeland security (Graduate Certificate); music (MM); music performance (MM); political science (MA, MS); public history (Graduate Certificate); sociology (MS); Spanish (MA); studies in children's and adolescent literature and culture (Graduate Certificate); teaching English to speakers of other languages (Graduate Certificate); theater (MA, MS); world history (Graduate Certificate). *Application deadline:* For fall admission, 6/1 priority date for international students; for spring admission, 10/15 priority date for international students; for summer admission, 3/15 priority date for international students. Applications are processed on a rolling basis. *Application fee:* $50 ($75 for international students). Electronic applications accepted. *Application Contact:* Vicky Turner, Doctoral Degree and Special Programs Coordinator, 903-886-5167, E-mail: vicky.turner@tamuc.edu. *Interim Dean,* Dr. William F. Kuracina, 903-886-5166, Fax: 903-886-5774, E-mail: william.kuracina@tamuc.edu.

College of Science and Engineering Students: 178 full-time (67 women), 234 part-time (104 women); includes 82 minority (19 Black or African American, non-Hispanic/Latino; 1 American Indian or Alaska Native, non-Hispanic/Latino; 14 Asian, non-Hispanic/Latino; 37 Hispanic/Latino; 11 Two or more races, non-Hispanic/Latino), 158 international. Average age 30. 481 applicants, 52% accepted, 105 enrolled. *Faculty:* 44 full-time (7 women), 7 part-time/adjunct (0 women). Expenses: Contact institution. *Financial support:* In 2018–19, 46 students received support, including 43 research assistantships with partial tuition reimbursements available (averaging $2,418 per year), 135 teaching assistantships with partial tuition reimbursements available (averaging $3,376 per year); scholarships/grants, health care benefits, and unspecified assistantships also available. Financial award application deadline: 5/1; financial award applicants required to submit FAFSA. In 2018, 218 master's awarded. *Program availability:* Part-time. Offers biological sciences (MS); broadfield science biology (MS); broadfield science chemistry (MS); broadfield science physics (MS); chemistry (MS); computational linguistics (Graduate Certificate); computational science (MS); computer science (MS); environmental science (Graduate Certificate); mathematics (MS); physics (MS); technology management (MS). *Application deadline:* For fall admission, 6/1 priority date for international students; for spring admission, 10/15 priority date for international students; for summer admission, 3/15 priority date for international students. Applications are processed on a rolling basis. *Application fee:* $50 ($75 for international students). Electronic applications accepted. *Application Contact:* Dayla Burgin, Graduate Student Services Coordinator, 903-886-5134, E-mail: dayla.burgin@tamuc.edu. *Dean,* Dr. Brent L. Donham, 903-886-5321, Fax: 903-886-5199, E-mail: brent.donham@tamuc.edu.

TEXAS A&M UNIVERSITY–CORPUS CHRISTI, Corpus Christi, TX 78412

General Information State-supported, coed, university. CGS member. *Graduate housing:* Room and/or apartments available on a first-come, first-served basis to single students; on-campus housing not available to married students. Housing application deadline: 5/1.

GRADUATE UNITS

College of Graduate Studies *Program availability:* Part-time, evening/weekend, 100% online, blended/hybrid learning. Electronic applications accepted.

College of Business *Program availability:* Part-time, evening/weekend, 100% online, blended/hybrid learning. Offers accounting (M Acc); business (MBA); finance (MBA); health care administration (MBA); international business (MBA). Electronic applications accepted.

College of Education and Human Development *Program availability:* Part-time, evening/weekend, blended/hybrid learning. Offers counseling (MS); counselor education (PhD); curriculum and instruction (MS, PhD); early childhood education (MS); educational administration (MS); educational leadership (Ed D); elementary education (MS); instructional design and educational technology (MS); kinesiology (MS); reading (MS); secondary education (MS); special education (MS). Electronic applications accepted.

College of Liberal Arts *Program availability:* Part-time, evening/weekend. Offers clinical psychology (MA); communication (MA); English (MA); general psychology (MA); history (MA); psychology (MA); public administration (MPA); studio art (MFA). Electronic applications accepted.

College of Nursing and Health Sciences *Program availability:* Part-time, evening/weekend, online only, 100% online. Offers family nurse practitioner (MSN); leadership in nursing systems (MSN); nurse educator (MSN); nursing practice (DNP). Electronic applications accepted.

College of Science and Engineering *Program availability:* Part-time, evening/weekend. Offers biology (MS, PhD); chemistry (MS); coastal and marine system science (MS); computer science (MS); environmental science (MS); fisheries and mariculture (MS); geospatial computing sciences (PhD); geospatial surveying engineering (MS); marine biology (MS, PhD); mathematics (MS). Electronic applications accepted.

TEXAS A&M UNIVERSITY–KINGSVILLE, Kingsville, TX 78363

General Information State-supported, coed, university. *Graduate housing:* Room and/or apartments available on a first-come, first-served basis to single students; on-campus housing not available to married students. Housing application deadline: 8/1. *Research affiliation:* American Chemical Society (chemistry: the use of terminally-functionalized atactic-polypropylene oligomers as supports for catalysis), Texas Citrus Producers Board (agriculture: citrus center grapefruit research), ExxonMobil, East Wildlife Foundation (agriculture: bird populations, deer research), The Brown Foundation (agriculture: invasive grass research), Wildlife Pharmaceuticals, Inc. (agriculture: deer).

GRADUATE UNITS

College of Graduate Studies *Program availability:* Part-time, online learning. Electronic applications accepted.

College of Arts and Sciences Offers arts and sciences (MA, MM, MS, MSW); biology (MS); chemistry (MS); communication sciences and disorders (MS); criminology (MS); cultural studies (MA); elementary music (MM); English (MA, MS); Hispanic culture (PhD); instrumental (MM); instrumental performance (MM); mathematics (MS); music (MM); music education (MM); psychology (MA, MS); social work (MSW); sociology (MA, MS); Spanish (MA); statistical analytics, computing and modeling (MS); vocal (MM); vocal performance (MM). Electronic applications accepted.

College of Business Administration *Program availability:* Online only, 100% online, blended/hybrid learning. Offers business administration (MBA). Electronic applications accepted.

College of Education and Human Performance *Program availability:* 100% online, blended/hybrid learning. Offers adult education (M Ed); bilingual education (M Ed, Ed D); counseling and guidance (MA, MS); early childhood education (M Ed); education and human performance (M Ed, MA, MS, Ed D, Certificate); educational administration (MA, MS); educational leadership (Ed D); health and kinesiology (MA, MS); instructional technology (MS); reading specialization (MS); science in education (MS); special education (M Ed). Electronic applications accepted.

Dick and Mary Lewis Kleberg College of Agriculture, Natural Resources and Human Sciences Offers agribusiness (MS); agricultural science (MS); agriculture, natural resources and human sciences (MS, PhD); animal science (MS); horticulture (PhD); human sciences (MS); plant and soil science (MS); ranch management (MS); range and wildlife management (MS); wildlife science (PhD). Electronic applications accepted.

Frank H. Dotterweich College of Engineering Offers chemical engineering (ME, MS); civil engineering (ME, MS); computer science (MS); electrical engineering (ME, MS); engineering (ME, MS, PhD); environmental engineering (ME, MS, PhD); industrial engineering (ME, MS); industrial management (MS); mechanical engineering (ME, MS); natural gas engineering (ME, MS); sustainable energy systems engineering (PhD). Electronic applications accepted.

TEXAS A&M UNIVERSITY–SAN ANTONIO, San Antonio, TX 78224

General Information State-supported, coed, comprehensive institution. *Graduate housing:* On-campus housing not available.

GRADUATE UNITS

Department of Counseling, Health and Kinesiology *Program availability:* Part-time, evening/weekend, online learning. Offers clinical mental health counseling (MA); counseling and guidance (MA); kinesiology (MS); marriage and family counseling (MA). Electronic applications accepted.

Department of Educator and Leadership Preparation *Program availability:* Part-time, evening/weekend, online learning. Offers bilingual education (MS); early childhood education (M Ed); educational administration (MA); reading specialization (MS); special education (M Ed). Electronic applications accepted.

School of Arts and Sciences *Program availability:* Part-time, evening/weekend, online learning. Offers English (MA). Electronic applications accepted.

School of Business *Program availability:* Part-time, evening/weekend, online learning. Offers business administration (MBA); professional accounting (MPA). Electronic applications accepted.

TEXAS A&M UNIVERSITY–TEXARKANA, Texarkana, TX 75503

General Information State-supported, coed, comprehensive institution. *Graduate housing:* On-campus housing not available.

GRADUATE UNITS

Graduate Studies and Research *Program availability:* Part-time, evening/weekend. Electronic applications accepted.

College of Business *Program availability:* Part-time, evening/weekend. Offers accounting (MSA); business administration (MBA, MS). Electronic applications accepted.

College of Education and Liberal Arts *Program availability:* Part-time, evening/weekend. Offers adult education (MS); curriculum and instruction (M Ed); education (MS); educational administration (M Ed); English (MA); instructional technology (MS); interdisciplinary studies (MA, MS); special education (MS). Electronic applications accepted.

College of Health and Behavioral Sciences *Program availability:* Part-time, evening/weekend. Offers counseling psychology (MS). Electronic applications accepted.

TEXAS CHIROPRACTIC COLLEGE, Pasadena, TX 77505-1699

General Information Independent, coed, graduate-only institution. *Graduate housing:* On-campus housing not available.

GRADUATE UNITS

Professional Program Offers chiropractic (DC).

TEXAS CHRISTIAN UNIVERSITY, Fort Worth, TX 76129-0002

General Information Independent-religious, coed, university. CGS member. *Graduate housing:* Rooms and/or apartments available on a first-come, first-served basis to single and married students. Housing application deadline: 5/1. *Research affiliation:* Lockheed Martin Corporation (business), Botanical Research Institute of Texas, Inc. (biology, environmental science, ranch management), The University of Texas Southwestern Medical School (health sciences), NextEra (environmental science, wind energy), University of North Texas Health Science Center at Fort Worth (physics, biology), Bell Helicopter (engineering).

GRADUATE UNITS

AddRan College of Liberal Arts Students: 208 full-time (108 women), 33 part-time (26 women); includes 70 minority (16 Black or African American, non-Hispanic/Latino; 1 American Indian or Alaska Native, non-Hispanic/Latino; 1 Asian, non-Hispanic/Latino; 41 Hispanic/Latino; 1 Native Hawaiian or other Pacific Islander, non-Hispanic/Latino; 10 Two or more races, non-Hispanic/Latino), 9 international. Average age 33. 76 applicants, 58% accepted, 38 enrolled. *Faculty:* 58 full-time (25 women), 9 part-time/adjunct (1 woman). Expenses: Contact institution. *Financial support:* Fellowships, research assistantships, teaching assistantships, career-related internships or fieldwork, Federal Work-Study, institutionally sponsored loans, traineeships, health care benefits, tuition waivers, and unspecified assistantships available. Support available to part-time students. In 2018, 19 master's, 11 doctorates awarded. Offers criminal justice and criminology (MS); English (MA, PhD); Latin America (MA, PhD); liberal arts (MA, MS, PhD); rhetoric and composition (PhD); United States (MA, PhD). *Application Contact:*

Admissions, TCU Graduate Studies Office, 817-257-7515, Fax: 817-257-7484, E-mail: frogmail@tcu.edu. *Associate Dean*, Dr. Don M. Coerver, 817-257-6290, Fax: 817-257-7709, E-mail: d.coerver@tcu.edu.

Bob Schieffer College of Communication Students: 21 full-time (18 women), 2 part-time (1 woman); includes 5 minority (1 Asian, non-Hispanic/Latino; 4 Hispanic/Latino). Average age 25. 24 applicants, 71% accepted, 12 enrolled. *Faculty:* 26 full-time (12 women). Expenses: Contact institution. *Financial support:* In 2018–19, 23 students received support, including 20 teaching assistantships with full tuition reimbursements available (averaging $12,500 per year); health care benefits, tuition waivers (full and partial), and unspecified assistantships also available. Financial award application deadline: 2/15. In 2018, 16 master's awarded. *Program availability:* Part-time. Offers communication studies (MS); strategic communication (MS). *Application deadline:* For fall admission, 2/15 for domestic and international students; for spring admission, 10/15 for domestic and international students. Applications are processed on a rolling basis. *Application fee:* $60. Electronic applications accepted. *Application Contact:* Ashley Tully, Coordinator of Degree of Certification, 817-257-4935, Fax: 817-257-5921, E-mail: A.TULLY@tcu.edu. *Associate Dean*, Dr. Julie O'Neil, 817-257-6966, Fax: 817-257-5921, E-mail: j.oneil@tcu.edu.

College of Education Students: 204 full-time (151 women), 40 part-time (25 women); includes 93 minority (29 Black or African American, non-Hispanic/Latino; 2 American Indian or Alaska Native, non-Hispanic/Latino; 9 Asian, non-Hispanic/Latino; 45 Hispanic/Latino; 8 Two or more races, non-Hispanic/Latino), 7 international. Average age 33. 195 applicants, 72% accepted, 109 enrolled. *Faculty:* 29 full-time (21 women), 3 part-time/adjunct (1 woman). Expenses: Contact institution. *Financial support:* In 2018–19, 201 students received support, including 1 fellowship with full tuition reimbursement available (averaging $18,500 per year), 9 research assistantships with full tuition reimbursements available (averaging $18,500 per year), 39 teaching assistantships with full tuition reimbursements available (averaging $15,000 per year); career-related internships or fieldwork, scholarships/grants, health care benefits, and unspecified assistantships also available. Support available to part-time students. Financial award application deadline: 2/1. In 2018, 62 master's, 12 doctorates awarded. *Program availability:* Part-time, evening/weekend. Offers counseling (M Ed); counseling and counselor education (PhD); curriculum and instruction (M Ed); curriculum studies (PhD); education (MAT); educational leadership (M Ed, Ed D); higher educational leadership (Ed D); science education (PhD); special education (M Ed). *Application deadline:* For fall admission, 2/1 for domestic and international students; for spring admission, 11/16 for domestic and international students; for summer admission, 2/1 for domestic and international students. *Application fee:* $60. Electronic applications accepted. *Application Contact:* Lori Kimball, Graduate Coordinator, 817-257-7661, Fax: 817-257-7466, E-mail: l.kimball@tcu.edu. *Interim Dean*, Dr. Jan Lacina, 817-257-6786, Fax: 817-257-7466, E-mail: j.lacina@tcu.edu.

College of Fine Arts Average age 27. 95 applicants, 44% accepted, 31 enrolled. Expenses: Contact institution. *Financial support:* In 2018–19, 66 students received support, including 88 teaching assistantships with full tuition reimbursements available (averaging $34,120 per year); career-related internships or fieldwork, scholarships/grants, health care benefits, tuition waivers (full and partial), and unspecified assistantships also available. Financial award application deadline: 2/15. In 2018, 25 master's, 3 doctorates awarded. Offers fine arts (M Mus, MA, MFA, MM Ed, DMA, Artist Diploma). *Application deadline:* For fall admission, 2/1 for domestic and international students; for spring admission, 10/1 for domestic and international students. *Application fee:* $60. Electronic applications accepted. *Application Contact:* Donna Smolik, TCU College of Fine Arts Graduate Office, 817-257-7603, Fax: 817-257-5672, E-mail: cfagradinfo@tcu.edu. *Associate Dean, College of Fine Arts*, Dr. H. Joseph Butler, 817-257-7603, Fax: 817-257-5672, E-mail: cfagradinfo@tcu.edu.

School of Art Students: 22 full-time (17 women); includes 3 minority (all Hispanic/Latino), 5 international. Average age 28. 31 applicants, 35% accepted, 9 enrolled. *Faculty:* 11 full-time (5 women). Expenses: Contact institution. *Financial support:* In 2018–19, 21 students received support, including 21 teaching assistantships (averaging $10,000 per year); institutionally sponsored loans, scholarships/grants, health care benefits, tuition waivers (full and partial), and unspecified assistantships also available. Financial award application deadline: 2/1. In 2018, 3 master's awarded. Offers art history (MA); studio art (MFA). *Application deadline:* For fall admission, 2/1 for domestic and international students. *Application fee:* $60. Electronic applications accepted. *Application Contact:* Donna Smolik, TCU College of Fine Arts Graduate Office, 817-257-7603, Fax: 817-257-5672, E-mail: cfagradinfo@tcu.edu. *Director*, Richard Lane, 817-257-7643, E-mail: r.lane@tcu.edu.

School of Music Average age 26. 64 applicants, 48% accepted, 22 enrolled. Expenses: Contact institution. *Financial support:* In 2018–19, 84 students received support, including 54 research assistantships with full tuition reimbursements available (averaging $9,000 per year); career-related internships or fieldwork, institutionally sponsored loans, scholarships/grants, tuition waivers (full and partial), and unspecified assistantships also available. Financial award application deadline: 12/1; financial award applicants required to submit CSS PROFILE or FAFSA. In 2018, 21 master's, 3 doctorates awarded. Offers composition (DMA); conducting (M Mus, DMA); music (M Mus, MM Ed, DMA); music education (MM Ed); percussion (Artist Diploma); performance (DMA); piano (Artist Diploma); piano pedagogy (DMA); voice (Artist Diploma); winds (Artist Diploma). *Application deadline:* For fall admission, 12/1 for domestic and international students; for spring admission, 9/1 for domestic and international students. *Application fee:* $60. Electronic applications accepted. *Application Contact:* Dr. Joseph Butler, Associate Dean, College of Fine Arts, 817-257-6629, Fax: 817-257-7602, E-mail: r.gipson@tcu.edu. *Director*, Dr. Richard C. Gipson, 817-257-7602, E-mail: r.gipson@tcu.edu.

College of Science and Engineering Students: 132 full-time (73 women), 3 part-time (1 woman); includes 23 minority (3 Black or African American, non-Hispanic/Latino; 1 American Indian or Alaska Native, non-Hispanic/Latino; 3 Asian, non-Hispanic/Latino; 10 Hispanic/Latino; 6 Two or more races, non-Hispanic/Latino), 20 international. Average age 27. 179 applicants, 40% accepted, 49 enrolled. *Faculty:* 87 full-time (26 women), 2 part-time/adjunct (both women). Expenses: Contact institution. *Financial support:* In 2018–19, 135 students received support, including 5 fellowships with full tuition reimbursements available (averaging $21,000 per year), 9 research assistantships with full tuition reimbursements available (averaging $21,000 per year), 94 teaching assistantships with full tuition reimbursements available (averaging $20,000 per year); health care benefits, tuition waivers (full and partial), and unspecified assistantships also available. Support available to part-time students. Financial award application deadline: 1/1. In 2018, 47 master's, 16 doctorates awarded. *Program availability:* Part-time. Offers applied mathematics (MS); biology (MA, MS, PhD); chemistry and biochemistry (MA, MS, PhD); developmental trauma (MS); environmental science (MA, MEM, MS); experimental psychology (PhD); mathematics (MAT, PhD); physics (MA, MS, PhD); pure mathematics (MS); science and engineering (MA, MAT, MEM, MS, PhD). *Application deadline:* For fall admission, 1/1 priority date for domestic

and international students; for spring admission, 9/15 priority date for domestic and international students. Applications are processed on a rolling basis. *Application fee:* $60. Electronic applications accepted. *Application Contact:* Sue Dolce, Director of Degree Certification, 817-257-7734, Fax: 817-257-7736, E-mail: s.dolce@tcu.edu. *Senior Associate Dean for Administration and Graduate Programs*, Dr. Magnus Rittby, 817-257-7729, Fax: 817-257-7736, E-mail: m.rittby@tcu.edu.

Harris College of Nursing and Health Sciences Average age 31. 582 applicants, 35% accepted, 166 enrolled. Expenses: Contact institution. *Financial support:* Application deadline: 5/1; applicants required to submit FAFSA. In 2018, 101 master's, 89 doctorates, 4 other advanced degrees awarded. *Program availability:* Part-time, 100% online, blended/hybrid learning. Offers administration and leadership (MSN); advanced generalist (MSW); clinical nurse leader (MSN, Certificate); clinical nurse specialist (MSN); clinical nurse specialist - adult/gerontology nursing (DNP); clinical nurse specialist - pediatrics (DNP); family nurse practitioner (DNP); general (DNP); kinesiology (MS); nursing administration (DNP); nursing and health sciences (MS, MSN, MSW, DNP, DNP-A, Certificate); nursing education (MSN). *Application fee:* $60. Electronic applications accepted. *Application Contact:* Debbie Rhea, Associate Dean, 817-257-5263, E-mail: d.rhea@tcu.edu. *Interim Dean*, Dr. Suzy Lockwood, 817-257-6749, E-mail: s.lockwood@tcu.edu.

Davies School of Communication Sciences and Disorders Average age 23. 220 applicants, 9% accepted, 20 enrolled. Expenses: Contact institution. *Financial support:* In 2018–19, 20 students received support, including 40 research assistantships (averaging $35,000 per year); tuition waivers (partial) and unspecified assistantships also available. Financial award application deadline: 1/15; financial award applicants required to submit FAFSA. In 2018, 20 master's awarded. Offers speech-language pathology (MS). *Application deadline:* For fall admission, 1/15 for domestic and international students. *Application fee:* $60. Electronic applications accepted. *Application Contact:* Janet Schwartz, Administrative Assistant, 817-257-7620, E-mail: janet.schwartz@tcu.edu. *Director*, Dr. Christopher Watts, 817-257-7620, E-mail: c.watts@tcu.edu.

School of Nurse Anesthesia Students: 192 full-time (115 women); includes 43 minority (6 Black or African American, non-Hispanic/Latino; 17 Asian, non-Hispanic/Latino; 15 Hispanic/Latino; 5 Two or more races, non-Hispanic/Latino). Average age 32. 253 applicants, 32% accepted, 72 enrolled. *Faculty:* 10 full-time (6 women), 1 part-time/adjunct (0 women). Expenses: Contact institution. *Financial support:* In 2018–19, 3 students received support. Scholarships/grants available. Financial award application deadline: 7/1; financial award applicants required to submit FAFSA. In 2018, 57 doctorates awarded. Offers nurse anesthesia (DNP-A). *Application deadline:* For fall and spring admission, 7/1 for domestic and international students. Applications are processed on a rolling basis. *Application fee:* $70. Electronic applications accepted. *Application Contact:* Kimberly Bowen, Administrative Assistant, 817-257-7887, Fax: 817-257-5472, E-mail: k.k.bowen@tcu.edu. *Director*, Dr. Robyn Ward, 817-257-7887, Fax: 817-257-5472, E-mail: r.ward@tcu.edu.

Master of Liberal Arts Program Students: 81 full-time (33 women), 30 part-time (22 women); includes 37 minority (21 Black or African American, non-Hispanic/Latino; 2 American Indian or Alaska Native, non-Hispanic/Latino; 8 Hispanic/Latino; 1 Native Hawaiian or other Pacific Islander, non-Hispanic/Latino; 5 Two or more races, non-Hispanic/Latino), 3 international. Average age 32. 85 applicants, 93% accepted, 57 enrolled. *Faculty:* 5 part-time/adjunct (0 women). Expenses: Contact institution. *Financial support:* In 2018–19, 55 students received support. Scholarships/grants, unspecified assistantships, and employee tuition benefits available. Financial award applicants required to submit FAFSA. In 2018, 33 master's awarded. *Program availability:* Part-time, evening/weekend, 100% online. Offers liberal arts (MLA). *Application deadline:* For fall admission, 8/15 for domestic students, 6/1 for international students; for spring admission, 1/15 for domestic students, 11/1 for international students. Applications are processed on a rolling basis. *Application fee:* $60. Electronic applications accepted. *Application Contact:* Anita Unger, Graduate Program Coordinator, 817-257-7515, Fax: 817-257-7484, E-mail: a.unger@tcu.edu. *Associate Dean, AddRan College of Liberal Arts*, Dr. Peter Worthing, 817-257-6656, Fax: 817-257-7484, E-mail: p.worthing@tcu.edu.

Neeley School of Business Students: 351 full-time (100 women), 23 part-time (6 women); includes 49 minority (12 Black or African American, non-Hispanic/Latino; 2 American Indian or Alaska Native, non-Hispanic/Latino; 7 Asian, non-Hispanic/Latino; 27 Hispanic/Latino; 1 Two or more races, non-Hispanic/Latino), 34 international. Average age 30. 394 applicants, 78% accepted, 214 enrolled. *Faculty:* 83 full-time (26 women), 14 part-time/adjunct (5 women). Expenses: Contact institution. *Financial support:* Career-related internships or fieldwork, scholarships/grants, and unspecified assistantships available. Financial award application deadline: 4/5; financial award applicants required to submit FAFSA. In 2018, 208 master's awarded. *Program availability:* Part-time, evening/weekend. Offers advisory and valuation (M Ac); audit & assurance services (M Ac); business (M Ac, MBA); business administration (MBA); general, energy, healthcare (MBA); taxation (M Ac). *Application deadline:* For fall admission, 10/15 priority date for domestic and international students. Applications are processed on a rolling basis. *Application fee:* $100. Electronic applications accepted. *Application Contact:* Graduate Programs Admissions Office, 817-257-7531, E-mail: mbainfo@tcu.edu. *Associate Dean Graduate Programs*, Dr. David Allen, 817-257-7535, E-mail: david.allen@tcu.edu.

TEXAS HEALTH AND SCIENCE UNIVERSITY, Austin, TX 78704
General Information Private, coed, graduate-only institution. *Graduate housing:* On-campus housing not available.
GRADUATE UNITS
Graduate Programs Offers acupuncture and Oriental medicine (MS, DAOM); business administration (MBA); healthcare management (MBA). Electronic applications accepted.

TEXAS LUTHERAN UNIVERSITY, Seguin, TX 78155-5999
General Information Independent-religious, coed, comprehensive institution.
GRADUATE UNITS
Program in Accounting Offers accounting (M Acy).

TEXAS SOUTHERN UNIVERSITY, Houston, TX 77004-4584
General Information State-supported, coed, university. CGS member. *Graduate housing:* Room and/or apartments available on a first-come, first-served basis to single students; on-campus housing not available to married students. Housing application deadline: 7/15. *Research affiliation:* Environmental Research and Technology Transfer Center (chemistry and environmental toxicology), Institute for International and Immigration Law/Center on Legal Pedagogy (law), Innovative Transportation Research Institute (transportation planning and management), NASA University Research Biotechnology & Environmental Health (biology), Economic Development Center/JP Chase Center for Financial Education (business), Gerald B. Smith Center for Entrepreneurship and Executive Development (business, urban planning and environmental policy).

GRADUATE UNITS

Barbara Jordan-Mickey Leland School of Public Affairs *Program availability:* Part-time. Offers administration of justice (MS, PhD); public administration (MPA); public affairs (MPA, MS, PhD); urban planning and environmental policy (MS, PhD). Electronic applications accepted.

College of Education *Program availability:* Part-time, evening/weekend. Offers bilingual education (M Ed); counseling (M Ed); counselor education (Ed D); curriculum and instruction (Ed D); education (M Ed, MS, Ed D); educational administration (M Ed, Ed D); health education (MS); human performance (MS); secondary education (M Ed). Electronic applications accepted.

College of Liberal Arts and Behavioral Sciences *Program availability:* Part-time, evening/weekend. Offers English (MA); fine arts (MA); history (MA); human services and consumer sciences (MS); liberal arts and behavioral sciences (MA, MS); music (MA); psychology (MA); sociology (MA). Electronic applications accepted.

College of Pharmacy and Health Sciences *Program availability:* Online learning. Offers health care administration (MS); pharmaceutical sciences (MS, PhD); pharmacy and health sciences (MS, PhD, Pharm D); pharmacy practice (Pharm D). Electronic applications accepted.

Jesse H. Jones School of Business *Program availability:* Part-time, evening/weekend. Offers business (MBA, MS); business administration (MBA); management information systems (MS). Electronic applications accepted.

School of Science and Technology *Program availability:* Part-time, evening/weekend. Offers biology (MS); chemistry (MS); computer science (MS); environmental toxicology (MS, PhD); industrial technology (MS); mathematics (MS); science and technology (MS, PhD); transportation, planning and management (MS). Electronic applications accepted.

Tavis Smiley School of Communication *Program availability:* Part-time. Offers communication (MA). Electronic applications accepted.

Thurgood Marshall School of Law Offers law (JD). Electronic applications accepted.

TEXAS STATE UNIVERSITY, San Marcos, TX 78666

General Information State-supported, coed, university. CGS member. *Enrollment:* 2,302 full-time matriculated graduate/professional students (1,515 women), 1,654 part-time matriculated graduate/professional students (1,074 women). *Enrollment by degree level:* 3,445 master's, 390 doctoral, 121 other advanced degrees. *Graduate faculty:* 923 full-time (437 women), 112 part-time/adjunct (66 women). *International tuition:* $18,229 full-time. Tuition, state resident: full-time $8102; part-time $4051 per semester. Tuition, nonresident: full-time $18,229; part-time $9115 per semester. *Required fees:* $2116; $120 per credit hour. Tuition and fees vary according to course load. *Graduate housing:* Room and/or apartments available on a first-come, first-served basis to single students; on-campus housing not available to married students. Typical cost: $10,288 (including board). Room and board charges vary according to board plan and housing facility selected. Housing application deadline: 7/1. *Student services:* Campus employment opportunities, campus safety program, career counseling, exercise/wellness program, free psychological counseling, grant writing training, international student services, low-cost health insurance, multicultural affairs office, services for students with disabilities, teacher training, writing training. *Library facilities:* Alkek Library plus 1 other. *Collection:* Books: 1.5 million (physical), 664,569 (digital/electronic); Serial titles: 32,501 (physical), 129,479 (digital/electronic); Databases: 503. Weekly public service hours: 103; students can reserve study rooms.

Computer facilities: Computer purchase and lease plans are available. 3,233 computers available on campus for general student use. A campuswide network can be accessed from student residence rooms and from off campus. Online class registration is available.
Website: http://www.txstate.edu/

General Application Contact: Dr. Andrea Golato, Dean of Graduate School, 512-245-2581, Fax: 512-245-8365, E-mail: gradcollege@txstate.edu.

GRADUATE UNITS

The Graduate College Students: 2,302 full-time (1,515 women), 1,654 part-time (1,074 women); includes 1,530 minority (283 Black or African American, non-Hispanic/Latino; 7 American Indian or Alaska Native, non-Hispanic/Latino; 122 Asian, non-Hispanic/Latino; 1,031 Hispanic/Latino; 1 Native Hawaiian or other Pacific Islander, non-Hispanic/Latino; 86 Two or more races, non-Hispanic/Latino), 346 international. Average age 30. 3,792 applicants, 49% accepted, 1164 enrolled. *Faculty:* 923 full-time (437 women), 112 part-time/adjunct (66 women). Expenses: Contact institution. *Financial support:* In 2018–19, 1,494 students received support, including 210 research assistantships (averaging $16,610 per year), 786 teaching assistantships (averaging $15,480 per year); fellowships, career-related internships or fieldwork, Federal Work-Study, institutionally sponsored loans, scholarships/grants, unspecified assistantships, and laboratory instructorships, stipends also available. Support available to part-time students. Financial award application deadline: 1/15; financial award applicants required to submit FAFSA. In 2018, 1,360 master's, 50 doctorates, 41 other advanced degrees awarded. *Program availability:* Part-time, evening/weekend, blended/hybrid learning. *Application deadline:* For fall admission, 1/15 for domestic students, 1/1 for international students; for spring admission, 10/15 for domestic students, 10/1 for international students. Applications are processed on a rolling basis. *Application fee:* $55 ($90 for international students). Electronic applications accepted. *Application Contact:* Dr. Andrea Golato, Dean of Graduate School, 512-245-2581, Fax: 512-245-8365, E-mail: gradcollege@txstate.edu. *Dean,* Dr. Andrea Golato, 512-245-2581, Fax: 512-245-8365, E-mail: gradcollege@txstate.edu.

College of Applied Arts Students: 321 full-time (262 women), 292 part-time (221 women); includes 295 minority (77 Black or African American, non-Hispanic/Latino; 2 American Indian or Alaska Native, non-Hispanic/Latino; 11 Asian, non-Hispanic/Latino; 188 Hispanic/Latino; 17 Two or more races, non-Hispanic/Latino), 11 international. Average age 31. 536 applicants, 43% accepted, 172 enrolled. *Faculty:* 96 full-time (52 women), 16 part-time/adjunct (14 women). Expenses: Contact institution. *Financial support:* In 2018–19, 328 students received support, including 39 research assistantships (averaging $13,888 per year), 46 teaching assistantships (averaging $16,148 per year); career-related internships or fieldwork, Federal Work-Study, scholarships/grants, and unspecified assistantships also available. Support available to part-time students. Financial award application deadline: 1/15; financial award applicants required to submit FAFSA. In 2018, 211 master's, 1 doctorate awarded. *Program availability:* Part-time, evening/weekend, blended/hybrid learning. Offers agricultural education (M Ed); applied arts (M Ed, MAIS, MS, MSCJ, MSIS, MSW, PhD); criminal justice (MSCJ, PhD); family and child studies (MS); human nutrition (MS); management of technical education (M Ed); merchandising and consumer studies (MS); occupational education (MAIS, MSIS); social work (MSW). *Application deadline:* For fall admission, 2/1 priority date for domestic and international students; for spring admission, 10/15 priority date for domestic students, 10/1 for international students. Applications are processed on a rolling basis.

Application fee: $55 ($90 for international students). Electronic applications accepted. *Application Contact:* Dr. Andrea Golato, Dean of Graduate School, 512-245-2581, Fax: 512-245-8365, E-mail: gradcollege@txstate.edu. *Dean,* Dr. T. Jaime Chahin, 512-245-3333, Fax: 512-245-3338, E-mail: tc03@txstate.edu.

College of Education Students: 541 full-time (413 women), 558 part-time (427 women); includes 486 minority (94 Black or African American, non-Hispanic/Latino; 1 American Indian or Alaska Native, non-Hispanic/Latino; 29 Asian, non-Hispanic/Latino; 338 Hispanic/Latino; 24 Two or more races, non-Hispanic/Latino), 26 international. Average age 31. 897 applicants, 56% accepted, 296 enrolled. *Faculty:* 129 full-time (85 women), 31 part-time/adjunct (21 women). Expenses: Contact institution. *Financial support:* In 2018–19, 549 students received support, including 71 research assistantships (averaging $17,177 per year), 75 teaching assistantships (averaging $14,778 per year); fellowships, career-related internships or fieldwork, Federal Work-Study, institutionally sponsored loans, and scholarships/grants also available. Support available to part-time students. Financial award application deadline: 1/15; financial award applicants required to submit FAFSA. In 2018, 363 master's, 27 doctorates awarded. *Program availability:* Part-time, evening/weekend. Offers adult education (MA); adult, professional and community education (PhD); athletic training (MS); clinical mental health counseling (MA); developmental education (MA, PhD); early childhood-12 reading specialist (M Ed); educational leadership (M Ed); elementary education (M Ed, MA); elementary education - bilingual/bicultural (M Ed, MA); health education (M Ed); instructional leadership (MA); marriage and family counseling (MA); recreation management (MSRLS); school counseling (MA); school improvement (PhD); school psychology (SSP); secondary education (M Ed, MA); special education (M Ed); student affairs in higher education (M Ed). *Application deadline:* For fall admission, 1/15 priority date for domestic and international students; for spring admission, 10/1 priority date for domestic and international students. Applications are processed on a rolling basis. *Application fee:* $55 ($90 for international students). Electronic applications accepted. *Application Contact:* Dr. Andrea Golato, Dean of Graduate School, 512-245-2581, Fax: 512-245-8365, E-mail: gradcollege@txstate.edu. *Dean,* Dr. Michael O'Malley, 512-245-2150, Fax: 512-245-3158, E-mail: mo20@txstate.edu.

College of Fine Arts and Communication Students: 144 full-time (72 women), 53 part-time (33 women); includes 76 minority (16 Black or African American, non-Hispanic/Latino; 2 Asian, non-Hispanic/Latino; 56 Hispanic/Latino; 2 Two or more races, non-Hispanic/Latino), 13 international. Average age 29. 184 applicants, 55% accepted, 66 enrolled. *Faculty:* 131 full-time (61 women), 19 part-time/adjunct (10 women). Expenses: Contact institution. *Financial support:* In 2018–19, 138 students received support, including 2 research assistantships (averaging $13,725 per year), 97 teaching assistantships (averaging $11,887 per year); career-related internships or fieldwork, Federal Work-Study, institutionally sponsored loans, scholarships/grants, and unspecified assistantships also available. Support available to part-time students. Financial award application deadline: 1/15; financial award applicants required to submit FAFSA. In 2018, 97 master's awarded. *Program availability:* Part-time, evening/weekend. Offers communication design (MFA); communication studies (MA); design (MFA); directing (MFA); dramatic writing (MFA); fine arts and communication (MA, MFA, MM); mass communication (MA); music (MM); music education (MM); theatre history, dramatic criticism and dramaturgy (MA). *Application deadline:* For fall admission, 2/1 priority date for domestic and international students; for spring admission, 10/15 for domestic students, 10/1 for international students; for summer admission, 4/15 for domestic students, 3/15 for international students. Applications are processed on a rolling basis. *Application fee:* $55 ($90 for international students). Electronic applications accepted. *Application Contact:* Dr. Andrea Golato, Dean of Graduate School, 512-245-2581, Fax: 512-245-8365, E-mail: gradcollege@txstate.edu. *Dean of the College of Fine Arts and Communication,* Dr. John Fleming, 512-245-2308, Fax: 512-245-8386, E-mail: jf18@txstate.edu.

College of Health Professions Students: 338 full-time (273 women), 53 part-time (39 women); includes 169 minority (33 Black or African American, non-Hispanic/Latino; 1 American Indian or Alaska Native, non-Hispanic/Latino; 20 Asian, non-Hispanic/Latino; 102 Hispanic/Latino; 13 Two or more races, non-Hispanic/Latino), 16 international. Average age 29. 561 applicants, 31% accepted, 115 enrolled. *Faculty:* 64 full-time (43 women), 17 part-time/adjunct (7 women). Expenses: Contact institution. *Financial support:* In 2018–19, 215 students received support, including 9 research assistantships (averaging $6,342 per year), 34 teaching assistantships (averaging $12,540 per year); fellowships, career-related internships or fieldwork, Federal Work-Study, institutionally sponsored loans, scholarships/grants, unspecified assistantships, and stipends also available. Support available to part-time students. Financial award application deadline: 1/15; financial award applicants required to submit FAFSA. In 2018, 117 master's awarded. *Program availability:* Part-time, evening/weekend, blended/hybrid learning. Offers communication disorders (MA, MSCD); family nurse practitioner (MSN); health information management (MHIIM); health professions (MA, MHA, MHIIM, MSCD, MSN, DPT); healthcare administration (MHA); physical therapy (DPT). *Application deadline:* For fall admission, 1/15 priority date for domestic and international students; for spring admission, 10/1 for domestic and international students. Applications are processed on a rolling basis. *Application fee:* $55 ($90 for international students). Electronic applications accepted. *Application Contact:* Dr. Andrea Golato, Dean of Graduate School, 512-245-2581, Fax: 512-245-8365, E-mail: gradcollege@txstate.edu. *Dean,* Dr. Ruth Welborn, 512-245-3300, Fax: 512-245-3791, E-mail: rw01@txstate.edu.

College of Liberal Arts Students: 476 full-time (282 women), 350 part-time (209 women); includes 293 minority (44 Black or African American, non-Hispanic/Latino; 1 American Indian or Alaska Native, non-Hispanic/Latino; 13 Asian, non-Hispanic/Latino; 215 Hispanic/Latino; 20 Two or more races, non-Hispanic/Latino), 39 international. Average age 30. 702 applicants, 54% accepted, 273 enrolled. *Faculty:* 253 full-time (114 women), 16 part-time/adjunct (9 women). Expenses: Contact institution. *Financial support:* In 2018–19, 506 students received support, including 25 research assistantships (averaging $13,486 per year), 259 teaching assistantships (averaging $14,681 per year); fellowships, career-related internships or fieldwork, Federal Work-Study, institutionally sponsored loans, scholarships/grants, and unspecified assistantships also available. Support available to part-time students. Financial award application deadline: 1/15; financial award applicants required to submit FAFSA. In 2018, 258 master's, 8 doctorates awarded. *Program availability:* Part-time, evening/weekend. Offers anthropology (MA); applied philosophy and ethics (MA); applied sociology (MS); creative writing (MFA); dementia and aging studies (MS); environmental geography (MS); geographic education (PhD); geographic information science (MAG); geography (MAG); history (M Ed, MA); international relations (MPA); international studies (MA); legal and judicial administration (MPA); legal studies (MA); liberal arts (M Ed, MA, MAG, MFA, MPA, MS, PhD); literature (MA); political science (MA); psychological research (MA); resources and environmental studies (MAG); rhetoric and composition (MA); sociology (MA);

Spanish (MA); sustainability (MA, MS); technical communication (MA). *Application deadline:* For fall admission, 1/15 priority date for domestic students, 1/1 priority date for international students; for spring admission, 10/15 for domestic students, 10/1 for international students; for summer admission, 4/15 for domestic students, 3/15 for international students. Applications are processed on a rolling basis. *Application fee:* $55 ($90 for international students). Electronic applications accepted. *Application Contact:* Dr. Andrea Golato, Dean of Graduate School, 512-245-2581, Fax: 512-245-8365, E-mail: gradcollege@txstate.edu. *Dean,* Dr. Mary Brennan, 512-245-2317, Fax: 512-245-8291, E-mail: liberalarts@txstate.edu.

College of Science and Engineering Students: 358 full-time (157 women), 172 part-time (78 women); includes 106 minority (6 Black or African American, non-Hispanic/Latino; 20 Asian, non-Hispanic/Latino; 73 Hispanic/Latino; 7 Two or more races, non-Hispanic/Latino), 225 international. Average age 29. 510 applicants, 60% accepted, 161 enrolled. *Faculty:* 177 full-time (52 women), 6 part-time/adjunct (1 woman). Expenses: Contact institution. *Financial support:* In 2018–19, 354 students received support, including 58 research assistantships (averaging $18,734 per year), 249 teaching assistantships (averaging $18,356 per year); career-related internships or fieldwork, Federal Work-Study, institutionally sponsored loans, scholarships/grants, health care benefits, unspecified assistantships, and laboratory instructorships also available. Support available to part-time students. Financial award application deadline: 1/15; financial award applicants required to submit FAFSA. In 2018, 146 master's, 14 doctorates awarded. *Program availability:* Part-time, evening/weekend. Offers aquatic resources (MS, PhD); biochemistry (MS); chemistry (MA, MS); civil engineering (MS); computer science (MA, MS, PhD); electrical engineering (MS); industrial engineering (MS); materials science, engineering, and commercialization (PhD); mathematics (M Ed); mathematics education (PhD); mechanical and manufacturing engineering (MS); physics (MS); population and conservation biology (MS); software engineering (MS); technology management (MS). *Application deadline:* For fall admission, 1/15 priority date for domestic and international students; for spring admission, 10/15 for domestic students, 10/1 for international students. Applications are processed on a rolling basis. *Application fee:* $55 ($90 for international students). Electronic applications accepted. *Application Contact:* Dr. Andrea Golato, Dean of Graduate School, 512-245-2581, Fax: 512-245-8365, E-mail: gradcollege@txstate.edu. *Dean,* Dr. Christine Hailey, 512-245-2119, Fax: 512-245-8095, E-mail: ceh138@txstate.edu.

Emmett and Miriam McCoy College of Business Administration Students: 124 full-time (56 women), 176 part-time (67 women); includes 105 minority (13 Black or African American, non-Hispanic/Latino; 2 American Indian or Alaska Native, non-Hispanic/Latino; 27 Asian, non-Hispanic/Latino; 59 Hispanic/Latino; 1 Native Hawaiian or other Pacific Islander, non-Hispanic/Latino; 3 Two or more races, non-Hispanic/Latino), 16 international. Average age 30. 396 applicants, 31% accepted, 81 enrolled. *Faculty:* 68 full-time (27 women), 3 part-time/adjunct. Expenses: Contact institution. *Financial support:* In 2018–19, 110 students received support, including 1 research assistantship (averaging $13,009 per year), 24 teaching assistantships (averaging $13,093 per year); Federal Work-Study, institutionally sponsored loans, scholarships/grants, health care benefits, and unspecified assistantships also available. Support available to part-time students. Financial award application deadline: 1/15; financial award applicants required to submit FAFSA. In 2018, 168 master's awarded. *Program availability:* Part-time. Offers accounting (M Acy); accounting and information technology (MS); business administration (M Acy, MBA, MS); human resource management (MS). *Application deadline:* For fall admission, 1/15 priority date for domestic and international students; for spring admission, 10/1 for domestic and international students; for summer admission, 4/1 for domestic students, 3/15 for international students. Applications are processed on a rolling basis. *Application fee:* $55 ($90 for international students). Electronic applications accepted. *Application Contact:* Dr. Andrea Golato, Dean of Graduate School, 512-245-2581, Fax: 512-245-8365, E-mail: gradcollege@txstate.edu. *Dean of the College of Business Administration,* Dr. Denise Smart, 512-245-2311, Fax: 512-245-8375, E-mail: businessgraduate@txstate.edu.

TEXAS TECH UNIVERSITY, Lubbock, TX 79409

General Information State-supported, coed, university. CGS member. *Enrollment:* 38,209 graduate, professional, and undergraduate students; 3,814 full-time matriculated graduate/professional students (1,845 women), 2,135 part-time matriculated graduate/professional students (1,296 women). *Enrollment by degree level:* 3,040 master's, 2,909 doctoral. *Graduate faculty:* 1,600 full-time (659 women), 188 part-time/adjunct (99 women). Tuition, state resident: full-time $7776; part-time $324 per credit hour. Tuition, nonresident: full-time $17,736; part-time $739 per credit hour. *Required fees:* $2504; $53.50 per credit hour. $610 per semester. Tuition and fees vary according to program. *Graduate housing:* Room and/or apartments available on a first-come, first-served basis to single students; on-campus housing not available to married students. Typical cost: $6236 per year ($9772 including board). Room and board charges vary according to board plan and housing facility selected. *Student services:* Campus employment opportunities, campus safety program, career counseling, exercise/wellness program, free psychological counseling, grant writing training, international student services, low-cost health insurance, multicultural affairs office, services for students with disabilities, teacher training, writing training. *Library facilities:* Texas Tech Library plus 3 others. *Collection:* Books: 2.9 million (physical), 159,373 (digital/electronic); Serial titles: 1,464 (physical), 200,332 (digital/electronic); Databases: 405. Weekly public service hours: 146; study areas open 24 hours, 5–7 days a week; students can reserve study rooms.

Computer facilities: Computer purchase and lease plans are available. 2,087 computers available on campus for general student use. A campuswide network can be accessed from student residence rooms and from off campus. Online class registration, online degree plans, accounts, transcripts, financial aid, course and instructor evaluations, scholarship applications and submissions are available. Website: http://www.ttu.edu/

General Application Contact: Jade Foerster, Director of Admissions, 806-834-5332, Fax: 806-742-4038, E-mail: graduate.admissions@ttu.edu.

GRADUATE UNITS

Graduate School Students: 3,402 full-time (1,672 women), 2,134 part-time (1,295 women); includes 1,377 minority (269 Black or African American, non-Hispanic/Latino; 11 American Indian or Alaska Native, non-Hispanic/Latino; 156 Asian, non-Hispanic/Latino; 798 Hispanic/Latino; 3 Native Hawaiian or other Pacific Islander, non-Hispanic/Latino; 140 Two or more races, non-Hispanic/Latino), 1,305 international. Average age 30. 4,130 applicants, 57% accepted, 1590 enrolled. *Faculty:* 1,567 full-time (645 women), 177 part-time/adjunct (95 women). Expenses: Contact institution. *Financial support:* In 2018–19, 4,252 students received support, including 3,904 fellowships (averaging $3,511 per year), 965 research assistantships (averaging $17,492 per year), 1,477 teaching assistantships (averaging $14,867 per year); career-

related internships or fieldwork, Federal Work-Study, scholarships/grants, traineeships, health care benefits, and unspecified assistantships also available. Support available to part-time students. Financial award application deadline: 4/15; financial award applicants required to submit FAFSA. In 2018, 1,629 master's, 349 doctorates awarded. *Program availability:* Part-time, evening/weekend, 100% online, blended/hybrid learning. Offers arid land studies (MS); biotechnology (MS); heritage and museum sciences (MA); interdisciplinary studies (MA, MS); wind science and engineering (PhD). *Application deadline:* For fall admission, 6/1 priority date for domestic students, 1/15 priority date for international students; for spring admission, 9/1 priority date for domestic students, 6/15 priority date for international students. Applications are processed on a rolling basis. *Application fee:* $65. Electronic applications accepted. *Application Contact:* Jade Foerster, Director of Admissions, 806-742-2787, E-mail: graduate.admissions@ttu.edu. *Vice Provost for Graduate and Postdoctoral Affairs/Dean of the Graduate School,* Dr. Mark A. Sheridan, 806-834-5537, Fax: 806-742-1746, E-mail: mark.sheridan@ttu.edu.

College of Agricultural Sciences and Natural Resources Students: 304 full-time (162 women), 118 part-time (57 women); includes 51 minority (2 Black or African American, non-Hispanic/Latino; 4 Asian, non-Hispanic/Latino; 34 Hispanic/Latino; 11 Two or more races, non-Hispanic/Latino), 121 international. Average age 29. 176 applicants, 65% accepted, 93 enrolled. *Faculty:* 125 full-time (44 women), 19 part-time/adjunct (4 women). Expenses: Contact institution. *Financial support:* In 2018–19, 372 students received support, including 310 fellowships (averaging $3,561 per year), 254 research assistantships (averaging $15,078 per year), 36 teaching assistantships (averaging $15,284 per year); scholarships/grants, health care benefits, and unspecified assistantships also available. Support available to part-time students. Financial award application deadline: 4/15; financial award applicants required to submit FAFSA. In 2018, 88 master's, 31 doctorates awarded. *Program availability:* Part-time, 100% online, blended/hybrid learning. Offers agribusiness (MAB); agricultural and applied economics (MS, PhD); agricultural communications (MS); agricultural communications and education (PhD); agricultural education (MS, Ed D); agricultural sciences and natural resources (MAB, MLA, MS, Ed D, PhD); animal science (MS, PhD); food science (MS); horticulture science (MS); landscape architecture (MLA); plant and soil science (MS, PhD); wildlife, aquatic, and wildlands science and management (MS, PhD). *Application deadline:* For fall admission, 6/1 priority date for domestic students, 1/15 priority date for international students; for spring admission, 9/1 priority date for domestic students, 6/15 priority date for international students. Applications are processed on a rolling basis. *Application fee:* $65. Electronic applications accepted. *Application Contact:* Dr. Christy Bratcher, Associate Dean for Research, 806-834-1364, Fax: 806-742-2836, E-mail: christy.bratcher@ttu.edu. *Dean,* Dr. William Brown, 806-742-2808, Fax: 806-742-2836, E-mail: william.f.brown@ttu.edu.

College of Architecture Students: 70 full-time (29 women), 13 part-time (1 woman); includes 31 minority (4 Black or African American, non-Hispanic/Latino; 1 Asian, non-Hispanic/Latino; 26 Hispanic/Latino), 16 international. Average age 26. 49 applicants, 57% accepted, 16 enrolled. *Faculty:* 34 full-time (13 women), 11 part-time/adjunct (3 women). Expenses: Contact institution. *Financial support:* In 2018–19, 70 students received support, including 70 fellowships (averaging $4,305 per year); research assistantships, teaching assistantships, career-related internships or fieldwork, Federal Work-Study, institutionally sponsored loans, scholarships/grants, traineeships, health care benefits, and unspecified assistantships also available. Support available to part-time students. Financial award application deadline: 2/1; financial award applicants required to submit FAFSA. In 2018, 41 master's, 1 doctorate awarded. *Program availability:* Part-time. Offers architecture (M Arch, MS); land-use planning, management, and design (PhD). *Application deadline:* For fall admission, 6/1 priority date for domestic students, 1/15 priority date for international students; for spring admission, 9/1 priority date for domestic students, 6/15 priority date for international students. Applications are processed on a rolling basis. *Application fee:* $65. Electronic applications accepted. *Application Contact:* Sarah Hatley, Unit Manager, College Advising, 806-834-5704, Fax: 806-742-1400, E-mail: sarah.hatley@ttu.edu. *Dean,* Prof. James P. Williamson, 806-742-3136, Fax: 806-742-1400, E-mail: james.p.williamson@ttu.edu.

College of Arts and Sciences Students: 1,029 full-time (526 women), 226 part-time (130 women); includes 265 minority (37 Black or African American, non-Hispanic/Latino; 4 American Indian or Alaska Native, non-Hispanic/Latino; 40 Asian, non-Hispanic/Latino; 150 Hispanic/Latino; 2 Native Hawaiian or other Pacific Islander, non-Hispanic/Latino; 32 Two or more races, non-Hispanic/Latino), 387 international. Average age 30. 1,099 applicants, 45% accepted, 329 enrolled. *Faculty:* 531 full-time (198 women), 28 part-time/adjunct (17 women). Expenses: Contact institution. *Financial support:* In 2018–19, 1,120 students received support, including 969 fellowships (averaging $2,582 per year), 233 research assistantships (averaging $16,449 per year), 785 teaching assistantships (averaging $15,262 per year); career-related internships or fieldwork, Federal Work-Study, institutionally sponsored loans, scholarships/grants, traineeships, health care benefits, and unspecified assistantships also available. Support available to part-time students. Financial award application deadline: 2/1; financial award applicants required to submit FAFSA. In 2018, 258 master's, 107 doctorates awarded. *Program availability:* Part-time, evening/weekend, 100% online, blended/hybrid learning. Offers anthropology (MA); arts and sciences (MA, MPA, MS, MSW, PSM, PhD); atmospheric science (MS); biology (MS, PhD); chemical biology (MS); chemistry (MS, PhD); clinical psychology (PhD); counseling psychology (MA, PhD); economics (MA, PhD); English (MA, PhD); environmental sustainability and natural resource management (PSM); environmental toxicology (MS, PhD); general experimental psychology (MA, PhD); geography (MS); geosciences (MS, PhD); history (MA, PhD); kinesiology (MS); languages and cultures (MA); mathematics (MA, MS, PhD); microbiology (MS); philosophy (MA); physics (MS, PhD); political science (MA, PhD); psychology (MA); public administration (MPA); Romance languages (MA); social work (MSW); sociology (MA); Spanish (PhD); sport management (MS); statistics (MS); technical communication (MA); technical communication and rhetoric (PhD); zoology (MS, PhD). *Application deadline:* For fall admission, 6/1 priority date for domestic students, 1/15 priority date for international students; for spring admission, 9/1 priority date for domestic students, 6/15 priority date for international students. Applications are processed on a rolling basis. *Application fee:* $65. Electronic applications accepted. *Application Contact:* Dr. Jorge Iber, Associate Dean, 806-834-5511, E-mail: jorge.iber@ttu.edu. *Dean,* Dr. W. Brent Lindquist, 806-742-3831, Fax: 806-742-3893, E-mail: brent.lindquist@ttu.edu.

College of Education Students: 309 full-time (225 women), 889 part-time (702 women); includes 428 minority (113 Black or African American, non-Hispanic/Latino; 3 American Indian or Alaska Native, non-Hispanic/Latino; 21 Asian, non-Hispanic/Latino; 256 Hispanic/Latino; 1 Native Hawaiian or other Pacific Islander, non-Hispanic/Latino; 34 Two or more races, non-Hispanic/Latino), 66 international. Average age 37. 538 applicants, 71% accepted, 303 enrolled. *Faculty:* 157 full-time (105 women), 5 part-time/adjunct (all women). Expenses: Contact institution.

Financial support: In 2018–19, 635 students received support, including 625 fellowships (averaging $3,215 per year), 89 research assistantships (averaging $12,476 per year), 12 teaching assistantships (averaging $13,752 per year); career-related internships or fieldwork, Federal Work-Study, institutionally sponsored loans, scholarships/grants, traineeships, health care benefits, and unspecified assistantships also available. Support available to part-time students. Financial award application deadline: 2/1; financial award applicants required to submit FAFSA. In 2018, 304 master's, 61 doctorates awarded. *Program availability:* Part-time, evening/weekend. Offers bilingual education (M Ed); counselor education (M Ed, PhD); curriculum and instruction (M Ed, Ed D, PhD); education (M Ed, MS, Ed D, PhD); educational leadership (M Ed, Ed D, PhD); educational psychology (M Ed, PhD); elementary education (M Ed); higher education administration (M Ed, Ed D); higher education research (PhD); instructional technology (M Ed, Ed D); language/literacy education (M Ed); multidisciplinary science (MS); secondary education (M Ed); special education (M Ed, Ed D, PhD). *Application deadline:* For fall admission, 6/1 priority date for domestic students, 1/15 priority date for international students; for spring admission, 9/1 priority date for domestic students, 6/15 priority date for international students. Applications are processed on a rolling basis. *Application fee:* $65. Electronic applications accepted. *Application Contact:* Beth Watson, Coordinator, 806-834-0429, Fax: 806-742-2179, E-mail: beth.watson@ttu.edu. *Dean,* Dr. Jesse Perez Mendez, 806-742-2377, Fax: 806-742-2179, E-mail: jp.mendez@ttu.edu.

College of Human Sciences Students: 275 full-time (165 women), 231 part-time (137 women); includes 129 minority (18 Black or African American, non-Hispanic/Latino; 20 Asian, non-Hispanic/Latino; 79 Hispanic/Latino; 12 Two or more races, non-Hispanic/Latino), 92 international. Average age 31. 285 applicants, 75% accepted, 183 enrolled. *Faculty:* 115 full-time (70 women), 27 part-time/adjunct (22 women). Expenses: Contact institution. *Financial support:* In 2018–19, 349 students received support, including 335 fellowships (averaging $4,360 per year), 70 research assistantships (averaging $13,847 per year), 116 teaching assistantships (averaging $12,596 per year); institutionally sponsored loans, scholarships/grants, and unspecified assistantships also available. Financial award application deadline: 1/15; financial award applicants required to submit FAFSA. In 2018, 106 master's, 34 doctorates awarded. *Program availability:* Part-time, 100% online, blended/hybrid learning. Offers couple, marriage, & family therapy (MS, PhD); environmental design (MS); family and consumer sciences education (MS, PhD); hospitality administration (PhD); hospitality and retail management (MS); human development and family studies (MS, PhD); human sciences (MS, PhD); interior and environmental design (PhD); nutrition and dietetics (MS); nutritional sciences (MS, PhD); personal financial planning (MS, PhD). *Application deadline:* For fall admission, 6/1 priority date for domestic students, 1/15 priority date for international students; for spring admission, 9/1 priority date for domestic students, 6/15 priority date for international students. Applications are processed on a rolling basis. *Application fee:* $65. Electronic applications accepted. *Application Contact:* Prof. Mitzi Lauderdale, Associate Dean for Students, 806-834-0529, Fax: 806-742-1849, E-mail: mitzi.lauderdale@ttu.edu. *AT&T Dean's Chair in Human Sciences,* Dr. Linda C. Hoover, 806-742-3031, Fax: 806-742-1849, E-mail: linda.hoover@ttu.edu.

College of Media and Communication Students: 129 full-time (81 women), 143 part-time (92 women); includes 67 minority (11 Black or African American, non-Hispanic/Latino; 1 American Indian or Alaska Native, non-Hispanic/Latino; 3 Asian, non-Hispanic/Latino; 43 Hispanic/Latino; 9 Two or more races, non-Hispanic/Latino), 23 international. Average age 30. 144 applicants, 69% accepted, 83 enrolled. *Faculty:* 76 full-time (36 women), 16 part-time/adjunct (9 women). Expenses: Contact institution. *Financial support:* In 2018–19, 172 students received support, including 137 fellowships (averaging $3,510 per year), 16 research assistantships (averaging $15,912 per year), 92 teaching assistantships (averaging $11,851 per year); career-related internships or fieldwork, scholarships/grants, and unspecified assistantships also available. Support available to part-time students. Financial award application deadline: 4/15; financial award applicants required to submit FAFSA. In 2018, 73 master's, 7 doctorates awarded. *Program availability:* Part-time, evening/weekend, 100% online, blended/hybrid learning. Offers communication studies (MA); mass communications (MA); media and communication (PhD); strategic communication and innovation (MA). *Application deadline:* For fall admission, 6/1 priority date for domestic students, 1/15 priority date for international students; for spring admission, 9/1 priority date for domestic students, 6/15 priority date for international students. Applications are processed on a rolling basis. *Application fee:* $65. Electronic applications accepted. *Application Contact:* Elaine Taylor, Graduate Program Administrative, 806-834-7064, Fax: 806-742-1085, E-mail: elaine.taylor@ttu.edu. *Professor & Associate Dean of Graduate Studies,* Dr. Coy Callison, 806-834-5344, E-mail: coy.callison@ttu.edu.

Edward E. Whitacre Jr. College of Engineering Students: 545 full-time (149 women), 226 part-time (38 women); includes 110 minority (22 Black or African American, non-Hispanic/Latino; 1 American Indian or Alaska Native, non-Hispanic/Latino; 29 Asian, non-Hispanic/Latino; 48 Hispanic/Latino; 10 Two or more races, non-Hispanic/Latino), 446 international. Average age 30. 914 applicants, 45% accepted, 185 enrolled. *Faculty:* 182 full-time (31 women), 19 part-time/adjunct (3 women). Expenses: Contact institution. *Financial support:* In 2018–19, 622 students received support, including 585 fellowships (averaging $4,151 per year), 265 research assistantships (averaging $23,462 per year), 140 teaching assistantships (averaging $20,404 per year); scholarships/grants, health care benefits, and unspecified assistantships also available. Financial award application deadline: 4/15; financial award applicants required to submit FAFSA. In 2018, 235 master's, 62 doctorates awarded. *Program availability:* Part-time, evening/weekend, 100% online, blended/hybrid learning. Offers bioengineering (MS); chemical engineering (MS Ch E, PhD); civil engineering (MSCE, PhD); computer science (MS, PhD); electrical engineering (MSEE, PhD); engineering (M Engr); environmental engineering (MENVEGR); industrial engineering (MSIE, PhD); manufacturing engineering (MS); mechanical engineering (MSME, PhD); petroleum engineering (MSPE, PhD); software engineering (MS); systems and engineering management (MSSEM). *Application deadline:* For fall admission, 6/1 priority date for domestic students, 1/15 priority date for international students; for spring admission, 9/1 priority date for domestic students, 6/15 priority date for international students. Applications are processed on a rolling basis. *Application fee:* $65. Electronic applications accepted. *Application Contact:* Dr. Brandon Weeks, Associate Dean of Research and Graduate Programs, Edward E. Whitacre Jr. College of Engineering, 806-834-7450, Fax: 806-742-3493, E-mail: brandon.weeks@ttu.edu. *Dean, Edward E. Whitacre Jr. College of Engineering,* Dr. Albert Sacco, Jr., 806-742-3451, Fax: 806-742-3493, E-mail: al.sacco-jr@ttu.edu.

J.T. and Margaret Talkington College of Visual and Performing Arts Students: 234 full-time (114 women), 69 part-time (46 women); includes 55 minority (8 Black or African American, non-Hispanic/Latino; 2 Asian, non-Hispanic/Latino; 34 Hispanic/Latino; 11 Two or more races, non-Hispanic/Latino), 71 international.

Average age 32. 177 applicants, 63% accepted, 79 enrolled. *Faculty:* 114 full-time (54 women), 14 part-time/adjunct (9 women). Expenses: Contact institution. *Financial support:* In 2018–19, 298 students received support, including 278 fellowships (averaging $4,006 per year), 8 research assistantships (averaging $15,381 per year), 215 teaching assistantships (averaging $10,782 per year); Federal Work-Study, institutionally sponsored loans, scholarships/grants, health care benefits, tuition waivers (partial), unspecified assistantships, and competitive grants to support graduate research also available. Financial award application deadline: 2/1; financial award applicants required to submit FAFSA. In 2018, 47 master's, 35 doctorates awarded. *Program availability:* Evening/weekend. Offers art (MFA); art education (MAE); art history (MA); dance studies (MA); fine arts (PhD); music (MM, DMA); music education (MM Ed); theatre arts (MA, MFA); visual and performing arts (MA, MAE, MFA, MM, MM Ed, DMA, PhD). *Application deadline:* For fall admission, 6/1 priority date for domestic students, 1/15 priority date for international students; for spring admission, 9/1 priority date for domestic students, 6/15 priority date for international students. Applications are processed on a rolling basis. *Application fee:* $65. Electronic applications accepted. *Application Contact:* Shannon Samson, Coordinator of Graduate School Recruitment, 806-834-5201, Fax: 806-742-1746, E-mail: gradschool@ttu.edu. *Dean & Professor,* Dr. Noel Zahler, 806-742-0700, Fax: 806-742-0695, E-mail: noel.zahler@ttu.edu.

Rawls College of Business Administration *Program availability:* Evening/weekend, 100% online, blended/hybrid learning. Offers accounting (MSA, PhD); data science (MS); finance (PhD); general business (MBA); healthcare management (MS); information systems and operations management (PhD); management (PhD); marketing (PhD); STEM (MBA). Electronic applications accepted.

School of Law Students: 412 full-time (173 women), 1 (woman) part-time; includes 118 minority (12 Black or African American, non-Hispanic/Latino; 1 American Indian or Alaska Native, non-Hispanic/Latino; 11 Asian, non-Hispanic/Latino; 61 Hispanic/Latino; 33 Two or more races, non-Hispanic/Latino). Average age 25. 1,164 applicants, 44% accepted, 150 enrolled. *Faculty:* 33 full-time (14 women), 11 part-time/adjunct (4 women). Expenses: Contact institution. *Financial support:* In 2018–19, 314 students received support. Federal Work-Study, scholarships/grants, and Tutor available. Financial award application deadline: 5/1; financial award applicants required to submit FAFSA. In 2018, 155 doctorates awarded. Offers law (JD); United States legal studies (LL M). *Application deadline:* For fall admission, 3/1 priority date for domestic and international students. Applications are processed on a rolling basis. *Application fee:* $0. Electronic applications accepted. *Application Contact:* Dean Danielle I. Saavedra, Assistant Dean of Admissions, 806-834-7092, Fax: 806-742-1629, E-mail: admissions.law@ttu.edu. *Dean and W. Frank Newton Professor of Law,* Dean Jack Wade Nowlin, 806-834-1504, Fax: 806-742-1629, E-mail: jack.nowlin@ttu.edu.

TEXAS TECH UNIVERSITY HEALTH SCIENCES CENTER, Lubbock, TX 79430

General Information State-supported, coed, graduate-only institution. *Graduate housing:* On-campus housing not available.

GRADUATE UNITS

Graduate School of Biomedical Sciences Offers biomedical sciences (MS, PhD); biotechnology (MS); pharmaceutical sciences (MS, PhD). Electronic applications accepted.

Pharm D Program Offers pharmacy (Pharm D).

School of Health Professions Students: 997 full-time (769 women), 171 part-time (94 women); includes 347 minority (99 Black or African American, non-Hispanic/Latino; 6 American Indian or Alaska Native, non-Hispanic/Latino; 101 Asian, non-Hispanic/Latino; 124 Hispanic/Latino; 4 Native Hawaiian or other Pacific Islander, non-Hispanic/Latino; 13 Two or more races, non-Hispanic/Latino). Average age 29. 4,112 applicants, 14% accepted, 481 enrolled. *Faculty:* 81 full-time (43 women), 44 part-time/adjunct (25 women). Expenses: Contact institution. *Financial support:* In 2018–19, 445 students received support. Research assistantships, teaching assistantships, institutionally sponsored loans, scholarships/grants, and health care benefits available. Support available to part-time students. Financial award application deadline: 9/1; financial award applicants required to submit FAFSA. In 2018, 279 master's, 114 doctorates awarded. *Program availability:* Part-time, 100% online, blended/hybrid learning. Offers addiction counseling (MS); athletic training (MAT); audiology (Au D); clinical mental health counseling (MS); clinical rehabilitation counseling (MRC); health professions (MAT, MOT, MPAS, MRC, MS, Au D, DPT, PhD, Sc D, TDPT); healthcare administration (MS); molecular pathology (MS); occupational therapy (MOT); physical therapy (DPT, Sc D, TDPT); physician assistant studies (MPAS); rehabilitation science (PhD); speech-language pathology (MS). *Application deadline:* Applications are processed on a rolling basis. *Application fee:* $75. Electronic applications accepted. *Application Contact:* Lindsay Johnson, Associate Dean for Admissions and Student Affairs, 806-743-3220, Fax: 806-743-2994, E-mail: health.professions@ttuhsc.edu. *Associate Dean for Admissions and Student Affairs,* Lindsay R. Johnson, 806-743-3220, Fax: 806-743-2994, E-mail: health.professions@ttuhsc.edu.

School of Medicine Offers medicine (MD). Open only to residents of Texas, eastern New Mexico, and southwestern Oklahoma; MD/PhD offered jointly with Texas Tech University; JD/MD with School of Law. Electronic applications accepted.

School of Nursing *Program availability:* Part-time, online learning. Offers acute care nurse practitioner (MSN, Certificate); administration (MSN); advanced practice (DNP); education (MSN); executive leadership (DNP); family nurse practitioner (MSN, Certificate); geriatric nurse practitioner (MSN, Certificate); pediatric nurse practitioner (MSN, Certificate).

TEXAS TECH UNIVERSITY HEALTH SCIENCES CENTER EL PASO, El Paso, TX 79905

General Information State-supported, coed, comprehensive institution.

GRADUATE UNITS

Gayle Greve Hunt School of Nursing Offers nursing (MSN).

Graduate School of Biomedical Sciences Offers biomedical sciences (MS).

Paul L. Foster School of Medicine Offers medicine (MD).

TEXAS WESLEYAN UNIVERSITY, Fort Worth, TX 76105

General Information Independent-religious, coed, university. *Graduate housing:* Room and/or apartments available on a first-come, first-served basis to single students; on-campus housing not available to married students.

GRADUATE UNITS

Graduate Programs *Program availability:* Part-time, evening/weekend, 100% online. Offers business (MBA); education (M Ed, Ed D); nurse anesthesia (MHS, MSNA, DNAP). Electronic applications accepted.

TEXAS WOMAN'S UNIVERSITY, Denton, TX 76204

General Information State-supported, coed, primarily women, university. CGS member. *Enrollment:* 15,520 graduate, professional, and undergraduate students; 2,114 full-time matriculated graduate/professional students (1,848 women), 2,927 part-time matriculated graduate/professional students (2,601 women). *Enrollment by degree level:* 3,928 master's, 1,001 doctoral, 112 other advanced degrees. *Graduate faculty:* 343 full-time (245 women), 152 part-time/adjunct (109 women). *International tuition:* $12,322 full-time. *Tuition, area resident:* Full-time $4852; part-time $270 per semester hour. Tuition, state resident: full-time $4852; part-time $270 per semester hour. Tuition, nonresident: full-time $12,322; part-time $685 per semester hour. *Required fees:* $2714; $113 per semester hour. $296 per semester. Tuition and fees vary according to course level, course load, degree level, campus/location and program. *Graduate housing:* Rooms and/or apartments available on a first-come, first-served basis to single and married students. Typical cost: $8000 per year for single students; $8400 per year for married students. Room charges vary according to housing facility selected. *Student services:* Campus employment opportunities, campus safety program, career counseling, exercise/wellness program, free psychological counseling, grant writing training, international student services, low-cost health insurance, services for students with disabilities, teacher training, writing training. *Library facilities:* Blagg-Huey Library. *Collection:* Books: 387,169 (physical), 504,151 (digital/electronic); Serial titles: 131,848 (physical), 209,764 (digital/electronic); Databases: 306. Weekly public service hours: 116; students can reserve study rooms.

Computer facilities: Computer purchase and lease plans are available. 296 computers available on campus for general student use. A campuswide network can be accessed from student residence rooms and from off campus. Online class registration is available.
Website: http://www.twu.edu/

General Application Contact: Korie Hawkins, Associate Director of Admissions, Graduate Recruitment, 940-898-3188, Fax: 940-898-3081, E-mail: admissions@twu.edu.

GRADUATE UNITS

Graduate School Students: 2,114 full-time (1,848 women), 2,927 part-time (2,601 women); includes 2,352 minority (828 Black or African American, non-Hispanic/Latino; 15 American Indian or Alaska Native, non-Hispanic/Latino; 470 Asian, non-Hispanic/Latino; 896 Hispanic/Latino; 3 Native Hawaiian or other Pacific Islander, non-Hispanic/Latino; 140 Two or more races, non-Hispanic/Latino), 146 international. Average age 33. 3,115 applicants, 51% accepted, 1233 enrolled. *Faculty:* 357 full-time (255 women), 159 part-time/adjunct (116 women). Expenses: Contact institution. *Financial support:* In 2018–19, 1,395 students received support, including 22 research assistantships (averaging $7,808 per year), 273 teaching assistantships (averaging $9,346 per year); career-related internships or fieldwork, Federal Work-Study, institutionally sponsored loans, scholarships/grants, traineeships, health care benefits, unspecified assistantships, and research associateships also available. Support available to part-time students. Financial award application deadline: 3/1; financial award applicants required to submit FAFSA. In 2018, 1,414 master's, 221 doctorates, 114 other advanced degrees awarded. *Program availability:* Part-time, evening/weekend, 100% online, blended/hybrid learning. MSW offered in cooperation with The University of North Texas. *Application deadline:* For fall admission, 3/1 priority date for domestic students, 9/1 priority date for international students; for spring admission, 11/1 priority date for domestic students, 5/1 priority date for international students. Applications are processed on a rolling basis. *Application fee:* $50 ($75 for international students). Electronic applications accepted. *Application Contact:* Korie Hawkins, Associate Director of Admissions, Graduate Recruitment, 940-898-3188, Fax: 940-898-3081, E-mail: admissions@twu.edu. *Interim Dean of Graduate School,* Dr. Claire Sahlin, 940-898-3415, Fax: 940-898-3412, E-mail: gradschool@twu.edu.

College of Arts and Sciences Students: 227 full-time (186 women), 406 part-time (327 women); includes 260 minority (90 Black or African American, non-Hispanic/Latino; 3 American Indian or Alaska Native, non-Hispanic/Latino; 43 Asian, non-Hispanic/Latino; 100 Hispanic/Latino; 24 Two or more races, non-Hispanic/Latino), 42 international. Average age 33. 409 applicants, 59% accepted, 186 enrolled. *Faculty:* 110 full-time (67 women), 24 part-time/adjunct (16 women). Expenses: Contact institution. *Financial support:* In 2018–19, 290 students received support, including 7 research assistantships (averaging $10,643 per year), 168 teaching assistantships (averaging $9,601 per year); career-related internships or fieldwork, Federal Work-Study, institutionally sponsored loans, scholarships/grants, traineeships, health care benefits, and unspecified assistantships also available. Support available to part-time students. Financial award application deadline: 3/1; financial award applicants required to submit FAFSA. In 2018, 94 master's, 30 doctorates, 6 other advanced degrees awarded. *Program availability:* Part-time, evening/weekend, 100% online, blended/hybrid learning. Offers all (MA, MAT, MFA); arts (MA, MAT, MFA, PhD); arts and sciences (MA, MAT, MFA, MS, PhD, SSP); biology (MS); chemistry (MS); counseling psychology (MA, PhD); dance (MA, MFA, PhD); drama (MA); emphasis in mathematics or computer science (MAT); English (MA, MAT); government (MA); history (MA); informatics (MS); mathematics (MS); mathematics teaching (MS); molecular biology (PhD); multicultural women's and gender studies (MA, PhD); music (MA); psychological science (MS); rhetoric (PhD); school psychology (PhD, SSP); social work (MS); sociology (MA, PhD). MSW offered in cooperation with The University of North Texas. *Application deadline:* For fall admission, 3/1 priority date for domestic and international students; for spring admission, 11/1 priority date for domestic students, 7/1 priority date for international students; for summer admission, 5/1 priority date for domestic students, 2/1 priority date for international students. Applications are processed on a rolling basis. *Application fee:* $50 ($75 for international students). Electronic applications accepted. *Application Contact:* Korie Hawkins, Associate Director of Admissions, Graduate Recruitment, 940-898-3188, Fax: 940-898-3081, E-mail: admissions@twu.edu. *Dean,* Dr. Abigail Tilton, 940-898-3326, Fax: 940-898-3366, E-mail: cas@twu.edu.

College of Business Students: 483 full-time (429 women), 445 part-time (373 women); includes 643 minority (325 Black or African American, non-Hispanic/Latino; 4 American Indian or Alaska Native, non-Hispanic/Latino; 134 Asian, non-Hispanic/Latino; 152 Hispanic/Latino; 1 Native Hawaiian or other Pacific Islander, non-Hispanic/Latino; 27 Two or more races, non-Hispanic/Latino), 38 international. Average age 33. 401 applicants, 84% accepted, 251 enrolled. *Faculty:* 26 full-time (9 women), 14 part-time/adjunct (7 women). Expenses: Contact institution. *Financial support:* In 2018–19, 138 students received support, including 12 teaching assistantships (averaging $10,666 per year); career-related internships or fieldwork, Federal Work-Study, institutionally sponsored loans, scholarships/grants, traineeships, health care benefits, and unspecified assistantships also available. Support available to part-time students. Financial award application deadline: 3/1; financial award applicants required to submit FAFSA. In 2018, 471 master's awarded. *Program availability:* Part-time, 100% online, blended/hybrid learning. Offers business

administration (MBA); health systems management (MHSM); healthcare administration (MHA). *Application deadline:* Applications are processed on a rolling basis. *Application fee:* $50 ($75 for international students). Electronic applications accepted. *Application Contact:* Korie Hawkins, Associate Director of Admissions, Graduate Recruitment, 940-898-3188, Fax: 940-898-3081, E-mail: admissions@twu.edu. *Dean,* Dr. James R. Lumpkin, 940-898-2458, Fax: 940-898-2120, E-mail: mba@twu.edu.

College of Health Sciences Students: 1,059 full-time (907 women), 371 part-time (313 women); includes 540 minority (110 Black or African American, non-Hispanic/Latino; 1 American Indian or Alaska Native, non-Hispanic/Latino; 111 Asian, non-Hispanic/Latino; 282 Hispanic/Latino; 36 Two or more races, non-Hispanic/Latino), 38 international. Average age 29. 1,546 applicants, 27% accepted, 360 enrolled. *Faculty:* 98 full-time (73 women), 22 part-time/adjunct (17 women). Expenses: Contact institution. *Financial support:* In 2018–19, 625 students received support, including 11 research assistantships (averaging $5,200 per year), 63 teaching assistantships (averaging $7,839 per year); career-related internships or fieldwork, Federal Work-Study, institutionally sponsored loans, scholarships/grants, traineeships, health care benefits, and unspecified assistantships also available. Support available to part-time students. Financial award application deadline: 3/1; financial award applicants required to submit FAFSA. In 2018, 301 master's, 131 doctorates awarded. *Program availability:* Part-time, evening/weekend, 100% online, blended/hybrid learning. Offers education of the deaf (MS); exercise and sports nutrition (MS); food science and flavor chemistry (MS); food systems administration (MS); health sciences (MA, MOT, MS, DPT, OTD, PhD); health studies (MS, PhD); nutrition (MS, PhD); occupational therapy (MOT, OTD, PhD); physical therapy (DPT, PhD); speech-language pathology (MS). *Application deadline:* For fall admission, 7/1 priority date for domestic students, 3/1 priority date for international students; for spring admission, 12/1 priority date for domestic students, 7/1 priority date for international students. Applications are processed on a rolling basis. *Application fee:* $50 ($75 for international students). Electronic applications accepted. *Application Contact:* Korie Hawkins, Associate Director of Admissions, Graduate Recruitment, 940-898-3188, Fax: 940-898-3081, E-mail: admissions@twu.edu. *Dean,* Dr. Christopher T. Ray, 940-898-2852, Fax: 940-898-2853.

College of Nursing Students: 29 full-time (27 women), 774 part-time (713 women); includes 443 minority (163 Black or African American, non-Hispanic/Latino; 6 American Indian or Alaska Native, non-Hispanic/Latino; 159 Asian, non-Hispanic/Latino; 90 Hispanic/Latino; 2 Native Hawaiian or other Pacific Islander, non-Hispanic/Latino; 23 Two or more races, non-Hispanic/Latino), 17 international. Average age 37. 278 applicants, 89% accepted, 179 enrolled. *Faculty:* 51 full-time (49 women), 35 part-time/adjunct (28 women). Expenses: Contact institution. *Financial support:* In 2018–19, 85 students received support, including 1 research assistantship, 6 teaching assistantships (averaging $13,821 per year); career-related internships or fieldwork, Federal Work-Study, institutionally sponsored loans, scholarships/grants, traineeships, health care benefits, and unspecified assistantships also available. Support available to part-time students. Financial award application deadline: 3/1; financial award applicants required to submit FAFSA. In 2018, 213 master's, 35 doctorates awarded. *Program availability:* Part-time, 100% online, blended/hybrid learning. Offers adult health clinical nurse specialist (MS); adult health nurse practitioner (MS); adult/gerontology acute care nurse practitioner (MS); child health clinical nurse specialist (MS); clinical nurse leader (MS); family nurse practitioner (MS); health systems management (MS); nursing education (MS); nursing practice (DNP); nursing science (PhD); pediatric nurse practitioner (MS); women's health clinical nurse specialist (MS); women's health nurse practitioner (MS). *Application deadline:* For fall admission, 5/1 for domestic students, 3/1 priority date for international students; for spring admission, 9/15 for domestic students, 7/1 priority date for international students. *Application fee:* $50 ($75 for international students). Electronic applications accepted. *Application Contact:* Korie Hawkins, Associate Director of Admissions, Graduate Recruitment, 940-898-3188, Fax: 940-898-3081, E-mail: admissions@twu.edu. *Dean,* Dr. Rosalie Mainous, 940-898-2401, Fax: 940-898-2437, E-mail: nursing@twu.edu.

College of Professional Education Students: 316 full-time (299 women), 931 part-time (875 women); includes 466 minority (140 Black or African American, non-Hispanic/Latino; 1 American Indian or Alaska Native, non-Hispanic/Latino; 23 Asian, non-Hispanic/Latino; 272 Hispanic/Latino; 30 Two or more races, non-Hispanic/Latino), 11 international. Average age 35. 481 applicants, 74% accepted, 257 enrolled. *Faculty:* 72 full-time (57 women), 64 part-time/adjunct (48 women). Expenses: Contact institution. *Financial support:* In 2018–19, 257 students received support, including 3 research assistantships, 24 teaching assistantships (averaging $9,735 per year); career-related internships or fieldwork, Federal Work-Study, institutionally sponsored loans, scholarships/grants, traineeships, health care benefits, and unspecified assistantships also available. Support available to part-time students. Financial award application deadline: 3/1; financial award applicants required to submit FAFSA. In 2018, 335 master's, 25 doctorates, 65 other advanced degrees awarded. *Program availability:* Part-time, evening/weekend, 100% online, blended/hybrid learning. Offers child development (MS); child life (MS); counseling and development (MS); early childhood development and education (PhD); early childhood education (M Ed); educational administration (M Ed, MA); family studies (MS, PhD); family therapy (MS, PhD); library science (MA, MLS); professional education (M Ed, MA, MAT, MLS, MS, PhD, Certificate); reading education (M Ed, MA, PhD); special education (M Ed, PhD); teaching, learning, and curriculum (M Ed, MA); Texas all-level (K-12) reading specialist (Certificate); Texas master reading teacher (Certificate). *Application deadline:* For fall admission, 3/1 priority date for domestic and international students; for spring admission, 11/1 priority date for domestic students, 7/1 priority date for international students. Applications are processed on a rolling basis. *Application fee:* $50 ($75 for international students). Electronic applications accepted. *Application Contact:* Korie Hawkins, Associate Director of Admissions, Graduate Recruitment, 940-898-3188, Fax: 940-898-3081, E-mail: admissions@twu.edu. *Dean,* Dr. Lisa Huffman, 940-898-2202, Fax: 940-898-2209, E-mail: cope@twu.edu.

THEOLOGICAL UNIVERSITY OF THE CARIBBEAN, Saint Just, PR 00978-0901

General Information Independent-religious, coed, comprehensive institution.

GRADUATE UNITS

Graduate Programs Offers childhood and adolescent education (MA); counseling and pastoral care (MA); ministry (D Min); missions (MA).

THOMAS COLLEGE, Waterville, ME 04901-5097

General Information Independent, coed, comprehensive institution. *Graduate housing:* On-campus housing not available.

GRADUATE UNITS

Graduate School *Program availability:* Part-time, evening/weekend. Offers business (MBA); computer technology education (MS); education (MS); human resource management (MBA). Electronic applications accepted.

THOMAS EDISON STATE UNIVERSITY, Trenton, NJ 08608

General Information State-supported, coed, comprehensive institution. *Graduate housing:* On-campus housing not available.

GRADUATE UNITS

Heavin School of Arts and Sciences *Program availability:* Part-time, online learning. Offers arts and sciences (MA, MAEL, MALS, Graduate Certificate); digital humanities (MALS, Graduate Certificate); educational leadership (MAEL, Graduate Certificate); educational technology and online learning (MA); geropsychology (MALS, Graduate Certificate); industrial-organizational psychology (MALS, Graduate Certificate); learner-designed area of study (MALS); online learning and teaching (Graduate Certificate); professional communications (MALS, Graduate Certificate). Electronic applications accepted.

John S. Watson School of Public Service and Continuing Studies *Program availability:* Part-time, online learning. Offers community and economic development (MSM); environmental policy/environmental justice (MSM); homeland security (MSHS, MSM); information and technology for public service (MSM); nonprofit management (MSM); public and municipal finance (MSM); public health (MSM); public service administration and leadership (MSM); public service leadership (MPSL). Electronic applications accepted.

School of Applied Science and Technology *Program availability:* Part-time, online learning. Offers clinical trials management (Graduate Certificate); cybersecurity (Graduate Certificate); information technology (MS); nuclear energy technology management (MS); technical studies (MS). Electronic applications accepted.

School of Business and Management *Program availability:* Part-time, online learning. Offers accounting (MSM); business administration (MBA); business and management (MBA, MS, MSHRM, MSM); hospitality management (MS); human resources management (MSHRM); international business finance (MS); organizational leadership (MSM); project management (MSM). Electronic applications accepted.

W. Cary Edwards School of Nursing *Program availability:* Part-time, online learning. Offers nurse educator (MSN); nursing (MSN, DNP); nursing administration (MSN); nursing informatics (MSN); systems-level leadership (DNP). Electronic applications accepted.

THOMAS JEFFERSON SCHOOL OF LAW, San Diego, CA 92110-2905

General Information Independent, coed, graduate-only institution. *Graduate housing:* Rooms and/or apartments available on a first-come, first-served basis to single and married students. Housing application deadline: 5/1.

GRADUATE UNITS

Graduate and Professional Programs *Program availability:* Part-time, evening/weekend. Offers law (JD). JD/MBA offered in partnership with San Diego State University. Electronic applications accepted.

THOMAS JEFFERSON UNIVERSITY, Philadelphia, PA 19107

General Information Independent, coed, university. CGS member. *Graduate housing:* Rooms and/or apartments available to single and married students. *Research affiliation:* Christiana Care Health Services (biomedical research), Lankenau Institute for Medical Research (biomedical research), A.I. du Pont for Children Nemours (biomedical research), University of Delaware (biomedical research).

GRADUATE UNITS

College of Architecture and the Built Environment Offers architecture (M Arch, MS); architecture and the built environment (MS); construction management (MS); geospatial technology for geodesign (MS); interior architecture (MS); real estate development (MS); sustainable design (MS).

Jefferson College of Health Professions Offers biotechnology (MS); community and trauma counseling (MS); couple and family therapy (MFT); cytotechnology (MS); disaster medicine and management (MS); health professions (MFT, MS, DPT, OTD); medical laboratory science (MS); medical physics (MS); midwifery (MS); physician assistant studies (MS); radiologic and imaging sciences (MS). Electronic applications accepted.

Jefferson College of Life Sciences *Program availability:* Part-time, evening/weekend. Offers biochemistry and molecular pharmacology (PhD); biomedical sciences (MS, Certificate); cell and developmental biology (MS); cell biology and regenerative medicine (PhD); clinical research (MS); clinical research and trials: implementation (Certificate); clinical research: operations (Certificate); forensic toxicology (MS); genetics, genomics and cancer biology (PhD); human clinical investigation: theory (Certificate); human genetics and genetic counseling (MS); immunology and microbial pathogenesis (PhD); infectious disease control (Certificate); life sciences (MS, PhD, Certificate); microbiology (MS); neuroscience (PhD); patient-centered research (Certificate); pharmacology (MS). Electronic applications accepted.

Jefferson College of Nursing *Program availability:* Part-time, online only, 100% online, blended/hybrid learning. Offers nursing (MS, DNP). Electronic applications accepted.

Jefferson College of Pharmacy Offers pharmacy (Pharm D). Electronic applications accepted.

Jefferson College of Population Health *Program availability:* Part-time, evening/weekend, online learning. Offers applied health economics and outcomes research (MS, PhD, Certificate); behavioral health science (MS); health policy (MS, PhD, Certificate); healthcare quality and safety (MS, PhD, Certificate); population health (Certificate); public health (MPH, Certificate). Electronic applications accepted.

Jefferson College of Rehabilitation Sciences *Program availability:* Part-time, evening/weekend, online learning. Offers athletic training (MS); occupational therapy (MS); physical therapy (DPT); rehabilitation sciences (MS, Postbaccalaureate Certificate). Electronic applications accepted.

Kanbar College of Design, Engineering and Commerce *Program availability:* Part-time. Offers business analytics (MBA); design, engineering and commerce (MS, PhD); fashion design management (MS); general business (MBA); global fashion enterprise (MS); industrial design (MS); management (MBA); marketing (MBA); strategy and design thinking (MBA); surface imaging (MS); taxation (MS); textile design (MS); textile engineering (MS); textile engineering and sciences (PhD); user experience and interaction design (MS). Electronic applications accepted.

School of Continuing and Professional Studies

Sidney Kimmel Medical College Offers medicine (MD). Electronic applications accepted.

THOMAS MORE UNIVERSITY, Crestview Hills, KY 41017-3495

General Information Independent-religious, coed, comprehensive institution. *Graduate housing:* On-campus housing not available.

GRADUATE UNITS

Program in Business Administration *Program availability:* Evening/weekend, 100% online. Offers business administration (MBA). Electronic applications accepted.

Program in Teacher Leader *Program availability:* Part-time, evening/weekend. Offers teacher leader (M Ed). Electronic applications accepted.

Program in Teaching *Program availability:* Part-time. Offers teaching (MAT). Electronic applications accepted.

THOMAS UNIVERSITY, Thomasville, GA 31792-7499

General Information Independent, coed, comprehensive institution. *Graduate housing:* Room and/or apartments available on a first-come, first-served basis to single students; on-campus housing not available to married students. Housing application deadline: 8/1.

GRADUATE UNITS

Department of Business Administration *Program availability:* Part-time. Offers business administration (MBA). Electronic applications accepted.

Department of Education *Program availability:* Part-time. Offers education (M Ed). Electronic applications accepted.

Department of Human Services *Program availability:* Part-time. Offers community counseling (MSCC); rehabilitation counseling (MRC). Electronic applications accepted.

Department of Nursing *Program availability:* Part-time. Offers nursing (MSN). Electronic applications accepted.

THOMPSON RIVERS UNIVERSITY, Kamloops, BC V2C 0C8, Canada

General Information Province-supported, coed, comprehensive institution. CGS member.

GRADUATE UNITS

Program in Business Administration *Program availability:* Part-time. Offers business administration (MBA).

Program in Education *Program availability:* Part-time. Offers education (M Ed).

Program in Environmental Science Offers environmental science (MS).

Program in Social Work Offers social work (MSW).

TIFFIN UNIVERSITY, Tiffin, OH 44883-2161

General Information Independent, coed, comprehensive institution. *Graduate housing:* Room and/or apartments available on a first-come, first-served basis to single students; on-campus housing not available to married students. Housing application deadline: 8/1.

GRADUATE UNITS

Program in Business Administration *Program availability:* Part-time, evening/weekend, online learning. Offers finance (MBA); general management (MBA); healthcare administration (MBA); human resource management (MBA); international business (MBA); leadership (MBA); marketing (MBA); non-profit management (MBA); sports management (MBA). Electronic applications accepted.

Program in Criminal Justice *Program availability:* Part-time, evening/weekend, 100% online, blended/hybrid learning. Offers criminal justice (MS). Electronic applications accepted.

Program in Education *Program availability:* Part-time, evening/weekend, online only, 100% online, blended/hybrid learning. Offers educational technology management (M Ed); higher education administration (M Ed). Electronic applications accepted.

Program in Humanities *Program availability:* Part-time, evening/weekend, online only, 100% online, blended/hybrid learning. Offers art and visual media (MH); communication (MH); creative writing (MH); English (MH); film studies (MH); humanities (MH); individualized studies (MH). Electronic applications accepted.

Program in Psychology *Program availability:* Part-time, evening/weekend, online only, 100% online. Offers psychology (MS). Electronic applications accepted.

TORONTO SCHOOL OF THEOLOGY, Toronto, ON M5S 2C3, Canada

General Information Independent-religious, coed, graduate-only institution.

GRADUATE UNITS

Graduate Programs *Program availability:* Online learning. Offers theology (M Div, MA, MAMS, MPS, MRE, MSM, MTS, Th M, D Min, PhD, Th D). Electronic applications accepted.

TOURO COLLEGE, New York, NY 10010

General Information Independent, coed, comprehensive institution.

GRADUATE UNITS

College of Dental Medicine

College of Osteopathic Medicine

College of Pharmacy

Graduate School of Education *Program availability:* Part-time, evening/weekend, online learning. Offers education and special education (MS); instructional technology (MS); mathematics education (MS); school leadership (MS); teaching English to speakers of other languages (MS); teaching literacy (MS).

Graduate School of Jewish Studies *Program availability:* Part-time. Offers Jewish studies (MA).

Graduate School of Social Work Offers social work (MSW).

Graduate School of Technology Offers information systems (MS); instructional technology (MS); Web and multimedia design (MA).

Jacob D. Fuchsberg Law Center *Program availability:* Part-time, evening/weekend. Offers general law (LL M); law (JD); U.S. legal studies (LL M). JD/MBA and JD/MPA offered with Long Island University-LIU Post; JD/MSW offered with Stony Brook University, State University of New York.

School of Health Sciences Offers industrial-organizational psychology (MS); mental health counseling (MS); occupational therapy (MS); physical therapy (DPT); physician assistant (MS); speech-language pathology (MS).

TOURO UNIVERSITY CALIFORNIA, Vallejo, CA 94592

General Information Independent, coed, graduate-only institution. *Graduate housing:* On-campus housing not available. *Research affiliation:* University of California San Francisco (cancer, HIV/AIDS), Genetech (cancer), National Institutes of Health (diabetes, cardiac arrest in teens).

GRADUATE UNITS

Graduate Programs *Program availability:* Part-time, evening/weekend. Offers education (MA); medical health sciences (MS); osteopathic medicine (DO); pharmacy (Pharm D); public health (MPH). Electronic applications accepted.

TOWSON UNIVERSITY, Towson, MD 21252-0001

General Information State-supported, coed, university. CGS member. *Enrollment:* 22,923 graduate, professional, and undergraduate students; 1,035 full-time matriculated graduate/professional students (737 women), 2,032 part-time matriculated graduate/professional students (1,510 women). *Enrollment by degree level:* 2,676 master's, 166 doctoral, 225 other advanced degrees. *Graduate faculty:* 300 full-time (174 women), 119 part-time/adjunct (71 women). *International tuition:* $19,030 full-time. *Tuition, area resident:* Full-time $9196; part-time $418 per unit. Tuition, state resident: full-time $9196; part-time $418 per unit. Tuition, nonresident: full-time $19,030; part-time $865 per unit. *Required fees:* $3102; $141 per year. $423 per term. Tuition and fees vary according to campus/location and program. *Graduate housing:* On-campus housing not available. *Student services:* Campus employment opportunities, campus safety program, career counseling, child daycare facilities, exercise/wellness program, free psychological counseling, international student services, low-cost health insurance, multicultural affairs office, services for students with disabilities, writing training. *Library facilities:* Cook Library. *Collection:* Books: 396,754 (physical), 520,928 (digital/electronic); Serial titles: 288 (physical), 79,916 (digital/electronic); Databases: 312. Weekly public service hours: 108; study areas open 24 hours, 5–7 days a week; students can reserve study rooms.

Computer facilities: 3,800 computers available on campus for general student use. A campuswide network can be accessed from student residence rooms and from off campus. Online class registration is available.
Website: http://www.towson.edu/

General Application Contact: Coverley Beidleman, Assistant Director of Graduate Admissions, 410-704-5630, Fax: 410-704-3030, E-mail: grads@towson.edu.

GRADUATE UNITS

College of Business and Economics Offers accounting (MS); business and economics (MS, Postbaccalaureate Certificate); marketing intelligence (MS, Postbaccalaureate Certificate); project, program and portfolio management (Postbaccalaureate Certificate); supply chain management (MS). Electronic applications accepted.

College of Education Offers early childhood education (MAT); education (M Ed, MAT, MS, Ed D, CAS, Postbaccalaureate Certificate); educational technology (MS); elementary education (M Ed); instructional design and development (MS); instructional leadership and professional development (CAS, Postbaccalaureate Certificate); reading (M Ed); reading education (CAS); school library media (MS); secondary education (MAT); special education (M Ed, MAT); teacher as leader in autism spectrum disorder (M Ed). Electronic applications accepted.

College of Fine Arts and Communication Offers art education (M Ed); arts integration (Postbaccalaureate Certificate); communication management (MS); fine arts and communication (M Ed, MA, MFA, MM, MS, Postbaccalaureate Certificate); interactive media design (Postbaccalaureate Certificate); interdisciplinary arts infusion (MA); music education (MS); music performance and composition (MM); studio art (MFA); theatre (MFA). Electronic applications accepted.

College of Health Professions Offers audiology (Au D); autism studies (Postbaccalaureate Certificate); clinician to administrator transition (MS, Postbaccalaureate Certificate); health professions (MS, Au D, Sc D, Postbaccalaureate Certificate); health science (MS); nursing education (Postbaccalaureate Certificate); occupational science (Sc D); occupational therapy (MS); physician assistant studies (MS); speech-language pathology (MS). Electronic applications accepted.

College of Liberal Arts Offers art history (MA); child life, administration and family collaboration (MS); clinical psychology (MA); counseling psychology (MA); education leadership (MS); experimental psychology (MA); family-professional collaboration (Postbaccalaureate Certificate); general human resource management (MS); geography and environmental planning (MA); global humanities (MS); individualized plan of study (MA); integrated homeland security management (MS); liberal arts (MA, MS, CAS, Postbaccalaureate Certificate); professional writing (MS); school psychology (MA); security assessment and management (Postbaccalaureate Certificate); social science (MS); women's studies (MS, Postbaccalaureate Certificate). Electronic applications accepted.

Program in Leadership and Jewish Studies Offers Jewish communal service (Postbaccalaureate Certificate). Electronic applications accepted.

Jess and Mildred Fisher College of Science and Mathematics Offers applied and industrial mathematics (MS); applied information technology (MS); applied physics (MS); biology (MS); computer science (MS); environmental science (MS, Postbaccalaureate Certificate); forensic science (MS); information technology (D Sc); integrated STEM instructional leadership (Postbaccalaureate Certificate); Internet application development (Postbaccalaureate Certificate); mathematics education (MS); science and mathematics (MS, D Sc, Postbaccalaureate Certificate). Electronic applications accepted.

TOYOTA TECHNOLOGICAL INSTITUTE AT CHICAGO, Chicago, IL 60637

General Information Proprietary, coed, graduate-only institution.

GRADUATE UNITS

Program in Computer Science Offers computer science (PhD).

TRENT UNIVERSITY, Peterborough, ON K9J 7B8, Canada

General Information Province-supported, coed, university. *Graduate housing:* Room and/or apartments available to single students; on-campus housing not available to married students. Housing application deadline: 7/10. *Research affiliation:* Watershed Science Centre (watershed studies), Ontario Power Generation, Inc. (acid rain deposition), Enbridge Consumers Gas (ozone depletion), Forensics Laboratory (DNA testing).

GRADUATE UNITS

Graduate Studies *Program availability:* Part-time. Offers anthropology (MA); applications of modeling in the natural and social sciences (MA); biology (M Sc, PhD); chemistry (M Sc); computer studies (M Sc); cultural studies (PhD); environmental and resource studies (M Sc, PhD); geography (M Sc, PhD); indigenous studies (PhD); materials science (M Sc); physics (M Sc).

The Frost Centre for Canadian Studies and Indigenous Studies *Program availability:* Part-time. Offers Canadian studies (PhD); Canadian studies and indigenous studies (MA).

TREVECCA NAZARENE UNIVERSITY, Nashville, TN 37210-2877

General Information Independent-religious, coed, comprehensive institution. *Graduate housing:* On-campus housing not available.

GRADUATE UNITS

Graduate Business Programs *Program availability:* Evening/weekend, online learning. Offers business administration (MBA); health care leadership and innovation (MS); management (MSM). Electronic applications accepted.

Graduate Counseling Program *Program availability:* Part-time, evening/weekend. Offers clinical counseling: teaching and supervision (PhD); clinical mental health counseling (MA); marriage and family counseling/therapy (MMFC/T). Electronic applications accepted.

Graduate Education Program *Program availability:* Part-time, evening/weekend, online learning. Offers accountability and instructional leadership (Ed S); curriculum and instruction for Christian school educators (M Ed); curriculum and instruction K-12 (M Ed); educational leadership (M Ed); English second language (M Ed); library and information science (MLI Sc); special education: visual impairments (M Ed); teaching (MAT). Electronic applications accepted.

Graduate Instructional Design and Technology Program *Program availability:* Online only. Offers instructional design and technology (MS). Electronic applications accepted.

Graduate Leadership Programs *Program availability:* Online learning. Offers leadership and professional practice (Ed D); organizational leadership (MOL). Electronic applications accepted.

Graduate Physician Assistant Program Offers physician assistant (MS).

Graduate Religion Programs *Program availability:* Part-time, online learning. Offers biblical and theological studies (MA); Christian ministry (MA); pastoral counseling (MA). Electronic applications accepted.

TRIDENT UNIVERSITY INTERNATIONAL, Cypress, CA 90630

General Information Independent, coed, university.

GRADUATE UNITS

College of Business Administration *Program availability:* Part-time, evening/weekend, online learning. Offers business administration (MBA, PhD); conflict and negotiation management (MBA); criminal justice administration (MBA); entrepreneurship (MBA); finance (MBA); general management (MBA); government accounting (MBA); human resource management (MBA); information security and digital assurance management (MBA); information technology management (MBA); international business (MBA); logistics management (MBA); marketing (MBA); project management (MBA); public management (MBA); quality management (MBA); strategic leadership (MBA). Electronic applications accepted.

College of Education *Program availability:* Part-time, evening/weekend, online learning. Offers adult education (MA Ed); aviation education (MA Ed); children's literacy development (MA Ed); e-learning (MA Ed); e-learning leadership (MA Ed, PhD); early childhood education (MA Ed); education (MA Ed, PhD); educational leadership (MA Ed); enrollment management (MA Ed); higher education (MA Ed); higher education leadership (PhD); K-12 leadership (PhD); teaching and instruction (MA Ed); training and development (MA Ed). Electronic applications accepted.

College of Health Sciences *Program availability:* Part-time, evening/weekend, online learning. Offers clinical research administration (MS, Certificate); emergency and disaster management (MS, Certificate); environmental health science (Certificate); health care administration (PhD); health care management (MS); health education (MS, Certificate); health informatics (Certificate); health sciences (MS, PhD, Certificate); international health (MS); international health: educator or researcher option (PhD); international health: practitioner option (PhD); law and expert witness studies (MS, Certificate); public health (MS); quality assurance (Certificate). Electronic applications accepted.

College of Information Systems *Program availability:* Part-time, evening/weekend, online learning. Offers business intelligence (Certificate); information technology management (MS). Electronic applications accepted.

TRINE UNIVERSITY, Angola, IN 46703-1764

General Information Independent, coed, comprehensive institution. *Graduate housing:* On-campus housing not available.

GRADUATE UNITS

Lou Holtz Program in Leadership Offers leadership (MS).

Program in Business Administration Offers business administration (MBA).

Program in Criminal Justice *Program availability:* Part-time, evening/weekend, online only, 100% online, blended/hybrid learning. Offers emergency management (MS). Electronic applications accepted.

Program in Engineering Management Offers engineering management (MS).

Program in Information Studies Offers information studies (MS).

Program in Physical Therapy Offers physical therapy (DPT).

Program in Physician Assistant Studies Offers physician assistant studies (MPAS).

TRINITY BAPTIST COLLEGE, Jacksonville, FL 32221

General Information Independent-religious, coed, comprehensive institution. *Graduate housing:* On-campus housing not available.

GRADUATE UNITS

Graduate Programs *Program availability:* Online learning. Offers Bible (MA); curriculum and instruction (M Ed); educational leadership (M Ed); special education (M Ed).

TRINITY BIBLE COLLEGE AND GRADUATE SCHOOL, Ellendale, ND 58436

General Information Independent-religious, coed, comprehensive institution.

GRADUATE UNITS

Graduate School Offers global theology (MA); missional leadership (MA); rural ministries (MA).

TRINITY CHRISTIAN COLLEGE, Palos Heights, IL 60463-0929

General Information Independent-religious, coed, comprehensive institution.

GRADUATE UNITS

Program in Counseling Psychology *Program availability:* Evening/weekend, online learning. Offers counseling psychology (MA).

Program in Special Education *Program availability:* Evening/weekend. Offers special education (MA). Electronic applications accepted.

TRINITY COLLEGE, Toronto, ON M5S 1H8, Canada

General Information Independent-religious, coed, graduate-only institution. *Graduate housing:* Room and/or apartments available on a first-come, first-served basis to single students; on-campus housing not available to married students. Housing application deadline: 7/15.

GRADUATE UNITS

Faculty of Divinity *Program availability:* Part-time. Offers ministry (Diploma); ministry for church musicians (Diploma); theology (M Div, MA, MTS, Th M, D Min, PhD, Th D, Diploma, L Th).

TRINITY COLLEGE, Hartford, CT 06106-3100

General Information Independent, coed, comprehensive institution. *Graduate housing:* On-campus housing not available.

GRADUATE UNITS

Graduate Programs *Program availability:* Part-time, evening/weekend. Offers American culture studies (MA); health care policy (MA); literary studies (MA); museums and communities (MA); public policy studies (MA); writing, rhetoric, and media arts (MA). Electronic applications accepted.

TRINITY INTERNATIONAL UNIVERSITY, Deerfield, IL 60015-1284

General Information Independent-religious, coed, university. *Graduate housing:* Rooms and/or apartments available on a first-come, first-served basis to single and married students.

GRADUATE UNITS

Trinity Evangelical Divinity School *Program availability:* Part-time, online learning. Offers academic ministry (M Div); Biblical and Near Eastern archaeology and languages (MA); chaplaincy and ministry care (MA); Christian studies (Certificate); church and parachurch ministry (M Div); church history (MA, Th M); counseling (Th M); educational ministries (MA); educational ministry (Th M); educational studies (PhD); intercultural studies (MA, PhD); leadership and management (D Min); mental health counseling (MA); military chaplaincy (D Min); ministry (MA); missions (Th M); missions and evangelism (D Min); New Testament (MA, Th M); Old Testament (Th M); Old Testament and Semitic languages (MA); pastoral ministry and care (D Min); pastoral theology (Th M); preaching and teaching (D Min); spiritual formation and education (D Min); systematic theology (MA, Th M); theological studies (MA, PhD); urban ministry (MA). Electronic applications accepted.

Trinity Graduate School *Program availability:* Part-time, evening/weekend, online learning. Offers athletic training (MA); bioethics (MA); counseling psychology (MA); diverse learning (M Ed); leadership (MA); teaching (MA). Electronic applications accepted.

Trinity Law School *Program availability:* Part-time, evening/weekend. Offers bioethics (MLS); church and ministry management (MLS); general legal studies (MLS); human resources management (MLS); human rights (MLS); law (JD); nonprofit organizations (MLS).

TRINITY INTERNATIONAL UNIVERSITY FLORIDA, Davie, FL 33324

General Information Independent-religious, coed, graduate-only institution. *Graduate housing:* On-campus housing not available.

GRADUATE UNITS

Divinity School Offers Christian studies (MA, Certificate).

Graduate School Offers counseling psychology (MA).

TRINITY SCHOOL FOR MINISTRY, Ambridge, PA 15003-2397

General Information Independent-religious, coed, graduate-only institution. *Graduate housing:* On-campus housing not available.

GRADUATE UNITS

Graduate Programs *Program availability:* Part-time. Offers Anglican studies (Diploma); basic Christian studies (Diploma); divinity (M Div); ministry (D Min); mission and evangelism (MAME, Diploma); religion (MAR); youth ministry (Diploma).

TRINITY UNIVERSITY, San Antonio, TX 78212-7200

General Information Independent-religious, coed, comprehensive institution. *Enrollment:* 115 full-time matriculated graduate/professional students (69 women), 48 part-time matriculated graduate/professional students (20 women). *Enrollment by degree level:* 163 master's. *Graduate faculty:* 18 full-time (11 women), 20 part-time/adjunct (10 women). Tuition and fees vary according to program and student level. *Graduate housing:* On-campus housing not available. *Student services:* Campus employment opportunities, campus safety program, career counseling, exercise/wellness program, free psychological counseling, grant writing training, international student services, services for students with disabilities, teacher training, writing training. *Library facilities:* Elizabeth Huth Coates Library plus 1 other. *Collection:* Books: 716,500 (physical); Serial titles: 1,907 (physical), 95,000 (digital/electronic); Databases: 297. Weekly public service hours: 96; students can reserve study rooms.

Computer facilities: Computer purchase and lease plans are available. 500 computers available on campus for general student use. A campuswide network can be accessed from student residence rooms and from off campus. Online class registration is available.
Website: http://www.trinity.edu/

GRADUATE UNITS

Department of Education Students: 40 full-time (30 women); includes 24 minority (2 Black or African American, non-Hispanic/Latino; 21 Hispanic/Latino; 1 Two or more races, non-Hispanic/Latino), 2 international. Average age 31. *Faculty:* 17 full-time (14 women), 12 part-time/adjunct (9 women). Expenses: Contact institution. *Financial support:* Application deadline: 5/1; applicants required to submit FAFSA. In 2018, 42 master's awarded. *Program availability:* Part-time, evening/weekend. Offers elementary education (MAT); school leadership (M Ed); school psychology (MA); teaching (MAT). *Application Contact:* Office of Admissions, 210-999-7207, Fax: 210-999-8164, E-mail: admissions@trinity.edu. *Interim Chair,* Norvella Carter, 210-999-7506, Fax: 210-999-7592, E-mail: ncarter1@trinity.edu.

Department of Health Care Administration Students: 46 full-time (25 women), 42 part-time (15 women); includes 33 minority (5 Black or African American, non-Hispanic/Latino; 8 Asian, non-Hispanic/Latino; 18 Hispanic/Latino; 2 Two or more races, non-Hispanic/Latino). Average age 28. *Faculty:* 5 full-time (0 women), 4 part-time/adjunct (1 woman). Expenses: Contact institution. *Financial support:* Fellowships, institutionally sponsored loans, scholarships/grants, and unspecified assistantships available. Support available to part-time students. Financial award application deadline: 5/1; financial award applicants required to submit FAFSA. In 2018, 34 master's awarded. *Program availability:* Part-time, online learning. Offers health care administration (MS).

Application deadline: For fall admission, 6/1 for domestic students. Applications are processed on a rolling basis. *Application fee:* $50. Electronic applications accepted. *Application Contact:* Dr. Ed Schumacher, Professor/Chair, 210-999-8137, E-mail: hca@trinity.edu. *Professor/Chair,* Dr. Ed Schumacher, 210-999-8137, E-mail: hca@trinity.edu.
School of Business Students: 17 full-time (5 women); includes 4 minority (1 Black or African American, non-Hispanic/Latino; 1 Asian, non-Hispanic/Latino; 1 Hispanic/Latino; 1 Two or more races, non-Hispanic/Latino), 3 international. Average age 22. *Faculty:* 2 full-time (both women), 3 part-time/adjunct (0 women). Expenses: Contact institution. *Financial support:* Institutionally sponsored loans and scholarships/grants available. Financial award application deadline: 5/1; financial award applicants required to submit FAFSA. In 2018, 16 master's awarded. Offers accounting (MS). *Application deadline:* For fall admission, 2/1 for domestic and international students. Electronic applications accepted. *Application Contact:* Dr. Julie Persellin, Chair, Department of Accounting, 210-999-7230, E-mail: jpersell@trinity.edu. *Chair, Department of Accounting,* Dr. Julie Persellin, 210-999-7230, E-mail: jpersell@trinity.edu.

TRINITY WASHINGTON UNIVERSITY, Washington, DC 20017-1094

General Information Independent-religious, women only, comprehensive institution. *Graduate housing:* Room and/or apartments available on a first-come, first-served basis to single students; on-campus housing not available to married students.

GRADUATE UNITS

School of Business and Graduate Studies *Program availability:* Part-time, evening/weekend. Offers business administration (MBA); communication (MA); international security studies (MA); organizational management (MSA).

School of Education *Program availability:* Part-time, evening/weekend. Offers clinical mental health counseling (MA); early childhood education (MAT); educating for change (M Ed); educational administration (MSA); elementary education (MAT); reading (M Ed); school counseling (MA); secondary education (MAT); special education (MAT).

School of Nursing and Health Professions Offers nursing (MSN); occupational therapy (MOT).

TRINITY WESTERN UNIVERSITY, Langley, BC V2Y 1Y1, Canada

General Information Independent-religious, coed, comprehensive institution. *Enrollment:* 478 full-time matriculated graduate/professional students (316 women). *Enrollment by degree level:* 478 master's. *Graduate housing:* On-campus housing not available. *Student services:* Campus employment opportunities, campus safety program, career counseling, exercise/wellness program, free psychological counseling, international student services, low-cost health insurance, services for students with disabilities, teacher training, writing training.

Computer facilities: A campuswide network can be accessed from student residence rooms and from off campus.
Website: http://www.twu.ca/

General Application Contact: Phil Kay, Director of Graduate and International Admissions, 604-513-2121 Ext. 3046, E-mail: phil.kay@twu.ca.

GRADUATE UNITS

ACTS Seminaries *Program availability:* Part-time. Offers Christian studies (MA); cross cultural ministry (MA); theology (M Div, M Th, MAMFT, MLE, MTS, D Min).

School of Graduate Studies Expenses: Contact institution. Offers biblical studies (MA); business (MA, Certificate); Christian ministry (MA); counseling psychology (MA); education (MA, Certificate); general humanities (MAIH); healthcare (MA, Certificate); international business (MBA); linguistics (MA); management of the growing enterprise (MBA); non-profit (MA, Certificate); non-profit and charitable organization management (MBA); specialized (MAIH); teaching English to speakers of other languages (TESOL) (MA). *Application Contact:* Phil Kay, Director of Graduate and International Admissions, 604-513-2121 Ext. 3444, E-mail: phil.kay@twu.ca.

School of Nursing Offers nursing (MSN).

TRI-STATE BIBLE COLLEGE, South Point, OH 45680-8402

General Information Independent-religious, coed, comprehensive institution.

GRADUATE UNITS

Graduate Program Offers Biblical studies (MA). Electronic applications accepted.

TROY UNIVERSITY, Troy, AL 36082

General Information State-supported, coed, comprehensive institution. *Enrollment:* 1,144 full-time matriculated graduate/professional students (854 women), 2,385 part-time matriculated graduate/professional students (1,498 women). *Enrollment by degree level:* 3,339 master's, 97 doctoral, 93 other advanced degrees. *Graduate faculty:* 196 full-time (94 women), 82 part-time/adjunct (46 women). *International tuition:* $850 full-time. *Tuition, area resident:* Full-time $425; part-time $425 per credit hour. Tuition, state resident: full-time $425; part-time $425 per credit hour. Tuition, nonresident: full-time $850; part-time $850 per credit hour. *Required fees:* $50 per semester. Tuition and fees vary according to campus/location and program. *Graduate housing:* Rooms and/or apartments available on a first-come, first-served basis to single and married students. Typical cost: $3300 per year ($6804 including board) for single students; $3300 per year ($6804 including board) for married students. Room and board charges vary according to housing facility selected. Housing application deadline: 7/31. *Student services:* Campus employment opportunities, campus safety program, career counseling, exercise/wellness program, free psychological counseling, international student services, low-cost health insurance, services for students with disabilities, teacher training, writing training. *Library facilities:* Lurleen B. Wallace Library (Troy Campus) plus 2 others. *Collection:* Books: 603,904 (physical), 277,690 (digital/electronic); Serial titles: 213 (physical), 134,396 (digital/electronic); Databases: 261.

Computer facilities: 1,935 computers available on campus for general student use. A campuswide network can be accessed from student residence rooms and from off campus. Online class registration is available.
Website: http://www.troy.edu/

General Application Contact: Jessica A Kimbro, Assistant Director of Graduate Programs, 334-670-3189, Fax: 334-670-3733, E-mail: jacord@troy.edu.

GRADUATE UNITS

Graduate School Students: 1,132 full-time (801 women), 2,290 part-time (1,460 women); includes 1,061 minority (879 Black or African American, non-Hispanic/Latino; 14 American Indian or Alaska Native, non-Hispanic/Latino; 44 Asian, non-Hispanic/Latino; 74 Hispanic/Latino; 3 Native Hawaiian or other Pacific Islander, non-Hispanic/Latino; 47 Two or more races, non-Hispanic/Latino). Average age 31. 2,237 applicants, 87% accepted, 1241 enrolled. *Faculty:* 215 full-time (99 women), 68 part-time/adjunct (34 women). Expenses: Contact institution. *Financial support:* Fellowships, career-related internships or fieldwork, and scholarships/grants available. Support available to part-time students. Financial award applicants required to submit FAFSA. In

2018, 1,174 master's, 21 doctorates, 42 other advanced degrees awarded. *Program availability:* Part-time, evening/weekend, 100% online, blended/hybrid learning. *Application deadline:* Applications are processed on a rolling basis. *Application fee:* $50. Electronic applications accepted. *Application Contact:* Jessica A. Kimbro, Assistant Director of Graduate Programs, 334-670-3189, Fax: 334-670-3912, E-mail: jacord@troy.edu. *Associate Provost/Dean,* Dr. Mary Anne C. Templeton, 334-670-3189, Fax: 334-670-3912, E-mail: mtempleton@troy.edu.

College of Arts and Sciences Students: 168 full-time (91 women), 695 part-time (352 women); includes 246 minority (213 Black or African American, non-Hispanic/Latino; 2 American Indian or Alaska Native, non-Hispanic/Latino; 6 Asian, non-Hispanic/Latino; 11 Hispanic/Latino; 1 Native Hawaiian or other Pacific Islander, non-Hispanic/Latino; 13 Two or more races, non-Hispanic/Latino), 49 international. Average age 33. 678 applicants, 89% accepted, 320 enrolled. *Faculty:* 59 full-time (20 women), 18 part-time/adjunct (6 women). Expenses: Contact institution. *Financial support:* Fellowships, career-related internships or fieldwork, and scholarships/grants available. Support available to part-time students. Financial award applicants required to submit FAFSA. In 2018, 328 master's, 2 other advanced degrees awarded. *Program availability:* Part-time, evening/weekend. Offers American history (MA); arts and sciences (MA, MPA, MS, MS Sc, Certificate); biomedical sciences (MS, Certificate); computer science (MS); criminal justice (MS); environmental and biological sciences (MS); European history (MA); government contracting (MPA); international relations (MS); social science (MS Sc). *Application deadline:* Applications are processed on a rolling basis. *Application fee:* $50. Electronic applications accepted. *Application Contact:* Jessica A. Kimbro, Assistant Director of Graduate Programs, 334-670-3189, E-mail: jacord@troy.edu. *Dean,* Dr. Steven Taylor, 334-670-3399, E-mail: sltaylor@troy.edu.

College of Business Students: 194 full-time (120 women), 778 part-time (431 women); includes 248 minority (218 Black or African American, non-Hispanic/Latino; 3 American Indian or Alaska Native, non-Hispanic/Latino; 3 Asian, non-Hispanic/Latino; 15 Hispanic/Latino; 9 Two or more races, non-Hispanic/Latino), 38 international. Average age 34. 584 applicants, 84% accepted, 324 enrolled. *Faculty:* 42 full-time (14 women), 2 part-time/adjunct (0 women). Expenses: Contact institution. *Financial support:* In 2018–19, 5 research assistantships were awarded; career-related internships or fieldwork and scholarships/grants also available. Support available to part-time students. Financial award applicants required to submit FAFSA. In 2018, 268 master's awarded. *Program availability:* Part-time, evening/weekend, 100% online, blended/hybrid learning. Offers accountancy (M Acc); accounting (EMBA, MBA); business (EMBA, M Acc, MA, MBA, MBAi, MS, MSM); criminal justice (EMBA); economics (MA); finance (MBA); general management (EMBA, MBA); healthcare management (EMBA); human resources management (MS); information systems (EMBA, MBA); international economic development (MBA); management (MS, MSM). *Application deadline:* Applications are processed on a rolling basis. *Application fee:* $50. Electronic applications accepted. *Application Contact:* Jessica A. Kimbro, Assistant Director of Graduate Programs, 334-670-3189, Fax: 334-670-3912, E-mail: jacord@troy.edu. *Dean,* Dr. Judson Edwards, 334-670-3989, Fax: 334-670-3708, E-mail: jcedwards@troy.edu.

College of Communication and Fine Arts Students: 33 full-time (22 women), 72 part-time (49 women); includes 24 minority (20 Black or African American, non-Hispanic/Latino; 1 American Indian or Alaska Native, non-Hispanic/Latino; 2 Hispanic/Latino; 1 Native Hawaiian or other Pacific Islander, non-Hispanic/Latino). Average age 32. 54 applicants, 85% accepted, 32 enrolled. *Faculty:* 19 full-time (9 women), 3 part-time/adjunct (2 women). Expenses: Contact institution. *Financial support:* Fellowships, career-related internships or fieldwork, and scholarships/grants available. Support available to part-time students. Financial award applicants required to submit FAFSA. In 2018, 53 master's awarded. *Program availability:* Part-time, evening/weekend. Offers strategic communication (MS). *Application deadline:* For fall admission, 6/1 for international students; for spring admission, 10/15 for international students. Applications are processed on a rolling basis. *Application fee:* $50. Electronic applications accepted. *Application Contact:* Jessica A. Kimbro, Assistant Director of Graduate Programs, 334-670-3189, E-mail: jacord@troy.edu. *Dean,* Dr. Larry Blocher, 334-670-3869, Fax: 334-670-3547, E-mail: lblocher@troy.edu.

College of Education Students: 392 full-time (319 women), 560 part-time (463 women); includes 316 minority (284 Black or African American, non-Hispanic/Latino; 4 American Indian or Alaska Native, non-Hispanic/Latino; 3 Asian, non-Hispanic/Latino; 12 Hispanic/Latino; 1 Native Hawaiian or other Pacific Islander, non-Hispanic/Latino; 12 Two or more races, non-Hispanic/Latino), 17 international. Average age 35. 524 applicants, 86% accepted, 288 enrolled. *Faculty:* 75 full-time (45 women), 26 part-time/adjunct (19 women). Expenses: Contact institution. *Financial support:* Fellowships, career-related internships or fieldwork, and scholarships/grants available. Support available to part-time students. Financial award applicants required to submit FAFSA. In 2018, 338 master's, 30 other advanced degrees awarded. *Program availability:* Part-time, evening/weekend. Offers adult education (MS); community counseling (MS); early childhood education (MS, Ed S); education (MS, MS Ed, Ed S); educational administration/leadership (MS, Ed S); K-6 elementary and collaborative education (MS, Ed S); postsecondary education (MS Ed); school counseling (MS, Ed S); second language instruction (MS); secondary education (MS); teacher education-multiple levels (MS). *Application deadline:* For fall admission, 1/1 for domestic students, 6/1 for international students; for spring admission, 10/15 for international students. Applications are processed on a rolling basis. *Application fee:* $50. Electronic applications accepted. *Application Contact:* Jessica A. Kimbro, Assistant Director of Graduate Programs, 334-670-3189, E-mail: jacord@troy.edu. *Dean,* Dr. Dionne Rosser-Mims, 334-670-3365, Fax: 334-670-3474, E-mail: drosser-mims@troy.edu.

College of Health and Human Services Students: 356 full-time (301 women), 251 part-time (181 women); includes 175 minority (156 Black or African American, non-Hispanic/Latino; 1 American Indian or Alaska Native, non-Hispanic/Latino; 1 Asian, non-Hispanic/Latino; 10 Hispanic/Latino; 7 Two or more races, non-Hispanic/Latino), 17 international. Average age 34. 360 applicants, 91% accepted, 256 enrolled. *Faculty:* 32 full-time (19 women), 14 part-time/adjunct (12 women). Expenses: Contact institution. *Financial support:* Tuition waivers and unspecified assistantships available. Support available to part-time students. Financial award application deadline: 4/5; financial award applicants required to submit FAFSA. In 2018, 187 master's, 21 doctorates, 10 other advanced degrees awarded. *Program availability:* Part-time, evening/weekend. Offers adult health (MSN); family nurse practitioner (DNP); health and human services (MS, MS Sc, MSN, MSW, DNP, DPH, PMC); maternal infant (MSN); nursing informatics specialist (MSN); social work (MSW); sport and fitness management (MS, DPH). *Application deadline:* Applications are processed on a rolling basis. *Application fee:* $50. Electronic applications accepted. *Application Contact:* Jessica A. Kimbro, Assistant Director of Graduate Programs,

334-670-3189, E-mail: jacord@troy.edu. *Dean,* Dr. Denise Green, 334-670-3712, Fax: 334-670-3743, E-mail: dmgreen@troy.edu.

TRUETT MCCONNELL UNIVERSITY, Cleveland, GA 30528
General Information Independent-religious, coed, comprehensive institution. *Graduate housing:* Rooms and/or apartments available on a first-come, first-served basis to single and married students. Housing application deadline: 7/1.

GRADUATE UNITS
Balthasar Hubmaier School of Theology and Missions *Program availability:* Part-time, 100% online. Offers theology (MA). Electronic applications accepted.
Hans Hut School of Business *Program availability:* Part-time, evening/weekend, 100% online. Offers business (MBA). Electronic applications accepted.
The Leonhard Schiemer School of Psychology and Biblical Counseling *Program availability:* Part-time. Offers professional counseling (MA). Electronic applications accepted.
Pilgram Marpeck School of Science, Technology, Engineering and Mathematics *Program availability:* Part-time. Offers biology (MS). Electronic applications accepted.

TRUMAN STATE UNIVERSITY, Kirksville, MO 63501-4221
General Information State-supported, coed, comprehensive institution. CGS member. *Enrollment:* 5,853 graduate, professional, and undergraduate students; 218 full-time matriculated graduate/professional students (153 women), 21 part-time matriculated graduate/professional students (17 women). *Enrollment by degree level:* 239 master's. *Graduate faculty:* 132 full-time (55 women). *International tuition:* $668 full-time. Tuition, state resident: full-time $385.50; part-time $385.50 per credit hour. Tuition, nonresident: full-time $668; part-time $668 per credit hour. *Required fees:* $648. *Graduate housing:* Rooms and/or apartments available on a first-come, first-served basis to single and married students. Housing application deadline: 5/1. *Student services:* Campus employment opportunities, campus safety program, career counseling, exercise/wellness program, free psychological counseling, grant writing training, international student services, multicultural affairs office, services for students with disabilities, teacher training, writing training. *Library facilities:* Pickler Memorial Library. *Collection:* Books: 495,980 (physical), 388,874 (digital/electronic); Serial titles: 355 (physical), 2,407 (digital/electronic); Databases: 107. Weekly public service hours: 105; students can reserve study rooms.
Computer facilities: 1,056 computers available on campus for general student use. A campuswide network can be accessed from student residence rooms and from off campus. Online class registration is available.
Website: http://www.truman.edu/
General Application Contact: Bethany Gibson, Graduate & Academic Offices Administrative Assistant, 660-785-4109, Fax: 660-785-7460, E-mail: gradinfo@truman.edu.

GRADUATE UNITS
Graduate School Electronic applications accepted.
School of Arts and Letters Students: 224 full-time (171 women); includes 16 minority (4 Asian, non-Hispanic/Latino; 7 Hispanic/Latino; 5 Two or more races, non-Hispanic/Latino). Average age 23. 45 applicants, 51% accepted, 17 enrolled. *Faculty:* 44 full-time (19 women). Expenses: Contact institution. *Financial support:* In 2018–19, research assistantships with tuition reimbursements (averaging $8,000 per year), teaching assistantships with tuition reimbursements (averaging $8,000 per year) were awarded; career-related internships or fieldwork and Federal Work-Study also available. Financial award application deadline: 5/1; financial award applicants required to submit FAFSA. In 2018, 10 master's awarded. Offers arts and letters (MA, MS); English (MA); music (MA). *Application deadline:* For fall admission, 6/1 priority date for domestic and international students; for spring admission, 11/1 priority date for domestic students, 11/1 for international students. Applications are processed on a rolling basis. *Application fee:* $40. Electronic applications accepted. *Application Contact:* Bethany Gibson, Graduate Office Administrative Assistant, 660-785-4109, Fax: 660-785-7460, E-mail: gradinfo@truman.edu. *Dean,* Jeanne Harding, 660-785-7777, Fax: 660-785-7109, E-mail: jharding@truman.edu.
School of Business Students: 27 full-time (7 women), 1 part-time; includes 4 minority (3 Asian, non-Hispanic/Latino; 1 Two or more races, non-Hispanic/Latino). Average age 23. 27 applicants, 93% accepted, 23 enrolled. *Faculty:* 11 full-time (4 women). Expenses: Contact institution. *Financial support:* In 2018–19, 10 teaching assistantships with full and partial tuition reimbursements (averaging $5,000 per year) were awarded; research assistantships with tuition reimbursements and career-related internships or fieldwork also available. Financial award application deadline: 4/1; financial award applicants required to submit FAFSA. In 2018, 26 master's awarded. Offers accounting (M Ac); business (M Ac). *Application deadline:* For fall admission, 6/1 for domestic and international students; for spring admission, 11/1 for domestic and international students; for summer admission, 4/1 for domestic and international students. Applications are processed on a rolling basis. *Application fee:* $40. Electronic applications accepted. *Application Contact:* Bethany Gibson, Graduate Office Secretary, 660-785-4109, Fax: 660-785-7460, E-mail: bethanyc@truman.edu. *Dean,* Dr. Debra Kerby, 660-785-4346, Fax: 660-785-7471, E-mail: dkerby@truman.edu.
School of Health Sciences and Education Offers communication disorders (MA); education (MAE); health sciences and education (MA, MAE). Electronic applications accepted.

TUFTS UNIVERSITY, Medford, MA 02155
General Information Independent, coed, university. CGS member. *Enrollment:* 5,194 full-time matriculated graduate/professional students (3,054 women), 554 part-time matriculated graduate/professional students (349 women). *Enrollment by degree level:* 2,396 master's, 3,013 doctoral, 339 other advanced degrees. *Graduate faculty:* 987 full-time (459 women), 544 part-time/adjunct (275 women). *Tuition:* Full-time $51,288; part-time $1710 per credit hour. *Required fees:* $904. Full-time tuition and fees vary according to degree level, program and student level. Part-time tuition and fees vary according to course load. *Graduate housing:* Room and/or apartments available on a first-come, first-served basis to single students; on-campus housing not available to married students. Housing application deadline: 4/15. *Student services:* Campus employment opportunities, campus safety program, career counseling, exercise/wellness program, international student services, services for students with disabilities, teacher training, writing training. *Library facilities:* Tisch Library plus 3 others. *Collection:* Books: 1.3 million (physical), 432,877 (digital/electronic); Serial titles: 1,012 (physical); Databases: 83,216. Weekly public service hours: 110; students can reserve study rooms.
Computer facilities: Computer purchase and lease plans are available. 1,039 computers available on campus for general student use. A campuswide network can be

accessed from student residence rooms and from off campus. Online class registration, Cloud storage for all students, staff, and faculty are available. Website: http://www.tufts.edu/

General Application Contact: Information Contact, 617-628-5000.

GRADUATE UNITS

Cummings School of Veterinary Medicine Offers animals and public policy (MS); biomedical sciences (PhD); conservation medicine (MS); veterinary medicine (DVM). Electronic applications accepted.

The Fletcher School of Law and Diplomacy *Program availability:* Online learning. Offers economics and public policy (PhD); international affairs (PhD); international business (MIB); international law (LL M); law and diplomacy (MA, MALD); transatlantic affairs (MA). MA in transatlantic affairs offered jointly with The College of Europe; PhD in economics and public policy with Tufts' Graduate School of Arts and Sciences. Electronic applications accepted.

The Gerald J. and Dorothy R. Friedman School of Nutrition Science and Policy *Program availability:* Part-time. Offers agriculture, food and environment (MS, PhD); biochemical and molecular nutrition (MS, PhD); dietetic internship (MS); food and nutrition policy (MS, PhD); humanitarian assistance (MAHA); nutrition (MS, PhD); nutrition data science (MS, PhD); nutrition interventions, communication, and behavior change (MS, PhD); sustainable water management (MS). Electronic applications accepted.

Graduate School of Arts and Sciences *Program availability:* Part-time. Offers art education (MAT); art history (MA); art history and museum studies (MA); arts and sciences (MA, MAT, MPP, MS, OTD, PhD, Certificate, Ed S); astrophysics (MS, PhD); bioengineering (Certificate); biology (MS, PhD); biotechnology (Certificate); biotechnology engineering (Certificate); chemical physics (PhD); chemistry (MS, PhD); chemistry/biotechnology (PhD); child study and human development (MA, PhD); classics (MA); classics with teaching licensure (MA); cognitive science (PhD); community development (MA); community environmental studies (Certificate); composition (MA); computer science (Certificate); computer science minor (Certificate); digital tools for premodern studies (MA); diversity and inclusion leadership (MA); economics (MS); economics and public policy (PhD); education (MA, MAT, MS, PhD); educational studies (MA); elementary education (MAT); English (MA, PhD); environmental management (Certificate); environmental policy (MA); epidemiology (Certificate); ethnomusicology (MA); French (MA); German (MA); German with teaching licensure (MA); health and human welfare (MA); history (MA, PhD); history and museum studies (MA); housing policy (MA); human-computer interaction (Certificate); interdisciplinary studies (PhD); international environment/development policy (MA); management of community organizations (Certificate); manufacturing engineering (Certificate); mathematics (MS, PhD); microwave and wireless engineering (Certificate); middle and secondary education (MAT); museum education (MA); museum studies (Certificate); music theory (MA); occupational therapy (Certificate); philosophy (MA); physics (MS, PhD); physics education (PhD); program evaluation (Certificate); psychology (MS, PhD); public policy (MPP); school psychology (MA, Ed S); secondary education (MA); soft materials robotics (PhD); STEM education (MS, PhD); theatre and performance studies (MA, PhD). Electronic applications accepted.

Sackler School of Graduate Biomedical Sciences Students: 221 full-time (126 women), 2 part-time; includes 50 minority (6 Black or African American, non-Hispanic/Latino; 26 Asian, non-Hispanic/Latino; 10 Hispanic/Latino; 8 Two or more races, non-Hispanic/Latino), 42 international. Average age 33. 734 applicants, 17% accepted, 56 enrolled. *Faculty:* 190 full-time (62 women), 26 part-time/adjunct (13 women). Expenses: Contact institution. *Financial support:* In 2018–19, 163 research assistantships with full tuition reimbursements (averaging $34,000 per year) were awarded; traineeships also available. Financial award application deadline: 12/1. In 2018, 24 master's, 34 doctorates awarded. Offers biomedical sciences (MS, PhD, Certificate); cancer biology (PhD); clinical and translational science (MS, PhD, Certificate); developmental and regenerative biology (PhD); genetics (PhD); immunology (PhD); mammalian genetics (PhD); medically-oriented research in graduate education (PhD); molecular and cellular medicine (PhD); molecular microbiology (PhD); neuroscience (PhD); structural and chemical biology (PhD). *Application deadline:* For fall admission, 12/1 priority date for domestic and international students. *Application fee:* $90. Electronic applications accepted. *Application Contact:* Jeff Miller, Admissions Coordinator, 617-636-6767, Fax: 617-636-0375, E-mail: SacklerAdmissions@tufts.edu. *Dean,* Dr. Dan Jay, 617-636-6767, Fax: 617-636-0375, E-mail: daniel.jay@tufts.edu.

School of Dental Medicine Offers dental medicine (MS, DMD, Certificate); dentistry (Certificate). DMD/MPH offered with School of Medicine.

School of Engineering *Program availability:* Part-time. Offers bioengineering (MS); biomedical engineering (MS, PhD); biotechnology (MS, PhD); chemical engineering (MS, PhD); civil and environmental engineering (MS, PhD); cognitive science/computer science (PhD); computer science (MS, PhD); electrical engineering (MS, PhD); engineering (MS, MSEM, PhD); human factors (MS); mechanical engineering (MS, PhD); soft material robotics (PhD). Electronic applications accepted.

The Gordon Institute *Program availability:* Part-time. Offers engineering management (MS); innovation and management (MS). Electronic applications accepted.

School of Medicine Offers biomedical sciences (MS); health communication (MS, Certificate); medicine (MPH, MS, Dr PH, MD, Certificate); pain research, education and policy (MS, Certificate); physician assistant (MS); public health (MPH, Dr PH).

School of the Museum of Fine Arts at Tufts University Offers art education (MAT); studio art (MFA, Postbaccalaureate Certificate). Electronic applications accepted.

TULANE UNIVERSITY, New Orleans, LA 70118-5669

General Information Independent, coed, university. CGS member. *Enrollment:* 11,722 graduate, professional, and undergraduate students; 4,166 full-time matriculated graduate/professional students (2,279 women), 1,150 part-time matriculated graduate/professional students (699 women). *Enrollment by degree level:* 2,470 master's, 2,809 doctoral, 37 other advanced degrees. *Graduate faculty:* 72 full-time (35 women), 59 part-time/adjunct (41 women). *Tuition:* Full-time $52,856; part-time $2937 per credit hour. *Required fees:* $2040; $44.50 per credit hour. $580 per term. Tuition and fees vary according to course load, degree level and program. *Graduate housing:* Rooms and/or apartments available on a first-come, first-served basis to single and married students. Typical cost: $9660 per year for single students; $19,200 per year for married students. Room charges vary according to board plan, campus/location and housing facility selected. *Student services:* Campus employment opportunities, campus safety program, career counseling, child daycare facilities, exercise/wellness program, free psychological counseling, grant writing training, international student services, low-cost health insurance, multicultural affairs office, services for students with disabilities, teacher training, writing training. *Library facilities:* Howard Tilton Memorial Library plus 8 others. *Collection:* Books: 4.6 million (physical); Serial titles: 77,251 (physical). Study areas open 24 hours, 5–7 days a week.

Computer facilities: 556 computers available on campus for general student use. A campuswide network can be accessed from student residence rooms and from off campus. Online class registration is available. Website: http://www.tulane.edu/

General Application Contact: Jennifer O'Brien, Program Manager, 504-247-1213, Fax: 504-865-6723, E-mail: ogps@tulane.edu.

GRADUATE UNITS

A. B. Freeman School of Business Students: 432 full-time (218 women), 533 part-time (262 women); includes 99 minority (32 Black or African American, non-Hispanic/Latino; 1 American Indian or Alaska Native, non-Hispanic/Latino; 26 Asian, non-Hispanic/Latino; 35 Hispanic/Latino; 5 Two or more races, non-Hispanic/Latino), 644 international. Average age 28. 1,911 applicants, 77% accepted, 411 enrolled. *Faculty:* 43 full-time (11 women), 45 part-time/adjunct (8 women). Expenses: Contact institution. *Financial support:* In 2018–19, 153 students received support. Fellowships with tuition reimbursements available, research assistantships, teaching assistantships, career-related internships or fieldwork, Federal Work-Study, tuition waivers (full and partial), and unspecified assistantships available. Support available to part-time students. Financial award application deadline: 4/15; financial award applicants required to submit FAFSA. In 2018, 728 master's, 4 doctorates awarded. *Program availability:* Part-time, evening/weekend. Offers accounting (M Acct); analytics (MBA); banking and financial services (M Fin); energy (M Fin, MBA); entrepreneurship (MBA); finance (MBA, PhD); financial accounting (PhD); international business (MBA); international management (MBA); strategic management and leadership (MBA). *Application deadline:* For fall admission, 11/1 priority date for domestic students, 11/1 for international students; for winter admission, 1/6 for domestic and international students; for spring admission, 3/1 priority date for domestic students, 3/1 for international students; for summer admission, 5/5 for domestic students. Applications are processed on a rolling basis. *Application fee:* $125. Electronic applications accepted. *Application Contact:* Melissa Booth, Assistant Dean for Graduate Admissions, 800-223-5402, E-mail: freeman.admissions@tulane.edu. *Dean,* Ira Solomon, PhD, 504-865-5407, Fax: 504-865-5491, E-mail: businessdean@tulane.edu.

School of Architecture *Program availability:* Part-time. Offers architecture (M Arch, M Arch II, MPS, MSRED).

School of Law Offers American business law (LL M); international development (MS, PhD); law (JD, SJD). Electronic applications accepted.

The Payson Center for International Development *Program availability:* Part-time. Offers international development (MS, PhD); law and development (LL M). Electronic applications accepted.

School of Liberal Arts *Program availability:* Part-time. Offers anthropology (PhD); classical studies (MA); design and technical production (MFA); economics (MA, PhD); English (MA); French (MA, PhD); history (MA, PhD); history of art (MA); liberal arts (MA, MFA, PhD); music (MA, MFA); philosophy (MA, PhD); political science (PhD); Portuguese (MA); sociology (MA); Spanish and Portuguese (PhD); studio art (MFA). Electronic applications accepted.

Roger Thayer Stone Center for Latin American Studies Offers Latin American studies (MA, PhD). Electronic applications accepted.

School of Medicine Offers medicine (MS, MD, PhD).

Graduate Programs in Biomedical Sciences Offers biochemistry and molecular biology (MS); biomedical sciences (MS, PhD); human genetics (MS); microbiology and immunology (MS); molecular and cellular biology (PhD); neuroscience (MS, PhD); pharmacology (MS); physiology (MS); structural and cellular biology (MS, PhD).

School of Professional Advancement *Program availability:* Part-time. Offers health and wellness management (MPS); homeland security studies (MPS); information technology management (MPS); liberal arts (MLA).

School of Public Health and Tropical Medicine *Program availability:* Part-time, evening/weekend, 100% online, synchronous sessions. Offers Clinical Tropical Medicine and Traveler's Health (Diploma); community health sciences (MPH); epidemiology (MPH, MS, Dr PH, PhD); global biostatistics and data science (MS, MSPH, PhD); global community health and behavioral sciences (Dr PH, PhD); global environmental health sciences (MPH, MSPH, PhD); health policy and management (MHA, MPH, PhD, Sc D); parasitology (PhD); public health (MSPH); public health and tropical medicine (MPHTM). Electronic applications accepted.

School of Science and Engineering *Program availability:* Part-time. Offers biomedical engineering (MS, PhD); cell and molecular biology (MS, PhD); chemical and biomolecular engineering (MS, PhD); chemistry (MS, PhD); ecology and evolutionary biology (MS, PhD); interdisciplinary studies (PhD); mathematics (MS, PhD); neuroscience (MS, PhD); physics (PhD); psychology (MS, PhD); science and engineering (MS, PhD). MS and PhD offered through the Graduate School. Electronic applications accepted.

School of Social Work *Program availability:* Part-time. Offers city, culture and community (PhD); disaster resilience leadership (MS); social work (MSW, DSW). Electronic applications accepted.

TUSCULUM UNIVERSITY, Greeneville, TN 37743-9997

General Information Independent-religious, coed, comprehensive institution. *Graduate housing:* On-campus housing not available.

GRADUATE UNITS

Program in Business Administration *Program availability:* Evening/weekend. Offers general management (MBA).

Program in Curriculum and Instruction *Program availability:* Evening/weekend. Offers special education (MA Ed).

Program in Nursing *Program availability:* Part-time. Offers family nurse practitioner (MSN).

Program in Talent Development *Program availability:* Online learning. Offers talent development (MA).

Program in Teaching *Program availability:* Evening/weekend. Offers teaching (MAT).

TUSKEGEE UNIVERSITY, Tuskegee, AL 36088

General Information Independent, coed, comprehensive institution. *Graduate housing:* Rooms and/or apartments available to single students and available on a first-come, first-served basis to married students. Housing application deadline: 5/1. *Research affiliation:* Boeing (engineering), Chevron (engineering), 3M Corporation (engineering), U.S. Department of Education (DOE) (agriculture), U.S. Department of Defense (agriculture).

GRADUATE UNITS

Graduate Programs *Program availability:* Part-time. Offers integrative biosciences (PhD).

Andrew F. Brimmer College of Business and Information Science Offers information systems and security management (MS).

College of Agriculture, Environment and Nutrition Sciences Offers agricultural and resource economics (MS); agriculture, environment and nutrition sciences (MS); animal and poultry breeding (MS); animal and poultry nutrition (MS); animal and poultry physiology (MS); animal and poultry sciences (MS); environmental sciences (MS); food and nutritional sciences (MS); plant and soil sciences (MS).

College of Arts and Sciences Offers arts and sciences (MS); biology (MS); chemistry (MS).

College of Engineering Offers electrical engineering (MSEE); engineering (MSEE, MSME, PhD); materials science and engineering (PhD); mechanical engineering (MSME).

College of Veterinary Medicine, Nursing and Allied Health Offers occupational therapy (MS); veterinary medicine (MS, DVM); veterinary medicine, nursing and allied health (MS, DVM).

TYNDALE UNIVERSITY COLLEGE & SEMINARY, Toronto, ON M2M 3S4, Canada

General Information Independent-religious, coed, comprehensive institution. *Graduate housing:* Room and/or apartments available on a first-come, first-served basis to single students; on-campus housing not available to married students.

GRADUATE UNITS

Graduate Programs *Program availability:* Part-time, online learning. Offers Biblical studies (M Div); Christian foundations (MTS); Christian studies (Diploma); counseling (M Div); educational ministry (M Div); missions (M Div, Diploma); pastoral and Chinese ministry (M Div); pastoral ministry (M Div); Pentecostal studies (MTS); spiritual formation (M Div, Diploma); theological studies (M Div); theology (Th M); worship and liturgy (M Div, MTS); youth and family ministry (M Div). Electronic applications accepted.

UNIFICATION THEOLOGICAL SEMINARY, Barrytown, NY 12507

General Information Independent-religious, coed, graduate-only institution. *Enrollment by degree level:* 72 master's, 32 doctoral. *Graduate faculty:* 4 full-time (1 woman), 9 part-time/adjunct (1 woman). *Tuition:* Full-time $9450; part-time $525 per credit. *Required fees:* $260; $210 per semester. $105 per semester. *Graduate housing:* On-campus housing not available. *Student services:* Campus employment opportunities, career counseling, free psychological counseling, international student services, writing training. *Library facilities:* Seminary Library plus 1 other. *Collection:* Books: 58,264 (physical), 69,025 (digital/electronic); Databases: 26. Weekly public service hours: 44.

Computer facilities: 10 computers available on campus for general student use. A campuswide network can be accessed. Online class registration is available. Website: http://www.uts.edu/

General Application Contact: Henry Christopher, Director of Admissions, 212-563-6647 Ext. 105, Fax: 212-563-6431, E-mail: h.christopher@uts.edu.

GRADUATE UNITS

Graduate Programs Students: 48 full-time (16 women), 56 part-time (21 women); includes 49 minority (26 Black or African American, non-Hispanic/Latino; 19 Asian, non-Hispanic/Latino; 2 Hispanic/Latino; 2 Two or more races, non-Hispanic/Latino), 38 international. Average age 46. *Faculty:* 3 full-time (1 woman), 9 part-time/adjunct (1 woman). Expenses: Contact institution. *Financial support:* In 2018–19, 104 students received support. Scholarships/grants available. Financial award application deadline: 6/15; financial award applicants required to submit FAFSA. In 2018, 8 master's, 3 doctorates awarded. *Program availability:* Part-time, evening/weekend. Offers family and educational ministry (D Min); interfaith peacebuilding (MRE); peace and justice ministry (D Min); religious education (MRE); religious studies (MA); theology (M Div). *Application deadline:* For fall admission, 3/15 priority date for domestic and international students; for spring admission, 9/15 priority date for domestic and international students. Applications are processed on a rolling basis. *Application fee:* $30. Electronic applications accepted. *Application Contact:* Henry Christopher, Director of Admissions and Financial Aid, 212-563-6647 Ext. 105, Fax: 845-752-3014, E-mail: admissions@uts.edu. *Vice-President*, Michael Mickler, 845-752-3235, Fax: 845-752-3014, E-mail: mm@uts.edu.

UNIFORMED SERVICES UNIVERSITY OF THE HEALTH SCIENCES, Bethesda, MD 20814-4799

General Information Federally supported, coed, graduate-only institution. *Enrollment by degree level:* 44 master's, 780 doctoral. *Graduate faculty:* 372 full-time (119 women), 4,044 part-time/adjunct (908 women). *Graduate housing:* On-campus housing not available. *Student services:* Campus safety program, career counseling, child daycare facilities, exercise/wellness program, free psychological counseling, grant writing training, low-cost health insurance, multicultural affairs office, teacher training, writing training. *Library facilities:* James A. Zimble Learning Resource Center. *Collection:* Study areas open 24 hours, 5–7 days a week; students can reserve study rooms.

Computer facilities: 100 computers available on campus for general student use. Online class registration is available. Website: http://www.usuhs.edu/

General Application Contact: Tina Finley, Program Administrative Specialist, 301-295-3642, Fax: 301-295-1996, E-mail: netina.finley@usuhs.edu.

GRADUATE UNITS

Daniel K. Inouye Graduate School of Nursing Offers adult-gerontology clinical nurse specialist (MSN, DNP); family nurse practitioner (DNP); nurse anesthesia (DNP); nursing science (PhD); psychiatric mental health nurse practitioner (DNP); women's health nurse practitioner (DNP). Electronic applications accepted.

F. Edward Hebert School of Medicine Offers medicine (MPH, MS, MSPH, MTMH, Dr PH, MD, PhD).

Graduate Programs in the Biomedical Sciences and Public Health Offers clinical psychology (PhD); emerging infectious diseases (PhD); environmental health sciences (PhD); healthcare administration and policy (MS); medical and clinical psychology (PhD); medical psychology (PhD); medical zoology (PhD); medicine (MS, PhD); molecular and cell biology (MS, PhD); neuroscience (PhD); preventive medicine and biometrics (MPH, MS, MSPH, MTMH, PhD); public health (MPH, MSPH); tropical medicine and hygiene (MTMH). Electronic applications accepted.

UNION COLLEGE, Barbourville, KY 40906-1499

General Information Independent-religious, coed, comprehensive institution. *Graduate housing:* Rooms and/or apartments available to single and married students.

GRADUATE UNITS

Graduate Programs *Program availability:* Part-time, evening/weekend. Offers clinical psychology (MA); counseling psychology (MA); elementary education (MA); health (MA Ed); health and physical education (MA); middle grades (MA); music education (MA); principalship (MA); reading specialist (MA); school psychology (MA); secondary education (MA); special education (MA).

UNION COLLEGE, Lincoln, NE 68506-4300

General Information Independent-religious, coed, comprehensive institution. *Graduate housing:* Rooms and/or apartments available on a first-come, first-served basis to single and married students.

GRADUATE UNITS

Physician Assistant Program Offers physician assistant (MPAS). Electronic applications accepted.

UNION INSTITUTE & UNIVERSITY, Cincinnati, OH 45206-1925

General Information Independent, coed, university.

GRADUATE UNITS

Master of Arts Program *Program availability:* Part-time, online only, 100% online. Offers creativity studies (MA); health and wellness (MA); history and culture (MA); leadership, public policy, and social issues (MA); literature and writing (MA). Electronic applications accepted.

Master of Arts Program in Clinical Mental Health Counseling *Program availability:* Part-time, online only, blended/hybrid learning. Offers clinical mental health counseling (MA). Electronic applications accepted.

Master of Science Program in Healthcare Leadership Offers healthcare leadership (MS).

Master of Science Program in Organizational Leadership *Program availability:* Part-time, online only, 100% online. Offers organizational leadership (MS). Electronic applications accepted.

PhD Program in Interdisciplinary Studies *Program availability:* Part-time, online only, blended/hybrid learning. Offers educational studies (PhD); ethical and creative leadership (PhD); humanities and culture (PhD); public policy and social change (PhD). Program requires participation in brief on-campus residencies twice each year (January and July). Electronic applications accepted.

UNION PRESBYTERIAN SEMINARY, Richmond, VA 23227-4597

General Information Independent-religious, coed, graduate-only institution. *Graduate housing:* Rooms and/or apartments available on a first-come, first-served basis to single and married students. Housing application deadline: 6/30.

GRADUATE UNITS

Graduate and Professional Programs *Program availability:* Part-time, evening/weekend, online learning. Electronic applications accepted.

UNION THEOLOGICAL SEMINARY IN THE CITY OF NEW YORK, New York, NY 10027-5710

General Information Independent-religious, coed, graduate-only institution. *Graduate housing:* Rooms and/or apartments available on a first-come, first-served basis to single and married students. Housing application deadline: 5/15.

GRADUATE UNITS

Graduate and Professional Programs *Program availability:* Part-time. Offers theology (M Div, MA, STM, D Min, PhD). M Div/MSSW with Columbia University.

UNION UNIVERSITY, Jackson, TN 38305-3697

General Information Independent-religious, coed, comprehensive institution. *Graduate housing:* Rooms and/or apartments available on a first-come, first-served basis to single and married students. Housing application deadline: 8/1.

GRADUATE UNITS

College of Pharmacy Offers pharmacy (Pharm D). Electronic applications accepted.

Institute for International and Intercultural Studies *Program availability:* Part-time, evening/weekend. Offers international and intercultural studies (MAIS). Electronic applications accepted.

McAfee School of Business Administration *Program availability:* Evening/weekend, online learning. Offers accountancy (M Acc). Program also available at Germantown campus. Electronic applications accepted.

School of Education *Program availability:* Part-time, evening/weekend, online learning. Offers education (M Ed, MA Ed); education administration generalist (Ed S); educational leadership (Ed D); educational supervision (Ed S); higher education (Ed D). M Ed also available at Germantown campus. Electronic applications accepted.

School of Nursing Offers executive leadership (DNP); nurse anesthesia (DNP); nurse practitioner (DNP); nursing education (MSN, PMC). Electronic applications accepted.

School of Social Work Offers social work (MSW).

School of Theology and Missions *Program availability:* Part-time, evening/weekend, online learning. Offers Christian studies (MCS); expository preaching (D Min). Electronic applications accepted.

UNITED LUTHERAN SEMINARY, Gettysburg, PA 17325-1795

General Information Independent-religious, coed, graduate-only institution. *Graduate housing:* Rooms and/or apartments available on a first-come, first-served basis to single and married students. Housing application deadline: 4/1.

GRADUATE UNITS

Graduate and Professional Programs *Program availability:* Part-time, online learning. Offers divinity (M Div); ministerial studies (MAMS); outdoor ministry (MAR); parish ministry (D Min); theology (STM). Electronic applications accepted.

UNITED LUTHERAN SEMINARY, Philadelphia, PA 19119-1794

General Information Independent-religious, coed, graduate-only institution. *Graduate housing:* Rooms and/or apartments available on a first-come, first-served basis to single and married students. Housing application deadline: 5/15.

GRADUATE UNITS

Graduate School *Program availability:* Part-time, evening/weekend. Offers divinity (M Div); ministry (D Min); public leadership (MA); religion (MAR); social ministry and church (Certificate); theology (STM, PhD). Electronic applications accepted.

UNITED STATES ARMY COMMAND AND GENERAL STAFF COLLEGE, Fort Leavenworth, KS 66027-2301

General Information Federally supported, coed, primarily men, graduate-only institution. *Graduate housing:* Rooms and/or apartments available to single and married students.

GRADUATE UNITS

Graduate Program Offers military art and science (MMAS). Only career military officers are selected to attend United States Army Command and General Staff College; Graduate Program is voluntary for first-year students, but mandatory for second-year students.

UNITED STATES INTERNATIONAL UNIVERSITY–AFRICA, Nairobi 00800, Kenya

General Information Independent, coed, comprehensive institution. *Graduate housing:* Room and/or apartments available on a first-come, first-served basis to single students; on-campus housing not available to married students. Housing application deadline: 7/31.

GRADUATE UNITS

School of Arts and Sciences *Program availability:* Part-time, evening/weekend. Offers counseling psychology (MA); international relations (MA).

School of Business Administration *Program availability:* Part-time, evening/weekend. Offers business administration (GEMBA); entrepreneurship (MBA); finance (MBA); human resource management (MBA); information technology management (MBA); integrated studies (MBA); international business administration (MBA); management and organizational development (MS); marketing (MBA); organizational development (EMS); strategic management (MBA).

UNITED STATES MERCHANT MARINE ACADEMY, Kings Point, NY 11024-1699

General Information Federally supported, coed, comprehensive institution.

GRADUATE UNITS

Graduate Program Offers marine engineering (MS).

UNITED STATES SPORTS ACADEMY, Daphne, AL 36526-7055

General Information Independent, coed, upper-level institution. *Graduate housing:* On-campus housing not available.

GRADUATE UNITS

Graduate Programs *Program availability:* Part-time, 100% online. Offers recreation management (MSS); sports coaching (MSS); sports health and fitness (MSS); sports management (MSS, Ed D); sports studies (MSS). Electronic applications accepted.

UNITED STATES UNIVERSITY, San Diego, CA 92108

General Information Proprietary, coed, comprehensive institution.

GRADUATE UNITS

Family Nurse Practitioner Program Offers family nurse practitioner (MSN).

UNITED TALMUDICAL SEMINARY, Brooklyn, NY 11211

General Information Independent-religious, men only, comprehensive institution.

GRADUATE UNITS

Graduate Programs

UNITED THEOLOGICAL SEMINARY, Dayton, OH 45426

General Information Independent-religious, coed, graduate-only institution.

GRADUATE UNITS

Graduate and Professional Programs *Program availability:* Part-time, evening/weekend, online learning. Offers Christian ministries (MA); ministry (M Div, D Min); theological studies (MTS). Electronic applications accepted.

UNITED THEOLOGICAL SEMINARY OF THE TWIN CITIES, New Brighton, MN 55112-2598

General Information Independent-religious, coed, graduate-only institution. *Graduate housing:* Rooms and/or apartments available on a first-come, first-served basis to single and married students.

GRADUATE UNITS

Graduate Programs *Program availability:* Part-time, evening/weekend. Offers advanced theological studies (Diploma); justice and peace studies (M Div, MA); leadership toward racial justice (M Div, MA, Certificate); Methodist studies (M Div, MA, Certificate); ministry (D Min); ministry renewal and professional development (Certificate); pastoral care and counseling (M Div, MA, MARL); religion and theology (MA); theological and religious studies (Certificate); theology and the arts (M Div, MA); urban ministry (M Div, MA, MARL); women's studies: religion, theology and ministry (M Div, MA).

UNITY COLLEGE, Unity, ME 04988

General Information Independent, coed, comprehensive institution.

GRADUATE UNITS

Program in Professional Science *Program availability:* Online learning. Offers sustainability science (MS); sustainable natural resource management (MS).

UNIVERSIDAD ADVENTISTA DE LAS ANTILLAS, Mayagüez, PR 00681-0118

General Information Independent-religious, coed, comprehensive institution. *Graduate housing:* Rooms and/or apartments available on a first-come, first-served basis to single and married students.

GRADUATE UNITS

EGECED Department Offers curriculum and instruction (M Ed); medical surgical nursing (MN); school administration and supervision (M Ed). Electronic applications accepted.

UNIVERSIDAD CENTRAL DEL CARIBE, Bayamón, PR 00960-6032

General Information Independent, coed, comprehensive institution. *Graduate housing:* On-campus housing not available.

GRADUATE UNITS

Program in Substance Abuse Counseling Offers substance abuse counseling (MHS).

School of Medicine Offers anatomy and cell biology (MA, MS); biochemistry (MS); biomedical sciences (MA); cellular and molecular biology (PhD); medicine (MA, MS, MD, PhD); microbiology and immunology (MA, MS); pharmacology (MS); physiology (MS).

UNIVERSIDAD DE LAS AMERICAS, A.C., 06700 Mexico City, Mexico

General Information Independent, coed, comprehensive institution.

GRADUATE UNITS

Program in Business Administration Offers finance (MBA); marketing research (MBA); production and quality (MBA).

Program in Education Offers education (M Ed).

Program in International Organizations and Institutions Offers international organizations and institutions (MA).

Program in Psychology Offers family therapy (MA).

UNIVERSIDAD DE LAS AMÉRICAS PUEBLA, Puebla CP 72810, Mexico

General Information Independent, coed, university. CGS member. *Graduate housing:* On-campus housing not available. *Research affiliation:* Empacadora San Marcos S. A. de C. U. (food service), Volkswagen de Mexico S. A. de C. U. (mechanical engineering), Institute Mexicano del Tecnologa del agua (electronic engineering), Frugosa S. A. de C. U. (chemical engineering).

GRADUATE UNITS

Division of Graduate Studies *Program availability:* Part-time, evening/weekend.

School of Business and Economics *Program availability:* Part-time, evening/weekend. Offers business administration (MBA); finance (M Adm).

School of Engineering *Program availability:* Part-time, evening/weekend. Offers chemical engineering (MS); computer science (PhD); construction management (M Adm); electronic engineering (MS); engineering (M Adm, MS, PhD); food sciences (MS); food technology (MS); industrial engineering (MS); manufacturing administration (MS); production management (M Adm).

School of Humanities *Program availability:* Part-time, evening/weekend. Offers humanities (MA); information design (MA); linguistics (MA); literature (MA).

School of Sciences *Program availability:* Part-time, evening/weekend. Offers biotechnology (MS); clinical analysis (biomedicine) (MS); sciences (MS).

School of Social Sciences *Program availability:* Part-time, evening/weekend. Offers American studies (MA); anthropology (MA); archaeology (MA); economics (MA); education (MA); finance (M Adm); psychology (MA); social sciences (M Adm, MA).

UNIVERSIDAD DEL ESTE, Carolina, PR 00984

General Information Independent, coed, comprehensive institution.

GRADUATE UNITS

Graduate School Offers accounting (MBA); adult education (M Ed); agribusiness (MBA); criminal justice and criminology (MA); curriculum and instruction - early education (M Ed); curriculum and instruction - elementary (M Ed); curriculum and instruction - English (M Ed); curriculum and Instruction - Spanish (M Ed); human resources (MBA); information security management (MBA); information technology and Web business development (MBA); management (MBA); public policy (MPA); social work (MA); special education (M Ed); strategic leadership (MBA).

UNIVERSIDAD DEL TURABO, Gurabo, PR 00778-3030

General Information Independent, coed, university. CGS member. *Graduate housing:* On-campus housing not available.

GRADUATE UNITS

Graduate Programs *Program availability:* Part-time, evening/weekend, 100% online, blended/hybrid learning. Offers athletic therapeutic (MPHE); coaching (MPHE); counseling (M Ed); curriculum and instruction and appropriate environment (D Ed); curriculum and teaching (M Ed); education (M Ed, MPHE, D Ed); educational administration (M Ed); educational leadership (D Ed); environmental analysis (MSE); environmental management (MSE); environmental science (D Sc); library service and information technology (M Ed); special education (M Ed); teaching at primary level (M Ed); teaching English as a second language (M Ed); teaching of fine arts (M Ed); wellness (MPHE). Electronic applications accepted.

School of Business and Entrepreneurship *Program availability:* Part-time, evening/weekend. Offers accounting (MBA); business and entrepreneurship (MBA, DBA); human resources (MBA); logistics and materials management (MBA); management (MBA, DBA); management of information systems (DBA); marketing (MBA); project management (MBA); quality management (MBA). Electronic applications accepted.

School of Engineering Offers computer engineering (M Eng); electrical engineering (M Eng); mechanical engineering (M Eng); telecommunications and network systems administration (M Eng). Electronic applications accepted.

School of Health Sciences Offers family nurse practitioner (MSN, Certificate); family nurse practitioner - adult nursing (MSN, Certificate); health sciences (MS, MSN, ND, Certificate); naturopathy (ND); speech and language pathology (MS). Electronic applications accepted.

School of Social Sciences and Humanities Offers arts administration (MPA); conflict and mediation studies (MPA); counseling psychology (M Psych, Psy D, Certificate); criminal justice studies (MPA); forensic psychology (Certificate); forensic science (MPA); human services administration (MPA); psychology (M Psych); social sciences and humanities (M Psych, MPA, Psy D, Certificate). Electronic applications accepted.

UNIVERSIDAD DE MONTERREY, 66238 San Pedro Garza Garcia, NL, Mexico

General Information Independent-religious, coed, comprehensive institution.

GRADUATE UNITS

Graduate Programs

UNIVERSIDAD METROPOLITANA, San Juan, PR 00928-1150

General Information Independent, coed, comprehensive institution. *Graduate housing:* On-campus housing not available. *Research affiliation:* Berkeley National Laboratories (bioremediation), University Corporation for Atmospheric Research (computer science, atmospheric science), University of Colorado Boulder (computer science, biology), University of Puerto Rico (physics, chemistry), University of Utah (computational chemistry), Howard University (computational chemistry).

GRADUATE UNITS

School of Business Administration *Program availability:* Part-time, evening/weekend. Offers accounting (MBA); finance (MBA); human resources management (MBA); international business (MBA); management (MBA); management information systems (MBA); marketing (MBA). Electronic applications accepted.

School of Education *Program availability:* Part-time, evening/weekend. Offers administration and supervision (M Ed); curriculum and teaching (M Ed); education (M Ed, Ed D); educational administration and supervision (M Ed); managing recreation and sports services (M Ed); pedagogy (PhD); pre-school centers administration (M Ed);

special education (M Ed); teaching of adult physical education (M Ed); teaching of elementary physical education (M Ed); teaching of physical education (M Ed); teaching of secondary physical education (M Ed). Electronic applications accepted.

School of Environmental Affairs *Program availability:* Part-time. Offers environmental management (MSEM); environmental planning (MP); environmental studies (MAES). Electronic applications accepted.

School of Health Sciences Offers case management (Certificate); health sciences (MSN, Certificate); nursing (MSN); oncology nursing (Certificate).

School of Social Sciences, Humanities and Communications Offers counseling psychology (MA).

UNIVERSITÉ DE MONCTON, Moncton, NB E1A 3E9, Canada

General Information Province-supported, coed, comprehensive institution. *Graduate housing:* Rooms and/or apartments available on a first-come, first-served basis to single and married students.

GRADUATE UNITS

Faculty of Administration *Program availability:* Part-time, evening/weekend, 100% online. Offers administration (MBA). Electronic applications accepted.

Faculty of Arts and Social Sciences *Program availability:* Part-time. Offers arts and social sciences (MA, MPA, MSW, PhD); economics (MA); French studies (MA, PhD); history (MA); public administration (MPA). Electronic applications accepted.

School of Social Work Offers social work (MSW).

Faculty of Education *Program availability:* Part-time. Offers education (M Ed, MA Ed).

Graduate Studies in Education *Program availability:* Part-time. Offers educational psychology (M Ed, MA Ed); guidance (M Ed, MA Ed); school administration (M Ed, MA Ed); teaching (M Ed, MA Ed).

Faculty of Engineering Offers civil engineering (M Sc A); electrical engineering (M Sc A); industrial engineering (M Sc A); mechanical engineering (M Sc A).

Faculty of Sciences *Program availability:* Part-time. Offers biochemistry (M Sc); biology (M Sc); chemistry (M Sc); information technology (M Sc, Certificate, Diploma); mathematics (M Sc); physics and astronomy (M Sc); sciences (M Sc, Certificate, Diploma). Electronic applications accepted.

School of Food Science, Nutrition and Family Studies *Program availability:* Part-time. Offers foods/nutrition (M Sc). Electronic applications accepted.

UNIVERSITÉ DE MONTRÉAL, Montréal, QC H3C 3J7, Canada

General Information Province-supported, coed, university. *Graduate housing:* Room and/or apartments available on a first-come, first-served basis to single students; on-campus housing not available to married students. Housing application deadline: 2/1. *Research affiliation:* Centre Hospitalier Universitaire Mere-Enfant de l'Hopital Sainte-Justine, Centre de Recherche de L'Hopital Sacre-Coeur, Institut de Recherches Cliniques de Montreal, Institut de Cardiologie de Montreal, Institut Universitaire de geriatrie de Montreal.

GRADUATE UNITS

Department of Kinesiology Offers kinesiology (M Sc, DESS); physical activity (M Sc, PhD). Electronic applications accepted.

Faculty of Arts and Sciences *Program availability:* Part-time. Offers anthropology (M Sc, PhD); applied human sciences (PhD); art history (MA, PhD); arts and sciences (M Sc, MA, MIS, PhD, DESS); biological sciences (M Sc, PhD); chemistry (M Sc, PhD); classical studies (MA); communication (PhD); communication sciences (M Sc); comparative literature (MA); computer systems (M Sc, PhD); demography (M Sc, PhD); economics (M Sc, PhD); electronic commerce (M Sc); English studies (MA, PhD); environment and durable development (DESS); film studies (MA, PhD); French literature (MA, PhD); geography (M Sc, PhD, DESS); German literature (PhD); German studies (MA); Hispanic literature (PhD); Hispanic studies (MA); history (MA, PhD); international studies (M Sc, DESS); linguistics (MA, PhD); literature (PhD); mathematical and computational finance (M Sc, DESS); mathematics (M Sc, PhD); museology (MA); philosophy (MA, PhD); physics (M Sc, PhD); political science (M Sc, PhD); psychology (M Sc, PhD); societies, public policies and health (DESS); sociology (M Sc, PhD); statistics (M Sc, PhD); translation (MA, PhD, DESS). Electronic applications accepted.

School of Criminology Offers criminology (M Sc, PhD). Electronic applications accepted.

School of Industrial Relations *Program availability:* Part-time. Offers industrial relations (M Sc, PhD, DESS). Electronic applications accepted.

School of Library and Information Sciences Offers information sciences (MIS, PhD). Electronic applications accepted.

School of Psychoeducation *Program availability:* Part-time. Offers psychoeducation (M Sc, PhD). Electronic applications accepted.

School of Social Service *Program availability:* Part-time. Offers social administration (DESS); social work (M Sc, PhD). M Sc and PhD offered jointly with McGill University. Electronic applications accepted.

Faculty of Dental Medicine Offers dental medicine (M Sc, Certificate); multidisciplinary residency (Certificate); oral and dental sciences (M Sc); orthodontics (M Sc); pediatric dentistry (M Sc); prosthodontics rehabilitation (M Sc); stomatology residency (Certificate). Electronic applications accepted.

Faculty of Education *Program availability:* Part-time, evening/weekend. Offers administration and foundations of education (M Ed, MA, PhD, DESS); didactics (M Ed, MA, PhD, DESS); education (M Ed, MA, PhD, DESS); psychopedagogy and andragogy (M Ed, MA, PhD, DESS). Electronic applications accepted.

Faculty of Environmental Design and Planning Offers environmental design and planning (M Sc A, PhD); environmental planning and design projects (DESS); game design (DESS); urban management for developing countries (DESS); urban planning (M Urb). DESS programs offered jointly with HEC Montreal and École Polytechnique de Montréal. Electronic applications accepted.

Faculty of Law *Program availability:* Part-time. Offers business law (DESS); common law (North America) (JD); international law (DESS); law (LL M, LL D, DDN, DESS, LL B); tax law (LL M). Electronic applications accepted.

Faculty of Medicine Offers biochemistry (M Sc, PhD, DEPD); bioethics (MA, DESS); bioinformatics (M Sc, PhD); biomedical sciences (M Sc, PhD); clinical biochemistry (DEPD); community health (M Sc, DESS); echography transoephagian perioperatoryenvironment, health and disaster management (DESS); environmental and occupational health (M Sc); genetic counseling (DESS); health administration (M Sc, DESS); health sciencesinsurance medicine and expertise (English) (DESS); insurance medicine and expertise in health sciences (DESS); medical genetics (DESS); medicine (M Sc, M Sc A, MA, PMS, DES, MD, PhD, DEPD, DESS); microbiology and immunology (M Sc, PhD); mobility and posture (DESS); molecular biology (M Sc); neurological sciences (M Sc, PhD); nutrition (M Sc, PhD, DESS); occupational therapy (DESS);

pathology and cellular biology (M Sc, PhD); pharmacology (M Sc, PhD); physiology (M Sc, PhD); public health (PhD); toxicology and risk analysis (DESS). Electronic applications accepted.

Institute of Biomedical Engineering Offers biomedical engineering (M Sc A, PhD, DESS). M Sc A and PhD programs offered jointly with École Polytechnique de Montréal. Electronic applications accepted.

School of Speech Therapy and Audiology Offers audiology (PMS); speech therapy (PMS, DESS). Electronic applications accepted.

Faculty of Music Offers composition (M Mus, D Mus); interpretation (M Mus, D Mus, DESS); music (MA, PhD); orchestral repertoire (DESS). Electronic applications accepted.

Faculty of Nursing *Program availability:* Part-time. Offers nursing (M Sc, PhD, Certificate, DESS). PhD offered jointly with McGill University. Electronic applications accepted.

Faculty of Pharmacy *Program availability:* Part-time. Offers drugs development (DESS); pharmaceutical care (DESS); pharmaceutical practice (M Sc); pharmaceutical sciences (M Sc, PhD); pharmacist-supervisor teacher (DESS). Electronic applications accepted.

Faculty of Theology and Sciences of Religions Offers health, spirituality and bioethics (DESS); practical theology (MA, PhD); religious sciences (MA, PhD); theology (MA, D Th, PhD, L Th); theology-Biblical studies (PhD). Electronic applications accepted.

Faculty of Veterinary Medicine Offers veterinary medicine (M Sc, DES, PhD); veterinary sciences (M Sc, PhD); virology and immunology (PhD). Electronic applications accepted.

School of Optometry *Program availability:* Part-time. Offers optometry (M Sc, OD, DESS); vision sciences (M Sc); visual impairment intervention-orientation and mobility (DESS); visual impairment intervention-readaptation (DESS). Electronic applications accepted.

UNIVERSITÉ DE SAINT-BONIFACE, Saint-Boniface, MB R2H 0H7, Canada

General Information Independent-religious, coed, comprehensive institution.

GRADUATE UNITS

Department of Education Offers education (M Ed).

Program in Canadian Studies Offers Canadian studies (MA).

UNIVERSITÉ DE SHERBROOKE, Sherbrooke, QC J1K 2R1, Canada

General Information Independent, coed, university. *Graduate housing:* Room and/or apartments available to single students; on-campus housing not available to married students. Housing application deadline: 6/1. *Research affiliation:* Societe de Microelectronique Industrielle.

GRADUATE UNITS

Faculty of Administration *Program availability:* Part-time, evening/weekend. Offers accounting (M Sc); administration (EMBA, M Adm, M Sc, M Tax, MBA, DBA, PhD, Diploma); business administration (EMBA, MBA, DBA); e-commerce (M Sc); economic development (PhD); economics (M Sc); executive business administration (EMBA); finance (M Sc); general management (MBA); governance, audit and security of information technology (M Adm); international business (M Sc); management and governance of cooperatives and mutuals (M Adm); management information systems (M Sc); marketing (M Sc); marketing communications (M Adm); organizational change and intervention (M Sc); public management (M Adm); taxation (M Tax, Diploma).

Faculty of Education *Program availability:* Part-time, evening/weekend. Offers education (M Ed, MA, Diploma); elementary education (M Ed, Diploma); postsecondary education training (M Ed, Diploma); school administration (M Ed); sciences of education (MA); special education (M Ed, Diploma).

Faculty of Engineering *Program availability:* Part-time. Offers chemical engineering (M Sc A, PhD); civil engineering (M Sc A, PhD); electrical engineering (M Sc A, PhD); engineering (M Eng, M Env, M Sc A, PhD, Diploma); engineering management (M Eng, Diploma); environment (M Env); mechanical engineering (M Sc A, PhD). Electronic applications accepted.

Faculty of Law *Program availability:* Part-time, evening/weekend. Offers alternative dispute resolution (LL M, Diploma); business law (Diploma); common law (JD); criminal and penal law (Diploma); health law (LL M, Diploma); international law (LL M); law (LL D); legal management (Diploma); notarial law (Diploma); transnational law (Diploma). Electronic applications accepted.

Faculty of Letters and Human Sciences *Program availability:* Part-time. Offers comparative Canadian literature (MA, PhD); economics (MA); French literature (MA, PhD); geography and remote sensing (M Sc, PhD); gerontology (MA); history (MA); letters and human sciences (M Psych, M Sc, MA, MSS, PhD, Diploma); linguistics (MA); philosophy (MA); social service (MSS); theatre (MA).

Institute of Management and Development of Cooperatives Offers management and development of cooperatives (MA, Diploma).

Faculty of Medicine and Health Sciences *Program availability:* Part-time. Offers medicine (MD); medicine and health sciences (M Sc, MD, PhD). Electronic applications accepted.

Graduate Programs in Medicine *Program availability:* Part-time. Offers biochemistry (M Sc, PhD); cell biology (M Sc, PhD); clinical sciences (M Sc, PhD); immunology (M Sc, PhD); medicine (M Sc, PhD); microbiology (M Sc, PhD); pharmacology (M Sc, PhD); physiology and biophysics (M Sc, PhD); radiobiology (M Sc, PhD). Electronic applications accepted.

Faculty of Physical Education and Sports *Program availability:* Part-time. Offers kinanthropology (M Sc); physical activity (Diploma); physical education (M Sc, Diploma).

Faculty of Sciences Offers biology (M Sc, PhD, Diploma); chemistry (M Sc, PhD, Diploma); informatics (M Sc, PhD); mathematics (M Sc, PhD); physics (M Sc, PhD); sciences (M Sc, PhD, Diploma).

Centre de Formation en Technologies de L'information Offers information technologies (M Sc, Diploma). Electronic applications accepted.

Centre Universitaire de Formation en Environnement *Program availability:* Online learning. Offers environment (M Sc, Diploma). Electronic applications accepted.

Faculty of Theology and Religious Studies *Program availability:* Part-time, evening/weekend, online learning. Offers applied ethics (Diploma); human science of religions (MA); intercultural training (Diploma); philosophy (MA, PhD); spiritual anthropology (Diploma); theology (MA, PhD, Diploma).

UNIVERSITÉ DU QUÉBEC À CHICOUTIMI, Chicoutimi, QC G7H 2B1, Canada

General Information Province-supported, coed, university. CGS member. *Graduate housing:* Room and/or apartments available to single students; on-campus housing not available to married students.

GRADUATE UNITS

Graduate Programs *Program availability:* Part-time. Offers didactics of French-mother tongue (Diploma); earth sciences (M Sc A); education (M Ed, MA, PhD); engineering (M Sc A, PhD); ethics (Diploma); fine arts (MA); genetics (M Sc); linguistics (MA); literary studies (MA); mineral resources (PhD); project management (MA); regional studies (MA); renewable resources (M Sc); small and medium-sized organization management (M Sc); theology (pastoral studies) (MA, PhD).

UNIVERSITÉ DU QUÉBEC À MONTRÉAL, Montréal, QC H3C 3P8, Canada

General Information Province-supported, coed, university. CGS member. *Graduate housing:* Room and/or apartments available to single students; on-campus housing not available to married students. *Research affiliation:* Labopharm, Inc. (pharmacology), Hydro-Quebec (environmental sciences), Bell (computer sciences), Microcreatif (computer sciences), University Corporation for Atmospheric Research.

GRADUATE UNITS

Graduate Programs *Program availability:* Part-time. Offers accounting (M Sc, MPA, Diploma); actuarial sciences (Diploma); art history (PhD); art studies (MA); atmospheric sciences (M Sc); biology (M Sc, PhD); business administration (PhD); business administration (research) (MBA); chemistry (M Sc, PhD); communications (MA, PhD); dance (MA); death (Diploma); Earth and atmospheric sciences (PhD); Earth science (M Sc); earth sciences (M Sc); economics (M Sc, PhD); education (M Ed, MA, PhD); education of the environmental sciences (Diploma); environmental sciences (M Sc, PhD); Certificate); ergonomics in occupational health and safety (Diploma); finance (Diploma); fine arts (MA); geographical information systems (Diploma); geography (M Sc); history (MA, PhD); human movement studies (M Sc); linguistics (MA, PhD); literary studies (MA, PhD); management consultant (Diploma); management information systems (M Sc, M Sc A); mathematics (M Sc, PhD); meteorology (PhD, Diploma); mineral resources (PhD); museology (MA); non-renewable resources (DESS); philosophy (MA, PhD); political science (MA, PhD); project management (MGP, Diploma); psychology (D Ps, PhD); religious sciences (MA, PhD); semiology (PhD); sexology (MA); social and labor law (Certificate); social intervention (MA); sociology (MA, PhD); study and practices of the arts (PhD); urban analysis and management (MA); urban studies (MA, PhD).

UNIVERSITÉ DU QUÉBEC À RIMOUSKI, Rimouski, QC G5L 3A1, Canada

General Information Province-supported, coed, comprehensive institution. CGS member. *Graduate housing:* Rooms and/or apartments available on a first-come, first-served basis to single and married students. *Research affiliation:* Institut des Sciences de la Mer de Rimouski (ISMER) (marine sciences), CRDT (territory development), Centre d'Etudes Nordiques (Nordicity), Quebec Ocean (oceans), Centre Recherche en Forestene (forestry).

GRADUATE UNITS

Graduate Programs *Program availability:* Part-time. Offers biology (PhD); business administration (MBA); education (M Ed, MA, PhD, Diploma); engineering (M Sc A); ethics (MA, Diploma); literary studies (MA, PhD); management of marine resources (M Sc, Diploma); management of people in working situation (M Sc, Diploma); nursing studies (M Sc, Diploma); oceanography (M Sc, PhD); project management (M Sc, Diploma); psychosocial studies (MA); regional development (MA, PhD, Diploma); wildlife resources management (M Sc, Diploma).

UNIVERSITÉ DU QUÉBEC À TROIS-RIVIÈRES, Trois-Rivières, QC G9A 5H7, Canada

General Information Province-supported, coed, university. CGS member. *Graduate housing:* Room and/or apartments available to single students; on-campus housing not available to married students. Housing application deadline: 2/1.

GRADUATE UNITS

Graduate Programs *Program availability:* Part-time. Offers accounting science (MBA); biophysics and cellular biology (M Sc, PhD); business administration (MBA, DBA); chemistry (M Sc); chiropractic (DC); education (M Ed, PhD); educational administration (DESS); electrical engineering (M Sc A, PhD); environmental sciences (M Sc, PhD); finance (DESS); industrial engineering (M Sc, DESS); labor relations (DESS); leisure, culture and tourism sciences (MA, DESS); literary studies (MA); mathematics and computer science (M Sc); matter and energy (MS, PhD); nursing sciences (M Sc, DESS); philosophy (MA, PhD); physical education (M Sc); psychoeducation (M Ed, PhD); psychology (PhD, Certificate); social communication (MA, DESS).

UNIVERSITÉ DU QUÉBEC, ÉCOLE DE TECHNOLOGIE SUPÉRIEURE, Montréal, QC H3C 1K3, Canada

General Information Province-supported, coed, primarily men, comprehensive institution. CGS member. *Graduate housing:* Rooms and/or apartments available on a first-come, first-served basis to single and married students.

GRADUATE UNITS

Graduate Programs *Program availability:* Online learning. Offers engineering (M Eng, PhD, Diploma).

UNIVERSITÉ DU QUÉBEC, ÉCOLE NATIONALE D'ADMINISTRATION PUBLIQUE, Quebec, QC G1K 9E5, Canada

General Information Province-supported, coed, graduate-only institution. CGS member. *Graduate housing:* On-campus housing not available.

GRADUATE UNITS

Graduate Programs in Public Administration *Program availability:* Part-time. Offers international administration (MAP, Diploma); public administration (MAGU, MAP, PhD, Diploma); urban analysis and management (MAGU).

UNIVERSITÉ DU QUÉBEC EN ABITIBI-TÉMISCAMINGUE, Rouyn-Noranda, QC J9X 5E4, Canada

General Information Province-supported, coed, comprehensive institution. CGS member. *Graduate housing:* Room and/or apartments available on a first-come, first-served basis to single students; on-campus housing not available to married students. Housing application deadline: 3/1.

GRADUATE UNITS

Graduate Programs *Program availability:* Part-time. Offers biology (MS); business administration (MBA); education (M Ed, MA, PhD, DESS); engineering (ME); environmental sciences (PhD); mineral engineering (ME); mining engineering (DESS); organization management (M Sc); project management (M Sc, DESS); social work (MSW); sustainable forest ecosystem management (MS).

UNIVERSITÉ DU QUÉBEC EN OUTAOUAIS, Gatineau, QC J8X 3X7, Canada

General Information Province-supported, coed, university. CGS member. *Graduate housing:* Rooms and/or apartments available on a first-come, first-served basis to single and married students.

GRADUATE UNITS

Graduate Programs *Program availability:* Part-time, evening/weekend. Offers accounting (MA, DESS, Diploma); computer science (M Sc, PhD, DESS); education (M Ed, MA, PhD, DESS, Diploma); executive certified management accounting (MA, MBA, DESS); financial services (MBA, DESS, Diploma); industrial relations (M Sc, MA, PhD, Diploma); nursing (M Sc, DESS, Diploma); project management (M Sc, MA, DESS, Diploma); psychoeducation (M Ed, MA); regional development (MA); second and foreign language teaching (Diploma); social work (MA). Electronic applications accepted.

UNIVERSITÉ DU QUÉBEC, INSTITUT NATIONAL DE LA RECHERCHE SCIENTIFIQUE, Québec, QC G1K 9A9, Canada

General Information Province-supported, coed, graduate-only institution. CGS member. *Enrollment by degree level:* 243 master's, 433 doctoral, 1 other advanced degree. *Graduate faculty:* 150 full-time. *Graduate housing:* On-campus housing not available. *Student services:* Exercise/wellness program, free psychological counseling, international student services, low-cost health insurance, services for students with disabilities. *Library facilities:* Service de documentation et d'information specialisees (SDIS) plus 3 others.

Computer facilities: 500 computers available on campus for general student use. A campuswide network can be accessed. Online class registration is available. Website: http://www.inrs.ca/

General Application Contact: Sean Otto, Registrar, 418-654-2518, Fax: 418-654-3858, E-mail: sean.otto@inrs.ca.

GRADUATE UNITS

Graduate Programs Students: 617 full-time (290 women), 60 part-time (29 women), 427 international. Average age 33. 172 applicants, 83% accepted, 109 enrolled. *Faculty:* 150 full-time. Expenses: Contact institution. *Financial support:* In 2018–19, fellowships (averaging $16,500 per year) were awarded; research assistantships and scholarships/grants also available. In 2018, 78 master's, 76 doctorates awarded. *Program availability:* Part-time. *Application deadline:* For fall admission, 3/30 for domestic and international students; for winter admission, 11/1 for domestic and international students; for spring admission, 3/1 for domestic and international students. *Application fee:* $45. Electronic applications accepted. *Application Contact:* Sean Otto, Registrar, 418-654-2518, Fax: 418-654-3858, E-mail: sean.otto@inrs.ca. *Acting Director of Research and Academic Affairs,* Jean-Francois Blais Begin, 418-654-2575, E-mail: jean-francois.blais@inrs.ca.

Armand-Frappier Santé Biotechnologie Students: 154 full-time (93 women), 14 part-time (6 women), 90 international. Average age 33. 30 applicants, 97% accepted, 22 enrolled. *Faculty:* 46 full-time. Expenses: Contact institution. *Financial support:* In 2018–19, fellowships (averaging $16,500 per year) were awarded; research assistantships also available. In 2018, 18 master's, 19 doctorates awarded. *Program availability:* Part-time. Offers applied microbiology (M Sc); biology (PhD); experimental health sciences (M Sc); virology and immunology (M Sc, PhD). *Application deadline:* For fall admission, 3/30 for domestic and international students; for winter admission, 11/1 for domestic and international students; for spring admission, 3/1 for domestic and international students. *Application fee:* $45 Canadian dollars. Electronic applications accepted. *Application Contact:* Sean Otto, Registrar, 418-654-2518, Fax: 418-654-3858, E-mail: sean.otto@inrs.ca. *Director,* Claude Guertin, 450-687-5010, Fax: 450-686-5501, E-mail: claude.guertin@iaf.inrs.ca.

Centre for Energie Materiaux Telecommunications Students: 207 full-time (60 women), 13 part-time (3 women), 186 international. Average age 34. 45 applicants, 87% accepted, 24 enrolled. *Faculty:* 38 full-time. Expenses: Contact institution. *Financial support:* In 2018–19, fellowships (averaging $16,500 per year) were awarded; research assistantships and scholarships/grants also available. In 2018, 13 master's, 30 doctorates awarded. *Program availability:* Part-time. Offers energy and materials science (M Sc, PhD); telecommunications (M Sc, PhD). *Application deadline:* For fall admission, 3/30 for domestic and international students; for winter admission, 11/1 for domestic and international students; for spring admission, 3/1 for domestic and international students. *Application fee:* $45. Electronic applications accepted. *Application Contact:* Sean Otto, Registrar, 418-654-2518, Fax: 418-654-3858, E-mail: sean.otto@inrs.ca. *Director,* Ana Tavares, 514-228-6947, Fax: 450-929-8102, E-mail: ana.tavares@emt.inrs.ca.

Centre for Urbanisation Culture Societe Students: 87 full-time (50 women), 14 part-time (9 women), 19 international. Average age 34. 39 applicants, 92% accepted, 31 enrolled. *Faculty:* 32 full-time. Expenses: Contact institution. *Financial support:* In 2018–19, fellowships (averaging $16,500 per year) were awarded; research assistantships also available. In 2018, 13 master's, 3 doctorates awarded. *Program availability:* Part-time. Offers demography (M Sc, PhD); research practices and public action (MA, DESS); urban studies (M Sc, PhD). *Application deadline:* For fall admission, 3/30 for domestic and international students; for winter admission, 11/1 for domestic and international students; for spring admission, 3/1 for domestic and international students. *Application fee:* $45. Electronic applications accepted. *Application Contact:* Sean Otto, Registrar, 418-654-2518, Fax: 418-654-3858, E-mail: sean.otto@inrs.ca. *Director,* Helene Belleau, 514-499-4001, Fax: 514-499-4065, E-mail: helene.belleau@ucs.inrs.ca.

Research Center–Water Earth Environment Students: 169 full-time (87 women), 19 part-time (11 women), 132 international. Average age 33. 58 applicants, 66% accepted, 32 enrolled. *Faculty:* 34 full-time. Expenses: Contact institution. *Financial support:* In 2018–19, fellowships (averaging $16,500 per year) were awarded; research assistantships also available. In 2018, 34 master's, 24 doctorates awarded. *Program availability:* Part-time. Offers earth sciences (M Sc, PhD); earth sciences - environmental technologies (M Sc); water sciences (M Sc, PhD). *Application deadline:* For fall admission, 3/30 for domestic and international students; for winter admission, 11/1 for domestic and international students; for spring admission, 3/1 for domestic and international students. *Application fee:* $45. Electronic applications accepted. *Application Contact:* Sean Otto, Registrar, 418-654-2518, Fax: 418-654-3858, E-mail: sean.otto@inrs.ca. *Director,* Jean-François Blais, 418-654-2575, Fax: 418-654-2600, E-mail: jean-francois.blais@ete.inrs.ca.

UNIVERSITÉ LAVAL, Québec, QC G1K 7P4, Canada

General Information Independent, coed, university. *Graduate housing:* Room and/or apartments available on a first-come, first-served basis to single students; on-campus housing not available to married students. *Research affiliation:* Centre Hospitalier Universitaire de Quebec (biomedical research), Institut National d'optique (optics and photonics), Centre de Developpement de la Geomatique (applied geomatics), Institut Maurice-Lamontagne (oceanography), Forintek Canada (forestry and wood processing), Societe des pades de Sciences Naturelles du Quebec (biology).

GRADUATE UNITS

Faculty of Administrative Sciences *Program availability:* Part-time, online learning. Offers accounting (MBA); administrative sciences (M Sc, MBA, PhD, Diploma); administrative studies (M Sc, PhD); agri-food management (MBA); electronic business (MBA, Diploma); factory management and logistics (MBA); finance (MBA); financial engineering (M Sc); firm management (MBA); geomatic management (MBA); information technology management (MBA); international management (MBA); management (MBA); management accounting (MBA, Diploma); marketing (MBA); modeling and organizational decision (MBA); occupational health and safety management (MBA); organizations management and development (Diploma); pharmacy management (MBA); public accountancy (MBA, Diploma); social and environmental responsibility (MBA); technological entrepreneurship (Diploma). Electronic applications accepted.

Faculty of Agricultural and Food Sciences *Program availability:* Part-time. Offers agri-food engineering (M Sc); agricultural and food sciences (M Sc, Diploma); agricultural economics (M Sc); agricultural microbiology (M Sc); agro-food microbiology (PhD); animal sciences (M Sc, PhD); consumer sciences (Diploma); environmental technology (M Sc); food sciences and technology (M Sc, PhD); integrated rural development (Diploma); nutrition (M Sc, PhD); plant biology (M Sc, PhD); soils and environment science (M Sc, PhD). Electronic applications accepted.

Faculty of Architecture, Planning and Visual Arts Offers architecture, planning and visual arts (M Arch, M Sc, MA, MATDR, PhD); planning and regional development (MATDR, PhD). Electronic applications accepted.

School of Architecture *Program availability:* Part-time. Offers architecture (M Arch, M Sc). Electronic applications accepted.

School of Visual Arts Offers graphic design and multimedia (MA); visual arts (MA). Electronic applications accepted.

Faculty of Dentistry Offers buccal and maxillofacial surgery (DESS); dentistry (M Sc, DMD, DESS); gerodontology (DESS); multidisciplinary dentistry (DESS); periodontics (DESS). Electronic applications accepted.

Faculty of Education *Program availability:* Part-time. Offers didactics (MA, PhD); education (MA, PhD, Diploma); educational administration and evaluation (MA, PhD); educational pedagogy (Diploma); educational practice (Diploma); educational psychology (MA, PhD); orientation sciences (MA, PhD); pedagogy management and development (Diploma); school adaptation (Diploma); teaching technology (MA, PhD). Electronic applications accepted.

Faculty of Forestry, Geography and Geomatics Offers agroforestry (M Sc); forestry sciences (M Sc, PhD); forestry, geography and geomatics (M Sc, M Sc Geogr, PhD); geographical sciences (M Sc Geogr, PhD); geography (M Sc Geogr, PhD); geomatics sciences (M Sc, PhD); wood sciences (M Sc, PhD). Electronic applications accepted.

Faculty of Law *Program availability:* Part-time. Offers environment, sustainable development and food safety (LL M); international and transnational law (LL M, Diploma); law (LL M, LL D, Diploma); law of business (LL M, Diploma); notarial law (Diploma). Electronic applications accepted.

Faculty of Letters *Program availability:* Part-time. Offers ancient civilization (MA, PhD); archaeology (MA, PhD); art history (MA, PhD); English literatures (MA, PhD); ethnology of French-speaking people in North America (MA, PhD); history (MA, PhD, Diploma); international journalism (Diploma); letters (MA, PhD, Diploma); linguistics (MA, PhD); literary studies (MA, PhD); literature and arts of the screen and stage (PhD); literature and arts of the screen and stage (MA); museology (Diploma); public communication (MA, PhD); public relations (Diploma); Spanish literature (MA, PhD); terminology and translation (MA, Diploma). Electronic applications accepted.

Faculty of Medicine *Program availability:* Part-time. Offers accident prevention and occupational health and safety management (Diploma); anatomy–pathology (DESS); anesthesiology (DESS); cardiology (DESS); care of older people (Diploma); cellular and molecular biology (M Sc, PhD); clinical research (DESS); community health (M Sc, PhD); dermatology (DESS); diagnostic radiology (DESS); emergency medicine (Diploma); epidemiology (M Sc, PhD); experimental medicine (M Sc, PhD); family medicine (DESS); general surgery (DESS); geriatrics (DESS); hematology (DESS); internal medicine (DESS); kinesiology (M Sc, PhD); maternal and fetal medicine (Diploma); medical biochemistry (DESS); medical microbiology and infectious diseases (DESS); medical oncology (DESS); medicine (M Sc, MD, PhD, DESS, Diploma); microbiology-immunology (M Sc, PhD); nephrology (DESS); neurobiology (M Sc, PhD); neurology (DESS); neurosurgery (DESS); obstetrics and gynecology (DESS); ophthalmology (DESS); orthopedic surgery (DESS); oto-rhino-laryngology (DESS); palliative medicine (Diploma); pediatrics (DESS); physiology-endocrinology (M Sc, PhD); plastic surgery (DESS); psychiatry (DESS); pulmonary medicine (DESS); radiology–oncology (DESS); speech therapy (M Sc); thoracic surgery (DESS); urology (DESS). Electronic applications accepted.

Faculty of Music Offers composition (M Mus); instrumental didactics (M Mus); interpretation (M Mus); music (M Mus, PhD); music education (M Mus, PhD); musicology (M Mus, PhD). Electronic applications accepted.

Faculty of Nursing Offers nursing (M Sc, PhD, DESS, Diploma). Electronic applications accepted.

Faculty of Pharmacy *Program availability:* Part-time. Offers community pharmacy (DESS); hospital pharmacy (M Sc); pharmacy (M Sc, PhD, DESS). Electronic applications accepted.

Faculty of Philosophy Offers philosophy (MA, PhD). Electronic applications accepted.

Faculty of Sciences and Engineering *Program availability:* Part-time. Offers aerospace engineering (M Sc); biochemistry (M Sc, PhD); biology (M Sc, PhD); chemical engineering (M Sc, PhD); chemistry (M Sc, PhD); civil engineering (M Sc, PhD); computer science (M Sc, PhD); earth sciences (M Sc, PhD); electrical engineering (M Sc, PhD); environmental technologies (M Sc); environmental technology (M Sc); geology (M Sc, PhD); industrial engineering (Diploma); mathematics (M Sc, PhD); mechanical engineering (M Sc, PhD); metallurgical engineering (M Sc, PhD); microbiology (M Sc, PhD); mining engineering (M Sc, PhD); oceanography (PhD); physics (M Sc, PhD); sciences and engineering (M Sc, PhD, Diploma); software engineering (Diploma); statistics (M Sc); urban infrastructure engineering (Diploma). Electronic applications accepted.

Faculty of Social Sciences *Program availability:* Part-time. Offers anthropology (MA, PhD); economics (MA, PhD); feminist studies (Diploma); industrial relations (MA, PhD); policy analysis (MA); political science (MA, PhD); social sciences (M Serv Soc, MA, PhD, Psy D, Diploma); sociology (MA, PhD). Electronic applications accepted.

School of Psychology Offers clinical psychology (PhD); community psychology (PhD); psychology (PhD, Psy D). Electronic applications accepted.

School of Social Work Offers social work (M Serv Soc, PhD). Electronic applications accepted.

Faculty of Theology and Religious Sciences Offers applied ethics (DESS); human sciences of religion (MA, PhD); practical theology (D Th P); theology (MA, PhD); theology and religious sciences (MA, D Th P, PhD, DESS). Electronic applications accepted.

Québec Institute for Advanced International Studies Offers advanced international studies (MA, PhD); international relations (MA, PhD). Electronic applications accepted.

UNIVERSITÉ SAINTE-ANNE, Church Point, NS B0W 1M0, Canada

General Information Province-supported, coed, comprehensive institution.

GRADUATE UNITS

Program in Education *Program availability:* Part-time. Offers education (M Ed).

UNIVERSITY AT ALBANY, STATE UNIVERSITY OF NEW YORK, Albany, NY 12222-0001

General Information State-supported, coed, university. CGS member. *Enrollment:* 2,176 full-time matriculated graduate/professional students (1,266 women), 2,171 part-time matriculated graduate/professional students (1,393 women). *Enrollment by degree level:* 2,639 master's, 1,452 doctoral, 256 other advanced degrees. *Graduate faculty:* 604 full-time (249 women), 219 part-time/adjunct (96 women). *Graduate housing:* On-campus housing not available. *Student services:* Campus employment opportunities, campus safety program, career counseling, child daycare facilities, exercise/wellness program, free psychological counseling, grant writing training, international student services, low-cost health insurance, multicultural affairs office, services for students with disabilities, teacher training, writing training. *Library facilities:* University Library plus 2 others. *Collection:* Books: 2.3 million (physical), 342,263 (digital/electronic); Serial titles: 97,614 (digital/electronic). Weekly public service hours: 113; students can reserve study rooms.

Computer facilities: Computer purchase and lease plans are available. 500 computers available on campus for general student use. A campuswide network can be accessed from student residence rooms and from off campus. Online class registration is available.
Website: http://www.albany.edu/

General Application Contact: Michael DeRensis, Director, Graduate Admissions, 518-442-3980, Fax: 518-442-3922, E-mail: graduate@albany.edu.

GRADUATE UNITS

College of Arts and Sciences Students: 623 full-time (322 women), 578 part-time (313 women); includes 235 minority (60 Black or African American, non-Hispanic/Latino; 3 American Indian or Alaska Native, non-Hispanic/Latino; 49 Asian, non-Hispanic/Latino; 94 Hispanic/Latino; 29 Two or more races, non-Hispanic/Latino), 303 international, 1,381 applicants, 43% accepted, 285 enrolled. *Faculty:* 284 full-time (95 women), 40 part-time/adjunct (15 women). Expenses: Contact institution. *Financial support:* Fellowships, research assistantships, teaching assistantships, career-related internships or fieldwork, Federal Work-Study, institutionally sponsored loans, traineeships, and unspecified assistantships available. Financial award applicants required to submit FAFSA. In 2018, 153 master's, 62 doctorates, 14 other advanced degrees awarded. *Program availability:* Part-time, evening/weekend, 100% online, blended/hybrid learning. Offers African studies (MA); Afro-American studies (MA); anthropology (MA, PhD); art (MA, MFA); arts and sciences (MA, MALS, MFA, MRP, MS, PhD, Certificate); atmospheric science (MS, PhD); behavioral neuroscience (PhD); chemistry (MS, PhD); clinical psychology (PhD); cognitive psychology (PhD); communication (MA); demography (Certificate); economic forecasting (MA); economics (MA, PhD); English (MA, PhD); forensic biology (MS); geographic information science (Certificate); geography (MA); history (MA, PhD); industrial/organizational psychology (MA, PhD); Latin American, Caribbean, and U.S. Latino studies (MA, PhD, Certificate); liberal studies (MALS); mathematics (MA, PhD); philosophy (MA, PhD); physics (MS, PhD); public history (Certificate); regional planning (MRP); social-personality psychology (PhD); sociology (MA, PhD); sociology and communication (PhD); Spanish (MA, PhD); urban policy (Certificate); women's, gender and sexuality studies (MA). *Application deadline:* Applications are processed on a rolling basis. *Application fee:* $75. Electronic applications accepted. *Application Contact:* Michael DeRensis, Director, Graduate Admissions, 518-442-3980, Fax: 518-442-3922, E-mail: graduate@albany.edu. *Dean,* Edelgard Wulfert, 518-442-4654, Fax: 518-442-4651.

College of Emergency Preparedness, Homeland Security and Cybersecurity Students: 50 full-time (35 women), 108 part-time (83 women); includes 27 minority (8 Black or African American, non-Hispanic/Latino; 5 Asian, non-Hispanic/Latino; 12 Hispanic/Latino; 2 Two or more races, non-Hispanic/Latino), 13 international. 90 applicants, 67% accepted, 36 enrolled. *Faculty:* 14 full-time (6 women), 7 part-time/adjunct (4 women). Expenses: Contact institution. In 2018, 30 master's, 1 doctorate, 24 other advanced degrees awarded. Offers cybersecurity (Certificate); emergency preparedness (Certificate); homeland security (Certificate); information science (MS, PhD). *Application Contact:* Michael DeRensis, Director, Graduate Admissions, 518-442-3980, Fax: 518-442-3922, E-mail: graduate@albany.edu. *Dean,* Dr. Robert Griffin, 518-442-5258.

College of Engineering and Applied Sciences Students: 188 full-time (48 women), 69 part-time (22 women); includes 14 minority (1 Black or African American, non-Hispanic/Latino; 9 Asian, non-Hispanic/Latino; 3 Hispanic/Latino; 1 Two or more races, non-Hispanic/Latino), 228 international. Average age 27. 552 applicants, 51% accepted, 193 enrolled. *Faculty:* 29 full-time (8 women), 19 part-time/adjunct (3 women). Expenses: Contact institution. *Financial support:* Fellowships and Federal Work-Study available. Financial award application deadline: 4/1. In 2018, 84 master's, 3 doctorates awarded. *Program availability:* Part-time. Offers computer science (MS, PhD); engineering and applied sciences (MS, PhD, CAS). *Application deadline:* For fall admission, 3/1 for domestic students. Applications are processed on a rolling basis. *Application fee:* $75. Electronic applications accepted. *Application Contact:* Kim L. Boyer, Dean, 518-956-8240, Fax: 518-442-5367, E-mail: ceasinfo@albany.edu. *Dean,* Kim L. Boyer, 518-956-8240, Fax: 518-442-5367, E-mail: ceasinfo@albany.edu.

Nelson A. Rockefeller College of Public Affairs and Policy Students: 147 full-time (75 women), 132 part-time (71 women); includes 61 minority (21 Black or African American, non-Hispanic/Latino; 10 Asian, non-Hispanic/Latino; 20 Hispanic/Latino; 10 Two or more races, non-Hispanic/Latino), 45 international. Average age 33. 288 applicants, 68% accepted, 94 enrolled. *Faculty:* 42 full-time (16 women), 19 part-time/adjunct (10 women). Expenses: Contact institution. *Financial support:* Fellowships, research assistantships, teaching assistantships, career-related internships or fieldwork, Federal Work-Study, and institutionally sponsored loans available. Financial award application deadline: 2/1. In 2018, 62 master's, 4 doctorates, 14 other advanced degrees awarded. *Program availability:* Part-time. Offers financial management and public economics (MPA); financial market regulation (MPA); health policy (MPA); healthcare management (MPA); homeland security (MPA); human resources management (MPA); information strategy and management (MPA); local government management (MPA); nonprofit management (MPA); nonprofit management and leadership (Certificate); organizational behavior and theory (MPA, PhD); planning and policy analysis (CAS); policy analysis (MPA); political science (MA, PhD); politics and administration (PhD); public affairs and policy (MA, MPA, PhD, CAS, Certificate); public finance (PhD); public management (PhD); public policy (PhD); public sector management (Certificate); women and public policy (Certificate). *Application deadline:* For fall admission, 2/1 priority date for domestic students, 5/1 for international students. Applications are processed on a rolling basis. *Application fee:* $75. Electronic applications accepted. *Application Contact:* Karl R. Rethemeyer, Dean, 518-442-5283, E-mail: krethme@albany.edu. *Dean,* Karl R. Rethemeyer, 518-442-5283, E-mail: krethme@albany.edu.

School of Business Students: 277 full-time (94 women), 192 part-time (74 women); includes 127 minority (44 Black or African American, non-Hispanic/Latino; 2 American Indian or Alaska Native, non-Hispanic/Latino; 36 Asian, non-Hispanic/Latino; 34 Hispanic/Latino; 11 Two or more races, non-Hispanic/Latino), 37 international. 485 applicants, 63% accepted, 236 enrolled. *Faculty:* 34 full-time (11 women), 21 part-time/adjunct (3 women). Expenses: Contact institution. *Financial support:* Fellowships, research assistantships, career-related internships or fieldwork, and Federal Work-Study available. In 2018, 221 master's awarded. *Program availability:* Part-time, evening/weekend. Offers business (MBA, MS); business administration (MBA); cyber security (MBA); entrepreneurship (MBA); finance (MBA); human resource information systems (MBA); information systems and business analytics (MBA); marketing (MBA). *Application deadline:* For fall admission, 3/1 for domestic students, 5/1 for international students. Applications are processed on a rolling basis. *Application fee:* $75. Electronic applications accepted. *Application Contact:* Michael DeRensis, Director, Graduate Admissions, 518-442-3980, Fax: 518-442-3922, E-mail: graduate@albany.edu. *Dean,* Nilanjan Sen, 518-956-8370, E-mail: nsen@albany.edu.

School of Criminal Justice Students: 73 full-time (44 women), 22 part-time (16 women); includes 29 minority (11 Black or African American, non-Hispanic/Latino; 4 Asian, non-Hispanic/Latino; 14 Hispanic/Latino), 12 international. 121 applicants, 55% accepted, 31 enrolled. *Faculty:* 16 full-time (8 women), 4 part-time/adjunct (2 women). Expenses: Contact institution. *Financial support:* Fellowships, research assistantships, teaching assistantships, career-related internships or fieldwork, and institutionally sponsored loans available. Financial award application deadline: 4/1. In 2018, 44 master's, 1 doctorate awarded. *Program availability:* Part-time. Offers criminal justice (MA, PhD). *Application deadline:* For fall admission, 7/1 for domestic students, 5/1 for international students. Applications are processed on a rolling basis. *Application fee:* $75. Electronic applications accepted. *Application Contact:* Jane Champagne, Director, Graduate Admissions, 518-442-3980, Fax: 518-442-3922, E-mail: graduate@albany.edu. *Dean,* William Alex Pridemore, 518-442-5210, E-mail: pridemore@albany.edu.

School of Education Students: 348 full-time (271 women), 632 part-time (496 women); includes 184 minority (59 Black or African American, non-Hispanic/Latino; 33 Asian, non-Hispanic/Latino; 69 Hispanic/Latino; 1 Native Hawaiian or other Pacific Islander, non-Hispanic/Latino; 22 Two or more races, non-Hispanic/Latino), 82 international. Average age 31. 588 applicants, 64% accepted, 310 enrolled. *Faculty:* 68 full-time (39 women), 38 part-time/adjunct (24 women). Expenses: Contact institution. *Financial support:* Fellowships, career-related internships or fieldwork, and Federal Work-Study available. In 2018, 192 master's, 18 doctorates, 24 other advanced degrees awarded. *Program availability:* Part-time, evening/weekend, 100% online, blended/hybrid learning. Offers counseling psychology (PhD, CAS); curriculum and instruction (PhD, CAS); curriculum development and instructional technology (MS); education (MS, PhD, Psy D, CAS); educational policy and leadership (MS, PhD); general education studies (MS); higher education (MS); international education management (CAS); literacy teaching and learning (MS, PhD, CAS); mental health counseling (MS). *Application fee:* $75. Electronic applications accepted. *Application Contact:* Jason Lane, Interim Dean, 518-442-4988, E-mail: jlane@albany.edu. *Interim Dean,* Jason Lane, 518-442-4988, E-mail: jlane@albany.edu.

School of Public Health Students: 195 full-time (141 women), 303 part-time (223 women); includes 163 minority (56 Black or African American, non-Hispanic/Latino; 53 Asian, non-Hispanic/Latino; 36 Hispanic/Latino; 18 Two or more races, non-Hispanic/Latino), 49 international. 375 applicants, 69% accepted, 181 enrolled. *Faculty:* 47 full-time (27 women), 47 part-time/adjunct (21 women). Expenses: Contact institution. *Financial support:* Fellowships and research assistantships available. In 2018, 81 master's, 12 doctorates, 47 other advanced degrees awarded. *Program availability:* Part-time, evening/weekend, 100% online, blended/hybrid learning. Offers biomedical sciences (MS, PhD); environmental and occupational health (MS, PhD); environmental chemistry (MS, PhD); epidemiology and biostatistics (MS, PhD); health policy, management, and behavior (MPH, MS, Dr PH, PhD); public health (MPH, MS, Dr PH, PhD, Certificate); toxicology (MS, PhD). *Application deadline:* For fall admission, 1/1 for domestic students. Applications are processed on a rolling basis. *Application fee:* $75. Electronic applications accepted. *Application Contact:* Michael DeRensis, Director, Graduate Admissions, 518-442-3980, Fax: 518-442-3922, E-mail: graduate@albany.edu. *Dean,* Dr. David Holtgrave, 518-485-5500, E-mail: dholtgrave@albany.edu.

School of Social Welfare Students: 274 full-time (236 women), 114 part-time (89 women); includes 115 minority (54 Black or African American, non-Hispanic/Latino; 8 Asian, non-Hispanic/Latino; 37 Hispanic/Latino; 16 Two or more races, non-Hispanic/Latino), 15 international. 435 applicants, 63% accepted, 192 enrolled. *Faculty:* 28 full-time (23 women), 14 part-time/adjunct (8 women). Expenses: Contact institution. *Financial support:* Fellowships, career-related internships or fieldwork, and Federal Work-Study available. Financial award application deadline: 2/15. In 2018, 144 master's, 7 doctorates awarded. *Program availability:* Part-time, evening/weekend. Offers social welfare (MSW, PhD). *Application deadline:* For fall admission, 2/15 for domestic and international students. *Application fee:* $75. Electronic applications accepted. *Application Contact:* Lynn Warner, Dean, 518-442-5324, E-mail: lwarner@albany.edu. *Dean,* Lynn Warner, 518-442-5324, E-mail: lwarner@albany.edu.

UNIVERSITY AT BUFFALO, THE STATE UNIVERSITY OF NEW YORK, Buffalo, NY 14260

General Information State-supported, coed, university. CGS member. *Enrollment:* 31,503 graduate, professional, and undergraduate students; 6,186 full-time matriculated graduate/professional students (3,182 women), 3,295 part-time matriculated graduate/professional students (1,634 women). *Enrollment by degree level:* 4,436

master's, 4,830 doctoral, 215 other advanced degrees. *Graduate faculty:* 1,675 full-time (624 women), 179 part-time/adjunct (64 women). *Graduate housing:* Rooms and/or apartments available on a first-come, first-served basis to single and married students. Housing application deadline: 5/1. *Student services:* Campus employment opportunities, campus safety program, career counseling, child daycare facilities, exercise/wellness program, free psychological counseling, international student services, low-cost health insurance, multicultural affairs office, services for students with disabilities, teacher training, writing training. *Library facilities:* Lockwood Memorial Library plus 11 others. *Collection:* Books: 3.4 million (physical), 826,650 (digital/electronic); Serial titles: 2,352 (physical), 175,278 (digital/electronic); Databases: 383. Weekly public service hours: 168; study areas open 24 hours, 5–7 days a week; students can reserve study rooms.

Computer facilities: 3,061 computers available on campus for general student use. A campuswide network can be accessed from student residence rooms and from off campus. Online class registration is available.
Website: http://www.buffalo.edu/

General Application Contact: Danielle D. Ianni, Director of Enrollment Operations, 716-645-3482, Fax: 716-645-6998, E-mail: ddianni@buffalo.edu.

GRADUATE UNITS

Graduate School Students: 6,186 full-time (3,182 women), 3,295 part-time (1,634 women); includes 1,553 minority (387 Black or African American, non-Hispanic/Latino; 27 American Indian or Alaska Native, non-Hispanic/Latino; 722 Asian, non-Hispanic/Latino; 276 Hispanic/Latino; 141 Two or more races, non-Hispanic/Latino), 2,918 international. 22,831 applicants, 35% accepted, 3397 enrolled. *Faculty:* 1,675 full-time (624 women), 179 part-time/adjunct (64 women). Expenses: Contact institution. *Financial support:* Fellowships with tuition reimbursements, research assistantships with tuition reimbursements, teaching assistantships with tuition reimbursements, career-related internships or fieldwork, Federal Work-Study, institutionally sponsored loans, scholarships/grants, traineeships, tuition waivers (full and partial), unspecified assistantships, and stipends available. Support available to part-time students. Financial award applicants required to submit FAFSA. In 2018, 2,340 master's, 426 doctorates, 638 other advanced degrees awarded. *Program availability:* Part-time, evening/weekend, 100% online, blended/hybrid learning. *Application deadline:* Applications are processed on a rolling basis. *Application fee:* $75. Electronic applications accepted. *Application Contact:* Lisa C. Coia, Associate Director, 716-645-3482, Fax: 716-645-6998, E-mail: grad@buffalo.edu. *Vice Provost for Graduate Education/Dean of the Graduate School,* Dr. Graham Hammill, 716-645-2939, Fax: 716-645-6142, E-mail: grad@buffalo.edu.

College of Arts and Sciences Program availability: Part-time. Offers American studies (MA, PhD); anthropology (MA, PhD); architecture and media (MAH, MFA, PhD, Certificate); arts and sciences (MA, MAH, MFA, MM, MS, Au D, PhD, Advanced Certificate, Certificate); arts management (MA); audiology (Au D); biological sciences (MA, MS, PhD); Canadian studies (MA); chemistry (MA, PhD); classics (MA, PhD); communication (MA, PhD); communicative disorders and sciences (MA, PhD); comparative literature (MA, PhD); computational science (Advanced Certificate); contemporary performance (Advanced Certificate); critical museum studies (MA); dance (MFA); earth systems science (MA, MS); econometrics and quantitative economics (MS); economic geography and business geographics (MS); economics (MA, PhD); English (MA, PhD); environmental modeling and analysis (MA); evolution, ecology and behavior (MS, PhD, Certificate); film and media study (MAH); financial economics (Certificate); French (MA, PhD); geographic information science (MA, MS); geography (MA, PhD); geology (MA, MS, PhD); global gender studies (MA, PhD); health geography (MS); health services (Certificate); historical musicology and music theory (PhD); history (MA, PhD, Advanced Certificate); humanities (MA); information and Internet economics (Certificate); interdisciplinary computational linguistics (MS); international economics (Certificate); international trade (MA); Latin (MA); law and regulation (Certificate); linguistics (MA, PhD); mathematics (MA, PhD); media arts production (MFA); media study (PhD); medicinal chemistry (MS, PhD); music composition (MA, PhD); music history (MA); music performance (MM); music theory (MA); natural sciences (MA); new media design (Certificate); philosophy (MA, PhD); physics (MS, PhD); political science (MA, PhD); psychology (MA, PhD); public history (MA); social media (MAH); social sciences (MS); sociology (MA, PhD); Spanish (MA, PhD); studio art (MFA); theatre and performance (MA, PhD); urban and regional analysis (MA); urban and regional economics (Certificate); visual studies (MA, PhD). Electronic applications accepted.

Graduate Programs in Cancer Research and Biomedical Sciences at Roswell Park Cancer Institute Offers cancer pathology and prevention (PhD); cellular and molecular biology (PhD); immunology (PhD); interdisciplinary natural sciences (MS); molecular and cellular biophysics and biochemistry (PhD); molecular pharmacology and cancer therapeutics (PhD). Electronic applications accepted.

Graduate School of Education Students: 467 full-time (343 women), 752 part-time (557 women); includes 182 minority (75 Black or African American, non-Hispanic/Latino; 4 American Indian or Alaska Native, non-Hispanic/Latino; 53 Asian, non-Hispanic/Latino; 40 Hispanic/Latino; 1 Native Hawaiian or other Pacific Islander, non-Hispanic/Latino; 9 Two or more races, non-Hispanic/Latino), 72 international. Average age 33. 981 applicants, 67% accepted, 451 enrolled. *Faculty:* 74 full-time (45 women), 81 part-time/adjunct (53 women). Expenses: Contact institution. *Financial support:* In 2018–19, 98 fellowships (averaging $5,401 per year), 125 research assistantships with tuition reimbursements (averaging $11,177 per year) were awarded; teaching assistantships, Federal Work-Study, institutionally sponsored loans, scholarships/grants, tuition waivers (full and partial), and unspecified assistantships also available. Support available to part-time students. Financial award applicants required to submit FAFSA. In 2018, 290 master's, 59 doctorates, 107 other advanced degrees awarded. *Program availability:* Part-time, 100% online. Offers applied statistical analysis (Advanced Certificate); biology education (Ed M, Certificate); chemistry education (Ed M, Certificate); childhood education (Ed M); childhood education with bilingual extension (Ed M); college teaching (Advanced Certificate); counseling/school psychology (PhD); counselor education (PhD); curriculum, instruction and the science of learning (PhD); early childhood education (Ed M); early childhood education with bilingual extension (Ed M); earth science education (Ed M, Certificate); economics and education policy analysis (MA); education (Ed M, MA, MS, Ed D, PhD, Advanced Certificate, Certificate); education and technology (Ed M); education studies (Ed M); educational administration (Ed M, Ed D, PhD); educational culture, policy and society (PhD); educational psychology (MA, PhD); educational technology and new literacies (Certificate); educational technology and new literacies (Advanced Certificate); elementary education (Ed D); English education (Ed M, Certificate); English education studies (Ed M); English for speakers of other languages (Ed M); foreign and second language education (PhD); French education (Ed M, Certificate); German education (Ed M, Certificate); gifted education (Certificate); higher education administration (Ed M, PhD); information and library science (MS); Latin education (Ed M, Certificate); library and information studies (Certificate); literacy education studies (Ed M); literacy specialist (Ed M); literacy teaching and learning (Certificate); mathematics education (Ed M, Certificate); mental health counseling (MS, Certificate); mindful counseling for wellness and engagement (Advanced Certificate); music education (Ed M, Certificate); music education studies (Ed M); music learning theory (Advanced Certificate); online education (Advanced Certificate); physics education (Ed M, Certificate); rehabilitation counseling (MS, Advanced Certificate); school building leadership (Certificate); school business and human resource administration (Certificate); school counseling (Ed M, Certificate); school district business leadership (Certificate); school district leadership (Certificate); school librarianship (MS); science and the public (Ed M); social studies education (Ed M, Certificate); Spanish education (Ed M, Certificate); special education (PhD); teaching English to speakers of other languages (Ed M). *Application deadline:* Applications are processed on a rolling basis. *Application fee:* $50. Electronic applications accepted. *Application Contact:* Cory Meyers, Assistant Dean for Enrollment Management, 716-645-2110, Fax: 716-645-7937, E-mail: gseinfo@buffalo.edu. *Dean,* Dr. Suzanne Rosenblith, 716-645-1354, Fax: 716-645-2479, E-mail: dean@ap.buffalo.edu.

Jacobs School of Medicine and Biomedical Sciences Offers anatomical sciences (MA, PhD); biochemistry (MA, PhD); bioinformatics and translational research informatics (PhD); biomedical informatics (MS); biomedical ontology (PhD); biomedical sciences (PhD); biophysics (MS, PhD); biotechnology (MS); clinical informatics and decision support (PhD); computational cell biology, anatomy, and pathology (PhD); genetics, genomics and bioinformatics (MS, PhD); medical physics (MS, PhD); medicine (MD); medicine and biomedical sciences (MA, MS, MD, PhD); microbiology and immunology (MS, PhD); neuroscience (MS, PhD); pathology (MA, PhD); pharmacology (MS, PhD); physiology (MA, PhD); structural biology (MS, PhD). Electronic applications accepted.

School of Architecture and Planning Students: 171 full-time (77 women), 35 part-time (15 women); includes 45 minority (18 Black or African American, non-Hispanic/Latino; 5 Asian, non-Hispanic/Latino; 14 Hispanic/Latino; 8 Two or more races, non-Hispanic/Latino; 36 international. Average age 27. 392 applicants, 25% accepted, 61 enrolled. *Faculty:* 41 full-time (15 women), 20 part-time/adjunct (9 women). Expenses: Contact institution. *Financial support:* In 2018–19, 87 students received support, including 9 fellowships with full tuition reimbursements available (averaging $15,600 per year), 5 research assistantships with partial tuition reimbursements available (averaging $13,728 per year), 54 teaching assistantships with partial tuition reimbursements available (averaging $5,609 per year); career-related internships or fieldwork, Federal Work-Study, institutionally sponsored loans, scholarships/grants, health care benefits, tuition waivers (full and partial), and unspecified assistantships also available. Support available to part-time students. Financial award application deadline: 3/1; financial award applicants required to submit FAFSA. In 2018, 100 master's, 2 doctorates, 4 other advanced degrees awarded. *Program availability:* Part-time. Offers architecture (M Arch); ecological practices, inclusive design, situated technologies, historic preservation (MS Arch); economic development (MUP); environment/land use (MUP); health and food systems (MUP); health and food systems, economic development, environment/land use, historic preservation, neighborhood/community development, urban design (MUP); historic preservation (MUP, Certificate); neighborhood/community development (MUP); real estate development (MSRED); real estate development (MSRED); urban and regional planning (MUP); urban design (MUP). *Application deadline:* For fall admission, 1/1 priority date for domestic and international students. Applications are processed on a rolling basis. *Application fee:* $75. Electronic applications accepted. *Application Contact:* Kevin P. Donovan, Director of Graduate Recruitment, 716-829-5224, Fax: 716-829-3256, E-mail: kpd2@buffalo.edu. *Dean,* Robert G. Shibley, 716-829-3981, Fax: 716-829-2297, E-mail: dean@ap.buffalo.edu.

School of Dental Medicine Students: 525 full-time (259 women); includes 147 minority (24 Black or African American, non-Hispanic/Latino; 1 American Indian or Alaska Native, non-Hispanic/Latino; 94 Asian, non-Hispanic/Latino; 28 Hispanic/Latino; 80 international. Average age 26. 2,023 applicants, 10% accepted, 139 enrolled. *Faculty:* 69 full-time (25 women), 99 part-time/adjunct (32 women). Expenses: Contact institution. *Financial support:* In 2018–19, 10 research assistantships with full and partial tuition reimbursements (averaging $24,000 per year) were awarded; fellowships with full and partial tuition reimbursements, career-related internships or fieldwork, institutionally sponsored loans, scholarships/grants, unspecified assistantships, and Graduate Medical Education Stipend also available. Financial award applicants required to submit FAFSA. In 2018, 18 master's, 111 doctorates, 36 other advanced degrees awarded. Offers biomaterials (MS); dental medicine (MS, DDS, PhD, Certificate); dental specialties (Certificate); oral biology (PhD); oral sciences (MS); orthodontics (MS, Certificate). *Application deadline:* For fall admission, 2/1 for domestic and international students. Applications are processed on a rolling basis. *Application fee:* $85. Electronic applications accepted. *Application Contact:* Dr. Pamela Jones, Associate Dean for Advanced Education, 716-829-6927, Fax: 716-829-2731, E-mail: sdmpg@buffalo.edu. *Dean,* Dr. Joseph Zambon, 716-829-2836, Fax: 716-833-3517, E-mail: sdm-dean@buffalo.edu.

School of Engineering and Applied Sciences Students: 2,062 full-time (512 women); includes 127 minority (22 Black or African American, non-Hispanic/Latino; 66 Asian, non-Hispanic/Latino; 23 Hispanic/Latino; 16 Two or more races, non-Hispanic/Latino), 1,663 international. Average age 25. 7,143 applicants, 38% accepted, 683 enrolled. *Faculty:* 236 full-time (35 women), 28 part-time/adjunct (3 women). Expenses: Contact institution. *Financial support:* In 2018–19, 520 students received support, including 38 fellowships with full and partial tuition reimbursements available (averaging $26,734 per year), 215 research assistantships with full and partial tuition reimbursements available (averaging $21,800 per year), 185 teaching assistantships with full and partial tuition reimbursements available (averaging $21,875 per year); scholarships/grants and unspecified assistantships also available. Support available to part-time students. In 2018, 613 master's, 76 doctorates awarded. *Program availability:* Part-time, evening/weekend, 100% online, blended/hybrid learning. Offers advanced manufacturing (Certificate); aerospace engineering (MS, PhD); bioengineering nanotechnology (Certificate); biomedical engineering (MS, PhD); chemical and biological engineering (ME, MS, PhD); civil engineering (MS, PhD); computational and data enabled sciences (MS, PhD); computer science and engineering (MS, PhD); electrical engineering (ME, MS, PhD); engineering and applied sciences (ME, MS, PhD, Certificate); engineering science (MS); environmental and water resources engineering (MS); industrial engineering (ME, MS, PhD); information assurance (Certificate); materials design and innovation (MS, PhD); mechanical engineering (MS, PhD); nanomaterials and materials informatics (Certificate); sustainable transportation and logistics (MS). *Application deadline:* For fall admission, 12/15 priority date for domestic and international students; for spring admission, 10/15 priority date for domestic and international students. Applications are processed on a rolling basis. *Application fee:* $85. Electronic applications accepted. *Application*

Contact: Jennifer Gammell, Associate Director of Graduate Enrollment Management, 716-645-9099, E-mail: gradeng@buffalo.edu.

School of Law Students: 451 full-time (250 women), 10 part-time (6 women); includes 91 minority (30 Black or African American, non-Hispanic/Latino; 2 American Indian or Alaska Native, non-Hispanic/Latino; 23 Asian, non-Hispanic/Latino; 23 Hispanic/Latino; 13 Two or more races, non-Hispanic/Latino), 18 international. Average age 26. 895 applicants, 60% accepted, 168 enrolled. *Faculty:* 56 full-time (29 women), 74 part-time/adjunct (30 women). Expenses: Contact institution. *Financial support:* In 2018–19, 350 students received support. Federal Work-Study, institutionally sponsored loans, scholarships/grants, tuition waivers (full and partial), and unspecified assistantships available. Financial award application deadline: 3/1; financial award applicants required to submit FAFSA. In 2018, 1 master's, 153 doctorates awarded. Offers criminal law (LL M); cross-border legal studies (LL M); environmental law (LL M); general law (LL M); law (JD). *Application deadline:* For fall admission, 3/1 priority date for domestic and international students. Applications are processed on a rolling basis. *Application fee:* $85. Electronic applications accepted. *Application Contact:* Lindsay Gladney, Vice Dean for Admissions, 716-645-2907, Fax: 716-645-6676, E-mail: law-admissions@buffalo.edu. *Dean,* Aviva Abramovsky, 716-645-2052, E-mail: aabramov@buffalo.edu.

School of Management *Program availability:* Part-time, evening/weekend. Offers accounting (MS); analytics (MBA); business administration (PMBA); consulting (MBA); finance (MBA, MS); healthcare (MBA); information assurance (MBA); information systems (MBA); international management (MBA); management (EMBA, PhD); management information systems (MS); marketing (MBA); supply chain and operations (MBA); supply chains and operations management (MS). Electronic applications accepted.

School of Nursing *Program availability:* Part-time, 100% online. Offers adult gerontology nurse practitioner (DNP); family nurse practitioner (DNP); health care systems and leadership (MS); nurse anesthetist (DNP); nursing (PhD); nursing education (Certificate); psychiatric/mental health nurse practitioner (DNP). Electronic applications accepted.

School of Pharmacy and Pharmaceutical Sciences Students: 537 full-time (325 women), 33 part-time (14 women); includes 214 minority (27 Black or African American, non-Hispanic/Latino; 186 Asian, non-Hispanic/Latino; 1 Hispanic/Latino), 57 international. Average age 23. 712 applicants, 24% accepted, 134 enrolled. *Faculty:* 39 full-time (10 women), 6 part-time/adjunct (4 women). Expenses: Contact institution. *Financial support:* In 2018–19, 361 students received support, including 42 research assistantships with full tuition reimbursements available (averaging $24,448 per year); scholarships/grants also available. Financial award application deadline: 3/1; financial award applicants required to submit FAFSA. In 2018, 9 master's, 144 doctorates awarded. Offers pharmaceutical sciences (MS); pharmacy (Pharm D). *Application deadline:* For fall admission, 2/1 priority date for domestic and international students. Applications are processed on a rolling basis. *Application fee:* $50. Electronic applications accepted. *Application Contact:* Dr. Jennifer M. Rosenberg, Associate Dean, 716-645-2825 Ext. 1, Fax: 716-829-6568, E-mail: prepharm@buffalo.edu. *Dean,* Dr. James M. O'Donnell, 716-645-2823, Fax: 716-829-6568.

School of Public Health and Health Professions *Program availability:* Part-time. Offers assistive and rehabilitation technology (Certificate); biostatistics (MA, MPH, MS, PhD); community health and health behavior (MPH, PhD); epidemiology (MS, PhD); exercise science (MS, PhD); nutrition (MS, Advanced Certificate); occupational therapy (MS); physical therapy (DPT); public health (MPH); public health and health professions (MA, MPH, MS, DPT, PhD, Advanced Certificate, Certificate); rehabilitation science (PhD). Electronic applications accepted.

School of Social Work Students: 290 full-time (238 women), 277 part-time (241 women); includes 100 minority (59 Black or African American, non-Hispanic/Latino; 5 American Indian or Alaska Native, non-Hispanic/Latino; 17 Asian, non-Hispanic/Latino; 19 Hispanic/Latino). Average age 30. 504 applicants, 66% accepted, 229 enrolled. *Faculty:* 33 full-time (24 women), 52 part-time/adjunct (41 women). Expenses: Contact institution. *Financial support:* In 2018–19, 10 fellowships with full tuition reimbursements (averaging $9,400 per year), 2 research assistantships with full tuition reimbursements (averaging $17,300 per year), 8 teaching assistantships with full tuition reimbursements (averaging $5,000 per year) were awarded; Federal Work-Study, scholarships/grants, health care benefits, tuition waivers (full and partial), unspecified assistantships, and instructorships and research grants (for PhD students) also available. Financial award application deadline: 4/30; financial award applicants required to submit FAFSA. In 2018, 207 master's, 6 doctorates awarded. *Program availability:* Part-time, blended/hybrid learning, Coursework Online & Field Education in Agency. Offers social welfare (PhD); social work (MSW). *Application deadline:* For fall admission, 3/1 priority date for domestic and international students; for spring admission, 9/15 for domestic and international students; for summer admission, 2/1 for domestic and international students. *Application fee:* $75. Electronic applications accepted. *Application Contact:* Maria Carey, Admissions Processor, 716-645-3381, Fax: 716-645-3456, E-mail: sw-info@buffalo.edu. *Dean,* Dr. Nancy J. Smyth, 716-645-3381, Fax: 716-645-3883, E-mail: sw-dean@buffalo.edu.

UNIVERSITY OF ADVANCING TECHNOLOGY, Tempe, AZ 85283-1042

General Information Proprietary, coed, primarily men, comprehensive institution. *Graduate housing:* Room and/or apartments available on a first-come, first-served basis to single students; on-campus housing not available to married students.

GRADUATE UNITS

Master of Science Program in Technology Offers advancing computer science (MS); emerging technologies (MS); game production and management (MS); information assurance (MS); technology leadership (MS). Electronic applications accepted.

THE UNIVERSITY OF AKRON, Akron, OH 44325

General Information State-supported, coed, university. CGS member. *Graduate housing:* Room and/or apartments available on a first-come, first-served basis to single students; on-campus housing not available to married students. Housing application deadline: 3/1.

GRADUATE UNITS

Graduate School *Program availability:* Part-time, evening/weekend. Electronic applications accepted.

Buchtel College of Arts and Sciences *Program availability:* Part-time, evening/weekend. Offers accompanying (MM); adult development and aging (PhD); applied mathematics (MS); applied politics (MAP); arts administration (MA); arts and sciences (MA, MAP, MFA, MM, MPA, MS, PhD); biology (MS); chemistry (MS, PhD); child development (MA); clothing, textiles and interiors (MA); communication (MA);

composition (MA, MM); computer science (MS); counseling psychology (MA, PhD); creative writing (MFA); earth science (MS); engineering geology (MS); environmental geology (MS); geology (MS); history (MA, PhD); industrial/organizational psychology (MA, PhD); integrated bioscience (PhD); literature (MA); mathematics (MS); music education (MM); music technology (MM); performance (MM); political science (MA, MAP); psychology (MA); public administration (MPA); statistics (MS); theatre arts (MA); theory (MM). Electronic applications accepted.

College of Business Administration Program availability: Part-time, evening/weekend. Offers accounting (MSA); business administration (MA, MBA, MS, MSA, MSM, MT); economics (MA); finance (MBA); global technological innovation (MBA); information systems management (MSM); management (MBA); marketing (MBA); supply chain management (MBA); taxation (MT). Electronic applications accepted.

College of Education Program availability: Part-time. Offers adolescent to young adult education (MS); art education (MS); chemistry (MS); chemistry and physics (MS); curriculum and instruction (MS); drama/theatre (MS); earth science (MS); earth science and chemistry (MS); earth science and physics (MS); education (MA, MS); elementary education - literacy (MA); integrated language arts (MS); integrated mathematics (MS); integrated social studies (MS); life science (MS); life science and chemistry (MS); life science and earth science (MS); life science and physics (MS); P-12 multi-age education (MS); physics (MS); principalship (MA, MS). Electronic applications accepted.

College of Engineering Program availability: Part-time, evening/weekend. Offers biomedical engineering (MS); chemical engineering (MS); civil engineering (MS); computer engineering (MS, PhD); electrical engineering (MS); engineering (PhD); mechanical engineering (MS). Electronic applications accepted.

College of Health Professions Offers audiology (Au D); clinical mental health counseling (MA); counselor education and supervision (PhD); exercise physiology/adult fitness (MS); health professions (MA, MS, MSN, MSW, Au D, DNP, PhD); marriage and family counseling/therapy (MA, PhD); nursing (MSN, DNP); school counseling (MA, MS); social work (MSW); speech-language pathology (MA); sport science/coaching (MA, MS). Electronic applications accepted.

College of Polymer Science and Polymer Engineering Program availability: Part-time, evening/weekend. Offers polymer engineering (MS, PhD); polymer science (MS, PhD). Electronic applications accepted.

School of Law Program availability: Part-time, evening/weekend. Offers law (LL M, JD). Electronic applications accepted.

THE UNIVERSITY OF ALABAMA, Tuscaloosa, AL 35487

General Information State-supported, coed, university. CGS member. *Graduate housing:* On-campus housing not available. *Research affiliation:* Mercedes-Benz (automotive engineering), Alabama Power (utilities), TDK Corp. (materials science), Nucor Steel (materials science), Boeing (aerospace, manufacturing), Lockheed Martin Corporation (business analytics).

GRADUATE UNITS

Graduate School Program availability: Part-time, evening/weekend, online learning. Electronic applications accepted.

Capstone College of Nursing Program availability: Part-time, online learning. Offers nursing (MSN, DNP). Electronic applications accepted.

College of Arts and Sciences Program availability: Part-time, online learning. Offers acting (MFA); American studies (MA); anthropology (MA, PhD); applied mathematics (PhD); arranging (MM); art history (MA); arts and sciences (MA, MATESOL, MFA, MM, MPA, MS, DMA, PhD); biological sciences (MS, PhD); chemistry (MS, PhD); choral conducting (MM, DMA); church music (MM); clinical psychology (PhD); composition (MM, DMA); composition and rhetoric (PhD); costume design (MFA); creative writing (MFA); criminal justice (MS); directing (MFA); earth system science (MS, PhD); environment and natural resources (MS, PhD); environment and society (MS, PhD); experimental psychology (PhD); French (MA, PhD); French and Spanish (PhD); geographic information science (MS, PhD); geological sciences (MS, PhD); German (MA); history (MA, PhD); literature (MA, PhD); mathematics (MA, PhD); music education (MA, PhD); musicology (MM); performance (MM, DMA); physics and astronomy (MS, PhD); political science (MA, PhD); public administration (MPA); pure mathematics (PhD); rhetoric and composition (MA); Romance languages (MA, PhD); scene design/technical production (MFA); Spanish (MA, PhD); speech language pathology (MS); stage management (MFA); studio art (MA, MFA); teaching English as a second language (MATESOL); theatre (MFA); theatre management/administration (MFA); theory (MM); wind conducting (MM, DMA); women's studies (MA). Electronic applications accepted.

College of Communication and Information Sciences Offers advertising and public relations (MA); book arts (MFA); communication and information sciences (MA, MFA, MLIS, PhD); communication studies (MA); journalism and creative media (MA); library and information studies (MLIS, PhD). Electronic applications accepted.

College of Education Program availability: Part-time, online learning. Offers alternative sport pedagogy (MA); choral music education (MA); collaborative special education (M Ed, Ed S); early intervention (M Ed, Ed S); education (M Ed, MA, Ed D, PhD, Ed S); educational administration (Ed D, PhD); educational leadership (MA, Ed S); educational studies in psychology, research methodology and counseling (MA, Ed D, PhD, Ed S); elementary education (MA, Ed D, PhD, Ed S); exercise science (PhD); gifted and talented education (M Ed, Ed S); higher education administration (MA, Ed D, PhD); instructional leadership (Ed D, PhD); instrumental music education (MA); multiple abilities (M Ed); music education (MA, Ed D, PhD, Ed S); secondary education (MA, Ed D, PhD, Ed S); special education (Ed D, PhD).

College of Engineering Program availability: Part-time, online learning. Offers aerospace engineering (MSAEM); chemical and biological engineering (MS Ch E, PhD); civil engineering (MSCE, PhD); computer science (MS, PhD); electrical engineering (MS, PhD); engineering (MS, MS Ch E, MS Met E, MSAEM, MSCE, PhD); engineering science and mechanics (PhD); environmental engineering (MS); materials science (PhD); mechanical engineering (MS, PhD); metallurgical and materials engineering (MS Met E, PhD). Electronic applications accepted.

College of Human Environmental Sciences Program availability: Part-time, evening/weekend, online learning. Offers apparel and textiles (MSHES); consumer sciences (MS); health education and promotion (PhD); health studies (MA); human development and family studies (MSHES); human environmental sciences (MA, MS, MSHES, PhD); human nutrition and hospitality management (MSHES); interactive technology (MS); marriage and family therapy (MSHES); parent and family life education (MSHES); quality management (MS); restaurant and meeting management (MS); rural community health (MS); sport management (MS). Electronic applications accepted.

Manderson Graduate School of Business Program availability: Part-time, evening/weekend, online learning. Offers accounting (M Acc); applied statistics (MS, PhD); business (EMBA, M Acc, MA, MBA, MS, MTA, PhD); economics (MA, PhD); finance (MS, PhD); general commerce and business (EMBA, MBA); management (MA, MS, PhD); marketing (MS, PhD); operations management (MS, PhD); tax accounting (MTA). Electronic applications accepted.

School of Social Work Program availability: Part-time, blended/hybrid learning. Offers social work (MSW, PhD). Electronic applications accepted.

Hugh F. Culverhouse Jr. School of Law Offers business transactions (LL M); comparative law (LL M, JSD); law (JD, JSD); taxation (LL M). Electronic applications accepted.

Interdisciplinary Programs Program availability: Part-time, evening/weekend. Offers interdisciplinary studies (PhD). Electronic applications accepted.

THE UNIVERSITY OF ALABAMA AT BIRMINGHAM, Birmingham, AL 35294

General Information State-supported, coed, university. CGS member. *Enrollment:* 4,073 full-time matriculated graduate/professional students (2,460 women), 3,718 part-time matriculated graduate/professional students (2,519 women). *Enrollment by degree level:* 4,914 master's, 2,639 doctoral, 238 other advanced degrees. *Graduate faculty:* 2,398 full-time (991 women), 217 part-time/adjunct (104 women). *Tuition, area resident:* Full-time $8100; part-time $8100 per year. Tuition, state resident: full-time $8100. Tuition, nonresident: full-time $19,188; part-time $19,188 per year. Tuition and fees vary according to program. *Graduate housing:* On-campus housing not available. *Student services:* Campus employment opportunities, campus safety program, career counseling, exercise/wellness program, free psychological counseling, grant writing training, international student services, low-cost health insurance, multicultural affairs office, services for students with disabilities, teacher training, writing training. *Library facilities:* Mervyn Sterne Library plus 2 others. *Collection:* Books: 1.3 million (physical). Students can reserve study rooms.

Computer facilities: A campuswide network can be accessed from student residence rooms and from off campus. Online class registration, transcript requests are available. Website: http://www.uab.edu/

General Application Contact: Jesse Keppley, Director of Student and Academic Services, 205-996-5696, E-mail: jkeppley@uab.edu.

GRADUATE UNITS

Collat School of Business Program availability: Part-time, evening/weekend, blended/hybrid learning. Offers accounting (M Acct); business (M Acct, MBA, MS); business administration (MBA); management information systems (MS). MD/MBA program offered in partnership with the School of Medicine. Electronic applications accepted.

College of Arts and Sciences Program availability: Part-time, evening/weekend, online learning. Offers anthropology (MA); applied mathematics (MS); art history (MA); arts and sciences (MA, MPA, MS, MSCJ, MSFS, MSW, PhD); behavioral neuroscience (PhD); biology (MS, PhD); chemistry (MS, PhD); communication management (MA); computer and information sciences (MS, PhD); computer forensics and security management (MS); creative writing (MA); criminal justice (MSCJ); forensic science (MSFS); history (MA); lifespan developmental psychology (PhD); literature (MA); mathematics (MS); medical sociology (PhD); medical/clinical psychology (PhD); physics (MS, PhD); psychology (MA); public administration (MPA); rhetoric and composition (MA); social work (MSW). Electronic applications accepted.

Joint Health Sciences Expenses: Contact institution. *Financial support:* Fellowships, research assistantships, and health care benefits available. Offers basic medical sciences (MSBMS); biochemistry, structural, and stem cell biology (PhD); cancer biology (PhD); cell, molecular, and developmental biology (PhD); genetics, genomics, and bioinformatics (PhD); health sciences (MSBMS, PhD); immunology (PhD); microbiology (PhD); neuroscience (PhD); pathobiology and molecular medicine (PhD); pharmacology and toxicology (PhD). Electronic applications accepted. *Application Contact:* Graduate School, 205-934-8227, E-mail: gradschool@uab.edu.

School of Dentistry Offers dentistry (MS, DMD).

School of Education Program availability: Part-time, evening/weekend, online learning. Offers arts education (MA Ed); community health and human services (MA Ed); counseling (MA); curriculum education (Ed S); early childhood education (MA Ed, PhD); education (MA, MA Ed, Ed D, PhD, Ed S); educational leadership (MA Ed, Ed D, Ed S); elementary education (MA Ed); English as a second language (MA Ed, Ed S); high school education (MA Ed); reading (MA Ed); special education (MA Ed). Electronic applications accepted.

School of Engineering Students: 176 full-time (45 women), 407 part-time (80 women); includes 129 minority (90 Black or African American, non-Hispanic/Latino; 1 American Indian or Alaska Native, non-Hispanic/Latino; 13 Asian, non-Hispanic/Latino; 16 Hispanic/Latino; 9 Two or more races, non-Hispanic/Latino), 151 international. Average age 34. 410 applicants, 68% accepted, 148 enrolled. *Faculty:* 41 full-time (6 women), 27 part-time/adjunct (5 women). Expenses: Contact institution. *Financial support:* In 2018–19, 126 students received support, including 40 fellowships with full tuition reimbursements available (averaging $27,017 per year), 57 research assistantships with full and partial tuition reimbursements available, 12 teaching assistantships; institutionally sponsored loans also available. Support available to part-time students. In 2018, 140 master's, 12 doctorates awarded. *Program availability:* Part-time, evening/weekend, 100% online, blended/hybrid learning. Offers advanced safety engineering and management (M Eng); biomedical engineering (MSBME, PhD); civil engineering (MSCE, PhD); computational engineering (PhD); computer engineering (PhD); construction engineering management (M Eng); design and commercialization (M Eng); electrical and computer engineering (MSEE); engineering (M Eng, MS Mt E, MSBME, MSCE, MSEE, MSME, PhD); information engineering management (M Eng); materials engineering (MS Mt E, PhD); mechanical engineering (MSME); structural engineering (M Eng); sustainable smart cities (M Eng). *Application deadline:* For fall admission, 8/1 for domestic and international students; for spring admission, 12/1 for domestic and international students; for summer admission, 5/1 for domestic and international students. Applications are processed on a rolling basis. *Application fee:* $50 ($60 for international students). Electronic applications accepted. *Application Contact:* Jesse Keppley, Director of Student and Academic Services, 205-996-5696, Fax: 205-934-8413, E-mail: gradschool@uab.edu. *Interim Dean,* Dr. Timothy M Wick, 205-975-5890, Fax: 205-934-8437, E-mail: tmwick@uab.edu.

School of Health Professions Program availability: Part-time, online learning. Offers administration/health services (D Sc, PhD); biotechnology (MS); clinical laboratory science (MS); data analytics user experience (MSHI); genetic counseling (MS); health administration (MSHA); health professions (MS, MSHA, MSHI, MSPAS, D Sc, DPT, PhD, Certificate); low vision rehabilitation (Certificate); nutrition sciences (MS, PhD); occupational therapy (MS); physical therapy (DPT); physician assistant studies (MSPAS); rehabilitation science (PhD). Electronic applications accepted.

School of Medicine Offers medicine (MD). Electronic applications accepted.

School of Nursing *Program availability:* Part-time, online only, blended/hybrid learning. Offers clinical nurse leader (MSN); nurse anesthesia (DNP); nurse practitioner (MSN, DNP); nursing (MSN, DNP, PhD); nursing health systems administration (MSN); nursing informatics (MSN). Electronic applications accepted.

School of Optometry Students: 211 full-time (147 women), 10 part-time (8 women); includes 49 minority (10 Black or African American, non-Hispanic/Latino; 2 American Indian or Alaska Native, non-Hispanic/Latino; 31 Asian, non-Hispanic/Latino; 6 Hispanic/Latino), 11 international. Average age 29. 342 applicants, 35% accepted, 52 enrolled. *Faculty:* 205 full-time (141 women). Expenses: Contact institution. *Financial support:* In 2018–19, 44 students received support. Federal Work-Study, scholarships/grants, and out-of-state tuition offsets available. Financial award application deadline: 5/1; financial award applicants required to submit FAFSA. In 2018, 3 master's, 50 doctorates awarded. Offers optometry (MS, OD, PhD); sensory impairment (PhD); vision science (MS, PhD). *Application deadline:* For fall admission, 4/1 for domestic students. Applications are processed on a rolling basis. Electronic applications accepted. *Application Contact:* Gerald Simon, Director, Optometry Student Affairs, 205-975-0739, Fax: 205-934-6458, E-mail: gsimonod@uab.edu. *Dean,* Dr. Kelly K. Nichols, 205-975-9935, Fax: 205-934-6758, E-mail: nicholsk@uab.edu.

School of Public Health Students: 277 full-time (194 women), 206 part-time (153 women); includes 140 minority (61 Black or African American, non-Hispanic/Latino; 6 American Indian or Alaska Native, non-Hispanic/Latino; 49 Asian, non-Hispanic/Latino; 9 Hispanic/Latino; 15 Two or more races, non-Hispanic/Latino), 85 international. Average age 31. *Faculty:* 67 full-time (38 women). Expenses: Contact institution. *Financial support:* Fellowships, research assistantships, teaching assistantships, career-related internships or fieldwork, traineeships, and unspecified assistantships available. Financial award application deadline: 3/1; financial award applicants required to submit FAFSA. In 2018, 133 master's, 19 doctorates awarded. *Program availability:* Part-time, 100% online, blended/hybrid learning. Offers applied epidemiology and pharmacoepidemiology (MSPH); biostatistics (MPH, MS, MSPH, Dr PH, PhD); clinical and translational science (MSPH); environmental & occupational health (MPH); environmental health (MPH); environmental health and toxicology (MSPH); environmental health sciences (PhD); epidemiology (MPH, PhD); general theory and practice (MPH); health behavior (MPH); health care organization (MPH, Dr PH); health education and health promotion (PhD); health policy (MPH); industrial hygiene (MPH, MSPH, PhD); maternal and child health policy (Dr PH); maternal and child health policy and leadership (MPH); occupational health and safety (MPH); outcomes research (MSPH, Dr PH); public health (PhD); public health preparedness management (MPH). *Application deadline:* For fall admission, 4/1 priority date for domestic and international students; for spring admission, 11/1 for domestic students; for summer admission, 4/1 for domestic students. Applications are processed on a rolling basis. *Application fee:* $0 ($60 for international students). Electronic applications accepted. *Application Contact:* Hannah VanSlambrouck, Director of Enrollment Management, 205-975-8688, Fax: 205-975-5484, E-mail: soph@uab.edu. *Dean,* Dr. Paul Erwin, 205-934-4993, Fax: 205-975-5484, E-mail: perwin@uab.edu.

THE UNIVERSITY OF ALABAMA IN HUNTSVILLE, Huntsville, AL 35899

General Information State-supported, coed, university. CGS member. *Enrollment:* 727 full-time matriculated graduate/professional students (335 women), 1,277 part-time matriculated graduate/professional students (707 women). *Enrollment by degree level:* 1,529 master's, 475 doctoral. *Graduate faculty:* 219 full-time (77 women), 41 part-time/adjunct (19 women). *Tuition, area resident:* Full-time $10,632; part-time $412 per credit hour. Tuition, state resident: full-time $10,632. Tuition, nonresident: full-time $23,604; part-time $412 per credit hour. *Required fees:* $582; $582. Tuition and fees vary according to course load and program. *Graduate housing:* Rooms and/or apartments available on a first-come, first-served basis to single and married students. Typical cost: $4385 (including board) for single students; $4385 (including board) for married students. Housing application deadline: 6/1. *Student services:* Campus employment opportunities, campus safety program, career counseling, child daycare facilities, exercise/wellness program, free psychological counseling, grant writing training, international student services, low-cost health insurance, multicultural affairs office, services for students with disabilities, teacher training, writing training. *Library facilities:* Louis Salmon Library. *Collection:* Books: 239,503 (physical), 387,481 (digital/electronic); Serial titles: 3,441 (physical), 42,868 (digital/electronic); Databases: 133.

Computer facilities: 1,227 computers available on campus for general student use. A campuswide network can be accessed from student residence rooms and from off campus. Online class registration is available. Website: http://www.uah.edu/

General Application Contact: Kim Gray, Admissions Coordinator, Graduate Studies, 256-824-6198, Fax: 256-824-6002, E-mail: deangrad@uah.edu.

GRADUATE UNITS

School of Graduate Studies Students: 727 full-time (335 women), 1,277 part-time (707 women); includes 333 minority (177 Black or African American, non-Hispanic/Latino; 21 American Indian or Alaska Native, non-Hispanic/Latino; 62 Asian, non-Hispanic/Latino; 53 Hispanic/Latino; 20 Two or more races, non-Hispanic/Latino), 269 international. Average age 34. 1,841 applicants, 69% accepted, 686 enrolled. *Faculty:* 219 full-time (77 women), 41 part-time/adjunct (19 women). Expenses: Contact institution. *Financial support:* In 2018–19, 185 research assistantships with full and partial tuition reimbursements (averaging $7,788 per year), 225 teaching assistantships with full and partial tuition reimbursements (averaging $5,611 per year) were awarded; career-related internships or fieldwork, Federal Work-Study, institutionally sponsored loans, scholarships/grants, traineeships, health care benefits, tuition waivers (full and partial), and unspecified assistantships also available. Support available to part-time students. Financial award application deadline: 4/1; financial award applicants required to submit FAFSA. In 2018, 528 master's, 72 doctorates, 40 other advanced degrees awarded. *Program availability:* Part-time. *Application deadline:* For fall admission, 7/16 priority date for domestic students, 4/1 priority date for international students; for spring admission, 11/30 priority date for domestic students, 9/1 priority date for international students. Applications are processed on a rolling basis. *Application fee:* $50. Electronic applications accepted. *Application Contact:* Kim Gray, Graduate Studies Admissions Coordinator, 256-824-6002, Fax: 256-824-6405, E-mail: deangrad@uah.edu. *Dean of Graduate Studies,* Dr. David Berkowitz, 256-824-6002, Fax: 256-824-6405, E-mail: deangrad@uah.edu.

College of Arts, Humanities, and Social Sciences Students: 49 full-time (30 women), 65 part-time (43 women); includes 23 minority (13 Black or African American, non-Hispanic/Latino; 1 American Indian or Alaska Native, non-Hispanic/Latino; 5 Hispanic/Latino; 4 Two or more races, non-Hispanic/Latino), 4 international. Average age 32. 58 applicants, 93% accepted, 35 enrolled. *Faculty:* 30 full-time (17 women). Expenses: Contact institution. *Financial support:* In 2018–19, 49 students received support, including 5 research assistantships with full and partial tuition reimbursements available (averaging $4,261 per year), 17 teaching assistantships with full tuition reimbursements available (averaging $4,147 per year); career-related internships or fieldwork, Federal Work-Study, institutionally sponsored loans, scholarships/grants, health care benefits, tuition waivers (full and partial), and unspecified assistantships also available. Support available to part-time students. Financial award application deadline: 4/1; financial award applicants required to submit FAFSA. In 2018, 37 master's, 12 other advanced degrees awarded. *Program availability:* Part-time. Offers arts, humanities, and social sciences (MA, Certificate); education (MA); English (MA); history (MA); industrial/organizational psychology (MA); psychology (MA); public affairs (MA); technical writing (Certificate); TESOL (Certificate). *Application deadline:* For fall admission, 7/15 priority date for domestic students, 4/1 priority date for international students; for spring admission, 11/30 priority date for domestic students, 9/1 priority date for international students. Applications are processed on a rolling basis. *Application fee:* $50. Electronic applications accepted. *Application Contact:* Kim Gray, Graduate Studies Admissions Coordinator, 256-824-6002, Fax: 256-824-6405, E-mail: deangrad@uah.edu. *Dean,* Dr. Sean Lane, 256-824-6200, Fax: 256-824-6949, E-mail: dean-ahs@uah.edu.

College of Business Administration Students: 104 full-time (40 women), 271 part-time (131 women); includes 67 minority (35 Black or African American, non-Hispanic/Latino; 2 American Indian or Alaska Native, non-Hispanic/Latino; 11 Asian, non-Hispanic/Latino; 14 Hispanic/Latino; 2 Native Hawaiian or other Pacific Islander, non-Hispanic/Latino; 3 Two or more races, non-Hispanic/Latino), 30 international. Average age 33. 352 applicants, 76% accepted, 159 enrolled. *Faculty:* 24 full-time (7 women). Expenses: Contact institution. *Financial support:* In 2018–19, 19 students received support, including 15 teaching assistantships with full tuition reimbursements available (averaging $4,434 per year); research assistantships with full tuition reimbursements available, career-related internships or fieldwork, Federal Work-Study, institutionally sponsored loans, scholarships/grants, health care benefits, tuition waivers (full and partial), and unspecified assistantships also available. Support available to part-time students. Financial award application deadline: 4/1; financial award applicants required to submit FAFSA. In 2018, 147 master's, 14 other advanced degrees awarded. *Program availability:* Part-time. Offers accounting (M Acc); business administration (M Acc, MBA, MS, MSIS, MSM, MSMS, Certificate); business analytics (MSMS); cybersecurity (MS, Certificate); enterprise resource planning (Certificate); federal contracting and procurement management (Certificate); human resource management (MSM); information systems (MSIS); management (MBA); supply chain and logistics management (MS); supply chain management (Certificate); technology and innovation management (Certificate). *Application deadline:* For fall admission, 7/15 priority date for domestic students, 4/1 priority date for international students; for spring admission, 11/30 priority date for domestic students, 9/1 priority date for international students. Applications are processed on a rolling basis. *Application fee:* $50. Electronic applications accepted. *Application Contact:* Jennifer Pettitt, Director of Advising, 256-824-6681, Fax: 256-824-7571, E-mail: jennifer.pettitt@uah.edu. *Dean,* Dr. Jason Greene, 256-824-4424, Fax: 256-824-7571, E-mail: jason.greene@uah.edu.

College of Education Students: 38 full-time (30 women), 39 part-time (37 women); includes 17 minority (10 Black or African American, non-Hispanic/Latino; 3 American Indian or Alaska Native, non-Hispanic/Latino; 2 Asian, non-Hispanic/Latino; 2 Two or more races, non-Hispanic/Latino). Average age 33. 47 applicants, 83% accepted, 29 enrolled. *Faculty:* 13 full-time (10 women). Expenses: Contact institution. *Financial support:* In 2018–19, 2 students received support, including 1 teaching assistantship with full tuition reimbursement available (averaging $4,500 per year); career-related internships or fieldwork, Federal Work-Study, institutionally sponsored loans, scholarships/grants, health care benefits, tuition waivers (full and partial), and unspecified assistantships also available. Support available to part-time students. Financial award application deadline: 4/1; financial award applicants required to submit FAFSA. In 2018, 31 master's awarded. *Program availability:* Part-time. Offers autism spectrum disorders (M Ed, Graduate Certificate); biology (MAT); chemistry (MAT); differentiated instruction in elementary education (M Ed); English language arts (MAT); English speakers of other languages (M Ed, MAT); history (MAT); mathematics (MAT); physics (MAT); reading education (M Ed); secondary education (M Ed). *Application deadline:* For fall admission, 7/15 priority date for domestic students, 4/1 priority date for international students; for spring admission, 11/30 priority date for domestic students, 9/1 priority date for international students. Applications are processed on a rolling basis. *Application fee:* $50. Electronic applications accepted. *Application Contact:* Kim Gray, Graduate Studies Admissions Coordinator, 256-824-6002, Fax: 256-824-6405, E-mail: deangrad@uah.edu. *Dean,* Dr. Beth Nason Quick, 256-824-2325, E-mail: beth.quick@uah.edu.

College of Engineering Students: 192 full-time (44 women), 302 part-time (46 women); includes 58 minority (21 Black or African American, non-Hispanic/Latino; 7 American Indian or Alaska Native, non-Hispanic/Latino; 20 Asian, non-Hispanic/Latino; 7 Hispanic/Latino; 3 Two or more races, non-Hispanic/Latino), 127 international. Average age 31. 511 applicants, 63% accepted, 113 enrolled. *Faculty:* 59 full-time (9 women), 6 part-time/adjunct (0 women). Expenses: Contact institution. *Financial support:* In 2018–19, 149 students received support, including 83 research assistantships with full tuition reimbursements available (averaging $6,729 per year), 66 teaching assistantships with full tuition reimbursements available (averaging $5,765 per year); career-related internships or fieldwork, Federal Work-Study, institutionally sponsored loans, scholarships/grants, health care benefits, tuition waivers (full and partial), and unspecified assistantships also available. Support available to part-time students. Financial award application deadline: 4/1; financial award applicants required to submit FAFSA. In 2018, 114 master's, 22 doctorates awarded. *Program availability:* Part-time. Offers aerospace systems engineering (MS, PhD); biotechnology science and engineering (PhD); chemical and materials engineering (MSE); civil and environmental engineering (PhD); civil engineering (MSE); computer engineering (MSE, PhD); electrical engineering (MSE, PhD); engineering (MS, MSE, MSOR, MSSE, PhD); engineering management (MSE, PhD); industrial engineering (MSE, PhD); materials science (PhD); mechanical engineering (PhD); operations research (MSOR); optical science and engineering (PhD); software engineering (MSSE); systems engineering (MSE, PhD). *Application deadline:* For fall admission, 7/15 priority date for domestic students, 4/1 priority date for international students; for spring admission, 11/30 priority date for domestic students, 9/1 priority date for international students. Applications are processed on a rolling basis. *Application fee:* $50. Electronic applications accepted. *Application Contact:* Kim Gray, Graduate Studies Admissions Coordinator, 256-824-6002, Fax: 256-824-6405, E-mail: deangrad@uah.edu. *Dean,* Dr. Shankar Mahalingam, 256-824-6474, Fax: 256-824-6843, E-mail: coedean@uah.edu.

College of Nursing Students: 117 full-time (101 women), 473 part-time (414 women); includes 132 minority (81 Black or African American, non-Hispanic/Latino; 7 American Indian or Alaska Native, non-Hispanic/Latino; 20 Asian, non-Hispanic/Latino; 19 Hispanic/Latino; 5 Two or more races, non-Hispanic/Latino), 5 international. Average age 40. 397 applicants, 56% accepted, 197 enrolled. *Faculty:* 25 full-time (23 women), 14 part-time/adjunct (all women). Expenses: Contact institution. *Financial support:* In 2018–19, 37 students received support, including 37 teaching assistantships with full tuition reimbursements available (averaging $3,633 per year); career-related internships or fieldwork, Federal Work-Study, institutionally sponsored loans, scholarships/grants, traineeships, health care benefits, and unspecified assistantships also available. Support available to part-time students. Financial award application deadline: 4/1; financial award applicants required to submit FAFSA. In 2018, 117 master's, 34 doctorates, 14 other advanced degrees awarded. *Program availability:* Part-time. Offers family nurse practitioner (Certificate); nursing (MSN, DNP); nursing education (Certificate). DNP offered jointly with The University of Alabama at Birmingham. *Application deadline:* For fall admission, 7/15 for domestic students, 4/1 for international students; for spring admission, 11/30 for domestic students, 9/1 for international students. Applications are processed on a rolling basis. *Application fee:* $50. Electronic applications accepted. *Application Contact:* Charles Davis, Director of Graduate Admission and Advisement, 256-824-6669, Fax: 256-824-6026, E-mail: charles.davis@uah.edu. *Dean,* Dr. Marsha Adams, 256-824-6345, Fax: 256-824-6026, E-mail: marsha.adams@uah.edu.

College of Science Students: 227 full-time (90 women), 127 part-time (36 women); includes 38 minority (17 Black or African American, non-Hispanic/Latino; 1 American Indian or Alaska Native, non-Hispanic/Latino; 9 Asian, non-Hispanic/Latino; 8 Hispanic/Latino; 3 Two or more races, non-Hispanic/Latino), 103 international. Average age 32. 383 applicants, 72% accepted, 100 enrolled. *Faculty:* 67 full-time (11 women), 9 part-time/adjunct (1 woman). Expenses: Contact institution. *Financial support:* In 2018–19, 188 students received support, including 94 research assistantships with full tuition reimbursements available (averaging $8,489 per year), 89 teaching assistantships with full tuition reimbursements available (averaging $6,578 per year); career-related internships or fieldwork, Federal Work-Study, institutionally sponsored loans, scholarships/grants, health care benefits, tuition waivers (full and partial), and unspecified assistantships also available. Support available to part-time students. Financial award application deadline: 4/1; financial award applicants required to submit FAFSA. In 2018, 82 master's, 16 doctorates awarded. *Program availability:* Part-time. Offers applied mathematics (PhD); atmospheric science (MS, PhD); biology (MS); biotechnology science and engineering (PhD); chemistry (MS); computer science (MS, PhD); cybersecurity (MS); earth system science (MS); education (MA, MS); materials science (MS, PhD); mathematics (MA, MS); modeling and simulation (MS, PhD, Certificate); optics and photonics technology (MS); physics (MS, PhD); science (MA, MS, MSSE, PhD, Certificate); software engineering (MSSE, Certificate); space science (MS, PhD). *Application deadline:* For fall admission, 7/15 priority date for domestic students, 4/1 priority date for international students; for spring admission, 11/30 priority date for domestic students, 9/1 priority date for international students. Applications are processed on a rolling basis. *Application fee:* $50. Electronic applications accepted. *Application Contact:* Kim Gray, Graduate Studies Admissions Coordinator, 256-824-6002, Fax: 256-824-6405, E-mail: deangrad@uah.edu. *Interim Dean,* Dr. John Christy, 256-824-6605, Fax: 256-824-6819, E-mail: cosdean@uah.edu.

UNIVERSITY OF ALASKA ANCHORAGE, Anchorage, AK 99508

General Information State-supported, coed, comprehensive institution. *Graduate housing:* Rooms and/or apartments available on a first-come, first-served basis to single and married students. Housing application deadline: 7/1. *Research affiliation:* Conoco Phillips (energy), Habitat for Humanity (project management), BP Alaska (energy), Municipality of Anchorage (government), Providence Hospital (health care).

GRADUATE UNITS

College of Arts and Sciences *Program availability:* Part-time. Offers anthropology (MA); arts and sciences (MA, MFA, MS, PhD); biological sciences (MS); clinical psychology (MS); clinical-community psychology with rural and indigenous emphasis (PhD); creative writing and literary arts (MFA); English (MA).

College of Business and Public Policy *Program availability:* Part-time, evening/weekend. Offers business administration (MBA); business and public policy (MBA, MPA, MS); global supply chain management (MS); public administration (MPA).

College of Health *Program availability:* Part-time, evening/weekend. Offers health (MPA, MPH, MS, MSW, DNP, Certificate, Graduate Certificate); physician assistant (MS); public health practice (MPH).

School of Nursing *Program availability:* Part-time, evening/weekend. Offers nursing (MS, DNP, Graduate Certificate).

School of Social Work *Program availability:* Part-time, evening/weekend, online learning. Offers children's mental health (Graduate Certificate); social work (MSW). Electronic applications accepted.

School of Education *Program availability:* Part-time. Offers early childhood special education (M Ed); education (M Ed, Certificate); educational leadership (M Ed); master teacher (M Ed); principal (Certificate); special education (M Ed, Certificate); teaching (M Ed).

UNIVERSITY OF ALASKA FAIRBANKS, Fairbanks, AK 99775-7520

General Information State-supported, coed, university. *Enrollment:* 433 full-time matriculated graduate/professional students (228 women), 484 part-time matriculated graduate/professional students (307 women). *Enrollment by degree level:* 610 master's, 263 doctoral, 44 other advanced degrees. *Graduate faculty:* 247 full-time (100 women), 12 part-time/adjunct (6 women). *International tuition:* $18,504 full-time. *Tuition, area resident:* Full-time $8802; part-time $5868 per credit hour. *Tuition, state resident:* full-time $8802; part-time $5868 per credit hour. *Tuition, nonresident:* full-time $18,504; part-time $12,336 per credit hour. *Required fees:* $1416; $944 per credit hour. $472 per semester. Tuition and fees vary according to course load and program. *Graduate housing:* Rooms and/or apartments available on a first-come, first-served basis to single and married students. Typical cost: $6000 per year ($12,050 including board) for single students; $13,050 per year for married students. Room and board charges vary according to board plan and housing facility selected. Housing application deadline: 7/31. *Student services:* Campus employment opportunities, campus safety program, career counseling, child daycare facilities, exercise/wellness program, free psychological counseling, grant writing training, international student services, low-cost health insurance, multicultural affairs office, services for students with disabilities, teacher training, writing training. *Library facilities:* Rasmuson Library plus 1 other. Collection: Books: 533,679 (physical), 324,260 (digital/electronic); Serial titles: 222,847 (physical), 30,490 (digital/electronic); Databases: 175. Weekly public service hours: 87; students can reserve study rooms. *Research affiliation:* Southcentral Foundation (Health

Research), Pollock Conservation Cooperative Research Center (Fisheries Research), Hilcorp (Oil Production), Cold Climate Housing Research Center (Cold Regions Housing), Alaska Native Tribal Health Consortium (Alaska Native Health), Alyeska (Oil Transport).

Computer facilities: 125 computers available on campus for general student use. A campuswide network can be accessed from student residence rooms and from off campus. Online class registration, university portal are available.
Website: http://www.uaf.edu/

General Application Contact: Samara Taber, Director of Admissions, 907-474-7034, E-mail: uaf-admissions@alaska.edu.

GRADUATE UNITS

College of Engineering and Mines Students: 44 full-time (8 women), 39 part-time (9 women); includes 12 minority (2 Black or African American, non-Hispanic/Latino; 2 Asian, non-Hispanic/Latino; 2 Hispanic/Latino; 6 Two or more races, non-Hispanic/Latino), 26 international. Average age 30. 94 applicants, 36% accepted, 17 enrolled. *Faculty:* 36 full-time (4 women), 1 (woman) part-time/adjunct. Expenses: Contact institution. *Financial support:* In 2018–19, 20 research assistantships with full tuition reimbursements (averaging $6,054 per year), 32 teaching assistantships with full tuition reimbursements (averaging $6,669 per year) were awarded; fellowships with full tuition reimbursements, career-related internships or fieldwork, Federal Work-Study, scholarships/grants, health care benefits, and unspecified assistantships also available. Support available to part-time students. Financial award application deadline: 7/1; financial award applicants required to submit FAFSA. In 2018, 26 master's, 3 doctorates awarded. *Program availability:* Part-time. Offers civil engineering (MS); computer science (MS); design and construction management (Graduate Certificate); electrical engineering (MEE, MS); engineering (PhD); engineering and mines (MCE, MEE, MS, PhD, Graduate Certificate); environmental engineering (PhD); geological engineering (MS); mechanical engineering (MS); mineral preparation engineering (MS); mining engineering (MS); petroleum engineering (MS). *Application deadline:* For fall admission, 6/1 for domestic students, 3/1 for international students; for spring admission, 10/15 for domestic students, 9/1 for international students. Applications are processed on a rolling basis. *Application fee:* $60. Electronic applications accepted. *Application Contact:* Samara Taber, Director of Admissions, 907-474-7500, E-mail: uaf-admissions@alaska.edu. *Dean,* Dr. William Schnabel, 907-474-7730, E-mail: fycem@uaf.edu.

College of Fisheries and Ocean Sciences Students: 51 full-time (37 women), 48 part-time (26 women); includes 8 minority (1 Black or African American, non-Hispanic/Latino; 1 American Indian or Alaska Native, non-Hispanic/Latino; 2 Asian, non-Hispanic/Latino; 3 Hispanic/Latino; 1 Two or more races, non-Hispanic/Latino), 9 international. Average age 32. 42 applicants, 38% accepted, 14 enrolled. *Faculty:* 41 full-time (20 women), 6 part-time/adjunct (3 women). Expenses: Contact institution. *Financial support:* In 2018–19, 28 research assistantships with full tuition reimbursements (averaging $11,456 per year), 9 teaching assistantships with full tuition reimbursements (averaging $11,469 per year) were awarded; fellowships with full tuition reimbursements, career-related internships or fieldwork, Federal Work-Study, scholarships/grants, health care benefits, and unspecified assistantships also available. Support available to part-time students. Financial award application deadline: 2/15; financial award applicants required to submit FAFSA. In 2018, 12 master's, 8 doctorates awarded. *Program availability:* Part-time, Zoom. Offers fisheries (MS, PhD); fisheries and ocean sciences (MS, PhD); marine biology (MS, PhD); oceanography (MS, PhD). *Application deadline:* For fall admission, 3/1 for international students; for spring admission, 8/15 for international students. Applications are processed on a rolling basis. *Application fee:* $60. Electronic applications accepted. *Application Contact:* Samara Taber, Director of Admissions, 907-474-7500, E-mail: uaf-admissions@alaska.edu. *Dean,* Dr. S. Bradley Moran, 907-474-7824, E-mail: info@cfos.uaf.edu.

College of Liberal Arts Students: 76 full-time (47 women), 91 part-time (69 women); includes 44 minority (1 Black or African American, non-Hispanic/Latino; 16 American Indian or Alaska Native, non-Hispanic/Latino; 3 Asian, non-Hispanic/Latino; 5 Hispanic/Latino; 1 Native Hawaiian or other Pacific Islander, non-Hispanic/Latino; 18 Two or more races, non-Hispanic/Latino), 10 international. Average age 37. 96 applicants, 42% accepted, 24 enrolled. *Faculty:* 91 full-time (45 women), 4 part-time/adjunct (1 woman). Expenses: Contact institution. *Financial support:* In 2018–19, 4 research assistantships with tuition reimbursements (averaging $11,274 per year), 54 teaching assistantships with tuition reimbursements (averaging $5,578 per year) were awarded; fellowships with tuition reimbursements, career-related internships or fieldwork, Federal Work-Study, scholarships/grants, health care benefits, and unspecified assistantships also available. Support available to part-time students. Financial award application deadline: 7/1; financial award applicants required to submit FAFSA. In 2018, 25 master's, 7 doctorates awarded. *Program availability:* Part-time, 100% online, blended/hybrid learning. Offers anthropology (MA, PhD); applied linguistics (MA); Arctic policy (MA); art (MFA); ceramics (MFA); computer art (MFA); creative writing (MFA); cross-cultural studies (MA); drawing (MFA); environmental politics and policy (MA); justice (MA); liberal arts (MA, MFA, MM, PhD); literature (MA); Northern history (MA); painting (MFA); photography (MFA); printmaking (MFA); professional communication (MA); sculpture (MFA). *Application deadline:* For fall admission, 6/1 for domestic students, 3/1 for international students; for spring admission, 10/15 for domestic students, 9/1 for international students. Applications are processed on a rolling basis. *Application fee:* $60. Electronic applications accepted. *Application Contact:* Samara Taber, Director of Admissions, 907-474-7500, E-mail: uaf-admissions@alaska.edu. *Dean,* Todd Sherman, 907-474-7231, E-mail: uaf-cla@alaska.edu.

College of Natural Science and Mathematics Students: 202 full-time (106 women), 178 part-time (123 women); includes 58 minority (1 Black or African American, non-Hispanic/Latino; 11 American Indian or Alaska Native, non-Hispanic/Latino; 8 Asian, non-Hispanic/Latino; 17 Hispanic/Latino; 2 Native Hawaiian or other Pacific Islander, non-Hispanic/Latino; 19 Two or more races, non-Hispanic/Latino), 44 international. Average age 34. 255 applicants, 32% accepted, 69 enrolled. *Faculty:* 124 full-time (57 women), 3 part-time/adjunct (1 woman). Expenses: Contact institution. *Financial support:* In 2018–19, 72 research assistantships with full tuition reimbursements (averaging $11,985 per year), 64 teaching assistantships with full tuition reimbursements (averaging $11,908 per year) were awarded; fellowships with full tuition reimbursements, career-related internships or fieldwork, Federal Work-Study, scholarships/grants, health care benefits, and unspecified assistantships also available. Support available to part-time students. Financial award application deadline: 7/1; financial award applicants required to submit FAFSA. In 2018, 81 master's, 28 doctorates, 35 other advanced degrees awarded. *Program availability:* Part-time. Offers atmospheric science (MS, PhD); biochemistry and neuroscience (PhD); biological sciences (MS, PhD); chemistry (MA, MS); computational physics (MS); environmental chemistry (PhD); geophysics (MS); mathematics (PhD); natural science and mathematics (MA, MS, PhD, Graduate Certificate); physics (MS, PhD); space physics (MS); statistics (MS, Graduate Certificate); wildlife biology and conservation (MS). DVM awarded through Colorado State University, PHD in Natural Resources and Environment joint between UAF College of Natural Sciences and Mathematics and UAF School of Management. *Application deadline:* For fall admission, 6/1 for domestic students, 3/1 for international students; for spring admission, 10/15 for domestic students, 9/1 for international students. Applications are processed on a rolling basis. *Application fee:* $60. Electronic applications accepted. *Application Contact:* Samara Taber, Director of Admissions, 907-474-7500, Fax: 907-474-7097, E-mail: admissions@uaf.edu. *Dean,* Dr. Kinchel Doerner, 907-474-7608, Fax: 907-474-5101, E-mail: fycnsm@uaf.edu.

College of Rural and Community Development Students: 5 full-time (1 woman), 15 part-time (13 women); includes 14 minority (7 American Indian or Alaska Native, non-Hispanic/Latino; 2 Hispanic/Latino; 5 Two or more races, non-Hispanic/Latino), 1 international. Average age 35. 13 applicants, 69% accepted, 7 enrolled. *Faculty:* 17 full-time (15 women). Expenses: Contact institution. *Financial support:* In 2018–19, 1 research assistantship with full tuition reimbursement (averaging $7,574 per year) was awarded; teaching assistantships with full tuition reimbursements, scholarships/grants, and health care benefits also available. Financial award application deadline: 2/15; financial award applicants required to submit FAFSA. *Program availability:* Part-time, evening/weekend, 100% online, blended/hybrid learning. Offers rural and community development (MA); rural development (MA). *Application deadline:* For fall admission, 6/1 for domestic students, 3/1 for international students; for spring admission, 10/15 for domestic students, 9/1 for international students. Applications are processed on a rolling basis. *Application fee:* $60. Electronic applications accepted. *Application Contact:* Samara Taber, Director of Admissions, 907-474-7500, Fax: 907-474-7097, E-mail: uaf-admissions@alaska.edu. *Vice Chancellor for Rural, Community and Native Education,* Evon Peter, 907-474-1865, Fax: 907-474-5824, E-mail: uaf-crcd-vice-chancellor@alaska.edu.

Graduate School for Interdisciplinary Studies Students: 8 full-time (all women), 17 part-time (14 women); includes 10 minority (9 American Indian or Alaska Native, non-Hispanic/Latino; 1 Two or more races, non-Hispanic/Latino), 3 international. Average age 47. 24 applicants, 38% accepted, 8 enrolled. Expenses: Contact institution. *Financial support:* In 2018–19, 1 teaching assistantship with full tuition reimbursement (averaging $6,203 per year) was awarded; fellowships with full tuition reimbursements, research assistantships with full tuition reimbursements, career-related internships or fieldwork, Federal Work-Study, scholarships/grants, health care benefits, and unspecified assistantships also available. Support available to part-time students. Financial award application deadline: 2/15; financial award applicants required to submit FAFSA. In 2018, 8 doctorates awarded. *Program availability:* Part-time. Offers indigenous studies (PhD); interdisciplinary studies (MA, MS, PhD). The UAF interdisciplinary program provides flexibility to students who have well-defined goals that do not fit into one of the established majors offered by the university. The proposed program must differ significantly from, and may not substitute for, an existing UAF graduate degree program. *Application deadline:* For fall admission, 3/1 for domestic and international students; for spring admission, 10/1 for domestic students, 9/1 for international students. Applications are processed on a rolling basis. *Application fee:* $60. Electronic applications accepted. *Application Contact:* Samara Taber, Director of Admissions, 907-474-7500, E-mail: uaf-admissions@alaska.edu. *Interim Dean,* Michael Castellini, 907-474-7319, E-mail: UAF-Grad-School@alaska.edu.

School of Education Students: 39 full-time (27 women), 105 part-time (89 women); includes 27 minority (8 American Indian or Alaska Native, non-Hispanic/Latino; 1 Asian, non-Hispanic/Latino; 9 Hispanic/Latino; 1 Native Hawaiian or other Pacific Islander, non-Hispanic/Latino; 8 Two or more races, non-Hispanic/Latino), 3 international. Average age 37. 63 applicants, 52% accepted, 29 enrolled. *Faculty:* 15 full-time (11 women), 1 part-time/adjunct (0 women). Expenses: Contact institution. *Financial support:* In 2018–19, 2 teaching assistantships with full tuition reimbursements (averaging $11,955 per year) were awarded; fellowships with full tuition reimbursements, research assistantships with full tuition reimbursements, career-related internships or fieldwork, Federal Work-Study, scholarships/grants, health care benefits, and unspecified assistantships also available. Support available to part-time students. Financial award application deadline: 6/1; financial award applicants required to submit FAFSA. In 2018, 49 master's, 34 other advanced degrees awarded. *Program availability:* 100% online, blended/hybrid learning. Offers community counseling (M Ed); education (M Ed, Graduate Certificate); special education (M Ed). *Application deadline:* For fall admission, 2/15 for domestic and international students; for spring admission, 10/1 for domestic students, 8/1 for international students. *Application fee:* $60. Electronic applications accepted. *Application Contact:* Samara Taber, Director of Admissions, 907-474-7500, E-mail: uaf-admissions@alaska.edu. *Director,* Dr. Amy Vinlove, 907-474-7341, E-mail: uaf-soe-school@alaska.edu.

School of Management Students: 46 full-time (21 women), 96 part-time (53 women); includes 36 minority (3 Black or African American, non-Hispanic/Latino; 4 American Indian or Alaska Native, non-Hispanic/Latino; 6 Asian, non-Hispanic/Latino; 13 Hispanic/Latino; 10 Two or more races, non-Hispanic/Latino), 3 international. Average age 33. 77 applicants, 57% accepted, 30 enrolled. *Faculty:* 23 full-time (7 women). Expenses: Contact institution. *Financial support:* In 2018–19, 1 research assistantship with full tuition reimbursement (averaging $7,600 per year), 11 teaching assistantships with full tuition reimbursements (averaging $14,075 per year) were awarded; fellowships with full tuition reimbursements, career-related internships or fieldwork, Federal Work-Study, scholarships/grants, health care benefits, and unspecified assistantships also available. Support available to part-time students. Financial award application deadline: 7/1; financial award applicants required to submit FAFSA. In 2018, 47 master's awarded. *Program availability:* Part-time, 100% online, blended/hybrid learning. Offers capital markets (MBA); general management (MBA); management (MBA, MS, MSDM); security and disaster management (MSDM). *Application deadline:* For fall admission, 6/1 for domestic students; for spring admission, 10/15 for domestic students; for summer admission, 5/1 for domestic students. Applications are processed on a rolling basis. *Application fee:* $60. Electronic applications accepted. *Application Contact:* Samara Taber, Director of Admissions, 907-474-7500, E-mail: uaf-admissions@alaska.edu. *Dean,* Dr. Mark Herrmann, 907-474-7461, E-mail: uaf-som@alaska.edu.

School of Natural Resources and Extension Students: 11 full-time (8 women), 15 part-time (7 women); includes 5 minority (1 Black or African American, non-Hispanic/Latino; 1 Hispanic/Latino; 3 Two or more races, non-Hispanic/Latino), 1 international. Average age 39. 11 applicants, 36% accepted, 3 enrolled. *Faculty:* 34 full-time (18 women), 1 (woman) part-time/adjunct. Expenses: Contact institution. *Financial support:* In 2018–19, 4 research assistantships with full tuition reimbursements (averaging $11,999 per year), 1 teaching assistantship with full tuition reimbursement (averaging $5,034 per year) were awarded; fellowships with full tuition reimbursements, career-related internships or fieldwork, Federal Work-Study, scholarships/grants, health care benefits, and unspecified assistantships also available. Support available to part-time students. Financial award application deadline: 2/15; financial award applicants required to submit FAFSA. In 2018, 7 master's, 2 doctorates awarded. *Program availability:* Part-time. Offers natural resources and sustainability (PhD); natural resources management (MS). *Application deadline:* For fall admission, 6/1 for domestic

students, 3/1 for international students; for spring admission, 10/15 for domestic students, 9/1 for international students. Applications are processed on a rolling basis. *Application fee:* $60. Electronic applications accepted. *Application Contact:* Samara Taber, Director of Admissions, 907-474-7500, E-mail: uaf-admissions@alaska.edu. *Director,* Milan Shipka, 907-474-7429, E-mail: uaf-snre@alaska.edu.

UNIVERSITY OF ALASKA SOUTHEAST, Juneau, AK 99801

General Information State-supported, coed, comprehensive institution. *Graduate housing:* Rooms and/or apartments available on a first-come, first-served basis to single and married students. Housing application deadline: 5/1. *Research affiliation:* National Park Service (environmental resources, cultural studies), North Pacific Research Board (marine biology, oceanography), U.S. Department of Education (DOE) (teaching, early childhood education), Natural Science Foundation (marine biology), U.S. Department of Agriculture (USDA) (forest service), Alaska Department of Education (teaching).

GRADUATE UNITS

Graduate Programs *Program availability:* Part-time, evening/weekend, online learning. Offers educational leadership (M Ed); elementary education (MAT); learning design and technology (M Ed); mathematics education (M Ed); public administration (MPA); reading specialist (M Ed); secondary education (MAT); special education (M Ed, MAT). Electronic applications accepted.

UNIVERSITY OF ALBERTA, Edmonton, AB T6G 2E1, Canada

General Information Province-supported, coed, university. CGS member. *Graduate housing:* Rooms and/or apartments available on a first-come, first-served basis to single and married students.

GRADUATE UNITS

Faculty of Extension Offers communications and technology (MA).

Faculty of Graduate Studies and Research *Program availability:* Part-time, evening/weekend. Offers accounting (PhD); adult education (M Ed, Ed D, PhD); agricultural economics (M Ag, M Sc, PhD); agricultural, food and nutritional science (M Ag, M Eng, M Sc, PhD); agroforestry (M Ag, M Sc, MF); ancient history (PhD); anthropology (MA, PhD); applied linguistics (Germanic, Romance, Slavic) (MA); applied mathematics (M Sc, PhD); applied music (M Mus); astrophysics (M Sc, PhD); biostatistics (M Sc); business administration (Exec MBA, MBA); chemical engineering (M Eng, M Sc, PhD); chemistry (M Sc, PhD); Chinese literature (MA); choral conducting (M Mus); classical archaeology (MA, PhD); classical literature (PhD); classics (MA); communications (M Eng, M Sc, PhD); communications and technology (MACT); composition (M Mus); computer engineering (M Eng, M Sc, PhD); computing science (M Sc, PhD); condensed matter (M Sc, PhD); conservation biology (M Sc, PhD); construction engineering and management (M Eng, M Sc, PhD); counseling psychology (M Ed, PhD); criminal justice (MA); demography (MA, PhD); design (MFA); directing (MFA); drama (MA); drawing (MFA); earth and atmospheric sciences (M Sc, MA, PhD); East Asian interdisciplinary studies (MA); economics (MA, PhD); economics and finance (MA); educational administration and leadership (M Ed, Ed D, PhD, Postgraduate Diploma); educational psychology (M Ed, PhD); electromagnetics (M Eng, M Sc, PhD); elementary education (M Ed, Ed D, PhD); engineering management (M Eng); English (MA, PhD); environmental and natural resource economics (PhD); environmental biology and ecology (M Sc, PhD); environmental engineering (M Eng, M Sc, PhD); environmental science (M Sc, PhD); experimental linguistics (M Sc, PhD); family ecology and practice (M Sc, PhD); finance (PhD); First Nations education (M Ed, Ed D, PhD); forest biology and management (M Sc, PhD); forest economics (M Ag, M Sc, PhD); French language, literatures and linguistics (PhD); French language, literatures, and linguistics (MA); geoenvironmental engineering (M Eng, M Sc, PhD); geophysics (M Sc, PhD); geotechnical engineering (M Eng, M Sc, PhD); Germanic languages, literatures and linguistics (PhD); Germanic languages, literatures, and linguistics (MA); history (MA, PhD); history of art, design, and visual culture (MA); human resources/industrial relations (PhD); industrial design (M Des); instructional technology (M Ed); international business (MBA); Italian studies (MA); Japanese literature (MA); land reclamation and remediation (M Sc, PhD); leisure and sport management (MBA); management science (PhD); marketing (PhD); materials engineering (M Eng, M Sc, PhD); mathematical finance (M Sc, PhD); mathematical physics (M Sc, PhD); mathematics (M Sc, PhD); mechanical engineering (M Eng, M Sc, PhD); medical physics (M Sc, PhD); microbiology and biotechnology (M Sc, PhD); mining engineering (M Eng, M Sc, PhD); molecular biology and genetics (M Sc, PhD); music (PhD); nanotechnology and microdevices (M Eng, M Sc, PhD); natural resources and energy (MBA); organ and choral conductors (D Mus); organizational analysis (PhD); painting (MFA); petroleum engineering (M Eng, M Sc, PhD); philosophy (MA, PhD); physiology and cell biology (M Sc, PhD); piano (D Mus); plant biology (M Sc, PhD); political science (MA, PhD); power/power electronics (M Eng, M Sc, PhD); printmaking (MFA); process control (M Eng, M Sc, PhD); protected areas and wildlands management (M Sc, PhD); psychology (M Sc, MA, PhD); rural sociology (M Ag, M Sc); school counseling (M Ed); school psychology (M Ed, PhD); sculpture (MFA); secondary education (M Ed, Ed D, PhD); Slavic languages and literatures (Russian, Ukrainian) (MA, PhD); Slavic linguistics (Russian, Ukrainian) (MA, PhD); sociology (MA, PhD); soil science (M Ag, M Sc, PhD); Spanish and Latin American studies (MA, PhD); special education (M Ed, PhD); special education-deafness studies (M Ed); statistics (M Sc, PhD, Postgraduate Diploma); structural engineering (M Eng, M Sc, PhD); subatomic physics (M Sc, PhD); systematics and evolution (M Sc, PhD); systems (M Eng, M Sc, PhD); teaching English as a second language (M Ed); technology commercialization (MBA); textiles and clothing (M Sc, MA, PhD); theoretical, cultural and international studies in education (M Ed, Ed D, PhD); Ukrainian folklore (MA, PhD); visual communication design (M Des); water and land resources (M Ag, M Sc, PhD); water resources (M Eng, M Sc, PhD); welding (M Eng); wildlife ecology and management (M Sc, PhD). Electronic applications accepted.

Facultè Saint Jean *Program availability:* Part-time, evening/weekend, online learning. Offers education (M Ed).

Faculty of Nursing *Program availability:* Part-time. Offers nursing (MN, PhD).

Faculty of Rehabilitation Medicine Offers occupational therapy (M Sc, PhD); physical therapy (M Sc, PhD); rehabilitation medicine (M Sc, PhD); speech-language pathology (M Sc). Electronic applications accepted.

School of Library and Information Studies Offers library and information studies (MLIS). Electronic applications accepted.

Faculty of Kinesiology, Sport, and Recreation *Program availability:* Part-time. Offers physical education (M Sc); recreation and physical education (MA, PhD).

Faculty of Law *Program availability:* Part-time. Offers law (LL M, PhD). Electronic applications accepted.

Faculty of Medicine and Dentistry Offers medicine (MD); medicine and dentistry (M Sc, DDS, MD, PhD, Diploma); pharmacology (M Sc, PhD). Electronic applications accepted.

Graduate Programs in Medicine *Program availability:* Part-time. Offers biochemistry (M Sc, PhD); biomedical engineering (M Sc); cell and molecular biology (M Sc, PhD); medical genetics (M Sc, PhD); medical microbiology and immunology (M Sc, PhD); medical sciences (M Sc, PhD); medicine (M Sc, MD, PhD); obstetrics and gynecology (MD); oncology (M Sc, PhD); ophthalmology (M Sc, PhD); pediatrics (M Sc, PhD); physiology (M Sc, PhD); psychiatry (M Sc, PhD); radiology and diagnostic imaging (M Sc); surgery (M Sc, PhD).

School of Dentistry Offers dental hygiene (Diploma); dentistry (DDS); orthodontics (M Sc, PhD); TMD/orofacial pain (M Sc).

Faculty of Pharmacy and Pharmaceutical Sciences Offers pharmacy and pharmaceutical sciences (M Sc, PhD). Electronic applications accepted.

Neuroscience and Mental Health Institute Offers neuroscience (M Sc, PhD). Electronic applications accepted.

School of Public Health Offers clinical epidemiology (M Sc, MPH); environmental and occupational health (MPH); environmental health sciences (M Sc); epidemiology (M Sc); global health (M Sc, MPH); health policy and management (MPH); health policy research (M Sc); health technology assessment (MPH); occupational health (M Sc); population health (M Sc); public health (M Sc, MPH, PhD, Postgraduate Diploma); public health leadership (MPH); public health sciences (PhD); quantitative methods (MPH).

Centre for Health Promotion Studies *Program availability:* Part-time, online learning. Offers health promotion (M Sc, Postgraduate Diploma).

UNIVERSITY OF ANTELOPE VALLEY, Lancaster, CA 93534
General Information Proprietary, coed, comprehensive institution.

GRADUATE UNITS

Program in Business Management Offers business management (MS).

Program in Criminal Justice Offers criminal justice (MS).

THE UNIVERSITY OF ARIZONA, Tucson, AZ 85721
General Information State-supported, coed, university. CGS member. *Graduate housing:* Rooms and/or apartments available on a first-come, first-served basis to single students and available to married students. Housing application deadline: 5/1. *Research affiliation:* Smithsonian Astrophysical Observatory (astronomy), Research Corporation (astronomy), National Center for Atmospheric Research (atmospheric physics), Kitt Peak National Observatory (astronomy), Argonne National Laboratory (physics).

GRADUATE UNITS

College of Agriculture and Life Sciences *Program availability:* Part-time. Offers agricultural and biosystems engineering (MS, PhD); agricultural education (MAE, MS, Graduate Certificate); agriculture and life sciences (MAE, MHE Ed, MS, PhD, Graduate Certificate); animal sciences (MS, PhD); applied econometrics and data analytics (MS); applied economics and policy analysis (MS); arid lands resource sciences (PhD); nutritional sciences (MS, PhD); soil, water and environmental science (MS, PhD, Graduate Certificate). Electronic applications accepted.

School of Animal and Comparative Biomedical Sciences Offers animal and comparative biomedical sciences (MS, PhD). Electronic applications accepted.

School of Family and Consumer Sciences *Program availability:* Part-time. Offers family and consumer sciences (PhD). Electronic applications accepted.

School of Natural Resources and the Environment Offers ecology and management of rangelands (MS, PhD); natural resources (MS, PhD); water, society, and policy (MS); watershed management (MS, PhD). Electronic applications accepted.

School of Plant Sciences *Program availability:* Part-time. Offers plant pathology (MS, PhD); plant sciences (MS, PhD). Electronic applications accepted.

College of Architecture, Planning, and Landscape Architecture *Program availability:* Part-time. Offers architecture, planning, and landscape architecture (M Ar, M Arch, ML Arch, MRED, MS, PhD, Graduate Certificate); landscape architecture (ML Arch); planning (MS). Electronic applications accepted.

School of Architecture Offers architecture (M Arch, MS). Electronic applications accepted.

College of Education *Program availability:* Part-time, online learning. Offers counseling and mental health (MA); cross-categorical special education (MA); deaf and hard of hearing (MA); education (M Ed, MA, MS, Ed D, PhD, Certificate, Ed S); educational leadership (M Ed, Ed D, Ed S); educational psychology (MA, PhD); educational research methodology (Certificate); family studies and human development (M Ed); higher education (MA, PhD); language, reading and culture (MA, Ed D, PhD, Ed S); learning disabilities (MA); motivating learning environments (Certificate); reading instruction (Graduate Certificate); rehabilitation counseling (MA, PhD); school counseling (MA); school psychology (PhD, Ed S); severe and multiple disabilities (MA); special education (MA, PhD); teaching and teacher education (M Ed, MA, PhD); visual impairment (MA). Electronic applications accepted.

College of Engineering *Program availability:* Part-time, online learning. Offers aerospace engineering (MS, PhD); chemical engineering (MS, PhD); civil engineering and engineering mechanics (MS, PhD); electrical and computer engineering (MS, PhD); engineering (ME, MS, PhD, Certificate); engineering management (Graduate Certificate); environmental engineering (MS, PhD); industrial engineering (MS); materials science and engineering (MS, PhD); mechanical engineering (MS, PhD); mining and geological engineering (MS, PhD); mining engineering (Certificate); systems and industrial engineering (MS, PhD); systems engineering (MS, PhD, Graduate Certificate). Electronic applications accepted.

College of Fine Arts *Program availability:* Part-time. Offers fine arts (MA, MFA, MM, PhD, Graduate Certificate). Electronic applications accepted.

School of Art *Program availability:* Part-time. Offers art (MA, MFA, PhD); art education (MA); art history (MA); art history and education (PhD); history and theory of art (PhD). Electronic applications accepted.

School of Dance Offers dance (MFA). Electronic applications accepted.

School of Music *Program availability:* Part-time. Offers composition (MM, DMA); conducting (MM, DMA); ethnomusicology (MM); music (MM, PhD); music education (MM, PhD); music theory (MM, PhD); musical arts (DMA); musicology (MM); performance (MM, DMA). Electronic applications accepted.

School of Theatre, Film and Television Offers theatre, film and television (MFA). Electronic applications accepted.

College of Humanities *Program availability:* Part-time. Offers classics (MA); creative writing (MFA); East Asian studies (MA, PhD); English (MA, PhD); English language/linguistics (MA, PhD); ESL (MA); French (MA); German (MA); humanities (MA, MFA, PhD); rhetoric, composition and the teaching of English (MA, PhD); Russian (MA); Spanish (MA, PhD); teaching English as a second language (Graduate Certificate); transcultural German (PhD). Electronic applications accepted.

College of Medicine *Program availability:* Part-time. Offers cellular and molecular medicine (MS, PhD); immunobiology (PhD); medical sciences (MS, PhD); medicine (MS, MD, PhD, Graduate Certificate). MD program open only to state residents.

College of Nursing *Program availability:* Part-time, online learning. Offers health care informatics (Certificate); nurse practitioner (MS); nursing (DNP, PhD). Electronic applications accepted.

College of Optical Sciences *Program availability:* Part-time. Offers optical sciences (MS, PhD, Graduate Certificate). Electronic applications accepted.

College of Pharmacy Offers medical pharmacology (MS, PhD); medicinal and natural products chemistry (MS, PhD); perfusion science (MS); pharmaceutical economics (MS, PhD); pharmaceutics and pharmacokinetics (MS, PhD); pharmacy (MS, PhD, Pharm D).

College of Science *Program availability:* Part-time. Offers applied biosciences (PSM); astronomy (PhD); atmospheric sciences (MS, PhD); biochemistry (PhD); biochemistry and molecular and cellular biology (PhD); chemistry (MA, MS, PhD); computer science (MS, PhD); ecology and evolutionary biology (MS, PhD); geosciences (MS, PSM, PhD); hydrology (PhD); mathematics (MA, MS, PhD); medical physics (PSM); physics (PhD); planetary sciences (MS, PhD); psychology (MA, PhD); science (MS, PSM, PhD, Certificate, Graduate Certificate); secondary mathematics education (MA); speech, language, and hearing sciences (MS, PhD, Certificate). Electronic applications accepted.

College of Social and Behavioral Sciences *Program availability:* Part-time, evening/weekend. Offers communication (MA, PhD); gender and women's studies (MA, PhD, Certificate); history (MA, PhD, Graduate Certificate); human language technology (MS); linguistics and anthropology (PhD); Native American linguistics (MA); philosophy (MA, PhD); political science (MA, PhD); public administration (MPA); public administration and policy (PhD); social and behavioral sciences (MA, MPA, MS, PhD, Certificate, Graduate Certificate); sociology (MA, PhD). Electronic applications accepted.

Center for Latin American Studies *Program availability:* Part-time. Offers Latin American studies (MA). Electronic applications accepted.

School of Anthropology *Program availability:* Part-time. Offers anthropology (MA, MS, PhD, Graduate Certificate). Electronic applications accepted.

School of Geography and Development *Program availability:* Part-time. Offers geographic information systems technology (MA); geography (PhD). Electronic applications accepted.

School of Information *Program availability:* Part-time. Offers information (MA, PhD). Electronic applications accepted.

School of Journalism *Program availability:* Part-time. Offers international journalism studies (MA); professional journalism (MA). Electronic applications accepted.

School of Middle Eastern and North African Studies *Program availability:* Part-time, evening/weekend. Offers Middle Eastern and North African studies (MA, PhD, Graduate Certificate). Electronic applications accepted.

Eller College of Management *Program availability:* Evening/weekend. Offers accounting (M Ac, MS); business administration (MBA); economics (MA, PhD); finance (MS); management (M Ac, MA, MBA, MS, PhD, Graduate Certificate); management and organization (MS, PhD); management information systems (MS, Graduate Certificate); marketing (MBA, MS, PhD). Electronic applications accepted.

Graduate Interdisciplinary Programs *Program availability:* Part-time. Offers American Indian studies (MA, PhD); applied mathematics (MS, PMS, PhD); biomedical engineering (MS, PhD); cancer biology (PhD); entomology (MA); entomology and insect science (MS, PhD); genetics (MS, PhD); mathematical sciences (PMS); neuroscience (PhD); physiological sciences (MS, PhD); second language acquisition and teaching (PhD); statistics (MS, PhD).

James E. Rogers College of Law Offers Indigenous people's law and policy (LL M); international trade and business law (LL M); law (JD). Electronic applications accepted.

Mel and Enid Zuckerman College of Public Health Offers biostatistics (MS, PhD); epidemiology (MS, PhD); public health (MPH, MS, MSPH, Dr PH, PhD, Graduate Certificate). Electronic applications accepted.

UNIVERSITY OF ARKANSAS, Fayetteville, AR 72701
General Information State-supported, coed, university. CGS member. *Graduate housing:* Room and/or apartments available on a first-come, first-served basis to single students; on-campus housing not available to married students. *Student services:* Campus employment opportunities, campus safety program, career counseling, exercise/wellness program, free psychological counseling, international student services, low-cost health insurance, multicultural affairs office, services for students with disabilities, teacher training, writing training. *Library facilities:* David W. Mullins Library plus 4 others. *Collection:* Books: 2 million (physical), 593,016 (digital/electronic); Serial titles: 60,187 (physical), 147,231 (digital/electronic); Databases: 331. Weekly public service hours: 109; students can reserve study rooms.

Computer facilities: Computer purchase and lease plans available. 675 computers available on campus for general student use. A campuswide network can be accessed from student residence rooms and from off campus. Online class registration is available.
Website: http://www.uark.edu/

GRADUATE UNITS

Graduate School Students: 2,060 full-time (1,040 women), 2,101 part-time (1,046 women); includes 627 minority (227 Black or African American, non-Hispanic/Latino; 54 American Indian or Alaska Native, non-Hispanic/Latino; 74 Asian, non-Hispanic/Latino; 189 Hispanic/Latino; 5 Native Hawaiian or other Pacific Islander, non-Hispanic/Latino; 78 Two or more races, non-Hispanic/Latino), 726 international. Average age 33. 4,608 applicants, 46% accepted, 1318 enrolled. *Faculty:* 685 full-time (216 women), 47 part-time/adjunct (32 women). Expenses: Contact institution. *Financial support:* In 2018–19, 761 research assistantships, 484 teaching assistantships with full tuition reimbursements were awarded; fellowships with tuition reimbursements, career-related internships or fieldwork, Federal Work-Study, institutionally sponsored loans, scholarships/grants, traineeships, and unspecified assistantships also available. Support available to part-time students. Financial award application deadline: 4/1; financial award applicants required to submit FAFSA. In 2018, 1,114 master's, 338 doctorates, 10 other advanced degrees awarded. *Program availability:* Part-time, online learning. Offers cell and molecular biology (MS, PhD); comparative literature and cultural studies (MA, PhD); environmental dynamics (PhD); microelectronics and photonics (MS, PhD); public policy (PhD); space and planetary sciences (MS, PhD). *Application deadline:* For fall admission, 8/1 for domestic students, 4/1 for international students; for spring admission, 12/1 for domestic students, 10/1 for international students; for summer admission, 4/15 for domestic students, 3/1 for international students. Applications are processed on a rolling basis. *Application fee:* $60. Electronic applications accepted. *Application Contact:* Lynn Mosesso, Director, Graduate and International Recruitment and Admissions, 479-575-6247, Fax: 479-575-5908, E-mail: mosesso@uark.edu. *Dean,* Dr. Kim L. Needy, 479-575-4401, Fax: 479-575-5908, E-mail: gradinfo@uark.edu.

College of Education and Health Professions Expenses: Contact institution. *Financial support:* In 2018–19, 110 research assistantships, 15 teaching assistantships were awarded; fellowships with tuition reimbursements, career-related internships or fieldwork, and Federal Work-Study also available. Support available to part-time students. Financial award application deadline: 4/1; financial award applicants required to submit FAFSA. In 2018, 211 master's, 56 doctorates, 10 other advanced degrees awarded. Offers adult and lifelong learning (M Ed, Ed D); athletic training (MAT); childhood education (MAT); communication disorders (MS); community health promotion (MS, PhD); counselor education (MS, PhD); curriculum and instruction (M Ed, MAT, MS, Ed D, PhD, Ed S); education and health professions (M Ed, MAT, MAT, MS, MSN, Ed D, PhD, Ed S); education policy (PhD); educational leadership (M Ed, Ed D, Ed S); educational statistics and research methods (MS, PhD); educational technology (M Ed); health science (MS, PhD); higher education (M Ed, Ed D, Ed S); human resource and workforce development education (M Ed, Ed D); kinesiology (MS, PhD); middle-level education (MAT); nursing (MSN); physical education (M Ed, MAT); recreation and sports management (M Ed, Ed D); rehabilitation (MS, PhD); secondary education (M Ed, MAT, Ed S); special education (M Ed, MAT); vocational education (M Ed, Ed D). *Application deadline:* For fall admission, 8/1 for domestic students, 4/1 for international students; for spring admission, 12/1 for domestic students, 10/1 for international students; for summer admission, 4/15 for domestic students, 3/1 for international students. Applications are processed on a rolling basis. *Application fee:* $60. Electronic applications accepted. *Application Contact:* Dr. Brian Primack, Dean, E-mail: bprimack@uark.edu. *Dean,* Dr. Brian Primack, E-mail: bprimack@uark.edu.

College of Engineering Expenses: Contact institution. *Financial support:* In 2018–19, 198 research assistantships, 21 teaching assistantships were awarded; fellowships with tuition reimbursements, career-related internships or fieldwork, and Federal Work-Study also available. Support available to part-time students. Financial award application deadline: 4/1; financial award applicants required to submit FAFSA. In 2018, 273 master's, 27 doctorates awarded. Offers biological and agricultural engineering (MSE, PhD); biological engineering (MSBE); biomedical engineering (MSBME); chemical engineering (MS Ch E, MSE, PhD); civil engineering (MSCE, MSE, PhD); computer engineering (MS Cmp E, MSE, PhD); computer science (MS, PhD); electrical engineering (MSEE, PhD); engineering (MS, MS Cmp E, MS Ch E, MS En E, MS Tc E, MSBE, MSBME, MSCE, MSE, MSEE, MSIE, MSME, MSTE, PhD); environmental engineering (MS En E, MSE); industrial engineering (MS, MSIE, PhD); mechanical engineering (MSE, MSME, PhD); operations management (MS); telecommunications engineering (MS Tc E); transportation engineering (MSE, MSTE). *Application deadline:* For fall admission, 8/1 for domestic students, 4/1 for international students; for spring admission, 12/1 for domestic students, 10/1 for international students; for summer admission, 4/15 for domestic students, 3/1 for international students. Applications are processed on a rolling basis. *Application fee:* $60. Electronic applications accepted. *Application Contact:* Dr. Norman Dennis, Senior Associate Dean and University Professor, 479-575-6011, E-mail: ndennis@uark.edu. *Dean,* Dr. John R. English, 479-575-7455, E-mail: jre@uark.edu.

Dale Bumpers College of Agricultural, Food and Life Sciences 164 applicants, 59% accepted. Expenses: Contact institution. *Financial support:* In 2018–19, 167 research assistantships, 7 teaching assistantships were awarded; fellowships with tuition reimbursements, career-related internships or fieldwork, Federal Work-Study, scholarships/grants, and unspecified assistantships also available. Support available to part-time students. Financial award application deadline: 4/1; financial award applicants required to submit FAFSA. In 2018, 80 master's, 16 doctorates awarded. Offers agricultural and extension education (MS); agricultural economics and agribusiness (MS); agricultural, food and life sciences (MS, PhD); agronomy (MS, PhD); animal science (MS, PhD); entomology (MS, PhD); food safety (MS); food science (MS, PhD); horticulture (MS); human environmental sciences (MS); plant pathology (MS); plant science (PhD); poultry science (MS, PhD). *Application deadline:* For fall admission, 8/1 for domestic students, 4/1 for international students; for spring admission, 12/1 for domestic students, 10/1 for international students; for summer admission, 4/15 for domestic students, 3/1 for international students. Applications are processed on a rolling basis. *Application fee:* $60. Electronic applications accepted. *Application Contact:* Dausen Garet Duncan, Coordinator of Recruitment, 479-575-2253, E-mail: dgduncan@uark.edu. *Dean,* Dr. Deacue Fields, 479-575-2034, E-mail: dcfields@uark.edu.

J. William Fulbright College of Arts and Sciences Expenses: Contact institution. *Financial support:* In 2018–19, 143 research assistantships, 373 teaching assistantships with full tuition reimbursements were awarded; fellowships, career-related internships or fieldwork, Federal Work-Study, institutionally sponsored loans, and traineeships also available. Support available to part-time students. Financial award application deadline: 4/1; financial award applicants required to submit FAFSA. In 2018, 242 master's, 69 doctorates awarded. Offers anthropology (MA, PhD); applied physics (MS); art (MFA); arts and sciences (MA, MFA, MM, MPA, MS, MSW, PhD); biological sciences (MA, MS, PhD); chemistry (MS, PhD); communication (MA); creative writing (MFA); English (MA, MFA, PhD); French (MA); geography (MA); geology (MS); German (MA); history (MA, PhD); journalism (MA); mathematics (MS, PhD); music (MM); philosophy (MA, PhD); physics (MS, PhD); physics education (MA); political science (MA); psychology (MA, PhD); public administration (MPA); secondary mathematics (MA); social work (MSW); sociology (MA); Spanish (MA); statistics (MS); theatre (MA, MFA). *Application deadline:* For fall admission, 8/1 for domestic students, 4/1 for international students; for spring admission, 12/1 for domestic students, 10/1 for international students; for summer admission, 4/15 for domestic students, 3/1 for international students. Applications are processed on a rolling basis. *Application fee:* $60. Electronic applications accepted. *Application Contact:* Dr. Todd G. Shields, Dean, 479-575-4804, Fax: 479-575-2642, E-mail: tshield@uark.edu. *Dean,* Dr. Todd G. Shields, 479-575-4804, Fax: 479-575-2642, E-mail: tshield@uark.edu.

Sam M. Walton College of Business Administration Expenses: Contact institution. *Financial support:* In 2018–19, 64 research assistantships, 17 teaching assistantships were awarded; fellowships, career-related internships or fieldwork, and Federal Work-Study also available. Support available to part-time students. Financial award application deadline: 4/1; financial award applicants required to submit FAFSA. In 2018, 216 master's, 13 doctorates awarded. Offers accounting (M Acc); business administration (M Acc, MA, MBA, MIS, PhD); economics (MA, PhD); information systems (MIS). *Application deadline:* For fall admission, 8/1 for domestic students, 4/1 for international students; for spring admission, 12/1 for domestic students, 10/1 for international students; for summer admission, 4/15 for domestic students, 3/1 for international students. *Application fee:* $60. Electronic applications accepted. *Application Contact:* Dr. Matt Waller, Dean, 479-575-5949, Fax: 479-575-4435, E-mail: mwaller@walton.uark.edu. *Dean,* Dr. Matt Waller, 479-575-5949, Fax: 479-575-4435, E-mail: mwaller@walton.uark.edu.

School of Law Expenses: Contact institution. *Financial support:* In 2018–19, fellowships with full tuition reimbursements (averaging $6,000 per year), 8 research assistantships (averaging $2,500 per year) were awarded; teaching assistantships, career-related internships or fieldwork, Federal Work-Study, and scholarships/grants also available. Support available to part-time students. Financial award application deadline: 4/1; financial award applicants required to submit FAFSA. In 2018, 5 master's, 119 doctorates awarded. Offers agricultural law (LL M); law (JD). *Application deadline:* For fall admission, 8/1 for domestic students, 4/1 for international students; for spring admission, 12/1 for domestic students, 10/1 for international students; for summer admission, 4/15 for domestic students, 3/1 for international students. Applications are processed on a rolling basis. *Application fee:* $60. Electronic applications accepted. *Application Contact:* Stacy L. Leeds, Dean, 479-575-3873, E-mail: sleeds@uark.edu. *Dean,* Stacy L. Leeds, 479-575-3873, E-mail: sleeds@uark.edu.

UNIVERSITY OF ARKANSAS AT LITTLE ROCK, Little Rock, AR 72204-1099

General Information State-supported, coed, university. CGS member. *Graduate housing:* Room and/or apartments available on a first-come, first-served basis to single students; on-campus housing not available to married students. Housing application deadline: 9/1.

GRADUATE UNITS

Graduate School *Program availability:* Part-time, evening/weekend, online learning. Electronic applications accepted.

Clinton School of Public Service Offers public service (MPS, Graduate Certificate).

College of Arts, Letters, and Sciences *Program availability:* Part-time, evening/weekend. Offers applied statistics (Graduate Certificate); art education (MA); art history (MA); arts, letters, and sciences (MA, MS, Graduate Certificate); biology (MS); chemistry (MA, MS); mathematical sciences (MS); philosophy and interdisciplinary studies (MA); public history (MA); second languages (MA); studio art (MA).

College of Business *Program availability:* Part-time, evening/weekend. Offers business administration (MBA); business information systems (MS, Graduate Certificate); management (Graduate Certificate).

College of Education and Health Professions *Program availability:* Part-time, evening/weekend. Offers administration (MA); adult education (M Ed); clinical social work (MSW); college student affairs (MA); counselor education (M Ed); curriculum and instruction (M Ed); education and health professions (M Ed, MA, MS, MSW, Ed D, Ed S, Graduate Certificate); educational administration and supervision (M Ed, Ed D, Ed S); exercise science (MS); gerontology (Graduate Certificate); gifted and talented education (M Ed, Graduate Certificate); health education and promotion (MS); health professions teaching and learning (MA); higher education (MA, Ed D); learning systems technology education (M Ed); management and community practice (MSW); middle childhood education (M Ed); reading education (M Ed, PhD, Ed S); rehabilitation counseling (MA, Graduate Certificate); rehabilitation for the blind: orientation and mobility (MA); secondary education (M Ed); social work (MSW, Graduate Certificate); special education (M Ed); sport management (MS); two-year college teaching (MA).

College of Social Sciences and Communication *Program availability:* Part-time, evening/weekend. Offers applied communication studies (MA); applied psychology (MAP); conflict mediation (Graduate Certificate); criminal justice (MA, MS, PhD); mass communication (MA); nonprofit management (Graduate Certificate); professional and technical writing (MA); public administration (MPA); social sciences and communication (MA, MAP, MPA, MS, PhD, Graduate Certificate).

George W. Donaghey College of Engineering and Information Technology *Program availability:* Part-time, evening/weekend. Offers applied science (MS, PhD); bioinformatics (MS, PhD); computer science (MS, PhD); construction management (MS); engineering and information technology (MS, PhD, Graduate Certificate); geospatial technology (Graduate Certificate); information quality (MS, PhD, Graduate Certificate); systems engineering (MS, PhD, Graduate Certificate); technology innovation (Graduate Certificate).

William H. Bowen School of Law *Program availability:* Part-time, evening/weekend. Offers law (JD). Electronic applications accepted.

UNIVERSITY OF ARKANSAS AT MONTICELLO, Monticello, AR 71656

General Information State-supported, coed, comprehensive institution. *Graduate housing:* Rooms and/or apartments guaranteed to single students and available on a first-come, first-served basis to married students. Housing application deadline: 8/15.

GRADUATE UNITS

School of Education *Program availability:* Part-time, evening/weekend, online learning. Offers education (M Ed, MAT); educational leadership (M Ed). Electronic applications accepted.

School of Forest Resources *Program availability:* Part-time. Offers forest resources (MS). Electronic applications accepted.

UNIVERSITY OF ARKANSAS AT PINE BLUFF, Pine Bluff, AR 71601-2799

General Information State-supported, coed, comprehensive institution. *Graduate housing:* Room and/or apartments available on a first-come, first-served basis to single students; on-campus housing not available to married students. Housing application deadline: 8/1.

GRADUATE UNITS

Division of Graduate Studies and Continuing Education Offers addiction studies (MS).

School of Agriculture, Fisheries and Human Sciences Offers agricultural regulations (MS); aquaculture and fisheries (MS, PhD).

School of Education *Program availability:* Part-time, evening/weekend. Offers elementary education (M Ed); secondary education (M Ed); teaching (MAT).

UNIVERSITY OF ARKANSAS FOR MEDICAL SCIENCES, Little Rock, AR 72205-7199

General Information State-supported, coed, university. *Graduate housing:* Rooms and/or apartments available on a first-come, first-served basis to single and married students. Housing application deadline: 7/15. *Research affiliation:* National Center for Toxicological Research, Veterans Administration Hospital, Oak Ridge Associated Universities, Arkansas Children's Hospital.

GRADUATE UNITS

College of Health Professions *Program availability:* Part-time, online learning. Offers audiology (Au D); communication sciences and disorders (MS, PhD); genetic counseling (MS); nuclear medicine advanced associate (MIS); physician assistant studies (MPAS); radiologist assistant (MIS). PhD offered through consortium with University of Arkansas at Little Rock and University of Central Arkansas. Electronic applications accepted.

College of Medicine Offers medicine (MD). Electronic applications accepted.

College of Nursing *Program availability:* Part-time. Offers nursing (PhD).

College of Pharmacy Offers pharmacy (MS, Pharm D). Electronic applications accepted.

Fay W. Boozman College of Public Health *Program availability:* Part-time. Offers biostatistics (MPH); environmental and occupational health (MPH, Certificate); epidemiology (MPH, PhD); health behavior and health education (MPH); health policy and management (MPH); health promotion and prevention research (PhD); health services administration (MHSA); health systems research (PhD); public health (Certificate); public health leadership (Dr PH). Electronic applications accepted.

Graduate School *Program availability:* Part-time. Offers biochemistry and molecular biology (MS, PhD); bioinformatics (MS, PhD); cellular physiology and molecular biophysics (MS, PhD); clinical nutrition (MS); interdisciplinary biomedical sciences (MS, PhD, Certificate); interdisciplinary toxicology (MS); microbiology and immunology (PhD); neurobiology and developmental sciences (PhD); pharmacology (PhD). Bioinformatics programs hosted jointly with the University of Arkansas at Little Rock. Electronic applications accepted.

UNIVERSITY OF ARKANSAS–FORT SMITH, Fort Smith, AR 72913-3649

General Information State and locally supported, coed, comprehensive institution.

GRADUATE UNITS

Program in Healthcare Administration *Program availability:* Online learning. Offers healthcare administration (MS).

UNIVERSITY OF BALTIMORE, Baltimore, MD 21201-5779

General Information State-supported, coed, comprehensive institution. *Graduate housing:* On-campus housing not available.

GRADUATE UNITS

Graduate School *Program availability:* Part-time, evening/weekend, online learning. Electronic applications accepted.

College of Public Affairs Offers criminal justice (MS); health systems management (MS); human services administration (MS); negotiations and conflict management (MS); public administration (MPA, DPA); public affairs (MPA, MS, DPA).

Merrick School of Business *Program availability:* Part-time, evening/weekend, online learning. Offers accounting and business advisory services (MS); accounting fundamentals (Graduate Certificate); business (MBA, MS, Graduate Certificate); business/finance (MS); forensic accounting (Graduate Certificate); global leadership (MS); innovation management and technology commercialization (MS); taxation (MS). Electronic applications accepted.

Yale Gordon College of Arts and Sciences *Program availability:* Part-time, evening/weekend. Offers arts and sciences (MA, MFA, MS, DS); counseling psychology (MS); creative writing and publishing arts (MFA); information and interaction design (DS); integrated design (MA, MFA); interaction design and information architecture (MS); legal studies (MA). Electronic applications accepted.

Joint University of Baltimore/Towson University (UB/Towson) MBA Program *Program availability:* Part-time, evening/weekend, online learning. Offers business administration (MBA). MBA/MSN, MBA/Pharm D offered jointly with University of Maryland, Baltimore.

School of Law *Program availability:* Part-time, evening/weekend. Offers business law (JD); criminal practice (JD); estate planning (JD); family law (JD); intellectual property (JD); international law (JD); law (JD); law of the United States (LL M); litigation and advocacy (JD); public service (JD); real estate practice (JD); taxation (LL M). JD/MS offered jointly with Division of Criminology, Criminal Justice, and Social Policy; JD/PhD with University of Maryland, Baltimore. Electronic applications accepted.

UNIVERSITY OF BRIDGEPORT, Bridgeport, CT 06604

General Information Independent, coed, comprehensive institution. CGS member. *Graduate housing:* Rooms and/or apartments guaranteed to single students and available on a first-come, first-served basis to married students. Housing application deadline: 8/15. *Research affiliation:* Connecticut Medicine Research Consortia, Marine Biology Station, Burndy Library.

GRADUATE UNITS

Acupuncture Institute *Program availability:* Part-time. Offers acupuncture (MS). Electronic applications accepted.

College of Chiropractic Offers chiropractic (DC). Electronic applications accepted.

College of Naturopathic Medicine Offers naturopathic medicine (ND). Electronic applications accepted.

College of Public and International Affairs *Program availability:* Part-time, evening/weekend. Offers East Asian and Pacific Rim studies (MA); global development and peace (MA); global media and communication studies (MA).

Fones School of Dental Hygiene *Program availability:* Part-time, evening/weekend, online learning. Offers dental hygiene (MS).

Nutrition Institute *Program availability:* Part-time, evening/weekend, online learning. Offers human nutrition (MS). Electronic applications accepted.

Physician Assistant Institute Offers physician assistant (MS).

School of Arts and Sciences *Program availability:* Part-time, evening/weekend. Offers arts and sciences (MS); clinical mental health counseling (MS); college student personnel (MS); community counseling (MS); human resource development (MS); human service (MS). Electronic applications accepted.

School of Business *Program availability:* Part-time, evening/weekend. Offers accounting (MBA); finance (MBA); general business (MBA); global financial services (MBA); human resource management (MBA); information systems and knowledge management (MBA); international business (MBA); management (MBA); marketing (MBA); operations management (MBA); small business and entrepreneurship (MBA); specialized business (MBA). Electronic applications accepted.

School of Education *Program availability:* Part-time, evening/weekend. Offers education (MS, Ed D, Diploma); educational management (Ed D, Diploma); elementary education (MS, Diploma); intermediate administrator or supervisor (Diploma); leadership (Ed D); middle school education (MS); music education (MS); remedial reading and

language arts (Diploma); secondary education (MS, Diploma). Electronic applications accepted.

School of Engineering *Program availability:* Part-time, evening/weekend, online learning. Offers biomedical engineering (MS); computer engineering (MS); computer science (MS); computer science and engineering (PhD); electrical engineering (MS); engineering (MS, PhD); mechanical engineering (MS); technology management (MS, PhD). Electronic applications accepted.

Shintaro Akatsu School of Design *Program availability:* Part-time, evening/weekend. Offers design management (MPS). Electronic applications accepted.

THE UNIVERSITY OF BRITISH COLUMBIA, Vancouver, BC V6T 1Z1, Canada

General Information Province-supported, coed, university. CGS member. *Graduate housing:* Rooms and/or apartments available on a first-come, first-served basis to single and married students. Housing application deadline: 3/1. *Research affiliation:* British Columbia Research (chemical and biological science technology), Forintek Canada (forest technology), National Research Council of Canada Institute of Machinery Research (machinery research), Pulp and Paper Research Institute of Canada, Pacific Environment Institute, Pacific Biological Station (fisheries and oceanography).

GRADUATE UNITS

Faculty of Applied Science *Program availability:* Part-time. Offers applied science (M Arch, M Eng, M Sc, M Sc P, MA Sc, MAP, MASA, MASLA, MCRP, MEL, MLA, MN, MSN, MUD, PhD); chemical and biological engineering (M Eng, M Sc, MA Sc, PhD); civil engineering (M Eng, MA Sc, PhD); electrical and computer engineering (M Eng, MA Sc, PhD); materials engineering (M Sc, MA Sc, PhD); mechanical engineering (M Eng, MA Sc, PhD); mining engineering (M Eng, MA Sc, PhD). Electronic applications accepted.

Clean Energy Research Center Offers clean energy engineering (MEL).

School of Architecture and Landscape Architecture Offers advanced studies in landscape architecture (MASLA); architecture (M Arch, MASA); landscape architecture (MASLA, MLA, MUD); urban design (MUD). Electronic applications accepted.

School of Biomedical Engineering Offers biomedical engineering (M Eng, MA Sc, PhD).

School of Community and Regional Planning Offers community and regional planning (M Sc P, MAP, MCRP, PhD). Electronic applications accepted.

School of Nursing *Program availability:* Part-time. Offers nurse practitioner (MN); nursing (MSN, PhD). Electronic applications accepted.

Faculty of Arts Offers ancient culture, religion and ethnicity (MA); ancient culture, religion, and ethnicity (MA, PhD); anthropology (MA, PhD); art history (MA, PhD); arts (M Mus, M Sc, MA, MAS, MDM, MFA, MJ, MLIS, MSW, DMA, PhD, CAS, Diploma); Asian studies (MA, PhD); behavioral neuroscience (MA, PhD); classical and Near Eastern archaeology (MA); classical and Near eastern archaeology (MA); classics (MA, PhD); clinical psychology (MA, PhD); cognitive science (MA, PhD); creative writing (MFA); creative writing and theatre (MFA); critical and curatorial studies (MA); developmental psychology (MA, PhD); English (MA, PhD); film (MA, MFA); film production (MFA); film production and creative writing (MFA); film studies (MA); French (MA, PhD); geography (M Sc, MA, PhD); Germanic studies (MA, PhD); health psychology (MA, PhD); Hispanic studies (MA, PhD); history (MA, PhD); linguistics (MA, PhD); philosophy (MA, PhD); political science (MA, PhD); quantitative methods (MA, PhD); religious studies (MA, PhD); social/personality psychology (MA, PhD); sociology (MA, PhD); theatre (MA, MFA, PhD); theatre design (MFA); theatre directing (MFA); visual art (MFA). Electronic applications accepted.

Center for Digital Media Offers digital media (MDM)

Institute for Gender, Race, Sexuality, and Social Justice Offers gender, race, sexuality, and social justice (MA, PhD).

School of Journalism Offers journalism (MJ). Electronic applications accepted.

School of Library, Archival and Information Studies *Program availability:* Part-time. Offers archival studies (MAS); children's literature (MA); library and information studies (MLIS); library, archival and information studies (PhD). Electronic applications accepted.

School of Music *Program availability:* Part-time. Offers music (M Mus, MA, DMA, PhD). Electronic applications accepted.

School of Social Work Offers social work (MSW, PhD). Electronic applications accepted.

Vancouver School of Economics Offers economics (MA, PhD). Electronic applications accepted.

Faculty of Dentistry *Program availability:* Part-time. Offers craniofacial science (M Sc, PhD); dentistry (M Sc, DMD, PhD). Electronic applications accepted.

Faculty of Education *Program availability:* Part-time, evening/weekend, online learning. Offers adult learning and education (M Ed); adult learning and global change (M Ed); art education (M Ed, MA); counseling psychology (M Ed, MA, PhD); curriculum and leadership (M Ed); curriculum studies (M Ed, MA, PhD); education (M Ed, M Kin, M Sc, MA, MET, MHPCTL, Ed D, PhD, Diploma); educational administration and leadership (M Ed); educational leadership and policy (Ed D); educational studies (M Ed, MA, PhD); guidance studies (Diploma); higher education (M Ed); home economics education (M Ed, MA); human development, learning and culture (M Ed, MA, PhD); literacy education (M Ed, MA, PhD); mathematics education (M Ed, MA); measurement, evaluation, and research methodology (M Ed, MA, PhD); media and technology studies education (M Ed, MA); modern languages education (M Ed, MA); music education (M Ed, MA); physical education (M Ed, MA); school psychology (M Ed, MA, PhD); science education (M Ed, MA); social studies education (M Ed, MA); society, culture and politics in education (M Ed); special education (M Ed, MA, PhD, Diploma); teaching English as a second language (M Ed, MA, PhD). Electronic applications accepted.

School of Kinesiology *Program availability:* Part-time. Offers high performance coaching and technical leadership (MHPCTL); kinesiology (M Kin, M Sc, MA, PhD). Electronic applications accepted.

Faculty of Forestry Offers forestry (M Sc, MA Sc, MF, MGEM, MIF, MSFM, PhD); geomatics for environmental management (MGEM); international forestry (MIF); sustainable forest management (MSFM). Electronic applications accepted.

Faculty of Land and Food Systems *Program availability:* Part-time. Offers applied animal biology (M Sc, PhD); food and resource economics (MFRE); food science (M Sc, MFS, PhD); human nutrition (M Sc, PhD); integrated studies in land and food systems (M Sc, PhD); land and food systems (M Sc, MFRE, MFS, MLWS, PhD); land and water systems (MLWS); plant science (M Sc, PhD); soil science (M Sc, PhD). Electronic applications accepted.

Faculty of Medicine *Program availability:* Part-time. Offers biochemistry and molecular biology (M Sc, PhD); bioinformatics (M Sc, PhD); cell and developmental biology (M Sc, PhD); experimental medicine (M Sc, PhD); genetic counselling (M Sc); genome science and technology (M Sc, PhD); medical genetics (M Sc, PhD); medicine (M Sc, MH Sc, MHA, MOT, MPH, MPT, MRSc, MD, PhD); neuroscience (M Sc, PhD); occupational therapy (MOT); pathology (M Sc, PhD); pharmacology (M Sc, PhD); physical therapy (MPT); reproductive and developmental sciences (M Sc, PhD); surgery (M Sc).

School of Audiology and Speech Sciences Offers audiology and speech sciences (M Sc, PhD). Electronic applications accepted.

School of Population and Public Health *Program availability:* Online learning. Offers health administration (MHA); health sciences (MH Sc); occupational and environmental hygiene (M Sc); population and public health (M Sc, MPH, PhD). Electronic applications accepted.

School of Rehabilitation Sciences Offers rehabilitation sciences (M Sc, MRSc, PhD). Electronic applications accepted.

Faculty of Pharmaceutical Sciences Offers pharmaceutical sciences (M Sc, PhD, Pharm D). Electronic applications accepted.

Faculty of Science *Program availability:* Part-time. Offers astronomy (M Sc, PhD); atmospheric science (M Sc, PhD); botany (M Sc, PhD); chemistry (M Sc, PhD); computer science (M Sc, PhD); data science (MDS); geological engineering (M Eng, MA Sc, PhD); geological sciences (M Sc, PhD); geophysics (M Sc, MA Sc, PhD); mathematics (M Sc, PhD); microbiology and immunology (M Sc, PhD); oceanography (M Sc, PhD); physics (M Sc, PhD); science (M Eng, M Sc, MA, MA Sc, MDS, PhD); statistics (M Sc, PhD); zoology (M Sc, PhD). Electronic applications accepted.

Institute for Resources, Environment and Sustainability Offers resources, environment and sustainability (M Sc, MA, PhD). Electronic applications accepted.

Institute of Asian Research Offers Asia Pacific policy studies (MAAPPS); public policy and global affairs (MPPGA). Electronic applications accepted.

Peter A. Allard School of Law *Program availability:* Part-time. Offers common law (LL M CL); law (LL M, PhD); taxation (LL M). Electronic applications accepted.

Sauder School of Business *Program availability:* Part-time, evening/weekend. Offers accounting (PhD); business (IMBA, M Sc, MBA, MM, MSBA, PhD); business administration (IMBA, MBA, PhD); business analytics (MSBA); finance (PhD); management information systems (PhD); management science (PhD); marketing (PhD); organizational behavior (PhD); strategy and business economics (PhD); transportation and logistics (PhD); urban land economics (PhD). Electronic applications accepted.

UNIVERSITY OF CALGARY, Calgary, AB T2N 1N4, Canada

General Information Province-supported, coed, university. CGS member. *Graduate housing:* Rooms and/or apartments available on a first-come, first-served basis to single and married students. Housing application deadline: 3/31. *Research affiliation:* Alta Telecommunications Research Centre, Alberta Sulphur Research, Calgary Society for Students with Learning Difficulties, Canadian Institute of Resources Law, Canadian Music Centre, Canadian Energy Research Institute.

GRADUATE UNITS

Cumming School of Medicine *Program availability:* Part-time. Offers biochemistry and molecular biology (M Sc, PhD); biomedical technology (MBT); cancer biology (M Sc, PhD); cardiovascular and respiratory sciences (M Sc, PhD); community health sciences (M Sc, PhD); critical care medicine (M Sc, PhD); gastrointestinal sciences (M Sc, PhD); joint injury and arthritis (M Sc, PhD); medicine (M Sc, MBT, MCM, MD, PhD); microbiology, immunology and infectious diseases (M Sc, PhD); molecular and medical genetics (M Sc, PhD); mountain medicine and high altitude physiology (M Sc, PhD); neuroscience (M Sc, PhD); pathologists' assistant (M Sc, PhD). Electronic applications accepted.

Faculty of Graduate Studies *Program availability:* Part-time, evening/weekend, blended/hybrid learning. Offers interdisciplinary research (M Sc, MA, PhD); resources and the environment (M Sc, MA, PhD). Electronic applications accepted.

Faculty of Arts *Program availability:* Part-time, evening/weekend. Offers arts (MA, PhD); clinical psychology (M Sc, PhD); geography (M Sc, MA, MGIS, PhD); German (MA); Greek and Roman studies (MA, PhD); history (MA, PhD); linguistics (MA, PhD); military and strategic studies (MSS); music (M Mus, MA, PhD); philosophy (MA, PhD); political science (MA, PhD); psychology (M Sc, PhD); religious studies (MA, PhD); sociology (MA, PhD). Electronic applications accepted.

Faculty of Kinesiology Offers kinesiology (M Kin, M Sc, PhD). Electronic applications accepted.

Faculty of Law Offers law (LL M, JD, Postbaccalaureate Certificate); natural resources, energy and environmental law (LL M, Postbaccalaureate Certificate).

Faculty of Nursing *Program availability:* Part-time. Offers nursing (MN, PhD, PMD). Electronic applications accepted.

Faculty of Science *Program availability:* Part-time. Offers analytical chemistry (M Sc, PhD); applied chemistry (M Sc, PhD); biological sciences (M Sc, PhD); computer science (M Sc, PhD); geology (M Sc, PhD); geophysics (M Sc, PhD); hydrology (M Sc, PhD); inorganic chemistry (M Sc, PhD); mathematics and statistics (M Sc, PhD); organic chemistry (M Sc, PhD); physical chemistry (M Sc, PhD); physics and astronomy (M Sc, PhD); polymer chemistry (M Sc, PhD); science (M Sc, PhD); software engineering (M Sc); theoretical chemistry (M Sc, PhD).

Faculty of Social Work Offers social work (MSW, PhD, Postgraduate Diploma). Electronic applications accepted.

Haskayne School of Business *Program availability:* Part-time, evening/weekend. Offers business (EMBA, GEMBA, MBA, PhD); business administration (EMBA, MBA); management (MBA, PhD).

The School of Public Policy *Program availability:* Part-time. Offers public policy (MPP).

Schulich School of Engineering *Program availability:* Part-time, evening/weekend. Offers avalanche mechanics (M Sc, PhD); biomedical engineering (M Sc, PhD); chemical engineering (M Eng, M Sc, PhD); civil engineering (M Eng, M Sc, PhD); electrical and computer engineering (M Eng, M Sc, PhD); energy and environment engineering (M Eng, M Sc, PhD); energy and environmental systems (M Eng, M Sc, PhD); engineering (M Eng, M Sc, MPM, PhD); environmental engineering (M Eng, M Sc, PhD); geomatics engineering (M Eng, M Sc, PhD); geotechnical engineering (M Eng, M Sc, PhD); materials science (M Eng, M Sc, PhD); mechanical and manufacturing engineering (M Eng, M Sc, PhD); petroleum engineering (M Eng, M Sc, PhD); project management (M Eng, M Sc); reservoir characterization (M Eng, M Sc); structures and solid mechanics (M Eng, M Sc, PhD); transportation engineering (M Eng, M Sc, PhD); water resources (M Eng, M Sc, PhD). Electronic applications accepted.

Werklund School of Education *Program availability:* Part-time, evening/weekend, online learning. Offers adult learning (M Ed, MA, Ed D, PhD); counseling psychology (M Sc, MC, PhD); curriculum and learning (M Ed, MA, Ed D, PhD); education (M Ed, M Sc, MA, MC, Ed D, PhD); educational leadership (M Ed, MA, Ed D, PhD); languages and diversity (M Ed, MA, Ed D, PhD); learning sciences (M Ed, MA, Ed D, PhD); school and applied child psychology (M Ed, M Sc, PhD). Electronic applications accepted.

Faculty of Veterinary Medicine

School of Architecture, Planning and Landscaping

Program in Environmental Design Offers architecture (M Arch); environmental design (M Env Des, PhD); landscape architecture (MLA); planning (M Plan).

UNIVERSITY OF CALIFORNIA, BERKELEY, Berkeley, CA 94720

General Information State-supported, coed, university. CGS member. *Graduate housing:* Rooms and/or apartments available to single and married students.

GRADUATE UNITS

Graduate Division *Program availability:* Part-time, blended/hybrid learning. Offers bioengineering (PhD); comparative biochemistry (PhD); East Asian studies (MA); global studies (MA); neuroscience (PhD); Northeast Asian studies (MA); South Asian studies (MA); Southeast Asian studies (MA); vision science (MS, PhD).

College of Chemistry Offers chemical engineering (PhD); chemistry (MS, PhD); product development (MS). Electronic applications accepted.

College of Engineering *Program availability:* Part-time, 100% online, blended/hybrid learning. Offers applied science and technology (PhD); bioengineering (M Eng, MTM); computer science (MS, PhD); decision analytics (M Eng); electrical engineering (M Eng, MS, PhD); engineering (M Eng, MS, MTM, PhD); engineering and project management (M Eng, MS, PhD); engineering science (M Eng, MS, PhD); environmental engineering (M Eng, MS, PhD); geoengineering (M Eng, MS, PhD); industrial engineering and operations research (M Eng, MS, PhD); mechanical engineering (M Eng, MS, PhD); nuclear engineering (M Eng, MS, PhD); structural engineering, mechanics and materials (M Eng, MS, PhD); transportation engineering (M Eng, MS, PhD). Electronic applications accepted.

College of Environmental Design Offers architecture (M Arch); building science (MS, PhD); building structures, construction and materials (MS, PhD); city and regional planning (MCP, PhD); design theories, methods, and practices (MS, PhD); environmental design (M Arch, MA, MCP, MLA, MS, MUD, PhD); environmental design in developing countries (MS, PhD); history of architecture and urbanism (MS, PhD); landscape architecture (MLA); landscape architecture and environmental planning (PhD); social and cultural processes in architecture and urbanism (MS, PhD); urban design (MUD). Electronic applications accepted.

College of Letters and Science Offers African American studies (PhD); ancient history and Mediterranean archaeology (MA, PhD); anthropology (MA, PhD); applied mathematics (PhD); art practice (MFA); astrophysics (PhD); biophysics (PhD); Buddhist studies (PhD); Chinese language (PhD); classical archaeology (MA, PhD); classics (MA, PhD); comparative literature (PhD); composition (PhD); Czech (PhD); demography (PhD); economics (PhD); endocrinology (MA, PhD); English (PhD); ethnic studies (PhD); ethnomusicology (PhD); film and media (PhD); folklore (MA); French (PhD); geography (PhD); geology (MA, MS, PhD); geophysics (MA, MS, PhD); German (PhD); Greek (MA); Hindi (MA, PhD); Hispanic languages and literatures (PhD); history (PhD); history of art (PhD); Indonesian (MA, PhD); integrative biology (PhD); Italian (PhD); Italian studies (PhD); Japanese language (PhD); Latin (MA); letters and science (MA, MFA, MS, PhD); linguistics (PhD); logic and the methodology of science (PhD); mathematics (MA, PhD); medical anthropology (PhD); molecular and cell biology (PhD); musicology (PhD); Near Eastern studies (MA, PhD); performance studies (PhD); philosophy (PhD); physics (PhD); Polish (PhD); political science (PhD); psychology (PhD); rhetoric (PhD); Russian (PhD); Sanskrit (MA, PhD); Scandinavian languages and literatures (PhD); Serbo-Croatian (MA); sociology (PhD); sociology and demography (MA, PhD); Spanish (PhD); statistics (MA, PhD); Tamil (MA, PhD). Electronic applications accepted.

College of Natural Resources Offers agricultural and resource economics (PhD); development practice (MDP); energy and resources (MA, MS, PhD); environmental science, policy, and management (MS, PhD); forestry (MF); metabolic biology (MS, PhD); microbiology (PhD); molecular toxicology (PhD); natural resources (MA, MDP, MF, MS, PhD); plant biology (PhD); range management (MS).

Graduate School of Journalism Offers journalism (MJ). Electronic applications accepted.

Graduate School of Public Policy Offers public affairs (MPA); public policy (MPA, MPP, PhD). Electronic applications accepted.

Haas School of Business *Program availability:* Part-time, evening/weekend. Offers accounting (PhD); business (EMBA, MBA, MFE, PhD); business administration (EMBA, MBA, PhD); business and public policy (PhD); finance (PhD); financial engineering (MFE); management of organizations (PhD); marketing (PhD); real estate (PhD).

School of Education Offers development in mathematics and science (MA); education (MA, PhD); education in mathematics, science, and technology (MA, PhD); human development and education (MA, PhD); leadership education (MA); science and mathematics education (PhD); special education (PhD); teacher education (MA). Electronic applications accepted.

School of Information Offers information (MIDS, MIMS, PhD); information and data science (MIDS); information management and systems (MIMS, PhD). Electronic applications accepted.

School of Public Health *Program availability:* Blended/hybrid learning. Offers biostatistics (MA, PhD); environmental health sciences (MS, PhD); epidemiology (MS, PhD); health policy (PhD); infectious diseases (PhD); infectious diseases and immunity (PhD); public health (MA, MPH, MS, Dr PH, PhD). Electronic applications accepted.

School of Social Welfare Offers social welfare (MSW, PhD). Electronic applications accepted.

School of Law Offers jurisprudence and social policy (PhD); law (LL M, JD, JSD).

School of Optometry Offers optometry (OD, Certificate). Electronic applications accepted.

UC Berkeley Extension *Program availability:* Part-time, evening/weekend, online learning. Offers accounting (Certificate); alcohol and drug abuse studies (Certificate); business administration (Certificate); clinical research conduct and management (Certificate); college admissions and career planning (Certificate); construction management (Certificate); finance (Certificate); global business management (Certificate); human resource management (Certificate); HVAC (Certificate); information systems and management (Postbaccalaureate Certificate); integrated circuit design and techniques (online) (Certificate); interior design and interior architecture (Certificate); landscape architecture (Certificate); leadership in sustainability and environmental management (Professional Certificate); management (Certificate); marketing

(Certificate); project management (Certificate); solar energy and green building (Professional Certificate); sustainable design (Professional Certificate); teaching English as a second language (Certificate); UNIX/LINUX system administration (Certificate); visual arts (Postbaccalaureate Certificate); writing (Postbaccalaureate Certificate).

UNIVERSITY OF CALIFORNIA, DAVIS, Davis, CA 95616

General Information State-supported, coed, university. CGS member. *Graduate housing:* Rooms and/or apartments available to single and married students. Housing application deadline: 4/1.

GRADUATE UNITS

College of Engineering *Program availability:* Part-time. Offers aeronautical engineering (M Engr, MS, D Engr, PhD, Certificate); applied science (MS, PhD); biological systems engineering (M Engr, MS, D Engr, PhD); biomedical engineering (MS, PhD); chemical engineering (MS, PhD); civil and environmental engineering (M Engr, MS, D Engr, PhD, Certificate); computer science (MS, PhD); electrical and computer engineering (MS, PhD); engineering (M Engr, MS, D Engr, PhD, Certificate); materials science and engineering (MS, PhD); mechanical engineering (M Engr, MS, D Engr, PhD, Certificate); transportation, technology and policy (MS, PhD). Electronic applications accepted.

Graduate School of Management Students: 203 full-time (108 women), 279 part-time (107 women); includes 207 minority (14 Black or African American, non-Hispanic/Latino; 3 American Indian or Alaska Native, non-Hispanic/Latino; 141 Asian, non-Hispanic/Latino; 49 Hispanic/Latino; 125 international. Average age 28. 1,653 applicants, 28% accepted, 237 enrolled. *Faculty:* 32 full-time (10 women), 70 part-time/adjunct (27 women). Expenses: Contact institution. *Financial support:* In 2018–19, 258 students received support. Fellowships with full and partial tuition reimbursements available, research assistantships with partial tuition reimbursements available, teaching assistantships with partial tuition reimbursements available, institutionally sponsored loans, scholarships/grants, health care benefits, tuition waivers (partial), and unspecified assistantships available. Support available to part-time students. Financial award application deadline: 3/1; financial award applicants required to submit FAFSA. In 2018, 238 master's awarded. *Program availability:* Part-time, evening/weekend, 100% online. Offers audit analytics (MP Ac); business analytics (MSBA); business analytics and technologies (MBA); entrepreneurship and innovation (MBA); finance and accounting (MBA); financial accounting (MP Ac); general management (MBA); management (MBA, MP Ac, MSBA); marketing (MBA); organizational behavior (MBA); public health management (MBA); strategy (MBA); technology management (MBA). *Application deadline:* For fall admission, 9/15 priority date for domestic and international students. Applications are processed on a rolling basis. *Application fee:* $125. Electronic applications accepted. *Application Contact:* Andrea Shaw, Senior Director of Admissions, 530-752-7658, Fax: 530-754-9355, E-mail: admissions@gsm.ucdavis.edu. *Assistant Dean of Student Affairs,* Amanda Opperman, 530-752-7658, Fax: 530-754-9355, E-mail: admissions@gsm.ucdavis.edu.

Graduate Studies Offers acting (MFA); agricultural and environmental chemistry (MS, PhD); agricultural and resource economics (MS, PhD); animal behavior (PhD); animal biology (MAM, MS, PhD); anthropology (MA, PhD); applied linguistics (MA, PhD); applied mathematics (MS, PhD); art (MFA); art history (MA, PhD); atmospheric sciences (MS, PhD); avian sciences (MS); biochemistry and molecular biology (MS, PhD); biophysics (MS, PhD); biostatistics (MS, PhD); cell and developmental biology (MS, PhD); chemistry (MS, PhD); child development (MS, PhD); clinical research (MAS); communication (MA); community development (MS); comparative literature (PhD); comparative pathology (MS, PhD); composition (MA, PhD); conducting (MA, PhD); creative writing (MA); cultural studies (MA, PhD); dramatic art (PhD); ecology (MS, PhD); economics (MA, PhD); education (MA, Ed D); English (MA, PhD); entomology (MS, PhD); epidemiology (MS, PhD); exercise science (MS); food science (MS, PhD); forensic science (MS); French (PhD); genetics (MS, PhD); geography (MS, PhD); geology (MS, PhD); German (MA, PhD); health informatics (MS); history (MA, PhD); horticulture and agronomy (MS); human development (PhD); hydrologic sciences (MS, PhD); immunology (MS, PhD); instructional studies (MS); integrated pest management (MS); international agricultural development (MS); linguistics (MA, MAT, PhD); mathematics (MA, MAT, PhD); microbiology (MS, PhD); molecular, cellular and integrative physiology (MS, PhD); musicology (MA, PhD); Native American studies (MA, PhD); neuroscience (PhD); nutrition (MS, PhD); pharmacology/toxicology (MS, PhD); philosophy (MA, PhD); physics (MS, PhD); plant biology (MS, PhD); plant pathology (MS, PhD); political science (MA, PhD); population biology (PhD); psychological studies (PhD); psychology (PhD); sociocultural studies (PhD); sociology (MA, PhD); soils and biogeochemistry (MS, PhD); Spanish (MA, PhD); statistics (MS, PhD); textile arts and costume design (MFA); textiles (MS); viticulture and enology (MS, PhD). Electronic applications accepted.

School of Law Offers law (LL M, JD). Electronic applications accepted.

School of Medicine Offers medicine (MD). Electronic applications accepted.

School of Veterinary Medicine Offers preventive veterinary medicine (MPVM); veterinary medicine (MPVM, DVM, Certificate).

UNIVERSITY OF CALIFORNIA, HASTINGS COLLEGE OF THE LAW, San Francisco, CA 94102-4978

General Information State-supported, coed, graduate-only institution. *Enrollment by degree level:* 55 master's, 947 doctoral. *Graduate faculty:* 70 full-time (36 women), 66 part-time/adjunct (26 women). *International tuition:* $49,486 full-time. *Tuition, area resident:* Full-time $43,486; part-time $1812 per credit. Tuition, state resident: full-time $43,486; part-time $1812 per credit. Tuition, nonresident: full-time $49,486; part-time $2062 per credit. *Required fees:* $840; $840 per unit. *Graduate housing:* Rooms and/or apartments available on a first-come, first-served basis to single and married students. Typical cost: $1550 per year for single students; $2040 per year for married students. Room charges vary according to housing facility selected. Housing application deadline: 7/1. *Student services:* Campus employment opportunities, campus safety program, career counseling, exercise/wellness program, free psychological counseling, international student services, low-cost health insurance, services for students with disabilities, writing training. *Library facilities:* UC Hastings Law Library. *Collection:* Books: 111,102 (physical), 230,048 (digital/electronic); Serial titles: 4,435 (physical), 21,861 (digital/electronic); Databases: 107. Weekly public service hours: 102; students can reserve study rooms.

Computer facilities: A campuswide network can be accessed from student residence rooms and from off campus. Online class registration is available. Website: http://www.uchastings.edu/

General Application Contact: Bryan Zerbe, Admissions Office, 415-565-4623, Fax: 415-565-4863, E-mail: admiss@uchastings.edu.

GRADUATE UNITS

Graduate Programs Students: 971 full-time (574 women), 31 part-time (20 women); includes 380 minority (21 Black or African American, non-Hispanic/Latino; 11 American Indian or Alaska Native, non-Hispanic/Latino; 171 Asian, non-Hispanic/Latino; 169 Hispanic/Latino; 2 Native Hawaiian or other Pacific Islander, non-Hispanic/Latino; 6 Two or more races, non-Hispanic/Latino), 60 international. Average age 24. 3,234 applicants, 45% accepted, 303 enrolled. *Faculty:* 70 full-time (36 women), 106 part-time/adjunct (66 women). Expenses: Contact institution. *Financial support:* In 2018–19, 844 students received support. Fellowships, research assistantships, teaching assistantships, career-related internships or fieldwork, Federal Work-Study, institutionally sponsored loans, scholarships/grants, traineeships, health care benefits, and unspecified assistantships available. Support available to part-time students. Financial award application deadline: 3/1; financial award applicants required to submit FAFSA. In 2018, 59 master's, 277 doctorates awarded. *Program availability:* 100% online, blended/hybrid learning. Offers law (LL M, MS, MSL, JD). MSL and MS offered jointly with University of California, San Francisco. *Application deadline:* For fall admission, 3/31 for domestic students, 5/1 for international students. Applications are processed on a rolling basis. *Application fee:* $0. Electronic applications accepted. *Application Contact:* Admissions Office, 415-565-4623, Fax: 415-565-4863, E-mail: admiss@uchastings.edu. *Admissions Office,* Bryan Zerbe, 415-565-4623, Fax: 415-581-8946, E-mail: admiss@uchastings.edu.

UNIVERSITY OF CALIFORNIA, IRVINE, Irvine, CA 92697

General Information State-supported, coed, university. CGS member. *Graduate housing:* Rooms and/or apartments available on a first-come, first-served basis to single and married students.

GRADUATE UNITS

Claire Trevor School of the Arts Average age 29. 432 applicants, 21% accepted, 64 enrolled. Expenses: Contact institution. *Financial support:* Fellowships, teaching assistantships, institutionally sponsored loans, traineeships, health care benefits, and unspecified assistantships available. Financial award application deadline: 3/1; financial award applicants required to submit FAFSA. In 2018, 45 master's, 1 doctorate awarded. Offers accompanying (MFA); acting (MFA); art (MFA); arts (MFA, PhD); choral conducting (MFA); composition and technology (MFA); dance (MFA); design and stage management (MFA); directing (MFA); drama (MFA); drama and theatre (PhD); guitar/lute performance (MFA); instrumental performance (MFA); piano performance (MFA); vocal performance (MFA). *Application deadline:* For fall admission, 1/15 for domestic and international students. Applications are processed on a rolling basis. *Application fee:* $105 ($125 for international students). Electronic applications accepted. *Application Contact:* Prof. Vincent Olivieri, Associate Dean, 949-824-5684, Fax: 949-824-2450, E-mail: olivieri@uci.edu. *Dean,* Dr. Stephen Barker, 949-824-8792, Fax: 949-824-2450, E-mail: barker@uci.edu.

Donald Bren School of Information and Computer Sciences Students: 503 full-time (177 women), 16 part-time (4 women); includes 77 minority (7 Black or African American, non-Hispanic/Latino; 1 American Indian or Alaska Native, non-Hispanic/Latino; 49 Asian, non-Hispanic/Latino; 11 Hispanic/Latino; 9 Two or more races, non-Hispanic/Latino), 340 international. Average age 27. 3,777 applicants, 13% accepted, 195 enrolled. Expenses: Contact institution. *Financial support:* Fellowships, research assistantships with full tuition reimbursements, teaching assistantships, institutionally sponsored loans, traineeships, health care benefits, and unspecified assistantships available. Financial award applicants required to submit FAFSA. In 2018, 256 master's, 38 doctorates awarded. Offers computer science (MS, PhD); informatics (MS, PhD); information and computer science (MS, PhD); networked systems (MS, PhD); statistics (MS, PhD). *Application deadline:* For fall admission, 12/15 for domestic and international students. *Application fee:* $105 ($125 for international students). Electronic applications accepted. *Application Contact:* Kristine Bolcer, Director of Student Affairs, 949-824-5156, Fax: 949-824-4163, E-mail: kbolcer@uci.edu. *Dean,* Marios C. Papaefthymiou, 949-824-7427, E-mail: marios@uci.edu.

Institute of Transportation Studies Students: 12 full-time (5 women), 11 international. Average age 29. 26 applicants, 35% accepted, 5 enrolled. Expenses: Contact institution. *Financial support:* Fellowships, research assistantships with full tuition reimbursements, teaching assistantships, institutionally sponsored loans, traineeships, health care benefits, and unspecified assistantships available. Financial award application deadline: 3/1. In 2018, 2 master's, 1 doctorate awarded. Offers transportation studies (MA, PhD). *Application deadline:* For fall admission, 1/15 for domestic and international students. *Application fee:* $105 ($125 for international students). *Application Contact:* Amelia Regan, Director, Transportation Science Program, 949-824-2611, E-mail: aregan@uci.edu. *Director,* Stephen G. Ritchie, 949-824-4214, E-mail: sritchie@uci.edu.

Interdisciplinary Studies

The Paul Merage School of Business Students: 718 full-time (332 women), 243 part-time (96 women); includes 499 minority (19 Black or African American, non-Hispanic/Latino; 21 American Indian or Alaska Native, non-Hispanic/Latino; 387 Asian, non-Hispanic/Latino; 68 Hispanic/Latino; 4 Native Hawaiian or other Pacific Islander, non-Hispanic/Latino), 236 international. Average age 31. 3,632 applicants, 27% accepted, 510 enrolled. Expenses: Contact institution. *Financial support:* Career-related internships or fieldwork, Federal Work-Study, institutionally sponsored loans, scholarships/grants, traineeships, health care benefits, and unspecified assistantships available. Support available to part-time students. Financial award application deadline: 3/1; financial award applicants required to submit FAFSA. In 2018, 528 master's, 7 doctorates awarded. *Program availability:* Part-time, evening/weekend. Offers business (EMBA, MBA, MPA, MS, PhD); business administration (EMBA, MBA); business analytics (MS); health care administration (MBA); management (MS); professional accountancy (MPA). *Application deadline:* For fall admission, 1/2 priority date for domestic and international students. Applications are processed on a rolling basis. *Application fee:* $105 ($125 for international students). Electronic applications accepted. *Application Contact:* Eric Spangenberg, Dean, 949-824-8470, E-mail: ers@uci.edu. *Dean,* Eric Spangenberg, 949-824-8470, E-mail: ers@uci.edu.

Programs in Health Sciences Students: 129 full-time (103 women), 4 part-time (3 women); includes 77 minority (4 Black or African American, non-Hispanic/Latino; 30 Asian, non-Hispanic/Latino; 34 Hispanic/Latino; 9 Two or more races, non-Hispanic/Latino), 11 international. Average age 28. 662 applicants, 25% accepted, 56 enrolled. Expenses: Contact institution. In 2018, 42 master's, 8 doctorates awarded. Offers health sciences (MPH, MSN, PhD); medicinal chemistry and pharmacology (PhD); nursing science (MSN); public health (MPH, PhD). *Application fee:* $105 ($125 for international students). *Application Contact:* Sheree McPeak, Graduate Division, 949-824-4611, Fax: 949-824-9096, E-mail: ogsfront@uci.edu.

Samueli School of Engineering Students: 863 full-time (287 women), 63 part-time (14 women); includes 164 minority (12 Black or African American, non-Hispanic/Latino; 106 Asian, non-Hispanic/Latino; 31 Hispanic/Latino; 15 Two or more races, non-Hispanic/Latino), 566 international. Average age 26. 3,561 applicants, 28% accepted, 288 enrolled. Expenses: Contact institution. *Financial support:* Fellowships with tuition reimbursements, research assistantships with full tuition reimbursements, teaching assistantships with tuition reimbursements, institutionally sponsored loans, traineeships, health care benefits, and unspecified assistantships available. Financial award application deadline: 3/1; financial award applicants required to submit FAFSA. In 2018, 262 master's,

97 doctorates awarded. *Program availability:* Part-time. Offers biomedical engineering (MS, PhD); chemical and biochemical engineering (MS, PhD); civil and environmental engineering (MS, PhD); electrical engineering and computer science (MS, PhD); engineering (MS, PhD); engineering management (MS); materials science and engineering (MS, PhD); mechanical and aerospace engineering (MS, PhD); networked systems (MS, PhD). *Application deadline:* For fall admission, 1/15 priority date for domestic students, 1/15 for international students. Applications are processed on a rolling basis. *Application fee:* $105 ($125 for international students). Electronic applications accepted. *Application Contact:* Jean Bennett, Director of Graduate Student Affairs, 949-824-6475, Fax: 949-824-8200, E-mail: jean.bennett@uci.edu. *Dean,* Gregory N. Washington, 949-824-4333, Fax: 949-824-8200, E-mail: engineering@uci.edu.

School of Biological Sciences Students: 316 full-time (177 women), 7 part-time (3 women); includes 131 minority (7 Black or African American, non-Hispanic/Latino; 1 American Indian or Alaska Native, non-Hispanic/Latino; 58 Asian, non-Hispanic/Latino; 54 Hispanic/Latino; 11 Two or more races, non-Hispanic/Latino), 59 international. Average age 26. 923 applicants, 23% accepted, 100 enrolled. Expenses: Contact institution. *Financial support:* Fellowships with full tuition reimbursements, research assistantships with full tuition reimbursements, teaching assistantships with full tuition reimbursements, career-related internships or fieldwork, institutionally sponsored loans, scholarships/grants, traineeships, health care benefits, and unspecified assistantships available. Financial award application deadline: 3/1; financial award applicants required to submit FAFSA. In 2018, 68 master's, 36 doctorates awarded. Offers biological science (MS); biological sciences (MS, PhD); biotechnology (MS); biotechnology management (MS); interdisciplinary cellular and molecular biosciences (PhD); mathematical, computational and systems biology (PhD); neuroscience (PhD). *Application deadline:* For fall admission, 12/15 for domestic and international students. Applications are processed on a rolling basis. *Application fee:* $105 ($125 for international students). Electronic applications accepted. *Application Contact:* Prof. R. Michael Mulligan, Associate Dean, 949-824-8433, Fax: 949-824-4709, E-mail: rmmullig@uci.edu. *Dean,* Prof. Frank Laferla, 949-824-5315, Fax: 949-824-3035, E-mail: laferla@uci.edu.

School of Education Students: 213 full-time (155 women), 3 part-time (2 women); includes 107 minority (1 Black or African American, non-Hispanic/Latino; 51 Asian, non-Hispanic/Latino; 40 Hispanic/Latino; 15 Two or more races, non-Hispanic/Latino), 23 international. Average age 28. 482 applicants, 47% accepted, 148 enrolled. Expenses: Contact institution. *Financial support:* Fellowships, research assistantships with full tuition reimbursements, institutionally sponsored loans, traineeships, health care benefits, and unspecified assistantships available. Financial award application deadline: 3/1; financial award applicants required to submit FAFSA. In 2018, 141 master's, 8 doctorates awarded. *Program availability:* Part-time, evening/weekend. Offers educational administration (Ed D); educational administration and leadership (Ed D); elementary and secondary education (MAT). *Application deadline:* For fall admission, 1/2 priority date for domestic students, 1/2 for international students. *Application fee:* $105 ($125 for international students). Electronic applications accepted. *Application Contact:* Denise Earley, Assistant Director of Student Affairs, 949-824-4022, E-mail: denise.earley@uci.edu. *Dean,* Richard Arum, 949-824-2534, E-mail: richard.arum@uci.edu.

School of Humanities Students: 279 full-time (143 women), 9 part-time (5 women); includes 88 minority (10 Black or African American, non-Hispanic/Latino; 21 Asian, non-Hispanic/Latino; 35 Hispanic/Latino; 22 Two or more races, non-Hispanic/Latino), 50 international. Average age 32. 925 applicants, 14% accepted, 72 enrolled. Expenses: Contact institution. *Financial support:* Fellowships with tuition reimbursements, research assistantships with full tuition reimbursements, teaching assistantships with tuition reimbursements, institutionally sponsored loans, traineeships, health care benefits, and unspecified assistantships available. Financial award application deadline: 3/1; financial award applicants required to submit FAFSA. In 2018, 52 master's, 44 doctorates awarded. Offers Chinese (MA, PhD); classics (MA, PhD); comparative literature (MA, PhD); creative writing (MFA); culture and theory (PhD); East Asian languages and literatures (MA, PhD); English (MA, PhD); English and American literature (PhD); French (MA, PhD); German (MA, PhD); history (MA, PhD); humanities (MA, MAT, MFA, PhD); Japanese (MA, PhD); philosophy (MA, PhD); Spanish (MA, MAT, PhD); visual studies (MA, PhD); writing (MFA). *Application deadline:* For fall, 1/15 for domestic and international students. Applications are processed on a rolling basis. *Application fee:* $105 ($125 for international students). Electronic applications accepted. *Application Contact:* Amy Fujitani, Director of Graduate Student Affairs, Fax: 949-824-1360, E-mail: amy.fujitani@uci.edu. *Dean,* Georges Van Den Abbeele, 949-824-5133, E-mail: gvandena@uci.edu.

School of Law Offers law (JD). Electronic applications accepted.

School of Medicine Students: 589 full-time (321 women), 42 part-time (20 women); includes 117 minority (7 Black or African American, non-Hispanic/Latino; 1 American Indian or Alaska Native, non-Hispanic/Latino; 69 Asian, non-Hispanic/Latino; 39 Hispanic/Latino; 1 Two or more races, non-Hispanic/Latino), 28 international. Average age 28. 297 applicants, 17% accepted, 29 enrolled. Expenses: Contact institution. *Financial support:* Fellowships, research assistantships with full tuition reimbursements, teaching assistantships, career-related internships or fieldwork, institutionally sponsored loans, traineeships, health care benefits, and unspecified assistantships available. Financial award application deadline: 3/1; financial award applicants required to submit FAFSA. In 2018, 47 master's, 115 doctorates awarded. Offers biological sciences (MS, PhD); biomedical and translational science (MS); environmental health sciences (MS); environmental toxicology (PhD); epidemiology (MS, PhD); experimental pathology (PhD); exposure sciences and risk assessment (PhD); genetic counseling (MS); medicine (MS, MD, PhD); pharmacological sciences (PhD). *Application deadline:* For fall admission, 1/15 for domestic and international students. *Application fee:* $105 ($125 for international students). Electronic applications accepted. *Application Contact:* Leora Fellus, Graduate Studies Director, 949-824-1028, E-mail: lfellus@uci.edu. *Dean,* Dr. Michael Stamos, 949-824-1046, E-mail: mstamos@uci.edu.

School of Physical Sciences Students: 514 full-time (172 women), 4 part-time (0 women); includes 146 minority (4 Black or African American, non-Hispanic/Latino; 1 American Indian or Alaska Native, non-Hispanic/Latino; 59 Asian, non-Hispanic/Latino; 51 Hispanic/Latino; 31 Two or more races, non-Hispanic/Latino), 107 international. Average age 27. 1,155 applicants, 31% accepted, 112 enrolled. Expenses: Contact institution. *Financial support:* Fellowships, research assistantships with full tuition reimbursements, teaching assistantships, career-related internships or fieldwork, institutionally sponsored loans, traineeships, and unspecified assistantships available. Financial award application deadline: 3/1; financial award applicants required to submit FAFSA. In 2018, 65 master's, 76 doctorates awarded. Offers chemical and materials physics (MS, PhD); chemistry (MS, PhD); earth system science (MS, PhD); mathematics (MS, PhD); physical sciences (MS, PhD); physics (MS, PhD). *Application deadline:* For fall admission, 1/15 priority date for domestic and international students. Applications are processed on a rolling basis. *Application fee:* $105 ($125 for international students). Electronic applications accepted. *Application*

Contact: Prof. Roger McWilliams, Associate Dean, 949-824-6228, Fax: 949-824-2174, E-mail: mcw@uci.edu. *Dean,* Kenneth C. Janda, 949-824-6022, Fax: 949-824-2261, E-mail: kcjanda@uci.edu.

School of Social Ecology Students: 343 full-time (240 women), 82 part-time (58 women); includes 214 minority (29 Black or African American, non-Hispanic/Latino; 40 Asian, non-Hispanic/Latino; 103 Hispanic/Latino; 2 Native Hawaiian or other Pacific Islander, non-Hispanic/Latino; 40 Two or more races, non-Hispanic/Latino), 60 international. Average age 29. 762 applicants, 42% accepted, 150 enrolled. Expenses: Contact institution. *Financial support:* Fellowships, research assistantships with full tuition reimbursements, teaching assistantships, institutionally sponsored loans, traineeships, health care benefits, and unspecified assistantships available. Financial award application deadline: 3/1; financial award applicants required to submit FAFSA. In 2018, 145 master's, 14 doctorates awarded. Offers criminology, law and society (MAS, PhD); environmental analysis and design (PhD); epidemiology and public health (PhD); planning, policy and design (PhD); psychology and social behavior (PhD); social ecology (PhD); urban and regional planning (MURP). *Application deadline:* For fall admission, 1/15 priority date for domestic students, 1/15 for international students. Applications are processed on a rolling basis. *Application fee:* $105 ($125 for international students). Electronic applications accepted. *Application Contact:* Jennifer Craig, Director of Graduate Student Services, 949-824-5918, E-mail: craigj@uci.edu. *Dean,* Nancy Guerra, 949-824-5466, Fax: 949-824-1845, E-mail: nguerra1@uci.edu.

School of Social Sciences Students: 439 full-time (202 women), 4 part-time (0 women); includes 139 minority (15 Black or African American, non-Hispanic/Latino; 2 American Indian or Alaska Native, non-Hispanic/Latino; 47 Asian, non-Hispanic/Latino; 46 Hispanic/Latino; 29 Two or more races, non-Hispanic/Latino), 110 international. Average age 30. 701 applicants, 33% accepted, 105 enrolled. Expenses: Contact institution. *Financial support:* Fellowships, research assistantships with full tuition reimbursements, teaching assistantships, institutionally sponsored loans, traineeships, health care benefits, and unspecified assistantships available. Financial award application deadline: 3/1; financial award applicants required to submit FAFSA. In 2018, 65 master's, 53 doctorates awarded. Offers anthropology (MA, PhD); demographic and social analysis (MA); economics (MA, PhD); philosophy (PhD); political psychology (PhD); political sciences (PhD); psychology (PhD); public choice (MA, PhD); social networks (PhD); social science (PhD); social sciences (MA, PhD); sociology and social relations (PhD); transportation economics (MA, PhD). *Application deadline:* For fall admission, 1/15 priority date for domestic students, 1/15 for international students. Applications are processed on a rolling basis. *Application fee:* $105 ($125 for international students). Electronic applications accepted. *Application Contact:* Michael McBride, Associate Dean for Research and Graduate Studies, 949-824-7417, Fax: 949-824-2182, E-mail: mcbride@uci.edu. *Dean,* William M. Maurer, 949-824-6802, Fax: 949-824-0646, E-mail: wmmaurer@uci.edu.

Institute for Mathematical Behavioral Sciences Students: 8 full-time (4 women), 2 part-time (0 women); includes 3 minority (1 Asian, non-Hispanic/Latino; 2 Two or more races, non-Hispanic/Latino), 2 international. Average age 36. 8 applicants, 13% accepted, 0 enrolled. Expenses: Contact institution. *Financial support:* Fellowships, research assistantships with full tuition reimbursements, teaching assistantships, institutionally sponsored loans, traineeships, health care benefits, and unspecified assistantships available. Financial award application deadline: 3/1; financial award applicants required to submit FAFSA. In 2018, 2 master's, 1 doctorate awarded. Offers games, decisions, and dynamical systems (PhD); mathematical behavioral sciences (MA). *Application deadline:* For fall admission, 1/15 priority date for domestic students, 1/15 for international students. Applications are processed on a rolling basis. *Application fee:* $105 ($125 for international students). Electronic applications accepted. *Application Contact:* Joanna Kerner, Administrative Manager, 949-824-8651, Fax: 949-824-3733, E-mail: kernerj@uci.edu. *Interim Director,* Jean-Paul Carvalho, 949-824-3417, Fax: 949-824-3733, E-mail: jpcarv@uci.edu.

UNIVERSITY OF CALIFORNIA, LOS ANGELES, Los Angeles, CA 90095

General Information State-supported, coed, university. CGS member. *Graduate housing:* Rooms and/or apartments available on a first-come, first-served basis to single and married students.

GRADUATE UNITS

David Geffen School of Medicine Offers biological chemistry (MS, PhD); biomathematics (MS, PhD); biomedical physics (MS, PhD); cellular and molecular pathology (MS, PhD); clinical research (MS); experimental pathology (MS, PhD); human genetics (MS, PhD); medicine (MS, MD, PhD); microbiology, immunology and molecular genetics (MS, PhD); molecular and medical pharmacology (MS, PhD); neurobiology (MS, PhD); neuroscience (PhD); physiology (PhD). Electronic applications accepted.

Graduate Division Electronic applications accepted.

College of Letters and Science Offers Afro-American studies (MA); American Indian studies (MA); anthropology (MA, PhD); applied economics (MAE); applied linguistics (PhD); applied linguistics and teaching English as a second language (MA); archaeology (MA, PhD); art history (MA, PhD); Asian languages and cultures (MA, PhD); Asian-American studies (MA); astronomy (MAT, MS, PhD); atmospheric and oceanic sciences (MS, PhD); biochemistry and molecular biology (MS, PhD); bioinformatics (MS, PhD); biological chemistry (PhD); cellular and molecular pathology (PhD); chemistry (MS, PhD); classics (MA, PhD); comparative literature (MA, PhD); conservation of archaeological and ethnographic materials (MA); ecology and evolutionary biology (MA, PhD); economics (MAE, PhD); English (MA, PhD); French and Francophone studies (MA, PhD); gender studies (MA, PhD); geochemistry (MS, PhD); geography (MA, PhD); geology (MS, PhD); geophysics and space physics (MS, PhD); Germanic languages (MA, PhD); Greek (MA); Hispanic languages and literature (PhD); history (MA, PhD); human genetics (PhD); Indo-European studies (PhD); Italian (MA, PhD); Latin (MA); letters and science (MA, MAT, MS, PhD, Certificate); linguistics (MA, PhD); mathematics (MA, MAT, MS, PhD); microbiology, immunology, and molecular genetics (PhD); molecular biology (PhD); molecular toxicology (PhD); molecular, cell and developmental biology (MA, PhD); molecular, cellular and integrative physiology (MA, PhD); musicology (MA, PhD); Near Eastern languages and cultures (MA, PhD); neurobiology (PhD); oral biology (PhD); philosophy (MA, PhD); physics (MA, PhD); physiological science (MS); physiology (PhD); political science (MA, PhD); Portuguese (MA); psychology (MA, PhD); Scandinavian (MA); Slavic languages and literatures (MA, PhD); sociology (MA, PhD); Spanish (MA, PhD); statistics (MS, PhD); teaching English as a second language (Certificate). Electronic applications accepted.

Fielding School of Public Health Offers biostatistics (MPH, MS, Dr PH, PhD); environmental health sciences (MS, PhD); environmental science and engineering (D Env); epidemiology (MPH, MS, Dr PH, PhD); health services (MPH, MS, Dr PH, PhD); molecular toxicology (PhD); public health (MPH, MS, D Env, Dr PH, PhD). Electronic applications accepted.

Graduate School of Education and Information Studies *Program availability:* Part-time, evening/weekend. Offers archival studies (MLIS); education (M Ed, MA, Ed D, PhD); education and information studies (M Ed, MA, MLIS, Ed D, PhD, Certificate); educational leadership (Ed D); informatics (MLIS); information studies (PhD); library and information science (Certificate); library studies (MLIS); moving image archive studies (MA); rare books, print and visual culture (MLIS); special education (PhD). Electronic applications accepted.

Henry Samueli School of Engineering and Applied Science *Program availability:* Evening/weekend, blended/hybrid learning. Offers aerospace engineering (MS, PhD); bioengineering (MS, PhD); chemical and biomolecular engineering (MS, PhD); civil and environmental engineering (MS, PhD); computer science (MS, PhD); electrical and computer engineering (MS, PhD); engineering (MS); engineering and applied science (MS, PhD); manufacturing engineering (MS); materials science and engineering (MS, PhD); mechanical engineering (MS, PhD). Electronic applications accepted.

Institute of the Environment and Sustainability Offers environmental science and engineering (D Env).

International Institute Offers African studies (MA); East Asian studies (MA); Islamic studies (MA, PhD); Latin American studies (MA). Electronic applications accepted.

Luskin School of Public Affairs Offers public affairs (MA, MPP, MSW, PhD); public policy (MPP); social welfare (MSW, PhD); urban planning (MA, PhD). Electronic applications accepted.

School of Nursing Offers nursing (MSN, PhD). Electronic applications accepted.

School of the Arts and Architecture Offers architecture and urban design (M Arch, MA, PhD); art (MFA); arts and architecture (M Arch, MA, MFA, MM, DMA, PhD); composition (MA, PhD); culture and performance (MA, PhD); dance (MFA); design media arts (MFA); ethnomusicology (MA, PhD); performance (MM, DMA). Electronic applications accepted.

School of Theater, Film and Television Offers animation (MFA); cinema and media studies (MA, PhD); cinematography (MFA); film and television (MA, MFA, PhD); moving image archive studies (MA); production (MFA); screenwriting (MFA); theater (MA, MFA); theater and performance studies (PhD); theater, film and television (MA, MFA, PhD). Electronic applications accepted.

UCLA Anderson School of Management Students: 1,040 full-time (378 women), 1,262 part-time (391 women); includes 784 minority (47 Black or African American, non-Hispanic/Latino; 1 American Indian or Alaska Native, non-Hispanic/Latino; 539 Asian, non-Hispanic/Latino; 116 Hispanic/Latino; 5 Native Hawaiian or other Pacific Islander, non-Hispanic/Latino; 76 Two or more races, non-Hispanic/Latino), 609 international. Average age 31. 6,708 applicants, 27% accepted, 949 enrolled. *Faculty:* 86 full-time (19 women), 102 part-time/adjunct (16 women). *Expenses:* Contact institution. *Financial support:* Fellowships, research assistantships with partial tuition reimbursements, teaching assistantships with partial tuition reimbursements, career-related internships or fieldwork, institutionally sponsored loans, and scholarships/grants available. Support available to part-time students. In 2018, 885 master's, 13 doctorates awarded. *Program availability:* Part-time, evening/weekend. Offers accounting (PhD); behavioral decision making (PhD); business administration (EMBA, MBA); business administration/computer science (EMBA, MBA, MFE, MSBA, PhD); business administration/latin american studies (EMBA, MBA, MFE, MSBA, PhD); business administration/law (EMBA, MBA, MFE, MSBA, PhD); business administration/library science (EMBA, MBA, MFE, MSBA, PhD); business administration/medicine (EMBA, MBA, MFE, MSBA, PhD); business administration/nursing (EMBA, MBA, MFE, MSBA, PhD); business administration/public health (EMBA, MBA, MFE, MSBA, PhD); business administration/public policy (EMBA, MBA, MFE, MSBA, PhD); business administration/urban and regional planning (EMBA, MBA, MFE, MSBA, PhD); business analytics (MSBA); decisions, operations, and technology management (PhD); finance (PhD); financial engineering (MFE); global economics and management (PhD); management and organizations (PhD); marketing (PhD); strategy and policy (PhD). UCLA-NUS EMBA: UCLA Anderson and the National University of Singapore. *Application deadline:* For fall admission, 10/2 for domestic and international students; for winter admission, 1/8 for domestic and international students; for spring admission, 4/16 for domestic and international students. Applications are processed on a rolling basis. *Application fee:* $200. Electronic applications accepted. *Application Contact:* Alex Lawrence, Assistant Dean and Director of MBA Admissions, 310-825-6944, Fax: 310-825-8582, E-mail: mba.admissions@anderson.ucla.edu. *Dean & John E. Anderson Chair in Management,* Dr. Antonio Bernardo, 310-825-7982, Fax: 310-206-2073, E-mail: a.bernardo@anderson.ucla.edu.

School of Dentistry Offers dentistry (MS, DDS, PhD, Certificate); oral biology (MS, PhD). Electronic applications accepted.

School of Law Students: 1,154 full-time (601 women); includes 319 minority (35 Black or African American, non-Hispanic/Latino; 3 American Indian or Alaska Native, non-Hispanic/Latino; 141 Asian, non-Hispanic/Latino; 101 Hispanic/Latino; 1 Native Hawaiian or other Pacific Islander, non-Hispanic/Latino; 38 Two or more races, non-Hispanic/Latino), 212 international. Average age 24. 6,243 applicants, 23% accepted, 311 enrolled. *Faculty:* 108 full-time (48 women), 113 part-time/adjunct (53 women). *Expenses:* Contact institution. *Financial support:* In 2018–19, 759 students received support. Career-related internships or fieldwork, scholarships/grants, health care benefits, tuition waivers (full and partial), and unspecified assistantships available. Financial award application deadline: 3/2. In 2018, 195 master's, 320 doctorates awarded. Offers law (LL M, JD, SJD). We offer the following formal joint degree programs: Law and African-American Studies; Law and American Indian Studies; Law and Management; Law and Philosophy; Law and Public Health; Law and Public Policy; Law and Social Welfare; Law and Urban Planning. *Application deadline:* For fall admission, 2/1 for domestic students. Applications are processed on a rolling basis. *Application fee:* $75. Electronic applications accepted. *Application Contact:* Admissions Office, 310-825-2080. *Dean/Professor of Law,* Jennifer L. Mnookin, 310-825-8202.

UNIVERSITY OF CALIFORNIA, MERCED, Merced, CA 95343

General Information State-supported, coed, university. CGS member. *Enrollment:* 8,540 graduate, professional, and undergraduate students; 656 full-time matriculated graduate/professional students (307 women), 7 part-time matriculated graduate/professional students (3 women). *Enrollment by degree level:* 56 master's, 607 doctoral. *Graduate faculty:* 250 full-time (103 women). *International tuition:* $26,544 full-time. *Tuition, area resident:* Full-time $11,442; part-time $5721 per year. *Tuition, state resident:* full-time $11,442; part-time $5721 per year. *Tuition, nonresident:* full-time $26,544; part-time $13,272 per year. *Required fees:* $1765; $1765 per unit. $883 per semester. *Graduate housing:* Rooms and/or apartments available on a first-come, first-served basis to single and married students. Typical cost: $9720 per year for single students; $13,452 per year for married students. Room charges vary according to board

plan and housing facility selected. *Student services:* Campus employment opportunities, campus safety program, career counseling, child daycare facilities, exercise/wellness program, free psychological counseling, grant writing training, international student services, low-cost health insurance, multicultural affairs office, services for students with disabilities, teacher training, writing training. *Library facilities:* Kolligian Library. *Collection:* Books: 140,278 (physical), 1.7 million (digital/electronic); Serial titles: 100,836 (physical). Weekly public service hours: 97; students can reserve study rooms.

Computer facilities: 220 computers available on campus for general student use. A campuswide network can be accessed from student residence rooms and from off campus. Online class registration, student calendar, 10Gb online cloud storage, free office software are available.
Website: http://www.ucmerced.edu/

General Application Contact: Tsu Ya, Director of Admissions and Academic Services, 209-228-4521, Fax: 209-228-6906, E-mail: tya@ucmerced.edu.

GRADUATE UNITS

Graduate Division Students: 656 full-time (307 women), 7 part-time (4 women); includes 212 minority (17 Black or African American, non-Hispanic/Latino; 61 Asian, non-Hispanic/Latino; 118 Hispanic/Latino; 2 Native Hawaiian or other Pacific Islander, non-Hispanic/Latino; 14 Two or more races, non-Hispanic/Latino), 245 international. Average age 29. 799 applicants, 45% accepted, 169 enrolled. *Faculty:* 250 full-time (103 women). *Expenses:* Contact institution. *Financial support:* In 2018–19, 622 students received support, including 34 fellowships with full tuition reimbursements available (averaging $21,245 per year), 142 research assistantships with full tuition reimbursements available (averaging $18,738 per year), 446 teaching assistantships with full tuition reimbursements available (averaging $20,809 per year); scholarships/grants, traineeships, and health care benefits also available. In 2018, 55 master's, 63 doctorates awarded. *Application deadline:* For fall admission, 1/15 for domestic and international students. *Application fee:* $105 ($125 for international students). Electronic applications accepted. *Application Contact:* Tsu Ya, Director of Admissions and Academic Services, 209-228-4521, Fax: 209-228-6906, E-mail: tya@ucmerced.edu. *Vice Provost and Graduate Dean,* Dr. Marjorie S. Zatz, 209-228-2408, Fax: 209-228-6906, E-mail: mzatz@ucmerced.edu.

School of Engineering Students: 219 full-time (72 women), 1 part-time (0 women); includes 43 minority (2 Black or African American, non-Hispanic/Latino; 17 Asian, non-Hispanic/Latino; 20 Hispanic/Latino; 1 Native Hawaiian or other Pacific Islander, non-Hispanic/Latino; 3 Two or more races, non-Hispanic/Latino), 145 international. Average age 28. 371 applicants, 46% accepted, 75 enrolled. *Faculty:* 60 full-time (16 women). *Expenses:* Contact institution. *Financial support:* In 2018–19, 200 students received support, including 14 fellowships with full tuition reimbursements available (averaging $20,851 per year), 70 research assistantships with full tuition reimbursements available (averaging $18,334 per year), 116 teaching assistantships with full tuition reimbursements available (averaging $19,841 per year); scholarships/grants, traineeships, and health care benefits also available. In 2018, 30 master's, 17 doctorates awarded. Offers biological engineering and small scale technologies (MS, PhD); electrical engineering and computer science (MS, PhD); environmental systems (MS, PhD); management of innovation, sustainability, and technology (MM); mechanical engineering (MS); mechanical engineering and applied mechanics (PhD). *Application deadline:* For fall admission, 1/15 priority date for domestic and international students. *Application fee:* $105 ($125 for international students). Electronic applications accepted. *Application Contact:* Tsu Ya, Director of Admissions and Academic Services, 209-228-4521, Fax: 209-228-6906, E-mail: tya@ucmerced.edu. *Dean,* Dr. Mark Matsumoto, 209-228-4047, Fax: 209-228-4047, E-mail: mmatsumoto@ucmerced.edu.

School of Natural Sciences Students: 232 full-time (98 women), 2 part-time (0 women); includes 79 minority (8 Black or African American, non-Hispanic/Latino; 22 Asian, non-Hispanic/Latino; 41 Hispanic/Latino; 8 Two or more races, non-Hispanic/Latino), 65 international. Average age 28. 302 applicants, 42% accepted, 58 enrolled. *Faculty:* 77 full-time (30 women). *Expenses:* Contact institution. *Financial support:* In 2018–19, 229 students received support, including 12 fellowships with full tuition reimbursements available (averaging $21,865 per year), 47 research assistantships with full tuition reimbursements available (averaging $19,123 per year), 170 teaching assistantships with full tuition reimbursements available (averaging $20,710 per year); scholarships/grants, traineeships, and health care benefits also available. In 2018, 13 master's, 23 doctorates awarded. Offers applied mathematics (MS, PhD); chemistry and chemical biology (MS, PhD); physics (MS, PhD); quantitative and systems biology (MS, PhD). *Application deadline:* For fall admission, 1/15 for domestic and international students. *Application fee:* $105 ($125 for international students). Electronic applications accepted. *Application Contact:* Tsu Ya, Director of Graduate Admissions and Academic Services, 209-228-4521, Fax: 209-228-6906, E-mail: tya@ucmerced.edu. *Dean,* Dr. Elizabeth Dumont, 209-228-4487, Fax: 209-228-4060, E-mail: edumont@ucmerced.edu.

School of Social Sciences, Humanities and Arts Students: 195 full-time (130 women), 4 part-time (3 women); includes 83 minority (6 Black or African American, non-Hispanic/Latino; 21 Asian, non-Hispanic/Latino; 52 Hispanic/Latino; 1 Native Hawaiian or other Pacific Islander, non-Hispanic/Latino; 3 Two or more races, non-Hispanic/Latino), 35 international. Average age 31. 150 applicants, 54% accepted, 36 enrolled. *Faculty:* 113 full-time (57 women). *Expenses:* Contact institution. *Financial support:* In 2018–19, 193 students received support, including 8 fellowships with full tuition reimbursements available (averaging $21,003 per year), 25 research assistantships with full tuition reimbursements available (averaging $19,145 per year), 160 teaching assistantships with full tuition reimbursements available (averaging $21,617 per year); scholarships/grants, traineeships, and health care benefits also available. In 2018, 12 master's, 23 doctorates awarded. Offers cognitive and information sciences (PhD); interdisciplinary humanities (MA, PhD); psychological sciences (MA, PhD); social sciences (MA, PhD); sociology (MA, PhD). *Application deadline:* For fall admission, 1/15 for domestic and international students. *Application fee:* $105 ($125 for international students). Electronic applications accepted. *Application Contact:* Tsu Ya, Director of Admissions and Academic Services, 209-228-4521, Fax: 209-228-6906, E-mail: tya@ucmerced.edu. *Interim Dean,* Dr. Jeffrey Gilger, 209-228-4343, E-mail: jgilger@ucmerced.edu.

UNIVERSITY OF CALIFORNIA, RIVERSIDE, Riverside, CA 92521-0102

General Information State-supported, coed, university. CGS member. *Graduate housing:* Rooms and/or apartments available on a first-come, first-served basis to single and married students. Housing application deadline: 6/1. *Research affiliation:* Los Alamos National Laboratory (botany and plant sciences, chemistry, earth sciences, physics), Brookhaven National Laboratory (chemistry, physics), U.S. Salinity Laboratory (environmental sciences, biochemistry), J. Paul Getty Museum (art history), Lawrence Livermore National Laboratory (anthropology), Fermi National Accelerator Laboratory (physics).

GRADUATE UNITS

Graduate Division *Program availability:* Part-time, evening/weekend. Offers anthropology (MA, MS, PhD); archival management (MA); art history (MA, PhD); biochemistry and molecular biology (MS, PhD); bioengineering (MS, PhD); biomedical sciences (PhD); cell, molecular, and developmental biology (MS, PhD); chemical and environmental engineering (MS, PhD); chemistry (MS, PhD); classics (PhD); comparative literature (MA, PhD); composition (PhD); computer engineering (MS); computer science (MS, PhD); creative writing and writing for the performing arts (MFA); cultural politics and production (PhD); economics (MA, PhD); electrical engineering (MS, PhD); English (MA, PhD); entomology (MS, PhD); environmental sciences (MS, PhD); environmental toxicology (MS, PhD); ethnomusicology (MA); evolution, ecology and organismal biology (MS, PhD); experimental choreography (MFA); genetics, genomics, and bioinformatics (PhD); geological sciences (MS, PhD); history (PhD); materials science and engineering (MS); mathematics (MS, PhD); mechanical engineering (MS, PhD); microbiology (MS, PhD); neuroscience (PhD); philosophy (MA, PhD); physics (MS, PhD); plant biology (MS, PhD); plant pathology (MS, PhD); political science (MA, PhD); psychology (PhD); religious studies (MA, PhD); sociology (MA, PhD); Southeast Asian studies (MA); Spanish (MA, PhD); statistics (MS); visual arts (MFA). Electronic applications accepted.

The A. Gary Anderson Graduate School of Management *Program availability:* Part-time, evening/weekend. Offers accounting (MPAC); business administration (MBA, PhD); finance (M Fin). Electronic applications accepted.

Graduate School of Education Offers applied behavior analysis (M Ed); diversity and equity (M Ed); education policy analysis and leadership (PhD); education specialist (Credential); education, society, and culture (MA, PhD); educational psychology (MA, PhD); general education (M Ed); higher education administration and policy (M Ed, PhD); multiple subject (Credential); research, evaluation, measurement and statistics (MA); school psychology (PhD); single subject (Credential); special education (M Ed, PhD); special education and autism (MA); TESOL (M Ed). Electronic applications accepted.

School of Public Policy Offers global health (MS); public policy (MPP, PhD). MD/MPP offered in partnership with School of Medicine.

School of Medicine Offers medicine (MD).

UNIVERSITY OF CALIFORNIA, SAN DIEGO, La Jolla, CA 92093

General Information State-supported, coed, university. CGS member. *Enrollment:* 5,577 full-time matriculated graduate/professional students (2,012 women), 356 part-time matriculated graduate/professional students (140 women). *Enrollment by degree level:* 2,507 master's, 3,426 doctoral. *Graduate housing:* Rooms and/or apartments available on a first-come, first-served basis to single and married students. *Student services:* Campus employment opportunities, campus safety program, career counseling, child daycare facilities, exercise/wellness program, free psychological counseling, grant writing training, international student services, low-cost health insurance, multicultural affairs office, services for students with disabilities, teacher training, writing training. *Library facilities:* Geisel Library plus 1 other. *Collection:* Books: 3.5 million (physical), 958,000 (digital/electronic). Study areas open 24 hours, 5–7 days a week; students can reserve study rooms.

Computer facilities: A campuswide network can be accessed from student residence rooms and from off campus. Online class registration is available. Website: http://www.ucsd.edu/

General Application Contact: Graduate Admissions Office, 858-534-3554, E-mail: gradadmissions@ucsd.edu.

GRADUATE UNITS

Graduate Division Students: 5,577 full-time (2,012 women), 356 part-time (140 women); includes 1,744 minority (88 Black or African American, non-Hispanic/Latino; 12 American Indian or Alaska Native, non-Hispanic/Latino; 691 Asian, non-Hispanic/Latino; 518 Hispanic/Latino; 1 Native Hawaiian or other Pacific Islander, non-Hispanic/Latino; 434 Two or more races, non-Hispanic/Latino), 3,205 international. 23,217 applicants, 28% accepted, 2513 enrolled. Expenses: Contact institution. *Financial support:* Fellowships with tuition reimbursements, research assistantships with tuition reimbursements, teaching assistantships with partial tuition reimbursements, career-related internships or fieldwork, institutionally sponsored loans, scholarships/grants, traineeships, health care benefits, and unspecified assistantships available. Support available to part-time students. Financial award applicants required to submit FAFSA. In 2018, 1,857 master's, 522 doctorates awarded. Offers acting (MFA); aerospace engineering (MS, PhD); anthropology (MA); applied mathematics (MA); applied mechanics (MS, PhD); applied ocean science (MS, PhD); applied physics (MS, PhD); architecture-based enterprise systems engineering (MAS); art history, theory, and criticism (PhD); bioengineering (M Eng, MS, PhD); bioinformatics and systems biology (PhD); biophysics (PhD); chemical engineering (MS, PhD); chemistry (MS, PhD); climate science and policy (MAS); clinical psychology (PhD); cognitive science (PhD); communication (PhD); communication of science (PhD); communication theory and systems (MS, PhD); computational neuroscience (PhD); computational science (PhD); computational science, mathematics and engineering (MS); computer engineering (MS, PhD); computer science (MS, PhD); contemporary music performance (DMA); dance theatre (MFA); data science and engineering (MAS); design (MFA); directing (MFA); drama and theatre (PhD); earth sciences (PhD); economics (PhD); education (M Ed, PhD); educational leadership (Ed D); electronic circuits and systems (MS, PhD); engineering physics (MS, PhD); engineering sciences (PhD); epidemiology (PhD); ethnic studies (PhD); geophysics (PhD); global health (PhD); health behavior (PhD); history (MA, PhD); history of science (PhD); intelligent systems, robotics and control (MS, PhD); Judaic studies (MA); language and communicative disorders (PhD); Latin American studies (MA); linguistics (PhD); literature (PhD); marine biodiversity and conservation (MAS); materials science and engineering (MS, PhD); mathematics (MA, PhD); mathematics and science education (PhD); mechanical engineering (MS, PhD); medical devices and systems (MS, PhD); multi-scale biology (PhD); music (MA, PhD); nanoengineering (MS, PhD); nanoscale devices and systems (PhD); oceanography (MS, PhD); philosophy (PhD); philosophy of science (PhD); photonics (MS, PhD); physics (MS, PhD); playwriting (MFA); political science (PhD); political science and international affairs (PhD); psychology (PhD); quantitative biology (PhD); signal and image processing (MS, PhD); sociology (PhD); sociology of science (PhD); stage management (MFA); statistics (MS, PhD); structural engineering (MS, PhD); structural health monitoring, prognosis, and validated simulations (MS); teaching and learning (MA, Ed D); visual arts (MFA); wireless embedded systems (MAS); writing (MFA). *Application fee:* $105 ($125 for international students). Electronic applications accepted. *Application Contact:* Graduate Admissions, 858-534-3554, E-mail: gradadmissions@ucsd.edu. *Dean,* Dr. James Antony, 858-534-6655, E-mail: graduatedean@ucsd.edu.

Division of Biological Sciences Students: 369 full-time (192 women), 7 part-time (2 women); includes 159 minority (5 Black or African American, non-Hispanic/Latino; 1 American Indian or Alaska Native, non-Hispanic/Latino; 91 Asian, non-Hispanic/Latino; 37 Hispanic/Latino; 25 Two or more races, non-Hispanic/Latino), 100 international. 705 applicants, 27% accepted, 125 enrolled. Expenses: Contact institution. *Financial support:* Fellowships with full tuition reimbursements, research assistantships with full tuition reimbursements, teaching assistantships with full tuition reimbursements, scholarships/grants, traineeships, and unspecified assistantships available. Financial award applicants required to submit FAFSA. In 2018, 24 doctorates awarded. Offers anthropogeny (PhD); bioinformatics (PhD); biology (PhD); interdisciplinary environmental research (PhD); multi-scale biology (PhD); quantitative biology (PhD). PhD in biology offered jointly with San Diego State University. *Application deadline:* For fall admission, 6/7 for domestic students. *Application fee:* $105 ($125 for international students). Electronic applications accepted. *Application Contact:* Melody Bayzar, Program Coordinator, 858-534-0181, E-mail: biogradprog@ucsd.edu. *Chair,* Andrew Chisholm, 858-534-7783.

Rady School of Management Students: 452 full-time (206 women), 158 part-time (91 women). 2,403 applicants, 34% accepted, 336 enrolled. *Faculty:* 28 full-time (5 women), 5 part-time/adjunct (1 woman). Expenses: Contact institution. *Financial support:* Fellowships, teaching assistantships, and scholarships/grants available. Financial award applicants required to submit FAFSA. In 2018, 297 master's, 3 doctorates awarded. *Program availability:* Part-time, evening/weekend. Offers business administration (MBA); business analytics (MF); finance (MF); management (PhD). *Application deadline:* Applications are processed on a rolling basis. *Application fee:* $200. Electronic applications accepted. *Application Contact:* Jay Bryant, Director of Graduate Recruitment and Admissions, 858-534-0864, E-mail: radygradadmissions@ucsd.edu. *Dean,* Robert Sullivan, 858-822-0830, E-mail: rssullivan@ucsd.edu.

School of Global Policy and Strategy *Program availability:* Part-time. Offers American policy in global context (MPP); business, government and regulation (MPP); Chinese economic and political affairs (MCEPA); energy and environmental policy (MPP); health policy (MPP); international affairs (MAS, MIA); international development and nonprofit management (MIA); international economics (MIA); international environmental policy (MIA); international management (MIA); international politics (MIA); political science and international affairs (PhD); program design and evaluation (MPP); public policy (MPP). Electronic applications accepted.

School of Medicine Students: 504. Expenses: Contact institution. Offers anthropogeny (PhD); audiology (Au D); bioinformatics (PhD); biomedical science (PhD); biostatistics (PhD); clinical research (MAS); leadership of healthcare organizations (MAS); medicine (MAS, Au D, MD, PhD); multi-scale biology (PhD); neurosciences (PhD). *Application Contact:* 858-534-3880, E-mail: somadmissions@ucsd.edu. *Associate Dean for Admissions,* Dr. Carolyn J. Kelly, MD.

Skaggs School of Pharmacy and Pharmaceutical Sciences Students: 254. Expenses: Contact institution. Offers pharmacy and pharmaceutical sciences (Pharm D). *Application Contact:* Dr. James McKerrow, Dean, 858-822-7801. *Dean,* Dr. James McKerrow, 858-822-7801.

UNIVERSITY OF CALIFORNIA, SAN FRANCISCO, San Francisco, CA 94143

General Information State-supported, coed, graduate-only institution. CGS member. *Graduate housing:* Rooms and/or apartments available to single and married students.

GRADUATE UNITS

Graduate Division *Program availability:* Part-time. Offers biochemistry and molecular biology (PhD); bioengineering (PhD); biomedical imaging (MS); biomedical sciences (PhD); cell biology (PhD); developmental biology (PhD); genetics (PhD); health policy and law (MS); history of health sciences (MA, PhD); medical anthropology (PhD); neuroscience (PhD); oral and craniofacial sciences (MS, PhD); physical therapy (DPT, DPTSc).

School of Nursing Offers nursing (MS, PhD); sociology (PhD).

School of Dentistry Offers dentistry (DDS).

School of Medicine Offers medicine (MD, PhD). Electronic applications accepted.

School of Pharmacy Offers bioinformatics (PhD); biophysics (PhD); chemistry and chemical biology (PhD); pharmaceutical sciences and pharmacogenomics (PhD); pharmacy (MS, PhD, Pharm D). Electronic applications accepted.

UNIVERSITY OF CALIFORNIA, SANTA BARBARA, Santa Barbara, CA 93106-2014

General Information State-supported, coed, university. CGS member. *Graduate housing:* Rooms and/or apartments guaranteed to single students and available on a first-come, first-served basis to married students. Housing application deadline: 6/1. *Research affiliation:* National Center for Ecological Analysis and Synthesis, The Institute for Collaborative Biotechnologies, Institute for Polymers and Organic Solids, Mitsubishi Chemical Center for Advanced Materials, California NanoSystems Institute, The Institute for Social, Behavioral and Economic Research.

GRADUATE UNITS

Graduate Division Electronic applications accepted.

College of Engineering Offers bioengineering (PhD); chemical engineering (MS, PhD); communications, control and signal processing (MS, PhD); computer engineering (MS, PhD); computer science (MS, PhD); electronics and photonics (MS, PhD); engineering (MS, MTM, PhD); materials (MS, PhD); mechanical engineering (MS); technology management (MTM). Electronic applications accepted.

College of Letters and Sciences Offers ancient history (PhD); ancient Mediterranean studies (PhD); applied linguistics (PhD); applied mathematics (MA); art (MFA); art history (PhD); astrophysics (PhD); biochemistry and molecular biology (PhD); bioengineering (PhD); brass (MM); chemistry (MA, MS, PhD); classics (MA, PhD); cognitive science (PhD); communication (PhD); comparative literature (PhD); composition (MA, PhD); conducting (MM, DMA); dynamical neuroscience (PhD); earth science (MS, PhD); East Asian languages and cultural studies (MA); East Asian literatures (PhD); ecology, evolution, and marine biology (MA, PhD); economics (MA); English (PhD); ethnomusicology (MA, PhD); European medieval studies (PhD); feminist studies (PhD); film and media studies (PhD); financial mathematics and statistics (PhD); French (PhD); geography (MA, PhD); global culture, ideology, and religion (MA, PhD); global government, human rights, and civil society (MA, PhD); global studies (PhD); Hispanic languages and literatures (PhD); Hispanic linguistics (MA); humanities and fine arts (MA, MFA, MM, MS, DMA, PhD); interdisciplinary emphasis: Black studies (PhD); interdisciplinary emphasis: environment and society (PhD); interdisciplinary emphasis: feminist studies (PhD); interdisciplinary emphasis: global studies (PhD); interdisciplinary emphasis: language, interaction and social organization (PhD); interdisciplinary emphasis: quantitative methods in the social sciences (PhD); interdisciplinary emphasis: technology and society (PhD); keyboard (MM, DMA); language, interaction and social organization (PhD); Latin American and

Iberian studies (MA); letters and sciences (MA, MFA, MM, MS, DMA, PhD); linguistics (PhD); literature and theory (MA); Luso-Brazilian literature (MA); marine science (MS, PhD); mathematical economics (PhD); mathematics (MA, PhD); mathematics, life, and physical sciences (MA, MS, PhD); media arts and technology (MS, PhD); molecular, cellular, and developmental biology (MA, PhD); musicology (MA, PhD); philosophy (PhD); physics (PhD); piano accompanying (MM); political economy, sustainable development, and the environment (MA, PhD); political science (PhD); psychology (PhD); public finance (PhD); public historical studies (PhD); quantitative methods in the social sciences (PhD); religious studies (MA, PhD); social sciences (MA, PhD); society and technology (PhD); sociocultural anthropology (PhD); sociology (PhD); Spanish or Spanish-American literature (MA); statistics (MA); statistics and applied probability (PhD); strings (MM, DMA); technology and society (PhD); theater studies (MA, PhD); theory (MA, PhD); translation studies (PhD); transportation (PhD); voice (MM, DMA); women's studies (PhD); woodwinds (MM). Electronic applications accepted.

Donald Bren School of Environmental Science and Management Offers economics and environmental science (PhD); environmental science and management (MESM, PhD); technology and society (PhD). Electronic applications accepted.

Gevirtz Graduate School of Education Offers counseling, clinical and school psychology (MA, PhD, Credential); education (MA, PhD); teacher education (M Ed, Credential). Electronic applications accepted.

UNIVERSITY OF CALIFORNIA, SANTA CRUZ, Santa Cruz, CA 95064

General Information State-supported, coed, university. CGS member. *Graduate housing:* Rooms and/or apartments available on a first-come, first-served basis to single and married students. Housing application deadline: 5/20. *Research affiliation:* Center for Biomimetic MicroElectronic Systems (science and engineering), Center for Information Technology Research in the Interest of Society (science and engineering), Institute for Regenerative Medicine (science and engineering), Center for Adaptive Optics (science and engineering), Center for Biomolecular Science and Engineering (science and engineering), Institute for Quantitative Biology (science and engineering).

GRADUATE UNITS

Division of Graduate Studies Electronic applications accepted.

Division of Humanities Offers history (MA, PhD); history of consciousness (PhD); humanities (MA, PhD); linguistics (MA, PhD); literature (MA, PhD); philosophy (MA, PhD). Electronic applications accepted.

Division of Physical and Biological Sciences Offers astronomy and astrophysics (PhD); chemistry and biochemistry (MS, PhD); earth and planetary sciences (MS, PhD); ecology and evolutionary biology (MA, PhD); mathematics (MA, PhD); microbiology and environmental toxicology (MS, PhD); molecular, cellular, and developmental biology (MA, PhD); ocean sciences (MS, PhD); physical and biological sciences (MA, MS, PhD, Certificate); physics (MS, PhD); science communication (Certificate). Electronic applications accepted.

Division of Social Sciences Offers applied economics and finance (MS); cultural anthropology (PhD); education (MA, PhD); environmental studies (PhD); international economics (PhD); politics (PhD); psychology (PhD); social documentation (MA); social sciences (MA, MS, PhD); sociology (PhD). Electronic applications accepted.

Division of the Arts Offers arts (MA, MFA, DMA, PhD, Certificate); digital arts and new media (MFA); ethnomusicology (MA); film and digital media (PhD); music (PhD); music composition (MA, DMA); music composition (DMA); performance practice (MA); theater arts (Certificate); visual studies (PhD). Electronic applications accepted.

Jack Baskin School of Engineering *Program availability:* Part-time. Offers biomolecular engineering and bioinformatics (MS, PhD); computational media (MS, PhD); computer engineering (MS, PhD); computer science (MS, PhD); electrical engineering (MS, PhD); engineering (MS, PhD); games and playable media (MS); scientific computing and applied mathematics (MS); statistics and applied mathematics (MS, PhD). Electronic applications accepted.

UNIVERSITY OF CENTRAL ARKANSAS, Conway, AR 72035-0001

General Information State-supported, coed, university. CGS member. *Graduate housing:* Rooms and/or apartments available on a first-come, first-served basis to single and married students. Housing application deadline: 7/1. *Research affiliation:* 3M Corporation, State Farm Foundation (insurance), Arkansas Game and Fish Commission, Acxiom (math, computers), Arkansas Educational Television Network.

GRADUATE UNITS

Graduate School *Program availability:* Part-time, evening/weekend, online learning. Offers leadership studies (PhD).

College of Business Administration *Program availability:* Part-time, evening/weekend. Offers accounting (M Acc); business administration (M Acc, MBA).

College of Education *Program availability:* Part-time, evening/weekend, online learning. Offers collaborative instructional specialist (ages 0-8) (MSE); collaborative instructional specialist (grades 4-12) (MSE); college student personnel (MS); district-level administration (PMC); education (MAT, MS, MSE, Ed S, Graduate Certificate, PMC); educational leadership - district level (Ed S); gifted and talented education (Graduate Certificate); instructional facilitator (Graduate Certificate); instructional technology (MS); library media and information technology (MS); reading education (MSE); school counseling (MS); school leadership (MS); school-based leadership adult education program administration (PMC); school-based leadership building administration (PMC); school-based leadership curriculum administration (PMC); school-based leadership gifted and talented program administration (PMC); school-based leadership special education program administration (PMC); special education (MSE, Graduate Certificate); special education instructional specialist grades 4-12 (Graduate Certificate); special education instructional specialist P-4 (Graduate Certificate); teaching (MAT); teaching and learning (MSE). Electronic applications accepted.

College of Fine Arts and Communication *Program availability:* Part-time. Offers choral conducting (MM); creative writing (MFA); digital filmmaking (MFA); fine arts and communication (MFA, MM, PC); instrumental conducting (MM); music (PC); music education (MM); music theory (MM); performance (MM). Electronic applications accepted.

College of Health and Behavioral Sciences *Program availability:* Part-time, evening/weekend, online learning. Offers adult nurse practitioner (PMC); clinical nurse leader (PMC); clinical nurse specialist (MSN); communication sciences and disorders (PhD); community counseling (MS); counseling psychology (MS); family and consumer sciences (MS); family nurse practitioner (PMC); health and behavioral sciences (MS, MSN, DPT, PhD, PMC); health education (MS); kinesiology (MS); nurse educator (PMC); nurse practitioner (MSN); nutrition (MS); occupational therapy (MS); physical therapy (DPT, PhD); school psychology (MS, PhD, PMC); speech-language pathology (MS). Electronic applications accepted.

College of Liberal Arts *Program availability:* Part-time. Offers English (MA); history (MA); liberal arts (MA); Spanish (MA). Electronic applications accepted.

College of Natural Sciences and Math *Program availability:* Part-time. Offers applied computing (MS); applied mathematics (MS); biological science (MS); community and economic development (MS); geographic information systems (MGIS, Certificate); math education (MA); natural sciences and math (MA, MGIS, MS, Certificate). Electronic applications accepted.

UNIVERSITY OF CENTRAL FLORIDA, Orlando, FL 32816

General Information State-supported, coed, university. CGS member. *Graduate housing:* Room and/or apartments available on a first-come, first-served basis to single students; on-campus housing not available to married students. Housing application deadline: 3/1.

GRADUATE UNITS

College of Arts and Humanities Students: 194 full-time (105 women), 185 part-time (117 women); includes 106 minority (20 Black or African American, non-Hispanic/Latino; 1 American Indian or Alaska Native, non-Hispanic/Latino; 10 Asian, non-Hispanic/Latino; 70 Hispanic/Latino; 5 Two or more races, non-Hispanic/Latino), 15 international. Average age 33. 338 applicants, 63% accepted, 119 enrolled. *Faculty:* 293 full-time (148 women), 90 part-time/adjunct (44 women). Expenses: Contact institution. *Financial support:* In 2018–19, 130 students received support, including 32 fellowships with partial tuition reimbursements available (averaging $7,875 per year), 36 research assistantships with partial tuition reimbursements available (averaging $7,650 per year), 99 teaching assistantships with partial tuition reimbursements available (averaging $8,543 per year); career-related internships or fieldwork, Federal Work-Study, institutionally sponsored loans, scholarships/grants, health care benefits, tuition waivers (partial), and unspecified assistantships also available. Financial award application deadline: 3/1; financial award applicants required to submit FAFSA. In 2018, 78 master's, 8 doctorates, 31 other advanced degrees awarded. *Program availability:* Part-time, evening/weekend. Offers arts and humanities (MA, MFA, MS, PhD, Certificate); English (MA, MFA, PhD, Certificate); history (MA); Spanish (MA); teaching English to speakers of other languages (MA, Certificate). *Application fee:* $30. Electronic applications accepted. *Application Contact:* Associate Director, Graduate Admissions, 407-823-2766, Fax: 407-823-6442, E-mail: gradadmissions@ucf.edu. *Dean,* Jeffrey Moore, 407-823-2573, E-mail: jeffrey.moore@ucf.edu.

School of Performing Arts Students: 37 full-time (18 women), 28 part-time (9 women); includes 12 minority (4 Black or African American, non-Hispanic/Latino; 1 Asian, non-Hispanic/Latino; 5 Hispanic/Latino; 2 Two or more races, non-Hispanic/Latino), 2 international. Average age 32. 63 applicants, 48% accepted, 16 enrolled. Expenses: Contact institution. *Financial support:* In 2018–19, 33 students received support, including 6 fellowships with partial tuition reimbursements available (averaging $8,333 per year), 10 research assistantships with partial tuition reimbursements available (averaging $7,267 per year), 23 teaching assistantships with partial tuition reimbursements available (averaging $8,152 per year); career-related internships or fieldwork, Federal Work-Study, institutionally sponsored loans, health care benefits, tuition waivers (partial), and unspecified assistantships also available. Financial award application deadline: 3/1; financial award applicants required to submit FAFSA. In 2018, 15 master's awarded. *Program availability:* Part-time. Offers music (MA); theatre (MA, MFA). *Application deadline:* For fall admission, 7/15 for domestic students; for spring admission, 12/1 for domestic students. *Application fee:* $30. Electronic applications accepted. *Application Contact:* Associate Director, Graduate Admissions, 407-823-2766, Fax: 407-823-6442, E-mail: gradadmissions@ucf.edu. *Director,* Dr. Michael Wainstein, 407-823-2519, Fax: 407-823-3378, E-mail: michael.wainstein@ucf.edu.

School of Visual Arts and Design Students: 24 full-time (11 women), 5 part-time (3 women); includes 12 minority (3 Black or African American, non-Hispanic/Latino; 1 Asian, non-Hispanic/Latino; 8 Hispanic/Latino), 3 international. Average age 32. 45 applicants, 64% accepted, 13 enrolled. Expenses: Contact institution. *Financial support:* In 2018–19, 14 students received support, including 7 fellowships with partial tuition reimbursements available (averaging $9,286 per year), 2 research assistantships with partial tuition reimbursements available (averaging $9,122 per year), 12 teaching assistantships with partial tuition reimbursements available (averaging $8,253 per year); scholarships/grants, health care benefits, and unspecified assistantships also available. Financial award application deadline: 3/1; financial award applicants required to submit FAFSA. In 2018, 7 master's awarded. *Program availability:* Part-time. Offers digital media (MA); emerging media (MFA). *Application deadline:* For fall admission, 7/1 for domestic students. *Application fee:* $30. Electronic applications accepted. *Application Contact:* Associate Director, Graduate Admissions, 407-823-2766, Fax: 407-823-6442, E-mail: gradadmissions@ucf.edu. *Director,* Dr. Rudy McDaniel, 407-823-3145, E-mail: rudy@ucf.edu.

College of Business Administration Students: 288 full-time (136 women), 685 part-time (328 women); includes 408 minority (104 Black or African American, non-Hispanic/Latino; 75 Asian, non-Hispanic/Latino; 209 Hispanic/Latino; 20 Two or more races, non-Hispanic/Latino), 46 international. Average age 30. 884 applicants, 53% accepted, 378 enrolled. *Faculty:* 136 full-time (36 women), 24 part-time/adjunct (9 women). Expenses: Contact institution. *Financial support:* In 2018–19, 112 students received support, including 6 fellowships with partial tuition reimbursements available (averaging $8,167 per year), 43 research assistantships with partial tuition reimbursements available (averaging $8,304 per year), 86 teaching assistantships with partial tuition reimbursements available (averaging $11,193 per year); career-related internships or fieldwork, Federal Work-Study, institutionally sponsored loans, health care benefits, and tuition waivers (partial) also available. Financial award application deadline: 3/1; financial award applicants required to submit FAFSA. In 2018, 399 master's, 5 doctorates, 16 other advanced degrees awarded. *Program availability:* Part-time, evening/weekend. Offers business administration (MBA, MSA, MSBM, MSM, MSRE, PhD, Graduate Certificate); economics (MS, PhD); entrepreneurship (Graduate Certificate); management (MSM); sport business management (MSBM); technology ventures (Graduate Certificate). *Application fee:* $30. Electronic applications accepted. *Application Contact:* Associate Director, Graduate Admissions, 407-823-2766, Fax: 407-823-6442, E-mail: gradadmissions@ucf.edu. *Dean,* Dr. Paul Jarley, 407-823-5133, E-mail: pjarley@bus.ucf.edu.

Dr. P. Phillips School of Real Estate Students: 9 part-time (2 women); includes 4 minority (1 Black or African American, non-Hispanic/Latino; 1 Asian, non-Hispanic/Latino; 1 Hispanic/Latino; 1 Two or more races, non-Hispanic/Latino). Average age 29. Expenses: Contact institution. *Financial support:* Application deadline: 3/1; applicants required to submit FAFSA. In 2018, 1 master's awarded. *Program availability:* Part-time. Offers real estate (MSRE). *Application deadline:* For fall admission, 7/1 for domestic students. *Application fee:* $30. Electronic applications accepted. *Application Contact:* Associate Director, Graduate Admissions, 407-823-2766, Fax: 407-823-6442, E-mail: gradadmissions@ucf.edu. *Chair and Director,* Dr. Ajai Singh, 407-823-5756, Fax: 407-823-6676, E-mail: ajai.singh@ucf.edu.

Kenneth G. Dixon School of Accounting Students: 89 full-time (42 women), 47 part-time (27 women); includes 51 minority (7 Black or African American, non-Hispanic/Latino; 16 Asian, non-Hispanic/Latino; 24 Hispanic/Latino; 4 Two or more races, non-Hispanic/Latino), 5 international. Average age 27. 91 applicants, 53% accepted, 37 enrolled. Expenses: Contact institution. *Financial support:* In 2018–19, 21 students received support, including 21 teaching assistantships with partial tuition reimbursements available (averaging $8,625 per year); career-related internships or fieldwork, Federal Work-Study, institutionally sponsored loans, health care benefits, tuition waivers (partial), and unspecified assistantships also available. Financial award application deadline: 3/1; financial award applicants required to submit FAFSA. In 2018, 89 master's awarded. *Program availability:* Part-time, evening/weekend. Offers accounting (MSA). *Application deadline:* For fall admission, 7/15 for domestic students; for spring admission, 12/1 for domestic students; for summer admission, 4/15 for domestic students. *Application fee:* $30. Electronic applications accepted. *Application Contact:* Associate Director, Graduate Admissions, 407-823-2766, Fax: 407-823-6442, E-mail: gradadmissions@ucf.edu. *Director,* Dr. Gregory Trompeter, 407-823-2876, Fax: 407-823-3881, E-mail: trompete@ucf.edu.

College of Community Innovation and Education *Program availability:* Part-time, evening/weekend. Offers applied learning and instruction (MA); career and technical education (MA); career counseling (Certificate); community innovation and education (M Ed, MA, MAT, MHA, MNM, MPA, MRA, MS, Ed D, PhD, Certificate, Ed S); corrections leadership (Certificate); counselor education (MA, Ed S); criminal justice (MS, PhD); curriculum and instruction (M Ed); e-learning (Certificate); educational leadership (M Ed, MA, Ed S); educational technology (Certificate); gifted education (M Ed, Graduate Certificate); health administration (MHA); health care informatics (MS); health information administration (Certificate); higher education/college teaching and leadership (MA); higher education/student personnel (MA); instructional design (Certificate); instructional design and technology (MA, Certificate); instructional design for simulations (Certificate); juvenile justice leadership (Certificate); marriage, couple, and family therapy (Certificate); methodology, measurement and analysis (Graduate Certificate); play therapy (Certificate); police leadership (Certificate); public affairs (PhD); school psychology (Ed S); sport and exercise science (MS). Electronic applications accepted.

School of Public Administration *Program availability:* Part-time, evening/weekend. Offers emergency management and homeland security (Certificate); fundraising (Certificate); nonprofit management (MNM, Certificate); public administration (MPA); research administration (MRA); urban and regional planning (MS). Electronic applications accepted.

School of Teacher Education *Program availability:* Part-time, evening/weekend. Offers applied learning and instruction (MA); autism spectrum disorders (Certificate); curriculum and instruction (M Ed, MA); elementary education (M Ed, MA); exceptional student education (M Ed, MA, Certificate); exceptional student education K-12 (MA); intervention specialist (Certificate); K-8 mathematics and science education (M Ed, Certificate); pre-kindergarten disabilities (Certificate); reading education (M Ed, Certificate); teacher education (M Ed, MA, MAT, Certificate); world languages education - English for speakers of other languages (ESOL) (Certificate); world languages education - languages other than English (LOTE) (Certificate). Electronic applications accepted.

College of Engineering and Computer Science Students: 953 full-time (215 women), 738 part-time (196 women); includes 456 minority (88 Black or African American, non-Hispanic/Latino; 2 American Indian or Alaska Native, non-Hispanic/Latino; 106 Asian, non-Hispanic/Latino; 241 Hispanic/Latino; 19 Two or more races, non-Hispanic/Latino), 648 international. Average age 30. 1,762 applicants, 61% accepted, 517 enrolled. *Faculty:* 205 full-time (31 women), 55 part-time/adjunct (4 women). Expenses: Contact institution. *Financial support:* In 2018–19, 599 students received support, including 182 fellowships with partial tuition reimbursements available (averaging $10,579 per year), 454 research assistantships with partial tuition reimbursements available (averaging $12,376 per year), 216 teaching assistantships with partial tuition reimbursements available (averaging $11,537 per year); career-related internships or fieldwork, Federal Work-Study, institutionally sponsored loans, tuition waivers (partial), and unspecified assistantships also available. Financial award application deadline: 3/1; financial award applicants required to submit FAFSA. In 2018, 401 master's, 100 doctorates, 23 other advanced degrees awarded. *Program availability:* Part-time, evening/weekend. Offers aerospace engineering (MSAE); civil engineering (MS, MSCE, PhD, Certificate); computer engineering (MS Cp E, PhD); computer science (MS, PhD); electrical engineering (MSEE, PhD); engineering and computer science (MS, MS Cp E, MS Env E, MSAE, MSCE, MSEE, MSEM, MSIE, MSME, MSMSE, PhD, Certificate); environmental engineering (MS, PhD); industrial engineering and management systems (MS, MSEM, MSIE, PhD, Certificate); materials science and engineering (MSMSE, PhD); mechanical and aerospace engineering (MSAE, MSME, PhD); mechanical engineering (MSME, PhD). *Application deadline:* For fall admission, 7/15 for domestic students; for spring admission, 12/1 for domestic students. *Application fee:* $30. Electronic applications accepted. *Application Contact:* Associate Director, Graduate Admissions, 407-823-2766, Fax: 407-823-6442, E-mail: gradadmissions@ucf.edu. *Dean,* Dr. Michael Georgiopoulos, 407-823-2156, E-mail: michaelg@ucf.edu.

College of Graduate Studies Students: 57 full-time (26 women), 74 part-time (38 women); includes 42 minority (10 Black or African American, non-Hispanic/Latino; 1 American Indian or Alaska Native, non-Hispanic/Latino; 12 Asian, non-Hispanic/Latino; 17 Hispanic/Latino; 2 Two or more races, non-Hispanic/Latino). Average age 31. 86 applicants, 80% accepted, 59 enrolled. *Faculty:* 4 full-time (2 women), 1 (woman) part-time/adjunct. Expenses: Contact institution. *Financial support:* In 2018–19, 12 students received support, including 6 fellowships with partial tuition reimbursements available (averaging $9,933 per year), 11 research assistantships with partial tuition reimbursements available (averaging $12,400 per year), 1 teaching assistantship with partial tuition reimbursement available (averaging $13,624 per year); health care benefits also available. Financial award application deadline: 3/1; financial award applicants required to submit FAFSA. In 2018, 21 master's, 16 other advanced degrees awarded. Offers interdisciplinary studies (MA); modeling and simulation (MS, PhD); modeling and simulation of behavioral cybersecurity (Certificate); modeling and simulation of technical systems (Certificate). *Application deadline:* For fall admission, 7/15 for domestic students; for spring admission, 12/1 for domestic students. *Application fee:* $30. Electronic applications accepted. *Application Contact:* Associate Director, Graduate Admissions, 407-823-2766, Fax: 407-823-6442, E-mail: gradadmissions@ucf.edu. *Vice President for Research/Dean, College of Graduate Studies,* Dr. Elizabeth Klonoff, 407-823-6432, Fax: 407-823-6442, E-mail: elizabeth.klonoff@ucf.edu.

College of Health Professions and Sciences Students: 468 full-time (391 women), 300 part-time (269 women); includes 299 minority (99 Black or African American, non-Hispanic/Latino; 2 American Indian or Alaska Native, non-Hispanic/Latino; 27 Asian, non-Hispanic/Latino; 155 Hispanic/Latino; 1 Native Hawaiian or other Pacific Islander, non-Hispanic/Latino; 15 Two or more races, non-Hispanic/Latino), 3 international. Average age 29. 692 applicants, 45% accepted, 151 enrolled. *Faculty:* 96 full-time (57 women), 81 part-time/adjunct (61 women). Expenses: Contact institution. *Financial support:* In 2018–19, 19 students received support, including 9 fellowships with partial tuition reimbursements available (averaging $3,400 per year), 6 research assistantships with partial tuition reimbursements available (averaging $5,639 per year), 9 teaching assistantships with partial tuition reimbursements available (averaging $7,355 per year); career-related internships or fieldwork, Federal Work-Study, institutionally sponsored loans, traineeships, health care benefits, tuition waivers (partial), and unspecified assistantships also available. Financial award application deadline: 3/1; financial award applicants required to submit FAFSA. In 2018, 236 master's, 32 doctorates, 8 other advanced degrees awarded. *Program availability:* Part-time, evening/weekend. Offers athletic training (MAT); health professions and sciences (MA, MAT, MHA, MNM, MRA, MS, MSW, DPT, PhD, Certificate); kinesiology (MS); physical therapy (DPT). *Application fee:* $30. Electronic applications accepted. *Application Contact:* Associate Director, Graduate Admissions, 407-823-2766, Fax: 407-823-6442, E-mail: gradadmissions@ucf.edu. *Interim Dean,* Dr. Jose Fernandez, 407-823-0171, E-mail: jose.fernandez@ucf.edu.

School of Communication Sciences and Disorders Students: 181 full-time (172 women), 1 (woman) part-time; includes 57 minority (8 Black or African American, non-Hispanic/Latino; 8 Asian, non-Hispanic/Latino; 36 Hispanic/Latino; 5 Two or more races, non-Hispanic/Latino), 2 international. Average age 25. 332 applicants, 33% accepted, 22 enrolled. Expenses: Contact institution. *Financial support:* In 2018–19, 13 students received support, including 4 fellowships with partial tuition reimbursements available (averaging $3,150 per year), 4 research assistantships with partial tuition reimbursements available (averaging $5,490 per year), 8 teaching assistantships with partial tuition reimbursements available (averaging $7,517 per year); career-related internships or fieldwork, Federal Work-Study, institutionally sponsored loans, and unspecified assistantships also available. Financial award application deadline: 3/1; financial award applicants required to submit FAFSA. In 2018, 93 master's awarded. *Program availability:* Part-time, evening/weekend. Offers communication sciences and disorders (MA, Certificate). *Application deadline:* For fall admission, 2/1 for domestic students; for spring admission, 10/1 for domestic students. *Application fee:* $30. Electronic applications accepted. *Application Contact:* Associate Director, Graduate Admissions, 407-823-2766, Fax: 407-823-6442, E-mail: gradadmissions@ucf.edu. *Program Coordinator,* Dr. Linda Rosa-Lugo, 407-823-4798, E-mail: csdgraduate@ucf.edu.

School of Kinesiology and Physical Therapy Students: 110 full-time (62 women), 1 (woman) part-time; includes 38 minority (4 Black or African American, non-Hispanic/Latino; 8 Asian, non-Hispanic/Latino; 25 Hispanic/Latino; 1 Two or more races, non-Hispanic/Latino), 1 international. Average age 25. 760 applicants, 8% accepted, 38 enrolled. Expenses: Contact institution. *Financial support:* In 2018–19, 5 students received support, including 4 fellowships (averaging $2,000 per year), 2 research assistantships (averaging $5,937 per year), 1 teaching assistantship (averaging $6,054 per year). *Application Contact:* Associate Director, Graduate Admissions, 407-823-2766, Fax: 407-823-6442, E-mail: gradadmissions@ucf.edu. *Interim Dean,* Dr. Jose Fernandez, 407-823-0171, E-mail: jose.fernandez@ucf.edu.

School of Social Work Students: 177 full-time (157 women), 298 part-time (267 women); includes 204 minority (87 Black or African American, non-Hispanic/Latino; 2 American Indian or Alaska Native, non-Hispanic/Latino; 11 Asian, non-Hispanic/Latino; 94 Hispanic/Latino; 1 Native Hawaiian or other Pacific Islander, non-Hispanic/Latino; 9 Two or more races, non-Hispanic/Latino). Average age 31. 359 applicants, 55% accepted, 128 enrolled. Expenses: Contact institution. *Financial support:* In 2018–19, 1 received support, including 1 fellowship (averaging $10,000 per year); career-related internships or fieldwork, institutionally sponsored loans, and unspecified assistantships also available. Financial award application deadline: 3/1; financial award applicants required to submit FAFSA. In 2018, 143 master's, 8 other advanced degrees awarded. *Program availability:* Part-time, evening/weekend. Offers military social work (Certificate); social work (MSW). *Application deadline:* For fall admission, 4/1 for domestic students. *Application fee:* $30. Electronic applications accepted. *Application Contact:* Associate Director, Graduate Admissions, 407-823-2766, Fax: 407-823-6442, E-mail: gradadmissions@ucf.edu. *Director,* Dr. Bonnie Yegidis, 407-823-2114, E-mail: bonnie.yegidis@ucf.edu.

College of Medicine Students: 131 full-time (79 women), 14 part-time (9 women); includes 55 minority (16 Black or African American, non-Hispanic/Latino; 8 Asian, non-Hispanic/Latino; 27 Hispanic/Latino; 4 Two or more races, non-Hispanic/Latino), 33 international. Average age 26. 281 applicants, 34% accepted, 51 enrolled. *Faculty:* 141 full-time (66 women), 27 part-time/adjunct (13 women). Expenses: Contact institution. *Financial support:* In 2018–19, 82 students received support, including 18 fellowships (averaging $14,005 per year), 79 research assistantships (averaging $9,003 per year), 53 teaching assistantships (averaging $7,707 per year). In 2018, 36 master's, 11 doctorates awarded. Offers medicine (MS, MD, PhD). *Application Contact:* Associate Director, Graduate Admissions, 407-823-2766, Fax: 407-823-6442, E-mail: gradadmissions@ucf.edu. *Vice President for Medical Affairs/Dean,* Dr. Deborah C. German, 407-266-1000, E-mail: deb@ucf.edu.

College of Nursing Students: 89 full-time (85 women), 320 part-time (280 women); includes 121 minority (35 Black or African American, non-Hispanic/Latino; 1 American Indian or Alaska Native, non-Hispanic/Latino; 23 Asian, non-Hispanic/Latino; 50 Hispanic/Latino; 12 Two or more races, non-Hispanic/Latino), 1 international. Average age 37. 191 applicants, 79% accepted, 107 enrolled. *Faculty:* 59 full-time (49 women), 87 part-time/adjunct (81 women). Expenses: Contact institution. *Financial support:* In 2018–19, 6 students received support, including 2 fellowships with partial tuition reimbursements available (averaging $7,431 per year), 2 research assistantships with partial tuition reimbursements available (averaging $13,010 per year), 2 teaching assistantships (averaging $12,650 per year); career-related internships or fieldwork, Federal Work-Study, institutionally sponsored loans, traineeships, and unspecified assistantships also available. Financial award application deadline: 3/1; financial award applicants required to submit FAFSA. In 2018, 101 master's, 14 doctorates, 16 other advanced degrees awarded. *Program availability:* Part-time, evening/weekend. Offers nursing (MSN, DNP, PhD, Certificate, Post-Master's Certificate). *Application deadline:* For fall admission, 3/15 for domestic students; for spring admission, 10/15 for domestic students. *Application fee:* $30. Electronic applications accepted. *Application Contact:* Associate Director, Graduate Admissions, 407-823-2766, Fax: 407-823-6442, E-mail: gradadmissions@ucf.edu. *Dean,* Dr. Mary Lou Sole, 407-823-5496, Fax: 407-823-5675, E-mail: mary.sole@ucf.edu.

College of Optics and Photonics Students: 121 full-time (28 women), 21 part-time (2 women); includes 14 minority (1 Black or African American, non-Hispanic/Latino; 4 Asian, non-Hispanic/Latino; 8 Hispanic/Latino; 1 Two or more races, non-

Hispanic/Latino), 90 international. Average age 28. 167 applicants, 43% accepted, 27 enrolled. *Faculty:* 41 full-time (3 women), 9 part-time/adjunct (1 woman). Expenses: Contact institution. *Financial support:* In 2018–19, 116 students received support, including 25 fellowships with partial tuition reimbursements available (averaging $22,304 per year), 106 research assistantships with partial tuition reimbursements available (averaging $15,182 per year), 9 teaching assistantships with partial tuition reimbursements available (averaging $14,404 per year); career-related internships or fieldwork, Federal Work-Study, institutionally sponsored loans, health care benefits, tuition waivers (partial), and unspecified assistantships also available. Financial award application deadline: 3/1; financial award applicants required to submit FAFSA. In 2018, 21 master's, 12 doctorates awarded. *Program availability:* Part-time, evening/weekend. Offers optics and photonics (MS, PhD). *Application deadline:* For fall admission, 7/15 for domestic students; for spring admission, 12/1 for domestic students. *Application fee:* $30. Electronic applications accepted. *Application Contact:* Associate Director, Graduate Admissions, 407-823-2766, Fax: 407-823-6442, E-mail: gradadmissions@ucf.edu. *Dean and Director,* Dr. Bahaa E. Saleh, 407-823-6817, E-mail: besaleh@creol.ucf.edu.

College of Sciences Students: 570 full-time (280 women), 116 part-time (62 women); includes 178 minority (42 Black or African American, non-Hispanic/Latino; 1 American Indian or Alaska Native, non-Hispanic/Latino; 42 Asian, non-Hispanic/Latino; 81 Hispanic/Latino; 12 Two or more races, non-Hispanic/Latino), 148 international. Average age 30. 982 applicants, 42% accepted, 197 enrolled. *Faculty:* 317 full-time (106 women), 41 part-time/adjunct (13 women). Expenses: Contact institution. *Financial support:* In 2018–19, 452 students received support, including 99 fellowships with partial tuition reimbursements available (averaging $8,537 per year), 197 research assistantships with partial tuition reimbursements available (averaging $9,056 per year), 373 teaching assistantships with partial tuition reimbursements available (averaging $12,411 per year); health care benefits also available. Financial award application deadline: 3/1; financial award applicants required to submit FAFSA. In 2018, 135 master's, 48 doctorates, 16 other advanced degrees awarded. Offers anthropology (MA); chemistry (MS, PhD, Certificate); clinical psychology (MA, PhD); conservation biology (Certificate); human factors and cognitive psychology (PhD); industrial/organizational psychology (MS, PhD); mathematics (MS, PhD, Certificate); physics (MS, PhD); sciences (MA, MS, PhD, Certificate); sociology (MA, PhD). *Application fee:* $30. Electronic applications accepted. *Application Contact:* Associate Director, Graduate Admissions, 407-823-2766, Fax: 407-823-6442, E-mail: gradadmissions@ucf.edu. *Dean,* Dr. Michael Johnson, 407-823-1911, E-mail: michael.johnson@ucf.edu.

School of Policy, Security, and International Affairs Students: 44 full-time (17 women), 19 part-time (10 women); includes 10 minority (3 Black or African American, non-Hispanic/Latino; 1 Asian, non-Hispanic/Latino; 6 Hispanic/Latino), 15 international. Average age 31. 45 applicants, 76% accepted, 19 enrolled. Expenses: Contact institution. *Financial support:* In 2018–19, 26 students received support, including 8 fellowships (averaging $6,900 per year), 2 research assistantships (averaging $12,195 per year), 26 teaching assistantships (averaging $10,940 per year). *Application Contact:* Associate Director, Graduate Admissions, 407-823-2766, Fax: 407-823-6442, E-mail: gradadmissions@ucf.edu. *Dean,* Dr. Michael Johnson, 407-823-1911, E-mail: michael.johnson@ucf.edu.

Nicholson School of Communication and Media Students: 116 full-time (54 women), 101 part-time (41 women); includes 70 minority (13 Black or African American, non-Hispanic/Latino; 11 Asian, non-Hispanic/Latino; 42 Hispanic/Latino; 4 Two or more races, non-Hispanic/Latino), 29 international. Average age 27. 215 applicants, 66% accepted, 95 enrolled. *Faculty:* 92 full-time (37 women), 18 part-time/adjunct (9 women). Expenses: Contact institution. *Financial support:* In 2018–19, 30 students received support, including 6 fellowships (averaging $3,833 per year), 5 research assistantships (averaging $7,724 per year), 29 teaching assistantships (averaging $7,898 per year). *Application Contact:* Associate Director, Graduate Admissions, 407-823-2766, Fax: 407-823-6442, E-mail: gradadmissions@ucf.edu.

Rosen College of Hospitality Management Students: 82 full-time (53 women), 168 part-time (113 women); includes 70 minority (30 Black or African American, non-Hispanic/Latino; 1 American Indian or Alaska Native, non-Hispanic/Latino; 8 Asian, non-Hispanic/Latino; 27 Hispanic/Latino; 4 Two or more races, non-Hispanic/Latino), 40 international. Average age 30. 226 applicants, 64% accepted, 92 enrolled. *Faculty:* 71 full-time (27 women), 26 part-time/adjunct (10 women). Expenses: Contact institution. *Financial support:* In 2018–19, 36 students received support, including 17 fellowships with partial tuition reimbursements available (averaging $14,760 per year), 1 research assistantship with partial tuition reimbursement available (averaging $9,882 per year), 26 teaching assistantships with partial tuition reimbursements available (averaging $11,242 per year); health care benefits also available. Financial award application deadline: 3/1; financial award applicants required to submit FAFSA. In 2018, 58 master's, 2 doctorates, 44 other advanced degrees awarded. *Program availability:* Part-time. Offers destination marketing and management (Certificate); event management (Certificate); hospitality and tourism management (MS); hospitality management (PhD). *Application deadline:* For fall admission, 7/15 for domestic students; for spring admission, 12/1 for domestic students. *Application fee:* $30. Electronic applications accepted. *Application Contact:* Associate Director, Graduate Admissions, 407-823-2766, Fax: 407-823-6442, E-mail: gradadmissions@ucf.edu. *Dean,* Dr. Abraham C. Pizam, 407-903-8010, E-mail: abraham.pizam@ucf.edu.

UNIVERSITY OF CENTRAL MISSOURI, Warrensburg, MO 64093

General Information State-supported, coed, comprehensive institution. CGS member. *Graduate housing:* Rooms and/or apartments available on a first-come, first-served basis to single and married students. Housing application deadline: 5/1.

GRADUATE UNITS

The Graduate School *Program availability:* Part-time, 100% online, blended/hybrid learning. Offers accountancy (MA); accounting (MBA); applied mathematics (MS); aviation safety (MS); biology (MS); business administration (MBA); career and technical education leadership (MS); college student personnel administration (MS); communication (MA); computer science (MS); counseling (MS); criminal justice (MS); educational leadership (Ed D); educational technology (MS); elementary and early childhood education (MSE); English (MA); environmental studies (MA); finance (MBA); history (MA); human services/educational technology (Ed S); human services/learning resources (Ed S); human services/professional counseling (Ed S); industrial hygiene (MS); industrial management (MS); information systems (MBA); information technology (MS); kinesiology (MS); library science and information services (MS); literacy education (MSE); marketing (MBA); mathematics (MS); music (MA); occupational safety management (MS); psychology (MS); rural family nursing (MS); school administration (MSE); social gerontology (MS); sociology (MA); special education (MSE); speech language pathology (MS); superintendency (Ed S); teaching (MAT); teaching English as a second language (MA); technology (MS); technology management (PhD); theatre (MA). Electronic applications accepted.

UNIVERSITY OF CENTRAL OKLAHOMA, Edmond, OK 73034-5209

General Information State-supported, coed, comprehensive institution. CGS member. *Graduate housing:* Rooms and/or apartments available on a first-come, first-served basis to single and married students. *Research affiliation:* National Science Foundation, U.S. Department of Education (DOE), U.S. Department of Veteran Affairs, Oklahoma Department of Human Services, Oklahoma Idea Network of Biomedical Research Excellence, Oklahoma Small Business Administration.

GRADUATE UNITS

The Jackson College of Graduate Studies *Program availability:* Part-time, evening/weekend. Electronic applications accepted.

College of Business *Program availability:* Part-time. Offers business administration (MBA); business analytics (MS). Electronic applications accepted.

College of Education and Professional Studies *Program availability:* Part-time. Offers adult and higher education (M Ed); athletic training (MS); bilingual education/teaching English as a second language (M Ed); early childhood education (M Ed); education and professional studies (M Ed, MA, MS); educational leadership (M Ed); elementary education (M Ed); family and child studies (MS); library media education (M Ed); nutrition-food science (MS); psychology (MA); reading (M Ed); school counseling (M Ed); secondary education (M Ed); special education (M Ed); speech-language pathology (MS); wellness management (MS). Electronic applications accepted.

College of Fine Arts and Design *Program availability:* Part-time, evening/weekend. Offers design (MFA); fine arts and design (MFA, MM); jazz studies (MM); music (MM). Electronic applications accepted.

College of Liberal Arts *Program availability:* Part-time. Offers composition and rhetoric (MA); creative writing (MA); crime and intelligence analysis (MA); criminal justice management and administration (MA); gerontology (MA); liberal arts (MA, MPA); liberal studies (MA); literature (MA); museum studies (MA); political science (MA); public administration (MPA); substance abuse studies (MA); teaching English as a second language (MA). Electronic applications accepted.

College of Mathematics and Science *Program availability:* Part-time. Offers applied mathematical science (MS); applied mathematics and computer science (MS); biology (MS); computational science (PSM); engineering physics (MS); mathematics and science (MS, PSM); nursing (MS). Electronic applications accepted.

Forensic Science Institute Offers biology/chemistry (MS); forensic science (MS). Electronic applications accepted.

UNIVERSITY OF CHARLESTON, Charleston, WV 25304-1099

General Information Independent, coed, comprehensive institution. *Graduate housing:* Rooms and/or apartments available on a first-come, first-served basis to single and married students. *Research affiliation:* Walmart (pharmacy).

GRADUATE UNITS

Doctor of Executive Leadership Program Offers leadership (DEL). Electronic applications accepted.

Master of Business Administration Program *Program availability:* Part-time, evening/weekend. Offers business administration (MBA). Electronic applications accepted.

Master of Forensic Accounting Program *Program availability:* Part-time, blended/hybrid learning. Offers forensic accounting (EMFA). Electronic applications accepted.

Master of Science in Strategic Leadership Program Offers strategic leadership (MS). Electronic applications accepted.

Physician Assistant Program Offers physician assistant (MPAS). Electronic applications accepted.

School of Pharmacy Offers pharmacy (Pharm D). Electronic applications accepted.

UNIVERSITY OF CHICAGO, Chicago, IL 60637-1513

General Information Independent, coed, university. CGS member. *Graduate housing:* Rooms and/or apartments available on a first-come, first-served basis to single and married students. *Research affiliation:* National Opinion Research Center (social science), Argonne National Laboratory (energy, materials), Marine Biological Laboratory (molecular biology), Fermilab (high-energy physics).

GRADUATE UNITS

Booth School of Business *Program availability:* Part-time, evening/weekend. Offers accounting (MBA); analytic finance (MBA); analytic management (MBA); business (MBA, PhD, Certificate); business administration (MBA, Certificate); econometrics and statistics (MBA); economics (MBA); entrepreneurship (MBA); executive business administration (MBA); finance (MBA); general management (MBA); health administration and policy (Certificate); international business (MBA); managerial and organizational behavior (MBA); marketing analytics (MBA); marketing management (MBA); operations management (MBA); strategic management (MBA). Electronic applications accepted.

Divinity School Offers anthropology and sociology of religions (PhD); Bible (PhD); divinity (M Div, MA, PhD); history of Christianity (PhD); history of Judaism (PhD); history of religions (PhD); Islamic studies (PhD); ministry (M Div); philosophy of religions (PhD); religion (MA, PhD); religion, literature, and visual culture (PhD); religions in America (PhD); religious ethics (PhD); religious studies (MA); theology (PhD). Electronic applications accepted.

Division of the Biological Sciences Offers biochemistry and molecular biology (PhD); biological sciences (MS, PhD); cancer biology (PhD); cell and molecular biology (PhD); computational neuroscience (PhD); development, regeneration, and stem cell biology (PhD); ecology and evolution (PhD); evolutionary biology (PhD); genetics, genomics and systems biology (PhD); human genetics (PhD); immunology (PhD); integrative biology (PhD); medical physics (PhD); microbiology (PhD); molecular metabolism and nutrition (PhD); neurobiology (PhD); public health sciences (MS, PhD). Electronic applications accepted.

Division of the Humanities Offers ancient Greek and Roman philosophy (PhD); ancient Mediterranean world (PhD); ancient philosophy (PhD); anthropology and linguistics (PhD); art history (MA); cinema and media studies (MA); classic languages (MA); classical languages and literatures (PhD); comparative literature (MA); composition (PhD); creative writing (MA); cultural policy studies (MA); digital humanities (MA); digital studies of language, culture, and history (MA); East Asian languages and civilizations (MA); English language and literature (PhD); ethnomusicology (PhD); French and Francophone studies (PhD); gender and sexuality studies (MA); Germanic studies (PhD); Hispanic and Luso-Brazilian studies (PhD); humanities (MA, MFA, PhD); Italian studies (PhD); linguistics (MA); music (MA); music history and theory (PhD); Near Eastern languages and civilizations (PhD); near Eastern languages and civilizations (MA); philosophy (MA, PhD); poetics (MA); race, politics and culture (MA); Renaissance and early modern studies (PhD); Romance languages and literatures

(MA); Slavic languages and literatures (MA); South Asian languages and civilizations (MA, PhD); theater and performance studies (MA); transformations in the classical tradition (PhD); visual arts (MFA). Electronic applications accepted.

Division of the Physical Sciences Offers astronomy and astrophysics (PhD); atmospheric sciences (PhD); biophysical sciences (PhD); chemistry (PhD); computational and applied mathematics (PhD); computer science (MS, PhD); earth sciences (PhD); financial mathematics (MS); mathematics (PhD); paleobiology (PhD); physical sciences (MS, PhD); physics (PhD); planetary and space sciences (PhD); statistics (MS, PhD). Electronic applications accepted.

Division of the Social Sciences Offers archaeology (PhD); comparative human development (PhD); computational social science (MA); conceptual and historical studies of science (PhD); economics (PhD); history (PhD); international relations (MA); political science (PhD); psychology (PhD); social sciences (MA, PhD); social thought (PhD); sociocultural and linguistic anthropology (PhD); sociology (PhD). Electronic applications accepted.

Center for Latin American Studies Offers Latin American studies (MA). Electronic applications accepted.

Center for Middle Eastern Studies Offers Middle Eastern studies (MA). Electronic applications accepted.

Graham School of Continuing Liberal and Professional Studies *Program availability:* Part-time, evening/weekend. Offers analytics (M Sc); biomedical informatics (M Sc); liberal arts (MLA); threat and response management (M Sc); urban teacher education (MAT). Electronic applications accepted.

Harris School of Public Policy *Program availability:* Part-time, evening/weekend. Offers computational analysis and public policy (MS); environmental science and policy (MS); public policy (AM, MPP, MS, PhD); public policy studies (AM). Electronic applications accepted.

Institute for Molecular Engineering Offers molecular engineering (PhD). Electronic applications accepted.

The Law School Offers law (LL M, MCL, DCL, JD, JSD). Electronic applications accepted.

Pritzker School of Medicine Offers medicine (MD). Electronic applications accepted.

School of Social Service Administration *Program availability:* Part-time, evening/weekend. Offers social service administration (AM, MA, PhD). AM/M Div offered jointly with the Divinity School, MBA/AM offered jointly with Booth School of Business, MPP/AM offered jointly with Harris School of Public Policy. Electronic applications accepted.

UNIVERSITY OF CINCINNATI, Cincinnati, OH 45221
General Information State-supported, coed, university. CGS member. *Graduate housing:* Rooms and/or apartments available on a first-come, first-served basis to single and married students. *Research affiliation:* Cincinnati Children's Hospital Medical Center, Cincinnati Department of Veterans Affairs Medical Center, Shriners Hospitals for Children-Cincinnati.
GRADUATE UNITS

Carl H. Lindner College of Business Students: 476 full-time (204 women), 680 part-time (287 women); includes 151 minority (55 Black or African American, non-Hispanic/Latino; 1 American Indian or Alaska Native, non-Hispanic/Latino; 52 Asian, non-Hispanic/Latino; 27 Hispanic/Latino; 3 Native Hawaiian or other Pacific Islander, non-Hispanic/Latino; 13 Two or more races, non-Hispanic/Latino), 395 international. Average age 30. 1,871 applicants, 49% accepted, 456 enrolled. *Faculty:* 117 full-time (37 women), 28 part-time/adjunct (4 women). Expenses: Contact institution. *Financial support:* In 2018–19, 395 students received support, including 25 research assistantships with full and partial tuition reimbursements available (averaging $23,250 per year); teaching assistantships, scholarships/grants, tuition waivers (full and partial), and unspecified assistantships also available. Financial award application deadline: 3/15; financial award applicants required to submit FAFSA. In 2018, 587 master's, 7 doctorates awarded. *Program availability:* Part-time, evening/weekend, 100% online, blended/hybrid learning. Offers accounting (MS, PhD); applied economics (MS); business (MA, MBA, MS, PhD); business administration (MBA); business analytics (MS, PhD); economics (PhD); finance (MS, PhD); human resources (MA); information systems (MS); management (MS); marketing (MS, PhD); operations and business analytics (PhD); operations research (PhD); taxation (MS). *Application deadline:* For fall admission, 6/30 priority date for domestic students, 3/15 for international students; for spring admission, 12/15 for domestic students, 9/15 for international students; for summer admission, 4/15 for domestic and international students. Applications are processed on a rolling basis. *Application fee:* $65 ($70 for international students). Electronic applications accepted. *Application Contact:* Dona Clary, Executive Director, Graduate Programs, 513-556-3546, Fax: 513-558-7006, E-mail: dona.clary@uc.edu. *Dean,* Dr. Marianne Lewis, 513-556-7001, Fax: 513-556-4891, E-mail: marianne.lewis@uc.edu.

College of Law Offers law (LL M, JD). Electronic applications accepted.

Graduate School *Program availability:* Part-time, evening/weekend, online learning. Offers neuroscience (PhD). Electronic applications accepted.

College-Conservatory of Music Offers arts administration (MA); choral conducting (MM, DMA); composition (MM, DMA); directing (MFA); keyboard studies (MM, DMA, AD); music (MA, MFA, MM, DMA, PhD, AD); music education (MM); music history (MM); music theory (MM); musicology (PhD); orchestral conducting (MM, DMA); performance (MM, DMA, AD); theater design and production (MFA); voice and opera (MM, DMA); wind conducting (MM, DMA). Electronic applications accepted.

College of Allied Health Sciences *Program availability:* Part-time. Offers allied health sciences (MA, MS, MSW, Au D, DPT, PhD); children and families, health and aging, mental health (MSW); communication sciences and disorders (MA, Au D, PhD); health informatics (MHI); medical genetics (MS); nutritional sciences (MS); physical therapy (DPT).

College of Design, Architecture, Art, and Planning 255 applicants, 59% accepted. Expenses: Contact institution. *Financial support:* Fellowships, career-related internships or fieldwork, Federal Work-Study, tuition waivers (full), and unspecified assistantships available. Support available to part-time students. In 2018, 119 master's awarded. *Program availability:* Part-time. Offers architecture (MS Arch); art history (MA); community planning (MCP); design, architecture, art, and planning (M Arch, M Des, MA, MCP, MFA, PhD); fashion design (M Des); fine arts (MFA); graphic design (M Des); industrial design (M Des); interaction design (M Des); interior design (M Des); product development (M Des); regional development planning (PhD); visual arts education (MA). *Application deadline:* For fall admission, 2/1 for domestic and international students. Applications are processed on a rolling basis. *Application fee:* $30. Electronic applications accepted. *Application Contact:* Prof. John E. Hancock, Associate Dean, 513-556-0223, E-mail: john.hancock@uc.edu. *Dean,* Dr. Robert Probst, 513-556-1204, Fax: 513-556-3288, E-mail: robert.probst@uc.edu.

College of Education, Criminal Justice, and Human Services *Program availability:* Part-time, online learning. Offers counselor education (Ed D); criminal justice (MS, PhD); curriculum and instruction (M Ed, Ed D); education (M Ed, Ed D, PhD, Ed S); education, criminal justice, and human services (M Ed, MA, MS, Ed D, PhD, CAGS, Certificate, Ed S, Graduate Certificate); educational leadership (M Ed, Ed S); educational studies (M Ed, PhD); exercise and fitness (MS); health education (PhD); human services (M Ed, MA, MPH, MS, Ed D, PhD, Ed S, Graduate Certificate); information technology (MS, Graduate Certificate); literacy and second language studies (M Ed, Ed D); mental health (MA); public and community health (MS); public health (MPH); school counseling (M Ed); school psychology (PhD, Ed S); special education (M Ed, Ed D); sport administration (MS); substance abuse prevention (Graduate Certificate); urban educational leadership (Ed D). Electronic applications accepted.

College of Engineering and Applied Science Students: 1,192 full-time (305 women), 65 part-time (6 women); includes 41 minority (15 Black or African American, non-Hispanic/Latino; 1 American Indian or Alaska Native, non-Hispanic/Latino; 14 Asian, non-Hispanic/Latino; 9 Hispanic/Latino; 2 Two or more races, non-Hispanic/Latino), 986 international. Average age 26. 1,803 applicants, 41% accepted, 448 enrolled. *Faculty:* 119 full-time (16 women), 15 part-time/adjunct (0 women). Expenses: Contact institution. *Financial support:* In 2018–19, 733 students received support, including 16 fellowships with tuition reimbursements available (averaging $23,400 per year), 396 research assistantships with tuition reimbursements available (averaging $23,400 per year), 248 teaching assistantships with tuition reimbursements available (averaging $23,400 per year); career-related internships or fieldwork, Federal Work-Study, scholarships/grants, tuition waivers (full and partial), and unspecified assistantships also available. Support available to part-time students. Financial award application deadline: 1/15. In 2018, 414 master's, 58 doctorates awarded. *Program availability:* Part-time, 100% online. Offers aerospace engineering and engineering mechanics (M Eng, MS, PhD); biomechanics (PhD); chemical engineering (MS, PhD); civil engineering (M Eng, MS, PhD); computer engineering (MS); computer science (MS); computer science and engineering (PhD); electrical engineering (MS, PhD); engineering and applied science (M Eng, MS, PhD); environmental engineering (MS, PhD); environmental sciences (MS, PhD); industrial engineering (PhD); materials science and engineering (MS, PhD); mechanical engineering (MS, PhD); medical imaging (PhD); nuclear engineering (PhD); tissue engineering (PhD). *Application deadline:* For fall admission, 3/15 priority date for domestic students, 1/15 priority date for international students. Applications are processed on a rolling basis. *Application fee:* $75 ($80 for international students). Electronic applications accepted. *Application Contact:* Julie Muenchen, Director, Academics, 513-556-3647, E-mail: julie.muenchen@uc.edu. *Senior Associate Dean,* Dr. Frank M. Gerner, 513-556-3647, E-mail: frank.gerner@uc.edu.

College of Medicine Offers biomedical informatics (PhD, Graduate Certificate); biomedical research (MS); biomedical sciences (MS, PhD, Graduate Certificate); cancer and cell biology (PhD); cell biophysics (PhD); environmental and industrial hygiene (MS, PhD); environmental and occupational medicine (MS); environmental genetics and molecular toxicology (MS, PhD); epidemiology and biostatistics (MS, PhD); immunobiology (PhD); immunology (MS, PhD); medical physics (MS); medicine (MS, MD, PhD, Graduate Certificate); molecular and developmental biology (PhD); molecular genetics, biochemistry and microbiology (PhD); occupational safety and ergonomics (MS, PhD); pathology (PhD); pharmacology (PhD); systems biology and physiology (PhD). Electronic applications accepted.

College of Nursing *Program availability:* Part-time, 100% online, blended/hybrid learning. Offers nurse midwifery (MSN); nurse practitioner (MSN, DNP); nursing (MSN, PhD). Electronic applications accepted.

McMicken College of Arts and Sciences *Program availability:* Part-time, evening/weekend. Offers analytical chemistry (MS, PhD); anthropology (MA); applied mathematics (MS, PhD); arts and sciences (MA, MALER, MAT, MS, PhD, Certificate); biochemistry (MS, PhD); biological sciences (MS, PhD); classics (MA, PhD); clinical psychology (PhD); communication (MA); English and comparative literature (MA, MAT, PhD); experimental psychology (PhD); French (MA, PhD); geography (MA, PhD); geology (MS, PhD); German studies (MA, PhD); history (MA, PhD); inorganic chemistry (MS, PhD); interdisciplinary studies (PhD); labor and employment relations (MALER); mathematics education (MAT); organic chemistry (MS, PhD); organizational leadership (MALER); philosophy (MA, PhD); physical chemistry (MS, PhD); physics (MS, PhD); political science (MA, PhD); polymer chemistry (MS, PhD); pure mathematics (MS, PhD); Romance languages and literatures (PhD); sensors (PhD); sociology (MA, PhD); Spanish (MA, PhD); statistics (MS, PhD); women's, gender, and sexuality studies (MA, Certificate).

James L. Winkle College of Pharmacy *Program availability:* Part-time. Offers pharmacy (MS, PhD, Pharm D).

Division of Pharmaceutical Sciences *Program availability:* Part-time, evening/weekend, 100% online, blended/hybrid learning. Offers biomembrane science (MS); biomembrane sciences (PhD); experiential therapeutics (MS). Electronic applications accepted.

Division of Pharmacy Practice Offers pharmacy practice (Pharm D).

UNIVERSITY OF COLORADO BOULDER, Boulder, CO 80309
General Information State-supported, coed, university. CGS member. *Graduate housing:* Rooms and/or apartments available to single and married students. *Research affiliation:* National Institute of Standards and Technology (NIST), National Oceanic and Atmospheric Administration (NOAA), U.S. West Advanced Technologies, NASA, National Center for Atmospheric Research.
GRADUATE UNITS

Graduate School Offers materials science and engineering (MS, PhD); museum and field studies (MS); organizational leadership. Electronic applications accepted.

College of Arts and Sciences Offers anthropology (MA, PhD); applied mathematics (MS, PhD); art history (MA); arts and sciences (MA, MFA, MS, Au D, PhD); Asian languages and civilizations (MA, PhD); astrophysics (MS, PhD); atmospheric and oceanic sciences (MS, PhD); cellular structure and function (MA, PhD); ceramics (MFA); chemistry and biochemistry (MS, PhD); classics (MA, PhD); dance (MFA); developmental biology (PhD); economics (MA); environmental studies (MS, PhD); ethnic studies (PhD); French and Italian (MA, PhD); geography (MA, PhD); geology (MS, PhD); geophysics (PhD); Germanic and Slavic languages and literatures (MA); Hispanic linguistics (MA); history (MA, PhD); integrative physiology (MS, PhD); linguistics (MA, PhD); literature (MA, PhD); mathematical physics (PhD); mathematics (MA, MS, PhD); medieval and early modern Hispanic literatures (PhD); molecular biology (PhD); peninsular and Latin American literature (MA); philosophy (MA, PhD); photography and media arts (MFA); planetary science (PhD); political science (MA, PhD); population biology (MA); printmaking (MFA); psychology and neuroscience (MA, PhD); religious studies (MA); Russian studies (MA); sculpture (MFA); sociology (PhD); speech, language and hearing sciences (MA, Au D, PhD); theatre (MA, PhD). Electronic applications accepted.

College of Engineering and Applied Science Offers aerospace engineering sciences (MS, PhD); chemical and biological engineering (ME, MS, PhD); civil, environmental, and architectural engineering (MS, PhD); computer science (ME, MS, PhD); electrical, computer and energy engineering (ME, MS, PhD); engineering and applied science (ME, MS, PhD); engineering management (ME); mechanical engineering (ME, MS, PhD); technology, learning, and society (MS, PhD); telecommunications (MS). Electronic applications accepted.

College of Media, Communication and Information Offers communication (MA, PhD); information science (PhD); interdisciplinary documentary media practices (MFA); intermedia art, writing and performance (PhD); journalism (MA); media research and practice (PhD); media studies (PhD); media, communication and information (MA, MFA, PhD); strategic communication design (MA). Electronic applications accepted.

College of Music Offers composition (M Mus, D Mus A); conducting (M Mus); instrumental conducting and literature (D Mus A); literature and performance of choral music (D Mus A); music education (M Mus Ed, PhD); music theory (M Mus); performance (M Mus, D Mus A); performance and pedagogy (M Mus, D Mus A). Electronic applications accepted.

School of Education Offers curriculum and instruction (MA, PhD); education (MA, PhD); educational and psychological studies (MA, PhD); educational equity and cultural diversity (PhD); educational foundations, policy, and practice (MA, PhD); multicultural education (MA); research and evaluation methodology (PhD). Electronic applications accepted.

Leeds School of Business Offers business (MBA, MS, PhD); business administration (MS, PhD). Electronic applications accepted.

MBA Program Offers business administration (MBA). Electronic applications accepted.

School of Law Offers law (JD). Electronic applications accepted.

UNIVERSITY OF COLORADO COLORADO SPRINGS, Colorado Springs, CO 80918

General Information State-supported, coed, university. CGS member. *Enrollment:* 436 full-time matriculated graduate/professional students (276 women), 1,529 part-time matriculated graduate/professional students (880 women). *Enrollment by degree level:* 1,591 master's, 243 doctoral, 131 other advanced degrees. *Graduate faculty:* 444 full-time (232 women), 330 part-time/adjunct (195 women). *International tuition:* $21,542 full-time. *Tuition, area resident:* Full-time $10,634; part-time $676 per credit. Tuition, state resident: full-time $10,634. Tuition, nonresident: full-time $21,542; part-time $1281 per credit. Tuition and fees vary according to course load, campus/location, program and reciprocity agreements. *Graduate housing:* Room and/or apartments available on a first-come, first-served basis to single students; on-campus housing not available to married students. Typical cost: $9116 per year ($12,592 including board). Room and board charges vary according to board plan, campus/location and housing facility selected. *Student services:* Campus employment opportunities, campus safety program, career counseling, child daycare facilities, exercise/wellness program, free psychological counseling, grant writing training, international student services, low-cost health insurance, multicultural affairs office, services for students with disabilities, teacher training, writing training. *Library facilities:* Kraemer Family Library. *Collection:* Books: 337,790 (physical), 168,770 (digital/electronic); Serial titles: 3,020 (physical); Databases: 154. Students can reserve study rooms.

Computer facilities: Computer purchase and lease plans are available. A campuswide network can be accessed from student residence rooms and from off campus. Online class registration, student portal, learning management system are available. Website: http://www.uccs.edu/

General Application Contact: Sarah Elsey, Program Manager, Graduate School, 719-255-3072, Fax: 719-255-3045, E-mail: gradinfo@uccs.edu.

GRADUATE UNITS

College of Business Students: 63 full-time (28 women), 304 part-time (140 women); includes 94 minority (12 Black or African American, non-Hispanic/Latino; 1 American Indian or Alaska Native, non-Hispanic/Latino; 16 Asian, non-Hispanic/Latino; 46 Hispanic/Latino; 19 Two or more races, non-Hispanic/Latino; 9 international. Average age 34. 161 applicants, 77% accepted, 92 enrolled. *Faculty:* 43 full-time (14 women), 85 part-time/adjunct (29 women). Expenses: Contact institution. *Financial support:* In 2018–19, 6 students received support. Career-related internships or fieldwork, Federal Work-Study, scholarships/grants, and unspecified assistantships available. Support available to part-time students. Financial award application deadline: 3/1; financial award applicants required to submit FAFSA. In 2018, 83 master's awarded. *Program availability:* Part-time, evening/weekend, 100% online, blended/hybrid learning. Offers business (MBA, MSA). *Application deadline:* For fall admission, 6/1 priority date for domestic students, 6/1 for international students; for spring admission, 11/1 priority date for domestic students, 11/1 for international students; for summer admission, 4/1 priority date for domestic students, 4/1 for international students. Applications are processed on a rolling basis. *Application fee:* $60 ($100 for international students). Electronic applications accepted. *Application Contact:* Janice Dowsett, Director of Graduate Programs, 719-255-3070, E-mail: cobgrad@uccs.edu. *Interim Dean,* Dr. Eric Olson, 719-255-3113, Fax: 719-255-3100, E-mail: eolson@uccs.edu.

College of Education Students: 208 full-time (149 women), 351 part-time (256 women); includes 136 minority (30 Black or African American, non-Hispanic/Latino; 1 American Indian or Alaska Native, non-Hispanic/Latino; 12 Asian, non-Hispanic/Latino; 64 Hispanic/Latino; 29 Two or more races, non-Hispanic/Latino; 8 international. Average age 36. 230 applicants, 80% accepted, 101 enrolled. *Faculty:* 31 full-time (22 women), 61 part-time/adjunct (47 women). Expenses: Contact institution. *Financial support:* In 2018–19, 15 students received support. Career-related internships or fieldwork, Federal Work-Study, scholarships/grants, and unspecified assistantships available. Support available to part-time students. Financial award application deadline: 3/1; financial award applicants required to submit FAFSA. In 2018, 186 master's, 9 doctorates awarded. *Program availability:* Part-time, evening/weekend, 100% online, blended/hybrid learning. Offers counseling and human services (MA); curriculum and instruction (MA); educational leadership (MA); educational leadership, research and policy (PhD); special education (MA); teaching English to speakers of other languages (MA). *Application deadline:* For fall admission, 1/28 priority date for domestic and international students; for spring admission, 11/1 priority date for domestic and international students. Applications are processed on a rolling basis. *Application fee:* $60 ($100 for international students). Electronic applications accepted. *Application Contact:* The College of Education Student Resource Office, 719-255-4996, E-mail: education@uccs.edu. *Dean,* Dr. Valerie Martin Conley, 719-255-4133, E-mail: vmconley@uccs.edu.

College of Engineering and Applied Science Students: 26 full-time (4 women), 267 part-time (50 women); includes 61 minority (6 Black or African American, non-Hispanic/Latino; 22 Asian, non-Hispanic/Latino; 20 Hispanic/Latino; 1 Native Hawaiian or other Pacific Islander, non-Hispanic/Latino; 12 Two or more races, non-Hispanic/Latino), 73 international. Average age 33. 162 applicants, 84% accepted, 52 enrolled. *Faculty:* 41 full-time (11 women), 48 part-time/adjunct (9 women). Expenses: Contact institution. *Financial support:* In 2018–19, 22 students received support, including 33 teaching assistantships (averaging $5,800 per year); career-related internships or fieldwork, Federal Work-Study, scholarships/grants, and unspecified assistantships also available. Support available to part-time students. Financial award application deadline: 3/1; financial award applicants required to submit FAFSA. In 2018, 58 master's, 15 doctorates awarded. *Program availability:* Part-time, evening/weekend. Offers computer science (ME); cybersecurity (ME); electrical engineering (MS, PhD); energy engineering (ME); engineering management (ME); engineering systems (ME); mechanical engineering (ME); software engineering (ME); space operations (ME). *Application deadline:* For fall admission, 6/1 for domestic students, 4/1 for international students; for spring admission, 11/1 for domestic students, 10/1 for international students. Applications are processed on a rolling basis. *Application fee:* $60 ($100 for international students). *Application Contact:* Ali Langfels, Office of Student Support, 719-255-3544, E-mail: alangfel@uccs.edu. *Dean,* Dr. Donald Rabern, 719-255-3543, E-mail: drabern@uccs.edu.

College of Letters, Arts and Sciences Students: 67 full-time (44 women), 192 part-time (104 women); includes 58 minority (8 Black or African American, non-Hispanic/Latino; 2 American Indian or Alaska Native, non-Hispanic/Latino; 6 Asian, non-Hispanic/Latino; 26 Hispanic/Latino; 16 Two or more races, non-Hispanic/Latino), 7 international. Average age 31. 467 applicants, 33% accepted, 80 enrolled. *Faculty:* 145 full-time (66 women), 143 part-time/adjunct (82 women). Expenses: Contact institution. *Financial support:* In 2018–19, 113 students received support, including 8 fellowships (averaging $5,000 per year), 7 research assistantships (averaging $3,500 per year), 6 teaching assistantships (averaging $3,500 per year); career-related internships or fieldwork, Federal Work-Study, scholarships/grants, and unspecified assistantships also available. Support available to part-time students. Financial award application deadline: 3/1; financial award applicants required to submit FAFSA. In 2018, 90 master's, 6 doctorates awarded. *Program availability:* Part-time, evening/weekend, 100% online, blended/hybrid learning. Offers applied mathematics (MS); applied sciences (PhD); communication (MA); geography and environmental studies (MA); history (MA); interdisciplinary sciences (M Sc); letters, arts and sciences (M Sc, MA, MS, PhD); psychology (MA, PhD); sociology (MA). *Application deadline:* For fall admission, 12/15 for domestic and international students. Applications are processed on a rolling basis. *Application fee:* $60 ($100 for international students). Electronic applications accepted. *Application Contact:* Sarah Elsey, Graduate Recruitment and Retention Specialist, 719-255-3072, E-mail: gradinfo@uccs.edu. *Dean of the Graduate School,* Dr. Kelli Klebe, 719-255-3779, Fax: 719-255-3045, E-mail: kklebe@uccs.edu.

Helen and Arthur E. Johnson Beth-El College of Nursing and Health Sciences Students: 16 full-time (12 women), 261 part-time (230 women); includes 62 minority (7 Black or African American, non-Hispanic/Latino; 1 American Indian or Alaska Native, non-Hispanic/Latino; 10 Asian, non-Hispanic/Latino; 28 Hispanic/Latino; 1 Native Hawaiian or other Pacific Islander, non-Hispanic/Latino; 15 Two or more races, non-Hispanic/Latino). Average age 36. 152 applicants, 67% accepted, 71 enrolled. *Faculty:* 53 full-time (45 women), 105 part-time/adjunct (94 women). Expenses: Contact institution. *Financial support:* In 2018–19, 6 students received support. Career-related internships or fieldwork, Federal Work-Study, and scholarships/grants available. Support available to part-time students. Financial award application deadline: 3/1; financial award applicants required to submit FAFSA. In 2018, 37 master's, 2 doctorates awarded. *Program availability:* Part-time, 100% online. Offers nursing practice (MSN, DNP). *Application deadline:* For fall admission, 3/15 priority date for domestic students, 3/15 for international students; for spring admission, 8/15 for domestic and international students. Applications are processed on a rolling basis. *Application fee:* $60 ($100 for international students). Electronic applications accepted. *Application Contact:* Diane Busch, Program Assistant II, 719-255-4416, E-mail: dbusch@uccs.edu. *Nursing Department Chair,* Dr. Deborah Pollard, 719-255-3577, Fax: 719-255-4416, E-mail: dpollard@uccs.edu.

School of Public Affairs Students: 28 full-time (17 women), 181 part-time (114 women); includes 81 minority (12 Black or African American, non-Hispanic/Latino; 2 American Indian or Alaska Native, non-Hispanic/Latino; 5 Asian, non-Hispanic/Latino; 47 Hispanic/Latino; 15 Two or more races, non-Hispanic/Latino). Average age 34. 84 applicants, 92% accepted, 45 enrolled. *Faculty:* 13 full-time (5 women), 26 part-time/adjunct (10 women). Expenses: Contact institution. *Financial support:* In 2018–19, 9 students received support. Career-related internships or fieldwork, scholarships/grants, and tuition waivers available. Support available to part-time students. Financial award application deadline: 3/1; financial award applicants required to submit FAFSA. In 2018, 41 master's awarded. *Program availability:* Part-time, evening/weekend, 100% online, blended/hybrid learning. Offers criminal justice (MCJ); public administration (MPA). *Application deadline:* Applications are processed on a rolling basis. *Application fee:* $60 ($100 for international students). Electronic applications accepted. *Application Contact:* Crista Hill, Graduate Recruitment and Retention Specialist, 719-255-4993, Fax: 719-255-4183, E-mail: chill12@uccs.edu. *Dean,* Dr. George Reed, 719-255-4109, E-mail: george.reed@uccs.edu.

UNIVERSITY OF COLORADO DENVER, Denver, CO 80217-3364

General Information State-supported, coed, university. CGS member. *Enrollment:* 25,645 graduate, professional, and undergraduate students; 6,686 full-time matriculated graduate/professional students (4,083 women), 1,567 part-time matriculated graduate/professional students (998 women). *Enrollment by degree level:* 4,876 master's, 3,275 doctoral, 102 other advanced degrees. Tuition, state resident: full-time $6786; part-time $337 per credit hour. Tuition, nonresident: full-time $22,590; part-time $1255 per credit hour. *Required fees:* $1231; $137 per credit hour. Tuition and fees vary according to program and reciprocity agreements. *Graduate housing:* Room and/or apartments available on a first-come, first-served basis to single students; on-campus housing not available to married students. *Student services:* Campus employment opportunities, campus safety program, career counseling, child daycare facilities, exercise/wellness program, free psychological counseling, international student services, low-cost health insurance, multicultural affairs office, services for students with disabilities, teacher training, writing training. *Library facilities:* Auraria Library plus 1 other. *Collection:* Books: 573,818 (physical), 325,936 (digital/electronic); Serial titles: 5,780 (physical), 92,591 (digital/electronic); Databases: 308. Weekly public service hours: 85; students can reserve study rooms.

Computer facilities: 750 computers available on campus for general student use. A campuswide network can be accessed from student residence rooms and from off campus. Online class registration is available. Website: http://www.ucdenver.edu/

General Application Contact: Graduate School Admissions, 303-556-2704, E-mail: admissions@ucdenver.edu.

GRADUATE UNITS

Business School Students: 893 full-time (364 women), 289 part-time (129 women); includes 248 minority (30 Black or African American, non-Hispanic/Latino; 6 American Indian or Alaska Native, non-Hispanic/Latino; 74 Asian, non-Hispanic/Latino; 107 Hispanic/Latino; 31 Two or more races, non-Hispanic/Latino), 202 international. Average age 33. 778 applicants, 65% accepted, 292 enrolled. Expenses: Contact institution. *Financial support:* In 2018–19, 377 students received support. Fellowships, research assistantships, teaching assistantships, Federal Work-Study, institutionally sponsored loans, scholarships/grants, and traineeships available. Financial award application deadline: 4/1; financial award applicants required to submit FAFSA. In 2018, 527 master's, 4 doctorates awarded. *Program availability:* Part-time, evening/weekend, 100% online, blended/hybrid learning. Offers accounting (MS); accounting and information systems audit and control (MS); accounting and information systems audit control (MS); advanced market analytics in a big data world (MS); auditing (MS); brand communication in the digital era (MS); business administration (MBA); business intelligence systems (MS); business strategy (MS); change and innovation (MS); computer science and information systems (PhD); controllership and financial leadership (MS); digital health entrepreneurship (MS); economics (MS); enterprise risk management (MS); enterprise technology management (MS); entrepreneurship and innovation (MS); finance (MS); financial analysis and management (MS); financial and commodities risk management (MS); geographic information systems (MS); global energy management (MS); global management (MS); global marketing (MS); health administration (MS); health information technology (MS); high-tech and entrepreneurial marketing (MS); international business (MS); leadership (MS); managing for sustainability (MS); managing human resources (MS); marketing and global sustainability (MS); marketing intelligence and strategy in the 21st century (MS); risk management and insurance (MS); sports and entertainment (MS); sports and entertainment business (MS); strategic management (MS); taxation (MS); technology innovation and entrepreneurship (MS); traditional mba, one year mba, executive mba in health admin, executive mba (MBA); Web and mobile computing (MS). *Application deadline:* For fall admission, 4/15 priority date for domestic students, 3/15 priority date for international students; for spring admission, 10/15 priority date for domestic students, 9/15 priority date for international students; for summer admission, 2/15 priority date for domestic students, 1/15 priority date for international students. Applications are processed on a rolling basis. Electronic applications accepted. *Application Contact:* Dr. Rohan Christie-David, Dean and Professor of Finance, 303-315-8000, E-mail: rohan.christie-david@ucdenver.edu. *Dean and Professor of Finance,* Dr. Rohan Christie-David, 303-315-8000, E-mail: rohan.christie-david@ucdenver.edu.

College of Architecture and Planning Students: 371 full-time (211 women), 22 part-time (13 women); includes 54 minority (7 Black or African American, non-Hispanic/Latino; 9 Asian, non-Hispanic/Latino; 30 Hispanic/Latino; 8 Two or more races, non-Hispanic/Latino), 35 international. Average age 31. 493 applicants, 43% accepted, 146 enrolled. Expenses: Contact institution. *Financial support:* In 2018–19, 114 students received support. Fellowships with tuition reimbursements available, research assistantships, teaching assistantships, Federal Work-Study, institutionally sponsored loans, scholarships/grants, and traineeships available. Financial award application deadline: 4/1; financial award applicants required to submit FAFSA. In 2018, 125 master's, 3 doctorates awarded. *Program availability:* Part-time. Offers architecture (M Arch); architecture and planning (M Arch, MLA, MS, MUD, MURP, PhD); economic and community development planning (MURP); historic preservation (MS); history of architecture, landscape and urbanism (PhD); land use and environmental planning (MURP); landscape architecture (MLA); sustainable and healthy environments (PhD); urban design (MUD); urban place making (MURP). *Application deadline:* For fall admission, 1/15 for domestic students, 1/1 for international students. Applications are processed on a rolling basis. *Application fee:* $0. Electronic applications accepted. *Application Contact:* Rachael Kuroiwa, Manager of Admissions and Outreach, 303-315-2325, E-mail: rachael.kuroiwa@ucdenver.edu. *Dean,* Dr. Nan Ellin, 303-315-1000, E-mail: mark.gelernter@ucdenver.edu.

College of Arts and Media Students: 21 full-time (5 women), 10 part-time (1 woman); includes 7 minority (5 Hispanic/Latino; 2 Two or more races, non-Hispanic/Latino), 1 international. Average age 31. 12 applicants, 92% accepted, 8 enrolled. Expenses: Contact institution. *Financial support:* In 2018–19, 4 students received support. Federal Work-Study, institutionally sponsored loans, scholarships/grants, traineeships, and unspecified assistantships available. Financial award application deadline: 4/1; financial award applicants required to submit FAFSA. In 2018, 12 master's awarded. *Program availability:* Part-time, evening/weekend. Offers recording arts (MS). *Application deadline:* For fall admission, 4/1 for domestic students, 3/1 for international students. *Application fee:* $50 ($75 for international students). Electronic applications accepted. *Application Contact:* Lisa Funderburg, Program Assistant, 303-352-3833, E-mail: lisa.funderburg@ucdenver.edu. *Dean, College of Arts and Media,* Laurence D. Kaptain, 303-556-2279, E-mail: laurence.kaptain@ucdenver.edu.

College of Engineering, Design and Computing Students: 296 full-time (88 women), 132 part-time (36 women); includes 74 minority (12 Black or African American, non-Hispanic/Latino; 22 Asian, non-Hispanic/Latino; 30 Hispanic/Latino; 10 Two or more races, non-Hispanic/Latino), 162 international. Average age 30. 702 applicants, 52% accepted, 111 enrolled. Expenses: Contact institution. *Financial support:* In 2018–19, 180 students received support. Federal Work-Study and scholarships/grants available. Support available to part-time students. Financial award applicants required to submit FAFSA. In 2018, 118 master's, 12 doctorates awarded. *Program availability:* Part-time, evening/weekend. Offers basic research (MS, PhD); biomedical device design (MS); civil engineering (M Eng, EASPh D); civil engineering systems (PhD); comp sci and info systems, bioengineering, civil engineering (PhD); computer science (MS); computer science and engineering (EASPh D); computer science and information systems (PhD); electrical engineering (MS, EASPh D); electrical, mechanical, civil engineering (M Eng); electrical, mechanical, civil, computer science, bioengineering (MS); entrepreneurship (PhD); entrepreneurship and regulatory affairs (MS); environmental and sustainability engineering (MS, PhD); geographic information systems (MS); geotechnical engineering (MS, PhD); hydrology and hydraulics (MS, PhD); mechanical engineering (M Eng, MS); mechanics (MS); structural engineering (MS, PhD); thermal sciences (MS); translational bioengineering (PhD); transportation engineering (MS, PhD). *Application fee:* $50 ($75 for international students). Electronic applications accepted. *Application Contact:* Graduate School Admissions, 303-556-2704, E-mail: admissions@ucdenver.edu. *Dean,* Martin Dunn, 303-315-7173, Fax: 303-315-7173, E-mail: martin.dunn@ucdenver.edu.

College of Liberal Arts and Sciences Students: 379 full-time (205 women), 170 part-time (101 women); includes 145 minority (20 Black or African American, non-Hispanic/Latino; 5 American Indian or Alaska Native, non-Hispanic/Latino; 27 Asian, non-Hispanic/Latino; 64 Hispanic/Latino; 29 Two or more races, non-Hispanic/Latino), 34 international. Average age 31. 644 applicants, 55% accepted, 160 enrolled. Expenses: Contact institution. *Financial support:* In 2018–19, 306 students received support. In 2018, 144 master's, 7 doctorates awarded. *Program availability:* Part-time, evening/weekend. Offers applied linguistics (MA); applied mathematics (MS, PhD); applied science (MIS); archaeological studies (MA); biological anthropology (MA); biology (MS); chemistry (MS); clinical health psychology (PhD); communication (MA); community health (MSS); computer science (MA); economics (MA); environmental sciences (MS); ethnic studies (MH, MSS); European history (MA); global history (MA); health and behavioral sciences (PhD); humanities (MH, Graduate Certificate); integrative and systems biology (PhD); international studies (MSS); liberal arts and sciences (MA, MH, MIS, MS, MSS, PhD, Graduate Certificate); mathematics (MIS); medical anthropology (MA); philosophy and theory (MH); political science (MA); public history (MA); social justice (MH, MSS); society and the environment (MSS); sociology (MA); Spanish (MA); sustainable development and political ecology (MA); U.S. history (MA); visual studies (MH); women's and gender studies (MH, MSS). *Application fee:* $50 ($75 for international students). Electronic applications accepted. *Application Contact:* College of Liberal Arts and Sciences, 303-315-5969, E-mail: clas@ucdenver.edu. *Dean,* Pamela Jansma, 303-315-7000, E-mail: pamela.jansma@ucdenver.edu.

College of Nursing Students: 468 full-time (407 women), 150 part-time (121 women); includes 111 minority (19 Black or African American, non-Hispanic/Latino; 3 American Indian or Alaska Native, non-Hispanic/Latino; 27 Asian, non-Hispanic/Latino; 47 Hispanic/Latino; 15 Two or more races, non-Hispanic/Latino), 2 international. Average age 38. 370 applicants, 51% accepted, 173 enrolled. Expenses: Contact institution. *Financial support:* In 2018–19, 232 students received support. In 2018, 157 master's, 25 doctorates awarded. *Program availability:* Part-time, evening/weekend, online learning. Offers adult clinical nurse specialist (MS); adult nurse practitioner (MS); family nurse practitioner (MS); family psychiatric mental health nurse practitioner (MS); health care informatics (MS); nurse-midwifery (MS); nursing (DNP, PhD); nursing leadership and health care systems (MS); pediatric nurse practitioner (MS); women's health (MS). *Application deadline:* For fall admission, 2/15 for domestic students, 1/15 for international students; for spring admission, 7/1 for domestic students, 6/1 for international students. *Application fee:* $50 ($75 for international students). Electronic applications accepted. *Application Contact:* Judy Campbell, Graduate Programs Advisor, 303-724-8503, E-mail: judy.campbell@ucdenver.edu. *Dean,* Dr. Elias Provencio-Vasquez, 303-724-1679, E-mail: Eli.Provencio-Vasquez@ucdenver.edu.

Colorado School of Public Health Students: 487 full-time (391 women), 99 part-time (80 women); includes 137 minority (20 Black or African American, non-Hispanic/Latino; 2 American Indian or Alaska Native, non-Hispanic/Latino; 42 Asian, non-Hispanic/Latino; 49 Hispanic/Latino; 1 Native Hawaiian or other Pacific Islander, non-Hispanic/Latino; 23 Two or more races, non-Hispanic/Latino), 21 international. Average age 31. 967 applicants, 24% accepted, 171 enrolled. Expenses: Contact institution. *Financial support:* In 2018–19, 472 students received support. In 2018, 210 master's, 13 doctorates awarded. *Program availability:* Part-time. Offers biostatistics and informatics (MS, PhD); community and behavioral health (MPH, Dr PH); epidemiology (MS, PhD); health services research (MS, PhD); public health (MPH, MS, Dr PH, PhD). *Application deadline:* For fall admission, 1/15 for domestic and international students. *Application fee:* $50 ($75 for international students). Electronic applications accepted. *Application Contact:* Office of Student Affairs, 303-724-4613, Fax: 303-724-4620, E-mail: admissions.csph@ucdenver.edu. *Dean,* Dr. Jon Samet, 303-724-4450, E-mail: elizabeth.a.wyatt@ucdenver.edu.

School of Dental Medicine Students: 444 full-time (223 women), 1 part-time (0 women); includes 175 minority (23 Black or African American, non-Hispanic/Latino; 2 American Indian or Alaska Native, non-Hispanic/Latino; 81 Asian, non-Hispanic/Latino; 53 Hispanic/Latino; 1 Native Hawaiian or other Pacific Islander, non-Hispanic/Latino; 15 Two or more races, non-Hispanic/Latino), 39 international. Average age 29. 2,022 applicants, 7% accepted, 95 enrolled. Expenses: Contact institution. *Financial support:* In 2018–19, 282 students received support. In 2018, 114 doctorates awarded. Offers dental surgery (DDS); orthodontics (Certificate); periodontics (Certificate). *Application deadline:* For fall admission, 10/15 for domestic and international students. *Application fee:* $0. Electronic applications accepted. *Application Contact:* Graduate Student Admissions, 303-724-7122, Fax: 303-724-7109, E-mail: ddsadmissioninquiries@ucdenver.edu. *Dean,* Dr. Denise K. Kassebaum, 303-724-7100, Fax: 303-724-7109, E-mail: denise.kassebaum@ucdenver.edu.

School of Education and Human Development Students: 896 full-time (724 women), 397 part-time (323 women); includes 323 minority (59 Black or African American, non-Hispanic/Latino; 5 American Indian or Alaska Native, non-Hispanic/Latino; 35 Asian, non-Hispanic/Latino; 190 Hispanic/Latino; 3 Native Hawaiian or other Pacific Islander, non-Hispanic/Latino; 31 Two or more races, non-Hispanic/Latino), 25 international. Average age 35. 803 applicants, 44% accepted, 275 enrolled. Expenses: Contact institution. *Financial support:* In 2018–19, 215 students received support. In 2018, 505 master's, 29 doctorates, 6 other advanced degrees awarded. *Program availability:* Part-time, evening/weekend, online learning. Offers administrative leadership and policy (PhD); administrative leadership and policy studies (MA, Ed S); assessment (MA); counseling (MA); e-learning design and implementation (MA); early childhood education (MA); early childhood special education/early childhood education (PhD); education and human development (MA, MS Ed, Ed D, PhD, Psy D, Ed S); educational studies and research (PhD); elementary linguistically diverse education (MA); elementary math and science education (MA); elementary math education (MA); elementary reading and writing (MA); elementary science education (MA); executive leadership (Ed D); family science and human development (PhD); human development and family relations (MA); instructional design and adult learning (MA); instructional leadership (Ed D); K-12 teaching (MA); learning (MA); mathematics education (MS Ed); research and evaluation methods (MA); research, assessment and evaluation (PhD); school counseling (MA); school psychology (Psy D); science education (PhD); secondary English education (MA); secondary linguistically diverse education (MA); secondary math education (MA); secondary reading and writing (MA); secondary science education (MA); special education (MA); urban ecologies (PhD). *Application fee:* $0. Electronic applications accepted. *Application Contact:* Student Services Center, 303-315-6300, Fax: 303-315-6311, E-mail: education@ucdenver.edu. *Dean,* Rebecca Kantor, 303-315-6343, E-mail: rebecca.kantor@ucdenver.edu.

School of Medicine Students: 1,553 full-time (909 women), 43 part-time (33 women); includes 345 minority (34 Black or African American, non-Hispanic/Latino; 4 American Indian or Alaska Native, non-Hispanic/Latino; 114 Asian, non-Hispanic/Latino; 120 Hispanic/Latino; 1 Native Hawaiian or other Pacific Islander, non-Hispanic/Latino; 72 Two or more races, non-Hispanic/Latino), 24 international. Average age 29. 1,471 applicants, 23% accepted, 322 enrolled. Expenses: Contact institution. *Financial support:* In 2018–19, 1,471 students received support. In 2018, 132 master's, 271 doctorates awarded. Offers anesthesiology (MS); biochemistry (PhD); biochemistry and molecular genetics (PhD); bioinformatics (PhD); biomedical sciences (MS, PhD); biomolecular structure (PhD); biophysics and genetics (MS); cancer biology (PhD); cell biology, stem cells, and developmental biology (PhD); child health associate (MPAS); clinical investigation (PhD); clinical sciences (MS); computational bioscience (PhD); health information technology (PhD); health services research (PhD); human medical genetics and genomics (PhD); immunology (PhD); medicine (MPAS, MS, DPT, MD, PhD); microbiology; microbiology and immunology (PhD); modern human anatomy (MS); neuroscience (PhD); physical therapy (DPT); rehabilitation science (PhD). *Application fee:* $0. Electronic applications accepted. *Application Contact:* Director of Student Life, 303-724-8025, E-mail: somadmin@ucdenver.edu. *Dean,* Dr. John Reilly, Jr., 303-724-5375, E-mail: john.reillyjr@ucdenver.edu.

School of Public Affairs Students: 244 full-time (158 women), 149 part-time (95 women); includes 61 minority (12 Black or African American, non-Hispanic/Latino; 2 American Indian or Alaska Native, non-Hispanic/Latino; 10 Asian, non-Hispanic/Latino; 32 Hispanic/Latino; 5 Two or more races, non-Hispanic/Latino), 32 international. Average age 33. 249 applicants, 80% accepted, 95 enrolled. Expenses: Contact institution. *Financial support:* In 2018–19, 90 students received support. In 2018, 147 master's, 6 doctorates awarded. *Program availability:* Part-time, evening/weekend, online learning. Offers criminal justice (MCJ); public administration (MPA); public affairs (PhD). *Application deadline:* For fall admission, 2/1 priority date for domestic students, 1/15 priority date for international students; for spring admission, 10/15 priority date for domestic students. *Application fee:* $50 ($75 for international students). Electronic applications accepted. *Application Contact:* Antoinette Sandoval, Student Service Specialist, 303-315-2487, Fax: 303-315-2229, E-mail: antoinette.sandoval@ucdenver.edu. *Dean,* Paul Teske, 303-315-2805, Fax: 303-315-2229, E-mail: paul.teske@ucdenver.edu.

Skaggs School of Pharmacy and Pharmaceutical Sciences Students: 635 full-time (396 women), 111 part-time (71 women); includes 301 minority (38 Black or African American, non-Hispanic/Latino; 5 American Indian or Alaska Native, non-Hispanic/Latino; 173 Asian, non-Hispanic/Latino; 80 Hispanic/Latino; 5 Two or more races, non-Hispanic/Latino), 23 international. Average age 29. 301 applicants, 69% accepted, 174 enrolled. Expenses: Contact institution. *Financial support:* In 2018–19, 519 students received support. In 2018, 197 doctorates awarded. *Program availability:* Online learning. Offers clinical pharmaceutical sciences (PhD); pharmacy (Pharm D); pharmacy and pharmaceutical sciences (PhD, Pharm D); toxicology (PhD). *Application fee:* $0. Electronic applications accepted. *Application Contact:* Jackie Milowski, Department of Pharmaceutical Sciences Administrative Assistant, 303-724-7263, E-mail: jackie.milowski@ucdenver.edu. *Dean,* Dr. Ralph Altiere, 303-724-2631, E-mail: ralph.altiere@ucdenver.edu.

UNIVERSITY OF CONNECTICUT, Storrs, CT 06269

General Information State-supported, coed, university. CGS member. *Graduate housing:* Rooms and/or apartments available on a first-come, first-served basis to single and married students. Housing application deadline: 4/1. *Research affiliation:* U.S. Navy–Submarine Medical Research Laboratory, Haskins Laboratories.

GRADUATE UNITS

Graduate School *Program availability:* Part-time, evening/weekend, online learning. Electronic applications accepted.

College of Agriculture, Health and Natural Resources Offers agricultural and resource economics (MS, PhD); agriculture, health and natural resources (MS, PhD); animal science (MS, PhD); exercise science (MS, PhD); natural resources and the environment (MS, PhD); nutritional sciences (MS, PhD); pathobiology (MS, PhD); physical therapy (DPT); plant science and landscape architecture (MS, PhD); sport management (MS). Electronic applications accepted.

College of Liberal Arts and Sciences Offers anthropology (MA, PhD); applied financial mathematics (MS); applied genomics (PSM); behavioral neuroscience (PhD); biopsychology (PhD); botany (MS, PhD); cell and developmental biology (MS, PhD); chemistry (MS, PhD); clinical psychology (MA, PhD); cognition and instruction (PhD); communication (MA, Au D, PhD); comparative physiology (MS, PhD); developmental psychology (MA, PhD); ecological psychology (PhD); economics (MA, PhD); English (MA, PhD); experimental psychology (PhD); general psychology (MA, PhD); genetics and genomics (MS, PhD); geography (MA, PhD); geological sciences (MS, PhD); history (MA, PhD); human development and family studies (MA, PhD); industrial/organizational psychology (PhD); Judaic studies (MA, PhD); language and cognition (PhD); Latino and Latin American studies (MA); liberal arts and sciences (MA, MPA, MS, Au D, PhD, Certificate, Graduate Certificate); linguistics (MA, PhD); medieval studies (MA, PhD); microbial systems analysis (PSM); microbiology (MS, PhD); neuroscience (PhD); philosophy (MA, PhD); physics (MS, PhD); political science (MA, PhD); public administration (MPA, Graduate Certificate); quantitative research methods (Graduate Certificate); social psychology (MA, PhD); sociology (MA, PhD); speech, language and hearing sciences (MA, Au D, PhD); statistics (MS, PhD); structural biology, biochemistry and biophysics (MS, PhD); survey research (MA, Graduate Certificate). Electronic applications accepted.

eCampus *Program availability:* Online learning. Offers continuing studies (MS, Certificate); human resource management (MS); occupational safety and health management (Certificate).

Neag School of Education Offers adult learning (MA, PhD); agriculture (MA); agriculture education (MA, PhD); bilingual and bicultural education (MA, PhD); cognition and instruction (MA, PhD); cognition, instruction, and learning technology (MA, PhD); counseling psychology (PhD); education (MA, PhD); educational administration (MA, PhD); elementary education (MA, PhD); English education (MA, PhD); gifted and talented education (Graduate Certificate); higher education and student affairs (MA); history and social sciences education (MA, PhD); mathematics education (MA, PhD); music education (MA, PhD); reading education (MA, PhD); school counseling (MA); science education (MA, PhD); secondary education (MA, PhD); world languages education (MA, PhD). Electronic applications accepted.

School of Business Offers accounting (MS, PhD); business (PhD); business administration (MBA); business analytics and project management (MS); finance (PhD); financial risk management (MS); health care management and insurance studies (MBA); human resource management (MS); management (PhD); management consulting (MBA); marketing (PhD); marketing intelligence (MBA); operations and information management (PhD). Electronic applications accepted.

School of Engineering Offers biomedical engineering (MS, PhD); chemical and biomolecular engineering (MS, PhD); civil engineering (MS, PhD); computer science (MS, PhD); electrical and computer engineering (MS, PhD); engineering (M Eng, MS, PhD); environmental engineering (MS, PhD); materials science and engineering (M Eng); mechanical engineering (MS, PhD). Electronic applications accepted.

School of Fine Arts Offers acting (MA, MFA); conducting (M Mus, DMA); design (MA, MFA); fine arts (M Mus, MA, MFA, DMA, PhD); historical musicology (MA); music theory (MA); music theory and history (PhD); performance (M Mus, DMA); puppetry (MA, MFA); technical direction (MA, MFA). Electronic applications accepted.

School of Nursing Offers adult gerontological acute care nurse practitioner (MS); adult gerontological primary care nurse practitioner (MS); adult gerontology acute care nurse practitioner (Post-Master's Certificate); adult gerontology primary care nurse practitioner (Post-Master's Certificate); family nurse practitioner (MS); neonatal nurse practitioner (MS, Post-Master's Certificate); nursing (MS, DNP, PhD, Post-Master's Certificate). Electronic applications accepted.

School of Pharmacy Offers medicinal chemistry (MS, PhD); pharmaceutics (MS, PhD); pharmacology (MS, PhD); pharmacology and toxicology (MS, PhD); pharmacy (MS, PhD, Pharm D); toxicology (MS, PhD). Electronic applications accepted.

School of Social Work Offers social work (MSW, PhD). Electronic applications accepted.

Institute of Materials Science Offers materials science (MS, PhD); polymer science and engineering (MS, PhD).

School of Law *Program availability:* Part-time. Offers law (JD). Electronic applications accepted.

UNIVERSITY OF CONNECTICUT HEALTH CENTER, Farmington, CT 06030

General Information State-supported, coed, graduate-only institution. *Graduate housing:* On-campus housing not available.

GRADUATE UNITS

Graduate School *Program availability:* Part-time, evening/weekend. Offers biomedical sciences (PhD); biomedical sciences - integrated (PhD); cell analysis and modeling (PhD); cell biology (PhD); clinical and translational research (MS); genetics and developmental biology (PhD); immunology (PhD); molecular biology and biochemistry (PhD); neuroscience (PhD); public health (MPH); skeletal biology and regeneration (PhD).

School of Dental Medicine Offers dental medicine (MDS, DMD, Certificate); dental science (MDS). Electronic applications accepted.

School of Medicine Offers medicine (MD). Electronic applications accepted.

UNIVERSITY OF DALLAS, Irving, TX 75062-4736

General Information Independent-religious, coed, university. *Enrollment:* 2,542 graduate, professional, and undergraduate students; 268 full-time matriculated graduate/professional students (111 women), 803 part-time matriculated graduate/professional students (336 women). *Enrollment by degree level:* 958 master's, 86 doctoral, 6 other advanced degrees. *Tuition:* Full-time $1250; part-time $1250 per credit hour. *Graduate housing:* On-campus housing not available. *Student services:* Campus employment opportunities, career counseling, exercise/wellness program, international student services, services for students with disabilities, teacher training, writing training. *Library facilities:* William A. Blakley Library. *Collection:* Books: 235,868 (physical), 237,409 (digital/electronic); Serial titles: 294 (physical), 179 (digital/electronic); Databases: 215. Weekly public service hours: 99.

Computer facilities: Computer purchase and lease plans are available. 125 computers available on campus for general student use. A campuswide network can be accessed from student residence rooms and from off campus. Online class registration is available.
Website: http://www.udallas.edu/

General Application Contact: Breonna Collins, Director, Graduate Admissions and College of Business Enrollment Management, 972-721-5304, E-mail: bcollins@udallas.edu.

GRADUATE UNITS

Ann and Joe O. Neuhoff School of Ministry Students: 81 part-time (40 women); includes 23 minority (1 Black or African American, non-Hispanic/Latino; 7 Asian, non-Hispanic/Latino; 15 Hispanic/Latino), 1 international. Average age 48. 76 applicants, 49% accepted, 27 enrolled. *Faculty:* 5 full-time (2 women), 8 part-time/adjunct (3 women). Expenses: Contact institution. *Financial support:* In 2018–19, 12 students received support, including 2 research assistantships (averaging $8,775 per year); scholarships/grants and unspecified assistantships also available. Financial award application deadline: 7/1; financial award applicants required to submit FAFSA. In 2018, 14 master's awarded. *Program availability:* Part-time, evening/weekend. Offers ministry (MCSL). Theology Department; Education Department; College of Business. *Application deadline:* For fall admission, 8/1 priority date for domestic and international students; for spring admission, 1/1 priority date for domestic and international students; for summer admission, 5/1 priority date for domestic and international students. Applications are processed on a rolling basis. *Application fee:* $25. Electronic applications accepted. *Application Contact:* Dr. Diana Dudoit Raiche, Director of Graduate Programs, 972-721-4081, E-mail: ddraiche@udallas.edu. *Dean,* Theodore J. Whapham, 972-721-4068, E-mail: twhapham@udallas.edu.

Braniff Graduate School of Liberal Arts Students: 116 full-time (53 women), 140 part-time (65 women); includes 32 minority (4 Black or African American, non-Hispanic/Latino; 3 Asian, non-Hispanic/Latino; 21 Hispanic/Latino; 4 Two or more races, non-Hispanic/Latino), 13 international. Average age 32. 247 applicants, 69% accepted. Expenses: Contact institution. *Financial support:* In 2018–19, 164 students received support. Research assistantships, teaching assistantships, scholarships/grants, tuition waivers (full and partial), and unspecified assistantships available. Financial award application deadline: 2/15; financial award applicants required to submit FAFSA. *Program availability:* Part-time. Offers liberal arts (M Hum, M Pol, M Psych, M Th, MA, MAS, MC, MCSL, MEL, MFA, PhD). *Application deadline:* For fall admission, 7/15 priority date for domestic and international students; for spring admission, 11/15 priority date for domestic and international students; for summer admission, 2/15 priority date for domestic and international students. Applications are processed on a rolling basis. *Application fee:* $50. Electronic applications accepted. *Application Contact:* Breonna Collins, Director, Graduate Admissions, 972-721-5304, E-mail: bcollins@udallas.edu. *Dean,* Dr. Joshua Parens, 972-721 5241, E-mail: parens@udallas.edu.

Satish and Yasmin Gupta College of Business Students: 147 full-time (56 women), 584 part-time (232 women); includes 402 minority (204 Black or African American, non-Hispanic/Latino; 95 Asian, non-Hispanic/Latino; 92 Hispanic/Latino; 2 Native Hawaiian or other Pacific Islander, non-Hispanic/Latino; 9 Two or more races, non-Hispanic/Latino), 113 international. Average age 34. 992 applicants, 30% accepted, 157 enrolled. Expenses: Contact institution. *Financial support:* In 2018–19, 291 students received support. Research assistantships, teaching assistantships, scholarships/grants, and unspecified assistantships available. Support available to part-time students. Financial award application deadline: 2/15; financial award applicants required to submit FAFSA. In 2018, 336 master's, 5 doctorates awarded. *Program availability:* Part-time, evening/weekend, 100% online. Offers accounting (MBA, MS); business administration (DBA); business analytics (MS); business management (MBA); corporate finance (MBA); cybersecurity (MS); finance (MS); financial services (MBA); global business (MBA, MS); health services management (MBA); human resource management (MBA); information and technology management (MS); information assurance (MBA); information technology (MBA); information technology service management (MBA); marketing management (MBA); organization development (MBA);

project management (MBA); sports and entertainment management (MBA); strategic leadership (MBA); supply chain management (MBA). *Application deadline:* Applications are processed on a rolling basis. *Application fee:* $50. Electronic applications accepted. *Application Contact:* Breonna Collins, Director, Graduate Admissions, 972-7215304, E-mail: bcollins@udallas.edu. *Dean,* Brett J.L. Landry, 972-721-5356, E-mail: blandry@udallas.edu.

UNIVERSITY OF DAYTON, Dayton, OH 45469

General Information Independent-religious, coed, university. CGS member. *Graduate housing:* Room and/or apartments available on a first-come, first-served basis to single students; on-campus housing not available to married students. *Research affiliation:* California Institute of Technology (materials development), Dayton Area Graduate Studies Institute (materials testing), Kern Family Foundation (curriculum development), Ohio Aerospace Institute (engine analysis), Riverside Research Institute (radar and materials research), Southwest Research Institute (engineering services).

GRADUATE UNITS

College of Arts and Sciences *Program availability:* Part-time, evening/weekend, online learning. Offers arts and sciences (MA, MAS, MCS, MFM, MME, MPA, MS, PhD). Electronic applications accepted.

Department of Biology Offers biology (MS, PhD). Electronic applications accepted.

Department of Chemical Engineering *Program availability:* Part-time, online learning. Offers bioengineering (MS); chemical engineering (MS Ch E). Electronic applications accepted.

Department of Chemistry and Biochemistry *Program availability:* Part-time. Offers chemistry and biochemistry (MS). Electronic applications accepted.

Department of Civil and Environmental Engineering and Engineering Mechanics *Program availability:* Part-time, blended/hybrid learning. Offers engineering mechanics (MSEM); environmental engineering (MSCE); geotechnical engineering (MSCE); structural engineering (MSCE); transportation engineering (MSCE); water resources engineering (MSCE). Electronic applications accepted.

Department of Communication *Program availability:* Part-time, 100% online. Offers communication (MA); interdisciplinary communication (MA). Electronic applications accepted.

Department of Computer Science *Program availability:* Part-time. Offers computer science (MCS). Electronic applications accepted.

Department of Counselor Education and Human Services *Program availability:* Part-time. Offers clinical mental health counseling (MS Ed); college student personnel (MS Ed); higher education administration (MS Ed); human services (MS Ed); school counseling (MS Ed); school psychology (MS Ed, Ed S). Electronic applications accepted.

Department of Educational Administration *Program availability:* Part-time, blended/hybrid learning. Offers Catholic school leadership (MS Ed); educational leadership (MS Ed, Ed S); leadership for educational systems (MS Ed). Ed S program in educational leadership offered jointly by the Graduate Schools of the University of Dayton and Wright State University. Electronic applications accepted.

Department of Electrical and Computer Engineering *Program availability:* Part-time, blended/hybrid learning. Offers computer engineering (MS); electrical engineering (MSEE, PhD). Electronic applications accepted.

Department of Electro-Optics and Photonics Offers electro-optics (MSEO, PhD). Electronic applications accepted.

Department of Engineering Management, Systems and Technology *Program availability:* Part-time, 100% online, blended/hybrid learning. Offers engineering management (MSEM); management science (MSMS). Electronic applications accepted.

Department of English *Program availability:* Part-time. Offers literary and cultural studies (MA); teaching English to speakers of other languages (TESOL) (MA); writing and rhetoric (MA). Electronic applications accepted.

Department of Health and Sport Science *Program availability:* Part-time, 100% online. Offers exercise science (MS Ed). Electronic applications accepted.

Department of Mathematics *Program availability:* Part-time. Offers applied mathematics (MAS); financial mathematics (MFM). Electronic applications accepted.

Department of Mechanical and Aerospace Engineering *Program availability:* Part-time, 100% online, blended/hybrid learning. Offers aerospace engineering (MSAE, PhD); mechanical engineering (MSME, PhD); renewable and clean energy (MS). Electronic applications accepted.

Department of Physical Therapy Offers physical therapy (DPT). Electronic applications accepted.

Department of Physician Assistant Education Offers physician assistant practice (MPAP). Electronic applications accepted.

Department of Religious Studies *Program availability:* Part-time. Offers pastoral ministry (MA); theological studies (MA); theology (PhD). Electronic applications accepted.

Department of Teacher Education *Program availability:* Part-time, 100% online. Offers adolescence to young adult education (MS Ed); early childhood leadership and advocacy (MS Ed); interdisciplinary education (MS Ed); interdisciplinary education studies (MS Ed); leadership in educational systems (MS Ed); literacy (MS Ed); mathematics education (MS Ed); middle childhood education (MS Ed); multi-age education (MS Ed); music education (MS Ed); teacher as leader (MS Ed); teacher education (MS Ed); technology-enhanced learning (MS Ed); trans-disciplinary early childhood education (MS Ed). Electronic applications accepted.

Master of Public Administration Program *Program availability:* Part-time, evening/weekend. Offers public administration (MPA). Electronic applications accepted.

PhD Program in Educational Leadership *Program availability:* Part-time. Offers educational leadership (PhD). Electronic applications accepted.

Program in Clinical Psychology Offers clinical psychology (MA). Electronic applications accepted.

Program in General Psychology Offers general psychology (MA). Electronic applications accepted.

Program in Materials Engineering *Program availability:* Part-time, evening/weekend, blended/hybrid learning. Offers materials engineering (MS, DE, PhD). Electronic applications accepted.

School of Business Administration *Program availability:* Part-time, evening/weekend, blended/hybrid learning. Offers accounting (MBA); cyber security (MBA); finance (MBA); marketing (MBA). Electronic applications accepted.

School of Education

School of Law *Program availability:* Part-time, 100% online. Offers American and transnational law (LL M); criminal law (JD); government contracting and procurement (MSL); intellectual property and technology (MSL).

UNIVERSITY OF DELAWARE, Newark, DE 19716

General Information State-related, coed, university. CGS member. *Graduate housing:* Rooms and/or apartments available to single and married students. Housing application deadline: 3/15. *Research affiliation:* Hagley Museum, Winterthur Museum, Longwood Gardens, Bartol Research Foundation.

GRADUATE UNITS

Alfred Lerner College of Business and Economics *Program availability:* Part-time, evening/weekend. Offers accounting (MS); business administration (MBA); business and economics (MA, MBA, MS, PhD); economic education (PhD); economics (MA, MS, PhD); economics for entrepreneurship and educators (MA); finance (MS); financial service analytics (MS); hospitality information management (MS); information systems and technology management (MS). Electronic applications accepted.

Center for Energy and Environmental Policy Offers energy and environmental policy (MA, MEEP, PhD); urban affairs and public policy (PhD). Electronic applications accepted.

College of Agriculture and Natural Resources *Program availability:* Part-time. Offers agricultural and resource economics (MS); agricultural education (MA); agriculture and natural resources (MA, MS, PhD); animal sciences (MS, PhD); bioresources engineering (MS); entomology and applied ecology (MS, PhD); food sciences (MS); operations research (MS); plant and soil sciences (MS, PhD); public horticulture (MS); statistics (MS). Electronic applications accepted.

College of Arts and Sciences *Program availability:* Part-time, evening/weekend. Offers acting (MFA); American material culture (MA); applied mathematics (MS, PhD); art (MA, MFA); art conservation (MS); art history (MA, PhD); arts and sciences (MA, MALS, MFA, MM, MS, DPT, PhD); behavioral neuroscience (PhD); biochemistry (MA, MS, PhD); biomechanics and movement science (MS, PhD); biotechnology (MS); cancer biology (MS, PhD); cell and extracellular matrix biology (MS, PhD); cell and systems physiology (MS, PhD); chemistry (MA, MS, PhD); clinical psychology (PhD); cognitive psychology (PhD); communication (MA); composition (MM); criminology (MA, PhD); developmental biology (MS, PhD); ecology and evolution (MS, PhD); English and American literature (MA, PhD); fashion and apparel studies (MS); foreign languages and literatures (MA); foreign languages pedagogy (MA); history (MA, PhD); history of technology and industrialization (MA, PhD); liberal studies (MALS); linguistics (PhD); linguistics and cognitive science (MA); mathematics (MS, PhD); microbiology (MS, PhD); molecular biology and genetics (MS, PhD); music education (MM); performance (MM); physics and astronomy (MS, PhD); political science and international relations (MA, PhD); preservation studies (PhD); social psychology (PhD); sociology (MA, PhD); stage management (MFA); technical Chinese translation (MA); technical production (MFA). Electronic applications accepted.

School of Public Policy and Administration *Program availability:* Part-time, evening/weekend. Offers disaster science and management (MS, PhD); governance planning and management (PhD); historic preservation (MA); public administration (MPA); public policy and administration (MA, MPA, PhD); social and urban policy (PhD); technology, environment and society (PhD); urban affairs and public policy (MA). Electronic applications accepted.

College of Earth, Ocean, and Environment Offers geography (MA, MS, PhD); geological sciences (MA, PhD); geology (MS, PhD); marine science and policy (MMP, MS, PhD); ocean engineering (MS, PhD). Electronic applications accepted.

School of Marine Science and Policy Offers marine policy (MMP); marine studies (MS, PhD); oceanography (PhD).

College of Education and Human Development *Program availability:* Part-time, evening/weekend. Offers education and human development (M Ed, MA, MEEP, MI, MPA, MS, Ed D, PhD, Ed S); human development and family studies (MS, PhD). Electronic applications accepted.

School of Education *Program availability:* Part-time, evening/weekend. Offers education (PhD); educational leadership (Ed D); higher education (MA, Ed); instruction (MI); reading (M Ed); school leadership (M Ed); school psychology (MA, Ed S); teaching English as a second language (TESL) (MA). Electronic applications accepted.

College of Engineering *Program availability:* Part-time, evening/weekend, online learning. Offers chemical engineering (M Ch E, PhD); computer and information sciences (MS, PhD); electrical and computer engineering (MSECE, PhD); engineering (M Ch E, MAS, MCE, MEM, MMSE, MS, MSECE, MSME, PhD); environmental engineering (MAS, MCE, PhD); geotechnical engineering (MAS, MCE, PhD); materials science and engineering (MMSE, PhD); mechanical engineering (MEM, MSME, PhD); ocean engineering (MAS, MCE, PhD); structural engineering (MAS, MCE, PhD); transportation engineering (MAS, MCE, PhD); water resource engineering (MAS, MCE, PhD). Electronic applications accepted.

College of Health Sciences *Program availability:* Part-time, evening/weekend, online learning. Offers adult nurse practitioner (MSN, PMC); cardiopulmonary clinical nurse specialist (MSN, PMC); cardiopulmonary clinical nurse specialist/adult nurse practitioner (MSN, PMC); family nurse practitioner (MSN, PMC); gerontology clinical nurse specialist (MSN, PMC); gerontology clinical nurse specialist geriatric nurse practitioner (PMC); gerontology clinical nurse specialist/geriatric nurse practitioner (MSN); health promotion (MS); health sciences (MS, MSN, DPT, PMC); health services administration (MSN, PMC); human nutrition (MS); kinesiology and applied physiology (MS, PhD); nursing of children clinical nurse specialist (MSN, PMC); nursing of children clinical nurse specialist/pediatric nurse practitioner (MSN, PMC); oncology/immune deficiency clinical nurse specialist (MSN, PMC); oncology/immune deficiency clinical nurse specialist/adult nurse practitioner (MSN, PMC); perinatal/women's health clinical nurse specialist (MSN, PMC); perinatal/women's health clinical nurse specialist/women's health nurse practitioner (MSN, PMC); physical therapy (DPT); psychiatric nursing clinical nurse specialist (MSN, PMC); speech-language pathology (MA). Electronic applications accepted.

UNIVERSITY OF DENVER, Denver, CO 80208

General Information Independent, coed, university. CGS member. *Enrollment:* 2,964 full-time matriculated graduate/professional students (1,994 women), 3,076 part-time matriculated graduate/professional students (1,731 women). *Enrollment by degree level:* 4,163 master's, 1,465 doctoral, 412 other advanced degrees. *Graduate faculty:* 748 full-time (358 women), 624 part-time/adjunct (344 women). *Graduate housing:* Rooms and/or apartments available on a first-come, first-served basis to single and married students. Housing application deadline: 5/1. *Student services:* Campus employment opportunities, campus safety program, career counseling, exercise/wellness program, free psychological counseling, international student services, low-cost health insurance, multicultural affairs office, services for students with disabilities, teacher training, writing training. *Library facilities:* Anderson Academic Commons plus 1 other. *Collection:* Books: 1.7 million (physical), 2.3 million (digital/electronic); Serial titles: 594,063 (physical), 218,954 (digital/electronic); Databases: 1,306. Weekly public service hours: 145; study areas open 24 hours, 5–7 days a week; students can reserve study rooms.

Computer facilities: Computer purchase and lease plans are available. 150 computers available on campus for general student use. A campuswide network can be accessed from student residence rooms and from off campus. Online class registration is available.
Website: http://www.du.edu/

General Application Contact: Office of Graduate Studies, 303-871-2706, Fax: 303-871-4942, E-mail: gradinfo@du.edu.

GRADUATE UNITS

Daniel Felix Ritchie School of Engineering and Computer Science Students: 32 full-time (9 women), 184 part-time (46 women); includes 30 minority (4 Black or African American, non-Hispanic/Latino; 1 American Indian or Alaska Native, non-Hispanic/Latino; 10 Asian, non-Hispanic/Latino; 6 Hispanic/Latino; 1 Native Hawaiian or other Pacific Islander, non-Hispanic/Latino; 8 Two or more races, non-Hispanic/Latino), 85 international. Average age 29. 425 applicants, 59% accepted, 113 enrolled. *Faculty:* 39 full-time (6 women), 5 part-time/adjunct (2 women). Expenses: Contact institution. *Financial support:* In 2018–19, 156 students received support, including 14 research assistantships with tuition reimbursements available (averaging $13,848 per year), 34 teaching assistantships with tuition reimbursements available (averaging $16,054 per year); Federal Work-Study, institutionally sponsored loans, scholarships/grants, health care benefits, and unspecified assistantships also available. Financial award application deadline: 2/15; financial award applicants required to submit FAFSA. In 2018, 39 master's, 14 doctorates awarded. Offers bioengineering (MS); computer engineering (MS); computer science (MS, PhD); cybersecurity (MS); data science (MS); electrical and computer engineering (PhD); electrical engineering (MS); engineering (MS, PhD); engineering and computer science (MS, PhD); materials science (MS, PhD); mechanical engineering (MS, PhD); mechatronic systems engineering (MS, PhD). *Application deadline:* Applications are processed on a rolling basis. *Application fee:* $65. Electronic applications accepted. *Application Contact:* Information Contact, 303-871-3787, E-mail: ritchieschool@du.edu. *Dean*, JB Holston, 303-871-3787, E-mail: jb.holston@du.edu.

Daniels College of Business Students: 305 full-time (125 women), 460 part-time (197 women); includes 130 minority (12 Black or African American, non-Hispanic/Latino; 1 American Indian or Alaska Native, non-Hispanic/Latino; 20 Asian, non-Hispanic/Latino; 73 Hispanic/Latino; 2 Native Hawaiian or other Pacific Islander, non-Hispanic/Latino; 22 Two or more races, non-Hispanic/Latino), 98 international. Average age 32. 1,185 applicants, 63% accepted, 376 enrolled. *Faculty:* 107 full-time (40 women), 36 part-time/adjunct (9 women). Expenses: Contact institution. *Financial support:* In 2018–19, 412 students received support. Teaching assistantships, career-related internships or fieldwork, Federal Work-Study, institutionally sponsored loans, scholarships/grants, and unspecified assistantships available. Support available to part-time students. Financial award application deadline: 2/15; financial award applicants required to submit FAFSA. In 2018, 406 master's awarded. *Program availability:* Part-time, evening/weekend, online learning. Offers business (M Acc, MBA, MS); business administration (MBA); business information and analytics (MBA, MS); general business administration (MBA); management (MS); marketing (MBA, MS). *Application deadline:* For fall admission, 10/15 priority date for domestic and international students; for spring admission, 9/15 priority date for domestic and international students. Applications are processed on a rolling basis. *Application fee:* $100. Electronic applications accepted. *Application Contact:* Information Contact, 303-732-6186, E-mail: daniels@du.edu. *Dean*, Dr. Vivek Choudhury, 303-871-3411, E-mail: vivek.choudhury@du.edu.

Franklin L. Burns School of Real Estate and Construction Management Students: 26 full-time (6 women), 50 part-time (16 women); includes 12 minority (1 Black or African American, non-Hispanic/Latino; 7 Hispanic/Latino; 4 Two or more races, non-Hispanic/Latino). Average age 33. 60 applicants, 78% accepted, 25 enrolled. *Faculty:* 7 full-time (1 woman), 5 part-time/adjunct (0 women). Expenses: Contact institution. *Financial support:* In 2018–19, 56 students received support. Teaching assistantships with tuition reimbursements available, Federal Work-Study, institutionally sponsored loans, scholarships/grants, and unspecified assistantships available. Support available to part-time students. Financial award application deadline: 2/15; financial award applicants required to submit FAFSA. In 2018, 47 master's awarded. *Program availability:* Part-time, evening/weekend. Offers real estate and the built environment (MBA, MS). *Application deadline:* For fall admission, 10/15 priority date for domestic and international students; for spring admission, 9/15 priority date for domestic and international students. Applications are processed on a rolling basis. *Application fee:* $100. Electronic applications accepted. *Application Contact:* Ceci Smith, Assistant to the Director, 303-871-2145, E-mail: ceci.smith@du.edu. *Associate Professor and Director*, Dr. Barbara Jackson, 303-871-3470, E-mail: barbara.jackson@du.edu.

Reiman School of Finance Students: 35 full-time (14 women), 26 part-time (12 women); includes 11 minority (1 American Indian or Alaska Native, non-Hispanic/Latino; 3 Asian, non-Hispanic/Latino; 4 Hispanic/Latino; 1 Native Hawaiian or other Pacific Islander, non-Hispanic/Latino; 2 Two or more races, non-Hispanic/Latino), 28 international. Average age 26. 144 applicants, 53% accepted, 32 enrolled. *Faculty:* 16 full-time (4 women). Expenses: Contact institution. *Financial support:* In 2018–19, 50 students received support. Teaching assistantships with tuition reimbursements available, career-related internships or fieldwork, Federal Work-Study, institutionally sponsored loans, scholarships/grants, tuition waivers, and unspecified assistantships available. Support available to part-time students. Financial award application deadline: 2/15; financial award applicants required to submit FAFSA. In 2018, 33 master's awarded. *Program availability:* Part-time, evening/weekend. Offers applied quantitative finance (MS); finance (MBA). *Application deadline:* For fall admission, 10/15 priority date for domestic and international students; for spring admission, 9/15 priority date for domestic and international students. Applications are processed on a rolling basis. *Application fee:* $100. Electronic applications accepted. *Application Contact:* Claudia Walinder, Office Manager, 303-871-3322, E-mail: claudia.walinder@du.edu. *Director*, Dr. Conrad Ciccotello, 303-871-2282, E-mail: conrad.ciccotello@du.edu.

School of Accountancy Students: 48 full-time (21 women), 26 part-time (15 women); includes 11 minority (1 Black or African American, non-Hispanic/Latino; 1 Asian, non-Hispanic/Latino; 8 Hispanic/Latino; 1 Two or more races, non-Hispanic/Latino), 27 international. Average age 26. 138 applicants, 56% accepted, 35 enrolled. *Faculty:* 17 full-time (8 women), 2 part-time/adjunct (1 woman). Expenses: Contact institution. *Financial support:* In 2018–19, 56 students received support. Teaching assistantships with tuition reimbursements available, career-related internships or fieldwork, Federal Work-Study, institutionally sponsored loans, scholarships/grants, and unspecified assistantships available. Support available to part-time students. Financial award application deadline: 2/15; financial award applicants required to submit FAFSA. In 2018, 75 master's awarded. *Program availability:* Part-time, evening/weekend. Offers accounting (M Acc, MBA). *Application deadline:* For fall admission, 10/15 priority date for domestic and international students; for spring admission, 9/15 priority date for domestic and international students. Applications are

processed on a rolling basis. *Application fee:* $100. Electronic applications accepted. *Application Contact:* Jacquelyn Villa, Assistant to the Director, 303-871-2032, E-mail: jacquelyn.villa@du.edu. *Professor/Director, School of Accountancy*, Dr. Sharon Lassar, 303-871-2032, E-mail: slassar@du.edu.

Division of Arts, Humanities and Social Sciences Students: 107 full-time (74 women), 197 part-time (108 women); includes 55 minority (11 Black or African American, non-Hispanic/Latino; 6 Asian, non-Hispanic/Latino; 22 Hispanic/Latino; 1 Native Hawaiian or other Pacific Islander, non-Hispanic/Latino; 15 Two or more races, non-Hispanic/Latino), 32 international. Average age 28. 1,101 applicants, 31% accepted, 137 enrolled. *Faculty:* 236 full-time (123 women), 4 part-time/adjunct (3 women). Expenses: Contact institution. *Financial support:* In 2018–19, 264 students received support, including 12 research assistantships with tuition reimbursements available (averaging $11,597 per year), 132 teaching assistantships with tuition reimbursements available (averaging $10,720 per year); career-related internships or fieldwork, Federal Work-Study, institutionally sponsored loans, scholarships/grants, and unspecified assistantships also available. Support available to part-time students. Financial award application deadline: 2/15; financial award applicants required to submit FAFSA. In 2018, 95 master's, 28 doctorates, 6 other advanced degrees awarded. *Program availability:* Part-time. Offers affective/cognitive/social psychology (PhD); archaeology (MA); arts, humanities and social sciences (MA, MFA, MM, MPP, MS, PhD, Certificate); clinical child psychology (PhD); creative writing (PhD); critical theory and religion (MA); cultural anthropology (MA); developmental psychology (PhD); economics (MA); emergent digital practices (MA, MFA); international and intercultural communication (MA); literary studies (MA, PhD); lived religions (MA); media and public communication (MA); museum and heritage studies (MA); philosophy of religion (MA); religion and international studies (MA); sacred texts (MA). *Application deadline:* Applications are processed on a rolling basis. *Application fee:* $65. Electronic applications accepted. *Application Contact:* Information Contact, 303-871-4449, E-mail: cahss@du.edu. *Dean*, Dr. Danny McIntosh, 303-871-4449, E-mail: daniel.mcintosh@du.edu.

Lamont School of Music Students: 20 full-time (8 women), 89 part-time (36 women); includes 20 minority (4 Black or African American, non-Hispanic/Latino; 3 Asian, non-Hispanic/Latino; 7 Hispanic/Latino; 6 Two or more races, non-Hispanic/Latino), 14 international. Average age 28. 162 applicants, 80% accepted, 59 enrolled. *Faculty:* 30 full-time (9 women), 33 part-time/adjunct (16 women). Expenses: Contact institution. *Financial support:* In 2018–19, 92 students received support, including 40 teaching assistantships with tuition reimbursements available (averaging $6,031 per year); career-related internships or fieldwork, Federal Work-Study, institutionally sponsored loans, scholarships/grants, tuition waivers, and unspecified assistantships also available. Support available to part-time students. Financial award application deadline: 2/15; financial award applicants required to submit FAFSA. In 2018, 26 master's awarded. *Program availability:* Part-time. Offers composition (MM); composition - jazz emphasis (MM); conducting (MM, Certificate); jazz studies (Certificate); music theory (MA); musicology (MA); orchestral studies (Certificate); pedagogy (MM); performance (MM, Certificate); performance - jazz emphasis (MM); Suzuki teaching (Certificate). *Application deadline:* For fall admission, 1/15 priority date for domestic and international students. Applications are processed on a rolling basis. *Application fee:* $65. Electronic applications accepted. *Application Contact:* Stephen Campbell, Director of Admission, 303-871-6973, E-mail: stephen.l.campbell@du.edu. *Professor and Director*, Dr. Nancy Cochran, 303-871-6986, E-mail: nancy.cochran@du.edu.

School of Art and Art History Students: 12 full-time (11 women), 9 part-time (all women); includes 4 minority (1 Black or African American, non-Hispanic/Latino; 3 Hispanic/Latino), 1 international. Average age 25. 25 applicants, 64% accepted, 8 enrolled. *Faculty:* 15 full-time (11 women), 5 part-time/adjunct (4 women). Expenses: Contact institution. *Financial support:* In 2018–19, 20 students received support, including 8 teaching assistantships with tuition reimbursements available (averaging $7,819 per year); research assistantships with tuition reimbursements available, career-related internships or fieldwork, Federal Work-Study, institutionally sponsored loans, scholarships/grants, and unspecified assistantships also available. Support available to part-time students. Financial award application deadline: 2/15; financial award applicants required to submit FAFSA. In 2018, 11 master's awarded. *Program availability:* Part-time. Offers art history (MA); museum studies (MA). *Application deadline:* For fall admission, 1/31 priority date for domestic and international students. Applications are processed on a rolling basis. *Application fee:* $65. Electronic applications accepted. *Application Contact:* Jason Kellermeyer, Coordinator of Academic Programs, 303-871-2846, E-mail: jason.kellermeyer@du.edu. *Associate Professor and Director*, Annabeth Headrick, 303-871-3574, E-mail: annabeth.headrick@du.edu.

Division of Natural Sciences and Mathematics Students: 25 full-time (11 women), 134 part-time (59 women); includes 26 minority (3 Black or African American, non-Hispanic/Latino; 3 Asian, non-Hispanic/Latino; 11 Hispanic/Latino; 9 Two or more races, non-Hispanic/Latino), 20 international. Average age 28. 352 applicants, 45% accepted, 68 enrolled. *Faculty:* 89 full-time (29 women), 12 part-time/adjunct (6 women). Expenses: Contact institution. *Financial support:* In 2018–19, 151 students received support, including 33 research assistantships with tuition reimbursements available (averaging $16,477 per year), 82 teaching assistantships with tuition reimbursements available (averaging $17,370 per year); career-related internships or fieldwork, institutionally sponsored loans, scholarships/grants, and unspecified assistantships also available. Support available to part-time students. Financial award application deadline: 2/15; financial award applicants required to submit FAFSA. In 2018, 46 master's, 12 doctorates awarded. *Program availability:* Part-time, evening/weekend. Offers biology, ecology and evolution (MS, PhD); biomedical sciences (PSM); cell and molecular biology (MS, PhD); chemistry (MA, MS, PhD); geographic information science (MS); geography (MA, PhD); mathematics (MA, MS, PhD); natural sciences and mathematics (MA, MS, PSM, PhD); physics (MS, PhD). *Application deadline:* Applications are processed on a rolling basis. *Application fee:* $65. Electronic applications accepted. *Application Contact:* Kirsten Norwood, Executive Assistant to the Dean, 303-871-2693, E-mail: kirsten.norwood@du.edu. *Dean*, Dr. Andrei Kutateladze, 303-871-2995, E-mail: andrei.kutateladze@du.edu.

DU/Iliff Joint PhD Program in the Study of Religion Students: 21 full-time (8 women), 21 part-time (5 women); includes 5 minority (1 Asian, non-Hispanic/Latino; 3 Hispanic/Latino; 1 Two or more races, non-Hispanic/Latino), 3 international. Average age 38. 33 applicants, 55% accepted, 9 enrolled. *Faculty:* 9 part-time/adjunct (4 women). Expenses: Contact institution. *Financial support:* In 2018–19, 26 students received support, including 11 teaching assistantships (averaging $2,727 per year); scholarships/grants and unspecified assistantships also available. Financial award application deadline: 1/15. In 2018, 14 doctorates awarded. *Program availability:* Part-time. Offers future faculty in religion (Certificate); Latinx studies (Certificate); study of religion (PhD). Program jointly offered with Iliff School of Theology. *Application deadline:*

For fall admission, 1/15 priority date for domestic and international students. Applications are processed on a rolling basis. *Application fee:* $65. Electronic applications accepted. *Application Contact:* Information Contact, 303-765-3136, E-mail: jointphd@iliff.edu. *Director,* Annette Stott, 303-871-3278.

Graduate School of Professional Psychology Students: 246 full-time (188 women), 84 part-time (47 women); includes 99 minority (24 Black or African American, non-Hispanic/Latino; 1 American Indian or Alaska Native, non-Hispanic/Latino; 13 Asian, non-Hispanic/Latino; 44 Hispanic/Latino; 1 Native Hawaiian or other Pacific Islander, non-Hispanic/Latino; 16 Two or more races, non-Hispanic/Latino), 9 international. Average age 27. 942 applicants, 28% accepted, 139 enrolled. *Faculty:* 24 full-time (15 women), 17 part-time/adjunct (10 women). Expenses: Contact institution. *Financial support:* In 2018–19, 239 students received support, including 17 teaching assistantships with tuition reimbursements available (averaging $2,213 per year); career-related internships or fieldwork, Federal Work-Study, institutionally sponsored loans, scholarships/grants, unspecified assistantships, and clinical assistantships also available. Support available to part-time students. Financial award application deadline: 2/15; financial award applicants required to submit FAFSA. In 2018, 98 master's, 34 doctorates awarded. Offers clinical psychology (Psy D); forensic psychology (MA); international disaster psychology (MA); sport and performance psychology (MA); sport coaching (MA); strength and conditioning and fitness coaching (Certificate). *Application deadline:* For fall admission, 1/11 for domestic and international students. *Application fee:* $65. Electronic applications accepted. *Application Contact:* Julie Schellman, Director of Admissions & Recruitment, 303-871-2908, E-mail: Julie.Schellman@du.edu. *Dean,* Dr. Shelly Smith-Acuna, 303-871-3880, Fax: 303-871-4220, E-mail: shelly.smith-acuna@du.edu.

Graduate School of Social Work Students: 687 full-time (619 women), 165 part-time (152 women); includes 209 minority (28 Black or African American, non-Hispanic/Latino; 6 American Indian or Alaska Native, non-Hispanic/Latino; 20 Asian, non-Hispanic/Latino; 133 Hispanic/Latino; 1 Native Hawaiian or other Pacific Islander, non-Hispanic/Latino; 21 Two or more races, non-Hispanic/Latino), 5 international. Average age 29. 1,332 applicants, 88% accepted, 523 enrolled. *Faculty:* 41 full-time (28 women), 85 part-time/adjunct (74 women). Expenses: Contact institution. *Financial support:* In 2018–19, 518 students received support, including 1 research assistantship (averaging $6,000 per year); teaching assistantships, scholarships/grants, and unspecified assistantships also available. Support available to part-time students. Financial award application deadline: 2/15; financial award applicants required to submit FAFSA. In 2018, 280 master's, 5 doctorates, 62 other advanced degrees awarded. *Program availability:* Part-time, evening/weekend, online learning. Offers animal-assisted social work (Certificate); couples and family therapy (Certificate); social work (MSW, PhD); social work with Latinos/as (Certificate). *Application deadline:* For fall admission, 1/15 priority date for domestic and international students. Applications are processed on a rolling basis. *Application fee:* $65. Electronic applications accepted. *Application Contact:* Roberto Garcia, Executive Director, Enrollment, 303-871-2602, E-mail: gsswadmission@du.edu. *Dean,* Dr. Amanda Moore McBride, 303-871-2203, E-mail: gssw.communications@du.edu.

Josef Korbel School of International Studies Students: 223 full-time (115 women), 36 part-time (17 women); includes 61 minority (13 Black or African American, non-Hispanic/Latino; 11 Asian, non-Hispanic/Latino; 23 Hispanic/Latino; 14 Two or more races, non-Hispanic/Latino), 16 international. Average age 27. 970 applicants, 66% accepted, 111 enrolled. *Faculty:* 45 full-time (15 women), 13 part-time/adjunct (3 women). Expenses: Contact institution. *Financial support:* In 2018–19, 189 students received support, including 1 teaching assistantship with tuition reimbursement available (averaging $7,500 per year); research assistantships with tuition reimbursements available, career-related internships or fieldwork, Federal Work-Study, institutionally sponsored loans, scholarships/grants, and unspecified assistantships also available. Support available to part-time students. Financial award application deadline: 2/15; financial award applicants required to submit FAFSA. In 2018, 171 master's, 8 doctorates, 37 other advanced degrees awarded. *Program availability:* Part-time. Offers conflict resolution (MA); global business and corporate social responsibility (Certificate); global finance, trade and economic integration (MA); global health affairs (Certificate); homeland security (Certificate); humanitarian assistance (Certificate); international administration (MA); international development (MA); international human rights (MA); international security (MA); international studies (MA, PhD); public policy studies (MPP); religion and international affairs (Certificate). *Application deadline:* For fall admission, 1/23 priority date for domestic and international students; for winter admission, 11/1 for domestic and international students. Applications are processed on a rolling basis. *Application fee:* $65. Electronic applications accepted. *Application Contact:* Admissions Contact, 303-871-2324, E-mail: korbeladm@du.edu. *Dean,* Dr. Fritz Mayer, 303-871-6338, E-mail: frederick.mayer@du.edu.

Institute for Public Policy Studies Students: 20 full-time (10 women), 3 part-time (1 woman); includes 6 minority (3 Black or African American, non-Hispanic/Latino; 3 Hispanic/Latino). Average age 27. 93 applicants, 54% accepted, 8 enrolled. *Faculty:* 3 full-time (0 women). Expenses: Contact institution. *Financial support:* In 2018–19, 13 students received support, including 1 teaching assistantship with tuition reimbursement available (averaging $7,500 per year); Federal Work-Study, scholarships/grants, and unspecified assistantships also available. Financial award application deadline: 2/15; financial award applicants required to submit FAFSA. In 2018, 8 master's awarded. Offers public policy studies (MPP). *Application deadline:* For fall admission, 1/23 priority date for domestic and international students; for winter admission, 11/1 priority date for domestic and international students. Applications are processed on a rolling basis. *Application fee:* $65. Electronic applications accepted. *Application Contact:* Institute for Public Policy Studies, E-mail: ipps@du.edu. *Director,* Dr. Richard Caldwell, 303-871-2468, Fax: 303-871-3066, E-mail: richard.caldwell@du.edu.

Morgridge College of Education Students: 509 full-time (400 women), 365 part-time (277 women); includes 236 minority (53 Black or African American, non-Hispanic/Latino; 6 American Indian or Alaska Native, non-Hispanic/Latino; 28 Asian, non-Hispanic/Latino; 116 Hispanic/Latino; 33 Two or more races, non-Hispanic/Latino), 56 international. Average age 31. 1,372 applicants, 57% accepted, 382 enrolled. *Faculty:* 49 full-time (35 women), 33 part-time/adjunct (20 women). Expenses: Contact institution. *Financial support:* In 2018–19, 690 students received support, including 29 research assistantships with tuition reimbursements available (averaging $11,465 per year), 9 teaching assistantships with tuition reimbursements available (averaging $2,527 per year); career-related internships or fieldwork, Federal Work-Study, institutionally sponsored loans, scholarships/grants, and unspecified assistantships also available. Support available to part-time students. Financial award application deadline: 2/15; financial award applicants required to submit FAFSA. In 2018, 258 master's, 41 doctorates, 162 other advanced degrees awarded. *Program availability:* Part-time, evening/weekend, online learning. Offers child, family and school psychology (MA, PhD, Ed S); counseling psychology (MA, PhD); curriculum and instruction (MA, Ed D, PhD);

curriculum instruction and teaching (Certificate); early childhood special education (MA, Certificate); educational leadership and policy studies (MA, Ed D, PhD, Certificate); higher education (Ed D, PhD); library and information science (MLIS); research methods and statistics (MA, PhD). *Application deadline:* Applications are processed on a rolling basis. *Application fee:* $65. Electronic applications accepted. *Application Contact:* Jodi Dye, Director of Admissions, 303-871-2510, E-mail: jodi.dye@du.edu. *Dean,* Dr. Karen Riley, 303-871-3665, E-mail: karen.riley@du.edu.

Sturm College of Law Students: 758 full-time (419 women), 139 part-time (90 women); includes 203 minority (22 Black or African American, non-Hispanic/Latino; 3 American Indian or Alaska Native, non-Hispanic/Latino; 33 Asian, non-Hispanic/Latino; 119 Hispanic/Latino; 26 Two or more races, non-Hispanic/Latino), 29 international. Average age 29. 2,773 applicants, 49% accepted, 316 enrolled. *Faculty:* 67 full-time (36 women), 36 part-time/adjunct (11 women). Expenses: Contact institution. *Financial support:* In 2018–19, 599 students received support, including 4 teaching assistantships with tuition reimbursements available (averaging $37,000 per year); career-related internships or fieldwork, Federal Work-Study, institutionally sponsored loans, scholarships/grants, unspecified assistantships, and tutorships also available. Support available to part-time students. Financial award application deadline: 2/15; financial award applicants required to submit FAFSA. In 2018, 109 master's, 245 doctorates, 87 Certificates awarded. *Program availability:* Part-time, evening/weekend. Offers environmental and natural resources law and policy (LL M, MLS); law (LL M, MLS, MRLS, MSLA, MT, JD, Certificate); legal administration (MSLA, Certificate); natural resources law and policy (Certificate); tax (LL M, MT). *Application deadline:* Applications are processed on a rolling basis. *Application fee:* $65. Electronic applications accepted. *Application Contact:* Yvonne Cherena-Pacheco, Associate Director of Admissions, 303-871-6151, E-mail: admissions@law.du.edu. *Dean,* Dr. Bruce Smith, 303-871-6103, E-mail: bsmith@law.du.edu.

University College Students: 51 full-time (26 women), 1,291 part-time (733 women); includes 337 minority (112 Black or African American, non-Hispanic/Latino; 6 American Indian or Alaska Native, non-Hispanic/Latino; 46 Asian, non-Hispanic/Latino; 132 Hispanic/Latino; 3 Native Hawaiian or other Pacific Islander, non-Hispanic/Latino; 38 Two or more races, non-Hispanic/Latino), 75 international. Average age 34. 834 applicants, 87% accepted, 423 enrolled. *Faculty:* 4 full-time (2 women), 108 part-time/adjunct (51 women). Expenses: Contact institution. *Financial support:* In 2018–19, 38 students received support. Teaching assistantships available. Financial award applicants required to submit FAFSA. In 2018, 443 master's, 232 other advanced degrees awarded. *Program availability:* Part-time, evening/weekend, 100% online, blended/hybrid learning. Offers arts and culture (MA, Certificate); communication management (MS, Certificate); environmental policy and management (MS); geographic information systems (MS); global affairs (MA, Certificate); healthcare leadership (MS); information communications and technology (MS); leadership and organizations (MS); professional creative writing (MA, Certificate); security management (MS, Certificate); strategic human resources (Certificate). *Application deadline:* For fall admission, 6/19 priority date for domestic students, 6/14 priority date for international students; for winter admission, 10/25 priority date for domestic students, 9/27 priority date for international students; for spring admission, 2/7 priority date for domestic students, 1/10 priority date for international students; for summer admission, 4/24 priority date for domestic students, 3/27 priority date for international students. Applications are processed on a rolling basis. *Application fee:* $75. Electronic applications accepted. *Application Contact:* Admission Team, 303-871-2291, E-mail: ucoladm@du.edu. *Dean,* Dr. Michael McGuire, 303-871-3518, E-mail: michael.mcguire@du.edu.

UNIVERSITY OF DETROIT MERCY, Detroit, MI 48221

General Information Independent-religious, coed, university. *Graduate housing:* Room and/or apartments available on a first-come, first-served basis to single students; on-campus housing not available to married students.

GRADUATE UNITS

College of Business Administration *Program availability:* Part-time, evening/weekend, 100% online, blended/hybrid learning. Offers business administration (MBA); business fundamentals (Certificate); business turnaround management (Certificate); ethical leadership and change management (Certificate); finance (Certificate); forensic accounting (Certificate). Electronic applications accepted.

College of Engineering and Science *Program availability:* Part-time, evening/weekend. Offers chemistry (MS); civil and environmental engineering (DE); electrical and computer engineering (ME); electrical engineering (DE); engineering management (M Eng Mgt); environmental engineering (MEE); mechanical engineering (MME, DE); product development (MS); software engineering (MSSE); teaching of mathematics (MATM). Electronic applications accepted.

College of Health Professions Offers clinical nurse leader (MSN); family nurse practitioner (MSN); health services administration (MHSA); health systems management (MSN); nurse anesthesia (MS); nursing (DNP); nursing education (MSN, Certificate); nursing leadership and financial management (Certificate); outcomes performance management (Certificate); physician assistant (MS).

College of Liberal Arts and Education *Program availability:* Part-time, evening/weekend. Offers addiction counseling (MA); addiction studies (Certificate); clinical mental health counseling (MA); clinical psychology (MA, PhD); computer and information systems (MS); criminal justice (MA); curriculum and instruction (MA); economics (MA); educational administration (MA); financial economics (MA); industrial/organizational psychology (MA); information assurance (MA); intelligence analysis (MA); liberal studies (MALS); religious studies (MA); school counseling (MA, Certificate); school psychology (Spec); security administration (MS); special education: emotionally impaired/behaviorally disordered (MA); special education: learning disabilities (MA).

School of Architecture Offers architecture (M Arch); community development (MA).

School of Dentistry Offers dentistry (MS, DDS, Certificate).

School of Law *Program availability:* Part-time. Offers law (JD).

UNIVERSITY OF DUBUQUE, Dubuque, IA 52001-5099

General Information Independent-religious, coed, comprehensive institution. *Graduate housing:* Rooms and/or apartments available on a first-come, first-served basis to single students and available to married students.

GRADUATE UNITS

Program in Business Administration *Program availability:* Part-time, evening/weekend. Offers business administration (MBA). Electronic applications accepted.

Program in Communication *Program availability:* Part-time, evening/weekend. Offers information technologies communication (MAC); leadership and management (MAC); strategic and corporate communication (MAC). Electronic applications accepted.

University of Dubuque Theological Seminary *Program availability:* Part-time, 100% online, blended/hybrid learning. Offers theology (M Div, D Min). Electronic applications accepted.

UNIVERSITY OF EAST-WEST MEDICINE, Sunnyvale, CA 94085-3922

General Information Proprietary, coed, graduate-only institution. *Graduate housing:* On-campus housing not available.

GRADUATE UNITS

Graduate Programs Offers acupuncture and Oriental medicine (DAOM); Tai Chi (MS); traditional Chinese medicine (MSTCM).

UNIVERSITY OF EVANSVILLE, Evansville, IN 47722

General Information Independent-religious, coed, comprehensive institution. *Graduate housing:* Room and/or apartments available to single students; on-campus housing not available to married students. *Research affiliation:* The New American Colleges and Universities (higher education administration), Independent Colleges of Indiana (higher education administration), Council of Independent Colleges (higher education administration), Military Family Research Institute (higher education administration).

GRADUATE UNITS

Center for Adult Education *Program availability:* Part-time, evening/weekend. Offers public service administration (MS).

College of Education and Health Sciences Offers education and health sciences (MPH, MS, MSAT, DPT); physical therapy (DPT).

School of Health Sciences *Program availability:* Part-time, evening/weekend. Offers athletic training (MSAT); health policy (MPH); health services administration (MS).

UNIVERSITY OF FAIRFAX, Vienna, VA 22182

General Information Proprietary, coed, graduate-only institution.

GRADUATE UNITS

Graduate Programs

THE UNIVERSITY OF FINDLAY, Findlay, OH 45840-3653

General Information Independent-religious, coed, comprehensive institution. *Graduate housing:* Room and/or apartments available on a first-come, first-served basis to single students; on-campus housing not available to married students. *Research affiliation:* The Ohio State University Research Foundation (biology), Rollin M. Gerstacker Foundation (environmental research), U.S. Department of Agriculture (USDA) (wildlife research), U.S. Department of Education (DOE) (technology innovation, bilingual teaching research), U.S. Department of Health and Human Services (terrorism preparedness).

GRADUATE UNITS

Office of Graduate Admissions *Program availability:* Part-time, evening/weekend, 100% online, blended/hybrid learning. Offers applied security and analytics (MSAS); athletic training (MAT); business (MBA); education (MA Ed, Ed D); environmental, safety, and health management (MSEM); health informatics (MS); occupational therapy (MOT); pharmacy (Pharm D); physician assistant (MPA); rhetoric and writing (MA); teaching English to speakers of other languages (TESOL) and applied linguistics (MA). Electronic applications accepted.

UNIVERSITY OF FLORIDA, Gainesville, FL 32611

General Information State-supported, coed, university. CGS member. *Graduate housing:* Rooms and/or apartments available on a first-come, first-served basis to single and married students. *Research affiliation:* Los Alamos National Laboratory (high magnetic field research), National Center for Automated Information Research (law and business data), Oracle Corporation (database management), IBM (information infrastructure), Association of Universities for Research in Astronomy (Gemini multinational telescope).

GRADUATE UNITS

College of Dentistry Offers dentistry (MS, DMD, PhD, Certificate); endodontics (MS, Certificate); foreign trained dentistry (Certificate); oral biology (PhD); orthodontics (MS, Certificate); periodontology (MS, Certificate); prosthodontics (MS, Certificate).

College of Medicine Offers biochemistry and molecular biology (PhD); biomedical sciences (MS, PhD); clinical investigation (MS); epidemiology (MS); genetics (PhD); immunology and microbiology (PhD); medicine (MPAS, MPH, MS, MD, PhD); molecular cell biology (PhD); molecular genetics and microbiology (PhD); neuroscience (PhD); physician assistant (MPAS); physiology and pharmacology (PhD); public health (MPH). Electronic applications accepted.

College of Veterinary Medicine *Program availability:* Part-time. Offers forensic toxicology (Certificate); veterinary medical sciences (MS, PhD); veterinary medicine (MS, DVM, PhD, Certificate).

Graduate School *Program availability:* Part-time, evening/weekend, online learning. Electronic applications accepted.

College of Agricultural and Life Sciences *Program availability:* Part-time. Offers agribusiness (MS); agricultural and life sciences (MAB, MFAS, MFRC, MS, DPM, PhD, Certificate); agricultural education and communication (MS, PhD); agroecology (MS); agronomy (MS, PhD); animal molecular and cellular biology (MS, PhD); animal sciences (MS, PhD); community studies (MS); environmental education and communications (Certificate); environmental horticulture (MS, PhD); family and youth development (MS); family, youth and community sciences (MS); fisheries and aquatic sciences (MFAS, MS, PhD); food and resource economics (MAB, MS, PhD); food science (PhD); food science and human nutrition (MS); forest resources and conservation (MFRC, MS, PhD); geographic information systems (MS); horticultural sciences (MS, PhD); hydrologic sciences (MS, PhD); microbiology and cell science (MS, PhD); nonprofit organization development (MS); nutritional sciences (MS, PhD); plant medicine (DPM); plant molecular and cellular biology (MS, PhD); plant pathology (MS, PhD); soil and water science (MS, PhD); toxicology (MS, PhD); tropical conservation and development (MAB, MS, DPM, PhD); wildlife ecology and conservation (MS, PhD). Electronic applications accepted.

College of Design, Construction and Planning *Program availability:* Part-time, online learning. Offers architecture (M Arch, MSAS); construction management (MSCM, PhD); design, construction and planning (M Arch, MAURP, MFES, MICM, MID, MLA, MSAS, MSCM, MURP, PhD); fire and emergency services (MFES); geographic information systems (MAURP, MLA, PhD); historic preservation (M Arch, MAURP, MID, MLA, MSAS, MSCM, PhD); interior design (MID, PhD); international construction (MICM); landscape architecture (MLA, PhD); sustainable architecture (M Arch, MSAS); sustainable construction (MSCM); sustainable design (M Arch, MAURP, MID, MLA, MSAS, MSCM); tropical conservation and development (MAURP); urban and regional planning (MAURP, MURP, PhD); wetland sciences (MAURP, MLA). Electronic applications accepted.

College of Education *Program availability:* Part-time, evening/weekend, online learning. Offers counseling and counselor education (Ed D, PhD); curriculum and instruction (M Ed, MAE, Ed D, PhD, Ed S); early childhood education (M Ed, MAE); education (M Ed, MAE, Ed D, PhD, Ed S); educational leadership (M Ed, MAE, Ed D, PhD, Ed S); elementary education (M Ed, MAE); English education (M Ed, MAE); higher education administration (Ed D, PhD); marriage and family counseling (M Ed, MAE, Ed D, PhD, Ed S); mathematics education (M Ed, MAE); mental health counseling (M Ed, MAE, Ed D, PhD, Ed S); reading education (M Ed, MAE); research and evaluation methodology (M Ed, MAE, Ed D, PhD); school counseling and guidance (M Ed, MAE, Ed D, PhD, Ed S); school psychology (M Ed, MAE, Ed D, PhD, Ed S); science education (M Ed, MAE); social studies education (M Ed, MAE); special education (M Ed, MAE, Ed D, PhD, Ed S); student personnel in higher education (M Ed, MAE). Electronic applications accepted.

College of Health and Human Performance *Program availability:* Part-time. Offers applied physiology and kinesiology (MS); athletic training/sports medicine (MS); biobehavioral science (MS); clinical exercise physiology (MS); exercise physiology (MS); health and human performance (PhD); health communication (Graduate Certificate); health education and behavior (MS); human performance (MS); recreation, parks and tourism (MS); sport management (MS). Electronic applications accepted.

College of Journalism and Communications *Program availability:* Part-time, online learning. Offers advertising (M Adv); international/intercultural communication (MAMC); journalism (MAMC); mass communication (MAMC, PhD); public relations (MAMC); science/health communication (MAMC); telecommunication (MAMC). Electronic applications accepted.

College of Liberal Arts and Sciences *Program availability:* Part-time. Offers anthropology (MA, MAT, PhD); applications of geographic technologies (MA, MS); astronomy (MS, MST, PhD); botany (MS, MST, PhD); chemistry (MS, MST, PhD); classical studies (MA, PhD); clinical and translational science (PhD); counseling psychology (PhD); creative writing (MFA); criminology, law, and society (MA, PhD); educational policy (PhD); English (MA, PhD); French and Francophone studies (MA, PhD); gender and development (Graduate Certificate); geographic information systems (MA, MS, PhD); geography (MA, MS, PhD); geology (MS, MST, PhD); German (MA, PhD); historic preservation (MA, PhD); history (MA, PhD); hydrologic sciences (MS, PhD); imaging science and technology (PhD); international development policy and administration (MA, Certificate); international relations (MA, MAT); Jewish studies (MA); Latin (MA, MAT, ML); Latin American studies (MA, Certificate); liberal arts and sciences (M Ag, M Stat, MA, MAT, MDP, MFA, ML, MS, MS Stat, MST, MWS, PhD, Certificate, Graduate Certificate); linguistics (MA, PhD); mathematics (MAT, MS, MST, PhD); philosophy (MA, PhD); physics (MS, MST, PhD); political campaigning (MA, Certificate); political science (MA, PhD); psychology (MA, MS, PhD); public affairs (MA, Certificate); quantitative finance (PhD); religion (MA, PhD); sociology (MA, PhD); Spanish (MA, MAT, PhD); statistics (M Stat, MS Stat, PhD); sustainable development practice (MDP); teaching English as a second language (Certificate); tropical conservation and development (MA, MS, MST, PhD); wetland sciences (MA, MS, MST, PhD); women's and gender studies (MA, PhD); women's studies (MA, Graduate Certificate); zoology (MS, MST, PhD). Electronic applications accepted.

College of Nursing *Program availability:* Part-time. Offers clinical and translational science (PhD); clinical nursing (DNP); nursing (MSN); nursing sciences (PhD). Electronic applications accepted.

College of Pharmacy *Program availability:* Part-time, evening/weekend, online learning. Offers clinical and translational sciences (PhD); clinical pharmaceutical sciences (PhD); clinical pharmacy (MSP); clinical toxicology (MSP, Certificate); drug chemistry (Certificate); environmental forensics (Certificate); forensic death investigation (Certificate); forensic DNA and serology (MSP, Certificate); forensic drug chemistry (MSP); forensic science (MSP); forensic toxicology (Certificate); medicinal chemistry (MSP, PhD); pharmaceutical chemistry (MSP); pharmaceutical outcomes and policy (MSP, PhD); pharmaceutical sciences (MSP, PhD); pharmacodynamics (MSP, PhD); pharmacy (MSP, PhD). Electronic applications accepted.

College of Public Health and Health Professions *Program availability:* Part-time. Offers audiology (Au D); biostatistics (MS, PhD); clinical and translational science (PhD); communication sciences and disorders (MA, PhD); environmental health (MPH, PhD); epidemiology (MPH, MS, PhD); health administration (MHA); health management and policy (MPH); health services research (PhD); occupational therapy (MHS, MOT); one health (MHS, PhD); physical therapy (DPT); psychology (MS); public health (MPH, PhD, Certificate); public health and health professions (MA, MHA, MHS, MHS, MOT, MPH, MS, Au D, DPT, PhD, Certificate); public health practice (MPH); rehabilitation science (PhD); social and behavioral sciences (MPH). Electronic applications accepted.

College of The Arts *Program availability:* Online learning. Offers art (MA); art education (MA); art history (MA, PhD); arts (MA, MFA, MM, PhD, Graduate Certificate); choral conducting (MM); composition (MM, PhD); electronic music (MM); ethnomusicology (MM); instrumental conducting (MM); museology (MA); music (MM, PhD); music education (MM, PhD); music history and literature (MM, PhD); music theory (MM); performance (MM); sacred music (MM); theatre (MFA). Electronic applications accepted.

Herbert Wertheim College of Engineering *Program availability:* Part-time, online learning. Offers aerospace engineering (ME, MS, PhD); agricultural and biological engineering (ME, MS, PhD, Certificate); biomedical engineering (ME, MS, PhD, Engr); chemical engineering (ME, MS, PhD, Engr); civil engineering (ME, MS, PhD); clinical and translational science (PhD); coastal and oceanographic engineering (ME, MS, PhD); computer engineering (ME, MS, PhD); computer science (MS); digital arts and sciences (MS); electrical and computer engineering (ME, MS, PhD); engineering (ME, MS, PhD, Certificate, Engr); environmental engineering sciences (ME, MS, PhD, Engr); geographic information systems (ME, MS, PhD); hydrologic sciences (ME, MS, PhD); imaging science and technology (PhD); industrial and systems engineering (ME, MS, PhD, Engr); material science and engineering (MS); materials science and engineering (ME, PhD); mechanical engineering (ME, MS, PhD); medical physics (MS, PhD); nuclear engineering (ME, PhD); nuclear engineering sciences (ME, MS, PhD); quantitative finance (PhD); structural engineering (ME, MS); wetland sciences (ME, MS, PhD). Electronic applications accepted.

School of Natural Resources and Environment Offers interdisciplinary ecology (MS, PhD). Electronic applications accepted.

Warrington College of Business Administration *Program availability:* Part-time, evening/weekend, online learning. Offers accounting (M Acc, PhD); business administration (M Acc, MA, MBA, MS, PhD, Certificate); competitive strategy (MBA); economics (MA, PhD); entrepreneurship (MS); finance (MBA, MS, PhD); financial services (Certificate); global management (MBA); Graham-Buffett security analysis

(MBA); health care risk management (MS); human resource management (MBA); information systems and operations management (MBA, PhD); insurance (PhD); international business (MA); international studies (MBA); management (MBA, MS, PhD); marketing (MIA, MS, PhD); quantitative finance (PhD); real estate (MBA, MS); real estate and urban analysis (PhD); supply chain management (Certificate). Electronic applications accepted.

Levin College of Law Offers comparative law (LL M); environmental and land use law (LL M); international taxation (LL M); law (JD); taxation (LL M, SJD). Electronic applications accepted.

UNIVERSITY OF FORT LAUDERDALE, Lauderhill, FL 33313

General Information Independent-religious, coed, comprehensive institution.

GRADUATE UNITS

Graduate Program Offers ministry (MS).

UNIVERSITY OF GEORGIA, Athens, GA 30602

General Information State-supported, coed, university. CGS member. *Graduate housing:* Rooms and/or apartments available on a first-come, first-served basis to single and married students. *Research affiliation:* Skidaway Institute of Oceanography, Southeast Water Laboratory, Russell Research Laboratory, Organization for Tropical Studies.

GRADUATE UNITS

Biomedical and Health Sciences Institute Offers neuroscience (PhD).

College of Agricultural and Environmental Sciences Offers agricultural and environmental sciences (MAE, MS, PhD); agricultural economics (MAE, MS, PhD); animal and dairy science (PhD); animal nutrition (PhD); animal science (MS); crop and soil sciences (MS, PhD); entomology (MS, PhD); environmental economics (MS); food science (MS, PhD); horticulture (MS, PhD); plant pathology (MS, PhD); poultry science (MS, PhD). Electronic applications accepted.

Institute of Plant Breeding, Genetics and Genomics Offers plant breeding, genetics and genomics (MS, PhD).

College of Education Offers adult education (Ed D, Ed S); college student affairs administration (M Ed, PhD); communication science and disorders (M Ed, MA, PhD, Ed S); education (M Ed, MA, MA Ed, MAT, MS, Ed D, PhD, Ed S); educational psychology (Ed S); English education (M Ed); higher education (M Ed, Ed D, PhD); kinesiology (MS, PhD); language and literacy education (PhD); learning, design, and technology (M Ed, PhD, Ed S); lifelong education, administration and policy (PhD); mathematics education (M Ed, PhD, Ed S); professional school counseling (Ed S); special education (Ed D); workforce education (MAT, Ed S). Electronic applications accepted.

College of Engineering Offers engineering (MS).

College of Environment and Design Offers environmental planning and design (MEPD); historic preservation (MHP); landscape architecture (MLA).

College of Family and Consumer Sciences Offers child and family development (MS); family and consumer sciences (MS, PhD); foods and nutrition (MS, PhD); historical and cultural aspects of dress and textiles (MS); interior environments (MS); international merchandising (PhD); merchandising and international trade (MS); polymer, fiber and textile science (MS); polymer, fiber, and textile sciences (PhD). Electronic applications accepted.

College of Pharmacy Offers clinical and experimental therapeutics (PhD); pharmaceutical and biomedical sciences (MS, PhD); pharmacy (MS, PhD, Pharm D, Certificate); pharmacy care administration (PhD). Electronic applications accepted.

College of Public Health Offers environmental health science (MPH, MS, PhD); health promotion and behavior (MA, MPH, Dr PH, PhD); public health (MA, MPH, MS, Dr PH, PhD, Certificate).

Institute of Gerontology Offers gerontology (Certificate).

College of Veterinary Medicine Offers infectious diseases (PhD); pharmacology (MS, PhD); veterinary medicine (MS, DVM, PhD); veterinary pathology (MS, PhD). Electronic applications accepted.

Eugene P. Odum School of Ecology Offers conservation ecology and sustainable development (MS); ecology (PhD). Electronic applications accepted.

Franklin College of Arts and Sciences Offers analytical chemistry (MS, PhD); anthropology (MA, PhD); applied mathematical science (MAMS); arts and sciences (MA, MAMS, MAT, MFA, MM, MM Ed, MS, DMA, PhD, Certificate); biochemistry and molecular biology (MS, PhD); cellular biology (MS, PhD); classical languages (MA); comparative literature (MA, PhD); computer science (MS, PhD); English (MA, MAT, PhD); French (PhD); genetics (MS, PhD); geography (MA, MS, PhD); geology (MS, PhD); German (MA); Greek (MA); history (MA, PhD); Italian (MA, PhD); Latin (MA); linguistics (MA, PhD); marine sciences (MS, PhD); mathematics (MA, PhD); microbiology (MS, PhD); philosophy (MA, PhD); physics (MS, PhD); plant biology (MS, PhD); Portuguese (MA, PhD); psychology (PhD); religion (MA); romance linguistics (MA); sociology (MA, PhD); Spanish (PhD); statistics (MS, PhD); theatre (MFA, PhD). Electronic applications accepted.

Artificial Intelligence Center Offers artificial intelligence (MS). Electronic applications accepted.

Hugh Hodgson School of Music Offers composition (MM, DMA); conducting (MM, DMA); music (PhD); music education (MM Ed, Ed D); musicology (MA); performance (MM, DMA). Ed D offered jointly with College of Education. Electronic applications accepted.

Institute for Women's Studies Offers women's studies (Certificate).

Lamar Dodd School of Art Offers art (MFA, PhD); art history (MA). Electronic applications accepted.

Grady College of Journalism and Mass Communication Offers journalism and mass communication (MA); mass communication (PhD). Electronic applications accepted.

Institute of Bioinformatics Offers bioinformatics (MS, PhD).

School of Law Offers law (LL M, MSL, JD). Electronic applications accepted.

School of Public and International Affairs Offers international affairs (MA, MIP, PhD); political science (MA, PhD); public administration (MPA, PhD); public and international affairs (MA, MIP, MPA, PhD). Electronic applications accepted.

School of Social Work *Program availability:* Part-time, evening/weekend. Offers social work (MA, MSW, PhD, Certificate). Electronic applications accepted.

Terry College of Business Offers business (Exec MBA, M Acc, MA, MBA, MMR, MSBA, PhD); business administration (Exec MBA, MBA); business analytics (MSBA); economics (MA, PhD). Electronic applications accepted.

J.M. Tull School of Accounting Offers accounting (M Acc). Electronic applications accepted.

Warnell School of Forestry and Natural Resources Offers forestry and natural resources (MFR, MS, PhD). Electronic applications accepted.

UNIVERSITY OF GUAM, Mangilao, GU 96923

General Information Territory-supported, coed, comprehensive institution. *Graduate housing:* Room and/or apartments available on a first-come, first-served basis to single students; on-campus housing not available to married students. Housing application deadline: 5/1. *Research affiliation:* Bernice Pauahi Bishop Museum (science, cultural preservation), Pilar Project, Inc. (salvage of artifacts, archaeology), Cancer Research Center of Hawaii (cancer research).

GRADUATE UNITS

Office of Graduate Studies *Program availability:* Part-time.

College of Liberal Arts and Social Sciences *Program availability:* Part-time. Offers ceramics (MA); English (MA); graphics (MA); liberal arts and social sciences (MA); Micronesian studies (MA); painting (MA).

College of Natural and Applied Sciences Offers environmental science (MS); natural and applied sciences (MS, MSW); social work (MSW); tropical marine biology (MS).

School of Business and Public Administration *Program availability:* Part-time. Offers business administration (PMBA); business and public administration (MPA, PMBA); public administration (MPA).

School of Education *Program availability:* Part-time. Offers administration and supervision (M Ed); counseling (MA); education (M Ed, MA); language and literacy (M Ed); secondary education (M Ed); special education (M Ed); teaching English to speakers of other languages (M Ed).

UNIVERSITY OF GUELPH, Guelph, ON N1G 2W1, Canada

General Information Province-supported, coed, university. *Graduate housing:* Rooms and/or apartments available to single and married students. Housing application deadline: 5/28.

GRADUATE UNITS

Office of Graduate and Postdoctoral Studies Students: 2,427 full-time (1,369 women), 195 part-time (124 women). *Faculty:* 736. Expenses: Contact institution. *Financial support:* Fellowships with full tuition reimbursements, research assistantships, teaching assistantships with full tuition reimbursements, career-related internships or fieldwork, Federal Work-Study, institutionally sponsored loans, scholarships/grants, tuition waivers (full), unspecified assistantships, and bursaries available. Support available to part-time students. *Program availability:* Part-time, evening/weekend, online learning. Offers biophysics (M Sc, PhD). *Application deadline:* Applications are processed on a rolling basis. *Application fee:* $110. Electronic applications accepted. *Application Contact:* Nick Pankerichan, Manager, Graduate Admission and Marketing, 519-824-4120 Ext. 56198, Fax: 519-766-0143, E-mail: gradonln@uoguelph.ca. *Assistant VP - Graduate Studies,* Dr. B Bradshaw, 519-824-4120 Ext. 58460, E-mail: bbradsha@uoguelph.ca.

Collaborative International Development Studies *Program availability:* Part-time. Offers international development studies (M Eng, M Sc, MA, MBA, PhD).

College of Arts *Program availability:* Part-time. Offers arts (MA, MFA, PhD); drama (MA); English (MA); European studies (MA); French studies (MA); history (MA, PhD); literary studies/theatre studies in English (PhD); philosophy (MA, PhD); studio art (MFA).

College of Biological Science *Program availability:* Part-time. Offers biochemistry (M Sc, PhD); biological science (M Sc, PhD); biophysics (M Sc, PhD); botany (M Sc, PhD); microbiology (M Sc, PhD); molecular biology and genetics (M Sc, PhD); nutritional sciences (M Sc, PhD); zoology (M Sc, PhD). Electronic applications accepted.

College of Management and Economics Offers economics (MA, PhD); food and agribusiness management (MBA); hospitality and tourism management (MBA); leadership (MA); management and economics (M Sc, MA, MBA, PhD); marketing and consumer studies (M Sc).

College of Physical and Engineering Science *Program availability:* Part-time. Offers applied computer science (M Sc); applied mathematics (PhD); applied statistics (PhD); biological engineering (M Eng, M Sc, MA Sc, PhD); chemistry and biochemistry (M Sc, PhD); computer science (PhD); engineering systems and computing (M Eng, M Sc, MA Sc, PhD); environmental engineering (M Eng, M Sc, MA Sc, PhD); mathematics and statistics (M Sc); physical and engineering science (M Eng, M Sc, MA Sc, PhD); physics (M Sc, PhD); water resources engineering (M Eng, M Sc, MA Sc, PhD).

College of Social and Applied Human Sciences *Program availability:* Part-time. Offers anthropology (MA); applied nutrition (MAN); applied social psychology (MA, PhD); clinical psychology: applied development emphasis (MA); clinical psychology: applied developmental emphasis (MA); comparative politics (MA); crime and criminal justice policy (MA); criminology and criminal justice policy (MA); family relations and human development (M Sc, PhD); geography (M Sc, MA, PhD); industrial/organizational psychology (MA, PhD); international development (MA); neuroscience and applied cognitive science (MA, PhD); political science (MA); public policy and public administration (MA); social and applied human sciences (M Sc, MA, MAN, PhD); sociology (MA, PhD); the Americas (Canada emphasis) (MA).

Ontario Agricultural College *Program availability:* Part-time, online learning. Offers agricultural economics (M Sc, PhD); agriculture (M Sc, MLA, PhD, Diploma); animal and poultry science (M Sc, PhD); aquaculture (M Sc, PhD); atmospheric science (M Sc, PhD); capacity development and extension (M Sc); entomology (M Sc, PhD); environmental and agricultural earth sciences (M Sc, PhD); environmental microbiology and biotechnology (M Sc, PhD); environmental toxicology (M Sc, PhD); food safety and quality assurance (M Sc); food science (M Sc, PhD); international rural planning and development (M Sc); land resources management (M Sc, PhD); landscape architecture (MLA); plant agriculture (M Sc, PhD); plant and forest systems (M Sc, PhD); plant pathology (M Sc, PhD); rural planning and development (M Sc); rural planning and development in Canada (M Sc); rural studies (PhD); soil science (M Sc, PhD).

Ontario Veterinary College Offers toxicology (M Sc, PhD); veterinary medicine (M Sc, DV Sc, PhD, Diploma).

Graduate Programs in Veterinary Sciences Offers anatomic pathology (DV Sc, Diploma); anesthesiology (M Sc, DV Sc); cardiology (DV Sc, Diploma); clinical pathology (Diploma); clinical studies (Diploma); comparative pathology (M Sc, PhD); dermatology (M Sc); diagnostic imaging (M Sc, DV Sc); emergency/critical care (M Sc, DV Sc, Diploma); epidemiology (M Sc, DV Sc, PhD); health management (DV Sc); immunology (M Sc, PhD); laboratory animal science (DV Sc); medicine (M Sc, DV Sc); morphology (M Sc, PhD); neurology (M Sc, DV Sc); neuroscience (M Sc, DV Sc, PhD); ophthalmology (M Sc, DV Sc); pathology (M Sc, PhD, Diploma); pharmacology (M Sc, DV Sc, PhD); physiology (M Sc, DV Sc, PhD);

population medicine and health management (M Sc); surgery (M Sc, DV Sc); swine health management (M Sc); theriogenology (M Sc, DV Sc); toxicology (M Sc, DV Sc, PhD); veterinary infectious diseases (M Sc, PhD); veterinary sciences (M Sc, DV Sc, PhD, Diploma); zoo animal/wildlife medicine (DV Sc).

UNIVERSITY OF HARTFORD, West Hartford, CT 06117-1599

General Information Independent, coed, comprehensive institution. CGS member. *Graduate housing:* On-campus housing not available.

GRADUATE UNITS

Barney School of Business *Program availability:* Part-time, evening/weekend. Offers business (MBA, MSAT, Certificate); business administration (MBA); professional accounting (Certificate); taxation (MSAT). Electronic applications accepted.

College of Arts and Sciences *Program availability:* Part-time, evening/weekend. Offers arts and sciences (MA, MS, Psy D); clinical practices (Psy D); communication (MA); neuroscience (MS); organizational behavior (MS); psychology (MA); school psychology (MS). Electronic applications accepted.

College of Education, Nursing, and Health Professions *Program availability:* Part-time, evening/weekend. Offers community/public health nursing (MSN); early childhood education (M Ed); education, nursing, and health professions (M Ed, MS, MSN, MSPT, DPT, Ed D, CAGS, Sixth Year Certificate); educational leadership (Ed D); elementary education (M Ed); nursing education (MSN); nursing management (MSN); physical therapy (MSPT, DPT). Electronic applications accepted.

College of Engineering, Technology and Architecture *Program availability:* Part-time, evening/weekend. Offers architecture (M Arch); engineering (M Eng); engineering, technology and architecture (M Arch, M Eng). Electronic applications accepted.

Hartford Art School *Program availability:* Part-time. Offers art (MFA). Electronic applications accepted.

The Hartt School *Program availability:* Part-time. Offers choral conducting (MM Ed); composition (MM, DMA, Artist Diploma, Diploma); conducting (MM, DMA, Artist Diploma, Diploma); early childhood education (MM Ed); instrumental conducting (MM Ed); Kodály (MM Ed); music (CAGS); music education (DMA, PhD); music history (MM); music theory (MM); pedagogy (MM Ed); performance (MM, MM Ed, DMA, Artist Diploma, Diploma); research (MM Ed); technology (MM Ed). Electronic applications accepted.

UNIVERSITY OF HAWAII AT HILO, Hilo, HI 96720-4091

General Information State-supported, coed, comprehensive institution. *Graduate housing:* Rooms and/or apartments available on a first-come, first-served basis to single and married students.

GRADUATE UNITS

Program in Clinical Psychopharmacology Offers clinical psychopharmacology (MS). Electronic applications accepted.

Program in Counseling Psychology Offers counseling psychology (MA).

Program in Education *Program availability:* Part-time, evening/weekend. Offers education (M Ed). Electronic applications accepted.

Program in Hawaiian and Indigenous Language and Culture Revitalization Offers Hawaiian and indigenous language and culture revitalization (PhD). Electronic applications accepted.

Program in Hawaiian Language and Literature Offers Hawaiian language and literature (MA). Electronic applications accepted.

Program in Indigenous Language and Culture Education Offers indigenous language and culture education (MA). Electronic applications accepted.

Program in Nursing Practice Offers nursing practice (DNP). Electronic applications accepted.

Program in Pharmaceutical Sciences Offers pharmaceutical sciences (PhD). Electronic applications accepted.

Program in Pharmacy Offers pharmacy (Pharm D). Electronic applications accepted.

Program in Teaching Offers teaching (MA). Electronic applications accepted.

Program in Tropical Conservation Biology and Environmental Science Offers tropical conservation biology and environmental science (MS). Electronic applications accepted.

UNIVERSITY OF HAWAII AT MANOA, Honolulu, HI 96822

General Information State-supported, coed, university. CGS member. *Graduate housing:* Rooms and/or apartments available to single and married students. Housing application deadline: 5/1. *Research affiliation:* Hawaiian Volcano Observatory (geology, geophysics), Honolulu Academy of Arts, East-West Center (communication, geography, economics), U.S. Geological Survey (USGS), Hawaii Agriculture Research Center, Bernice Pauahi Bishop Museum (anthropology, zoology).

GRADUATE UNITS

John A. Burns School of Medicine *Program availability:* Part-time. Offers cell and molecular biology (MS, PhD); communication sciences and disorders (MS); developmental and reproductive biology (MS, PhD); epidemiology (PhD); global health and population studies (Graduate Certificate); medicine (MPH, MS, Dr PH, MD, PhD, Graduate Certificate); public health (MPH, MS, Dr PH).

Graduate Programs in Biomedical Sciences *Program availability:* Part-time. Offers biomedical sciences (MS, PhD); tropical medicine (MS, PhD).

Office of Graduate Education *Program availability:* Part-time. Offers communication and information sciences (PhD); international cultural studies (Graduate Certificate). Electronic applications accepted.

College of Arts and Humanities *Program availability:* Part-time. Offers American studies (MA); art history (MA); arts and humanities (M Mus, MA, MFA, PhD, Graduate Certificate); communicology (MA); dance (MA, MFA); historic preservation (Graduate Certificate); history (MA, PhD); museum studies (Graduate Certificate); music (M Mus, MA, PhD); philosophy (MA, PhD); religion (MA); theatre (MA, MFA, PhD); visual arts (MFA).

College of Education *Program availability:* Part-time, evening/weekend. Offers curriculum and instruction (PhD); curriculum studies (M Ed); disability and diversity studies (Graduate Certificate); early childhood education (M Ed); education (M Ed, M Ed T, MS, Ed D, PhD, Graduate Certificate); educational administration (M Ed); educational foundations (M Ed); educational policy studies (PhD); educational psychology (PhD); educational technology (M Ed); exceptionalities (PhD); kinesiology (MS, PhD); learning design and technology (PhD); professional practice (Ed D); special education (M Ed); teaching (M Ed T).

College of Engineering *Program availability:* Part-time. Offers civil and environmental engineering (MS, PhD); electrical engineering (MS, PhD); engineering (MS, PhD); mechanical engineering (MS, PhD).

College of Languages, Linguistics and Literature *Program availability:* Part-time. Offers Chinese (MA, PhD); English (MA, PhD); English as a second language (MA, Graduate Certificate); French (MA); Japanese (MA, PhD); Korean (MA); languages, linguistics and literature (MA, PhD, Graduate Certificate); linguistics (MA, PhD); second language acquisition (PhD); Spanish (MA).

College of Natural Sciences *Program availability:* Part-time. Offers advanced library and information science (Graduate Certificate); astronomy (MS, PhD); botany (MS, PhD); chemistry (MS, PhD); computer science (MS, PhD); library and information science (MLI Sc, Graduate Certificate); mathematics (MA, PhD); microbiology (MS, PhD); natural sciences (MA, MLI Sc, MS, PhD, Graduate Certificate); physics (MS, PhD); zoology (MS, PhD).

College of Social Sciences *Program availability:* Part-time, evening/weekend. Offers advanced women's studies (Graduate Certificate); anthropology (MA, PhD); clinical psychology (PhD); communication (MA); community and cultural psychology (PhD); community and culture (MA); community planning (MURP); conflict resolution (Graduate Certificate); disaster management and humanitarian assistance (Graduate Certificate); disaster preparedness and emergency management (Graduate Certificate); economics (MA, PhD); environmental planning and sustainability (MURP); geography (MA, PhD); international development planning (MURP); land use, transportation and infrastructure planning (MURP); ocean policy (Graduate Certificate); planning studies (Graduate Certificate); political science (MA, PhD); psychology (MA, PhD, Graduate Certificate); public administration (MPA, Graduate Certificate); public policy (Graduate Certificate); social sciences (MA, MPA, MURP, PhD, Graduate Certificate); sociology (MA, PhD); telecommunication and information resource management (Graduate Certificate); urban and regional planning (PhD, Graduate Certificate).

College of Tropical Agriculture and Human Resources *Program availability:* Part-time. Offers animal sciences (MS); bioengineering (MS); entomology (MS, PhD); food science (MS); molecular bioscience and bioengineering (MS); molecular biosciences and bioengineering (PhD); natural resources and environmental management (MS, PhD); nutrition (PhD); nutritional sciences (MS, PhD); tropical agriculture and human resources (MS, PhD); tropical plant and soil sciences (MS, PhD); tropical plant pathology (MS, PhD).

Hawai'inuiakea School of Hawaiian Knowledge *Program availability:* Part-time. Offers Hawaiian (MA); Hawaiian studies (MA).

School of Nursing and Dental Hygiene *Program availability:* Part-time, online learning. Offers clinical nurse specialist (MS); nurse practitioner (MS); nursing (PhD, Graduate Certificate); nursing administration (MS).

School of Ocean and Earth Science and Technology *Program availability:* Part-time. Offers high-pressure geophysics and geochemistry (MS, PhD); hydrogeology and engineering geology (MS, PhD); marine biology (MS, PhD); marine geology and geophysics (MS, PhD); meteorology (MS, PhD); ocean and earth science and technology (MS, PhD); ocean and resources engineering (MS, PhD); oceanography (MS, PhD); planetary geosciences and remote sensing (MS, PhD); seismology and solid-earth geophysics (MS, PhD); volcanology, petrology, and geochemistry (MS, PhD).

School of Pacific and Asian Studies *Program availability:* Part-time. Offers Asian studies (MA, Graduate Certificate); Chinese studies (Graduate Certificate); Japanese studies (Graduate Certificate); Korean studies (Graduate Certificate); Pacific and Asian studies (MA, Graduate Certificate); Pacific Island studies (MA, Graduate Certificate); Philippine studies (Graduate Certificate); Southeast Asian studies (Graduate Certificate).

School of Social Work *Program availability:* Part-time. Offers social welfare (PhD); social work (MSW).

School of Travel Industry Management *Program availability:* Part-time. Offers travel industry management (MS). Electronic applications accepted.

Shidler College of Business *Program availability:* Part-time, evening/weekend. Offers accounting (M Acc); accounting law (M Acc); Asian business studies (MBA); Asian finance (PhD); business (EMBA, M Acc, MBA, MHRM, MS, PhD, Graduate Certificate); Chinese business studies (MBA); decision sciences (MBA); entrepreneurship (MBA, Graduate Certificate); executive business administration (EMBA); finance (MBA); finance and banking (MBA); global information technology management (PhD); human resources management (MHRM); information management (MBA); information systems (M Acc); information technology (MBA); international accounting (PhD); international business (MBA); international marketing (PhD); international organization and strategy (PhD); Japanese business studies (MBA); marketing (MBA); organizational behavior (MBA); organizational management (MBA); real estate (MBA); student-designed track (MBA); taxation (M Acc); Vietnam focused business administration (EMBA).

School of Architecture *Program availability:* Part-time. Offers architecture (D Arch).

William S. Richardson School of Law Offers law (LL M, JD, Graduate Certificate).

UNIVERSITY OF HOLY CROSS, New Orleans, LA 70131-7399

General Information Independent-religious, coed, comprehensive institution. *Graduate housing:* On-campus housing not available.

GRADUATE UNITS

Graduate Programs *Program availability:* Part-time, evening/weekend, online learning. Offers biomedical sciences (MS); Catholic theology (MA); counseling (MA, PhD); educational leadership (M Ed); executive leadership (Ed D); management (MS); teaching and learning (M Ed).

UNIVERSITY OF HOUSTON, Houston, TX 77204

General Information State-supported, coed, university. CGS member. *Graduate housing:* Rooms and/or apartments available on a first-come, first-served basis to single and married students. *Research affiliation:* Keck Consortium.

GRADUATE UNITS

Bauer College of Business *Program availability:* Part-time, evening/weekend. Offers accountancy (MS Accy); accountancy and taxation (PhD); business (MBA, MS, MS Accy, PhD); decision and information sciences (PhD); finance (MS); management (PhD); marketing (PhD). Electronic applications accepted.

College of Education Students: 388 full-time (314 women), 543 part-time (409 women); includes 535 minority (219 Black or African American, non-Hispanic/Latino; 5 American Indian or Alaska Native, non-Hispanic/Latino; 64 Asian, non-Hispanic/Latino; 225 Hispanic/Latino; 1 Native Hawaiian or other Pacific Islander, non-Hispanic/Latino; 21 Two or more races, non-Hispanic/Latino), 49 international. Average age 35. 614 applicants, 73% accepted, 227 enrolled. *Faculty:* 89 full-time (64 women), 9 part-time/adjunct (5 women). Expenses: Contact institution. *Financial support:* In 2018–19, 34 students received support, including 2 fellowships with full tuition reimbursements available (averaging $2,000 per year), 17 research assistantships with full tuition reimbursements available (averaging $8,634 per year), 82 teaching assistantships with full tuition reimbursements available (averaging $8,697 per year); career-related internships or fieldwork, Federal Work-Study, institutionally sponsored loans, scholarships/grants, health care benefits, and unspecified assistantships also available. Support available to part-time students. Financial award application deadline: 2/1; financial award applicants required to submit FAFSA. In 2018, 167 master's, 72 doctorates awarded. *Program availability:* Part-time, evening/weekend, 100% online, blended/hybrid learning. Offers administration & supervision (M Ed); administration and supervision (M Ed, Ed D); administration and supervision - higher education (M Ed); counseling (M Ed); counseling psychology (PhD); curriculum and instruction (M Ed, Ed D); educational psychology (M Ed); higher education (M Ed); historical, social, and cultural foundations of education (M Ed); professional leadership (Ed D); school psychology (PhD); school psychology and individual differences (PhD); special education (M Ed). None. *Application fee:* $80 ($75 for international students). Electronic applications accepted. *Application Contact:* Bridgette Jones, Director of Student Affairs, 713-743-2978, E-mail: bajones5@uh.edu. *Dean,* Dr. Robert H. McPherson, 713-743-5003, Fax: 713-743-9870, E-mail: bmcph@uh.edu.

College of Liberal Arts and Social Sciences *Program availability:* Part-time, online learning. Offers anthropology (MA); applied economics (MA); applied English linguistics (MA); clinical psychology (PhD); communication sciences and disorders (MA); creative writing (MFA); creative writing and literature (MA, PhD); developmental psychology (PhD); economics (MA, PhD); English (MA, PhD); exercise science (MS); Hispanic literature and linguistics (PhD); history (MA, PhD); human nutrition (MS); human space exploration sciences (MS); industrial/organizational psychology (PhD); kinesiology (PhD); liberal arts and social sciences (M Ed, MA, MFA, MM, MS, DMA, PhD); philosophy (MA); physical education (M Ed); political science (MA, PhD); psychology (MA); public administration (MA); social psychology (PhD); sociology (MA); Spanish (MA, PhD); world cultures and literatures (MA). Electronic applications accepted.

Jack J. Valenti School of Communication *Program availability:* Part-time. Offers health communication (MA); mass communication studies (MA); public relations studies (MA); speech communication (MA). Electronic applications accepted.

College of Natural Sciences and Mathematics *Program availability:* Part-time, online learning. Offers applied mathematics (MS); atmospheric science (PhD); biochemistry (MA, PhD); biology (MA); chemistry (MA, PhD); computer science (MA, PhD); geology (MA, PhD); geophysics (PhD); mathematics (MA, PhD); natural sciences and mathematics (MA, MS, PhD); physics (MA, PhD). Electronic applications accepted.

College of Nursing Offers family nurse practitioner (MSN); nursing administration (MSN); nursing education (MSN). Electronic applications accepted.

College of Optometry *Program availability:* Part-time. Offers optometry (MS, OD, PhD); physiological optics (MS, PhD). Electronic applications accepted.

College of Pharmacy *Program availability:* Part-time. Offers pharmaceutics (MSPHR, PhD); pharmacology (MSPHR, PhD); pharmacy (Pharm D); pharmacy administration (MSPHR, PhD). Electronic applications accepted.

College of Technology Students: 173 full-time (74 women), 167 part-time (73 women); includes 93 minority (37 Black or African American, non-Hispanic/Latino; 1 American Indian or Alaska Native, non-Hispanic/Latino; 24 Asian, non-Hispanic/Latino; 28 Hispanic/Latino; 1 Native Hawaiian or other Pacific Islander, non-Hispanic/Latino; 2 Two or more races, non-Hispanic/Latino), 132 international. Average age 30. 163 applicants, 90% accepted, 99 enrolled. *Faculty:* 24 full-time (11 women), 17 part-time/adjunct (8 women). Expenses: Contact institution. *Financial support:* In 2018–19, 17 research assistantships with partial tuition reimbursements (averaging $9,266 per year), 44 teaching assistantships with partial tuition reimbursements (averaging $7,791 per year) were awarded; career-related internships or fieldwork, Federal Work-Study, institutionally sponsored loans, scholarships/grants, health care benefits, and unspecified assistantships also available. Support available to part-time students. Financial award application deadline: 2/1. In 2018, 71 master's awarded. *Program availability:* Part-time. Offers construction management (MS); engineering technology (MS); future studies in commerce (MS); human resources development (MS); information security (MS); network communications (M Tech); supply chain and logistics technology (MS); technology (M Tech, MS); technology project management (MS). *Application deadline:* For fall admission, 7/1 for domestic students, 4/1 for international students; for spring admission, 12/1 for domestic students, 10/1 for international students. Applications are processed on a rolling basis. *Application fee:* $75 ($150 for international students). Electronic applications accepted. *Application Contact:* Tiffany Roosa, Graduate Advisor, 713-743-4100, Fax: 713-743-4151, E-mail: troosa@uh.edu. *Dean,* Dr. William Fitzgibbon, 713-743-3465, Fax: 713-743-4994, E-mail: fitz@uh.edu.

Conrad N. Hilton College of Hotel and Restaurant Management *Program availability:* Part-time. Offers hospitality management (MS). Electronic applications accepted.

Cullen College of Engineering *Program availability:* Part-time. Offers biomedical engineering (PhD); chemical engineering (MChE, PhD); civil engineering (MCE, PhD); electrical engineering (MEE, MSEE, PhD); engineering (M Pet E, MCE, MChE, MEE, MIE, MME, MSEE, MSME, PhD); industrial engineering (MIE, PhD); mechanical engineering (MME, MSME, PhD); petroleum engineering (M Pet E).

Gerald D. Hines College of Architecture and Design Offers architectural studies (MA); architecture (M Arch, MS); industrial design (MS). Electronic applications accepted.

Graduate College of Social Work *Program availability:* Part-time. Offers social work (MSW, PhD).

Hobby School of Public Affairs Students: 35 full-time (27 women), 5 part-time (2 women); includes 22 minority (7 Black or African American, non-Hispanic/Latino; 1 American Indian or Alaska Native, non-Hispanic/Latino; 6 Asian, non-Hispanic/Latino; 7 Hispanic/Latino; 1 Two or more races, non-Hispanic/Latino). Average age 25. 35 applicants, 80% accepted, 21 enrolled. *Faculty:* 5 full-time (0 women), 4 part-time/adjunct (2 women). Expenses: Contact institution. *Financial support:* In 2018–19, 40 students received support. Career-related internships or fieldwork, Federal Work-Study, institutionally sponsored loans, scholarships/grants, traineeships, health care benefits, and unspecified assistantships available. Support available to part-time students. Financial award application deadline: 6/15; financial award applicants required to submit FAFSA. In 2018, 10 master's awarded. *Program availability:* Part-time. Offers public policy (MPP). University of Houston (Graduate Dual Degrees): MSW/MPP, JD/MPP; University of Houston (Accelerated Pathway Programs): Honors College–BA/BS Liberal Studies/MPP, Philosophy/MPP, Psychology/MPP. *Application deadline:* For fall admission, 6/15 for domestic and international students; for spring admission, 12/1 for domestic and international students. Applications are processed on a rolling basis. *Application fee:* $75 ($125 for international students). Electronic applications accepted. *Application Contact:* Scott Mason, Program Manager 2, 713-743-5572, E-mail: smason@uh.edu. *Executive Director,* Dr. Jim Granato, 713-743-3887, Fax: 713-743-3978, E-mail: jgranato@uh.edu.

Kathrine G. McGovern College of the Arts Offers arts (MA, MFA, MM, DMA).

Moores School of Music *Program availability:* Part-time. Offers accompanying and chamber music (MM); applied music (MM); composition (MM); music education (DMA); music theory (MM); performance (DMA). Electronic applications accepted.

School of Art Offers art history (MA); interdisciplinary practice and emerging forms (MFA); painting (MFA); studio art (MFA). Electronic applications accepted.

School of Theatre and Dance *Program availability:* Part-time. Offers theatre (MA, MFA). Electronic applications accepted.

University of Houston Law Center Students: 606 full-time (303 women), 98 part-time (41 women); includes 260 minority (43 Black or African American, non-Hispanic/Latino; 6 American Indian or Alaska Native, non-Hispanic/Latino; 72 Asian, non-Hispanic/Latino; 137 Hispanic/Latino; 2 Native Hawaiian or other Pacific Islander, non-Hispanic/Latino; 14 international. Average age 26. 2,596 applicants, 33% accepted, 202 enrolled. *Faculty:* 58 full-time (22 women), 148 part-time/adjunct (45 women). Expenses: Contact institution. *Financial support:* In 2018–19, 573 students received support, including 47 fellowships (averaging $3,768 per year); research assistantships, career-related internships or fieldwork, Federal Work-Study, scholarships/grants, and tuition waivers (full and partial) also available. Support available to part-time students. Financial award application deadline: 3/15; financial award applicants required to submit FAFSA. In 2018, 75 master's awarded. *Program availability:* Part-time, evening/weekend. Offers energy, environment, and natural resources (LL M); health law (LL M); intellectual property and information law (LL M); international law (LL M); law (JD); tax law (LL M); U.S. law (LL M). *Application deadline:* For fall admission, 2/15 for domestic and international students. Applications are processed on a rolling basis. *Application fee:* $0. Electronic applications accepted. *Application Contact:* Pilar Mensah, Assistant Dean for Admissions, 713-743-2280, Fax: 713-743-2194, E-mail: lpmensah@central.uh.edu. *Dean and Professor of Law,* Leonard M. Baynes, 713-743-2100, Fax: 713-743-2122, E-mail: lbaynes@central.uh.edu.

UNIVERSITY OF HOUSTON–CLEAR LAKE, Houston, TX 77058-1002

General Information State-supported, coed, comprehensive institution. CGS member. *Graduate housing:* Rooms and/or apartments available on a first-come, first-served basis to single students and available to married students. *Research affiliation:* Baylor College of Medicine (life sciences), NASA–Johnson Space Center (computer science, computer engineering), Schlumberger (ergonomic software).

GRADUATE UNITS

School of Business *Program availability:* Part-time, evening/weekend. Offers accounting (MS); business (MA, MBA, MHA, MS); business administration (MBA); environmental management (MS); finance (MS); healthcare administration (MHA); human resource management (MS); management information systems (MS); professional accounting (MS). Electronic applications accepted.

School of Education *Program availability:* Part-time, evening/weekend. Offers counseling (MS); curriculum and instruction (MS); early childhood education (MS); education (MS, Ed D); educational leadership (Ed D); educational management (MS); instructional technology (MS); multicultural studies (MS); reading (MS); school library and information science (MS). Electronic applications accepted.

School of Human Sciences and Humanities *Program availability:* Part-time, evening/weekend. Offers behavioral sciences (MA); clinical psychology (MA); criminology (MA); cross cultural studies (MA); family therapy (MA); fitness and human performance (MA); history (MA); human sciences and humanities (MA); humanities (MA); literature (MA); school psychology (MA).

School of Science and Computer Engineering *Program availability:* Part-time, evening/weekend. Offers biological sciences (MS); biotechnology (MS); chemistry (MS); computer engineering (MS); computer information systems (MS); computer science (MS); environmental science (MS); mathematical sciences (MS); physics (MS); science and computer engineering (MS); software engineering (MS); statistics (MS); system engineering (MS).

UNIVERSITY OF HOUSTON–DOWNTOWN, Houston, TX 77002

General Information State-supported, coed, comprehensive institution. *Graduate housing:* On-campus housing not available.

GRADUATE UNITS

College of Humanities and Social Sciences *Program availability:* Part-time, evening/weekend, 100% online. Offers humanities and social sciences (MA, MS); non-profit management (MA); rhetoric and composition (MA); technical communication (MS). Electronic applications accepted.

College of Public Service *Program availability:* Part-time, evening/weekend, 100% online. Offers criminal justice and social work (MS); curriculum and instruction (MAT); public service (MAT, MS). Electronic applications accepted.

College of Sciences and Technology *Program availability:* Part-time, evening/weekend. Offers data analytics (MS). Electronic applications accepted.

Marilyn Davies College of Business *Program availability:* Part-time, evening/weekend, 100% online. Offers accounting (MBA); business (MBA, MSM); finance (MBA); human resource management (MBA); international business (MBA); investment management (MBA); leadership (MBA); project management and process improvement (MBA); sales management and business development (MBA); security management (MSM); supply chain management (MBA). Electronic applications accepted.

UNIVERSITY OF HOUSTON–VICTORIA, Victoria, TX 77901-4450

General Information State-supported, coed, upper-level institution. *Enrollment:* 345 full-time matriculated graduate/professional students (247 women), 793 part-time matriculated graduate/professional students (514 women). *Enrollment by degree level:* 1,138 master's. *Graduate faculty:* 19 full-time (8 women), 29 part-time/adjunct (18 women). *International tuition:* $13,624 full-time. *Tuition, area resident:* Full-time $6154; part-time $3077 per semester. Tuition, state resident: full-time $6154; part-time $3077 per semester. Tuition, nonresident: full-time $13,624; part-time $6812 per semester. *Required fees:* $1405; $847 per semester. Tuition and fees vary according to program. *Graduate housing:* On-campus housing not available. *Student services:* Campus employment opportunities, campus safety program, career counseling, exercise/wellness program, free psychological counseling, grant writing training, international student services, low-cost health insurance, multicultural affairs office, services for students with disabilities, teacher training, writing training. *Library facilities:* VC/UHV Library.

Computer facilities: A campuswide network can be accessed from student residence rooms and from off campus. Online class registration is available. Website: http://www.uhv.edu/

General Application Contact: Admissions and Records, 361-570-4359, Fax: 361-580-5500, E-mail: admissions@uhv.edu.

GRADUATE UNITS

School of Arts and Sciences Students: 112 full-time (83 women), 120 part-time (81 women); includes 126 minority (54 Black or African American, non-Hispanic/Latino; 1 American Indian or Alaska Native, non-Hispanic/Latino; 14 Asian, non-Hispanic/Latino; 50 Hispanic/Latino; 7 Two or more races, non-Hispanic/Latino), 23 international. Average age 33. *Faculty:* 20 full-time (8 women), 28 part-time/adjunct (18 women). Expenses: Contact institution. *Financial support:* Research assistantships with partial tuition reimbursements, teaching assistantships with partial tuition reimbursements, Federal Work-Study, scholarships/grants, and unspecified assistantships available. Support available to part-time students. Financial award application deadline: 4/15; financial award applicants required to submit FAFSA. In 2018, 342 master's awarded. *Program availability:* Part-time, evening/weekend, 100% online, blended/hybrid learning. Offers biological sciences (MS); biomedical sciences (MS); computer information systems (MS); computer science (MS); counseling psychology (MA); creative writing (MFA); forensic psychology (MA); forensic science (MS); interdisciplinary studies (MAIS); publishing (MS); school psychology (MA). *Application deadline:* For fall admission, 8/10 for domestic students, 7/1 for international students; for spring admission, 1/3 for domestic students, 11/1 for international students; for summer admission, 5/10 for domestic students, 3/1 for international students. Applications are processed on a rolling basis. *Application fee:* $25. Electronic applications accepted. *Application Contact:* Tracey Fox, Director of Services, 361-570-4233, Fax: 361-580-5507, E-mail: foxt@uhv.edu. *Dean,* Dr. Jeffrey Dileo, 361-570-4200, Fax: 361-580-5507, E-mail: dileoj@uhv.edu.

School of Business Administration *Program availability:* Part-time, evening/weekend, online learning. Offers accounting (MBA); economic development and entrepreneurship (MS); finance (GMBA, MBA); general business (MBA); international business (MBA); management (GMBA, MBA); marketing (MBA). Electronic applications accepted.

School of Education, Health Professions and Human Development *Program availability:* Part-time, evening/weekend, online learning. Offers administration and supervision (M Ed); adult and higher education (M Ed); counselor education (M Ed); curriculum and instruction (M Ed); dyslexia education (Certificate); educational technology (M Ed); special education (M Ed). Electronic applications accepted.

UNIVERSITY OF IDAHO, Moscow, ID 83844-2282

General Information State-supported, coed, university. CGS member. *Enrollment:* 11,841 graduate, professional, and undergraduate students; 1,364 full-time matriculated graduate/professional students (597 women), 671 part-time matriculated graduate/professional students (302 women). *Enrollment by degree level:* 1,234 master's, 788 doctoral, 37 other advanced degrees. *Graduate faculty:* 468 full-time (153 women), 37 part-time/adjunct (18 women). Tuition, state resident: full-time $7266.44; part-time $474.50 per credit hour. Tuition, nonresident: full-time $24,902; part-time $1453.50 per credit hour. *Required fees:* $2085.56; $45.50 per credit hour. *Graduate housing:* Rooms and/or apartments available on a first-come, first-served basis to single and married students. *Student services:* Campus employment opportunities, campus safety program, career counseling, exercise/wellness program, free psychological counseling, grant writing training, international student services, low-cost health insurance, multicultural affairs office, services for students with disabilities, writing training. *Library facilities:* University of Idaho Library plus 1 other. *Collection:* Books: 1.5 million (physical), 1.3 million (digital/electronic); Serial titles: 109,553 (physical), 177,970 (digital/electronic).

Computer facilities: 510 computers available on campus for general student use. A campuswide network can be accessed from student residence rooms and from off campus. Online class registration is available.
Website: http://www.uidaho.edu/

GRADUATE UNITS

College of Graduate Studies Students: 1,057 full-time (461 women), 663 part-time (300 women); includes 198 minority (19 Black or African American, non-Hispanic/Latino; 24 American Indian or Alaska Native, non-Hispanic/Latino; 24 Asian, non-Hispanic/Latino; 101 Hispanic/Latino; 30 Two or more races, non-Hispanic/Latino), 318 international. Average age 32. 1,469 applicants, 59% accepted, 546 enrolled. *Faculty:* 435 full-time (136 women), 28 part-time/adjunct (14 women). Expenses: Contact institution. *Financial support:* Fellowships, research assistantships, teaching assistantships, career-related internships or fieldwork, Federal Work-Study, institutionally sponsored loans, scholarships/grants, and tuition waivers (full and partial) available. Support available to part-time students. Financial award applicants required to submit FAFSA. In 2018, 487 master's, 54 doctorates, 36 other advanced degrees awarded. *Program availability:* Online learning. Offers interdisciplinary studies (MA, MS). *Application deadline:* For fall admission, 8/1 for domestic students, 5/1 for international students; for spring admission, 12/15 for domestic students, 10/1 for international students. Applications are processed on a rolling basis. *Application fee:* $60 ($70 for international students). Electronic applications accepted. *Application Contact:* Dr. Jerry McMurtry, Dean of the College of Graduate Studies, 208-885-2647, E-mail: cogs@uidaho.edu. *Dean of the College of Graduate Studies,* Dr. Jerry McMurtry, 208-885-2647, E-mail: cogs@uidaho.edu.

College of Agricultural and Life Sciences Students: 133 full-time (76 women), 44 part-time (25 women). Average age 30. 138 applicants, 46% accepted, 46 enrolled. *Faculty:* 89 full-time (30 women). Expenses: Contact institution. *Financial support:* Research assistantships, teaching assistantships, career-related internships or fieldwork, and Federal Work-Study available. Support available to part-time students. Financial award application deadline: 12/1; financial award applicants required to submit FAFSA. In 2018, 40 master's, 9 doctorates awarded. Offers agricultural and life sciences (MS, PhD); agricultural economics and rural sociology (MS); animal and veterinary science (MS, PhD); engineering and science (MS, PhD); family and consumer sciences (MS); food science (MS, PhD); law, management and policy (MS, PhD); plant science (MS); plant sciences (MS, PhD); science and management (MS, PhD); soil and land resources (MS, PhD). *Application deadline:* For fall admission, 8/1 for domestic students; for spring admission, 12/15 for domestic students. Applications are processed on a rolling basis. *Application fee:* $60 ($70 for international students). Electronic applications accepted. *Application Contact:* Dr. Michael Parrella, Dean, 208-885-6681, E-mail: ag@uidaho.edu. *Dean,* Dr. Michael Parrella, 208-885-6681, E-mail: ag@uidaho.edu.

College of Art and Architecture Students: 63 full-time, 9 part-time. Average age 29. 70 applicants, 79% accepted, 27 enrolled. Expenses: Contact institution. *Financial support:* Applicants required to submit FAFSA. In 2018, 32 master's awarded. Offers architecture (M Arch); art and design (MFA); bioregional planning and community design (MS); integrated architecture and design (MS); landscape architecture (MLA). *Application deadline:* For fall admission, 8/1 for domestic students; for spring admission, 12/15 for domestic students. Applications are processed on a rolling basis. *Application fee:* $60. Electronic applications accepted. *Application Contact:* Dr.

Shauna Corry, Dean, 208-885-4409, E-mail: caa@uidaho.edu. *Dean,* Dr. Shauna Corry, 208-885-4409, E-mail: caa@uidaho.edu.

College of Business and Economics Students: 48. Average age 31. 56 applicants, 77% accepted, 34 enrolled. *Faculty:* 11. Expenses: Contact institution. *Financial support:* Research assistantships, teaching assistantships, Federal Work-Study, and scholarships/grants available. Support available to part-time students. Financial award applicants required to submit FAFSA. In 2018, 33 master's awarded. Offers accountancy (M Acct); business and economics (M Acct, MBA); general management (MBA). *Application deadline:* For fall admission, 8/1 for domestic students; for spring admission, 12/15 for domestic students. Applications are processed on a rolling basis. *Application fee:* $60. Electronic applications accepted. *Application Contact:* Dr. Marc Chopin, Dean, 208-885-6478, E-mail: cbe@uidaho.edu. *Dean,* Dr. Marc Chopin, 208-885-6478, E-mail: cbe@uidaho.edu.

College of Education, Health and Human Sciences Students: 175 full-time (102 women), 216 part-time (136 women). Average age 35. 221 applicants, 83% accepted, 130 enrolled. *Faculty:* 57 full-time, 6 part-time/adjunct. Expenses: Contact institution. *Financial support:* Teaching assistantships and Federal Work-Study available. Support available to part-time students. Financial award applicants required to submit FAFSA. In 2018, 128 master's, 14 doctorates, 33 other advanced degrees awarded. Offers adult/organizational learning and leadership (Ed S); athletic training (MSAT, DAT); career and technology education (M Ed); curriculum and instruction (M Ed, Ed S); education (Ed D, PhD); education, health and human sciences (M Ed, MS, MSAT, DAT, Ed D, PhD, Ed S); educational leadership (Ed S); exercise science and health (MS); physical education teacher education (M Ed, MS); recreation, sport, and tourism management (MS); rehabilitation counseling and human services (M Ed); school counseling (M Ed, MS); special education (M Ed). *Application deadline:* For fall admission, 8/1 for domestic students; for spring admission, 12/15 for domestic students. Applications are processed on a rolling basis. *Application fee:* $60. Electronic applications accepted. *Application Contact:* Dr. Alison Carr-Chellman, Dean, 208-885-6772, E-mail: ehhs@uidaho.edu. *Dean,* Dr. Alison Carr-Chellman, 208-885-6772, E-mail: ehhs@uidaho.edu.

College of Engineering Students: 220 full-time (32 women), 182 part-time (30 women). Average age 32. 390 applicants, 56% accepted, 116 enrolled. *Faculty:* 81 full-time, 8 part-time/adjunct. Expenses: Contact institution. *Financial support:* Fellowships, research assistantships, teaching assistantships, career-related internships or fieldwork, and Federal Work-Study available. Support available to part-time students. Financial award applicants required to submit FAFSA. In 2018, 81 master's, 11 doctorates awarded. Offers biological engineering (M Engr, MS, PhD); chemical engineering (M Engr, MS, PhD); civil and environmental engineering (M Engr, PhD); computer science (MS, PhD); electrical and computer engineering (MS, PhD); electrical engineering (M Engr); engineering (M Engr, MS, PhD); geological engineering (MS); materials science and engineering (PhD); mechanical engineering (M Engr, MS, PhD); nuclear engineering (M Engr, MS, PhD). *Application deadline:* For fall admission, 8/1 for domestic students; for spring admission, 12/15 for domestic students. Applications are processed on a rolling basis. *Application fee:* $60. Electronic applications accepted. *Application Contact:* Dr. Larry Stauffer, Dean, 208-885-6470, E-mail: deanengr@uidaho.edu. *Dean,* Dr. Larry Stauffer, 208-885-6470, E-mail: deanengr@uidaho.edu.

College of Letters, Arts and Social Sciences Students: 162 full-time (77 women), 38 part-time (24 women). Average age 32. 194 applicants, 57% accepted, 76 enrolled. *Faculty:* 70. Expenses: Contact institution. *Financial support:* Fellowships, research assistantships, teaching assistantships, and Federal Work-Study available. Support available to part-time students. Financial award applicants required to submit FAFSA. In 2018, 72 master's, 1 doctorate awarded. Offers anthropology (MA); creative writing (MFA); English (MA, MAT); experimental psychology (PhD); history (MA, PhD); letters, arts and social sciences (M Mus, MA, MAT, MFA, MPA, MS, PhD); music (M Mus, MA); political science (MA, PhD); psychology and communication studies (MS); public administration (MPA); theatre arts (MFA). *Application deadline:* For fall admission, 8/1 for domestic students; for spring admission, 12/15 for domestic students. Applications are processed on a rolling basis. *Application fee:* $60. Electronic applications accepted. *Application Contact:* Dr. Sean Quinlan, Dean, 208-885-6426, E-mail: class@uidaho.edu. *Dean,* Dr. Sean Quinlan, 208-885-6426, E-mail: class@uidaho.edu.

College of Natural Resources Students: 130 full-time (77 women), 146 part-time (67 women). Average age 33. 146 applicants, 67% accepted, 74 enrolled. *Faculty:* 60. Expenses: Contact institution. *Financial support:* Fellowships, research assistantships, teaching assistantships, and Federal Work-Study available. Support available to part-time students. Financial award applicants required to submit FAFSA. In 2018, 79 master's, 6 doctorates awarded. Offers environmental science (MS, PhD); natural resources (MNR, MS, PSM, PhD). *Application deadline:* For fall admission, 8/1 for domestic students; for spring admission, 12/15 for domestic students. Applications are processed on a rolling basis. *Application fee:* $60. Electronic applications accepted. *Application Contact:* Dr. Dennis Becker, Dean, 208-885-8981, Fax: 208-885-5534, E-mail: cnr@uidaho.edu. *Dean,* Dr. Dennis Becker, 208-885-8981, Fax: 208-885-5534, E-mail: cnr@uidaho.edu.

College of Science Students: 135 full-time (49 women), 26 part-time (12 women). Average age 30. 253 applicants, 40% accepted, 43 enrolled. *Faculty:* 79. Expenses: Contact institution. *Financial support:* Applicants required to submit FAFSA. In 2018, 21 master's, 13 doctorates awarded. Offers bioinformatics and computational biology (MS, PhD); biology (MS, PhD); chemistry (MS, PhD); geography (MS, PhD); geology (MS, PhD); mathematics (MAT, MS, PhD); microbiology, molecular biology and biochemistry (PhD); physics (MS, PhD); science (MAT, MS, PhD); statistical science (MS). *Application deadline:* Applications are processed on a rolling basis. *Application fee:* $60. Electronic applications accepted. *Application Contact:* Dr. Ginger Carney, Dean, 208-885-6195, E-mail: science@uidaho.edu. *Dean,* Dr. Ginger Carney, 208-885-6195, E-mail: science@uidaho.edu.

College of Law Students: 308 full-time, 7 part-time. Average age 29. *Faculty:* 34 full-time, 9 part-time/adjunct. Expenses: Contact institution. *Financial support:* Career-related internships or fieldwork, Federal Work-Study, and institutionally sponsored loans available. Financial award applicants required to submit FAFSA. Offers law (LL M, JD). *Application deadline:* For fall admission, 3/15 priority date for domestic students. Applications are processed on a rolling basis. Electronic applications accepted. *Application Contact:* Carole Wells, Director of Admissions, 208-885-2300, E-mail: lawadmit@uidaho.edu. *Term Dean,* Jerrold Long, 208-885-4977, E-mail: uilaw@uidaho.edu.

UNIVERSITY OF ILLINOIS AT CHICAGO, Chicago, IL 60607-7128

General Information State-supported, coed, university. CGS member. *Graduate housing:* Room and/or apartments available on a first-come, first-served basis to single students; on-campus housing not available to married students. Housing application deadline: 3/1. *Research affiliation:* Chicago Manufacturing Technology Extension Center (manufacturing research and development, industrial research), Eastern Cooperative Oncology Group (clinical cancer research), Argonne National Laboratory (battery performance), National Surgical Adjuvant Breast and Bowel Project (prevention of breast cancer).

GRADUATE UNITS

College of Applied Health Sciences *Program availability:* Part-time. Offers applied health sciences (MS, DPT, OTD, PhD, CAS, Certificate); biomedical visualization (MS); disability and human development (MS, PhD); health informatics (MS, CAS); health information management (Certificate); kinesiology (MS, PhD); nutrition (MS, PhD); occupational therapy (MS, OTD); physical therapy (MS, DPT). Electronic applications accepted.

College of Architecture, Design and the Arts *Program availability:* Part-time, evening/weekend. Offers architecture, design and the arts (M Arch, M Des, MA, MFA, MS, MS Arch, PhD). Electronic applications accepted.

School of Architecture Offers architecture (M Arch, MA, MS, MS Arch). Electronic applications accepted.

School of Art and Art History *Program availability:* Part-time, evening/weekend. Offers art history (MA); electronic visualization (MFA); museum and exhibition studies (MA); new media arts (MFA). Electronic applications accepted.

School of Design Offers graphic design (M Des); industrial design (M Des). Electronic applications accepted.

College of Dentistry Offers dentistry (MS, DDS, DMD, PhD); oral sciences (MS, PhD). Electronic applications accepted.

College of Education *Program availability:* Part-time, evening/weekend. Offers curriculum studies (PhD); early childhood education (M Ed); education (M Ed, Ed D, PhD); educational psychology (PhD); elementary education (M Ed); measurement, evaluation, statistics, and assessment (M Ed); policy studies (M Ed); policy studies in urban education (PhD); secondary education (M Ed); special education (M Ed, PhD); urban education leadership (Ed D); youth development (M Ed). Electronic applications accepted.

College of Engineering *Program availability:* Part-time, evening/weekend. Offers bioengineering (MS, PhD); chemical engineering (MS, PhD); civil and materials engineering (MS, PhD); computer science (MS, PhD); electrical and computer engineering (MS, PhD); energy engineering (MEE); engineering (M Eng, MEE, MS, PhD); fluids engineering (MS, PhD); industrial engineering (MS, PhD); industrial engineering and operations research (PhD); mechanical analysis and design (MS, PhD); mechanical engineering (MS, PhD); thermomechanical and power engineering (MS, PhD). Electronic applications accepted.

College of Liberal Arts and Sciences *Program availability:* Part-time, evening/weekend. Offers anthropology (MA, PhD); biological sciences (MS, PhD); chemistry (MS, PhD); communication (MA, PhD); criminology, law, and justice (MA, PhD); earth and environmental sciences (MS, PhD); economics (MA, PhD); English (MA, PhD); environmental and urban geography (MA); history (MA, MAT, PhD); Latin American and Latino studies (MA, MAT, MS, MST, DA, PhD); mathematics (DA); philosophy (MA, PhD); physics (MS, PhD); political science (MA, PhD); probability and statistics (PhD); psychology (MA, PhD); secondary school mathematics (MST); sociology (MA, PhD); statistics (MS). Electronic applications accepted.

School of Literatures, Cultural Studies and Linguistics *Program availability:* Part-time. Offers French and Francophone studies (MA); Germanic studies (MA, PhD); Hispanic and Italian studies (MAT, PhD); Hispanic linguistics (PhD); linguistics (MA); Slavic and Baltic languages and literatures (MA); Slavic and Baltic languages and literatures (PhD); Slavic studies (MA, PhD). Electronic applications accepted.

College of Medicine *Program availability:* Part-time. Offers anatomy and cell biology (MS); biochemistry and molecular genetics (PhD); medical education (MHPE); medicine (MHPE, MS, MD, PhD); microbiology and immunology (PhD); pharmacology (PhD); physiology and biophysics (MS, PhD); surgery (MS).

College of Nursing *Program availability:* Part-time. Offers acute care clinical nurse specialist (MS); administrative nursing leadership (Certificate); adult nurse practitioner (MS); adult/geriatric nurse practitioner (MS); advanced community health nurse specialist (MS); family nurse practitioner (MS); geriatric clinical nurse specialist (MS); geriatric nurse practitioner (MS); nurse midwifery (MS); nursing (MS, DNP, PhD, Certificate); nursing practice (DNP); nursing science (PhD); occupational health/advanced community health nurse specialist (MS); occupational health/family nurse practitioner (MS); pediatric nurse practitioner (MS); perinatal clinical nurse specialist (MS); school/advanced community health nurse specialist (MS); school/family nurse practitioner (MS); women's health nurse practitioner (MS). Electronic applications accepted.

College of Pharmacy Offers biopharmaceutical sciences (PhD); comparative effectiveness research (MS); forensic science (MS); forensic toxicology (MS); medicinal chemistry (MS, PhD); pharmacognosy (MS, PhD); pharmacy (PhD).

College of Urban Planning and Public Affairs *Program availability:* Part-time, evening/weekend. Offers public administration (MPA, PhD); urban planning and policy (MUPP, PhD); urban planning and public affairs (MPA, MUPP, PhD). Electronic applications accepted.

Jane Addams College of Social Work *Program availability:* Part-time. Offers social work (MSW, PhD, Certificate). Electronic applications accepted.

Liautaud Graduate School of Business *Program availability:* Part-time, evening/weekend. Offers accounting (MS); business (MA, MBA, MS, PhD); business administration (MBA, PhD); finance (MS); management information systems (PhD); real estate (MA). Electronic applications accepted.

Program in Learning Sciences Offers learning sciences (PhD).

Program in Neuroscience Offers cellular and systems neuroscience and cell biology (PhD); neuroscience (MS).

School of Public Health *Program availability:* Part-time. Offers public health (MHA, MPH, MS, Dr PH, PhD). Electronic applications accepted.

Division of Community Health Sciences *Program availability:* Part-time. Offers community health sciences (MPH, MS, Dr PH, PhD). Electronic applications accepted.

Division of Environmental and Occupational Health Sciences *Program availability:* Part-time. Offers environmental and occupational health sciences (MPH, MS, Dr PH, PhD). Electronic applications accepted.

Division of Health Policy and Administration *Program availability:* Part-time. Offers clinical and translational science (MS); health policy (PhD); health services research (PhD); healthcare administration (MHA); public health policy management (MPH). Electronic applications accepted.

Epidemiology and Biostatistics Division *Program availability:* Part-time. Offers biostatistics (MPH, MS, PhD); epidemiology (MPH, MS, PhD). Electronic applications accepted.

UNIVERSITY OF ILLINOIS AT SPRINGFIELD, Springfield, IL 62703-5407

General Information State-supported, coed, comprehensive institution. CGS member. *Enrollment:* 4,575 graduate, professional, and undergraduate students; 568 full-time matriculated graduate/professional students (274 women), 1,082 part-time matriculated graduate/professional students (527 women). *Enrollment by degree level:* 1,589 master's, 30 doctoral, 31 other advanced degrees. *Graduate faculty:* 158 full-time (68 women), 37 part-time/adjunct (22 women). *Graduate housing:* Rooms and/or apartments available on a first-come, first-served basis to single and married students. Housing application deadline: 5/1. *Student services:* Campus employment opportunities, campus safety program, career counseling, child daycare facilities, exercise/wellness program, free psychological counseling, international student services, low-cost health insurance, multicultural affairs office, services for students with disabilities, teacher training, writing training. *Library facilities:* Norris L Brookens Library plus 1 other. *Collection:* Books: 352,668 (physical), 215,723 (digital/electronic); Serial titles: 9,513 (physical), 14,928 (digital/electronic); Databases: 176. Weekly public service hours: 90; students can reserve study rooms.

Computer facilities: 560 computers available on campus for general student use. A campuswide network can be accessed from student residence rooms and from off campus. Online class registration is available.
Website: http://www.uis.edu/

General Application Contact: Dr. Cecelia Cornell, Associate Vice Chancellor for Graduate Education, 888-977-4847, Fax: 217-206-7230, E-mail: ccorn1@uis.edu.

GRADUATE UNITS

Graduate Programs Students: 568 full-time (274 women), 1,082 part-time (527 women); includes 367 minority (167 Black or African American, non-Hispanic/Latino; 87 Asian, non-Hispanic/Latino; 74 Hispanic/Latino; 2 Native Hawaiian or other Pacific Islander, non-Hispanic/Latino; 37 Two or more races, non-Hispanic/Latino), 338 international. Average age 32. 1,893 applicants, 49% accepted, 470 enrolled. *Faculty:* 211 full-time (97 women), 36 part-time/adjunct (19 women). Expenses: Contact institution. *Financial support:* In 2018–19, 5 research assistantships with full tuition reimbursements (averaging $10,384 per year), 7 teaching assistantships with full tuition reimbursements (averaging $10,303 per year) were awarded; fellowships, career-related internships or fieldwork, Federal Work-Study, scholarships/grants, health care benefits, and unspecified assistantships also available. Support available to part-time students. Financial award application deadline: 11/15; financial award applicants required to submit FAFSA. In 2018, 805 master's, 2 doctorates, 25 other advanced degrees awarded. *Program availability:* Part-time, evening/weekend, 100% online, blended/hybrid learning. *Application deadline:* Applications are processed on a rolling basis. *Application fee:* $60 ($75 for international students). Electronic applications accepted. *Application Contact:* Dr. Cecelia Cornell, Associate Vice Chancellor for Graduate Education, 217-206-7230, Fax: 217-206-7623, E-mail: ccorn1@uis.edu. *Associate Vice Chancellor for Graduate Education,* Dr. Cecelia Cornell, 217-206-7230, Fax: 217-206-7623, E-mail: ccorn1@uis.edu.

College of Business and Management Students: 185 full-time (87 women), 165 part-time (69 women); includes 64 minority (19 Black or African American, non-Hispanic/Latino; 24 Asian, non-Hispanic/Latino; 12 Hispanic/Latino; 9 Two or more races, non-Hispanic/Latino), 127 international. Average age 31. 512 applicants, 43% accepted, 95 enrolled. *Faculty:* 34 full-time (7 women), 5 part-time/adjunct (1 woman). Expenses: Contact institution. *Financial support:* In 2018–19, research assistantships with full tuition reimbursements (averaging $10,384 per year), teaching assistantships with full tuition reimbursements (averaging $10,303 per year) were awarded; fellowships, career-related internships or fieldwork, Federal Work-Study, scholarships/grants, health care benefits, and unspecified assistantships also available. Support available to part-time students. Financial award application deadline: 11/15; financial award applicants required to submit FAFSA. In 2018, 209 master's awarded. *Program availability:* Part-time, evening/weekend, 100% online, blended/hybrid learning. Offers accountancy (MA); business administration (MBA); business and management (MA, MBA, MS); management information systems (MS). *Application deadline:* Applications are processed on a rolling basis. *Application fee:* $60 ($75 for international students). Electronic applications accepted. *Application Contact:* Dr. Somnath Bhattacharya, Dean, 217-206-6533, Fax: 217-206-7541, E-mail: cbmdean@uis.edu. *Dean,* Dr. Somnath Bhattacharya, 217-206-6533, Fax: 217-206-7541, E-mail: cbmdean@uis.edu.

College of Education and Human Services Students: 59 full-time (50 women), 204 part-time (155 women); includes 64 minority (42 Black or African American, non-Hispanic/Latino; 1 Asian, non-Hispanic/Latino; 12 Hispanic/Latino; 9 Two or more races, non-Hispanic/Latino), 5 international. Average age 32. 146 applicants, 42% accepted, 53 enrolled. *Faculty:* 22 full-time (14 women), 12 part-time/adjunct (9 women). Expenses: Contact institution. *Financial support:* In 2018–19, research assistantships with full tuition reimbursements (averaging $10,384 per year), teaching assistantships with full tuition reimbursements (averaging $10,303 per year) were awarded; fellowships, career-related internships or fieldwork, Federal Work-Study, scholarships/grants, health care benefits, and unspecified assistantships also available. Support available to part-time students. Financial award application deadline: 11/15; financial award applicants required to submit FAFSA. In 2018, 72 master's, 4 other advanced degrees awarded. *Program availability:* Part-time, evening/weekend, 100% online, blended/hybrid learning. Offers alcohol and substance abuse (Graduate Certificate); alcoholism and substance abuse (MA); child and family studies (MA); education and human services (MA, CAS, Certificate, Graduate Certificate); educational leadership (MA, CAS, Graduate Certificate); gerontology (MA); human development counseling (MA); social services administration (MA). *Application deadline:* Applications are processed on a rolling basis. *Application fee:* $60 ($75 for international students). Electronic applications accepted. *Application Contact:* Dr. Hanfu Mi, Dean, 217-206-6784, Fax: 217-206-6775, E-mail: hmi2@uis.edu. *Dean,* Dr. Hanfu Mi, 217-206-6784, Fax: 217-206-6775, E-mail: hmi2@uis.edu.

College of Liberal Arts and Sciences Students: 181 full-time (59 women), 339 part-time (95 women); includes 105 minority (30 Black or African American, non-Hispanic/Latino; 45 Asian, non-Hispanic/Latino; 20 Hispanic/Latino; 2 Native Hawaiian or other Pacific Islander, non-Hispanic/Latino; 8 Two or more races, non-Hispanic/Latino), 170 international. Average age 31. 814 applicants, 54% accepted, 188 enrolled. *Faculty:* 102 full-time (48 women), 4 part-time/adjunct (1 woman). Expenses: Contact institution. *Financial support:* In 2018–19, research assistantships with full tuition reimbursements (averaging $10,384 per year), teaching assistantships with full tuition reimbursements (averaging $10,303 per year) were awarded;

fellowships, career-related internships or fieldwork, Federal Work-Study, scholarships/grants, health care benefits, and unspecified assistantships also available. Support available to part-time students. Financial award application deadline: 11/15; financial award applicants required to submit FAFSA. In 2018, 366 master's awarded. *Program availability:* Part-time, evening/weekend, 100% online, blended/hybrid learning. Offers biology (MS); communication (MA); computer science (MS); data analytics (MS); English and modern languages (MA, Graduate Certificate); history (MA); liberal and integrative studies (MA); liberal arts and sciences (MA, MS, Graduate Certificate). *Application deadline:* Applications are processed on a rolling basis. *Application fee:* $60 ($75 for international students). Electronic applications accepted. *Application Contact:* Dr. James Ermatinger, Dean, 217-206-6512, Fax: 217-206-6217, E-mail: jerma2@uis.edu. *Dean,* Dr. James Ermatinger, 217-206-6512, Fax: 217-206-6217, E-mail: jerma2@uis.edu.

College of Public Affairs and Administration Students: 143 full-time (78 women), 374 part-time (208 women); includes 134 minority (76 Black or African American, non-Hispanic/Latino; 17 Asian, non-Hispanic/Latino; 30 Hispanic/Latino; 11 Two or more races, non-Hispanic/Latino), 36 international. Average age 34. 421 applicants, 48% accepted, 134 enrolled. *Faculty:* 43 full-time (21 women), 14 part-time/adjunct (7 women). Expenses: Contact institution. *Financial support:* In 2018–19, research assistantships with full tuition reimbursements (averaging $10,384 per year), teaching assistantships with full tuition reimbursements (averaging $10,303 per year) were awarded; fellowships, career-related internships or fieldwork, Federal Work-Study, scholarships/grants, health care benefits, and unspecified assistantships also available. Support available to part-time students. Financial award application deadline: 11/15; financial award applicants required to submit FAFSA. In 2018, 158 master's, 2 doctorates, 21 other advanced degrees awarded. *Program availability:* Part-time, evening/weekend, 100% online, blended/hybrid learning. Offers community health education (Graduate Certificate); emergency preparedness and homeland security (Graduate Certificate); environmental health (MPH, Graduate Certificate); environmental risk assessment (Graduate Certificate); environmental science (MS); environmental studies (MA); epidemiology (Graduate Certificate); legal studies (MA); political science (MA); public administration (MPA, DPA, Graduate Certificate); public affairs and administration (MA, MPA, MPH, MS, DPA, Graduate Certificate); public affairs reporting (MA); public health (MPH). *Application deadline:* Applications are processed on a rolling basis. *Application fee:* $60 ($75 for international students). Electronic applications accepted. *Application Contact:* Dr. Robert Smith, Dean, 217-206-6523, Fax: 217-206-7807, E-mail: cpaa@uis.edu. *Dean,* Dr. Robert Smith, 217-206-6523, Fax: 217-206-7807, E-mail: cpaa@uis.edu.

UNIVERSITY OF ILLINOIS AT URBANA–CHAMPAIGN, Champaign, IL 61820

General Information State-supported, coed, university. CGS member. *Graduate housing:* Rooms and/or apartments available to single and married students. *Research affiliation:* Midwest Universities Research Association, Sandia National Laboratories, National Center for Atmospheric Research.

GRADUATE UNITS

College of Law Offers law (LL M, MCL, JD, JSD).

College of Veterinary Medicine Offers comparative biosciences (MS, PhD); pathobiology (MS, PhD); veterinary clinical medicine (MS, PhD); veterinary medical science (DVM); veterinary medicine (MS, DVM, PhD).

Graduate College Offers strategic brand communication (MS).

College of Agricultural, Consumer and Environmental Sciences Offers agricultural and applied economics (MS, PhD); agricultural and biological engineering (MS, PhD); agricultural education (MS); agricultural production (MS); agricultural, consumer and environmental sciences (MS, PSM, PhD); animal sciences (MS, PhD); bioenergy (PSM); bioinformatics: animal sciences (MS); bioinformatics: crop sciences (MS); crop sciences (MS, PhD); food science (MS); food science and human nutrition (MS, PhD); human and community development (MS, PhD); human nutrition (MS); natural resources and environmental science (MS, PhD); nutritional sciences (MS, PhD); technical systems management (MS, PSM).

College of Applied Health Sciences Offers applied health sciences (MA, MPH, MS, MSPH, Au D, PhD); audiology (Au D); community health (MS, MSPH, PhD); kinesiology (MS, PhD); public health (MPH); recreation, sport and tourism (MS, PhD); rehabilitation (MS); speech and hearing science (MA, PhD).

College of Education *Program availability:* Part-time, online learning. Offers curriculum and instruction (Ed M, MA, MS, Ed D, PhD, CAS); early childhood education (Ed M); education (Ed M, MA, MS, Ed D, PhD, CAS); educational organization and leadership (Ed M, MS, Ed D, PhD, CAS); educational policy studies (Ed M, MA, PhD); educational psychology (Ed M, MA, MS, PhD, CAS); elementary education (Ed M); human resource education (Ed M, MS, Ed D, PhD, CAS); secondary education (Ed M); special education (Ed M, MS, Ed D, PhD, CAS).

College of Engineering *Program availability:* Part-time, evening/weekend, online learning. Offers aerospace engineering (MS, PhD); bioengineering (MS, PhD); bioinformatics (MS); civil engineering (MS, PhD); computer science (MCS, PhD); electrical and computer engineering (MS, PhD); energy systems (M Eng); engineering (M Eng, MCS, MS, PhD); environmental engineering in civil engineering (MS, PhD); financial engineering (MS); industrial engineering (MS, PhD); materials science and engineering (M Eng, MS, PhD); mechanical engineering (MS, PhD); nuclear, plasma, and radiological engineering (MS, PhD); physics (MS, PhD); systems and entrepreneurial engineering (MS, PhD); teaching of physics (MS); theoretical and applied mechanics (MS, PhD).

College of Fine and Applied Arts Offers architectural studies (MS); architecture (M Arch, PhD); art and design (MFA); art education (Ed M, MA, PhD); art history (MA, PhD); crafts (MFA); dance (MFA); fine and applied arts (Ed M, M Arch, M Mus, MA, MFA, MLA, MME, MS, MUP, AD, DMA, PhD); graphic design (MFA); industrial design (MFA); landscape architecture (MLA, PhD); metals (MFA); music (M Mus, AD, DMA); music education (MME, PhD); musicology (PhD); painting (MFA); photography (MFA); regional planning (PhD); sculpture (MFA); theatre (MA, MFA, PhD); urban planning (MUP).

College of Liberal Arts and Sciences *Program availability:* Online learning. Offers African studies (MA); analytics (MS); animal biology (ecology, ethology and evolution) (MS, PhD); anthropology (MA, PhD); applied mathematics (MS); applied mathematics: actuarial science (MS); applied statistics (MS); astrochemistry (PhD); astronomy (MS, PhD); atmospheric sciences (MS, PhD); biochemistry (MS, PhD); bioinformatics: chemical and biomolecular engineering (MS); biophysics and computational biology (MS, PhD); cell and developmental biology (PhD); chemical engineering (MS, PhD); chemical physics (PhD); chemical sciences (MA, MS, PhD); chemistry (MA, MS, PhD); classical philology (PhD); classics (MA); communication (MA, PhD); comparative literature (MA, PhD); creative writing (MFA); earth, society

and environment (MA, MS, PhD); East Asian languages and cultures (PhD); East Asian studies (MA); ecology, evolution and conservation biology (MS, PhD); economics (MS, PhD); English (MA, PhD); entomology (MS, PhD); European Union studies (MA); French (MA, PhD); geography and geographic information science (MA, MS, PhD); geology (MS, PhD); German (MA, PhD); history (MA, PhD); integrative biology (MS, MST, PSM, PhD); Italian (MA, PhD); Latin American studies (MA); liberal arts and sciences (MA, MFA, MS, MST, PSM, PhD); linguistics (MA, PhD); literatures, cultures and linguistics (MA, MS, PhD); mathematics (MS, PhD); microbiology (MS, PhD); molecular and cellular biology (MS, PhD); molecular and integrative physiology (MS, PhD); neuroscience (PhD); philosophy (MA, PhD); plant biology (MS, PhD); plant biotechnology (PSM); policy economics (MS); political science (MA, PhD); Portuguese (MA, PhD); psychology (MA, MS, PhD); religious studies (MA); romance linguistics (PhD); Russian, East European, and Eurasian studies (MA); second language acquisition and teacher education (MA, PhD); Slavic languages and literatures (MA, PhD); sociology (MA, PhD); south Asian and Middle Eastern studies (MA); Spanish (MA, PhD); statistics (MS, PhD); teaching of chemistry (MS); teaching of earth sciences (MS); teaching of English as a second language (MS); teaching of Latin (MA); teaching of mathematics (MS); translation and interpreting (MA).

College of Media Offers advertising (MS); communications and media (PhD); journalism (MS); media (MS, PhD).

Gies College of Business *Program availability:* Online learning. Offers accountancy (MS, PhD); accounting science (MAS); business (MAS, MBA, MS, PhD); business administration (MS, PhD); finance (MS, PhD); technology management (MS).

School of Information Sciences *Program availability:* Part-time, online learning. Offers bioinformatics (MS); digital libraries (CAS); information management (MS); library and information science (MS, PhD, CAS).

School of Labor and Employment Relations Offers human resources and industrial relations (MHRIR, PhD).

School of Social Work Offers advocacy, leadership, and social change (MSW); children, youth and family services (MSW); health care (MSW); mental health (MSW); school social work (MSW); social work (PhD).

Illinois Informatics Institute Offers informatics (PhD).

UNIVERSITY OF INDIANAPOLIS, Indianapolis, IN 46227-3697

General Information Independent-religious, coed, comprehensive institution. CGS member. *Graduate housing:* Rooms and/or apartments available on a first-come, first-served basis to single and married students.

GRADUATE UNITS

Graduate Programs *Program availability:* Part-time, evening/weekend, online learning.

Center for Aging and Community *Program availability:* Part-time, evening/weekend, online learning. Offers gerontology (MS, Certificate).

College of Applied Behavioral Sciences Offers addictions counseling (MA); clinical psychology (Psy D); mental health counseling (MA); psychology (MA); social work (MSW).

College of Health Sciences Offers health sciences (MHS, MOT, MPH, MS, DHS, DPT, OTD); occupational therapy (MOT, DHS, OTD); physical therapy (MHS, DHS, DPT); public health (MPH); sport management (MS).

School of Business *Program availability:* Part-time, evening/weekend. Offers business (EMBA, MBA, Graduate Certificate).

School of Education *Program availability:* Part-time, evening/weekend. Offers art education (MAT); biology (MAT); chemistry (MAT); curriculum and instruction (MA); earth sciences (MAT); education (MA, MAT); educational leadership (MA); elementary education (MA); English (MAT); French (MAT); math (MAT); physical education (MAT); physics (MAT); secondary education (MAT); social studies (MAT); Spanish (MAT).

School of Nursing Offers advanced practice nursing (DNP); family nurse practitioner (MSN); gerontological nurse practitioner (MSN); neonatal nurse practitioner (MSN); nurse-midwifery (MSN); nursing (MSN); nursing and health systems leadership (MSN); nursing education (MSN); women's health nurse practitioner (MSN). Electronic applications accepted.

Shaheen College of Arts and Sciences *Program availability:* Part-time, evening/weekend. Offers anthropology (MS); applied sociology (MA); art (MA); arts and sciences (MA, MS); English (MA); history (MA); human biology (MS); international relations (MA).

THE UNIVERSITY OF IOWA, Iowa City, IA 52242-1316

General Information State-supported, coed, university. CGS member. *Graduate housing:* Rooms and/or apartments available on a first-come, first-served basis to single and married students.

GRADUATE UNITS

College of Dentistry Offers dental public health (MS); dentistry (MS, DDS, PhD, Certificate); endodontics (MS, Certificate); operative dentistry (MS, Certificate); oral and maxillofacial surgery (MS, PhD, Certificate); oral pathology, radiology and medicine (MS, PhD, Certificate); oral science (MS, PhD); orthodontics (MS, Certificate); pediatric dentistry (Certificate); periodontics (MS, Certificate); preventive and community dentistry (MS); prosthodontics (MS, Certificate).

College of Law Students: 437 full-time (193 women); includes 93 minority (17 Black or African American, non-Hispanic/Latino; 2 American Indian or Alaska Native, non-Hispanic/Latino; 18 Asian, non-Hispanic/Latino; 39 Hispanic/Latino; 17 Two or more races, non-Hispanic/Latino), 31 international. Average age 24. 1,823 applicants, 46% accepted, 163 enrolled. *Faculty:* 49 full-time (22 women), 38 part-time/adjunct (15 women). Expenses: Contact institution. *Financial support:* In 2018–19, 345 students received support, including 345 fellowships with tuition reimbursements available (averaging $18,769 per year), 127 research assistantships with partial tuition reimbursements available (averaging $2,175 per year); career-related internships or fieldwork, scholarships/grants, and health care benefits also available. Financial award applicants required to submit FAFSA. In 2018, 3 master's, 141 doctorates awarded. Offers law (LL M, MSL, JD, SJD). *Application deadline:* For fall admission, 5/1 priority date for domestic and international students. Applications are processed on a rolling basis. *Application fee:* $0. Electronic applications accepted. *Application Contact:* Collins Byrd, Assistant Dean of Enrollment Management, 319-335-9095, Fax: 319-335-9646, E-mail: law-admissions@uiowa.edu. *Dean,* Kevin Washburn, 319-335-9034, Fax: 319-335-9019, E-mail: kevin-washburn@uiowa.edu.

College of Pharmacy Offers clinical pharmaceutical sciences (PhD); medicinal and natural products chemistry (PhD); pharmaceutical socioeconomics (PhD); pharmaceutics (MS, PhD); pharmacy (Pharm D). Electronic applications accepted.

Graduate College *Program availability:* Part-time, evening/weekend, online learning. Offers applied mathematical and computational sciences (PhD); bioinformatics (MS); bioinformatics and computational biology (Certificate); genetics (PhD);

geoinformatics (MS, PhD, Certificate); health informatics (MS, PhD, Certificate); human toxicology (MS, PhD); immunology (PhD); information science (MS, PhD, Certificate); molecular and cellular biology (PhD); neuroscience (PhD); translational biomedicine (MS, PhD); urban and regional planning (MA, MS). Electronic applications accepted.

College of Education Offers art education (MA); counseling psychology (PhD); counselor education and supervision (PhD); couple and family therapy (PhD); developmental reading (MA); education (MA, MAT, MM, PhD); educational leadership (MA, PhD, Ed S); educational measurement and statistics (MA, PhD); educational psychology (MA, PhD); elementary education (MA); English education (MA, MAT); foreign and second language education (MAT); foreign language education (MA); foreign language/ESL education (PhD); higher education and student affairs (MA, PhD); language, literacy and culture (PhD); mathematics education (MA, MAT, PhD); music education (MM, PhD); rehabilitation and mental health counseling (MA); rehabilitation counselor education (PhD); school counseling (MA); school psychology (PhD, Ed S); schools, culture, and society (MA, PhD); science education (MA); secondary education (MA); social studies (MA, PhD); special education (MA, PhD). Electronic applications accepted.

College of Engineering Offers biomedical engineering (MS, PhD); chemical and biochemical engineering (MS, PhD); electrical and computer engineering (MS, PhD); energy systems (MS, PhD); engineering (MS, PhD); engineering design (MS, PhD); engineering design and manufacturing (MS, PhD); environmental engineering and science (MS, PhD); fluid dynamics (MS, PhD); healthcare systems (MS, PhD); human factors (MS, PhD); hydraulics and water resources (MS, PhD); information and engineering management (MS, PhD); materials and manufacturing (MS, PhD); operations research (MS, PhD); structures, mechanics and materials (MS, PhD); sustainable water development (MS, PhD); transportation engineering (MS, PhD); wind energy (MS, PhD). Electronic applications accepted.

College of Liberal Arts and Sciences *Program availability:* Part-time, online learning. Offers actuarial science (MS); American studies (MA, PhD); anthropology (MA, PhD); art (MA, MFA); art history (MA, PhD); astronomy (MS); athletic training (MS); biology (MS, PhD); cell and developmental biology (MS, PhD); chemistry (PhD); Chinese (MA); classics (MA, PhD); clinical exercise physiology (MS); communication sciences and disorders (MA, Au D, PhD); computer science (MCS, PhD); dance (MFA); earth and environmental science (MS, PhD); English (PhD); evolution (MS, PhD); film and video production (MFA); film studies (MA, PhD); French (MA, PhD); gender, women's and sexuality studies (Certificate); genetics (MS, PhD); geographical and sustainability sciences (MA, PhD, Certificate); Greek (MA); health and human physiology (PhD); Hindi (MA); history (MA, PhD); interpersonal communication and relationships (MA, PhD); journalism and media communication (MA); Latin (MA); leisure studies (MA, PhD); liberal arts and sciences (MA, MCS, MFA, MS, MSW, Au D, DMA, PhD, Certificate); linguistics (MA, PhD); literary studies (MA); mass communication (PhD); mathematics (MS, PhD); media studies (MA, PhD); music (MA, MFA, DMA, PhD); neurobiology (MS, PhD); nonfiction writing (MFA); philosophy (PhD); physics (MS, PhD); political science (PhD); psychology (MA, PhD); religious studies (MA, PhD); rhetoric and public advocacy (MA, PhD); Sanskrit (MA); second language acquisition (PhD); social work (MSW, PhD); sociology (MA, PhD); South Asian studies (MA, PhD); Spanish (MA, PhD); Spanish creative writing (MFA); statistics (MS, PhD); strategic communication (MA); theatre arts (MFA). Electronic applications accepted.

College of Nursing Offers nursing (MSN, DNP, PhD). Electronic applications accepted.

College of Public Health Offers agricultural safety and health (MS, PhD); biostatistics (MS, PhD, Certificate); clinical investigation (MS); community and behavioral health (MPH, MS, PhD); epidemiology (MPH, MS, PhD); ergonomics (MPH); health management and policy (MHA, PhD); industrial hygiene (MS, PhD); occupational and environmental health (MPH, MS, PhD, Certificate); public health (MHA, MPH, MS, PhD, Certificate); quantitative methods (MPH). Electronic applications accepted.

School of Library and Information Science Offers library and information science (MA, PhD). Electronic applications accepted.

Roy J. and Lucille A. Carver College of Medicine *Program availability:* Part-time. Offers medicine (MA, MPAS, MS, DPT, MD, PhD). Electronic applications accepted.

Graduate Programs in Medicine *Program availability:* Part-time. Offers anatomy and cell biology (PhD); biochemistry (MS, PhD); free radical and radiation biology (MS); general microbiology and microbial physiology (MS, PhD); immunology (MS, PhD); medicine (MA, MPAS, MS, DPT, PhD); microbial genetics (MS, PhD); molecular physiology and biophysics (MS, PhD); pathogenic bacteriology (MS, PhD); pathology (MS); pharmacology (MS, PhD); physical rehabilitation science (MA, PhD); physical therapy (DPT); physician assistant studies and services (MPAS); virology (MS, PhD). Electronic applications accepted.

Tippie College of Business Offers accounting (M Ac, PhD); business (EMBA, M Ac, MBA, MS, PhD); business administration (EMBA, MBA); business analytics (MBA); economics (PhD); finance (MBA); leadership (MBA); management and organizations (PhD); management sciences (PhD); marketing (MBA). Electronic applications accepted.

UNIVERSITY OF JAMESTOWN, Jamestown, ND 58405

General Information Independent-religious, coed, comprehensive institution.

GRADUATE UNITS

Program in Education Offers curriculum and instruction (M Ed).

Program in Physical Therapy Offers physical therapy (DPT).

THE UNIVERSITY OF KANSAS, Lawrence, KS 66045

General Information State-supported, coed, university. CGS member. *Enrollment:* 5,654 full-time matriculated graduate/professional students (3,074 women), 2,443 part-time matriculated graduate/professional students (1,493 women). *Enrollment by degree level:* 3,575 master's, 4,283 doctoral, 239 other advanced degrees. *Graduate housing:* Rooms and/or apartments available on a first-come, first-served basis to single and married students. Housing application deadline: 3/1. *Student services:* Campus employment opportunities, campus safety program, career counseling, child daycare facilities, exercise/wellness program, free psychological counseling, grant writing training, international student services, low-cost health insurance, multicultural affairs office, services for students with disabilities, teacher training, writing training. *Library facilities:* Watson Library plus 11 others. Collection: Books: 4.7 million (physical), 1 million (digital/electronic). Weekly public service hours: 168; study areas open 24 hours, 5–7 days a week; students can reserve study rooms.

Computer facilities: 1,500 computers available on campus for general student use. A campuswide network can be accessed from student residence rooms and from off campus. Online class registration, online payments are available.
Website: http://www.ku.edu/

General Application Contact: Graduate Studies, 785-864-8040, Fax: 785-864-7209, E-mail: graduate@ku.edu.

GRADUATE UNITS

Graduate Studies Students: 3,280 full-time (1,742 women), 1,787 part-time (1,051 women); includes 834 minority (226 Black or African American, non-Hispanic/Latino; 46 American Indian or Alaska Native, non-Hispanic/Latino; 152 Asian, non-Hispanic/Latino; 231 Hispanic/Latino; 4 Native Hawaiian or other Pacific Islander, non-Hispanic/Latino; 175 Two or more races, non-Hispanic/Latino), 895 international. Average age 31. 4,831 applicants, 56% accepted, 1708 enrolled. Expenses: Contact institution. *Financial support:* Fellowships, research assistantships, teaching assistantships, career-related internships or fieldwork, Federal Work-Study, institutionally sponsored loans, scholarships/grants, traineeships, and unspecified assistantships available. Support available to part-time students. Financial award application deadline: 4/15; financial award applicants required to submit FAFSA. In 2018, 1,754 master's, 368 doctorates, 599 other advanced degrees awarded. *Program availability:* Part-time, evening/weekend, online learning. *Application fee:* $65 ($85 for international students). Electronic applications accepted. *Application Contact:* Abby Ehling, Assistant Director of Graduate Admissions, 785-864-3140, Fax: 785-864-7209, E-mail: graduate@ku.edu. *Dean of Graduate Studies,* Audrey Lamb, 785-864-8040, E-mail: lamb@ku.edu.

College of Liberal Arts and Sciences Students: 1,496 full-time (803 women), 209 part-time (136 women); includes 256 minority (52 Black or African American, non-Hispanic/Latino; 26 American Indian or Alaska Native, non-Hispanic/Latino; 46 Asian, non-Hispanic/Latino; 79 Hispanic/Latino; 1 Native Hawaiian or other Pacific Islander, non-Hispanic/Latino; 52 Two or more races, non-Hispanic/Latino), 370 international. Average age 30. 2,000 applicants, 42% accepted, 443 enrolled. Expenses: Contact institution. *Financial support:* Fellowships, research assistantships with partial tuition reimbursements, teaching assistantships with tuition reimbursements, career-related internships or fieldwork, Federal Work-Study, institutionally sponsored loans, scholarships/grants, traineeships, and unspecified assistantships available. Support available to part-time students. Financial award applicants required to submit FAFSA. In 2018, 317 master's, 140 doctorates, 55 other advanced degrees awarded. *Program availability:* Part-time, evening/weekend, online learning. Offers African and African-American studies (MA); African studies (Graduate Certificate); American studies (MA, PhD); anthropology (MA, PhD); applied behavioral science (MA); applied mathematics (Graduate Certificate); art history (MA, PhD); atmospheric science (MS); audiology (PhD); behavioral psychology (PhD); biochemistry and biophysics (PhD); Brazilian studies (Graduate Certificate); Central American and Mexican studies (Graduate Certificate); ceramics (MFA); chemistry (MS, PhD); child language (MA, PhD); city and county management (Graduate Certificate); classics (PhD); clinical psychology (MA, PhD); cognitive and brain sciences (MA, PhD); communication studies (MA, PhD); community health and development (Graduate Certificate); computational biology (PhD); creative writing (MFA); developmental psychology (MA, PhD); drawing and painting (MFA); East Asian languages and cultures (MA, Graduate Certificate); ecology and evolutionary biology (MA, PhD); economics (MA, PhD); English (MA, PhD); expanded media (MFA); film and media studies (MA, PhD); foreign area officer (MA); French (MA, PhD); geographic information science (Graduate Certificate); geography (MA, PhD); geology (MS, PhD); gerontology (MA, PhD); global and international studies (MA); history (MA, PhD); indigenous studies (MA, Graduate Certificate); Latin American and Caribbean studies (Graduate Certificate); Latin American studies (MA); liberal arts and sciences (MA, MFA, MPA, MS, MUP, PhD, Graduate Certificate); linguistics (MA, PhD); mathematics (MA, PhD); metalsmithing/jewelry (MFA); microbiology (PhD); molecular, cellular, and developmental biology (PhD); museum studies (MA, Graduate Certificate); performance management (Graduate Certificate); philosophy (MA, PhD); physics and astronomy (MS, PhD); political science (MA, PhD); professional workplace communication (Graduate Certificate); public administration (MPA, PhD); quantitative psychology (PhD); religious studies (MA, Graduate Certificate); Russian, East European and EurAsian studies (MA, Graduate Certificate); scenography (MFA); sculpture (MFA); Slavic languages and literatures (MA, PhD); social psychology (MA, PhD); sociology (PhD); Spanish and Portuguese (MA, PhD); speech-language pathology (MA, PhD); textiles/fibers (MFA); theatre studies (MA, PhD); urban planning (MUP); visual art education (MA). *Application fee:* $65 ($85 for international students). Electronic applications accepted. *Application Contact:* Kristine Latta, Director of the College Office of Graduate Affairs, 785-864-1784, E-mail: klatta@ku.edu. *Dean, College of Liberal Arts and Sciences,* Carl W. Lejuez, 785-864-3661, E-mail: clejuez@ku.edu.

School of Architecture and Design Students: 91 full-time (44 women), 35 part-time (18 women); includes 23 minority (5 Black or African American, non-Hispanic/Latino; 4 Asian, non-Hispanic/Latino; 9 Hispanic/Latino; 5 Two or more races, non-Hispanic/Latino), 24 international. Average age 27. 101 applicants, 70% accepted, 30 enrolled. Expenses: Contact institution. *Financial support:* Fellowships, research assistantships, teaching assistantships, career-related internships or fieldwork, scholarships/grants, health care benefits, and unspecified assistantships available. Financial award application deadline: 1/15; financial award applicants required to submit FAFSA. In 2018, 74 master's, 3 doctorates, 11 other advanced degrees awarded. *Program availability:* Part-time. Offers architectural acoustics (Certificate); architecture (M Arch, PhD); architecture and design (M Arch, MA, PhD, Certificate, Graduate Certificate); design management (MA); health and wellness (Certificate); historic preservation (Certificate); interaction design (MA); urban design (Certificate). *Application deadline:* For fall admission, 1/15 priority date for domestic and international students; for summer admission, 1/15 priority date for domestic and international students. *Application fee:* $65 ($85 for international students). Electronic applications accepted. *Application Contact:* Joan Weaver, Graduate Admissions Contact, 785-864-3709, E-mail: jweaver@ku.edu. *Dean,* Frank Zilm, 816-561-7186, E-mail: frankzilm@ku.edu.

School of Business Students: 274 full-time (108 women), 412 part-time (156 women); includes 121 minority (29 Black or African American, non-Hispanic/Latino; 4 American Indian or Alaska Native, non-Hispanic/Latino; 28 Asian, non-Hispanic/Latino; 24 Hispanic/Latino; 2 Native Hawaiian or other Pacific Islander, non-Hispanic/Latino; 34 Two or more races, non-Hispanic/Latino), 48 international. Average age 31. 625 applicants, 65% accepted, 349 enrolled. Expenses: Contact institution. *Financial support:* Fellowships, research assistantships, teaching assistantships, career-related internships or fieldwork, Federal Work-Study, and unspecified assistantships available. Financial award application deadline: 1/15; financial award applicants required to submit FAFSA. In 2018, 311 master's, 7 doctorates awarded. *Program availability:* Part-time, evening/weekend. Offers accounting (M Acc); business (M Acc, MBA, MS, PhD); business administration and management (MBA); business and organizational leadership (MS); decision sciences and supply chain management (PhD); finance (PhD); human resources management (PhD); marketing (PhD); organizational behavior (PhD); strategic management (PhD); supply chain management and logistics (MS). *Application deadline:* For fall admission, 1/15 priority date for domestic and international students. *Application fee:* $65 ($85 for international students). Electronic applications accepted. *Application Contact:* Andrea Noltner, Graduate Admissions Contact, 785-864-7556, E-mail: anoltner@ku.edu. *Dean,* Dr. L. Paige Fields, 785-864-7546, E-mail: paige.fields@ku.edu.

School of Education Students: 487 full-time (315 women), 745 part-time (576 women); includes 222 minority (79 Black or African American, non-Hispanic/Latino; 8 American Indian or Alaska Native, non-Hispanic/Latino; 31 Asian, non-Hispanic/Latino; 60 Hispanic/Latino; 1 Native Hawaiian or other Pacific Islander, non-Hispanic/Latino; 43 Two or more races, non-Hispanic/Latino), 104 international. Average age 33. 821 applicants, 71% accepted, 416 enrolled. Expenses: Contact institution. *Financial support:* Fellowships, research assistantships, teaching assistantships, career-related internships or fieldwork, scholarships/grants, and unspecified assistantships available. Financial award application deadline: 2/1. In 2018, 446 master's, 77 doctorates, 110 other advanced degrees awarded. *Program availability:* Part-time, online learning. Offers autism spectrum disorder (Certificate); counseling psychology (MS, PhD); curriculum and teaching (MA, MS Ed, PhD); early childhood unified (MS Ed); education (MA, MS, MS Ed, MSE, Ed D, PhD, Certificate, Ed S); education leadership and policy (MSE, PhD); educational administration (MSE, Ed D, PhD); educational psychology and research (MS Ed, PhD); educational technology (MS Ed, PhD); exercise science (MS Ed); health, sport, and exercise sciences (PhD); higher education administration (MS Ed, Ed D, PhD); policy studies (PhD); school psychology (PhD, Ed S); social and cultural studies in education (MSE, PhD); special and inclusive education leadership (Certificate); special education (PhD); sport management (MS Ed). *Application fee:* $65 ($85 for international students). Electronic applications accepted. *Application Contact:* Kim Huggett, Graduate Student Services Manager, 785-864-4510, E-mail: khuggett@ku.edu. *Dean,* Dr. Rick J. Ginsberg, 785-864-4297, E-mail: ginsberg@ku.edu.

School of Engineering Students: 401 full-time (99 women), 239 part-time (58 women); includes 86 minority (24 Black or African American, non-Hispanic/Latino; 1 American Indian or Alaska Native, non-Hispanic/Latino; 24 Asian, non-Hispanic/Latino; 20 Hispanic/Latino; 17 Two or more races, non-Hispanic/Latino), 262 international. Average age 29. 585 applicants, 61% accepted, 150 enrolled. Expenses: Contact institution. *Financial support:* Fellowships, research assistantships, teaching assistantships, career-related internships or fieldwork, Federal Work-Study, scholarships/grants, and unspecified assistantships available. In 2018, 164 master's, 32 doctorates, 2 other advanced degrees awarded. *Program availability:* Part-time, evening/weekend, online learning. Offers aerospace engineering (ME, MS, DE, PhD); architectural engineering (MS); bioengineering (MS, PhD); chemical and petroleum engineering (PhD); chemical engineering (MS); civil engineering (MCE, MS, PhD); computer engineering (MS); computer science (MS, PhD); construction management (MCM); electrical engineering (MS, PhD); engineering (MCE, MCM, ME, MS, DE, PhD, Certificate); engineering management (MS, Certificate); environmental engineering (MS, PhD); environmental science (MS, PhD); information technology (MS); mechanical engineering (MS, PhD); petroleum engineering (MS); petroleum management (Certificate); project management (ME, MS). *Application fee:* $65 ($85 for international students). Electronic applications accepted. *Application Contact:* Amy Wierman, Assistant to the Dean, 785-864-2930, E-mail: awierman@ku.edu. *Dean,* Dr. Arvin Agah, 785-864-2930, E-mail: agah@ku.edu.

School of Music Students: 150 full-time (72 women), 28 part-time (19 women); includes 12 minority (3 Black or African American, non-Hispanic/Latino; 5 Asian, non-Hispanic/Latino; 2 Hispanic/Latino; 2 Two or more races, non-Hispanic/Latino), 41 international. Average age 30. 199 applicants, 58% accepted, 59 enrolled. Expenses: Contact institution. *Financial support:* Fellowships, research assistantships, teaching assistantships, scholarships/grants, and unspecified assistantships available. In 2018, 38 master's, 37 doctorates awarded. Offers music (MM, MME, DMA, PhD); music education (MME, PhD); music therapy (MME, PhD). *Application fee:* $65 ($85 for international students). Electronic applications accepted. *Application Contact:* Terri Morris, Graduate Services Coordinator, 785-864-3422, E-mail: tlmorris@ku.edu. *Dean,* Dr. Robert Walzel, 785-864-3421, E-mail: robert.walzel@ku.edu.

School of Pharmacy Students: 86 full-time (39 women), 19 part-time (8 women); includes 13 minority (2 Black or African American, non-Hispanic/Latino; 1 American Indian or Alaska Native, non-Hispanic/Latino; 6 Asian, non-Hispanic/Latino; 2 Hispanic/Latino; 2 Two or more races, non-Hispanic/Latino), 40 international. Average age 28. 148 applicants, 28% accepted, 24 enrolled. Expenses: Contact institution. *Financial support:* Fellowships, research assistantships, teaching assistantships, career-related internships or fieldwork, scholarships/grants, traineeships, and unspecified assistantships available. In 2018, 21 master's, 22 doctorates awarded. Offers medicinal chemistry (MS, PhD); neurosciences (MS, PhD); pharmaceutical chemistry (MS, PhD); pharmacology and toxicology (MS, PhD); pharmacy (MS, PhD). *Application fee:* $65 ($85 for international students). Electronic applications accepted. *Application Contact:* Patti Steffan, Graduate Admissions Contact, 785-864-3893, E-mail: psteffan@ku.edu. *Dean,* Kenneth L. Audus, 785-864-3591, E-mail: audus@ku.edu.

School of Social Welfare Students: 301 full-time (262 women), 45 part-time (41 women); includes 87 minority (25 Black or African American, non-Hispanic/Latino; 6 American Indian or Alaska Native, non-Hispanic/Latino; 7 Asian, non-Hispanic/Latino; 34 Hispanic/Latino; 15 Two or more races, non-Hispanic/Latino), 4 international. Average age 30. 279 applicants, 92% accepted, 190 enrolled. Expenses: Contact institution. *Financial support:* Fellowships, research assistantships, teaching assistantships, Federal Work-Study, scholarships/grants, and tuition waivers (partial) available. Support available to part-time students. Financial award application deadline: 1/17; financial award applicants required to submit FAFSA. In 2018, 204 master's, 3 doctorates awarded. *Program availability:* Part-time, online learning. Offers social welfare (MSW, PhD). *Application deadline:* For fall admission, 1/15 for domestic and international students. *Application fee:* $65 ($85 for international students). Electronic applications accepted. *Application Contact:* Georgiana Spear, Graduate Admissions Contact, 785-864-0115, E-mail: gspear@ku.edu. *Dean,* Michelle Carney, 785-864-5975, E-mail: mmcarney@ku.edu.

William Allen White School of Journalism and Mass Communications Students: 29 full-time (18 women), 63 part-time (45 women); includes 17 minority (7 Black or African American, non-Hispanic/Latino; 1 Asian, non-Hispanic/Latino; 2 Hispanic/Latino; 1 Native Hawaiian or other Pacific Islander, non-Hispanic/Latino; 6 Two or more races, non-Hispanic/Latino), 8 international. Average age 33. 60 applicants, 78% accepted, 39 enrolled. Expenses: Contact institution. *Financial support:* Fellowships, research assistantships, teaching assistantships, career-related internships or fieldwork, scholarships/grants, and unspecified assistantships available. Support available to part-time students. Financial award application deadline: 2/1; financial award applicants required to submit FAFSA. In 2018, 39 master's, 2 doctorates awarded. *Program availability:* Part-time. Offers journalism

(MS); journalism and mass communications (PhD). *Application deadline:* For fall admission, 1/1 priority date for domestic and international students; for spring admission, 8/1 for domestic and international students; for summer admission, 5/15 for domestic and international students. *Application fee:* $65 ($85 for international students). Electronic applications accepted. *Application Contact:* Jammie A. Johnson, Graduate Advisor/Administrative Assistant, 785-864-7649, E-mail: jamjohn@ku.edu. *Dean,* Ann Brill, 785-864-4755, E-mail: abrill@ku.edu.

School of Law Students: 317 full-time (152 women), 32 part-time (10 women); includes 62 minority (16 Black or African American, non-Hispanic/Latino; 4 American Indian or Alaska Native, non-Hispanic/Latino; 12 Asian, non-Hispanic/Latino; 24 Hispanic/Latino; 6 Two or more races, non-Hispanic/Latino), 21 international. Average age 24. 731 applicants, 51% accepted, 107 enrolled. *Faculty:* 31 full-time (18 women), 20 part-time/adjunct (8 women). Expenses: Contact institution. *Financial support:* In 2018–19, 6 fellowships (averaging $1,310 per year), 70 research assistantships (averaging $1,215 per year), 7 teaching assistantships (averaging $800 per year) were awarded; career-related internships or fieldwork, Federal Work-Study, institutionally sponsored loans, scholarships/grants, and unspecified assistantships also available. Financial award application deadline: 2/15; financial award applicants required to submit FAFSA. In 2018, 102 doctorates awarded. *Program availability:* Part-time. Offers law (JD). *Application deadline:* For fall admission, 4/1 priority date for domestic students, 4/1 for international students. Applications are processed on a rolling basis. *Application fee:* $55. Electronic applications accepted. *Application Contact:* Steven Freedman, Assistant Dean for Admissions, 866-220-3654, E-mail: admitlaw@ku.edu. *Dean,* Stephen W. Mazza, 785-864-4550, Fax: 785-864-5054.

University of Kansas Medical Center Students: 1,594 full-time (919 women), 495 part-time (386 women); includes 416 minority (58 Black or African American, non-Hispanic/Latino; 7 American Indian or Alaska Native, non-Hispanic/Latino; 144 Asian, non-Hispanic/Latino; 100 Hispanic/Latino; 1 Native Hawaiian or other Pacific Islander, non-Hispanic/Latino; 106 Two or more races, non-Hispanic/Latino), 94 international. Average age 28. *Faculty:* 1,431. Expenses: Contact institution. In 2018, 150 master's, 371 doctorates, 25 other advanced degrees awarded. Offers health informatics (MS, Post Master's Certificate). *Application Contact:* Dr. Robert Simari, Executive Vice Chancellor, 913-588-1440, E-mail: rsimari@kumc.edu. *Executive Vice Chancellor,* Dr. Robert Simari, 913-588-1440, E-mail: rsimari@kumc.edu.

School of Health Professions Students: 461 full-time (332 women), 68 part-time (61 women); includes 57 minority (10 Black or African American, non-Hispanic/Latino; 2 American Indian or Alaska Native, non-Hispanic/Latino; 9 Asian, non-Hispanic/Latino; 20 Hispanic/Latino; 1 Native Hawaiian or other Pacific Islander, non-Hispanic/Latino; 15 Two or more races, non-Hispanic/Latino), 21 international. Average age 27. *Faculty:* 117. Expenses: Contact institution. In 2018, 59 master's, 102 doctorates, 17 other advanced degrees awarded. Offers audiology (Au D); dietetic internship (Graduate Certificate); dietetics and nutrition (MS); health professions (MOT, MS, Au D, DNAP, DPT, OTD, PhD, SLPD, Graduate Certificate); medical nutrition science (PhD); molecular biotechnology (MS); nurse anesthesia education (DNAP); occupational therapy (MOT, OTD); physical therapy (DPT); rehabilitation science (PhD); speech-language pathology (SLPD); therapeutic science (PhD). *Application Contact:* Dr. Abiodun Akinwuntan, Dean, 913-588-5235, Fax: 913-588-5254, E-mail: aakinwuntan@kumc.edu. *Dean,* Dr. Abiodun Akinwuntan, 913-588-5235, Fax: 913-588-5254, E-mail: aakinwuntan@kumc.edu.

School of Medicine Students: 1,078 full-time (538 women), 148 part-time (77 women); includes 293 minority (30 Black or African American, non-Hispanic/Latino; 3 American Indian or Alaska Native, non-Hispanic/Latino; 113 Asian, non-Hispanic/Latino; 71 Hispanic/Latino; 76 Two or more races, non-Hispanic/Latino), 71 international. Average age 27. *Faculty:* 1,258. Expenses: Contact institution. In 2018, 69 master's, 241 doctorates, 1 other advanced degree awarded. Offers anatomy and cell biology (MS, PhD); applied statistics and analytics (MS); biochemistry and molecular biology (PhD); biomedical sciences (PhD); biostatistics (MS, PhD, Graduate Certificate); cancer biology (MS, PhD); clinical research (MS); epidemiology (MPH); health policy and management (PhD); health services administration (MHSA); medicine (MHSA, MPH, MS, MD, PhD, Graduate Certificate); microbiology, molecular genetics and immunology (MS, PhD); molecular and integrative physiology (PhD); neuroscience (PhD); pathology and laboratory medicine (MS, PhD); pharmacology (PhD); public health management (MPH); social and behavioral health (MPH); statistical applications (Graduate Certificate); toxicology (PhD). *Application Contact:* Dr. Robert Simari, Executive Dean, 913-588-7201, E-mail: rsimari@kumc.edu. *Executive Dean,* Dr. Robert Simari, 913-588-7201, E-mail: rsimari@kumc.edu.

School of Nursing Students: 55 full-time (49 women), 273 part-time (246 women); includes 62 minority (16 Black or African American, non-Hispanic/Latino; 2 American Indian or Alaska Native, non-Hispanic/Latino; 21 Asian, non-Hispanic/Latino; 9 Hispanic/Latino; 14 Two or more races, non-Hispanic/Latino), 1 international. Average age 36. 76 applicants, 93% accepted, 60 enrolled. *Faculty:* 56. Expenses: Contact institution. *Financial support:* In 2018–19, 5 research assistantships with tuition reimbursements (averaging $20,000 per year), 30 teaching assistantships with tuition reimbursements (averaging $20,000 per year) were awarded; scholarships/grants and traineeships also available. Financial award application deadline: 3/1; financial award applicants required to submit FAFSA. In 2018, 19 master's, 28 doctorates, 7 other advanced degrees awarded. *Program availability:* Part-time, 100% online, blended/hybrid learning. Offers adult/gerontological clinical nurse specialist (PMC); adult/gerontological nurse practitioner (PMC); health care informatics (PMC); health professions educator (PMC); nurse midwife (PMC); nursing (MS, DNP, PhD); organizational leadership (PMC); psychiatric/mental health nurse practitioner (PMC); public health nursing (PMC). *Application deadline:* For fall admission, 4/1 for domestic and international students; for spring admission, 9/1 for domestic and international students. *Application fee:* $75. Electronic applications accepted. *Application Contact:* Dr. Pamela K. Barnes, Associate Dean, Student Affairs, 913-588-1619, Fax: 913-588-1615, E-mail: pbarnes2@kumc.edu. *Dean,* Dr. Sally Maliski, 913-588-1601, Fax: 913-588-1660, E-mail: smaliski@kumc.edu.

UNIVERSITY OF KENTUCKY, Lexington, KY 40506-0032

General Information State-supported, coed, university. CGS member. *Graduate housing:* Rooms and/or apartments available to single and married students. *Research affiliation:* Continuous Electron Beam Accelerator Facility (high-energy physics), Battelle–Pacific Northwest National Laboratory (environmental sciences), Oak Ridge National Laboratory (nuclear physics), National Institute of Occupational Health and Safety (environmental health), National Drug Addiction Center (drug abuse and prevention).

GRADUATE UNITS

College of Dentistry Students: 254 full-time (131 women); includes 76 minority (16 Black or African American, non-Hispanic/Latino; 35 Asian, non-Hispanic/Latino; 16 Hispanic/Latino; 9 Two or more races, non-Hispanic/Latino), 2 international. Average

age 29. 1,273 applicants, 11% accepted, 65 enrolled. *Faculty:* 69 full-time (25 women), 53 part-time/adjunct (18 women). Expenses: Contact institution. *Financial support:* In 2018–19, 158 students received support. Institutionally sponsored loans and scholarships/grants available. Financial award application deadline: 3/1; financial award applicants required to submit FAFSA. In 2018, 66 doctorates awarded. Offers dentistry (DMD). *Application deadline:* For fall admission, 12/1 priority date for domestic students. Applications are processed on a rolling basis. *Application fee:* $75. Electronic applications accepted. *Application Contact:* Rebekah Huff, Student Affairs Officer, 859-323-6071, Fax: 859-257-5550, E-mail: rebekah.huff@uky.edu. *Interim Dean,* Dr. Lawrence Holloway, 859-323-1884, Fax: 859-323-1042, E-mail: larry.holloway@uky.edu.

College of Law Offers law (JD). Electronic applications accepted.

College of Medicine Offers medicine (MD). Electronic applications accepted.

Graduate School *Program availability:* Part-time, evening/weekend. Offers dentistry (MS); pharmaceutical sciences (MS, PhD); pharmacy (Pharm D). Electronic applications accepted.

College of Agriculture, Food and Environment *Program availability:* Part-time. Offers agricultural economics (MS, PhD); agriculture, food and environment (MS, MSFOR, PhD); animal and food sciences (MS, PhD); biosystems and agricultural engineering (MS, PhD); entomology (MS, PhD); family studies, human development, and resource management (MS, PhD); forestry (MSFOR); hospitality and dietetics administration (MS); integrated plant and soil sciences (MS, PhD); plant pathology (MS, PhD); veterinary science (MS, PhD). Electronic applications accepted.

College of Arts and Sciences *Program availability:* Part-time. Offers anthropology (MA, PhD); applied mathematics (MS); arts and sciences (MA, MS, PhD); biology (MS, PhD); chemistry (MS, PhD); English (MA, PhD); geography (MA, PhD); geology (MS, PhD); German (MA); Hispanic studies (MA, PhD); history (MA, PhD); mathematics (MA, MS, PhD); modern and classical languages and literatures (MA); philosophy (MA, PhD); physics and astronomy (MS, PhD); political science (MA, PhD); psychology (MA, PhD); sociology (MA, MS, PhD); statistics (MS, PhD); teaching world languages (MA). Electronic applications accepted.

College of Communication and Information *Program availability:* Part-time. Offers communication and information (MA, MSLS, PhD); information communication technology (MA, PhD); library science (MA, MSLS). Electronic applications accepted.

College of Design Offers architecture (M Arch); design (M Arch, MAIDM, MHP, MSIDM); historic preservation (MHP); interior design (MA). Electronic applications accepted.

College of Education *Program availability:* Part-time, evening/weekend. Offers biomechanics (MS); counseling psychology (MS, PhD, Ed S); curriculum and instruction (Ed D, PhD); early childhood (MS Ed); education (M Ed, MA Ed, MRC, MS, MS Ed, Ed D, PhD, Ed S); educational leadership (M Ed, Ed D, PhD, Ed S); educational policy studies and evaluation (Ed D); educational psychology (MS, PhD); educational sciences (PhD); elementary education (MA Ed); exercise physiology (MS, PhD); exercise science (PhD); family resource and youth services (M Ed, Ed S); health promotion (MS, Ed D); higher education (MS Ed, PhD); instructional system design (MS Ed); literacy (MA Ed); middle school education (MA Ed, MS Ed); physical education training (Ed D); principalship (Ed D, Ed S); rehabilitation counseling (MRC, PhD); school psychology (PhD, Ed S); school technology leadership (M Ed, PhD, Ed S); secondary education (MA Ed, MS Ed); social and philosophical studies (MS Ed); special education (MS Ed, PhD); sport leadership (MS); teacher leadership (M Ed, Ed S); teaching and coaching (MS). Electronic applications accepted.

College of Engineering *Program availability:* Part-time. Offers biomedical engineering (MSBE, PBME, PhD); chemical engineering (MS, PhD); civil engineering (MSCE, PhD); computer science (MS, PhD); electrical engineering (MSEE, PhD); engineering (M Eng, MCE, MME, MS, MS Ch E, MS Min, MSCE, MSEE, MSEM, MSMAE, MSME, MSMSE, PhD); manufacturing systems engineering (MSMSE); materials science and engineering (MS, PhD); mechanical engineering (MSME, PhD); mining engineering (MME, MS Min, PhD). Electronic applications accepted.

College of Fine Arts *Program availability:* Part-time, evening/weekend. Offers art education (MA); art history (MA); art studio (MFA); arts administration (MA); composition (MM, DMA); conducting (MM, DMA); fine arts (MA, MFA, MM, DMA, PhD); music education (MM, PhD); music theory (MA, PhD); music therapy (MM); musicology (MA, PhD); performance (MM, DMA); sacred music (MM). Electronic applications accepted.

College of Health Sciences *Program availability:* Part-time. Offers athletic training (MS); communication disorders (MS); health administration (MHA); health sciences (MHA, MS, MSCD, MSHP, MSNS, MSPAS, MSPT, MSRMP, DS, PhD); nutritional sciences (MSNS, PhD); physical therapy (DPT); physician assistant studies (MSPAS); rehabilitation sciences (PhD). Electronic applications accepted.

College of Nursing Offers nursing (DNP, PhD). Electronic applications accepted.

College of Public Health Offers clinical research design (MS); epidemiology and biostatistics (PhD); gerontology (PhD, Graduate Certificate); public health (MPH, Dr PH, PhD). Electronic applications accepted.

College of Social Work Offers social work (MSW, PhD). Electronic applications accepted.

Gatton College of Business and Economics *Program availability:* Part-time, evening/weekend. Offers accounting (MSACC); business administration (MBA, PhD); business and economics (MBA, MS, MSACC, PhD); economics (MS, PhD). Electronic applications accepted.

Graduate School Programs from the College of Medicine Offers anatomy and neurobiology (PhD); medical science (MS); medicine (MS, PhD); microbiology and immunology (PhD); molecular and biomedical pharmacology (PhD); molecular and cellular biochemistry (PhD); physiology (PhD); radiation sciences (MSRMP); toxicology (MS, PhD). Electronic applications accepted.

Martin School of Public Policy and Administration *Program availability:* Part-time, evening/weekend, 100% online. Offers public administration (MPA); public financial management (MPFM, Graduate Certificate); public policy (MPP); public policy and administration (PhD). Electronic applications accepted.

Patterson School of Diplomacy and International Commerce Offers diplomacy and international commerce (MA). Electronic applications accepted.

UNIVERSITY OF KING'S COLLEGE, Halifax, NS B3H 2A1, Canada

General Information Province-supported, coed, comprehensive institution. *Graduate housing:* Room and/or apartments available on a first-come, first-served basis to single students; on-campus housing not available to married students. Housing application deadline: 4/1.

GRADUATE UNITS

Graduate and Advanced Programs Offers creative nonfiction (MFA); journalism (MJ).

UNIVERSITY OF LA VERNE, La Verne, CA 91750-4443

General Information Independent, coed, university. *Graduate housing:* Room and/or apartments available on a first-come, first-served basis to single students; on-campus housing not available to married students. *Research affiliation:* San Antonio Community Hospital, Riverside Community Hospital, Presbyterian Intercommunity Hospital, Huntington Memorial Hospital (health services management), Southern California Healthcare Systems, Methodist Hospital of Southern California.

GRADUATE UNITS

College of Arts and Sciences *Program availability:* Part-time. Offers arts and sciences (MFT, MS, Psy D); clinical psychology (Psy D); marriage and family therapy (MFT, MS).

College of Business and Public Management *Program availability:* Part-time, evening/weekend, online learning. Offers accounting (MS); business and public management (MBA, MBA-EP, MHA, MPA, MS, DPA, Certificate); finance (MS); financial management (MHA); gerontology (MS, Certificate); health services management (MBA); human resource management (Certificate); information technology (MBA, MBA-EP); international business (MBA, MBA-EP); leadership and management (MS); management and leadership (MBA, MBA-EP, MHA); marketing (MBA, MBA-EP); marketing and business development (MHA); nonprofit (MPA); nonprofit management (Certificate); organizational leadership (Certificate); public administration (MPA, DPA); public health (MPA); supply chain management (MBA, MBA-EP); urban management and affairs (MPA). Electronic applications accepted.

College of Law *Program availability:* Part-time, evening/weekend. Offers law (JD). Electronic applications accepted.

LaFetra College of Education *Program availability:* Part-time, evening/weekend, 100% online, blended/hybrid learning. Offers advanced teaching skills (M Ed); child development (MS); child life (MS); education (M Ed, MA, MS, Ed D, Certificate, Credential); educational counseling (MS); educational leadership (M Ed); mild/moderate education specialist (Credential); multiple subject (Credential); organizational leadership (Ed D); pupil personnel services (Credential); reading (M Ed, Certificate); reading and language arts specialist (Credential); school psychology (MS); single subject (Credential); social justice higher education administration (MA); special education studies (MS); special emphasis (M Ed); teaching (MA).

Regional and Online Campuses *Program availability:* Part-time, evening/weekend. Offers administration services (preliminary) (Credential); business administration (MBA, MBA-EP); business administration for experienced professionals (MBA, MBA-EP, MS); child development (MS); education (special emphasis) (M Ed); education specialist: mild/moderate (Credential); educational (special emphasis) (M Ed); educational counseling (MS); educational leadership (M Ed); English (Certificate); health administration (MHA); leadership and management (MS); mild/moderate education specialist (Credential); multiple subject (elementary) (Credential); multiple subject teaching (Credential); organizational leadership (Ed D); preliminary administrative services (Credential); pupil personnel services (Credential); pupil personnel services: school counseling (Credential); single subject (secondary) (Credential); single subject teaching (Credential); special education (MS); special education studies (MS); special emphasis (M Ed).

UNIVERSITY OF LETHBRIDGE, Lethbridge, AB T1K 3M4, Canada

General Information Province-supported, coed, university. *Graduate housing:* Rooms and/or apartments available on a first-come, first-served basis to single and married students. Housing application deadline: 4/1. *Research affiliation:* Plains Midstream Canada ULC, Pacific Forestry Institution.

GRADUATE UNITS

School of Graduate Studies *Program availability:* Part-time, evening/weekend. Offers addictions counseling (M Sc); agricultural biotechnology (M Sc); agricultural studies (M Sc, MA); anthropology (MA); archaeology (M Sc, MA); art (MA, MFA); biochemistry (M Sc); biological sciences (M Sc); biomolecular science (PhD); biosystems and biodiversity (PhD); Canadian studies (MA); chemistry (M Sc); computer science (M Sc); computer science and geographical information science (M Sc); counseling (MC); counseling psychology (M Ed); dramatic arts (MA); earth, space, and physical science (PhD); economics (MA); education (MA, PhD); educational leadership (M Ed); English (MA); environmental science (M Sc); evolution and behavior (PhD); exercise science (M Sc); French (MA); French/German (MA); French/Spanish (MA); general education (M Ed); geography (M Sc, MA); German (MA); health sciences (M Sc); individualized multidisciplinary (M Sc, MA); kinesiology (M Sc, MA); management (M Sc); mathematics (M Sc); music (M Mus, MA); Native American studies (MA); neuroscience (M Sc, PhD); new media (MA, MFA); nursing (M Sc, MN); philosophy (MA); physics (M Sc); political science (MA); psychology (MA); religious studies (MA); sociology (MA); theatre and dramatic arts (MFA); theoretical and computational science (PhD); urban and regional studies (MA); women and gender studies (MA). Electronic applications accepted.

UNIVERSITY OF LOUISIANA AT LAFAYETTE, Lafayette, LA 70504

General Information State-supported, coed, university. CGS member. *Graduate housing:* Rooms and/or apartments available on a first-come, first-served basis to single and married students. Housing application deadline: 66/15. *Research affiliation:* National Wetlands Research Center (biology, wetlands restoration), Louisiana Universities Marine Consortium (marine biology), U.S. Fish and Wildlife Service (ecology), Army Corps of Engineers (wetlands), U.S. Geological Survey (USGS), U.S. Department of Agriculture (USDA).

GRADUATE UNITS

BI Moody III College of Business Administration *Program availability:* Part-time, evening/weekend. Offers accounting (MS); business administration (MBA); entrepreneurship (MBA); finance (MBA); global management (MBA); health care administration (MBA); hospitality management (MBA); human resource management (MBA); project management (MBA); sales leadership (MBA).

College of Education *Program availability:* Part-time. Offers counselor education (MS); curriculum and instruction (M Ed); education (M Ed, MS, Ed D); education of the gifted (M Ed); educational foundations and leadership (M Ed, Ed D); instructional specialist (M Ed); K-8 mathematics education (M Ed); non-public school administration (M Ed); special education diagnostics (M Ed); teacher researcher (M Ed). Electronic applications accepted.

College of Engineering *Program availability:* Part-time, evening/weekend. Offers chemical engineering (MSE); civil engineering (MSE); electrical engineering (MS); engineering (MS, MSE, MSTC, PhD); mechanical engineering (MSE); petroleum engineering (MSE); systems engineering (PhD); systems technology (MRE). Electronic applications accepted.

College of Liberal Arts *Program availability:* Part-time. Offers American culture (MA, PhD); American literature and language (PhD); applied language and speech sciences (PhD); communication (MS); creative writing (MA, PhD); folklore (MA, PhD);

Francophone studies (PhD); French (MA); history (MA); liberal arts (MA, MS, PhD); linguistic studies (MA, PhD); professional writing (PhD); psychology (MS); rhetoric (MA, PhD); speech pathology and audiology (MS); TESOL studies (MA, PhD). Electronic applications accepted.

College of Nursing and Allied Health Professions Offers family nurse practitioner (MSN); nursing (DNP); nursing education (MSN). Electronic applications accepted.

College of Sciences *Program availability:* Part-time. Offers biology (MS); environmental and evolutionary biology (PhD); mathematics (MS, PhD); physics (MS); sciences (MS, PhD). Electronic applications accepted.

School of Geosciences *Program availability:* Part-time. Offers environmental resource science (MS); geosciences (MS). Electronic applications accepted.

College of the Arts Offers arts (M Arch, MM). Electronic applications accepted.

School of Architecture and Design Offers architecture and design (M Arch). Electronic applications accepted.

School of Music Offers conducting (MM); music education (MM); performance (MM); performance pedagogy (MM); theory/composition (MM). Electronic applications accepted.

UNIVERSITY OF LOUISIANA AT MONROE, Monroe, LA 71209-0001

General Information State-supported, coed, university. *Enrollment:* 883 full-time matriculated graduate/professional students (626 women), 473 part-time matriculated graduate/professional students (361 women). *Enrollment by degree level:* 774 master's, 526 doctoral, 54 other advanced degrees. *Graduate faculty:* 102 full-time (51 women), 20 part-time/adjunct (14 women). *Graduate housing:* Room and/or apartments available on a first-come, first-served basis to single students; on-campus housing not available to married students. Housing application deadline: 5/1. *Student services:* Campus employment opportunities, career counseling, child daycare facilities, exercise/wellness program, free psychological counseling, international student services, services for students with disabilities. *Library facilities:* University Library. *Collection:* Books: 150,255 (physical), 293,246 (digital/electronic); Serial titles: 245 (physical), 93,407 (digital/electronic); Databases: 101. Students can reserve study rooms.

Computer facilities: Computer purchase and lease plans are available. A campuswide network can be accessed from student residence rooms and from off campus. Online class registration is available.
Website: http://www.ulm.edu/

General Application Contact: Karen Higuera, Coordinator of Graduate Admissions, 318-342-1753, Fax: 318-342-1042, E-mail: gradadmissions@ulm.edu.

GRADUATE UNITS

Graduate School Students: 883 full-time (626 women), 473 part-time (361 women); includes 371 minority (247 Black or African American, non-Hispanic/Latino; 4 American Indian or Alaska Native, non-Hispanic/Latino; 44 Asian, non-Hispanic/Latino; 42 Hispanic/Latino; 1 Native Hawaiian or other Pacific Islander, non-Hispanic/Latino; 33 Two or more races, non-Hispanic/Latino), 67 international. Average age 29. 439 applicants, 64% accepted, 194 enrolled. *Faculty:* 102 full-time (51 women), 19 part-time/adjunct (14 women). Expenses: Contact institution. *Financial support:* In 2018–19, 411 students received support. Research assistantships, teaching assistantships, career-related internships or fieldwork, Federal Work-Study, institutionally sponsored loans, tuition waivers (full and partial), and unspecified assistantships available. Support available to part-time students. Financial award application deadline: 4/1; financial award applicants required to submit FAFSA. In 2018, 274 master's, 113 doctorates, 387 other advanced degrees awarded. *Program availability:* Part-time, evening/weekend, 100% online, blended/hybrid learning. *Application deadline:* For fall admission, 3/1 priority date for domestic and international students; for winter admission, 4/1 priority date for domestic students, 4/1 for international students; for spring admission, 8/1 priority date for domestic and international students. Applications are processed on a rolling basis. *Application fee:* $20 ($30 for international students). Electronic applications accepted. *Application Contact:* Karen Higuera, Coordinator of Graduate Admissions, 318-342-1038, Fax: 318-342-1042, E-mail: higuera@ulm.edu. *Dean,* Dr. Sushma Krishnamurthy, 318-342-1036, Fax: 318-342-1042, E-mail: krishnamurthy@ulm.edu.

College of Arts, Education, and Sciences Students: 81 full-time (60 women), 119 part-time (92 women); includes 48 minority (34 Black or African American, non-Hispanic/Latino; 1 Asian, non-Hispanic/Latino; 7 Hispanic/Latino; 6 Two or more races, non-Hispanic/Latino), 10 international. Average age 31. 86 applicants, 85% accepted, 56 enrolled. *Faculty:* 30 full-time (14 women), 4 part-time/adjunct (3 women). Expenses: Contact institution. *Financial support:* Research assistantships with full tuition reimbursements, teaching assistantships with full tuition reimbursements, career-related internships or fieldwork, Federal Work-Study, institutionally sponsored loans, and unspecified assistantships available. Support available to part-time students. Financial award application deadline: 4/1; financial award applicants required to submit FAFSA. In 2018, 63 master's, 7 doctorates awarded. *Program availability:* Part-time, evening/weekend. Offers arts, education, and sciences (M Ed, MA, MAT, MS, Ed D); biology (MS); communication (MA); curriculum and instruction (M Ed, Ed D); education (M Ed, MAT, Ed D); elementary education (MAT); English (MA); history (MA); secondary education (MAT); special education (MAT). *Application deadline:* For fall admission, 8/24 priority date for domestic students, 3/1 priority date for international students; for winter admission, 12/14 priority date for domestic students, 4/1 priority date for international students; for spring admission, 1/19 priority date for domestic students, 8/1 priority date for international students. Applications are processed on a rolling basis. *Application fee:* $20 ($30 for international students). Electronic applications accepted. *Application Contact:* Dr. Jeffrey Anderson, Interim Associate Dean, 318-342-1243, Fax: 318-342-1755, E-mail: jeanderson@ulm.edu. *Interim Dean,* Dr. Chris Michaelides, 318-342-1235, Fax: 318-342-1755, E-mail: cmichaelides@ulm.edu.

College of Business and Social Sciences Students: 111 full-time (89 women), 118 part-time (79 women); includes 93 minority (71 Black or African American, non-Hispanic/Latino; 3 Asian, non-Hispanic/Latino; 11 Hispanic/Latino; 8 Two or more races, non-Hispanic/Latino), 21 international. Average age 28. 118 applicants, 77% accepted, 59 enrolled. *Faculty:* 23 full-time (8 women), 4 part-time/adjunct (2 women). Expenses: Contact institution. *Financial support:* In 2018–19, 69 students received support. Research assistantships, career-related internships or fieldwork, Federal Work-Study, and unspecified assistantships available. Financial award application deadline: 4/1; financial award applicants required to submit FAFSA. In 2018, 86 master's awarded. *Program availability:* Part-time, evening/weekend, online learning. Offers aging studies (MA); business administration (MBA); business and social sciences (MA, MBA, MPA, MS, CGS); criminal justice (MA); forensic psychology (MS); general psychology (MS); gerontology (CGS); grief care management (MA); long-term care administration (MA); mental health (MA); program administration (MA); psychometrics (MS); public administration (MPA); small business management (MA). *Application deadline:* For fall admission, 8/24 for domestic students, 7/1 for

international students; for winter admission, 12/14 for domestic students; for spring admission, 1/19 for domestic students, 11/1 for international students. Applications are processed on a rolling basis. *Application fee:* $20 ($30 for international students). Electronic applications accepted. *Application Contact:* Dr. Ronald Berry, Dean, 318-342-1103, E-mail: rberry@ulm.edu. *Dean,* Dr. Ronald Berry, 318-342-1103, E-mail: rberry@ulm.edu.

College of Health Sciences Students: 211 full-time (161 women), 110 part-time (86 women); includes 83 minority (56 Black or African American, non-Hispanic/Latino; 3 American Indian or Alaska Native, non-Hispanic/Latino; 2 Asian, non-Hispanic/Latino; 14 Hispanic/Latino; 1 Native Hawaiian or other Pacific Islander, non-Hispanic/Latino; 7 Two or more races, non-Hispanic/Latino), 3 international. Average age 30. 112 applicants, 87% accepted, 90 enrolled. Expenses: Contact institution. *Financial support:* In 2018–19, 165 students received support. Research assistantships, career-related internships or fieldwork, Federal Work-Study, and unspecified assistantships available. Financial award application deadline: 4/1; financial award applicants required to submit FAFSA. In 2018, 97 master's, 2 doctorates awarded. Offers applied exercise science (MS); clinical exercise physiology (MS); clinical mental health counseling (MS); health sciences (MA, MOT, MS, PhD, CGS); marriage and family therapy (MA, PhD); occupational therapy (MOT); school counseling (MS); speech-language pathology (MS); sports, fitness and recreation management (MS). *Application deadline:* For fall admission, 8/24 priority date for domestic students, 7/1 for international students; for winter admission, 12/14 priority date for domestic students; for spring admission, 1/19 for domestic students, 11/1 for international students. Applications are processed on a rolling basis. *Application fee:* $20 ($30 for international students). Electronic applications accepted. *Application Contact:* Dr. Glenn Anderson, Jr., Dean, 318-342-1600, E-mail: ganderson@ulm.edu. *Dean,* Dr. Glenn Anderson, Jr., 318-342-1600, E-mail: ganderson@ulm.edu.

College of Pharmacy Students: 384 full-time (237 women), 3 part-time (1 woman); includes 90 minority (40 Black or African American, non-Hispanic/Latino; 1 American Indian or Alaska Native, non-Hispanic/Latino; 35 Asian, non-Hispanic/Latino; 6 Hispanic/Latino; 8 Two or more races, non-Hispanic/Latino), 33 international. Average age 24. 49 applicants, 98% accepted, 48 enrolled. *Faculty:* 22 full-time (10 women). Expenses: Contact institution. *Financial support:* In 2018–19, 63 students received support. Research assistantships, Federal Work-Study, and unspecified assistantships available. Financial award application deadline: 4/1; financial award applicants required to submit FAFSA. In 2018, 104 doctorates awarded. Offers pharmacy (PhD); toxicology (PhD). *Application deadline:* For fall admission, 3/1 for domestic and international students; for winter admission, 12/14 for domestic students; for spring admission, 9/1 for domestic and international students. Applications are processed on a rolling basis. *Application fee:* $20 ($30 for international students). Electronic applications accepted. *Application Contact:* Dr. Paul W. Sylvester, Director, Research and Graduate Studies, 318-342-1958, Fax: 318-342-1606, E-mail: sylvester@ulm.edu. *Dean,* Dr. Glenn Anderson, 318-342-1600, E-mail: ganderson@ulm.edu.

UNIVERSITY OF LOUISVILLE, Louisville, KY 40292-0001

General Information State-supported, coed, university. CGS member. *Enrollment:* 21,431 graduate, professional, and undergraduate students; 4,024 full-time matriculated graduate/professional students (2,153 women), 1,649 part-time matriculated graduate/professional students (824 women). *Enrollment by degree level:* 2,824 master's, 2,692 doctoral, 157 other advanced degrees. *Graduate faculty:* 1,776 full-time (740 women), 764 part-time/adjunct (427 women). *Tuition, area resident:* Full-time $6500; part-time $723 per credit hour. Tuition, state resident: full-time $6500. Tuition, nonresident: full-time $13,557; part-time $1507 per credit hour. Tuition and fees vary according to course load and program. *Graduate housing:* Rooms and/or apartments available on a first-come, first-served basis to single and married students. Typical cost: $9600 per year ($11,016 including board) for single students; $9600 per year ($11,016 including board) for married students. Room and board charges vary according to board plan, campus/location and housing facility selected. Housing application deadline: 2/1. *Student services:* Campus employment opportunities, campus safety program, career counseling, child daycare facilities, exercise/wellness program, free psychological counseling, grant writing training, international student services, low-cost health insurance, multicultural affairs office, services for students with disabilities, teacher training, writing training. *Library facilities:* William F. Ekstrom Library plus 6 others. *Collection:* Books: 1.6 million (physical), 367,856 (digital/electronic); Serial titles: 2,158 (physical), 90,689 (digital/electronic); Databases: 345. Weekly public service hours: 97; study areas open 24 hours, 5–7 days a week; students can reserve study rooms.

Computer facilities: Computer purchase and lease plans are available. 400 computers available on campus for general student use. A campuswide network can be accessed from student residence rooms and from off campus. Online class registration is available.
Website: http://www.louisville.edu/

General Application Contact: Tamekka Cornelius, Director of Graduate Recruitment and Diversity Retention, 502-852-5207, E-mail: gradadm@louisville.edu.

GRADUATE UNITS

Graduate School Students: 4,024 full-time (2,153 women), 1,649 part-time (824 women); includes 1,248 minority (509 Black or African American, non-Hispanic/Latino; 5 American Indian or Alaska Native, non-Hispanic/Latino; 274 Asian, non-Hispanic/Latino; 242 Hispanic/Latino; 4 Native Hawaiian or other Pacific Islander, non-Hispanic/Latino; 214 Two or more races, non-Hispanic/Latino), 482 international. Average age 30. 7,250 applicants, 31% accepted, 1634 enrolled. *Faculty:* 1,776 full-time (740 women), 764 part-time/adjunct (427 women). Expenses: Contact institution. *Financial support:* In 2018–19, 80 students received support, including 80 fellowships with full tuition reimbursements available (averaging $20,000 per year); diversity scholarships also available. Financial award application deadline: 1/1; financial award applicants required to submit FAFSA. In 2018, 858 master's, 432 doctorates, 75 other advanced degrees awarded. *Program availability:* Part-time. *Application deadline:* For fall admission, 12/1 priority date for domestic and international students; for winter admission, 11/1 for domestic students, 6/1 for international students; for spring admission, 11/1 for domestic students, 6/1 for international students; for summer admission, 4/1 for domestic students, 1/1 for international students. Applications are processed on a rolling basis. *Application fee:* $65. Electronic applications accepted. *Application Contact:* Dr. Barbara Clark, Acting Associate Dean, 502-852-6498, Fax: 502-852-3111, E-mail: gradadm@louisville.edu. *Acting Dean and Acting Vice Provost for Graduate Affairs,* Dr. Paul J. DeMarco, 502-852-0788, Fax: 502-852-2365, E-mail: paul.demarco@louisville.edu.

College of Arts and Sciences Students: 474 full-time (239 women), 217 part-time (99 women); includes 140 minority (55 Black or African American, non-Hispanic/Latino; 17 Asian, non-Hispanic/Latino; 31 Hispanic/Latino; 37 Two or more races, non-Hispanic/Latino), 99 international. Average age 33. 519 applicants, 47% accepted, 164 enrolled. *Faculty:* 386 full-time (162 women), 217 part-time/adjunct (120 women).

Expenses: Contact institution. *Financial support:* In 2018–19, 495 students received support, including 10 research assistantships with full tuition reimbursements available (averaging $18,000 per year), 240 teaching assistantships with full tuition reimbursements available (averaging $18,000 per year); scholarships/grants, health care benefits, tuition waivers, and unspecified assistantships also available. In 2018, 94 master's, 19 doctorates, 40 other advanced degrees awarded. *Program availability:* Part-time, 100% online. Offers African and Diaspora studies (MA); African-American studies (MA); analytical chemistry (MS, PhD); anthropology (MA); applied and industrial mathematics (PhD); applied geography (MS); applied sociology (PhD); art history (MA, PhD); arts and sciences (MA, MFA, MPA, MS, MUP, PhD, Certificate); biochemistry (MS, PhD); biology (MS); chemical physics (PhD); civic leadership (MA); clinical psychology (PhD); communication (MA); criminal justice (MS, PhD); culture, criticism, and contemporary thought (PhD); curatorial studies (MA); design (MFA); digital politics (MA); English (MA); environmental biology (PhD); experimental psychology (PhD); French (MA); history (MA); humanities (MA, PhD); inorganic chemistry (MS, PhD); linguistics (MA); mathematics (MA); organic chemistry (MS, PhD); performance (MFA); physical chemistry (MS, PhD); physics (MS, PhD); political science (MA); public administration (MPA); public arts and letters (PhD); public history (Certificate); rhetoric and composition (PhD); sociology (MA); Spanish (MA); studio art (MFA); traditional humanities (MA); translation and interpretation (Certificate); urban and public affairs (PhD); urban planning (MUP); women's and gender studies (MA, Certificate). *Application deadline:* Applications are processed on a rolling basis. *Application fee:* $65. Electronic applications accepted. *Application Contact:* Dr. David Norvil Brown, Associate Dean for Graduate Education, 502-852-8966, Fax: 502-852-6888, E-mail: david.brown@louisville.edu. *Dean,* Dr. Kimberly Kempf-Leonard, 502-852-6490, Fax: 502-852-6888, E-mail: kleonard@louisville.edu.

College of Business Students: 288 full-time (100 women), 80 part-time (50 women); includes 78 minority (39 Black or African American, non-Hispanic/Latino; 1 American Indian or Alaska Native, non-Hispanic/Latino; 17 Asian, non-Hispanic/Latino; 12 Hispanic/Latino; 9 Two or more races, non-Hispanic/Latino; 37 international. Average age 32. 301 applicants, 71% accepted, 175 enrolled. *Faculty:* 79 full-time (21 women), 41 part-time/adjunct (14 women). Expenses: Contact institution. *Financial support:* In 2018–19, 139 students received support. Fellowships with full tuition reimbursements available, research assistantships with full tuition reimbursements available, teaching assistantships with full tuition reimbursements available, scholarships/grants, health care benefits, and unspecified assistantships available. Financial award application deadline: 3/15; financial award applicants required to submit FAFSA. In 2018, 102 master's, 2 doctorates awarded. *Program availability:* Part-time, 100% online, blended/hybrid learning. Offers accountancy (MAC); business (MAC, MBA, PhD); entrepreneurship (PhD); global business (MBA); health sector management (MBA). *Application deadline:* For fall admission, 3/31 for domestic students, 5/1 priority date for international students; for spring admission, 12/1 for domestic students, 11/1 priority date for international students; for summer admission, 4/1 priority date for international students. Applications are processed on a rolling basis. *Application fee:* $65. *Application Contact:* Susan E. Hildebrand, Program Director, 502-852-7257, Fax: 502-852-4901, E-mail: s.hildebrand@louisville.edu. *Dean,* Dr. Todd Mooradian, 502-852-6443, Fax: 502-852-7557, E-mail: todd.mooradian@louisville.edu.

College of Education and Human Development Students: 475 full-time (272 women), 669 part-time (389 women); includes 309 minority (178 Black or African American, non-Hispanic/Latino; 2 American Indian or Alaska Native, non-Hispanic/Latino; 25 Asian, non-Hispanic/Latino; 64 Hispanic/Latino; 2 Native Hawaiian or other Pacific Islander, non-Hispanic/Latino; 38 Two or more races, non-Hispanic/Latino), 18 international. Average age 33. 586 applicants, 66% accepted, 304 enrolled. *Faculty:* 97 full-time (64 women), 131 part-time/adjunct (86 women). Expenses: Contact institution. *Financial support:* In 2018–19, 5 fellowships with full tuition reimbursements (averaging $21,024 per year), 32 research assistantships with full tuition reimbursements (averaging $21,024 per year), 18 teaching assistantships with full tuition reimbursements (averaging $21,024 per year) were awarded; Federal Work-Study, scholarships/grants, health care benefits, tuition waivers (full), and unspecified assistantships also available. Financial award application deadline: 3/1; financial award applicants required to submit FAFSA. In 2018, 235 master's, 10 doctorates, 22 other advanced degrees awarded. *Program availability:* Part-time, evening/weekend, 100% online, blended/hybrid learning. Offers art education (MAT); autism and applied behavior analysis (Certificate); community health education (M Ed); counseling and personnel services (M Ed, PhD); curriculum and instruction (PhD); early elementary education (MAT); education and human development (M Ed, MA, MAT, MS, Ed D, PhD, Certificate, Ed S); educational leadership and organizational development (Ed D, PhD); exercise physiology (MS); health and physical education (MAT); health professions education (Certificate); higher education (MA); higher education administration (MA); human resources and organization development (MS); instructional technology (M Ed); interdisciplinary early childhood education (MAT); middle school education (MAT); music education (MAT); P-12 educational administration (Ed S); secondary education (MAT); special education (MAT); sport administration (MAT); teacher leadership (M Ed). *Application deadline:* For fall admission, 6/1 priority date for domestic students, 5/1 priority date for international students; for spring admission, 10/1 priority date for domestic students, 11/1 priority date for international students; for summer admission, 3/1 priority date for domestic students, 4/1 priority date for international students. *Application fee:* $65. *Application Contact:* Margaret Penetcost, Assistant Dean for Graduate Student Success, 502-852-6437, Fax: 502-852-1417, E-mail: gedadm@louisville.edu. *Interim Dean,* Dr. Amy A. Lingo, 502-852-3235, E-mail: cehdinfo@louisville.edu.

Kent School of Social Work Students: 413 full-time (369 women), 107 part-time (85 women); includes 149 minority (83 Black or African American, non-Hispanic/Latino; 1 American Indian or Alaska Native, non-Hispanic/Latino; 9 Asian, non-Hispanic/Latino; 26 Hispanic/Latino; 1 Native Hawaiian or other Pacific Islander, non-Hispanic/Latino; 29 Two or more races, non-Hispanic/Latino), 7 international. Average age 31. 406 applicants, 69% accepted, 184 enrolled. *Faculty:* 33 full-time (22 women), 63 part-time/adjunct (49 women). Expenses: Contact institution. *Financial support:* In 2018–19, 99 students received support, including 1 fellowship (averaging $19,000 per year), 8 research assistantships with full tuition reimbursements available (averaging $21,500 per year), teaching assistantships with full tuition reimbursements available (averaging $19,000 per year); scholarships/grants, health care benefits, and unspecified assistantships also available. Financial award application deadline: 2/15; financial award applicants required to submit FAFSA. In 2018, 175 master's, 2 doctorates awarded. *Program availability:* Part-time, evening/weekend, 100% online, blended/hybrid learning. Offers marriage and family therapy (PMC); social work (MSSW, PhD). *Application deadline:* For fall admission, 5/30 for domestic and international students; for spring admission, 9/30 for domestic and international students; for summer admission, 2/28 for domestic and international students. Applications are processed on a rolling basis. *Application fee:* $65. Electronic applications accepted. *Application Contact:* Misty Kupka, Program Manager for

Admissions and Recruitment, 502-852-0414, Fax: 502-852-0422, E-mail: misty.kupka@louisville.edu. *Dean,* Dr. David Jenkins, 502-852-3944, Fax: 502-852-0422, E-mail: d.jenkins@louisville.edu.

School of Music Students: 54 full-time (20 women), 4 part-time (1 woman); includes 10 minority (2 Black or African American, non-Hispanic/Latino; 1 American Indian or Alaska Native, non-Hispanic/Latino; 4 Asian, non-Hispanic/Latino; 2 Hispanic/Latino; 1 Two or more races, non-Hispanic/Latino), 8 international. Average age 27. 87 applicants, 63% accepted, 32 enrolled. *Faculty:* 42 full-time (13 women), 37 part-time/adjunct (17 women). Expenses: Contact institution. *Financial support:* In 2018–19, 52 students received support, including 1 fellowship with full tuition reimbursement available (averaging $12,000 per year), 12 teaching assistantships with full tuition reimbursements available (averaging $12,000 per year); Federal Work-Study, scholarships/grants, health care benefits, tuition waivers (full), and unspecified assistantships also available. Financial award application deadline: 3/1. In 2018, 23 master's awarded. *Program availability:* Part-time, evening/weekend. Offers composition (MM); electronic composition (MM); music education (MME); music history and literature (MM); music performance (MM); music theory (MM). *Application fee:* $65. Electronic applications accepted. *Application Contact:* Laura Angermeier, Admissions Counselor/Senior Advising Counselor, 502-852-1623, Fax: 502-852-0520, E-mail: leange01@louisville.edu. *Dean,* Dr. Teresa L. Reed, 502-852-6907, Fax: 502-852-0520, E-mail: teresa.reed@louisville.edu.

School of Nursing Students: 158 full-time (133 women), 45 part-time (37 women); includes 42 minority (18 Black or African American, non-Hispanic/Latino; 7 Asian, non-Hispanic/Latino; 7 Hispanic/Latino; 10 Two or more races, non-Hispanic/Latino), 3 international. Average age 33. 85 applicants, 62% accepted, 39 enrolled. *Faculty:* 47 full-time (42 women), 72 part-time/adjunct (67 women). Expenses: Contact institution. *Financial support:* In 2018–19, 47 students received support, including 8 research assistantships with full tuition reimbursements available (averaging $20,000 per year), 4 teaching assistantships with full tuition reimbursements available (averaging $15,000 per year); fellowships, scholarships/grants, and unspecified assistantships also available. Financial award application deadline: 10/1; financial award applicants required to submit FAFSA. In 2018, 27 master's, 1 doctorate awarded. *Program availability:* Part-time. Offers adult gerontology nurse practitioner (MSN, DNP); education and administration (MSN); family nurse practitioner (MSN, DNP); neonatal nurse practitioner (MSN, DNP); nursing research (PhD); psychiatric/mental health nurse practitioner (MSN, DNP); women's health nurse practitioner (MSN). *Application deadline:* For fall admission, 1/15 priority date for domestic students, 1/15 for international students; for summer admission, 10/15 priority date for domestic students. *Application fee:* $60. Electronic applications accepted. *Application Contact:* Trish Hart, MA, Assistant Dean for Student Affairs, 502-852-5825, Fax: 502-852-8783, E-mail: trish.hart@louisville.edu.

School of Public Health and Information Sciences Students: 133 full-time (88 women), 88 part-time (55 women); includes 69 minority (35 Black or African American, non-Hispanic/Latino; 19 Asian, non-Hispanic/Latino; 7 Hispanic/Latino; 8 Two or more races, non-Hispanic/Latino), 49 international. Average age 32. 219 applicants, 61% accepted, 94 enrolled. *Faculty:* 40 full-time (17 women), 8 part-time/adjunct (3 women). Expenses: Contact institution. *Financial support:* In 2018–19, 129 students received support, including 4 fellowships with full tuition reimbursements available (averaging $20,000 per year), 37 research assistantships with full tuition reimbursements available (averaging $20,000 per year), 2 teaching assistantships with full tuition reimbursements available (averaging $20,000 per year); career-related internships or fieldwork, Federal Work-Study, scholarships/grants, health care benefits, tuition waivers (full), and unspecified assistantships also available. Support available to part-time students. Financial award application deadline: 5/1; financial award applicants required to submit FAFSA. In 2018, 34 master's, 2 doctorates awarded. *Program availability:* Part-time, evening/weekend, 100% online. Offers biostatistics (MPH, MS, PhD); decision science (MS); environmental and occupational health sciences (MPH); epidemiology (MPH, MS); health policy (MPH); health promotion (PhD); population health management (MPH); public health (PhD); public health sciences (PhD). *Application deadline:* For fall admission, 7/1 for domestic students, 3/1 for international students; for spring admission, 11/1 for domestic students, 10/1 for international students; for summer admission, 4/1 for domestic students, 3/1 for international students. Applications are processed on a rolling basis. *Application fee:* $60. Electronic applications accepted. *Application Contact:* Vicki Lewis, Administrative Assistant, 502-852-1798, Fax: 502-852-3294, E-mail: vicki.lewis@louisville.edu. *Professor and Dean,* Dr. Craig Elliot Blakely, 502-852-3297, Fax: 502-852-3291, E-mail: craig.blakely@louisville.edu.

J. B. Speed School of Engineering Students: 296 full-time (73 women), 396 part-time (93 women); includes 105 minority (26 Black or African American, non-Hispanic/Latino; 38 Asian, non-Hispanic/Latino; 21 Hispanic/Latino; 20 Two or more races, non-Hispanic/Latino), 201 international. Average age 29. 266 applicants, 51% accepted, 108 enrolled. *Faculty:* 111 full-time (21 women), 23 part-time/adjunct (4 women). Expenses: Contact institution. *Financial support:* In 2018–19, 293 students received support. Fellowships, research assistantships, teaching assistantships, scholarships/grants, health care benefits, tuition waivers (full), and unspecified assistantships available. Financial award application deadline: 2/1. In 2018, 122 master's, 15 doctorates, 8 other advanced degrees awarded. *Program availability:* 100% online, blended/hybrid learning. Offers advancing bioengineering technologies through entrepreneurship (PhD); bioengineering (M Eng); chemical engineering (M Eng, MS, PhD); civil engineering (M Eng, MS, PhD); computer engineering and computer science (M Eng); computer science (MS, PhD); cybersecurity (Certificate); data science (Certificate); engineering (M Eng, MS, PhD, Certificate); engineering management (M Eng); industrial engineering (M Eng, MS, PhD); logistics and distribution (Certificate). *Application deadline:* For fall admission, 5/1 priority date for domestic and international students; for spring admission, 11/1 priority date for domestic and international students; for summer admission, 3/1 priority date for domestic students, 4/1 priority date for international students. Applications are processed on a rolling basis. *Application fee:* $65. Electronic applications accepted. *Application Contact:* Dr. Katherine Markuson, Director of Graduate Affairs, 502-852-6278, E-mail: katherine.markuson@louisville.edu. *Associate Dean for Research and Graduate Studies,* Dr. Kevin Walsh, 502-852-0826, E-mail: kevin.walsh@louisville.edu.

Louis D. Brandeis School of Law *Program availability:* Part-time. Offers law (JD). Electronic applications accepted.

School of Dentistry Students: 507 full-time (228 women), 15 part-time (11 women); includes 122 minority (20 Black or African American, non-Hispanic/Latino; 60 Asian, non-Hispanic/Latino; 26 Hispanic/Latino; 16 Two or more races, non-Hispanic/Latino), 16 international. Average age 26. 183 applicants, 93% accepted, 137 enrolled. *Faculty:* 77 full-time (32 women), 70 part-time/adjunct (18 women). Expenses: Contact institution. *Financial support:* In 2018–19, 1 research assistantship with full tuition reimbursement (averaging $20,000 per year) was awarded. Financial award application deadline: 3/15; financial award applicants required to submit FAFSA. In 2018, 7 master's, 113 doctorates awarded. *Program availability:* Part-time. Offers dentistry (DMD); oral biology (MS). *Application deadline:* For fall admission, 1/1 for domestic and international students. Applications are processed on a rolling basis. *Application fee:* $65. Electronic applications accepted. *Application Contact:* Robin Benningfield, Admissions Counselor, 502-852-5081, Fax: 502-852-1210, E-mail: dmdadms@louisville.edu. *Dean*, Dr. T. Gerry Bradley, 502-852-5295, E-mail: t0brad03@exchange.louisville.edu.

School of Interdisciplinary and Graduate Studies Students: 27 full-time (13 women), 11 part-time (5 women); includes 4 minority (1 Black or African American, non-Hispanic/Latino; 2 Hispanic/Latino; 1 Two or more races, non-Hispanic/Latino), 11 international. Average age 32. 19 applicants, 68% accepted, 8 enrolled. Expenses: Contact institution. *Financial support:* In 2018–19, 30 students received support, including 120 fellowships with full tuition reimbursements available (averaging $20,000 per year). Financial award application deadline: 1/15. In 2018, 2 master's awarded. *Program availability:* Part-time. Offers interdisciplinary studies (MA, MS, PhD). *Application deadline:* For fall admission, 12/1 priority date for domestic and international students; for winter admission, 11/1 for domestic students, 6/1 for international students; for spring admission, 11/1 for domestic students, 6/1 for international students; for summer admission, 4/1 for domestic students, 1/1 for international students. Applications are processed on a rolling basis. *Application fee:* $65. Electronic applications accepted. *Application Contact:* Dr. Barbara Clark, Acting Associate Dean, 502-852-6498, E-mail: gradadm@louisville.edu. *Acting Dean and Acting Vice Provost for Graduate Affairs*, Dr. Paul DeMarco, 502-852-5110, E-mail: paul.demarco@louisville.edu.

School of Medicine Students: 863 full-time (438 women), 40 part-time (18 women); includes 182 minority (45 Black or African American, non-Hispanic/Latino; 73 Asian, non-Hispanic/Latino; 32 Hispanic/Latino; 32 Two or more races, non-Hispanic/Latino; 32 international. Average age 26. 3,900 applicants, 11% accepted, 255 enrolled. *Faculty:* 797 full-time (308 women), 85 part-time/adjunct (41 women). Expenses: Contact institution. *Financial support:* In 2018–19, 412 students received support, including 25 research assistantships with full tuition reimbursements available (averaging $25,000 per year); fellowships, scholarships/grants, health care benefits, and unspecified assistantships also available. Financial award application deadline: 7/1; financial award applicants required to submit FAFSA. In 2018, 37 master's, 168 doctorates awarded. Offers anatomical sciences and neurobiology (MS, PhD); audiology (Au D); biochemistry and molecular genetics (MS, PhD); medicine (MS, Au D, MD, PhD); microbiology and immunology (MS, PhD); pharmacology and toxicology (MS); physiology (MS); speech-language pathology (MS). *Application deadline:* For fall admission, 10/15 priority date for domestic students. Applications are processed on a rolling basis. *Application fee:* $75. *Application Contact:* Dr. Stephen F. Wheeler, Associate Dean for Admissions, 502-852-5193, Fax: 502-852-0302, E-mail: sfwhee01@louisville.edu. *Dean*, Dr. Toni M. Ganzel, 502-852-1499, Fax: 502-852-1484, E-mail: meddean@louisville.edu.

UNIVERSITY OF LYNCHBURG, Lynchburg, VA 24501-3199

General Information Independent-religious, coed, comprehensive institution. *Graduate housing:* Room and/or apartments available on a first-come, first-served basis to single students; on-campus housing not available to married students.

GRADUATE UNITS

Graduate Studies *Program availability:* Part-time, evening/weekend. Offers athletic training (MS); business administration (MBA); clinical mental health counseling (M Ed); criminal justice leadership (MA); educational leadership (Ed D); health informatics management (Certificate); higher education (M Ed); instructional leadership (M Ed); non-profit leadership (MA); physical therapy (DPT); physician assistant medicine (MA); physician assisted medicine (D Med Sc); PK-12 administrative and supervisory (M Ed); public health (MPH); reading instruction (M Ed); reading specialist (M Ed); school counseling (M Ed); science education (M Ed); special education (M Ed); teacher licensure (M Ed). Electronic applications accepted.

UNIVERSITY OF MAINE, Orono, ME 04469

General Information State-supported, coed, university. CGS member. *Graduate housing:* Rooms and/or apartments available on a first-come, first-served basis to single and married students. Housing application deadline: 8/1. *Research affiliation:* Jackson Laboratory (medical genetics), Bigelow Laboratories for Ocean Sciences (marine science), Mount Desert Island Biological Laboratory (marine molecular biology), Sensor Research Development Corporation (electrical sensors), Maine Medical Center Research Institute (clinical medicine), Maine Institute for Human Genetics (medical genetics).

GRADUATE UNITS

Graduate School Students: 1,224 full-time (722 women), 449 part-time (318 women); includes 124 minority (16 Black or African American, non-Hispanic/Latino; 25 American Indian or Alaska Native, non-Hispanic/Latino; 31 Asian, non-Hispanic/Latino; 32 Hispanic/Latino; 20 Two or more races, non-Hispanic/Latino), 186 international. Average age 33. 1,664 applicants, 58% accepted, 557 enrolled. *Faculty:* 652 full-time (227 women), 232 part-time/adjunct (100 women). Expenses: Contact institution. *Financial support:* In 2018–19, 868 students received support, including 28 fellowships with full tuition reimbursements available (averaging $22,400 per year), 305 research assistantships with full tuition reimbursements available (averaging $18,200 per year), 312 teaching assistantships with full tuition reimbursements available (averaging $16,000 per year); career-related internships or fieldwork, Federal Work-Study, institutionally sponsored loans, scholarships/grants, tuition waivers (full and partial), and unspecified assistantships also available. Support available to part-time students. Financial award application deadline: 3/1; financial award applicants required to submit FAFSA. In 2018, 375 master's, 55 doctorates, 90 other advanced degrees awarded. *Program availability:* Part-time, evening/weekend, 100% online, blended/hybrid learning. Offers interdisciplinary studies (MA, PhD); intermedia (MFA). *Application deadline:* For fall admission, 1/15 priority date for domestic and international students; for spring admission, 11/15 priority date for domestic and international students. Applications are processed on a rolling basis. *Application fee:* $65. Electronic applications accepted. *Application Contact:* Scott G. Delcourt, Assistant Vice President for Graduate Studies/Senior Associate Dean, 207-581-3291, Fax: 207-581-3232, E-mail: graduate@maine.edu. *Assistant Vice President for Graduate Studies/Senior Associate Dean*, Scott G. Delcourt, 207-581-3291, Fax: 207-581-3232, E-mail: graduate@maine.edu.

Climate Change Institute Students: 8 full-time (6 women), 3 part-time (2 women); includes 1 minority (American Indian or Alaska Native, non-Hispanic/Latino), 1 international. Average age 28. 17 applicants, 47% accepted, 1 enrolled. *Faculty:* 39 full-time (11 women). Expenses: Contact institution. *Financial support:* In 2018–19, 28 students received support, including 24 research assistantships with full tuition reimbursements available (averaging $15,200 per year), 1 teaching assistantship with

full tuition reimbursement available (averaging $15,200 per year); institutionally sponsored loans, tuition waivers (full and partial), and unspecified assistantships also available. Financial award application deadline: 3/1. In 2018, 2 master's awarded. *Program availability:* Part-time. Offers climate change (MS, CGS). *Application deadline:* For fall admission, 11/1 priority date for domestic and international students; for spring admission, 2/1 priority date for domestic and international students. Applications are processed on a rolling basis. *Application fee:* $65. Electronic applications accepted. *Application Contact:* Dr. Karl Kreutz, Graduate Coordinator, 207-581-3011, E-mail: karl.kreutz@maine.edu. *Director*, Dr. Paul Mayewski, 207-581-3019, Fax: 207-581-1203, E-mail: paul.mayewski@maine.edu.

College of Education and Human Development Students: 194 full-time (154 women), 290 part-time (235 women); includes 21 minority (7 Black or African American, non-Hispanic/Latino; 4 American Indian or Alaska Native, non-Hispanic/Latino; 6 Asian, non-Hispanic/Latino; 3 Hispanic/Latino; 1 Two or more races, non-Hispanic/Latino), 4 international. Average age 37. 318 applicants, 93% accepted, 206 enrolled. *Faculty:* 35 full-time (19 women), 47 part-time/adjunct (34 women). Expenses: Contact institution. *Financial support:* In 2018–19, 18 students received support, including 9 teaching assistantships with full tuition reimbursements available (averaging $15,200 per year); career-related internships or fieldwork, Federal Work-Study, institutionally sponsored loans, scholarships/grants, and unspecified assistantships also available. Support available to part-time students. Financial award application deadline: 3/1. In 2018, 103 master's, 6 doctorates, 59 other advanced degrees awarded. *Program availability:* Part-time, evening/weekend. Offers classroom technology integrationist (CGS); counselor education (M Ed, MA, MS, CAS); early childhood teacher (CGS); education (PhD); education and human development (M Ed, MA, MAT, MS, Ed D, PhD, CAS, CGS); education data specialist (CGS); educational leadership (M Ed, CAS); educational technology coordinator (CGS); elementary education (M Ed, CAS); higher education (CAS); human development (MS); individualized education (M Ed, CAS); kinesiology and physical education (M Ed, MS); literacy education (CAS); response to intervention for behavior (CGS); science education (M Ed, MS); secondary education (M Ed, CAS); social studies education (M Ed); special education (M Ed, CAS); STEM education (PhD). *Application deadline:* For fall admission, 1/15 priority date for domestic students. Applications are processed on a rolling basis. *Application fee:* $65. Electronic applications accepted. *Application Contact:* Scott G. Delcourt, Senior Associate Dean of the Graduate School, 207-581-3291, Fax: 207-581-3232, E-mail: graduate@maine.edu. *Dean*, Dr. Timothy Reagan, 207-581-2441, Fax: 207-581-2423.

College of Engineering Students: 111 full-time (30 women), 29 part-time (2 women); includes 11 minority (1 Black or African American, non-Hispanic/Latino; 2 American Indian or Alaska Native, non-Hispanic/Latino; 4 Asian, non-Hispanic/Latino; 3 Hispanic/Latino; 1 Two or more races, non-Hispanic/Latino), 50 international. Average age 29. 123 applicants, 70% accepted, 34 enrolled. *Faculty:* 52 full-time (8 women), 5 part-time/adjunct (0 women). Expenses: Contact institution. *Financial support:* In 2018–19, 120 students received support, including 4 fellowships (averaging $22,650 per year), 48 research assistantships (averaging $20,700 per year), 22 teaching assistantships (averaging $16,300 per year); Federal Work-Study, institutionally sponsored loans, scholarships/grants, tuition waivers (full and partial), and unspecified assistantships also available. Financial award application deadline: 3/1. In 2018, 42 master's, 9 doctorates awarded. *Program availability:* Part-time. Offers chemical engineering (MS, PhD); civil and environmental engineering (MS, PSM, PhD); computer engineering (MS); electrical engineering (MS, PhD); engineering (ME, MS, PSM, PhD); mechanical engineering (MS, PSM, PhD). *Application deadline:* For fall admission, 2/1 priority date for domestic students. Applications are processed on a rolling basis. *Application fee:* $65. Electronic applications accepted. *Application Contact:* Scott G. Delcourt, Assistant Vice President for Graduate Studies and Senior Associate Dean, 207-581-3291, Fax: 207-581-3232, E-mail: graduate@maine.edu. *Dean*, Dr. Dana Humphrey, 207-581-2217, Fax: 207-581-2220, E-mail: dana.humphrey@umit.maine.edu.

College of Liberal Arts and Sciences Students: 242 full-time (117 women), 45 part-time (20 women); includes 27 minority (4 Black or African American, non-Hispanic/Latino; 4 American Indian or Alaska Native, non-Hispanic/Latino; 5 Asian, non-Hispanic/Latino; 8 Hispanic/Latino; 6 Two or more races, non-Hispanic/Latino), 45 international. Average age 31. 365 applicants, 41% accepted, 77 enrolled. *Faculty:* 147 full-time (46 women), 42 part-time/adjunct (14 women). Expenses: Contact institution. *Financial support:* In 2018–19, 250 students received support, including 13 fellowships (averaging $19,200 per year), 35 research assistantships (averaging $17,500 per year), 160 teaching assistantships (averaging $16,200 per year); career-related internships or fieldwork, Federal Work-Study, institutionally sponsored loans, scholarships/grants, and tuition waivers (full and partial) also available. Support available to part-time students. Financial award application deadline: 3/1. In 2018, 58 master's, 9 doctorates, 2 other advanced degrees awarded. *Program availability:* Part-time, evening/weekend. Offers anthropology and environmental policy (PhD); chemistry (MS, PhD); communication and journalism (MA, PhD); computing and information science (MS, PhD, CGS); English (MA); French (MA, MAT); global policy (MA); history (MA, PhD); liberal arts and sciences (MA, MAT, ME, MM, MS, MST, PhD, CGS); mathematics (MA); performing arts (MM); physics and astronomy (ME, MS, PhD); psychological sciences (PhD); Spanish (MAT). *Application deadline:* For fall admission, 2/1 priority date for domestic students. Applications are processed on a rolling basis. *Application fee:* $65. Electronic applications accepted. *Application Contact:* Scott G. Delcourt, Assistant Vice President for Graduate Studies and Senior Associate Dean, 207-581-3291, Fax: 207-581-3232, E-mail: graduate@maine.edu. *Dean*, Dr. Emily Haddad, 207-581-1954, Fax: 207-581-1947, E-mail: emily.haddad@maine.edu.

College of Natural Sciences, Forestry, and Agriculture Students: 500 full-time (339 women), 59 part-time (45 women); includes 46 minority (4 Black or African American, non-Hispanic/Latino; 10 American Indian or Alaska Native, non-Hispanic/Latino; 11 Asian, non-Hispanic/Latino; 13 Hispanic/Latino; 8 Two or more races, non-Hispanic/Latino), 72 international. Average age 30. 562 applicants, 56% accepted, 188 enrolled. *Faculty:* 193 full-time (86 women), 122 part-time/adjunct (45 women). Expenses: Contact institution. *Financial support:* In 2018–19, 347 students received support, including 7 fellowships (averaging $23,900 per year), 190 research assistantships (averaging $19,700 per year), 93 teaching assistantships (averaging $16,000 per year); career-related internships or fieldwork, Federal Work-Study, institutionally sponsored loans, scholarships/grants, health care benefits, tuition waivers (full and partial), and unspecified assistantships also available. Support available to part-time students. Financial award application deadline: 3/1. In 2018, 129 master's, 21 doctorates, 9 other advanced degrees awarded. *Program availability:* Part-time, evening/weekend. Offers biological sciences (PhD); botany and plant pathology (MS); communication sciences and disorders (MA); earth and climate sciences (MS, PhD); economics (MA); entomology (MS); financial economics (MA);

forest resources (MF, MS, PhD); horticulture (MS); individualized (MS); marine sciences (MS, PSM, PhD); microbiology (PhD); natural sciences, forestry, and agriculture (MA, MF, MPS, MS, MSW, MWC, PSM, PhD, CAS, CGS); nursing education (CGS); resource economics and policy (MS); rural health family nurse practitioner (MS, CAS); social work (MSW, CGS); wildlife ecology (PhD); zoology (MS, PhD). *Application deadline:* For fall admission, 2/1 priority date for domestic students. Applications are processed on a rolling basis. *Application fee:* $65. Electronic applications accepted. *Application Contact:* Scott G. Delcourt, Assistant Vice President for Graduate Studies and Senior Associate Dean, 207-581-3291, Fax: 207-581-3232, E-mail: graduate@maine.edu. *Interim Dean,* Dr. Fred Servello, 207-581-3206, Fax: 207-581-3207.

Graduate School of Biomedical Science and Engineering Students: 46 full-time (25 women), 6 part-time (3 women); includes 2 minority (1 Asian, non-Hispanic/Latino; 1 Two or more races, non-Hispanic/Latino), 9 international. Average age 30. 54 applicants, 20% accepted, 8 enrolled. *Faculty:* 182 full-time (60 women). Expenses: Contact institution. *Financial support:* In 2018–19, 4 students received support, including 1 research assistantship with full tuition reimbursement available (averaging $18,000 per year), 4 teaching assistantships with full tuition reimbursements available (averaging $15,600 per year); scholarships/grants and unspecified assistantships also available. Financial award application deadline: 3/1. In 2018, 5 doctorates awarded. Offers bioinformatics (PSM); biomedical engineering (PhD); biomedical science (PhD). *Application deadline:* For fall admission, 1/1 priority date for domestic and international students. Applications are processed on a rolling basis. *Application fee:* $65. Electronic applications accepted. *Application Contact:* Scott G. Delcourt, Assistant Vice President for Graduate Studies and Senior Associate Dean, 207-581-3291, Fax: 207-581-3232, E-mail: graduate@maine.edu. *Director,* Dr. David Neivandt, 207-581-2803.

The Maine Business School Students: 44 full-time (13 women), 53 part-time (25 women); includes 10 minority (1 Black or African American, non-Hispanic/Latino; 2 American Indian or Alaska Native, non-Hispanic/Latino; 4 Asian, non-Hispanic/Latino; 1 Hispanic/Latino; 2 Two or more races, non-Hispanic/Latino), 5 international. Average age 32. 70 applicants, 93% accepted, 40 enrolled. *Faculty:* 14 full-time (4 women), 6 part-time/adjunct (1 woman). Expenses: Contact institution. *Financial support:* In 2018–19, 15 students received support, including 1 fellowship with full tuition reimbursement available (averaging $10,000 per year), 3 teaching assistantships with full tuition reimbursements available (averaging $15,600 per year); career-related internships or fieldwork, Federal Work-Study, institutionally sponsored loans, scholarships/grants, tuition waivers (full and partial), and unspecified assistantships also available. Financial award application deadline: 3/1. In 2018, 28 master's, 9 other advanced degrees awarded. *Program availability:* Part-time, evening/weekend, online learning. Offers business (MBA, CGS). *Application deadline:* For fall admission, 7/1 priority date for domestic and international students; for spring admission, 12/1 priority date for domestic and international students; for summer admission, 4/1 priority date for domestic and international students. Applications are processed on a rolling basis. *Application fee:* $65. Electronic applications accepted. *Application Contact:* Scott G. Delcourt, Assistant Vice President for Graduate Studies and Senior Associate Dean, 207-581-3291, Fax: 207-581-3232, E-mail: graduate@maine.edu. *MBA Director and Lecturer in Management,* Scott Spolan, 207-581-1973, E-mail: scott.spolan@maine.edu.

University of Maine School of Law Students: 241 full-time (135 women), 9 part-time (4 women); includes 25 minority (6 Black or African American, non-Hispanic/Latino; 3 American Indian or Alaska Native, non-Hispanic/Latino; 7 Asian, non-Hispanic/Latino; 9 Hispanic/Latino), 2 international. Average age 27. 592 applicants, 53% accepted, 80 enrolled. *Faculty:* 23 full-time (12 women), 52 part-time/adjunct (21 women). Expenses: Contact institution. *Financial support:* In 2018–19, 165 students received support, including 20 fellowships (averaging $5,000 per year), 5 research assistantships (averaging $1,000 per year), 6 teaching assistantships with partial tuition reimbursements available (averaging $2,500 per year); Federal Work-Study, scholarships/grants, and unspecified assistantships also available. Financial award application deadline: 2/15; financial award applicants required to submit FAFSA. In 2018, 77 doctorates awarded. *Program availability:* Part-time. Offers law (JD). JD/MBA offered in conjunction with the University of Maine and University of Southern Maine; JD/MPH and JD/MPPM offered with the Muskie School of Public Service. *Application deadline:* For fall admission, 7/31 for domestic students, 6/1 for international students; for spring admission, 11/15 for international students. Applications are processed on a rolling basis. *Application fee:* $0. Electronic applications accepted. *Application Contact:* Caroline Wilshusen, Associate Dean of Admissions, 207-780-4341, Fax: 207-780-4239, E-mail: lawadmissions@maine.edu. *Dean,* Dmitry Bam, 207-780-4344, Fax: 207-780-4239.

UNIVERSITY OF MAINE AT FARMINGTON, Farmington, ME 04938
General Information State-supported, coed, comprehensive institution.

GRADUATE UNITS

Graduate Programs in Education *Program availability:* Part-time-only, evening/weekend, 100% online, blended/hybrid learning. Offers early childhood education (MS Ed); educational leadership (MS Ed); instructional technology (M Ed). M Ed offered in collaboration with University of Maine and University of Southern Maine. Electronic applications accepted.

UNIVERSITY OF MANAGEMENT AND TECHNOLOGY, Arlington, VA 22209-1609
General Information Proprietary, coed, comprehensive institution. *Enrollment:* 113 full-time matriculated graduate/professional students (32 women), 73 part-time matriculated graduate/professional students (36 women). *Graduate faculty:* 74 full-time (10 women). *Tuition:* Full-time $7020; part-time $1170 per course. *Graduate housing:* On-campus housing not available. *Student services:* Career counseling, international student services. *Collection:* Books: 9,149 (physical), 35 (digital/electronic).

Computer facilities: A campuswide network can be accessed. Online class registration is available.
Website: http://www.umtweb.edu/

General Application Contact: Kenny Hickey, Admissions, 703-516-0035, Fax: 703-516-0985, E-mail: admissions@umtweb.edu.

GRADUATE UNITS

Program in Business Administration *Program availability:* Part-time, 100% online. Offers general management (MBA, DBA); project management (MBA). Electronic applications accepted.

Program in Computer Science *Program availability:* Part-time, evening/weekend, online learning. Offers computer science (MS); information technology (AC); project management (AC); software engineering (MS). Electronic applications accepted.

Program in Criminal Justice *Program availability:* Part-time, evening/weekend, online learning. Offers homeland security (MS).

Program in Engineering Management Offers engineering management (MS).

Program in Health Administration Offers health administration (MHA).

Program in Homeland Security Offers homeland security (MS).

Program in Information Technology Offers information technology (MS, Advanced Certificate).

Program in Management *Program availability:* Part-time, evening/weekend, online learning. Offers acquisition management (MS, AC); criminal justice administration (MS); general management (MS); project management (MS, AC). Electronic applications accepted.

Program in Public Administration Offers public administration (MPA, Advanced Certificate).

THE UNIVERSITY OF MANCHESTER, Manchester M13 9PL, United Kingdom
General Information Public, coed, comprehensive institution.

GRADUATE UNITS

Alliance Manchester Business School Offers accounting and finance (M Sc); business (M Ent); business analysis and strategic management (M Sc); business analytics: operational research and risk analysis (M Sc); business psychology (M Sc); corporate communications and reputation management (M Sc); finance (M Sc); finance and business economics (M Sc); human resource management and industrial relations (M Sc); innovation management and entrepreneurship (M Sc); international business and management (M Sc); international human resource management and comparative industrial relations (M Sc); management (M Sc); marketing (M Sc); operations, project and supply chain management (M Sc); organizational psychology (M Sc); quantitative finance (M Sc). Electronic applications accepted.

Manchester Institute of Education Offers counseling (D Couns); counseling psychology (D Couns); education (M Phil, Ed D, PhD); educational and child psychology (Ed D); educational psychology (Ed D).

School of Arts, Languages and Cultures Offers anthropology, media and performance (PhD); applied theatre (PhD); Arab world studies (PhD); archaeology (PhD); art history and visual studies (PhD); arts and cultural management (PhD); arts management and cultural policy (PhD); Chinese studies (PhD); classics and ancient history (PhD); composition (PhD); creative writing (PhD); drama (PhD); East Asian studies (PhD); electroacoustic composition (PhD); English and American studies (PhD); English language (PhD); French studies (PhD); German studies (PhD); history (PhD); humanitarianism and conflict response (PhD); interpreting studies (PhD); Japanese studies (PhD); Latin American cultural studies (PhD); linguistics (PhD); Middle Eastern studies (PhD); museology (PhD); museum practice (PhD); music (PhD); musicology (PhD); Polish studies (PhD); Portuguese studies (PhD); religions and theology (PhD); Russian studies (PhD); Spanish studies (PhD); translation and intercultural studies (PhD).

School of Biological Sciences Offers adaptive organismal biology (M Phil, PhD); animal biology (M Phil, PhD); biochemistry (M Phil, PhD); bioinformatics (M Phil, PhD); biomolecular sciences (M Phil, PhD); biotechnology (M Phil, PhD); cell biology (M Phil, PhD); cell matrix research (M Phil, PhD); channels and transporters (M Phil, PhD); developmental biology (M Phil, PhD); environmental biology (M Phil, PhD); evolutionary biology (M Phil, PhD); gene expression (M Phil, PhD); genetics (M Phil, PhD); history of science, technology and medicine (M Phil, PhD); immunology (M Phil, PhD); integrative neurobiology and behavior (M Phil, PhD); membrane trafficking (M Phil, PhD); microbiology (M Phil, PhD); molecular and cellular neuroscience (M Phil, PhD); molecular biology (M Phil, PhD); molecular cancer studies (M Phil, PhD); neuroscience (M Phil, PhD); ophthalmology (M Phil, PhD); optometry (M Phil, PhD); organelle function (M Phil, PhD); pharmacology (M Phil, PhD); physiology (M Phil, PhD); plant sciences (M Phil, PhD); stem cell research (M Phil, PhD); structural biology (M Phil, PhD); systems neuroscience (M Phil, PhD); toxicology (M Phil, PhD).

School of Chemical Engineering and Analytical Science Offers biocatalysis (M Phil, PhD); chemical engineering (M Phil, PhD); chemical engineering and analytical science (M Phil, D Eng, PhD); colloids, crystals, interfaces and materials (M Phil, PhD); environment and sustainable technology (M Phil, PhD); instrumentation (M Phil, PhD); multi-scale modeling (M Phil, PhD); process integration (M Phil, PhD); systems biology (M Phil, PhD).

School of Chemistry Offers biological chemistry (PhD); chemistry (M Ent, M Phil, M Sc, D Ent, PhD); inorganic chemistry (PhD); materials chemistry (PhD); nanoscience (PhD); nuclear fission (PhD); organic chemistry (PhD); physical chemistry (PhD); theoretical chemistry (PhD).

School of Computer Science Offers computer science (M Phil, PhD).

School of Dentistry Offers basic dental sciences (cancer studies) (M Phil, PhD); basic dental sciences (molecular genetics) (M Phil, PhD); basic dental sciences (stem cell biology) (M Phil, PhD); biomaterials sciences and dental technology (M Phil, PhD); dental public health/community dentistry (M Phil, PhD); dental science (clinical) (PhD); endodontology (M Phil, PhD); fixed and removable prosthodontics (M Phil, PhD); operative dentistry (M Phil, PhD); oral and maxillofacial surgery (M Phil, PhD); oral radiology (M Phil, PhD); orthodontics (M Phil, PhD); restorative dentistry (M Phil, PhD).

School of Earth and Environmental Sciences Offers atmospheric sciences (M Phil, M Sc, PhD); basin studies and petroleum geosciences (M Phil, M Sc, PhD); earth, atmospheric and environmental sciences (M Phil, M Sc, PhD); environmental geochemistry and cosmochemistry (M Phil, M Sc, PhD); isotope geochemistry and cosmochemistry (M Phil, M Sc, PhD); paleontology (M Phil, M Sc, PhD); physics and chemistry of minerals and fluids (M Phil, M Sc, PhD); structural and petrological geosciences (M Phil, M Sc, PhD).

School of Electrical and Electronic Engineering Offers electrical and electronic engineering (M Phil, PhD).

School of Environment, Education and Development Offers architecture (M Phil, PhD); development policy and management (M Phil, PhD); human geography (M Phil, PhD); physical geography (M Phil, PhD); planning and landscape (M Phil, PhD).

School of Law Offers bioethics and medical jurisprudence (PhD); criminology (M Phil, PhD); law (PhD).

School of Materials Offers advanced aerospace materials engineering (M Sc); advanced metallic systems (M Phil, M Sc, PhD); biomedical materials (M Phil, M Sc, PhD); ceramics and glass (M Phil, M Sc, PhD); composite materials (M Sc, PhD); corrosion and protection (M Phil, M Sc, PhD); materials (M Phil, PhD); metallic materials (M Phil, M Sc, PhD); nanostructural materials (M Phil, M Sc, PhD); paper science (M Phil, M Sc, PhD); polymer science and engineering (M Phil, M Sc, PhD); technical textiles (M Sc); textile design, fashion and management (M Phil, M Sc, PhD); textile science and technology (M Phil, M Sc, PhD); textiles (M Phil, PhD); textiles and fashion (M Ent).

School of Mathematics Offers actuarial science (PhD); applied mathematics (M Phil, PhD); applied numerical computing (M Phil, PhD); financial mathematics (M Phil, PhD); mathematical logic (M Phil); probability (M Phil, PhD); pure mathematics (M Phil, PhD); statistics (M Phil, PhD).

School of Mechanical, Aerospace and Civil Engineering Offers advanced manufacturing technology (M Ent); aerospace engineering (M Phil, M Sc, PhD); civil engineering (M Phil, M Sc, PhD); environmental engineering (M Phil, PhD); management of projects (M Phil, M Sc, PhD); mechanical engineering (M Phil, M Sc, PhD); mechanical engineering design (M Ent); nuclear engineering (M Phil, D Eng, PhD).

School of Medicine Offers medicine (M Phil, PhD).

School of Nursing, Midwifery and Social Work Offers nursing (M Phil, PhD); social work (M Phil, PhD).

School of Pharmacy and Pharmaceutical Sciences Offers pharmacy and pharmaceutical sciences (M Phil, PhD).

School of Physics and Astronomy Offers astronomy and astrophysics (M Sc, PhD); biological physics (M Sc, PhD); condensed matter physics (M Sc, PhD); nonlinear and liquid crystals physics (M Sc, PhD); nuclear physics (M Sc, PhD); particle physics (M Sc, PhD); photon physics (M Sc, PhD); physics (M Sc, PhD); theoretical physics (M Sc, PhD).

School of Psychological Sciences Offers audiology (M Phil, PhD); clinical psychology (M Phil, PhD, Psy D); psychology (M Phil, PhD).

School of Social Sciences Offers ethnographic documentary (M Phil); interdisciplinary study of culture (PhD); philosophy (PhD); politics (PhD); social anthropology (PhD); social anthropology with visual media (PhD); social change (PhD); social statistics (PhD); sociology (PhD); visual anthropology (M Phil).

UNIVERSITY OF MANITOBA, Winnipeg, MB R3T 2N2, Canada

General Information Province-supported, coed, university. CGS member. *Graduate housing:* Rooms and/or apartments available to single and married students. *Research affiliation:* Canada Department of Agriculture Research Station, Freshwater Institute, Atomic Energy of Canada, Manitoba Department of Mines, Resources, and Environmental Management, Northern Scientific Training Program (Northern studies), Taiga Biological Research Trust.

GRADUATE UNITS

Dr. Gerald Niznick College of Dentistry Offers dental diagnostic and surgical sciences (M Dent); dentistry (M Dent, M Sc, DMD, PhD); oral and maxillofacial surgery (M Dent); oral biology (M Sc, PhD); orthodontics (M Sc); periodontology (M Dent); preventive dental science (M Sc); restorative dentistry (M Dent).

Faculty of Graduate Studies *Program availability:* Part-time.

Asper School of Business Offers business (M Sc, MBA, PhD).

Clayton H. Riddell Faculty of Environment, Earth, and Resources Offers environment (M Env); environment and geography (M Sc); environment, earth, and resources (M Env, M Sc, MA, MNRM, PhD); geography (MA, PhD); geology (M Sc, PhD); geophysics (M Sc, PhD); natural resources and environmental management (PhD); natural resources management (MNRM).

College of Nursing Offers cancer nursing (MN); nursing (MN).

College of Pharmacy Offers pharmacy (M Sc, PhD).

College of Rehabilitation Sciences Offers applied health sciences (PhD); occupational therapy (MOT); physical therapy (MPT); rehabilitation sciences (M Sc).

College Universitaire de Saint Boniface Offers Canadian studies (MA); education (M Ed).

Desautels Faculty of Music Offers music (M Mus).

Faculty of Agricultural and Food Sciences Offers agribusiness (M Sc, PhD); agricultural and food sciences (M Sc, PhD); agronomy and plant protection (M Sc, PhD); animal science (M Sc, PhD); entomology (M Sc, PhD); food science (M Sc, PhD); horticulture (M Sc, PhD); human nutritional sciences (M Sc, PhD); plant breeding and genetics (M Sc, PhD); plant physiology-biochemistry (M Sc, PhD); soil science (M Sc, PhD).

Faculty of Architecture Offers architecture (M Arch, M Land Arch, MCP, MID); city planning (MCP); interior design (MID); landscape architecture (M Land Arch).

Faculty of Arts Offers anthropology (MA, PhD); archival studies (MA); arts (MA, MPA, PhD); classics (MA); clinical psychology (PhD); economics (MA, PhD); English (MA, PhD); French (MA, PhD); German language and literature (MA); history (MA, PhD); Icelandic language and literature (MA); linguistics (MA, PhD); native studies (MA); philosophy (MA); political studies (MA, PhD); psychology (MA, PhD); public administration (MPA); religion (MA, PhD); school psychology (MA) Slavic languages and literatures (MA); sociology (MA, PhD).

Faculty of Education Offers adult and post-secondary education (M Ed); education (M Ed, PhD); educational administration (M Ed); guidance and counseling (M Ed); inclusive special education (M Ed); language and literacy (M Ed); second language education (M Ed); social foundations of education (M Ed); studies in curriculum, teaching and learning (M Ed).

Faculty of Engineering Offers biosystems engineering (M Eng, M Sc, PhD); civil engineering (M Eng, M Sc, PhD); electrical and computer engineering (M Eng, M Sc, PhD); engineering (M Eng, M Sc, PhD); mechanical and manufacturing engineering (M Eng, M Sc, PhD).

Faculty of Kinesiology and Recreation Management Offers kinesiology and recreation (M Sc, MA).

Faculty of Law Offers law (LL M). Electronic applications accepted.

Faculty of Science Offers botany (M Sc, PhD); chemistry (M Sc, PhD); computer science (M Sc, PhD); ecology (M Sc, PhD); mathematical, computational and statistical sciences (MMCSS); mathematics (M Sc, PhD); microbiology (M Sc, PhD); physics and astronomy (M Sc, PhD); science (M Sc, MMCSS, PhD); statistics (M Sc, PhD); zoology (M Sc, PhD).

Faculty of Social Work Offers social work (MSW, PhD).

Interdisciplinary Programs Offers disability studies (M Sc, MA); individual interdisciplinary studies (M Sc, MA, PhD); interdisciplinary studies (M Sc, MA, PhD).

Max Rady College of Medicine *Program availability:* Part-time. Offers medicine (M Sc, PhD). Electronic applications accepted.

Graduate Programs in Medicine *Program availability:* Part-time. Offers biochemistry and medical genetics (M Sc, PhD); community health sciences (M Sc, MPH, PhD, G Dip); genetic counseling (M Sc); human anatomy and cell science (M Sc, PhD); immunology (M Sc, PhD); medical microbiology and infectious diseases (M Sc, PhD); medicine (M Sc, MPH, PhD, G Dip); pathology (M Sc); pediatrics and child health (M Sc); pharmacology and therapeutics (M Sc, PhD); physiology and pathophysiology (M Sc, PhD); psychiatry (M Sc); surgery (M Sc).

UNIVERSITY OF MARY, Bismarck, ND 58504-9652

General Information Independent-religious, coed, comprehensive institution. *Graduate housing:* Room and/or apartments available on a first-come, first-served basis to single students; on-campus housing not available to married students. Housing application deadline: 7/15.

GRADUATE UNITS

Gary Tharaldson School of Business *Program availability:* Part-time, evening/weekend. Offers business administration (MBA); energy management (MBA, MS); executive (MBA, MS); health care (MBA, MS); human resource management (MBA); project management (MBA, MPM); virtuous leadership (MBA, MPM, MS). Electronic applications accepted.

Liffrig Family School of Education and Behavioral Sciences Offers curriculum, instruction and assessment (M Ed); education (Ed D); education and behavioral sciences (M Ed, Ed D); elementary administration (M Ed); reading (M Ed); secondary administration (M Ed); special education strategist (M Ed).

School of Health Sciences Offers bioethics (MS); clinical exercise physiology (MS); health sciences (MS, MSN, MSOT, DNP, DPT); kinesiology (MS); occupational therapy (MSOT); physical therapy (DPT); respiratory therapy (MS); speech-language pathology (MS); sports and physical education administration (MS). Electronic applications accepted.

Division of Nursing *Program availability:* Part-time, evening/weekend, online learning. Offers family nurse practitioner (DNP); nurse administrator (MSN); nursing educator (MSN). Electronic applications accepted.

UNIVERSITY OF MARY HARDIN-BAYLOR, Belton, TX 76513

General Information Independent-religious, coed, comprehensive institution. *Graduate housing:* On-campus housing not available.

GRADUATE UNITS

Graduate Studies in Business Administration *Program availability:* Part-time, evening/weekend. Offers accounting (MBA); information systems management (MBA); international business (MBA); management (MBA). Electronic applications accepted.

Graduate Studies in Counseling *Program availability:* Part-time, evening/weekend. Offers clinical and mental health counseling (MA); marriage, family and child counseling (MA); non-clinical professional studies (MA). Electronic applications accepted.

Graduate Studies in Education *Program availability:* Part-time, evening/weekend. Offers curriculum and instruction (M Ed); educational administration (M Ed, Ed D). Electronic applications accepted.

Graduate Studies in Exercise Physiology *Program availability:* Part-time, 100% online. Offers exercise physiology (MS Ed); sport administration (MS Ed). Electronic applications accepted.

Graduate Studies in Information Systems *Program availability:* Part-time, evening/weekend. Offers information systems (MS). Electronic applications accepted.

Graduate Studies in Nursing *Program availability:* Evening/weekend. Offers family nurse practitioner (MSN, Post-Master's Certificate); nursing education (MSN); nursing practice (DNP). Electronic applications accepted.

Graduate Studies in Physical Therapy Offers physical therapy (DPT). Electronic applications accepted.

UNIVERSITY OF MARYLAND, BALTIMORE, Baltimore, MD 21201

General Information State-supported, coed, graduate-only institution. CGS member. *Graduate housing:* Rooms and/or apartments available on a first-come, first-served basis to single and married students. *Research affiliation:* University of Maryland Medical System (medical research), University of Maryland Biotechnology Institute (biology), University of Maryland BioPark (biology).

GRADUATE UNITS

Francis King Carey School of Law Students: 556 full-time (318 women), 200 part-time (116 women); includes 263 minority (123 Black or African American, non-Hispanic/Latino; 1 American Indian or Alaska Native, non-Hispanic/Latino; 60 Asian, non-Hispanic/Latino; 53 Hispanic/Latino; 26 Two or more races, non-Hispanic/Latino), 16 international. Average age 27. 2,323 applicants, 50% accepted, 281 enrolled. *Faculty:* 48 full-time (23 women), 64 part-time/adjunct (22 women). Expenses: Contact institution. *Financial support:* In 2018–19, 536 students received support, including 23 fellowships (averaging $5,000 per year); Federal Work-Study, institutionally sponsored loans, and scholarships/grants also available. Support available to part-time students. Financial award application deadline: 3/1; financial award applicants required to submit FAFSA. In 2018, 68 master's, 192 doctorates awarded. *Program availability:* Part-time, evening/weekend, 100% online. Offers law (LL M, JD). *Application deadline:* For fall admission, 4/1 priority date for domestic and international students. Applications are processed on a rolling basis. *Application fee:* $70. Electronic applications accepted. *Application Contact:* Katrin Hussmann Schroll, Assistant Dean for Admissions, 410-706-3492, Fax: 410-706-1793, E-mail: admissions@law.umaryland.edu. *Dean/Professor,* Donald B. Tobin, 410-706-7214, Fax: 410-706-4045, E-mail: dtobin@law.umaryland.edu.

Graduate School *Program availability:* Part-time, evening/weekend, online learning. Offers applied pharmacology and toxicology (PhD); biochemistry (MS, PhD); biochemistry and molecular biology (MS, PhD); biomedical sciences (MS, PhD); cancer biology (PhD); cellular and molecular biomedical science (MS); clinical research (Postbaccalaureate Certificate); epidemiology (MS, PhD); forensic medicine (MS); genome biology (PhD); gerontology (PhD); health science (MS); marine-estuarine-environmental sciences (MS, PhD); medical and research technology (MS); molecular and cellular physiology (PhD); molecular medicine (PhD); molecular microbiology and immunology (PhD); neuroscience (PhD); oral pathology (PhD); pharmaceutical health service research (MS, PhD); pharmaceutical sciences (PhD); pharmacometrics (MS); pharmacy administration (PhD); physical rehabilitation science (PhD); regulatory science (MS); research ethics (Certificate); thanatology (Certificate); toxicology (MS, PhD). Electronic applications accepted.

School of Social Work Offers social work (MSW, PhD). MSW/MA offered jointly with Baltimore Hebrew University; MBA/MSW with University of Maryland, College Park; MSW/MPH with The Johns Hopkins University. Electronic applications accepted.

Professional and Advanced Education Programs in Dentistry Offers advanced general dentistry (Certificate); dentistry (DDS); endodontics (Certificate); oral-maxillofacial surgery (Certificate); orthodontics (Certificate); pediatric dentistry (Certificate); periodontics (Certificate); prosthodontics (Certificate). Electronic applications accepted.

Professional Program in Pharmacy Offers pharmacy (Pharm D). Electronic applications accepted.

School of Medicine *Program availability:* Part-time. Offers biostatistics (MS); clinical research (MS); epidemiology and preventive medicine (MPH, MS, PhD); genetic counseling (MGC); gerontology (PhD); human genetics and genomic medicine (MS, PhD); medicine (MGC, MPH, MS, DPT, MD, PhD); molecular epidemiology (MS, PhD); pathologists' assistant (MS); physical rehabilitation science (PhD); physical therapy and rehabilitation science (DPT); toxicology (MS, PhD). Electronic applications accepted.

University of Maryland School of Nursing Students: 528 full-time (457 women), 554 part-time (499 women); includes 466 minority (264 Black or African American, non-Hispanic/Latino; 2 American Indian or Alaska Native, non-Hispanic/Latino; 116 Asian, non-Hispanic/Latino; 56 Hispanic/Latino; 28 Two or more races, non-Hispanic/Latino), 16 international. Average age 34. 812 applicants, 57% accepted, 322 enrolled. *Faculty:* 130 full-time (117 women), 125 part-time/adjunct (114 women). Expenses: Contact institution. *Financial support:* In 2018–19, 257 students received support, including 31 research assistantships with full and partial tuition reimbursements available (averaging $25,000 per year), 21 teaching assistantships with full and partial tuition reimbursements available (averaging $19,000 per year); scholarships/grants, traineeships, and unspecified assistantships also available. Support available to part-time students. Financial award application deadline: 3/1; financial award applicants required to submit FAFSA. In 2018, 189 master's, 135 doctorates, 12 other advanced degrees awarded. *Program availability:* Part-time. Offers adult-gerontology acute care nurse practitioner (DNP); adult-gerontology primary care nurse practitioner (DNP); clinical nurse leader (MS); community/public health nursing (MS); family nurse practitioner (DNP); global health (Postbaccalaureate Certificate); health services leadership and management (MS); neonatal nurse practitioner (DNP); nurse anesthesia (DNP); nursing (PhD); nursing informatics (MS, Postbaccalaureate Certificate); pediatric acute/primary care nurse practitioner (DNP); psychiatric mental health nurse practitioner (DNP); teaching in nursing and health professions (Postbaccalaureate Certificate). MS/MBA offered jointly with University of Baltimore. *Application deadline:* For fall admission, 11/1 for domestic and international students; for spring admission, 8/1 for domestic and international students. *Application fee:* $75. Electronic applications accepted. *Application Contact:* Larry Fillian, Associate Dean of Student and Academic Services, 410-706-6298, E-mail: lfillian@umaryland.edu. *Dean,* Dr. Jane Kirschling, 410-706-4359, E-mail: kirschling@umaryland.edu.

UNIVERSITY OF MARYLAND, BALTIMORE COUNTY, Baltimore, MD 21250

General Information State-supported, coed, university. CGS member. *Graduate housing:* Room and/or apartments available on a first-come, first-served basis to single students; on-campus housing not available to married students. Housing application deadline: 6/1. *Research affiliation:* Sciences Applications International Corporation (information systems and technology), Halliburton Energy Services, IBM (computers and information technology), BouMatic (dairy industry), Pfizer, Inc. (pharmaceuticals), Fujitsu Laboratories of America (information technology and communications).

GRADUATE UNITS

The Graduate School Offers engineering management (MS, Postbaccalaureate Certificate); marine-estuarine-environmental sciences (MS, PhD); systems engineering (MS, Postbaccalaureate Certificate). Electronic applications accepted.

College of Arts, Humanities and Social Sciences Program availability: Part-time, evening/weekend, online learning. Offers aging policy issues (PhD); American contemporary music (Postbaccalaureate Certificate); applied behavioral analysis (MA); applied developmental psychology (PhD); applied sociology (MA); arts, humanities and social science (MA, MAE, MAE, MAT, MFA, MPP, MPS, MS, PhD, Certificate, Graduate Certificate, Postbaccalaureate Certificate); distance education (Graduate Certificate); early childhood education (MAT); economic policy analysis (MA); education (MAE, MAE); elementary education (MAT); emergency health services (MS); emergency management (Postbaccalaureate Certificate); English: texts, technologies, and literature (MA); epidemiology of aging (PhD); gender and women's studies (Postbaccalaureate Certificate); geographic information systems (MPS, Certificate); geography and environmental systems (MS, PhD); historical studies (MA); human services psychology (MA, PhD); industrial/organizational psychology (MPS); instructional systems development (MA, Graduate Certificate); instructional technology (Graduate Certificate); intercultural communication (MA); intermedia and digital arts (MFA); K-8 mathematics instructional leadership (MAE); K-8 science education (MAE); K-8 STEM education (MAE); language, literacy, and culture (PhD); nonprofit sector (Postbaccalaureate Certificate); public policy (MPP, PhD); secondary mathematics education (MAE); secondary science education (MAE); secondary STEM education (MAE); social, cultural, and behavioral sciences (PhD); teaching (MAT); teaching English to speakers of other languages (MA, Postbaccalaureate Certificate). Electronic applications accepted.

College of Engineering and Information Technology Program availability: Part-time. Offers biochemical regulatory engineering (Postbaccalaureate Certificate); chemical and biochemical engineering (MS, PhD); computational thermal fluid dynamics (Postbaccalaureate Certificate); computer engineering (MS, PhD); computer science (MS, PhD); cybersecurity (MPS, Postbaccalaureate Certificate); cybersecurity operations (Postbaccalaureate Certificate); cybersecurity strategy and policy (Postbaccalaureate Certificate); data science (MPS); electrical engineering (MS, PhD); engineering and information technology (MPS, MS, PhD, Postbaccalaureate Certificate); environmental engineering (MS, PhD); health information technology (MPS); human-centered computing (MS, PhD); information systems (MPS, MS, PhD); mechanical engineering (MS, PhD, Postbaccalaureate Certificate); mechatronics (Postbaccalaureate Certificate); technical management (MPS). Electronic applications accepted.

College of Natural and Mathematical Sciences Program availability: Part-time. Offers applied mathematics (MS, PhD); applied molecular biology (MS); atmospheric physics (MS, PhD); biological sciences (MPS, MS, PhD, Graduate Certificate); biostatistics (PhD); biotechnology (MPS); biotechnology (Graduate Certificate); biotechnology management (Graduate Certificate); chemistry (MS, PhD); chemistry and biochemistry (Postbaccalaureate Certificate); environmental statistics (MS); molecular and cell biology (PhD); natural and mathematical sciences (MPS, MS, PhD, Graduate Certificate, Postbaccalaureate Certificate); neuroscience and cognitive sciences (PhD); physics (MS, PhD); statistics (MS, PhD). Electronic applications accepted.

Erickson School of Aging Studies Program availability: Part-time. Offers management of aging services (MA). Electronic applications accepted.

UNIVERSITY OF MARYLAND, COLLEGE PARK, College Park, MD 20742

General Information State-supported, coed, university. CGS member. *Graduate housing:* On-campus housing not available. *Research affiliation:* Battelle–Pacific Northwest National Laboratory, Canon U.S. Life Sciences, Inc. (technology development and analysis), Bill and Melinda Gates Foundation (international aid and outreach),

Lockheed Martin Corporation (science and technology), BAE Systems (science and technology).

GRADUATE UNITS

Academic Affairs *Program availability:* Part-time, evening/weekend, online learning. Offers history, library, and information services. Electronic applications accepted.

A. James Clark School of Engineering Program availability: Part-time, evening/weekend, online learning. Offers advanced engineering education (M Eng); aerospace engineering (M Eng, MS, PhD); bioengineering (MS, PhD); chemical engineering (M Eng, MS, PhD); civil and environmental engineering (M Eng, MS, PhD); electrical and computer engineering (M Eng, MS, PhD); electrical engineering (MS, PhD); electronic packaging and reliability (MS, PhD); engineering (M Eng, ME, MS, PhD, Certificate); engineering and public policy (MS); fire protection engineering (M Eng, MS); manufacturing and design (MS, PhD); materials science and engineering (MS, PhD); mechanics and materials (MS, PhD); nuclear engineering (ME, MS, PhD); reliability engineering (M Eng, MS, PhD); systems engineering (M Eng, MS); telecommunications (MS); thermal and fluid sciences (MS, PhD).

College of Agriculture and Natural Resources Program availability: Part-time, evening/weekend. Offers agriculture and natural resources (MS, DVM, PhD); agriculture economics (MS, PhD); animal sciences (MS, PhD); environmental science and technology (MS, PhD); food science (MS, PhD); landscape architecture (MLA); natural resource sciences (MS, PhD); nutrition (MS, PhD); plant science (MS, PhD); resource economics (MS, PhD); veterinary medical sciences (MS, PhD); veterinary medicine (MS, DVM, PhD). Electronic applications accepted.

College of Arts and Humanities Program availability: Part-time, evening/weekend. Offers American studies (MA, PhD); art (MFA); art history (MA, PhD); arts and humanities (M Ed, MA, MFA, MM, DMA, Ed D, PhD); classics (MA); communication (MA, PhD); comparative literature (MA, PhD); creative writing (MA, MFA, PhD); dance (MFA); English language and literature (MA, PhD); ethnomusicology (MA); French language and literature (MA); Germanic language and literature (MA, PhD); history (MA, PhD); Jewish studies (MA); languages, literatures, and cultures (MA, PhD); linguistics (MA, PhD); modern French studies (PhD); music (M Ed, MA, MM, DMA, Ed D, PhD); performance (MFA); philosophy (MA, PhD); second language instruction (PhD); second language learning (PhD); second language measurement and assessment (PhD); second language use (PhD); Spanish language and literatures (MA, PhD); theatre (MA, MFA, PhD); theatre and performance studies (MA, PhD); theatre design (MFA); women's studies (MA, PhD). Electronic applications accepted.

College of Behavioral and Social Sciences Program availability: Part-time, evening/weekend. Offers American politics (PhD); applied anthropology (MAA); audiology (MA, PhD); behavioral and social sciences (MA, MAA, MS, Au D, PhD); clinical psychology (PhD); comparative politics (PhD); criminology and criminal justice (MA, PhD); developmental psychology (PhD); economics (MA, PhD); experimental psychology (PhD); geography (MA, PhD); hearing and speech sciences (Au D); industrial psychology (MA, MS, PhD); international relations (PhD); language pathology (MA, PhD); neuroscience (PhD); neurosciences and cognitive sciences (PhD); political economy (PhD); political theory (PhD); social psychology (PhD); sociology (MA, PhD); speech (MA, PhD); survey methodology (MS, PhD). Electronic applications accepted.

College of Computer, Mathematical and Natural Sciences Program availability: Part-time, evening/weekend, online learning. Offers analytical chemistry (MS, PhD); applied mathematics (MS, PhD); astronomy (MS, PhD); atmospheric and oceanic science (MS, PMS, PhD); behavior, ecology, and systematics (PhD); behavior, ecology, evolution, and systematics (MS, PhD); biochemistry (MS, PhD); biological sciences (PhD); biology (MS, PhD); biophysics (PhD); cell biology and molecular genetics (MS, PhD); chemical physics (MS, PhD); chemistry (MS, PhD); computational biology, bioinformatics, and genomics (PhD); computer science (MS, PhD); computer, mathematical and natural sciences (MA, MLS, MS, PMS, PhD); entomology (MS, PhD); geology (MS, PhD); inorganic chemistry (MS, PhD); life sciences (MLS); marine-estuarine-environmental sciences (MS, PhD); mathematical statistics (MA, PhD); mathematics (MA, PhD); molecular and cellular biology (PhD); organic chemistry (MS, PhD); physical chemistry (MS, PhD); physics (MS, PhD); physiological systems (MS, PhD); plant biology (MS, PhD); sustainable development and conservation biology (MS).

College of Education Program availability: Part-time, evening/weekend, online learning. Offers college student personnel (M Ed, MA); college student personnel administration (PhD); community counseling (CAGS); community/career counseling (M Ed, MA); counseling and personnel services (M Ed, MA, PhD); counseling psychology (PhD); counselor education (PhD); curriculum and educational communications (M Ed, MA, Ed D, PhD); education (M Ed, MA, Ed D, PhD, AGSC, CAGS); human development and quantitative methodology (MA, Ed D, PhD); reading (M Ed, MA, PhD, CAGS); rehabilitation counseling (M Ed, MA, AGSC); school counseling (M Ed, MA); school psychology (M Ed, MA, PhD); secondary education (M Ed, MA, Ed D, PhD, CAGS); social foundations of education (M Ed, MA, Ed D, PhD, CAGS); teaching English to speakers of other languages (M Ed). Electronic applications accepted.

College of Information Studies Program availability: Part-time, evening/weekend. Offers information studies (MIM, MLS, PhD). Electronic applications accepted.

Philip Merrill College of Journalism Program availability: Part-time, evening/weekend. Offers broadcast journalism (MA); journalism (MA); journalism and media studies (PhD); online news (MA); public affairs reporting (MA). Electronic applications accepted.

Robert H. Smith School of Business Program availability: Part-time, evening/weekend, online learning. Offers business (EMBA, MBA, MS, PhD); business administration (MBA); business and management (MS, PhD); executive business administration (EMBA). Electronic applications accepted.

School of Architecture, Planning and Preservation Program availability: Part-time, evening/weekend. Offers architecture (M Arch); architecture, planning and preservation (M Arch, MCP, MHP, MRED, PhD, Certificate); historic preservation (MHP, Certificate); real estate development (MRED); urban and regional planning/design (PhD); urban studies and planning (MCP). Electronic applications accepted.

School of Public Health Program availability: Part-time, evening/weekend. Offers biostatistics (MPH); community health education (MPH); environmental health sciences (MPH); epidemiology (MPH, PhD); family studies (PhD); health services administration (MHA, PhD); kinesiology (MA, PhD); marriage and family therapy (MS); maternal and child health (PhD); public health (MA, MHA, MPH, MS, PhD); public/community health (PhD). Electronic applications accepted.

School of Public Policy Program availability: Part-time, evening/weekend, online learning. Offers policy studies (PhD); public management (MPM); public policy (MPM, MPP, PhD). Electronic applications accepted.

UNIVERSITY OF MARYLAND EASTERN SHORE, Princess Anne, MD 21853

General Information State-supported, coed, university. CGS member. *Graduate housing:* Room and/or apartments available to single students; on-campus housing not available to married students.

GRADUATE UNITS

Graduate Programs *Program availability:* Part-time, evening/weekend. Offers applied computer science (MS); career and technology education (M Ed); chemistry (MS); criminal justice (MS); education leadership (Ed D); food and agricultural sciences (MS); food science and technology (PhD); guidance and counseling (M Ed); marine-estuarine-environmental sciences (MS, PhD); organizational leadership (MS); physical therapy (DPT); quantitative fisheries and resource economics (PMS); rehabilitation counseling (MS); special education (M Ed); teaching (MAT); toxicology (MS, PhD). Electronic applications accepted.

School of Pharmacy Offers pharmaceutical sciences (MS, PhD); pharmacy (Pharm D).

UNIVERSITY OF MARYLAND UNIVERSITY COLLEGE, Adelphi, MD 20783

General Information State-supported, coed, comprehensive institution. *Enrollment:* 60,603 graduate, professional, and undergraduate students; 3,999 full-time matriculated graduate/professional students (1,847 women), 9,631 part-time matriculated graduate/professional students (5,446 women). *Enrollment by degree level:* 12,925 master's, 170 doctoral, 535 other advanced degrees. *Graduate faculty:* 189 full-time (84 women), 3,502 part-time/adjunct (1,611 women). *Graduate housing:* On-campus housing not available. *Student services:* Career counseling, international student services, services for students with disabilities, writing training. *Library facilities:* Library plus 1 other. *Collection:* Books: 1,234 (physical), 129,937 (digital/electronic); Serial titles: 161,585 (digital/electronic); Databases: 96. Weekly public service hours: 95.

Computer facilities: Computer purchase and lease plans are available. 510 computers available on campus for general student use. A campuswide network can be accessed from off campus. Online class registration is available.
Website: http://www.umuc.edu/

General Application Contact: Admissions, 800-888-UMUC, E-mail: Studentsfirst@umuc.edu.

GRADUATE UNITS

The Graduate School Students: 97 full-time (57 women), 13,253 part-time (7,258 women); includes 7,547 minority (5,218 Black or African American, non-Hispanic/Latino; 38 American Indian or Alaska Native, non-Hispanic/Latino; 853 Asian, non-Hispanic/Latino; 980 Hispanic/Latino; 34 Native Hawaiian or other Pacific Islander, non-Hispanic/Latino; 424 Two or more races, non-Hispanic/Latino), 313 international. Average age 36. 6,005 applicants, 100% accepted, 2580 enrolled. *Faculty:* 193 full-time (86 women), 3,653 part-time/adjunct (1,681 women). Expenses: Contact institution. *Financial support:* Scholarships/grants available. Support available to part-time students. Financial award application deadline: 6/1; financial award applicants required to submit FAFSA. In 2018, 4,456 master's, 46 doctorates, 481 other advanced degrees awarded. *Program availability:* Part-time, evening/weekend, online learning. Offers accounting and financial management (MS); accounting and information systems (MS, Certificate); biotechnology (MS, Certificate); business administration (MBA); cloud computing architecture (MS); cybersecurity management and policy (MS, Certificate); cybersecurity technology (MS, Certificate); data analytics (MS, Certificate); digital forensics and cyber investigation (MS, Certificate); distance education and e-learning (MDE); environmental management (MS); health care administration (MS); health informatics administration (MS); information technology (MS); instructional technology (M Ed); learning design and technology (MS); management (MS, DM, Certificate); management and technology (MAT, MBA, MDE, MS, DM, Certificate); teaching (MAT). *Application deadline:* Applications are processed on a rolling basis. *Application fee:* $50. Electronic applications accepted. *Application Contact:* Admissions, 800-888-8682, E-mail: studentsfirst@umuc.edu. *Dean and Vice Provost,* Kathryn Klose, 240-684-2406, E-mail: kathryn.klose@umuc.edu.

UNIVERSITY OF MARY WASHINGTON, Fredericksburg, VA 22401-5358

General Information State-supported, coed, comprehensive institution. *Graduate housing:* Room and/or apartments available on a first-come, first-served basis to single students; on-campus housing not available to married students.

GRADUATE UNITS

College of Business *Program availability:* Part-time-only, evening/weekend. Offers business (MBA). Electronic applications accepted.

College of Education *Program availability:* Part-time, evening/weekend. Offers education (M Ed); elementary education (MS). Electronic applications accepted.

UNIVERSITY OF MASSACHUSETTS AMHERST, Amherst, MA 01003

General Information State-supported, coed, university. CGS member. *Graduate housing:* Rooms and/or apartments available on a first-come, first-served basis to single and married students. Housing application deadline: 6/15.

GRADUATE UNITS

Graduate School *Program availability:* Part-time, evening/weekend. Electronic applications accepted.

College of Education *Program availability:* Part-time, online learning. Offers bilingual, English as a second language, and multicultural education (M Ed, Ed S); child study and early education (M Ed); children, families and schools (Ed D, Ed S); early childhood and elementary teacher education (M Ed); education (M Ed, Ed D, PhD, Ed S); educational leadership (M Ed); educational policy and leadership (Ed D); higher education (M Ed); international education (M Ed); language, literacy and culture (Ed D); learning, media and technology (M Ed, Ed S); mathematics, science, and learning technologies (Ed D); reading and writing (M Ed); research, educational measurement and psychometrics (Ed D); school counselor education (M Ed, Ed S); school psychology (M Ed, PhD, Ed S); science education (Ed S); secondary teacher education (M Ed); social justice education (M Ed, Ed D, Ed S); special education (M Ed, Ed D, Ed S); teacher education and school improvement (Ed D, Ed S). Electronic applications accepted.

College of Engineering *Program availability:* Part-time. Offers chemical engineering (MSChE, PhD); civil engineering (MSCE, PhD); electrical and computer engineering (MSECE, PhD); engineering (MS, MS Env E, MSCE, MSChE, MSECE, MSEM, MSIE, MSME, PhD); environmental and water resources engineering (MSCE); geotechnical engineering (MSCE); industrial engineering and operations research (MS, PhD); mechanical engineering (MSME, PhD); structural engineering and mechanics (MSCE); transportation engineering (MSCE). Electronic applications accepted.

College of Humanities and Fine Arts *Program availability:* Part-time. Offers Afro-American studies (MA, PhD); American studies (PhD); architecture (M Arch); art (MA, MFA); Asian languages and literatures (MA); Chinese (MA); collaborative piano (MM); comparative literature (MA, PhD); composition (MM); composition and rhetoric (PhD); conducting (MM); costume design (MFA); creative writing (MFA); design (MS); design in historic preservation (MS); directing (MFA); dramaturgy (MFA); English and American literature (MA, PhD); French (MAT); French and Francophone studies (MA, MAT); German and Scandinavian studies (MA, PhD); Hispanic literatures, cultures and linguistics (MA, PhD); history (MA, PhD); history of art and architecture (MA); humanities and fine arts (M Arch, MA, MAT, MFA, MM, MS, PhD); Italian studies (MAT); Japanese (MA); jazz composition/arranging (MM); Latin and classical humanities (MAT); lighting design (MFA); linguistics (MA, PhD); music education (MM, PhD); music history (MM); music theory (PhD); performance (MM); philosophy (MA, PhD); scenic design (MFA); Spanish and Portuguese studies (MA, MAT, PhD); teaching Spanish (MAT). Electronic applications accepted.

College of Natural Sciences *Program availability:* Part-time. Offers animal biotechnology and biomedical sciences (MS, PhD); applied mathematics (MS); astronomy (MS, PhD); biochemistry and molecular biology (MS, PhD); building systems (MS, PhD); chemistry (MS, PhD); clinical psychology (MS, PhD); cognitive psychology (MS, PhD); computer science (MS, PhD); developmental science (MS, PhD); environmental policy and human dimensions (MS, PhD); food science (MS, PhD); forest resources (MS, PhD); geography (MS); geosciences (MS, PhD); mathematics (MS, PhD); microbiology (MS, PhD); natural sciences (MA, PhD); physics (MS, PhD); polymer science and engineering (MS, PhD); psychology of peace and violence (MS, PhD); social psychology (MS, PhD); statistics (MS, PhD); sustainability science (MS); water, wetlands and watersheds (MS, PhD); wildlife and fisheries conservation (MS, PhD). Electronic applications accepted.

College of Nursing *Program availability:* Part-time, online learning. Offers adult gerontology primary care nurse practitioner (DNP); clinical nurse leader (MS); family nurse practitioner (DNP); nursing (PhD); public health nurse leader (DNP). Electronic applications accepted.

College of Social and Behavioral Sciences *Program availability:* Part-time. Offers anthropology (MA, PhD); communication (MA, PhD); economics (MA, PhD); labor studies (MS); landscape architecture (MLA); political science (MA, PhD); public policy and administration (MPP, MPPA); regional planning (MRP, PhD); resource economics (MS, PhD); social and behavioral sciences (MA, MLA, MPP, MPPA, MRP, MS, PhD); sociology (MA, PhD); union leadership and administration (MS). Electronic applications accepted.

Interdisciplinary Programs *Program availability:* Part-time. Offers animal behavior and learning (PhD); biochemistry and metabolism (MS, PhD); biological chemistry and molecular biophysics (PhD); biomedicine (PhD); cell biology and physiology (MS, PhD); cellular and developmental biology (PhD); environmental, ecological and integrative biology (MS, PhD); genetics and evolution (MS, PhD); interdisciplinary studies (MS, PhD); marine science and technology (MS, PhD); molecular and cellular neuroscience (PhD); neural and behavioral development (PhD); neuroendocrinology (PhD); neuroscience and behavior (MS); organismic and evolutionary biology (MS, PhD); sensorimotor, cognitive, and computational neuroscience (PhD). Electronic applications accepted.

Isenberg School of Management *Program availability:* Part-time, evening/weekend, online learning. Offers accounting (MSA); business administration (MBA); entrepreneurship (MBA); finance (MBA, PhD); healthcare administration (MBA); hospitality and tourism management (PhD); management (MBA, MS, MSA, PhD); management science (PhD); marketing (MBA, PhD); organization studies (PhD); sport management (PhD); strategic management (PhD). Electronic applications accepted.

School of Public Health and Health Sciences *Program availability:* Part-time, evening/weekend, online learning. Offers audiology (Au D, PhD); biostatistics (MPH, MS, PhD); clinical audiology (MS); community health education (MPH, MS, PhD); community nutrition (MS); environmental health sciences (MPH, MS, PhD); epidemiology (MPH, MS, PhD); health policy and management (MPH, MS, PhD); kinesiology (MS, PhD); nutrition (MPH, MS, PhD); nutrition science (MS); public health and health sciences (MA, MPH, MS, Au D, PhD); public health practice (MPH); speech-language pathology (MA, PhD). Electronic applications accepted.

UNIVERSITY OF MASSACHUSETTS BOSTON, Boston, MA 02125-3393

General Information State-supported, coed, university. CGS member. *Enrollment:* 16,155 graduate, professional, and undergraduate students; 1,228 full-time matriculated graduate/professional students (805 women), 1,943 part-time matriculated graduate/professional students (1,351 women). *Enrollment by degree level:* 2,076 master's, 806 doctoral, 289 other advanced degrees. *Graduate faculty:* 718 full-time (371 women), 445 part-time/adjunct (270 women). *International tuition:* $34,932 full-time. *Tuition, area resident:* Full-time $17,896. Tuition, state resident: full-time $17,896. Tuition, nonresident: full-time $34,932. *Required fees:* $355. *Graduate housing:* On-campus housing not available. *Student services:* Campus employment opportunities, campus safety program, career counseling, child daycare facilities, exercise/wellness program, free psychological counseling, international student services, low-cost health insurance, multicultural affairs office, services for students with disabilities, teacher training, writing training. *Library facilities:* Joseph P. Healey Library. *Collection:* Books: 459,163 (physical), 547,086 (digital/electronic); Databases: 124.

Computer facilities: 350 computers available on campus for general student use. A campuswide network can be accessed from off campus. Online class registration is available.
Website: http://www.umb.edu/

General Application Contact: Graduate Admissions Coordinator, 617-287-6400, Fax: 617-287-6236, E-mail: graduate.admissions@umb.edu.

GRADUATE UNITS

College of Advancing and Professional Studies Students: 22 full-time (17 women), 119 part-time (94 women); includes 2 minority (1 American Indian or Alaska Native, non-Hispanic/Latino; 1 Hispanic/Latino), 1 international. Average age 40. 53 applicants, 60% accepted, 38 enrolled. *Faculty:* 2 full-time (1 woman), 35 part-time/adjunct (18 women). Expenses: Contact institution. In 2018, 36 master's, 48 other advanced degrees awarded. *Program availability:* Online learning. Offers critical and creative thinking (MA, Certificate); instructional design (M Ed, Certificate). *Application fee:* $60 ($100 for international students). Electronic applications accepted. *Application Contact:* Graduate Admissions Coordinator, 617-287-6400, Fax: 617-287-6236, E-mail: graduate.admissions@umb.edu. *Dean,* Dr. Philip DiSalvio, 617-287-7926, Fax: 617-287-5699, E-mail: philip.disalvio@umb.edu.

College of Education and Human Development Students: 339 full-time (269 women), 384 part-time (280 women); includes 21 minority (10 Black or African American, non-Hispanic/Latino; 6 Asian, non-Hispanic/Latino; 5 Hispanic/Latino), 1 international. Average age 33. 779 applicants, 56% accepted, 300 enrolled. *Faculty:* 50 full-time (35 women), 42 part-time/adjunct (31 women). Expenses: Contact institution. *Financial support:* Research assistantships, teaching assistantships, career-related internships or fieldwork, Federal Work-Study, and unspecified assistantships available. Support available to part-time students. Financial award application deadline: 3/1; financial award applicants required to submit FAFSA. In 2018, 226 master's, 16 doctorates, 43 other advanced degrees awarded. *Program availability:* Part-time, evening/weekend. Offers counseling and school psychology (PhD); early childhood education and care (PhD); education (M Ed, Ed D, PhD); education and human development (M Ed, MS, Ed D, PhD, CAGS); educational administration (M Ed, CAGS); family therapy (MS); higher education (Ed D, PhD); mental health counseling (MS); school counseling (M Ed); school psychology (M Ed); special education (M Ed); urban education, leadership, and policy studies (Ed D, PhD). *Application deadline:* For fall admission, 3/1 for domestic students. *Application fee:* $60 ($100 for international students). Electronic applications accepted. *Application Contact:* Graduate Admissions Coordinator, 617-287-6400, Fax: 617-287-6236, E-mail: graduate.admissions@umb.edu. *Dean,* Dr. Joseph B Berger, 617-287-7600, E-mail: Joseph.Berger@umb.edu.

College of Liberal Arts Students: 215 full-time (152 women), 340 part-time (220 women); includes 91 minority (27 Black or African American, non-Hispanic/Latino; 1 American Indian or Alaska Native, non-Hispanic/Latino; 35 Asian, non-Hispanic/Latino; 27 Hispanic/Latino; 1 Two or more races, non-Hispanic/Latino), 15 international. Average age 32. 641 applicants, 41% accepted, 153 enrolled. *Faculty:* 330 full-time (186 women), 151 part-time/adjunct (76 women). Expenses: Contact institution. *Financial support:* Research assistantships, teaching assistantships, career-related internships or fieldwork, Federal Work-Study, and unspecified assistantships available. Support available to part-time students. Financial award application deadline: 3/1. In 2018, 148 master's, 13 doctorates awarded. *Program availability:* Part-time, evening/weekend. Offers American studies (MA); applied economics (MA); applied linguistics (MA, PhD); applied sociology (MA); archival methods (MA); clinical psychology (PhD); creative writing (MFA); developmental and brain sciences (MA); English (MA); historical archaeology (MA); Latin and classical humanities (MA); liberal arts (MA, MFA, MS, PhD); sociology (PhD); transnational, cultural, and community studies (MS). *Application fee:* $60 ($100 for international students). Electronic applications accepted. *Application Contact:* Graduate Admissions Coordinator, 617-287-6400, Fax: 617-287-6236, E-mail: graduate.admissions@ umb.edu. *Dean,* David Terkla, 617-287-6500, E-mail: david.terkla@umb.edu.

College of Management Students: 208 full-time (101 women), 268 part-time (135 women); includes 24 minority (3 Black or African American, non-Hispanic/Latino; 19 Asian, non-Hispanic/Latino; 2 Hispanic/Latino), 11 international. Average age 31. 346 applicants, 73% accepted, 172 enrolled. *Faculty:* 72 full-time (25 women), 29 part-time/adjunct (8 women). Expenses: Contact institution. *Financial support:* Research assistantships, teaching assistantships, career-related internships or fieldwork, Federal Work-Study, and unspecified assistantships available. Support available to part-time students. Financial award application deadline: 3/1; financial award applicants required to submit FAFSA. In 2018, 241 master's awarded. *Program availability:* Part-time, evening/weekend. Offers accounting (MS); business administration (MBA); business analytics (MS); finance (MS); information technology (MS); international management (MS); management (MBA, MS). *Application fee:* $60 ($100 for international students). Electronic applications accepted. *Application Contact:* Graduate Admissions Coordinator, 617-287-6400, Fax: 617-287-6236, E-mail: graduate.admissions@ umb.edu. *Associate Professor,* Dr. Nardia Haigh, 617-287.7731, E-mail: Nardia.Haigh@ umb.edu.

College of Nursing and Health Sciences Students: 83 full-time (65 women), 282 part-time (253 women); includes 15 minority (6 Black or African American, non-Hispanic/Latino; 8 Asian, non-Hispanic/Latino; 1 Hispanic/Latino), 4 international. Average age 36. 211 applicants, 92% accepted, 122 enrolled. *Faculty:* 57 full-time (49 women), 92 part-time/adjunct (84 women). Expenses: Contact institution. *Financial support:* Research assistantships, teaching assistantships, career-related internships or fieldwork, Federal Work-Study, and unspecified assistantships available. Support available to part-time students. Financial award application deadline: 3/1; financial award applicants required to submit FAFSA. In 2018, 62 master's, 17 doctorates awarded. *Program availability:* Part-time, evening/weekend. Offers exercise and health sciences (MS, PhD); nursing (MS, DNP, MS); nursing practice (DNP). *Application fee:* $60 ($100 for international students). Electronic applications accepted. *Application Contact:* Graduate Admissions Coordinator, 617-287-6400, Fax: 617-287-6236, E-mail: graduate.admissions@umb.edu. *Dean and Professor,* Dr. Linda S. Thompson, 617-287-7500, E-mail: linda.thompson@umb.edu.

College of Public and Community Service 2 applicants, 0% accepted. Expenses: Contact institution. *Financial support:* Research assistantships, teaching assistantships, career-related internships or fieldwork, Federal Work-Study, and unspecified assistantships available. Support available to part-time students. Financial award application deadline: 3/1; financial award applicants required to submit FAFSA. *Program availability:* Part-time, evening/weekend. Offers human services (MS); public and community service (MS). *Application deadline:* For fall admission, 3/1 for domestic students. Applications are processed on a rolling basis. *Application Contact:* Stephanie Hartwell, Interim Dean, 617-287-6288, E-mail: stephanie.hartwell@umb.edu. *Dean,* Dr. Adenrele Awotona, 617-287-7112, Fax: 617-287-5544, E-mail: adenrele.awotona@umb.edu.

College of Science and Mathematics Students: 169 full-time (78 women), 98 part-time (28 women); includes 37 minority (5 Black or African American, non-Hispanic/Latino; 27 Asian, non-Hispanic/Latino; 5 Hispanic/Latino), 10 international. Average age 30. 268 applicants, 50% accepted, 60 enrolled. *Faculty:* 131 full-time (38 women), 36 part-time/adjunct (15 women). Expenses: Contact institution. *Financial support:* Research assistantships, teaching assistantships, career-related internships or fieldwork, Federal Work-Study, institutionally sponsored loans, and unspecified assistantships available. Support available to part-time students. Financial award application deadline: 3/1; financial award applicants required to submit FAFSA. In 2018, 71 master's, 16 doctorates awarded. *Program availability:* Part-time, evening/weekend. Offers applied physics (MS); biology (MS, PhD); biomedical engineering and biotechnology (PhD); biotechnology and biomedical sciences (MS); chemistry (MS, PhD); computational sciences (PhD); computer science (MS, PhD); integrative biosciences (PhD); science and mathematics (MS, PhD). *Application deadline:* Applications are processed on a rolling basis. *Application fee:* $60 ($100 for international students). Electronic applications accepted. *Application Contact:* Dr. William Hagar, Associate Dean, 617-287-5776, E-mail: William.Hagar@umb.edu. *Associate Dean,* Dr. William Hagar, 617-287-5776, E-mail: William.Hagar@umb.edu.

Graduate School of Global Inclusion and Social Development Students: 33 full-time (26 women), 217 part-time (183 women); includes 8 minority (1 Black or African American, non-Hispanic/Latino; 6 Asian, non-Hispanic/Latino; 1 Hispanic/Latino). Average age 38. 141 applicants, 79% accepted, 88 enrolled. *Faculty:* 9 full-time (8 women), 16 part-time/adjunct (12 women). Expenses: Contact institution. In 2018, 66 master's, 1 doctorate awarded. Offers global inclusion and social development (M Ed, MA, MS, PhD); rehabilitation counseling (MS); vision studies (M Ed). *Application fee:* $60 ($100 for international students). Electronic applications accepted. *Application Contact:* Graduate Admissions Coordinator, 617-287-6400, Fax: 617-287-6236, E-mail: graduate.admissions@umb.edu. *Program Coordinator,* Kaitlyn Siner-Cappas, 617-287.3070, E-mail: Kaitlyn.Siner@umb.edu.

McCormack Graduate School of Policy and Global Studies Students: 113 full-time (73 women), 200 part-time (138 women); includes 5 minority (3 Black or African American, non-Hispanic/Latino; 2 Asian, non-Hispanic/Latino), 3 international. Average age 36. 167 applicants, 72% accepted, 78 enrolled. *Faculty:* 33 full-time (19 women), 19 part-time/adjunct (13 women). Expenses: Contact institution. *Financial support:* Research assistantships, teaching assistantships, career-related internships or fieldwork, Federal Work-Study, and unspecified assistantships available. Support available to part-time students. Financial award application deadline: 3/1; financial award applicants required to submit FAFSA. In 2018, 99 master's, 12 doctorates, 19 other advanced degrees awarded. *Program availability:* Part-time, evening/weekend. Offers conflict resolution (MA, Certificate); gerontology (PhD); global comparative public administration (MPA); global governance and human security (MA); international relations (MA); policy and global studies (MA, MPA, MS, PhD, Certificate); public administration (MPA); public policy (MS, PhD). *Application fee:* $60 ($100 for international students). Electronic applications accepted. *Application Contact:* Graduate Admissions Coordinator, 617-287-6400, Fax: 617-287-6236, E-mail: graduate.admissions@umb.edu. *Dean,* Dr. David Cash, 617-287-5511, E-mail: david.cash@umb.edu.

School for the Environment Students: 46 full-time (24 women), 35 part-time (20 women); includes 5 minority (all Asian, non-Hispanic/Latino), 6 international. Average age 30. 36 applicants, 64% accepted, 14 enrolled. *Faculty:* 24 full-time (6 women), 9 part-time/adjunct (3 women). Expenses: Contact institution. In 2018, 18 master's, 5 doctorates awarded. Offers environment (MS, PSM, PhD); environmental sciences (MS, PhD); marine science and technology (MS, PhD); urban planning and community development (MS). *Application fee:* $60 ($100 for international students). Electronic applications accepted. *Application Contact:* Graduate Admissions Coordinator, 617-287-6400, Fax: 617-287-6236, E-mail: graduate.admissions@umb.edu. *Professor,* Dr. Adenrele Awotona, 617-287.5544, Fax: 617-287.7112, E-mail: adenrele.awotona@umb.edu.

UNIVERSITY OF MASSACHUSETTS DARTMOUTH, North Dartmouth, MA 02747-2300

General Information State-supported, coed, university. *Enrollment:* 8,513 graduate, professional, and undergraduate students; 636 full-time matriculated graduate/professional students (333 women), 1,036 part-time matriculated graduate/professional students (586 women). *Enrollment by degree level:* 1,017 master's, 490 doctoral, 94 other advanced degrees. *Graduate faculty:* 306 full-time (144 women), 128 part-time/adjunct (70 women). *Graduate housing:* Room and/or apartments available on a first-come, first-served basis to single students; on-campus housing not available to married students. Housing application deadline: 3/14. *Student services:* Campus employment opportunities, campus safety program, career counseling, exercise/wellness program, free psychological counseling, grant writing training, international student services, low-cost health insurance, multicultural affairs office, services for students with disabilities, teacher training, writing training. *Library facilities:* Claire T. Carney Library. *Collection:* Books: 242,682 (physical), 80,828 (digital/electronic); Serial titles: 1,348 (physical), 110,141 (digital/electronic); Databases: 142. Students can reserve study rooms.

Computer facilities: Computer purchase and lease plans are available. 400 computers available on campus for general student use. A campuswide network can be accessed from student residence rooms and from off campus. Online class registration is available.

Website: http://www.umassd.edu/

General Application Contact: Scott Webster, Director of Graduate Studies and Admission, 508-999-8604, Fax: 508-999-8183, E-mail: graduate@umassd.edu.

GRADUATE UNITS

Graduate School Students: 609 full-time (319 women), 957 part-time (531 women); includes 305 minority (75 Black or African American, non-Hispanic/Latino; 4 American Indian or Alaska Native, non-Hispanic/Latino; 68 Asian, non-Hispanic/Latino; 111 Hispanic/Latino; 1 Native Hawaiian or other Pacific Islander, non-Hispanic/Latino; 46 Two or more races, non-Hispanic/Latino), 254 international. Average age 32. 2,027 applicants, 68% accepted, 555 enrolled. *Faculty:* 317 full-time (146 women), 123 part-time/adjunct (77 women). Expenses: Contact institution. *Financial support:* In 2018–19, 42 fellowships (averaging $10,281 per year), 97 research assistantships (averaging $14,441 per year), 121 teaching assistantships (averaging $11,206 per year) were awarded; tuition waivers (full and partial) and instructional assistantships, dissertation writing support, doctoral support, studio assistantships also available. Financial award application deadline: 3/1; financial award applicants required to submit FAFSA. In 2018, 461 master's, 92 doctorates, 69 other advanced degrees awarded. *Program availability:* Part-time, 100% online, blended/hybrid learning. Offers data science (MS); nursing (MS, DNP, PhD). *Application fee:* $60. Electronic applications accepted. *Application Contact:* Scott Webster, Director of Graduate Studies and Admissions, 508-999-8604, Fax: 508-999-8183, E-mail: graduate@umassd.edu. *Director of Graduate Studies and Admissions,* Scott Webster, 508-999-8202, Fax: 508-999-8183, E-mail: graduate@umassd.edu.

Charlton College of Business Average age 32. 233 applicants, 86% accepted, 145 enrolled. Expenses: Contact institution. *Financial support:* In 2018–19, 2 research assistantships (averaging $8,000 per year) were awarded; teaching assistantships, tuition waivers (full and partial), and unspecified assistantships also available. Support available to part-time students. Financial award application deadline: 3/1; financial award applicants required to submit FAFSA. In 2018, 190 master's, 21 other advanced degrees awarded. *Program availability:* Part-time, 100% online, blended/hybrid learning. Offers accounting (MS, Postbaccalaureate Certificate); accounting and finance (MS, Postbaccalaureate Certificate); business administration (MBA); decision and information sciences (MS); finance (Postbaccalaureate Certificate); healthcare management (MS); technology management (MS). *Application deadline:* For fall admission, 8/1 priority date for domestic students, 7/1 priority date for international students; for spring admission, 11/15 priority date for domestic students, 10/15 priority date for international students. *Application fee:* $60. Electronic applications accepted. *Application Contact:* Steven Briggs, Director of

Recruitment and Marketing for Graduate Studies, 508-999-8604, Fax: 508-999-8183, E-mail: graduate@umassd.edu. *Assistant Dean of Graduate Programs*, Melissa Pacheco, 508-999-8543, Fax: 508-999-8646, E-mail: mpacheco@umassd.edu.

College of Arts and Sciences Students: 103 full-time (68 women), 162 part-time (113 women); includes 44 minority (10 Black or African American, non-Hispanic/Latino; 9 Asian, non-Hispanic/Latino; 19 Hispanic/Latino; 6 Two or more races, non-Hispanic/Latino), 26 international. Average age 31. 229 applicants, 64% accepted, 88 enrolled. *Faculty:* 103 full-time (51 women), 31 part-time/adjunct (20 women). Expenses: Contact institution. *Financial support:* In 2018–19, fellowships (averaging $3,000 per year), 15 research assistantships (averaging $11,399 per year), 48 teaching assistantships (averaging $13,927 per year) were awarded; career-related internships or fieldwork, traineeships, tuition waivers (full and partial), unspecified assistantships, and dissertation writing support also available. Financial award application deadline: 3/1; financial award applicants required to submit FAFSA. In 2018, 69 master's, 3 doctorates, 25 other advanced degrees awarded. *Program availability:* Part-time, 100% online, blended/hybrid learning. Offers arts and sciences (MA, MAT, MPP, MS, Ed D, PhD, Graduate Certificate, Post-Master's Certificate, Postbaccalaureate Certificate); autism studies (Graduate Certificate); biology (MS); chemistry (MS, PhD); educational leadership (Ed D, PhD); educational leadership and policy studies (Ed D, PhD); educational policy (Graduate Certificate); English as a second language (Postbaccalaureate Certificate); environmental policy (Graduate Certificate); integrative biology (PhD); Luso-Afro Brazilian studies and theory (PhD); marine biology (MS); mathematics education (PhD); middle school education (MAT); Portuguese studies (MA); professional writing (MA, Postbaccalaureate Certificate); psychology - applied behavioral analysis (MA, Post-Master's Certificate); psychology - clinical (MA); psychology - research (MA); public management (Graduate Certificate); public policy (MPP); secondary school education (MAT); STEM education and teacher development (MAT, PhD, Postbaccalaureate Certificate). *Application fee:* $60. *Application Contact:* Scott Webster, Director of Graduate Studies & Admissions, 508-999-8604, Fax: 508-999-8183, E-mail: graduate@umassd.edu. *Interim Dean, College of Arts and Sciences,* Amy Shapiro, 508-910-9101, E-mail: ashapiro@umassd.edu.

College of Engineering Students: 133 full-time (40 women), 150 part-time (35 women); includes 36 minority (7 Black or African American, non-Hispanic/Latino; 8 Asian, non-Hispanic/Latino; 14 Hispanic/Latino; 7 Two or more races, non-Hispanic/Latino), 135 international. Average age 28. 317 applicants, 78% accepted, 82 enrolled. *Faculty:* 61 full-time (16 women), 5 part-time/adjunct (0 women). Expenses: Contact institution. *Financial support:* In 2018–19, 12 fellowships (averaging $18,583 per year), 49 research assistantships (averaging $13,426 per year), 50 teaching assistantships (averaging $10,546 per year) were awarded; tuition waivers (full and partial), unspecified assistantships, and doctoral support, dissertation writing support also available. Financial award application deadline: 3/1; financial award applicants required to submit FAFSA. In 2018, 106 master's, 11 doctorates, 5 other advanced degrees awarded. *Program availability:* Part-time, 100% online, blended/hybrid learning. Offers biomedical engineering/biotechnology (PhD); civil engineering (MS); communications (Postbaccalaureate Certificate); computer science (MS, Graduate Certificate); computing infrastructure security (Postbaccalaureate Certificate); digital signal processing (Postbaccalaureate Certificate); electrical engineering (MS, PhD); electrical engineering systems (Postbaccalaureate Certificate); engineering (MS, PhD, Graduate Certificate, Postbaccalaureate Certificate); engineering and applied science (PhD); industrial and systems engineering (Postbaccalaureate Certificate); mechanical engineering (MS); physics (MS); software development and design (Postbaccalaureate Certificate). *Application fee:* $60. Electronic applications accepted. *Application Contact:* Scott Webster, Director of Graduate Studies & Admissions, 508-999-8406, Fax: 508-999-8183, E-mail: graduate@umassd.edu. *Dean, College of Engineering,* Jean VanderGheynst, 508-999-8539, Fax: 508-999-9137, E-mail: jvandergheynst@umassd.edu.

College of Visual and Performing Arts Students: 28 full-time (19 women), 33 part-time (25 women); includes 7 minority (1 Black or African American, non-Hispanic/Latino; 1 Asian, non-Hispanic/Latino; 4 Hispanic/Latino; 1 Two or more races, non-Hispanic/Latino), 6 international. Average age 34. 68 applicants, 56% accepted, 15 enrolled. *Faculty:* 40 full-time (22 women), 15 part-time/adjunct (9 women). Expenses: Contact institution. *Financial support:* In 2018–19, 16 fellowships (averaging $5,175 per year), 2 teaching assistantships (averaging $2,700 per year) were awarded; tuition waivers (full and partial) also available. Financial award application deadline: 3/1; financial award applicants required to submit FAFSA. In 2018, 19 master's, 6 other advanced degrees awarded. *Program availability:* Part-time. Offers art education, art history and media studies (MAE); artisanry (MFA, Postbaccalaureate Certificate); fine arts (MFA, Postbaccalaureate Certificate); visual and performing arts (MAE, MFA, Postbaccalaureate Certificate); visual design (MFA). *Application fee:* $60. Electronic applications accepted. *Application Contact:* Scott Webster, Director of Graduate Studies and Admissions, 508-999-8604, Fax: 508-999-8183, E-mail: graduate@umassd.edu. *Dean, College of Visual and Performing Arts,* Lawrence Jenkens, 508-999-9286, E-mail: lawrence.jenkens@umassd.edu.

School for Marine Science and Technology Students: 21 full-time (13 women), 31 part-time (15 women); includes 3 minority (1 Asian, non-Hispanic/Latino; 2 Two or more races, non-Hispanic/Latino), 8 international. Average age 31. 30 applicants, 73% accepted, 10 enrolled. *Faculty:* 14 full-time (1 woman). Expenses: Contact institution. *Financial support:* In 2018–19, 3 fellowships (averaging $14,000 per year), 30 research assistantships (averaging $17,994 per year), 1 teaching assistantship (averaging $9,250 per year) were awarded; tuition waivers (full and partial) and doctoral support, dissertation writing support also available. Financial award application deadline: 3/1; financial award applicants required to submit FAFSA. In 2018, 7 master's, 4 doctorates awarded. *Program availability:* Part-time. Offers coastal and ocean administration science and technology (MS); marine science and technology (MS, PhD). *Application deadline:* For fall admission, 2/15 priority date for domestic students, 1/15 priority date for international students; for spring admission, 11/15 priority date for domestic students, 10/15 priority date for international students. *Application fee:* $60. Electronic applications accepted. *Application Contact:* Scott Webster, Director of Graduate Studies and Admissions, 508-999-8604, Fax: 508-999-8183, E-mail: graduate@umassd.edu. *Dean, School for Marine Science and Technology,* Steven Lohrenz, 508-910-6550, E-mail: slohrenz@umassd.edu.

University of Massachusetts School of Law–Dartmouth Students: 169 full-time (91 women), 55 part-time (29 women); includes 69 minority (19 Black or African American, non-Hispanic/Latino; 2 American Indian or Alaska Native, non-Hispanic/Latino; 9 Asian, non-Hispanic/Latino; 28 Hispanic/Latino; 1 Native Hawaiian or other Pacific Islander, non-Hispanic/Latino; 10 Two or more races, non-Hispanic/Latino), 4 international. Average age 30. 958 applicants, 57% accepted, 94 enrolled. *Faculty:* 15 full-time (7 women), 11 part-time/adjunct (2 women). Expenses: Contact institution. *Financial support:* Fellowships, research assistantships, teaching assistantships, and tuition waivers available. Financial award application deadline:

3/1; financial award applicants required to submit FAFSA. In 2018, 49 doctorates awarded. *Program availability:* Part-time, evening/weekend. Offers law (JD). *Application deadline:* For fall admission, 6/30 priority date for domestic students, 5/30 priority date for international students. *Application fee:* $60. Electronic applications accepted. *Application Contact:* Nancy Hebert, Assistant Director of Law School Recruiting & Marketing, 508-985-1110, Fax: 508-985-1175, E-mail: lawadmissions@umassd.edu. *Assistant Dean,* Daniel Fitzpatrick, 508-985-1109, Fax: 508-985-1175, E-mail: lawadmissions@umassd.edu.

UNIVERSITY OF MASSACHUSETTS LOWELL, Lowell, MA 01854

General Information State-supported, coed, university. CGS member. *Graduate housing:* Rooms and/or apartments available on a first-come, first-served basis to single students and available to married students. Housing application deadline: 4/1.

GRADUATE UNITS

College of Fine Arts, Humanities and Social Sciences Offers community social psychology (MA); fine arts, humanities and social sciences (MA, MM, PhD); music education (MM); peace and conflict studies (MA); regional economic and social development (MA, Graduate Certificate).

School of Criminology and Justice Studies *Program availability:* Part-time, evening/weekend. Offers criminal justice (MA). Electronic applications accepted.

College of Health Sciences *Program availability:* Part-time. Offers cleaner production and pollution prevention (Sc D); clinical laboratory sciences (MS); health sciences (MS, DNP, DPT, PhD); physical therapy (DPT).

School of Nursing Offers adult/gerontological nursing (MS); family health nursing (MS); nursing (DNP, PhD).

College of Sciences *Program availability:* Part-time, evening/weekend. Offers analytical chemistry (PhD); biochemistry (PhD); biological sciences (MS); chemistry (MS, PhD); computer science (MS, PhD); environmental studies (PhD); green chemistry (PhD); inorganic chemistry (PhD); mathematical sciences (Ed D); organic chemistry (PhD); physics (MS, PhD); polymer science (MS); radiological sciences and protection (MS, PSM); sciences (MA, MM, MS, Ed D, PhD).

Francis College of Engineering *Program availability:* Part-time, evening/weekend. Offers chemical engineering (MS Eng, PhD); computer engineering (MS Eng, PhD); electrical engineering (MS Eng, PhD); energy engineering (MS Eng, PhD); engineering (MS, MS Eng, PhD); environmental studies (PhD); mechanical engineering (MS Eng, PhD); plastics engineering (MS Eng, PhD).

Graduate School of Education *Program availability:* Part-time, evening/weekend, online learning. Offers curriculum and instruction (M Ed). Electronic applications accepted.

Manning School of Business *Program availability:* Part-time, evening/weekend. Offers business administration (MBA, PhD); healthcare innovation and entrepreneurship (MS).

UNIVERSITY OF MASSACHUSETTS MEDICAL SCHOOL, Worcester, MA 01655-0115

General Information State-supported, coed, graduate-only institution. CGS member. *Graduate housing:* On-campus housing not available. *Research affiliation:* Abbott Bioresearch Center (biomedical research and training), Charles River Laboratories (pre-clinical biomedical research).

GRADUATE UNITS

Graduate School of Biomedical Sciences Offers biomedical sciences (PhD); biomedical sciences (millennium program) (PhD); clinical and population health research (PhD); clinical investigation (MS). Electronic applications accepted.

Graduate School of Nursing Offers adult gerontological acute care nurse practitioner (DNP, Post Master's Certificate); adult gerontological primary care nurse practitioner (DNP, Post Master's Certificate); family nursing practitioner (DNP); nurse administrator (DNP); nurse educator (MS, Post Master's Certificate); nursing (PhD). Electronic applications accepted.

School of Medicine Offers medicine (MD). Electronic applications accepted.

UNIVERSITY OF MEMPHIS, Memphis, TN 38152

General Information State-supported, coed, university. CGS member. *Enrollment:* 21,458 graduate, professional, and undergraduate students; 1,908 full-time matriculated graduate/professional students (1,110 women), 2,118 part-time matriculated graduate/professional students (1,349 women). *Enrollment by degree level:* 2,508 master's, 1,364 doctoral, 154 other advanced degrees. *Graduate faculty:* 546 full-time (223 women), 108 part-time/adjunct (44 women). *Tuition, area resident:* Full-time $10,240; part-time $503 per credit hour. *Tuition, state resident:* full-time $10,464. *Tuition, nonresident:* full-time $20,224; part-time $991 per credit hour. *Required fees:* $850; $106 per credit hour. *Graduate housing:* Rooms and/or apartments available on a first-come, first-served basis to single and married students. *Student services:* Campus employment opportunities, campus safety program, career counseling, child daycare facilities, exercise/wellness program, free psychological counseling, grant writing training, international student services, multicultural affairs office, services for students with disabilities, teacher training, writing training. *Library facilities:* McWherter Library plus 4 others. *Collection:* Books: 1.4 million (physical), 315,573 (digital/electronic); Serial titles: 17,630 (physical), 256,700 (digital/electronic); Databases: 400. Weekly public service hours: 91; students can reserve study rooms.

Computer facilities: 1,255 computers available on campus for general student use. A campuswide network can be accessed from student residence rooms and from off campus. Online class registration is available. Website: http://www.memphis.edu/

General Application Contact: Dr. Robin Poston, Dean of the Graduate School, 901-678-5739, Fax: 901-678-0378, E-mail: graduateschool@memphis.edu.

GRADUATE UNITS

Cecil C. Humphreys School of Law Students: 312 (137 women); includes 79 minority (60 Black or African American, non-Hispanic/Latino; 5 American Indian or Alaska Native, non-Hispanic/Latino; 5 Asian, non-Hispanic/Latino; 9 Hispanic/Latino). Average age 25. 647 applicants, 52% accepted, 107 enrolled. *Faculty:* 27 full-time (13 women), 31 part-time/adjunct (5 women). Expenses: Contact institution. *Financial support:* In 2018–19, 140 students received support, including 26 fellowships (averaging $12,118 per year), 20 research assistantships (averaging $5,000 per year); teaching assistantships, career-related internships or fieldwork, Federal Work-Study, scholarships/grants, and tuition waivers (partial) also available. Support available to part-time students. Financial award application deadline: 5/1; financial award applicants required to submit FAFSA. In 2018, 1 doctorate awarded. *Program availability:* Part-time. Offers law (JD). *Application deadline:* For fall admission, 3/15 priority date for domestic and international students. Applications are processed on a rolling basis. *Application fee:* $0 ($40 for international students). Electronic applications accepted. *Application Contact:* Dr. Sue Ann McClellan,

Assistant Dean for Law Admissions, Recruiting and Scholarships, 901-678-5403, Fax: 901-678-0741, E-mail: smcclell@memphis.edu. *Dean,* Katharine Traylor Schaffzin, 901-678-1623, Fax: 901-678-5210, E-mail: ktschffz@memphis.edu.

Graduate School Students: 1,908 full-time (1,110 women), 2,118 part-time (1,349 women); includes 1,381 minority (973 Black or African American, non-Hispanic/Latino; 5 American Indian or Alaska Native, non-Hispanic/Latino; 194 Asian, non-Hispanic/Latino; 130 Hispanic/Latino; 79 Two or more races, non-Hispanic/Latino; 420 international. Average age 32. 3,040 applicants, 69% accepted, 1169 enrolled. *Faculty:* 546 full-time (223 women), 108 part-time/adjunct (44 women). Expenses: Contact institution. *Financial support:* Fellowships with full tuition reimbursements, research assistantships with full tuition reimbursements, teaching assistantships with full tuition reimbursements, career-related internships or fieldwork, Federal Work-Study, institutionally sponsored loans, scholarships/grants, and unspecified assistantships available. Support available to part-time students. Financial award application deadline: 2/1; financial award applicants required to submit FAFSA. In 2018, 952 master's, 241 doctorates, 177 other advanced degrees awarded. *Program availability:* Part-time, evening/weekend, 100% online, blended/hybrid learning. *Application deadline:* For fall admission, 7/1 for domestic students, 5/1 for international students; for spring admission, 12/1 for domestic students, 9/15 for international students. Applications are processed on a rolling basis. *Application fee:* $35 ($60 for international students). Electronic applications accepted. *Application Contact:* Dr. James Kierulff, Director of Graduate Student Services, 901-678-4370, Fax: 901-678-0378, E-mail: graduateadmission@memphis.edu. *Dean of the Graduate School,* Dr. Robin Poston, 901-678-5739, Fax: 901-678-0378, E-mail: graduateschool@memphis.edu.

College of Arts and Sciences Students: 689 full-time (390 women), 399 part-time (226 women); includes 346 minority (222 Black or African American, non-Hispanic/Latino; 51 Asian, non-Hispanic/Latino; 43 Hispanic/Latino; 30 Two or more races, non-Hispanic/Latino; 192 international. Average age 31. 695 applicants, 62% accepted, 266 enrolled. *Faculty:* 210 full-time (79 women), 29 part-time/adjunct (15 women). Expenses: Contact institution. *Financial support:* Fellowships with full tuition reimbursements, research assistantships with full tuition reimbursements, teaching assistantships with full tuition reimbursements, career-related internships or fieldwork, Federal Work-Study, institutionally sponsored loans, scholarships/grants, tuition waivers (full and partial), and unspecified assistantships available. Financial award application deadline: 2/1; financial award applicants required to submit FAFSA. In 2018, 226 master's, 58 doctorates, 36 other advanced degrees awarded. *Program availability:* Part-time, evening/weekend. Offers adults and families (MSW); African-American literature (Graduate Certificate); analytical chemistry (MS, PhD); ancient Egyptian history (MA, PhD); applied linguistics (PhD); applied mathematics (MS); applied statistics (PhD); arts and sciences (MA, MCRP, MFA, MPA, MS, MSW, PhD, Ed S, Graduate Certificate); bioinformatics (MS); biology (MS, PhD); children, youth, and families (MSW); city and regional planning (MCRP); clinical psychology (PhD); composition studies (PhD); computational chemistry (MS, PhD); computational physics (MS); computer science (MS, PhD); creative writing (MFA); criminology and criminal justice (MA); earth sciences (MA, MS, PhD); English as a second language (MA); experimental psychology (PhD); general physics (MS); general psychology (MS); geographic information systems (Graduate Certificate); inorganic chemistry (MS, PhD); linguistics (MA); literary and cultural studies (PhD); literature (MA); local government management (Graduate Certificate); material science (MS); mathematics (MS, PhD); medical anthropology (MA); museum studies (Graduate Certificate); organic chemistry (MS, PhD); philanthropy and nonprofit leadership (Graduate Certificate); philosophy (MA, PhD); physical chemistry (PhD); political science (MA); professional writing (MA, PhD); romance languages (MA); school psychology (MA, PhD, Ed S); sociology (MA); statistics (MS); teaching English as a second/foreign language (Graduate Certificate); teaching of mathematics (MS); women's and gender studies (Graduate Certificate). *Application deadline:* Applications are processed on a rolling basis. *Application fee:* $35 ($60 for international students). Electronic applications accepted. *Application Contact:* Dr. Abby Parrill-Baker, Dean, 901-678-2251, Fax: 901-678-4831, E-mail: aparrill@memphis.edu. *Dean,* Dr. Abby Parrill-Baker, 901-678-2251, Fax: 901-678-4831, E-mail: aparrill@memphis.edu.

College of Communication and Fine Arts Students: 129 full-time (55 women), 118 part-time (65 women); includes 71 minority (36 Black or African American, non-Hispanic/Latino; 7 Asian, non-Hispanic/Latino; 17 Hispanic/Latino; 11 Two or more races, non-Hispanic/Latino; 17 international. Average age 32. 188 applicants, 74% accepted, 73 enrolled. *Faculty:* 91 full-time (36 women), 6 part-time/adjunct (1 woman). Expenses: Contact institution. *Financial support:* Research assistantships with full tuition reimbursements, teaching assistantships with full tuition reimbursements, career-related internships or fieldwork, Federal Work-Study, institutionally sponsored loans, scholarships/grants, and unspecified assistantships available. Financial award application deadline: 2/1; financial award applicants required to submit FAFSA. In 2018, 59 master's, 10 doctorates, 5 other advanced degrees awarded. *Program availability:* Part-time, online learning. Offers architecture (M Arch); art history (MA); ceramics (MFA); communication (MA); communication and fine arts (M Arch, M Mu, MA, MFA, DMA, PhD, Graduate Certificate); communication arts (PhD); composition (M Mu, DMA); conducting (M Mu, DMA); entrepreneurial journalism (Graduate Certificate); film and video production (MA); graphic design (MFA); jazz and studio music (M Mu); journalism and strategic media (MA); museum studies (Graduate Certificate); music education (M Mu, PhD); music theory (DCC); musicology (PhD); Orff-Schulwerk (M Mu); painting (MFA); pedagogy (M Mu); performance (M Mu, DMA); printmaking/photography (MFA); sculpture (MFA); theatre (MFA). *Application deadline:* Applications are processed on a rolling basis. *Application fee:* $35 ($60 for international students). Electronic applications accepted. *Application Contact:* Dr. Anne Hogan, Dean, 901-678-2350, Fax: 901-678-5118, E-mail: anne.hogan@memphis.edu. *Dean,* Dr. Anne Hogan, 901-678-2350, Fax: 901-678-5118, E-mail: anne.hogan@memphis.edu.

College of Education Students: 219 full-time (172 women), 689 part-time (521 women); includes 396 minority (337 Black or African American, non-Hispanic/Latino; 1 American Indian or Alaska Native, non-Hispanic/Latino; 13 Asian, non-Hispanic/Latino; 32 Hispanic/Latino; 13 Two or more races, non-Hispanic/Latino; 10 international. Average age 35. 344 applicants, 83% accepted, 240 enrolled. *Faculty:* 60 full-time (38 women), 28 part-time/adjunct (18 women). Expenses: Contact institution. *Financial support:* Research assistantships with full tuition reimbursements, teaching assistantships with full tuition reimbursements, career-related internships or fieldwork, Federal Work-Study, scholarships/grants, tuition waivers (partial), and unspecified assistantships available. Financial award application deadline: 2/1; financial award applicants required to submit FAFSA. In 2018, 163 master's, 49 doctorates, 63 other advanced degrees awarded. *Program availability:* Part-time, evening/weekend, 100% online, blended/hybrid learning. Offers adult education (Ed D); advanced studies in teaching and learning (M Ed); applied behavior

analysis (Graduate Certificate); autism studies (Graduate Certificate); community college teaching and leadership (Graduate Certificate); community education (Ed D); counseling (MS, Ed D); counseling psychology (PhD); early childhood education (MAT, MS, Ed D); education (M Ed, MAT, MS, Ed D, PhD, Graduate Certificate); educational leadership (Ed D); educational psychology and research (MS, PhD); elementary education (MAT); higher education (Ed D); instruction and curriculum (MS, Ed D); instruction design and technology (MS, Ed D); instructional design and technology (Graduate Certificate); leadership (MS); literacy, leadership, and coaching (Graduate Certificate); policy studies (Ed D); reading (MS, Ed D); school administration and supervision (MS); school library information specialist (Graduate Certificate); secondary education (MAT); special education (MAT, MS, Ed D); STEM teacher leadership (Graduate Certificate); student personnel (MS); urban education (Graduate Certificate). *Application deadline:* Applications are processed on a rolling basis. *Application fee:* $35 ($60 for international students). Electronic applications accepted. *Application Contact:* Stormey Warren, Graduate Programs, 901-678-2363, Fax: 901-678-4778, E-mail: shutsell@memphis.edu. *Dean,* Dr. Kandi Hill-Clarke, 901-678-5495, Fax: 901-678-4778, E-mail: k.hill-clarke@memphis.edu.

Fogelman College of Business and Economics Students: 256 full-time (132 women), 454 part-time (188 women); includes 236 minority (129 Black or African American, non-Hispanic/Latino; 1 American Indian or Alaska Native, non-Hispanic/Latino; 80 Asian, non-Hispanic/Latino; 14 Hispanic/Latino; 12 Two or more races, non-Hispanic/Latino; 132 international. Average age 32. 382 applicants, 77% accepted, 182 enrolled. *Faculty:* 47 full-time (6 women), 13 part-time/adjunct (all women). Expenses: Contact institution. *Financial support:* Fellowships, research assistantships with full tuition reimbursements, teaching assistantships with full tuition reimbursements, career-related internships or fieldwork, Federal Work-Study, scholarships/grants, and unspecified assistantships available. Financial award application deadline: 2/1; financial award applicants required to submit FAFSA. In 2018, 245 master's, 3 doctorates, 50 other advanced degrees awarded. *Program availability:* Part-time, evening/weekend, online learning. Offers accountancy (MS); accounting (MBA, MS, PhD); business administration (IMBA, MBA, MS, PhD); business information and technology (MS, PhD, Graduate Certificate); economics (MA, PhD); executive business administration (MBA); finance (PhD); management (PhD); marketing (MS); marketing and supply chain management (PhD); real estate development (MS). *Application deadline:* For fall admission, 7/1 for domestic students, 5/1 for international students; for winter admission, 9/15 for international students; for spring admission, 12/1 for domestic students. *Application fee:* $35 ($60 for international students). Electronic applications accepted. *Application Contact:* Dr. Chuck Pierce, Associate Dean for Academic Programs and Research, 901-678-4620, Fax: 901-678-3759, E-mail: capierce@memphis.edu. *Dean,* Dr. Damon Fleming, 901-678-2457, Fax: 901-678-4705, E-mail: mstaffrd@memphis.edu.

Herff College of Engineering Students: 90 full-time (22 women), 75 part-time (20 women); includes 29 minority (8 Black or African American, non-Hispanic/Latino; 1 American Indian or Alaska Native, non-Hispanic/Latino; 15 Asian, non-Hispanic/Latino; 4 Hispanic/Latino; 1 Two or more races, non-Hispanic/Latino; 86 international. Average age 31. 151 applicants, 68% accepted, 38 enrolled. *Faculty:* 31 full-time (5 women), 4 part-time/adjunct (0 women). Expenses: Contact institution. *Financial support:* Fellowships with full tuition reimbursements, research assistantships with full tuition reimbursements, teaching assistantships with full tuition reimbursements, career-related internships or fieldwork, Federal Work-Study, scholarships/grants, tuition waivers (full and partial), and unspecified assistantships available. Financial award application deadline: 2/1; financial award applicants required to submit FAFSA. In 2018, 27 master's, 7 doctorates, 3 other advanced degrees awarded. *Program availability:* Part-time. Offers applied lean leadership (Graduate Certificate); biomedical engineering (MS, PhD); civil engineering (PhD); computer engineering (MS, PhD); electrical engineering (MS, PhD); engineering (MS, PhD, Graduate Certificate); engineering seismology (MS); engineering technology (MS); environmental engineering (MS); freight transportation (Graduate Certificate); geotechnical engineering (MS); imaging and signal processing (Graduate Certificate); power systems (MS); structural engineering (MS); transportation engineering (MS); water resources engineering (MS). *Application deadline:* For fall admission, 8/1 for domestic students, 5/1 for international students; for spring admission, 12/1 for domestic students, 9/15 for international students; for summer admission, 5/1 for domestic students. *Application fee:* $35 ($60 for international students). Electronic applications accepted. *Application Contact:* Dr. Russell Deaton, Associate Dean of Academic Affairs and Administration, 901-678-2175, Fax: 901-678-5030, E-mail: rjdeaton@memphis.edu. *Dean,* Dr. Richard Joseph Sweigard, 901-678-4306, Fax: 901-678-4180, E-mail: rjswgard@memphis.edu.

Kemmons Wilson School of Hospitality and Resort Management Students: 33 full-time (13 women), 28 part-time (8 women); includes 26 minority (23 Black or African American, non-Hispanic/Latino; 1 Asian, non-Hispanic/Latino; 2 Two or more races, non-Hispanic/Latino; 2 international. Average age 28. 35 applicants, 80% accepted, 28 enrolled. *Faculty:* 9 full-time (3 women), 3 part-time/adjunct (1 woman). Expenses: Contact institution. *Financial support:* Research assistantships, teaching assistantships, career-related internships or fieldwork, Federal Work-Study, scholarships/grants, and unspecified assistantships available. Support available to part-time students. Financial award application deadline: 2/1; financial award applicants required to submit FAFSA. In 2018, 30 master's awarded. *Program availability:* Part-time. Offers hospitality management specialist (Graduate Certificate); sports commerce (MS). *Application deadline:* For fall admission, 7/1 for domestic students, 5/1 for international students; for spring admission, 12/1 for domestic students, 9/1 for international students; for summer admission, 5/1 for domestic students, 2/1 for international students. *Application fee:* $35 ($60 for international students). Electronic applications accepted. *Application Contact:* Dr. Tim Ryan, Coordinator of Graduate Studies, 901-678-5003, E-mail: tdryan@memphis.edu. *Dean,* Dr. Radesh Palakurthi, 901-678-3430, E-mail: rplkrthi@memphis.edu.

School of Communication Sciences and Disorders Students: 112 full-time (102 women), 15 part-time (all women); includes 16 minority (5 Black or African American, non-Hispanic/Latino; 7 Asian, non-Hispanic/Latino; 2 Hispanic/Latino; 2 Two or more races, non-Hispanic/Latino; 3 international. Average age 25. 462 applicants, 32% accepted, 51 enrolled. *Faculty:* 15 full-time (12 women), 3 part-time/adjunct (2 women). Expenses: Contact institution. *Financial support:* Research assistantships with full tuition reimbursements, Federal Work-Study, scholarships/grants, and unspecified assistantships available. Financial award application deadline: 2/1; financial award applicants required to submit FAFSA. In 2018, 21 master's, 17 doctorates awarded. *Program availability:* Part-time. Offers audiology (Au D); communication sciences and disorders (PhD); speech-language pathology (MA). *Application deadline:* For fall admission, 2/1 priority date for domestic students. Applications are processed on a rolling basis. *Application fee:* $35 ($60 for international students). Electronic applications accepted. *Application Contact:* Dr. Lisa

Mendel, Interim Associate Dean of Graduate Studies, 901-678-5800, E-mail: lmendel@memphis.edu. *Dean*, Dr. Linda Jarmulowicz, 901-678-5800, Fax: 901-525-1282, E-mail: ljrmlwcz@memphis.edu.

School of Health Studies Students: 55 full-time (41 women), 49 part-time (33 women); includes 40 minority (34 Black or African American, non-Hispanic/Latino; 1 Asian, non-Hispanic/Latino; 4 Hispanic/Latino; 1 Two or more races, non-Hispanic/Latino), 6 international. Average age 31. 74 applicants, 64% accepted, 42 enrolled. *Faculty:* 20 full-time (11 women), 3 part-time/adjunct (all women). Expenses: Contact institution. *Financial support:* Research assistantships, teaching assistantships, career-related internships or fieldwork, Federal Work-Study, scholarships/grants, and unspecified assistantships available. Financial award application deadline: 2/1; financial award applicants required to submit FAFSA. In 2018, 38 master's, 2 other advanced degrees awarded. *Program availability:* 100% online. Offers faith and health (Graduate Certificate); health studies (MS); nutrition (MS); sport nutrition and dietary supplementation (Graduate Certificate). *Application deadline:* For fall admission, 4/15 priority date for domestic students; for spring admission, 10/15 priority date for domestic students; for summer admission, 4/15 priority date for domestic students. *Application fee:* $35 ($60 for international students). *Application Contact:* Dr. Richard Bloomer, Dean, 901-678-4316, Fax: 901-678-3591, E-mail: rbloomer@memphis.edu. *Dean*, Dr. Richard Bloomer, 901-678-4316, Fax: 901-678-3591, E-mail: rbloomer@memphis.edu.

School of Public Health Students: 123 full-time (84 women), 75 part-time (54 women); includes 77 minority (46 Black or African American, non-Hispanic/Latino; 20 Asian, non-Hispanic/Latino; 7 Hispanic/Latino; 4 Two or more races, non-Hispanic/Latino), 31 international. Average age 31. 109 applicants, 93% accepted, 76 enrolled. *Faculty:* 19 full-time (5 women), 7 part-time/adjunct (2 women). Expenses: Contact institution. *Financial support:* Research assistantships with full tuition reimbursements, Federal Work-Study, scholarships/grants, and unspecified assistantships available. Financial award application deadline: 2/1; financial award applicants required to submit FAFSA. In 2018, 47 master's, 9 doctorates awarded. *Program availability:* Part-time, evening/weekend. Offers biostatistics (MPH); environmental health (MPH); epidemiology (MPH, PhD); health systems and policy (PhD); health systems management (MPH); public health (MHA); social and behavioral sciences (MPH, PhD). *Application deadline:* For fall admission, 4/1 for domestic students; for spring admission, 11/1 for domestic students. *Application fee:* $35 ($60 for international students). Electronic applications accepted. *Application Contact:* Dr. Marian Levy, Associate Dean, 901-678-4514, E-mail: mlevy@memphis.edu. *Dean*, Dr. James Gurney, 901-678-1673, E-mail: jggurney@memphis.edu.

University College Students: 15 full-time (9 women), 85 part-time (63 women); includes 71 minority (67 Black or African American, non-Hispanic/Latino; 2 Hispanic/Latino; 2 Two or more races, non-Hispanic/Latino), 1 International. Average age 40. 57 applicants, 77% accepted, 44 enrolled. *Faculty:* 3 full-time (2 women). Expenses: Contact institution. *Financial support:* Research assistantships with full tuition reimbursements, teaching assistantships with tuition reimbursements, Federal Work-Study, scholarships/grants, and unspecified assistantships available. Financial award application deadline: 2/3; financial award applicants required to submit FAFSA. In 2018, 25 master's, 5 other advanced degrees awarded. *Program availability:* Part-time, evening/weekend. Offers human resources leadership (MPS); liberal studies (MALS, Graduate Certificate); strategic leadership (MPS, Graduate Certificate); training and development (MPS). *Application deadline:* For fall admission, 7/1 for domestic students, 5/1 for international students; for spring admission, 11/1 for domestic students, 9/15 for international students. Applications are processed on a rolling basis. *Application fee:* $35 ($60 for international students). Electronic applications accepted. *Application Contact:* Dr. Colin Chapell, Graduate Advisor, 901-678-3066, E-mail: cbchpell@memphis.edu. *Executive Dean*, Dr. Richard Irwin, 901-678-2716, E-mail: rirwin@memphis.edu.

Loewenberg College of Nursing Students: 23 full-time (20 women), 264 part-time (238 women); includes 104 minority (85 Black or African American, non-Hispanic/Latino; 8 Asian, non-Hispanic/Latino; 7 Hispanic/Latino; 4 Two or more races, non-Hispanic/Latino), 4 international. Average age 35. 146 applicants, 70% accepted, 64 enrolled. *Faculty:* 19 full-time (17 women), 1 (woman) part-time/adjunct. Expenses: Contact institution. *Financial support:* Federal Work-Study and scholarships/grants available. Financial award application deadline: 2/1; financial award applicants required to submit FAFSA. In 2018, 71 master's, 3 other advanced degrees awarded. *Program availability:* Part-time, evening/weekend, online learning. Offers advanced practice nursing (Graduate Certificate); executive leadership (MSN); family nurse practitioner (MSN); nursing administration (MSN, Graduate Certificate); nursing education (MSN, Graduate Certificate). *Application deadline:* For fall admission, 2/15 for domestic and international students; for spring admission, 10/1 for domestic and international students. *Application fee:* $35 ($60 for international students). *Application Contact:* Dr. Lin Zhan, Dean, 901-678-2020, E-mail: lzhan@memphis.edu. *Dean*, Dr. Lin Zhan, 901-678-2020, E-mail: lzhan@memphis.edu.

UNIVERSITY OF MIAMI, Coral Gables, FL 33124

General Information Independent, coed, university. CGS member. *Graduate housing:* On-campus housing not available. *Research affiliation:* Howard Hughes Medical Institute (biology), The Buoniconti Fund: Miami Project to Cure Paralysis (paralysis research), Organization for Tropical Studies, National Center for Atmospheric Research (atmospheric science).

GRADUATE UNITS

Graduate School *Program availability:* Part-time, evening/weekend, online learning. Electronic applications accepted.

College of Arts and Sciences *Program availability:* Part-time, evening/weekend. Offers adult clinical (PhD); art history (MA); arts and sciences (MA, MAIA, MALS, MFA, MPA, MS, PhD); behavioral neuroscience (PhD); biology (MS, PhD); ceramics/glass (MFA); chemistry (MS); child clinical (PhD); computer science (MS, PhD); creative writing (MFA); developmental psychology (PhD); English (MA, PhD); genetics and evolution (MS, PhD); geography (MA); graphic design/multimedia (MFA); health clinical (PhD); history (MA, PhD); inorganic chemistry (PhD); international administration (MAIA); international studies (MA, PhD); Latin American studies (MA); liberal studies (MALS); mathematical finance (MS); mathematics (MA, MS, PhD); organic chemistry (PhD); painting (MFA); philosophy (MA, PhD); photography/digital imaging (MFA); physical chemistry (PhD); physics (MS, PhD); political science (MPA); printmaking (MFA); psychology (MS); romance studies (PhD); sculpture (MFA); sociology (MA, PhD). Electronic applications accepted.

College of Engineering *Program availability:* Part-time, evening/weekend. Offers architectural engineering (MSAE); biomedical engineering (MSBE, PhD); civil engineering (MSCE, PhD); electrical and computer engineering (MSECE, PhD); engineering (MS, MSAE, MSBE, MSCE, MSECE, MSIE, MSME, MSOES, PhD); environmental health and safety (MS); ergonomics (PhD); industrial engineering

(MSIE, PhD); management of technology (MS); mechanical and aerospace engineering (MSME, PhD); occupational ergonomics and safety (MS, MSOES). Electronic applications accepted.

Frost School of Music Offers accompanying and chamber music (MM, DMA); choral conducting (MM, DMA); composition (MM, DMA); electronic music (MM); instrumental conducting (MM, DMA); instrumental performance (MM, DMA, AD); jazz composition (DMA); jazz pedagogy (MM); jazz performance (MM, DMA); keyboard performance and pedagogy (MM, DMA); media writing and production (MM); multiple woodwinds (MM, DMA); music (MM, MS, DMA, PhD, AD, Spec M); music business and entertainment industries (MM); music education (MM, PhD, Spec M); music engineering (MS); music theory (MM); music therapy (MM); musicology (MM); piano performance (MM, DMA, AD); studio jazz writing (MM); vocal pedagogy (DMA); vocal performance (MM, DMA, AD). Electronic applications accepted.

Miller School of Medicine Students: 1,347 full-time (765 women), 38 part-time (25 women); includes 596 minority (65 Black or African American, non-Hispanic/Latino; 173 Asian, non-Hispanic/Latino; 239 Hispanic/Latino; 119 Two or more races, non-Hispanic/Latino), 97 international. Average age 26. *Faculty:* 1,459 full-time (538 women), 90 part-time/adjunct (50 women). Expenses: Contact institution. *Financial support:* Fellowships with partial tuition reimbursements, research assistantships with partial tuition reimbursements, teaching assistantships, Federal Work-Study, institutionally sponsored loans, scholarships/grants, and health care benefits available. Financial award applicants required to submit FAFSA. In 2018, 149 master's, 302 doctorates awarded. Offers biochemistry and molecular biology (PhD); biostatistics (MS, PhD); cancer biology (PhD); cellular physiology and molecular biophysics (PhD); climate and health (MS); epidemiology (PhD); epidemiology, biostatistics, prevention science and community health (MPH, MS, MSPH, PhD); generalist (MPH, MSPH); medicine (MPH, MSPH, DPT, MD, PhD); microbiology and immunology (PhD); molecular and cellular pharmacology (PhD); molecular cell and developmental biology (PhD); neuroscience (PhD); physical therapy (DPT, PhD); prevention science and community health (MS, PhD). *Application deadline:* Applications are processed on a rolling basis. Electronic applications accepted. *Application Contact:* Dr. John L. Bixby, Vice Provost, 305-243-7587, Fax: 305-243-3593, E-mail: jbixby@med.miami.edu. *Executive Vice President & CEO of UHealth*, Dr. Henri Ford, 305-243-5677, Fax: 305-243-1698, E-mail: eabraham@miami.edu.

Rosenstiel School of Marine and Atmospheric Science *Program availability:* Part-time. Offers applied marine physics (MS, PhD); marine affairs and policy (MA, MS); marine and atmospheric chemistry (MS, PhD); marine and atmospheric science (MA, MS, PhD); marine biology and fisheries (MA, MS, PhD); marine geology and geophysics (MS, PhD); meteorology (MS, PhD); physical oceanography (MS, PhD). Electronic applications accepted.

School of Architecture Offers architecture (M Arch); suburb and town design (M Arch). Electronic applications accepted.

School of Communication *Program availability:* Part-time. Offers communication (PhD); communication studies (MA); film studies (MA, PhD); motion pictures (MFA); print journalism (MA); public relations (MA); Spanish language journalism (MA); television broadcast journalism (MA). Electronic applications accepted.

School of Education and Human Development Students: 314 full-time (164 women), 131 part-time (88 women); includes 239 minority (84 Black or African American, non-Hispanic/Latino; 2 American Indian or Alaska Native, non-Hispanic/Latino; 11 Asian, non-Hispanic/Latino; 127 Hispanic/Latino; 15 Two or more races, non-Hispanic/Latino), 39 international. Average age 30. 560 applicants, 54% accepted, 177 enrolled. *Faculty:* 78 full-time (42 women), 38 part-time/adjunct (23 women). Expenses: Contact institution. *Financial support:* Fellowships, research assistantships, teaching assistantships, career-related internships or fieldwork, institutionally sponsored loans, scholarships/grants, health care benefits, tuition waivers (full and partial), and unspecified assistantships available. Support available to part-time students. Financial award application deadline: 3/1; financial award applicants required to submit FAFSA. In 2018, 192 master's, 25 doctorates, 2 other advanced degrees awarded. *Program availability:* Online only, 100% online. Offers athletic training (MS Ed); community and social change (MS Ed); community well-being (PhD); counseling (MS Ed, Certificate); counseling and research (MS Ed); counseling psychology (PhD); early childhood special education (MS Ed, Ed S); education and human development (MS Ed, Ed D, PhD, Certificate, Ed S); education and social change (MS Ed); enrollment management (MS Ed, Certificate); exercise physiology (MS Ed, PhD); higher education administration (MS Ed, Ed D, Certificate); higher education leadership (Ed D); language and literacy learning in multilingual settings (PhD); Latino mental health (Certificate); marriage and family therapy (MS Ed); mental health counseling (MS Ed); nutrition for health and human performance (MS Ed); research, measurement, and evaluation (MS Ed, PhD); science, technology, engineering and mathematics (stem) (PhD); special education (PhD); sport administration (MS Ed); strength and conditioning (MS Ed); student life and development (MS Ed, Certificate); teaching and learning (PhD); women's health (Certificate). *Application deadline:* For fall admission, 10/1 for international students. *Application fee:* $85. Electronic applications accepted. *Application Contact:* Lois Heffernan, Graduate Admissions Coordinator, 305-284-2167, Fax: 305-284-9395, E-mail: lheffernan@miami.edu. *Vice Dean*, Dr. Walter Secada, 305-284-2102, Fax: 305-284-9395, E-mail: wsecada@miami.edu.

School of Nursing and Health Studies *Program availability:* Part-time. Offers acute care (MSN); nursing (PhD); primary care (MSN). Electronic applications accepted.

University of Miami School of Law Students: 1,101 full-time (544 women), 89 part-time (43 women); includes 544 minority (68 Black or African American, non-Hispanic/Latino; 3 American Indian or Alaska Native, non-Hispanic/Latino; 27 Asian, non-Hispanic/Latino; 406 Hispanic/Latino; 40 Two or more races, non-Hispanic/Latino), 102 international. Average age 25. 2,576 applicants, 62% accepted, 360 enrolled. *Faculty:* 83 full-time (45 women), 93 part-time/adjunct (20 women). Expenses: Contact institution. *Financial support:* Fellowships, research assistantships, career-related internships or fieldwork, Federal Work-Study, institutionally sponsored loans, scholarships/grants, and unspecified assistantships available. Financial award application deadline: 3/1; financial award applicants required to submit FAFSA. Offers law (LL M, JD). *Application deadline:* For fall admission, 7/31 for domestic and international students. Applications are processed on a rolling basis. *Application fee:* $60. Electronic applications accepted. *Application Contact:* Therese Lambert, Director of Student Recruitment, 305-284-6746, Fax: 305-284-3084, E-mail: tlambert@law.miami.edu. *Associate Dean of Admissions and Enrollment Management*, Michael Goodnight, 305-284-2527, Fax: 305-284-3084, E-mail: mgoodnig@law.miami.edu.

Miami Business School Students: 1,083 full-time (469 women); includes 422 minority (79 Black or African American, non-Hispanic/Latino; 1 American Indian or Alaska Native, non-Hispanic/Latino; 43 Asian, non-Hispanic/Latino; 274 Hispanic/Latino; 3 Native Hawaiian or other Pacific Islander, non-Hispanic/Latino; 22 Two or more races, non-

Hispanic/Latino), 282 international. Average age 30. 2,564 applicants, 38% accepted, 450 enrolled. *Faculty:* 155 full-time (47 women), 14 part-time/adjunct (5 women). Expenses: Contact institution. *Financial support:* In 2018–19, 643 students received support, including 1 fellowship with full tuition reimbursement available (averaging $20,000 per year), 47 research assistantships with full and partial tuition reimbursements available (averaging $28,826 per year), 6 teaching assistantships with full and partial tuition reimbursements available (averaging $2,183 per year); career-related internships or fieldwork, Federal Work-Study, institutionally sponsored loans, scholarships/grants, and unspecified assistantships also available. Support available to part-time students. Financial award application deadline: 3/26; financial award applicants required to submit FAFSA. In 2018, 558 master's, 5 doctorates awarded. *Program availability:* Part-time, evening/weekend, 100% online, blended/hybrid learning. Offers accounting (M Acc); business (PhD); business administration (MBA); business analytics (MSBA); economics (PhD); finance (MSF); health administration (MHA); international business (MIBS); real estate (MBA); taxation (MS Tax). *Application deadline:* For fall admission, 6/30 priority date for domestic students, 5/30 priority date for international students; for spring admission, 10/31 priority date for domestic students, 9/30 priority date for international students. Applications are processed on a rolling basis. *Application fee:* $48. Electronic applications accepted. *Application Contact:* Loubna Bouamane, Director of Graduate Business Recruiting and Admissions, 305-284-2510, Fax: 305-284-5905, E-mail: loubna@miami.edu. *Dean,* Dr. John Quelch, 305-284-6515, Fax: 305-284-6526, E-mail: jquelch@miami.edu.

UNIVERSITY OF MICHIGAN, Ann Arbor, MI 48109

General Information State-supported, coed, university. CGS member. *Graduate housing:* Rooms and/or apartments available on a first-come, first-served basis to single and married students.

GRADUATE UNITS

College of Engineering Students: 3,285 full-time (888 women), 323 part-time (56 women). 11,153 applicants, 26% accepted, 1099 enrolled. *Faculty:* 426 full-time (86 women). Expenses: Contact institution. *Financial support:* Fellowships, research assistantships, teaching assistantships, career-related internships or fieldwork, Federal Work-Study, institutionally sponsored loans, scholarships/grants, traineeships, health care benefits, tuition waivers (full and partial), and unspecified assistantships available. Support available to part-time students. Financial award applicants required to submit FAFSA. In 2018, 1,244 master's, 289 doctorates awarded. *Program availability:* Part-time, 100% online, blended/hybrid learning. Offers aerospace engineering (M Eng, MS, MSE, PhD); applied climate (M Eng); atmospheric, oceanic and space sciences (MS, PhD); automotive engineering (M Eng); biomedical engineering (MS, MSE, PhD); chemical engineering (MSE, PhD, Ch E); civil engineering (MSE, PhD, CE); computer science and engineering (MS, MSE, PhD); construction engineering and management (M Eng, MSE); design science (MS, PhD); electrical and computer engineering (MS, MSE, PhD); energy systems engineering (M Eng, MS); engineering (M Eng, MS, MSE, D Eng, PhD, CE, Certificate, Ch E, Mar Eng, Nav Arch, Nuc E); environmental engineering (MSE, PhD); geoscience and remote sensing (PhD); global automotive and manufacturing engineering (M Eng); industrial and operations engineering (MS, MSE, PhD); manufacturing engineering (M Eng, D Eng); materials science and engineering (MS, MSE, PhD); mechanical engineering (MSE, PhD); naval architecture and marine engineering (MS, MSE, PhD, Mar Eng, Nav Arch); nuclear engineering (Nuc E); nuclear engineering and radiological sciences (MSE, PhD); nuclear science (MS, PhD); pharmaceutical engineering (M Eng); robotics (MS, PhD); robotics and autonomous vehicles (M Eng); space and planetary sciences (PhD); space engineering (M Eng); structural engineering (M Eng); systems engineering and design (M Eng). *Application deadline:* Applications are processed on a rolling basis. Electronic applications accepted. *Application Contact:* Jeanne Murabito, Executive Director for Student Affairs, 734-647-7118, E-mail: coe-studentaffairs@umich.edu. *Dean of Engineering,* Prof. Alec D. Gallimore, 734-647-7008, Fax: 734-647-7009, E-mail: alec.gallimore@umich.edu.

College of Pharmacy Offers clinical pharmacy (PhD); medicinal chemistry (PhD); pharmaceutical sciences (PhD); pharmacy (PhD, Pharm D). Electronic applications accepted.

Gerald R. Ford School of Public Policy Students: 282 full-time (149 women); includes 91 minority (23 Black or African American, non-Hispanic/Latino; 1 American Indian or Alaska Native, non-Hispanic/Latino; 26 Asian, non-Hispanic/Latino; 30 Hispanic/Latino; 11 Two or more races, non-Hispanic/Latino), 38 international. Average age 27. 663 applicants, 65% accepted, 114 enrolled. *Faculty:* 43 full-time (17 women), 36 part-time/adjunct (14 women). Expenses: Contact institution. *Financial support:* In 2018–19, 203 students received support, including 169 fellowships with tuition reimbursements available, 33 teaching assistantships with tuition reimbursements available; research assistantships, career-related internships or fieldwork, traineeships, health care benefits, and unspecified assistantships also available. Financial award application deadline: 1/15; financial award applicants required to submit FAFSA. In 2018, 116 master's, 3 doctorates awarded. Offers public policy (MPA, MPP, PhD). *Application deadline:* For fall admission, 1/15 priority date for domestic students, 1/15 for international students. *Application fee:* $75 ($90 for international students). Electronic applications accepted. *Application Contact:* Beth Soboleski, Director, Admissions and Recruiting, 734-764-0453, Fax: 734-647-7486, E-mail: fspp-admissions@umich.edu. *Dean of Public Policy,* Michael S. Barr, 734-764-2258, E-mail: ford.school.dean@umich.edu.

Law School Students: 1,012 full-time (490 women); includes 238 minority (45 Black or African American, non-Hispanic/Latino; 6 American Indian or Alaska Native, non-Hispanic/Latino; 77 Asian, non-Hispanic/Latino; 63 Hispanic/Latino; 47 Two or more races, non-Hispanic/Latino), 39 international. 5,698 applicants, 20% accepted, 362 enrolled. *Faculty:* 106 full-time (37 women), 89 part-time/adjunct (23 women). Expenses: Contact institution. *Financial support:* In 2018–19, 876 students received support. Career-related internships or fieldwork, Federal Work-Study, institutionally sponsored loans, and scholarships/grants available. Financial award applicants required to submit FAFSA. In 2018, 37 master's, 291 doctorates awarded. Offers comparative law (MCL); international tax (LL M); law (LL M, JD, SJD). *Application deadline:* For fall admission, 2/15 for domestic students. Applications are processed on a rolling basis. *Application fee:* $75. Electronic applications accepted. *Application Contact:* Sarah C. Zearfoss, Assistant Dean and Director of Admissions, 734-764-0537, Fax: 734-647-3218, E-mail: law.jd.admissions@umich.edu. *Dean,* Mark D. West, 734-764-1358.

Medical School Students: 721 full-time (417 women); includes 265 minority (45 Black or African American, non-Hispanic/Latino; 3 American Indian or Alaska Native, non-Hispanic/Latino; 130 Asian, non-Hispanic/Latino; 51 Hispanic/Latino; 36 Two or more races, non-Hispanic/Latino). Average age 27. 6,771 applicants, 5% accepted, 168 enrolled. *Faculty:* 2,766 full-time (1,085 women), 1,299 part-time/adjunct (643 women). Expenses: Contact institution. *Financial support:* Institutionally sponsored loans and scholarships/grants available. Financial award application deadline: 9/30; financial award applicants required to submit FAFSA. In 2018, 164 doctorates awarded. Offers medicine (MD). *Application deadline:* For fall admission, 9/30 for domestic students.

Applications are processed on a rolling basis. Electronic applications accepted. *Application Contact:* Carol Teener, Director of Admissions, 734-764-6317, Fax: 734-936-3510, E-mail: cteener@umich.edu. *Dean,* Dr. Marschall S. Runge, MD, 734-764-8175, E-mail: mrunge@umich.edu.

Rackham Graduate School Students: 7,971 full-time (3,574 women), 706 part-time (287 women); includes 1,715 minority (339 Black or African American, non-Hispanic/Latino; 14 American Indian or Alaska Native, non-Hispanic/Latino; 591 Asian, non-Hispanic/Latino; 563 Hispanic/Latino; 3 Native Hawaiian or other Pacific Islander, non-Hispanic/Latino; 205 Two or more races, non-Hispanic/Latino), 3,473 international. Average age 26. 28,417 applicants, 27% accepted, 3000 enrolled. Expenses: Contact institution. *Financial support:* Fellowships with full and partial tuition reimbursements, research assistantships with full and partial tuition reimbursements, teaching assistantships with full and partial tuition reimbursements, career-related internships or fieldwork, Federal Work-Study, scholarships/grants, traineeships, health care benefits, and unspecified assistantships available. Support available to part-time students. In 2018, 2,220 master's, 871 doctorates awarded. Offers cancer chemical biology (MS); chemical biology (PhD); data science (MS, PhD); education and psychology (PhD); English and education (PhD); social and psychological (MS, PhD); statistical (MS, PhD); survey methodology (Certificate). *Application deadline:* Applications are processed on a rolling basis. *Application fee:* $75 ($90 for international students). Electronic applications accepted. *Application Contact:* Admissions Office, 734-764-8129, E-mail: rackadmis@umich.edu. *Dean/Vice Provost for Academic Affairs, Graduate Studies,* Dr. Michael J. Solomon, 734-764-4400.

College of Literature, Science, and the Arts Offers American culture (AM, PhD); analytical chemistry (PhD); ancient Near Eastern studies (AM, PhD); anthropological archaeology (PhD); anthropology and history (PhD); applied and interdisciplinary mathematics (AM, MS, PhD); applied economics (AM); applied physics (PhD); applied statistics (MS); Arabic for professional purposes (AM); Arabic language and literature (AM, PhD); Armenian studies (AM, PhD); Asian languages and cultures (PhD); astronomy and astrophysics (PhD); biological anthropology (PhD); biophysics (PhD); biopsychology (PhD); chemical biology (PhD); chemical sciences (MS); Chinese studies (MA, Graduate Certificate); Christianity in late antiquity (AM, PhD); classical art and archaeology (MA, PhD); classical studies (MA, PhD); clinical science (PhD); cognition and cognitive neuroscience (PhD); communication studies (PhD); comparative literature (PhD); creative writing (MFA); data science (MS); developmental psychology (PhD); earth and environmental sciences (MS, PhD); ecology and evolutionary biology (MS, PhD); economics (AM, PhD); Egyptology (AM, PhD); English and education (PhD); English and women's studies (PhD); English language and literature (PhD); French (PhD); German (AM, PhD); German studies (Certificate); Greek and Roman history (PhD); Hebrew Bible and ancient Israel (AM, PhD); Hebrew literature (AM, PhD); history (PhD); history and women's studies (PhD); history of art (PhD); inorganic chemistry (PhD); Islamic studies (AM, PhD); Italian (PhD); Japanese studies (AM); Jewish cultural studies (AM, PhD); Jewish mysticism (AM, PhD); Judaic studies (MA, Graduate Certificate); Latin (MA); Latin with teaching certification (MAT); LGBTQ studies (Certificate); linguistic anthropology (PhD); linguistics (PhD); literature, science, and the arts (AM, MA, MAT, MFA, MS, PhD, Certificate, Graduate Certificate); materials chemistry (PhD); mathematics (AM, MS, PhD); Middle Eastern and North African studies (AM); molecular, cellular, and developmental biology (MS, PhD); organic chemistry (PhD); Persian and Iranian studies (AM, PhD); personality and social contexts (PhD); philosophy (AM, PhD); physical chemistry (PhD); physics (PhD); political science (PhD); political science and public policy (PhD); psychology and women's studies (PhD); public policy and economics (PhD); public policy and sociology (PhD); quantitative finance and risk management (MS); Rabbinic literature (AM, PhD); Russian, East European, and Eurasian studies (AM, Certificate); screen arts and cultures (PhD, Certificate); Second Temple Judaism (AM, PhD); Slavic languages and literatures (AM, PhD); social psychology (PhD); social work and economics (PhD); social work and political science (PhD); social work and sociology (PhD); sociocultural anthropology (PhD); sociology (PhD); South Asian studies (MA, Certificate); Southeast Asian studies (MA, Graduate Certificate); Spanish (PhD); statistics (AM, PhD); teaching Arabic as a foreign language (AM); Turkish studies (AM, PhD); women's studies (Certificate). Electronic applications accepted.

Penny W. Stamps School of Art and Design Students: 18 (12 women). 179 applicants, 6% accepted, 10 enrolled. *Faculty:* 37. Expenses: Contact institution. *Financial support:* In 2018–19, 19 students received support, including 10 research assistantships with partial tuition reimbursements available, 10 teaching assistantships with full and partial tuition reimbursements available; fellowships with full tuition reimbursements available, career-related internships or fieldwork, Federal Work-Study, institutionally sponsored loans, scholarships/grants, health care benefits, tuition waivers (full and partial), and unspecified assistantships also available. Support available to part-time students. Financial award application deadline: 1/1. In 2018, 10 master's awarded. Offers art and design (MFA); integrative design (M Des). *Application deadline:* For fall admission, 1/1 for domestic and international students. *Application fee:* $75 ($90 for international students). Electronic applications accepted. *Application Contact:* Meghan Jellema, Graduate Programs Coordinator, 734-763-5247, E-mail: stamps-graduate-info@umich.edu. *Dean,* Gunalan Nadarajan, 734-764-0397, E-mail: artdes-dean@umich.edu.

Program in Biomedical Sciences (PIBS) Students: 76 full-time (44 women); includes 27 minority (1 Black or African American, non-Hispanic/Latino; 10 Asian, non-Hispanic/Latino; 8 Hispanic/Latino; 8 Two or more races, non-Hispanic/Latino), 14 international. Average age 24. 1,058 applicants, 22% accepted, 84 enrolled. *Faculty:* 565 full-time. Expenses: Contact institution. *Financial support:* In 2018–19, 84 students received support, including 84 fellowships with full tuition reimbursements available (averaging $30,600 per year); scholarships/grants, health care benefits, and unspecified assistantships also available. Financial award application deadline: 12/1. Offers bioinformatics (MS, PhD); biological chemistry (MS, PhD); biomedical sciences (MS, PhD); cancer biology (PhD); cell and developmental biology (PhD); cellular and molecular biology (PhD); genetic counseling (MS); human genetics (MS, PhD); immunology (PhD); microbiology and immunology (MS, PhD); molecular and cellular pathology (PhD); molecular and integrative physiology (MS, PhD); neuroscience (PhD); pharmacology (MS, PhD). *Application deadline:* For fall admission, 12/1 for domestic and international students. *Application fee:* $75 ($90 for international students). Electronic applications accepted. *Application Contact:* Jim Musgrave, Director of Graduate Enrollment Management, 734-647-7005, Fax: 734-647-7022, E-mail: jdmusg@umich.edu. *Associate Professor, Cell and Developmental Biology/Director of the Program in Biomedical Sciences,* Dr. Scott Barolo, Dr. 734-615-7005, Fax: 734-647-7022, E-mail: sbarolo@umich.edu.

School of Kinesiology Students: 115 full-time (56 women); includes 31 minority (13 Black or African American, non-Hispanic/Latino; 4 Asian, non-Hispanic/Latino; 11 Hispanic/Latino; 3 Two or more races, non-Hispanic/Latino). Average age 26. 223

applicants, 51% accepted, 64 enrolled. *Faculty:* 30 full-time (15 women). Expenses: Contact institution. *Financial support:* In 2018–19, 34 students received support, including 13 fellowships with full tuition reimbursements available, 9 research assistantships with full tuition reimbursements available, 14 teaching assistantships with full tuition reimbursements available; Federal Work-Study, scholarships/grants, traineeships, health care benefits, and unspecified assistantships also available. Financial award application deadline: 12/1. In 2018, 47 master's, 4 doctorates awarded. Offers movement science (MS, PhD); sport management (MS, PhD). *Application deadline:* For fall admission, 12/1 priority date for domestic students, 12/1 for international students. Applications are processed on a rolling basis. *Application fee:* $75 ($90 for international students). Electronic applications accepted. *Application Contact:* Charlene F. Ruloff, Graduate Program Coordinator, 734-764-1343, Fax: 734-647-2808, E-mail: cruloff@umich.edu. *Associate Dean for Graduate Affairs,* Dr. Ketra L. Armstrong, 734-647-3027, Fax: 734-647-2808, E-mail: ketra@umich.edu.

School of Music, Theatre, and Dance Offers composition (MA, MM, A Mus D); composition and theory (PhD); conducting (MM, A Mus D); media arts (MA); modern dance performance and choreography (MFA); music education (MM, PhD, Spec M); music theory (PhD); music, theatre, and dance (MA, MFA, MM, A Mus D, PhD, Spec M); musicology (MA, PhD); performance (MM, A Mus D, Spec M). Electronic applications accepted.

School of Nursing *Program availability:* Part-time, online learning. Offers acute care pediatric nurse practitioner (MS); nursing (DNP, PhD, Post Master's Certificate).

Ross School of Business *Program availability:* Part-time, evening/weekend. Offers accounting (M Acc); business (MBA); business administration (PhD); supply chain management (MSCM). Electronic applications accepted.

School for Environment and Sustainability Students: 369 full-time (214 women); includes 55 minority (7 Black or African American, non-Hispanic/Latino; 1 American Indian or Alaska Native, non-Hispanic/Latino; 15 Asian, non-Hispanic/Latino; 18 Hispanic/Latino; 1 Native Hawaiian or other Pacific Islander, non-Hispanic/Latino; 13 Two or more races, non-Hispanic/Latino), 80 international. Average age 26. 579 applicants. *Faculty:* 44 full-time (17 women), 27 part-time/adjunct (7 women). Expenses: Contact institution. *Financial support:* Fellowships, research assistantships, teaching assistantships, career-related internships or fieldwork, Federal Work-Study, scholarships/grants, health care benefits, and unspecified assistantships available. Financial award application deadline: 1/7; financial award applicants required to submit FAFSA. In 2018, 123 master's, 4 doctorates awarded. Offers behavior, education and communication (MS); conservation ecology (MS); environment and sustainability (MS, PhD); environmental informatics (MS); environmental justice (MS, Certificate); environmental policy and planning (MS); industrial ecology (Certificate); landscape architecture (MLA); spatial analysis (Certificate); sustainability (Certificate); sustainable systems (MS). *Application deadline:* For fall admission, 4/30 for domestic and international students. Applications are processed on a rolling basis. *Application fee:* $75 ($90 for international students). Electronic applications accepted. *Application Contact:* Jung Koral, Associate Director of Enrollment Services, 734-764-6453, Fax: 734-936-2195, E-mail: seas-admissions@umich.edu. *Samuel A. Graham Dean,* Dr. Jonathan Overpeck, 734-764-2550, Fax: 734-763-8965, E-mail: overpeck@umich.edu.

School of Dentistry Students: 601 full-time (306 women); includes 212 minority (25 Black or African American, non-Hispanic/Latino; 3 American Indian or Alaska Native, non-Hispanic/Latino; 145 Asian, non-Hispanic/Latino; 25 Hispanic/Latino; 14 Two or more races, non-Hispanic/Latino), 100 international. 2,437 applicants, 10% accepted, 157 enrolled. Expenses: Contact institution. Offers dental hygiene (MS); dentistry (MS, DDS, PhD); endodontics (MS); oral health sciences (PhD); orthodontics (MS); pediatric dentistry (MS); periodontics (MS); prosthodontics (MS); restorative dentistry (MS). *Application deadline:* Applications are processed on a rolling basis. *Application fee:* $75 ($90 for international students). Electronic applications accepted. *Application Contact:* Patricia Katcher, Admissions Associate Director, 734-763-3316, Fax: 734-764-1922, E-mail: ddsadmissions@umich.edu. *Dean,* Dr. Laurie McCauley, 734-763-3311, E-mail: mccauley@umich.edu.

School of Education Offers education (MA, MS, PhD). Electronic applications accepted.

School of Information Students: 453 full-time (270 women), 32 part-time (20 women); includes 99 minority (16 Black or African American, non-Hispanic/Latino; 49 Asian, non-Hispanic/Latino; 21 Hispanic/Latino; 13 Two or more races, non-Hispanic/Latino), 212 international. Average age 27. 829 applicants, 53% accepted, 199 enrolled. Expenses: Contact institution. *Financial support:* In 2018–19, 122 students received support, including 2 fellowships (averaging $28,200 per year), 33 research assistantships (averaging $28,200 per year), 41 teaching assistantships (averaging $28,200 per year); scholarships/grants and tuition waivers (full and partial) also available. In 2018, 179 master's, 7 doctorates awarded. *Program availability:* Part-time. Offers health informatics (MHI); information (MSI, PhD). *Application deadline:* Applications are processed on a rolling basis. *Application fee:* $75 ($90 for international students). Electronic applications accepted. *Application Contact:* School of Information Admissions, 734-763-2285, Fax: 734-615-3587, E-mail: umsi.admissions@umich.edu. *Dean, School of Information,* Dr. Thomas A. Finholt, 734-647-3576.

School of Public Health *Program availability:* Evening/weekend. Offers biostatistics (MPH, MS, PhD); clinical research design and statistical analysis (MS); dietetics (MPH); environmental health policy and promotion (MPH); environmental health sciences (MS, PhD); environmental quality, sustainability and health (MPH); epidemiological science (PhD); general epidemiology (MPH); global health epidemiology (MPH); health behavior and health education (MPH, PhD); health management and policy (MHSA, MPH); health services organization and policy (PhD); hospital and molecular epidemiology (MPH); industrial hygiene (MPH, MS); nutritional sciences (MPH, MS, PhD); occupational and environmental epidemiology (MPH); public health (MHSA, MPH, MS, PhD); toxicology (MPH, MS, PhD). MS and PhD offered through the Rackham Graduate School. Electronic applications accepted.

School of Social Work Offers social work (MSW, PhD); social work and anthropology (PhD); social work and economics (PhD); social work and political science (PhD); social work and psychology (PhD); social work and sociology (PhD). PhD offered through the Rackham Graduate School. Electronic applications accepted.

Taubman College of Architecture and Urban Planning 1,152 applicants, 60% accepted, 225 enrolled. *Faculty:* 108. Expenses: Contact institution. Offers architecture (M Arch); business (M Arch, MS, MUD, MURP, PhD, Graduate Certificate); design and health (MS); digital materials technologies (MS); engineering (M Arch, MS, MUD, MURP, PhD, Graduate Certificate); master of science in architecture design and research (MS); material systems (MS); real estate development (Graduate Certificate); urban and regional planning (MURP, PhD); urban design (MUD); urban regional planning (MURP). *Application fee:* $75 ($90 for international students). Electronic applications accepted. *Application Contact:* Lisa Hauser, Assistant Director for Admissions and Recruiting, 734-763-1275, E-mail: taubmancollegeadmissions@umich.edu. *Dean,* Jonathan Massey.

UNIVERSITY OF MICHIGAN–DEARBORN, Dearborn, MI 48128

General Information State-supported, coed, comprehensive institution. *Enrollment:* 9,468 graduate, professional, and undergraduate students; 505 full-time matriculated graduate/professional students (197 women), 1,744 part-time matriculated graduate/professional students (576 women). *Enrollment by degree level:* 2,141 master's, 92 doctoral, 16 other advanced degrees. *Graduate faculty:* 323 full-time (132 women), 230 part-time/adjunct (99 women). Tuition, state resident: full-time $15,380; part-time $88 per credit hour. Tuition, nonresident: full-time $23,948; part-time $1377 per credit hour. *Required fees:* $780; $780 390. Tuition and fees vary according to course level, course load, degree level, program, reciprocity agreements and student level. *Student services:* Campus employment opportunities, campus safety program, career counseling, child daycare facilities, exercise/wellness program, free psychological counseling, grant writing training, international student services, low-cost health insurance, multicultural affairs office, services for students with disabilities, teacher training, writing training. *Library facilities:* Mardigian Library. *Collection:* Books: 189,907 (physical), 662,503 (digital/electronic); Serial titles: 387 (physical), 103,160 (digital/electronic); Databases: 795. Weekly public service hours: 95; students can reserve study rooms.

Computer facilities: Computer purchase and lease plans are available. 1,060 computers available on campus for general student use. A campuswide network can be accessed from off campus. Online class registration, tuition and application payments accepted online are available. Website: http://www.umdearborn.edu/

General Application Contact: Office of Graduate Studies, 313-583-6321, E-mail: umd-graduatestudies@umich.edu.

GRADUATE UNITS

College of Arts, Sciences, and Letters Students: 40 full-time (33 women), 73 part-time (42 women); includes 39 minority (18 Black or African American, non-Hispanic/Latino; 12 Asian, non-Hispanic/Latino; 8 Hispanic/Latino; 1 Two or more races, non-Hispanic/Latino), 1 international. Average age 31. 100 applicants, 60% accepted, 38 enrolled. *Faculty:* 55 full-time (28 women), 20 part-time/adjunct (10 women). Expenses: Contact institution. *Financial support:* In 2018–19, 56 students received support. Scholarships/grants and non-resident tuition scholarships available. Financial award application deadline: 3/1; financial award applicants required to submit FAFSA. In 2018, 42 master's awarded. *Program availability:* Part-time, evening/weekend. Offers applied and computational mathematics (MS); arts, sciences, and letters (MPA, MS); clinical health psychology (MS); criminology and criminal justice (MS); environmental science (MS); health psychology (MS); public administration (MPA). *Application deadline:* For fall admission, 8/1 priority date for domestic students, 5/1 priority date for international students; for winter admission, 12/1 priority date for domestic students, 9/1 priority date for international students; for spring admission, 4/1 priority date for domestic students, 1/1 priority date for international students. Applications are processed on a rolling basis. *Application fee:* $60. Electronic applications accepted. *Application Contact:* Office of Graduate Studies, 313-583-6321, E-mail: umd-graduatestudies@umich.edu. *Dean,* Dr. Martin Hershock, 313-593-5490, E-mail: mhershoc@umich.edu.

College of Business Students: 99 full-time (45 women), 441 part-time (173 women); includes 111 minority (22 Black or African American, non-Hispanic/Latino; 2 American Indian or Alaska Native, non-Hispanic/Latino; 55 Asian, non-Hispanic/Latino; 18 Hispanic/Latino; 14 Two or more races, non-Hispanic/Latino), 91 international. Average age 30. 492 applicants, 54% accepted, 153 enrolled. *Faculty:* 40 full-time (17 women), 9 part-time/adjunct (6 women). Expenses: Contact institution. *Financial support:* In 2018–19, 148 students received support. Scholarships/grants and non-resident tuition scholarships available. Financial award application deadline: 3/1; financial award applicants required to submit FAFSA. In 2018, 158 master's awarded. *Program availability:* Part-time, evening/weekend, 100% online. Offers accounting (MS); business (MBA, MS); business administration (MBA); business analytics (MS); finance (MS); information systems (MS); supply chain management (MS). *Application deadline:* For fall admission, 8/1 priority date for domestic students, 5/1 priority date for international students; for winter admission, 12/1 priority date for domestic students, 9/1 priority date for international students; for spring admission, 4/1 priority date for domestic students, 1/1 priority date for international students. Applications are processed on a rolling basis. *Application fee:* $60. Electronic applications accepted. *Application Contact:* Joan Doherty, Academic Advisor/Counselor, 313-593-5460, E-mail: umd-gradbusiness@umich.edu. *Dean,* Dr. Raju Balakrishnan, 313-593-5460, E-mail: umd-cob-dean@umich.edu.

College of Education, Health, and Human Services Students: 23 full-time (21 women), 207 part-time (172 women); includes 49 minority (29 Black or African American, non-Hispanic/Latino; 5 Asian, non-Hispanic/Latino; 10 Hispanic/Latino; 1 Native Hawaiian or other Pacific Islander, non-Hispanic/Latino; 4 Two or more races, non-Hispanic/Latino), 3 international. Average age 34. 106 applicants, 75% accepted, 53 enrolled. *Faculty:* 16 full-time (11 women), 18 part-time/adjunct (12 women). Expenses: Contact institution. *Financial support:* In 2018–19, 45 students received support. Career-related internships or fieldwork and scholarships/grants available. Financial award application deadline: 3/1; financial award applicants required to submit FAFSA. In 2018, 84 master's, 5 doctorates awarded. *Program availability:* Part-time, evening/weekend, 100% online, blended/hybrid learning. Offers applied behavior analysis (MS); community based education (MA); curriculum and practice (Ed D, Ed S); early childhood education (MA); education (MA, Ed D, Ed S); education, health, and human services (M Ed, MA, MAT, MS, Ed D, Certificate, Ed S); educational leadership (MA); educational technology (MS); health information technology (MS); metropolitan education (Ed D, Ed S); program evaluation and assessment (MA); teaching (MAT). *Application deadline:* For fall admission, 8/1 priority date for domestic students, 5/1 priority date for international students; for winter admission, 12/1 priority date for domestic students, 9/1 priority date for international students; for spring admission, 4/1 priority date for domestic students, 1/1 priority date for international students. Applications are processed on a rolling basis. *Application fee:* $60. Electronic applications accepted. *Application Contact:* Dr. Paul Fossum, Director, Master's Programs, 313-593-0982, E-mail: pfossum@umich.edu. *Dean,* Dr. Ann Lampkin-Williams, 313-593-5090, E-mail: lampkin@umich.edu.

College of Engineering and Computer Science Students: 343 full-time (98 women), 1,023 part-time (189 women); includes 193 minority (46 Black or African American, non-Hispanic/Latino; 3 American Indian or Alaska Native, non-Hispanic/Latino; 90 Asian, non-Hispanic/Latino; 38 Hispanic/Latino; 1 Native Hawaiian or other Pacific Islander, non-Hispanic/Latino; 15 Two or more races, non-Hispanic/Latino), 514 international. Average age 28. 1,641 applicants, 47% accepted, 369 enrolled. *Faculty:* 80 full-time (11 women), 42 part-time/adjunct (4 women). Expenses: Contact institution. *Financial support:* In 2018–19, 327 students received support. Research assistantships with full tuition reimbursements available, teaching assistantships with full tuition reimbursements available, career-related internships or fieldwork, scholarships/grants, health care benefits, and non-residential student scholarships available. Support available to part-time students. Financial award application deadline: 3/1; financial award applicants required to submit FAFSA. In 2018, 471 master's, 4 doctorates awarded. *Program availability:* Part-time, evening/weekend, 100% online. Offers automotive systems engineering (MSE); bioengineering (MSE); computer and information science (MS, PhD); computer engineering (MSE); data management (PhD); data science (MS); electrical and computer engineering (PhD); electrical engineering (MSE); energy systems engineering (MSE); engineering and computer science (MS, MSE, PhD); engineering management (MS); industrial and systems engineering (MSE, PhD); information systems and technology (MS); manufacturing systems engineering (MSE); mechanical engineering (MSE); mechanical sciences and engineering (PhD); program and project management (MS); software engineering (MS); systems and security (PhD). *Application deadline:* For fall admission, 8/1 priority date for domestic students, 5/1 priority date for international students; for winter admission, 12/1 priority date for domestic students, 9/1 priority date for international students; for spring admission, 4/1 priority date for domestic students, 1/1 priority date for international students. Applications are processed on a rolling basis. *Application fee:* $60. Electronic applications accepted. *Application Contact:* Office of Graduate Studies Staff, 313-583-6321, E-mail: umd-graduatestudies@umich.edu. *Dean,* Dr. Anthony England, 313-593-5290, E-mail: cecsdeansoffice@umich.edu.

UNIVERSITY OF MICHIGAN–FLINT, Flint, MI 48502-1950

General Information State-supported, coed, comprehensive institution. CGS member. *Enrollment by degree level:* 863 master's, 499 doctoral, 40 other advanced degrees. *Graduate housing:* Room and/or apartments available on a first-come, first-served basis to single students; on-campus housing not available to married students. *Student services:* Campus employment opportunities, campus safety program, career counseling, child daycare facilities, exercise/wellness program, free psychological counseling, international student services, services for students with disabilities, teacher training, writing training. *Library facilities:* Frances Willson Thompson Library plus 1 other. *Collection:* Books: 251,483 (physical), 981,065 (digital/electronic); Serial titles: 1,862 (physical), 163,338 (digital/electronic); Databases: 1,387. Weekly public service hours: 96; students can reserve study rooms.

Computer facilities: Computer purchase and lease plans are available. 512 computers available on campus for general student use. A campuswide network can be accessed from student residence rooms and from off campus. Online class registration is available.

Website: http://www.umflint.edu/

General Application Contact: Bradley T. Maki, Director of Graduate Admissions, 810-762-3171, Fax: 810-766-6789, E-mail: bmaki@umflint.edu.

GRADUATE UNITS

College of Arts and Sciences Students: 48 full-time (28 women), 138 part-time (68 women); includes 43 minority (19 Black or African American, non-Hispanic/Latino; 3 Asian, non-Hispanic/Latino; 16 Hispanic/Latino; 1 Native Hawaiian or other Pacific Islander, non-Hispanic/Latino; 4 Two or more races, non-Hispanic/Latino), 46 international. Average age 33. 424 applicants, 55% accepted, 70 enrolled. *Faculty:* 101 full-time (50 women), 36 part-time/adjunct (19 women). Expenses: Contact institution. *Financial support:* Federal Work-Study, scholarships/grants, and unspecified assistantships available. Support available to part-time students. Financial award application deadline: 3/1; financial award applicants required to submit FAFSA. In 2018, 118 master's awarded. *Program availability:* Part-time. Offers applied communication (MA); arts and sciences (MA, MS, MSE); biology (MS); computer science (MS); gender studies (MA); global studies (MA); information systems (MS); literature (MA); mathematics (MA); mechanical engineering (MSE); U.S. history and politics (MA); writing and rhetoric (MA). *Application deadline:* For fall admission, 8/1 for domestic students, 5/1 for international students; for winter admission, 11/15 for domestic students, 9/1 for international students; for spring admission, 3/15 for domestic students, 1/1 for international students; for summer admission, 5/15 for domestic students. Applications are processed on a rolling basis. *Application fee:* $55. Electronic applications accepted. *Application Contact:* Bradley T. Maki, Director of Graduate Admissions, 810-762-3171, Fax: 810-766-6789, E-mail: bmaki@umflint.edu. *Dean,* Dr. Susan Gano-Phillips, 810-762-3234, Fax: 810-762-3006, E-mail: sganop@umflint.edu.

College of Health Sciences Students: 241 full-time (152 women), 96 part-time (60 women); includes 47 minority (10 Black or African American, non-Hispanic/Latino; 1 American Indian or Alaska Native, non-Hispanic/Latino; 19 Asian, non-Hispanic/Latino; 10 Hispanic/Latino; 7 Two or more races, non-Hispanic/Latino), 29 international. Average age 30. 519 applicants, 43% accepted, 107 enrolled. *Faculty:* 32 full-time (24 women), 49 part-time/adjunct (27 women). Expenses: Contact institution. *Financial support:* Federal Work-Study, scholarships/grants, and unspecified assistantships available. Support available to part-time students. Financial award application deadline: 3/1; financial award applicants required to submit FAFSA. In 2018, 43 master's, 77 doctorates awarded. *Program availability:* Part-time, 100% online. Offers adult neurology (PhD); anesthesia (DNAP); health administration (MPH); health education (MPH); health professions and studies (MPH, DNAP, DPT, PhD, Certificate); neurology (Certificate); orthopedics (PhD, Certificate); pediatrics (PhD, Certificate); physical therapy (DPT). *Application deadline:* For fall admission, 8/1 for domestic students, 5/1 for international students; for winter admission, 11/15 for domestic students, 9/1 for international students; for spring admission, 3/15 for domestic students, 1/1 for international students. Applications are processed on a rolling basis. *Application fee:* $55. Electronic applications accepted. *Application Contact:* Matt Bohlen, Director of Graduate Admissions, 810-762-3171, Fax: 810-766-6789, E-mail: mbohlen@umflint.edu. *Dean,* Dr. Donna Fry, 810-237-6503, Fax: 810-237-6532, E-mail: donnafry@umflint.edu.

Graduate Programs Students: 15 full-time (10 women), 121 part-time (77 women); includes 45 minority (33 Black or African American, non-Hispanic/Latino; 5 American Indian or Alaska Native, non-Hispanic/Latino; 2 Asian, non-Hispanic/Latino; 2 Hispanic/Latino; 3 Two or more races, non-Hispanic/Latino), 3 international. Average age 38. 95 applicants, 67% accepted, 38 enrolled. *Faculty:* 7 full-time (4 women), 14 part-time/adjunct (8 women). Expenses: Contact institution. *Financial support:* Fellowships, Federal Work-Study, scholarships/grants, and unspecified assistantships available. Support available to part-time students. Financial award application deadline: 3/1; financial award applicants required to submit FAFSA. In 2018, 48 master's awarded. *Program availability:* Part-time, evening/weekend, online learning. Offers administration of non-profit agencies (MPA); criminal justice administration (MPA); educational administration (MPA); general public administration (MPA); healthcare administration (MPA); liberal studies in American culture (MA, MLS); performance (MA). *Application deadline:* For fall admission, 8/1 for domestic students, 5/1 for international students; for winter admission, 11/15 for domestic students, 9/1 for international students; for spring admission, 3/15 for domestic students, 1/1 for international students; for summer admission, 5/15 for domestic students. Applications are processed on a rolling basis. *Application fee:* $55. Electronic applications accepted. *Application Contact:* Matt Bohlen,

Director of Graduate Admissions, 810-762-3171, Fax: 810-766-6789, E-mail: mbohlen@umflint.edu. *Dean of Graduate Programs,* Stephen W Turner, 810-762-3171, Fax: 810-766-6789, E-mail: swturner@umflint.edu.

School of Education and Human Services Students: 31 full-time (23 women), 179 part-time (135 women); includes 54 minority (42 Black or African American, non-Hispanic/Latino; 3 Asian, non-Hispanic/Latino; 4 Hispanic/Latino; 1 Native Hawaiian or other Pacific Islander, non-Hispanic/Latino; 4 Two or more races, non-Hispanic/Latino), 1 international. Average age 39. 133 applicants, 72% accepted, 61 enrolled. *Faculty:* 16 full-time (10 women), 28 part-time/adjunct (14 women). Expenses: Contact institution. *Financial support:* Federal Work-Study and unspecified assistantships available. Support available to part-time students. Financial award application deadline: 3/1; financial award applicants required to submit FAFSA. In 2018, 60 master's awarded. *Program availability:* Part-time, mixed mode format. Offers curriculum and instruction (Ed S); early childhood education (MA); education (Ed D); education and human services (MA, Ed D, Ed S); educational leadership (Ed S); educational technology (MA); literacy education (MA); secondary education with certification (MA). *Application deadline:* For fall admission, 7/1 for domestic students, 4/1 for international students; for winter admission, 11/15 for domestic students, 9/1 for international students; for spring admission, 3/15 for domestic students, 1/1 for international students. Applications are processed on a rolling basis. *Application fee:* $55. Electronic applications accepted. *Application Contact:* Matt Bohlen, Director of Graduate Admissions, 810-762-3171, Fax: 810-766-6789, E-mail: mbohlen@umflint.edu. *Dean,* Dr. Bob Barnett, 810-766-6878, Fax: 810-766-6891, E-mail: rbarnett@umflint.edu.

School of Management Students: 28 full-time (16 women), 193 part-time (77 women); includes 56 minority (27 Black or African American, non-Hispanic/Latino; 4 American Indian or Alaska Native, non-Hispanic/Latino; 10 Asian, non-Hispanic/Latino; 9 Hispanic/Latino; 6 Two or more races, non-Hispanic/Latino), 27 international. Average age 35. 182 applicants, 78% accepted, 73 enrolled. *Faculty:* 30 full-time (4 women), 10 part-time/adjunct (2 women). Expenses: Contact institution. *Financial support:* Federal Work-Study, scholarships/grants, and unspecified assistantships available. Support available to part-time students. Financial award application deadline: 3/1; financial award applicants required to submit FAFSA. In 2018, 75 master's, 1 other advanced degree awarded. *Program availability:* Part-time, evening/weekend, mixed mode format. Offers accounting (MBA); computer information systems (MBA); finance (MBA, Post-Master's Certificate); general business (Graduate Certificate); general business administration (MBA); health care management (MBA); international business (MBA, Post-Master's Certificate); leadership and organizational dynamics (MS); lean manufacturing (MBA); management (MBA, MS, MSA, Graduate Certificate, Post-Master's Certificate); marketing (Post-Master's Certificate); marketing and innovation management (MBA); organizational leadership (MBA, Post-Master's Certificate). *Application deadline:* For fall admission, 8/1 for domestic students, 5/1 for international students; for winter admission, 11/15 for domestic students, 9/1 for international students; for spring admission, 3/15 for domestic students, 1/1 for international students; for summer admission, 5/15 for domestic students. Applications are processed on a rolling basis. *Application fee:* $55. Electronic applications accepted. *Application Contact:* Matt Bohlen, Director of Graduate Admissions, 810-762-3171, Fax: 810-766-6789, E-mail: mbohlen@umflint.edu. *Dean, School of Management,* Dr. Scott Johnson, 810-762-6579, Fax: 810-237-6685, E-mail: scotjohn@umflint.edu.

School of Nursing Students: 167 full-time (146 women), 177 part-time (148 women); includes 87 minority (50 Black or African American, non-Hispanic/Latino; 2 American Indian or Alaska Native, non-Hispanic/Latino; 17 Asian, non-Hispanic/Latino; 11 Hispanic/Latino; 7 Two or more races, non-Hispanic/Latino), 2 international. Average age 37. 147 applicants, 82% accepted, 69 enrolled. *Faculty:* 32 full-time (all women), 79 part-time/adjunct (72 women). Expenses: Contact institution. *Financial support:* Federal Work-Study, scholarships/grants, and unspecified assistantships available. Support available to part-time students. Financial award application deadline: 3/1; financial award applicants required to submit FAFSA. In 2018, 52 master's, 22 doctorates, 8 other advanced degrees awarded. *Program availability:* Part-time, evening/weekend, 100% online. Offers adult-gerontology acute care (DNP); adult-gerontology primary care (DNP); family nurse practitioner (DNP); nursing (MSN); psychiatric mental health (DNP); psychiatric mental health nurse practitioner (Certificate). *Application deadline:* For fall admission, 7/1 for domestic students, 5/1 for international students; for winter admission, 11/1 for domestic students, 9/1 for international students; for spring admission, 3/15 for domestic students, 1/1 for international students. Applications are processed on a rolling basis. *Application fee:* $55. Electronic applications accepted. *Application Contact:* Matt Bohlen, Director of Graduate Admissions, 810-762-3171, Fax: 810-766-6789, E-mail: mbohlen@umflint.edu. *Director,* Dr. Constance J. Creech, 810-762-3420, Fax: 810-766-6851, E-mail: ccreech@umflint.edu.

UNIVERSITY OF MINNESOTA, DULUTH, Duluth, MN 55812-2496

General Information State-supported, coed, comprehensive institution. *Graduate housing:* Room and/or apartments available to single students; on-campus housing not available to married students. Housing application deadline: 3/1. *Research affiliation:* Environmental Protection Agency Environmental Research Laboratory (aquatic biology), Minnesota Geological Survey, Northeastern Minnesota National Historical Center (local history), U.S. Forest Service, Northcentral Forest Experiment Station.

GRADUATE UNITS

Graduate School *Program availability:* Part-time, evening/weekend, online learning. Offers toxicology (MS, PhD).

College of Education and Human Service Professions *Program availability:* Part-time, evening/weekend, online learning. Offers communication sciences and disorders (MA); education (M Ed, Ed D); education and human service professions (M Ed, MA, MSW, Ed D); social work (MSW).

College of Liberal Arts *Program availability:* Part-time. Offers criminology (MA); English (MA); liberal arts (MA, MLS); liberal studies (MLS).

Labovitz School of Business and Economics *Program availability:* Part-time, evening/weekend. Offers business administration (MBA); business and economics (MBA).

School of Fine Arts *Program availability:* Part-time. Offers fine arts (MFA, MM); graphic design (MFA); music education (MM); performance (MM).

Swenson College of Science and Engineering *Program availability:* Part-time, evening/weekend, online learning. Offers applied and computational mathematics (MS); chemistry and biochemistry (MS); computer science (MS); electrical and computer engineering (MSECE); engineering management (MSEM); environmental health and safety (MEHS); geological sciences (MS, PhD); integrated biosciences (MS, PhD); physics (MS); science and engineering (MEHS, MS, MSECE, MSEM, PhD).

Medical School *Program availability:* Part-time. Offers biochemistry, molecular biology and biophysics (MS); biology and biophysics (PhD); medicine (MS, MD, PhD);

microbiology, immunology and molecular pathobiology (MS, PhD); pharmacology (MS, PhD); physiology (MS, PhD); social, administrative, and clinical pharmacy (MS, PhD); toxicology (MS, PhD).

UNIVERSITY OF MINNESOTA ROCHESTER, Rochester, MN 55904
General Information State-supported, coed, comprehensive institution.
GRADUATE UNITS
Graduate Programs

UNIVERSITY OF MINNESOTA, TWIN CITIES CAMPUS, Minneapolis, MN 55455-0213

General Information State-supported, coed, university. CGS member. *Graduate housing:* Rooms and/or apartments available on a first-come, first-served basis to single and married students. Housing application deadline: 5/1.

GRADUATE UNITS
Carlson School of Management Students: 537 full-time (232 women), 949 part-time (326 women); includes 210 minority (33 Black or African American, non-Hispanic/Latino; 18 American Indian or Alaska Native, non-Hispanic/Latino; 116 Asian, non-Hispanic/Latino; 41 Hispanic/Latino; 2 Native Hawaiian or other Pacific Islander, non-Hispanic/Latino, 305 international. Average age 28. 1,956 applicants, 45% accepted, 498 enrolled. *Faculty:* 150 full-time (43 women), 57 part-time/adjunct (18 women). Expenses: Contact institution. *Financial support:* Fellowships with full and partial tuition reimbursements, research assistantships with full tuition reimbursements, teaching assistantships with full and partial tuition reimbursements, career-related internships or fieldwork, Federal Work-Study, institutionally sponsored loans, scholarships/grants, health care benefits, tuition waivers (full and partial), and unspecified assistantships available. Support available to part-time students. Financial award application deadline: 4/1; financial award applicants required to submit FAFSA. In 2018, 565 master's, 14 doctorates awarded. *Program availability:* Part-time, evening/weekend, 100% online, blended/hybrid learning. Offers accountancy (M Acc); accounting (PhD); business analytics (MS); business taxation (MBT); finance (MBA, PhD); human resources and industrial relations (MA); information and decision sciences (PhD); information technology (MBA); management (MBA); marketing (MBA, PhD); medical industry orientation (MBA); strategic management and entrepreneurship (PhD); supply chain and operations (MBA, PhD); work and organizations (PhD). *Application fee:* $75 ($95 for international students). Electronic applications accepted. *Application Contact:* Graduate School Admissions, 612-625-3014, Fax: 612-625-6002, E-mail: gsquest@umn.edu. *Associate Dean of Faculty and Research,* Prof. Alok Gupta, 612-626-0276, Fax: 612-624-6374, E-mail: gupta037@umn.edu.

College of Pharmacy *Program availability:* Part-time. Offers experimental and clinical pharmacology (MS, PhD); medicinal chemistry (MS, PhD); pharmaceutics (MS, PhD); pharmacy (MS, PhD, Pharm D); social and administrative pharmacy (MS, PhD).

College of Science and Engineering Students: 2,250 full-time, 379 part-time; includes 273 minority (38 Black or African American, non-Hispanic/Latino; 5 American Indian or Alaska Native, non-Hispanic/Latino; 114 Asian, non-Hispanic/Latino; 73 Hispanic/Latino; 1 Native Hawaiian or other Pacific Islander, non-Hispanic/Latino; 42 Two or more races, non-Hispanic/Latino), 1,286 international. Average age 25. 5,478 applicants, 32% accepted, 721 enrolled. *Faculty:* 428 full-time (67 women). Expenses: Contact institution. *Financial support:* Fellowships, research assistantships, teaching assistantships, and unspecified assistantships available. Financial award applicants required to submit FAFSA. In 2018, 586 master's, 255 doctorates awarded. *Program availability:* Part-time, evening/weekend, 100% online, blended/hybrid learning. Offers aerospace engineering and mechanics (MS, PhD); biomedical engineering (MS, PhD); chemical engineering (M Ch E, MS Ch E, PhD); chemical physics (MS, PhD); chemistry (MS, PhD); civil engineering (MCE, MS, PhD); computer science (MCS, MS, PhD); data science (MS); earth sciences (MS, PhD); electrical and computer engineering (MSEE, PhD); geological engineering (M Geo E, MS); history of science, technology and medicine (MA, PhD); industrial and systems engineering (MS, PhD); materials science and engineering (M Mat SE, MS Mat SE, PhD); mechanical engineering (MSME, PhD); science and engineering (M Ch E, M Geo E, M Mat SE, MA, MCE, MCS, MFM, MS, MS Ch E, MS Mat SE, MSEE, MSME, MSMOT, MSSE, MSST, PhD, Certificate); scientific computation (MS); software engineering (MSSE); stream restoration science and engineering (Certificate). *Application deadline:* Applications are processed on a rolling basis. *Application fee:* $75 ($95 for international students). Electronic applications accepted. *Application Contact:* Graduate Admissions Office, 612-625-3014. *Dean,* Mostafa Kaveh, 612-624-2006, Fax: 612-624-2841, E-mail: mos@umn.edu.

School of Mathematics *Program availability:* Part-time. Offers mathematics (MS, PhD); quantitative finance (Certificate). Electronic applications accepted.

School of Physics and Astronomy *Program availability:* Part-time. Offers astrophysics (MS, PhD); physics (MS, PhD).

Technological Leadership Institute *Program availability:* Evening/weekend. Offers management of technology (MSMOT); medical device innovation (MS); security technologies (MSST). Electronic applications accepted.

College of Veterinary Medicine *Program availability:* Part-time. Offers comparative and molecular bioscience (MS, PhD); veterinary medicine (MS, PhD). Electronic applications accepted.

Graduate School *Program availability:* Part-time, evening/weekend, online learning. Offers biophysical sciences and medical physics (MS, PhD); genetic counseling (MS); health informatics (MHI, MS, PhD); history of science, technology and medicine (MA, PhD); integrative biology and physiology (PhD); microbial engineering (MS); microbiology, immunology and cancer biology (PhD); molecular, cellular, developmental biology and genetics (PhD); neuroscience (MS, PhD); occupational therapy (MOT); stem cell biology (MS). Electronic applications accepted.

College of Biological Sciences *Program availability:* Part-time. Offers biochemistry, molecular biology and biophysics (PhD); biological science (MBS); biological sciences (MBS, MS, PhD); ecology, evolution, and behavior (MS, PhD); plant biological sciences (MS, PhD). Electronic applications accepted.

College of Design Offers apparel (MA, MS, PhD); architecture (M Arch); design (M Arch, MA, MFA, MLA, MS, PhD, Postbaccalaureate Certificate); design communication (MA, MS, PhD); housing studies (MA, MS, PhD, Postbaccalaureate Certificate); interactive design (MFA); interior design (MA, MS, PhD); landscape architecture (MLA, MS); sustainable design (MS). Electronic applications accepted.

College of Education and Human Development Students: 1,485 full-time (1,079 women), 571 part-time (404 women); includes 458 minority (119 Black or African American, non-Hispanic/Latino; 12 American Indian or Alaska Native, non-Hispanic/Latino; 123 Asian, non-Hispanic/Latino; 115 Hispanic/Latino; 89 Two or more races, non-Hispanic/Latino), 221 international. Average age 32. 2,070 applicants, 58% accepted, 936 enrolled. *Faculty:* 167 full-time (89 women). Expenses: Contact institution. *Financial support:* In 2018–19, 108 fellowships, 249 research

assistantships with full tuition reimbursements (averaging $12,642 per year), 223 teaching assistantships with full tuition reimbursements (averaging $12,068 per year) were awarded; scholarships/grants and tuition waivers (partial) also available. Financial award applicants required to submit FAFSA. In 2018, 765 master's, 113 doctorates, 124 other advanced degrees awarded. *Program availability:* Part-time. Offers adult literacy (Certificate); applied child and adolescent development (MA); art education (M Ed, MA, PhD); autism spectrum disorder (Certificate); comparative and international development education (MA, PhD); counseling and student personnel psychology (MA); curriculum and instruction (M Ed, MA, PhD); developmental psychology (PhD); disability policy and services (Certificate); early childhood education (M Ed); early childhood special education (M Ed); education and human development (M Ed, MA, MS, MSW, Ed D, PhD, Certificate, Ed S); education policy and leadership (M Ed, MA, Ed D, PhD); educational policy and leadership (MA, Ed D, PhD); elementary education (MA, PhD); English education (PhD); evaluation studies (MA, PhD); family education (M Ed); higher education (MA, Ed D, PhD); human resource development (M Ed, MA, Ed D, PhD, Certificate); kinesiology (MS, PhD); language and immersion education (Certificate); leadership in education (M Ed); learning technologies (MA, PhD); literacy education (MA, PhD); marriage and family therapy (MA, PhD); multicultural college teaching and learning (MA); PK-12 administrative licensure (Certificate); prevention science (MA); private college leadership (Certificate); professional development (Certificate); program evaluation (Certificate); psychological foundations of education (MA, PhD); quantitative methods in education (MA, PhD); school psychology (MA, PhD, Ed S); second language education (MA, PhD); social studies education (MA, PhD); social work (MSW, PhD); special education (M Ed, MA, PhD); sport and exercise science (M Ed); sport management (M Ed, MA); STEM education (MA, PhD); talent development and gifted education (Certificate); teaching (M Ed); teaching English to speakers of other languages (MA); technical education (Certificate); technology enhanced learning (Certificate); undergraduate multicultural teaching and learning (Certificate); youth development leadership (M Ed). *Application fee:* $75 ($95 for international students). *Application Contact:* Schee Moua, Director of Graduate Education, 612-626-7356, E-mail: scmoua@umn.edu. *Dean,* Dr. Jean K. Quam, 612-626-9252, Fax: 612-626-7496, E-mail: jquam@umn.edu.

College of Food, Agricultural and Natural Resource Sciences *Program availability:* Part-time. Offers animal sciences (MS, PhD); applied economics (MS, PhD); applied plant sciences (MS, PhD); assessment, monitoring, and geospatial analysis (MS, PhD); bioproducts and biosystems science, engineering and management (MS, PhD); conservation sciences (MS); economics, policy, management, and society (MS, PhD); entomology (MS, PhD); food science (MS, PhD); food, agricultural and natural resource sciences (MS, PhD); forest hydrology and watershed management (MS, PhD); forest products (MS, PhD); forests: biology, ecology, conservation, and management (MS, PhD); land and atmospheric science (MS, PhD); natural resources science and management (MS, PhD); nutrition (MS, PhD); paper science and engineering (MS, PhD); plant pathology (MS, PhD); recreation resources, tourism, and environmental education (MS, PhD); water resources science (MS, PhD). Electronic applications accepted.

College of Liberal Arts *Program availability:* Part-time, evening/weekend. Offers American studies (PhD); ancient and medieval art and archaeology (MA, PhD); anthropology (MA, PhD); art (MFA); art history (MA, PhD); Asian literatures, cultures, and media (PhD); audiology (Au D); biological psychopathology (PhD); classics (MA, PhD); clinical psychology (PhD); cognitive and biological psychology (PhD); communication studies (MA, PhD); comparative literature (PhD); comparative studies in discourse and society (PhD); counseling psychology (PhD); design technology (MFA); economics (MA, PhD); English (MA, PhD); English as a second language (MA); feminist studies (PhD); French (MA, PhD); geographic information science (MGIS); geography, environment and society (MA, PhD); Germanic studies (MA, PhD); Greek (MA, PhD); Hispanic and Lusophone literatures, cultures and linguistics (PhD); Hispanic linguistics (MA); Hispanic literature (MA); history (MA, PhD); industrial/organizational psychology (PhD); Latin (MA); liberal arts (MA, MFA, MGIS, MM, MS, Au D, DMA, PhD); linguistics (MA, PhD); Lusophone literature (MA); mass communication (MA, PhD); music (MA, MM, DMA, PhD); personality, individual differences, and behavior genetics (PhD); philosophy (MA, PhD); political science (PhD); quantitative/psychometric methods (PhD); religions in antiquity (MA); school psychology (PhD); social psychology (PhD); sociology (MA, PhD); speech-language pathology (MA); speech-language-hearing sciences (PhD); statistics (MS, PhD); strategic communication (professional program) (MA); theatre arts (MA, PhD). Electronic applications accepted.

Humphrey School of Public Affairs *Program availability:* Part-time, evening/weekend. Offers development practice (MDP); management and governance (PhD); public affairs (MDP, MPA, MPP, MS, MURP, PhD); public policy (PhD); science, technology, and environmental policy (PhD); urban and regional planning (MURP); urban planning (PhD). Electronic applications accepted.

School of Nursing *Program availability:* Part-time, online learning. Offers adult/gerontological clinical nurse specialist (DNP); adult/gerontological primary care nurse practitioner (DNP); family nurse practitioner (DNP); health innovation and leadership (DNP); integrative health and healing (DNP); nurse anesthesia (DNP); nurse midwifery (DNP); nursing (MN, PhD); nursing informatics (DNP); pediatric clinical nurse specialist (DNP); primary care certified pediatric nurse practitioner (DNP); psychiatric/mental health nurse practitioner (DNP); women's health nurse practitioner (DNP).

Law School Students: 590 full-time (299 women); includes 92 minority (5 Black or African American, non-Hispanic/Latino; 6 American Indian or Alaska Native, non-Hispanic/Latino; 33 Asian, non-Hispanic/Latino; 31 Hispanic/Latino; 1 Native Hawaiian or other Pacific Islander, non-Hispanic/Latino; 16 Two or more races, non-Hispanic/Latino), 55 international. 1,966 applicants, 35% accepted, 220 enrolled. *Faculty:* 62 full-time (25 women), 138 part-time/adjunct (44 women). Expenses: Contact institution. *Financial support:* In 2018–19, 577 students received support. Fellowships, research assistantships, career-related internships or fieldwork, Federal Work-Study, institutionally sponsored loans, and scholarships/grants available. Financial award application deadline: 7/1; financial award applicants required to submit FAFSA. In 2018, 193 doctorates awarded. Offers law (LL M, MS, JD, SJD). *Application deadline:* For fall admission, 7/15 for domestic students. Applications are processed on a rolling basis. *Application fee:* $60. Electronic applications accepted. *Application Contact:* Robin Ingli, Director of Admissions, 612-625-3487, Fax: 612-625-2011, E-mail: jdadmissions@umn.edu. *Dean,* Garry W. Jenkins, 612-625-4841.

Medical School *Program availability:* Part-time, evening/weekend. Offers medicine (MA, MS, DPT, MD, PhD); pharmacology (MS, PhD).

School of Dentistry Offers dentistry (MS, DDS, PhD, Certificate); endodontics (MS, Certificate); oral biology (MS, PhD); oral health services for older adults (geriatrics) (MS, Certificate); orthodontics (MS); pediatric dentistry (MS); periodontology (MS); prosthodontics (MS); temporomandibular joint disorders (MS).

School of Public Health *Program availability:* Part-time, online learning. Offers biostatistics (MPH, MS, PhD); clinical research (MS); community health education (MPH); core concepts (Certificate); epidemiology (MPH, PhD); food safety and biosecurity (Certificate); health services research, policy, and administration (MS, PhD); healthcare administration (MHA); maternal and child health (MPH); occupational health and safety (Certificate); preparedness, response and recovery (Certificate); public health (MHA, MPH, MS, PhD, Certificate); public health administration and policy (MPH); public health nutrition (MPH); public health practice (MPH). Electronic applications accepted.

Division of Environmental Health Sciences *Program availability:* Part-time. Offers environmental and occupational epidemiology (MPH, MS, PhD); environmental chemistry (MS, PhD); environmental health policy (MPH, MS, PhD); environmental infectious diseases (MPH, MS, PhD); environmental toxicology (MPH, MS, PhD); exposure sciences (MS); general environmental health (MPH, MS); global environmental health (MPH, MS, PhD); industrial hygiene (MPH, MS, PhD); occupational health nursing (MPH, MS, PhD); occupational medicine (MPH). Electronic applications accepted.

UNIVERSITY OF MISSISSIPPI, University, MS 38677

General Information State-supported, coed, university. CGS member. *Graduate housing:* Rooms and/or apartments available to single and married students. *Research affiliation:* Mississippi Geographic Alliance, Mississippi Research Consortium, Mississippi-Alabama Sea Grant Consortium, Oak Ridge Associated Universities, Southeastern Universities Research Association, Mississippi Space Grant Consortium.

GRADUATE UNITS

Graduate School *Program availability:* Part-time. Electronic applications accepted.

College of Liberal Arts Students: 471 full-time (241 women), 80 part-time (39 women); includes 90 minority (43 Black or African American, non-Hispanic/Latino; 14 Asian, non-Hispanic/Latino; 23 Hispanic/Latino; 10 Two or more races, non-Hispanic/Latino), 136 international. *Faculty:* 474 full-time (209 women), 71 part-time/adjunct (38 women). Expenses: Contact institution. *Financial support:* Fellowships, research assistantships, teaching assistantships, career-related internships or fieldwork, Federal Work-Study, institutionally sponsored loans, scholarships/grants, and unspecified assistantships available. Financial award application deadline: 3/1; financial award applicants required to submit FAFSA. *Program availability:* Part-time. Offers anthropology (MA); biology (MS, PhD); chemistry (MS, DA, PhD); creative writing (MFA); documentary expression (MFA); economics (MA, PhD); English (MA, PhD); experimental psychology (PhD); history (MA, PhD); mathematics (MS, PhD); modern languages (MA); music (MM); philosophy (MA); physics (MA, MS, PhD); political science (MA, PhD); Southern studies (MA); studio art (MFA). *Application deadline:* Applications are processed on a rolling basis. *Application fee:* $50. Electronic applications accepted. *Application Contact:* Tameka Smith, Graduate Activities Specialist for Admissions, 662-915-7474, Fax: 662-915-7577, E-mail: gschool@olemiss.edu. *Dean,* Dr. Lee Michael Cohen, 662-915-7177, Fax: 662-915-5792, E-mail: libarts@olemiss.edu.

School of Accountancy Students: 228 full-time (102 women), 4 part-time (2 women); includes 32 minority (16 Black or African American, non-Hispanic/Latino; 4 Asian, non-Hispanic/Latino; 5 Hispanic/Latino; 1 Native Hawaiian or other Pacific Islander, non-Hispanic/Latino; 6 Two or more races, non-Hispanic/Latino), 7 international. Average age 24. *Faculty:* 20 full-time (6 women), 2 part-time/adjunct (both women). Expenses: Contact institution. *Financial support:* Scholarships/grants available. Financial award application deadline: 3/1; financial award applicants required to submit FAFSA. In 2018, 131 master's, 2 doctorates awarded. Offers accountancy (M Acc, PhD); accounting and data analytics (MA); taxation accounting (M Tax). *Application deadline:* Applications are processed on a rolling basis. *Application fee:* $50. Electronic applications accepted. *Application Contact:* Tameka Smith, Graduate Activities Specialist for Admissions, 662-915-7474, Fax: 662-915-7577, E-mail: gschool@olemiss.edu. *Dean, School of Accountancy,* Dr. W. Mark Wilder, 662-915-7468, Fax: 662-915-7483, E-mail: umaccy@olemiss.edu.

School of Applied Sciences Students: 192 full-time (148 women), 40 part-time (25 women); includes 50 minority (41 Black or African American, non-Hispanic/Latino; 1 American Indian or Alaska Native, non-Hispanic/Latino; 1 Asian, non-Hispanic/Latino; 5 Hispanic/Latino; 2 Two or more races, non-Hispanic/Latino), 16 international. Average age 26. *Faculty:* 66 full-time (36 women), 27 part-time/adjunct (13 women). Expenses: Contact institution. *Financial support:* Scholarships/grants available. Financial award application deadline: 3/1; financial award applicants required to submit FAFSA. In 2018, 72 master's, 5 doctorates awarded. Offers communicative disorders (MS); criminal justice (MCJ); exercise science (MS); food and nutrition services (MS); health and kinesiology (MS); health promotion (MS); nutrition and hospitality management (PhD); park and recreation management (MA); social welfare (PhD); social work (MSW). *Application deadline:* Applications are processed on a rolling basis. *Application fee:* $50. Electronic applications accepted. *Application Contact:* Temeka Smith, Graduate Activities Specialist for Admissions, 662-915-7474, Fax: 662-915-7577, E-mail: gschool@olemiss.edu. *Dean of Applied Sciences,* Dr. Peter Grandjean, 662-915-7900, Fax: 662-915-7901, E-mail: applsci@olemiss.edu.

School of Business Administration Students: 62 full-time (18 women), 83 part-time (20 women); includes 13 minority (4 Black or African American, non-Hispanic/Latino; 3 Asian, non-Hispanic/Latino; 4 Hispanic/Latino; 2 Two or more races, non-Hispanic/Latino), 14 international. Average age 30. *Faculty:* 60 full-time (18 women), 7 part-time/adjunct (1 woman). Expenses: Contact institution. *Financial support:* Fellowships, career-related internships or fieldwork, scholarships/grants, tuition waivers (full), and unspecified assistantships available. Financial award application deadline: 3/1; financial award applicants required to submit FAFSA. In 2018, 180 master's, 11 doctorates awarded. Offers business administration (MBA, PhD); finance (PhD); management (PhD); management information systems (PhD); marketing (PhD). *Application deadline:* Applications are processed on a rolling basis. *Application fee:* $50. Electronic applications accepted. *Application Contact:* Temeka Smith, Graduate Activities Specialist for Admissions, 662-915-7474, Fax: 662-915-7577, E-mail: gschool@olemiss.edu. *Dean,* Dr. Ken Cyree, 662-915-5820, Fax: 662-915-5821, E-mail: info@bus.olemiss.edu.

School of Education Students: 169 full-time (137 women), 461 part-time (329 women); includes 199 minority (185 Black or African American, non-Hispanic/Latino; 3 Asian, non-Hispanic/Latino; 7 Hispanic/Latino; 4 Two or more races, non-Hispanic/Latino), 5 international. Average age 33. *Faculty:* 59 full-time (35 women), 34 part-time/adjunct (26 women). Expenses: Contact institution. *Financial support:* Scholarships/grants available. Financial award application deadline: 3/1; financial award applicants required to submit FAFSA. In 2018, 180 master's, 5 doctorates, 37 other advanced degrees awarded. Offers counselor education (M Ed, PhD); counselor education - play therapy (Ed S); early childhood (M Ed); educational leadership K-12 (M Ed, Ed D, PhD, Ed S); elementary education (M Ed, Ed D, Ed S); higher education/student personnel (Ed D, PhD); literacy education (M Ed); math education (Ed D); secondary education (M Ed, PhD, Ed S); special education (M Ed, PhD, Ed S); teacher corporations (MA); teacher education (MA). *Application deadline:* Applications are processed on a rolling basis. *Application fee:* $50. Electronic applications accepted. *Application Contact:* Temeka Smith, Graduate Activities Specialist for Admissions, 662-915-7474, Fax: 662-915-7577, E-mail: gschool@olemiss.edu. *Dean,* Dr. David Rock, 662-915-7063, Fax: 662-915-7249, E-mail: soe@olemiss.edu.

School of Engineering Students: 129 full-time (33 women), 21 part-time (5 women); includes 15 minority (7 Black or African American, non-Hispanic/Latino; 6 Asian, non-Hispanic/Latino; 1 Hispanic/Latino; 1 Two or more races, non-Hispanic/Latino), 73 international. Average age 29. *Faculty:* 76 full-time (16 women), 3 part-time/adjunct (1 woman). Expenses: Contact institution. *Financial support:* Scholarships/grants available. Financial award application deadline: 3/1; financial award applicants required to submit FAFSA. In 2018, 36 master's, 17 doctorates awarded. Offers aeroacoustics (MS, PhD); chemical engineering (MS, PhD); civil engineering (MS, PhD); computational hydroscience (MS, PhD); computer science (MS, PhD); electrical engineering (MS, PhD); electromagnetics (MS, PhD); environmental engineering (MS, PhD); geology and geological engineering (MS, PhD); hydrology (MS); material science (MS); mechanical engineering (MS, PhD); telecommunications (MS). *Application deadline:* Applications are processed on a rolling basis. *Application fee:* $50. Electronic applications accepted. *Application Contact:* Temeka Smith, Graduate Activities Specialist for Admissions, 662-915-7474, Fax: 662-915-7577, E-mail: gschool@olemiss.edu. *Dean,* Dr. David Puleo, 662-915-5780, Fax: 662-915-5387, E-mail: engineer@olemiss.edu.

School of Journalism and New Media Students: 44 full-time (23 women), 7 part-time (6 women); includes 10 minority (6 Black or African American, non-Hispanic/Latino; 2 Hispanic/Latino; 2 Two or more races, non-Hispanic/Latino), 5 international. Average age 25. *Faculty:* 34 full-time (14 women), 18 part-time/adjunct (9 women). Expenses: Contact institution. In 2018, 18 master's awarded. Offers integrated marketing communications (MA); journalism (MA). *Application deadline:* Applications are processed on a rolling basis. *Application fee:* $50. Electronic applications accepted. *Application Contact:* Tameka Smith, Graduate Activities Specialist for Admission, 662-915-7474, Fax: 662-915-7577, E-mail: gschool@olemiss.edu. *Dean,* Dr. Will Norton, Jr., 662-915-7146, Fax: 662-915-7765, E-mail: meekschool@olemiss.edu.

School of Pharmacy Students: 336 full-time (207 women), 125 part-time (73 women); includes 73 minority (27 Black or African American, non-Hispanic/Latino; 1 American Indian or Alaska Native, non-Hispanic/Latino; 32 Asian, non-Hispanic/Latino; 7 Hispanic/Latino; 6 Two or more races, non-Hispanic/Latino), 99 international. Average age 25. *Faculty:* 69 full-time (31 women), 18 part-time/adjunct (7 women). Expenses: Contact institution. *Financial support:* Fellowships, research assistantships, teaching assistantships, career-related internships or fieldwork, Federal Work-Study, institutionally sponsored loans, scholarships/grants, tuition waivers (full), and unspecified assistantships available. Financial award application deadline: 3/1; financial award applicants required to submit FAFSA. In 2018, 29 master's, 128 doctorates awarded. *Program availability:* Part-time. Offers environmental toxicology (MS, PhD); industrial pharmacy (MS); medicinal chemistry (MS, PhD); pharmaceutics (MS, PhD); pharmacognosy (MS, PhD); pharmacology (MS, PhD); pharmacy (Pharm D); pharmacy administration (MS, PhD). *Application deadline:* Applications are processed on a rolling basis. *Application fee:* $50. Electronic applications accepted. *Application Contact:* Temeka Smith, Graduate Activities Specialist for Admissions, 662-915-7474, Fax: 662-915-7577, E-mail: gschool@olemiss.edu. *Dean, School of Pharmacy,* Dr. David Allen, 662-915-7265, Fax: 662-9155704, E-mail: sopdean@olemiss.edu.

School of Law Students: 363 full-time (162 women), 3 part-time (2 women); includes 94 minority (56 Black or African American, non-Hispanic/Latino; 1 American Indian or Alaska Native, non-Hispanic/Latino; 5 Asian, non-Hispanic/Latino; 24 Hispanic/Latino; 8 Two or more races, non-Hispanic/Latino), 2 international. Average age 25. *Faculty:* 31 full-time (12 women), 10 part-time/adjunct (4 women). Expenses: Contact institution. *Financial support:* Fellowships, research assistantships, teaching assistantships, career-related internships or fieldwork, Federal Work-Study, institutionally sponsored loans, and scholarships/grants available. Support available to part-time students. Financial award application deadline: 3/1; financial award applicants required to submit FAFSA. In 2018, 1 master's, 108 doctorates awarded. Offers law (LL M, JD). *Application deadline:* Applications are processed on a rolling basis. *Application fee:* $50. Electronic applications accepted. *Application Contact:* Temeka Smith, Graduate Activities Specialist for Admissions, 662-915-7474, Fax: 662-915-7577, E-mail: gschool@olemiss.edu. *Dean, School of Law,* Dr. Susan Duncan, 662-915-7361, Fax: 662-915-6895, E-mail: lawadmin@olemiss.edu.

UNIVERSITY OF MISSISSIPPI MEDICAL CENTER, Jackson, MS 39216-4505

General Information State-supported, coed, upper-level institution. *Graduate housing:* On-campus housing not available. *Research affiliation:* NASA-Stennis Space Center (imaging technology), Catfish Genetics Research Unit (immunology), Oak Ridge National Laboratory (physiology, biomedical engineering), Gulf Coast Research Laboratory (microbiology).

GRADUATE UNITS

School of Dentistry Offers craniofacial and dental research (MS, PhD); dentistry (MS, DMD, PhD).

School of Graduate Studies in Health Sciences *Program availability:* Part-time. Offers biochemistry (PhD); biomedical materials science (MS, PhD); biomedical sciences (MS); clinical anatomy (MS, PhD); health sciences (MS, PhD); microbiology (PhD); neuroscience (PhD); pathology (PhD); pharmacology and toxicology (PhD); physiology and biophysics (PhD).

School of Health Related Professions *Program availability:* Part-time. Offers health related professions (MOT, MPT); occupational therapy (MOT); physical therapy (MPT).

School of Medicine *Program availability:* Part-time. Offers medicine (MD). Electronic applications accepted.

School of Nursing *Program availability:* Part-time, evening/weekend, online learning. Offers nursing (MSN, DNP, PhD). Electronic applications accepted.

UNIVERSITY OF MISSOURI, Columbia, MO 65211

General Information State-supported, coed, university. CGS member. *Graduate housing:* Rooms and/or apartments available on a first-come, first-served basis to single and married students. Housing application deadline: 12/1.

GRADUATE UNITS

College of Veterinary Medicine Offers veterinary medicine (MS, DVM, PhD).

Graduate Programs in Veterinary Medicine Offers biomedical sciences (MS, PhD); comparative medicine (MS); pathobiology (MS, PhD); veterinary medicine (MS, PhD); veterinary medicine and surgery (MS).

Office of Research and Graduate Studies *Program availability:* Part-time, evening/weekend. Offers neuroscience (MS, PhD, Graduate Certificate).

College of Agriculture, Food and Natural Resources *Program availability:* Part-time. Offers agricultural economics (MS, PhD); agricultural education (MS, PhD); agriculture, food and natural resources (MS, PhD); agroforestry (MS, Certificate); animal sciences (MS, PhD); biochemistry (MS, PhD); conservation biology (Certificate); crop, soil and pest management (MS, PhD); entomology (MS, PhD); fisheries and wildlife sciences (MS, PhD); food science (MS, PhD); forestry (MS, PhD); geographical information science (Certificate); horticulture (MS, PhD); human dimensions of natural resources (MS, PhD); parks, recreation and tourism (MS); plant breeding, genetics and genomics (MS, PhD); plant stress biology (MS, PhD); rural sociology (MS, PhD); society and ecosystems (Certificate); soil, environmental and atmospheric sciences (MS, PhD); water resources (MS, PhD).

College of Arts and Science *Program availability:* Part-time. Offers analytical chemistry (PhD); anthropology (MA, PhD); applied mathematics (MS); art (MFA); art history and archaeology (MA, PhD); arts and science (MA, MFA, MS, PhD, Certificate, Graduate Certificate); classical languages (MA, PhD); classical studies (MA, PhD); communication (MA, PhD); economics (MA, PhD); English (MA, PhD); evolutionary biology and ecology (MA, PhD); French (MA, PhD); geographic information science (Graduate Certificate); geography (MA); geological sciences (MS, PhD); German and Russian studies (MA); history (MA, PhD); mathematics (MA, PhD); music (MA, Certificate); philosophy (MA, PhD); physics and astronomy (MS, PhD); political science (MA, PhD, Certificate); psychological sciences (MA, PhD, Certificate); religious studies (MA); sociology (MA, PhD); statistics (MA, PhD); theatre (MA, PhD).

College of Education *Program availability:* Part-time, evening/weekend. Offers administration and supervision of special education (PhD); agricultural education (M Ed, PhD, Ed S); art education (M Ed, PhD, Ed S); business and office education (M Ed, PhD, Ed S); counseling psychology (M Ed, MA, PhD, Ed S); early childhood education (M Ed, PhD, Ed S); education (M Ed, MA, Ed D, PhD, Ed S); education administration (M Ed, MA, Ed D, PhD, Ed S); educational psychology (M Ed, MA, PhD, Ed S); elementary education (M Ed, PhD, Ed S); English education (M Ed, PhD, Ed S); foreign language education (M Ed, PhD, Ed S); health education and promotion (M Ed, PhD); higher and adult education (M Ed, MA, Ed D, PhD, Ed S); information science and learning technology (PhD); learning and instruction (M Ed); marketing education (M Ed, PhD, Ed S); mathematics education (M Ed, PhD, Ed S); music education (M Ed, Ed S); reading education (M Ed, Ed S); school psychology (M Ed, MA, PhD, Ed S); science education (M Ed, PhD, Ed S); social studies education (M Ed, PhD, Ed S); vocational education (M Ed, PhD, Ed S).

College of Engineering *Program availability:* Part-time. Offers biological engineering (MS, PhD); chemical engineering (MS, PhD); civil engineering (MS, PhD); computer engineering (MSCE); computer science (MS, PhD); electrical and computer engineering (PhD); electrical engineering (MSEE); engineering (ME, MS, MSCE, MSEE, PhD, Certificate); industrial and manufacturing systems engineering (ME, MS, PhD); mechanical and aerospace engineering (ME, MS, PhD).

College of Human Environmental Sciences *Program availability:* Part-time. Offers architectural studies (MS, PhD); exercise physiology (MS, PhD); human development and family sciences (MA, MS, PhD); human environmental sciences (MA, MS, PhD, Certificate, Graduate Certificate); nutritional sciences (MS, PhD); personal financial planning (PhD); textile and apparel management (MS, PhD).

Harry S Truman School of Public Affairs Offers grantsmanship (Graduate Certificate); nonprofit management (Graduate Certificate); organizational change (Graduate Certificate); public affairs (MPA, PhD); public management (Graduate Certificate); science and public policy (Graduate Certificate). Electronic applications accepted.

Informatics Institute Offers informatics (MS). Electronic applications accepted.

Robert J. Trulaske, Sr. College of Business *Program availability:* Part-time. Offers accountancy (M Acc, PhD); business (Exec MBA, M Acc, MBA, PhD, Certificate); business administration (MBA); finance (PhD); taxation (Certificate).

School of Journalism *Program availability:* Part-time. Offers health communications (MA); journalism (PhD). Electronic applications accepted.

School of Social Work *Program availability:* Part-time. Offers gerontological social work (Graduate Certificate); social work (MSW, PhD). Electronic applications accepted.

Sinclair School of Nursing *Program availability:* Part-time. Offers adult-gerontology clinical nurse specialist (DNP, Certificate); family nurse practitioner (DNP); family psychiatric and mental health nurse practitioner (DNP); nursing (MS, PhD); nursing leadership and innovations in health care (DNP); pediatric clinical nurse specialist (DNP, Certificate); pediatric nurse practitioner (DNP). Electronic applications accepted.

School of Health Professions Offers communication science and disorders (MHS, PhD); diagnostic medical ultrasound (MHS); global public health (Graduate Certificate); health professions (MHS, MOT, MPH, DPT, PhD, Graduate Certificate); health promotion and policy (MPH); occupational therapy (MOT); physical therapy (DPT); public health (Graduate Certificate); veterinary public health (MPH).

School of Law Offers dispute resolution (LL M); law (JD).

School of Medicine *Program availability:* Part-time. Offers medicine (MHA, MS, MD, PhD, Certificate, Graduate Certificate).

Graduate Programs in Medicine *Program availability:* Part-time. Offers health administration (MHA); health informatics (MS, Certificate); medical pharmacology and physiology (MS, PhD); medicine (MHA, MS, PhD, Certificate); molecular microbiology and immunology (PhD); pathology and anatomical sciences (MS, PhD).

UNIVERSITY OF MISSOURI–KANSAS CITY, Kansas City, MO 64110-2499

General Information State-supported, coed, university. CGS member. *Graduate housing:* Room and/or apartments available on a first-come, first-served basis to single students; on-campus housing not available to married students. *Research affiliation:* St. Luke's Hospital (health sciences), Children's Mercy Hospital (health sciences), Truman Medical Center (health sciences), Veterans Administration Hospital (health sciences), Midwest Research Institute (health sciences).

GRADUATE UNITS

College of Arts and Sciences *Program availability:* Part-time, evening/weekend. Offers analytical chemistry (PhD); art and art history (MA, PhD); arts and sciences (MA, MFA, MS, MSW, PhD); community psychology (PhD); criminal justice and criminology (MS); economics (MA, PhD); English (MA, PhD); geosciences (MS, PhD); history (MA, PhD); inorganic chemistry (PhD); mathematics and statistics (MA, MS, PhD); organic chemistry (PhD); physical chemistry (PhD); physics (MS, PhD); political science (MA); polymer chemistry (MS, PhD); romance languages and literatures (MA); sociology (MA); theatre (MA, MFA). Electronic applications accepted.

School of Social Work *Program availability:* Part-time, evening/weekend. Offers social work (MSW).

Conservatory of Music and Dance *Program availability:* Part-time. Offers composition (MM, DMA); conducting (MM, DMA); music (MA); music education (MME, PhD); music history and literature (MM); music theory (MM); music therapy (MA); performance (MM, DMA). PhD (interdisciplinary) offered through the School of Graduate Studies.

Henry W. Bloch School of Management *Program availability:* Part-time, evening/weekend. Offers accounting (MS); finance (MS); public affairs (MPA, PhD). PhD (interdisciplinary) offered through the School of Graduate Studies. Electronic applications accepted.

School of Biological Sciences *Program availability:* Part-time, evening/weekend. Offers biology (MA); cell biology and biophysics (PhD); cellular and molecular biology (MS); molecular biology and biochemistry (PhD). PhD (interdisciplinary) offered through the School of Graduate Studies.

School of Computing and Engineering *Program availability:* Part-time. Offers civil engineering (MS); computer and electrical engineering (PhD); computer science (MS); computer science and informatics (PhD); computing (PhD); electrical engineering (MS); engineering (PhD); engineering and construction management (Graduate Certificate); mechanical engineering (MS); telecommunications and computer networking (PhD). PhD (interdisciplinary) offered through the School of Graduate Studies.

School of Dentistry Offers advanced education in dentistry (Graduate Dental Certificate); dental hygiene education (MS); endodontics (Graduate Dental Certificate); oral and maxillofacial surgery (Graduate Dental Certificate); oral biology (MS, PhD); orthodontics and dentofacial orthopedics (Graduate Dental Certificate); periodontics (Graduate Dental Certificate). PhD (interdisciplinary) offered through the School of Graduate Studies.

School of Education *Program availability:* Part-time, evening/weekend. Offers administration (Ed D); counseling and guidance (MA, Ed S); counseling psychology (PhD); curriculum and instruction (MA, Ed S); education (PhD); educational administration (MA, Ed S); reading education (MA); special education (MA). PhD in education offered through the School of Graduate Studies.

School of Graduate Studies Offers interdisciplinary studies (PhD). Electronic applications accepted.

School of Law *Program availability:* Part-time. Offers law (LL M, JD). Electronic applications accepted.

School of Medicine Offers health professions education (MS).

School of Nursing and Health Studies *Program availability:* Part-time, online learning. Offers adult clinical nurse specialist (MSN); adult clinical nursing practice (DNP); clinical nursing practice (DNP); neonatal nurse practitioner (MSN); nurse educator (MSN); nurse executive (MSN); nursing practice (DNP); pediatric clinical nursing practice (DNP); pediatric nurse practitioner (MSN).

School of Pharmacy *Program availability:* Online learning. Offers pharmacy (PhD, Pharm D). PhD offered through School of Graduate Studies. Electronic applications accepted.

UNIVERSITY OF MISSOURI–ST. LOUIS, St. Louis, MO 63121

General Information State-supported, coed, university. CGS member. *Graduate housing:* Rooms and/or apartments available on a first-come, first-served basis to single and married students. Housing application deadline: 7/1. *Research affiliation:* Express Scripts (business), St. Louis Zoo (biology), Missouri Botanical Garden (biology), Donald Danforth Plant Science Center (biology).

GRADUATE UNITS

College of Arts and Sciences *Program availability:* Part-time, evening/weekend. Offers American politics (MA); applied physics (MS); arts and sciences (MA, MFA, MS, PhD, Certificate); astrophysics (MS); behavioral neuroscience (MA, PhD); biochemistry and biotechnology (MS); biology (MS, PhD, Certificate); chemistry (MS, PhD); clinical psychology (PhD); communication (MA); comparative politics (MA); computer science (MS); creative writing (MFA); criminology and criminal justice (MA, PhD); economics (MA); English (MA); history (MA); history education (Certificate); international politics (MA); mathematical and computational sciences (PhD); mathematics (MA); museum studies (MA, Certificate); philosophy (MA); physics (PhD); political process and behavior (MA); political science (PhD); public administration and public policy (MA); trauma studies (Certificate); urban and regional politics (MA). Electronic applications accepted.

College of Business Administration *Program availability:* Part-time, evening/weekend. Offers accounting (M Acc); business administration (MBA, DBA, PhD, Certificate); business intelligence (Certificate); cybersecurity (Certificate); digital and social media marketing (Certificate); human resources management (Certificate); information systems (MS); logistics and supply chain management (Certificate); marketing management (Certificate). Electronic applications accepted.

College of Education *Program availability:* Part-time, evening/weekend. Offers adult and higher education (M Ed); counseling (PhD); education (M Ed, Ed D, PhD, Certificate, Ed S); educational leadership and policy studies (PhD); educational psychology (M Ed, PhD); elementary education (M Ed); leadership in educational practice (Ed D); program evaluation (Certificate); school psychology (Ed S); secondary education (M Ed); special education (M Ed); teaching-learning processes (PhD). Electronic applications accepted.

College of Nursing *Program availability:* Part-time. Offers adult/geriatric nurse practitioner (Post Master's Certificate); family nurse practitioner (Post Master's Certificate); nursing (DNP, PhD); pediatric acute care nurse practitioner (Post Master's Certificate); pediatric nurse practitioner (Post Master's Certificate); psychiatric-mental health nurse practitioner (Post Master's Certificate); women's health nurse practitioner (Post Master's Certificate). Electronic applications accepted.

College of Optometry Offers optometry (OD). Electronic applications accepted.

Graduate School *Program availability:* Part-time, evening/weekend. Offers local government management (MPPA, Certificate); nonprofit management and leadership (MPPA, Certificate); policy and program evaluation (MPPA, Certificate). Electronic applications accepted.

School of Social Work *Program availability:* Part-time. Offers social work (MSW). Electronic applications accepted.

UNIVERSITY OF MOBILE, Mobile, AL 36613

General Information Independent-religious, coed, comprehensive institution. *Enrollment:* 193 full-time matriculated graduate/professional students (151 women), 8 part-time matriculated graduate/professional students (5 women). *Enrollment by degree level:* 186 master's, 15 doctoral. *Tuition:* Full-time $453; part-time $453 per credit hour. *Required fees:* $320; $320. Tuition and fees vary according to degree level and program. *Graduate housing:* Room and/or apartments available on a first-come, first-served basis to single students; on-campus housing not available to married students. Housing application deadline: 8/15. *Student services:* Campus employment opportunities, career counseling, free psychological counseling, international student services, low-cost health insurance. *Library facilities:* J. L. Bedsole Library. *Collection:* Books: 66,089 (physical), 157,420 (digital/electronic); Serial titles: 153 (physical), 151,115 (digital/electronic); Databases: 80.

Computer facilities: 100 computers available on campus for general student use. A campuswide network can be accessed. Online class registration is available. Website: http://www.umobile.edu/

General Application Contact: Brian Boyle, 251-442-2287.

GRADUATE UNITS

Graduate Studies *Program availability:* Part-time, evening/weekend, online learning. Offers biblical and theological studies (MA); business administration (MBA); education (MA); education/administration (MSN); higher education leadership and policy (M Ed); marriage and family counseling (MA); nurse practitioner (DNP); piano performance (MM); vocal performance (MM, DMA); worship leadership and theology (MA). Electronic applications accepted.

UNIVERSITY OF MONTANA, Missoula, MT 59812

General Information State-supported, coed, university. CGS member. *Graduate housing:* Rooms and/or apartments available on a first-served basis to single and married students. *Research affiliation:* Arthur Carhart National Wilderness Training Center (environmental research), Nature Center at Ft. Missoula Museum (environmental research), Rocky Mountain National Laboratories (medical research), Community Hospital Medical Center (medical research), Aldo Leopold Wilderness Institute (forestry).

GRADUATE UNITS

Alexander Blewett III School of Law Offers law (JD).

Graduate School *Program availability:* Part-time. Offers individualized interdisciplinary studies (PhD); interdisciplinary studies (MIS).

College of Forestry and Conservation Offers fish and wildlife biology (PhD); forest and conservation sciences (PhD); forestry (MS); recreation management (MS); resource conservation (MS); systems ecology (MS, PhD); wildlife biology (MS).

College of Health Professions and Biomedical Sciences Offers biomedical and pharmaceutical sciences (MS, PhD); biomedical sciences (PhD); health professions and biomedical sciences (MPH, MS, MSW, DPT, PhD, Pharm D, CPH); medicinal chemistry (MS, PhD); molecular and cellular toxicology (MS, PhD); neuroscience (PhD); pharmaceutical sciences (MS); pharmacy (Pharm D); physical therapy (DPT); public health (MPH, CPH); social work (MSW).

College of Humanities and Sciences *Program availability:* Part-time. Offers anthropology (MA, PhD); applied anthropology (PhD); applied medical anthropology (MA); cellular and developmental biology (PhD); cellular, molecular and microbial biology (PhD); chemistry (MS, PhD); clinical psychology (PhD); communication studies (MA); community and environmental planning (MA); computer science (MS); creative writing (MFA); criminology (MA); cultural heritage (MA, PhD); economics (MA); environmental studies (MS); experimental psychology (PhD); fiction (MFA); forensic anthropology (MA); French (MA); geography (MA, MS); geosciences (MS, PhD); German (MA); history (MA, PhD); humanities and sciences (MA, MFA, MPA, MS, PhD, Ed S); inequality and social justice (MA); linguistic anthropology (MA); linguistics (MA); literature (MA); mathematics (MA, PhD); mathematics education (MA); microbial evolution and ecology (PhD); microbiology and immunology (PhD); molecular biology and biochemistry (PhD); non-fiction (MFA); organismal biology and ecology (MS, PhD); philosophy (MA); poetry (MFA); political science (MA); public administration (MPA); rural and environmental change (MA); school psychology (MA, PhD, Ed S); sociology (MA); Spanish (MA); systems ecology (MS, PhD); teaching (MA).

College of Visual and Performing Arts Offers design/technology (MFA); digital filmmaking (MFA); fine arts (MA); integrated arts and education (MA); integrated digital media (MFA); performance (MM); photography (MFA); theatre (MA); visual and performing arts (MA, MFA, MM).

Phyllis J. Washington College of Education and Human Sciences *Program availability:* Part-time. Offers clinical mental health counseling (MA); community health (MS); counseling and supervision (Ed D); counselor education (Ed S); curriculum and instruction (M Ed, Ed D); early childhood education (M Ed); education (MA); education and human sciences (M Ed, MA, MS, Ed D, Ed S); educational leadership (M Ed, Ed D, Ed S); exercise science (MS); health and human performance generalist (MS); intercultural youth and family development (MA); school counseling (MA); speech-language pathology (MS, Postbaccalaureate Certificate); teaching and learning (PhD).

School of Business Administration *Program availability:* Part-time, evening/weekend, online learning. Offers accounting (M Acct); business administration (M Acct, MBA).

School of Journalism Offers journalism (MA). Electronic applications accepted.

UNIVERSITY OF MONTEVALLO, Montevallo, AL 35115

General Information State-supported, coed, comprehensive institution. *Enrollment:* 2,616 graduate, professional, and undergraduate students; 139 full-time matriculated graduate/professional students (119 women), 180 part-time matriculated graduate/professional students (135 women). *International tuition:* $22,464 full-time. *Tuition, area resident:* Full-time $10,512. Tuition, state resident: full-time $10,512. Tuition, nonresident: full-time $22,464. *Graduate housing:* Rooms and/or apartments guaranteed to single students and available on a first-come, first-served basis to married students. Typical cost: $6695 per year ($9810 including board) for single students. *Student services:* Campus employment opportunities, campus safety program, career counseling, free psychological counseling, international student services, low-cost health insurance, services for students with disabilities, writing training. *Library facilities:* Carmichael Library. *Collection:* Students can reserve study rooms.

Computer facilities: 340 computers available on campus for general student use. A campuswide network can be accessed from student residence rooms and from off campus. Online class registration is available. Website: http://www.montevallo.edu/

GRADUATE UNITS

College of Arts and Sciences Students: 53 full-time (51 women), 4 part-time (all women); includes 4 minority (2 Black or African American, non-Hispanic/Latino; 1 Hispanic/Latino; 1 Native Hawaiian or other Pacific Islander, non-Hispanic/Latino). Expenses: Contact institution. *Financial support:* Federal Work-Study, scholarships/grants, and unspecified assistantships available. In 2018, 27 master's awarded. *Program availability:* Part-time, evening/weekend. Offers arts and sciences (MA, MS); communication science and disorders (MS); English (MA). *Application deadline:* For fall admission, 7/15 for domestic students; for spring admission, 11/15 for

domestic students. *Application fee:* $30. *Application Contact:* Tonja Battle, Administrative Assistant, 205-665-6508, E-mail: battletl@montevallo.edu. *Dean*, Dr. Mary Beth Armstrong, 205-665-6508.

College of Education Students: 76 full-time (61 women), 151 part-time (113 women); includes 51 minority (41 Black or African American, non-Hispanic/Latino; 4 Hispanic/Latino; 6 Two or more races, non-Hispanic/Latino), 1 international. Expenses: Contact institution. *Financial support:* Federal Work-Study, scholarships/grants, and unspecified assistantships available. In 2018, 114 master's awarded. *Program availability:* Part-time, evening/weekend. Offers counseling (M Ed); education (M Ed, Ed S); educational administration (M Ed, Ed S); elementary education (M Ed); secondary/high school education (M Ed). *Application deadline:* For fall admission, 7/15 for domestic students; for spring admission, 11/15 for domestic students. *Application fee:* $30. *Application Contact:* Colleen Kennedy, Graduate Program Assistant, 205-665-6350, E-mail: ckennedy@montevallo.edu. *Interim Dean*, Dr. Charlotte Daughhetee, 205-665-6360, E-mail: daughc@montevallo.edu.

Stephens College of Business Students: 10 full-time (7 women), 25 part-time (18 women); includes 10 minority (6 Black or African American, non-Hispanic/Latino; 2 Asian, non-Hispanic/Latino; 2 Hispanic/Latino), 2 international. Expenses: Contact institution. In 2018, 19 master's awarded. *Program availability:* Part-time, evening/weekend. Offers business (MBA). *Application deadline:* For fall admission, 7/15 for domestic students; for spring admission, 11/15 for domestic students. *Application fee:* $30. *Application Contact:* Dr. Stephen H. Craft, Dean, 205-665-6540, E-mail: scob@montevallo.edu. *Dean*, Dr. Stephen H. Craft, 205-665-6540, E-mail: scob@montevallo.edu.

UNIVERSITY OF MOUNT OLIVE, Mount Olive, NC 28365

General Information Independent-religious, coed, comprehensive institution.

GRADUATE UNITS

Graduate Programs *Program availability:* Online learning.

UNIVERSITY OF MOUNT UNION, Alliance, OH 44601-3993

General Information Independent-religious, coed, comprehensive institution. *Graduate housing:* Rooms and/or apartments available on a first-come, first-served basis to single and married students. Housing application deadline: 4/13.

GRADUATE UNITS

Program in Educational Leadership *Program availability:* Part-time, online only, 100% online. Offers educational leadership (MA). Electronic applications accepted.

Program in Physical Therapy Offers physical therapy (DPT). Electronic applications accepted.

Program in Physician Assistant Studies Offers physician assistant studies (MS). Electronic applications accepted.

UNIVERSITY OF NEBRASKA AT KEARNEY, Kearney, NE 68849-0001

General Information State-supported, coed, comprehensive institution. CGS member. *Graduate housing:* Room and/or apartments available on a first-come, first-served basis to single students; on-campus housing not available to married students. Housing application deadline: 6/15.

GRADUATE UNITS

College of Business and Technology *Program availability:* Part-time, evening/weekend. Offers accounting (MBA); business and technology (MBA); generalist (MBA); human resources (MBA); human services (MBA); marketing (MBA). Electronic applications accepted.

College of Education *Program availability:* Part-time, evening/weekend, 100% online. Offers clinical mental health counseling (MS Ed); curriculum and instruction (MA Ed); curriculum supervisor of academic area (MA Ed); education (MA Ed, MS Ed, Ed S); general physical education (MA Ed); instructional technology (MS Ed); physical education exercise science (MA Ed); physical education master teacher (MA Ed); reading PK-12 (MA Ed); school counseling (MS Ed); school principalship 7-12 (MA Ed); school principalship PK-8 (MA Ed); school psychology (Ed S); school superintendent (Ed S); special education (MA Ed); speech/language pathology (MS Ed); student affairs (MS Ed); supervisor of special education (MA Ed). Electronic applications accepted.

College of Fine Arts and Humanities *Program availability:* Part-time, evening/weekend, 100% online. Offers art education (MA Ed); creative writing (MA); fine arts and humanities (MA, MA Ed); literature (MA); music education (MA Ed); Spanish education (MA Ed); writing (MA). Electronic applications accepted.

College of Natural and Social Sciences *Program availability:* Part-time, evening/weekend, online learning. Offers biology (MS); history (MA); natural and social sciences (MA, MA Ed, MS); science/math education (MA Ed). Electronic applications accepted.

UNIVERSITY OF NEBRASKA AT OMAHA, Omaha, NE 68182

General Information State-supported, coed, university. CGS member. *Graduate housing:* Room and/or apartments available on a first-come, first-served basis to single students; on-campus housing not available to married students.

GRADUATE UNITS

Graduate Studies *Program availability:* Part-time, evening/weekend, online learning. Electronic applications accepted.

College of Arts and Sciences *Program availability:* Part-time, evening/weekend, online learning. Offers advanced writing (Certificate); American government (Certificate); applied behavior analysis (Certificate); arts and sciences (MA, MAT, MS, PhD, Certificate, Ed S); biology (MS); business for bioscientists (Certificate); critical and creative thinking (MA); English (MA); geographic information science (Certificate); geography (MA); global information operations (Certificate); history (MA); human resources and training (Certificate); industrial/organizational psychology (MS); intelligence and national security (Certificate); language teaching (MA); mathematics (MA, MAT, MS); political science (MS); psychology (MA, PhD); school psychology (MS, Ed S); sociology (MA); teaching English to speakers of other languages (Certificate); technical communication (Certificate). Electronic applications accepted.

College of Business Administration *Program availability:* Part-time, evening/weekend. Offers accounting (M Acc); business administration (MBA); business for bioscientists (Certificate); economics (MA, MS); executive business administration (EMBA); human resources and training (Certificate). Electronic applications accepted.

College of Communication, Fine Arts and Media *Program availability:* Part-time, evening/weekend. Offers arts (MA); communication (MA); communication, fine arts and media (MA, MFA, MM, Certificate); human resources and training (Certificate); music (MM); technical communication (Certificate); writing (MFA). Electronic applications accepted.

College of Education *Program availability:* Part-time, evening/weekend. Offers athletic training (MA); counseling (MA, MS); education (MA, MS, Ed D, PhD, Certificate, Ed S); educational administration and supervision (Ed D); educational leadership (MS, Ed S); elementary education (MS); exercise science (PhD); health, physical education, and recreation (MA, MS); instruction in urban schools (Certificate); secondary education (MS, Certificate); special education (MS); speech-language pathology (MS). Electronic applications accepted.

College of Information Science and Technology *Program availability:* Part-time, evening/weekend. Offers artificial intelligence (Certificate); biomedical informatics (MS, PhD); communication networks (Certificate); computer science (MA, MS); computer science education (MS, Certificate); data analytics (Certificate); information assurance (MS, Certificate); information science and technology (MA, MIT, MS, PhD, Certificate); information technology (MIT, PhD); management information systems (MS); project management (Certificate); software engineering (Certificate); system and architecture (Certificate); systems analysis and design (Certificate). Electronic applications accepted.

College of Public Affairs and Community Service *Program availability:* Part-time, evening/weekend, online learning. Offers criminology and criminal justice (MA, MS, PhD); gerontology (PhD, Certificate); managing juvenile and adult populations (Certificate); public administration (MPA, PhD); public affairs and community service (MA, MPA, MS, MSW, PhD, Certificate); public management (Certificate); social gerontology (MA); social work (MSW); urban studies (MS). Electronic applications accepted.

UNIVERSITY OF NEBRASKA–LINCOLN, Lincoln, NE 68588

General Information State-supported, coed, university. CGS member. *Graduate housing:* Rooms and/or apartments available on a first-come, first-served basis to single and married students. Housing application deadline: 7/1. *Research affiliation:* U.S. Department of Agriculture (USDA), U.S. Department of Defense, NASA, National Science Foundation, National Institutes of Health, U.S. Meat Animal Research Center.

GRADUATE UNITS

College of Law Offers law (JD); legal studies (MLS); space and telecommunications law (LL M). Electronic applications accepted.

Graduate College *Program availability:* Part-time, evening/weekend, online learning. Offers environmental health, occupational health and toxicology (MS, PhD); survey research and methodology (MS, PhD). Electronic applications accepted.

College of Agricultural Sciences and Natural Resources Offers agribusiness (MBA); agricultural economics (MS, PhD); agricultural sciences and natural resources (M Ag, MA, MBA, MS, PhD); agronomy (MS, PhD); animal science (MS, PhD); biochemistry (MS, PhD); community development (M Ag); entomology (MS, PhD); food science and technology (MS, PhD); geography (PhD); horticulture (MS, PhD); leadership development (MS); leadership education (MS); mechanized systems management (MS); natural resources (MS, PhD); nutrition (MS, PhD); statistics (MS, PhD); teaching and extension education (MS); veterinary science (MS). Electronic applications accepted.

College of Architecture Offers architecture (M Arch, MS, PhD); community and regional planning (MCRP); interior design (MS). Electronic applications accepted.

College of Arts and Sciences Offers analytical chemistry (PhD); anthropology (MA); arts and sciences (M Sc T, MA, MAT, MS, PhD, Graduate Certificate); astronomy (MS, PhD); biochemistry (PhD); bioinformatics (MS, PhD); biological sciences (MA, MS, PhD); biopsychology (PhD); chemistry (MS); classics and religious studies (MA); clinical psychology (PhD); cognitive psychology (PhD); composition and rhetoric (MA, PhD); computer engineering (MS, PhD); computer science (MS, PhD); creative writing (MA, PhD); developmental psychology (PhD); French (MA, PhD); geography (MA, PhD); geosciences (MS, PhD); German (MA, PhD); history (MA, PhD); information technology (PhD); inorganic chemistry (PhD); instructional communication (MA, PhD); interpersonal communication (MA, PhD); literature studies (MA, PhD); marketing, communication studies, and advertising (MA, PhD); materials chemistry (PhD); mathematics (MA, MAT, MS, PhD); mathematics and computer science (PhD); organic chemistry (PhD); organizational communication (MA, PhD); philosophy (MA, PhD); physical chemistry (PhD); physics (MS, PhD); political science (MA, PhD); professional archaeology (MA); psychology (MA); public policy analysis (Graduate Certificate); rhetoric and culture (MA, PhD); social/personality psychology (PhD); sociology (MA, PhD); Spanish (MA, PhD). Electronic applications accepted.

College of Business Administration *Program availability:* Part-time, evening/weekend. Offers accountancy (MPA, PhD); actuarial science (MS); business (MA, MBA, PhD); business administration (MA, MBA, MPA, MS, PhD); economics (MA, PhD); finance (MA, PhD); management (MA, PhD); marketing (MA, PhD). Electronic applications accepted.

College of Education and Human Sciences Offers administration, curriculum and instruction (Ed D, PhD); adult and continuing education (MA); audiology and hearing science (Au D); audiology research (PhD); child development/early childhood education (MS, PhD); child, youth and family studies (MS); clinical audiology (Au D); cognition, learning and development (MA); community nutrition and health promotion (MS); counseling psychology (MA); education and human sciences (M Ed, MA, MS, MST, Au D, Ed D, PhD, Certificate, Ed S); educational administration (M Ed, MA, Ed D, Certificate); educational psychology (MA, Ed S); educational studies (Ed D, PhD); family and consumer sciences education (MS, PhD); family financial planning (MS); family science (MS); gerontology (PhD); human sciences (PhD); marriage and family therapy (MS); medical family therapy (PhD); merchandising (MS); nutrition (MS, PhD); nutrition and exercise (MS); nutrition and health sciences (PhD); psychological studies in education (PhD); quantitative, qualitative, and psychometric methods (MA); school psychology (MA, Ed S); special education (M Ed, MA, Ed S); speech-language pathology and audiology (MS, Au D); teaching, learning and teacher education (M Ed, MA, MST, Ed D, PhD); textile history/quilt studies (MA); textile science (MS); textile-apparel (MA); textiles, clothing and design (MA, MS); vocational and adult education (M Ed, MA); youth development (MS). Electronic applications accepted.

College of Engineering Offers agricultural and biological systems engineering (MS, PhD); architectural engineering (M Eng, MAE, MS, PhD); biological engineering (PhD); biomedical engineering (PhD); chemical and biomolecular engineering (MS, PhD); civil engineering (MS, PhD); electrical engineering (MS, PhD); engineering (M Eng, MAE, MEE, MS, PhD); engineering management (M Eng); engineering mechanics (MS, PhD); environmental engineering (MS, PhD); industrial and management systems engineering (MS, PhD); manufacturing systems engineering (MS); materials engineering (PhD); mechanical engineering (MS); mechanical engineering and applied mechanics (PhD); mechanized systems management (MS). Electronic applications accepted.

College of Fine and Performing Arts Offers acting (MFA); art history (MA); composition (MM, DMA); conducting (MM, DMA); costume (MFA); directing (MFA); fine and performing arts (MA, MFA, MM, DMA, PhD); music education (MM, PhD); music history (MM); music theory (MM); performance (MM, DMA); piano pedagogy (MM); stage design (MFA); studio art (MFA); woodwind specialties (MM). Electronic applications accepted.

College of Journalism and Mass Communications *Program availability:* Online learning. Offers marketing, communication and advertising (MA); professional journalism (MA). Electronic applications accepted.

UNIVERSITY OF NEBRASKA MEDICAL CENTER, Omaha, NE 68198

General Information State-supported, coed, upper-level institution. CGS member. *Enrollment:* 2,164 full-time matriculated graduate/professional students (1,300 women), 348 part-time matriculated graduate/professional students (260 women). *Enrollment by degree level:* 704 master's, 1,704 doctoral, 104 other advanced degrees. *Graduate faculty:* 468 full-time (195 women), 148 part-time/adjunct (22 women). *International tuition:* $24,975 full-time. *Tuition, area resident:* Full-time $8721; part-time $2907 per credit hour. Tuition, state resident: full-time $8721; part-time $2907 per credit hour. Tuition, nonresident: full-time $24,975; part-time $8325 per credit hour. *Required fees:* $582. *Student services:* Campus safety program, child daycare facilities, exercise/wellness program, free psychological counseling, grant writing training, international student services, low-cost health insurance, multicultural affairs office, services for students with disabilities. *Library facilities:* McGoogan Library of Medicine.

Computer facilities: 120 computers available on campus for general student use. A campuswide network can be accessed from off campus. Online class registration is available.
Website: http://www.unmc.edu/

General Application Contact: Cody Phillips, Graduate Studies Specialist, 402-559-4476, E-mail: cody.phillips@unmc.edu.

GRADUATE UNITS

College of Allied Health Professions Offers allied health professions (MPAS, MPS, DPT, Certificate); clinical perfusion education (MPS); cytotechnology (Certificate); medical nutrition (Certificate).

Division of Physical Therapy Education Offers physical therapy education (DPT).

Division of Physician Assistant Education Offers physician assistant education (MPAS). Electronic applications accepted.

College of Dentistry Offers dentistry (MS, DDS, PhD, Certificate). Electronic applications accepted.

College of Medicine Offers medicine (MD, Certificate). Electronic applications accepted.

College of Pharmacy Offers pharmacy (Pharm D). Electronic applications accepted.

College of Public Health *Program availability:* Part-time, online learning. Offers public health (MPH). Electronic applications accepted.

Department of Biostatistics Students: 5 full-time (0 women), 5 part-time (2 women); includes 3 minority (2 Black or African American, non-Hispanic/Latino; 1 Asian, non-Hispanic/Latino), 3 international. Average age 37. 5 applicants, 60% accepted, 2 enrolled. *Faculty:* 7 full-time (4 women). Expenses: Contact institution. *Financial support:* In 2018–19, 1 research assistantship with full tuition reimbursement, 4 teaching assistantships with full tuition reimbursements were awarded; health care benefits and unspecified assistantships also available. Financial award application deadline: 4/1. *Program availability:* Part-time. Offers biostatistics (PhD). *Application deadline:* For fall admission, 6/1 for domestic students, 4/1 for international students. Applications are processed on a rolling basis. *Application fee:* $60. Electronic applications accepted. *Application Contact:* Dr. Gleb Haynatzki, Graduate Program Director/Professor, 402-559-3294, E-mail: ghaynatzki@unmc.edu. *Campus Director of Assessment, Assistant Dean Graduate Studies, Professor and Interim Chair,* Dr. Kendra Schmid, 402-559-8117, E-mail: kkschmid@unmc.edu.

Department of Epidemiology *Program availability:* Part-time. Offers epidemiology (PhD). Electronic applications accepted.

Department of Health Promotion, Social and Behavioral Health Students: 13 full-time (9 women), 5 part-time (4 women); includes 4 minority (1 Black or African American, non-Hispanic/Latino; 1 Asian, non-Hispanic/Latino; 1 Hispanic/Latino; 1 Two or more races, non-Hispanic/Latino), 4 international. Average age 34. 12 applicants, 33% accepted, 4 enrolled. *Faculty:* 15 full-time (7 women), 2 part-time/adjunct (both women). Expenses: Contact institution. *Financial support:* In 2018–19, research assistantships with full tuition reimbursements (averaging $23,100 per year) were awarded; scholarships/grants also available. Support available to part-time students. Financial award application deadline: 2/15; financial award applicants required to submit FAFSA. In 2018, 2 doctorates awarded. *Program availability:* Part-time. Offers health promotion and disease prevention research (PhD). *Application deadline:* For fall admission, 4/1 for domestic and international students. *Application fee:* $45. Electronic applications accepted. *Application Contact:* Kate Kusnerik, Coordinator, 402-559-4325, E-mail: kate.kusnerik@unmc.edu. *Graduate Program Director,* Dr. Ghada Soliman, 402-559-5157, E-mail: ghada.soliman@unmc.edu.

Department of Health Services Research and Administration Students: 8 full-time (6 women), 7 international. Average age 31. 12 applicants, 42% accepted, 3 enrolled. *Faculty:* 5 full-time (2 women), 2 part-time/adjunct (1 woman). Expenses: Contact institution. *Financial support:* In 2018–19, 5 students received support. Federal Work-Study, scholarships/grants, and unspecified assistantships available. Financial award application deadline: 2/15; financial award applicants required to submit FAFSA. In 2018, 5 doctorates awarded. *Program availability:* Part-time, 100% online, blended/hybrid learning. Offers health administration (MHA); health services research, administration, and policy (PhD); public health administration and policy (MPH). *Application deadline:* For fall admission, 6/1 for domestic students, 4/1 for international students. *Application fee:* $60. Electronic applications accepted. *Application Contact:* Denise Howard, Coordinator, 402-559-5260, E-mail: denise.howard@unmc.edu. *Associate Professor,* Dr. Fernando Wilson, 402-552-6948, E-mail: fernando.wilson@unmc.edu.

Department of Pharmaceutical Sciences Students: 60 full-time (27 women), 1 (woman) part-time; includes 3 minority (all Asian, non-Hispanic/Latino), 48 international. Average age 27. 65 applicants, 18% accepted, 12 enrolled. *Faculty:* 27 full-time (3 women), 1 part-time/adjunct (0 women). Expenses: Contact institution. *Financial support:* In 2018–19, 95 students received support, including 10 fellowships with full tuition reimbursements available (averaging $25,000 per year), 35 research assistantships with full tuition reimbursements available (averaging $24,500 per year); scholarships/grants and unspecified assistantships also available. Financial award application deadline: 4/1. In 2018, 9 doctorates awarded. Offers pharmaceutical sciences (MS, PhD). *Application deadline:* For fall admission, 6/1 priority date for domestic students, 4/1 priority date for international students; for spring admission, 10/1 for domestic students, 8/1 for international students. Applications are processed on a rolling basis. *Application fee:* $60. Electronic applications accepted. *Application Contact:* Renee Kaszynski, Office Associate, 402-559-5320, E-mail: renee.kaszynski@unmc.edu. *Chair, Pharmaceutical Sciences Graduate Program Committee,* Dr. Ram Mahato, 402-559-5422, E-mail: ram.mahato@unmc.edu.

Environmental Health, Occupational Health and Toxicology Graduate Program Offers environmental health, occupational health and toxicology (PhD). Electronic applications accepted.

Interdisciplinary Graduate Program in Biomedical Sciences Offers biochemistry and molecular biology (MS); biomedical sciences (MS, PhD); cancer research (PhD); genetics, cell biology and anatomy (PhD); immunology, pathology and infectious disease (MS, PhD); integrative physiology and molecular medicine (PhD); medical anatomy (MS); molecular genetics and cell biology (MS); pharmacology and experimental neuroscience (PhD). Electronic applications accepted.

Medical Sciences Interdepartmental Area Students: 68 full-time (39 women), 43 part-time (25 women); includes 15 minority (1 Black or African American, non-Hispanic/Latino; 1 American Indian or Alaska Native, non-Hispanic/Latino; 8 Asian, non-Hispanic/Latino; 4 Hispanic/Latino; 1 Native Hawaiian or other Pacific Islander, non-Hispanic/Latino), 230 international. Average age 34. 68 applicants, 34% accepted, 23 enrolled. *Faculty:* 170 full-time, 20 part-time/adjunct. Expenses: Contact institution. *Financial support:* In 2018–19, 72 students received support, including 1 fellowship with full tuition reimbursement available (averaging $25,000 per year), 37 research assistantships with full tuition reimbursements available (averaging $25,000 per year), 2 teaching assistantships with full tuition reimbursements available (averaging $25,000 per year); scholarships/grants, health care benefits, and unspecified assistantships also available. Financial award application deadline: 2/15; financial award applicants required to submit FAFSA. In 2018, 26 master's, 915 doctorates awarded. *Program availability:* Part-time. Offers applied behavior analysis (PhD); clinical translational research (MS, PhD); health practice and medical education research (MS); oral biology (MS, PhD). *Application deadline:* For fall admission, 6/1 for domestic students, 4/1 for international students; for spring admission, 10/1 for domestic and international students. Applications are processed on a rolling basis. *Application fee:* $60. Electronic applications accepted. *Application Contact:* Jennifer Escher, Interdisciplinary Programs Coordinator, 402-559-5141, E-mail: msia@unmc.edu. *Graduate Committee Chair,* Dr. Laura Bilek, 402-559-6923, E-mail: lbilek@unmc.edu.

PhD in Nursing Program Students: 14 full-time (13 women), 9 part-time (all women); includes 3 minority (1 Black or African American, non-Hispanic/Latino; 1 Asian, non-Hispanic/Latino; 1 Hispanic/Latino), 1 international. Average age 39. 8 applicants, 88% accepted, 7 enrolled. *Faculty:* 16 full-time (all women). Expenses: Contact institution. *Financial support:* In 2018–19, 12 students received support. Scholarships/grants and unspecified assistantships available. Financial award application deadline: 5/1; financial award applicants required to submit FAFSA. In 2018, 3 doctorates awarded. *Program availability:* Part-time, blended/hybrid learning. Offers nursing (PhD). *Application deadline:* For spring admission, 5/1 for domestic and international students. *Application fee:* $65. Electronic applications accepted. *Application Contact:* Rolee Kelly, Graduate Coordinator, Student Services, 402-559-4120, E-mail: rolee.kelly@unmc.edu. *Professor,* Dr. Carol Pullen, 402-559-6548, E-mail: chpullen@unmc.edu.

Program in Biomedical Informatics Students: 1 full-time (0 women), 6 part-time (2 women); includes 1 minority (Asian, non-Hispanic/Latino), 5 international. Average age 37. *Faculty:* 29 full-time (7 women). Expenses: Contact institution. *Financial support:* In 2018–19, 9 students received support, including 1 fellowship with full tuition reimbursement available (averaging $25,000 per year), 4 research assistantships with full tuition reimbursements available (averaging $25,000 per year); scholarships/grants and unspecified assistantships also available. Financial award application deadline: 2/15; financial award applicants required to submit FAFSA. In 2018, 2 doctorates awarded. *Program availability:* Part-time. Offers biomedical informatics (MS, PhD). *Application deadline:* For fall admission, 6/1 for domestic students, 4/1 for international students; for spring admission, 10/1 for domestic and international students. Applications are processed on a rolling basis. *Application fee:* $60. Electronic applications accepted. *Application Contact:* Rhonda Sheibal-Carver, Academic Program Coordinator, 402-559-5141, E-mail: rhonda.sheibalcarver@unmc.edu. *Director,* Dr. Jim McClay, 402-559-3587, E-mail: jmcclay@unmc.edu.

Program in Emergency Preparedness *Program availability:* Part-time, 100% online, blended/hybrid learning. Offers emergency preparedness (MS). Electronic applications accepted.

UNIVERSITY OF NEVADA, LAS VEGAS, Las Vegas, NV 89154

General Information State-supported, coed, university. CGS member. *Graduate housing:* Room and/or apartments available on a first-come, first-served basis to single students; on-campus housing not available to married students. Housing application deadline: 7/1. *Research affiliation:* Tesla (effluent remediation), Teledyne Brown Engineering (aerospace engineering), Eli Lilly and Company (clinical trials), Cryolife (clinical trials), Metawater (water treatment).

GRADUATE UNITS

Graduate College Students: 2,328 full-time (1,379 women), 1,463 part-time (924 women); includes 1,455 minority (284 Black or African American, non-Hispanic/Latino; 15 American Indian or Alaska Native, non-Hispanic/Latino; 306 Asian, non-Hispanic/Latino; 625 Hispanic/Latino; 11 Native Hawaiian or other Pacific Islander, non-Hispanic/Latino; 214 Two or more races, non-Hispanic/Latino), 361 international. Average age 33. 2,851 applicants, 53% accepted, 1082 enrolled. *Faculty:* 517 full-time (180 women), 163 part-time/adjunct (86 women). Expenses: Contact institution. *Financial support:* In 2018–19, 1,060 students received support, including 9 fellowships with full tuition reimbursements available (averaging $22,222 per year), 348 research assistantships with full tuition reimbursements available (averaging $15,245 per year), 712 teaching assistantships with full tuition reimbursements available (averaging $15,931 per year); institutionally sponsored loans, scholarships/grants, health care benefits, and unspecified assistantships also available. Financial award application deadline: 3/15; financial award applicants required to submit FAFSA. In 2018, 1,049 master's, 163 doctorates, 60 other advanced degrees awarded. *Program availability:* Part-time. *Application deadline:* For fall admission, 8/1 for domestic students, 5/1 for international students; for spring admission, 11/1 for domestic students, 10/1 for international students. *Application fee:* $60 ($95 for international students). Electronic applications accepted. *Application Contact:* Elizabeth Jost, Senior Admissions Analyst, 702-895-5412, E-mail: elizabeth.jost@unlv.edu. *Dean,* Dr. Kathryn Korgan, 702-895-0446, Fax: 702-895-4180, E-mail: kate.korgan@unlv.edu.

College of Education *Program availability:* Part-time. Offers addiction studies (Advanced Certificate); chief diversity officer in higher education (Certificate); college sport leadership (Certificate); counselor education (M Ed, MS); curriculum and instruction (M Ed, MS, Ed D, PhD, Ed S); early childhood education (M Ed); early childhood special education (Certificate); education (M Ed, MS, Ed D, PhD, Advanced Certificate, Certificate, Ed S); educational policy and leadership (M Ed); educational psychology (MS, PhD, Ed S); educational psychology/law (M Ed, MS, PhD, Certificate, Ed S); elementary teaching (Certificate); English language learning (M Ed); higher education (M Ed, PhD, Certificate); mental health counseling (Advanced Certificate); online teaching and training (Certificate); psychology/learning and technology (PhD); secondary teaching (Certificate); social justice studies (Certificate); special education (M Ed, PhD); teaching and learning (PhD); workforce development/educational leadership (PhD). Electronic applications accepted.

College of Fine Arts Students: 143 full-time (74 women), 37 part-time (24 women); includes 55 minority (11 Black or African American, non-Hispanic/Latino; 1 American Indian or Alaska Native, non-Hispanic/Latino; 15 Asian, non-Hispanic/Latino; 21 Hispanic/Latino; 1 Native Hawaiian or other Pacific Islander, non-Hispanic/Latino; 6 Two or more races, non-Hispanic/Latino), 26 international. Average age 32. 154 applicants, 58% accepted, 62 enrolled. *Faculty:* 56 full-time (16 women), 28 part-time/adjunct (9 women). Expenses: Contact institution. *Financial support:* In 2018–19, 98 students received support, including 19 research assistantships with full tuition reimbursements available (averaging $15,013 per year), 79 teaching assistantships with full tuition reimbursements available (averaging $14,421 per year); institutionally sponsored loans, scholarships/grants, health care benefits, and unspecified assistantships also available. Financial award application deadline: 3/15; financial award applicants required to submit FAFSA. In 2018, 40 master's, 7 doctorates, 2 other advanced degrees awarded. *Program availability:* Part-time. Offers architecture (M Arch); art (MFA); film/writing for dramatic media (MFA); fine arts (M Arch, MA, MFA, MHID, MM, DMA, Certificate); healthcare interior design (MHID); hospitality design (Certificate); K-12 music (Certificate); music (MM); musical arts (DMA); theatre (MA, MFA); writing for dramatic media (Certificate). *Application fee:* $60 ($95 for international students). Electronic applications accepted. *Application Contact:* Dr. Nancy J. Uscher, Dean/Professor, 702-895-4210, Fax: 702-895-4194, E-mail: fine.arts.dean@unlv.edu. *Dean/Professor,* Dr. Nancy J. Uscher, 702-895-4210, Fax: 702-895-4194, E-mail: fine.arts.dean@unlv.edu.

College of Liberal Arts Students: 223 full-time (135 women), 101 part-time (50 women); includes 92 minority (8 Black or African American, non-Hispanic/Latino; 2 American Indian or Alaska Native, non-Hispanic/Latino; 10 Asian, non-Hispanic/Latino; 49 Hispanic/Latino; 1 Native Hawaiian or other Pacific Islander, non-Hispanic/Latino; 22 Two or more races, non-Hispanic/Latino), 17 international. Average age 32. 525 applicants, 23% accepted, 72 enrolled. *Faculty:* 102 full-time (41 women), 6 part-time/adjunct (2 women). Expenses: Contact institution. *Financial support:* In 2018–19, 216 students received support, including 4 fellowships with full tuition reimbursements available (averaging $22,500 per year), 58 research assistantships with full tuition reimbursements available (averaging $15,843 per year), 158 teaching assistantships with full tuition reimbursements available (averaging $15,204 per year); institutionally sponsored loans, scholarships/grants, health care benefits, and unspecified assistantships also available. Financial award application deadline: 3/15; financial award applicants required to submit FAFSA. In 2018, 53 master's, 32 doctorates, 7 other advanced degrees awarded. *Program availability:* Part-time. Offers anthropology (MA, PhD); creative writing (MFA); English (MA, PhD); Hispanic studies (MA); history (MA, PhD); liberal arts (MA, MFA, PhD, Certificate); political science (MA, PhD); quantitative psychology (Certificate); sociology (MA, PhD); Spanish translation (Certificate). *Application fee:* $60 ($95 for international students). Electronic applications accepted. *Application Contact:* Dr. Jennifer Keene, Dean, 702-895-3401, Fax: 702-895-4097, E-mail: liberalarts.dean@unlv.edu. *Dean,* Dr. Jennifer Keene, 702-895-3401, Fax: 702-895-4097, E-mail: liberalarts.dean@unlv.edu.

College of Sciences Students: 178 full-time (75 women), 42 part-time (17 women); includes 53 minority (3 Black or African American, non-Hispanic/Latino; 2 American Indian or Alaska Native, non-Hispanic/Latino; 22 Asian, non-Hispanic/Latino; 18 Hispanic/Latino; 8 Two or more races, non-Hispanic/Latino), 33 international. Average age 30. 183 applicants, 35% accepted, 46 enrolled. *Faculty:* 79 full-time (16 women), 4 part-time/adjunct (1 woman). Expenses: Contact institution. *Financial support:* In 2018–19, 179 students received support, including 1 fellowship with full tuition reimbursement available (averaging $25,000 per year), 38 research assistantships with full tuition reimbursements available (averaging $18,745 per year), 141 teaching assistantships with full tuition reimbursements available (averaging $19,728 per year); institutionally sponsored loans, scholarships/grants, health care benefits, and unspecified assistantships also available. Financial award application deadline: 3/15; financial award applicants required to submit FAFSA. In 2018, 25 master's, 25 doctorates awarded. *Program availability:* Part-time. Offers astronomy (MS, PhD); biochemistry (MS); biological sciences (MS, PhD); chemistry (MS, PhD); geoscience (MS, PhD); mathematical sciences (MS, PhD); physics (MS, PhD); radio chemistry (PhD); sciences (MA, MS, PhD); water resources management (MS). *Application fee:* $60 ($95 for international students). Electronic applications accepted. *Application Contact:* Dr. Eric Chronister, Dean, 702-895-3487, Fax: 702-895-4159, E-mail: sciences.dean@unlv.edu. *Dean,* Dr. Eric Chronister, 702-895-3487, Fax: 702-895-4159, E-mail: sciences.dean@unlv.edu.

Greenspun College of Urban Affairs Students: 306 full-time (219 women), 206 part-time (142 women); includes 271 minority (75 Black or African American, non-Hispanic/Latino; 2 American Indian or Alaska Native, non-Hispanic/Latino; 26 Asian, non-Hispanic/Latino; 129 Hispanic/Latino; 4 Native Hawaiian or other Pacific Islander, non-Hispanic/Latino; 35 Two or more races, non-Hispanic/Latino), 9 international. Average age 33. 338 applicants, 71% accepted, 172 enrolled. *Faculty:* 39 full-time (19 women), 22 part-time/adjunct (10 women). Expenses: Contact institution. *Financial support:* In 2018–19, 101 students received support, including 29 research assistantships with full tuition reimbursements available (averaging $14,600 per year), 72 teaching assistantships with full tuition reimbursements available (averaging $13,257 per year); institutionally sponsored loans, scholarships/grants, health care benefits, and unspecified assistantships also available. Financial award application deadline: 3/15; financial award applicants required to submit FAFSA. In 2018, 194 master's, 7 doctorates, 19 other advanced degrees awarded. *Program availability:* Part-time. Offers communication studies (MA); couple and family therapy (MS); criminal justice (MA); criminology and criminal justice (PhD); crisis and emergency management (MS); emergency crisis management cybersecurity (Certificate); environmental science (MS, PhD); journalism and media studies (MA); non-profit management (Certificate); public administration (MPA); public affairs (PhD); public management (Certificate); social work/law (MSW); urban affairs (MA, MPA, MS, MSW, PhD, Certificate); urban leadership (MA). *Application fee:* $60 ($95 for international students). Electronic applications accepted. *Application Contact:* Dr. Robert Ulmer, Dean, 702-895-0628, Fax: 702-895-3291, E-mail: urbanaffairs.dean@unlv.edu. *Dean,* Dr. Robert Ulmer, 702-895-0628, Fax: 702-895-3291, E-mail: urbanaffairs.dean@unlv.edu.

Howard R. Hughes College of Engineering Students: 162 full-time (44 women), 84 part-time (17 women); includes 64 minority (6 Black or African American, non-Hispanic/Latino; 1 American Indian or Alaska Native, non-Hispanic/Latino; 20 Asian, non-Hispanic/Latino; 27 Hispanic/Latino; 10 Two or more races, non-Hispanic/Latino), 110 international. Average age 30. 178 applicants, 66% accepted, 58 enrolled. *Faculty:* 62 full-time (9 women), 5 part-time/adjunct (0 women). Expenses: Contact institution. *Financial support:* In 2018–19, 156 students received support, including 2 fellowships with full tuition reimbursements available (averaging $20,000 per year), 48 research assistantships with full tuition reimbursements available (averaging $16,373 per year), 108 teaching assistantships with full tuition reimbursements available (averaging $15,832 per year); institutionally sponsored loans, scholarships/grants, health care benefits, and unspecified assistantships also available. Financial award application deadline: 3/15; financial award applicants required to submit FAFSA. In 2018, 50 master's, 17 doctorates, 2 other advanced degrees awarded. *Program availability:* Part-time. Offers aerospace engineering (MS); biomedical engineering (MS); civil & environmental engineering and construction, computer science, electrical and computer engineering, mechanical engineering (PhD); civil and environmental engineering (MS, PhD); civil and environmental engineering /transportation (MS); computer science (MS, PhD); construction management (MS); electrical and computer engineering (MS); electrical and computer engineering / mathematical sciences (PhD); materials and nuclear engineering (MS); mechanical engineering (MS, PhD); nuclear criticality safety engineering (Certificate); nuclear safeguards and security (Certificate); solar and renewable energy (Certificate). *Application fee:* $60 ($95 for international students). Electronic applications accepted. *Application Contact:* Dr. Rama Venkat, Dean, 702-895-3699, Fax: 702-895-4059, E-mail: engineering.dean@unlv.edu. *Dean,* Dr. Rama Venkat, 702-895-3699, Fax: 702-895-4059, E-mail: engineering.dean@unlv.edu.

Lee Business School Students: 250 full-time (105 women), 163 part-time (69 women); includes 149 minority (15 Black or African American, non-Hispanic/Latino; 1 American Indian or Alaska Native, non-Hispanic/Latino; 64 Asian, non-Hispanic/Latino; 50 Hispanic/Latino; 19 Two or more races, non-Hispanic/Latino), 68 international. Average age 31. 250 applicants, 65% accepted, 106 enrolled. *Faculty:* 38 full-time (7 women), 11 part-time/adjunct (3 women). Expenses: Contact institution. *Financial support:* In 2018–19, 62 students received support, including 35 research assistantships with full tuition reimbursements available (averaging $11,426 per year), 27 teaching assistantships with full tuition reimbursements available (averaging $11,519 per year); institutionally sponsored loans, scholarships/grants, health care benefits, and unspecified assistantships also available. Financial award application deadline: 3/15; financial award applicants required to submit FAFSA. In 2018, 173 master's, 5 other advanced degrees awarded. *Program availability:* Part-time. Offers accountancy (MS); accounting (Advanced Certificate, Certificate); applied economics (MA); business (Exec MBA, MA, MBA, MS, Advanced Certificate, Certificate); business administration (Certificate); business administration/dental (Exec MBA, MBA, Certificate); business administration/law (Exec MBA, MBA, Certificate); business administration/management information system (Exec MBA, MBA, Certificate); data analytics (Certificate); data analytics and applied economics (MS); economics/mathematical science (MA); hotel administration/management information systems (MS, Certificate); management (Certificate); management information systems (MS, Certificate); new venture management (Certificate). *Application fee:* $60 ($95 for international students). Electronic applications accepted. *Application Contact:* Dr. Brent Hathaway, Dean, 702-895-3362, Fax: 702-895-4090, E-mail: business.dean@unlv.edu. *Dean,* Dr. Brent Hathaway, 702-895-3362, Fax: 702-895-4090, E-mail: business.dean@unlv.edu.

School of Integrated Health Sciences Students: 192 full-time (85 women), 20 part-time (12 women); includes 72 minority (6 Black or African American, non-Hispanic/Latino; 1 American Indian or Alaska Native, non-Hispanic/Latino; 28 Asian, non-Hispanic/Latino; 24 Hispanic/Latino; 13 Two or more races, non-Hispanic/Latino), 9 international. Average age 28. 121 applicants, 38% accepted, 30 enrolled. *Faculty:* 20 full-time (8 women), 11 part-time/adjunct (7 women). Expenses: Contact institution. *Financial support:* In 2018–19, 56 students received support, including 1 fellowship with partial tuition reimbursement available (averaging $20,000 per year), 26 research assistantships with full tuition reimbursements available (averaging $15,971 per year), 30 teaching assistantships with full tuition reimbursements available (averaging $15,775 per year); institutionally sponsored loans, scholarships/grants, health care benefits, and unspecified assistantships also available. Financial award application deadline: 3/15; financial award applicants required to submit FAFSA. In 2018, 17 master's, 41 doctorates awarded. *Program availability:* Part-time. Offers allied health sciences (MS, DMP, DPT, PhD, Advanced Certificate); exercise kinesiology (MS); health physics (MS); interdisciplinary health sciences (PhD); kinesiology (PhD); medical physics (DMP, Advanced Certificate); nutrition sciences (MS); physical therapy (DPT). *Application fee:* $60 ($95 for international students). Electronic applications accepted. *Application Contact:* Dr. Ronald T. Brown, Dean, 702-895-3693, Fax: 702-895-1356, E-mail: ihs.dean@unlv.edu. *Dean,* Dr. Ronald T. Brown, 702-895-3693, Fax: 702-895-1356, E-mail: ihs.dean@unlv.edu.

School of Nursing Students: 38 full-time (35 women), 110 part-time (99 women); includes 44 minority (10 Black or African American, non-Hispanic/Latino; 14 Asian, non-Hispanic/Latino; 12 Hispanic/Latino; 8 Two or more races, non-Hispanic/Latino). Average age 39. 198 applicants, 42% accepted, 72 enrolled. *Faculty:* 14 full-time (12 women), 10 part-time/adjunct (8 women). Expenses: Contact institution. *Financial support:* In 2018–19, 5 students received support, including 5 research assistantships with full tuition reimbursements available (averaging $18,450 per year); institutionally sponsored loans, scholarships/grants, health care benefits, and unspecified assistantships also available. Financial award application deadline: 3/15; financial award applicants required to submit FAFSA. In 2018, 31 master's, 7 doctorates awarded. *Program availability:* Part-time, 100% online, blended/hybrid learning. Offers biobehavioral nursing (Advanced Certificate); family nurse practitioner (Advanced Certificate); nursing (MS, DNP, PhD); nursing education (Advanced Certificate). *Application fee:* $60 ($95 for international students). Electronic applications accepted. *Application Contact:* Dr. Angela Amar, Dean/Professor, 702-895-3906, Fax: 702-895-4807, E-mail: nursing.dean@unlv.edu. *Dean/Professor,* Dr. Angela Amar, 702-895-3906, Fax: 702-895-4807, E-mail: nursing.dean@unlv.edu.

School of Public Health Students: 86 full-time (59 women), 70 part-time (50 women); includes 81 minority (17 Black or African American, non-Hispanic/Latino; 2 American Indian or Alaska Native, non-Hispanic/Latino; 22 Asian, non-Hispanic/Latino; 25 Hispanic/Latino; 2 Native Hawaiian or other Pacific Islander, non-Hispanic/Latino; 13 Two or more races, non-Hispanic/Latino), 12 international. Average age 32. 86 applicants, 65% accepted, 36 enrolled. *Faculty:* 21 full-time (9 women), 11 part-time/adjunct (5 women). Expenses: Contact institution. *Financial support:* In 2018–19, 38 students received support, including 1 fellowship with full tuition reimbursement available (averaging $25,000 per year), 35 research assistantships with full tuition reimbursements available (averaging $13,399 per year), 3 teaching assistantships with full tuition reimbursements available (averaging $12,700 per year); institutionally sponsored loans, scholarships/grants, health care benefits, and unspecified assistantships also available. Financial award application deadline: 3/15; financial award applicants required to submit FAFSA. In 2018, 40 master's, 2 doctorates, 3 other advanced degrees awarded. *Program availability:* Part-time. Offers community health sciences (Exec MHA, MHA, MPH, PhD, Certificate); health care administration (Exec MHA, MHA); infection prevention (Certificate); public health (MPH, PhD, Certificate). *Application fee:* $60 ($95 for international students). Electronic applications accepted. *Application Contact:* Dr. Shawn Gerstenberger, Dean, 702-895-5090, Fax: 702-895-5184, E-mail: sph.dean@unlv.edu. *Dean,* Dr. Shawn Gerstenberger, 702-895-5090, Fax: 702-895-5184, E-mail: sph.dean@unlv.edu.

William F. Harrah College of Hospitality Students: 43 full-time (24 women), 51 part-time (28 women); includes 20 minority (4 Black or African American, non-Hispanic/Latino; 9 Asian, non-Hispanic/Latino; 4 Hispanic/Latino; 3 Two or more races, non-Hispanic/Latino), 32 international. Average age 34. 118 applicants, 40% accepted, 28 enrolled. *Faculty:* 16 full-time (6 women), 3 part-time/adjunct (0 women). Expenses: Contact institution. *Financial support:* In 2018–19, 35 students received support, including 4 research assistantships with full tuition reimbursements available (averaging $12,188 per year), 31 teaching assistantships with full tuition reimbursements available (averaging $13,306 per year); institutionally sponsored loans, scholarships/grants, health care benefits, and unspecified assistantships also available. Financial award application deadline: 3/15; financial award applicants required to submit FAFSA. In 2018, 36 master's, 1 doctorate awarded. *Program availability:* Part-time, evening/weekend, 100% online, blended/hybrid learning. Offers hospitality administration (MHA, PhD); hotel administration (MS). *Application fee:* $60 ($95 for international students). Electronic applications accepted. *Application Contact:* Dr. Stowe Shoemaker, Dean, 702-895-3308, Fax: 702-895-4109, E-mail: hospitality.dean@unlv.edu. *Dean,* Dr. Stowe Shoemaker, 702-895-3308, Fax: 702-895-4109, E-mail: hospitality.dean@unlv.edu.

School of Dental Medicine Students: 366 full-time (160 women), 1 part-time (0 women); includes 137 minority (4 Black or African American, non-Hispanic/Latino; 1 American Indian or Alaska Native, non-Hispanic/Latino; 77 Asian, non-Hispanic/Latino; 34 Hispanic/Latino; 2 Native Hawaiian or other Pacific Islander, non-Hispanic/Latino; 19 Two or more races, non-Hispanic/Latino), 3 international. Average age 29. 1,622 applicants, 9% accepted, 85 enrolled. Expenses: Contact institution. *Financial support:* Federal Work-Study, institutionally sponsored loans, scholarships/grants, health care benefits, and unspecified assistantships available. Support available to part-time students. Financial award application deadline: 3/15; financial award applicants required to submit FAFSA. In 2018, 6 master's, 70 doctorates, 5 other advanced degrees awarded. *Program availability:* Part-time, evening/weekend, online learning. Offers dental medicine (DMD); dental surgery (DDS); dentistry (DMD); oral biology (MS); orthodontics and dentofacial orthopedics (Certificate). *Application deadline:* For fall admission, 1/1 for domestic and international students; for summer admission, 3/1 for domestic students. Applications are processed on a rolling basis. *Application fee:* $75. Electronic applications accepted. *Application Contact:* Dr. Christine C. Ancajas, Assistant Dean of Admissions and Student Affairs, 702-774-2522, Fax: 702-774-2521, E-mail: christine.ancajas@unlv.edu. *Assistant Dean of Admissions and Student Affairs,* Dr. Christine C. Ancajas, 702-774-2522, Fax: 702-774-2521, E-mail: christine.ancajas@unlv.edu.

School of Medicine Expenses: Contact institution. *Application Contact:* Sebern Coleman, Graduate Recruitment and CRM Specialist, 702-895-3423, Fax: 702-895-4180, E-mail: sebern.coleman@unlv.edu.

William S. Boyd School of Law Students: 354 full-time (182 women), 63 part-time (28 women); includes 150 minority (32 Black or African American, non-Hispanic/Latino; 20 Asian, non-Hispanic/Latino; 78 Hispanic/Latino; 20 Two or more races, non-Hispanic/Latino), 1 international. Average age 29. 883 applicants, 31% accepted, 157 enrolled. *Faculty:* 43 full-time (27 women), 46 part-time/adjunct (11 women). Expenses: Contact institution. *Financial support:* In 2018–19, 331 students received support, including 10 fellowships (averaging $4,750 per year); scholarships/grants also available. Support available to part-time students. Financial award application deadline: 3/15. In 2018, 18 master's, 106 doctorates awarded. *Program availability:* Part-time, evening/weekend. Offers gaming law and regulation (LL M); law (JD). *Application deadline:* For fall admission, 3/15 for domestic and international students. Applications are processed on a rolling basis. *Application fee:* $50. Electronic applications accepted. *Application Contact:* Dr. Brain Wall, Assistant Dean for Admissions and Financial Aid, 702-895-1350, Fax: 702-895-2414, E-mail: brian.wall@unlv.edu. *Dean,* Dr. Daniel W. Hamilton, 702-895-1876, Fax: 702-895-1095, E-mail: daniel.hamilton@unlv.edu.

UNIVERSITY OF NEVADA, RENO, Reno, NV 89557

General Information State-supported, coed, university. CGS member. *Graduate housing:* Rooms and/or apartments available on a first-come, first-served basis to single and married students. Housing application deadline: 5/16. *Research affiliation:* National Institutes of Health (nursing), Desert Research Institute (natural resource sciences, environmental sciences).

GRADUATE UNITS

Graduate School *Program availability:* Part-time, evening/weekend, online learning. Offers atmospheric sciences (MS, PhD); Basque studies (PhD); biomedical engineering (MS, PhD); cell and molecular biology (MS, PhD); cellular and molecular pharmacology and physiology (PhD); chemical physics (PhD); ecology, evolution, and conservation biology (PhD); environmental sciences and health (MS, PhD); hydrogeology (MS, PhD); hydrology (MS, PhD); social psychology (PhD); speech pathology (PhD); speech pathology and audiology (MS). Electronic applications accepted.

College of Agriculture, Biotechnology and Natural Resources Offers agriculture, biotechnology and natural resources (MS, PhD); animal and rangeland science (MS); biochemistry (MS, PhD); biotechnology (MS); natural resources and environmental science (MS); nutrition (MS). Electronic applications accepted.

College of Business *Program availability:* Part-time, online learning. Offers accounting (M Acc); business (M Acc, MA, MBA, MS); business administration (MBA); economics (MA, MS); finance (MS); information systems (MS). Electronic applications accepted.

College of Education Offers counseling and educational psychology (M Ed, MA, MS, Ed D, PhD, Ed S); curriculum and instruction (PhD); curriculum, teaching and learning (Ed D, PhD); education (M Ed, MA, MS, Ed D, PhD, Ed S); educational leadership (M Ed, MA, MS, Ed D, PhD, Ed S); educational specialties (M Ed, MS, Ed D, PhD); elementary education (M Ed, MA, MS); human development and family studies (MS); literacy studies (M Ed, MA, Ed D, PhD); secondary education (M Ed, MA, MS); special education (M Ed, MA, MS, Ed D, PhD); special education and disability studies (PhD); teaching English to speakers of other languages (MA). Electronic applications accepted.

College of Engineering Offers chemical engineering (MS, PhD); civil and environmental engineering (MS, PhD); computer science and engineering (MS, PhD); electrical and biomedical engineering (MS, PhD); engineering (MS, PhD); materials science and engineering (MS, PhD); mechanical engineering (MS, PhD). Electronic applications accepted.

College of Liberal Arts *Program availability:* Part-time, evening/weekend, online learning. Offers anthropology (MA, PhD); behavior analysis (MA, PhD); clinical psychology (PhD); cognitive brain science (MA, PhD); communication studies (MA); criminal justice (MA); English (MA, MATE, PhD); fine arts (MFA); history (MA, PhD); judicial studies (MJS, PhD); justice management (MJM); liberal arts (MA, MATE, MFA, MJM, MJS, MM, MPA, PhD); music (MA, MM); philosophy (MA); political science (MA, PhD); public administration (MPA); public administration and policy (MPA); social research and justice studies (MA, MJM, MJS, PhD); sociology (MA); Spanish (MA). Electronic applications accepted.

College of Science Offers biology (MS); chemistry (MS, PhD); earth sciences and engineering (MS, PhD); geochemistry (MS, PhD); geography (MS, PhD); geological engineering (MS, PhD); geology (MS, PhD); geophysics (MS, PhD); land use planning (MS); mathematics (MS); metallurgical engineering (MS); mining engineering (MS, PhD); physics (MS, PhD); science (MATM, MS, PhD); teaching mathematics (MATM). Electronic applications accepted.

Division of Health Sciences Offers community health sciences (MPH, PhD); health sciences (MPH, MS, MSN, MSW, DNP, PhD); nursing (MSN, DNP); social work (MSW). Electronic applications accepted.

Donald W. Reynolds School of Journalism Offers journalism (MA). Electronic applications accepted.

School of Medicine Offers medicine (MD).

UNIVERSITY OF NEW BRUNSWICK FREDERICTON, Fredericton, NB E3B 5A3, Canada

General Information Province-supported, coed, university. *Graduate housing:* Rooms and/or apartments available on a first-come, first-served basis to single and married students. Housing application deadline: 5/31. *Research affiliation:* Petroleum Research Atlantic Canada (petroleum), Atlantic Associate for Research in the Mathematical Sciences (mathematical sciences), Atlantic Hydrogen, Inc. (hydrogen), Pulp and Paper Research Institute of Canada (pulp and paper), National Research Council Institute for Information Technology (information technology), Huntsman Marine Science Centre (marine sciences).

GRADUATE UNITS

School of Graduate Studies *Program availability:* Part-time, evening/weekend, online learning. Offers applied health services (MAHSR); citizen engagement/dispute resolution (M Phil); community development (M Phil); interdisciplinary studies (M IDST, PhD); international development (M Phil); leadership (M Phil); sustainability/environmental issues (M Phil); worldviews (M Phil).

Faculty of Arts *Program availability:* Part-time. Offers anthropology (MA); applied economics and finance (M Sc); arts (M Sc, MA, PhD); classics (MA); economics (MA); English (MA, PhD); history (MA, PhD); political science (MA); psychology (MA, PhD); sociology (MA, PhD). Electronic applications accepted.

Faculty of Business Administration *Program availability:* Part-time. Offers business administration (MBA); engineering management (MBA); entrepreneurship (MBA); sports and recreation management (MBA). Electronic applications accepted.

Faculty of Computer Science *Program availability:* Part-time. Offers computer science (M Sc CS, PhD). Electronic applications accepted.

Faculty of Education *Program availability:* Part-time, online learning. Offers education (M Ed, PhD). Electronic applications accepted.

Faculty of Engineering *Program availability:* Part-time. Offers applied mechanics (M Eng, M Sc E, PhD); chemical engineering (M Eng, M Sc E, PhD); construction engineering and management (M Eng, M Sc E, PhD); electrical and computer engineering (M Eng, M Sc E, PhD); engineering (M Eng, M Sc E, PhD, Certificate); environmental engineering (M Eng, M Sc E, PhD); environmental studies (M Eng); geodesy and geomatics engineering (M Eng, M Sc E, PhD); geotechnical engineering (M Eng, M Sc E, PhD); groundwater/hydrology (M Eng, M Sc E, PhD); materials (M Eng, M Sc E, PhD); mechanical engineering (M Eng, M Sc E, PhD); pavements (M Eng, M Sc E, PhD); structures (M Eng, M Sc E, PhD); transportation (M Eng, M Sc E, PhD). Electronic applications accepted.

Faculty of Forestry and Environmental Management *Program availability:* Part-time. Offers ecological foundations of forest management (PhD); environmental management (MEM); forest engineering (M Sc FE, MFE); forest products marketing (MBA); forest resources (M Sc F, MF, PhD). Electronic applications accepted.

Faculty of Kinesiology *Program availability:* Part-time. Offers exercise and sport science (M Sc); sport and recreation management (MBA); sport and recreation studies (MA). Electronic applications accepted.

Faculty of Nursing *Program availability:* Part-time, online learning. Offers nurse educator (MN); nurse practitioner (MN); nursing (MN). Electronic applications accepted.

Faculty of Science *Program availability:* Part-time. Offers biology (M Sc, PhD); chemistry (M Sc, PhD); earth sciences (M Sc, PhD); mathematics and statistics (M Sc, PhD); physics (M Sc, PhD); science (M Sc, PhD). Electronic applications accepted.

UNIVERSITY OF NEW BRUNSWICK SAINT JOHN, Saint John, NB E2L 4L5, Canada

General Information Province-supported, coed, comprehensive institution. *Graduate housing:* Rooms and/or apartments available on a first-come, first-served basis to single and married students. Housing application deadline: 3/31. *Research affiliation:* Cook Aquaculture (aquaculture), Horizon Health (health research), Dalhousie Medicine New Brunswick (cancer and general health), Fisheries and Oceans Canada (biology/ecology), New Brunswick Community College (health research).

GRADUATE UNITS

Department of Biology *Program availability:* Part-time. Offers biology (M Sc, PhD). Electronic applications accepted.

Department of Psychology *Program availability:* Part-time. Offers clinical psychology (PhD); experimental psychology (MA, PhD). Electronic applications accepted.

Faculty of Business *Program availability:* Part-time. Offers administration (MBA); electronic commerce (MBA); international business (MBA); natural resource management (MBA). Electronic applications accepted.

UNIVERSITY OF NEW ENGLAND, Biddeford, ME 04005-9526

General Information Independent, coed, comprehensive institution. *Enrollment:* 2,945 full-time matriculated graduate/professional students (2,018 women), 569 part-time matriculated graduate/professional students (458 women). *Enrollment by degree level:* 1,674 master's, 1,677 doctoral, 163 other advanced degrees. *Graduate faculty:* 137 full-time (72 women), 204 part-time/adjunct (117 women). *Graduate housing:* On-campus housing not available. *Student services:* Campus employment opportunities, campus safety program, career counseling, exercise/wellness program, free psychological counseling, international student services, low-cost health insurance, multicultural affairs office, services for students with disabilities, teacher training, writing training. *Library facilities:* Jack S. Ketchum Library plus 1 other. *Collection:* Books: 135,000 (physical), 1.2 million (digital/electronic); Serial titles: 140,000 (digital/electronic); Databases: 200. Weekly public service hours: 146; study areas open 24 hours, 5–7 days a week; students can reserve study rooms.

Computer facilities: Computer purchase and lease plans are available. 91 computers available on campus for general student use. A campuswide network can be accessed from student residence rooms and from off campus. Online class registration is available.
Website: http://www.une.edu/

General Application Contact: Scott Steinberg, Vice President of University Admissions, 207-221-4225, Fax: 207-523-1925, E-mail: ssteinberg@une.edu.

GRADUATE UNITS

College of Arts and Sciences Students: 13 full-time (9 women), 3 part-time (all women). Average age 26. 46 applicants, 37% accepted, 12 enrolled. *Faculty:* 13 full-time (5 women). Expenses: Contact institution. *Financial support:* Fellowships, research assistantships, teaching assistantships, career-related internships or fieldwork, scholarships/grants, traineeships, and unspecified assistantships available. Financial award application deadline: 5/1; financial award applicants required to submit FAFSA. In 2018, 8 master's awarded. *Program availability:* Part-time. Offers biological sciences (MS); marine sciences (MS). *Application deadline:* Applications are processed on a rolling basis. Electronic applications accepted. *Application Contact:* Scott Steinberg, Vice President of University Admissions, 207-221-4225, Fax: 207-523-1925, E-mail: ssteinberg@une.edu. *Dean, College of Arts and Sciences,* Dr. Jonathan H. Millen, 207-602-2371, E-mail: jmillen@une.edu.

College of Dental Medicine Students: 251 full-time (133 women); includes 61 minority (6 Black or African American, non-Hispanic/Latino; 4 American Indian or Alaska Native, non-Hispanic/Latino; 33 Asian, non-Hispanic/Latino; 11 Hispanic/Latino; 1 Native Hawaiian or other Pacific Islander, non-Hispanic/Latino; 6 Two or more races, non-Hispanic/Latino), 10 international. Average age 27. 1,007 applicants, 17% accepted, 64 enrolled. *Faculty:* 28 full-time (13 women), 30 part-time/adjunct (6 women). Expenses: Contact institution. *Financial support:* Application deadline: 5/1; applicants required to submit FAFSA. In 2018, 63 doctorates awarded. Offers dental medicine (DMD). *Application deadline:* For fall admission, 11/1 for domestic and international students. Electronic applications accepted. *Application Contact:* Scott Steinberg, Vice President of University Admissions, 207-221-4225, Fax: 207-523-1925, E-mail: ssteinberg@une.edu. *Dean, College of Dental Medicine,* Dr. Jon Ryder, 207-221-4702, Fax: 207-523-1915, E-mail: jryder2@une.edu.

College of Graduate and Professional Studies Students: 1,207 full-time (972 women), 561 part-time (450 women); includes 411 minority (280 Black or African American, non-Hispanic/Latino; 17 American Indian or Alaska Native, non-Hispanic/Latino; 74 Asian, non-Hispanic/Latino; 25 Hispanic/Latino; 9 Native Hawaiian or other Pacific Islander, non-Hispanic/Latino; 6 Two or more races, non-Hispanic/Latino). Average age 36. 740 applicants, 92% accepted, 494 enrolled. *Faculty:* 109 part-time/adjunct (78 women). Expenses: Contact institution. *Financial support:* Application deadline: 5/1; applicants required to submit FAFSA. In 2018, 586 master's, 44 doctorates, 85 other advanced degrees awarded. *Program availability:* Part-time, evening/weekend, online only, 100% online. Offers advanced educational leadership (CAGS); applied nutrition (MS); career and technical education (MS Ed); curriculum and instruction (MS Ed); education (CAGS, Post-Master's Certificate); educational leadership (MS Ed, Ed D); generalist (MS Ed); health informatics (MS, Graduate Certificate); inclusion education (MS Ed); literacy K-12 (MS Ed); medical education leadership (MMEL); public health (MPH, Graduate Certificate); reading specialist (MS Ed); social work (MSW). *Application deadline:* Applications are processed on a rolling basis. Electronic applications accepted. *Application Contact:* Nicole Lindsay, Director of Online Admissions, 207-221-4966, E-mail: nlindsay1@une.edu. *Dean of the College of Graduate and Professional Studies,* Dr. Martha Wilson, 207-221-4985, E-mail: mwilson13@une.edu.

College of Osteopathic Medicine Students: 701 full-time (372 women); includes 123 minority (3 Black or African American, non-Hispanic/Latino; 3 American Indian or Alaska Native, non-Hispanic/Latino; 106 Asian, non-Hispanic/Latino; 4 Hispanic/Latino; 7 Two or more races, non-Hispanic/Latino), 24 international. Average age 26. 1,425 applicants, 29% accepted, 179 enrolled. *Faculty:* 38 full-time (17 women), 35 part-time/adjunct (15 women). Expenses: Contact institution. *Financial support:* Application deadline: 5/1; applicants required to submit FAFSA. In 2018, 175 doctorates awarded. Offers osteopathic medicine (DO). *Application deadline:* For fall admission, 3/1 for domestic students. *Application Contact:* Scott Steinberg, Vice President of University Admissions, 207-221-4225, Fax: 207-523-1925, E-mail: ssteinberg@une.edu. *Dean, College of Osteopathic Medicine,* Dr. Jane Carreiro, 207-602-2460, E-mail: jcarreiro@une.edu.

College of Pharmacy Students: 273 full-time (172 women); includes 75 minority (30 Black or African American, non-Hispanic/Latino; 1 American Indian or Alaska Native, non-Hispanic/Latino; 35 Asian, non-Hispanic/Latino; 6 Hispanic/Latino; 3 Two or more races, non-Hispanic/Latino), 1 international. Average age 25. 251 applicants, 41% accepted, 59 enrolled. *Faculty:* 21 full-time (11 women), 7 part-time/adjunct (3 women). Expenses: Contact institution. *Financial support:* Application deadline: 5/1; applicants required to submit FAFSA. In 2018, 99 doctorates awarded. Offers pharmacy (Pharm D). *Application deadline:* For fall admission, 3/1 for domestic students. Applications are processed on a rolling basis. Electronic applications accepted. *Application Contact:* Scott Steinberg, Vice President of University Admissions, 207-221-4225, Fax: 207-523-1925, E-mail: ssteinberg@une.edu. *Dean, College of Pharmacy,* Dr. Robert L. McCarthy, 207-221-4365, E-mail: rmccarthy2@une.edu.

Westbrook College of Health Professions Students: 500 full-time (360 women), 5 part-time (all women); includes 52 minority (3 Black or African American, non-Hispanic/Latino; 30 Asian, non-Hispanic/Latino; 10 Hispanic/Latino; 2 Native Hawaiian or other Pacific Islander, non-Hispanic/Latino; 7 Two or more races, non-Hispanic/Latino), 1 international. Average age 27. 2,512 applicants, 18% accepted, 227 enrolled. *Faculty:* 37 full-time (26 women), 23 part-time/adjunct (15 women). Expenses: Contact institution. *Financial support:* Application deadline: 5/1; applicants required to submit FAFSA. In 2018, 176 master's, 63 doctorates awarded. *Program availability:* Part-time. Offers nurse anesthesia (MSNA); occupational therapy (MS); physical therapy

(DPT); physician assistant (MS); social work (MSW). *Application deadline:* Applications are processed on a rolling basis. Electronic applications accepted. *Application Contact:* Scott Steinberg, Vice President of University Admissions, 207-221-4225, Fax: 207-523-1925, E-mail: ssteinberg@une.edu. *Dean, Westbrook College of Health Professions,* Dr. Karen T. Pardue, 207-221-4361, E-mail: kpardue@une.edu.

UNIVERSITY OF NEW HAMPSHIRE, Durham, NH 03824

General Information State-supported, coed, university. CGS member. *Graduate housing:* Rooms and/or apartments available on a first-come, first-served basis to single and married students. Housing application deadline: 7/15.

GRADUATE UNITS

Graduate School *Program availability:* Part-time, evening/weekend. Electronic applications accepted.

Carsey School of Public Policy *Program availability:* Part-time. Offers community development policy and practice (MA); public administration (MPA); public policy (MA, MPA, MPP). Electronic applications accepted.

College of Engineering and Physical Sciences *Program availability:* Part-time, evening/weekend. Offers applied mathematics (PhD); chemical engineering (M Engr, MS, PhD); chemistry (MS, PhD); chemistry education (PhD); civil and environmental engineering (M Engr, MS, PhD); computer science (MS, PhD); electrical and computer engineering (MS); electrical engineering (M Engr, MS, PhD); engineering and physical sciences (M Engr, MS, MST, PhD, Certificate, Postbaccalaureate Certificate); geochemical systems (MS); geology (MS); hydrology (MS); industrial statistics (Certificate); materials science (MS); materials science and engineering (PhD); mathematics (MS, MST, PhD); mathematics education (PhD); mathematics: applied mathematics (MS); mathematics: statistics (MS, PhD); mechanical engineering (M Engr, MS, PhD); ocean mapping (MS); oceanography (MS); physics (MS, PhD); ubiquitous computing (Certificate); wireless communication systems (Certificate). Electronic applications accepted.

College of Health and Human Services *Program availability:* Part-time, evening/weekend. Offers adapted physical education (Postbaccalaureate Certificate); adaptive sports (MS); adolescent development (Postbaccalaureate Certificate); adult neurogenic communication (MS); assistive technology (Postbaccalaureate Certificate); child welfare (Postbaccalaureate Certificate); communication sciences and disorders (MS); early childhood intervention (MS); family nurse practitioner (Postbaccalaureate Certificate); health and human services (MPH, MS, MSW, DNP, Postbaccalaureate Certificate); human development and family studies (MS); intellectual and development disabilities (Postbaccalaureate Certificate); kinesiology (MS); kinesiology and social work (MS); language and literacy disorders (MS); marriage and family therapy (MS, DNP); occupational therapy (MS); psychiatric mental health (Postbaccalaureate Certificate); public health (MPH, Postbaccalaureate Certificate); recreation administration (MS); social work (MSW); substance use disorders (Postbaccalaureate Certificate); therapeutic recreation administration (MS). Electronic applications accepted.

College of Liberal Arts *Program availability:* Part-time. Offers assessment evaluation and policy (Postbaccalaureate Certificate); autism spectrum disorders (Postbaccalaureate Certificate); children and youth in communities (PhD); curriculum and instruction leadership (Postbaccalaureate Certificate); early childhood education (M Ed); early childhood education: special needs (M Ed); education (PhD, Postbaccalaureate Certificate); educational administration and supervision (Ed S); educational studies (M Ed); elementary education (M Ed); English (MST, PhD); history (MA, PhD); history: museum studies (MA); justice studies (MA); language and linguistics (MA); liberal arts (M Ed, MA, MALS, MAT, MFA, MPA, MST, PhD, Ed S, Postbaccalaureate Certificate); liberal studies (MALS); literature (MA); mentoring teachers (Postbaccalaureate Certificate); music composition (MA); music conducting (MA); musicology (MA); political science (MA, Postbaccalaureate Certificate); psychology (PhD); secondary education (M Ed, MAT); sociology (MA, PhD); Spanish (MA, Postbaccalaureate Certificate); special education (M Ed, Postbaccalaureate Certificate); special education administration (Postbaccalaureate Certificate); technology integration (Postbaccalaureate Certificate); writing (MFA). Electronic applications accepted.

College of Life Sciences and Agriculture *Program availability:* Part-time. Offers agricultural sciences (MS, PhD); animal and nutritional sciences (MS, PhD); biochemistry (MS, PhD); environmental conservation (MS); environmental economics (MS); forestry (MS); genetics (MS, PhD); integrative and organismal biology (MS, PhD); life sciences and agriculture (MS, PhD); marine biology (MS, PhD); microbiology (MS, PhD); molecular and evolutionary systems biology (PhD); natural resources (MS); nutritional sciences (MS, PhD); resource administration and management (MS); soil and water resource management (MS); wildlife and conservation biology (MS). Electronic applications accepted.

Interdisciplinary Programs *Program availability:* Part-time. Offers analytics (MS, Postbaccalaureate Certificate); college teaching (Postbaccalaureate Certificate); earth and environmental sciences (PhD); feminist studies (Postbaccalaureate Certificate); geospatial science (Postbaccalaureate Certificate); natural resources and environmental studies (PhD). Electronic applications accepted.

Graduate School Manchester Campus *Program availability:* Part-time, evening/weekend. Offers business administration (MBA); cybersecurity policy and risk management (MS); educational administration and supervision (Ed S); educational studies (M Ed); elementary education (M Ed); information technology (MS); public administration (MPA); public health (MPH, Certificate); secondary education (M Ed, MAT); social work (MSW); substance use disorders (Certificate). Electronic applications accepted.

Peter T. Paul College of Business and Economics *Program availability:* Part-time, evening/weekend. Offers accounting (MS); business administration (MBA); business and economics (MA, MBA, MS, PhD); economics (MA, PhD). Electronic applications accepted.

School of Marine Science and Ocean Engineering Offers ocean engineering (MS, PhD); ocean mapping (MS, Postbaccalaureate Certificate). Electronic applications accepted.

School of Law *Program availability:* Part-time, 100% online, limited residential. Offers business law (JD); commerce and technology (LL M, MCT, Diploma); criminal law (JD); intellectual property (LL M, MIP, JD, Diploma); international criminal law and justice (LL M, MICLJ); litigation (JD); public interest and social justice (JD); sports and entertainment law (JD). Electronic applications accepted.

UNIVERSITY OF NEW HAVEN, West Haven, CT 06516

General Information Independent, coed, comprehensive institution. CGS member. *Enrollment:* 6,867 graduate, professional, and undergraduate students; 1,139 full-time matriculated graduate/professional students (571 women), 636 part-time matriculated graduate/professional students (298 women). *Enrollment by degree level:* 1,722 master's, 32 doctoral, 19 other advanced degrees. *Graduate faculty:* 128 full-time (39 women), 98 part-time/adjunct (28 women). *Tuition:* Full-time $16,470; part-time $915 per credit hour. *Required fees:* $230; $95 per term. *Graduate housing:* Room and/or apartments available on a first-come, first-served basis to single students; on-campus housing not available to married students. *Student services:* Campus employment opportunities, campus safety program, career counseling, free psychological counseling, international student services, low-cost health insurance, multicultural affairs office, services for students with disabilities, writing training. *Library facilities:* Marvin K. Peterson Library.

Computer facilities: Computer purchase and lease plans are available. A campuswide network can be accessed from student residence rooms. Online class registration, computer repair services are available.
Website: http://www.newhaven.edu/

General Application Contact: Steven Boyd, Executive Director of Graduate Admissions, 203-932-7463, E-mail: gradinfo@newhaven.edu.

GRADUATE UNITS

Graduate School Students: 1,285 full-time (612 women), 591 part-time (267 women); includes 383 minority (177 Black or African American, non-Hispanic/Latino; 3 American Indian or Alaska Native, non-Hispanic/Latino; 79 Asian, non-Hispanic/Latino; 116 Hispanic/Latino; 3 Native Hawaiian or other Pacific Islander, non-Hispanic/Latino; 5 Two or more races, non-Hispanic/Latino), 682 international. Average age 28. 3,175 applicants, 77% accepted, 711 enrolled. Expenses: Contact institution. *Financial support:* Research assistantships with partial tuition reimbursements, teaching assistantships with partial tuition reimbursements, Federal Work-Study, scholarships/grants, and unspecified assistantships available. Financial award applicants required to submit FAFSA. In 2018, 731 master's, 3 doctorates, 19 other advanced degrees awarded. *Program availability:* Part-time, evening/weekend. *Application deadline:* Applications are processed on a rolling basis. *Application fee:* $50. Electronic applications accepted. *Application Contact:* Selina O'Toole, Senior Associate Director of Graduate Admissions, 203-932-7337, E-mail: SOToole@newhaven.edu.

College of Arts and Sciences Students: 172 full-time (120 women), 35 part-time (23 women); includes 51 minority (25 Black or African American, non-Hispanic/Latino; 7 Asian, non-Hispanic/Latino; 18 Hispanic/Latino; 1 Native Hawaiian or other Pacific Islander, non-Hispanic/Latino), 41 international. Average age 27. 291 applicants, 77% accepted, 88 enrolled. Expenses: Contact institution. *Financial support:* Research assistantships with partial tuition reimbursements, teaching assistantships with partial tuition reimbursements, Federal Work-Study, scholarships/grants, and unspecified assistantships available. Support available to part-time students. Financial award application deadline: 5/1; financial award applicants required to submit FAFSA. In 2018, 85 master's, 2 other advanced degrees awarded. *Program availability:* Part-time, evening/weekend. Offers applications of psychology (Graduate Certificate); arts and sciences (MA, MS, Graduate Certificate); cellular and molecular biology (MS); community clinical services (MA); community psychology (MA); conflict management (MA); environmental ecology (MS); environmental geoscience (MS); environmental health and management (MS); environmental science (MS); forensic psychology (MA); geographical information systems (MS); industrial organizational psychology (MA); industrial-human resources psychology (MA); organizational development and consultation (MA); program development (MA); psychology of conflict management (Graduate Certificate). *Application deadline:* Applications are processed on a rolling basis. *Application fee:* $50. Electronic applications accepted. *Application Contact:* Selina O'Toole, Senior Associate Director of Graduate Admissions, 203-932-7337, E-mail: SOToole@newhaven.edu. *Interim Dean,* Dr. Elizabeth A. Beaulieu, 203-932-7257, E-mail: EBeaulieu@newhaven.edu.

College of Business Students: 261 full-time (117 women), 89 part-time (35 women); includes 89 minority (38 Black or African American, non-Hispanic/Latino; 1 American Indian or Alaska Native, non-Hispanic/Latino; 27 Asian, non-Hispanic/Latino; 22 Hispanic/Latino; 1 Two or more races, non-Hispanic/Latino), 110 international. Average age 28. 351 applicants, 93% accepted, 151 enrolled. Expenses: Contact institution. *Financial support:* Research assistantships with partial tuition reimbursements, teaching assistantships with partial tuition reimbursements, Federal Work-Study, scholarships/grants, and unspecified assistantships available. Support available to part-time students. Financial award application deadline: 5/1; financial award applicants required to submit FAFSA. In 2018, 126 master's, 4 other advanced degrees awarded. *Program availability:* Part-time, evening/weekend. Offers accounting (MS, Graduate Certificate); business (EMBA, MBA, MS, Graduate Certificate); business administration (EMBA, MBA); business intelligence (MBA); business policy and strategic leadership (MBA); collegiate athletic administration (MS); facility management (MBA); finance (MBA); global marketing (MBA); human resources management (MBA); sport analytics (MS); sport management (MBA, Graduate Certificate); taxation (MS, Graduate Certificate). *Application deadline:* Applications are processed on a rolling basis. *Application fee:* $50. Electronic applications accepted. *Application Contact:* Selina O'Toole, Senior Associate Director of Graduate Admissions, 203-932-7337, E-mail: SOToole@newhaven.edu. *Dean,* Dr. Brian Kench, 203-932-7115, E-mail: bkench@newhaven.edu.

Henry C. Lee College of Criminal Justice and Forensic Sciences Students: 294 full-time (172 women), 250 part-time (113 women); includes 134 minority (63 Black or African American, non-Hispanic/Latino; 1 American Indian or Alaska Native, non-Hispanic/Latino; 15 Asian, non-Hispanic/Latino; 51 Hispanic/Latino; 2 Native Hawaiian or other Pacific Islander, non-Hispanic/Latino; 2 Two or more races, non-Hispanic/Latino), 47 international. Average age 31. 471 applicants, 82% accepted, 206 enrolled. Expenses: Contact institution. *Financial support:* Research assistantships with partial tuition reimbursements, teaching assistantships with partial tuition reimbursements, Federal Work-Study, scholarships/grants, and unspecified assistantships available. Support available to part-time students. Financial award applicants required to submit FAFSA. In 2018, 233 master's, 3 doctorates, 11 other advanced degrees awarded. *Program availability:* Part-time, evening/weekend, 100% online, blended/hybrid learning. Offers criminal investigations (MS); criminal justice (MS, PhD); criminal justice and forensic sciences (MPA, MS, PhD, Graduate Certificate); criminal justice management (Graduate Certificate); digital forensic investigations (MS); emergency management (MS, Graduate Certificate); financial crimes investigations (MS); fire and emergency medical services (MPA); fire science (MS); fire/arson investigation (MS, Graduate Certificate); forensic computer investigation (Graduate Certificate); forensic science (MS, Graduate Certificate); forensic science/fire science (Graduate Certificate); forensic technology (MS); municipal management (MPA); national security (MS, Graduate Certificate); national security administration (Graduate Certificate); nonprofit organization management (MPA); public administration (MPA, Graduate Certificate); public finance (MPA); public safety (MPA); public safety management (MS). *Application deadline:* Applications are processed on a rolling basis. *Application fee:* $50. Electronic applications accepted.

University of New Haven

Application Contact: Selina O'Toole, Senior Associate Director of Graduate Admissions, 203-932-7337, E-mail: SOToole@newhaven.edu. *Acting Dean,* Dr. David Schroeder, 203-931-2959, E-mail: DSchroeder@newhaven.edu.

Tagliatela College of Engineering Students: 463 full-time (129 women), 143 part-time (41 women); includes 50 minority (16 Black or African American, non-Hispanic/Latino; 1 American Indian or Alaska Native, non-Hispanic/Latino; 22 Asian, non-Hispanic/Latino; 10 Hispanic/Latino; 1 Two or more races, non-Hispanic/Latino), 445 international. Average age 26. 1,825 applicants, 72% accepted, 188 enrolled. Expenses: Contact institution. *Financial support:* Research assistantships with partial tuition reimbursements, teaching assistantships with partial tuition reimbursements, Federal Work-Study, scholarships/grants, and unspecified assistantships available. Support available to part-time students. Financial award application deadline: Submit FAFSA. In 2018, 213 master's, 1 other advanced degree awarded. *Program availability:* Part-time, evening/weekend. Offers biomedical engineering (MS); civil engineering (MS); computer engineering (MS); computer programming (Graduate Certificate); computer science (MS); control systems (MS); cybersecurity and networks (MS); digital signal processing and communication (MS); electrical engineering (MS); engineering (MS, MSIE, Graduate Certificate); engineering and operations management (MS); engineering management (MS); environmental engineering (MS); industrial and hazardous waste (MS); industrial engineering (MSIE); Lean Six Sigma (Graduate Certificate); mechanical engineering (MS); network systems (MS); quality engineering (Graduate Certificate); software development (MS); water and wastewater treatment (MS); water resources (MS). *Application deadline:* Applications are processed on a rolling basis. *Application fee:* $50. Electronic applications accepted. *Application Contact:* Selina O'Toole, Senior Associate Director of Graduate Admissions, 203-932-7337, E-mail: SOToole@newhaven.edu. *Dean and Vice Provost for Research,* Dr. Ronald Harichandran, 203-932-7167, E-mail: rharichandran@newhaven.edu.

School of Health Sciences Students: 95 full-time (74 women), 74 part-time (55 women); includes 59 minority (35 Black or African American, non-Hispanic/Latino; 8 Asian, non-Hispanic/Latino; 15 Hispanic/Latino; 1 Two or more races, non-Hispanic/Latino), 39 international. Average age 32. 237 applicants, 84% accepted, 78 enrolled. Expenses: Contact institution. *Application deadline:* Applications are processed on a rolling basis. *Application fee:* $50. Electronic applications accepted. *Application Contact:* Selina O'Toole, Senior Associate Director of Graduate Admissions, 203-932-7337, E-mail: SOToole@newhaven.edu. *Dean,* Dr. Summer McGee, 203-479-4104, E-mail: SMcGee@newhaven.edu.

UNIVERSITY OF NEW MEXICO, Albuquerque, NM 87131-2039

General Information State-supported, coed, university. CGS member. *Enrollment:* 24,393 graduate, professional, and undergraduate students; 2,073 full-time matriculated graduate/professional students, 1,979 part-time matriculated graduate/professional students. *Enrollment by degree level:* 2,135 master's, 1,734 doctoral, 183 other advanced degrees. *Graduate faculty:* 758 full-time (346 women), 72 part-time/adjunct (37 women). *Graduate housing:* Rooms and/or apartments available on a first-come, first-served basis to single and married students. Housing application deadline: 7/16. *Student services:* Campus employment opportunities, campus safety program, career counseling, child daycare facilities, exercise/wellness program, free psychological counseling, grant writing training, international student services, low-cost health insurance, multicultural affairs office, services for students with disabilities, teacher training, writing training. *Library facilities:* College of University Libraries and Learning Sciences plus 7 others. *Collection:* Students can reserve study rooms.

Computer facilities: Computer purchase and lease plans are available. 990 computers available on campus for general student use. A campuswide network can be accessed from student residence rooms and from off campus. Online class registration is available.
Website: http://www.unm.edu/

General Application Contact: Deborah Kieltyka, Associate Director, Admissions, 505-277-3140, Fax: 505-277-6686, E-mail: deborahk@unm.edu.

GRADUATE UNITS

Anderson School of Management Students: 392 part-time (201 women); includes 186 minority (5 Black or African American, non-Hispanic/Latino; 9 American Indian or Alaska Native, non-Hispanic/Latino; 18 Asian, non-Hispanic/Latino; 145 Hispanic/Latino; 9 Two or more races, non-Hispanic/Latino), 38 international. Average age 28. 329 applicants, 53% accepted, 141 enrolled. Faculty: 62 full-time (27 women), 41 part-time/adjunct (17 women). Expenses: Contact institution. *Financial support:* In 2018–19, 79 students received support, including 50 fellowships (averaging $15,746 per year), 52 research assistantships with partial tuition reimbursements available (averaging $15,400 per year); career-related internships or fieldwork, Federal Work-Study, scholarships/grants, and unspecified assistantships also available. Support available to part-time students. Financial award application deadline: 6/1; financial award applicants required to submit FAFSA. In 2018, 330 master's awarded. *Program availability:* Part-time, evening/weekend. Offers accounting (MBA); advanced accounting (M Acct); entrepreneurship (MBA); finance (MBA); information assurance (M Acct); information systems and assurance (MS); international management (MBA); international management in Latin America (MBA); management information systems (MBA); management of technology (MBA); marketing management (MBA); operations management (MBA); organizational behavior and human resources management (MBA); professional accounting (M Acct); strategic management and policy (MBA); tax accounting (M Acct). *Application deadline:* For fall admission, 3/1 priority date for domestic students, 5/1 priority date for international students; for spring admission, 9/1 priority date for domestic students, 10/1 priority date for international students. Applications are processed on a rolling basis. *Application fee:* $50 ($70 for international students). Electronic applications accepted. *Application Contact:* Lisa Beauchene-Lawson, Supervisor, Graduate Admissions & Advisement, 505-277-3290, E-mail: andersongrad@unm.edu. *Interim Dean,* Dr. Shawn Berman, 505-277-1792, E-mail: sberman@unm.edu.

Graduate Studies Students: 2,073 full-time (1,117 women), 1,979 part-time (1,117 women); includes 1,459 minority (82 Black or African American, non-Hispanic/Latino; 171 American Indian or Alaska Native, non-Hispanic/Latino; 105 Asian, non-Hispanic/Latino; 984 Hispanic/Latino; 5 Native Hawaiian or other Pacific Islander, non-Hispanic/Latino; 112 Two or more races, non-Hispanic/Latino), 657 international. Average age 34. 3,340 applicants, 40% accepted, 1021 enrolled. Faculty: 758 full-time (346 women), 72 part-time/adjunct (37 women). Expenses: Contact institution. *Financial support:* Fellowships, research assistantships, teaching assistantships, career-related internships or fieldwork, Federal Work-Study, institutionally sponsored loans, scholarships/grants, health care benefits, tuition waivers (full and partial), and project assistantships, residencies available. Support available to part-time students. Financial award application deadline: 3/1; financial award applicants required to submit FAFSA. In 2018, 975 master's, 257 doctorates, 57 other advanced degrees awarded. *Program*

availability: Part-time, evening/weekend, online only, 100% online, blended/hybrid learning. Offers hydroscience (MWR); policy management (MWR). *Application fee:* $50. Electronic applications accepted. *Application Contact:* Deborah Kieltyka, Associate Director, Admissions, 505-277-3140, Fax: 505-277-6686, E-mail: deborahk@unm.edu. *Dean,* Dr. Julie A. Coonrod, 505-277-2711, Fax: 505-277-7405, E-mail: jcoonrod@unm.edu.

College of Arts and Sciences Average age 32. 1,345 applicants, 29% accepted, 303 enrolled. Expenses: Contact institution. *Financial support:* Scholarships/grants, health care benefits, tuition waivers (full and partial), and unspecified assistantships available. Financial award application deadline: 3/1; financial award applicants required to submit FAFSA. In 2018, 225 master's, 114 doctorates awarded. *Program availability:* Part-time. Offers American studies (MA, PhD); archaeology (MA, MS, PhD); arts and sciences (MA, MFA, MS, PhD); behavioral neuroscience (PhD); biology (MS, PhD); chemistry (MS, PhD); clinical psychology (PhD); cognitive neuroimaging (PhD); communication (MA, PhD); comparative literature and cultural studies (MA); creative writing (MFA); developmental psychology (PhD); earth and planetary sciences (MS, PhD); econometrics (MA); economic theory (MA); English (MA, PhD); environmental/natural resource economics (MA, PhD); ethnology (MA, MS, PhD); evolution (PhD); evolutionary anthropology (PhD); French (MA); French studies (PhD); geography and environmental studies (MS); German studies (MA); health psychology (PhD); history (MA, PhD); imaging science (MS, PhD); international/development and sustainability economics (MA, PhD); Latin American studies (MA, PhD); linguistics (MA, PhD); mathematics (MS, PhD); optical science and engineering (MS, PhD); philosophy (MA, PhD); photonics (MS, PhD); physics (MS, PhD); political science (MA, PhD); Portuguese (MA); public archaeology (MA, MS, PhD); public economics (MA, PhD); quantitative methodology (PhD); sociology (MA, PhD); Spanish (MA); Spanish and Portuguese (PhD); speech-language pathology (MS); statistics (MS, PhD). *Application fee:* $50. Electronic applications accepted. *Application Contact:* Vicki Hall, Academic Administrator III, 505-277-6131, Fax: 505-277-0351, E-mail: vhall@unm.edu. *Dean,* Dr. Brenda J. Claiborne, 505-277-6131, Fax: 505-277-0351, E-mail: brendac@unm.edu.

College of Education Average age 37. 398 applicants, 56% accepted, 212 enrolled. Expenses: Contact institution. *Financial support:* Career-related internships or fieldwork, Federal Work-Study, scholarships/grants, health care benefits, and unspecified assistantships available. Support available to part-time students. Financial award application deadline: 3/1; financial award applicants required to submit FAFSA. In 2018, 288 master's, 33 doctorates, 39 other advanced degrees awarded. *Program availability:* Part-time, evening/weekend. Offers American Indian education (MA); art education (MA); bilingual education (MA, PhD); community health education (MS); counseling (MA); counselor education (PhD); curriculum and instruction (PhD); education (MA, MS, Ed D, PhD, Ed S, Graduate Certificate); educational leadership (MA, Ed D, Ed S); educational linguistics (PhD); educational psychology (MA, PhD); educational thought and sociocultural studies (MA, PhD); exercise science (PhD); family life education (MA); family relations (MA); family studies (PhD); human development in families (MA); intellectual disability and severe disabilities (MA); intensive social, language and behavioral needs (Graduate Certificate); learning and behavioral exceptionalities (MA); literacy/language arts (MA, PhD); math, science, and educational technology (MA); multicultural teacher and childhood education (Ed D, PhD); nutrition (MS); social studies (MA); special education (Ed D, PhD, Ed S); sports administration (PhD); TESOL (MA, PhD). *Application deadline:* For fall admission, 3/1 for international students; for spring admission, 8/1 for international students. *Application fee:* $50. Electronic applications accepted. *Application Contact:* Academic Graduate Coordinator, 505-277-3190, E-mail: coeac@unm.edu. *Dean,* Dr. Richard Howell, 505-277-2231, Fax: 505-277-8427, E-mail: rhowell@unm.edu.

College of Fine Arts Average age 31. 200 applicants, 52% accepted, 63 enrolled. Expenses: Contact institution. *Financial support:* Unspecified assistantships available. Financial award application deadline: 3/1; financial award applicants required to submit FAFSA. In 2018, 41 master's awarded. *Program availability:* Part-time. Offers art history (MA); art of the Americas (MA); collaborative piano (M Mu); conducting (M Mu); dance (MFA); dance history (MA); dramatic writing (MFA); fine arts (M Mu, MA, MFA, PhD); history of architecture (PhD); history of graphic arts (PhD); history of photography (PhD); modern Latin American art (PhD); music education (M Mu); music history and literature (M Mu); Native American art (PhD); performance (M Mu); Pre-Columbian art and architecture (PhD); Spanish colonial art (PhD); studio art (MFA); theatre education and outreach (MA); theory and composition (M Mu). *Application fee:* $50. *Application Contact:* Deanna Sanchez-Mulcahy, Associate Director, Admissions, 505-277-0708, E-mail: dmulcahy@unm.edu. *Dean,* Dr. Jim Linnell, 505-277-2112, Fax: 505-277-0708, E-mail: jlinnell@unm.edu.

College of Pharmacy *Program availability:* Part-time. Offers pharmaceutical sciences (MS, PhD); pharmacy (MS, PhD, Pharm D). Electronic applications accepted.

College of University Libraries and Learning Sciences Average age 45. 30 applicants, 80% accepted, 21 enrolled. Expenses: Contact institution. *Financial support:* Fellowships, research assistantships, teaching assistantships, and career-related internships or fieldwork available. Financial award application deadline: 3/1; financial award applicants required to submit FAFSA. In 2018, 19 master's, 4 doctorates awarded. *Program availability:* Part-time, evening/weekend, online learning. Offers organization, information and learning sciences (MA, PhD, Ed S). *Application deadline:* For fall admission, 3/15 for domestic and international students; for spring admission, 10/15 for domestic and international students. *Application fee:* $50. Electronic applications accepted. *Application Contact:* Linda Wood, Program Coordinator, 505-277-4131, Fax: 505-277-1427, E-mail: woodl@unm.edu. *Program Director,* Dr. Charlotte Gunawardens, 505-277-5046, Fax: 505-277-1427, E-mail: lani@unm.edu.

Health Sciences Center Average age 30. 218 applicants, 47% accepted, 94 enrolled. Expenses: Contact institution. Offers biochemistry and molecular biology (MS, PhD); cell biology and physiology (MS, PhD); clinical and translational science (Certificate); community health (MPH); dental hygiene (MS); education (MS); epidemiology (MPH); health sciences (MOT, MPH, MPT, MS, MSN, DNP, DPT, MD, Pharm D, Certificate); health systems, services and policy (MPH); laboratory management (MS); molecular genetics and microbiology (MS); neuroscience (MS, PhD); nursing (MSN, DNP, PhD); occupational therapy (MOT); pathology (MS, PhD); physical therapy (DPT); physician assistant studies (MS); research and development (MS); toxicology (MS, PhD). *Application Contact:* Deborah Kieltyka, Associate Director, Admissions, 505-277-3140, Fax: 505-277-6686, E-mail: deborahk@unm.edu. *Interim Vice President,* Dr. R. Philip Eaton, 505-272-5849.

School of Architecture and Planning Average age 32. 148 applicants, 56% accepted, 71 enrolled. Expenses: Contact institution. *Financial support:* Application deadline: 3/1; applicants required to submit FAFSA. In 2018, 73 master's, 11 other advanced degrees awarded. Offers architecture (M Arch); architecture and planning (M Arch, MCRP, MLA, Graduate Certificate); community and regional planning (MCRP); historic preservation and regionalism (Graduate Certificate); landscape architecture (MLA). *Application deadline:* For fall admission, 2/1 for domestic and international students. *Application fee:* $50. Electronic applications accepted. *Application Contact:* Elizabeth M. Rowe, Senior Academic Adviser, 505-277-1303, Fax: 505-277-0076, E-mail: erowe@unm.edu. *Dean*, Geraldine Forbes Isais, 505-277-2053, E-mail: gforbes@unm.edu.

School of Engineering *Program availability:* Part-time. Offers biomedical engineering (MS, PhD); chemical engineering (MS, PhD); civil engineering (M Eng, MSCE); computer engineering (MS, PhD); computer science (MS, PhD); construction management (MCM); electrical and computer engineering (MS, PhD); engineering (M Eng, MCM, MEME, MS, MSCE, PhD); manufacturing engineering (MEME); mechanical engineering (MS, PhD); nanoscience and microsystems engineering (MS, PhD); nuclear engineering (MS, PhD). Electronic applications accepted.

School of Public Administration Average age 36. 94 applicants, 80% accepted, 64 enrolled. *Expenses:* Contact institution. *Financial support:* Fellowships with partial tuition reimbursements, research assistantships with partial tuition reimbursements, career-related internships or fieldwork, scholarships/grants, health care benefits, and unspecified assistantships available. Financial award application deadline: 3/31; financial award applicants required to submit FAFSA. In 2018, 95 master's awarded. *Program availability:* Part-time, evening/weekend, online learning. Offers health administration (MHA); public administration (MHA, MPA). *Application deadline:* For fall admission, 4/1 for domestic students, 3/1 for international students; for spring admission, 10/1 for domestic students, 8/1 for international students. *Application fee:* $50. Electronic applications accepted. *Application Contact:* Gene V. Henley, Associate Director and Graduate Academic Advisor, 505-277-9196, Fax: 505-277-2529, E-mail: spadvise@unm.edu. *Director*, Dr. Uday Desai, 505-277-1092, Fax: 505-277-2529, E-mail: ucdesai@unm.edu.

School of Law Offers law (JD). Electronic applications accepted.

School of Medicine Offers medicine (MOT, MPH, MS, DPT, MD, PhD, Certificate); university science teaching (Certificate). Electronic applications accepted.

UNIVERSITY OF NEW ORLEANS, New Orleans, LA 70148

General Information State-supported, coed, university. *Graduate housing:* Rooms and/or apartments available on a first-come, first-served basis to single and married students. *Research affiliation:* John C. Stennis Space Center (acoustics, computer science), Northrop Grumman Corporation (engineering), TJ Watson Research Center-IBM (chemistry), Paratek Microwave, Inc. (nanotechnology), Applied Research Lab-Penn State University (engineering), Lockheed Martin Corporation (materials).

GRADUATE UNITS

Graduate School *Program availability:* Part-time, evening/weekend. Electronic applications accepted.

College of Business Administration *Program availability:* Part-time, evening/weekend. Offers accounting (MS); business administration (MBA, MS, PhD); finance (MS); financial economics (PhD); health care management (MS); hospitality and tourism management (MS); taxation (MS). Electronic applications accepted.

College of Engineering *Program availability:* Part-time. Offers civil engineering (MS); electrical engineering (MS); engineering (MS, PhD); engineering and applied science (PhD); engineering management (MS); mechanical engineering (MS); naval architecture and marine engineering (MS). Electronic applications accepted.

College of Liberal Arts, Education and Human Development *Program availability:* Part-time, evening/weekend. Offers arts administration (MA); counseling (M Ed); counselor education (M Ed, PhD); creative writing (MFA); curriculum and instruction (M Ed); design (MFA); educational administration (PhD); educational leadership (M Ed, PhD); English (MA, MFA); film production (MFA); fine arts (MFA); higher education (M Ed); history (MA); liberal arts, education and human development (M Ed, MA, MAT, MFA, MM, MPA, MS, MURP, PhD); music (MM); political science (MA, PhD); public administration (MPA); Romance languages (MA); sociology (MA); teaching (MAT); theatre performance (MFA); transportation (MS); urban and regional planning (MURP); urban studies (MS, PhD). Electronic applications accepted.

College of Sciences *Program availability:* Part-time, evening/weekend. Offers biological sciences (MS); chemistry (MS, PhD); computer science (MS, PhD); earth and environmental sciences (MS, PhD); mathematics (MS); physics (MS, PhD); psychology (MS, PhD); sciences (MS, PhD). Electronic applications accepted.

UNIVERSITY OF NORTH ALABAMA, Florence, AL 35632-0001

General Information State-supported, coed, comprehensive institution. *Graduate housing:* Rooms and/or apartments available on a first-come, first-served basis to single and married students.

GRADUATE UNITS

Anderson College of Nursing *Program availability:* Part-time, online only, 100% online, blended/hybrid learning. Offers nursing (MSN). Electronic applications accepted.

College of Arts and Sciences *Program availability:* Part-time, 100% online. Offers arts and sciences (MA, MPS, MS, MSCJ); creative writing (MA); criminal justice (MSCJ); English (MA); family studies (MA); geospatial science (MS); historic preservation (MA); historical administration (MA); history (MA); professional studies (MPS); public history (MA); rhetoric and composition (MA); technical writing (MA); writing (MA). Electronic applications accepted.

College of Business *Program availability:* Part-time, 100% online, blended/hybrid learning. Offers business administration (MBA). Electronic applications accepted.

College of Education *Program availability:* Part-time, 100% online, blended/hybrid learning. Offers clinical mental health counseling (MA); collaborative teacher special education (MA Ed); counseling (MA Ed); education (MA, MA Ed, MS, Ed S); elementary education (MA Ed, Ed S); health and human performance (MS); instructional leadership (MA Ed, Ed S); secondary education (MA Ed); special education (MA Ed); teacher leader (Ed S). Electronic applications accepted.

UNIVERSITY OF NORTH CAROLINA AT ASHEVILLE, Asheville, NC 28804-3299

General Information State-supported, coed, comprehensive institution. *Enrollment:* 3,762 graduate, professional, and undergraduate students; 1 (woman) full-time matriculated graduate/professional student, 18 part-time matriculated graduate/professional students (9 women). *Enrollment by degree level:* 19 master's. *Graduate faculty:* 4 full-time (2 women), 3 part-time/adjunct (1 woman). *International tuition:* $21,236 full-time. *Tuition, area resident:* Full-time $4914. Tuition, state resident: full-time $4914. Tuition, nonresident: full-time $21,236. *Required fees:* $3023. *Graduate housing:* Room and/or apartments available on a first-come, first-served basis to single students; on-campus housing not available to married students. Typical cost: $7000 per

year ($11,000 including board). Room and board charges vary according to housing facility selected. Housing application deadline: 5/1. *Student services:* Campus employment opportunities, career counseling, exercise/wellness program, free psychological counseling, international student services, low-cost health insurance, multicultural affairs office, services for students with disabilities, writing training. *Library facilities:* Ramsey Library. *Collection:* Books: 306,273 (physical), 487,660 (digital/electronic); Serial titles: 113 (physical), 82,954 (digital/electronic); Databases: 138. Weekly public service hours: 99; students can reserve study rooms.

Computer facilities: Computer purchase and lease plans are available. 500 computers available on campus for general student use. A campuswide network can be accessed. Online class registration is available.
Website: http://www.unca.edu/

General Application Contact: Lilly Augspurger, Administrative Assistant, 828-251-6099, E-mail: laugspur@unca.edu.

GRADUATE UNITS

Master of Liberal Arts and Sciences Program Students: 1 (woman) full-time, 18 part-time (9 women); includes 1 minority (Two or more races, non-Hispanic/Latino), 1 international. Average age 39. 11 applicants, 64% accepted, 5 enrolled. *Faculty:* 4 full-time (2 women), 3 part-time/adjunct (1 woman). *Expenses:* Contact institution. *Financial support:* In 2018–19, 1 student received support. Tuition waivers for UNC faculty/staff available. Financial award applicants required to submit FAFSA. In 2018, 8 master's, 4 Graduate Certificates awarded. *Program availability:* Part-time. Offers climate change and society (Graduate Certificate); environmental and cultural sustainability (Graduate Certificate). *Application deadline:* For fall admission, 5/15 priority date for domestic students, 7/1 priority date for international students; for spring admission, 12/15 priority date for domestic students, 12/1 priority date for international students. Applications are processed on a rolling basis. *Application fee:* $60. Electronic applications accepted. *Application Contact:* Lilly Augspurger, Administrative Assistant, 828-251-6099, E-mail: laugspur@unca.edu. *Director, Master of Liberal Arts and Sciences Program and the Asheville Graduate Center*, Gerard Voos, 828-232-5040, E-mail: gvoos@unca.edu.

THE UNIVERSITY OF NORTH CAROLINA AT CHAPEL HILL, Chapel Hill, NC 27599

General Information State-supported, coed, university. CGS member. *Graduate housing:* Rooms and/or apartments available on a first-come, first-served basis to single and married students. *Research affiliation:* Research Triangle Institute, Centers for Disease Control (CDC), Triangle Universities Nuclear Laboratory.

GRADUATE UNITS

Eshelman School of Pharmacy Offers pharmaceutical sciences (PhD); pharmaceutical sciences - health system pharmacy administration (MS); pharmacy (Pharm D). Electronic applications accepted.

Graduate School *Program availability:* Online learning. Electronic applications accepted.

College of Arts and Sciences *Program availability:* Part-time. Offers acting (MFA); anthropology (MA, PhD); art history (MA, PhD); arts and sciences (MA, MCRP, MFA, MPA, MRP, MS, MSRA, PhD, Certificate); athletic training (MA); behavioral neuroscience psychology (PhD); botany (MA, MS, PhD); cell biology, development, and physiology (MA, MS, PhD); cell motility and cytoskeleton (PhD); chemistry (MA, MS, PhD); city and regional planning (MCRP); classical archaeology (MA, PhD); classics (MA, PhD); clinical psychology (PhD); cognitive psychology (PhD); communication studies (PhD); computer science (MS, PhD); costume production (MFA); developmental psychology (PhD); ecology (MA, MS, PhD); ecology and behavior (MA, MS, PhD); economics (MS, PhD); English (MA, PhD); exercise physiology (MA); folklore (MA); French (MA, PhD); genetics and molecular biology (MA, MS, PhD); geography (MA, PhD); geological sciences (MS, PhD); German studies (PhD); global studies (MA); history (MA, PhD); Italian (MA, PhD); Latin American studies (Certificate); linguistics (MA); marine sciences (MS, PhD); mathematics (MA, MS, PhD); morphology, systematics, and evolution (MA, MS, PhD); music (MA, PhD); operations research (MS, PhD); philosophy (MA, PhD); physics (MS, PhD); planning (PhD); political science (MA, PhD); Portuguese (MA, PhD); public policy (PhD); public policy analysis (PhD); quantitative psychology (PhD); religious studies (MA, PhD); Romance languages (MA, PhD); Romance philology (MA, PhD); social psychology (PhD); sociology (MA, PhD); Spanish (MA, PhD); sport administration (MA); statistics (MS, PhD); studio art (MFA); technical production (MFA); trans-Atlantic studies (MA). Electronic applications accepted.

Gillings School of Global Public Health Students: 831 full-time (616 women), 488 part-time (345 women); includes 393 minority (123 Black or African American, non-Hispanic/Latino; 1 American Indian or Alaska Native, non-Hispanic/Latino; 132 Asian, non-Hispanic/Latino; 76 Hispanic/Latino; 1 Native Hawaiian or other Pacific Islander, non-Hispanic/Latino; 60 Two or more races, non-Hispanic/Latino), 157 international. Average age 30. 2,102 applicants, 44% accepted, 523 enrolled. *Faculty:* 236 full-time (138 women), 389 part-time/adjunct (206 women). *Expenses:* Contact institution. *Financial support:* Fellowships, research assistantships, teaching assistantships, career-related internships or fieldwork, Federal Work-Study, scholarships/grants, traineeships, health care benefits, and unspecified assistantships available. Financial award application deadline: 12/11; financial award applicants required to submit FAFSA. In 2018, 345 master's, 95 doctorates awarded. *Program availability:* Part-time, 100% online, blended/hybrid learning. Offers biostatistics (MPH, MS, Dr PH, PhD); clinical research (MSCR); environmental engineering (MPH, MS, MSEE, MSPH); environmental health sciences (MPH, MS, MSPH, PhD); epidemiology (MPH, PhD); global public health (MHA, MPH, MS, MSCR, MSEE, MSPH, Dr PH, PhD); health behavior (MPH, PhD); health care and prevention (MPH); health policy and management (MHA, MPH, MSPH, Dr PH, PhD); leadership (MPH); maternal and child health (MPH, MSPH, Dr PH, PhD); nutrition (MPH, PhD); nutrition/registered dietitian (MPH); nutritional biochemistry (MS); occupational health nursing (MPH); veterinary epidemiology (MPH). *Application deadline:* For fall admission, 2/1 for domestic and international students. *Application fee:* $90. Electronic applications accepted. *Application Contact:* Johnston King, Enrollment Management Coordinator, 919-962-6314, Fax: 919-966-6352, E-mail: sph-osa@unc.edu. *Dean*, Dr. Barbara K. Rimer, 919-966-3215, Fax: 919-966-7678.

Hussman School of Journalism and Media *Program availability:* Part-time, all course instruction online, plus two on-campus experiences totaling seven days. Offers digital communication (MA, Certificate); media and communication (MA, PhD). MA/JD and JD/PhD offered jointly with School of Law. Electronic applications accepted.

School of Education *Program availability:* Part-time. Offers culture, curriculum and change (MA, PhD); early childhood intervention and family support (M Ed); early childhood, intervention and literacy (MA, PhD); education (M Ed, MA, MAT, MSA, Ed D, PhD); education for experienced teachers (K-12) (M Ed); educational leadership (Ed D); educational psychology, measurement and evaluation (MA, PhD);

English (Grades 9-12) (MAT); English as a second language (MAT); French (Grades K-12) (MAT); German (Grades K-12) (MAT); Japanese (Grades K-12) (MAT); Latin (Grades 9-12) (MAT); mathematics (Grades 9-12) (MAT); music (Grades K-12) (MAT); school administration (MSA); school counseling (M Ed); school psychology (M Ed, MA, PhD); science (Grades 9-12) (MAT); social studies (Grades 9-12) (MAT); Spanish (Grades K-12) (MAT). Electronic applications accepted.

School of Government Offers government (MPA). Electronic applications accepted.

School of Information and Library Science Students: 255 full-time (188 women), 29 part-time (18 women); includes 34 minority (11 Black or African American, non-Hispanic/Latino; 6 Asian, non-Hispanic/Latino; 8 Hispanic/Latino; 9 Two or more races, non-Hispanic/Latino), 62 international. Average age 28. 303 applicants, 69% accepted, 98 enrolled. *Faculty:* 31 full-time (13 women), 46 part-time/adjunct (23 women). Expenses: Contact institution. *Financial support:* In 2018–19, 59 fellowships with full tuition reimbursements (averaging $2,565 per year), 46 research assistantships with full tuition reimbursements (averaging $3,528 per year), 7 teaching assistantships with full tuition reimbursements (averaging $22,917 per year) were awarded; career-related internships or fieldwork, Federal Work-Study, scholarships/grants, health care benefits, and unspecified assistantships also available. Financial award application deadline: 12/12. In 2018, 125 master's, 17 doctorates, 2 other advanced degrees awarded. *Program availability:* Part-time, 100% online, blended/hybrid learning. Offers data curation (PMC); digital curation and management (PSM); information and library science (PhD); information science (MSIS); library science (MSLS). *Application deadline:* For fall admission, 12/10 priority date for domestic and international students; for spring admission, 10/8 for domestic and international students; for summer admission, 3/10 for domestic and international students. Applications are processed on a rolling basis. *Application fee:* $90. Electronic applications accepted. *Application Contact:* Lara Bailey, Student Services Coordinator, 919-962-7601, Fax: 919-962-8071, E-mail: bailey@email.unc.edu. *Dean,* Dr. Gary Marchionini, 919-962-8363, Fax: 919-962-8071, E-mail: gary@ils.unc.edu.

School of Social Work *Program availability:* Part-time. Offers social work (MSW, PhD). Electronic applications accepted.

Kenan-Flagler Business School *Program availability:* Evening/weekend, online learning. Offers accounting (MAC); business (MAC, MBA, PhD); business administration (MBA, PhD); finance (PhD); marketing (PhD); operations management (PhD); organizational behavior (PhD); strategy (PhD). Electronic applications accepted.

School of Dentistry Offers dental hygiene (MS); dentistry (MS, DDS, PhD); endodontics (MS); epidemiology (PhD); operative dentistry (MS); oral and maxillofacial pathology (MS); oral and maxillofacial radiology (MS); oral biology (PhD); orthodontics (MS); pediatric dentistry (MS); periodontology (MS); prosthodontics (MS). Electronic applications accepted.

School of Law Offers law (LL M, JD). Electronic applications accepted.

School of Medicine Offers audiology (Au D); biochemistry and biophysics (MS, PhD); bioinformatics and computational biology (PhD); biomedical engineering (MS, PhD); cell and developmental biology (PhD); cell and molecular physiology (PhD); clinical rehabilitation and mental health counseling (MS); experimental pathology (PhD); genetics and molecular biology (MS, PhD); human movement science (PhD); immunology (MS, PhD); medicine (MPT, MS, Au D, DPT, MD, PhD); microbiology (MS, PhD); neurobiology (PhD); occupational science (PhD); occupational science and occupational therapy (MS, PhD); occupational therapy (MS); pharmacology (PhD); physical therapy (DPT); speech and hearing sciences (MS, Au D, PhD); speech-language pathology (MS); toxicology (MS, PhD). Electronic applications accepted.

School of Nursing *Program availability:* Part-time. Offers advanced practice registered nurse (DNP); nursing (MSN, PhD, PMC). Electronic applications accepted.

THE UNIVERSITY OF NORTH CAROLINA AT CHARLOTTE, Charlotte, NC 28223-0001

General Information State-supported, coed, university. CGS member. *Enrollment:* 29,710 graduate, professional, and undergraduate students; 2,564 full-time matriculated graduate/professional students (1,361 women), 2,759 part-time matriculated graduate/professional students (1,669 women). *Enrollment by degree level:* 3,410 master's, 1,019 doctoral, 894 other advanced degrees. Tuition and fees vary according to course load and program. *Graduate housing:* Room and/or apartments available on a first-come, first-served basis to single students; on-campus housing not available to married students. Typical cost: $4750 per year ($11,310 including board). Room and board charges vary according to board plan and housing facility selected. Housing application deadline: 6/1. *Student services:* Campus employment opportunities, campus safety program, career counseling, exercise/wellness program, free psychological counseling, international student services, low-cost health insurance, multicultural affairs office, services for students with disabilities, teacher training, writing training. *Library facilities:* J. Murrey Atkins Library plus 1 other. *Collection:* Books: 812,959 (physical), 980,416 (digital/electronic); Serial titles: 4,578 (physical), 92,904 (digital/electronic); Databases: 675. Study areas open 24 hours, 5–7 days a week; students can reserve study rooms.

Computer facilities: 1,600 computers available on campus for general student use. A campuswide network can be accessed from student residence rooms and from off campus. Online class registration is available. Website: http://www.uncc.edu.

General Application Contact: Kathy B. Giddings, Director of Graduate Admissions, 704-687-5503, Fax: 704-687-1668, E-mail: gradadm@uncc.edu.

GRADUATE UNITS

Belk College of Business Students: 277 full-time (124 women), 373 part-time (113 women); includes 171 minority (59 Black or African American, non-Hispanic/Latino; 1 American Indian or Alaska Native, non-Hispanic/Latino; 52 Asian, non-Hispanic/Latino; 41 Hispanic/Latino; 18 Two or more races, non-Hispanic/Latino), 167 international. Average age 31. 584 applicants, 75% accepted, 268 enrolled. Expenses: Contact institution. *Financial support:* Research assistantships, teaching assistantships, career-related internships or fieldwork, institutionally sponsored loans, scholarships/grants, and unspecified assistantships available. Support available to part-time students. Financial award application deadline: 3/1; financial award applicants required to submit FAFSA. In 2018, 256 master's, 3 doctorates, 9 other advanced degrees awarded. *Program availability:* Part-time, evening/weekend. Offers applied econometrics (Graduate Certificate); business (M Acct, MBA, MS, DBA, Graduate Certificate, Post-Master's Certificate, Postbaccalaureate Certificate); business administration (MBA, DBA, PhD); business analytics (Graduate Certificate); economics (MS); management (MS); mathematical finance (MS); real estate (MS, Graduate Certificate). *Application deadline:* Applications are processed on a rolling basis. *Application fee:* $75. Electronic applications accepted. *Application Contact:* Kathy B. Giddings, Director of Graduate

Admissions, 704-687-5503, Fax: 704-687-1668, E-mail: gradadm@uncc.edu. *Dean,* Dr. Steven Ott, 704-687-7577, Fax: 704-687-1393, E-mail: cob-dean@uncc.edu.

Turner School of Accountancy Students: 65 full-time (35 women), 30 part-time (12 women); includes 24 minority (3 Black or African American, non-Hispanic/Latino; 8 Asian, non-Hispanic/Latino; 11 Hispanic/Latino; 2 Two or more races, non-Hispanic/Latino), 6 international. Average age 26. 101 applicants, 76% accepted, 60 enrolled. Expenses: Contact institution. *Financial support:* Research assistantships, teaching assistantships, career-related internships or fieldwork, institutionally sponsored loans, scholarships/grants, and unspecified assistantships available. Support available to part-time students. Financial award application deadline: 3/1; financial award applicants required to submit FAFSA. In 2018, 68 master's awarded. *Program availability:* Part-time, evening/weekend. Offers accountancy (M Acct). *Application deadline:* Applications are processed on a rolling basis. *Application fee:* $75. Electronic applications accepted. *Application Contact:* Kathy B. Giddings, Director of Graduate Admissions, 704-687-5503, Fax: 704-687-1668, E-mail: gradadm@uncc.edu. *Chair,* Dr. Hughlene Burton, 704-687-7701, Fax: 704-687-1382, E-mail: haburton@uncc.edu.

Cato College of Education Students: 248 full-time (204 women), 1,051 part-time (846 women); includes 449 minority (327 Black or African American, non-Hispanic/Latino; 2 American Indian or Alaska Native, non-Hispanic/Latino; 20 Asian, non-Hispanic/Latino; 72 Hispanic/Latino; 28 Two or more races, non-Hispanic/Latino), 26 international. Average age 34. 918 applicants, 74% accepted, 487 enrolled. Expenses: Contact institution. *Financial support:* Research assistantships, teaching assistantships, career-related internships or fieldwork, institutionally sponsored loans, scholarships/grants, unspecified assistantships, and administrative assistantships available. Support available to part-time students. Financial award application deadline: 3/1; financial award applicants required to submit FAFSA. In 2018, 229 master's, 42 doctorates, 311 other advanced degrees awarded. *Program availability:* Part-time, evening/weekend, 100% online, blended/hybrid learning. Offers academically or intellectually gifted (Graduate Certificate); art education (Graduate Certificate); autism spectrum disorders (Graduate Certificate); child and family development: birth through kindergarten (Graduate Certificate); child and family development: early childhood education (MAT); child and family studies: early education (M Ed); counseling (MA); counselor education and supervision (PhD); curriculum and instruction (PhD); education (M Ed, MA, MAT, MSA, Ed D, PhD, Graduate Certificate, Post-Master's Certificate, Postbaccalaureate Certificate); education research, measurement, and evaluation (PhD); educational leadership (Ed D); elementary education (M Ed, MAT, Graduate Certificate); elementary mathematics education (Graduate Certificate); foreign language education (MAT); instructional systems technology M Ed, Graduate Certificate); middle grades and secondary education (M Ed); middle grades education (MAT); play therapy (Postbaccalaureate Certificate); quantitative analysis (Graduate Certificate); reading education (M Ed); school administration (MSA, Post-Master's Certificate); school counseling (Post-Master's Certificate); secondary education (MAT); special education (M Ed, MAT, PhD, Graduate Certificate); substance abuse counseling (Postbaccalaureate Certificate); teaching (Graduate Certificate); teaching English as a second language (M Ed, MAT, Graduate Certificate); theatre education (Graduate Certificate); university and college teaching (Graduate Certificate). *Application deadline:* Applications are processed on a rolling basis. *Application fee:* $75. Electronic applications accepted. *Application Contact:* Kathy B. Giddings, Director of Graduate Admissions, 704-687-5503, Fax: 704-687-1668, E-mail: gradadm@uncc.edu. *Dean,* Dr. Ellen McIntyre, 704-687-8722, E-mail: ellen.mcintyre@uncc.edu.

College of Arts and Architecture Students: 83 full-time (36 women), 5 part-time (1 woman); includes 24 minority (8 Black or African American, non-Hispanic/Latino; 4 Asian, non-Hispanic/Latino; 10 Hispanic/Latino; 2 Two or more races, non-Hispanic/Latino), 20 international. Average age 26. 117 applicants, 87% accepted, 32 enrolled. Expenses: Contact institution. *Financial support:* Research assistantships, teaching assistantships, career-related internships or fieldwork, institutionally sponsored loans, unspecified assistantships, and administrative assistantship available. Support available to part-time students. Financial award application deadline: 3/1; financial award applicants required to submit FAFSA. In 2018, 37 master's awarded. *Program availability:* Part-time. Offers arts and architecture (M Arch I, M Arch II, MS, MUD, Graduate Certificate); vocal pedagogy (Graduate Certificate). *Application deadline:* Applications are processed on a rolling basis. *Application fee:* $75. Electronic applications accepted. *Application Contact:* Kathy B. Giddings, Director of Graduate Admissions, 704-687-5503, Fax: 704-687-1668, E-mail: gradadm@uncc.edu. *Dean,* Kenneth A. Lambla, 704-687-0090, E-mail: kalambla@uncc.edu.

School of Architecture Students: 83 full-time (36 women), 5 part-time (1 woman); includes 24 minority (8 Black or African American, non-Hispanic/Latino; 4 Asian, non-Hispanic/Latino; 10 Hispanic/Latino; 2 Two or more races, non-Hispanic/Latino), 20 international. Average age 26. 116 applicants, 88% accepted, 32 enrolled. Expenses: Contact institution. *Financial support:* Research assistantships, teaching assistantships, institutionally sponsored loans, scholarships/grants, unspecified assistantships, and administrative assistantship available. Financial award application deadline: 3/1; financial award applicants required to submit FAFSA. In 2018, 37 master's awarded. Offers architecture (M Arch I, M Arch II, MS); urban design (MUD). *Application deadline:* Applications are processed on a rolling basis. *Application fee:* $75. Electronic applications accepted. *Application Contact:* Kathy B. Giddings, Director of Graduate Admissions, 704-687-5503, Fax: 704-687-1668, E-mail: gradadm@uncc.edu. *Dean,* Kenneth A. Lambla, 704-687-0090, E-mail: kalambla@uncc.edu.

College of Computing and Informatics Students: 571 full-time (216 women), 234 part-time (91 women); includes 88 minority (29 Black or African American, non-Hispanic/Latino; 32 Asian, non-Hispanic/Latino; 21 Hispanic/Latino; 1 Native Hawaiian or other Pacific Islander, non-Hispanic/Latino; 5 Two or more races, non-Hispanic/Latino), 588 international. Average age 26. 1,584 applicants, 65% accepted, 352 enrolled. Expenses: Contact institution. *Financial support:* Fellowships, research assistantships, teaching assistantships, career-related internships or fieldwork, institutionally sponsored loans, scholarships/grants, and unspecified assistantships available. Support available to part-time students. Financial award application deadline: 3/1; financial award applicants required to submit FAFSA. In 2018, 357 master's, 19 doctorates, 23 other advanced degrees awarded. *Program availability:* Part-time, evening/weekend. Offers advanced databases and knowledge discovery (Graduate Certificate); bioinformatics (PSM); bioinformatics and computational biology (PhD); bioinformatics applications (Graduate Certificate); bioinformatics technology (Graduate Certificate); computer science (MS); computing and informatics (MS, PSM, PhD, Graduate Certificate); computing and information systems (PhD); game design and development (Graduate Certificate); information security and privacy (Graduate Certificate); information technology (MS); management of information technology (Graduate Certificate); network security (Graduate Certificate); secure software development (Graduate Certificate). *Application deadline:* Applications are processed on a rolling basis. *Application fee:* $75. Electronic applications accepted. *Application Contact:* Kathy B. Giddings, Director of Graduate Admissions, 704-687-5503, Fax: 704-687-1668, E-mail: gradadm@uncc.edu. *Dean,* Dr. Fatma Mili, 704-687-8450, E-mail: fmili@uncc.edu.

College of Health and Human Services Students: 416 full-time (353 women), 249 part-time (203 women); includes 246 minority (153 Black or African American, non-Hispanic/Latino; 2 American Indian or Alaska Native, non-Hispanic/Latino; 29 Asian, non-Hispanic/Latino; 42 Hispanic/Latino; 1 Native Hawaiian or other Pacific Islander, non-Hispanic/Latino; 19 Two or more races, non-Hispanic/Latino), 18 international. Average age 32. 858 applicants, 49% accepted, 271 enrolled. Expenses: Contact institution. *Financial support:* Fellowships, research assistantships, teaching assistantships, career-related internships or fieldwork, institutionally sponsored loans, scholarships/grants, traineeships, unspecified assistantships, and administrative assistantships available. Support available to part-time students. Financial award application deadline: 3/1; financial award applicants required to submit FAFSA. In 2018, 221 master's, 9 doctorates, 16 other advanced degrees awarded. *Program availability:* Part-time, evening/weekend, 100% online, blended/hybrid learning. Offers community health (Certificate); health administration (MHA); health and human services (MHA, MPH, MS, MSN, MSW, DNP, PhD, Certificate, Graduate Certificate, Post-Master's Certificate); health services research (PhD); kinesiology (MS); public health (MPH); public health core concepts (Graduate Certificate); public health sciences (PhD); respiratory care (MS). *Application deadline:* Applications are processed on a rolling basis. *Application fee:* $75. Electronic applications accepted. *Application Contact:* Kathy B. Giddings, Director of Graduate Admissions, 704-687-5503, Fax: 704-687-1668, E-mail: gradadm@uncc.edu. *Dean,* Dr. Nancy Fey-Yensan, 704-687-7917, E-mail: fey-yensan@uncc.edu.

School of Nursing Students: 119 full-time (96 women), 159 part-time (142 women); includes 75 minority (52 Black or African American, non-Hispanic/Latino; 10 Asian, non-Hispanic/Latino; 6 Hispanic/Latino; 7 Two or more races, non-Hispanic/Latino), 2 international. Average age 35. 361 applicants, 37% accepted, 98 enrolled. Expenses: Contact institution. *Financial support:* Research assistantships, teaching assistantships, career-related internships or fieldwork, institutionally sponsored loans, scholarships/grants, traineeships, and unspecified assistantships available. Support available to part-time students. Financial award application deadline: 3/1; financial award applicants required to submit FAFSA. In 2018, 81 master's, 6 doctorates, 6 other advanced degrees awarded. *Program availability:* Part-time, blended/hybrid learning. Offers adult-gerontology acute care nurse practitioner (Post-Master's Certificate); advanced clinical nursing (MSN); family nurse practitioner across the lifespan (Post-Master's Certificate); nurse anesthesia (MSN); nurse anesthesia across the lifespan (Post-Master's Certificate); nursing (DNP); nursing administration (Graduate Certificate); nursing education (Graduate Certificate); systems/population nursing (MSN). *Application deadline:* Applications are processed on a rolling basis. *Application fee:* $75. Electronic applications accepted. *Application Contact:* Kathy B. Giddings, Director of Graduate Admissions, 704-687-5503, Fax: 704-687-1668, E-mail: gradadm@uncc.edu. *Director,* Dr. Dena Evans, 704-687-7974, E-mail: devans37@uncc.edu.

School of Social Work Students: 166 full-time (151 women), 15 part-time (14 women); includes 98 minority (56 Black or African American, non-Hispanic/Latino; 11 Asian, non-Hispanic/Latino; 26 Hispanic/Latino; 5 Two or more races, non-Hispanic/Latino), 3 international. Average age 29. 299 applicants, 47% accepted, 94 enrolled. Expenses: Contact institution. *Financial support:* Research assistantships, career-related internships or fieldwork, Federal Work-Study, institutionally sponsored loans, scholarships/grants, unspecified assistantships, and administrative assistantship available. Support available to part-time students. Financial award application deadline: 3/1; financial award applicants required to submit FAFSA. In 2018, 79 master's awarded. *Program availability:* Part-time. Offers social work (MSW). *Application deadline:* Applications are processed on a rolling basis. *Application fee:* $75. Electronic applications accepted. *Application Contact:* Kathy B. Giddings, Director of Graduate Admissions, 704-687-5503, Fax: 704-687-1668, E-mail: gradadm@uncc.edu. *Associate Professor and MSW Director,* Dr. Diana Rowan, 704-687-7934, E-mail: drowan@uncc.edu.

College of Liberal Arts and Sciences Students: 462 full-time (275 women), 326 part-time (200 women); includes 174 minority (67 Black or African American, non-Hispanic/Latino; 1 American Indian or Alaska Native, non-Hispanic/Latino; 29 Asian, non-Hispanic/Latino; 52 Hispanic/Latino; 25 Two or more races, non-Hispanic/Latino), 130 international. Average age 29. 846 applicants, 46% accepted, 232 enrolled. Expenses: Contact institution. *Financial support:* Fellowships, research assistantships, teaching assistantships, career-related internships or fieldwork, institutionally sponsored loans, scholarships/grants, and administrative assistantships available. Support available to part-time students. Financial award application deadline: 3/1; financial award applicants required to submit FAFSA. In 2018, 196 master's, 43 doctorates, 36 other advanced degrees awarded. *Program availability:* Part-time, evening/weekend. Offers Africana studies (Graduate Certificate); anthropology (MA); applied linguistics (Graduate Certificate); applied mathematics (PhD); applied physics (MS); biological sciences (MS, PhD); chemistry (MS); cognitive science (Graduate Certificate); communication studies (MA); criminal justice and criminology (MS); earth sciences (MS); emergency management (Graduate Certificate); English (MA); ethics and applied philosophy (MA, Graduate Certificate); gender, sexuality, and women's studies (Graduate Certificate); geography (MA); geography and urban regional analysis (PhD); gerontology (MA, Graduate Certificate); health psychology (PhD); history (MA); industrial/organizational psychology (MA); languages and culture studies: translating (Graduate Certificate); Latin American studies (MA); liberal arts and sciences (MA, MPA, MS, PhD, Graduate Certificate); liberal studies (MA); mathematics (MS); nanoscale science (PhD); non-profit management (Graduate Certificate); optical science and engineering (MS, PhD); organizational science (PhD); psychology (MA); public administration (MPA); public budgeting and finance (Graduate Certificate); public policy (PhD); religious studies (MA); sociology (MA); Spanish (MA); technical and professional writing (Graduate Certificate); urban management and policy (Graduate Certificate). *Application deadline:* Applications are processed on a rolling basis. *Application fee:* $75. Electronic applications accepted. *Application Contact:* Kathy B. Giddings, Director of Graduate Admissions, 704-687-5503, Fax: 704-687-1668, E-mail: gradadm@uncc.edu. *Dean,* Dr. Nancy A. Gutierrez, 704-687-0081, E-mail: ngutierr@uncc.edu.

The Graduate School Students: 83 full-time (48 women), 124 part-time (51 women); includes 62 minority (25 Black or African American, non-Hispanic/Latino; 23 Asian, non-Hispanic/Latino; 10 Hispanic/Latino; 4 Two or more races, non-Hispanic/Latino), 65 international. Average age 31. 495 applicants, 36% accepted, 102 enrolled. Expenses: Contact institution. *Financial support:* Research assistantships, teaching assistantships, career-related internships or fieldwork, institutionally sponsored loans, scholarships/grants, traineeships, unspecified assistantships, and administrative assistantships available. Support available to part-time students. Financial award

application deadline: 3/1; financial award applicants required to submit FAFSA. In 2018, 82 master's, 21 other advanced degrees awarded. *Program availability:* Part-time, evening/weekend. Offers data science and business analytics (MS, PSM, Graduate Certificate); health informatics (PSM). *Application deadline:* Applications are processed on a rolling basis. *Application fee:* $75. Electronic applications accepted. *Application Contact:* Kathy B. Giddings, Director of Graduate Admissions, 704-687-5503, Fax: 704-687-1668, E-mail: gradadm@uncc.edu. *Dean and Associate Provost,* Dr. Thomas L. Reynolds, 704-687-7248, E-mail: gradadm@uncc.edu.

William States Lee College of Engineering Students: 393 full-time (89 women), 198 part-time (35 women); includes 47 minority (13 Black or African American, non-Hispanic/Latino; 1 American Indian or Alaska Native, non-Hispanic/Latino; 16 Asian, non-Hispanic/Latino; 11 Hispanic/Latino; 6 Two or more races, non-Hispanic/Latino), 370 international. Average age 28. 738 applicants, 72% accepted, 150 enrolled. Expenses: Contact institution. *Financial support:* Fellowships, research assistantships, teaching assistantships, career-related internships or fieldwork, institutionally sponsored loans, scholarships/grants, and unspecified assistantships available. Support available to part-time students. Financial award application deadline: 3/1; financial award applicants required to submit FAFSA. In 2018, 193 master's, 33 doctorates, 3 other advanced degrees awarded. *Program availability:* Part-time, evening/weekend, blended/hybrid learning. Offers applied energy (Graduate Certificate); applied energy and electromechanical systems (MS); civil engineering (MSCE); construction and facilities management (MS); electrical engineering (MSEE, PhD); energy analytics (Graduate Certificate); engineering (MS, MSCE, MSE, MSEE, MSEM, MSME, PhD, Graduate Certificate); engineering management (MSEM); fire protection and administration (MS); infrastructure and environmental systems (PhD); Lean Six Sigma (Graduate Certificate); logistics and supply chains (Graduate Certificate); mechanical engineering (MSME, PhD); systems analytics (Graduate Certificate). *Application deadline:* Applications are processed on a rolling basis. *Application fee:* $75. Electronic applications accepted. *Application Contact:* Kathy B. Giddings, Director of Graduate Admissions, 704-687-5503, Fax: 704-687-1668, E-mail: gradadm@uncc.edu. *Dean,* Dr. Robert E. Johnson, 704-687-8242, E-mail: robejohn@uncc.edu.

THE UNIVERSITY OF NORTH CAROLINA AT GREENSBORO, Greensboro, NC 27412-5001

General Information State-supported, coed, university. CGS member. *Graduate housing:* Room and/or apartments available to single students; on-campus housing not available to married students. Housing application deadline: 5/15. *Research affiliation:* Moses Cone Memorial Hospital, North Carolina Zoological Park, North Carolina Baptist Hospital.

GRADUATE UNITS

Graduate School *Program availability:* Part-time, evening/weekend, online learning. Offers liberal studies (MALS). Electronic applications accepted.

Bryan School of Business and Economics *Program availability:* Part-time. Offers accounting (MS); applied economics (MA); business administration (MBA, PMC, Postbaccalaureate Certificate); business and economics (MA, MBA, MS, PhD, Certificate, PMC, Postbaccalaureate Certificate); consumer, apparel, and retail studies (MS, PhD); economics (MA, PhD); financial analysis (PMC); financial economics (MA); information systems (PhD); information technology (Certificate); information technology and management (MS); supply chain management (Certificate). Electronic applications accepted.

College of Arts and Sciences *Program availability:* Part-time. Offers advanced Spanish language and Hispanic cultural studies (Certificate); American literature (PhD); applied geography (MA); arts and sciences (M Ed, MA, MFA, MPA, MS, PhD, Certificate); biochemistry (MS); biology (MS); chemistry (MS); clinical psychology (MA, PhD); cognitive psychology (MA, PhD); communication studies (MA); computer science (MS); creative writing (MFA); criminology (MA); developmental psychology (MA, PhD); English (M Ed, MA, PhD, Certificate); English literature (PhD); film and video production (MFA); French (MA); geographic information science (Certificate); geography (PhD); historic preservation (Certificate); history (MA); interior architecture (MS); Latin (M Ed); mathematics (MA, PhD); museum studies (Certificate); nonprofit management (Certificate); public affairs (MPA); rhetoric and composition (PhD); social psychology (MA, PhD); sociology (MA); Spanish (MA, Certificate); studio arts (MFA); U.S. history (MA); urban and economic development (Certificate); women's and gender studies (MA, Certificate). Electronic applications accepted.

School of Education *Program availability:* Part-time, evening/weekend. Offers advanced school counseling (PMC); college teaching and adult learning (Certificate); counseling and counselor education (PhD); counseling and educational development (MS); couple and family counseling (PMC); cross-categorical special education (M Ed); curriculum and instruction (M Ed); curriculum and teaching (PhD); education (M Ed, MLIS, MS, MSA, Ed D, PhD, Certificate, Ed S, PMC); educational leadership (Ed D, Ed S); educational research, measurement and evaluation (PhD); English as a second language (Certificate); higher education (M Ed, PhD); interdisciplinary studies in special education (M Ed); leadership early care and education (Certificate); library and information studies (MLIS); school administration (MSA); school counseling (PMC); special education (M Ed, PhD); supervision (M Ed); teacher education and development (PhD). Electronic applications accepted.

School of Health and Human Sciences Offers athletic training (MSAT); community health education (MPH, Dr PH); community recreation management (MS); genetic counseling (MS); gerontology (MS, Certificate); health and human sciences (M Ed, MA, MFA, MPH, MS, Dr PH, Ed D, PhD); human development and family studies (M Ed, MS, PhD); kinesiology (MS, Ed D, PhD); nutrition (MS, PhD); peace and conflict studies (MA, Certificate); social work (MSW); speech language pathology (PhD); speech pathology and audiology (MS); therapeutic recreation (MS). Electronic applications accepted.

School of Music, Theatre and Dance Offers acting (MFA); composition (MM); dance (MA, MFA); design (MFA); directing (MFA); education (MM); music education (PhD); performance (MM, DMA); theater education (M Ed); theater for youth (MFA); theatre (M Ed, MFA); theory (MM). Electronic applications accepted.

School of Nursing Offers adult clinical nurse specialist (MSN, PMC); adult/gerontological nurse practitioner (MSN, PMC); nurse anesthesia (MSN, PMC); nursing (PhD); nursing administration (MSN); nursing education (MSN). Electronic applications accepted.

THE UNIVERSITY OF NORTH CAROLINA AT PEMBROKE, Pembroke, NC 28372-1510

General Information State-supported, coed, comprehensive institution. CGS member. *Graduate housing:* Room and/or apartments available to single students; on-campus housing not available to married students. Housing application deadline: 4/15.

GRADUATE UNITS

The Graduate School *Program availability:* Part-time, evening/weekend, 100% online, blended/hybrid learning. Offers art (MAT); art education (MA); clinical nurse leader (MSN); criminal justice (MPA); emergency management (MPA); English education (MA, MAT); health administration (MPA); mathematics education (MA); nurse educator (MSN); public management (MPA); rural case manager (MSN); science education (MA, MAT); social studies education (MA, MAT); social work (MSW). Electronic applications accepted.

School of Business *Program availability:* Part-time, evening/weekend. Offers business (MBA).

School of Education *Program availability:* Part-time, evening/weekend. Offers clinical mental health counseling (MA Ed); education (MA, MA Ed, MAT, MSA); elementary education (MA Ed, MAT); health/physical education (MAT); physical education (MA); professional school counseling (MA Ed); reading education (MA Ed); school administration (MSA).

UNIVERSITY OF NORTH CAROLINA SCHOOL OF THE ARTS, Winston-Salem, NC 27127-2738

General Information State-supported, coed, comprehensive institution. *Graduate housing:* Room and/or apartments available on a first-come, first-served basis to single students. Housing application deadline: 5/1.

GRADUATE UNITS

School of Design and Production Offers costume design (MFA); costume technology (MFA); scene design (MFA); scenic art (MFA); sound design (MFA); stage automation (MFA); stage properties (MFA); technical direction (MFA); wig and makeup design (MFA). Electronic applications accepted.

School of Filmmaking Offers creative producing (MFA); film music composition (MFA); screenwriting (MFA). Electronic applications accepted.

School of Music Offers music (Artist Certificate); music performance (MM); vocal performance (MM). Electronic applications accepted.

THE UNIVERSITY OF NORTH CAROLINA WILMINGTON, Wilmington, NC 28403-3297

General Information State-supported, coed, comprehensive institution. CGS member. *Graduate housing:* Room and/or apartments available on a first-come, first-served basis to single students; on-campus housing not available to married students. Housing application deadline: 4/30. *Research affiliation:* Seatox Research Inc. (biotechnology research and development), CMS Technology (seafood technology and safety), A-1 Biochem Labs (pharmaceuticals development), O.TM Biotech (environmental testing), OCIS Biotechnology (pharmaceuticals development).

GRADUATE UNITS

Cameron School of Business *Program availability:* Part-time. Offers accountancy (MSA); business administration (MBA); business administration - international (MBA); business administration - professional (MBA). Electronic applications accepted.

Center for Marine Science *Program availability:* Part-time. Offers marine science (MS). Electronic applications accepted.

College of Arts and Sciences *Program availability:* Part-time. Offers applied statistics (Professional Certificate); arts and sciences (MA, MFA, MPA, MS, PhD, Graduate Certificate, Postbaccalaureate Certificate, Professional Certificate); biology (MS); chemistry (MS); clinical psychology (PhD); coastal and ocean policy (MS); conflict management and resolution (MA); creative writing (MFA); English (MA); environmental studies (MS); geographic information science (Graduate Certificate); geoscience (MS); Hispanic studies (Postbaccalaureate Certificate); history (MA); liberal studies (MA); marine biology (MS, PhD); mathematics (MS); psychology (MA); public administration (MPA); sociology and criminology (MA); Spanish (MA). Electronic applications accepted.

Interdisciplinary Program in Computer Science and Information Systems Offers computer science and information systems (MS); data science (MS). Electronic applications accepted.

School of Health and Applied Human Sciences *Program availability:* Part-time. Offers applied gerontology (MS). Electronic applications accepted.

School of Nursing *Program availability:* Part-time, 100% online. Offers clinical research and product development (MS); family nurse practitioner (Post-Master's Certificate); nurse educator (Post-Master's Certificate); nursing (MSN); nursing practice (DNP). Electronic applications accepted.

School of Social Work *Program availability:* Part-time. Offers social work (MSW). Electronic applications accepted.

Watson College of Education *Program availability:* Part-time. Offers curriculum, instruction and supervision (M Ed); education (M Ed, MAT, MS, MSA, Ed D); educational leadership and administration (Ed D); educational leadership, policy, and advocacy (M Ed); elementary education (M Ed, MAT); English as a second language (M Ed, MAT); higher education (M Ed); instructional technology (MS); language and literacy (M Ed); middle grades education (MAT); school administration (MSA); secondary education (M Ed, MAT). Electronic applications accepted.

UNIVERSITY OF NORTH DAKOTA, Grand Forks, ND 58202

General Information State-supported, coed, university. CGS member. *Graduate housing:* Rooms and/or apartments guaranteed to single students and available on a first-come, first-served basis to married students. *Research affiliation:* U.S. Department of Agriculture (USDA), Human Nutrition Research Center, Neuropsychiatric Research Institute (neurosciences), Environmental Energy Research Center.

GRADUATE UNITS

Graduate School *Program availability:* Part-time, evening/weekend, online learning. Offers clinical translation science (MS, PhD); medicine (MOT, MPAS, MS, DPT, PhD); occupational therapy (MOT); physical therapy (DPT); physician assistant (MPAS). Electronic applications accepted.

College of Arts and Sciences *Program availability:* Part-time, online learning. Offers arts and sciences (M Ed, MA, MFA, MM, MS, DA, PhD); biology (MS); chemistry (MS, PhD); clinical psychology (PhD); communication and public discourse (PhD); criminal justice (PhD); English (MA, PhD); fisheries/wildlife (PhD); forensic psychology (MA, MS); genetics (PhD); geography and geographic information science (MA, MS); history (M Ed, MA, DA, PhD); linguistics (MA); mathematics (M Ed, MS); music (MM); music education (PhD); physics and astrophysics (MA, MS, PhD); sociology (MA); speech-language pathology (MS); visual arts (MFA); zoology (PhD). Electronic applications accepted.

College of Business and Public Administration *Program availability:* Part-time, evening/weekend, online learning. Offers applied economics (MSAE); business administration (MBA); business and public administration (MBA, MPA, MSAE, MSIT); public administration (MPA). Electronic applications accepted.

College of Education and Human Development *Program availability:* Part-time, evening/weekend, online learning. Offers counseling (MA); counseling psychology (PhD); early childhood education (MS); education and human development (M Ed, MA, MS, MSW, Ed D, PhD, Ed S); education/general studies (MS); educational leadership (M Ed, Ed D, PhD, Ed S); elementary education (M Ed, MS); instructional design and technology (M Ed, MS); kinesiology (MS); reading education (M Ed, MS); special education (M Ed, MS). Electronic applications accepted.

College of Nursing and Professional Disciplines *Program availability:* Part-time, evening/weekend, online learning. Offers adult-gerontological nurse practitioner (MS); advanced public health nurse (MS); family nurse practitioner (MS); nurse anesthesia (MS); nurse educator (MS); nursing (PhD, Post-Master's Certificate); nursing and professional disciplines (MS, MSW, DNP, PhD, Post-Master's Certificate); nursing practice (DNP); psychiatric and mental health nurse practitioner (MS); social work (MSW). Electronic applications accepted.

John D. Odegard School of Aerospace Sciences *Program availability:* Part-time, evening/weekend, online learning. Offers aerospace sciences (MEM, MS, PhD); atmospheric sciences (MS, PhD); aviation (MS); computer science (MS); earth system science and policy (MEM, MS, PhD); space studies (MS). Electronic applications accepted.

School of Engineering and Mines *Program availability:* Part-time. Offers chemical engineering (M Engr, MS, PhD); civil engineering (M Engr); electrical engineering (M Engr, MS, PhD); engineering (PhD); engineering and mines (M Engr, MA, MS, PhD); environmental engineering (M Engr, MS, PhD); geological engineering (MS, PhD); geology (MA, MS, PhD); mechanical engineering (M Engr, MS, PhD). Electronic applications accepted.

School of Law Offers law (JD).

School of Medicine and Health Sciences *Program availability:* Online learning. Offers medicine and health sciences (MPH); public health (MPH).

UNIVERSITY OF NORTHERN BRITISH COLUMBIA, Prince George, BC V2N 4Z9, Canada

General Information Province-supported, coed, university. *Graduate housing:* Room and/or apartments available on a first-come, first-served basis to single students; on-campus housing not available to married students. Housing application deadline: 2/15. *Research affiliation:* Insurance Corporation of British Columbia (moose involved in highway traffic accidents), Houston Forest Products (forestry–wood debris management), TRC Cedar Ltd. (forestry–cyanolicen growth rate study), Remote Law Online Systems Corporation (computer science), Canadian Natural Oils Ltd. (chemistry–oil fractionation), Stella Jones, Inc. (forestry–Douglas fir cores).

GRADUATE UNITS

Office of Graduate Studies *Program availability:* Part-time, evening/weekend, online learning.

UNIVERSITY OF NORTHERN COLORADO, Greeley, CO 80639

General Information State-supported, coed, university. CGS member. *Graduate housing:* Rooms and/or apartments available on a first-come, first-served basis to single and married students. Housing application deadline: 5/30.

GRADUATE UNITS

Graduate School *Program availability:* Part-time, evening/weekend, online learning. Electronic applications accepted.

College of Education and Behavioral Sciences *Program availability:* Part-time, online learning. Offers applied statistics and research methods (MS, PhD); clinical counseling (MA); counseling psychology (PhD); counselor education and supervision (PhD); curriculum studies (MAT); deaf/hard of hearing (MA); early childhood special education (MA); education and behavioral sciences (MA, MAT, MS, Ed D, PhD, Ed S); educational leadership (MA, Ed S); educational leadership and policy studies (MA, Ed D, Ed S); educational psychology (MA, PhD); educational studies (Ed D); elementary education (MAT); English education (MAT); gifted and talented (MA); higher education and student affairs leadership (PhD); literacy (MA); multilingual education (MA); school counseling (MA); school psychology (Ed S); special education (MA, PhD); teaching American Sign Language (MA); teaching diverse learners (MA); visual impairment (MA).

College of Humanities and Social Sciences *Program availability:* Part-time. Offers communication (MA); criminal justice (MA); English (MA); history (MA); humanities and social sciences (MA); sociology (MA). Electronic applications accepted.

College of Natural and Health Sciences Offers adult-gerontology acute care nurse practitioner (MSN, DNP); audiology (Au D); biological sciences (MS); biology education (PhD); biomedical sciences (MBS); chemical education (MS, PhD); chemistry (MS); community health education (MPH); earth sciences (MA); educational mathematics (PhD); exercise science (MS, PhD); family nurse practitioner (MSN, DNP); gerontology (MA); global health and community health education (MPH); healthy aging and community health education (MPH); human sciences (MA, MPH, Au D, PhD); mathematical teaching (MA); mathematics (MA); natural and health sciences (MA, MAT, MBS, MPH, MS, MSN, Au D, DNP, PhD); nursing education (PhD); nursing practice (DNP); physical education and physical activity leadership (MAT); rehabilitation counseling (MA); rehabilitation sciences (PhD); speech-language pathology (MA); sport administration (MS, PhD); sport pedagogy (MS, PhD); sports coaching (MA). Electronic applications accepted.

College of Performing and Visual Arts *Program availability:* Part-time. Offers art education (MA); art history (MA); collaborative piano (MM, DA); composition (DA); conducting (MM, DA); instrumental performance (MM); jazz studies (MM, DA); music education (MM, DA); music history and literature (MM, DA); music theory and composition (MM); performance (DA); performing and visual arts (MA, MM, DA); studio art (MA); vocal performance (MM). Electronic applications accepted.

Monfort College of Business Offers accounting (MA); general business management (MBA); healthcare administration (MBA); human resources management (MBA).

UNIVERSITY OF NORTHERN IOWA, Cedar Falls, IA 50614

General Information State-supported, coed, comprehensive institution. CGS member. *Graduate housing:* Rooms and/or apartments available on a first-come, first-served basis to single and married students.

GRADUATE UNITS

Graduate College *Program availability:* Part-time, evening/weekend. Offers philanthropy and nonprofit development (MA); women's and gender studies (MA). Electronic applications accepted.

College of Business Administration *Program availability:* Part-time, evening/weekend. Offers accounting (M Acc); business administration (M Acc, MBA).

College of Education *Program availability:* Part-time, evening/weekend. Offers allied health, recreation, and community services (Ed D); athletic training (MS); career/vocational programming and transition (MAE); community health education (MA); consultant (MAE); curriculum and instruction (Ed D); early childhood education (MAE); education (MA, MAE, MS, Ed D, Ed S); educational leadership (Ed D); educational psychology: context and techniques of assessment (MAE); educational psychology: context and techniques of assessment (MAE); educational psychology: professional development for teachers (MAE); elementary education (MAE); field specialization (MAE); health education (MA); health promotion/fitness management (MA); instructional technology (MA); kinesiology (MA); leisure, youth and human services (MA); literacy education (MAE); performance and training technology (MA); physical education (MA); postsecondary education: student affairs (MA); principalship (MAE); school health education (MA); school library endorsement (MA); school library studies (MA); school psychology (Ed S); special education (MAE); teaching/coaching (MA). Electronic applications accepted.

College of Humanities, Arts and Sciences *Program availability:* Part-time, evening/weekend. Offers art education (MA); biology (MS); communication studies (MA); community college teaching (MA); composition (MM); conducting (MM); creative writing (MA); earth science education (MA); English (MA); humanities, arts and sciences (MA, MM, MS, PSM, DIT); industrial mathematics (PSM); industrial technology (DIT); jazz pedagogy (MM); literature (MA); mathematics (MA); mathematics for the middle grades (MA); music (MA, MM); music education (MM); music history (MM); percussion (MM); performance (MM); physics education (MM); piano performance and pedagogy (MM); piano/organ (MM); science education (MA); secondary teaching (MA); Spanish (MA); Spanish teaching (MA); speech-language pathology (MA); strings (MM); teaching English in secondary schools (MA); teaching English to speakers of other languages (MA); technology (MS, DIT); TESOL/Spanish (MA); voice (MM); woodwind (MM). Electronic applications accepted.

College of Social and Behavioral Sciences *Program availability:* Part-time, evening/weekend. Offers counseling (MA); geography (MA); history (MA); mental health counseling (MA); psychology (MA); public history (MA); public policy (MPP); school counseling (MA); social and behavioral sciences (MA, MPP, MSW); social science (MA); social work (MSW). Electronic applications accepted.

UNIVERSITY OF NORTH FLORIDA, Jacksonville, FL 32224

General Information State-supported, coed, comprehensive institution. CGS member. *Enrollment:* 16,775 graduate, professional, and undergraduate students; 961 full-time matriculated graduate/professional students (664 women), 1,194 part-time matriculated graduate/professional students (785 women). *Enrollment by degree level:* 1,623 master's, 562 doctoral. *Graduate faculty:* 433 full-time (203 women), 33 part-time/adjunct (17 women). *Tuition, area resident:* Part-time $408.10 per credit hour. Tuition, state resident: part-time $408.10 per credit hour. Tuition, nonresident: part-time $932.61 per credit hour. *Required fees:* $111.81 per credit hour. Tuition and fees vary according to course load, campus/location and program. *Graduate housing:* Room and/or apartments available on a first-come, first-served basis to single students; on-campus housing not available to married students. Typical cost: $6020 per year ($9720 including board). Room and board charges vary according to board plan, campus/location and housing facility selected. Housing application deadline: 6/1. *Student services:* Campus employment opportunities, campus safety program, career counseling, child daycare facilities, exercise/wellness program, free psychological counseling, international student services, low-cost health insurance, multicultural affairs office, services for students with disabilities, teacher training, writing training. *Library facilities:* Thomas G. Carpenter Library. *Collection:* Books: 568,299 (physical), 543,121 (digital/electronic); Serial titles: 12,479 (physical), 211,959 (digital/electronic); Databases: 284. Students can reserve study rooms.

Computer facilities: Computer purchase and lease plans are available. 700 computers available on campus for general student use. A campuswide network can be accessed from student residence rooms and from off campus. Online class registration, reduced prices for students on certain business and design software are available. Website: http://www.unf.edu/

General Application Contact: Dr. Amanda Pascale, Director, The Graduate School, 904-620-1360, Fax: 904-620-1362, E-mail: graduateschool@unf.edu.

GRADUATE UNITS

Brooks College of Health Students: 435 full-time (331 women), 268 part-time (231 women); includes 239 minority (105 Black or African American, non-Hispanic/Latino; 4 American Indian or Alaska Native, non-Hispanic/Latino; 39 Asian, non-Hispanic/Latino; 61 Hispanic/Latino; 2 Native Hawaiian or other Pacific Islander, non-Hispanic/Latino; 28 Two or more races, non-Hispanic/Latino), 8 international. Average age 34. 910 applicants, 33% accepted, 197 enrolled. *Faculty:* 75 full-time (57 women), 13 part-time/adjunct (7 women). Expenses: Contact institution. *Financial support:* In 2018–19, 112 students received support, including 38 research assistantships (averaging $2,234 per year), 9 teaching assistantships (averaging $4,940 per year); career-related internships or fieldwork, Federal Work-Study, scholarships/grants, and tuition waivers also available. Support available to part-time students. Financial award application deadline: 4/1; financial award applicants required to submit FAFSA. In 2018, 104 master's, 135 doctorates awarded. *Program availability:* Part-time, evening/weekend. Offers aging services (Certificate); clinical and applied movement sciences (MSH, DPT); health (MHA, MPH, MS, MSH, MSN, DNP, DPT, Certificate); health administration (MHA); nutrition and dietetics (MSH); public health (MPH). *Application deadline:* For fall admission, 7/1 priority date for domestic students, 5/1 for international students; for spring admission, 11/1 priority date for domestic students, 10/1 for international students. *Application fee:* $30. Electronic applications accepted. *Application Contact:* Miwa Nguyen, Director of Advising, 904-620-2810, Fax: 904-620-1030, E-mail: cohadvis@unf.edu. *Dean,* Dr. Curt Lox, 904-620-1204, E-mail: c.lox@unf.edu.

School of Nursing Students: 171 full-time (143 women), 178 part-time (154 women); includes 142 minority (73 Black or African American, non-Hispanic/Latino; 1 American Indian or Alaska Native, non-Hispanic/Latino; 28 Asian, non-Hispanic/Latino; 27 Hispanic/Latino; 1 Native Hawaiian or other Pacific Islander, non-Hispanic/Latino; 12 Two or more races, non-Hispanic/Latino), 1 international. Average age 40. 163 applicants, 66% accepted, 60 enrolled. *Faculty:* 31 full-time (27 women), 1 (woman) part-time/adjunct. Expenses: Contact institution. *Financial support:* In 2018–19, 47 students received support, including 8 teaching assistantships (averaging $5,277 per year). Financial award application deadline: 4/1; financial award applicants required to submit FAFSA. In 2018, 109 doctorates awarded. *Program availability:* Part-time. Offers family nurse practitioner (Certificate); nurse anesthetist (MSN). *Application deadline:* For fall admission, 4/1 for domestic students, 5/1 for international students. *Application fee:* $30. Electronic applications accepted. *Application Contact:* Beth Dibble, Assistant Director of Admissions for Nursing and Physical Therapy, 904-620-2684, Fax: 904-620-1832, E-mail: nursingadmissions@unf.edu. *Chair,* Dr. Li Loriz, 904-620-1053, E-mail: lloriz@unf.edu.

Coggin College of Business Students: 193 full-time (98 women), 394 part-time (196 women); includes 146 minority (58 Black or African American, non-Hispanic/Latino; 31 Asian, non-Hispanic/Latino; 32 Hispanic/Latino; 25 Two or more races, non-Hispanic/Latino), 37 international. Average age 29. 473 applicants, 56% accepted, 178 enrolled. *Faculty:* 56 full-time (17 women), 1 part-time/adjunct (0 women). Expenses: Contact institution. *Financial support:* In 2018–19, 36 students received support, including 1 research assistantship (averaging $2,501 per year); career-related internships or fieldwork, Federal Work-Study, scholarships/grants, and tuition waivers (partial) also available. Financial award application deadline: 4/1; financial award applicants required to submit FAFSA. In 2018, 223 master's awarded. *Program availability:* Part-time, evening/weekend. Offers accountancy (M Acc); accounting (MBA); business (M Acc, MBA); construction management (MBA); e-commerce (MBA); economics (MBA); finance (MBA); human resource management (MBA); international business (MBA); logistics (MBA); management applications (MBA). *Application deadline:* For fall admission, 8/1 priority date for domestic students, 5/1 for international students; for spring admission, 12/1 priority date for domestic students, 10/1 for international students. *Application fee:* $30. Electronic applications accepted. *Application Contact:* Paul Schreier, Interim Director of Student Services, 904-620-2575, Fax: 904-620-2832, E-mail: coggin.students@unf.edu. *Dean,* Dr. Mark Dawkins, 904-620-5280, Fax: 904-620-2594, E-mail: mark.dawkins@unf.edu.

College of Arts and Sciences Students: 192 full-time (134 women), 175 part-time (113 women); includes 102 minority (51 Black or African American, non-Hispanic/Latino; 4 Asian, non-Hispanic/Latino; 34 Hispanic/Latino; 1 Native Hawaiian or other Pacific Islander, non-Hispanic/Latino; 12 Two or more races, non-Hispanic/Latino), 15 international. Average age 30. 402 applicants, 45% accepted, 130 enrolled. *Faculty:* 209 full-time (90 women), 6 part-time/adjunct (3 women). Expenses: Contact institution. *Financial support:* In 2018–19, 83 students received support, including 4 research assistantships (averaging $3,657 per year), 18 teaching assistantships (averaging $3,876 per year); career-related internships or fieldwork, Federal Work-Study, scholarships/grants, and tuition waivers (partial) also available. Support available to part-time students. Financial award application deadline: 4/1; financial award applicants required to submit FAFSA. In 2018, 112 master's awarded. *Program availability:* Part-time, evening/weekend. Offers applied ethics (Graduate Certificate); arts and sciences (MA, MAC, MPA, MS, MSW, Graduate Certificate); biology (MA, MS); counseling psychology (MAC); criminal justice (MS); English (MA); European history (MA); general psychology (MA); mathematical sciences (MS); nonprofit management (Graduate Certificate); practical philosophy and applied ethics (MA); public administration (MPA); social work (MSW); statistics (MS); U.S. history (MA). *Application deadline:* For fall admission, 7/1 priority date for domestic students, 5/1 for international students; for spring admission, 11/1 priority date for domestic students, 10/1 for international students. *Application fee:* $30. Electronic applications accepted. *Application Contact:* Dr. Amanda Pascale, Director, The Graduate School, 904-620-1360, Fax: 904-620-1362, E-mail: graduateschool@unf.edu. *Interim Dean,* Dr. Daniel Moon, 904-620-2560, Fax: 904-620-2929, E-mail: dmoon@unf.edu.

College of Computing, Engineering, and Construction Students: 31 full-time (9 women), 67 part-time (14 women); includes 27 minority (2 Black or African American, non-Hispanic/Latino; 13 Asian, non-Hispanic/Latino; 8 Hispanic/Latino; 4 Two or more races, non-Hispanic/Latino), 17 international. Average age 32. 69 applicants, 52% accepted, 27 enrolled. *Faculty:* 40 full-time (6 women), 1 part-time/adjunct (0 women). Expenses: Contact institution. *Financial support:* In 2018–19, 33 students received support, including 4 research assistantships (averaging $3,657 per year), 3 teaching assistantships (averaging $3,852 per year); Federal Work-Study, scholarships/grants, tuition waivers (partial), and unspecified assistantships also available. Support available to part-time students. Financial award application deadline: 4/1; financial award applicants required to submit FAFSA. In 2018, 67 master's awarded. *Program availability:* Part-time. Offers computing, engineering, and construction (MS, MSCE, MSEE, MSME). *Application deadline:* For fall admission, 7/1 priority date for domestic students, 5/1 for international students; for spring admission, 11/1 priority date for domestic students, 10/1 for international students. *Application fee:* $30. Electronic applications accepted. *Application Contact:* Dr. Amanda Pascale, Director, The Graduate School, 904-620-1360, Fax: 904-620-1362, E-mail: graduateschool@unf.edu. *Dean,* Dr. Mark Tumeo, 904-620-1350, E-mail: m.tumeo@unf.edu.

School of Computing Students: 14 full-time (4 women), 35 part-time (9 women); includes 14 minority (1 Black or African American, non-Hispanic/Latino; 8 Asian, non-Hispanic/Latino; 3 Hispanic/Latino; 2 Two or more races, non-Hispanic/Latino), 8 international. Average age 33. 33 applicants, 45% accepted, 11 enrolled. *Faculty:* 13 full-time (1 woman). Expenses: Contact institution. *Financial support:* In 2018–19, 8 students received support, including 6 research assistantships (averaging $3,134 per year), 1 teaching assistantship (averaging $2,666 per year); Federal Work-Study, scholarships/grants, and unspecified assistantships also available. Financial award application deadline: 4/1; financial award applicants required to submit FAFSA. In 2018, 48 master's awarded. *Program availability:* Part-time. Offers computer science (MS); information systems (MS); software engineering (MS). *Application deadline:* For fall admission, 8/1 priority date for domestic students, 5/1 for international students; for spring admission, 12/1 priority date for domestic students, 10/1 for international students; for summer admission, 3/15 priority date for domestic students, 2/1 for international students. *Application fee:* $30. Electronic applications accepted. *Application Contact:* Dr. Amanda Pascale, Director, The Graduate School, 904-620-1360, Fax: 904-620-1362, E-mail: graduateschool@unf.edu. *Director/Professor,* Dr. Sherif Elfayoumy, 904-620-2985, E-mail: selfayou@unf.edu.

School of Engineering Students: 17 full-time (5 women), 32 part-time (5 women); includes 13 minority (1 Black or African American, non-Hispanic/Latino; 5 Asian, non-Hispanic/Latino; 5 Hispanic/Latino; 2 Two or more races, non-Hispanic/Latino), 9 international. Average age 30. 36 applicants, 58% accepted, 16 enrolled. *Faculty:* 19 full-time (4 women). Expenses: Contact institution. *Financial support:* In 2018–19, 25 students received support, including 4 research assistantships (averaging $3,161 per year), 2 teaching assistantships (averaging $4,445 per year); Federal Work-Study, scholarships/grants, tuition waivers, and unspecified assistantships also available. Financial award application deadline: 4/1; financial award applicants required to submit FAFSA. In 2018, 19 master's awarded. *Program availability:* Part-time. Offers engineering (MSCE, MSEE, MSME). *Application deadline:* For fall admission, 8/1 priority date for domestic students, 5/1 for international students; for spring admission, 12/1 priority date for domestic students, 10/1 for international students; for summer admission, 3/15 priority date for domestic students, 2/1 for international students. *Application fee:* $30. *Application Contact:* Dr. Amanda Pascale, Director, The Graduate School, 904-320-1360, Fax: 904-620-1362, E-mail: graduateschool@unf.edu. *Director,* Dr. Murat Tiryakioglu, 904-620-1393, E-mail: m.tiryakioglu@unf.edu.

College of Education and Human Services Students: 110 full-time (92 women), 290 part-time (231 women); includes 138 minority (78 Black or African American, non-

Hispanic/Latino; 8 Asian, non-Hispanic/Latino; 32 Hispanic/Latino; 1 Native Hawaiian or other Pacific Islander, non-Hispanic/Latino; 19 Two or more races, non-Hispanic/Latino; 15 international. Average age 36. 244 applicants, 59% accepted, 101 enrolled. *Faculty:* 53 full-time (33 women), 12 part-time/adjunct (7 women). Expenses: Contact institution. *Financial support:* In 2018–19, 52 students received support, including 1 research assistantship (averaging $8,096 per year), 1 teaching assistantship (averaging $5,824 per year); career-related internships or fieldwork, Federal Work-Study, scholarships/grants, and tuition waivers (partial) also available. Support available to part-time students. Financial award application deadline: 4/1; financial award applicants required to submit FAFSA. In 2018, 115 master's, 20 doctorates awarded. *Program availability:* Part-time, evening/weekend. Offers adult learning (M Ed); American Sign Language (MS); American Sign Language/English interpreting (M Ed); applied behavior analysis (M Ed); autism (M Ed); counselor education (M Ed); deaf education (M Ed); disability services (M Ed); education and human services (M Ed, MS, Ed D); educational leadership (M Ed, Ed D); exceptional student education (M Ed); literacy (M Ed); professional education (M Ed); TESOL (M Ed). *Application deadline:* For fall admission, 7/1 priority date for domestic students, 5/1 for international students; for spring admission, 11/1 priority date for domestic students, 10/1 for international students. *Application fee:* $30. Electronic applications accepted. *Application Contact:* Dr. John Kemppainen, Director, Office of Student Services, 904-620-2530, Fax: 904-620-1135, E-mail: jkemppai@unf.edu. *Dean,* Dr. Diane Yendol-Hoppey, 904-620-2520, E-mail: diane.yendol-hoppey@unf.edu.

UNIVERSITY OF NORTH GEORGIA, Dahlonega, GA 30597

General Information State-supported, coed, comprehensive institution. *Graduate housing:* Room and/or apartments available on a first-come, first-served basis to single students; on-campus housing not available to married students. Housing application deadline: 2/1. *Research affiliation:* Northeast Georgia Medical Center, Morehouse School of Medicine, St. Joseph's Hospital, Mettler Electronic Corporation.

GRADUATE UNITS

Department of Counseling *Program availability:* Part-time. Offers counseling (MS). Electronic applications accepted.

Department of Criminal Justice *Program availability:* Part-time, evening/weekend, online only, 100% online. Offers criminal justice (MS). Electronic applications accepted.

Department of History, Anthropology and Philosophy *Program availability:* Part-time, evening/weekend. Offers history (MA). Electronic applications accepted.

Department of Physical Therapy Offers physical therapy (DPT). Electronic applications accepted.

Doctor of Education Program in Higher Education Leadership and Practice *Program availability:* Part-time, evening/weekend, online only, 100% online. Offers higher education leadership and practice (Ed D). Electronic applications accepted.

Ed S in Educational Leadership Program *Program availability:* Part-time, evening/weekend, blended/hybrid learning. Offers educational leadership (Certificate, Ed S). Electronic applications accepted.

Master of Arts in Teaching Program Offers physical education (MAT); secondary education - English (MAT); secondary education - history (MAT); secondary education - mathematics (MAT); secondary education - middle grades (MAT). Electronic applications accepted.

Mike Cottrell College of Business *Program availability:* Part-time-only, evening/weekend. Offers business (MBA). Electronic applications accepted.

Program in Athletic Training Offers athletic training (MS). Electronic applications accepted.

Program in Curriculum and Instruction *Program availability:* Part-time. Offers curriculum and instruction (M Ed). Electronic applications accepted.

Program in Early Childhood Education *Program availability:* Part-time, blended/hybrid learning. Offers early childhood education (M Ed). Electronic applications accepted.

Program in Family Nurse Practitioner *Program availability:* Part-time. Offers family nurse practitioner (MS, Certificate). Electronic applications accepted.

Program in Human Services and Delivery Administration *Program availability:* Evening/weekend. Offers human services and delivery administration (MS). Electronic applications accepted.

Program in International Affairs *Program availability:* Part-time, evening/weekend, 100% online. Offers international affairs (MAIA). Electronic applications accepted.

Program in Kinesiology *Program availability:* Part-time, evening/weekend, online only, 100% online. Offers kinesiology (MS). Electronic applications accepted.

Program in Middle Grades Math and Science *Program availability:* Part-time, evening/weekend, online only, 100% online. Offers middle grades math and science (M Ed). Electronic applications accepted.

Program in Nursing Education *Program availability:* Part-time, evening/weekend, online only, 100% online. Offers nursing education (MS). Electronic applications accepted.

Program in Public Administration *Program availability:* Part-time, evening/weekend, online only, 100% online. Offers public administration (MPA). Electronic applications accepted.

UNIVERSITY OF NORTH TEXAS, Denton, TX 76203

General Information State-supported, coed, university. CGS member. *Graduate housing:* Rooms and/or apartments available on a first-come, first-served basis to single and married students. Housing application deadline: 9/1. *Research affiliation:* Delta and Pine Land Company (natural science), Semiconductor Research Corporation (materials science), Tech America (technology transfer), National Business Incubation Association (entrepreneurship), International Economic Development Council (economic growth).

GRADUATE UNITS

Toulouse Graduate School *Program availability:* Part-time, evening/weekend, online learning. Offers accounting (MS); applied anthropology (MA, MS); applied behavior analysis (Certificate); applied geography (MA); applied technology and performance improvement (M Ed, MS); art education (MA); art history (MA); arts leadership (Certificate); audiology (Au D); behavior analysis (MS); behavioral science (PhD); biochemistry and molecular biology (MS); biology (MA, MS); biomedical engineering (MS); business analysis (MS); chemistry (MS); clinical health psychology (PhD); communication studies (MA, MS); computer engineering (MS); computer science (MS); counseling (M Ed, MS); creative writing (MA); criminal justice (MS); curriculum and instruction (M Ed); decision sciences (MBA); design (MA, MFA); early childhood studies (MS); economics (MS); educational leadership (M Ed, Ed D); educational psychology (MS, PhD); electrical engineering (MS); emergency management (MPA); engineering technology (MS); English (MA); English as a second language (MA); environmental science (MS); finance (MBA, MS); financial management (MPA); French (MA); health services management (MBA); higher education (M Ed, Ed D); history (MA, MS);

hospitality management (MS); human resources management (MPA); information science (MS); information systems (PhD); information technologies (MBA); interdisciplinary studies (MA, MS); international studies (MA); international sustainable tourism (MS); jazz studies (MM); journalism (MA, MJ, Graduate Certificate); kinesiology (MS); linguistics (MA); local government management (MPA); logistics (PhD); logistics and supply chain management (MBA); long-term care, senior housing, and aging services (MA); management (PhD); marketing (MBA); mathematics (MA, MS); mechanical and energy engineering (MS, PhD); music (MA); music composition (PhD); music education (MM Ed, PhD); nonprofit management (MPA); operations and supply chain management (MBA); performance (MM, DMA); philosophy (MA); political science (MA); professional and technical communication (MA); radio, television and film (MA, MFA); rehabilitation counseling (Certificate); sociology (MA); Spanish (MA); special education (M Ed); speech-language pathology (MA); strategic management (MBA); studio art (MFA); teaching (M Ed). Electronic applications accepted.

UNIVERSITY OF NORTH TEXAS AT DALLAS, Dallas, TX 75241

General Information State-supported, coed, comprehensive institution.

GRADUATE UNITS

College of Law Offers law (JD).

Graduate School

UNIVERSITY OF NORTH TEXAS HEALTH SCIENCE CENTER AT FORT WORTH, Fort Worth, TX 76107-2699

General Information State-supported, coed, graduate-only institution. CGS member. *Graduate housing:* On-campus housing not available. *Research affiliation:* Myogen, Inc. (cardiac research), My-tech, Inc. (cardiovascular research), Novopharm, Inc. (gene control), Ethnobotanical Product Investigation Consortium (natural plant products), Genelink (familial DNA depository), Botanical Research Institutions of Texas.

GRADUATE UNITS

Graduate School of Biomedical Sciences Offers biochemistry and cancer biology (MS, PhD); biotechnology (MS); cell biology, immunology and microbiology (MS, PhD); clinical research management (MS); forensic genetics (MS); genetics (MS, PhD); integrative physiology (MS, PhD); medical sciences (MS); pharmaceutical sciences and pharmacotherapy (MS, PhD); pharmacology and neuroscience (MS, PhD); structural anatomy and rehabilitation sciences (MS, PhD).

School of Health Professions Offers physical therapy (DPT); physician assistant studies (MPAS).

School of Public Health *Program availability:* Part-time, evening/weekend, 100% online. Offers biostatistics (MS); epidemiology (MPH, MS, PhD); food security and public health (Graduate Certificate); GIS in public health (Graduate Certificate); global health (Graduate Certificate); global health for medical professionals (Graduate Certificate); health administration (MHA); health behavior research (MS, PhD); maternal and child health (MPH); public health (Graduate Certificate); public health practice (MPH). Electronic applications accepted.

Texas College of Osteopathic Medicine Offers osteopathic medicine (DO). Electronic applications accepted.

UNIVERSITY OF NORTHWESTERN OHIO, Lima, OH 45805-1498

General Information Independent, coed, comprehensive institution.

GRADUATE UNITS

Graduate College *Program availability:* Evening/weekend, online learning.

UNIVERSITY OF NORTHWESTERN–ST. PAUL, St. Paul, MN 55113-1598

General Information Independent-religious, coed, comprehensive institution. *Graduate housing:* On-campus housing not available.

GRADUATE UNITS

Master of Arts in Education Program *Program availability:* Part-time, evening/weekend, online learning. Offers education (MA Ed). Electronic applications accepted.

Master of Arts in Human Services Program *Program availability:* Part-time, evening/weekend, online learning. Offers human services (MAHS). Electronic applications accepted.

Master of Arts in Theological Studies Program *Program availability:* Part-time, evening/weekend, online learning. Offers theological studies (MATS). Electronic applications accepted.

Master of Business Administration Program *Program availability:* Part-time, evening/weekend, online learning. Offers business administration (MBA). Electronic applications accepted.

Master of Divinity Program *Program availability:* Part-time, evening/weekend, online learning. Offers theology and Christian ministry (M Div). Electronic applications accepted.

Master of Organizational Leadership Program *Program availability:* Part-time, evening/weekend, online learning. Offers organizational leadership (MOL). Electronic applications accepted.

UNIVERSITY OF NOTRE DAME, Notre Dame, IN 46556

General Information Independent-religious, coed, university. CGS member. *Graduate housing:* Rooms and/or apartments available on a first-come, first-served basis to single and married students. Housing application deadline: 5/1. *Research affiliation:* Space Telescope Science Institute, Brookhaven National Laboratory, Fermi National Accelerator Laboratory, Argonne National Laboratory.

GRADUATE UNITS

The Graduate School *Program availability:* Part-time. Electronic applications accepted.

College of Arts and Letters *Program availability:* Part-time. Offers art history (MA); arts and letters (M Div, M Ed, MA, MFA, MMS, MSM, MTS, PhD); cognitive psychology (PhD); counseling psychology (PhD); creative writing (MFA); design (MFA); developmental psychology (PhD); early Christian studies (MA); economics (PhD); English (MA, PhD); French and Francophone studies (MA); history (MA, PhD); history and philosophy of science (MA); humanities (M Div, MA, MFA, MMS, MSM, MTS, PhD); Iberian and Latin American studies (MA); Italian studies (MA); literature (PhD); medieval studies (MMS, PhD); philosophy (PhD); political science (PhD); quantitative psychology (PhD); Romance literatures (MA); social sciences (M Ed, MA, PhD); sociology (PhD); studio art (MFA); theology (M Div, MA, MSM, MTS, PhD); theology and science (PhD). Electronic applications accepted.

College of Engineering Offers aerospace and mechanical engineering (M Eng, PhD); aerospace engineering (MS Aero E); bioengineering (MS Bio E); chemical and biomolecular engineering (MS Ch E, PhD); civil engineering (MSCE); civil engineering and geological sciences (PhD); computer science and engineering (MSCSE, PhD); earth sciences (MS); electrical engineering (MSEE, PhD); engineering (M Eng, MEME, MS, MS Aero E, MS Bio E, MS Ch E, MS Env E, MSCE, MSCSE, MSEE, MSME, PhD); environmental engineering (MS Env E); mechanical engineering (MEME, MSME). Electronic applications accepted.

College of Science Offers algebra (PhD); algebraic geometry (PhD); applied and computational mathematics and statistics (PhD); applied mathematics (MSAM); applied statistics (MS); aquatic ecology, evolution and environmental biology (MS, PhD); biochemistry (MS, PhD); cellular and molecular biology (MS, PhD); complex analysis (PhD); computational finance (MS); differential geometry (PhD); genetics (MS, PhD); inorganic chemistry (MS, PhD); logic (PhD); organic chemistry (MS, PhD); partial differential equations (PhD); physical chemistry (MS, PhD); physics (MS, PhD); physiology (MS, PhD); science (MS, MSAM, PhD); topology (PhD); vector biology and parasitology (MS, PhD). Electronic applications accepted.

Keough School of Global Affairs Offers global affairs (MGA); sustainable development (MGA).

Kroc Institute for International Peace Studies Offers international peace studies (MA, PhD). Electronic applications accepted.

School of Architecture Offers architectural design and urbanism (M ADU); architecture (M Arch). Electronic applications accepted.

Institute for Educational Initiatives Offers educational initiatives (M Ed, MA). Enrollment restricted to participants in the Alliance for Catholic Education (ACE) program. Electronic applications accepted.

The Law School Offers human rights (LL M, JSD); international and comparative law (LL M); law (JD). Electronic applications accepted.

Mendoza College of Business Offers assurance and advisory services (MSA); business (MBA, MNA, MSA, MSBA, MSF, MSM); business analytics (MSBA); business leadership (MBA); consulting (MBA); corporate finance (MBA); executive business administration (MBA); finance (MSF); innovation and entrepreneurship (MBA); investments (MBA); management (MSM); marketing (MBA); nonprofit administration (MNA); tax services (MSA). Electronic applications accepted.

UNIVERSITY OF OKLAHOMA, Norman, OK 73019-0390

General Information State-supported, coed, university. CGS member. *Enrollment:* 2,936 full-time matriculated graduate/professional students (1,544 women), 3,365 part-time matriculated graduate/professional students (1,759 women). *Enrollment by degree level:* 4,594 master's, 1,678 doctoral, 29 other advanced degrees. *Graduate faculty:* 1,034 full-time (365 women), 50 part-time/adjunct (19 women). *International tuition:* $20,342.40 full-time. Tuition, state resident: full-time $5683.20; part-time $236.80 per credit hour. Tuition, nonresident: full-time $20,342; part-time $847.60 per credit hour. *Required fees:* $2894.20; $110.05 per credit hour. $126.50 per semester. Tuition and fees vary according to course load and program. *Graduate housing:* Rooms and/or apartments available on a first-come, first-served basis to single and married students. Typical cost: $5123 per year ($9739 including board) for single students; $8472 per year ($13,088 including board) for married students. Room and board charges vary according to board plan, campus/location and housing facility selected. Housing application deadline: 5/10. *Student services:* Campus employment opportunities, campus safety program, career counseling, child daycare facilities, exercise/wellness program, free psychological counseling, grant writing training, international student services, low-cost health insurance, multicultural affairs office, services for students with disabilities, teacher training, writing training. *Library facilities:* Bizzell Memorial Library plus 5 others. *Collection:* Books: 4.4 million (physical), 1.4 million (digital/electronic); Serial titles: 71,289 (physical), 128,934 (digital/electronic); Databases: 311. Weekly public service hours: 114; students can reserve study rooms.

Computer facilities: Computer purchase and lease plans are available. 4,500 computers available on campus for general student use. A campuswide network can be accessed from student residence rooms and from off campus. Online class registration is available.
Website: http://www.ou.edu/

General Application Contact: Dr. Randall S. Hewes, Dean, Graduate College, 405-325-3811, Fax: 405-325-5346, E-mail: gradinfo@ou.edu.

GRADUATE UNITS

Christopher C. Gibbs College of Architecture Students: 86 full-time (47 women), 31 part-time (12 women); includes 19 minority (5 Black or African American, non-Hispanic/Latino; 3 American Indian or Alaska Native, non-Hispanic/Latino; 1 Asian, non-Hispanic/Latino; 4 Hispanic/Latino; 6 Two or more races, non-Hispanic/Latino), 43 international. Average age 29. 77 applicants, 75% accepted, 34 enrolled. *Faculty:* 31 full-time (14 women), 2 part-time/adjunct (1 woman). Expenses: Contact institution. *Financial support:* Fellowships, research assistantships, teaching assistantships, scholarships/grants, and unspecified assistantships available. Financial award application deadline: 6/1; financial award applicants required to submit FAFSA. In 2018, 43 master's, 1 other advanced degree awarded. *Program availability:* Part-time. Offers architecture (MS); data systems and digital design (Graduate Certificate); planning, design and construction (PhD). *Application deadline:* For fall admission, 3/1 for international students. *Application fee:* $50 ($100 for international students). Electronic applications accepted. *Application Contact:* Dr. Charlie Warnken, Associate Dean for Instructional Services, 405-325-2444, Fax: 405-325-7558, E-mail: cwarnken@ou.edu. *Dean,* Hans Butzer, 405-325-2444, Fax: 405-325-7558, E-mail: butzer@ou.edu.

Division of Architecture Students: 22 full-time (8 women), 11 part-time (3 women); includes 2 minority (1 Hispanic/Latino; 1 Two or more races, non-Hispanic/Latino), 9 international. Average age 28. 15 applicants, 93% accepted, 8 enrolled. *Faculty:* 32 full-time (15 women), 1 part-time/adjunct (0 women). Expenses: Contact institution. *Financial support:* Research assistantships, teaching assistantships, career-related internships or fieldwork, scholarships/grants, health care benefits, tuition waivers, and unspecified assistantships available. Financial award application deadline: 6/1; financial award applicants required to submit FAFSA. In 2018, 16 master's awarded. *Program availability:* Part-time. Offers architecture (MS); data and digital representation (M Arch); design entrepreneurship and real estate (M Arch); planning, design and construction (PhD); resilient planning, design, and construction (M Arch). *Application deadline:* For spring admission, 5/1 for domestic students, 3/1 for international students. Applications are processed on a rolling basis. *Application fee:* $50 ($100 for international students). Electronic applications accepted. *Application Contact:* Marjorie Callahan, Graduate Liaison, Fax: 405-325-7588, E-mail: mcallahan@ou.edu. *Director,* Dr. Stephanie Pilat, 405-325-9352, Fax: 405-325-7588, E-mail: architecture.director@ou.edu.

Division of Interior Design Students: 12 full-time (11 women); includes 4 minority (2 American Indian or Alaska Native, non-Hispanic/Latino; 1 Hispanic/Latino; 1 Two or more races, non-Hispanic/Latino), 1 international. Average age 32. 12 applicants, 83% accepted, 6 enrolled. *Faculty:* 1 (woman) full-time. Expenses: Contact institution.

Financial support: Research assistantships, teaching assistantships, career-related internships or fieldwork, scholarships/grants, and unspecified assistantships available. Financial award application deadline: 6/1; financial award applicants required to submit FAFSA. In 2018, 2 master's awarded. *Program availability:* Part-time. Offers interior design (MS); professional applications of interior design (Graduate Certificate). *Application deadline:* Applications are processed on a rolling basis. *Application fee:* $50 ($100 for international students). Electronic applications accepted. *Application Contact:* Dr. Suchismita Bhattacharjee, Assistant Professor and Graduate Liaison, 405-325-2548, Fax: 405-325-7558, E-mail: suchi@ou.edu. *Academic Director and Associate Professor,* Elizabeth Pober, 405-325-6764, Fax: 405-325-7558, E-mail: epober@ou.edu.

Division of Landscape Architecture Students: 19 full-time (12 women), 3 part-time (2 women); includes 2 minority (both Two or more races, non-Hispanic/Latino), 18 international. Average age 27. 14 applicants, 100% accepted, 10 enrolled. Expenses: Contact institution. *Financial support:* Research assistantships, scholarships/grants, and unspecified assistantships available. Financial award application deadline: 6/1; financial award applicants required to submit FAFSA. In 2018, 6 master's awarded. Offers landscape architectural studies (MLA); landscape architecture (MLA). *Application deadline:* For fall admission, 2/15 priority date for domestic and international students. Applications are processed on a rolling basis. *Application fee:* $50 ($100 for international students). Electronic applications accepted. *Application Contact:* Leehu Loon, Associate Dean and Director, 405-325-1519, Fax: 405-325-7558, E-mail: lloon@ou.edu. *Associate Dean and Director,* Leehu Loon, 405-325-1519, Fax: 405-325-7558, E-mail: lloon@ou.edu.

Division of Regional and City Planning Students: 18 full-time (5 women), 3 part-time (1 woman); includes 3 minority (1 American Indian or Alaska Native, non-Hispanic/Latino; 1 Two or more races, non-Hispanic/Latino), 5 international. Average age 26. 7 applicants, 100% accepted, 4 enrolled. Expenses: Contact institution. *Financial support:* Fellowships, research assistantships, teaching assistantships, career-related internships or fieldwork, Federal Work-Study, scholarships/grants, health care benefits, tuition waivers, and unspecified assistantships available. Financial award application deadline: 6/1; financial award applicants required to submit FAFSA. In 2018, 10 master's awarded. *Program availability:* Part-time. Offers community development (MRCP); physical planning (MRCP). *Application deadline:* For fall admission, 4/1 priority date for international students. Applications are processed on a rolling basis. *Application fee:* $50 ($100 for international students). Electronic applications accepted. *Application Contact:* Dr. Charles Warnken, Director, 405-325-2444, Fax: 405-325-7558, E-mail: cwarnken@ou.edu. *Director,* Dr. Charles Warnken, 405-325-2444, Fax: 405-325-7558, E-mail: cwarnken@ou.edu.

Haskell and Irene Lemon Division of Construction Science Students: 10 full-time (5 women), 7 part-time (3 women); includes 5 minority (3 Black or African American, non-Hispanic/Latino; 1 Asian, non-Hispanic/Latino; 1 Two or more races, non-Hispanic/Latino), 4 international. Average age 32. 15 applicants, 60% accepted, 5 enrolled. Expenses: Contact institution. *Financial support:* Fellowships, research assistantships, teaching assistantships, career-related internships or fieldwork, and scholarships/grants available. Financial award application deadline: 6/1; financial award applicants required to submit FAFSA. In 2018, 8 master's awarded. *Program availability:* Part-time. Offers construction management (MS); construction science (MCM); planning, design, and construction (PhD). *Application fee:* $50 ($100 for international students). Electronic applications accepted. *Application Contact:* Anthony Perrenoud, Graduate Liaison, 405-325-2674, E-mail: perrenoud@ou.edu. *Director,* Ben Bigelow, 405-325-6404, E-mail: bigelow@ou.edu.

College of Arts and Sciences Students: 1,093 full-time (690 women), 1,043 part-time (656 women); includes 711 minority (208 Black or African American, non-Hispanic/Latino; 94 American Indian or Alaska Native, non-Hispanic/Latino; 62 Asian, non-Hispanic/Latino; 189 Hispanic/Latino; 5 Native Hawaiian or other Pacific Islander, non-Hispanic/Latino; 153 Two or more races, non-Hispanic/Latino), 201 international. Average age 32. 1,073 applicants, 63% accepted, 444 enrolled. *Faculty:* 461 full-time (192 women), 19 part-time/adjunct (10 women). Expenses: Contact institution. *Financial support:* Fellowships, research assistantships, teaching assistantships, career-related internships or fieldwork, Federal Work-Study, institutionally sponsored loans, scholarships/grants, traineeships, health care benefits, and unspecified assistantships available. Support available to part-time students. Financial award application deadline: 6/1; financial award applicants required to submit FAFSA. In 2018, 611 master's, 95 doctorates, 130 other advanced degrees awarded. *Program availability:* Part-time, evening/weekend, online learning. Offers anthropology (MA, PhD); applied linguistic anthropology (MA); archaeology (PhD); arts and sciences (MA, MHR, MLIS, MPA, MS, MSW, PhD, Graduate Certificate); biology (MS, PhD); cellular and behavioral neurobiology (MS, PhD); chemistry (MS, PhD); clinical mental health (MHR); communication (MA); communication technology (PhD); ecology and evolutionary biology (PhD); economics (MA, PhD); engineering physics (MS); exercise physiology (MS, PhD); French (MA, PhD); German (MA); health and exercise science (MS); health and human biology (PhD); health communication (PhD); health promotion (MS, PhD); helping skills in human relations (Graduate Certificate); history (MA, PhD); history of science, technology and medicine (MA); human relations (MHR); human resource diversity and development (Graduate Certificate); human resources (MHR); intercultural/international communication (PhD); licensed professional counselor (MHR); literary and cultural studies (MA); mathematics (MA, MS, PhD); microbiology (MS, PhD); Native American studies (MA); organizational communication (PhD); organizational dynamics (MA, Graduate Certificate); philosophy (MA, PhD); physics (MS, PhD); plant biology (MS, PhD); political science (MA, PhD); political/mass communication (PhD); psychology (MS, PhD); public administration (MPA); social influence/interpersonal communication (PhD); socio-cultural and linguistics (PhD); socio-cultural anthropology (MA, PhD); sociology (MA, PhD); Spanish (MA, PhD); women's and gender studies (Graduate Certificate); writing and rhetoric studies (MA, PhD). *Application fee:* $50 ($100 for international students). Electronic applications accepted. *Application Contact:* David Wrobel, Dean, 405-325-2077, Fax: 405-325-7709, E-mail: david.wrobel@ou.edu. *Dean,* David Wrobel, 405-325-2077, Fax: 405-325-7709, E-mail: david.wrobel@ou.edu.

Anne and Henry Zarrow School of Social Work Students: 220 full-time (188 women), 202 part-time (166 women); includes 183 minority (53 Black or African American, non-Hispanic/Latino; 38 American Indian or Alaska Native, non-Hispanic/Latino; 8 Asian, non-Hispanic/Latino; 38 Hispanic/Latino; 46 Two or more races, non-Hispanic/Latino), 3 international. Average age 32. 181 applicants, 86% accepted, 124 enrolled. *Faculty:* 27 full-time (19 women), 4 part-time/adjunct (2 women). Expenses: Contact institution. *Financial support:* Research assistantships, teaching assistantships, career-related internships or fieldwork, scholarships/grants, traineeships, health care benefits, tuition waivers, and unspecified assistantships available. Support available to part-time students. Financial award application deadline: 6/1; financial award applicants required to submit FAFSA. In 2018, 170 master's awarded. *Program availability:* Part-time, evening/weekend. Offers direct practice (MSW). *Application deadline:* For fall admission, 2/1 priority date for domestic and international students; for summer admission, 2/1 priority date for domestic and international students. *Application fee:* $50 ($100 for international students). Electronic applications accepted. *Application Contact:* Amy Ann Arnold, Admissions and Enrollment Coordinator, 918-660-3385, Fax: 918-660-3383, E-mail: aarnold@ou.edu. *Director,* Dr. Julie Miller-Cribbs, 918-660-3378, Fax: 918-660-3383, E-mail: jmcribbs@ou.edu.

School of Library and Information Studies Students: 63 full-time (53 women), 133 part-time (108 women); includes 48 minority (8 Black or African American, non-Hispanic/Latino; 4 American Indian or Alaska Native, non-Hispanic/Latino; 5 Asian, non-Hispanic/Latino; 14 Hispanic/Latino; 1 Native Hawaiian or other Pacific Islander, non-Hispanic/Latino; 16 Two or more races, non-Hispanic/Latino), 2 international. Average age 32. 60 applicants, 93% accepted, 41 enrolled. *Faculty:* 7 full-time (6 women), 2 part-time/adjunct (1 woman). Expenses: Contact institution. *Financial support:* Research assistantships, teaching assistantships, scholarships/grants, health care benefits, and unspecified assistantships available. Financial award application deadline: 6/1; financial award applicants required to submit FAFSA. In 2018, 54 master's, 9 other advanced degrees awarded. *Program availability:* Part-time, evening/weekend, 100% online, blended/hybrid learning. Offers archival studies (Graduate Certificate); digital humanities (Graduate Certificate); information studies (PhD); library and information studies (MLIS). *Application deadline:* Applications are processed on a rolling basis. *Application fee:* $50 ($100 for international students). Electronic applications accepted. *Application Contact:* Sarah Connelly, Admissions and Student Services Coordinator, 405-325-3921, E-mail: sarahee@ou.edu. *Director,* Dr. Susan K. Burke, 405-325-3921, E-mail: sburke@ou.edu.

College of Atmospheric and Geographic Sciences Students: 82 full-time (31 women), 42 part-time (19 women); includes 13 minority (3 Black or African American, non-Hispanic/Latino; 2 Asian, non-Hispanic/Latino; 7 Hispanic/Latino; 1 Two or more races, non-Hispanic/Latino), 27 international. Average age 26. 115 applicants, 37% accepted, 35 enrolled. *Faculty:* 64 full-time (15 women). Expenses: Contact institution. *Financial support:* Fellowships, research assistantships, teaching assistantships, scholarships/grants, health care benefits, and unspecified assistantships available. Support available to part-time students. Financial award application deadline: 6/1; financial award applicants required to submit FAFSA. In 2018, 21 master's, 7 doctorates awarded. *Program availability:* Part-time. Offers atmospheric and geographic sciences (MA, MS, PhD); environmental sustainability (MS); geography (MA, MS, PhD). *Application deadline:* For fall admission, 1/15 for domestic and international students. *Application fee:* $50 ($100 for international students). Electronic applications accepted. *Application Contact:* Mary Anne Hempe, Assistant Dean for Student Services, 405-325-3095, Fax: 405-325-3148, E-mail: mahempe@ou.edu. *Dean,* Dr. Berrien Moore, 405-325-3095, Fax: 405-325-1180, E-mail: berrien@ou.edu.

School of Meteorology Students: 50 full-time (12 women), 29 part-time (10 women); includes 7 minority (1 Black or African American, non-Hispanic/Latino; 2 Asian, non-Hispanic/Latino; 4 Hispanic/Latino), 13 international. Average age 25. 86 applicants, 27% accepted, 22 enrolled. *Faculty:* 43 full-time (8 women). Expenses: Contact institution. *Financial support:* In 2018–19, 70 students received support, including 2 fellowships with tuition reimbursements available (averaging $4,500 per year), 41 research assistantships with full tuition reimbursements available (averaging $20,415 per year), 19 teaching assistantships with full tuition reimbursements available (averaging $20,837 per year); health care benefits, tuition waivers (full and partial), and unspecified assistantships also available. Support available to part-time students. Financial award application deadline: 6/1; financial award applicants required to submit FAFSA. In 2018, 12 master's, 7 doctorates awarded. Offers meteorology (MS, PhD). *Application deadline:* For fall admission, 1/15 for domestic students, 2/1 for international students; for spring admission, 10/1 for domestic and international students. Applications are processed on a rolling basis. *Application fee:* $50 ($100 for international students). Electronic applications accepted. *Application Contact:* Christie Upchurch, Academic Coordinator, Graduate Program, 405-325-6571, Fax: 405-325-7689, E-mail: cupchurch@ou.edu. *Director,* Dr. David Parsons, 405-325-6561, Fax: 405-325-7689, E-mail: dparsons@ou.edu.

College of Law Students: 608 full-time (302 women), 291 part-time (193 women); includes 307 minority (32 Black or African American, non-Hispanic/Latino; 150 American Indian or Alaska Native, non-Hispanic/Latino; 13 Asian, non-Hispanic/Latino; 66 Hispanic/Latino; 1 Native Hawaiian or other Pacific Islander, non-Hispanic/Latino; 45 Two or more races, non-Hispanic/Latino), 7 international. Average age 32. 896 applicants, 55% accepted, 264 enrolled. *Faculty:* 33 full-time (15 women), 10 part-time/adjunct (3 women). Expenses: Contact institution. *Financial support:* In 2018–19, 472 students received support. Career-related internships or fieldwork, Federal Work-Study, scholarships/grants, and tuition waivers (full and partial) available. Financial award application deadline: 6/1; financial award applicants required to submit FAFSA. In 2018, 182 master's, 178 doctorates awarded. *Program availability:* Part-time, 100% online. Offers law (LL M, JD). *Application deadline:* For fall admission, 3/15 for domestic and international students. Applications are processed on a rolling basis. *Application fee:* $50. Electronic applications accepted. *Application Contact:* Madeline Farris, Assoc. Director of Admissions, 405-325-8521, Fax: 405-325-0502, E-mail: admissions@law.ou.edu. *Interim Dean,* Katheleen Guzman, 405-325-4884, Fax: 405-325-7712, E-mail: kguzman@ou.edu.

College of Professional and Continuing Studies *Program availability:* Part-time, 100% online, blended/hybrid learning. Offers administrative leadership (MA, Graduate Certificate); corrections management (Graduate Certificate); criminal justice (MS); integrated studies (MA); museum studies (MA); prevention science (MPS); restorative justice administration (Graduate Certificate). Electronic applications accepted.

David L. Boren College of International Studies Students: 65 full-time (29 women), 322 part-time (101 women); includes 127 minority (34 Black or African American, non-Hispanic/Latino; 2 American Indian or Alaska Native, non-Hispanic/Latino; 21 Asian, non-Hispanic/Latino; 48 Hispanic/Latino; 2 Native Hawaiian or other Pacific Islander, non-Hispanic/Latino; 20 Two or more races, non-Hispanic/Latino), 4 international. Average age 33. 108 applicants, 81% accepted, 51 enrolled. *Faculty:* 17 full-time (7 women), 1 (woman) part-time/adjunct. Expenses: Contact institution. *Financial support:* Fellowships, research assistantships, teaching assistantships, career-related internships or fieldwork, scholarships/grants, health care benefits, and unspecified assistantships available. Financial award application deadline: 6/1; financial award applicants required to submit FAFSA. In 2018, 146 master's awarded. *Program availability:* Part-time, online courses with an 8-10 day study abroad. Offers economics and development (MAIS); global affairs (MA). *Application deadline:* For fall admission, 2/15 for domestic and international students. Applications are processed on a rolling basis. *Application fee:* $50 ($100 for international students). Electronic applications accepted. *Application Contact:* Katie Watkins, Academic Advisor, 405-325-2337, Fax: 405-325-7738, E-mail: kwatkins@ou.edu. *VP for Faculty/Interim Dean,* Dr. Jill Irvine, 405-325-3221, E-mail: jill.irvine@ou.edu.

Gallogly College of Engineering Students: 318 full-time (91 women), 257 part-time (77 women); includes 92 minority (16 Black or African American, non-Hispanic/Latino; 4 American Indian or Alaska Native, non-Hispanic/Latino; 28 Asian, non-Hispanic/Latino; 28 Hispanic/Latino; 16 Two or more races, non-Hispanic/Latino), 196 international. Average age 29. 507 applicants, 62% accepted, 143 enrolled. *Faculty:* 146 full-time (21 women), 4 part-time/adjunct (2 women). Expenses: Contact institution. *Financial support:* Fellowships, research assistantships, teaching assistantships, career-related internships or fieldwork, institutionally sponsored loans, tuition waivers, and unspecified assistantships available. Support available to part-time students. Financial award application deadline: 6/1; financial award applicants required to submit FAFSA. In 2018, 128 master's, 40 doctorates awarded. *Program availability:* Part-time. Offers aerospace engineering (PhD). *Application fee:* $50 ($100 for international students). Electronic applications accepted. *Application Contact:* Dr. John Antonio, Senior Associate Dean, 405-325-7508, Fax: 405-325-7508, E-mail: antonio@ou.edu. *Interim Dean,* Dr. John Antonio, 405-325-4397, Fax: 405-325-7508, E-mail: antonio@ou.edu.

School of Aerospace and Mechanical Engineering Students: 46 full-time (12 women), 18 part-time (5 women); includes 8 minority (1 Black or African American, non-Hispanic/Latino; 1 American Indian or Alaska Native, non-Hispanic/Latino; 2 Asian, non-Hispanic/Latino; 1 Hispanic/Latino; 3 Two or more races, non-Hispanic/Latino), 38 international. Average age 28. 33 applicants, 73% accepted, 14 enrolled. *Faculty:* 28 full-time (3 women). Expenses: Contact institution. *Financial support:* Fellowships, research assistantships, teaching assistantships, and scholarships/grants available. Financial award application deadline: 6/1; financial award applicants required to submit FAFSA. In 2018, 15 master's, 8 doctorates awarded. *Program availability:* Part-time. Offers aerospace engineering (MS, PhD); mechanical engineering (MS, PhD). *Application deadline:* For fall admission, 1/15 for domestic and international students; for spring admission, 9/1 for domestic and international students. *Application fee:* $50 ($100 for international students). Electronic applications accepted. *Application Contact:* Bethany Burklund, AME Student Services Coordinator, 405-325-5013, Fax: 405-325-1088, E-mail: bethanyhb@ou.edu. *Director,* Zahed Siddique, 405-325-5011, Fax: 405-325-1088, E-mail: zsiddique@ou.edu.

School of Chemical, Biological and Materials Engineering Students: 25 full-time (9 women), 8 part-time (3 women); includes 3 minority (2 Hispanic/Latino; 1 Two or more races, non-Hispanic/Latino), 22 international. Average age 27. 51 applicants, 47% accepted, 11 enrolled. *Faculty:* 17 full-time (3 women). Expenses: Contact institution. *Financial support:* Research assistantships and teaching assistantships available. Financial award application deadline: 6/1; financial award applicants required to submit FAFSA. In 2018, 1 master's, 8 doctorates awarded. *Program availability:* Part-time. Offers chemical engineering (MS, PhD). *Application deadline:* For fall admission, 4/1 for international students; for spring admission, 9/1 for international students; for summer admission, 2/1 for international students. Applications are processed on a rolling basis. *Application fee:* $50 ($100 for international students). Electronic applications accepted. *Application Contact:* Rett Norman, Graduate Program Staff Assistant, 405-325-5814, Fax: 405-325-5813, E-mail: Rett.Norman@ou.edu. *Director,* Dr. Brian Grady, 405-325-5814, Fax: 405-325-5813, E-mail: cbme@ou.edu.

School of Civil Engineering and Environmental Science Students: 33 full-time (11 women), 61 part-time (22 women); includes 21 minority (6 Black or African American, non-Hispanic/Latino; 2 American Indian or Alaska Native, non-Hispanic/Latino; 2 Asian, non-Hispanic/Latino; 7 Hispanic/Latino; 4 Two or more races, non-Hispanic/Latino), 27 international. Average age 30. 154 applicants, 68% accepted, 52 enrolled. *Faculty:* 24 full-time (4 women), 3 part-time/adjunct (2 women). Expenses: Contact institution. *Financial support:* Fellowships, research assistantships, teaching assistantships, and scholarships/grants available. Financial award application deadline: 6/1; financial award applicants required to submit FAFSA. In 2018, 9 master's, 4 doctorates awarded. *Program availability:* Part-time. Offers civil engineering (MS, PhD); environmental engineering (MS, PhD); environmental science (M Env Sc, PhD). *Application deadline:* For fall admission, 1/15 for domestic and international students; for spring admission, 5/15 for domestic and international students. *Application fee:* $50 ($100 for international students). Electronic applications accepted. *Application Contact:* Graduate Studies Coordinator, 405-325-2344, Fax: 405-325-4217, E-mail: ceesgradstudies@ou.edu. *Director,* Dr. Randall Kolar, 405-325-4267, Fax: 405-325-4217, E-mail: kolar@ou.edu.

School of Computer Science Students: 51 full-time (19 women), 11 part-time (6 women); includes 6 minority (2 Black or African American, non-Hispanic/Latino; 3 Asian, non-Hispanic/Latino; 1 Two or more races, non-Hispanic/Latino), 49 international. Average age 27. 89 applicants, 45% accepted, 13 enrolled. *Faculty:* 17 full-time (3 women). Expenses: Contact institution. *Financial support:* Fellowships, research assistantships, teaching assistantships, scholarships/grants, and unspecified assistantships available. Financial award application deadline: 6/1; financial award applicants required to submit FAFSA. In 2018, 24 master's, 1 doctorate awarded. *Program availability:* Part-time. Offers computer science (PhD). *Application deadline:* For fall admission, 4/1 for domestic students, 3/1 for international students; for spring admission, 10/1 for domestic students, 9/1 for international students. Applications are processed on a rolling basis. *Application fee:* $50 ($100 for international students). Electronic applications accepted. *Application Contact:* Virginie Perez Woods, Academic Programs Coordinator, 405-325-0145, Fax: 405-325-4044, E-mail: vpw@cs.ou.edu. *Director,* Dr. Sridhar Radhakrishnan, 405-325-4042, Fax: 405-325-4044, E-mail: sridhar@ou.edu.

School of Electrical and Computer Engineering Students: 83 full-time (16 women), 40 part-time (9 women); includes 11 minority (1 Black or African American, non-Hispanic/Latino; 1 American Indian or Alaska Native, non-Hispanic/Latino; 3 Asian, non-Hispanic/Latino; 5 Hispanic/Latino; 1 Two or more races, non-Hispanic/Latino), 76 international. Average age 29. 61 applicants, 67% accepted, 14 enrolled. *Faculty:* 44 full-time (3 women), 1 part-time/adjunct (0 women). Expenses: Contact institution. *Financial support:* Fellowships, research assistantships, teaching assistantships, career-related internships or fieldwork, scholarships/grants, and health care benefits available. Financial award application deadline: 6/1; financial award applicants required to submit FAFSA. In 2018, 21 master's, 15 doctorates awarded. *Program availability:* Part-time. Offers electrical and computer engineering (MS, PhD); telecommunications engineering (MS). *Application deadline:* For fall admission, 4/1 for domestic students, 3/1 for international students; for spring admission, 11/1 for domestic students, 10/1 for international students. Applications are processed on a rolling basis. *Application fee:* $50 ($100 for international students). Electronic applications accepted. *Application Contact:* Emily Benton Wilkins, Graduate Programs Coordinator, 405-325-7334, Fax: 405-325-7066, E-mail: emily.d.benton-1@ou.edu. *Director,* Dr. J.R. Cruz, 405-325-8131, Fax: 405-325-7066, E-mail: jcruz@ou.edu.

School of Industrial and Systems Engineering Students: 26 full-time (10 women), 24 part-time (12 women); includes 7 minority (1 Black or African American, non-Hispanic/Latino; 2 Asian, non-Hispanic/Latino; 3 Hispanic/Latino; 1 Two or more races, non-Hispanic/Latino; 35 international. Average age 29. 39 applicants, 77% accepted, 8 enrolled. *Faculty:* 12 full-time (2 women). Expenses: Contact institution. *Financial support:* Research assistantships, teaching assistantships, Federal Work-Study, institutionally sponsored loans, scholarships/grants, and health care benefits available. Financial award application deadline: 6/1; financial award applicants required to submit FAFSA. In 2018, 15 master's, 2 doctorates awarded. Offers industrial and systems engineering (MS, PhD). *Application deadline:* For fall admission, 6/1 priority date for domestic students, 4/1 priority date for international students; for spring admission, 11/1 priority date for domestic students, 9/1 priority date for international students. Applications are processed on a rolling basis. *Application fee:* $50 ($100 for international students). Electronic applications accepted. *Application Contact:* Dr. Janet Allen, Chair/Graduate Liaison, 405-550-3969, Fax: 405-325-7555, E-mail: janet.allen@ou.edu. *Professor/Interim Director,* Dr. Shivakumar Raman, 405-819-3710, Fax: 405-325-7555, E-mail: raman@ou.edu.

Stephenson School of Biomedical Engineering Students: 12 full-time (4 women), 7 part-time (3 women); includes 4 minority (1 Asian, non-Hispanic/Latino; 1 Hispanic/Latino; 2 Two or more races, non-Hispanic/Latino); 7 international. Average age 26. 22 applicants, 18% accepted, 4 enrolled. *Faculty:* 24 full-time (4 women). Expenses: Contact institution. *Financial support:* Fellowships, research assistantships, teaching assistantships, scholarships/grants, health care benefits, and unspecified assistantships available. Financial award application deadline: 6/1; financial award applicants required to submit FAFSA. In 2018, 1 master's, 2 doctorates awarded. *Program availability:* Part-time. Offers biomedical engineering (MS, PhD). *Application deadline:* For fall admission, 1/15 priority date for domestic and international students; for spring admission, 9/15 priority date for domestic and international students. *Application fee:* $50 ($100 for international students). Electronic applications accepted. *Application Contact:* Shayla Glover, University Programs Specialist, 405-325-3947, E-mail: shaylaglover@ou.edu. *Director,* Dr. Michael Detamore, 405-325-2144, E-mail: detamore@ou.edu.

Gaylord College of Journalism and Mass Communication Students: 37 full-time (18 women), 39 part-time (13 women); includes 17 minority (3 Black or African American, non-Hispanic/Latino; 1 American Indian or Alaska Native, non-Hispanic/Latino; 3 Asian, non-Hispanic/Latino; 5 Hispanic/Latino; 5 Two or more races, non-Hispanic/Latino), 12 international. Average age 32. 34 applicants, 68% accepted, 17 enrolled. *Faculty:* 25 full-time (11 women), 1 part-time/adjunct (0 women). Expenses: Contact institution. *Financial support:* Fellowships, research assistantships, teaching assistantships, career-related internships or fieldwork, scholarships/grants, health care benefits, unspecified assistantships, and research and research travel awards available. Financial award application deadline: 6/1; financial award applicants required to submit FAFSA. In 2018, 14 master's, 10 doctorates awarded. *Program availability:* Part-time. Offers journalism and mass communication (MA); mass communication (PhD); professional writing (MPW). *Application deadline:* For fall admission, 2/1 priority date for domestic students, 2/1 for international students; for spring admission, 11/1 for domestic students, 9/1 for international students; for summer admission, 3/1 for domestic students. Applications are processed on a rolling basis. *Application fee:* $50 ($100 for international students). Electronic applications accepted. *Application Contact:* Larry Laneer, Graduate Advisor, 405-325-2722, Fax: 405-325-7565, E-mail: llaneer@ou.edu. *Dean,* Dr. Ed Kelley, 405-325-4094, Fax: 405-325-7565, E-mail: ekelley@ou.edu.

Graduate College Students: 37 full-time (18 women), 39 part-time (13 women); includes 22 minority (9 Black or African American, non-Hispanic/Latino; 2 American Indian or Alaska Native, non-Hispanic/Latino; 8 Hispanic/Latino; 3 Two or more races, non-Hispanic/Latino), 10 international. Average age 34. 2 applicants, 100% accepted, 2 enrolled. *Faculty:* 29 full-time (13 women), 1 part-time/adjunct (0 women). Expenses: Contact institution. *Financial support:* Fellowships, research assistantships, teaching assistantships, scholarships/grants, health care benefits, tuition waivers, and unspecified assistantships available. Financial award application deadline: 6/1; financial award applicants required to submit FAFSA. In 2018, 17 master's, 7 doctorates, 1 other advanced degree awarded. *Program availability:* Part-time, evening/weekend, blended/hybrid learning. Offers earth observation science for society and sustainability (Graduate Certificate); interdisciplinary programs (MA); interdisciplinary studies (PhD). *Application deadline:* For fall admission, 4/1 for international students; for spring admission, 9/1 for international students; for summer admission, 2/1 for international students. Applications are processed on a rolling basis. *Application fee:* $50 ($100 for international students). Electronic applications accepted. *Application Contact:* Amy Shaw, Director, Office of Graduate Admissions, 405-325-6765, Fax: 405-325-5345, E-mail: ashaw@ou.edu. *Dean and Professor,* Dr. Randall S. Hewes, 405-325-3811, Fax: 405-325-5343, E-mail: hewes@ou.edu.

Jeannine Rainbolt College of Education Students: 248 full-time (167 women), 443 part-time (332 women); includes 218 minority (66 Black or African American, non-Hispanic/Latino; 37 American Indian or Alaska Native, non-Hispanic/Latino; 17 Asian, non-Hispanic/Latino; 44 Hispanic/Latino; 1 Native Hawaiian or other Pacific Islander, non-Hispanic/Latino; 53 Two or more races, non-Hispanic/Latino), 26 international. Average age 34. 257 applicants, 72% accepted, 140 enrolled. *Faculty:* 56 full-time (33 women), 4 part-time/adjunct (2 women). Expenses: Contact institution. *Financial support:* Fellowships, research assistantships, teaching assistantships, career-related internships or fieldwork, Federal Work-Study, institutionally sponsored loans, scholarships/grants, traineeships, health care benefits, and unspecified assistantships available. Support available to part-time students. Financial award application deadline: 6/1; financial award applicants required to submit FAFSA. In 2018, 175 master's, 42 doctorates, 42 other advanced degrees awarded. *Program availability:* Part-time, evening/weekend. Offers adult and higher education (M Ed, PhD); communication, culture and pedagogy for Hispanic (ESL/ELL) populations in educational settings (Graduate Certificate); educational administration, curriculum and supervision (M Ed, Ed D, PhD); educational studies (M Ed, PhD); instructional leadership and academic curriculum (M Ed, PhD); instructional psychology and technology (M Ed, PhD); professional counseling (M Ed); reading specialist (M Ed); special education (M Ed, PhD). *Application fee:* $50 ($100 for international students). Electronic applications accepted. *Application Contact:* Mike Jenkins, Graduate Programs Specialist, 405-325-4525, E-mail: mjenkins@ou.edu. *Dean,* Dr. Gregg Garn, 405-325-1082, Fax: 405-325-7390, E-mail: garn@ou.edu.

Mewbourne College of Earth and Energy Students: 125 full-time (33 women), 107 part-time (21 women); includes 26 minority (4 Black or African American, non-Hispanic/Latino; 2 American Indian or Alaska Native, non-Hispanic/Latino; 3 Asian, non-Hispanic/Latino; 13 Hispanic/Latino; 4 Two or more races, non-Hispanic/Latino), 126 international. Average age 30. 282 applicants, 29% accepted, 53 enrolled. *Faculty:* 45 full-time (6 women), 3 part-time/adjunct (0 women). Expenses: Contact institution. *Financial support:* Research assistantships, teaching assistantships, scholarships/grants, health care benefits, and unspecified assistantships available. Financial award application deadline: 6/1; financial award applicants required to submit FAFSA. In 2018, 56 master's, 16 doctorates awarded. *Program availability:* Part-time, evening/weekend. Offers earth and energy (MS, PhD, Graduate Certificate). *Application fee:* $50 ($100 for international students). Electronic applications accepted. *Application Contact:* Dr. J. Mike Stice, Dean, 405-325-3821, Fax: 405-325-3180, E-mail: mstice@ou.edu. *Dean,* Dr. J. Mike Stice, 405-325-3821, Fax: 405-325-3180, E-mail: mstice@ou.edu.

ConocoPhillips School of Geology and Geophysics *Program availability:* Part-time. Offers geology (MS, PhD); geophysics (MS, PhD). Electronic applications accepted.

Mewbourne School of Petroleum and Geological Engineering Students: 67 full-time (11 women), 65 part-time (11 women); includes 16 minority (3 Black or African American, non-Hispanic/Latino; 1 American Indian or Alaska Native, non-Hispanic/Latino; 1 Asian, non-Hispanic/Latino; 7 Hispanic/Latino; 4 Two or more races, non-Hispanic/Latino), 86 international. Average age 31. 147 applicants, 39% accepted, 31 enrolled. *Faculty:* 19 full-time (1 woman), 1 part-time/adjunct (0 women). Expenses: Contact institution. *Financial support:* Fellowships, research assistantships, teaching assistantships, and scholarships/grants available. Financial award application deadline: 6/1; financial award applicants required to submit FAFSA. In 2018, 27 master's, 10 doctorates awarded. *Program availability:* Part-time, evening/weekend. Offers geological engineering (MS, PhD); natural gas engineering and management (MS); natural gas technology (Graduate Certificate); petroleum engineering (MS, PhD). *Application deadline:* For fall admission, 3/1 for domestic and international students; for spring admission, 9/1 for domestic and international students. *Application fee:* $50 ($100 for international students). Electronic applications accepted. *Application Contact:* Danika Hines-Barnett, Graduate Programs Coordinator, 405-325-2921, E-mail: danika@ou.edu. *Director,* Dr. Runar Nygaard, 405-325-2921, E-mail: runar.nygaard@ou.edu.

Price College of Business Students: 108 full-time (31 women), 267 part-time (84 women); includes 92 minority (16 Black or African American, non-Hispanic/Latino; 9 American Indian or Alaska Native, non-Hispanic/Latino; 16 Asian, non-Hispanic/Latino; 33 Hispanic/Latino; 1 Native Hawaiian or other Pacific Islander, non-Hispanic/Latino; 17 Two or more races, non-Hispanic/Latino), 38 international. Average age 33. 265 applicants, 44% accepted, 83 enrolled. *Faculty:* 58 full-time (16 women), 6 part-time/adjunct (0 women). Expenses: Contact institution. *Financial support:* Fellowships, research assistantships, teaching assistantships, career-related internships or fieldwork, scholarships/grants, health care benefits, and unspecified assistantships available. Support available to part-time students. Financial award application deadline: 6/1; financial award applicants required to submit FAFSA. In 2018, 132 master's, 5 doctorates, 41 other advanced degrees awarded. *Program availability:* Part-time, evening/weekend, 100% online. Offers accounting (M Acc); business administration (MBA, PMBA, PhD); business entrepreneurship (Graduate Certificate); digital technologies (Graduate Certificate); energy (EMBA); foundations of business (Graduate Certificate); management information technology (MS); the business of energy (Graduate Certificate). *Application deadline:* Applications are processed on a rolling basis. *Application fee:* $50 ($100 for international students). Electronic applications accepted. *Application Contact:* Amber Hasbrook, Academic Counselor, 405-325-5815, Fax: 405-325-7753, E-mail: ahasbrook@ou.edu. *Interim Dean,* Wayne Thomas, 405-325-0100, Fax: 405-325-3421, E-mail: wthomas@ou.edu.

Division of Management Information Systems Students: 23 full-time (8 women), 15 part-time (8 women); includes 8 minority (1 Black or African American, non-Hispanic/Latino; 2 Asian, non-Hispanic/Latino; 2 Hispanic/Latino; 3 Two or more races, non-Hispanic/Latino), 10 international. Average age 27. 28 applicants, 25% accepted, 5 enrolled. *Faculty:* 9 full-time (6 women), 1 part-time/adjunct (0 women). Expenses: Contact institution. *Financial support:* Research assistantships, teaching assistantships, career-related internships or fieldwork, scholarships/grants, and unspecified assistantships available. Support available to part-time students. Financial award application deadline: 6/1; financial award applicants required to submit FAFSA. In 2018, 17 master's, 4 other advanced degrees awarded. *Program availability:* Part-time, evening/weekend. Offers digital technologies (Graduate Certificate); management of information technology (MS). *Application deadline:* For fall admission, 6/15 for domestic students, 3/1 for international students; for spring admission, 10/1 for domestic students, 8/1 for international students. Applications are processed on a rolling basis. *Application fee:* $50 ($100 for international students). Electronic applications accepted. *Application Contact:* Jennifer Aragon, Academic Advisor, 405-325-2074, Fax: 405-325-7118, E-mail: jhardman@ou.edu. *Chair/Division Director,* Radhika Santhanam, 405-325-0791, E-mail: radhika@ou.edu.

John T. Steed School of Accounting Students: 10 full-time (7 women), 76 part-time (39 women); includes 33 minority (12 Black or African American, non-Hispanic/Latino; 1 American Indian or Alaska Native, non-Hispanic/Latino; 4 Asian, non-Hispanic/Latino; 12 Hispanic/Latino; 1 Native Hawaiian or other Pacific Islander, non-Hispanic/Latino; 3 Two or more races, non-Hispanic/Latino), 2 international. Average age 35. 71 applicants, 73% accepted, 33 enrolled. *Faculty:* 13 full-time (4 women). Expenses: Contact institution. *Financial support:* In 2018–19, 15 students received support, including 1 fellowship (averaging $5,000 per year), 5 research assistantships (averaging $14,940 per year), 9 teaching assistantships (averaging $13,701 per year); career-related internships or fieldwork, scholarships/grants, and unspecified assistantships also available. Support available to part-time students. Financial award application deadline: 6/1; financial award applicants required to submit FAFSA. In 2018, 19 master's awarded. *Program availability:* Part-time, 100% online. Offers accounting (M Acc). *Application deadline:* For fall admission, 6/15 for domestic students, 3/1 for international students; for spring admission, 11/15 for domestic students, 8/1 for international students; for summer admission, 3/15 for domestic students, 1/1 for international students. Applications are processed on a rolling basis. *Application fee:* $50 ($100 for international students). Electronic applications accepted. *Application Contact:* Jennifer Aragon, Academic Advisor, 405-325-2074, Fax: 405-325-7118, E-mail: jhardman@ou.edu. *Director/Chair,* Wayne Thomas, 405-325-5799, Fax: 405-325-7348, E-mail: wthomas@ou.edu.

Weitzenhoffer Family College of Fine Arts Students: 121 full-time (65 women), 74 part-time (35 women); includes 35 minority (3 Black or African American, non-Hispanic/Latino; 6 American Indian or Alaska Native, non-Hispanic/Latino; 4 Asian, non-Hispanic/Latino; 13 Hispanic/Latino; 9 Two or more races, non-Hispanic/Latino), 32 international. Average age 30. 174 applicants, 55% accepted, 53 enrolled. *Faculty:* 87 full-time (28 women), 1 part-time/adjunct (0 women). Expenses: Contact institution. *Financial support:* Fellowships, research assistantships, teaching assistantships, career-related internships or fieldwork, Federal Work-Study, institutionally sponsored loans, scholarships/grants, health care benefits, tuition waivers, and unspecified assistantships available. Support available to part-time students. Financial award application deadline: 6/1; financial award applicants required to submit FAFSA. In 2018, 50 master's, 11 doctorates awarded. Offers fine arts (M Mus, M Mus Ed, MA, MFA,

DMA, PhD, Graduate Certificate). *Application fee:* $50 ($100 for international students). Electronic applications accepted. *Application Contact:* Dr. Mary Margaret Holt, Dean, 405-325-7370, Fax: 405-325-1667, E-mail: marymholt@ou.edu. *Dean,* Dr. Mary Margaret Holt, 405-325-7370, Fax: 405-325-1667, E-mail: marymholt@ou.edu.

Helmerich School of Drama Offers drama (MA). Electronic applications accepted.

School of Dance Students: 5 full-time (all women), 1 (woman) part-time; includes 1 minority (Two or more races, non-Hispanic/Latino). Average age 40. 1 applicant, 100% accepted, 1 enrolled. *Faculty:* 6 full-time (2 women). Expenses: Contact institution. *Financial support:* Fellowships, teaching assistantships, health care benefits, and unspecified assistantships available. Financial award application deadline: 6/1; financial award applicants required to submit FAFSA. In 2018, 5 master's awarded. Offers dance (MFA); modern dance (MFA). *Application deadline:* For fall admission, 4/15 for domestic students, 3/1 for international students. Applications are processed on a rolling basis. *Application fee:* $50 ($100 for international students). Electronic applications accepted. *Application Contact:* Roxanne Lyst, Graduate Liaison, 405-325-4051, E-mail: rlyst@ou.edu. *Director,* Michael R. Bearden, 405-325-4461, E-mail: mrbearden@ou.edu.

School of Music Students: 97 full-time (47 women), 65 part-time (26 women); includes 22 minority (3 Black or African American, non-Hispanic/Latino; 3 American Indian or Alaska Native, non-Hispanic/Latino; 3 Asian, non-Hispanic/Latino; 8 Hispanic/Latino; 5 Two or more races, non-Hispanic/Latino), 30 international. Average age 29. 157 applicants, 56% accepted, 47 enrolled. *Faculty:* 53 full-time (15 women). Expenses: Contact institution. *Financial support:* Fellowships, research assistantships, teaching assistantships, health care benefits, tuition waivers, and unspecified assistantships available. Financial award application deadline: 6/1; financial award applicants required to submit FAFSA. In 2018, 37 master's, 10 doctorates awarded. Offers choral conducting (M Mus); composition (M Mus); conducting (M Mus Ed, DMA); general (M Mus Ed); instrumental (M Mus Ed); instrumental conducting (M Mus); music composition (DMA); music education (PhD); music performance (Graduate Certificate); music theory (M Mus); musicology (M Mus); organ (M Mus, DMA); piano (M Mus, DMA); piano pedagogy (M Mus Ed); voice (M Mus, DMA); wind/percussion/string (M Mus); wind/percussion/string instruments (DMA). *Application deadline:* For fall admission, 2/1 for domestic and international students; for spring admission, 10/1 for domestic students, 9/1 for international students; for summer admission, 2/1 for domestic and international students. Applications are processed on a rolling basis. *Application fee:* $50 ($100 for international students). Electronic applications accepted. *Application Contact:* Jan Russell, Graduate Admissions and Recruiting Advisor, 405-325-5393, Fax: 405-325-7574, E-mail: jrussell@ou.edu. *Director,* Dr. Roland Barrett, 405-325-2081, Fax: 405-325-7574, E-mail: rcbarrett@ou.edu.

School of Visual Arts Students: 19 full-time (13 women), 8 part-time (all women); includes 12 minority (3 American Indian or Alaska Native, non-Hispanic/Latino; 1 Asian, non-Hispanic/Latino; 5 Hispanic/Latino; 3 Two or more races, non-Hispanic/Latino), 1 international. Average age 34. 16 applicants, 44% accepted, 5 enrolled. *Faculty:* 24 full-time (8 women). Expenses: Contact institution. *Financial support:* Fellowships, research assistantships, teaching assistantships, career-related internships or fieldwork, Federal Work-Study, institutionally sponsored loans, scholarships/grants, health care benefits, tuition waivers, and unspecified assistantships available. Support available to part-time students. Financial award application deadline: 6/1; financial award applicants required to submit FAFSA. In 2018, 7 master's, 1 doctorate awarded. Offers art (MFA); art history (MA, PhD); design (MFA). *Application deadline:* For fall admission, 2/1 for domestic and international students. *Application fee:* $50 ($100 for international students). Electronic applications accepted. *Application Contact:* Curtis Jones, MFA Coordinator, 405-325-2691, E-mail: chivo@ou.edu. *Interim Director,* Pete Froslie, E-mail: froslie@ou.edu.

UNIVERSITY OF OKLAHOMA HEALTH SCIENCES CENTER, Oklahoma City, OK 73190

General Information State-supported, coed, upper-level institution. CGS member. *Graduate housing:* Rooms and/or apartments available on a first-come, first-served basis to single and married students. *Research affiliation:* Oklahoma Medical Research Foundation, Dean A. McGee Eye Institute (ophthalmology), Oklahoma Children's Memorial Hospital (pediatrics), Veterans Administration Medical Center (clinical and applied medicine), University of Oklahoma Medical Center, Peggy and Charles Stephenson Oklahoma Cancer Center (cancer research).

GRADUATE UNITS

College of Dentistry Offers dentistry (MS, DDS, Certificate); general dentistry (Certificate); orthodontics (MS); periodontics (MS). Electronic applications accepted.

College of Medicine Offers biochemistry (MS, PhD); biochemistry and molecular biology (MS, PhD); biological psychology (MS, PhD); cell biology (MS, PhD); genetic counseling (MS); immunology (MS, PhD); medical radiation physics (MS, PhD); medical sciences (MS); medicine (MHS, MS, MD, PhD); microbiology (MS, PhD); microbiology and immunology (MS, PhD); molecular biology (MS, PhD); neuroscience (MS, PhD); pathology (PhD); physician associate (MHS); physiology (MS, PhD); psychiatry and behavioral sciences (MS); radiological sciences (MS, PhD). Electronic applications accepted.

College of Pharmacy Offers pharmacy (MS, PhD, Pharm D).

Graduate College *Program availability:* Part-time, evening/weekend.

College of Allied Health *Program availability:* Part-time. Offers allied health (MOT, MPT, MS, Au D, PhD, Certificate); allied health sciences (PhD); audiology (MS, Au D, PhD); communication sciences and disorders (Certificate); education of the deaf (MS); nutritional sciences (MS); occupational therapy (MOT); physical therapy (MPT); rehabilitation sciences (MS); speech-language pathology (MS, PhD).

College of Nursing *Program availability:* Part-time. Offers nursing (MS). MS/MBA offered jointly with Oklahoma State University and University of Oklahoma.

Hudson College of Public Health *Program availability:* Part-time. Offers biostatistics (MPH, MS, Dr PH, PhD); epidemiology (MPH, MS, Dr PH, PhD); general public health (MPH, Dr PH); health administration and policy (MHA, MPH, MS, Dr PH, PhD); health promotion sciences (MPH, MS, Dr PH, PhD); occupational and environmental health (MPH, MS, Dr PH, PhD); preparedness and terrorism (MPH); public health (MHA, MPH, MS, Dr PH, PhD).

UNIVERSITY OF OREGON, Eugene, OR 97403

General Information State-supported, coed, university. CGS member. *Graduate housing:* Rooms or apartments available to single and married students. *Research affiliation:* Oregon Research Institute, Battelle–Pacific Northwest National Laboratory, National Renewable Energy Laboratory (NREL), Stanford Linear Accelerator Center, Naval Research Laboratories.

GRADUATE UNITS

Graduate School *Program availability:* Part-time, evening/weekend. Offers applied information management (MS).

Charles H. Lundquist College of Business *Program availability:* Part-time, evening/weekend. Offers accounting (M Actg, PhD); business (M Actg, MA, MBA, MS, PhD); decision sciences (MA, MS); finance (PhD); management (PhD); management: general business (MBA); marketing (PhD); sports product management (MS).

College of Arts and Sciences *Program availability:* Part-time, evening/weekend. Offers anthropology (MA, MS, PhD); arts and sciences (MA, MFA, MS, PhD); Asian studies (MA); biochemistry (MA, MS, PhD); chemistry (MA, MS, PhD); Chinese (MA, PhD); classical civilization (MA); classics (MA); clinical psychology (PhD); cognitive psychology (MA, MS, PhD); comparative literature (MA, PhD); computer and information science (MA, MS, PhD); creative writing (MFA); developmental psychology (MA, MS, PhD); ecology and evolution (MA, MS, PhD); economics (MA, MS, PhD); English (MA, PhD); environmental science, studies, and policy (PhD); environmental studies (MA, MS); French (MA); geography (MA, MS, PhD); geological sciences (MA, MS, PhD); Germanic languages and literatures (MA, PhD); Greek (MA); history (MA, PhD); human physiology (MS); independent study: folklore (MA, MS); international studies (MA); Italian (MA); Japanese (MA, PhD); language teaching studies (MA); Latin (MA); linguistics (MA, PhD); marine biology (MA, MS, PhD); mathematics (MA, MS, PhD); molecular, cellular and genetic biology (PhD); neuroscience and development (PhD); philosophy (MA, PhD); physics (MA, MS, PhD); physiological psychology (MA, MS, PhD); political science (MA, MS, PhD); psychology (MA, MS, PhD); Romance languages (MA, PhD); Russian and East European Studies (MA); social/personality psychology (MA, MS, PhD); sociology (MA, MS, PhD); Spanish (MA); theater arts (MA, MFA, MS, PhD).

College of Design *Program availability:* Part-time, evening/weekend. Offers architecture (M Arch); art (MFA); art history (MA, PhD); community and regional planning (MCRP); design (M Arch, MA, MCRP, MFA, MI Arch, MLA, MNM, MPA, MS, PhD, Graduate Certificate); historic preservation (MS); interior architecture (MI Arch, MS); landscape architecture (MLA, PhD); nonprofit management (MNM, Graduate Certificate); public administration (MPA); sports product design (MS).

College of Education *Program availability:* Part-time. Offers communication disorders and sciences (MA, MS, PhD); counseling psychology (PhD); couples and family therapy (MS); critical and sociocultural studies in education (PhD); curriculum and teacher education (MA, MS); educational leadership (MS, D Ed, PhD); prevention science (M Ed, MS, PhD); school psychology (MS, PhD); special education (M Ed, MA, MS, PhD).

School of Journalism and Communication *Program availability:* Part-time. Offers journalism (MA, MS); media studies (MA, MS, PhD); multimedia journalism (MA, MS); strategic communication (MA, MS).

School of Music *Program availability:* Part-time. Offers composition (M Mus, DMA, PhD); conducting (M Mus); dance (MA, MS); jazz studies (M Mus); music (M Mus, MA, MS, DMA, PhD); music education (M Mus, DMA, PhD); music history (PhD); music theory (PhD); performance (M Mus, DMA); piano pedagogy (M Mus).

School of Law Offers law (MA, MS, JD).

UNIVERSITY OF OTTAWA, Ottawa, ON K1N 6N5, Canada

General Information Province-supported, coed, university. *Graduate housing:* Rooms and/or apartments available on a first-come, first-served basis to single and married students. Housing application deadline: 3/15. *Research affiliation:* IBM (performance analytics software, supercomputing), General Electric Company (GE) (hardware, imaging, medical devices), Rio Tinto Alcan (aluminum and aluminum products), Pratt and Whitney Canada (turbine engines, advanced materials, aerospace), Wright Medical Technology Canada (orthopedic medical devices), Air Products and Chemicals Inc. (industrial gases (hydrogen), performance materials, equipment and technology).

GRADUATE UNITS

Faculty of Graduate and Postdoctoral Studies *Program availability:* Part-time, evening/weekend. Offers biomedical engineering (MA Sc); e-business technologies (M Sc, MEBT); globalization and international development (MA); population health (PhD); systems science (M Sc, M Sys Sc, Certificate). MCL, MRE, MP Th offered jointly with Saint Paul University. Electronic applications accepted.

Faculty of Arts *Program availability:* Part-time, evening/weekend. Offers arts (M Geog, M Mus, M Sc, MA, PhD, Certificate); classical studies (MA); communication (MA); directing for theatre (MA); economics (PhD); English (MA, PhD); geography (M Geog, M Sc, MA, PhD); history (PhD); interpreting (MA); lettres Françaises (MA, PhD); linguistics (MA, PhD); music (M Mus, MA); orchestral studies (Certificate); philosophy (PhD); piano pedagogy research (Certificate); political science (PhD); psychology (PhD); religious studies (PhD); Spanish (MA, PhD); Spanish translation (MA); translation (MA); translation studies (PhD). Electronic applications accepted.

Faculty of Education *Program availability:* Online learning. Offers education (M Ed, MA Ed, PhD, Certificate). Electronic applications accepted.

Faculty of Engineering Offers chemical and biological engineering (M Eng, MA Sc, PhD); civil engineering (M Eng, MA Sc, PhD); computer science (MCS, PhD); electrical and computer engineering (M Eng, MA Sc, PhD); engineering (M Eng, MA Sc, MCS, PhD, Certificate); engineering management (M Eng); information technology (Certificate); mechanical and aerospace engineering (M Eng, MA Sc, PhD); project management (Certificate). Electronic applications accepted.

Faculty of Health Sciences *Program availability:* Part-time, evening/weekend. Offers audiology (M Sc); health sciences (M Sc, MA, PhD, Certificate); human kinetics (MA); nurse practitioner (Certificate); nursing (M Sc, PhD); nursing/primary health care (M Sc); orthophony (M Sc). Electronic applications accepted.

Faculty of Law *Program availability:* Part-time, evening/weekend. Offers law (LL M, LL D). Electronic applications accepted.

Faculty of Medicine Offers biochemistry (M Sc, PhD); cellular and molecular medicine (M Sc, PhD); epidemiology (M Sc); medicine (M Sc, MD, PhD); microbiology and immunology (M Sc, PhD). Electronic applications accepted.

Faculty of Science *Program availability:* Part-time, evening/weekend. Offers biology (M Sc, PhD); chemistry (M Sc, PhD); earth sciences (M Sc, PhD); mathematics and statistics (M Sc, PhD); physics (M Sc, PhD); science (M Sc, PhD). Electronic applications accepted.

Faculty of Social Sciences *Program availability:* Part-time, evening/weekend. Offers criminology (MA, MCA); economics (MA, PhD); education (MA); English (MA); history (MA); human kinetics (MA); law (LL M); lettres Françaises (MA); nursing (M Sc); pastoral studies (MA); political science (MA); political studies (MA, PhD); psychology (PhD); religious studies (MA); social sciences (LL M, M Sc, MA, MCA, MSS, PhD); social work (MSS); sociology (MA); sociology and anthropology (MA). Electronic applications accepted.

Telfer School of Management Program availability: Part-time, evening/weekend. Offers business administration (MBA); executive business administration (EMBA); health administration (MHA); management (EMBA, MBA, MHA). Electronic applications accepted.

UNIVERSITY OF PENNSYLVANIA, Philadelphia, PA 19104

General Information Independent, coed, university. CGS member. Enrollment: 22,376 graduate, professional, and undergraduate students; 11,053 full-time matriculated graduate/professional students (5,787 women), 1,959 part-time matriculated graduate/professional students (1,269 women). Enrollment by degree level: 7,003 master's, 5,843 doctoral, 166 other advanced degrees. Graduate faculty: 2,666 full-time (898 women), 2,453 part-time/adjunct (1,027 women). Graduate housing: Rooms and/or apartments available on a first-come, first-served basis to single and married students. Student services: Campus employment opportunities, campus safety program, career counseling, child daycare facilities, exercise/wellness program, free psychological counseling, international student services, low-cost health insurance, multicultural affairs office, services for students with disabilities, writing training. Library facilities: Van Pelt Library plus 14 others. Collection: Books: 6.4 million (physical); Serial titles: 188,604 (physical). Study areas open 24 hours, 5–7 days a week; students can reserve study rooms.

Computer facilities: Computer purchase and lease plans are available. A campuswide network can be accessed. Online class registration, billing information, financial aid application, status, academic records, student services are available.
Website: http://www.upenn.edu/

GRADUATE UNITS

Annenberg School for Communication Average age 30. 257 applicants, 7% accepted, 11 enrolled. Expenses: Contact institution. Financial support: In 2018–19, 80 students received support. In 2018, 6 doctorates awarded. Offers communication (PhD). Application Contact: Joanne Murray, Assistant Dean for Graduate Studies, 215-573-6349, Fax: 215-898-2024, E-mail: joanne.murray@asc.upenn.edu.

Graduate School of Education Average age 31. 3,105 applicants, 51% accepted, 888 enrolled. Expenses: Contact institution. In 2018, 559 master's, 77 doctorates awarded. Program availability: Part-time, evening/weekend, online learning. Offers education (M Phil, MS, MS Ed, Ed D, PhD, Certificate); educational leadership (Ed D); learning leadership (Ed D); medical education (MS Ed, Certificate); teaching (MS Ed); urban teaching (MS Ed). Application fee: $80. Electronic applications accepted. Application Contact: Dr. Pam Grossman, Dean, 215-898-7014, Fax: 215-746-6884, E-mail: admissions@gse.upenn.edu. Dean, Dr. Pam Grossman, 215-898-7014, Fax: 215-746-6884, E-mail: admissions@gse.upenn.edu.

Division of Educational Linguistics Average age 25. 554 applicants, 34% accepted, 98 enrolled. Expenses: Contact institution. Financial support: In 2018–19, 55 students received support. Fellowships, research assistantships, teaching assistantships, Federal Work-Study, scholarships/grants, health care benefits, and unspecified assistantships available. In 2018, 91 master's, 6 doctorates awarded. Program availability: Part-time. Offers educational linguistics (MS Ed, PhD); intercultural communication (MS Ed); teaching English to speakers of other languages (MS Ed). Application deadline: For fall admission, 12/8 priority date for domestic and international students. Applications are processed on a rolling basis. Application fee: $75. Electronic applications accepted. Application Contact: Kristina Lewis, Program Manager, 215-898-5212, E-mail: klewi@upenn.edu. Program Manager, Kristina Lewis, 215-898-5212, E-mail: klewi@upenn.edu.

Division of Education Policy Average age 28. 250 applicants, 50% accepted, 34 enrolled. Expenses: Contact institution. Financial support: In 2018–19, 13 students received support. Fellowships, research assistantships, teaching assistantships, Federal Work-Study, scholarships/grants, and health care benefits available. In 2018, 16 master's, 2 doctorates awarded. Program availability: Part-time. Offers education policy (MS Ed, PhD). Application deadline: For fall admission, 12/8 priority date for domestic and international students. Applications are processed on a rolling basis. Application fee: $75. Electronic applications accepted. Application Contact: Krista Featherstone, Program Manager, 215-573-8075, E-mail: kfeat@upenn.edu. Program Manager, Krista Featherstone, 215-573-8075, E-mail: kfeat@upenn.edu.

Division of Higher Education Students: 106 full-time (57 women), 44 part-time (31 women); includes 67 minority (32 Black or African American, non-Hispanic/Latino; 15 Asian, non-Hispanic/Latino; 15 Hispanic/Latino; 5 Two or more races, non-Hispanic/Latino), 4 international. Average age 35. 334 applicants, 55% accepted, 96 enrolled. Expenses: Contact institution. Financial support: In 2018–19, 24 students received support. Fellowships, research assistantships, teaching assistantships, Federal Work-Study, scholarships/grants, health care benefits, and unspecified assistantships available. In 2018, 53 master's, 33 doctorates awarded. Program availability: Part-time. Offers higher education (MS Ed, Ed D, PhD); higher education management (Ed D). Application deadline: For fall admission, 12/8 priority date for domestic and international students. Application fee: $80. Electronic applications accepted. Application Contact: Dr. Ross Aikins, Program Manager, 215-898-8398, E-mail: raikins@upenn.edu. Program Manager, Dr. Ross Aikins, 215-898-8398, E-mail: raikins@upenn.edu.

Division of Human Development and Quantitative Methods Students: 192 full-time (160 women), 11 part-time (8 women); includes 61 minority (25 Black or African American, non-Hispanic/Latino; 17 Asian, non-Hispanic/Latino; 11 Hispanic/Latino; 8 Two or more races, non-Hispanic/Latino), 76 international. Average age 27. 622 applicants, 52% accepted, 192 enrolled. Expenses: Contact institution. Financial support: In 2018–19, 95 students received support. Fellowships, research assistantships, teaching assistantships, career-related internships or fieldwork, Federal Work-Study, scholarships/grants, health care benefits, and unspecified assistantships available. In 2018, 152 master's, 6 doctorates awarded. Program availability: Part-time-only, evening/weekend. Offers counseling and mental health services (M Phil, MS Ed); human development (MS Ed, PhD); quantitative methods (M Phil, MS, PhD); school and mental health counseling (MS Ed); statistics, measurement, assessment, and research technology (MS). Application deadline: For fall admission, 12/8 priority date for domestic and international students. Applications are processed on a rolling basis. Application fee: $75. Electronic applications accepted. Application Contact: Dr. Elizabeth Mackenzie, Program Manager, 215-898-4176, E-mail: emackenz@upenn.edu. Program Manager, Dr. Elizabeth Mackenzie, 215-898-4176, E-mail: emackenz@upenn.edu.

Division of Literacy, Culture, and International Education Students: 80 full-time (68 women), 16 part-time (13 women); includes 28 minority (6 Black or African American, non-Hispanic/Latino; 9 Asian, non-Hispanic/Latino; 7 Hispanic/Latino; 6 Two or more races, non-Hispanic/Latino), 30 international. Average age 30. 462 applicants, 47% accepted, 95 enrolled. Expenses: Contact institution. Financial support: In 2018–19, 44 students received support. Fellowships, research assistantships, teaching assistantships, Federal Work-Study, scholarships/grants, and health care benefits

available. In 2018, 71 master's, 6 doctorates awarded. Program availability: Part-time. Offers education, culture and society (MS Ed, PhD); international educational development (MS Ed); language and literacy (MS Ed); reading/writing/literacy (MS Ed, Ed D, PhD). Application deadline: For fall admission, 12/8 priority date for domestic and international students. Applications are processed on a rolling basis. Application fee: $75. Electronic applications accepted. Application Contact: Dr. Alex Posecznick, Program Manager, 215-573-3947, E-mail: alpos@upenn.edu. Program Manager, Dr. Alex Posecznick, 215-573-3947, E-mail: alpos@upenn.edu.

Division of Teaching, Learning, and Leadership Students: 198 full-time (139 women), 68 part-time (46 women); includes 81 minority (31 Black or African American, non-Hispanic/Latino; 20 Asian, non-Hispanic/Latino; 10 Hispanic/Latino; 20 Two or more races, non-Hispanic/Latino), 46 international. Average age 32. 746 applicants, 62% accepted, 269 enrolled. Expenses: Contact institution. Financial support: In 2018–19, 13 students received support. Fellowships, research assistantships, teaching assistantships, Federal Work-Study, scholarships/grants, health care benefits, and unspecified assistantships available. In 2018, 125 master's, 5 doctorates awarded. Program availability: Part-time. Offers education entrepreneurship (MS Ed); educational leadership (MS Ed, Ed D, PhD); elementary education (MS Ed); learning sciences and technologies (MS Ed); school leadership (MS Ed); secondary education (MS Ed); teacher education (MS Ed); teaching and learning (MS Ed); teaching, learning, and leadership (MS Ed); teaching, learning, and teacher education (Ed D, PhD). Application deadline: For fall admission, 12/8 priority date for domestic and international students. Applications are processed on a rolling basis. Application fee: $80. Electronic applications accepted. Application Contact: Administrative Coordinator, 215-898-4176. Program Manager, Dr. Veronica Aplenc, 215-898-2566, E-mail: vaplenc@upenn.edu.

Law School Students: 755 full-time (386 women); includes 226 minority (53 Black or African American, non-Hispanic/Latino; 2 American Indian or Alaska Native, non-Hispanic/Latino; 81 Asian, non-Hispanic/Latino; 51 Hispanic/Latino; 39 Two or more races, non-Hispanic/Latino), 39 international. Average age 27. 6,413 applicants, 15% accepted, 238 enrolled. Faculty: 87 full-time (34 women), 155 part-time/adjunct (52 women). Expenses: Contact institution. Financial support: In 2018–19, 390 students received support, including 56 research assistantships (averaging $1,166 per year), 13 teaching assistantships (averaging $3,501 per year); fellowships, career-related internships or fieldwork, Federal Work-Study, institutionally sponsored loans, and scholarships/grants also available. Financial award application deadline: 3/1; financial award applicants required to submit CSS PROFILE or FAFSA. In 2018, 24 master's, 250 doctorates awarded. Offers law (LL CM, LL M, ML, JD, SJD). JD/LLM offered jointly with Hong Kong University; JD/MA Global Governance Studies with Sciences Po (Paris); JD/LLM Transnational Arbitration with Sciences Po (Paris). Application deadline: For fall admission, 3/1 for domestic and international students. Applications are processed on a rolling basis. Application fee: $80. Electronic applications accepted. Application Contact: Renee Post, Associate Dean of Admissions and Financial Aid, 215-898-7400, Fax: 215-898-9606, E-mail: contactadmissions@law.upenn.edu. Dean, Theodore W. Ruger, 215-898-7463, Fax: 215-573-2025, E-mail: deanruger@law.upenn.edu.

Perelman School of Medicine Offers environmental health (MPH); generalist (MPH); global health (MPH); health policy research (MSHP); medical ethics and health policy (MBE, MSME); medicine (MBE, MPH, MRA, MS, MSCE, MSHP, MSME, MTR, MD, PhD); regulatory affairs (MRA); translational research (MTR).

Biomedical Graduate Studies Offers biochemistry and molecular biophysics (PhD); biomedical studies (MS, PhD); biostatistics (MS, PhD); cancer biology (PhD); cell biology, physiology, and metabolism (PhD); developmental stem cell regenerative biology (PhD); epidemiology (PhD); gene therapy and vaccines (PhD); genetics and gene regulation (PhD); genomics and computational biology (PhD); immunology (PhD); microbiology, virology, and parasitology (PhD); neuroscience (PhD); pharmacology (PhD).

Center for Clinical Epidemiology and Biostatistics Program availability: Part-time. Offers clinical epidemiology (MSCE). Electronic applications accepted.

School of Arts and Sciences Students: 1,648 full-time (796 women), 390 part-time (228 women); includes 359 minority (87 Black or African American, non-Hispanic/Latino; 1 American Indian or Alaska Native, non-Hispanic/Latino; 127 Asian, non-Hispanic/Latino; 87 Hispanic/Latino; 1 Native Hawaiian or other Pacific Islander, non-Hispanic/Latino; 56 Two or more races, non-Hispanic/Latino), 689 international. Average age 30. 6,438 applicants, 17% accepted, 610 enrolled. Faculty: 501 full-time (178 women), 22 part-time/adjunct (10 women). Expenses: Contact institution. In 2018, 517 master's, 185 doctorates, 11 other advanced degrees awarded. Program availability: Part-time, evening/weekend. Offers Africana studies (MA, PhD); ancient history (AM, PhD); anthropology (AM, MS, PhD); applied mathematics and computational science (PhD); art and archaeology of the Mediterranean world (AM, PhD); arts and sciences (AM, MA, MBA, MES, MGA, MGA, MLA, MPA, MS, PhD, Certificate); biology (PhD); chemistry (MS, PhD); classical studies (AM, PhD); comparative literature (AM, PhD); criminology (MA, MS, PhD); demography (AM, PhD); earth and environmental science (MS, PhD); East Asian languages and civilizations (AM, PhD); economics (AM, PhD); English (AM, PhD); French (AM, PhD); Germanic languages (AM, PhD); history (AM, PhD); history and sociology of science (AM, PhD); history of art (AM, PhD); international studies (AM); Italian (AM, PhD); linguistics (AM, PhD); literary theory (AM, PhD); mathematics (AM, PhD); medical physics (MS); music (AM, PhD); Near Eastern languages and civilizations (AM, PhD); philosophy (AM, PhD); physics (PhD); political science (AM, PhD); psychology (PhD); religious studies (PhD); sociology (AM, PhD); South Asian regional studies (AM, PhD); Spanish (AM, PhD). Application fee: $80.

College of Liberal and Professional Studies Students: 219 full-time (144 women), 295 part-time (178 women); includes 101 minority (31 Black or African American, non-Hispanic/Latino; 1 American Indian or Alaska Native, non-Hispanic/Latino; 35 Asian, non-Hispanic/Latino; 16 Hispanic/Latino; 1 Native Hawaiian or other Pacific Islander, non-Hispanic/Latino; 17 Two or more races, non-Hispanic/Latino), 103 international. Average age 34. 633 applicants, 52% accepted, 249 enrolled. Expenses: Contact institution. In 2018, 180 master's awarded. Offers applied geosciences (MSAG); applied positive psychology (MAP); chemical sciences (MCS); environmental studies (MES); individualized study (MLA); liberal arts (M Phil); medical physics (MMP); organization dynamics (M Phil). Application Contact: Nora Lewis, Vice Dean, Professional and Liberal Education, 215-898-7326, E-mail: nlewis@sas.upenn.edu. Vice Dean, Professional and Liberal Education, Nora Lewis, 215-898-7326, E-mail: nlewis@sas.upenn.edu.

Fels Institute of Government Students: 30 full-time (15 women), 60 part-time (33 women); includes 25 minority (4 Black or African American, non-Hispanic/Latino; 10 Asian, non-Hispanic/Latino; 8 Hispanic/Latino; 3 Two or more races, non-Hispanic/Latino), 4 international. Average age 32. 757 applicants, 41% accepted, 240 enrolled. Expenses: Contact institution. Financial support: Application deadline: 1/1. In 2018, 48 master's, 10 other advanced degrees awarded. Program availability: Part-time, evening/weekend. Offers economic development and growth (Certificate);

government administration (MGA); nonprofit administration (Certificate); organization dynamics (MS); politics (Certificate); public administration (MPA); public finance (Certificate).

Joseph H. Lauder Institute of Management and International Studies Offers international studies (MA); management and international studies (MBA). Applications must be made concurrently and separately to the Wharton MBA program. Electronic applications accepted.

School of Dental Medicine Offers dental medicine (DMD).

School of Engineering and Applied Science Students: 1,283 full-time (420 women), 407 part-time (131 women); includes 234 minority (15 Black or African American, non-Hispanic/Latino; 1 American Indian or Alaska Native, non-Hispanic/Latino; 141 Asian, non-Hispanic/Latino; 45 Hispanic/Latino; 32 Two or more races, non-Hispanic/Latino), 1,048 international. Average age 25. 9,042 applicants, 20% accepted, 928 enrolled. *Faculty:* 124 full-time (22 women), 27 part-time/adjunct (4 women). Expenses: Contact institution. In 2018, 647 master's, 73 doctorates awarded. *Program availability:* Part-time. Offers bioengineering (MSE, PhD); biotechnology (MBT); chemical and biomolecular engineering (MSE, PhD); computer and information science (MSE, PhD); computer and information technology (MCIT); computer graphics and game technology (MSE); data science (MSE); electrical and systems engineering (MSE, PhD); embedded systems (MSE); engineering and applied science (MBT, MCIT, MIPD, MSE, PhD); integrated product design (MIPD, MSE); materials science and engineering (MSE, PhD); mechanical engineering and applied mechanics (MSE, PhD); nanotechnology (MSE); robotics (MSE); scientific computing (MSE). *Application deadline:* For fall admission, 12/15 for domestic and international students. *Application fee:* $80. Electronic applications accepted. *Application Contact:* William Fenton, Assistant Director of Graduate Admissions, 215-898-4542, Fax: 215-573-5577, E-mail: gradstudies@seas.upenn.edu.

School of Nursing Students: 250 full-time (205 women), 474 part-time (426 women); includes 204 minority (47 Black or African American, non-Hispanic/Latino; 84 Asian, non-Hispanic/Latino; 41 Hispanic/Latino; 32 Two or more races, non-Hispanic/Latino), 14 international. Average age 32. 593 applicants, 54% accepted, 290 enrolled. *Faculty:* 60 full-time (52 women), 33 part-time/adjunct (29 women). Expenses: Contact institution. In 2018, 321 master's, 15 doctorates awarded. *Program availability:* Part-time, online learning. Offers adult and special populations (MSN); adult gerontology clinical nurse specialist (MSN); adult-gerontology acute care nurse practitioner (MSN); adult-gerontology primary care nurse practitioner (MSN); child and family (MSN); family nurse practitioner (MSN, Certificate); geropsychiatrics (MSN); health leadership (MSN); neonatal clinical nurse specialist (MSN); neonatal nurse practitioner (MSN); nurse anesthesia (MSN); nurse midwifery (MSN); nursing (MSN, PhD, Certificate); nursing and health care administration (MSN, PhD); pediatric acute care nurse practitioner (MSN); pediatric clinical nurse specialist (MSN); pediatric primary care nurse practitioner (MSN); women's health/gender related nurse practitioner (MSN). *Application Contact:* Sylvia English, Enrollment Management Coordinator, 215-898-8439, Fax: 215-573-8439, E-mail: sylviaj@nursing.upenn.edu. *Assistant Dean for Admissions and Academic Affairs,* Dr. Christina Costanzo Clark, 215-898-4271, Fax: 215-573-8439, E-mail: costanzo@nursing.upenn.edu.

School of Social Policy and Practice Students: 454 full-time (385 women), 100 part-time (86 women); includes 176 minority (65 Black or African American, non-Hispanic/Latino; 3 American Indian or Alaska Native, non-Hispanic/Latino; 44 Asian, non-Hispanic/Latino; 10 Hispanic/Latino; 54 Two or more races, non-Hispanic/Latino), 38 international. Average age 30. 1,035 applicants, 304 enrolled. *Faculty:* 26 full-time (14 women), 58 part-time/adjunct (33 women). Expenses: Contact institution. *Financial support:* In 2018–19, 336 students received support, including 24 fellowships (averaging $24,378 per year); career-related internships or fieldwork, Federal Work-Study, institutionally sponsored loans, scholarships/grants, tuition waivers (partial), and unspecified assistantships also available. Support available to part-time students. Financial award applicants required to submit FAFSA. In 2018, 252 master's, 17 doctorates awarded. *Program availability:* Part-time, 100% online, blended/hybrid learning. Offers social policy and practice (MNPL, MSSP, MSW, DSW, PhD); social welfare (PhD); social work (MNPL, MSSP, MSW, DSW). *Application deadline:* For fall admission, 2/1 priority date for domestic and international students. Applications are processed on a rolling basis. *Application fee:* $65. Electronic applications accepted. *Application Contact:* Dr. Mary C. Mazzola, Associate Dean, Enrollment Management, 215-898-5550, Fax: 215-573-2099, E-mail: mmazzola@sp2.upenn.edu. *Dean,* Dr. Sara S. Bachman, 215-898-5541, Fax: 215-573-2099, E-mail: deansoffice@sp2.upenn.edu.

School of Veterinary Medicine Students: 478 full-time (398 women), 4 part-time (all women); includes 67 minority (4 Black or African American, non-Hispanic/Latino; 25 Asian, non-Hispanic/Latino; 27 Hispanic/Latino; 11 Two or more races, non-Hispanic/Latino), 4 international. Average age 26. 1,146 applicants, 11% accepted, 121 enrolled. *Faculty:* 110 full-time (54 women), 58 part-time/adjunct (41 women). Expenses: Contact institution. In 2018, 114 doctorates awarded. Offers veterinary medicine (VMD).

Stuart Weitzman School of Design Students: 700 full-time (409 women), 12 part-time (5 women); includes 98 minority (14 Black or African American, non-Hispanic/Latino; 1 American Indian or Alaska Native, non-Hispanic/Latino; 36 Asian, non-Hispanic/Latino; 35 Hispanic/Latino; 1 Native Hawaiian or other Pacific Islander, non-Hispanic/Latino; 11 Two or more races, non-Hispanic/Latino), 406 international. Average age 27. 1,861 applicants, 47% accepted, 361 enrolled. *Faculty:* 41 full-time (16 women), 17 part-time/adjunct (5 women). Expenses: Contact institution. *Financial support:* In 2018–19, 29 students received support. In 2018, 291 master's, 6 doctorates, 53 other advanced degrees awarded. *Program availability:* Part-time. Offers architecture (M Arch, PhD); city and regional planning (PhD); city planning (MCP); design (M Arch, MCP, MEBD, MFA, MLA, MS, MUSA, PhD, Advanced Certificate, Certificate); ecological architecture (Certificate); emerging design and research (Certificate); environmental building design (MEBD); fine arts (MFA); GIS and spatial analysis (Certificate); historic preservation (MS, Certificate); land preservation (Certificate); landscape architecture (MLA); landscape studies (Certificate); time-based and interactive media (Certificate); urban design (Certificate); urban redevelopment (Certificate); urban spatial analytics (MUSA). *Application fee:* $80.

Wharton School *Program availability:* Evening/weekend. Offers accounting (PhD); applied economics (PhD); business (MBA, PhD); business administration (MBA); business and public policy (MBA, PhD); ethics and legal studies (PhD); finance (PhD); health care management (MBA, PhD); health care management and economics (PhD); insurance and risk management (MBA, PhD); legal studies and business ethics (MBA, PhD); management (PhD); marketing (PhD); operations and information management (PhD); real estate (MBA, PhD); statistics (MBA, PhD). Electronic applications accepted.

The Wharton MBA Program for Executives *Program availability:* Evening/weekend. Offers executive business administration (MBA).

UNIVERSITY OF PHILOSOPHICAL RESEARCH, Los Angeles, CA 90027

General Information Proprietary, coed, graduate-only institution.

GRADUATE UNITS

Master's in Consciousness Studies Program Offers consciousness studies (MA). Electronic applications accepted.

Master's in Transformational Psychology Program Offers transformational psychology (MA). Electronic applications accepted.

UNIVERSITY OF PHOENIX–BAY AREA CAMPUS, San Jose, CA 95134-1805

General Information Proprietary, coed, comprehensive institution. *Graduate housing:* On-campus housing not available.

GRADUATE UNITS

College of Criminal Justice and Security Offers administration of justice and security (MS).

College of Education *Program availability:* Evening/weekend, online learning. Offers administration and supervision (MA Ed); adult education and training (MA Ed); early childhood education (MA Ed); education (Ed S); educational leadership (Ed D); elementary teacher education (MA Ed); higher education administration (PhD); secondary teacher education (MA Ed); special education (MA Ed); teacher leadership (MA Ed). Electronic applications accepted.

College of Information Systems and Technology *Program availability:* Evening/weekend. Offers information systems (MIS); organizational leadership/information systems and technology (DM). Electronic applications accepted.

College of Nursing *Program availability:* Evening/weekend, online learning. Offers education (MHA); gerontology (MHA); health administration (MHA, DHA); informatics (MHA, MSN); nursing (MSN, PhD); nursing/health care education (MSN). Electronic applications accepted.

College of Social Sciences *Program availability:* Evening/weekend. Offers marriage, family, and child therapy (MSC).

School of Business *Program availability:* Evening/weekend, online learning. Offers accountancy (MS); accounting (MBA); business administration (MBA, DBA); energy management (MBA); global management (MBA); health care management (MBA); human resource management (MBA); human resources management (MM); management (MM); marketing (MBA); organizational leadership (DM); project management (MBA); public administration (MPA); technology management (MBA). Electronic applications accepted.

UNIVERSITY OF PHOENIX–CENTRAL VALLEY CAMPUS, Fresno, CA 93720-1552

General Information Proprietary, coed, comprehensive institution.

GRADUATE UNITS

College of Education Offers curriculum and instruction (MA Ed); curriculum and instruction-computer education (MA Ed); elementary teacher education (MA Ed); secondary teacher education (MA Ed).

College of Human Services Offers marriage, family and child therapy (MSC).

College of Information Systems and Technology Offers information systems (MIS); technology management (MBA).

College of Nursing Offers education (MHA); gerontology (MHA); health administration (MHA); nursing (MSN).

School of Business Offers accounting (MBA); business administration (MBA); global management (MBA); human resources management (MBA, MM); management (MM); marketing (MBA); public administration (MBA, MM).

UNIVERSITY OF PHOENIX–DALLAS CAMPUS, Dallas, TX 75251

General Information Proprietary, coed, comprehensive institution. *Graduate housing:* On-campus housing not available.

GRADUATE UNITS

College of Criminal Justice and Security *Program availability:* Online learning. Offers administration of justice and security (MS). Electronic applications accepted.

College of Education Offers curriculum and instruction (MA Ed).

College of Information Systems and Technology *Program availability:* Evening/weekend. Offers e-business (MBA); information systems (MIS); technology management (MBA). Electronic applications accepted.

School of Business *Program availability:* Evening/weekend, online learning. Offers accounting (MBA); business administration (MBA); global management (MBA); human resources management (MBA, MM); management (MM); marketing (MBA); public administration (MBA, MM). Electronic applications accepted.

UNIVERSITY OF PHOENIX–HAWAII CAMPUS, Honolulu, HI 96813-3800

General Information Proprietary, coed, comprehensive institution. *Graduate housing:* On-campus housing not available.

GRADUATE UNITS

College of Education *Program availability:* Evening/weekend. Offers administration and supervision (MA Ed); curriculum and instruction (MA Ed); elementary education (MA Ed); secondary education (MA Ed); special education (MA Ed); teacher education for elementary licensure (MA Ed). Electronic applications accepted.

College of Information Systems and Technology *Program availability:* Evening/weekend. Offers information systems (MIS); technology management (MBA). Electronic applications accepted.

College of Nursing *Program availability:* Evening/weekend. Offers education (MHA); family nurse practitioner (MSN); gerontology (MHA); health administration (MHA); nursing (MSN); nursing/health care education (MSN). Electronic applications accepted.

School of Business *Program availability:* Evening/weekend. Offers accounting (MBA); business administration (MBA); global management (MBA); human resources management (MBA, MM); management (MM); marketing (MBA); public administration (MBA, MM). Electronic applications accepted.

UNIVERSITY OF PHOENIX–HOUSTON CAMPUS, Houston, TX 77079-2004

General Information Proprietary, coed, comprehensive institution. *Graduate housing:* On-campus housing not available.

GRADUATE UNITS

College of Education Offers curriculum and instruction (MA Ed).

College of Information Systems and Technology *Program availability:* Evening/weekend, online learning. Offers e-business (MBA); information systems (MIS); technology management (MBA). Electronic applications accepted.

College of Nursing *Program availability:* Online learning. Offers health administration (MHA). Electronic applications accepted.

School of Business *Program availability:* Evening/weekend, online learning. Offers accounting (MBA); business administration (MBA); global management (MBA); human resources management (MBA, MM); management (MM); marketing (MBA); public administration (MBA, MM). Electronic applications accepted.

UNIVERSITY OF PHOENIX–LAS VEGAS CAMPUS, Las Vegas, NV 89135

General Information Proprietary, coed, comprehensive institution. *Graduate housing:* On-campus housing not available.

GRADUATE UNITS

College of Education *Program availability:* Evening/weekend. Offers administration and supervision (MA Ed); curriculum and instruction (MA Ed); school counseling (MSC); teacher education-elementary licensure (MA Ed). Electronic applications accepted.

College of Human Services *Program availability:* Online learning. Offers marriage, family, and child therapy (MSC); mental health counseling (MSC); school counseling (MSC). Electronic applications accepted.

College of Information Systems and Technology *Program availability:* Evening/weekend. Offers information systems (MIS); technology management (MBA). Electronic applications accepted.

School of Business *Program availability:* Evening/weekend, online learning. Offers accounting (MBA); business administration (MBA); global management (MBA); human resources management (MBA, MM); management (MM); marketing (MBA); public administration (MM). Electronic applications accepted.

UNIVERSITY OF PHOENIX–ONLINE CAMPUS, Phoenix, AZ 85034-7209

General Information Proprietary, coed, comprehensive institution. *Graduate housing:* On-campus housing not available.

GRADUATE UNITS

College of Education *Program availability:* Evening/weekend, online learning. Offers administration and supervision (MAEd, Certificate); adult education and training (MAEd); curriculum and instruction (MAEd); early childhood education (MAEd); educational studies (MAEd); elementary teacher education (MAEd); principal licensure (Certificate); secondary teacher education (MAEd); special education (MAEd, Certificate); teacher education (MAEd); teacher education middle level mathematics (MAEd); teacher education middle level science (MAEd); teacher education secondary mathematics (MAEd); teacher education secondary science (MAEd); teacher leadership (MAEd); teachers of English learners (Certificate); transition to teaching (Certificate). Electronic applications accepted.

College of Health Sciences and Nursing *Program availability:* Evening/weekend, online learning. Offers family nurse practitioner (Certificate); health care (Certificate); health care education (Certificate); health care informatics (Certificate); informatics (MSN); nursing (MSN); nursing and health care education (MSN). Electronic applications accepted.

College of Information Systems and Technology *Program availability:* Evening/weekend, online learning. Offers information systems and technology (MIS). Electronic applications accepted.

College of Justice and Security *Program availability:* Evening/weekend, online learning. Offers administration of justice and security (MS); public administration (MPA). Electronic applications accepted.

College of Social Science *Program availability:* Evening/weekend, online learning. Offers mediation (Certificate); psychology (MS). Electronic applications accepted.

School of Advanced Studies *Program availability:* Evening/weekend, online learning. Offers business administration (DBA); education (Ed S); educational leadership (Ed D); health administration (DHA); higher education administration (PhD); industrial/organizational psychology (PhD); nursing (PhD); organizational leadership (DM). Electronic applications accepted.

School of Business *Program availability:* Evening/weekend, online learning. Offers accountancy (MS); accounting (MBA, Certificate); business administration (MBA); energy management (MBA); global management (MBA); health care management (MBA); human resource management (MBA, Certificate); human resources management (MM); management (MM); marketing (MBA, Certificate); project management (MBA, Certificate); public administration (MBA, MM); technology management (MBA). Electronic applications accepted.

UNIVERSITY OF PHOENIX–PHOENIX CAMPUS, Tempe, AZ 85282-2371

General Information Proprietary, coed, comprehensive institution. CGS member. *Graduate housing:* On-campus housing not available.

GRADUATE UNITS

College of Criminal Justice and Security *Program availability:* Evening/weekend, online learning. Offers administration of justice and security (MS); global and homeland security (MS); law enforcement organizations (MS); public administration (MPA). Electronic applications accepted.

College of Education *Program availability:* Evening/weekend, online learning. Offers administration and supervision (MA Ed); adult education and training (MA Ed); curriculum and instruction reading (MA Ed); early childhood education (MA Ed); education studies (MA Ed); elementary teacher education (MA Ed); secondary teacher education (MA Ed); special education (MA Ed); teacher leadership (MA Ed). Electronic applications accepted.

College of Health Sciences and Nursing *Program availability:* Evening/weekend, online learning. Offers family nurse practitioner (MSN, Certificate); gerontology health care (Certificate); health care education (MSN, Certificate); health care informatics (Certificate); informatics (MSN); nursing (MSN). Electronic applications accepted.

College of Social Sciences *Program availability:* Evening/weekend, online learning. Offers counseling (MS); psychology (MS). Electronic applications accepted.

School of Business *Program availability:* Evening/weekend, online learning. Offers accounting (MBA, MS, Certificate); business administration (MBA); energy management (MBA); global management (MBA); health care management (MBA); human resource management (MBA, Certificate); management (MM); marketing (MBA); project management (MBA); technology management (MBA). Electronic applications accepted.

UNIVERSITY OF PHOENIX–SACRAMENTO VALLEY CAMPUS, Sacramento, CA 95833-4334

General Information Proprietary, coed, comprehensive institution. *Graduate housing:* On-campus housing not available.

GRADUATE UNITS

College of Education *Program availability:* Evening/weekend. Offers adult education (MA Ed); curriculum instruction (MA Ed); elementary teacher education (MA Ed); secondary teacher education (MA Ed); teacher education (Certificate). Electronic applications accepted.

College of Information Systems and Technology *Program availability:* Evening/weekend. Offers management (MIS); technology management (MBA). Electronic applications accepted.

College of Nursing *Program availability:* Evening/weekend. Offers family nurse practitioner (MSN); health administration (MHA); health care education (MSN); nursing (MSN). Electronic applications accepted.

School of Business *Program availability:* Evening/weekend. Offers accounting (MBA); business administration (MBA); global management (MBA); human resources management (MBA, MM); management (MM); marketing (MBA); public administration (MBA, MM). Electronic applications accepted.

UNIVERSITY OF PHOENIX–SAN ANTONIO CAMPUS, San Antonio, TX 78230

General Information Proprietary, coed, comprehensive institution.

GRADUATE UNITS

College of Criminal Justice and Security Offers administration of justice and security (MS).

College of Education Offers curriculum and instruction (MA Ed).

College of Information Systems and Technology Offers information systems (MIS); technology management (MBA).

College of Nursing Offers health administration (MHA).

School of Business Offers accounting (MBA); business administration (MBA); e-business (MBA); global management (MBA); human resources management (MBA, MM); management (MM); marketing (MBA); public administration (MBA, MM).

UNIVERSITY OF PHOENIX–SAN DIEGO CAMPUS, San Diego, CA 92123

General Information Proprietary, coed, comprehensive institution. *Graduate housing:* On-campus housing not available.

GRADUATE UNITS

College of Education *Program availability:* Evening/weekend. Offers curriculum and instruction (MA Ed); elementary teacher education (MA Ed); secondary teacher education (MA Ed). Electronic applications accepted.

College of Information Systems and Technology *Program availability:* Evening/weekend. Offers management (MIS); technology management (MBA). Electronic applications accepted.

College of Nursing *Program availability:* Evening/weekend. Offers health care education (MSN); nursing (MSN). Electronic applications accepted.

School of Business *Program availability:* Evening/weekend. Offers accounting (MBA); business administration (MBA); global management (MBA); human resources management (MBA, MM); management (MM); marketing (MBA); public administration (MBA). Electronic applications accepted.

UNIVERSITY OF PIKEVILLE, Pikeville, KY 41501

General Information Independent-religious, coed, comprehensive institution. *Graduate housing:* Room and/or apartments available on a first-come, first-served basis to single students; on-campus housing not available to married students. Housing application deadline: 5/1.

GRADUATE UNITS

Coleman College of Business *Program availability:* Part-time, evening/weekend. Offers business (MBA); entrepreneurship (MBA); healthcare (MBA).

Kentucky College of Optometry Offers optometry (OD).

Kentucky College of Osteopathic Medicine Offers osteopathic medicine (DO).

Patton College of Education *Program availability:* Part-time, evening/weekend. Offers teacher leader (MA).

UNIVERSITY OF PITTSBURGH, Pittsburgh, PA 15260

General Information State-related, coed, university. CGS member. *Research affiliation:* National Institutes of Health, National Science Foundation, General Electric Company (GE), Shire, Phillips.

GRADUATE UNITS

Graduate School of Public and International Affairs *Program availability:* Part-time, evening/weekend, 100% online. Offers energy and environment (MID, MPA); governance and international public management (MID, MPA); human security (MID, MPIA); international affairs (PhD); international development (PhD); international political economy (MPIA); nongovernmental organizations and civil society (MID); policy research and analysis (MPA); public administration (PhD); public and international affairs (MID, MPA, MPPM, PhD); public and nonprofit management (MPA); public policy (PhD); public policy and management (MPPM); security and intelligence studies (MPIA); urban affairs and planning (MID, MPA).

Graduate School of Public Health *Program availability:* Part-time. Offers applied research and leadership in behavioral and community health sciences (Dr PH); applied social and behavioral concepts in public health (MPH); biostatistics (MS, PhD); community-based participatory research (Certificate); decision sciences (MS); environmental and occupational health (MPH, MS, PhD); epidemiology (MPH, MS, PhD); evaluation of public health programs (Certificate); genetic counseling (MS); global health (Certificate); health equity (Certificate); health policy and economics (MS); health policy and management (MHA, MPH, PhD); human genetics (MS, PhD); infectious diseases and microbiology (MS, PhD); LGBT health and wellness (Certificate); management, intervention, and community practice (MPH); maternal and child health (MPH); pathogenesis, eradication, and laboratory practice (MPH); public health (MHA, MPH, MS, Dr PH, PhD, Certificate); public health genetics (MPH, Certificate); theory and research methods (Dr PH). Electronic applications accepted.

Katz Graduate School of Business *Program availability:* Part-time, evening/weekend, blended/hybrid learning. Offers accounting (PhD); business (EMBA, MBA, MS, PhD, Certificate); business administration (EMBA, MBA, PhD); business analytics and operations (PhD); finance (MS); information systems (MBA); information systems and technology management (PhD); international business administration (Certificate);

management information systems (MS); marketing (MBA, PhD); marketing science (MS); operations (MBA); organizational behavior and human resources (MBA, PhD); public and international affairsstrategic management (PhD); strategy, environment and organizations (MBA); supply chain management (MS). Electronic applications accepted.

Kenneth P. Dietrich School of Arts and Sciences *Program availability:* Part-time. Offers anthropology (MA, PhD); applied linguistics (MA); applied linguistics with TESOL (MA); applied mathematics (MA, MS); applied statistics (MA, MS); arts and sciences (MA, MFA, MS, Pro-MS, PhD, Certificate, Doctoral Certificate, Master's Certificate); biological and health psychology (PhD); chemistry (MS, PhD); Chinese (MA); clinical psychology (PhD); cognitive psychology (PhD); communication (MA, PhD); composition and theory (PhD); cultural studies (Certificate); developmental psychology (PhD); ecology and evolution (PhD); economics (MA, PhD); English (MA, PhD); ethnomusicology (PhD); film and media studies (PhD, Certificate); film studies (PhD); French (MA, PhD); gender, sexuality, and women's studies (Doctoral Certificate, Master's Certificate); geographical information systems and remote sensing (Pro-MS); geology and environmental science (MS, PhD); historical musicology (PhD); history (MA, PhD); history and philosophy of science (PhD); history of art and architecture (MA, PhD); Italian (MA); Japanese (MA); jazz studies (PhD); mathematics (MA, MS, PhD); medieval and Renaissance studies (Doctoral Certificate, Master's Certificate); molecular, cellular, and developmental biology (PhD); music (MA); philosophy (PhD); physics and astronomy (MS, PhD); political science (MA, PhD); Russian literature and culture (MA, PhD); social psychology (PhD); sociolinguistics (PhD); sociology (MA, PhD); statistics (MA, MS, PhD); teaching English to speakers of other languages (Certificate); TESOL (PhD); theatre arts (MA, MFA, PhD); writing (MFA). Electronic applications accepted.

Center for Bioethics and Health Law *Program availability:* Part-time. Offers bioethics (MA). Electronic applications accepted.

Center for Neuroscience Offers neuroscience (PhD). Program held jointly with School of Medicine. Electronic applications accepted.

School of Computing and Information *Program availability:* Part-time, evening/weekend, 100% online. Offers big data analytics (Certificate); biological science (PhD); computer science (MS, PhD); computing and information (MLIS, MS, MSIS, MST, PhD, Certificate); information science (MSIS, PhD, Certificate); intelligent systems (MS, PhD); library and information science (MLIS, PhD); security assurance/information systems (Certificate); telecommunications (MST, Certificate). Electronic applications accepted.

School of Dental Medicine Offers dental anesthesiology (Certificate); dental medicine (MDS, MPH, MS, DMD, PhD, Certificate); dental science (MDS); endodontics (Certificate); general dentistry (Certificate); general practice (Certificate); multidisciplinary public health (MPH); oral and maxillofacial pathology (Certificate); oral and maxillofacial surgery (Certificate); oral biology (MS, PhD); orthodontics (MDS, Certificate); pediatric cranio-maxillofacial surgery (Certificate); pediatric dentistry (Certificate); periodontics (MDS, Certificate); prosthodontics (MDS, Certificate). Electronic applications accepted.

School of Education *Program availability:* Part-time, evening/weekend, online learning. Offers applied behavior analysis (M Ed); applied developmental psychology (M Ed, MS, PhD); developmental movement (MS); early childhood education (M Ed); early intervention (M Ed, PhD); education (M Ed, MA, MAT, MS, Ed D, PhD); elementary education (M Ed, MAT); elementary education (MAT); English and communications education (M Ed, MAT); exercise physiology (MS, PhD); foreign language education (M Ed, MAT); general special education (M Ed, Ed D); higher education management (M Ed, Ed D, PhD); language, literacy and culture education (Ed D, PhD); learning sciences and policy (PhD); mathematics education (M Ed, MAT, Ed D, PhD); reading education (PhD); research methodology (M Ed, MA, PhD); school leadership (M Ed, Ed D, PhD); science education (M Ed, MAT, Ed D, PhD); secondary education (M Ed, MAT, Ed D, PhD); social and comparative analysis in education (M Ed, MA, Ed D, PhD); social studies education (M Ed, MAT); special education (M Ed, PhD); special education (Ed D); special education teacher preparation (M Ed); STEM education (Ed D); vision studies (M Ed, PhD). Electronic applications accepted.

School of Health and Rehabilitation Sciences *Program availability:* Part-time, evening/weekend. Offers audiology (MA, MS, Au D); clinical rehabilitation and mental health counseling (MS); communication science and disorders (PhD); health and rehabilitation sciences (MS); medical speech language pathology (CScD); nutrition and dietetics (MS); occupational therapy (MS, CScD, OTD); physical therapy (MS, DPT); physician assistant studies (MS); prosthetics and orthotics (DPT); rehabilitation science (PhD); rehabilitation technology (MS); speech language pathology (MA, MS). Electronic applications accepted.

School of Law *Program availability:* Part-time, online learning. Offers biomedical and health services research (MSL); business law (MSL); Constitutional law (MSL); criminal law and justice (MSL); disability law (MSL); disability legal studies (Certificate); elder and estate planning law (MSL); employment and labor law (MSL); energy law (MSL); environmental and real estate law (MSL); family law (MSL); health law (MSL); intellectual property and technology law (MSL); international and human rights law (MSL); jurisprudence (MSL); law (LL M, MSL, JD, SJD, Certificate); regulatory law (MSL); self-designed (MSL); U.S. law (LL M). Electronic applications accepted.

School of Medicine *Program availability:* Part-time, blended/hybrid learning. Offers biomedical informatics (MS, PhD, Certificate); biomedical sciences (MS); cell biology and molecular physiology (PhD); cellular and molecular pathology (PhD); clinical and translational science (PhD); clinical research (MS, Certificate); computational biology (PhD); integrative systems biology (PhD); interdisciplinary biomedical sciences (PhD); medical education (MS, Certificate); medicine (MS, MD, PhD, Certificate); microbiology and immunology (PhD); molecular biophysics and structural biology (PhD); molecular genetics and developmental biology (PhD); molecular pharmacology (PhD). Electronic applications accepted.

School of Nursing Students: 195 full-time (152 women), 143 part-time (124 women); includes 45 minority (13 Black or African American, non-Hispanic/Latino; 28 Asian, non-Hispanic/Latino; 4 Hispanic/Latino), 13 international. Average age 31. 291 applicants, 55% accepted, 131 enrolled. *Faculty:* 45 full-time (40 women), 6 part-time/adjunct (5 women). Expenses: Contact institution. *Financial support:* In 2018–19, 165 students received support, including 19 fellowships (averaging $15,691 per year), 11 research assistantships (averaging $19,253 per year), 44 teaching assistantships (averaging $11,335 per year); scholarships/grants, unspecified assistantships, and Matching Funds also available. Financial award applicants required to submit FAFSA. In 2018, 158 master's, 52 doctorates awarded. *Program availability:* Part-time. Offers anesthesia (DNP); clinical nurse specialist (DNP); doctor of philosophy (PhD); nurse midwife (DNP); nurse practitioner (MSN, DNP); nurse specialty role (DNP). *Application deadline:* For fall admission, 6/1 priority date for domestic students, 2/15 priority date for international students. *Application fee:* $50. Electronic applications accepted. *Application Contact:* Laurie Lapsley, Graduate Administrator, 412-624-9670, Fax: 412-624-2409, E-mail:

lapsleyl@pitt.edu. *Dean/Professor*, Dr. Jacqueline Dunbar-Jacob, 412-624-7838, Fax: 412-624-2401, E-mail: dunbar@pitt.edu.

School of Pharmacy *Program availability:* Part-time. Offers community, leadership, innovation, and practice (Pharm D); global health (Pharm D); pediatrics (Pharm D); pharmaceutical sciences (MS, PhD); pharmacotherapy (Pharm D); pharmacy (MS, PhD, Pharm D); pharmacy business administration (MS). Electronic applications accepted.

School of Social Work *Program availability:* Part-time. Offers social work (MSW, PhD, Certificate). Electronic applications accepted.

Swanson School of Engineering *Program availability:* Part-time. Offers bioengineering (MSBENG); chemical engineering (MS Ch E, PhD); civil and environmental engineering (MSCEE, PhD); electrical and computer engineering (MS, PhD); engineering (MS, MS Ch E, MSBENG, MSCEE, MSIE, MSME, MSNE, MSPE, PhD); industrial engineering (MSIE, PhD); mechanical engineering and materials science (MSME, MSNE, PhD); petroleum engineering (MSPE). Electronic applications accepted.

University Center for International Studies *Program availability:* Part-time, evening/weekend, online learning. Offers African studies (Certificate); Asian studies (Certificate); European Union studies (Certificate); global studies (Certificate); Latin American studies (Certificate); Russian and East European studies (Certificate); West European studies (Certificate).

UNIVERSITY OF PORTLAND, Portland, OR 97203-5798

General Information Independent-religious, coed, comprehensive institution. *Enrollment:* 117 full-time matriculated graduate/professional students (63 women), 352 part-time matriculated graduate/professional students (233 women). *Enrollment by degree level:* 358 master's, 75 doctoral, 36 other advanced degrees. *Graduate faculty:* 60 full-time (31 women), 31 part-time/adjunct (13 women). *Graduate housing:* Room and/or apartments available on a first-come, first-served basis to single students; on-campus housing not available to married students. *Student services:* Campus employment opportunities, campus safety program, career counseling, exercise/wellness program, free psychological counseling, international student services, low-cost health insurance, multicultural affairs office, services for students with disabilities, teacher training, writing training. *Library facilities:* Wilson M. Clark Library plus 1 other. *Collection:* Books: 191,219 (physical), 138,108 (digital/electronic); Serial titles: 1,080 (digital/electronic); Databases: 153. Weekly public service hours: 117; students can reserve study rooms.

Computer facilities: 157 computers available on campus for general student use. A campuswide network can be accessed from student residence rooms and from off campus. Online class registration is available. Website: http://www.up.edu/

General Application Contact: Caitlin Biddulph, Graduate Programs and Admissions Specialist, 503-943-7107, E-mail: gradschl@up.edu.

GRADUATE UNITS

Department of Communication Studies Students: 4 full-time (2 women), 4 part-time (2 women). Average age 34. 14 applicants, 57% accepted, 6 enrolled. Expenses: Contact institution. *Financial support:* Career-related internships or fieldwork, Federal Work-Study, and scholarships/grants available. Financial award application deadline: 3/1; financial award applicants required to submit FAFSA. In 2018, 4 master's awarded. *Program availability:* Part-time, evening/weekend. Offers communication (MA); management communication (MS). *Application deadline:* For fall admission, 7/15 priority date for domestic and international students; for spring admission, 12/15 priority date for domestic and international students; for summer admission, 4/15 for domestic and international students. Applications are processed on a rolling basis. Electronic applications accepted. *Application Contact:* Caitlin Biddulph, Graduate Programs and Admissions Specialist, 503-943-7107, E-mail: biddulph@up.edu. *Director*, Dr. Jennette Lovejoy, 503-943-7358, E-mail: lovejoy@up.edu.

Dr. Robert B. Pamplin, Jr. School of Business Students: 35 full-time (16 women), 114 part-time (47 women); includes 21 minority (3 Black or African American, non-Hispanic/Latino; 2 American Indian or Alaska Native, non-Hispanic/Latino; 8 Asian, non-Hispanic/Latino; 8 Hispanic/Latino), 24 international. Average age 32. *Faculty:* 26 full-time (5 women), 8 part-time/adjunct (1 woman). Expenses: Contact institution. *Financial support:* Application deadline: 3/1; applicants required to submit FAFSA. In 2018, 55 master's awarded. *Program availability:* Part-time, evening/weekend. Offers entrepreneurship (MBA); finance (MBA, MS); health care management (MBA); marketing (MBA); nonprofit management (EMBA); operations and technology management (MBA, MS); sustainability (MBA). *Application deadline:* For fall admission, 7/19 priority date for domestic and international students; for spring admission, 12/7 priority date for domestic and international students; for summer admission, 4/12 priority date for domestic and international students. Applications are processed on a rolling basis. *Application fee:* $0. Electronic applications accepted. *Application Contact:* Melissa McCarthy, Director, 503-943-7224, E-mail: mba-up@up.edu. *Director*, Melissa McCarthy, 503-943-7224, E-mail: mba-up@up.edu.

School of Education Students: 32 full-time (30 women), 239 part-time (187 women); includes 33 minority (7 Black or African American, non-Hispanic/Latino; 3 American Indian or Alaska Native, non-Hispanic/Latino; 13 Asian, non-Hispanic/Latino; 1 Native Hawaiian or other Pacific Islander, non-Hispanic/Latino; 9 Two or more races, non-Hispanic/Latino). Average age 34. 92 applicants, 60% accepted, 42 enrolled. Expenses: Contact institution. *Financial support:* Fellowships, Federal Work-Study, and scholarships/grants available. Support available to part-time students. Financial award application deadline: 3/1; financial award applicants required to submit FAFSA. In 2018, 57 master's, 16 doctorates awarded. *Program availability:* Part-time, evening/weekend. Offers education (MA, MAT); educational leadership (M Ed); English for speakers of other languages (M Ed); initial administrator licensure (M Ed); neuroeducation (M Ed, Ed D); organizational leadership and development (Ed D); reading (M Ed); school leadership and development (Ed D); special education (M Ed). *Application deadline:* For fall admission, 7/15 priority date for domestic and international students; for spring admission, 12/15 priority date for domestic and international students; for summer admission, 4/15 for domestic and international students. Applications are processed on a rolling basis. Electronic applications accepted. *Application Contact:* Caitlin Biddulph, Graduate Programs and Admissions Specialist, 503-943-7107, E-mail: biddulph@up.edu. *Associate Dean*, Dr. Bruce Weitzel, 503-943-7135, E-mail: soed@up.edu.

School of Nursing Students: 64 part-time (48 women); includes 9 minority (3 Black or African American, non-Hispanic/Latino; 1 American Indian or Alaska Native, non-Hispanic/Latino; 5 Hispanic/Latino). Average age 40. *Faculty:* 16 full-time (15 women), 10 part-time/adjunct (8 women). Expenses: Contact institution. *Financial support:* Federal Work-Study and scholarships/grants available. Support available to part-time students. Financial award application deadline: 3/1; financial award applicants required to submit FAFSA. In 2018, 9 doctorates awarded. *Program availability:* Part-time, evening/weekend. Offers clinical nurse leader (MS); family nurse practitioner (DNP); nurse educator (MS). *Application deadline:* For fall admission, 7/19 priority date for domestic and international students; for spring admission, 12/12 priority date for domestic and international students. Applications are processed on a rolling basis. Electronic applications accepted. *Application Contact:* Caitlin Biddulph, Graduate Programs and Admissions Specialist, 503-943-7107. *Graduate Program Coordinator,* Becca Fischer, 503-943-7211, E-mail: fischer@up.edu.

Shiley School of Engineering Students: 12 full-time (4 women), 2 part-time (both women); includes 1 minority (Black or African American, non-Hispanic/Latino), 2 international. Average age 24. 43 applicants, 49% accepted, 10 enrolled. Expenses: Contact institution. *Financial support:* Research assistantships, career-related internships or fieldwork, Federal Work-Study, and scholarships/grants available. Support available to part-time students. Financial award application deadline: 3/1; financial award applicants required to submit FAFSA. In 2018, 6 master's awarded. *Program availability:* Part-time, evening/weekend. Offers biomedical engineering (MBME); civil engineering (ME); computer science (ME); electrical engineering (ME); mechanical engineering (ME). *Application deadline:* For fall admission, 7/15 priority date for domestic and international students; for spring admission, 12/15 priority date for domestic and international students; for summer admission, 4/15 for domestic and international students. Applications are processed on a rolling basis. Electronic applications accepted. *Application Contact:* Caitlin Biddulph, Graduate Programs and Admissions Specialist, 503-943-7107. *Dean,* Dr. Matthew Kuhn, 503-943-7361, E-mail: kuhn@up.edu.

UNIVERSITY OF PRINCE EDWARD ISLAND, Charlottetown, PE C1A 4P3, Canada

General Information Province-supported, coed, comprehensive institution. *Graduate housing:* Room and/or apartments available on a first-come, first-served basis to single students; on-campus housing not available to married students. *Research affiliation:* National Research Council of Canada Institute for Nutrisciences and Health, PEI Food Technology Centre, Agriculture Canada Research Station, Diagnostic Chemicals, Ltd., Canadian Food Inspection Agency, AquaHealth.

GRADUATE UNITS

Atlantic Veterinary College *Program availability:* Part-time. Offers anatomy (M Sc, PhD); bacteriology (M Sc, PhD); clinical pharmacology (M Sc, PhD); clinical sciences (M Sc, PhD); epidemiology (M Sc, PhD); fish health (M Sc, PhD); food animal nutrition (M Sc, PhD); immunology (M Sc, PhD); microanatomy (M Sc, PhD); parasitology (M Sc, PhD); pathology (M Sc, PhD); pharmacology (M Sc, PhD); physiology (M Sc, PhD); toxicology (M Sc, PhD); veterinary medicine (M Sc, M Vet Sc, DVM, PhD); veterinary science (M Vet Sc); virology (M Sc, PhD).

Faculty of Arts *Program availability:* Part-time. Offers island studies (MA).

Faculty of Education *Program availability:* Part-time. Offers educational studies (PhD); leadership in learning (M Ed).

Faculty of Science Offers environmental sciences (M Sc, PhD); human biology (M Sc); molecular and macromolecular sciences (M Sc, PhD); sustainable design engineering (M Sc).

UNIVERSITY OF PROVIDENCE, Great Falls, MT 59405

General Information Independent-religious, coed, comprehensive institution. *Graduate housing:* On-campus housing not available.

GRADUATE UNITS

Graduate Studies *Program availability:* Part-time, online learning. Offers counseling (MSC); criminal justice (MSM); human development (MSM); management (MSM). Electronic applications accepted.

UNIVERSITY OF PUERTO RICO–MAYAGÜEZ, Mayagüez, PR 00681-9000

General Information Commonwealth-supported, coed, university. *Graduate housing:* On-campus housing not available. *Research affiliation:* U.S. Department of Education (DOE) (STEM education), National Endowment for the Humanities, Tropical Agriculture Research Station (agriculture), Corporation for the Development and Administration of Marine Resources of Puerto Rico (marine science), National Science Foundation.

GRADUATE UNITS

Graduate Studies *Program availability:* Part-time, evening/weekend. Electronic applications accepted.

College of Agricultural Sciences *Program availability:* Part-time. Offers agricultural economics and rural sociology (MS); agricultural education (MS); agricultural extension (MS); agricultural sciences (MS); agronomy (MS); animal science (MS); crop protection (MS); food science and technology (MS); horticulture (MS); soils (MS).

College of Arts and Sciences *Program availability:* Part-time. Offers applied chemistry (MS, PhD); applied mathematics (MS); arts and sciences (MA, MS, PhD); biology (MS); English education (MA); geology (MS); Hispanic studies (MA); kinesiology (MA); marine sciences (MS, PhD); physics (MS); pre-college math education (MS); pure mathematics (MS); scientific computing (MS); statistics (MS).

College of Business Administration *Program availability:* Part-time, evening/weekend. Offers business administration (MBA); finance (MBA); human resources (MBA); industrial management (MBA). Electronic applications accepted.

College of Engineering *Program availability:* Part-time. Offers chemical engineering (ME, MS, PhD); civil engineering (ME, MS, PhD); computer engineering (ME, MS); computer science and engineering (PhD); computing and information sciences and engineering (PhD); electrical engineering (ME, MS); engineering (ME, MS, PhD); industrial engineering (ME, MS); materials science and engineering (MS); mechanical engineering (ME, MS, PhD). Electronic applications accepted.

UNIVERSITY OF PUERTO RICO–MEDICAL SCIENCES CAMPUS, San Juan, PR 00936-5067

General Information Commonwealth-supported, coed, primarily women, university. *Graduate housing:* On-campus housing not available.

GRADUATE UNITS

Graduate School of Public Health *Program availability:* Part-time. Offers biostatistics (MPH); demography (MS); developmental disabilities-early intervention (Certificate); environmental health (MS, Dr PH); epidemiology (MPH, MS); evaluative research of health systems (MS); gerontology (MPH, Certificate); health services administration (MHSA, MS); industrial hygiene (MS); maternal and child health (MPH); nurse midwifery (MPH, Certificate); nutrition (MS); public health (MHSA, MPH, MPHE, MS, Dr PH, Certificate); public health education (MPHE); school health promotion (Certificate).

School of Dental Medicine Offers dental medicine (DMD, Certificate); dentistry (DMD, Certificate); general dentistry (Certificate); oral and maxillofacial surgery (Certificate); orthodontics (Certificate); pediatric dentistry (Certificate); prosthodontics (Certificate). Electronic applications accepted.

School of Health Professions Offers audiology (Au D); clinical laboratory science (MS); clinical research (MS, Graduate Certificate); cytotechnology (Certificate); dietetics (Certificate); health information administration (MS); health professions (MS, Au D, Certificate); medical technology (Certificate); occupational therapy (MS); physical therapy (MS); speech-language pathology (MS). Electronic applications accepted.

School of Medicine Offers medicine (MS, MD, PhD). Electronic applications accepted.

Biomedical Sciences Graduate Program Offers anatomy (MS, PhD); biochemistry (MS, PhD); biomedical sciences (MS, PhD); microbiology and medical zoology (MS, PhD); pharmacology and toxicology (MS, PhD); physiology (MS, PhD). Electronic applications accepted.

School of Nursing Offers adult and elderly nursing (MSN); child and adolescent nursing (MSN); critical care nursing (MSN); family and community nursing (MSN); family nurse practitioner (MSN); maternity nursing (MSN); mental health and psychiatric nursing (MSN). Electronic applications accepted.

School of Pharmacy *Program availability:* Part-time, evening/weekend. Offers industrial pharmacy (MS); pharmaceutical sciences (MS); pharmacy (Pharm D). Electronic applications accepted.

UNIVERSITY OF PUERTO RICO–RÍO PIEDRAS, San Juan, PR 00931-3300

General Information Commonwealth-supported, coed, university. *Graduate housing:* Room and/or apartments available to single students; on-campus housing not available to married students. Housing application deadline: 6/15. *Research affiliation:* U.S. Department of Education (DOE) (social sciences, general studies, physics, biology), U.S. Department of Health and Human Services (social sciences, biology), National Science Foundation (ecology, biology), Ocean Conservancy (ecology, biology), Ford International (ecology).

GRADUATE UNITS

College of Business Administration *Program availability:* Part-time. Offers accounting (MBA); finance (MBA, PhD); general business (MBA); human resources management (MBA); international trade and business (MBA, PhD); marketing (MBA); operations management (MBA); quantitative methods (MBA).

College of Education *Program availability:* Part-time. Offers biology education (M Ed); chemistry education (M Ed); curriculum and teaching (Ed D); early child education (M Ed); education (M Ed, MS, Ed D); educational research and evaluation (M Ed); exercise sciences (MS); family ecology and nutrition (M Ed); guidance and counseling (M Ed, Ed D); history education (M Ed); mathematics education (M Ed); physics education (M Ed); school administration and supervision (M Ed, Ed D); Spanish education (M Ed); special and differentiated education (M Ed); teaching English as a second language (M Ed).

College of Humanities *Program availability:* Part-time. Offers Caribbean history (PhD); Caribbean linguistics (PhD); Caribbean literature (PhD); comparative literature (MA); English (MA); Hispanic linguistics (PhD); Hispanic studies (MA); history (MA); humanities (MA, PhD, Certificate); Latin American literature (PhD); linguistics (MA); philosophy (MA); Puerto Rican history (PhD); Puerto Rican literature (PhD); Spanish literature (PhD); translation (MA, Certificate).

College of Natural Sciences *Program availability:* Part-time. Offers chemical physics (PhD); chemistry (MS, PhD); ecology/systematics (MS, PhD); environmental sciences (MS, PhD); evolution/genetics (MS, PhD); mathematics (MS, PhD); molecular/cellular biology (MS, PhD); natural sciences (MS, PhD); neuroscience (MS, PhD); physics (MS).

College of Social Sciences *Program availability:* Part-time. Offers clinical psychology (MA); economics (MA); industrial organizational psychology (MA); investigative academic psychology (MA); psychology (PhD); social sciences (MA, MPA, MRC, MSW, PhD); social-community psychology (MA); sociology (MA).

Graduate School of Rehabilitation Counseling *Program availability:* Part-time. Offers rehabilitation counseling (MRC).

Graduate School of Social Work *Program availability:* Part-time. Offers social work (MSW, PhD).

School of Public Administration *Program availability:* Part-time. Offers public administration (MPA).

Graduate School of Information Sciences and Technologies *Program availability:* Part-time. Offers administration of academic libraries (PMC); administration of public libraries (PMC); administration of special libraries (PMC); consultant in information services (PMC); documents and files administration (Post-Graduate Certificate); electronic information resources analyst (Post-Graduate Certificate); information science (MIS); librarianship and information services (MLS); school librarian (Post-Graduate Certificate); school librarian distance education mode (Post-Graduate Certificate); specialist in legal information (PMC).

Graduate School of Planning *Program availability:* Part-time. Offers economic planning systems (MP); environmental planning (MP); social policy and planning (MP); urban and territorial planning (MP).

School of Architecture *Program availability:* Part-time. Offers architecture (M Arch).

School of Communication *Program availability:* Part-time. Offers communication (MA); communication theory and research (MA); journalism (MA).

School of Law *Program availability:* Part-time, evening/weekend. Offers law (LL M, JD).

UNIVERSITY OF PUGET SOUND, Tacoma, WA 98416

General Information Independent, coed, comprehensive institution. *Graduate housing:* On-campus housing not available.

GRADUATE UNITS

School of Education *Program availability:* Part-time. Offers education (M Ed, MAT); elementary education (MAT); mental health counseling (M Ed); school counseling (M Ed); secondary education (MAT). Electronic applications accepted.

School of Occupational Therapy Offers occupational therapy (MSOT, Dr OT). Electronic applications accepted.

School of Physical Therapy Offers physical therapy (DPT). Electronic applications accepted.

UNIVERSITY OF REDLANDS, Redlands, CA 92373-0999

General Information Independent, coed, comprehensive institution. *Graduate housing:* Rooms and/or apartments available on a first-come, first-served basis to single students and available to married students. Housing application deadline: 8/19. *Research affiliation:* Environmental Systems Research Institute (geographic information systems).

GRADUATE UNITS

College of Arts and Sciences Offers arts and sciences (MM, MS); communication sciences and disorders (MS); geographic information science (MS). Electronic applications accepted.

School of Music *Program availability:* Part-time. Offers music (MM).

School of Business *Program availability:* Evening/weekend. Offers business (MBA); information technology (MS); management (MA).

School of Education *Program availability:* Part-time, evening/weekend. Offers education (MA, Ed D, Certificate).

UNIVERSITY OF REGINA, Regina, SK S4S 0A2, Canada

General Information Province-supported, coed, university. *Enrollment:* 15,568 graduate, professional, and undergraduate students; 968 full-time matriculated graduate/professional students (497 women), 539 part-time matriculated graduate/professional students (376 women). *Enrollment by degree level:* 1,238 master's, 291 doctoral, 69 other advanced degrees. *Graduate faculty:* 472 full-time (195 women), 243 part-time/adjunct (85 women). Tuition and fees vary according to course level, course load, degree level and program. *Graduate housing:* Rooms and/or apartments available on a first-come, first-served basis to single and married students. Typical cost: $11,652 Canadian dollars per year for single students; $15,108 Canadian dollars per year for married students. Room charges vary according to board plan, campus/location and housing facility selected. *Student services:* Campus employment opportunities, campus safety program, career counseling, child daycare facilities, exercise/wellness program, free psychological counseling, grant writing training, international student services, low-cost health insurance, multicultural affairs office, services for students with disabilities, teacher training, writing training. *Library facilities:* Dr. John Archer Library plus 5 others. *Collection:* Books: 806,988 (physical), 802,795 (digital/electronic); Serial titles: 163,120 (physical), 131,946 (digital/electronic); Databases: 519. Weekly public service hours: 105; students can reserve study rooms.

Computer facilities: 412 computers available on campus for general student use. A campuswide network can be accessed from student residence rooms and from off campus. Online class registration is available.
Website: http://www.uregina.ca/

General Application Contact: Mandy Kiel, Faculty Administrator, 306-585-5187, Fax: 306-337-2444, E-mail: grad.studies@uregina.ca.

GRADUATE UNITS

Faculty of Graduate Studies and Research Students: 965 full-time (494 women), 657 part-time (454 women). Average age 30. 2,543 applicants, 26% accepted, 356 enrolled. *Faculty:* 456 full-time (182 women), 204 part-time/adjunct (67 women). *Expenses:* Contact institution. *Financial support:* Fellowships, research assistantships, teaching assistantships, career-related internships or fieldwork, institutionally sponsored loans, scholarships/grants, unspecified assistantships, and travel awards available. Financial award application deadline: 9/30. In 2018, 446 master's, 37 doctorates, 41 other advanced degrees awarded. *Program availability:* Part-time, evening/weekend. First Nations University, University of Saskatchewan and Sask Polytechnic. *Application deadline:* For fall admission, 2/15 for domestic and international students; for winter admission, 7/15 for domestic and international students; for spring admission, 10/15 for domestic and international students. Applications are processed on a rolling basis. *Application fee:* $100. Electronic applications accepted. *Application Contact:* Mandy Kiel, Faculty Administrator, 306-585-5187, Fax: 306-337-2444, E-mail: grad.admin@uregina.ca. *Dean,* Dr. Nick Jones, 306-585-5185, Fax: 306-337-2444, E-mail: grad.dean@uregina.ca.

Faculty of Arts Students: 100 full-time (77 women), 25 part-time (14 women). Average age 30. 168 applicants, 30% accepted, 33 enrolled. *Faculty:* 144 full-time (59 women), 50 part-time/adjunct (20 women). *Expenses:* Contact institution. *Financial support:* In 2018–19, 147 students received support, including 66 fellowships, 43 teaching assistantships (averaging $2,552 per year); research assistantships, career-related internships or fieldwork, Federal Work-Study, scholarships/grants, unspecified assistantships, and travel award and Graduate Scholarship Base funds also available. Support available to part-time students. Financial award application deadline: 9/30. In 2018, 37 master's, 7 doctorates awarded. *Program availability:* Part-time. Offers anthropology (MA); arts (M Sc, MA, MJ, PhD); clinical psychology (MA, PhD); creative writing (MA); English (MA, PhD); experimental and applied psychology (MA, PhD); French (MA); geography (M Sc, MA, PhD); gerontology (M Sc, MA); history (MA); journalism (MJ); justice studies (MA); philosophy (MA); police studies (MA); religious studies (MA); social studies (MA); sociology (MA); women's and gender studies (MA). *Application deadline:* Applications are processed on a rolling basis. *Application fee:* $100. Electronic applications accepted. *Application Contact:* Dr. Troni Grande, Acting Assoc Dean, Graduate Studies, 306-585-4570, E-mail: troni.grande@uregina.ca. *Dean,* Dr. Richard Kleer, 306-585-4895, Fax: 306-585-5368, E-mail: arts.dean@uregina.ca.

Faculty of Education Students: 98 full-time (72 women), 200 part-time (160 women). Average age 30. 88 applicants, 56% accepted, 26 enrolled. *Faculty:* 52 full-time (36 women), 28 part-time/adjunct (15 women). *Expenses:* Contact institution. *Financial support:* In 2018–19, 120 students received support, including 87 fellowships, 27 teaching assistantships (averaging $2,552 per year); research assistantships, career-related internships or fieldwork, Federal Work-Study, scholarships/grants, unspecified assistantships, and travel award and Graduate Scholarship Base funds also available. Support available to part-time students. Financial award application deadline: 9/30. In 2018, 102 master's, 5 doctorates, 3 other advanced degrees awarded. *Program availability:* Part-time. Offers adult education (MA Ed); curriculum and instruction (M Ed); education (M Ed, MA Ed, MHRD, PhD, Master's Certificate); educational administration (M Ed); educational psychology (M Ed); human resource development (MHRD). Joint with Gabriel Dumont Institute in Community Based Master program. *Application deadline:* For fall admission, 2/15 for domestic and international students; for winter admission, 10/15 for domestic and international students; for spring admission, 2/15 for domestic and international students. *Application fee:* $100. Electronic applications accepted. *Application Contact:* Linda Jiang, Graduate Program Coordinator, 306-585-4506, Fax: 306-585-5387, E-mail: edgrad@uregina.ca. *Dean,* Dr. Jarome Cranston, 306-585-4500, Fax: 306-585-5387, E-mail: Jerome.Cranston@uregina.ca.

Faculty of Engineering and Applied Science Students: 255 full-time (69 women), 32 part-time (7 women). Average age 30. 154 applicants, 33% accepted. *Faculty:* 44 full-time (6 women), 26 part-time/adjunct (2 women). *Expenses:* Contact institution. *Financial support:* In 2018–19, 24 fellowships (averaging $6,000 per year), 70 teaching assistantships (averaging $2,562 per year) were awarded; research assistantships, career-related internships or fieldwork, scholarships/grants, and unspecified assistantships also available. Financial award application deadline: 6/15. In 2018, 88 master's, 14 doctorates awarded. *Program availability:* Part-time. Offers electronic systems (M Eng, MA Sc, PhD); electronic systems engineering (M Eng, MA Sc, PhD); environmental systems (M Eng, MA Sc, PhD); environmental systems engineering (M Eng, MA Sc, PhD); industrial systems (M Eng, MA Sc, PhD); industrial systems engineering (M Eng, MA Sc, PhD); petroleum systems (M Eng, MA Sc,

PhD); petroleum systems engineering (M Eng, MA Sc, PhD); process systems (M Eng, MA Sc, PhD); process systems engineering (M Eng, MA Sc, PhD); software systems (M Eng, MA Sc, PhD); software systems engineering (M Eng, MA Sc, PhD). *Application deadline:* For fall admission, 3/31 for domestic and international students; for winter admission, 7/31 for domestic and international students; for spring admission, 11/30 for domestic and international students. *Application fee:* $100. Electronic applications accepted. *Application Contact:* Colleen Walsh, Graduate and Co-operative Education Coordinator, 306-585-5416, Fax: 306-585-4556, E-mail: colleen.walsh@uregina.ca. *Acting Dean,* Dr. Amr Henni, 306-585-4960, Fax: 306-585-4556, E-mail: Amr.Henni@uregina.ca.

Faculty of Kinesiology and Health Studies Students: 24 full-time (9 women), 14 part-time (7 women). Average age 30. 14 applicants, 36% accepted, 3 enrolled. *Faculty:* 18 full-time (9 women), 24 part-time/adjunct (10 women). *Expenses:* Contact institution. *Financial support:* In 2018–19, 31 students received support, including 12 fellowships, 9 teaching assistantships (averaging $2,552 per year); research assistantships, career-related internships or fieldwork, scholarships/grants, unspecified assistantships, and Travel Award and Graduate Scholarship Base funds also available. Support available to part-time students. Financial award application deadline: 9/30. In 2018, 3 master's, 1 doctorate awarded. *Program availability:* Part-time. Offers kinesiology and health studies (M Sc, PhD). *Application deadline:* Applications are processed on a rolling basis. *Application fee:* $100 Canadian dollars. Electronic applications accepted. *Application Contact:* Dr. Darren Candow, Associate Dean, Graduate Studies and Research, 306-585-4906, Fax: 306-585-4854, E-mail: darren.candow@uregina.ca. *Dean,* Dr. Harold Riemer, 306-585-4535, Fax: 306-585-4854, E-mail: khs.dean@uregina.ca.

Faculty of Media, Art, and Performance Students: 36 full-time (23 women), 7 part-time (6 women). Average age 30. 49 applicants, 31% accepted, 10 enrolled. *Faculty:* 40 full-time (24 women), 3 part-time/adjunct (1 woman). *Expenses:* Contact institution. *Financial support:* In 2018–19, 71 students received support, including 52 fellowships, 12 teaching assistantships (averaging $2,552 per year); research assistantships, career-related internships or fieldwork, scholarships/grants, and travel award and Graduate Scholarship Base funds also available. Support available to part-time students. Financial award application deadline: 9/30. In 2018, 4 master's awarded. *Program availability:* Part-time. Offers ceramics (MFA); composition (MMus); conducting (MMus); drawing (MFA); interdisciplinary studies (MA, MFA); intermedia (MFA); media production (MFA); media studies (MA); media, art, and performance (MA, MFA, MMus); music theory (MA); musicology (MA); painting (MFA); performance (MMus); sculpture (MFA). *Application deadline:* For fall admission, 1/15 for domestic and international students. Applications are processed on a rolling basis. *Application fee:* $100. Electronic applications accepted. *Application Contact:* Dr. Kathleen Irwin, Associate Dean, Graduate and Research, 306-585-5519, Fax: 306-585-5544, E-mail: kathleen.irwin@uregina.ca. *Dean,* Dr. Rae Staseson, 306-585-5510, Fax: 306-585-5544, E-mail: Map.Dean@uregina.ca.

Faculty of Nursing Students: 20 full-time (19 women), 32 part-time (29 women). 48 applicants, 56% accepted, 24 enrolled. *Faculty:* 17 full-time (13 women), 8 part-time/adjunct (all women). *Expenses:* Contact institution. *Financial support:* In 2018–19, 27 students received support, including 26 fellowships, 2 teaching assistantships (averaging $2,552 per year); career-related internships or fieldwork, Federal Work-Study, scholarships/grants, unspecified assistantships, and travel Award and Graduate Scholarship Base Funds also available. Support available to part-time students. Financial award application deadline: 9/30. In 2018, 9 master's awarded. Offers nurse practitioner clinical nurse specialist (MN); nursing (M Sc, PhD). *Application deadline:* For fall admission, 3/15 for domestic and international students. *Application fee:* $100 Canadian dollars. Electronic applications accepted. *Application Contact:* Gillian Borys, Graduate Program Assistant, 306-337-3355, Fax: 306-337-8493, E-mail: gillian.borys@uregina.ca. *Associate Dean, Graduate Programs and Research,* Dr. David Gregory, 306-585-5608, Fax: 306-337-8493, E-mail: david.gregory@uregina.ca.

Faculty of Science Students: 253 full-time (108 women), 36 part-time (10 women). Average age 25. 526 applicants, 27% accepted, 46 enrolled. *Faculty:* 89 full-time (20 women), 50 part-time/adjunct (7 women). *Expenses:* Contact institution. *Financial support:* In 2018–19, 168 students received support, including 115 fellowships, 62 teaching assistantships (averaging $2,552 per year); research assistantships, career-related internships or fieldwork, Federal Work-Study, scholarships/grants, unspecified assistantships, and travel award and Graduate Scholarship Base funds also available. Support available to part-time students. Financial award application deadline: 9/30. In 2018, 37 master's, 10 doctorates awarded. *Program availability:* Part-time. Offers biology (M Sc, PhD); biophysics of biological interfaces (M Sc, PhD); computational chemistry (M Sc, PhD); computer science (M Sc, PhD); environmental analytical chemistry (M Sc, PhD); enzymology/chemical biology (M Sc, PhD); geology (M Sc, PhD); inorganic/organometallic chemistry (M Sc, PhD); mathematics (M Sc, PhD); physics (M Sc, PhD); science (M Sc, PhD); signal transduction and mechanisms of cancer cell regulation (M Sc, PhD); statistics (M Sc, PhD); supramolecular organic photochemistry and photophysics (M Sc, PhD); synthetic organic chemistry (M Sc, PhD). *Application deadline:* Applications are processed on a rolling basis. *Application fee:* $100. Electronic applications accepted. *Application Contact:* Dr. Cory Butz, Associate Dean for Research, 306-585-4201, Fax: 306-585-4291, E-mail: cory.butz@uregina.ca. *Dean,* Dr. Douglas Farenick, 306-337-2110, Fax: 306-585-4291, E-mail: douglas.farenick@uregina.ca.

Faculty of Social Work Students: 10 full-time (all women), 1 (woman) part-time. Average age 30. 76 applicants, 25% accepted, 17 enrolled. *Faculty:* 25 full-time (17 women), 8 part-time/adjunct (3 women). *Expenses:* Contact institution. *Financial support:* In 2018–19, 38 students received support, including 32 fellowships, 6 teaching assistantships (averaging $2,552 per year); research assistantships, career-related internships or fieldwork, Federal Work-Study, scholarships/grants, unspecified assistantships, and travel award and Graduate Scholarship Base funds also available. Support available to part-time students. Financial award application deadline: 9/30. In 2018, 20 master's awarded. *Program availability:* Part-time. Offers indigenous social work (MISW); social work (MSW, PhD). PhD offered as a special case program. *Application deadline:* For fall admission, 1/31 for domestic and international students. *Application fee:* $100. Electronic applications accepted. *Application Contact:* Dr. Nuelle Novik, Graduate Program Coordinator, 306-585-4573, Fax: 306-585-4872, E-mail: nuelle.novik@uregina.ca. *Dean,* Dr. Judy White, 306-585-4037, Fax: 306-585-5691, E-mail: sw.dean@uregina.ca.

Johnson-Shoyama Graduate School of Public Policy Students: 102 full-time (62 women), 147 part-time (107 women). Average age 30. 260 applicants, 53% accepted, 92 enrolled. *Faculty:* 9 full-time (4 women), 19 part-time/adjunct (9 women). *Expenses:* Contact institution. *Financial support:* In 2018–19, 43 fellowships, 16 teaching assistantships (averaging $2,552 per year) were awarded; research assistantships, career-related internships or fieldwork, Federal Work-Study, scholarships/grants, unspecified assistantships, and travel award and Graduate Scholarship Base funds also available. Support available to part-time students. Financial award application deadline: 9/30. In 2018, 78 master's, 29 other advanced degrees awarded. *Program availability:* Part-time. Offers economic analysis for public policy (Master's Certificate); health administration (MHA); health systems management (Master's Certificate); public management (MPA, Master's Certificate); public policy (MPA, MPP, PhD); public policy analysis (Master's Certificate). *Application deadline:* For fall admission, 5/1 for domestic and international students; for winter admission, 11/1 for domestic students; for spring admission, 3/1 for domestic students. *Application fee:* $100. Electronic applications accepted. *Application Contact:* John Bird, Academic Advisor, 306-585-5469, Fax: 306-585-5461, E-mail: john.bird@uregina.ca. *Executive Director,* Dr. Doug Moen, 306-585-4921, Fax: 306-585-5461, E-mail: doeg.moen@uregina.ca.

Kenneth Levene Graduate School of Business Students: 72 full-time (52 women), 47 part-time (34 women). Average age 30. 271 applicants, 31% accepted, 36 enrolled. *Faculty:* 41 full-time (15 women), 7 part-time/adjunct (3 women). Expenses: Contact institution. *Financial support:* In 2018–19, 58 students received support, including 37 fellowships, 9 teaching assistantships (averaging $2,552 per year); research assistantships, career-related internships or fieldwork, Federal Work-Study, scholarships/grants, unspecified assistantships, and travel award and Graduate Scholarship Base funds also available. Support available to part-time students. Financial award application deadline: 9/30. In 2018, 62 master's, 9 other advanced degrees awarded. *Program availability:* Part-time. Offers business (EMBA, M Admin, MBA, MHRM, Master's Certificate, PGD); business foundations (PGD); engineering management (MBA); executive business administration (EMBA); human resources management (MHRM, Master's Certificate); international business (MBA); leadership (M Admin); organizational leadership (Master's Certificate); project management (Master's Certificate); public safety management (MBA). *Application deadline:* For fall admission, 3/1 for domestic and international students; for winter admission, 7/1 for domestic and international students; for spring admission, 10/1 for domestic and international students; for summer admission, 10/1 for domestic and international students. *Application fee:* $100. Electronic applications accepted. *Application Contact:* Dr. Adrian Pitariu, Associate Dean, Research and Graduate Programs, 306-585-6294, Fax: 306-585-5361, E-mail: business.AD.levene@uregina.ca. *Dean,* Dr. Gina Grandy, 306-585-4435, Fax: 306-585-5361, E-mail: business.levene@uregina.ca.

UNIVERSITY OF RHODE ISLAND, Kingston, RI 02881

General Information State-supported, coed, university. CGS member. *Enrollment:* 1,875 full-time matriculated graduate/professional students (1,164 women), 933 part-time matriculated graduate/professional students (534 women). *Enrollment by degree level:* 1,309 master's, 1,449 doctoral, 50 other advanced degrees. *Graduate faculty:* 670 full-time (329 women), 4 part-time/adjunct (2 women). *International tuition:* $25,854 full-time. *Tuition, area resident:* Full-time $13,226; part-time $735 per credit. Tuition, state resident: full-time $13,226; part-time $735 per credit. Tuition, nonresident: full-time $25,854; part-time $1436 per credit. *Required fees:* $1698; $50 per credit. $35 per semester. One-time fee: $165. *Graduate housing:* Rooms and/or apartments available on a first-come, first-served basis to single and married students. Housing application deadline: 5/1. *Student services:* Campus employment opportunities, campus safety program, career counseling, free psychological counseling, international student services, low-cost health insurance, multicultural affairs office, services for students with disabilities. *Library facilities:* Robert L. Carothers Library and Learning Commons plus 3 others. *Collection:* Study areas open 24 hours, 5–7 days a week; students can reserve study rooms.

Computer facilities: Computer purchase and lease plans are available. 2,500 computers available on campus for general student use. A campuswide network can be accessed from student residence rooms and from off campus. Online class registration is available.
Website: http://www.uri.edu/

General Application Contact: Graduate School Main Number, 401-874-2262, E-mail: urigrad@etal.uri.edu.

GRADUATE UNITS

Graduate School Students: 1,875 full-time (1,164 women), 933 part-time (534 women); includes 380 minority (83 Black or African American, non-Hispanic/Latino; 8 American Indian or Alaska Native, non-Hispanic/Latino; 140 Asian, non-Hispanic/Latino; 107 Hispanic/Latino; 6 Native Hawaiian or other Pacific Islander, non-Hispanic/Latino; 36 Two or more races, non-Hispanic/Latino), 289 international. 2,487 applicants, 55% accepted, 781 enrolled. *Faculty:* 670 full-time (329 women), 4 part-time/adjunct (2 women). Expenses: Contact institution. *Financial support:* In 2018–19, 145 research assistantships with full tuition reimbursements (averaging $10,341 per year), 325 teaching assistantships with full tuition reimbursements (averaging $13,356 per year) were awarded; unspecified assistantships also available. Financial award application deadline: 2/1; financial award applicants required to submit FAFSA. In 2018, 581 master's, 269 doctorates, 93 other advanced degrees awarded. *Program availability:* Part-time, evening/weekend, 100% online, blended/hybrid learning. *Application deadline:* For fall admission, 7/15 for domestic students, 2/1 for international students; for spring admission, 11/15 for domestic students, 7/15 for international students. *Application fee:* $65. Electronic applications accepted. *Application Contact:* Graduate Admissions, 401-874-2262, E-mail: urigrad@etal.uri.edu. *Dean of the Graduate School,* Dr. Nasser H. Zawia, 401-874-5909, Fax: 401-874-5787, E-mail: nzawia@uri.edu.

Alan Shawn Feinstein College of Education and Professional Studies Students: 53 full-time (35 women), 151 part-time (124 women); includes 28 minority (13 Black or African American, non-Hispanic/Latino; 3 American Indian or Alaska Native, non-Hispanic/Latino; 4 Asian, non-Hispanic/Latino; 5 Hispanic/Latino; 3 Two or more races, non-Hispanic/Latino), 6 international. 79 applicants, 71% accepted, 44 enrolled. *Faculty:* 24 full-time (5 women). Expenses: Contact institution. *Financial support:* In 2018–19, 1 research assistantship with tuition reimbursement (averaging $9,040 per year), 4 teaching assistantships with tuition reimbursements (averaging $15,776 per year) were awarded; unspecified assistantships also available. In 2018, 54 master's, 6 doctorates awarded. Offers education (PhD); education and professional studies (MA, MM, MS, PhD); reading (MA); special education (MA). *Application Contact:* R. Anthony Rolle, Dean, 401-277-5489, E-mail: anthony_rolle@uri.edu. *Dean,* R. Anthony Rolle, 401-277-5489, E-mail: anthony_rolle@uri.edu.

College of Arts and Sciences Students: 217 full-time (110 women), 255 part-time (129 women); includes 52 minority (12 Black or African American, non-Hispanic/Latino; 13 Asian, non-Hispanic/Latino; 21 Hispanic/Latino; 2 Native Hawaiian or other Pacific Islander, non-Hispanic/Latino; 4 Two or more races, non-Hispanic/Latino), 49 international. 299 applicants, 86% accepted, 155 enrolled. *Faculty:* 221 full-time (99 women). Expenses: Contact institution. *Financial support:* In 2018–19, 8 research assistantships with tuition reimbursements (averaging $8,545 per year), 131 teaching

assistantships with tuition reimbursements (averaging $15,812 per year) were awarded; unspecified assistantships also available. Financial award applicants required to submit FAFSA. In 2018, 127 master's, 32 doctorates, 28 other advanced degrees awarded. *Program availability:* Part-time, evening/weekend. Offers American literature and culture (PhD); applied analysis (MS); applied mathematical sciences (PhD); archaeology and anthropology (MA); arts and sciences (MA, MLIS, MM, MPA, MS, PSM, PhD, Graduate Certificate); British literature and culture (PhD); chemistry (MS, PhD); combinatorics and graph theory (MS); communication studies (MA); complex dynamical systems (MS); computer science (MS, PhD); creative writing (PhD); critical theories (PhD); cyber security (PSM, Graduate Certificate); difference equations (MS); digital forensics (Graduate Certificate); English (MA); European history (MA); film (MA); gender and women's studies (Graduate Certificate); gender studies (PhD); international relations (MA); libraries, leadership and transforming communities (MLIS); medical physics (MS); music education (MM); music performance (MM); numerical analysis (MS); organization of digital media (MLIS); physics (MS, PhD); public policy and administration (MPA); pure mathematics (MS); school library media (MLIS); Spanish (MA). *Application fee:* $65. Electronic applications accepted. *Application Contact:* Dr. Jeannette Riley, Dean, 401-874-4101, E-mail: jen_riley@uri.edu. *Dean,* Dr. Jeannette Riley, 401-874-4101, E-mail: jen_riley@uri.edu.

College of Business Students: 85 full-time (35 women), 196 part-time (89 women); includes 43 minority (14 Black or African American, non-Hispanic/Latino; 1 American Indian or Alaska Native, non-Hispanic/Latino; 14 Asian, non-Hispanic/Latino; 10 Hispanic/Latino; 1 Native Hawaiian or other Pacific Islander, non-Hispanic/Latino; 3 Two or more races, non-Hispanic/Latino), 23 international. 155 applicants, 85% accepted, 105 enrolled. *Faculty:* 61 full-time (30 women), 1 (woman) part-time/adjunct. Expenses: Contact institution. *Financial support:* In 2018–19, 15 teaching assistantships with tuition reimbursements (averaging $17,739 per year) were awarded; research assistantships also available. Financial award applicants required to submit FAFSA. In 2018, 127 master's, 5 doctorates, 23 other advanced degrees awarded. *Program availability:* Part-time, evening/weekend. Offers accounting (MS); business administration (MBA, PhD); fashion merchandising (Certificate); finance (MBA, MS, PhD); general business (MBA); health care management (MBA); labor relations and human resources (MS, Graduate Certificate); labor research (MS, Graduate Certificate); management (MBA); marketing (MBA, PhD); master seamstress (Certificate); operations and supply chain management (PhD); strategic innovation (MBA); supply chain management (MBA); textiles, fashion merchandising and design (MS, Certificate). *Application fee:* $65. Electronic applications accepted. *Application Contact:* Lisa Lancellotta, Coordinator, MBA Programs, 401-874-4241, Fax: 401-874-4312, E-mail: mba@uri.edu. *Dean,* Dr. Maling Ebrahimpour, 401-874-4348, Fax: 401-874-4312, E-mail: mebrahimpour@uri.edu.

College of Engineering Students: 137 full-time (35 women), 88 part-time (13 women); includes 26 minority (6 Black or African American, non-Hispanic/Latino; 1 American Indian or Alaska Native, non-Hispanic/Latino; 9 Asian, non-Hispanic/Latino; 9 Hispanic/Latino; 1 Two or more races, non-Hispanic/Latino), 78 international. 170 applicants, 68% accepted, 67 enrolled. *Faculty:* 72 full-time (14 women), 1 part-time/adjunct (0 women). Expenses: Contact institution. *Financial support:* In 2018–19, 50 research assistantships with full tuition reimbursements (averaging $10,164 per year), 30 teaching assistantships with full tuition reimbursements (averaging $9,283 per year) were awarded. Financial award applicants required to submit FAFSA. In 2018, 49 master's, 16 doctorates, 1 other advanced degree awarded. *Program availability:* Part-time. Offers acoustics and underwater acoustics (MS, PhD); biomedical engineering (MS, PhD); chemical engineering (MS, PhD); circuits and devices (MS); civil and environmental engineering (MS, PhD); communication theory (MS, PhD); computer architectures and digital systems (MS, PhD); computer networks (MS, PhD); digital signal processing (MS); embedded systems and computer applications (MS, PhD); engineering (MS, PhD, Graduate Certificate, Postbaccalaureate Certificate); fault-tolerant computing (MS, PhD); industrial and systems engineering (MS, PhD); materials and optics (MS, PhD); ocean engineering (MS, PhD); polymer (Postbaccalaureate Certificate); systems theory (MS, PhD). *Application fee:* $65. Electronic applications accepted. *Application Contact:* Dr. Raymond Wright, Dean, 401-874-2186, Fax: 401-782-1066, E-mail: dean@egr.uri.edu. *Dean,* Dr. Raymond Wright, 401-874-2186, Fax: 401-782-1066, E-mail: dean@egr.uri.edu.

College of Health Sciences Students: 266 full-time (211 women), 96 part-time (73 women); includes 50 minority (11 Black or African American, non-Hispanic/Latino; 1 American Indian or Alaska Native, non-Hispanic/Latino; 25 Asian, non-Hispanic/Latino; 10 Hispanic/Latino; 3 Two or more races, non-Hispanic/Latino), 11 international. 556 applicants, 30% accepted, 113 enrolled. *Faculty:* 84 full-time (57 women), 2 part-time/adjunct (1 woman). Expenses: Contact institution. *Financial support:* In 2018–19, 11 research assistantships with tuition reimbursements (averaging $10,920 per year), 45 teaching assistantships with tuition reimbursements (averaging $11,410 per year) were awarded. Financial award applicants required to submit FAFSA. In 2018, 95 master's, 41 doctorates awarded. *Program availability:* Part-time, evening/weekend, 100% online, blended/hybrid learning. Offers behavioral science (PhD); clinical psychology (PhD); college student personnel (MS); cultural studies of sport and physical culture (MS); dietetic internship (MS); exercise science (MS); health sciences (MA, MM, MS, DPT, PhD); human development and family studies (MS); marriage and family therapy (MS); nutrition (MS); online dietetics (MS); physical therapy (DPT); psychosocial/behavioral aspects of physical activity (MS); school psychology (MS, PhD); speech-language pathology (MS). *Application fee:* $65. Electronic applications accepted. *Application Contact:* Dr. Gary Liguori, Dean, 401-874-9330, E-mail: gliguori@uri.edu. *Dean,* Dr. Gary Liguori, 401-874-9330, E-mail: gliguori@uri.edu.

College of Nursing Students: 48 full-time (44 women), 80 part-time (71 women); includes 18 minority (9 Black or African American, non-Hispanic/Latino; 2 Asian, non-Hispanic/Latino; 4 Hispanic/Latino; 2 Native Hawaiian or other Pacific Islander, non-Hispanic/Latino; 1 Two or more races, non-Hispanic/Latino), 6 international. 35 applicants, 71% accepted, 21 enrolled. *Faculty:* 32 full-time (31 women). Expenses: Contact institution. *Financial support:* In 2018–19, 5 teaching assistantships with tuition reimbursements (averaging $13,412 per year) were awarded. Financial award application deadline: 2/1; financial award applicants required to submit FAFSA. In 2018, 26 master's, 7 doctorates, 4 other advanced degrees awarded. *Program availability:* Part-time, evening/weekend, 100% online, blended/hybrid learning. Offers acute care nurse practitioner (adult-gerontology focus) (Post Master's Certificate); adult gerontology nurse practitioner/clinical nurse specialist (Post Master's Certificate); adult-gerontological acute care nurse practitioner (MS); adult-gerontological nurse practitioner/clinical nurse specialist (MS); family nurse practitioner (MS, Post Master's Certificate); nursing (DNP, PhD); nursing education

(MS, Post Master's Certificate). *Application deadline:* For fall admission, 2/15 for domestic students, 2/1 for international students; for spring admission, 10/15 for domestic students, 7/15 for international students. *Application fee:* $65. Electronic applications accepted. *Application Contact:* Dr. Denise Coppa, Associate Professor/Interim Associate Dean for Graduate Programs, 401-874-5036, E-mail: dcoppa@uri.edu. *Dean,* Dr. Barbara Wolfe, 401-874-5324, E-mail: bwolfe@uri.edu.

College of Pharmacy Students: 812 full-time (543 women), 16 part-time (10 women); includes 138 minority (10 Black or African American, non-Hispanic/Latino; 1 American Indian or Alaska Native, non-Hispanic/Latino; 66 Asian, non-Hispanic/Latino; 43 Hispanic/Latino; 18 Two or more races, non-Hispanic/Latino), 61 international. 782 applicants, 55% accepted, 183 enrolled. *Faculty:* 51 full-time (34 women). Expenses: Contact institution. *Financial support:* In 2018–19, 17 research assistantships with tuition reimbursements (averaging $11,834 per year), 17 teaching assistantships with tuition reimbursements (averaging $13,526 per year) were awarded. Financial award application deadline: 2/1; financial award applicants required to submit FAFSA. In 2018, 5 master's, 138 doctorates awarded. *Program availability:* Part-time. Offers health outcomes (MS, PhD); medicinal chemistry and pharmacognosy (MS, PhD); pharmaceutics and pharmacokinetics (MS, PhD); pharmacology and toxicology (MS, PhD); pharmacy (MS, PhD, Pharm D); pharmacy practice (Pharm D). *Application fee:* $65. Electronic applications accepted. *Application Contact:* Dr. E. Paul Larrat, Dean/Professor, 401-874-5003, Fax: 401-874-2181, E-mail: larrat@uri.edu. *Dean/Professor,* Dr. E. Paul Larrat, 401-874-5003, Fax: 401-874-2181, E-mail: larrat@uri.edu.

College of the Environment and Life Sciences Students: 201 full-time (118 women), 41 part-time (20 women); includes 24 minority (8 Black or African American, non-Hispanic/Latino; 1 American Indian or Alaska Native, non-Hispanic/Latino; 6 Asian, non-Hispanic/Latino; 5 Hispanic/Latino; 1 Native Hawaiian or other Pacific Islander, non-Hispanic/Latino; 3 Two or more races, non-Hispanic/Latino), 45 international. 235 applicants, 57% accepted, 76 enrolled. *Faculty:* 96 full-time (39 women). Expenses: Contact institution. *Financial support:* In 2018–19, 28 research assistantships with tuition reimbursements (averaging $11,197 per year), 64 teaching assistantships with tuition reimbursements (averaging $13,212 per year) were awarded. Financial award applicants required to submit FAFSA. In 2018, 83 master's, 19 doctorates, 25 other advanced degrees awarded. *Program availability:* Part-time. Offers animal health and disease (MS); animal science (MS); aquaculture (MS); aquatic pathology (MS); biochemistry (MS, PhD); cell and molecular biology (MS, PhD); clinical laboratory sciences (MS); earth and environmental sciences (MS, PhD); ecology and ecosystem sciences (MS, PhD); environment and life sciences (MA, MESM, MMA, MS, PhD, Graduate Certificate); environmental and earth sciences (MS, PhD); environmental and natural resource economics (MS, PhD); environmental science and management (MESM); environmental sciences (PhD); evolutionary and marine biology (MS, PhD); fisheries (MS); hydrology (Graduate Certificate); marine affairs (MA, MMA, PhD); microbiology (MS, PhD); molecular genetics (MS, PhD); natural resources science (MS, PhD); sustainable agriculture and food systems (MS, PhD). *Application fee:* $65. Electronic applications accepted. *Application Contact:* Dr. John Kirby, Dean, 401-874-2957, Fax: 401-874-4017, E-mail: jdkirby@uri.edu. *Dean,* Dr. John Kirby, 401-874-2957, Fax: 401-874-4017, E-mail: jdkirby@uri.edu.

Graduate School of Oceanography Students: 56 full-time (33 women), 10 part-time (5 women); includes 1 minority (Asian, non-Hispanic/Latino), 10 international. 76 applicants, 72% accepted, 17 enrolled. *Faculty:* 29 full-time (10 women). Expenses: Contact institution. *Financial support:* In 2018–19, 31 research assistantships with tuition reimbursements (averaging $9,647 per year), 14 teaching assistantships with tuition reimbursements (averaging $10,563 per year) were awarded. Financial award application deadline: 1/15; financial award applicants required to submit FAFSA. In 2018, 15 master's, 5 doctorates awarded. *Program availability:* Part-time. Offers biological oceanography (MS, PhD); coastal ocean management (MO); coastal systems (MO); fisheries (MO); general oceanography (MO); marine and atmospheric chemistry (MS, PhD); marine fisheries management (MO); marine geology and geophysics (MS, PhD); ocean technology and data (MO); physical oceanography (MS, PhD). *Application deadline:* For fall admission, 1/15 for domestic and international students. *Application fee:* $65. Electronic applications accepted. *Application Contact:* Dr. David Smith, Professor of Oceanography/Associate Dean for Academic Affairs, 401-874-6172, E-mail: dcsmith@uri.edu. *Dean,* Dr. Bruce Corliss, 401-874-6222, Fax: 401-874-6931, E-mail: bruce.corliss@gso.uri.edu.

UNIVERSITY OF RICHMOND, University of Richmond, VA 23173

General Information Independent, coed, comprehensive institution. *Graduate housing:* On-campus housing not available.

GRADUATE UNITS

Robins School of Business *Program availability:* Part-time, evening/weekend. Offers business (MBA). Electronic applications accepted.

School of Law Offers law (JD). JD/MSW, JD/MHA, JD/MPA offered jointly with Virginia Commonwealth University; JD/MURP with Virginia Commonwealth University; JD/MA with Department of History; JD/MS with Department of Biology. Electronic applications accepted.

UNIVERSITY OF RIO GRANDE, Rio Grande, OH 45674

General Information Independent, coed, comprehensive institution. *Graduate housing:* Room and/or apartments available on a first-come, first-served basis to single students; on-campus housing not available to married students.

GRADUATE UNITS

Graduate School *Program availability:* Part-time. Offers athletic coaching leadership (M Ed); educational leadership (M Ed); integrated arts (M Ed); intervention specialist in early childhood (M Ed); intervention specialist in mild/moderate (M Ed).

UNIVERSITY OF ROCHESTER, Rochester, NY 14627

General Information Independent, coed, university. CGS member. *Enrollment:* 3,644 full-time matriculated graduate/professional students (1,710 women), 1,638 part-time matriculated graduate/professional students (1,090 women). *Tuition:* Full-time $52,974; part-time $1654 per credit hour. *Required fees:* $612. One-time fee: $30 part-time. Tuition and fees vary according to campus/location and program. *Graduate housing:* Rooms and/or apartments available on a first-come, first-served basis to single and married students. *Student services:* Campus employment opportunities, campus safety program, career counseling, exercise/wellness program, free psychological counseling, grant writing training, international student services, low-cost health insurance, multicultural affairs office, services for students with disabilities, teacher training, writing training. *Library facilities:* Rush Rhees Library plus 7 others. *Collection:* Study areas open 24 hours, 5–7 days a week; students can reserve study rooms.

Computer facilities: Computer purchase and lease plans are available. 700 computers available on campus for general student use. A campuswide network can be accessed. Online class registration is available. Website: http://www.rochester.edu/

General Application Contact: Melissa Sturge-Apple, PhD, Vice Provost and University Dean of Graduate Education, 585-275-3540, E-mail: melissa.sturge-apple@rochester.edu.

GRADUATE UNITS

Eastman School of Music *Program availability:* Part-time. Offers conducting (MM, DMA); ethnomusicology (MA); jazz studies/contemporary media (MM); music composition (MA, MM, DMA, PhD); music education (MA, MM, DMA, PhD); music theory (PhD); music theory pedagogy (MA); musicology (PhD); performance and literature (MM, DMA); piano accompanying and chamber music (MM, DMA).

Hajim School of Engineering and Applied Sciences Students: 630 full-time (159 women), 21 part-time (4 women); includes 73 minority (18 Black or African American, non-Hispanic/Latino; 1 American Indian or Alaska Native, non-Hispanic/Latino; 29 Asian, non-Hispanic/Latino; 18 Hispanic/Latino; 7 Two or more races, non-Hispanic/Latino), 411 international. Average age 26. 2,490 applicants, 40% accepted, 245 enrolled. *Faculty:* 97 full-time (13 women). Expenses: Contact institution. *Financial support:* Fellowships, research assistantships, teaching assistantships, career-related internships or fieldwork, scholarships/grants, traineeships, health care benefits, tuition waivers, and unspecified assistantships available. Support available to part-time students. In 2018, 167 master's, 49 doctorates awarded. Offers algorithms and complexity (MS); artificial intelligence and machine learning (MS); biomedical engineering (MS); biomedical ultrasound and biomedical engineering (MS); chemical engineering (MS, PhD); computer architecture (MS); computer science (PhD); engineering and applied sciences (MS, PhD); human computer interaction (MS); integrated electronics and computer engineering (MS, PhD); materials science (MS, PhD); mechanical engineering (MS, PhD); music acoustics and signal processing (MS); natural language processing (MS); physical electronics, electron magnetism, and acoustics (PhD); programming languages and computer systems (MS); signal and image processing and communications (MS); signal processing and communications (PhD). *Application fee:* $60. Electronic applications accepted. *Application Contact:* Gretchen Briscoe, Director of Graduate Enrollment, 585-275-2059, E-mail: gretchen.briscoe@rochester.edu. *Dean, Hajim School of Engineering and Applied Sciences/Professor of Electrical and Computer Engineering,* Dr. Wendi Heinzelman, 585-273-3958, E-mail: wendi.heinzelman@rochester.edu.

Institute of Optics Students: 127 full-time (27 women), 6 part-time (1 woman); includes 21 minority (2 Black or African American, non-Hispanic/Latino; 10 Asian, non-Hispanic/Latino; 6 Hispanic/Latino; 3 Two or more races, non-Hispanic/Latino), 67 international. Average age 26. 275 applicants, 55% accepted, 45 enrolled. *Faculty:* 19 full-time (1 woman). Expenses: Contact institution. *Financial support:* In 2018–19, 154 students received support, including 26 fellowships with full and partial tuition reimbursements available (averaging $30,000 per year), 86 research assistantships with full and partial tuition reimbursements available (averaging $30,000 per year), 42 teaching assistantships with full and partial tuition reimbursements available (averaging $9,996 per year); health care benefits and tuition waivers (full and partial) also available. In 2018, 31 master's, 16 doctorates awarded. *Program availability:* Part-time. Offers optics (MS, PhD). *Application fee:* $60. Electronic applications accepted. *Application Contact:* Kai Davies, Graduate Program Coordinator, 585-275-7629, E-mail: kai.davies@rochester.edu. *Director/Professor of Optics,* Scott Carney, 585-274-0113, E-mail: scott.carney@rochester.edu.

Margaret Warner Graduate School of Education and Human Development *Program availability:* Part-time, evening/weekend. Offers counseling (Ed D); education and human development (MS, Ed D, PhD); educational administration (Ed D); educational policy (MS); educational policy and theory (PhD); higher education (MS, PhD); higher education student affairs (MS); human development (MS); human development in educational context (PhD); school and community counseling (MS); school counseling (MS); school leadership (MS); teaching and curriculum (MS); teaching, curriculum, and change (PhD).

School of Arts and Sciences Students: 703 full-time (305 women), 14 part-time (8 women); includes 86 minority (10 Black or African American, non-Hispanic/Latino; 1 American Indian or Alaska Native, non-Hispanic/Latino; 21 Asian, non-Hispanic/Latino; 40 Hispanic/Latino; 14 Two or more races, non-Hispanic/Latino), 279 international. Average age 28. 2,268 applicants, 27% accepted, 181 enrolled. *Faculty:* 272 full-time (80 women). Expenses: Contact institution. *Financial support:* Fellowships, research assistantships, teaching assistantships, career-related internships or fieldwork, Federal Work-Study, institutionally sponsored loans, scholarships/grants, traineeships, health care benefits, tuition waivers, and unspecified assistantships available. Support available to part-time students. In 2018, 118 master's, 69 doctorates awarded. Offers arts and sciences (MA, MS, PhD, AC); biology (MS); brain and cognitive sciences (PhD); clinical psychology (PhD); computational linguistics (MS); developmental psychology (PhD); ecology, genetics, and genomics (PhD); economics (PhD); English (MA, PhD); epistemology (PhD); ethics (PhD); geological sciences (MS); geosciences (PhD); history (MA, PhD); history of ancient philosophy (PhD); history of modern philosophy (PhD); inorganic chemistry (PhD); language documentation and description (MA); linguistics (MA); literary translation studies (MA, AC); mathematics (PhD); metaphysics (PhD); molecular, cellular, and developmental biology evolution (PhD); organic chemistry (PhD); philosophy of language (PhD); philosophy of mind (PhD); photographic preservation and collections management (MA); physical chemistry (PhD); physics and astronomy (PhD); political science (PhD); social-personality psychology (PhD); visual and cultural studies (PhD). Electronic applications accepted. *Application Contact:* Gretchen Briscoe, Director of Graduate Enrollment, 585-275-5029, E-mail: gretchen.briscoe@rochester.edu. *Dean of the School of Arts and Sciences/Professor of Biology,* Gloria Culver, 585-273-5000, E-mail: gloria.culver@rochester.edu.

Goergen Institute for Data Science Students: 49 full-time (25 women), 7 part-time (3 women); includes 5 minority (1 Black or African American, non-Hispanic/Latino; 2 Asian, non-Hispanic/Latino; 2 Hispanic/Latino), 43 international. Average age 27. 351 applicants, 46% accepted, 37 enrolled. Expenses: Contact institution. *Financial support:* In 2018–19, 5 students received support, including 1 fellowship with partial tuition reimbursement available (averaging $2,100 per year), 6 teaching assistantships (averaging $500 per year); tuition waivers (full and partial) also available. In 2018, 6 master's awarded. Offers business and social science (MS); computational and statistical methods (MS); health and biomedical sciences (MS). *Application deadline:* For fall admission, 4/15 priority date for domestic and international students. *Application fee:* $60. Electronic applications accepted. *Application Contact:* Lisa Altman, Education Program Coordinator, 585-275-5288, E-mail: lisa.altman@rochester.edu. *Deputy Director,* Ajay Anand, 585-276-3149, E-mail: ajay.anand@rochester.edu.

School of Medicine and Dentistry *Program availability:* Part-time. Offers medicine (MD); medicine and dentistry (MA, MPH, MS, MD, PhD, Certificate). Electronic applications accepted.

Graduate Programs in Medicine and Dentistry *Program availability:* Part-time. Offers biochemistry (PhD); biochemistry and molecular biology (PhD); bioinformatics and computational biology (PhD); biophysics (PhD); biophysics, structural and computational biology (PhD); clinical investigation (MS); clinical translational research (MS); dental science (MS); epidemiology (PhD); genetics, genomics and development (PhD); health services research and policy (PhD); marriage and family therapy (MS); medical microbiology (MS, PhD); medical statistics (MS); medicine and dentistry (MA, MPH, MS, PhD); microbiology and immunology (MS, PhD); neurobiology and anatomy (PhD); neuroscience (PhD); pathology (PhD); pharmacology (MS, PhD); physiology (MS, PhD); public health (MPH, MS); statistics (MA, PhD); toxicology (PhD); translational biomedical science (PhD). Electronic applications accepted.

School of Nursing Students: 17 full-time (12 women), 306 part-time (252 women); includes 46 minority (16 Black or African American, non-Hispanic/Latino; 1 American Indian or Alaska Native, non-Hispanic/Latino; 7 Asian, non-Hispanic/Latino; 17 Hispanic/Latino; 5 Two or more races, non-Hispanic/Latino), 3 international. Average age 34. 121 applicants, 57% accepted, 53 enrolled. *Faculty:* 42 full-time (35 women), 58 part-time/adjunct (32 women). Expenses: Contact institution. *Financial support:* In 2018–19, 88 students received support, including 4 fellowships with full and partial tuition reimbursements available (averaging $25,000 per year); scholarships/grants, traineeships, health care benefits, and tuition waivers (full and partial) also available. Support available to part-time students. Financial award application deadline: 6/30; financial award applicants required to submit FAFSA. In 2018, 70 master's, 3 doctorates awarded. *Program availability:* Part-time, 100% online, blended/hybrid learning. Offers adult gerontological acute care nurse practitioner (MS); adult gerontological primary care nurse practitioner (MS); clinical nurse leader (MS); family nurse practitioner (MS); family psychiatric mental health nurse practitioner (MS); health care organization management and leadership (MS); nursing (DNP); nursing and health science (PhD); nursing education (MS); pediatric nurse practitioner (MS); pediatric nurse practitioner/neonatal nurse practitioner (MS). *Application deadline:* For fall admission, 4/1 for domestic and international students; for spring admission, 9/1 for domestic and international students; for summer admission, 1/2 for domestic and international students. Applications are processed on a rolling basis. *Application fee:* $50. Electronic applications accepted. *Application Contact:* Peter Bertoldo, Asst Director of Enrollment, 585-275-1939, Fax: 585-756-8299, E-mail: peter_bertoldo@urmc.rochester.edu. *Dean,* Dr. Kathy H. Rideout, 585-273-8902, Fax: 585-273-1268, E-mail: kathy_rideout@urmc.rochester.edu.

Simon Business School *Program availability:* Part-time, evening/weekend. Offers accountancy (MS); accounting (PhD); business (MBA, MS, PhD); business administration (MBA, PhD); business analytics (MS); business systems consulting (MBA); competitive and organizational strategy (MBA); computer information systems (PhD); computers and information systems (MBA); corporate accounting (MBA); entrepreneurship (MBA); finance (MS); health sciences management (MBA); marketing (MBA, PhD); marketing analytics (MS); operations management (MBA, PhD); public accounting (MBA); strategy and organizations (MBA). Electronic applications accepted.

UNIVERSITY OF ST. AUGUSTINE FOR HEALTH SCIENCES, San Marcos, CA 92069

General Information Proprietary, coed, graduate-only institution. *Graduate housing:* On-campus housing not available.

GRADUATE UNITS

Graduate Programs *Program availability:* Part-time, evening/weekend, online learning. Offers athletic training (MHS); executive leadership (MHS); health administration (MHA); health science (DH Sc); health sciences education (Ed D); informatics (MHS); nurse educator (MSN); nurse executive (MSN); nurse informatics (MSN); nursing (MSN, DNP); occupational therapy (TOTD); physical therapy (DPT); teaching and learning (MHS).

UNIVERSITY OF ST. FRANCIS, Joliet, IL 60435-6169

General Information Independent-religious, coed, comprehensive institution. *Enrollment:* 360 full-time matriculated graduate/professional students (276 women), 972 part-time matriculated graduate/professional students (799 women). *Enrollment by degree level:* 1,100 master's, 147 doctoral, 85 other advanced degrees. *Graduate faculty:* 42 full-time (32 women), 94 part-time/adjunct (59 women). *Tuition:* $748 per credit. Tuition and fees vary according to degree level and program. *Graduate housing:* Room and/or apartments available on a first-come, first-served basis to single students; on-campus housing not available to married students. Typical cost: $9544 (including board). *Student services:* Campus employment opportunities, campus safety program, career counseling, exercise/wellness program, free psychological counseling, international student services, multicultural affairs office, services for students with disabilities, teacher training. *Library facilities:* Brown Library. *Collection:* Books: 113,077 (physical), 4,118 (digital/electronic); Serial titles: 605 (physical), 113 (digital/electronic); Databases: 76. Weekly public service hours: 74; students can reserve study rooms.

Computer facilities: 560 computers available on campus for general student use. A campuswide network can be accessed from student residence rooms and from off campus. Online class registration, billing/payment are available.
Website: http://www.stfrancis.edu/

General Application Contact: Sandee Sloka, Director Adult & Graduate Admissions, 800-735-7500, Fax: 815-740-3431, E-mail: ssloka@stfrancis.edu.

GRADUATE UNITS

College of Arts and Sciences Students: 119 full-time (95 women), 20 part-time (19 women); includes 46 minority (12 Black or African American, non-Hispanic/Latino; 1 American Indian or Alaska Native, non-Hispanic/Latino; 6 Asian, non-Hispanic/Latino; 21 Hispanic/Latino; 1 Native Hawaiian or other Pacific Islander, non-Hispanic/Latino; 5 Two or more races, non-Hispanic/Latino), 6 international. Average age 37. 60 applicants, 42% accepted, 17 enrolled. *Faculty:* 12 full-time (10 women), 3 part-time/adjunct (1 woman). Expenses: Contact institution. *Financial support:* In 2018–19, 13 students received support. Scholarships/grants and tuition waivers (partial) available. Support available to part-time students. Financial award applicants required to submit FAFSA. In 2018, 48 master's awarded. *Program availability:* Part-time. Offers forensic social work (Post-Master's Certificate); physician assistant practice (MS); social work (MSW). *Application deadline:* Applications are processed on a rolling basis. Electronic applications accepted. *Application Contact:* Sandee Sloka, Director Adult & Graduate Admissions, 800-735-7500, E-mail: ssloka@stfrancis.edu. *Dean,* Dr. Elizabeth Davies, 815-740-3819, E-mail: edavies@stfrancis.edu.

College of Business and Health Administration Students: 139 full-time (94 women), 206 part-time (159 women); includes 86 minority (51 Black or African American, non-Hispanic/Latino; 1 American Indian or Alaska Native, non-Hispanic/Latino; 11 Asian,

non-Hispanic/Latino; 21 Hispanic/Latino; 2 Two or more races, non-Hispanic/Latino), 24 international. Average age 37. 261 applicants, 63% accepted, 98 enrolled. *Faculty:* 13 full-time (6 women), 20 part-time/adjunct (7 women). Expenses: Contact institution. *Financial support:* In 2018–19, 126 students received support. Scholarships/grants and tuition waivers (partial) available. Support available to part-time students. Financial award applicants required to submit FAFSA. In 2018, 129 master's, 3 other advanced degrees awarded. *Program availability:* Part-time, evening/weekend, 100% online, blended/hybrid learning. Offers accounting (MBA, Certificate); business analytics (MBA, Certificate); e-learning (Certificate); finance (MBA, Certificate); health administration (MBA, MS); human resource management (MBA, Certificate); logistics (Certificate); management (MBA, MSM); supply chain management (MBA); training and development (Certificate); supply chain management (MBA); training and development (MBA); training specialist (Certificate). *Application deadline:* Applications are processed on a rolling basis. Electronic applications accepted. *Application Contact:* Sandee Sloka, Director Adult & Graduate Admissions, 800-735-7500, E-mail: ssloka@stfrancis.edu. *Dean,* Dr. Orlando Griego, 815-740-3395, Fax: 815-740-3452, E-mail: ogriego@stfrancis.edu.

College of Education Students: 43 full-time (35 women), 453 part-time (354 women); includes 110 minority (48 Black or African American, non-Hispanic/Latino; 7 Asian, non-Hispanic/Latino; 52 Hispanic/Latino; 3 Two or more races, non-Hispanic/Latino), 3 international. Average age 37. 300 applicants, 66% accepted, 164 enrolled. *Faculty:* 11 full-time (8 women), 58 part-time/adjunct (38 women). Expenses: Contact institution. *Financial support:* In 2018–19, 33 students received support. Scholarships/grants and tuition waivers (partial) available. Support available to part-time students. Financial award applicants required to submit FAFSA. In 2018, 151 master's, 42 doctorates, 4 other advanced degrees awarded. *Program availability:* Part-time, evening/weekend, 100% online, blended/hybrid learning. Offers educational leadership (MS, Ed D); elementary education (M Ed); reading (MS); secondary education (M Ed); special education (M Ed); teaching and learning (MS); TESOL (Certificate). *Application deadline:* Applications are processed on a rolling basis. Electronic applications accepted. *Application Contact:* Sandee Sloka, Director Adult & Graduate Admissions, 800-735-7500, E-mail: ssloka@stfrancis.edu. *Dean,* Dr. John Gambro, 815-740-3456, E-mail: jgambro@stfrancis.edu.

Leach College of Nursing Students: 59 full-time (52 women), 293 part-time (267 women); includes 125 minority (61 Black or African American, non-Hispanic/Latino; 29 Asian, non-Hispanic/Latino; 25 Hispanic/Latino; 5 Native Hawaiian or other Pacific Islander, non-Hispanic/Latino; 5 Two or more races, non-Hispanic/Latino). Average age 41. 331 applicants, 47% accepted, 102 enrolled. *Faculty:* 8 full-time (all women), 12 part-time/adjunct (all women). Expenses: Contact institution. *Financial support:* In 2018–19, 134 students received support. Scholarships/grants and tuition waivers (partial) available. Support available to part-time students. Financial award applicants required to submit FAFSA. In 2018, 61 master's, 9 doctorates, 15 other advanced degrees awarded. *Program availability:* Part-time, evening/weekend, 100% online. Offers family nurse practitioner (MSN); nursing administration (MSN); nursing education (MSN); nursing practice (DNP); psychology/mental health nurse practitioner (MSN, Post-Master's Certificate); teaching in nursing (Certificate). *Application deadline:* Applications are processed on a rolling basis. Electronic applications accepted. *Application Contact:* Sandee Sloka, Director Adult & Graduate Admissions, 800-735-7500, E-mail: ssloka@stfrancis.edu. *Dean,* Dr. Ebere Ume, 815-740-3492, E-mail: eume@stfrancis.edu.

UNIVERSITY OF SAINT FRANCIS, Fort Wayne, IN 46808-3994

General Information Independent-religious, coed, comprehensive institution. *Enrollment:* 2,199 graduate, professional, and undergraduate students; 184 full-time matriculated graduate/professional students (123 women), 208 part-time matriculated graduate/professional students (147 women). *Enrollment by degree level:* 366 master's, 25 doctoral, 1 other advanced degree. *Graduate faculty:* 35 full-time (22 women), 32 part-time/adjunct (19 women). *Tuition:* Full-time $22,440; part-time $935 per credit hour. *Required fees:* $330 per semester. Tuition and fees vary according to degree level, campus/location and program. *Graduate housing:* Room and/or apartments available on a first-come, first-served basis to single students; on-campus housing not available to married students. Typical cost: $10,600 (including board). Housing application deadline: 7/1. *Student services:* Campus employment opportunities, campus safety program, career counseling, exercise/wellness program, free psychological counseling, multicultural affairs office, services for students with disabilities. *Library facilities:* Lee and Jim Vann Library. *Collection:* Books: 64,241 (physical), 163,451 (digital/electronic); Serial titles: 798 (physical), 41,820 (digital/electronic); Databases: 110. Weekly public service hours: 86; study areas open 24 hours, 5–7 days a week; students can reserve study rooms.

Computer facilities: Computer purchase and lease plans are available. 120 computers available on campus for general student use. A campuswide network can be accessed from student residence rooms and from off campus. Online class registration is available.
Website: http://www.sf.edu/

General Application Contact: Kyle Richardson, Associate Director of Enrollment Services for Adult Learning, 260-399-7700 Ext. 6310, E-mail: krichardson@sf.edu.

GRADUATE UNITS

Graduate School Students: 184 full-time (123 women), 208 part-time (147 women); includes 69 minority (36 Black or African American, non-Hispanic/Latino; 1 American Indian or Alaska Native, non-Hispanic/Latino; 3 Asian, non-Hispanic/Latino; 20 Hispanic/Latino; 1 Native Hawaiian or other Pacific Islander, non-Hispanic/Latino; 8 Two or more races, non-Hispanic/Latino), 1 international. Average age 32. 172 applicants, 94% accepted, 124 enrolled. *Faculty:* 35 full-time (22 women), 32 part-time/adjunct (19 women). Expenses: Contact institution. *Financial support:* Federal Work-Study, scholarships/grants, and unspecified assistantships available. Financial award application deadline: 4/15; financial award applicants required to submit FAFSA. In 2018, 197 master's awarded. *Program availability:* Part-time, evening/weekend, 100% online, blended/hybrid learning. Offers clinical mental health counseling (MS, Post Master's Certificate); family nurse practitioner (MSN, Post Master's Certificate); nurse anesthesia (DNP); nursing practice (DNP); physician assistant studies (MS); psychology (MS); school counseling (MS Ed); secondary education (MAT); special education (MS Ed); studio art (MA, MFA). *Application deadline:* For fall admission, 7/1 for international students; for spring admission, 11/1 for international students; for summer admission, 3/1 for international students. Applications are processed on a rolling basis. *Application fee:* $0. Electronic applications accepted. *Application Contact:* Kyle Richardson, Associate Director of Enrollment Services for Adult Learning, 260-399-7700 Ext. 6310, E-mail: krichardson@sf.edu. *Associate Vice President of Academic Affairs,* Tricia Bugajski, 260-399-7700 Ext. 6008, E-mail: tbugajski@sf.edu.

Keith Busse School of Business and Entrepreneurial Leadership Students: 62 full-time (33 women), 94 part-time (53 women); includes 40 minority (23 Black or African American, non-Hispanic/Latino; 1 American Indian or Alaska Native, non-

Hispanic/Latino; 10 Hispanic/Latino; 1 Native Hawaiian or other Pacific Islander, non-Hispanic/Latino; 5 Two or more races, non-Hispanic/Latino. Average age 33. 72 applicants, 96% accepted, 51 enrolled. *Faculty:* 4 full-time (3 women), 11 part-time/adjunct (1 woman). Expenses: Contact institution. In 2018, 112 master's awarded. *Program availability:* Part-time, evening/weekend, online only, 100% online. Offers business administration (MBA); environmental health (MEH); healthcare administration (MHA); organizational leadership (MOL). *Application deadline:* For fall admission, 7/1 for international students; for spring admission, 11/1 for international students; for summer admission, 3/1 for international students. Applications are processed on a rolling basis. *Application fee:* $0. Electronic applications accepted. *Application Contact:* Kyle Richardson, Associate Director of Enrollment Services for Adult Learning, 260-399-7700 Ext. 6310, Fax: 260-399-8152, E-mail: krichardson@sf.edu. *Dean,* Dr. Robert W. Lee, 260-399-7700 Ext. 8304, Fax: 260-399-8174, E-mail: rlee@sf.edu.

UNIVERSITY OF SAINT JOSEPH, West Hartford, CT 06117-2700

General Information Independent-religious, coed, primarily women, comprehensive institution. *Graduate housing:* Room and/or apartments available on a first-come, first-served basis to single students; on-campus housing not available to married students. Housing application deadline: 6/1.

GRADUATE UNITS

Department of Biology *Program availability:* Part-time, online learning. Offers biology (MS). Electronic applications accepted.

Department of Business Administration *Program availability:* Part-time, evening/weekend. Offers management (MS). Electronic applications accepted.

Department of Chemistry *Program availability:* Part-time, evening/weekend, online learning. Offers biochemistry (MS); chemistry (MS). Electronic applications accepted.

Department of Counseling and Applied Behavioral Studies *Program availability:* Part-time, evening/weekend. Offers clinical mental health counseling (MA); school counseling (MA). Electronic applications accepted.

Department of Education *Program availability:* Part-time, evening/weekend. Offers curriculum and instruction (MA); elementary education (MAT); instructional technology (MA); literacy (MA); secondary education (MAT); TESOL (MA). Electronic applications accepted.

Department of Nursing *Program availability:* Part-time, evening/weekend. Offers family nurse practitioner (MS); nurse educator (MS); nursing practice (DNP); psychiatric/mental health nurse practitioner (MS). Electronic applications accepted.

Department of Nutrition and Public Health *Program availability:* Part-time, evening/weekend, online learning. Offers nutrition (MS); public health (MPH). Electronic applications accepted.

Program in Marriage and Family Therapy *Program availability:* Part-time, evening/weekend. Offers marriage and family therapy (MA). Electronic applications accepted.

Program in Social Work Offers social work (MSW).

Program in Special Education *Program availability:* Part-time, evening/weekend. Offers autism spectrum disorders (Graduate Certificate); special education (MA). Electronic applications accepted.

School of Pharmacy and Physician Assistant Studies Offers pharmacy (Pharm D). Electronic applications accepted.

UNIVERSITY OF SAINT MARY, Leavenworth, KS 66048-5082

General Information Independent-religious, coed, comprehensive institution. *Graduate housing:* Room and/or apartments available on a first-come, first-served basis to single students; on-campus housing not available to married students.

GRADUATE UNITS

Graduate Programs *Program availability:* Part-time, evening/weekend, online learning. Offers counseling psychology (MA); education (MA); elementary education (MA); enterprise risk management (MBA); finance (MBA); general management (MBA); health care management (MBA); human resources management (MBA); marketing and advertising management (MBA); nurse administrator (MSN); nurse educator (MSN); physical therapy (DPT); psychology (MA); special education (MA). Electronic applications accepted.

UNIVERSITY OF SAINT MARY OF THE LAKE–MUNDELEIN SEMINARY, Mundelein, IL 60060

General Information Independent-religious, men only, graduate-only institution. *Graduate housing:* Room and/or apartments guaranteed to single students; on-campus housing not available to married students. Housing application deadline: 8/1.

GRADUATE UNITS

Graduate and Professional Programs Offers liturgical studies (MA); ministry (D Min); pastoral studies (MA); theology (M Div). Electronic applications accepted.

UNIVERSITY OF ST. MICHAEL'S COLLEGE, Toronto, ON M5S 1J4, Canada

General Information Independent-religious, coed, graduate-only institution. *Graduate housing:* Rooms and/or apartments available on a first-come, first-served basis to single and married students. Housing application deadline: 8/15.

GRADUATE UNITS

Faculty of Theology *Program availability:* Part-time. Offers Catholic leadership (MA); eastern Christian studies (Diploma); religious education (Diploma); theological studies (Diploma); theology (M Div, MA, MRE, MTS, D Min, PhD, Th D); theology and Jewish studies (MA). Th D offered jointly with University of Toronto. Electronic applications accepted.

UNIVERSITY OF ST. THOMAS, St. Paul, MN 55105-1096

General Information Independent-religious, coed, university. *Enrollment:* 10,035 graduate, professional, and undergraduate students; 1,210 full-time matriculated graduate/professional students (674 women), 2,430 part-time matriculated graduate/professional students (1,242 women). *Enrollment by degree level:* 2,751 master's, 624 doctoral, 215 other advanced degrees. *Graduate faculty:* 172 full-time (68 women), 279 part-time/adjunct (137 women). Tuition and fees vary according to course load, degree level and program. *Graduate housing:* Room and/or apartments available on a first-come, first-served basis to single students; on-campus housing not available to married students. Housing application deadline: 5/1. *Student services:* Campus employment opportunities, campus safety program, career counseling, child daycare facilities, exercise/wellness program, free psychological counseling, international student services, low-cost health insurance, multicultural affairs office, services for students with disabilities, writing training. *Library facilities:* O'Shaughnessy-Frey Library plus 7 others.

Collection: Books: 399,594 (physical), 1.2 million (digital/electronic); Serial titles: 1,701 (physical), 76,726 (digital/electronic); Databases: 308. Students can reserve study rooms.

Computer facilities: Computer purchase and lease plans are available. A campuswide network can be accessed from student residence rooms and from off campus. Online class registration is available.
Website: http://www.stthomas.edu/

GRADUATE UNITS

College of Arts and Sciences *Program availability:* Part-time, evening/weekend. Offers art history (MA); arts and sciences (MA, Ed D, Certificate, Graduate Certificate); Catholic studies (MA); choral (MA); english literature (MA); instrumental (MA); Kodaly (MA); leadership in music education (Ed D); museum studies (Graduate Certificate); Orff Schulwerk (MA); piano pedagogy (MA); teaching college english (Certificate).

College of Education, Leadership and Counseling *Program availability:* Part-time, evening/weekend, 100% online, blended/hybrid learning. Offers education leadership and administration (MA); education, leadership and counseling (MA, Ed D, Psy D, Certificate, Ed S); educational leadership and learning (Ed D); executive coaching (Certificate); K-12 administration (Ed S); leadership in student affairs (MA); organization development and change (Ed D); special education (MA, Certificate, Ed S); teacher education (MA). Electronic applications accepted.

Graduate School of Professional Psychology *Program availability:* Part-time, evening/weekend. Offers counseling psychology (MA, Psy D). Electronic applications accepted.

Opus College of Business Expenses: Contact institution. Offers accountancy (MS); business (MBA, MS, MSBA); business administration (MBA); business analytics (MS); executive business administration (MBA); health care business administration (MBA); health care communication (MS). *Application Contact:* Tiffany Cork, Director of Recruiting and Admissions, 651-962-8801, Fax: 651-962-4129, E-mail: ustmba@stthomas.edu. *Dean,* Dr. Stefanie Lenway, 651-962-4200, Fax: 651-962-4129, E-mail: ocbdean@stthomas.edu.

The Saint Paul Seminary School of Divinity *Program availability:* Part-time, evening/weekend. Offers pastoral ministry (MAPM); religious education (MARE); theology (MA). Electronic applications accepted.

School of Engineering *Program availability:* Part-time, evening/weekend. Offers data science (MS); electrical engineering (MS); information technology (MS); manufacturing engineering (MS); manufacturing systems (Certificate); mechanical engineering (MS); medical device development (Certificate); regulatory science (MS); software engineering (MS); software management (MS); systems engineering (MS); technology leadership (Certificate); technology management (MS). Electronic applications accepted.

School of Law Students: 434 full-time (228 women); includes 70 minority (24 Black or African American, non-Hispanic/Latino; 1 American Indian or Alaska Native, non-Hispanic/Latino; 12 Asian, non-Hispanic/Latino; 21 Hispanic/Latino; 12 Two or more races, non-Hispanic/Latino), 13 international. Average age 26. 699 applicants, 61% accepted, 149 enrolled. *Faculty:* 27 full-time (6 women), 70 part-time/adjunct (29 women). Expenses: Contact institution. *Financial support:* In 2018–19, 385 students received support. Scholarships/grants available. Financial award application deadline: 7/1; financial award applicants required to submit FAFSA. In 2018, 2 master's, 101 doctorates awarded. *Program availability:* 100% online. Offers law (JD); law/business administration (LL M, MSL, JD); law/catholic studies (LL M, MSL, JD); law/organizational ethics and compliance (LL M, MSL, JD); law/social work (LL M, MSL, JD); organizational ethics and compliance (LL M, MSL); U.S. law (LL M). *Application deadline:* For fall admission, 8/1 priority date for domestic and international students. Applications are processed on a rolling basis. *Application fee:* $0. Electronic applications accepted. *Application Contact:* Cari Haaland, Assistant Dean for Admissions, 651-962-4872, Fax: 651-962-4876, E-mail: lawschool@stthomas.edu. *Dean,* Robert K. Vischer, 651-962-4838, Fax: 651-962-4881, E-mail: rkvischer@stthomas.edu.

School of Social Work Students: 180 full-time, 188 part-time; includes 69 minority (28 Black or African American, non-Hispanic/Latino; 1 American Indian or Alaska Native, non-Hispanic/Latino; 11 Asian, non-Hispanic/Latino; 19 Hispanic/Latino; 10 Two or more races, non-Hispanic/Latino), 3 international. Average age 36. *Faculty:* 19 full-time, 42 part-time/adjunct. Expenses: Contact institution. *Financial support:* In 2018–19, 8 research assistantships with partial tuition reimbursements (averaging $1,425 per year) were awarded; career-related internships or fieldwork, Federal Work-Study, scholarships/grants, and unspecified assistantships also available. Financial award application deadline: 7/1; financial award applicants required to submit FAFSA. In 2018, 118 master's awarded. *Program availability:* Part-time, evening/weekend, 100% online, blended/hybrid learning. Offers social work (MSW). *Application deadline:* For fall admission, 1/10 for domestic and international students. *Application fee:* $0. Electronic applications accepted. *Application Contact:* Dr. Corrine Carvalho, Interim Dean and Professor, 651-962-6031, Fax: 651-962-6031, E-mail: clcarvalho@stthomas.edu. *Interim Dean and Professor,* Dr. Corrine Carvalho, 651-962-6031, Fax: 651-962-6031, E-mail: clcarvalho@stthomas.edu.

UNIVERSITY OF ST. THOMAS, Houston, TX 77006-4696

General Information Independent-religious, coed, comprehensive institution. *Graduate housing:* Room and/or apartments available on a first-come, first-served basis to single students; on-campus housing not available to married students.

GRADUATE UNITS

Cameron School of Business *Program availability:* Part-time, evening/weekend. Offers business (MBA, MCTM, MIB, MSA, MSF). Electronic applications accepted.

Center for Faith and Culture *Program availability:* Part-time. Offers faith and culture (MA). Electronic applications accepted.

Center for Thomistic Studies *Program availability:* Part-time. Offers philosophy (MA, PhD). Electronic applications accepted.

Program in Liberal Arts *Program availability:* Part-time, evening/weekend. Offers liberal arts (MLA). Electronic applications accepted.

School of Arts and Sciences *Program availability:* Part-time. Offers public policy administration (MPPA); sacred music (MSM). Electronic applications accepted.

School of Education and Human Services *Program availability:* Part-time, evening/weekend, online learning. Offers all level education (M Ed); bilingual/dual language (M Ed); Catholic school teaching (M Ed); Catholic/private school leadership (M Ed); counselor education (M Ed); curriculum and instruction (M Ed); education (Ed D); educational leadership (M Ed); elementary teaching (M Ed); English as a second language (M Ed); exceptionality/educational diagnostician (M Ed); exceptionality/special education (M Ed); generalist (M Ed); reading (M Ed); secondary teaching (M Ed); teaching (MAT). Electronic applications accepted.

School of Theology *Program availability:* Part-time. Offers divinity (M Div); pastoral studies (MAPS); theological studies (MA). Electronic applications accepted.

UNIVERSITY OF SAN DIEGO, San Diego, CA 92110-2492

General Information Independent-religious, coed, university. *Enrollment:* 9,073 graduate, professional, and undergraduate students; 1,588 full-time matriculated graduate/professional students (1,017 women), 1,481 part-time matriculated graduate/professional students (824 women). *Enrollment by degree level:* 2,110 master's, 959 doctoral. *Graduate faculty:* 161 full-time (73 women), 278 part-time/adjunct (136 women). *Graduate housing:* Room and/or apartments available on a first-come, first-served basis to single students; on-campus housing not available to married students. Housing application deadline: 5/1. *Student services:* Campus employment opportunities, campus safety program, career counseling, child daycare facilities, exercise/wellness program, free psychological counseling, international student services, low-cost health insurance, multicultural affairs office, services for students with disabilities, teacher training. *Library facilities:* Helen K. and James S. Copley Library plus 1 other. *Collection:* Books: 455,753 (physical), 870,474 (digital/electronic); Serial titles: 10,446 (physical), 146,831 (digital/electronic); Databases: 391. Weekly public service hours: 116; students can reserve study rooms.

Computer facilities: Computer purchase and lease plans are available. 1,066 computers available on campus for general student use. A campuswide network can be accessed from student residence rooms and from off campus. Online class registration is available.
Website: http://www.sandiego.edu/

General Application Contact: Erika Garwood, Associate Director of Graduate Admissions, 619-260-4524, Fax: 619-260-4158, E-mail: grads@sandiego.edu.

GRADUATE UNITS

College of Arts and Sciences Students: 32 full-time (16 women), 35 part-time (20 women); includes 24 minority (3 Black or African American, non-Hispanic/Latino; 3 Asian, non-Hispanic/Latino; 13 Hispanic/Latino; 5 Two or more races, non-Hispanic/Latino), 4 international. Average age 29. *Faculty:* 17 full-time (7 women), 5 part-time/adjunct (2 women). Expenses: Contact institution. *Financial support:* In 2018–19, 56 students received support, including 14 fellowships with full tuition reimbursements available; career-related internships or fieldwork, Federal Work-Study, institutionally sponsored loans, scholarships/grants, and unspecified assistantships also available. Support available to part-time students. Financial award application deadline: 4/1; financial award applicants required to submit FAFSA. In 2018, 18 master's awarded. *Program availability:* Part-time, evening/weekend. Offers acting (MFA); arts and sciences (MA, MFA, MS); environmental and ocean sciences (MS); international relations (MA). *Application deadline:* Applications are processed on a rolling basis. *Application fee:* $45. Electronic applications accepted. *Application Contact:* Erika Garwood, Associate Director of Graduate Admissions, 619-260-4524, Fax: 619-260-4158, E-mail: grads@sandiego.edu. *Dean,* Dr. Noelle Norton, 619-260-4545.

Division of Professional and Continuing Education Students: 331 part-time (83 women); includes 117 minority (16 Black or African American, non-Hispanic/Latino; 1 American Indian or Alaska Native, non-Hispanic/Latino; 22 Asian, non-Hispanic/Latino; 73 Hispanic/Latino; 1 Native Hawaiian or other Pacific Islander, non-Hispanic/Latino; 4 Two or more races, non-Hispanic/Latino), 1 international. Average age 39. 224 applicants, 98% accepted, 159 enrolled. *Faculty:* 1 full-time (0 women), 25 part-time/adjunct (1 woman). Expenses: Contact institution. *Financial support:* Application deadline: 4/1; applicants required to submit FAFSA. *Program availability:* Part-time-only, evening/weekend, 100% online. Offers cyber security operations and leadership (MS); law enforcement and public safety leadership (MS). *Application deadline:* For fall admission, 8/7 for domestic students; for spring admission, 12/3 for domestic students; for summer admission, 4/24 for domestic students. Applications are processed on a rolling basis. *Application fee:* $45. Electronic applications accepted. *Application Contact:* Erika Garwood, Associate Director of Graduate Admissions, 619-260-4524, Fax: 619-260-4158, E-mail: grads@sandiego.edu. *Assoc. Provost for Professional Education and Online Dev.,* Dr. Chell Roberts, 619-260-4585, Fax: 619-260-2961, E-mail: continuinged@sandiego.edu.

Hahn School of Nursing and Health Science Students: 260 full-time (219 women), 282 part-time (205 women); includes 273 minority (47 Black or African American, non-Hispanic/Latino; 1 American Indian or Alaska Native, non-Hispanic/Latino; 118 Asian, non-Hispanic/Latino; 82 Hispanic/Latino; 25 Two or more races, non-Hispanic/Latino), 19 international. Average age 34. *Faculty:* 28 full-time (24 women), 58 part-time/adjunct (47 women). Expenses: Contact institution. *Financial support:* In 2018–19, 260 students received support. Institutionally sponsored loans, scholarships/grants, and traineeships available. Support available to part-time students. Financial award application deadline: 4/1; financial award applicants required to submit FAFSA. In 2018, 122 master's, 33 doctorates awarded. *Program availability:* Part-time, evening/weekend. Offers adult-gerontology clinical nurse specialist (MSN); adult-gerontology nurse practitioner/family nurse practitioner (MSN); clinical nurse leader (MSN); executive nurse leader (MSN); family nurse practitioner (MSN); healthcare informatics (MS); master's entry program in clinical nursing (for non-rns) (MSN); nursing (PhD); nursing informatics (MSN); nursing practice (DNP); psychiatric-mental health nurse practitioner (MSN). *Application deadline:* Applications are processed on a rolling basis. *Application fee:* $45. Electronic applications accepted. *Application Contact:* Erika Garwood, Associate Director of Graduate Admissions, 619-260-4524, Fax: 619-260-4158, E-mail: grads@sandiego.edu. *Dean,* Dr. Jane Georges, 619-260-4550, Fax: 619-260-6814, E-mail: nursing@sandiego.edu.

Joan B. Kroc School of Peace Studies Students: 73 full-time (58 women), 18 part-time (16 women); includes 35 minority (6 Black or African American, non-Hispanic/Latino; 5 Asian, non-Hispanic/Latino; 20 Hispanic/Latino; 4 Two or more races, non-Hispanic/Latino), 15 international. Average age 31. *Faculty:* 7 full-time (2 women), 5 part-time/adjunct (2 women). Expenses: Contact institution. *Financial support:* In 2018–19, 75 students received support. Career-related internships or fieldwork, Federal Work-Study, institutionally sponsored loans, scholarships/grants, and unspecified assistantships available. Support available to part-time students. Financial award application deadline: 4/1; financial award applicants required to submit FAFSA. In 2018, 28 master's awarded. Offers conflict management and resolution (MS); peace and justice (MA); social innovation (MA). *Application fee:* $45. Electronic applications accepted. *Application Contact:* Erika Garwood, Associate Director of Graduate Admissions, 619-260-4524, Fax: 619-260-4158, E-mail: grads@sandiego.edu. *Dean,* Dr. Patricia Marquez, 619-260-7919, E-mail: krocschool@sandiego.edu.

School of Business Students: 201 full-time (71 women), 169 part-time (75 women); includes 105 minority (9 Black or African American, non-Hispanic/Latino; 22 Asian, non-Hispanic/Latino; 64 Hispanic/Latino; 2 Native Hawaiian or other Pacific Islander, non-Hispanic/Latino; 8 Two or more races, non-Hispanic/Latino), 69 international. Average age 31. *Faculty:* 32 full-time (7 women), 27 part-time/adjunct (8 women). Expenses: Contact institution. *Financial support:* In 2018–19, 215 students received support. Career-related internships or fieldwork, Federal Work-Study, institutionally sponsored loans, and scholarships/grants available. Support available to part-time students.

Financial award application deadline: 4/1; financial award applicants required to submit FAFSA. In 2018, 230 master's awarded. *Program availability:* Part-time, evening/weekend. Offers accountancy (MS); business administration (MBA); executive leadership (MS); finance (MSF); global leadership (MS); real estate (MS); supply chain management (MS, Certificate); taxation (MS). *Application fee:* $80. Electronic applications accepted. *Application Contact:* Erika Garwood, Associate Director of Graduate Admissions, 619-260-4524, Fax: 619-260-4158, E-mail: grads@sandiego.edu. *Interim Dean,* Dr. Barbara Lougee, 619-260-4886, E-mail: sbadean@sandiego.edu.

School of Law Students: 661 full-time (363 women), 92 part-time (49 women); includes 244 minority (31 Black or African American, non-Hispanic/Latino; 12 American Indian or Alaska Native, non-Hispanic/Latino; 75 Asian, non-Hispanic/Latino; 110 Hispanic/Latino; 4 Native Hawaiian or other Pacific Islander, non-Hispanic/Latino; 12 Two or more races, non-Hispanic/Latino), 31 international. Average age 27. 3,511 applicants, 240 enrolled. *Faculty:* 45 full-time (16 women), 72 part-time/adjunct (21 women). Expenses: Contact institution. *Financial support:* In 2018–19, 640 students received support. Career-related internships or fieldwork, Federal Work-Study, institutionally sponsored loans, and scholarships/grants available. Support available to part-time students. Financial award application deadline: 3/1; financial award applicants required to submit FAFSA. In 2018, 59 master's, 264 doctorates awarded. *Program availability:* Part-time, evening/weekend. Offers business and corporate law (LL M); comparative law (LL M); general studies (LL M); international law (LL M); law (JD); legal studies (MS); peace and law (LL M, MS, JD, Diploma); taxation (LL M, Diploma). *Application deadline:* For fall admission, 2/1 priority date for domestic students. Applications are processed on a rolling basis. *Application fee:* $0. Electronic applications accepted. *Application Contact:* Jorge Garcia, Assistant Dean, JD Admissions, 619-260-4528, Fax: 619-260-2218, E-mail: jdinfo@sandiego.edu. *Dean,* Dr. Stephen C. Ferruolo, 619-260-4527, E-mail: lawdean@sandiego.edu.

School of Leadership and Education Sciences Students: 361 full-time (290 women), 497 part-time (367 women); includes 373 minority (47 Black or African American, non-Hispanic/Latino; 66 Asian, non-Hispanic/Latino; 207 Hispanic/Latino; 3 Native Hawaiian or other Pacific Islander, non-Hispanic/Latino; 50 Two or more races, non-Hispanic/Latino), 32 international. Average age 31. *Faculty:* 30 full-time (17 women), 84 part-time/adjunct (54 women). Expenses: Contact institution. *Financial support:* In 2018–19, 512 students received support. Career-related internships or fieldwork, Federal Work-Study, institutionally sponsored loans, scholarships/grants, unspecified assistantships, and stipends available. Support available to part-time students. Financial award application deadline: 4/1; financial award applicants required to submit FAFSA. In 2018, 365 master's, 17 doctorates awarded. *Program availability:* Part-time, evening/weekend. Offers clinical mental health counseling (MA); curriculum and instruction (M Ed); higher education leadership (MA); inclusive learning (M Ed); leadership and education sciences (M Ed, MA, PhD, Certificate); leadership studies (MA, PhD, Certificate); literacy and digital learning (M Ed); marital and family therapy (MA); nonprofit leadership and management (MA); school counseling (MA); school leadership (M Ed); special education (M Ed); STEAM (science, technology, engineering, arts, and mathematics) (M Ed); TESOL, literacy and culture (M Ed). *Application fee:* $45. *Application Contact:* Erika Garwood, Associate Director of Graduate Admissions, 619-260-4524, Fax: 619-260-4158, E-mail: grads@sandiego.edu. *Dean,* Dr. Nicholas Ladany, 619-260-4540, Fax: 619-260-6835, E-mail: nladany@sandiego.edu.

Shiley-Marcos School of Engineering Students: 57 part-time (9 women); includes 34 minority (6 Black or African American, non-Hispanic/Latino; 10 Asian, non-Hispanic/Latino; 16 Hispanic/Latino; 1 Native Hawaiian or other Pacific Islander, non-Hispanic/Latino; 1 Two or more races, non-Hispanic/Latino), 1 international. Average age 33. 47 applicants, 79% accepted, 23 enrolled. *Faculty:* 2 full-time (0 women), 2 part-time/adjunct (1 woman). Expenses: Contact institution. *Financial support:* In 2018–19, 15 students received support. Institutionally sponsored loans and scholarships/grants available. Financial award application deadline: 4/1; financial award applicants required to submit FAFSA. In 2018, 3 master's awarded. *Program availability:* Part-time, evening/weekend. Offers cyber security engineering (MS). *Application deadline:* For fall admission, 8/5 for domestic students; for spring admission, 12/2 for domestic students; for summer admission, 4/24 for domestic students. Applications are processed on a rolling basis. *Application fee:* $45. Electronic applications accepted. *Application Contact:* Erika Garwood, Associate Director of Graduate Admissions, 619-260-4524, Fax: 619-260-4158, E-mail: grads@sandiego.edu. *Dean,* Dr. Chell Roberts, 619-260-4627, E-mail: croberts@sandiego.edu.

UNIVERSITY OF SAN FRANCISCO, San Francisco, CA 94117

General Information Independent-religious, coed, university. *Enrollment:* 10,714 graduate, professional, and undergraduate students; 3,346 full-time matriculated graduate/professional students (2,166 women), 637 part-time matriculated graduate/professional students (433 women). *Enrollment by degree level:* 3,195 master's, 788 doctoral. *Graduate housing:* Room and/or apartments available on a first-come, first-served basis to single students; on-campus housing not available to married students. Housing application deadline: 5/1. *Student services:* Campus employment opportunities, career counseling, exercise/wellness program, free psychological counseling, international student services, low-cost health insurance, multicultural affairs office, services for students with disabilities, teacher training, writing training. *Library facilities:* Gleeson Library/Geschke Center plus 1 other. *Collection:* Books: 580,130 (physical), 664,362 (digital/electronic); Serial titles: 7,960 (physical), 135,406 (digital/electronic); Databases: 348. Weekly public service hours: 136; study areas open 24 hours, 5–7 days a week; students can reserve study rooms.

Computer facilities: Computer purchase and lease plans are available. 257 computers available on campus for general student use. A campuswide network can be accessed. Online class registration is available.
Website: http://www.usfca.edu/

General Application Contact: Office of Graduate Enrollment, 415-422-2090, E-mail: graduate@usfca.edu.

GRADUATE UNITS

College of Arts and Sciences Students: 894 full-time (449 women), 124 part-time (84 women); includes 372 minority (64 Black or African American, non-Hispanic/Latino; 2 American Indian or Alaska Native, non-Hispanic/Latino; 104 Asian, non-Hispanic/Latino; 152 Hispanic/Latino; 5 Native Hawaiian or other Pacific Islander, non-Hispanic/Latino; 45 Two or more races, non-Hispanic/Latino), 286 international. Average age 27. 2,420 applicants, 52% accepted, 496 enrolled. Expenses: Contact institution. *Financial support:* Fellowships, research assistantships, teaching assistantships, career-related internships or fieldwork, Federal Work-Study, institutionally sponsored loans, scholarships/grants, and tuition waivers (partial) available. Support available to part-time students. Financial award application deadline: 8/1; financial award applicants required to submit FAFSA. In 2018, 419 master's awarded. *Program availability:* Part-time, evening/weekend. Offers arts and sciences (MA, MFA, MMS, MPA, MS, PSM); Asia Pacific studies (MA); biology (MS); biotechnology (PSM); chemistry (MS); computer science (MS); data science (MS); economics (MA, MS); energy systems management (MS); environmental management (MS); international and development economics (MA); international studies (MA); migration studies (MMS); museum studies (MA); professional communication (MA); sport management (MA); urban and public affairs (MA); writing (MFA). *Application fee:* $55. Electronic applications accepted. *Application Contact:* Mark Landerghini, Information Contact, 415-422-5101, Fax: 415-422-5134, E-mail: asgraduate@usfca.edu. *Dean*, Dr. Marcelo Camperi, 415-422-6373.

School of Education Students: 845 full-time (641 women), 199 part-time (151 women); includes 584 minority (91 Black or African American, non-Hispanic/Latino; 2 American Indian or Alaska Native, non-Hispanic/Latino; 150 Asian, non-Hispanic/Latino; 289 Hispanic/Latino; 7 Native Hawaiian or other Pacific Islander, non-Hispanic/Latino; 45 Two or more races, non-Hispanic/Latino), 64 international. Average age 31. 1,076 applicants, 73% accepted, 404 enrolled. Expenses: Contact institution. *Financial support:* Fellowships, research assistantships, and teaching assistantships available. Financial award application deadline: 3/2; financial award applicants required to submit FAFSA. In 2018, 355 master's, 37 doctorates awarded. *Program availability:* Part-time, evening/weekend. Offers Catholic school leadership (Ed D); counseling (MA); digital media and learning (MA); digital technologies for teaching and learning (MA); education (MA, Ed D); international and multicultural education (MA, Ed D); leadership studies (MA, Ed D); learning and instruction (MA, Ed D); special education (MA, Ed D); teaching (MA); teaching reading (MA); teaching urban education and social justice (MA). *Application deadline:* For fall admission, 3/1 priority date for domestic and international students; for spring admission, 10/15 priority date for domestic and international students. Applications are processed on a rolling basis. *Application fee:* $55. Electronic applications accepted. *Application Contact:* Amy Fogliani, Director of Admission, 415-422-5467, E-mail: schoolofeducation@usfca.edu. *Dean*, Dr. Shabnam Koirala-Azad, 415-422-6525.

School of Law Students: 347 full-time (192 women), 159 part-time (83 women); includes 242 minority (31 Black or African American, non-Hispanic/Latino; 64 Asian, non-Hispanic/Latino; 113 Hispanic/Latino; 3 Native Hawaiian or other Pacific Islander, non-Hispanic/Latino; 31 Two or more races, non-Hispanic/Latino), 37 international. Average age 29. 1,861 applicants, 58% accepted, 195 enrolled. Expenses: Contact institution. *Financial support:* Career-related internships or fieldwork, Federal Work-Study, and institutionally sponsored loans available. Support available to part-time students. Financial award application deadline: 3/2; financial award applicants required to submit FAFSA. In 2018, 39 master's, 173 doctorates awarded. *Program availability:* Part-time, evening/weekend. Offers intellectual property and technology law (LL M); international transactions and comparative law (LL M); law (LL M, JD). *Application deadline:* For fall admission, 4/1 for domestic students. Applications are processed on a rolling basis. *Application fee:* $60. Electronic applications accepted. *Application Contact:* Alan P. Guerrero, Director of Admissions, 415-422-2975, E-mail: lawadmissions@usfca.edu. *Dean*, Susan Freiwald.

School of Management Students: 596 full-time (335 women), 21 part-time (15 women); includes 289 minority (34 Black or African American, non-Hispanic/Latino; 1 American Indian or Alaska Native, non-Hispanic/Latino; 115 Asian, non-Hispanic/Latino; 99 Hispanic/Latino; 6 Native Hawaiian or other Pacific Islander, non-Hispanic/Latino; 34 Two or more races, non-Hispanic/Latino), 123 international. Average age 31. 927 applicants, 71% accepted, 293 enrolled. Expenses: Contact institution. *Financial support:* Federal Work-Study and scholarships/grants available. Financial award application deadline: 3/2; financial award applicants required to submit FAFSA. In 2018, 390 master's awarded. *Program availability:* Part-time, evening/weekend, online learning. Offers entrepreneurship and innovation (MBA); executive business administration (MBA); finance (MBA); financial analysis (MSFA); global entrepreneurial management (MGEM); health services administration (MPA); information systems (MS); management (MBA, MGEM, MNA, MPA, MS, MSFA, MSOD, MSRM); marketing (MBA); nonprofit administration (MNA); organization development (MSOD); public administration (MPA). *Application fee:* $55. Electronic applications accepted. *Application Contact:* Terra Cole Brown, Assistant Director of Graduate Recruiting & Admissions, E-mail: tcolebrown@usfca.edu. *Interim Dean*, Dr. Charles T. Moses, E-mail: management@usfca.edu.

School of Nursing and Health Professions Students: 664 full-time (549 women), 134 part-time (100 women); includes 496 minority (78 Black or African American, non-Hispanic/Latino; 204 Asian, non-Hispanic/Latino; 160 Hispanic/Latino; 12 Native Hawaiian or other Pacific Islander, non-Hispanic/Latino; 42 Two or more races, non-Hispanic/Latino), 32 international. Average age 33. 1,193 applicants, 37% accepted, 223 enrolled. Expenses: Contact institution. *Financial support:* Institutionally sponsored loans available. Financial award application deadline: 3/2. In 2018, 310 master's, 48 doctorates awarded. *Program availability:* Part-time, 100% online, blended/hybrid learning. Offers clinical psychology (Psy D); health informatics (MS); nursing and health professions (MPH, MS, MSBH, MSN, DNP, Psy D); nursing practice (DNP); public health (MPH). *Application deadline:* Applications are processed on a rolling basis. Electronic applications accepted. *Application Contact:* Dr. Margaret Baker, Dean, 415-422-6681, Fax: 415-422-6877, E-mail: nursing@usfca.edu. *Dean*, Dr. Margaret Baker, 415-422-6681, Fax: 415-422-6877, E-mail: nursing@usfca.edu.

UNIVERSITY OF SASKATCHEWAN, Saskatoon, SK S7N 5A2, Canada

General Information Province-supported, coed, university. *Graduate housing:* Rooms and/or apartments available on a first-come, first-served basis to single and married students. *Research affiliation:* Canada Agriculture (agriculture research), Saskatchewan Research Council, University Hospital (cancer research), Innovation Place, Vaccine and Infectious Disease Organization/InterVac Laboratory (vaccinology and immunotherapeutics), Canadian Light Source.

GRADUATE UNITS

College of Dentistry Offers dentistry (DMD). Electronic applications accepted.

College of Graduate and Postdoctoral Studies *Program availability:* Part-time. Electronic applications accepted.

College of Agriculture and Bioresources *Program availability:* Part-time. Offers agricultural and resource economics (M Sc, PhD, PGD); agriculture and bioresources (M Ag, M Sc, MA, PhD, PGD); animal and poultry science (M Sc, PhD); applied microbiology (M Sc, PhD); food science (M Sc, PhD); plant sciences (M Sc, PhD); soil science (M Sc, PhD).

College of Arts and Science *Program availability:* Part-time. Offers applied linguistics (MA); archaeology and anthropology (MA); arts and science (M Math, M Mus, M Sc, MA, MFA, PhD, Diploma); biology (M Sc, PhD); chemistry (M Sc, PhD); computer science (M Sc, PhD); drama (MA); economics (MA, Diploma); English (MA, PhD); French (MA); geography and planning (M Sc, MA, PhD); geological sciences (M Sc, PhD, Diploma); history (MA, PhD); indigenous studies (MA, PhD); mathematics and statistics (M Math, M Sc, PhD); music (M Mus, MA); philosophy (MA); physics and engineering physics (M Sc, PhD); political studies (MA); psychology (MA, PhD);

religion and culture (MA); sociology (MA, PhD); studio (MFA); teaching English to speakers of other languages (MA). Electronic applications accepted.

College of Education *Program availability:* Part-time. Offers curriculum studies (M Ed, PhD, Diploma); education (M Ed, PhD, Diploma); educational administration (M Ed, PhD, Diploma); educational foundations (M Ed, PhD, Diploma); measurement and evaluation (M Ed, PhD); school and counseling psychology (M Ed, PhD); special education (M Ed, PhD). Electronic applications accepted.

College of Engineering *Program availability:* Part-time. Offers biological engineering (M Sc, PhD); biomedical engineering (M Eng, M Sc, PhD, PGD); chemical engineering (M Eng, M Sc, PhD); civil and geological engineering (M Eng, M Sc, PhD); electrical engineering (M Eng, M Sc, PhD, PGD); engineering (M Eng, M Sc, PhD, PGD); mechanical engineering (M Eng, M Sc, PhD). Electronic applications accepted.

College of Kinesiology Offers kinesiology (M Sc, PhD).

College of Law *Program availability:* Part-time. Offers law (LL M, JD).

College of Nursing *Program availability:* Part-time. Offers nursing (MN, PhD).

College of Pharmacy and Nutrition Offers nutrition (M Sc, PhD); pharmacy (M Sc, PhD).

Edwards School of Business *Program availability:* Part-time. Offers accounting (MP Acc); agribusiness management (MBA); business (M Sc, MBA, MP Acc, PhD); finance (M Sc); marketing (M Sc).

School of Environment and Sustainability Offers environment and sustainability (MES, PhD).

School of Public Policy Offers public policy (MPP, PhD).

Toxicology Centre Offers toxicology (M Sc, PhD, Diploma).

College of Medicine Offers anatomy and cell biology (M Sc, PhD); biochemistry (M Sc, PhD); community health and epidemiology (M Sc, PhD); medicine (M Sc, DPT, MD, PhD); microbiology and immunology (M Sc, PhD); obstetrics and gynecology (M Sc, PhD); pathology and lab medicine (M Sc, PhD); pharmacology (M Sc, PhD); physiology (M Sc, PhD); psychiatry (M Sc, PhD); surgery (M Sc).

Western College of Veterinary Medicine Offers large animal clinical sciences (M Sc, M Vet Sc, PhD); small animal clinical sciences (M Sc, M Vet Sc, PhD); veterinary anatomy (M Sc); veterinary anesthesiology, radiology and surgery (M Vet Sc); veterinary biomedical sciences (M Sc, M Vet Sc, PhD); veterinary internal medicine (M Vet Sc); veterinary medicine (M Sc, M Vet Sc, DVM, PhD); veterinary microbiology (M Sc, M Vet Sc, PhD); veterinary pathology (M Sc, M Vet Sc, PhD); veterinary physiological sciences (M Sc, PhD).

THE UNIVERSITY OF SCRANTON, Scranton, PA 18510

General Information Independent-religious, coed, comprehensive institution. CGS member. *Graduate housing:* Room and/or apartments available on a first-come, first-served basis to single students; on-campus housing not available to married students. *Research affiliation:* Wyoming Valley Health Care System (nursing), Community Medical Center (health services), National Health Management Center (health care management), Allied Services (rehabilitation), Lackawanna River Corridor Association (environment), Universidad Iberoamericana (counseling and human services).

GRADUATE UNITS

College of Arts and Sciences *Program availability:* Part-time, evening/weekend, 100% online. Offers arts and sciences (MA, MS); biochemistry (MS); chemistry (MS); clinical chemistry (MS); theology (MA). Electronic applications accepted.

Kania School of Management Offers accountancy (M Acc); accounting (MBA); finance (MBA); general business administration (MBA); health care management (MBA); international business (MBA); management (M Acc, MBA, MS); management information systems (MBA); marketing (MBA); operations management (MBA); software engineering (MS).

Panuska College of Professional Studies Offers clinical mental health counseling (MS); curriculum and instruction (MS); educational administration (MS); family nurse practitioner (MSN, PMC); health administration (MHA); human resources (MS); nurse anesthesia (MSN, PMC); nursing leadership (DNP); occupational therapy (MS); physical therapy (DPT); professional counseling (CAGS); reading education (MS); rehabilitation counseling (MS); school counseling (MS); secondary education (MS); special education (MS).

UNIVERSITY OF SIOUX FALLS, Sioux Falls, SD 57105-1699

General Information Independent-religious, coed, comprehensive institution. *Graduate housing:* Rooms and/or apartments available on a first-come, first-served basis to single and married students.

GRADUATE UNITS

Fredrikson School of Education *Program availability:* Part-time, evening/weekend. Offers educational administration (Ed S); leadership in reading (M Ed); leadership in schools (M Ed); leadership in technology (M Ed); teaching (M Ed). Admission in summer only.

Vucurevich School of Business *Program availability:* Part-time, evening/weekend. Offers entrepreneurial leadership (MBA); general management (MBA); health care management (MBA); marketing (MBA).

UNIVERSITY OF SOUTH AFRICA, Pretoria 0003, South Africa

General Information Private, coed, university.

GRADUATE UNITS

College of Agriculture and Environmental Sciences Offers agriculture (MS); consumer science (MCS); environmental management (MA, MS, PhD); environmental science (MA, MS, PhD); geography (MA, MS, PhD); horticulture (M Tech); human ecology (MHE); life sciences (MS); nature conservation (M Tech).

College of Economic and Management Sciences Offers accounting (D Admin, D Com); accounting science (DA); auditing (D Admin, D Com); business administration (M Tech); business economics (D Admin); business leadership (DBL); business management (D Admin, D Com); economic management analysis (M Tech); economics (D Admin, D Com, PhD); human resource development (M Tech); industrial psychology (D Admin, D Com, PhD); logistics (D Com); marketing (M Tech); public administration (D Admin, D Com, DPA, PhD); public management (M Tech); quantitative management (D Admin, D Com); real estate (M Tech); statistics (D Admin, PhD); tourism management (D Admin, D Com); transport economics (D Admin, D Com).

College of Human Sciences Offers adult education (M Ed); African languages (MA, PhD); African politics (MA, PhD); Afrikaans (MA, PhD); ancient history (MA, PhD); ancient Near Eastern studies (MA, PhD); anthropology (MA, PhD); applied linguistics (MA); Arabic (MA, PhD); archaeology (MA); art history (MA); Biblical archaeology (MA); Biblical studies (M Th, D Th, PhD); Christian spirituality (M Th, D Th); church history (M Th, D Th); classical studies (MA, PhD); clinical psychology (MA); communication

(MA, PhD); comparative education (M Ed, Ed D); consulting psychology (D Admin, D Com, PhD); curriculum studies (M Ed, Ed D); development studies (M Admin, MA, D Admin, PhD); didactics (M Ed, Ed D); education (M Tech); education management (M Ed, Ed D); educational psychology (M Ed); English (MA); environmental education (M Ed); French (MA, PhD); German (MA, PhD); Greek (MA); guidance and counseling (M Ed); health studies (MA, PhD); history (MA, PhD); history of education (Ed D); inclusive education (M Ed, Ed D); information and communications technology policy and regulation (MA); information science (MA, MIS, PhD); international politics (MA, PhD); Islamic studies (MA, PhD); Italian (MA, PhD); Judaica (MA, PhD); linguistics (MA, PhD); mathematical education (M Ed); mathematics education (MA); missiology (M Th, D Th); modern Hebrew (MA, PhD); musicology (MA, MMus, D Mus, PhD); natural science education (M Ed); New Testament (M Th, D Th); Old Testament (D Th); pastoral therapy (M Th, D Th); philosophy (MA); philosophy of education (M Ed, Ed D); politics (MA, PhD); Portuguese (MA, PhD); practical theology (M Th, D Th); psychology (MA, MS, PhD); psychology of education (M Ed, Ed D); public health (MA); religious studies (MA, D Th, PhD); Romance languages (MA); Russian (MA, PhD); Semitic languages (MA, PhD); social behavior studies in HIV/AIDS (MA); social science (mental health) (MA); social science in development studies (MA); social science in psychology (MA); social science in social work (MA); social science in sociology (MA); social work (MSW, DSW, PhD); socio-education (M Ed, Ed D); sociolinguistics (MA); sociology (MA, PhD); Spanish (MA, PhD); systematic theology (M Th, D Th); TESOL (teaching English to speakers of other languages) (MA); theological ethics (M Th, D Th); theory of literature (MA, PhD); urban ministries (D Th); urban ministry (M Th).

College of Law Offers correctional services management (M Tech); criminology (MA, PhD); law (LL M, LL D); penology (MA, PhD); police science (MA, PhD); policing (M Tech); security risk management (M Tech); social science in criminology (MA).

College of Science, Engineering and Technology Offers chemical engineering (M Tech); information technology (M Tech).

Graduate School of Business Leadership Offers business leadership (MBA, MBL, DBL).

Institute for Science and Technology Education Offers mathematics, science and technology education (M Sc, PhD).

UNIVERSITY OF SOUTH ALABAMA, Mobile, AL 36688-0002

General Information State-supported, coed, university. CGS member. *Graduate housing:* Room and/or apartments available on a first-come, first-served basis to single students; on-campus housing not available to married students. Housing application deadline: 3/1. *Research affiliation:* Dauphin Island Marine Laboratory (marine sciences), Gynecologic Oncology Group (oncology), Eastern Cooperative Oncology Group (oncology), Radiation Therapy Oncology Group (oncology), National Institutes of Health (biomedical science), American College of Surgeons Oncology Group (oncology).

GRADUATE UNITS

College of Arts and Sciences *Program availability:* Part-time, evening/weekend. Offers arts and sciences (MA, MFA, MM, MPA, MS, PhD); biological sciences (MS); collaborative keyboard (MM); communication (MA); creative technologies and practice (MFA); creative writing (MA); history (MA); literature (MA); marine conservation and resource management (MS); marine sciences (MS, PhD); mathematics (MS); music education (MM); performance (MM); psychology (MS); public administration (MPA); sociology (MA). Electronic applications accepted.

College of Education and Professional Studies *Program availability:* Part-time, evening/weekend. Offers art education (M Ed); clinical mental health counseling (MS); early childhood education (M Ed); education and professional studies (M Ed, MS, Ed D, PhD, Ed S); educational leadership (M Ed, Ed D); educational media (M Ed); educational media and technology (MS); elementary education (M Ed); exercise science (MS); health education (M Ed, MS); instructional design and development (MS, PhD); instructional leadership (Ed S); physical education (M Ed); reading education (M Ed); school counseling (M Ed); science education (M Ed); secondary education (M Ed); special education (M Ed); sport management (MS). Electronic applications accepted.

College of Engineering *Program availability:* Part-time. Offers chemical and biomolecular engineering (MS Ch E); civil, coastal, and environmental engineering (MSCE); computer engineering (MSEE); electrical engineering (MSEE); engineering (MS Ch E, MSCE, MSEE, MSME, D Sc); mechanical engineering (MSME); systems engineering (D Sc). Electronic applications accepted.

College of Medicine Offers basic medical sciences (PhD); medicine (MD). Electronic applications accepted.

College of Nursing *Program availability:* Part-time, online learning. Offers nursing (MSN, DNP); nursing administration (Certificate); nursing education (Certificate); nursing practice (Certificate). Electronic applications accepted.

Graduate School *Program availability:* Part-time, evening/weekend. Offers basic medical sciences (MS); biology (MS); chemistry (MS); clinical and counseling psychology (PhD); environmental toxicology (MS); exposure route and chemical transport (MS). Electronic applications accepted.

Mitchell College of Business *Program availability:* Part-time, evening/weekend. Offers accounting (M Acc); business administration (MBA, DBA); management (DBA); marketing (DBA). Electronic applications accepted.

Pat Capps Covey College of Allied Health Professions Offers allied health professions (MHS, MS, Au D, DPT, PhD); audiology (Au D); communication sciences and disorders (PhD); occupational therapy (MS); physical therapy (DPT); physician assistant studies (MHS); speech-language pathology (MS). Electronic applications accepted.

School of Computing *Program availability:* Part-time, evening/weekend. Offers computer science (MS); information systems (MS). Electronic applications accepted.

UNIVERSITY OF SOUTH CAROLINA, Columbia, SC 29208

General Information State-supported, coed, university. CGS member. *Graduate housing:* Rooms and/or apartments available to single and married students. *Research affiliation:* E.I. du Pont de Nemours and Company (engineering, chemical engineering), Westinghouse/Savannah River Corporation (environmental restoration, hazardous waste remediation), Motorola Corporation–Energy Production Division (electrochemical engineering), Glaxo-Wellcome (pharmaceuticals), NCR Corporation (electrical and computer engineering).

GRADUATE UNITS

The Graduate School *Program availability:* Part-time, evening/weekend, online learning. Offers gerontology (Certificate). Electronic applications accepted.

Arnold School of Public Health *Program availability:* Part-time, online learning. Offers biostatistics (MPH, MSPH, Dr PH, PhD); communication sciences and disorders (MCD, MSP, PhD); environmental health science (MS); environmental quality (MPH, MS, MSPH, PhD); epidemiology (MPH, MSPH, Dr PH, PhD); exercise science (MS, DPT, PhD); general public health (MPH); hazardous materials management (MPH, MSPH, PhD); health education (MAT); health promotion, education, and behavior (MPH, MS, MSPH, Dr PH, PhD); health services policy and management (MHA, MPH, Dr PH, PhD); industrial hygiene (MPH, MSPH, PhD); physical activity and public health (MPH); public health (MAT, MCD, MHA, MPH, MS, MSP, MSPH, DPT, Dr PH, PhD, Certificate); school health education (Certificate). Electronic applications accepted.

College of Arts and Sciences *Program availability:* Part-time, evening/weekend. Offers anthropology (MA, PhD); applied statistics (CAS); archive management (MA); art education (IMA, MA, MAT); art history (MA); art studio (MA); arts and sciences (IMA, M Math, MA, MAT, MFA, MIS, MMA, MPA, MS, PSM, PhD, CAS, Certificate); biology (MS, PhD); biology education (IMA, MAT); chemistry and biochemistry (IMA, MAT, MS, PhD); clinical/community psychology (MA, PhD); comparative literature (MA, PhD); creative writing (MFA); criminology and criminal justice (MA, PhD); ecology, evolution and organismal biology (MS, PhD); English (MA, PhD); English education (MAT); experimental psychology (MA, PhD); foreign languages (MAT); French (MA); general psychology (MA); geography (MA, MS, PhD); geography education (IMA); geological sciences (MS, PhD); German (MA); historic preservation (MA); history (MA, PhD); industrial statistics (MIS); international studies (MA, PhD); linguistics (MA, PhD); marine science (MS, PhD); mathematics (MA, MS, PhD); mathematics education (M Math, MAT); media arts (MMA); molecular, cellular, and developmental biology (MS, PhD); museum administration (MA); museum management (Certificate); philosophy (MA, PhD); physics and astronomy (IMA, MAT, MS, PSM, PhD); political science (MA, MPA, PhD); public administration (MPA); public history (MA, Certificate); religious studies (MA); school psychology (PhD); sociology (MA, PhD); Spanish (MA); statistics (MS, PhD); studio art (MFA); teaching English to speakers of other languages (Certificate); theatre (MA, MAT, MFA); women's studies (Certificate). Electronic applications accepted.

College of Education *Program availability:* Part-time, evening/weekend, online learning. Offers art education (IMA, MAT); business education (IMA, MAT); counseling education (PhD, Ed S); curriculum and instruction (Ed D); early childhood education (M Ed, Ed D, PhD); education (IMA, M Ed, MAT, MS, MT, Ed D, PhD, Certificate, Ed S); educational administration (M Ed, PhD, Ed S); educational psychology, research (M Ed, PhD); educational technology (M Ed); elementary education (MAT, Ed D, PhD); English (MAT); foreign language (MAT); foundations in education (PhD); health education (MAT); higher education and student affairs (M Ed); higher education leadership (Certificate); language and literacy (M Ed, Ed D); mathematics (MAT); physical education (IMA, MAT, MS, PhD); science (IMA, MAT); secondary (Ed D); secondary education (IMA, MAT, MT, Ed D, PhD); social studies (MAT); special education (M Ed, MAT, PhD); teaching (M Ed, Ed S); theatre and speech (MAT). Electronic applications accepted.

College of Engineering and Computing *Program availability:* Part-time, evening/weekend, online learning. Offers chemical engineering (ME, MS, PhD); civil engineering (ME, MS, PhD); computer science and engineering (ME, MS, PhD); electrical engineering (ME, MS, PhD); engineering and computing (ME, MS, PhD); mechanical engineering (ME, MS, PhD); nuclear engineering (ME, MS, PhD); software engineering (MS). Electronic applications accepted.

College of Hospitality, Retail, and Sport Management *Program availability:* Part-time, online learning. Offers hospitality, retail, and sport management (MIHTM, MR, MS); hotel, restaurant and tourism management (MIHTM); live sport and entertainment events (MS); public assembly facilities management (MS); retailing (MR). Electronic applications accepted.

College of Information and Communications Offers information and communications (MA, MLIS, MMC, PhD, Certificate, Specialist); journalism and mass communications (MA, MMC, PhD); library and information science (MLIS, PhD, Certificate, Specialist).

College of Nursing *Program availability:* Part-time, online learning. Offers acute care clinical specialist (MSN); acute care nurse practitioner (MSN, Certificate); adult nurse practitioner (MSN); advanced practice clinical nursing (MSN, Certificate); advanced practice nursing in primary care (MSN, Certificate); advanced practice nursing in psychiatric mental health (MSN, Certificate); clinical nursing (MSN); community mental health and psychiatric health nursing (MSN); community/public health clinical nurse specialist (MSN); family nurse practitioner (MSN); health nursing (MSN); nursing administration (MSN); nursing practice (DNP); nursing science (PhD); pediatric nurse practitioner (MSN); psychiatric/mental health nurse practitioner (MSN); psychiatric/mental health specialist (MSN); women's health nurse practitioner (MSN). Electronic applications accepted.

College of Social Work *Program availability:* Part-time. Offers social work (MSW, PhD). Electronic applications accepted.

Darla Moore School of Business *Program availability:* Part-time, evening/weekend, online learning. Offers accountancy (M Acc); business administration (MBA, PhD); business measurement and assurance (M Acc); economics (MA, PhD); human resources (MHR); international business administration (IMBA). Electronic applications accepted.

School of Music *Program availability:* Part-time. Offers composition (MM, DMA); conducting (MM, DMA); jazz studies (MM); music education (MM Ed, PhD); music history (MM); music performance (Certificate); music theory (MM); opera theater (MM); performance (MM, DMA); piano pedagogy (MM, DMA). Electronic applications accepted.

School of the Environment *Program availability:* Part-time, online learning. Offers earth and environmental resources management (MEERM); environment (MEERM). Electronic applications accepted.

School of Law Offers law (JD).

School of Medicine Offers biomedical science (MBS, PhD); genetic counseling (MS); medicine (MBS, MNA, MRC, MS, MD, PhD, Certificate); nurse anesthesia (MNA); psychiatric rehabilitation (Certificate); rehabilitation counseling (MRC, Certificate). Electronic applications accepted.

South Carolina College of Pharmacy *Program availability:* Part-time. Offers pharmaceutical sciences (MS, PhD); pharmacy (MS, PhD, Pharm D). Electronic applications accepted.

UNIVERSITY OF SOUTH CAROLINA AIKEN, Aiken, SC 29801

General Information State-supported, coed, comprehensive institution. *Enrollment:* 3,699 graduate, professional, and undergraduate students; 43 full-time matriculated graduate/professional students (31 women), 105 part-time matriculated graduate/professional students (51 women). *Enrollment by degree level:* 148 master's. *Graduate faculty:* 16 full-time (11 women), 6 part-time/adjunct (2 women). Tuition, state resident: full-time $13,650; part-time $568.75 per credit hour. Tuition, nonresident: full-time $29,196; part-time $1216.50 per credit hour. *Required fees:* $13 per credit hour. $25 per semester. Full-time tuition and fees vary according to course load and program. *Graduate housing:* Room and/or apartments available on a first-come, first-served basis to single students; on-campus housing not available to married students. Typical cost: $5066 per year ($7766 including board). Room and board charges vary according to board plan. Housing application deadline: 5/1. *Student services:* Campus employment opportunities, campus safety program, career counseling, child daycare facilities, exercise/wellness program, free psychological counseling, grant writing training, international student services, multicultural affairs office, services for students with disabilities, teacher training, writing training. *Library facilities:* Gregg-Graniteville Library. *Collection:* Books: 133,161 (physical), 407,453 (digital/electronic); Serial titles: 16,034 (physical), 125,380 (digital/electronic); Databases: 217. Weekly public service hours: 78; students can reserve study rooms.

Computer facilities: 550 computers available on campus for general student use. A campuswide network can be accessed from student residence rooms and from off campus. Online class registration is available.
Website: http://www.usca.edu/

General Application Contact: Dan Robb, Associate Vice Chancellor for Enrollment Management, 803-641-3487, Fax: 803-641-3727, E-mail: danr@usca.edu.

GRADUATE UNITS

Program in Applied Clinical Psychology Students: 17 full-time (16 women), 10 part-time (8 women); includes 2 minority (1 Black or African American, non-Hispanic/Latino; 1 Two or more races, non-Hispanic/Latino), 1 international. Average age 25. 48 applicants, 44% accepted, 10 enrolled. *Faculty:* 8 full-time (6 women). Expenses: Contact institution. *Financial support:* In 2018–19, 25 students received support, including 17 research assistantships with partial tuition reimbursements available (averaging $2,510 per year), 5 teaching assistantships with partial tuition reimbursements available (averaging $2,125 per year); career-related internships or fieldwork, Federal Work-Study, scholarships/grants, tuition waivers (partial), and unspecified assistantships also available. Financial award application deadline: 3/1; financial award applicants required to submit FAFSA. In 2018, 2 master's awarded. *Program availability:* Part-time. Offers applied clinical psychology (MS). *Application deadline:* For fall admission, 4/1 priority date for domestic and international students. Applications are processed on a rolling basis. *Application fee:* $45 ($100 for international students). Electronic applications accepted. *Application Contact:* Dan Robb, Associate Vice Chancellor for Enrollment Management, 803-641-3487, Fax: 803-641-3727, E-mail: danr@usca.edu. *Director,* Dr. Jane Stafford, 803-641-3358, Fax: 803-641-3720, E-mail: jstafford@usca.edu.

Program in Business Administration Students: 26 full-time (15 women), 86 part-time (38 women); includes 34 minority (25 Black or African American, non-Hispanic/Latino; 2 Asian, non-Hispanic/Latino; 4 Hispanic/Latino; 3 Two or more races, non-Hispanic/Latino), 4 international. Average age 36. 198 applicants, 55% accepted, 76 enrolled. *Faculty:* 6 full-time (4 women), 5 part-time/adjunct (1 woman). Expenses: Contact institution. *Financial support:* In 2018–19, 7 students received support. Scholarships/grants and tuition waivers (partial) available. Support available to part-time students. Financial award application deadline: 3/1; financial award applicants required to submit FAFSA. In 2018, 14 master's awarded. *Program availability:* Part-time, evening/weekend, online only, 100% online. Offers business administration (MBA). *Application deadline:* For fall admission, 7/31 for domestic and international students; for spring admission, 12/16 for domestic and international students. Applications are processed on a rolling basis. *Application fee:* $45 ($100 for international students). Electronic applications accepted. *Application Contact:* Dan Robb, Associate Vice Chancellor for Enrollment Management, 803-641-3487, Fax: 803-641-3727, E-mail: danr@usca.edu. *Dean for School of Business Administration,* Dr. Michael J. Fekula, 803-641-3340, E-mail: mickf@usca.edu.

Program in Educational Technology Students: 9 part-time (5 women); includes 1 minority (Hispanic/Latino). Average age 37. 9 applicants, 67% accepted, 5 enrolled. *Faculty:* 2 full-time (1 woman), 1 (woman) part-time/adjunct. Expenses: Contact institution. *Financial support:* In 2018–19, 5 students received support. Fellowships with partial tuition reimbursements available, career-related internships or fieldwork, Federal Work-Study, scholarships/grants, tuition waivers (partial), and unspecified assistantships available. Support available to part-time students. Financial award application deadline: 3/1; financial award applicants required to submit FAFSA. In 2018, 4 master's awarded. *Program availability:* Part-time, evening/weekend, online only, 100% online. Offers educational technology (M Ed). Program offered with University of South Carolina in Columbia. *Application deadline:* Applications are processed on a rolling basis. *Application fee:* $45 ($100 for international students). Electronic applications accepted. *Application Contact:* Dan Robb, Associate Vice Chancellor for Enrollment Management, 803-641-3487, Fax: 803-641-3727, E-mail: danr@usca.edu. *Educational Technology Program Coordinator,* Dr. Erin Besser, 803-641-3712, E-mail: erinbe@usca.edu.

UNIVERSITY OF SOUTH CAROLINA UPSTATE, Spartanburg, SC 29303-4999

General Information State-supported, coed, comprehensive institution. *Graduate housing:* On-campus housing not available.

GRADUATE UNITS

Graduate Programs *Program availability:* Part-time, evening/weekend. Offers early childhood education (M Ed); elementary education (M Ed); informatics (MS); special education: visual impairment (M Ed).

UNIVERSITY OF SOUTH DAKOTA, Vermillion, SD 57069

General Information State-supported, coed, university. CGS member. *Enrollment:* 10,066 graduate, professional, and undergraduate students; 1,283 full-time matriculated graduate/professional students (745 women), 1,012 part-time matriculated graduate/professional students (586 women). *Enrollment by degree level:* 1,211 master's, 1,084 doctoral, 181 other advanced degrees. *Graduate faculty:* 364 full-time (163 women), 54 part-time/adjunct (31 women). *Graduate housing:* Room and/or apartments available on a first-come, first-served basis to single students; on-campus housing not available to married students. Typical cost: $3751 per year ($4280 including board). Room and board charges vary according to board plan, campus/location and housing facility selected. Housing application deadline: 5/1. *Student services:* Campus employment opportunities, campus safety program, career counseling, child daycare facilities, exercise/wellness program, free psychological counseling, grant writing training, international student services, low-cost health insurance, multicultural affairs office, services for students with disabilities, teacher training, writing training. *Library facilities:* I. D. Weeks Library plus 2 others. *Collection:* Books: 528,075 (physical), 152,540 (digital/electronic); Serial titles: 4,739 (physical), 154,738 (digital/electronic); Databases: 230. Weekly public service hours: 103; students can reserve study rooms.

Computer facilities: 975 computers available on campus for general student use. A campuswide network can be accessed from student residence rooms and from off campus. Online class registration is available.
Website: http://www.usd.edu/

General Application Contact: Travis Vlasman, Director of Graduate Admissions, 605-658-6228, Fax: 605-677-6118, E-mail: gradadmissions@usd.edu.

GRADUATE UNITS

Graduate School *Program availability:* Part-time, evening/weekend, 100% online, blended/hybrid learning. Offers interdisciplinary studies (MA). Electronic applications accepted.

Beacom School of Business *Program availability:* Part-time, evening/weekend, 100% online, blended/hybrid learning. Offers accounting (MP Acc); business administration (MBA, Graduate Certificate); business analytics (MBA, Graduate Certificate); health services administration (MBA); long term care management (Graduate Certificate); marketing (MBA, Graduate Certificate); operations and supply chain management (MBA, Graduate Certificate); professional accountancy (MP Acc). Electronic applications accepted.

College of Arts and Sciences *Program availability:* Part-time, online learning. Offers addiction studies (MSA); arts and sciences (MA, MNS, MS, MSA, Au D, PhD); audiology (Au D); biology (MS, PhD); chemistry (MS, PhD); clinical psychology (MA, PhD); communication studies (MA); computer science (MS); criminal justice studies (MSA); English (MA, PhD); health services administration (MA); history (MA); human factors (MA, PhD); human resources (MSA); interdisciplinary studies (MSA); long term care administration (MSA); mathematics (MA, MS); organizational leadership (MSA); physics (MS, PhD); speech-language pathology (MA); sustainability (MS). Electronic applications accepted.

College of Fine Arts Offers art education (MFA); ceramics (MFA); collaborative piano (MM); conducting (MM); design/technology (MFA); directing (MFA); fine arts (MA, MFA, MM); graphic design (MFA); history of musical instruments (MM); music education (MM); music history (MM); music performance (MM); painting (MFA); photography (MFA); printmaking (MFA); sculpture (MFA); theatre (MA). Electronic applications accepted.

Sanford School of Medicine *Program availability:* Part-time. Offers bioethics (Certificate); cardiovascular research (MS, PhD); cellular and molecular biology (MS, PhD); medicine (MS, MD, PhD, Certificate); molecular microbiology and immunology (MS, PhD); neuroscience (MS, PhD); physiology and pharmacology (MS, PhD).

School of Education *Program availability:* Part-time, evening/weekend, 100% online, blended/hybrid learning. Offers American Indian education (Certificate); counseling (MA, PhD, Ed S); curriculum and instruction (Ed D, Ed S); education (MA, MS, Ed D, PhD, Certificate, Ed S); educational administration (MA, Ed D, Ed S); elementary education (MA); English language learners (Certificate); exercise science (MA); human development and educational psychology (MA, PhD, Ed S); literacy leadership and coaching (Certificate); mental health counseling (Certificate); reading interventionist (Certificate); school psychology (PhD, Ed S); science, technology and math pedagogy (Certificate); secondary education (MA); special education (MA); sport management (MA); technology for education and training (MS). Electronic applications accepted.

School of Health Sciences *Program availability:* Part-time. Offers health sciences (MA, MPH, MS, MSW, DPT, OTD, PhD, Graduate Certificate); occupational therapy (OTD); physical therapy (DPT); physician assistant studies (MS); post-professional clinical occupational therapy (OTD); public health (MPH); social work (MSW).

School of Law *Program availability:* Part-time. Offers law (JD). Electronic applications accepted.

UNIVERSITY OF SOUTHERN CALIFORNIA, Los Angeles, CA 90089

General Information Independent, coed, university. CGS member. *Graduate housing:* Rooms and/or apartments available on a first-come, first-served basis to single and married students. *Research affiliation:* SETI Institute (astronomy/astrobiology), Rancho Los Amigos Medical Center (medicine), Children's Hospital Los Angeles (medicine), Doheny Eye Institute (medicine), House Ear Institute (medicine), Jet Propulsion Laboratory (engineering and technology).

GRADUATE UNITS

Graduate School Electronic applications accepted.

Annenberg School for Communication and Journalism Students: 702 full-time, 147 part-time; includes 349 minority (96 Black or African American, non-Hispanic/Latino; 62 Asian, non-Hispanic/Latino; 154 Hispanic/Latino; 3 Native Hawaiian or other Pacific Islander, non-Hispanic/Latino; 34 Two or more races, non-Hispanic/Latino), 256 international. Average age 27. 1,776 applicants, 47% accepted, 403 enrolled. *Faculty:* 98 full-time, 100 part-time/adjunct. Expenses: Contact institution. *Financial support:* In 2018–19, 28 fellowships with full tuition reimbursements (averaging $22,287 per year), 16 research assistantships with partial tuition reimbursements (averaging $15,000 per year), 6 teaching assistantships with full tuition reimbursements (averaging $22,287 per year) were awarded; career-related internships or fieldwork, Federal Work-Study, institutionally sponsored loans, scholarships/grants, health care benefits, tuition waivers (partial), and unspecified assistantships also available. Support available to part-time students. Financial award application deadline: 1/1; financial award applicants required to submit FAFSA. In 2018, 445 master's, 19 doctorates awarded. *Program availability:* Part-time, evening/weekend, online learning. Offers communication (MA, MCM, MPD, MS, PhD); communication management (MCM); culture and community (PhD); digital social media (MS); global and transnational communication (PhD); groups, organizations and networks (PhD); health communication and social dynamics (PhD); information, political economy and entertainment (PhD); journalism (MA, MS); journalism, digital social media (MS); new media and technology (PhD); public diplomacy (MPD); rhetoric, politics and public media (PhD); specialized journalism (MA); specialized journalism (the arts) (MA); strategic public relations (MA). *Application deadline:* For fall admission, 12/1 priority date for domestic and international students; for spring admission, 3/1 priority date for domestic students, 1/1 priority date for international students; for summer admission, 1/1 priority date for domestic and international students. Applications are processed on a rolling basis. *Application fee:* $90. Electronic applications accepted. *Application Contact:* Allyson Hill, Associate Dean for Admissions, 213-821-0770, Fax: 213-740-1933, E-mail: ascadm@usc.edu. *Dean,* Willow Bay, 213-740-6180, Fax: 213-740-3772, E-mail: ascdean@usc.edu.

Dana and David Dornsife College of Letters, Arts and Sciences Offers American studies and ethnicity (PhD); applied mathematics (MA, MS, PhD); art history (MA, PhD); biology (MS); brain and cognitive science (PhD); chemistry (PhD); classical Chinese literature (MA, PhD); classical Japanese literature (MA, PhD); classics (MA, PhD); clinical science (PhD); comparative literature (PhD); comparative media and culture (PhD); computational biology and bioinformatics (PhD); computational molecular biology (MS); developmental psychology (PhD); earth sciences (MS, PhD); East Asian linguistics (PhD); East Asian studies (MA); economic development programming (MA, PhD); English (MA, PhD); geographic information science and technology (MS, Graduate Certificate); Hispanic linguistics (PhD); history (PhD);

human behavior (MHB); integrative and evolutionary biology (PhD); letters, arts and sciences (MA, MHB, MMM, MPW, MS, PhD, Graduate Certificate); linguistics (MA, PhD); literature and creative writing (PhD); marine and environmental biology (MS); marine biology and biological oceanography (MS, PhD); mathematical finance (MS); mathematics (MS, PhD); modern Chinese literature (MA, PhD); modern Japanese literature (MA, PhD); modern Korean literature (MA, PhD); molecular and computational biology (PhD); molecular biology (PhD); neurobiology (PhD); ocean sciences (MS, PhD); philosophy (PhD); physical chemistry (PhD); physics (MA, MS, PhD); political science and international relations (PhD); quantitative methods (PhD); Slavic languages and literatures (MA, PhD); Slavic linguistics (PhD); social psychology (PhD); sociology (PhD); Spanish and Latin American studies (PhD); statistics (MS); visual studies (Graduate Certificate). Electronic applications accepted.

Gould School of Law Offers comparative law for foreign attorneys (MCL); law (JD); law for foreign-educated attorneys (LL M).

Herman Ostrow School of Dentistry Offers biokinesiology (MS, PhD); craniofacial biology (MS, PhD, Graduate Certificate); dentistry (MA, MS, DDS, DPT, OTD, PhD, Graduate Certificate); occupational science (PhD); occupational therapy (MA, OTD); physical therapy (DPT). Electronic applications accepted.

Leonard Davis School of Gerontology *Program availability:* Part-time, online learning. Offers aging services management (MASM); biology of aging (PhD); gerontology (MA, MS, PhD, Graduate Certificate); long term care administration (MLTCA). PhD in biology of aging offered jointly with Buck Institute for Research on Aging. Electronic applications accepted.

Marshall School of Business Offers accounting (M Acc); business (M Acc, MBA, MBT, MBV, MMM, MS, PhD); business administration (MBA, MMM, MS, PhD); business taxation (MBT); entrepreneurship and innovation (MS). Electronic applications accepted.

Roski School of Art and Design Offers art and curatorial practices in the public sphere (MA); art and design (MA, MFA); new genres (MFA); painting/drawing (MFA); photography (MFA); sculpture (MFA). Electronic applications accepted.

Rossier School of Education Offers education (MAT, ME, MMFT, Ed D, PhD); educational counseling (ME); educational psychology (Ed D, PhD); higher education administration (Ed D); higher education administration and policy (PhD); K-12 leadership in urban school settings (Ed D); K-12 policy and practice (PhD); marriage, family and child counseling (MMFT); postsecondary administration and student affairs [PASA] (ME); school counseling (ME); teacher education in multicultural societies (Ed D); teaching (online) (MAT); teaching and teaching credential (MAT); teaching English to speakers of other languages (MAT). Electronic applications accepted.

School of Architecture Offers architecture (M Arch); building science (MBS); heritage conservation (MHP); landscape architecture and urbanism (MLA). Electronic applications accepted.

School of Cinematic Arts Offers animation and digital arts (MFA); cinema and media studies (MA, PhD); cinematic arts (MA, MFA, PhD); film and television production (MFA); interactive media (MFA); media arts and practice (PhD); motion picture producing (MFA); writing for screen and television (MFA). Electronic applications accepted.

School of Dramatic Arts Offers acting (MFA); dramatic writing (MFA). Electronic applications accepted.

School of Pharmacy Offers clinical and experimental therapeutics (PhD); clinical research design and management (Graduate Certificate); food safety (Graduate Certificate); healthcare decision analysis (MS); patient and product safety (Graduate Certificate); pharmaceutical economics and policy (MS, PhD); pharmaceutical sciences (MS, PhD); pharmacology and pharmaceutical sciences (MS, PhD); pharmacy (MS, DRSc, PhD, Pharm D, Graduate Certificate); preclinical drug development (Graduate Certificate); regulatory and clinical affairs (Graduate Certificate); regulatory science (MS, DRSc).

Sol Price School of Public Policy Offers ambulatory care (Graduate Certificate); health administration (EMHA, MHA, Graduate Certificate); homeland security and public policy (Graduate Certificate); international public policy and management (MPPM); leadership (EML); long-term care (Graduate Certificate); nonprofit management and policy (Graduate Certificate); policy, planning, and development (DPPD); political management (Graduate Certificate); public administration (MPA); public management (Graduate Certificate); public policy (EMHA, EML, M PI, MHA, MPA, MPP, MPPM, MRED, DPPD, PhD, Graduate Certificate); public policy and management (MRED); real estate development (MRED); sustainable cities (Graduate Certificate); transportation systems (Graduate Certificate); urban planning (M PI); urban planning and development (PhD). Electronic applications accepted.

Suzanne Dworak-Peck School of Social Work Offers community organization, planning and administration (MSW); families and children (MSW); health (MSW); mental health (MSW); Military Social Work and Veterans Services (MSW); older adults (MSW); public child welfare (MSW); school settings (MSW); social work (MSW, PhD); systems of mental illness recovery (MSW); work and life (MSW). Electronic applications accepted.

Thornton School of Music *Program availability:* Part-time, evening/weekend. Offers brass performance (MM, DMA, Graduate Certificate); choral and sacred music (MM, DMA); classical guitar (MM, DMA, Graduate Certificate); composition (MM, DMA); early music (MA, DMA); harp performance (MM, DMA, Graduate Certificate); historical musicology (PhD); jazz studies (MM, DMA, Graduate Certificate); keyboard collaborative arts (MM, DMA, Graduate Certificate); music education (MM, DMA); organ performance (MM, DMA, Graduate Certificate); percussion performance (MM, DMA, Graduate Certificate); piano performance (MM, DMA, Graduate Certificate); scoring for motion pictures and television (Graduate Certificate); strings performance (MM, DMA, Graduate Certificate); studio jazz guitar (MM, DMA, Graduate Certificate); teaching music (MA); vocal arts (classical voice/opera) (MM, DMA, Graduate Certificate); woodwind performance (MM, DMA, Graduate Certificate). Electronic applications accepted.

Viterbi School of Engineering *Program availability:* Part-time, online learning. Offers aerospace and mechanical engineering: computational fluid and solid mechanics (MS); aerospace and mechanical engineering: dynamics and control (MS); aerospace engineering (MS, PhD, Engr); applied mechanics (MS); astronautical engineering (MS, PhD, Engr, Graduate Certificate); biomedical engineering (PhD); chemical engineering (MS, PhD, Engr); civil engineering (MS, PhD); computer engineering (MS, PhD); computer networks (MS); computer science (MS, PhD); computer security (MS); computer-aided engineering (ME, Graduate Certificate); construction management (MCM); digital supply chain management (MS); electric power (MS); electrical engineering (MS, PhD, Engr); engineering (MCM, ME, MS, PhD, Engr, Graduate Certificate); engineering management (MS); engineering technology commercialization (Graduate Certificate); engineering technology communication (Graduate Certificate); environmental engineering (MS, PhD); environmental quality

management (ME); game development (MS); geoscience technologies (MS); green technologies (MS); health systems operations (Graduate Certificate); high performance computing and simulations (MS); human language technology (MS); industrial and systems engineering (MS, PhD, Engr); intelligent robotics (MS); manufacturing engineering (MS); materials engineering (MS); materials science (MS, PhD, Engr); mechanical engineering (MS, PhD, Engr); medical device and diagnostic engineering (MS); medical imaging and imaging informatics (MS); multimedia and creative technologies (MS); operations research engineering (MS); optimization and supply chain management (Graduate Certificate); petroleum engineering (MS, PhD, Engr); product development engineering (MS); safety systems and security (MS); smart oilfield technologies (MS, Graduate Certificate); software engineering (MS); structural design (ME); sustainable cities (Graduate Certificate); systems architecting and engineering (MS, Graduate Certificate); systems safety and security (Graduate Certificate); telecommunications (MS); transportation systems (MS, Graduate Certificate); VLSI design (MS); water and waste management (MS); wireless health technology (MS). Electronic applications accepted.

Keck School of Medicine Students: 1,650 full-time (980 women), 134 part-time (100 women); includes 975 minority (126 Black or African American, non-Hispanic/Latino; 5 American Indian or Alaska Native, non-Hispanic/Latino; 544 Asian, non-Hispanic/Latino; 237 Hispanic/Latino; 8 Native Hawaiian or other Pacific Islander, non-Hispanic/Latino; 55 Two or more races, non-Hispanic/Latino), 163 international. Average age 25. 10,835 applicants, 12% accepted, 589 enrolled. *Faculty:* 474 full-time (170 women). Expenses: Contact institution. *Financial support:* In 2018–19, 211 students received support. Fellowships, research assistantships, teaching assistantships, career-related internships or fieldwork, Federal Work-Study, institutionally sponsored loans, scholarships/grants, traineeships, and health care benefits available. Support available to part-time students. Financial award applicants required to submit FAFSA. In 2018, 397 master's, 231 doctorates awarded. Offers anesthesia (DNAP); medicine (MPAP, MPH, MS, DNAP, MD, PhD, Certificate). *Application deadline:* Applications are processed on a rolling basis. *Application fee:* $90. Electronic applications accepted. *Application Contact:* Marisela Zuniga, Department Business Administrator, 323-442-1607, Fax: 323-442-1199, E-mail: mzuniga@usc.edu. *Dean,* Dr. Rohit Varma, 323-442-1900.

Graduate Programs in Medicine Students: 930 full-time (641 women), 134 part-time (100 women); includes 562 minority (81 Black or African American, non-Hispanic/Latino; 4 American Indian or Alaska Native, non-Hispanic/Latino; 286 Asian, non-Hispanic/Latino; 162 Hispanic/Latino; 7 Native Hawaiian or other Pacific Islander, non-Hispanic/Latino; 22 Two or more races, non-Hispanic/Latino), 162 international. Average age 26. 2,736 applicants, 32% accepted, 403 enrolled. *Faculty:* 474 full-time (170 women), 45 part-time/adjunct (24 women). Expenses: Contact institution. *Financial support:* Fellowships, research assistantships, teaching assistantships, career-related internships or fieldwork, Federal Work-Study, institutionally sponsored loans, scholarships/grants, traineeships, and health care benefits available. Support available to part-time students. Financial award applicants required to submit CSS PROFILE or FAFSA. In 2018, 397 master's, 32 doctorates awarded. Offers applied biostatistics and epidemiology (MS); biochemistry and molecular medicine (MS); biomedical and biological sciences (PhD); biostatistics (MS, PhD); biostatistics and epidemiology (MPH); biotechnology (MS); cancer biology and genomics (PhD); child and family health (MPH); community health promotion (MPH); development, stem cell and regenerative medicine (PhD); environmental health (MPH); epidemiology (PhD); experimental and molecular pathology (MS); geohealth (MPH); global health leadership (MPH); global medicine (MS, Certificate); health behavior research (PhD); health communication (MPH); health services and policy (MPH); medical biology (PhD); medical biophysics (MS); medical physiology (MS); medicine (MPAP, MPH, MS, PhD, Certificate); molecular epidemiology (MS); molecular microbiology and immunology (MS); primary care physician assistant (MPAP); public health (MPH); stem cell biology and regenerative medicine (MS). *Application deadline:* Applications are processed on a rolling basis. *Application fee:* $90. Electronic applications accepted. *Application Contact:* Marisela Zuniga, Administrative Coordinator, 323-442-1607, Fax: 323-442-1199, E-mail: mzuniga@usc.edu. *Associate Dean for Graduate Affairs,* Dr. Ite Offringa, 323-442-1607, Fax: 323-442-1199, E-mail: ilaird@usc.edu.

Program in Neuroscience Offers neuroscience (MS, PhD). M.S. degree is terminal degree only. Electronic applications accepted.

UNIVERSITY OF SOUTHERN INDIANA, Evansville, IN 47712-3590

General Information State-supported, coed, comprehensive institution. CGS member. *Graduate housing:* Room and/or apartments available on a first-come, first-served basis to single students; on-campus housing not available to married students. Housing application deadline: 3/1.

GRADUATE UNITS

Graduate Studies *Program availability:* Part-time, evening/weekend. Electronic applications accepted.

College of Liberal Arts *Program availability:* Part-time, evening/weekend. Offers communication (MA); English (MA); liberal arts (MA, MALS, MPA, MSW); liberal studies (MALS); nonprofit administration (MPA); public sector administration (MPA); second language acquisition, policy, and culture (MA); social work (MSW). Electronic applications accepted.

College of Nursing and Health Professions *Program availability:* Part-time, blended/hybrid learning. Offers adult-gerontology acute care nurse practitioner (MSN, PMC); adult-gerontology clinical nurse specialist (MSN, PMC); adult-gerontology primary care nurse practitioner (MSN, PMC); advanced nursing practice (DNP); family nurse practitioner (MSN, PMC); health administration (MHA); nursing and health professions (MHA, MSN, MSOT, DNP, PMC); nursing education (MSN, PMC); nursing management and leadership (MSN, PMC); occupational therapy (MSOT); organizational and systems leadership (DNP); psychiatric mental health nurse practitioner (MSN, PMC). Electronic applications accepted.

Pott College of Science, Engineering, and Education *Program availability:* Part-time, evening/weekend. Offers administrative leadership (Ed D); educational leadership (Ed D); elementary education (MSE); industrial management (MSIM); pedagogical leadership (Ed D); school administration and leadership (MSE); science, engineering, and education (MSE, MSIM, MSSM, Ed D); secondary education (MSE); sport management (MSSM). Electronic applications accepted.

Romain College of Business *Program availability:* Part-time, evening/weekend. Offers accounting (MBA); business (MBA); data analytics (MBA); engineering management (MBA); general business administration (MBA); healthcare administration (MBA); human resource management (MBA). Electronic applications accepted.

UNIVERSITY OF SOUTHERN MAINE, Portland, ME 04103

General Information State-supported, coed, comprehensive institution. CGS member. *Graduate housing:* Rooms and/or apartments available on a first-come, first-served basis to single and married students. Housing application deadline: 5/1.

GRADUATE UNITS

College of Arts, Humanities, and Social Sciences *Program availability:* Part-time, evening/weekend, online learning. Offers American and New England studies (MA, CGS); arts, humanities, and social sciences (MA, MFA, MM, CGS); creative writing (MFA). Electronic applications accepted.

School of Music Offers composition (MM); conducting (MM); jazz studies (MM); music education (MM); performance (MM).

College of Management and Human Service Offers management and human service (MBA, MCPD, MPH, MPPM, MS, MS Ed, MSW, Psy D, CAS, CGS).

Muskie School of Public Service *Program availability:* Part-time, evening/weekend, online learning. Offers community planning and development (MCPD, CGS); health policy and management (MPH, CGS); public policy and management (MPPM). Electronic applications accepted.

School of Business *Program availability:* Part-time, evening/weekend. Offers accounting (MBA); business administration (MBA); finance (MBA); health management and policy (MBA); sustainability (MBA). Electronic applications accepted.

School of Education and Human Development *Program availability:* Part-time, evening/weekend, online learning. Offers adult and higher education (MS); adult learning (CAS); applied behavior analysis (MS, CGS); applied literacy (MS Ed); assistant principal (CGS); clinical mental health counseling (MS); counseling (CAS); culturally responsive practices in education and human development (CGS); education and human development (MS, MS Ed, Psy D, CAS, CGS); educational leadership (MS Ed, CAS); English as a second language (MS Ed, CAS, CGS); gifted and talented education (CGS); literacy education (MS Ed, CAS, CGS); mental health rehabilitation technician/community (CGS); professional educator (MS Ed); professional teacher (MS Ed); rehabilitation counseling (MS); school counseling (MS); school psychology (MS, Psy D); special education (MS); substance abuse counseling (CGS); teaching all students (CGS); teaching and learning (MS Ed). Electronic applications accepted.

School of Social Work *Program availability:* Part-time, evening/weekend. Offers social work (MSW). Electronic applications accepted.

College of Science, Technology, and Health *Program availability:* Part-time, evening/weekend. Offers applied medical sciences (MS); biology (MS); computer science (MS); science, technology, and health (MS, DNP, CAS, CGS, PMC); software systems (CGS); statistics (MS, CGS). Electronic applications accepted.

School of Nursing *Program availability:* Part-time. Offers adult-gerontology primary care nurse practitioner (MS, PMC); education (MS); family nurse practitioner (MS, PMC); family psychiatric/mental health nurse practitioner (MS); management (MS); nursing (CAS, CGS); psychiatric-mental health nurse practitioner (PMC). Electronic applications accepted.

Lewiston-Auburn College Offers creative leadership/global strategies (CGS); leadership studies (MA); occupational therapy (MOT).

UNIVERSITY OF SOUTHERN MISSISSIPPI, Hattiesburg, MS 39406-0001

General Information State-supported, coed, university. CGS member. *Graduate housing:* On-campus housing not available. *Research affiliation:* Oak Ridge Associated Universities.

GRADUATE UNITS

College of Arts and Sciences *Program availability:* Part-time, evening/weekend, online learning. Offers anthropology and sociology (MA); arts and sciences (MA, MATL, MFA, MM, MME, MS, DMA, PhD); biological sciences (MS, PhD); chemistry and biochemistry (MS, PhD); computational science (PhD); costume design (MFA); creative writing (MA, PhD); directing (MFA); English education (MA); French (MATL); geography (PhD); geography and geology (MS, PhD); history (MA, MS, PhD); lighting and sound design (MFA); literature (MA, PhD); mathematics (MS); performance (MFA); physics (MS); political science, international development and international affairs (MA, PhD); scenic design (MFA); Spanish (MATL); teaching English to speakers of other languages (MATL). Electronic applications accepted.

Division of Coastal Sciences *Program availability:* Part-time. Offers coastal sciences (MS, PhD). Electronic applications accepted.

Division of Marine Science *Program availability:* Part-time. Offers hydrographic science (MS); marine science (MS, PhD). Electronic applications accepted.

School of Communication *Program availability:* Part-time. Offers communication (MA, MS, PhD); public relations (MS). Electronic applications accepted.

School of Computing Sciences and Computer Engineering Offers computational science (MS, PhD); computer science (MS). Electronic applications accepted.

School of Construction and Design *Program availability:* Part-time, online learning. Offers logistics, trade and transportation (MS).

School of Criminal Justice, Forensic Science, and Security *Program availability:* Part-time. Offers criminal justice (MA, MS, PhD); forensic science (MS). Electronic applications accepted.

School of Music *Program availability:* Blended/hybrid learning. Offers conducting (DMA); music education (MME); performance and pedagogy (DMA); piano accompanying (MM); theory (MM); woodwind performance and pedagogy (MM).

School of Polymer Science and Engineering Offers polymer science and engineering (MS, PhD). Electronic applications accepted.

College of Business and Economic Development *Program availability:* Part-time, evening/weekend. Offers business administration (MBA); business and economic development (MBA, MPA, MS); sport security management (MBA). Electronic applications accepted.

School of Accountancy *Program availability:* Part-time, evening/weekend. Offers accountancy (MPA). Electronic applications accepted.

School of Finance *Program availability:* Part-time. Offers economic development (MS).

School of Marketing *Program availability:* Part-time, evening/weekend. Offers sport management (MS). Electronic applications accepted.

College of Education and Human Sciences *Program availability:* Part-time. Offers education and human sciences (M Ed, MA, MAT, MLIS, MS, MSW, Ed D, PhD, Ed S, Graduate Certificate); educational administration (M Ed, Ed D, PhD, Ed S); educational administration and supervision (M Ed); educational studies and research (MS); elementary education (M Ed, PhD); higher education (Ed D); higher education administration (PhD); higher education: student affairs (M Ed); instructional technology (MS); instructional technology and design (PhD); nutrition and food systems (MS); research, evaluation, statistics, assessment (PhD); secondary education (MAT); special education (M Ed, PhD). Electronic applications accepted.

School of Child and Family Sciences *Program availability:* Part-time, online learning. Offers child and family studies (MS); marriage and family therapy (MS); school counseling (M Ed). Electronic applications accepted.

School of Kinesiology *Program availability:* Part-time, evening/weekend. Offers kinesiology (MS, PhD). Electronic applications accepted.

School of Library and Information Science *Program availability:* Part-time, evening/weekend, online learning. Offers library and information science (MLIS); youth services and literature (Graduate Certificate). Electronic applications accepted.

School of Psychology Offers psychology (MS, PhD).

School of Social Work *Program availability:* Part-time. Offers social work (MSW). Electronic applications accepted.

College of Nursing and Health Professions *Program availability:* Part-time, evening/weekend. Offers medical laboratory science (MLS); nursing and health professions (MA, MLS, MPH, MS, MSN, MSW, Au D, DNP, PhD, Graduate Certificate). Electronic applications accepted.

School of Health Professions *Program availability:* Part-time, evening/weekend. Offers epidemiology and biostatistics (MPH); health policy and administration (MPH). Electronic applications accepted.

School of Leadership and Advanced Practice Nursing *Program availability:* Part-time, evening/weekend. Offers leadership and advanced practice nursing (MSN, DNP, PhD, Graduate Certificate). Electronic applications accepted.

School of Speech and Hearing Sciences Offers speech and hearing sciences (MA, MS, Au D). Electronic applications accepted.

UNIVERSITY OF SOUTH FLORIDA, Tampa, FL 33620-9951

General Information State-supported, coed, university. CGS member. *Enrollment:* 43,838 graduate, professional, and undergraduate students; 6,752 full-time matriculated graduate/professional students (3,668 women), 3,976 part-time matriculated graduate/professional students (2,516 women). *Enrollment by degree level:* 6,748 master's, 3,943 doctoral, 37 other advanced degrees. *Graduate faculty:* 1,185 full-time (493 women), 65 part-time/adjunct (27 women). *International tuition:* $19,048 full-time. Tuition, state resident: full-time $6350. Tuition, nonresident: full-time $19,048. *Required fees:* $2079. *Graduate housing:* Room and/or apartments available on a first-come, first-served basis to single students; on-campus housing not available to married students. Typical cost: $8756 per year ($12,614 including board). Room and board charges vary according to board plan and housing facility selected. Housing application deadline: 8/22. *Student services:* Campus employment opportunities, campus safety program, career counseling, child daycare facilities, exercise/wellness program, free psychological counseling, grant writing training, international student services, low-cost health insurance, multicultural affairs office, services for students with disabilities, teacher training, writing training. *Library facilities:* Tampa Campus Library plus 5 others. *Collection:* Books: 1.8 million (physical), 652,513 (digital/electronic); Serial titles: 537 (physical), 58,975 (digital/electronic); Databases: 939. Weekly public service hours: 116; study areas open 24 hours, 5–7 days a week; students can reserve study rooms.

Computer facilities: 825 computers available on campus for general student use. A campuswide network can be accessed from student residence rooms and from off campus. Online class registration is available. Website: http://www.usf.edu/

General Application Contact: Dr. Dwayne Smith, Senior Vice Provost and Dean, Office of Graduate Studies, 813-974-2846, Fax: 813-974-5762, E-mail: mdsmith3@usf.edu.

GRADUATE UNITS

College of Arts and Sciences Students: 1,184 full-time (616 women), 525 part-time (340 women); includes 367 minority (92 Black or African American, non-Hispanic/Latino; 2 American Indian or Alaska Native, non-Hispanic/Latino; 52 Asian, non-Hispanic/Latino; 181 Hispanic/Latino; 40 Two or more races, non-Hispanic/Latino), 350 international. Average age 30. 1,846 applicants, 40% accepted, 426 enrolled. *Faculty:* 369 full-time (135 women), 4 part-time/adjunct (2 women). *Expenses:* Contact institution. *Financial support:* In 2018–19, 420 students received support, including 2 research assistantships with tuition reimbursements available (averaging $13,650 per year); career-related internships or fieldwork, Federal Work-Study, institutionally sponsored loans, scholarships/grants, tuition waivers (full and partial), and unspecified assistantships also available. Support available to part-time students. Financial award applicants required to submit FAFSA. In 2018, 372 master's, 116 doctorates awarded. *Program availability:* Part-time, evening/weekend, online learning. Offers applied anthropology (MA, PhD); applied physics (PhD); arts and sciences (MA, MFA, MPA, MS, PhD, Graduate Certificate); biology (MS); cancer biology (PhD); cancer chemical biology (PhD); cancer immunology and immunotherapy (PhD); cell and molecular biology (PhD); chemistry (MA, MS, PhD); communication (MA, PhD); creative writing (MFA); economics (MA, PhD); English (MA, PhD); French (MA); history (MA, PhD); integrative biology (PhD); liberal arts (MA); linguistics (MA); linguistics and applied linguistics studies (PhD); linguistics: English as a second language (MA); mathematics (MA, PhD); medical anthropology (Graduate Certificate); microbiology (MS); philosophy (MA, PhD); physics (MS); psychology (PhD); religious studies (MA); sociology (MA, PhD); Spanish (MA); statistics (MA); women's and gender studies (MA). *Application fee:* $30. Electronic applications accepted. *Application Contact:* Susan Hall, Executive Assistant to the Dean, 813-974-0853, Fax: 813-974-5911, E-mail: hall@usf.edu. *Dean,* Dr. Eric Eisenberg, 813-974-2804, Fax: 813-974-5911, E-mail: eisenberg@usf.edu.

School of Geosciences Students: 93 full-time (43 women), 48 part-time (23 women); includes 24 minority (8 Black or African American, non-Hispanic/Latino; 6 Asian, non-Hispanic/Latino; 5 Hispanic/Latino; 5 Two or more races, non-Hispanic/Latino), 42 international. Average age 31. 107 applicants, 50% accepted, 23 enrolled. *Faculty:* 33 full-time (6 women). *Expenses:* Contact institution. *Financial support:* In 2018–19, 45 students received support, including 3 research assistantships (averaging $12,345 per year), 25 teaching assistantships with tuition reimbursements available (averaging $12,807 per year); unspecified assistantships also available. Financial award application deadline: 3/1. In 2018, 14 master's, 11 doctorates awarded. *Program availability:* Part-time, evening/weekend. Offers environmental science and policy (MS); geography (MA); geography and environmental science and policy (PhD); geology (MS, PhD). *Application deadline:* For fall admission, 2/15 priority date for domestic students, 2/15 for international students; for spring admission, 10/15 priority date for domestic students, 9/15 for international students; for summer admission, 2/15 priority date for domestic students, 1/15 for international students. *Application fee:* $30. Electronic applications accepted. *Application Contact:* Dr. Ruiliang Pu, Associate Professor and Graduate Program Coordinator, 813-974-1508, Fax: 813-974-5911, E-mail: rpu@usf.edu. *Professor and Chair,* Dr. Mark Rains, 813-974-3310, Fax: 813-974-5911, E-mail: mrains@usf.edu.

School of Information Students: 108 full-time (77 women), 182 part-time (137 women); includes 83 minority (23 Black or African American, non-Hispanic/Latino; 7 Asian, non-Hispanic/Latino; 49 Hispanic/Latino; 4 Two or more races, non-Hispanic/Latino).

Average age 32. 141 applicants, 86% accepted, 71 enrolled. *Faculty:* 15 full-time (7 women). Expenses: Contact institution. *Financial support:* In 2018–19, 62 students received support. Unspecified assistantships available. Financial award application deadline: 6/30. In 2018, 128 master's awarded. *Program availability:* Part-time, evening/weekend, online learning. Offers intelligence studies (MS); library and information science (MA). *Application deadline:* For fall admission, 6/1 priority date for domestic students, 5/1 for international students; for spring admission, 10/15 priority date for domestic students, 9/15 for international students. Applications are processed on a rolling basis. *Application fee:* $30. Electronic applications accepted. *Application Contact:* Dr. Randy Borum, Graduate Program Director, 813-974-3520, Fax: 813-974-6840, E-mail: wborum@usf.edu. *Director and Associate Professor,* Dr. Jim Andrews, 813-974-2108, Fax: 813-974-6840, E-mail: jimandrews@usf.edu.

School of Interdisciplinary Global Studies Students: 37 full-time (10 women), 20 part-time (10 women); includes 12 minority (5 Black or African American, non-Hispanic/Latino; 2 Asian, non-Hispanic/Latino; 4 Hispanic/Latino; 1 Two or more races, non-Hispanic/Latino), 17 international. Average age 34. 48 applicants, 67% accepted, 20 enrolled. *Faculty:* 14 full-time (3 women). Expenses: Contact institution. *Financial support:* In 2018–19, 9 students received support, including 18 teaching assistantships with tuition reimbursements available (averaging $12,390 per year); unspecified assistantships also available. Financial award application deadline: 4/1. In 2018, 7 master's, 2 doctorates awarded. *Program availability:* Part-time, evening/weekend. Offers government (PhD); Latin American, Caribbean and Latino studies (MA); liberal arts (MA); political science (MA). *Application deadline:* For fall admission, 1/5 for domestic and international students; for spring admission, 10/15 for domestic students, 9/15 for international students. Applications are processed on a rolling basis. *Application fee:* $30. Electronic applications accepted. *Application Contact:* Dr. Steven Roach, Professor and Director of Graduate Studies, 813-974-9753, E-mail: sroach@usf.edu. *Associate Professor and SIGS Director,* Dr. Scott Solomon, 813-974-6394, E-mail: msolomon@usf.edu.

Zimmerman School of Advertising and Mass Communications Students: 24 full-time (20 women), 20 part-time (17 women); includes 8 minority (4 Black or African American, non-Hispanic/Latino; 4 Hispanic/Latino), 20 international. Average age 26. 28 applicants, 79% accepted, 14 enrolled. *Faculty:* 11 full-time (6 women). Expenses: Contact institution. *Financial support:* In 2018–19, 6 students received support, including 10 teaching assistantships with tuition reimbursements available (averaging $10,513 per year); unspecified assistantships also available. Financial award application deadline: 2/28. In 2018, 12 master's awarded. *Program availability:* Part-time, evening/weekend. Offers mass communications (MA). *Application deadline:* For fall admission, 2/15 priority date for domestic and international students. *Application fee:* $30. Electronic applications accepted. *Application Contact:* Dr. Art Ramirez, Jr., Associate Director, 813-974-2591, Fax: 813-974-2592, E-mail: aramirez2@usf.edu. *Director and Senior Instructor,* Dr. Wayne Garcia, 813-498-1925, Fax: 813-974-2592, E-mail: wgarcia@usf.edu.

College of Behavioral and Community Sciences Students: 585 full-time (500 women), 307 part-time (251 women); includes 281 minority (105 Black or African American, non-Hispanic/Latino; 1 American Indian or Alaska Native, non-Hispanic/Latino; 20 Asian, non-Hispanic/Latino; 132 Hispanic/Latino; 1 Native Hawaiian or other Pacific Islander, non-Hispanic/Latino; 22 Two or more races, non-Hispanic/Latino), 20 international. Average age 28. 1,265 applicants, 34% accepted, 294 enrolled. *Faculty:* 106 full-time (72 women), 4 part-time/adjunct (3 women). Expenses: Contact institution. *Financial support:* In 2018–19, 240 students received support. In 2018, 374 master's, 32 doctorates awarded. Offers applied behavior analysis (MA, MS, PhD); audiology (Au D); behavioral and community sciences (MA, MS, MSW, Au D, PhD, Graduate Certificate); child and adolescent behavioral health (MS); communication sciences and disorders (PhD); criminal justice administration (MA); criminology (MA, PhD); cybercrime (MS); rehabilitation and mental health counseling (MA); speech-language pathology (MS). *Application Contact:* Francisco Vera, Assistant Director for Graduate Admissions, 813-974-2829, E-mail: fvera@usf.edu. *Dean,* Dr. Julianne Serovich, 813-974-1990, Fax: 813-974-2365, E-mail: jserovich@usf.edu.

School of Aging Studies Students: 23 full-time (16 women), 4 part-time (all women); includes 4 minority (1 Black or African American, non-Hispanic/Latino; 1 Asian, non-Hispanic/Latino; 2 Two or more races, non-Hispanic/Latino). Average age 28. 25 applicants, 48% accepted, 6 enrolled. *Faculty:* 9 full-time (4 women). Expenses: Contact institution. *Financial support:* In 2018–19, 6 students received support, including 2 research assistantships with tuition reimbursements available (averaging $15,690 per year), 13 teaching assistantships with tuition reimbursements available (averaging $13,503 per year). Financial award application deadline: 2/3. In 2018, 6 master's, 3 doctorates awarded. *Program availability:* Part-time, evening/weekend. Offers aging studies (PhD); gerontology (MA). *Application deadline:* For fall admission, 12/11 priority date for domestic and international students; for spring admission, 10/15 for domestic students, 9/15 for international students; for summer admission, 2/15 for domestic students, 1/15 for international students. *Application fee:* $30. Electronic applications accepted. *Application Contact:* Brent Small, Professor, 813-974-9746, Fax: 813-974-9754, E-mail: bsmall@usf.edu. *Director and Professor,* Dr. Cathy L. McEvoy, 813-974-1940, Fax: 813-974-9754, E-mail: cmcevoy@usf.edu.

School of Social Work Students: 143 full-time (132 women), 79 part-time (69 women); includes 86 minority (42 Black or African American, non-Hispanic/Latino; 1 American Indian or Alaska Native, non-Hispanic/Latino; 7 Asian, non-Hispanic/Latino; 34 Hispanic/Latino; 2 Two or more races, non-Hispanic/Latino), 3 international. Average age 30. 184 applicants, 42% accepted, 48 enrolled. *Faculty:* 14 full-time (13 women). Expenses: Contact institution. *Financial support:* In 2018–19, 53 students received support, including 1 research assistantship with tuition reimbursement available (averaging $9,001 per year); unspecified assistantships also available. Financial award application deadline: 3/15; financial award applicants required to submit FAFSA. In 2018, 138 master's awarded. *Program availability:* Part-time, evening/weekend. Offers social work (MSW, PhD). *Application deadline:* For fall admission, 2/15 priority date for domestic students, 2/15 for international students; for spring admission, 10/15 for domestic students, 9/15 for international students; for summer admission, 2/15 for domestic students, 1/15 for international students. Applications are processed on a rolling basis. *Application fee:* $30. Electronic applications accepted. *Application Contact:* Dr. Chris Simmons, MSW Chair and Instructor, 813-974-4306, E-mail: csimmon4@usf.edu. *Professor and Director,* Dr. Riaan van Zyl, 813-974-4194, Fax: 813-974-4675, E-mail: nanpark@usf.edu.

College of Education Students: 486 full-time (368 women), 675 part-time (472 women); includes 349 minority (152 Black or African American, non-Hispanic/Latino; 4 American Indian or Alaska Native, non-Hispanic/Latino; 27 Asian, non-Hispanic/Latino; 144 Hispanic/Latino; 1 Native Hawaiian or other Pacific Islander, non-Hispanic/Latino; 21 Two or more races, non-Hispanic/Latino), 113 international. Average age 35. 824

applicants, 55% accepted, 289 enrolled. *Faculty:* 87 full-time (54 women). Expenses: Contact institution. *Financial support:* In 2018–19, 260 students received support, including 9 fellowships with full tuition reimbursements available (averaging $15,000 per year), 2 research assistantships with full tuition reimbursements available (averaging $15,000 per year); career-related internships or fieldwork, Federal Work-Study, institutionally sponsored loans, scholarships/grants, health care benefits, and unspecified assistantships also available. Support available to part-time students. Financial award applicants required to submit FAFSA. In 2018, 240 master's, 64 doctorates, 15 other advanced degrees awarded. *Program availability:* Part-time, evening/weekend, online learning. Offers adult education (MA, Ed D, PhD, Ed S); career and technical education (MA); career and workforce education (PhD); college student affairs (M Ed); counselor education (MA, PhD, Ed S); early childhood education (M Ed, MA, PhD); education (M Ed, MA, MAT, Ed D, PhD, Ed S); elementary education (MA, MAT, PhD); higher education/community college teaching (MA, Ed D, PhD); interdisciplinary education (PhD, Ed S); reading/language arts (MA, PhD, Ed S); school psychology (PhD, Ed S); vocational education (Ed S). *Application deadline:* For fall admission, 2/15 for domestic students, 1/2 for international students; for spring admission, 10/15 for domestic students, 6/1 for international students. *Application fee:* $30. Electronic applications accepted. *Application Contact:* Dr. Diane Briscoe, Coordinator of Graduate Studies, 813-974-1804, Fax: 813-974-3391, E-mail: briscoe@usf.edu. *Dean,* Dr. Colleen S. Kennedy, 813-974-3400, Fax: 813-974-3826.

College of Engineering Students: 879 full-time (221 women), 302 part-time (66 women); includes 141 minority (35 Black or African American, non-Hispanic/Latino; 27 Asian, non-Hispanic/Latino; 69 Hispanic/Latino; 10 Two or more races, non-Hispanic/Latino), 832 international. Average age 27. 1,773 applicants, 50% accepted, 311 enrolled. *Faculty:* 136 full-time (22 women), 1 part-time/adjunct (0 women). Expenses: Contact institution. *Financial support:* In 2018–19, 169 students received support. Career-related internships or fieldwork, Federal Work-Study, scholarships/grants, health care benefits, and unspecified assistantships available. Financial award application deadline: 3/1. In 2018, 450 master's, 62 doctorates awarded. *Program availability:* Part-time, evening/weekend. Offers biomedical engineering (MSBE); chemical engineering (MSCH, PhD); civil engineering (MCE, MSCE, PhD); computer engineering (MSCP); computer science (MSCS); computer science and engineering (PhD); electrical engineering (MSEE, PhD); engineering (MCE, MEVE, MSBE, MSCE, MSCH, MSCP, MSCS, MSEE, MSEM, MSEV, MSIE, MSIT, MSME, MSMSE, PhD, Graduate Certificate); engineering management (MSEM); environmental engineering (MEVE, MSEV, PhD); industrial engineering (MSIE, PhD); information technology (MSIT); materials science and engineering (MSMSE); mechanical engineering (MSME, PhD). *Application deadline:* For fall admission, 2/15 for domestic students, 1/2 priority date for international students; for spring admission, 10/15 for domestic students, 6/1 priority date for international students. Applications are processed on a rolling basis. *Application fee:* $30. Electronic applications accepted. *Application Contact:* Dr. Sanjukta Bhanja, Associate Dean for Academic Affairs, 813-974-4755, Fax: 813-974-5094, E-mail: bhanja@usf.edu. *Dean,* Dr. Robert Bishop, 813-974-3864, Fax: 813-974-5094, E-mail: robertbishop@usf.edu.

College of Graduate Studies Students: 69 full-time (19 women), 157 part-time (41 women); includes 103 minority (22 Black or African American, non-Hispanic/Latino; 1 American Indian or Alaska Native, non-Hispanic/Latino; 18 Asian, non-Hispanic/Latino; 55 Hispanic/Latino; 7 Two or more races, non-Hispanic/Latino), 2 international. Average age 35. 135 applicants, 67% accepted, 64 enrolled. *Faculty:* 1 (woman) full-time. Expenses: Contact institution. *Financial support:* In 2018–19, 20 students received support. Teaching assistantships available. Financial award application deadline: 2/1; financial award applicants required to submit FAFSA. In 2018, 124 master's awarded. *Program availability:* Part-time, evening/weekend, online learning. Offers cybersecurity (MS). *Application deadline:* For fall admission, 2/15 for domestic and international students; for spring admission, 10/15 for domestic students, 9/15 for international students; for summer admission, 2/15 for domestic and international students. *Application fee:* $30. Electronic applications accepted. *Application Contact:* Paul Crawford, Associate Director for Graduate Admissions, 813-974-8800, E-mail: pjcrawford@usf.edu. *Senior Vice Provost and Dean of the Office of Graduate Studies,* Dr. Dwayne Smith, 813-974-7359, Fax: 813-974-5762, E-mail: mdsmith8@usf.edu.

College of Marine Science Students: 67 full-time (39 women), 21 part-time (12 women); includes 10 minority (1 Black or African American, non-Hispanic/Latino; 6 Hispanic/Latino; 3 Two or more races, non-Hispanic/Latino), 16 international. Average age 30. 79 applicants, 25% accepted, 17 enrolled. *Faculty:* 27 full-time (8 women). Expenses: Contact institution. *Financial support:* In 2018–19, 41 students received support, including 45 research assistantships with partial tuition reimbursements available (averaging $14,199 per year), 10 teaching assistantships with partial tuition reimbursements available (averaging $14,196 per year); health care benefits and unspecified assistantships also available. Financial award application deadline: 1/15. In 2018, 14 master's, 14 doctorates awarded. *Program availability:* Part-time. Offers marine science (MS, PhD). *Application deadline:* For fall admission, 1/10 for domestic and international students; for spring admission, 10/1 for domestic and international students. Applications are processed on a rolling basis. *Application fee:* $30. Electronic applications accepted. *Application Contact:* Dr. David F. Naar, Associate Professor and Director of Academic Affairs, 727-553-1637, Fax: 727-553-1189, E-mail: naar@usf.edu. *Dean,* Dr. Jacqueline E. Dixon, 727-553-3369, Fax: 727-553-1189, E-mail: jdixon@usf.edu.

College of Nursing Students: 265 full-time (207 women), 687 part-time (594 women); includes 343 minority (113 Black or African American, non-Hispanic/Latino; 1 American Indian or Alaska Native, non-Hispanic/Latino; 60 Asian, non-Hispanic/Latino; 141 Hispanic/Latino; 1 Native Hawaiian or other Pacific Islander, non-Hispanic/Latino; 27 Two or more races, non-Hispanic/Latino), 2 international. Average age 33. 955 applicants, 44% accepted, 343 enrolled. *Faculty:* 34 full-time (28 women), 2 part-time/adjunct (1 woman). Expenses: Contact institution. *Financial support:* In 2018–19, 181 students received support, including 7 research assistantships with tuition reimbursements available (averaging $18,935 per year), 29 teaching assistantships with tuition reimbursements available (averaging $30,814 per year); tuition waivers (partial) and unspecified assistantships also available. Financial award application deadline: 2/1; financial award applicants required to submit FAFSA. In 2018, 281 master's, 80 doctorates awarded. *Program availability:* Part-time. Offers nurse anesthesia (DNP); nursing (MS, DNP); nursing education (Post Master's Certificate); nursing science (PhD); simulation based academic fellowship in advanced pain management (Graduate Certificate). *Application deadline:* For fall admission, 12/15 for domestic and international students; for spring admission, 10/1 for domestic students, 9/15 for international students. *Application fee:* $30. Electronic applications accepted. *Application Contact:* Dr. Denise Maguire, Vice Dean, Graduate Programs, 813-396-9962, E-mail: dmaguire@health.usf.edu. *Dean, College of Nursing,* Dr. Victoria Rich, 813-974-8939, Fax: 813-974-5418, E-mail: victoriarich@health.usf.edu.

College of Public Health *Program availability:* Part-time, evening/weekend, 100% online, blended/hybrid learning. Offers public health (MHA, MPH, MSPH, Dr PH, PhD). Electronic applications accepted.

College of The Arts Students: 177 full-time (92 women), 38 part-time (18 women); includes 55 minority (11 Black or African American, non-Hispanic/Latino; 9 Asian, non-Hispanic/Latino; 25 Hispanic/Latino; 10 Two or more races, non-Hispanic/Latino), 52 international. Average age 27. 204 applicants, 43% accepted, 65 enrolled. *Faculty:* 50 full-time (17 women), 3 part-time/adjunct (0 women). Expenses: Contact institution. *Financial support:* In 2018–19, 125 students received support. Unspecified assistantships available. In 2018, 89 master's, 2 doctorates awarded. *Program availability:* Part-time, evening/weekend. Offers the arts (M Arch, MA, MFA, MM, MUCD, PhD). *Application deadline:* For fall admission, 1/15 for domestic and international students; for spring admission, 10/15 for domestic students, 9/15 for international students; for summer admission, 2/15 for domestic students, 1/15 for international students. *Application fee:* $30. Electronic applications accepted. *Application Contact:* Prof. Barton Lee, Senior Associate Dean, 813-974-2301, Fax: 813-974-2091, E-mail: blee@usf.edu. *Dean,* Dr. James S. Moy, 813-974-7380, Fax: 813-974-2091, E-mail: moy@usf.edu.

School of Architecture and Community Design Students: 74 full-time (40 women), 19 part-time (8 women); includes 33 minority (7 Black or African American, non-Hispanic/Latino; 9 Asian, non-Hispanic/Latino; 14 Hispanic/Latino; 3 Two or more races, non-Hispanic/Latino), 19 international. Average age 26. 59 applicants, 39% accepted, 17 enrolled. *Faculty:* 8 full-time (0 women). Expenses: Contact institution. *Financial support:* In 2018–19, 43 students received support, including 3 teaching assistantships with tuition reimbursements available (averaging $9,360 per year); Federal Work-Study, scholarships/grants, and unspecified assistantships also available. In 2018, 42 master's awarded. Offers architecture (M Arch); urban and community design (MUCD). *Application deadline:* For fall admission, 2/1 priority date for domestic students, 2/1 for international students. Applications are processed on a rolling basis. *Application fee:* $30. Electronic applications accepted. *Application Contact:* Mildred Abreu, Academic Advisor, 813-974-1216, Fax: 813-974-2557, E-mail: abreu@arch.usf.edu. *Director and Professor, School of Architecture and Community Design,* Dr. Robert MacLeod, 813-974-6015, Fax: 813-974-2557, E-mail: rmacleod@arch.usf.edu.

School of Art and Art History Students: 45 full-time (25 women), 1 (woman) part-time; includes 11 minority (1 Black or African American, non-Hispanic/Latino; 8 Hispanic/Latino; 2 Two or more races, non-Hispanic/Latino), 4 international. Average age 30. 69 applicants, 32% accepted, 20 enrolled. *Faculty:* 17 full-time (8 women). Expenses: Contact institution. *Financial support:* In 2018–19, 42 students received support, including 37 teaching assistantships with partial tuition reimbursements available (averaging $9,440 per year); scholarships/grants, health care benefits, and unspecified assistantships also available. Support available to part-time students. Financial award application deadline: 2/15; financial award applicants required to submit FAFSA. In 2018, 13 master's awarded. *Program availability:* Part-time. Offers art history (MA); studio art (MFA). *Application deadline:* For fall admission, 1/15 priority date for domestic students, 2/1 for international students. *Application fee:* $30. Electronic applications accepted. *Application Contact:* Prof. Neil Bender, Associate Professor and Graduate Program Director, 813-974-2360, Fax: 813-974-9226, E-mail: nb2@usf.edu. *Director,* Prof. Wallace Wilson, 813-974-2360, Fax: 813-974-9226, E-mail: wwilson2@usf.edu.

School of Music Students: 58 full-time (27 women), 18 part-time (9 women); includes 11 minority (3 Black or African American, non-Hispanic/Latino; 3 Hispanic/Latino; 5 Two or more races, non-Hispanic/Latino), 29 international. Average age 28. 76 applicants, 55% accepted, 28 enrolled. *Faculty:* 23 full-time (7 women), 1 part-time/adjunct (0 women). Expenses: Contact institution. *Financial support:* In 2018–19, 40 students received support, including 1 research assistantship with tuition reimbursement available (averaging $15,724 per year), 46 teaching assistantships with tuition reimbursements available (averaging $10,099 per year); unspecified assistantships also available. Financial award application deadline: 2/15. In 2018, 34 master's, 2 doctorates awarded. *Program availability:* Part-time, evening/weekend. Offers music (MM, PhD); music education (MA). *Application deadline:* For fall admission, 2/15 priority date for domestic students, 2/1 for international students; for spring admission, 10/15 for domestic students, 9/15 for international students; for summer admission, 2/15 for domestic students, 1/15 for international students. *Application fee:* $30. Electronic applications accepted. *Application Contact:* Dr. David Williams, Associate Director/Associate Professor of Music Education, 813-974-9166, Fax: 813-974-8721, E-mail: davidw@usf.edu. *Director,* Dr. Karen Bryan, 813-974-2311, Fax: 813-974-8721, E-mail: kmbryan@usf.edu.

Innovative Education Expenses: Contact institution. Offers adult, career and higher education (Graduate Certificate); Africana studies (Graduate Certificate); aging studies (Graduate Certificate); art research (Graduate Certificate); business foundations (Graduate Certificate); chemical and biomedical engineering (Graduate Certificate); child and family studies (Graduate Certificate); civil and industrial engineering (Graduate Certificate); community and family health (Graduate Certificate); criminology (Graduate Certificate); data science for public administration (Graduate Certificate); digital humanities (Graduate Certificate); educational measurement and research (Graduate Certificate); English (Graduate Certificate); entrepreneurship (Graduate Certificate); environmental health (Graduate Certificate); epidemiology and biostatistics (Graduate Certificate); geography, environment and planning (Graduate Certificate); geology (Graduate Certificate); global health (Graduate Certificate); government and international affairs (Graduate Certificate); health policy and management (Graduate Certificate); hearing specialist: early intervention (Graduate Certificate); industrial and management systems engineering (Graduate Certificate); information studies (Graduate Certificate); information systems/decision sciences (Graduate Certificate); instructional technology (Graduate Certificate); internal medicine, bioethics and medical humanities (Graduate Certificate); Latin American and Caribbean studies (Graduate Certificate); leadership for coastal resiliency planning (Graduate Certificate); mass communications (Graduate Certificate); mathematics and statistics (Graduate Certificate); medicine (Graduate Certificate); national and competitive intelligence (Graduate Certificate); nursing (Graduate Certificate); psychological and social foundations (Graduate Certificate); public affairs (Graduate Certificate); public health (Graduate Certificate); public health practices (Graduate Certificate); rehabilitation and mental health counseling (Graduate Certificate); secondary education (Graduate Certificate); social work (Graduate Certificate); special education (Graduate Certificate); world languages (Graduate Certificate). *Application Contact:* Owen Hooper, Director, Summer and Alternative Calendar Programs, 813-974-6917, E-mail: hooper@usf.edu. *Associate Vice President and Assistant Vice Provost,* Dr. Cynthia DeLuca, 813-974-3077, Fax: 813-974-7061, E-mail: deluca@usf.edu.

Morsani College of Medicine Students: 1,314 full-time (694 women), 272 part-time (172 women); includes 634 minority (112 Black or African American, non-

Hispanic/Latino; 7 American Indian or Alaska Native, non-Hispanic/Latino; 289 Asian, non-Hispanic/Latino; 194 Hispanic/Latino; 2 Native Hawaiian or other Pacific Islander, non-Hispanic/Latino; 30 Two or more races, non-Hispanic/Latino), 50 international. Average age 26. 8,974 applicants, 11% accepted, 567 enrolled. *Faculty:* 200 full-time (85 women), 39 part-time/adjunct (17 women). Expenses: Contact institution. *Financial support:* In 2018–19, 749 students received support. In 2018, 362 master's, 226 doctorates awarded. *Program availability:* Part-time. Offers advanced athletic training (MS); athletic training (MS); bioinformatics and computational biology (MSBCB); biotechnology (MSB); health informatics (MSHI); medical sciences (MSMS, PhD); medicine (MS, MSB, MSBCB, MSHI, MSMS, DPT, MD, PhD). *Application deadline:* For fall admission, 2/1 priority date for domestic students, 2/1 for international students. *Application fee:* $30. Electronic applications accepted. *Application Contact:* Dr. Bob Deschenes, Vice Dean, Educational Affairs, 813-974-6393, E-mail: rdeschen@health.usf.edu. *Dean,* Dr. Charles J. Lockwood, 813-974-0533, Fax: 813-974-4990, E-mail: cjlockwood@health.usf.edu.

School of Physical Therapy Students: 137 full-time (86 women); includes 29 minority (6 Black or African American, non-Hispanic/Latino; 9 Asian, non-Hispanic/Latino; 13 Hispanic/Latino; 1 Two or more races, non-Hispanic/Latino). Average age 24. 1,190 applicants, 4% accepted, 46 enrolled. *Faculty:* 12 full-time (7 women). Expenses: Contact institution. *Financial support:* In 2018–19, 64 students received support. Teaching assistantships available. In 2018, 44 doctorates awarded. Offers physical therapy (DPT); rehabilitation sciences (PhD). *Application deadline:* For fall admission, 6/1 for domestic students, 1/1 for international students; for spring admission, 10/15 for domestic students, 9/15 for international students. *Application fee:* $30. Electronic applications accepted. *Application Contact:* Dr. Gina Maria Musolino, Associate Professor and Coordinator for Clinical Education, 813-974-2254, Fax: 813-974-8915, E-mail: gmusolin@health.usf.edu. *Director,* Dr. William S. Quillen, 813-974-9863, Fax: 813-974-8915, E-mail: wquillen@health.usf.edu.

Muma College of Business Students: 854 full-time (332 women), 485 part-time (191 women); includes 281 minority (78 Black or African American, non-Hispanic/Latino; 2 American Indian or Alaska Native, non-Hispanic/Latino; 65 Asian, non-Hispanic/Latino; 117 Hispanic/Latino; 1 Native Hawaiian or other Pacific Islander, non-Hispanic/Latino; 18 Two or more races, non-Hispanic/Latino), 517 international. Average age 30. 1,720 applicants, 57% accepted, 492 enrolled. *Faculty:* 76 full-time (21 women), 2 part-time/adjunct (0 women). Expenses: Contact institution. *Financial support:* In 2018–19, 300 students received support. Career-related internships or fieldwork, scholarships/grants, health care benefits, and unspecified assistantships available. Financial award applicants required to submit FAFSA. In 2018, 602 master's, 42 doctorates awarded. *Program availability:* Part-time, evening/weekend. Offers business (M Acc, MS, MSM, MSRE, DBA, PhD); business administration (PhD); business analytics and information systems (MS); finance (MS); management (MS); marketing (MSM); real estate (MSRE); sport and entertainment management (MS) *Application deadline:* For fall admission, 1/2 for domestic and international students; for spring admission, 10/1 for domestic students, 9/15 for international students. *Application fee:* $30. Electronic applications accepted. *Application Contact:* Dr. Jacqueline Reck, Professor/Interim Associate Dean, 813-974-6721, Fax: 813-974-6528, E-mail: jreck@usf.edu. *Dean,* Dr. Moez Limayem, 813-974-4281, Fax: 813-974-3030, E-mail: mlimayem@usf.edu.

Center for Entrepreneurship Students: 3. *Faculty:* 4 full-time (2 women), 1 part-time/adjunct (0 women). Expenses: Contact institution. In 2018, 55 master's awarded. *Program availability:* Part-time, evening/weekend. Offers entrepreneurship and applied technologies (MS). *Application deadline:* For fall admission, 6/1 for domestic students, 2/1 for international students; for spring admission, 10/15 for domestic students, 7/1 for international students. Applications are processed on a rolling basis. *Application fee:* $30. Electronic applications accepted. *Application Contact:* Dr. Tapas Das, Assistant Director/Professor, 813-974-5585, Fax: 813-974-5953, E-mail: das@usf.edu. *Director, Center for Entrepreneurship,* Dr. Michael W. Fountain, 813-974-7825, Fax: 813-974-6175, E-mail: fountain@usf.edu.

Lynn Pippenger School of Accountancy Students: 69 full-time (31 women), 28 part-time (14 women); includes 34 minority (2 Black or African American, non-Hispanic/Latino; 1 American Indian or Alaska Native, non-Hispanic/Latino; 7 Asian, non-Hispanic/Latino; 18 Hispanic/Latino; 6 Two or more races, non-Hispanic/Latino), 8 international. Average age 24. 104 applicants, 59% accepted, 49 enrolled. *Faculty:* 11 full-time (5 women). Expenses: Contact institution. *Financial support:* In 2018–19, 55 students received support, including 18 teaching assistantships with tuition reimbursements available (averaging $12,273 per year); scholarships/grants, health care benefits, and unspecified assistantships also available. Financial award applicants required to submit FAFSA. In 2018, 50 master's awarded. *Program availability:* Part-time, evening/weekend. Offers accountancy (M Acc, PhD). *Application deadline:* For fall admission, 3/1 priority date for domestic students, 3/1 for international students; for spring admission, 10/1 for domestic students, 9/15 for international students; for summer admission, 2/15 for domestic and international students. *Application fee:* $30. Electronic applications accepted. *Application Contact:* Stacee Bender, Academic Services Administrator, 813-974-4516, E-mail: staceebender@usf.edu. *Interim Director, School of Accountancy,* Dr. Uday Murthy, 813-974-6516, Fax: 813-974-6528, E-mail: umurthy@usf.edu.

Patel College of Global Sustainability Students: 64 full-time (33 women), 92 part-time (57 women); includes 32 minority (8 Black or African American, non-Hispanic/Latino; 3 Asian, non-Hispanic/Latino; 15 Hispanic/Latino; 6 Two or more races, non-Hispanic/Latino), 50 international. Average age 29. 119 applicants, 75% accepted, 60 enrolled. *Faculty:* 1 full-time (0 women). Expenses: Contact institution. *Financial support:* In 2018–19, 35 students received support. In 2018, 91 master's awarded. Offers energy, global, water and sustainable tourism (Graduate Certificate); global sustainability (MA). *Application deadline:* For fall admission, 6/1 for domestic students, 5/1 for international students; for spring admission, 10/15 for domestic students, 9/15 for international students. Electronic applications accepted. *Application Contact:* Dr. Govindan Parayil, Dean, 813-974-9694, E-mail: gparayil@usf.edu. *Dean,* Dr. Govindan Parayil, 813-974-9694, E-mail: gparayil@usf.edu.

Taneja College of Pharmacy Students: 398 full-time (234 women), 7 part-time (3 women); includes 180 minority (33 Black or African American, non-Hispanic/Latino; 72 Asian, non-Hispanic/Latino; 59 Hispanic/Latino; 2 Native Hawaiian or other Pacific Islander, non-Hispanic/Latino; 14 Two or more races, non-Hispanic/Latino), 13 international. Average age 25. 465 applicants, 44% accepted, 112 enrolled. *Faculty:* 32 full-time (18 women), 1 part-time/adjunct (0 women). Expenses: Contact institution. *Financial support:* In 2018–19, 159 students received support. In 2018, 11 master's, 91 doctorates awarded. Offers pharmaceutical nanotechnology (MS); pharmacy (Pharm D). *Application deadline:* For fall admission, 6/1 for domestic and international students; for spring admission, 10/15 for domestic students, 9/15 for international students; for summer admission, 2/15 for domestic and international students. Electronic applications accepted. *Application Contact:* Dr. Amy Schwartz, Associate Dean, 813-974-2251, E-mail: aschwar1@health.usf.edu.

UNIVERSITY OF SOUTH FLORIDA, ST. PETERSBURG, St. Petersburg, FL 33701

General Information State-supported, coed, comprehensive institution. *Graduate housing:* Rooms and/or apartments available on a first-come, first-served basis to single and married students.

GRADUATE UNITS

College of Arts and Sciences *Program availability:* Part-time, online learning. Offers digital journalism and design (MA); environmental science and policy (MA, MS); Florida studies (MLA); journalism and media studies (MA); liberal studies (MLA); psychology (MA). Electronic applications accepted.

College of Education *Program availability:* Part-time. Offers educational leadership development (M Ed); elementary education (MA); English education (MA); middle grades STEM education (MS); reading education (MA). Electronic applications accepted.

Kate Tiedemann College of Business *Program availability:* Part-time. Offers business (MBA). Electronic applications accepted.

UNIVERSITY OF SOUTH FLORIDA SARASOTA-MANATEE, Sarasota, FL 34243

General Information State-supported, coed, comprehensive institution. *Enrollment:* 2,069 graduate, professional, and undergraduate students; 42 full-time matriculated graduate/professional students (23 women), 100 part-time matriculated graduate/professional students (63 women). *Enrollment by degree level:* 142 master's. *Graduate faculty:* 26 full-time (11 women), 6 part-time/adjunct (5 women). *Tuition, area resident:* Full-time $8350; part-time $348 per credit hour. Tuition, state resident: full-time $8350; part-time $348 per credit hour. Tuition, nonresident: full-time $19,048; part-time $794 per credit hour. *Required fees:* $1689; $70 per credit hour. $5 per semester. Tuition and fees vary according to program. *Student services:* Campus employment opportunities, campus safety program, career counseling, exercise/wellness program, free psychological counseling, international student services, low-cost health insurance, multicultural affairs office, services for students with disabilities, teacher training, writing training. *Library facilities:* USF Libraries. *Collection:* Books: 1,231 (physical), 721,020 (digital/electronic); Serial titles: 65,050 (digital/electronic); Databases: 941. Weekly public service hours: 96; students can reserve study rooms.

Computer facilities: Computer purchase and lease plans are available. 61 computers available on campus for general student use. A campuswide network can be accessed from off campus. Online class registration is available. Website: http://www.usfsm.edu/

General Application Contact: Brandon Avery, Director, Admissions, 941-359-4331, E-mail: bavery@sar.usf.edu.

GRADUATE UNITS

College of Business Students: 24 full-time (9 women), 47 part-time (20 women); includes 26 minority (5 Black or African American, non-Hispanic/Latino; 4 Asian, non-Hispanic/Latino; 16 Hispanic/Latino; 1 Two or more races, non-Hispanic/Latino). Average age 33. 41 applicants, 34% accepted, 10 enrolled. *Faculty:* 8 full-time (1 woman). Expenses: Contact institution. *Financial support:* Federal Work-Study, scholarships/grants, health care benefits, and unspecified assistantships available. Support available to part-time students. Financial award application deadline: 6/30; financial award applicants required to submit FAFSA. In 2018, 25 master's awarded. *Program availability:* Part-time, evening/weekend. Offers business (MBA). *Application deadline:* For fall admission, 6/1 priority date for domestic students, 6/1 for international students; for spring admission, 10/1 priority date for domestic students, 10/1 for international students; for summer admission, 3/1 for domestic and international students. Applications are processed on a rolling basis. *Application fee:* $30. Electronic applications accepted. *Application Contact:* Brandon Avery, Interim Director, Admissions, 941-359-4331, E-mail: bavery@sar.usf.edu. Interim Dean, Dr. Thomas Becker, 941-359-4245, E-mail: teb1@sar.usf.edu.

College of Hospitality and Technology Leadership Students: 8 full-time (6 women), 7 part-time (3 women); includes 3 minority (1 Asian, non-Hispanic/Latino; 2 Hispanic/Latino), 4 international. Average age 35. 18 applicants, 33% accepted, 5 enrolled. *Faculty:* 4 full-time (1 woman). Expenses: Contact institution. *Financial support:* In 2018–19, 3 research assistantships (averaging $13,478 per year) were awarded; teaching assistantships with tuition reimbursements, career-related internships or fieldwork, institutionally sponsored loans, health care benefits, and unspecified assistantships also available. Support available to part-time students. Financial award application deadline: 6/30; financial award applicants required to submit FAFSA. In 2018, 7 master's awarded. *Program availability:* Part-time. Offers hospitality management (MS). *Application deadline:* For fall admission, 6/1 priority date for domestic students, 6/1 for international students; for spring admission, 10/1 priority date for domestic students, 10/1 for international students; for summer admission, 3/1 priority date for domestic students, 3/1 for international students. Applications are processed on a rolling basis. *Application fee:* $30. Electronic applications accepted. *Application Contact:* Brandon Avery, Director, Admissions, 941-359-4331, E-mail: bavery@sar.usf.edu. Dean, Dr. Pat Moreo, 941-359-4327, E-mail: pmoreo@sar.usf.edu.

College of Liberal Arts and Social Sciences Students: 10 full-time (8 women), 46 part-time (40 women); includes 17 minority (6 Black or African American, non-Hispanic/Latino; 7 Hispanic/Latino; 4 Two or more races, non-Hispanic/Latino). Average age 33. 57 applicants, 46% accepted, 24 enrolled. *Faculty:* 14 full-time (9 women), 6 part-time/adjunct (5 women). Expenses: Contact institution. *Financial support:* Career-related internships or fieldwork, institutionally sponsored loans, scholarships/grants, health care benefits, and unspecified assistantships available. Support available to part-time students. Financial award application deadline: 6/30; financial award applicants required to submit FAFSA. In 2018, 12 master's awarded. *Program availability:* Part-time, 100% online, blended/hybrid learning. Offers criminal justice (MA); education (MA); educational leadership (M Ed); elementary education (MAT); English education (MA); social work (MSW). *Application deadline:* For fall admission, 3/1 priority date for domestic students, 3/1 for international students; for spring admission, 10/1 priority date for domestic students, 10/1 for international students. Applications are processed on a rolling basis. *Application fee:* $30. Electronic applications accepted. *Application Contact:* Brandon Avery, Assistant Director, Admissions, 941-359-4331, E-mail: bavery@sar.usf.edu. Dean, Dr. Jane Rose, 941-359-4469, Fax: 941-359-4778, E-mail: jane.rose@sar.usf.edu.

THE UNIVERSITY OF TAMPA, Tampa, FL 33606-1490

General Information Independent, coed, comprehensive institution. *Enrollment:* 9,335 graduate, professional, and undergraduate students; 324 full-time matriculated graduate/professional students (154 women), 568 part-time matriculated graduate/professional students (366 women). *Enrollment by degree level:* 880 master's, 12 other advanced degrees. *Graduate faculty:* 124 full-time (58 women), 17 part-time/adjunct (7 women). *Tuition:* Full-time $10,192. *Graduate housing:* Rooms and/or apartments available on a first-come, first-served basis to single and married students. Typical cost: $8920 per year ($11,549 including board) for single students. Housing application deadline: 5/1. *Student services:* Campus employment opportunities, campus safety program, career counseling, international student services, services for students with disabilities. *Library facilities:* Macdonald Kelce Library. *Collection:* Books: 195,067 (physical), 145,016 (digital/electronic); Serial titles: 1,214 (physical), 190,560 (digital/electronic); Databases: 214. Weekly public service hours: 100; students can reserve study rooms.

Computer facilities: Computer purchase and lease plans are available. 791 computers available on campus for general student use. A campuswide network can be accessed from student residence rooms and from off campus. Online class registration is available. Website: http://www.ut.edu/

General Application Contact: Rachel Sutton, Assistant Director of Graduate Admissions, 813-422-3738, Fax: 813-258-7451, E-mail: rsutton@ut.edu.

GRADUATE UNITS

Program in Creative Writing Students: 34 full-time (19 women); includes 11 minority (5 Black or African American, non-Hispanic/Latino; 3 Hispanic/Latino; 3 Two or more races, non-Hispanic/Latino), 1 international. Average age 40. 16 applicants, 31% accepted, 3 enrolled. Expenses: Contact institution. *Financial support:* In 2018–19, 18 students received support. Career-related internships or fieldwork, scholarships/grants, and unspecified assistantships available. Financial award applicants required to submit FAFSA. In 2018, 23 master's awarded. *Program availability:* Part-time. Offers creative writing (MFA). *Application deadline:* Applications are processed on a rolling basis. *Application fee:* $40. Electronic applications accepted. *Application Contact:* Ashley Russell, Staff Assistant, Graduate and Continuing Studies, 813-253-6249, E-mail: arussell@ut.edu. *Director,* Dr. Erica Dawson, 813-257-6311, E-mail: edawson@ut.edu.

Program in Criminology and Criminal Justice Students: 13 full-time (10 women), 14 part-time (11 women); includes 10 minority (5 Black or African American, non-Hispanic/Latino; 5 Hispanic/Latino). Average age 26. 10 applicants, 40% accepted, 4 enrolled. *Faculty:* 1 full-time (0 women), 5 part-time/adjunct (2 women). Expenses: Contact institution. *Financial support:* In 2018–19, 16 students received support. Fellowships, career-related internships or fieldwork, scholarships/grants, and unspecified assistantships available. Financial award applicants required to submit FAFSA. Offers criminology and criminal justice (MS). *Application deadline:* Applications are processed on a rolling basis. *Application fee:* $40. Electronic applications accepted. *Application Contact:* Dr. Joshua Stagner, Director of Graduate and Continuing Studies, 813-257-3016, Fax: 813-258-7451, E-mail: jstagner@ut.edu. *Coordinator,* Christopher R. Capsambelis, 813-257-3348, E-mail: ccapsambelis@ut.edu.

Program in Exercise and Nutrition Science Students: 46 full-time (18 women), 10 part-time (7 women); includes 12 minority (6 Black or African American, non-Hispanic/Latino; 1 American Indian or Alaska Native, non-Hispanic/Latino; 3 Hispanic/Latino; 2 Two or more races, non-Hispanic/Latino), 3 international. Average age 25. 165 applicants, 57% accepted, 56 enrolled. *Faculty:* 10 part-time/adjunct (2 women). Expenses: Contact institution. *Financial support:* In 2018–19, 6 students received support. Career-related internships or fieldwork, scholarships/grants, and unspecified assistantships available. Financial award applicants required to submit FAFSA. In 2018, 39 master's awarded. *Program availability:* Part-time, evening/weekend. Offers exercise and nutrition science (MS). *Application deadline:* Applications are processed on a rolling basis. *Application fee:* $40. Electronic applications accepted. *Application Contact:* Ashley Russell, Staff Assistant, Admissions for Graduate and Continuing Studies, 813-253-6249, E-mail: arussell@ut.edu. *Associate Professor, Health Sciences and Human Performance,* Dr. Ronda C. Sturgill, 813-257-3445, E-mail: rsturgill@ut.edu.

Program in Nursing Students: 8 full-time (7 women), 180 part-time (172 women); includes 49 minority (15 Black or African American, non-Hispanic/Latino; 1 American Indian or Alaska Native, non-Hispanic/Latino; 9 Asian, non-Hispanic/Latino; 19 Hispanic/Latino; 5 Two or more races, non-Hispanic/Latino), 2 international. Average age 33. 173 applicants, 62% accepted, 58 enrolled. *Faculty:* 2 full-time (both women), 29 part-time/adjunct (26 women). Expenses: Contact institution. *Financial support:* In 2018–19, 23 students received support. Career-related internships or fieldwork, scholarships/grants, and unspecified assistantships available. Financial award applicants required to submit FAFSA. In 2018, 47 master's awarded. *Program availability:* Part-time, evening/weekend. Offers adult nursing practitioner (MSN); family nursing practitioner (MSN); nursing (MS). *Application deadline:* Applications are processed on a rolling basis. *Application fee:* $40. Electronic applications accepted. *Application Contact:* Ashley Russell, Staff Assistant, Admissions for Graduate and Continuing Studies, 813-253-6249, E-mail: arussell@ut.edu. *Director,* Michele Wolf, 813-257-3179, E-mail: mwolf@ut.edu.

Programs in Education Students: 52 full-time (38 women), 238 part-time (211 women); includes 86 minority (36 Black or African American, non-Hispanic/Latino; 1 American Indian or Alaska Native, non-Hispanic/Latino; 9 Asian, non-Hispanic/Latino; 32 Hispanic/Latino; 8 Two or more races, non-Hispanic/Latino), 15 international. Average age 33. 119 applicants, 71% accepted, 48 enrolled. *Faculty:* 2 full-time (both women), 19 part-time/adjunct (15 women). Expenses: Contact institution. *Financial support:* In 2018–19, 28 students received support. Career-related internships or fieldwork, scholarships/grants, and unspecified assistantships available. Financial award applicants required to submit FAFSA. In 2018, 37 master's awarded. *Program availability:* Part-time, evening/weekend. Offers curriculum and instruction (M Ed); educational leadership (M Ed); instructional design and technology (MS). *Application deadline:* Applications are processed on a rolling basis. *Application fee:* $40. Electronic applications accepted. *Application Contact:* Ashley Russell, Staff Assistant, Admissions for Graduate and Continuing Studies, 813-253-6249, E-mail: arussell@ut.edu. *Chair,* Dr. Antony Erben, 813-257-3414, E-mail: terben@ut.edu.

Sykes College of Business Students: 361 full-time (153 women), 122 part-time (52 women); includes 101 minority (31 Black or African American, non-Hispanic/Latino; 5 Asian, non-Hispanic/Latino; 57 Hispanic/Latino; 1 Native Hawaiian or other Pacific Islander, non-Hispanic/Latino; 7 Two or more races, non-Hispanic/Latino), 144 international. Average age 29. 1,079 applicants, 57% accepted, 263 enrolled. *Faculty:* 61 full-time (13 women), 11 part-time/adjunct (3 women). Expenses: Contact institution. *Financial support:* In 2018–19, 123 students received support. Career-related internships or fieldwork, scholarships/grants, and unspecified assistantships available. Financial award applicants required to submit FAFSA. In 2018, 281 master's, 12 other advanced degrees awarded. *Program availability:* Part-time, evening/weekend. Offers accounting (MS); business analytics (MBA); cybersecurity (MBA, MS); entrepreneurship (MBA, MS); finance (MBA, MS); information systems management (MBA); innovation management (MBA); international business (MBA); marketing (MBA, MS); nonprofit management (MBA, Certificate). *Application deadline:* Applications are processed on a rolling basis. *Application fee:* $40. Electronic applications accepted. *Application Contact:* Ashley Russell, Staff Assistant, Admissions for Graduate and Continuing Studies, 813-253-6249, E-mail: arussell@ut.edu. *Associate Dean,* Dr. Natasha F. Veltri, 813-253-6289, E-mail: nveltri@ut.edu.

See Display below and Close-Up on page 745.

THE UNIVERSITY OF TENNESSEE, Knoxville, TN 37996

General Information State-supported, coed, university. CGS member. *Graduate housing:* Room and/or apartments available on a first-come, first-served basis to single students; on-campus housing not available to married students. Housing application deadline: 2/1. *Research affiliation:* Intel Corporation (computational science), Boeing (mechanical and aerospace engineering), Eastman Chemical (chemical engineering, chemistry), Mars, Inc. (materials science and engineering, polymer science, food science), DuPont (biofuels), Goodyear (chemical engineering; materials science and engineering; polymer science).

GRADUATE UNITS

College of Law Students: 360 full-time (165 women); includes 71 minority (28 Black or African American, non-Hispanic/Latino; 4 American Indian or Alaska Native, non-Hispanic/Latino; 2 Asian, non-Hispanic/Latino; 26 Hispanic/Latino; 11 Two or more races, non-Hispanic/Latino), 2 international. Average age 24. 1,006 applicants, 37% accepted, 124 enrolled. *Faculty:* 45 full-time (20 women), 84 part-time/adjunct (31 women). Expenses: Contact institution. *Financial support:* In 2018–19, 249 students received support, including 13 research assistantships with full tuition reimbursements available (averaging $27,928 per year); career-related internships or fieldwork, Federal Work-Study, institutionally sponsored loans, scholarships/grants, and unspecified assistantships also available. Support available to part-time students. Financial award application deadline: 3/1; financial award applicants required to submit FAFSA. In 2018, 100 doctorates awarded. Offers business transactions (JD); law (JD); trial advocacy and dispute resolution (JD). *Application deadline:* For fall admission, 3/1 priority date for domestic and international students. Applications are processed on a rolling basis. *Application fee:* $35. Electronic applications accepted. *Application Contact:* Sarah Busse, Director, Admissions and Financial Aid, 865-974-4131, Fax: 865-974-1572, E-mail: lawadmit@utk.edu. *Director, Admissions and Financial Aid,* Sarah Busse, 865-974-4131, Fax: 865-974-1572, E-mail: lawadmit@utk.edu.

Graduate School *Program availability:* Part-time, evening/weekend, online learning. Offers aviation systems (MS); comparative and experimental medicine (MS, PhD). Electronic applications accepted.

College of Agricultural Sciences and Natural Resources *Program availability:* Part-time, online learning. Offers agricultural education (MS); agricultural extension education (MS); agricultural sciences and natural resources (MS, PhD); animal anatomy (PhD); biosystems engineering (MS, PhD); biosystems engineering technology (MS); breeding (MS, PhD); entomology (MS, PhD); floriculture (MS); food science and technology (MS, PhD); forestry (MS); integrated pest management and bioactive natural products (PhD); landscape design (MS); management (MS, PhD); nutrition (MS, PhD); physiology (MS, PhD); plant pathology (MS, PhD); public horticulture (MS); turfgrass (MS); wildlife and fisheries science (MS); woody ornamentals (MS). Electronic applications accepted.

College of Architecture and Design Offers architecture (professional) (M Arch); architecture (research) (M Arch); architecture and design (M Arch, MA, MLA, MS); landscape architecture (MLA); landscape architecture (research) (MA, MS). Electronic applications accepted.

College of Arts and Sciences *Program availability:* Part-time, evening/weekend. Offers accompanying (MM); acting (MFA); American history (PhD); analytical chemistry (MS, PhD); applied linguistics (PhD); applied mathematics (MS); archaeology (MA, PhD); arts and sciences (M Math, MA, MFA, MM, MPA, MS, PhD); audiology (MA); behavior (MS, PhD); biochemistry, cellular and molecular biology (MS, PhD); biological anthropology (MA, PhD); ceramics (MFA); chemical physics (PhD); choral conducting (MM); clinical psychology (PhD); composition (MM); computer science (MS, PhD); costume design (MFA); criminology (MA, PhD); cultural anthropology (MA, PhD); drawing (MFA); ecology (MS, PhD); energy, environment, and resource policy (MA, PhD); English (MA, PhD); environmental chemistry (MS, PhD); European history (PhD); evolutionary biology (MS, PhD); experimental psychology (MA, PhD); French (MA, PhD); genome science and technology (MS, PhD); geography (MS, PhD); geology (MS, PhD); German (MA); graphic design (MFA); hearing science (PhD); history (MA); inorganic chemistry (MS, PhD); instrumental conducting (MM); inter-area studies (MFA); Italian (PhD); jazz (MM); lighting design (MFA); mathematical ecology (PhD); mathematics (M Math, MS, PhD); media arts (MFA); medical ethics (MA, PhD); microbiology (MS, PhD); modern foreign languages (PhD); music education (MM); music theory (MM); musicology (MM); organic chemistry (MS, PhD); painting (MFA); performance (MM); philosophy (MA, PhD); physical chemistry (MS, PhD); physics (MS, PhD); piano pedagogy and literature (MM); plant physiology and genetics (MS, PhD); political economy (MA, PhD); political science (MA, PhD); polymer chemistry (MS, PhD); Portuguese (PhD); printmaking (MFA); psychology (MA); public administration (MPA); religious studies (MA); Russian (PhD); scene design (MFA); sculpture (MFA); Spanish (MA); speech and hearing science (PhD); speech and language pathology (PhD); speech and language science (PhD); speech pathology (MA); theoretical chemistry (PhD); watercolor (MFA); zoo-archaeology (MA, PhD). Electronic applications accepted.

College of Business Administration *Program availability:* Part-time, online learning. Offers accounting (M Acc, PhD); business administration (M Acc, MA, MBA, MS, PhD); economics (MA, PhD); finance (MBA, PhD); industrial and organizational psychology (PhD); industrial statistics (MS); logistics and transportation (MBA, PhD); management (PhD); management science (MS, PhD); marketing (MBA, PhD); operations management (MBA); professional business administration (MBA); statistics (MS, PhD); systems (M Acc); taxation (M Acc); teacher licensure (MS); training and development (MS). Electronic applications accepted.

College of Communication and Information *Program availability:* Part-time, evening/weekend, online learning. Offers advertising (MS, PhD); communications (MS, PhD); information sciences (MS, PhD); journalism and electronic media (MS, PhD); public relations (MS, PhD). Electronic applications accepted.

College of Education, Health and Human Sciences *Program availability:* Part-time, evening/weekend, online learning. Offers adult education (MS); applied educational psychology (MS); art education (MS); biomechanics/sports medicine (MS, PhD); child and family studies (MS, PhD); collaborative learning (Ed D); college student personnel (MS); community health (PhD); community health education (MPH); consumer services management (MS); counseling education (PhD); cultural studies in education (PhD); curriculum (MS, Ed S); curriculum, educational research and evaluation (Ed D, PhD); early childhood education (MS, PhD); early childhood special education (MS); education of deaf and hard of hearing (MS); education, health and

WE GIVE YOU DIRECTION.
YOU LEAD THE WAY.

THE UNIVERSITY OF TAMPA

You're ready to fast-track your growth, stand out from your peers and pave the way to a career you love. Become a part of our vibrant community and you'll build lifelong relationships with fellow students, professors and potential employers. At UT, you'll have direct access to a team of proven mentors with the real-world experience to help you make your dream job a reality.

LEARN MORE: UT.EDU/GRADINFO

human sciences (MPH, MS, Ed D, PhD, Ed S); educational administration and policy studies (Ed D, PhD); educational administration and supervision (MS, Ed S); educational psychology (Ed D, PhD); elementary education (MS, Ed S); elementary teaching (MS); English education (MS, Ed S); exercise physiology (MS, PhD); exercise science (MS, PhD); foreign language/ESL education (MS, Ed S); gerontology (MPH); health planning/administration (MPH); health promotion and health education (MS); hospitality management (MS); hotel, restaurant, and tourism management (MS); instructional technology (MS, Ed D, PhD, Ed S); literacy, language and ESL education (PhD); literacy, language education, and ESL education (Ed D); mathematics education (MS, Ed S); mental health counseling (MS); modified and comprehensive special education (MS); nutrition (MS); nutrition science (PhD); reading education (MS, Ed S); recreation and leisure studies (MS); rehabilitation counseling (MS); retail and consumer sciences (MS); retailing and consumer sciences (PhD); safety (MS); school counseling (MS, Ed S); school psychology (PhD, Ed S); science education (MS, Ed S); secondary teaching (MS); social foundations (MS); social science education (MS, Ed S); socio-cultural foundations of sports and education (PhD); special education (Ed S); sport management (MS); sport studies (MS, PhD); teacher education (Ed D, PhD); textile science (MS, PhD); therapeutic recreation (MS); tourism (MS). Electronic applications accepted.

College of Nursing *Program availability:* Part-time. Offers nursing (MSN, PhD). Electronic applications accepted.

College of Social Work *Program availability:* Part-time, online learning. Offers clinical practice and leadership (DSW); evidenced-based interpersonal practice (MSSW); management leadership and community practice (MSSW); social work (MSSW, DSW, PhD). Electronic applications accepted.

College of Veterinary Medicine Offers veterinary medicine (DVM).

Tickle College of Engineering Students: 847 full-time (192 women), 264 part-time (51 women); includes 120 minority (26 Black or African American, non-Hispanic/Latino; 1 American Indian or Alaska Native, non-Hispanic/Latino; 42 Asian, non-Hispanic/Latino; 37 Hispanic/Latino; 1 Native Hawaiian or other Pacific Islander, non-Hispanic/Latino; 13 Two or more races, non-Hispanic/Latino), 388 international. Average age 28. 1,139 applicants, 50% accepted, 272 enrolled. *Faculty:* 222 full-time (28 women), 24 part-time/adjunct (4 women). Expenses: Contact institution. *Financial support:* In 2018–19, 949 students received support, including 176 fellowships with full tuition reimbursements available (averaging $18,134 per year), 561 research assistantships with full tuition reimbursements available (averaging $23,396 per year), 212 teaching assistantships with full tuition reimbursements available (averaging $19,998 per year); career-related internships or fieldwork, Federal Work-Study, institutionally sponsored loans, health care benefits, and unspecified assistantships also available. Financial award application deadline: 2/1; financial award applicants required to submit FAFSA. In 2018, 234 master's, 116 doctorates awarded. *Program availability:* Part-time, online learning. Offers aerospace engineering (MS, PhD); biomedical engineering (MS, PhD); chemical engineering (MS, PhD); civil engineering (MS, PhD); computer engineering (MS, PhD); computer science (MS, PhD); data science and engineering (PhD); electrical engineering (MS, PhD); energy science and engineering (PhD); engineering (MS, PhD); engineering management (MS); engineering science (MS, PhD); environmental engineering (MS); industrial engineering (MS, PhD); materials science and engineering (MS, PhD); mechanical engineering (MS, PhD); nuclear engineering (MS, PhD); reliability and maintainability engineering (MS). *Application deadline:* For fall admission, 2/1 priority date for domestic and international students; for spring admission, 6/15 for domestic and international students; for summer admission, 10/15 for domestic and international students. Applications are processed on a rolling basis. *Application fee:* $60. Electronic applications accepted. *Application Contact:* Dr. Ozlem Kilic, Associate Dean of Student Affairs, 865-974-2454, Fax: 865-974-9871, E-mail: okilic@utk.edu. *Dean,* Dr. Janis P. Terpenny, 865-974-5321, Fax: 865-974-8890, E-mail: terpenny@utk.edu.

The University of Tennessee Space Institute *Program availability:* Part-time, blended/hybrid learning. Offers aerospace engineering (MS, PhD); biomedical engineering (MS, PhD); engineering science (MS, PhD); industrial and systems engineering/engineering management (MS, PhD); mechanical engineering (MS, PhD); physics (MS, PhD). Electronic applications accepted.

THE UNIVERSITY OF TENNESSEE AT CHATTANOOGA, Chattanooga, TN 37403-2598

General Information State-supported, coed, comprehensive institution. CGS member. *Graduate housing:* Room and/or apartments available on a first-come, first-served basis to single students; on-campus housing not available to married students. Housing application deadline: 6/1. *Research affiliation:* UT Law Enforcement Innovation Center (criminal justice), Highland Biological Field Station (biology and environmental science), Tennessee Valley Authority (engineering), Gulf Coast Research Laboratory (biology and environmental science), Tennessee Coalition against Domestic and Sexual Violence (criminal justice).

GRADUATE UNITS

Department of Health and Human Performance Offers athletic training (MSAT); health and human performance (MS). Electronic applications accepted.

Department of Occupational Therapy Offers occupational therapy (OTD). Electronic applications accepted.

Department of Political Science and Public Service *Program availability:* Part-time, evening/weekend. Offers local government management (MPA); non-profit management (MPA); public administration (MPA); public administration and non-profit management (Postbaccalaureate Certificate). Electronic applications accepted.

Engineering Management and Technology Program *Program availability:* 100% online, blended/hybrid learning. Offers construction management (Graduate Certificate); engineering management (MS); fundamentals of engineering management (Graduate Certificate); leadership and ethics (Graduate Certificate); logistics and supply chain management (Graduate Certificate); power systems management (Graduate Certificate); project and technology management (Graduate Certificate); quality management (Graduate Certificate). Electronic applications accepted.

Program in Accountancy *Program availability:* Part-time, evening/weekend. Offers accountancy (M Acc). Electronic applications accepted.

Program in Business Administration *Program availability:* Part-time, evening/weekend. Offers business administration (EMBA, MBA, PMBA). Electronic applications accepted.

Program in Computational Science Offers computational science (PhD). Electronic applications accepted.

Program in Computer Science *Program availability:* Part-time. Offers biomedical informatics (Post Master's Certificate); computer science (MS). Electronic applications accepted.

Program in Counseling Offers mental health (M Ed); school counseling (M Ed, Post Master's Certificate). Electronic applications accepted.

Program in Criminal Justice *Program availability:* Part-time. Offers criminal justice (MSCJ). Electronic applications accepted.

Program in Engineering *Program availability:* Part-time. Offers automotive (MS Engr); chemical (MS Engr); civil (MS Engr); electrical (MS Engr); mechanical (MS Engr). Electronic applications accepted.

Program in English *Program availability:* Part-time. Offers creative writing (MA); literary study (MA); rhetoric and writing (MA). Electronic applications accepted.

Program in Environmental Science *Program availability:* Part-time. Offers environmental science (MS). Electronic applications accepted.

Program in Interior Design Offers interior design (MID, MS). Electronic applications accepted.

Program in Learning and Leadership Offers educational leadership (Ed D, PhD). Electronic applications accepted.

Program in Mathematics *Program availability:* Part-time. Offers applied mathematics (MS); applied statistics (MS); mathematics education (MS); pre-professional mathematics (MS). Electronic applications accepted.

Program in Music Offers music education (MM); performance (MM). Electronic applications accepted.

Program in Physical Therapy Offers physical therapy (DPT). Electronic applications accepted.

Program in Psychology *Program availability:* Part-time. Offers industrial/organizational psychology (MS); research psychology (MS). Electronic applications accepted.

Program in Social Work Offers social work (MSW). Electronic applications accepted.

School of Education *Program availability:* Part-time. Offers counseling (M Ed); education (M Ed, Post-Master's Certificate); elementary education (M Ed); learning and leadership (Ed D); school leadership (Post-Master's Certificate); school leadership: principal licensure (Ed S); secondary education (M Ed); special education (M Ed). Electronic applications accepted.

School of Nursing Offers certified nurse anesthetist (Post-Master's Certificate); family nurse practitioner (MSN, Post-Master's Certificate); gerontology acute care (MSN, Post-Master's Certificate); nurse anesthesia (MSN); nurse education (Post-Master's Certificate); nursing (DNP). Electronic applications accepted.

THE UNIVERSITY OF TENNESSEE AT MARTIN, Martin, TN 38238

General Information State-supported, coed, comprehensive institution. *Enrollment:* 7,069 graduate, professional, and undergraduate students; 58 full-time matriculated graduate/professional students (42 women), 317 part-time matriculated graduate/professional students (232 women). *Enrollment by degree level:* 375 master's. *Graduate faculty:* 127. *International tuition:* $22,862 full-time. *Tuition, area resident:* Full-time $8918; part-time $495 per credit hour. Tuition, state resident: full-time $8918; part-time $485 per credit hour. Tuition, nonresident: full-time $14,958; part-time $831 per credit hour. *Required fees:* $1446; $81 per credit hour. Part-time tuition and fees vary according to course load. *Graduate housing:* Rooms and/or apartments available on a first-come, first-served basis to single and married students. Typical cost: $2820 per year ($6194 including board) for single students; $4510 per year for married students. Housing application deadline: 3/1. *Student services:* Campus employment opportunities, campus safety program, career counseling, child daycare facilities, exercise/wellness program, free psychological counseling, international student services, low-cost health insurance, multicultural affairs office, services for students with disabilities, teacher training, writing training. *Library facilities:* Paul Meek Library. *Collection:* Books: 302,341 (physical), 92,351 (digital/electronic); Serial titles: 47,314 (physical), 350,984 (digital/electronic); Databases: 231. Weekly public service hours: 92; study areas open 24 hours, 5–7 days a week.

Computer facilities: 1,214 computers available on campus for general student use. A campuswide network can be accessed from student residence rooms and from off campus. Online class registration, online fee payments, degree progress, financial aid data, housing applications, transcripts are available.
Website: http://www.utm.edu/

General Application Contact: Jolene L. Cunningham, Student Services Specialist, 731-881-7012, Fax: 731-881-7499, E-mail: jcunningham@utm.edu.

GRADUATE UNITS

Graduate Programs Students: 58 full-time (42 women), 317 part-time (232 women); includes 40 minority (28 Black or African American, non-Hispanic/Latino; 6 Hispanic/Latino; 6 Two or more races, non-Hispanic/Latino). Average age 34. 286 applicants, 47% accepted, 83 enrolled. *Faculty:* 127. Expenses: Contact institution. *Financial support:* In 2018–19, 103 students received support, including 7 research assistantships with full tuition reimbursements available (averaging $7,396 per year), 18 teaching assistantships with full tuition reimbursements available (averaging $7,159 per year); scholarships/grants and tuition waivers (full and partial) also available. Financial award application deadline: 2/1; financial award applicants required to submit FAFSA. In 2018, 109 master's awarded. *Program availability:* Part-time, 100% online, blended/hybrid learning. *Application deadline:* For fall admission, 7/27 priority date for domestic and international students; for spring admission, 12/17 priority date for domestic and international students; for summer admission, 5/10 priority date for domestic and international students. Applications are processed on a rolling basis. *Application fee:* $30 ($130 for international students). Electronic applications accepted. *Application Contact:* Jolene L. Cunningham, Student Services Specialist, 731-881-7012, Fax: 731-881-7499, E-mail: jcunningham@utm.edu. *Associate Vice Chancellor and Dean of Graduate Studies,* Dr. Victoria S. Seng, 731-881-7012, Fax: 731-881-7499, E-mail: vseng@utm.edu.

College of Agriculture and Applied Sciences Students: 8 full-time (4 women), 48 part-time (36 women); includes 2 minority (both Black or African American, non-Hispanic/Latino). Average age 29. 76 applicants, 62% accepted, 23 enrolled. *Faculty:* 22. Expenses: Contact institution. *Financial support:* In 2018–19, 20 students received support, including 5 teaching assistantships with full tuition reimbursements available (averaging $6,356 per year); research assistantships, scholarships/grants, and tuition waivers (full and partial) also available. Financial award application deadline: 2/1; financial award applicants required to submit FAFSA. In 2018, 18 master's awarded. *Program availability:* Part-time, 100% online, blended/hybrid learning. Offers agricultural and natural resources management (MSANR); agriculture and applied sciences (MSANR, MSFCS); dietetics (MSFCS); general family and consumer sciences (MSFCS). *Application deadline:* For fall admission, 7/27 priority date for domestic and international students; for spring admission, 12/17 priority date for domestic and international students; for summer admission, 5/10 priority date for domestic and international students. Applications are processed on a rolling basis. *Application fee:* $30 ($130 for international students). Electronic applications accepted. *Application Contact:* Jolene L. Cunningham, Student Services Specialist, 731-881-7012, Fax: 731-881-7499, E-mail: jcunningham@utm.edu. *Dean,* Dr. Todd Winters, 731-881-7250, E-mail: winters@utm.edu.

College of Business and Global Affairs Students: 8 full-time (2 women), 58 part-time (32 women); includes 5 minority (3 Black or African American, non-Hispanic/Latino; 1 Hispanic/Latino; 1 Two or more races, non-Hispanic/Latino). Average age 36. 65 applicants, 28% accepted, 13 enrolled. *Faculty:* 33. Expenses: Contact institution. *Financial support:* In 2018–19, 30 students received support, including 5 research assistantships with full tuition reimbursements available (averaging $7,289 per year), 4 teaching assistantships with full tuition reimbursements available (averaging $8,187 per year); scholarships/grants and tuition waivers (full and partial) also available. Financial award application deadline: 2/1; financial award applicants required to submit FAFSA. In 2018, 39 master's awarded. *Program availability:* Part-time, 100% online, blended/hybrid learning. Offers agricultural business (MBA); business and global affairs (MBA); financial services (MBA); general business (MBA). *Application deadline:* For fall admission, 7/27 priority date for domestic and international students; for spring admission, 12/17 priority date for domestic and international students; for summer admission, 5/10 priority date for domestic and international students. Applications are processed on a rolling basis. *Application fee:* $30 ($130 for international students). Electronic applications accepted. *Application Contact:* Jolene L. Cunningham, Student Services Specialist, 731-881-7012, Fax: 731-881-7499, E-mail: jcunningham@utm.edu. *Dean,* Dr. Ross Dickens, 731-881-7227, Fax: 731-881-7241, E-mail: rdicken2@utm.edu.

College of Education, Health and Behavioral Sciences Students: 42 full-time (36 women), 196 part-time (154 women); includes 32 minority (22 Black or African American, non-Hispanic/Latino; 5 Hispanic/Latino; 5 Two or more races, non-Hispanic/Latino). Average age 34. 135 applicants, 45% accepted, 40 enrolled. *Faculty:* 42. Expenses: Contact institution. *Financial support:* In 2018–19, 50 students received support, including 1 research assistantship with full tuition reimbursement available (averaging $6,283 per year), 7 teaching assistantships with full tuition reimbursements available (averaging $7,126 per year); scholarships/grants and tuition waivers (full and partial) also available. Financial award application deadline: 2/1; financial award applicants required to submit FAFSA. In 2018, 51 master's awarded. *Program availability:* Part-time, online only, 100% online. Offers addictions counseling (MS Ed); community counseling (MS Ed); curriculum and instruction (MS Ed); education, health and behavioral sciences (MS Ed); educational leadership (MS Ed); initial licensure (MS Ed); initial licensure k-8 (MS Ed); interdisciplinary (MS Ed); school counseling (MS Ed); student affairs and college counseling (MS Ed). *Application deadline:* For fall admission, 7/27 priority date for domestic and international students; for spring admission, 12/17 priority date for domestic and international students; for summer admission, 5/10 priority date for domestic and international students. Applications are processed on a rolling basis. *Application fee:* $30 ($130 for international students). Electronic applications accepted. *Application Contact:* Jolene L. Cunningham, Student Services Specialist, 731-881-7012, Fax: 731-881-7499, E-mail: jcunningham@utm.edu. *Dean,* Cynthia West, 731-881-7127, Fax: 731-881-7975, E-mail: cwest@utm.edu.

College of Humanities and Fine Arts Students: 15 part-time (10 women); includes 1 minority (Black or African American, non-Hispanic/Latino). Average age 39. 10 applicants, 70% accepted, 7 enrolled. *Faculty:* 18 full-time (7 women). Expenses: Contact institution. *Financial support:* In 2018–19, 13 students received support, including 1 research assistantship with full tuition reimbursement available (averaging $9,048 per year), 2 teaching assistantships with full tuition reimbursements available (averaging $7,226 per year); scholarships/grants and tuition waivers (full and partial) also available. Financial award application deadline: 2/1; financial award applicants required to submit FAFSA. In 2018, 1 master's awarded. *Program availability:* Part-time, blended/hybrid learning. Offers strategic communication (MASC). *Application deadline:* For fall admission, 7/27 priority date for domestic and international students; for spring admission, 12/15 priority date for domestic and international students; for summer admission, 5/10 priority date for domestic and international students. Applications are processed on a rolling basis. *Application fee:* $30 ($130 for international students). Electronic applications accepted. *Application Contact:* Jolene L. Cunningham, Student Services Specialist, 731-881-7012, Fax: 731-881-7499, E-mail: jcunningham@utm.edu. *Dean,* Dr. Lynn Alexander, 731-881-7490, Fax: 731-881-7276, E-mail: lalexand@utm.edu.

THE UNIVERSITY OF TENNESSEE HEALTH SCIENCE CENTER, Memphis, TN 38163-0002

General Information State-supported, coed, upper-level institution. CGS member. *Graduate housing:* On-campus housing not available. *Research affiliation:* Saint Jude's Children's Research Hospital, Veterans Administration Medical Center, University of Memphis, LeBonheur Children's Medical Center.

GRADUATE UNITS

College of Dentistry Offers dentistry (DDS). Electronic applications accepted.

College of Graduate Health Sciences Offers biomedical engineering (MS, PhD); biomedical sciences (PhD); dental sciences (MDS); epidemiology (MS); health outcomes and policy research (PhD); laboratory research and management (MS); nursing science (PhD); pharmaceutical sciences (PhD); pharmacology (MS); speech and hearing science (PhD). MS and PhD programs in biomedical engineering offered jointly with University of Memphis. Electronic applications accepted.

College of Health Professions *Program availability:* Part-time, evening/weekend, online learning. Offers audiology (MS, Au D); clinical laboratory science (MSCLS); cytopathology practice (MCP); health informatics and information management (MHIIM); occupational therapy (MOT); physical therapy (DPT, ScDPT); physician assistant (MMS); speech-language pathology (MS). Electronic applications accepted.

College of Medicine Offers medicine (MD). Electronic applications accepted.

College of Nursing Students: 230 full-time (196 women), 20 part-time (19 women); includes 74 minority (61 Black or African American, non-Hispanic/Latino; 8 Asian, non-Hispanic/Latino; 5 Hispanic/Latino). Average age 33. 218 applicants, 54% accepted, 101 enrolled. *Faculty:* 52 full-time (47 women), 11 part-time/adjunct (4 women). Expenses: Contact institution. *Financial support:* In 2018–19, 112 students received support, including 9 research assistantships (averaging $24,783 per year); Federal Work-Study, institutionally sponsored loans, scholarships/grants, and tuition waivers (partial) also available. Financial award application deadline: 3/15; financial award applicants required to submit FAFSA. In 2018, 88 doctorates, 1 Certificate awarded. *Program availability:* Part-time, blended/hybrid learning. Offers adult-gerontology acute care nurse practitioner (Post Master's Certificate); advance practice nursing (DNP); family nurse practitioner (Post-Doctoral Certificate); pediatric acute care nurse practitioner (Post-Doctoral Certificate); pediatric primary care nurse practitioner (Post-Doctoral Certificate); psychiatric/mental health nurse practitioner (Post-Doctoral Certificate); registered nurse first assistant (Certificate). *Application deadline:* For fall admission,

1/15 for domestic students; for spring admission, 8/15 for domestic students. *Application fee:* $70. Electronic applications accepted. *Application Contact:* Jamie Overton, Director, Student Affairs, 901-448-6139, Fax: 901-448-4121, E-mail: joverton@uthsc.edu. *Dean,* Dr. Wendy Likes, 901-448-6135, Fax: 901-448-4121, E-mail: wlikes@uthsc.edu.

College of Pharmacy Offers pharmacy (MS, PhD, Pharm D). Electronic applications accepted.

THE UNIVERSITY OF TENNESSEE–OAK RIDGE NATIONAL LABORATORY, Oak Ridge, TN 37830-8026

General Information State-supported, coed, graduate-only institution. *Research affiliation:* Oak Ridge National Laboratory.

GRADUATE UNITS

Graduate Program in Genome Science and Technology Offers life sciences (MS, PhD). Electronic applications accepted.

THE UNIVERSITY OF TEXAS AT ARLINGTON, Arlington, TX 76019

General Information State-supported, coed, university. CGS member. *Graduate housing:* Rooms and/or apartments available on a first-come, first-served basis to single and married students. *Research affiliation:* Texas Health Resources (medical technologies), Center for Innovation (technology development and commercialization), Facebook (energy efficient electronic systems), U.S. Department of Energy (bioengineering), National Science Foundation (materials science and engineering), Texas Instruments (medical technologies).

GRADUATE UNITS

Graduate School *Program availability:* Part-time, evening/weekend, online learning.

College of Architecture, Planning and Public Affairs *Program availability:* Part-time, evening/weekend, online learning. Offers architecture (M Arch); architecture, planning and public affairs (M Arch, MLA, MPA, MPP, PhD); landscape architecture (MLA); public administration (MPA); public and urban administration (PhD); public policy (MPP); urban planning and public policy (PhD). Electronic applications accepted.

College of Business *Program availability:* Part-time, evening/weekend, online learning. Offers accounting (MP Acc, MS, PhD); business (MA, MBA, MP Acc, MS, MSHRM, PhD); economics (MA); finance (PhD); health care administration (MS); human resources (MSHRM); information systems (MS, PhD); marketing (MBA); marketing research (MS); quantitative finance (MS); real estate (MS); taxation (MS). Electronic applications accepted.

College of Education Offers curriculum and instruction (M Ed); education (M Ed, M Ed T, PhD); educational leadership (PhD); higher education (M Ed); principal certification (M Ed); teaching (with certification) (M Ed T).

College of Engineering *Program availability:* Part-time, evening/weekend, online learning. Offers aerospace engineering (M Engr, MS, PhD); bioengineering (MS, PhD); civil engineering (M Engr, MS, PhD); computer engineering (MS, PhD); computer science (MS, PhD); construction management (MCM); electrical engineering (M Engr, MS, PhD); engineering (M Engr, MCM, MS, PhD); engineering management (MS); industrial engineering (MS, PhD); logistics (MS); materials science and engineering (M Engr, MS, PhD); mechanical engineering (M Engr, MS, PhD); software engineering (MS); systems engineering (MS).

College of Liberal Arts *Program availability:* Part-time, evening/weekend. Offers anthropology (MA); communication (MA); criminology and criminal justice (MA); education (MM); English (MA); film and video (MFA); French (MA); glass (MFA); history (MA); intermedia (MFA); liberal arts (MA, MFA, MM, PhD); linguistics (MA, PhD); literature (PhD); performance (MM); political science (MA); sociology (MA); Spanish (MA); teaching English to speakers of other languages (MA); transatlantic history (PhD); visual communication (MFA).

College of Nursing and Health Innovation *Program availability:* Part-time, evening/weekend, online learning. Offers athletic training (MS); exercise science (MS); kinesiology (PhD); nurse practitioner (MSN); nursing (PhD); nursing administration (MSN); nursing education (MSN); nursing practice (DNP).

College of Science *Program availability:* Part-time, evening/weekend. Offers applied math (MS); biology (MS); chemistry (MS, PhD); earth and environmental sciences (MS, PhD); experimental health psychology (PhD); experimental psychology (MS, PhD); health/neuroscience psychology (MS, PhD); industrial and organizational psychology (MS); mathematics (PhD); mathematics education (MA); physics (MS); physics and applied physics (PhD); quantitative biology (PhD); science (MA, MS, PhD).

School of Social Work *Program availability:* Part-time, evening/weekend, online learning. Offers social work (MSW, PhD). Electronic applications accepted.

THE UNIVERSITY OF TEXAS AT AUSTIN, Austin, TX 78712-1111

General Information State-supported, coed, university. CGS member. *Graduate housing:* Rooms and/or apartments available to single students and available on a first-come, first-served basis to married students.

GRADUATE UNITS

Dell Medical School Offers medicine (MD).

Graduate School *Program availability:* Part-time, evening/weekend. Offers computational science, engineering, and mathematics (MS, PhD). Electronic applications accepted.

Cockrell School of Engineering *Program availability:* Part-time, evening/weekend. Offers aerospace engineering (MSE, PhD); architectural engineering (MSE); biomedical engineering (MS, PhD); chemical engineering (MSE, PhD); civil engineering (MS, PhD); electrical and computer engineering (MS, PhD); energy and earth resources (MA); engineering (MA, MS, MSE, PhD); engineering mechanics (MS, PhD); environmental and water resources engineering (MS, PhD); materials science and engineering (MS, PhD); mechanical engineering (MS, PhD); operations research and industrial engineering (MS, PhD); petroleum engineering (MS, PhD). Electronic applications accepted.

College of Communication *Program availability:* Part-time. Offers advertising (MA, PhD); audiology (Au D); communication (MA, MFA, Au D, PhD); communication sciences and disorders (PhD); communication studies (MA); film and media production (MFA); journalism (MA, PhD); media studies (MA, PhD); screenwriting (MFA); speech language pathology (MA). Electronic applications accepted.

College of Education *Program availability:* Part-time. Offers academic educational psychology (M Ed, MA); autism and developmental disabilities (Ed D, PhD); autism and developmental disability (M Ed, MA); behavioral health (PhD); bilingual/bicultural education (M Ed, MA, PhD); counseling psychology (PhD); counselor education (M Ed); cultural studies in education (M Ed, MA, PhD); early childhood education (M Ed, MA, PhD); early childhood special education (M Ed, MA, Ed D, PhD); education (M Ed, MA, MS, Ed D, PhD); educational administration (M Ed, Ed D, PhD);

exercise and sport psychology (M Ed, MA); exercise science (M Ed, MS, PhD); health education (M Ed, MS, Ed D, PhD); human development, culture and learning sciences (PhD); language and literacy studies (M Ed, PhD); learning disabilities (Ed D, PhD); learning disabilities/behavior disorders (M Ed, MA); learning technologies (M Ed, MA, PhD); multicultural special education (M Ed, MA, Ed D, PhD); physical education (M Ed, MA, PhD); program evaluation (MA); quantitative methods (M Ed, MA, PhD); rehabilitation counselor (M Ed); rehabilitation counselor education (Ed D, PhD); school psychology (MA, PhD); special education administration (Ed D, PhD). Electronic applications accepted.

College of Fine Arts *Program availability:* Part-time. Offers acting (MFA); art education (MA); art history (MA, PhD); band and wind conducting (M Music, DMA); brass/woodwind/percussion (MM, DMA); chamber music (MM); choral conducting (MM, DMA); collaborative piano (MM, DMA); composition (MM, DMA); dance (MFA); design (MFA); directing (MFA); drama and theatre for youth (MFA); ethnomusicology (MM, PhD); fine arts (M Music, MA, MFA, MM, DMA, PhD); literature and pedagogy (MM); music and human learning (MM, PhD); music and human learning (DMA); musicology (MM, PhD); opera performance (MM, DMA); orchestral conducting (MM, DMA); organ (MM); organ performance (MM, DMA); performance (MM); performance (DMA); performance as public practice (MA, MFA, PhD); piano (DMA); piano literature and pedagogy (MM); piano performance (MM, DMA); playwriting (MFA); string performance (MM, DMA); studio art (MFA); theatre technology (MFA); theatrical design (MFA); theory (MM, PhD); vocal performance (MM, DMA); voice (DMA); voice performance pedagogy (DMA); woodwind, brass, percussion performance (MM). Electronic applications accepted.

College of Liberal Arts *Program availability:* Part-time. Offers African Diaspora studies (MA, PhD); American studies (MA, PhD); applied linguistics/pedagogy (PhD); archaeology (MA, PhD); Asian cultures and languages (MA, PhD); Asian studies (MA); behavioral neuroscience (PhD); classics (MA, PhD); clinical psychology (PhD); cognitive systems (PhD); comparative literature (MA, PhD); creative writing (MFA); cultural forms (MA, PhD); cultural politics of Afro-Latin and indigenous peoples (MA); development studies (MA); developmental psychology (PhD); economics (MA, MS Econ, PhD); English (MA, PhD); environmental studies (MA); French linguistics (MA, PhD); French studies (MA, PhD); geography and the environment (MA, PhD); Germanic studies (MA, PhD); government (MA, PhD); Hispanic linguistics (MA, PhD); Hispanic literature (MA, PhD); history (MA, PhD); human dimensions of organizations (MA); human rights (MA); Ibero-romance philology and linguistics (PhD); individual differences and evolutionary psychology (PhD); Italian studies (MA, PhD); Latin American and international law (LL M); liberal arts (LL M, MA, MFA, MS Econ, PhD); linguistic anthropology (MA, PhD); linguistics (MA, PhD); literature and culture (PhD); Luso-Brazilian literature (MA, PhD); Mexican American studies (MA); Middle Eastern languages and cultures (MA, PhD); Middle Eastern studies (MA); perceptual systems (PhD); philosophy (PhD); physical anthropology (MA, PhD); Romance linguistics (PhD); Russian, East European, and Eurasian studies (MA); Slavic languages (MA); Slavic linguistics (PhD); social anthropology (MA, PhD); social psychology (PhD); sociology (MA, PhD). Electronic applications accepted.

College of Natural Sciences *Program availability:* Part-time. Offers analytical chemistry (PhD); astronomy (MA, PhD); biochemistry (PhD); computer science (MSCS, PhD); ecology, evolution and behavior (PhD); human development and family sciences (MA, PhD); inorganic chemistry (PhD); marine science (MS, PhD); mathematics (MA, PhD); microbiology (PhD); natural sciences (MA, MSCS, PhD); nutrition (MA); nutritional sciences (MA, MS, PhD); organic chemistry (PhD); physical chemistry (PhD); physics (MA, MS, PhD); plant biology (MA, PhD); statistics (MS, PhD); textile and apparel technology (MS). Electronic applications accepted.

College of Pharmacy Offers health outcomes and pharmacy practice (PhD); health outcomes and pharmacy practice (MS); medicinal chemistry (PhD); pharmaceutics (PhD); pharmacology and toxicology (PhD); pharmacotherapy (MS, PhD); pharmacy (MS, PhD, Pharm D); translational science (PhD). Electronic applications accepted.

Institute for Cellular and Molecular Biology Offers cellular and molecular biology (PhD).

The Institute for Neuroscience Offers neuroscience (PhD). Electronic applications accepted.

Jackson School of Geosciences *Program availability:* Part-time. Offers geosciences (MA, MS, PhD). Electronic applications accepted.

Lyndon B. Johnson School of Public Affairs *Program availability:* Part-time. Offers global policy studies (MGPS); public affairs (MP Aff); public leadership (EMPL); public policy (PhD). Electronic applications accepted.

McCombs School of Business Offers accounting (MPA, PhD); business (MBA, MPA, MS, MSF, PhD); business administration (MBA); executive business administration (MBA); finance (MSF, PhD); information management (MBA); information systems (PhD); information technology and management (MS); management (PhD); marketing (MBA, MS, PhD); risk analysis and decision making (PhD); risk management (MBA); supply chain and operations management (MBA, PhD); technology commercialization (MS). Electronic applications accepted.

Michener Center for Writers Offers fiction (MFA); playwriting (MFA); poetry (MFA); screenwriting (MFA). Electronic applications accepted.

School of Architecture Offers architectural history (MA, PhD); architecture (M Arch, M Arch I, M Arch II, MA, MID, MLA, MS, MSAS, MSCRP, MSSD, MSUD, PhD); community and regional planning (MSCRP, PhD); historic preservation (M Arch, MS, MSCRP); interior design (MID); landscape architecture (MLA); sustainable design (M Arch I, M Arch II, MSSD); urban design (M Arch, MSUD). Electronic applications accepted.

School of Information *Program availability:* Part-time. Offers identity management and security (MSIMS); information (PhD); information studies (MSIS). MSIMS program offered in conjunction with the Center for Identity. Electronic applications accepted.

School of Nursing *Program availability:* Part-time. Offers adult - gerontology clinical nurse specialist (MSN); child health (MSN); family nurse practitioner (MSN); family psychiatric/mental health nurse practitioner (MSN); holistic adult health (MSN); maternity (MSN); nursing (PhD); nursing administration and healthcare systems management (MSN); nursing practice (DNP); pediatric nurse practitioner (MSN); public health nursing (MSN). Electronic applications accepted.

Steve Hicks School of Social Work *Program availability:* Part-time. Offers social work (MSSW, PhD).

School of Law Offers law (LL M, JD). Electronic applications accepted.

THE UNIVERSITY OF TEXAS AT DALLAS, Richardson, TX 75080

General Information State-supported, coed, university. CGS member. *Enrollment:* 5,967 full-time matriculated graduate/professional students (2,540 women), 2,789 part-time matriculated graduate/professional students (1,238 women). *Enrollment by degree level:* 7,261 master's, 1,495 doctoral. *Graduate faculty:* 556 full-time (123 women), 239

part-time/adjunct (79 women). *International tuition:* $26,852 full-time. *Tuition, area resident:* Full-time $13,458. Tuition, state resident: full-time $13,458. Tuition, nonresident: full-time $26,852. Tuition and fees vary according to course load. *Graduate housing:* Rooms and/or apartments available on a first-come, first-served basis to single and married students. Typical cost: $7442 per year ($11,532 including board) for single students; $7442 per year ($11,532 including board) for married students. Housing application deadline: 5/31. *Student services:* Campus employment opportunities, campus safety program, career counseling, child daycare facilities, exercise/wellness program, free psychological counseling, grant writing training, international student services, low-cost health insurance, multicultural affairs office, services for students with disabilities, teacher training, writing training. *Library facilities:* Eugene McDermott Library plus 1 other. *Collection:* Books: 652,018 (physical), 1.5 million (digital/electronic); Serial titles: 135,287 (physical), 149,406 (digital/electronic); Databases: 530. Weekly public service hours: 152; study areas open 24 hours, 5–7 days a week; students can reserve study rooms.

Computer facilities: Computer purchase and lease plans are available. 170 computers available on campus for general student use. A campuswide network can be accessed from student residence rooms and from off campus. Online class registration is available.
Website: http://www.utdallas.edu/

General Application Contact: Dr. Juan E González, Dean of Graduate Studies, 972-883-2234, Fax: 972-883-4308, E-mail: graduatestudies@utdallas.edu.

GRADUATE UNITS

Erik Jonsson School of Engineering and Computer Science Students: 1,726 full-time (487 women), 530 part-time (142 women); includes 177 minority (18 Black or African American, non-Hispanic/Latino; 96 Asian, non-Hispanic/Latino; 49 Hispanic/Latino; 14 Two or more races, non-Hispanic/Latino), 1,851 international. Average age 27. 5,913 applicants, 40% accepted, 709 enrolled. *Faculty:* 151 full-time (16 women), 40 part-time/adjunct (7 women). *Expenses:* Contact institution. *Financial support:* In 2018–19, 494 students received support, including 34 fellowships (averaging $3,054 per year), 382 research assistantships with partial tuition reimbursements available (averaging $24,085 per year), 186 teaching assistantships with partial tuition reimbursements available (averaging $17,393 per year); career-related internships or fieldwork, Federal Work-Study, institutionally sponsored loans, scholarships/grants, and unspecified assistantships also available. Support available to part-time students. Financial award application deadline: 4/30; financial award applicants required to submit FAFSA. In 2018, 825 master's, 89 doctorates awarded. *Program availability:* Part-time, evening/weekend. Offers biomedical engineering (MS, PhD); computer engineering (MS, PhD); computer science (MSCS, PhD); electrical engineering (MSEE, PhD); engineering and computer science (MS, MSCS, MSEE, MSTE, PhD); materials science and engineering (MS, PhD); mechanical engineering (MS, PhD); software engineering (MS, PhD); systems engineering and management (MS); telecommunications engineering (MSTE, PhD). *Application deadline:* For fall admission, 7/15 for domestic students, 5/1 priority date for international students; for spring admission, 11/15 for domestic students, 9/1 priority date for international students. Applications are processed on a rolling basis. *Application fee:* $50 ($100 for international students). Electronic applications accepted. *Application Contact:* Leiane Davis, Administrative Associate, 972-883-6851, Fax: 972-883-2813, E-mail: leiane.davis@utdallas.edu. *Dean,* Dr. Stephanie G Adams, 972-883-2557, Fax: 972-883-2813.

Naveen Jindal School of Management Students: 2,848 full-time (1,224 women), 1,723 part-time (789 women); includes 952 minority (129 Black or African American, non-Hispanic/Latino; 4 American Indian or Alaska Native, non-Hispanic/Latino; 524 Asian, non-Hispanic/Latino; 224 Hispanic/Latino; 71 Two or more races, non-Hispanic/Latino), 2,614 international. Average age 30. 5,382 applicants, 64% accepted, 1575 enrolled. *Faculty:* 108 full-time (22 women), 132 part-time/adjunct (38 women). *Expenses:* Contact institution. *Financial support:* In 2018–19, 104 students received support, including 25 research assistantships with partial tuition reimbursements available (averaging $36,440 per year), 149 teaching assistantships with partial tuition reimbursements available (averaging $18,444 per year); fellowships, career-related internships or fieldwork, Federal Work-Study, institutionally sponsored loans, scholarships/grants, and unspecified assistantships also available. Support available to part-time students. Financial award application deadline: 4/30; financial award applicants required to submit FAFSA. In 2018, 2,300 master's, 23 doctorates awarded. *Program availability:* Part-time, evening/weekend, online learning. Offers accounting (MS); business administration (MBA); business analytics (MS); executive business administration (EMBA); finance (MS); global leadership (EMBA); healthcare leadership and management (MS); healthcare management (EMBA); information technology and management (MS); innovation and entrepreneurship (MS); international management studies (MS, PhD); management (EMBA, MBA, MS, PhD); management science (MS, PhD); marketing (MS); project management (EMBA); supply chain management (MS); systems engineering and management (MS). *Application deadline:* For fall admission, 7/15 for domestic students, 5/1 priority date for international students; for spring admission, 11/15 for domestic students, 9/1 priority date for international students. Applications are processed on a rolling basis. *Application fee:* $50 ($100 for international students). Electronic applications accepted. *Application Contact:* Dr. Hasan Pirkul, Dean, 972-883-2705, Fax: 972-883-2799, E-mail: hpirkul@utdallas.edu. *Dean,* Dr. Hasan Pirkul, 972-883-2705, Fax: 972-883-2799, E-mail: hpirkul@utdallas.edu.

School of Arts and Humanities Students: 126 full-time (77 women), 116 part-time (73 women); includes 67 minority (13 Black or African American, non-Hispanic/Latino; 1 American Indian or Alaska Native, non-Hispanic/Latino; 13 Asian, non-Hispanic/Latino; 26 Hispanic/Latino; 14 Two or more races, non-Hispanic/Latino), 26 international. Average age 41. 133 applicants, 52% accepted, 50 enrolled. *Faculty:* 45 full-time (15 women), 10 part-time/adjunct (6 women). *Expenses:* Contact institution. *Financial support:* In 2018–19, 66 students received support, including 2 fellowships (averaging $1,500 per year), 10 research assistantships with partial tuition reimbursements available (averaging $22,697 per year), 67 teaching assistantships with partial tuition reimbursements available (averaging $14,986 per year); Federal Work-Study, institutionally sponsored loans, scholarships/grants, and unspecified assistantships also available. Support available to part-time students. Financial award application deadline: 4/30; financial award applicants required to submit FAFSA. In 2018, 29 master's, 15 doctorates awarded. *Program availability:* Part-time, evening/weekend. Offers art history (MA); humanities (MA, PhD); Latin American studies (MA). *Application deadline:* For fall admission, 7/15 for domestic students, 5/1 priority date for international students; for spring admission, 11/15 for domestic students, 9/1 priority date for international students. Applications are processed on a rolling basis. *Application fee:* $50 ($100 for international students). Electronic applications accepted. *Application Contact:* Dr. John Gooch, Associate Dean of Graduate Studies, 972-883-2989, E-mail: john.gooch@utdallas.edu. *Dean,* Dr. Dennis M. Kratz, 972-883-2984, Fax: 972-883-2989, E-mail: dkratz@utdallas.edu.

School of Arts, Technology, and Emerging Communication Students: 41 full-time (15 women), 21 part-time (10 women); includes 20 minority (5 Black or African American, non-Hispanic/Latino; 7 Asian, non-Hispanic/Latino; 2 Two or more races, non-Hispanic/Latino), 12 international. Average age 35. 125 applicants, 21% accepted, 17 enrolled. *Faculty:* 23 full-time (11 women), 2 part-time/adjunct (0 women). Expenses: Contact institution. *Financial support:* In 2018–19, 29 students received support, including 10 research assistantships with partial tuition reimbursements available (averaging $25,278 per year), 20 teaching assistantships with partial tuition reimbursements available (averaging $15,612 per year); career-related internships or fieldwork, Federal Work-Study, institutionally sponsored loans, scholarships/grants, and unspecified assistantships also available. Support available to part-time students. Financial award application deadline: 4/30; financial award applicants required to submit FAFSA. In 2018, 38 master's, 5 doctorates awarded. Offers arts and technology (MA, MFA, PhD); emerging media and communication (MA). *Application deadline:* For fall admission, 7/15 for domestic students, 5/1 priority date for international students; for spring admission, 11/15 for domestic students, 9/1 priority date for international students. Applications are processed on a rolling basis. *Application fee:* $50 ($100 for international students). Electronic applications accepted. *Application Contact:* Dr. Kim Knight, Associate Dean for Graduate Studies, 972-883-4346, E-mail: kak102020@utdallas.edu. *Dean,* Dr. Anne Balsamo, 972-883-4376, E-mail: atecdean@utdallas.edu.

School of Behavioral and Brain Sciences Students: 511 full-time (415 women), 81 part-time (58 women); includes 173 minority (23 Black or African American, non-Hispanic/Latino; 2 American Indian or Alaska Native, non-Hispanic/Latino; 48 Asian, non-Hispanic/Latino; 73 Hispanic/Latino; 27 Two or more races, non-Hispanic/Latino), 74 international. Average age 27. 906 applicants, 27% accepted, 178 enrolled. *Faculty:* 56 full-time (27 women), 24 part-time/adjunct (21 women). Expenses: Contact institution. *Financial support:* In 2018–19, 108 students received support, including 45 research assistantships with partial tuition reimbursements available (averaging $27,865 per year), 64 teaching assistantships with partial tuition reimbursements available (averaging $18,598 per year); fellowships, career-related internships or fieldwork, Federal Work-Study, institutionally sponsored loans, scholarships/grants, and unspecified assistantships also available. Support available to part-time students. Financial award application deadline: 4/30; financial award applicants required to submit FAFSA. In 2018, 217 master's, 28 doctorates awarded. *Program availability:* Part-time, evening/weekend. Offers applied cognition and neuroscience (MS); audiology (Au D); behavioral and brain sciences (MS, Au D, PhD); cognition and neuroscience (PhD); communication disorders (MS); communication sciences and disorders (PhD); early childhood disorders (MS); psychological sciences (MS, PhD). *Application deadline:* For fall admission, 7/15 for domestic students, 5/1 priority date for international students; for spring admission, 11/15 for domestic students, 9/1 priority date for international students. Applications are processed on a rolling basis. *Application fee:* $50 ($100 for international students). Electronic applications accepted. *Application Contact:* Dr. Robert D. Stillman, Associate Dean of Graduate Programs, 214-905-3106, Fax: 972-883-2491, E-mail: stillman@utdallas.edu. *Dean,* Dr. Steven L Small, 972-883-2355, Fax: 972-883-2491, E-mail: small@utdallas.edu.

School of Economic, Political and Policy Sciences Students: 197 full-time (103 women), 177 part-time (92 women); includes 132 minority (37 Black or African American, non-Hispanic/Latino; 1 American Indian or Alaska Native, non-Hispanic/Latino; 32 Asian, non-Hispanic/Latino; 49 Hispanic/Latino; 13 Two or more races, non-Hispanic/Latino), 91 international. Average age 39. 355 applicants, 43% accepted, 76 enrolled. *Faculty:* 62 full-time (14 women), 14 part-time/adjunct (1 woman). Expenses: Contact institution. *Financial support:* In 2018–19, 77 students received support, including 16 research assistantships with partial tuition reimbursements available (averaging $18,830 per year), 76 teaching assistantships with partial tuition reimbursements available (averaging $13,501 per year); fellowships, career-related internships or fieldwork, Federal Work-Study, institutionally sponsored loans, scholarships/grants, and unspecified assistantships also available. Support available to part-time students. Financial award application deadline: 4/30; financial award applicants required to submit FAFSA. In 2018, 122 master's, 31 doctorates awarded. *Program availability:* Part-time, evening/weekend. Offers applied sociology (MS); Constitutional law (MA); criminology (MS, PhD); economic, political and policy sciences (MA, MPA, MPP, MS, PhD); economics (MS, PhD); geospatial information sciences (MS, PhD); international political economy (MS); justice administration and leadership (MS); legislative studies (MA); political science (MA, PhD); public affairs (MPA, PhD); public policy (MPP); public policy and political economy (PhD); social data analytics and research (MS). *Application deadline:* For fall admission, 7/15 for domestic students, 5/1 priority date for international students; for spring admission, 11/15 for domestic students, 9/1 priority date for international students. Applications are processed on a rolling basis. *Application fee:* $50 ($100 for international students). Electronic applications accepted. *Application Contact:* Dr. Alex Piquero, Associate Dean for Graduate Programs, 972-883-2482, Fax: 972-883-6297, E-mail: apiquero@utdallas.edu. *Interim Dean,* Dr. Jennifer S Holmes, 972-883-6852, Fax: 972-883-6297, E-mail: jholmes@utdallas.edu.

School of Interdisciplinary Studies Students: 6 full-time (3 women), 9 part-time (5 women); includes 19 minority (6 Black or African American, non-Hispanic/Latino; 5 Asian, non-Hispanic/Latino; 7 Hispanic/Latino; 1 Native Hawaiian or other Pacific Islander, non-Hispanic/Latino), 1 international. Average age 37. 42 applicants, 81% accepted, 23 enrolled. *Faculty:* 3 full-time (2 women), 3 part-time/adjunct (2 women). Expenses: Contact institution. *Financial support:* Research assistantships with partial tuition reimbursements, teaching assistantships with partial tuition reimbursements, career-related internships or fieldwork, Federal Work-Study, institutionally sponsored loans, and scholarships/grants available. Support available to part-time students. Financial award application deadline: 4/30; financial award applicants required to submit FAFSA. In 2018, 2 master's awarded. *Program availability:* Part-time, evening/weekend. Offers interdisciplinary studies (MA). *Application deadline:* For fall admission, 7/15 for domestic students, 5/1 priority date for international students; for spring admission, 11/15 for domestic students, 9/1 priority date for international students. Applications are processed on a rolling basis. *Application fee:* $50 ($100 for international students). Electronic applications accepted. *Application Contact:* Becky Wiser, Academic Support Coordinator, 972-883-2354, Fax: 972-883-2440, E-mail: rwiser@utdallas.edu. *Dean,* Dr. George Fair, 972-883-2350, Fax: 972-883-2440, E-mail: gwfair@utdallas.edu.

School of Natural Sciences and Mathematics Students: 494 full-time (206 women), 115 part-time (56 women); includes 121 minority (15 Black or African American, non-Hispanic/Latino; 1 American Indian or Alaska Native, non-Hispanic/Latino; 63 Asian, non-Hispanic/Latino; 32 Hispanic/Latino; 10 Two or more races, non-Hispanic/Latino), 324 international. Average age 30. 891 applicants, 30% accepted, 153 enrolled. *Faculty:* 108 full-time (16 women), 14 part-time/adjunct (4 women). Expenses: Contact institution. *Financial support:* In 2018–19, 322 students received support, including 97 research assistantships with partial tuition reimbursements available (averaging $23,666 per year), 255 teaching assistantships with partial tuition reimbursements available

(averaging $17,193 per year); fellowships with partial tuition reimbursements available, career-related internships or fieldwork, Federal Work-Study, institutionally sponsored loans, scholarships/grants, and unspecified assistantships also available. Support available to part-time students. Financial award application deadline: 4/30. In 2018, 116 master's, 60 doctorates awarded. *Program availability:* Part-time, evening/weekend. Offers actuarial science (MS); bioinformatics and computational biology (MS); biotechnology (MS); chemistry and biochemistry (MS, PhD); geosciences (MS, PhD); geosciences - petrology and mineralogy (MS, PhD); geosciences - sedimentology (MS, PhD); geosciences - stratigraphy (MS, PhD); mathematics (MS, PhD); mathematics education (MAT); molecular and cell biology (MS, PhD); natural sciences and mathematics (MAT, MS, PhD); physics (MS, PhD); science education (MAT); statistics (MS, PhD). *Application deadline:* For fall admission, 7/15 for domestic students, 5/1 priority date for international students; for spring admission, 11/15 for domestic students, 9/1 priority date for international students. Applications are processed on a rolling basis. *Application fee:* $50 ($100 for international students). Electronic applications accepted. *Application Contact:* Dr. Mihaela Stefan, Associate Dean for Graduate Studies, 972-883-6581, Fax: 972-883-6371, E-mail: mihaela@utdallas.edu. *Dean,* Dr. Bruce Novak, 972-883-2416, Fax: 972-883-6371, E-mail: bruce.novak@utdallas.edu.

THE UNIVERSITY OF TEXAS AT EL PASO, El Paso, TX 79968-0001

General Information State-supported, coed, university. CGS member. *Graduate housing:* Room and/or apartments available on a first-come, first-served basis to single students; on-campus housing not available to married students.

GRADUATE UNITS

Graduate School *Program availability:* Part-time, evening/weekend, online learning. Electronic applications accepted.

College of Business Administration Program availability: Part-time, evening/weekend, online learning. Offers accounting (M Acc); business administration (M Acc, MBA, MS, PhD, Certificate); economics (MS); international business (PhD). Electronic applications accepted.

College of Education Program availability: Part-time, evening/weekend, online learning. Offers education (M Ed, MA, Ed D, PhD); educational administration (M Ed); educational diagnostics (M Ed); educational leadership and administration (Ed D); guidance and counseling (M Ed); instruction (M Ed); reading education (M Ed); special education (M Ed); teaching, learning, and culture (PhD). Electronic applications accepted.

College of Engineering Program availability: Part-time, evening/weekend. Offers civil engineering (MS, PhD); computer engineering (MS); computer science (MS, PhD); construction management (MS, Certificate); cyber security (Graduate Certificate); electric power and energy systems (Graduate Certificate); electrical and computer engineering (PhD); electrical engineering (MS); engineering (M Eng, MEENE, MS, MSENE, MSIT, PhD, Certificate, Graduate Certificate); environmental engineering (MEENE, MSENE); environmental science and engineering (PhD); industrial engineering (MS); information technology (MSIT); manufacturing engineering (MS); materials science and engineering (PhD); mechanical engineering (MS); metallurgical and materials engineering (MS); software engineering (MS); systems engineering (MS). Electronic applications accepted.

College of Health Sciences Program availability: Part-time, evening/weekend, online learning. Offers health sciences (MOT, MPH, MRC, MS, MSN, MSW, DPT, PhD, Graduate Certificate); interdisciplinary health sciences (PhD); kinesiology (MS); occupational therapy (MOT); physical therapy (DPT); public health sciences (MPH, Graduate Certificate); rehabilitation counseling (MRC); social work in the border region (MSW); speech-language pathology (MS). Electronic applications accepted.

College of Liberal Arts Program availability: Part-time, evening/weekend, online learning. Offers applied anthropology (Certificate); applied social sciences (Certificate); art education (MA); bilingual professional writing (Certificate); borderlands history (MA, PhD); clinical psychology (MA); communication (MA); creative writing (MFA); creative writing of the Americas (MFA); English and American literature (MA); experimental psychology (MA); history (MA); interdisciplinary studies (MAIS); liberal arts (MA, MAIS, MAT, MFA, MM, PhD, Certificate); linguistics (MA); music education (MM); music performance (MM); philosophy (MA); political science (MA); psychology (PhD); rhetoric and composition (PhD); rhetoric and writing studies (MA); sociology (MA); Spanish (MA); studio art (MA); teaching English (MAT); teaching English to speakers of other languages (Certificate). Electronic applications accepted.

College of Science Program availability: Part-time, evening/weekend. Offers bioinformatics (MS); biological sciences (MS, PhD); chemistry (MS, PhD); geological sciences (MS, PhD); geophysics (MS); mathematics (MAT, MS); physics (MS); science (MAT, MS, PhD); statistics (MS). Electronic applications accepted.

School of Nursing Program availability: Online learning. Offers family nurse practitioner (MSN); health care leadership and management (Certificate); interdisciplinary health sciences (PhD); nursing (DNP); nursing education (MSN, Certificate); nursing systems management (MSN). Electronic applications accepted.

THE UNIVERSITY OF TEXAS AT SAN ANTONIO, San Antonio, TX 78249-0617

General Information State-supported, coed, university. CGS member. *Graduate housing:* Room and/or apartments available on a first-come, first-served basis to single students; on-campus housing not available to married students. *Research affiliation:* Air Force Research Laboratory (information assurance and security), Carnegie Mellon University/National Security Agency (computer security), National Science Foundation (virtual reality, computer architecture, real-time systems), Cancer Prevention and Research Institute of Texas (chemistry), Army Research Laboratory (computer science, management science and statistics, electrical engineering), CPS Energy (engineering).

GRADUATE UNITS

College of Architecture, Construction and Planning *Program availability:* Part-time. Offers architecture (M Arch, MS Arch); architecture, construction and planning (M Arch, MS, MS Arch); urban and regional planning (MS). Electronic applications accepted.

College of Business *Program availability:* Part-time, evening/weekend. Offers accounting (M Acy, PhD); applied statistics (MS, PhD); business (M Acy, MA, MBA, MS, MSIT, PhD, Certificate); business economics (MBA); cyber security (MSIT); economics (MA); finance (MBA, MS, PhD); information technology (MS, PhD); management and organization studies (PhD); management of technology (MBA); management science (MBA); marketing (PhD); marketing management (MBA); technology entrepreneurship and management (Certificate); tourism destination development (MBA). Electronic applications accepted.

College of Education and Human Development *Program availability:* Part-time, evening/weekend, online learning. Offers applied behavior analysis (Certificate); bicultural and bilingual studies (MA); counselor education and supervision (PhD);

culture, literacy, and language (PhD); education (MA); education and human development (M Ed, MA, MS, Ed D, PhD, Certificate); educational leadership (Ed D); educational leadership and policy studies (M Ed); educational psychology (MA); health and kinesiology (MS); interdisciplinary learning and teaching (PhD); language acquisition and bilingual psychoeducational assessment (Certificate); school counseling (M Ed); school psychology (MA); teaching English as a second language (MA). Electronic applications accepted.

College of Engineering *Program availability:* Part-time, evening/weekend. Offers advanced manufacturing and enterprise engineering (MS); advanced materials engineering (MS); biomedical engineering (MS, PhD); civil engineering (MCE, MSCE); computer engineering (MS); electrical engineering (MSEE, PhD); engineering (MCE, MS, MSCE, MSEE, PhD); environmental science and engineering (PhD); mechanical engineering (MS, PhD). Electronic applications accepted.

College of Liberal and Fine Arts Offers anthropology (MA, PhD); art (MFA); art history (MA); communication (MA); English (MA, PhD); geography (MA); history (MA); liberal and fine arts (MA, MFA, MM, MS, PhD); music (MM); philosophy and classics (MA); political science (MA); psychology (MS, PhD); sociology (MS); Spanish (MA). Electronic applications accepted.

College of Public Policy *Program availability:* Part-time, evening/weekend. Offers applied demography (PhD); criminology (MS); public administration (MPA); public policy (MPA, MS, MSW, PhD); social work (MSW). Electronic applications accepted.

College of Sciences Offers applied mathematics (MS); biology (MS); biotechnology (MS); cell and molecular biology (PhD); chemistry (MS, PhD); computer science (MS, PhD); environmental science and ecology (MS); geological sciences (MS); mathematics (MS); mathematics education (MS); neurobiology (PhD); physics (MS, PhD); sciences (MS, PhD). Electronic applications accepted.

Joint PhD Program in Translational Science *Program availability:* Part-time. Offers translational science (PhD). Program offered in partnership with The University of Texas Health Science Center at San Antonio, The University of Texas at Austin, and The University of Texas Health Science Center at Houston. Electronic applications accepted.

THE UNIVERSITY OF TEXAS AT TYLER, Tyler, TX 75799-0001

General Information State-supported, coed, comprehensive institution. *Enrollment:* 287 full-time matriculated graduate/professional students (168 women), 642 part-time matriculated graduate/professional students (414 women). *Enrollment by degree level:* 890 master's, 39 doctoral. *Graduate faculty:* 165 full-time (63 women). *Graduate housing:* Rooms and/or apartments available on a first-come, first-served basis to single and married students. *Student services:* Campus employment opportunities, campus safety program, career counseling, exercise/wellness program, free psychological counseling, grant writing training, services for students with disabilities, teacher training, writing training. *Library facilities:* Robert Muntz Library.

Computer facilities: A campuswide network can be accessed from student residence rooms and from off campus. Online class registration is available.
Website: http://www.uttyler.edu/

General Application Contact: Office of Graduate Admissions, 903-566-7457, Fax: 903-566-7492, E-mail: ogs@uttyler.edu.

GRADUATE UNITS

Ben and Maytee Fisch College of Pharmacy Expenses: Contact institution. Offers pharmacy (Pharm D). *Application Contact:* Jennifer Engel, Admissions Representative, 903-565-5777, E-mail: pharmacy@uttyler.edu. *Dean,* Dr. Lane J. Brunner, 903-566-6153, E-mail: lbrunner@uttyler.edu.

College of Arts and Sciences Average age 31. 60 applicants, 90% accepted, 39 enrolled. Expenses: Contact institution. *Financial support:* In 2018–19, 7 students received support. Fellowships, research assistantships, teaching assistantships, and Federal Work-Study available. Support available to part-time students. Financial award application deadline: 7/1; financial award applicants required to submit FAFSA. In 2018, 29 master's awarded. *Program availability:* Part-time, evening/weekend, online learning. Offers art history (MA); arts and sciences (MA, MAIS, MAT, MFA, MPA, MS, MSIS); biology (MS); communication (MA); criminal justice (MS); English (MA); history (MA); interdisciplinary (MAIS); interdisciplinary studies (MAIS, MSIS); mathematics (MS, MSIS); public administration (MPA); sociology (MS); studio art (MFA). *Application deadline:* Applications are processed on a rolling basis. *Application fee:* $0. Electronic applications accepted. *Application Contact:* Dr. Neil Gray, Dean, 903-566-7368. *Dean,* Dr. Neil Gray, 903-566-7368.

College of Education and Psychology Students: 87 full-time (69 women), 162 part-time (118 women); includes 20 minority (14 Black or African American, non-Hispanic/Latino; 2 American Indian or Alaska Native, non-Hispanic/Latino; 4 Hispanic/Latino), 2 international. Average age 34. 134 applicants, 89% accepted, 80 enrolled. Expenses: Contact institution. *Financial support:* Research assistantships, teaching assistantships, career-related internships or fieldwork, Federal Work-Study, institutionally sponsored loans, and scholarships/grants available. Support available to part-time students. Financial award application deadline: 4/1; financial award applicants required to submit FAFSA. In 2018, 75 master's awarded. *Program availability:* Part-time, evening/weekend. Offers clinical psychology (MS); counseling psychology (MA); education and psychology (M Ed, MA, MS, MSIS); interdisciplinary studies (MSIS); school counseling (MA). *Application fee:* $0 ($50 for international students). *Application Contact:* Dr. Wes Hickey, Dean, 903-565-5669, E-mail: whickey@uttyler.edu. *Dean,* Dr. Wes Hickey, 903-565-5669, E-mail: whickey@uttyler.edu.

School of Education Students: 4 full-time (3 women), 30 part-time (all women); includes 4 minority (3 Black or African American, non-Hispanic/Latino; 1 Hispanic/Latino), 2 international. Average age 37. 13 applicants, 100% accepted, 6 enrolled. Expenses: Contact institution. *Financial support:* In 2018–19, 2 research assistantships (averaging $12,000 per year) were awarded; scholarships/grants also available. Financial award application deadline: 7/1. In 2018, 14 master's awarded. *Program availability:* Part-time, evening/weekend. Offers early childhood education (M Ed, MA); reading (M Ed, MA); special education (M Ed, MA). *Application deadline:* For fall admission, 8/17 priority date for domestic students, 7/1 priority date for international students; for spring admission, 12/21 priority date for domestic students, 11/1 priority date for international students. Applications are processed on a rolling basis. *Application fee:* $25 ($50 for international students). Electronic applications accepted. *Application Contact:* Dr. Wes Hickey, Dean, 903-565-5669, E-mail: whickey@uttyler.edu. *Dean,* Dr. Wes Hickey, 903-565-5669, E-mail: whickey@uttyler.edu.

College of Engineering Average age 27. 67 applicants, 82% accepted, 12 enrolled. Expenses: Contact institution. *Financial support:* In 2018–19, 9 research assistantships with tuition reimbursements (averaging $2,333 per year), 11 teaching assistantships (averaging $2,333 per year) were awarded. Financial award application deadline: 7/1; financial award applicants required to submit FAFSA. In 2018, 14 master's awarded. *Program availability:* Part-time. Offers electrical engineering (MS); engineering (MS,

MSIS); environmental engineering (MS); industrial safety (MS); mechanical engineering (MS); structural engineering (MS); transportation engineering (MS); water resources engineering (MS). *Application deadline:* Applications are processed on a rolling basis. *Application fee:* $25 ($50 for international students). Electronic applications accepted. *Application Contact:* Dr. Javier Kypuros, Dean, 903-566-6121, E-mail: jkypuros@uttyler.edu. *Dean,* Dr. Javier Kypuros, 903-566-6121, E-mail: jkypuros@uttyler.edu.

College of Nursing and Health Sciences Students: 49 full-time (40 women), 194 part-time (163 women); includes 45 minority (25 Black or African American, non-Hispanic/Latino; 3 American Indian or Alaska Native, non-Hispanic/Latino; 7 Asian, non-Hispanic/Latino; 10 Hispanic/Latino). Average age 35. 95 applicants, 77% accepted, 42 enrolled. Expenses: Contact institution. *Financial support:* Fellowships, research assistantships, and teaching assistantships available. In 2018, 45 master's awarded. *Program availability:* Part-time, evening/weekend, online learning. Offers health and kinesiology (M Ed, MA); health sciences (MS); kinesiology (MS); nurse practitioner (MSN); nursing (PhD); nursing administration (MSN); nursing and health sciences (M Ed, MA, MS, MSN, PhD); nursing education (MSN). *Application deadline:* Applications are processed on a rolling basis. *Application fee:* $0. Electronic applications accepted. *Application Contact:* Dr. Yong Tai Wang, Dean, 903-566-7075, Fax: 903-566-7075, E-mail: ywang@uttyler.edu. *Dean,* Dr. Yong Tai Wang, 903-566-7075, Fax: 903-566-7075, E-mail: ywang@uttyler.edu.

Soules College of Business Average age 32. 107 applicants, 96% accepted, 58 enrolled. Expenses: Contact institution. *Financial support:* Research assistantships and career-related internships or fieldwork available. Financial award application deadline: 7/1. In 2018, 68 master's awarded. *Program availability:* Part-time, evening/weekend, online learning. Offers accountancy (M Acc); business (M Acc, MBA, MS, PhD); computer science (MS); cyber security (MBA); engineering management (MBA); general management (MBA); healthcare management (MBA); human resource development (MS, PhD); industrial management (MS); internal assurance and consulting (MBA); marketing (MBA); oil, gas and energy (MBA); organizational development (MBA); quality management (MBA). *Application deadline:* Applications are processed on a rolling basis. *Application fee:* $0 ($50 for international students). Electronic applications accepted. *Application Contact:* Dr. Robert Beatty, Dean, 903-566-7360. *Dean,* Dr. Robert Beatty, 903-566-7360.

THE UNIVERSITY OF TEXAS HEALTH SCIENCE CENTER AT HOUSTON, Houston, TX 77225-0036

General Information State-supported, coed, upper-level institution. *Graduate housing:* On-campus housing not available.

GRADUATE UNITS

Cizik School of Nursing *Program availability:* Part-time. Offers nursing (MSN, DNP, PhD). Electronic applications accepted.

McGovern Medical School Offers medicine (MD). Electronic applications accepted.

MD Anderson UTHealth Graduate School Offers biochemistry and cell biology (PhD); biomedical sciences (MS); cancer biology (PhD); genetic counseling (MS); genetics and epigenetics (PhD); immunology (PhD); medical physics (MS, PhD); microbiology and infectious diseases (PhD); neuroscience (PhD); quantitative sciences (PhD); therapeutics and pharmacology (PhD). Electronic applications accepted.

School of Biomedical Informatics Students: 62 full-time (42 women), 224 part-time (120 women); includes 152 minority (43 Black or African American, non-Hispanic/Latino; 2 American Indian or Alaska Native, non-Hispanic/Latino; 59 Asian, non-Hispanic/Latino; 42 Hispanic/Latino; 3 Native Hawaiian or other Pacific Islander, non-Hispanic/Latino; 3 Two or more races, non-Hispanic/Latino). Average age 36. 136 applicants, 77% accepted, 52 enrolled. *Faculty:* 29 full-time (10 women), 11 part-time/adjunct (2 women). Expenses: Contact institution. *Financial support:* In 2018–19, 59 students received support, including 50 research assistantships (averaging $22,376 per year), 10 teaching assistantships (averaging $11,600 per year); career-related internships or fieldwork, institutionally sponsored loans, scholarships/grants, health care benefits, and unspecified assistantships also available. Support available to part-time students. Financial award application deadline: 5/1; financial award applicants required to submit FAFSA. In 2018, 48 master's, 4 doctorates awarded. *Program availability:* Part-time, 100% online, blended/hybrid learning. Offers applied biomedical informatics (MS, Certificate); biomedical informatics (MS, PhD, Certificate); health data science (Certificate); public health informatics (Certificate). *Application deadline:* For fall admission, 7/1 for domestic and international students; for spring admission, 11/1 for domestic and international students; for summer admission, 3/1 for domestic and international students. Applications are processed on a rolling basis. *Application fee:* $60. Electronic applications accepted. *Application Contact:* Jaime Hargrave, Director, Student Affairs, 713-500-3920, Fax: 713-500-0360, E-mail: jaime.n.hargrave@uth.tmc.edu. *Dean/Chair in Informatics Excellence,* Dr. Jiajie Zhang, 713-500-3922, E-mail: jiajie.zhang@uth.tmc.edu.

School of Dentistry Offers dentistry (MS, DDS). Electronic applications accepted.

School of Public Health *Program availability:* Part-time. Offers behavioral science (PhD); biostatistics (MPH, MS, PhD); environmental health (MPH); epidemiology (MPH, MS, PhD); general public health (Certificate); genomics and bioinformatics (Certificate); health disparities (Certificate); health promotion/health education (MPH, Dr PH); healthcare management (Certificate); management, policy and community health (MPH, Dr PH, PhD); maternal and child health (Certificate); public health informatics (Certificate). Specific programs are offered at each of our six campuses in Texas (Austin, Brownsville, Dallas, El Paso, Houston, and San Antonio). Electronic applications accepted.

THE UNIVERSITY OF TEXAS HEALTH SCIENCE CENTER AT SAN ANTONIO, San Antonio, TX 78229-3900

General Information State-supported, coed, upper-level institution. CGS member. *Research affiliation:* University Hospital, Southwest Research Institute, Southwest Foundation for Biomedical Research, Veterans Administration Hospital.

GRADUATE UNITS

Graduate School of Biomedical Sciences Offers biochemistry (MS, PhD); biomedical engineering (MS, PhD); biomedical sciences (MS, PhD); cellular and structural biology (MS, PhD); clinical investigation (MS); dental science (MS); integrated biomedical sciences (PhD); microbiology and immunology (MS, PhD); molecular medicine (MS, PhD); neuroscience (PhD); nursing science (PhD); radiological sciences (PhD); toxicology (MS); translational science (PhD).

Joe R. and Teresa Lozano Long School of Medicine Offers deaf education and hearing (MS); medicine (MD). Electronic applications accepted.

School of Health Professions Offers occupational therapy (MOT); physical therapy (DPT); physician assistant studies (MS); speech language pathology (MS).

School of Nursing *Program availability:* Part-time. Offers administrative management (MSN); adult-gerontology acute care nurse practitioner (PGC); advanced practice leadership (DNP); clinical nurse leader (MSN); executive administrative management (DNP); family nurse practitioner (MSN, PGC); nursing (MSN, PhD); nursing education (MSN, PGC); pediatric nurse practitioner care (PGC); psychiatric mental health nurse practitioner (PGC); public health nurse leader (DNP).

UT Health San Antonio School of Dentistry Students: 497 full-time (261 women), 33 part-time (13 women); includes 247 minority (17 Black or African American, non-Hispanic/Latino; 94 Asian, non-Hispanic/Latino; 126 Hispanic/Latino; 10 Two or more races, non-Hispanic/Latino), 23 international. Average age 27. 1,433 applicants, 15% accepted, 100 enrolled. *Faculty:* 96 full-time (35 women), 84 part-time/adjunct (19 women). Expenses: Contact institution. *Financial support:* In 2018–19, 89 students received support, including 3 research assistantships (averaging $5,836 per year), 86 teaching assistantships (averaging $14,893 per year). Financial award application deadline: 3/1; financial award applicants required to submit FAFSA. In 2018, 17 master's, 113 doctorates, 42 other advanced degrees awarded. Offers dentistry (MS, DDS, Certificate). *Application deadline:* For fall admission, 10/1 for domestic students. Applications are processed on a rolling basis. *Application fee:* $150. Electronic applications accepted. *Application Contact:* Dr. Kay Malone, Director of Admissions, 210-567-3180, Fax: 210-567-6721, E-mail: dsadmissions@uthscsa.edu. *Director of Admissions*, Dr. Kay Malone, 210-567-3180, Fax: 210-567-6721, E-mail: dsadmissions@uthscsa.edu.

THE UNIVERSITY OF TEXAS HEALTH SCIENCE CENTER AT TYLER, Tyler, TX 75708

General Information State-supported, coed, graduate-only institution.

GRADUATE UNITS

School of Community and Rural Health Offers health administration (MHA); public health (MPH).

School of Medical Biological Sciences Offers biotechnology (MS).

THE UNIVERSITY OF TEXAS MD ANDERSON CANCER CENTER, Houston, TX 77030

General Information State-supported, coed, upper-level institution. CGS member.

GRADUATE UNITS

School of Health Professions Offers diagnostic genetics (MS).

THE UNIVERSITY OF TEXAS MEDICAL BRANCH, Galveston, TX 77555

General Information State-supported, coed, comprehensive institution. CGS member. *Graduate housing:* Rooms and/or apartments available on a first-come, first-served basis to single and married students. *Research affiliation:* Shriners Hospitals (burns and wound healing).

GRADUATE UNITS

Graduate School of Biomedical Sciences Offers biochemistry (PhD); bioinformatics (PhD); biomedical sciences (MA, MMS, MPH, MS, PhD); biophysics (PhD); cell biology (PhD); clinical science (MS, PhD); computational biology (PhD); experimental pathology (PhD); human pathophysiology and translational medicine (MS, PhD); medical humanities (MA, PhD); medical science (MMS); microbiology and immunology (MS, PhD); molecular biophysics education (PhD); neuroscience (PhD); nursing (PhD); pharmacology (MS); pharmacology and toxicology (PhD); population health sciences (PhD); public health (MPH); rehabilitation sciences (PhD); structural biology (PhD). Electronic applications accepted.

School of Health Professions Offers health professions (MOT, MPAS, MPT, DPT); occupational therapy (MOT); physical therapy (MPT, DPT); physician assistant studies (MPAS). Electronic applications accepted.

School of Medicine Offers medicine (MD).

School of Nursing *Program availability:* Part-time, online learning. Offers nursing (MSN, PhD). Electronic applications accepted.

THE UNIVERSITY OF TEXAS OF THE PERMIAN BASIN, Odessa, TX 79762-0001

General Information State-supported, coed, comprehensive institution. *Graduate housing:* Rooms and/or apartments available on a first-come, first-served basis to single and married students. Housing application deadline: 6/15.

GRADUATE UNITS

Office of Graduate Studies *Program availability:* Part-time, evening/weekend.

College of Arts and Sciences Program availability: Part-time, evening/weekend. Offers arts and sciences (MA, MS); biology (MS); clinical psychology (MA); computer science (MS); criminal justice administration (MS); English (MA); experimental psychology (MA); geology (MS); history (MA); kinesiology (MS); political science (MPA); Spanish (MA).

College of Business Program availability: Part-time, evening/weekend. Offers accountancy (MPA); business (MBA, MPA); management (MBA).

School of Education Offers bilingual/English as a second language education (MA); counseling (MA); early childhood education (MA); education (MA); educational leadership (MA); professional education (MA); reading (MA); special education (MA).

THE UNIVERSITY OF TEXAS RIO GRANDE VALLEY, Edinburg, TX 78539

General Information State-supported, coed, university. CGS member. *Enrollment:* 28,644 graduate, professional, and undergraduate students; 1,062 full-time matriculated graduate/professional students (659 women), 2,460 part-time matriculated graduate/professional students (1,602 women). *Enrollment by degree level:* 3,083 master's, 439 doctoral. *Graduate faculty:* 421 full-time (193 women), 49 part-time/adjunct (18 women). *International tuition:* $14,484 full-time. *Tuition, area resident:* Full-time $6888. Tuition, state resident: full-time $6888. Tuition, nonresident: full-time $14,484. *Required fees:* $1468. *Graduate housing:* Rooms and/or apartments available on a first-come, first-served basis to single and married students. Housing application deadline: 7/1. *Student services:* Campus employment opportunities, campus safety program, career counseling, child daycare facilities, exercise/wellness program, free psychological counseling, international student services, services for students with disabilities, teacher training, writing training. *Library facilities:* University Library. *Collection:* Students can reserve study rooms.

Computer facilities: A campuswide network can be accessed from student residence rooms and from off campus. Online class registration is available. Website: http://www.utrgv.edu.

General Application Contact: Stephanie Ozuna, Assoc Dir Graduate Studies, 956-665-3558, E-mail: stephanie.ozuna@utrgv.edu.

GRADUATE UNITS

College of Education and P-16 Integration *Program availability:* Part-time, evening/weekend. Offers bilingual education (M Ed); clinical mental health counseling (M Ed); curriculum and instruction (M Ed, Ed D); early childhood education (M Ed); early childhood special education (M Ed); education and P-16 integration (M Ed, MA, Ed D); educational leadership (M Ed, Ed D); educational technology (M Ed); reading and literacy (M Ed); school counseling (M Ed); school psychology (MA); special education (M Ed). Electronic applications accepted.

College of Engineering and Computer Science *Program availability:* Part-time, blended/hybrid learning. Offers computer science (MS); electrical engineering (MSE); engineering and computer science (MS, MSE); engineering management (MS); information technology (MS); manufacturing engineering (MS); mechanical engineering (MSE). Electronic applications accepted.

College of Fine Arts Offers creative writing (MFA); fine arts (MFA, MM).

School of Art Program availability: Part-time. Offers art (MFA).

School of Music Program availability: Part-time. Offers music (MM).

College of Health Affairs *Program availability:* Part-time, evening/weekend. Offers clinical laboratory sciences (MSHS); communication sciences and disorders (MS); exercise science (MS); health affairs (MPAS, MS, MSHS, MSN, MSSW, PhD, Post Master's Certificate); health care administration (MSHS); kinesiology (MS); nutrition (MSHS); occupational therapy (MS); primary care (MPAS).

School of Rehabilitation Services and Counseling Students: 100 full-time (21 women), 91 part-time (20 women); includes 170 minority (3 Black or African American, non-Hispanic/Latino; 1 Asian, non-Hispanic/Latino; 166 Hispanic/Latino), 3 international. 88 applicants, 67% accepted, 54 enrolled. *Faculty:* 16 full-time (8 women), 1 (woman) part-time/adjunct. Expenses: Contact institution. *Financial support:* In 2018–19, 60 students received support, including 12 research assistantships (averaging $25,500 per year), 10 teaching assistantships (averaging $12,600 per year); career-related internships or fieldwork, Federal Work-Study, institutionally sponsored loans, scholarships/grants, traineeships, and unspecified assistantships also available. In 2018, 54 master's, 8 doctorates awarded. *Program availability:* Part-time, evening/weekend. Offers rehabilitation services and counseling (MS, PhD). *Application deadline:* For fall admission, 2/15 for domestic and international students; for spring admission, 10/15 for domestic and international students; for summer admission, 2/15 for domestic and international students. *Application fee:* $50. Electronic applications accepted. *Application Contact:* Dr. Elizabeth Chavez-Palacios, Clinical Assistant Professor/Graduate Coordinator, 956-665-3734, Fax: 956-665-5237, E-mail: elizabeth.palacios@utrgv.edu. *Director/Professor*, Dr. Bruce Reed, 956-665-3734, Fax: 956-665-5237, E-mail: bruce.reed@utrgv.edu.

College of Liberal Arts *Program availability:* Part-time, evening/weekend. Offers communication (MA); criminal justice (MS); disaster studies (MA); English (MA); English as a second language (MA); global security studies and leadership (MPA); history (MA, MAIS); interdisciplinary studies (MAIS, MSIS); liberal arts (MA, MAIS, MPA, MS, MSIS); psychology (MA); public administration (MPA); public policy and management (MPA); sociology (MS); Spanish (MA); Spanish translation and interpreting (MA).

College of Sciences *Program availability:* Part-time, evening/weekend. Offers biology (MS); chemistry (MS); physics (MS); sciences (MS, MSIS). Electronic applications accepted.

School of Earth, Environmental, and Marine Sciences Offers agricultural, environmental, and sustainability sciences (MS); ocean, coastal, and earth sciences (MS).

School of Mathematical and Statistical Sciences Program availability: Part-time, evening/weekend. Offers mathematics (MS). Electronic applications accepted.

Robert C. Vackar College of Business and Entrepreneurship *Program availability:* Part-time, evening/weekend. Offers accounting (M Acc, MS); business administration (MBA); business and entrepreneurship (M Acc, MBA, MS, PhD); finance (PhD); management (PhD); marketing (PhD).

School of Medicine *Program availability:* Part-time, evening/weekend, online learning. Offers medicine (MD).

THE UNIVERSITY OF TEXAS SOUTHWESTERN MEDICAL CENTER, Dallas, TX 75390

General Information State-supported, coed, graduate-only institution. CGS member. *Graduate housing:* Rooms and/or apartments available on a first-come, first-served basis to single and married students.

GRADUATE UNITS

Southwestern Graduate School of Biomedical Sciences Offers biomedical sciences (MCS, MS, MSCS, PhD); clinical psychology (PhD); clinical science (MCS, MSCS); medical scientist training (PhD). Electronic applications accepted.

Division of Basic Science Offers biological chemistry (PhD); biomedical engineering (MS, PhD); cancer biology (PhD); cell regulation (PhD); genetics and development (PhD); immunology (PhD); integrative biology (PhD); molecular biophysics (PhD); molecular microbiology (PhD); neuroscience (PhD). Electronic applications accepted.

Southwestern Medical School Offers medicine (MD). Electronic applications accepted.

Southwestern School of Health Professions Offers clinical nutrition (MCN); health professions (MCN, MPAS, MPO, MRC, DPT); physical therapy (DPT); physician assistant studies (MPAS); prosthetics - orthotics (MPO); rehabilitation counseling psychology (MRC).

THE UNIVERSITY OF THE ARTS, Philadelphia, PA 19102-4944

General Information Independent, coed, comprehensive institution. *Graduate housing:* Room and/or apartments available to single students; on-campus housing not available to married students. Housing application deadline: 6/1. *Research affiliation:* The Franklin Institute (general science education), Philadelphia Museum of Art (arts and culture), School District of Philadelphia (education), Ben Franklin Technology Partners (high tech department and creative/cultural production in Philadelphia).

GRADUATE UNITS

College of Art, Media and Design *Program availability:* Part-time. Offers art, media and design (M Des, MA, MAT, MFA); book arts and printmaking (MFA); museum education (MA); museum exhibition planning and design (MFA); museum studies (MA); product design (M Des); studio art (MFA); visual arts (MAT). Electronic applications accepted.

College of Performing Arts *Program availability:* Part-time. Offers devised performance (MFA, Certificate); performing arts (MAT, MFA, MM, Certificate).

School of Dance Offers dance (MFA).

School of Music Program availability: Part-time. Offers jazz studies (MM); music education (MAT, MM). Electronic applications accepted.

UNIVERSITY OF THE CUMBERLANDS, Williamsburg, KY 40769-1372

General Information Independent-religious, coed, university. *Graduate housing:* Room and/or apartments available on a first-come, first-served basis to single students; on-campus housing not available to married students.

GRADUATE UNITS

Graduate Programs in Education *Program availability:* Part-time, evening/weekend, online learning. Offers all grades (P-12) (M Ed); business and marketing (MA Ed, MAT); counselor education and supervision (Ed D); director of pupil personnel (Certificate); director of special education (Certificate); educational administration and supervision (Ed S); educational leadership (Ed D); elementary education (MA Ed, MAT); instructional leadership - principalship (MA Ed); instructional leadership - school principal (Certificate); middle school education (MA Ed, MAT); reading and writing (MA Ed); school counseling (MA Ed); school superintendent (Certificate); secondary education (MA Ed, MAT); special education (MAT); supervisor of instruction (Certificate); teacher leader (MA Ed). Electronic applications accepted.

Hutton School of Business *Program availability:* Part-time, online learning. Offers accounting (MBA); business (MBA). Electronic applications accepted.

Program in Christian Studies *Program availability:* Part-time, evening/weekend, online learning. Offers Christian studies (MA). Electronic applications accepted.

Program in Clinical Psychology *Program availability:* Part-time, evening/weekend, online learning. Offers clinical psychology (PhD).

Program in Physician Assistant Studies Offers physician assistant studies (MPAS). Electronic applications accepted.

Program in Professional Counseling *Program availability:* Part-time, evening/weekend, online learning. Offers professional counseling (MA). Program also offered in San Francisco. Electronic applications accepted.

UNIVERSITY OF THE DISTRICT OF COLUMBIA, Washington, DC 20008-1175

General Information District-supported, coed, comprehensive institution. CGS member.

GRADUATE UNITS

College of Agriculture, Urban Sustainability and Environmental Sciences Offers agriculture, urban sustainability and environmental sciences (M Arch, M Arch II, MS, PSM); architecture (M Arch, M Arch II); nutrition and dietetics (MS); water resources management (PSM).

College of Arts and Sciences *Program availability:* Part-time, evening/weekend. Offers adult education (Graduate Certificate); arts and sciences (MA, MAT, MS, Graduate Certificate); cancer biology, prevention and control (MS); counseling (MS); early childhood education (MA); elementary education (MAT); homeland security (MS); middle school mathematics (MAT); rehabilitation counseling (MA); secondary English language arts (MAT); secondary social studies (MAT); speech-language pathology (MS).

David A. Clarke School of Law Students: 123 full-time (83 women), 133 part-time (80 women); includes 158 minority (100 Black or African American, non-Hispanic/Latino; 1 American Indian or Alaska Native, non-Hispanic/Latino; 25 Asian, non-Hispanic/Latino; 32 Hispanic/Latino), 2 international. Average age 28. 675 applicants, 20% accepted, 94 enrolled. *Faculty:* 21 full-time (9 women), 22 part-time/adjunct (12 women). Expenses: Contact institution. *Financial support:* In 2018–19, 172 students received support, including 46 fellowships (averaging $4,250 per year), 4 research assistantships (averaging $3,000 per year), 39 teaching assistantships (averaging $3,000 per year); Federal Work-Study and scholarships/grants also available. Financial award application deadline: 3/15; financial award applicants required to submit FAFSA. In 2018, 64 doctorates awarded. *Program availability:* Part-time, evening/weekend. Offers clinical teaching and social justice (LL M); law (JD). *Application deadline:* For fall admission, 3/15 priority date for domestic and international students. Applications are processed on a rolling basis. *Application fee:* $35. Electronic applications accepted. *Application Contact:* Jino Ray, Associate Dean of Admission, 202-274-7336, Fax: 202-274-5583, E-mail: jino.ray@udc.edu. *Dean,* Renee M. Hutchins, 202-274-7346, Fax: 202-274-5583, E-mail: renee.hutchins@udc.edu.

School of Business and Public Administration *Program availability:* Part-time, evening/weekend. Offers business administration (MBA); business and public administration (MBA, MPA); public administration (MPA).

School of Engineering and Applied Sciences Offers computer science (MS, MSCS); electrical engineering (MSEE); engineering and applied sciences (MSCS, MSEE).

UNIVERSITY OF THE FRASER VALLEY, Abbotsford, BC V2S 7M8, Canada

General Information Province-supported, coed, comprehensive institution. *Enrollment:* 46 full-time matriculated graduate/professional students (32 women), 38 part-time matriculated graduate/professional students (27 women). *Enrollment by degree level:* 75 master's, 9 advanced degrees. *Graduate faculty:* 23 full-time (13 women). *International tuition:* $16,850 Canadian dollars full-time. *Tuition, area resident:* Full-time $7056 Canadian dollars. Tuition, province resident: full-time $7056 Canadian dollars. Tuition, Canadian resident: full-time $8925 Canadian dollars. *Required fees:* $558 Canadian dollars. One-time fee: $78 Canadian dollars full-time. *Graduate housing:* Room and/or apartments available on a first-come, first-served basis to single students; on-campus housing not available to married students. Typical cost: $6040 Canadian dollars per year ($8040 Canadian dollars including board). Housing application deadline: 5/15. *Student services:* Campus employment opportunities, campus safety program, career counseling, exercise/wellness program, free psychological counseling, grant writing training, international student services, low-cost health insurance, services for students with disabilities, writing training. *Library facilities:* Peter Jones Library plus 3 others. Collection: Books: 181,000 (physical), 37,000 (digital/electronic). Students can reserve study rooms.

Computer facilities: Online class registration is available.
Website: http://www.ufv.ca/

General Application Contact: Educational Advisors, 604-854-4528, Fax: 604-855-7614, E-mail: advising@ufv.ca.

GRADUATE UNITS

Graduate Studies Students: 46 full-time (32 women), 38 part-time (27 women); includes 26 minority (all American Indian or Alaska Native, non-Hispanic/Latino). Average age 40. 65 applicants, 89% accepted, 58 enrolled. *Faculty:* 23 full-time (13 women). Expenses: Contact institution. *Financial support:* Research assistantships, scholarships/grants, health care benefits, and bursaries available. Financial award application deadline: 5/10. In 2018, 27 master's awarded. *Program availability:* Evening/weekend. Offers criminal justice (MA); social work (MSW). *Application deadline:*

For fall admission, 1/31 priority date for domestic students, 4/1 priority date for international students; for winter admission, 8/31 priority date for domestic students; for spring admission, 12/31 priority date for domestic students. *Application fee:* $75 ($250 for international students). Electronic applications accepted. *Application Contact:* Educational Advisors, 604-854-4528, Fax: 604-855-7614, E-mail: advising@ufv.ca. *Associate Vice President for Research, Engagement and Graduate Studies,* Dr. Garry Fehr, 604-504-4074, Fax: 778-880-0356, E-mail: Garry.Fehr@ufv.ca.

UNIVERSITY OF THE INCARNATE WORD, San Antonio, TX 78209-6397

General Information Independent-religious, coed, comprehensive institution. *Enrollment:* 8,263 graduate, professional, and undergraduate students; 2,098 full-time matriculated graduate/professional students (1,245 women), 588 part-time matriculated graduate/professional students (289 women). *Enrollment by degree level:* 1,263 master's, 1,423 doctoral. *Graduate faculty:* 153 full-time (84 women), 75 part-time/adjunct (39 women). *Tuition:* Full-time $22,560; part-time $940 per credit hour. *Required fees:* $2484; $94 per credit hour. Tuition and fees vary according to degree level, program and student level. *Graduate housing:* Room and/or apartments available on a first-come, first-served basis to single students; on-campus housing not available to married students. Typical cost: $12,716 (including board). Room and board charges vary according to board plan and housing facility selected. Housing application deadline: 5/1. *Student services:* Campus employment opportunities, campus safety program, career counseling, exercise/wellness program, free psychological counseling, grant writing training, international student services, low-cost health insurance, multicultural affairs office, services for students with disabilities, teacher training, writing training. *Library facilities:* J. E. and M. E. Mabee Library plus 1 other. Collection: Books: 159,953 (physical), 60,292 (digital/electronic); Serial titles: 1,063 (physical), 86,652 (digital/electronic); Databases: 206. Weekly public service hours: 105.

Computer facilities: Computer purchase and lease plans are available. 406 computers available on campus for general student use. A campuswide network can be accessed from student residence rooms and from off campus. Online class registration is available.
Website: http://www.uiw.edu/

General Application Contact: Jessica Delarosa, Associate Director of Admissions, 210-805-2543, Fax: 210-829-3921, E-mail: jsdelaro@uiwtx.edu.

GRADUATE UNITS

College of Humanities, Arts, and Social Sciences Students: 7 full-time (3 women), 2 part-time (1 woman); includes 8 minority (all Hispanic/Latino). 3 applicants, 100% accepted, 1 enrolled. *Faculty:* 3 full-time (2 women). Expenses: Contact institution. *Financial support:* Research assistantships, scholarships/grants, tuition waivers (full and partial), and unspecified assistantships available. Financial award applicants required to submit FAFSA. In 2018, 1 master's awarded. *Program availability:* Part-time, evening/weekend. Offers multidisciplinary studies (MA); pastoral ministry (MA). *Application deadline:* Applications are processed on a rolling basis. *Application fee:* $20. Electronic applications accepted. *Application Contact:* Jessica Delarosa, Associate Director of Admissions, 210-829-6005, Fax: 210-829-3921, E-mail: admis@uiwtx.edu. *Dean,* Dr. Kevin Vichcales, 210-829-2759, Fax: 210-829-3830, E-mail: vichcale@uiwtx.edu.

Dreeben School of Education Students: 110 full-time (72 women), 101 part-time (59 women); includes 127 minority (23 Black or African American, non-Hispanic/Latino; 3 Asian, non-Hispanic/Latino; 97 Hispanic/Latino; 4 Two or more races, non-Hispanic/Latino), 29 international. 82 applicants, 96% accepted, 48 enrolled. *Faculty:* 9 full-time (5 women), 3 part-time/adjunct (2 women). Expenses: Contact institution. *Financial support:* In 2018–19, 4 research assistantships were awarded; Federal Work-Study, scholarships/grants, tuition waivers (partial), and unspecified assistantships also available. Financial award applicants required to submit FAFSA. In 2018, 21 master's, 12 doctorates awarded. *Program availability:* Part-time, evening/weekend. Offers education (M Ed, MA, MAT, PhD). *Application deadline:* Applications are processed on a rolling basis. *Application fee:* $20. Electronic applications accepted. *Application Contact:* Jessica Delarosa, Associate Director of Admissions, 210-829-6005, Fax: 210-829-3921, E-mail: staudt@uiwtx.edu. *Dean,* Dr. Denise Staudt, 210-829-2761, Fax: 210-829-2765, E-mail: staudt@uiwtx.edu.

Feik School of Pharmacy Students: 375 full-time (255 women), 7 part-time (6 women); includes 279 minority (25 Black or African American, non-Hispanic/Latino; 78 Asian, non-Hispanic/Latino; 164 Hispanic/Latino; 1 Native Hawaiian or other Pacific Islander, non-Hispanic/Latino; 11 Two or more races, non-Hispanic/Latino), 3 international. 148 applicants, 100% accepted, 115 enrolled. *Faculty:* 20 full-time (14 women), 1 (woman) part-time/adjunct. Expenses: Contact institution. *Financial support:* Research assistantships, Federal Work-Study, scholarships/grants, and unspecified assistantships available. Financial award applicants required to submit FAFSA. In 2018, 87 doctorates awarded. Offers pharmacy (Pharm D). *Application deadline:* For fall admission, 12/1 for domestic and international students. *Application fee:* $50. Electronic applications accepted. *Application Contact:* Dr. Amy Diepenbrock, Assistant Dean, Student Affairs, 210-883-1060, Fax: 210-822-1521, E-mail: diepenbr@uiwtx.edu. *Dean,* Dr. David Maize, 210-883-1000, Fax: 210-822-1521, E-mail: maize@uiwtx.edu.

H-E-B School of Business and Administration Students: 249 full-time (120 women), 27 part-time (12 women); includes 162 minority (24 Black or African American, non-Hispanic/Latino; 1 American Indian or Alaska Native, non-Hispanic/Latino; 8 Asian, non-Hispanic/Latino; 124 Hispanic/Latino; 1 Native Hawaiian or other Pacific Islander, non-Hispanic/Latino; 4 Two or more races, non-Hispanic/Latino), 40 international. 202 applicants, 98% accepted, 108 enrolled. *Faculty:* 22 full-time (12 women), 13 part-time/adjunct (5 women). Expenses: Contact institution. *Financial support:* Research assistantships, Federal Work-Study, scholarships/grants, tuition waivers (partial), and unspecified assistantships available. Financial award applicants required to submit FAFSA. In 2018, 142 master's awarded. *Program availability:* Part-time, evening/weekend. Offers accounting (MS); business administration (MBA); health administration (MHA). *Application deadline:* Applications are processed on a rolling basis. *Application fee:* $20. Electronic applications accepted. *Application Contact:* Jessica Delarosa, Associate Director of Admissions, 210-8296005, Fax: 210-829-3921, E-mail: admis@uiwtx.edu. *Dean,* Dr. Forrest Aven, 210-805-5884, Fax: 210-805-3564, E-mail: aven@uiwtx.edu.

Ila Faye Miller School of Nursing and Health Professions Students: 106 full-time (74 women), 13 part-time (12 women); includes 80 minority (26 Black or African American, non-Hispanic/Latino; 1 American Indian or Alaska Native, non-Hispanic/Latino; 3 Asian, non-Hispanic/Latino; 47 Hispanic/Latino; 3 Two or more races, non-Hispanic/Latino), 3 international. 43 applicants, 95% accepted, 28 enrolled. *Faculty:* 15 full-time (10 women). Expenses: Contact institution. *Financial support:* Research assistantships, Federal Work-Study, scholarships/grants, tuition waivers (partial), and unspecified assistantships available. Financial award applicants required to submit FAFSA. In 2018,

26 master's, 19 doctorates awarded. *Program availability:* Part-time, evening/weekend. Offers kinesiology (MS); nursing (MSN, DNP); sport management (MS). *Application deadline:* Applications are processed on a rolling basis. *Application fee:* $20. Electronic applications accepted. *Application Contact:* Jessica Delarosa, Associate Director of Admissions, 210-8296005, Fax: 210-829-3921, E-mail: admis@uiwtx.edu. *Dean*, Dr. Mary Hoke, 210-829-3982, Fax: 210-829-3174, E-mail: mhoke@uiwtx.edu.

Rosenberg School of Optometry Students: 259 full-time (181 women); includes 153 minority (7 Black or African American, non-Hispanic/Latino; 1 American Indian or Alaska Native, non-Hispanic/Latino; 91 Asian, non-Hispanic/Latino; 54 Hispanic/Latino), 3 international. 94 applicants, 100% accepted, 65 enrolled. *Faculty:* 17 full-time (5 women). Expenses: Contact institution. *Financial support:* Fellowships, Federal Work-Study, and scholarships/grants available. Financial award applicants required to submit FAFSA. In 2018, 62 doctorates awarded. Offers optometry (OD). *Application deadline:* For fall admission, 5/1 for domestic students. *Application fee:* $50. Electronic applications accepted. *Application Contact:* Jill Mohr, Director of Admissions and Student Services, 210-883-1190, Fax: 210-883-1191, E-mail: mohr@uiwtx.edu. *Dean*, Dr. Timothy Wingert, 210-883-1195, Fax: 210-283-6890, E-mail: twingert@uiwtx.edu.

School of Mathematics, Science, and Engineering Students: 30 full-time (24 women), 9 part-time (7 women); includes 20 minority (1 Black or African American, non-Hispanic/Latino; 1 American Indian or Alaska Native, non-Hispanic/Latino; 1 Asian, non-Hispanic/Latino; 17 Hispanic/Latino), 5 international. 34 applicants, 88% accepted, 13 enrolled. *Faculty:* 6 full-time (4 women), 1 (woman) part-time/adjunct. Expenses: Contact institution. *Financial support:* Research assistantships, Federal Work-Study, scholarships/grants, tuition waivers (partial), and unspecified assistantships available. Financial award applicants required to submit FAFSA. In 2018, 10 master's awarded. *Program availability:* Part-time, evening/weekend. Offers applied statistics (MS); biology (MA, MS); mathematics (MA); multidisciplinary sciences (MA); nutrition (MS). *Application deadline:* Applications are processed on a rolling basis. *Application fee:* $20. Electronic applications accepted. *Application Contact:* Jessica Delarosa, Associate Director of Admissions, 210-8296005, Fax: 210-829-3921, E-mail: admis@uiwtx.edu. *Dean*, Dr. Carlos A. Garcia, 210-829-2717, Fax: 210-829-3153, E-mail: cagarci9@uiwtx.edu.

School of Media and Design Students: 22 full-time (14 women), 6 part-time (2 women); includes 16 minority (1 Black or African American, non-Hispanic/Latino; 15 Hispanic/Latino), 3 international. 15 applicants, 87% accepted, 10 enrolled. *Faculty:* 5 full-time (3 women), 2 part-time/adjunct (0 women). Expenses: Contact institution. *Financial support:* Federal Work-Study, scholarships/grants, tuition waivers (partial), and unspecified assistantships available. Financial award applicants required to submit FAFSA. In 2018, 19 master's awarded. *Program availability:* Part-time, evening/weekend. Offers communication arts (MA); fashion design (MA). *Application deadline:* Applications are processed on a rolling basis. *Application fee:* $20. Electronic applications accepted. *Application Contact:* Jessica Delarosa, Associate Director of Admissions, 210-829-3921, Fax: 210-829-3921, E-mail: admis@uiwtx.edu. *Dean*, Dr. Sharon Welkey, 210-829-6091, Fax: 210-829-3196, E-mail: welkey@uiwtx.edu.

School of Osteopathic Medicine Students: 359 full-time (210 women); includes 214 minority (23 Black or African American, non-Hispanic/Latino; 1 American Indian or Alaska Native, non-Hispanic/Latino; 79 Asian, non-Hispanic/Latino; 95 Hispanic/Latino; 16 Two or more races, non-Hispanic/Latino). 490 applicants, 100% accepted, 203 enrolled. *Faculty:* 7 full-time (4 women), 2 part-time/adjunct (0 women). Expenses: Contact institution. *Financial support:* Research assistantships, career-related internships or fieldwork, scholarships/grants, and unspecified assistantships available. Financial award applicants required to submit FAFSA. In 2018, 49 master's awarded. Offers osteopathic medicine (MBS, DO). *Application deadline:* For fall admission, 9/1 for domestic students; for spring admission, 3/15 for domestic students. Applications are processed on a rolling basis. *Application fee:* $50. Electronic applications accepted. *Application Contact:* Sonia Winney, Admissions Coordinator, 210-283-6998, E-mail: winney@uiwtx.edu. *Dean*, Dr. Robyn Phillips-Madson, E-mail: rmadson@uiwtx.edu.

School of Physical Therapy Students: 106 full-time (63 women), 65 part-time (40 women); includes 94 minority (14 Black or African American, non-Hispanic/Latino; 29 Asian, non-Hispanic/Latino; 49 Hispanic/Latino; 2 Two or more races, non-Hispanic/Latino), 1 international. 66 applicants, 100% accepted, 53 enrolled. *Faculty:* 17 full-time (5 women). Expenses: Contact institution. *Financial support:* Scholarships/grants and unspecified assistantships available. Financial award applicants required to submit FAFSA. In 2018, 46 doctorates awarded. Offers physical therapy (DPT). *Application deadline:* For fall admission, 10/1 priority date for domestic students. *Application fee:* $50. *Application Contact:* Christina Immel, Director of Enrollment, 210-283-6918, E-mail: cimmel@uiwtx.edu. *Dean*, Dr. Caroline Goulet, 210-283-6924, E-mail: goulet@uiwtx.edu.

School of Professional Studies Students: 475 full-time (229 women), 358 part-time (151 women); includes 536 minority (122 Black or African American, non-Hispanic/Latino; 5 American Indian or Alaska Native, non-Hispanic/Latino; 19 Asian, non-Hispanic/Latino; 366 Hispanic/Latino; 3 Native Hawaiian or other Pacific Islander, non-Hispanic/Latino; 21 Two or more races, non-Hispanic/Latino). 593 applicants, 91% accepted, 287 enrolled. *Faculty:* 9 full-time (3 women), 26 part-time/adjunct (10 women). Expenses: Contact institution. *Financial support:* Scholarships/grants and unspecified assistantships available. Financial award applicants required to submit FAFSA. In 2018, 488 master's, 11 doctorates awarded. *Program availability:* Part-time, evening/weekend, 100% online, blended/hybrid learning. Offers communication arts (MAA); organizational development and leadership (MS); professional studies (DBA). *Application deadline:* Applications are processed on a rolling basis. Electronic applications accepted. *Application Contact:* Julie Weber, Director of Marketing and Recruitment, 210-318-1876, Fax: 210-829-2756, E-mail: eapadmission@uiwtx.edu. *Dean*, Vincent Porter, 210-8292770, E-mail: porterv@uiwtx.edu.

UNIVERSITY OF THE PACIFIC, Stockton, CA 95211-0197
General Information Independent, coed, university. CGS member. *Graduate housing:* Rooms and/or apartments available on a first-come, first-served basis to single and married students. Housing application deadline: 7/1. *Research affiliation:* Lawrence Hall of Science.

GRADUATE UNITS
Arthur A. Dugoni School of Dentistry Offers dentistry (MSD, DDS, Certificate). Electronic applications accepted.

College of the Pacific Offers biological sciences (MS); communication (MA); food studies (MA); health, exercise and sport science (MA); psychology (MA).

Conservatory of Music Offers music education (MM); music therapy (MA).

Eberhardt School of Business *Program availability:* Part-time. Offers business (M Acc, MBA).

Gladys L. Benerd School of Education Offers curriculum and instruction (MA, Ed D); education (M Ed); educational administration and leadership (MA, Ed D); educational and school psychology (MA, Ed D); educational entrepreneurship (MA); school psychology (Ed S); special education (MA); teacher education (MA).

McGeorge School of Law *Program availability:* Part-time, evening/weekend. Offers advocacy (JD); international water resources law (JSD); public policy and law (LL M). Electronic applications accepted.

School of Engineering and Computer Science Offers engineering science (MS). Electronic applications accepted.

Thomas J. Long School of Pharmacy and Health Sciences Offers audiology (Au D); pharmaceutical and chemical sciences (MS, PhD); pharmacy (Pharm D); pharmacy and health sciences (MS, Au D, DPT, PhD, Pharm D); physical therapy (MS, DPT); speech-language pathology (MS).

UNIVERSITY OF THE PEOPLE, Pasadena, CA 91101
General Information Private, coed, comprehensive institution.

GRADUATE UNITS
Master of Business Administration Program *Program availability:* Online learning. Offers business administration (MBA).

UNIVERSITY OF THE POTOMAC, Washington, DC 20005
General Information Proprietary, coed, comprehensive institution.

GRADUATE UNITS
Program in Business Administration *Program availability:* Online learning. Offers business administration (MBA). Program also offered at Vienna, VA campus.

UNIVERSITY OF THE SACRED HEART, San Juan, PR 00914-0383
General Information Independent-religious, coed, comprehensive institution. *Graduate housing:* Room and/or apartments available on a first-come, first-served basis to single students; on-campus housing not available to married students. Housing application deadline: 5/31.

GRADUATE UNITS
Graduate Programs *Program availability:* Part-time, evening/weekend. Offers contemporary culture and media (MA); creative writing (MFA, Certificate); digital journalism (MA, Certificate); early childhood education (M Ed); editing for media (MA, Certificate); human resource management (MBA); human rights and anti-discriminatory processes (MASJ); information systems auditing (MS); information systems management (MBA); information technology (Certificate); information technology and multimedia (Certificate); instruction systems and education technology (M Ed); international marketing (MBA); management information systems (MBA); mediation and transformation of conflicts (MASJ); nonprofit organization administration (MBA); occupational health and safety (MS); occupational nursing (MSN); production and marketing of special events (Certificate); public relations (MA, Certificate); publicity (MA, Certificate); scriptwriting (MA, Certificate); taxation (MBA).

UNIVERSITY OF THE SCIENCES, Philadelphia, PA 19104-4495
General Information Independent, coed, university. CGS member. *Graduate housing:* On-campus housing not available. *Research affiliation:* Progenra (molecular biology), Encapsulation Systems (analytical chemistry), Johnson & Johnson (cell biology), Ortho-McNeil Pharmaceuticals, Inc. (pharmacy), Polymedix (computational chemistry).

GRADUATE UNITS
Doctor of Physical Therapy Program *Program availability:* Part-time, evening/weekend, online learning. Offers physical therapy (DPT).

Philadelphia College of Pharmacy Offers pharmacy (Pharm D).

Program in Bioinformatics *Program availability:* Part-time, evening/weekend. Offers bioinformatics (MS).

Program in Biomedical Writing *Program availability:* Part-time, evening/weekend, online learning. Offers biomedical writing (MS); medical marketing writing (Certificate); regulatory affairs writing (Certificate).

Program in Cell Biology and Biotechnology *Program availability:* Part-time, evening/weekend. Offers cell biology and biotechnology (MS).

Program in Chemistry, Biochemistry and Pharmacognosy *Program availability:* Part-time. Offers biochemistry (MS, PhD); chemistry (MS, PhD); pharmacognosy (MS, PhD).

Program in Health Policy *Program availability:* Part-time, evening/weekend, online learning. Offers health policy (MS, PhD).

Program in Health Psychology Offers health psychology (MS).

Program in Occupational Therapy *Program availability:* Online learning. Offers occupational therapy (MOT, Dr OT). Electronic applications accepted.

Program in Pharmaceutical and Healthcare Business *Program availability:* Part-time, evening/weekend, online learning. Offers pharmaceutical and healthcare business (MBA).

Program in Pharmaceutics *Program availability:* Part-time. Offers pharmaceutics (MS, PhD).

Program in Pharmacology and Toxicology Offers pharmacology (MS, PhD); toxicology (MS, PhD).

Program in Pharmacy Administration *Program availability:* Part-time. Offers pharmacy administration (MS).

Program in Public Health *Program availability:* Part-time, evening/weekend, online learning. Offers public health (MPH).

THE UNIVERSITY OF THE SOUTH, Sewanee, TN 37383-1000
General Information Independent-religious, coed, comprehensive institution. *Enrollment:* 1,785 graduate, professional, and undergraduate students; 66 full-time matriculated graduate/professional students (30 women), 17 part-time matriculated graduate/professional students (9 women). *Enrollment by degree level:* 81 master's, 2 other advanced degrees. *Graduate faculty:* 10 full-time (4 women), 9 part-time/adjunct (1 woman). *Graduate housing:* Rooms and/or apartments available on a first-come, first-served basis to single and married students. Housing application deadline: 33/44. *Student services:* Campus employment opportunities, campus safety program, career counseling, child daycare facilities, free psychological counseling, international student services, multicultural affairs office, writing training. *Library facilities:* Jessie Ball duPont Library. *Collection:* Books: 512,993 (physical), 563,193 (digital/electronic); Serial titles: 4,034 (physical), 22,304 (digital/electronic); Databases: 382. Study areas open 24 hours, 5–7 days a week; students can reserve study rooms.

Computer facilities: 150 computers available on campus for general student use. A campuswide network can be accessed from student residence rooms and from off campus. Online class registration is available.
Website: http://www.sewanee.edu/

GRADUATE UNITS

School of Theology Students: 66 full-time (30 women), 3 part-time (1 woman); includes 4 minority (3 Black or African American, non-Hispanic/Latino; 1 Hispanic/Latino), 6 international. Average age 38. *Faculty:* 10 full-time (4 women), 9 part-time/adjunct (1 woman). Expenses: Contact institution. *Financial support:* Institutionally sponsored loans and scholarships/grants available. Support available to part-time students. Financial award application deadline: 4/30. In 2018, 21 master's, 4 doctorates awarded. *Program availability:* Part-time. Offers theology (M Div, MA, STM, D Min). *Application deadline:* For fall admission, 7/1 for domestic students, 1/15 for international students. Applications are processed on a rolling basis. *Application fee:* $0. Electronic applications accepted. *Application Contact:* Stephanie Borne, Administrative Assistant for Recruitment and Admission, 931-598-1283, E-mail: theologyadmissions@ sewanee.edu. *Dean,* Very Rev. Dr. J. Neil Alexander, 931-598-1288, Fax: 931-598-1412, E-mail: deansot@sewanee.edu.

Sewanee School of Letters Students: 46 part-time (27 women); includes 5 minority (1 Black or African American, non-Hispanic/Latino; 1 Asian, non-Hispanic/Latino; 3 Two or more races, non-Hispanic/Latino), 1 international. Average age 39. *Faculty:* 10 part-time/adjunct (7 women). Expenses: Contact institution. *Financial support:* Institutionally sponsored loans and scholarships/grants available. In 2018, 11 master's awarded. *Program availability:* Part-time. Offers American and English literature (MA); creative writing (MFA). *Application deadline:* For summer admission, 4/15 for domestic students. Applications are processed on a rolling basis. *Application fee:* $0. Electronic applications accepted. *Application Contact:* April R. Alvarez, Administrator, 931-598-1636, E-mail: sletters@sewanee.edu. *Interim Director,* Dr. John Gatta, 931-598-1636, E-mail: sletters@sewanee.edu.

UNIVERSITY OF THE SOUTHWEST, Hobbs, NM 88240-9129

General Information Independent-religious, coed, comprehensive institution. *Graduate housing:* On-campus housing not available.

GRADUATE UNITS

Graduate Programs *Program availability:* Part-time, evening/weekend, online learning. Offers business administration (MBA); curriculum and instruction (MSE); curriculum and instruction: bilingual (MSE); curriculum and instruction: TESOL (MSE); early childhood education (MSE); educational administration (MSE); mental health counseling (MSE); school counseling (MSE); special education (MSE); sports management (MBA). Electronic applications accepted.

UNIVERSITY OF THE VIRGIN ISLANDS, St. Thomas, VI 00802

General Information Territory-supported, coed, comprehensive institution. *Enrollment:* 81 full-time matriculated graduate/professional students (66 women), 156 part-time matriculated graduate/professional students (123 women). *Enrollment by degree level:* 149 master's, 86 doctoral. *International tuition:* $13,230 full-time. Tuition, territory resident: full-time $6948; part-time $386 per credit. Tuition, nonresident: full-time $13,230; part-time $735 per credit. *Required fees:* $508. *Graduate housing:* On-campus housing not available. *Student services:* Campus employment opportunities, career counseling, child daycare facilities, exercise/wellness program. *Library facilities:* Ralph M. Paiewonsky Library. *Collection:* Students can reserve study rooms.

Computer facilities: 500 computers available on campus for general student use. A campuswide network can be accessed from student residence rooms. Online class registration is available.
Website: http://www.uvi.edu/

General Application Contact: Charmaine L. Smith, Director of Admissions, 340-692-4070, E-mail: hsmithc@uvi.edu.

GRADUATE UNITS

College of Liberal Arts and Social Sciences Students: 23 full-time (19 women), 13 part-time (9 women); includes 27 minority (24 Black or African American, non-Hispanic/Latino; 1 Asian, non-Hispanic/Latino; 1 Hispanic/Latino; 1 Two or more races, non-Hispanic/Latino), 6 international. Average age 34. 13 applicants, 85% accepted, 10 enrolled. *Faculty:* 7 full-time (5 women), 4 part-time/adjunct (0 women). Expenses: Contact institution. *Financial support:* Career-related internships or fieldwork and scholarships/grants available. Financial award application deadline: 4/15; financial award applicants required to submit FAFSA. In 2018, 4 master's awarded. *Program availability:* Part-time, evening/weekend. Offers liberal arts and social sciences (M Psych, MPA). *Application deadline:* For fall admission, 4/30 for domestic and international students; for spring admission, 10/30 for domestic and international students. *Application fee:* $30. Electronic applications accepted. *Application Contact:* Dr. Xuri M. Allen, Director of Admissions, 340-693-1224, Fax: 340-693-1167, E-mail: xallen@uvi.edu. *Dean,* Dr. Emily Allen-Williams, 340-693-1261, Fax: 340-693-1265, E-mail: emily.allenwilliams@uvi.edu.

College of Science and Mathematics Students: 16 full-time (13 women), 19 part-time (13 women); includes 10 minority (4 Black or African American, non-Hispanic/Latino; 1 American Indian or Alaska Native, non-Hispanic/Latino; 2 Hispanic/Latino; 1 Native Hawaiian or other Pacific Islander, non-Hispanic/Latino; 2 Two or more races, non-Hispanic/Latino), 1 international. Average age 27. *Faculty:* 5 full-time (4 women), 7 part-time/adjunct (2 women). Expenses: Contact institution. *Financial support:* Fellowships, research assistantships, teaching assistantships, career-related internships or fieldwork, and scholarships/grants available. Financial award application deadline: 4/15; financial award applicants required to submit FAFSA. In 2018, 8 master's awarded. Offers marine and environmental science (MS); mathematics for secondary teachers (MA). *Application deadline:* For fall admission, 4/30 for domestic and international students; for spring admission, 10/30 for domestic and international students. *Application fee:* $30. Electronic applications accepted. *Application Contact:* Charmaine Smith, Director of Admissions, 340-690-4070, E-mail: csmith@uvi.edu. *Dean,* Dr. Sandra Romano, 340-693-1230, Fax: 340-693-1245, E-mail: sromano@uvi.edu.

School of Business Students: 5 full-time (4 women), 29 part-time (18 women); includes 27 minority (23 Black or African American, non-Hispanic/Latino; 1 Asian, non-Hispanic/Latino; 3 Hispanic/Latino), 5 international. Average age 31. Expenses: Contact institution. *Financial support:* Application deadline: 4/15; applicants required to submit FAFSA. In 2018, 5 master's awarded. *Program availability:* Part-time, evening/weekend. Offers business (EMBA, MBA). *Application deadline:* For fall admission, 4/30 for domestic and international students; for spring admission, 10/30 for domestic and international students. Applications are processed on a rolling basis. *Application fee:* $30. Electronic applications accepted. *Application Contact:* Charmaine M Smith, Director of Admissions, 340-692-4070, E-mail: csmith@uvi.edu. *Dean,* Dr. Kendra Harris, 340-693-1301, Fax: 340-693-1305, E-mail: kendra.harris@uvi.edu.

School of Education Students: 41 full-time (34 women), 95 part-time (75 women); includes 80 minority (79 Black or African American, non-Hispanic/Latino; 1 Hispanic/Latino), 24 international. Average age 43. Expenses: Contact institution. *Financial support:* Fellowships, research assistantships, teaching assistantships, and scholarships/grants available. Financial award application deadline: 4/15; financial award applicants required to submit FAFSA. In 2018, 6 master's, 7 doctorates awarded. *Program availability:* Part-time, evening/weekend. Offers creative leadership for innovation and change (PhD); educational leadership (MA); school counseling (MA); school psychology (Ed S). *Application deadline:* For fall admission, 4/30 for domestic and international students; for spring admission, 10/30 for domestic and international students. *Application fee:* $25. Electronic applications accepted. *Application Contact:* Charmaine M. Smith, Director of Admissions, 340-692-4070, E-mail: csmith@uvi.edu. *Dean,* Dr. Karen Brown, 340-693-1321, Fax: 340-693-1335, E-mail: karen.brown@uvi.edu.

UNIVERSITY OF THE WEST, Rosemead, CA 91770

General Information Independent, coed, comprehensive institution. *Graduate housing:* Rooms and/or apartments guaranteed to single students and available on a first-come, first-served basis to married students. Housing application deadline: 9/22.

GRADUATE UNITS

Department of Business Administration *Program availability:* Part-time, evening/weekend. Offers business administration (EMBA); computer information systems (MBA); finance (MBA); international business (MBA); nonprofit organization management (MBA).

Department of Psychology *Program availability:* Part-time, evening/weekend. Offers Buddhist psychology (MA); multicultural counseling (MA).

Department of Religious Studies *Program availability:* Part-time, evening/weekend. Offers religious studies (MA, PhD).

Program in Buddhist Chaplaincy Offers Buddhist chaplaincy (M Div).

THE UNIVERSITY OF TOLEDO, Toledo, OH 43606-3390

General Information State-supported, coed, university. CGS member. *Graduate housing:* Room and/or apartments available to single students; on-campus housing not available to married students. *Research affiliation:* NASA–Glen Research Center at Lewis Field (aerospace engineering), Merck & Company, Inc. (pharmaceutical research), Midwest Astronomical Data Reduction and Analysis Facility (astronomy), Edison Industrial Systems Center (systems integration, quality control, mathematical modeling), Ohio Aerospace Institute (aerospace research), National Renewable Energy Laboratory (NREL) (thin films, photovoltaics).

GRADUATE UNITS

College of Graduate Studies *Program availability:* Part-time, evening/weekend, online learning. Electronic applications accepted.

College of Business and Innovation *Program availability:* Part-time, evening/weekend. Offers accounting (MBA, MSA); business administration-general (MBA); business and innovation (EMBA, MBA, MSA, DME, PhD, Certificate); finance (MBA); information operations and technology management (MBA, DME, PhD, Certificate); management (MBA); marketing and international business (MBA). Electronic applications accepted.

College of Communication and the Arts Offers communication (Certificate); communication and the arts (ME, MME, MMP, Certificate); music (Certificate); music performance (MMP). Electronic applications accepted.

College of Engineering *Program availability:* Part-time, evening/weekend, online learning. Offers bioengineering (MS, PhD); biomedical engineering (PhD); chemical engineering (MS, PhD); civil engineering (MS, PhD); computer science (MS, PhD); electrical engineering (MS, PhD); engineering (MS, PhD); general engineering (MS); industrial engineering (MS, PhD); mechanical engineering (MS, PhD). Electronic applications accepted.

College of Health and Human Services Offers athletic training (MSES); counselor education (MA, PhD); criminal justice (MA); exercise physiology (MSES); exercise science (PhD); health and human services (MA, MPH, MS, MSES, MSW, DPT, OTD, PhD, Ed S); health education (PhD); occupational health-industrial hygiene (MS); occupational therapy (OTD); physical therapy (DPT); public health (MPH); recreation and leisure studies (MA); school psychology (Ed S); social work (MSW); speech-language pathology (MA). Electronic applications accepted.

College of Languages, Literature and Social Sciences *Program availability:* Part-time. Offers applied econometric specialization (MA); clinical psychology (MA, PhD); economics (MA); English as a second language (MA); experimental psychology (MA, PhD); French (MA); geographic information science and applied geographics (Certificate); geography and planning (MA); German (MA); health care policy and administration (Certificate); history (MA, PhD); languages, literature and social sciences (MA, MLS, MPA, PhD, Certificate); liberal studies (MLS); management of non-profit organizations (Certificate); municipal administration (Certificate); philosophy (MA); political science (MA); public administration (MPA); sociology (MA); Spanish (MA); spatially-integrated social science (PhD); teaching of writing (Certificate); women's and gender studies (Certificate). Electronic applications accepted.

College of Medicine and Life Sciences *Program availability:* Part-time, evening/weekend. Offers bioinformatics and proteomics/genomics (MSBS); biomarkers and bioinformatics (Certificate); biomarkers and diagnostics (PSM); biostatistics and epidemiology (Certificate); cancer biology (MSBS, PhD); cardiovascular and metabolic diseases (MSBS, PhD); contemporary gerontological practice (Certificate); environmental and occupational health and safety (MPH); epidemiology (Certificate); global public health (Certificate); health promotion and education (MPH); human donation sciences (MSBS); industrial hygiene (MSOH); infection, immunity, and transplantation (MSBS, PhD); medical and health science teaching and learning (Certificate); medical physics (MSBS); medical sciences (MSBS); medicine and life sciences (MPH, MS, MSBS, MSOH, MD, Certificate); neurosciences (MSBS, PhD); occupational health (Certificate); oral biology (MSBS); orthopedic surgery (MSBS); pathology (Certificate); pathology assistant (MSBS); physician assistant studies (MSBS); public health administration (MPH); public health and emergency response (Certificate); public health epidemiology (MPH); public health nutrition (MPH). Electronic applications accepted.

College of Natural Sciences and Mathematics *Program availability:* Part-time. Offers analytical chemistry (MS, PhD); applied mathematics (MS, PhD); biological chemistry (MS, PhD); biology (MS, PhD); geology (MS); inorganic chemistry (MS, PhD); natural sciences and mathematics (MS, PSM, PhD); organic chemistry (MS, PhD); photovoltaics (PSM); physical chemistry (MS, PhD); physics (MS, PhD); statistics (MS, PhD). Electronic applications accepted.

College of Nursing *Program availability:* Part-time, online learning. Offers clinical nurse leader (MSN); family nurse practitioner (MSN, Certificate); health promotions, outcomes, systems, and policy (MSN, DNP); nurse educator (MSN, Certificate); nursing (MSN, DNP, Certificate); pediatric nurse practitioner (MSN, Certificate). Electronic applications accepted.

College of Pharmacy and Pharmaceutical Sciences Offers administrative pharmacy (MSPS); experimental therapeutics (PhD); industrial pharmacy (MSPS); medicinal and biological chemistry (MS, PhD); pharmacology toxicology (MSPS); pharmacy and pharmaceutical sciences (MS, MSPS, PhD, Pharm D). Electronic applications accepted.

College of Social Justice and Human Service Offers child advocacy (Certificate); counselor education (MA, PhD); criminal justice (MA); elder law (Certificate); higher education (ME, PhD, Certificate); juvenile justice (Certificate); patient advocacy (Certificate); school psychology (MA, Ed S); social justice and human service (MA, ME, MSW, PhD, Certificate, Ed S); social work (MSW).

Judith Herb College of Education *Program availability:* Part-time, evening/weekend. Offers art education (ME); career and technical education (ME, Ed S); curriculum and instruction (ME, PhD, Ed S); early childhood education (ME, Ed S); education (MAE, ME, MES, MME, DE, PhD, Certificate, Ed S); education and anthropology (MAE); education and biology (MES); education and chemistry (MES); education and classics (MAE); education and economics (MAE); education and English (MAE); education and French (MAE); education and geology (MES); education and German (MAE); education and history (MAE); education and mathematics (MAE, MES); education and physics (MES); education and political science (MAE); education and sociology (MAE); education and Spanish (MAE); educational administration and supervision (ME, DE, Ed S); educational media (PhD); educational psychology (ME, PhD); educational research and measurement (ME); educational sociology (PhD); educational technology (ME); educational technology: virtual educator (Certificate); educational theory and social foundations (ME); elementary education (PhD); English as a second language (MAE); foundations of education (DE, PhD); gifted and talented education (ME); history of education (PhD); middle childhood education (ME); philosophy of education (PhD); physical education (ME); secondary education (ME, PhD); special education (PhD). Electronic applications accepted.

College of Law Students: 231 full-time (119 women), 63 part-time (40 women); includes 49 minority (13 Black or African American, non-Hispanic/Latino; 1 American Indian or Alaska Native, non-Hispanic/Latino; 10 Asian, non-Hispanic/Latino; 19 Hispanic/Latino; 1 Native Hawaiian or other Pacific Islander, non-Hispanic/Latino; 5 Two or more races, non-Hispanic/Latino). Average age 29. 422 applicants, 62% accepted, 97 enrolled. *Faculty:* 20 full-time (9 women), 11 part-time/adjunct (5 women). Expenses: Contact institution. *Financial support:* In 2018–19, 226 students received support. Research assistantships, career-related internships or fieldwork, Federal Work-Study, and scholarships/grants available. Support available to part-time students. Financial award application deadline: 8/1; financial award applicants required to submit FAFSA. In 2018, 6 master's, 55 doctorates, 3 Certificates awarded. *Program availability:* Part-time, evening/weekend, 100% online. Offers compliance (Certificate); health care compliance (Certificate); higher education compliance (Certificate); law (MLW, JD). *Application deadline:* For fall admission, 8/1 priority date for domestic students, 7/31 for international students; for winter admission, 11/15 for domestic students. Applications are processed on a rolling basis. *Application fee:* $0. Electronic applications accepted. *Application Contact:* Jessica Mehl, Assistant Dean of Law Admissions, 419-530-4131, Fax: 419-530-4345, E-mail: law.admissions@utoledo.edu. *Dean,* D. Benjamin Barros, 419-530-2379, Fax: 419-530-4526, E-mail: ben.barros@utoledo.edu.

UNIVERSITY OF TORONTO, Toronto, ON M5S 1A1, Canada

General Information Province-supported, coed, university. CGS member. *Graduate housing:* Rooms and/or apartments available on a first-come, first-served basis to single students and available to married students. *Research affiliation:* Fields Institute for Research in Mathematical Sciences, Canadian Institute for Theoretical Astrophysics, Royal Ontario Museum, Pontifical Institute of Medieval Studies, Hospital for Sick Children, Center for Addiction and Mental Health.

GRADUATE UNITS

Faculty of Medicine Offers biochemistry (M Sc, PhD); genetic counseling (M Sc); immunology (M Sc, PhD); laboratory medicine and pathobiology (M Sc, PhD); management of innovation (MMI); medical biophysics (M Sc, PhD); medicine (M Sc, M Sc BMC, M Sc OT, M Sc PT, MH Sc, MD, PhD); molecular genetics (M Sc, PhD); nutritional sciences (M Sc, PhD); occupational therapy (M Sc OT); pharmacology (M Sc, PhD); physical therapy (M Sc PT); physiology (M Sc, PhD); rehabilitation science (M Sc, PhD); speech-language pathology (M Sc, MH Sc, PhD). Electronic applications accepted.

Institute of Health Policy, Management and Evaluation Offers health administration (MH Sc); health informatics (MHI); health policy, management and evaluation (PhD). Electronic applications accepted.

Institute of Medical Science Offers bioethics (MH Sc); biomedical communications (M Sc BMC); medical radiation science (MH Sc); medical science (PhD). Electronic applications accepted.

School of Graduate Studies *Program availability:* Part-time, evening/weekend. Offers biotechnology (MBiotech); environmental science (M Env Sc, PhD). Electronic applications accepted.

Advanced Design and Manufacturing Institute *Program availability:* Part-time. Offers design and manufacturing (M Eng). Program offered jointly with McMaster University, Queen's University, and The University of Western Ontario; available only to Canadian citizens and permanent residents of Canada. Electronic applications accepted.

Department of Nursing Science *Program availability:* Part-time. Offers nursing (MN, PhD). Electronic applications accepted.

Department of Public Health Sciences *Program availability:* Part-time. Offers biostatistics (M Sc, PhD); community health (M Sc); community nutrition (MPH); epidemiology (MPH, PhD); family and community medicine (MPH); occupational and environmental health (MPH); social and behavioral health science (PhD); social and behavioral health sciences (MPH). Electronic applications accepted.

Faculty of Applied Science and Engineering *Program availability:* Part-time. Offers aerospace studies (M Eng, MA Sc, PhD); applied science and engineering (M Eng, MA Sc, MH Sc, PhD); biomedical engineering (MA Sc, PhD); chemical engineering and applied chemistry (M Eng, MA Sc, PhD); civil engineering (M Eng, MA Sc, PhD); clinical engineering (MH Sc, PhD); electrical and computer engineering (M Eng, MA Sc, PhD); materials science and engineering (M Eng, MA Sc, PhD); mechanical and industrial engineering (M Eng, MA Sc, PhD).

Faculty of Arts and Science *Program availability:* Part-time. Offers anthropology (M Sc, MA, PhD); applied computing (M Sc AC); art history (MA, PhD); arts and science (M Sc, M Sc AC, M Sc Pl, MA, MA Sc, MFE, MIRHR, MMF, MUD, MUDS, MVS, PhD); astronomy and astrophysics (M Sc, PhD); cell and systems biology (M Sc, PhD); chemistry (M Sc, PhD); cinema studies (MA, PhD); classics (MA, PhD); comparative literature (MA, PhD); computer science (M Sc, PhD); creative writing (MA); criminology and sociolegal studies (MA, PhD); drama, theatre and performance studies (MA, PhD); earth sciences (M Sc, MA Sc, PhD); East Asian studies (MA, PhD); ecology and evolutionary biology (M Sc, PhD); economics (MA, PhD); English (MA, PhD); financial economics (MFE); French language and literature (MA, PhD); geography (M Sc, MA, PhD); German (MA, PhD); history (MA, PhD); history and philosophy of science and technology (MA, PhD); industrial relations and human resources (MIRHR, PhD); Italian studies (MA, PhD); linguistics (MA, PhD); mathematical finance (MMF); mathematics (M Sc, PhD); medieval studies (MA, PhD); Near and Middle Eastern civilizations (MA, PhD); philosophy (MA, PhD); physics (M Sc, PhD); planning (M Sc Pl, MUDS, PhD); political science (MA, PhD); psychology (MA, PhD); religion (MA, PhD); Slavic languages and literatures (MA, PhD); sociology (MA, PhD); Spanish and Portuguese (MA, PhD); statistical sciences (M Sc, PhD); urban design (MUD); women and gender studies (MA, PhD). Electronic applications accepted.

Faculty of Dentistry Offers dental public health (M Sc); dentistry (M Sc, DDS, PhD); endodontics (M Sc); oral and maxillofacial radiology (M Sc); oral and maxillofacial surgery (M Sc); oral medicine (M Sc); orthodontics and dentofacial orthopedics (M Sc); pediatric dentistry (M Sc); periodontology (M Sc). Electronic applications accepted.

Faculty of Forestry Offers forestry (M Sc F, MFC, PhD). Electronic applications accepted.

Faculty of Information *Program availability:* Part-time. Offers information (MI, PhD); museum studies (MM St). Electronic applications accepted.

Faculty of Kinesiology and Physical Education Offers kinesiology and physical education (M Sc, PhD). Electronic applications accepted.

Faculty of Law *Program availability:* Part-time. Offers law (LL M, MSL, JD, SJD). Electronic applications accepted.

Faculty of Music *Program availability:* Part-time. Offers composition (M Mus, DMA); ethnomusicology (MA, PhD); jazz (M Mus); music education (MA, PhD); musicology/theory (MA, PhD); opera (M Mus); performance (M Mus, DMA). Electronic applications accepted.

Faculty of Social Work *Program availability:* Part-time. Offers social work (MSW, PhD). Electronic applications accepted.

John H. Daniels Faculty of Architecture, Landscape, and Design Offers architecture, landscape, and design (M Arch, MLA, MUD, MVS). Electronic applications accepted.

Leslie Dan Faculty of Pharmacy *Program availability:* Part-time. Offers pharmacy (M Sc, PhD, Pharm D). Electronic applications accepted.

Munk School of Global Affairs Offers European, Russian and Eurasian studies (MA); European, Russian and EurAsian studies (MA); global affairs (MGA). Electronic applications accepted.

Ontario Institute for Studies in Education *Program availability:* Part-time, evening/weekend. Offers education (M Ed, MA, MT, Ed D, PhD).

Rotman School of Management *Program availability:* Part-time, evening/weekend. Offers management (MBA, MF, PhD).

THE UNIVERSITY OF TULSA, Tulsa, OK 74104-3189

General Information Independent, coed, university. CGS member. *Enrollment:* 4,399 graduate, professional, and undergraduate students; 474 full-time matriculated graduate/professional students (216 women), 295 part-time matriculated graduate/professional students (109 women). *Enrollment by degree level:* 478 master's, 291 doctoral. *Graduate faculty:* 194 full-time (54 women), 11 part-time/adjunct (5 women). *Tuition:* Full-time $22,230; part-time $1235 per credit hour. *Required fees:* $2100; $6 per credit hour. One-time fee: $400 full-time. Tuition and fees vary according to course level, course load and program. *Graduate housing:* Rooms and/or apartments available on a first-come, first-served basis to single and married students. Housing application deadline: 2/1. *Student services:* Campus employment opportunities, campus safety program, career counseling, child daycare facilities, exercise/wellness program, free psychological counseling, grant writing training, international student services, low-cost health insurance, multicultural affairs office, services for students with disabilities, teacher training, writing training. *Library facilities:* McFarlin Library plus 1 other. *Collection:* Books: 1.2 million (physical), 460,240 (digital/electronic); Serial titles: 59,171 (digital/electronic); Databases: 289. Weekly public service hours: 94; study areas open 24 hours, 5–7 days a week; students can reserve study rooms.

Computer facilities: Computer purchase and lease plans are available. 710 computers available on campus for general student use. A campuswide network can be accessed. Online class registration is available.
Website: http://www.utulsa.edu/

General Application Contact: Dr. Brenton McLaury, Vice Provost for Research/Dean of the Graduate School, 918-631-2336, Fax: 918-631-2156, E-mail: grad@utulsa.edu.

GRADUATE UNITS

College of Law Students: 250 full-time (110 women), 31 part-time (14 women); includes 80 minority (10 Black or African American, non-Hispanic/Latino; 17 American Indian or Alaska Native, non-Hispanic/Latino; 4 Asian, non-Hispanic/Latino; 12 Hispanic/Latino; 37 Two or more races, non-Hispanic/Latino; 5 international. Average age 28. 581 applicants, 42% accepted, 100 enrolled. *Faculty:* 27 full-time (15 women), 19 part-time/adjunct (7 women). Expenses: Contact institution. *Financial support:* In 2018–19, 251 students received support. Scholarships/grants available. Support available to part-time students. Financial award application deadline: 8/1; financial award applicants required to submit FAFSA. In 2018, 1 master's, 81 doctorates, 14 Certificates awarded. *Program availability:* Part-time. Offers American Indian and indigenous law (LL M); American law for foreign lawyers (LL M); energy and natural resources law (LL M); energy law (MJ); health law (Certificate); Indian law (MJ); law (JD); Native American law (Certificate); sustainable energy and resources law (Certificate). *Application deadline:* For fall admission, 7/31 priority date for domestic and international students; for spring admission, 12/1 priority date for domestic students, 12/1 for international students; for summer admission, 4/13 for domestic and international students. Applications are processed on a rolling basis. *Application fee:* $30. Electronic applications accepted. *Application Contact:* April M. Fox, Associate Dean of Admissions and Financial Aid, 918-631-2406, Fax: 918-631-3630, E-mail: april-fox@utulsa.edu. *Dean,* Prof. Lyn Suzanne Entzeroth, 918-631-2400, Fax: 918-631-3126, E-mail: lyn-entzeroth@utulsa.edu.

Graduate School Students: 486 full-time (228 women), 283 part-time (97 women); includes 110 minority (18 Black or African American, non-Hispanic/Latino; 24 American Indian or Alaska Native, non-Hispanic/Latino; 19 Asian, non-Hispanic/Latino; 27 Hispanic/Latino; 2 Native Hawaiian or other Pacific Islander, non-Hispanic/Latino; 20 Two or more races, non-Hispanic/Latino), 197 international. Average age 29. 1,337 applicants, 39% accepted, 217 enrolled. *Faculty:* 194 full-time (54 women), 11 part-time/adjunct (5 women). Expenses: Contact institution. *Financial support:* Fellowships with full tuition reimbursements, research assistantships with full tuition reimbursements, teaching assistantships with full tuition reimbursements, career-related internships or fieldwork, Federal Work-Study, institutionally sponsored loans, scholarships/grants, traineeships, health care benefits, tuition waivers (partial), and unspecified assistantships available. Support available to part-time students. Financial award application deadline: 2/1; financial award applicants required to submit FAFSA. In 2018, 223 master's, 37 doctorates awarded. *Program availability:* Part-time, evening/weekend. Offers museum science and management (MA). *Application deadline:* Applications are processed on a rolling basis. *Application fee:* $55. Electronic applications accepted. *Application Contact:* Graduate School, 918-631-2336, Fax: 918-631-2156, E-mail: grad@utulsa.edu. *Vice Provost for Research/Dean of the Graduate School,* Dr. Brenton McLaury, 918-631-2336, Fax: 918-631-2156, E-mail: grad@utulsa.edu.

College of Engineering and Natural Sciences Students: 210 full-time (46 women), 96 part-time (23 women); includes 29 minority (6 Black or African American, non-Hispanic/Latino; 7 American Indian or Alaska Native, non-Hispanic/Latino; 2 Asian, non-Hispanic/Latino; 8 Hispanic/Latino; 6 Two or more races, non-Hispanic/Latino), 151 international. Average age 28. 563 applicants, 40% accepted, 71 enrolled. *Faculty:* 102 full-time (11 women), 2 part-time/adjunct (1 woman). Expenses: Contact institution. *Financial support:* Fellowships with full tuition reimbursements, research assistantships with full tuition reimbursements, teaching assistantships with full tuition reimbursements, career-related internships or fieldwork, Federal Work-Study, scholarships/grants, health care benefits, tuition waivers (full and partial), and unspecified assistantships available. Support available to part-time students. Financial award application deadline: 2/1; financial award applicants required to submit FAFSA. In 2018, 92 master's, 22 doctorates awarded. *Program availability:* Part-time. Offers biological science (MS, MTA, PhD); chemical engineering (ME, MSE, PhD); computer engineering (ME, MSE, PhD); computer science (MS, PhD); cyber security (MS); electrical engineering (ME, MSE); engineering and natural sciences (ME, MS, MSE, MTA, PhD); geophysics (MS); geosciences (MS, PhD); mathematics (MS, MTA, PhD); mechanical engineering (ME, MSE, PhD); petroleum engineering (ME, MSE, PhD). *Application deadline:* Applications are processed on a rolling basis. *Application fee:* $55. Electronic applications accepted. *Application Contact:* Graduate School, 918-631-2336, Fax: 918-631-2156, E-mail: grad@utulsa.edu. *Dean,* Dr. James Sorem, 918-631-2288, E-mail: james-sorem@utulsa.edu.

Collins College of Business Students: 80 full-time (32 women), 128 part-time (35 women); includes 29 minority (2 Black or African American, non-Hispanic/Latino; 7 American Indian or Alaska Native, non-Hispanic/Latino; 8 Asian, non-Hispanic/Latino; 7 Hispanic/Latino; 5 Two or more races, non-Hispanic/Latino), 35 international. Average age 31. 269 applicants, 43% accepted, 70 enrolled. *Faculty:* 42 full-time (27 women), 2 part-time/adjunct (0 women). Expenses: Contact institution. *Financial support:* Fellowships with full tuition reimbursements, research assistantships with full tuition reimbursements, teaching assistantships with full tuition reimbursements, career-related internships or fieldwork, Federal Work-Study, institutionally sponsored loans, scholarships/grants, health care benefits, tuition waivers (full and partial), and unspecified assistantships available. Support available to part-time students. Financial award application deadline: 2/1; financial award applicants required to submit FAFSA. In 2018, 84 master's awarded. *Program availability:* Part-time, evening/weekend, 100% online. Offers accounting (M Acc); business (M Acc, MBA, MEB, MS); business administration (MBA); business analytics (MS); energy business (MEB). *Application deadline:* Applications are processed on a rolling basis. *Application fee:* $55. Electronic applications accepted. *Application Contact:* Information Contact, 918-631-2242, E-mail: graduate-business@utulsa.edu. *Dean,* Dr. Linda Nichols, 918-631-2213, E-mail: linda-nichols@utulsa.edu.

Kendall College of Arts and Sciences Students: 95 full-time (59 women), 49 part-time (34 women); includes 25 minority (5 Black or African American, non-Hispanic/Latino; 3 American Indian or Alaska Native, non-Hispanic/Latino; 5 Asian, non-Hispanic/Latino; 6 Hispanic/Latino; 1 Native Hawaiian or other Pacific Islander, non-Hispanic/Latino; 5 Two or more races, non-Hispanic/Latino), 6 international. Average age 30. 330 applicants, 25% accepted, 34 enrolled. *Faculty:* 65 full-time (30 women), 9 part-time/adjunct (5 women). Expenses: Contact institution. *Financial support:* Fellowships with full tuition reimbursements, research assistantships with full tuition reimbursements, teaching assistantships with full tuition reimbursements, career-related internships or fieldwork, Federal Work-Study, scholarships/grants, traineeships, health care benefits, tuition waivers (full and partial), and unspecified assistantships available. Support available to part-time students. Financial award application deadline: 2/1; financial award applicants required to submit FAFSA. In 2018, 38 master's, 15 doctorates awarded. *Program availability:* Part-time, evening/weekend. Offers anthropology (MA, PhD); arts and sciences (MA, MFA, MS, MSMSE, MTA, PhD); clinical psychology (MA, PhD); English language and literature (MA, PhD); industrial/organizational psychology (MA, PhD). *Application deadline:* Applications are processed on a rolling basis. *Application fee:* $55. Electronic applications accepted. *Application Contact:* Graduate School, 918-631-2336, Fax: 918-631-2156, E-mail: grad@utulsa.edu. *Dean,* Dr. Kalpana Misra, 918-631-2222, Fax: 918-631-3721, E-mail: kalpana-misra@utulsa.edu.

Oxley College of Health Sciences Students: 86 full-time (78 women), 7 part-time (5 women); includes 23 minority (3 Black or African American, non-Hispanic/Latino; 6 American Indian or Alaska Native, non-Hispanic/Latino; 4 Asian, non-Hispanic/Latino; 6 Hispanic/Latino; 1 Native Hawaiian or other Pacific Islander, non-Hispanic/Latino; 3 Two or more races, non-Hispanic/Latino), 3 international. Average age 28. 176 applicants, 54% accepted, 42 enrolled. Expenses: Contact institution. *Financial support:* Fellowships with full tuition reimbursements, teaching assistantships with full tuition reimbursements, career-related internships or fieldwork, Federal Work-Study, scholarships/grants, traineeships, health care benefits, tuition waivers (full and partial), and unspecified assistantships available. Support available to part-time students. In 2018, 17 master's awarded. Offers adult-gerontology acute care nurse practitioner (DNP); communication sciences and disorders (MS); family nurse practitioner (DNP); health sciences (MAT, MS, DNP); kinesiology and rehabilitative sciences (MAT). *Application fee:* $55. Electronic applications accepted. *Application Contact:* Graduate School, 918-631-2336, Fax: 918-631-2156, E-mail: grad@utulsa.edu. *Dean,* Robin Ploeger, 918-631-3170, E-mail: robin-ploeger@utulsa.edu.

UNIVERSITY OF UTAH, Salt Lake City, UT 84112-1107

General Information State-supported, coed, university. CGS member. *Enrollment:* 6,366 full-time matriculated graduate/professional students (3,016 women), 1,885 part-time matriculated graduate/professional students (832 women). *Enrollment by degree level:* 4,275 master's, 3,976 doctoral. *Graduate faculty:* 1,504 full-time (520 women), 2,485 part-time/adjunct (1,074 women). *Tuition, area resident:* Full-time $7190.66; part-time $2112.48 per year. Tuition, state resident: full-time $7190.66. Tuition, nonresident: full-time $25,195. *Required fees:* $558; $555.04 per unit. Tuition and fees vary according to course level, course load, degree level, program and student level. *Graduate housing:* Rooms and/or apartments available on a first-come, first-served basis to single and married students. Housing application deadline: 4/1. *Student services:* Campus employment opportunities, campus safety program, career counseling, child daycare facilities, exercise/wellness program, free psychological counseling, grant writing training, international student services, low-cost health insurance, multicultural affairs office, services for students with disabilities, teacher training, writing training. *Library facilities:* J. Willard Marriott Library plus 3 others. *Collection:* Books: 3.2 million (physical), 460,000 (digital/electronic); Serial titles: 500 (physical), 11,500 (digital/electronic); Databases: 325. Weekly public service hours: 111; students can reserve study rooms.

Computer facilities: 1,099 computers available on campus for general student use. A campuswide network can be accessed from student residence rooms and from off campus. Online class registration, online classes are available. Website: http://www.utah.edu/

General Application Contact: E-mail: graduate@sa.utah.edu.

GRADUATE UNITS

Graduate School Students: 6,366 full-time (3,016 women), 1,885 part-time (832 women); includes 1,417 minority (103 Black or African American, non-Hispanic/Latino; 27 American Indian or Alaska Native, non-Hispanic/Latino; 401 Asian, non-Hispanic/Latino; 613 Hispanic/Latino; 20 Native Hawaiian or other Pacific Islander, non-Hispanic/Latino; 253 Two or more races, non-Hispanic/Latino), 1,207 international. Average age 30. *Faculty:* 1,504 full-time (520 women), 2,485 part-time/adjunct (1,074 women). Expenses: Contact institution. *Financial support:* Fellowships with tuition reimbursements, research assistantships with tuition reimbursements, teaching assistantships with tuition reimbursements, career-related internships or fieldwork, Federal Work-Study, institutionally sponsored loans, scholarships/grants, traineeships, health care benefits, tuition waivers (full and partial), and unspecified assistantships available. Support available to part-time students. Financial award application deadline: 2/1; financial award applicants required to submit FAFSA. In 2018, 2,155 master's, 756 doctorates awarded. *Program availability:* Part-time, evening/weekend, 100% online, blended/hybrid learning. Offers biotechnology (PSM); computational science (PSM); environmental science (PSM); science instrumentation (PSM). *Application deadline:* For fall admission, 4/1 for domestic and international students; for spring admission, 11/1 for domestic and international students; for summer admission, 3/15 for domestic and international students. *Application fee:* $55 ($65 for international students). Electronic applications accepted. *Application Contact:* Admissions Office, 801-581-7283, Fax: 801-585-7864, E-mail: graduate@sa.utah.edu. *Dean,* Dr. David Kieda, 801-585-5529, Fax: 801-585-7864, E-mail: dave.kieda@utah.edu.

College of Architecture and Planning Students: 91 full-time (37 women), 19 part-time (6 women); includes 27 minority (5 Asian, non-Hispanic/Latino; 16 Hispanic/Latino; 6 Two or more races, non-Hispanic/Latino), 16 international. Average age 29. *Faculty:* 16 full-time (10 women), 24 part-time/adjunct (5 women). Expenses: Contact institution. *Financial support:* Application deadline: 2/1; applicants required to submit FAFSA. In 2018, 47 master's, 3 doctorates awarded. Offers architectural studies (MS); architecture (M Arch); city and metropolitan planning (MCMP); metropolitan planning, policy and design (PhD); metropolitan planning, policy, & design (PhD). *Application deadline:* For fall admission, 1/10 for domestic students, 12/1 for international students. *Application fee:* $0. Electronic applications accepted. *Application Contact:* Lorilie Spegar, Academic Advisor, Recruitment and Admissions, 801-585-2361, Fax: 801-581-8217, E-mail: recruitment@arch.utah.edu. *Dean,* Dr. Keith Diaz Moore, 801-585-1766, Fax: 801-581-8217, E-mail: diazmoore@utah.edu.

College of Education Students: 304 full-time (221 women), 285 part-time (189 women); includes 153 minority (14 Black or African American, non-Hispanic/Latino; 1 American Indian or Alaska Native, non-Hispanic/Latino; 18 Asian, non-Hispanic/Latino; 98 Hispanic/Latino; 3 Native Hawaiian or other Pacific Islander, non-Hispanic/Latino; 19 Two or more races, non-Hispanic/Latino), 11 international. Average age 33. *Faculty:* 48 full-time (31 women), 68 part-time/adjunct (48 women). Expenses: Contact institution. *Financial support:* Application deadline: 2/1; applicants required to submit FAFSA. In 2018, 213 master's, 28 doctorates awarded. Offers board certified behavior analyst (M Ed, MS, PhD); clinical mental health counseling (M Ed); counseling psychology (PhD); deaf and hard of hearing (M Ed); deafblind (M Ed, MS); early childhood deaf and hard of hearing (MS); early childhood special education (M Ed, MS, PhD); early childhood visual impairments (M Ed); education, culture & society (MA); educational leadership & policy (Ed D); educational leadership and policy (Ed D, PhD); educational psychology (Ed S); educational psychology - statistics (M Stat); elementary education (M Ed); history, sociology, and philosophy of education, language culture, curriculum, educational theory, social justice inquiry (PhD); instructional design and educational technology (M Ed); instructional design and technology (MS); interdisciplinary inquiry, reflexive praxis, and reflexive praxis with esl endorsement, secondary licensure, esl endorsement (M Ed); K-12 school administration (M Ed); k-12 teacher leadership (M Ed); learning and cognition (MS, PhD); mild/moderate disabilities (M Ed, MS, PhD); reading and literacy (M Ed, PhD); school counseling (M Ed); school psychology (M Ed, PhD, Ed S); severe disabilities (M Ed, MS, PhD); statistics (M Stat); student affairs (M Ed); visual impairments (M Ed, MS). Electronic applications accepted. *Application Contact:* Elaine Clark, Dean, 801-581-8221, E-mail: el.clark@utah.edu. *Dean,* Elaine Clark, 801-581-8221, E-mail: el.clark@utah.edu.

College of Engineering Students: 966 full-time (214 women), 301 part-time (47 women); includes 135 minority (12 Black or African American, non-Hispanic/Latino; 59 Asian, non-Hispanic/Latino; 40 Hispanic/Latino; 1 Native Hawaiian or other Pacific Islander, non-Hispanic/Latino; 23 Two or more races, non-Hispanic/Latino), 528 international. Average age 28. *Faculty:* 177 full-time (28 women), 90 part-time/adjunct (13 women). Expenses: Contact institution. *Financial support:* Research assistantships with tuition reimbursements, career-related internships or fieldwork, Federal Work-Study, institutionally sponsored loans, scholarships/grants, and unspecified assistantships available. Financial award application deadline: 2/1; financial award applicants required to submit FAFSA. In 2018, 332 master's, 88 doctorates awarded. Offers bioengineering (MS, PhD); chemical engineering (MS, PhD); civil and environmental engineering (MS, PhD); computer science (MS, PhD); computing (MS, PhD); electrical and computer engineering (MS, PhD); electrical engineering (ME); engineering (ME, MEAE, MS, PhD); game art (MEAE); game engineering (MEAE); game production (MEAE); materials science and engineering (MS, PhD); mechanical engineering (MS, PhD); nuclear engineering (MS, PhD); petroleum engineering (MS); software development (MS); technical art (MEAE). Electronic applications accepted. *Application Contact:* Jeff Bates, Assistant Professor, 801-581-8737, E-mail: jeff.bates@utah.edu. *Dean,* Dr. Richard B. Brown, 801-585-7498, E-mail: brown@utah.edu.

College of Fine Arts Students: 120 full-time (67 women), 48 part-time (30 women); includes 30 minority (2 Black or African American, non-Hispanic/Latino; 1 American Indian or Alaska Native, non-Hispanic/Latino; 10 Asian, non-Hispanic/Latino; 12 Hispanic/Latino; 1 Native Hawaiian or other Pacific Islander, non-Hispanic/Latino; 4 Two or more races, non-Hispanic/Latino), 24 international. Average age 32. *Faculty:* 82 full-time (34 women), 128 part-time/adjunct (57 women). Expenses: Contact institution. *Financial support:* Career-related internships or fieldwork, Federal Work-Study, institutionally sponsored loans, and scholarships/grants available. Financial award application deadline: 2/1; financial award applicants required to submit FAFSA. In 2018, 32 master's, 12 doctorates awarded. Offers art history (MA); ceramics (MFA); choral conducting (M Mus, DMA); collaborative piano (M Mus); community-based art education (MFA); composition (M Mus, PhD); dance (MFA, Certificate); drawing (MFA); film and media arts (MFA); graphic design (MFA); instrumental conducting (M Mus, DMA); instrumental performance (M Mus, DMA); jazz studies (M Mus); music (PhD); music education (M Mus, PhD); music history and literature (M Mus); musicology (MA); organ performance (M Mus); painting (MFA); photography/digital imaging (MFA); piano performance (M Mus, DMA); piano performance and pedagogy (M Mus); printmaking (MFA); sculpture/intermedia (MFA); string performance and pedagogy (M Mus); theory (M Mus); vocal performance (DMA). Electronic applications accepted. *Application Contact:* Sarah Reichel, Academic Coordinator, Graduate Studies, 801-585-6972, E-mail: sarah.reichel@utah.edu. *Dean,* John W. Scheib, 801-581-3887, Fax: 801-581-3066.

College of Health Students: 537 full-time (379 women), 66 part-time (46 women); includes 91 minority (8 Black or African American, non-Hispanic/Latino; 2 American Indian or Alaska Native, non-Hispanic/Latino; 18 Asian, non-Hispanic/Latino; 44 Hispanic/Latino; 2 Native Hawaiian or other Pacific Islander, non-Hispanic/Latino; 17 Two or more races, non-Hispanic/Latino; 20 international. Average age 28. *Faculty:* 53 full-time (25 women), 99 part-time/adjunct (71 women). Expenses: Contact institution. *Financial support:* Fellowships with tuition reimbursements, research assistantships with tuition reimbursements, teaching assistantships with tuition reimbursements, career-related internships or fieldwork, Federal Work-Study, institutionally sponsored loans, scholarships/grants, traineeships, health care benefits, tuition waivers (full and partial), and unspecified assistantships available. Financial award application deadline: 2/1; financial award applicants required to submit FAFSA. In 2018, 137 master's, 68 doctorates awarded. Offers audiology (Au D); audiology/speech-language pathology (PhD); health (M Phil, MA, MOT, MS, Au D, DPT, Ed D, OTD, PhD); health promotion and education (M Phil, MA, PhD); kinesiology (MS, PhD); nutrition and integrative physiology (MS, PhD); occupational and recreational therapies (MOT, OTD); parks, recreation, and tourism (MS, PhD); physical therapy (DPT); rehabilitation science (PhD); speech-language pathology (MA, MS, PhD). Electronic applications accepted. *Application Contact:* Dr. Shari Lindsey, Assistant Dean of Students, 801-581-5580, Fax: 801-581-5580, E-mail: shari.lindsey@health.utah.edu. *Dean,* Dr. David H. Perrin, 801-581-8537, Fax: 801-581-5580, E-mail: david.perrin@health.utah.edu.

College of Humanities Students: 167 full-time (94 women), 69 part-time (35 women); includes 42 minority (3 Black or African American, non-Hispanic/Latino; 3 American Indian or Alaska Native, non-Hispanic/Latino; 12 Asian, non-Hispanic/Latino; 17 Hispanic/Latino; 7 Two or more races, non-Hispanic/Latino; 25 international. Average age 33. *Faculty:* 141 full-time (72 women), 57 part-time/adjunct (21 women). Expenses: Contact institution. *Financial support:* Fellowships with full tuition reimbursements, teaching assistantships with tuition reimbursements, Federal Work-Study, scholarships/grants, health care benefits, and unspecified assistantships available. Financial award application deadline: 2/1; financial award applicants required to submit FAFSA. In 2018, 49 master's, 21 doctorates awarded. Offers Arabic (MA, PhD); Asian studies (MA); communicating science, health, environment and risk (MA, MS, PhD); comparative literary and cultural studies (MA, PhD); critical cultural studies (MA, MS, PhD); digital media (MA, MS, PhD); English (MA, MFA, PhD); environmental humanities (MA, MS); French (MA); Hebrew (MA); history (MA, MS, PhD); humanities (MA, MALP, MFA, MS, PhD); Latin American studies (MA); linguistics (MA, PhD); Persian (MA, PhD); philosophy (MA, MS, PhD); political science (MA, PhD); rhetoric (MA, MS, PhD); Spanish (MA, MALP); world languages (MA). Electronic applications accepted. *Application Contact:* Dr. Stuart Culver, Dean, 801-581-6214. *Dean,* Dr. Stuart Culver, 801-581-6214.

College of Mines and Earth Sciences Students: 115 full-time (35 women), 28 part-time (7 women); includes 20 minority (2 Black or African American, non-Hispanic/Latino; 1 American Indian or Alaska Native, non-Hispanic/Latino; 4 Asian, non-Hispanic/Latino; 10 Hispanic/Latino; 3 Two or more races, non-Hispanic/Latino; 40 international. Average age 28. *Faculty:* 50 full-time (10 women), 34 part-time/adjunct (8 women). Expenses: Contact institution. *Financial support:* Federal Work-Study, institutionally sponsored loans, and scholarships/grants available. Financial award application deadline: 2/15; financial award applicants required to submit FAFSA. In 2018, 33 master's, 14 doctorates awarded. Offers atmospheric sciences (MS, PhD); geological engineering (ME, MS, PhD); geology (MS, PhD); geophysics (MS, PhD); metallurgical engineering (ME, MS, PhD); mines and earth sciences (ME, MS, PhD); mining engineering (ME, MS, PhD). Electronic applications accepted. *Application Contact:* Anita Austin Tromp, Executive Assistant, 801-585-9344, E-mail: anita.austin@utah.edu. *Dean,* Dr. Darryl P. Butt, 801-581-8767, E-mail: darryl.butt@utah.edu.

College of Nursing Students: 340 full-time (267 women), 67 part-time (60 women); includes 72 minority (10 Black or African American, non-Hispanic/Latino; 20 Asian, non-Hispanic/Latino; 22 Hispanic/Latino; 2 Native Hawaiian or other Pacific Islander, non-Hispanic/Latino; 18 Two or more races, non-Hispanic/Latino; 6 international. Average age 35. 260 applicants, 72% accepted, 161 enrolled. *Faculty:* 61 full-time (55 women), 33 part-time/adjunct (24 women). Expenses: Contact institution. *Financial support:* In 2018–19, 166 students received support, including 75 fellowships with partial tuition reimbursements available (averaging $10,295 per year), 7 research assistantships with partial tuition reimbursements available (averaging $13,008 per year), 18 teaching assistantships with partial tuition reimbursements available (averaging $17,423 per year); Federal Work-Study, institutionally sponsored loans, scholarships/grants, traineeships, health care benefits, and unspecified assistantships also available. Support available to part-time students. Financial award application deadline: 1/20; financial award applicants required to submit FAFSA. In 2018, 19 master's, 101 doctorates awarded. *Program availability:* Part-time, 100% online, blended/hybrid learning. Offers gerontology (MS, Certificate); nursing (MS, DNP, PhD, Certificate). *Application deadline:* For fall admission, 12/1 for domestic and international students. *Application fee:* $55 ($65 for international students). Electronic applications accepted. *Application Contact:* Carrie Radmall, Associate Director of Student Services, 801-581-3414, E-mail: carrie.radmall@nurs.utah.edu. *Dean,* Barbara Wilson, PhD, 801-581-8262, E-mail: barbara.wilson@nurs.utah.edu.

College of Pharmacy Students: 256 full-time (145 women), 15 part-time (9 women); includes 92 minority (5 Black or African American, non-Hispanic/Latino; 57 Asian, non-Hispanic/Latino; 13 Hispanic/Latino; 17 Two or more races, non-Hispanic/Latino; 20 international. Average age 27. *Faculty:* 28 full-time (10 women), 44 part-time/adjunct (19 women). Expenses: Contact institution. *Financial support:* Institutionally sponsored loans and scholarships/grants available. Financial award application deadline: 2/1; financial award applicants required to submit FAFSA. In 2018, 1 master's, 62 doctorates awarded. Offers health system pharmacy administration (MS); medicinal chemistry (MS, PhD); outcomes research and health policy (PhD); pharmaceutics and pharmaceutical chemistry (PhD); pharmacology and toxicology (PhD); pharmacy (MS, PhD, Pharm D). Electronic applications accepted. *Application Contact:* Dallas Nelson, Senior Academic Advisor, 801-581-5384, E-mail: dallas.nelson@pharm.utah.edu. *Dean,* Dr. Randall T. Peterson, 801-587-3064, E-mail: randall.peterson@pharm.utah.edu.

College of Science Students: 355 full-time (155 women), 134 part-time (56 women); includes 50 minority (1 Black or African American, non-Hispanic/Latino; 1 American Indian or Alaska Native, non-Hispanic/Latino; 21 Asian, non-Hispanic/Latino; 19 Hispanic/Latino; 8 Two or more races, non-Hispanic/Latino; 140 international. Average age 28. *Faculty:* 143 full-time (26 women), 106 part-time/adjunct (34 women). Expenses: Contact institution. *Financial support:* Federal Work-Study, institutionally sponsored loans, and scholarships/grants available. Financial award application deadline: 2/1; financial award applicants required to submit FAFSA. In 2018, 60 master's, 65 doctorates awarded. Offers chemical physics (PhD); chemistry (MS, PhD); doctor of philosophy (PhD); masters of science (MS); mathematics (MA, MS, PhD); mathematics teaching (MS); medical physics (MS, PhD); physics (MA, MS, PhD); physics teaching (PhD); science (M Stat, MA, MS, PhD); science teacher education (MS); statistics (M Stat). Electronic applications accepted. *Application Contact:* Lisa Batchelder, Student Services and Administration Manager, 801-581-3374, E-mail: office@science.utah.edu. *Dean,* Dr. Peter Trapa, 801-581-6958, E-mail: ptrapa@math.utah.edu.

College of Social and Behavioral Science Students: 276 full-time (154 women), 224 part-time (118 women); includes 87 minority (5 Black or African American, non-Hispanic/Latino; 2 American Indian or Alaska Native, non-Hispanic/Latino; 10 Asian, non-Hispanic/Latino; 47 Hispanic/Latino; 1 Native Hawaiian or other Pacific Islander, non-Hispanic/Latino; 22 Two or more races, non-Hispanic/Latino; 58 international. Average age 32. *Faculty:* 131 full-time (51 women), 108 part-time/adjunct (46 women). Expenses: Contact institution. *Financial support:* Fellowships, Federal Work-Study, and scholarships/grants available. Financial award application deadline: 2/1; financial award applicants required to submit FAFSA. In 2018, 108 master's, 25 doctorates awarded. Offers American politics (MA, MS, PhD); anthropology (MA, MS, PhD); clinical psychology (PhD); comparative politics (MA, MS, PhD); econometrics (M Stat); economics (M Phil, MA, MS, PhD); geographic information science (MS); geography (MS, PhD); human development and social policy (MS); international affairs and global enterprise (MS); international relations (MA, MS, PhD); political science (MA, MS, PhD); political theory (MA, MS, PhD); psychology (PhD); public administration (Exec MPA, MPA); public policy (MPP); social and behavioral science (Exec MPA, M Phil, M Stat, MA, MPA, MPP, MS, PhD); sociology (M Stat, MA, MS, PhD). Electronic applications accepted. *Application Contact:* Bobbi Davis, Student Services Director, 801-581-7579, E-mail: bobbi.davis@utah.edu. *Dean,* Cynthia Berg, 801-581-8620, E-mail: cynthia.berg@csbs.utah.edu.

College of Social Work Students: 299 full-time (238 women), 26 part-time (22 women); includes 84 minority (12 Black or African American, non-Hispanic/Latino; 5 American Indian or Alaska Native, non-Hispanic/Latino; 10 Asian, non-Hispanic/Latino; 41 Hispanic/Latino; 2 Native Hawaiian or other Pacific Islander, non-Hispanic/Latino; 14 Two or more races, non-Hispanic/Latino; 2 international. Average age 32. *Faculty:* 17 full-time (8 women), 52 part-time/adjunct (35 women). Expenses: Contact institution. *Financial support:* Federal Work-Study, institutionally sponsored loans, and scholarships/grants available. Financial award application deadline: 4/30; financial award applicants required to submit FAFSA. In 2018, 164 master's, 5 doctorates awarded. *Program availability:* Part-time, evening/weekend. Offers social work (MSW, PhD). Electronic applications accepted. *Application Contact:* Elizabeth Perez, Director of Academic Advising, 801-585-1596, E-mail: elizabeth.perez@utah.edu. *Dean,* Dr. Martell L. Teasley, 801-581-6194, E-mail: martell.teasley@utah.edu.

David Eccles School of Business *Program availability:* Part-time, evening/weekend. Offers accounting (PhD); accounting information systems (M Acc); business (EMBA, M Acc, MBA, MHA, MRED, MS, MSF, PMBA, PhD, Graduate Certificate); business administration (EMBA, MBA, PMBA); finance (MSF); financial/audit (M Acc); healthcare administration (MHA); information systems (MS, PhD, Graduate Certificate); marketing (PhD); operations management (PhD); organizational behavior (PhD); real estate development (MRED); strategic management (PhD); tax (M Acc). Electronic applications accepted.

School of Dentistry Students: 174 full-time (54 women); includes 34 minority (2 Black or African American, non-Hispanic/Latino; 15 Asian, non-Hispanic/Latino; 13 Hispanic/Latino; 4 Two or more races, non-Hispanic/Latino. Average age 26. 450 applicants, 11% accepted, 50 enrolled. *Faculty:* 33 full-time (12 women), 55 part-time/adjunct (6 women). Expenses: Contact institution. *Financial support:* Scholarships/grants available. Financial award application deadline: 4/1; financial award applicants required to submit FAFSA. In 2018, 23 doctorates awarded. Offers dentistry (DDS). *Application deadline:* For fall admission, 10/1 priority date for domestic students. *Application fee:* $75. Electronic applications accepted. *Application Contact:* Gary W. Lowder, DDS, Office of Admissions, 801-213-3506, Fax: 801-585-6485, E-mail: dental.admissions@hsc.utah.edu. *Dean,* Dr. Wyatt R. Hume, DDS, 801-587-1208, E-mail: wyatt.hume@hsc.utah.edu.

School of Medicine Offers biochemistry (MS, PhD); biostatistics (M Stat); experimental pathology (PhD); human genetics (MS, PhD); laboratory medicine and biomedical science (MS); medical informatics (MS, PhD, Certificate); medicine (M Phil, M Stat, MPAS, MPH, MS, MSPH, MD, PhD, Certificate); molecular biology (PhD); neurobiology and anatomy (PhD); neuroscience (PhD); oncological sciences (M Phil, MS, PhD); physician assistant (MPAS); physiology (PhD); public health (MPH, MSPH, PhD).

S.J. Quinney College of Law Students: 295 full-time (130 women), 3 part-time (2 women); includes 43 minority (1 Black or African American, non-Hispanic/Latino; 3 American Indian or Alaska Native, non-Hispanic/Latino; 8 Asian, non-Hispanic/Latino; 28 Hispanic/Latino; 1 Native Hawaiian or other Pacific Islander, non-Hispanic/Latino; 2 Two or more races, non-Hispanic/Latino; 3 international. Average age 29. *Faculty:* 25 full-time (11 women), 42 part-time/adjunct (17 women). Expenses: Contact institution. *Financial support:* Fellowships with partial tuition reimbursements, Federal Work-Study, institutionally sponsored loans, scholarships/grants, and tuition waivers (full and partial) available. Financial award application deadline: 2/1; financial award applicants required to submit FAFSA. In 2018, 1 master's, 93 doctorates awarded. *Program availability:* Part-time, evening/weekend. Offers law (LL M, MLS, JD). *Application deadline:* For fall admission, 1/15 priority date for domestic students, 2/15 priority date for international students. Applications are processed on a rolling basis. *Application fee:* $60. Electronic applications accepted. *Application Contact:* Reyes Aguilar, Associate Director for Admission and Financial Aid, 801-581-6563, E-mail: reyes.aguilar@law.utah.edu. *Dean,* Elizabeth K. Warner, 801-585-9318, E-mail: elizabeth.warner@law.utah.edu.

UNIVERSITY OF VALLEY FORGE, Phoenixville, PA 19460

General Information Independent-religious, coed, comprehensive institution.

GRADUATE UNITS

Program in Christian Leadership Offers Christian leadership (MA).

Program in Music Technology *Program availability:* Online learning. Offers music technology (MM).

Program in Theology Offers theology (MA).

Program in Worship Studies Offers worship studies (MA).

UNIVERSITY OF VERMONT, Burlington, VT 05405

General Information State-supported, coed, university. CGS member. *Graduate housing:* On-campus housing not available. *Research affiliation:* Miner Institute (animal sciences).

GRADUATE UNITS

Graduate College *Program availability:* Part-time, 100% online, blended/hybrid learning. Offers bioengineering (PhD); cellular, molecular and biomedical sciences (PhD); food systems (MS, PhD); materials science (MS, PhD); neuroscience (PhD). Electronic applications accepted.

College of Agriculture and Life Sciences *Program availability:* Part-time. Offers agriculture and life sciences (MPA, MS, PhD, Graduate Certificate); agroecology (Graduate Certificate); animal science (MS); animal, nutrition and food sciences (PhD); community development and applied economics (MS); dietetics (MS); nutrition and food sciences (MS); plant and soil science (MS, PhD); plant biology (MS, PhD); public administration (MPA). Electronic applications accepted.

College of Arts and Sciences *Program availability:* Part-time. Offers arts and sciences (MA, MAT, MS, MST, PhD, Graduate Certificate); biology (MS, PhD); biology education (MST); chemistry (MS, PhD); clinical developmental psychology (PhD); clinical psychology (PhD); English (MA); geology (MS); German (MA); Greek and Latin (MA); Greek and Latin languages (Graduate Certificate); historic preservation (MS); history (MA); Latin (MAT); physics (MS); psychology (PhD). Electronic applications accepted.

College of Education and Social Services *Program availability:* Part-time, evening/weekend. Offers counseling (MS); curriculum and instruction (MAT); early childhood special education (M Ed); education and social services (M Ed, MAT, MS, MSW, Ed D); educational leadership (M Ed); educational leadership and policy studies (Ed D, PhD); higher education and student affairs administration (M Ed); interdisciplinary studies (M Ed); social work (MSW); special education, grades K-12 (M Ed). Electronic applications accepted.

College of Engineering and Mathematical Sciences *Program availability:* Part-time. Offers biomedical engineering (MS); biostatistics (MS); civil and environmental engineering (MS, PhD); complex systems and data science (MS, PhD); computer science (MS, PhD); electrical engineering (MS, PhD); engineering and mathematical sciences (MS, MST, PhD); engineering management (MS); mathematics (MS, MST, PhD); mechanical engineering (MS, PhD); statistics (MS). Electronic applications accepted.

College of Nursing and Health Sciences Offers communication sciences and disorders (MS); human functioning and rehabilitation science (PhD); medical laboratory science (MS); nursing (MS, DNP, Post-Graduate Certificate); nursing and health sciences (MS, DNP, DPT, PhD, Post-Graduate Certificate); physical activity and wellness science (MS); physical therapy (DPT). Electronic applications accepted.

Grossman School of Business *Program availability:* Part-time. Offers accountancy (M Acc); business (M Acc, MBA); sustainable innovation (MBA). Electronic applications accepted.

The Rubenstein School of Environment and Natural Resources *Program availability:* Part-time. Offers ecological economics (Certificate); environment and natural resources (MPS, MS, PhD, Certificate); leadership for sustainability (MPS); natural resources (MS); natural resources (PhD). MELP/MS offered in collaboration with Vermont Law School. Electronic applications accepted.

The Robert Larner, MD College of Medicine Offers medicine (MPH, MS, MD, PhD, Certificate, Graduate Certificate). Electronic applications accepted.

Graduate Programs in Medicine *Program availability:* 100% online. Offers biochemistry (MS, PhD); clinical and translational science (MS, PhD, Certificate); epidemiology (Graduate Certificate); global and environmental health (Graduate Certificate); healthcare management and policy (Graduate Certificate); medical science (MS); medicine (MPH, MS, PhD, Certificate, Graduate Certificate); pathology and laboratory medicine (MS); pharmacology (MS, PhD); public health (MPH). Electronic applications accepted.

UNIVERSITY OF VICTORIA, Victoria, BC V8W 2Y2, Canada

General Information Province-supported, coed, university. *Graduate housing:* Rooms and/or apartments available on a first-come, first-served basis to single and married students. Housing application deadline: 2/1. *Research affiliation:* Dominion Astrophysical Observatory, Bamfield Marine Research Station (marine biology), Tri-University Meson Facility, Canada/France/Hawaii Telescope Observatory, Institute of Ocean Sciences (geography, oceanography).

GRADUATE UNITS

Faculty of Graduate Studies *Program availability:* Part-time, online learning. Electronic applications accepted.

Faculty of Education Offers aboriginal communities counseling (M Ed); art education (M Ed, PhD); coaching studies (co-operative education) (M Ed); counseling (M Ed, MA); curriculum studies (M Ed, PhD); early childhood education (M Ed, PhD); education (M Ed, M Sc, MA, PhD); educational psychology (M Ed, MA, PhD); educational studies (PhD); kinesiology (M Sc, MA); language and literacy (M Ed, MA, PhD); leadership studies (M Ed, MA); leisure service administration (MA); mathematics (M Ed, MA, PhD); music education (M Ed, MA, PhD); physical education (MA); science (M Ed, MA, PhD); social studies (M Ed, MA); social, cultural and foundational studies (MA, PhD); technology and environmental education (PhD).

Faculty of Engineering Offers computer science (M Sc, PhD); electrical and computer engineering (M Eng, MA Sc, PhD); engineering (M Eng, M Sc, MA Sc, PhD); mechanical engineering (M Eng, MA Sc, PhD).

Faculty of Fine Arts Offers composition (M Mus); design (MFA); digital multimedia (MFA); directing (MFA); drawing (MFA); fine arts (M Mus, MA, MFA, PhD); history in art (MA, PhD); musicology (MA, PhD); musicology with performance (MA); painting (MFA); performance (M Mus); photography (MFA); sculpture (MFA); theatre history (MA); video (MFA); writing (MFA).

Faculty of Human and Social Development Offers advanced nursing practice (advanced practice leadership option) (MN); advanced nursing practice (nurse educator option) (MN); advanced nursing practice (nurse practitioner option) (MN); child and youth care (MA, PhD); dispute resolution (MADR); health information science (M Sc); human and social development (M Sc, MA, MADR, MN, MPA, MSW,

PhD); indigenous governance (MA); nursing (PhD); public administration (MPA, PhD); social work (MSW); studies in policy and practice (MA).

Faculty of Humanities Offers applied linguistics (MA); English (MA, PhD); German studies (MA); Greek and Roman studies (MA, PhD); Hispanic and Italian studies (MA); Hispanic studies (MA); history (MA, PhD); humanities (MA, PhD); linguistics (MA, PhD); literature (MA); Pacific and Asian studies (MA); philosophy (MA); teaching emphasis (MA).

Faculty of Science Offers astronomy and astrophysics (M Sc, PhD); biochemistry (M Sc, PhD); biology (M Sc, PhD); chemistry (M Sc, PhD); condensed matter physics (M Sc, PhD); earth and ocean sciences (M Sc, PhD); experimental particle physics (M Sc, PhD); mathematics and statistics (M Sc, MA, PhD); medical physics (M Sc, PhD); microbiology (M Sc, PhD); ocean physics (M Sc, PhD); science (M Sc, MA, PhD); theoretical physics (M Sc, PhD). Electronic applications accepted.

Faculty of Social Sciences Offers anthropology (MA); clinical psychology (PhD); clinical psychology (neuropsychology) (M Sc); cognition and brain science (M Sc, PhD); economics (MA, PhD); experimental neuropsychology (M Sc, PhD); geography (M Sc, MA, PhD); individualized study (M Sc); life span development psychology (PhD); life span developmental psychology (M Sc); political science (MA, PhD); social psychology (M Sc, PhD); social sciences (M Sc, MA, PhD); sociology (MA, PhD).

Peter B. Gustavson School of Business *Program availability:* Part-time. Offers business (MBA). Electronic applications accepted.

Faculty of Law *Program availability:* Part-time. Offers law (LL M, JD, PhD). Electronic applications accepted.

UNIVERSITY OF VIRGINIA, Charlottesville, VA 22903

General Information State-supported, coed, university. CGS member. *Graduate housing:* Rooms and/or apartments available on a first-come, first-served basis to single and married students. Housing application deadline: 6/1. *Research affiliation:* Oak Ridge National Laboratory (energy), National Institute of Aerospace, Jefferson National Accelerator Facility (nuclear physics), Federal Executive Institute (leadership development), National Radio Astronomy Observatory, The Judge Advocate General's School, U.S. Army (law).

GRADUATE UNITS

College and Graduate School of Arts and Sciences *Program availability:* Part-time. Offers anthropology (MA, PhD); art and architectural history (MA, PhD); arts and sciences (MA, MAPE, MFA, MS, PhD); astronomy (MS, PhD); biology (MA, MS, PhD); chemistry (MA, MS, PhD); classics (MA, PhD); creative writing (MFA); drama (MFA); East Asian studies (MA); economics (MA, PhD); English (MA, PhD); environmental sciences (MA, MS, PhD); European studies (MA); foreign affairs (MA, PhD); French (MA, PhD); German (MA); government (MA, PhD); history (MA, PhD); linguistics (MA); math education (MA); mathematics (MA, MS, PhD); Middle Eastern and South Asian studies (MA); music (MA, PhD); philosophy (MA, PhD); physics (MA, MS, PhD); physics education (MAPE); psychology (MA, PhD); religion, politics and global society (MA); religious studies (MA, PhD); Slavic languages and literatures (MA, PhD); sociology (MA, PhD); Spanish (MA, PhD); statistics (MS, PhD). Electronic applications accepted.

Curry School of Education Offers administration and supervision (M Ed, Ed D, PhD, Ed S); applied developmental science (M Ed, PhD); clinical and school psychology (PhD); counselor education (M Ed, Ed D, PhD, Ed S); curriculum and instruction (M Ed, Ed D, PhD, Ed S); early childhood special education (MT); education (M Ed, MS, MT, Ed D, PhD, Ed S); education evaluation (PhD); educational evaluation (M Ed); educational policy (PhD); educational psychology (M Ed, Ed D, PhD, Ed S); educational research (Ed D, PhD); elementary education (M Ed, MT, M Ed D); English education (M Ed, MT, Ed D, PhD); foreign language education (M Ed, MT); gifted education (M Ed); higher education (M Ed, Ed D, PhD, Ed S); instructional technology (M Ed, PhD, Ed S); kinesiology (MT, PhD); math education (PhD); mathematics education (M Ed, Ed D); reading education (PhD); research statistics and evaluation (Ed D); research, statistics and evaluation (PhD); school psychology (Ed D, PhD); science education (Ed D, PhD); social studies education (M Ed, MT, PhD); special education (M Ed, Ed D, PhD, Ed S); speech communication disorders (M Ed, PhD); student affairs practice (M Ed); world languages education (MT). Electronic applications accepted.

Darden School of Business Offers business (MBA, MSBA, PhD). Electronic applications accepted.

Data Science Institute Offers data science (MS).

Frank Batten Sr. School of Leadership and Public Policy Offers leadership and public policy (MPP). Electronic applications accepted.

McIntire School of Commerce Students: 342 full-time (134 women); includes 59 minority (16 Black or African American, non-Hispanic/Latino; 31 Asian, non-Hispanic/Latino; 12 Hispanic/Latino), 77 international. Average age 23. *Faculty:* 76 full-time (23 women), 1 (woman) part-time/adjunct. *Expenses:* Contact institution. *Financial support:* Federal Work-Study, scholarships/grants, and unspecified assistantships available. Financial award application deadline: 2/1; financial award applicants required to submit FAFSA. Offers accounting (MS); business analytics (MSC); commerce (MS, MSC, Certificate); finance (MSC); global commerce (MS); global strategic management (MS); international management (Certificate); management of information technology (MS); marketing and management (MSC). *Application deadline:* Applications are processed on a rolling basis. *Application fee:* $75. Electronic applications accepted. *Application Contact:* Emma Candelier, Assistant Dean of Graduate Recruiting, 434-243-4992, Fax: 434-924-4511, E-mail: ecandelier@virginia.edu. *Dean,* Carl Zeithaml, 877-349-2620, Fax: 434-924-7074, E-mail: mcintiregrad@virginia.edu.

School of Architecture Offers architectural history (M Arch H, PhD); architecture (M Arch, M Arch H, M Land Arch, MUEP, PhD); landscape architecture (M Land Arch); the constructed environment (PhD); urban and environmental planning (MUEP). Electronic applications accepted.

School of Engineering and Applied Science *Program availability:* Part-time, online learning. Offers biomedical engineering (ME, MS, PhD); chemical engineering (ME, MS, PhD); civil and environmental engineering (ME, MS, PhD); computer engineering (ME, MS, PhD); computer science (MCS, MS, PhD); electrical engineering (ME, MS, PhD); engineering and applied science (MCS, ME, MEP, MMSE, MS, PhD); engineering physics (ME, MS, PhD); materials science (MMSE, MS, PhD); mechanical and aerospace engineering (ME, MS, PhD); systems and information engineering (ME, MS, PhD). Electronic applications accepted.

School of Law Offers law (LL M, JD, SJD). JD/MA in international relations offered jointly with The Johns Hopkins University. Electronic applications accepted.

School of Medicine Offers biochemistry (PhD); biological and physical sciences (MS); biophysics (PhD); cell biology (PhD); clinical investigation and patient-oriented research (MS); clinical research (MS); informatics in medicine (MS); medicine (MPH, MS, MD, PhD); microbiology, immunology, and cancer biology (PhD); neuroscience (PhD); pathology (PhD); pharmacology (PhD); physiology (PhD); public health (MPH). Electronic applications accepted.

School of Nursing *Program availability:* Part-time. Offers acute and specialty care (MSN); acute care nurse practitioner (MSN); clinical nurse leadership (MSN); community-public health leadership (MSN); nursing (DNP, PhD); psychiatric mental health counseling (MSN). Electronic applications accepted.

UNIVERSITY OF WASHINGTON, Seattle, WA 98195

General Information State-supported, coed, university. CGS member. *Graduate housing:* Rooms and/or apartments available on a first-come, first-served basis to single and married students. Housing application deadline: 5/1. *Research affiliation:* Fred Hutchinson Cancer Research Center, Children's Hospital and Regional Medical Center (pediatric research).

GRADUATE UNITS

Graduate School *Program availability:* Part-time, evening/weekend, online learning. Offers biology for teachers (MS); global trade, transportation and logistics studies (Certificate); museum evaluation (MA); Near and Middle Eastern studies (PhD); quantitative ecology and resource management (MS, PhD). Electronic applications accepted.

College of Arts and Sciences *Program availability:* Part-time, evening/weekend. Offers acting (MFA); animal behavior (PhD); anthropology (MA, PhD); applied child and adolescent psychology: prevention and treatment (MA); applied mathematics (MS, PhD); art (MFA); art history (MA, PhD); arts and sciences (MA, MAIS, MAT, MC, MFA, MM, MS, Au D, DMA, PhD); astronomy (MS, PhD); audiology (Au D); behavioral neuroscience (PhD); biology (PhD); Buddhist studies (MA, PhD); Central Asian studies (MAIS); chemistry (MS, PhD); China studies (MAIS); Chinese language and literature (MA, PhD); choral conducting (MM, DMA); classics (MA, PhD); classics and philosophy (PhD); clinical psychology (PhD); cognition and perception (PhD); communication (MA, MC, PhD); comparative literature (MA, PhD); comparative religion (MAIS); computational linguistics (MA); costume design (MFA); creative writing (MFA); dance (MFA); design (MFA); developmental psychology (PhD); directing (MFA); dramatic theory (PhD); East European studies (MAIS); economics (PhD); English as a second language (MAT); English literature and language (MA, MAT, PhD); ethnomusicology (MA, PhD); French (MA, PhD); gender, women and sexuality studies (PhD); geography (MA, PhD); Germanics (MA, PhD); Hispanic literary and cultural studies (MA); history (MA, PhD); industrial design (MFA); international studies (MAIS, PhD); Italian (MA); Japan studies (MAIS); Japanese language and literature (MA, PhD); Korea studies (MAIS); Korean language and literature (MA, PhD); lighting design (MFA); linguistics (MA, PhD); mathematics (MA, MS, PhD); Middle East studies (MAIS); music (MA, MM, DMA, PhD); music education (MA, PhD); music history (MA, PhD); Near Eastern languages and civilization (MA); numerical analysis (MS); optimization (MS); painting and drawing (MFA); philosophy (MA, PhD); photography (MFA); physics (MS, PhD); political science (MA, PhD); quantitative psychology (PhD); Romance linguistics (MA, PhD); Russian literature (MA, PhD); Russian studies (MAIS); Russian, East European and Central Asian studies (MAIS); Scandinavian studies (MA, PhD); scenic design (MFA); Slavic linguistics (MA, PhD); social psychology and personality (PhD); sociology (MA, PhD); South Asian language and literature (MA, PhD); South Asian studies (MAIS); Southeast Asian studies (MAIS); speech and hearing sciences (PhD); speech-language pathology (MS); statistics (MS, PhD); theatre and performance history (PhD); visual communication design (MFA). Electronic applications accepted.

College of Built Environments *Program availability:* Part-time, evening/weekend. Offers architecture (M Arch, MS); built environment (PhD); built environments (M Arch, MLA, MS, MSCM, MUP, PhD, Certificate); construction management (MSCM); design computing (Certificate); design firm leadership and management (Certificate); historic preservation (Certificate); landscape architecture (MLA); lighting (Certificate); urban design (Certificate); urban design and planning (PhD); urban planning (MUP). Electronic applications accepted.

College of Education *Program availability:* Part-time, evening/weekend. Offers curriculum and instruction (M Ed, Ed D, PhD); early childhood special education (M Ed); educational leadership and policy studies (M Ed, Ed D, PhD); educational psychology (M Ed, PhD); emotional and behavioral disabilities (M Ed); human development and cognition (M Ed); instructional leadership (M Ed); intercollegiate athletic leadership (M Ed); learning disabilities (M Ed); learning sciences (M Ed, PhD); low-incidence disabilities (M Ed); measurement, statistics and research design (M Ed); school psychology (M Ed); special education (M Ed, Ed D, PhD); teacher education (MIT). Electronic applications accepted.

College of Engineering Students: 1,679 full-time (535 women), 989 part-time (298 women); includes 575 minority (39 Black or African American, non-Hispanic/Latino; 5 American Indian or Alaska Native, non-Hispanic/Latino; 323 Asian, non-Hispanic/Latino; 121 Hispanic/Latino; 3 Native Hawaiian or other Pacific Islander, non-Hispanic/Latino; 84 Two or more races, non-Hispanic/Latino; 996 international. Average age 27. 7,345 applicants, 32% accepted, 838 enrolled. *Faculty:* 264 full-time (64 women). Expenses: Contact institution. *Financial support:* In 2018–19, 1,126 students received support, including 130 fellowships with full tuition reimbursements available (averaging $33,722 per year), 727 research assistantships with full tuition reimbursements available (averaging $33,722 per year), 312 teaching assistantships with full tuition reimbursements available (averaging $33,722 per year); career-related internships or fieldwork, Federal Work-Study, institutionally sponsored loans, scholarships/grants, traineeships, health care benefits, tuition waivers (full), unspecified assistantships, and stipend supplements also available. Financial award application deadline: 2/28; financial award applicants required to submit FAFSA. In 2018, 736 master's, 112 doctorates awarded. *Program availability:* Part-time, online learning. Offers aeronautics and astronautics (MAE, MSAA, PhD); applied bioengineering (MAB); applied materials science and engineering (MS); bioengineering (MS, PhD); bioengineering and nanotechnology (PhD); chemical engineering (MS, PhD); chemical engineering and advanced data science (PhD); chemical engineering and nanotechnology (PhD); computer science and engineering (MS, PhD); construction engineering (MSCE, PhD); electrical engineering (MS, PhD); electrical engineering and nanotechnology (PhD); engineering (MAB, MAE, MISE, MS, MSAA, MSCE, MSE, MSME, PhD, Certificate); environmental engineering (MSCE, PhD); geotechnical engineering (MSCE, PhD); human centered design and engineering (MS, PhD); hydrology and hydrodynamics (MSCE, PhD); industrial and systems engineering (MISE, MS, PhD); materials science and engineering (MS, PhD); materials science and engineering and nanotechnology (PhD); materials science and engineering, nanotechnology, and molecular engineering (PhD); mechanical engineering (MSE, MSME, PhD); pharmaceutical bioengineering (MS); structural engineering and mechanics (MSCE); transportation engineering (MSCE, PhD); user centered design (Certificate). *Application deadline:* For fall admission, 12/1 for domestic and international students. *Application fee:* $85. Electronic applications accepted. *Application Contact:* Mike Engh, Assistant Director, Academic Affairs, 206-685-3714, Fax: 206-685-0666, E-mail: enghmw@uw.edu.

Interim Dean of Engineering, Dr. Greg Miller, 206-543-1829, Fax: 206-685-0666, E-mail: gmiller@uw.edu.

College of the Environment Offers aquatic and fishery sciences (MS, PhD); atmospheric sciences (MS, PhD); biological oceanography (MS, PhD); bioresource science and engineering (MS, PhD); chemical oceanography (MS, PhD); environment (MEH, MFR, MMA, MS, PhD, Graduate Certificate); environmental horticulture (MEH); forest ecology (MS, PhD); forest management (MFR); forest soils (MS, PhD); geology (MS, PhD); geophysics (MS, PhD); marine and environmental affairs (MMA, Graduate Certificate); marine geology and geophysics (MS, PhD); physical oceanography (MS, PhD); restoration ecology (MS, PhD); restoration ecology and environmental horticulture (MS, PhD); social sciences (MS, PhD); sustainable resource management (MS, PhD); wildlife science (MS, PhD). Electronic applications accepted.

Evans School of Public Policy and Governance *Program availability:* Part-time, evening/weekend. Offers public administration (MPA); public policy and management (PhD). Electronic applications accepted.

Information School Students: 347 full-time (229 women), 259 part-time (195 women); includes 129 minority (23 Black or African American, non-Hispanic/Latino; 7 American Indian or Alaska Native, non-Hispanic/Latino; 59 Asian, non-Hispanic/Latino; 36 Hispanic/Latino; 4 Native Hawaiian or other Pacific Islander, non-Hispanic/Latino), 160 international. Average age 32. 1,190 applicants, 42% accepted, 264 enrolled. *Faculty:* 51 full-time (23 women), 38 part-time/adjunct (21 women). Expenses: Contact institution. *Financial support:* In 2018–19, 73 students received support. Fellowships with full tuition reimbursements available, research assistantships with full tuition reimbursements available, teaching assistantships with full tuition reimbursements available, Federal Work-Study, institutionally sponsored loans, scholarships/grants, health care benefits, tuition waivers (full and partial), and unspecified assistantships available. Support available to part-time students. Financial award application deadline: 10/1; financial award applicants required to submit FAFSA. In 2018, 231 master's, 10 doctorates awarded. *Program availability:* Part-time, evening/weekend, 100% online coursework with required attendance at on-campus orientation at start of program. *Application deadline:* For fall admission, 12/1 priority date for domestic and international students. *Application fee:* $85. Electronic applications accepted. *Application Contact:* Kari Brothers, Admissions Counselor, 206-616-5541, Fax: 206-616-3152, E-mail: kari683@uw.edu. *Dean,* Dr. Anind Dey, E-mail: anind@uw.edu.

Michael G. Foster School of Business *Program availability:* Part-time, evening/weekend, blended/hybrid learning. Offers auditing and assurance (MP Acc); business administration (MBA, PhD); entrepreneurship (MS); executive business administration (MBA); global executive business administration (MBA); information systems (MSIS); supply chain management (MSSCM); taxation (MP Acc); technology management (MBA). Electronic applications accepted.

School of Dentistry Offers dental surgery (DDS); dentistry (MS, MSD, DDS, PhD, Certificate); endodontics (MSD, Certificate); oral biology (MS, MSD, PhD); oral medicine (MSD); orthodontics (MSD, Certificate); pediatric dentistry (MSD, Certificate); periodontics (MSD, PhD, Certificate); prosthodontics (MSD, Certificate).

School of Law Offers Asian law (LL M, PhD); intellectual property law and policy (LL M); law (JD); law of sustainable international development (LL M); taxation (LL M).

School of Medicine *Program availability:* Part-time. Offers biochemistry (PhD); bioethics (MA); biological structure (PhD); biomedical and health informatics (MS, PhD); comparative medicine (MS); genome sciences (PhD); immunology (PhD); laboratory medicine (MS); medicine (MA, MOT, MPO, MS, DPT, MD, PhD); microbiology (PhD); molecular and cellular biology (PhD); molecular medicine and mechanisms of disease (PhD); neurobiology and behavior (PhD); occupational therapy (MOT); pharmacology (PhD); physical therapy (DPT); physiology and biophysics (PhD); prosthetics and orthotics (MPO); rehabilitation science (PhD). Electronic applications accepted.

School of Nursing *Program availability:* Part-time. Offers nursing (MN, MS, DNP, PhD, Graduate Certificate).

School of Public Health Students: 789 full-time (575 women), 201 part-time (130 women); includes 327 minority (60 Black or African American, non-Hispanic/Latino; 15 American Indian or Alaska Native, non-Hispanic/Latino; 181 Asian, non-Hispanic/Latino; 63 Hispanic/Latino; 8 Native Hawaiian or other Pacific Islander, non-Hispanic/Latino), 132 international. Average age 31. 1,918 applicants, 40% accepted, 384 enrolled. *Faculty:* 264 full-time (123 women), 203 part-time/adjunct (101 women). Expenses: Contact institution. *Financial support:* Fellowships with full and partial tuition reimbursements, research assistantships with full and partial tuition reimbursements, teaching assistantships with full and partial tuition reimbursements, career-related internships or fieldwork, Federal Work-Study, institutionally sponsored loans, scholarships/grants, traineeships, health care benefits, tuition waivers (full and partial), and unspecified assistantships available. Support available to part-time students. In 2018, 298 master's, 40 doctorates awarded. *Program availability:* Part-time, evening/weekend, blended/hybrid learning. Offers applied toxicology (MS); biostatistics (MPH, MS, PhD); clinical and translational research methods (MS); community-oriented public health practice (MPH); environmental and occupational health (MPH); environmental and occupational hygiene (PhD); environmental health (MS); environmental toxicology (MS, PhD); epidemiology (PhD); general epidemiology (MPH, MS); genetic epidemiology (MS); global health (MPH); global health metrics and implementation science (PhD); health administration (EMHA, MHA); health informatics and health information management (MHIHIM); health metrics and evaluation (MPH); health services (MPH, MS, PhD); health systems and policy (MPH); leadership, policy and management (MPH); maternal and child health (MPH); nutritional sciences (PhD); nutritional sciences, dietetics practice (MS); occupational and environmental exposure sciences (MS); occupational and environmental medicine (MPH); pathobiology (PhD); public health (EMHA, MHA, MHIHIM, MPH, MS, PhD, Graduate Certificate); public health genetics (MPH, PhD, Graduate Certificate); public health nutrition, public health nutrition practice (MPH); social and behavioral sciences (MPH); statistical genetics (PhD). *Application fee:* $85. Electronic applications accepted. *Application Contact:* Student and Academic Services, 206-685-3057, E-mail: sphsas@uw.edu. *Dean,* Hilary Godwin.

School of Social Work *Program availability:* Evening/weekend, online learning. Offers social work (MSW, PhD).

School of Pharmacy Offers biomedical regulatory affairs (MS); medicinal chemistry (PhD); pharmaceutical outcomes research and policy (PhD); pharmaceutics (PhD); pharmacy (MS, PhD, Pharm D).

UNIVERSITY OF WASHINGTON, BOTHELL, Bothell, WA 98011

General Information State-supported, coed, comprehensive institution. *Graduate housing:* Room and/or apartments available on a first-come, first-served basis to single students; on-campus housing not available to married students. Housing application deadline: 5/1. *Research affiliation:* Bill and Melinda Gates Foundation (improving health and reducing poverty in developing countries, providing opportunities to succeed in school and life in the U.S.), Carnegie Corporation of New York (doing real and permanent good in this world by creating ladders on which the aspiring can rise), American Institutes for Research (labor market success), Michael and Susan Dell Foundation (portfolio network scale-up project), William and Flora Hewlett Foundation (planning for the state education agency of the future), Walton Family Foundation (student-based allocation systems).

GRADUATE UNITS

Master of Arts in Cultural Studies Program *Program availability:* Evening/weekend. Offers cultural studies (MA). Electronic applications accepted.

Master of Arts in Policy Studies Program *Program availability:* Evening/weekend. Offers policy studies (MA). Electronic applications accepted.

Program in Computing and Software Systems *Program availability:* Part-time, evening/weekend. Offers computing and software systems (MS). Electronic applications accepted.

Program in Creative Writing and Poetics Offers creative writing and poetics (MFA).

Program in Education *Program availability:* Part-time, evening/weekend. Offers education (M Ed); leadership development for educators (M Ed); secondary/middle level endorsement (M Ed). Electronic applications accepted.

Program in Nursing *Program availability:* Part-time. Offers nursing (MN). Electronic applications accepted.

School of Business *Program availability:* Part-time, evening/weekend. Offers leadership (MBA); technology (MBA). Electronic applications accepted.

UNIVERSITY OF WASHINGTON, TACOMA, Tacoma, WA 98402-3100

General Information State-supported, coed, comprehensive institution. *Graduate housing:* Room and/or apartments available on a first-come, first-served basis to single students; on-campus housing not available to married students. Housing application deadline: 5/14. *Research affiliation:* City of Tacoma/Port of Tacoma (water quality and sustainability studies), South Sound Public and Private Schools (internships and educational research).

GRADUATE UNITS

Graduate Programs *Program availability:* Part-time, evening/weekend. Offers accounting (MBA); advanced integrative practice (MSW); business administration (MBA); certified financial analyst (MBA); communities, populations and health (MN); computing and software systems (MS); education (M Ed); educational administration (principal or program administrator certification) (M Ed); elementary education teacher certification (M Ed); elementary education/special education teacher certification (M Ed); interdisciplinary studies (MA); leadership in healthcare (MN); nurse educator (MN); secondary science or math teacher certification (M Ed); social work (MSW). Electronic applications accepted.

UNIVERSITY OF WATERLOO, Waterloo, ON N2L 3G1, Canada

General Information Province-supported, coed, university. *Enrollment:* 4,728 full-time matriculated graduate/professional students, 1,264 part-time matriculated graduate/professional students. *Enrollment by degree level:* 3,835 master's, 2,127 doctoral. *Graduate housing:* Rooms and/or apartments available on a first-come, first-served basis to single and married students. *Student services:* Campus employment opportunities, campus safety program, career counseling, child daycare facilities, exercise/wellness program, free psychological counseling, international student services, low-cost health insurance, services for students with disabilities, teacher training, writing training. *Library facilities:* Dana Porter Library plus 11 others. *Collection:* Students can reserve study rooms.

Computer facilities: 6,000 computers available on campus for general student use. A campuswide network can be accessed from student residence rooms and from off campus. Online class registration is available.
Website: http://www.uwaterloo.ca/

General Application Contact: Graduate Studies and Postdoctoral Affairs, 519-888-4567 Ext. 35209, Fax: 519-746-3051, E-mail: askthecentre@uwaterloo.ca.

GRADUATE UNITS

Graduate Studies and Postdoctoral Affairs Students: 4,728 full-time, 1,264 part-time. Expenses: Contact institution. *Financial support:* Fellowships with partial tuition reimbursements, research assistantships with partial tuition reimbursements, teaching assistantships with partial tuition reimbursements, career-related internships or fieldwork, Federal Work-Study, institutionally sponsored loans, scholarships/grants, and tuition waivers (partial) available. Support available to part-time students. In 2018, 1,898 master's, 331 doctorates awarded. *Program availability:* Part-time, evening/weekend, online learning. *Application deadline:* Applications are processed on a rolling basis. *Application fee:* $125 Canadian dollars. Electronic applications accepted. *Application Contact:* Graduate Studies, 519-888-4567, Fax: 519-746-3051, E-mail: askthecentre@uwaterloo.ca.

Faculty of Applied Health Sciences Expenses: Contact institution. *Financial support:* Research assistantships, teaching assistantships, career-related internships or fieldwork, Federal Work-Study, institutionally sponsored loans, scholarships/grants, and university-sponsored bursaries available. *Program availability:* Part-time. Offers applied health sciences (M Sc, MA, MHE, MHI, MPH, PhD); health evaluation (MHE); health informatics (MHI); health studies and gerontology (M Sc, PhD); kinesiology (M Sc, PhD); public health (MPH); recreation and leisure studies (MA, PhD). *Application deadline:* For fall admission, 2/1 for domestic and international students. *Application fee:* $125 Canadian dollars. Electronic applications accepted. *Application Contact:* Tracy Taves, Graduate Studies Coordinator, 519-888-4567 Ext. 36149, Fax: 519-746-6776, E-mail: tltaves@uwaterloo.ca. *Associate Dean,* Dr. Rhona Hanning, 519-888-4567 Ext. 36585, Fax: 519-746-6776, E-mail: rhanning@uwaterloo.ca.

Faculty of Arts Expenses: Contact institution. *Financial support:* Fellowships, research assistantships, teaching assistantships, career-related internships or fieldwork, and scholarships/grants available. *Program availability:* Part-time, evening/weekend. Offers accounting (M Acc); ancient Mediterranean cultures (MA); anthropology (MA); arts (M Acc, M Tax, MA, MA Sc, MFA, MPS, PhD); economics (MA, PhD); English language and literature (PhD); finance (M Acc); French (MA, PhD); German (MA, PhD); global governance (MA, PhD); history (MA, PhD); literary studies (MA); philosophy (MA, PhD); psychology (MA, MA Sc, PhD); public issues (MA); religious diversity in North America (PhD); rhetoric and communication design (MA); Russian (MA); sociology (MA, PhD); studio art (MFA); taxation (M Tax). *Application deadline:* Applications are processed on a rolling basis. *Application fee:* $100 Canadian dollars. Electronic applications accepted.

Faculty of Engineering Expenses: Contact institution. *Financial support:* Fellowships, research assistantships, teaching assistantships, career-related internships or fieldwork, Federal Work-Study, and institutionally sponsored loans available. *Program availability:* Part-time, evening/weekend, online learning. Offers applied operations research (MA Sc, MMS, PhD); architecture (M Arch); business, entrepreneurship and technology (MBET); chemical engineering (M Eng, MA Sc, PhD); civil and environmental engineering (M Eng, MA Sc, PhD); electrical and computer engineering (M Eng, MA Sc, PhD); engineering (M Arch, M Eng, MA Sc, MBET, MMS, PhD); information systems (MA Sc, MMS, PhD); management of technology (MA Sc, MMS, PhD); mechanical engineering (M Eng, MA Sc, PhD); mechanical engineering design and manufacturing (M Eng); systems design engineering (M Eng, MA Sc, PhD). *Application deadline:* Applications are processed on a rolling basis. *Application fee:* $125 Canadian dollars. Electronic applications accepted.

Faculty of Environment Expenses: Contact institution. *Financial support:* Fellowships, research assistantships, teaching assistantships, career-related internships or fieldwork, institutionally sponsored loans, and scholarships/grants available. Support available to part-time students. *Program availability:* Part-time. Offers environment (M Plan, MA, MAES, MES, PhD); environment, resources and sustainability (MES, PhD); geography and environmental management (MA, PhD); planning (M Plan, MA, MAES, MES, PhD). *Application fee:* $125 Canadian dollars. Electronic applications accepted.

Faculty of Mathematics Expenses: Contact institution. *Financial support:* Research assistantships, teaching assistantships, career-related internships or fieldwork, and scholarships/grants available. Offers actuarial science (M Math, MAS, PhD); applied mathematics (M Math, PhD); biostatistics (PhD); combinatorics and optimization (M Math, PhD); computer science (M Math, PhD); mathematics (M Math, MAS, MMT, PhD); pure mathematics (M Math, PhD); software engineering (M Math); statistics (M Math, PhD); statistics and computing (M Math); statistics-biostatistics (M Math); statistics-computing (M Math); statistics-finance (M Math). *Application deadline:* For fall admission, 2/1 for domestic and international students. *Application fee:* $125 Canadian dollars. Electronic applications accepted.

Faculty of Science Expenses: Contact institution. *Financial support:* Fellowships, research assistantships, teaching assistantships, career-related internships or fieldwork, and institutionally sponsored loans available. *Program availability:* Part-time. Offers biology (M Sc, PhD); chemistry and biochemistry (M Sc, PhD); earth and environmental sciences (M Sc, PhD); optometry (OD); physics (M Sc, PhD); science (M Sc, OD, PhD); vision science (M Sc, PhD). *Application deadline:* Applications are processed on a rolling basis. Electronic applications accepted.

THE UNIVERSITY OF WEST ALABAMA, Livingston, AL 35470

General Information State-supported, coed, comprehensive institution. *Enrollment:* 5,206 graduate, professional, and undergraduate students; 2,919 full-time matriculated graduate/professional students (2,394 women), 128 part-time matriculated graduate/professional students (88 women). *Enrollment by degree level:* 2,654 master's, 31 doctoral, 362 other advanced degrees. *Graduate faculty:* 47 full-time (27 women), 101 part-time/adjunct (60 women). *Tuition, area resident:* Full-time $9100. Tuition, state resident: full-time $9100. Tuition, nonresident: full-time $19,200. *Required fees:* $1890; $130. *Graduate housing:* Room and/or apartments available on a first-come, first-served basis to single students; on-campus housing not available to married students. Housing application deadline: 5/1. *Student services:* Campus employment opportunities, campus safety program, career counseling, exercise/wellness program, free psychological counseling, international student services, services for students with disabilities. *Library facilities:* Julia Tutwiler Library plus 1 other. *Collection:* Books: 176,910 (physical), 1,789 (digital/electronic); Serial titles: 11 (physical); Databases: 39. Weekly public service hours: 96; students can reserve study rooms.

Computer facilities: 600 computers available on campus for general student use. A campuswide network can be accessed from student residence rooms. Online class registration is available.
Website: http://www.uwa.edu/

General Application Contact: Dr. B. J. Kimbrough, Dean of Graduate Studies, 205-652-3647, Fax: 205-652-3670, E-mail: bkimbrough@uwa.edu.

GRADUATE UNITS

School of Graduate Studies Students: 2,919 full-time (2,394 women), 128 part-time (88 women); includes 1,102 minority (1,016 Black or African American, non-Hispanic/Latino; 17 American Indian or Alaska Native, non-Hispanic/Latino; 4 Asian, non-Hispanic/Latino; 24 Hispanic/Latino; 3 Native Hawaiian or other Pacific Islander, non-Hispanic/Latino; 38 Two or more races, non-Hispanic/Latino), 31 international. Average age 34. 1,059 applicants, 95% accepted, 770 enrolled. *Faculty:* 47 full-time (27 women), 101 part-time/adjunct (60 women). Expenses: Contact institution. *Financial support:* In 2018–19, 22 teaching assistantships (averaging $7,344 per year) were awarded; Federal Work-Study, scholarships/grants, and unspecified assistantships also available. Support available to part-time students. Financial award application deadline: 3/1; financial award applicants required to submit FAFSA. In 2018, 726 master's, 119 other advanced degrees awarded. *Program availability:* Part-time, evening/weekend, 100% online. *Application deadline:* Applications are processed on a rolling basis. *Application fee:* $40. Electronic applications accepted. *Application Contact:* Dr. B. J. Kimbrough, Dean of Graduate Studies, 205-652-3647, Fax: 205-652-3670, E-mail: bkimbrough@uwa.edu. *Dean of Graduate Studies,* Dr. B. J. Kimbrough, 205-652-3647, Fax: 205-652-3670, E-mail: bkimbrough@uwa.edu.

College of Business and Technology Students: 169 full-time (124 women), 8 part-time (0 women); includes 97 minority (87 Black or African American, non-Hispanic/Latino; 1 American Indian or Alaska Native, non-Hispanic/Latino; 2 Asian, non-Hispanic/Latino; 1 Hispanic/Latino; 6 Two or more races, non-Hispanic/Latino). Average age 30. 110 applicants, 95% accepted, 78 enrolled. *Faculty:* 1 full-time (0 women), 15 part-time/adjunct (11 women). Expenses: Contact institution. *Financial support:* Federal Work-Study and scholarships/grants available. Support available to part-time students. Financial award application deadline: 3/1; financial award applicants required to submit FAFSA. In 2018, 16 master's awarded. *Program availability:* Part-time, evening/weekend, 100% online. Offers finance (MBA); general business (MBA). *Application deadline:* Applications are processed on a rolling basis. *Application fee:* $40. Electronic applications accepted. *Application Contact:* Dr. Aliquippa Allen, Dean of College of Business and Technology, 205-652-3564, Fax: 205-652-3776, E-mail: aallen@uwa.edu. *Dean of College of Business and Technology,* Dr. Aliquippa Allen, 205-652-3564, Fax: 205-652-3776, E-mail: aallen@uwa.edu.

College of Education Students: 2,601 full-time (2,202 women), 106 part-time (85 women); includes 953 minority (882 Black or African American, non-Hispanic/Latino; 15 American Indian or Alaska Native, non-Hispanic/Latino; 3 Asian, non-Hispanic/Latino; 21 Hispanic/Latino; 2 Native Hawaiian or other Pacific Islander, non-

Hispanic/Latino; 30 Two or more races, non-Hispanic/Latino), 17 international. Average age 35. 891 applicants, 95% accepted, 645 enrolled. *Faculty:* 46 full-time (27 women), 86 part-time/adjunct (49 women). Expenses: Contact institution. *Financial support:* In 2018–19, 2 teaching assistantships (averaging $7,344 per year) were awarded; Federal Work-Study, scholarships/grants, and unspecified assistantships also available. Support available to part-time students. Financial award application deadline: 3/1; financial award applicants required to submit FAFSA. In 2018, 657 master's, 119 other advanced degrees awarded. *Program availability:* Part-time, evening/weekend, 100% online. Offers biology (MAT); clinical mental health counseling (MS); collaborative special education 6-12 (Ed S); collaborative special education K-6 (Ed S); counseling and psychology (MSCE); early childhood development (M Ed); early childhood education P-3 (M Ed); education (M Ed, MAT, MS, MSCE, Ed S); elementary education (Ed S); elementary education K-6 (M Ed); English language arts (MAT); family counseling (MS); general (MSCE); guidance and counseling (MS); high school 6-12 (M Ed); history (MAT); instructional leadership (M Ed, Ed S); learning, design, and technology (M Ed); library media (M Ed, MSCE, Ed S); mathematics (MAT); school counseling (M Ed, Ed S); science (MAT); social science (MAT); special education collaborative teacher 6-12 (M Ed); special education collaborative teacher K-6 (M Ed); student affairs in higher education (M Ed); teacher leader (Ed S). *Application deadline:* Applications are processed on a rolling basis. *Application fee:* $40. Electronic applications accepted. *Application Contact:* Dr. B. J. Kimbrough, Dean of Graduate Studies, 205-652-3647, Fax: 205-652-3670, E-mail: bkimbrough@uwa.edu. *Dean of Graduate Studies,* Dr. B. J. Kimbrough, 205-652-3647, Fax: 205-652-3670, E-mail: bkimbrough@uwa.edu.

College of Liberal Arts Students: 19 full-time (16 women); includes 6 minority (4 Black or African American, non-Hispanic/Latino; 1 Hispanic/Latino; 1 Two or more races, non-Hispanic/Latino), 1 international. Average age 26. 11 applicants, 82% accepted, 9 enrolled. *Faculty:* 3 full-time (1 woman), 5 part-time/adjunct (3 women). Expenses: Contact institution. *Financial support:* In 2018–19, 3 teaching assistantships (averaging $7,344 per year) were awarded; Federal Work-Study, scholarships/grants, and unspecified assistantships also available. Support available to part-time students. Financial award application deadline: 3/1; financial award applicants required to submit FAFSA. In 2018, 5 master's awarded. *Program availability:* Part-time, evening/weekend, 100% online. Offers experimental psychology (MS). *Application deadline:* Applications are processed on a rolling basis. *Application fee:* $40. Electronic applications accepted. *Application Contact:* Dr. Mark Davis, Dean, 205-652-3570, Fax: 205-652-3717, E-mail: mdavis@uwa.edu. *Dean,* Dr. Mark Davis, 205-652-3570, Fax: 205-652-3717, E-mail: mdavis@uwa.edu.

College of Natural Sciences and Mathematics Students: 130 full-time (52 women), 14 part-time (3 women); includes 47 minority (43 Black or African American, non-Hispanic/Latino; 1 American Indian or Alaska Native, non-Hispanic/Latino; 1 Hispanic/Latino; 2 Two or more races, non-Hispanic/Latino), 6 international. Average age 29. 47 applicants, 91% accepted, 38 enrolled. *Faculty:* 10 full-time (3 women), 5 part-time/adjunct (0 women). Expenses: Contact institution. *Financial support:* In 2018–19, 8 teaching assistantships (averaging $7,344 per year) were awarded; Federal Work-Study, scholarships/grants, and unspecified assistantships also available. Support available to part-time students. Financial award application deadline: 3/1; financial award applicants required to submit FAFSA. In 2018, 48 master's awarded. *Program availability:* Part-time, evening/weekend, 100% online. Offers conservation biology (MS); physical education (M Ed, MAT, MS). *Application deadline:* Applications are processed on a rolling basis. *Application fee:* $40. Electronic applications accepted. *Application Contact:* Dr. John McCall, Dean of College of Natural Sciences and Mathematics, 205-652-3412, Fax: 205-652-3831, E-mail: jmccall@uwa.edu. *Dean of College of Natural Sciences and Mathematics,* Dr. John McCall, 205-652-3412, Fax: 205-652-3831, E-mail: jmccall@uwa.edu.

THE UNIVERSITY OF WESTERN ONTARIO, London, ON N6A 3K7, Canada

General Information Province-supported, coed, university. CGS member. *Graduate housing:* Rooms and/or apartments available on a first-come, first-served basis to single and married students.

GRADUATE UNITS

Faculty of Law Offers law (LL M, MLS, JD, Diploma).

Ivey Business School Offers business (EMBA, PhD); corporate strategy and leadership elective (MBA); entrepreneurship elective (MBA); finance elective (MBA); health sector stream (MBA); international management elective (MBA); marketing elective (MBA). Electronic applications accepted.

School of Graduate and Postdoctoral Studies *Program availability:* Part-time, evening/weekend, online learning. Offers chemical and biochemical engineering (ME Sc, PhD); civil and environmental engineering (M Eng, ME Sc, PhD); electrical and computer engineering (M Eng, ME Sc, PhD); mechanical and materials engineering (M Eng, ME Sc, PhD). Electronic applications accepted.

Center for the Study of Theory and Criticism Offers theory and criticism (MA, PhD).

Don Wright Faculty of Music *Program availability:* Part-time. Offers music (M Mus, PhD); popular music and culture (MA).

Faculty of Arts and Humanities *Program availability:* Part-time. Offers arts and humanities (M Mus, MA, PhD); Canadian literature (MA); classical studies (MA); comparative literature (MA, PhD); English (PhD); English literature (MA); French studies (MA, PhD); Hispanic studies (MA, PhD); philosophy (MA, PhD).

Faculty of Health Sciences *Program availability:* Part-time. Offers health sciences (M Cl Sc, M Sc, M Sc N, MA, MCTS, MN NP, MPT, PhD); kinesiology (M Sc, MA, PhD); manipulative therapy (CAS); nurse practitioner (MN NP); nursing (M Sc N, MN NP, PhD); occupational therapy (M Sc); physical therapy (MPT); speech-language pathology (M Cl Sc, M Sc); wound healing (CAS).

Faculty of Information and Media Studies Offers journalism (MA); library and information science (MLIS, PhD); media studies (MA, PhD).

Faculty of Science *Program availability:* Part-time, online learning. Offers applied mathematics (M Sc, PhD); astronomy (M Sc, PhD); biology (M Sc, PhD); chemistry (M Sc, PhD); computer science (M Sc, PhD); environment and sustainability (MES); geology (M Sc, PhD); geology and environmental science (M Sc, PhD); geophysics (M Sc, PhD); geophysics and environmental science (M Sc, PhD); mathematics (M Sc, PhD); physics (M Sc, PhD); psychology (M Sc, PhD); science (M Sc, MA, PhD, CAS); statistical and actuarial sciences (M Sc, PhD); theoretical physics (PhD).

Faculty of Social Science *Program availability:* Part-time, evening/weekend. Offers anthropology (MA, PhD); counseling psychology (M Ed); curriculum studies (M Ed); economics (MA, PhD); education (M Ed); educational policy studies (M Ed); educational psychology/special education (M Ed); geography (M Sc, MA, PhD); history (MA, PhD); political science (MA, MPA, PhD); social science (M Ed, M Sc, MA, MPA, PhD); sociology (MA, PhD).

Schulich School of Medicine and Dentistry Offers anatomy and cell biology (M Sc, PhD); biochemistry (M Sc, PhD); clinical anatomy (M Sc); clinical neurological sciences (M Sc, PhD); dentistry (M Cl D, DDS); epidemiology and biostatistics (M Sc, PhD); family medicine (M Cl Sc); medical biophysics (M Sc, PhD); medicine (MD); medicine and dentistry (M Cl D, M Cl Sc, M Sc, MA, DDS, MD, PhD); microbiology and immunology (M Sc, PhD); orthodontics (M Cl D); pathology (M Sc, PhD); physiology (M Sc, PhD).

UNIVERSITY OF WESTERN STATES, Portland, OR 97230-3099

General Information Independent, coed, graduate-only institution. *Graduate housing:* On-campus housing not available. *Research affiliation:* Oregon Center for Complimentary and Alternative Medicine in Craniofacial Disorders (complimentary and alternative medicine), Consortial Center for Chiropractic Research (Palmer College of Chiropractic) (chiropractic).

GRADUATE UNITS

Professional Program Offers chiropractic (DC).

UNIVERSITY OF WEST FLORIDA, Pensacola, FL 32514-5750

General Information State-supported, coed, comprehensive institution. CGS member. *Graduate housing:* Room and/or apartments available on a first-come, first-served basis to single students; on-campus housing not available to married students. *Research affiliation:* Pensacola Bay Area Convention and Visitors Bureau (Pensacola tourism study), Software Engineering Research Consortium (Motorola, Northrup Grumman through Ball State University) (software engineering), University of Southern Mississippi Consortium on Coastal Estuarine Research (microbial biofilms and coastal estuarine research).

GRADUATE UNITS

College of Arts, Social Sciences, and Humanities *Program availability:* Part-time, evening/weekend. Offers arts, social sciences, and humanities (MA); creative writing (MA); early American studies (MA); literature (MA); political science (MA); public history (MA); strategic communication and leadership (MA); traditional history (MA).

Division of Anthropology and Archaeology Offers anthropology (MA); historical archaeology (MA).

College of Business *Program availability:* Part-time, evening/weekend. Offers accounting (M Acc); business (M Acc, MBA); business administration (MBA).

College of Education and Professional Studies *Program availability:* Part-time, evening/weekend. Offers applied behavior analysis (MA); college student affairs administration (M Ed); criminal justice (MS); curriculum and assessment (Ed D); curriculum and instruction (M Ed, Ed S); education and professional studies (M Ed, MA, MS, MSA, MSW, Ed D, Ed S); educational leadership (M Ed); elementary education (M Ed); exceptional student education (MA); instructional design and technology (M Ed, Ed D); legal studies, public administration and sport management (MSA); middle level education (M Ed); network operations, performance and security (M Ed); reading education (M Ed); secondary education (M Ed); social work (MSW); special and alternative education (MA).

Ed D Programs *Program availability:* Part-time, evening/weekend. Offers administrative and leadership studies (Ed D); education (Ed D); instructional design and technology (Ed D); physical education and health (Ed D).

Hal Marcus College of Science and Engineering *Program availability:* Part-time, evening/weekend. Offers biology (MS); computer science (MS); environmental science (MS); geographic information science administration (MS); information technology (MS); mathematical sciences (MS); science and engineering (MPH, MS, MSN, MST).

Usha Kundu, MD College of Health *Program availability:* Part-time. Offers applied experimental (MA); counseling (MA); health (MA, MHA, MPH, MS, MSN); health promotion (MS); health, leisure, and exercise science (MS); healthcare administration (MHA); industrial-organizational (MA); public health (MPH).

School of Nursing *Program availability:* Part-time, evening/weekend. Offers nursing (MSN).

UNIVERSITY OF WEST GEORGIA, Carrollton, GA 30118

General Information State-supported, coed, comprehensive institution. CGS member. *Enrollment:* 13,733 graduate, professional, and undergraduate students; 598 full-time matriculated graduate/professional students (471 women), 1,595 part-time matriculated graduate/professional students (1,243 women). *Enrollment by degree level:* 1,515 master's, 177 doctoral, 501 other advanced degrees. *Graduate faculty:* 251 full-time (124 women). Tuition and fees vary according to course load, degree level, campus/location and program. *Graduate housing:* Rooms and/or apartments available on a first-come, first-served basis to single and married students. Typical cost: $5600 per year ($10,488 including board) for single students. Room and board charges vary according to board plan, campus/location and housing facility selected. Housing application deadline: 6/1. *Student services:* Campus employment opportunities, campus safety program, career counseling, exercise/wellness program, free psychological counseling, international student services, multicultural affairs office, services for students with disabilities, teacher training, writing training. *Library facilities:* Irvine Sullivan Ingram Library plus 1 other. *Collection:* Weekly public service hours: 109; study areas open 24 hours, 5–7 days a week; students can reserve study rooms.

Computer facilities: 1,200 computers available on campus for general student use. A campuswide network can be accessed from student residence rooms and from off campus. Online class registration is available.
Website: http://www.westga.edu/

General Application Contact: Dr. Toby Ziglar, Assistant Dean of the Graduate School, 678-839-1394, Fax: 678-839-1395, E-mail: graduate@westga.edu.

GRADUATE UNITS

College of Arts and Humanities Students: 22 full-time (11 women), 71 part-time (48 women); includes 13 minority (7 Black or African American, non-Hispanic/Latino; 1 American Indian or Alaska Native, non-Hispanic/Latino; 1 Asian, non-Hispanic/Latino; 1 Hispanic/Latino; 3 Two or more races, non-Hispanic/Latino). Average age 30. 44 applicants, 95% accepted, 32 enrolled. *Faculty:* 67 full-time (36 women). Expenses: Contact institution. *Financial support:* Fellowships, research assistantships, teaching assistantships, career-related internships or fieldwork, Federal Work-Study, institutionally sponsored loans, scholarships/grants, and unspecified assistantships available. Support available to part-time students. Financial award application deadline: 4/1; financial award applicants required to submit FAFSA. In 2018, 24 master's, 8 other advanced degrees awarded. *Program availability:* Part-time, evening/weekend, 100% online, blended/hybrid learning. Offers English (MA); history (MA); museum studies (Postbaccalaureate Certificate); music performance (M Mus); music teacher education (M Mus); public history (Postbaccalaureate Certificate). *Application deadline:* For fall admission, 8/1 for domestic students, 6/1 for international students; for spring admission, 11/15 for domestic students, 10/15 for international students; for summer admission, 5/15 for domestic students, 3/30 for international students. Applications are processed on a rolling basis. *Application fee:*

$40. Electronic applications accepted. *Application Contact:* Dr. Toby Ziglar, Assistant Dean of the Graduate School, 678-839-1394, Fax: 678-839-1395, E-mail: graduate@westga.edu. *Dean of Arts and Humanities, Interim Dean COSM,* Dr. Pauline D. Gagnon, 678-839-5450, Fax: 678-839-5451, E-mail: pgagnon@westga.edu.

College of Education Students: 368 full-time (316 women), 1,140 part-time (960 women); includes 460 minority (376 Black or African American, non-Hispanic/Latino; 1 American Indian or Alaska Native, non-Hispanic/Latino; 11 Asian, non-Hispanic/Latino; 44 Hispanic/Latino; 28 Two or more races, non-Hispanic/Latino), 6 international. Average age 35. 625 applicants, 77% accepted, 401 enrolled. *Faculty:* 39 full-time (23 women). Expenses: Contact institution. *Financial support:* Fellowships, research assistantships, teaching assistantships, career-related internships or fieldwork, Federal Work-Study, institutionally sponsored loans, scholarships/grants, and unspecified assistantships available. Support available to part-time students. Financial award application deadline: 4/1; financial award applicants required to submit FAFSA. In 2018, 399 master's, 25 doctorates, 273 other advanced degrees awarded. *Program availability:* Part-time, evening/weekend, 100% online, blended/hybrid learning. Offers business education (M Ed); early childhood education (M Ed, Ed S); educational leadership (M Ed, Ed S); media (M Ed, Ed S); professional counseling (M Ed, Ed S); professional counseling and supervision (Ed D); reading instruction (M Ed); school improvement (Ed D); secondary education (M Ed); special education (M Ed, Ed S); speech language pathology (M Ed); teaching (MAT). *Application deadline:* For fall admission, 7/21 for domestic students, 6/1 for international students; for spring admission, 11/30 for domestic students, 10/15 for international students; for summer admission, 4/15 for domestic students, 3/30 for international students. Applications are processed on a rolling basis. *Application fee:* $40. Electronic applications accepted. *Application Contact:* Dr. Toby Ziglar, Assistant Dean of the Graduate School, 678-839-1394, Fax: 678-839-1395, E-mail: graduate@westga.edu. *Dean, College of Education,* Dr. Diane Hoff, 678-839-6570, Fax: 678-839-6098, E-mail: dhoff@westga.edu.

College of Science and Mathematics Students: 14 full-time (12 women), 93 part-time (26 women); includes 35 minority (21 Black or African American, non-Hispanic/Latino; 1 American Indian or Alaska Native, non-Hispanic/Latino; 7 Asian, non-Hispanic/Latino; 3 Hispanic/Latino; 3 Two or more races, non-Hispanic/Latino), 11 international. Average age 34. 97 applicants, 91% accepted, 71 enrolled. *Faculty:* 47 full-time (16 women). Expenses: Contact institution. *Financial support:* Fellowships, research assistantships, teaching assistantships, career-related internships or fieldwork, Federal Work-Study, institutionally sponsored loans, scholarships/grants, and unspecified assistantships available. Support available to part-time students. Financial award application deadline: 4/1; financial award applicants required to submit FAFSA. In 2018, 27 master's, 4 other advanced degrees awarded. *Program availability:* Part-time, evening/weekend, 100% online, blended/hybrid learning. Offers biology (MS); computer science (MS); geographic information systems (Postbaccalaureate Certificate); mathematics (MS). *Application deadline:* For fall admission, 6/1 for domestic and international students; for spring admission, 11/15 for domestic students, 10/15 for international students; for summer admission, 4/1 for domestic students, 3/30 for international students. Applications are processed on a rolling basis. *Application fee:* $40. Electronic applications accepted. *Application Contact:* Dr. Toby Ziglar, Assistant Dean of the Graduate School, 678-839-1394, Fax: 678-839-1395, E-mail: graduate@westga.edu. *Interim Dean of Science and Mathematics, Dean of COAH,* Dr. Pauline Gagnon, 678-839-5190, Fax: 678-839-5191, E-mail: pgagnon@westga.edu.

College of Social Sciences Students: 105 full-time (68 women), 69 part-time (41 women); includes 66 minority (55 Black or African American, non-Hispanic/Latino; 1 Asian, non-Hispanic/Latino; 6 Hispanic/Latino; 4 Two or more races, non-Hispanic/Latino), 7 international. Average age 32. 97 applicants, 75% accepted, 57 enrolled. *Faculty:* 48 full-time (22 women). Expenses: Contact institution. *Financial support:* Fellowships, research assistantships, teaching assistantships, career-related internships or fieldwork, Federal Work-Study, institutionally sponsored loans, scholarships/grants, and unspecified assistantships available. Support available to part-time students. Financial award application deadline: 4/1; financial award applicants required to submit FAFSA. In 2018, 50 master's, 7 doctorates, 10 other advanced degrees awarded. *Program availability:* Part-time, evening/weekend, 100% online, blended/hybrid learning. Offers criminology (MA); data analysis and evaluation methods (Postbaccalaureate Certificate); European Union studies (Postbaccalaureate Certificate); integrative health systems (Postbaccalaureate Certificate); nonprofit management and community development (Postbaccalaureate Certificate); psychology (MA, PhD); public administration (MPA); public management (Postbaccalaureate Certificate); sociology (MA). *Application deadline:* For fall admission, 7/15 for domestic students, 6/1 for international students; for spring admission, 11/30 for domestic students, 10/15 for international students; for summer admission, 5/15 for domestic students, 3/30 for international students. Applications are processed on a rolling basis. *Application fee:* $40. Electronic applications accepted. *Application Contact:* Dr. Toby Ziglar, Assistant Dean of the Graduate School, 678-839-1394, Fax: 678-839-1395, E-mail: graduate@westga.edu. *Interim Dean of Social Sciences,* Dr. Amber Smallwood, 678-839-5170, Fax: 678-839-5171, E-mail: amksmall@westga.edu.

Richards College of Business Students: 57 full-time (34 women), 118 part-time (68 women); includes 60 minority (45 Black or African American, non-Hispanic/Latino; 3 Asian, non-Hispanic/Latino; 10 Hispanic/Latino; 2 Two or more races, non-Hispanic/Latino), 9 international. Average age 30. 123 applicants, 96% accepted, 73 enrolled. *Faculty:* 38 full-time (15 women). Expenses: Contact institution. *Financial support:* Fellowships, research assistantships, teaching assistantships, career-related internships or fieldwork, Federal Work-Study, institutionally sponsored loans, scholarships/grants, and unspecified assistantships available. Support available to part-time students. Financial award application deadline: 4/1; financial award applicants required to submit FAFSA. In 2018, 112 master's awarded. *Program availability:* Part-time, evening/weekend, 100% online, blended/hybrid learning. Offers accounting (MP Acc); business administration (MBA). *Application deadline:* For fall admission, 7/15 for domestic students, 6/1 for international students; for spring admission, 11/15 for domestic students, 10/15 for international students; for summer admission, 5/15 for domestic students, 3/30 for international students. Applications are processed on a rolling basis. *Application fee:* $40. Electronic applications accepted. *Application Contact:* Dr. Toby Ziglar, Assistant Dean of the Graduate School, 678-839-1394, Fax: 678-839-1395, E-mail: graduate@westga.edu. *Dean of Richards College of Business,* Dr. Faye S. McIntyre, 678-839-6467, Fax: 678-839-5040, E-mail: fmcintyr@westga.edu.

Tanner Health System School of Nursing Students: 32 full-time (30 women), 104 part-time (100 women); includes 28 minority (21 Black or African American, non-Hispanic/Latino; 1 Asian, non-Hispanic/Latino; 3 Hispanic/Latino; 3 Two or more races, non-Hispanic/Latino). Average age 40. 104 applicants, 95% accepted, 61 enrolled. *Faculty:* 12 full-time (all women). Expenses: Contact institution. *Financial support:* Fellowships, research assistantships, teaching assistantships, career-related internships or fieldwork, Federal Work-Study, institutionally sponsored loans, scholarships/grants, and unspecified assistantships available. Support available to part-time students. Financial award application deadline: 4/1; financial award applicants required to submit

FAFSA. In 2018, 37 master's, 4 doctorates, 2 other advanced degrees awarded. *Program availability:* Part-time, evening/weekend, 100% online, blended/hybrid learning. Offers health systems leadership (Post-Master's Certificate); nursing (MSN); nursing education (Ed D, Post-Master's Certificate). *Application deadline:* For fall admission, 2/1 priority date for domestic and international students. Applications are processed on a rolling basis. *Application fee:* $40. Electronic applications accepted. *Application Contact:* Dr. Toby Ziglar, Assistant Dean of the Graduate School, 678-839-1390, Fax: 678-839-1395, E-mail: graduate@westga.edu. *Dean of the School of Nursing,* Dr. Jennifer Schuessler, 678-839-6553, E-mail: jschuess@westga.edu.

UNIVERSITY OF WEST LOS ANGELES, Inglewood, CA 90301

General Information Proprietary, coed, upper-level institution. *Graduate housing:* On-campus housing not available.

GRADUATE UNITS

School of Business Offers organizational leadership and business innovation (MS).

School of Law *Program availability:* Part-time, evening/weekend. Offers law (JD). Electronic applications accepted.

UNIVERSITY OF WINDSOR, Windsor, ON N9B 3P4, Canada

General Information Province-supported, coed, university. *Graduate housing:* Rooms and/or apartments available on a first-come, first-served basis to single and married students. Housing application deadline: 6/7. *Research affiliation:* Daimler/Chrysler Automotive Research and Development Centre.

GRADUATE UNITS

Faculty of Graduate Studies *Program availability:* Part-time, evening/weekend. Electronic applications accepted.

Faculty of Arts and Social Sciences *Program availability:* Part-time. Offers adult clinical (MA, PhD); applied social psychology (MA, PhD); arts and social sciences (MA, MFA, MSW, PhD); child clinical (MA, PhD); clinical neuropsychology (MA, PhD); communication and social justice (MA); criminology (MA); English: creative writing and language and literature (MA); English: language and literature (MA); history (MA); philosophy (MA); political science (MA); social work (MSW); sociology (MA); sociology-social justice (PhD); visual arts (MFA). Electronic applications accepted.

Faculty of Education *Program availability:* Part-time, evening/weekend. Offers education (M Ed); educational studies (PhD). Electronic applications accepted.

Faculty of Engineering *Program availability:* Part-time. Offers civil engineering (M Eng, MA Sc, PhD); electrical engineering (M Eng, MA Sc, PhD); engineering (M Eng, MA Sc, PhD); engineering materials (M Eng, MA Sc, PhD); environmental engineering (M Eng, MA Sc, PhD); industrial engineering (M Eng, MA Sc); manufacturing systems engineering (PhD); mechanical engineering (M Eng, MA Sc, PhD). Electronic applications accepted.

Faculty of Human Kinetics *Program availability:* Part-time. Offers human kinetics (MHK). Electronic applications accepted.

Faculty of Nursing Offers nursing (M Sc, MN). Electronic applications accepted.

Faculty of Science *Program availability:* Part-time. Offers biological sciences (M Sc, PhD); chemistry and biochemistry (M Sc, PhD); computer science (M Sc, PhD); earth sciences (M Sc, PhD); economics (MA); mathematics (M Sc); physics (M Sc, PhD); science (M Sc, MA, PhD); statistics (M Sc). Electronic applications accepted.

GLIER-Great Lakes Institute for Environmental Research Offers environmental science (M Sc, PhD). Electronic applications accepted.

Odette School of Business *Program availability:* Evening/weekend. Offers business (MBA, MM). Electronic applications accepted.

THE UNIVERSITY OF WINNIPEG, Winnipeg, MB R3B 2E9, Canada

General Information Province-supported, coed, comprehensive institution. *Graduate housing:* On-campus housing not available.

GRADUATE UNITS

Faculty of Theology *Program availability:* Part-time. Offers marriage and family therapy (MMFT, Certificate); sacred theology (STM); theology (M Div).

Graduate Studies *Program availability:* Part-time, evening/weekend. Offers history (MA); public administration (MPA); religious studies (MA).

UNIVERSITY OF WISCONSIN–EAU CLAIRE, Eau Claire, WI 54702-4004

General Information State-supported, coed, comprehensive institution. CGS member. *Graduate housing:* Room and/or apartments available on a first-come, first-served basis to single students; on-campus housing not available to married students. Housing application deadline: 5/1. *Research affiliation:* Geological Survey of Canada (geology), Chevron Phillips Chemical Company (chemistry), Excel Energy (geography), American Chemical Society Petroleum Research Fund (chemistry, geology), ASIANetwork (anthropology, biology, geography), Research Corporation (chemistry).

GRADUATE UNITS

College of Arts and Sciences Offers arts and sciences (MA, MSE, Ed S); literature and textual interpretation (MA); public history (MA); school psychology (MSE, Ed S); writing (MA). Electronic applications accepted.

College of Business Offers business (MBA); business administration (MBA). Electronic applications accepted.

College of Education and Human Sciences Offers communication sciences and disorders (MS); education and human sciences (ME-PD, MS, MSE, MST); professional development (ME-PD); reading (MST); special education (MSE). Electronic applications accepted.

College of Nursing and Health Sciences Offers adult-gerontological administration (DNP); adult-gerontological clinical nurse specialist (DNP); adult-gerontological education (MSN); adult-gerontological primary care nurse practitioner (DNP); family health administration (DNP); family health in education (MSN); family health nurse practitioner (DNP); nursing (MSN); nursing and health sciences (MSN, DNP); nursing practice (DNP). Electronic applications accepted.

UNIVERSITY OF WISCONSIN–GREEN BAY, Green Bay, WI 54311-7001

General Information State-supported, coed, comprehensive institution. *Graduate housing:* Room and/or apartments available on a first-come, first-served basis to single students; on-campus housing not available to married students. Housing application deadline: 5/1. *Research affiliation:* Wisconsin Space Grant Consortium (space and aerospace science), UW Sea Grant Institute (Great Lakes and ocean sustainability and stewardship), UW System Applied Research Program (biogas generation), UW Extension Solid and Hazardous Waste Education Center (sustainable use of natural resources), Abbott Laboratories (anaerobic digestion systems).

GRADUATE UNITS

Graduate Studies *Program availability:* Part-time, evening/weekend, 100% online. Offers applied leadership for teaching and learning (MS Ed); environmental science and policy (MS); health and wellness management (MS); management (MS); nursing (MSN); social work (MSW); sustainable management (MS). Electronic applications accepted.

UNIVERSITY OF WISCONSIN–LA CROSSE, La Crosse, WI 54601-3742

General Information State-supported, coed, comprehensive institution. CGS member. *Graduate housing:* Room and/or apartments available on a first-come, first-served basis to single students; on-campus housing not available to married students. Housing application deadline: 5/1.

GRADUATE UNITS

College of Liberal Studies Offers liberal studies (MS Ed, Ed D, Ed S); school psychology (MS Ed, Ed S); student affairs administration (MS Ed, Ed D). Electronic applications accepted.

College of Science and Health Offers aquatic sciences (MS); biology (MS); cellular and molecular biology (MS); clinical exercise physiology (MS); clinical microbiology (MS); community health education (MPH, MS); data science (MS); exercise sport science: human performance (MS); exercise sport science: physical education teaching (MS); human performance (MS); medical dosimetry (MS); microbiology (MS); nurse anesthesia (MS); occupational therapy (MS); physical education teaching (MS); physical therapy (DPT); physician assistant studies (MS); physiology (MS); public health (MPH); recreation management (MS); school health education (MS); science and health (MPH, MS, MSE, DPT); software engineering (MSE); therapeutic recreation (MS). Electronic applications accepted.

School of Education *Program availability:* Part-time, evening/weekend. Offers English language arts elementary (Graduate Certificate); professional development in education (ME-PD); reading (MS Ed); special education (MS Ed). Electronic applications accepted.

UNIVERSITY OF WISCONSIN–MADISON, Madison, WI 53706-1380

General Information State-supported, coed, university. CGS member. *Graduate housing:* Rooms and/or apartments available on a first-come, first-served basis to single and married students. *Research affiliation:* Morgridge Institute for Research (life sciences: biological sciences), WiCell Research Institute (life sciences: biological sciences), University of Wisconsin Hospitals and Clinics (life sciences: health and medical sciences), William S. Middleton Memorial Veterans Hospital (life sciences: health and medical sciences), Universities Research Association, Inc. (physical and earth sciences: physics and astronomy), U.S. Department of Agriculture (USDA), Dairy Forage Center (life sciences: agriculture).

GRADUATE UNITS

Graduate School *Program availability:* Part-time, evening/weekend, 100% online, blended/hybrid learning. Offers biophysics (PhD); cellular and molecular biology (PhD). Electronic applications accepted.

College of Agricultural and Life Sciences *Program availability:* Part-time. Offers agricultural and applied economics (MA, MS, PhD); agricultural and life sciences (MA, MPS, MS, PhD); agroecology (MS); agronomy (MS, PhD); animal sciences (MS, PhD); bacteriology (MS); biochemistry (MS, PhD); biological systems engineering (MS, PhD); dairy science (MS, PhD); entomology (MS, PhD); food science (MS, PhD); forestry (MS, PhD); genetic counseling (MS); genetics (PhD); horticulture (MS, PhD); life sciences communication (MPS, MS); mass communications (PhD); microbiology (PhD); nutritional sciences (MS, PhD); plant breeding and plant genetics (MS, PhD); plant pathology (MS, PhD); soil science (MS, PhD); wildlife ecology (MS, PhD). Electronic applications accepted.

College of Engineering Students: 1,384 full-time (334 women), 460 part-time (102 women); includes 208 minority (31 Black or African American, non-Hispanic/Latino; 1 American Indian or Alaska Native, non-Hispanic/Latino; 77 Asian, non-Hispanic/Latino; 74 Hispanic/Latino; 2 Native Hawaiian or other Pacific Islander, non-Hispanic/Latino; 23 Two or more races, non-Hispanic/Latino), 902 international. Average age 27. 5,591 applicants, 25% accepted, 453 enrolled. *Faculty:* 194 full-time (40 women). Expenses: Contact institution. *Financial support:* In 2018–19, 1,199 students received support, including 64 fellowships with full tuition reimbursements available, 765 research assistantships with full tuition reimbursements available, 335 teaching assistantships with full tuition reimbursements available; career-related internships or fieldwork, Federal Work-Study, institutionally sponsored loans, scholarships/grants, health care benefits, and unspecified assistantships also available. Support available to part-time students. Financial award application deadline: 12/1; financial award applicants required to submit FAFSA. In 2018, 416 master's, 157 doctorates awarded. *Program availability:* Part-time, 100% online, blended/hybrid learning. Offers biomedical engineering (MS, PhD); chemical engineering (PhD); construction engineering and management (MS); electrical engineering (MS, PhD); engineering (MS, PhD); engineering mechanics (MS, PhD); environmental chemistry and technology (MS); environmental science and engineering (MS); geological engineering (MS); geological/geotechnical engineering (MS); industrial engineering (MS, PhD); machine learning and signal processing (MS); manufacturing systems engineering (MS); materials science and engineering (MS); mechanical engineering (MS, PhD); nuclear engineering and engineering physics (MS, PhD); structural engineering (MS); transportation engineering (MS); water resources engineering (MS). *Application deadline:* Applications are processed on a rolling basis. *Application fee:* $75 ($81 for international students). Electronic applications accepted. *Application Contact:* Information Contact, 608-262-2433, Fax: 608-265-9505, E-mail: admissions@grad.wisc.edu. *Dean,* Dr. Ian M. Robertson, 608-262-3482, Fax: 608-262-6400, E-mail: engr-dean_engr@wisc.edu.

College of Letters and Science *Program availability:* Part-time, evening/weekend, online learning. Offers African history (MA, PhD); African languages and literature (MA, PhD); Afro-American studies (MA); applied English linguistics (MA); archaeology (PhD); art history (MA, PhD); astronomy (PhD); atmospheric and oceanic sciences (MS, PhD); audiology (Au D); biological anthropology (PhD); biology of brain and behavior (PhD); biometry (MS); botany (MS, PhD); cartography and geographic information systems (MS); Central Asian history (MA, PhD); chemistry (MS, PhD); Chinese literature (MA, PhD); Chinese thought (MA, PhD); choral (MM, DMA); civilizations and cultures (MA, PhD); classics (MA, PhD); clinical psychology (PhD); cognitive neurosciences (PhD); communication science (MA, PhD); comparative literature (MA, PhD); comparative world history (MA, PhD); composition (MM, DMA); composition and rhetoric (PhD); computer sciences (MS, PhD); creative writing (MFA); cultural anthropology (PhD); curriculum and instruction (MS, PhD); developmental psychology (PhD); East Asian history (PhD); economics (PhD); English language and linguistics (MA, PhD); ethnomusicology (MA, PhD); European history (MA, PhD); family and consumer journalism (PhD); film (MA, PhD); French

(MA, PhD); French studies (MFS, Certificate); gender and women's history (MA, PhD); geographic information systems (Certificate); geography (MS, PhD); geology (MS, PhD); geophysics (MS, PhD); German (MA, PhD); Greek (MA); Hebrew and Semitic studies (MA, PhD); historical musicology (PhD); history of science, medicine, and technology (MA, PhD); information (MA, PhD); instrumental (MM, DMA); Italian (MA, PhD); Japanese linguistics (MA, PhD); Japanese literature (MA, PhD); journalism and mass communication (MA); landscape architecture (MS); languages and cultures of Asia (MA); languages and literatures (PhD); Latin (MA); Latin American and Caribbean history (MA, PhD); Latin American, Caribbean and Iberian studies (MA); letters and science (MA, MFA, MFS, MIPA, MM, MPA, MS, MSW, DMA, PhD, Certificate); linguistics (MA, PhD); literary studies (MA, PhD); mass communication (PhD); mathematics (PhD); media and cultural studies (MA, PhD); Middle Eastern history (MA, PhD); music (MA, MM, DMA, PhD); music education (MM); music history (MA); music performance (MM, DMA); music theory (MA, PhD); normal aspects of speech, language and hearing (MS, PhD); orchestral (MM, DMA); perception (PhD); philosophy (MA, PhD); physics (MA, MS, PhD); political science (PhD); Portuguese (MA, PhD); psychology (PhD); public policy and administration (MIPA, MPA); religions of Asia (PhD); rhetoric (MA, PhD); rural sociology (MS); Scandinavian studies (MA, PhD); Slavic languages and literature (MA, PhD); social and personality psychology (PhD); social welfare (PhD); social work (MSW); sociology (MS, PhD); South Asian history (MA, PhD); Southeast Asian history (MA, PhD); Southeast Asian studies (MA); Spanish (MA, PhD); speech-language pathology (MS, PhD); statistics (MA, PhD); theatre and drama (MA, MFA, PhD); United States history (MA, PhD); urban and regional planning (MS, PhD); zoology (MA, MS, PhD). Electronic applications accepted.

Gaylord Nelson Institute for Environmental Studies *Program availability:* Part-time. Offers environment and resources (MS, PhD); environmental conservation (MS); environmental studies (MS, PhD); water resources management (MS). Electronic applications accepted.

School of Education Offers administration (Certificate); art (MFA); counseling (MS); counseling psychology (PhD); curriculum and instruction (MS, PhD); education (MA, MFA, MS, PhD, Certificate); educational policy (MS, PhD); educational policy studies (MA, PhD); educational psychology (MS, PhD); English as a second language (MS, PhD); global higher education (MS); kinesiology (MS, PhD); occupational therapy (MS, PhD); rehabilitation psychology (MA, MS, PhD); special education (MA, MS, PhD).

School of Human Ecology Offers consumer behavior and family economics (MS, PhD); design studies (MFA, MS, PhD); human development and family studies (MS, PhD). Electronic applications accepted.

Wisconsin School of Business *Program availability:* Part-time, evening/weekend. Offers accountancy (M Acc); accounting and information systems (PhD); actuarial science, risk management and insurance (PhD); applied security analysis (MBA); arts administration (MBA); brand and product management (MBA); business (M Acc, MBA, PhD); corporate finance and investment banking (MBA); finance, investment and banking (PhD); general management (MBA); information systems (PhD); management and human resources (PhD); marketing (PhD); marketing research (MBA); operations and technology management (MBA); operations management (PhD); real estate (MBA); real estate and urban land economics (PhD); risk management and insurance (MBA); strategic human resource management (MBA); supply chain management (MBA); taxation (M Acc). Electronic applications accepted.

Law School Students: 617 full-time (294 women), 36 part-time (21 women); includes 124 minority (26 Black or African American, non-Hispanic/Latino; 2 American Indian or Alaska Native, non-Hispanic/Latino; 22 Asian, non-Hispanic/Latino; 53 Hispanic/Latino; 1 Native Hawaiian or other Pacific Islander, non-Hispanic/Latino; 20 Two or more races, non-Hispanic/Latino), 66 international. Average age 26. 1,712 applicants, 46% accepted, 271 enrolled. *Faculty:* 64 full-time (38 women), 56 part-time/adjunct (20 women). Expenses: Contact institution. *Financial support:* In 2018–19, 485 students received support. Fellowships, research assistantships, teaching assistantships, career-related internships or fieldwork, Federal Work-Study, scholarships/grants, health care benefits, tuition waivers (full and partial), and unspecified assistantships available. Support available to part-time students. Financial award application deadline: 4/1. In 2018, 41 master's, 158 doctorates awarded. *Program availability:* Part-time, evening/weekend. Offers law (LL M, JD, SJD). *Application deadline:* For fall admission, 4/1 for domestic and international students. Applications are processed on a rolling basis. *Application fee:* $60. Electronic applications accepted. *Application Contact:* Rebecca L. Scheller, Assistant Dean for Admissions and Financial Aid, 608-262-5914, Fax: 608-263-3190, E-mail: admissions@law.wisc.edu. *Dean,* Margaret Raymond, 608-265-3750, Fax: 608-890-0134.

School of Medicine and Public Health Offers biomedical data science (MS, PhD); cancer biology (PhD); cellular and molecular pathology (PhD); clinical investigation (MS, PhD); endocrinology-reproductive physiology (MS, PhD); epidemiology (MS, PhD); genetic counselor studies (MGCS); medical physics (MS, PhD); medicine (MD); medicine and public health (MGCS, MPA, MPH, MS, DPT, MD); molecular and cellular pharmacology (PhD); molecular and environmental toxicology (MS, PhD); neuroscience (PhD); physical therapy (DPT); physician assistant (MPA); population health (PhD); public health (MPH). Electronic applications accepted.

School of Nursing Students: 76 full-time (67 women), 57 part-time (48 women); includes 15 minority (3 Black or African American, non-Hispanic/Latino; 3 American Indian or Alaska Native, non-Hispanic/Latino; 5 Asian, non-Hispanic/Latino; 4 Hispanic/Latino), 14 international. Average age 34. 75 applicants, 56% accepted, 23 enrolled. *Faculty:* 30 full-time (29 women), 13 part-time/adjunct (12 women). Expenses: Contact institution. *Financial support:* In 2018–19, 70 students received support, including 4 fellowships with full tuition reimbursements available (averaging $20,000 per year), 2 research assistantships with full tuition reimbursements available (averaging $19,000 per year), 15 teaching assistantships with full tuition reimbursements available (averaging $15,000 per year); career-related internships or fieldwork, Federal Work-Study, institutionally sponsored loans, scholarships/grants, traineeships, health care benefits, and unspecified assistantships also available. Support available to part-time students. Financial award application deadline: 3/1; financial award applicants required to submit FAFSA. In 2018, 43 doctorates awarded. *Program availability:* Part-time. Offers adult/gerontology (DNP); adult/gerontology acute care (DNP); adult/gerontology primary care (DNP); nursing (PhD). *Application deadline:* For fall admission, 12/1 priority date for domestic and international students. Applications are processed on a rolling basis. *Application fee:* $45. Electronic applications accepted. *Application Contact:* Mandi Moy, Director of Admissions and Recruitment, 608-263-5180, E-mail: admissions@nursing.wisc.edu. *Dean and Professor,* Dr. Linda D. Scott, 608-263-9725, E-mail: ldscott@wisc.edu.

School of Pharmacy Offers pharmaceutical sciences (PhD); pharmacy (MS, PhD, Pharm D); social and administrative sciences in pharmacy (MS, PhD). Electronic applications accepted.

School of Veterinary Medicine Offers veterinary medicine (MS, DVM, PhD).

UNIVERSITY OF WISCONSIN–MILWAUKEE, Milwaukee, WI 53201-0413

General Information State-supported, coed, university. CGS member. *Enrollment:* 24,933 graduate, professional, and undergraduate students; 2,703 full-time matriculated graduate/professional students (1,617 women), 1,789 part-time matriculated graduate/professional students (1,104 women). *Enrollment by degree level:* 3,032 master's, 1,337 doctoral, 123 other advanced degrees. *Graduate housing:* Rooms and/or apartments available on a first-come, first-served basis to single and married students. Housing application deadline: 5/1. *Student services:* Campus employment opportunities, campus safety program, career counseling, child daycare facilities, exercise/wellness program, free psychological counseling, grant writing training, international student services, low-cost health insurance, multicultural affairs office, services for students with disabilities, writing training. *Library facilities:* Golda Meir Library. *Collection:* Books: 2.5 million (physical), 178,268 (digital/electronic); Serial titles: 112,752 (physical). Students can reserve study rooms.

Computer facilities: Computer purchase and lease plans are available. 500 computers available on campus for general student use. A campuswide network can be accessed from student residence rooms and from off campus. Online class registration is available.
Website: http://www.uwm.edu/

General Application Contact: General Information Contact, 414-229-6569, Fax: 414-229-6967, E-mail: gradschool-staff@uwm.edu.

GRADUATE UNITS

Graduate School Students: 2,703 full-time (1,617 women), 1,789 part-time (1,104 women); includes 832 minority (238 Black or African American, non-Hispanic/Latino; 27 American Indian or Alaska Native, non-Hispanic/Latino; 181 Asian, non-Hispanic/Latino; 55 Hispanic/Latino; 4 Native Hawaiian or other Pacific Islander, non-Hispanic/Latino; 327 Two or more races, non-Hispanic/Latino), 650 international. Average age 32. 4,511 applicants, 48% accepted, 1430 enrolled. Expenses: Contact institution. *Financial support:* Fellowships with partial tuition reimbursements, research assistantships with full tuition reimbursements, teaching assistantships with full tuition reimbursements, career-related internships or fieldwork, Federal Work-Study, scholarships/grants, health care benefits, tuition waivers (partial), and unspecified assistantships available. Support available to part-time students. Financial award application deadline: 6/30; financial award applicants required to submit FAFSA. In 2018, 1,036 master's, 168 doctorates, 99 other advanced degrees awarded. *Program availability:* Part-time, evening/weekend. *Application deadline:* Applications are processed on a rolling basis. *Application fee:* $56 ($96 for international students). Electronic applications accepted. *Application Contact:* General Information Contact, 414-229-6569, Fax: 414-229-6967, E-mail: gradschool-staff@uwm.edu. *Dean,* Marija Gajdardziska-Josifovska, 414-229-5220, E-mail: mgj@uwm.edu.

College of Engineering and Applied Science Students: 219 full-time (54 women), 177 part-time (34 women); includes 42 minority (4 Black or African American, non-Hispanic/Latino; 1 American Indian or Alaska Native, non-Hispanic/Latino; 21 Asian, non-Hispanic/Latino; 5 Hispanic/Latino; 11 Two or more races, non-Hispanic/Latino), 243 international. Average age 31. 485 applicants, 54% accepted, 98 enrolled. Expenses: Contact institution. *Financial support:* Fellowships, research assistantships, teaching assistantships, career-related internships or fieldwork, Federal Work-Study, and unspecified assistantships available. Support available to part-time students. Financial award application deadline: 4/15. In 2018, 87 master's, 25 doctorates awarded. *Program availability:* Part-time. Offers biomedical engineering (MS); civil engineering (MS, PhD); computer science (PhD); electrical and computer engineering (MS); electrical engineering (PhD); engineering and applied science (MS, PhD); engineering mechanics (MS); health information systems (PhD); health services management and policy (PhD); industrial and management engineering (MS); industrial engineering (PhD); knowledge based systems (PhD); manufacturing engineering (MS); materials (PhD); materials engineering (MS); mechanical engineering (MS); medical imaging and instrumentation (PhD); public health informatics (PhD). *Application deadline:* For fall admission, 1/1 for domestic students; for spring admission, 9/1 for domestic students. Applications are processed on a rolling basis. *Application fee:* $56 ($96 for international students). Electronic applications accepted. *Application Contact:* Betty Warras, General Information Contact, 414-229-6169, Fax: 414-229-6958, E-mail: ceas-graduate@uwm.edu. *Dean,* Dr. Brett Peters, 414-229-4126, E-mail: ceas-deans-office@uwm.edu.

College of Health Sciences Students: 332 full-time (239 women), 44 part-time (30 women); includes 53 minority (9 Black or African American, non-Hispanic/Latino; 1 American Indian or Alaska Native, non-Hispanic/Latino; 12 Asian, non-Hispanic/Latino; 5 Hispanic/Latino; 26 Two or more races, non-Hispanic/Latino), 29 international. Average age 29. 319 applicants, 47% accepted, 112 enrolled. Expenses: Contact institution. *Financial support:* Research assistantships, teaching assistantships, career-related internships or fieldwork, Federal Work-Study, and unspecified assistantships available. Support available to part-time students. Financial award application deadline: 3/30. In 2018, 83 master's, 23 doctorates, 2 other advanced degrees awarded. *Program availability:* Part-time. Offers assistive technology and design (MS); athletic training (MS); biomedical sciences (MS); communication sciences and disorders (MS); disability and occupation (MS); ergonomics (MS); health care informatics (MS); health sciences (MHA, MS, DPT, PhD, Graduate Certificate); healthcare administration (MHA); kinesiology (MS, PhD); physical therapy (DPT); therapeutic recreation (MS). *Application deadline:* For fall admission, 1/1 priority date for domestic students; for spring admission, 9/1 for domestic students. Applications are processed on a rolling basis. *Application fee:* $56 ($96 for international students). *Application Contact:* Office of Student Affairs, 414-229-2758, Fax: 414-229-3373, E-mail: chs-info@uwm.edu. *Dean,* Ron A. Cisler, PhD, 414-229-5663, E-mail: rac@uwm.edu.

College of Letters and Science Students: 715 full-time (355 women), 347 part-time (197 women); includes 132 minority (31 Black or African American, non-Hispanic/Latino; 5 American Indian or Alaska Native, non-Hispanic/Latino; 11 Hispanic/Latino; 28 Native Hawaiian or other Pacific Islander, non-Hispanic/Latino; 57 Two or more races, non-Hispanic/Latino), 228 international. Average age 31. 1,481 applicants, 33% accepted, 306 enrolled. Expenses: Contact institution. *Financial support:* Fellowships, research assistantships, teaching assistantships, career-related internships or fieldwork, Federal Work-Study, unspecified assistantships, and project assistantships available. Support available to part-time students. Financial award application deadline: 4/15. In 2018, 173 master's, 49 doctorates, 14 other advanced degrees awarded. *Program availability:* Part-time. Offers Africology (MS); anthropology (MS, PhD); art history (MA); art history and criticism (MA); art museum studies (MA); cellular and molecular biology (MS, PhD); chemistry and biochemistry (MS, PhD); communication (MA, PhD); economics (MA, PhD); English (MA, PhD); foreign languages and literature (MA); geological sciences (MS, PhD); history (MA,

PhD); human resources and labor relations (MHRLR); international human resources and labor relations (Graduate Certificate); international interests (MA, MS, PhD); interpreting (Graduate Certificate); language, literature, and translation (MA, MALLT); letters and science (MA, MALLT, MHRLR, MLS, MPA, MS, MSP, PhD, Graduate Certificate); liberal studies (MLS); linguistics (MA, PhD); mathematics (MS, PhD); media studies (MA); mediation and negotiation (Graduate Certificate); microbiology (MS, PhD); museum studies (Graduate Certificate); philosophy (MA); physical geography and environmental studies (MA, MS, PhD); physics (MS, PhD); political science (MA, PhD); psychology (MS, PhD); public administration (MPA); rhetorical leadership (Graduate Certificate); sociology (MA, PhD); Spanish and Portuguese (MA); teaching English to speakers of other languages, adult- and university-level (Graduate Certificate); translation (Graduate Certificate); urban development (MA, MS, PhD); urban studies (MS, PhD); women's and gender studies (MA, Graduate Certificate). *Application deadline:* For fall admission, 1/1 priority date for domestic students; for spring admission, 9/1 for domestic students. *Application fee:* $56 ($96 for international students). Electronic applications accepted. *Application Contact:* General Letters and Science Support, 414-229-7711, E-mail: let-sci@uwm.edu. *Acting Dean,* Dave Clark, 414-375-0457, E-mail: dclark@uwm.edu.

College of Nursing Students: 188 full-time (155 women), 139 part-time (126 women); includes 84 minority (26 Black or African American, non-Hispanic/Latino; 1 American Indian or Alaska Native, non-Hispanic/Latino; 19 Asian, non-Hispanic/Latino; 3 Hispanic/Latino; 1 Native Hawaiian or other Pacific Islander, non-Hispanic/Latino; 34 Two or more races, non-Hispanic/Latino), 7 international. Average age 36. 179 applicants, 59% accepted, 85 enrolled. Expenses: Contact institution. *Financial support:* Fellowships, research assistantships, teaching assistantships, career-related internships or fieldwork, Federal Work-Study, health care benefits, unspecified assistantships, and project assistantships available. Support available to part-time students. Financial award application deadline: 4/15; financial award applicants required to submit FAFSA. In 2018, 25 master's, 46 doctorates, 1 other advanced degree awarded. *Program availability:* Part-time. Offers clinical nurse specialist (Graduate Certificate); family nurse practitioner (Graduate Certificate); nursing (MN, DNP, PhD); sustainable peacebuilding (MSP). *Application deadline:* For fall admission, 1/1 priority date for domestic students; for spring admission, 9/1 for domestic students. *Application fee:* $56 ($96 for international students). Electronic applications accepted. *Application Contact:* Student Affairs Office, 414-229-5047, E-mail: uwmnurse@uwm.edu. *Interim Dean,* Dr. Kim Litwack, 414-229-4189, E-mail: litwack@uwm.edu.

Helen Bader School of Social Welfare Students: 239 full-time (207 women), 107 part-time (88 women); includes 115 minority (50 Black or African American, non-Hispanic/Latino; 5 American Indian or Alaska Native, non-Hispanic/Latino; 14 Asian, non-Hispanic/Latino; 3 Hispanic/Latino; 43 Two or more races, non-Hispanic/Latino), 4 international. Average age 30. 415 applicants, 59% accepted, 189 enrolled. Expenses: Contact institution. *Financial support:* Fellowships with full tuition reimbursements, research assistantships with full tuition reimbursements, teaching assistantships with full tuition reimbursements, career-related internships or fieldwork, Federal Work-Study, health care benefits, unspecified assistantships, and project assistantships available. Support available to part-time students. Financial award application deadline: 4/15; financial award applicants required to submit FAFSA. In 2018, 100 master's, 2 other advanced degrees awarded. *Program availability:* Part-time. Offers applied data analysis using SAS (Graduate Certificate); applied gerontology (Graduate Certificate); crime analytics (MS); criminal justice (MS); nonprofit management (Graduate Certificate); social welfare (PhD); social work (MSW, PhD). *Application deadline:* For fall admission, 1/1 priority date for domestic students; for spring admission, 9/1 for domestic students. *Application fee:* $56 ($96 for international students). Electronic applications accepted. *Application Contact:* Deb Padgett, Associate Professor, Social Work, 414-229-6452, E-mail: dpadgett@uwm.edu. *Dean and Professor,* Stan Stojkovic, PhD, 414-229-4400, E-mail: stojkovi@uwm.edu.

Joseph J. Zilber School of Public Health Students: 82 full-time (65 women), 21 part-time (14 women); includes 28 minority (5 Black or African American, non-Hispanic/Latino; 12 Asian, non-Hispanic/Latino; 11 Two or more races, non-Hispanic/Latino), 9 international. Average age 32. 88 applicants, 76% accepted, 59 enrolled. Expenses: Contact institution. *Financial support:* Fellowships and scholarships/grants available. In 2018, 18 master's awarded. *Program availability:* Part-time. Offers biostatistics (MPH); community and behavioral health promotion (MPH); environmental health sciences (MPH); epidemiology (MPH, PhD); public and population health (Graduate Certificate); public health (MPH, PhD, Graduate Certificate); public health policy and administration (MPH); public health: biostatistics (PhD); public health: community and behavioral health promotion (PhD). Electronic applications accepted. *Application Contact:* Advisor, 414-227-3001, Fax: 414-227-3002, E-mail: applyph@uwm.edu. *Interim Dean,* Ronald Perez, 414-229-4587, E-mail: perez@uwm.edu.

Lubar School of Business Students: 282 full-time (122 women), 280 part-time (115 women); includes 95 minority (19 Black or African American, non-Hispanic/Latino; 2 American Indian or Alaska Native, non-Hispanic/Latino; 35 Asian, non-Hispanic/Latino; 7 Hispanic/Latino; 32 Two or more races, non-Hispanic/Latino), 65 international. Average age 32. 389 applicants, 66% accepted, 191 enrolled. Expenses: Contact institution. *Financial support:* Fellowships with full tuition reimbursements, research assistantships with full tuition reimbursements, teaching assistantships with full tuition reimbursements, career-related internships or fieldwork, Federal Work-Study, health care benefits, unspecified assistantships, and project assistantships available. Support available to part-time students. Financial award application deadline: 4/15; financial award applicants required to submit FAFSA. In 2018, 212 master's, 2 doctorates, 18 other advanced degrees awarded. *Program availability:* Part-time, evening/weekend. Offers business administration (MBA); business analytics (Graduate Certificate); enterprise resource planning (Graduate Certificate); executive business administration (EMBA); information technology management (MS); investment management (Graduate Certificate); management science (MS, PhD, Graduate Certificate); nonprofit management (Graduate Certificate); nonprofit management and leadership (MS); state and local taxation (Graduate Certificate); technology entrepreneurship (Graduate Certificate). *Application deadline:* For fall admission, 1/1 priority date for domestic students; for spring admission, 9/1 for domestic students. *Application fee:* $56 ($96 for international students). Electronic applications accepted. *Application Contact:* Business Graduate Student Services, 414-229-5403, E-mail: mba-ms@uwm.edu. *Dean,* V. Kanti Prasad, 414-229-6256, E-mail: dean-prasad@uwm.edu.

Peck School of the Arts Students: 85 full-time (52 women), 18 part-time (12 women); includes 15 minority (1 Black or African American, non-Hispanic/Latino; 2 Asian, non-Hispanic/Latino; 3 Hispanic/Latino; 1 Native Hawaiian or other Pacific Islander, non-Hispanic/Latino; 8 Two or more races, non-Hispanic/Latino), 22 international. Average

age 31. 140 applicants, 36% accepted, 37 enrolled. Expenses: Contact institution. *Financial support:* Teaching assistantships, career-related internships or fieldwork, Federal Work-Study, health care benefits, unspecified assistantships, and project assistantships available. Support available to part-time students. Financial award application deadline: 4/15; financial award applicants required to submit FAFSA. In 2018, 39 master's, 2 other advanced degrees awarded. *Program availability:* Part-time. Offers art education (MS); chamber music (CAS); conducting (MM); dance (MFA); design entrepreneurship and innovation (MA); film, video, animation, and new genres (MFA); music education (MM); music history and literature (MM); performance (MM); string pedagogy (MM); studio art (MA, MFA); theory and composition (MM). *Application deadline:* For fall admission, 1/1 priority date for domestic students; for spring admission, 9/1 for domestic students. *Application fee:* $56 ($96 for international students). Electronic applications accepted. *Application Contact:* Arts Student Services, 414-229-4763, E-mail: uwmpsoa@uwm.edu. *Dean,* Scott Emmons, 414-229-4762, E-mail: semm@uwm.edu.

School of Architecture and Urban Planning Students: 109 full-time (45 women), 14 part-time (7 women); includes 21 minority (6 Black or African American, non-Hispanic/Latino; 3 Asian, non-Hispanic/Latino; 1 Hispanic/Latino; 11 Two or more races, non-Hispanic/Latino), 14 international. Average age 30. 122 applicants, 64% accepted, 39 enrolled. Expenses: Contact institution. *Financial support:* Fellowships, research assistantships, teaching assistantships, career-related internships or fieldwork, Federal Work-Study, health care benefits, unspecified assistantships, and project assistantships available. Support available to part-time students. Financial award application deadline: 4/15; financial award applicants required to submit FAFSA. In 2018, 45 master's, 4 doctorates, 8 other advanced degrees awarded. *Program availability:* Part-time. Offers architecture (M Arch, MS Arch, PhD); architecture and urban planning (M Arch, MS Arch, MUP, PhD, Graduate Certificate); geographic information systems (Graduate Certificate); urban planning (MUP). *Application deadline:* For fall admission, 1/1 priority date for domestic students; for spring admission, 9/1 for domestic students. *Application fee:* $56 ($96 for international students). Electronic applications accepted. *Application Contact:* Student Advising Office, 414-229-4015, E-mail: sarup-grad@uwm.edu. *Dean,* Robert Greenstreet, 414-229-4016, E-mail: bobg@uwm.edu.

School of Education Students: 259 full-time (199 women), 361 part-time (279 women); includes 173 minority (64 Black or African American, non-Hispanic/Latino; 11 American Indian or Alaska Native, non-Hispanic/Latino; 18 Asian, non-Hispanic/Latino; 10 Hispanic/Latino; 1 Native Hawaiian or other Pacific Islander, non-Hispanic/Latino; 69 Two or more races, non-Hispanic/Latino), 11 international. Average age 34. 517 applicants, 43% accepted, 148 enrolled. Expenses: Contact institution. *Financial support:* Fellowships, teaching assistantships, career-related internships or fieldwork, Federal Work-Study, health care benefits, unspecified assistantships, and project assistantships available. Support available to part-time students. Financial award application deadline: 4/15; financial award applicants required to submit FAFSA. In 2018, 129 master's, 16 doctorates, 24 other advanced degrees awarded. *Program availability:* Part-time. Offers administrative leadership (MS); autism spectrum disorders (Graduate Certificate); children's mental health for school professionals (Graduate Certificate); counseling psychology (PhD); cultural foundations of community engagement and education (MS); curriculum and instruction (MS, PhD, CAS, Ed S, Graduate Certificate); educational policy (Graduate Certificate); educational statistics and measurement (MS, PhD); exceptional education (MS); learning and development (MS, PhD); multicultural knowledge of mental health practices (Graduate Certificate); school counseling (MS, Graduate Certificate); school psychology (MS, PhD, Ed S); support services for online students in higher education (Graduate Certificate); teaching and learning in higher education (Graduate Certificate); transition for students with disabilities (Graduate Certificate); urban education (PhD). *Application deadline:* For fall admission, 1/1 priority date for domestic students; for spring admission, 9/1 for domestic students. *Application fee:* $56 ($96 for international students). Electronic applications accepted. *Application Contact:* Education Office of Student Services, 414-229-4721, E-mail: soeoss@uwm.edu. *Dean,* Alan Shoho, 414-229-4181, E-mail: shoho@uwm.edu.

School of Freshwater Sciences Students: 36 full-time (23 women), 19 part-time (8 women); includes 3 minority (1 Hispanic/Latino; 2 Two or more races, non-Hispanic/Latino), 2 international. Average age 31. 54 applicants, 56% accepted, 25 enrolled. Expenses: Contact institution. *Financial support:* Fellowships, research assistantships, teaching assistantships, and unspecified assistantships available. Financial award applicants required to submit FAFSA. In 2018, 21 master's awarded. Offers freshwater sciences (MS, PhD). *Application fee:* $56 ($96 for international students). Electronic applications accepted. *Application Contact:* Dr. Harvey Bootsma, Graduate Program Representative, 414-382-1717, E-mail: hbootsma@uwm.edu. *Dean,* J. Val Klump, 414-382-1715, E-mail: vklump@uwm.edu.

School of Information Studies Students: 157 full-time (101 women), 257 part-time (191 women); includes 71 minority (23 Black or African American, non-Hispanic/Latino; 1 American Indian or Alaska Native, non-Hispanic/Latino; 17 Asian, non-Hispanic/Latino; 6 Hispanic/Latino; 1 Native Hawaiian or other Pacific Islander, non-Hispanic/Latino; 23 Two or more races, non-Hispanic/Latino), 16 international. Average age 34. 310 applicants, 64% accepted, 138 enrolled. Expenses: Contact institution. *Financial support:* Fellowships, research assistantships, teaching assistantships, career-related internships or fieldwork, Federal Work-Study, health care benefits, unspecified assistantships, and project assistantships available. Support available to part-time students. Financial award application deadline: 4/15; financial award applicants required to submit FAFSA. In 2018, 104 master's, 2 doctorates awarded. *Program availability:* Part-time. Offers information studies (MLIS, MS, PhD, CAS). *Application deadline:* For fall admission, 1/1 priority date for domestic students; for spring admission, 9/1 for domestic students. *Application fee:* $56 ($96 for international students). Electronic applications accepted. *Application Contact:* Linda Barajas, Admissions Coordinator, 414-229-3316, E-mail: barajas@uwm.edu. *Dean/Professor,* Tomas A. Lipinski, 414-229-4707, E-mail: tlipinsk@uwm.edu.

UNIVERSITY OF WISCONSIN–OSHKOSH, Oshkosh, WI 54901

General Information State-supported, coed, comprehensive institution. *Graduate housing:* Room and/or apartments available on a first-come, first-served basis to single students; on-campus housing not available to married students.

GRADUATE UNITS

Graduate Studies *Program availability:* Part-time, evening/weekend. Offers social work (MSW). Electronic applications accepted.

College of Business *Program availability:* Part-time. Offers business (GMBA, MBA); business administration (MBA); global business administration (GMBA). Electronic applications accepted.

College of Education and Human Services *Program availability:* Part-time, evening/weekend. Offers counseling (MSE); cross-categorical (MSE); curriculum and instruction (MSE); early childhood: exceptional education needs (MSE); education and human services (MS, MSE); educational leadership (MS); non-licensure (MSE); reading education (MSE). Electronic applications accepted.

College of Letters and Science *Program availability:* Part-time, evening/weekend. Offers biology (MS); English (MA); experimental psychology (MS); general agency (MPA); health care (MPA); industrial/organizational psychology (MS); letters and science (MA, MPA, MS, MSW); mathematics education (MS). Electronic applications accepted.

College of Nursing *Program availability:* Part-time. Offers adult health and illness (MSN); family nurse practitioner (MSN). Electronic applications accepted.

UNIVERSITY OF WISCONSIN–PARKSIDE, Kenosha, WI 53141-2000

General Information State-supported, coed, comprehensive institution. *Graduate housing:* Room and/or apartments available on a first-come, first-served basis to single students; on-campus housing not available to married students.

GRADUATE UNITS

College of Business, Economics, and Computing *Program availability:* Part-time, evening/weekend. Offers business administration (MBA); business, economics, and computing (MBA, MSCIS); computer and information systems (MSCIS). Electronic applications accepted.

College of Natural and Health Sciences *Program availability:* Part-time. Offers applied molecular biology (MSBS); clinical mental health counseling (MS); health and wellness management (MS); natural and health sciences (MS, MSBS); sport management (MS); sustainable management (MS). Electronic applications accepted.

UNIVERSITY OF WISCONSIN–PLATTEVILLE, Platteville, WI 53818-3099

General Information State-supported, coed, comprehensive institution. *Graduate housing:* On-campus housing not available.

GRADUATE UNITS

School of Graduate Studies *Program availability:* Part-time, evening/weekend, online learning. Electronic applications accepted.

College of Engineering, Mathematics and Science *Program availability:* Part-time. Offers computer science (MS); engineering, mathematics and science (MS).

College of Liberal Arts and Education *Program availability:* Part-time, evening/weekend. Offers adult education (MSE); liberal arts and education (MSE). Electronic applications accepted.

Distance Learning Center *Program availability:* Part-time, evening/weekend. Offers criminal justice (MS); engineering (MS); integrated supply chain management (MS); organizational change leadership (MS); project management (MS). Electronic applications accepted.

UNIVERSITY OF WISCONSIN–RIVER FALLS, River Falls, WI 54022

General Information State-supported, coed, comprehensive institution. *Graduate housing:* Room and/or apartments available on a first-come, first-served basis to single students; on-campus housing not available to married students.

GRADUATE UNITS

Outreach and Graduate Studies *Program availability:* Part-time. Electronic applications accepted.

College of Agriculture, Food, and Environmental Sciences *Program availability:* Part-time. Offers agricultural education (MS); agriculture, food, and environmental sciences (MS). Electronic applications accepted.

College of Arts and Science *Program availability:* Part-time. Offers arts and science (MA, MSE); fine arts (MSE); mathematics education (MSE); science education (MSE); social science education (MSE); teaching English to speakers of other languages (MA). Electronic applications accepted.

College of Business and Economics Offers business and economics (MBA, MM). Electronic applications accepted.

College of Education and Professional Studies *Program availability:* Part-time. Offers communicative disorders (MS); counseling (MSE); education and professional studies (MS, MSE, Ed S); elementary education (MSE); professional development shared inquiry communities (MSE); reading (MSE); school psychology (MSE, Ed S); secondary education-communicative disorders (MSE).

UNIVERSITY OF WISCONSIN–STEVENS POINT, Stevens Point, WI 54481-3897

General Information State-supported, coed, comprehensive institution. *Graduate housing:* Room and/or apartments available on a first-come, first-served basis to single students; on-campus housing not available to married students.

GRADUATE UNITS

College of Fine Arts and Communication *Program availability:* Part-time. Offers elementary/secondary music education (MM Ed); fine arts and communication (MA, MM Ed); studio pedagogy (MM Ed); Suzuki talent education (MM Ed).

Division of Communication *Program availability:* Part-time. Offers interpersonal communication (MA); media studies (MA); organizational communication (MA); public relations (MA).

College of Letters and Science Offers biology (MST); data science (MS); English (MST); history (MST); letters and science (MS, MST).

College of Natural Resources *Program availability:* Part-time. Offers natural resources (MNR, MS).

College of Professional Studies *Program availability:* Part-time.

School of Communication Sciences and Disorders Offers audiology (Au D); speech and language pathology (MS).

School of Education *Program availability:* Part-time. Offers education—general/reading (MSE); education—general/special (MSE); educational administration (MSE); educational sustainability (Ed D); elementary education (MSE).

School of Health Care Professions Offers athletic training (MS).

School of Health Promotion and Human Development *Program availability:* Part-time. Offers family and consumer sciences (Graduate Certificate); health and wellness management (MS); sustainable and resilient food systems (MS).

UNIVERSITY OF WISCONSIN–STOUT, Menomonie, WI 54751

General Information State-supported, coed, comprehensive institution. *Graduate housing:* Room and/or apartments available on a first-come, first-served basis to single students; on-campus housing not available to married students.

GRADUATE UNITS

Graduate School *Program availability:* Part-time, online learning. Electronic applications accepted.

College of Arts, Humanities and Social Sciences Offers design (MFA); technical and professional communication (MS).

College of Education, Health and Human Sciences *Program availability:* Part-time, online learning. Offers applied psychology (MS); career and technical education (MS, Ed D, Ed S); clinical mental health counseling (MS); education (MS, MS Ed, Ed D, Ed S); education, health and human sciences (MS, Ed S); food and nutritional sciences (MS); marriage and family therapy (MS); school counseling (MS); school psychology (MS Ed, Ed S); vocational rehabilitation (MS). Electronic applications accepted.

College of Management Offers management (MS); operations management (MS); project management (MS); quality management (MS); risk control (MS); supply chain management (MS); sustainable management (MS); training and human resource development (MS).

College of Science, Technology, Engineering and Mathematics *Program availability:* Part-time, online learning. Offers conservation biology (PSM); construction management (MS); industrial and applied mathematics (PSM); information and communication technologies (MS); manufacturing engineering (MS); science, technology, engineering and mathematics (MS). Electronic applications accepted.

UNIVERSITY OF WISCONSIN–SUPERIOR, Superior, WI 54880-4500

General Information State-supported, coed, comprehensive institution. *Graduate housing:* Rooms and/or apartments available on a first-come, first-served basis to single students and available to married students. Housing application deadline: 7/1. *Research affiliation:* Great Lakes Indian Fish and Wildlife Commission, Wisconsin Department of Natural Resources (biology), Environmental Protection Agency (biology), The Mexican National Institute for Ecology (biology), The Mexican Marine National Park Service (biology), Coastal Zone Management Institute and Authority of Belize (biology), Fisheries Department, Government of Belize (biology).

GRADUATE UNITS

Graduate Division *Program availability:* Part-time, evening/weekend, online learning. Offers art education (MA); art history (MA); art therapy (MA); community counseling (MSE); educational administration (MSE, Ed S); emotional/behavior disabilities (MSE); human relations (MSE); instruction (MSE); learning disabilities (MSE); mass communication (MA); school counseling (MSE); special education (MSE); speech communication (MA); studio arts (MA); sustainable management (MS); teaching reading (MSE); theater (MA). Electronic applications accepted.

UNIVERSITY OF WISCONSIN–WHITEWATER, Whitewater, WI 53190-1790

General Information State-supported, coed, comprehensive institution. CGS member. *Graduate housing:* Rooms and/or apartments available on a first-come, first-served basis to single students and available to married students. Housing application deadline: 9/1. *Research affiliation:* Generac Power Systems (manufacturing), American Ag-Tec International (international marketing), American Family Insurance (insurance), R.A. Smith and Associates (civil engineering), Sho-Deen (property management and development), Webco Industries, Inc. (lightning radioactive transfer).

GRADUATE UNITS

School of Graduate Studies *Program availability:* Part-time, evening/weekend, online learning. Electronic applications accepted.

College of Arts and Communications *Program availability:* Part-time, evening/weekend, online learning. Offers arts and communications (MS); corporate communication (MS); mass communication (MS). Electronic applications accepted.

College of Business and Economics *Program availability:* Part-time, evening/weekend, online learning. Offers accounting (MPA); business and economics (MBA, MPA, MS, MSE); business and marketing education (MS); finance (MBA); school business management (MSE). Electronic applications accepted.

College of Education and Professional Studies *Program availability:* Part-time, evening/weekend, online learning. Offers communication sciences and disorders (MS); cross categorical licensure (MSE); education and professional studies (MS, MSE, Postbaccalaureate Certificate); professional development (MSE); safety (MS); special education (Postbaccalaureate Certificate). Electronic applications accepted.

College of Letters and Sciences *Program availability:* Part-time, evening/weekend. Offers letters and sciences (MSE, Ed S); school psychology (MSE, Ed S). Electronic applications accepted.

UNIVERSITY OF WYOMING, Laramie, WY 82071

General Information State-supported, coed, university. CGS member. *Enrollment:* 12,450 graduate, professional, and undergraduate students; 1,498 full-time matriculated graduate/professional students (763 women), 954 part-time matriculated graduate/professional students (535 women). *Enrollment by degree level:* 1,230 master's, 1,113 doctoral, 109 other advanced degrees. *Graduate faculty:* 673 full-time (275 women), 7 part-time/adjunct (5 women). *International tuition:* $19,464 full-time. *Tuition, area resident:* Full-time $6504; part-time $271 per credit hour. Tuition, state resident: full-time $6504; part-time $271 per credit hour. Tuition, nonresident: full-time $19,464; part-time $811 per credit hour. *Required fees:* $1410.94; $343.82 per semester. $343.82 per semester. Tuition and fees vary according to course load, program and reciprocity agreements. *Graduate housing:* Rooms and/or apartments available on a first-come, first-served basis to single and married students. Typical cost: $6876 per year ($12,820 including board) for single students; $6876 per year ($12,820 including board) for married students. Room and board charges vary according to board plan and housing facility selected. *Student services:* Campus employment opportunities, campus safety program, career counseling, child daycare facilities, exercise/wellness program, free psychological counseling, international student services, low-cost health insurance, multicultural affairs office, services for students with disabilities, teacher training, writing training. *Library facilities:* William Robertson Coe Library plus 4 others. *Collection:* Books: 1.8 million (physical), 1.2 million (digital/electronic); Serial titles: 14,085 (physical), 96,240 (digital/electronic); Databases: 1,043. Study areas open 24 hours, 5–7 days a week; students can reserve study rooms.

Computer facilities Computer purchase and lease plans are available. 1,683 computers available on campus for general student use. A campuswide network can be accessed from student residence rooms and from off campus. Online class registration is available.
Website: http://www.uwyo.edu/

General Application Contact: Office of Graduate Education, E-mail: graded@uwyo.edu.

GRADUATE UNITS

College of Agriculture and Natural Resources *Program availability:* Part-time. Offers agricultural and applied economics (MS); agriculture and natural resources (MA, MS, PhD); agronomy (MS, PhD); animal sciences (MS, PhD); early childhood development (MS); ecology (MS); entomology (MS, PhD); family and consumer sciences (MS); food science and human nutrition (MA, MS, PhD); molecular biology (MA, MS, PhD); pathobiology (MS); rangeland ecology and watershed management (MS, PhD); reproductive biology (MS, PhD); soil science (MS, PhD); water resources (MS, PhD). Electronic applications accepted.

College of Arts and Sciences *Program availability:* Part-time. Offers American studies (MA); anthropology (MA, PhD); applied statistics (MS); arts and sciences (MA, MAT, MFA, MM, MME, MP, MPA, MS, MST, PhD); botany (MS, PhD); botany/water resources (MS); chemistry (MS, PhD); communication (MA); community and regional planning and natural resources (MP); creative writing (MFA); English (MA); French (MA); geography (MA, MP, MST); geography/water resources (MA); geology (MS, PhD); geophysics (MS, PhD); German (MA); history (MA, MAT); mathematics (MA, MAT, MS, MST, PhD); music education (MME); performance (MM); philosophy (MA); psychology (MA, MS, PhD); rural planning and natural resources (MP); sociology (MA); Spanish (MA); zoology and physiology (MS, PhD). Electronic applications accepted.

School of Politics, Public Affairs and International Studies *Program availability:* Part-time. Offers international peace corps (MA); international studies (MA); political science (MA); public administration (MPA). Electronic applications accepted.

College of Business *Program availability:* Part-time, evening/weekend, online learning. Offers accounting (MS); business (MBA, MS, PhD); business administration (MBA); economics (MS, PhD); finance (MS).

College of Education *Program availability:* Online learning. Offers community mental health (MS); counselor education and supervision (PhD); curriculum and instruction (MA, Ed D, Ed S); education (MA, MS, MST, Ed D, PhD, Certificate, Ed S); educational leadership (MA, Ed D, Certificate); instructional technology (MS, Ed D, PhD); school counseling (MS); special education (MA, PhD, Ed S); student affairs (MS). Electronic applications accepted.

Science and Mathematics Teaching Center Offers science and mathematics teaching (MS, MST). Electronic applications accepted.

College of Engineering and Applied Science *Program availability:* Part-time. Offers architectural engineering (MS); atmospheric science (MS, PhD); chemical engineering (MS, PhD); civil engineering (MS, PhD); computer science (MS, PhD); electrical engineering (MS, PhD); engineering and applied science (MS, PhD); environmental engineering (MS); mechanical and energy systems engineering (MS, PhD); petroleum engineering (MS, PhD). Electronic applications accepted.

College of Health Sciences *Program availability:* Part-time, online learning. Offers health sciences (MS, MSW, Pharm D). Electronic applications accepted.

Division of Communication Disorders *Program availability:* Part-time, online learning. Offers speech-language pathology (MS). Electronic applications accepted.

Division of Kinesiology and Health *Program availability:* Part-time, online learning. Offers kinesiology and health (MS). Electronic applications accepted.

Division of Social Work Offers social work (MSW).

Fay W. Whitney School of Nursing *Program availability:* Part-time, online learning. Offers nursing (MS).

School of Pharmacy *Program availability:* Online learning. Offers health services administration (MS); pharmacy (Pharm D).

College of Law Offers law (JD). Electronic applications accepted.

Graduate Program in Molecular and Cellular Life Sciences Offers molecular and cellular life sciences (PhD).

Program in Ecology Offers ecology (MS, PhD).

UPPER IOWA UNIVERSITY, Fayette, IA 52142-1857

General Information Independent, coed, comprehensive institution. *Graduate housing:* Room and/or apartments available to single students.

GRADUATE UNITS

Master of Education Program Offers early childhood (M Ed); English as a second language (M Ed); higher education (M Ed); instructional strategist (M Ed); reading (M Ed); teacher leadership (M Ed).

Online Master's Programs *Program availability:* Part-time, online learning. Offers accounting (MBA); corporate financial management (MBA); emergency management and homeland security (MPA); general management (MBA); general studies (MPA); government administration (MPA); health and human services (MPA); human resources management (MBA); nonprofit organizational management (MPA); organizational development (MBA); public management (MPA); sport administration (MSA). MBA also available at Madison, WI campus. Electronic applications accepted.

URBANA UNIVERSITY–A BRANCH CAMPUS OF FRANKLIN UNIVERSITY, Urbana, OH 43078-2091

General Information Independent, coed, comprehensive institution. *Graduate housing:* Room and/or apartments available on a first-come, first-served basis to single students; on-campus housing not available to married students.

GRADUATE UNITS

College of Education and Sports Studies *Program availability:* Part-time, evening/weekend. Offers classroom education (M Ed).

College of Nursing and Allied Health Offers nursing (MSN).

College of Social and Behavioral Sciences Offers criminal justice administration (MA).

Division of Business Administration *Program availability:* Part-time, evening/weekend. Offers business administration (MBA).

URSHAN GRADUATE SCHOOL OF THEOLOGY, Florissant, MO 63031

General Information Independent-religious, coed, graduate-only institution.

GRADUATE UNITS

Graduate Programs *Program availability:* Online learning. Offers theology (M Div, MACM, MTS).

URSULINE COLLEGE, Pepper Pike, OH 44124-4398

General Information Independent-religious, coed, primarily women, comprehensive institution. *Enrollment:* 247 full-time matriculated graduate/professional students (220 women), 191 part-time matriculated graduate/professional students (162 women).

Enrollment by degree level: 365 master's, 12 doctoral, 61 other advanced degrees. *Graduate faculty:* 19 full-time (15 women), 45 part-time/adjunct (29 women). *Tuition:* Full-time $14,088; part-time $7044 per credit hour. Tuition and fees vary according to course load and program. *Graduate housing:* Room and/or apartments guaranteed to single students; on-campus housing not available to married students. Typical cost: $8142 per year ($12,980 including board). Room and board charges vary according to board plan. Housing application deadline: 8/20. *Student services:* Campus employment opportunities, career counseling, exercise/wellness program, free psychological counseling, multicultural affairs office, services for students with disabilities, teacher training, writing training. *Library facilities:* Ralph M. Besse Library. *Collection:* Books: 132,089 (physical), 137,533 (digital/electronic); Serial titles: 902 (physical), 14,413 (digital/electronic); Databases: 162. Weekly public service hours: 91; students can reserve study rooms.

Computer facilities: 72 computers available on campus for general student use. A campuswide network can be accessed from student residence rooms. Online class registration is available.
Website: http://www.ursuline.edu/

General Application Contact: Melanie Steele, Director, Graduate Admission, 440-646-8119, Fax: 440-684-6138, E-mail: graduateadmissions@ursuline.edu.

GRADUATE UNITS

School of Graduate and Professional Studies Students: 247 full-time (220 women), 191 part-time (162 women); includes 122 minority (94 Black or African American, non-Hispanic/Latino; 2 American Indian or Alaska Native, non-Hispanic/Latino; 9 Asian, non-Hispanic/Latino; 9 Hispanic/Latino; 8 Two or more races, non-Hispanic/Latino), 2 international. Average age 36. 774 applicants, 99% accepted, 142 enrolled. *Faculty:* 19 full-time (15 women), 45 part-time/adjunct (29 women). Expenses: Contact institution. *Financial support:* In 2018–19, 48 students received support. Federal Work-Study, scholarships/grants, tuition waivers (partial), and campus work-study available. Financial award application deadline: 3/1; financial award applicants required to submit FAFSA. In 2018, 136 master's, 6 doctorates awarded. *Program availability:* Part-time, 100% online. Offers acute-care nurse practitioner (MSN); adult nurse practitioner (MSN); adult-gerontology acute care nurse practitioner (MSN); adult-gerontology clinical nurse specialist (MSN); adult-gerontology nurse practitioner (MSN); care management (MSN); clinical nurse specialist (MSN); counseling and art therapy (MA); education (MA); educational administration (MA); ethical and entrepreneurial leadership (MBA); family nurse practitioner (MSN); financial planning and accounting (MBA); health services management (MBA); historic preservation (MA); management (MBA); management and leadership (MBA); marketing and communications management (MBA); nursing (DNP); nursing education (MSN); palliative care (MSN); theological and pastoral studies (MA). Avg program cost excluded Counseling and Art Therapy; some programs require fewer hours and thus cost less. *Application deadline:* For fall admission, 8/1 priority date for domestic students. Applications are processed on a rolling basis. *Application fee:* $25. Electronic applications accepted. *Application Contact:* Melanie Steele, Director, Graduate Admission, 440-646-8146, Fax: 440-684-6138, E-mail: graduateadmissions@ursuline.edu. *Dean,* Dr. James Connell, 440-646-8120, Fax: 440-684-6088, E-mail: jconnell@ursuline.edu.

UTAH STATE UNIVERSITY, Logan, UT 84322

General Information State-supported, coed, university. CGS member. *Graduate housing:* Rooms and/or apartments available on a first-come, first-served basis to single and married students. *Research affiliation:* Boeing Aerospace and Engineering (science and engineering), Duke Energy Corporation (engineering), Kennecott Copper Corporation (natural resources), Kraft Foods, Inc. (agriculture), National Endowment for Financial Education (education).

GRADUATE UNITS

School of Graduate Studies *Program availability:* Part-time, evening/weekend, online learning.

Caine College of the Arts Offers art and design (MFA); arts (MFA, MM); design (MFA); guitar performance (MM); piano performance and pedagogy (MM).

College of Agriculture and Applied Sciences *Program availability:* Part-time, online learning. Offers agricultural extension and education (MS); agriculture and applied sciences (MAE, MDA, MLA, MPS, MS, PhD); animal science (MS, PhD); applied economics (MAE, MS, PhD); bioregional planning (MS); bioveterinary science (MS, PhD); climate sciences (MS, PhD); dairy science (MS); dietetic administration (MDA); ecology (MS, PhD); family and consumer sciences education and extension (MS); horticulture (MPS); international food and agribusiness (MS); landscape architecture (MLA); nutrition and food sciences (MS, PhD); plant science (MS, PhD); soil science (MS, PhD); technology and engineering education (MS); toxicology (MS, PhD).

College of Engineering *Program availability:* Part-time, evening/weekend. Offers aerospace engineering (MS, PhD); biological engineering (MS, PhD); civil and environmental engineering (ME, MS, PhD, CE); computer science (MCS, MS, PhD); electrical engineering (ME, MS, PhD); engineering (MCS, ME, MS, PhD, CE); engineering education (PhD); mechanical engineering (ME, MS, PhD). Electronic applications accepted.

College of Humanities and Social Sciences *Program availability:* Part-time, evening/weekend, online learning. Offers American studies (MA, MS); anthropology (MS); English (MA, MS); folklore (MA, MS); history (MA, MS); humanities and social sciences (MA, MS, MSLT, MSW, PhD); journalism and communication (MA, MS); political science (MS); second language teaching (MSLT); social work (MSW); sociology (MS, PhD); western American literature and culture (MA, MS).

College of Science *Program availability:* Part-time, evening/weekend. Offers biochemistry (MS, PhD); biology (MS, PhD); chemistry (MS, PhD); ecology (MS, PhD); geology (MS); industrial mathematics (MS); mathematical sciences (PhD); mathematics (M Math, MS); physics (MS, PhD); science (M Math, MCS, MS, PhD); statistics (MS).

Emma Eccles Jones College of Education and Human Services *Program availability:* Part-time, evening/weekend, online learning. Offers audiology (Au D, Ed S); business information systems (Ed D, PhD); clinical/counseling/school psychology (PhD); communication disorders and deaf education (M Ed); communicative disorders and deaf education (MA, MS); curriculum and instruction (Ed D, PhD); disability disciplines (PhD); education and human services (M Ed, MA, MFHD, MRC, MS, Au D, Ed D, PhD, Ed S); elementary education (M Ed, MA, MS); family and human development (MFHD); family, consumer, and human development (MS, PhD); fitness promotion (MS); health and human movement (MS); instructional technology and learning sciences (M Ed, MS, PhD, Ed S); pathokinesiology (PhD); physical and sport education (M Ed); public health (MPH); rehabilitation counseling (MRC); research and evaluation (PhD); research and evaluation methodology (PhD); school counseling (MS); school psychology (MS); secondary education (M Ed, MA, MS); special education (M Ed, MS, Ed S).

Jon M. Huntsman School of Business *Program availability:* Part-time, evening/weekend, online learning. Offers accountancy (M Acc); business (M Acc, MA, MBA, MHR, MMIS, MS); business administration (MBA); economics (MS); financial economics (MS); human resources (MHR); management information systems (MMIS).

S.J. and Jessie E. Quinney College of Natural Resources *Program availability:* Part-time. Offers bioregional planning (MS); ecology (MS, PhD); fisheries biology (MS, PhD); forestry (MS, PhD); geography (MA, MS); human dimensions of ecosystem science and management (MS, PhD); natural resources (MA, MNR, MS, PhD); range science (MS, PhD); recreation resource management (MS, PhD); watershed science (MS, PhD); wildlife biology (MS, PhD).

UTAH VALLEY UNIVERSITY, Orem, UT 84058-5999

General Information State-supported, coed, comprehensive institution. *Enrollment:* 39,931 graduate, professional, and undergraduate students; 185 full-time matriculated graduate/professional students (103 women), 333 part-time matriculated graduate/professional students (108 women). *Enrollment by degree level:* 510 master's, 8 other advanced degrees. *International tuition:* $19,781 full-time. *Tuition, area resident:* Full-time $7932. Tuition, state resident: full-time $7932. Tuition, nonresident: full-time $19,781. *Required fees:* $700. Tuition and fees vary according to course load and program. *Graduate housing:* On-campus housing not available. *Student services:* Campus employment opportunities, campus safety program, career counseling, child daycare facilities, exercise/wellness program, free psychological counseling, grant writing training, international student services, low-cost health insurance, multicultural affairs office, services for students with disabilities, teacher training. *Library facilities:* Utah Valley University Library plus 1 other. *Collection:* Students can reserve study rooms.

Computer facilities: A campuswide network can be accessed from off campus. Online class registration is available.
Website: http://www.uvu.edu/

General Application Contact: Shauna Reher, Administrative Assistant, 801-863-7348, E-mail: graduate_studies@uvu.edu.

GRADUATE UNITS

MBA Program *Program availability:* Part-time, evening/weekend. Offers accounting (MBA); management (MBA). Electronic applications accepted.

Program in Cybersecurity Offers cybersecurity (Graduate Certificate).

Program in Education *Program availability:* Part-time. Offers educational technology (M Ed); elementary mathematics (M Ed); elementary STEM (M Ed); English as a second language (M Ed); reading (M Ed); teachers as leaders (M Ed). Electronic applications accepted.

Program in Nursing *Program availability:* Part-time, online learning. Offers nursing (MSN). Electronic applications accepted.

Program in Social Work Offers social work (MSW).

UTICA COLLEGE, Utica, NY 13502-4892

General Information Independent, coed, comprehensive institution. *Enrollment:* 5,196 graduate, professional, and undergraduate students; 990 full-time matriculated graduate/professional students (538 women), 484 part-time matriculated graduate/professional students (265 women). *Enrollment by degree level:* 1,086 master's, 339 doctoral, 36 other advanced degrees. *Graduate faculty:* 65 full-time (28 women). *Tuition:* Full-time $35,254; part-time $10,284 per credit. *Required fees:* $550; $70 per course. Tuition and fees vary according to course load, degree level, campus/location and program. *Graduate housing:* Room and/or apartments available on a first-come, first-served basis to single students; on-campus housing not available to married students. Housing application deadline; 3/1. *Student services:* Campus employment opportunities, campus safety program, career counseling, international student services, low-cost health insurance, services for students with disabilities. *Library facilities:* Frank E. Gannett Memorial Library. *Collection:* Books: 307,523 (physical); Serial titles: 267,023 (physical). Students can reserve study rooms.

Computer facilities: 430 computers available on campus for general student use. A campuswide network can be accessed from student residence rooms. Online class registration is available.
Website: http://www.utica.edu/

General Application Contact: John D. Rowe, Director of Graduate Admissions, 315-792-3824, Fax: 315-792-3003, E-mail: jrowe@utica.edu.

GRADUATE UNITS

Department of Physical Therapy Students: 86 full-time (46 women), 386 part-time (253 women); includes 246 minority (17 Black or African American, non-Hispanic/Latino; 220 Asian, non-Hispanic/Latino; 8 Hispanic/Latino; 1 Native Hawaiian or other Pacific Islander, non-Hispanic/Latino), 4 international. Average age 34. 240 applicants, 98% accepted, 232 enrolled. *Faculty:* 10 full-time (4 women). Expenses: Contact institution. *Financial support:* Career-related internships or fieldwork, scholarships/grants, tuition waivers (partial), and unspecified assistantships available. Support available to part-time students. Financial award application deadline: 3/15; financial award applicants required to submit FAFSA. In 2018, 299 doctorates awarded. *Program availability:* Part-time, evening/weekend, online learning. Offers physical therapy (DPT, TDPT). *Application deadline:* Applications are processed on a rolling basis. *Application fee:* $50. Electronic applications accepted. *Application Contact:* John D. Rowe, Director of Graduate Admissions, 315-792-3824, Fax: 315-792-3003, E-mail: jrowe@utica.edu. *Director,* Dr. Ashraf Elazzazi, 315-792-3313, E-mail: aelazza@utica.edu.

MBA in Economic Crime and Fraud Management Students: 50 full-time (35 women), 14 part-time (6 women); includes 17 minority (6 Black or African American, non-Hispanic/Latino; 1 American Indian or Alaska Native, non-Hispanic/Latino; 5 Asian, non-Hispanic/Latino; 4 Hispanic/Latino; 1 Two or more races, non-Hispanic/Latino). Average age 33. 31 applicants, 61% accepted, 17 enrolled. *Faculty:* 4 full-time (0 women). Expenses: Contact institution. *Financial support:* Career-related internships or fieldwork, scholarships/grants, tuition waivers (partial), and unspecified assistantships available. Support available to part-time students. Financial award application deadline: 3/15; financial award applicants required to submit FAFSA. In 2018, 49 master's awarded. *Program availability:* Part-time, evening/weekend, online learning. Offers economic crime management (MBA). *Application deadline:* Applications are processed on a rolling basis. *Application fee:* $50. Electronic applications accepted. *Application Contact:* John D. Rowe, Director of Graduate Admissions, 315-792-3824, Fax: 315-792-3003, E-mail: jrowe@utica.edu. *Director of Economic Crime Graduate Programs,* Dr. R. Bruce McBride, 315-792-3808, E-mail: rmcbride@utica.edu.

Program in Accountancy Students: 9 full-time (6 women), 3 part-time (2 women); includes 5 minority (1 Black or African American, non-Hispanic/Latino; 1 Asian, non-Hispanic/Latino; 3 Hispanic/Latino). Average age 25. 11 applicants, 64% accepted, 6 enrolled. *Faculty:* 3 full-time (1 woman). Expenses: Contact institution. *Financial support:* Career-related internships or fieldwork, scholarships/grants, tuition waivers (partial), and unspecified assistantships available. Support available to part-time students. Financial award application deadline: 3/15; financial award applicants required to submit FAFSA. In 2018, 13 master's awarded. *Program availability:* Part-time, evening/weekend. *Application deadline:* Applications are processed on a rolling basis. *Application fee:* $50. Electronic applications accepted. *Application Contact:* John D. Rowe, Director of Graduate Admissions, 315-792-3824, Fax: 315-792-3003, E-mail: jrowe@utica.edu. *MBA Director,* Dr. Zhaodan Huang, 315-792-3247, E-mail: zhuang@utica.edu.

Program in Cybersecurity Students: 280 full-time (75 women), 88 part-time (32 women); includes 97 minority (52 Black or African American, non-Hispanic/Latino; 1 American Indian or Alaska Native, non-Hispanic/Latino; 15 Asian, non-Hispanic/Latino; 23 Hispanic/Latino; 6 Two or more races, non-Hispanic/Latino). Average age 34. 232 applicants, 78% accepted, 148 enrolled. *Faculty:* 5 full-time (0 women), 8 part-time/adjunct (0 women). Expenses: Contact institution. *Financial support:* Application deadline: 3/15; applicants required to submit FAFSA. In 2018, 155 master's awarded. *Program availability:* Part-time, evening/weekend, 100% online. Offers cybersecurity (MPS, MS). *Application deadline:* Applications are processed on a rolling basis. Electronic applications accepted. *Application Contact:* John D. Rowe, Director of Graduate Admissions, 315-792-3824, Fax: 315-792-3003, E-mail: jrowe@utica.edu. *Chair,* Joseph Giordano, 315-792-2521.

Program in Economic Crime and Fraud Management Students: 44 full-time (27 women), 14 part-time (5 women); includes 15 minority (6 Black or African American, non-Hispanic/Latino; 2 Asian, non-Hispanic/Latino; 5 Hispanic/Latino; 1 Native Hawaiian or other Pacific Islander, non-Hispanic/Latino; 1 Two or more races, non-Hispanic/Latino). Average age 37. 36 applicants, 64% accepted, 17 enrolled. *Faculty:* 7 full-time (0 women). Expenses: Contact institution. *Financial support:* Career-related internships or fieldwork, scholarships/grants, tuition waivers (partial), and unspecified assistantships available. Support available to part-time students. Financial award application deadline: 3/15; financial award applicants required to submit FAFSA. In 2018, 28 master's awarded. *Program availability:* Part-time, evening/weekend, 100% online. Offers economic crime and fraud management (MS). *Application deadline:* Applications are processed on a rolling basis. *Application fee:* $50. Electronic applications accepted. *Application Contact:* John D. Rowe, Director of Graduate Admissions, 315-792-3824, Fax: 315-792-3003, E-mail: jrowe@utica.edu. *Director of Economic Crime Graduate Programs,* Dr. R. Bruce McBride, 315-792-3808, E-mail: rmcbride@utica.edu.

Program in Health Care Administration Students: 179 full-time (137 women), 24 part-time (18 women); includes 54 minority (31 Black or African American, non-Hispanic/Latino; 2 American Indian or Alaska Native, non-Hispanic/Latino; 9 Asian, non-Hispanic/Latino; 8 Hispanic/Latino; 1 Native Hawaiian or other Pacific Islander, non-Hispanic/Latino; 3 Two or more races, non-Hispanic/Latino). Average age 33. 134 applicants, 69% accepted, 78 enrolled. *Faculty:* 2 full-time (both women), 11 part-time/adjunct (4 women). Expenses: Contact institution. *Financial support:* Application deadline: 3/15; applicants required to submit FAFSA. In 2018, 92 master's awarded. *Program availability:* Part-time, evening/weekend, online learning. Offers health care administration (MS). *Application deadline:* Applications are processed on a rolling basis. *Application fee:* $50. Electronic applications accepted. *Application Contact:* John D. Rowe, Director of Graduate Admissions, 315-792-3824, Fax: 315-792-3003, E-mail: jrowe@utica.edu. *Program Director,* Dr. Jamie Cuda, 315-792-3540, E-mail: jlcuda@utica.edu.

Program in Occupational Therapy Students: 88 full-time (80 women), 1 part-time (0 women); includes 10 minority (2 Black or African American, non-Hispanic/Latino; 2 Asian, non-Hispanic/Latino; 5 Hispanic/Latino; 1 Two or more races, non-Hispanic/Latino), 1 international. Average age 25. 65 applicants, 98% accepted, 57 enrolled. *Faculty:* 7 full-time (all women). Expenses: Contact institution. *Financial support:* Career-related internships or fieldwork, scholarships/grants, tuition waivers (partial), and unspecified assistantships available. Support available to part-time students. Financial award application deadline: 3/15; financial award applicants required to submit FAFSA. In 2018, 59 master's awarded. *Program availability:* Part-time, evening/weekend. Offers occupational therapy (MS). *Application deadline:* Applications are processed on a rolling basis. *Application fee:* $50. Electronic applications accepted. *Application Contact:* John D. Rowe, Director of Graduate Admissions, 315-792-3824, Fax: 315-792-3003, E-mail: jrowe@utica.edu. *Director,* Cora Bruns, 315-792-3125, E-mail: cbruns@utica.edu.

Teacher Education Programs Students: 58 full-time (36 women), 20 part-time (13 women); includes 10 minority (3 Black or African American, non-Hispanic/Latino; 1 Asian, non-Hispanic/Latino; 4 Hispanic/Latino; 2 Two or more races, non-Hispanic/Latino). Average age 28. 85 applicants, 65% accepted, 46 enrolled. *Faculty:* 10 full-time (7 women). Expenses: Contact institution. *Financial support:* Career-related internships or fieldwork, scholarships/grants, tuition waivers (partial), and unspecified assistantships available. Support available to part-time students. Financial award application deadline: 3/15; financial award applicants required to submit FAFSA. In 2018, 17 master's awarded. Offers teacher education (MS, MS Ed, CAS). *Application deadline:* Applications are processed on a rolling basis. *Application fee:* $50. Electronic applications accepted. *Application Contact:* John D. Rowe, Director of Graduate Admissions, 315-792-3824, Fax: 315-792-3003, E-mail: jrowe@utica.edu. *Dean of Health Professions and Education,* Dr. Patrice Hallock, 315-792-3162, E-mail: phallock@utica.edu.

VALDOSTA STATE UNIVERSITY, Valdosta, GA 31698

General Information State-supported, coed, university. CGS member. *Graduate housing:* Rooms and/or apartments available on a first-come, first-served basis to single and married students. Housing application deadline: 7/1.

GRADUATE UNITS

College of Nursing and Health Sciences *Program availability:* Part-time, online learning. Offers adult gerontology nurse practitioner (MSN); exercise physiology (MS); family nurse practitioner (MSN); family psychiatric mental health nurse practitioner (MSN). Electronic applications accepted.

Department of Communication Sciences and Disorders Offers communication disorders (M Ed); communication sciences and disorders (SLPD); special education (MAT, Ed S). Electronic applications accepted.

Department of Curriculum, Leadership, and Technology *Program availability:* 100% online, blended/hybrid learning. Offers leadership (Ed D); P-12 school leadership (M Ed); performance-based leadership (Ed S). Electronic applications accepted.

Department of Elementary Education *Program availability:* Part-time, evening/weekend, blended/hybrid learning. Offers elementary education (M Ed). Electronic applications accepted.

Department of English *Program availability:* Part-time, 100% online, blended/hybrid learning. Offers English (MA); English studies for language arts teachers (MA). Electronic applications accepted.

Department of Political Science *Program availability:* Part-time, evening/weekend, online learning. Offers public administration (MPA, DPA). Electronic applications accepted.

Department of Psychology, Counseling, and Family Therapy *Program availability:* Part-time, evening/weekend, 100% online, blended/hybrid learning. Offers industrial/organizational psychology (MS); marriage and family therapy (MS); school counseling (M Ed, Ed S). Electronic applications accepted.

Department of Social Work *Program availability:* Part-time, evening/weekend, online learning. Offers social work (MSW).

Langdale College of Business *Program availability:* Part-time, evening/weekend, 100% online, blended/hybrid learning. Offers accountancy (M Acc); business administration (MBA); healthcare administration (MBA). MBA program is a member of the Georgia WebMBA. Electronic applications accepted.

Program in Library and Information Science *Program availability:* 100% online. Offers library and information science (MLIS).

VALLEY CITY STATE UNIVERSITY, Valley City, ND 58072

General Information State-supported, coed, comprehensive institution.

GRADUATE UNITS

Online Graduate Programs Students: 5 full-time (2 women), 133 part-time (100 women); includes 8 minority (1 Black or African American, non-Hispanic/Latino; 3 American Indian or Alaska Native, non-Hispanic/Latino; 2 Asian, non-Hispanic/Latino; 2 Hispanic/Latino). Average age 36. 23 applicants, 74% accepted, 12 enrolled. *Faculty:* 20 full-time (11 women), 13 part-time/adjunct (8 women). Expenses: Contact institution. *Financial support:* In 2018–19, 16 students received support. Scholarships/grants, tuition waivers (full and partial), and unspecified assistantships available. Financial award applicants required to submit FAFSA. In 2018, 47 master's awarded. *Program availability:* Part-time, evening/weekend, online only, 100% online. Offers elementary education (M Ed); English education (M Ed); library and information technologies (M Ed); teaching (MAT); teaching and technology (M Ed); teaching English language learners (M Ed); technology education (M Ed). *Application deadline:* For fall admission, 7/26 for domestic and international students; for spring admission, 12/13 for domestic and international students; for summer admission, 5/18 for domestic and international students. Applications are processed on a rolling basis. *Application fee:* $35. Electronic applications accepted. *Application Contact:* Misty Lindgren, Graduate Studies, 701-845-7303, Fax: 701-845-7190, E-mail: misty.lindgren@vcsu.edu. *Dean,* Dr. Sheri Okland, 701-845-7184, E-mail: sheri.l.okland@vcsu.edu.

VALPARAISO UNIVERSITY, Valparaiso, IN 46383

General Information Independent-religious, coed, comprehensive institution. CGS member. *Graduate housing:* Rooms and/or apartments available on a first-come, first-served basis to single and married students. Housing application deadline: 8/1.

GRADUATE UNITS

College of Business Students: 7 full-time (5 women), 43 part-time (16 women); includes 5 minority (4 Black or African American, non-Hispanic/Latino; 1 Two or more races, non-Hispanic/Latino). Average age 31. Expenses: Contact institution. *Financial support:* Available to part-time students. Applicants required to submit FAFSA. *Program availability:* Part-time, evening/weekend, online learning. Offers business administration (MBA); business decision-making (Certificate); business intelligence (Certificate); engineering management (Certificate); finance (Certificate); general business (Certificate); leading the global enterprise (Certificate); management (Certificate). *Application deadline:* Applications are processed on a rolling basis. *Application fee:* $30 ($50 for international students). Electronic applications accepted. *Application Contact:* Cindy Scanlan, Director of Graduate Programs in Management, 219-465-7952, Fax: 219-464-5789, E-mail: cindy.scanlan@valpo.edu. *Dean,* Jim Brodzinski, 219-464-5035, E-mail: jim.brodzinski@valpo.edu.

College of Nursing and Health Professions *Program availability:* Part-time, evening/weekend, online learning. Offers nursing (DNP); nursing education (MSN, Certificate); physician assistant (MSPA); public health (MPH). Electronic applications accepted.

VAN ANDEL INSTITUTE GRADUATE SCHOOL, Grand Rapids, MI 49503

General Information Private, coed, graduate-only institution.

GRADUATE UNITS

PhD Program Offers cell and molecular genetics (PhD). Electronic applications accepted.

VANCOUVER ISLAND UNIVERSITY, Nanaimo, BC V9R 5S5, Canada

General Information Province-supported, coed, comprehensive institution. *Graduate housing:* Room and/or apartments available on a first-come, first-served basis to single students; on-campus housing not available to married students. Housing application deadline: 3/5.

GRADUATE UNITS

Master of Business Administration Program *Program availability:* Part-time. Offers international business (MBA). Program offered jointly with University of Hertfordshire. Electronic applications accepted.

VANCOUVER SCHOOL OF THEOLOGY, Vancouver, BC V6T 1L4, Canada

General Information Independent-religious, coed, graduate-only institution. *Enrollment by degree level:* 76 master's, 41 other advanced degrees. *Graduate faculty:* 12 full-time (4 women), 12 part-time/adjunct (9 women). *Graduate housing:* Rooms and/or apartments available on a first-come, first-served basis to single and married students. Housing application deadline: 3/15. *Student services:* Campus employment opportunities, career counseling, low-cost health insurance, services for students with disabilities. *Library facilities:* H.R. MacMillan Library.

Computer facilities: A campuswide network can be accessed from student residence rooms.
Website: http://www.vst.edu/

General Application Contact: Julie Lees, Recruitment, 604-822-6502, E-mail: jlees@vst.edu.

GRADUATE UNITS

Graduate and Professional Programs *Program availability:* Part-time, online learning. Offers denominational studies (Diploma); indigenous and inter-religious studies (MA, Diploma); public and pastoral leadership (MA); public and pastoral leadership in spiritual care (MA); theological studies (MATS, Diploma, Graduate Diploma); theology (M Div, Th M). Electronic applications accepted.

VANDERBILT UNIVERSITY, Nashville, TN 37240-1001

General Information Independent, coed, university. CGS member. *Enrollment:* 5,120 full-time matriculated graduate/professional students (2,885 women), 889 part-time matriculated graduate/professional students (671 women). *Enrollment by degree level:* 2,542 master's, 3,429 doctoral, 38 other advanced degrees. *Graduate faculty:* 1,084 full-time (351 women), 14 part-time/adjunct (5 women). *Tuition:* Full-time $47,208; part-time $2026 per credit hour. *Required fees:* $478. *Graduate housing:* On-campus housing not available. *Student services:* Campus employment opportunities, campus safety program, career counseling, child daycare facilities, exercise/wellness program, free psychological counseling, grant writing training, international student services, low-cost health insurance, multicultural affairs office, services for students with disabilities, teacher training, writing training. *Library facilities:* Jean and Alexander Heard Library plus 7 others. *Collection:* Books: 3.1 million (physical), 1.7 million (digital/electronic); Databases: 3,700.

Computer facilities: A campuswide network can be accessed from student residence rooms and from off campus. Online class registration, productivity and educational software are available.
Website: http://www.vanderbilt.edu/

General Application Contact: Walter B. Bieschke, Program Coordinator for Graduate Admissions, 615-322-0236, Fax: 615-343-9936, E-mail: vandygrad@vanderbilt.edu.

GRADUATE UNITS

Center for Medicine, Health, and Society Students: 18 full-time (13 women), 4 part-time (2 women); includes 11 minority (3 Black or African American, non-Hispanic/Latino; 4 Asian, non-Hispanic/Latino; 1 Hispanic/Latino; 3 Two or more races, non-Hispanic/Latino), 1 international. Average age 22. 30 applicants, 80% accepted, 18 enrolled. *Faculty:* 9 full-time (5 women). Expenses: Contact institution. *Financial support:* Federal Work-Study, scholarships/grants, and health care benefits available. Financial award application deadline: 1/15; financial award applicants required to submit CSS PROFILE or FAFSA. In 2018, 13 master's awarded. Offers medicine, health, and society (MA). *Application deadline:* For fall admission, 1/15 for domestic and international students. Electronic applications accepted. *Application Contact:* JuLeigh Petty, Acting Director/Director of Graduate Studies, 615-322-6725, Fax: 615-322-2731, E-mail: juleigh.petty@vanderbilt.edu. *Director,* Dr. Jonathan Metzl, 615-343-2504, Fax: 615-343-8889, E-mail: jonathan.metzl@vanderbilt.edu.

Department of Anthropology Students: 30 full-time (20 women); includes 5 minority (1 Black or African American, non-Hispanic/Latino; 4 Hispanic/Latino), 12 international. Average age 33. 49 applicants, 6% accepted, 3 enrolled. *Faculty:* 14 full-time (4 women). Expenses: Contact institution. *Financial support:* Fellowships with tuition reimbursements, research assistantships with full tuition reimbursements, teaching assistantships with full tuition reimbursements, career-related internships or fieldwork, Federal Work-Study, institutionally sponsored loans, scholarships/grants, and health care benefits available. Financial award application deadline: 1/15; financial award applicants required to submit CSS PROFILE or FAFSA. In 2018, 4 master's, 2 doctorates awarded. Offers anthropology (MA, PhD). *Application deadline:* For fall admission, 1/15 for domestic and international students. *Application fee:* $0. Electronic applications accepted. *Application Contact:* John Janusek, Director of Graduate Studies, 615-343-6120, E-mail: john.w.janusek@vanderbilt.edu. *Chair,* Dr. Beth Conklin, 615-343-6120, Fax: 615-343-0230, E-mail: beth.a.conklin@vanderbilt.edu.

Department of Biological Sciences Students: 59 full-time (29 women); includes 16 minority (4 Black or African American, non-Hispanic/Latino; 5 Asian, non-Hispanic/Latino; 4 Hispanic/Latino; 3 Two or more races, non-Hispanic/Latino), 14 international. Average age 27. 63 applicants, 22% accepted, 10 enrolled. *Faculty:* 20 full-time (4 women). Expenses: Contact institution. *Financial support:* Fellowships with tuition reimbursements, research assistantships with full tuition reimbursements, teaching assistantships with full tuition reimbursements, Federal Work-Study, institutionally sponsored loans, scholarships/grants, traineeships, and health care benefits available. Financial award application deadline: 1/15; financial award applicants required to submit CSS PROFILE or FAFSA. In 2018, 6 doctorates awarded. Offers biological sciences (MS, PhD). *Application deadline:* For fall admission, 1/15 for domestic and international students. Electronic applications accepted. *Application Contact:* Julian Hillyer, Director of Graduate Studies, 615-343-2065, E-mail: julian.hillyer@vanderbilt.edu. *Chair,* Dr. Douglas McMahon, 615-322-2008, Fax: 615-343-6707, E-mail: douglas.g.mcmahon@vanderbilt.edu.

Department of Biomedical Informatics Students: 18 full-time (6 women); includes 4 minority (1 Black or African American, non-Hispanic/Latino; 3 Asian, non-Hispanic/Latino), 1 international. Average age 31. 51 applicants, 12% accepted, 3 enrolled. *Faculty:* 26 full-time (6 women). Expenses: Contact institution. *Financial support:* Fellowships with tuition reimbursements, research assistantships with tuition reimbursements, teaching assistantships with tuition reimbursements, Federal Work-Study, institutionally sponsored loans, scholarships/grants, traineeships, and health care benefits available. Financial award application deadline: 1/15; financial award applicants required to submit CSS PROFILE or FAFSA. In 2018, 5 master's, 2 doctorates awarded. *Program availability:* Part-time. Offers biomedical informatics (MS, PhD). *Application deadline:* For fall admission, 1/15 for domestic and international students. Electronic applications accepted. *Application Contact:* Cynthia Gadd, Director of Graduate Studies, 615-936-1050, Fax: 615-936-1427, E-mail: cindy.gadd@vanderbilt.edu. *Chair,* Dr. Kevin Johnson, 615-936-1423, Fax: 615-936-1427, E-mail: kevin.johnson@vanderbilt.edu.

Department of Chemistry Students: 111 full-time (54 women); includes 29 minority (8 Black or African American, non-Hispanic/Latino; 6 Asian, non-Hispanic/Latino; 10 Hispanic/Latino; 5 Two or more races, non-Hispanic/Latino). Average age 26. 227 applicants, 24% accepted, 13 enrolled. *Faculty:* 21 full-time (4 women). Expenses: Contact institution. *Financial support:* Fellowships with tuition reimbursements, research assistantships with full tuition reimbursements, teaching assistantships with full tuition reimbursements, Federal Work-Study, institutionally sponsored loans, scholarships/grants, traineeships, and health care benefits available. Financial award application deadline: 1/15; financial award applicants required to submit CSS PROFILE or FAFSA. In 2018, 3 master's, 20 doctorates awarded. Offers chemistry (MAT, MS, PhD). *Application deadline:* For fall admission, 1/15 for domestic and international students. *Application fee:* $0. Electronic applications accepted. *Application Contact:* Carmello Rizzo, Director of Graduate Studies, 615-322-2861, Fax: 615-322-4936, E-mail: c.rizzo@vanderbilt.edu. *Chair,* Dr. David Cliffel, 615-343-3937, Fax: 615-322-4936, E-mail: d.cliffel@vanderbilt.edu.

Department of Earth and Environmental Sciences Students: 13 full-time (8 women), 4 part-time (1 woman); includes 2 minority (both Hispanic/Latino). Average age 26. 39 applicants, 13% accepted, 4 enrolled. *Faculty:* 9 full-time (2 women), 1 part-time/adjunct. Expenses: Contact institution. *Financial support:* Fellowships with tuition reimbursements, research assistantships with tuition reimbursements, teaching assistantships with full tuition reimbursements, career-related internships or fieldwork, Federal Work-Study, institutionally sponsored loans, and health care benefits available. Financial award application deadline: 1/15; financial award applicants required to submit CSS PROFILE or FAFSA. In 2018, 5 master's awarded. Offers earth and environmental sciences (MAT, MS). *Application deadline:* For fall admission, 1/15 for domestic and international students. *Application fee:* $0. Electronic applications accepted. *Application Contact:* David Furbish, Director of Graduate Studies, 615-322-2137, E-mail: david.j.furbish@vanderbilt.edu. *Chair,* Dr. Steven Goodbred, 615-322-2976, E-mail: g.gualda@vanderbilt.edu.

Department of Economics Students: 90 full-time (34 women), 2 part-time (both women); includes 8 minority (2 Asian, non-Hispanic/Latino; 3 Hispanic/Latino; 3 Two or more races, non-Hispanic/Latino), 59 international. Average age 26. 598 applicants, 31% accepted, 35 enrolled. *Faculty:* 31 full-time (5 women). Expenses: Contact institution. *Financial support:* Fellowships, teaching assistantships, career-related internships or fieldwork, Federal Work-Study, institutionally sponsored loans, scholarships/grants, and health care benefits available. Financial award application deadline: 1/15; financial award applicants required to submit CSS PROFILE or FAFSA. In 2018, 35 master's, 2 doctorates awarded. Offers economic development (MA); economics (PhD). *Application deadline:* For fall admission, 1/15 for domestic and international students; for spring admission, 11/1 for domestic students. Applications are processed on a rolling basis. Electronic applications accepted. *Application Contact:* Mattias Polborn, Director of Graduate Studies, 615-322-8113, Fax: 615-343-8495, E-mail: mattias.polborn@vanderbilt.edu. *Chair,* Dr. Peter Rousseau, 615-343-2466, Fax: 615-343-8495, E-mail: peter.l.rousseau@vanderbilt.edu.

Department of English Students: 31 full-time (21 women), 2 part-time (1 woman); includes 13 minority (10 Black or African American, non-Hispanic/Latino; 1 Asian, non-Hispanic/Latino; 2 Two or more races, non-Hispanic/Latino), 3 international. Average age 29. 178 applicants, 8% accepted, 7 enrolled. *Faculty:* 29 full-time (20 women). Expenses: Contact institution. *Financial support:* Fellowships, research assistantships, teaching assistantships with full tuition reimbursements, Federal Work-Study, institutionally sponsored loans, scholarships/grants, and health care benefits available. Financial award application deadline: 1/15; financial award applicants required to submit CSS PROFILE or FAFSA. In 2018, 4 master's, 6 doctorates awarded. Offers English (MA, MAT, PhD). *Application deadline:* For fall admission, 1/15 for domestic and international students. Electronic applications accepted. *Application Contact:* Vera Kutzinski, Director of Graduate Studies, 615-322-2541, Fax: 615-343-8028, E-mail: vera.kutzinski@vanderbilt.edu. *Chair,* Dr. Dana Nelson, 615-322-2541, Fax: 615-343-8028, E-mail: dana.d.nelson@vanderbilt.edu.

Department of French and Italian Students: 14 full-time (8 women); includes 2 minority (1 Hispanic/Latino; 1 Two or more races, non-Hispanic/Latino), 3 international. Average age 29. 19 applicants, 11% accepted, 2 enrolled. *Faculty:* 15 full-time (10 women). Expenses: Contact institution. *Financial support:* Fellowships, teaching assistantships, career-related internships or fieldwork, Federal Work-Study, institutionally sponsored loans, scholarships/grants, and health care benefits available. Financial award application deadline: 1/15; financial award applicants required to submit CSS PROFILE or FAFSA. In 2018, 2 doctorates awarded. Offers French (MA, MAT, PhD). *Application deadline:* For fall admission, 1/15 for domestic and international students. Electronic applications accepted. *Application Contact:* Nathalie Debrauwere-Miller, Director of Graduate Studies, 615-322-6900, Fax: 615-343-6909, E-mail: n.debrau@vanderbilt.edu. *Chair,* Dr. Lynn Ramey, 615-322-6900, Fax: 615-343-6909, E-mail: lynn.ramey@vanderbilt.edu.

Department of Germanic and Slavic Languages Students: 18 full-time (12 women); includes 3 minority (1 Black or African American, non-Hispanic/Latino; 1 Hispanic/Latino; 1 Two or more races, non-Hispanic/Latino), 4 international. Average age 30. 7 applicants, 71% accepted, 4 enrolled. *Faculty:* 7 full-time (4 women). Expenses: Contact institution. *Financial support:* Fellowships, teaching assistantships, career-related internships or fieldwork, Federal Work-Study, institutionally sponsored loans, scholarships/grants, and health care benefits available. Financial award application deadline: 1/15; financial award applicants required to submit CSS PROFILE or FAFSA. In 2018, 1 master's, 3 doctorates awarded. Offers Germanic and Slavic languages (MA, MAT, PhD). *Application deadline:* For fall admission, 1/15 for domestic and international students. Electronic applications accepted. *Application Contact:* Meike Werner, Director of Graduate Studies, 615-875-9065, Fax: 615-343-7258, E-mail: meike.werner@Vanderbilt.Edu. *Chair,* Dr. Lutz Koepnick, 615-322-2611, Fax: 615-343-7258, E-mail: lutz.koepnick@vanderbilt.edu.

Department of History Students: 54 full-time (30 women); includes 8 minority (2 Black or African American, non-Hispanic/Latino; 1 American Indian or Alaska Native, non-Hispanic/Latino; 3 Hispanic/Latino; 2 Two or more races, non-Hispanic/Latino), 14 international. Average age 29. 134 applicants, 13% accepted, 9 enrolled. *Faculty:* 38 full-time (12 women). Expenses: Contact institution. *Financial support:* Fellowships with full tuition reimbursements, teaching assistantships with full tuition reimbursements, Federal Work-Study, institutionally sponsored loans, scholarships/grants, and health care benefits available. Financial award application deadline: 1/15; financial award applicants required to submit CSS PROFILE or FAFSA. In 2018, 4 master's, 5 doctorates awarded. Offers history (MA, MAT, PhD). *Application deadline:* For fall admission, 1/15 for domestic and international students. *Application fee:* $0. Electronic applications accepted. *Application Contact:* Samira Sheikh, Director of Graduate Studies, 615-322-4740, Fax: 615-343-6002, E-mail: samira.sheikh@vanderbilt.edu. *Chair,* Dr. Joel Harrington, 615-322-2575, Fax: 615-343-6002, E-mail: joel.harrington@vanderbilt.edu.

Department of Mathematics Students: 40 full-time (5 women); includes 2 minority (1 Black or African American, non-Hispanic/Latino; 1 Two or more races, non-Hispanic/Latino), 22 international. Average age 26. 85 applicants, 21% accepted, 10 enrolled. *Faculty:* 30 full-time (2 women). Expenses: Contact institution. *Financial support:* Fellowships, research assistantships with full tuition reimbursements, teaching assistantships with full tuition reimbursements, Federal Work-Study, institutionally sponsored loans, scholarships/grants, and health care benefits available. Financial award application deadline: 1/15; financial award applicants required to submit CSS PROFILE or FAFSA. In 2018, 2 master's, 8 doctorates awarded. Offers mathematics (MA, MAT, MS, PhD). *Application deadline:* For fall admission, 1/1 for domestic and international students. *Application fee:* $0. Electronic applications accepted. *Application Contact:* Alexander Powell, Director of Graduate Studies, 615-322-6650, Fax: 315-343-0215, E-mail: alexander.m.powell@vanderbilt.edu. *Chair,* Dr. Mike Neamtu, 615-322-6672, Fax: 615-343-0215, E-mail: mike.neamtu@vanderbilt.edu.

Department of Philosophy Students: 26 full-time (16 women); includes 8 minority (1 Black or African American, non-Hispanic/Latino; 1 Asian, non-Hispanic/Latino; 3

Hispanic/Latino; 3 Two or more races, non-Hispanic/Latino), 3 international. Average age 28. 113 applicants, 6% accepted, 5 enrolled. *Faculty:* 12 full-time (3 women). Expenses: Contact institution. *Financial support:* Fellowships with full tuition reimbursements, teaching assistantships with full tuition reimbursements, Federal Work-Study, institutionally sponsored loans, scholarships/grants, and health care benefits available. Financial award application deadline: 1/15; financial award applicants required to submit CSS PROFILE or FAFSA. In 2018, 1 master's, 2 doctorates awarded. Offers philosophy (MA, PhD). *Application deadline:* For fall admission, 1/15 for domestic and international students. Electronic applications accepted. *Application Contact:* Kelly Oliver, Director of Graduate Studies, 615-343-0334, Fax: 615-343-7259, E-mail: kelly.oliver@vanderbilt.edu. *Chair,* Dr. Robert Talisse, 615-343-5349, Fax: 615-343-7259, E-mail: robert.talisse@vanderbilt.edu.

Department of Physics and Astronomy Students: 40 full-time (7 women); includes 8 minority (2 Black or African American, non-Hispanic/Latino; 1 Asian, non-Hispanic/Latino; 4 Hispanic/Latino; 1 Two or more races, non-Hispanic/Latino), 8 international. Average age 27. 61 applicants, 28% accepted, 8 enrolled. *Faculty:* 25 full-time (5 women). Expenses: Contact institution. *Financial support:* Fellowships, research assistantships with full tuition reimbursements, teaching assistantships with full tuition reimbursements, career-related internships or fieldwork, Federal Work-Study, and institutionally sponsored loans available. Financial award application deadline: 1/15; financial award applicants required to submit CSS PROFILE or FAFSA. In 2018, 6 master's, 8 doctorates awarded. Offers physics and astronomy (MA, MAT, MS, PhD). *Application deadline:* For fall admission, 1/1 for domestic and international students. Electronic applications accepted. *Application Contact:* Julia Velkovska, Director of Graduate Studies, 615-322-2828, E-mail: julia.velkovska@vanderbilt.edu. *Chair,* Dr. Shane Hutson, 615-343-9980, E-mail: shane.hutson@Vanderbilt.Edu.

Department of Political Science Students: 42 full-time (20 women), 1 (woman) part-time; includes 3 minority (1 Black or African American, non-Hispanic/Latino; 1 Asian, non-Hispanic/Latino; 1 Two or more races, non-Hispanic/Latino), 13 international. Average age 28. 166 applicants, 15% accepted, 14 enrolled. *Faculty:* 22 full-time (7 women). Expenses: Contact institution. *Financial support:* Fellowships with full tuition reimbursements, research assistantships with full tuition reimbursements, teaching assistantships with full tuition reimbursements, Federal Work-Study, institutionally sponsored loans, scholarships/grants, and health care benefits available. Financial award application deadline: 1/15; financial award applicants required to submit CSS PROFILE or FAFSA. In 2018, 7 doctorates awarded. Offers political science (MA, MAT, PhD). *Application deadline:* For fall admission, 1/15 for domestic and international students. Electronic applications accepted. *Application Contact:* Emily Ritter, Director of Graduate Studies, 615-936-9795, Fax: 615-343-6003, Email: emily.h.ritter@vanderbilt.edu. *Chair,* Dr. Alan Wiseman, 615-322-6222, Fax: 615-343-6003, E-mail: alan.wiseman@vanderbilt.edu.

Department of Religion Students: 59 full-time (37 women), 1 (woman) part-time; includes 19 minority (12 Black or African American, non-Hispanic/Latino; 3 Asian, non-Hispanic/Latino; 3 Hispanic/Latino; 1 Two or more races, non-Hispanic/Latino), 7 international. Average age 34. 129 applicants, 12% accepted, 8 enrolled. *Faculty:* 29 full-time (9 women). Expenses: Contact institution. *Financial support:* Fellowships, teaching assistantships, Federal Work-Study, institutionally sponsored loans, health care benefits, and tuition waivers (full and partial) available. Support available to part-time students. Financial award application deadline: 1/15; financial award applicants required to submit CSS PROFILE or FAFSA. In 2018, 7 master's, 7 doctorates awarded. Offers religion (MA, PhD). *Application deadline:* For fall admission, 12/15 for domestic and international students. Electronic applications accepted. *Application Contact:* Karen Eardley, Administrative Assistant, 615-343-3977, Fax: 615-343-9957, E-mail: karen.eardley@vanderbilt.edu. *Chair and Director of Graduate Studies,* Dr. James Byrd, Jr., 615-343-9977, Fax: 615-343-9957, E-mail: james.p.byrd@vanderbilt.edu.

Department of Sociology Students: 30 full-time (24 women); includes 10 minority (5 Black or African American, non-Hispanic/Latino; 4 Asian, non-Hispanic/Latino; 1 Hispanic/Latino), 2 international. Average age 28. 82 applicants, 15% accepted, 5 enrolled. *Faculty:* 16 full-time (6 women). Expenses: Contact institution. *Financial support:* Fellowships with full tuition reimbursements, research assistantships, teaching assistantships with full tuition reimbursements, Federal Work-Study, institutionally sponsored loans, scholarships/grants, and health care benefits available. Financial award application deadline: 1/15; financial award applicants required to submit CSS PROFILE or FAFSA. In 2018, 10 master's, 8 doctorates awarded. Offers sociology (MA, PhD). *Application deadline:* For fall admission, 1/15 for domestic and international students. Electronic applications accepted. *Application Contact:* Lijun Song, Director of Graduate Studies, 615-322-1731, Fax: 615-322-7505, E-mail: lijun.song@vanderbilt.edu. *Chair,* Dr. Larry Isaac, 615-322-7626, Fax: 615-322-7505, E-mail: larry.isaac@vanderbilt.edu.

Department of Spanish and Portuguese Students: 26 full-time (13 women); includes 7 minority (2 Black or African American, non-Hispanic/Latino; 5 Hispanic/Latino), 13 international. Average age 31. 28 applicants, 21% accepted, 4 enrolled. *Faculty:* 11 full-time (4 women). Expenses: Contact institution. *Financial support:* Fellowships, teaching assistantships with full tuition reimbursements, Federal Work-Study, institutionally sponsored loans, and health care benefits available. Financial award application deadline: 1/15; financial award applicants required to submit CSS PROFILE or FAFSA. In 2018, 5 master's, 7 doctorates awarded. Offers Portuguese (MA); Spanish (PhD). *Application deadline:* For fall admission, 1/15 for domestic and international students. Electronic applications accepted. *Application Contact:* Jose Cardenas Bunsen, Director of Graduate Studies, 615-322-6930, Fax: 615-343-7260, E-mail: jose.cardenas-bunsen@Vanderbilt.Edu. *Chair,* Andres Zamora, 615-322-6930, Fax: 615-343-7260, E-mail: andres.zamora@vanderbilt.edu.

Divinity School *Program availability:* Part-time. Offers divinity (M Div, MTS). Electronic applications accepted.

Peabody College Students: 520 full-time (423 women), 442 part-time (312 women); includes 232 minority (132 Black or African American, non-Hispanic/Latino; 4 American Indian or Alaska Native, non-Hispanic/Latino; 37 Asian, non-Hispanic/Latino; 45 Hispanic/Latino; 14 Two or more races, non-Hispanic/Latino), 88 international. Average age 30. 1,878 applicants, 56% accepted, 561 enrolled. *Faculty:* 170 full-time (111 women), 83 part-time/adjunct (59 women). Expenses: Contact institution. *Financial support:* In 2018–19, 574 students received support. Fellowships with partial tuition reimbursements available, research assistantships with partial tuition reimbursements available, career-related internships or fieldwork, Federal Work-Study, institutionally sponsored loans, scholarships/grants, traineeships, tuition waivers (partial), and unspecified assistantships available. Support available to part-time students. Financial award application deadline: 1/15; financial award applicants required to submit FAFSA. In 2018, 357 master's, 20 doctorates awarded. *Program availability:* Part-time, evening/weekend, online courses with semester immersions on campus. Offers child studies (M Ed); clinical psychological assessment (M Ed); community development and action (M Ed); early childhood special education (M Ed); education policy (MPP); elementary education (M Ed); English language learners (M Ed); higher education administration (M Ed); human development counseling (M Ed); quantitative methods (M Ed); reading education (M Ed); secondary education (M Ed). *Application deadline:* For fall admission, 12/31 priority date for domestic and international students; for spring admission, 11/1 priority date for domestic and international students. Applications are processed on a rolling basis. *Application fee:* $0. Electronic applications accepted. *Application Contact:* Kimberly Brazil, Director of Graduate and Professional Admissions, 615-332-8410, Fax: 615-343-3474, E-mail: kim.brazil@vanderbilt.edu. *Dean,* Dr. Camilla P. Benbow, 615-322-8407, Fax: 615-322-8501, E-mail: camilla.benbow@vanderbilt.edu.

PhD Program in Special Education Students: 145 full-time (134 women), 10 part-time (all women); includes 28 minority (1 Black or African American, non-Hispanic/Latino; 7 Asian, non-Hispanic/Latino; 10 Hispanic/Latino; 10 Two or more races, non-Hispanic/Latino), 9 international. Average age 27. 62 applicants, 23% accepted, 13 enrolled. *Faculty:* 16 full-time (10 women). Expenses: Contact institution. *Financial support:* Fellowships with full tuition reimbursements, research assistantships with full tuition reimbursements, teaching assistantships with full tuition reimbursements, Federal Work-Study, institutionally sponsored loans, traineeships, and health care benefits available. Financial award application deadline: 1/15; financial award applicants required to submit CSS PROFILE or FAFSA. In 2018, 5 doctorates awarded. Offers special education (PhD). *Application deadline:* For fall admission, 12/1 for domestic and international students. *Application fee:* $0. Electronic applications accepted. *Application Contact:* Dr. Robert Hodapp, Director of Graduate Studies, 615-322-8150, Fax: 615-343-1570, E-mail: robert.hodapp@vanderbilt.edu. *Chair,* Dr. Joseph Wehby, 615-322-8150, Fax: 615-343-1570, E-mail: joseph.wehby@vanderbilt.edu.

Program in Community Research and Action Students: 29 full-time (21 women), 1 (woman) part-time; includes 14 minority (6 Black or African American, non-Hispanic/Latino; 4 Asian, non-Hispanic/Latino; 1 Hispanic/Latino; 3 Two or more races, non-Hispanic/Latino), 5 international. Average age 30. 92 applicants, 13% accepted, 8 enrolled. Expenses: Contact institution. *Financial support:* In 2018–19, 16 students received support. Fellowships, research assistantships with full tuition reimbursements available, teaching assistantships with full tuition reimbursements available, Federal Work-Study, scholarships/grants, health care benefits, tuition waivers, and unspecified assistantships available. Financial award application deadline: 1/15; financial award applicants required to submit FAFSA. In 2018, 2 doctorates awarded. Offers community research and action (PhD). *Application deadline:* For fall admission, 12/1 for domestic and international students. *Application fee:* $0. Electronic applications accepted. *Application Contact:* Brian Christens, Director of Graduate Studies, 615-322-6881, Fax: 615-322-1141, E-mail: b.christens@vanderbilt.edu. *Chair,* Paul Speer, 615-322-3117, Fax: 615-322-1769, E-mail: paul.w.speer@vanderbilt.edu.

Program in Creative Writing Students: 17 full-time (12 women); includes 8 minority (2 Black or African American, non-Hispanic/Latino; 2 Asian, non-Hispanic/Latino; 4 Hispanic/Latino), 2 international. Average age 27. 322 applicants, 3% accepted, 6 enrolled. *Faculty:* 29 full-time (20 women). Expenses: Contact institution. *Financial support:* Fellowships, teaching assistantships, Federal Work-Study, institutionally sponsored loans, and health care benefits available. Financial award application deadline: 1/15; financial award applicants required to submit CSS PROFILE or FAFSA. In 2018, 6 master's awarded. Offers creative writing (MFA). *Application deadline:* For fall admission, 1/15 for domestic and international students. Electronic applications accepted. *Application Contact:* Katherine Daniels, Director of Graduate Studies, 615-322-2541, E-mail: kate.daniels@vanderbilt.edu. *Chair,* Dr. Dana Nelson, 615-322-2541, E-mail: dana.d.nelson@vanderbilt.edu.

Program in Human Genetics Students: 15 full-time (10 women); includes 3 minority (2 Asian, non-Hispanic/Latino; 1 Two or more races, non-Hispanic/Latino), 4 international. Average age 26. *Faculty:* 33 full-time (10 women). Expenses: Contact institution. *Financial support:* Fellowships, research assistantships, Federal Work-Study, institutionally sponsored loans, traineeships, and health care benefits available. Financial award application deadline: 1/15; financial award applicants required to submit CSS PROFILE or FAFSA. In 2018, 3 doctorates awarded. Offers human genetics (PhD). *Application deadline:* For fall admission, 1/15 for domestic and international students. *Application fee:* $0. Electronic applications accepted. *Application Contact:* Todd Edwards, Director of Graduate Studies, 615-322-3652, E-mail: todd.l.edwards@vanderbilt.edu. *Director,* Dr. David Samuels, 615-343-7870, Fax: 615-322-1453, E-mail: david.c.samuels@vanderbilt.edu.

Program in Latin American Studies Students: 5 full-time (2 women); includes 1 minority (Black or African American, non-Hispanic/Latino), 1 international. Average age 29. 17 applicants, 35% accepted, 1 enrolled. *Faculty:* 19 full-time (20 women). Expenses: Contact institution. *Financial support:* Teaching assistantships with full tuition reimbursements, Federal Work-Study, institutionally sponsored loans, and health care benefits available. Financial award application deadline: 1/15; financial award applicants required to submit CSS PROFILE or FAFSA. In 2018, 5 master's awarded. Offers Latin American studies (MA). *Application deadline:* For fall admission, 1/15 for domestic and international students. *Application fee:* $0. Electronic applications accepted. *Application Contact:* Nicolette M. Kostiw, Assistant Director/Director of Graduate Studies, 615-322-2527, Fax: 615-343-6002, E-mail: nicolette.m.wilhide@vanderbilt.edu. *Director,* Dr. Edward Fischer, 615-322-2527, Fax: 615-343-6002, E-mail: edward.f.fischer@vanderbilt.edu.

Program in Leadership and Policy Studies Students: 31 full-time (19 women), 2 part-time (both women); includes 12 minority (4 Black or African American, non-Hispanic/Latino; 5 Asian, non-Hispanic/Latino; 1 Hispanic/Latino; 2 Two or more races, non-Hispanic/Latino). Average age 30. 73 applicants, 14% accepted, 6 enrolled. *Faculty:* 14 full-time (7 women). Expenses: Contact institution. *Financial support:* Fellowships with full tuition reimbursements, research assistantships with full tuition reimbursements, teaching assistantships with full tuition reimbursements, Federal Work-Study, institutionally sponsored loans, scholarships/grants, traineeships, and health care benefits available. Financial award application deadline: 1/15; financial award applicants required to submit CSS PROFILE or FAFSA. In 2018, 5 doctorates awarded. Offers higher education leadership and policy (PhD); K-12 educational leadership and policy (PhD). *Application deadline:* For fall admission, 12/1 for domestic and international students. *Application fee:* $0. Electronic applications accepted. *Application Contact:* Sean Corcoran, Director of Graduate Studies, 615-322-8021, Fax: 615-343-7094, E-mail: sean.corcoran@vanderbilt.edu. *Chair,* Carolyn Heinrich, 615-322-1169, Fax: 615-343-7094, E-mail: carolyn.j.heinrich@vanderbilt.edu.

Program in Learning, Teaching and Diversity Students: 38 full-time (31 women); includes 12 minority (3 Black or African American, non-Hispanic/Latino; 4 Asian, non-Hispanic/Latino; 1 Hispanic/Latino; 4 Two or more races, non-Hispanic/Latino), 3 international. Average age 32. 91 applicants, 12% accepted, 6 enrolled. *Faculty:* 19 full-time (10 women), 2 part-time/adjunct (both women). Expenses: Contact institution. *Financial support:* Fellowships with partial tuition reimbursements, research assistantships with full tuition reimbursements, teaching assistantships with full tuition reimbursements, Federal Work-Study, institutionally sponsored loans, scholarships/grants, traineeships, and health care benefits available. Financial award application deadline: 1/15; financial award applicants required to submit CSS PROFILE or FAFSA. In 2018, 8 doctorates awarded. Offers learning, teaching and diversity (PhD). *Application deadline:* For fall admission, 12/1 for domestic and international students. *Application fee:* $0. Electronic applications accepted. *Application Contact:* Llana Horn, Director of Graduate Studies, 615-322-5884, Fax: 615-322-8014, E-mail: llana.horn@vanderbilt.edu. *Chair,* Dr. Deborah Rowe, 615-322-8044, Fax: 615-322-8014, E-mail: deborah.w.rowe@vanderbilt.edu.

Program in Liberal Arts and Science Students: 34 part-time (24 women); includes 5 minority (4 Black or African American, non-Hispanic/Latino; 1 Two or more races, non-Hispanic/Latino). Average age 40. 24 applicants, 54% accepted, 9 enrolled. Expenses: Contact institution. *Financial support:* Institutionally sponsored loans and tuition waivers (partial) available. In 2018, 7 master's awarded. *Program availability:* Part-time. Offers liberal arts and science (MLAS). *Application deadline:* For fall admission, 1/15 priority date for domestic students, 1/15 for international students; for spring admission, 11/15 for domestic and international students. Applications are processed on a rolling basis. *Application Contact:* Andrea Hearn, Director, 615-875-5831, Fax: 615-343-8702, E-mail: andrea.l.hearn@vanderbilt.edu. *Director,* Andrea Hearn, 615-875-5831, Fax: 615-343-8702, E-mail: andrea.l.hearn@vanderbilt.edu.

Program in Nursing Science Students: 26 full-time (23 women), 2 part-time (both women); includes 7 minority (1 Black or African American, non-Hispanic/Latino; 4 Hispanic/Latino; 1 Native Hawaiian or other Pacific Islander, non-Hispanic/Latino; 1 Two or more races, non-Hispanic/Latino). Average age 38. 24 applicants, 38% accepted, 8 enrolled. *Faculty:* 22 full-time (20 women), 3 part-time/adjunct (all women). Expenses: Contact institution. *Financial support:* Fellowships with full tuition reimbursements, research assistantships with full tuition reimbursements, teaching assistantships with full tuition reimbursements, career-related internships or fieldwork, Federal Work-Study, institutionally sponsored loans, scholarships/grants, health care benefits, and tuition waivers (full and partial) available. Financial award application deadline: 1/15; financial award applicants required to submit CSS PROFILE or FAFSA. In 2018, 5 doctorates awarded. Offers nursing science (PhD). *Application deadline:* For fall admission, 1/15 for domestic and international students. Electronic applications accepted. *Application Contact:* Judy Vesterfelt, Program Manager, 615-322-7410, E-mail: judy.vesterfelt@vanderbilt.edu. *Director of Graduate Studies,* Sheila Ridner, 615-322-3800, Fax: 615-343-5898, E-mail: sheila.ridner@vanderbilt.edu.

Program in Psychological Sciences Students: 75 full-time (46 women), 1 part-time (0 women); includes 7 minority (1 Black or African American, non-Hispanic/Latino; 1 Asian, non-Hispanic/Latino; 3 Hispanic/Latino; 2 Two or more races, non-Hispanic/Latino), 24 international. Average age 26. 513 applicants, 4% accepted, 11 enrolled. *Faculty:* 51 full-time (21 women). Expenses: Contact institution. *Financial support:* Fellowships with full tuition reimbursements, research assistantships with full tuition reimbursements, teaching assistantships with full tuition reimbursements, career-related internships or fieldwork, Federal Work-Study, institutionally sponsored loans, scholarships/grants, traineeships, and health care benefits available. Financial award application deadline: 1/15; financial award applicants required to submit CSS PROFILE or FAFSA. In 2018, 18 doctorates awarded. Offers psychological sciences (PhD). *Application deadline:* For fall admission, 12/1 for domestic and international students. *Application fee:* $0. Electronic applications accepted. *Application Contact:* Dr. Rene Marois, Chair, 615-322-2874, Fax: 615-343-5027, E-mail: r.marois@vanderbilt.edu. *Chair,* Bethany Rittle-Johnson, 615-322-8301, Fax: 615-343-9494, E-mail: Bethany.rittle-johnson@vanderbilt.edu.

School of Engineering *Program availability:* Part-time. Offers biomedical engineering (M Eng, MS, PhD); chemical and biomolecular engineering (M Eng, MS, PhD); civil engineering (M Eng, MS, PhD); computer science (M Eng, MS, PhD); cyber-physical systems (M Eng); electrical engineering (M Eng, MS, PhD); engineering (M Eng, MS, PhD); environmental engineering (M Eng, MS, PhD); environmental management (MS, PhD); materials science (M Eng, MS, PhD); mechanical engineering (M Eng, MS, PhD). MS and PhD offered through the Graduate School. Electronic applications accepted.

School of Medicine *Faculty:* 108 full-time (38 women), 1 part-time/adjunct (0 women). Expenses: Contact institution. *Financial support:* Institutionally sponsored loans and scholarships/grants available. Financial award application deadline: 3/1; financial award applicants required to submit FAFSA. Offers audiology (Au D); biochemistry (MS, PhD); cell and developmental biology (MS, PhD); chemical and physical biology (PhD); medicine (MDE, MMP, MS, MSCI, Au D, DMP, MD, PhD); microbiology and immunology (MS, PhD); molecular physiology and biophysics (MS, PhD); pathology and immunology (PhD); pharmacology (PhD). *Application deadline:* For fall admission, 11/15 for domestic and international students. *Application fee:* $50. *Application Contact:* Dr. Jeffrey R. Balser, Dean, School of Medicine, 615-936-3030, E-mail: jeffrey.balser@vanderbilt.edu. *Dean, School of Medicine,* Dr. Jeffrey R. Balser, 615-936-3030, E-mail: jeffrey.balser@vanderbilt.edu.

Vanderbilt Law School Offers law (LL M, JD); law and economics (PhD). Electronic applications accepted.

Vanderbilt University Owen Graduate School of Management *Program availability:* Evening/weekend. Offers accountancy (M Acc); accounting (MBA); business administration (EMBA, MBA); finance (MS); general management (MBA); health care (MBA); human and organizational performance (MBA); management (EMBA, M Acc, M Mark, MBA, MM, MS); marketing (MBA); operations (MBA); strategy (MBA); valuation (M Acc).

Vanderbilt University School of Nursing Students: 501 full-time (435 women), 387 part-time (355 women); includes 153 minority (40 Black or African American, non-Hispanic/Latino; 1 American Indian or Alaska Native, non-Hispanic/Latino; 27 Asian, non-Hispanic/Latino; 48 Hispanic/Latino; 4 Native Hawaiian or other Pacific Islander, non-Hispanic/Latino; 33 Two or more races, non-Hispanic/Latino), 9 international. Average age 31. 1,210 applicants, 57% accepted, 473 enrolled. *Faculty:* 134 full-time (120 women), 30 part-time/adjunct (26 women). Expenses: Contact institution. *Financial support:* In 2018–19, 645 students received support. Scholarships/grants available. Financial award application deadline: 3/15; financial award applicants required to submit FAFSA. In 2018, 357 master's, 63 doctorates, 3 other advanced degrees awarded. *Program availability:* Part-time, blended/hybrid learning. Offers advanced clinical practice, advanced systems practice; executive leadership (DNP); agacnp; agpcnp; enp; fnp; enp/fnp; nhcl; ni; nnp; nm; nm;fnp; pmhnp; pnp-ac; pnp-pc; whnp; whnp/agpacnp (MSN); clinical research; health services research (PhD). *Application deadline:* For fall admission, 11/1 priority date for domestic and international students. Applications are processed on a rolling basis. *Application fee:* $50. Electronic applications accepted. *Application Contact:* Patricia Peerman, Assistant Dean for Enrollment Management, 615-322-3800, Fax: 615-343-0333, E-mail: vusn-admissions@vanderbilt.edu. *Dean,* Dr. Linda Norman, 615-343-8876, Fax: 615-343-7711, E-mail: linda.norman@vanderbilt.edu.

VANDERCOOK COLLEGE OF MUSIC, Chicago, IL 60616-3731

General Information Independent, coed, comprehensive institution. *Graduate housing:* Rooms and/or apartments available on a first-come, first-served basis to single and married students. Housing application deadline: 6/1.

GRADUATE UNITS

Master of Music Education Program Students: 115 full-time (57 women), 25 part-time (12 women); includes 17 minority (10 Black or African American, non-Hispanic/Latino; 4 Asian, non-Hispanic/Latino; 1 Hispanic/Latino; 2 Two or more races, non-Hispanic/Latino). Average age 30. *Faculty:* 11 full-time (6 women), 66 part-time/adjunct (17 women). Expenses: Contact institution. *Financial support:* Federal Work-Study, scholarships/grants, and unspecified assistantships available. Financial award application deadline: 5/1; financial award applicants required to submit FAFSA. In 2018, 38 master's awarded. *Program availability:* Part-time. Offers music education (MM Ed). *Application deadline:* For fall admission, 4/1 for domestic and international students; for spring admission, 11/1 for domestic and international students. Applications are processed on a rolling basis. *Application fee:* $50. *Application Contact:* Cindy Tovar, Director of Admissions and Alumni Relations, 312-788-1122, Fax: 312-225-5211, E-mail: ctovar@vandercook.edu. *Dean of Graduate Studies,* Dr. Robert L. Sinclair, 312-788-1144, Fax: 312-225-5211, E-mail: rsinclair@vandercook.edu.

VANGUARD UNIVERSITY OF SOUTHERN CALIFORNIA, Costa Mesa, CA 92626

General Information Independent-religious, coed, comprehensive institution. *Graduate housing:* On-campus housing not available.

GRADUATE UNITS

Graduate Program in Clinical Psychology *Program availability:* Part-time, evening/weekend. Offers clinical psychology (MS). Electronic applications accepted.

Graduate Program in Nursing *Program availability:* Part-time, evening/weekend, blended/hybrid learning. Offers nursing (MSN).

Graduate Program in Organizational Psychology Offers intercultural studies (MS); training and development in organizations (MS).

Graduate Programs in Education *Program availability:* Evening/weekend. Offers Christian education leadership (MA); curriculum and instruction (MA); teacher leadership (MA). Electronic applications accepted.

Graduate Programs in Religion *Program availability:* Part-time, evening/weekend, 100% online, blended/hybrid learning. Offers leadership studies (MA); theology (MA). Electronic applications accepted.

VAUGHN COLLEGE OF AERONAUTICS AND TECHNOLOGY, Flushing, NY 11369

General Information Independent, coed, primarily men, comprehensive institution.

GRADUATE UNITS

Graduate Programs Offers airport management (MS).

VERMONT COLLEGE OF FINE ARTS, Montpelier, VT 05602

General Information Independent, coed, graduate-only institution. *Graduate housing:* Rooms and/or apartments available on a first-come, first-served basis to single and married students.

GRADUATE UNITS

Graduate Studies in Art and Design Education Offers art and design education (MA, MAT). Electronic applications accepted.

International MFA in Creative Writing and Literary Translation Program Offers creative writing and literary translation (MFA).

MFA in Film Program Offers film (MFA). Electronic applications accepted.

MFA in Graphic Design Program Offers graphic design (MFA). Electronic applications accepted.

MFA in Music Composition Program Offers music composition (MFA).

MFA in Visual Art Program Offers visual art (MFA). Electronic applications accepted.

MFA in Writing and Publishing Program Offers writing and publishing (MFA).

MFA in Writing for Children and Young Adults Program Offers writing for children and young adults (MFA). Electronic applications accepted.

MFA in Writing Program Offers writing (MFA).

VERMONT LAW SCHOOL, South Royalton, VT 05068-0096

General Information Independent, coed, graduate-only institution. *Graduate housing:* On-campus housing not available.

GRADUATE UNITS

Graduate and Professional Programs *Program availability:* Part-time. Offers law (LL M, MELP, MERL, MFALP, JD). Electronic applications accepted.

Master's Programs *Program availability:* Part-time, 100% online, blended/hybrid learning. Offers American legal studies (LL M); energy law (LL M); energy regulation and law (MERL); environmental law (LL M); environmental law and policy (MELP); food and agriculture law (LL M); food and agriculture law and policy (MFALP).

VERMONT TECHNICAL COLLEGE, Randolph Center, VT 05061-0500

General Information State-supported, coed, comprehensive institution.

GRADUATE UNITS

Program in Computer Software Engineering Offers computer software engineering (MS).

VICTORIA UNIVERSITY, Toronto, ON M5S 1K7, Canada

General Information Independent-religious, coed, graduate-only institution. *Graduate housing:* Rooms and/or apartments available on a first-come, first-served basis to single and married students. Housing application deadline: 6/30.

GRADUATE UNITS

Emmanuel College Offers theology (M Div, MA, MPS, MRE, MSMus, MTS, Th M, D Min, PhD, Th D, Certificate, Diploma, L Th). M Div, MRE, Th M, Th D, M Div/MA, M Div/MRE, M Div/MPS offered jointly with University of Toronto; MA, PhD with University of St. Michael's College. Electronic applications accepted.

VILLANOVA UNIVERSITY, Villanova, PA 19085-1699

General Information Independent-religious, coed, university. CGS member. *Graduate housing:* On-campus housing not available.

GRADUATE UNITS

Charles Widger School of Law *Program availability:* Part-time, evening/weekend. Offers law (LL M, JD); tax (LL M). Electronic applications accepted.

College of Engineering *Program availability:* Part-time, evening/weekend, online learning. Offers biochemical engineering (Certificate); chemical engineering (MSChE); civil engineering (MSCE); computer architectures (Certificate); computer engineering (MSCPE, Certificate); electric power systems (Certificate); electrical engineering (MSEE, Certificate); electro mechanical systems (Certificate); electro-mechanical systems (Certificate); engineering (MSCPE, MSChE, MSEE, MSME, MSWREE, PhD, Certificate); environmental protection in the chemical process industries (Certificate); high frequency systems (Certificate); intelligent control systems (Certificate); machinery dynamics (Certificate); mechanical engineering (MSME); nonlinear dynamics and control (Certificate); thermofluid systems (Certificate); urban water resources design (Certificate); water resources and environmental engineering (MSWREE, Certificate); wireless and digital communications (Certificate). Electronic applications accepted.

Graduate School of Liberal Arts and Sciences *Program availability:* Part-time, evening/weekend, 100% online. Offers applied statistics (MS); biology (MA, MS); chemistry (MS); city management (Certificate); classical studies (MA); communication (MA); computer science (MS); elementary school counseling (MS); English (MA); Hispanic studies (MA); history (MA); human resource development (MS); liberal arts and sciences (MA, MPA, MS, PhD, Certificate); liberal studies (MA); mathematics (MA); nonprofit management (Certificate); philosophy (PhD); political science (MA); psychology (MA, MS); public administration (MPA, Certificate); teacher leadership (MA); theatre (MA); theology (MA, PhD). Electronic applications accepted.

M. Louise Fitzpatrick College of Nursing *Program availability:* Part-time, online learning. Offers adult-gerontology primary care nurse practitioner (MSN, Post Master's Certificate); family primary care nurse practitioner (MSN, Post Master's Certificate); nurse anesthesia (DNP); nursing (PhD); nursing education (MSN, Post Master's Certificate); nursing practice (DNP); pediatric primary care nurse practitioner (MSN, Post Master's Certificate). Electronic applications accepted.

Villanova School of Business Students: 36 full-time (10 women), 1,112 part-time (424 women); includes 223 minority (50 Black or African American, non-Hispanic/Latino; 2 American Indian or Alaska Native, non-Hispanic/Latino; 78 Asian, non-Hispanic/Latino; 67 Hispanic/Latino; 26 Two or more races, non-Hispanic/Latino), 34 international. Average age 32. 835 applicants, 78% accepted, 504 enrolled. *Faculty:* 101 full-time (38 women), 36 part-time/adjunct (9 women). Expenses: Contact institution. *Financial support:* Research assistantships with tuition reimbursements, institutionally sponsored loans, and scholarships/grants available. Support available to part-time students. Financial award application deadline: 6/30; financial award applicants required to submit FAFSA. In 2018, 447 master's awarded. *Program availability:* 100% online, blended/hybrid learning. Offers accountancy (MAC); analytics (MSA); business (EMBA, MAC, MBA, MSA, MSCM, MSF); business administration (MBA); church management (MSCM); executive business administration (EMBA); finance (MSF); healthcare (MBA); international business (MBA); marketing (MBA); real estate (MBA); strategic management (MBA). *Application deadline:* For fall admission, 7/31 for domestic and international students; for spring admission, 11/30 for domestic and international students; for summer admission, 4/30 for domestic and international students. Applications are processed on a rolling basis. *Application fee:* $65. Electronic applications accepted. *Application Contact:* Claire Bruno, Director of Recruitment and Enrollment Management, 610-519-4336, Fax: 610-519-6273, E-mail: claire.bruno@villanova.edu. *Dean,* Dr. Joyce E. A. Russell, 610-519-6082, Fax: 610-519-6273, E-mail: joyce.russell@villanova.edu.

VIRGINIA BAPTIST COLLEGE, Fredericksburg, VA 22407

General Information Independent, coed, comprehensive institution.

GRADUATE UNITS

Graduate Programs Offers theology (MBS, MCE, MM).

VIRGINIA BEACH THEOLOGICAL SEMINARY, Virginia Beach, VA 23464

General Information Independent-religious, coed, graduate-only institution. *Graduate housing:* On-campus housing not available.

GRADUATE UNITS

Graduate Programs *Program availability:* Online learning. Offers Biblical studies (MBS, Th M); chaplaincy (MBS); ministry (M Div). Electronic applications accepted.

VIRGINIA COMMONWEALTH UNIVERSITY, Richmond, VA 23284-9005

General Information State-supported, coed, university. CGS member. *Graduate housing:* Room and/or apartments available on a first-come, first-served basis to single students; on-campus housing not available to married students. *Research affiliation:* Virginia Biotechnology Research Park.

GRADUATE UNITS

Graduate School *Program availability:* Part-time, evening/weekend. Offers interdisciplinary studies (MIS). Electronic applications accepted.

College of Humanities and Sciences *Program availability:* Part-time, evening/weekend. Offers analytical chemistry (MS, PhD); applied mathematics (MS); behavioral medicine (PhD); biology (MS); chemical physics (PhD); clinical child psychology (PhD); clinical psychology (PhD); counseling psychology (PhD); creative writing (MFA); digital sociology (MS); dual genre (MFA); English (MA); fiction (MFA); forensic biology (MS); forensic chemistry/drugs and toxicology (MS); forensic chemistry/trace evidence (MS); forensic physical analysis (MS); health and movement sciences (MS); health psychology (PhD); history (MA); humanities and sciences (MA, MFA, MPA, MS, MURP, PhD, Certificate, Graduate Certificate, Postbaccalaureate Certificate); inorganic chemistry (MS, PhD); literature (MA); media and culture (MS, PhD); media, art, and text (PhD); medical physics (MS, PhD); multimedia journalism (MS); nanoscience and nanotechnology (PhD); nanosciences (PhD); nonprofit management (Graduate Certificate); organic chemistry (MS, PhD); physical chemistry (MS, PhD); physics and applied physics (MS); poetry (MFA); rehabilitation and movement science (PhD); strategic public relations (MS). Electronic applications accepted.

L. Douglas Wilder School of Government and Public Affairs Offers criminal justice (MS, Postbaccalaureate Certificate); financial management (MPA); geographic information systems (Certificate); government and public affairs (MA, MPA, MS, MURP, PhD, Certificate, Graduate Certificate, Postbaccalaureate Certificate); homeland security and emergency preparedness (MA, Graduate Certificate); human resource management (MPA); public policy and administration (PhD); state and local government management (MPA); urban and regional studies and planning (MURP).

School of Allied Health Professions *Program availability:* Part-time. Offers allied health professions (MHA, MS, MSHA, MSNA, MSOT, DNAP, DPT, OTD, PhD, CAS); clinical laboratory sciences (PhD); gerontology (MS, PhD); health administration (MHA, MSHA, PhD); health services organization and research (PhD); nurse anesthesia (PhD); occupational therapy (MSOT, OTD); patient counseling (MS); physical therapy (PhD); radiation sciences (PhD); rehabilitation counseling (MS); rehabilitation leadership (PhD). Electronic applications accepted.

School of Business *Program availability:* Part-time, evening/weekend. Offers accounting (M Acc); business (M Acc, MA, MBA, MS, PhD, Postbaccalaureate Certificate); business administration (MBA, PhD); economics (MA); information systems (MS); real estate and urban land development (Postbaccalaureate Certificate). Electronic applications accepted.

School of Education *Program availability:* Part-time. Offers adult literacy (M Ed); art education (PhD); college student development and counseling (M Ed); counselor education and supervision (PhD); curriculum, culture and change (PhD); early and elementary education (MT); early childhood (M Ed); education (M Ed, MT, Ed D, PhD, Certificate); educational leadership (M Ed); educational psychology (PhD); general education (M Ed); human resource development (M Ed); leadership (Ed D); reading (M Ed); reading specialist (Certificate); research and evaluation (PhD); school counseling (M Ed); severe disabilities (M Ed); special education and disability leadership (PhD); sport leadership (M Ed); teaching and learning with technology (M Ed); urban services leadership (PhD). Electronic applications accepted.

School of Engineering Offers biomedical engineering (MS, PhD); computer science (MS); engineering (MS, PhD); mechanical and nuclear engineering (MS, PhD). Electronic applications accepted.

School of Life Sciences Offers environmental studies (M Env Sc, MS); integrative life sciences (PhD); life sciences (M Env Sc, MS, PhD). Electronic applications accepted.

School of Nursing *Program availability:* Part-time, evening/weekend, online learning. Offers adult health acute nursing (MS); adult health primary nursing (MS); biobehavioral clinical research (PhD); child health nursing (MS); clinical nurse leader (MS); family health nursing (MS); nurse educator (MS); nurse practitioner (MS); nursing (Certificate); nursing administration (MS); psychiatric-mental health nursing (MS); quality and safety in health care (DNP); women's health nursing (MS). Electronic applications accepted.

School of Social Work Offers social work (MSW, PhD). Electronic applications accepted.

School of the Arts *Program availability:* Part-time. Offers art education (MAE, PhD); art history (MA, PhD); ceramics (MFA); costume design (MFA); curatorial (PhD); design (MFA); fibers (MFA); furniture design (MFA); glassworking (MFA); historical studies (MA, PhD); jewelry/metalworking (MFA); kinetic imaging (MFA); museum studies (MA); music (MM); music education (MM); painting (MFA); pedagogy/literature (MFA); pedagogy/performance (MFA); photography and film (MFA); printmaking (MFA); scene design/technical theatre (MFA); sculpture (MFA); theatre (MFA). Electronic applications accepted.

Medical College of Virginia-Professional Programs *Program availability:* Part-time. Offers medicine (MPH, MS, MSD, DDS, MD, PhD, Pharm D, Certificate). Electronic applications accepted.

School of Dentistry Offers dentistry (MS, DDS). Electronic applications accepted.

School of Medicine Offers anatomy and neurobiology (MS); biochemistry and molecular biology (MS, PhD); biostatistics (MS, PhD); epidemiology (MPH, PhD); genetic counseling (MS); healthcare policy and research (PhD); human genetics (PhD); medicine (MPH, MS, MD, PhD, Certificate); microbiology and immunology (MS, PhD); molecular biology and genetics (MS); neuroscience (PhD); pharmacology (Certificate); pharmacology and toxicology (MS, PhD); physical therapy (PhD); physiology (MS, PhD); public health practice (MPH); social and behavioral science (MPH); social and behavioral sciences (PhD). Electronic applications accepted.

School of Pharmacy *Program availability:* Part-time. Offers medicinal chemistry (MS); pharmaceutical sciences (PhD); pharmaceutics (MS); pharmacotherapy and pharmacy administration (MS); pharmacy (MS, PhD, Pharm D). Electronic applications accepted.

Program in Pre-Medical Basic Health Sciences Offers pre-medical basic health sciences (Postbaccalaureate Certificate). Electronic applications accepted.

VIRGINIA INTERNATIONAL UNIVERSITY, Fairfax, VA 22030

General Information Proprietary, coed, comprehensive institution. *Research affiliation:* Apple Federal Credit Union (financial management).

GRADUATE UNITS

School of Business *Program availability:* Part-time, online learning. Offers accounting (MBA, MS); entrepreneurship (MBA); executive management (Graduate Certificate); global logistics (MBA); health care management (MBA); hospitality and tourism management (MBA); human resources management (MBA); international business management (MBA); international finance (MBA); marketing management (MBA); mass media and public relations (MBA); project management (MBA, MS). Electronic applications accepted.

School of Computer Information Systems *Program availability:* Part-time, online learning. Offers business intelligence (Graduate Certificate); business intelligence and data analytics (MIS); computer science (MS); cybersecurity (MIS); data management (MIS); enterprise project management (MIS); health informatics (MIS); information assurance (MIS); information systems (Graduate Certificate); information systems management (MS, Graduate Certificate); information technology (MIS); information technology audit and compliance (Graduate Certificate); knowledge management (MIS); software engineering (MS). Electronic applications accepted.

School of Education *Program availability:* Part-time, online learning. Offers applied linguistics (MS); education (M Ed); teaching English to speakers of other languages (MA). Electronic applications accepted.

School of Public and International Affairs Offers international relations (MS); public administration (MPA).

VIRGINIA POLYTECHNIC INSTITUTE AND STATE UNIVERSITY, Blacksburg, VA 24061

General Information State-supported, coed, university. CGS member. *Enrollment:* 34,850 graduate, professional, and undergraduate students; 4,959 full-time matriculated graduate/professional students (2,215 women), 2,080 part-time matriculated graduate/professional students (840 women). *Enrollment by degree level:* 3,414 master's, 3,625 doctoral. *Graduate faculty:* 1,938 full-time (674 women), 19 part-time/adjunct (12 women). Tuition, state resident: full-time $15,510; part-time $739.50 per credit hour. Tuition, nonresident: full-time $29,629; part-time $1490.25 per credit hour. *Required fees:* $2804; $550 per semester. Tuition and fees vary according to course load, campus/location and program. *Graduate housing:* Room and/or apartments available on a first-come, first-served basis to single students; on-campus housing not available to married students. Typical cost: $13,334 (including board). *Student services:* Campus employment opportunities, campus safety program, career counseling, exercise/wellness program, free psychological counseling, grant writing training, international student services, low-cost health insurance, multicultural affairs office, services for students with disabilities, teacher training, writing training. *Library facilities:* Newman Library plus 2 others. *Collection:* Study areas open 24 hours, 5–7 days a week.

Computer facilities: A campuswide network can be accessed from student residence rooms and from off campus. Online class registration is available.
Website: http://www.vt.edu/

General Application Contact: Graduate Admissions and Academic Progress, 540-231-8636, E-mail: grads@vt.edu.

GRADUATE UNITS

Graduate School Students: 4,959 full-time (2,215 women), 2,080 part-time (840 women); includes 1,373 minority (356 Black or African American, non-Hispanic/Latino; 53 American Indian or Alaska Native, non-Hispanic/Latino; 402 Asian, non-Hispanic/Latino; 298 Hispanic/Latino; 7 Native Hawaiian or other Pacific Islander, non-Hispanic/Latino; 257 Two or more races, non-Hispanic/Latino), 1,966 international. Average age 30. 7,523 applicants, 44% accepted, 1612 enrolled. *Faculty:* 1,938 full-time (674 women), 19 part-time/adjunct (12 women). Expenses: Contact institution. *Application deadline:* For fall admission, 8/1 for domestic students, 4/1 for international students; for spring admission, 1/1 for domestic students, 9/1 for international students. Applications are processed on a rolling basis. *Application fee:* $75. Electronic applications accepted. *Application Contact:* Graduate Admissions and Academic Progress, E-mail: grads@vt.edu. *Vice President and Dean for Graduate Education,* Dr. Karen P. DePauw, 540-231-6691, E-mail: grads@vt.edu.

College of Agriculture and Life Sciences Students: 360 full-time (195 women), 110 part-time (73 women); includes 70 minority (24 Black or African American, non-Hispanic/Latino; 1 American Indian or Alaska Native, non-Hispanic/Latino; 15 Asian, non-Hispanic/Latino; 12 Hispanic/Latino; 18 Two or more races, non-Hispanic/Latino), 110 international. Average age 28. 296 applicants, 54% accepted, 105 enrolled. *Faculty:* 244 full-time (79 women), 1 (woman) part-time/adjunct. Expenses: Contact institution. *Financial support:* In 2018–19, 3 fellowships with full tuition reimbursements (averaging $25,731 per year), 249 research assistantships with full tuition reimbursements (averaging $19,826 per year), 105 teaching assistantships with full tuition reimbursements (averaging $19,277 per year) were awarded; scholarships/grants and unspecified assistantships also available. Financial award application deadline: 3/1; financial award applicants required to submit FAFSA. In 2018, 92 master's, 59 doctorates awarded. Offers agricultural and applied economics (MS, PhD); agricultural and life sciences (MS); agriculture, leadership, and community education (MS, PhD); animal and poultry science (MS, PhD); biochemistry (MS, PhD); crop and soil environmental sciences (MS, PhD); dairy science (MS, PhD); entomology (MS, PhD); food science and technology (MS, PhD); horticulture (MS, PhD); human nutrition, foods and exercise (MS, PhD); plant pathology, physiology, and weed science (MS, PhD). *Application deadline:* For fall admission, 8/1 for domestic students, 4/1 for international students; for spring admission, 1/1 for domestic students, 9/1 for international students. Applications are processed on a rolling basis. *Application fee:* $75. Electronic applications accepted. *Application Contact:* Crystal Tawney, Administrative Assistant, 540-231-4152, Fax: 540-231-4163, E-mail: cdtawney@vt.edu. *Dean,* Dr. Alan L. Grant, 540-231-4152, Fax: 540-231-4163, E-mail: algrant@vt.edu.

College of Architecture and Urban Studies Students: 334 full-time (167 women), 188 part-time (99 women); includes 112 minority (43 Black or African American, non-Hispanic/Latino; 1 American Indian or Alaska Native, non-Hispanic/Latino; 26 Asian, non-Hispanic/Latino; 30 Hispanic/Latino; 12 Two or more races, non-Hispanic/Latino), 134 international. Average age 33. 521 applicants, 65% accepted, 111 enrolled. *Faculty:* 145 full-time (56 women), 2 part-time/adjunct (1 woman). Expenses: Contact institution. *Financial support:* In 2018–19, 1 fellowship with full tuition reimbursement (averaging $28,977 per year), 34 research assistantships with full tuition reimbursements (averaging $15,814 per year), 148 teaching assistantships with full tuition reimbursements (averaging $10,971 per year) were awarded; scholarships/grants and unspecified assistantships also available. Financial award application deadline: 3/1; financial award applicants required to submit FAFSA. In 2018, 130 master's, 23 doctorates awarded. Offers architecture (M Arch, MS); architecture and design research (PhD); building construction science management (MS); creative technologies (MFA); environmental design and planning (PhD); government and international affairs (MPIA); landscape architecture (MLA, PhD); planning, governance, and globalization (PhD); public administration and public affairs (MPA, PhD); urban and regional planning (MURPL). *Application deadline:* For fall admission, 8/1 for domestic students, 4/1 for international students; for spring admission, 1/1 for domestic students, 9/1 for international students. Applications are processed on a rolling basis. *Application fee:* $75. Electronic applications accepted. *Application Contact:* Christine Mattsson-Coon, Executive Assistant, 540-231-6416, Fax: 540-231-6332, E-mail: cmattsso@vt.edu. *Dean,* Dr. Richard Blythe, 540-231-6416, Fax: 540-231-6332, E-mail: richbl1@vt.edu.

College of Engineering Students: 1,776 full-time (471 women), 367 part-time (62 women); includes 260 minority (50 Black or African American, non-Hispanic/Latino; 3 American Indian or Alaska Native, non-Hispanic/Latino; 99 Asian, non-Hispanic/Latino; 67 Hispanic/Latino; 41 Two or more races, non-Hispanic/Latino), 1,178 international. Average age 27. 3,798 applicants, 37% accepted, 507 enrolled. *Faculty:* 446 full-time (87 women), 7 part-time/adjunct (3 women). Expenses: Contact institution. *Financial support:* In 2018–19, 37 fellowships with full tuition reimbursements (averaging $24,951 per year), 1,110 research assistantships with full tuition reimbursements (averaging $20,129 per year), 486 teaching assistantships with full tuition reimbursements (averaging $16,192 per year) were awarded; scholarships/grants and unspecified assistantships also available. Financial award application deadline: 3/1; financial award applicants required to submit FAFSA. In 2018, 489 master's, 200 doctorates awarded. Offers aerospace engineering (PhD); biological systems engineering (PhD); biomedical engineering (MS, PhD); chemical engineering (PhD); civil engineering (PhD); computer engineering (PhD); computer science and applications (MS); electrical engineering (PhD); engineering education (PhD). *Application deadline:* For fall admission, 8/1 for domestic students, 4/1 for international students; for spring admission, 1/1 for domestic students, 9/1 for international students. Applications are processed on a rolling basis. *Application fee:* $75. Electronic applications accepted. *Application Contact:* Linda Perkins, Executive Assistant, 540-231-9752, Fax: 540-231-3031, E-mail: lperkins@vt.edu. *Dean,* Dr. Julia Ross, 540-231-9752, Fax: 540-231-3031, E-mail: rjulie@vt.edu.

College of Liberal Arts and Human Sciences Students: 603 full-time (428 women), 359 part-time (237 women); includes 189 minority (107 Black or African American, non-Hispanic/Latino; 4 American Indian or Alaska Native, non-Hispanic/Latino; 24 Asian, non-Hispanic/Latino; 27 Hispanic/Latino; 2 Native Hawaiian or other Pacific Islander, non-Hispanic/Latino; 25 Two or more races, non-Hispanic/Latino), 84 international. Average age 33. 856 applicants, 48% accepted, 262 enrolled. *Faculty:* 420 full-time (221 women), 1 (woman) part-time/adjunct. Expenses: Contact institution. *Financial support:* In 2018–19, 4 fellowships with full tuition reimbursements (averaging $23,122 per year), 28 research assistantships with full tuition reimbursements (averaging $15,605 per year), 245 teaching assistantships with full tuition reimbursements (averaging $16,046 per year) were awarded; scholarships/grants and unspecified assistantships also available. Financial award application deadline: 3/1; financial award applicants required to submit FAFSA. In 2018, 270 master's, 63 doctorates awarded. Offers career and technical education (MS Ed, Ed S); communication (MA); counselor education (MA); creative writing (MFA); curriculum and instruction (MA Ed, Ed S); educational leadership and policy studies (Ed S); educational research and evaluation (PhD); English (MA); social, political, ethical, and cultural thought (PhD). *Application deadline:* For fall admission, 8/1 for domestic students, 4/1 for international students; for spring admission, 1/1 for domestic students, 9/1 for international students. Applications are processed on a rolling basis. *Application fee:* $75. Electronic applications accepted. *Application Contact:* Chelsea Blanchet, Executive Assistant, 540-231-6779, Fax: 540-231-7157, E-mail: bchels1@vt.edu. *Dean,* Dr. Laura Belmonte, 540-231-6779, Fax: 540-231-7157, E-mail: belmonte@vt.edu.

College of Natural Resources and Environment Students: 179 full-time (80 women), 75 part-time (40 women); includes 34 minority (3 Black or African American, non-Hispanic/Latino; 7 Asian, non-Hispanic/Latino; 17 Hispanic/Latino; 1 Native Hawaiian or other Pacific Islander, non-Hispanic/Latino; 6 Two or more races, non-Hispanic/Latino), 33 international. Average age 32. 110 applicants, 58% accepted, 50 enrolled. *Faculty:* 80 full-time (18 women). Expenses: Contact institution. *Financial support:* In 2018–19, 4 fellowships with full tuition reimbursements (averaging $29,791 per year), 97 research assistantships with full tuition reimbursements (averaging $18,686 per year), 47 teaching assistantships with full tuition reimbursements (averaging $17,302 per year) were awarded; scholarships/grants also available. Financial award application deadline: 3/1; financial award applicants required to submit FAFSA. In 2018, 93 master's, 13 doctorates awarded. Offers fisheries and wildlife (MS, PhD); forest products (MNR, MS, PhD); forestry (PhD); geography (MS); geospatial and environmental analysis (PhD); natural resources (MNR). *Application deadline:* For fall admission, 8/1 for domestic students, 4/1 for international students; for spring admission, 1/1 for domestic students, 9/1 for international students. Applications are processed on a rolling basis. *Application fee:* $75. Electronic applications accepted. *Application Contact:* Arlice Banks, Executive Assistant, 540-231-7051, Fax: 540-231-7664, E-mail: arbanks@vt.edu. *Dean,* Dr. Paul M. Winistorfer, 540-231-5481, Fax: 540-231-7664, E-mail: pstorfer@vt.edu.

College of Science Students: 542 full-time (202 women), 39 part-time (19 women); includes 71 minority (11 Black or African American, non-Hispanic/Latino; 1 American Indian or Alaska Native, non-Hispanic/Latino; 18 Asian, non-Hispanic/Latino; 32 Hispanic/Latino; 9 Two or more races, non-Hispanic/Latino), 220 international. Average age 27. 977 applicants, 25% accepted, 110 enrolled. *Faculty:* 349 full-time (109 women), 3 part-time/adjunct (2 women). Expenses: Contact institution. *Financial support:* In 2018–19, 7 fellowships with full tuition reimbursements (averaging $29,657 per year), 260 research assistantships with full tuition reimbursements (averaging $15,888 per year), 383 teaching assistantships with full tuition reimbursements (averaging $18,063 per year) were awarded; unspecified assistantships also available. Financial award application deadline: 3/1; financial award applicants required to submit FAFSA. In 2018, 75 master's, 69 doctorates awarded. Offers biological sciences (MS, PhD); biomedical technology development and management (MS); chemistry (MS, PhD); data analysis and applied statistics (MA); economics (PhD); geosciences (MS, PhD); mathematics (MS, PhD); physics (MS, PhD); psychology (MS, PhD); statistics (MS, PhD). *Application deadline:* For fall admission, 8/1 for domestic students, 4/1 for international students; for spring admission, 1/1 for domestic students, 9/1 for international students. Applications are processed on a rolling basis. *Application fee:* $75. Electronic applications accepted. *Application Contact:* Allison Craft, Executive Assistant, 540-231-6394, Fax: 540-231-3380, E-mail: crafta@vt.edu. *Dean,* Dr. Sally C. Morton, 540-231-5422, Fax: 540-231-3380, E-mail: scmorton@vt.edu.

Intercollege Students: 189 full-time (92 women), 685 part-time (206 women); includes 260 minority (65 Black or African American, non-Hispanic/Latino; 106 Asian, non-Hispanic/Latino; 54 Hispanic/Latino; 2 Native Hawaiian or other Pacific Islander, non-Hispanic/Latino; 33 Two or more races, non-Hispanic/Latino), 98 international. Average age 33. 531 applicants, 75% accepted, 274 enrolled. Expenses: Contact institution. *Financial support:* In 2018–19, 3 fellowships with full and partial tuition reimbursements (averaging $18,380 per year), 158 research assistantships with full tuition reimbursements (averaging $22,336 per year), 21 teaching assistantships with full tuition reimbursements (averaging $19,355 per year) were awarded; scholarships/grants also available. Financial award application deadline: 3/1; financial award applicants required to submit FAFSA. In 2018, 138 master's, 20 doctorates awarded. Offers genetics, bioinformatics, and computational biology (PhD); information technology (MIT); macromolecular science and engineering (MS, PhD); translational biology, medicine, and health (PhD). *Application deadline:* For fall admission, 8/1 for domestic students, 4/1 for international students; for spring admission, 1/1 for domestic students, 9/1 for international students. Applications are processed on a rolling basis. *Application fee:* $75. Electronic applications accepted. *Application Contact:* Dr. Karen P. DePauw, Vice President and Dean for Graduate Education, 540-231-7581, Fax: 540-231-1670, E-mail: kpdepauw@vt.edu. *Vice President and Dean for Graduate Education,* Dr. Karen P. DePauw, 540-231-7581, Fax: 540-231-1670, E-mail: kpdepauw@vt.edu.

Pamplin College of Business Students: 227 full-time (89 women), 217 part-time (75 women); includes 131 minority (30 Black or African American, non-Hispanic/Latino; 58 Asian, non-Hispanic/Latino; 25 Hispanic/Latino; 18 Two or more races, non-Hispanic/Latino), 81 international. Average age 32. 361 applicants, 55% accepted, 152 enrolled. *Faculty:* 141 full-time (42 women), 2 part-time/adjunct (1 woman). Expenses: Contact institution. *Financial support:* In 2018–19, 1 fellowship with full tuition reimbursement (averaging $3,999 per year), 4 research assistantships with full tuition reimbursements (averaging $20,163 per year), 66 teaching assistantships with full tuition reimbursements (averaging $19,822 per year) were awarded; scholarships/grants and unspecified assistantships also available. Financial award application deadline: 3/1; financial award applicants required to submit FAFSA. In 2018, 181 master's, 8 doctorates awarded. Offers accounting and information systems (MACIS, PhD); business administration (MS); business information technology (PhD); executive business research (PhD); finance (PhD); marketing (PhD). *Application deadline:* For fall admission, 8/1 for domestic students, 4/1 for international students; for spring admission, 1/1 for domestic students, 9/1 for international students. Applications are processed on a rolling basis. *Application fee:* $75. Electronic applications accepted. *Application Contact:* Kimberly Ridpath, Executive Assistant, 540-231-9647, Fax: 540-231-4487, E-mail: ridpathk@vt.edu. *Dean,* Dr. Robert T. Sumichrast, 540-231-6601, Fax: 540-231-4487, E-mail: busdean@vt.edu.

Virginia-Maryland College of Veterinary Medicine Students: 582 full-time (417 women), 40 part-time (29 women); includes 225 minority (20 Black or African American, non-Hispanic/Latino; 43 American Indian or Alaska Native, non-Hispanic/Latino; 31 Asian, non-Hispanic/Latino; 34 Hispanic/Latino; 2 Native Hawaiian or other Pacific Islander, non-Hispanic/Latino; 95 Two or more races, non-Hispanic/Latino), 28 international. Average age 26. 73 applicants, 88% accepted, 41 enrolled. *Faculty:* 103 full-time (56 women), 2 part-time/adjunct (both women). Expenses: Contact institution. *Financial support:* In 2018–19, 13 fellowships with full and partial tuition reimbursements (averaging $7,108 per year), 31 research assistantships with full tuition reimbursements (averaging $18,931 per year), 22 teaching assistantships with full tuition reimbursements (averaging $21,014 per year) were awarded; scholarships/grants also available. Financial award application deadline: 3/1; financial award applicants required to submit FAFSA. In 2018, 33 master's, 137 doctorates awarded. Offers biomedical and veterinary sciences (MS, PhD); public health (MPH); veterinary medicine (DVM). *Application deadline:* For fall admission, 8/1 for domestic students, 4/1 for international students; for spring admission, 1/1 for domestic students, 9/1 for international students. Applications are processed on a rolling basis. *Application fee:* $75. Electronic applications accepted. *Application Contact:* Sheila Steele, Executive Assistant, 540-231-7910, Fax: 540-231-3505, E-mail: ssteele@vt.edu. *Interim Dean,* Dr. Gregory B. Daniel, 540-231-7910, Fax: 540-231-3505, E-mail: gdaniel@vt.edu.

Virginia Tech Carilion School of Medicine and Research Institute Students: 167 full-time (74 women); includes 21 minority (3 Black or African American, non-Hispanic/Latino; 18 Asian, non-Hispanic/Latino). Average age 25. *Faculty:* 10 full-time (6 women), 1 (woman) part-time/adjunct. Expenses: Contact institution. *Financial support:* Scholarships/grants available. Offers medicine (MD). *Application deadline:* For fall admission, 12/1 for domestic students. *Application fee:* $70. Electronic applications accepted. *Application Contact:* Cynda Ann Johnson, MD, Founding Dean, 540-526-2559, E-mail: cajohnson@vt.edu. *Founding Dean,* Cynda Ann Johnson, MD, 540-526-2559, E-mail: cajohnson@vt.edu.

VT Online Expenses: Contact institution. Offers advanced transportation systems (Certificate); aerospace engineering (MS); agricultural and life sciences (MSLFS); business information systems (Graduate Certificate); career and technical education (MS); civil engineering (MS); computer engineering (M Eng, MS); decision support systems (Graduate Certificate); eLearning leadership (MA); electrical engineering (M Eng, MS); engineering administration (MEA); environmental engineering (Certificate); environmental politics and policy (Graduate Certificate); environmental sciences and engineering (MS); foundations of political analysis (Graduate Certificate); health product risk management (Graduate Certificate); industrial and systems engineering (MS); information policy and society (Graduate Certificate); information security (Graduate Certificate); information technology (MIT); instructional technology (MA); integrative STEM education (MA Ed); liberal arts (Graduate Certificate); life sciences: health product risk management (MS); natural resources (MNR, Graduate Certificate); networking (Graduate Certificate); nonprofit and nongovernmental organization management (Graduate Certificate); ocean engineering (MS); political science (MA); security studies (Graduate Certificate); software development (Graduate Certificate). *Application Contact:* Graduate Admissions and Academic Progress, 540-231-8636, E-mail: grads@vt.edu.

VIRGINIA STATE UNIVERSITY, Petersburg, VA 23806-0001

General Information State-supported, coed, comprehensive institution. *Enrollment by degree level:* 459 master's, 36 doctoral, 13 other advanced degrees. *Graduate housing:* Room and/or apartments available on a first-come, first-served basis to single students; on-campus housing not available to married students. Housing application deadline: 5/1. *Student services:* Career counseling, international student services, services for students with disabilities. *Library facilities:* Johnston Memorial Library. *Collection:* Books: 434,496 (physical); Serial titles: 5,805 (physical); Databases: 245. Weekly public service hours: 82.

Computer facilities: 1,400 computers available on campus for general student use. A campuswide network can be accessed from student residence rooms and from off campus. Online class registration is available. Website: http://www.vsu.edu/

General Application Contact: Patrice Randall, Graduate Programs Coordinator, 804-524-5385, Fax: 804-524-5104, E-mail: prandall@vsu.edu.

GRADUATE UNITS

College of Graduate Studies *Program availability:* Part-time, evening/weekend. Offers interdisciplinary studies (MIS).
College of Education Offers administration and supervision (M Ed); education (M Ed, MS, Ed D); school and community counseling (M Ed, MS).
College of Engineering and Technology Offers economics (MA); engineering and technology (M Ed, MS); mathematics (MS).
College of Humanities and Social Sciences *Program availability:* Part-time, evening/weekend. Offers criminal justice (MS); humanities and social sciences (M Ed, MA, MS); media management (MA).
College of Natural and Health Sciences Offers behavioral and community health sciences (PhD); biology (MS); clinical health psychology (PhD); clinical psychology (MS); general psychology (MS); natural and health sciences (MS, PhD).

VIRGINIA THEOLOGICAL SEMINARY, Alexandria, VA 22304

General Information Independent-religious, coed, graduate-only institution. *Graduate housing:* Rooms and/or apartments available on a first-come, first-served basis to single and married students. Housing application deadline: 5/1.

GRADUATE UNITS

Graduate and Professional Programs *Program availability:* Part-time. Offers Christian spirituality (D Min); educational leadership (D Ed Min, D Min); ministry development (D Min); theology (M Div, MA).

VIRGINIA UNION UNIVERSITY, Richmond, VA 23220-1170

General Information Independent-religious, coed, comprehensive institution. *Graduate housing:* Room and/or apartments available on a first-come, first-served basis to single students; on-campus housing not available to married students.

GRADUATE UNITS

Evelyn R. Syphax School of Education, Psychology and Interdisciplinary Studies Offers curriculum and instruction (MA).
Samuel DeWitt Proctor School of Theology *Program availability:* Part-time, evening/weekend. Offers theology (M Div, D Min).

VIRGINIA UNIVERSITY OF INTEGRATIVE MEDICINE, Fairfax, VA 22031

General Information Private, coed, graduate-only institution.

GRADUATE UNITS

Graduate Programs

VIRGINIA UNIVERSITY OF LYNCHBURG, Lynchburg, VA 24501-6417

General Information Independent-religious, coed, comprehensive institution. *Graduate housing:* Room and/or apartments available on a first-come, first-served basis to single students; on-campus housing not available to married students. Housing application deadline: 9/5.

GRADUATE UNITS

Graduate Programs *Program availability:* Online learning. Offers Christian ministry (M Div); ministry (D Min).

VIRGINIA WESLEYAN UNIVERSITY, Virginia Beach, VA 23455

General Information Independent-religious, coed, comprehensive institution.

GRADUATE UNITS

Graduate Studies *Program availability:* Online learning.

VITERBO UNIVERSITY, La Crosse, WI 54601-4797

General Information Independent-religious, coed, comprehensive institution. *Graduate housing:* Room and/or apartments available on a first-come, first-served basis to single students; on-campus housing not available to married students. Housing application deadline: 4/2.

GRADUATE UNITS

Graduate Program in Nursing *Program availability:* Part-time. Offers nursing (DNP). Electronic applications accepted.
Graduate Programs in Education *Program availability:* Part-time, evening/weekend. Offers cross-categorical special education (Certificate); director of instruction (Certificate); director of special education and pupil services (Certificate); early childhood (Certificate); education (MAE); literacy coaching (Certificate); PreK-12 principal/supervisor of special education (Certificate); principal (Certificate); reading specialist endorsement (Certificate); reading teacher (Certificate); reading teacher 5-12 endorsement (Certificate); reading teacher K-8 endorsement (Certificate); superintendent (Certificate); talented and gifted endorsement (Certificate); Wisconsin school business administrator (Certificate). Weekend courses available in summer. Electronic applications accepted.
Master of Arts in Servant Leadership Program *Program availability:* Part-time, evening/weekend. Offers ethical leadership in organizations (Certificate); servant leadership (MA). Electronic applications accepted.
Master of Business Administration Program *Program availability:* Part-time, evening/weekend. Offers general business administration (MBA); health care management (MBA); international business (MBA); leadership (MBA); project management (MBA). Electronic applications accepted.
Master of Science in Mental Health Counseling Program *Program availability:* Part-time, evening/weekend. Offers addiction counseling (MS); child and adolescent counseling (MS); complementary health and wellness counseling (MS). Electronic applications accepted.

WAGNER COLLEGE, Staten Island, NY 10301-4495

General Information Independent, coed, comprehensive institution. *Graduate housing:* Room and/or apartments available on a first-come, first-served basis to single students; on-campus housing not available to married students. Housing application deadline: 4/1. *Research affiliation:* Staten Island University Hospital.

GRADUATE UNITS

Division of Graduate Studies *Program availability:* Part-time, evening/weekend. Offers childhood education (MS Ed); childhood education/students with disabilities (MS Ed); early childhood education/students with disabilities (birth-grade 2) (MS Ed); higher education and learning organizations leadership (MA); microbiology (MS); secondary education 7-12 (MS Ed); secondary education/students with disabilities (MS Ed). Electronic applications accepted.
Evelyn L. Spiro School of Nursing *Program availability:* Part-time, evening/weekend. Offers family nurse practitioner (MS, Certificate); nurse educator (MS); nursing (DNP). Electronic applications accepted.
Nicolais School of Business *Program availability:* Part-time, evening/weekend. Offers accounting (MS); business administration (MBA); finance (MBA); management (Exec MBA); marketing (MBA); media management (MS).

WAKE FOREST UNIVERSITY, Winston-Salem, NC 27109

General Information Independent, coed, university. CGS member. *Graduate housing:* On-campus housing not available.

GRADUATE UNITS

Graduate School of Arts and Sciences *Program availability:* Part-time. Offers analytical chemistry (MS, PhD); arts and sciences (MA, MA Ed, MALS, MS, MSA, PhD); biology (MS, PhD); computer science (MA); counseling (MA); English (MA); health and exercise science (MS); inorganic chemistry (MS, PhD); liberal studies (MALS); mathematics (MA); organic chemistry (MS, PhD); physical chemistry (MS, PhD); physics (MS, PhD); psychology (MA); religious studies (MA); secondary education (MA Ed); speech communication (MA). Electronic applications accepted.
School of Business *Program availability:* Evening/weekend. Offers assurance services (MSA); business (MA, MBA, MSA, MSBA); business administration (MBA); business analytics (MSBA); management (MA); tax consulting (MSA); transaction services (MSA). Electronic applications accepted.
School of Law Offers law (LL M, MSL, JD, SJD). LL M program is designed for foreign law graduates in American law. Electronic applications accepted.
School of Medicine Offers medicine (MS, MD, PhD). Electronic applications accepted.
Graduate Programs in Medicine Offers biochemistry (PhD); cancer biology (PhD); comparative medicine (MS); medicine (MS, PhD); microbiology and immunology (PhD); molecular genetics and genomics (PhD); molecular medicine and translational

science (MS, PhD); neurobiology and anatomy (PhD); neuroscience (PhD); nurse anesthesia (MS); pharmacology (PhD); physiology (PhD). Electronic applications accepted.

Virginia Tech-Wake Forest University School of Biomedical Engineering and Sciences Offers biomedical engineering (MS, PhD). Electronic applications accepted.

WALDEN UNIVERSITY, Minneapolis, MN 55401

General Information Proprietary, coed, university. CGS member.

GRADUATE UNITS

Graduate Programs *Program availability:* Part-time, evening/weekend, online only, 100% online. Electronic applications accepted.

Richard W. Riley College of Education and Leadership *Program availability:* Part-time, evening/weekend, online only, 100% online. Offers adult education (Post-Master's Certificate); adult learning (Graduate Certificate); college teaching and learning (Graduate Certificate); community college leadership (Ed D); curriculum, instruction and assessment (Ed D, Ed S, Graduate Certificate); developmental education (Graduate Certificate); early childhood administration, management, and leadership (Graduate Certificate); early childhood education (Ed D, Ed S); early childhood public policy and advocacy (Graduate Certificate); early childhood studies (MS); education (MS, PhD); educational administration and leadership (Ed D); educational leadership and administration (principal preparation) (Ed S); educational technology (Ed D, Ed S, Post Master's Certificate); elementary reading and literacy (Graduate Certificate); engaging culturally diverse learners (Graduate Certificate); enrollment management and institutional marketing (Graduate Certificate); higher education (MS); higher education and adult learning (Ed D); higher education leadership and management (Ed D); higher education leadership for student success (Graduate Certificate); instructional design and technology (MS, Postbaccalaureate Certificate); integrating technology in the classroom (Graduate Certificate); mathematics 5-8 (Graduate Certificate); mathematics K-6 (Graduate Certificate); online teaching for adult educators (Graduate Certificate); reading, literacy, and assessment (Ed D, Ed S); science K-8 (Graduate Certificate); special education (Ed D, Ed S, Graduate Certificate); special education (K-age 21) (MAT); teacher leadership (Graduate Certificate); teaching adults English as a second language (Graduate Certificate); teaching adults in the early childhood field (Graduate Certificate); teaching and diversity in early childhood education (Graduate Certificate); teaching English language learners (grades K-12) (Graduate Certificate); teaching K-12 students online (Graduate Certificate). Electronic applications accepted.

School of Counseling *Program availability:* Part-time, evening/weekend, online only, 100% online. Offers addiction counseling (MS); clinical mental health counseling (MS); counselor education and supervision (PhD); marriage, couple, and family counseling (MS); school counseling (MS). Electronic applications accepted.

School of Health Sciences *Program availability:* Part-time, evening/weekend, online only, 100% online. Offers clinical research administration (MS, Graduate Certificate); health education and promotion (MS, PhD); health informatics (MS); health services (PhD); healthcare administration (MHA, DHA); leadership and organizational development (MHA); public health (MPH, Dr PH, PhD, Graduate Certificate); systems policy (MHA). Electronic applications accepted.

School of Information Systems and Technology *Program availability:* Part-time, evening/weekend, online only, 100% online. Offers information systems (Graduate Certificate); information systems management (MISM); information technology (MS, DIT). Electronic applications accepted.

School of Management *Program availability:* Part-time, evening/weekend, online only, 100% online. Offers accounting (MBA, MS, DBA); advanced project management (Graduate Certificate); applied project management (Graduate Certificate); auditing (Graduate Certificate); bridge to business administration (Post-Doctoral Certificate); bridge to management (Post-Doctoral Certificate); business management (Graduate Certificate); communication (MBA); corporate finance (MBA); digital marketing (Graduate Certificate); entrepreneurship (DBA); entrepreneurship and small business (MBA); finance (MS, DBA); global supply chain management (DBA); healthcare management (MBA, DBA); human resource management (MBA, MS, Graduate Certificate); human resources management (DBA); information systems management (DBA); international business (MBA, DBA); leadership (MBA, MS, DBA, Graduate Certificate); management (MS, PhD); managerial accounting (Graduate Certificate); marketing (MBA, MS, DBA); project management (MBA, MS, DBA); self-designed (MBA, DBA); social impact management (DBA); technology entrepreneurship (DBA). Electronic applications accepted.

School of Nursing *Program availability:* Part-time, evening/weekend, online only, 100% online. Offers adult-gerontology acute care nurse practitioner (MSN); adult-gerontology nurse practitioner (MSN); education (MSN); family nurse practitioner (MSN); informatics (MSN); leadership and management (MSN); nursing (PhD, Post-Master's Certificate); nursing practice (DNP); psychiatric mental health (MSN). Electronic applications accepted.

School of Psychology *Program availability:* Part-time, evening/weekend, online only, 100% online. Offers clinical psychology (MS); forensic psychology (MS); industrial organizational (MS, PhD); online teaching in psychology (Post-Master's Certificate); organizational psychology and development (Postbaccalaureate Certificate); psychology (MS, PhD); psychology respecialization (Post-Doctoral Certificate). Electronic applications accepted.

School of Public Policy and Administration *Program availability:* Part-time, evening/weekend, online only, 100% online. Offers criminal justice (MPA, MPP, MS, Graduate Certificate); criminal justice and executive management (MS); criminal justice leadership and executive management (MS); emergency management (MPA, MPP, MS); general program (MPA, MPP); global leadership (MPA, MPP); government management (Graduate Certificate); health policy (MPA, MPP); homeland security (Graduate Certificate); homeland security and policy coordination (MPA, MPP); international nongovernmental organizations (MPA, MPP); law and public policy (MPA, MPP); local government management for sustainable communities (MPA, MPP); nonprofit management (Graduate Certificate); nonprofit management and leadership (MPA, MPP, MS); online teaching in higher education (Post-Master's Certificate); policy analysis (MPA); public management and leadership (MPA, MPP, Graduate Certificate); public policy (Graduate Certificate); public policy and administration (PhD); strategic planning and public policy (Graduate Certificate); terrorism, mediation, and peace (MPA, MPP). Electronic applications accepted.

School of Social Work and Human Services *Program availability:* Part-time, evening/weekend, online only, 100% online. Offers addictions and social work (DSW); advanced clinical practice (MSW); clinical expertise (DSW); criminal justice (DSW); disaster, crisis, and intervention (DSW); family studies and interventions (DSW); human and social services (PhD); medical social work (DSW); military social work (MSW); policy practice (DSW); social work (PhD); social work administration (DSW);

social work in healthcare (MSW); social work with children and families (MSW). Electronic applications accepted.

WALDORF UNIVERSITY, Forest City, IA 50436

General Information Independent-religious, coed, comprehensive institution.

GRADUATE UNITS

Program in Organizational Leadership Offers criminal justice leadership (MA); emergency management leadership (MA); fire/rescue executive leadership (MA); human resource development (MA); public administration (MA); sport management (MA); teacher leader (MA).

WALLA WALLA UNIVERSITY, College Place, WA 99324

General Information Independent-religious, coed, comprehensive institution. *Graduate housing:* Rooms and/or apartments available on a first-come, first-served basis to single and married students.

GRADUATE UNITS

Graduate Studies *Program availability:* Part-time, evening/weekend. Offers biology (MS). Electronic applications accepted.

Center for Cinema, Religion, and Worldview Offers Web and interactive media (MA).

School of Education and Psychology *Program availability:* Part-time. Offers curriculum and instruction (M Ed, MAT); educational leadership (M Ed, MAT); literacy instruction (M Ed, MAT); special education (M Ed, MAT). Electronic applications accepted.

Wilma Hepker School of Social Work and Sociology *Program availability:* Part-time. Offers social work (MSW). Electronic applications accepted.

WALSH COLLEGE OF ACCOUNTANCY AND BUSINESS ADMINISTRATION, Troy, MI 48083

General Information Independent, coed, upper-level institution. *Enrollment:* 38 full-time matriculated graduate/professional students (16 women), 1,164 part-time matriculated graduate/professional students (573 women). *Enrollment by degree level:* 1,188 master's, 14 other advanced degrees. *Graduate faculty:* 17 full-time (7 women), 44 part-time/adjunct (14 women). *Tuition:* Full-time $21,195; part-time $14,130 per credit hour. *Required fees:* $525; $525 per semester. $175 per semester. *Graduate housing:* On-campus housing not available. *Student services:* Campus employment opportunities, career counseling, international student services, services for students with disabilities, writing training. *Library facilities:* Vollbrecht Library plus 1 other. *Collection:* Books: 27,985 (physical), 18,425 (digital/electronic); Serial titles: 2,262 (physical), 71,676 (digital/electronic); Databases: 79. Weekly public service hours: 113.

Computer facilities: 400 computers available on campus for general student use. A campuswide network can be accessed from off campus. Online class registration, Campus Wifi are available.
Website: http://www.walshcollege.edu/

General Application Contact: Karen Mahaffy, Executive Director, Admissions and Enrollment Services, 248-823-1216, Fax: 248-823-1611, E-mail: kmahaffy@walshcollege.edu.

GRADUATE UNITS

Graduate Programs Students: 38 full-time (16 women), 1,164 part-time (573 women); includes 278 minority (153 Black or African American, non-Hispanic/Latino; 3 American Indian or Alaska Native, non-Hispanic/Latino; 74 Asian, non-Hispanic/Latino; 30 Hispanic/Latino; 1 Native Hawaiian or other Pacific Islander, non-Hispanic/Latino; 17 Two or more races, non-Hispanic/Latino), 65 international. Average age 34. 373 applicants, 88% accepted, 190 enrolled. *Faculty:* 17 full-time (7 women), 44 part-time/adjunct (14 women). Expenses: Contact institution. *Financial support:* In 2018–19, 71 students received support. Career-related internships or fieldwork and scholarships/grants available. Financial award application deadline: 6/30; financial award applicants required to submit FAFSA. In 2018, 380 master's awarded. *Program availability:* Part-time, evening/weekend, 100% online, blended/hybrid learning, on-ground. Offers business (MAB); business administration (MBA); chief information officer (MS, MSIT); chief information officer, chief security officer, project management officechief information officer, cybersecurity, data science, global project and program management (MSIT); chief security officer (MS); cybersecurity (MSIT); data analytics (MAC); data analytics, finance, taxation (MAC); data science (MSIT); finance (MAC); financial investments (MSF); financial management (MSF); financial management, financial services (MSF); financial services (MSF); global project and program management (MSIT); human resources management (MS); human resources management, strategic managementinternational business (MS); marketing (MS); program management office (MS); strategic management (MS); taxation (MAC). *Application deadline:* Applications are processed on a rolling basis. *Application fee:* $35. Electronic applications accepted. *Application Contact:* Karen Mahaffy, Executive Director, Admissions and Enrollment Services, 248-823-1600, Fax: 248-823-1611, E-mail: kmahaffy@walshcollege.edu. *Chief Academic Officer/Executive Vice President,* Dr. Michael Rinkus, 248-823-1269, Fax: 248-689-0920, E-mail: mrinkus@walshcollege.edu.

WALSH UNIVERSITY, North Canton, OH 44720-3396

General Information Independent-religious, coed, comprehensive institution. CGS member. *Graduate housing:* Room and/or apartments available on a first-come, first-served basis to single students; on-campus housing not available to married students. Housing application deadline: 7/15. *Research affiliation:* North Canton Public Schools (straight A grants (student development)), Research Foundation of the Carolinas (surgery), Akron General Health System (patient satisfaction), Mercy Medical Center (orthopedics, nursing, physical therapy), Akron Children's Hospital (orthopedics).

GRADUATE UNITS

Graduate Programs *Program availability:* Part-time, evening/weekend, online learning. Offers clinical mental health counseling (MA); healthcare management (MBA); leadership with principal license (MA Ed); management (MBA); marketing (MBA); parish administration (MA); pastoral ministry (MA); physical therapy (DPT); reading literacy (MA Ed); religious education (MA); school counseling (MA); student affairs in higher education (MA). Electronic applications accepted.

Gary and Linda Byers School of Nursing *Program availability:* Part-time, evening/weekend, online only, 100% online. Offers academic nurse educator (MSN); adult acute care nurse practitioner (MSN); clinical nurse leader (MSN); nursing practice (DNP). Electronic applications accepted.

WARNER PACIFIC UNIVERSITY, Portland, OR 97215-4099

General Information Independent-religious, coed, comprehensive institution. *Graduate housing:* On-campus housing not available.

GRADUATE UNITS

Graduate Programs *Program availability:* Part-time, evening/weekend. Offers human services (MA); not-for-profit leadership (MS); organizational leadership (MS); teaching (MAT).

WARNER UNIVERSITY, Lake Wales, FL 33859

General Information Independent-religious, coed, comprehensive institution. *Graduate housing:* Room and/or apartments available on a first-come, first-served basis to single students; on-campus housing not available to married students.

GRADUATE UNITS

School of Business *Program availability:* Part-time, evening/weekend, online learning. Offers accounting (MBA); business administration (MBA); human resource management (MBA); international business (MBA); management (MSMC). Electronic applications accepted.

School of Education *Program availability:* Part-time, evening/weekend, online learning. Offers curriculum and instruction (MAEd); elementary education (MAEd); science, technology, engineering, and mathematics (STEM) (MAEd). Electronic applications accepted.

WARREN WILSON COLLEGE, Asheville, NC 28815-9000

General Information Independent-religious, coed, comprehensive institution. *Graduate housing:* Room and/or apartments guaranteed to single students; on-campus housing not available to married students.

GRADUATE UNITS

Master of Arts Program in Critical and Historical Craft Studies Offers critical and historical craft studies (MA). Electronic applications accepted.

MFA Program for Writers Students: 78 full-time (54 women); includes 20 minority (2 Black or African American, non-Hispanic/Latino; 1 American Indian or Alaska Native, non-Hispanic/Latino; 8 Asian, non-Hispanic/Latino; 6 Hispanic/Latino; 3 Two or more races, non-Hispanic/Latino). Average age 37. 80 applicants, 33% accepted, 20 enrolled. *Faculty:* 28 full-time (14 women). Expenses: Contact institution. *Financial support:* In 2018–19, 33 students received support, including 2 fellowships with full tuition reimbursements available (averaging $18,800 per year); scholarships/grants also available. Financial award application deadline: 3/1; financial award applicants required to submit FAFSA. In 2018, 28 master's awarded. Offers creative writing (MFA). *Application deadline:* For fall admission, 9/1 for domestic and international students; for spring admission, 3/1 for domestic and international students. *Application fee:* $75. Electronic applications accepted. *Application Contact:* Trish Marshall, MFA Project Manager, 828-771-3717, Fax: 828-771-7005, E-mail: pmarshall@warren-wilson.edu. *Director,* Prof. Debra Allbery, 828-771-3716, Fax: 828-771-3716, E-mail: dallbery@warren-wilson.edu.

WARTBURG THEOLOGICAL SEMINARY, Dubuque, IA 52004-5004

General Information Independent-religious, coed, graduate-only institution. *Graduate housing:* Rooms and/or apartments available on a first-come, first-served basis to single and married students. Housing application deadline: 4/30. *Research affiliation:* Menighetsfakultet, Augustana Theologische Hochschule.

GRADUATE UNITS

Graduate and Professional Programs *Program availability:* Online learning. Offers diaconal ministry (MA); ministry (M Div); theology (MA). Electronic applications accepted.

WASHBURN UNIVERSITY, Topeka, KS 66621

General Information City-supported, coed, comprehensive institution. *Graduate housing:* Room and/or apartments available on a first-come, first-served basis to single students; on-campus housing not available to married students.

GRADUATE UNITS

College of Arts and Sciences *Program availability:* Part-time, evening/weekend. Offers arts and sciences (M Ed, MA, MLS); clinical psychology (MA); curriculum and instruction (M Ed); educational leadership (M Ed); liberal studies (MLS); reading (M Ed); special education (M Ed). Electronic applications accepted.

School of Applied Studies *Program availability:* Part-time, evening/weekend, online learning. Offers addiction counseling (MA); applied studies (MA, MCJ, MHS, MSW); clinical social work (MSW); criminal justice and legal studies (MCJ); health care education (MHS).

School of Business *Program availability:* Part-time, evening/weekend. Offers accountancy (M Acc). Electronic applications accepted.

School of Law Offers global legal studies (LL M); law (MSL, JD). Electronic applications accepted.

School of Nursing *Program availability:* Part-time. Offers clinical nurse leader (MSN); nursing (DNP); psychiatric mental health nurse practitioner (Post-Graduate Certificate).

WASHINGTON ADVENTIST UNIVERSITY, Takoma Park, MD 20912

General Information Independent-religious, coed, comprehensive institution. *Graduate housing:* Rooms and/or apartments available on a first-come, first-served basis to single and married students. Housing application deadline: 8/1.

GRADUATE UNITS

MBA Program *Program availability:* Part-time, evening/weekend, online learning. Offers business administration (MBA).

Program in Counseling Psychology *Program availability:* Part-time. Offers counseling psychology (MA).

Program in Health Care Administration *Program availability:* Part-time. Offers health care administration (MA). Electronic applications accepted.

Program in Nursing - Business Leadership *Program availability:* Part-time. Offers nursing - business leadership (MSN).

Program in Nursing - Education *Program availability:* Part-time. Offers nursing - education (MS).

Program in Professional Counseling Psychology *Program availability:* Part-time. Offers professional counseling psychology (MA).

Program in Public Administration *Program availability:* Part-time. Offers public administration (MPA).

Program in Religion *Program availability:* Part-time. Offers religion (MAR).

WASHINGTON & JEFFERSON COLLEGE, Washington, PA 15301

General Information Independent, coed, comprehensive institution.

GRADUATE UNITS

Graduate and Continuing Studies

WASHINGTON AND LEE UNIVERSITY, Lexington, VA 24450

General Information Independent, coed, comprehensive institution. *Research affiliation:* Future of Privacy Forum (data privacy, data security, and related fields).

GRADUATE UNITS

School of Law Offers law (JD). Electronic applications accepted.

WASHINGTON STATE UNIVERSITY, Pullman, WA 99164

General Information State-supported, coed, university. CGS member. *Graduate housing:* Rooms and/or apartments available on a first-come, first-served basis to single and married students. Housing application deadline: 3/1. *Research affiliation:* Battelle–Pacific Northwest National Laboratory (biochemistry, engineering).

GRADUATE UNITS

Carson College of Business *Program availability:* Online learning. Offers accounting (M Acc); business (M Acc, MBA, PhD). Programs also offered at the Tri-Cities, Vancouver, and Global (online) campuses.

College of Agricultural, Human, and Natural Resource Sciences *Program availability:* Part-time, online learning. Offers agricultural, human, and natural resource sciences (MA, MS, PhD, Graduate Certificate); animal sciences (MS, PhD); apparel, merchandising, design, and textiles (MA); biological and agricultural engineering (MS, PhD); crop sciences (MS, PhD); entomology (MS, PhD); horticulture (MS, PhD); interior design and landscape architecture (MA, MS); plant pathology (MS, PhD); prevention science (PhD); soil sciences (MS, PhD). Programs also offered at the Global (online) campuses. Electronic applications accepted.

School of Economic Sciences Offers agricultural economics (PhD); economics (PhD). Programs offered at the Pullman campus. Electronic applications accepted.

School of Food Science *Program availability:* Part-time. Offers food science (MS, PhD). Programs offered at the Pullman campus. Electronic applications accepted.

School of the Environment Offers environmental and natural resource sciences (PhD); natural resource sciences (MS). Program applications must be made through the Pullman campus.

College of Arts and Sciences Offers American studies (MA, PhD); applied mathematics (MS, PhD); archaeology (MA, PhD); arts and sciences (MA, MFA, MPA, MS, PhD, Graduate Certificate); chemistry (MS, PhD); clinical psychology (PhD); criminal justice and criminology (MA, PhD); cultural anthropology (PhD); English (MA, PhD); evolutionary anthropology (MA, PhD); experimental psychology (PhD); fine arts (MFA); foreign languages and cultures (MA); history (MA, PhD); mathematics (MS, PhD); mathematics teaching (MS, PhD); physics and astronomy (MS, PhD); sociology (MA, PhD). Electronic applications accepted.

School of Biological Sciences Offers biological sciences (MS, PhD). Programs are offered at the Pullman campus.

School of Music *Program availability:* Part-time. Offers music (MA). Electronic applications accepted.

School of Politics, Philosophy and Public Affairs *Program availability:* Online learning. Offers bioethics (Graduate Certificate); political science (MA, PhD); public affairs (MPA). MPA, MA, and PhD programs also offered at the Vancouver campus; Graduate Certificate offered through Global (online) campus. Electronic applications accepted.

School of the Environment Offers environmental and natural resource sciences (PhD); environmental science (MS); geology (MS, PhD); natural resource science (MS).

College of Education Offers counseling psychology (PhD); cultural studies and social thought in education (PhD); curriculum and instruction (Ed M, MA); education (Ed M, MA, MIT, Ed D, PhD); educational leadership (Ed M, MA, Ed D, PhD); educational psychology (MA, PhD); English language learners (Ed M, MA); language, literacy and technology (PhD); literacy education (Ed M, MA); mathematics education (MA); special education (Ed M, MA, PhD); sport management (MA); teacher leadership (Ed D); teaching (MIT). Electronic applications accepted.

College of Nursing Offers advanced population health (MN, DNP); family nurse practitioner (MN, DNP); nursing (PhD); psychiatric/mental health nurse practitioner (DNP); psychiatric/mental health practitioner (MN). Programs offered at the Spokane, Tri-Cities, and Vancouver campuses.

College of Pharmacy and Pharmaceutical Sciences Offers health policy and administration (MHPA); nutrition and exercise physiology (MS); pharmacy (Pharm D). Programs offered at the Spokane campus.

College of Veterinary Medicine Offers clinical and translational science (MS, PhD); immunology and infectious diseases (MS, PhD); molecular biosciences (MS, PhD); neuroscience (MS, PhD); veterinary medicine (MS, DVM, PhD). Electronic applications accepted.

The Edward R. Murrow College of Communication Offers communication (MA, PhD); strategic communication (MA). MA in strategic communication offered at the Global (online) campus. Electronic applications accepted.

Elson S. Floyd College of Medicine Offers medicine (MS, MD); speech and hearing sciences (MS).

Voiland College of Engineering and Architecture Offers architecture (M Arch); civil engineering (MS, PhD); engineering and architecture (M Arch, METM, MS, PhD, Certificate); engineering and computer science (MS); engineering and technology management (METM, Certificate); environmental engineering (MS).

The Gene and Linda Voiland School of Chemical Engineering and Bioengineering Offers chemical engineering and bioengineering (MS, PhD).

School of Electrical Engineering and Computer Science *Program availability:* Part-time. Offers computer engineering (MS); computer science (MS); electrical engineering (MS); electrical engineering and computer science (PhD); electrical power engineering (MS). MS programs in computer engineering, computer science and electrical engineering also offered at Tri-Cities campus; MS in electrical power engineering offered at the Global (online) campus.

School of Mechanical and Materials Engineering *Program availability:* Part-time. Offers materials science and engineering (MS, PhD); mechanical engineering (MS, PhD). MS programs also offered at Tri-Cities campus. Electronic applications accepted.

WASHINGTON UNIVERSITY IN ST. LOUIS, St. Louis, MO 63130-4899

General Information Independent, coed, university. CGS member. *Graduate housing:* Rooms and/or apartments available on a first-come, first-served basis to single and married students.

GRADUATE UNITS

Brown School Offers American Indian/Alaska native (MSW); children, youth and families (MSW); epidemiology/biostatistics (MPH); generalist (MPH); global health

(MPH); health (MSW); health policy analysis (MPH); individualized (MSW); mental health (MSW); older adults and aging societies (MSW); public health sciences (PhD); social and economic development (MSW); social work (MSW); urban design (MPH); violence and injury prevention (MSW). MSW/M Div and MSW/MAPS offered in partnership with Eden Theological Seminary. Electronic applications accepted.

The Graduate School Offers aging and development (PhD); anthropology (PhD); art history and archaeology (AM, PhD); chemistry (PhD); Chinese (MA); Chinese and comparative literature (PhD); Chinese language and literature (PhD); classics (MA, PhD); comparative literature (PhD); dance (MFA); earth and planetary sciences (PhD); East Asian studies (MA); economics (PhD); educational research (PhD); elementary education (MA Ed); English and American literature (PhD); French (PhD); French and comparative literature (PhD); French language and literature (PhD); Germanic languages and literatures (PhD); Hispanic languages and literatures (PhD); history (PhD); Islamic and Near Eastern studies (MA); Japanese (MA); Japanese and comparative literature (PhD); Japanese language and literature (PhD); Jewish studies (MA); mathematics (MA, PhD); music (MA, PhD); philosophy (PhD); philosophy-neuroscience-psychology (PhD); physics (PhD); political science (PhD); secondary education (MAT); Spanish (PhD); Spanish and comparative literature (PhD); statistics (MA, PhD); theater and performance studies (MA); writing (MFA). Electronic applications accepted.

Division of Biology and Biomedical Sciences Offers biochemistry (PhD); computational and molecular biophysics (PhD); computational and systems biology (PhD); developmental, regenerative, and stem cell biology (PhD); ecology (PhD); evolution, ecology and population biology (PhD); human and statistical genetics (PhD); immunology (PhD); molecular cell biology (PhD); molecular genetics and genomics (PhD); molecular microbiology and microbial pathogenesis (PhD); neurosciences (PhD); plant and microbial biosciences (PhD). Electronic applications accepted.

Olin Business School Students: 904 full-time (487 women), 541 part-time (189 women); includes 260 minority (52 Black or African American, non-Hispanic/Latino; 160 Asian, non-Hispanic/Latino; 31 Hispanic/Latino; 2 Native Hawaiian or other Pacific Islander, non-Hispanic/Latino; 15 Two or more races, non-Hispanic/Latino), 698 international. 4,556 applicants, 31% accepted, 644 enrolled. *Faculty*: 85 full-time (16 women), 46 part-time/adjunct (13 women). Expenses: Contact institution. Offers accounting (MS); business (EMBA, M Acc, MBA, MS, DBA, PhD); business administration (EMBA, MBA, PhD); corporate finance and investments (MS); customer analytics (MS); leadership (MS); marketing (DBA); quantitative finance (MS); supply chain management (MS). Electronic applications accepted. *Application Contact:* Graduate Admissions, 314-935-7301, Fax: 314-935-4464, E-mail: OlinGradAdmissions@wustl.edu. *Dean*, Dr. Mark P. Taylor, 314-935-6344, Fax: 314-300-0827.

Sam Fox School of Design and Visual Arts Offers architecture (M Arch, MLA); design and visual arts (M Arch, MFA, MLA, MUD); landscape architecture (MLA); urban design (MUD).

Graduate School of Art Offers visual art (MFA). Electronic applications accepted.

School of Engineering and Applied Science *Program availability:* Part-time, evening/weekend. Offers aerospace engineering (MS, PhD); biomedical engineering (MS, D Sc, PhD); chemical engineering (MS, D Sc); computer engineering (MS, PhD); computer science (MS, PhD); computer science and engineering (M Eng); engineering and applied science (M Eng, MCE, MCM, MEM, MIM, MPM, MS, MSEE, MSEE, MSI, D Sc, PhD); environmental engineering (MS, D Sc); materials science (MS); mechanical engineering (M Eng, MS, PhD). Electronic applications accepted.

School of Law Offers law (LL M, MJS, JD, JSD). Electronic applications accepted.

School of Medicine Students: 1,173 full-time (790 women), 93 part-time (49 women); includes 370 minority (34 Black or African American, non-Hispanic/Latino; 4 American Indian or Alaska Native, non-Hispanic/Latino; 211 Asian, non-Hispanic/Latino; 54 Hispanic/Latino; 1 Native Hawaiian or other Pacific Islander, non-Hispanic/Latino; 66 Two or more races, non-Hispanic/Latino), 66 international. Average age 23. 5,032 applicants, 7% accepted, 124 enrolled. Expenses: Contact institution. *Financial support:* Applicants required to submit FAFSA. In 2018, 133 master's, 207 doctorates awarded. Offers applied health behavior research (MS); audiology (Au D); clinical epidemiology (MPHS); clinical investigation (MS); deaf education (MS); health behavior planning and evaluation (Graduate Certificate); health services (MPHS); medicine (MS, MSOT, Au D, DPT, MD, OTD, PPDPT, PhD, Graduate Certificate); movement science (PhD); occupational therapy (MSOT, OTD); physical therapy (DPT); psychiatric and behavioral health sciences (MPHS); quantitative methods (MPHS); rehabilitation and participation science (PhD); speech and hearing sciences (PhD). MD/MPH offered jointly with Brown School. *Application deadline:* For fall admission, 12/31 for domestic and international students. Applications are processed on a rolling basis. *Application fee:* $100. Electronic applications accepted. *Application Contact:* Dr. Valerie Ratts, Associate Dean for Admissions, 314-362-6844, Fax: 314-362-4658, E-mail: wusmcoa@wustl.edu. *Executive Vice Chancellor for Medical Affairs/Dean of the School of Medicine*, Dr. David H. Perlmutter, 314-362-6828.

Division of Biostatistics *Program availability:* Part-time. Offers biostatistics (MS); genetic epidemiology (Certificate). Electronic applications accepted.

See Close-Up on page 747.

WATKINS COLLEGE OF ART, DESIGN, & FILM, Nashville, TN 37228

General Information Independent, coed, comprehensive institution.

GRADUATE UNITS

Program in Film *Program availability:* Evening/weekend. Offers film (MFA).

WAYLAND BAPTIST UNIVERSITY, Plainview, TX 79072-6998

General Information Independent-religious, coed, comprehensive institution. *Graduate housing:* Rooms and/or apartments available on a first-come, first-served basis to single and married students.

GRADUATE UNITS

Graduate Programs *Program availability:* Part-time, evening/weekend, 100% online, blended/hybrid learning. Offers accounting (MBA); Christian ministry (MCM); counseling (MA); criminal justice (MACJ); divinity (M Div); education administration (M Ed); education diagnostics (M Ed); education literacy (M Ed); elementary certification (M Ed); English (M Ed); English as a second language (M Ed); general business (MBA); government administration (MPA); health care administration (MAM, MBA); higher education administration (M Ed); history (MA); homeland security (MPA); human resource management (MAM, MBA); human resources (M Ed); humanities (MAH); instructional leadership (M Ed); instructional technology (M Ed); international management (MBA); justice administration (MPA); leadership training and development (M Ed); management (MBA, D Mgt); management information systems (MBA);

organization management (MAM); project management (MBA); religion (MA); science education (M Ed); secondary certification (M Ed); social studies (M Ed); special education (M Ed); sports administration and management (M Ed). Electronic applications accepted.

WAYNESBURG UNIVERSITY, Waynesburg, PA 15370-1222

General Information Independent-religious, coed, comprehensive institution. *Graduate housing:* Room and/or apartments available on a first-come, first-served basis to single students; on-campus housing not available to married students. Housing application deadline: 8/1.

GRADUATE UNITS

Graduate and Professional Studies *Program availability:* Part-time, evening/weekend. Offers business (MBA); counseling (MA); counselor education and supervision (PhD); criminal investigation (MA); education (M Ed); nursing (MSN); nursing practice (DNP); special education (M Ed); technology (M Ed). Electronic applications accepted.

WAYNE STATE COLLEGE, Wayne, NE 68787

General Information State-supported, coed, comprehensive institution. CGS member. *Graduate housing:* Room or apartments available on a first-come, first-served basis to single students; on-campus housing not available to married students. *Research affiliation:* Social Sciences Research Center, Nebraska Business Development Center.

GRADUATE UNITS

Department of Health, Human Performance and Sport *Program availability:* Part-time, evening/weekend. Offers exercise science (MSE); organizational management (MS). Electronic applications accepted.

School of Business and Technology *Program availability:* Part-time, evening/weekend, online learning. Offers business and technology (MBA).

School of Education and Counseling *Program availability:* Part-time, evening/weekend. Offers alternative education (MSE); business and information technology education (MSE); communication arts education (MSE); counseling (MSE); counselor education (MSE); curriculum and instruction (MSE); early childhood education (MSE); education and counseling (MSE, Ed S); educational administration (MSE, Ed S); elementary administration (MSE); elementary and secondary administration (MSE); elementary education (MSE); English as a second language (MSE); English education (MSE); family and consumer sciences education (MSE); guidance and counseling (MSE); industrial technology and vocational education (MSE); learning communities (MSE); mathematics education (MSE); music education (MSE); school counseling (MSE); science education (MSE); secondary administration (MSE); social science education (MSE); special education (MSE).

WAYNE STATE UNIVERSITY, Detroit, MI 48202

General Information State-supported, coed, university. CGS member. *Enrollment:* 5,777 full-time matriculated graduate/professional students (3,256 women), 3,601 part-time matriculated graduate/professional students (2,126 women). *Enrollment by degree level:* 5,431 master's, 3,689 doctoral, 258 other advanced degrees. *Graduate faculty:* 804. *Graduate housing:* Rooms and/or apartments available on a first-come, first-served basis to single and married students. *Student services:* Campus employment opportunities, campus safety program, career counseling, child daycare facilities, exercise/wellness program, free psychological counseling, grant writing training, international student services, multicultural affairs office, services for students with disabilities, teacher training, writing training. *Library facilities:* David Adamany Undergraduate Library plus 5 others. *Collection:* Books: 1.7 million (physical), 1 million (digital/electronic); Serial titles: 60,832 (physical), 112,521 (digital/electronic); Databases: 700. Weekly public service hours: 138; study areas open 24 hours, 5–7 days a week.

Computer facilities: A campuswide network can be accessed from student residence rooms. Online class registration is available.
Website: http://www.wayne.edu/

General Application Contact: Sherry Quinn, Office of Graduate Admissions, 313-577-8141, Fax: 313-625-6053, E-mail: gradadmissions@wayne.edu.

GRADUATE UNITS

College of Education Students: 426 full-time (307 women), 926 part-time (692 women); includes 511 minority (382 Black or African American, non-Hispanic/Latino; 3 American Indian or Alaska Native, non-Hispanic/Latino; 22 Asian, non-Hispanic/Latino; 44 Hispanic/Latino; 2 Native Hawaiian or other Pacific Islander, non-Hispanic/Latino; 58 Two or more races, non-Hispanic/Latino), 52 international. Average age 35. 919 applicants, 36% accepted, 228 enrolled. *Faculty*: 46. Expenses: Contact institution. *Financial support:* In 2018–19, 303 students received support, including 4 fellowships with tuition reimbursements available (averaging $13,500 per year), 13 research assistantships with tuition reimbursements available (averaging $18,339 per year), 5 teaching assistantships with tuition reimbursements available (averaging $18,534 per year); Federal Work-Study, scholarships/grants, traineeships, health care benefits, and unspecified assistantships also available. Support available to part-time students. Financial award applicants required to submit FAFSA. In 2018, 322 master's, 53 doctorates, 64 other advanced degrees awarded. *Program availability:* Part-time, evening/weekend, 100% online, blended/hybrid learning. Offers athletic training (MSAT); education (M Ed, MA, MAT, MSAT, Ed D, PhD, Certificate, Ed S); health education (M Ed); kinesiology (M Ed, PhD); sports administration (MA). *Application deadline:* For fall admission, 6/1 priority date for domestic students, 5/1 for international students; for winter admission, 10/1 priority date for domestic students, 9/1 priority date for international students; for spring admission, 2/1 priority date for domestic students, 1/1 priority date for international students. *Application fee:* $50. Electronic applications accepted. *Application Contact:* Paul W. Johnson, Assistant Dean of Academic Services, 313-577-1606, E-mail: askcoe@wayne.edu. *Dean*, Dr. R. Douglas Whitman, 313-577-1620, E-mail: dwhitman@wayne.edu.

Division of Administrative and Organizational Studies Students: 77 full-time (53 women), 223 part-time (160 women); includes 155 minority (126 Black or African American, non-Hispanic/Latino; 7 Asian, non-Hispanic/Latino; 11 Hispanic/Latino; 1 Native Hawaiian or other Pacific Islander, non-Hispanic/Latino; 10 Two or more races, non-Hispanic/Latino), 9 international. Average age 39. 239 applicants, 33% accepted, 58 enrolled. *Faculty*: 9. Expenses: Contact institution. *Financial support:* In 2018–19, 87 students received support, including 1 fellowship with tuition reimbursement available (averaging $20,000 per year), 4 research assistantships with tuition reimbursements available (averaging $19,267 per year); scholarships/grants and unspecified assistantships also available. Support available to part-time students. Financial award applicants required to submit FAFSA. In 2018, 51 master's, 10 doctorates, 54 other advanced degrees awarded. *Program availability:* Part-time, evening/weekend. Offers educational administration and supervision (Ed S); educational leadership (M Ed); educational leadership and policy studies (Ed D, PhD);

educational technology (Certificate); learning design and technology (M Ed, Ed D, PhD, Ed S); online teaching (Certificate). *Application deadline:* Applications are processed on a rolling basis. *Application fee:* $50. Electronic applications accepted. *Application Contact:* Dr. Mary L. Waker, Graduate Admissions Officer, 313-577-1601, Fax: 313-577-7904, E-mail: m.waker@wayne.edu. *Assistant Dean,* Dr. William Hill, 313-577-9316, E-mail: ad2107@wayne.edu.

Division of Teacher Education Students: 121 full-time (94 women), 251 part-time (209 women); includes 116 minority (83 Black or African American, non-Hispanic/Latino; 3 American Indian or Alaska Native, non-Hispanic/Latino; 3 Asian, non-Hispanic/Latino; 14 Hispanic/Latino; 13 Two or more races, non-Hispanic/Latino; 11 international. Average age 37. 171 applicants, 23% accepted, 32 enrolled. *Faculty:* 20. Expenses: Contact institution. *Financial support:* In 2018–19, 85 students received support, including 3 fellowships (averaging $14,275 per year); research assistantships with tuition reimbursements available, Federal Work-Study, scholarships/grants, and unspecified assistantships also available. Support available to part-time students. Financial award applicants required to submit FAFSA. In 2018, 112 master's, 8 doctorates, 11 other advanced degrees awarded. *Program availability:* Part-time, evening/weekend. Offers art education (M Ed); bilingual/bicultural education (Certificate); curriculum and instruction (Ed D, PhD, Ed S); elementary education (MAT); elementary mathematics specialist (Certificate); English as a second language (Certificate); reading (M Ed, Ed S); reading, language and literature (Ed D); secondary education (MAT); special education (MAT); teaching and learning (M Ed). *Application deadline:* Applications are processed on a rolling basis. *Application fee:* $50. Electronic applications accepted. *Application Contact:* Dr. Mary L. Waker, Graduate Admissions Officer, 313-577-1601, Fax: 313-577-7904, E-mail: m.waker@wayne.edu. *Assistant Dean for Teacher Education,* Dr. Roland Coloma, 313-577-0902, E-mail: rscoloma@wayne.edu.

Division of Theoretical and Behavioral Foundations Students: 168 full-time (136 women), 200 part-time (171 women); includes 128 minority (82 Black or African American, non-Hispanic/Latino; 2 American Indian or Alaska Native, non-Hispanic/Latino; 8 Asian, non-Hispanic/Latino; 12 Hispanic/Latino; 24 Two or more races, non-Hispanic/Latino), 14 international. Average age 32. 340 applicants, 24% accepted, 66 enrolled. *Faculty:* 9. Expenses: Contact institution. *Financial support:* In 2018–19, 86 students received support, including 2 research assistantships with tuition reimbursements available (averaging $19,267 per year); fellowships, teaching assistantships, Federal Work-Study, scholarships/grants, health care benefits, and unspecified assistantships also available. Support available to part-time students. Financial award applicants required to submit FAFSA. In 2018, 103 master's, 6 doctorates, 18 other advanced degrees awarded. *Program availability:* Part-time, evening/weekend. Offers applied behavior analysis (Certificate); counseling (M Ed, MA, Ed D, Ed S); counseling psychology (MA, PhD); education evaluation and research (M Ed, Ed D); educational psychology (M Ed, PhD); rehabilitation counseling and community inclusion (MA); school and community psychology (MA, Certificate). *Application deadline:* Applications are processed on a rolling basis. *Application fee:* $50. Electronic applications accepted. *Application Contact:* Dr. Mary L Waker, Graduate Admissions Officer, 313-577-1601, Fax: 313-577-7904, E-mail: m.waker@wayne.edu. *Assistant Dean,* Dr. Cheryl Somers, 313-577-1670, E-mail: c.somers@wayne.edu.

College of Engineering Students: 741 full-time (196 women), 390 part-time (99 women); includes 139 minority (49 Black or African American, non-Hispanic/Latino; 65 Asian, non-Hispanic/Latino; 21 Hispanic/Latino; 4 Two or more races, non-Hispanic/Latino), 655 international. Average age 28. 1,916 applicants, 40% accepted, 289 enrolled. *Faculty:* 110. Expenses: Contact institution. *Financial support:* In 2018–19, 538 students received support, including 23 fellowships with tuition reimbursements available (averaging $20,935 per year), 66 research assistantships with tuition reimbursements available (averaging $20,907 per year), 82 teaching assistantships with tuition reimbursements available (averaging $20,204 per year); Federal Work-Study, scholarships/grants, health care benefits, tuition waivers (full and partial), and unspecified assistantships also available. Support available to part-time students. Financial award applicants required to submit FAFSA. In 2018, 584 master's, 47 doctorates, 1 other advanced degree awarded. *Program availability:* Part-time, evening/weekend. Offers alternative energy technology (MS, Graduate Certificate); biomedical engineering (MS, PhD); chemical engineering (MS, PhD); civil engineering (MS); computer engineering (MS, PhD); computer science (MS, PhD); data science and business analytics (MS); electric-drive vehicle engineering (MS, Graduate Certificate); electrical engineering (MS, PhD); engineering (MS, MSET, PhD, Certificate, Graduate Certificate, Postbaccalaureate Certificate); engineering management (MS); industrial engineering (MS, PhD); injury biomechanics (Graduate Certificate); manufacturing engineering (MS); materials science and engineering (MS, PhD); mechanical engineering (MS, PhD); polymer engineering (Graduate Certificate); systems engineering (Certificate). *Application deadline:* For fall admission, 7/15 priority date for domestic students, 5/15 priority date for international students; for winter admission, 11/1 priority date for domestic students, 10/1 priority date for international students; for spring admission, 2/1 priority date for domestic students, 1/1 priority date for international students. Applications are processed on a rolling basis. *Application fee:* $50. Electronic applications accepted. *Application Contact:* Graduate Program Coordinator, E-mail: engineeringgradadmissions@eng.wayne.edu. *Dean,* Dr. Farshad Fotouhi, 313-577-3776, E-mail: fotouhi@wayne.edu.

Division of Engineering Technology Students: 10 full-time (0 women), 8 part-time (1 woman); includes 7 minority (5 Black or African American, non-Hispanic/Latino; 1 Asian, non-Hispanic/Latino; 1 Hispanic/Latino), 4 international. Average age 35. 23 applicants, 57% accepted, 6 enrolled. *Faculty:* 4. Expenses: Contact institution. *Financial support:* In 2018–19, 7 students received support. Career-related internships or fieldwork and scholarships/grants available. Financial award applicants required to submit FAFSA. In 2018, 6 master's awarded. Offers engineering technology (MSET). *Application deadline:* For fall admission, 6/1 priority date for domestic students, 5/1 priority date for international students; for winter admission, 10/1 priority date for domestic students, 9/1 priority date for international students; for spring admission, 2/1 priority date for domestic students, 1/1 priority date for international students. Applications are processed on a rolling basis. *Application fee:* $50. Electronic applications accepted. *Application Contact:* Ellen Cope, Graduate Program Coordinator, 313-577-0409, E-mail: escope@wayne.edu. *Division Chair,* Dr. Ece Yaprak, 313-577-0875, E-mail: yaprak@eng.wayne.edu.

College of Fine, Performing and Communication Arts Students: 130 full-time (76 women), 109 part-time (75 women); includes 68 minority (51 Black or African American, non-Hispanic/Latino; 1 Asian, non-Hispanic/Latino; 6 Hispanic/Latino; 10 Two or more races, non-Hispanic/Latino), 15 international. Average age 33. 341 applicants, 35% accepted, 77 enrolled. *Faculty:* 28. Expenses: Contact institution. *Financial support:* In 2018–19, 123 students received support, including 6 fellowships with tuition reimbursements available (averaging $21,250 per year), 32 research assistantships with

tuition reimbursements available (averaging $19,373 per year), 28 teaching assistantships with tuition reimbursements available (averaging $19,356 per year); career-related internships or fieldwork, scholarships/grants, health care benefits, and unspecified assistantships also available. Financial award applicants required to submit FAFSA. In 2018, 74 master's, 8 doctorates, 3 other advanced degrees awarded. *Program availability:* Online learning. Offers art (MA, MFA); art history (MA); communication (PhD); communication and new media (Graduate Certificate); communication studies (MA); composition/theory (MA, MM); conducting (MA, MM); dispute resolution (MADR, Graduate Certificate); fine, performing and communication arts (MA, MADR, MFA, MM, PhD, Graduate Certificate); health communication (Graduate Certificate); jazz performance (MA, MM); journalism (MA); media arts (MA); media studies (MA); music education (MA, MM); orchestral studies (Certificate); performance (MA, MM); public relations and organizational communication (MA); theatre (MFA); theatre and dance (MA). *Application deadline:* For fall admission, 6/1 priority date for domestic students, 5/1 priority date for international students; for winter admission, 10/1 priority date for domestic students, 9/1 priority date for international students; for spring admission, 2/1 priority date for domestic students, 1/1 priority date for international students. Applications are processed on a rolling basis. *Application fee:* $50. Electronic applications accepted. *Application Contact:* Lezlie Hart, Associate Director of Student Services, 313-577-5337, E-mail: aa3266@wayne.edu. *Dean,* Dr. Matthew Seeger, 313-577-5342, Fax: 313-577-5342, E-mail: matthew.seeger@wayne.edu.

College of Liberal Arts and Sciences Students: 838 full-time (474 women), 326 part-time (193 women); includes 216 minority (108 Black or African American, non-Hispanic/Latino; 2 American Indian or Alaska Native, non-Hispanic/Latino; 26 Asian, non-Hispanic/Latino; 43 Hispanic/Latino; 2 Native Hawaiian or other Pacific Islander, non-Hispanic/Latino; 35 Two or more races, non-Hispanic/Latino), 239 international. Average age 31. 2,216 applicants, 25% accepted, 304 enrolled. *Faculty:* 279. Expenses: Contact institution. *Financial support:* In 2018–19, 674 students received support, including 79 fellowships with tuition reimbursements available (averaging $17,231 per year), 92 research assistantships with tuition reimbursements available (averaging $21,265 per year), 329 teaching assistantships with tuition reimbursements available (averaging $20,203 per year); scholarships/grants, health care benefits, and unspecified assistantships also available. Support available to part-time students. Financial award applicants required to submit FAFSA. In 2018, 225 master's, 93 doctorates, 2 other advanced degrees awarded. *Program availability:* Part-time, evening/weekend, online learning. Offers analytical chemistry (PhD); anthropology (MA, PhD); applied macroeconomics (MA, PhD); applied mathematics (MA); applied sociological research methodology (MA); audiology (Au D); behavioral and cognitive neuroscience (PhD); biological sciences (MA, MS, PhD); chemistry (MA, MS); classics (MA); clinical psychology (PhD); communication disorders and science (PhD); criminal justice (MS); developmental science (PhD); dietetics (Postbaccalaureate Certificate); economic development (Graduate Certificate); English (PhD); film and media studies (PhD); food science (PhD); geology (MS); German (MA); health economics (MA, PhD); history (MA, PhD); industrial organization (MA, PhD); industrial/organizational psychology (MA, PhD); international economics (MA, PhD); labor and human resources (MA, PhD); language learning (MALL); liberal arts and sciences (MA, MALL, MPA, MS, MUP, Au D, PhD, Graduate Certificate, Postbaccalaureate Certificate); linguistics (MA); literary and cultural studies (PhD); mathematical statistics (MA); mathematics (MA, MS, PhD); medical sociology/health (PhD); modern languages (PhD); molecular biotechnology (MS); Near Eastern languages (MA); nutrition (PhD); nutrition and food science (MA, MS); philosophy (MA, PhD); physics (MA, MS, PhD); political science (MA, PhD); public administration (MPA); public history (MA); race/gender inequality (PhD); rhetoric and composition studies (PhD); Romance languages (MA); social personality (PhD); social work (PhD); sociology (MA); speech-language pathology (MA); urban studies and planning (MUP); urban/labor studies (PhD); world history (Graduate Certificate). *Application deadline:* For fall admission, 6/1 priority date for domestic students, 5/1 priority date for international students; for winter admission, 10/1 priority date for domestic students, 9/1 priority date for international students; for spring admission, 2/1 priority date for domestic students, 1/1 priority date for international students. Applications are processed on a rolling basis. *Application fee:* $50. Electronic applications accepted. *Application Contact:* Deirdre Baker, Director, Graduate Admissions, 313-577-8141, E-mail: gradadmissions@wayne.edu. *Dean,* Wayne Raskind, 313-577-2519, E-mail: raskind@wayne.edu.

College of Nursing Students: 138 full-time (127 women), 181 part-time (159 women); includes 80 minority (46 Black or African American, non-Hispanic/Latino; 1 American Indian or Alaska Native, non-Hispanic/Latino; 18 Asian, non-Hispanic/Latino; 5 Hispanic/Latino; 10 Two or more races, non-Hispanic/Latino), 19 international. Average age 34. 423 applicants, 35% accepted, 90 enrolled. *Faculty:* 32. Expenses: Contact institution. *Financial support:* In 2018–19, 80 students received support, including 34 fellowships with tuition reimbursements available (averaging $7,305 per year), 1 research assistantship (averaging $23,472 per year), 5 teaching assistantships with tuition reimbursements available (averaging $25,000 per year); scholarships/grants, health care benefits, and unspecified assistantships also available. Support available to part-time students. Financial award applicants required to submit FAFSA. In 2018, 60 master's, 27 doctorates awarded. *Program availability:* Part-time. Offers adult gerontology acute care nurse practitioner (MSN); adult gerontology primary care nurse practitioner (MSN); advanced public health nursing (MSN); infant and mental health (DNP, PhD); neonatal nurse practitioner (MSN); nurse-midwifery (MSN); pediatric acute care nurse practitioner (MSN); pediatric primary care nurse practitioner (MSN); psychiatric mental health nurse practitioner (MSN); women's health nurse practitioner (MSN). Doctoral program admits for fall only. *Application fee:* $50. Electronic applications accepted. *Application Contact:* Dr. Laurie Lauzon Clabo, Dean, College of Nursing, 313-577-4082, E-mail: laurie.lauzon.clabo@wayne.edu. *Dean, College of Nursing,* Dr. Laurie Lauzon Clabo, 313-577-4082, E-mail: laurie.lauzon.clabo@wayne.edu.

Eugene Applebaum College of Pharmacy and Health Sciences Students: 772 full-time (494 women), 10 part-time (5 women); includes 112 minority (23 Black or African American, non-Hispanic/Latino; 60 Asian, non-Hispanic/Latino; 18 Hispanic/Latino; 1 Native Hawaiian or other Pacific Islander, non-Hispanic/Latino; 10 Two or more races, non-Hispanic/Latino), 57 international. Average age 25. 544 applicants, 37% accepted, 157 enrolled. *Faculty:* 26. Expenses: Contact institution. *Financial support:* In 2018–19, 236 students received support, including 2 fellowships with tuition reimbursements available (averaging $39,750 per year), 15 research assistantships with tuition reimbursements available (averaging $25,000 per year); scholarships/grants, health care benefits, and unspecified assistantships also available. Financial award application deadline: 3/31; financial award applicants required to submit FAFSA. In 2018, 112 master's, 142 doctorates awarded. *Program availability:* Part-time, evening/weekend. Offers anesthesia (MS); medicinal chemistry (MS, PhD); nurse anesthesia (MS, DNP-A, Certificate); nurse anesthesia practice (DNP-A); occupational therapy (MOT); pediatric anesthesia (Certificate); pharmaceutics (MS, PhD); pharmacology and toxicology (MS, PhD); pharmacy (Pharm D); pharmacy and health sciences (MOT, MS, DPT, PhD,

Pharm D, Certificate); physical therapy (DPT); physician assistant studies (MS). *Application fee:* $50. Electronic applications accepted. *Application Contact:* Dr. Mary K. Clark, Assistant Dean, Office of Student and Alumni Affairs, 313-577-1716, E-mail: cphsinfo@wayne.edu. *Interim Dean,* Dr. Catherine Lysack, 313-577-1716, E-mail: c.lysack@wayne.edu.

Law School Students: 406 full-time (198 women), 38 part-time (9 women); includes 51 minority (35 Black or African American, non-Hispanic/Latino; 3 American Indian or Alaska Native, non-Hispanic/Latino; 7 Asian, non-Hispanic/Latino; 1 Hispanic/Latino; 5 Two or more races, non-Hispanic/Latino), 15 international. Average age 26. 859 applicants, 49% accepted, 137 enrolled. *Faculty:* 43 full-time (18 women), 17 part-time/adjunct (9 women). Expenses: Contact institution. *Financial support:* In 2018–19, 365 students received support. Fellowships, Federal Work-Study, and scholarships/grants available. Support available to part-time students. Financial award application deadline: 6/30; financial award applicants required to submit FAFSA. In 2018, 6 master's awarded. *Program availability:* Part-time, evening/weekend. Offers corporate and finance law (LL M); labor and employment law (LL M); law (JD); taxation (LL M); United States law (LL M). *Application deadline:* For fall admission, 7/1 for domestic students. Applications are processed on a rolling basis. *Application fee:* $0. Electronic applications accepted. *Application Contact:* Kathy Fox, Assistant Dean of Admissions, 313-577-3937, Fax: 313-993-8129, E-mail: lawinquire@wayne.edu. *Dean and Professor of Law,* Richard A. Bierschbach, 313-577-3933, E-mail: rbierschbach@wayne.edu.

Mike Ilitch School of Business Students: 286 full-time (152 women), 1,166 part-time (533 women); includes 409 minority (236 Black or African American, non-Hispanic/Latino; 83 Asian, non-Hispanic/Latino; 53 Hispanic/Latino; 37 Two or more races, non-Hispanic/Latino), 74 international. Average age 30. 1,212 applicants, 38% accepted, 294 enrolled. *Faculty:* 31. Expenses: Contact institution. *Financial support:* In 2018–19, 175 students received support, including 1 fellowship with tuition reimbursement available (averaging $20,000 per year), 5 research assistantships with tuition reimbursements available (averaging $21,393 per year); teaching assistantships with tuition reimbursements available, scholarships/grants, health care benefits, and unspecified assistantships also available. Support available to part-time students. Financial award applicants required to submit FAFSA. In 2018, 285 master's, 6 doctorates, 7 other advanced degrees awarded. *Program availability:* Part-time, evening/weekend. Offers accounting (MS, MSA, Postbaccalaureate Certificate); business (EMS, Graduate Certificate); business administration (MBA, PhD); data science (MS); entrepreneurship and innovation (Postbaccalaureate Certificate); finance (MS); information systems management (Postbaccalaureate Certificate); taxation (MST). Application deadline for PhD is February 15. *Application deadline:* For fall admission, 7/1 for domestic students, 5/1 priority date for international students; for winter admission, 11/1 for domestic students, 9/1 priority date for international students; for spring admission, 3/1 for domestic students, 1/1 priority date for international students. Applications are processed on a rolling basis. *Application fee:* $50. Electronic applications accepted. *Application Contact:* Kiantee N. Rupert-Jones, Director, 313-577-4511, Fax: 313-577-9442, E-mail: gradbusiness@wayne.edu. *Dean, School of Business Administration,* Dr. Robert Forsythe, 313-577-4501, E-mail: robert.forsythe@wayne.edu.

School of Information Sciences Students: 85 full-time (74 women), 316 part-time (258 women); includes 77 minority (42 Black or African American, non-Hispanic/Latino; 2 American Indian or Alaska Native, non-Hispanic/Latino; 3 Asian, non-Hispanic/Latino; 19 Hispanic/Latino; 1 Native Hawaiian or other Pacific Islander, non-Hispanic/Latino; 10 Two or more races, non-Hispanic/Latino), 1 international. Average age 33. 258 applicants, 60% accepted, 100 enrolled. *Faculty:* 12 full-time (9 women), 17 part-time/adjunct (12 women). Expenses: Contact institution. *Financial support:* In 2018–19, 133 students received support. Fellowships with tuition reimbursements available, scholarships/grants, health care benefits, and unspecified assistantships available. Support available to part-time students. Financial award applicants required to submit FAFSA. In 2018, 149 master's, 34 other advanced degrees awarded. *Program availability:* Part-time, evening/weekend, 100% online, blended/hybrid learning. Offers archival administration (Graduate Certificate); information management (MS, Graduate Certificate); library and information science (MLIS, Graduate Certificate, Spec); public library services to children and young adults (Graduate Certificate). WSU History Department. *Application deadline:* For fall admission, 7/1 for domestic students, 5/1 priority date for international students; for winter admission, 10/1 priority date for domestic students, 9/1 priority date for international students; for spring admission, 2/1 priority date for domestic students, 1/1 priority date for international students. Applications are processed on a rolling basis. *Application fee:* $50. Electronic applications accepted. *Application Contact:* Academic Services Officer II, 313-577-1825, E-mail: asklis@wayne.edu. *Dean,* Dr. Jon Cawthorne, 313-577-4020, E-mail: jon.cawthorne@wayne.edu.

School of Medicine Students: 1,425 full-time (687 women), 139 part-time (80 women); includes 545 minority (116 Black or African American, non-Hispanic/Latino; 4 American Indian or Alaska Native, non-Hispanic/Latino; 290 Asian, non-Hispanic/Latino; 89 Hispanic/Latino; 36 Two or more races, non-Hispanic/Latino), 100 international. Average age 26. 9,782 applicants, 6% accepted, 432 enrolled. Expenses: Contact institution. *Financial support:* In 2018–19, 1,150 students received support, including 54 fellowships with tuition reimbursements available (averaging $24,438 per year), 102 research assistantships with tuition reimbursements available (averaging $26,944 per year), 1 teaching assistantship (averaging $19,267 per year); Federal Work-Study, scholarships/grants, health care benefits, and unspecified assistantships also available. Support available to part-time students. Financial award applicants required to submit FAFSA. In 2018, 96 master's, 29 doctorates, 307 other advanced degrees awarded. Offers anatomy and cell biology (MS, PhD); basic medical sciences (MS); biochemistry and molecular biology (MS, PhD); cancer biology (MS, PhD); clinical and translational science (Graduate Certificate); family medicine and public health sciences (MPH, Graduate Certificate); genetic counseling (MS); immunology and microbiology (MS, PhD); medical physics (MS, PhD, Graduate Certificate); medical research (MS); medicine (MPH, MS, MD, PhD, Graduate Certificate); molecular medicine and genomics (MS, PhD); pathology (PhD); pharmacology (MS, PhD); physiology (MS, PhD); psychiatry and behavioral neurosciences (PhD). Electronic applications accepted. *Application Contact:* Dr. Kevin Sprague, Associate Dean of Admissions, 313-577-1466. *Dean,* Dr. Jack Sobel, 313-577-1335, Fax: 313-577-8777, E-mail: ad6283@wayne.edu.

School of Social Work Students: 484 full-time, 162 part-time. 708 applicants, 41% accepted. Expenses: Contact institution. *Financial support:* Fellowships with tuition reimbursements, research assistantships with tuition reimbursements, teaching assistantships with tuition reimbursements, scholarships/grants, and unspecified assistantships available. Financial award applicants required to submit FAFSA. *Program availability:* Part-time, evening/weekend. Offers gerontology (Certificate); social work (MSW, PhD). Application deadlines: April 1 for MSW, December 19 for PhD. *Application deadline:* For spring admission, 4/1 for domestic students. Applications are processed on a rolling basis. *Application fee:* $50. Electronic applications accepted. *Application*

Contact: Anwar Najor-Durack, Assistant Dean for Student Affairs, 313-577-4409, E-mail: ac1724@wayne.edu. *Dean and Professor,* Sheryl Kubiak, 313-577-4409, E-mail: spk@wayne.edu.

WEBBER INTERNATIONAL UNIVERSITY, Babson Park, FL 33827-0096

General Information Independent, coed, comprehensive institution. *Enrollment:* 50 full-time matriculated graduate/professional students (29 women), 6 part-time matriculated graduate/professional students (2 women). *Enrollment by degree level:* 56 master's. *Graduate faculty:* 10 full-time (4 women), 1 part-time/adjunct (0 women). *Graduate housing:* Room and/or apartments guaranteed to single students; on-campus housing not available to married students. *Student services:* Campus employment opportunities, campus safety program, career counseling, exercise/wellness program, international student services, services for students with disabilities. *Library facilities:* Grace and Roger Babson Library. *Collection:* Books: 1,041 (physical); Databases: 127. Weekly public service hours: 70; students can reserve study rooms.

Computer facilities: 92 computers available on campus for general student use. A campuswide network can be accessed from off campus. Online class registration is available.

Website: http://www.webber.edu/

General Application Contact: Lacy Edwards, Admissions Counselor/MBA Coordinator, 863-638-2910, Fax: 863-638-1591, E-mail: admissions@webber.edu.

GRADUATE UNITS

Graduate School of Business Students: 69 full-time (34 women), 11 part-time (5 women); includes 26 minority (17 Black or African American, non-Hispanic/Latino; 1 Asian, non-Hispanic/Latino; 8 Hispanic/Latino), 10 international. Average age 24. 64 applicants, 61% accepted, 32 enrolled. *Faculty:* 11 full-time (5 women), 1 part-time/adjunct (0 women). Expenses: Contact institution. *Financial support:* In 2018–19, 11 students received support. Scholarships/grants and unspecified assistantships available. Financial award application deadline: 8/1; financial award applicants required to submit FAFSA. In 2018, 17 master's awarded. *Program availability:* Part-time, evening/weekend, 100% online, blended/hybrid learning. Offers accounting (MBA); business (MBA); criminal justice management (MBA); international business (MBA); sport business management (MBA). *Application deadline:* For fall admission, 8/1 for domestic students, 6/1 for international students; for spring admission, 1/1 for domestic students. Applications are processed on a rolling basis. *Application fee:* $0. Electronic applications accepted. *Application Contact:* Lacy Edwards, Admissions Counselor and MBA Coordinator, 863-638-2910, Fax: 863-638-1591, E-mail: admissions@webber.edu. *Dean,* Dr. Nikos Orphanoudakis, 863-638-2910, Fax: 863-638-1591, E-mail: orphanoudakisn@webber.edu.

WEBER STATE UNIVERSITY, Ogden, UT 84408-1001

General Information State-supported, coed, comprehensive institution. *Enrollment:* 28,247 graduate, professional, and undergraduate students; 330 full-time matriculated graduate/professional students (194 women), 452 part-time matriculated graduate/professional students (245 women). *Enrollment by degree level:* 782 master's. *Graduate faculty:* 110 full-time (53 women), 6 part-time/adjunct (2 women). *Graduate housing:* Room and/or apartments available on a first-come, first-served basis to single students; on-campus housing not available to married students. *Student services:* Campus employment opportunities, campus safety program, career counseling, child daycare facilities, exercise/wellness program, free psychological counseling, grant writing training, international student services, low-cost health insurance, multicultural affairs office, services for students with disabilities, teacher training, writing training. *Library facilities:* Stewart Library. *Collection:* Books: 498,531 (physical); Serial titles: 425 (physical); Databases: 223,410.

Computer facilities: Computer purchase and lease plans are available. 650 computers available on campus for general student use. A campuswide network can be accessed from student residence rooms and from off campus. Online class registration is available.

Website: http://www.weber.edu/

General Application Contact: Scott Teichert, Director of Admissions, 801-626-7670, Fax: 801-626-6045, E-mail: scottteichert@weber.edu.

GRADUATE UNITS

College of Engineering, Applied Science and Technology Students: 6 full-time (1 woman), 9 part-time (0 women); includes 1 minority (Asian, non-Hispanic/Latino), 1 international. Average age 28. *Faculty:* 9 full-time (1 woman). Expenses: Contact institution. *Financial support:* In 2018–19, 1 student received support. In 2018, 3 master's awarded. *Program availability:* Part-time. Offers computer engineering (MS). *Application deadline:* For fall admission, 5/7 for domestic and international students; for spring admission, 11/7 for domestic and international students. Electronic applications accepted. *Application Contact:* Scott Teichert, Director of Admissions, 801-626-7670, Fax: 801-626-6045, E-mail: scottteichert@weber.edu. *Dean,* Dr. David L. Ferro, 801-626-6303, E-mail: dferro@weber.edu.

College of Social and Behavioral Sciences Students: 5 full-time (4 women), 22 part-time (10 women); includes 5 minority (1 American Indian or Alaska Native, non-Hispanic/Latino; 3 Hispanic/Latino; 1 Native Hawaiian or other Pacific Islander, non-Hispanic/Latino). Average age 34. *Faculty:* 6 full-time (1 woman). Expenses: Contact institution. *Financial support:* In 2018–19, 4 students received support. Scholarships/grants available. Financial award application deadline: 4/1; financial award applicants required to submit FAFSA. In 2018, 15 master's awarded. *Program availability:* Part-time, evening/weekend, online only, 100% online. Offers criminal justice (MCJ); social and behavioral sciences (MCJ). *Application deadline:* For fall admission, 7/29 for domestic students; for spring admission, 12/11 for domestic students; for summer admission, 4/1 for domestic students. Applications are processed on a rolling basis. *Application fee:* $60 ($90 for international students). *Application Contact:* Faye Medd, Enrollment Director, 801-626-6146, Fax: 801-626-6145, E-mail: fmedd@weber.edu. *Dean,* Dr. Francis Harrold, 801-626-6232, Fax: 801-626-7130, E-mail: francisharrold@weber.edu.

Dumke College of Health Professions Students: 176 full-time (113 women), 31 part-time (15 women); includes 11 minority (1 Asian, non-Hispanic/Latino; 8 Hispanic/Latino; 2 Two or more races, non-Hispanic/Latino), 1 international. Average age 36. *Faculty:* 21 full-time (15 women), 1 part-time/adjunct (0 women). Expenses: Contact institution. *Financial support:* In 2018–19, 41 students received support. Scholarships/grants available. Financial award application deadline: 4/1; financial award applicants required to submit FAFSA. In 2018, 107 master's awarded. *Program availability:* Part-time, evening/weekend, 100% online. Offers health administration (MHA); health professions (MHA, MSN, MSRS); radiologic sciences (MSRS). *Application deadline:* For fall admission, 3/15 for domestic students, 2/20 for international students. *Application fee:* $60 ($90 for international students). Electronic applications accepted. *Application*

Contact: Ann Gessel, Office Manager, 801-626-7127, Fax: 801-626-7683, E-mail: anngessel@weber.edu. *Dean,* Dr. Yasmin Simonian, 801-626-7117, Fax: 801-626-7683, E-mail: ysimonian@weber.edu.

School of Nursing Students: 87 full-time (72 women), 6 part-time (5 women); includes 5 minority (4 Hispanic/Latino; 1 Two or more races, non-Hispanic/Latino), 1 international. Average age 38. *Faculty:* 10 full-time (all women). Expenses: Contact institution. *Financial support:* In 2018–19, 39 students received support. Scholarships/grants available. Financial award application deadline: 4/1; financial award applicants required to submit FAFSA. In 2018, 39 master's awarded. *Program availability:* Part-time, evening/weekend, 100% online. Offers educator (MSN); executive (MSN); nurse practitioner (MSN). *Application deadline:* For fall admission, 4/1 priority date for domestic students. *Application fee:* $60 ($90 for international students). Electronic applications accepted. *Application Contact:* Robert Holt, Director of Enrollment, 801-626-7774, Fax: 801-626-6397, E-mail: rholt@weber.edu. *MSN Program Director,* Dr. Melissa Neville, 801-626-6204, Fax: 801-626-6397, E-mail: mneville@weber.edu.

Goddard School of Business and Economics Students: 87 full-time (36 women), 168 part-time (56 women); includes 15 minority (1 Black or African American, non-Hispanic/Latino; 1 American Indian or Alaska Native, non-Hispanic/Latino; 3 Asian, non-Hispanic/Latino; 8 Hispanic/Latino; 2 Two or more races, non-Hispanic/Latino), 7 international. Average age 35. *Faculty:* 18 full-time (6 women), 2 part-time/adjunct (0 women). Expenses: Contact institution. *Financial support:* In 2018–19, 36 students received support. Scholarships/grants available. Financial award application deadline: 4/1; financial award applicants required to submit FAFSA. In 2018, 132 master's, 38 other advanced degrees awarded. *Program availability:* Part-time, evening/weekend. Offers business administration (MBA, Graduate Certificate); business and economics (M Acc, M Tax, MBA, Graduate Certificate). *Application deadline:* For fall admission, 5/1 for domestic students; for spring admission, 9/1 for domestic students. *Application fee:* $60 ($90 for international students). Electronic applications accepted. *Application Contact:* Mara Sikkink, Coordinator of Academic Advisement, 801-626-6534, Fax: 801-626-6747, E-mail: marasikkink@weber.edu. *Dean,* Dr. Jeffery W. Steagall, 801-626-7253, Fax: 801-626-6687, E-mail: jeffsteagall@weber.edu.

School of Accounting and Taxation Students: 29 full-time (16 women), 25 part-time (10 women); includes 5 minority (2 Asian, non-Hispanic/Latino; 3 Hispanic/Latino), 1 international. Average age 32. *Faculty:* 7 full-time (3 women), 1 part-time/adjunct (0 women). Expenses: Contact institution. *Financial support:* In 2018–19, 20 students received support. Scholarships/grants available. Financial award application deadline: 4/1; financial award applicants required to submit FAFSA. In 2018, 44 master's awarded. *Program availability:* Part-time, evening/weekend. Offers accounting (M Acc); taxation (M Tax). *Application deadline:* For fall admission, 8/1 for domestic students; for spring admission, 12/1 for domestic students; for summer admission, 4/1 for domestic students. *Application fee:* $60 ($90 for international students). Electronic applications accepted. *Application Contact:* Dr. Larry A. Deppe, Graduate Coordinator, 801-626-7838, Fax: 801-626-7423, E-mail: ldeppe1@weber.edu. *Program Director,* Dr. Ryan Pace, 801-626-7562, Fax: 801-626-7423, E-mail: rpace@weber.edu.

Jerry and Vickie Moyes College of Education Students: 43 full-time (30 women), 146 part-time (116 women); includes 13 minority (1 Black or African American, non-Hispanic/Latino; 2 American Indian or Alaska Native, non-Hispanic/Latino; 2 Asian, non-Hispanic/Latino; 7 Hispanic/Latino; 1 Two or more races, non-Hispanic/Latino), 8 international. Average age 35. *Faculty:* 27 full-time (15 women), 1 part-time/adjunct (0 women). Expenses: Contact institution. *Financial support:* In 2018–19, 33 students received support. Institutionally sponsored loans, scholarships/grants, tuition waivers (full and partial), and unspecified assistantships available. Support available to part-time students. Financial award application deadline: 4/1; financial award applicants required to submit FAFSA. In 2018, 50 master's awarded. *Program availability:* Part-time, evening/weekend. Offers athletic training (MSAT); curriculum and instruction (M Ed); education (M Ed, MSAT). *Application deadline:* For fall admission, 5/15 for domestic students; for spring admission, 9/15 for domestic students; for summer admission, 1/15 for domestic students. *Application fee:* $60 ($90 for international students). *Application Contact:* Nathan Alexander, College of Education Recruiter, 801-626-8124, Fax: 801-626-7427, E-mail: nathanalexander@weber.edu. *Dean,* Dr. Jack Rasmussen, 801-626-6273, Fax: 801-626-7427, E-mail: jrasmussen@weber.edu.

Telitha E. Lindquist College of Arts and Humanities Students: 13 full-time (10 women), 75 part-time (47 women); includes 11 minority (1 American Indian or Alaska Native, non-Hispanic/Latino; 4 Asian, non-Hispanic/Latino; 6 Hispanic/Latino). Average age 36. *Faculty:* 20 full-time (10 women). Expenses: Contact institution. *Financial support:* In 2018–19, 20 students received support. Scholarships/grants and tuition waivers (full and partial) available. Financial award application deadline: 4/1; financial award applicants required to submit FAFSA. In 2018, 42 master's awarded. *Program availability:* Part-time, evening/weekend. Offers arts and humanities (MA, MPC); communication (MPC); English (MA). *Application deadline:* For fall admission, 4/1 for domestic students. *Application fee:* $60 ($90 for international students). Electronic applications accepted. *Application Contact:* Scott Teichert, Director of Admissions, 801-626-7670, Fax: 801-626-6045, E-mail: scottteichert@weber.edu. *Dean, College of Arts and Humanities,* Dr. Scott Springer, 801-626-6424, Fax: 801-626-7422, E-mail: arts_humanities@weber.edu.

WEBSTER UNIVERSITY, St. Louis, MO 63119-3194

General Information Independent, coed, comprehensive institution. *Enrollment:* 2,263 full-time matriculated graduate/professional students (1,277 women), 6,798 part-time matriculated graduate/professional students (3,921 women). *Enrollment by degree level:* 8,763 master's, 72 doctoral, 226 other advanced degrees. *Graduate faculty:* 185 full-time (82 women), 1,022 part-time/adjunct (390 women). *Tuition:* Full-time $22,500; part-time $750 per credit hour. Tuition and fees vary according to degree level, campus/location and program. *Graduate housing:* Room and/or apartments available on a first-come, first-served basis to single students; on-campus housing not available to married students. Typical cost: $7680 per year. Room charges vary according to housing facility selected. Housing application deadline: 4/1. *Student services:* Campus employment opportunities, campus safety program, career counseling, exercise/wellness program, free psychological counseling, international student services, multicultural affairs office, services for students with disabilities, teacher training, writing training. *Library facilities:* Emerson Library. *Collection:* Study areas open 24 hours, 5–7 days a week; students can reserve study rooms.

Computer facilities: Computer purchase and lease plans are available. A campuswide network can be accessed from student residence rooms and from off campus. Online class registration is available. Website: http://www.webster.edu/

General Application Contact: Sarah Nandor, Director of Graduate Admission, 314-246-7109, E-mail: nandor@webster.edu.

GRADUATE UNITS

College of Arts and Sciences *Program availability:* Part-time, evening/weekend, online learning. Offers arts and sciences (GM Acc, MA, MS, MSN, DNAP, Graduate Certificate); biological sciences (MS); counseling (MA); counseling psychology (MS); environmental management (MS); gerontology (MS); human services (MA); international nongovernmental organizations (MA); international relations (MA); legal studies (MA, Graduate Certificate); nurse anesthesia (DNAP); nurse educator (MSN).

Institute for Human Rights and Humanitarian Studies Offers international human rights (MA).

George Herbert Walker School of Business and Technology *Program availability:* Part-time, evening/weekend, online learning. Offers business and organizational security management (MA, MBA); business and technology (MA, MBA, MHA, MHA, MPA, MS, D Mgt, DM, Graduate Certificate); cybersecurity (MS); decision support systems (MBA); digital marketing management (Graduate Certificate); environmental management (MBA); finance (MBA, MS); forensic accounting (MS); gerontology (MBA); government contracting (Graduate Certificate); health administration (MHA); health care management (MA); health services management (MA); human resources development (MA, MBA); human resources management (MA, MBA); information technology management (MA, MBA, MS); international business (MA, MBA); international relations (MBA); management (D Mgt); management and leadership (MA, MBA); marketing (MA, MBA); media communications (MBA); nonprofit leadership (MA); nonprofit revenue development (Graduate Certificate); organizational development (Graduate Certificate); procurement and acquisitions management (MA, MBA); public administration (MPA); space systems operations management (MS); Web services (MBA).

Leigh Gerdine College of Fine Arts *Program availability:* Part-time, evening/weekend. Offers art history and criticism (MA); church music (MM); composition (MM); fine arts (MA, MFA, MM); jazz studies (MM); music (MA); music education (MM); organ (MM); performance (MM); piano (MM); voice (MM).

School of Communications *Program availability:* Part-time, evening/weekend, online learning. Offers advertising and marketing communications (MA); communications (MA); communications management (MA); media communications (MA); media literacy (MA); new media production (MA); public relations (MA).

School of Education *Program availability:* Part-time, online learning. Offers applied educational psychology (MA, Ed S); communication arts (MA, MAT); early childhood education (MA, MAT); education (MA, MAT, MET, Ed S); education and innovation (MA); educational technology (MET); elementary education (MAT); mathematics for educators (MA); middle school education (MAT); multidisciplinary studies (MAT); multimodal literacy for global impact (MA); reading (MA); secondary school education (MAT); special education (MA, MAT); teaching English as a second language (MA); transformative learning in the global community (Ed S).

WEILL CORNELL MEDICINE, New York, NY 10065

General Information Independent, coed, graduate-only institution. *Graduate housing:* Rooms and/or apartments guaranteed to single students and available on a first-come, first-served basis to married students. Housing application deadline: 4/30. *Research affiliation:* Memorial Sloan-Kettering Cancer Center (cancer), Houston Methodist Hospital (general medicine and surgery), The Rockefeller University (biomedical research), New York Methodist (general medicine and surgery), Hospital for Special Surgery (orthopedics), Burke Medical Research Institute (neurology).

GRADUATE UNITS

Weill Cornell Graduate School of Medical Sciences Offers biochemistry, cell and molecular biology (MS, PhD); biostatistics and data science (MS); chemical biology (PhD); clinical epidemiology and health services research (MS); computational biology and medicine (PhD); health informatics (MS); health policy and economics (MS); health sciences (MS); immunology (MS, PhD); medical sciences (MS, PhD); neuroscience (MS, PhD); pharmacology (MS, PhD); physiology, biophysics and systems biology (MS, PhD). Electronic applications accepted.

Weill Cornell/Rockefeller/Sloan-Kettering Tri-Institutional MD-PhD Program Offered jointly with The Rockefeller University and Sloan-Kettering Institute. Electronic applications accepted.

WELCH COLLEGE, Gallatin, TN 37066

General Information Independent-religious, coed, comprehensive institution.

GRADUATE UNITS

Program in Theology and Ministry *Program availability:* Online learning. Offers theology and ministry (MA).

WENTWORTH INSTITUTE OF TECHNOLOGY, Boston, MA 02115-5998

General Information Independent, coed, comprehensive institution. *Graduate housing:* Room and/or apartments available on a first-come, first-served basis to single students; on-campus housing not available to married students. Housing application deadline: 5/1.

GRADUATE UNITS

Department of Architecture Offers architecture (M Arch). Electronic applications accepted.

Master of Engineering in Civil Engineering Program *Program availability:* Part-time-only, evening/weekend. Offers construction engineering (M Eng); infrastructure engineering (M Eng). Electronic applications accepted.

Master of Science in Applied Computer Science Program *Program availability:* Part-time, online only, 100% online. Offers applied computer science (MS). Electronic applications accepted.

Master of Science in Construction Management Program *Program availability:* Part-time-only, evening/weekend, 100% online, blended/hybrid learning. Offers construction management (MS). Electronic applications accepted.

Master of Science in Facility Management Program *Program availability:* Part-time, evening/weekend, online only, 100% online, blended/hybrid learning. Offers facility management (MS). Electronic applications accepted.

Online Master of Science in Technology Management Program *Program availability:* Part-time-only, evening/weekend, online only, 100% online. Offers technology management (MS). Electronic applications accepted.

WESLEYAN COLLEGE, Macon, GA 31210-4462

General Information Independent-religious, Undergraduate: women only; graduate: coed, comprehensive institution. *Enrollment:* 707 graduate, professional, and undergraduate students; 33 full-time matriculated graduate/professional students (29 women), 7 part-time matriculated graduate/professional students (5 women). *Enrollment by degree level:* 40 master's. *Tuition:* Full-time $27,250; part-time $757 per credit hour. Tuition and fees vary according to program. *Graduate housing:* On-campus housing not available. *Student services:* Campus safety program, career counseling, exercise/wellness program, international student services, low-cost health insurance, services for students with disabilities, teacher training, writing training. *Library facilities:* Willet Memorial Library. *Collection:* Books: 88,108 (physical), 260,161 (digital/electronic); Serial titles: 646 (physical), 24,701 (digital/electronic); Databases: 294. Study areas open 24 hours, 5–7 days a week; students can reserve study rooms.

Computer facilities: 63 computers available on campus for general student use. A campuswide network can be accessed from student residence rooms and from off campus. Online class registration, online payment are available.
Website: http://www.wesleyancollege.edu/

General Application Contact: Mariana Furlin, Assessment Coordinator for Education Department, Program Assistant to the EMBA, 478-7572801, E-mail: mfurlin@wesleyancollege.edu.

GRADUATE UNITS

Department of Business and Economics Expenses: Contact institution. Offers business administration (EMBA); business and economics (EMBA). *Application Contact:* Mariana Furlin, Program Assistant to the EMBA, 478-7572801, E-mail: mfurlin@wesleyancollege.edu. *EMBA Program Director,* Dwight Hines, 478-757-5184, E-mail: dhines@wesleyancollege.edu.

Department of Education Expenses: Contact institution. *Program availability:* Part-time. Offers early childhood education (MA). Electronic applications accepted. *Application Contact:* Mariana Furlin, Assessment Coordinator for Education Department, Program Assistant to the EMBA, 478-7572801, E-mail: mfurlin@wesleyancollege.edu. *Associate Professor of Education,* Dr. Virginia Wilcox, 478-7575279, E-mail: vwilcox@wesleyancollege.edu.

WESLEYAN UNIVERSITY, Middletown, CT 06459

General Information Independent, coed, university. CGS member. *Graduate housing:* Rooms and/or apartments available on a first-come, first-served basis to single and married students. Housing application deadline: 7/1. *Research affiliation:* Woods Hole Oceanographic Institution, Cold Spring Harbor Laboratory.

GRADUATE UNITS

Graduate Liberal Studies Program Expenses: Contact institution. *Financial support:* Scholarships/grants available. Support available to part-time students. *Program availability:* Part-time, evening/weekend. Offers liberal arts (M Phil); liberal studies (MALS); writing (Graduate Certificate). *Application deadline:* For fall admission, 7/15 for domestic students; for spring admission, 11/14 for domestic students; for summer admission, 4/15 for domestic students. Applications are processed on a rolling basis. *Application fee:* $100. Electronic applications accepted. *Application Contact:* Glenn Knight, Assistant Director, Continuing Studies, 860-685-3345, E-mail: gknight01@wesleyan.edu. *Director,* Jennifer Curran, 860-685-3338, Fax: 860-685-2901, E-mail: jcurran@wesleyan.edu.

Graduate Studies Offers astronomy (MA); biochemistry (PhD); cell and developmental biology (PhD); chemical physics (PhD); composition (MA); computer science (MA); earth and environmental sciences (MA); ethnomusicology (MA, PhD); evolution and ecology (PhD); genetics and genomics (PhD); inorganic chemistry (PhD); mathematics (MA, PhD); molecular biology and biochemistry (PhD); molecular biophysics (PhD); neurobiology and behavior (PhD); organic chemistry (PhD); physical chemistry (PhD); physics (PhD); theoretical chemistry (PhD). Electronic applications accepted.

WESLEY BIBLICAL SEMINARY, Jackson, MS 39206

General Information Independent-religious, coed, graduate-only institution.

GRADUATE UNITS

Graduate Programs *Program availability:* Part-time. Offers apologetics (MA); Biblical languages (M Div); Biblical literature (MA); Christian studies (MA); context and mission (M Div); honors research (M Div); interpretation (M Div); ministry (M Div); spiritual formation (M Div); teaching (M Div); theology (MA). Electronic applications accepted.

WESLEY COLLEGE, Dover, DE 19901-3875

General Information Independent-religious, coed, comprehensive institution. *Graduate housing:* On-campus housing not available.

GRADUATE UNITS

Business Program *Program availability:* Part-time, evening/weekend. Offers environmental management (MBA); executive leadership (MBA); management (MBA). Executive leadership concentration also offered at New Castle, DE location.

Education Program *Program availability:* Part-time, evening/weekend. Offers education (M Ed, MA Ed, MAT).

Environmental Studies Program *Program availability:* Part-time, evening/weekend. Offers environmental studies (MS).

Nursing Program *Program availability:* Part-time, evening/weekend. Offers nursing (MSN). Electronic applications accepted.

Occupational Therapy Program Offers occupational therapy (MOT).

WESLEY THEOLOGICAL SEMINARY, Washington, DC 20016-5690

General Information Independent-religious, coed, graduate-only institution. *Graduate housing:* Rooms and/or apartments available to single and married students. Housing application deadline: 7/1.

GRADUATE UNITS

Graduate and Professional Programs *Program availability:* Part-time. Offers theology (M Div, MA, MTS, D Min).

WEST CHESTER UNIVERSITY OF PENNSYLVANIA, West Chester, PA 19383

General Information State-supported, coed, comprehensive institution. CGS member. *Graduate housing:* Room and/or apartments available on a first-come, first-served basis to single students; on-campus housing not available to married students. Housing application deadline: 5/1. *Research affiliation:* Pennsylvania Equine Toxicology and Research Laboratory (chemistry), Temple University Collaborative on Community Inclusion of Individuals with Psychiatric Disabilities (social work), University of Pennsylvania (social work), University of Connecticut Human Rights Institute Research Program on Economic and Social Rights (social work), The Soldier's Project (social work), Independent Blue Cross (IBC) (nursing).

GRADUATE UNITS

College of Arts and Humanities *Program availability:* Part-time, evening/weekend. Offers arts and humanities (M Ed, MA, MS, Certificate, Teaching Certificate); business ethics (Certificate); communication studies (MA); English (MA); French (Teaching Certificate); German (Teaching Certificate); health care ethics (Certificate); history (M Ed, MA); Holocaust and genocide studies (MA, Certificate); languages and cultures (MA); philosophy (MA); philosophy: applied ethics (MA); publishing (Certificate);

secondary English (Teaching Certificate); Spanish (Teaching Certificate); teaching English as a second language (MA, Certificate). Electronic applications accepted.

College of Business and Public Management *Program availability:* Part-time, evening/weekend, 100% online, blended/hybrid learning. Offers administration (Certificate); business and public management (MA, MBA, MPA, MS, MURP, Certificate, DPA); criminal justice (MS); geographic information systems (Certificate); geography (MS); geography and planning (MURP); human resource management (MS, Certificate); non-profit administration (Certificate); nonprofit administration (MPA); public administration (MPA); public policy and administration (MPA, DPA); urban and regional planning (Certificate). Electronic applications accepted.

School of Business *Program availability:* Part-time, evening/weekend, online only, 100% online. Offers business analytics (Certificate); business education (MBA). Electronic applications accepted.

College of Education and Social Work *Program availability:* Part-time, evening/weekend, 100% online, blended/hybrid learning. Offers applied studies in teaching and learning (M Ed); autism (Certificate); clinical mental health counseling (MS); counseling (Certificate); early childhood education (M Ed); education and social work (M Ed, MS, MSW, Ed D, Certificate, Post Master's Certificate, Teaching Certificate); education for sustainability (Certificate); educational technology (Certificate); gerontology (Certificate); grades 4-8 (Teaching Certificate); grades preK-4 (Teaching Certificate); higher education counseling (Post Master's Certificate); higher education counseling/student affairs (MS, Certificate); higher education policy and student affairs (MS); literacy (Certificate); literacy coaching (Certificate); policy, planning, and administration (Ed D); reading (M Ed); reading specialist (Teaching Certificate); school counseling (M Ed); social work (MSW); special education (Teaching Certificate); special education (M Ed); transformative education and social change (MS); universal design for learning and assistive technology (Certificate). Electronic applications accepted.

College of Health Sciences *Program availability:* Part-time, evening/weekend. Offers adapted physical education (Certificate); adult-gerontology clinical nurse specialist (MSN); athletic training (MS); community nutrition (MS); exercise and sport physiology (MS); health care management (Certificate); health sciences (MA, MPA, MPH, MS, MSN, DNP, Certificate, Teaching Certificate); integrative health (Certificate); nursing (DNP); nursing education (MSN); public health (MPH); school nurse (Certificate); speech-language pathology (MA); sport management and athletics (MPA). Electronic applications accepted.

College of the Sciences and Mathematics *Program availability:* Part-time, 100% online. Offers applied and computational mathematics (MS); applied statistics (MS, Certificate); biology (MS, Teaching Certificate); chemistry (Teaching Certificate); clinical psychology (Psy D); computer science (MS); computer security (information assurance) (Certificate); general science (Teaching Certificate); geoscience (MS); industrial/organizational psychology (Certificate); information systems (Certificate); mathematics (MA, Teaching Certificate); mathematics education (MA); physics (Teaching Certificate); psychology (MA); sciences and mathematics (MA, MS, Psy D, Certificate, Teaching Certificate); Web technology (Certificate). Electronic applications accepted.

School of Music *Program availability:* Part-time, evening/weekend. Offers history and literature (MM); Kodaly methodology (Certificate); music (MM, Certificate, Teaching Certificate); music education (MM, Teaching Certificate); music technology (Certificate); music theory, history, and composition (MM); Orff-Schulwerk (Certificate); performance (MM); piano pedagogy (MM, Certificate).

WESTCLIFF UNIVERSITY, Irvine, CA 92606

General Information Proprietary, coed, comprehensive institution.

GRADUATE UNITS

College of Business Offers business (MBA, DBA).

College of Education Offers teaching English to speakers of other languages (MA).

WEST COAST UNIVERSITY, North Hollywood, CA 91606

General Information Proprietary, coed, comprehensive institution.

GRADUATE UNITS

Graduate Programs

WESTERN CAROLINA UNIVERSITY, Cullowhee, NC 28723

General Information State-supported, coed, university. CGS member. *Enrollment:* 762 full-time matriculated graduate/professional students (523 women), 784 part-time matriculated graduate/professional students (536 women). *Enrollment by degree level:* 1,328 master's, 157 doctoral, 56 other advanced degrees. *Graduate faculty:* 233 full-time (110 women), 36 part-time/adjunct (17 women). *International tuition:* $14,842 full-time. *Tuition, area resident:* Full-time $4435. Tuition, state resident: full-time $4435. Tuition, nonresident: full-time $14,842. *Required fees:* $2979. Part-time tuition and fees vary according to course load, degree level and program. *Graduate housing:* Room and/or apartments available on a first-come, first-served basis to single students; on-campus housing not available to married students. Typical cost: $6744 per year ($11,170 including board). Room and board charges vary according to board plan and housing facility selected. Housing application deadline: 5/1. *Student services:* Campus employment opportunities, campus safety program, career counseling, child daycare facilities, exercise/wellness program, free psychological counseling, international student services, low-cost health insurance, multicultural affairs office, services for students with disabilities, teacher training, writing training. *Library facilities:* Hunter Library. *Collection:* Weekly public service hours: 96; study areas open 24 hours, 5–7 days a week; students can reserve study rooms.

Computer facilities: Computer purchase and lease plans are available. A campuswide network can be accessed from student residence rooms and from off campus. Online class registration is available.
Website: http://www.wcu.edu/

General Application Contact: Admissions Specialist, 828-227-7398, Fax: 828-227-7480, E-mail: grad@email.wcu.edu.

GRADUATE UNITS

Graduate School Students: 762 full-time (523 women), 784 part-time (536 women); includes 292 minority (133 Black or African American, non-Hispanic/Latino; 19 American Indian or Alaska Native, non-Hispanic/Latino; 16 Asian, non-Hispanic/Latino; 86 Hispanic/Latino; 38 Two or more races, non-Hispanic/Latino; 33 international). Average age 33. *Faculty:* 233 full-time (110 women), 36 part-time/adjunct (17 women). Expenses: Contact institution. *Financial support:* Fellowships, research assistantships with tuition reimbursements, teaching assistantships with tuition reimbursements, career-related internships or fieldwork, institutionally sponsored loans, scholarships/grants, and unspecified assistantships available. Financial award application deadline: 3/31; financial award applicants required to submit FAFSA. In 2018, 555 master's, 42 doctorates, 25 other advanced degrees awarded. *Program availability:* Part-time, evening/weekend, 100% online, blended/hybrid learning. *Application deadline:* For fall admission, 5/1 priority date for domestic students, 4/1 for international students; for spring admission, 9/1 priority date for domestic students, 9/1 for international students. Applications are processed on a rolling basis. *Application fee:* $50. *Application Contact:* Admissions Specialist, 828-227-7398, Fax: 828-227-7480, E-mail: gradsch@email.wcu.edu. *Dean,* Dr. Brian Kloeppel, 828-227-3174, Fax: 828-227-7480, E-mail: bkloeppel@wcu.edu.

College of Arts and Sciences *Program availability:* Part-time, evening/weekend. Offers arts and sciences (MA, MPA, MS, Certificate, Graduate Certificate); biology (MS); chemistry (MS); history (MA); literature (MA); political science and public affairs (MPA); professional writing (MA); rhetoric and composition (MA); teaching English to speakers of other languages (Certificate); technical and professional writing (Certificate). Electronic applications accepted.

College of Business *Program availability:* Part-time, evening/weekend, online learning. Offers accountancy (M Ac); business administration (MBA); entrepreneurship (ME); project management (MPM).

College of Education and Allied Professions *Program availability:* Part-time, evening/weekend, online learning. Offers education and allied professions (MA); general psychology (MA).

College of Engineering and Technology *Program availability:* Part-time, evening/weekend, online learning. Offers construction management (MCM); engineering and technology (MCM, MS); technology (MS).

College of Fine and Performing Arts *Program availability:* Part-time. Offers art and design (MFA); fine and performing arts (MFA).

College of Health and Human Sciences *Program availability:* Part-time, evening/weekend. Offers communication sciences and disorders (MS); health and human sciences (MHS, MPT, MS, MSN, MSW, DPT, PMC); health sciences (MHS); nursing (MS, DNP, Post-Master's Certificate, Postbaccalaureate Certificate); physical therapy (DPT); social work (MSW).

WESTERN CONNECTICUT STATE UNIVERSITY, Danbury, CT 06810-6885

General Information State-supported, coed, comprehensive institution. *Enrollment:* 5,642 graduate, professional, and undergraduate students; 53 full-time matriculated graduate/professional students (39 women), 561 part-time matriculated graduate/professional students (421 women). *Enrollment by degree level:* 419 master's, 66 doctoral, 21 other advanced degrees. *Graduate housing:* Rooms and/or apartments available on a first-come, first-served basis to single and married students. Housing application deadline: 4/1. *Student services:* Campus employment opportunities, career counseling, child daycare facilities, exercise/wellness program, free psychological counseling, international student services, low-cost health insurance, multicultural affairs office, services for students with disabilities, teacher training, writing training. *Library facilities:* Ruth Haas Library plus 2 others. *Collection:* Books: 204,701 (physical), 240,140 (digital/electronic); Serial titles: 302 (physical), 67,162 (digital/electronic); Databases: 188. Weekly public service hours: 144; students can reserve study rooms.

Computer facilities: 1,034 computers available on campus for general student use. A campuswide network can be accessed from student residence rooms and from off campus. Online class registration, online payment are available. Website: http://www.wcsu.edu/

General Application Contact: Dr. Chris Shankle, Associate Director of Graduate Studies, 203-837-9005, Fax: 203-837-8326, E-mail: shanklec@wcsu.edu.

GRADUATE UNITS

Division of Graduate Studies Students: 54 full-time (40 women), 560 part-time (420 women). Average age 35. Expenses: Contact institution. *Financial support:* Scholarships/grants available. Financial award application deadline: 5/1; financial award applicants required to submit FAFSA. *Program availability:* Part-time. *Application deadline:* For fall admission, 8/5 priority date for domestic students, 3/1 priority date for international students; for spring admission, 1/5 priority date for domestic students, 10/1 for international students. Applications are processed on a rolling basis. *Application fee:* $50. *Application Contact:* Chris Shankle, Associate Director of Graduate Studies, 203-837-9005, Fax: 203-837-8326, E-mail: shanklec@wcsu.edu. *Provost and Vice President for Academic Affairs,* Dr. Missy Alexander, 203-837-8400, Fax: 203-837-8525, E-mail: alexanderm@wcsu.edu.

Ancell School of Business Students: 9 full-time (6 women), 60 part-time (34 women). Average age 33. Expenses: Contact institution. *Financial support:* Scholarships/grants available. Financial award application deadline: 5/1; financial award applicants required to submit FAFSA. *Program availability:* Part-time. Offers accounting (MBA); business (MBA, MHA, MS); business administration (MBA); health administration (MHA). *Application deadline:* For fall admission, 8/5 priority date for domestic students; for spring admission, 1/5 priority date for domestic students. Applications are processed on a rolling basis. *Application fee:* $50. *Application Contact:* Chris Shankle, Associate Director of Graduate Studies, 203-837-9005, Fax: 203-837-8326, E-mail: shanklec@wcsu.edu. *Dean,* David Martin, 203-837-9600, Fax: 203-837-8527, E-mail: martindg@wcsu.edu.

Maricostas School of Arts and Sciences Students: 20 full-time (13 women), 147 part-time (91 women). Average age 39. Expenses: Contact institution. *Financial support:* Scholarships/grants available. Financial award application deadline: 5/1; financial award applicants required to submit FAFSA. *Program availability:* Part-time. Offers arts and sciences (MA, MAT, MFA); creative and professional writing (MFA); earth and planetary sciences (MA); history and non-Western cultures (MA); literature (MA); mathematics (MA). *Application deadline:* For fall admission, 8/5 priority date for domestic students; for spring admission, 1/5 priority date for domestic students. Applications are processed on a rolling basis. *Application fee:* $50. *Application Contact:* Chris Shankle, Associate Director of Graduate Studies, 203-837-9005, Fax: 203-837-8326, E-mail: shanklec@wcsu.edu. *Dean,* Dr. Michelle Brown, 203-837-9400, Fax: 203-837-8525, E-mail: brownml@wcsu.edu.

School of Professional Studies Students: 14 full-time (12 women), 348 part-time (291 women). Average age 36. Expenses: Contact institution. *Financial support:* Scholarships/grants available. Financial award application deadline: 5/1; financial award applicants required to submit FAFSA. *Program availability:* Part-time. Offers adult gerontology clinical nurse specialist (MSN); adult gerontology nurse practitioner (MSN); clinical mental health counseling (MS); curriculum (MS); instructional leadership (Ed D); instructional technology (MS); nursing education (Ed D); reading (MS); school counseling (MS); special education (MS). *Application deadline:* For fall admission, 8/5 priority date for domestic students; for spring admission, 1/5 priority date for domestic students. Applications are processed on a rolling basis. *Application fee:* $50. *Application Contact:* Dr. Chris Shankle, Associate Director of Graduate Admissions, 203-837-9005, Fax: 203-837-8326, E-mail: shanklec@wcsu.edu. *Interim*

Dean, Dr. Joan Palladino, 203-837-9500, Fax: 203-837-8526, E-mail: palladinoj@wcsu.edu.

School of Visual and Performing Arts Students: 11 full-time (9 women), 5 part-time (4 women). Average age 31. Expenses: Contact institution. *Financial support:* Scholarships/grants available. Financial award applicants required to submit FAFSA. *Program availability:* Part-time. Offers illustration (MFA); music education (MS); painting (MFA); visual and performing arts (MFA, MS). *Application deadline:* For fall admission, 8/5 priority date for domestic students; for spring admission, 1/5 priority date for domestic students. *Application fee:* $50. *Application Contact:* Dr. Chris Shankle, Associate Director of Graduate Studies, 203-837-9005, Fax: 203-837-8326, E-mail: shanklec@wcsu.edu. *Dean,* Brian Vernon, 203-837-8851, Fax: 203-837-3223, E-mail: begianj@wcsu.edu.

WESTERN GOVERNORS UNIVERSITY, Salt Lake City, UT 84107

General Information Independent, coed, comprehensive institution. *Graduate housing:* On-campus housing not available.

GRADUATE UNITS

College of Business *Program availability:* Evening/weekend, online learning. Offers accounting (MS); information technology management (MBA); management and leadership (MS); management and strategy (MBA); strategic leadership (MBA). Electronic applications accepted.

College of Health Professions *Program availability:* Evening/weekend, online learning. Offers healthcare management (MBA); leadership and management (MSN); nursing education (MSN); nursing informatics (MSN). Electronic applications accepted.

College of Information Technology *Program availability:* Online learning. Offers cybersecurity and information assurance (MS); data analytics (MS); information technology management (MS).

Teachers College *Program availability:* Evening/weekend, online learning. Offers curriculum and instruction (MS); educational leadership (MS); elementary education (MAT, Postbaccalaureate Certificate); English education (5-12) (MAT); English language learning (PreK-12) (MA); instructional design (M Ed); learning and technology (M Ed); mathematics (5-12) (MAT); mathematics (5-9) (MAT); mathematics education (5-12) (MA); mathematics education (5-9) (MA); mathematics education (K-6) (MA); science (5-12) (MAT); science education (5-12) (MA); science education (5-9) (MA); special education (MS). Electronic applications accepted.

WESTERN ILLINOIS UNIVERSITY, Macomb, IL 61455-1390

General Information State-supported, coed, comprehensive institution. CGS member. *Graduate housing:* Rooms and/or apartments available on a first-come, first-served basis to single and married students. *Research affiliation:* National Council of Teachers of English (English and journalism), Petroleum Research Fund (chemistry), Bayer Crop Services (agriculture), McDonald's Corporation (education), The Ceres Trust (agriculture), Quad Cities Manufacturing Lab (engineering).

GRADUATE UNITS

School of Graduate Studies *Program availability:* Part-time, online learning. Electronic applications accepted.

College of Arts and Sciences *Program availability:* Part-time. Offers arts and sciences (MA, MLAS, MS, PhD, Certificate, SSP); biology (MS); chemistry (MS); clinical/community mental health (MS); English (MA); environmental GIS (Certificate); environmental science: large river ecosystems (PhD); general experimental psychology (MS); geography (MA); GIS analysis: GIS applications (Certificate); history (MA); liberal arts and sciences (MLAS); literary studies (Certificate); mathematics (MS); physics (MS); political science (MA); school psychology (SSP); sociology (MA); zoo and aquarium studies (Certificate). Electronic applications accepted.

College of Business and Technology *Program availability:* Part-time. Offers accountancy (M Acct); applied statistics and decision analytics (MS); business administration (MBA, Certificate); business analytics (Certificate); business and technology (M Acct, MA, MBA, MS, Certificate); computer science (MS); economics (MA); educational technology specialist (Certificate); engineering technology leadership (MS); instructional design and technology (MS); instructional media development (Certificate); online and distance learning development (Certificate); supply chain management (Certificate); technology integration in education (Certificate); workplace learning and performance (Certificate). Electronic applications accepted.

College of Education and Human Services *Program availability:* Part-time, evening/weekend, online learning. Offers college student personnel (MS); counseling (MS Ed); curriculum and instruction (MS Ed); education and human services (MA, MS, MS Ed, Ed D, Certificate, Ed S); educational and interdisciplinary studies (MS Ed, Certificate); educational leadership (MS Ed, Ed D, Ed S); health sciences (MS); kinesiology (MS); law enforcement and justice administration (MA); police executive administration (Certificate); reading (MS Ed); recreation, park, and tourism administration (MS); special education (MS Ed); sport management (MS); teaching English to speakers of other languages (Certificate). Electronic applications accepted.

College of Fine Arts and Communication *Program availability:* Part-time. Offers communication (MA); fine arts and communication (MA, MFA, MM, MS, Certificate); museum studies (MA, Certificate); music (MM); speech pathology and audiology (MS); theatre (MFA). Electronic applications accepted.

Illinois Institute for Rural Affairs Students: 13 full-time (9 women), 7 part-time (5 women); includes 6 minority (3 Black or African American, non-Hispanic/Latino; 1 Asian, non-Hispanic/Latino; 2 Hispanic/Latino). Average age 37. 7 applicants, 100% accepted, 6 enrolled. Expenses: Contact institution. Offers community and economic development (MA). *Application deadline:* Applications are processed on a rolling basis. *Application fee:* $30. Electronic applications accepted. *Application Contact:* Dr. Mark Mossman, Associate Provost and Director of Graduate Studies, 309-298-1806, Fax: 309-298-2345, E-mail: grad-office@wiu.edu. *Director,* Dr. Christopher Merrett, 309-298-2281, E-mail: cd-merrett@wiu.edu.

WESTERN KENTUCKY UNIVERSITY, Bowling Green, KY 42101

General Information State-supported, coed, comprehensive institution. CGS member. *Graduate housing:* Room and/or apartments guaranteed to single students; on-campus housing not available to married students. Housing application deadline: 4/1. *Research affiliation:* Bowling Green Field Station for Animal Studies (U.S. Fish and Wildlife Service), Roybal Center (gerontology).

GRADUATE UNITS

Graduate School *Program availability:* Part-time, evening/weekend, online learning.

College of Education and Behavioral Sciences *Program availability:* Part-time, evening/weekend, online learning. Offers adult education (MAE); clinical psychology (MA); counseling (MA Ed); education and behavioral sciences (MA, MAE, MS, Ed D, Ed S); educational leadership (Ed D); elementary education (MAE, Ed S); exceptional education: learning and behavioral disorders (MAE); experimental psychology (MA); general psychology (MA); industrial/organizational psychology (MA); instructional design (MS); interdisciplinary early childhood education (MAE); library media education (MS); literacy education (MAE); middle grades education (MAE); school administration (Ed S); school counseling (P-12) (MA Ed); school principal (MAE); school psychology (Ed S); secondary education (MAE, Ed S); special education: moderate and severe disabilities (MAE); student affairs in higher education (MA Ed).

College of Health and Human Services *Program availability:* Part-time, evening/weekend. Offers athletic administration and coaching (MS); communication sciences and disorders (MS); health and human services (MHA, MPH, MS, MSN, MSW, DPT); healthcare administration (MHA); nursing (MSN); physical education (MS); physical therapy (DPT); public health (MPH); recreation and sport administration (MS); social work (MSW).

Gordon Ford College of Business *Program availability:* Part-time, evening/weekend. Offers applied economics (MA); business (MA, MBA); business administration (MBA).

Ogden College of Science and Engineering *Program availability:* Part-time, evening/weekend. Offers agriculture (MA Ed, MS); biology (MS); chemistry (MA Ed, MS); computer science (MS); engineering technology management (MS); geoscience (MS); homeland security sciences (MS); mathematics (MA, MS); physics (MA Ed); science and engineering (MA Ed, MS).

Potter College of Arts and Letters *Program availability:* Part-time, evening/weekend, online learning. Offers art education (MA Ed); arts and letters (MA, MA Ed, MPA); communication (MA); criminology (MA); education (MA Ed); English (MA Ed); folk studies (MA); French (MA Ed); German (MA Ed); history (MA, MA Ed); literature (MA); music (MA Ed); organizational communication (Graduate Certificate); political science (MPA); sociology (MA); Spanish (MA Ed); teaching English as a second language (MA); writing (MA).

WESTERN MICHIGAN UNIVERSITY, Kalamazoo, MI 49008

General Information State-supported, coed, university. CGS member. *Graduate housing:* Rooms and/or apartments available on a first-come, first-served basis to single and married students. Housing application deadline: 7/1. *Research affiliation:* Argonne National Laboratory (particle physics), Central States Universities, Inc., Ames Research Center (manufacturing education), Copper Development Association, Inc. (plastics extrusion), Pharmacia and Upjohn Company (electron microscopy), Flowserve Corporation (mechanical pumps and seals).

GRADUATE UNITS

Graduate College *Program availability:* Part-time, evening/weekend.

College of Arts and Sciences *Program availability:* Part-time. Offers anthropology (MA); applied and computational mathematics (MS); applied economics (MA, PhD); arts and sciences (MA, MFA, MIDA, MPA, MS, PhD, Graduate Certificate); behavior analysis (MA, PhD); biological sciences (MS, PhD); chemistry (MS, PhD); clinical psychology (PhD); communication (MA); comparative religion (MA, Graduate Certificate); creative writing (MFA, PhD); earth science (MS); English (MA, PhD); English teaching (MA); geographic information science (Graduate Certificate); geography (MA); geosciences (MS, PhD); health care administration (MPA, Graduate Certificate); history (MA, PhD); industrial/organizational behavior management (MA); international development administration (MIDA); mathematics education (MA, PhD); nonprofit leadership and administration (Graduate Certificate); philosophy (MA); physics (MA, PhD); political science (MA, PhD); public administration (PhD); science education (MA, PhD); sociology (MA, PhD); Spanish (MA, PhD); statistics (MS, PhD, Graduate Certificate).

College of Education and Human Development *Program availability:* Part-time. Offers athletic training (MS); career and technical education (MA); counseling psychology (MA, PhD); counselor education (MA, PhD); education and human development (MA, MS, Ed D, PhD, Ed S, Graduate Certificate); educational leadership (MA, PhD, Ed S); educational technology (MA, Graduate Certificate); evaluation, measurement and research (MA, PhD); family and consumer sciences (MA); interdisciplinary education (PhD); literacy studies (MA); organizational learning and performance (MA); practice of teaching (MA); socio-cultural studies of education (MA); special education (MA, Ed D); sport management (MA); teaching children with visual impairments (MA).

College of Engineering and Applied Sciences *Program availability:* Part-time. Offers chemical and paper engineering (MS, MSE, PhD); civil and construction engineering (MSE); computer engineering (MSE); computer science (MS, PhD); electrical and computer engineering (PhD); electrical engineering (MSE); engineering and applied sciences (MS, MSE, PhD); engineering design, manufacturing, and management systems (MS); engineering management (MS); industrial engineering (MSE, PhD); mechanical engineering (MSE, PhD).

College of Fine Arts *Program availability:* Part-time. Offers art education (MA); fine arts (MA, MM, Graduate Certificate); music (MA); music composition (MM); music conducting (MM); music education (MM); music performance (MM); music therapy (MM).

College of Health and Human Services *Program availability:* Part-time. Offers audiology (Au D); health and human services (MA, MS, MSM, MSN, MSW, Au D, PhD, Graduate Certificate); interdisciplinary health services (PhD); nursing (MSN); occupational therapy (MS); orientation and mobility (MA); orientation and mobility of children (MA); physician assistant (MSM); social work (MSW); speech pathology and audiology (MA); vision rehabilitation therapy (MA).

Haworth College of Business *Program availability:* Part-time. Offers accountancy (MSA); business (MBA, MSA); business administration (MBA).

WESTERN MICHIGAN UNIVERSITY HOMER STRYKER MD SCHOOL OF MEDICINE, Kalamazoo, MI 49007

General Information Graduate-only institution.

GRADUATE UNITS

MD Program Offers medicine (MD).

WESTERN MICHIGAN UNIVERSITY THOMAS M. COOLEY LAW SCHOOL, Lansing, MI 48901-3038

General Information Independent, coed, graduate-only institution. *Graduate housing:* On-campus housing not available.

GRADUATE UNITS

Graduate Programs *Program availability:* Part-time, evening/weekend, 100% online, blended/hybrid learning. Offers administrative law (public law) (JD); business transactions (JD); Canadian law practice (JD); corporate law and finance (LL M); environmental law (public law) (JD); general practice (JD); general studies (LL M); homeland and national security law (LL M); insurance law (LL M); intellectual property (JD); intellectual property law (LL M); international law (JD); litigation (JD); taxation (LL M); U.S. legal studies for foreign attorneys (LL M). Electronic applications accepted.

WESTERN NEW ENGLAND UNIVERSITY, Springfield, MA 01119

General Information Independent, coed, university. *Enrollment:* 500 full-time matriculated graduate/professional students (320 women), 529 part-time matriculated graduate/professional students (302 women). *Enrollment by degree level:* 398 master's, 615 doctoral, 16 other advanced degrees. *Graduate faculty:* 237 full-time (101 women), 25 part-time/adjunct (13 women). Full-time tuition and fees vary according to degree level, program and student level. *Graduate housing:* Rooms and/or apartments available to single and married students. Housing application deadline: 3/9. *Student services:* Campus employment opportunities, campus safety program, career counseling, exercise/wellness program, free psychological counseling, international student services, services for students with disabilities, teacher training, writing training. *Library facilities:* D'Amour Library plus 1 other. *Collection:* Books: 106,500 (physical), 31,912 (digital/electronic); Serial titles: 46 (physical), 109,440 (digital/electronic); Databases: 128. Weekly public service hours: 97; study areas open 24 hours, 5–7 days a week.

Computer facilities: 530 computers available on campus for general student use. A campuswide network can be accessed from student residence rooms and from off campus. Online class registration is available. Website: http://www.wne.edu/

General Application Contact: Matthew Fox, Executive Director of Graduate Admissions, 413-782-1410, Fax: 413-782-1777, E-mail: study@wne.edu.

GRADUATE UNITS

College of Arts and Sciences Students: 214 part-time (168 women); includes 33 minority (6 Black or African American, non-Hispanic/Latino; 1 American Indian or Alaska Native, non-Hispanic/Latino; 13 Asian, non-Hispanic/Latino; 11 Hispanic/Latino; 2 Two or more races, non-Hispanic/Latino), 7 international. Average age 29. 145 applicants, 77% accepted, 67 enrolled. *Faculty:* 113 full-time (53 women). Expenses: Contact institution. *Financial support:* In 2018–19, 6 fellowships with tuition reimbursements were awarded. Support available to part-time students. Financial award application deadline: 4/15; financial award applicants required to submit FAFSA. In 2018, 67 master's, 2 doctorates awarded. *Program availability:* Part-time-only, evening/weekend, online learning. Offers applied behavior analysis (MS); arts and sciences (M Ed, MA, MAET, MAMT, MFA, MS, PhD); behavior analysis (PhD); creative writing (MFA); curriculum and instruction (M Ed); English for teachers (MAET); mathematics for teachers (MAMT); public relations (MA). *Application fee:* $30. Electronic applications accepted. *Application Contact:* Matthew Fox, Executive Director of Graduate Admissions, 413-782-1410, Fax: 413-782-1777, E-mail: study@wne.edu. *Dean,* Dr. Saeed Ghahramani, 413-782-1218, Fax: 413-796-2118, E-mail: sghahram@wne.edu.

College of Business Students: 137 part-time (64 women); includes 13 minority (3 Black or African American, non-Hispanic/Latino; 6 Asian, non-Hispanic/Latino; 4 Hispanic/Latino), 2 international. Average age 30. 95 applicants, 85% accepted, 62 enrolled. *Faculty:* 36 full-time (12 women). Expenses: Contact institution. *Financial support:* Application deadline: 4/15; applicants required to submit FAFSA. In 2018, 71 master's awarded. *Program availability:* Part-time, evening/weekend, online learning. Offers accounting (MSA); business (MBA, MS, MSA); business administration (MBA); organizational leadership (MS); sport leadership and coaching (MS). *Application deadline:* Applications are processed on a rolling basis. *Application fee:* $30. Electronic applications accepted. *Application Contact:* Matthew Fox, Executive Director of Graduate Admissions, 413-782-1410, Fax: 413-782-1777, E-mail: study@wne.edu. *Dean,* Dr. Sharianne Walker, 413-782-1389, Fax: 413-796-2068, E-mail: swalker@wne.edu.

College of Engineering Students: 78 part-time (13 women); includes 6 minority (1 Black or African American, non-Hispanic/Latino; 2 Asian, non-Hispanic/Latino; 3 Hispanic/Latino), 18 international. Average age 29. 300 applicants, 73% accepted, 37 enrolled. *Faculty:* 33 full-time (3 women). Expenses: Contact institution. *Financial support:* In 2018–19, 6 fellowships with tuition reimbursements were awarded. Financial award application deadline: 4/15; financial award applicants required to submit FAFSA. In 2018, 41 master's, 2 doctorates awarded. *Program availability:* Part-time, evening/weekend, online learning. Offers business and engineering information systems (MSEM); civil engineering (MS); electrical engineering (MSEE); engineering (MS, MSEE, MSEM, MSME, PhD); engineering management (MSEM, PhD); general engineering management (MSEM); industrial engineering (MS); mechanical engineering (MSME); production and manufacturing systems (MSEM); quality engineering (MSEM). *Application deadline:* For fall admission, 1/15 priority date for domestic students. Applications are processed on a rolling basis. *Application fee:* $30. Electronic applications accepted. *Application Contact:* Matthew Fox, Executive Director of Graduate Admissions, 413-782-1410, Fax: 413-782-1777, E-mail: study@wne.edu. *Dean,* Dr. S. Hossein Cheraghi, 413-796-2302, Fax: 413-796-2116, E-mail: cheraghi@wne.edu.

College of Pharmacy and Health Sciences Students: 316 full-time (218 women); includes 70 minority (20 Black or African American, non-Hispanic/Latino; 2 American Indian or Alaska Native, non-Hispanic/Latino; 27 Asian, non-Hispanic/Latino; 20 Hispanic/Latino; 1 Two or more races, non-Hispanic/Latino), 3 international. Average age 24. 369 applicants, 54% accepted, 99 enrolled. *Faculty:* 34 full-time (20 women). Expenses: Contact institution. *Financial support:* Scholarships/grants and unspecified assistantships available. Financial award application deadline: 4/15; financial award applicants required to submit FAFSA. In 2018, 73 doctorates awarded. Offers occupational therapy (OTD); pharmacy (Pharm D); pharmacy and health sciences (OTD, Pharm D). *Application deadline:* Applications are processed on a rolling basis. Electronic applications accepted. *Application Contact:* Lori Berg, Dir of Admissions & Recruitment Health Professional Programs, 413-796-2073, Fax: 413-796-2266, E-mail: rxadmissions@wne.edu. *Dean,* Dr. Evan T. Robinson, 413-796-2323, E-mail: erobinson@wne.edu.

School of Law Students: 184 full-time (102 women), 100 part-time (57 women); includes 67 minority (28 Black or African American, non-Hispanic/Latino; 3 American Indian or Alaska Native, non-Hispanic/Latino; 9 Asian, non-Hispanic/Latino; 27 Hispanic/Latino), 2 international. Average age 30. 638 applicants, 59% accepted, 88 enrolled. *Faculty:* 19 full-time (11 women), 18 part-time/adjunct (6 women). Expenses: Contact institution. *Financial support:* Career-related internships or fieldwork, Federal Work-Study, and scholarships/grants available. Support available to part-time students. Financial award application deadline: 4/15; financial award applicants required to submit FAFSA. In 2018, 2 master's, 79 doctorates awarded. *Program availability:* Part-time, evening/weekend. Offers law (LL M, MS, JD). *Application deadline:* For fall admission, 3/15 priority date for domestic students. Applications are processed on a rolling basis. *Application fee:* $0. Electronic applications accepted. *Application Contact:* Anthony Orlando, Director of Law Admissions, 413-782-1281, Fax: 413-796-2067, E-mail: admissions@law.wne.edu. *Dean and Professor of Law,* Sudha Setty, 413-782-1431, E-mail: sudha.setty@law.wne.edu.

See Display on the next page and Close-Up on page 749.

WESTERN NEW MEXICO UNIVERSITY, Silver City, NM 88062-0680

General Information State-supported, coed, comprehensive institution. *Graduate housing:* Rooms and/or apartments available on a first-come, first-served basis to single and married students. Housing application deadline: 6/30.

GRADUATE UNITS

Graduate Division *Program availability:* Part-time, evening/weekend, online learning. Offers interdisciplinary studies (MA); occupational therapy (MOT); social work (MSW). Electronic applications accepted.

School of Business *Program availability:* Part-time, online learning. Offers business administration (MBA). Electronic applications accepted.

School of Education *Program availability:* Part-time, online learning. Offers bilingual education (MAT); educational leadership (MA); elementary education (MAT); reading (MAT); secondary education (MAT); special education (MAT); TESOL (teaching English to speakers of other languages) (MAT). Electronic applications accepted.

WESTERN OREGON UNIVERSITY, Monmouth, OR 97361

General Information State-supported, coed, comprehensive institution. *Graduate housing:* Room and/or apartments available on a first-come, first-served basis to single students; on-campus housing not available to married students. *Research affiliation:* Teaching Research Institute (education).

GRADUATE UNITS

Graduate Programs *Program availability:* Part-time, evening/weekend, online learning.

College of Education *Program availability:* Part-time, evening/weekend, online learning. Offers bilingual education (MS Ed); deaf education (MS Ed); early childhood special education (MS Ed); education (MAT, MS, MS Ed); health (MS Ed); humanities (MAT, MS Ed); information technology (MS Ed); initial licensure (MAT); mathematics (MAT, MS Ed); rehabilitation counseling (MS); science (MAT, MS Ed); secondary education (MAT, MS Ed); social science (MAT, MS Ed); special education (MS, MS Ed).

College of Liberal Arts and Sciences *Program availability:* Part-time, evening/weekend. Offers contemporary music (MM); criminal justice (MA, MS); liberal arts and sciences (MA, MM, MS).

WESTERN SEMINARY, Portland, OR 97215-3367

General Information Independent-religious, coed, graduate-only institution. *Graduate housing:* On-campus housing not available.

GRADUATE UNITS

Graduate Programs *Program availability:* Part-time, evening/weekend, online learning. Offers biblical and theological studies (MA, G Dip); biblical studies (Certificate); chaplaincy (MA); coaching (MA); counseling (MA, Certificate); divinity (M Div); intercultural studies (MA, D Miss, Certificate, G Dip); Jewish ministry (MA); pastoral care to women (MA); pastoral counseling (M Div); theology (Th M); youth ministry (MA).

WESTERN SEMINARY–SACRAMENTO CAMPUS, Rocklin, CA 95765

General Information Independent-religious, coed, graduate-only institution.

GRADUATE UNITS

Graduate Certificate Programs *Program availability:* Online learning. Offers Bible (Graduate Certificate); coaching (Graduate Certificate); pastoral care to women (Graduate Certificate); theology (Graduate Certificate); youth and family (Graduate Certificate).

Graduate Diploma Programs Offers Bible and theology (Graduate Diploma); ministry (Graduate Diploma); pastoral care to women (Graduate Diploma).

Master of Divinity Program Offers divinity (M Div).

Program in Biblical and Theological Studies Offers biblical and theological studies (MA).

Program in Marital and Family Therapy Offers marital and family therapy (MA).

Program in Ministry and Leadership Offers ministry and leadership (MA).

WESTERN SEMINARY–SAN JOSE CAMPUS, Milpitas, CA 95035

General Information Independent-religious, coed, graduate-only institution. *Graduate housing:* On-campus housing not available.

GRADUATE UNITS

Graduate Programs *Program availability:* Part-time, evening/weekend, online learning. Offers Bible and theology (Graduate Diploma); Bible, camp and conference ministry (CGS); Biblical and theological studies (MA); coaching (CGS); expositional ministry (M Div); marital and family therapy (MA); ministry (Graduate Diploma); ministry and leadership (MA); pastoral care to women (CGS, Graduate Diploma); pastoral ministry (M Div); theology (CGS); youth and family (CGS). Electronic applications accepted.

WESTERN STATE COLLEGE OF LAW AT ARGOSY UNIVERSITY, Irvine, CA 92618-3601

General Information Proprietary, coed, graduate-only institution. *Graduate housing:* On-campus housing not available.

GRADUATE UNITS

Professional Program *Program availability:* Part-time, evening/weekend. Offers law (JD). Electronic applications accepted.

WESTERN STATE COLORADO UNIVERSITY, Gunnison, CO 81231

General Information State-supported, coed, comprehensive institution.

GRADUATE UNITS

Graduate Programs in Education *Program availability:* Online learning. Offers education administrator leadership (MA); reading leadership (MA); teacher leadership (MA).

Program in Creative Writing *Program availability:* Online learning. Offers mainstream genre fiction (MFA); poetry (MFA); screenwriting (MFA).

Program in Environmental Management *Program availability:* Online learning. Offers integrative land management (MEM); sustainable and resilient communities (MEM).

WESTERN THEOLOGICAL SEMINARY, Holland, MI 49423-3622

General Information Independent-religious, coed, graduate-only institution. *Graduate housing:* Rooms and/or apartments available on a first-come, first-served basis to single and married students. Housing application deadline: 5/1.

GRADUATE UNITS

Graduate and Professional Programs *Program availability:* Part-time, 100% online, blended/hybrid learning. Offers divinity (M Div); ministry (D Min); theology (M Th, MA); urban pastoral ministry (Graduate Certificate). Electronic applications accepted.

WESTERN UNIVERSITY OF HEALTH SCIENCES, Pomona, CA 91766-1854

General Information Independent, coed, graduate-only institution. *Enrollment by degree level:* 566 master's, 3,267 doctoral. *Graduate faculty:* 306 full-time (156 women), 99 part-time/adjunct (51 women). *Tuition:* Full-time $23,502. *Required fees:* $40. One-time fee: $350 full-time. *Graduate housing:* Rooms and/or apartments available on a first-come, first-served basis to single and married students. Typical cost $1000 per year for single students; $1000 per year for married students. Room charges vary according to housing facility selected. *Student services:* Campus employment opportunities, campus safety program, career counseling, exercise/wellness program, free psychological counseling, grant writing training, international student services, low-cost health insurance, services for students with disabilities, teacher training. *Library facilities:* Pumerantz Library plus 1 other. *Collection:* Books: 18,534 (physical), 2,288 (digital/electronic); Serial titles: 581 (physical), 10,567 (digital/electronic); Databases: 70. Weekly public service hours: 91; students can reserve study rooms.

Computer facilities: 56 computers available on campus for general student use. A campuswide network can be accessed. Online class registration is available. Website: http://www.westernu.edu/

General Application Contact: Admissions Office, 909-469-5335, Fax: 909-469-5570, E-mail: admissions@westernu.edu.

GRADUATE UNITS

College of Dental Medicine Students: 276 full-time (144 women); includes 187 minority (8 Black or African American, non-Hispanic/Latino; 3 American Indian or Alaska Native, non-Hispanic/Latino; 104 Asian, non-Hispanic/Latino; 45 Hispanic/Latino; 27 Two or more races, non-Hispanic/Latino), 3 international. Average age 28. 2,514 applicants, 7% accepted, 67 enrolled. *Faculty:* 44 full-time (20 women), 19 part-time/adjunct (10 women). Expenses: Contact institution. *Financial support:* In 2018–19, 20 students received support. Scholarships/grants available. Financial award application deadline: 3/2; financial award applicants required to submit FAFSA. In 2018, 66 doctorates awarded. Offers dental medicine (DMD). *Application deadline:* For fall admission, 12/1 for domestic and international students. Applications are processed on a rolling basis. *Application fee:* $60. Electronic applications accepted. *Application Contact:* Marie Anderson, Director of Admissions, 909-469-5485, Fax: 909-469-5570, E-mail: admissions@westernu.edu. *Dean,* Dr. Steven Friedrichsen, 909-706-3911, E-mail: sfriedrichsen@westernu.edu.

College of Graduate Nursing Students: 267 full-time (209 women), 50 part-time (46 women); includes 216 minority (12 Black or African American, non-Hispanic/Latino; 4 American Indian or Alaska Native, non-Hispanic/Latino; 95 Asian, non-Hispanic/Latino; 78 Hispanic/Latino; 1 Native Hawaiian or other Pacific Islander, non-Hispanic/Latino; 26 Two or more races, non-Hispanic/Latino), 4 international. Average age 33. 571 applicants, 35% accepted, 126 enrolled. *Faculty:* 20 full-time (16 women), 26 part-time/adjunct (17 women). Expenses: Contact institution. *Financial support:* In 2018–19, 30 students received support. Career-related internships or fieldwork and scholarships/grants available. Support available to part-time students. Financial award application deadline: 3/2; financial award applicants required to submit FAFSA. In 2018, 79 master's, 9 doctorates awarded. *Program availability:* Part-time, evening/weekend, blended/hybrid learning. Offers administrative nurse leader (MSN); adn to msn (MSN); ambulatory care nurse (MSN); clinical nurse leader (MSN); nursing practice (DNP). *Application fee:* $60. Electronic applications accepted. *Application Contact:* Daniell Mendoza, Assistant Director of Admissions, 909-469-5541, Fax: 909-469-5570, E-mail: dmendoza@westernu.edu. *Dean,* Dr. Mary Lopez, 909-706-3860, Fax: 909-469-5521, E-mail: mlopez@westernu.edu.

College of Health Sciences Students: 365 full-time (239 women), 21 part-time (14 women); includes 249 minority (26 Black or African American, non-Hispanic/Latino; 2 American Indian or Alaska Native, non-Hispanic/Latino; 65 Asian, non-Hispanic/Latino; 109 Hispanic/Latino; 3 Native Hawaiian or other Pacific Islander, non-Hispanic/Latino; 44 Two or more races, non-Hispanic/Latino), 1 international. Average age 28. 3,159 applicants, 8% accepted, 154 enrolled. *Faculty:* 27 full-time (20 women), 13 part-time/adjunct (9 women). Expenses: Contact institution. *Financial support:* In 2018–19, 105 students received support. Career-related internships or fieldwork, scholarships/grants, and traineeships available. Financial award application deadline: 3/2; financial award applicants required to submit FAFSA. In 2018, 106 master's, 64 doctorates awarded. *Program availability:* Blended/hybrid learning. Offers health sciences (MS, DPT); physical therapy (DPT); physician assistant studies (MS). Electronic applications accepted. *Application Contact:* Karen Hutton-Lopez, Director of Admissions, 909-469-5650, Fax: 909-469-5570, E-mail: admissions@westernu.edu. *Interim Dean,* Dr. Dee Schilling, 909-469-5300, Fax: 909-469-5438, E-mail: dschilling@westernu.edu.

College of Optometry Students: 336 full-time (246 women); includes 219 minority (6 Black or African American, non-Hispanic/Latino; 1 American Indian or Alaska Native, non-Hispanic/Latino; 127 Asian, non-Hispanic/Latino; 42 Hispanic/Latino; 4 Native Hawaiian or other Pacific Islander, non-Hispanic/Latino; 39 Two or more races, non-Hispanic/Latino), 14 international. Average age 27. 693 applicants, 30% accepted, 80 enrolled. *Faculty:* 31 full-time (16 women), 4 part-time/adjunct (3 women). Expenses: Contact institution. *Financial support:* In 2018–19, 31 students received support. Career-related internships or fieldwork, scholarships/grants, and traineeships available. Financial award application deadline: 3/2; financial award applicants required to submit FAFSA. In 2018, 62 doctorates awarded. Offers optometry (OD). *Application deadline:* For fall admission, 5/1 for domestic and international students. Applications are processed on a rolling basis. *Application fee:* $65. Electronic applications accepted. *Application Contact:* Marie Anderson, Director of Admissions, 909-469-5485, Fax: 909-469-5570, E-mail: ehoppe@westernu.edu. *Dean,* Dr. Elizabeth Hoppe, 909-706-3497, E-mail: ehoppe@westernu.edu.

College of Osteopathic Medicine of the Pacific Students: 1,352 full-time (653 women); includes 656 minority (18 Black or African American, non-Hispanic/Latino; 1 American Indian or Alaska Native, non-Hispanic/Latino; 439 Asian, non-Hispanic/Latino; 87 Hispanic/Latino; 1 Native Hawaiian or other Pacific Islander, non-Hispanic/Latino; 110 Two or more races, non-Hispanic/Latino), 16 international. Average age 27. 6,103 applicants, 12% accepted, 329 enrolled. *Faculty:* 66 full-time (30 women), 22 part-time/adjunct (7 women). Expenses: Contact institution. *Financial support:* In 2018–19, 240 students received support. Career-related internships or fieldwork and scholarships/grants available. Financial award application deadline: 3/2; financial award applicants required to submit FAFSA. In 2018, 323 doctorates awarded. Offers osteopathic medicine (DO). *Application deadline:* For fall admission, 2/1 for domestic and international students. Applications are processed on a rolling basis. *Application fee:* $65. Electronic applications accepted. *Application Contact:* Susan Hanson, Director of Admissions, 909-469-5329, Fax: 909-469-5570, E-mail: admissions@westernu.edu. *Dean,* Dr. Paula Crone, 541-259-0206, Fax: 541-259-0201, E-mail: pcrone@westernu.edu.

College of Pharmacy Students: 549 full-time (368 women), 7 part-time (4 women); includes 397 minority (23 Black or African American, non-Hispanic/Latino; 276 Asian, non-Hispanic/Latino; 45 Hispanic/Latino; 53 Two or more races, non-Hispanic/Latino), 23 international. Average age 27. 691 applicants, 46% accepted, 143 enrolled. *Faculty:* 36 full-time (15 women), 5 part-time/adjunct (2 women). Expenses: Contact institution. *Financial support:* In 2018–19, 52 students received support, including 15 teaching assistantships with full tuition reimbursements available (averaging $21,000 per year); research assistantships and scholarships/grants also available. Financial award application deadline: 3/2; financial award applicants required to submit FAFSA. In 2018, 6 master's, 132 doctorates awarded. Offers pharmaceutical sciences (MS); pharmacy (MS, Pharm D). Electronic applications accepted. *Application Contact:* Daniell Mendoza, Assistant Director of Admissions, 909-469-5541, Fax: 909-469-5570, E-mail: dmendoza@westernu.edu. *Dean,* Dr. Daniel Robinson, 909-469-5533, Fax: 909-469-5539, E-mail: drobinson@westernu.edu.

College of Podiatric Medicine Students: 139 full-time (49 women); includes 82 minority (4 Black or African American, non-Hispanic/Latino; 53 Asian, non-Hispanic/Latino; 14 Hispanic/Latino; 1 Native Hawaiian or other Pacific Islander, non-Hispanic/Latino; 10 Two or more races, non-Hispanic/Latino), 2 international. Average age 27. 376 applicants, 23% accepted, 30 enrolled. *Faculty:* 10 full-time (6 women), 6 part-time/adjunct (1 woman). Expenses: Contact institution. *Financial support:* In 2018–19, 17 students received support. Career-related internships or fieldwork, scholarships/grants, and traineeships available. Financial award application deadline: 3/2; financial award applicants required to submit FAFSA. In 2018, 34 doctorates awarded. Offers podiatric medicine (DPM). *Application deadline:* For fall admission, 6/30 for domestic and international students. Applications are processed on a rolling basis. *Application fee:* $0. Electronic applications accepted. *Application Contact:* Marie Anderson, Director of Admissions, 909-469-5485, Fax: 909-469-5570, E-mail: admissions@westernu.edu. *Dean,* Dr. Kathleen Satterfield, 909-706-3933, E-mail: vsatterfield@westernu.edu.

College of Veterinary Medicine Students: 414 full-time (320 women); includes 201 minority (14 Black or African American, non-Hispanic/Latino; 1 American Indian or Alaska Native, non-Hispanic/Latino; 55 Asian, non-Hispanic/Latino; 88 Hispanic/Latino; 1 Native Hawaiian or other Pacific Islander, non-Hispanic/Latino; 42 Two or more races, non-Hispanic/Latino), 5 international. Average age 27. 745 applicants, 33% accepted, 105 enrolled. *Faculty:* 56 full-time (27 women), 6 part-time/adjunct (3 women). Expenses: Contact institution. *Financial support:* In 2018–19, 41 students received support. Career-related internships or fieldwork, institutionally sponsored loans, scholarships/grants, and veterans' educational benefits available. Financial award application deadline: 3/2; financial award applicants required to submit FAFSA. In 2018, 105 doctorates awarded. Offers veterinary medicine (DVM). *Application deadline:* For fall admission, 9/17 for domestic and international students. Electronic applications accepted. *Application Contact:* Karen Hutton-Lopez, Director of Admissions, 909-469-5650, Fax: 909-469-5570, E-mail: admissions@westernu.edu. *Dean,* Dr. Phil Nelson, 909-469-5661, Fax: 909-469-5635, E-mail: pnelson@westernu.edu.

Graduate College of Biomedical Sciences Students: 54 full-time (32 women), 3 part-time (1 woman); includes 46 minority (7 Black or African American, non-Hispanic/Latino; 15 Asian, non-Hispanic/Latino; 15 Hispanic/Latino; 1 Native Hawaiian or other Pacific Islander, non-Hispanic/Latino; 8 Two or more races, non-Hispanic/Latino), 1 international. Average age 26. 336 applicants, 18% accepted, 46 enrolled. *Faculty:* 9 full-time (2 women), 5 part-time/adjunct (1 woman). Expenses: Contact institution. *Financial support:* In 2018–19, 7 students received support. Scholarships/grants available. Financial award application deadline: 3/2; financial award applicants required to submit FAFSA. In 2018, 40 master's awarded. Offers biomedical sciences (MS); medical sciences (MS). *Application deadline:* Applications are processed on a rolling basis. *Application fee:* $50. Electronic applications accepted. *Application Contact:* Daniell Mendoza, Assistant Director of Admissions, 909-469-5541, Fax: 909-469-5570, E-mail: dmendoza@westernu.edu. *Acting Dean of Graduate College of Biomedical Sciences,* Dr. Guru Betageri, 909-469-5682, E-mail: gbetageri@westernu.edu.

WESTERN WASHINGTON UNIVERSITY, Bellingham, WA 98225-5996

General Information State-supported, coed, comprehensive institution. CGS member. *Graduate housing:* Rooms and/or apartments available on a first-come, first-served basis to single and married students. Housing application deadline: 5/1. *Research affiliation:* Golden Associates, American Metals Technology, Teck Cominco Ltd., Research Corporation, Dreyfus Foundation, NARSAD (mental health).

GRADUATE UNITS

Graduate School *Program availability:* Part-time. Electronic applications accepted.

College of Business and Economics *Program availability:* Part-time, evening/weekend. Offers business and economics (MBA, MP Acc). Electronic applications accepted.

College of Fine and Performing Arts *Program availability:* Part-time. Offers fine and performing arts (M Mus, MA); music (M Mus). Electronic applications accepted.

College of Humanities and Social Sciences *Program availability:* Part-time. Offers anthropology (MA); communication sciences and disorders (MA); English (MA); exercise science (MS); experimental psychology (MS); history (MA); humanities and social sciences (M Ed, MA); mental health counseling (MS); political science (MA); school counseling (M Ed); sport psychology (MS). Electronic applications accepted.

College of Sciences and Technology Offers biology (MS); chemistry (MS); computer science (MS); geology (MS); mathematics (MS); natural science/science education (M Ed); sciences and technology (M Ed, MS). Electronic applications accepted.

Huxley College of the Environment *Program availability:* Part-time. Offers environment (M Ed, MS); environmental education (M Ed); environmental science (MS); geography (MS); marine and estuarine science (MS). Electronic applications accepted.

Woodring College of Education *Program availability:* Part-time, online learning. Offers continuing and college education (M Ed); education (M Ed, MA, MIT); educational administration (M Ed); elementary education (M Ed); rehabilitation counseling (MA); secondary education (MIT); special education (M Ed); student affairs administration (M Ed). Electronic applications accepted.

WESTFIELD STATE UNIVERSITY, Westfield, MA 01086

General Information State-supported, coed, comprehensive institution. *Graduate housing:* On-campus housing not available.

GRADUATE UNITS

College of Graduate and Continuing Education *Program availability:* Part-time, evening/weekend. Offers accounting (MS); applied behavior analysis (MA); biology teacher education (M Ed); counseling (MA); criminal justice (MS); criminal justice administration (MPA); early childhood education (M Ed); elementary education (M Ed);

English (MA); forensic mental health counseling (MA); history teacher education (M Ed); mathematics teacher education (M Ed); mental health counseling (MA); moderate disabilities, 5-12 (M Ed); moderate disabilities, preK-8 (M Ed); non-profit management (MPA); physical education teacher education (M Ed); physician assistant studies (MS); public management (MPA); reading specialist (M Ed); school adjustment counseling (MA); school guidance counseling (MA); secondary education (M Ed); secondary education-biology (M Ed); secondary education-history (M Ed); secondary education-mathematics (M Ed); secondary education-physical education (M Ed); social work (MSW); special education (M Ed); vocational technical education (M Ed).

WEST LIBERTY UNIVERSITY, West Liberty, WV 26074

General Information State-supported, coed, comprehensive institution. *Graduate housing:* Room and/or apartments available on a first-come, first-served basis to single students; on-campus housing not available to married students.

GRADUATE UNITS

College of Education and Human Performance *Program availability:* Part-time, evening/weekend. Offers community education research and leadership (MA Ed); innovative instruction (MA Ed); leadership in disability services (MA Ed); leadership studies (MA Ed); multi-categorical special education (MA Ed); reading specialist (MA Ed); sports leadership and coaching (MA Ed). Electronic applications accepted.

College of Sciences Offers biology (MA, MS); biomedical science (MA); physician assistant studies (MS); zoo science (MA, MS).

Gary E. West College of Business Offers accounting (MBA); management (MBA).

School of Professional Studies Offers organizational leadership (MPS).

WESTMINSTER COLLEGE, New Wilmington, PA 16172-0001

General Information Independent-religious, coed, comprehensive institution. *Graduate housing:* On-campus housing not available.

GRADUATE UNITS

Graduate School *Program availability:* Part-time, evening/weekend. Offers clinical mental health counseling (MA); school counselor (M Ed); school principal K-12 (M Ed); school superintendent (M Ed); special education and reading specialist (M Ed).

WESTMINSTER COLLEGE, Salt Lake City, UT 84105-3697

General Information Independent, coed, comprehensive institution. *Graduate housing:* Room and/or apartments available on a first-come, first-served basis to single students; on-campus housing not available to married students. *Research affiliation:* International Psychotherapy Institute (clinical training), Zions Bank (entrepreneurship).

GRADUATE UNITS

The Bill and Vieve Gore School of Business *Program availability:* Part-time, evening/weekend, blended/hybrid learning. Offers accountancy (M Acc); business administration (MBA, Certificate); technology commercialization (MBA). Electronic applications accepted.

Master of Science in Mental Health Counseling Program Offers mental health counseling (MSMHC). Electronic applications accepted.

Program in Professional Communication Offers professional communication (MPC, MSC). Electronic applications accepted.

School of Education *Program availability:* Part-time, evening/weekend. Offers community leadership (MACL); education (M Ed); teaching (MAT). Electronic applications accepted.

School of Nursing and Health Sciences Offers family nurse practitioner (MSN); nurse anesthesia (MSNA); public health (MPH). Electronic applications accepted.

WESTMINSTER SEMINARY CALIFORNIA, Escondido, CA 92027-4128

General Information Independent-religious, coed, primarily men, graduate-only institution. *Graduate housing:* On-campus housing not available.

GRADUATE UNITS

Programs in Theology *Program availability:* Part-time, evening/weekend. Offers Biblical studies (MA); historical theology (MA); theological studies (M Div, MA).

WESTMINSTER THEOLOGICAL SEMINARY, Philadelphia, PA 19118

General Information Independent-religious, coed, primarily men, graduate-only institution. *Graduate housing:* Room and/or apartments available on a first-come, first-served basis to single students; on-campus housing not available to married students.

GRADUATE UNITS

Graduate and Professional Programs *Program availability:* Part-time. Offers apologetics (Th M); Biblical and urban studies (Certificate); Biblical counseling (MA); biblical studies (MAR); Christian studies (Certificate); church history (Th M); counseling (M Div); general studies (M Div, MAR); hermeneutics and Bible interpretations (PhD); historical and theological studies (PhD); historical theology (Th M); New Testament (Th M); Old Testament (Th M); pastoral counseling (D Min); pastoral ministry (M Div, D Min); systematic theology (Th M); theological studies (MAR); urban missions (M Div, MA, MAR, D Min).

WEST TEXAS A&M UNIVERSITY, Canyon, TX 79015

General Information State-supported, coed, comprehensive institution. CGS member. *Graduate housing:* Room and/or apartments available on a first-come, first-served basis to single students; on-campus housing not available to married students. *Research affiliation:* Owens Corning (sports exercise), Pantex (chemistry), Agriculture Experiment Station (agriculture), Engineering Experiment Station (math, science).

GRADUATE UNITS

College of Agriculture and Natural Sciences *Program availability:* Part-time. Offers agricultural business and economics (MS); agriculture (MS, PhD); agriculture and natural sciences (MS, PhD); animal science (MS); biology (MS); chemistry (MS); environmental science (MS); plant, soil and environmental science (MS). Electronic applications accepted.

College of Business *Program availability:* Part-time, evening/weekend, 100% online, blended/hybrid learning. Offers accounting (MPA); business (MBA, MPA, MS); business administration (MBA); finance and economics (MS). Electronic applications accepted.

College of Education and Social Sciences *Program availability:* Part-time, evening/weekend, online learning. Offers counseling (MA); criminal justice (MA); curriculum and instruction (M Ed); education and social sciences (M Ed, MA, MAT, MS); educational diagnostician (M Ed); educational leadership (M Ed); instructional design and technology (M Ed); psychology (MA); reading education (M Ed); school counseling (M Ed); social work (MS); teaching (MAT). Electronic applications accepted.

College of Fine Arts and Humanities *Program availability:* Part-time, evening/weekend. Offers communication (MA); English (MA); fine arts and humanities (MA, MFA, MM); history (MA); studio art (MFA). Electronic applications accepted.

School of Music *Program availability:* Part-time. Offers music (MA); performance (MM). Electronic applications accepted.

College of Nursing and Health Sciences *Program availability:* Part-time, evening/weekend. Offers communication disorders (MS); family nurse practitioner (MSN); nursing (MSN); nursing and health sciences (MS, MSN); sport management (MS); sports and exercise sciences (MS). Electronic applications accepted.

Program in Interdisciplinary Studies *Program availability:* Part-time, evening/weekend. Offers interdisciplinary studies (MA, MS). Electronic applications accepted.

School of Engineering, Computer Science and Mathematics *Program availability:* Part-time. Offers engineering technology (MS); mathematics (MS). Electronic applications accepted.

WEST VIRGINIA SCHOOL OF OSTEOPATHIC MEDICINE, Lewisburg, WV 24901-1196

General Information State-supported, coed, graduate-only institution. *Graduate housing:* On-campus housing not available.

GRADUATE UNITS

Professional Program Offers osteopathic medicine (DO). Electronic applications accepted.

WEST VIRGINIA STATE UNIVERSITY, Institute, WV 25112-1000

General Information State-supported, coed, comprehensive institution. *Graduate housing:* Rooms and/or apartments available on a first-come, first-served basis to single and married students. Housing application deadline: 9/1.

GRADUATE UNITS

Biotechnology Graduate Program Offers biotechnology (MA, MS). Electronic applications accepted.

Master of Science Program in Law Enforcement and Administration Offers law enforcement and administration (MS). Electronic applications accepted.

Media Studies Graduate Program Offers media studies (MA). Electronic applications accepted.

WEST VIRGINIA UNIVERSITY, Morgantown, WV 26506

General Information State-supported, coed, university. CGS member. *Enrollment:* 4,278 full-time matriculated graduate/professional students (2,243 women), 1,431 part-time matriculated graduate/professional students (912 women). *Enrollment by degree level:* 3,125 master's, 1,242 doctoral, 1,520 other advanced degrees. *Graduate faculty:* 355. *Graduate housing:* Rooms and/or apartments available on a first-come, first-served basis to single and married students. Housing application deadline: 1/22. *Student services:* Campus employment opportunities, campus safety program, career counseling, child daycare facilities, exercise/wellness program, free psychological counseling, grant writing training, international student services, low-cost health insurance, multicultural affairs office, services for students with disabilities, teacher training, writing training. *Library facilities:* Downtown Library Complex plus 5 others. *Collection:* Books: 1.1 million (physical), 621,166 (digital/electronic); Serial titles: 56,340 (physical), 96,553 (digital/electronic); Databases: 975. Study areas open 24 hours, 5–7 days a week; students can reserve study rooms.

Computer facilities: Computer purchase and lease plans are available. 1,800 computers available on campus for general student use. A campuswide network can be accessed from student residence rooms and from off campus. Online class registration is available.

Website: http://www.wvu.edu/

General Application Contact: Dr. Betty Mei, Program Director for Graduate Student Success, 304-293-7173, E-mail: bmei@mail.wvu.edu.

GRADUATE UNITS

College of Business and Economics Students: 341 full-time (139 women), 44 part-time (13 women); includes 39 minority (10 Black or African American, non-Hispanic/Latino; 12 Asian, non-Hispanic/Latino; 7 Hispanic/Latino; 10 Two or more races, non-Hispanic/Latino), 40 international. Expenses: Contact institution. *Financial support:* Fellowships, research assistantships, teaching assistantships, career-related internships or fieldwork, Federal Work-Study, institutionally sponsored loans, scholarships/grants, health care benefits, tuition waivers (full and partial), unspecified assistantships, and administrative assistantships available. Financial award application deadline: 2/1; financial award applicants required to submit FAFSA. In 2018, 208 master's, 20 doctorates awarded. *Program availability:* Part-time, online learning. Offers accountancy (M Acc); accounting (PhD); business administration (MBA); business cyber security management (MS); business data analytics (MS); economics (MA, PhD); finance (MS, PhD); forensic and fraud examination (MS); industrial relations (MS); management (PhD); marketing (PhD). *Application deadline:* For fall admission, 10/15 priority date for domestic and international students; for spring admission, 3/1 priority date for domestic and international students. Applications are processed on a rolling basis. *Application fee:* $60. Electronic applications accepted. *Application Contact:* Dr. Virginia F Kleist, Associate Dean for Graduate Programs, 304-293-7939, Fax: 304-293-7188, E-mail: Virginia.Kleist@mail.wvu.edu. *Dean,* Dr. Javier Reyes, 304-293-7800, Fax: 304-293-4056, E-mail: javier.reyes@mail.wvu.edu.

College of Creative Arts Students: 110 full-time (58 women), 30 part-time (15 women); includes 15 minority (5 Black or African American, non-Hispanic/Latino; 4 Asian, non-Hispanic/Latino; 6 Hispanic/Latino), 29 international. Expenses: Contact institution. *Financial support:* Research assistantships, teaching assistantships, career-related internships or fieldwork, Federal Work-Study, institutionally sponsored loans, scholarships/grants, health care benefits, tuition waivers (partial), and administrative assistantships available. Financial award applicants required to submit FAFSA. In 2018, 29 master's, 14 doctorates awarded. *Program availability:* Part-time. Offers acting (MFA); art education (MA); art history (MA); ceramics (MFA); collaborative piano (MM, DMA); composition (MM, DMA); conducting (MM, DMA); costume design and technology (MFA); graphic design (MFA); intermedia and photography (MFA); jazz pedagogy (MM); lighting design and technology (MFA); music (PhD); music education (MM, PhD); music industry (MA); music theory (MM); musicology (MA); painting and printmaking (MFA); performance (MM, DMA); piano pedagogy (MM); scenic design and technology (MFA); sculpture (MFA); studio art (MA); technical direction (MFA); vocal pedagogy and performance (DMA). *Application deadline:* For fall admission, 3/1 priority date for domestic students, 2/15 for international students; for spring admission, 11/1 for domestic students, 9/15 for international students. Applications are processed on a rolling basis. *Application fee:* $60. Electronic applications accepted. *Application*

Contact: Dr. Keith Jackson, Dean, 304-293-4351, Fax: 304-293-6896, E-mail: Keith.jackson@mail.wvu.edu. *Dean,* Dr. Keith Jackson, 304-293-4351, Fax: 304-293-6896, E-mail: Keith.jackson@mail.wvu.edu.

College of Education and Human Services Students: 392 full-time (325 women), 337 part-time (285 women); includes 44 minority (16 Black or African American, non-Hispanic/Latino; 16 Hispanic/Latino; 12 Two or more races, non-Hispanic/Latino), 11 international. Expenses: Contact institution. *Financial support:* Fellowships, research assistantships, teaching assistantships, career-related internships or fieldwork, Federal Work-Study, institutionally sponsored loans, health care benefits, tuition waivers (full and partial), and administrative assistantships available. Financial award applicants required to submit FAFSA. In 2018, 303 master's, 6 doctorates awarded. *Program availability:* Part-time, evening/weekend, online learning. Offers audiology (Au D); autism spectrum disorder (MA); clinical rehabilitation and mental health counseling (MS); communication science and disorders (PhD); counseling (MA); counseling psychology (PhD); curriculum and instruction (Ed D); early childhood education (MA); early intervention/ early childhood special education (MA); education (PhD); educational leadership (MA); educational leadership/ public school administration (Ed D); educational leadership/public school administration (MA); educational psychology (MA, Ed D); elementary education (MA); gifted education (MA); higher education administration (MA, Ed D); higher education curriculum and teaching (MA); institutional design and technology (MA); instructional design and technology (Ed D); literacy education (MA); secondary education (MA); secondary education/English (MA); special education (Ed D); speech pathology (MS). *Application deadline:* For fall admission, 8/1 for domestic students; for spring admission, 1/1 for domestic students; for summer admission, 5/1 for domestic students. *Application fee:* $60. Electronic applications accepted. *Application Contact:* Dr. Melissa Luna, Associate Dean for Research, 304-293-2174, Fax: 304-293-3802, E-mail: Melissa.Luna@mail.wvu.edu. *Interim Dean,* Dr. Tracy L. Morris, 304-293-0816, Fax: 304-293-7565, E-mail: Tracy.Morris@mail.wvu.edu.

College of Law Students: 324 full-time (146 women), 5 part-time (2 women); includes 40 minority (12 Black or African American, non-Hispanic/Latino; 4 Asian, non-Hispanic/Latino; 10 Hispanic/Latino; 14 Two or more races, non-Hispanic/Latino). Expenses: Contact institution. *Financial support:* Fellowships, research assistantships, teaching assistantships, career-related internships or fieldwork, Federal Work-Study, institutionally sponsored loans, scholarships/grants, health care benefits, tuition waivers (full), unspecified assistantships, and administrative assistantships, resident assistantships available. Support available to part-time students. Financial award application deadline: 3/1; financial award applicants required to submit FAFSA. In 2018, 4 master's awarded. *Program availability:* Part-time. Offers energy law and sustainable development (LL M); forensic justice (LL M); law (JD); white collar forensic justice (LL M). *Application deadline:* For fall admission, 2/1 for domestic and international students. Applications are processed on a rolling basis. *Application fee:* $60. Electronic applications accepted. *Application Contact:* Gregory W. Bowman, Dean, College of Law, 304-293-3199, Fax: 304-293-8102, E-mail: gregory.bowman@mail.wvu.edu. *Dean,* College of Law, Gregory W. Bowman, 304-293-3199, Fax: 304-293-8102, E-mail: gregory.bowman@mail.wvu.edu.

College of Physical Activity and Sport Sciences Students: 98 full-time (40 women), 122 part-time (42 women); includes 38 minority (18 Black or African American, non-Hispanic/Latino; 4 Asian, non-Hispanic/Latino; 10 Hispanic/Latino; 6 Two or more races, non-Hispanic/Latino), 13 international. Expenses: Contact institution. *Financial support:* Research assistantships, teaching assistantships, career-related internships or fieldwork, Federal Work-Study, institutionally sponsored loans, health care benefits, tuition waivers (full and partial), and administrative assistantships available. Support available to part-time students. Financial award application deadline: 2/1; financial award applicants required to submit FAFSA. In 2018, 74 master's, 5 doctorates awarded. Offers athletic training (MS); coaching and sport education (MS); coaching and teaching studies (Ed D, PhD); physical education/teacher education (MS); sport coaching (MS); sport management (MS); sport, exercise & performance psychology (MS). *Application deadline:* For fall admission, 12/15 for domestic students, 10/1 for international students. *Application fee:* $60. Electronic applications accepted. *Application Contact:* Sean Bulger, Online Program Coordinator, 304-293-0845, Fax: 304-293-4641, E-mail: sean.bulger@mail.wvu.edu. *Online Program Coordinator,* Sean Bulger, 304-293-0845, Fax: 304-293-4641, E-mail: sean.bulger@mail.wvu.edu.

Davis College of Agriculture, Forestry and Consumer Sciences Students: 188 full-time (86 women), 47 part-time (30 women); includes 22 minority (5 Black or African American, non-Hispanic/Latino; 5 Asian, non-Hispanic/Latino; 8 Hispanic/Latino; 4 Two or more races, non-Hispanic/Latino), 60 international. Expenses: Contact institution. *Financial support:* Fellowships, research assistantships, teaching assistantships, career-related internships or fieldwork, Federal Work-Study, institutionally sponsored loans, tuition waivers (full and partial), and unspecified assistantships available. Financial award application deadline: 2/1; financial award applicants required to submit FAFSA. In 2018, 56 master's, 14 doctorates awarded. *Program availability:* Part-time. Offers agricultural and extension education (MS, PhD); agriculture and resource management (MS); agriculture, natural resources and design (M Agr); agronomy (MS); animal and food science (PhD); animal physiology (MS); applied and environmental microbiology (MS); design and merchandising (MS); entomology (MS); forest resource science (PhD); forestry (MSF); genetics and developmental biology (MS, PhD); horticulture (MS); human and community development (PhD); landscape architecture (MLA); natural resource economics (PhD); nutritional and food science (MS); plant and soil science (PhD); plant pathology (MS); recreation, parks and tourism resources (MS); reproductive physiology (MS, PhD); wildlife and fisheries resources (PhD). *Application deadline:* For fall admission, 6/1 priority date for domestic students, 6/1 for international students; for spring admission, 1/5 for domestic and international students. Applications are processed on a rolling basis. *Application fee:* $60. Electronic applications accepted. *Application Contact:* Dr. J. Todd Petty, Associate Dean, 304-293-2278, Fax: 304-293-3740, E-mail: jtpetty@mail.wvu.edu. *Interim Dean,* Dr. Ken Blemings, 304-293-2395, Fax: 304-293-3740, E-mail: ken.blemings@mail.wvu.edu.

Eberly College of Arts and Sciences Students: 803 full-time (434 women), 237 part-time (138 women); includes 99 minority (31 Black or African American, non-Hispanic/Latino; 1 American Indian or Alaska Native, non-Hispanic/Latino; 16 Asian, non-Hispanic/Latino; 25 Hispanic/Latino; 26 Two or more races, non-Hispanic/Latino), 208 international. Expenses: Contact institution. *Financial support:* Fellowships with full tuition reimbursements, research assistantships with full tuition reimbursements, teaching assistantships with full tuition reimbursements, career-related internships or fieldwork, Federal Work-Study, institutionally sponsored loans, scholarships/grants, health care benefits, tuition waivers (full and partial), unspecified assistantships, and administrative assistantships available. Financial award application deadline: 2/1; financial award applicants required to submit FAFSA. In 2018, 285 master's, 63 doctorates awarded. *Program availability:* Part-time, evening/weekend, online learning. Offers biology (MS, PhD); chemistry (MS, PhD); communication studies (MA, PhD); computational statistics (PhD); creative writing (MFA); English (MA, PhD); forensic and

investigative science (MS); forensic science (PhD); geography (MA); geology (MA, PhD); history (MA, PhD); legal studies (MLS); mathematics (MS); physics (MS, PhD); political science (MA, PhD); professional writing and editing (MA); psychology (MA); public administration (MPA); social work (MSW); sociology (MA, PhD); statistics (MS). *Application deadline:* For spring admission, 2/15 priority date for domestic and international students. Applications are processed on a rolling basis. *Application fee:* $45. Electronic applications accepted. *Application Contact:* Dr. Jessica Queener, Director of Graduate Studies, 304-293-7476 Ext. 5205, Fax: 304-293-6858, E-mail: Jessica.queener@mail.wvu.edu. *Dean,* Dr. Gregory Dunaway, 304-293-4611, Fax: 304-293-6858, E-mail: gregory.dunaway@mail.wvu.edu.

School of Social Work *Program availability:* Part-time. Offers aging and health care (MSW); children and families (MSW); community mental health (MSW); community organization and social administration (MSW); direct (clinical) social work practice (MSW).

Reed College of Media Students: 128 full-time (97 women), 192 part-time (147 women); includes 58 minority (34 Black or African American, non-Hispanic/Latino; 1 Asian, non-Hispanic/Latino; 18 Hispanic/Latino; 5 Two or more races, non-Hispanic/Latino), 2 international. Expenses: Contact institution. *Financial support:* Research assistantships, teaching assistantships, career-related internships or fieldwork, Federal Work-Study, institutionally sponsored loans, health care benefits, tuition waivers (full and partial), and administrative assistantships available. Financial award application deadline: 2/1; financial award applicants required to submit FAFSA. In 2018, 165 master's awarded. *Program availability:* Part-time, online learning. Offers data marketing communications (MS); integrated marketing communications (MS, Graduate Certificate); journalism (MSJ); media solutions and innovation (MSJ). *Application deadline:* For fall admission, 3/1 priority date for domestic students, 3/1 for international students. *Application fee:* $60. Electronic applications accepted. *Application Contact:* Dr. Steve Urbanski, Director of Graduate Studies/Associate Professor, 304-293-6797, Fax: 304-293-3072, E-mail: steve.urbanski@mail.wvu.edu. *Dean,* Dr. Diana Knott Martinelli, 304-293-6561 Ext. 5409, Fax: 304-293-3072, E-mail: Diana.Martinelli@mail.wvu.edu.

School of Dentistry Students: 214 full-time (108 women); includes 23 minority (1 Black or African American, non-Hispanic/Latino; 15 Asian, non-Hispanic/Latino; 4 Hispanic/Latino; 3 Two or more races, non-Hispanic/Latino), 12 international. Expenses: Contact institution. *Financial support:* Research assistantships, teaching assistantships, Federal Work-Study, institutionally sponsored loans, scholarships/grants, health care benefits, and tuition waivers (partial) available. Financial award application deadline: 3/1; financial award applicants required to submit FAFSA. In 2018, 7 master's, 55 doctorates awarded. Offers dental hygiene (MS); dentistry (DDS); endodontics (MS); orthodontics (MS); periodontics (MS); prosthodontics (MS). *Application deadline:* For fall admission, 11/1 for domestic and international students. Applications are processed on a rolling basis. *Application fee:* $60. Electronic applications accepted. *Application Contact:* Dr. Sheila Price, Associate Dean for Admissions, Recruitment, and Access, 304-293-6646, E-mail: sprice@hsc.wvu.edu. *Dean,* Dr. Tom Borgia, 304-293-2521, E-mail: aborgia@hsc.wvu.edu.

School of Medicine Students: 798 full-time (440 women), 24 part-time (13 women); includes 141 minority (15 Black or African American, non-Hispanic/Latino; 1 American Indian or Alaska Native, non-Hispanic/Latino; 64 Asian, non-Hispanic/Latino; 40 Hispanic/Latino; 1 Native Hawaiian or other Pacific Islander, non-Hispanic/Latino; 20 Two or more races, non-Hispanic/Latino), 36 international. Expenses: Contact institution. *Financial support:* Fellowships, research assistantships, teaching assistantships, career-related internships or fieldwork, Federal Work-Study, institutionally sponsored loans, health care benefits, tuition waivers (full and partial), and administrative assistantships available. Financial award applicants required to submit FAFSA. In 2018, 93 master's, 11 doctorates awarded. *Program availability:* Part-time, evening/weekend. Offers biochemistry and molecular biology (PhD); biomedical science (MS); cancer cell biology (PhD); cellular and integrative physiology (PhD); exercise physiology (MS, PhD); health sciences (MS); immunology (PhD); medicine (MD); occupational therapy (MOT); pathologists assistant' (MHS); physical therapy (DPT). *Application deadline:* Applications are processed on a rolling basis. *Application fee:* $60. Electronic applications accepted. *Application Contact:* Lisa M. Salati, Assistant Vice President, Graduate Education, 304-293-7759, Fax: 304-293-3080, E-mail: lsalati@hsc.wvu.edu. *Executive Dean,* Dr. Clay Marsh, 304-293-6607, Fax: 304-293-6627, E-mail: clay.marsh@hsc.wvu.edu.

School of Nursing Students: 25 full-time (21 women), 159 part-time (142 women); includes 12 minority (2 Black or African American, non-Hispanic/Latino; 2 Asian, non-Hispanic/Latino; 3 Hispanic/Latino; 1 Native Hawaiian or other Pacific Islander, non-Hispanic/Latino; 4 Two or more races, non-Hispanic/Latino). Expenses: Contact institution. *Financial support:* Teaching assistantships, Federal Work-Study, institutionally sponsored loans, health care benefits, tuition waivers (partial), and administrative assistantships available. Financial award application deadline: 2/1; financial award applicants required to submit FAFSA. In 2018, 38 master's, 1 doctorate, 3 other advanced degrees awarded. *Program availability:* Part-time, online learning. Offers nurse practitioner (Certificate); nursing (MSN, DNP, PhD). *Application deadline:* For fall admission, 6/1 for domestic students. *Application fee:* $60. Electronic applications accepted. *Application Contact:* Brandy Sue Toothman, Program Assistant III, 304-293-4298, Fax: 304-293-2546, E-mail: btoothman@hsc.wvu.edu. *Dean,* Dr. Tara Hulsey, 304-293-6521, Fax: 304-293-6826, E-mail: tmhulsey@hsc.wvu.edu.

School of Pharmacy Students: 338 full-time (202 women); includes 37 minority (7 Black or African American, non-Hispanic/Latino; 1 American Indian or Alaska Native, non-Hispanic/Latino; 14 Asian, non-Hispanic/Latino; 7 Hispanic/Latino; 8 Two or more races, non-Hispanic/Latino), 23 international. Expenses: Contact institution. *Financial support:* Research assistantships, teaching assistantships, career-related internships or fieldwork, Federal Work-Study, institutionally sponsored loans, health care benefits, tuition waivers (full and partial), and unspecified assistantships available. Financial award application deadline: 3/1; financial award applicants required to submit FAFSA. In 2018, 8 doctorates awarded. Offers health services and outcomes research (PhD); pharmaceutical and pharmacological sciences (PhD); professional pharmacy (Pharm D). *Application deadline:* For fall admission, 3/1 priority date for domestic and international students. *Application fee:* $60. Electronic applications accepted. *Application Contact:* Dr. Mary L. Euler, Associate Dean for Student Services, 304-293-7806, Fax: 304-293-5483, E-mail: mleuler@hsc.wvu.edu. *Dean,* Dr. Willaim P Petros, 304-293-5212, Fax: 304-293-5483, E-mail: wpetros@hsc.wvu.edu.

School of Public Health Students: 52 full-time (34 women), 26 part-time (15 women); includes 13 minority (4 Black or African American, non-Hispanic/Latino; 5 Asian, non-Hispanic/Latino; 2 Hispanic/Latino; 2 Two or more races, non-Hispanic/Latino), 10 international. Expenses: Contact institution. *Financial support:* Research assistantships, teaching assistantships, scholarships/grants, and health care benefits available. Financial award application deadline: 2/1; financial award applicants required to submit FAFSA. In 2018, 38 master's, 9 doctorates awarded. *Program availability:* Part-time, online learning. Offers biostatistics (MPH, MS, PhD); epidemiology (MPH, PhD);

health policy (MPH); occupational and environmental health sciences (MPH, PhD); public health (MPH); school health education (MS); social and behavioral science (MPH, PhD). *Application deadline:* For fall admission, 4/15 priority date for domestic students; for spring admission, 12/1 for domestic students. Applications are processed on a rolling basis. *Application fee:* $60. *Application Contact:* Leah Adkins, Senior Program Coordinator, 304-293-1097, E-mail: leadkins@hsc.wvu.edu. *Dean,* Dr. Jeffrey Coben, 304-293-5775, E-mail: jcoben@hsc.wvu.edu.

Statler College of Engineering and Mineral Resources Students: 466 full-time (113 women), 154 part-time (27 women); includes 57 minority (22 Black or African American, non-Hispanic/Latino; 1 American Indian or Alaska Native, non-Hispanic/Latino; 8 Asian, non-Hispanic/Latino; 12 Hispanic/Latino; 14 Two or more races, non-Hispanic/Latino), 283 international. Expenses: Contact institution. *Financial support:* Fellowships, research assistantships, teaching assistantships, career-related internships or fieldwork, Federal Work-Study, institutionally sponsored loans, health care benefits, tuition waivers (full and partial), unspecified assistantships, and administrative assistantships available. Financial award application deadline: 2/1; financial award applicants required to submit FAFSA. In 2018, 179 master's, 19 doctorates awarded. *Program availability:* Part-time. Offers aerospace engineering (MSAE, PhD); chemical engineering (MS Ch E, PhD); civil engineering (MSCE, PhD); computer engineering (PhD); computer science (MSCS, PhD); electrical engineering (MSEE, PhD); energy systems engineering (MSESE); engineering (MSE); industrial engineering (MSIE, PhD); industrial hygiene (MS); material science and engineering (MSMSE, PhD); mechanical engineering (MSME, PhD); mining engineering (MS Min E, PhD); petroleum and natural gas engineering (MSPNGE, PhD); safety management (MS); software engineering (MSSE). *Application deadline:* For fall admission, 4/1 for international students; for winter admission, 4/1 for international students; for spring admission, 10/1 for international students. Applications are processed on a rolling basis. *Application fee:* $60. Electronic applications accepted. *Application Contact:* Dr. David A. Wyrick, Associate Dean, Academic Affairs, 304-293-4334, Fax: 304-293-5024, E-mail: david.wyrick@mail.wvu.edu. *Interim Dean,* Dr. Earl Scime, 304-293-4157 Ext. 2237, Fax: 304-293-2037, E-mail: earl.scime@mail.wvu.edu.

WEST VIRGINIA WESLEYAN COLLEGE, Buckhannon, WV 26201

General Information Independent-religious, coed, comprehensive institution. *Graduate housing:* Room and/or apartments available to single students; on-campus housing not available to married students.

GRADUATE UNITS

MBA Program *Program availability:* Part-time, evening/weekend. Offers business administration (MBA).

Program in Creative Writing Offers creative writing (MFA).

School of Exercise Science and Athletic Training Offers athletic training (MS).

School of Nursing Offers family nurse practitioner (MS, Post Master's Certificate); nurse-midwifery (MS); nursing (DNP); nursing leadership (MS); psychiatric mental health nurse practitioner (MS).

WHEATON COLLEGE, Wheaton, IL 60187-5593

General Information Independent-religious, coed, comprehensive institution. CGS member. *Enrollment:* 2,944 graduate, professional, and undergraduate students; 274 full-time matriculated graduate/professional students (159 women), 201 part-time matriculated graduate/professional students (109 women). *Enrollment by degree level:* 356 master's, 119 doctoral. *Graduate faculty:* 40 full-time (12 women), 21 part-time/adjunct (12 women). *Tuition:* Full-time $20,400; part-time $850 per credit hour. Tuition and fees vary according to degree level and program. *Graduate housing:* Rooms and/or apartments available on a first-come, first-served basis to single and married students. Typical cost: $6210 per year for single students; $11,024 per year for married students. Room charges vary according to board plan and housing facility selected. *Student services:* Campus employment opportunities, campus safety program, career counseling, exercise/wellness program, free psychological counseling, grant writing training, international student services, multicultural affairs office, services for students with disabilities, writing training. *Library facilities:* Buswell Memorial Library. *Collection:* Books: 357,263 (physical), 162,503 (digital/electronic); Serial titles: 371 (physical), 6,140 (digital/electronic); Databases: 214. Weekly public service hours: 94; students can reserve study rooms.

Computer facilities: 325 computers available on campus for general student use. A campuswide network can be accessed from student residence rooms and from off campus. Online class registration, financial information, degree requirements evaluation are available.

Website: http://www.wheaton.edu/

General Application Contact: Terrance Campbell, Director of Graduate Admissions, 630-752-5195, Fax: 630-752-7047, E-mail: graduate.admissions@wheaton.edu.

GRADUATE UNITS

Graduate School Students: 274 full-time (159 women), 201 part-time (109 women); includes 92 minority (24 Black or African American, non-Hispanic/Latino; 3 American Indian or Alaska Native, non-Hispanic/Latino; 34 Asian, non-Hispanic/Latino; 14 Hispanic/Latino; 17 Two or more races, non-Hispanic/Latino), 99 international. Average age 31. 316 applicants, 78% accepted, 142 enrolled. *Faculty:* 40 full-time (12 women), 21 part-time/adjunct (12 women). Expenses: Contact institution. *Financial support:* Fellowships, career-related internships or fieldwork, Federal Work-Study, scholarships/grants, and unspecified assistantships available. Financial award application deadline: 3/1; financial award applicants required to submit FAFSA. In 2018, 139 master's, 21 doctorates awarded. *Program availability:* Part-time. Offers Biblical and theological studies (PhD); Biblical archaeology (MA); Biblical exegesis (MA); Biblical studies (MA); Christian formation and ministry (MA); clinical mental health counseling (MA); clinical psychology (Psy D); elementary education (MAT); evangelism and leadership (MA); general theological studies (MA); historical and systematic theology (MA); history of Christianity (MA); marriage and family therapy (MA); missional church movements (MA); secondary education (MAT). *Application deadline:* For fall admission, 1/1 priority date for domestic and international students; for spring admission, 11/1 for domestic students. Applications are processed on a rolling basis. *Application fee:* $30. Electronic applications accepted. *Application Contact:* Terrance Campbell, Director of Graduate Admissions, 630-752-5195, E-mail: graduate.admissions@wheaton.edu. *Dean,* Dr. Scott Moreau, 630-752-5933, E-mail: graduate.dean@wheaton.edu.

Humanitarian and Disaster Leadership Program Students: 8 full-time (6 women), 8 part-time (all women); includes 1 minority (Two or more races, non-Hispanic/Latino), 1 international. Average age 35. *Faculty:* 1 full-time (0 women), 4 part-time/adjunct (2 women). Expenses: Contact institution. *Financial support:* Federal Work-Study and scholarships/grants available. Financial award applicants required to submit FAFSA. *Program availability:* Part-time. Offers humanitarian and disaster leadership (MA). *Application deadline:* For fall admission, 3/1 priority date for domestic students.

Applications are processed on a rolling basis. *Application fee:* $30. Electronic applications accepted. *Application Contact:* Terrance Campbell, Director of Graduate Admissions, 630-752-5195, Fax: 630-752-7047, E-mail: graduate.admissions@wheaton.edu. *Executive Director,* Dr. Jamie Aten, 630-752-7659, E-mail: jamie.aten@wheaton.edu.

WHEELING JESUIT UNIVERSITY, Wheeling, WV 26003-6295

General Information Independent-religious, coed, comprehensive institution. *Graduate housing:* Rooms and/or apartments available on a first-come, first-served basis to single and married students.

GRADUATE UNITS

Department of Business *Program availability:* Part-time, evening/weekend. Offers accounting (MSA); business administration (MBA). Electronic applications accepted.

Department of Education *Program availability:* Part-time, evening/weekend, online learning. Offers education (MEL). Electronic applications accepted.

Department of Nursing *Program availability:* Part-time, evening/weekend, online learning. Offers nursing (MSN). Electronic applications accepted.

Department of Physical Therapy Offers physical therapy (DPT). Electronic applications accepted.

Department of Social Sciences *Program availability:* Part-time, evening/weekend. Offers social sciences (MSOL). Electronic applications accepted.

WHITTIER COLLEGE, Whittier, CA 90608-0634

General Information Independent, coed, comprehensive institution. *Graduate housing:* On-campus housing not available.

GRADUATE UNITS

Graduate Programs *Program availability:* Part-time, evening/weekend. Offers educational administration (MA Ed); elementary education (MA Ed); secondary education (MA Ed).

WHITWORTH UNIVERSITY, Spokane, WA 99251-0001

General Information Independent-religious, coed, comprehensive institution. *Graduate housing:* Room and/or apartments available on a first-come, first-served basis to single students; on-campus housing not available to married students. Housing application deadline: 5/1.

GRADUATE UNITS

Graduate Studies in Theology *Program availability:* Part-time, evening/weekend. Offers Christian ministry (MA); mission and culture (MA); theology (MA). Electronic applications accepted.

School of Business *Program availability:* Part-time, evening/weekend. Offers business (MBA). Electronic applications accepted.

School of Education *Program availability:* Part-time, evening/weekend, online learning. Offers administration (M Ed); counseling (M Ed); education (M Ed, MAT, MIT); elementary education (M Ed); gifted and talented (MAT); school counselors (M Ed); secondary education (M Ed); social agency/church setting (M Ed); special education (MAT); teaching (MIT).

WICHITA STATE UNIVERSITY, Wichita, KS 67260

General Information State-supported, coed, university. CGS member. *Enrollment:* 1,200 full-time matriculated graduate/professional students (693 women), 1,572 part-time matriculated graduate/professional students (821 women). *Enrollment by degree level:* 1,816 master's, 488 doctoral, 468 other advanced degrees. *Graduate faculty:* 399 full-time (159 women), 20 part-time/adjunct (12 women). *Graduate housing:* Rooms and/or apartments available on a first-come, first-served basis to single and married students. *Student services:* Campus employment opportunities, campus safety program, career counseling, child daycare facilities, exercise/wellness program, free psychological counseling, grant writing training, international student services, low-cost health insurance, multicultural affairs office, services for students with disabilities, teacher training, writing training. *Library facilities:* Ablah Library plus 2 others. *Collection:* Books: 1.9 million (physical), 475,186 (digital/electronic); Serial titles: 460 (physical), 94,566 (digital/electronic); Databases: 269. Study areas open 24 hours, 5–7 days a week; students can reserve study rooms.

Computer facilities: 1,500 computers available on campus for general student use. A campuswide network can be accessed from student residence rooms and from off campus. Online class registration, learning management system are available.

Website: http://www.wichita.edu/

General Application Contact: Jordan Oleson, Assistant Director of Graduate Admissions, 316-978-3095, Fax: 316-978-3253, E-mail: jordan.oleson@wichita.edu.

GRADUATE UNITS

Graduate School Students: 1,200 full-time (693 women), 1,572 part-time (821 women); includes 529 minority (142 Black or African American, non-Hispanic/Latino; 22 American Indian or Alaska Native, non-Hispanic/Latino; 107 Asian, non-Hispanic/Latino; 197 Hispanic/Latino; 1 Native Hawaiian or other Pacific Islander, non-Hispanic/Latino; 60 Two or more races, non-Hispanic/Latino), 469 international. Average age 32. 1,950 applicants, 77% accepted, 798 enrolled. *Faculty:* 399 full-time (159 women), 20 part-time/adjunct (12 women). Expenses: Contact institution. *Financial support:* In 2018–19, 579 research assistantships with partial tuition reimbursements (averaging $11,664 per year), 497 teaching assistantships with partial tuition reimbursements (averaging $9,720 per year) were awarded; fellowships, career-related internships or fieldwork, Federal Work-Study, institutionally sponsored loans, scholarships/grants, traineeships, health care benefits, and unspecified assistantships also available. Support available to part-time students. Financial award application deadline: 4/1; financial award applicants required to submit FAFSA. In 2018, 712 master's, 123 doctorates, 6 other advanced degrees awarded. *Program availability:* Part-time, evening/weekend, 100% online, blended/hybrid learning. *Application deadline:* For fall admission, 7/15 priority date for domestic students, 5/1 for international students; for spring admission, 12/1 priority date for domestic students, 9/1 for international students. Applications are processed on a rolling basis. *Application fee:* $60 ($75 for international students). Electronic applications accepted. *Application Contact:* Jordan Oleson, Assistant Director of Graduate Admissions, 316-978-3095, Fax: 316-978-3253, E-mail: jordan.oleson@wichita.edu. *Dean of the Graduate School/Associate Vice President of Research and Technology Transfer,* Dr. Coleen Pugh, 316-978-3095, Fax: 316-978-3253, E-mail: coleen.pugh@wichita.edu.

College of Applied Studies Expenses: Contact institution. *Program availability:* Part-time, evening/weekend, 100% online, blended/hybrid learning. Offers counseling (M Ed); education (M Ed, MAT, Ed D, Ed S); educational leadership (M Ed, Ed D); educational psychology (M Ed); exercise science (M Ed); learning and instructional design (M Ed); school psychology (Ed S); special education (M Ed); sport management (M Ed); teaching (MAT). *Application Contact:* Jordan Oleson, Admissions Coordinator, 316-978-3095, Fax: 316-978-3253, E-mail: jordan.oleson@wichita.edu. *Dean,* Dr. Shirley Lefever, 316-978-3301, Fax: 316-978-3302, E-mail: shirley.lefever@wichita.edu.

College of Engineering Expenses: Contact institution. *Program availability:* Part-time, evening/weekend. Offers aerospace engineering (MS, PhD); biomedical engineering (MS); computer networking (MS); computer science (MS); electrical and computer engineering (MS); electrical engineering and computer science (PhD); engineering (MEM, MS, PhD); engineering management (MEM); industrial engineering (MS, PhD); mechanical engineering (MS, PhD). *Application Contact:* Jordan Oleson, Admissions Coordinator, 316-978-3095, Fax: 316-978-3253, E-mail: jordan.oleson@wichita.edu. *Dean,* Dr. Dennis R. Livesay, 316-978-3400, Fax: 316-978-3853, E-mail: dennis.livesay@wichita.edu.

College of Fine Arts Expenses: Contact institution. *Program availability:* Part-time. Offers fine arts (MFA, MM, MME); music (MM); music education (MME); studio arts (MFA). *Application Contact:* Jordan Oleson, Admissions Coordinator, 316-978-3095, Fax: 316-978-3253, E-mail: jordan.oleson@wichita.edu. *Dean,* Dr. Rodney E. Miller, 316-978-3389, Fax: 316-978-3951, E-mail: rodney.miller@wichita.edu.

College of Health Professions Expenses: Contact institution. *Program availability:* Part-time. Offers aging studies (MA); communication sciences and disorders (MA, Au D, PhD); health professions (MA, MPA, MSN, Au D, DNP, DPT, PhD); nursing (MSN); nursing practice (DNP); physical therapy (DPT); physician assistant (MPA). *Application Contact:* Jordan Oleson, Admissions Coordinator, 316-978-3095, Fax: 316-978-3253, E-mail: jordan.oleson@wichita.edu. *Dean,* Dr. Sandra C. Bibb, 316-978-3600, Fax: 316-978-3025, E-mail: sandra.bibb@wichita.edu.

Fairmount College of Liberal Arts and Sciences Expenses: Contact institution. *Program availability:* Part-time, evening/weekend, 100% online, blended/hybrid learning. Offers anthropology (MA); applied mathematics (PhD); biological sciences (MS); chemistry (MS, PhD); clinical (PhD); communication (MA); community (PhD); creative writing (MFA); criminal justice (MA); earth, environmental, and physical sciences (MS); English (MA); history (MA); human factors (PhD); liberal arts and sciences (MA, MFA, MPA, MS, MSW, PhD); liberal studies (MA); mathematics (MS); physics (MS); public administration (MPA); social work (MSW); sociology (MA); Spanish (MA). *Application Contact:* Jordan Oleson, Admissions Coordinator, 316-978-3095, Fax: 316-978-3253, E-mail: jordan.oleson@wichita.edu. *Dean,* Dr. Andrew Hippisley, 316-978-3100, Fax: 316-978-3234, E-mail: andrew.hippisley@wichita.edu.

Institute for Interdisciplinary Creativity Expenses: Contact institution. Offers innovation design (MID). *Application Contact:* Jordan Oleson, Admissions Coordinator, 316-978-3095, Fax: 316-978-3253, E-mail: jordan.oleson@wichita.edu. *Graduate Coordinator,* Dr. Jeremy Patterson, 316-978-3010, E-mail: jeremy.patterson@wichita.edu.

W. Frank Barton School of Business Expenses: Contact institution. *Program availability:* Part-time, evening/weekend. Offers accounting information systems (M Acc); applied economics (MA); business (EMBA, M Acc, MA, MBA, MS); global supply chain management (MS); taxation (M Acc). *Application Contact:* Jordan Oleson, Admissions Coordinator, 316-978-3095, Fax: 316-978-3253, E-mail: jordan.oleson@wichita.edu. *Dean,* Dr. Larisa Genin, 316-978-3200, Fax: 316-978-3845, E-mail: larisa.genin@wichita.edu.

WIDENER UNIVERSITY, Chester, PA 19013-5792

General Information Independent, coed, comprehensive institution. CGS member. *Graduate housing:* Rooms and/or apartments available on a first-come, first-served basis to single students and available to married students. Housing application deadline: 5/30. *Research affiliation:* Small Business Administration, Riverfront Development Corporation (engineering, management), Advanced Technology Center (engineering).

GRADUATE UNITS

College of Arts and Sciences *Program availability:* Part-time, evening/weekend. Offers arts and sciences (MA, MPA); criminal justice (MA); public administration (MPA).

Commonwealth Law School *Program availability:* Part-time. Offers law (JD). Electronic applications accepted.

Delaware Law School *Program availability:* Part-time, 100% online. Offers corporate and business law (MJ); corporate law and finance (LL M); higher education compliance (MJ); higher education compliance (MJ); juridical science (SJD); law (JD).

Graduate Programs in Engineering *Program availability:* Part-time, evening/weekend. Offers biomedical engineering (M Eng); chemical engineering (M Eng); civil engineering (M Eng); electrical engineering (M Eng); engineering (M Eng); engineering management (M Eng); mechanical engineering (M Eng). Electronic applications accepted.

School of Business Administration *Program availability:* Part-time, evening/weekend, 100% online, blended/hybrid learning. Offers business administration (MBA, MHA, MS); health and medical services administration (MBA, MHA); taxation (MS). Electronic applications accepted.

School of Human Service Professions *Program availability:* Part-time, evening/weekend, 100% online, blended/hybrid learning. Offers human service professions (M Ed, MS, MSW, DPT, Ed D, PhD, Psy D).

Center for Education *Program availability:* Part-time, evening/weekend. Offers adult education (M Ed); counseling in higher education (M Ed); counselor education (M Ed); early childhood education (M Ed); educational foundations (M Ed); educational leadership (M Ed); educational psychology (M Ed); elementary education (M Ed); English and language arts (M Ed); health education (M Ed); higher education leadership (Ed D); home and school visitor (M Ed); human sexuality (M Ed, PhD); mathematics education (M Ed); middle school education (M Ed); principalship (M Ed); reading and language arts (M Ed); reading education (M Ed); school administration (Ed D); science education (M Ed); social studies education (M Ed); special education (M Ed); technology education (M Ed). Electronic applications accepted.

Center for Social Work Education Offers social work education (MSW, PhD).

Institute for Graduate Clinical Psychology Offers clinical psychology (Psy D). Electronic applications accepted.

Institute for Physical Therapy Education Offers physical therapy education (MS, DPT).

School of Nursing *Program availability:* Part-time, evening/weekend. Offers nursing (MSN, DN Sc, PhD, PMC). Electronic applications accepted.

WILBERFORCE UNIVERSITY, Wilberforce, OH 45384

General Information Independent-religious, coed, comprehensive institution.

GRADUATE UNITS

Program in Rehabilitation Counseling Offers rehabilitation counseling (MS).

WILFRID LAURIER UNIVERSITY, Waterloo, ON N2L 3C5, Canada

General Information Province-supported, coed, comprehensive institution.

GRADUATE UNITS

Faculty of Graduate and Postdoctoral Studies *Program availability:* Part-time, evening/weekend. Electronic applications accepted.

Faculty of Arts *Program availability:* Part-time. Offers agency (MA); arts (M Sc, MA, MES, MIPP, PhD); body politics (MA); Canadian political studies (MA); community (MA); comparative politics/international relations (MA); cultural representation and social theory (MA); English (MA); English and film (PhD); environmental and resource management (MA, MES, PhD); environmental science (M Sc, MES, PhD); gender, sexuality and embodiment (MA); geomatics (M Sc, MES, PhD); globalization, identity and social movements (MA); health, family and well-being (MA); history (MA, PhD); human geography (MES, PhD); internationalization, migration and human rights (MA); media, technology and culture (MA); religion and culture (MA); religious diversity of North America (PhD); self (MA); visual communication and culture (MA). Electronic applications accepted.

Faculty of Music Offers music (MMT). Electronic applications accepted.

Faculty of Science Offers behavioral neuroscience (M Sc, PhD); chemistry (M Sc); cognitive neuroscience (M Sc, PhD); community psychology (MA, PhD); integrative biology (M Sc); mathematics for science and finance (M Sc); physical activity and health (M Sc); science (M Sc, MA, PhD); social and developmental psychology (MA, PhD). Electronic applications accepted.

Lazaridis School of Business and Economics *Program availability:* Part-time, evening/weekend. Offers accounting (PhD); business and economics (EMTM, M Fin, M Sc, MA, MBA, PhD); co-op (MBA); economics (MA); finance (M Fin); financial economics (PhD); full-time (MBA); marketing (PhD); operations and supply chain management (PhD); organizational behavior and human resource management (M Sc); organizational behaviour and human resource management (PhD); part-time (MBA); supply chain management (M Sc); technology management (EMTM). Electronic applications accepted.

Lyle S. Hallman Faculty of Social Work *Program availability:* Part-time. Offers Aboriginal studies (MSW); community, policy, planning and organizations (MSW); critical social policy and organizational studies (PhD); individuals, families and groups (MSW); social work practice (individuals, families, groups and communities) (PhD); social work practice: individuals, families, groups and communities (PhD). Electronic applications accepted.

School of International Policy and Governance Offers conflict and security (PhD); global environment (PhD); global governance (MIPP); global justice and human rights (PhD); global political economy (PhD); global social governance (PhD); human security (MIPP); international economic relations (MIPP); international environmental policy (MIPP); international policy and governance (MIPP, PhD); multilateral institutions and diplomacy (PhD).

Laurier Brantford Offers criminology (MA). Electronic applications accepted.

Waterloo Lutheran Seminary *Program availability:* Part-time. Offers divinity (M Div); multifaith spiritual care and counseling (Diploma); pastoral leadership (D Min); spiritual care and counseling (D Min); theology (M Th, MTS). Electronic applications accepted.

WILKES UNIVERSITY, Wilkes-Barre, PA 18766-0002

General Information Independent, coed, comprehensive institution. *Enrollment:* 5,132 graduate, professional, and undergraduate students; 481 full-time matriculated graduate/professional students (334 women), 2,196 part-time matriculated graduate/professional students (1,719 women). *Enrollment by degree level:* 2,104 master's, 573 doctoral. Tuition and fees vary according to course load, degree level and program. *Graduate housing:* On-campus housing not available. *Student services:* Campus employment opportunities, career counseling, free psychological counseling, international student services, low-cost health insurance, multicultural affairs office, services for students with disabilities. *Library facilities:* Eugene S. Farley Library. *Collection:* Books: 184,565 (physical), 8,000 (digital/electronic); Serial titles: 60,000 (digital/electronic); Databases: 88. Students can reserve study rooms.

Computer facilities: Computer purchase and lease plans are available. 860 computers available on campus for general student use. A campuswide network can be accessed from student residence rooms and from off campus. Online class registration is available.
Website: http://www.wilkes.edu/

GRADUATE UNITS

College of Graduate and Professional Studies Students: 481 full-time (334 women), 2,196 part-time (1,719 women); includes 383 minority (165 Black or African American, non-Hispanic/Latino; 4 American Indian or Alaska Native, non-Hispanic/Latino; 79 Asian, non-Hispanic/Latino; 81 Hispanic/Latino; 54 Two or more races, non-Hispanic/Latino), 10 international. Average age 35. Expenses: Contact institution. *Financial support:* Unspecified assistantships available. Financial award application deadline: 3/1; financial award applicants required to submit FAFSA. In 2018, 907 master's, 165 doctorates awarded. *Program availability:* Part-time, evening/weekend, 100% online, blended/hybrid learning. Offers creative writing (MA, MFA). *Application deadline:* Applications are processed on a rolling basis. *Application fee:* $45 ($65 for international students). Electronic applications accepted.

College of Science and Engineering Students: 12 full-time (2 women), 7 part-time (1 woman); includes 5 minority (2 Asian, non-Hispanic/Latino; 3 Hispanic/Latino), 1 international. Average age 26. Expenses: Contact institution. *Financial support:* Unspecified assistantships available. Financial award application deadline: 3/1; financial award applicants required to submit FAFSA. In 2018, 28 master's awarded. *Program availability:* Part-time. Offers bioengineering (MS); electrical engineering (MSEE); engineering management (MS); mathematics (MS); mechanical engineering (MS); science and engineering (MS, MSEE). *Application deadline:* Applications are processed on a rolling basis. *Application fee:* $45 ($65 for international students). Electronic applications accepted. *Application Contact:* Kristin Donati, Associate Director of Graduate Admissions, 570-408-3338, Fax: 570-408-7846, E-mail: kristin.donati@wilkes.edu. *Interim Dean,* Dr. Prahlad Murthy, 570-408-4600, Fax: 570-408-7860, E-mail: prahlad.murthy@wilkes.edu.

Jay S. Sidhu School of Business and Leadership Students: 16 full-time (9 women), 64 part-time (33 women); includes 11 minority (3 Black or African American, non-Hispanic/Latino; 3 Asian, non-Hispanic/Latino; 3 Hispanic/Latino; 2 Two or more races, non-Hispanic/Latino), 7 international. Average age 30. Expenses: Contact institution. *Financial support:* Unspecified assistantships available. Financial award application deadline: 3/1; financial award applicants required to submit FAFSA. In 2018, 49 master's awarded. *Program availability:* Part-time, evening/weekend. Offers accounting (MBA); global business (MBA); human resource management (MBA); international business (MBA); leadership (MBA); management (MBA); operations management (MBA); organizational leadership and development (MBA). *Application deadline:* Applications are processed on a rolling basis. *Application fee:* $45 ($65 for international students). Electronic applications accepted. *Application Contact:* Kristin Donati, Associate Director of Graduate Admissions, 570-408-3338, Fax: 570-408-7846, E-mail: kristin.donati@wilkes.edu. *Dean*, Dr. Abel Adekola, 570-408-4701, Fax: 570-408-7846, E-mail: abel.adekola@wilkes.edu.

Nesbitt School of Pharmacy Students: 283 full-time (188 women); includes 46 minority (1 Black or African American, non-Hispanic/Latino; 2 American Indian or Alaska Native, non-Hispanic/Latino; 22 Asian, non-Hispanic/Latino; 5 Hispanic/Latino; 16 Two or more races, non-Hispanic/Latino), 2 international. Average age 23. Expenses: Contact institution. *Financial support:* Federal Work-Study and unspecified assistantships available. Financial award application deadline: 3/1; financial award applicants required to submit FAFSA. In 2018, 72 doctorates awarded. Offers pharmacy (Pharm D). *Application deadline:* Applications are processed on a rolling basis. *Application Contact:* Dr. Scott Stolte, Dean, 570-408-4280, Fax: 570-408-7828, E-mail: scott.stolte@wilkes.edu. *Dean*, Dr. Scott Stolte, 570-408-4280, Fax: 570-408-7828, E-mail: scott.stolte@wilkes.edu.

Passan School of Nursing Students: 38 full-time (32 women), 625 part-time (545 women); includes 224 minority (145 Black or African American, non-Hispanic/Latino; 1 American Indian or Alaska Native, non-Hispanic/Latino; 39 Asian, non-Hispanic/Latino; 27 Hispanic/Latino; 12 Two or more races, non-Hispanic/Latino). Average age 42. Expenses: Contact institution. *Financial support:* Unspecified assistantships available. Financial award application deadline: 3/1; financial award applicants required to submit FAFSA. In 2018, 183 master's, 84 doctorates awarded. *Program availability:* Part-time, online only, 100% online. Offers nursing (MSN, DNP, PhD). *Application deadline:* Applications are processed on a rolling basis. *Application fee:* $45. Electronic applications accepted. *Application Contact:* Director of Graduate Enrollment, 570-408-4234, Fax: 570-408-7846. *Dean*, Dr. Deborah Zbegner, 570-408-4086, Fax: 570-408-7807, E-mail: deborah.zbegner@wilkes.edu.

School of Education Students: 87 full-time (67 women), 1,418 part-time (1,078 women); includes 87 minority (13 Black or African American, non-Hispanic/Latino; 1 American Indian or Alaska Native, non-Hispanic/Latino; 11 Asian, non-Hispanic/Latino; 40 Hispanic/Latino; 22 Two or more races, non-Hispanic/Latino). Average age 35. Expenses: Contact institution. *Financial support:* Unspecified assistantships available. Financial award application deadline: 3/1; financial award applicants required to submit FAFSA. In 2018, 611 master's, 9 doctorates awarded. *Program availability:* Part-time, evening/weekend, 100% online, blended/hybrid learning. Offers educational development and strategies (MS Ed); educational leadership (MS Ed, Ed D); effective teaching (MS Ed); instructional media (MS Ed); instructional technology (MS Ed); international school leadership (MS Ed); international teaching and learning (MS Ed); literacy (MS Ed); middle level education (MS Ed); online teaching (MS Ed); school business leadership (MS Ed); special education (MS Ed); teaching English to speakers of other languages (MS Ed). *Application deadline:* Applications are processed on a rolling basis. *Application fee:* $45 ($65 for international students). Electronic applications accepted. *Application Contact:* Stephanie Wasmanski, Associate Director of Graduate Admissions, 570-408-5535, Fax: 570-408-7846, E-mail: stephanie.wasmanski@wilkes.edu. *Dean*, Dr. Rhonda Rabbitt, 570-408-4680, Fax: 570-408-7872, E-mail: rhonda.rabbitt@wilkes.edu.

WILLAMETTE UNIVERSITY, Salem, OR 97301-3931

General Information Independent-religious, coed, comprehensive institution. *Graduate housing:* Room and/or apartments available on a first-come, first-served basis to single students; on-campus housing not available to married students. Housing application deadline: 6/1.

GRADUATE UNITS

Atkinson Graduate School of Management Students: 126 full-time (52 women), 111 part-time (55 women); includes 67 minority (16 Black or African American, non-Hispanic/Latino; 12 Asian, non-Hispanic/Latino; 26 Hispanic/Latino; 1 Native Hawaiian or other Pacific Islander, non-Hispanic/Latino; 12 Two or more races, non-Hispanic/Latino), 17 international. Average age 28. 261 applicants, 67% accepted, 105 enrolled. *Faculty:* 18 full-time (5 women), 19 part-time/adjunct (7 women). Expenses: Contact institution. *Financial support:* In 2018-19, 232 students received support. Federal Work-Study, scholarships/grants, and unspecified assistantships available. Financial award application deadline: 5/1; financial award applicants required to submit FAFSA. In 2018, 118 master's awarded. *Program availability:* Part-time, evening/weekend. Offers accounting, entrepreneurship, finance, global management, human resources, management science and quantitative methods (stem), marketing, operations (MBA). JD/MBA offered jointly with Willamette University College of Law. *Application deadline:* 5/1 priority date for domestic and international students. Applications are processed on a rolling basis. *Application fee:* $0. Electronic applications accepted. *Application Contact:* Juliet Valdez, Director of Recruitment, 503-370-6792, Fax: 503-370-3011, E-mail: jvaldez@willamette.edu. *Interim Dean, Professor of Applied Statistics and Information Systems*, Dr. Michael L. Hand, 503-370-6790, Fax: 503-370-3011, E-mail: mhand@willamette.edu.

College of Law *Program availability:* Part-time. Offers dispute resolution (LL M); law (MLS, JD); transnational law (LL M). Electronic applications accepted.

WILLIAM CAREY UNIVERSITY, Hattiesburg, MS 39401

General Information Independent-religious, coed, comprehensive institution. *Graduate housing:* Room and/or apartments available on a first-come, first-served basis to single students; on-campus housing not available to married students. Housing application deadline: 8/15.

GRADUATE UNITS

College of Osteopathic Medicine Offers osteopathic medicine (DO).

Department of Psychology and Graduate Counseling *Program availability:* Part-time. Offers counseling psychology (MS).

School of Business *Program availability:* Part-time. Offers business (MBA).

School of Education *Program availability:* Part-time. Offers art education (M Ed); art of teaching (M Ed); elementary education (M Ed, Ed S); English education (M Ed); gifted education (M Ed); history and social science (M Ed); mild/moderate disabilities (M Ed); secondary education (M Ed).

School of Nursing *Program availability:* Part-time. Offers nursing (MSN).

School of Pharmacy Offers pharmacy (Pharm D).

WILLIAM JAMES COLLEGE, Newton, MA 02459

General Information Independent, coed, primarily women, upper-level institution. *Enrollment:* 765 graduate, professional, and undergraduate students; 515 matriculated graduate/professional students. *Tuition:* Full-time $33,000. *Required fees:* $960.

Graduate housing: On-campus housing not available. *Student services:* Campus employment opportunities, career counseling, international student services, low-cost health insurance, multicultural affairs office, services for students with disabilities, writing training.

Website: http://www.williamjames.edu/

General Application Contact: Kristen Frady, Admissions Counselor, 617-327-6777 Ext. 1506, Fax: 617-327-4447, E-mail: Kristen_Frady@williamjames.edu.

GRADUATE UNITS

Graduate Programs Offers applied psychology in higher education student personnel administration (MA); clinical psychology (Psy D); counseling psychology (MA); counseling psychology and community mental health (MA); counseling psychology and global mental health (MA); executive coaching (Graduate Certificate); forensic and counseling psychology (MA); leadership psychology (Psy D); organizational psychology (MA); primary care psychology (MA); respecialization in clinical psychology (Certificate); school psychology (Psy D). Electronic applications accepted.

WILLIAM JESSUP UNIVERSITY, Rocklin, CA 95765

General Information Independent-religious, coed, comprehensive institution.

GRADUATE UNITS

Program in Teaching *Program availability:* Evening/weekend. Offers single subject English (MAT); single subject math (MAT).

WILLIAM JEWELL COLLEGE, Liberty, MO 64068-1843

General Information Independent, coed, comprehensive institution.

GRADUATE UNITS

Department of Education Offers differentiated instruction (MS Ed).

WILLIAM PATERSON UNIVERSITY OF NEW JERSEY, Wayne, NJ 07470-8420

General Information State-supported, coed, comprehensive institution. CGS member. *Enrollment:* 322 full-time matriculated graduate/professional students (207 women), 1,064 part-time matriculated graduate/professional students (799 women). *Enrollment by degree level:* 1,000 master's, 49 doctoral, 337 other advanced degrees. *Graduate faculty:* 148 full-time (82 women), 86 part-time/adjunct (48 women). *International tuition:* $22,952 full-time. *Tuition, area resident:* Full-time $14,714; part-time $727 per credit. Tuition, state resident: full-time $14,714; part-time $727 per credit. Tuition, nonresident: full-time $22,952; part-time $727 per credit. *Required fees:* $4 per semester. Tuition and fees vary according to course load, degree level and program. *Graduate housing:* Room and/or apartments available on a first-come, first-served basis to single students; on-campus housing not available to married students. Typical cost: $9570 per year ($11,570 including board). Housing application deadline: 5/1. *Student services:* Campus employment opportunities, campus safety program, career counseling, exercise/wellness program, free psychological counseling, international student services, services for students with disabilities, teacher training, writing training. *Library facilities:* David and Lorraine Cheng Library. *Collection:* Books: 369,216 (physical), 116,597 (digital/electronic); Serial titles: 3,772 (physical), 164,249 (digital/electronic); Databases: 126. Weekly public service hours: 102; students can reserve study rooms.

Computer facilities: Computer purchase and lease plans are available. 1,271 computers available on campus for general student use. A campuswide network can be accessed from student residence rooms and from off campus. Online class registration is available.

Website: http://www.wpunj.edu/

General Application Contact: Atinuke Adeniran, Senior Associate Director, Graduate Admissions, 973-720-2764, E-mail: adenirant@wpunj.edu.

GRADUATE UNITS

College of Education Average age 35. 347 applicants, 87% accepted, 226 enrolled. Expenses: Contact institution. *Financial support:* In 2018–19, 8,416 students received support. Career-related internships or fieldwork, Federal Work-Study, scholarships/grants, and unspecified assistantships available. Support available to part-time students. Financial award application deadline: 3/15; financial award applicants required to submit FAFSA. In 2018, 136 master's awarded. *Program availability:* Part-time, evening/weekend. Offers curriculum and learning (M Ed); early childhood education (Certificate); educational leadership (M Ed); educational media specialist (Certificate); elementary education (MAT, Certificate); elementary education subject area (Certificate); higher education administration (MA); learning disabilities consultant (Certificate); literacy (M Ed); middle level education (M Ed); middle school education subject area (Certificate); professional counseling (M Ed); reading specialist (Certificate); school library media specialist (Certificate); school principal (Certificate); school supervisor (Certificate); secondary education (MAT); special education (M Ed); teacher of students with disabilities (Certificate). *Application deadline:* For fall admission, 6/1 for domestic students, 3/1 for international students; for spring admission, 11/1 for domestic students, 10/1 for international students. Applications are processed on a rolling basis. *Application fee:* $50. Electronic applications accepted. *Application Contact:* Liana Fornarotto, Director of Education Enrollment and Certification, 973-720-2206, Fax: 973-720-2989, E-mail: fornarottol@wpunj.edu. *Dean*, Dr. Dorothy Feola, 973-720-2138, Fax: 973-720-3647, E-mail: feolad@wpunj.edu.

College of Humanities and Social Sciences Students: 69 full-time (49 women), 65 part-time (42 women); includes 55 minority (6 Black or African American, non-Hispanic/Latino; 2 Asian, non-Hispanic/Latino; 41 Hispanic/Latino; 6 Two or more races, non-Hispanic/Latino), 3 international. Average age 32. 152 applicants, 47% accepted, 44 enrolled. *Faculty:* 41 full-time (25 women), 7 part-time/adjunct (5 women). Expenses: Contact institution. *Financial support:* In 2018–19, 16 students received support. Career-related internships or fieldwork, Federal Work-Study, scholarships/grants, tuition waivers, and unspecified assistantships available. Support available to part-time students. Financial award application deadline: 3/15; financial award applicants required to submit FAFSA. In 2018, 46 master's awarded. *Program availability:* Part-time. Offers applied sociology (MA); assessment and evaluation research (Certificate); bilingual education (Certificate); clinical and counseling psychology (MA); clinical psychology (Psy D); creative and professional writing (MFA); English (MA); history (MA); public policy and international affairs (MA); teaching English as a second language (Certificate). *Application deadline:* For fall admission, 6/1 for domestic students, 3/1 for international students; for spring admission, 11/1 for domestic students, 10/1 for international students. Applications are processed on a rolling basis. *Application fee:* $50. Electronic applications accepted. *Application Contact:* Tinu Adeniran, Associate Director, Graduate Admissions, 973-720-2764, Fax: 973-720-2035, E-mail: adenirant@wpunj.edu. *Dean*, Dr. Kara Rabbitt, 973-720-2180, Fax: 973-720-2955, E-mail: rabbittk@wpunj.edu.

College of Science and Health Students: 62 full-time (49 women), 236 part-time (203 women); includes 135 minority (22 Black or African American, non-Hispanic/Latino; 48

Asian, non-Hispanic/Latino; 57 Hispanic/Latino; 8 Two or more races, non-Hispanic/Latino; 4 international. Average age 33. 546 applicants, 47% accepted, 151 enrolled. *Faculty:* 34 full-time (20 women), 24 part-time/adjunct (19 women). Expenses: Contact institution. *Financial support:* In 2018–19, 18 students received support. Career-related internships or fieldwork, Federal Work-Study, scholarships/grants, tuition waivers, and unspecified assistantships available. Support available to part-time students. Financial award application deadline: 3/15; financial award applicants required to submit FAFSA. In 2018, 75 master's, 8 doctorates awarded. *Program availability:* Part-time. Offers adult gerontology nurse practitioner (Certificate); adult nurse practitioner (Certificate); biology (MS); biotechnology (MS); communication disorders (MS); exercise and sport studies (MS); materials chemistry (MS); nursing (MSN); nursing education (Certificate); nursing practice (DNP); school nurse instructional (Certificate). *Application deadline:* For fall admission, 6/1 for domestic students, 3/1 for international students; for spring admission, 11/1 for domestic students, 10/1 for international students. Applications are processed on a rolling basis. *Application fee:* $50. Electronic applications accepted. *Application Contact:* Christina Aiello, Assistant Director, Graduate Admissions, 973-720-2506, Fax: 973-720-2035, E-mail: aielloc@wpunj.edu. *Dean,* Dr. Venkat Sharma, 973-720-2194, Fax: 973-720-3414, E-mail: sharmav@wpunj.edu.

College of the Arts and Communication Students: 44 full-time (19 women), 14 part-time (11 women); includes 19 minority (7 Black or African American, non-Hispanic/Latino; 8 Hispanic/Latino; 4 Two or more races, non-Hispanic/Latino), 14 international. Average age 30. 81 applicants, 62% accepted, 26 enrolled. *Faculty:* 20 full-time (9 women), 22 part-time/adjunct (5 women). Expenses: Contact institution. *Financial support:* In 2018–19, 10 students received support. Career-related internships or fieldwork, Federal Work-Study, scholarships/grants, tuition waivers, and unspecified assistantships available. Support available to part-time students. Financial award application deadline: 3/15; financial award applicants required to submit FAFSA. In 2018, 32 master's awarded. *Program availability:* Part-time. Offers art (MFA); music (MM); professional communication (MA). *Application deadline:* For fall admission, 6/1 for domestic students, 3/1 for international students; for spring admission, 11/1 for domestic students, 10/1 for international students. Applications are processed on a rolling basis. *Application fee:* $50. Electronic applications accepted. *Application Contact:* Christina Aiello, Assistant Director, Graduate Admissions, 973-720-2506, Fax: 973-720-2035, E-mail: aielloc@wpunj.edu. *Dean,* Daryl Moore, 973-720-2232, E-mail: moored@wpunj.edu.

Cotsakos College of Business Students: 78 full-time (40 women), 250 part-time (113 women); includes 161 minority (39 Black or African American, non-Hispanic/Latino; 1 American Indian or Alaska Native, non-Hispanic/Latino; 23 Asian, non-Hispanic/Latino; 82 Hispanic/Latino; 16 Two or more races, non-Hispanic/Latino), 14 international. Average age 31. 222 applicants, 86% accepted, 136 enrolled. *Faculty:* 21 full-time (6 women), 5 part-time/adjunct (1 woman). Expenses: Contact institution. *Financial support:* In 2018–19, 18 students received support. Career-related internships or fieldwork, Federal Work-Study, scholarships/grants, tuition waivers, and unspecified assistantships available. Support available to part-time students. Financial award application deadline: 3/15; financial award applicants required to submit FAFSA. In 2018, 95 master's awarded. *Program availability:* Part-time, evening/weekend. Offers applied business analytics (MS); business administration (MBA); MBA pathways (Certificate); sales leadership (MS). *Application deadline:* For fall admission, 6/1 for domestic students, 3/1 for international students; for spring admission, 11/1 for domestic students, 10/1 for international students. Applications are processed on a rolling basis. *Application fee:* $50. Electronic applications accepted. *Application Contact:* Tinu Adeniran, Assistant Director, Graduate Admissions, 973-720-2764, Fax: 973-720-2035, E-mail: adenirant@wpunj.edu. *Dean,* Dr. Siamack Shojai, 973-720-2964, Fax: 973-720-2809, E-mail: shojais@wpunj.edu.

WILLIAM PENN UNIVERSITY, Oskaloosa, IA 52577-1799
General Information Independent-religious, coed, comprehensive institution.
GRADUATE UNITS
College for Working Adults *Program availability:* Online learning.

WILLIAMS BAPTIST COLLEGE, Walnut Ridge, AR 72476
General Information Independent-religious, coed, comprehensive institution.
GRADUATE UNITS
Graduate Programs

WILLIAMS COLLEGE, Williamstown, MA 01267
General Information Independent, coed, comprehensive institution. *Graduate housing:* Room and/or apartments available on a first-come, first-served basis to single students; on-campus housing not available to married students. *Research affiliation:* Clark Art Institute.
GRADUATE UNITS
Graduate Program in the History of Art Offers development economics (MA); history of art (MA). MA in history of art offered jointly with Sterling and Francine Clark Art Institute. Electronic applications accepted.

WILLIAMSON COLLEGE, Franklin, TN 37067
General Information Independent-religious, coed, comprehensive institution.
GRADUATE UNITS
Program in Organizational Leadership *Program availability:* Evening/weekend. Offers organizational leadership (MA).

WILLIAM WOODS UNIVERSITY, Fulton, MO 65251-1098
General Information Independent-religious, coed, comprehensive institution. *Graduate housing:* On-campus housing not available.
GRADUATE UNITS
Graduate and Adult Studies *Program availability:* Part-time, evening/weekend. Offers administration (M Ed, Ed S); athletic/activities administration (M Ed); curriculum and instruction (M Ed, Ed S); educational leadership (Ed D); equestrian education (M Ed); health management (MBA); human resources (MBA); leadership (MBA); marketing, advertising, and public relations (MBA); teaching and technology (M Ed). Electronic applications accepted.

WILMINGTON COLLEGE, Wilmington, OH 45177
General Information Independent-religious, coed, comprehensive institution. *Graduate housing:* On-campus housing not available.
GRADUATE UNITS
Department of Education *Program availability:* Part-time. Offers reading (M Ed); special education (M Ed).

WILMINGTON UNIVERSITY, New Castle, DE 19720-6491
General Information Independent, coed, university. *Graduate housing:* On-campus housing not available.
GRADUATE UNITS
College of Business *Program availability:* Part-time, evening/weekend. Offers accounting (MBA, MS); business administration (MBA, DBA); environmental stewardship (MBA); finance (MBA); health care administration (MBA, MSM); homeland security (MBA, MSM); human resource management (MSM); management information systems (MBA, MSN); marketing (MSM); marketing management (MBA); military leadership (MSM); organizational leadership (MBA, MSM); public administration (MSM). Electronic applications accepted.
College of Education *Program availability:* Part-time, evening/weekend. Offers applied technology in education (M Ed); career and technical education (M Ed); educational leadership (Ed D); elementary and secondary school counseling (M Ed); elementary studies (M Ed); ESOL literacy (M Ed); higher education leadership (Ed D); instruction: gifted and talented (M Ed); instruction: teacher of reading (M Ed); instruction: teaching and learning (M Ed); organizational leadership (Ed D); school leadership (M Ed); secondary education (MAT); special education (M Ed). Electronic applications accepted.
College of Health Professions *Program availability:* Part-time. Offers adult nurse practitioner (MSN); family nurse practitioner (MSN); gerontology nurse practitioner (MSN); nursing (MSN); nursing leadership (MSN); nursing practice (DNP). Electronic applications accepted.
College of Social and Behavioral Sciences *Program availability:* Part-time, evening/weekend. Offers administration of human services (MS); administration of justice (MS); clinical mental health counseling (MS); homeland security (MS). Electronic applications accepted.
College of Technology *Program availability:* Part-time, evening/weekend. Offers cybersecurity (MS); information assurance (MS); information systems technologies (MS); management and management information systems (MS); technology project management (MS); Web design (MS). Electronic applications accepted.

WILSON COLLEGE, Chambersburg, PA 17201-1285
General Information Independent-religious, coed, primarily women, comprehensive institution.
GRADUATE UNITS
Graduate Programs *Program availability:* Evening/weekend. Offers accounting (M Acc); choreography and visual art (MFA); education (M Ed); educational technology (MET); healthcare administration (MHA); humanities (MA); management (MSM); nursing (MSN); special education (MSE). Electronic applications accepted.

WINEBRENNER THEOLOGICAL SEMINARY, Findlay, OH 45840
General Information Independent-religious, coed, graduate-only institution. *Enrollment by degree level:* 46 master's, 2 doctoral. *Graduate faculty:* 6 full-time (3 women), 5 part-time/adjunct (0 women). *Tuition:* Full-time $16,500; part-time $555 per credit hour. *Required fees:* $495; $300 per unit. Tuition and fees vary according to degree level. *Graduate housing:* On-campus housing not available. *Student services:* Campus safety program, career counseling, free psychological counseling, international student services, multicultural affairs office, services for students with disabilities, writing training. *Library facilities:* Shafer Library plus 1 other. *Collection:* Books: 42,350 (physical), 43 (digital/electronic); Serial titles: 2 (physical), 4 (digital/electronic). Weekly public service hours: 95; study areas open 24 hours, 5–7 days a week; students can reserve study rooms.

Computer facilities: 224 computers available on campus for general student use. A campuswide network can be accessed from student residence rooms and from off campus. Online class registration is available.
Website: http://www.winebrenner.edu/

General Application Contact: Amy Kinney, Director of Enrollment Management, 419-434-4241, E-mail: admissions@winebrenner.edu.

GRADUATE UNITS
Graduate Programs Students: 16 full-time (10 women), 50 part-time (23 women); includes 12 minority (8 Black or African American, non-Hispanic/Latino; 2 Asian, non-Hispanic/Latino; 2 Two or more races, non-Hispanic/Latino), 2 international. Average age 41. 25 applicants, 76% accepted, 12 enrolled. *Faculty:* 7 full-time (2 women), 22 part-time/adjunct (8 women). Expenses: Contact institution. *Financial support:* In 2018–19, 32 students received support, including 3 teaching assistantships with partial tuition reimbursements available (averaging $1,575 per year); research assistantships, institutionally sponsored loans, scholarships/grants, unspecified assistantships, and denominational discounts, spousal discounts also available. Financial award application deadline: 7/1; financial award applicants required to submit FAFSA. In 2018, 8 master's, 2 doctorates awarded. *Program availability:* Part-time, 100% online, blended/hybrid learning. Offers clinical counseling (MA); family ministry (MA); practical theology (MA); theological and ministerial studies (M Div, D Min); theological studies (MA). *Application deadline:* For fall admission, 8/15 priority date for domestic students, 7/15 priority date for international students; for winter admission, 12/15 priority date for domestic students, 11/15 priority date for international students; for spring admission, 4/15 priority date for domestic students, 3/15 priority date for international students. Applications are processed on a rolling basis. *Application fee:* $30. Electronic applications accepted. *Application Contact:* Jim Smarkel, Director of Enrollment Management, 419-434-4220, Fax: 419-434-4267, E-mail: admissions@winebrenner.edu. *Academic Dean,* Dr. Joel W. Cocklin, 419-434-4250, Fax: 419-434-4267, E-mail: jcocklin@winebrenner.edu.

WINGATE UNIVERSITY, Wingate, NC 28174
General Information Independent-religious, coed, comprehensive institution. *Graduate housing:* Rooms and/or apartments available on a first-come, first-served basis to single and married students. Housing application deadline: 8/15.
GRADUATE UNITS
Department of Physical Therapy Offers physical therapy (DPT).
Harris Department of Physician Assistant Studies Offers physician assistant studies (MPAS).
Porter B. Byrum School of Business *Program availability:* Part-time, evening/weekend. Offers accounting (MAC); corporate innovation (MBA); finance (MBA); general management (MBA); healthcare management (MBA); marketing (MBA); project management (MBA). Electronic applications accepted.
School of Pharmacy Offers pharmacy (Pharm D). Electronic applications accepted.
School of Sport Sciences Offers sport management (MA). Electronic applications accepted.

Thayer School of Education *Program availability:* Part-time, evening/weekend. Offers community college executive leadership (Ed D); educational leadership (MA Ed, Ed S); elementary education (MA Ed, MAT).

WINONA STATE UNIVERSITY, Winona, MN 55987
General Information State-supported, coed, comprehensive institution. *Graduate housing:* Room and/or apartments available to single students; on-campus housing not available to married students. Housing application deadline: 3/2.

GRADUATE UNITS

College of Education *Program availability:* Part-time, evening/weekend. Offers addiction counseling (Certificate); clinical mental health counseling (MS); education (MS, Certificate, Ed S); education leadership (MS, Ed S); human services (MS); multicultural education (Certificate); organizational leadership (MS); professional leadership (MS); school counseling (MS); special education (MS); sport management (MS).

College of Liberal Arts *Program availability:* Part-time. Offers English (MS); liberal arts (MA, MS); literature and language (MA); TESOL (MA).

College of Nursing and Health Sciences *Program availability:* Part-time, online learning. Offers adult-gerontology acute care nurse practitioner (MS, DNP, Post Master's Certificate); adult-gerontology clinical nurse specialist (MS, DNP, Post Master's Certificate); adult-gerontology primary care nurse practitioner (MS, DNP, Post Master's Certificate); family nurse practitioner (MS, DNP, Post Master's Certificate); nurse educator (MS); nursing and organizational leadership (MS, DNP, Post Master's Certificate); practice and leadership innovations (DNP, Post Master's Certificate).

WINSTON-SALEM STATE UNIVERSITY, Winston-Salem, NC 27110-0003
General Information State-supported, coed, comprehensive institution. *Graduate housing:* On-campus housing not available.

GRADUATE UNITS

Department of Occupational Therapy Offers occupational therapy (MS). Electronic applications accepted.

Department of Physical Therapy Offers physical therapy (DPT). Electronic applications accepted.

MAT Program *Program availability:* Part-time, evening/weekend, online learning. Offers middle grades education (MAT); special education (MAT). Electronic applications accepted.

Program in Business Administration *Program availability:* Part-time, evening/weekend, online learning. Offers business administration (MBA). Electronic applications accepted.

Program in Computer Science and Information Technology *Program availability:* Part-time. Offers computer science and information technology (MS). Electronic applications accepted.

Program in Health Administration Offers health administration (MHA).

Program in Nursing *Program availability:* Part-time, evening/weekend, online learning. Offers advanced nurse educator (MSN); family nurse practitioner (MSN); nursing (DNP). Electronic applications accepted.

Program in Rehabilitation Counseling *Program availability:* Part-time, online learning. Offers rehabilitation counseling (MRC). Electronic applications accepted.

WINTHROP UNIVERSITY, Rock Hill, SC 29733
General Information State-supported, coed, comprehensive institution. CGS member. *Enrollment:* 5,813 graduate, professional, and undergraduate students; 465 full-time matriculated graduate/professional students (355 women), 594 part-time matriculated graduate/professional students (460 women). *Enrollment by degree level:* 1,059 master's. Tuition, state resident: full-time $15,166; part-time $635 per credit hour. Tuition, nonresident: full-time $29,214. *Required fees:* $500; $180 per semester. *Graduate housing:* Rooms and/or apartments available on a first-come, first-served basis to single and married students. Housing application deadline: 3/1. *Student services:* Campus employment opportunities, campus safety program, career counseling, exercise/wellness program, free psychological counseling, international student services, low-cost health insurance, multicultural affairs office, services for students with disabilities. *Library facilities:* Dacus Library plus 1 other. *Collection:* 356,611 (physical), 281,972 (digital/electronic); Serial titles: 540 (physical), 36,003 (digital/electronic); Databases: 133. Weekly public service hours: 144; study areas open 24 hours, 5–7 days a week; students can reserve study rooms.

Computer facilities: Computer purchase and lease plans are available. 620 computers available on campus for general student use. A campuswide network can be accessed from student residence rooms and from off campus. Online class registration, university services are available.
Website: http://www.winthrop.edu/

General Application Contact: The Graduate School, 800-411-7041, Fax: 803-323-2204, E-mail: gradschool@winthrop.edu.

GRADUATE UNITS

College of Arts and Sciences Students: 185 full-time (156 women), 144 part-time (114 women); includes 110 minority (85 Black or African American, non-Hispanic/Latino; 3 American Indian or Alaska Native, non-Hispanic/Latino; 4 Asian, non-Hispanic/Latino; 14 Hispanic/Latino; 4 Two or more races, non-Hispanic/Latino), 2 international. Average age 28. Expenses: Contact institution. *Financial support:* Research assistantships with full tuition reimbursements, career-related internships or fieldwork, Federal Work-Study, scholarships/grants, and unspecified assistantships available. Support available to part-time students. Financial award application deadline: 2/1; financial award applicants required to submit FAFSA. In 2018, 109 master's, 26 other advanced degrees awarded. *Program availability:* Part-time. Offers arts and sciences (MA, MLA, MS, MSW, Certificate, SSP); biology (MS); dietetics (Certificate); English (MA); history (MA); human nutrition (MS); liberal arts (MLA); psychology (MS, SSP); social work (MSW). *Application deadline:* Applications are processed on a rolling basis. *Application fee:* $50. Electronic applications accepted. *Application Contact:* 800-411-7041, Fax: 803-323-2292, E-mail: gradschool@winthrop.edu. *Dean,* Takita Sumter, 803-323-2160, E-mail: sumtert@winthrop.edu.

College of Business Administration Students: 29 full-time (16 women), 103 part-time (56 women); includes 32 minority (25 Black or African American, non-Hispanic/Latino; 2 Asian, non-Hispanic/Latino; 4 Hispanic/Latino; 1 Two or more races, non-Hispanic/Latino), 29 international. Average age 29. Expenses: Contact institution. *Financial support:* Research assistantships with full tuition reimbursements, Federal Work-Study, scholarships/grants, and unspecified assistantships available. Support available to part-time students. Financial award application deadline: 2/1; financial award applicants required to submit FAFSA. In 2018, 36 master's awarded. *Program*

availability: Part-time, evening/weekend, online learning. Offers business administration (MBA). *Application deadline:* For fall admission, 7/15 priority date for domestic students; for spring admission, 12/1 for domestic students. Applications are processed on a rolling basis. *Application fee:* $50. Electronic applications accepted. *Application Contact:* 800-411-7041, Fax: 803-323-2292, E-mail: gradschool@winthrop.edu. *Dean,* Dr. PN Saksena, 803-323-2186, Fax: 803-323-3960, E-mail: saksenapn@winthrop.edu.

College of Education Students: 116 full-time (89 women), 271 part-time (224 women); includes 105 minority (85 Black or African American, non-Hispanic/Latino; 1 American Indian or Alaska Native, non-Hispanic/Latino; 1 Asian, non-Hispanic/Latino; 13 Hispanic/Latino; 5 Two or more races, non-Hispanic/Latino), 12 international. Average age 30. Expenses: Contact institution. *Financial support:* Research assistantships with full tuition reimbursements, career-related internships or fieldwork, Federal Work-Study, scholarships/grants, and unspecified assistantships available. Support available to part-time students. Financial award application deadline: 2/1; financial award applicants required to submit FAFSA. In 2018, 99 master's awarded. *Program availability:* Part-time. Offers agency counseling (M Ed); education (M Ed, MAT); educational leadership (M Ed); physical education (M Ed); school counseling (M Ed); secondary education (M Ed); special education (M Ed). *Application deadline:* For fall admission, 7/15 priority date for domestic students; for spring admission, 12/1 for domestic students. Applications are processed on a rolling basis. *Application fee:* $50. Electronic applications accepted. *Application Contact:* 800-411-7041, Fax: 803-323-2292, E-mail: gradschool@winthrop.edu. *Dean,* Dr. Jeannie Rakestraw, 803-323-2151, Fax: 803-323-4369, E-mail: rakestrawj@winthrop.edu.

College of Visual and Performing Arts Students: 9 full-time (6 women), 29 part-time (24 women); includes 10 minority (7 Black or African American, non-Hispanic/Latino; 2 Hispanic/Latino; 1 Two or more races, non-Hispanic/Latino). Average age 36. Expenses: Contact institution. *Financial support:* Research assistantships with full tuition reimbursements, Federal Work-Study, scholarships/grants, and unspecified assistantships available. Support available to part-time students. Financial award application deadline: 2/1; financial award applicants required to submit FAFSA. In 2018, 4 master's awarded. *Program availability:* Part-time. Offers art (MFA); art administration (MA); art education (MA); conducting (MM); music education (MME); performance (MM); visual and performing arts (MA, MFA, MM, MME). *Application deadline:* Applications are processed on a rolling basis. *Application fee:* $50. Electronic applications accepted. *Application Contact:* 800-411-7041, Fax: 803-323-2292, E-mail: gradschool@winthrop.edu. *Dean,* Dr. Jeff Bellantoni, 803-323-2323, Fax: 803-323-2333, E-mail: wohld@winthrop.edu.

WISCONSIN LUTHERAN COLLEGE, Milwaukee, WI 53226-9942
General Information Independent-religious, coed, comprehensive institution.

GRADUATE UNITS
College of Adult and Graduate Studies

WISCONSIN SCHOOL OF PROFESSIONAL PSYCHOLOGY, Milwaukee, WI 53225-4960
General Information Independent, coed, graduate-only institution. *Graduate housing:* On-campus housing not available.

GRADUATE UNITS
Program in Clinical Psychology *Program availability:* Part-time, evening/weekend. Offers clinical psychology (MA, Psy D).

WITTENBERG UNIVERSITY, Springfield, OH 45501-0720
General Information Independent-religious, coed, comprehensive institution.
GRADUATE UNITS
Graduate Program

WONGU UNIVERSITY OF ORIENTAL MEDICINE, Las Vegas, NV 89123
General Information Private, coed, graduate-only institution.
GRADUATE UNITS
Graduate Program Offers Oriental medicine (MSOM).

WON INSTITUTE OF GRADUATE STUDIES, Glenside, PA 19038
General Information Proprietary, coed, graduate-only institution. *Enrollment by degree level:* 51 master's, 27 other advanced degrees. *Graduate faculty:* 5 full-time (3 women), 46 part-time/adjunct (34 women). *Tuition:* Full-time $19,716; part-time $5436 per credit. *Required fees:* $100 per term. Tuition and fees vary according to course load and program. *Student services:* Career counseling, writing training. *Library facilities:* Won Institute Library plus 1 other. *Collection:* Books: 4,987 (physical), 5 (digital/electronic); Databases: 3. Students can reserve study rooms.

Computer facilities: 4 computers available on campus for general student use. A campuswide network can be accessed. Online class registration is available.
Website: http://www.woninstitute.edu/

General Application Contact: Jennifer Cake, Enrollment Management Counselor, 215-884-8942 Ext. 219, Fax: 215-884-9002, E-mail: jennifer.cake@woninstitute.edu.

GRADUATE UNITS

Acupuncture Studies Program Students: 43 full-time (32 women); includes 12 minority (1 Black or African American, non-Hispanic/Latino; 8 Asian, non-Hispanic/Latino; 2 Hispanic/Latino; 1 Two or more races, non-Hispanic/Latino), 2 international. Average age 40. Expenses: Contact institution. Offers acupuncture studies (M Ac). *Application deadline:* For fall admission, 6/15 for domestic students. Applications are processed on a rolling basis. *Application fee:* $75. Electronic applications accepted. *Application Contact:* Jennifer Cake, Lead Enrollment Management Counselor, 215-884-8942 Ext. 212, E-mail: jennifer.cake@woninstitute.edu. *Chair,* Ben Griffith, 215-884-8942, Fax: 215-884-8942, E-mail: acupuncturechair@woninstitute.edu.

Program in Chinese Herbal Medicine Students: 24 full-time (18 women); includes 7 minority (1 Black or African American, non-Hispanic/Latino; 4 Asian, non-Hispanic/Latino; 1 Hispanic/Latino; 1 Two or more races, non-Hispanic/Latino), 2 international. Average age 42. Expenses: Contact institution. *Financial support:* Scholarships/grants available. Offers Chinese herbal medicine (Certificate). *Application deadline:* For fall admission, 8/1 for domestic students. Applications are processed on a rolling basis. *Application fee:* $75. Electronic applications accepted. *Application Contact:* Jennifer Cake, Enrollment Management Counselor, 215-884-8942 Ext. 219, Fax: 215-884-9002, E-mail: jennifer.cake@woninstitute.edu. *Acupuncture and Chinese Herbal Medicine Chair,* Jacqueline Lacava, 215-884-8942, Fax: 215-884-9002, E-mail: jacqueline.lacava@woninstitute.edu.

Won Buddhist Studies Program Students: 2 full-time (1 woman), 3 part-time (2 women), 3 international. Average age 40. Expenses: Contact institution. *Financial* *support:* Scholarships/grants available. Financial award application deadline: 8/1. *Program availability:* Part-time. Offers Won Buddhist studies (MWBS). *Application deadline:* For fall admission, 8/1 for domestic students; for spring admission, 12/1 for domestic students. Applications are processed on a rolling basis. *Application fee:* $75. *Application Contact:* Jennifer Cake, Enrollment Management Counselor, 215-884-8942 Ext. 219, E-mail: jennifer.cake@woninstitute.edu. *Chair,* Rev. Dr. Hye Sung Park, 215-884-8942, E-mail: wbschair@woninstitute.edu.

WOODBURY UNIVERSITY, Burbank, CA 91504-1052

General Information Independent, coed, comprehensive institution. *Graduate housing:* Room and/or apartments available on a first-come, first-served basis to single students; on-campus housing not available to married students.

GRADUATE UNITS

School of Architecture Offers architecture (M Arch, MIA, MS Arch).

School of Business *Program availability:* Part-time, evening/weekend. Offers business administration (MBA); organizational leadership (MA).

WOODS HOLE OCEANOGRAPHIC INSTITUTION, Woods Hole, MA 02543-1541

General Information Independent, coed, graduate-only institution. CGS member. *Graduate housing:* Rooms and/or apartments guaranteed to single students and available on a first-come, first-served basis to married students.

GRADUATE UNITS

MIT/WHOI Joint Program in Oceanography/Applied Ocean Science and Engineering Offers applied ocean science and engineering (PhD); biological oceanography (PhD); chemical oceanography (PhD); marine geology and geophysics (PhD); physical oceanography (PhD). Program offered jointly with Massachusetts Institute of Technology. Electronic applications accepted.

WORCESTER POLYTECHNIC INSTITUTE, Worcester, MA 01609-2280

General Information Independent, coed, university. CGS member. *Enrollment:* 6,874 graduate, professional, and undergraduate students. *Enrollment by degree level:* 1,595 master's, 419 doctoral, 77 other advanced degrees. *Graduate housing:* Rooms and/or apartments available on a first-come, first-served basis to single and married students. *Student services:* Campus employment opportunities, campus safety program, career counseling, exercise/wellness program, free psychological counseling, grant writing training, international student services, low-cost health insurance, multicultural affairs office, services for students with disabilities, teacher training, writing training. *Library facilities:* George C. Gordon Library plus 1 other. *Collection:* Books: 192,701 (physical), 750,858 (digital/electronic); Serial titles: 5,371 (physical), 143,312 (digital/electronic); Databases: 215. Weekly public service hours: 107; students can reserve study rooms.

Computer facilities: Computer purchase and lease plans are available. 860 computers available on campus for general student use. A campuswide network can be accessed from student residence rooms and from off campus. Online class registration, online course content are available.
Website: http://www.wpi.edu/

General Application Contact: Lynne Dougherty, Administrative Assistant, 508-831-5301, Fax: 508-831-5717, E-mail: grad@wpi.edu.

GRADUATE UNITS

Graduate Admissions Students: 839 full-time (291 women), 1,247 part-time (331 women); includes 278 minority (55 Black or African American, non-Hispanic/Latino; 2 American Indian or Alaska Native, non-Hispanic/Latino; 106 Asian, non-Hispanic/Latino; 87 Hispanic/Latino; 1 Native Hawaiian or other Pacific Islander, non-Hispanic/Latino; 27 Two or more races, non-Hispanic/Latino), 839 international. Average age 29. 4,194 applicants, 54% accepted, 735 enrolled. Expenses: Contact institution. *Financial support:* Fellowships, research assistantships, teaching assistantships, career-related internships or fieldwork, institutionally sponsored loans, scholarships/grants, health care benefits, tuition waivers, and unspecified assistantships available. Financial award application deadline: 1/1. In 2018, 791 master's, 60 doctorates, 67 other advanced degrees awarded. *Program availability:* Part-time, evening/weekend, 100% online, blended/hybrid learning. Offers aerospace engineering (MS); applied mathematics (MS); applied statistics (MS); biochemistry (MS, PhD); bioinformatics & computational biology (PhD); biology and biotechnology (MS, PhD); biomedical engineering (M Eng, MS, PhD, Graduate Certificate); bioscience administration (MS); chemical engineering (MS, PhD); chemistry (MS, PhD); civil engineering (MS, PhD, Advanced Certificate, Graduate Certificate); construction project management (Graduate Certificate); data science (Graduate Certificate); electrical and computer engineering (Advanced Certificate, Graduate Certificate); electrical engineering (M Eng, MS, PhD); financial mathematics (MS); fire protection engineering (MS, PhD, Advanced Certificate, Graduate Certificate); industrial mathematics (MS); interactive media & game development (MS); interdisciplinary social science (PhD); learning sciences & technologies (PhD); manufacturing engineering (MS, PhD); materials process engineering (MS); materials science & engineering (MS); materials science and engineering (PhD); mathematical sciences (PhD, Graduate Certificate); mathematics for educators (MME); nuclear science and engineering (Graduate Certificate); physics (MS); power systems engineering (MS); power systems management (MS); robotics engineering (MS); social science (PhD); system dynamics (MS, Graduate Certificate); system dynamics and innovation management (MS, Graduate Certificate); systems engineering (Graduate Certificate); systems modeling (MS). *Application deadline:* For fall admission, 1/1 priority date for domestic and international students; for spring admission, 10/1 priority date for domestic and international students. Applications are processed on a rolling basis. *Application fee:* $70. Electronic applications accepted. *Application Contact:* Lynne Dougherty, Administrative Assistant, 508-831-5301, Fax: 508-831-5717, E-mail: grad@wpi.edu. *Dean of Graduate Studies,* Dr. Terri Camesano, 508-831-5380, E-mail: grad@wpi.edu.

Foisie Business School Students: 136 full-time (74 women), 214 part-time (85 women); includes 29 minority (4 Black or African American, non-Hispanic/Latino; 11 Asian, non-Hispanic/Latino; 9 Hispanic/Latino; 5 Two or more races, non-Hispanic/Latino), 189 international. Average age 29. 636 applicants, 64% accepted, 104 enrolled. Expenses: Contact institution. *Financial support:* Career-related internships or fieldwork, institutionally sponsored loans, scholarships/grants, and unspecified assistantships available. Financial award application deadline: 6/1. In 2018, 165 master's, 1 doctorate, 10 other advanced degrees awarded. *Program availability:* Part-time, evening/weekend, 100% online, blended/hybrid learning. Offers business administration (MBA); information technology (MS); management (MS, Graduate Certificate); marketing and innovation (MS); operations analytics and management (MS); supply chain management (MS). *Application deadline:* For fall admission, 6/1 priority date for domestic and international students; for spring

admission, 11/1 priority date for domestic students, 10/1 priority date for international students. Applications are processed on a rolling basis. *Application fee:* $70. Electronic applications accepted. *Application Contact:* Amy Trakimas, Associate Director of Graduate Recruitment & Admissions, 508-831-4665, Fax: 508-831-5866, E-mail: atrakimas@wpi.edu. *Director of Graduate Recruitment & Admissions,* Melissa Terrio, 508-831-4665, Fax: 508-831-5866, E-mail: biz@wpi.edu.

WORCESTER STATE UNIVERSITY, Worcester, MA 01602-2597

General Information State-supported, coed, comprehensive institution. *Enrollment:* 6,217 graduate, professional, and undergraduate students; 167 full-time matriculated graduate/professional students (137 women), 670 part-time matriculated graduate/professional students (501 women). *Enrollment by degree level:* 646 master's, 191 other advanced degrees. *Graduate faculty:* 47 full-time (33 women), 36 part-time/adjunct (18 women). *International tuition:* $3042 full-time. *Tuition, area resident:* Full-time $3042; part-time $169 per credit hour. Tuition, state resident: full-time $3042; part-time $169 per credit hour. Tuition, nonresident: full-time $3042; part-time $169 per credit hour. *Required fees:* $2754; $153 per credit hour. *Graduate housing:* On-campus housing not available. *Student services:* Campus employment opportunities, campus safety program, career counseling, exercise/wellness program, free psychological counseling, international student services, low-cost health insurance, multicultural affairs office, services for students with disabilities, teacher training, writing training. *Library facilities:* Learning Resource Center. *Collection:* Books: 128,798 (physical), 1.6 million (digital/electronic); Serial titles: 202 (physical), 144,391 (digital/electronic); Databases: 273. Weekly public service hours: 100.

Computer facilities: Computer purchase and lease plans are available. A campuswide network can be accessed from student residence rooms and from off campus. Online class registration is available.
Website: http://www.worcester.edu/

General Application Contact: Sara Grady, Associate Dean, Graduate and Continuing Education, 508-929-8130, Fax: 508-929-8100, E-mail: sara.grady@worcester.edu.

GRADUATE UNITS

Graduate School Students: 166 full-time (137 women), 480 part-time (364 women); includes 77 minority (20 Black or African American, non-Hispanic/Latino; 5 American Indian or Alaska Native, non-Hispanic/Latino; 11 Asian, non-Hispanic/Latino; 33 Hispanic/Latino; 8 Two or more races, non-Hispanic/Latino), 15 international. Average age 35. 278 applicants, 91% accepted, 209 enrolled. *Faculty:* 47 full-time (33 women), 36 part-time/adjunct (18 women). Expenses: Contact institution. *Financial support:* Career-related internships or fieldwork, scholarships/grants, and unspecified assistantships available. Support available to part-time students. Financial award application deadline: 3/1; financial award applicants required to submit FAFSA. In 2018, 239 master's, 52 other advanced degrees awarded. Offers accounting (MS); adult English as a esl (Postbaccalaureate Certificate); biotechnology (MS); community and public health nursing (MSN); curriculum and instruction (Ed S); early childhood education (M Ed); education (M Ed, Ed S, Postbaccalaureate Certificate); elementary education (M Ed); English (MA); English as a second language (M Ed, Postbaccalaureate Certificate); health care administration (MS); health education (M Ed); history (MA); leadership (MS); leadership and administration (M Ed); marketing (MS); middle or secondary school education (Postbaccalaureate Certificate); middle school education (M Ed); middle/secondary school education (Postbaccalaureate Certificate); moderate disabilities (M Ed, Postbaccalaureate Certificate); non-profit management (MS); nurse educator (MSN); occupational therapy (MOT); reading (M Ed, Postbaccalaureate Certificate); reading specialist (Postbaccalaureate Certificate); school leadership and education administration (M Ed); school psychology (M Ed, Ed S); secondary education (M Ed, Ed S, Postbaccalaureate Certificate); Spanish (MA); speech-language pathology (MS). *Application deadline:* For fall admission, 3/1 for domestic and international students; for spring admission, 11/1 for domestic and international students; for summer admission, 3/1 for domestic and international students. Applications are processed on a rolling basis. *Application fee:* $50. Electronic applications accepted. *Application Contact:* Sara Grady, Associate Dean, Graduate Studies and Professional Development, 508-929-8130, Fax: 508-929-8100, E-mail: sara.grady@worcester.edu. *Associate Vice President for Continuing Education/Dean of the Graduate Studies,* Dr. Roberta Kyle, 508-929-8811, Fax: 508-929-8100, E-mail: rkyle@worcester.edu.

WORLD MISSION UNIVERSITY, Los Angeles, CA 90020

General Information Independent-religious, coed, comprehensive institution.

GRADUATE UNITS

Graduate Programs *Program availability:* Online learning.

WRIGHT GRADUATE UNIVERSITY FOR THE REALIZATION OF HUMAN POTENTIAL, Elkhorn, WI 53121

General Information Independent, coed, graduate-only institution.

GRADUATE UNITS

Graduate Programs

THE WRIGHT INSTITUTE, Berkeley, CA 94704-1796

General Information Independent, coed, graduate-only institution. *Graduate housing:* On-campus housing not available.

GRADUATE UNITS

Doctoral Program in Clinical Psychology Offers clinical psychology (Psy D). Electronic applications accepted.

Master of Arts in Counseling Psychology Program *Program availability:* Part-time, evening/weekend. Offers counseling psychology (MA). Electronic applications accepted.

WRIGHT STATE UNIVERSITY, Dayton, OH 45435

General Information State-supported, coed, university. CGS member. *Graduate housing:* Rooms and/or apartments available on a first-come, first-served basis to single and married students. *Research affiliation:* Wright-Patterson Air Force Base (research and development, systems and logistics), Veterans Administration Medical Center, Scott-Kettering Magnetic Resonance Research Laboratory (medical science), Edison Biotechnology Center, Edison Materials Technology Center (processing).

GRADUATE UNITS

Boonshoft School of Medicine Offers aerospace medicine (MS); health promotion and education (MPH); medicine (MPH, MS, MD, PhD); pharmacology and toxicology (MS).

Graduate School *Program availability:* Part-time, evening/weekend, 100% online, blended/hybrid learning. Electronic applications accepted.

College of Education and Human Services *Program availability:* Part-time, evening/weekend. Offers adolescent to young adult education (M Ed); advanced curriculum and instruction (Ed S); advanced educational leadership (Ed S); chemical dependency (MRC); classroom teacher education (M Ed, MA); counseling (M Ed, MA, MS); education and human services (M Ed, MA, MRC, MS, Ed S); intervention specialist (M Ed); pupil personnel services (M Ed); rehabilitation counseling (MRC).

College of Engineering and Computer Science *Program availability:* Part-time, evening/weekend. Offers aerospace systems engineering (MS); biomedical engineering (MS); computer engineering (MS); computer science (MS); computer science and engineering (MS, PhD); electrical engineering (MS); engineering (PhD); engineering and computer science (MS, PhD); industrial and human factors engineering (MS); materials science and engineering (MS); mechanical engineering (MS); renewable and clean energy (MS).

College of Liberal Arts *Program availability:* Part-time. Offers criminal justice and social problems (MA); English (MA); history (MA); humanities (M Hum); liberal arts (M Hum, MA, MM, MPA); music (MM); public administration (MPA).

College of Nursing and Health *Program availability:* Part-time, evening/weekend. Offers administration of nursing and health care systems (MS); adult gerontology clinical nurse specialist (MS); adult-gerontology acute care nurse practitioner (MS); family nurse practitioner (MS); neonatal nurse practitioner (MS); nursing and health (MS); pediatric nurse practitioner-acute care (MS); pediatric nurse practitioner-primary care (MS); psychiatric mental health nurse practitioner (MS); school nurse (MS).

College of Science and Mathematics *Program availability:* Part-time, evening/weekend. Offers anatomy (MS); applied mathematics (MS); applied statistics (MS); biochemistry and molecular biology (MS); biological sciences (MS); biomedical sciences (PhD); chemistry (MS); earth science education (MST); environmental sciences (PhD); geological sciences (Graduate Certificate); geophysics (MS); human factors and industrial/organizational psychology (MS, PhD); mathematics (MS); microbiology and immunology (MS); physics (MS, MST); physiology and neuroscience (MS); science and mathematics (MS, MST, PhD, Graduate Certificate).

Raj Soin College of Business *Program availability:* Part-time, evening/weekend. Offers accountancy (M Acc); business (M Acc, MBA, MIS, MS); business administration (MBA); information systems (MIS); logistics and supply chain management (MS); management information technology (MBA); social and applied economics (MS).

School of Professional Psychology Offers clinical psychology (Psy D).

WYCLIFFE COLLEGE, Toronto, ON M5S 1H7, Canada
General Information Independent-religious, coed, graduate-only institution. *Graduate housing:* Rooms and/or apartments guaranteed to single students and available on a first-come, first-served basis to married students. Housing application deadline: 5/1.

GRADUATE UNITS

Division of Advanced Degree Studies *Program availability:* Part-time. Offers theology (MA, Th M, D Min, PhD, Th D). PhD, D Min, MA offered jointly with Toronto School of Theology; Th D, Th M with University of Toronto.

Division of Basic Degree Studies *Program availability:* Part-time. Offers Christian Studies (Diploma); theology (M Div, M Rel, MTS). M Div, M Rel, MTS offered jointly with University of Toronto.

XAVIER UNIVERSITY, Cincinnati, OH 45207
General Information Independent-religious, coed, university. *Graduate housing:* On-campus housing not available.

GRADUATE UNITS

College of Arts and Sciences *Program availability:* Part-time. Offers arts and sciences (MA); English (MA); health care mission integration (MA); theology (MA); urban sustainability and resilience (MA). Electronic applications accepted.

College of Professional Sciences Offers clinical psychology (Psy D); coaching education and athlete development (M Ed); criminal justice (MS); health services administration (MHSA); industrial-organizational psychology (MA); occupational therapy (MOT); sport administration (M Ed).

School of Education Offers children's multicultural literature (M Ed); clinical mental health counseling (MA); education (M Ed, MA, MS, Ed D); educational administration (M Ed); elementary education (M Ed); human resource development (MS); Montessori education (M Ed); reading (M Ed); school counseling (MA); secondary education (M Ed); special education (M Ed). Electronic applications accepted.

School of Nursing *Program availability:* Part-time, evening/weekend. Offers nursing (MSN, DNP, PMC). Electronic applications accepted.

Williams College of Business *Program availability:* Part-time, evening/weekend. Offers accountancy (MS); business (Exec MBA, MBA, MS); business administration (Exec MBA, MBA); business intelligence (MBA); finance (MBA); health industry (MBA); international business (MBA); marketing (MBA); values-based leadership (MBA). Electronic applications accepted.

XAVIER UNIVERSITY OF LOUISIANA, New Orleans, LA 70125
General Information Independent-religious, coed, comprehensive institution. *Enrollment:* 723 full-time matriculated graduate/professional students (533 women), 30 part-time matriculated graduate/professional students (17 women). *Enrollment by degree level:* 138 master's, 615 doctoral. *Graduate faculty:* 57 full-time (34 women), 5 part-time/adjunct (2 women). *Tuition:* Full-time $2652; part-time $1326 per credit hour. *Required fees:* $531; $323 per semester. $258 per semester. Tuition and fees vary according to degree level and program. *Graduate housing:* Room and/or apartments available on a first-come, first-served basis to single students; on-campus housing not available to married students. Typical cost: $9709 (including board). Room and board charges vary according to board plan and housing facility selected. Housing application deadline: 5/1. *Student services:* Campus employment opportunities, campus safety program, career counseling, exercise/wellness program, free psychological counseling, international student services, low-cost health insurance, services for students with disabilities, teacher training. *Library facilities:* Xavier Library.

Computer facilities: A campuswide network can be accessed from student residence rooms and from off campus. Online class registration is available. Website: http://www.xula.edu/

General Application Contact: Dr. Marcus Cox, Associate Dean, College of Arts & Sciences, Director of the Center for Continuing Studies, Professor of History, 504-5207648, Fax: 504-5207896, E-mail: mcox1@xula.edu.

GRADUATE UNITS

College of Pharmacy Offers pharmacy (Pharm D). Electronic applications accepted.

Graduate School Students: 723 full-time (533 women), 30 part-time (17 women); includes 583 minority (356 Black or African American, non-Hispanic/Latino; 165 Asian, non-Hispanic/Latino; 40 Hispanic/Latino; 22 Two or more races, non-Hispanic/Latino), 27 international. Average age 26. 101 applicants, 100% accepted, 101 enrolled. *Faculty:* 7 full-time (5 women), 8 part-time/adjunct (5 women). Expenses: Contact institution.

Financial support: Career-related internships or fieldwork, scholarships/grants, and tuition waivers (partial) available. Support available to part-time students. Financial award application deadline: 6/30; financial award applicants required to submit FAFSA. In 2018, 32 master's awarded. *Program availability:* Part-time, evening/weekend. Offers counseling (MA); curriculum and instruction (MA); educational leadership (MA); theology (Th M). *Application deadline:* For fall admission, 7/1 for domestic students, 3/1 priority date for international students; for spring admission, 12/1 for domestic students, 9/15 priority date for international students; for summer admission, 3/1 for domestic students. Applications are processed on a rolling basis. *Application fee:* $30. Electronic applications accepted. *Application Contact:* Marcus Cox, Associate Dean, 504-5207896, Fax: 504-520-7896, E-mail: mcox1@xula.edu. *Associate Dean,* Dr. Marcus S Cox, 504-520-7487, Fax: 504-520-7896, E-mail: mcox1@xula.edu.

Institute for Black Catholic Studies Students: 25 full-time (5 women); includes 21 minority (19 Black or African American, non-Hispanic/Latino; 2 Hispanic/Latino). Average age 40. 3 applicants, 100% accepted, 3 enrolled. *Faculty:* 8 part-time/adjunct (4 women). Expenses: Contact institution. *Financial support:* Career-related internships or fieldwork and scholarships/grants available. Financial award application deadline: 3/1. In 2018, 4 master's awarded. *Program availability:* Part-time. Offers pastoral theology (Th M). *Application deadline:* For winter admission, 3/15 priority date for domestic students. Applications are processed on a rolling basis. *Application fee:* $30. Electronic applications accepted. *Application Contact:* Dana Lockett, Program Specialist, 504-520-7567, Fax: 504-520-7912, E-mail: dlocket1@xula.edu. *Director,* Dr. Kathleen D. Bellow, 504-520-7567, Fax: 504-520-7912, E-mail: kdbellow@xula.edu.

YALE UNIVERSITY, New Haven, CT 06520
General Information Independent, coed, university. CGS member. *Graduate housing:* Rooms and/or apartments available on a first-come, first-served basis to single and married students. Housing application deadline: 6/1. *Research affiliation:* Howard Hughes Medical Institute, J.B. Pierce Foundation (environmental physiology), Haskins Laboratories (speech, hearing, reading).

GRADUATE UNITS

Graduate School of Arts and Sciences *Program availability:* Part-time. Offers African studies (MA); African-American studies (PhD); American studies (PhD); anthropology (M Phil, MA, PhD); applied mathematics (M Phil, MS, PhD); Arabic humanities (MA, PhD); archaeological studies (MA); arts and sciences (M Phil, MA, MS, PhD); Assyriology (MA, PhD); astronomy (PhD); behavioral neuroscience (PhD); biochemistry, molecular biology and chemical biology (PhD); biogeochemistry (PhD); biophysical chemistry (PhD); cell biology (PhD); cellular and developmental biology (PhD); cellular and molecular physiology (PhD); classics (M Phil, MA, PhD); climate dynamics (PhD); clinical psychology (PhD); cognitive psychology (PhD); comparative and historical sociology (PhD); comparative literature (PhD); computer science (MS, PhD); cultural sociology and social theory (PhD); developmental psychology (PhD); East Asian languages and literatures (PhD); East Asian languages and literatures and film studies (PhD); East Asian studies (MA); ecology and evolutionary biology (PhD); economics (PhD); Egyptology (MA, PhD); English language and literature (MA, PhD); environmental sciences (PhD); experimental pathology (MS, PhD); film studies (PhD); forestry (PhD); French (M Phil, MA, PhD); genetics (PhD); geochemistry (PhD); geophysics (PhD); German (PhD); global affairs (MA); history (M Phil, MA, PhD); history of art (PhD); history of science and medicine (MS, PhD); immunobiology (PhD); inorganic chemistry (PhD); international and development economics (MA); Italian language and literature (PhD); Latin American literature (PhD); linguistics (PhD); Luso-Brazilian and Spanish/Spanish American literatures (PhD); mathematics (M Phil, MS, PhD); medieval Slavic literature and philology (PhD); medieval studies (M Phil, PhD); meteorology (PhD); molecular biophysics and biochemistry (PhD); music history (MA); music theory (MA); neurobiology (PhD); neuroscience (PhD); oceanography (PhD); organic chemistry (PhD); paleontology (PhD); paleooceanography (PhD); petrology (PhD); philosophy (PhD); physical and theoretical chemistry (PhD); physics (PhD); plant sciences (PhD); Polish literature (PhD); political science (PhD); religious studies (PhD); Renaissance studies (PhD); Russian and East European studies (MA); Russian literature (PhD); Slavic languages and literatures and film studies (PhD); social stratification and the life course (PhD); social/personality psychology (PhD); solar and terrestrial physics (PhD); Spanish peninsular literature (PhD); statistics (MA, PhD); tectonics (PhD); the Classical Near East (MA, PhD).

School of Engineering and Applied Science *Program availability:* Part-time. Offers applied physics (MS, PhD); biomedical engineering (MS, PhD); chemical engineering (MS, PhD); electrical engineering (MS, PhD); engineering and applied science (MS, PhD); environmental engineering (MS, PhD); mechanical engineering (MS, PhD).

School of Architecture Offers architecture (M Arch, M Env Des, MEM, PhD). Electronic applications accepted.

School of Art Offers graphic design (MFA); painting/printmaking (MFA); photography (MFA); sculpture (MFA). Electronic applications accepted.

School of Drama Offers acting (MFA, Certificate); design (MFA, Certificate); directing (MFA, Certificate); dramaturgy and dramatic criticism (MFA, DFA); playwriting (MFA, Certificate); sound design (MFA, Certificate); stage management (MFA, Certificate); technical design and production (MFA, Certificate); theater management (MFA). Electronic applications accepted.

School of Forestry and Environmental Studies *Program availability:* Part-time. Offers environmental management (MEM); environmental science (MES); forest science (MFS); forestry (MF); forestry and environmental studies (PhD). Electronic applications accepted.

School of Music Students: 232 full-time (100 women); includes 49 minority (3 Black or African American, non-Hispanic/Latino; 22 Asian, non-Hispanic/Latino; 12 Hispanic/Latino; 12 Two or more races, non-Hispanic/Latino), 82 international. Average age 24. 1,481 applicants, 12% accepted, 116 enrolled. *Faculty:* 29 full-time (9 women), 31 part-time/adjunct (7 women). Expenses: Contact institution. *Financial support:* In 2018–19, 232 students received support, including 232 fellowships (averaging $37,000 per year); Federal Work-Study, scholarships/grants, and unspecified assistantships also available. Financial award application deadline: 5/30; financial award applicants required to submit FAFSA. In 2018, 75 master's, 6 doctorates, 31 ADs awarded. Offers music (MM, MMA, DMA, AD, Certificate). *Application deadline:* For fall admission, 12/1 for domestic and international students. *Application fee:* $150. Electronic applications accepted. *Application Contact:* Suzanne M. Stringer, Director of Student Services, 203-432-1962, Fax: 203-432-7448, E-mail: suzanne.stringer@yale.edu. *Dean,* Robert Blocker, 203-432-4160, Fax: 203-432-7542.

School of Nursing *Program availability:* Part-time, online learning. Offers nursing (MSN, DNP, PhD, Post Master's Certificate). Electronic applications accepted.

Yale Divinity School *Program availability:* Part-time. Offers divinity (M Div, MAR, STM). Electronic applications accepted.

Yale Law School Students: 620 full-time (309 women). Average age 25. 3,473 applicants, 7% accepted, 204 enrolled. *Faculty:* 93 full-time, 164 part-time/adjunct. Expenses: Contact institution. *Financial support:* Application deadline: 3/15; applicants required to submit FAFSA. Offers law (LL M, MSL, JD, JSD, PhD). *Application deadline:* For fall admission, 2/28 for domestic students. Applications are processed on a rolling basis. *Application fee:* $85. Electronic applications accepted. *Application Contact:* Craig Janecek, Assistant Dean of Admissions, 203-432-4995, E-mail: admissions.law@yale.edu. *Dean,* Heather Gerken, 203-432-1660.

Yale School of Management Offers accounting (PhD); business administration (MBA); financial economics (PhD); management (MBA, PhD); marketing (PhD); organizations and management (PhD).

Yale School of Medicine *Program availability:* Part-time. Offers biological and biomedical sciences (PhD); computational biology and bioinformatics (PhD); immunology (PhD); medicine (APMPH, MM Sc, MPH, MS, MD, PhD); microbiology (PhD); molecular biophysics and biochemistry (PhD); molecular cell biology, genetics, and development (PhD); neurobiology (PhD); neuroscience (PhD); pharmacological sciences and molecular medicine (PhD); pharmacology (PhD); physician associate (MM Sc); physiology and integrative medical biology (PhD). Electronic applications accepted.

Yale School of Public Health *Program availability:* Part-time. Offers applied biostatistics and epidemiology (APMPH); biostatistics (MPH, MS, PhD); chronic disease epidemiology (MPH, PhD); environmental health sciences (MPH, PhD); epidemiology of microbial diseases (MPH, PhD); global health (APMPH); health management (MPH); health policy (MPH); health policy and administration (APMPH, PhD); occupational and environmental medicine (APMPH); preventive medicine (APMPH, MPH); social and behavioral sciences (APMPH, MPH). MS and PhD offered through the Graduate School. Electronic applications accepted.

YESHIVA BETH MOSHE, Scranton, PA 18505-2124

General Information Independent-religious, men only, comprehensive institution.
GRADUATE UNITS
Graduate Programs

YESHIVA DERECH CHAIM, Brooklyn, NY 11218

General Information Independent-religious, men only, comprehensive institution.
GRADUATE UNITS
Graduate Program Offers Talmudic studies (PhD).

YESHIVA KARLIN STOLIN, Brooklyn, NY 11204

General Information Independent-religious, men only, comprehensive institution. *Graduate housing:* On-campus housing not available.
GRADUATE UNITS
Graduate Programs

YESHIVA OF NITRA RABBINICAL COLLEGE, Mount Kisco, NY 10549

General Information Independent-religious, men only, comprehensive institution.
GRADUATE UNITS
Graduate Programs Offers theology (First Talmudic Degree, Second Talmudic Degree).

YESHIVA SHAAR HATORAH TALMUDIC RESEARCH INSTITUTE, Kew Gardens, NY 11418-1469

General Information Independent-religious, men only, comprehensive institution.
GRADUATE UNITS
Graduate Programs

YESHIVATH VIZNITZ, Monsey, NY 10952

General Information Independent-religious, men only, comprehensive institution.
GRADUATE UNITS
Graduate Programs

YESHIVATH ZICHRON MOSHE, South Fallsburg, NY 12779

General Information Independent-religious, men only, comprehensive institution.
GRADUATE UNITS
Graduate Programs *Program availability:* Part-time.

YESHIVA UNIVERSITY, New York, NY 10033-3201

General Information Independent, coed, university. *Graduate housing:* On-campus housing not available.
GRADUATE UNITS
Azrieli Graduate School of Jewish Education and Administration *Program availability:* Part-time, evening/weekend. Offers Jewish education and administration (MS, Ed D, Specialist).

Benjamin N. Cardozo School of Law Students: 960 full-time (537 women), 85 part-time (46 women); includes 229 minority (38 Black or African American, non-Hispanic/Latino; 83 Asian, non-Hispanic/Latino; 83 Hispanic/Latino; 25 Two or more races, non-Hispanic/Latino), 86 international. 2,584 applicants, 49% accepted, 365 enrolled. *Faculty:* 61 full-time (25 women), 111 part-time/adjunct (46 women). Expenses: Contact institution. *Financial support:* In 2018–19, 831 students received support, including 114 research assistantships (averaging $1,512 per year); career-related internships or fieldwork, Federal Work-Study, institutionally sponsored loans, scholarships/grants, health care benefits, and tuition waivers (full and partial) also available. Support available to part-time students. Financial award application deadline: 3/1; financial award applicants required to submit FAFSA. In 2018, 75 master's, 282 doctorates awarded. *Program availability:* 100% online. Offers comparative legal thought (LL M); dispute resolution and advocacy (LL M); general studies (LL M); intellectual property law (LL M); law (JD). Joint JD/MSW (Masters in Social Work) with Benjamin N. Cardozo School of Law & the Wurzweiler School of Social Work; joint JD/MBE (Masters in Bioethics) with Benjamin N. Cardozo School of Law and the Albert Einstein College of Medicine. *Application deadline:* For fall admission, 4/1 priority date for domestic students, 6/15 priority date for international students; for spring admission, 12/1 for domestic students, 12/1 priority date for international students. Applications are processed on a rolling basis. *Application fee:* $0 ($50 for international students). Electronic applications accepted. *Application Contact:* David G. Martinidez, Dean of Admissions, 212-790-0274, Fax: 212-790-0482, E-mail: lawinfo@yu.edu. *Dean and Samuel Belkin Professor of Law,* Dean Melanie Leslie, 212-790-0310, Fax: 212-790-0203, E-mail: DeansOfficeCardozo@yu.edu.

Bernard Revel Graduate School of Jewish Studies *Program availability:* Part-time. Offers Jewish studies (MA, PhD).

Ferkauf Graduate School of Psychology *Program availability:* Part-time. Offers clinical health psychology (PhD); clinical psychology (Psy D); mental health counseling psychology (MA); psychology (MA, PhD, Psy D); school/clinical-child psychology (Psy D).

The Katz School *Program availability:* Part-time, online learning. Offers biotechnology management and entrepreneurship (MS); data analytics and visualization (MS); enterprise risk management (MS); marketing (MS); mathematics (MA); quantitative economics (MS); speech-language pathology (MS).

Sy Syms School of Business *Program availability:* Part-time. Offers accounting (MS); business (EMBA); marketing (MS); taxation (MS).

Wurzweiler School of Social Work *Program availability:* Part-time, evening/weekend. Offers social work (MSW, PhD).

YORK COLLEGE OF PENNSYLVANIA, York, PA 17403-3651

General Information Independent, coed, comprehensive institution. *Enrollment:* 53 full-time matriculated graduate/professional students (27 women), 214 part-time matriculated graduate/professional students (140 women). *Enrollment by degree level:* 241 master's, 26 doctoral. *Graduate faculty:* 20 full-time (13 women), 18 part-time/adjunct (13 women). Tuition and fees vary according to program. *Graduate housing:* On-campus housing not available. *Student services:* Campus employment opportunities, campus safety program, career counseling, exercise/wellness program, free psychological counseling, international student services, services for students with disabilities, writing training. *Library facilities:* Schmidt Library.

Computer facilities: A campuswide network can be accessed from student residence rooms and from off campus. Online class registration is available. Website: http://www.ycp.edu/

General Application Contact: Michael Thorp, Director of Admissions, 717-815-2240, Fax: 717-849-1607, E-mail: admissions@ycp.edu.

GRADUATE UNITS
Graduate Programs in Behavioral Sciences and Education Students: 1 full-time (0 women), 107 part-time (77 women); includes 3 minority (1 Hispanic/Latino; 2 Two or more races, non-Hispanic/Latino). Average age 34. 35 applicants, 69% accepted, 23 enrolled. *Faculty:* 1 full-time (0 women), 10 part-time/adjunct (8 women). Expenses: Contact institution. *Financial support:* Scholarships/grants available. Financial award applicants required to submit FAFSA. In 2018, 10 master's awarded. *Program availability:* Part-time-only, evening/weekend. Offers educational leadership (M Ed); educational technology (M Ed); reading specialist (M Ed). *Application deadline:* For fall admission, 7/15 priority date for domestic students; for spring admission, 11/15 priority date for domestic students; for summer admission, 4/15 priority date for domestic students. Applications are processed on a rolling basis. *Application fee:* $0. Electronic applications accepted. *Application Contact:* Dr. Joshua D. DeSantis, Director, Graduate Programs in Behavioral Science and Education, 717-815-1936, E-mail: jdesant1@ycp.edu. *Director, Graduate Programs in Behavioral Science and Education,* Dr. Joshua D. DeSantis, 717-815-1936, E-mail: jdesant1@ycp.edu.

Graham School of Business Students: 13 full-time (4 women), 73 part-time (32 women); includes 11 minority (5 Black or African American, non-Hispanic/Latino; 2 Asian, non-Hispanic/Latino; 2 Hispanic/Latino; 2 Two or more races, non-Hispanic/Latino), 1 international. Average age 35. 57 applicants, 65% accepted, 25 enrolled. *Faculty:* 11 full-time (5 women), 3 part-time/adjunct (1 woman). Expenses: Contact institution. *Financial support:* In 2018–19, 3 students received support. Scholarships/grants available. Financial award applicants required to submit FAFSA. In 2018, 8 master's awarded. *Program availability:* Part-time, evening/weekend. Offers accounting (M Acc); business (MBA); continuous improvement (MBA); financial management (MBA); health care management (MBA); management (MBA); marketing (MBA); self-designed (MBA). *Application deadline:* For fall admission, 7/15 priority date for domestic students, 5/1 for international students; for spring admission, 11/15 priority date for domestic students, 9/1 for international students; for summer admission, 4/15 priority date for domestic students. Applications are processed on a rolling basis. *Application fee:* $0. Electronic applications accepted. *Application Contact:* MBA Office, 717-815-1491, Fax: 717-600-3999, E-mail: mba@ycp.edu. *MBA Director,* Nicole Cornell Sadowski, 717-815-1491, Fax: 717-600-3999, E-mail: ncornell@ycp.edu.

The Stabler Department of Nursing *Program availability:* Part-time. Offers adult gerontology clinical nurse specialist (MS); nurse anesthetist (MS). Electronic applications accepted.

YORK COLLEGE OF THE CITY UNIVERSITY OF NEW YORK, Jamaica, NY 11451

General Information State and locally supported, coed, comprehensive institution.
GRADUATE UNITS
School of Arts and Sciences Offers pharmaceutcal science and business (MS).
School of Health Sciences and Professional Programs Offers physician assistant (MSPAS).

YORK UNIVERSITY, Toronto, ON M3J 1P3, Canada

General Information Province-supported, coed, university. CGS member. *Graduate housing:* Rooms and/or apartments available on a first-come, first-served basis to single and married students. *Research affiliation:* Imperial Oil Limited, National Palace Museum, Unicorn Children's Foundation (developmental and learning disorders), Smithsonian Institution (astronomy, physics, space), Beijing Municipality (management training), German Academic Exchange (German studies).

GRADUATE UNITS
Faculty of Graduate Studies *Program availability:* Part-time, evening/weekend. Offers communication and culture (MA, PhD); environmental studies (MES, PhD); interdisciplinary studies (MA); social and political thought (MA, PhD). Electronic applications accepted.

Faculty of Education *Program availability:* Part-time. Offers education (M Ed, PhD). Electronic applications accepted.

Faculty of Fine Arts *Program availability:* Part-time. Offers art history (MA, PhD); composition (MA); dance (MA, MFA, PhD); design (M Des); film (MA, MFA, PhD); fine arts (M Des, MA, MFA, PhD); music (PhD); musicology and ethnomusicology (MA); theatre (MFA); theatre and performance studies (MA, PhD); visual arts (MFA, PhD). Electronic applications accepted.

Faculty of Health Offers critical disability studies (MA, PhD); health (M Sc, M Sc N, MA, PhD); kinesiology and health science (M Sc, MA, PhD); nursing (M Sc N); psychology (MA, PhD).

Faculty of Liberal Arts and Professional Studies Offers disaster and emergency management (MA); economics (MA, PhD); English (MA, PhD); gender, feminist and women's studies (MA, PhD); geography (M Sc, MA, PhD); history (MA, PhD); human resources management (MHRM, PhD); humanities (MA, PhD); liberal arts and professional studies (M Sc, MA, MHRM, MPPAL, MSW, PhD); linguistics and applied linguistics (MA, PhD); philosophy (MA, PhD); political science (MA, PhD); public policy, administration and law (MPPAL); social anthropology (MA, PhD); social work (MSW, PhD); sociology (MA, PhD).

Faculty of Science *Program availability:* Part-time, evening/weekend. Offers biology (M Sc, PhD); chemistry (M Sc, PhD); industrial and applied mathematics (M Sc); mathematics and statistics (MA, PhD); physics and astronomy (M Sc, PhD); science (M Sc, MA, PhD).

Glendon Campus Offers French studies (MA, PhD); public and international affairs (MA); translation (MA).

Lassonde School of Engineering Offers computer science (M Sc, PhD); earth and space science (M Sc, PhD); engineering (M Sc, PhD).

Osgoode Hall Law School *Program availability:* Part-time, evening/weekend. Offers law (LL M, JD, PhD). Electronic applications accepted.

Schulich School of Business *Program availability:* Part-time, evening/weekend. Offers accounting (M Acc); administration (PhD); business (MBA); business analytics (MBA); finance (MF); international business (IMBA). Electronic applications accepted.

YO SAN UNIVERSITY OF TRADITIONAL CHINESE MEDICINE, Los Angeles, CA 90066

General Information Private, coed, graduate-only institution. *Graduate housing:* On-campus housing not available.

GRADUATE UNITS

Program in Acupuncture and Traditional Chinese Medicine *Program availability:* Part-time, online learning. Offers acupuncture and traditional Chinese medicine (MATCM).

YOUNGSTOWN STATE UNIVERSITY, Youngstown, OH 44555-0001

General Information State-supported, coed, comprehensive institution. CGS member. *Graduate housing:* Room and/or apartments available on a first-come, first-served basis to single students; on-campus housing not available to married students. *Research affiliation:* Ohio Supercomputer Center (computational chemistry and physics), Northeast Ohio Medical University (medicine), Parker-Hannifin Corporation (engineering technology), Ohio Mass Spectrometry Consortium (chemistry and biology), BioRemedial Technologies Inc. (environmental bioremediation).

GRADUATE UNITS

College of Graduate Studies *Program availability:* Part-time, evening/weekend.

Beeghly College of Education *Program availability:* Part-time, evening/weekend. Offers content area concentration (MS Ed); counseling (MS Ed); curriculum and instruction (MS Ed); education (MS Ed, Ed D, Ed S); educational administration (MS Ed); educational leadership (Ed D); literacy (MS Ed); school psychology (Ed S); special education (MS Ed).

Bitonte College of Health and Human Services *Program availability:* Part-time, evening/weekend. Offers athletic training (MAT); criminal justice (MS); health and human services (MHHS); nursing (MSN); physical therapy (DPT); public health (MPH); social work (MSW).

Cliffe College of Creative Arts and Communication *Program availability:* Part-time, evening/weekend. Offers creative arts and communication (MM); jazz studies (MM); music education (MM); music history and literature (MM); music theory and composition (MM); performance (MM).

College of Liberal Arts and Social Sciences *Program availability:* Part-time. Offers American studies (MA); economics (MA); English (MA); financial economics (MA); gerontology (MA); history (MA); liberal arts and social sciences (MA).

College of Science, Technology, Engineering and Mathematics *Program availability:* Part-time, evening/weekend. Offers actuarial science (MS); analytical chemistry (MS); applied mathematics (MS); biochemistry (MS); chemistry education (MS); civil and environmental engineering (MSE); computer engineering (MSE); computer science (MS); computing and information systems (MCIS); electrical engineering (MSE); environmental biology (MS); environmental studies (MS); industrial and systems engineering (MSE); industrial/institutional management (Certificate); inorganic chemistry (MS); mathematics (MS); mechanical engineering (MSE); molecular biology, microbiology, and genetics (MS); organic chemistry (MS); physical chemistry (MS); physiology and anatomy (MS); risk management (Certificate); science, technology, engineering and mathematics (MCIS, MS, MSE, Certificate); secondary/community college mathematics (MS); statistics (MS).

Williamson College of Business Administration *Program availability:* Part-time, evening/weekend. Offers accountancy (M Acc); business administration (M Acc, MBA, Certificate); enterprise resource planning (Certificate).

CLOSE-UPS OF INSTITUTIONS OFFERING GRADUATE AND PROFESSIONAL WORK

THE COLLEGE OF NEW JERSEY
Graduate Programs

Programs of Study

The College of New Jersey (TCNJ) offers the following advanced degrees: Master of Arts (M.A.) in counselor education (areas include school counseling; clinical mental health counseling) or English (literature); Master of Arts in Teaching (M.A.T.) in early childhood education, elementary education, secondary education (iSTEM math, iSTEM science, and iSTEM technology education), special education/elementary; five-year programs (for TCNJ undergraduate students only) in education of the deaf and hard of hearing/elementary education, special education, urban education, and English; Master of Education (M.Ed.) in educational leadership–principal certification, educational leadership: instruction (a collaborative program in conjunction with the Regional Training Center), elementary and secondary education (off-site Global Program only), reading K–12, special education, special education/teacher of the blind or visually impaired, Integrative Science, Technology, Engineering, and Math (iSTEM), teaching English as a second language, or Urban Secondary Education; Master of Science in Nursing (M.S.N.) in adult/gerontological primary care nurse practitioner studies, clinical nurse leader studies, family nurse practitioner studies, neonatal nurse practitioner studies, or school nurse certification (instructional option); Master of Public Health (M.P.H.); Master of Business Administration.

Graduate certificate programs and/or post-master's programs are offered in adult/gerontological primary care nurse practitioner studies, family nurse practitioner studies, school nurse certification (instructional and non-instructional options), bilingual education (main campus and off-site Global Program), educational leadership–principal certification, instructional licensure-teacher of preschool–grade 3, learning disabilities teacher/consultant studies, teacher of students with blindness and visual impairments studies, reading specialist studies, student assistance coordinator studies, teacher certification for international schools (off-site Global Program only), teacher of students with disabilities, teaching English as a second language, or gender studies.

Global opportunities in education are also available for graduate students. Graduate global programs at TCNJ have been in existence for over thirty-five years and provide course work leading toward master's-level degrees in education and certification in teaching, administration, and substance abuse counseling. Courses are taught by TCNJ faculty members and other internationally recognized professors. Courses are offered June through July at TCNJ sites in Mallorca, Spain; Bangkok, Thailand; Lisbon, Portugal; and Johannesburg, South Africa. During the academic year, courses are available in Cairo, Egypt; Hsinchu, Taiwan; and Ho Chi Minh City, Vietnam.

For the convenience of the majority of graduate students who pursue degrees while employed full-time, graduate courses held on the Ewing campus are offered during the day and in the evening.

Research Facilities

TCNJ offers a state-of-the-art library that serves as an exciting intellectual, cultural, and social center for the College community. The five-story, 135,000-square-foot facility will provide cutting-edge services to the TCNJ community well into the twenty-first century. In addition to housing traditional library collections and services in an atmosphere that is both friendly and elegant, a key feature of the recently built library is its wide array of carefully considered and thoughtful amenities, which make using the facility both a pleasure and a convenience. The library provides twenty-four group-study rooms (one reserved for graduate students), ample and comfortable seating, tables and carrels, and both WiFi and LAN Internet access throughout, with power connections available at every carrel and study table. Special design features include a café, a secure, late night/24-hour study area, and a 105-seat multipurpose auditorium. The library also houses the Instructional Technology Services facility, creating ideal one-stop shopping for students working on projects.

Library collections include more than 560,000 volumes and 200,000 microforms as well as subscriptions to more than 1,400 periodicals. The library also subscribes to more than seventy-five electronic indexes covering more than 14,000 scholarly journals, including full-text resources. A media facility offers viewing and listening equipment as well as sound recordings, videos, and interactive computer software. PCs are available for public access to electronic resources. Collections are constantly augmented by new acquisitions, and interlibrary loan and document delivery services are available to students. The library is also an active participant in a number of library networks and maintains cooperative arrangements with many regional academic libraries, from which students may borrow directly. TCNJ librarians are an important resource in and of themselves. In addition to advanced studies in library and information science, each subject librarian has additional graduate degrees in one of the major academic areas, and students are encouraged to consult them in person and online.

In addition to providing new library facilities for the College community, TCNJ has met the challenge of the computer field's phenomenal growth with installations of computer facilities in each of its seven schools.

Financial Aid

The College of New Jersey offers financial aid to qualified matriculated students through a combination of loans, assistantships, and/or student employment opportunities. To be considered for all financial aid programs, students must submit the Free Application for Federal Student Aid (FAFSA) to the College Financial Assistance Office. Graduate assistantships are available to qualified full-time students on a competitive basis. Prospective students must apply through the Office of Graduate Studies by April 15 to be considered for a graduate assistantship.

Cost of Study

Tuition for graduate courses for the 2019–20 academic year is $959.06 per semester hour of credit for New Jersey residents and $1,398.62 per semester hour of credit for out-of-state residents. Additional fees include ID, student center, computer access and service fees, and health insurance (for full-time students). Tuition and fees are subject to change by action of the New Jersey State Legislature.

Living and Housing Costs

As the majority of TCNJ's graduate students attend classes part-time in the evenings, the College does not offer on-campus housing for graduate students. Graduate students who seek housing in the area may obtain assistance from the Office of Residence Life.

Student Group

The College of New Jersey has an enrollment of approximately 6,500 undergraduate students and 1,000 graduate students.

Student Outcomes

The College of New Jersey's excellent reputation has afforded graduates outstanding opportunities when entering their professional fields. Many TCNJ graduates receive job placements through various on-campus recruitment programs sponsored by the Office of Career Services.

Location

The College of New Jersey is located on 289 tree-lined acres in suburban Ewing, New Jersey, 7 miles from the state capital in Trenton. Woodlands and two lakes surround the academic and residential buildings. More than thirty-five buildings make up the physical plant, most of which are built in the classic Georgian Colonial architecture. The campus is 30 miles from Philadelphia and 60 miles from New York's theaters, museums, and other attractions. The nearby towns of Princeton and New Hope offer additional cultural activities.

The College

Founded in 1855, the College has grown from its early years as a teachers' college to a multipurpose institution comprising seven schools: Arts and Communication; Business; Education; Engineering; Humanities and Social Sciences; Nursing, Health, and Exercise Science; and Science. Graduate study is available in the Schools of Education, Humanities and Social Sciences, and Nursing, Health, and Exercise Science.

TCNJ introduced its first advanced degree program, a Master of Science in elementary education, in 1947. Over the years, the number of graduate programs has steadily increased. At present, there are more than fifty specialized graduate degree and certificate programs.

TCNJ's academic programs are accredited by the Middle States Association of Colleges and Schools, the National Council for Accreditation of Teacher Education (NCATE)/Council for the Accreditation of Educator Preparation (CAEP), the Council for the Accreditation of Counseling and Related Educational Programs (CACREP), Commission on Collegiate Nursing Education (CCNE), and other appropriate professional associations.

Applying

Students of proven ability with undergraduate degrees in appropriate fields are eligible to apply for graduate study. Applications should be submitted online (http://graduate.tcnj.edu/apply) along with a $75 nonrefundable application fee. Transcripts of all previous college or university work and other supporting documentation, as noted on the website, should be forwarded to the Office of Graduate and Advancing Education. Acceptable

The College of New Jersey

scores on the appropriate national standardized tests are required for most degree and initial teacher certificate programs.

Application deadlines for matriculation and non-matriculation for the various graduate programs are located on the Graduate Studies website (http://graduate.tcnj.edu/apply).

Correspondence and Information
Office of Graduate and Advancing Education
Green Hall, Room 111
The College of New Jersey
P.O. Box 7718
2000 Pennington Road
Ewing, New Jersey 08628
United States
Phone: 609-771-2300
Fax: 609-637-5105
E-mail: graduate@tcnj.edu
Website: http://graduate.tcnj.edu

DEANS AND PROGRAM COORDINATORS

SCHOOL OF HUMANITIES AND SOCIAL SCIENCES
Jane Wong, Dean; Ph.D.

Graduate Program Coordinator
English: Jo Carney, Ph.D., Iowa.

SCHOOL OF EDUCATION
Suzanne McCotter, Dean; Ph.D., Georgia.

Graduate Program Coordinators
Counselor Education: Mark Woodford, Ph.D., Virginia. Marion Cavallaro, Ph.D., Ohio State. Atsuko Seto, Ph.D., Wyoming. Stuart Roe, Ph.D., Penn State.
Deaf and Hard of Hearing/Elementary Education Five-Year Program: Barbara Strassman, Ed.D., Columbia Teachers College.
Early Childhood Education: Jody Eberly, Ph.D., Rutgers.
Educational Leadership–Instruction: Alan Amtzis, Ph.D., Boston College.
Educational Leadership–Principal: Linda Mayger, Ph.D., Lehigh University.
Elementary and Early Childhood Education (M.A.T.): Arti Joshi, Ph.D., Syracuse.
Instructional Licensure–Teacher of Preschool–Grade 3: Jody Eberly, Ph.D., Rutgers.
Reading K–12: David Bwire, Ph.D.
Secondary Education: Donald Leake, Ph.D., Ohio State.
Special Education: Dr. Shridevi Rao, Ph.D., Syracuse University.
TESOL/Bilingual Education: Yiqiang Wu, Ph.D., Texas A&M.

SCHOOL OF NURSING, HEALTH, AND EXERCISE SCIENCE
Carole Kenner, Dean; Ph.D., Indiana.

Graduate Program Coordinators
Nursing: Dara Whalen, Ph.D.

MAJOR RESEARCH PROJECTS, AWARDS, GRANTS, AND INITIATIVES

School of Education
Intoxicated Drivers' Resource Center (IDRC); Dr. Cassandra Gibson and the TCNJ Clinic, School of Education.
Community Reinforcement and Family Training (CRAFT); Dr. Cassandra Gibson and Dr. Mark Woodford, School of Education.
Collegiate Recovery Support and Environmental Change (CRC); Dr. Cassandra Gibson, School of Education.
Trenton Violence Reduction Strategy (TVRS); Dr. Cassandra Gibson, School of Education.
LifeChoices; Dr. Cassandra Gibson and Dr. Stuart Roe, School of Education.
Creating a team of highly qualified professionals for English language learners (CTHQP) grant; Dr. Yiqiang Wu, School of Education.
Adaptive Technology Center grant; Dr. Amy G. Dell, School of Education.
Preparing special and elementary educators to use inquiry and design-based learning; Dr. Amy Dell, School of Education.
Provisional Teacher Program; Dr. Anthony Evangelisto, School of Education.
TECH-NJ (Technology, Educators, and Children with Disabilities–New Jersey); Dr. Amy G. Dell, School of Education.
Deaf/Blind Family and Community Educational Support; Dr. Jerry Petroff, School of Education.
Conversation analysis of native/non-native speakers; Dr. Jean Wong, School of Education.
Facilitating transition from school to employment for individuals with challenging behavior; Dr. Shridevi Rao, School of Education.
Issues of literacy and teaching elementary students of color; Dr. Deborah Thompson, School of Education.
Fulbright Scholar Award to teach at the University of Bahrain, Bahrain Teachers College; Dr. Lynnette Mawhinney, School of Education

School of Nursing, Health and Exercise Science
Advanced education nursing traineeship program; Dr. Claire Lindberg, School of Nursing
HIV symptom distress project; Dr. Claire Lindberg, School of Nursing.

School of Humanities and Social Sciences
The reception of Dante and Chaucer within the work of their literary successors; Dr. Glenn Steinberg, School of Culture and Society.
Book-length research project in family memoir based on research and interviews: "The Seven: A Family Holocaust Story"; Ellen Friedman, School of Humanities and Social Sciences.
Research in Early Modern Grammars and Spelling Books; Felicia Steele, School of Humanities and Social Sciences.
"'Universal Mixing' and Interpenetrating Standing: Disability and Community in Melville's Moby-Dick"; Harriet Hustis, School of Humanities and Social Sciences.
Executive Director of the Thornton Wilder Society, which is headquartered at TCNJ, and co-founder and officer of the Edward Albee Society; Lincoln Konkle, School of Humanities and Social Sciences.
Thornton Wilder: New Perspectives; Lincoln Konkle, School of Humanities and Social Sciences.
Thornton Wilder and The Puritan Narrative Tradition; Lincoln Konkle, School of Humanities and Social Sciences.
National Endowment for the Humanities Fellowship; Michael Robertson, School of Humanities and Social Sciences.
Worshipping Walt: The Whitman Disciples; Michael Robertson, School of Humanities and Social Sciences.
Walt Whitman, Where the Future Becomes Present; David Blake and Michael Robertson, School of Humanities and Social Sciences.

The clock tower above Green Hall, the main administrative building on campus, is a well-known symbol of TCNJ tradition.

TCNJ offers a state-of-the-art library that serves as an exciting intellectual, cultural, and social center for the College community.

COLLEGE OF STATEN ISLAND
OF THE CITY UNIVERSITY OF NEW YORK

Graduate Degree Programs

Programs of Study

The College of Staten Island (CSI) offers master's degrees in Accounting (M.S.); Biology (M.S.); Business Management (M.S.); Cinema and Media Studies (M.A.); Clinical Mental Health Counseling (M.A.); Computer Science (M.S.); Education: Childhood (elementary) Education (M.S.Ed.), Adolescence (secondary) Education (M.S.Ed.), Special Education (grades 1–6) (M.S.Ed.), Special Education (grades 7–12) (M.S.Ed.), Teaching of English to Speakers of other Languages (M.S.Ed.); English (M.A.); Environmental Science (M.S.); History (M.A.); Liberal Studies (M.A.); Neuroscience and Developmental Disabilities (M.S.); Nursing: Adult-Gerontological Health Nursing (M.S.); Social Work (M.S.W.); Healthcare Management (M.S.); and Electrical Engineering (M.E.).

Post-master's degrees are awarded in Education: School District Leader, School Building Leader and School District Leader (dual certificate) and in Nursing: Adult-Gerontological Health Nursing. Advanced certificates are offered in Autism Spectrum Disorders, Business Analytics of Large-Scale Data, Cultural Competence, Bilingual Education, Public History, Special Education, and Teaching of English to Speakers of other Languages (online and in-classroom). The College of Staten Island offers an Adult-Gerontological Health Nursing (D.N.P.) program and a Clinical Doctorate in Physical Therapy (D.P.T.).

In addition, the College offers the following doctoral programs jointly with the Graduate Center of the City University of New York (CUNY): Biochemistry (Ph.D.), Biology (Ph.D.), Computer Science (Ph.D.), Nursing (Ph.D.), Physics (Ph.D.), and Polymer Chemistry (Ph.D.).

Research Facilities

The Center for Developmental Neuroscience and Developmental Disabilities is supported jointly with the New York State Institute for Basic Research (IBR). The center conducts, promotes, and sponsors research, education, and training in the developmental neurosciences, with special emphasis on research and educational programs in the specific field of developmental disabilities. The center provides for collaborative efforts between the College and IBR in offering the master's degree in Neuroscience and Developmental Disabilities, as well as with the University's doctoral programs in biology (subprogram in neuroscience), and in psychology (subprogram in learning processes). The center provides advanced research training for graduate students.

The Center for Environmental Science provides support for research and policy recommendations concerning environmental problems. One of the major purposes of the center is to define and solve environmental problems on Staten Island and its environs through research that includes studies of respiratory diseases, toxic and carcinogenic chemicals in the air, and the population at risk for lung cancer.

The Center for the Study of Staten Island: Staten Island Project (SIP) is designed to integrate the work of the College with the public affairs concerns of the people of Staten Island. To that end, it mediates and facilitates the collaboration of the College's faculty, students, and staff with government, civic organizations, and businesses in order to identify and assist in finding solutions to the borough's pressing public issues. The center serves as an information and consultation resource to prepare citizens and leaders to make better-informed decisions about public life; it fosters the development of faculty research and graduate education through engagement with the community; and it builds bridges to other public affairs institutes and local communities as a spur to innovations in public life on Staten Island.

The Center for Interdisciplinary Applied Mathematics and Computational Sciences brings together a diverse group of research faculty members and students with interests in interdisciplinary applications of mathematics and computational science. The center's activities include the use of the campus supercomputer, faculty collaboration, grant writing, student mentoring and research, and sponsored lectures.

The CUNY High-Performance Computing Center (HPCC) is located on the CSI campus. Goals of the HPCC are to: support the scientific computing needs of university faculty, student, staff, and their public and private sector partners; create opportunities for the CUNY research community to develop new partnerships with the government and private sectors; and leverage the center's capabilities to acquire additional research resources for its faculty and graduate students in existing and major new programs.

Financial Aid

The Office of Student Financial Aid administers federal and state grant, loan, and work-study programs to assist students with financial need to attend the College of Staten Island. Students should contact the Office of Student Financial Aid early in the admission process to discuss eligibility requirements and responsibilities. Graduate assistant positions are available for full-time graduate students in some departments. Information about these positions may be obtained from the individual program departments. The College of Staten Island also recognizes academic excellence through scholarship programs which offer assistance to students as well. For more information about the scholarship programs, prospective students can visit www.csi.cuny.edu/advancement/scholarships.html.

Cost of Study

For the 2019–20 academic year, tuition for master's programs for New York State residents is $470 per credit, or $5,545 per semester for 12 or more credits. Tuition for non-state residents is $855 per credit. Tuition for the Master in Social Work program is $620 per credit, or $7,315 per semester for New York State residents. Tuition for non-state residents is $1000 per credit. Tuition for the Master of Engineering program is $550 per credit, or $6,485 per semester for New York State residents. Tuition for non-state residents is $945 per credit. Tuition for the Clinical Doctorate in Physical Therapy program for New York State residents is $685 per credit, or $6,595 per semester. Tuition for non-state residents is $1,075 per credit. Tuition for the Doctorate in Nursing Practice program for New York State residents is $620

College of Staten Island of the City University of New York

per credit, or $7,315 per semester. Tuition for non-state residents is $1000 per credit.

Living and Housing Costs

For the 2019–20 academic year, students living with parents budget a minimum of $1,364 for books and supplies, $1,088 for local transportation, $3,019 for meals and personal expenses, and $4,450 for housing. Students living away from parents budget the same amounts for books, supplies, and transportation, plus $19,993 for food, housing, and personal expenses for a nine-month academic year. The College of Staten Island's first on-campus student housing is now open. Floor plans and rates are available online at www.csi.cuny.edu/housing.

Student Group

Nearly 1,000 graduate students enrolled at the College of Staten Island in the 2016 fall semester. The graduate population reflects a wide range of ethnicity, social and economic backgrounds, educational and professional experiences, and aspirations.

Location

The College of Staten Island is located in New York City in the Borough of Staten Island. Completed in 1994, the 204-acre campus of the College of Staten Island is the largest one for a college in New York City. Set in a park-like landscape, the campus is centrally located on Staten Island and is accessible by automobile and public transportation.

The College

The College of Staten Island is a college of the City University of New York that offers exceptional opportunities to all its students. Programs in the liberal arts and sciences and professional studies lead to bachelor's and associate degrees, in addition to the graduate programs previously listed.

Graduate Program Faculty Heads

A full listing of graduate program directors, contact information, and office hours is available at the College website. Please visit http://www.csi.cuny.edu/graduatestudies and click on "Graduate Programs and Requirements."

Applying

Requirements for admission and application deadlines vary by program and department. Students should contact the Graduate Admissions' Office for additional information or to arrange an admissions interview or campus tour.

Correspondence and Information

Sasha Spence, Associate Director for Graduate Admissions
Office of Recruitment and Admissions
North Administration Building (2A), Room 103
College of Staten Island
2800 Victory Boulevard
Staten Island, New York 10314
Phone: 718-982-2019
Fax: 718-982-2500

E-mail: masterit@csi.cuny.edu
Website: http://www.csi.cuny.edu/graduatestudies

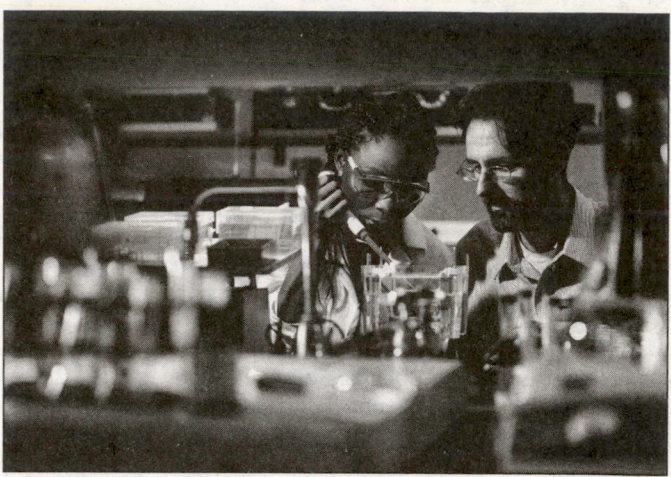

Graduate students at the College of Staten Island are provided with the tools and opportunities they need to make positive contributions to society. CSI students perform research with faculty from every academic discipline on campus, using the College's state-of-the-art equipment and facilities.

Instructors at the College of Staten Island are committed to each graduate student's success. Whether offering guidance on a rigorous course of study, engaging students in stimulating research, or sharing their professional experiences, CSI faculty members help students shape and achieve their goals.

ROBERT MORRIS UNIVERSITY
Graduate Programs

Programs of Study

Robert Morris University (RMU) offers more than thirty graduate degree programs and a Doctor of Philosophy (Ph.D.) in instructional management and leadership, and the Doctor of Nursing Practice (D.N.P.) offered as an adult nurse practitioner, family nurse practitioner, or psychiatric and mental health nurse practitioner. Master's programs available include the Master of Business Administration (M.B.A.) as well as Master of Science (M.S.) degrees in business education, cybersecurity & information assurance, data analytics, engineering management, instructional leadership, Internet information systems, healthcare administration, human resource management, nonprofit leadership, nursing education, nursing leadership, and organizational leadership. On-campus programs include a Master of Education (M.Ed.) degrees in literacy and special education and M.S. programs in cyber security and information assurance, information systems management, IT project management, cyber investigations, counseling psychology, data analytics, web & mobile information systems, healthcare analytics, and taxation. The university also offers a variety of online graduate certificates.

The University is accredited by the Middle States Association of Colleges and Schools. RMU schools and programs are also accredited by the Association to Advance Collegiate Schools of Business International, the Teacher Education Accreditation Council, ABET Inc., and the Commission on Collegiate Nursing Education.

Research Facilities

Facilities supporting the graduate programs at Robert Morris University include nine open-access computer laboratories, two physical libraries, and an electronic library offering an array of research databases. Classrooms have been equipped with advanced computer and presentation technology equipment to facilitate teaching and learning.

To support a large number of holdings, the library has a state-of-the-art searchable catalog system. The RMU Electronic Library offers continual off-campus access to more than 100 major research databases. The library is a member of numerous resource-sharing consortia that greatly extend the amount of materials available to support graduate education.

Financial Aid

Graduate loans are available for those who qualify. Students are encouraged to file the Free Application for Federal Student Aid (FAFSA). Robert Morris University participates in the Federal Family Education Loan (FFEL) Program and also offers various interest-free payment plans, as well as third-party billing and corporate reimbursement programs.

Cost of Study

Tuition varies by program. Visit http://sfs.rmu.edu/tuition-fee-schedules/2019-2020-tuition-fees for current tuition rates and fees.

Student Group

RMU enrolls approximately 1,000 students in its graduate degree programs, with an equal number of men and women. Students come from diverse professional and academic backgrounds.

Location

Robert Morris University is located on a 230-acre campus in suburban Moon Township, 17 miles west of downtown Pittsburgh and 15 minutes from Pittsburgh International Airport. Many graduate programs and classes are also offered online or at the RMU downtown campus at the Heinz 57 Center.

The University

Robert Morris University is located on a 230-acre campus in suburban Moon Township, 17 miles west of downtown Pittsburgh and 15 minutes from Pittsburgh International Airport. The city is an important corporate hub for financial and banking industries, health care, and industrial and high-tech engineering and manufacturing, providing a wide selection of employment opportunities as well as the cultural and commercial opportunities of a major city. Many graduate programs and classes are also offered online to help drive positive change locally, nationally, and globally.

Applying

The graduate programs admit students on a rolling admission basis. However, students are encouraged to submit all required materials at least two months prior to the start of their desired term of entry. Applications can be filed for free through the University's website.

Correspondence and Information

Office of Graduate Admissions
Robert Morris University
6001 University Boulevard
Moon Township, Pennsylvania 15108-1189
United States
Phone: 800-762-0097 (toll-free)
graduateadmissions@rmu.edu
Website: http://www.rmu.edu/graduate

FULL-TIME FACULTY (2019)
SCHOOL OF BUSINESS
Michelle Patrick, Dean; Ph.D., Kent State.
Patrick J. Litzinger, Interim Associate Dean; Ph.D., Pittsburgh.
Lois D. Bryan, Senior Associate Dean, Academic Excellence; D.Sc., Robert Morris.

Accounting and Taxation Faculty
Ira Abdullah, Ph.D., Virginia Commonwealth.
William G. Brucker, M.B.A., J.D., Duquesne.
Lois D. Bryan, D.Sc., Robert Morris.
Victoria A. Fratto, D.Ed., Robert Morris.
Fei Han, Ph.D., Connecticut.
David Hess, M.B.A., Ohio State.
Steven Hodaszy, J.D., L.L.M., NYU.
James E. Rebele, Ph.D., Indiana.
Ronald R. Rubenfield, M.B.A., Shippensburg.
Zhaoyun Shangguan, Ph.D., Connecticut.
Carol MacPhail, M.S., Robert Morris.
Gregory Krivacek, M.P.M., Carnegie Mellon.

Finance Faculty
Robert G. Beaves, Ph.D., Iowa.
Zane Dennick-Ream, M.B.A., Iowa.
Riza Emekter, Ph.D., Nebraska.
Frank Flanegin, Ph.D., Central Florida.
Denise C. Letterman, M.B.A., Shippensburg.
Jianyu Ma, Ph.D., Texas–Pan American.
Stanko Racic, Ph.D., Pittsburgh.

Management Faculty
Gregory Dell'Omo, President; Ph.D., Wisconsin–Madison.
Michele T. Cole, J.D., Ph.D., Pittsburgh.
Daria C. Crawley, Ph.D., Michigan.
Jeffery K. Guiler, Ph.D., Pittsburgh.
Nell T. Hartley, Ph.D., Vanderbilt.
Albena Ivanova, Ph.D., Minnesota.
Chia-Jung Lin, Ph.D., Southern Illinois Carbondale.
Marcel C. Minutolo, Ph.D., Pittsburgh.
Jodi A. Potter, Ph.D., Pittsburgh.
Yasmin S. Purohit, Ph.D., Drexel.
William F. Repack, M.S., Loyola.
Michael A. Yahr, M.B.A., Pittsburgh.
Qin Yang, Ph.D., Temple.
Derya A. Jacobs, Ph.D., Missouri–Rolla.
Mark Haney, Ph.D., Pittsburgh.
KiHyun Park, Ph.D., University of Toledo.

Marketing Faculty
Yun Chu, Ph.D., Texas–Pan American.
Steven R. Clinton, Ph.D., Michigan State.
Cathleen S. Jones, D.Sc., Robert Morris.
Ersem Karadag, Ph.D., Oklahoma State.
Jill K. Maher, Ph.D., Kent State.
Dean R. Manna, Ph.D., Pittsburgh.
Gayle J. Marco, Ph.D., Pittsburgh.
Richard Mills, Ph.D., Duquesne
Denis P. Rudd, Ed.D., Nevada, Las Vegas; CHA, FMP.
Norman V. Schnurr, M.B.A., Pittsburgh.
Alan D. Smith, Ph.D., Akron; CPGS.
Yanbin Tu, Ph.D., Connecticut.

Sport Management Faculty
Artemisia Apostolopoulou, Ph.D., Massachusetts.
Scott Branvold, Ed.D., Utah.
John S. Clark, Ph.D., Massachusetts Amherst.
David P. Synowka, Ph.D., Pittsburgh.

SCHOOL OF COMMUNICATIONS AND INFORMATION SYSTEMS
David Jamison, Acting Dean; J.D.
David F. Wood, Associate Dean; Ph.D., Pittsburgh.
Jon A. Radermacher, Associate Dean; M.F.A., Indiana.

Communication Faculty
Barbara J. Levine, Ph.D., Wisconsin–Madison.
Barbara Burgess-Lefebvre, M.F.A., Illinois State.
Michele Reese Edwards, Ph.D., Ohio State.
Kenneth V. Gargaro, Ph.D., Pittsburgh.
Jeeyun Oh, Ph.D., Penn State.
Ann D. Jabro, Ph.D., Penn State.
Heather Pinson, Ph.D., Ohio.
Sun-A Park, Ph.D., Missouri–Columbia.
Wenli Wang, Ph.D., Texas at Austin.
Anthony Moretti, Ph.D., Ohio.

Robert Morris University

Computer and Information Systems Faculty
Jeanne M. Baugh, Ed.D., West Virginia.
Donald J. Caputo, Ph.D., Pittsburgh.
Donna Cellante, Ed.D., Pittsburgh.
Gary A. Davis, D.Sc., Robert Morris.
Peter J. Draus, Ed.D., Pittsburgh.
Natalya Goreva, Ph.D., Utah State.
Linda Kavanaugh, Ph.D., Pittsburgh.
Fred G. Kohun, Ph.D., Carnegie Mellon.
Paul J. Kovacs, Ph.D., Pittsburgh.
Joseph Laverty, Ph.D., Pittsburgh.
G. James Leone, Ph.D., Pittsburgh.
Sushma Mishra, Ph.D., Virginia Commonwealth.
Karen Paullet, D.Sc., Robert Morris.
Walter Pilof, M.B.A., Xavier (Cincinnati).
Jamie Pinchot, D.Sc., Robert Morris.
Valerie J. Powell, Ph.D., Texas at Austin.
Robert J. Skovira, Ph.D., Pittsburgh.
John Turchek, M.Ed., Duquesne.
Charles R. Woratschek, Ph.D., Pittsburgh.
Peter Wu, Ph.D., Rensselaer.

English Faculty
Diane Todd Bucci, Ph.D., Indiana of Pennsylvania.
Roger Gillan, M.A., Bucknell.
Edward Karshner, Ph.D., Bowling Green State.
John Lawson, Ph.D., Northern Illinois.
John D. O'Banion, Ph.D., Northern Illinois.
Sylvia A. Pamboukian, Ph.D., Indiana Bloomington.
Constance M. Ruzich, Ph.D., Pennsylvania.
H. James Vincent, M.A., Indiana.

Media Arts Faculty
Andrew Ames, M.F.A., Rhode Island School of Design.
Ferris Crane, M.F.A., Academy of Arts.
Timothy J. Hadfield, M.F.A., Chelsea College of Art and Design (London).
Christine Holtz, M.F.A., RIT.
Carolina Loyola-Garcia, M.F.A., Carnegie Mellon.
Helena Vanhala, Ph.D., Oregon.
Hyla J. Willis, M.F.A., Carnegie Mellon.
Michael DiLauro, M.F.A., Ohio.

Organizational Studies Faculty
Stuart Allen, Ph.D., Regent.
Arthur J. Grant, Ph.D., Wheaton (Illinois).
Beatrice Kunka, Ed.D., University of the Pacific.
Anthony Petroy, D.M., Phoenix.
Michael Quigley, Ph.D., Pittsburgh.
Elizabeth M. Stork, Ph.D., Pittsburgh.

SCHOOL OF EDUCATION AND SOCIAL SCIENCES
Philip J. Harold, Acting Dean, Ph.D., Catholic University.

Education Faculty
Carianne Bernadowski, Ph.D., Pittsburgh.
James Bernauer, Ed.D., Pittsburgh.
Robert DelGreco, Ed.D., Pittsburgh.
Vicki Donne, Ed.D., Pittsburgh.
Richard G. Fuller, D.Ed., Penn State.
Bruce Golmic, Ed.D., Indiana of Pennsylvania.
Mary A. Hansen, Ph.D., Pittsburgh.
Carla Haser, Ph.D., Catholic University.
Michele N. Hipsky, Ed.D., Duquesne.
E. Gregory Holdan, Ph.D., Penn State.
Susan Parker, Ph.D., Pittsburgh.
Ronald Perry, Ph.D., Pittsburgh.
George W. Semich, Ed.D., Pittsburgh.
Daniel J. Shelley, Ph.D., Pittsburgh.
Darcy Tannehill, Ed.D., Pittsburgh.
Nathan Taylor, Ph.D., Ohio State.
Lawrence A. Tomei, Ed.D., USC.
Fan-Yu Lin, Ph.D., Penn State.
Ying Zhang, Ph.D., Purdue.
John A. Zeanchock, Ed.D., Indiana of Pennsylvania.

Social Sciences Faculty
Daniel P. Barr, Ph.D., Kent State.
William R. Beaver, Ph.D., Carnegie Mellon.
Kathryn Dennick-Brecht, Ed.D., Duquesne.
Soren Fanning, Ph.D., Bowling Green State.
Philip J. Harold, Ph.D., Catholic University.
William E. Kelly, Ph.D., Louisiana Tech.
John M. McCarthy, Ph.D., Marquette.
Samantha Monda, Ph.D., West Virginia.
Stephen T. Paul, Ph.D., Kansas.
Melinda Rauscher, Ph.D., Emory.
David Wheeler, Ph.D., Washington (Seattle).

SCHOOL OF ENGINEERING, MATHEMATICS, AND SCIENCE
Maria V. Kalevitch, Dean; Ph.D., Academy of Sciences (Lithuania).
Jeffrey J. Mitchell, Associate Dean; Ph.D., Cornell.

Engineering Faculty
Sushil Acharya, D.Eng., Asian Institute of Technology (Thailand).
Won Joo, Ph.D., Case Western Reserve.
Tony Kerzmann, Ph.D., Pittsburgh.
Priyadarshan A. Manohar, Ph.D., Wollongong (Australia).
Louis Moterrubio, Ph.D., Waikato.
Arif Sirinterlikci, Ph.D., Ohio State.
Benjamin Campbell, Ph.D., Robert Morris.
Tamiko Youngblood, Ph.D., Missouri University of Science and Technology.

Mathematics Faculty
Len Asimow, Ph.D., Washington (Seattle).
Liang Hong, Ph.D., Purdue.
David G. Hudak, Ph.D., Carnegie Mellon.
Allen R. Lias, Ph.D., Pittsburgh.
Andris Niedra, Ph.D., Pittsburgh.
Monica M. VanDieren, Ph.D., Carnegie Mellon.
Charles W. Zimmerman, Ph.D., Ohio State.
Chistophe Groendyke, Ph.D., Penn State.

Science Faculty
Paul D. Badger, Ph.D., Pittsburgh.
Gavin Buxton, Ph.D., Sheffield Hallam (UK).
William J. Dress, Ph.D., Ohio State.
Catherine Hanna, Ph.D., Louisville.
Kenneth A. Lasota, Ph.D., Pittsburgh.
Matthew Maurer, Ph.D., Ohio State.
Daniel Short, Ph.D., Liverpool (England).
Melissa Hillwig, Ph.D., Iowa State.

SCHOOL OF NURSING AND HEALTH SCIENCES
Nadine C. Englert, Acting Dean; Ph.D., Pittsburgh.

Nuclear Medicine Faculty
Angela M. Bires, Ed.D., Duquesne.
Donna L. Mason, M.S., Carlow.
William Wentling, M.S., Buffalo State, SUNY.

Nursing Faculty
Joseph Angelelli, Ph.D., USC.
Marcel C. Minutolo, Ph.D., Pittsburgh.
Lynda J. Davidson, Ph.D., Pittsburgh.
Stephen Foreman, Ph.D., Berkeley.
Susan Hellier, Ph.D., Waynesburg.
Valerie M. Howard, Ed.D., Pittsburgh.
Pamela Jackson, M.S., Robert Morris.
Judith A. Kaufmann, Dr.PH., Pittsburgh.
Kirstyn K. Kameg, D.N.P., Case Western Reserve.
Lisa W. Locasto, D.N.P., Robert Morris.
Donna McDermott, M.S.N., Robert Morris.
Joyce Ott, D.N.P., Robert Morris.
Catherine Pyo, Ph.D., Robert Morris.
Denise Ramponi, D.N.P., Waynesburg.
Katherine Perozzi, M.S.N., Pittsburgh.
Carl A. Ross, Ph.D., Duquesne; RN.
Janice Sarasnick, M.S.N., Robert Morris
Janice Shade, M.S.N., Pittsburgh.
Janene Szpak, D.N.P., Robert Morris.
Susan Van Cleve, D.N.P., Robert Morris.

RMU's suburban Pittsburgh campus spreads across 230 scenic acres that were once the grounds of a country estate.

SALISBURY UNIVERSITY
Graduate Studies and Research

Programs of Study

Graduate study at Salisbury University (SU) provides baccalaureate degree holders from the United States and abroad with opportunities for professional advancement and personal enrichment. The graduate curriculum is designed to assist students in attaining greater mastery of their fields of specialization, improving skills in pursuing independent study, and increasing professional knowledge and ability through the study of new findings in areas of special interest.

Master's degree programs available at SU include the following: applied biology (M.S.), applied health physiology (M.S.), athletic training (M.S.), business administration (M.B.A.), conflict analysis and dispute resolution (M.A.), education (M.Ed.: curriculum and instruction; educational leadership; post-secondary education track; reading specialist), English (M.A.), geographic information systems management (M.S.), history (M.A.), mathematics education (M.S.M.E.), nursing (M.S.: clinical nurse educator; health care leadership), social work (M.S.W.), and teaching (M.A.T.).

Doctoral programs are available in education (Ed.D.: contemporary curriculum theory and instruction in literacy) and nursing (D.N.P.: post-B.S.; post-masters).

A graduate certificate program is offered in Teaching English to Speakers of Other Languages (TESOL); also available are a post-master's Literacy Educator certificate, a post-master's Educational Leadership certificate and a post-master's Certificate of Advanced Study in Educational Leadership and a post-baccalaureate certificate in Higher Education..

Research Facilities

Salisbury University is home to Henson Science Hall a $42-million science education and research building, and the new $117 million Patricia R. Guerrieri Academic Commons, the largest academic building in University history. An epicenter for learning, research and creativity, it houses SU Libraries, the Nabb Research Center for Delmarva History and Culture, a Graduate Student Commons and numerous academic centers and services.

Financial Aid

A limited amount of financial aid in the form of graduate assistantships from the University and scholarships from the Maryland State Scholarship Administration (Maryland residents only) are available each year to selected graduate students. Students applying for aid must complete the Free Application for Federal Student Aid (FAFSA) and indicate Salisbury University (title IV code of 002091). Students may also apply online at www.fafsa.ed.gov. For more information about financial assistance, prospective students should contact the Financial Aid Office at 410-543-6165 or finaid@salisbury.edu, or visit www.salisbury.edu/admissions/finaid/graduate.html.

Graduate assistants are eligible to receive a stipend and tuition waiver of up to 18 credits per fiscal year. To be eligible for the tuition waiver, students must enroll for a minimum of 6 credits in both the fall and spring terms. Tuition is waived only for graduate courses applicable toward master's degree requirements. The tuition waiver does not include waiver of fees. A full-time assistantship requires a time commitment of approximately 20 hours per week, and a half-time assistantship requires 10 hours per week. For specific details, prospective students should visit www.salisbury.edu/gsr/gradstudies/grad_assistantships.html or consult the Graduate Assistantship section of the Graduate Student Handbook.

Enrolled graduate students are eligible for competitive research and funding opportunities within their academic schools and for Research and Presentation Grants providing up to $500 to support scholarly projects and presentations.

Cost of Study

All graduate tuition rates are charged on a per credit-hour basis; there is no full-time tuition rate. Prospective students should visit www.salisbury.edu/cashiers for information and an updated listing of tuition, fees, special course fees, and other related expenses. Tuition and fees for each semester may be changed and new ones established at any time by action of the Board of Regents of the University System of Maryland.

Living and Housing Costs

Salisbury University offers limited on-campus housing for graduate students at the Honors College Global Village. Interested students can visit https://salisbury.abroadoffice.net/internal-program-description-Honors-College-Global-Village-188092-245.html for additional information. There are also numerous off-campus housing options nearby. Prospective students should visit SU's Commuter and Connections' website at www.salisbury.edu/commuters.

Student Group

The Graduate Student Council (GSC) at SU provides opportunities for intellectual, professional, personal, and social development through grants, advocacy, public presentation of research, graduate community events, and campus service. The GSC is part of the campus' Governance Consortium.

Student Outcomes

SU offers a network of over 55,000 alumni nationwide.

Location

With a regional population of roughly 99,000, Salisbury is the cultural and economic hub of Delmarva (containing portions of Delaware, Maryland, and Virginia), a historically and ecologically rich peninsula located between the Atlantic Ocean and Chesapeake Bay. The city is 30 minutes west of the beaches of Assateague and Ocean City, Maryland; about 2 hours from Baltimore, Maryland; Wilmington, Delaware; Norfolk, Virginia; and Washington, D.C.; and 4½ hours from New York City.

The University

A member of the University System of Maryland, SU is a regionally accredited four-year comprehensive institution offering 60 distinct graduate and undergraduate programs.

Applying

To be considered for admission, the Salisbury University application, all transcripts and supporting documents, and $65 non-refundable application fee must be submitted. For questions regarding the application process, prospective students should call the Office of Graduate Studies and Research at 410-548-3546. For more information about specific program admission requirements, including priority application deadlines, applicants should contact the appropriate graduate program director. Additional information can be found online at www.salisbury.edu/gsr/gradstudies/admissions.html.

Correspondence and Information

Graduate Studies and Research
Holloway Hall 266-267
Salisbury University
1101 Camden Avenue
Salisbury, Maryland 21801
Phone: 410-548-3546
Fax: 410-677-0052

E-mail: graduateadmissions@salisbury.edu Website: https://www.salisbury.edu/administration/academic-affairs/graduate-studies-and-research/graduate-studies/index.aspx

GRADUATE PROGRAMS AND THEIR DIRECTORS

Applied Biology (M.S.)
Dana Price, Ph.D., Graduate Program Director
410-543-6498, dlprice@salisbury.edu
https://www.salisbury.edu/explore-academics/programs/graduate-degree-programs/applied-biology-masters/index.aspx.

Applied Health Physiology (M.S.)
Thomas Pellinger, Ph.D., Graduate Program Director
410-677-0144, tkpellinger@salisbury.edu
https://www.salisbury.edu/explore-academics/programs/graduate-degree-programs/applied-health-physiology-master/index.aspx.

Athletic Training (M.S.A.T.)
Laura Marinaro, Ph.D., Graduate Program Director
410-548-3529, lmmarinaro@salisbury.edu
https://www.salisbury.edu/explore-academics/programs/graduate-degree-programs/athletic-training-master/index.aspx.

Business Administration (M.B.A.)
Yvonne Downie, Ph.D., Graduate Program Director
410-548-3983, yxdownie@salisbury.edu
https://www.salisbury.edu/explore-academics/programs/graduate-degree-programs/business-admin-master/index.aspx.

Conflict Analysis and Dispute Resolution (M.A.)
Ignaciyas Soosaipillai, Ph.D., Graduate Program Director
410-543-6435, iksoosaipillai@salisbury.edu
https://www.salisbury.edu/explore-academics/programs/graduate-degree-programs/cadr-masters/index.aspx.

Education (Ed.D., M.Ed)
Ed.D.: Judith Franzak, Ph.D., Graduate Program Director: 410-677-0238, jkfranzak@salisbury.edu. https://www.salisbury.edu/explore-academics/programs/graduate-degree-programs/contemporary-curriculum-doctor/index.aspx

M.Ed. Curriculum and Instruction: Doug DeWitt, Ph.D., Graduate Program Director: 410-543-6286, dmdewitt@salisbury.edu. https://www.salisbury.edu/explore-academics/programs/graduate-degree-programs/med-programs/curriculum-instruction-masters/index.aspx

M.Ed. Education Leadership: Doug Dewitt, Ph.D.,Dr. Ted Gilkey, Graduate Program Director:
410-543-6286, dmdewitt@salisbury.edu. https://www.salisbury.edu/explore-academics/programs/graduate-degree-programs/med-programs/educational-leadership-masters/index.aspx

M.Ed. Reading Specialist: Joyce Wiencek, Ph.D., Graduate Program Director:
410-543-6288, bjwiencek@salisbury.edu. https://www.salisbury.edu/explore-academics/programs/graduate-degree-programs/med-programs/reading-specialist-masters/index.aspx

English (M.A.)
John Nieves, Ph.D., Graduate Program Director
410-677-6511, janieves@salisbury.edu
https://www.salisbury.edu/explore-academics/programs/graduate-degree-programs/english-masters/index.aspx.

Geographic Information Systems Management (M.S.)
Stuart Hamilton, PhD., Graduate Program Director
410-548-3518, sehamilton@salisbury.edu
https://www.salisbury.edu/explore-academics/programs/graduate-degree-programs/geo-info-sys-masters/index.aspx.

History (M.A.)
Celine Carayon, Ph.D., Graduate Program Director:
410-677-4601, cxcarayon@salisbury.edu
https://www.salisbury.edu/explore-academics/programs/graduate-degree-programs/history-masters/index.aspx.

Mathematics Education (M.S.M.E.)
Jennifer Bergner, Ph.D., Graduate Program Director
410-677-5429, jabergner@salisbury.edu
https://www.salisbury.edu/explore-academics/programs/graduate-degree-programs/mathematics-education-masters/index.aspx.

Nursing
D.N.P.: Dorothea Winter, Ph.D., Graduate Program Director
410-548-5562, dmwinter@salisbury.edu
https://www.salisbury.edu/explore-academics/programs/graduate-degree-programs/nursing-practice-doctor/index.aspx.
M.S.: Dorothea Winter, Ph.D., Graduate Program Director
410-548-5562, dmwinter@salisbury.edu
https://www.salisbury.edu/explore-academics/programs/graduate-degree-programs/nursing-master/index.aspx.

Social Work (M.S.W.)
Mary Hylton, Ph.D., Graduate Program Director:
410-677-5346, mehylton@salisbury.edu
http://www.salisbury.edu/gsr/gradstudies/MSWpage.html.

Teaching (M.A.T.)
Gwen Beegle, Ph.D., Graduate Program Director:
410-543-6393, gpbeegle@salisbury.edu
https://www.salisbury.edu/explore-academics/programs/graduate-degree-programs/teaching-masters/index.aspx.

Teaching English to Speakers of Other Languages (TESOL)
http://www.salisbury.edu/english/grad/tesolD.html#tesol.

Holloway Hall, which opened in 1925, is the oldest building on campus.

SU's Patricia R. Guerrieri Academic Commons, opened fall 2016, houses SU Libraries, the Nabb Research Center and a Graduate Student Commons.

THE UNIVERSITY OF TAMPA

Graduate Programs

Programs of Study

The University of Tampa (UT) is a private nonprofit institution located on the west coast of Florida that offers graduate programs in business, criminology, education, nursing, physician assistant medicine, creative writing, and exercise and nutrition science. U.S. News & World Report ranks UT among the Best Business Schools (with a Best Full-Time M.B.A. program) and Best Nursing Schools, as well as among the Top 25 Regional Universities in the South. UT has also been included in the Forbes annual ranking of America's Best Colleges every year since 2010. Likewise, The Princeton Review includes UT in its lists of Best Southeastern Colleges and Best 384 Colleges.

Graduate Business Programs for Full-Time and Working Students: The University of Tampa offers nine graduate degree programs in business including an M.B.A., Professional M.B.A., and Executive M.B.A. and six specialized master's programs. The Master of Business Administration gives students eight concentration options:

- Business analytics
- Cybersecurity
- Entrepreneurship
- Finance
- Information systems management
- International business
- Marketing
- Nonprofit management

M.B.A. students may choose to enroll in the full-time/day program or part-time/evening program. Full-time business students typically complete the program in as few as twelve months. This schedule also applies to UT's M.S. in Accounting, M.S. in Business Analytics, M.S. in Cybersecurity, M.S. in Entrepreneurship, M.S. in Finance, and M.S. in Marketing programs.

Working professionals who want to earn their M.B.A. may choose to apply for UT's part-time Professional M.B.A. (P.M.B.A.) or the unique Executive M.B.A. (E.M.B.A.), which is designed for professionals with seven or more years of work experience. E.M.B.A. classes are held on alternate Saturdays and focus on the most current problem-solving and decision-making practices. The program takes two years to complete and includes a ten-day study abroad trip during the second year.

The Sykes College of Business is AACSB (Association to Advance Collegiate Schools of Business) accredited.

Graduate Programs in Education and Instructional Design: UT's Master of Education (M.Ed.) in Curriculum and Instruction program enjoys a solid, long-established relationship with Tampa Bay area school districts and administrators. The program helps develop and extend the teaching and leadership skills of certified teachers. The M.Ed. in Educational Leadership prepares educators for administrative roles and covers topics such as instructional leadership, school budgeting and finance, and community relations. Education classes are offered in the evenings, on weekends, and during summers, allowing students to complete either M.Ed. program in as little as a year.

The M.S. in Instructional Design and Technology program addresses a growing field in learning and human performance, providing an interdisciplinary approach to its study. It emphasizes theories of learning and cognition, multimedia development, systematic instructional design, technology, and open learning environments. The hybrid classroom-online curriculum allows students to complete the program within two years.

Master of Science in Criminology and Criminal Justice: UT's M.S. in Criminology and Criminal Justice prepares students for both practitioner and management careers in criminal justice and public safety. It is ideal for those embarking on a new career or seeking advancement in law enforcement, corrections, victim advocacy, or criminal justice management. It also provides preparation for doctoral studies. Students may choose between thesis and non-thesis tracks, with degree completion in two years.

Master of Science in Exercise and Nutrition Science: This internationally recognized program focuses on the relationship between exercise physiology and nutrition, with the goal of optimizing athletic performance. During a one-year course of study, students undertake numerous hands-on experiences in UT's Human Performance Research Lab, combined with rigorous classroom learning. Students may begin the program in the summer, fall, or spring semester.

Master of Physician Assistant Medicine: UT's 27-month Master of Physician Assistant Medicine (M.P.A.M.) program prepares graduates to provide medical care as part of an intercollaborative, physician-led team. The curriculum consists of four semesters of classroom training in UT's state-of-the-art facilities, followed by three semesters of clinical rotations, all of which are located within 80 miles of campus.

Graduate Programs in Nursing: The M.S.N. program at UT offers graduate-level study with adult/gerontology and family nurse practitioner concentrations, all in a part-time format. Students benefit from UT's numerous clinical affiliations and are well equipped to serve as primary care providers in a variety of settings. Admission to the program is competitive. UT also offers an online Doctor of Nursing Practice (D.N.P.) designed for working nurse practitioners who wish to advance their skills in administration, research and clinical leadership.

Master of Fine Arts in Creative Writing: UT's Master of Fine Arts in Creative Writing is a low-residency program intended to develop the skills of poets, fiction, and creative nonfiction writers through supportive critique and mentoring. Students attend four ten-day working residencies on campus, followed by semester-long faculty mentorships designed to support an individualized plan of study. The program takes approximately two years to complete.

Research Opportunities for Graduate Students

UT faculty members conduct and coordinate research in numerous fields across the disciplines. The Naimoli Institute for Business Strategy connects groups of students with more than 600 Tampa Bay area enterprises to conduct strategic evaluations and make performance improvement recommendations. Research done by students in UT's renowned Human Performance Research Lab has been presented at the National Strength and Conditioning Conference. Graduate students also have opportunities to conduct research independently or with faculty in the criminology, cybersecurity, instructional design, and nursing programs.

Financial Aid and Scholarship Opportunities

The University of Tampa prides itself on its competitive graduate tuition rates. UT offers a limited number of merit-based scholarships for graduate students. Each program also offers graduate assistantship positions, which provide a tuition waiver for up to 12 credit hours per semester, plus a stipend. Reimbursement and stipend amounts vary by program. Graduate assistants are expected to work 20 hours per week for an academic or administrative office and to carry a full course load. Part-time employment is also available on campus.

Cost of Study

For the 2018–19 academic year, tuition for most graduate programs is $637 per credit hour. The cost for the Executive M.B.A. program is $48,715 for the entire two-year program. The M.F.A. in Creative Writing program is $8,570 per semester.

Living and Housing Costs

Most UT graduate students choose to live off campus. However, on-campus housing is also available, primarily in Urso or Straz halls. Costs for on-campus housing range from $3,966 to $5,130 per semester, depending on the room chosen. Students living on campus are also required to purchase a meal plan, with costs ranging from $1,460 to $2,629 per semester.

Student Life

UT's graduate student body reflects the global nature of the city and the school. For example, about 40 percent of the University's graduate business students come from outside the United States. UT enrolls students from 135 countries and all 50 states, providing opportunities for diverse cultural and educational exchange.

Location

The University's 110-acre campus is located in downtown Tampa, just north of Hillsborough Bay and a short drive from Gulf Coast beaches. The city is a cultural crossroads where national and global corporations offer opportunities for internships, networking, and job recruitment.

The University

Known for academic excellence, personal attention, and real-world experience in its undergraduate and graduate programs, UT offers more than 200 programs of study, including 17 graduate degree programs and numerous study-abroad opportunities. Boasting a $330 million annual budget and a $1.1 billion estimated annual economic impact, UT serves approximately 9,600 undergraduate and graduate students.

Applying

The University of Tampa has rolling admissions. Applicants are advised to submit applications and supporting documents by June 1 for the fall semester, which begins in August. The deadline for the spring semester is November 1.

In general, applicants should submit a complete online application, the application fee, completed bachelor's degree official transcripts, two recommendation letters, and a personal statement and resume. For most graduate business programs, a GMAT or GRE score is required; TOEFL or IELTS scores are required for international applicants.

Correspondence Information

Arthur Goon
Director of Graduate and Continuing Studies
The University of Tampa
401 West Kennedy Boulevard
Tampa, Florida 33606-1490
United States
Phone: 813-257-3016
E-mail: agoon@ut.edu
Website: www.ut.edu/graduate

Programs of Study

The Graduate School offers more than thirty programs leading to the doctorate (Ph.D.) and to the Master of Arts (A.M.). In addition, programs are offered leading to the Master of Arts in Education (M.A.Ed.), Master of Arts in Teaching (M.A.T.), and Master of Fine Arts (M.F.A.).

Opportunities for combining a degree available through the Graduate School with a degree from one of the University's professional schools (business, law, medicine) are also available.

Research Facilities

The Washington University community is served by a network of libraries designed to meet the instructional and research needs of faculty members, students, and staff members. Washington University libraries contain the largest collection of any private academic library system between the Mississippi River and California. John M. Olin Library, the central University library, and twelve school and departmental libraries house many important and unique collections and provide state-of-the-art computerized information retrieval. The combined holdings include more than 3 million books and bound periodicals, 18,000 current serial subscriptions, and access to thousands of electronic journals and databases. For more information, students can visit http://library.wustl.edu.

More than thirty centers and institutes provide a spectrum of research opportunities. They include the Center for Air Pollution Impact and Trend Analysis; Center for the Study of American Business; Center for American Indian Studies; Business, Law, and Economics Center; Arts and Sciences Computing Center; Institutes for Biomedical Computing; McDonnell Center for Cellular and Molecular Neurobiology; Construction Management Center; Carolyne Roehm Electronic Media Center; Center for Engineering Computing; Center for Genetics in Medicine; McDonnell Center for Studies of Higher Brain Function; Center for the History of Freedom; Office of International Studies; International Writers Center; Center for the Study of Islamic Societies and Civilizations; Management Center; Fred Gasche Laboratory for Microstructured Materials Technologies; Markey Center for Research in Molecular Biology of Human Disease; Center for Optimization and Semantic Control; Center for Plant Science and Biotechnology; Center for the Study of Public Affairs; Center for Robotics and Automation; Social Work Research Development Center; McDonnell Center for Space Sciences; Center for the Application of Information Technology; and Urban Research and Design Center.

Financial Aid

The majority of full-time students receive financial support. Financial assistance in the form of scholarships, fellowships, and traineeships is offered annually on a competitive basis through the Graduate School from government, private, or endowed sources. Also available are scholarships and, in applied social sciences, clinical internships; grants and fellowships in national competition; and loans. Specific information may be obtained from the departmental or administrative unit to which the student intends to apply.

Cost of Study

Tuition for the 2018–19 academic year for the Graduate School is $52,400. The cost per credit unit is $2,183.

Living and Housing Costs

Many graduate students live in University-owned apartments, some with data connections and shuttle bus service. Listing information for these units as well as non-University housing is available through the University's Apartment Referral Service (http://offcampushousing.wustl.edu/). Average rent ranges from $700 to $2,000 per month.

Student Group

Of the more than 15,000 people attending Washington University, more than 7,000 are graduate students; approximately 1,400 of them are enrolled in the Graduate School. Students come to Washington University from all fifty states and more than eighty international locations.

Location

Washington University has two campuses that lie at opposite ends of Forest Park (one of the largest municipal parks in the nation). The campuses are approximately 5 miles west of downtown St. Louis. The Danforth campus is the location of the Graduate School and all other schools of the University except Medicine. The latter is located on the east, or medical campus. The Division of Biology and Biomedical Sciences is also located on the medical campus. Free shuttle buses run between the campuses on a regular schedule.

The St. Louis area has nearly 2.4 million residents. The cost of living is affordable. The University's central location provides easy access to the zoo, museums, Science Center, Missouri Botanical Gardens, St. Louis Symphony, Opera Theatre, St. Louis Repertory Theatre, Black Repertory Theatre, Blues hockey, and Cardinals baseball. Outdoor adventure beyond the city can be found in the Ozark Mountains and on the rivers of Missouri. Camping, hiking, floating, rock climbing, and spelunking are among the many possibilities within a few hours' drive of St. Louis.

The Graduate School

The Graduate School is a charter member of both the Association of Graduate Schools and the Council of Graduate Schools. The School provides a physical and academic environment in which inquiry, intellectual growth, and discovery can thrive and flourish.

Applying

Prospective students may apply online. Applicants should check with the department or program to which they are applying, as application deadlines vary. Most programs require GRE scores. For international students whose native language is not English, most programs require an official copy of a TOEFL score.

Correspondence and Information

Graduate School
Campus Box 1187
Washington University in St. Louis
One Brookings Drive
St. Louis, Missouri 63130-4899
United States
Phone: 314-935-6880
Fax: 314-935-4887
E-mail: GraduateSchool@wustl.edu
Website: http://graduateschool.wustl.edu

FACULTY HEADS, DEGREES OFFERED, AND DEPARTMENTAL INTERESTS

Anthropology (Ph.D.): T. R. Kidder (trkidder@wustl.edu). Sociocultural anthropology (including medical anthropology), archaeology, physical anthropology (including primate studies, paleontology and human biology).

Art History and Archaeology (A.M., Ph.D.): Liz Childs (ecchilds@wustl.edu). Ancient, medieval, Renaissance, early modern, European, modern and contemporary European and American, Asian art history; classical archaeology.

Division of Biology and Biomedical Sciences (Ph.D.): John Russell (800-852-9074, toll-free); e-mail: DBBSPhDAdmissions@wustl.edu).

Biochemistry: Peter Burgers (DBBSPhDAdmissions@wustl.edu). Metabolic regulation, signal transduction, receptors, membrane channels and transporters, membrane structure and dynamics, membrane trafficking, cholesterol and lipid metabolism, nucleic acid-protein structure interactions and function, DNA replication and repair, recombination, transcription, translation, enzyme kinetics, cancer biology, cell cycle regulation, apoptosis, cell motility, cytoskeleton, cell division, extracellular matrix, vascular biology, aging, senescence, telomere biology, heat-shock proteins, prion proteins, gene expression, RNA editing and binding proteins, microbial pathogenesis, parasitology, virology, drug design and metabolism, plant natural products, photosynthesis and plant energy production, molecular imaging in cells and tissues, carbohydrate metabolism, proteases.

Computational and Molecular Biophysics: Daved Fremont (DBBSPhDAdmissions@wustl.edu). Structural biology, protein and nucleic acid kinetics and thermodynamics, single-molecule enzymology, protein design, nanoscience, ion channels and lipid membranes, computational biophysics.

Computational and Systems Biology: Barak Cohen (DBBSPhDAdmissions@wustl.edu). Systems biology, genomics, sequence analysis, regulatory networks, synthetic biology, metagenomics, metabolomics, proteomics, single cell dynamics, high-throughput technology development, applied math and mathematical models of biological processes, computational biology, comparative genomics, personalized medicine, next generation sequencing and its applications, bioinformatics.

Developmental, Regenerative, and Stem Cell Biology: Kerry Kornfeld and James Skeath (DBBSPhDAdmissions@wustl.edu). Development, stem cell biology, regenerative biology, cell biology, genetics, cell signaling, the biology of cancer, epigenetics, circadian rhythms, systems biology.

Evolution, Ecology, and Population Biology: David Queller (DBBSPhDAdmissions@wustl.edu). Population ecology, community ecology, plant and animal evolution, microbial evolution, evolution of behavior, phylogenetics, systematics, theoretical and experimental population genetics.

Human and Statistical Genetics: Patrick Jay and John Rice (DBBSPhDAdmissions@wustl.edu). Human genetics, statistical genetics, functional genomics, molecular genetics, Mendelian disease, complex disease, Mammalian genetics, systems biology.

Immunology: Eugene Otiz (DBBSPhDAdmissions@wustl.edu). Cellular immunology; molecular immunology; lineage development; autoimmunity; cancer immunotherapy; transcription factors; epigenomics; mucosal immunity; innate immunity; bacterial, viral, and parasite immunity; immune evasion; antigen processing and presentation; dendritic cells; T cell signaling; antigen receptor diversification.

Molecular Cell Biology: Heather True-Krob and Jason Weber (DBBSPhDAdmissions@wustl.edu). Cell adhesion, protein trafficking and organelle biogenesis, cell cycle, receptors, signal transduction, gene expression, metabolism, cytoskeleton and motility, membrane excitability, molecular basis of diseases.

Molecular Genetics and Genomics: Tim Schedl and James Skeath (DBBSPhDAdmissions@wustl.edu). Genetics, genetic basis of disease, genomics, epigenetics, genetic engineering, genome editing, model organism genetics, development, cell biology, molecular biology, complex traits, bioinformatics, systems biology.

Molecular Microbiology and Microbial Pathogenesis: David Sibley (DBBSPhDAdmissions@wustl.edu). Host-pathogen interactions, cellular microbiology, comparative genomics, molecular microbiology, microbial pathogenesis, pathogen discovery, emerging infectious diseases, microbial physiology, microbial ecology and engergetics, virology, bacteriology, mycology, parasitology.

Neurosciences: Lawrence Snyder and Erik Herzog (DBBSPhDAdmissions@wustl.edu). Neurobiology, neurology, functional imaging, behavior, cognition, computational neuroscience, electrophysiology, sensory systems, motor systems, neuroglia, neuronal development, learning, memory, language, synaptic plasticity, mind, consciousness, neurodegeneration, diseases of the nervous system, neuronal injury, clinical neuroscience, motor control, biological rhythms, connectivity mapping.

Plant and Microbial Bioscience: Joseph Jez and Petra Levin (DBBSPhDAdmissions@wustl.edu). Cell biology, development, physiology, signaling, development, metabolic regulation, photosynthesis, bioenergy, protein structure-function, synthetic biology, biogeochemistry, environmental microbiology, ecology, population genetics, molecular evolution.

Business (Ph.D.): Anjan Thakor (phdinfo@olin.wustl.edu). Accounting, business economics, finance, marketing, organizational behavior, strategy, operations and manufacturing management.

Chemistry (Ph.D.): Bill Buhro (chemistry-admissions@wustl.edu). Bioinorganic, biological, bioorganic, biophysical, materials, nuclear, organic, organometallic, physical, polymer, radiochemistry, spectroscopy, theoretical.

Classics (A.M., Ph.D.): Timothy Moore (classics@wustl.edu). Greek and Latin language and literature, ancient performance, philosophy, history, and material culture.

Comparative Literature (Ph.D.): Lynne Tatlock (ltatlock@wustl.edu). World literature; literary theory; translation studies; global and multicultural theory; comparative drama; comparative arts; studies in literature, politics, and society; narrative theory; media ecologies, histories, and poetics.

Earth and Planetary Sciences (Ph.D.): Viatcheslav Solomatov (mwysession@wustl.edu). Planetary sciences, geology, geobiology, geochemistry, geodynamics.

East Asian Languages and Cultures (A.M., J.D./A.M., Ph.D.): Rebecca Copeland (ealc@wustl.edu). Chinese; Japanese; Chinese fiction, theater, poetry, modern literature; Japanese modern and classical fiction; translation theory; East Asian studies.

Economics (Ph.D.): John Nachbar (nachbar@wustl.edu). Economic theory, industrial organization, political economy, public economics, macroeconomics, public finance, development economics.

Education (M.A.Ed., M.A.T., Ph.D.): Kit Wellmon (kwellman@wustl.edu). Teacher education, educational studies, urban education, policy studies, science and math education, second language research.

English and American Literature (Ph.D.): Wolfram Schmidgen (wschmidg@wustl.edu). Medieval, early modern, early American, eighteenth-century British, nineteenth-century British, nineteenth-century American, twentieth-century British, twentieth-century American, African-American literature and culture, Irish literature, Anglophone postcolonial literature, gender and sexuality studies, modernism, poetry and poetics, theory.

Film and Media Studies (A.M.): Gaylyn Studlar (gstudlar@wustl.edu). Criticism, history, and theories of film and electronic media; all moving image forms of visual culture.

Germanic Languages and Literatures (A.M., Ph.D.): Matt Erlin (merlin@wustl.edu). German literature and culture from the Middle Ages through the twenty-first century, intellectual history, film and media studies, gender studies, Holocaust studies, history of the book, digital humanities.

History (Ph.D.): Peter Kastor (pjkastor@wustl.edu). Seventeenth- through nineteenth-century America, twentieth-century America, African history, central Europe, early modern Europe, East Asian history, history of American political culture, international urban history, Middle East, religion in the medieval Mediterranean world.

Institute of Materials Science and Engineering (Ph.D.): Kathy Flores (floresk@wustl.edu). Materials structure, properties, processing, and performance, particularly as related to materials for energy harvesting and storage; materials for environmental remediation and sustainability; materials for regenerative medicine; metallic glasses and other structurally complex materials; plasmonics, photonics, and materials for sensors and imaging; and computational materials science.

Jewish, Islamic, and Near Eastern Languages and Cultures (A.M.): Nancy Berg (nberg@wustl.edu). Islamic and Near Eastern studies (Islamic history, Arabic language and literature, modern Middle East history), Jewish studies (Hebrew Bible, Rabbinic literature, Jewish history, modern Hebrew literature).

Mathematics (A.M., Ph.D.): John McCarthy (mccarthy@wustl.edu). Algebra, algebraic geometry, real and complex analysis, differential geometry, topology, mathematical statistics, survival analysis, modeling, statistical computing for massive data, Bayesian regularization, bioinformatics, longitudinal and functional data analysis, statistical computation, application of statistics to medicine.

Movement Science (Ph.D.): Gammon Earhart (earhartg@wustl.edu). Philosophy of human movement function and dysfunction, with special emphasis on bioenergetics, biomechanics, and biocontrol.

Music (A.M., Ph.D.): Todd Decker (tdecker@wustl.edu). Musicology, ethnomusicology, theory, piano performance and pedagogy.

Performing Arts (A.M., M.F.A.): Mark Rollins (mark@wustl.edu). Theater studies, performance studies, dance.

Philosophy (Ph.D.): Ron Mallon (rmallon@wustl.edu). Ethics, social and political philosophy, history of philosophy, philosophy of law, philosophy of science, philosophy of mind, philosophy of language, theory of knowledge, aesthetics.

Philosophy/Neuroscience/Psychology (Ph.D.): Ron Mallon (pnp@wustl.edu). Philosophy of mind and language, with a special emphasis on the philosophical dimensions of psychology, neuroscience, and linguistics.

Physics (A.M., Ph.D.): Mark Alford (alford@wustl.edu). Experimental: astrophysics and space sciences, condensed matter and material physics, applications in biology and medicine, nuclear physics. Theoretical: astrophysics, biophysics, condensed matter and materials physics, elementary particles, many-body theory.

Political Science (Ph.D.): Jim Spriggs (jspriggs@wustl.edu). American politics, comparative politics, formal theory, international politics, law and courts, normative theory, political methodology.

Psychological & Brain Sciences (Ph.D.): Deanna Barch (dbarch@wustl.edu). Behavior/brain/cognition, clinical, development and aging, social/personality.

Rehabilitation and Participation Science (Ph.D.): Carolyn Baum (baumc@wustl.edu). Science of rehabilitation and participation with special emphasis placed on neurorehabilitation, performance, and community participation.

Romance Languages and Literatures (Ph.D.): Michael Sherberg (sherberg@wustl.edu). French language and literature, Latin American and Iberian literature and languages, Spanish and comparative literature.

Social Work (Ph.D.): Renee Cunningham Williams (williamsr@wustl.edu). Mental health, disparities, social and economic development, addictions, aging, child welfare, civic service, disabilities, health, poverty and social policy. Social determinants of health, health disparities, health promotion and disease prevention, health policy, dissemination and implementation, epidemiology, global health.

Speech and Hearing Sciences (Ph.D.): William Clark (elliottb@wustl.edu). Speech and hearing sciences, clinical audiology, deaf education, speech and language, sensory neuroscience.

The Writing Program (M.F.A.): David Schuman (dschuman@wustl.edu). Fiction, creative nonfiction, poetry-writing workshops and academic courses.

Programs of Study

A better job, financial security, and personal satisfaction are just some of the end goals for students seeking to earn an advanced degree through graduate study at Western New England University. From business to communication, creative writing to behavior analysis, and programs for teachers and engineers, students gain essential skills and expertise for success in their careers.

Programs in Communication, Accounting, and Curriculum and Instruction are offered entirely online and were developed specifically for that delivery model. Most of the Business and Engineering master's programs follow a blended model, allowing students to study completely online or attend select live sessions on campus. This flexibility enables working professionals to learn at their own pace. Education programs are offered in late afternoon and early evening to accommodate the schedules of working teachers. The low-residency M.F.A. in Creative Writing program includes four short-term residencies with author mentors, and the M.S. in Sport Leadership and Coaching includes two short-term residencies.

The University is regionally accredited by the New England Commission of Higher Education.

The **College of Arts and Sciences** offers the following graduate programs:

- Master of Arts in Communication with a public relations concentration
- Master of Arts in English for Teachers
- Master of Arts in Mathematics for Teachers
- Master of Education in Curriculum and Instruction
- Master of Fine Arts in Creative Writing
- Master of Science in Applied Behavior Analysis
- Ph.D. in Behavior Analysis

The **College of Business** offers the following graduate programs:

- Master of Business Administration (M.B.A.)
- Master of Science in Accounting (M.S.A.)
- M.S.A. with Forensic Accounting and Fraud Investigation concentration
- Master of Science in Organizational Leadership (M.S.O.L.)
- Master of Science in Sport Leadership and Coaching (M.S.L.C)
- J.D./M.B.A. dual degree program
- J.D./M.S.A. dual degree program
- J.D./M.S.O.L. dual degree program
- J.D./M.S.L.C. dual degree program
- Pharm.D./M.B.A. dual degree program
- Pharm.D./M.S.O.L. dual degree program

The **College of Engineering** offers these graduate programs:

- Master of Science in Civil Engineering (M.S.C.E.)
- Master of Science in Electrical Engineering (M.S.E.E.)
- M.S.E.E. with Mechatronics concentration
- Master of Science in Engineering Management (M.S.E.M.)
- Master of Science in Industrial Engineering (M.S.I.E.)
- Master of Science in Mechanical Engineering (M.S.M.E.)

- M.S.M.E. with Mechatronics concentration
- M.S.E.M./M.B.A. combined degree program
- Ph.D. in Engineering Management
- J.D./M.S.E.M. dual degree program

The University also offers programs though the College of Pharmacy and Health Sciences and the Law School. These include the Juris Doctor, the Doctor of Pharmacy, and the Doctor of Occupational Therapy.

Financial Aid

To be considered for financial aid, a student must have final approval into a degree program and be enrolled in a minimum of 3 credits per term. Financial need-based resources, including grants and low-interest federal loans, may be available for eligible students.

Cost of Study

Western New England University is committed to keeping a high-quality private education affordable for its students. Western New England's graduate tuition rates are some of the most affordable in the region. Tuition for graduate programs is as follows:

College of Arts and Sciences:

- Online M.Ed.: $703 per credit
- M.A.E.T., and M.A.M.T.: $389 per credit
- M.A. in Communication: $816 per credit
- M.F.A. in Creative Writing: $653 per credit
- M.S. in Applied Behavior Analysis: $1,168 per credit
- Ph.D. in Behavior Analysis: $1,392 per credit

College of Business:

- M.B.A., M.S.A., M.S.O.L., and M.S.L.C.: $892 per credit

College of Engineering:

- M.S.C.E., M.S.E.E., M.S.E.M., M.S.I.E., and M.S.M.E.: $1,168 per credit
- Ph.D. in Engineering Management: $1,392 per credit

Living and Housing Costs

Graduate students have the option of living on campus. Housing costs range between $9,600 and $12,432, depending upon the apartment type and duration (10 to 12 months).

Career Development

The Career Development Center assists students and alumni with career planning, occupational exploration, and job search strategies. The center's staff members implement the University's strong commitment to the development of a student's career decision-making by providing individual career advising and assistance in identifying career options.

The Career Development Center staff brings students in contact with employers through dynamic on-campus recruiting, employer information sessions, and career fairs. In addition, students are assisted with resources for part-time and summer employment. A weekly newsletter is published online at www.wne.edu/careercenter and serves as one tool for alerting students to employment opportunities, internships, recruiting schedules, and career-related workshops and activities.

Location

Western New England University's beautiful 215-acre suburban campus is located in Springfield, Massachusetts, the cultural urban center of the western part of the state. Perhaps best known as the birthplace of basketball and home of the Naismith Memorial Basketball Hall of Fame, Springfield is midway between New York and Boston and on the road between New York and Canada. Springfield is ideally located for travel in all directions, and there is convenient access from the University to both the Mass Pike and Interstate 91.

Faculty

With an average class size of 20, students work closely with the University's full-time faculty members who bring outstanding professional and academic credentials to the classroom. On average, 85 percent of graduate courses are taught by full-time faculty members. Ninety percent of the faculty hold terminal degrees in their field.

Additional details about the faculty for specific departments/programs can be found at wne.edu.

The University

Originally established in 1919 to serve working adults, Western New England University is renowned for its innovative programs, culture of collaboration, and faculty members who are focused on student success. Today that commitment continues through the University's graduate programs on campus and online.

Accredited by AACSB International, the College of Business is widely respected throughout the region for the caliber of its flagship M.B.A. program, sought-after M.S.A. degree, and dynamic new offering in organizational leadership. The College of Arts and Sciences offers high-quality master's programs for teachers at an affordable tuition rate and an immersive M.F.A. in Creative Writing program. The College's master's and doctoral programs in Behavior Analysis have positioned the University as a global leader in research and education in that discipline. Accredited by the Association of Behavior Analysis International (ABAI), the Ph.D. in Behavior Analysis program has been cited by the ABAI as ranking third in total scholarly publications out of 74 programs. The thriving College of Engineering is recognized as an educational leader by major corporations in the northeast who seek out graduates of the University's master's and combined engineering/business and law degree programs.

Applying

Western New England University has a rolling admissions policy for most programs, not a set admission deadline. Admission decisions are typically released within two to three weeks of an application being complete. The University urges prospective students to apply as early as possible in relation to the anticipated start date. Most of the graduate programs offer multiple entry points annually. Graduate students can apply online at www.wne.edu/gradapp.

Correspondence and Information

Office of Graduate Admissions
Western New England University
1215 Wilbraham Road
Springfield, Massachusetts 01119
United States
Phone: 413-782-1517
       800-325-1122, Ext. 1517 (toll-free)
E-mail: study@wne.edu
Website: wne.edu/grad

APPENDIXES

Institutional Changes
Since the 2019 Edition

Following is an alphabetical listing of institutions that have recently closed, merged with other institutions, or changed their names or status. In the case of a name change, the former name appears first, followed by the new name.

Argosy University, Dallas (Farmers Branch, TX): *closed.*

Argosy University, Denver (Denver, CO): *closed.*

Argosy University, Inland Empire (Ontario, CA): *closed.*

Argosy University, Nashville (Nashville, TN): *closed.*

Argosy University, Salt Lake City (Draper, UT): *closed.*

Argosy University, San Diego (San Diego, CA): *closed.*

Argosy University, San Francisco Bay Area (Alameda, CA): *closed.*

Argosy University, Sarasota (Sarasota, FL): *closed.*

Argosy University, Schaumburg (Schaumburg, IL): *closed.*

Arlington Baptist College (Arlington, TX): *name changed to Arlington Baptist University.*

Armstrong State University (Savannah, GA): *name changed to Georgia Southern University–Armstrong Campus.*

Art Center College of Design (Pasadena, CA): *name changed to ArtCenter College of Design.*

The Art Institute of California–San Francisco, a campus of Argosy University (San Francisco, CA): *closed.*

Augsburg College (Minneapolis, MN): *name changed to Augsburg University.*

Bristol University (Anaheim, CA): *closed.*

Claremont McKenna College (Claremont, CA): *merged into The Claremont Colleges (Claremont, CA).*

Coleman University (San Diego, CA): *closed.*

Digital Media Arts College (Boca Raton, FL): *closed.*

Everest University (Tampa, FL): *no longer offers graduate degrees.*

Fairleigh Dickinson University, College at Florham (Madison, NJ): *name changed to Fairleigh Dickinson University, Florham Campus.*

Faith Evangelical College & Seminary (Tacoma, WA): *name changed to Faith International University.*

Frank Lloyd Wright School of Architecture (Scottsdale, AZ): *name changed to School of Architecture at Taliesin.*

Future Generations Graduate School (Franklin, WV): *name changed to Future Generations University.*

Grace University (Omaha, NE): *closed.*

Greenville College (Greenville, IL): *name changed to Greenville University.*

Hazelden Graduate School of Addiction Studies (Center City, MN): *name changed to Hazelden Betty Ford Graduate School of Addiction.*

Henley-Putnam University (San Jose, CA): *name changed to Henley-Putnam School of Strategic Security.*

Huntington College of Health Sciences (Knoxville, TN): *name changed to Huntington University of Health Sciences.*

The Institute for the Psychological Sciences (Arlington, VA): *name changed to Divine Mercy University.*

International College of the Cayman Islands (Newlands, Cayman Islands): *not accredited by an agency recognized by USDE or CHEA at the time of publication.*

Johnson State College (Johnson, VT): *name changed to Northern Vermont University–Johnson.*

John Wesley University (High Point, NC): *closed.*

Kaplan University, Davenport Campus (Davenport, IA): *name changed to Purdue University Global.*

Knowledge Systems Institute (Skokie, IL): no longer degree granting.

Long Island University–Hudson at Westchester (Purchase, NY): *name changed to Long Island University–Hudson.*

Lutheran Theological Seminary at Gettysburg (Gettysburg, PA): *name changed to United Lutheran Seminary.*

Lynchburg College (Lynchburg, VA): *name changed to University of Lynchburg.*

Lyndon State College (Lyndonville, VT): *name changed to Northern Vermont University–Lyndon.*

Marylhurst University (Marylhurst, OR): *closed.*

McNally Smith College of Music (Saint Paul, MN): *closed.*

Memphis College of Art (Memphis, TN): *closed.*

Mirrer Yeshiva (Brooklyn, NY): *name changed to Mirrer Yeshiva Central Institute.*

Moody Theological Seminary–Michigan (Plymouth, MI): *name changed to Moody Theological Seminary Michigan.*

Mount Ida College (Newton, MA): *closed.*

National American University (Rapid City, SD): *no longer offers graduate degrees.*

The Ohio State University–Mansfield Campus (Mansfield, OH): *name changed to The Ohio State University at Mansfield.*

The Ohio State University–Newark Campus (Newark, OH): *name changed to The Ohio State University at Newark.*

Our Lady of the Lake College (Baton Rouge, LA): *name changed to Franciscan Missionaries of Our Lady University.*

Philadelphia University (Philadelphia, PA): *closed.*

Rudolf Steiner College (Fair Oaks, CA): *not accredited by an agency recognized by USDE or CHEA at the time of publication.*

Sacred Heart School of Theology (Hales Corners, WI): *name changed to Sacred Heart Seminary and School of Theology.*

Sewanee: The University of the South (Sewanee, TN): *name changed to The University of the South.*

Shepherd University (Los Angeles, CA): *closed.*

Silicon Valley University (San Jose, CA): *closed.*

South University (Novi, MI): *closed.*

South University (High Point, NC): *closed.*

South University (Cleveland, OH): *closed.*

University of Great Falls (Great Falls, MT): *name changed to University of Providence.*

University of Phoenix–Atlanta Campus (Sandy Springs, GA): *closed.*

University of Phoenix–Augusta Campus (Augusta, GA): *closed.*

University of Phoenix–Central Florida Campus (Orlando, FL): *closed.*

University of Phoenix–Charlotte Campus (Charlotte, NC): *closed.*

University of Phoenix–Colorado Campus (Lone Tree, CO): *closed.*

University of Phoenix–Colorado Springs Downtown Campus (Colorado Springs, CO): *closed.*

University of Phoenix–Columbus Georgia Campus (Columbus, GA): *closed.*

University of Phoenix–Jersey City Campus (Jersey City, NJ): *closed.*

University of Phoenix–New Mexico Campus (Albuquerque, NM): *closed.*

University of Phoenix–North Florida Campus (Jacksonville, FL): *closed.*

University of Phoenix–Southern Arizona Campus (Tucson, AZ): *closed.*

University of Phoenix–Southern California Campus (Costa Mesa, CA): *closed.*

University of Phoenix–South Florida Campus (Miramar, FL): *closed.*

University of Phoenix–Utah Campus (Salt Lake City, UT): *closed.*

University of Phoenix–Washington D.C. Campus (Washington, DC): *closed.*

University of Phoenix–Western Washington Campus (Tukwila, WA): *closed.*

University of Puerto Rico, Mayagüez Campus (Mayagüez, PR): *name changed to University of Puerto Rico–Mayagüez.*

University of Puerto Rico, Medical Sciences Campus (San Juan, PR): *name changed to University of Puerto Rico–Medical Sciences Campus.*

University of Puerto Rico, Río Piedras Campus (San Juan, PR): *name changed to University of Puerto Rico–Río Piedras.*

The University of South Dakota (Vermillion, SD): *name changed to University of South Dakota.*

Urbana University (Urbana, OH): *name changed to Urbana University–A Branch Campus of Franklin University.*

Virginia College in Birmingham (Birmingham, AL): *closed.*

Warner Pacific College (Portland, OR): *name changed to Warner Pacific University.*

Wheelock College (Boston, MA): *merged into Boston University (Boston, MA).*

Wright Institute (Berkeley, CA): *name changed to The Wright Institute.*

Yeshiva Karlin Stolin Rabbinical Institute (Brooklyn, NY): *name changed to Yeshiva Karlin Stolin.*

Abbreviations Used in the Guides

The following list includes abbreviations of degree names used in the profiles in the 2020 edition of the guides. Because some degrees (e.g., Doctor of Education) can be abbreviated in more than one way (e.g., D.Ed. or Ed.D.), and because the abbreviations used in the guides reflect the preferences of the individual colleges and universities, the list may include two or more abbreviations for a single degree.

DEGREES

A Mus D	Doctor of Musical Arts
AC	Advanced Certificate
AD	Artist's Diploma
	Doctor of Arts
ADP	Artist's Diploma
Adv C	Advanced Certificate
AGC	Advanced Graduate Certificate
AGSC	Advanced Graduate Specialist Certificate
ALM	Master of Liberal Arts
AM	Master of Arts
AMBA	Accelerated Master of Business Administration
APC	Advanced Professional Certificate
APMPH	Advanced Professional Master of Public Health
App Sc	Applied Scientist
App Sc D	Doctor of Applied Science
AstE	Astronautical Engineer
ATC	Advanced Training Certificate
Au D	Doctor of Audiology
B Th	Bachelor of Theology
CAES	Certificate of Advanced Educational Specialization
CAGS	Certificate of Advanced Graduate Studies
CAL	Certificate in Applied Linguistics
CAPS	Certificate of Advanced Professional Studies
CAS	Certificate of Advanced Studies
CATS	Certificate of Achievement in Theological Studies
CE	Civil Engineer
CEM	Certificate of Environmental Management
CET	Certificate in Educational Technologies
CGS	Certificate of Graduate Studies
Ch E	Chemical Engineer
Clin Sc D	Doctor of Clinical Science
CM	Certificate in Management
CMH	Certificate in Medical Humanities
CMM	Master of Church Ministries
CMS	Certificate in Ministerial Studies
CNM	Certificate in Nonprofit Management
CPC	Certificate in Publication and Communication
CPH	Certificate in Public Health
CPS	Certificate of Professional Studies
CScD	Doctor of Clinical Science
CSD	Certificate in Spiritual Direction
CSS	Certificate of Special Studies
CTS	Certificate of Theological Studies
D Ac	Doctor of Acupuncture
D Admin	Doctor of Administration
D Arch	Doctor of Architecture
D Be	Doctor in Bioethics
D Com	Doctor of Commerce
D Couns	Doctor of Counseling
D Des	Doctorate of Design
D Div	Doctor of Divinity
D Ed	Doctor of Education
D Ed Min	Doctor of Educational Ministry
D Eng	Doctor of Engineering
D Engr	Doctor of Engineering
D Ent	Doctor of Enterprise
D Env	Doctor of Environment
D Law	Doctor of Law
D Litt	Doctor of Letters
D Med Sc	Doctor of Medical Science
D Mgt	Doctor of Management
D Min	Doctor of Ministry

D Miss	Doctor of Missiology
D Mus	Doctor of Music
D Mus A	Doctor of Musical Arts
D Phil	Doctor of Philosophy
D Prof	Doctor of Professional Studies
D Ps	Doctor of Psychology
D Sc	Doctor of Science
D Sc D	Doctor of Science in Dentistry
D Sc IS	Doctor of Science in Information Systems
D Sc PA	Doctor of Science in Physician Assistant Studies
D Th	Doctor of Theology
D Th P	Doctor of Practical Theology
DA	Doctor of Accounting
	Doctor of Arts
DACM	Doctor of Acupuncture and Chinese Medicine
DAIS	Doctor of Applied Intercultural Studies
DAOM	Doctorate in Acupuncture and Oriental Medicine
DAT	Doctorate of Athletic Training
	Professional Doctor of Art Therapy
DBA	Doctor of Business Administration
DBH	Doctor of Behavioral Health
DBL	Doctor of Business Leadership
DC	Doctor of Chiropractic
DCC	Doctor of Computer Science
DCD	Doctor of Communications Design
DCE	Doctor of Computer Engineering
DCJ	Doctor of Criminal Justice
DCL	Doctor of Civil Law
	Doctor of Comparative Law
DCM	Doctor of Church Music
DCN	Doctor of Clinical Nutrition
DCS	Doctor of Computer Science
DDN	Diplôme du Droit Notarial
DDS	Doctor of Dental Surgery
DE	Doctor of Education
	Doctor of Engineering
DED	Doctor of Economic Development
DEIT	Doctor of Educational Innovation and Technology
DEL	Doctor of Executive Leadership
DEM	Doctor of Educational Ministry
DEPD	Diplôme Études Spécialisées
DES	Doctor of Engineering Science
DESS	Diplôme Études Supérieures Spécialisées
DET	Doctor of Educational Technology
DFA	Doctor of Fine Arts
DGP	Diploma in Graduate and Professional Studies
DGS	Doctor of Global Security
DH Sc	Doctor of Health Sciences
DHA	Doctor of Health Administration
DHCE	Doctor of Health Care Ethics
DHL	Doctor of Hebrew Letters
DHPE	Doctorate of Health Professionals Education
DHS	Doctor of Health Science
DHSc	Doctor of Health Science
DIT	Doctor of Industrial Technology
	Doctor of Information Technology
DJS	Doctor of Jewish Studies
DLS	Doctor of Liberal Studies
DM	Doctor of Management
	Doctor of Music
DMA	Doctor of Musical Arts
DMD	Doctor of Dental Medicine
DME	Doctor of Manufacturing Management
	Doctor of Music Education
DMFT	Doctor of Marital and Family Therapy
DMH	Doctor of Medical Humanities
DML	Doctor of Modern Languages
DMP	Doctorate in Medical Physics
DMPNA	Doctor of Management Practice in Nurse Anesthesia
DN Sc	Doctor of Nursing Science

DNAP	Doctor of Nurse Anesthesia Practice
DNP	Doctor of Nursing Practice
DNP-A	Doctor of Nursing Practice - Anesthesia
DNS	Doctor of Nursing Science
DO	Doctor of Osteopathy
DOL	Doctorate of Organizational Leadership
DOM	Doctor of Oriental Medicine
DOT	Doctor of Occupational Therapy
DPA	Diploma in Public Administration
	Doctor of Public Administration
DPDS	Doctor of Planning and Development Studies
DPH	Doctor of Public Health
DPM	Doctor of Plant Medicine
	Doctor of Podiatric Medicine
DPPD	Doctor of Policy, Planning, and Development
DPS	Doctor of Professional Studies
DPT	Doctor of Physical Therapy
DPTSc	Doctor of Physical Therapy Science
Dr DES	Doctor of Design
Dr NP	Doctor of Nursing Practice
Dr OT	Doctor of Occupational Therapy
Dr PH	Doctor of Public Health
Dr Sc PT	Doctor of Science in Physical Therapy
DRSc	Doctor of Regulatory Science
DS	Doctor of Science
DS Sc	Doctor of Social Science
DScPT	Doctor of Science in Physical Therapy
DSI	Doctor of Strategic Intelligence
DSJS	Doctor of Science in Jewish Studies
DSL	Doctor of Strategic Leadership
DSNS	Doctorate of Statecraft and National Security
DSS	Doctor of Strategic Security
DSW	Doctor of Social Work
DTL	Doctor of Talmudic Law
	Doctor of Transformational Leadership
DV Sc	Doctor of Veterinary Science
DVM	Doctor of Veterinary Medicine
DWS	Doctor of Worship Studies
EAA	Engineer in Aeronautics and Astronautics
EASPh D	Engineering and Applied Science Doctor of Philosophy
ECS	Engineer in Computer Science
Ed D	Doctor of Education
Ed DCT	Doctor of Education in College Teaching
Ed L D	Doctor of Education Leadership
Ed M	Master of Education
Ed S	Specialist in Education
Ed Sp	Specialist in Education
EDB	Executive Doctorate in Business
EDM	Executive Doctorate in Management
EE	Electrical Engineer
EJD	Executive Juris Doctor
EMBA	Executive Master of Business Administration
EMFA	Executive Master of Forensic Accounting
EMHA	Executive Master of Health Administration
EMHCL	Executive Master in Healthcare Leadership
EMIB	Executive Master of International Business
EMIR	Executive Master in International Relations
EML	Executive Master of Leadership
EMPA	Executive Master of Public Administration
EMPL	Executive Master in Policy Leadership
	Executive Master in Public Leadership
EMS	Executive Master of Science
EMTM	Executive Master of Technology Management
Eng	Engineer
Eng Sc D	Doctor of Engineering Science
Engr	Engineer
Exec MHA	Executive Master of Health Administration
Exec Ed D	Executive Doctor of Education
Exec MBA	Executive Master of Business Administration
Exec MPA	Executive Master of Public Administration
Exec MPH	Executive Master of Public Health
Exec MS	Executive Master of Science
Executive MA	Executive Master of Arts
G Dip	Graduate Diploma
GBC	Graduate Business Certificate
GDM	Graduate Diploma in Management
GDPA	Graduate Diploma in Public Administration
GEMBA	Global Executive Master of Business Administration
GM Acc	Graduate Master of Accountancy
GMBA	Global Master of Business Administration
GP LL M	Global Professional Master of Laws
GPD	Graduate Performance Diploma
GSS	Graduate Special Certificate for Students in Special Situations
IEMBA	International Executive Master of Business Administration
IMA	Interdisciplinary Master of Arts
IMBA	International Master of Business Administration
IMES	International Master's in Environmental Studies
Ingeniero	Engineer
JCD	Doctor of Canon Law
JCL	Licentiate in Canon Law
JD	Juris Doctor
JM	Juris Master
JSD	Doctor of Juridical Science
	Doctor of Jurisprudence
	Doctor of the Science of Law
JSM	Master of the Science of Law
L Th	Licentiate in Theology
LL B	Bachelor of Laws
LL CM	Master of Comparative Law
LL D	Doctor of Laws
LL M	Master of Laws
LL M in Tax	Master of Laws in Taxation
LL M CL	Master of Laws in Common Law
M Ac	Master of Accountancy
	Master of Accounting
	Master of Acupuncture
M Ac OM	Master of Acupuncture and Oriental Medicine
M Acc	Master of Accountancy
	Master of Accounting
M Acct	Master of Accountancy
	Master of Accounting
M Accy	Master of Accountancy
M Actg	Master of Accounting
M Acy	Master of Accountancy
M Ad	Master of Administration
M Ad Ed	Master of Adult Education
M Adm	Master of Administration
M Adm Mgt	Master of Administrative Management
M Admin	Master of Administration
M ADU	Master of Architectural Design and Urbanism
M Adv	Master of Advertising
M Ag	Master of Agriculture
M Ag Ed	Master of Agricultural Education
M Agr	Master of Agriculture
M App Comp Sc	Master of Applied Computer Science
M App St	Master of Applied Statistics
M Appl Stat	Master of Applied Statistics
M Aq	Master of Aquaculture
M Ar	Master of Architecture
M Arch	Master of Architecture
M Arch I	Master of Architecture I
M Arch II	Master of Architecture II
M Arch E	Master of Architectural Engineering
M Arch H	Master of Architectural History
M Bioethics	Master in Bioethics
M Cat	Master of Catechesis
M Ch E	Master of Chemical Engineering
M Cl D	Master of Clinical Dentistry
M Cl Sc	Master of Clinical Science
M Comm	Master of Communication
M Comp	Master of Computing
M Comp Sc	Master of Computer Science
M Coun	Master of Counseling
M Dent	Master of Dentistry
M Dent Sc	Master of Dental Sciences
M Des	Master of Design
M Des S	Master of Design Studies
M Div	Master of Divinity
M E Sci	Master of Earth Science
M Ec	Master of Economics

M Econ	Master of Economics	M Th	Master of Theology
M Ed	Master of Education	M Trans E	Master of Transportation Engineering
M Ed T	Master of Education in Teaching	M U Ed	Master of Urban Education
M En	Master of Engineering	M Urb	Master of Urban Planning
M En S	Master of Environmental Sciences	M Vet Sc	Master of Veterinary Science
M Eng	Master of Engineering	MA	Master of Accounting
M Eng Mgt	Master of Engineering Management		Master of Administration
M Engr	Master of Engineering		Master of Arts
M Ent	Master of Enterprise	MA Comm	Master of Arts in Communication
M Env	Master of Environment	MA Ed	Master of Arts in Education
M Env Des	Master of Environmental Design	MA Ed/HD	Master of Arts in Education and Human Development
M Env E	Master of Environmental Engineering		
M Env Sc	Master of Environmental Science	MA Islamic	Master of Arts in Islamic Studies
M Ext Ed	Master of Extension Education	MA Min	Master of Arts in Ministry
M Fin	Master of Finance	MA Miss	Master of Arts in Missiology
M Geo E	Master of Geological Engineering	MA Past St	Master of Arts in Pastoral Studies
M Geoenv E	Master of Geoenvironmental Engineering	MA Ph	Master of Arts in Philosophy
M Geog	Master of Geography	MA Psych	Master of Arts in Psychology
M Hum	Master of Humanities	MA Sc	Master of Applied Science
M IDST	Master's in Interdisciplinary Studies	MA Sp	Master of Arts (Spirituality)
M Jur	Master of Jurisprudence	MA Th	Master of Arts in Theology
M Kin	Master of Kinesiology	MA-R	Master of Arts (Research)
M Land Arch	Master of Landscape Architecture	MAA	Master of Applied Anthropology
M Litt	Master of Letters		Master of Applied Arts
M Mark	Master of Marketing		Master of Arts in Administration
M Mat SE	Master of Material Science and Engineering	MAAA	Master of Arts in Arts Administration
M Math	Master of Mathematics	MAAD	Master of Advanced Architectural Design
M Mech E	Master of Mechanical Engineering	MAAE	Master of Arts in Art Education
M Med Sc	Master of Medical Science	MAAPPS	Master of Arts in Asia Pacific Policy Studies
M Mgmt	Master of Management	MAAS	Master of Arts in Aging and Spirituality
M Mgt	Master of Management	MAASJ	Master of Arts in Applied Social Justice
M Min	Master of Ministries	MAAT	Master of Arts in Applied Theology
M Mtl E	Master of Materials Engineering	MAB	Master of Agribusiness
M Mu	Master of Music		Master of Applied Bioengineering
M Mus	Master of Music		Master of Arts in Business
M Mus Ed	Master of Music Education	MABA	Master's in Applied Behavior Analysis
M Music	Master of Music	MABC	Master of Arts in Biblical Counseling
M Pet E	Master of Petroleum Engineering	MABE	Master of Arts in Bible Exposition
M Pharm	Master of Pharmacy	MABL	Master of Arts in Biblical Languages
M Phil	Master of Philosophy	MABM	Master of Agribusiness Management
M Phil F	Master of Philosophical Foundations	MABS	Master of Arts in Biblical Studies
M Pl	Master of Planning	MABT	Master of Arts in Bible Teaching
M Plan	Master of Planning	MAC	Master of Accountancy
M Pol	Master of Political Science		Master of Accounting
M Pr Met	Master of Professional Meteorology		Master of Arts in Communication
M Prob S	Master of Probability and Statistics		Master of Arts in Counseling
M Psych	Master of Psychology	MACC	Master of Arts in Christian Counseling
M Pub	Master of Publishing	MACCT	Master of Accounting
M Rel	Master of Religion	MACD	Master of Arts in Christian Doctrine
M Sc	Master of Science	MACE	Master of Arts in Christian Education
M Sc A	Master of Science (Applied)	MACH	Master of Arts in Church History
M Sc AC	Master of Science in Applied Computing	MACI	Master of Arts in Curriculum and Instruction
M Sc AHN	Master of Science in Applied Human Nutrition	MACIS	Master of Accounting and Information Systems
M Sc BMC	Master of Science in Biomedical Communications	MACJ	Master of Arts in Criminal Justice
		MACL	Master of Arts in Christian Leadership
M Sc CS	Master of Science in Computer Science		Master of Arts in Community Leadership
M Sc E	Master of Science in Engineering	MACM	Master of Arts in Christian Ministries
M Sc Eng	Master of Science in Engineering		Master of Arts in Christian Ministry
M Sc Engr	Master of Science in Engineering		Master of Arts in Church Music
M Sc F	Master of Science in Forestry		Master of Arts in Counseling Ministries
M Sc FE	Master of Science in Forest Engineering	MACML	Master of Arts in Christian Ministry and Leadership
M Sc Geogr	Master of Science in Geography		
M Sc N	Master of Science in Nursing	MACN	Master of Arts in Counseling
M Sc OT	Master of Science in Occupational Therapy	MACO	Master of Arts in Counseling
M Sc P	Master of Science in Planning	MAcOM	Master of Acupuncture and Oriental Medicine
M Sc Pl	Master of Science in Planning	MACP	Master of Arts in Christian Practice
M Sc PT	Master of Science in Physical Therapy		Master of Arts in Church Planting
M Sc T	Master of Science in Teaching		Master of Arts in Counseling Psychology
M SEM	Master of Sustainable Environmental Management	MACS	Master of Applied Computer Science
			Master of Arts in Catholic Studies
M Serv Soc	Master of Social Service		Master of Arts in Christian Studies
M Soc	Master of Sociology	MACSE	Master of Arts in Christian School Education
M Sp Ed	Master of Special Education	MACT	Master of Arts in Communications and Technology
M Stat	Master of Statistics		
M Sys E	Master of Systems Engineering	MAD	Master in Educational Institution Administration
M Sys Sc	Master of Systems Science		
M Tax	Master of Taxation		Master of Art and Design
M Tech	Master of Technology	MADR	Master of Arts in Dispute Resolution

MADS	Master of Applied Disability Studies
MAE	Master of Aerospace Engineering
	Master of Agricultural Economics
	Master of Agricultural Education
	Master of Applied Economics
	Master of Architectural Engineering
	Master of Art Education
	Master of Arts in Education
	Master of Arts in English
MAEd	Master of Arts Education
MAEE	Master of Agricultural and Extension Education
MAEL	Master of Arts in Educational Leadership
MAEM	Master of Arts in Educational Ministries
MAEP	Master of Arts in Economic Policy
	Master of Arts in Educational Psychology
MAES	Master of Arts in Environmental Sciences
MAET	Master of Arts in English Teaching
MAF	Master of Arts in Finance
MAFE	Master of Arts in Financial Economics
MAFM	Master of Accounting and Financial Management
MAFS	Master of Arts in Family Studies
MAG	Master of Applied Geography
MAGU	Master of Urban Analysis and Management
MAH	Master of Arts in Humanities
MAHA	Master of Arts in Humanitarian Assistance
MAHCM	Master of Arts in Health Care Mission
MAHG	Master of American History and Government
MAHL	Master of Arts in Hebrew Letters
MAHN	Master of Applied Human Nutrition
MAHR	Master of Applied Historical Research
MAHS	Master of Arts in Human Services
MAHSR	Master in Applied Health Services Research
MAIA	Master of Arts in International Administration
	Master of Arts in International Affairs
MAICS	Master of Arts in Intercultural Studies
MAIDM	Master of Arts in Interior Design and Merchandising
MAIH	Master of Arts in Interdisciplinary Humanities
MAIOP	Master of Applied Industrial/Organizational Psychology
MAIS	Master of Arts in Intercultural Studies
	Master of Arts in Interdisciplinary Studies
	Master of Arts in International Studies
MAIT	Master of Administration in Information Technology
MAJ	Master of Arts in Journalism
MAJCS	Master of Arts in Jewish Communal Service
MAJPS	Master of Arts in Jewish Professional Studies
MAJS	Master of Arts in Jewish Studies
MAL	Master of Athletic Leadership
MALA	Master of Arts in Liberal Arts
MALCM	Master in Arts Leadership and Cultural Management
MALD	Master of Arts in Law and Diplomacy
MALER	Master of Arts in Labor and Employment Relations
MALL	Master of Arts in Language Learning
MALLT	Master of Arts in Language, Literature, and Translation
MALP	Master of Arts in Language Pedagogy
MALS	Master of Arts in Liberal Studies
MAM	Master of Acquisition Management
	Master of Agriculture and Management
	Master of Applied Mathematics
	Master of Arts in Management
	Master of Arts in Ministry
	Master of Arts Management
	Master of Aviation Management
MAMC	Master of Arts in Mass Communication
	Master of Arts in Ministry and Culture
	Master of Arts in Ministry for a Multicultural Church
MAME	Master of Arts in Missions/Evangelism
MAMFC	Master of Arts in Marriage and Family Counseling
MAMFT	Master of Arts in Marriage and Family Therapy
MAMHC	Master of Arts in Mental Health Counseling

MAMS	Master of Applied Mathematical Sciences
	Master of Arts in Ministerial Studies
	Master of Arts in Ministry and Spirituality
MAMT	Master of Arts in Mathematics Teaching
MAN	Master of Applied Nutrition
MANT	Master of Arts in New Testament
MAOL	Master of Arts in Organizational Leadership
MAOM	Master of Acupuncture and Oriental Medicine
	Master of Arts in Organizational Management
MAOT	Master of Arts in Old Testament
MAP	Master of Applied Politics
	Master of Applied Psychology
	Master of Arts in Planning
	Master of Psychology
	Master of Public Administration
MAP Min	Master of Arts in Pastoral Ministry
MAPA	Master of Arts in Public Administration
MAPC	Master of Arts in Pastoral Counseling
MAPE	Master of Arts in Physics Education
MAPM	Master of Arts in Pastoral Ministry
	Master of Arts in Pastoral Music
	Master of Arts in Practical Ministry
MAPP	Master of Arts in Public Policy
MAPS	Master of Applied Psychological Sciences
	Master of Arts in Pastoral Studies
	Master of Arts in Public Service
MAPW	Master of Arts in Professional Writing
MAQRM	Master's of Actuarial and Quantitative Risk Management
MAR	Master of Arts in Reading
	Master of Arts in Religion
Mar Eng	Marine Engineer
MARC	Master of Arts in Rehabilitation Counseling
MARE	Master of Arts in Religious Education
MARL	Master of Arts in Religious Leadership
MARS	Master of Arts in Religious Studies
MAS	Master of Accounting Science
	Master of Actuarial Science
	Master of Administrative Science
	Master of Advanced Study
	Master of American Studies
	Master of Animal Science
	Master of Applied Science
	Master of Applied Statistics
	Master of Archival Studies
MASA	Master of Advanced Studies in Architecture
MASC	Master of Arts in School Counseling
MASD	Master of Arts in Spiritual Direction
MASE	Master of Arts in Special Education
MASF	Master of Arts in Spiritual Formation
MASJ	Master of Arts in Systems of Justice
MASLA	Master of Advanced Studies in Landscape Architecture
MASM	Master of Aging Services Management
	Master of Arts in Specialized Ministries
MASS	Master of Applied Social Science
MASW	Master of Aboriginal Social Work
MAT	Master of Arts in Teaching
	Master of Arts in Theology
	Master of Athletic Training
	Master's in Administration of Telecommunications
Mat E	Materials Engineer
MATCM	Master of Acupuncture and Traditional Chinese Medicine
MATDE	Master of Arts in Theology, Development, and Evangelism
MATDR	Master of Territorial Management and Regional Development
MATE	Master of Arts for the Teaching of English
MATESL	Master of Arts in Teaching English as a Second Language
MATESOL	Master of Arts in Teaching English to Speakers of Other Languages
MATF	Master of Arts in Teaching English as a Foreign Language/Intercultural Studies
MATFL	Master of Arts in Teaching Foreign Language
MATH	Master of Arts in Therapy

MATI	Master of Administration of Information Technology
MATL	Master of Arts in Teaching of Languages
	Master of Arts in Transformational Leadership
MATM	Master of Arts in Teaching of Mathematics
MATRN	Master of Athletic Training
MATS	Master of Arts in Theological Studies
	Master of Arts in Transforming Spirituality
MAUA	Master of Arts in Urban Affairs
MAUD	Master of Arts in Urban Design
MAURP	Master of Arts in Urban and Regional Planning
MAW	Master of Arts in Worship
MAWSHP	Master of Arts in Worship
MAYM	Master of Arts in Youth Ministry
MB	Master of Bioinformatics
MBA	Master of Business Administration
MBA-AM	Master of Business Administration in Aviation Management
MBA-EP	Master of Business Administration–Experienced Professionals
MBAA	Master of Business Administration in Aviation
MBAE	Master of Biological and Agricultural Engineering
	Master of Biosystems and Agricultural Engineering
MBAH	Master of Business Administration in Health
MBAi	Master of Business Administration–International
MBAICT	Master of Business Administration in Information and Communication Technology
MBC	Master of Building Construction
MBE	Master of Bilingual Education
	Master of Bioengineering
	Master of Bioethics
	Master of Biomedical Engineering
	Master of Business Economics
	Master of Business Education
MBEE	Master in Biotechnology Enterprise and Entrepreneurship
MBET	Master of Business, Entrepreneurship and Technology
MBI	Master in Business Informatics
MBIOT	Master of Biotechnology
MBiotech	Master of Biotechnology
MBL	Master of Business Leadership
MBLE	Master in Business Logistics Engineering
MBME	Master's in Biomedical Engineering
MBMSE	Master of Business Management and Software Engineering
MBOE	Master of Business Operational Excellence
MBS	Master of Biblical Studies
	Master of Biological Science
	Master of Biomedical Sciences
	Master of Bioscience
	Master of Building Science
	Master of Business and Science
	Master of Business Statistics
MBST	Master of Biostatistics
MBT	Master of Biomedical Technology
	Master of Biotechnology
	Master of Business Taxation
MBV	Master of Business for Veterans
MC	Master of Classics
	Master of Communication
	Master of Counseling
MC Ed	Master of Continuing Education
MC Sc	Master of Computer Science
MCA	Master of Commercial Aviation
	Master of Communication Arts
	Master of Criminology (Applied)
MCAM	Master of Computational and Applied Mathematics
MCC	Master of Computer Science
MCD	Master of Communications Disorders
	Master of Community Development
MCE	Master in Electronic Commerce
	Master of Chemistry Education
	Master of Christian Education
	Master of Civil Engineering

	Master of Control Engineering
MCEM	Master of Construction Engineering Management
MCEPA	Master of Chinese Economic and Political Affairs
MCHE	Master of Chemical Engineering
MCIS	Master of Communication and Information Studies
	Master of Computer and Information Science
	Master of Computer Information Systems
MCIT	Master of Computer and Information Technology
MCJ	Master of Criminal Justice
MCL	Master in Communication Leadership
	Master of Canon Law
	Master of Christian Leadership
	Master of Comparative Law
MCM	Master of Christian Ministry
	Master of Church Music
	Master of Communication Management
	Master of Community Medicine
	Master of Construction Management
	Master of Contract Management
MCMin	Master of Christian Ministry
MCMM	Master in Communications and Media Management
MCMP	Master of City and Metropolitan Planning
MCMS	Master of Clinical Medical Science
MCN	Master of Clinical Nutrition
MCOL	Master of Arts in Community and Organizational Leadership
MCP	Master of City Planning
	Master of Community Planning
	Master of Counseling Psychology
	Master of Cytopathology Practice
	Master of Science in Quality Systems and Productivity
MCPD	Master of Community Planning and Development
MCR	Master in Clinical Research
MCRP	Master of City and Regional Planning
	Master of Community and Regional Planning
MCRS	Master of City and Regional Studies
MCS	Master of Chemical Sciences
	Master of Christian Studies
	Master of Clinical Science
	Master of Combined Sciences
	Master of Communication Studies
	Master of Computer Science
	Master of Consumer Science
MCSE	Master of Computer Science and Engineering
MCSL	Master of Catholic School Leadership
MCSM	Master of Construction Science and Management
MCT	Master of Commerce and Technology
MCTM	Master of Clinical Translation Management
MCTP	Master of Communication Technology and Policy
MCTS	Master of Clinical and Translational Science
MCVS	Master of Cardiovascular Science
MD	Doctor of Medicine
MDA	Master of Dietetic Administration
MDB	Master of Design-Build
MDE	Master in Design Engineering
	Master of Developmental Economics
	Master of Distance Education
	Master of the Education of the Deaf
MDH	Master of Dental Hygiene
MDI	Master of Disruptive Innovation
MDM	Master of Design Methods
	Master of Digital Media
MDP	Master in Sustainable Development Practice
	Master of Development Practice
MDR	Master of Dispute Resolution
MDS	Master in Data Science
	Master of Dental Surgery
	Master of Design Studies
	Master of Digital Sciences
MDSPP	Master in Data Science for Public Policy

ME	Master of Education		Master of Forest Engineering
	Master of Engineering	MFES	Master of Fire and Emergency Services
	Master of Entrepreneurship	MFG	Master of Functional Genomics
ME Sc	Master of Engineering Science	MFHD	Master of Family and Human Development
ME-PD	Master of Education–Professional Development	MFM	Master of Financial Management
MEA	Master of Educational Administration		Master of Financial Mathematics
	Master of Engineering Administration	MFPE	Master of Food Process Engineering
MEAE	Master of Entertainment Arts and Engineering	MFR	Master of Forest Resources
MEAP	Master of Environmental Administration and Planning	MFRC	Master of Forest Resources and Conservation
		MFRE	Master of Food and Resource Economics
MEB	Master of Energy Business	MFS	Master of Food Science
MEBD	Master in Environmental Building Design		Master of Forensic Sciences
MEBT	Master in Electronic Business Technologies		Master of Forest Science
MEC	Master of Electronic Commerce		Master of Forest Studies
Mech E	Mechanical Engineer		Master of French Studies
MEDS	Master of Environmental Design Studies	MFST	Master of Food Safety and Technology
MEE	Master in Education	MFT	Master of Family Therapy
	Master of Electrical Engineering	MFWCB	Master of Fish, Wildlife and Conservation Biology
	Master of Energy Engineering		
	Master of Environmental Engineering	MFYCS	Master of Family, Youth and Community Sciences
MEECON	Master of Energy Economics		
MEEM	Master of Environmental Engineering and Management	MGA	Master of Global Affairs
			Master of Government Administration
MEENE	Master of Engineering in Environmental Engineering		Master of Governmental Administration
		MGBA	Master of Global Business Administration
MEEP	Master of Environmental and Energy Policy	MGC	Master of Genetic Counseling
MEERM	Master of Earth and Environmental Resource Management	MGCS	Master of Genetic Counselor Studies
		MGD	Master of Graphic Design
MEH	Master in Humanistic Studies	MGE	Master of Geotechnical Engineering
	Master of Environmental Health	MGEM	Master of Geomatics for Environmental Management
	Master of Environmental Horticulture		
MEHS	Master of Environmental Health and Safety		Master of Global Entrepreneurship and Management
MEIM	Master of Entertainment Industry Management		
	Master of Equine Industry Management	MGIS	Master of Geographic Information Science
MEL	Master of Educational Leadership		Master of Geographic Information Systems
	Master of Engineering Leadership	MGM	Master of Global Management
	Master of English Literature	MGMA	Master of Greenhouse Gas Management and Accounting
MELP	Master of Environmental Law and Policy		
MEM	Master of Engineering Management	MGP	Master of Gestion de Projet
	Master of Environmental Management	MGPS	Master of Global Policy Studies
	Master of Marketing	MGREM	Master of Global Real Estate Management
MEME	Master of Engineering in Manufacturing Engineering	MGS	Master of Gender Studies
			Master of Gerontological Studies
	Master of Engineering in Mechanical Engineering		Master of Global Studies
		MH	Master of Humanities
MENR	Master of Environment and Natural Resources	MH Sc	Master of Health Sciences
MENVEGR	Master of Environmental Engineering	MHA	Master of Health Administration
MEP	Master of Engineering Physics		Master of Healthcare Administration
MEPC	Master of Environmental Pollution Control		Master of Hospital Administration
MEPD	Master of Environmental Planning and Design		Master of Hospitality Administration
MER	Master of Employment Relations	MHB	Master of Human Behavior
MERE	Master of Entrepreneurial Real Estate	MHC	Master of Mental Health Counseling
MERL	Master of Energy Regulation and Law	MHCA	Master of Health Care Administration
MES	Master of Education and Science	MHCD	Master of Health Care Design
	Master of Engineering Science	MHCI	Master of Human-Computer Interaction
	Master of Environment and Sustainability	MHCL	Master of Health Care Leadership
	Master of Environmental Science	MHCM	Master of Health Care Management
	Master of Environmental Studies	MHE	Master of Health Education
	Master of Environmental Systems		Master of Higher Education
MESM	Master of Environmental Science and Management		Master of Human Ecology
		MHE Ed	Master of Home Economics Education
MET	Master of Educational Technology	MHEA	Master of Higher Education Administration
	Master of Engineering Technology	MHHS	Master of Health and Human Services
	Master of Entertainment Technology	MHI	Master of Health Informatics
	Master of Environmental Toxicology		Master of Healthcare Innovation
METM	Master of Engineering and Technology Management	MHID	Master of Healthcare Interior Design
		MHIHIM	Master of Health Informatics and Health Information Management
MEVE	Master of Environmental Engineering		
MF	Master of Finance	MHIIM	Master of Health Informatics and Information Management
	Master of Forestry		
MFA	Master of Financial Administration	MHK	Master of Human Kinetics
	Master of Fine Arts	MHM	Master of Healthcare Management
MFALP	Master of Food and Agriculture Law and Policy	MHMS	Master of Health Management Systems
MFAS	Master of Fisheries and Aquatic Science	MHP	Master of Health Physics
MFC	Master of Forest Conservation		Master of Heritage Preservation
MFCS	Master of Family and Consumer Sciences		Master of Historic Preservation
MFE	Master of Financial Economics		
	Master of Financial Engineering	MHPA	Master of Heath Policy and Administration

MHPCTL	Master of High Performance Coaching and Technical Leadership
MHPE	Master of Health Professions Education
MHR	Master of Human Resources
MHRD	Master in Human Resource Development
MHRIR	Master of Human Resources and Industrial Relations
MHRLR	Master of Human Resources and Labor Relations
MHRM	Master of Human Resources Management
MHS	Master of Health Science
	Master of Health Sciences
	Master of Health Studies
	Master of Hispanic Studies
	Master of Human Services
	Master of Humanistic Studies
MHSA	Master of Health Services Administration
MHSM	Master of Health Systems Management
MI	Master of Information
	Master of Instruction
MI Arch	Master of Interior Architecture
MIA	Master of Interior Architecture
	Master of International Affairs
MIAA	Master of International Affairs and Administration
MIAM	Master of International Agribusiness Management
MIAPD	Master of Interior Architecture and Product Design
MIB	Master of International Business
MIBS	Master of International Business Studies
MICLJ	Master of International Criminal Law and Justice
MICM	Master of International Construction Management
MID	Master of Industrial Design
	Master of Industrial Distribution
	Master of Innovation Design
	Master of Interior Design
	Master of International Development
MIDA	Master of International Development Administration
MIDP	Master of International Development Policy
MIDS	Master of Information and Data Science
MIE	Master of Industrial Engineering
MIF	Master of International Forestry
MIHTM	Master of International Hospitality and Tourism Management
MIJ	Master of International Journalism
MILR	Master of Industrial and Labor Relations
MIM	Master in Ministry
	Master of Information Management
	Master of International Management
	Master of International Marketing
MIMFA	Master of Investment Management and Financial Analysis
MIMLAE	Master of International Management for Latin American Executives
MIMS	Master of Information Management and Systems
	Master of Integrated Manufacturing Systems
MIP	Master of Infrastructure Planning
	Master of Intellectual Property
	Master of International Policy
MIPA	Master of International Public Affairs
MIPD	Master of Integrated Product Design
MIPER	Master of International Political Economy of Resources
MIPM	Master of International Policy Management
MIPP	Master of International Policy and Practice
	Master of International Public Policy
MIPS	Master of International Planning Studies
MIR	Master of Industrial Relations
	Master of International Relations
MIRD	Master of International Relations and Diplomacy
MIRHR	Master of Industrial Relations and Human Resources
MIS	Master of Imaging Science

	Master of Industrial Statistics
	Master of Information Science
	Master of Information Systems
	Master of Integrated Science
	Master of Interdisciplinary Studies
	Master of International Service
	Master of International Studies
MISE	Master of Industrial and Systems Engineering
MISKM	Master of Information Sciences and Knowledge Management
MISM	Master of Information Systems Management
MISW	Master of Indigenous Social Work
MIT	Master in Teaching
	Master of Industrial Technology
	Master of Information Technology
	Master of Initial Teaching
	Master of International Trade
MITA	Master of Information Technology Administration
MITM	Master of Information Technology and Management
MJ	Master of Journalism
	Master of Jurisprudence
MJ Ed	Master of Jewish Education
MJA	Master of Justice Administration
MJM	Master of Justice Management
MJS	Master of Judaic Studies
	Master of Judicial Studies
	Master of Juridical Studies
MK	Master of Kinesiology
MKM	Master of Knowledge Management
ML	Master of Latin
	Master of Law
ML Arch	Master of Landscape Architecture
MLA	Master of Landscape Architecture
	Master of Liberal Arts
MLAS	Master of Laboratory Animal Science
	Master of Liberal Arts and Sciences
MLAUD	Master of Landscape Architecture in Urban Development
MLD	Master of Leadership Development
	Master of Leadership Studies
MLE	Master of Applied Linguistics and Exegesis
MLER	Master of Labor and Employment Relations
MLI Sc	Master of Library and Information Science
MLIS	Master of Library and Information Science
	Master of Library and Information Studies
MLM	Master of Leadership in Ministry
MLPD	Master of Land and Property Development
MLRHR	Master of Labor Relations and Human Resources
MLS	Master of Leadership Studies
	Master of Legal Studies
	Master of Liberal Studies
	Master of Library Science
	Master of Life Sciences
	Master of Medical Laboratory Sciences
MLSCM	Master of Logistics and Supply Chain Management
MLT	Master of Language Technologies
MLTCA	Master of Long Term Care Administration
MLW	Master of Studies in Law
MLWS	Master of Land and Water Systems
MM	Master of Management
	Master of Mediation
	Master of Ministry
	Master of Music
MM Ed	Master of Music Education
MM Sc	Master of Medical Science
MM St	Master of Museum Studies
MMA	Master of Marine Affairs
	Master of Media Arts
	Master of Musical Arts
MMAL	Master of Maritime Administration and Logistics
MMAS	Master of Military Art and Science
MMB	Master of Microbial Biotechnology
MMC	Master of Manufacturing Competitiveness

	Master of Mass Communications	MO	Master of Oceanography
MMCM	Master of Music in Church Music	MOD	Master of Organizational Development
MMCSS	Master of Mathematical Computational and Statistical Sciences	MOGS	Master of Oil and Gas Studies
		MOL	Master of Organizational Leadership
MME	Master of Management in Energy	MOM	Master of Organizational Management
	Master of Manufacturing Engineering		Master of Oriental Medicine
	Master of Mathematics Education	MOR	Master of Operations Research
	Master of Mathematics for Educators	MOT	Master of Occupational Therapy
	Master of Mechanical Engineering	MP	Master of Physiology
	Master of Mining Engineering		Master of Planning
	Master of Music Education	MP Ac	Master of Professional Accountancy
MMEL	Master's in Medical Education Leadership	MP Acc	Master of Professional Accountancy
MMF	Master of Mathematical Finance		Master of Professional Accounting
MMFC/T	Master of Marriage and Family Counseling/ Therapy		Master of Public Accounting
		MP Aff	Master of Public Affairs
MMFT	Master of Marriage and Family Therapy	MP Th	Master of Pastoral Theology
MMG	Master of Management	MPA	Master of Performing Arts
MMH	Master of Management in Hospitality		Master of Physician Assistant
	Master of Medical Humanities		Master of Professional Accountancy
MMI	Master of Management of Innovation		Master of Professional Accounting
MMIS	Master of Management Information Systems		Master of Public Administration
MML	Master of Managerial Logistics		Master of Public Affairs
MMM	Master of Manufacturing Management	MPAC	Master of Professional Accounting
	Master of Marine Management	MPAID	Master of Public Administration and International Development
	Master of Medical Management		
MMP	Master of Marine Policy	MPAP	Master of Physician Assistant Practice
	Master of Medical Physics		Master of Public Administration and Policy
	Master of Music Performance		Master of Public Affairs and Politics
MMPA	Master of Management and Professional Accounting	MPAS	Master of Physician Assistant Science
			Master of Physician Assistant Studies
MMQM	Master of Manufacturing Quality Management	MPC	Master of Professional Communication
MMR	Master of Marketing Research	MPD	Master of Product Development
MMRM	Master of Marine Resources Management		Master of Public Diplomacy
MMS	Master in Migration Studies	MPDS	Master of Planning and Development Studies
	Master of Management Science	MPE	Master of Physical Education
	Master of Management Studies	MPEM	Master of Project Engineering and Management
	Master of Manufacturing Systems		
	Master of Marine Studies	MPFM	Master of Public Financial Management
	Master of Materials Science	MPH	Master of Public Health
	Master of Mathematical Sciences	MPHE	Master of Public Health Education
	Master of Medical Science	MPHM	Master in Plant Health Management
	Master of Medieval Studies	MPHS	Master of Population Health Sciences
MMSE	Master of Manufacturing Systems Engineering	MPHTM	Master of Public Health and Tropical Medicine
MMSM	Master of Music in Sacred Music	MPI	Master of Public Informatics
MMT	Master in Marketing	MPIA	Master of Public and International Affairs
	Master of Math for Teaching	MPL	Master of Pastoral Leadership
	Master of Music Therapy	MPM	Master of Pastoral Ministry
	Master's in Marketing Technology		Master of Pest Management
MMus	Master of Music		Master of Policy Management
MN	Master of Nursing		Master of Practical Ministries
	Master of Nutrition		Master of Professional Management
MN NP	Master of Nursing in Nurse Practitioner		Master of Project Management
MNA	Master of Nonprofit Administration		Master of Public Management
	Master of Nurse Anesthesia	MPNA	Master of Public and Nonprofit Administration
MNAE	Master of Nanoengineering	MPNL	Master of Philanthropy and Nonprofit Leadership
MNAL	Master of Nonprofit Administration and Leadership		
		MPO	Master of Prosthetics and Orthotics
MNAS	Master of Natural and Applied Science	MPOD	Master of Positive Organizational Development
MNCL	Master of Nonprofit and Civic Leadership	MPP	Master of Public Policy
MNCM	Master of Network and Communications Management	MPPA	Master of Public Policy Administration
			Master of Public Policy and Administration
MNE	Master of Nuclear Engineering	MPPAL	Master of Public Policy, Administration and Law
MNL	Master in International Business for Latin America	MPPGA	Master of Public Policy and Global Affairs
		MPPM	Master of Public Policy and Management
MNM	Master of Nonprofit Management	MPR	Master of Public Relations
MNO	Master of Nonprofit Organization	MPRTM	Master of Parks, Recreation, and Tourism Management
MNPL	Master of Not-for-Profit Leadership		
MNpS	Master of Nonprofit Studies	MPS	Master of Pastoral Studies
MNR	Master of Natural Resources		Master of Perfusion Science
MNRD	Master of Natural Resources Development		Master of Planning Studies
MNRES	Master of Natural Resources and Environmental Studies		Master of Political Science
			Master of Preservation Studies
MNRM	Master of Natural Resource Management		Master of Prevention Science
MNRMG	Master of Natural Resource Management and Geography		Master of Professional Studies
			Master of Public Service
MNRS	Master of Natural Resource Stewardship	MPSA	Master of Public Service Administration
MNS	Master of Natural Science	MPSG	Master of Population and Social Gerontology
MNSE	Master of Natural Sciences Education		

MPSIA	Master of Political Science and International Affairs
MPSL	Master of Public Safety Leadership
MPT	Master of Pastoral Theology
	Master of Physical Therapy
	Master of Practical Theology
MPVM	Master of Preventive Veterinary Medicine
MPW	Master of Professional Writing
	Master of Public Works
MQF	Master of Quantitative Finance
MQM	Master of Quality Management
	Master of Quantitative Management
MQS	Master of Quality Systems
MR	Master of Recreation
	Master of Retailing
MRA	Master in Research Administration
	Master of Regulatory Affairs
MRC	Master of Rehabilitation Counseling
MRCP	Master of Regional and City Planning
	Master of Regional and Community Planning
MRD	Master of Rural Development
MRE	Master of Real Estate
	Master of Religious Education
MRED	Master of Real Estate Development
MREM	Master of Resource and Environmental Management
MRLS	Master of Resources Law Studies
MRM	Master of Resources Management
MRP	Master of Regional Planning
MRRD	Master in Recreation Resource Development
MRS	Master of Religious Studies
MRSc	Master of Rehabilitation Science
MRUD	Master of Resilient Design
MS	Master of Science
MS Cmp E	Master of Science in Computer Engineering
MS Kin	Master of Science in Kinesiology
MS Acct	Master of Science in Accounting
MS Accy	Master of Science in Accountancy
MS Aero E	Master of Science in Aerospace Engineering
MS Ag	Master of Science in Agriculture
MS Arch	Master of Science in Architecture
MS Arch St	Master of Science in Architectural Studies
MS Bio E	Master of Science in Bioengineering
MS Bm E	Master of Science in Biomedical Engineering
MS Ch E	Master of Science in Chemical Engineering
MS Cp E	Master of Science in Computer Engineering
MS Eco	Master of Science in Economics
MS Econ	Master of Science in Economics
MS Ed	Master of Science in Education
MS Ed Admin	Master of Science in Educational Administration
MS El	Master of Science in Educational Leadership and Administration
MS En E	Master of Science in Environmental Engineering
MS Eng	Master of Science in Engineering
MS Engr	Master of Science in Engineering
MS Env E	Master of Science in Environmental Engineering
MS Exp Surg	Master of Science in Experimental Surgery
MS Mat SE	Master of Science in Material Science and Engineering
MS Met E	Master of Science in Metallurgical Engineering
MS Mgt	Master of Science in Management
MS Min	Master of Science in Mining
MS Min E	Master of Science in Mining Engineering
MS Mt E	Master of Science in Materials Engineering
MS Otol	Master of Science in Otolaryngology
MS Pet E	Master of Science in Petroleum Engineering
MS Sc	Master of Social Science
MS Sp Ed	Master of Science in Special Education
MS Stat	Master of Science in Statistics
MS Surg	Master of Science in Surgery
MS Tax	Master of Science in Taxation
MS Tc E	Master of Science in Telecommunications Engineering
MS-R	Master of Science (Research)
MSA	Master of School Administration

	Master of Science in Accountancy
	Master of Science in Accounting
	Master of Science in Administration
	Master of Science in Aeronautics
	Master of Science in Agriculture
	Master of Science in Analytics
	Master of Science in Anesthesia
	Master of Science in Architecture
	Master of Science in Aviation
	Master of Sports Administration
	Master of Surgical Assisting
MSAA	Master of Science in Astronautics and Aeronautics
MSABE	Master of Science in Agricultural and Biological Engineering
MSAC	Master of Science in Acupuncture
MSACC	Master of Science in Accounting
MSACS	Master of Science in Applied Computer Science
MSAE	Master of Science in Aeronautical Engineering
	Master of Science in Aerospace Engineering
	Master of Science in Applied Economics
	Master of Science in Applied Engineering
	Master of Science in Architectural Engineering
MSAEM	Master of Science in Aerospace Engineering and Mechanics
MSAF	Master of Science in Aviation Finance
MSAG	Master of Science in Applied Geosciences
MSAH	Master of Science in Allied Health
MSAL	Master of Sport Administration and Leadership
MSAM	Master of Science in Applied Mathematics
MSANR	Master of Science in Agriculture and Natural Resources
MSAS	Master of Science in Administrative Studies
	Master of Science in Applied Statistics
	Master of Science in Architectural Studies
MSAT	Master of Science in Accounting and Taxation
	Master of Science in Advanced Technology
	Master of Science in Athletic Training
MSB	Master of Science in Biotechnology
MSBA	Master of Science in Business Administration
	Master of Science in Business Analysis
MSBAE	Master of Science in Biological and Agricultural Engineering
	Master of Science in Biosystems and Agricultural Engineering
MSBCB	Master's in Bioinformatics and Computational Biology
MSBE	Master of Science in Biological Engineering
	Master of Science in Biomedical Engineering
MSBENG	Master of Science in Bioengineering
MSBH	Master of Science in Behavioral Health
MSBM	Master of Sport Business Management
MSBME	Master of Science in Biomedical Engineering
MSBMS	Master of Science in Basic Medical Science
MSBS	Master of Science in Biomedical Sciences
MSBTM	Master of Science in Biotechnology and Management
MSC	Master of Science in Commerce
	Master of Science in Communication
	Master of Science in Counseling
	Master of Science in Criminology
	Master of Strategic Communication
MSCC	Master of Science in Community Counseling
MSCD	Master of Science in Communication Disorders
	Master of Science in Community Development
MSCE	Master of Science in Chemistry Education
	Master of Science in Civil Engineering
	Master of Science in Clinical Epidemiology
	Master of Science in Computer Engineering
	Master of Science in Continuing Education
MSCEE	Master of Science in Civil and Environmental Engineering
MSCF	Master of Science in Computational Finance
MSCH	Master of Science in Chemical Engineering
MSChE	Master of Science in Chemical Engineering
MSCI	Master of Science in Clinical Investigation
MSCID	Master of Science in Community and International Development

MSCIS	Master of Science in Computer and Information Science
	Master of Science in Computer and Information Systems
	Master of Science in Computer Information Science
	Master of Science in Computer Information Systems
MSCIT	Master of Science in Computer Information Technology
MSCJ	Master of Science in Criminal Justice
MSCJA	Master of Science in Criminal Justice Administration
MSCJS	Master of Science in Crime and Justice Studies
MSCLS	Master of Science in Clinical Laboratory Studies
MSCM	Master of Science in Church Management
	Master of Science in Conflict Management
	Master of Science in Construction Management
	Master of Supply Chain Management
MSCMP	Master of Science in Cybersecurity Management and Policy
MSCNU	Master of Science in Clinical Nutrition
MSCP	Master of Science in Clinical Psychology
	Master of Science in Community Psychology
	Master of Science in Computer Engineering
	Master of Science in Counseling Psychology
MSCPE	Master of Science in Computer Engineering
MSCPharm	Master of Science in Pharmacy
MSCR	Master of Science in Clinical Research
MSCRP	Master of Science in City and Regional Planning
	Master of Science in Community and Regional Planning
MSCS	Master of Science in Clinical Science
	Master of Science in Computer Science
	Master of Science in Cyber Security
MSCSD	Master of Science in Communication Sciences and Disorders
MSCSE	Master of Science in Computer Science and Engineering
MSCTE	Master of Science in Career and Technical Education
MSD	Master of Science in Dentistry
	Master of Science in Design
	Master of Science in Dietetics
MSDM	Master of Security and Disaster Management
MSE	Master of Science Education
	Master of Science in Economics
	Master of Science in Education
	Master of Science in Engineering
	Master of Science in Engineering Management
	Master of Software Engineering
	Master of Special Education
	Master of Structural Engineering
MSECE	Master of Science in Electrical and Computer Engineering
MSED	Master of Sustainable Economic Development
MSEE	Master of Science in Electrical Engineering
	Master of Science in Environmental Engineering
MSEH	Master of Science in Environmental Health
MSEL	Master of Science in Educational Leadership
MSEM	Master of Science in Engineering and Management
	Master of Science in Engineering Management
	Master of Science in Engineering Mechanics
	Master of Science in Environmental Management
MSENE	Master of Science in Environmental Engineering
MSEO	Master of Science in Electro-Optics
MSES	Master of Science in Embedded Software Engineering
	Master of Science in Engineering Science
	Master of Science in Environmental Science
	Master of Science in Environmental Studies
	Master of Science in Exercise Science
MSESE	Master of Science in Energy Systems Engineering
MSET	Master of Science in Educational Technology

	Master of Science in Engineering Technology
MSEV	Master of Science in Environmental Engineering
MSF	Master of Science in Finance
	Master of Science in Forestry
MSFA	Master of Science in Financial Analysis
MSFCS	Master of Science in Family and Consumer Science
MSFE	Master of Science in Financial Engineering
MSFM	Master of Sustainable Forest Management
MSFOR	Master of Science in Forestry
MSFP	Master of Science in Financial Planning
MSFS	Master of Science in Financial Sciences
	Master of Science in Forensic Science
MSFSB	Master of Science in Financial Services and Banking
MSFT	Master of Science in Family Therapy
MSGC	Master of Science in Genetic Counseling
MSH	Master of Science in Health
	Master of Science in Hospice
MSHA	Master of Science in Health Administration
MSHCA	Master of Science in Health Care Administration
MSHCPM	Master of Science in Health Care Policy and Management
MSHE	Master of Science in Health Education
MSHES	Master of Science in Human Environmental Sciences
MSHFID	Master of Science in Human Factors in Information Design
MSHFS	Master of Science in Human Factors and Systems
MSHI	Master of Science in Health Informatics
MSHP	Master of Science in Health Professions
MSHR	Master of Science in Human Resources
MSHRL	Master of Science in Human Resource Leadership
MSHRM	Master of Science in Human Resource Management
MSHROD	Master of Science in Human Resources and Organizational Development
MSHS	Master of Science in Health Science
	Master of Science in Health Services
	Master of Science in Homeland Security
MSHSR	Master of Science in Human Security and Resilience
MSI	Master of Science in Information
	Master of Science in Instruction
	Master of System Integration
MSIA	Master of Science in Industrial Administration
	Master of Science in Information Assurance
MSIDM	Master of Science in Interior Design and Merchandising
MSIE	Master of Science in Industrial Engineering
MSIEM	Master of Science in Information Engineering and Management
MSIM	Master of Science in Industrial Management
	Master of Science in Information Management
	Master of Science in International Management
MSIMC	Master of Science in Integrated Marketing Communications
MSIMS	Master of Science in Identity Management and Security
MSIS	Master of Science in Information Science
	Master of Science in Information Studies
	Master of Science in Information Systems
	Master of Science in Interdisciplinary Studies
MSISE	Master of Science in Infrastructure Systems Engineering
MSISM	Master of Science in Information Systems Management
MSISPM	Master of Science in Information Security Policy and Management
MSIST	Master of Science in Information Systems Technology
MSIT	Master of Science in Industrial Technology
	Master of Science in Information Technology
	Master of Science in Instructional Technology
MSITM	Master of Science in Information Technology Management

MSJ	Master of Science in Journalism		Master of Science in Occupational Therapy
	Master of Science in Jurisprudence	MSP	Master of Science in Pharmacy
MSJC	Master of Social Justice and Criminology		Master of Science in Planning
MSJFP	Master of Science in Juvenile Forensic Psychology		Master of Speech Pathology
			Master of Sustainable Peacebuilding
MSJJ	Master of Science in Juvenile Justice	MSPA	Master of Science in Physician Assistant
MSJPS	Master of Science in Justice and Public Safety	MSPAS	Master of Science in Physician Assistant Studies
MSK	Master of Science in Kinesiology	MSPC	Master of Science in Professional Communications
MSL	Master in the Study of Law		
	Master of School Leadership	MSPE	Master of Science in Petroleum Engineering
	Master of Science in Leadership	MSPH	Master of Science in Public Health
	Master of Science in Limnology	MSPHR	Master of Science in Pharmacy
	Master of Sports Leadership	MSPM	Master of Science in Professional Management
	Master of Strategic Leadership		Master of Science in Project Management
	Master of Studies in Law	MSPNGE	Master of Science in Petroleum and Natural Gas Engineering
MSLA	Master of Science in Legal Administration		
MSLB	Master of Sports Law and Business	MSPPM	Master of Science in Public Policy and Management
MSLFS	Master of Science in Life Sciences	MSPS	Master of Science in Pharmaceutical Science
MSLP	Master of Speech-Language Pathology		Master of Science in Political Science
MSLS	Master of Science in Library Science		Master of Science in Psychological Services
MSLSCM	Master of Science in Logistics and Supply Chain Management	MSPT	Master of Science in Physical Therapy
MSLT	Master of Second Language Teaching	MSRA	Master of Science in Recreation Administration
MSM	Master of Sacred Ministry	MSRE	Master of Science in Real Estate
	Master of Sacred Music		Master of Science in Religious Education
	Master of School Mathematics	MSRED	Master of Science in Real Estate Development
	Master of Science in Management		Master of Sustainable Real Estate Development
	Master of Science in Medicine	MSRLS	Master of Science in Recreation and Leisure Studies
	Master of Science in Organization Management		
	Master of Security Management	MSRM	Master of Science in Risk Management
	Master of Strategic Ministry	MSRMP	Master of Science in Radiological Medical Physics
	Master of Supply Management		
MSMA	Master of Science in Marketing Analysis	MSRS	Master of Science in Radiological Sciences
MSMAE	Master of Science in Materials Engineering		Master of Science in Rehabilitation Science
MSMC	Master of Science in Management and Communications	MSS	Master of Security Studies
			Master of Social Science
	Master of Science in Mass Communications		Master of Social Services
MSME	Master of Science in Mathematics Education		Master of Sports Science
	Master of Science in Mechanical Engineering		Master of Strategic Studies
	Master of Science in Medical Ethics		Master's in Statistical Science
MSMHC	Master of Science in Mental Health Counseling	MSSA	Master of Science in Social Administration
MSMIT	Master of Science in Management and Information Technology	MSSCM	Master of Science in Supply Chain Management
		MSSD	Master of Arts in Software Driven Systems Design
MSMLS	Master of Science in Medical Laboratory Science		
			Master of Science in Sustainable Design
MSMOT	Master of Science in Management of Technology	MSSE	Master of Science in Software Engineering
			Master of Science in Special Education
MSMP	Master of Science in Medical Physics	MSSEM	Master of Science in Systems and Engineering Management
	Master of Science in Molecular Pathology		
MSMS	Master of Science in Management Science	MSSI	Master of Science in Security Informatics
	Master of Science in Marine Science		Master of Science in Strategic Intelligence
	Master of Science in Medical Sciences	MSSIS	Master of Science in Security and Intelligence Studies
MSMSE	Master of Science in Manufacturing Systems Engineering		
		MSSL	Master of Science in School Leadership
	Master of Science in Material Science and Engineering	MSSLP	Master of Science in Speech-Language Pathology
	Master of Science in Material Science Engineering	MSSM	Master of Science in Sports Medicine
			Master of Science in Systems Management
	Master of Science in Mathematics and Science Education	MSSP	Master of Science in Social Policy
		MSSS	Master of Science in Safety Science
MSMus	Master of Sacred Music		Master of Science in Systems Science
MSN	Master of Science in Nursing	MSST	Master of Science in Security Technologies
MSNA	Master of Science in Nurse Anesthesia	MSSW	Master of Science in Social Work
MSNE	Master of Science in Nuclear Engineering	MSSWE	Master of Science in Software Engineering
MSNS	Master of Science in Natural Science	MST	Master of Science and Technology
	Master of Science in Nutritional Science		Master of Science in Taxation
MSOD	Master of Science in Organization Development		Master of Science in Teaching
			Master of Science in Technology
	Master of Science in Organizational Development		Master of Science in Telecommunications
			Master of Science Teaching
MSOEE	Master of Science in Outdoor and Environmental Education	MSTC	Master of Science in Technical Communication
			Master of Science in Telecommunications
MSOES	Master of Science in Occupational Ergonomics and Safety	MSTCM	Master of Science in Traditional Chinese Medicine
MSOH	Master of Science in Occupational Health	MSTE	Master of Science in Telecommunications Engineering
MSOL	Master of Science in Organizational Leadership		
MSOM	Master of Science in Oriental Medicine		Master of Science in Transportation Engineering
MSOR	Master of Science in Operations Research		
MSOT	Master of Science in Occupational Technology	MSTL	Master of Science in Teacher Leadership

MSTM	Master of Science in Technology Management
	Master of Science in Transfusion Medicine
MSTOM	Master of Science in Traditional Oriental Medicine
MSUASE	Master of Science in Unmanned and Autonomous Systems Engineering
MSUD	Master of Science in Urban Design
MSUS	Master of Science in Urban Studies
MSW	Master of Social Work
MSWE	Master of Software Engineering
MSWREE	Master of Science in Water Resources and Environmental Engineering
MT	Master of Taxation
	Master of Teaching
	Master of Technology
	Master of Textiles
MTA	Master of Tax Accounting
	Master of Teaching Arts
	Master of Tourism Administration
MTC	Master of Technical Communications
MTCM	Master of Traditional Chinese Medicine
MTD	Master of Training and Development
MTE	Master in Educational Technology
	Master of Technological Entrepreneurship
MTESOL	Master in Teaching English to Speakers of Other Languages
MTHM	Master of Tourism and Hospitality Management
MTI	Master of Information Technology
MTID	Master of Tangible Interaction Design
MTL	Master of Talmudic Law
MTM	Master of Technology Management
	Master of Telecommunications Management
	Master of the Teaching of Mathematics
	Master of Transformative Ministry
	Master of Translational Medicine
MTMH	Master of Tropical Medicine and Hygiene
MTMS	Master in Teaching Mathematics and Science
MTOM	Master of Traditional Oriental Medicine
MTPC	Master of Technical and Professional Communication
MTR	Master of Translational Research
MTS	Master of Theatre Studies
	Master of Theological Studies
MTW	Master of Teaching Writing
MTWM	Master of Trust and Wealth Management
MUA	Master of Urban Affairs
MUAP	Master's of Urban Affairs and Policy
MUCD	Master of Urban and Community Design
MUD	Master of Urban Design
MUDS	Master of Urban Design Studies
MUEP	Master of Urban and Environmental Planning
MUP	Master of Urban Planning
MUPD	Master of Urban Planning and Development
MUPP	Master of Urban Planning and Policy
MUPRED	Master of Urban Planning and Real Estate Development
MURP	Master of Urban and Regional Planning
	Master of Urban and Rural Planning
MURPL	Master of Urban and Regional Planning
MUS	Master of Urban Studies
Mus M	Master of Music
MUSA	Master of Urban Spatial Analytics
MVP	Master of Voice Pedagogy
MVS	Master of Visual Studies
MWBS	Master of Won Buddhist Studies
MWC	Master of Wildlife Conservation
MWR	Master of Water Resources
MWS	Master of Women's Studies
	Master of Worship Studies
MWSc	Master of Wildlife Science
Nav Arch	Naval Architecture
Naval E	Naval Engineer
ND	Doctor of Naturopathic Medicine
	Doctor of Nursing
NE	Nuclear Engineer
Nuc E	Nuclear Engineer
OD	Doctor of Optometry
OTD	Doctor of Occupational Therapy
PBME	Professional Master of Biomedical Engineering
PC	Performer's Certificate
PD	Professional Diploma
PGC	Post-Graduate Certificate
PGD	Postgraduate Diploma
Ph L	Licentiate of Philosophy
Pharm D	Doctor of Pharmacy
PhD	Doctor of Philosophy
PhD Otol	Doctor of Philosophy in Otolaryngology
PhD Surg	Doctor of Philosophy in Surgery
PhDEE	Doctor of Philosophy in Electrical Engineering
PMBA	Professional Master of Business Administration
PMC	Post Master Certificate
PMD	Post-Master's Diploma
PMS	Professional Master of Science
	Professional Master's
Post-Doctoral MS	Post-Doctoral Master of Science
Post-MSN Certificate	Post-Master of Science in Nursing Certificate
PPDPT	Postprofessional Doctor of Physical Therapy
Pro-MS	Professional Science Master's
Professional MA	Professional Master of Arts
Professional MBA	Professional Master of Business Administration
Professional MS	Professional Master of Science
PSM	Professional Master of Science
	Professional Science Master's
Psy D	Doctor of Psychology
Psy M	Master of Psychology
Psy S	Specialist in Psychology
Psya D	Doctor of Psychoanalysis
S Psy S	Specialist in Psychological Services
Sc D	Doctor of Science
Sc M	Master of Science
SCCT	Specialist in Community College Teaching
ScDPT	Doctor of Physical Therapy Science
SD	Specialist Degree
SJD	Doctor of Juridical Sciences
SLPD	Doctor of Speech-Language Pathology
SM	Master of Science
SM Arch S	Master of Science in Architectural Studies
SMACT	Master of Science in Art, Culture and Technology
SMBT	Master of Science in Building Technology
SP	Specialist Degree
Sp Ed	Specialist in Education
Sp LIS	Specialist in Library and Information Science
SPA	Specialist in Arts
Spec	Specialist's Certificate
Spec M	Specialist in Music
Spt	Specialist Degree
SSP	Specialist in School Psychology
STB	Bachelor of Sacred Theology
STD	Doctor of Sacred Theology
STL	Licentiate of Sacred Theology
STM	Master of Sacred Theology
tDACM	Transitional Doctor of Acupuncture and Chinese Medicine
TDPT	Transitional Doctor of Physical Therapy
Th D	Doctor of Theology
Th M	Master of Theology
TOTD	Transitional Doctor of Occupational Therapy
VMD	Doctor of Veterinary Medicine
WEMBA	Weekend Executive Master of Business Administration
XMA	Executive Master of Arts

INDEXES

Profiles, Displays, and Close-Ups

Peterson's Graduate & Professional Programs: An Overview 2020

Directories and Subject Areas

Following is an alphabetical listing of directories and subject areas. Also listed are cross-references for subject area names not used in the directory structure of the guides, for example, "City and Regional Planning (see Urban and Regional Planning)"

Graduate Programs in the Humanities, Arts & Social Sciences

Addictions/Substance Abuse Counseling
Administration (see Arts Administration; Public Administration)
African-American Studies
African Languages and Literatures (see African Studies)
African Studies
Agribusiness (see Agricultural Economics and Agribusiness)
Agricultural Economics and Agribusiness
Alcohol Abuse Counseling (see Addictions/Substance Abuse Counseling)
American Indian/Native American Studies
American Studies
Anthropology
Applied Arts and Design—General
Applied Behavior Analysis
Applied Economics
Applied History (see Public History)
Applied Psychology
Applied Social Research
Arabic (see Near and Middle Eastern Languages)
Arab Studies (see Near and Middle Eastern Studies)
Archaeology
Architectural History
Architecture
Archives Administration (see Public History)
Area and Cultural Studies (see African-American Studies; African Studies; American Indian/Native American Studies; American Studies; Asian-American Studies; Asian Studies; Canadian Studies; Cultural Studies; East European and Russian Studies; Ethnic Studies; Folklore; Gender Studies; Hispanic Studies; Holocaust Studies; Jewish Studies; Latin American Studies; Near and Middle Eastern Studies; Northern Studies; Pacific Area/Pacific Rim Studies; Western European Studies; Women's Studies)
Art/Fine Arts
Art History
Arts Administration
Arts Journalism
Art Therapy
Asian-American Studies
Asian Languages
Asian Studies
Behavioral Sciences (see Psychology)
Bible Studies (see Religion; Theology)
Biological Anthropology
Black Studies (see African-American Studies)
Broadcasting (see Communication; Film, Television, and Video Production)
Broadcast Journalism
Building Science
Canadian Studies
Celtic Languages
Ceramics (see Art/Fine Arts)
Child and Family Studies
Child Development
Chinese
Chinese Studies (see Asian Languages; Asian Studies)
Christian Studies (see Missions and Missiology; Religion; Theology)
Cinema (see Film, Television, and Video Production)
City and Regional Planning (see Urban and Regional Planning)

Classical Languages and Literatures (see Classics)
Classics
Clinical Psychology
Clothing and Textiles
Cognitive Psychology (see Psychology—General; Cognitive Sciences)
Cognitive Sciences
Communication—General
Community Affairs (see Urban and Regional Planning; Urban Studies)
Community Planning (see Architecture; Environmental Design; Urban and Regional Planning; Urban Design; Urban Studies)
Community Psychology (see Social Psychology)
Comparative and Interdisciplinary Arts
Comparative Literature
Composition (see Music)
Computer Art and Design
Conflict Resolution and Mediation/Peace Studies
Consumer Economics
Corporate and Organizational Communication
Corrections (see Criminal Justice and Criminology)
Counseling (see Counseling Psychology; Pastoral Ministry and Counseling)
Counseling Psychology
Crafts (see Art/Fine Arts)
Creative Arts Therapies (see Art Therapy; Therapies—Dance, Drama, and Music)
Criminal Justice and Criminology
Cultural Anthropology
Cultural Studies
Dance
Decorative Arts
Demography and Population Studies
Design (see Applied Arts and Design; Architecture; Art/Fine Arts; Environmental Design; Graphic Design; Industrial Design; Interior Design; Textile Design; Urban Design)
Developmental Psychology
Diplomacy (see International Affairs)
Disability Studies
Drama Therapy (see Therapies—Dance, Drama, and Music)
Dramatic Arts (see Theater)
Drawing (see Art/Fine Arts)
Drug Abuse Counseling (see Addictions/Substance Abuse Counseling)
Drug and Alcohol Abuse Counseling (see Addictions/Substance Abuse Counseling)
East Asian Studies (see Asian Studies)
East European and Russian Studies
Economic Development
Economics
Educational Theater (see Theater; Therapies—Dance, Drama, and Music)
Emergency Management
English
Environmental Design
Ethics
Ethnic Studies
Ethnomusicology (see Music)
Experimental Psychology
Family and Consumer Sciences—General
Family Studies (see Child and Family Studies)
Family Therapy (see Child and Family Studies; Clinical Psychology; Counseling Psychology; Marriage and Family Therapy)
Filmmaking (see Film, Television, and Video Production)
Film Studies (see Film, Television, and Video Production)
Film, Television, and Video Production
Film, Television, and Video Theory and Criticism
Fine Arts (see Art/Fine Arts)
Folklore
Foreign Languages (see specific language)

Foreign Service (*see* International Affairs; International Development)
Forensic Psychology
Forensic Sciences
Forensics (*see* Speech and Interpersonal Communication)
French
Gender Studies
General Studies (*see* Liberal Studies)
Genetic Counseling
Geographic Information Systems
Geography
German
Gerontology
Graphic Design
Greek (*see* Classics)
Health Communication
Health Psychology
Hebrew (*see* Near and Middle Eastern Languages)
Hebrew Studies (*see* Jewish Studies)
Hispanic and Latin American Languages
Hispanic Studies
Historic Preservation
History
History of Art (*see* Art History)
History of Medicine
History of Science and Technology
Holocaust and Genocide Studies
Home Economics (*see* Family and Consumer Sciences—General)
Homeland Security
Household Economics, Sciences, and Management (*see* Family and Consumer Sciences—General)
Human Development
Humanities
Illustration
Industrial and Labor Relations
Industrial and Organizational Psychology
Industrial Design
Interdisciplinary Studies
Interior Design
International Affairs
International Development
International Economics
International Service (*see* International Affairs; International Development)
International Trade Policy
Internet and Interactive Multimedia
Interpersonal Communication (*see* Speech and Interpersonal Communication)
Interpretation (*see* Translation and Interpretation)
Islamic Studies (*see* Near and Middle Eastern Studies; Religion)
Italian
Japanese
Japanese Studies (*see* Asian Languages; Asian Studies; Japanese)
Jewelry (*see* Art/Fine Arts)
Jewish Studies
Journalism
Judaic Studies (*see* Jewish Studies; Religion)
Labor Relations (*see* Industrial and Labor Relations)
Landscape Architecture
Latin American Studies
Latin (*see* Classics)
Law Enforcement (*see* Criminal Justice and Criminology)
Liberal Studies
Lighting Design
Linguistics
Literature (*see* Classics; Comparative Literature; specific language)
Marriage and Family Therapy
Mass Communication
Media Studies
Medical Illustration
Medieval and Renaissance Studies
Metalsmithing (*see* Art/Fine Arts)
Middle Eastern Studies (*see* Near and Middle Eastern Studies)
Military and Defense Studies

Mineral Economics
Ministry (*see* Pastoral Ministry and Counseling; Theology)
Missions and Missiology
Motion Pictures (*see* Film, Television, and Video Production)
Museum Studies
Music
Musicology (*see* Music)
Music Therapy (*see* Therapies—Dance, Drama, and Music)
National Security
Native American Studies (*see* American Indian/Native American Studies)
Near and Middle Eastern Languages
Near and Middle Eastern Studies
Northern Studies
Organizational Psychology (*see* Industrial and Organizational Psychology)
Oriental Languages (*see* Asian Languages)
Oriental Studies (*see* Asian Studies)
Pacific Area/Pacific Rim Studies
Painting (*see* Art/Fine Arts)
Pastoral Ministry and Counseling
Philanthropic Studies
Philosophy
Photography
Playwriting (*see* Theater; Writing)
Policy Studies (*see* Public Policy)
Political Science
Population Studies (*see* Demography and Population Studies)
Portuguese
Printmaking (*see* Art/Fine Arts)
Product Design (*see* Industrial Design)
Psychoanalysis and Psychotherapy
Psychology—General
Public Administration
Public Affairs
Public History
Public Policy
Public Speaking (*see* Mass Communication; Rhetoric; Speech and Interpersonal Communication)
Publishing
Regional Planning (*see* Architecture; Urban and Regional Planning; Urban Design; Urban Studies)
Rehabilitation Counseling
Religion
Renaissance Studies (*see* Medieval and Renaissance Studies)
Rhetoric
Romance Languages
Romance Literatures (*see* Romance Languages)
Rural Planning and Studies
Rural Sociology
Russian
Scandinavian Languages
School Psychology
Sculpture (*see* Art/Fine Arts)
Security Administration (*see* Criminal Justice and Criminology)
Slavic Languages
Slavic Studies (*see* East European and Russian Studies; Slavic Languages)
Social Psychology
Social Sciences
Sociology
Southeast Asian Studies (*see* Asian Studies)
Soviet Studies (*see* East European and Russian Studies; Russian)
Spanish
Speech and Interpersonal Communication
Sport Psychology
Studio Art (*see* Art/Fine Arts)
Substance Abuse Counseling (*see* Addictions/Substance Abuse Counseling)
Survey Methodology
Sustainable Development
Technical Communication
Technical Writing

Telecommunications (*see* Film, Television, and Video Production)
Television (*see* Film, Television, and Video Production)
Textile Design
Textiles (*see* Clothing and Textiles; Textile Design)
Thanatology
Theater
Theater Arts (*see* Theater)
Theology
Therapies—Dance, Drama, and Music
Translation and Interpretation
Transpersonal and Humanistic Psychology
Urban and Regional Planning
Urban Design
Urban Planning (*see* Architecture; Urban and Regional Planning; Urban Design; Urban Studies)
Urban Studies
Video (*see* Film, Television, and Video Production)
Visual Arts (*see* Applied Arts and Design; Art/Fine Arts; Film, Television, and Video Production; Graphic Design; Illustration; Photography)
Western European Studies
Women's Studies
World Wide Web (*see* Internet and Interactive Multimedia)
Writing

Graduate Programs in the Biological/Biomedical Sciences & Health-Related Medical Professions

Acupuncture and Oriental Medicine
Acute Care/Critical Care Nursing Administration (*see* Health Services Management and Hospital Administration; Nursing and Healthcare Administration; Pharmaceutical Administration)
Adult Nursing
Advanced Practice Nursing (*see* Family Nurse Practitioner Studies)
Allied Health—General
Allied Health Professions (*see* Clinical Laboratory Sciences/Medical Technology; Clinical Research; Communication Disorders; Dental Hygiene; Emergency Medical Services; Occupational Therapy; Physical Therapy; Physician Assistant Studies; Rehabilitation Sciences)
Allopathic Medicine
Anatomy
Anesthesiologist Assistant Studies
Animal Behavior
Bacteriology
Behavioral Sciences (*see* Biopsychology; Neuroscience; Zoology)
Biochemistry
Bioethics
Biological and Biomedical Sciences—General Biological Chemistry (*see* Biochemistry)
Biological Oceanography (*see* Marine Biology)
Biophysics
Biopsychology
Botany
Breeding (*see* Botany; Plant Biology; Genetics)
Cancer Biology/Oncology
Cardiovascular Sciences
Cell Biology
Cellular Physiology (*see* Cell Biology; Physiology)
Child-Care Nursing (*see* Maternal and Child/Neonatal Nursing)
Chiropractic
Clinical Laboratory Sciences/Medical Technology
Clinical Research
Community Health
Community Health Nursing
Computational Biology
Conservation (*see* Conservation Biology; Environmental Biology)
Conservation Biology
Crop Sciences (*see* Botany; Plant Biology)

Cytology (*see* Cell Biology)
Dental and Oral Surgery (*see* Oral and Dental Sciences)
Dental Assistant Studies (*see* Dental Hygiene)
Dental Hygiene
Dental Services (*see* Dental Hygiene)
Dentistry
Developmental Biology Dietetics (*see* Nutrition)
Ecology
Embryology (*see* Developmental Biology)
Emergency Medical Services
Endocrinology (*see* Physiology)
Entomology
Environmental Biology
Environmental and Occupational Health
Epidemiology
Evolutionary Biology
Family Nurse Practitioner Studies
Foods (*see* Nutrition)
Forensic Nursing
Genetics
Genomic Sciences
Gerontological Nursing
Health Physics/Radiological Health
Health Promotion
Health-Related Professions (*see* individual allied health professions)
Health Services Management and Hospital Administration
Health Services Research
Histology (*see* Anatomy; Cell Biology)
HIV/AIDS Nursing
Hospice Nursing
Hospital Administration (*see* Health Services Management and Hospital Administration)
Human Genetics
Immunology
Industrial Hygiene
Infectious Diseases
International Health
Laboratory Medicine (*see* Clinical Laboratory Sciences/Medical Technology; Immunology; Microbiology; Pathology)
Life Sciences (*see* Biological and Biomedical Sciences)
Marine Biology
Maternal and Child Health
Maternal and Child/Neonatal Nursing
Medical Imaging
Medical Microbiology
Medical Nursing (*see* Medical/Surgical Nursing)
Medical Physics
Medical/Surgical Nursing
Medical Technology (*see* Clinical Laboratory Sciences/Medical Technology)
Medical Sciences (*see* Biological and Biomedical Sciences)
Medical Science Training Programs (*see* Biological and Biomedical Sciences)
Medicinal and Pharmaceutical Chemistry
Medicinal Chemistry (*see* Medicinal and Pharmaceutical Chemistry)
Medicine (*see* Allopathic Medicine; Naturopathic Medicine; Osteopathic Medicine; Podiatric Medicine)
Microbiology
Midwifery (*see* Nurse Midwifery)
Molecular Biology
Molecular Biophysics
Molecular Genetics
Molecular Medicine
Molecular Pathogenesis
Molecular Pathology
Molecular Pharmacology
Molecular Physiology
Molecular Toxicology
Naturopathic Medicine
Neural Sciences (*see* Biopsychology; Neurobiology; Neuroscience)
Neurobiology
Neuroendocrinology (*see* Biopsychology; Neurobiology; Neuroscience; Physiology)

Neuropharmacology (*see* Biopsychology; Neurobiology; Neuroscience; Pharmacology)

Neurophysiology (*see* Biopsychology; Neurobiology; Neuroscience; Physiology)

Neuroscience

Nuclear Medical Technology (*see* Clinical Laboratory Sciences/ Medical Technology)

Nurse Anesthesia

Nurse Midwifery

Nurse Practitioner Studies (*see* Family Nurse Practitioner Studies)

Nursing Administration (*see* Nursing and Healthcare Administration)

Nursing and Healthcare Administration

Nursing Education

Nursing—General

Nursing Informatics

Nutrition

Occupational Health (*see* Environmental and Occupational Health; Occupational Health Nursing)

Occupational Health Nursing

Occupational Therapy

Oncology (*see* Cancer Biology/Oncology)

Oncology Nursing

Optometry

Oral and Dental Sciences

Oral Biology (*see* Oral and Dental Sciences)

Oral Pathology (*see* Oral and Dental Sciences)

Organismal Biology (*see* Biological and Biomedical Sciences; Zoology)

Oriental Medicine and Acupuncture (*see* Acupuncture and Oriental Medicine)

Orthodontics (*see* Oral and Dental Sciences)

Osteopathic Medicine

Parasitology

Pathobiology

Pathology

Pediatric Nursing

Pedontics (*see* Oral and Dental Sciences)

Perfusion

Pharmaceutical Administration

Pharmaceutical Chemistry (*see* Medicinal and Pharmaceutical Chemistry)

Pharmaceutical Sciences

Pharmacology

Pharmacy

Photobiology of Cells and Organelles (*see* Botany; Cell Biology; Plant Biology)

Physical Therapy

Physician Assistant Studies

Physiological Optics (*see* Vision Sciences)

Podiatric Medicine

Preventive Medicine (*see* Community Health and Public Health)

Physiological Optics (*see* Physiology)

Physiology

Plant Biology

Plant Molecular Biology

Plant Pathology

Plant Physiology

Pomology (*see* Botany; Plant Biology)

Psychiatric Nursing

Public Health—General

Public Health Nursing (*see* Community Health Nursing)

Psychiatric Nursing

Psychobiology (*see* Biopsychology)

Psychopharmacology (*see* Biopsychology; Neuroscience; Pharmacology)

Radiation Biology

Radiological Health (*see* Health Physics/Radiological Health)

Rehabilitation Nursing

Rehabilitation Sciences

Rehabilitation Therapy (*see* Physical Therapy)

Reproductive Biology

School Nursing

Sociobiology (*see* Evolutionary Biology)

Structural Biology

Surgical Nursing (*see* Medical/Surgical Nursing)

Systems Biology

Teratology

Therapeutics

Theoretical Biology (*see* Biological and Biomedical Sciences)

Therapeutics (*see* Pharmaceutical Sciences; Pharmacology; Pharmacy)

Toxicology

Transcultural Nursing

Translational Biology

Tropical Medicine (*see* Parasitology)

Veterinary Medicine

Veterinary Sciences

Virology

Vision Sciences

Wildlife Biology (*see* Zoology)

Women's Health Nursing

Zoology

Graduate Programs in the Physical Sciences, Mathematics, Agricultural Sciences, the Environment & Natural Resources

Acoustics

Agricultural Sciences

Agronomy and Soil Sciences

Analytical Chemistry

Animal Sciences

Applied Mathematics

Applied Physics

Applied Statistics

Aquaculture

Astronomy

Astrophysical Sciences (*see* Astrophysics; Atmospheric Sciences; Meteorology; Planetary and Space Sciences)

Astrophysics

Atmospheric Sciences

Biological Oceanography (*see* Marine Affairs; Marine Sciences; Oceanography)

Biomathematics

Biometry

Biostatistics

Chemical Physics

Chemistry

Computational Sciences

Condensed Matter Physics

Dairy Science (*see* Animal Sciences)

Earth Sciences (*see* Geosciences)

Environmental Management and Policy

Environmental Sciences

Environmental Studies (*see* Environmental Management and Policy)

Experimental Statistics (*see* Statistics)

Fish, Game, and Wildlife Management

Food Science and Technology

Forestry

General Science (*see* specific topics)

Geochemistry

Geodetic Sciences

Geological Engineering (*see* Geology)

Geological Sciences (*see* Geology)

Geology

Geophysical Fluid Dynamics (*see* Geophysics)

Geophysics

Geosciences

Horticulture

Hydrogeology

Hydrology

Inorganic Chemistry

Limnology

Marine Affairs

Marine Geology

Marine Sciences

Marine Studies (*see* Marine Affairs; Marine Geology; Marine Sciences; Oceanography)
Mathematical and Computational Finance
Mathematical Physics
Mathematical Statistics (*see* Applied Statistics; Statistics)
Mathematics
Meteorology
Mineralogy
Natural Resource Management (*see* Environmental Management and Policy; Natural Resources)
Natural Resources
Nuclear Physics (*see* Physics)
Ocean Engineering (*see* Marine Affairs; Marine Geology; Marine Sciences; Oceanography)
Oceanography
Optical Sciences
Optical Technologies (*see* Optical Sciences)
Optics (*see* Applied Physics; Optical Sciences; Physics)
Organic Chemistry
Paleontology
Paper Chemistry (*see* Chemistry)
Photonics
Physical Chemistry
Physics
Planetary and Space Sciences
Plant Sciences
Plasma Physics
Poultry Science (*see* Animal Sciences)
Radiological Physics (*see* Physics)
Range Management (*see* Range Science)
Range Science
Resource Management (*see* Environmental Management and Policy; Natural Resources)
Solid-Earth Sciences (*see* Geosciences)
Space Sciences (*see* Planetary and Space Sciences)
Statistics
Theoretical Chemistry
Theoretical Physics
Viticulture and Enology
Water Resources

Graduate Programs in Engineering & Applied Sciences

Aeronautical Engineering (*see* Aerospace/Aeronautical Engineering)
Aerospace/Aeronautical Engineering
Aerospace Studies (*see* Aerospace/Aeronautical Engineering)
Agricultural Engineering
Applied Mechanics (*see* Mechanics)
Applied Science and Technology
Architectural Engineering
Artificial Intelligence/Robotics
Astronautical Engineering (*see* Aerospace/Aeronautical Engineering)
Automotive Engineering
Aviation
Biochemical Engineering
Bioengineering
Bioinformatics
Biological Engineering (*see* Bioengineering)
Biomedical Engineering
Biosystems Engineering
Biotechnology
Ceramic Engineering (*see* Ceramic Sciences and Engineering)
Ceramic Sciences and Engineering
Ceramics (*see* Ceramic Sciences and Engineering)
Chemical Engineering
Civil Engineering
Computer and Information Systems Security
Computer Engineering
Computer Science
Computing Technology (*see* Computer Science)
Construction Engineering

Construction Management
Database Systems
Electrical Engineering
Electronic Materials
Electronics Engineering (*see* Electrical Engineering)
Energy and Power Engineering
Energy Management and Policy
Engineering and Applied Sciences
Engineering and Public Affairs (*see* Technology and Public Policy)
Engineering and Public Policy (*see* Energy Management and Policy; Technology and Public Policy)
Engineering Design
Engineering Management
Engineering Mechanics (*see* Mechanics)
Engineering Metallurgy (*see* Metallurgical Engineering and Metallurgy)
Engineering Physics
Environmental Design (*see* Environmental Engineering)
Environmental Engineering
Ergonomics and Human Factors
Financial Engineering
Fire Protection Engineering
Food Engineering (*see* Agricultural Engineering)
Game Design and Development
Gas Engineering (*see* Petroleum Engineering)
Geological Engineering
Geophysics Engineering (*see* Geological Engineering)
Geotechnical Engineering
Hazardous Materials Management
Health Informatics
Health Systems (*see* Safety Engineering; Systems Engineering)
Highway Engineering (*see* Transportation and Highway Engineering)
Human-Computer Interaction
Human Factors (*see* Ergonomics and Human Factors)
Hydraulics
Hydrology (*see* Water Resources Engineering)
Industrial Engineering (*see* Industrial/Management Engineering)
Industrial/Management Engineering
Information Science
Internet Engineering
Macromolecular Science (*see* Polymer Science and Engineering)
Management Engineering (*see* Engineering Management; Industrial/Management Engineering)
Management of Technology
Manufacturing Engineering
Marine Engineering (*see* Civil Engineering)
Materials Engineering
Materials Sciences
Mechanical Engineering
Mechanics
Medical Informatics
Metallurgical Engineering and Metallurgy
Metallurgy (*see* Metallurgical Engineering and Metallurgy)
Mineral/Mining Engineering
Modeling and Simulation
Nanotechnology
Nuclear Engineering
Ocean Engineering
Operations Research
Paper and Pulp Engineering
Petroleum Engineering
Pharmaceutical Engineering
Plastics Engineering (*see* Polymer Science and Engineering)
Polymer Science and Engineering
Public Policy (*see* Energy Management and Policy; Technology and Public Policy)
Reliability Engineering
Robotics (*see* Artificial Intelligence/Robotics)
Safety Engineering
Software Engineering
Solid-State Sciences (*see* Materials Sciences)
Structural Engineering
Surveying Science and Engineering

Systems Analysis (*see* Systems Engineering)
Systems Engineering
Systems Science
Technology and Public Policy
Telecommunications
Telecommunications Management
Textile Sciences and Engineering
Textiles (*see* Textile Sciences and Engineering)
Transportation and Highway Engineering
Urban Systems Engineering (*see* Systems Engineering)
Waste Management (*see* Hazardous Materials Management)
Water Resources Engineering

Graduate Programs in Business, Education, Information Studies, Law & Social Work

Accounting
Actuarial Science
Adult Education
Advertising and Public Relations
Agricultural Education
Alcohol Abuse Counseling (*see* Counselor Education)
Archival Management and Studies
Art Education
Athletics Administration (*see* Kinesiology and Movement Studies)
Athletic Training and Sports Medicine
Audiology (*see* Communication Disorders)
Aviation Management
Banking (*see* Finance and Banking)
Business Administration and Management—General
Business Education
Communication Disorders
Community College Education
Computer Education
Continuing Education (*see* Adult Education)
Counseling (*see* Counselor Education)
Counselor Education
Curriculum and Instruction
Developmental Education
Distance Education Development
Drug Abuse Counseling (*see* Counselor Education)
Early Childhood Education
Educational Leadership and Administration
Educational Measurement and Evaluation
Educational Media/Instructional Technology
Educational Policy
Educational Psychology
Education—General
Education of the Blind (*see* Special Education)
Education of the Deaf (*see* Special Education)
Education of the Gifted
Education of the Hearing Impaired (*see* Special Education)
Education of the Learning Disabled (*see* Special Education)
Education of the Mentally Retarded (*see* Special Education)
Education of the Physically Handicapped (*see* Special Education)
Education of Students with Severe/Multiple Disabilities
Education of the Visually Handicapped (*see* Special Education)
Electronic Commerce
Elementary Education
English as a Second Language
English Education
Entertainment Management
Entrepreneurship
Environmental Education
Environmental Law
Exercise and Sports Science
Exercise Physiology (*see* Kinesiology and Movement Studies)
Facilities and Entertainment Management
Finance and Banking

Food Services Management (*see* Hospitality Management)
Foreign Languages Education
Foundations and Philosophy of Education
Guidance and Counseling (*see* Counselor Education)
Health Education
Health Law
Hearing Sciences (*see* Communication Disorders)
Higher Education
Home Economics Education
Hospitality Management
Hotel Management (*see* Travel and Tourism)
Human Resources Development
Human Resources Management
Human Services
Industrial Administration (*see* Industrial and Manufacturing Management)
Industrial and Manufacturing Management
Industrial Education (*see* Vocational and Technical Education)
Information Studies
Instructional Technology (*see* Educational Media/Instructional Technology)
Insurance
Intellectual Property Law
International and Comparative Education
International Business
International Commerce (*see* International Business)
International Economics (*see* International Business)
International Trade (*see* International Business)
Investment and Securities (*see* Business Administration and Management; Finance and Banking; Investment Management)
Investment Management
Junior College Education (*see* Community College Education)
Kinesiology and Movement Studies
Law
Legal and Justice Studies
Leisure Services (*see* Recreation and Park Management)
Leisure Studies
Library Science
Logistics
Management (*see* Business Administration and Management)
Management Information Systems
Management Strategy and Policy
Marketing
Marketing Research
Mathematics Education
Middle School Education
Movement Studies (*see* Kinesiology and Movement Studies)
Multilingual and Multicultural Education
Museum Education
Music Education
Nonprofit Management
Nursery School Education (*see* Early Childhood Education)
Occupational Education (*see* Vocational and Technical Education)
Organizational Behavior
Organizational Management
Parks Administration (*see* Recreation and Park Management)
Personnel (*see* Human Resources Development; Human Resources Management; Organizational Behavior; Organizational Management; Student Affairs)
Philosophy of Education (*see* Foundations and Philosophy of Education)
Physical Education
Project Management
Public Relations (*see* Advertising and Public Relations)
Quality Management
Quantitative Analysis
Reading Education
Real Estate
Recreation and Park Management
Recreation Therapy (*see* Recreation and Park Management)
Religious Education
Remedial Education (*see* Special Education)
Restaurant Administration (*see* Hospitality Management)

Science Education
Secondary Education
Social Sciences Education
Social Studies Education (*see* Social Sciences Education)
Social Work
Special Education
Speech-Language Pathology and Audiology (*see* Communication Disorders)
Sports Management
Sports Medicine (*see* Athletic Training and Sports Medicine)
Sports Psychology and Sociology (*see* Kinesiology and Movement Studies)
Student Affairs
Substance Abuse Counseling (*see* Counselor Education)

Supply Chain Management
Sustainability Management
Systems Management (*see* Management Information Systems)
Taxation
Teacher Education (*see* specific subject areas)
Teaching English as a Second Language (*see* English as a Second Language)
Technical Education (*see* Vocational and Technical Education)
Transportation Management
Travel and Tourism
Urban Education
Vocational and Technical Education
Vocational Counseling (*see* Counselor Education)

NOTES

NOTES

NOTES

NOTES

NOTES

NOTES

NOTES

NOTES

NOTES

NOTES

NOTES

NOTES

NOTES

NOTES

NOTES

NOTES